P9-CBM-208

NIV Archaeological STUDY BIBLE

NEW INTERNATIONAL VERSION

NIV *Archaeological* STUDY BIBLE

AN ILLUSTRATED WALK THROUGH BIBLICAL HISTORY AND CULTURE

GRAND RAPIDS, MICHIGAN 49530 USA

The Holy Bible, New International Version ®
Copyright © 1973, 1978, 1984 by International Bible Society

ZONDERVAN™

NIV Archaeological Study Bible
Copyright © 2005 by The Zondervan Corporation
All rights reserved

Published by Zondervan
Grand Rapids, Michigan 49530, U.S.A.

www.zondervan.com

Library of Congress Catalog Card Number 2005934075

The NIV Side-Column Cross-reference System, copyright © 1984.
The NIV Concordance, copyright © 1982, 1984.
Color Maps, copyright © 2000, 2005 by Zondervan.

Photography:
See Acknowledgements and Photographic Permissions on page xvii.
Cover image displays the ruins of Ephesus.

The "NIV" and "New International Version" trademarks are registered in the United States Patent and Trademark Office by International Bible Society. Use of either trademark requires the permission of International Bible Society.

The NIV text may be quoted in any form (written, visual, electronic or audio), up to and inclusive of five hundred (500) verses without express written permission of the publisher, providing the verses quoted do not amount to a complete book of the Bible nor do the verses quoted account for 25 percent or more of the total text of the work in which they are quoted.

Notice of copyright must appear on the title or copyright page of the work as follows:

Scripture taken from the HOLY BIBLE, NEW INTERNATIONAL VERSION ®. Copyright © 1973, 1978, 1984 by International Bible Society. Used by permission of Zondervan. All rights reserved.

When quotations from the NIV text are used in non-saleable media, such as church bulletins, orders of service, posters, transparencies or similar media, a complete copyright notice is not required, but the initials (NIV) must appear at the end of each quotation.

Any commentary or other Biblical reference work produced for commercial sale that uses the New International Version must obtain written permission for use of the NIV text.

Permission requests for commercial use within the U.S. and Canada that exceed the above guidelines must be directed to, and approved in writing by, Zondervan, 5300 Patterson Avenue, S.E., Grand Rapids, MI 49530.

Permission requests for commercial use within the U.K., EEC, and EFTA countries that exceed the above guidelines must be directed to, and approved in writing by, Hodder & Stoughton Ltd., a member of the Hodder Headline Plc. Group, 338 Euston Road, London NW1 3BH, England.

Permission requests for non-commercial use that exceed the above guidelines must be directed to, and approved in writing by, International Bible Society, 1820 Jet Stream Drive, Colorado Springs, CO 80921.

Printed in China

06 07 08 09 10 11 12 /CTC/ 9 8 7 6 5 4 3 2 1

You will be pleased to know that a portion of the purchase price of your new NIV Bible has been provided to International Bible Society to help spread the gospel of Jesus Christ around the world!

www.ibs.org

The purpose and passion of International Bible Society is to faithfully translate, publish and reach out with God's Word so that people around the world may become disciples of Jesus Christ and members of his Body.

TABLE OF *Contents*

OLD TESTAMENT

NEW TESTAMENT

ALPHABETICAL ORDER OF THE *Books of the Bible*

The books of the New Testament are indicated by italics.

Abbreviations

The following abbreviations appear in this Bible within parentheses only.

BIBLE BOOKS

Genesis	Ge
Exodus	Ex
Leviticus	Lev
Numbers	Nu
Deuteronomy	Dt
Joshua	Jos
Judges	Jdg
Ruth	Ru
1 Samuel	1Sa
2 Samuel	2Sa
1 Kings	1Ki
2 Kings	2Ki
1 Chronicles	1Ch
2 Chronicles	2Ch
Ezra	Ezr
Nehemiah	Ne
Esther	Est
Job	Job
Psalms	Ps
Proverbs	Pr
Ecclesiastes	Ecc
Song of Songs	SS
Isaiah	Isa
Jeremiah	Jer
Lamentations	La
Ezekiel	Eze
Daniel	Da
Hosea	Hos
Joel	Joel
Amos	Am
Obadiah	Ob
Jonah	Jnh
Micah	Mic
Nahum	Na
Habakkuk	Hab
Zephaniah	Zep
Haggai	Hag
Zechariah	Zec
Malachi	Mal
Matthew	Mt
Mark	Mk
Luke	Lk
John	Jn
Acts	Ac
Romans	Ro
1 Corinthians	1Co
2 Corinthians	2Co
Galatians	Gal
Ephesians	Eph
Philippians	Php
Colossians	Col
1 Thessalonians	1Th
2 Thessalonians	2Th
1 Timothy	1Ti
2 Timothy	2Ti
Titus	Tit
Philemon	Phm
Hebrews	Heb
James	Jas
1 Peter	1Pe
2 Peter	2Pe
1 John	1Jn
2 John	2Jn
3 John	3Jn
Jude	Jude
Revelation	Rev

APOCRYPHAL BOOKS AND PORTIONS OF BOOKS

1 Esdras	1Es
2 Esdras	2Es
Baruch	Bar
Judith	Jth
1 Maccabees	1Mc
2 Maccabees	2Mc
3 Maccabees	3Mc
4 Maccabees	4Mc
Sirach	Sir
or Ecclesiasticus	Eccus
Tobit	Tb
Wisdom of Solomon	WS
The Rest of Esther	RE
or Additions to Esther	AE
Prayer of Azariah	PrAz
Epistle of Jeremiah	Ep Jer
Susanna	Sus
Bel and the Dragon	Bel
The Song of the Three Holy Children	STHC
or Song of the Three Young Men	STYM
Prayer of Manasseh	PrM

OTHER ABBREVIATIONS

c.	(circa): *about, approximately*
cf.	*compare, confer*
ch., chs.	*chapter, chapters*
d.	*died*
e.g.	*for example*
etc.	*and so on*
ff.	*and following (and the verses following)*
i.e.	*that is*
lit.	*literally, literal*
NT	*New Testament*
OT	*Old Testament*
p., pp.	*page, pages*
r.	*reigned*
v., vv.	*verse, verses*

Note: Various standard abbreviations are used within parentheses for measures of volume, length and distance.

Introduction

Gordon-Conwell Theological Seminary is pleased to join with Zondervan in offering this unique study Bible. Together we believe that its release marks one of the most important events in recent publishing history. The *NIV Archaeological Study Bible* represents a remarkable achievement, with its intriguing subject matter, archaeological/cultural focus and aesthetic presentation coupled with the widely accepted New International Version text. Rarely has the publisher seen so high a degree of enthusiasm greet the introduction of a publishing concept as that which the prototype for the *NIV Archaeological Study Bible* received from such diverse groups as lay Christians, scholars and pastors who lent their valuable feedback.

No previous generation has witnessed so high a degree of collaboration of Biblical events, persons and historical settings as we have during the past century of ongoing, successful archaeological exploration. The quantity, quality and relevancy of the artifacts and epigraphical materials impinging upon the story of the Bible from the ancient Near East have been so staggering that few have been able to incorporate them into one place, let alone link them side by side with relevant Scriptures. We have before us a unique opportunity to see firsthand how archaeological discovery helps us to make sense of some of the heretofore difficult texts of Scripture. The role of Biblical archaeology as a hermeneutical tool is invaluable in situations in which cultural allusions and settings have in the past plainly eluded us—simply because the context belonged to another, completely "foreign," place and time. Add full-color photographs of the artifacts and documents being referenced, and you begin to see how this Bible sets a new standard for Bibles in the study genre.

Our prayer is that the *NIV Archaeological Study Bible* will bring much praise and glory to our heavenly Father, as well as that it might be used by God to entice an increasingly Biblically illiterate public back into the text of Scripture. The Biblical narrative comprises the greatest story ever told, but that story is so much more than an impersonal, third-person, ancient account. Indeed, it is both *about* and *for* each of us. Engaging it with the eyes of renewed understanding constitutes the most substantial reality check any of us can experience. These events and persons truly are part of the real world, happenings that actually took place and individuals who truly lived within the spaces and times of which we are now the linear descendants.

We invite you to join us in a personal encounter with this epic-making Bible from Gordon-Conwell Theological Seminary and Zondervan. The seminary is pleased to pioneer this venture and trusts that there will be more to come in the great days that lie ahead.

Walter C. Kaiser, Jr., President
Colman M. Mockler Distinguished Professor of Old Testament

May 17, 2005

ABOUT THIS *Bible*

The Bible is not a book of abstract religious teaching. If it were, understanding its historical context would be of relatively minor importance, although even then questions about the circumstances of its composition could not be ignored. Furthermore, the Bible did not arise out of a single cultural and historical environment; it certainly is not the product of revelations given to a single man, as the Koran claims to be. If it were, understanding its historical background would be far simpler.

As it is, the writing of the Bible took place over a period of more than 1,000 years. Although most if not all the writers of Scripture were Israelite or Jewish, these authors lived in a wide variety of circumstances. The cultural backdrop to the Biblical stories includes Egypt of the pharaohs, Mesopotamia, Canaanite culture, Israel across the Late Bronze and Iron Ages, the royal court of Persia, the expansive Hellenistic civilization and the Roman Empire. The languages of the Bible are Hebrew, Greek and Aramaic, but there are traces as well of the influence of Egyptian, Ugaritic, Akkadian, Sumerian, Persian and Latin. Portions of the Bible were composed in Israel, Egypt, Babylon, Asia Minor (Turkey), Greece and Rome. The writers of Scripture were sages, kings, farmers, exiles, governors, fishermen and traveling preachers.

The literature of the Bible is itself of a wide variety, and a given genre is likely to have much in common with the literature of its day. Narratives that tell the story of God's people in simple yet absorbing tales run through the Bible in books as diverse as Genesis, Judges, Ruth, Esther and Acts. Legislative texts that have parallels in the law codes of Mesopotamia emerge in books such as Numbers and Deuteronomy. Hymns and devotional songs appear in the Psalms, and when set in comparison to the hymns and religious poems of Egypt, Ugarit and Mesopotamia, they display both striking similarities and telling dissimilarities to their counterparts. The Bible even contains love poetry (Song of Songs), and this, too, is both like and unlike contemporary Egyptian love poetry. Like the Egyptians and Mesopotamians, the people of Israel composed many proverbs.

Of course, differences can be as significant as similarities, and not every type of literature in the Bible has strong parallels outside its pages. The proclamations of the Hebrew prophets have limited parallels in ancient Mesopotamia, and it is difficult to find anything else that compares with the four Gospels of the New Testament. On the other hand, the apocalyptic visions of Revelation can be compared to the apocalyptic texts of "Second Temple" Judaism, just as the letters of Paul may be evaluated over against other epistolary literature of the Greco-Roman period. In short, the Bible is an amazingly diverse collection of texts, none of which originated in a vacuum.

The *NIV Archaeological Study Bible* focuses on the historical, literary and cultural context of the Bible. This context includes the history of peoples and places populating its pages, daily life in various periods and under widely diverse circumstances during Biblical times, and ancient texts that illuminate the Bible and the archaeology of the Biblical world. In addition, the articles in this Bible devote particular attention to challenges archaeologists and Biblical scholars face on the critical issue of the trustworthiness of Scripture. But why is there a need for a tool that focuses on historical context? Several answers apply:

1. *Context is crucial to interpretation.* Imagine reading the words of a political or religious debate without the benefit of any knowledge of the circumstances, customs or beliefs of those involved in the discussion/dispute. The reader would either be bewildered or would run the risk of grossly misinterpreting the issues and positions people were taking. It is foolish, even arrogant, to think that we can rightly understand the Biblical writers without knowing anything of their environment.
2. As described above, *the Biblical world is complex and spans a great deal of history.* The ancient world is simply too extensive and too diverse for us to expect a few passing comments on "background" to give us a meaningful awareness of the cultures that the Biblical writers inhabited.
3. *A study of the context of the Bible is an encouragement to faith.* Many modern Christians shun the study of the ancient world for fear that scholars will make them aware of troubling facts that will serve only to undermine their faith in the Bible. In reality, a careful study of the world of the Bible enhances our confidence in its historical accuracy and in its distinctiveness as the Word of God. Set against the astonishing variety of cultures that made up the Biblical world, the unity of the message of the Bible is remarkable. The writers of Scripture spoke in diverse times and places, but they were inspired by one changeless Spirit. And, of course, the only way to answer those who claim that historical facts undermine Biblical credibility is to take a firsthand look at those very facts.

4. *Awareness of the context of the Bible is an antidote to the dangerous dismissal of history that we see too often in both the church and the academy.* In our day the postmodern outlook all but rejects history and context. Under the influence of this movement readers simply refuse to hear the writers of Scripture on their own terms and instead assert that it is up to each reader to make whatever he or she will of the ancient texts. Many reject outright the suggestion that we are obligated to attempt to understand the objective of a passage's original writer. The author's intended meaning is thus rendered irrelevant to the modern reader, who feels free to interpret a text in any manner whatsoever. Such an approach makes a mockery of Biblical authority. Further, many well-intentioned Christian readers, although not fully committed to a postmodern way of thinking, tend to interpret the Bible strictly in terms of their own experiences and standards, without ever considering what a prophet or apostle was saying to the people of his own day. An awareness of the beliefs, conflicts, history and habits of the people of Biblical times forces us to confront questions like, "What did Paul actually mean when he wrote these words to the Corinthian church?"
5. *Awareness of the world of the Bible instills within us a deeper appreciation for the writers of Scripture and a deeper love for the Bible itself.* It is difficult for us to genuinely love someone we do not really know, and we cannot enter into the experiences and perspectives of Biblical people without first relating to their world. By looking at the tools with which they worked, the struggles they faced, the literature they knew and the customs under which they lived, we acquire a profound admiration for their faith and wisdom.

The *NIV Archaeological Study Bible* includes the following features:

- Over 500 insightful and accessible articles, many including full-color photographs, covering the following five general categories: Archaeological Sites; Cultural and Historical Notes; Ancient Peoples, Lands and Rulers; The Reliability of the Bible; and Ancient Texts and Artifacts.
- Bottom-of-the-page study notes geared to archaeological, cultural and historical themes and frequently cross-referenced to relevant articles and other notes.
- Detailed book introductions, including helpful, at-a-glance timelines and outlines.
- Charts and graphs on pertinent topics.
- Periodic citations (quotations) from the ancients, each tied to a particular article.
- Side-column cross references.
- Full-color interior throughout.
- Sixteen pages of full-color maps, along with an index for ease in location of the many place-names referenced in the articles and notes.
- Indexes to articles and photographs.
- Subject guide.
- Concordance.
- A glossary, cross-referenced to pertinent, bolded words within the articles.

Preface TO THE NIV

THE NEW INTERNATIONAL VERSION is a completely new translation of the Holy Bible made by over a hundred scholars working directly from the best available Hebrew, Aramaic and Greek texts. It had its beginning in 1965 when, after several years of exploratory study by committees from the Christian Reformed Church and the National Association of Evangelicals, a group of scholars met at Palos Heights, Illinois, and concurred in the need for a new translation of the Bible in contemporary English. This group, though not made up of official church representatives, was transdenominational. Its conclusion was endorsed by a large number of leaders from many denominations who met in Chicago in 1966.

Responsibility for the new version was delegated by the Palos Heights group to a self-governing body of fifteen, the Committee on Bible Translation, composed for the most part of biblical scholars from colleges, universities and seminaries. In 1967 the New York Bible Society (now the International Bible Society) generously undertook the financial sponsorship of the project—a sponsorship that made it possible to enlist the help of many distinguished scholars. The fact that participants from the United States, Great Britain, Canada, Australia and New Zealand worked together gave the project its international scope. That they were from many denominations—including Anglican, Assemblies of God, Baptist, Brethren, Christian Reformed, Church of Christ, Evangelical Free, Lutheran, Mennonite, Methodist, Nazarene, Presbyterian, Wesleyan and other churches—helped to safeguard the translation from sectarian bias.

How it was made helps to give the New International Version its distinctiveness. The translation of each book was assigned to a team of scholars. Next, one of the Intermediate Editorial Committees revised the initial translation, with constant reference to the Hebrew, Aramaic or Greek. Their work then went to one of the General Editorial Committees, which checked it in detail and made another thorough revision. This revision in turn was carefully reviewed by the Committee on Bible Translation, which made further changes and then released the final version for publication. In this way the entire Bible underwent three revisions, during each of which the translation was examined for its faithfulness to the original languages and for its English style.

All this involved many thousands of hours of research and discussion regarding the meaning of the texts and the precise way of putting them into English. It may well be that no other translation has been made by a more thorough process of review and revision from committee to committee than this one.

From the beginning of the project, the Committee on Bible Translation held to certain goals for the New International Version: that it would be an accurate translation and one that would have clarity and literary quality and so prove suitable for public and private reading, teaching, preaching, memorizing and liturgical use. The Committee also sought to preserve some measure of continuity with the long tradition of translating the Scriptures into English.

In working toward these goals, the translators were united in their commitment to the authority and infallibility of the Bible as God's Word in written form. They believe that it contains the divine answer to the deepest needs of humanity, that it sheds unique light on our path in a dark world, and that it sets forth the way to our eternal well-being.

The first concern of the translators has been the accuracy of the translation and its fidelity to the thought of the biblical writers. They have weighed the significance of the lexical and grammatical details of the Hebrew, Aramaic and Greek texts. At the same time, they have striven for more than a word-for-word translation. Because thought patterns and syntax differ from language to language, faithful communication of the meaning of the writers of the Bible demands frequent modifications in sentence structure and constant regard for the contextual meanings of words.

A sensitive feeling for style does not always accompany scholarship. Accordingly the Committee on Bible Translation submitted the developing version to a number of stylistic consultants. Two of them read every book of both Old and New Testaments twice—once before and once after the last major revision—and made invaluable suggestions. Samples of the translation were tested for clarity and ease of reading by various kinds of people—young and old, highly educated and less well educated, ministers and laymen.

Concern for clear and natural English—that the New International Version should be idiomatic but not idiosyncratic, contemporary but not dated—motivated the translators and consultants. At the same time, they tried to reflect the differing styles of the biblical writers. In view of the international use of English, the translators sought to avoid obvious Americanisms on the one hand and obvious Anglicisms on the other. A British edition reflects the comparatively few differences of significant idiom and of spelling.

As for the traditional pronouns "thou," "thee" and "thine" in reference to the Deity, the translators judged that to use these archaisms (along with the old verb forms such as "doest," "wouldest" and "hadst") would violate accuracy in translation. Neither Hebrew, Aramaic nor Greek uses special pronouns for the persons of the Godhead. A present-day translation is not enhanced by forms that in the time of the King James Version were used in everyday speech, whether referring to God or man.

For the Old Testament the standard Hebrew text, the Masoretic Text as published in the latest editions of *Biblia Hebraica*, was used throughout. The Dead Sea Scrolls contain material bearing on an earlier stage of the Hebrew text. They were consulted, as were the Samaritan Pentateuch and the ancient scribal traditions relating to textual changes. Sometimes a variant Hebrew reading in the margin of the Masoretic Text was followed instead of the text itself. Such instances, being variants within the Masoretic tradition, are not specified by footnotes. In rare cases, words in the consonantal text were divided differently from the way they appear in the Masoretic Text. Footnotes indicate this. The translators also consulted the more important early versions—the Septuagint; Aquila, Symmachus and Theodotion; the Vulgate; the Syriac Peshitta; the Targums; and for the Psalms the *Juxta Hebraica* of Jerome. Readings from these versions were occasionally followed where the Masoretic Text seemed doubtful and where accepted principles of textual criticism showed that one or more of these textual witnesses appeared to provide the correct reading. Such instances are footnoted. Sometimes vowel letters and vowel signs did not, in the judgment of the translators, represent the correct vowels for the original consonantal text. Accordingly some words were read with a different set of vowels. These instances are usually not indicated by footnotes.

The Greek text used in translating the New Testament was an eclectic one. No other piece of ancient literature has such an abundance of manuscript witnesses as does the New Testament. Where existing manuscripts differ, the translators made their choice of readings according to accepted principles of New Testament textual criticism. Footnotes call attention to places where there was uncertainty about what the original text was. The best current printed texts of the Greek New Testament were used.

There is a sense in which the work of translation is never wholly finished. This applies to all great literature and uniquely so to the Bible. In 1973 the New Testament in the New International Version was published. Since then, suggestions for corrections and revisions have been received from various sources. The Committee on Bible Translation carefully considered the suggestions and adopted a number of them. These were incorporated in the first printing of the entire Bible in 1978. Additional revisions were made by the Committee on Bible Translation in 1983 and appear in printings after that date.

As in other ancient documents, the precise meaning of the biblical texts is sometimes uncertain. This is more often the case with the Hebrew and Aramaic texts than with the Greek text. Although archaeological and linguistic discoveries in this century aid in understanding difficult passages, some uncertainties remain. The more significant of these have been called to the reader's attention in the footnotes.

In regard to the divine name *YHWH*, commonly referred to as the *Tetragrammaton*, the translators adopted the device used in most English versions of rendering that name as "LORD" in capital letters to distinguish it from *Adonai*, another Hebrew word rendered "Lord," for which small letters are used. Wherever the two names stand together in the Old Testament as a compound name of God, they are rendered "Sovereign LORD."

Because for most readers today the phrases "the LORD of hosts" and "God of hosts" have little meaning, this version renders them "the LORD Almighty" and "God Almighty." These renderings convey the sense of the Hebrew, namely, "he who is sovereign over all the 'hosts' (powers) in heaven and on earth, especially over the 'hosts' (armies) of Israel." For readers unacquainted with Hebrew this does not make clear the distinction between *Sabaoth* ("hosts" or "Almighty") and *Shaddai* (which can also be translated "Almighty"), but the latter occurs infrequently and is always footnoted. When *Adonai* and *YHWH Sabaoth* occur together, they are rendered "the Lord, the LORD Almighty."

As for other proper nouns, the familiar spellings of the King James Version are generally retained. Names traditionally spelled with "ch," except where it is final, are usually spelled in this translation with "k" or "c," since the biblical languages do not have the sound that "ch" frequently indicates in English—for example, in *chant.* For well-known names such as Zechariah, however, the traditional spelling has been retained. Variation in the spelling of names in the original languages has usually not been indicated. Where a person or place has two or more different names in the Hebrew, Aramaic or Greek texts, the more familiar one has generally been used, with footnotes where needed.

To achieve clarity the translators sometimes supplied words not in the original texts but required by the context. If there was uncertainty about such material, it is enclosed in brackets. Also for the sake of clarity or style, nouns, including some proper nouns, are sometimes substituted for pronouns, and vice versa. And though the Hebrew writers often shifted back and forth between first, second and third personal pronouns without change of antecedent, this translation often makes them uniform, in accordance with English style and without the use of footnotes.

Poetical passages are printed as poetry, that is, with indentation of lines and with separate stanzas. These are generally designed to reflect the structure of Hebrew poetry. This poetry is normally characterized by parallelism in balanced lines. Most of the poetry in the Bible is in the Old Testament, and scholars differ regarding the scansion of Hebrew lines. The translators determined the stanza divisions for the most part by analysis of the subject matter. The stanzas therefore serve as poetic paragraphs.

As an aid to the reader, italicized sectional headings are inserted in most of the books. They are not to be regarded as part of the NIV text, are not for oral reading, and are not intended to dictate the interpretation of the sections they head.

The footnotes in this version are of several kinds, most of which need no explanation. Those giving alternative translations begin with "Or" and generally introduce the alternative with the last word preceding it in the text, except when it is a single-word alternative; in poetry quoted in a footnote a slant mark indicates a line division. Footnotes introduced by "Or" do not have uniform significance. In some cases two possible translations were considered to have about equal validity. In other cases, though the translators were convinced that the translation in the text was correct, they judged that another interpretation was possible and of sufficient importance to be represented in a footnote.

In the New Testament, footnotes that refer to uncertainty regarding the original text are introduced by "Some manuscripts" or similar expressions. In the Old Testament, evidence for the reading chosen is given first and evidence for the alternative is added after a semicolon (for example: Septuagint; Hebrew *father*). In such notes the term "Hebrew" refers to the Masoretic Text.

It should be noted that minerals, flora and fauna, architectural details, articles of clothing and jewelry, musical instruments and other articles cannot always be identified with precision. Also measures of capacity in the biblical period are particularly uncertain (see the table of weights and measures following the text).

Like all translations of the Bible, made as they are by imperfect man, this one undoubtedly falls short of its goals. Yet we are grateful to God for the extent to which he has enabled us to realize these goals and for the strength he has given us and our colleagues to complete our task. We offer this version of the Bible to him in whose name and for whose glory it has been made. We pray that it will lead many into a better understanding of the Holy Scriptures and a fuller knowledge of Jesus Christ the incarnate Word, of whom the Scriptures so faithfully testify.

The Committee on Bible Translation

June 1978
(Revised Aug 1983)

Names of the translators and editors may be secured from the
International Bible Society translation sponsors of the
New International Version, 1820 Jet Stream Drive,
Colorado Springs, Colorado 08921-3696 U.S.A.

ACKNOWLEDGEMENTS AND PHOTOGRAPHIC 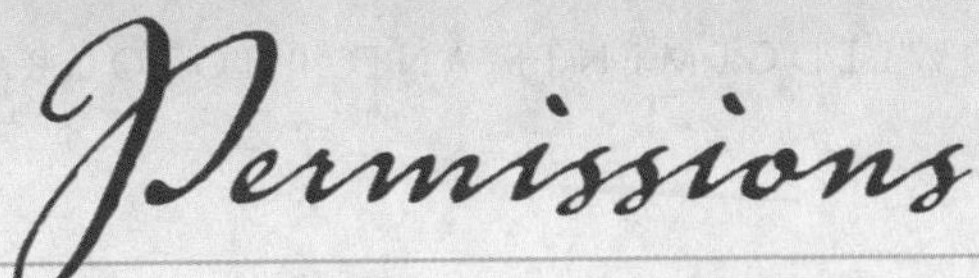

The *NIV Archaeological Study Bible* is a production of Gordon-Conwell Theological Seminary, Dr. Walter C. Kaiser, Jr., president and executive editor. The general editor is Dr. Duane A. Garrett, currently John R. Sampey Professor of Old Testament Literature, the Southern Baptist Seminary.

ABOUT GORDON-CONWELL THEOLOGICAL SEMINARY

Since the 1880s, Gordon-Conwell Theological Seminary and its founders have stood with historic Christianity and based its educational task on three main objectives: the pursuit of Christlikeness, the proclamation of the Gospel, and the probing of Scripture. Today, no less than over a century ago, the urgent task for the rising generation of Christian leaders is to raise the standard of the truth of God's Word with confidence, relevance and compassion to a culture adrift in doubt. The seminary's vision is to raise up men and women who will stand in the gap, who will equip the saints, who will ground and deepen believers in the Word of God, and who will pray fervently that out of these efforts a mighty spiritual awakening and a Biblical reformation will come to our culture. In doing so, we are preparing students to courageously confront the crisis of today's disoriented, empty and fractured lives, and to lead others toward a fuller knowledge of Jesus Christ. With the generous support of The Grace Foundation and the Van Kampen Family, and with the contributions of more than one hundred scholars, Gordon-Conwell is pleased to offer, along with Zondervan, this *NIV Archaeological Study Bible* as a testimony to the efficacy and fullness of God's Word. It is our sincere hope that with this Bible, your probing of Scripture will be deepened, your proclamation of the Gospel will become more vigorous, and your pursuit of Christ will lead you to deeper intimacy with our Savior and Lord.

The following photographic permissions and publishing rights granted to the *NIV Archaeological Study Bible* are in association with Dr. James C. Martin and Preserving Bible Times, Inc. and provided by:

Dr. James C. Martin
Bible World Seminars
P.O. Box 2687
Amarillo, Texas 79105
www.bibleworldphotos.com

Preserving Bible Times, Inc.
P.O. Box 83357
Gaithersburg, MD 20883
www.preservingbibletimes.org

The Amman Museum
The Hashemite Kingdom of Jordan, Ministry of Tourism & Antiquities
Press and Publication Department
Amman, Jordan

The British Museum
Media Relations Great Russell Street
London WC 1B 3DG
media@thebritishmuseum.ac.uk

The Egyptian Museum
Ministry of Antiquities and Culture
Cairo, Egypt

Collection of the Israel Museum, Jerusalem, and courtesy of the Israel Antiquities Authority, Exhibited at the Israel Museum, Jerusalem

Collection of the Israel Museum, Jerusalem, and courtesy of the Israel Angiquities authority, Exhibited at the Shrine of the Book, The Israel Museum, Jerusalem

Collection of the Israel Museum, Jerusalem, and courtesy of the Israel Antiquities Authority, exhibited at the Rockefeller Museum, Jerusalem

Eretz Israel Museum
2 Haim Levanon St.
Tel Aviv, Israel 69975

The Galilee Boat
The Yigal Allon Center
Kibbutz Ginosar, on the
Western shore of the Sea of Galilee
Israel

House of Anchors
Kibbutz En Gev, on the
Eastern shore of the Sea of Galilee
Israel

Reproduction of the City of Jerusalem at the time of the
Second Temple, located on the grounds of the Holyland Hotel, Jerusalem.
Photographing the site was done with the hotel's permission.

The Wohl Museum and Burnt House
The Jewish Quarter
Jerusalem, Israel

Musée de Louvre
Service de la Communication
34–36 Quai du Louvre
75058 Paris Cedex 01

Roman Forum and House of Nero
On licence Ministero per i Beni le Attivita Culturali
Soprintendza Archeologica di Roma

Museums in Turkey
The Ministry of Antiquities and Culture
II. Meclis Binasi 06100 Ulus
Ankara, Turkey

In addition, the creators of the *NIV Archaeological Study Bible* have acquired rights to publish text or photographs from the following individuals or associations not associated with Preserving Bible Times:

Todd Bolen
Producer, Pictorial Library of Bible Lands
D. N. Harei Yehuda
Israel
Todd Bolen/BiblePlaces.com

Dr. Gary Pratico
Gordon-Conwell Theological Seminary

Duane Garrett
Southern Baptist Seminary

Martin Schøyen
Owner, The Schøyen Collection
In association with the Nasjonalbiblioteket, Norway
Victoria Terrasse 11
P.O. Box 2674 Solli
NO–0203
NO–0255 Oslo
Norway

The enormous generosity of Mr. Schøyen in allowing us to publish photographs of his magnificent manuscript collection is hereby gratefully acknowledged.

Excerpts ("Ancient Voices" citations) from *The Context of Scripture*, edited by William W. Hallow and K. Lawson Younger and published by E. J. Brill (Leiden and New York, 1997–2002), are reprinted by permission of the publisher. The generosity of Brill Academic Publishers and the assistance of Dr. K. Lawson Younger are gratefully acknowledged. Detail is as follows (includes page number where the citation can be found):

From a Ramesside Stela (Inscribed Stone Monument) (*CS*, 1.13), Vol. I, p. 20 4
Gilgamesh (*CS*, 1.132), Vol. I, p. 460 14
The Zukru Festival (*CS*, 1.123), Vol. I, p. 433 131
Rituals From Emar (*CS*, 1.132), Vol. I, p. 428 137
Establishing a New Temple for the Goddess of the Night (*CS*, 1.70), Vol. I, p. 174 147
The Middle Assyrian Laws (*CS*, 2.132), Vol. II, p. 355 178
Instructions to Priests and Temple Officials (*CS*, 1.83), Vol. I, p. 217 209
Ugaritic Liturgy Against Venomous Snakes (*CS*, 1.94), Vol. I, p. 295 227
The Deir Alla Plaster Inscriptions (*CS*, 2.27), Vol. II, p. 142 228
The Laws of Eshnunna (*CS*, 2.130), Vol. II, p. 333 270
Mesopotamian Omens (*CS*, 1.120), Vol. I, p. 424 278
Hittite Laws (*CS*, 2.19), Vol. II, p. 108 280
The Descent of Ishtar to the Underworld (*CS*, 1.108), Vol. I, p. 381 357
Excerpt From the Hurro-Hittite Bilingual Wisdom Text (*CS*, 1.82), Vol. I, p. 216 458
The Proclamation Of Telipinu (*CS*, 1.76), Vol. I, p. 197 468
The Cylinders of Gudea (*CS*, 2.155), Vol. II, p. 419 484
The Balu (Baal) Myth (*CS*, 1.86), Vol. I, pp. 267–268 516
The Inscpription of King Mesha (*CS*, 2.23), Vol. II, p. 137 531
The Black Obelisk (*CS*, 2.113F), Vol. II, p. 269 545
The Eridu Genesis (*CS*, 1.158), Vol. I, p. 515 577
The Dialogue Between Two Scribes (*CS*, 1.184), Vol. I, p. 589 580
Assyrian King Lists (*CS*, 1.135), Vol. I, p. 465 651
The Sippar Cylinder of Nabonidus (*CS*, 2.123A), Vol. II, p. 313 665
Proclamation of Anitta of Kussar (*CS*, 1.72), Vol. I, p. 182 674
The Kirta Epic (*CS*, 1.102), Vol. I, p. 333 735
The Poem of the Righteous Sufferer (*CS*, 1.153), Vol. I, p. 487 759
The Aqhatu Legend (*CS*, 1.103), Vol. I, pp. 347–348 760
Dialogue Between a Man and His God (*CS*, 1.151), Vol. I, p. 485 770
Enki and Ninmah (*CS*, 1.159), Vol. I, pp. 517–518 799
Erra and Ishum (*CS*, 1.113), Vol. I, p. 406 827
Prayer to Marduk (*CS*, 1.114), Vol. I, p. 416 830
Ashurbanipal's Coronation Hymn (*CS*, 1.142), Vol. I, p. 473 867
Epic of Creation (*CS*, 1.111), Vol. I, p. 392 889
The Balu Myth (*CS*, 1.86), Vol. I, p. 246 906
A Sufferer's Salvation (*CS*, 1.152), Vol. I, p. 486 923
The Shamash Hymn (*CS*, 1.117), Vol. I, p. 418 976
Instruction of Anii (*CS*, 1.46), Vol. I, p. 111 991
Instruction of Amenemope (*CS*, 1.47), Vol. I, p. 116 995
The Song From the Tomb of King Intef (*CS*, 1.30), Vol. I, p. 49 1019
Papyrus Harris (*CS*, 1.49), Vol. I, p. 126 1036
Sargon II: The Annals (*CS*, 2.118A), Vol. II, p. 293 1073
The Letter-Prayer of King Sin-Iddinam to Nin-Isina (*CS*, 1.164), Vol. I, p. 533 1122
Atra-Hasis (*CS*, 1.130), Vol. I, p. 451 1177
The Admonitions of an Egyptian Sage: The Admonitions of Ipuwer (*CS*, 1.42), Vol. I, p. 94 1308
A Neo-Babylonian Lament for Tammmuz (*CS*, 1.118), Vol. I, p. 420 1321

Other sources used for study notes, charts, graphs, in-text maps and illustrations are:

Douglas, J.D., Revising Ed.; Tenney, Merrill C., General Ed., *New International Bible Dictionary* (Grand Rapids: Zondervan, 1963, 1964, 1967, 1987)

NIV Study Bible (Fully Revised) (Grand Rapids: Zondervan, 1985, 1995, 2002)

Faith in Action Study Bible (Grand Rapids: Zondervan, 2005)

John H. Walton, *Chronological and Background Charts of the Old Testament, Rev. Ed.* (Grand Rapids: Zondervan, 1997)

H. Wayne House, *Chronological and Background Charts of the New Testament, Rev. Ed.* (Grand Rapids: Zondervan, 1997)

John H. Walton and Andrew E. Hill, *Old Testament Today* (Grand Rapids: Zondervan, 2004)

Carl G. Rasmussen, *Zondervan NIV Atlas of the Bible* (Grand Rapids: Zondervan, 1989)

ARCHAEOLOGICAL PERIODS 

Neolithic	8300–4500 B.C.
Chalcolithic	4500–3200 B.C.
Early Bronze Age	3200–2200 B.C.
Middle Bronze Age	2200–1550 B.C.
Late Bronze Age	1550–1200 B.C.
Iron Age I	1200–1000 B.C.
Iron Age II	1000–586 B.C.
Babylonian/Exilic Period	586–539 B.C.
Persian Period	539–332 B.C.
Hellenistic Period	332–141 B.C.
Hasmonean Period	141–37 B.C.
Roman Period	37 B.C.–A.D. 133
Byzantine Period	A.D. 324–638
Arab Period	A.D. 638–1516
Crusader Period	A.D. 1099–1291
Ottoman Period	A.D. 1517–1917
British Mandate	A.D. 1917–1948
Modern Israel	A.D. 1948–present

Prepared by Duane A. Garrett

THE HISTORY OF THE *Holy Land*

The Holy Land, at times variously named **Canaan**,[1] Israel, the Levant or Palestine, has changed hands many times and has often been the center of conflict. The archaeology of Palestine is complex, in that it reflects all eras of the region's long history.

PRE-ISRAELITE CULTURE

Prehistoric and Early Bronze Age

Canaan was inhabited from prehistoric times. The earliest Stone Age culture was discovered at Mount Carmel, and remains of a later Stone Age culture, called the Natufian, were unearthed at Jericho. Agriculture and the production of pottery began during the **Neolithic period**,[2] which is divided into "pre-pottery" and "pottery" periods. During the late fifth and fourth millenniums B.C. a culture called "Ghassulian" emerged in the southern Jordan Valley. Along with a site in Beersheba, this marked the beginning of the **Chalcolithic Age** in the region. Ghassulian pottery is remarkably advanced and attests to the sophistication of these early people.

The beginning of the **Early Bronze Age** (3400–2000 B.C.) in the Levant corresponds with late predynastic and early dynastic Egypt, around 3400–3000 B.C. Important Early Bronze I sites include **Megiddo**, Jericho, Ai and Beth Shan, all in northern or central Palestine; a more advanced culture developed in the southern part of the region somewhat later. An important Early Bronze II site in the south is Arad.[3] The Early Bronze Age saw the beginning of urban culture in the land, with more or less autonomous city-states developing around major walled cities.

Around 2650–2350 B.C. a breakdown of unspecified origin occurred in urban culture, especially in the north. One suggested reason is that nomadic **Amorites** invaded the land and disrupted the culture. It is questionable, however, whether this change in culture can be attributed to an Amorite migration or invasion, and today many scholars reject this suggestion. Some believe that environmental problems were a more likely cause; Abraham is said to have gone down to Egypt because of a famine (Ge 12:10). The decline of Early Bronze culture in Canaan may be related to the end of the **Old Kingdom** in Egypt in the twenty-second century B.C., as "**Asiatics**" (Semitic peoples from Canaan and Syria) pushed their way into Egypt.

Middle Bronze and Late Bronze Ages

A new urban culture, contemporary with the beginning of the Middle Kingdom in Egypt, arose at the start of the **Middle Bronze Age** (c. 2000–1550 B.C.). Prominent cities included Tel Aphek, Byblos, Acco, Megiddo, Jericho and Beth Shan. The art of pottery-making advanced significantly as potters learned to use the fast wheel to fashion fine vessels. The Egyptian Tale of Sinuhe provides a portrait of Canaanite life at this time. The Middle Bronze Age in Canaan also spans the **Hyksos** era of the **Second Intermediate period** in Egypt; some have argued for a Hyksos presence in Canaan, but this is unlikely.[4]

There was a decline in the quality of material culture (especially pottery) in Canaan at the beginning of the **Late Bronze Age** (c. 1550–1200 B.C.), and there appears to have been a great deal of destruction during Late Bronze I (c. 1550–1400 B.C.). Egyptian rulers, especially Thutmose III (c. 1479–1425 B.C.), made forays into Canaan to keep the city-states there subservient to Egyptian demands, and Egyptian influence is evident at a number of sites (e.g., Megiddo). Many scholars, on the basis of destruction levels for various Late Bronze II sites, have argued that the Israelite invasion under Joshua occurred around 1250 B.C., but this argument has largely collapsed since in fact no cities, with the possible exception of **Hazor**,[5] have destruction levels that fit this interpretation.

ISRAELITE CULTURE

Although the Israelites appear to have invaded Canaan around 1400 B.C., they left almost no archaeological footprint until about 1200 B.C.[5] During **Iron** I (usually dated c. 1200–1000 B.C.) the nation of Israel began to take shape. Examples of what appears to be Israelite material culture, such as the "four-room house" and "collar-rim" pottery, appear in the archaeology of this time. Hundreds of villages in central Canaan dated to this period may be regarded as Israelite. The Philistines first appeared in Canaan

[1]See Glossary on page 2080 for definitions of bolded words. [2]See "Archaeological Periods chart" on page xx. [3]See "Arad" on page 247. [4]See "The Hyksos and the Old Testament" on page 121. [5]See "Hazor" on page 322. [6]See "Changes in Canaan" on page 358.

at this time as a part of the migration of the "**Sea Peoples**," and examples of their material culture (such as a distinctive bichrome pottery that is comparable to a type of Mycenaean Greek pottery) began to appear.

Inasmuch as the Biblical record indicates that Israel was in the land and contending with various other enemies long before the Philistines became a threat, the argument that the Philistines and Israelites emerged in Canaan at about the same time is erroneous. Indeed, the presence of "Israel" on the Merneptah Stele (c. 1210 B.C.) strongly suggests that Israel was well established in the land prior to 1200 B.C., the beginning of the Iron I Age.[7]

During the Judges period the Israelites were held together by their common covenant with God, but constant pressure from outside enemies led them to seek protection in stronger political unity (1Sa 8:19–20). Saul was Israel's first king, but the nation reached its cultural and political apex under David and Solomon (tenth century B.C.), when Israel dominated the entire Levant. Important physical remains from the united monarchy have been excavated at Hazor, Megiddo and Gezer, where triple-gated city entryways and **casemate walls** illustrate the fortification work described in 1 Kings 9:15.[8]

Israelite supremacy was weakened by the division of the kingdom between Rehoboam and Jeroboam I (1Ki 12) and shattered by the raid of the Egyptian Shishak (1Ki 14:25–26). Indeed, Shishak's attack seems to have been little more than a slash-and-burn campaign aimed at reducing Israel's power vis-à-vis Egypt.[9] The fortunes of **Samaria** (the northern kingdom of Israel)[10] vacillated during the next two centuries. Samaria was sometimes powerful, under kings such as Omri and Jeroboam II, but notably weak at other times, as when under pressure from kings such as Hazael of Damascus.[11] Samaria finally succumbed to **Assyria** around 720 B.C., and Judah, a relatively minor state, hung on until it was destroyed by **Nebuchadnezzar** of Babylon in 586 B.C.[12]

THE PERSIAN PERIOD

The land was fairly desolate during the **exile**, with all but the poorest Jews scattered across the Near East from Egypt to **Babylonia**. Other peoples began to migrate into the land. Edomites, perhaps impelled by Arabs exerting pressure from the south, moved north. The Samaritans, a people of partly Israelite and partly pagan origin, soon emerged.[13] In 539 B.C. Cyrus II of Persia conquered Babylon, and by 500 B.C. all of the Near East was in Persian hands.[14] Jews began to return to the land, but the situation was discouraging and little progress was made until Ezra and Nehemiah arrived during the fifth century to rebuild Jerusalem and reestablish the temple.

Archaeologically, this has been a somewhat dark period, but there have been some important finds. For example, **papyri** from Samaria containing legal documents dating to approximately 375–335 B.C. have been discovered at Wadi ed-Daliyeh in the central hill country of Israel. Numerous locations in the land have yielded evidence of Persian-era occupation levels, but, beyond the use of Persian royal names for dating purposes, little direct evidence of Persian influence has been found.

THE GREEK AND HASMONEAN PERIODS

Greek Rule

When Alexander the Great marched through the Levant in 333 B.C., he kept to the coastline in order to destroy the Persian navy and so bypassed Jewish areas. All of the Persian Empire fell under Greek control. After the death of Alexander (323 B.C.), a Greek family known as the **Ptolemies** took control of Egypt.[15] The Levant fell under the control of the Ptolemies as well. The letters of Zenon, a business manager under Ptolemy II Philadelphus (285–246 B.C.), reveal that there was active trade between the Levant and Egypt in various food staples and in slave girls (used as prostitutes). Meanwhile, the process of **Hellenization** moved forward, with many societal leaders embracing Greek culture and religion.

Ptolemaic rule in the region continued until 200 B.C., when it fell under the rule of the **Seleucids**, the Greek rulers of Syria.[16]

[7]See "The Merneptah Stele" on page 360. [8]See "The Building Activity of Solomon" on page 497. [9]See "The Campaign of Shishak" on page 635. [10]See "Omri and Samaria" on page 512. [11]See "Hazael, the Nemesis of Israel" on page 539. [12]See "The Last Days of Jerusalem" on page 1197. [13]See "The Samaritans" on page 1737. [14]See "Cyrus the Great" on page 669. [15]See "The Ptolemies" on page 1399. [16]See "The Seleucids" on page 1408.

The Seleucid who took the Levant from the Ptolemies was Antiochus III (223–187 B.C.). After losing **Asia Minor** to Rome in 189 B.C., however, Antiochus III found his kingdom in financial straits. His son, Seleucus IV (187–175 B.C.) failed in an attempt to plunder the riches of the Jewish temple, but Antiochus IV (175–164 B.C.) did so around 170 B.C. Antiochus IV is the best remembered Seleucid in Jewish history. Around 168 B.C. he destroyed much of Jerusalem, set up an altar to Zeus in the temple and forbade the observance of Judaism.[17] The Jews, under Judas Maccabeus and his brothers, defeated the Seleucids in successive campaigns. Judas died in battle in 160 B.C., but his brother Jonathan took the lead until his death in approximately 142 B.C. He was in turn followed by a third brother, Simon (rulers in the Maccabean line are referred to as "**Hasmoneans**").

Hasmonean Rule

By this time Judea had become all but independent (Simon became in effect both king and high priest, although the Hasmonean rulers typically presented themselves as high priests only). Simon was followed by his son John Hyrcanus I (134–104 B.C.), who extended the domain of Judah. After the brief reign of Aristobulus I (104–103 B.C.), the next Hasmonean leader was Alexander Jannaeus (103–76 B.C.), who continued to expand Judah's domain through military means. Enormous ideological divisions developed in Jewish society, however—primarily between the more conservative and religious groups, led by the Pharisees, and the more Hellenized and aristocratic groups, led by the Sadducees.[18] Alexander Jannaeus's widow, Salome Alexandra, ruled after him, and with her death in 67 B.C. her sons Aristobulus II and Hyrcanus II fought for the throne.

THE ROMAN AND BYZANTINE PERIODS

Roman Rule

By this time Rome had moved into the area. Pompey the Great destroyed the Seleucid kingdom, captured Jerusalem and set up the Decapolis as a region independent of Judean control. Hyrcanus II gained the high priesthood, but his political clout disappeared. The Idumean (i.e., Edomite) Antipater was given the title of "Procurator of Judaea" for services to Julius Caesar. In 40 B.C. the Parthians seized Jerusalem and reinstated Hasmonean rule in the person of Antigonus. Herod (the Great), son of the Idumean Antipater, escaped to Rome and returned with Roman forces to seize control of Jerusalem and, with Roman support, to claim the title of king.

Relief commemorating Roman victory over Judea
Preserving Bible Times; © Dr. James C. Martin; permission of Eretz Israel Museum

Herod ruled until 4 B.C., during which time he engaged in numerous building projects, including the port city of Caesarea Maritima, the palace-fortresses at Masada and Herodium, the Antonia fortress and the Jerusalem temple. Paranoid and vicious near the end of his life, he murdered several sons and left no clear heir.[19] Emperor Augustus divided Herod's domain among three of his surviving sons (Archelaus, Herod Antipas and Philip). The region was briefly united again under Herod Agrippa I, but with his death in A.D. 44 Herodian rule ended, and the Holy Land came under direct Roman control.

The mixture of Roman arrogance and Jewish antagonism to pagan rule proved lethal. The incompetent and heavy-handed

[17]See "Antiochus IV Epiphanes" on page 1406. [18]See "The Pharisees" on page 1566 and "The Sadducees" on page 1600. [19]See "Herod the Great" on page 1627.

administration of Gessius Florus, procurator in A.D. 64–66, proved to be intolerable, and the Jews revolted in A.D. 66. After initial successes they were crushed by a Roman army led by Vespasian and his son Titus. In A.D. 70 Jerusalem and the temple were destroyed amid horrific Jewish casualties.[20] Caesarea Maritima, the governor's city, became a Roman colony,[21] and the center of Jewish religious life moved to Jamnia, a town located west of Jerusalem near the Mediterranean. In A.D. 132 Emperor Hadrian decided to rebuild Jerusalem as a Roman colony, Aelia Capitolina. This provoked a rebellion under Simeon Bar Kosba, who was hailed as the messiah and called Bar Kokhba ("the son of the star") by Rabbi Akiba. The fighting was ferocious and ended in the near extermination of Jews in the region and in an edict forbidding them from entering Jerusalem. Christians, who did not join in the revolt, faired better.

Byzantine Rule

The Roman Empire eventually split into two parts, with the eastern portion governed from the city of Byzantium (also called Constantinople and now Istanbul). Thus, the region now known as Palestine fell under **Byzantine** control. The conversion of the Byzantine Emperor Constantine I to Christianity (A.D. 312) greatly enhanced the prestige of the region as shrines, pilgrimage sites and churches were built with imperial patronage.[22] Archaeology has recovered remains from many of these sites, and archaeological reports frequently mention finds from the Byzantine period. Except for the occasional revolt, the region enjoyed a prolonged period of peace under Byzantine rule.

Islamic Rule

The rise of Islam brought an Arab invasion from the east. The first caliph, Abu Bakr, called for a jihad to take the region and, after a bloody conflict with Byzantine forces, the land fell to Umar I in A.D. 636. Thereafter, the Holy Land came under the rule of the Umayyads, and the process of Arabizing the region and converting it to Islam began. In A.D. 691 Muslims built the Dome of the Rock on the temple mount, claiming this to be the spot from which Mohammed had ascended to heaven. Other Muslim dynasties (the Abbasid, the Ikhshidid and the Fatimid) successively seized control of the area.

The Fatimid rulers, and in particular the Caliph al-Hakim (A.D. 996–1021), were harsh toward Christians. In reaction, the western churches began the crusades. By A.D. 1100 Jerusalem was in crusader hands. Prolonged wars between Muslims and crusaders ensued. The Muslims won decisive victories under the leadership of Saladin (A.D. 1137–1193), and by A.D. 1291 the Holy Land was again securely in Muslim hands. Meanwhile, a Turkish-speaking military aristocracy called the Mamelukes had wrested power in Egypt and became rulers as well in the Levant. The Near East was then convulsed by the invasion of the Mongols, and the weakened Mamelukes fell to the Ottoman Turks in A.D. 1516.

The otherwise highly contested region was more or less isolated during 300 years of Ottoman rule, although it was often troubled internally by revolts and massacres, as well as by wars among factions vying for power in the empire. Direct European involvement began again with Napoleon's campaign in Egypt (A.D. 1798–1801). Thereafter, a weakened Ottoman Empire was at times propped up by European support. French, Russian and German settlements appeared in the region, and the first Zionist settlement sprang up in A.D. 1882. In 1896 Theodor Herzl wrote a pamphlet advocating the establishment of a Jewish state in Palestine.

THE BRITISH MANDATE

World War I brought about decisive changes. There was extensive fighting in Palestine itself during the war, and the decrepit Ottoman Empire finally expired. In 1917 British Foreign Secretary Arthur Balfour, hoping for Jewish support in the war effort, issued the "Balfour Declaration," which advocated a Jewish state in Palestine. In the aftermath of the war, Arabs rejected the Balfour Declaration and elected Faysal to rule a united Syria, Lebanon and Palestine. However, a conference in 1920 mandated Syria and Lebanon to the French and Palestine to the British. Faysal's short-lived kingdom ended, and Arabs referred to 1920 as "the year of catastrophe." During the 1930s, with the rise of Nazism, large numbers of Jews began immigrating to Palestine, and

[20]See "Josephus and the Fall of Jerusalem" on page 1606. [21]See "Caesarea Maritima" on page 1786. [22]See "Constantine and Queen Helena's Role in Preserving Holy Sites" on page 1758.

serious conflicts between Jews and Arabs began to occur. British policy vacillated between support for the Jews and for the Arabs.

World War II and the holocaust led to massive Jewish immigration into the region. The Arab League officially opposed a Zionist state in Palestine, but western powers, especially the United States, were sympathetic to the Jewish position, and the Jews themselves were determined never again to allow themselves to be in a position where a pogrom or holocaust could devastate their numbers. In 1947 the United Nations voted to partition Palestine into two states, one Jewish and the other Arab, but the plan met with armed resistance from Palestinian Arabs. Zionists routed the Arabs in early 1948, however, and the British Mandate came to an end. On May 14, 1948, the modern state of Israel was created. By the end of the year all opposing Arab armies had been defeated, and Israel was a member of the United Nations.

ISRAEL AND PALESTINE

During the ensuing years many Palestinian Arabs left the Israeli territory for either the Palestinian area (the West Bank and the Gaza Strip) or for other lands. In 1964 the Palestinian Liberation Organization emerged, and guerilla movements such as Fatah began their activities. In the 1967 war the Israeli military decisively defeated all Arab forces arrayed against the nation and took control of the West Bank and Gaza Strip (also the Sinai, which returned to Egyptian hands after the Yom Kippur war of 1973). Jordan drove Palestinian guerrilla units out of its territory, and the Palestinians fled into Lebanon, with the result that Lebanon itself was convulsed by civil wars. Israelis continued to battle Palestinian guerrillas and terrorists based in the occupied territories and in Lebanon.

The archaeology of this land, then, is not just concerned with Biblical history but with all eras, from the Stone Age to the modern. At any given site archaeologists may find Chalcolithic, Middle Bronze, Iron I, Hellenistic, Byzantine, Crusader and/or Ottoman occupation levels, as well as artifacts from the countless invaders who had passed through. The progress of archaeology is, of course, seriously hindered by modern conflicts. The history of the promised land has long been written in blood.

A CHRONOLOGICAL HISTORY OF 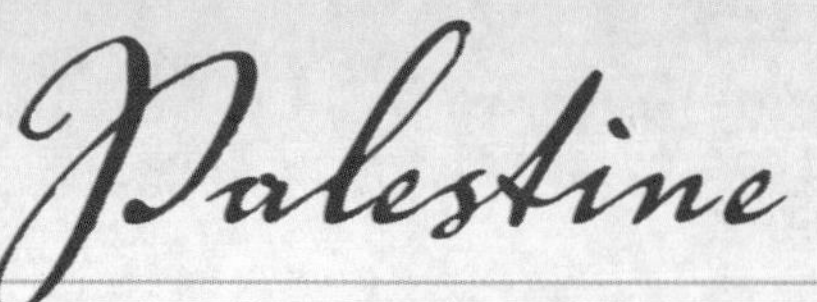

FROM JUDAH'S BABYLONIAN EXILE THROUGH ROMAN RULE

	Events	Persons
600 B.C.	Jerusalem destroyed by Nebuchadnezzar (587)	
	Cyrus's defeat by Media (549)	
	Babylon's fall to Cyrus II of Persia (539)	
	Darius I ruler of Persian Empire (522–486)	
		Haggai (520)
		Zechariah (520)
	Second temple in Jerusalem completed (515)	
500	Xerxes I's rule (486–464)	Esther
	Artaxerxes I's rule (464–423)	Nehemiah
		Malachi (450)
		Ezra (c. 400)
400	Samaritan schism: Samaritan temple built on Mount Gerizim	
	Alexander's conquering of Palestine (c. 330)	
	Control of Judah by Ptolemy I (Soter) (323–285)	
300	Translation of the Pentateuch into Greek under Ptolemy II (c. 250)	
	Capture of Jerusalem by Antiochus III (203)	
200	Palestine under Seleucid control (198)	
	Antiochus IV (Epiphanes) king of Syria (175–163)	
	Jerusalem made a Hellenistic city (172)	
	Antiochus IV forced by Rome to withdraw from Egypt (168)	
	Persecution of the Jews begun by Antiochus and "abomination that causes desolation" set up in temple (December, 168)	
	Maccabean Revolt (167)	
	Jews' defeat of Syria at Beth-Zur; rededication of temple (December, 164)	Mattathias (d. 166)
	Death of Antiochus IV (163)	Hasmonean
	Judas's siege of Syrian garrison in Jerusalem (163–162)	Judas Hasmonean
	Jonathan's succession to Judas (158–142)	(Maccabeus) (d. 161)
	Simon's succession to Jonathan (142–135)	Jonathan (d. c. 142)
	Jewish independence gained (142)	
	Judean independence recognized by Roman senate (139)	
	John Hyrcanus I's succession to Simon (135–105)	Simon (d. 135)
	Emergence of the Pharisees and Sadducees (135)	
	Destruction of the Samaritan temple on Mount Gerizim by John Hyrcanus (109–108)	
100	Civil war, Aristobulus II vs. Hyrcanus II in Judea (67–63)	

	Events	Persons
100 B.C. con't		
	Pompey the Great's conquering of Jerusalem (63)	
	Hyrcanus II installed as ruler (63)	
	Antipater procurator of Judea (47)	
	Herod governor of Galilee (47)	
	Herod crowned king of the Jews (40)	
	Invasion of Syria and Palestine by Parthians (40)	
	Parthians drive out; Herod's assumption of kingdom (37–34)	
	Rebuilding of temple begun by Herod (20)	
	Building of Caesarea completed by Herod (10)	
	Death of Herod the Great (4)	
	Archelaus, ethnarch of Judea, Samarian and Idumea (4 B.C.–A.D. 6)	
1 B.C.		
A.D. 1		
	Judea made a Roman imperial province	
	Jewish uprising (7)	
	Founding of Tiberias (18)	
	Pilate's arrival in Judea (26)	Pilate (26–36)
	Pilate dismissed as procurator of Judea (36)	
	Birth of Josephus (37)	Josephus (37–c. 95)
	Anti-Jewish riots in Alexandria (38)	
	Herod Antipas exiled (39)	
	Anti-Jewish riots in Antioch (40)	
	A group of Alexandrian Jews led by Philo to Caligula	
	Death of Herod Agrippa I (44)	
	Rise of the Zealots and Sicarii(?) (50–52)	
	Josephus's pleading of Jewish interests before Nero (64)	Paul (d. 64)
	Jewish revolt against Rome (66–70)	Peter (d. 64)
	Josephus's surrender to Vespasian (67)	
	Fall of Jerusalem (70)	
	Fall of Masada (73)	
	Josephus's completion of *Jewish War* (76–79)	
	Josephus's completion of *Antiquities* (93–94)	
	Synod of Jamnia (100?)	John (d. 100)
	Jewish revolt of Bar Kokhba (Cochba) (132–135)	
	Final Jewish revolt against Rome put down and Jerusalem made a Gentile city (135)	
	Martyrdom of Rabban (Rabbi) Akiba (135?)	

Adapted from *Chronological and Background Charts of the New Testament*, pp. 52–53

THE Old Testament

INTRODUCTION TO *Genesis*

AUTHOR, PLACE AND DATE OF WRITING

Genesis is, strictly speaking, an anonymous work. Historical tradition, however, as well as Biblical attestation, assigns authorship to Moses (see, e.g., Mk 12:26; Lk 24:27; Jn 1:45; Ro 10:5; 2Co 3:15). Moses' authorship would not have required him to write the entire book. In fact, all of the Genesis events took place long before Moses was born, indicating that he must have used sources. We might view Moses as an editor/historian who, in addition to receiving God's direct and supernatural communication, drew together details of the family histories of Abraham and his descendants, as they existed in the Israelite community in Egypt, into a single text.

Scholars who question Mosaic authorship of the Pentateuch (Ge–Dt) generally support one or another variant of the Documentary Hypothesis (see "The Documentary Hypothesis" on p. 15).

If Moses did indeed write/compile Genesis, he must have done so during the Israelites' exodus wandering period, probably between 1440 and 1400 B.C. (see "The Store Cities of Pithom and Rameses" on p. 86, "The Pharaoh of the Exodus" on p. 98, "The Date of the Exodus" on p. 106, "The Hyksos and the Old Testament" on p. 121 and "The Conquest of Canaan" on p. 310). Those scholars who suggest that the Pentateuch was written as a single work during the exile typically place the date of authorship at about 550 B.C.

AUDIENCE

Genesis records the stories of the creation, the fall into sin, the flood, the call of Abraham and the early history of the ancestors of Israel. The Genesis stories were probably circulated among the Israelites living in Egypt, reminding them of their familial and spiritual heritage and explaining their current situation. Genesis preserved individual stories (like those about Joseph) that could afford hope to God's enslaved people. Promises to Abraham about the future of his progeny (e.g., 15:1–7) also would have encouraged them. Later, Israelites directly involved in the exodus, as well as their succeeding generations, no doubt read Genesis in order to understand this piece of the great saga of their national origin. The fulfillment of God's historical promises to the patriarchs served as a testimony to his continuing faithfulness.

CULTURAL FACTS AND HIGHLIGHTS

Genesis records the birth and early history of humankind. Not only did God create the physical world, but he also formed man and woman in his own image and endowed them with the gift of free will. Over time changes took place, including humanity's fall into sin and the resultant great flood.

Tribes, cities and civilizations ebbed and flowed, rising and declining in a rhythm that has characterized human history ever since. Centuries passed, and at some point God chose to concentrate his particular attention on one individual from an ordinary, idol-worshiping family—who in his turn opted to listen and obey. From such unimpressive roots began the triumphant—if often temporarily tragic—saga of redemption history.

TIMELINE

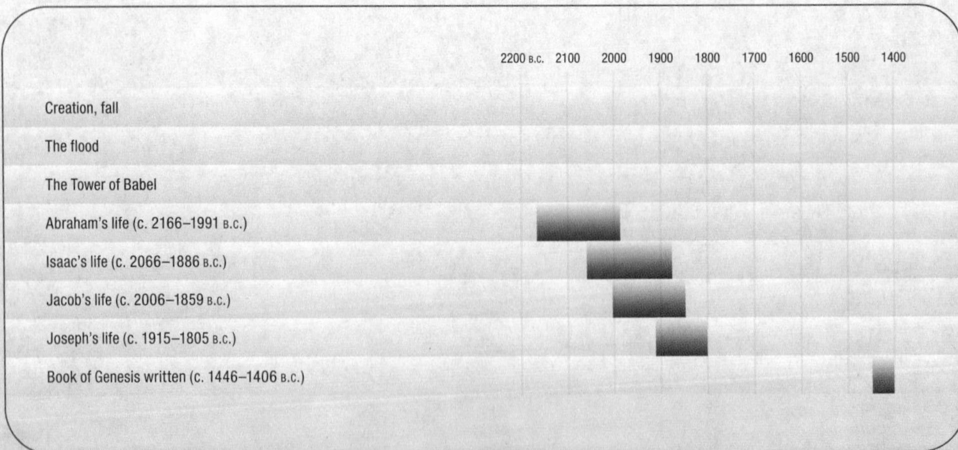

AS YOU READ

Note how quickly and irreversibly the human race turned its back on Eden and on perfect fellowship with God (chs. 2–3) and how God responded (chs. 4–8). Then, through the unlikely choice of a still-childless patriarch, God began to form the family from which the Israelite nation would spring (chs. 11–30; 49). Study the life of Joseph, from his years of slavery to his meteoric rise to power in a strange land to his revelation to his unsuspecting brothers (chs. 42–45). This book explains how and why the Israelites came to live in Egypt, setting the stage for what would happen to this special people in Exodus and beyond.

DID YOU KNOW?

- An individual in the ancient Near East could claim rights to a well on someone else's land (21:25–30).
- The bride price paid by a husband's family was to be held in trust to provide for the wife if she were to find herself abandoned or widowed (31:14–16).
- A man's seal, cord and staff were symbols of his individual and corporate identity—the ancient equivalent of an I.D. card or signature (38:17–18).
- Both the Egyptians and the Babylonians compiled "dream books," containing sample dreams with keys to their interpretation (40:8).
- The philosophy behind the Egyptian practice of embalming was a belief that the body was to be preserved as a repository for the soul after death (50:2–3).

THEMES

Genesis, the book of beginnings, includes the following themes:

1. *Creation.* God created the world "very good" (1:31). There was wholeness and harmony between God and humanity, among humans and between people and the rest of the created order.

2. *Sin.* Sin entered the world through one man, Adam (3:1–19; Ro 5:12). Unbelief, human conflict, sickness and environmental degradation are its results.

3. *The image of God.* All human beings are created in the image of God; each person *is* God's likeness as a personal, rational, creative, moral being. Men and women were created equal.

4. *God's global plan of redemption.* Although God chose to work through one ethnic group in the Old Testament, his divine intention was that all nations would come to know him through Abraham's descendants (12:1–3). Abraham was chosen because of his faith, making him the father of all who come to God on the same basis.

OUTLINE

- I. Primeval History: Four Great Events (1:1—11:26)
  - A. The Creation of the Universe; Adam and Eve (1–2)
  - B. The Fall and the Results of Sin (3–5)
  - C. The Flood (6–9)
  - D. The Scattering of the Nations (10:1—11:26)
- II. Patriarchal History: Four Great Characters (11:27—50:26)
  - A. Abraham (11:27—20:18)
  - B. Isaac (21–26)
  - C. Jacob (27:1—37:1)
  - D. Joseph (37:2—50:26)

ANCIENT VOICES

Noble god of the first occasion,
who built people and gave birth
to the gods,
original one who made it possible for
all to live;
in whose heart it was spoken, who saw
them evolve,
who foretold what was not and thought
of what is.

—FROM A RAMESSIDE STELA
(INSCRIBED STONE MONUMENT)

See "Ancient Creation Narratives" article.

The Beginning

1 In the beginning[a] God created the heavens and the earth.[b]
2Now the earth was[a] formless and empty,[c] darkness was over
the surface of the deep, and the Spirit of God[d] was hovering over the
waters.

3And God said,[e] "Let there be light," and there was light.[f] 4God saw
that the light was good, and he separated the light from the
darkness. 5God called the light "day," and the darkness he
called "night."[g] And there was evening, and there was morn-
ing—the first day.
6And God said, "Let there be an expanse[h] between the waters to sep-
arate water from water." 7So God made the expanse and sep-
arated the water under the expanse from the water above it.[i]
And it was so. 8God called the expanse "sky." And there was
evening, and there was morning—the second day.
9And God said, "Let the water under the sky be gathered to one place,[j] and let dry ground appear." And
it was so. 10God called the dry ground "land," and the gathered waters he called "seas." And God saw
that it was good.
11Then God said, "Let the land produce vegetation:[k] seed-bearing plants and trees on the land
that bear fruit with seed in it, according to their various kinds." And it was so. 12The land produced
vegetation: plants bearing seed according to their kinds and trees bearing fruit with seed in it ac-
cording to their kinds. And God saw that it was good. 13And there was evening, and there was
morning—the third day.
14And God said, "Let there be lights[l] in the expanse of the sky to separate the day from the night, and let
them serve as signs[m] to mark seasons[n] and days and years, 15and let them be lights in the expanse
of the sky to give light on the earth." And it was so. 16God made two great lights—the greater light
to govern[o] the day and the lesser light to govern[p] the night. He also made the stars.[q] 17God set
them in the expanse of the sky to give light on the earth, 18to govern the day and the night,[r] and
to separate light from darkness. And God saw that it was good. 19And there was evening, and there
was morning—the fourth day.
20And God said, "Let the water teem with living creatures, and let birds fly above the earth across the ex-
panse of the sky." 21So God created the great creatures of the sea and every living and moving thing
with which the water teems,[s] according to their kinds, and every winged bird according to its kind.
And God saw that it was good. 22God blessed them and said, "Be fruitful and increase in number
and fill the water in the seas, and let the birds increase on the earth."[t] 23And there was evening, and
there was morning—the fifth day.
24And God said, "Let the land produce living creatures according to their kinds: livestock, creatures that
move along the ground, and wild animals, each according to its kind." And it was so. 25God made

1:1 [a]Jn 1:1-2 [b]Job 38:4; Ps 90:2; Isa 42:5; 44:24; 45:12,18; Ac 17:24; Heb 11:3; Rev 4:11
1:2 [c]Jer 4:23 [d]Ps 104:30
1:3 [e]Ps 33:6,9; 148:5; Heb 11:3 [f]2Co 4:6*
1:5 [g]Ps 74:16
1:6 [h]Jer 10:12
1:7 [i]Job 38:8-11, 16; Ps 148:4
1:9 [j]Job 38:8-11; Ps 104:6-9; Pr 8:29; Jer 5:22; 2Pe 3:5
1:11 [k]Ps 65:9-13; 104:14
1:14 [l]Ps 74:16 [m]Jer 10:2 [n]Ps 104:19
1:16 [o]Ps 136:8 [p]Ps 136:9 [q]Job 38:7,31-32; Ps 8:3; Isa 40:26
1:18 [r]Jer 33:20, 25
1:21 [s]Ps 104:25-26
1:22 [t]ver 28; Ge 8:17

[a] 2 Or possibly *became*

1:1–31 The length of the creative days of Genesis 1 is not specified in the Bible. The Hebrew word for "day" may mean a period of light between two periods of darkness, a period of light together with the preceding period of darkness or a prolonged period of time. All three usages occur in the Bible. No one of them equates to exactly 24 hours, although the second one is near it. There is no indisputable indication as to which of the three is meant in Genesis 1. The Bible provides no specific statement as to how long ago matter was created, when the first day or creation began or when the sixth day ended.

1:1–2 Some scholars hold that there is a long gap between verses 1 and 2, during which God's perfect creation came into a period of chaos through a great catastrophe. Hebrew syntax, however, leaves no room for such a view.

1:5 In ancient times, when a king named something or someone, he was thereby claiming dominion or ownership over that possession or individual (see 17:5,15; 41:45; 2Ki 23:34; 24:17; Da 1:7).

1:12 There is much discussion about the question of "evolution" with relation to the creation, but the word *evolution* may be used in several different ways. If taken in the historical sense (the theory that everything now existing has come into its present condition as a result of natural development, all of it having proceeded by natural causes from one rudimentary beginning), such a theory is sharply contradicted by the divine facts revealed in Genesis 1–2. It is explicitly stated several times that plants and animals are to reproduce "according to their kinds." Moses nowhere stated how large a "kind" is, and there is no ground for equating it with any particular modern definition of "species." Yet Genesis teaches that there are a number (perhaps a large number) of "kinds" of plants and animals, which cannot reproduce in such a way as to evolve from one into another. Nothing in the Bible denies the possibility, however, of change and development within the limits of a particular "kind."

Moreover, the creation of Adam is sharply distinguished from other aspects of creation, and the creation of Eve is described as a distinct act of God. Genesis 2:7 (in the Hebrew) clearly teaches that Adam did not exist as an animate being before he was a man, created after the image of God.

1:21 The phrase "creatures of the sea" refers to the name of a dreaded sea monster in Canaanite mythology (see "The *Enuma Elish* and the Biblical Concept of Creation" on p. 888). Old Testament poetry often refers to him as one of God's most powerful opponents. In Genesis, however, the creatures of the sea are portrayed as part of God's good creation, all of which is to be appreciated.

1:25 [u]Jer 27:5
the wild animals[u] according to their kinds, the livestock according to their kinds, and all the creatures that move along the ground according to their kinds. And God saw that it was good.

1:26 [v]Ps 100:3 [w]Ge 9:6; Jas 3:9 [x]Ps 8:6-8
26 Then God said, "Let us[v] make man in our image,[w] in our likeness, and let them rule[x] over the fish of the sea and the birds of the air, over the livestock, over all the earth,[a] and over all the creatures that move along the ground."

1:27 [y]1Co 11:7 [z]Ge 5:2; Mt 19:4*; Mk 10:6*
27 So God created man in his own image,[y]
in the image of God he created him;
male and female[z] he created them.

[a] 26 Hebrew; Syriac *all the wild animals*

ANCIENT TEXTS AND ARTIFACTS

Ancient Creation Narratives

GENESIS 1 In contrast to the Biblical creation narratives, ancient creation stories from **Mesopotamia**,[1] Egypt and Syria-Palestine do far more than try to explain how the physical world came into being. Creation myths often elevated the particular god of a particular shrine to supremacy over all other gods in order to validate the prestige of that deity, that shrine or the city in which the shrine was located.

For example, Egyptian creation myths tend to assert that a primordial mound or "Island of Creation" arose from a primeval ocean and that a specific god created all things from that location. Several Egyptian shrines, however, claimed to be the site of that primordial mound and asserted that the god of their respective shrine was the great creator god.

At Memphis, it was Ptah. At Hermopolis, it was Thoth. At Heliopolis, it was Re-Atum. Here a sacred stone was said to mark the very spot where Re-Atum, in the form of a "Bennu" bird, alighted and initiated the creative process.

Common motifs in creation myths include a spontaneous generation of gods, sexual reproduction among gods and the deification of nature (e.g., of the sun and moon). A creation myth often focuses on geographic and other elements unique to the shrine associated with the myth. An Egyptian myth, for example, may pay special attention to the creation of the Nile.

Sometimes creation myths relate battles between gods and the monsters of a primeval, watery chaos, through which one or more deities rises to supremacy. Sometimes creation occurs when a god defeats a primeval monster and divides its body into two parts, which become heaven and earth or earth and sea, etc. The Babylonian creation myth *Enuma Elish* describes the god Marduk's defeat of Tiamat, the mother-goddess and sea monster.[2] After a terrible battle in which Marduk slays Tiamat, he cuts her body in half like "a fish for drying" and uses it to form the heavenly dome. This victory purportedly establishes Marduk's supremacy among the gods.

Greek creation myths are similar. After initial chaos, the primordial deities Gaia (earth-goddess) and Uranus (sky-god) emerge. A series of monster-like gods (such as Cronos, Typhon and the Titans) is born to them, but Zeus (son of Cronos) defeats these beings and establishes the present world order.

Humans in creation myths from various sources are typically created as drudges to perform the gods' "dirty work." Some myths depict humans as the gods' slaves, whose primary function it is to feed them with their sacrifices.[3]

The Genesis account implicitly challenges the claims of these ancient creation myths by affirming God's unity and sovereignty, by portraying the heavenly bodies and great sea creatures as his creations and by presenting humans as God's stewards—and indeed image bearers—rather than as an afterthought born of divine need or laziness.

The Genesis creation narrative refers to the sun and moon as the "great light" and the "small light." Why? By describing these celestial bodies in this way, the Bible reduces them to the status of mere physical objects that "rule" only in the sense that they emit light and demarcate the calendar. In contrast, in many ancient languages the words translated "sun" and "moon" also refer to the sun god(dess) or moon god(dess). For instance, the Hebrew word translated "sun" is *shemesh,* but *Shamash* is also the name of the Mesopotamian sun god. The Greek word translated "moon," *selene*, is also the proper name of a Greek moon goddess. Similarly, the ancients regarded the stars (or constellations) as divine beings. In contrast, the terse Biblical statement "He also made the stars" (Ge 1:16) demotes these bodies to the status of created objects.

The Genesis account rejects the central motif of pagan religion: the deification of nature. Interestingly, it does not seek to elevate Yahweh over other gods. Indeed, in the seven-day creation account (Ge 1:1—2:3) Yahweh is not named; the Creator is simply referred to as "God" (*Elohim*), a more generic term. Even Genesis 2–3 provides no sense that Yahweh needed to establish his supremacy over other deities. There is no conquest of other gods or monsters, and no shrine or city is said to be the place from which God began the creative process. No sacred object is mentioned. The God of Genesis 1 is indeed the universal God.

See also "Cosmology in the Ancient Near East" on page 1139.

[1]See Glossary on page 2080 for definitions of bolded words. [2]See "The *Enuma Elish* and the Biblical Concept of Creation" on page 888. [3]See "The Creation of Humans in the Sumerian Myth of Enki" on page 800.

28 God blessed them and said to them, "Be fruitful and increase in number; fill the earth[a] and 1:28 [a]Ge 9:1,7; Lev 26:9
subdue it. Rule over the fish of the sea and the birds of the air and over every living creature that
moves on the ground."
29 Then God said, "I give you every seed-bearing plant on the face of the whole earth and every
tree that has fruit with seed in it. They will be yours for food.[b] 30 And to all the beasts of the earth 1:29 [b]Ps 104:14
and all the birds of the air and all the creatures that move on the ground—everything that has the
breath of life in it—I give every green plant for food.[c]" And it was so. 1:30 [c]Ps 104:14, 27; 145:15
31 God saw all that he had made,[d] and it was very good.[e] And there was evening, and there was 1:31 [d]Ps 104:24 [e]1Ti 4:4
morning—the sixth day.

2 Thus the heavens and the earth were completed in all their vast array.

2 By the seventh day God had finished the work he had been doing; so on the seventh day he rested[a]
from all his work.[f] 3 And God blessed the seventh day and made it holy,[g] because on it he rested 2:2 [f]Ex 20:11; 31:17; Heb 4:4* 2:3 [g]Lev 23:3; Isa 58:13
from all the work of creating that he had done.

Adam and Eve

4 This is the account of the heavens and the earth when they were created.

[a] 2 Or *ceased*; also in verse 3

2:2–3 On the seventh day God ceased from his labors, later referring to this as an example for Israel to follow six days of labor with one of rest (Ex 20:11). No end to the rest of the seventh day is mentioned. As far as what the Bible tells us is concerned, God's rest from creating still continues.

2:4–25 While Genesis 1 describes the creation of the universe as a whole, 2:4–25 covers one special segment of that creation. The linking word (v. 4) is translated in the NIV as "account," but it means more—something like "subsequent/emergent account": The Hebrew *tôledôth,* both in its individual meaning and in its Old

The Location of Eden

GENESIS 2 The name Eden might have had one of two origins: the **Sumerian** word *eden*, which means "steppe" or "open field," or the identical Semitic word, denoting "luxury" or "delight." In Scripture, Eden is not only the name of the garden in which the first humans resided but also a metaphorical representation of the Garden of God (i.e., **Yahweh**'s dwelling place; Isa 51:3; Eze 28:12–15; 31:8–18).

Eden's precise location remains a mystery. Genesis 2:8 indicates that the Lord planted the garden "in the east, in Eden." This suggests a location east of Canaan. In addition, the Bible associates four rivers with Eden: the Pishon, the Gihon, the Tigris and the Euphrates (vv. 10–14).

The Tigris and Euphrates are undoubtedly the two **Mesopotamian** rivers that still bear those names today.[1] The Gihon (possibly Hebrew for "to gush") and Pishon (usually understood to be a form of the Semitic verb "to spring up") are more difficult to identify.

A spring named the Gihon waters Jerusalem, but this location does not match the description of its route through the land of Cush (v. 13). Many scholars identify the Gihon as the Nile, since Cush is sometimes associated with Nubia, south of Egypt. If this association is correct, it is all but impossible to make sense of the description of Eden's location, since this region nowhere converges with the Tigris and Euphrates.

Others identify Cush as the land of the Kassites, east of the Tigris, also known as Kush during ancient times. This theory makes better geographical sense. Finally, still other scholars posit that the Gihon and the Pishon were canals or tributaries of the Tigris and Euphrates.

Another challenge is determining the relationship of the four rivers to the single river that flowed through and watered Eden. Most scholars believe that they were downstream of the river of Eden, implying that all four rivers shared a common source and placing Eden in northern Mesopotamia or Armenia.

This supposition poses a problem, however, since the Tigris and Euphrates lack a common source. To suggest that the four rivers were upstream of the river of Eden makes some sense because these two rivers converge in southern Mesopotamia before emptying into the Persian Gulf. In this scenario Eden may still, as above, have been located in northern Mesopotamia or in the mountains in Armenia, from which the Tigris and Euphrates spring. Another possible setting would have been southern Mesopotamia, where they converge and end.

[1] See "The Tigris and Euphrates Rivers" on page 604.

When the LORD God made the earth and the heavens— 5and no shrub of the field had yet appeared
on the earth[a] and no plant of the field had yet sprung up,[h] for the LORD God had not sent rain on the
earth[a][i] and there was no man to work the ground, 6but streams[b] came up from the earth and watered
the whole surface of the ground— 7the LORD God formed the man[c] from the dust[j] of the ground[k] and
breathed into his nostrils the breath[l] of life,[m] and the man became a living being.[n]
8Now the LORD God had planted a garden in the east, in Eden;[o] and there he put the man he had
formed. 9And the LORD God made all kinds of trees grow out of the ground—trees that were pleasing to
the eye and good for food. In the middle of the garden were the tree of life[p] and the tree of the knowl-
edge of good and evil.[q]
10A river watering the garden flowed from Eden; from there it was separated into four headwaters.
11The name of the first is the Pishon; it winds through the entire land of Havilah, where there is gold.
12(The gold of that land is good; aromatic resin[d] and onyx are also there.) 13The name of the second riv-
er is the Gihon; it winds through the entire land of Cush.[e] 14The name of the third river is the Tigris;[r] it
runs along the east side of Asshur. And the fourth river is the Euphrates.
15The LORD God took the man and put him in the Garden of Eden to work it and take care of it. 16And
the LORD God commanded the man, "You are free to eat from any tree in the garden; 17but you must not
eat from the tree of the knowledge of good and evil, for when you eat of it you will surely die."[s]
18The LORD God said, "It is not good for the man to be alone. I will make a helper suitable for him."[t]
19Now the LORD God had formed out of the ground all the beasts of the field[u] and all the birds of the
air. He brought them to the man to see what he would name them; and whatever the man called each
living creature,[v] that was its name. 20So the man gave names to all the livestock, the birds of the air and
all the beasts of the field.
But for Adam[f] no suitable helper was found. 21So the LORD God caused the man to fall into a deep
sleep; and while he was sleeping, he took one of the man's ribs[g] and closed up the place with flesh. 22Then
the LORD God made a woman from the rib[h][w] he had taken out of the man, and he brought her to the man.
23The man said,

"This is now bone of my bones
and flesh of my flesh;[x]
she shall be called 'woman,[i]'
for she was taken out of man."

24For this reason a man will leave his father and mother and be united[y] to his wife, and they will become
one flesh.[z]
25The man and his wife were both naked,[a] and they felt no shame.

The Fall of Man

3 Now the serpent[b] was more crafty than any of the wild animals the LORD God had made. He said to
the woman, "Did God really say, 'You must not eat from any tree in the garden'?"
2The woman said to the serpent, "We may eat fruit from the trees in the garden, 3but God did say, 'You
must not eat fruit from the tree that is in the middle of the garden, and you must not touch it, or you will
die.' "
4"You will not surely die," the serpent said to the woman.[c] 5"For God knows that when you eat of it
your eyes will be opened, and you will be like God,[d] knowing good and evil."

2:5 [h]Ge 1:11 [i]Ps 65:9-10 **2:7** [j]Ge 3:19 [k]Ps 103:14 [l]Job 33:4 [m]Ac 17:25 [n]1Co 15:45* **2:8** [o]Ge 3:23,24; Isa 51:3 **2:9** [p]Ge 3:22,24; Rev 2:7; 22:2,14, 19 [q]Eze 47:12 **2:14** [r]Da 10:4 **2:17** [s]Dt 30:15, 19; Ro 5:12; 6:23; Jas 1:15 **2:18** [t]1Co 11:9 **2:19** [u]Ps 8:7 [v]Ge 1:24 **2:22** [w]1Co 11:8, 9,12 **2:23** [x]Ge 29:14; Eph 5:28-30 **2:24** [y]Mal 2:15 [z]Mt 19:5*; Mk 10:7-8*; 1Co 6:16*; Eph 5:31* **2:25** [a]Ge 3:7,10-11 **3:1** [b]2Co 11:3; Rev 12:9; 20:2 **3:4** [c]Jn 8:44; 2Co 11:3 **3:5** [d]Isa 14:14; Eze 28:2

[a] 5 Or *land*; also in verse 6 [b] 6 Or *mist* [c] 7 The Hebrew for *man (adam)* sounds like and may be related to the Hebrew for *ground (adamah)*; it is also the name *Adam* (see Gen. 2:20). [d] 12 Or *good; pearls* [e] 13 Possibly southeast Mesopotamia [f] 20 Or *the man* [g] 21 Or *took part of the man's side* [h] 22 Or *part* [i] 23 The Hebrew for *woman* sounds like the Hebrew for *man.*

Testament use, tells how something emerges from what has preceded. Genesis 2:4, then, steps back into Genesis 1 to begin the study of what happened next, how out of God's creative work there came the beginnings of human life and creation on Earth. This explains the often-alleged differences and supposed contradictions between the chapters. It is reasonable that chapter 2 gives a more detailed account of the creation of man while saying nothing about that of matter, light, heavenly bodies, plants and other animals. See "The Documentary Hypothesis" on page 15.

2:8 At the site of Eridu, situated near what was considered to be an ancient shoreline at the head of the Persian Gulf, clay tablets have been found that tell of a garden in the neighborhood in which grew a sacred palm tree. Further upstream, a short distance north of ancient Babylon, the Tigris and Euphrates flow close together so that canals connect them. Some consider this area to be the location of ancient Eden. See "The Location of Eden" on page 6.

2:9 Adam and Eve possessed from God's hand both life and moral discernment. While ancient pagans believed that the gods intended for human beings to remain mortal, Adam and Eve's access to the tree of life revealed that God's will and intention for them was life. See "The Tree of Life in Jewish Imagery" on page 2075.

2:18–22 This is the only full account of the creation of woman in all of ancient Near Eastern literature.

[6]When the woman saw that the fruit of the tree was good for food and pleasing to the eye, and also
desirable[e] for gaining wisdom, she took some and ate it. She also gave some to her husband, who was with
her, and he ate it.[f] [7]Then the eyes of both of them were opened, and they realized they were naked; so they
sewed fig leaves together and made coverings for themselves.

[8]Then the man and his wife heard the sound of the LORD God as he was walking[g] in the garden in the
cool of the day, and they hid[h] from the LORD God among the trees of the garden. [9]But the LORD God called
to the man, "Where are you?"

[10]He answered, "I heard you in the garden, and I was afraid because I was naked; so I hid."

[11]And he said, "Who told you that you were naked? Have you eaten from the tree that I commanded
you not to eat from?"

[12]The man said, "The woman you put here with me—she gave me some fruit from the tree, and I
ate it."

[13]Then the LORD God said to the woman, "What is this you have done?"

The woman said, "The serpent deceived me,[i] and I ate."

[14]So the LORD God said to the serpent, "Because you have done this,

"Cursed[j] are you above all the livestock
and all the wild animals!
You will crawl on your belly
and you will eat dust[k]
all the days of your life.
[15]And I will put enmity
between you and the woman,

3:6 [e]Jas 1:14-15; 1Jn 2:16 [f]1Ti 2:14
3:8 [g]Dt 23:14 [h]Job 31:33; Ps 139:7-12; Jer 23:24
3:13 [i]2Co 11:3; 1Ti 2:14
3:14 [j]Dt 28:15-20
3:14 [k]Isa 65:25; Mic 7:17

ANCIENT TEXTS AND ARTIFACTS

The Serpent Motif in Other Ancient Near Eastern Literature

GENESIS 3 Throughout most of the ancient Near East, people revered and often worshiped serpents as symbols of royalty, wisdom, healing,[1] fertility, death and other forces, both harmful and beneficent. However, in ancient writings serpents and serpentine creatures played their most prominent roles as adversaries of both humans and gods:[2]

✣ In the Egyptian Myth of Osiris[3] the sun god Ra (sometimes spelled Re) has to contend with Apophis, a demon serpent who attempts each morning to overthrow Ra and thereby enfold the world in darkness. Consequently, Egyptian texts liken the pharaoh's enemies to Apophis, thus calling down curses upon their heads.

✣ The snake of the **Sumerian** Epic of Gilgamesh is somewhat reminiscent of the serpent in Genesis 3 in that it deprives the hero, Gilgamesh, of immortality. While Gilgamesh is bathing in a pond, a serpent robs him of the Plant of Rejuvenation which, if eaten, would have granted him eternal life. The serpent devours the plant and is rejuvenated as it sheds its old skin. Gilgamesh, however, is consigned to die as a mortal.[4]

✣ Serpents similarly oppose humans and gods in other **Mesopotamian** stories, such as the Etana Myth, *Enuma Elish* and Inanna and the Huluppu Tree.[5]

✣ In **Ugarit**'s Baal-Anat Cycle, Baal and his consort, Anat,[6] defeat the seven-headed "twisting serpent," Lotan. The word *Lotan* is related to *Leviathan* (crushed by God at the time of creation [see Ps 74:14] but prophesied to reassert itself temporarily during the end times [Isa 27:1]). See a discussion of God's dealings with a similar monster, Rahab, in Job 9:13, 26:12, Psalm 89:10 and Isaiah 51:9.

✣ The serpent of Genesis 3 plays an adversarial role, as do those in other ancient Near Eastern literature, but it is introduced simply as one of the creatures "the LORD God had made" (v. 1). God the Creator is omnipotent; his purposes cannot be thwarted by any creature. Although the serpent or sea monster motif in the Bible reflects the fact that Biblical writers incorporated well-known images from the ancient world into their writings, other Biblical material clearly demonstrates that these inspired authors did not accept the mythology behind the Mesopotamian or Egyptian stories.

[1]See "Ugaritic Liturgy Against Venomous Snakes" on page 226. [2]See "The Hittite Storm Gods" on page 784. [3]See "The Mystery Religions" on page 1939. [4]See "Ancient Flood Narratives" on page 13 and "Ecclesiastes and the Epic of Gilgamesh" on page 1027. [5]See "The *Enuma Elish* and the Biblical Concept of Creation" on page 888. [6]See "The Queen of Heaven" on page 1267.

and between your offspring[a][l] and hers;[m]
he will crush[b] your head,[n]
and you will strike his heel."

16 To the woman he said,

"I will greatly increase your pains in childbearing;
with pain you will give birth to children.
Your desire will be for your husband,
and he will rule over you.[o]"

17 To Adam he said, "Because you listened to your wife and ate from the tree about which I command-
ed you, 'You must not eat of it,'

"Cursed[p] is the ground because of you;
through painful toil you will eat of it
all the days of your life.[q]
18 It will produce thorns and thistles for you,
and you will eat the plants of the field.[r]
19 By the sweat of your brow
you will eat your food[s]
until you return to the ground,
since from it you were taken;
for dust you are
and to dust you will return."[t]

20 Adam[c] named his wife Eve,[d] because she would become the mother of all the living.
21 The LORD God made garments of skin for Adam and his wife and clothed them. 22 And the LORD God
said, "The man has now become like one of us, knowing good and evil. He must not be allowed to reach
out his hand and take also from the tree of life[u] and eat, and live forever." 23 So the LORD God banished him
from the Garden of Eden[v] to work the ground[w] from which he had been taken. 24 After he drove the man
out, he placed on the east side[e] of the Garden of Eden cherubim[x] and a flaming sword[y] flashing back and
forth to guard the way to the tree of life.[z]

Cain and Abel

4 Adam[c] lay with his wife Eve, and she became pregnant and gave birth to Cain.[f] She said, "With the
help of the LORD I have brought forth[g] a man." 2 Later she gave birth to his brother Abel.[a]
Now Abel kept flocks, and Cain worked the soil. 3 In the course of time Cain brought some of the fruits
of the soil as an offering to the LORD.[b] 4 But Abel brought fat portions[c] from some of the firstborn of his
flock.[d] The LORD looked with favor on Abel and his offering,[e] 5 but on Cain and his offering he did not look
with favor. So Cain was very angry, and his face was downcast.
6 Then the LORD said to Cain, "Why are you angry? Why is your face downcast? 7 If you do what is right,

3:15 [l]Jn 8:44; Ac 13:10; 1Jn 3:8 [m]Isa 7:14; Mt 1:23; Rev 12:17 [n]Ro 16:20; Heb 2:14
3:16 [o]1Co 11:3; Eph 5:22
3:17 [p]Ge 5:29; Ro 8:20-22 [q]Job 5:7; 14:1; Ecc 2:23
3:18 [r]Ps 104:14
3:19 [s]2Th 3:10 [t]Ge 2:7; Ps 90:3; 104:29; Ecc 12:7
3:22 [u]Rev 22:14
3:23 [v]Ge 2:8 [w]Ge 4:2
3:24 [x]Ex 25:18-22 [y]Ps 104:4 [z]Ge 2:9
4:2 [a]Lk 11:51
4:3 [b]Nu 18:12
4:4 [c]Lev 3:16 [d]Ex 13:2,12 [e]Heb 11:4

[a] *15* Or *seed* [b] *15* Or *strike* [c] *20,1* Or *The man* [d] *20* *Eve* probably means *living.* [e] *24* Or *placed in front* [f] *1* *Cain* sounds like the Hebrew for *brought forth* or *acquired.* [g] *1* Or *have acquired*

3:20 When God named what he had made, he described for man the essence of each thing (1:5,8,10; 2:11–14). By allowing Adam to assign names, God enabled him to express his relationships to his fellow creatures: Adam named the animals (2:19–20) and the woman (2:23). Eve's personal name stems from her function as mother of all "living" (human) beings (3:20).

In Hebrew *adam* is both a personal name and a general noun, standing for "mankind" or "humankind." The latter meaning is found over 500 times in the Old Testament. Both usages occur in Genesis 1–3, where Adam as a personal name appears at 2:20 (cf. 3:17,21; 4:25; 5:2–5; 1Ch 1:1).

3:24 This description of the cherubim is similar to that of the winged sphinxes that adorned the armrests of royal thrones in many parts of the ancient Near East, as well as of the statues of winged, human-headed bulls or lions that guarded the entrances to palaces and temples in ancient Mesopotamia (see "Angels and Guardian Spirits in the Bible and the Ancient Near East" on p. 1529).

4:4–5 The origin of sacrifice is a matter of dispute. The question is, Did sacrifice arise from the natural religious instinct of humankind, whether or not guided by the Spirit of God, or did it originate in a distinct divine appointment? Genesis records the first sacrifice, by Cain and Abel, but gives no account of the origin of the practice. The custom was clearly approved by God, and in the Mosaic Law it was adopted and elaborately developed. The view that the rite was initiated by an expressed command of God is based primarily on Genesis 4:4–5, which states that Abel offered God an acceptable sacrifice, as well as on Hebrews 11:4, which clarifies that Abel's sacrifice was acceptable to God because of his faith. It is argued that Abel's faith was based upon a specific command of God in the past, without which the sacrifice would have been a response to mere superstition.

4:7 The Hebrew word translated "crouching" is the same as an ancient Babylonian word used to describe a demon lurking behind a door, threatening the people inside. On the other hand, the term can simply mean to lie down.

Sumer

GENESIS 4 To the Israelites of Biblical times Sumer was an ancient, classical civilization, similar to what ancient Rome is to us. **Sumer** (Biblical Shinar) refers to that region of **Mesopotamia** ("Map 14" in the back of this Bible), south of modern Baghdad that enormously influenced the Biblical world. The term *Sumerian* applies to people who lived there from the mid-fourth millennium B.C. (and possibly much earlier). Their principle cities were **Uruk** (Biblical Erech), Agade (Biblical Accad), Ur, Nippur, Kish, Lagash, Isin and Larsa. Sumerian civilization and culture came to an end around 1750 B.C. The Sumerians' racial identity and origin are unknown, but they were not Semites (they did not belong to the racial group that included Israelites, Canaanites, **Assyrians**, Arameans and Arabs).

The Sumerians created the world's earliest writing system, **cuneiform**, a method also used with another ancient language, **Akkadian**. Sumerian cuneiform was in fact the basis for the creation of Akkadian cuneiform.[1] Cuneiform appears on about 250,000 known tablets dating from approximately 3200 B.C. to the first century A.D.[2]

Deciphering Sumerian has proven difficult because this language was linguistically isolated. Whereas English and German are related (an English speaker might guess that the German *apfel* means "apple"), there is no language related to Sumerian that helps to elucidate the meanings of its words. However, bilingual tablets containing both Akkadian and Sumerian have enabled scholars to gain a working knowledge of Sumerian.

Sumerians contributed in numerous other significant ways to other ancient Near Eastern cultures. They invented the wheel, the potter's wheel and the sexagesimal numbering system (based on the number 60) and compiled collections of laws. In architecture they developed the arch, dome and vault. Incredibly, 100-foot-tall (30.5 m) Sumerian ziggurats—pyramidal, multistoried temple towers—still survive. Their form seems similar to the structure described in the Tower of Babel narrative of Genesis 11, but a direct connection has not been established.

Sumerian mythology also strongly influenced ancient Near Eastern religion, including worship of the sun, moon, stars and several "dying gods," like Dumuzi (also called Tammuz).[3] Sumerian literature includes hymns,[4] proverbs, love poems, laments and epic myths,[5] and there are interesting Biblical parallels in these Sumerian texts.

[1]See "Languages of the Old Testament World" on page 672. [2]See "Cuneiform and Clay Tablets in the Ancient Near East" on page 1108. [3]See "Mourning for Tammuz" on page 1320. [4]See "Sexuality and Religion in the Sumerian Hymns to Ishtar" on page 1340. [5]See "The Sumerian *Eridu Genesis*" on page 576, "The Creation of Humans in the Sumerian Myth of Enki" on page 800 and "The Exaltation of a Holy City in the Psalms and in the Myths" on page 917.

Board game played at Ur, c. 2600 B.C.
Preserving Bible Times; © Dr. James C. Martin; permission of The British Museum

He-goat caught in thicket from Sumerian Ur
Preserving Bible Times; © Dr. James C. Martin; permission of The British Museum

4:7 [f]Nu 32:23 [g]Ro 6:16 will you not be accepted? But if you do not do what is right, sin is crouching at your door;[f] it desires to
have you, but you must master it.[g]"
8 Now Cain said to his brother Abel, "Let's go out to the field."[a] And while they were in the field, Cain
4:8 [h]Mt 23:35; 1Jn 3:12 attacked his brother Abel and killed him.[h]
9 Then the LORD said to Cain, "Where is your brother Abel?"
"I don't know," he replied. "Am I my brother's keeper?"
4:10 [i]Ge 9:5; Nu 35:33; Heb 12:24; Rev 6:9-10 10 The LORD said, "What have you done? Listen! Your brother's blood cries out to me from the ground.[i]
11 Now you are under a curse and driven from the ground, which opened its mouth to receive your broth-
er's blood from your hand. 12 When you work the ground, it will no longer yield its crops for you. You will
be a restless wanderer on the earth."
13 Cain said to the LORD, "My punishment is more than I can bear. 14 Today you are driving me from the
4:14 [j]2Ki 17:18; Ps 51:11; 139:7-12; Jer 7:15; 52:3 [k]Ge 9:6; Nu 35:19,21,27,33 land, and I will be hidden from your presence;[j] I will be a restless wanderer on the earth, and whoever
finds me will kill me."[k]
15 But the LORD said to him, "Not so[b]; if anyone kills Cain[l], he will suffer vengeance seven times over.[m]"
4:15 [l]Eze 9:4,6 [m]ver 24; Ps 79:12 Then the LORD put a mark on Cain so that no one who found him would kill him. 16 So Cain went out
4:16 [n]Ge 2:8 from the LORD's presence and lived in the land of Nod,[c] east of Eden.[n]
17 Cain lay with his wife, and she became pregnant and gave birth to Enoch. Cain was then building a
4:17 [o]Ps 49:11 city, and he named it after his son[o] Enoch. 18 To Enoch was born Irad, and Irad was the father of Mehu-
jael, and Mehujael was the father of Methushael, and Methushael was the father of Lamech.
19 Lamech married two women, one named Adah and the other Zillah. 20 Adah gave birth to Jabal; he
was the father of those who live in tents and raise livestock. 21 His brother's name was Jubal; he was the
father of all who play the harp and flute. 22 Zillah also had a son, Tubal-Cain, who forged all kinds of tools
out of[d] bronze and iron. Tubal-Cain's sister was Naamah.
23 Lamech said to his wives,

"Adah and Zillah, listen to me;
wives of Lamech, hear my words.
4:23 [p]Ex 20:13; Lev 19:18 I have killed[e][p] a man for wounding me,
a young man for injuring me.
4:24 [q]Dt 32:35 [r]ver 15 24 If Cain is avenged[q] seven times,[r]
then Lamech seventy-seven times."

4:25 [s]Ge 5:3 [t]ver 8 25 Adam lay with his wife again, and she gave birth to a son and named him Seth,[f][s] saying, "God has
granted me another child in place of Abel, since Cain killed him."[t] 26 Seth also had a son, and he named
him Enosh.
4:26 [u]Ge 12:8; 1Ki 18:24; Ps 116:17; Joel 2:32; Zep 3:9; Ac 2:21; 1Co 1:2 At that time men began to call on[g] the name of the LORD.[u]

From Adam to Noah

5 This is the written account of Adam's line.

5:1 [v]Ge 1:27; Eph 4:24; Col 3:10 When God created man, he made him in the likeness of God.[v] 2 He created them male and female[w] and
5:2 [w]Ge 1:27; Mt 19:4; Mk 10:6; Gal 3:28 blessed them. And when they were created, he called them "man.[h]"
3 When Adam had lived 130 years, he had a son in his own likeness, in his own image;[x] and he named
5:3 [x]Ge 1:26; 1Co 15:49 him Seth. 4 After Seth was born, Adam lived 800 years and had other sons and daughters. 5 Altogether,
5:5 [y]Ge 3:19 Adam lived 930 years, and then he died.[y]
6 When Seth had lived 105 years, he became the father[i] of Enosh. 7 And after he became the father of

[a] 8 Samaritan Pentateuch, Septuagint, Vulgate and Syriac; Masoretic Text does not have *"Let's go out to the field."*
[b] 15 Septuagint, Vulgate and Syriac; Hebrew *Very well* [c] 16 *Nod* means *wandering* (see verses 12 and 14). [d] 22 Or *who instructed all who work in* [e] 23 Or *I will kill* [f] 25 *Seth* probably means *granted.* [g] 26 Or *to proclaim* [h] 2 Hebrew *adam*
[i] 6 *Father* may mean *ancestor*; also in verses 7-26.

4:21–22 It is difficult to date the beginnings of art. If some human being found pleasure in the shape of a stone axe or flint sickle, this might be described as an awakening of aesthetic sensitivity. For many reasons it seems reasonable to date the beginnings of art in historical cultures to some point during the mid-fourth millennium. The origin of the arts may be intended in verses 21–22, where Jubal and Tubal-Cain are mentioned.

5:5 It is uncertain whether the large numbers describing human longevity in the early chapters of Genesis are literal, serve a literary function, or both. The fact that there are exactly ten names in the list (as in the genealogy of 11:10–26) indicates that it almost certainly contains gaps, the lengths of which are summarized in the large numbers. Other ancient genealogies outside the Bible exhibit similarly unrealistic figures and also contain exactly ten names (see "The Sumerian King List" on p. 12).

Enosh, Seth lived 807 years and had other sons and daughters. [8]Altogether, Seth lived 912 years, and then
he died.
[9]When Enosh had lived 90 years, he became the father of Kenan. [10]And after he became the father of
Kenan, Enosh lived 815 years and had other sons and daughters. [11]Altogether, Enosh lived 905 years, and
then he died.
[12]When Kenan had lived 70 years, he became the father of Mahalalel. [13]And after he became the fa-
ther of Mahalalel, Kenan lived 840 years and had other sons and daughters. [14]Altogether, Kenan lived
910 years, and then he died.
[15]When Mahalalel had lived 65 years, he became the father of Jared. [16]And after he became the father
of Jared, Mahalalel lived 830 years and had other sons and daughters. [17]Altogether, Mahalalel lived 895
years, and then he died.
[18]When Jared had lived 162 years, he became the father of Enoch.[z] [19]And after he became the father **5:18** [z]Jude 1:14
of Enoch, Jared lived 800 years and had other sons and daughters. [20]Altogether, Jared lived 962 years,
and then he died.
[21]When Enoch had lived 65 years, he became the father of Methuselah. [22]And after he became the fa-
ther of Methuselah, Enoch walked with God[a] 300 years and had other sons and daughters. [23]Altogether, **5:22** [a]ver 24;
Enoch lived 365 years. [24]Enoch walked with God;[b] then he was no more, because God took him away.[c] Ge 6:9; 17:1; 48:15; Mic 6:8;
[25]When Methuselah had lived 187 years, he became the father of Lamech. [26]And after he became the Mal 2:6 **5:24** [b]ver 22
father of Lamech, Methuselah lived 782 years and had other sons and daughters. [27]Altogether, Methuse- [c]2Ki 2:1,11;
lah lived 969 years, and then he died. Heb 11:5
[28]When Lamech had lived 182 years, he had a son. [29]He named him Noah[a] and said, "He will comfort
us in the labor and painful toil of our hands caused by the ground the LORD has cursed.[d]" [30]After Noah **5:29** [d]Ge 3:17;
was born, Lamech lived 595 years and had other sons and daughters. [31]Altogether, Lamech lived 777 Ro 8:20
years, and then he died.
[32]After Noah was 500 years old, he became the father of Shem, Ham and Japheth.

[a] 29 *Noah* sounds like the Hebrew for *comfort.*

5:24 Abram would later walk "before" God (17:1), but of Enoch and Noah alone it is written that they walked "*with* God" (5:24; 6:9; emphasis added). Walking with God is a relic of the first Paradise when people walked and talked with God in holy familiarity, and it anticipates a new paradise (Rev 21:3; 22:3–40).

ANCIENT TEXTS AND ARTIFACTS

The Sumerian King List

The Ur-Isin King List; Babylonia, c. 1812 B.C.

© The Schøyen Collection; photography courtesy of Mr. Martin Schøyen

GENESIS 5 The Sumerian King List, an ancient record of the kings of **Sumer** and **Akkad**, was originally composed in the late third millennium B.C. during the reign of Utu-hegal of **Uruk** ("Map 1" in the back of this Bible), in order to legitimize the ruling dynasty. It displays striking similarities to the genealogies of Genesis.

The preamble begins with intriguing terminology: "when kingship was lowered from heaven." It goes on to list the succession of kings, the lengths of their reigns and the respective cities from which they ruled. The kings are recorded to have enjoyed extraordinarily long reigns. For example, "En-men-lu-Anna ruled 43,200 years; En-men-gal-Anna ruled 28,800 years." A great flood is then purported to have covered the land, after which kings were recorded as having significantly shorter reigns, though still of incredible duration (140 to 1,200 years). The genealogies in Genesis are also divided into pre- and post-flood periods, with longer life spans prior to the catastrophic deluge of Genesis 5 and significantly lesser longevity after it (ch. 11). Unlike the King List, however, the early Genesis genealogies do not serve to legitimate later kings.

The Flood

6:1 eGe 1:28 6 When men began to increase in number on the earth[e] and daughters were born to them, [2]the sons of
God saw that the daughters of men were beautiful, and they married any of them they chose. [3]Then
6:3 fIsa 57:16 gPs 78:39 the LORD said, "My Spirit will not contend with[a] man forever,[f] for he is mortal[b];[g] his days will be a hundred
and twenty years."
6:4 hNu 13:33 [4]The Nephilim[h] were on the earth in those days—and also afterward—when the sons of God went
to the daughters of men and had children by them. They were the heroes of old, men of renown.

[a] 3 Or *My spirit will not remain in* [b] 3 Or *corrupt*

ANCIENT TEXTS AND ARTIFACTS

Ancient Flood Narratives

GENESIS 6 The traditions of ancient peoples throughout the world share in common the inclusion of flood stories. The **Mesopotamian** accounts have garnered the most discussion since they are culturally closer to the Biblical material than any of the other non-Scriptural narratives. The most famous Mesopotamian flood account is the Babylonian version, found in the library of the **Assyrian** king Ashurbanipal (seventh century B.C.) as part of the larger Epic of Gilgamesh.[1]

In this epic, Gilgamesh searches for a man named Utnapishtum (the equivalent of the Biblical Noah), whose story is then recounted. When one of the highest gods, Enlil, becomes annoyed by the cacophony of noise coming from human beings, he decides to inundate and destroy them all in a catastrophic deluge. Enki, the god of waters, reveals Enlil's intent to the mortal Utnapishtum, directing him to construct an enormous boat and load it with pairs of animals. Instructed not to reveal the reason for this mystifying building project, Utnapishtum is further commanded at a critical point to take his wife on board with him. For seven harried days and nights Utnapishtum and his wife are tossed about in this vessel as floodwaters engulf the earth. When the waters finally subside, the boat lodges atop a tall mountain. Utnapishtum sends out a dove, a swallow and a raven, the last of which fails to return, apparently having located nourishment. The man then disembarks and offers lavish sacrifices to the gods, who in turn bestow eternal life upon him and his wife for having safeguarded the future of humans and animals.

An **Akkadian** account dating to around 1600 B.C. recounts basically the same tale as that embedded in the Babylonian Epic of Gilgamesh, except that the Noah-character is named Atra-hasis.[2] An even earlier **Sumerian** version, known as the *Eridu Genesis,* contains the stories of creation and the development of the first cities, along with an account of the great flood. Here the hero is Ziusudra.[3]

Sumerian flood story; Babylonia, 19th–18th centuries B.C.

© The Schøyen Collection; photography courtesy of Mr. Martin Schøyen

Bible readers will immediately recognize the similarities between the Mesopotamian and Biblical accounts. But there are significant differences, too. According to the Bible God was not simply irritated by the din of humanity; he was profoundly grieved, to the point that "his heart was filled with pain" by the magnitude of human sin (6:5–7). Nor was his plan thwarted by the cunning of another deity; God himself chose to preserve both humanity and animal life through Noah (vv. 13–22). Genesis also attests to a longer flood period and, although God made a covenant with Noah, he did not grant him immortality.

Assuming a later date for the Biblical composition, some scholars have suggested that Mesopotamian accounts may have served as a prototype for the narrative in Genesis. But most researchers believe that the Biblical account is not simply a modification of the Mesopotamian stories but one of several versions of a common story. The differences can be attributed to the special revelation God gave the Biblical authors, including the writer of Genesis, by which he made known his plan of redemption. The other versions provide extrabiblical confirmation of the story of a great flood rather than demonstrating, as some have suggested, that the Biblical account is a myth.

[1]See also "The Serpent Motif in Other Ancient Near Eastern Literature" on page 8 and "Ecclesiastes and the Epic of Gilgamesh" on page 1027. [2]See "Humanity and the Divine: Comparing the Bible to the Myth of Atra-Hasis" on page 1176. [3]See "The Sumerian *Eridu Genesis*" on page 576.

ANCIENT VOICES

When the seventh day arrived,
I released a dove to go free,
The dove went and returned,
No landing place came into view,
it turned back.
I released a swallow to go free,
The swallow went and returned,
No landing place came to view,
it turned back.
I sent a raven to go free,
The raven went forth, saw the ebbing
of the waters,
It ate, circled, left droppings, did not
turn back.

—GILGAMESH

See "Ancient Flood Narratives" article on previous page.

5The LORD saw how great man's wickedness on the earth had become, and that every inclination of the thoughts of his heart was only evil all the time.[i] 6The LORD was grieved[j] that he had made man on the earth, and his heart was filled with pain. 7So the LORD said, "I will wipe mankind, whom I have created, from the face of the earth—men and animals, and creatures that move along the ground, and birds of the air—for I am grieved that I have made them." 8But Noah found favor in the eyes of the LORD.[k]

9This is the account of Noah.

Noah was a righteous man, blameless among the people of his time,[l] and he walked with God.[m] 10Noah had three sons: Shem, Ham and Japheth.[n]

11Now the earth was corrupt in God's sight and was full of violence.[o] 12God saw how corrupt the earth had become, for all the people on earth had corrupted their ways.[p] 13So God said to Noah, "I am going to put an end to all people, for the earth is filled with violence because of them. I am surely going to destroy both them and the earth.[q] 14So make yourself an ark of cypress[a] wood;[r] make rooms in it and coat it with pitch[s] inside and out. 15This is how you are to build it: The ark is to be 450 feet long, 75 feet wide and 45 feet high.[b] 16Make a roof for it and finish[c] the ark to within 18 inches[d] of the top. Put a door in the side of the ark and make lower, middle and upper decks. 17I am going to bring floodwaters on the earth to destroy all life under the heavens, every creature that has the breath of life in it. Everything on earth will perish.[t] 18But I will establish my covenant with you,[u] and you will enter the ark[v]—you and your sons and your wife and your sons' wives with you. 19You are to bring into the ark two of all living creatures, male and female, to keep them alive with you. 20Two[w] of every kind of bird, of every kind of animal and of every kind of creature that moves along the ground will come to you to be kept alive. 21You are to take every kind of food that is to be eaten and store it away as food for you and for them."

22Noah did everything just as God commanded him.[x]

7 The LORD then said to Noah, "Go into the ark, you and your whole family,[y] because I have found you righteous[z] in this generation. 2Take with you seven[e] of every kind of clean[a] animal, a male and its mate, and two of every kind of unclean animal, a male and its mate, 3and also seven of every kind of bird, male and female, to keep their various kinds alive throughout the earth. 4Seven days from now I will send rain on the earth for forty days and forty nights, and I will wipe from the face of the earth every living creature I have made."

5And Noah did all that the LORD commanded him.[b]

6Noah was six hundred years old when the floodwaters came on the earth. 7And Noah and his sons and his wife and his sons' wives entered the ark to escape the waters of the flood. 8Pairs of clean and unclean animals, of birds and of all creatures that move along the ground, 9male and female, came to Noah and entered the ark, as God had commanded Noah. 10And after the seven days the floodwaters came on the earth.

11In the six hundredth year of Noah's life, on the seventeenth day of the second month—on that day all the springs of the great deep[c] burst forth, and the floodgates of the heavens[d] were opened. 12And rain fell on the earth forty days and forty nights.[e]

13On that very day Noah and his sons, Shem, Ham and Japheth, together with his wife and the wives of his three sons, entered the ark. 14They had with them every wild animal according to its kind, all live-

6:5 [i]Ge 8:21; Ps 14:1-3
6:6 [j]1Sa 15:11, 35; Isa 63:10
6:8 [k]Ge 19:19; Ex 33:12,13,17; Lk 1:30; Ac 7:46
6:9 [l]Ge 7:1; Eze 14:14,20; Heb 11:7; 2Pe 2:5 [m]Ge 5:22
6:10 [n]Ge 5:32
6:11 [o]Eze 7:23; 8:17
6:12 [p]Ps 14:1-3
6:13 [q]ver 17; Eze 7:2-3
6:14 [r]Heb 11:7; 1Pe 3:20 [s]Ex 2:3
6:17 [t]Ge 7:4,21-23; 2Pe 2:5
6:18 [u]Ge 9:9-16 [v]Ge 7:1,7,13
6:20 [w]Ge 7:15
6:22 [x]Ge 7:5,9, 16
7:1 [y]Mt 24:38 [z]Ge 6:9; Eze 14:14
7:2 [a]ver 8; Ge 8:20; Lev 10:10; 11:1-47
7:5 [b]Ge 6:22
7:11 [c]Eze 26:19 [d]Ge 8:2
7:12 [e]ver 4

[a] *14* The meaning of the Hebrew for this word is uncertain. [b] *15* Hebrew *300 cubits long, 50 cubits wide and 30 cubits high* (about 140 meters long, 23 meters wide and 13.5 meters high) [c] *16* Or *Make an opening for light by finishing* [d] *16* Hebrew *a cubit* (about 0.5 meter) [e] *2* Or *seven pairs*; also in verse 3

7:11 To attribute volcanic activity to verse 11 is highly speculative. The fact that igneous rock (rock formed by the cooling of molten rock materials) is found between layers of sedimentary rock is not good evidence in and of itself for volcanic activity at the time of the flood. Sediments that have been laid down during historic time have been cut by lava from present-day volcanoes, and it has been observed that the oldest layers are also cut by igneous rocks. It is impossible to designate any particular rock body as being coincident with the flood.

THE DOCUMENTARY HYPOTHESIS

GENESIS 7 Until fairly recently a majority of scholars espoused the Documentary Hypothesis to explain the composition of the **Pentateuch**, the first five Old Testament books. This theory asserts that these writings were actually based on four books, none still extant, referred to (for ease of identification) as J (Yahwist or Jahwist), E (Elohist), D (Deuteronomist) and P (Priestly Code). The main arguments for this theory are the existence of repetition and apparent contradiction within these five books, as well as the use of different names for God.

According to this hypothesis:

J, the oldest document, included large portions of Genesis, passages from Exodus and Numbers and a few short texts from Deuteronomy. In Genesis, J referred to God as **Yahweh** ("the LORD") because the Biblical author believed that people began using the name Yahweh early in human history (see 4:26, a "J" text).

E, written somewhat later, followed the same story line as J. In Genesis, E referred to God as **Elohim** (the more generic "God") rather than as Yahweh because, according to adherents of E, the name Yahweh was not revealed until the **exodus period** (see Ex 3:15, an "E" text).[1]

D was essentially the book of Deuteronomy. Second Kings records that Hilkiah the priest located a copy of the Law of Moses when the Jerusalem temple was being restored.[2] According to the Documentary Hypothesis, however, Deuteronomy was drafted at this time as a pious fraud to justify Josiah's reformation.

P, written during the **postexilic period** following the return from the exile, included large portions of Genesis, Exodus, Leviticus and Numbers. In Genesis, P referred to God as Elohim since, like E, its author(s) assumed that the divine name, Yahweh, was first revealed at the time of the exodus (see Ex 6:3, a "P" text).

According to this theory the four documents were composed independently of one another but were over a prolonged period of time compiled and edited into the present Pentateuch, with much of the original E material deleted. Still, they argued, the Pentateuch retains significant redundancy and contradiction because the four documents often tell the same or similar stories with inconsistent details. Thus, for example, Genesis 1:1—2:4a was identified as the P account of creation, while the rest of Genesis 2 was seen as a throwback to the earlier J rendition.

In refuting these arguments it is helpful to recognize that repetition was an essential part of ancient Near Eastern narrative. Storytellers often repeated details two or more times (sometimes from a different perspective or with differing details), and narrators often recounted parallel stories (cf. the three instances of a **patriarch** passing off his wife as his sister: Abraham in chs. 12 and 20 and Isaac in ch. 26). For a much later example, see the accounts of Paul's conversion in Acts 9, 22 and 26. In an ancient narrative, repetition was viewed not as evidence of multiple authorship but as confirmation of a single author.

The argument about the names Yahweh and Elohim may be based on a misunderstanding of certain passages, such as Exodus 6:2–3. This passage appears in the NIV as "I am the LORD. I appeared to Abraham, to Isaac and to Jacob as God Almighty, but by my name the LORD I did not make myself known to them." This rendering makes it sound (in line with the P portion of the Documentary Hypothesis) as though the patriarchs did not know the name Yahweh ("the LORD"), thus allowing such scholars to attribute to J the passages in Genesis referring to Yahweh. But the text may alternatively be translated, "I am the LORD. I appeared to Abraham, to Isaac and to Jacob as God Almighty. And my name is the LORD. Did I not make myself known to them?" Rendered in this way, these verses do not assert that Abraham had never heard of "the LORD."

Many scholars today have abandoned the Documentary Hypothesis, agreeing that it is based on a faulty understanding of ancient Near Eastern literature and that it contributes nothing helpful to our understanding of the Pentateuch.

[1]See also "YHWH: The Name of God in the Old Testament" on page 89. [2]See "The Huldah Delegation and Nathan-Melech, the Official" on page 567.

stock according to their kinds, every creature that moves along the ground according to its kind and ev-
ery bird according to its kind, everything with wings. 15 Pairs of all creatures that have the breath of life
in them came to Noah and entered the ark.[f] 16 The animals going in were male and female of every liv- **7:15** [f]Ge 6:19
ing thing, as God had commanded Noah. Then the LORD shut him in.

17 For forty days[g] the flood kept coming on the earth, and as the waters increased they lifted the ark **7:17** [g]ver 4
high above the earth. 18 The waters rose and increased greatly on the earth, and the ark floated on the
surface of the water. 19 They rose greatly on the earth, and all the high mountains under the entire heav-
ens were covered.[h] 20 The waters rose and covered the mountains to a depth of more than twenty feet.[a,b] **7:19** [h]Ps 104:6
21 Every living thing that moved on the earth perished—birds, livestock, wild animals, all the creatures
that swarm over the earth, and all mankind.[i] 22 Everything on dry land that had the breath of life[j] in its **7:21** [i]Ge 6:7,13
nostrils died. 23 Every living thing on the face of the earth was wiped out; men and animals and the crea- **7:22** [j]Ge 1:30
tures that move along the ground and the birds of the air were wiped from the earth.[k] Only Noah was left, **7:23** [k]Mt 24:39;
and those with him in the ark.[l] Lk 17:27; 1Pe 3:20; 2Pe 2:5 [l]Heb 11:7

24 The waters flooded the earth for a hundred and fifty days.[m] **7:24** [m]Ge 8:3

8 But God remembered[n] Noah and all the wild animals and the livestock that were with him in the ark, **8:1** [n]Ge 9:15;
and he sent a wind over the earth,[o] and the waters receded. 2 Now the springs of the deep and the 19:29; Ex 2:24; 1Sa 1:11,19 [o]Ex 14:21
floodgates of the heavens[p] had been closed, and the rain had stopped falling from the sky. 3 The water re- **8:2** [p]Ge 7:11
ceded steadily from the earth. At the end of the hundred and fifty days the water had gone down, 4 and
on the seventeenth day of the seventh month the ark came to rest on the mountains of Ararat. 5 The wa-
ters continued to recede until the tenth month, and on the first day of the tenth month the tops of the
mountains became visible.

6 After forty days Noah opened the window he had made in the ark 7 and sent out a raven, and it kept
flying back and forth until the water had dried up from the earth. 8 Then he sent out a dove to see if the
water had receded from the surface of the ground. 9 But the dove could find no place to set its feet because
there was water over all the surface of the earth; so it returned to Noah in the ark. He reached out his
hand and took the dove and brought it back to himself in the ark. 10 He waited seven more days and again
sent out the dove from the ark. 11 When the dove returned to him in the evening, there in its beak was a
freshly plucked olive leaf! Then Noah knew that the water had receded from the earth. 12 He waited sev-
en more days and sent the dove out again, but this time it did not return to him.

13 By the first day of the first month of Noah's six hundred and first year, the water had dried up from
the earth. Noah then removed the covering from the ark and saw that the surface of the ground was dry.
14 By the twenty-seventh day of the second month the earth was completely dry.

15 Then God said to Noah, 16 "Come out of the ark, you and your wife and your sons and their wives.[q] **8:16** [q]Ge 7:13
17 Bring out every kind of living creature that is with you—the birds, the animals, and all the creatures that
move along the ground—so they can multiply on the earth and be fruitful and increase in number upon it."[r] **8:17** [r]Ge 1:22

18 So Noah came out, together with his sons and his wife and his sons' wives. 19 All the animals and all
the creatures that move along the ground and all the birds—everything that moves on the earth—came
out of the ark, one kind after another.

20 Then Noah built an altar to the LORD[s] and, taking some of all the clean animals and clean[t] birds, he **8:20** [s]Ge 12:7-8;
sacrificed burnt offerings[u] on it. 21 The LORD smelled the pleasing aroma[v] and said in his heart: "Never 13:18; 22:9 [t]Ge 7:8; Lev 11:1-
again will I curse the ground[w] because of man, even though[c] every inclination of his heart is evil from 47 [u]Ge 22:2,13; Ex 10:25
childhood.[x] And never again will I destroy all living creatures,[y] as I have done. **8:21** [v]Lev 1:9,13; 2Co 2:15 [w]Ge 3:17 [x]Ge 6:5; Ps 51:5; Jer 17:9 [y]Ge 9:11,15; Isa 54:9

[a] 20 Hebrew *fifteen cubits* (about 6.9 meters) [b] 20 Or *rose more than twenty feet, and the mountains were covered*
[c] 21 Or *man, for*

7:19 Arguments for a universal flood have cited the inclusive language of verses 19 and 21 ("*all* the high mountains"; "*every* living thing"; emphasis added). Today, for various reasons, many conservative scholars defend a local flood. The crux of their arguments centers in the covenant relationship of God to people. Noah was not a preacher of righteousness (2Pe 2:5) to peoples of other areas but was concerned with the culture from which Abraham would eventually come. In addition, physical arguments have been raised against a universal flood: origin and disposal of the amount of water necessary to form a layer six miles (ten km) thick over the whole world; the effect on plant life of being covered for a year; the effect on fresh water life of a sea that contained salt from the ocean; and the fact that many topographical features of the earth (such as cinder cones) show no evidence of erosion by a flood and are thought to be much more ancient than the flood could possibly have been.

8:1 This verse implies that God did not leave the task of caring for the creatures aboard the ark entirely to Noah.

8:4 The name Ararat is related to the Assyrian region of Urartu, which became an extensive and mountainous kingdom (see Isa 37:38; Jer 51:27). It included much of the territory north of Mesopotamia and east of modern Turkey. The ark probably came to rest in southern Urartu.

8:13–14 The length of the flood is generally agreed upon within a few days. The Hebrews used a solar calendar, in contrast to the Babylonian lunar month and the Egyptian arbitrary 365-day year (see "The Jewish Calendar" on p. 241). Most authorities would put the number of days from the time the rain started (7:11) to the time Noah left the ark (8:14) between 371 and 376.

22 "As long as the earth endures,
seedtime and harvest,
cold and heat,
summer and winter,
day and night
will never cease."[z]

God's Covenant With Noah

9 Then God blessed Noah and his sons, saying to them, "Be fruitful and increase in number and fill
the earth.[a] 2 The fear and dread of you will fall upon all the beasts of the earth and all the birds of
the air, upon every creature that moves along the ground, and upon all the fish of the sea; they are given
into your hands. 3 Everything that lives and moves will be food for you.[b] Just as I gave you the green
plants, I now give you everything.

4 "But you must not eat meat that has its lifeblood still in it.[c] 5 And for your lifeblood I will surely de-
mand an accounting. I will demand an accounting from every animal.[d] And from each man, too, I will
demand an accounting for the life of his fellow man.[e]

6 "Whoever sheds the blood of man,
by man shall his blood be shed;[f]
for in the image of God[g]
has God made man.

7 As for you, be fruitful and increase in number; multiply on the earth and increase upon it."[h]

8 Then God said to Noah and to his sons with him: 9 "I now establish my covenant with you[i] and with
your descendants after you 10 and with every living creature that was with you—the birds, the livestock
and all the wild animals, all those that came out of the ark with you—every living creature on earth. 11 I
establish my covenant[j] with you: Never again will all life be cut off by the waters of a flood; never again
will there be a flood to destroy the earth.[k]"

12 And God said, "This is the sign of the covenant[l] I am making between me and you and every living
creature with you, a covenant for all generations to come: 13 I have set my rainbow in the clouds, and it
will be the sign of the covenant between me and the earth. 14 Whenever I bring clouds over the earth and
the rainbow appears in the clouds, 15 I will remember my covenant[m] between me and you and all living
creatures of every kind. Never again will the waters become a flood to destroy all life. 16 Whenever the
rainbow appears in the clouds, I will see it and remember the everlasting covenant[n] between God and
all living creatures of every kind on the earth."

17 So God said to Noah, "This is the sign of the covenant[o] I have established between me and all life
on the earth."

The Sons of Noah

18 The sons of Noah who came out of the ark were Shem, Ham and Japheth. (Ham was the father of
Canaan.)[p] 19 These were the three sons of Noah, and from them came the people who were scattered over
the earth.[q]

20 Noah, a man of the soil, proceeded[a] to plant a vineyard. 21 When he drank some of its wine, he

8:22 [z]Ge 1:14; Jer 33:20,25
9:1 [a]Ge 1:22
9:3 [b]Ge 1:29
9:4 [c]Lev 3:17; 17:10-14; Dt 12:16,23-25; 1Sa 14:33
9:5 [d]Ex 21:28-32 [e]Ge 4:10
9:6 [f]Ge 4:14; Ex 21:12,14; Lev 24:17; Mt 26:52 [g]Ge 1:26
9:7 [h]Ge 1:22
9:9 [i]Ge 6:18
9:11 [j]ver 16; Isa 24:5 [k]Ge 8:21; Isa 54:9
9:12 [l]ver 17; Ge 17:11
9:15 [m]Ex 2:24; Lev 26:42,45; Dt 7:9; Eze 16:60
9:16 [n]ver 11; Ge 17:7,13,19; 2Sa 7:13; 23:5
9:17 [o]ver 12; Ge 17:11
9:18 [p]ver 25-27; Ge 10:6,15
9:19 [q]Ge 10:32

[a] 20 Or *soil, was the first*

9:1–17 The rainbow feature in the Biblical flood account is unique in that none of the stories from Babylon or elsewhere make mention of this covenantal sign. In the Bible the rainbow is the first of the covenant signs and provides the key to understanding all of them, including those of baptism and the Lord's Supper in the new covenant. The rainbow in the clouds speaks to humankind from God. God allowed Noah to understand what the bow meant to him: a visible declaration that the Lord will never again destroy the earth by flood. The rainbow, then, is God's promise made visible. Covenant signs express covenant promises to covenant people.
9:2–4 From now on animals would fear people and were given to be food for them, except for their blood.
9:5–6 Human government was instituted by the provision of capital punishment for murderers.
9:8–17 The sacrifices of Cain and Abel (4:4–5) demonstrate that the rite of sacrifice goes back almost to the beginnings of the human race. No priest was needed in these early sacrifices. The sacrifice of Noah after the flood (8:20–21) is called a burnt offering and is closely connected with the covenant of God described in 9:8–17. In the sacrifices of Abraham, several of which are mentioned (12:7–8; 13:4,18; 15:4ff), he acted as his own priest, making offerings to express his adoration of God and probably to atone for sin. In Genesis 22 God revealed to Abraham that he did not desire human sacrifices, a common practice in those days (see "Human Sacrifice in the Ancient Near East" on p. 182).
9:18–19 The term *Semite* is derived from Noah's son Shem (vv. 18–19; 10:21–31) and is used to identify a diverse group of ancient peoples whose languages were related. It is not certain, however, that they themselves were related by blood. See "The Hyksos and the Old Testament" on page 121 for a discussion of a particular Semitic people who settled in Egypt.

became drunk and lay uncovered inside his tent. 22 Ham, the father of Canaan, saw his father's naked-
ness and told his two brothers outside. 23 But Shem and Japheth took a garment and laid it across their
shoulders; then they walked in backward and covered their father's nakedness. Their faces were turned
the other way so that they would not see their father's nakedness.
24 When Noah awoke from his wine and found out what his youngest son had done to him, 25 he said,

"Cursed be Canaan![r] — **9:25** [r]ver 18
The lowest of slaves
will he be to his brothers.[s]" — [s]Ge 25:23; Jos 9:23

26 He also said,

"Blessed be the LORD, the God of Shem!
May Canaan be the slave of Shem.[a]
27 May God extend the territory of Japheth[b];
may Japheth live in the tents of Shem,
and may Canaan be his[c] slave."

28 After the flood Noah lived 350 years. 29 Altogether, Noah lived 950 years, and then he died.

The Table of Nations

10 This is the account[t] of Shem, Ham and Japheth, Noah's sons, who themselves had sons after the — **10:1** [t]Ge 2:4
flood.

The Japhethites

2 The sons[d] of Japheth:
Gomer,[u] Magog,[v] Madai, Javan, Tubal,[w] Meshech and Tiras. — **10:2** [u]Eze 38:6 [v]Eze 38:2; Rev 20:8 [w]Isa 66:19
3 The sons of Gomer:
Ashkenaz,[x] Riphath and Togarmah.[y] — **10:3** [x]Jer 51:27 [y]Eze 27:14; 38:6
4 The sons of Javan:
Elishah, Tarshish,[z] the Kittim and the Rodanim.[e] 5 (From these the maritime peoples spread — **10:4** [z]Eze 27:12, 25; Jnh 1:3
out into their territories by their clans within their nations, each with its own language.)

The Hamites

6 The sons of Ham:
Cush, Mizraim,[f] Put and Canaan.[a] — **10:6** [a]ver 15; Ge 9:18
7 The sons of Cush:
Seba, Havilah, Sabtah, Raamah and Sabteca.
The sons of Raamah:
Sheba and Dedan.
8 Cush was the father[g] of Nimrod, who grew to be a mighty warrior on the earth. 9 He was a mighty
hunter before the LORD; that is why it is said, "Like Nimrod, a mighty hunter before the LORD." 10 The first
centers of his kingdom were Babylon,[b] Erech, Akkad and Calneh, in[h] Shinar.[i][c] 11 From that land he went — **10:10** [b]Ge 11:9 [c]Ge 11:2

[a] 26 Or *be his slave* [b] 27 *Japheth* sounds like the Hebrew for *extend.* [c] 27 Or *their* [d] 2 *Sons* may mean *descendants* or *successors* or *nations*; also in verses 3, 4, 6, 7, 20-23, 29 and 31. [e] 4 Some manuscripts of the Masoretic Text and Samaritan Pentateuch (see also Septuagint and 1 Chron. 1:7); most manuscripts of the Masoretic Text *Dodanim* [f] 6 That is, Egypt; also in verse 13 [g] 8 *Father* may mean *ancestor* or *predecessor* or *founder*; also in verses 13, 15, 24 and 26. [h] 10 Or *Erech and Akkad—all of them in* [i] 10 That is, Babylonia

---

9:27 A tent was the typical dwelling of nomadic peoples. Tents in ancient times were of various shapes—round and tapering, flat and oblong. All of a nomadic family's belongings could normally be carried on one pack animal. A sheik would have had several tents. "Tent" in the Old Testament is often a reference to any habitation (v. 27; Job 8:22; Ps 84:10) and is frequently used figuratively as well (Isa 13:20; 54:2; Jer 10:20).

10:1 The list of Noah's descendants contains 70 names—a number that symbolized for the ancients totality and completion. It should be noted that the list is incomplete and apparently representative. The author penetrated selectively into various lines in order to achieve his final number.

Knowledge of the peoples and countries of the world was considered just as much an indication of wisdom for the ancients as knowledge of plants and animals. The "wisdom" represented by this catalog of known peoples was more than just academic. The point was that all these people groups had resulted from God's early blessing.

10:8–9 Nimrod is an enigma. Claims that he is to be equated with Gilgamesh or Hercules or other figures, or that he built the Tower of Babel (11:1–9), are without historical foundation. Some have suggested that Nimrod was a Mesopotamian god (such as Marduk) or king (such as Sargon), but this is pure speculation.

Later the Canaanite[k] clans scattered 19and the borders of Canaan[l] reached from Sidon[m] toward Ge- 10:18 [k]Ge 12:6; Ex 13:11
rar as far as Gaza, and then toward Sodom, Gomorrah, Admah and Zeboiim, as far as Lasha. 10:19 [l]Ge 11:31; 13:12; 17:8
20These are the sons of Ham by their clans and languages, in their territories and nations. [m]ver 15

The Semites

21Sons were also born to Shem, whose older brother was[a] Japheth; Shem was the ancestor of all the
sons of Eber.[n] 10:21 [n]ver 24; Nu 24:24

22The sons of Shem:
Elam,[o] Asshur, Arphaxad,[p] Lud and Aram. 10:22 [o]Jer 49:34 [p]Lk 3:36
23The sons of Aram:
Uz,[q] Hul, Gether and Meshech.[b] 10:23 [q]Job 1:1
24Arphaxad was the father of[c] Shelah,
and Shelah the father of Eber.[r] 10:24 [r]ver 21
25Two sons were born to Eber:
One was named Peleg,[d] because in his time the earth was divided; his brother was named
Joktan.
26Joktan was the father of
Almodad, Sheleph, Hazarmaveth, Jerah, 27Hadoram, Uzal, Diklah, 28Obal, Abimael, Sheba,
29Ophir, Havilah and Jobab. All these were sons of Joktan.

30The region where they lived stretched from Mesha toward Sephar, in the eastern hill country.
31These are the sons of Shem by their clans and languages, in their territories and nations.

32These are the clans of Noah's sons,[s] according to their lines of descent, within their nations. From 10:32 [s]ver 1 [t]Ge 9:19
these the nations spread out over the earth[t] after the flood.

The Tower of Babel

11 Now the whole world had one language and a common speech. 2As men moved eastward,[e] they
found a plain in Shinar[f][u] and settled there. 11:2 [u]Ge 10:10
3They said to each other, "Come, let's make bricks[v] and bake them thoroughly." They used brick in- 11:3 [v]Ex 1:14 [w]Ge 14:10
stead of stone, and tar[w] for mortar. 4Then they said, "Come, let us build ourselves a city, with a tower that
reaches to the heavens,[x] so that we may make a name[y] for ourselves and not be scattered over the face 11:4 [x]Dt 1:28; 9:1 [y]Ge 6:4 [z]Dt 4:27
of the whole earth."[z]
5But the LORD came down[a] to see the city and the tower that the men were building. 6The LORD said, 11:5 [a]ver 7; Ge 18:21; Ex 3:8; 19:11,18,20
"If as one people speaking the same language they have begun to do this, then nothing they plan to do
will be impossible for them. 7Come, let us[b] go down and confuse their language so they will not under- 11:7 [b]Ge 1:26 [c]Ge 42:23
stand each other."[c]
8So the LORD scattered them from there over all the earth,[d] and they stopped building the city. 9That 11:8 [d]Ge 9:19; Lk 1:51
is why it was called Babel[g][e]—because there the LORD confused the language of the whole world. From 11:9 [e]Ge 10:10
there the LORD scattered them over the face of the whole earth.

[a] 21 Or *Shem, the older brother of* [b] 23 See Septuagint and 1 Chron. 1:17; Hebrew *Mash* [c] 24 Hebrew; Septuagint *father of Cainan, and Cainan was the father of* [d] 25 *Peleg* means *division.* [e] 2 Or *from the east*; or *in the east* [f] 2 That is, Babylonia [g] 9 That is, Babylon; *Babel* sounds like the Hebrew for *confused.*

10:21 "Eber" is thought by some to be the origin of the word for "Hebrew." Although Eber was a distant descendant of Shem (see vv. 24–25; 11:14–17), his importance as the ancestor of the Hebrews is hinted at here. The Ebla tablets—(see "Ebla" on p. 19)—frequently refer to a king named Ebrium, who ruled Ebla for 28 years.
10:32 The text accounts only for people groups of which the Israelites were aware, with no hint at a world beyond the ancient Near East. The author made no attempt to provide a comprehensive list of all the peoples descended from Noah but addressed only how the known groups and nations of his day were related to Israel.
11:3 While stone and mortar were common building materials in Canaan, stone was scarce in Mesopotamia. Archaeological excavations indicate that mud brick and tar were more frequently utilized there.

11:4 Ancient cities were dominated by a temple complex, including a tower. The typical Mesopotamian temple tower, known as a ziggurat, was square at the base and had sloping, stepped sides that led upward to a small shrine at the top. Ziggurats were dedicated to particular deities. Their design made it convenient for a god to "come down" to his temple, receive worship from his people and bless them. In this case God did come down—and he was not pleased!

Mesopotamian ziggurats were given names demonstrating that they were intended to serve as staircases from Earth to heaven: The House of the Link between Heaven and Earth (at Larsa), The House of the Seven Guides of Heaven and Earth (at Borsippa), The House of the Foundation-Platform of Heaven and Earth (at Babylon) and The House of the Mountain of the Universe (at Asshur).

10:11 [d]Ps 83:8; Mic 5:6 [e]Jnh 1:2; 4:11; Na 1:1

to Assyria,[d] where he built Nineveh,[e] Rehoboth Ir,[a] Calah 12 and Resen, which is between Nineveh and Ca-
lah; that is the great city.

13 Mizraim was the father of
the Ludites, Anamites, Lehabites, Naphtuhites, 14 Pathrusites, Casluhites (from whom the Phi-
listines[f] came) and Caphtorites.
15 Canaan[g] was the father of
Sidon[h] his firstborn,[b] and of the Hittites,[i] 16 Jebusites,[j] Amorites, Girgashites, 17 Hivites, Arkites,
Sinites, 18 Arvadites, Zemarites and Hamathites.

10:14 [f]Ge 21:32, 34; 26:1,8
10:15 [g]ver 6; Ge 9:18 [h]Eze 28:21 [i]Ge 23:3,20
10:16 [j]1Ch 11:4

[a] 11 Or *Nineveh with its city squares* [b] 15 Or *of the Sidonians, the foremost*

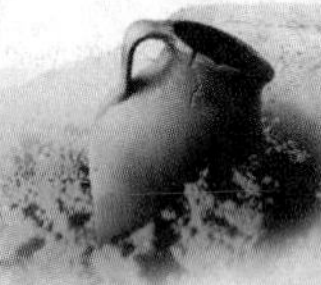

ARCHAEOLOGICAL SITES

EBLA

GENESIS 10 Excavating the city of **Ebla** (modern Tell Mardikh)—see "Map 1" in the back of this Bible—in northwestern Syria, archaeologists have discovered the single largest collection of third-millennium B.C. cuneiform tablets unearthed to date. Immensely important in the study of the ancient Near East, this site has yielded tens of thousands of complete texts and fragments. These texts, which include administrative, lexical, literary and diplomatic tablets, were discovered in the palace, which had been destroyed by fire. Ironically, the conflagration may have helped to preserve the tablets by baking them, although some more important tablets would have been purposely hard-baked when created in order to preserve their information for generations.[1]

The Eblaites utilized the **Sumerian** cuneiform writing system, adapting it to their Semitic language.[2] This has made decipherment and translation of the texts both difficult and tedious. In fact, early translations often vary drastically from more recent ones as more is learned about the Eblaite language. As a result, earlier scholars believed they had found a text parallel to the familiar Biblical proverbs, while today this so-called proverbial text is considered to be merely a list of Sumerian terms for cuts of meat! Some scholars had thought they saw references to the **patriarchs** (Abraham, Isaac and Jacob/Israel) in the Ebla tablets, but this also has turned out to be a false lead. At one point, ancient historians believed that information in the Ebla texts indicated that the city, during its zenith, controlled a vast empire from Egypt to the Persian Gulf. Many of these early readings have now come under renewed scrutiny as well, with the result that the extent of Ebla's former power remains in question.

The importance of the Ebla documents for Biblical studies probably lies in what they can tell us in general about life in third-millennium B.C. Syria-Palestine, as opposed to their providing any specific parallels to the Bible, as had been hoped. The history of these documents again reminds archaeologists to exercise caution when attempting to link ancient historical and literary finds to Biblical material.

Words for "King" in Various Scripts

The word *king* (*lugal*) in Sumerian script

The word *king* (*nesu*) in Egyptian Hieroglyphic script

The word *king* (*melek*) in Iron Age Hebrew script

The word king (*šarru*) in Neo-Assyrian Akkadian script

Old Testament Today, p. 19.

[1]See "Cuneiform and Clay Tablets in the Ancient Near East" on page 1108. [2]See "Languages of the Old Testament World" on page 672.

From Shem to Abram

10 This is the account of Shem.

Two years after the flood, when Shem was 100 years old, he became the father[a] of Arphaxad. 11 And
after he became the father of Arphaxad, Shem lived 500 years and had other sons and daughters.
11:12 [f]Lk 3:35 12 When Arphaxad had lived 35 years, he became the father of Shelah.[f] 13 And after he became the fa-
ther of Shelah, Arphaxad lived 403 years and had other sons and daughters.[b]
14 When Shelah had lived 30 years, he became the father of Eber. 15 And after he became the father of
Eber, Shelah lived 403 years and had other sons and daughters.
16 When Eber had lived 34 years, he became the father of Peleg. 17 And after he became the father of
Peleg, Eber lived 430 years and had other sons and daughters.
18 When Peleg had lived 30 years, he became the father of Reu. 19 And after he became the father of
Reu, Peleg lived 209 years and had other sons and daughters.
11:20 [g]Lk 3:35 20 When Reu had lived 32 years, he became the father of Serug.[g] 21 And after he became the father of
Serug, Reu lived 207 years and had other sons and daughters.
22 When Serug had lived 30 years, he became the father of Nahor. 23 And after he became the father of
Nahor, Serug lived 200 years and had other sons and daughters.
11:24 [h]Lk 3:34 24 When Nahor had lived 29 years, he became the father of Terah.[h] 25 And after he became the father
of Terah, Nahor lived 119 years and had other sons and daughters.
11:26 [i]Lk 3:34 [j]Jos 24:2 26 After Terah had lived 70 years, he became the father of Abram,[i] Nahor[j] and Haran.

27 This is the account of Terah.

11:27 [k]ver 31; Ge 12:4; 14:12; 19:1; 2Pe 2:7 Terah became the father of Abram, Nahor and Haran. And Haran became the father of Lot.[k] 28 While
his father Terah was still alive, Haran died in Ur of the Chaldeans,[l] in the land of his birth. 29 Abram and
11:28 [l]ver 31; Ge 15:7 Nahor both married. The name of Abram's wife was Sarai,[m] and the name of Nahor's wife was Milcah;[n]
11:29 [m]Ge 17:15 [n]Ge 22:20 she was the daughter of Haran, the father of both Milcah and Iscah. 30 Now Sarai was barren; she had no
11:30 [o]Ge 16:1; 18:11 children.[o]
31 Terah took his son Abram, his grandson Lot son of Haran, and his daughter-in-law Sarai, the wife
11:31 [p]Ge 15:7; Ne 9:7; Ac 7:4 [q]Ge 10:19 of his son Abram, and together they set out from Ur of the Chaldeans[p] to go to Canaan.[q] But when they
came to Haran, they settled there.
32 Terah lived 205 years, and he died in Haran.

The Call of Abram

12:1 [r]Ac 7:3*; Heb 11:8 12 The LORD had said to Abram, "Leave your country, your people and your father's household and
go to the land I will show you.[r]

12:2 [s]Ge 15:5; 17:2,4; 18:18; 22:17; Dt 26:5 [t]Ge 24:1,35 2 "I will make you into a great nation[s]
and I will bless you;[t]
I will make your name great,
and you will be a blessing.
3 I will bless those who bless you,
12:3 [u]Ge 27:29; Ex 23:22; Nu 24:9 and whoever curses you I will curse;[u]
and all peoples on earth
[v]Ge 18:18; 22:18; 26:4; Ac 3:25; Gal 3:8* will be blessed through you.[v]"

4 So Abram left, as the LORD had told him; and Lot went with him. Abram was seventy-five years old
12:4 [w]Ge 11:31 when he set out from Haran.[w] 5 He took his wife Sarai, his nephew Lot, all the possessions they had

[a] *10 Father* may mean *ancestor*; also in verses 11-25. [b] *12,13* Hebrew; Septuagint (see also Luke 3:35, 36 and note at Gen. 10:24) *35 years, he became the father of Cainan. 13 And after he became the father of Cainan, Arphaxad lived 430 years and had other sons and daughters, and then he died. When Cainan had lived 130 years, he became the father of Shelah. And after he became the father of Shelah, Cainan lived 330 years and had other sons and daughters*

11:10–26 Pre-flood and post-flood genealogies seem to be schematic and incomplete. If 11:10–26 has no gaps, Shem outlived Abraham, but no other hint of this is given in the Biblical picture (see "Genealogies in Ancient Israel" on p. 1559).

In general, the time period from Adam to Abraham appears to have been extensive, and the genealogical lists in Genesis hardly serve as a timetable.

12:5 At a normal caravan pace of 20 miles (32 km) per day, the trip from Haran to Canaan (about 500 miles or 800 km) would have taken the better part of a month. Shechem and Bethel, located in the central hill country, were often rest stops along the way. They became major sacred sites in later Israelite history. See "Haran" on page 47, "Bethel" on page 59 and "Shechem" on page 340.

EVIDENCE FOR SERUG, NAHOR AND TERAH

GENESIS 12 According to the Old Testament the patriarchs' original homeland was in south-central Turkey, in an area known as Aram Naharaim (Ge 24:10) or Paddan-Aram (25:20).[1] Among the genealogical names of individuals listed in Genesis 11, three—Serug, Nahor and Terah—have survived from antiquity also as names of towns in this region. The names of these Biblical characters have been preserved in the very area from which the Bible specifies the patriarchs to have originated.[2]

Serug, Abram's great-grandfather, fathered Nahor at age 30 and died at age 230 (11:22–23). His name, which corresponds to the place called Sargi in **Assyrian** inscriptions of the seventh century B.C., lives on as modern Sürüc, 35 miles (56.5 km) northwest of Haran[3] (see "Map 1" in the back of this Bible).

Nahor, Abram's grandfather, fathered Terah at age 29 and died at age 148 (11:24–25). A town called Nahor is mentioned in 24:10 as the home of the descendants of Bethuel, another son of Nahor (24:24). This particular town also is mentioned in texts from **Mari**[4] and Cappadocia from the nineteenth through the eighteenth centuries B.C., as well as in Assyrian inscriptions from the fourteenth century B.C. Later Assyrian records from the seventh century B.C. refer to it as Til Nakhiri, which means "Mound of Nahor." Although Nahor's exact location is unknown today, numerous references in ancient texts place it in the Balikh River valley south of Haran.

Terah fathered Abram at age 70 and died at age 205 (11:26,32). A town named Til Turahi ("Mound of Terah") is mentioned in ninth-century B.C. Assyrian texts as being north of Haran ("Map 1"), also on the Balikh River.

[1]See "Paddan Aram" on page 48. [2]See also "The Historicity of the Patriarchal Narratives" on page 73. [3]See "Haran" on page 47. [4]See "Mari" on page 54.

accumulated and the people[x] they had acquired in Haran, and they set out for the land of Canaan, and
they arrived there.
6 Abram traveled through the land[y] as far as the site of the great tree of Moreh[z] at Shechem. At that time
the Canaanites[a] were in the land. 7 The LORD appeared to Abram[b] and said, "To your offspring[a] I will give
this land."[c] So he built an altar there to the LORD,[d] who had appeared to him.
8 From there he went on toward the hills east of Bethel[e] and pitched his tent, with Bethel on the west
and Ai on the east. There he built an altar to the LORD and called on the name of the LORD. 9 Then Abram
set out and continued toward the Negev.[f]

Abram in Egypt

10 Now there was a famine in the land, and Abram went down to Egypt to live there for a while be-
cause the famine was severe. 11 As he was about to enter Egypt, he said to his wife Sarai, "I know what a

12:5 [x]Ge 14:14; 17:23
12:6 [y]Heb 11:9 [z]Ge 35:4; Dt 11:30 [a]Ge 10:18
12:7 [b]Ge 17:1; 18:1; Ex 6:3 [c]Ge 13:15,17; 15:18; 17:8; Ps 105:9-11 [d]Ge 13:4
12:8 [e]Ge 13:3
12:9 [f]Ge 13:1,3

[a] 7 Or *seed*

12:6 A large tree was often a prominent feature at a sacred place, and the "great tree of Moreh" was located at a famous pagan sanctuary at Shechem in central Canaan. Abram built an altar to the true God there.
12:10 Famine was common in Canaan, since the region's productivity depended on rainfall. Egypt was less susceptible to drought and famine because of its dependence on the annual flooding of the Nile. Modern archaeologists and geologists have found evidence of a massive, 300-year drought cycle that occurred during the end of the third millennium B.C. and the beginning of the second—the time period to which Abram/Abraham traditionally is dated. See "Famine in the Ancient Near East" on page 70. See also the note on Ruth 1:1.
12:11 Sarai's beauty is praised in the Genesis Apocryphon (one of the Dead Sea Scrolls). The criteria for beauty, particularly in the case of older women, may have been substantially different in the ancient Near East from the standards we value today.

beautiful woman you are. 12When the Egyptians see you, they will say, 'This is his wife.' Then they will
12:13 [g]Ge 20:2; 26:7 kill me but will let you live. 13Say you are my sister,[g] so that I will be treated well for your sake and my
life will be spared because of you."
14When Abram came to Egypt, the Egyptians saw that she was a very beautiful woman. 15And when
Pharaoh's officials saw her, they praised her to Pharaoh, and she was taken into his palace. 16He treated
Abram well for her sake, and Abram acquired sheep and cattle, male and female donkeys, menservants
and maidservants, and camels.
12:17 [h]1Ch 16:21 17But the LORD inflicted serious diseases on Pharaoh and his household[h] because of Abram's wife Sa-
12:18 [i]Ge 20:9; 26:10 rai. 18So Pharaoh summoned Abram. "What have you done to me?"[i] he said. "Why didn't you tell me she
was your wife? 19Why did you say, 'She is my sister,' so that I took her to be my wife? Now then, here is your
wife. Take her and go!" 20Then Pharaoh gave orders about Abram to his men, and they sent him on his
way, with his wife and everything he had.

Abram and Lot Separate

13:1 [j]Ge 12:9 13 So Abram went up from Egypt to the Negev,[j] with his wife and everything he had, and Lot went
with him. 2Abram had become very wealthy in livestock and in silver and gold.
13:3 [k]Ge 12:8 3From the Negev he went from place to place until he came to Bethel,[k] to the place between Bethel and
13:4 [l]Ge 12:7 Ai where his tent had been earlier 4and where he had first built an altar.[l] There Abram called on the name
of the LORD.
5Now Lot, who was moving about with Abram, also had flocks and herds and tents. 6But the land
could not support them while they stayed together, for their possessions were so great that they were not
13:6 [m]Ge 36:7 13:7 [n]Ge 26:20, 21 [o]Ge 12:6 able to stay together.[m] 7And quarreling[n] arose between Abram's herdsmen and the herdsmen of Lot. The
Canaanites and Perizzites were also living in the land[o] at that time.
13:8 [p]Pr 15:18; 20:3 [q]Ps 133:1 8So Abram said to Lot, "Let's not have any quarreling between you and me,[p] or between your herds-
men and mine, for we are brothers.[q] 9Is not the whole land before you? Let's part company. If you go to
the left, I'll go to the right; if you go to the right, I'll go to the left."

12:19 Absolute truthfulness was an important feature of Egyptian ethics.

13:2 Cattle are mentioned already in the first chapter of the Bible (1:24–26; "livestock" in the NIV), symbolic of their importance to the well-being of the human race. Eleven Hebrew and two Greek words are translated to indicate cattle, the species descended from wild members of the family *Bovidae*.

The Cities of the Plain

GENESIS 13 Sodom, where Lot chose to live, was one of five cities (Sodom, Gomorrah, Zoar, Admah and Zeboiim) referred to in the Old Testament as the "Cities of the Plain" (see Ge 13:12; 14:2). These cities were not mythical places but historical sites, and there is evidence of their destruction precisely as described in the Bible.[1]

Zoar ("Map 1") was the city to which Lot fled at the time of the annihilation of Sodom and Gomorrah (19:18–22). We know its location from the **Madaba map**, a mosaic map on the floor of a church in Madaba, Jordan, depicting the Holy Land (only much later called Palestine) during the sixth century B.C. Ancient Zoar was on the southeastern shore of the Dead Sea, just south of the Zared River (Wadi Hesa) near modern Safi. Zoar has a long history. It is mentioned a number of times in the Bible (e.g., Isa 15:5; Jer 48:34) and was the site of the prosperous, Arab-controlled city of Zugar during the Middle Ages.

Approximately 8 miles (13 km) north of Safi lies the archaeological site of Numeira, which was also occupied during the days of Lot. The consonants of the Arabic name Numeira are similar to those of the Hebrew name Gomorrah. Quite possibly the ancient Hebrew name is preserved in this modern Arabic name.

The archaeological site of Bab edh-Dhra, 10 miles (16 km) north of Numeira, also was occupied during the days of Lot. This location had a significant settlement during the Early Bronze period.[2] Since Bab edh-Dhra is the largest ancient ruin in the region, it stands to reason that it should be identified as Sodom, the most famous of the Cities of the Plain where Lot "pitched his tents" (Ge 13:12).

[1]See "The Destruction of Sodom and Gomorrah" on page 32. [2]See "Archaeological Periods" chart on page xx in the front of this Bible.

10 Lot looked up and saw that the whole plain of the Jordan was well watered, like the garden of the
LORD,[r] like the land of Egypt, toward Zoar.[s] (This was before the LORD destroyed Sodom and Gomorrah.)[t]
11 So Lot chose for himself the whole plain of the Jordan and set out toward the east. The two men part-
ed company: 12 Abram lived in the land of Canaan, while Lot lived among the cities of the plain[u] and
pitched his tents near Sodom.[v] 13 Now the men of Sodom were wicked and were sinning greatly against
the LORD.[w]
14 The LORD said to Abram after Lot had parted from him, "Lift up your eyes from where you are and
look north and south, east and west.[x] 15 All the land that you see I will give to you and your offspring[a] for-
ever.[y] 16 I will make your offspring like the dust of the earth, so that if anyone could count the dust, then
your offspring could be counted. 17 Go, walk through the length and breadth of the land,[z] for I am giving
it to you."
18 So Abram moved his tents and went to live near the great trees of Mamre[a] at Hebron,[b] where he
built an altar to the LORD.[c]

13:10 [r]Ge 2:8-10; Isa 51:3 [s]Ge 19:22,30 [t]Ge 14:8; 19:17-29
13:12 [u]Ge 19:17, 25,29 [v]Ge 14:12
13:13 [w]Ge 18:20; Eze 16:49-50; 2Pe 2:8
13:14 [x]Ge 28:14; Dt 3:27
13:15 [y]Ge 12:7; Gal 3:16*
13:17 [z]ver 15; Nu 13:17-25
13:18 [a]Ge 14:13, 24; 18:1 [b]Ge 35:27 [c]Ge 8:20

Abram Rescues Lot

14 At this time Amraphel king of Shinar,[b][d] Arioch king of Ellasar, Kedorlaomer king of Elam and
Tidal king of Goiim 2 went to war against Bera king of Sodom, Birsha king of Gomorrah, Shinab

14:1 [d]Ge 10:10

[a] *15* Or *seed*; also in verse 16 [b] *1* That is, Babylonia; also in verse 9

13:10 Already in these ancient times the names of Sodom and Gomorrah had become synonymous with vile wickedness and divine judgment on sin. Archaeological evidence has confirmed that the now dry area east and southeast of the Dead Sea enjoyed an ample water supply and was well populated prior to this catastrophe. See "The Cities of the Plain" on page 23.
13:18 Regarding "great trees," see the note on 12:6.

The Coalition of Mesopotamian Kings

GENESIS 14 None of the invading kings or events mentioned in Genesis 14 have been identified or confirmed from archaeological evidence, but circumstantial evidence in extra-biblical sources does shed light on this text and supports its historicity. There is no reason to treat it as fiction, as many scholars do.[1]

"Amraphel, king of Shinar" (i.e., southern **Mesopotamia**) is no longer identified, as he once was, with **Hammurabi** of **Babylon**, but the area from which Amraphel is said to have come, Shinar, is Babylonia.[2]

The name Arioch is rendered as Arriyuk or Arriwuk in eighteenth- through fifteenth-century texts discovered at **Mari**[3] and **Nuzi**[4] in Mesopotamia. Both of these place-names are listed on "Map 1."

Ellasar may represent either Asshur or Larsa, a city in southern Mesopotamia.

Kedorlaomer, the Hebrew version of Kudur-Lagamar, is comprised of known **Elamite** elements. *Kudur* means "servant of" and is included in the names of five other Elamite kings, and Lagamar was an Elamite goddess. Thus Kedorlaomer may be interpreted as "servant of Lagamar."

Tidal is a form of Tudkhalia, the name of five **Hittite** kings who perhaps all lived later than this king. His title, "king of Goiim" (meaning "nations"), essentially means that he was the principal chief of a loose confederation of tribes, reflecting the decentralized nature of **Antatolian** politics in the nineteenth through eighteenth centuries B.C.

Contemporary records trace similar Mesopotamian confederations that formed after the fall of the Ur III Dynasty (c. 2000 B.C.) and before King Hammurabi rose to power (c. 1750 B.C.). Immediately thereafter **Assyria** and Babylon controlled the entire region.

Curiously, King Yahdun-Lim of Mari (c. 1820 B.C.) left behind an account of a series of raids he made into Syria-Palestine in order to enforce the submission of local kings to himself, and this record is quite similar to what we see in Genesis 14. This does not mean that the Biblical episode and the raids conducted by Yahdun-Lim are one and the same, but it does make the point that the Biblical narrative fits in well with what we see in the history of the time.

[1]See also "The Historicity of the Patriarchal Narratives" on page 73. [2]See "Sumer" on page 10 [3]See "Mari" on page 54. [4]See "Nuzi" on page 52.

14:2 [e]Ge 10:19 [f]Ge 13:10 king of Admah, Shemeber king of Zeboiim,[e] and the king of Bela (that is, Zoar).[f] 3All these latter kings
14:3 [g]Nu 34:3, 12; Dt 3:17; joined forces in the Valley of Siddim (the Salt Sea[a][g]). 4For twelve years they had been subject to Kedor-
Jos 3:16; 15:2,5 laomer, but in the thirteenth year they rebelled.

5In the fourteenth year, Kedorlaomer and the kings allied with him went out and defeated the Reph-
14:5 [h]Ge 15:20; Dt 2:11,20 aites[h] in Ashteroth Karnaim, the Zuzites in Ham, the Emites[i] in Shaveh Kiriathaim 6and the Horites[j] in
[i]Dt 2:10 14:6 [j]Dt 2:12,22 the hill country of Seir,[k] as far as El Paran[l] near the desert. 7Then they turned back and went to En Mish-
[k]Dt 2:1,5,22 pat (that is, Kadesh), and they conquered the whole territory of the Amalekites, as well as the Amorites
[l]Ge 21:21; Nu 10:12 who were living in Hazazon Tamar.[m]
14:7 [m]2Ch 20:2 8Then the king of Sodom, the king of Gomorrah,[n] the king of Admah, the king of Zeboiim[o] and the
14:8 [n]Ge 13:10; 19:17-29 king of Bela (that is, Zoar) marched out and drew up their battle lines in the Valley of Siddim 9against
[o]Dt 29:23 Kedorlaomer king of Elam, Tidal king of Goiim, Amraphel king of Shinar and Arioch king of Ellasar—
four kings against five. 10Now the Valley of Siddim was full of tar pits, and when the kings of Sodom and
14:10 [p]Ge 19:17, 30 Gomorrah fled, some of the men fell into them and the rest fled to the hills.[p] 11The four kings seized all
the goods of Sodom and Gomorrah and all their food; then they went away. 12They also carried off
Abram's nephew Lot and his possessions, since he was living in Sodom.

13One who had escaped came and reported this to Abram the Hebrew. Now Abram was living near the
14:13 [q]ver 24; Ge 13:18 great trees of Mamre[q] the Amorite, a brother[b] of Eshcol and Aner, all of whom were allied with Abram.
14When Abram heard that his relative had been taken captive, he called out the 318 trained men born in
14:14 [r]Ge 15:3 [s]Dt 34:1; his household[r] and went in pursuit as far as Dan.[s] 15During the night Abram divided his men to attack
Jdg 18:29 them and he routed them, pursuing them as far as Hobah, north of Damascus. 16He recovered all the
goods and brought back his relative Lot and his possessions, together with the women and the other
people.

17After Abram returned from defeating Kedorlaomer and the kings allied with him, the king of Sod-
14:17 [t]2Sa 18:18 om came out to meet him in the Valley of Shaveh (that is, the King's Valley).[t]
14:18 [u]Ps 110:4; Heb 5:6 [v]Ps 76:2; Heb 7:2 18Then Melchizedek[u] king of Salem[c][v] brought out bread and wine. He was priest of God Most High,
14:19 [w]Heb 7:6 19and he blessed Abram,[w] saying,

"Blessed be Abram by God Most High,
[x]ver 22 Creator[d] of heaven and earth.[x]
14:20 [y]Ge 24:27 20And blessed be[e] God Most High,[y]
who delivered your enemies into your hand."

[z]Ge 28:22; Dt 26:12; Heb 7:4 Then Abram gave him a tenth of everything.[z]
21The king of Sodom said to Abram, "Give me the people and keep the goods for yourself."
14:22 [a]Ex 6:8; Da 12:7; 22But Abram said to the king of Sodom, "I have raised my hand[a] to the LORD, God Most High, Creator
Rev 10:5-6 [b]ver 19 of heaven and earth,[b] and have taken an oath 23that I will accept nothing belonging to you,[c] not even a
14:23 [c]2Ki 5:16 thread or the thong of a sandal, so that you will never be able to say, 'I made Abram rich.' 24I will accept
nothing but what my men have eaten and the share that belongs to the men who went with me—to Aner,
Eshcol and Mamre. Let them have their share."

[a] *3* That is, the Dead Sea [b] *13* Or *a relative*; or *an ally* [c] *18* That is, Jerusalem [d] *19* Or *Possessor*; also in verse 22 [e] *20* Or *And praise be to*

14:10 Even today lumps of asphalt are often seen floating in the southern end of the Dead Sea. Flanked by hills on both sides, the Dead Sea is the lowest body of water on Earth (about 1,300 ft—396 m—below sea level).

14:13 Abram, the father of the Hebrew people, was the first Biblical character to be called a Hebrew (see the note on 10:21). Usually an ethnic term in the Bible, it was normally used by non-Israelites in a disparaging sense (see, e.g., 39:17). Outside the Bible, people known as the Habiru/Apiru (a word probably related to "Hebrew") are referred to as a property-less, dependent, immigrant (foreign) social class rather than as a specific ethnic group. The Amarna Letters (clay tablets found in Egypt) contain negative descriptions of them. See "The Amarna Tablets and the Habiru" on page 347.

14:14 The home was the first and most effective agency for religious training. During the nomadic life of the patriarchs education was purely a domestic activity, and the parents were the teachers. God called Abraham as the father of the chosen people and put upon him the responsibility of training his children and his household to walk in the ways of the Lord (18:19; cf. Ps 78:5–7). The reference in Genesis 14:14 to Abram's "trained men" implies a definite training program supervised by him. This is the only occurrence of the Hebrew term for "trained men" in the Bible. A related word used elsewhere in very ancient texts means "armed retainers."

14:19 In ancient times the chief Canaanite deity was frequently referred to as the "most high," "lord of heaven" and "creator of earth." Based upon the terminology and location (Jerusalem was in central Canaan), Melchizedek was probably a Canaanite king-priest. By identifying Melchizedek's "God Most High" with "the LORD" (v. 22), Abram bore testimony to the one true God, whom Melchizedek also had come to know.

14:22 In ancient times raising one's hand was a standard oath-taking practice (see Dt 32:40; Rev 10:5–6).

The Patriarchal Period: Mesopotamia During the Time of Abraham

A well and tamarisk tree at Beersheba
Photograph: © Todd Bolen/Bible Places.com

GENESIS 15 Near the end of the third millennium B.C., the **Sumerian** Third Dynasty of Ur lost the predominate influence it had enjoyed over most of **Mesopotamia**. The entire region experienced severe political instability as its city-states continually challenged one another, as well as those in northern Syria, and power frequently changed hands.

Kings with **Amorite** names ruled many of these city-states during the **patriarchal period**. The Amorites comprised a large and diverse group of northwestern Semitic tribes from Syria-Arabia. Many scholars once thought them to have been mostly nomadic invaders who brought with them the widespread political instability mentioned above, as well as the urban decline characterizing the end of the third millennium B.C. However, texts from **Mari**[1] and elsewhere indicate that the Amorites included both semi-nomadic pastoralists (raisers of livestock) and sedentary groups, generally organized around patriarchal figures who began settling in Mesopotamian villages and urban centers as early as the middle of the third millenium B.C. This cultural pattern is similar to the one we see occurring in portraits of the **patriarchs** of the Bible.

By the turn of the third millennium B.C. even larger numbers of Amorites had migrated south into **Canaan**[2] and southeast into Mesopotamia, perhaps pressured by the **Hurrians** from the north.[3] Many Amorites worked their way into positions of leadership. The most famous of these were Shamshi-Adad I in **Assyria** (late nineteenth to early eighteenth centuries B.C.) and **Hammurabi** in **Babylon** (early to mid eighteenth century B.C.).

The Biblical patriarchs most likely lived within this early second-millennium period. The cross-cultural interaction taking place among the Sumerians, **Akkadians** and Amorites, as well as the Hurrians and **Hittites** to the north, is clearly reflected in the patriarchal narratives in terms of social customs, laws and languages.[4] Far from being anachronistic, the details of the Biblical stories of the patriarchs fit well into the historical environment of the late second millennium B.C. There is no evidence that should lead scholars to question their authenticity.[5] See "Map 1" at the back of this Bible.

[1]See "Mari" on page 54. [2]See "Canaan" on page 324. [3]See "The Hurrians" on page 57. [4]See "Custom and Law in Ancient Mesopotamia" on page 36. [5]See "The Historicity of the Patriarchal Narratives" on page 73.

God's Covenant With Abram

15 After this, the word of the LORD came to Abram[d] in a vision:

> "Do not be afraid,[e] Abram.
> I am your shield,[a][f]
> your very great reward.[b]"

2 But Abram said, "O Sovereign LORD, what can you give me since I remain childless[g] and the one who will inherit[c] my estate is Eliezer of Damascus?" 3 And Abram said, "You have given me no children; so a servant[h] in my household will be my heir."

4 Then the word of the LORD came to him: "This man will not be your heir, but a son coming from your own body will be your heir.[i]" 5 He took him outside and said, "Look up at the heavens and count the stars[j]—if indeed you can count them." Then he said to him, "So shall your offspring be."[k]

6 Abram believed the LORD, and he credited it to him as righteousness.[l]

7 He also said to him, "I am the LORD, who brought you out of Ur of the Chaldeans to give you this land to take possession of it."

8 But Abram said, "O Sovereign LORD, how can I know[m] that I will gain possession of it?"

9 So the LORD said to him, "Bring me a heifer, a goat and a ram, each three years old, along with a dove and a young pigeon."

10 Abram brought all these to him, cut them in two and arranged the halves opposite each other;[n] the birds, however, he did not cut in half.[o] 11 Then birds of prey came down on the carcasses, but Abram drove them away.

12 As the sun was setting, Abram fell into a deep sleep,[p] and a thick and dreadful darkness came over him. 13 Then the LORD said to him, "Know for certain that your descendants will be strangers in a country not their own, and they will be enslaved[q] and mistreated four hundred years.[r] 14 But I will punish the nation they serve as slaves, and afterward they will come out[s] with great possessions.[t] 15 You, however, will go to your fathers in peace and be buried at a good old age.[u] 16 In the fourth generation your descendants will come back here, for the sin of the Amorites[v] has not yet reached its full measure."

17 When the sun had set and darkness had fallen, a smoking firepot with a blazing torch appeared and passed between the pieces.[w] 18 On that day the LORD made a covenant with Abram and said, "To your descendants I give this land,[x] from the river[d] of Egypt[y] to the great river, the Euphrates— 19 the land of the Kenites, Kenizzites, Kadmonites, 20 Hittites, Perizzites, Rephaites, 21 Amorites, Canaanites, Girgashites and Jebusites."

Hagar and Ishmael

16 Now Sarai, Abram's wife, had borne him no children.[z] But she had an Egyptian maidservant[a] named Hagar; 2 so she said to Abram, "The LORD has kept me from having children. Go, sleep with my maidservant; perhaps I can build a family through her."[b]

Abram agreed to what Sarai said. 3 So after Abram had been living in Canaan[c] ten years, Sarai his wife took her Egyptian maidservant Hagar and gave her to her husband to be his wife. 4 He slept with Hagar, and she conceived.

a *1* Or *sovereign* *b* *1* Or *shield; / your reward will be very great* *c* *2* The meaning of the Hebrew for this phrase is uncertain. *d* *18* Or *Wadi*

15:1 [d]Da 10:1 [e]Ge 21:17; 26:24; 46:3; 2Ki 6:16; Ps 27:1; Isa 41:10,13-14 [f]Dt 33:29; 2Sa 22:3,31; Ps 3:3 **15:2** [g]Ac 7:5 **15:3** [h]Ge 24:2,34 **15:4** [i]Gal 4:28 **15:5** [j]Ps 147:4; Jer 33:22 [k]Ge 12:2; 22:17; Ex 32:13; Ro 4:18*; Heb 11:12 **15:6** [l]Ps 106:31; Ro 4:3*,20-24*; Gal 3:6*; Jas 2:23* **15:8** [m]Lk 1:18 **15:10** [n]ver 17; Jer 34:18 [o]Lev 1:17 **15:12** [p]Ge 2:21 **15:13** [q]Ex 1:11 [r]ver 16; Ex 12:40; Ac 7:6,17 **15:14** [s]Ac 7:7* [t]Ex 12:32-38 **15:15** [u]Ge 25:8 **15:16** [v]1Ki 21:26 **15:17** [w]ver 10 **15:18** [x]Ge 12:7 [y]Nu 34:5 **16:1** [z]Ge 11:30; Gal 4:24-25 [a]Ge 21:9 **16:2** [b]Ge 30:3-4, 9-10 **16:3** [c]Ge 12:5

15:2 The term *servant* in ancient times applied to anyone under the authority of another, implying that not all servants were domestics or slaves. In some passages of Scripture the word properly means "young man" or "minister." It is applied to the relationship of men to others occupying high position—men such as Eliezer, whose place in the household of Abraham compared with that of a prime minister (v. 2; 24:2; Pr 14:35; Jn 18:20).

15:3 Ancient Nuzi law permitted a childless man to adopt one of his own male servants to be heir and guardian of his estate. It also allowed inheritance rights to be transferred to a son born to the primary wife *after* she had adopted her surrogate's son. See "Custom and Law in Ancient Mesopotamia" on page 36, "The Rights of the Firstborn" on page 43 and "Nuzi" on page 52.

15:7 Ancient royal covenants often began with the self-identification of the king and a brief historical prologue.

15:17 In ancient times parties solemnized a covenant by walking down an aisle flanked by the pieces of slaughtered animals (see Jer 34:18–19), perhaps signifying a self-maledictory oath. See "The Hittite Ritual of Passing Between the Pieces of a Sacrifice" on page 146.

16:1–2 The privilege of childbearing was appropriately viewed to be in God's hands. Conversely, the inability to bear children was seen as his punishment. Ancient people often considered a barren woman accursed, and in some cases her condition served as ground for divorce. Marriage contracts of the time were based on the Code of Hammurabi (an ancient Babylonian law code) and stipulated that an infertile wife should provide her husband with a surrogate childbearer. See "Custom and Law in Ancient Mesopotamia" on page 36 and "Nuzi" on page 52.

When she knew she was pregnant, she began to despise her mistress. 5Then Sarai said to Abram, "You
are responsible for the wrong I am suffering. I put my servant in your arms, and now that she knows she
is pregnant, she despises me. May the LORD judge between you and me."[d] 16:5 [d]Ge 31:53
6"Your servant is in your hands," Abram said. "Do with her whatever you think best." Then Sarai mis-
treated Hagar; so she fled from her.
7The angel of the LORD[e] found Hagar near a spring in the desert; it was the spring that is beside 16:7 [e]Ge 21:17;
the road to Shur.[f] 8And he said, "Hagar, servant of Sarai, where have you come from, and where are 22:11,15; 31:11
you going?" [f]Ge 20:1
"I'm running away from my mistress Sarai," she answered.
9Then the angel of the LORD told her, "Go back to your mistress and submit to her." 10The angel add-
ed, "I will so increase your descendants that they will be too numerous to count."[g] 16:10 [g]Ge 13:16;
11The angel of the LORD also said to her: 17:20

"You are now with child
and you will have a son.
You shall name him Ishmael,[a]
for the LORD has heard of your misery.[h] 16:11 [h]Ex 2:24;
12He will be a wild donkey of a man; 3:7,9
his hand will be against everyone
and everyone's hand against him,
and he will live in hostility
toward[b] all his brothers."[i] 16:12 [i]Ge 25:18

13She gave this name to the LORD who spoke to her: "You are the God who sees me," for she said, "I
have now seen[c] the One who sees me."[j] 14That is why the well was called Beer Lahai Roi[d]; it is still there, 16:13 [j]Ge 32:30
between Kadesh and Bered.
15So Hagar bore Abram a son,[k] and Abram gave the name Ishmael to the son she had borne. 16Abram 16:15 [k]Gal 4:22
was eighty-six years old when Hagar bore him Ishmael.

[a] 11 *Ishmael* means *God hears.* [b] 12 Or *live to the east / of* [c] 13 Or *seen the back of* [d] 14 *Beer Lahai Roi* means *well of the Living One who sees me.*

Naming of Children

GENESIS 16 Ancient Near Eastern peoples attached a deep significance to the naming of children. Unlike modern parents, who typically choose names, often long before a child's birth, on the basis of cultural popularity, family tradition, personal preference or sound, Israelite parents tended to select names based upon circumstances surrounding the birth or words spoken near the time of birth. For example, in Genesis 35:18 we read that Rachel, dying in childbirth, named her son Ben-Oni ("my painful son"), although Jacob renamed the baby Benjamin ("son of the right hand").

On rare occasions God revealed a name to a child's parents before birth, signifying the divinely established role that child would play in history. For example, God specified the name Isaac, meaning "he laughs." This name may reflect not only Abraham's and Sarah's laughter of disbelief upon learning that they were indeed to have a son in their old age (17:17; 18:12; 21:6) but also the ultimate joy Isaac would bring as the beginning of the fulfillment of God's longstanding promise to Abraham (17:4–8; 21:1–2). Another clear example of God naming a child is his own Son Jesus (the Greek version of Joshua, meaning "he saves"), whose divinely revealed purpose was to "save his people from their sins" (Mt 1:20–21). See also Hosea 1:4, 6 and 9 for some more sobering names God designated for the offspring of the prophet Hosea.

The Covenant of Circumcision

17 When Abram was ninety-nine years old, the LORD appeared to him and said, "I am God Almighty[a];[l] walk before me and be blameless.[m] 2 I will confirm my covenant between me and you[n] and will greatly increase your numbers."

3 Abram fell facedown, and God said to him, 4 "As for me, this is my covenant with you:[o] You will be the father of many nations.[p] 5 No longer will you be called Abram[b]; your name will be Abraham,[c][q] for I have made you a father of many nations.[r] 6 I will make you very fruitful;[s] I will make nations of you, and kings will come from you.[t] 7 I will establish my covenant as an everlasting covenant between me and you and your descendants after you for the generations to come, to be your God[u] and the God of your descendants after you.[v] 8 The whole land of Canaan,[w] where you are now an alien,[x] I will give as an everlasting possession to you and your descendants after you;[y] and I will be their God."

9 Then God said to Abraham, "As for you, you must keep my covenant, you and your descendants after you for the generations to come. 10 This is my covenant with you and your descendants after you, the covenant you are to keep: Every male among you shall be circumcised.[z] 11 You are to undergo circumcision,[a] and it will be the sign of the covenant[b] between me and you. 12 For the generations to come every male among you who is eight days old must be circumcised,[c] including those born in your household or bought with money from a foreigner—those who are not your offspring. 13 Whether born in your household or bought with your money, they must be circumcised. My covenant in your flesh is to be an everlasting covenant. 14 Any uncircumcised male, who has not been circumcised in the flesh, will be cut off from his people;[d] he has broken my covenant."

15 God also said to Abraham, "As for Sarai your wife, you are no longer to call her Sarai; her name will be Sarah. 16 I will bless her and will surely give you a son by her.[e] I will bless her so that she will be the mother of nations;[f] kings of peoples will come from her."

17 Abraham fell facedown; he laughed[g] and said to himself, "Will a son be born to a man a hundred years old? Will Sarah bear a child at the age of ninety?" 18 And Abraham said to God, "If only Ishmael might live under your blessing!"

19 Then God said, "Yes, but your wife Sarah will bear you a son,[h] and you will call him Isaac.[d] I will establish my covenant with him[i] as an everlasting covenant for his descendants after him. 20 And as for Ishmael, I have heard you: I will surely bless him; I will make him fruitful and will greatly increase his numbers.[j] He will be the father of twelve rulers,[k] and I will make him into a great nation.[l] 21 But my covenant I will establish with Isaac, whom Sarah will bear to you by this time next year."[m] 22 When he had finished speaking with Abraham, God went up from him.

23 On that very day Abraham took his son Ishmael and all those born in his household or bought with his money, every male in his household, and circumcised them, as God told him. 24 Abraham was ninety-nine years old when he was circumcised,[n] 25 and his son Ishmael was thirteen; 26 Abraham and his son Ishmael were both circumcised on that same day. 27 And every male in Abraham's household, including those born in his household or bought from a foreigner, was circumcised with him.

The Three Visitors

18 The LORD appeared to Abraham near the great trees of Mamre[o] while he was sitting at the entrance to his tent in the heat of the day. 2 Abraham looked up and saw three men[p] standing nearby. When he saw them, he hurried from the entrance of his tent to meet them and bowed low to the ground.

17:1 [l]Ge 28:3; Ex 6:3 [m]Dt 18:13 **17:2** [n]Ge 15:18
17:4 [o]Ge 15:18 [p]ver 16; Ge 12:2; 35:11; 48:19 **17:5** [q]ver 15; Ne 9:7 [r]Ro 4:17* **17:6** [s]Ge 35:11 [t]Mt 1:6
17:7 [u]Ex 29:45, 46 [v]Ro 9:8; Gal 3:16 **17:8** [w]Ps 105:9, 11 [x]Ge 23:4; 28:4; Ex 6:4 [y]Ge 12:7
17:10 [z]ver 23; Ge 21:4; Jn 7:22; Ac 7:8; Ro 4:11 **17:11** [a]Ex 12:48; Dt 10:16 [b]Ro 4:11 **17:12** [c]Lev 12:3; Lk 2:21
17:14 [d]Ex 4:24-26
17:16 [e]Ge 18:10 [f]Ge 35:11; Gal 4:31 **17:17** [g]Ge 18:12; 21:6
17:19 [h]Ge 18:14; 21:2 [i]Ge 26:3
17:20 [j]Ge 16:10 [k]Ge 25:12-16 [l]Ge 21:18 **17:21** [m]Ge 21:2
17:24 [n]Ro 4:11
18:1 [o]Ge 13:18; 14:13 **18:2** [p]ver 16,22; Ge 32:24; Jos 5:13; Jdg 13:6-11; Heb 13:2

[a] *1* Hebrew *El-Shaddai* [b] *5* *Abram* means *exalted father.* [c] *5* *Abraham* means *father of many.* [d] *19* *Isaac* means *he laughs.*

17:5 Ancient Near Eastern peoples attached a deep significance to names, and Israelite parents tended to select a child's name based upon circumstances surrounding the birth or words spoken near the time of birth. By giving Abram a new name God marked him in a special way as his servant. See "Naming of Children" on page 28.

17:10 Although circumcision was practiced elsewhere in antiquity (see Jer 9:25–26; Eze 32:18–19), infant circumcision seems to have been unique. It was to be a sign of both the material and the spiritual aspects of God's covenant with Abraham (see "Circumcision in the Ancient World" on p. 1840).

18:1–33 In the early days of humanity, before people had the written Word, before the incarnation and before the Holy Spirit had come to make his abode in human hearts, God sometimes appeared and talked with people. One of the loveliest and most instructive of the theophanies (visible appearances of God) is found in Genesis 18. From Abraham's time on theophanies generally occurred when recipients were asleep, as in Jacob's vision at Bethel (28:10–17). But God addressed Moses "face to face" (Ex 33:11). There is good reason to believe that theophanies before the incarnation of Christ were visible manifestations of the pre-incarnate Son of God.

18:1–8 Hospitality was one of the most highly regarded virtues of the ancient world. Social protocol required an actual meal to exceed what was first offered. Thus Abraham ordered fresh bread, a calf and a mixture of milk and yogurt. The fresh meat was particularly generous—not a normal staple in the ancients' daily diet.

3 He said, "If I have found favor in your eyes, my lord,[a] do not pass your servant by. 4 Let a little water
be brought, and then you may all wash your feet[q] and rest under this tree. 5 Let me get you something to 18:4 [q]Ge 19:2; 43:24
eat,[r] so you can be refreshed and then go on your way—now that you have come to your servant." 18:5 [r]Jdg 13:15
"Very well," they answered, "do as you say."
6 So Abraham hurried into the tent to Sarah. "Quick," he said, "get three seahs[b] of fine flour and knead
it and bake some bread."
7 Then he ran to the herd and selected a choice, tender calf and gave it to a servant, who hurried to pre-
pare it. 8 He then brought some curds and milk and the calf that had been prepared, and set these before
them.[s] While they ate, he stood near them under a tree. 18:8 [s]Ge 19:3
9 "Where is your wife Sarah?" they asked him.
"There, in the tent," he said.
10 Then the LORD[c] said, "I will surely return to you about this time next year, and Sarah your wife will
have a son."[t] 18:10 [t]Ro 9:9*
Now Sarah was listening at the entrance to the tent, which was behind him. 11 Abraham and Sarah were
already old and well advanced in years,[u] and Sarah was past the age of childbearing.[v] 12 So Sarah laughed[w] 18:11 [u]Ge 17:17 [v]Ro 4:19
to herself as she thought, "After I am worn out and my master[d][x] is old, will I now have this pleasure?" 18:12 [w]Ge 17:17; 21:6 [x]1Pe 3:6
13 Then the LORD said to Abraham, "Why did Sarah laugh and say, 'Will I really have a child, now that
I am old?' 14 Is anything too hard for the LORD?[y] I will return to you at the appointed time next year and 18:14 [y]Jer 32:17, 27; Zec 8:6; Mt 19:26; Lk 1:37; Ro 4:21
Sarah will have a son."
15 Sarah was afraid, so she lied and said, "I did not laugh."
But he said, "Yes, you did laugh."

[a] 3 Or *O Lord* [b] 6 That is, probably about 20 quarts (about 22 liters) [c] 10 Hebrew *Then he* [d] 12 Or *husband*

CULTURAL AND HISTORICAL NOTES

The Role of the Patriarch in Family Life

GENESIS 18 In order to understand the description of Abraham as the founding father of Israel's faith, we do well to recognize the key role a **patriarch** such as Abraham played in family life during this **pre-monarchic period.** The social structure of the time had three tiers: tribe, clan and family/household (Jos 7:14). The fundamental unit was the household (Hebrew *bet av*, meaning "house of a father"). It consisted of a patriarch—responsible adult male—his wife, his sons and their wives, his grandchildren and various other dependents. Since lineage/descent in patriarchal societies was passed along through sons, married daughters joined their husbands' households.

Exploration of **Iron Age** I[1] settlements, although they existed later than the patriarchal period, tells us much about Israelite patriarchal society. They indicate that such social units likely inhabited clusters of compounds with a few houses around a courtyard, encircled by a low wall. The elder patriarch and his immediate descendants would occupy one of the homes, with his married sons and their families living in other houses within the compound. In like manner Jacob, along with his sons and their families, sojourned as a small, patriarchal clan (Ge 46:5–7).

Various Biblical passages reveal much about Abraham's patriarchal household. The patriarch was responsible for the socioeconomic and religious well-being of his entire household (14:13–16). In Genesis 18, for example, Abraham's hospitality toward his three visitors reflected kinship responsibilities that even included the protection of vulnerable sojourners or resident aliens (cf. Lev. 19:33–34). Providing water for dusty feet and serving an elaborate meal conferred honor upon guests, and, as in Abraham's case, indicated his generosity.

At the same time, Abraham in Genesis 18 may have realized that he was entertaining heavenly guests and thus have been especially hospitable. The bond established during their subsequent table fellowship engendered a blessing from one of the guests and established a basis for Abraham's intercession for Sodom.[2]

The sacrosanct nature of patriarchal hospitality recurs as a metaphor for God as the host of a feast in Psalm 23:5–6 (cf. Mt 8:11; Lk 13:29).

[1]See "Archaeological Periods" chart on page xx in the front of this Bible. [2]See "The Cities of the Plain" on page 23 and "The Destruction of Sodom and Gomorrah" on page 32.

Abraham Pleads for Sodom

16 When the men got up to leave, they looked down toward Sodom, and Abraham walked along with
18:17 [z]Am 3:7 [a]Ge 19:24 them to see them on their way. 17 Then the LORD said, "Shall I hide from Abraham[z] what I am about to do?[a]
18:18 [b]Gal 3:8* 18 Abraham will surely become a great and powerful nation,[b] and all nations on earth will be blessed
18:19 [c]Dt 4:9-10; 6:7 [d]Jos 24:15; through him. 19 For I have chosen him, so that he will direct his children[c] and his household after him to
Eph 6:4 keep the way of the LORD[d] by doing what is right and just, so that the LORD will bring about for Abraham
what he has promised him."

20 Then the LORD said, "The outcry against Sodom and Gomorrah is so great and their sin so grievous
18:21 [e]Ge 11:5 21 that I will go down[e] and see if what they have done is as bad as the outcry that has reached me. If not,
I will know."

18:22 [f]Ge 19:1 22 The men turned away and went toward Sodom,[f] but Abraham remained standing before the LORD.[a]
18:23 [g]Nu 16:22 23 Then Abraham approached him and said: "Will you sweep away the righteous with the wicked?[g] 24 What
if there are fifty righteous people in the city? Will you really sweep it away and not spare[b] the place for
18:24 [h]Jer 5:1 the sake of the fifty righteous people in it?[h] 25 Far be it from you to do such a thing—to kill the righteous
with the wicked, treating the righteous and the wicked alike. Far be it from you! Will not the Judge[c] of all
18:25 [i]Job 8:3, 20; Ps 58:11; 94:2; Isa 3:10-11; Ro 3:6 the earth do right?"[i]

26 The LORD said, "If I find fifty righteous people in the city of Sodom, I will spare the whole place for
18:26 [j]Jer 5:1 their sake.[j]"

27 Then Abraham spoke up again: "Now that I have been so bold as to speak to the Lord, though I am
18:27 [k]Ge 2:7; 3:19; Job 30:19; 42:6 nothing but dust and ashes,[k] 28 what if the number of the righteous is five less than fifty? Will you destroy
the whole city because of five people?"

"If I find forty-five there," he said, "I will not destroy it."

29 Once again he spoke to him, "What if only forty are found there?"

He said, "For the sake of forty, I will not do it."

30 Then he said, "May the Lord not be angry, but let me speak. What if only thirty can be found there?"

He answered, "I will not do it if I find thirty there."

31 Abraham said, "Now that I have been so bold as to speak to the Lord, what if only twenty can be
found there?"

He said, "For the sake of twenty, I will not destroy it."

18:32 [l]Jdg 6:39 32 Then he said, "May the Lord not be angry, but let me speak just once more.[l] What if only ten can be
found there?"

[m]Jer 5:1 He answered, "For the sake of ten,[m] I will not destroy it."

33 When the LORD had finished speaking with Abraham, he left, and Abraham returned home.

Sodom and Gomorrah Destroyed

19:1 [n]Ge 18:22 [o]Ge 18:1 **19** The two angels arrived at Sodom[n] in the evening, and Lot was sitting in the gateway of the city.[o]
When he saw them, he got up to meet them and bowed down with his face to the ground. 2 "My
19:2 [p]Ge 18:4; Lk 7:44 lords," he said, "please turn aside to your servant's house. You can wash your feet[p] and spend the night
and then go on your way early in the morning."

"No," they answered, "we will spend the night in the square."

3 But he insisted so strongly that they did go with him and entered his house. He prepared a meal for
19:3 [q]Ge 18:6 them, baking bread without yeast, and they ate.[q] 4 Before they had gone to bed, all the men from every
part of the city of Sodom—both young and old—surrounded the house. 5 They called to Lot, "Where are
19:5 [r]Jdg 19:22; Isa 3:9; Ro 1:24-27 the men who came to you tonight? Bring them out to us so that we can have sex with them."[r]

19:6 [s]Jdg 19:23 6 Lot went outside to meet them[s] and shut the door behind him 7 and said, "No, my friends. Don't do

[a] *22* Masoretic Text; an ancient Hebrew scribal tradition *but the LORD remained standing before Abraham* [b] *24* Or *forgive*; also in verse 26 [c] *25* Or *Ruler*

18:27 The expression "dust and ashes" is a play on words (*aphar* and *epher*) that signifies the origin of the human body from the ordinary chemical elements, contrasting the lowliness of a human being with the dignity of God.

19:1 The city gateway served as the administrative and judicial center where legal matters were discussed and prosecuted (see Ru 4:1–12; Pr 31:23; see also "The City Gate" on p. 392). Treaties witnessed by the city elders at the gate were as legally binding as written contracts are today.

19:2 The square was a large, open space near the main city gateway used for public gatherings. Important cities could have two or more squares (see Ne 8:16).

19:5 A sodomite was one who practiced that unnatural vice for which Sodom became noted. Although not named as such, the practice is referred to in Romans 1:27, and God strictly forbade it (Dt 23:17). Usually the practice was in connection with heathen worship, and its presence was a sign of departure from the Lord (1Ki 14:24).

THE RELIABILITY OF THE BIBLE

THE DESTRUCTION OF SODOM AND GOMORRAH

GENESIS 19 According to Genesis 19:24 burning sulfur "rained down" on Sodom and Gomorrah, obliterating both of these cities, as well as the surrounding region (vv. 25,29). To date, the location of Sodom is still disputed (but note possible location of Sodom and Gomorrah indicated by a box and arrow on "Map 1" in the back of this Bible). Some people place it on the southwestern side of the Dead Sea, others on the north side of this body of water near the mouth of the Jordan and still others at modern Bab edh-Dhra on the southeastern side of the Dead Sea.[1]

Recently archaeologists have focused significant attention upon Bab edh-Dhra, where they have found evidence of several **Early Bronze Age**[2] occupation levels. Although a layer of ash and burned debris has been discovered in excavations there, the most dramatic evidence that this may indeed be the site of ancient Sodom comes from a nearby cemetery. The dead had been interred in charnel houses, or mausoleums, constructed above ground. Five of these structures were excavated and found to have been burned. A detailed examination of the largest of these (26 ft x 51 ft [8 m x 15.5 m]) indicated that the fire had begun on the roof. Geological investigations determined that an earthquake had added to the devastation.

Since there were several distinct occupation levels at Bab edh-Dhra (evidence of habitation at the site during various time periods), evidence had to be handled carefully. For example, there is a substantial ash layer associated with the occupation in Early Bronze I (the oldest of the Early Bronze occupation levels), but this cannot be associated with the Biblical destruction of Sodom because its ruins point to a date far earlier than the time of Abraham. In fact, this earlier, fire-related damage appears to have been the work of invaders. The Early Bronze III city is more likely to be the Biblical Sodom. A much larger city, evidence points to its destruction by a combination of earthquake and fire in approximately 2350 B.C. People evidently reoccupied this site in Early Bronze IV, but it appears to have been permanently abandoned for some reason around 2150 B.C.

[1]See "The Cities of the Plain" on page 23. [2]See "Archaeological Periods" chart on page xx in the front of this Bible.

this wicked thing. 8Look, I have two daughters who have never slept with a man. Let me bring them out
to you, and you can do what you like with them. But don't do anything to these men, for they have come
under the protection of my roof."[t] **19:8** [t]Jdg 19:24
9"Get out of our way," they replied. "This fellow came here as an alien, and now he wants
to play the judge![u] We'll treat you worse than them." They kept bringing pressure on Lot and moved for- **19:9** [u]Ex 2:14; Ac 7:27
ward to break down the door.
10But the men inside reached out and pulled Lot back into the house and shut the door. 11Then they
struck the men who were at the door of the house, young and old, with blindness[v] so that they could not **19:11** [v]Dt 28:28-29; 2Ki 6:18; Ac 13:11
find the door.
12The two men said to Lot, "Do you have anyone else here—sons-in-law, sons or daughters, or any-
one else in the city who belongs to you?[w] Get them out of here, 13because we are going to destroy this **19:12** [w]Ge 7:1
place. The outcry to the LORD against its people is so great that he has sent us to destroy it."[x] **19:13** [x]1Ch 21:15
14So Lot went out and spoke to his sons-in-law, who were pledged to marry[a] his daughters. He said,
"Hurry and get out of this place, because the LORD is about to destroy the city![y]" But his sons-in-law **19:14** [y]Nu 16:21
thought he was joking.[z] [z]Ex 9:21; Lk 17:28
15With the coming of dawn, the angels urged Lot, saying, "Hurry! Take your wife and your two daugh-
ters who are here, or you will be swept away[a] when the city is punished.[b]" **19:15** [a]Nu 16:26 [b]Rev 18:4

[a] *14 Or were married to*

19:8 In ancient times a host was obliged to protect his guests in every situation.

16When he hesitated, the men grasped his hand and the hands of his wife and of his two daughters
and led them safely out of the city, for the LORD was merciful to them. 17As soon as they had brought
19:17 [c]Jer 48:6 them out, one of them said, "Flee for your lives![c] Don't look back,[d] and don't stop anywhere in the plain!
[d]ver 26 Flee to the mountains or you will be swept away!"
18But Lot said to them, "No, my lords,[a] please! 19Your[b] servant has found favor in your[b] eyes, and you[b]
have shown great kindness to me in sparing my life. But I can't flee to the mountains; this disaster will
overtake me, and I'll die. 20Look, here is a town near enough to run to, and it is small. Let me flee to it—
it is very small, isn't it? Then my life will be spared."
21He said to him, "Very well, I will grant this request too; I will not overthrow the town you speak of. 22But
flee there quickly, because I cannot do anything until you reach it." (That is why the town was called Zoar.[c])
23By the time Lot reached Zoar, the sun had risen over the land. 24Then the LORD rained down burn-
19:24 [e]Dt 29:23; Isa 1:9; 13:19 ing sulfur on Sodom and Gomorrah[e]—from the LORD out of the heavens.[f] 25Thus he overthrew those cit-
[f]Lk 17:29; 2Pe 2:6; Jude 7 ies and the entire plain, including all those living in the cities—and also the vegetation in the land.[g]
19:25 26But Lot's wife looked back,[h] and she became a pillar of salt.[i]
[g]Ps 107:34; Eze 16:48 27Early the next morning Abraham got up and returned to the place where he had stood before the
19:26 [h]ver 17 [i]Lk 17:32 LORD.[j] 28He looked down toward Sodom and Gomorrah, toward all the land of the plain, and he saw dense
19:27 [j]Ge 18:22 19:28 [k]Rev 9:2; smoke rising from the land, like smoke from a furnace.[k]
18:9 19:29 [l]2Pe 2:7 29So when God destroyed the cities of the plain, he remembered Abraham, and he brought Lot out of
the catastrophe[l] that overthrew the cities where Lot had lived.

Lot and His Daughters

19:30 [m]ver 19 30Lot and his two daughters left Zoar and settled in the mountains,[m] for he was afraid to stay in Zoar.
He and his two daughters lived in a cave. 31One day the older daughter said to the younger, "Our father
is old, and there is no man around here to lie with us, as is the custom all over the earth. 32Let's get our
father to drink wine and then lie with him and preserve our family line through our father."
33That night they got their father to drink wine, and the older daughter went in and lay with him. He
was not aware of it when she lay down or when she got up.
34The next day the older daughter said to the younger, "Last night I lay with my father. Let's get him
to drink wine again tonight, and you go in and lie with him so we can preserve our family line through
our father." 35So they got their father to drink wine that night also, and the younger daughter went and
lay with him. Again he was not aware of it when she lay down or when she got up.
36So both of Lot's daughters became pregnant by their father. 37The older daughter had a son, and she
19:37 [n]Dt 2:9 named him Moab[d]; he is the father of the Moabites[n] of today. 38The younger daughter also had a son, and
19:38 [o]Dt 2:19 she named him Ben-Ammi[e]; he is the father of the Ammonites[o] of today.

Abraham and Abimelech

20:1 [p]Ge 18:1 20 Now Abraham moved on from there[p] into the region of the Negev and lived between Kadesh and
[q]Ge 26:1,6,17 Shur. For a while he stayed in Gerar,[q] 2and there Abraham said of his wife Sarah, "She is my sis-
20:2 [r]ver 12; Ge 12:13; 26:7 ter.[r]" Then Abimelech king of Gerar sent for Sarah and took her.[s]
[s]Ge 12:15 3But God came to Abimelech in a dream[t] one night and said to him, "You are as good as dead because
20:3 [t]Job 33:15; Mt 27:19 of the woman you have taken; she is a married woman."[u]
[u]Ps 105:14 20:4 [v]Ge 18:25 4Now Abimelech had not gone near her, so he said, "Lord, will you destroy an innocent nation?[v] 5Did
he not say to me, 'She is my sister,' and didn't she also say, 'He is my brother'? I have done this with a clear
conscience and clean hands."
6Then God said to him in the dream, "Yes, I know you did this with a clear conscience, and so I have
20:6 [w]1Sa 25:26, 34 kept[w] you from sinning against me. That is why I did not let you touch her. 7Now return the man's wife,
20:7 [x]ver 17; 1Sa 7:5; Job 42:8 for he is a prophet, and he will pray for you[x] and you will live. But if you do not return her, you may be
sure that you and all yours will die."
8Early the next morning Abimelech summoned all his officials, and when he told them all that had

[a] *18* Or *No, Lord*; or *No, my lord* [b] *19* The Hebrew is singular. [c] *22* *Zoar* means *small.* [d] *37* *Moab* sounds like the Hebrew for *from father.* [e] *38* *Ben-Ammi* means *son of my people.*

19:31–38 Entirely unsupported is the critical view held by some scholars that this infamous incident in the cave was "created" by a later writer to justify the inferior position of the Moabites and Ammonites in their relationship with Israel (see "Moab" on p. 292 and "Ammon" on p. 364). At any rate, the almost buried faith of Lot reappeared much later in Ruth, the Moabitess who was also the great-grandmother of David and thus a member of the Messianic line (Ru 1:16–18; 4:13–21).

happened, they were very much afraid. 9 Then Abimelech called Abraham in and said, "What have you
done to us? How have I wronged you that you have brought such great guilt upon me and my kingdom?
You have done things to me that should not be done.[y]" 10 And Abimelech asked Abraham, "What was your
reason for doing this?"

11 Abraham replied, "I said to myself, 'There is surely no fear of God[z] in this place, and they will
kill me because of my wife.'[a] 12 Besides, she really is my sister, the daughter of my father though not

20:9 [y]Ge 12:18; 26:10; 34:7
20:11 [z]Ge 42:18; Ps 36:1
20:11 [a]Ge 12:12; 26:7

20:12 The word for "sister" (Hebrew *'āhôth*, Greek *adelphē*) is used in the Bible with varying meanings. In the Old Testament it refers to females having the same parents, females having one parent in common, a female relative or a woman of the same country (v. 12;

The Negev: Its Climate and Features

GENESIS 20 For thousands of years people have grazed their flocks and herds seasonally in the Negev (see "Map 2" in the back of this Bible), the southern region of Israel sandwiched between the hill country of Judah to the north and the deserts of Zin, Shur and Paran to the south. In fact, the seminomadic **patriarchs** (Abraham, Isaac and Jacob/Israel) grazed their livestock in the desert-like Negev during the winter and migrated north to Judah's hill country, around Bethel and Shechem, for the summer months ("Map 1").[1] During the New Testament period the Negev was known as **Idumea** (Mk 3:8).

In Biblical times the Negev was mostly south of the Dead Sea, some 30 miles (48 km) from east to west and centered around Beersheba (again see "Map 1"). Open, rugged and sparsely populated, the region supports scrub brush but no forests. It has two seasons: a milder winter with periodic rains and a hot, dry summer. Because less than 8 inches (200 mm) of rain falls annually in the Negev, the area is unsuitable for farming.

[1] See "Bethel" on page 59 and "Shechem" on page 340.

Negev landscape
Photograph courtesy of © Dr. Gary Pratico

of my mother; and she became my wife. [13]And when God had me wander from my father's house-
hold, I said to her, 'This is how you can show your love to me: Everywhere we go, say of me, "He is
my brother." ' "
20:14 [b]Ge 12:16 [14]Then Abimelech brought sheep and cattle and male and female slaves and gave them to Abraham,[b] and
20:15 [c]Ge 13:9 he returned Sarah his wife to him. [15]And Abimelech said, "My land is before you; live wherever you like."[c]
[16]To Sarah he said, "I am giving your brother a thousand shekels[a] of silver. This is to cover the offense
against you before all who are with you; you are completely vindicated."
20:17 [d]Job 42:9 [17]Then Abraham prayed to God,[d] and God healed Abimelech, his wife and his slave girls so they could
have children again, [18]for the LORD had closed up every womb in Abimelech's household because of Abra-
20:18 [e]Ge 12:17 ham's wife Sarah.[e]

The Birth of Isaac

21:1 [f]1Sa 2:21 [g]Ge 8:1; 17:16, 21; Gal 4:23 21 Now the LORD was gracious to Sarah[f] as he had said, and the LORD did for Sarah what he had
promised.[g] [2]Sarah became pregnant and bore a son[h] to Abraham in his old age,[i] at the very time
21:2 [h]Ge 17:19 [i]Gal 4:22; Heb 11:11 God had promised him. [3]Abraham gave the name Isaac[b][j] to the son Sarah bore him. [4]When his son Isaac
21:3 [j]Ge 17:19 was eight days old, Abraham circumcised him,[k] as God commanded him. [5]Abraham was a hundred years
21:4 [k]Ge 17:10, 12; Ac 7:8 old when his son Isaac was born to him.
21:6 [l]Ge 17:17; Isa 54:1 [6]Sarah said, "God has brought me laughter,[l] and everyone who hears about this will laugh with me."
[7]And she added, "Who would have said to Abraham that Sarah would nurse children? Yet I have borne
him a son in his old age."

Hagar and Ishmael Sent Away

[8]The child grew and was weaned, and on the day Isaac was weaned Abraham held a great feast. [9]But
21:9 [m]Ge 16:15 [n]Gal 4:29 Sarah saw that the son whom Hagar the Egyptian had borne to Abraham[m] was mocking,[n] [10]and she said
to Abraham, "Get rid of that slave woman and her son, for that slave woman's son will never share in the
21:10 [o]Gal 4:30* inheritance with my son Isaac."[o]
21:11 [p]Ge 17:18 [11]The matter distressed Abraham greatly because it concerned his son.[p] [12]But God said to him, "Do
not be so distressed about the boy and your maidservant. Listen to whatever Sarah tells you, because it
21:12 [q]Ro 9:7*; Heb 11:18* is through Isaac that your offspring[c] will be reckoned.[q] [13]I will make the son of the maidservant into a
21:13 [r]ver 18 nation[r] also, because he is your offspring."
[14]Early the next morning Abraham took some food and a skin of water and gave them to Hagar. He
set them on her shoulders and then sent her off with the boy. She went on her way and wandered in the
21:14 [s]ver 31,32 desert of Beersheba.[s]
[15]When the water in the skin was gone, she put the boy under one of the bushes. [16]Then she went off
and sat down nearby, about a bowshot away, for she thought, "I cannot watch the boy die." And as she sat
there nearby, she[d] began to sob.
21:17 [t]Ex 3:7 [17]God heard the boy crying,[t] and the angel of God called to Hagar from heaven and said to her, "What
is the matter, Hagar? Do not be afraid; God has heard the boy crying as he lies there. [18]Lift the boy up and
21:18 [u]ver 13 take him by the hand, for I will make him into a great nation.[u]"
21:19 [v]Nu 22:31 [19]Then God opened her eyes[v] and she saw a well of water. So she went and filled the skin with water
and gave the boy a drink.
21:20 [w]Ge 26:3, 24; 28:15; 39:2, 21,23 [20]God was with the boy[w] as he grew up. He lived in the desert and became an archer. [21]While he was
21:21 [x]Ge 24:4, 38 living in the Desert of Paran, his mother got a wife for him[x] from Egypt.

[a] 16 That is, about 25 pounds (about 11.5 kilograms) [b] 3 *Isaac* means *he laughs.* [c] 12 Or *seed* [d] 16 Hebrew; Septuagint *the child*

Lev 18:18; Nu 25:18; Job 42:11). In the New Testament it is used of girls belonging to the same family or simply of female blood relatives (Mt 13:56; Mk 6:3; Lk 10:39). The word is also used figuratively in Scripture (Eze 16:45; Ro 16:1; 2Jn 13).

In this case Sarah was Abraham's half sister, the daughter of his father but not of his mother. Marriage to half sisters was not uncommon in ancient times.

20:16 The word "shekels," though not included in the Hebrew text, is correctly supplied here as the most common unit of weight in ancient times. Originally the shekel was only a weight, not a coin, since coinage was not invented until the seventh century B.C.

21:8 In the ancient Near East many children died before they reached the age of two or three (the usual age for a child to be weaned), so a child's weaning was a celebrated rite of passage.

21:11 Abraham's distress was due not only to love but also to legal custom. The tradition of his day, illustrated later in the Nuzi tablets, prohibited the arbitrary expulsion of a servant girl's son (whose legal status was relatively weak in any case). See "Custom and Law in Ancient Mesopotamia" on page 36, "The Rights of the Firstborn" on page 43 and "Nuzi" on page 52.

The Treaty at Beersheba

22 At that time Abimelech and Phicol the commander of his forces said to Abraham, "God is with you
in everything you do. 23 Now swear[y] to me here before God that you will not deal falsely with me or my
children or my descendants. Show to me and the country where you are living as an alien the same kind-
ness I have shown to you."
24 Abraham said, "I swear it."

21:23 [y]ver 31; Jos 2:12

21:25–30 In a land of seasonal rainfall, wells were extremely important to the welfare of the human population and of their flocks and herds. The area in which Abraham had dug a well was under Abimelech's political control but was owned by no one. Abraham

Custom and Law in Ancient Mesopotamia

GENESIS 21 Laws from ancient **Mesopotamia** provide various interesting parallels to the Genesis stories. In particular, numerous regulations illustrate the marriage and inheritance issues found in the accounts of the **patriarchs**. For example:

Just as Sarai procured an heir for Abram through her maid (Ge 16; cf. ch. 30), the **Sumerian** laws of Ur-Nammu (founder and ruler of Ur's Third Dynasty, c. 2044–2007 B.C.) allowed a husband to take a concubine after waiting in vain for his primary wife to bear children. As in Sarai's case, the primary wife might even have initiated the arrangement.

Hurrian law at **Nuzi**[1] (mid-second millennium B.C.) and the **Code of Hammurabi** in **Babylonia** (early eighteenth century B.C.) allowed a man to adopt as legitimate heirs any children he may have fathered through a slave woman (see 17:18).

In Sumer, the eldest son inherited the whole of his father's estate and assumed responsibility for his siblings. But in **Assyria** and Nuzi brothers divided their father's estate, with the eldest son receiving a double portion.[2]

Nuzi law permitted inheritance rights to be transferred to a son born to the primary wife *after* she had adopted her surrogate's son. In a similar manner Isaac (although born after Ishmael) had the right to be Abraham's chief heir (21:12).

Neo-Babylonian law included the provision that sons born to a concubine would be subordinate to any sons born to the primary wife and that the combined sons of the primary wife would inherit two-thirds of the estate.

The disinheritance of a son, a practice allowed in certain societies, generally required a court order that might be officially overturned if the father were found to have acted unfairly. Some scholars, based upon such a prohibition in Nuzi law, have questioned the legality of Sarah's demand to expel Hagar and Ishmael (ch. 21), which by analogy may indicate that Abraham lived under similar customs and laws. Indeed, Abraham was hesitant to comply with Sarah's wish and did so only after divine intervention (vv. 10–13).[3]

In addition to family legislation, certain laws and customs concerning contracts and other agreements mentioned in Genesis had parallels in Mesopotamia. Treaties discovered at **Mari**[4] and modern Tell Leilan (from the early second millennium B.C.) are strikingly similar to the treaty reports in Genesis 21, 26 and 31:

In each case a formal oath was requested and given.

The oaths were followed by reports of stipulations, frequently including a pledge of nonhostility.

The oaths generally involved ceremonial feasts or sacrifices (26:30) and a gift exchange of sorts, particularly if the parties to the agreement had met in person (cf. 21:27–30).

The Ur-Nammu Law Code (oldest known code of laws; Sumer, twenty-first century B.C.)

© The Schøyen Collection; photography courtesy of Mr. Martin Schøyen

The Mesopotamian cultural milieu from which the patriarchs emerged helps us to understand patriarchal social structures and practices reported throughout Genesis.[5]

[1]See "Nuzi" on page 52. [2]See "Inheritance in the Ancient Near East" on page 250. [3]See "The Rights of the Firstborn" on page 43. [4]See "Mari" on page 54.
[5]See "The Patriarchal Period: Mesopotamia During the Time of Abraham" on page 26 and "The Historicity of the Patriarchal Narratives" on page 73.

25 Then Abraham complained to Abimelech about a well of water that Abimelech's servants had
21:25 [z]Ge 26:15, 18,20-22 seized.[z] 26 But Abimelech said, "I don't know who has done this. You did not tell me, and I heard about it
only today."
27 So Abraham brought sheep and cattle and gave them to Abimelech, and the two men made a trea-
21:27 [a]Ge 26:28, 31 ty.[a] 28 Abraham set apart seven ewe lambs from the flock, 29 and Abimelech asked Abraham, "What is the
meaning of these seven ewe lambs you have set apart by themselves?"
21:30 [b]Ge 31:44, 47,48,50,52 30 He replied, "Accept these seven lambs from my hand as a witness[b] that I dug this well."
21:31 [c]Ge 26:33 31 So that place was called Beersheba,[a] [c] because the two men swore an oath there.
32 After the treaty had been made at Beersheba, Abimelech and Phicol the commander of his forces re-
turned to the land of the Philistines. 33 Abraham planted a tamarisk tree in Beersheba, and there he called
21:33 [d]Ge 4:26 [e]Dt 33:27 upon the name of the LORD,[d] the Eternal God.[e] 34 And Abraham stayed in the land of the Philistines for a
long time.

Abraham Tested

22:1 [f]Dt 8:2,16; Heb 11:17; Jas 1:12-13 **22** Some time later God tested[f] Abraham. He said to him, "Abraham!"
"Here I am," he replied.
22:2 [g]ver 12,16; Jn 3:16; Heb 11:17; 1Jn 4:9 [h]2Ch 3:1 2 Then God said, "Take your son[g], your only son, Isaac, whom you love, and go to the region of Mori-
ah.[h] Sacrifice him there as a burnt offering on one of the mountains I will tell you about."
3 Early the next morning Abraham got up and saddled his donkey. He took with him two of his ser-
vants and his son Isaac. When he had cut enough wood for the burnt offering, he set out for the place God
had told him about. 4 On the third day Abraham looked up and saw the place in the distance. 5 He said to

[a] *31 Beersheba* can mean *well of seven* or *well of the oath.*

was claiming ownership not of the land but of the right to the water in the well. Such squatter's rights were available to a resident alien. See "The Negev: Its Climate and Features" on page 34 and "Wells, Cisterns and Aqueducks in the Ancient World" on page 1259.

21:31 Beersheba, an important town in the northern Negev, marked the southernmost boundary of the Israelite monarchy in later times (see, e.g., 2Sa 17:11; see also "Beersheba" on p. 518). Though its authenticity is uncertain, there is an ancient well there called "Abraham's well" (see Ge. 21:25).

21:32 Abimelech is a Semitic, not a Philistine name. So it may be that the reference to the "land of the Philistines" is anachronistic and merely intended to indicate the location, not the race of Abimelech.

22:2 The author of Chronicles identified the "region of Moriah" as the temple mount in Jerusalem (2Ch 3:1). Today Mount Moriah is occupied by the Dome of the Rock, an impressive Muslim structure erected in A.D. 691. A large outcropping of rock inside the building is still pointed to as the traditional site of the intended sacrifice of Isaac. See "Mount Moriah" on page 37.

Mount Moriah

GENESIS 22 "Mount Moriah," according to 2 Chronicles 3:1, was the location in Jerusalem where **Yahweh** appeared to David, inspiring him to build an altar and make a sacrifice. Solomon later constructed the temple on the same site.[1]

Some scholars are hesitant to identify this location as being synonymous with the site where God tested Abraham's faith by the near-sacrifice of Isaac because Genesis 22:2 names Moriah as a region, not a specific mountain. Also, it seems incongruous that Abraham would have carried wood to Jerusalem, a forested area, rather than gathering it at the site of the planned sacrifice. On the other hand, it may not seem surprising that Abraham would have gone prepared to make the sacrifice and would not have wanted to go to the trouble of seeking out suitably dried wood after his arrival. Also, Moriah at Jerusalem can reasonably be described as about a three-day trek from Beersheba (see vv. 4,19).

Genesis 22:14 indicates that later generations would know this site as "the mountain [or hill] of the LORD," language commonly used elsewhere for Zion/Jerusalem (see Ps 24:3; Isa 2:3; Zec 8:3). The name Moriah might be associated with a Hebrew verb meaning "to see" or "to provide," a theologically significant term appearing repeatedly throughout Genesis 22:1–19. In Jerusalem, as in no other place, the Lord would subsequently be "seen" and would "provide" for his people through the benefits of the sacrifices he would ordain. Based upon this association the Biblical authors may have assumed that Abraham was prepared to offer his sacrifice on the same mountain on which the Israelites would later offer theirs—Mount Zion in Jerusalem.

[1] See "Solomon's Temple and Other Ancient Temples" on page 620.

his servants, "Stay here with the donkey while I and the boy go over there. We will worship and then we
will come back to you."

6 Abraham took the wood for the burnt offering and placed it on his son Isaac,[i] and he himself carried 22:6 [i]Jn 19:17
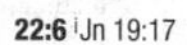
the fire and the knife. As the two of them went on together, 7 Isaac spoke up and said to his father Abra-
ham, "Father?"

"Yes, my son?" Abraham replied.

"The fire and wood are here," Isaac said, "but where is the lamb[j] for the burnt offering?" 22:7 [j]Lev 1:10

8 Abraham answered, "God himself will provide the lamb for the burnt offering, my son." And the two
of them went on together.

9 When they reached the place God had told him about, Abraham built an altar there and arranged the
wood on it. He bound his son Isaac and laid him on the altar,[k] on top of the wood. 10 Then he reached out 22:9 [k]Heb 11:17-
his hand and took the knife to slay his son. 11 But the angel of the LORD called out to him from heaven, 19; Jas 2:21
"Abraham! Abraham!"

"Here I am," he replied.

12 "Do not lay a hand on the boy," he said. "Do not do anything to him. Now I know that you fear God,[l] 22:12
because you have not withheld from me your son, your only son.[m]" [l]1Sa 15:22; Jas 2:21-22 [m]ver 2; Jn 3:16

13 Abraham looked up and there in a thicket he saw a ram[a] caught by its horns. He went over and took
the ram and sacrificed it as a burnt offering instead of his son.[n] 14 So Abraham called that place The LORD 22:13 [n]Ro 8:32
Will Provide. And to this day it is said, "On the mountain of the LORD it will be provided.[o]" 22:14 [o]ver 8

15 The angel of the LORD called to Abraham from heaven a second time 16 and said, "I swear by 22:16 [p]Lk 1:73;
myself,[p] declares the LORD, that because you have done this and have not withheld your son, your Heb 6:13 22:17 [q]Heb 6:14*
only son, 17 I will surely bless you and make your descendants[q] as numerous as the stars in the sky[r] [r]Ge 15:5 [s]Ge 26:24; 32:12
and as the sand on the seashore.[s] Your descendants will take possession of the cities of their ene- [t]Ge 24:60 22:18 [u]Ge 12:2,
mies,[t] 18 and through your offspring[b] all nations on earth will be blessed,[u] because you have 3; Ac 3:25*;
obeyed me."[v] Gal 3:8* [v]ver 10

19 Then Abraham returned to his servants, and they set off together for Beersheba. And Abraham
stayed in Beersheba.

[a] *13* Many manuscripts of the Masoretic Text, Samaritan Pentateuch, Septuagint and Syriac; most manuscripts of the Masoretic Text *a ram behind* ⌞*him*⌟ [b] *18* Or *seed*

ARCHAEOLOGICAL SITES

THE CAVE OF MACHPELAH

GENESIS 23 Until his wife's death Abraham wandered through **Canaan** as a nomadic herdsman.[1] Needing a burial plot for Sarah, he purchased his first small slice of the vast territory God had promised his descendants (Ge 15:18). The purchase included the burial cave and the field in which it was located, both known as Machpelah and located in Hebron[2] (see "Map 1" in the back of this Bible). The writer of Genesis carefully noted that Sarah, Abraham (25:9–10) and Isaac (35:27–29) were all buried in this cave. Later, upon his deathbed in Egypt, Jacob/Israel instructed that his bones were to be brought to Canaan and buried at this location along with those of his grandfather (Abraham), grandmother (Sarah), father (Isaac), mother (Rebekah) and wife (Leah). See 49:29–32; 50:13.

Not surprisingly, the Israelites remembered this cave throughout the ages. A monumental enclosure was built over the site during the days of Herod the Great.[3] This beautiful 200 by 110 foot (61 x 33.5 m) structure, bearing a remarkable architectural similarity to Herod's temple mount in Jerusalem,[4] is still intact today. Inside it, above ground, six large, medieval cenotaphs (empty tombs serving as monuments) commemorate the **patriarchs** and **matriarchs** buried there.

A **Byzantine** church later constructed inside this enclosure has been converted back and forth from church to mosque following successive changes of rule (and thereby of religion) in the area. During the fourteenth century A.D. Muslims sealed the subterranean structures beneath the compound, but clandestine investigations have since been carried out. One twentieth-century examination, under the direction of Israel's Moshe Dayan, involved the nighttime lowering of a twelve-year-old girl, equipped with a camera, into the tomb area! Investigators reported the existence of a staircase, a long hallway and a simple room.

[1]See "Canaan" on page 324. [2]See "Hebron" on page 446. [3]See "Herod the Great" on page 1627. [4]See "Herod's Temple" on page 1648.

Nahor's Sons

20Some time later Abraham was told, "Milcah is also a mother; she has borne sons to your brother Na-
22:20 [w]Ge 11:29 hor:[w] 21Uz the firstborn, Buz his brother, Kemuel (the father of Aram), 22Kesed, Hazo, Pildash, Jidlaph and
22:23 [x]Ge 24:15 Bethuel." 23Bethuel became the father of Rebekah.[x] Milcah bore these eight sons to Abraham's brother Na-
hor. 24His concubine, whose name was Reumah, also had sons: Tebah, Gaham, Tahash and Maacah.

The Death of Sarah

23:2 [y]Jos 14:15 **23** Sarah lived to be a hundred and twenty-seven years old. 2She died at Kiriath Arba[y] (that is, He-
[z]ver 19; Ge 13:18 bron)[z] in the land of Canaan, and Abraham went to mourn for Sarah and to weep over her.
3Then Abraham rose from beside his dead wife and spoke to the Hittites.[a] He said, 4"I am an alien and
23:4 [a]Ge 17:8; 1Ch 29:15; Ps 105:12; Heb 11:9,13 a stranger[a] among you. Sell me some property for a burial site here so I can bury my dead."
5The Hittites replied to Abraham, 6"Sir, listen to us. You are a mighty prince[b] among us. Bury your
23:6 [b]Ge 14:14-16; 24:35 dead in the choicest of our tombs. None of us will refuse you his tomb for burying your dead."
7Then Abraham rose and bowed down before the people of the land, the Hittites. 8He said to them,
23:8 [c]Ge 25:9 "If you are willing to let me bury my dead, then listen to me and intercede with Ephron son of Zohar[c] on
my behalf 9so he will sell me the cave of Machpelah, which belongs to him and is at the end of his field.
Ask him to sell it to me for the full price as a burial site among you."
10Ephron the Hittite was sitting among his people and he replied to Abraham in the hearing of all the
23:10 [d]Ge 34:20-24; Ru 4:4 Hittites who had come to the gate[d] of his city. 11"No, my lord," he said. "Listen to me; I give[b][e] you the field,
23:11 [e]2Sa 24:23 and I give[b] you the cave that is in it. I give[b] it to you in the presence of my people. Bury your dead."
12Again Abraham bowed down before the people of the land 13and he said to Ephron in their hearing,
"Listen to me, if you will. I will pay the price of the field. Accept it from me so I can bury my dead there."
14Ephron answered Abraham, 15"Listen to me, my lord; the land is worth four hundred shekels[c] of sil-
23:15 [f]Eze 45:12 ver,[f] but what is that between me and you? Bury your dead."
16Abraham agreed to Ephron's terms and weighed out for him the price he had named in the hearing
23:16 [g]Jer 32:9; Zec 11:12 of the Hittites: four hundred shekels of silver,[g] according to the weight current among the merchants.
23:17 [h]Ge 25:9; 49:30-32; 50:13; Ac 7:16 17So Ephron's field in Machpelah near Mamre[h]—both the field and the cave in it, and all the trees
within the borders of the field—was deeded 18to Abraham as his property in the presence of all the Hit-
tites who had come to the gate of the city. 19Afterward Abraham buried his wife Sarah in the cave in the
field of Machpelah near Mamre (which is at Hebron) in the land of Canaan. 20So the field and the cave
23:20 [i]Jer 32:10 in it were deeded[i] to Abraham by the Hittites as a burial site.

Isaac and Rebekah

24:1 [j]ver 35 **24** Abraham was now old and well advanced in years, and the LORD had blessed him in every way.[j]
24:2 [k]Ge 39:4-6 2He said to the chief[d] servant in his household, the one in charge of all that he had,[k] "Put your
[l]ver 9; Ge 47:29 hand under my thigh.[l] 3I want you to swear by the LORD, the God of heaven and the God of earth,[m] that
24:3 [m]Ge 14:19 [n]Ge 28:1; Dt 7:3 [o]Ge 10:15-19 you will not get a wife for my son[n] from the daughters of the Canaanites,[o] among whom I am living, 4but
24:4 [p]Ge 12:1; 28:2 will go to my country and my own relatives[p] and get a wife for my son Isaac."
5The servant asked him, "What if the woman is unwilling to come back with me to this land? Shall I
then take your son back to the country you came from?"
6"Make sure that you do not take my son back there," Abraham said. 7"The LORD, the God of heaven,
who brought me out of my father's household and my native land and who spoke to me and promised

[a] 3 Or *the sons of Heth*; also in verses 5, 7, 10, 16, 18 and 20 [b] *11* Or *sell* [c] *15* That is, about 10 pounds (about 4.5 kilograms)
[d] *2* Or *oldest*

22:20–24 Abraham's brother Nahor (11:26) fathered eight sons by his wife and four by his concubine. They would become the ancestors of 12 Aramean tribes, just as Abraham's son Ishmael would become the ancestor of 12 tribes (17:20; 25:12–16) and his grandson Jacob the ancestor of the 12 tribes of Israel (35:22–26; 49:28). See "Evidence for Serug, Nahor and Terah" on page 22.

23:4 Land suitable for farming was so precious in the ancient world that owners typically refused to sell it outside the family. But Abraham was not trying to buy farmland, only a burial site.

Village cultures used burial chambers (see "The Cave of Machpelah" on p. 38). A family tomb was used by several generations. A body was laid on a shelf along with grave goods (food, pottery, trinkets, weapons, tools). Later the skeletal remains were placed in another chamber or box to accommodate another burial.

23:9 Abraham wanted to buy only a small part of the field because purchasing the entire field would have entailed certain additional financial and social obligations. Hittite laws stipulated that if a property owner sold only part of his property, he (the original and principal landowner) was still required to pay all dues (taxes) on the land. But if he sold the entire tract, the new owner had to pay the dues.

24:2 One of the most frequently used words in Scripture, occurring over 1,600 times, is "hand." Besides its literal use, it occurs in numerous figurative senses as well. To put one's hand under another's thigh as in verses 2, 9 and 48:29 meant to take a solemn oath, evidently related to covenant obligations.

me on oath, saying, 'To your offspring[a][q] I will give this land'[r]—he will send his angel before you[s] so that
you can get a wife for my son from there. 8 If the woman is unwilling to come back with you, then you will
be released from this oath of mine. Only do not take my son back there." 9 So the servant put his hand un-
der the thigh[t] of his master Abraham and swore an oath to him concerning this matter.
10 Then the servant took ten of his master's camels and left, taking with him all kinds of good things
from his master. He set out for Aram Naharaim[b] and made his way to the town of Nahor. 11 He had the
camels kneel down near the well[u] outside the town; it was toward evening, the time the women go out
to draw water.[v]
12 Then he prayed, "O LORD, God of my master Abraham,[w] give me success today, and show kindness
to my master Abraham. 13 See, I am standing beside this spring, and the daughters of the townspeople are
coming out to draw water. 14 May it be that when I say to a girl, 'Please let down your jar that I may have
a drink,' and she says, 'Drink, and I'll water your camels too'—let her be the one you have chosen for
your servant Isaac. By this I will know[x] that you have shown kindness to my master."
15 Before he had finished praying,[y] Rebekah[z] came out with her jar on her shoulder. She was the daugh-
ter of Bethuel son of Milcah,[a] who was the wife of Abraham's brother Nahor.[b] 16 The girl was very beau-
tiful,[c] a virgin; no man had ever lain with her. She went down to the spring, filled her jar and came up
again.
17 The servant hurried to meet her and said, "Please give me a little water from your jar."
18 "Drink,[d] my lord," she said, and quickly lowered the jar to her hands and gave him a drink.
19 After she had given him a drink, she said, "I'll draw water for your camels too,[e] until they have fin-
ished drinking." 20 So she quickly emptied her jar into the trough, ran back to the well to draw more wa-
ter, and drew enough for all his camels. 21 Without saying a word, the man watched her closely to learn
whether or not the LORD had made his journey successful.[f]
22 When the camels had finished drinking, the man took out a gold nose ring[g] weighing a beka[c] and
two gold bracelets weighing ten shekels.[d] 23 Then he asked, "Whose daughter are you? Please tell me, is
there room in your father's house for us to spend the night?"
24 She answered him, "I am the daughter of Bethuel, the son that Milcah bore to Nahor.[h]" 25 And she
added, "We have plenty of straw and fodder, as well as room for you to spend the night."
26 Then the man bowed down and worshiped the LORD,[i] 27 saying, "Praise be to the LORD,[j] the God of
my master Abraham, who has not abandoned his kindness and faithfulness[k] to my master. As for me, the
LORD has led me on the journey[l] to the house of my master's relatives."[m]
28 The girl ran and told her mother's household about these things. 29 Now Rebekah had a brother
named Laban,[n] and he hurried out to the man at the spring. 30 As soon as he had seen the nose ring, and
the bracelets on his sister's arms, and had heard Rebekah tell what the man said to her, he went out to
the man and found him standing by the camels near the spring. 31 "Come, you who are blessed by the
LORD,"[o] he said. "Why are you standing out here? I have prepared the house and a place for the camels."
32 So the man went to the house, and the camels were unloaded. Straw and fodder were brought for
the camels, and water for him and his men to wash their feet.[p] 33 Then food was set before him, but he
said, "I will not eat until I have told you what I have to say."
"Then tell us," ⌞Laban⌟ said.
34 So he said, "I am Abraham's servant. 35 The LORD has blessed my master abundantly,[q] and he has
become wealthy. He has given him sheep and cattle, silver and gold, menservants and maidservants, and
camels and donkeys.[r] 36 My master's wife Sarah has borne him a son in her[e] old age,[s] and he has given
him everything he owns.[t] 37 And my master made me swear an oath, and said, 'You must not get a wife
for my son from the daughters of the Canaanites, in whose land I live,[u] 38 but go to my father's family and
to my own clan, and get a wife for my son.'[v]

24:7 [q]Gal 3:16* [r]Ge 12:7; 13:15 [s]Ex 23:20,23
24:9 [t]ver 2
24:11 [u]Ex 2:15 [v]ver 13; 1Sa 9:11
24:12 [w]ver 27, 42,48; Ge 26:24; Ex 3:6,15,16
24:14 [x]Jdg 6:17, 37
24:15 [y]ver 45 [z]Ge 22:23 [a]Ge 22:20 [b]Ge 11:29
24:16 [c]Ge 26:7
24:18 [d]ver 14
24:19 [e]ver 14
24:21 [f]ver 12
24:22 [g]ver 47
24:24 [h]ver 15
24:26 [i]ver 48,52; Ex 4:31
24:27 [j]Ex 18:10; Ru 4:14; 1Sa 25:32 [k]ver 49; Ge 32:10; Ps 98:3 [l]ver 21 [m]ver 12,48
24:29 [n]ver 4; Ge 29:5,12,13
24:31 [o]Ge 26:29; Ru 3:10; Ps 115:15
24:32 [p]Ge 43:24; Jdg 19:21
24:35 [q]ver 1 [r]Ge 13:2
24:36 [s]Ge 21:2, 10 [t]Ge 25:5
24:37 [u]ver 3
24:38 [v]ver 4

[a] *7* Or *seed* [b] *10* That is, Northwest Mesopotamia [c] *22* That is, about 1/5 ounce (about 5.5 grams) [d] *22* That is, about 4 ounces (about 110 grams) [e] *36* Or *his*

24:10 Naharaim was the northern part of the area later called Mesopotamia by the Greeks (lit., "between the rivers"). Perhaps named after Abraham's brother (see v. 15; 11:26), the town of Nahor is mentioned in clay tablets excavated by the French beginning in 1933 at the ancient city of Mari on the Euphrates River. Nahor was located in the Haran district and was ruled by an Amorite prince in the eighteenth century B.C. See "Evidence for Serug, Nahor and Terah" on page 22, "Haran" on page 47 and "Mari" on page 54.

24:14 An oracle posed a yes/no question to a deity, and a mechanism (cf. Jdg 6:36–40; 1Sa 6:7–12) was provided so that the deity could answer.

A camel (see "Camels" on p. 41) that has gone a few days without water can drink as much as 25 gallons (23.7 l; up to 100 drawings from the well for all the servant's camels). It is evident that Abraham's servant intentionally selected an extreme action as a sign to avoid any doubt that God was controlling the situation.

24:39 [w]ver 5 [39]"Then I asked my master, 'What if the woman will not come back with me?'[w]
24:40 [x]ver 7 [40]"He replied, 'The LORD, before whom I have walked, will send his angel with you[x] and make your
journey a success, so that you can get a wife for my son from my own clan and from my father's family.
[41]Then, when you go to my clan, you will be released from my oath even if they refuse to give her to
24:41 [y]ver 8 you—you will be released from my oath.'[y]
[42]"When I came to the spring today, I said, 'O LORD, God of my master Abraham, if you will, please
24:42 [z]ver 12 grant success[z] to the journey on which I have come. [43]See, I am standing beside this spring;[a] if a maid-
24:43 [a]ver 13 [b]ver 14 en comes out to draw water and I say to her, "Please let me drink a little water from your jar,"[b] [44]and if
she says to me, "Drink, and I'll draw water for your camels too," let her be the one the LORD has chosen
for my master's son.'

Camels

GENESIS 24 The first Biblical references to domesticated camels occur in the stories of Abraham. He owned them (Ge 12:16), and his servant used them as pack animals (24:10). Camels are also mentioned in the stories of Jacob (30:43; 31:34; 32:15) and Joseph (37:25) and were found among the Amalekites, Ishmaelites and Midianites.[1]

Scholars have debated the historicity of these references to camels because most believe that these animals were not widely domesticated until approximately 1200 B.C., long after the time of Abraham. Arguments in support of later domestication of the camel include:

Neither the **Mari** tablets from the eighteenth century B.C. nor the fourteenth-century B.C. **Amarna** correspondence mentions domesticated camels.[2]

During the patriarchal period the donkey appears to have been the animal primarily used for transport. For example, the "Beni Hasan painting," which depicts Semites bringing goods to Egypt during the Twelfth Dynasty (1900 B.C.), pictures donkeys rather than camels being used in caravans.[3]

On the other hand, we do see clear evidence of camel domestication in the first millennium, much later than the time of the patriarchs. For example, Assyrian wall relief artwork depicts men riding camels into war.

Other evidence does suggest that at least some camels were domesticated earlier. Bone fragments and other archaeological remains have led some scholars to postulate a third millennium date for camel domestication. Although many scholars regard this evidence as inconclusive because it is difficult to distinguish wild from domesticated animals using only bone samples, other evidence, as described below, suggests that people were relying on camels in some manner:

- A braided cord of camel hair from predynastic Egypt has been discovered.
- A **Sumerian** text refers to camel's milk.
- An **Old Babylonian** text from the early second-millennium **Ugarit** describes the camel as a domestic animal.

Thus, the evidence does not force us to regard the appearance of domesticated camels in Genesis as anachronistic. Such tamed animals probably were rare during the second millennium, however, and may have been owned almost exclusively by wealthy people.

[1]See "The Amalekites" on page 120 and "Midian" on page 92. [2]See "Mari" on page 54 and "The Amarna Tablets and the Habiru" on page 347.
[3]See "Caravan Trading and Routes in the Ancient Near East" on page 63.

Camels in the first millennium B.C. in an Assyrian battle scene

Preserving Bible Times; © Dr. James C. Martin; permission of The British Museum

45 "Before I finished praying in my heart,[c] Rebekah came out, with her jar on her shoulder.[d] She went down to the spring and drew water, and I said to her, 'Please give me a drink.'[e]

46 "She quickly lowered her jar from her shoulder and said, 'Drink, and I'll water your camels too.'[f] So I drank, and she watered the camels also.

47 "I asked her, 'Whose daughter are you?'[g]

"She said, 'The daughter of Bethuel son of Nahor, whom Milcah bore to him.'[h]

"Then I put the ring in her nose and the bracelets on her arms,[i] 48 and I bowed down and worshiped the LORD.[j] I praised the LORD, the God of my master Abraham, who had led me on the right road to get the granddaughter of my master's brother for his son.[k] 49 Now if you will show kindness and faithfulness[l] to my master, tell me; and if not, tell me, so I may know which way to turn."

50 Laban and Bethuel answered, "This is from the LORD;[m] we can say nothing to you one way or the other.[n] 51 Here is Rebekah; take her and go, and let her become the wife of your master's son, as the LORD has directed."

52 When Abraham's servant heard what they said, he bowed down to the ground before the LORD.[o] 53 Then the servant brought out gold and silver jewelry and articles of clothing and gave them to Rebekah; he also gave costly gifts[p] to her brother and to her mother. 54 Then he and the men who were with him ate and drank and spent the night there.

When they got up the next morning, he said, "Send me on my way[q] to my master."

55 But her brother and her mother replied, "Let the girl remain with us ten days or so; then you[a] may go."

56 But he said to them, "Do not detain me, now that the LORD has granted success to my journey. Send me on my way so I may go to my master."

57 Then they said, "Let's call the girl and ask her about it." 58 So they called Rebekah and asked her, "Will you go with this man?"

"I will go," she said.

59 So they sent their sister Rebekah on her way, along with her nurse[r] and Abraham's servant and his men. 60 And they blessed Rebekah and said to her,

> "Our sister, may you increase
> to thousands upon thousands;[s]
> may your offspring possess
> the gates of their enemies."[t]

61 Then Rebekah and her maids got ready and mounted their camels and went back with the man. So the servant took Rebekah and left.

62 Now Isaac had come from Beer Lahai Roi,[u] for he was living in the Negev.[v] 63 He went out to the field one evening to meditate,[b][w] and as he looked up, he saw camels approaching. 64 Rebekah also looked up and saw Isaac. She got down from her camel 65 and asked the servant, "Who is that man in the field coming to meet us?"

"He is my master," the servant answered. So she took her veil and covered herself.

66 Then the servant told Isaac all he had done. 67 Isaac brought her into the tent of his mother Sarah, and he married Rebekah.[x] So she became his wife, and he loved her;[y] and Isaac was comforted after his mother's death.[z]

The Death of Abraham

25 Abraham took[c] another wife, whose name was Keturah. 2 She bore him Zimran, Jokshan, Medan, Midian, Ishbak and Shuah.[a] 3 Jokshan was the father of Sheba and Dedan; the descendants of Dedan were the Asshurites, the Letushites and the Leummites. 4 The sons of Midian were Ephah, Epher, Hanoch, Abida and Eldaah. All these were descendants of Keturah.

5 Abraham left everything he owned to Isaac.[b] 6 But while he was still living, he gave gifts to the sons of his concubines[c] and sent them away from his son Isaac[d] to the land of the east.

24:45 [c] 1Sa 1:13 [d] ver 15 [e] ver 17
24:46 [f] ver 18-19
24:47 [g] ver 23 [h] ver 24 [i] Eze 16:11-12
24:48 [j] ver 26 [k] ver 27
24:49 [l] Ge 47:29; Jos 2:14
24:50 [m] Ps 118:23 [n] Ge 31:7,24,29, 42
24:52 [o] ver 26
24:53 [p] ver 10,22
24:54 [q] ver 56,59
24:59 [r] Ge 35:8
24:60 [s] Ge 17:16 [t] Ge 22:17
24:62 [u] Ge 16:14; 25:11 [v] Ge 20:1
24:63 [w] Ps 1:2; 77:12; 119:15,27, 48,97,148; 143:5; 145:5
24:67 [x] Ge 25:20 [y] Ge 29:18,20 [z] Ge 23:1-2
25:2 [a] 1Ch 1:32, 33
25:5 [b] Ge 24:36
25:6 [c] Ge 22:24 [d] Ge 21:10,14

[a] 55 Or *she* [b] 63 The meaning of the Hebrew for this word is uncertain. [c] 1 Or *had taken*

25:5 The law of primogeniture provided that a double share of a father's property be given to the firstborn son when the father died (Dt 21:15–17). Parallels to this practice come from Nuzi, from Larsa in the Old Babylonian period and from Assyria in the Middle Assyrian period. Isaac was Abraham's firstborn son according to law. See "Custom and Law in Ancient Mesopotamia" on page 36, "The Rights of the Firstborn" on page 43 and "Nuzi" on page 52.

25:6 A concubine in Old Testament times was not a paramour or

7Altogether, Abraham lived a hundred and seventy-five years. 8Then Abraham breathed his last and
25:8 [e]Ge 15:15 died at a good old age,[e] an old man and full of years; and he was gathered to his people.[f] 9His sons Isaac
[f]ver 17; Ge 35:29; 49:29,33 and Ishmael buried him[g] in the cave of Machpelah near Mamre, in the field of Ephron son of Zohar the
25:9 [g]Ge 35:29 [h]Ge 50:13 Hittite,[h] 10the field Abraham had bought from the Hittites.[a][i] There Abraham was buried with his wife Sar-
25:10 [i]Ge 23:16 25:11 [j]Ge 16:14 ah. 11After Abraham's death, God blessed his son Isaac, who then lived near Beer Lahai Roi.[j]

Ishmael's Sons

25:12 [k]Ge 16:1 [l]Ge 16:15 12This is the account of Abraham's son Ishmael, whom Sarah's maidservant, Hagar[k] the Egyptian,
bore to Abraham.[l]

13These are the names of the sons of Ishmael, listed in the order of their birth: Nebaioth the firstborn of
Ishmael, Kedar, Adbeel, Mibsam, 14Mishma, Dumah, Massa, 15Hadad, Tema, Jetur, Naphish and Kedemah.
25:16 [m]Ge 17:20 16These were the sons of Ishmael, and these are the names of the twelve tribal rulers[m] according to their set-
tlements and camps. 17Altogether, Ishmael lived a hundred and thirty-seven years. He breathed his last and
25:17 [n]ver 8 died, and he was gathered to his people.[n] 18His descendants settled in the area from Havilah to Shur, near
25:18 [o]Ge 16:12 the border of Egypt, as you go toward Asshur. And they lived in hostility toward[b] all their brothers.[o]

[a] 10 Or *the sons of Heth* [b] 18 Or *lived to the east of*

illicit lover but a woman lawfully united in marriage to a man in a relationship inferior to that of a regular wife. No moral stigma was attached to this status, which was considered a natural part of a polygamous social system. Concubines enjoyed no other right than that of lawful cohabitation. They exercised no authority within the family or in household affairs, and their husbands could send them away at any time with a small present. Their children as well, by means of small presents, could be excluded from the family heritage (v. 6), even though they were regarded as legitimate. In patriarchal times, at least, the immediate cause of concubinage was often the barrenness of the lawful wife, who would herself suggest that her husband have children by her maidservant (chs. 16; 30).

25:12–18 Many of the names of Ishmael's sons are Arabic, giving credence to the Arab tradition that Ishmael was their ancestor.

CULTURAL AND HISTORICAL NOTES

The Rights of the Firstborn

GENESIS 25 The Hebrew term *bet av* ("paternal household") reflects the fact that in ancient Israel the family was patrilineal: Inheritances were passed through the male line. The **patriarch** had authority over the entire household, including sons, daughters-in-law, unmarried daughters and grandchildren.[1] Upon the patriarch's death the firstborn son became the new head of the family, and the paternal lineage of the extended family continued through him. This firstborn son, therefore, exercised both special privileges and unique responsibilities.

Several Biblical texts stipulate that the firstborn belonged to the Lord and needed to be redeemed (since all firstborn sons belonged to God after the plague on the firstborn in Egypt, Israelites had to symbolically buy them back with animal sacrifices, according to Ex 13:2,12–16; 22:29; Nu 3:13). The firstborn took precedence over his younger brothers (Ge 43:33) and received a double portion of the inheritance,[2] as well as a special blessing (ch. 27; 48:14ff.).

The patriarch/father was not free to arbitrarily assign the first son's birthright to a younger sibling (Dt 21:15–17), although the birthright could pass to another son in exceptional circumstances (e.g., Reuben lost his birthright because he had defiled his father's bed; cf. 1Ch 5:1–2). Documents from **Nuzi** and **Mari**[3] reveal that if a concubine bore the first son, his birthright could be withdrawn if the primary wife subsequently gave birth to a son. This occurred in the case of Ishmael and Isaac.[4]

We also have access to Nuzi documents called "tablet of brotherhood" contracts. These concern the sale of a birthright to someone outside the family (based on a legal loophole of adopting the outsider as a family member) for the purpose of transferring property. Although not identical in concept to what we see in Genesis 25:27 and following, these Nuzi texts do indicate that the birthright could be sold or traded and provide some precedent for Esau's sale of his birthright to Jacob.

The concept underlying the rights of the firstborn son has theological implications. The nation of Israel enjoyed a special relationship with the Lord as his firstborn (Ex 4:22ff.). But Psalm 89:27 indicates that Christ is the Lord's firstborn. This is not to be seen as a contradiction. Believers who are in Christ share in the privileges his intimate relationship with the Father entails (Heb 12:23–24), and we are warned not to spurn or devalue our birthright as Esau did (Heb 12:16–17).

[1]See "The Role of the Patriarch in Family Life" on page 30. [2]See "Inheritance in the Ancient Near East" on page 250. [3]See "Nuzi" on page 52 and "Mari" on page 54. [4]See "Custom and Law in Ancient Mesopotamia" on page 36.

Jacob and Esau

19This is the account of Abraham's son Isaac.
Abraham became the father of Isaac, 20and Isaac was forty years old[p] when he married Rebekah[q]
daughter of Bethuel the Aramean from Paddan Aram[a] and sister of Laban[r] the Aramean.
21Isaac prayed to the LORD on behalf of his wife, because she was barren. The LORD answered his
prayer,[s] and his wife Rebekah became pregnant. 22The babies jostled each other within her, and she said,
"Why is this happening to me?" So she went to inquire of the LORD.[t]
23The LORD said to her,

> "Two nations[u] are in your womb,
> and two peoples from within you will be separated;
> one people will be stronger than the other,
> and the older will serve the younger.[v]"

24When the time came for her to give birth, there were twin boys in her womb. 25The first to come out
was red, and his whole body was like a hairy garment;[w] so they named him Esau.[b] 26After this, his broth-
er came out, with his hand grasping Esau's heel;[x] so he was named Jacob.[c][y] Isaac was sixty years old
when Rebekah gave birth to them.
27The boys grew up, and Esau became a skillful hunter, a man of the open country,[z] while Jacob was
a quiet man, staying among the tents. 28Isaac, who had a taste for wild game,[a] loved Esau, but Rebekah
loved Jacob.[b]
29Once when Jacob was cooking some stew, Esau came in from the open country, famished. 30He said
to Jacob, "Quick, let me have some of that red stew! I'm famished!" (That is why he was also called Edom.[d])
31Jacob replied, "First sell me your birthright."
32"Look, I am about to die," Esau said. "What good is the birthright to me?"
33But Jacob said, "Swear to me first." So he swore an oath to him, selling his birthright[c] to Jacob.
34Then Jacob gave Esau some bread and some lentil stew. He ate and drank, and then got up and left.
So Esau despised his birthright.

Isaac and Abimelech

26 Now there was a famine in the land[d]—besides the earlier famine of Abraham's time—and Isaac
went to Abimelech king of the Philistines in Gerar.[e] 2The LORD appeared[f] to Isaac and said, "Do
not go down to Egypt; live in the land where I tell you to live.[g] 3Stay in this land for a while,[h] and I will
be with you and will bless you.[i] For to you and your descendants I will give all these lands[j] and will con-
firm the oath I swore to your father Abraham. 4I will make your descendants as numerous as the stars
in the sky[k] and will give them all these lands, and through your offspring[e] all nations on earth will be
blessed,[l] 5because Abraham obeyed me[m] and kept my requirements, my commands, my decrees and my
laws." 6So Isaac stayed in Gerar.
7When the men of that place asked him about his wife, he said, "She is my sister,[n]" because he was
afraid to say, "She is my wife." He thought, "The men of this place might kill me on account of Rebekah,
because she is beautiful."
8When Isaac had been there a long time, Abimelech king of the Philistines looked down from a win-
dow and saw Isaac caressing his wife Rebekah. 9So Abimelech summoned Isaac and said, "She is really
your wife! Why did you say, 'She is my sister'?"
Isaac answered him, "Because I thought I might lose my life on account of her."

25:20 [p]ver 26; Ge 26:34 [q]Ge 24:67 [r]Ge 24:29
25:21 [s]1Ch 5:20; 2Ch 33:13; Ezr 8:23; Ps 127:3; Ro 9:10
25:22 [t]1Sa 9:9; 10:22
25:23 [u]Ge 17:4 [v]Ge 27:29,40; Mal 1:3; Ro 9:11-12*
25:25 [w]Ge 27:11
25:26 [x]Hos 12:3 [y]Ge 27:36
25:27 [z]Ge 27:3,5
25:28 [a]Ge 27:19 [b]Ge 27:6
25:33 [c]Ge 27:36; Heb 12:16
26:1 [d]Ge 12:10 [e]Ge 20:1
26:2 [f]Ge 12:7; 17:1; 18:1 [g]Ge 12:1
26:3 [h]Ge 20:1; 28:15 [i]Ge 12:2; 22:16-18 [j]Ge 12:7; 13:15; 15:18
26:4 [k]Ge 15:5; 22:17; Ex 32:13 [l]Ge 12:3; 22:18; Gal 3:8
26:5 [m]Ge 22:16
26:7 [n]Ge 12:13; 20:2,12; Pr 29:25

[a] *20* That is, Northwest Mesopotamia [b] *25 Esau* may mean *hairy*; he was also called Edom, which means *red.* [c] *26 Jacob* means *he grasps the heel* (figuratively, *he deceives*). [d] *30 Edom* means *red.* [e] *4* Or *seed*

25:23 The ancient law of primogeniture (see note on v. 5) also provided that, under ordinary circumstances, the younger of two sons would be subservient to the older. See also the note on verse 5.

25:26 Jacob's name was an old one among the Semitic people. As early as 2000 B.C. it occurs among writings of Hammurabi as *Yakibula.* That it was a well-known name among the Canaanites of pre-Abrahamic days is attested by records in the temple at Karnak. The name of a city captured by Thutmose III is similar to the Hebrew word: Jakob-el.

25:31 The birthright was the oldest son's share of the family's estate. In the ancient world the firstborn typically received a double share of the inheritance (see the note on v. 5). See "Custom and Law in Ancient Mesopotamia" on page 36, "The Rights of the Firstborn" on page 43 and "Nuzi" on page 52.

25:34 A lentil is a small, pea-like, annual plant that grows well even in nutrient-poor soil. Its pods turn reddish-brown when boiled. It has provided an important source of nourishment in the Near East since ancient times (see 2Sa 17:28; 23:11; Eze 4:9).

26:10 [o]Ge 20:9 10 Then Abimelech said, "What is this you have done to us?[o] One of the men might well have slept with
your wife, and you would have brought guilt upon us."
26:11 [p]Ps 105:15 11 So Abimelech gave orders to all the people: "Anyone who molests[p] this man or his wife shall surely
be put to death."
12 Isaac planted crops in that land and the same year reaped a hundredfold, because the LORD blessed
26:12 [q]ver 3; Job 42:12 him.[q] 13 The man became rich, and his wealth continued to grow until he became very wealthy.[r] 14 He had
26:13 [r]Pr 10:22 so many flocks and herds and servants[s] that the Philistines envied him.[t] 15 So all the wells[u] that his father's
26:14 [s]Ge 24:36 [t]Ge 37:11 servants had dug in the time of his father Abraham, the Philistines stopped up,[v] filling them with earth.
26:15 [u]Ge 21:30 [v]Ge 21:25 16 Then Abimelech said to Isaac, "Move away from us; you have become too powerful for us.[w]"
26:16 [w]Ex 1:9 17 So Isaac moved away from there and encamped in the Valley of Gerar and settled there. 18 Isaac re-
26:18 [x]Ge 21:30 opened the wells[x] that had been dug in the time of his father Abraham, which the Philistines had stopped
up after Abraham died, and he gave them the same names his father had given them.
19 Isaac's servants dug in the valley and discovered a well of fresh water there. 20 But the herdsmen of
26:20 [y]Ge 21:25 Gerar quarreled with Isaac's herdsmen and said, "The water is ours!"[y] So he named the well Esek,[a] be-
cause they disputed with him. 21 Then they dug another well, but they quarreled over that one also; so he
named it Sitnah.[b] 22 He moved on from there and dug another well, and no one quarreled over it. He
26:22 [z]Ge 17:6; Ex 1:7 named it Rehoboth,[c] saying, "Now the LORD has given us room and we will flourish[z] in the land."
23 From there he went up to Beersheba. 24 That night the LORD appeared to him and said, "I am the God
26:24 [a]Ge 24:12; Ex 3:6 [b]Ge 15:1 [c]ver 4 [d]Ge 17:7 of your father Abraham.[a] Do not be afraid,[b] for I am with you; I will bless you and will increase the num-
ber of your descendants[c] for the sake of my servant Abraham."[d]
26:25 [e]Ge 12:7, 8; 13:4,18; Ps 116:17 25 Isaac built an altar[e] there and called on the name of the LORD. There he pitched his tent, and there
his servants dug a well.
26 Meanwhile, Abimelech had come to him from Gerar, with Ahuzzath his personal adviser and Phi-
26:26 [f]Ge 21:22 col the commander of his forces.[f] 27 Isaac asked them, "Why have you come to me, since you were hostile
26:27 [g]ver 16 to me and sent me away?[g]"
26:28 [h]Ge 21:22 28 They answered, "We saw clearly that the LORD was with you;[h] so we said, 'There ought to be a sworn
agreement between us'—between us and you. Let us make a treaty with you 29 that you will do us no
harm, just as we did not molest you but always treated you well and sent you away in peace. And now you
26:29 [i]Ge 24:31; Ps 115:15 are blessed by the LORD."[i]

[a] 20 *Esek* means *dispute.* [b] 21 *Sitnah* means *opposition.* [c] 22 *Rehoboth* means *room.*

ANCIENT TEXTS AND ARTIFACTS

The Tale of Appu's Two Sons

GENESIS 26 In many respects the Neo-Hittite Tale of Appu's Two Sons is similar to the Biblical story of Isaac's twins, Jacob and Esau. Like Isaac (Ge 25:24), Appu, wealthy but aging and childless, prayed for an heir. The sun god granted the request, but Appu named the child Wrong because the gods in his opinion had unjustly withheld a child from him for so long. When Appu's wife became pregnant a second time and bore another son, he named the infant Right, implying that the gods had acted fairly this time.

When the boys had matured, Wrong attempted to defraud Right of his legitimate portion of the estate by giving him the sick livestock and keeping the healthy animals for himself. Upon perceiving Wrong's actions, the sun god summoned the brothers before him for judgment, awarding the legal settlement to the younger.

In both the Appu and Isaac narratives the younger son emerged the victor. In Appu's tale the deceptive elder brother was punished but his honest younger sibling appropriately rewarded. In the Genesis account the younger brother was the deceptive one, but he nevertheless came away with both the birthright and the blessing because, despite his character flaws, he was God's chosen.[1]

Although Jacob and Esau reconciled years later, Genesis 27 clearly demonstrates that God's choice was not based on any merit Jacob had to offer but solely upon God's plan for his people. The Tale of Appu's Two Sons appears to have been a kind of morality play, as indicated by the sons' artificial names. In contrast, the Biblical story of Isaac and his sons is historically true and strangely counterintuitive. Similarly, a first-time reader would not expect the saga of Jacob and Esau to turn out as it does; indeed, it reveals a surprising look at our God, whose unexpected and seemingly "upside-down" value system continues to amaze us anew.

[1] See "The Rights of the Firstborn" on page 43.

30 Isaac then made a feast[j] for them, and they ate and drank. 31 Early the next morning the men swore
an oath[k] to each other. Then Isaac sent them on their way, and they left him in peace.
32 That day Isaac's servants came and told him about the well they had dug. They said, "We've found
water!" 33 He called it Shibah,[a] and to this day the name of the town has been Beersheba.[b][l]
34 When Esau was forty years old,[m] he married Judith daughter of Beeri the Hittite, and also Base-
math daughter of Elon the Hittite.[n] 35 They were a source of grief to Isaac and Rebekah.[o]

Jacob Gets Isaac's Blessing

27 When Isaac was old and his eyes were so weak that he could no longer see,[p] he called for Esau
his older son[q] and said to him, "My son."
"Here I am," he answered.
2 Isaac said, "I am now an old man and don't know the day of my death.[r] 3 Now then, get your weap-
ons—your quiver and bow—and go out to the open country[s] to hunt some wild game for me. 4 Prepare
me the kind of tasty food I like and bring it to me to eat, so that I may give you my blessing[t] before I die."
5 Now Rebekah was listening as Isaac spoke to his son Esau. When Esau left for the open country to
hunt game and bring it back, 6 Rebekah said to her son Jacob,[u] "Look, I overheard your father say to your
brother Esau, 7 'Bring me some game and prepare me some tasty food to eat, so that I may give you my
blessing in the presence of the LORD before I die.' 8 Now, my son, listen carefully and do what I tell you:[v]
9 Go out to the flock and bring me two choice young goats, so I can prepare some tasty food for your fa-
ther, just the way he likes it. 10 Then take it to your father to eat, so that he may give you his blessing be-
fore he dies."
11 Jacob said to Rebekah his mother, "But my brother Esau is a hairy man,[w] and I'm a man with smooth
skin. 12 What if my father touches me?[x] I would appear to be tricking him and would bring down a curse
on myself rather than a blessing."
13 His mother said to him, "My son, let the curse fall on me.[y] Just do what I say;[z] go and get them
for me."
14 So he went and got them and brought them to his mother, and she prepared some tasty food, just the
way his father liked it. 15 Then Rebekah took the best clothes[a] of Esau her older son, which she had in the
house, and put them on her younger son Jacob. 16 She also covered his hands and the smooth part of his
neck with the goatskins. 17 Then she handed to her son Jacob the tasty food and the bread she had made.
18 He went to his father and said, "My father."
"Yes, my son," he answered. "Who is it?"
19 Jacob said to his father, "I am Esau your firstborn. I have done as you told me. Please sit up and eat
some of my game so that you may give me your blessing."[b]
20 Isaac asked his son, "How did you find it so quickly, my son?"
"The LORD your God gave me success,[c]" he replied.
21 Then Isaac said to Jacob, "Come near so I can touch you,[d] my son, to know whether you really are
my son Esau or not."
22 Jacob went close to his father Isaac, who touched him and said, "The voice is the voice of Jacob, but
the hands are the hands of Esau." 23 He did not recognize him, for his hands were hairy like those of his
brother Esau;[e] so he blessed him. 24 "Are you really my son Esau?" he asked.
"I am," he replied.
25 Then he said, "My son, bring me some of your game to eat, so that I may give you my blessing."[f]
Jacob brought it to him and he ate; and he brought some wine and he drank. 26 Then his father Isaac
said to him, "Come here, my son, and kiss me."
27 So he went to him and kissed him[g]. When Isaac caught the smell of his clothes,[h] he blessed him
and said,

"Ah, the smell of my son
is like the smell of a field
that the LORD has blessed.[i]

26:30 [j]Ge 19:3
26:31 [k]Ge 21:31
26:33 [l]Ge 21:14
26:34 [m]Ge 25:20 [n]Ge 28:9; 36:2
26:35 [o]Ge 27:46
27:1 [p]Ge 48:10; 1Sa 3:2 [q]Ge 25:25
27:2 [r]Ge 47:29
27:3 [s]Ge 25:27
27:4 [t]ver 10,25, 31; Ge 49:28; Dt 33:1; Heb 11:20
27:6 [u]Ge 25:28
27:8 [v]ver 13,43
27:11 [w]Ge 25:25
27:12 [x]ver 22
27:13 [y]Mt 27:25 [z]ver 8
27:15 [a]ver 27
27:19 [b]ver 4
27:20 [c]Ge 24:12
27:21 [d]ver 12
27:23 [e]ver 16
27:25 [f]ver 4
27:27 [g]Heb 11:20 [h]SS 4:11
[i]Ps 65:9-13

[a] 33 *Shibah* can mean *oath* or *seven*. [b] 33 *Beersheba* can mean *well of the oath* or *well of seven*.

27:1 Blindness and near-blindness were common conditions among elderly persons in ancient times (see 48:10; 1Sa 4:15).

27:4 Oral statements, including deathbed bequests (see 49:28–33), were legally enforceable by ancient Near Eastern law.

27:28 [j]Dt 33:13 [k]ver 39 [l]Ge 45:18; Nu 18:12; Dt 33:28

28 May God give you of heaven's dew[j]
and of earth's richness[k]—
an abundance of grain and new wine.[l]
29 May nations serve you
and peoples bow down to you.[m]
Be lord over your brothers,
and may the sons of your mother bow down to you.[n]
May those who curse you be cursed
and those who bless you be blessed.[o]"

27:29 [m]Isa 45:14,23; 49:7,23 [n]Ge 9:25; 25:23; 37:7 [o]Ge 12:3; Nu 24:9; Zep 2:8

30 After Isaac finished blessing him and Jacob had scarcely left his father's presence, his brother Esau
came in from hunting. 31 He too prepared some tasty food and brought it to his father. Then he said to him,
"My father, sit up and eat some of my game, so that you may give me your blessing."[p]
32 His father Isaac asked him, "Who are you?"[q]
"I am your son," he answered, "your firstborn, Esau."
33 Isaac trembled violently and said, "Who was it, then, that hunted game and brought it to me? I ate
it just before you came and I blessed him—and indeed he will be blessed![r]"
34 When Esau heard his father's words, he burst out with a loud and bitter cry[s] and said to his father,
"Bless me—me too, my father!"
35 But he said, "Your brother came deceitfully[t] and took your blessing."
36 Esau said, "Isn't he rightly named Jacob[a]?[u] He has deceived me these two times: He took my birth-
right,[v] and now he's taken my blessing!" Then he asked, "Haven't you reserved any blessing for me?"
37 Isaac answered Esau, "I have made him lord over you and have made all his relatives his servants,
and I have sustained him with grain and new wine.[w] So what can I possibly do for you, my son?"

27:31 [p]ver 4
27:32 [q]ver 18
27:33 [r]ver 29; Ge 28:3,4; Ro 11:29
27:34 [s]Heb 12:17
27:35 [t]Jer 9:4; 12:6
27:36 [u]Ge 25:26 [v]Ge 25:33
27:37 [w]ver 28

[a] *36 Jacob* means *he grasps the heel* (figuratively, *he deceives*).

27:33 Peoples of the ancient world believed that blessings and curses had a kind of magical power to accomplish what they pronounced (see "Curses and Imprecations" on p. 883. But Isaac, as heir and steward of God's covenant blessing, acknowledged that he had solemnly transmitted that heritage to Jacob by way of a legally binding bequest (see the note on v. 4). See "The Rights of the Firstborn" on page 43 and "The Tale of Appu's Two Sons" on page 45.

ARCHAEOLOGICAL SITES

HARAN

GENESIS 27 The ancient city of Haran ("Map 1"), which probably derived its name from the Akkadian word *harranu* ("highway"), is located in modern-day Turkey about 10 miles (16 km) north of the Syrian border. Strategically situated on the historic east-west trade route that linked the Tigris, River with the Mediterranean Sea, Haran was one of northern **Mesopotamia**'s important commercial and religious centers, widely known for its dedicated worship of the moon god, Sin.

Occupied from the mid-third millennium B.C. until several centuries after the New Testament period, this city is best known for its links with the Biblical patriarchs, who lived during the **Middle Bronze Age** (first half of the second millennium B.C.). **Mari** texts attest that Haran was thriving[1] during this time. En route to Canaan[2] Abram and his family lived there for a time, perhaps to care for Terah, Abram's ailing father who eventually died there (Ge 11:31–32).[3] Abram (now Abraham) later found a wife for his son Isaac from among relatives in Haran (cf. 24:1–7,24), and Isaac's son Jacob eventually secured refuge in the region with his uncle Laban (27:42—28:5), for whom he worked for 20 years. Before returning to Canaan Jacob married both Leah and Rachel (Laban's two daughters) and fathered 11 sons in Haran (chs. 29–31).

For approximately one thousand years after the patriarchs, Haran continued to flourish on the basis of its trade with other nations and activities related to the moon god, Sin. Following a civic revolt, **Assyrian** forces captured the city in 763 B.C. Assyrian officials later used this victory to intimidate the Judean king Hezekiah, after which Assyria destroyed the northern kingdom of Israel (Isa 37:11–12). Haran became the last capital of Assyria in 612 B.C. but was captured in 609 B.C. by the **Babylonians**, who revived the declining worship of Sin and restored Haran as a thriving trade center (cf. Eze 27:23).

[1]See "Mari" on page 54. [2]See "Canaan" on page 324. [3]See "Evidence for Serug, Nahor and Terah" on page 22.

[38]Esau said to his father, "Do you have only one blessing, my father? Bless me too, my father!" Then
Esau wept aloud.[x] 27:38 [x]Heb 12:17
[39]His father Isaac answered him,

"Your dwelling will be
away from the earth's richness,
away from the dew[y] of heaven above. 27:39 [y]ver 28
[40]You will live by the sword
and you will serve[z] your brother.[a] 27:40 [z]2Sa 8:14 [a]Ge 25:23
But when you grow restless,
you will throw his yoke
from off your neck.[b]" [b]2Ki 8:20-22

Jacob Flees to Laban

[41]Esau held a grudge[c] against Jacob[d] because of the blessing his father had given him. He said to him-
self, "The days of mourning[e] for my father are near; then I will kill my brother Jacob."[f] 27:41 [c]Ge 37:4 [d]Ge 32:11 [e]Ge 50:4,10 [f]Ob 1:10
[42]When Rebekah was told what her older son Esau had said, she sent for her younger son Jacob and
said to him, "Your brother Esau is consoling himself with the thought of killing you. [43]Now then, my son,
do what I say:[g] Flee at once to my brother Laban[h] in Haran.[i] [44]Stay with him for a while[j] until your broth-
er's fury subsides. [45]When your brother is no longer angry with you and forgets what you did to him,[k]
I'll send word for you to come back from there. Why should I lose both of you in one day?" 27:43 [g]ver 8 [h]Ge 24:29 [i]Ge 11:31 27:44 [j]Ge 31:38, 41 27:45 [k]ver 35
[46]Then Rebekah said to Isaac, "I'm disgusted with living because of these Hittite women. If Jacob takes
a wife from among the women of this land, from Hittite women like these, my life will not be worth living."[l] 27:46 [l]Ge 26:35
28 So Isaac called for Jacob and blessed[a] him and commanded him: "Do not marry a Canaanite
woman.[m] [2]Go at once to Paddan Aram,[b] to the house of your mother's father Bethuel.[n] Take a wife
for yourself there, from among the daughters of Laban, your mother's brother. [3]May God Almighty[c][o] 28:1 [m]Ge 24:3 28:2 [n]Ge 25:20 28:3 [o]Ge 17:1

[a] 1 Or *greeted* [b] 2 That is, Northwest Mesopotamia; also in verses 5, 6 and 7 [c] 3 Hebrew *El-Shaddai*

27:45 Because the nostrils quiver in anger, the word for nostril is rendered in 171 Old Testament instances as "anger," almost akin to "snorting." This applies not only to Esau (v. 45) but also to Moses (Ex 32:19) and even to the Lord (Nu 11:1,10). A tempestuous wind is described poetically in the Old Testament as "the blast of [God's] nostrils" (Ex 15:8; cf. 2Sa 22:16).

ARCHAEOLOGICAL SITES

PADDAN ARAM

GENESIS 28 The geographical name Paddan Aram has been found only in Genesis (e.g., 28:2), and its meaning and exact location are uncertain. Many scholars believe that Paddan Aram is an alternate name for Aram Naharaim ("Aram of the two rivers"; 24:10), the northern region of the Euphrates River, in the vicinity of Haran, which figures prominently in Genesis as the patriarchs' ancestral home[1] ("Map 1").

The prophet Hosea referred to Jacob's journey to the "country [or field] of Aram" (Hos 12:12). Some scholars believe this phrase to be Hosea's translation of *Paddan Aram*, based upon the facts that a **Ugaritic** text refers to "fields of Aram" and that an Arabic noun, *paddan*, sometimes means "field." This argument remains, however, inconclusive.

Others suggest that *Paddan* means "road," based on the similar Akkadian word *paddanu* ("highway"). Thus Paddan Aram would mean "road of Aram." A synonym of *paddanu* is the word *harranu*, which may have been the source of Haran, the city from which Abram departed for Canaan[2] (see Ge 12:4–5). Understood in this light, Paddan Aram would in fact be an alternative name for Haran. Although uncertainty about the name remains, scholars are confident that Paddan Aram refers either to the region around Haran or to Haran itself.

[1]See "The Patriarchal Period: Mesopotamia During the Time of Abraham" on page 26. [2]See "Haran" on page 47.

28:3 [p]Ge 17:6
28:4 [q]Ge 12:2,3 [r]Ge 17:8
28:5 [s]Hos 12:12 [t]Ge 24:29
28:6 [u]ver 1
28:8 [v]Ge 24:3 [w]Ge 26:35
28:9 [x]Ge 25:13 [y]Ge 26:34
28:10 [z]Ge 11:31
28:12 [a]Ge 20:3 [b]Jn 1:51
28:13 [c]Ge 12:7; 35:7,9; 48:3 [d]Ge 26:24 [e]Ge 13:15; 35:12
28:14 [f]Ge 26:4 [g]Ge 13:14 **28:14** [h]Ge 12:3; 18:18; 22:18; Gal 3:8
28:15 [i]Ge 26:3; 48:21 [j]Nu 6:24; Ps 121:5,7-8 [k]Dt 31:6,8 [l]Nu 23:19
28:17 [m]Ex 3:5; Jos 5:15
28:18 [n]Ge 35:14 [o]Lev 8:11
28:19 [p]Jdg 1:23, 26
28:20 [q]Ge 31:13; Jdg 11:30; 2Sa 15:8 [r]ver 15
28:21 [s]Jdg 11:31 [t]Dt 26:17
28:22 [u]Ge 35:7, 14 [v]Ge 14:20; Lev 27:30
29:1 [w]Jdg 6:3,33
29:4 [x]Ge 28:10
29:9 [y]Ex 2:16

bless you and make you fruitful[p] and increase your numbers until you become a community of peoples. 4 May he give you and your descendants the blessing given to Abraham,[q] so that you may take possession of the land where you now live as an alien,[r] the land God gave to Abraham." 5 Then Isaac sent Jacob on his way, and he went to Paddan Aram,[s] to Laban son of Bethuel the Aramean, the brother of Rebekah,[t] who was the mother of Jacob and Esau.

6 Now Esau learned that Isaac had blessed Jacob and had sent him to Paddan Aram to take a wife from there, and that when he blessed him he commanded him, "Do not marry a Canaanite woman,"[u] 7 and that Jacob had obeyed his father and mother and had gone to Paddan Aram. 8 Esau then realized how displeasing the Canaanite women[v] were to his father Isaac;[w] 9 so he went to Ishmael and married Mahalath, the sister of Nebaioth[x] and daughter of Ishmael son of Abraham, in addition to the wives he already had.[y]

Jacob's Dream at Bethel

10 Jacob left Beersheba and set out for Haran.[z] 11 When he reached a certain place, he stopped for the night because the sun had set. Taking one of the stones there, he put it under his head and lay down to sleep. 12 He had a dream[a] in which he saw a stairway[*a*] resting on the earth, with its top reaching to heaven, and the angels of God were ascending and descending on it.[b] 13 There above it[*b*] stood the LORD,[c] and he said: "I am the LORD, the God of your father Abraham and the God of Isaac.[d] I will give you and your descendants the land[e] on which you are lying. 14 Your descendants will be like the dust of the earth, and you[f] will spread out to the west and to the east, to the north and to the south.[g] All peoples on earth will be blessed through you and your offspring.[h] 15 I am with you[i] and will watch over you[j] wherever you go, and I will bring you back to this land. I will not leave you[k] until I have done what I have promised you."[l]

16 When Jacob awoke from his sleep, he thought, "Surely the LORD is in this place, and I was not aware of it." 17 He was afraid and said, "How awesome is this place![m] This is none other than the house of God; this is the gate of heaven."

18 Early the next morning Jacob took the stone he had placed under his head and set it up as a pillar[n] and poured oil on top of it.[o] 19 He called that place Bethel,[*c*] though the city used to be called Luz.[p]

20 Then Jacob made a vow,[q] saying, "If God will be with me and will watch over me[r] on this journey I am taking and will give me food to eat and clothes to wear 21 so that I return safely[s] to my father's house, then the LORD[*d*] will be my God[t] 22 and[*e*] this stone that I have set up as a pillar will be God's house,[u] and of all that you give me I will give you a tenth.[v]"

Jacob Arrives in Paddan Aram

29 Then Jacob continued on his journey and came to the land of the eastern peoples.[w] 2 There he saw a well in the field, with three flocks of sheep lying near it because the flocks were watered from that well. The stone over the mouth of the well was large. 3 When all the flocks were gathered there, the shepherds would roll the stone away from the well's mouth and water the sheep. Then they would return the stone to its place over the mouth of the well.

4 Jacob asked the shepherds, "My brothers, where are you from?"

"We're from Haran,[x]" they replied.

5 He said to them, "Do you know Laban, Nahor's grandson?"

"Yes, we know him," they answered.

6 Then Jacob asked them, "Is he well?"

"Yes, he is," they said, "and here comes his daughter Rachel with the sheep."

7 "Look," he said, "the sun is still high; it is not time for the flocks to be gathered. Water the sheep and take them back to pasture."

8 "We can't," they replied, "until all the flocks are gathered and the stone has been rolled away from the mouth of the well. Then we will water the sheep."

9 While he was still talking with them, Rachel came with her father's sheep,[y] for she was a shepherdess.

[*a*] 12 Or *ladder* [*b*] 13 Or *There beside him* [*c*] 19 *Bethel* means *house of God.* [*d*] 20,21 Or *Since God . . . father's house, the LORD* [*e*] 21,22 Or *house, and the LORD will be my God,* [22]*then*

28:11 In ancient times people were accustomed to sleeping on the ground. Their headrests were often quite hard and were sometimes made of metal.

28:12 This "stairway" was probably not a ladder with rungs but was more likely similar to the steps mounting the sloping side of a ziggurat (see the note on 11:4).

28:18 In ancient times memorials of worship or of communion with God were common.

10 When Jacob saw Rachel daughter of Laban, his mother's brother, and Laban's sheep, he went over and
rolled the stone away from the mouth of the well and watered his uncle's sheep.[z] 11 Then Jacob kissed Ra-
chel and began to weep aloud.[a] 12 He had told Rachel that he was a relative[b] of her father and a son of
Rebekah. So she ran and told her father.[c]
13 As soon as Laban[d] heard the news about Jacob, his sister's son, he hurried to meet him. He em-
braced him and kissed him and brought him to his home, and there Jacob told him all these things.
14 Then Laban said to him, "You are my own flesh and blood."[e]

Jacob Marries Leah and Rachel

After Jacob had stayed with him for a whole month, 15 Laban said to him, "Just because you are a rel-
ative of mine, should you work for me for nothing? Tell me what your wages should be."
16 Now Laban had two daughters; the name of the older was Leah, and the name of the younger was
Rachel. 17 Leah had weak[a] eyes, but Rachel was lovely in form, and beautiful. 18 Jacob was in love with Ra-
chel and said, "I'll work for you seven years in return for your younger daughter Rachel."[f]
19 Laban said, "It's better that I give her to you than to some other man. Stay here with me." 20 So Jacob
served seven years to get Rachel, but they seemed like only a few days to him because of his love for her.[g]
21 Then Jacob said to Laban, "Give me my wife. My time is completed, and I want to lie with her.[h]"
22 So Laban brought together all the people of the place and gave a feast.[i] 23 But when evening came,
he took his daughter Leah and gave her to Jacob, and Jacob lay with her. 24 And Laban gave his servant
girl Zilpah to his daughter as her maidservant.
25 When morning came, there was Leah! So Jacob said to Laban, "What is this you have done to me?[j]
I served you for Rachel, didn't I? Why have you deceived me?[k]"
26 Laban replied, "It is not our custom here to give the younger daughter in marriage before the older
one. 27 Finish this daughter's bridal week;[l] then we will give you the younger one also, in return for an-
other seven years of work."
28 And Jacob did so. He finished the week with Leah, and then Laban gave him his daughter Rachel to
be his wife. 29 Laban gave his servant girl Bilhah[m] to his daughter Rachel as her maidservant.[n] 30 Jacob lay
with Rachel also, and he loved Rachel more than Leah.[o] And he worked for Laban another seven years.[p]

Jacob's Children

31 When the LORD saw that Leah was not loved,[q] he opened her womb,[r] but Rachel was barren. 32 Leah
became pregnant and gave birth to a son. She named him Reuben,[b] for she said, "It is because the LORD
has seen my misery.[s] Surely my husband will love me now."
33 She conceived again, and when she gave birth to a son she said, "Because the LORD heard that I am
not loved, he gave me this one too." So she named him Simeon.[c][t]
34 Again she conceived, and when she gave birth to a son she said, "Now at last my husband will be-
come attached to me,[u] because I have borne him three sons." So he was named Levi.[d][v]
35 She conceived again, and when she gave birth to a son she said, "This time I will praise the LORD."
So she named him Judah.[e][w] Then she stopped having children.

30 When Rachel saw that she was not bearing Jacob any children,[x] she became jealous of her sis-
ter.[y] So she said to Jacob, "Give me children, or I'll die!"
2 Jacob became angry with her and said, "Am I in the place of God, who has kept you from having
children?"[z]
3 Then she said, "Here is Bilhah, my maidservant. Sleep with her so that she can bear children for me
and that through her I too can build a family."[a]
4 So she gave him her servant Bilhah as a wife.[b] Jacob slept with her,[c] 5 and she became pregnant and
bore him a son. 6 Then Rachel said, "God has vindicated me;[d] he has listened to my plea and given me a
son." Because of this she named him Dan.[f][e]

29:10 [z]Ex 2:17
29:11 [a]Ge 33:4
29:12 [b]Ge 13:8; 14:14,16 [c]Ge 24:28
29:13 [d]Ge 24:29
29:14 [e]Ge 2:23; Jdg 9:2; 2Sa 19:12-13
29:18 [f]Hos 12:12
29:20 [g]SS 8:7; Hos 12:12
29:21 [h]Jdg 15:1
29:22 [i]Jdg 14:10; Jn 2:1-2
29:25 [j]Ge 12:18 [k]Ge 27:36
29:27 [l]Jdg 14:12
29:29 [m]Ge 30:3 [n]Ge 16:1
29:30 [o]ver 16 [p]Ge 31:41
29:31 [q]Dt 21:15-17 [r]Ge 11:30; 30:1; Ps 127:3
29:32 [s]Ge 16:11; 31:42; Ex 4:31; Dt 26:7; Ps 25:18
29:33 [t]Ge 34:25; 49:5
29:34 [u]Ge 30:20; 1Sa 1:2-4 [v]Ge 49:5-7
29:35 [w]Ge 49:8; Mt 1:2-3
30:1 [x]Ge 29:31; 1Sa 1:5-6 [y]Lev 18:18
30:2 [z]Ge 16:2; 20:18; 29:31
30:3 [a]Ge 16:2
30:4 [b]ver 9,18 [c]Ge 16:3-4
30:6 [d]Ps 35:24; 43:1; La 3:59 [e]Ge 49:16-17

[a] 17 Or *delicate* [b] 32 *Reuben* sounds like the Hebrew for *he has seen my misery*; the name means *see, a son.* [c] 33 *Simeon* probably means *one who hears.* [d] 34 *Levi* sounds like and may be derived from the Hebrew for *attached.* [e] 35 *Judah* sounds like and may be derived from the Hebrew for *praise.* [f] 6 *Dan* here means *he has vindicated.*

29:24 This wedding custom is well documented in Old Babylonian marriage contracts. See "Nuzi" on page 52.

7 Rachel's servant Bilhah conceived again and bore Jacob a second son. 8 Then Rachel said, "I have had
30:8 [f]Hos 12:3-4 [g]Ge 49:21 a great struggle with my sister, and I have won."[f] So she named him Naphtali.[a][g]
9 When Leah saw that she had stopped having children, she took her maidservant Zilpah and gave her
30:9 [h]ver 4 to Jacob as a wife.[h] 10 Leah's servant Zilpah bore Jacob a son. 11 Then Leah said, "What good fortune!"[b] So
30:11 [i]Ge 49:19 she named him Gad.[c][i]
12 Leah's servant Zilpah bore Jacob a second son. 13 Then Leah said, "How happy I am! The women will
30:13 [j]Ps 127:3 [k]Pr 31:28; Lk 1:48 [l]Ge 49:20 call me[j] happy."[k] So she named him Asher.[d][l]
14 During wheat harvest, Reuben went out into the fields and found some mandrake plants,[m] which
30:14 [m]SS 7:13 he brought to his mother Leah. Rachel said to Leah, "Please give me some of your son's mandrakes."
30:15 [n]Nu 16:9, 13 15 But she said to her, "Wasn't it enough[n] that you took away my husband? Will you take my son's man-
drakes too?"
"Very well," Rachel said, "he can sleep with you tonight in return for your son's mandrakes."
16 So when Jacob came in from the fields that evening, Leah went out to meet him. "You must sleep with
me," she said. "I have hired you with my son's mandrakes." So he slept with her that night.
30:17 [o]Ge 25:21 17 God listened to Leah,[o] and she became pregnant and bore Jacob a fifth son. 18 Then Leah said, "God
30:18 [p]Ge 49:14 has rewarded me for giving my maidservant to my husband." So she named him Issachar.[e][p]
19 Leah conceived again and bore Jacob a sixth son. 20 Then Leah said, "God has presented me with a
precious gift. This time my husband will treat me with honor, because I have borne him six sons." So she
30:20 [q]Ge 35:23; 49:13; Mt 4:13 named him Zebulun.[f][q]
21 Some time later she gave birth to a daughter and named her Dinah.
30:22 [r]Ge 8:1; 1Sa 1:19-20 22 Then God remembered Rachel;[r] he listened to her and opened her womb.[s] 23 She became pregnant
[s]Ge 29:31 30:23 [t]ver 6 and gave birth to a son[t] and said, "God has taken away my disgrace."[u] 24 She named him Joseph,[g][v] and
[u]Isa 4:1; Lk 1:25 said, "May the LORD add to me another son."[w]

30:24 [v]Ge 35:24; 37:2; 39:1; 49:22-26 [w]Ge 35:17

Jacob's Flocks Increase

30:25 [x]Ge 24:54 25 After Rachel gave birth to Joseph, Jacob said to Laban, "Send me on my way[x] so I can go back to my
30:26 [y]Ge 29:20, 30; Hos 12:12 own homeland. 26 Give me my wives and children, for whom I have served you,[y] and I will be on my way.
You know how much work I've done for you."
27 But Laban said to him, "If I have found favor in your eyes, please stay. I have learned by divination
30:27 [z]Ge 26:24; 39:3,5 that[h] the LORD has blessed me because of you."[z] 28 He added, "Name your wages,[a] and I will pay them."
30:28 [a]Ge 29:15 29 Jacob said to him, "You know how I have worked for you[b] and how your livestock has fared under
30:29 [b]Ge 31:6 [c]Ge 31:38-40 my care.[c] 30 The little you had before I came has increased greatly, and the LORD has blessed you wherev-
30:30 [d]1Ti 5:8 er I have been. But now, when may I do something for my own household?[d]"
31 "What shall I give you?" he asked.
"Don't give me anything," Jacob replied. "But if you will do this one thing for me, I will go on tending
your flocks and watching over them: 32 Let me go through all your flocks today and remove from them
30:32 [e]Ge 31:8, 12 every speckled or spotted sheep, every dark-colored lamb and every spotted or speckled goat.[e] They will
be my wages. 33 And my honesty will testify for me in the future, whenever you check on the wages you
have paid me. Any goat in my possession that is not speckled or spotted, or any lamb that is not dark-
colored, will be considered stolen."
34 "Agreed," said Laban. "Let it be as you have said." 35 That same day he removed all the male goats
that were streaked or spotted, and all the speckled or spotted female goats (all that had white on them)
30:35 [f]Ge 31:1 and all the dark-colored lambs, and he placed them in the care of his sons.[f] 36 Then he put a three-day
journey between himself and Jacob, while Jacob continued to tend the rest of Laban's flocks.
37 Jacob, however, took fresh-cut branches from poplar, almond and plane trees and made white stripes
on them by peeling the bark and exposing the white inner wood of the branches. 38 Then he placed the
peeled branches in all the watering troughs, so that they would be directly in front of the flocks when they

[a] 8 *Naphtali* means *my struggle.* [b] 11 Or *"A troop is coming!"* [c] 11 *Gad* can mean *good fortune* or *a troop.* [d] 13 *Asher* means *happy.* [e] 18 *Issachar* sounds like the Hebrew for *reward.* [f] 20 *Zebulun* probably means *honor.* [g] 24 *Joseph* means *may he add.* [h] 27 Or possibly *have become rich and*

30:14 Mandrakes were thought to induce pregnancy when eaten (see SS 7:13).

30:32 Ancient shepherding contracts provided for a share of between 10 and 20 percent of the flock, along with a percentage of the wool and milk by-products. Dark and spotted animals typically represented a smaller proportion, ostensibly giving Laban the better deal. Jacob proposed to remove the designated sheep from Laban's flock for his wages, so Laban's actions (vv. 35–36) appeared to violate the agreement.

came to drink. When the flocks were in heat and came to drink, [39]they mated in front of the branches.
And they bore young that were streaked or speckled or spotted. [40]Jacob set apart the young of the flock by
themselves, but made the rest face the streaked and dark-colored animals that belonged to Laban. Thus
he made separate flocks for himself and did not put them with Laban's animals. [41]Whenever the stronger
females were in heat, Jacob would place the branches in the troughs in front of the animals so they would
mate near the branches, [42]but if the animals were weak, he would not place them there. So the weak ani-
mals went to Laban and the strong ones to Jacob. [43]In this way the man grew exceedingly prosperous and
came to own large flocks, and maidservants and menservants, and camels and donkeys.[g]

30:43 [g]ver 30; Ge 12:16; 13:2; 24:35; 26:13-14

ARCHAEOLOGICAL SITES

NUZI

GENESIS 30 The ancient city of **Nuzi** (modern Yorghan Tepe; find Nuzi on "Map 1"), located a few miles southwest of Kirkuk in Iraq, has provided archaeologists with a wealth of material. Estates of the nobility have yielded exquisite wall paintings, figurines, cylinder seals[1] and ceramics in a style dubbed "Nuzi ware." The most significant discovery to date, however, has been extensive archives dating to approximately 1500–1350 B.C., during which the **Mitanni** kingdom controlled Nuzi. Most of the 3,500 tablets in these archives originated from private homes and document the lives of the city's ruling families, as well as providing information regarding the political structure and social conditions of this region and time.

Several Nuzi texts parallel and illuminate Biblical accounts of the **patriarchs**. Not all of the alleged correspondences between the Bible and information gleaned from Nuzi are certain, but at the very least they demonstrate that the context of Genesis is in fact rooted in ancient customs. Some of the more famous of the proposed congruencies include:

A childless couple in Nuzi could adopt a servant as an heir (cf. Abram's assumption that his slave, Eliezer, would inherit his estate since Abram had not yet sired a son; 15:2–3).

Legal tablets demonstrate that an infertile primary wife could give her maidservant to her husband for the expressed purpose of providing him an heir, who could subsequently be adopted by the primary wife. According to these texts, if she later gave birth to her own son, he would displace the maidservant's son, as the rightful heir (cf. the accounts of Sarah and Hagar in 16:1–4; 21:8–10 and of the maidservants of Leah and Rachel in 30:1–13).

Marriage contracts discovered in Nuzi demonstrate that brothers could arrange for their sister's marriage, although she often had the option to agree or disagree with the proposed union (cf. 24:29–60). Marriage contracts formulated by a father, however, did not require his daughter's consent (cf. 29:16–30). There are also parallels to the institution of levirate marriage[2] (cf. Judah and Tamar's story).

Prior to discovery of the Nuzi tablets, scholars had assumed that a later editor had added the notes that Laban gave named maidservants to his daughters when they married (29:22–24,28–29). But researchers have discovered Nuzi marriage contracts stipulating that the bride was to be given a handmaiden, whose name was duly recorded in the contract.

An individual family's household idols were considered highly important in Nuzi and were handed down to the principal heir. If the inheritance were disputed in court, possession of the family idols could be accepted as proof that the deceased had intended the possessor to be his heir. Thus, Rachel's theft of the family idols could have been construed as a serious crime, an attempt to secure Laban's wealth for her husband and possible future children (31:22–37).

Some historians have argued that Nuzi arrangements allowing a man to adopt a young woman as his daughter for the purpose of giving her in marriage to his son shed light upon Abraham's two separate protestations that his wife was in reality his sister (12:10–20; 20:1–18). There is some doubt that this is a true parallel, but these incidents at least suggest that the patriarchs' stories likely had roots in ancient customs of which we may now know little or nothing.

Although the city of Haran ("Map 1"), in which Abraham had lived before journeying to Canaan,[3] is some distance from Nuzi, the Hurrians controlled both cities during the second millennium B.C.[4] Therefore it is not surprising that the Nuzi archives and the Biblical stories of the patriarchs reflect common customs and legal arrangements. Future discoveries of relics such as these tablets may shed additional light on some perplexing Biblical issues.[5]

[1]See "Signet Rings" and photographs of a cylinder seal impressions on page 728. [2]See "Levirate Marriage" on page 64. [3]See "Haran" on page 47 and "Canaan" on page 324. [4]See "The Hurrians" on page 57. [5]See "The Patriarchal Period: Mesopotamia During the Time of Abraham" on page 26, "Custom and Law in Ancient Mesopotamia" on page 36 and "The Historicity of the Patriarchal Narratives" on page 73.

Jacob Flees From Laban

31 Jacob heard that Laban's sons were saying, "Jacob has taken everything our father owned and
has gained all this wealth from what belonged to our father." 2And Jacob noticed that Laban's at-
titude toward him was not what it had been.
31:3 [h]ver 13; Ge 32:9 [i]Ge 21:22; 26:3; 28:15 3Then the LORD said to Jacob, "Go back[h] to the land of your fathers and to your relatives, and I will be
with you."[i]
4So Jacob sent word to Rachel and Leah to come out to the fields where his flocks were. 5He said to
them, "I see that your father's attitude toward me is not what it was before, but the God of my father has
31:5 [j]Ge 21:22; 26:3 been with me.[j] 6You know that I've worked for your father with all my strength,[k] 7yet your father has
31:6 [k]Ge 30:29 cheated me by changing my wages ten times.[l] However, God has not allowed him to harm me.[m] 8If he
31:7 [l]ver 41; Job 19:3 [m]ver 52; Ps 37:28; 105:14 said, 'The speckled ones will be your wages,' then all the flocks gave birth to speckled young; and if he said,
31:8 [n]Ge 30:32 'The streaked ones will be your wages,'[n] then all the flocks bore streaked young. 9So God has taken away
31:9 [o]ver 1,16; Ge 30:42 your father's livestock and has given them to me.[o]
10"In breeding season I once had a dream in which I looked up and saw that the male goats mating
31:11 [p]Ge 16:7; 48:16 with the flock were streaked, speckled or spotted. 11The angel of God[p] said to me in the dream, 'Jacob.' I
answered, 'Here I am.' 12And he said, 'Look up and see that all the male goats mating with the flock are
31:12 [q]Ex 3:7 streaked, speckled or spotted, for I have seen all that Laban has been doing to you.[q] 13I am the God of
31:13 [r]Ge 28:10-22 [s]ver 3; Ge 32:9 Bethel,[r] where you anointed a pillar and where you made a vow to me. Now leave this land at once and
go back to your native land.[s]' "
14Then Rachel and Leah replied, "Do we still have any share in the inheritance of our father's estate?
31:15 [t]Ge 29:20 15Does he not regard us as foreigners? Not only has he sold us, but he has used up what was paid for us.[t]
16Surely all the wealth that God took away from our father belongs to us and our children. So do what-
ever God has told you."
17Then Jacob put his children and his wives on camels, 18and he drove all his livestock ahead of him, along
31:18 [u]Ge 35:27 [v]Ge 10:19 with all the goods he had accumulated in Paddan Aram,[a] to go to his father Isaac[u] in the land of Canaan.[v]
19When Laban had gone to shear his sheep, Rachel stole her father's household gods.[w] 20Moreover, Ja-
31:19 [w]ver 30, 32,34-35; Ge 35:2; Jdg 17:5; 1Sa 19:13; Hos 3:4 cob deceived[x] Laban the Aramean by not telling him he was running away.[y] 21So he fled with all he had,
and crossing the River,[b] he headed for the hill country of Gilead.[z]

Laban Pursues Jacob

31:20 [x]Ge 27:36 [y]ver 27 31:21 [z]Ge 37:25 22On the third day Laban was told that Jacob had fled. 23Taking his relatives with him, he pursued Jacob
for seven days and caught up with him in the hill country of Gilead. 24Then God came to Laban the Ara-
31:24 [a]Ge 20:3; Job 33:15 [b]Ge 24:50 mean in a dream at night and said to him,[a] "Be careful not to say anything to Jacob, either good or bad."[b]
25Jacob had pitched his tent in the hill country of Gilead when Laban overtook him, and Laban and
31:26 [c]Ge 27:36 [d]1Sa 30:2-3 his relatives camped there too. 26Then Laban said to Jacob, "What have you done? You've deceived me,[c]
and you've carried off my daughters like captives in war.[d] 27Why did you run off secretly and deceive me?
31:27 [e]Ex 15:20 [f]Ge 4:21 Why didn't you tell me, so I could send you away with joy and singing to the music of tambourines[e] and
31:28 [g]ver 55 harps?[f] 28You didn't even let me kiss my grandchildren and my daughters good-by.[g] You have done a fool-
31:29 [h]ver 7 [i]ver 53 ish thing. 29I have the power to harm you;[h] but last night the God of your father[i] said to me, 'Be careful
not to say anything to Jacob, either good or bad.' 30Now you have gone off because you longed to return
31:30 [j]ver 19; Jdg 18:24 to your father's house. But why did you steal my gods?[j]"

[a] *18* That is, Northwest Mesopotamia [b] *21* That is, the Euphrates

---

31:14–16 In ancient times contracts for marriages were formal business transactions. The groom usually paid the father of the bride the bride price, which was supposed to be held in trust to provide for the wife if she were abandoned or widowed. In this case Jacob had given no bride price, so Laban should have set aside the equivalent of his wages for the women. If their father's house held no economic security for them, Laban's daughters had no reason to stay.

31:19 These "household gods" were small, portable idols, probably images of either ancestors or the patron gods of ancestors, believed to bring prosperity and protection. Such gods had no temples but were likely provided with a shrine area in the home. Rachel may have wanted something tangible to worship on the long journey ahead, a practice referred to much later in the writings of Josephus, a first-century Jewish historian. A family's household idols were considered highly important in Nuzi and were handed down to the principal heir. If the inheritance were disputed in court, possession of the family idols could be accepted as proof that the deceased had intended the possessor to be his heir (see "Nuzi" on p. 52).

31:30–31 It appears that according to Nuzian customs (see "Nuzi" on p. 52), Jacob had become Laban's male heir after Laban had adopted him as his son. Laban had then given Jacob both Leah and her sister Rachel as his wives. After having become prosperous, Jacob took his departure (v. 21). One reason "Laban's attitude toward him was not what it had been" (v. 2) is that Laban by now apparently had sons by birth, who regarded Jacob as an interloper (v. 1). Thus arose the dispute over the right of the possession of the teraphim, the household gods that Rachel concealed in the baggage as she, together with her husband and Jacob's extended family, fled (vv. 30–31). These household deities, about the size of miniature dolls, were regarded as indisputable evidence of the rights and privileges of family ownership and inheritance. Note Laban's indignant query, "But why did you steal my gods?" (v. 30).

[31]Jacob answered Laban, "I was afraid, because I thought you would take your daughters away from
me by force. [32]But if you find anyone who has your gods, he shall not live.[k] In the presence of our rela- **31:32** [k]Ge 44:9
tives, see for yourself whether there is anything of yours here with me; and if so, take it." Now Jacob did
not know that Rachel had stolen the gods.
[33]So Laban went into Jacob's tent and into Leah's tent and into the tent of the two maidservants, but
he found nothing. After he came out of Leah's tent, he entered Rachel's tent. [34]Now Rachel had taken the
household gods and put them inside her camel's saddle and was sitting on them. Laban searched[l] through **31:34** [l]ver 37; Ge 44:12
everything in the tent but found nothing.
[35]Rachel said to her father, "Don't be angry, my lord, that I cannot stand up in your presence;[m] I'm **31:35** [m]Ex 20:12; Lev 19:3,32
having my period." So he searched but could not find the household gods.
[36]Jacob was angry and took Laban to task. "What is my crime?" he asked Laban. "What sin have I
committed that you hunt me down? [37]Now that you have searched through all my goods, what have you
found that belongs to your household? Put it here in front of your relatives[n] and mine, and let them judge **31:37** [n]ver 23
between the two of us.
[38]"I have been with you for twenty years now. Your sheep and goats have not miscarried, nor have I
eaten rams from your flocks. [39]I did not bring you animals torn by wild beasts; I bore the loss myself. And
you demanded payment from me for whatever was stolen by day or night.[o] [40]This was my situation: The **31:39** [o]Ex 22:13
heat consumed me in the daytime and the cold at night, and sleep fled from my eyes. [41]It was like this
for the twenty years I was in your household. I worked for you fourteen years for your two daughters[p] and **31:41** [p]Ge 29:30 [q]ver 7
six years for your flocks, and you changed my wages ten times.[q] [42]If the God of my father,[r] the God of **31:42** [r]ver 5; Ex 3:15; 1Ch 12:17
Abraham and the Fear of Isaac,[s] had not been with me,[t] you would surely have sent me away empty- [s]ver 53; Isa 8:13 [t]Ps 124:1-2
handed. But God has seen my hardship and the toil of my hands,[u] and last night he rebuked you." [u]Ge 29:32

ARCHAEOLOGICAL SITES

MARI

GENESIS 31 **Mari** ("Map 1"), known today as Tell Hariri, is located on the Euphrates River just downstream from its confluence with the Habur River.[1] Ideally situated at the convergence of several trade routes connecting **Sumer** to **Assyria** and **Mesopotamia** to Syria-Palestine, cosmopolitan Mari was an ideal spot for trade and communications between kingdoms. The city served as a buffer zone between the Sumerian city-states to the southeast and the lands of the pastoral tribes, called **Amorites**, to the north. These livestock-raising nomads seem to have been particularly concentrated around the city of Haran (cf. Abram's sojourn there mentioned in Ge 11:31—12:5).[2] Swarming in from Mesopotamia, they settled down there between 2400–2200 B.C. In fact, people from northwestern Syria ruled Mari after this period, so the city's most famous kings were of Amorite descent.

Much of Mari's early history is obscure. Founded around 2900–2700 B.C., the city acquired wealth and importance but periodically was controlled by such great third-millenium B.C. powers as Sargon of Akkad and the Third Dynasty of Ur.[3] In 1775 B.C. Zimri-Lim of Mari broke free of Assyrian domination, but Hammurabi of Babylon burned the city in 1761 B.C.

Begun in 1933, excavations of Mari have uncovered a large palace and several temples, including a ziggurat. The excavations have also yielded tens of thousands of clay, **cuneiform** tablets that had become hardened from the heat of conflagrations inflicted by the Babylonians. Well preserved, these tablets address a wide variety of issues, such as palace administration, provincial administration, harems, expenses, gift registries, literary works, letters and treaties.

These Mari documents shed light upon Old Testament study in several ways:

They describe the Amorites and their culture, helping us to understand the broader cultural environment of the early Israelites.

They showcase similarities between many Amorite and Biblical names, although there are few, if any, direct links to specific Biblical characters.

They mention the towns of Laish, which the Danites destroyed and rebuilt (Jdg 18), and **Hazor**, an important city even before the Israelites entered the promised land (Jos 11:10).[4]

They refer to pagan prophets who functioned in some ways similarly to their Biblical counterparts.[5]

[1]See "The Tigris and Euphrates Rivers" on page 604. [2]See "Haran" on page 47. [3]See "Ur" on page 705. [4]See "Hazor" on page 322. [5]See "Prophets in the Bible and Pagan Nations" on page 1457.

43 Laban answered Jacob, "The women are my daughters, the children are my children, and the flocks are
my flocks. All you see is mine. Yet what can I do today about these daughters of mine, or about the children
31:44 [v]Ge 21:27; 26:28 [w]Jos 24:27
they have borne? 44 Come now, let's make a covenant,[v] you and I, and let it serve as a witness between us."[w]
31:45 [x]Ge 28:18
45 So Jacob took a stone and set it up as a pillar.[x] 46 He said to his relatives, "Gather some stones." So they
took stones and piled them in a heap, and they ate there by the heap. 47 Laban called it Jegar Sahadutha,[a]
and Jacob called it Galeed.[b]

48 Laban said, "This heap is a witness between you and me today." That is why it was called Galeed. 49 It
31:49 [y]Jdg 11:29; 1Sa 7:5-6
was also called Mizpah,[c] [y] because he said, "May the LORD keep watch between you and me when we are
away from each other. 50 If you mistreat my daughters or if you take any wives besides my daughters, even
31:50 [z]Jer 29:23; 42:5
though no one is with us, remember that God is a witness[z] between you and me."
31:51 [a]Ge 28:18
51 Laban also said to Jacob, "Here is this heap, and here is this pillar[a] I have set up between you and
31:52 [b]Ge 21:30 [c]ver 7; Ge 26:29
me. 52 This heap is a witness, and this pillar is a witness,[b] that I will not go past this heap to your side to
harm you and that you will not go past this heap and pillar to my side to harm me.[c] 53 May the God of
31:53 [d]Ge 28:13 [e]Ge 16:5 [f]Ge 21:23,27 [g]ver 42
Abraham[d] and the God of Nahor, the God of their father, judge between us."[e]
So Jacob took an oath[f] in the name of the Fear of his father Isaac.[g] 54 He offered a sacrifice there in the
hill country and invited his relatives to a meal. After they had eaten, they spent the night there.
31:55 [h]ver 28 [i]Ge 18:33; 30:25
55 Early the next morning Laban kissed his grandchildren and his daughters[h] and blessed them. Then
he left and returned home.[i]

Jacob Prepares to Meet Esau

32:1 [j]Ge 16:11; 2Ki 6:16-17; Ps 34:7; 91:11; Heb 1:14
32 Jacob also went on his way, and the angels of God[j] met him. 2 When Jacob saw them, he said,
32:2 [k]Ge 28:17 [l]2Sa 2:8,29
"This is the camp of God!"[k] So he named that place Mahanaim.[d] [l]
32:3 [m]Ge 27:41-42 [n]Ge 25:30; 36:8,9
3 Jacob sent messengers ahead of him to his brother Esau[m] in the land of Seir, the country of Edom.[n]
4 He instructed them: "This is what you are to say to my master Esau: 'Your servant Jacob says, I have
been staying with Laban and have remained there till now. 5 I have cattle and donkeys, sheep and goats,
32:5 [o]Ge 12:16; 30:43 [p]Ge 33:8, 10,15
menservants and maidservants.[o] Now I am sending this message to my lord, that I may find favor in
your eyes.[p]' "

6 When the messengers returned to Jacob, they said, "We went to your brother Esau, and now he is
32:6 [q]Ge 33:1
coming to meet you, and four hundred men are with him."[q]
32:7 [r]ver 11
7 In great fear[r] and distress Jacob divided the people who were with him into two groups,[e] and the
flocks and herds and camels as well. 8 He thought, "If Esau comes and attacks one group,[f] the group[f] that
is left may escape."

32:9 [s]Ge 28:13; 31:42 [t]Ge 31:13
9 Then Jacob prayed, "O God of my father Abraham, God of my father Isaac,[s] O LORD, who said to me,
'Go back to your country and your relatives, and I will make you prosper,'[t] 10 I am unworthy of all the kind-
32:10 [u]Ge 24:27
ness and faithfulness[u] you have shown your servant. I had only my staff when I crossed this Jordan, but
now I have become two groups. 11 Save me, I pray, from the hand of my brother Esau, for I am afraid he will
32:11 [v]Ps 59:2 [w]Ge 27:41
come and attack me,[v] and also the mothers with their children.[w] 12 But you have said, 'I will surely make
32:12 [x]Ge 22:17 [y]Ge 28:13-15; Hos 1:10; Ro 9:27
you prosper and will make your descendants like the sand[x] of the sea, which cannot be counted.[y]' "
32:13 [z]Ge 43:11, 15,25,26; Pr 18:16
13 He spent the night there, and from what he had with him he selected a gift[z] for his brother Esau:
14 two hundred female goats and twenty male goats, two hundred ewes and twenty rams, 15 thirty female
camels with their young, forty cows and ten bulls, and twenty female donkeys and ten male donkeys.
16 He put them in the care of his servants, each herd by itself, and said to his servants, "Go ahead of me,
and keep some space between the herds."

17 He instructed the one in the lead: "When my brother Esau meets you and asks, 'To whom do you be-
long, and where are you going, and who owns all these animals in front of you?' 18 then you are to say,
32:18 [a]Ge 18:3
'They belong to your servant[a] Jacob. They are a gift sent to my lord Esau, and he is coming behind us.' "
19 He also instructed the second, the third and all the others who followed the herds: "You are to say the
same thing to Esau when you meet him. 20 And be sure to say, 'Your servant Jacob is coming behind us.' "
For he thought, "I will pacify him with these gifts I am sending on ahead; later, when I see him, perhaps
32:20 [b]Ge 33:10; Pr 21:14
he will receive me."[b] 21 So Jacob's gifts went on ahead of him, but he himself spent the night in the camp.

[a] 47 The Aramaic *Jegar Sahadutha* means *witness heap.* [b] 47 The Hebrew *Galeed* means *witness heap.* [c] 49 *Mizpah* means *watchtower.* [d] 2 *Mahanaim* means *two camps.* [e] 7 Or *camps*; also in verse 10 [f] 8 Or *camp*

31:47 A western Semitic language, Aramaic is closely related to Hebrew and developed various dialects. Verse 47, while not explicitly stating Laban's use of Aramaic, calls attention to the fact that he used different wording than Jacob did.

Jacob Wrestles With God

22 That night Jacob got up and took his two wives, his two maidservants and his eleven sons and
crossed the ford of the Jabbok.[c] 23 After he had sent them across the stream, he sent over all his posses- **32:22** [c]Dt 2:37;
sions. 24 So Jacob was left alone, and a man[d] wrestled with him till daybreak. 25 When the man saw that 3:16; Jos 12:2 **32:24** [d]Ge 18:2
he could not overpower him, he touched the socket of Jacob's hip[e] so that his hip was wrenched as he **32:25** [e]ver 32
wrestled with the man. 26 Then the man said, "Let me go, for it is daybreak."
But Jacob replied, "I will not let you go unless you bless me."[f] **32:26** [f]Hos 12:4
27 The man asked him, "What is your name?"
"Jacob," he answered.
28 Then the man said, "Your name will no longer be Jacob, but Israel,[a][g] because you have struggled **32:28** [g]Ge 17:5;
with God and with men and have overcome." 35:10; 1Ki 18:31
29 Jacob said, "Please tell me your name."[h] **32:29** [h]Jdg 13:17
But he replied, "Why do you ask my name?"[i] Then he blessed[j] him there. [i]Jdg 13:18 [j]Ge 35:9
30 So Jacob called the place Peniel,[b] saying, "It is because I saw God face to face,[k] and yet my life was **32:30** [k]Ge 16:13;
spared." Ex 24:11; Nu 12:8;
31 The sun rose above him as he passed Peniel,[c] and he was limping because of his hip. 32 Therefore to Jdg 6:22; 13:22
this day the Israelites do not eat the tendon attached to the socket of the hip, because the socket of Ja-
cob's hip was touched near the tendon.

Jacob Meets Esau

33 Jacob looked up and there was Esau, coming with his four hundred men;[l] so he divided the chil- **33:1** [l]Ge 32:6
dren among Leah, Rachel and the two maidservants. 2 He put the maidservants and their chil-
dren in front, Leah and her children next, and Rachel and Joseph in the rear. 3 He himself went on ahead
and bowed down to the ground[m] seven times as he approached his brother. **33:3** [m]Ge 18:2; 42:6
4 But Esau ran to meet Jacob and embraced him; he threw his arms around his neck and kissed him.

[a] *28 Israel* means *he struggles with God.* [b] *30 Peniel* means *face of God.* [c] *31* Hebrew *Penuel,* a variant of *Peniel*

33:3 Bowing down to the ground seven times was a sign of total submission, documented also in texts found at Tell el-Amarna in Egypt and dating to the fourteenth century B.C.

ARCHAEOLOGICAL SITES

SUCCOTH/TELL DEIR ALLA

GENESIS 33 Succoth, located just east of the Jordan River, is mentioned in several Biblical contexts (but note that the Succoth of Ex 12–13 and Nu 33 ["Map 1"] was a different place):

After meeting Esau near the Jabbok River, Jacob proceeded toward the Jordan River near Penuel and built livestock enclosures there (Ge 33:17; the rivers, but not the names of these towns, are indicated on "Map 2"). Jacob named this place Succoth ("shelters").

Gideon followed Jacob's route in reverse (Jdg 8) while pursuing Midianite raiders.[1] The people of Succoth refused to feed his troops, and in retaliation they later sacked the town (Jdg 8:13–17).

Most scholars identify Succoth with modern Tell Deir Alla. A significant temple existed here during the **Late Bronze Age.**[2] Remains discovered at Succoth include jar fragments from 1209–1201 B.C., ornamented with a **cartouche** of an Egyptian queen, and three clay tablets in a script yet to be deciphered.

The Late Bronze-era Succoth was destroyed around 1200 B.C., possibly by Gideon and his troops. Excavation of **Iron Age** I strata offers no evidence of a permanent settlement there at that time (with the exception of minor structures dated near the end of this period), but remains do exist of furnaces used to smelt bronze. According to 1 Kings 7:46 Solomon arranged for bronze-casting in the Succoth area for the making of items designated for the temple.

The site was once again built up during the **Iron Age** II. A plastered wall from this era contains an **Aramaic** inscription in ink mentioning Balaam.[3] An earthquake probably destroyed the city during the eighth century B.C. (cf. Am 1:1). The site was inhabited, however, until the late **Persian period**, perhaps only seasonally due to the extreme summer temperatures.

[1]See "Midian" on page 92. [2]See "Archaeological Periods" chart on page xx in the front of this Bible. [3]See "Balaam, the Son of Beor" on page 229.

And they wept.[n] 5Then Esau looked up and saw the women and children. "Who are these with you?" he
asked.
Jacob answered, "They are the children God has graciously given your servant.[o]"
6Then the maidservants and their children approached and bowed down. 7Next, Leah and her chil-
dren came and bowed down. Last of all came Joseph and Rachel, and they too bowed down.
8Esau asked, "What do you mean by all these droves I met?"[p]
"To find favor in your eyes, my lord,"[q] he said.
9But Esau said, "I already have plenty, my brother. Keep what you have for yourself."
10"No, please!" said Jacob. "If I have found favor in your eyes, accept this gift from me. For to see your
face is like seeing the face of God,[r] now that you have received me favorably.[s] 11Please accept the pres-
ent[t] that was brought to you, for God has been gracious to me[u] and I have all I need." And because Jacob
insisted, Esau accepted it.
12Then Esau said, "Let us be on our way; I'll accompany you."
13But Jacob said to him, "My lord knows that the children are tender and that I must care for the ewes
and cows that are nursing their young. If they are driven hard just one day, all the animals will die. 14So
let my lord go on ahead of his servant, while I move along slowly at the pace of the droves before me and
that of the children, until I come to my lord in Seir.[v]"
15Esau said, "Then let me leave some of my men with you."
"But why do that?" Jacob asked. "Just let me find favor in the eyes of my lord."[w]
16So that day Esau started on his way back to Seir. 17Jacob, however, went to Succoth,[x] where he built
a place for himself and made shelters for his livestock. That is why the place is called Succoth.[a]
18After Jacob came from Paddan Aram,[b][y] he arrived safely at the[c] city of Shechem[z] in Canaan and
camped within sight of the city. 19For a hundred pieces of silver,[d] he bought from the sons of Hamor, the
father of Shechem,[a] the plot of ground[b] where he pitched his tent. 20There he set up an altar and called
it El Elohe Israel.[e]

33:4 [n]Ge 45:14-15
33:5 [o]Ge 48:9; Ps 127:3; Isa 8:18
33:8 [p]Ge 32:14-16 [q]Ge 24:9; 32:5
33:10 [r]Ge 16:13 [s]Ge 32:20
33:11 [t]1Sa 25:27 [u]Ge 30:43
33:14 [v]Ge 32:3
33:15 [w]Ge 34:11; 47:25; Ru 2:13
33:17 [x]Jos 13:27; Jdg 8:5,6,8,14-16; Ps 60:6
33:18 [y]Ge 25:20; 28:2 [z]Jos 24:1; Jdg 9:1
33:19 [a]Jos 24:32 [b]Jn 4:5

[a] *17 Succoth* means *shelters.* [b] *18* That is, Northwest Mesopotamia [c] *18* Or *arrived at Shalem, a* [d] *19* Hebrew *hundred kesitahs*; a kesitah was a unit of money of unknown weight and value. [e] *20 El Elohe Israel* can mean *God, the God of Israel* or *mighty is the God of Israel.*

33:19 Modern Bir Ya'kub is doubtless the well mentioned in John 4:6 as the well of Jacob. For many centuries Samaritans and Jews have believed this to be the case. The ground mentioned by John had been purchased by Jacob (v. 19). The area was later wrested by

The Hurrians

GENESIS 34 The **Hurrians** entered northern **Mesopotamia**, apparently from the Caucasus region, during the third millennium B.C. and scattered across the ancient Near East. They were well established in the area by the eighteenth century B.C. and created the kingdom of **Mitanni** in the northern territory between the Tigris and Euphrates Rivers by the mid-sixteenth century B.C.[1] This kingdom became a major international player during the mid-second millennium B.C., but its location between the areas inhabited by the Egyptians, **Hittites** and **Assyrians** rendered it vulnerable to attack. By about 1250 B.C. Mitanni had ceased to exist as a kingdom.

Little is known about the Hurrian language because most of the documents these people left behind are in **Akkadian**[2] rather than in their own language. It is certain, however, that the Hurrians were not Semitic.

In **Nuzi**, a Hurrian city east of the Tigris River, archaeologists have discovered an archive of **cuneiform** texts that reveal much about ancient Mesopotamian culture.[3] The Hurrians worshiped such deities as a storm god, a sun god and a moon god in a Mesopotamian temple/pantheon (temple dedicated to multiple gods). Excelling in metallurgy and glassmaking, they also were known for an intricately decorated pottery now called "Nuzi ware." Some scholars have suggested that the Biblical Horites (Ge 36:20–21; 14:6) were Hurrians, but this is most likely incorrect. The Horites were a late third-millennium tribal group indigenous to the region of Seir, south of the Dead Sea, whereas the Hurrians were a people who entered northern Mesopotamia from the north during the second millennium.

[1]See "The Tigris and Euphrates Rivers" on page 604. [2]See "Languages of the Old Testament World" on page 672. [3]See "Nuzi" on page 52.

Dinah and the Shechemites

34 Now Dinah,[c] the daughter Leah had borne to Jacob, went out to visit the women of the land.
2 When Shechem son of Hamor the Hivite, the ruler of that area, saw her, he took her and violat-
ed her. 3 His heart was drawn to Dinah daughter of Jacob, and he loved the girl and spoke tenderly to her.
4 And Shechem said to his father Hamor, "Get me this girl as my wife."

5 When Jacob heard that his daughter Dinah had been defiled, his sons were in the fields with his live-
stock; so he kept quiet about it until they came home.

6 Then Shechem's father Hamor went out to talk with Jacob.[d] 7 Now Jacob's sons had come in from the
fields as soon as they heard what had happened. They were filled with grief and fury, because Shechem
had done a disgraceful thing in[a] Israel[e] by lying with Jacob's daughter—a thing that should not be done.[f]

8 But Hamor said to them, "My son Shechem has his heart set on your daughter. Please give her to him
as his wife. 9 Intermarry with us; give us your daughters and take our daughters for yourselves. 10 You can
settle among us;[g] the land is open to you.[h] Live in it, trade[b] in it,[i] and acquire property in it."

11 Then Shechem said to Dinah's father and brothers, "Let me find favor in your eyes, and I will give
you whatever you ask. 12 Make the price for the bride[j] and the gift I am to bring as great as you like, and
I'll pay whatever you ask me. Only give me the girl as my wife."

13 Because their sister Dinah had been defiled, Jacob's sons replied deceitfully as they spoke to Shechem
and his father Hamor. 14 They said to them, "We can't do such a thing; we can't give our sister to a man
who is not circumcised.[k] That would be a disgrace to us. 15 We will give our consent to you on one con-
dition only: that you become like us by circumcising all your males.[l] 16 Then we will give you our
daughters and take your daughters for ourselves. We'll settle among you and become one people with
you. 17 But if you will not agree to be circumcised, we'll take our sister[c] and go."

18 Their proposal seemed good to Hamor and his son Shechem. 19 The young man, who was the most
honored of all his father's household, lost no time in doing what they said, because he was delighted with
Jacob's daughter.[m] 20 So Hamor and his son Shechem went to the gate of their city[n] to speak to their fel-
low townsmen. 21 "These men are friendly toward us," they said. "Let them live in our land and trade in
it; the land has plenty of room for them. We can marry their daughters and they can marry ours. 22 But
the men will consent to live with us as one people only on the condition that our males be circumcised,
as they themselves are. 23 Won't their livestock, their property and all their other animals become ours?
So let us give our consent to them, and they will settle among us."

24 All the men who went out of the city gate[o] agreed with Hamor and his son Shechem, and every male
in the city was circumcised.

25 Three days later, while all of them were still in pain, two of Jacob's sons, Simeon and Levi, Dinah's
brothers, took their swords[p] and attacked the unsuspecting city, killing every male.[q] 26 They put Ha-
mor and his son Shechem to the sword and took Dinah from Shechem's house and left. 27 The sons of
Jacob came upon the dead bodies and looted the city where[d] their sister had been defiled. 28 They
seized their flocks and herds and donkeys and everything else of theirs in the city and out in the
fields. 29 They carried off all their wealth and all their women and children, taking as plunder every-
thing in the houses.

30 Then Jacob said to Simeon and Levi, "You have brought trouble on me by making me a stench[r] to
the Canaanites and Perizzites, the people living in this land.[s] We are few in number,[t] and if they join forc-
es against me and attack me, I and my household will be destroyed."

31 But they replied, "Should he have treated our sister like a prostitute?"

Jacob Returns to Bethel

35 Then God said to Jacob, "Go up to Bethel[u] and settle there, and build an altar there to God, who
appeared to you when you were fleeing from your brother Esau."[v]

2 So Jacob said to his household[w] and to all who were with him, "Get rid of the foreign gods[x] you have
with you, and purify yourselves and change your clothes.[y] 3 Then come, let us go up to Bethel, where I will

34:1 [c]Ge 30:21
34:6 [d]Jdg 14:2-5
34:7 [e]Dt 22:21; Jdg 20:6; 2Sa 13:12 [f]Jos 7:15
34:10 [g]Ge 47:6, 27 [h]Ge 13:9; 20:15 [i]Ge 42:34
34:12 [j]Ex 22:16; Dt 22:29; 1Sa 18:25
34:14 [k]Ge 17:14; Jdg 14:3
34:15 [l]Ex 12:48
34:19 [m]ver 3
34:20 [n]Ru 4:1; 2Sa 15:2
34:24 [o]Ge 23:10
34:25 [p]Ge 49:5 [q]Ge 49:7
34:30 [r]Ex 5:21; 1Sa 13:4 [s]Ge 13:7 [t]Ge 46:27; 1Ch 16:19; Ps 105:12
35:1 [u]Ge 28:19 [v]Ge 27:43
35:2 [w]Ge 18:19; Jos 24:15 [x]Ge 31:19 [y]Ex 19:10,14

[a] 7 Or *against* [b] 10 Or *move about freely*; also in verse 21 [c] 17 Hebrew *daughter* [d] 27 Or *because*

---

force from the Amorites (48:22). The well is near the base of Mount Gerizim, whose bluffs may have been intended in Jesus' phrase "this mountain" (Jn 4:21). A narrow opening 4 feet (1.2 m) long led from the floor of the vault into the well, which had been dug through limestone. The depth of the well has not been determined. For centuries tourists cast pebbles into it, until Greek Catholics purchased the site and put it under guard.

34:20 See the note on 19:1.

35:3 [z]Ge 32:7 [a]Ge 28:15,20-22; 31:3,42
35:4 [b]Jos 24:25-26
35:5 [c]Ex 15:16; 23:27; Jos 2:9
35:6 [d]Ge 28:19; 48:3
35:7 [e]Ge 28:13
35:8 [f]Ge 24:59

build an altar to God, who answered me in the day of my distress[z] and who has been with me wherever
I have gone.[a]" 4So they gave Jacob all the foreign gods they had and the rings in their ears, and Jacob bur-
ied them under the oak at Shechem.[b] 5Then they set out, and the terror of God[c] fell upon the towns all
around them so that no one pursued them.
6Jacob and all the people with him came to Luz[d] (that is, Bethel) in the land of Canaan. 7There he
built an altar, and he called the place El Bethel,[a] because it was there that God revealed himself to him[e]
when he was fleeing from his brother.
8Now Deborah, Rebekah's nurse,[f] died and was buried under the oak below Bethel. So it was named
Allon Bacuth.[b]

[a] 7 *El Bethel* means *God of Bethel.* [b] 8 *Allon Bacuth* means *oak of weeping.*

ARCHAEOLOGICAL SITES

BETHEL

GENESIS 35 The holy site of Bethel ("Map 1") played an important role in the lives of Abraham and Jacob/Israel, as well as in later Israelite history. Abraham built an altar between Bethel and Ai (Ge 12:8), and Jacob, en route to Haran while fleeing from Esau, experienced a vivid dream at Bethel[1] (28:10–17). Before moving on, he set up a commemorative stone at the spot. In addition to serving as places of remembrance, such stones occasionally marked burial sites (35:20).

Biblical scholars have long debated Bethel's precise location. Most have placed it at modern Tell Beitin, 8 miles (13 km) north of Jerusalem, but el Bireh, a few miles farther south, has also been suggested. Clearly Bethel was located within the area north of Jerusalem now referred to as the West Bank.

Tell Beitin, which shows signs of occupation beginning with the **Chalcolithic** period,[2] was continuously occupied during the **Middle Bronze Age**s I and II, until the city was destroyed around 1550 B.C. A **Late Bronze Age** city located on the same site, dating from the fourteenth century B.C., boasted high-quality houses, streets with flagstone pavements, and sewers. There is evidence of its destruction at the end of the Bronze Age, and a later, **Iron Age** I settlement at the location reflects an impoverished community. This city continued to exist through the Iron Age, but no remains of Jeroboam's temple—which the Babylonian army destroyed in 586 B.C.—have been found here.

According to the *Onomasticon*, written by Eusebius (A.D. 269–339) and revised by Jerome (A.D. 345–419), Bethel was located at the twelfth Roman milestone on the eastern side of the road leading north to Neapolis (called Shechem in the Old Testament; modern Nablus). In this ancient manuscript Tell Beitin is described as being located at the fourteenth milestone, indicating that, if Eusebius's information was correct, it could not have been Bethel. Bethel may, then, have been situated a little to the south, at modern el Bireh, near the city of Ramallah. No excavation has been done at el Bireh, a town currently occupied by Palestinians.

During the period of Israel's monarchy, Bethel ("house of God") came to be embroiled in a controversy. Associations with its sacred history and monuments led the people to transform it into a center of idolatrous worship.

Jeroboam I, for example, took advantage of the holy traditions associated with Bethel and, against God's will, set up a shrine there to serve as an alternative worship site to Solomon's temple[3] (1Ki 12:26–30). As a result the prophets severely censured worship at Bethel. Hosea (Hos 4:15; 5:8; 10:5) went so far as to refer to Bethel as *Beth Aven*, a disparaging pun meaning "house of wickedness."[4] Such texts indicate that there was a debate during ancient times over whether Bethel was a sacred site or a center of apostasy.

The name Bethel was at the center of debate in another context. Bethel appears as a god's name in a seventh-century B.C. **Assyrian** treaty and in some texts from Elephantine, located in southern Egypt.[5] Based upon these discoveries, some scholars have argued that the word *Bethel* is used in the Old Testament as a divine name rather than as a place-name. Most interpreters remain unconvinced of the validity of this theory, since it appears quite evident that the Biblical Bethel was a specific place. In fact, certain Biblical texts seem to attest that Bethel in its early days was a city formerly known as Luz (mentioned in Ge 28:19; 35:6; 48:3) but renamed by Jacob (Jdg 1:23).

[1]See "Haran" on page 47. [2]See "Archaeological Periods" chart on page xx in the front of this Bible. [3]See "The High Place at Dan" on page 504. [4]See "Beth Aven: A Lesson in the Difficulty of Biblical Geography" on page 1417. [5]See "The Elephantine Community" on page 1264.

9 After Jacob returned from Paddan Aram,[a] God appeared to him again and blessed him.[g] 10 God said
to him, "Your name is Jacob,[b] but you will no longer be called Jacob; your name will be Israel.[c]"[h] So he
named him Israel.
11 And God said to him, "I am God Almighty[d];[i] be fruitful and increase in number. A nation[j] and a
community of nations will come from you, and kings will come from your body.[k] 12 The land I gave to
Abraham and Isaac I also give to you, and I will give this land to your descendants after you."[m] 13 Then
God went up from him[n] at the place where he had talked with him.
14 Jacob set up a stone pillar at the place where God had talked with him, and he poured out a drink
offering on it; he also poured oil on it.[o] 15 Jacob called the place where God had talked with him Bethel.[e][p]

The Deaths of Rachel and Isaac

16 Then they moved on from Bethel. While they were still some distance from Ephrath, Rachel began
to give birth and had great difficulty. 17 And as she was having great difficulty in childbirth, the midwife
said to her, "Don't be afraid, for you have another son."[q] 18 As she breathed her last—for she was dying—
she named her son Ben-Oni.[f] But his father named him Benjamin.[g]
19 So Rachel died and was buried on the way to Ephrath (that is, Bethlehem[r]). 20 Over her tomb Jacob
set up a pillar, and to this day that pillar marks Rachel's tomb.[s]
21 Israel moved on again and pitched his tent beyond Migdal Eder. 22 While Israel was living in that re-
gion, Reuben went in and slept with his father's concubine[t] Bilhah,[u] and Israel heard of it.

Jacob had twelve sons:
23 The sons of Leah:
Reuben the firstborn[v] of Jacob,
Simeon, Levi, Judah,[w] Issachar and Zebulun.[x]
24 The sons of Rachel:
Joseph[y] and Benjamin.[z]
25 The sons of Rachel's maidservant Bilhah:
Dan and Naphtali.[a]
26 The sons of Leah's maidservant Zilpah:
Gad[b] and Asher.[c]
These were the sons of Jacob, who were born to him in Paddan Aram.

27 Jacob came home to his father Isaac in Mamre,[d] near Kiriath Arba[e] (that is, Hebron), where Abra-
ham and Isaac had stayed. 28 Isaac lived a hundred and eighty years.[f] 29 Then he breathed his last and died
and was gathered to his people,[g] old and full of years.[h] And his sons Esau and Jacob buried him.[i]

Esau's Descendants

36 This is the account of Esau (that is, Edom).[j]
2 Esau took his wives from the women of Canaan:[k] Adah daughter of Elon the Hittite,[l] and Ohol-
ibamah daughter of Anah[m] and granddaughter of Zibeon the Hivite— 3 also Basemath daughter
of Ishmael and sister of Nebaioth.
4 Adah bore Eliphaz to Esau, Basemath bore Reuel,[n] 5 and Oholibamah bore Jeush, Jalam and
Korah. These were the sons of Esau, who were born to him in Canaan.
6 Esau took his wives and sons and daughters and all the members of his household, as well as
his livestock and all his other animals and all the goods he had acquired in Canaan,[o] and moved
to a land some distance from his brother Jacob. 7 Their possessions were too great for them to re-
main together; the land where they were staying could not support them both because of their
livestock.[p] 8 So Esau[q] (that is, Edom) settled in the hill country of Seir.[r]

35:9 [g]Ge 32:29
35:10 [h]Ge 17:5
35:11 [i]Ge 17:1; Ex 6:3 [j]Ge 28:3; 48:4 [k]Ge 17:6
35:12 [l]Ge 13:15; 28:13 [m]Ge 12:7; 26:3
35:13 [n]Ge 17:22
35:14 [o]Ge 28:18
35:15 [p]Ge 28:19
35:17 [q]Ge 30:24
35:19 [r]Ge 48:7; Ru 1:1,19; Mic 5:2; Mt 2:16
35:20 [s]1Sa 10:2
35:22 [t]Ge 49:4; 1Ch 5:1 [u]Ge 29:29; Lev 18:8
35:23 [v]Ge 46:8 [w]Ge 29:35 [x]Ge 30:20
35:24 [y]Ge 30:24 [z]ver 18
35:25 [a]Ge 30:8
35:26 [b]Ge 30:11 [c]Ge 30:13
35:27 [d]Ge 13:18; 18:1 [e]Jos 14:15
35:28 [f]Ge 25:7, 20
35:29 [g]Ge 25:8; 49:33 [h]Ge 15:15 [i]Ge 25:9
36:1 [j]Ge 25:30
36:2 [k]Ge 28:8-9 [l]Ge 26:34 [m]ver 25
36:4 [n]1Ch 1:35
36:6 [o]Ge 12:5
36:7 [p]Ge 13:6; 17:8; 28:4
36:8 [q]Dt 2:4 [r]Ge 32:3

[a] 9 That is, Northwest Mesopotamia; also in verse 26 [b] 10 *Jacob* means *he grasps the heel* (figuratively, *he deceives*). [c] 10 *Israel* means *he struggles with God.* [d] 11 Hebrew *El-Shaddai* [e] 15 *Bethel* means *house of God.* [f] 18 *Ben-Oni* means *son of my trouble.* [g] 18 *Benjamin* means *son of my right hand.*

35:22 Slaves, servants and concubines were considered part of the inheritance passed along from father to son. The oldest son would inherit with his birthright the human members of the household. When inheritance was seized prior to a father's death, the father's role was usurped (cf. e.g., 49:3–4 with 35:22).

36:8 Seir is another name for Edom (see "Edom" on p. 1467).

9 This is the account of Esau the father of the Edomites in the hill country of Seir.

10 These are the names of Esau's sons:
Eliphaz, the son of Esau's wife Adah, and Reuel, the son of Esau's wife Basemath.

36:11 [s]ver 15-16; Job 2:11 [t]Am 1:12; Hab 3:3

11 The sons of Eliphaz:[s]
Teman,[t] Omar, Zepho, Gatam and Kenaz.

36:12 [u]Ex 17:8, 16; Nu 24:20; 1Sa 15:2 [v]ver 16

12 Esau's son Eliphaz also had a concubine named Timna, who bore him Amalek.[u] These were
grandsons of Esau's wife Adah.[v]
13 The sons of Reuel:
Nahath, Zerah, Shammah and Mizzah. These were grandsons of Esau's wife Basemath.
14 The sons of Esau's wife Oholibamah daughter of Anah and granddaughter of Zibeon, whom she
bore to Esau:
Jeush, Jalam and Korah.

36:15 [w]Ex 15:15 [x]Job 2:11

15 These were the chiefs[w] among Esau's descendants:
The sons of Eliphaz the firstborn of Esau:
Chiefs Teman,[x] Omar, Zepho, Kenaz, 16 Korah,[a] Gatam and Amalek. These were the chiefs de-
scended from Eliphaz in Edom; they were grandsons of Adah.[y]

36:16 [y]ver 12

36:17 [z]1Ch 1:37

17 The sons of Esau's son Reuel:[z]
Chiefs Nahath, Zerah, Shammah and Mizzah. These were the chiefs descended from Reuel in
Edom; they were grandsons of Esau's wife Basemath.
18 The sons of Esau's wife Oholibamah:
Chiefs Jeush, Jalam and Korah. These were the chiefs descended from Esau's wife Oholibamah
daughter of Anah.

36:19 [a]Ge 25:30

19 These were the sons of Esau (that is, Edom),[a] and these were their chiefs.

36:20 [b]Ge 14:6; Dt 2:12,22; 1Ch 1:38

20 These were the sons of Seir the Horite,[b] who were living in the region:
Lotan, Shobal, Zibeon, Anah, 21 Dishon, Ezer and Dishan. These sons of Seir in Edom were Ho-
rite chiefs.
22 The sons of Lotan:
Hori and Homam.[b] Timna was Lotan's sister.
23 The sons of Shobal:
Alvan, Manahath, Ebal, Shepho and Onam.
24 The sons of Zibeon:
Aiah and Anah. This is the Anah who discovered the hot springs[c] in the desert while he was
grazing the donkeys of his father Zibeon.
25 The children of Anah:
Dishon and Oholibamah daughter of Anah.
26 The sons of Dishon[d]:
Hemdan, Eshban, Ithran and Keran.
27 The sons of Ezer:
Bilhan, Zaavan and Akan.
28 The sons of Dishan:
Uz and Aran.
29 These were the Horite chiefs:
Lotan, Shobal, Zibeon, Anah, 30 Dishon, Ezer and Dishan. These were the Horite chiefs, accord-
ing to their divisions, in the land of Seir.

The Rulers of Edom

36:31 [c]Ge 17:6; 1Ch 1:43

31 These were the kings who reigned in Edom before any Israelite king[c] reigned[e]:
32 Bela son of Beor became king of Edom. His city was named Dinhabah.

36:33 [d]Jer 49:13, 22
36:34 [e]Eze 25:13

33 When Bela died, Jobab son of Zerah from Bozrah[d] succeeded him as king.
34 When Jobab died, Husham from the land of the Temanites[e] succeeded him as king.

[a] *16* Masoretic Text; Samaritan Pentateuch (see also Gen. 36:11 and 1 Chron. 1:36) does not have *Korah.* [b] *22* Hebrew *Hemam,* a variant of *Homam* (see 1 Chron. 1:39) [c] *24* Vulgate; Syriac *discovered water;* the meaning of the Hebrew for this word is uncertain. [d] *26* Hebrew *Dishan,* a variant of *Dishon* [e] *31* Or *before an Israelite king reigned over them*

35 When Husham died, Hadad son of Bedad, who defeated Midian in the country of Moab,[f] succeed- 36:35 [f]Ge 19:37;
ed him as king. His city was named Avith. Nu 22:1; Dt 1:5; Ru 1:1,6
36 When Hadad died, Samlah from Masrekah succeeded him as king.
37 When Samlah died, Shaul from Rehoboth on the river[a] succeeded him as king.
38 When Shaul died, Baal-Hanan son of Acbor succeeded him as king.
39 When Baal-Hanan son of Acbor died, Hadad[b] succeeded him as king. His city was named Pau,
and his wife's name was Mehetabel daughter of Matred, the daughter of Me-Zahab.

40 These were the chiefs descended from Esau, by name, according to their clans and regions:
Timna, Alvah, Jetheth, 41 Oholibamah, Elah, Pinon, 42 Kenaz, Teman, Mibzar, 43 Magdiel and Iram.
These were the chiefs of Edom, according to their settlements in the land they occupied.

This was Esau the father of the Edomites.

Joseph's Dreams

37 Jacob lived in the land where his father had stayed,[g] the land of Canaan.[h] 37:1 [g]Ge 17:8 [h]Ge 10:19
2 This is the account of Jacob.

Joseph, a young man of seventeen, was tending the flocks[i] with his brothers, the sons of Bilhah[j] and 37:2 [i]Ps 78:71 [j]Ge 35:25
the sons of Zilpah,[k] his father's wives, and he brought their father a bad report[l] about them. [k]Ge 35:26 [l]1Sa 2:24
3 Now Israel loved Joseph more than any of his other sons,[m] because he had been born to him in his 37:3 [m]Ge 25:28
old age;[n] and he made a richly ornamented[c] robe[o] for him. 4 When his brothers saw that their father loved [n]Ge 44:20 [o]2Sa 13:18-19
him more than any of them, they hated him[p] and could not speak a kind word to him. 37:4 [p]Ge 27:41; 49:22-23; Ac 7:9
5 Joseph had a dream,[q] and when he told it to his brothers, they hated him all the more. 6 He said to 37:5 [q]Ge 20:3; 28:12
them, "Listen to this dream I had: 7 We were binding sheaves of grain out in the field when suddenly my
sheaf rose and stood upright, while your sheaves gathered around mine and bowed down to it."[r] 37:7 [r]Ge 42:6,9; 43:26,28; 44:14; 50:18
8 His brothers said to him, "Do you intend to reign over us? Will you actually rule us?"[s] And they hat-
ed him all the more because of his dream and what he had said. 37:8 [s]Ge 49:26
9 Then he had another dream, and he told it to his brothers. "Listen," he said, "I had another dream,
and this time the sun and moon and eleven stars were bowing down to me."
10 When he told his father as well as his brothers,[t] his father rebuked him and said, "What is this dream 37:10 [t]ver 5
you had? Will your mother and I and your brothers actually come and bow down to the ground before [u]ver 7; Ge 27:29
you?"[u] 11 His brothers were jealous of him,[v] but his father kept the matter in mind.[w] 37:11 [v]Ac 7:9 [w]Lk 2:19,51

Joseph Sold by His Brothers

12 Now his brothers had gone to graze their father's flocks near Shechem, 13 and Israel said to Joseph,
"As you know, your brothers are grazing the flocks near Shechem. Come, I am going to send you to them."
"Very well," he replied.
14 So he said to him, "Go and see if all is well with your brothers and with the flocks, and bring word
back to me." Then he sent him off from the Valley of Hebron.[x] 37:14 [x]Ge 13:18; 35:27
When Joseph arrived at Shechem, 15 a man found him wandering around in the fields and asked him,
"What are you looking for?"
16 He replied, "I'm looking for my brothers. Can you tell me where they are grazing their flocks?"
17 "They have moved on from here," the man answered. "I heard them say, 'Let's go to Dothan.[y]' " 37:17 [y]2Ki 6:13
So Joseph went after his brothers and found them near Dothan. 18 But they saw him in the distance,
and before he reached them, they plotted to kill him.[z] 37:18 [z]1Sa 19:1; Mk 14:1; Ac 23:12
19 "Here comes that dreamer!" they said to each other. 20 "Come now, let's kill him and throw him into
one of these cisterns[a] and say that a ferocious animal devoured him. Then we'll see what comes of his 37:20 [a]Jer 38:6,9
dreams."[b] [b]Ge 50:20
21 When Reuben heard this, he tried to rescue him from their hands. "Let's not take his life," he said.[c] 37:21 [c]Ge 42:22
22 "Don't shed any blood. Throw him into this cistern here in the desert, but don't lay a hand on him."
Reuben said this to rescue him from them and take him back to his father.
23 So when Joseph came to his brothers, they stripped him of his robe—the richly ornamented robe

[a] *37* Possibly the Euphrates [b] *39* Many manuscripts of the Masoretic Text, Samaritan Pentateuch and Syriac (see also 1 Chron. 1:50); most manuscripts of the Masoretic Text *Hadar* [c] *3* The meaning of the Hebrew for *richly ornamented* is uncertain; also in verses 23 and 32.

37:24 [d]Jer 41:7 he was wearing— [24]and they took him and threw him into the cistern.[d] Now the cistern was empty;
there was no water in it.
[25]As they sat down to eat their meal, they looked up and saw a caravan of Ishmaelites coming from
37:25 [e]Ge 43:11 [f]ver 28 Gilead. Their camels were loaded with spices, balm and myrrh,[e] and they were on their way to take them
down to Egypt.[f]

37:25 The caravan was made up of Midianites and Ishmaelites. Midianites were descendants of Abraham through Keturah, Ishmaelites his descendants through Hagar. The forebears of these two peoples were Jacob's uncles, making these traders second or third cousins to Joseph and his brothers. See "Caravan Trading and Routes in the Ancient Near East" on page 63.

The "balm" was an oil or gum used for its healing properties. The balm of Gilead was especially effective (see Jer 8:22; 46:11). See "Perfumes and Anointing Oils" on page 1746.

Caravan Trading and Routes in the Ancient Near East

GENESIS 37 According to Genesis 37 Joseph found his brothers near Dothan[1] (see "Map 1" at the back of this Bible). Overcome by jealousy based on their father's favoritism of this younger brother, they seized him and eventually sold him to a passing caravan of Ishmaelites bound for Egypt. Such a caravan probably was headed toward the "Way of the Sea" (**Via Maris**), an ancient roadway that began in Egypt, hugged the Mediterranean coast of **Canaan** as it meandered north, then passed just west of Dothan and on to Megiddo.[2] From there travelers could continue north beyond the coastal areas of **Phoenicia** or veer to the northeast toward Damascus[3] and on to **Mesopotamia**. The **King's Highway**, another great roadway during Old Testament times, allowed people to travel from north to south through the **Transjordan** and connected Damascus to the Gulf of Aqaba.

Ancient Babylonian map

Preserving Bible Times; © Dr. James C. Martin; permission of The British Museum

During ancient times merchants usually traveled in caravans, seeking protection in numbers on account of the many dangers and the lack of accommodations along the way. Caravans tended to be quite large (a column with three hundred donkeys was not extraordinary) and often included armed guards. Ancient texts from the Assyrians, Egyptians and **Hittites**[4] often refer to the hardships of travel. Wild animals, including lions, were a source of danger,[5] and a lone merchant transporting his wares was a tempting target for bandits. Extreme weather conditions, from drought to snow, also made travel hazardous.

The Romans' elaborate road system (exemplified by the celebrated Appian Way) did not yet exist during Old Testament times.[6] Roads were unpaved, often little more than dirt tracks from earlier caravans. Indeed, for many years scholars could only surmise the precise locations of these paths, making assumptions from the shape of the terrain and drawing from references to routes found in ancient documents. Recently, however, satellite photography has proven to be a useful tool for locating these beaten paths. Understandably, merchants transported their goods by sea or on navigable rivers whenever possible.

Despite all these difficulties merchants traded over great distances in the ancient Near East; goods found their way to the land of Israel from as far away as India and southern Arabia.

[1]See "Dothan, Ben-Hadad and a Chronological Problem" on page 536. [2]See "Megiddo" on page 1541. [3]See "Damascus" on page 1087. [4]See "Anatolia and the Hittites" on page 144. [5]See "Lions and Other Wild Beasts in Ancient Israel" on page 813. [6]But see "Travel in the Greco-Roman World" on page 1946.

26 Judah said to his brothers, "What will we gain if we kill our brother and cover up his blood?[g] 27 Come, 37:26 [g]ver 20; Ge 4:10
let's sell him to the Ishmaelites and not lay our hands on him; after all, he is our brother,[h] our own flesh 37:27 [h]Ge 42:21
and blood." His brothers agreed.
28 So when the Midianite[i] merchants came by, his brothers pulled Joseph up out of the cistern and 37:28 [i]Ge 25:2; Jdg 6:1-3
sold him for twenty shekels[a] of silver to the Ishmaelites, who took him to Egypt.[j] [j]Ge 45:4-5; Ps 105:17; Ac 7:9
29 When Reuben returned to the cistern and saw that Joseph was not there, he tore his clothes.[k] 30 He 37:29 [k]ver 34; Ge 44:13; Job 1:20
went back to his brothers and said, "The boy isn't there! Where can I turn now?"[l] 37:30 [l]ver 22; Ge 42:13,36
31 Then they got Joseph's robe,[m] slaughtered a goat and dipped the robe in the blood. 32 They took the 37:31 [m]ver 3,23
ornamented robe back to their father and said, "We found this. Examine it to see whether it is your son's
robe."
33 He recognized it and said, "It is my son's robe! Some ferocious animal[n] has devoured him. Joseph 37:33 [n]ver 20
has surely been torn to pieces."[o] [o]Ge 44:20,28
34 Then Jacob tore his clothes,[p] put on sackcloth[q] and mourned for his son many days.[r] 35 All his sons 37:34 [p]ver 29
and daughters came to comfort him, but he refused to be comforted. "No," he said, "in mourning will I [q]2Sa 3:31 [r]Ge 50:3,10,11
go down to the grave[b][s] to my son." So his father wept for him. 37:35 [s]Ge 42:38; 44:22,29,31
36 Meanwhile, the Midianites[c] sold Joseph in Egypt to Potiphar, one of Pharaoh's officials, the captain
of the guard.[t] 37:36 [t]Ge 39:1

Judah and Tamar

38 At that time, Judah left his brothers and went down to stay with a man of Adullam named Hi-
rah. 2 There Judah met the daughter of a Canaanite man named Shua.[u] He married her and lay 38:2 [u]1Ch 2:3
with her; 3 she became pregnant and gave birth to a son, who was named Er.[v] 4 She conceived again and 38:3 [v]ver 6; Ge 46:12; Nu 26:19
gave birth to a son and named him Onan. 5 She gave birth to still another son and named him Shelah. It
was at Kezib that she gave birth to him.

[a] *28* That is, about 8 ounces (about 0.2 kilogram) [b] *35* Hebrew *Sheol* [c] *36* Samaritan Pentateuch, Septuagint, Vulgate and Syriac (see also verse 28); Masoretic Text *Medanites*

38:3–4 Mesopotamian documents of this time include the tribal names Er and Onan.

Levirate Marriage

GENESIS 38 The "duty . . . as a brother-in-law" mentioned in Genesis 38:8 refers to the social and legal obligations of the *levir* (Latin for "husband's brother") to marry his widowed sister-in-law in the event his brother had died and left her childless.

This otherwise forbidden marriage arrangement (see Lev 18:16; 20:21) secured the inheritance of the deceased husband[1] and perpetuated his name (see Dt 25:6), thus reflecting the common desire among ancient Israelites to maintain a presence in the land after their deaths in the persons of their offspring.

In addition, this arrangement provided "social security" for the childless widow, who was effectively helpless and socially disadvantaged in the ancient Near East.[2] The **Hittites** and **Assyrians** also practiced levirate marriage.

In the event the deceased husband had no brothers (Ru 1:10–13), or if they had declined to fulfill their duty (Ge 38), other relatives might elect to assume the responsibility of the levir. It appears that this regulation was more strictly applied during the **patriarchal period** than it was several centuries later under the Mosaic Law (Dt 25:5–10). This is not surprising, since Genesis 38 narrates a period in Israel's history when "being fruitful" and "multiplying" were critical to the young nation's existence. Consequences for a brother-in-law's failure to fulfill this duty in these early days were severe (e.g., Onan's death; vv. 8–10). Tamar, in desperation, used her father-in-law to provide a legitimate heir. It is possible that her culture regarded her act as legally justified; by analogy, Hittite law stipulated that should the brother of a deceased man also perish and so be unable to fulfill his duty to the widow, she should marry her late husband's father.

[1]See "Inheritance in the Ancient Near East" on page 250. [2]See "The Kinsman-Redeemer" on page 391.

6 Judah got a wife for Er, his firstborn, and her name was Tamar. 7 But Er, Judah's firstborn, was wick-
38:7 [w]ver 10; Ge 46:12; 1Ch 2:3 — ed in the LORD's sight; so the LORD put him to death.[w]
8 Then Judah said to Onan, "Lie with your brother's wife and fulfill your duty to her as a brother-
38:8 [x]Dt 25:5-6; Mt 22:24-28 — in-law to produce offspring for your brother."[x] 9 But Onan knew that the offspring would not be his;
so whenever he lay with his brother's wife, he spilled his semen on the ground to keep from produc-
ing offspring for his brother. 10 What he did was wicked in the LORD's sight; so he put him to death
38:10 [y]Ge 46:12; Dt 25:7-10 — also.[y]
11 Judah then said to his daughter-in-law Tamar, "Live as a widow in your father's house until my son
38:11 [z]Ru 1:13 — Shelah grows up."[z] For he thought, "He may die too, just like his brothers." So Tamar went to live in her
father's house.
12 After a long time Judah's wife, the daughter of Shua, died. When Judah had recovered from his grief,
38:12 [a]ver 14; Jos 15:10,57 — he went up to Timnah,[a] to the men who were shearing his sheep, and his friend Hirah the Adullamite
went with him.
13 When Tamar was told, "Your father-in-law is on his way to Timnah to shear his sheep," 14 she took
off her widow's clothes, covered herself with a veil to disguise herself, and then sat down at the entrance
38:14 [b]ver 11 — to Enaim, which is on the road to Timnah. For she saw that, though Shelah[b] had now grown up, she had
not been given to him as his wife.
15 When Judah saw her, he thought she was a prostitute, for she had covered her face. 16 Not realizing
38:16 [c]Lev 18:15; 20:12 — that she was his daughter-in-law,[c] he went over to her by the roadside and said, "Come now, let me sleep
with you."
"And what will you give me to sleep with you?" she asked.
38:17 [d]Eze 16:33 [e]ver 20 — 17 "I'll send you a young goat[d] from my flock," he said.
"Will you give me something as a pledge[e] until you send it?" she asked.
18 He said, "What pledge should I give you?"
38:18 [f]ver 25 — "Your seal[f] and its cord, and the staff in your hand," she answered. So he gave them to her and slept
with her, and she became pregnant by him. 19 After she left, she took off her veil and put on her widow's
38:19 [g]ver 14 — clothes[g] again.
38:21 [h]Lev 19:29; Hos 4:14 — 20 Meanwhile Judah sent the young goat by his friend the Adullamite in order to get his pledge back
from the woman, but he did not find her. 21 He asked the men who lived there, "Where is the shrine pros-
titute[h] who was beside the road at Enaim?"
"There hasn't been any shrine prostitute here," they said.
22 So he went back to Judah and said, "I didn't find her. Besides, the men who lived there said, 'There
hasn't been any shrine prostitute here.' "
23 Then Judah said, "Let her keep what she has, or we will become a laughingstock. After all, I did send
her this young goat, but you didn't find her."
24 About three months later Judah was told, "Your daughter-in-law Tamar is guilty of prostitution, and
as a result she is now pregnant."
38:24 [i]Lev 21:9; Dt 22:21,22 — Judah said, "Bring her out and have her burned to death!"[i]
25 As she was being brought out, she sent a message to her father-in-law. "I am pregnant by the man
38:25 [j]ver 18 — who owns these," she said. And she added, "See if you recognize whose seal and cord and staff these are."[j]
38:26 [k]1Sa 24:17 [l]ver 11 — 26 Judah recognized them and said, "She is more righteous than I,[k] since I wouldn't give her to my son
Shelah.[l]" And he did not sleep with her again.
38:27 [m]Ge 25:24 — 27 When the time came for her to give birth, there were twin boys in her womb.[m] 28 As she was giving
birth, one of them put out his hand; so the midwife took a scarlet thread and tied it on his wrist and said,
"This one came out first." 29 But when he drew back his hand, his brother came out, and she said, "So this
38:29 [n]Ge 46:12; Nu 26:20,21; Ru 4:12,18; 1Ch 2:4; Mt 1:3 — is how you have broken out!" And he was named Perez.[a][n] 30 Then his brother, who had the scarlet thread
38:30 [o]1Ch 2:4 — on his wrist, came out and he was given the name Zerah.[b][o]

[a] *29 Perez* means *breaking out.* [b] *30 Zerah* can mean *scarlet* or *brightness.*

38:6–10 If a man died childless, his brother was duty bound to raise heirs to him by his widow (the Levirate law of Dt 25:5; see also "Levirate Marriage" on p. 64). Onan's action and resulting punishment had nothing to do with contraception or masturbation but everything to do with rightful inheritance.

38:11–14 A Hittite law stipulated that when a widow married her late husband's brother and *he* died, she was to marry his father. This was apparently the procedure Tamar was following. See the note on verses 6–10; see also "Nuzi" on page 52 and "Levirate Marriage" on page 64.

38:17–18 When Tamar accepted as guarantee of payment Jacob's seal, cord and staff, she held symbols of his individual and corporate identity—the equivalent of an I.D. card or signature.

Joseph and Potiphar's Wife

39 Now Joseph had been taken down to Egypt. Potiphar, an Egyptian who was one of Pharaoh's of-
ficials, the captain of the guard,[p] bought him from the Ishmaelites who had taken him there.[q]
2 The LORD was with Joseph[r] and he prospered, and he lived in the house of his Egyptian master. 3 When
his master saw that the LORD was with him[s] and that the LORD gave him success in everything he did,[t]
4 Joseph found favor in his eyes and became his attendant. Potiphar put him in charge of his household,
and he entrusted to his care everything he owned.[u] 5 From the time he put him in charge of his house-
hold and of all that he owned, the LORD blessed the household of the Egyptian because of Joseph.[v] The
blessing of the LORD was on everything Potiphar had, both in the house and in the field. 6 So he left in Jo-
seph's care everything he had; with Joseph in charge, he did not concern himself with anything except
the food he ate.
Now Joseph was well-built and handsome,[w] 7 and after a while his master's wife took notice of Joseph
and said, "Come to bed with me!"[x]
8 But he refused.[y] "With me in charge," he told her, "my master does not concern himself with any-
thing in the house; everything he owns he has entrusted to my care. 9 No one is greater in this house than
I am.[z] My master has withheld nothing from me except you, because you are his wife. How then could I
do such a wicked thing and sin against God?"[a] 10 And though she spoke to Joseph day after day, he refused
to go to bed with her or even be with her.
11 One day he went into the house to attend to his duties, and none of the household servants was in-
side. 12 She caught him by his cloak[b] and said, "Come to bed with me!" But he left his cloak in her hand
and ran out of the house.
13 When she saw that he had left his cloak in her hand and had run out of the house, 14 she called her

39:1 [p]Ge 37:36 [q]Ge 37:25; Ps 105:17
39:2 [r]Ge 21:20, 22; Ac 7:9
39:3 [s]Ge 21:22; 26:28 [t]Ps 1:3
39:4 [u]ver 8,22; Ge 24:2
39:5 [v]Ge 26:24; 30:27
39:6 [w]1Sa 16:12
39:7 [x]2Sa 13:11; Pr 7:15-18
39:8 [y]Pr 6:23-24
39:9 [z]Ge 41:33, 40 [a]Ge 20:6; 42:18; 2Sa 12:13
39:12 [b]Pr 7:13

ANCIENT TEXTS AND ARTIFACTS

The Two Brothers

GENESIS 39 An Egyptian text called Papyrus D'Orbiney, dating to approximately 1225 B.C., contains a story titled The Two Brothers. Vividly illustrating the fantastic nature of ancient storytelling, this tale is a curious example of a nonbiblical story having striking similarities to a Biblical text.

In this fictional account, Bata lived with and faithfully served his older brother, Anubis. One day Anubis's wife tried to seduce Bata, who rejected her advances. Furious, she accused him of attempted rape, and the enraged Anubis prepared to kill Bata. But Bata, forewarned by a cow, fled in the nick of time. A lake filled with crocodiles magically appeared between the brothers, cutting off Anubis's pursuit. Anubis returned home—and proceeded to kill his wife!

Meanwhile, Bata cut out his own heart and placed it high in a pine tree, an act rendering him nearly immortal. The gods fashioned a beautiful wife for Bata. An immoral woman, however, she entered Pharaoh's harem and divulged to the Egyptians that Bata could be killed by cutting down the pine tree. They followed through, but Anubis, apparently prepared to reconcile with Bata, found his brother's heart and restored him to life.

Bata in turn transformed himself into a bull and carried Anubis to Pharaoh's court, where Bata's alarmed wife persuaded Pharaoh to sacrifice the bull. Its blood caused two trees to sprout. Realizing that Bata still lived, his wife arranged to have the trees cut down, but a splinter flew into her mouth and she became pregnant. She bore a son, whom Pharaoh raised as his crown prince. The boy—Bata himself—in due course became the pharaoh and appointed Anubis to be his viceroy.

Outlandish as this tale may seem to us, many scholars have noted the amazing similarities between it and the Biblical account of Joseph. Obvious parallels include a rivalry between brothers, a false accusation of rape and an ascent to power in Egypt. There is no reason, however, to surmise that the Biblical story may have been derived from this Egyptian tale. The bizarre quality of the Egyptian story contrasts strongly with the factual tone of the historical, Biblical narrative. At the same time, parallels between the stories may not have been accidental.

If composed after the time of Joseph, the Egyptian tale may have been influenced by the Biblical reality.

If the Egyptian story existed prior to the time of Joseph (assuming that Papyrus D'Orbiney was not its earliest iteration), the obvious parallels included in the Joseph narrative may have been intended to signal the fact that the God of Israel could elevate a son of Israel to power, even in an Egyptian context. The argument could be made that the Biblical account shows that Joseph fulfilled even the Egyptian ideal of a hero.

It is impossible, in the final analysis, to speak definitively of literary dependence going in either direction in this instance; there is simply not enough evidence to make an accurate judgment.

For another parallel to a Biblical story, see "The Tale of Appu's Two Sons" on page 45.

household servants. "Look," she said to them, "this Hebrew has been brought to us to make sport of us!
39:14 [c]Dt 22:24, 27 He came in here to sleep with me, but I screamed.[c] 15When he heard me scream for help, he left his cloak
beside me and ran out of the house."
39:17 [d]Ex 23:1,7; Ps 101:5 16She kept his cloak beside her until his master came home. 17Then she told him this story:[d] "That He-
brew slave you brought us came to me to make sport of me. 18But as soon as I screamed for help, he left
his cloak beside me and ran out of the house."
19When his master heard the story his wife told him, saying, "This is how your slave treated me," he
39:19 [e]Pr 6:34 burned with anger.[e] 20Joseph's master took him and put him in prison,[f] the place where the king's pris-
39:20 [f]Ge 40:3; Ps 105:18 oners were confined.
But while Joseph was there in the prison, 21the LORD was with him; he showed him kindness and
39:21 [g]Ex 3:21 granted him favor in the eyes of the prison warden.[g] 22So the warden put Joseph in charge of all those
39:22 [h]ver 4 held in the prison, and he was made responsible for all that was done there.[h] 23The warden paid no at-
tention to anything under Joseph's care, because the LORD was with Joseph and gave him success in what-
39:23 [i]ver 3 ever he did.[i]

The Cupbearer and the Baker

40:1 [j]Ne 1:11 **40** Some time later, the cupbearer[j] and the baker of the king of Egypt offended their master, the
40:2 [k]Pr 16:14, 15 king of Egypt. 2Pharaoh was angry[k] with his two officials, the chief cupbearer and the chief bak-
40:3 [l]Ge 39:20 er, 3and put them in custody in the house of the captain of the guard,[l] in the same prison where Joseph
40:4 [m]Ge 39:4 was confined. 4The captain of the guard assigned them to Joseph,[m] and he attended them.
After they had been in custody for some time, 5each of the two men—the cupbearer and the baker
of the king of Egypt, who were being held in prison—had a dream the same night, and each dream had
40:5 [n]Ge 41:11 a meaning of its own.[n]
6When Joseph came to them the next morning, he saw that they were dejected. 7So he asked Pharaoh's
40:7 [o]Ne 2:2 officials who were in custody with him in his master's house, "Why are your faces so sad today?"[o]
40:8 [p]Ge 41:8,15 8"We both had dreams," they answered, "but there is no one to interpret them."[p]
[q]Ge 41:16; Da 2:22,28,47 Then Joseph said to them, "Do not interpretations belong to God?[q] Tell me your dreams."
9So the chief cupbearer told Joseph his dream. He said to him, "In my dream I saw a vine in front of
me, 10and on the vine were three branches. As soon as it budded, it blossomed, and its clusters ripened
into grapes. 11Pharaoh's cup was in my hand, and I took the grapes, squeezed them into Pharaoh's cup
and put the cup in his hand."
40:12 [r]Ge 41:12, 15,25; Da 2:36; 4:19 12"This is what it means,[r]" Joseph said to him. "The three branches are three days. 13Within three days
Pharaoh will lift up your head and restore you to your position, and you will put Pharaoh's cup in his
40:14 [s]Lk 23:42 hand, just as you used to do when you were his cupbearer. 14But when all goes well with you, remember
[t]Jos 2:12; 1Sa 20:14,42; 1Ki 2:7 me[s] and show me kindness;[t] mention me to Pharaoh and get me out of this prison. 15For I was forcibly
40:15 [u]Ge 37:26-28 carried off from the land of the Hebrews,[u] and even here I have done nothing to deserve being put in a
dungeon."
16When the chief baker saw that Joseph had given a favorable interpretation, he said to Joseph, "I too
had a dream: On my head were three baskets of bread.[a] 17In the top basket were all kinds of baked goods
for Pharaoh, but the birds were eating them out of the basket on my head."
40:18 [v]ver 12 18"This is what it means," Joseph said. "The three baskets are three days.[v] 19Within three days Phar-
40:19 [w]ver 13 aoh will lift off your head[w] and hang you on a tree.[b] And the birds will eat away your flesh."
40:20 [x]Mt 14:6-10 [y]Mk 6:21 20Now the third day was Pharaoh's birthday,[x] and he gave a feast for all his officials.[y] He lifted up the
heads of the chief cupbearer and the chief baker in the presence of his officials: 21He restored the chief
40:21 [z]ver 13 cupbearer to his position, so that he once again put the cup into Pharaoh's hand,[z] 22but he hanged[c] the
40:22 [a]ver 19 [b]Ps 105:19 chief baker,[a] just as Joseph had said to them in his interpretation.[b]
40:23 [c]Job 19:14; Ecc 9:15 23The chief cupbearer, however, did not remember Joseph; he forgot him.[c]

[a] 16 Or *three wicker baskets* [b] 19 Or *and impale you on a pole* [c] 22 Or *impaled*

40:8 In the ancient Near East great significance was given to dreams, and dream interpretations were sought from experts trained in the techniques and methods of the day. Both the Egyptians and the Babylonians compiled "dream books," which contained sample dreams with a key to their interpretation. These books preserved the data concerning past dreams and interpretations, providing the security of "scientific" documentation. Joseph consulted God, but his interpretation followed the way Egyptian dream literature interpreted comparable symbols. See "Dream Oracles in the Ancient World" on page 741.

40:20 The date of one's birth is, in a sense, the most important day of one's life, for without it the individual would not have experienced life in the world. So the celebration of birthdays goes back to very ancient times (cf. Mt 14:6).

Pharaoh's Dreams

41 When two full years had passed, Pharaoh had a dream:[d] He was standing by the Nile, 2when out 41:1 [d]Ge 20:3
of the river there came up seven cows, sleek and fat,[e] and they grazed among the reeds.[f] 3After 41:2 [e]ver 26
them, seven other cows, ugly and gaunt, came up out of the Nile and stood beside those on the river- [f]Isa 19:6
bank. 4And the cows that were ugly and gaunt ate up the seven sleek, fat cows. Then Pharaoh woke up.
5He fell asleep again and had a second dream: Seven heads of grain, healthy and good, were growing
on a single stalk. 6After them, seven other heads of grain sprouted—thin and scorched by the east wind.
7The thin heads of grain swallowed up the seven healthy, full heads. Then Pharaoh woke up; it had been
a dream.
8In the morning his mind was troubled,[g] so he sent for all the magicians[h] and wise men of Egypt. 41:8 [g]Da 2:1,3;
Pharaoh told them his dreams, but no one could interpret them for him. 4:5,19 [h]Ex 7:11,
9Then the chief cupbearer said to Pharaoh, "Today I am reminded of my shortcomings. 10Pharaoh 22; Da 1:20; 2:2, 27; 4:7
was once angry with his servants,[i] and he imprisoned me and the chief baker in the house of the cap- 41:10 [i]Ge 40:2
tain of the guard.[j] 11Each of us had a dream the same night, and each dream had a meaning of its own.[k] [j]Ge 39:20 41:11 [k]Ge 40:5
12Now a young Hebrew was there with us, a servant of the captain of the guard. We told him our dreams,
and he interpreted them for us, giving each man the interpretation of his dream.[l] 13And things turned 41:12 [l]Ge 40:12
out exactly as he interpreted them to us: I was restored to my position, and the other man was hanged.[a][m]" 41:13 [m]Ge 40:22
14So Pharaoh sent for Joseph, and he was quickly brought from the dungeon.[n] When he had shaved 41:14 [n]Ps 105:20;
and changed his clothes, he came before Pharaoh. Da 2:25
15Pharaoh said to Joseph, "I had a dream, and no one can interpret it. But I have heard it said of you
that when you hear a dream you can interpret it."[o] 41:15 [o]Da 5:16
16"I cannot do it," Joseph replied to Pharaoh, "but God will give Pharaoh the answer he desires."[p] 41:16 [p]Ge 40:8; Da 2:30; Ac 3:12; 2Co 3:5
17Then Pharaoh said to Joseph, "In my dream I was standing on the bank of the Nile, 18when out of
the river there came up seven cows, fat and sleek, and they grazed among the reeds. 19After them, seven
other cows came up—scrawny and very ugly and lean. I had never seen such ugly cows in all the land
of Egypt. 20The lean, ugly cows ate up the seven fat cows that came up first. 21But even after they ate them,
no one could tell that they had done so; they looked just as ugly as before. Then I woke up.
22"In my dreams I also saw seven heads of grain, full and good, growing on a single stalk. 23After them,
seven other heads sprouted—withered and thin and scorched by the east wind. 24The thin heads of grain
swallowed up the seven good heads. I told this to the magicians, but none could explain it to me.[q]" 41:24 [q]ver 8
25Then Joseph said to Pharaoh, "The dreams of Pharaoh are one and the same. God has revealed to
Pharaoh what he is about to do.[r] 26The seven good cows[s] are seven years, and the seven good heads of 41:25 [r]Da 2:45
grain are seven years; it is one and the same dream. 27The seven lean, ugly cows that came up afterward 41:26 [s]ver 2
are seven years, and so are the seven worthless heads of grain scorched by the east wind: They are sev-
en years of famine.[t] 41:27 [t]Ge 12:10; 2Ki 8:1
28"It is just as I said to Pharaoh: God has shown Pharaoh what he is about to do. 29Seven years of great
abundance[u] are coming throughout the land of Egypt, 30but seven years of famine[v] will follow them. 41:29 [u]ver 47
Then all the abundance in Egypt will be forgotten, and the famine will ravage the land.[w] 31The abun- 41:30 [v]ver 54; Ge 47:13 [w]ver 56
dance in the land will not be remembered, because the famine that follows it will be so severe. 32The rea-
son the dream was given to Pharaoh in two forms is that the matter has been firmly decided[x] by God, 41:32 [x]Nu 23:19;
and God will do it soon. Isa 46:10-11
33"And now let Pharaoh look for a discerning and wise man[y] and put him in charge of the land of 41:33 [y]ver 39
Egypt. 34Let Pharaoh appoint commissioners over the land to take a fifth[z] of the harvest of Egypt dur- 41:34 [z]1Sa 8:15
ing the seven years of abundance.[a] 35They should collect all the food of these good years that are com- [a]ver 48
ing and store up the grain under the authority of Pharaoh, to be kept in the cities for food.[b] 36This food 41:35 [b]ver 48
should be held in reserve for the country, to be used during the seven years of famine that will come
upon Egypt,[c] so that the country may not be ruined by the famine." 41:36 [c]ver 56
37The plan seemed good to Pharaoh and to all his officials.[d] 38So Pharaoh asked them, "Can we find 41:37 [d]Ge 45:16
anyone like this man, one in whom is the spirit of God[b]?"[e] 41:38 [e]Nu 27:18; Job 32:8; Da 4:8-9,18; 5:11,14

[a] 13 Or *impaled* [b] 38 Or *of the gods*

41:14 Egyptians were normally smooth-shaven, while Hebrews/Israelites wore beards (see 2Sa 10:5; Jer 41:5). See "Beards and Hairstyles in the Biblical World" on page 1084.

41:30 The Nile was the lifeline of Egypt; its annual flooding provided essential water and produced the only fertile soil there. Long famines were therefore rare in Egypt, but not uncommon elsewhere. See "Famine in the Ancient Near East" on page 70.

39 Then Pharaoh said to Joseph, "Since God has made all this known to you, there is no one so dis-
cerning and wise as you. 40 You shall be in charge of my palace, and all my people are to submit to your
41:40 [f]Ps 105:21-22; Ac 7:10 orders.[f] Only with respect to the throne will I be greater than you."

Joseph in Charge of Egypt

41:41 [g]Ge 42:6; Da 6:3 41 So Pharaoh said to Joseph, "I hereby put you in charge of the whole land of Egypt."[g] 42 Then Phar-
41:42 [h]Est 3:10 aoh took his signet ring[h] from his finger and put it on Joseph's finger. He dressed him in robes of fine lin-
[i]Da 5:7,16,29 en and put a gold chain around his neck.[i] 43 He had him ride in a chariot as his second-in-command,[a]
41:43 [j]Est 6:9 and men shouted before him, "Make way[b]!"[j] Thus he put him in charge of the whole land of Egypt.
44 Then Pharaoh said to Joseph, "I am Pharaoh, but without your word no one will lift hand or foot in
41:44 [k]Ps 105:22 all Egypt."[k] 45 Pharaoh gave Joseph the name Zaphenath-Paneah and gave him Asenath daughter of Po-
41:45 [l]ver 50; Ge 46:20,27 tiphera, priest of On,[c] to be his wife.[l] And Joseph went throughout the land of Egypt.
41:46 [m]Ge 37:2 46 Joseph was thirty years old[m] when he entered the service[n] of Pharaoh king of Egypt. And Joseph
[n]1Sa 16:21; Da 1:19 went out from Pharaoh's presence and traveled throughout Egypt. 47 During the seven years of abundance
the land produced plentifully. 48 Joseph collected all the food produced in those seven years of abundance
in Egypt and stored it in the cities. In each city he put the food grown in the fields surrounding it. 49 Jo-
seph stored up huge quantities of grain, like the sand of the sea; it was so much that he stopped keeping
records because it was beyond measure.
50 Before the years of famine came, two sons were born to Joseph by Asenath daughter of Potiphera,
41:50 [o]Ge 46:20; 48:5 priest of On.[o] 51 Joseph named his firstborn[p] Manasseh[d] and said, "It is because God has made me for-
41:51 [p]Ge 48:14, 18,20 get all my trouble and all my father's household." 52 The second son he named Ephraim[e][q] and said, "It is
41:52 [q]Ge 48:1, 5; 50:23 [r]Ge 17:6; 28:3; 49:22 because God has made me fruitful[r] in the land of my suffering."
53 The seven years of abundance in Egypt came to an end, 54 and the seven years of famine began,[s]
41:54 [s]ver 30; Ps 105:11; Ac 7:11 just as Joseph had said. There was famine in all the other lands, but in the whole land of Egypt there was
41:55 [t]Dt 32:24 food. 55 When all Egypt began to feel the famine,[t] the people cried to Pharaoh for food. Then Pharaoh
[u]ver 41 told all the Egyptians, "Go to Joseph and do what he tells you."[u]
56 When the famine had spread over the whole country, Joseph opened the storehouses and sold grain
41:56 [v]Ge 12:10 to the Egyptians, for the famine[v] was severe throughout Egypt. 57 And all the countries came to Egypt to
41:57 [w]Ge 42:5; 47:15 buy grain from Joseph,[w] because the famine was severe in all the world.

Joseph's Brothers Go to Egypt

42:1 [x]Ac 7:12 **42** When Jacob learned that there was grain in Egypt,[x] he said to his sons, "Why do you just keep
looking at each other?" 2 He continued, "I have heard that there is grain in Egypt. Go down there
42:2 [y]Ge 43:8 and buy some for us, so that we may live and not die."[y]
3 Then ten of Joseph's brothers went down to buy grain from Egypt. 4 But Jacob did not send Benjamin,
42:4 [z]ver 38 Joseph's brother, with the others, because he was afraid that harm might come to him.[z] 5 So Israel's sons
42:5 [a]Ge 41:57 [b]Ge 12:10; Ac 7:11 were among those who went to buy grain,[a] for the famine was in the land of Canaan also.[b]
6 Now Joseph was the governor of the land,[c] the one who sold grain to all its people. So when Joseph's
42:6 [c]Ge 41:41 [d]Ge 37:7-10 brothers arrived, they bowed down to him with their faces to the ground.[d] 7 As soon as Joseph saw his
42:7 [e]ver 30 brothers, he recognized them, but he pretended to be a stranger and spoke harshly to them.[e] "Where do
you come from?" he asked.
"From the land of Canaan," they replied, "to buy food."
42:8 [f]Ge 37:2 8 Although Joseph recognized his brothers, they did not recognize him.[f] 9 Then he remembered his
42:9 [g]Ge 37:7 dreams[g] about them and said to them, "You are spies! You have come to see where our land is un-
protected."

[a] *43* Or *in the chariot of his second-in-command*; or *in his second chariot* [b] *43* Or *Bow down* [c] *45* That is, Heliopolis; also in verse 50 [d] *51* *Manasseh* sounds like and may be derived from the Hebrew for *forget.* [e] *52* *Ephraim* sounds like the Hebrew for *twice fruitful.*

41:40–43 There were three symbols of power in the ancient Near East: the signet ring (Est 3:10), the robe (Est 6:11) and the gold chain (Da 5:7,16,29).
41:41–57 In the years that followed, Joseph brought about a permanent change in the Egyptian system of land tenure because of the famine and the consequent poverty of the people: Almost all the land became the property of the pharaoh, and the previous owners became his tenants.

41:56 See the note on famine at Ruth 1:1. Also see "Famine in the Ancient Near East" on page 70.
42:9 The custom of sending secret agents to discover facts about an enemy is age-old. The Hebrew word for a spy is suggested by the secrecy with which such an individual did his work. In this verse Joseph accused his brothers of being spies.

10"No, my lord," they answered. "Your servants have come to buy food. 11We are all the sons of one
man. Your servants are honest men, not spies."
12"No!" he said to them. "You have come to see where our land is unprotected."
13But they replied, "Your servants were twelve brothers, the sons of one man, who lives in the land of
Canaan. The youngest is now with our father, and one is no more."[h]
14Joseph said to them, "It is just as I told you: You are spies! 15And this is how you will be tested: As
surely as Pharaoh lives,[i] you will not leave this place unless your youngest brother comes here. 16Send one
of your number to get your brother; the rest of you will be kept in prison, so that your words may be test-
ed to see if you are telling the truth.[j] If you are not, then as surely as Pharaoh lives, you are spies!" 17And
he put them all in custody[k] for three days.

42:13 [h]Ge 37:30, 33; 44:20
42:15 [i]1Sa 17:55
42:16 [j]ver 11
42:17 [k]Ge 40:4

Famine in the Ancient Near East

GENESIS 42 Subsistence farming and chronic malnutrition were common in the ancient world, and many people perceived themselves at any given time as being only a step ahead of starvation. Natural causes (drought, locusts and blight) brought about frequent famines, as did human actions, from siege warfare to destruction of fields by invading armies to the exacerbating of food shortages by hoarding.[1] Joel 1 recounts the desolation brought about by a locust plague,[2] while Isaiah 7 records the devastation of Judah's agricultural economy by invading Assyrians.

Usually famines in this part of the world were temporary and local, but some long-term and widespread occurrences have been recorded. A protracted and extensive drought and consequent intermittent famines centered in Egypt occurred from the twenty-second to the twentieth centuries B.C., as Egyptian texts from this time period attest. For example, The Admonitions of Ipuwer describes famine-related social chaos in Egypt, indicating that during this time people languished from thirst and desert-like conditions prevailed.[3] This period of frequent famines corresponds to the **patriarchal age**; the Bible records famines during the lifetimes of Abraham (Ge 12:10), Isaac (26:1) and Joseph[4] (chs. 41–42).

Centuries later, according to Acts 11:28, Agabus predicted a worldwide famine, which did indeed occur between A.D. 44 and 48, during Claudius's reign. This is attested by extra-biblical sources. For example, Tacitus, in *The Annals*, 12.43, mentioned "scanty crops" during that period.[5]

[1]See "Siege Warfare" on page 465. [2]See "Locusts in the Ancient Near East" on page 1438. [3]See "Calamity and Distress in Ipuwer" on page 1309. [4]See also "Food and Agriculture" on page 390. [5]See "Claudius, Emperor of Rome" on page 1788.

The region of Edom
Photograph courtesy of © Dr. Gary Pratico

42:18 [l]Ge 20:11; Lev 25:43 18 On the third day, Joseph said to them, "Do this and you will live, for I fear God:[l] 19 If you are honest
men, let one of your brothers stay here in prison, while the rest of you go and take grain back for your
42:20 [m]ver 15, 34; Ge 43:5; 44:23 starving households. 20 But you must bring your youngest brother to me,[m] so that your words may be
verified and that you may not die." This they proceeded to do.
42:21 [n]Ge 37:26-28 [o]Hos 5:15 21 They said to one another, "Surely we are being punished because of our brother.[n] We saw how dis-
tressed he was when he pleaded with us for his life, but we would not listen; that's why this distress[o] has
come upon us."
42:22 [p]Ge 37:21-22 [q]Ge 9:5 [r]1Ki 2:32; 2Ch 24:22; Ps 9:12 22 Reuben replied, "Didn't I tell you not to sin against the boy?[p] But you wouldn't listen! Now we must
give an accounting[q] for his blood."[r] 23 They did not realize that Joseph could understand them, since he
was using an interpreter.
24 He turned away from them and began to weep, but then turned back and spoke to them again. He
42:24 [s]ver 13; Ge 43:14,23; 45:14-15 had Simeon taken from them and bound before their eyes.[s]
42:25 [t]Ge 43:2 [u]Ge 44:1,8 [v]Ro 12:17,20-21 25 Joseph gave orders to fill their bags with grain,[t] to put each man's silver back in his sack,[u] and to give
them provisions for their journey.[v] After this was done for them, 26 they loaded their grain on their don-
keys and left.
27 At the place where they stopped for the night one of them opened his sack to get feed for his don-
42:27 [w]Ge 43:21-22 key, and he saw his silver in the mouth of his sack.[w] 28 "My silver has been returned," he said to his broth-
ers. "Here it is in my sack."
Their hearts sank and they turned to each other trembling and said, "What is this that God has done
42:28 [x]Ge 43:23 to us?"[x]
29 When they came to their father Jacob in the land of Canaan, they told him all that had happened to
42:30 [y]ver 7 them. They said, 30 "The man who is lord over the land spoke harshly to us[y] and treated us as though we
42:31 [z]ver 11 were spying on the land. 31 But we said to him, 'We are honest men; we are not spies.[z] 32 We were twelve
brothers, sons of one father. One is no more, and the youngest is now with our father in Canaan.'
33 "Then the man who is lord over the land said to us, 'This is how I will know whether you are hon-
42:33 [a]ver 19,20 est men: Leave one of your brothers here with me, and take food for your starving households and go.[a]
34 But bring your youngest brother to me so I will know that you are not spies but honest men. Then I
42:34 [b]Ge 34:10 will give your brother back to you, and you can trade[a] in the land.[b]' "
35 As they were emptying their sacks, there in each man's sack was his pouch of silver! When they and
42:35 [c]Ge 43:12,15,18 their father saw the money pouches, they were frightened.[c] 36 Their father Jacob said to them, "You have
deprived me of my children. Joseph is no more and Simeon is no more, and now you want to take Ben-
42:36 [d]Ge 43:14 jamin.[d] Everything is against me!"
37 Then Reuben said to his father, "You may put both of my sons to death if I do not bring him back
to you. Entrust him to my care, and I will bring him back."
42:38 [e]Ge 37:33 [f]ver 4 [g]Ge 37:35 [h]Ge 44:29,34 38 But Jacob said, "My son will not go down there with you; his brother is dead[e] and he is the only one
left. If harm comes to him[f] on the journey you are taking, you will bring my gray head down to the grave[b][g]
in sorrow.[h]"

The Second Journey to Egypt

43:1 [i]Ge 12:10; 41:56-57 **43** Now the famine was still severe in the land.[i] 2 So when they had eaten all the grain they had
brought from Egypt, their father said to them, "Go back and buy us a little more food."
3 But Judah said to him, "The man warned us solemnly, 'You will not see my face again unless your
43:3 [j]Ge 42:15; 44:23 brother is with you.'[j] 4 If you will send our brother along with us, we will go down and buy food for you.
5 But if you will not send him, we will not go down, because the man said to us, 'You will not see my face
43:5 [k]Ge 42:15; 2Sa 3:13 again unless your brother is with you.[k]' "
6 Israel asked, "Why did you bring this trouble on me by telling the man you had another brother?"
7 They replied, "The man questioned us closely about ourselves and our family. 'Is your father still liv-
43:7 [l]ver 27 [m]Ge 42:13 ing?'[l] he asked us. 'Do you have another brother?'[m] We simply answered his questions. How were we to
know he would say, 'Bring your brother down here'?"
8 Then Judah said to Israel his father, "Send the boy along with me and we will go at once, so that we
43:8 [n]Ge 42:2; Ps 33:18-19 and you and our children may live and not die.[n] 9 I myself will guarantee his safety; you can hold me per-
sonally responsible for him. If I do not bring him back to you and set him here before you, I will bear the
43:9 [o]Ge 42:37; 44:32; Phm 1:18-19 blame before you all my life.[o] 10 As it is, if we had not delayed, we could have gone and returned twice."

[a] 34 Or *move about freely* [b] 38 Hebrew *Sheol*

11 Then their father Israel said to them, "If it must be, then do this: Put some of the best products of the land in your bags and take them down to the man as a gift[p]—a little balm[q] and a little honey, some spices[r] and myrrh, some pistachio nuts and almonds. 12 Take double the amount of silver with you, for you must return the silver that was put back into the mouths of your sacks.[s] Perhaps it was a mistake. 13 Take your brother also and go back to the man at once. 14 And may God Almighty[a][t] grant you mercy before the man so that he will let your other brother and Benjamin come back with you.[u] As for me, if I am bereaved, I am bereaved."[v]

15 So the men took the gifts and double the amount of silver, and Benjamin also. They hurried[w] down to Egypt and presented themselves[x] to Joseph. 16 When Joseph saw Benjamin with them, he said to the steward of his house,[y] "Take these men to my house, slaughter an animal and prepare dinner;[z] they are to eat with me at noon."

17 The man did as Joseph told him and took the men to Joseph's house. 18 Now the men were frightened[a] when they were taken to his house. They thought, "We were brought here because of the silver that was put back into our sacks the first time. He wants to attack us and overpower us and seize us as slaves and take our donkeys."

19 So they went up to Joseph's steward and spoke to him at the entrance to the house. 20 "Please, sir," they said, "we came down here the first time to buy food.[b] 21 But at the place where we stopped for the night we opened our sacks and each of us found his silver—the exact weight—in the mouth of his sack. So we have brought it back with us.[c] 22 We have also brought additional silver with us to buy food. We don't know who put our silver in our sacks."

23 "It's all right," he said. "Don't be afraid. Your God, the God of your father, has given you treasure in your sacks;[d] I received your silver." Then he brought Simeon out to them.[e]

24 The steward took the men into Joseph's house,[f] gave them water to wash their feet[g] and provided fodder for their donkeys. 25 They prepared their gifts for Joseph's arrival at noon, because they had heard that they were to eat there.

26 When Joseph came home, they presented to him the gifts[h] they had brought into the house, and they bowed down before him to the ground.[i] 27 He asked them how they were, and then he said, "How is your aged father you told me about? Is he still living?"[j]

28 They replied, "Your servant our father is still alive and well." And they bowed low to pay him honor.[k]

29 As he looked about and saw his brother Benjamin, his own mother's son, he asked, "Is this your youngest brother, the one you told me about?"[l] And he said, "God be gracious to you,[m] my son." 30 Deeply moved[n] at the sight of his brother, Joseph hurried out and looked for a place to weep. He went into his private room and wept[o] there.

31 After he had washed his face, he came out and, controlling himself,[p] said, "Serve the food."

32 They served him by himself, the brothers by themselves, and the Egyptians who ate with him by themselves, because Egyptians could not eat with Hebrews,[q] for that is detestable to Egyptians.[r] 33 The men had been seated before him in the order of their ages, from the firstborn to the youngest; and they looked at each other in astonishment. 34 When portions were served to them from Joseph's table, Benjamin's portion was five times as much as anyone else's.[s] So they feasted and drank freely with him.

A Silver Cup in a Sack

44 Now Joseph gave these instructions to the steward of his house: "Fill the men's sacks with as much food as they can carry, and put each man's silver in the mouth of his sack.[t] 2 Then put my cup, the silver one, in the mouth of the youngest one's sack, along with the silver for his grain." And he did as Joseph said.

3 As morning dawned, the men were sent on their way with their donkeys. 4 They had not gone far from the city when Joseph said to his steward, "Go after those men at once, and when you catch up with them, say to them, 'Why have you repaid good with evil?[u] 5 Isn't this the cup my master drinks from and also uses for divination?[v] This is a wicked thing you have done.' "

43:11 [p]Ge 32:20; Pr 18:16 [q]Ge 37:25; Jer 8:22 [r]1Ki 10:2
43:12 [s]Ge 42:25
43:14 [t]Ge 17:1; 28:3; 35:11 [u]Ge 42:24 [v]Est 4:16
43:15 [w]Ge 45:9, 13 [x]Ge 47:2,7
43:16 [y]Ge 44:1, 4,12 [z]ver 31; Lk 15:23
43:18 [a]Ge 42:35
43:20 [b]Ge 42:3
43:21 [c]ver 15; Ge 42:27,35
43:23 [d]Ge 42:28 [e]Ge 42:24
43:24 [f]ver 16 [g]Ge 18:4; 24:32
43:26 [h]Mt 2:11 [i]Ge 37:7,10
43:27 [j]ver 7
43:28 [k]Ge 37:7
43:29 [l]Ge 42:13 [m]Nu 6:25; Ps 67:1
43:30 [n]Jn 11:33, 38 [o]Ge 42:24; 45:2,14,15; 46:29
43:31 [p]Ge 45:1
43:32 [q]Gal 2:12 [r]Ge 46:34; Ex 8:26
43:34 [s]Ge 37:3; 45:22
44:1 [t]Ge 42:25
44:4 [u]Ps 35:12
44:5 [v]Ge 30:27; Dt 18:10-14

[a] 14 Hebrew *El-Shaddai*

43:29 For a discussion of salutations in the Bible, see the note at Ruth 2:4.
43:32 The taboo against eating with Hebrews was probably based upon ritual or religious reasons (see Ex 8:26), unlike the Egyptian refusal to associate with shepherds (see Ge 46:34), which was more likely tied to social custom.

THE HISTORICITY OF THE PATRIARCHAL NARRATIVES

GENESIS 44 No mention of the **patriarchs** (Abraham, Isaac and Jacob/Israel) has been found in extrabiblical documents from their era (c. 1950–1550 B.C.), nor should we expect to find such references. Living as nomads on the fringes of populated areas, the patriarchs wandered between the great empires of **Mesopotamia** and Egypt, and their activities would have been insignificant to scribes and annalists of that period. The Biblical narratives, which from their side make few references to political events of those times, nevertheless are historical, not myth or fiction. Biblical writers simply selected material appropriate to their theological objectives.

There are various reasons (above and beyond basic faith commitment) for us to accept the Biblical accounts as historically reliable, among them:

Because writing systems were in use by the third millennium B.C., it is unnecessary to assume that a long period of oral transmission existed between the events themselves and their documentation in written records. People of the late third millennium and early second millennium B.C. maintained written records and did not depend on memory for matters they considered to be important.[1] The events of the **patriarchal period** may have been recorded soon after their occurrence in texts that the Biblical writer later utilized as sources.

Names similar to Serug, Nahor, Terah, Abram/Abraham (Ge 11) and Jacob (ch. 25) appear in documents of the first half of the second millennium B.C., showing that these names were common during that period.[2] The names of the kings mentioned in Genesis 14 are difficult to account for, but evidence does collaborate the story itself.[3]

The homilies of Origen on Genesis and Exodus (Austria: twelfth century A.D.)

© The Schøyen Collection; photography courtesy of Mr. Martin Schøyen

Apparently some locations mentioned in the patriarchal narrative were sparsely inhabited during the time of the patriarchs and thus are difficult to account for archaeologically.[4] Other locations, however, had larger populations and are known from archaeology and/or texts contemporary to the lives of the patriarchs.[5] There is strong evidence, for example, related to the location of the cities of the plain.[6]

The patriarchs' travel is not to be regarded as improbable. Texts from **Ebla** (c. 2300 B.C.; see "Ebla" on p. 19) and Cappadocia (c. 2000 B.C.) indicate that travel, commerce and trade regularly occurred throughout the ancient Near East.

Hurrian family law, in force in Haran (see chs. 12; 24) and **Nuzi**, shed light on some of the activities of Abraham's family that might otherwise perplex us.[7] Another parallel has been found in a letter from Larsa (an ancient **Sumerian** city on the Euphrates River), indicating that a childless man could indeed adopt his slave as his heir (see 15:2).

The patriarchal stories faithfully reflect customs that were not practiced and institutions that did not exist during later periods, some of which were even prohibited under the religious norms of later Israel. For example, marriage to a half sister (cf. Lev 18:9) or to two sisters simultaneously (cf. Lev 18:18) was permissible during patriarchal times but forbidden in later Israelite society. This fact argues against the idea claimed by some critics that these stories were invented during the period of the Israelite **monarchy**.

Thus, various contemporary Near Eastern sources lend support to the historicity of the Genesis narrative. God, as we know and believe, revealed himself to real persons within the contexts of time and space.

[1]See "Cuneiform and Clay Tablets in the Ancient Near East" on page 1108. [2]See "Evidence for Serug, Nahor and Terah" on page 22. [3]See "The Coalition of Mesopotamian Kings" on page 24. [4]See "Beersheba" on page 518. [5]See "Haran" on page 47. [6]See "The Cities of the Plain" on page 23. [7]See "Nuzi" on page 52.

[6]When he caught up with them, he repeated these words to them. [7]But they said to him, "Why does
my lord say such things? Far be it from your servants to do anything like that! [8]We even brought back to
you from the land of Canaan the silver we found inside the mouths of our sacks.[w] So why would we steal — **44:8** [w]Ge 42:25; 43:21
silver or gold from your master's house? [9]If any of your servants is found to have it, he will die;[x] and the — **44:9** [x]Ge 31:32
rest of us will become my lord's slaves."

[10]"Very well, then," he said, "let it be as you say. Whoever is found to have it will become my slave; the
rest of you will be free from blame."

[11]Each of them quickly lowered his sack to the ground and opened it. [12]Then the steward proceeded
to search, beginning with the oldest and ending with the youngest. And the cup was found in Benjamin's
sack.[y] [13]At this, they tore their clothes.[z] Then they all loaded their donkeys and returned to the city. — **44:12** [y]ver 2
[14]Joseph was still in the house when Judah and his brothers came in, and they threw themselves to — **44:13** [z]Ge 37:29; Nu 14:6; 2Sa 1:11
the ground before him.[a] [15]Joseph said to them, "What is this you have done? Don't you know that a man — **44:14** [a]Ge 37:7, 10
like me can find things out by divination?[b]" — **44:15** [b]ver 5; Ge 30:27

[16]"What can we say to my lord?" Judah replied. "What can we say? How can we prove our innocence?
God has uncovered your servants' guilt. We are now my lord's slaves[c]—we ourselves and the one who was — **44:16** [c]ver 9; Ge 43:18 [d]ver 2
found to have the cup.[d]"

[17]But Joseph said, "Far be it from me to do such a thing! Only the man who was found to have the cup
will become my slave. The rest of you, go back to your father in peace."

[18]Then Judah went up to him and said: "Please, my lord, let your servant speak a word to my lord. Do
not be angry[e] with your servant, though you are equal to Pharaoh himself. [19]My lord asked his servants, — **44:18** [e]Ge 18:30; Ex 32:22
'Do you have a father or a brother?'[f] [20]And we answered, 'We have an aged father, and there is a young son — **44:19** [f]Ge 43:7
born to him in his old age.[g] His brother is dead,[h] and he is the only one of his mother's sons left, and his — **44:20** [g]Ge 37:3 [h]Ge 37:33 [i]Ge 42:13
father loves him.'[i]

[21]"Then you said to your servants, 'Bring him down to me so I can see him for myself.'[j] [22]And we said — **44:21** [j]Ge 42:15
to my lord, 'The boy cannot leave his father; if he leaves him, his father will die.'[k] [23]But you told your ser- — **44:22** [k]Ge 37:35
vants, 'Unless your youngest brother comes down with you, you will not see my face again.'[l] [24]When we — **44:23** [l]Ge 43:5
went back to your servant my father, we told him what my lord had said.

[25]"Then our father said, 'Go back and buy a little more food.'[m] [26]But we said, 'We cannot go down. — **44:25** [m]Ge 43:2
Only if our youngest brother is with us will we go. We cannot see the man's face unless our youngest
brother is with us.'

[27]"Your servant my father said to us, 'You know that my wife bore me two sons.[n] [28]One of them went — **44:27** [n]Ge 46:19
away from me, and I said, "He has surely been torn to pieces."[o] And I have not seen him since. [29]If you take — **44:28** [o]Ge 37:33
this one from me too and harm comes to him, you will bring my gray head down to the grave[a] in misery.'[p] — **44:29** [p]Ge 42:38

[30]"So now, if the boy is not with us when I go back to your servant my father and if my father, whose
life is closely bound up with the boy's life,[q] [31]sees that the boy isn't there, he will die. Your servants will bring — **44:30** [q]1Sa 18:1
the gray head of our father down to the grave in sorrow. [32]Your servant guaranteed the boy's safety to my
father. I said, 'If I do not bring him back to you, I will bear the blame before you, my father, all my life!'[r] — **44:32** [r]Ge 43:9

[33]"Now then, please let your servant remain here as my lord's slave[s] in place of the boy,[t] and let the — **44:33** [s]Ge 43:18 [t]Jn 15:13
boy return with his brothers. [34]How can I go back to my father if the boy is not with me? No! Do not let
me see the misery that would come upon my father."[u] — **44:34** [u]Est 8:6

Joseph Makes Himself Known

45 Then Joseph could no longer control himself[v] before all his attendants, and he cried out, "Have — **45:1** [v]Ge 43:31
everyone leave my presence!" So there was no one with Joseph when he made himself known to
his brothers. [2]And he wept[w] so loudly that the Egyptians heard him, and Pharaoh's household heard — **45:2** [w]Ge 29:11 [x]ver 16; Ge 46:29
about it.[x]

[3]Joseph said to his brothers, "I am Joseph! Is my father still living?"[y] But his brothers were not able to — **45:3** [y]Ac 7:13 [z]ver 15
answer him,[z] because they were terrified at his presence.

[4]Then Joseph said to his brothers, "Come close to me." When they had done so, he said, "I am your
brother Joseph, the one you sold into Egypt![a] [5]And now, do not be distressed[b] and do not be angry with — **45:4** [a]Ge 37:28
yourselves for selling me here,[c] because it was to save lives that God sent me ahead of you.[d] [6]For two — **45:5** [b]Ge 42:21 [c]Ge 42:22 [d]ver 7-8; Ge 50:20; Ps 105:17
years now there has been famine in the land, and for the next five years there will not be plowing and
reaping. [7]But God sent me ahead of you to preserve for you a remnant[e] on earth and to save your lives — **45:7** [e]2Ki 19:4, 30,31; Isa 10:20, 21; Mic 4:7; Zep 2:7 [f]Ex 15:2; Est 4:14; Isa 25:9
by a great deliverance.[b][f]

[a] 29 Hebrew *Sheol*; also in verse 31 [b] 7 Or *save you as a great band of survivors*

45:8 [g]Jdg 17:10 8“So then, it was not you who sent me here, but God. He made me father[g] to Pharaoh, lord of his en-
[h]Ge 41:41 45:9 [i]Ge 43:10 tire household and ruler of all Egypt.[h] 9Now hurry back to my father and say to him, ‘This is what your
son Joseph says: God has made me lord of all Egypt. Come down to me; don’t delay.[i] 10You shall live in
45:10 [j]Ge 46:28, 34; 47:1 the region of Goshen[j] and be near me—you, your children and grandchildren, your flocks and herds, and
45:11 [k]Ge 47:12 all you have. 11I will provide for you there,[k] because five years of famine are still to come. Otherwise you
and your household and all who belong to you will become destitute.’

12“You can see for yourselves, and so can my brother Benjamin, that it is really I who am speaking to
you. 13Tell my father about all the honor accorded me in Egypt and about everything you have seen. And
45:13 [l]Ac 7:14 bring my father down here quickly.[l]”

14Then he threw his arms around his brother Benjamin and wept, and Benjamin embraced him, weep-
45:15 [m]Lk 15:20 ing. 15And he kissed[m] all his brothers and wept over them. Afterward his brothers talked with him.[n]
[n]ver 3 45:16 [o]Ac 7:13 16When the news reached Pharaoh’s palace that Joseph’s brothers had come,[o] Pharaoh and all his of-
ficials were pleased. 17Pharaoh said to Joseph, “Tell your brothers, ‘Do this: Load your animals and return
to the land of Canaan, 18and bring your father and your families back to me. I will give you the best of
45:18 [p]Ge 27:28; 46:34; 47:6,11, 27; Nu 18:12,29 the land of Egypt[p] and you can enjoy the fat of the land.’[q]

19“You are also directed to tell them, ‘Do this: Take some carts[r] from Egypt for your children and your
[q]Ps 37:19 45:19 [r]Ge 46:5 wives, and get your father and come. 20Never mind about your belongings, because the best of all Egypt
will be yours.’ ”

21So the sons of Israel did this. Joseph gave them carts, as Pharaoh had commanded, and he also gave
45:21 [s]Ge 42:25 them provisions for their journey.[s] 22To each of them he gave new clothing, but to Benjamin he gave three
45:22 [t]Ge 37:3; 43:34 hundred shekels[a] of silver and five sets of clothes.[t] 23And this is what he sent to his father: ten donkeys
loaded with the best things of Egypt, and ten female donkeys loaded with grain and bread and other
provisions for his journey. 24Then he sent his brothers away, and as they were leaving he said to them,
45:24 [u]Ge 42:21-22 “Don’t quarrel on the way!”[u]

25So they went up out of Egypt and came to their father Jacob in the land of Canaan. 26They told him,
45:26 [v]Ge 44:28 “Joseph is still alive! In fact, he is ruler of all Egypt.” Jacob was stunned; he did not believe them.[v] 27But
45:27 [w]ver 19 when they told him everything Joseph had said to them, and when he saw the carts[w] Joseph had sent to
carry him back, the spirit of their father Jacob revived. 28And Israel said, “I’m convinced! My son Joseph
is still alive. I will go and see him before I die.”

Jacob Goes to Egypt

46:1 [x]Ge 21:14; 28:10 [y]Ge 26:24; 28:13; 31:42 **46** So Israel set out with all that was his, and when he reached Beersheba,[x] he offered sacrifices to
the God of his father Isaac.[y]

46:2 [z]Ge 15:1; Job 33:14-15 2And God spoke to Israel in a vision at night[z] and said, “Jacob! Jacob!”

[a]Ge 22:1; 31:11 “Here I am,”[a] he replied.

46:3 [b]Ge 28:13 [c]Ge 12:2; Dt 26:5 3“I am God, the God of your father,”[b] he said. “Do not be afraid to go down to Egypt, for I will make
[d]Ex 1:7 you into a great nation[c] there.[d] 4I will go down to Egypt with you, and I will surely bring you back again.[e]
46:4 [e]Ge 28:15; 48:21; Ex 3:8 [f]Ge 50:1,24 And Joseph’s own hand will close your eyes.[f]”

5Then Jacob left Beersheba, and Israel’s sons took their father Jacob and their children and their wives
46:5 [g]Ge 45:19 in the carts[g] that Pharaoh had sent to transport him. 6They also took with them their livestock and the
46:6 [h]Dt 26:5; Jos 24:4; possessions they had acquired in Canaan, and Jacob and all his offspring went to Egypt.[h] 7He took with
Ps 105:23; Isa 52:4; Ac 7:15 him to Egypt his sons and grandsons and his daughters and granddaughters—all his offspring.[i]

46:7 [i]Ge 45:10 46:8 [j]Ex 1:1; Nu 26:4 8These are the names of the sons of Israel[j] (Jacob and his descendants) who went to Egypt:

Reuben the firstborn of Jacob.

46:9 [k]1Ch 5:3 9The sons of Reuben:[k]

Hanoch, Pallu, Hezron and Carmi.

46:10 [l]Ge 29:33; Nu 26:14 10The sons of Simeon:[l]

[m]Ex 6:15 Jemuel,[m] Jamin, Ohad, Jakin, Zohar and Shaul the son of a Canaanite woman.

46:11 [n]Ge 29:34; Nu 3:17 11The sons of Levi:[n]

Gershon, Kohath and Merari.

[a] *22* That is, about 7 1/2 pounds (about 3.5 kilograms)

45:19 Ancient wagons or carts were crude, with wheels made of wood. They were covered or uncovered, usually drawn by oxen but sometimes by horses. Carts are first mentioned in 45:19—46:5, when Pharaoh sent them to help move Jacob and his family.

12 The sons of Judah:[o]
Er, Onan, Shelah, Perez and Zerah (but Er and Onan had died in the land of Canaan).
The sons of Perez:[p]
Hezron and Hamul.
13 The sons of Issachar:[q]
Tola, Puah,[a][r] Jashub[b] and Shimron.
14 The sons of Zebulun:[s]
Sered, Elon and Jahleel.
15 These were the sons Leah bore to Jacob in Paddan Aram,[c] besides his daughter Dinah. These sons
and daughters of his were thirty-three in all.

16 The sons of Gad:[t]
Zephon,[d][u] Haggi, Shuni, Ezbon, Eri, Arodi and Areli.
17 The sons of Asher:[v]
Imnah, Ishvah, Ishvi and Beriah.
Their sister was Serah.
The sons of Beriah:
Heber and Malkiel.
18 These were the children born to Jacob by Zilpah,[w] whom Laban had given to his daughter Leah[x]—
sixteen in all.

19 The sons of Jacob's wife Rachel:
Joseph and Benjamin.[y] 20 In Egypt, Manasseh[z] and Ephraim[a] were born to Joseph by Asenath
daughter of Potiphera, priest of On.[e]
21 The sons of Benjamin:[b]
Bela, Beker, Ashbel, Gera, Naaman, Ehi, Rosh, Muppim, Huppim and Ard.
22 These were the sons of Rachel who were born to Jacob—fourteen in all.

23 The son of Dan:
Hushim.
24 The sons of Naphtali:
Jahziel, Guni, Jezer and Shillem.
25 These were the sons born to Jacob by Bilhah,[c] whom Laban had given to his daughter Rachel[d]—
seven in all.

26 All those who went to Egypt with Jacob—those who were his direct descendants, not counting his
sons' wives—numbered sixty-six persons.[e] 27 With the two sons[f] who had been born to Joseph in Egypt,
the members of Jacob's family, which went to Egypt, were seventy[g] in all.[f]

28 Now Jacob sent Judah ahead of him to Joseph to get directions to Goshen.[g] When they arrived in the
region of Goshen, 29 Joseph had his chariot made ready and went to Goshen to meet his father Israel. As
soon as Joseph appeared before him, he threw his arms around his father[h] and wept for a long time.[h]
30 Israel said to Joseph, "Now I am ready to die, since I have seen for myself that you are still alive."
31 Then Joseph said to his brothers and to his father's household, "I will go up and speak to Pharaoh
and will say to him, 'My brothers and my father's household, who were living in the land of Canaan, have
come to me.[i] 32 The men are shepherds; they tend livestock, and they have brought along their flocks and
herds and everything they own.' 33 When Pharaoh calls you in and asks, 'What is your occupation?'[j] 34 you
should answer, 'Your servants have tended livestock from our boyhood on, just as our fathers did.' Then
you will be allowed to settle in the region of Goshen,[k] for all shepherds are detestable to the Egyptians.[l]"

46:12 [o]Ge 29:35 [p]1Ch 2:5; Mt 1:3
46:13 [q]Ge 30:18 [r]1Ch 7:1
46:14 [s]Ge 30:20
46:16 [t]Ge 30:11 [u]Nu 26:15
46:17 [v]Ge 30:13; 1Ch 7:30-31
46:18 [w]Ge 30:10 [x]Ge 29:24
46:19 [y]Ge 44:27
46:20 [z]Ge 41:51 [a]Ge 41:52
46:21 [b]Nu 26:38-41; 1Ch 7:6-12; 8:1
46:25 [c]Ge 30:8 [d]Ge 29:29
46:26 [e]ver 5-7; Ex 1:5; Dt 10:22
46:27 [f]Ac 7:14
46:28 [g]Ge 45:10
46:29 [h]Ge 45:14-15; Lk 15:20
46:31 [i]Ge 47:1
46:33 [j]Ge 47:3
46:34 [k]Ge 45:10 [l]Ge 43:32; Ex 8:26

[a] *13* Samaritan Pentateuch and Syriac (see also 1 Chron. 7:1); Masoretic Text *Puvah* [b] *13* Samaritan Pentateuch and some Septuagint manuscripts (see also Num. 26:24 and 1 Chron. 7:1); Masoretic Text *Iob* [c] *15* That is, Northwest Mesopotamia [d] *16* Samaritan Pentateuch and Septuagint (see also Num. 26:15); Masoretic Text *Ziphion* [e] *20* That is, Heliopolis [f] *27* Hebrew; Septuagint *the nine children* [g] *27* Hebrew (see also Exodus 1:5 and footnote); Septuagint (see also Acts 7:14) *seventy-five* [h] *29* Hebrew *around him*

46:32 The shepherd's equipment consisted of a bag made of goat's skin with legs tied, in which food and other articles were placed; a sling for protection against wild animals; a rod (stick) about 30 inches (77 cm) in length with a knob on one end; a staff, usually with a crook on one end; a flute made of reeds for entertainment and for calming the sheep; and a cloak used for bedding at night.

47 Joseph went and told Pharaoh, "My father and brothers, with their flocks and herds and everything they own, have come from the land of Canaan and are now in Goshen."[m] 2 He chose five of his brothers and presented them before Pharaoh.

3 Pharaoh asked the brothers, "What is your occupation?"[n]

"Your servants are shepherds," they replied to Pharaoh, "just as our fathers were." 4 They also said to him, "We have come to live here awhile,[o] because the famine is severe in Canaan[p] and your servants' flocks have no pasture. So now, please let your servants settle in Goshen."[q]

5 Pharaoh said to Joseph, "Your father and your brothers have come to you, 6 and the land of Egypt is before you; settle your father and your brothers in the best part of the land.[r] Let them live in Goshen. And if you know of any among them with special ability,[s] put them in charge of my own livestock."

7 Then Joseph brought his father Jacob in and presented him before Pharaoh. After Jacob blessed[a] Pharaoh,[t] 8 Pharaoh asked him, "How old are you?"

9 And Jacob said to Pharaoh, "The years of my pilgrimage are a hundred and thirty.[u] My years have been few and difficult,[v] and they do not equal the years of the pilgrimage of my fathers.[w]" 10 Then Jacob blessed[b] Pharaoh[x] and went out from his presence.

11 So Joseph settled his father and his brothers in Egypt and gave them property in the best part of the land, the district of Rameses,[y] as Pharaoh directed. 12 Joseph also provided his father and his brothers and all his father's household with food, according to the number of their children.[z]

Joseph and the Famine

13 There was no food, however, in the whole region because the famine was severe; both Egypt and Canaan wasted away because of the famine.[a] 14 Joseph collected all the money that was to be found in Egypt and Canaan in payment for the grain they were buying, and he brought it to Pharaoh's palace.[b] 15 When the money of the people of Egypt and Canaan was gone, all Egypt came to Joseph and said, "Give us food. Why should we die before your eyes?[c] Our money is used up."

16 "Then bring your livestock," said Joseph. "I will sell you food in exchange for your livestock, since your money is gone." 17 So they brought their livestock to Joseph, and he gave them food in exchange for their horses,[d] their sheep and goats, their cattle and donkeys. And he brought them through that year with food in exchange for all their livestock.

18 When that year was over, they came to him the following year and said, "We cannot hide from our lord the fact that since our money is gone and our livestock belongs to you, there is nothing left for our lord except our bodies and our land. 19 Why should we perish before your eyes—we and our land as well? Buy us and our land in exchange for food, and we with our land will be in bondage to Pharaoh. Give us seed so that we may live and not die, and that the land may not become desolate."

20 So Joseph bought all the land in Egypt for Pharaoh. The Egyptians, one and all, sold their fields, because the famine was too severe for them. The land became Pharaoh's, 21 and Joseph reduced the people to servitude,[c] from one end of Egypt to the other. 22 However, he did not buy the land of the priests, because they received a regular allotment from Pharaoh and had food enough from the allotment[e] Pharaoh gave them. That is why they did not sell their land.

23 Joseph said to the people, "Now that I have bought you and your land today for Pharaoh, here is seed for you so you can plant the ground. 24 But when the crop comes in, give a fifth[f] of it to Pharaoh. The other four-fifths you may keep as seed for the fields and as food for yourselves and your households and your children."

25 "You have saved our lives," they said. "May we find favor in the eyes of our lord;[g] we will be in bondage to Pharaoh."

26 So Joseph established it as a law concerning land in Egypt—still in force today—that a fifth of the produce belongs to Pharaoh. It was only the land of the priests that did not become Pharaoh's.[h]

27 Now the Israelites settled in Egypt in the region of Goshen. They acquired property there and were fruitful and increased greatly in number.[i]

47:1 [m]Ge 46:31
47:3 [n]Ge 46:33
47:4 [o]Ge 15:13; Dt 26:5 [p]Ge 43:1 [q]Ge 46:34
47:6 [r]Ge 45:18 [s]Ex 18:21,25
47:7 [t]ver 10; 2Sa 14:22
47:9 [u]Ge 25:7 [v]Heb 11:9,13 [w]Ge 35:28
47:10 [x]ver 7
47:11 [y]Ex 1:11; 12:37
47:12 [z]Ge 45:11
47:13 [a]Ge 41:30; Ac 7:11
47:14 [b]Ge 41:56
47:15 [c]ver 19; Ex 16:3
47:17 [d]Ex 14:9
47:22 [e]Dt 14:28-29; Ezr 7:24
47:24 [f]Ge 41:34
47:25 [g]Ge 32:5
47:26 [h]ver 22
47:27 [i]Ge 17:6; 46:3; Ex 1:7

[a] *7* Or *greeted* [b] *10* Or *said farewell to* [c] *21* Samaritan Pentateuch and Septuagint (see also Vulgate); Masoretic Text *and he moved the people into the cities*

47:5–6 The district of Goshen is not large, covering an area of some 900 square miles (2,368 sq km), but because of irrigation it is considered some of the best land in Egypt, excellent for grazing and for certain types of agriculture.

28 Jacob lived in Egypt[j] seventeen years, and the years of his life were a hundred and forty-seven. **47:28** [j]Ps 105:23
29 When the time drew near for Israel to die,[k] he called for his son Joseph and said to him, "If I have found **47:29** [k]Dt 31:14
favor in your eyes, put your hand under my thigh[l] and promise that you will show me kindness and faith- [l]Ge 24:2
fulness.[m] Do not bury me in Egypt, 30 but when I rest with my fathers, carry me out of Egypt and bury [m]Ge 24:49
me where they are buried."[n] **47:30** [n]Ge 49:29-32; 50:5,13; Ac 7:15-16

"I will do as you say," he said.

31 "Swear to me,"[o] he said. Then Joseph swore to him,[p] and Israel worshiped as he leaned on the top **47:31** [o]Ge 21:23 [p]Ge 24:3
of his staff.[a][q] [q]Heb 11:21 *fn*; 1Ki 1:47

Manasseh and Ephraim

48 Some time later Joseph was told, "Your father is ill." So he took his two sons Manasseh and Ephra-
im[r] along with him. 2 When Jacob was told, "Your son Joseph has come to you," Israel rallied his **48:1** [r]Ge 41:52
strength and sat up on the bed.

3 Jacob said to Joseph, "God Almighty[b] appeared to me at Luz[s] in the land of Canaan, and there he **48:3** [s]Ge 28:19
blessed me[t] 4 and said to me, 'I am going to make you fruitful and will increase your numbers.[u] I will [t]Ge 28:13; 35:9-12
make you a community of peoples, and I will give this land as an everlasting possession to your descen- **48:4** [u]Ge 17:6
dants after you.'

5 "Now then, your two sons born to you in Egypt[v] before I came to you here will be reckoned as mine; **48:5** [v]Ge 41:50-52; 46:20
Ephraim and Manasseh will be mine,[w] just as Reuben and Simeon are mine. 6 Any children born to you [w]1Ch 5:1;
after them will be yours; in the territory they inherit they will be reckoned under the names of their Jos 14:4
brothers. 7 As I was returning from Paddan,[c] to my sorrow Rachel died in the land of Canaan while we
were still on the way, a little distance from Ephrath. So I buried her there beside the road to Ephrath"
(that is, Bethlehem).[x] **48:7** [x]Ge 35:19

8 When Israel saw the sons of Joseph, he asked, "Who are these?"

9 "They are the sons God has given me here,"[y] Joseph said to his father. **48:9** [y]Ge 33:5

Then Israel said, "Bring them to me so I may bless[z] them." [z]Ge 27:4

10 Now Israel's eyes were failing because of old age, and he could hardly see.[a] So Joseph brought his **48:10** [a]Ge 27:1
sons close to him, and his father kissed them[b] and embraced them. [b]Ge 27:27

11 Israel said to Joseph, "I never expected to see your face again, and now God has allowed me to see
your children too."[c] **48:11** [c]Ge 50:23; Ps 128:6

12 Then Joseph removed them from Israel's knees and bowed down with his face to the ground. 13 And
Joseph took both of them, Ephraim on his right toward Israel's left hand and Manasseh on his left to-
ward Israel's right hand,[d] and brought them close to him. 14 But Israel reached out his right hand and put **48:13** [d]Ps 110:1
it on Ephraim's head, though he was the younger, and crossing his arms, he put his left hand on Manas-
seh's head, even though Manasseh was the firstborn.[e] **48:14** [e]Ge 41:51

15 Then he blessed[f] Joseph and said, **48:15** [f]Ge 17:1

"May the God before whom my fathers
 Abraham and Isaac walked,
the God who has been my shepherd[g] [g]Ge 49:24
 all my life to this day,
16 the Angel who has delivered me from all harm
 —may he bless these boys.[h] **48:16** [h]Heb 11:21
May they be called by my name
 and the names of my fathers Abraham and Isaac,[i] [i]Ge 28:13
and may they increase greatly
 upon the earth."

17 When Joseph saw his father placing his right hand on Ephraim's head[j] he was displeased; so he took **48:17** [j]ver 14
hold of his father's hand to move it from Ephraim's head to Manasseh's head. 18 Joseph said to him, "No,
my father, this one is the firstborn; put your right hand on his head."

[a] 31 Or *Israel bowed down at the head of his bed* [b] 3 Hebrew *El-Shaddai* [c] 7 That is, Northwest Mesopotamia

---

48:5 Jacob "adopted" Ephraim and Manasseh, in a sense replacing Reuben and Simeon (his oldest sons). A literal translation of the final Hebrew clause in this verse might read: "Like Reuben and Simeon they will be to me." Joseph's sons "became" Jacob's firstborn sons.

19 But his father refused and said, "I know, my son, I know. He too will become a people, and he too will
48:19 [k]Ge 17:20 [l]Ge 25:23
become great.[k] Nevertheless, his younger brother will be greater than he,[l] and his descendants will be-
come a group of nations." 20 He blessed them that day and said,

> "In your[a] name will Israel pronounce this blessing:
> 'May God make you like Ephraim[m] and Manasseh.[n]' "

48:20 [m]Nu 2:18 [n]Nu 2:20; Ru 4:11

So he put Ephraim ahead of Manasseh.
21 Then Israel said to Joseph, "I am about to die, but God will be with you[b][o] and take you[b] back to the
48:21 [o]Ge 26:3; 46:4 [p]Ge 28:13; 50:24
land of your[b] fathers.[p] 22 And to you, as one who is over your brothers,[q] I give the ridge of land[c][r] I took
48:22 [q]Ge 37:8 [r]Jos 24:32; Jn 4:5
from the Amorites with my sword and my bow."

Jacob Blesses His Sons

49 Then Jacob called for his sons and said: "Gather around so I can tell you what will happen to you
in days to come.[s]

49:1 [s]Nu 24:14; Jer 23:20

2 "Assemble and listen, sons of Jacob;
listen to your father Israel.[t]

49:2 [t]Ps 34:11

3 "Reuben, you are my firstborn,[u]
my might, the first sign of my strength,[v]
excelling in honor, excelling in power.
4 Turbulent as the waters,[w] you will no longer excel,
for you went up onto your father's bed,
onto my couch and defiled it.[x]

49:3 [u]Ge 29:32 [v]Dt 21:17; Ps 78:51
49:4 [w]Isa 57:20 [x]Ge 35:22; Dt 27:20

5 "Simeon and Levi are brothers—
their swords[d] are weapons of violence.[y]
6 Let me not enter their council,
let me not join their assembly,[z]
for they have killed men in their anger[a]
and hamstrung oxen as they pleased.
7 Cursed be their anger, so fierce,
and their fury, so cruel!
I will scatter them in Jacob
and disperse them in Israel.[b]

49:5 [y]Ge 34:25; Pr 4:17
49:6 [z]Pr 1:15; Eph 5:11 [a]Ge 34:26
49:7 [b]Jos 19:1,9; 21:1-42

8 "Judah,[e] your brothers will praise you;
your hand will be on the neck of your enemies;
your father's sons will bow down to you.[c]
9 You are a lion's[d] cub, O Judah;[e]
you return from the prey, my son.
Like a lion he crouches and lies down,
like a lioness—who dares to rouse him?
10 The scepter will not depart from Judah,[f]
nor the ruler's staff from between his feet,
until he comes to whom it belongs[f]
and the obedience of the nations is his.[g]
11 He will tether his donkey to a vine,
his colt to the choicest branch;
he will wash his garments in wine,
his robes in the blood of grapes.
12 His eyes will be darker than wine,
his teeth whiter than milk.[g]

49:8 [c]Dt 33:7; 1Ch 5:2
49:9 [d]Nu 24:9; Eze 19:5; Mic 5:8 [e]Rev 5:5
49:10 [f]Nu 24:17, 19; Ps 60:7 [g]Ps 2:9; Isa 42:1,4

[a] 20 The Hebrew is singular. [b] 21 The Hebrew is plural. [c] 22 Or *And to you I give one portion more than to your brothers—the portion* [d] 5 The meaning of the Hebrew for this word is uncertain. [e] 8 *Judah* sounds like and may be derived from the Hebrew for *praise.* [f] 10 Or *until Shiloh comes*; or *until he comes to whom tribute belongs* [g] 12 Or *will be dull from wine, / his teeth white from milk*

13 "Zebulun[h] will live by the seashore
and become a haven for ships;
his border will extend toward Sidon.

14 "Issachar[i] is a rawboned[a] donkey
lying down between two saddlebags.[b]
15 When he sees how good is his resting place
and how pleasant is his land,
he will bend his shoulder to the burden
and submit to forced labor.

16 "Dan[c][j] will provide justice for his people
as one of the tribes of Israel.
17 Dan[k] will be a serpent by the roadside,
a viper along the path,
that bites the horse's heels
so that its rider tumbles backward.

18 "I look for your deliverance, O LORD.[l]

19 "Gad[d][m] will be attacked by a band of raiders,
but he will attack them at their heels.

20 "Asher's[n] food will be rich;
he will provide delicacies fit for a king.

21 "Naphtali[o] is a doe set free
that bears beautiful fawns.[e]

22 "Joseph[p] is a fruitful vine,
a fruitful vine near a spring,
whose branches climb over a wall.[f]
23 With bitterness archers attacked him;
they shot at him with hostility.[q]
24 But his bow remained steady,
his strong arms[r] stayed[g] limber,
because of the hand of the Mighty One of Jacob,[s]
because of the Shepherd, the Rock of Israel,[t]
25 because of your father's God,[u] who helps you,
because of the Almighty,[h] who blesses you
with blessings of the heavens above,
blessings of the deep that lies below,[v]
blessings of the breast and womb.
26 Your father's blessings are greater
than the blessings of the ancient mountains,
than[i] the bounty of the age-old hills.
Let all these rest on the head of Joseph,
on the brow of the prince among[j] his brothers.[w]

27 "Benjamin[x] is a ravenous wolf;
in the morning he devours the prey,
in the evening he divides the plunder."

49:13 [h]Ge 30:20; Dt 33:18-19; Jos 19:10-11
49:14 [i]Ge 30:18
49:16 [j]Ge 30:6; Dt 33:22; Jdg 18:26-27
49:17 [k]Jdg 18:27
49:18 [l]Ps 119:166,174
49:19 [m]Ge 30:11; Dt 33:20; 1Ch 5:18
49:20 [n]Ge 30:13; Dt 33:24
49:21 [o]Ge 30:8; Dt 33:23
49:22 [p]Ge 30:24; Dt 33:13-17
49:23 [q]Ge 37:24
49:24 [r]Ps 18:34 [s]Ps 132:2,5; Isa 1:24; 41:10 [t]Isa 28:16
49:25 [u]Ge 28:13 [v]Ge 27:28
49:26 [w]Dt 33:15-16
49:27 [x]Ge 35:18; Jdg 20:12-13

[a] 14 Or *strong* [b] 14 Or *campfires* [c] 16 *Dan* here means *he provides justice.* [d] 19 *Gad* can mean *attack* and *band of raiders.* [e] 21 Or *free; / he utters beautiful words* [f] 22 Or *Joseph is a wild colt, / a wild colt near a spring, / a wild donkey on a terraced hill* [g] 23,24 Or *archers will attack . . . will shoot . . . will remain . . . will stay* [h] 25 Hebrew *Shaddai* [i] 26 Or *of my progenitors, / as great as* [j] 26 Or *the one separated from*

49:13 The territory of Zebulun, though landlocked by the tribes of Asher and Manasseh, was within 10 miles (16 km) of the Mediterranean.
49:19 Gad was located east of the Jordan River (see Jos 13:24–27). The Mesha (see 2Ki 3:4) Stele (a Moabite inscription dating from the late ninth century B.C.) describes the vulnerability of the descendants of Gad to raids by the Moabites to the south.

THE SONS OF JACOB

Mother	Son	*Meaning of Name	Reference of Birth (Genesis)	Order of Blessing	Symbol of Blessing	Reference of Blessing (Genesis)
Leah	Reuben	Behold, a son	29:32	1	Reckless	49:3–4
	Simeon	Hearing	29:33	2	Violence	49:5–7
	Levi	Attachment	29:34	3	Violence	49:5–7
	Judah	Praise	29:35	4	Lion	49:8–12
Bilhah	Dan	Judgment	30:6	7	Serpent	49:16–18
	Naphtali	Wrestle	30:8	10	Doe	49:21
Zilpah	Gad	Good fortune	30:11	8	Raider	49:19
	Asher	Happy	30:13	9	Rich food	49:20
Leah	Issachar	Reward	30:18	6	Donkey	49:14–15
	Zebulun	Abode	30:20	5	Ships	49:13
Rachel	Joseph	May he add	30:24	11	Fruitful	49:22–26
	Benjamin	Son of the right hand	35:18	12	Wolf	49:27

*See "Naming of Children" on page 28.

Chronological and Background Charts of the Old Testament, p. 18

28 All these are the twelve tribes of Israel, and this is what their father said to them when he blessed
them, giving each the blessing appropriate to him.

The Death of Jacob

49:29 [y]Ge 50:16 [z]Ge 25:8 [a]Ge 15:15; 47:30; 50:13 **49:30** [b]Ge 23:9 [c]Ge 23:20 **49:31** [d]Ge 25:9 [e]Ge 23:19 [f]Ge 35:29 **49:33** [g]ver 29; Ge 25:8; Ac 7:15 **50:1** [h]Ge 46:4 **50:2** [i]ver 26; 2Ch 16:14 **50:3** [j]Ge 37:34; Nu 20:29; Dt 34:8 **50:5** [k]Ge 47:31 **50:5** [l]2Ch 16:14; Isa 22:16 [m]Ge 47:31

29 Then he gave them these instructions:[y] "I am about to be gathered to my people.[z] Bury me with my
fathers[a] in the cave in the field of Ephron the Hittite, 30 the cave in the field of Machpelah,[b] near Mamre
in Canaan, which Abraham bought as a burial place from Ephron the Hittite, along with the field.[c] 31 There
Abraham[d] and his wife Sarah[e] were buried, there Isaac and his wife Rebekah[f] were buried, and there I
buried Leah. 32 The field and the cave in it were bought from the Hittites.[a]"
33 When Jacob had finished giving instructions to his sons, he drew his feet up into the bed, breathed
his last and was gathered to his people.[g]

50 Joseph threw himself upon his father and wept over him and kissed him.[h] 2 Then Joseph direct-
ed the physicians in his service to embalm his father Israel. So the physicians embalmed him,[i]
3 taking a full forty days, for that was the time required for embalming. And the Egyptians mourned for
him seventy days.[j]
4 When the days of mourning had passed, Joseph said to Pharaoh's court, "If I have found favor in your
eyes, speak to Pharaoh for me. Tell him, 5 'My father made me swear an oath[k] and said, "I am about to die;
bury me in the tomb I dug for myself[l] in the land of Canaan."[m] Now let me go up and bury my father;
then I will return.' "
6 Pharaoh said, "Go up and bury your father, as he made you swear to do."

[a] 32 Or *the sons of Heth*

50:2–3 Although it was common practice in Egypt, embalming of Israelites is found only in this chapter. The philosophy behind the Egyptian practice of embalming was a belief that the body was to be preserved as a repository for the soul after death. See "The Khu-Sebek Inscription and the Burial of Jacob" on page 82.

[7]So Joseph went up to bury his father. All Pharaoh's officials accompanied him—the dignitaries of his
court and all the dignitaries of Egypt— [8]besides all the members of Joseph's household and his broth-
ers and those belonging to his father's household. Only their children and their flocks and herds were
left in Goshen. [9]Chariots and horsemen[a] also went up with him. It was a very large company.
[10]When they reached the threshing floor of Atad, near the Jordan, they lamented loudly and bitterly;[n]
and there Joseph observed a seven-day period[o] of mourning for his father. [11]When the Canaanites who
lived there saw the mourning at the threshing floor of Atad, they said, "The Egyptians are holding a sol-
emn ceremony of mourning." That is why that place near the Jordan is called Abel Mizraim.[b]

50:10 [n]2Sa 1:17; Ac 8:2 [o]1Sa 31:13; Job 2:13

[a] 9 Or *charioteers* [b] 11 *Abel Mizraim* means *mourning of the Egyptians.*

ANCIENT TEXTS AND ARTIFACTS

The Khu-Sebek Inscription and the Burial of Jacob

GENESIS 50 The Khu-Sebek inscription, discovered at Abydos in Egypt, dates to the reign of Senwosret III (mid-nineteenth century B.C.) during the **Middle Kingdom** period of Egyptian history. It contains a first-person account of the career of Khu-Sebek, who rose to power while in the pharaoh's service (apparently as a member of his bodyguard). Khu-Sebek boasts of his zealous service to the pharaoh, particularly highlighting his heroic bravery during a campaign in **Canaan** against the city of Shechem.[1]

The inscription justifies Khu-Sebek's cenotaph (memorial monument) at the Osiris shrine in Abydos,[2] while also shedding light on two aspects of the Biblical account of Joseph's career. First, someone whose outstanding service caught the pharaoh's eye could be elevated to a high rank within the Egyptian government or military. Second, the most conclusive verification that an individual had earned the pharaoh's favor was a distinguished burial or a memorial erected in his honor. Fittingly, Genesis 50 describes the elaborate funeral of Joseph's father, Jacob/Israel, and mentions the embalming of Joseph.

[1]See "Shechem" on page 340. [2]For a brief description of the Osiris cult, see "The Mystery Religions" on page 1939.

Egyptian sarcophagus
Preserving Bible Times; © Dr. James C. Martin

12So Jacob's sons did as he had commanded them: 13They carried him to the land of Canaan and bur-
ied him in the cave in the field of Machpelah, near Mamre, which Abraham had bought as a burial place
50:13 [p]Ge 23:20; from Ephron the Hittite, along with the field.[p] 14After burying his father, Joseph returned to Egypt, to-
Ac 7:16 gether with his brothers and all the others who had gone with him to bury his father.

Joseph Reassures His Brothers

15When Joseph's brothers saw that their father was dead, they said, "What if Joseph holds a grudge
50:15 [q]Ge 37:28; against us and pays us back for all the wrongs we did to him?"[q] 16So they sent word to Joseph, saying,
42:21-22 "Your father left these instructions before he died: 17'This is what you are to say to Joseph: I ask you to
forgive your brothers the sins and the wrongs they committed in treating you so badly.' Now please for-
give the sins of the servants of the God of your father." When their message came to him, Joseph wept.
50:18 [r]Ge 37:7 18His brothers then came and threw themselves down before him.[r] "We are your slaves,"[s] they said.
[s]Ge 43:18 **50:19** [t]Ro 12:19; 19But Joseph said to them, "Don't be afraid. Am I in the place of God?[t] 20You intended to harm me,[u]
Heb 10:30 **50:20** [u]Ge 37:20 but God intended[v] it for good[w] to accomplish what is now being done, the saving of many lives.[x] 21So
[v]Mic 4:11-12 [w]Ro 8:28 then, don't be afraid. I will provide for you and your children.[y]" And he reassured them and spoke kind-
[x]Ge 45:5 **50:21** [y]Ge 45:11; ly to them.

47:12

The Death of Joseph

50:22 [z]Ge 25:7; 22Joseph stayed in Egypt, along with all his father's family. He lived a hundred and ten years[z] 23and saw
Jos 24:29 **50:23** [a]Job 42:16 the third generation[a] of Ephraim's children. Also the children of Makir[b] son of Manasseh were placed at
[b]Nu 32:39,40 birth on Joseph's knees.[a]
50:24 [c]Ge 48:21 24Then Joseph said to his brothers, "I am about to die.[c] But God will surely come to your aid[d] and take
[d]Ex 3:16-17 [e]Ge 15:14 you up out of this land to the land[e] he promised on oath to Abraham, Isaac and Jacob."[f] 25And Joseph
[f]Ge 12:7; 26:3; 28:13; 35:12 made the sons of Israel swear an oath and said, "God will surely come to your aid, and then you must car-
50:25 [g]Ge 47:29- ry my bones up from this place."[g]
30; Ex 13:19; Jos 24:32; 26So Joseph died at the age of a hundred and ten. And after they embalmed him,[h] he was placed in a
Heb 11:22 **50:26** [h]ver 2 coffin in Egypt.

[a] *23* That is, were counted as his

50:24–26 Joseph died at age one hundred ten. Egyptians considered this an ideal length of life, even though mummies have demonstrated that the average life expectancy in Egypt was between 40 and 50 years. To the Egyptians, Joseph's ripe old age would have been a witness of divine blessing.

INTRODUCTION TO *Exodus*

AUTHOR, PLACE AND DATE OF WRITING

While research has not unequivocally confirmed Mosaic authorship for this book, its adherents take the traditional evangelistic view of assigning most of its writing and compiling to Moses. This position is substantiated by several passages in Genesis (Ge 17:14; 24:3–4; 34:27) and in the New Testament (e.g., Lk 16:29; Jn 7:19). This does not necessarily imply that Moses composed Exodus in its present form, since editorial updating of the book probably occurred. Interpreters have claimed to find other sources for the Pentateuch (the first five books of the OT), but theories that deny a Mosaic origin for Exodus have significant weaknesses.

Moses almost certainly wrote/compiled Exodus at some point during the exodus period (most likely c. 1440–1400 B.C.).

AUDIENCE

Israelites who took part in the exodus, as well as their succeeding generations, most likely read Exodus in order to understand the great saga surrounding their national origin (see Ge 12:25–27). Not only did God miraculously deliver his people from slavery in Egypt and continue to fulfill his promises to the patriarchs, but his Presence returned to Israel and set the nation apart from all other peoples. God also gave the Israelites the gift of the law, the stipulations of the covenant by which Israel bound itself to him. Exodus records much about matters that defined the Israelites in terms of their relationship to God.

CULTURAL FACTS AND HIGHLIGHTS

Exodus recounts one of the greatest events recorded in the Bible, the miraculous departure of the Israelites from Egypt. Not only did God liberate his people from slavery, but in the process he demonstrated his mighty power over the gods of Egypt. Afterward he guided the Israelites step-by-step toward Canaan—the promised land. God was beginning to transform this unruly group of former slaves into a united nation of 12 tribes devoted to himself—but they had so much to learn!

God stepped directly into his people's daily lives in various ways:

Recognizing their physical needs, he provided them daily bread and water and made them victorious over their enemies.

In the desert of Sinai he gave them his law and established a special covenant with them. They became his holy people, with a solemn obligation to trust and obey him.

God made plans to live among them, even in the desert as they traveled, in the portable tabernacle he instructed them to build.

TIMELINE

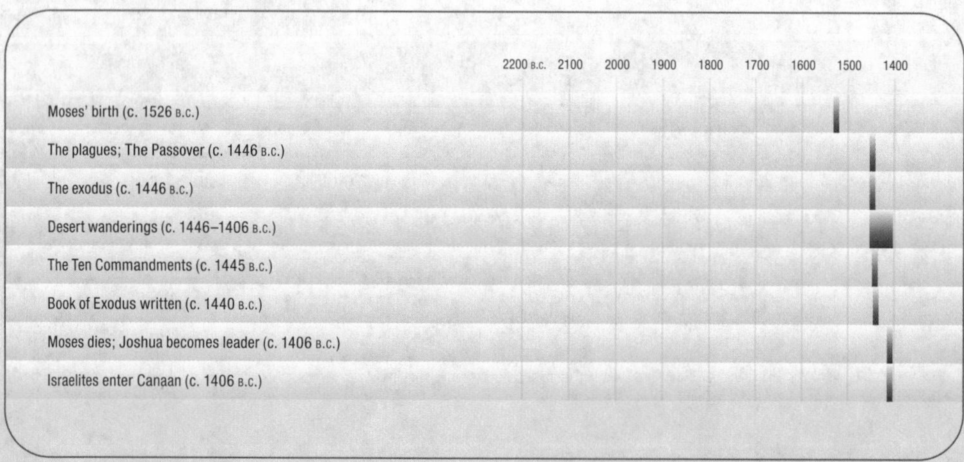

AS YOU READ

Notice how God unfolded his plans through Moses, who had fled from Pharaoh's anger until God commissioned him to return to Egypt (chs. 1–4). Watch Moses' strides in gaining trust in God, who demonstrated miraculous power in Egypt, during the Red Sea crossing (chs. 5–14) and beyond. Observe God's reaction when, after he had performed miracle after miracle to meet the Israelites' needs, they still doubted, complained and even turned to idol worship at the very point at which he was engaged in establishing a covenant with them (chs. 15–34). Yet God forgave them and stipulated detailed instructions for building his tabernacle—his earthly dwelling place among his own (35:1—40:33). After its completion God filled it with his Presence, again demonstrating his desire to be with his children and to form them into a united nation that would serve and glorify him (40:34–38).

DID YOU KNOW?

- The plague of darkness was almost certainly a challenge against Ra, an Egyptian sun god. This would also have been a direct challenge to Pharaoh, since Egyptian kings were referred to as sons of Ra (10:21–23).
- In the treaty language of the ancient Near East, the "love" owed to the great king was a conventional term for total allegiance and implicit trust expressing itself in obedient service (20:6).

THEMES

Exodus includes the following themes:

1. *Deliverance.* Through the deliverance of his people from Egypt (1:1—18:27), God revealed his involvement in human activity, his entrance into history to rescue his people. Exodus reveals God's power (6:1; 9:13–16) and compassionate love for them (15:13), attributes that are still evident today as he offers deliverance to all from the bondage of sin (Jn 8:34–36; Ro 6:20–22).

2. *The covenant.* The Ten Commandments (20:1–17) and the larger Book of the Covenant (19:1—24:18) reveal God's justice and righteousness; basic principles of ethics and morality; people's choice and responsibility (obedience brings blessing; disobedience brings punishment); and God's concern for the poor, helpless and oppressed.

3. *The tabernacle.* God's desire to be present among his people is revealed in the construction and regulations regarding the tabernacle and worship (25:1—40:38). Exodus emphasizes God's holiness and, by extension, that of the tabernacle (40:9).

4. *Moses.* The central human character of the book is Moses, the mediator between God and his people (20:19). Moses points ahead to Christ, our own great mediator (1Ti 2:5; Heb 9:15).

OUTLINE

- I. Preparation for Israel's Deliverance From Bondage (1–4)
- II. Israel's Deliverance From Bondage (5–18)
  - A. Pharaoh's Resistance and the Lord's Reassurance (5:1—6:27)
  - B. Plagues on Egypt (6:28—12:36)
  - C. The Exodus From Egypt to Mount Sinai (12:37—18:27)
- III. The Covenant at Sinai (19–24)
- IV. The Tabernacle for Worship (25–40)
  - A. Instructions for Tabernacle Construction and Furnishings (25–31)
  - B. The Golden Calf (32–34)
  - C. Tabernacle Construction (35–40)

The Israelites Oppressed

1 These are the names of the sons of Israel[a] who went to Egypt with Jacob, each with his family: 2 Reu- 1:1 [a]Ge 46:8
ben, Simeon, Levi and Judah; 3 Issachar, Zebulun and Benjamin; 4 Dan and Naphtali; Gad and Ash-
er. 5 The descendants of Jacob numbered seventy[a] in all;[b] Joseph was already in Egypt. 1:5 [b]Ge 46:26
6 Now Joseph and all his brothers and all that generation died,[c] 7 but the Israelites were fruitful and 1:6 [c]Ge 50:26
multiplied greatly and became exceedingly numerous,[d] so that the land was filled with them.
8 Then a new king, who did not know about Joseph, came to power in Egypt. 9 "Look," he said to his 1:7 [d]Ge 46:3; Dt 26:5; Ac 7:17
people, "the Israelites have become much too numerous[e] for us. 10 Come, we must deal shrewdly[f] with 1:9 [e]Ps 105:24-25

1:10 [f]Ps 83:3

[a] 5 Masoretic Text (see also Gen. 46:27); Dead Sea Scrolls and Septuagint (see also Acts 7:14 and note at Gen. 46:27) *seventy-five*

ARCHAEOLOGICAL SITES

THE STORE CITIES OF PITHOM AND RAMESES

EXODUS 1 During their Egyptian sojourn the enslaved Israelites were forced by the pharaoh to build the store cities of Pithom and Rameses (Ex 1:11). Scholars have long disagreed as to their locations, and this dispute is important. This knowledge would help to date the exodus, but uncertainty about the issue has led some historians to go so far as to suggest that this pivotal event never happened!

Note that some, but not all, of the possible locations for these cities discussed below are located on the map of Egypt on page 346.

Possible Sites of the City of Pithom

Modern Tell er-Retaba, the most likely location, faces Sinai.[1] It sits on the eastern fringe of the Nile delta on the Wadi Tumilat, about 60 miles (97 km) east-northeast of Cairo. The only major, fortified city in the area, Tell er-Retaba was occupied for a long time, including the Egyptian New Kingdom period—generally thought to be the time of Israel's oppression and exodus.

Modern Tell el-Maskhuta, a few miles further east, is considered by some scholars to be the site of ancient Pithom. But this is unlikely given the fact that this city was occupied only later, during the eighteenth to sixteenth centuries B.C., during the latter part of the Egyptian Middle Kingdom and the early Second Intermediate periods.[2] Pottery unearthed at this site leaves little doubt that Semitic people did indeed occupy this city, but they were probably related to the Hyksos, who dominated part of Egypt for a time.[3]

Tell el-Maskhuta evidently lay abandoned from the sixteenth century B.C. until approximately 610 B.C., when rebuilding took place under Pharaoh Neco II.[4]

Modern Heliopolis, another proposed site, this one in Egypt's southern delta region, also is an unlikely location for Pithom. Heliopolis is referred to as On in the Old Testament (Ge 41:50; Eze 30:17; it is called Beth Shemesh elsewhere), but we have no reason to suspect that it would have been called Pithom in Exodus 1:11.

Possible Sites of the City of Rameses

This city is named for Rameses II, who lived from 1279–1213 B.C., long after the generally accepted date for the exodus. It is highly probable that mention of this name in the Bible is anachronistic (the city may not have been known by this name when the Israelites lived there). Later Biblical writers may have referred to it as Rameses because their readers knew it as such.

Qantir is the most likely location for ancient Rameses. Egyptian texts record that this later city was located on the "waters of the Ra"—the Pelusiac or easternmost branch of the Nile River. Tanis (see discussion to follow) was on the Tanitic branch just west of the Pelusiac.

Qantir, which boasts a long history, was in the vicinity of modern Tell ed-Dab'a. It is also the likely site of an earlier Hyksos capital, Avaris. Many Semites, called Asiatics by the Egyptians, lived in this area. So it may have been a center of occupation for the Israelites, who comprised part of the Semite population. If this were the case, Israelite slave labor would have been readily available when the pharaoh of the oppression chose to build his store cities.

Tanis was once considered the best candidate for the location of Rameses, based largely on the fact that a number of statues dating from the time of Rameses II have been discovered here. For a long time scholars believed that Rameses II had taken a massive rebuilding program in Tanis. If this were true, and the Israelites had been involved in the reconstruction of the city then renamed Rameses, they would have labored under Rameses II around 1250 B.C., necessitating a much later date for the exodus.

Recent archaeological findings, however, overturn the suggestion that Tanis might have been the site of Rameses. Tanis has been found to be the principal residence of pharaohs living during the Twenty-first and Twenty-second Dynasties, *after* the time of Rameses II and much too late for the exodus. Ramesside statuary found in Tanis is now understood to have been moved there from Qantir long after the lifetime of Rameses II.

[1]See "The Location of Mount Sinai" on page 123. [2]See "A Breakdown of Ancient Egyptian History" on page 104. [3]See "The Hyksos and the Exodus" on page 99 and "The Hyksos and the Old Testament" on page 121. [4]See "Josiah, Zechariah and Neco II" on page 663.

them or they will become even more numerous and, if war breaks out, will join our enemies, fight against
us and leave the country."[g]
11 So they put slave masters[h] over them to oppress them with forced labor,[i] and they built Pithom and
Rameses[j] as store cities[k] for Pharaoh. 12 But the more they were oppressed, the more they multiplied and
spread; so the Egyptians came to dread the Israelites 13 and worked them ruthlessly.[l] 14 They made their
lives bitter with hard labor in brick and mortar and with all kinds of work in the fields; in all their hard
labor the Egyptians used them ruthlessly.[m]
15 The king of Egypt said to the Hebrew midwives, whose names were Shiphrah and Puah, 16 "When
you help the Hebrew women in childbirth and observe them on the delivery stool, if it is a boy, kill him;
but if it is a girl, let her live." 17 The midwives, however, feared[n] God and did not do what the king of Egypt
had told them to do;[o] they let the boys live. 18 Then the king of Egypt summoned the midwives and asked
them, "Why have you done this? Why have you let the boys live?"
19 The midwives answered Pharaoh, "Hebrew women are not like Egyptian women; they are vigorous
and give birth before the midwives arrive."[p]
20 So God was kind to the midwives[q] and the people increased and became even more numerous.
21 And because the midwives feared God, he gave them families[r] of their own.
22 Then Pharaoh gave this order to all his people: "Every boy that is born[a] you must throw into the
Nile, but let every girl live."[s]

The Birth of Moses

2 Now a man of the house of Levi married a Levite woman,[t] 2 and she became pregnant and gave birth
to a son. When she saw that he was a fine child, she hid him for three months.[u] 3 But when she could
hide him no longer, she got a papyrus basket for him and coated it with tar and pitch. Then she placed

1:10 [g]Ac 7:17-19
1:11 [h]Ex 3:7 [i]Ge 15:13; Ex 2:11; 5:4; 6:6-7 [j]Ge 47:11 [k]1Ki 9:19; 2Ch 8:4
1:13 [l]Dt 4:20
1:14 [m]Ex 2:23; 6:9; Nu 20:15; Ps 81:6; Ac 7:19
1:17 [n]ver 21; Pr 16:6 [o]Da 3:16-18; Ac 4:18-20; 5:29
1:19 [p]Jos 2:4-6; 2Sa 17:20
1:20 [q]ver 12; Pr 11:18; Isa 3:10
1:21 [r]1Sa 2:35; 2Sa 7:11,27-29; 1Ki 11:38
1:22 [s]Ac 7:19
2:1 [t]Ex 6:20; Nu 26:59
2:2 [u]Ac 7:20; Heb 11:23

[a] 22 Masoretic Text; Samaritan Pentateuch, Septuagint and Targums *born to the Hebrews*

1:11–14 Ancient bricks were generally square instead of oblong and were much larger than ours, about 13 x 13 x 3.5 inches (33 x 33 x 9 cm). Before being baked they were often stamped with the name of the monarch (e.g., Sargon or Nebuchadnezzar). Much ancient brickwork was comprised of bricks merely baked in the sun, especially in Egypt, but in Babylon the bricks were thoroughly burned.

2:3 Bitumen, a mineral pitch widely scattered over the earth, is one of the best waterproofing substances known. It was used with tar to cover Moses' papyrus basket (v. 3) and to waterproof Noah's ark (Ge 6:14). It was also used for mortar in the tower of Babel (Ge 11:3) and to represent a curse on Edom (Isa 34:9). There were great deposits near the Dead Sea and at different places in Mesopotamia. The principal modern source is a great lake of pitch on the islands of Trinidad.

ANCIENT TEXTS AND ARTIFACTS

Taken From a River: The Legend of Sargon and the Story of Moses

EXODUS 2 Discovered in the **Assyrian**[1] archive in Nineveh,[2] the Legend of Sargon recounts in fantastic language the birth, ascension and rule of Sargon of **Akkad**, who established his empire in **Mesopotamia** around 2300 B.C. Sargon II (721–705 B.C.), a later Assyrian king who sought to emulate his namesake's meteoric rise to power, probably commissioned the writing of this legend.[3]

The Legend of Sargon resonates with a number of features also found in Moses' birth narrative (Ex 2:1–10). Sargon's mother was a high priestess (reminiscent of Moses' Levitical lineage). After his secretive birth, Sargon was placed in a "reed basket," which was "sealed with pitch" and set adrift on a river. "Aqqi, drawer of water," rescued the infant, adopted him and raised him to be a farmer. Eventually, he found favor with the goddess Ishtar and was crowned king.

Moses' and Sargon's birth accounts employ a common ancient literary motif, in which a hero is exposed to death during infancy, only to be rescued and to achieve greatness. The plot of the Sargon legend emphasizes the stunning, and often miraculous, nature of the hero's rise from obscurity to honor. In the case of Sargon II, use of the device may have been a deliberate attempt after the fact to legitimize his own power grab. The Biblical narrative, however, includes many unique features, such as the threat of national genocide, the attempt to hide the child and his temporary return to his mother. Although the relationship between the Sargonic and Mosaic narratives is still being debated, the details of Moses' birth unquestionably signify his heroic role in God's plan. It is helpful to bear in mind that the fictional tale commissioned by Sargon II was written much later than the factual, Biblical account of Moses' early life.

[1]See Glossary on page 2080 for definitions of bolded words. [2]See "Nineveh" on page 1497. [3]See "The Annals of Sargon II" on page 1072.

the child in it and put it among the reeds along the bank of the Nile. 4 His sister[v] stood at a distance to
see what would happen to him.
5 Then Pharaoh's daughter went down to the Nile to bathe, and her attendants were walking along the
river bank.[w] She saw the basket among the reeds and sent her slave girl to get it. 6 She opened it and saw
the baby. He was crying, and she felt sorry for him. "This is one of the Hebrew babies," she said.
7 Then his sister asked Pharaoh's daughter, "Shall I go and get one of the Hebrew women to nurse the
baby for you?"
8 "Yes, go," she answered. And the girl went and got the baby's mother. 9 Pharaoh's daughter said to her,
"Take this baby and nurse him for me, and I will pay you." So the woman took the baby and nursed him.
10 When the child grew older, she took him to Pharaoh's daughter and he became her son. She named
him Moses,[a] saying, "I drew him out of the water."

Moses Flees to Midian

11 One day, after Moses had grown up, he went out to where his own people[x] were and watched
them at their hard labor. He saw an Egyptian beating a Hebrew, one of his own people. 12 Glancing
this way and that and seeing no one, he killed the Egyptian and hid him in the sand. 13 The next day
he went out and saw two Hebrews fighting. He asked the one in the wrong, "Why are you hitting your
fellow Hebrew?"[y]
14 The man said, "Who made you ruler and judge over us?[z] Are you thinking of killing me as you killed
the Egyptian?" Then Moses was afraid and thought, "What I did must have become known."
15 When Pharaoh heard of this, he tried to kill Moses, but Moses fled from Pharaoh and went to live
in Midian,[a] where he sat down by a well. 16 Now a priest of Midian[b] had seven daughters, and they came
to draw water[c] and fill the troughs to water their father's flock. 17 Some shepherds came along and drove
them away, but Moses got up and came to their rescue and watered their flock.[d]
18 When the girls returned to Reuel[e] their father, he asked them, "Why have you returned so early today?"
19 They answered, "An Egyptian rescued us from the shepherds. He even drew water for us and watered
the flock."
20 "And where is he?" he asked his daughters. "Why did you leave him? Invite him to have something
to eat."[f]
21 Moses agreed to stay with the man, who gave his daughter Zipporah[g] to Moses in marriage. 22 Zip-
porah gave birth to a son, and Moses named him Gershom,[b] saying, "I have become an alien[h] in a for-
eign land."
23 During that long period,[i] the king of Egypt died. The Israelites groaned in their slavery and cried
out, and their cry[j] for help because of their slavery went up to God. 24 God heard their groaning and he
remembered his covenant[k] with Abraham, with Isaac and with Jacob. 25 So God looked on the Israelites
and was concerned[l] about them.

Moses and the Burning Bush

3 Now Moses was tending the flock of Jethro[m] his father-in-law, the priest of Midian, and he led the flock
to the far side of the desert and came to Horeb,[n] the mountain[o] of God. 2 There the angel of the LORD[p]
appeared to him in flames of fire from within a bush.[q] Moses saw that though the bush was on fire it did
not burn up. 3 So Moses thought, "I will go over and see this strange sight—why the bush does not burn up."
4 When the LORD saw that he had gone over to look, God called to him from within the bush, "Moses!
Moses!"
And Moses said, "Here I am."

2:4 [v]Ex 15:20; Nu 26:59
2:5 [w]Ex 7:15; 8:20
2:11 [x]Ac 7:23; Heb 11:24-26
2:13 [y]Ac 7:26
2:14 [z]Ac 7:27*
2:15 [a]Ac 7:29; Heb 11:27
2:16 [b]Ex 3:1 [c]Ge 24:11
2:17 [d]Ge 29:10
2:18 [e]Nu 10:29
2:20 [f]Ge 31:54
2:21 [g]Ex 18:2
2:22 [h]Ex 18:3-4; Heb 11:13
2:23 [i]Ac 7:30 [j]Ex 3:7,9; Dt 26:7; Jas 5:4
2:24 [k]Ex 6:5; Ps 105:10,42
2:25 [l]Ex 3:7; 4:31
3:1 [m]Ex 2:18 [n]1Ki 19:8 [o]Ex 18:5
3:2 [p]Ge 16:7 [q]Dt 33:16; Mk 12:26; Ac 7:30

[a] 10 *Moses* sounds like the Hebrew for *draw out.* [b] 22 *Gershom* sounds like the Hebrew for *an alien there.*

2:11 Little is narrated in the book of Exodus regarding the early period of the life of Moses. Stephen in his address to the Sanhedrin (Ac 7:22) asserted that Moses was not only instructed in the science and learning of the Egyptians but also was endowed with oratorical ability and distinctive leadership qualities. The court of Egypt provided educational facilities for royal heirs or tributary princes from city-states of the Syro-Palestinian territory subject to the Egyptian rulers. Consequently Moses may have had classmates from as far north as the Euphrates River in his educational experiences in the Egyptian court.

2:14 While the Hebrew word for "judge" could also refer to a deliverer (see Ac 7:35), it was often used for "ruler" in the Old Testament (e.g., Ge 18:25) and in ancient Canaan.

2:15 The Midianites were named after one of Abraham's younger sons by his wife Keturah (see Ge 25:2). See also "Midian" on page 92.

3:1 As shepherd of his father-in-law's flocks, Moses gained first-hand geographical knowledge of the territory surrounding the Gulf of Aqabah. Little did he realize that through this area he would one day lead the great nation of Israel!

5 "Do not come any closer," God said. "Take off your sandals, for the place where you are standing is
holy ground."[r] 6 Then he said, "I am the God of your father, the God of Abraham, the God of Isaac and the
God of Jacob."[s] At this, Moses hid his face, because he was afraid to look at God.
7 The LORD said, "I have indeed seen the misery of my people in Egypt. I have heard them crying out
because of their slave drivers, and I am concerned[t] about their suffering. 8 So I have come down[u] to res-
cue them from the hand of the Egyptians and to bring them up out of that land into a good and spacious
land, a land flowing with milk and honey[v]—the home of the Canaanites, Hittites, Amorites, Perizzites,
Hivites and Jebusites.[w] 9 And now the cry of the Israelites has reached me, and I have seen the way the

3:5 [r]Ge 28:17; Jos 5:15; Ac 7:33* **3:6** [s]Ex 4:5; Mt 22:32*; Mk 12:26*; Lk 20:37*; Ac 7:32* **3:7** [t]Ex 2:25 **3:8** [u]Ge 50:24 [v]ver 17; Ex 13:5; Dt 1:25 [w]Ge 15:18-21

YHWH: The Name of God in the Old Testament

EXODUS 3 Known by many titles in Scripture, the God of Israel has but one personal name—**YHWH** (the original, written Hebrew language contained no vowels). This name is commonly referred to as the *Tetragrammaton*, which is derived from a Greek word meaning "four letters." Virtually every aspect of YHWH (its pronunciation, origin and significance) is widely debated.

The exact pronunciation of YHWH is unknown, but many today favor "Yahweh." This conclusion is based upon theophoric names—names that contain all or part of a divine name.[1] Examples include Jehoshaphat (*"AYHWH* [*Jeho*] judges [*shaphat*]") and Adonijah ("my Lord [*adoni*] is *YHWH* [*jah*]"). Although widely accepted, the pronunciation "Yahweh" remains uncertain.

In Exodus 3:14 God referred to himself as "I AM." The Hebrew word translated "I AM," a third-person form of the verb for "to be," is *ehyeh*, which looks like and may have sounded like YHWH. Accordingly, many linguists argue that the name YHWH was derived from this verb. Working from this premise, some scholars go on to argue that YHWH means "he is," "he will be" or "he causes to be." It is unlikely, however, that God intended to disclose the etymology (linguistic origin) of his name in this verse. A divine name in Hebrew is seldom merely an inflection of a verb, as would be the case if this argument were true.

Name of YHWH in ancient Hebrew script

Old Testament Today, p. 33

Frequently Hebrew texts use wordplays or puns. Some Biblical passages, for example, make their point based on the similar sounds of words in the original language (this often occurs when God is the speaker). Such puns were not intended to be humorous, clever or lighthearted, nor did they imply that a word's origin was being divulged. In Jeremiah 1:11–12, for example, God asked Jeremiah what he saw, and the prophet replied that he saw the rod of an almond tree (Hebrew *shaqed*). God responded by asserting that he was keeping watch (Hebrew *shoqed*) over his word (his revelation in Scripture). This wordplay does not suggest that *shaqed* ("almond tree") and *shoqed* ("keeping watch") are linguistically related. In a similar vein, it is possible that the similarity between the word translated "I AM" (*tehyeh*) and YHWH/Yahweh represents a deliberate wordplay, while not intended to address the origin of the name YHWH/Yahweh.

The context of Exodus 3 further suggests that etymology was not God's intended emphasis. Moses was worried about his response were the Hebrews to ask him with regard to his conversation with God "What is his name?" (v. 13). His anxiety implies that the Israelites tended to be skeptical and suggests that they might have been inclined to lower YHWH to the level of other gods, each of whom had a distinctive name. "I AM WHO I AM" was an assertion that YHWH is the one and only true God.

As early as the **Second Temple** period following Israel's return from exile, the name YHWH came to be regarded as so holy that its public pronunciation was forbidden. When readers came across the name, they would say either *shema* (**Aramaic** "the name") or *adonai* (Hebrew "my Lord"). Following the convention within Judaism of saying "My Lord" when readers came upon the divine name, the Jewish translators of the Septuagint (early Greek translation of the OT) rendered the divine name YHWH as *kuriost*, Greek for "Lord." This tradition continues in many modern English translations, where YHWH is translated "LORD."

[1]See "Theophoric Names and Their Significance" on page 243.

THE NAMES OF GOD

God (Heb. *Elohim*)	Names the transcendent Creator of all that exists (Ge 1:2).
God Most High (Heb. *El-Elyon*)	Indicates God's superior position above all the other gods of the nations (Ge 14:18–20).
LORD (Heb. *YHWH* or *Yahweh*)	Names the "I AM" God of the burning bush episode (Ex 3:14–15). The name is associated with God's covenant with Israel and speaks to the personal and relational nature of his character.
Lord (Heb. *Adonai*)	Reveals God as owner and master of all his creation (Jos 3:11).
God Almighty (Heb. *El-Shaddai*)	Recalls God's power in creating and sustaining all life (Ge 17:1).
God Everlasting (Heb. *El-Olam*)	Emphasizes God's immensity and eternality (Ge 21:33).
God, the One Who Sees (Heb. *El-Roeh*)	Reveals God's beneficent omniscience, a God who sees the needs of his people and cares enough to respond with help and deliverance (Ge 16:13).
God, the God of Israel (Heb. *El Elohe Israel*)	Attests God's sovereignty and providential watch and care over Israel as his elect people (Ge 33:19–20).
The LORD Our Provision (Heb. *YHWH/Yahweh-Yireh* or *Jehovah Jireh*)	Witnesses to God's ability to sustain the faithful in trial and testing (Ge 22:13–14).
The LORD of Hosts (Heb. *YHWH/Yahweh-Sabaoth*)	Designates God as the creator and leader of the angel armies of heaven (1Sa 17:45).

Old Testament Today, p. 73

Egyptians are oppressing[x] them. 10 So now, go. I am sending you to Pharaoh to bring my people the Isra- **3:9** [x]Ex 1:14; 2:23
elites out of Egypt."[y] **3:10** [y]Mic 6:4
11 But Moses said to God, "Who am I,[z] that I should go to Pharaoh and bring the Israelites out of **3:11** [z]Ex 6:12,30; 1Sa 18:18
Egypt?"
12 And God said, "I will be with you.[a] And this will be the sign to you that it is I who have sent you: **3:12** [a]Ge 31:3; Jos 1:5; Ro 8:31
When you have brought the people out of Egypt, you[a] will worship God on this mountain."
13 Moses said to God, "Suppose I go to the Israelites and say to them, 'The God of your fathers has sent
me to you,' and they ask me, 'What is his name?' Then what shall I tell them?"
14 God said to Moses, "I AM WHO I AM.[b] This is what you are to say to the Israelites: 'I AM[b] has sent me **3:14** [b]Ex 6:2-3; Jn 8:58; Heb 13:8
to you.' "
15 God also said to Moses, "Say to the Israelites, 'The LORD,[c] the God of your fathers—the God of Abra-

[a] *12* The Hebrew is plural. [b] *14* Or *I WILL BE WHAT I WILL BE* [c] *15* The Hebrew for *LORD* sounds like and may be derived from the Hebrew for *I AM* in verse 14.

3:15 cPs 135:13; Hos 12:5 ham, the God of Isaac and the God of Jacob—has sent me to you.' This is my name[c] forever, the name
by which I am to be remembered from generation to generation.

3:16 dEx 4:29 16"Go, assemble the elders[d] of Israel and say to them, 'The LORD, the God of your fathers—the God
of Abraham, Isaac and Jacob—appeared to me and said: I have watched over you and have seen what
3:17 eGe 15:16; Jos 24:11 has been done to you in Egypt. 17And I have promised to bring you up out of your misery in Egypt[e] into
the land of the Canaanites, Hittites, Amorites, Perizzites, Hivites and Jebusites—a land flowing with milk
and honey.'

3:18 fEx 4:1,8,31 18"The elders of Israel will listen[f] to you. Then you and the elders are to go to the king of Egypt and
say to him, 'The LORD, the God of the Hebrews, has met with us. Let us take a three-day journey into the
gEx 5:1,3 desert to offer sacrifices[g] to the LORD our God.' 19But I know that the king of Egypt will not let you go un-
3:19 hEx 4:21; 5:2 less a mighty hand[h] compels him. 20So I will stretch out my hand[i] and strike the Egyptians with all the
3:20 iEx 6:1,6; 9:15 jDt 6:22; Ne 9:10; Ac 7:36 kEx 12:31-33 wonders[j] that I will perform among them. After that, he will let you go.[k]

21"And I will make the Egyptians favorably disposed[l] toward this people, so that when you leave you
3:21 lEx 12:36 mPs 105:37 will not go empty-handed.[m] 22Every woman is to ask her neighbor and any woman living in her house
3:22 nEx 11:2 oEze 39:10 for articles of silver and gold[n] and for clothing, which you will put on your sons and daughters. And so
you will plunder[o] the Egyptians."

Signs for Moses

4:1 pEx 3:18; 6:30 4 Moses answered, "What if they do not believe me or listen[p] to me and say, 'The LORD did not appear
to you'?"

2Then the LORD said to him, "What is that in your hand?"

4:2 qver 17,20 "A staff,"[q] he replied.

3The LORD said, "Throw it on the ground."

Moses threw it on the ground and it became a snake, and he ran from it. 4Then the LORD said to him,
"Reach out your hand and take it by the tail." So Moses reached out and took hold of the snake and it
4:5 rEx 19:9 turned back into a staff in his hand. 5"This," said the LORD, "is so that they may believe[r] that the LORD, the
God of their fathers—the God of Abraham, the God of Isaac and the God of Jacob—has appeared to
you."

6Then the LORD said, "Put your hand inside your cloak." So Moses put his hand into his cloak, and
4:6 sNu 12:10; 2Ki 5:1,27 when he took it out, it was leprous,[a] like snow.[s]

7"Now put it back into your cloak," he said. So Moses put his hand back into his cloak, and when he
4:7 tNu 12:13-15; Dt 32:39; 2Ki 5:14; Mt 8:3 took it out, it was restored,[t] like the rest of his flesh.

8Then the LORD said, "If they do not believe you or pay attention to the first miraculous sign, they may
believe the second. 9But if they do not believe these two signs or listen to you, take some water from the
4:9 uEx 7:17-21 Nile and pour it on the dry ground. The water you take from the river will become blood[u] on the
ground."

10Moses said to the LORD, "O Lord, I have never been eloquent, neither in the past nor since you have
4:10 vEx 6:12; Jer 1:6 spoken to your servant. I am slow of speech and tongue."[v]

11The LORD said to him, "Who gave man his mouth? Who makes him deaf or mute? Who gives him
4:11 wPs 94:9; Mt 11:5 sight or makes him blind?[w] Is it not I, the LORD? 12Now go; I will help you speak and will teach you what
4:12 xIsa 50:4; Jer 1:9; Mt 10:19-20; Mk 13:11; Lk 12:12; 21:14-15 to say."[x]

13But Moses said, "O Lord, please send someone else to do it."

14Then the LORD's anger burned against Moses and he said, "What about your brother, Aaron the Le-
4:14 yver 27 vite? I know he can speak well. He is already on his way to meet[y] you, and his heart will be glad when he
4:15 zNu 23:5,12,16 sees you. 15You shall speak to him and put words in his mouth;[z] I will help both of you speak and will
4:16 aEx 7:1-2 teach you what to do. 16He will speak to the people for you, and it will be as if he were your mouth[a] and
4:17 bver 2 cEx 7:9-21 as if you were God to him. 17But take this staff[b] in your hand so you can perform miraculous signs[c]
with it."

Moses Returns to Egypt

18Then Moses went back to Jethro his father-in-law and said to him, "Let me go back to my own peo-
ple in Egypt to see if any of them are still alive."

Jethro said, "Go, and I wish you well."

[a] 6 The Hebrew word was used for various diseases affecting the skin—not necessarily leprosy.

Midian

EXODUS 4 The Midianites were descendants of one of the six sons Keturah bore to Abraham some time after Sarah's death (Ge 25:1–2). Our first Biblical encounter with this people group occurs in Genesis 37:25–36, when Midianite merchants purchased Joseph from his brothers and led him off in captivity to Egypt. The text interchanges the terms Midianites and Ishmaelites, suggesting either a close connection between the two groups or the possibility that the Midianites comprised a smaller group within the larger Ishmaelite tribal structure (cf. the seemingly random substitution of these terms in a later passage, Jdg 8:22–26).

When Moses fled for the first time from Egypt, he settled in Midian and married Zipporah, the daughter of a Midianite priest named Reuel (Ex 2:15–21). Later Reuel (also known as Jethro) advised Moses to organize the Israelites into groups of "thousands, hundreds, fifties and tens" (18:21) for the purpose of delegating administrative and judicial responsibilities, perhaps representative of the organizational structure of the Midianite culture. Many Kenites, probably from the Midianite clan to which Jethro belonged, joined the Israelites, integrating seamlessly into their society (Nu 10:29–33; Jdg 1:16; 4:11).

Not all of Israel's encounters with Midian were cordial, however. When the Israelites attempted to cross through the **Transjordan** during their journey toward the promised land, the leaders of **Moab**[1] and Midian dispatched a joint delegation to the prophet Balaam, requesting him to curse the traveling band[2] (Nu 22:1–7). Soon afterward Moabite and Midianite women enticed Israelite men to worship Baal of Peor and to engage in sexual immorality (Nu 25:1–6). As punishment for this treachery, the Lord ordered Moses to declare war on the Midianites (Nu 25:16–18; 31:1–18). All five of the Midianite kings named in Numbers 31:8 (cf. Jos 13:21) appear as genuine, early Arabic names in extrabiblical literature of the time.

During the period of the judges the Midianites and Amalekites[3] oppressed the Israelites by conducting raids into their territory during their harvests (Jdg 6:3–6). The Midianites successfully used domesticated camels to move swiftly during such military incursions.[4] Gideon's miraculous defeat of Midian (Jdg 7), which was long remembered in Israel, provided a solid basis for trust in the Lord's future deliverance of his people from other powerful enemies (cf. Ps 83:9–12; Isa 9:4; 10:26; Hab 3:7).

The Location of Midian

Genesis 25:6 tells us that Abraham sent Keturah's sons "to the land of the east," although this text does not define the boundaries of Midian. Passages that associate the Midianites with the Moabites, however, suggest that both groups lived in the southern part of the Transjordan. The Midianite soldiers also fled in this direction after Gideon's victory. Evidence from ancient scholars such as **Ptolemy**, Josephus and Eusebius, as well as information from classical and medieval Arabic geographers, indicates that the Midianite homeland was on the Gulf of Aqaba. This would place Midian in northwestern Arabia, one proposed site of Mount Sinai.[5]

Archaeology of Midian

Excavations east of the Gulf of Aqaba have uncovered large, walled towns and numerous villages dating to the Late Bronze[6] and early Iron Ages. A distinct variety of bichrome (two-colored) pottery, with motifs similar to those found on Mycenaean ceramics, seems to have been manufactured locally during the thirteenth through twelfth centuries B.C.[7] This distinctive type of pottery also has been unearthed at Timna, a mining site a few miles north of the gulf; a Midianite shrine was discovered on the same site. Whereas the painted motifs suggest a connection between the Midianites and the Greek world, the method of manufacturing compares with that used in Egypt. From this and other factors scholars have surmised that, rather than being an impoverished, disorganized, nomadic people, the Midianites seem to have developed a well-organized society, conducting trade with foreign nations and productively engaging in copper mining, smelting and ceramic production.

Timna graffiti
Photograph courtesy of © Dr. Gary Pratico

[1]See "Moab" on page 292. [2]See "Balaam, the Son of Beor" on page 229. [3]See "The Amalekites" on page 120. [4]See "Camels" on page 41. [5]See "The Location of Mount Sinai" on page 123. [6]See "Archaeological Periods" chart on page xx in the front of this Bible. [7]See "Greece: From the Prehistoric Period Through the Mycenean Empire" on page 1810.

4:19 [d]Ex 2:15 19 Now the LORD had said to Moses in Midian, "Go back to Egypt, for all the men who wanted to kill[d]
4:19 [e]Ex 2:23 you are dead."[e] 20 So Moses took his wife and sons, put them on a donkey and started back to Egypt. And
4:20 [f]Ex 17:9; Nu 20:8-9,11 he took the staff[f] of God in his hand.
21 The LORD said to Moses, "When you return to Egypt, see that you perform before Pharaoh all the
4:21 [g]Ex 3:19,20 [h]Ex 7:3,13; 9:12, wonders[g] I have given you the power to do. But I will harden his heart[h] so that he will not let the peo-
35; 14:4,8; Dt 2:30; ple go. 22 Then say to Pharaoh, 'This is what the LORD says: Israel is my firstborn son,[i] 23 and I told you,
Isa 63:17; Jn 12:40; Ro 9:18 "Let my son go,[j] so he may worship me." But you refused to let him go; so I will kill your firstborn
4:22 [i]Isa 63:16; son.' "[k]
64:8; Jer 31:9; Hos 11:1; Ro 9:4 24 At a lodging place on the way, the LORD met ⌊Moses⌋[a] and was about to kill[l] him. 25 But Zipporah
4:23 [j]Ex 5:1; 7:16 [k]Ex 11:5; 12:12, took a flint knife, cut off her son's foreskin[m] and touched ⌊Moses'⌋ feet with it.[b] "Surely you are a bride-
29 **4:24** [l]Nu 22:22 groom of blood to me," she said. 26 So the LORD let him alone. (At that time she said "bridegroom of blood,"
4:25 [m]Ge 17:14; Jos 5:2,3 referring to circumcision.)
4:27 [n]Ex 3:1 [o]ver 14 27 The LORD said to Aaron, "Go into the desert to meet Moses." So he met Moses at the mountain[n] of
4:28 [p]ver 8-9,16 God and kissed[o] him. 28 Then Moses told Aaron everything the LORD had sent him to say,[p] and also about
4:29 [q]Ex 3:16 all the miraculous signs he had commanded him to perform.
4:31 [r]ver 8; Ex 3:18 [s]Ex 2:25 29 Moses and Aaron brought together all the elders[q] of the Israelites, 30 and Aaron told them every-
thing the LORD had said to Moses. He also performed the signs before the people, 31 and they believed.[r]
And when they heard that the LORD was concerned[s] about them and had seen their misery, they bowed
down and worshiped.

Bricks Without Straw

5 Afterward Moses and Aaron went to Pharaoh and said, "This is what the LORD, the God of Israel,
5:1 [t]Ex 3:18 says: 'Let my people go, so that they may hold a festival[t] to me in the desert.' "
5:2 [u]2Ki 18:35; Job 21:15 2 Pharaoh said, "Who is the LORD,[u] that I should obey him and let Israel go? I do not know the LORD
[v]Ex 3:19 and I will not let Israel go."[v]
3 Then they said, "The God of the Hebrews has met with us. Now let us take a three-day journey into
5:3 [w]Ex 3:18 the desert to offer sacrifices to the LORD our God, or he may strike us with plagues[w] or with the sword."
5:4 [x]Ex 1:11 4 But the king of Egypt said, "Moses and Aaron, why are you taking the people away from their labor?[x]
5:5 [y]Ex 1:7,9 Get back to your work!" 5 Then Pharaoh said, "Look, the people of the land are now numerous,[y] and you
are stopping them from working."
6 That same day Pharaoh gave this order to the slave drivers and foremen in charge of the people:
7 "You are no longer to supply the people with straw for making bricks; let them go and gather their own
straw. 8 But require them to make the same number of bricks as before; don't reduce the quota. They are
lazy; that is why they are crying out, 'Let us go and sacrifice to our God.' 9 Make the work harder for the
men so that they keep working and pay no attention to lies."
10 Then the slave drivers and the foremen went out and said to the people, "This is what Pharaoh says:
'I will not give you any more straw. 11 Go and get your own straw wherever you can find it, but your work
will not be reduced at all.' " 12 So the people scattered all over Egypt to gather stubble to use for straw.
13 The slave drivers kept pressing them, saying, "Complete the work required of you for each day, just as
5:14 [z]Isa 10:24 when you had straw." 14 The Israelite foremen appointed by Pharaoh's slave drivers were beaten[z] and were
asked, "Why didn't you meet your quota of bricks yesterday or today, as before?"
15 Then the Israelite foremen went and appealed to Pharaoh: "Why have you treated your servants this
way? 16 Your servants are given no straw, yet we are told, 'Make bricks!' Your servants are being beaten, but
the fault is with your own people."
5:17 [a]ver 8 17 Pharaoh said, "Lazy, that's what you are—lazy![a] That is why you keep saying, 'Let us go and sacri-
fice to the LORD.' 18 Now get to work. You will not be given any straw, yet you must produce your full quo-
ta of bricks."
19 The Israelite foremen realized they were in trouble when they were told, "You are not to reduce the

[a] *24* Or ⌊*Moses' son*⌋; Hebrew *him* [b] *25* Or *and drew near* ⌊*Moses'*⌋ *feet*

4:25–26 Circumcision was practiced for various reasons among many peoples of the ancient Near East. See the note on Genesis 17:10. Originally the father performed the rite of circumcision, but in exceptional cases a woman could do so. (See "Circumcision in the Ancient World" on p. 1840.)

5:1 The Israelites had to leave Egypt in order to sacrifice because the Egyptians found their sacrifices "detestable" (8:26).

number of bricks required of you for each day." [20]When they left Pharaoh, they found Moses and Aaron
waiting to meet them, [21]and they said, "May the LORD look upon you and judge you! You have made us a
stench[b] to Pharaoh and his officials and have put a sword in their hand to kill us."[c] 5:21 [b]Ge 34:30 [c]Ex 14:11

God Promises Deliverance

[22]Moses returned to the LORD and said, "O Lord, why have you brought trouble upon this people?[d] Is 5:22 [d]Nu 11:11
this why you sent me? [23]Ever since I went to Pharaoh to speak in your name, he has brought trouble upon
this people, and you have not rescued[e] your people at all." 5:23 [e]Jer 4:10

ANCIENT TEXTS AND ARTIFACTS

The Soleb Hieroglyph

EXODUS 5 In Exodus 5:2 the pharaoh scoffed, "Who is the LORD, that I should obey him and let Israel go?" It is not clear whether this pharaoh had never heard of Yahweh or whether he was simply dismissing him as the insignificant god of an enslaved people. Amazingly, though, one of the first references to Yahweh besides those in the Bible has been discovered in an Egyptian temple.

The Eighteenth-Dynasty pharaoh Amenhotep III (c. 1390–1352 B.C.) built this temple at Soleb, in upper Nubia along the western bank of the Nile. This temple was dedicated to Amenhotep III, who was viewed as a divine king associated with the god Amon. Its **hieroglyphics** memorialize Amenhotep III's domination of foreign peoples; subjugated peoples are depicted with their arms bound behind their backs. The historical accuracy of his claims is doubtful, given that Egyptian pharaohs routinely made such boasts, whether or not they were true. Although long-lived and otherwise successful, Amenhotep III was not a notable warrior.

Even so, one remarkable inscription at the Soleb temple speaks of "the land of the Shasu, (those of) Yhw." The term *Shasu* refers to Bedouin peoples of the Levant (the region encompassing Syria and the area now known as Palestine). Scholars almost universally acknowledge that *Yhw* refers to Yahweh, the God of Israel. But what might be the significance of this inscription for Old Testament studies?

Evidently Amenhotep III was aware of a land in the Levant peopled by "Shasu" who worshiped Yahweh. This is not to imply that all Shasu were Israelites; the pharaoh may have been using a generic or shorthand term.

If the Shasu of the inscription were indeed the Israelites, the implication is that the exodus from Egypt to the Levant (Syria/Palestine) occurred prior to the time of Amenhotep III. The traditional date for the exodus is understood to be approximately 1445 B.C.,[1] or a little more than half a century prior to the reign of Amenhotep III. As with other such discoveries, however, we do well to treat this "evidence" cautiously. The Soleb inscription does not unambiguously refer to Israelites, and some have argued that the Shasu who worshiped YHWH were simply a small Bedouin group.

Egyptian victory inscription, showing enemies with arms bound behind backs

Preserving Bible Times; © Dr. James C. Martin

[1]But see "The Pharaoh of the Exodus" on page 98 for a more complete discussion.

6 Then the LORD said to Moses, "Now you will see what I will do to Pharaoh: Because of my mighty
6:1 [f]Ex 3:19 [g]Ex 3:20 hand[f] he will let them go;[g] because of my mighty hand he will drive them out of his country."[h]
[h]Ex 12:31,33,39 2 God also said to Moses, "I am the LORD. 3 I appeared to Abraham, to Isaac and to Jacob as God
6:3 [i]Ge 17:1 [j]Ps 68:4; 83:18; Almighty,[a][i] but by my name[j] the LORD[b][k] I did not make myself known to them.[c] 4 I also established my
Isa 52:6 [k]Ex 3:14 6:4 [l]Ge 15:18 covenant[l] with them to give them the land of Canaan, where they lived as aliens.[m] 5 Moreover, I have heard
[m]Ge 28:4,13 6:5 [n]Ex 2:23 the groaning[n] of the Israelites, whom the Egyptians are enslaving, and I have remembered my covenant.
6 "Therefore, say to the Israelites: 'I am the LORD, and I will bring you out from under the yoke of the
6:6 [o]Dt 7:8; 1Ch 17:21 Egyptians. I will free you from being slaves to them, and I will redeem[o] you with an outstretched arm[p]
[p]Dt 26:8 and with mighty acts of judgment. 7 I will take you as my own people, and I will be your God.[q] Then you
6:7 [q]Dt 4:20; 2Sa 7:24 will know[r] that I am the LORD your God, who brought you out from under the yoke of the Egyptians.
[r]Ex 16:12; Isa 41:20 8 And I will bring you to the land[s] I swore with uplifted hand[t] to give to Abraham, to Isaac and to Jacob.[u]
6:8 [s]Ge 15:18; 26:3 [t]Ge 14:22 I will give it to you as a possession. I am the LORD.' "
[u]Ps 136:21-22 9 Moses reported this to the Israelites, but they did not listen to him because of their discouragement and cruel bondage.
10 Then the LORD said to Moses, 11 "Go, tell Pharaoh king of Egypt to let the Israelites go out of his country."
12 But Moses said to the LORD, "If the Israelites will not listen to me, why would Pharaoh listen to me,
6:12 [v]ver 30; Ex 4:10; Jer 1:6 since I speak with faltering lips[d]?"[v]

Family Record of Moses and Aaron

13 Now the LORD spoke to Moses and Aaron about the Israelites and Pharaoh king of Egypt, and he commanded them to bring the Israelites out of Egypt.

6:14 [w]Ge 46:9 14 These were the heads of their families[e]:[w]

The sons of Reuben the firstborn son of Israel were Hanoch and Pallu, Hezron and Carmi. These were the clans of Reuben.

6:15 [x]Ge 46:10; 1Ch 4:24 15 The sons of Simeon[x] were Jemuel, Jamin, Ohad, Jakin, Zohar and Shaul the son of a Canaanite woman. These were the clans of Simeon.

6:16 [y]Ge 46:11 [z]Nu 3:17 16 These were the names of the sons of Levi according to their records: Gershon,[y] Kohath and Merari.[z] Levi lived 137 years.

6:17 [a]1Ch 6:17 17 The sons of Gershon, by clans, were Libni and Shimei.[a]

6:18 [b]1Ch 6:2,18 18 The sons of Kohath were Amram, Izhar, Hebron and Uzziel.[b] Kohath lived 133 years.

6:19 [c]Nu 3:20, 33; 1Ch 6:19; 23:21 19 The sons of Merari were Mahli and Mushi.[c]

These were the clans of Levi according to their records.

6:20 [d]Ex 2:1-2; Nu 26:59 20 Amram married his father's sister Jochebed, who bore him Aaron and Moses.[d] Amram lived 137 years.

6:21 [e]1Ch 6:38 21 The sons of Izhar[e] were Korah, Nepheg and Zicri.

6:22 [f]Lev 10:4; Nu 3:30 22 The sons of Uzziel were Mishael, Elzaphan[f] and Sithri.

6:23 [g]Ru 4:19,20 [h]Lev 10:1 [i]Nu 3:2, 32 [j]Nu 26:60 23 Aaron married Elisheba, daughter of Amminadab[g] and sister of Nahshon, and she bore him Nadab and Abihu,[h] Eleazar[i] and Ithamar.[j]

6:24 [k]Nu 26:11 24 The sons of Korah[k] were Assir, Elkanah and Abiasaph. These were the Korahite clans.

6:25 [l]Nu 25:7,11; Jos 24:33; Ps 106:30 25 Eleazar son of Aaron married one of the daughters of Putiel, and she bore him Phinehas.[l]

These were the heads of the Levite families, clan by clan.

26 It was this same Aaron and Moses to whom the LORD said, "Bring the Israelites out of Egypt by their
6:26 [m]Ex 7:4; 12:17,41,51 divisions."[m] 27 They were the ones who spoke to Pharaoh king of Egypt about bringing the Israelites out of Egypt. It was the same Moses and Aaron.

Aaron to Speak for Moses

6:29 [n]ver 11; Ex 7:2 28 Now when the LORD spoke to Moses in Egypt, 29 he said to him, "I am the LORD.[n] Tell Pharaoh king of Egypt everything I tell you."

6:30 [o]ver 12; Ex 4:10 30 But Moses said to the LORD, "Since I speak with faltering lips,[o] why would Pharaoh listen to me?"

[a] 3 Hebrew *El-Shaddai* [b] 3 See note at Exodus 3:15. [c] 3 Or *Almighty, and by my name the LORD did I not let myself be known to them?* [d] 12 Hebrew *I am uncircumcised of lips*; also in verse 30 [e] 14 The Hebrew for *families* here and in verse 25 refers to units larger than clans.

7 Then the LORD said to Moses, "See, I have made you like God[p] to Pharaoh, and your brother Aaron will 7:1 [p]Ex 4:16
be your prophet. [2]You are to say everything I command you, and your brother Aaron is to tell Pharaoh
to let the Israelites go out of his country. [3]But I will harden Pharaoh's heart,[q] and though I multiply my mi- 7:3 [q]Ex 4:21; 11:9
raculous signs and wonders in Egypt, [4]he will not listen[r] to you. Then I will lay my hand on Egypt and with 7:4 [r]Ex 11:9
mighty acts of judgment[s] I will bring out my divisions, my people the Israelites. [5]And the Egyptians will [s]Ex 3:20; 6:6
know that I am the LORD[t] when I stretch out my hand[u] against Egypt and bring the Israelites out of it." 7:5 [t]ver 17; Ex 8:19,22 [u]Ex 3:20
[6]Moses and Aaron did just as the LORD commanded[v] them. [7]Moses was eighty years old[w] and Aaron
eighty-three when they spoke to Pharaoh. 7:6 [v]ver 2 7:7 [w]Dt 31:2; 34:7; Ac 7:23,30

Aaron's Staff Becomes a Snake

[8]The LORD said to Moses and Aaron, [9]"When Pharaoh says to you, 'Perform a miracle,'[x] then say to Aar- 7:9 [x]Isa 7:11; Jn 2:18 [y]Ex 4:2-5
on, 'Take your staff and throw it down before Pharaoh,' and it will become a snake."[y]
[10]So Moses and Aaron went to Pharaoh and did just as the LORD commanded. Aaron threw his staff
down in front of Pharaoh and his officials, and it became a snake. [11]Pharaoh then summoned wise men
and sorcerers, and the Egyptian magicians[z] also did the same things by their secret arts:[a] [12]Each one 7:11 [z]Ge 41:8; 2Ti 3:8 [a]ver 22; Ex 8:7,18
threw down his staff and it became a snake. But Aaron's staff swallowed up their staffs. [13]Yet Pharaoh's
heart[b] became hard and he would not listen to them, just as the LORD had said. 7:13 [b]Ex 4:21

The Plague of Blood

[14]Then the LORD said to Moses, "Pharaoh's heart is unyielding;[c] he refuses to let the people go. [15]Go 7:14 [c]Ex 8:15,32; 10:1,20,27
to Pharaoh in the morning as he goes out to the water. Wait on the bank of the Nile to meet him, and take
in your hand the staff that was changed into a snake. [16]Then say to him, 'The LORD, the God of the He-

---

7:1 In Egypt, the pharaoh was considered divine. So by calling Moses "God," the Lord was beating Pharaoh at his own game. Moses was "God" to Pharaoh in that God was acting through him, and Moses would be the one through whom God would bring salvation to Israel.

7:11 Through his or her use of magic the wonder-worker possesses a formula that causes a predicted result. The alleged supernatural power is controlled by the performer. In miracles of God, on the other hand, the results depend wholly upon the divine will; the one who works the miracle is simply an agent for the Lord.

According to tradition, two of the magicians who opposed Moses were named Jannes and Jambres (see 2Ti 3:8; Jannes is also mentioned in the Dead Sea Scrolls). See "The Egyptian Priests and Their Snakes" on page 96.

7:14–24 When the Nile is at flood stage in June, its water turns red from soil brought down from Ethiopia. The water is still fit to drink, and the fish do not die. When the river is at its lowest, in May, the water is sometimes red and unfit to drink, and fish do die. The Egyptians had to dig wells, into which the river water would filter through sand. Evidently God directed Moses to lift up his rod at precisely the right time. Once the time was disclosed the Egyptian magicians were able to do likewise.

The Egyptian Priests and Their Snakes

EXODUS 7 The Bible frequently records particular events without explaining how they happened. Exodus 7, for example, reveals that Egyptian magicians mimicked Moses' changing of his staff into a snake "by their secret arts" (v. 11). This could mean that they employed supernatural power and actually changed staffs into snakes. The Bible, however, does not explicitly state whether or not supernatural agents, either divine (Nu 22:21ff.) or demonic (Dt 18:10–11; Job 2:7), were involved.

The majority of scholars believe that the Egyptians used mere trickery on this occasion. Throughout the ancient world pagan priests regularly deceived gullible people (e.g., a priest would hide in a large, hollowed-out idol and speak for the god). So the Egyptians could have used sleight of hand (analogous to modern stage magicians performing tricks with animals). Evidence also reveals that Egyptians regularly practiced a method of snake charming that allowed them to put snakes into a kind of catalepsy, whereby they would remain as stiff as a rod until awakened. This trick is still practiced in Egypt today.

It is helpful to recognize that the purpose of this Biblical text was not to debunk Egyptian magic but to show that the power of Israel's God was greater than any power Egypt possessed. When Moses' snake swallowed the Egyptians' snakes, the event predicted disaster for the pharaoh. A representative snake from Israel's God had defeated one of Egypt's national symbols—the serpent—an animal considered sacred in Lower Egypt where Moses' confrontation with the pharaoh was taking place.

7:16 [d]Ex 3:18; 5:1,3 — brews, has sent me to say to you: Let my people go, so that they may worship[d] me in the desert. But un-
7:17 [e]Ex 5:2 — til now you have not listened. 17 This is what the LORD says: By this you will know that I am the LORD:[e] With
[f]Ex 4:9; Rev 11:6; 16:4 — the staff that is in my hand I will strike the water of the Nile, and it will be changed into blood.[f] 18 The fish
7:18 [g]ver 21,24 — in the Nile will die, and the river will stink; the Egyptians will not be able to drink its water.' "[g]
7:19 [h]Ex 8:5-6, — 19 The LORD said to Moses, "Tell Aaron, 'Take your staff and stretch out your hand[h] over the waters of
16; 9:22; 10:12, 21; 14:21 — Egypt—over the streams and canals, over the ponds and all the reservoirs'—and they will turn to blood.
Blood will be everywhere in Egypt, even in the wooden buckets and stone jars."
20 Moses and Aaron did just as the LORD had commanded. He raised his staff in the presence of Phar-
7:20 [i]Ex 17:5 — aoh and his officials and struck the water of the Nile,[i] and all the water was changed into blood.[j] 21 The
[j]Ps 78:44; 105:29 — fish in the Nile died, and the river smelled so bad that the Egyptians could not drink its water. Blood was
everywhere in Egypt.
7:22 [k]ver 11 — 22 But the Egyptian magicians did the same things by their secret arts,[k] and Pharaoh's heart became
hard; he would not listen to Moses and Aaron, just as the LORD had said. 23 Instead, he turned and went
into his palace, and did not take even this to heart. 24 And all the Egyptians dug along the Nile to get
drinking water, because they could not drink the water of the river.

The Plague of Frogs

8 25 Seven days passed after the LORD struck the Nile. 1 Then the LORD said to Moses, "Go to Pharaoh and
8:1 [l]Ex 3:12,18; 4:23 — say to him, 'This is what the LORD says: Let my people go, so that they may worship[l] me. 2 If you re-
fuse to let them go, I will plague your whole country with frogs. 3 The Nile will teem with frogs. They will
come up into your palace and your bedroom and onto your bed, into the houses of your officials and on
8:3 [m]Ex 10:6 — your people,[m] and into your ovens and kneading troughs. 4 The frogs will go up on you and your people
and all your officials.' "
8:5 [n]Ex 7:19 — 5 Then the LORD said to Moses, "Tell Aaron, 'Stretch out your hand with your staff[n] over the streams and
canals and ponds, and make frogs come up on the land of Egypt.' "
8:6 [o]Ps 78:45; — 6 So Aaron stretched out his hand over the waters of Egypt, and the frogs[o] came up and covered the
105:30 8:7 [p]Ex 7:11 — land. 7 But the magicians did the same things by their secret arts;[p] they also made frogs come up on the
land of Egypt.
8:8 [q]ver 28; — 8 Pharaoh summoned Moses and Aaron and said, "Pray[q] to the LORD to take the frogs away from me
Ex 9:28; 10:17 [r]ver 25 — and my people, and I will let your people go to offer sacrifices[r] to the LORD."
9 Moses said to Pharaoh, "I leave to you the honor of setting the time for me to pray for you and your
officials and your people that you and your houses may be rid of the frogs, except for those that remain
in the Nile."
10 "Tomorrow," Pharaoh said.
8:10 [s]Ex 9:14; — Moses replied, "It will be as you say, so that you may know there is no one like the LORD our God.[s] 11 The
Dt 4:35; 33:26; 2Sa 7:22; — frogs will leave you and your houses, your officials and your people; they will remain only in the Nile."
1Ch 17:20; Ps 86:8; Isa 46:9; — 12 After Moses and Aaron left Pharaoh, Moses cried out to the LORD about the frogs he had brought on
Jer 10:6 — Pharaoh. 13 And the LORD did what Moses asked. The frogs died in the houses, in the courtyards and in
the fields. 14 They were piled into heaps, and the land reeked of them. 15 But when Pharaoh saw that there
8:15 [t]Ex 7:14 — was relief, he hardened his heart[t] and would not listen to Moses and Aaron, just as the LORD had said.

The Plague of Gnats

16 Then the LORD said to Moses, "Tell Aaron, 'Stretch out your staff and strike the dust of the ground,'
and throughout the land of Egypt the dust will become gnats." 17 They did this, and when Aaron stretched
8:17 [u]Ps 105:31 — out his hand with the staff and struck the dust of the ground, gnats[u] came upon men and animals. All
8:18 [v]Ex 9:11; — the dust throughout the land of Egypt became gnats. 18 But when the magicians[v] tried to produce gnats
Da 5:8 [w]Ex 7:11 — by their secret arts,[w] they could not. And the gnats were on men and animals.
8:19 [x]Ex 7:5; — 19 The magicians said to Pharaoh, "This is the finger[x] of God." But Pharaoh's heart was hard and he
10:7; Ps 8:3; Lk 11:20 — would not listen, just as the LORD had said.

7:20–21 The Nile's life-giving water was the source of Egypt's greatness as a civilization, and the Egyptians worshiped it. An attack on the Nile was nothing less than an attack on Egypt and its gods.
7:24 The sandy soil near the river bank filtered the water (see the note on vv. 14–24). Literal blood would not have been filtered by sand.
8:1–15 When the annual flood waters recede, frogs spawn in the marshes and invade the dry ground. God apparently directed Moses to lift up his rod at such a time. This sign the Egyptian magicians also claimed to produce (see again the note on 7:14–24).
8:16–19 The precise insect intended here is uncertain. So many biting, stinging pests abound in Egypt that people might not have been discriminating in naming them. The magicians failed, by their own admission, to reproduce this plague.

The Pharaoh of the Exodus

EXODUS 8 The Bible describes the **exodus** in great detail but eliminates mention of the one fact that would have proven most helpful in linking the event to a particular time period in Egyptian history: the name of the reigning pharaoh. Most researchers believe the pharaoh of the oppression and exodus to have been either **Rameses II** (c. 1279–1213 B.C.), Thutmose III (c. 1479–1425 B.C.) or Amenhotep II (c. 1427–1400 B.C.).

Rameses II

Rameses II remains a popular candidate,[1] primarily because the earliest evidence for Israelite settlements in the Holy Land come from the early twelfth century B.C. Also, the name of the store city Rameses (Ex 1:11) fits well with a pharaoh by this name.

But little evidence suggests a conquest of Canaan during this period. And the dates for Rameses II are too late for a conventional reading of the Old Testament that places the exodus at around 1445 B.C.[2] Also, the Biblical use of the name Rameses for the store city could be anachronistic; the text may use a later name for the location, known to a later reading audience.

Thutmose III

Thutmose III was a child pharaoh whose early years were overshadowed by the influence of the princess Hatshepsut, who acted as his regent, in effect taking upon herself the role of pharaoh. Some have identified Hatshepsut as the pharaoh's daughter who discovered baby Moses in the Nile (2:5–6), but this is pure speculation.

After Hatshepsut's death, Thutmose III proved to be a formidable warrior, conducting 17 military campaigns and consolidating Egyptian control over the Levant (Syria-Palestine). Thutmose maintained on the walls of the temple of Karnak at Thebes a record of events from his first campaign on. Some historians have suggested that he perished with his chariot corps while pursuing the Israelites into the Red Sea.

Amenhotep II

Amenhotep II inherited from Thutmose III a kingdom at the zenith of its power. Amenhotep excelled in running, rowing, archery, chariotry and equestrian arts, boasting on the Elephantine Stele (an inscribed stone monument) that his strength was greater than that of any other king who had ever lived. He also was an expert in warfare, demonstrating reckless gallantry in battle. Amenhotep received tribute from Mitanni and **Babylon**, as well as from the Hittites.[3] A brief campaign in Galilee during his ninth year as pharaoh is his last recorded military operation.

The dates most widely accepted for Amenhotep's reign (1427–1400 B.C.) are too late for an exodus of around 1445 B.C. Some historians suggest that Thutmose III was the pharaoh of the *oppression* since he is said to have been the first pharaoh to build a store city at the site only later known as Rameses. If so, his son Amenhotep II could still have been the pharaoh of the *exodus*.

Others hypothesize that Amenhotep's lack of military activity during the latter part of his reign may have resulted from a military catastrophe during the exodus. And some historians speculate that because Amenhotep II's successor (Thutmose IV) was not his firstborn or heir apparent, his firstborn son may have died during the final plague.

The archaeological evidence for a conquest of Canaan during the reigns of either Thutmose III or Amenhotep II is scanty. In fact, some argue that the end of the **Middle Bronze Age**[4] (c. 1550 B.C.) looks much more promising as the setting for the conquest of Canaan, though this paradigm would place the exodus much earlier than the Bible seems to indicate and is difficult to reconcile with our current understanding of Egyptian chronology. It is impossible to be dogmatic about the identity of the pharaoh of the exodus, but Thutmose III and Amenhotep II remain the most likely candidates.

Ramesses II
Preserving Bible Times; © Dr. James C. Martin; permission of The British Museum

[1]But see "The Store Cities of Pithom and Rameses" on page 86. [2]See "The Date of the Exodus" on page 106. [3]See "Anatolia and the Hittites" on page 144. [4]See "Archaeological Periods" chart on page xx in the front of this Bible.

The Hyksos and the Exodus

The Temple of Hatshepsut
Photograph: © Todd Bolen/Bible Places.com

EXODUS 8 The **Hyksos**, foreign rulers in Egypt from approximately 1637 to 1529 B.C., were of Semitic origin and thus related to the Israelites.[1] For this reason some Biblical historians have tried to establish a connection between the Hyksos and the Israelites. Three different theories seek to tie the history of the Hyksos directly to the Biblical record of Israel in Egypt.

Theory One: A Hyksos Pharaoh Promoted Joseph

Proponents of this view assert that the Hyksos ruled Egypt at the time Joseph was sold into slavery. The Hyksos, they surmise, being ethnically and linguistically related to Joseph, would have been inclined to empathize with him and promote him to power. This theory impacts the proposed date structure for the lives of the **patriarchs**, who are conventionally reckoned to have lived during the late third and early second millenniums B.C. It requires adherents to espouse the "late date" for the **exodus** (**Late Bronze** III Age, c. 1250 B.C.)[2] in order to build in sufficient time for Israel's sojourn in Egypt.

Apart from basic problems with this date in terms of the exodus,[3] this theory seems incompatible with the Biblical narrative. The Bible records only that the pharaoh promoted Joseph because of the young man's exceptional ability; his ethnicity is never mentioned as a factor. The Bible also presents the ruling class as Egyptians who instinctively reacted with scorn toward foreign shepherds (see Ge 46:28–34).

Theory Two: A Hyksos Was the Pharaoh of the Oppression

Adherents to this view propose that a Hyksos pharaoh enslaved the Israelites. Although advocated by some scholars who see this as a good chronological match with the Biblical account, this conjecture makes little sense. The Hyksos as Semitic foreigners were no doubt keenly aware of their tenuous control over a large, native Egyptian population. Why would they have persecuted a group they would have viewed as natural allies? Exodus 1:8–10 in fact shows that the pharaoh of the oppression shared the Egyptian hatred toward Semites in general.

Theory Three: The Expulsion of the Hyksos and the Israelite Exodus Are a Single Event

The Egyptians ultimately drove out the Hyksos after a protracted campaign during the latter sixteenth century B.C. The theory of the exodus based on this reality asserts that the story of the Hyksos' expulsion is simply the Egyptian version of the Israelite exodus account (i.e., the two narratives relate the same events from diametrically opposed perspectives—each presenting Israel's departure from Egypt as a victory for its side). This view, which necessitates a very early date for the exodus, does work well with the chronology of Jericho, in that this city is widely regarded to have suffered major destruction at the end of the **Middle Bronze** Age, not long after the expulsion of the Hyksos.[4]

Nevertheless, this position is open to serious challenge. The stories of the Hyksos' expulsion and that of the Israelites' exodus have nothing in common, except that in both cases a large group of foreigners departed from Egypt. The Egyptians drove out the Hyksos during a lengthy military campaign, while the Biblical exodus took place during a period of weeks, involving no military action whatsoever until the very end, after the Israelites had already left Egypt.

Any attempt to tie the Hyksos directly to the Biblical narrative ultimately falters. In all probability Hyksos rule relates to Israel's history only indirectly in that it gave the Egyptians a seemingly good reason to hate and distrust all Semites.

[1]See "The Hyksos and the Old Testament" on page 121. [2]See "Archaeological Periods" chart on page xx in the front of this Bible. [3]See "The Date of the Exodus" on page 106. [4]See "The Walls of Jericho" on page 312.

The Plague of Flies

20 Then the LORD said to Moses, "Get up early in the morning[y] and confront Pharaoh as he goes to
the water and say to him, 'This is what the LORD says: Let my people go, so that they may worship[z] me.
21 If you do not let my people go, I will send swarms of flies on you and your officials, on your people
and into your houses. The houses of the Egyptians will be full of flies, and even the ground where they
are.
22 " 'But on that day I will deal differently with the land of Goshen, where my people live;[a] no swarms
of flies will be there, so that you will know[b] that I, the LORD, am in this land. 23 I will make a distinction[a]
between my people and your people. This miraculous sign will occur tomorrow.' "
24 And the LORD did this. Dense swarms of flies poured into Pharaoh's palace and into the houses of
his officials, and throughout Egypt the land was ruined by the flies.[c]
25 Then Pharaoh summoned[d] Moses and Aaron and said, "Go, sacrifice to your God here in the land."
26 But Moses said, "That would not be right. The sacrifices we offer the LORD our God would be detestable
to the Egyptians.[e] And if we offer sacrifices that are detestable in their eyes, will they not stone us? 27 We must
take a three-day journey into the desert to offer sacrifices[f] to the LORD our God, as he commands us."
28 Pharaoh said, "I will let you go to offer sacrifices to the LORD your God in the desert, but you must
not go very far. Now pray[g] for me."
29 Moses answered, "As soon as I leave you, I will pray to the LORD, and tomorrow the flies will leave
Pharaoh and his officials and his people. Only be sure that Pharaoh does not act deceitfully[h] again by
not letting the people go to offer sacrifices to the LORD."
30 Then Moses left Pharaoh and prayed to the LORD,[i] 31 and the LORD did what Moses asked: The flies
left Pharaoh and his officials and his people; not a fly remained. 32 But this time also Pharaoh hardened
his heart[j] and would not let the people go.

The Plague on Livestock

9 Then the LORD said to Moses, "Go to Pharaoh and say to him, 'This is what the LORD, the God of the
Hebrews, says: "Let my people go, so that they may worship[k] me." 2 If you refuse to let them go and
continue to hold them back, 3 the hand[l] of the LORD will bring a terrible plague on your livestock in the
field—on your horses and donkeys and camels and on your cattle and sheep and goats. 4 But the LORD
will make a distinction between the livestock of Israel and that of Egypt,[m] so that no animal belonging
to the Israelites will die.' "
5 The LORD set a time and said, "Tomorrow the LORD will do this in the land." 6 And the next day the LORD
did it: All the livestock[n] of the Egyptians died,[o] but not one animal belonging to the Israelites died. 7 Phar-
aoh sent men to investigate and found that not even one of the animals of the Israelites had died. Yet his
heart was unyielding and he would not let the people go.[p]

The Plague of Boils

8 Then the LORD said to Moses and Aaron, "Take handfuls of soot from a furnace and have Moses toss
it into the air in the presence of Pharaoh. 9 It will become fine dust over the whole land of Egypt, and fes-
tering boils[q] will break out on men and animals throughout the land."
10 So they took soot from a furnace and stood before Pharaoh. Moses tossed it into the air, and fester-
ing boils broke out on men and animals. 11 The magicians[r] could not stand before Moses because of the
boils that were on them and on all the Egyptians. 12 But the LORD hardened Pharaoh's heart[s] and he would
not listen to Moses and Aaron, just as the LORD had said to Moses.

8:20 [y]Ex 7:15; 9:13 [z]ver 1; Ex 3:18
8:22 [a]Ex 9:4,6, 26; 10:23; 11:7 [b]Ex 7:5; 9:29
8:24 [c]Ps 78:45; 105:31
8:25 [d]ver 8; Ex 9:27
8:26 [e]Ge 43:32; 46:34
8:27 [f]Ex 3:18
8:28 [g]ver 8; Ex 9:28; 1Ki 13:6
8:29 [h]ver 15
8:30 [i]ver 12
8:32 [j]ver 8,15; Ex 4:21
9:1 [k]Ex 8:1
9:3 [l]Ex 7:4
9:4 [m]ver 26; Ex 8:22
9:6 [n]ver 19-21; Ex 11:5 [o]Ps 78:48-50
9:7 [p]Ex 7:14; 8:32
9:9 [q]Dt 28:27,35; Rev 16:2
9:11 [r]Ex 8:18
9:12 [s]Ex 4:21

[a] 23 Septuagint and Vulgate; Hebrew *will put a deliverance*

8:20–31 Moses' rod is no longer mentioned. Swarms of flies enveloped Egypt in unusual density to feed on the dead frogs. Once again, God directed Moses as to the time. The magicians no longer competed with Moses, and now there was a differentiation between Goshen and the rest of Egypt. Pharaoh tentatively offered to let the people go to sacrifice to their God, but only in the land of Egypt (v. 25). Moses protested that their sacrifice would involve an animal the Egyptians thought it improper to sacrifice and insisted that they must travel a three days' journey into the wilderness.

9:1–11 The plague on cattle was announced with a set time for its occurrence, and there is no record of its removal. Presumably it wore itself out. The Israelite cattle were spared, as evidence of God's favor and power.

9:9 The precise nature of the "festering boils" has provoked much speculation and two alternative explanations: (1) People and livestock were infected with virtually the same disease, called smallpox in humans and cowpox in cattle, the germ of cowpox being originally utilized for vaccination against smallpox. (2) The "terrible plague" (v. 3) was anthrax in animals, later transmitted to people as malignant pustule (anthrax). Untreated, anthrax is a fatal, infectious disease, chiefly of cattle and sheep, characterized by the formulation of hard lumps and ulcers and symptoms of collapse. In humans, without modern therapy, it is often fatal.

The Plague of Hail

13 Then the LORD said to Moses, "Get up early in the morning, confront Pharaoh and say to him, 'This is
what the LORD, the God of the Hebrews, says: Let my people go, so that they may worship[t] me, 14 or this time I
will send the full force of my plagues against you and against your officials and your people, so you may know[u]
that there is no one like[v] me in all the earth. 15 For by now I could have stretched out my hand and struck you
and your people[w] with a plague that would have wiped you off the earth. 16 But I have raised you up[a] for this
very purpose,[x] that I might show you my power[y] and that my name might be proclaimed in all the earth. 17 You
still set yourself against my people and will not let them go. 18 Therefore, at this time tomorrow I will send the
worst hailstorm[z] that has ever fallen on Egypt, from the day it was founded till now.[a] 19 Give an order now to
bring your livestock and everything you have in the field to a place of shelter, because the hail will fall on every man and animal that has not been brought in and is still out in the field, and they will die.' "
20 Those officials of Pharaoh who feared[b] the word of the LORD hurried to bring their slaves and their
livestock inside. 21 But those who ignored the word of the LORD left their slaves and livestock in the field.
22 Then the LORD said to Moses, "Stretch out your hand toward the sky so that hail will fall all over
Egypt—on men and animals and on everything growing in the fields of Egypt." 23 When Moses stretched
out his staff toward the sky, the LORD sent thunder[c] and hail,[d] and lightning flashed down to the ground.

9:13 [t]Ex 8:20
9:14 [u]Ex 8:10 [v]2Sa 7:22; 1Ch 17:20; Ps 86:8; Isa 46:9; Jer 10:6
9:15 [w]Ex 3:20
9:16 [x]Pr 16:4 [y]Ro 9:17*
9:18 [z]ver 23
9:18 [a]ver 24
9:20 [b]Pr 13:13
9:23 [c]Ps 18:13 [d]Jos 10:11; Ps 78:47; 105:32; Isa 30:30; Eze 38:22; Rev 8:7; 16:21

[a] 16 Or *have spared you*

9:13–35 Hail (which rarely occurs in Egypt) descended in unusual violence. Egyptians who feared the word of the Lord brought their cattle in out of the coming storm. Those who did not do so lost them all to the violent hail. The hand of God directed its local incidence. The season must have been January or February.

9:23–24 Hailstorms, though rare, sometimes take place in the Near East in the spring and summer and do considerable damage to crops, even harming property and endangering life. Plagues of hail are mentioned here and in Joshua 10:11. The prophets spoke of hail as a means of punishing the wicked (Isa 28:2; Eze 38:22; Rev 8:7; 11:19).

ANCIENT TEXTS AND ARTIFACTS

The Rosetta Stone and the Deciphering of Hieroglyphs

The Rosetta Stone
Preserving Bible Times; © Dr. James C. Martin; permission of The British Museum

EXODUS 9 In 1799 Napoleon's soldiers discovered an inscribed stone near the town of Rosetta on the Nile delta (see the delta region in the upper left of the "Egypt" map on p. 346, just south of the Mediterranean Sea). Known as the Rosetta Stone, this **stele** helped to solve the mystery of the Egyptian writing system known as **hieroglyphics**, thereby providing the key to understanding much of the Egyptian history and culture recorded on ancient monuments.

Originally inscribed to honor **Ptolemy** V Epiphanes (203–181 B.C.), this stone is divided into three sections called **registers**, each of which contains the same text but in a different writing system (**hieroglyphics**, **demotic** and Greek). At the time of its discovery only the bottom, Greek register could be read. It described how Egyptian priests, in gratitude for how Ptolemy had endowed their temple, declared him to be a god and ruler of Egypt forever. Soon several scholars isolated the royal names mentioned in the stone's hieroglyphics on the basis of their Greek equivalents. The most exciting breakthrough in decoding the stele's hieroglyphics, however, occurred when a historian named J.F. Champollion realized that the writing included symbols not only for letters but also for syllable-like sounds and even for entire words. Champollion announced in 1822 that he had substantially solved the riddle. Since then Egyptologists have steadily enhanced our knowledge of hieroglyphics and, as a consequence, of ancient Egypt.

So the LORD rained hail on the land of Egypt; 24 hail fell and lightning flashed back and forth. It was the
worst storm in all the land of Egypt since it had become a nation. 25 Throughout Egypt hail struck every-
thing in the fields—both men and animals; it beat down everything growing in the fields and stripped
every tree.[e] 26 The only place it did not hail was the land of Goshen,[f] where the Israelites were.[g]
27 Then Pharaoh summoned Moses and Aaron. "This time I have sinned,"[h] he said to them. "The LORD
is in the right,[i] and I and my people are in the wrong. 28 Pray[j] to the LORD, for we have had enough thun-
der and hail. I will let you go;[k] you don't have to stay any longer."
29 Moses replied, "When I have gone out of the city, I will spread out my hands[l] in prayer to the LORD.
The thunder will stop and there will be no more hail, so you may know that the earth[m] is the LORD's. 30 But
I know that you and your officials still do not fear the LORD God."
31 (The flax and barley[n] were destroyed, since the barley had headed and the flax was in bloom. 32 The
wheat and spelt, however, were not destroyed, because they ripen later.)
33 Then Moses left Pharaoh and went out of the city. He spread out his hands toward the LORD; the thun-
der and hail stopped, and the rain no longer poured down on the land. 34 When Pharaoh saw that the rain
and hail and thunder had stopped, he sinned again: He and his officials hardened their hearts. 35 So Phar-
aoh's heart[o] was hard and he would not let the Israelites go, just as the LORD had said through Moses.

The Plague of Locusts

10 Then the LORD said to Moses, "Go to Pharaoh, for I have hardened his heart[p] and the hearts of his
officials so that I may perform these miraculous signs[q] of mine among them 2 that you may tell
your children[r] and grandchildren how I dealt harshly with the Egyptians and how I performed my signs
among them, and that you may know that I am the LORD."
3 So Moses and Aaron went to Pharaoh and said to him, "This is what the LORD, the God of the He-
brews, says: 'How long will you refuse to humble[s] yourself before me? Let my people go, so that they may
worship me. 4 If you refuse to let them go, I will bring locusts[t] into your country tomorrow. 5 They will
cover the face of the ground so that it cannot be seen. They will devour what little you have left[u] after the
hail, including every tree that is growing in your fields. 6 They will fill your houses and those of all your
officials and all the Egyptians—something neither your fathers nor your forefathers have ever seen from
the day they settled in this land till now.' " Then Moses turned and left Pharaoh.
7 Pharaoh's officials said to him, "How long will this man be a snare[v] to us? Let the people go, so that
they may worship the LORD their God. Do you not yet realize that Egypt is ruined?"[w]
8 Then Moses and Aaron were brought back to Pharaoh. "Go, worship[x] the LORD your God," he said.
"But just who will be going?"
9 Moses answered, "We will go with our young and old, with our sons and daughters, and with our
flocks and herds, because we are to celebrate a festival to the LORD."
10 Pharaoh said, "The LORD be with you—if I let you go, along with your women and children! Clear-
ly you are bent on evil.[a] 11 No! Have only the men go; and worship the LORD, since that's what you have
been asking for." Then Moses and Aaron were driven out of Pharaoh's presence.
12 And the LORD said to Moses, "Stretch out your hand[y] over Egypt so that locusts will swarm over the
land and devour everything growing in the fields, everything left by the hail."
13 So Moses stretched out his staff over Egypt, and the LORD made an east wind blow across the land
all that day and all that night. By morning the wind had brought the locusts;[z] 14 they invaded all Egypt
and settled down in every area of the country in great numbers. Never before had there been such a
plague of locusts,[a] nor will there ever be again. 15 They covered all the ground until it was black. They de-
voured[b] all that was left after the hail—everything growing in the fields and the fruit on the trees. Noth-
ing green remained on tree or plant in all the land of Egypt.
16 Pharaoh quickly summoned Moses and Aaron and said, "I have sinned[c] against the LORD your God
and against you. 17 Now forgive my sin once more and pray[d] to the LORD your God to take this deadly
plague away from me."

9:25 [e] Ps 105:32-33
9:26 [f] ver 4 [g] Ex 8:22; 10:23; 11:7; 12:13
9:27 [h] Ex 10:16 [i] 2Ch 12:6; Ps 129:4; La 1:18
9:28 [j] Ex 10:17 [k] Ex 8:8
9:29 [l] 1Ki 8:22, 38; Ps 143:6; Isa 1:15 [m] Ex 19:5; Ps 24:1; 1Co 10:26
9:31 [n] Ru 1:22; 2:23
9:35 [o] Ex 4:21
10:1 [p] Ex 4:21 [q] Ex 7:3
10:2 [r] Ex 12:26-27; 13:8,14; Dt 4:9; Ps 44:1; 78:4,5; Joel 1:3
10:3 [s] 1Ki 21:29; Jas 4:10; 1Pe 5:6
10:4 [t] Rev 9:3
10:5 [u] Ex 9:32; Joel 1:4
10:7 [v] Ex 23:33; Jos 23:13; 1Sa 18:21; Ecc 7:26 [w] Ex 8:19
10:8 [x] Ex 8:8
10:12 [y] Ex 7:19
10:13 [z] Ps 105:34
10:14 [a] Ps 78:46; Joel 2:1-11,25
10:15 [b] ver 5; Ps 105:34-35
10:16 [c] Ex 9:27
10:17 [d] Ex 8:8

[a] 10 Or *Be careful, trouble is in store for you!*

9:29 Archaeologists have found statues of men praying with hands upraised at several ancient sites in the Middle East.
9:32 Grains of spelt, a member of the grass family, have been discovered in ancient Egyptian tombs. Although spelt is inferior to wheat, it grows well in poorer, drier soil.
10:4 In March or April swarms of migratory locusts were carried in by the prevailing east winds (see v. 13). At this phase (see "Locusts in the Ancient Near East" on p. 1438) locusts are immature and at their most voracious stage. As is true of susceptible areas today, locust plagues were greatly feared in ancient times. They became a symbol of divine judgment (see Joel 1:4–7; 2:1–11; Am 7:1–3).

10:18 [e]Ex 8:30 18Moses then left Pharaoh and prayed to the LORD.[e] 19And the LORD changed the wind to a very strong
west wind, which caught up the locusts and carried them into the Red Sea.[a] Not a locust was left any-
10:20 [f]Ex 4:21; 11:10 where in Egypt. 20But the LORD hardened Pharaoh's heart,[f] and he would not let the Israelites go.

The Plague of Darkness

10:21 [g]Dt 28:29 21Then the LORD said to Moses, "Stretch out your hand toward the sky so that darkness[g] will spread
over Egypt—darkness that can be felt." 22So Moses stretched out his hand toward the sky, and total dark-
10:22 [h]Ps 105:28; Rev 16:10 ness[h] covered all Egypt for three days. 23No one could see anyone else or leave his place for three days.
Yet all the Israelites had light in the places where they lived.[i]
10:23 [i]Ex 8:22 10:24 [j]ver 8-10 24Then Pharaoh summoned Moses and said, "Go, worship the LORD. Even your women and children[j]
may go with you; only leave your flocks and herds behind."
25But Moses said, "You must allow us to have sacrifices and burnt offerings to present to the LORD our God.
26Our livestock too must go with us; not a hoof is to be left behind. We have to use some of them in worship-
ing the LORD our God, and until we get there we will not know what we are to use to worship the LORD."
10:27 [k]ver 20; Ex 4:21 27But the LORD hardened Pharaoh's heart,[k] and he was not willing to let them go. 28Pharaoh said to Mo-
ses, "Get out of my sight! Make sure you do not appear before me again! The day you see my face you will die."
10:29 [l]Heb 11:27 29"Just as you say," Moses replied, "I will never appear[l] before you again."

[a] *19* Hebrew *Yam Suph*; that is, Sea of Reeds

10:21–23 A sandstorm, accentuated by the dust-bowl condition of the land and borne on the west wind that drove off the locusts, may well have brought a tawny, choking darkness. The plague of darkness was almost certainly a challenge against Ra (sometimes spelled Re), an Egyptian sun god. This would have been a direct confrontation against Pharaoh, since Egyptian kings were referred to as sons of Ra.

Some suggest that the ninth plague was meant to demonstrate Yahweh's superiority over Ra (or Re), the sun god (12:21–23). It is interesting that Joseph, after having been made food administrator of the land of Egypt, married the daughter of the priest of On of the cult of Ra (Ge 41:45).

ARCHAEOLOGICAL SITES

THE PALACE OF RAMESES

EXODUS 10 During their Egyptian sojourn the Israelites lived at Rameses, whether or not the city was called by this name at the time or only later[1] (Ge 47:11; Ex 1:11; 12:37). Various Biblical references suggest that a royal residence was located nearby:

- Pharaoh's daughter, who regularly bathed in the Nile River, with the help of her slave girl discovered the infant Moses in the water in a "basket among the reeds" (Ex 2:5; Ac 7:20–21).
- Moses, after having been reared in the palace as a prince, easily wandered to the area where the Israelites were laboring (Ex 2:11).
- The Israelite foremen were able to meet face-to-face with Pharaoh (5:14–15).
- Moses often held audience with the pharaoh during the plagues, and there is no indication that he had to travel any great distance to do so.

Critics once believed that the royal residence was located in Memphis, the administrative capital of Egypt approximately 75 miles (121 km) southwest of the site of Rameses (see Memphis on "Egypt" map on p. 346).

Excavations have revealed, however, that the region where Rameses was likely located served as an important commercial and military center.[2] During the 1990s an enormous royal compound was discovered on the southern bank of the eastern branch of the Nile River. Used throughout the Eighteenth Dynasty (c. 1550–1300 B.C.), the compound consisted of a fortress and a palace. The fortress was constructed on a 230 foot by 150 foot (61 x 46 m) platform approximately 100 feet (30.5 m) from the riverbank. A ramp on the east side led to a gate in a fortification wall, providing ready access to the river. The palace, south of the fortress, boasted thick walls, storage magazines (areas for storing weapons), corridors and even bathrooms. Both structures were located inside a walled compound that included a temple, workshops and a military camp. Moses probably meandered the halls of these buildings, and the pharaoh quite likely mobilized his 600 chariots to pursue the Israelites from this location (14:7).

[1]See "The Store Cities of Pithom and Rameses" on page 86. [2]But see again "The Store Cities of Pithom and Rameses" on page 86 for a discussion of uncertainty regarding their precise locations.

A Breakdown of Ancient Egyptian History

Pharaoh Tutankhamen (King Tut)
Preserving Bible Times; © Dr. James C. Martin; permission of The Cairo Museum

EXODUS 11 It is helpful for understanding the history of ancient Egypt to divide this enormously protracted time span into shorter, more manageable segments. Following the lead of a third-century B.C. Egyptian historian named Manetho, Egyptian history is typically divided into 30 dynasties.

Pre-Dynastic Egypt (prior to 3000 B.C.)

During this era regional societies and cultures began to emerge. Agriculture, pottery making and the construction of stone monuments were well established by the end of this period.[1] Loose confederations eventually gave way to more centralized power.

Archaic Egypt (First and Second Dynasties; 3000–2700 B.C.)

Meni (or Menes), a semi-legendary ruler from southern Egypt, established the First Dynasty. Memphis became the capital city,[2] and the pharaohs were preoccupied with holding together their extensive kingdom. **Hieroglyphics**, the distinctive Egyptian style in art and writing, became well established.

Old Kingdom Period (Third through Sixth Dynasties; 2700–2160 B.C.)

The pyramids and the great sphinx were built, the study of medicine flourished and works such as the Proverbs of Ptahhotep were produced.[3] Pharaohs ventured outside Egypt on military campaigns to the Sinai and Libya.

First Intermediate Period (Seventh through Tenth Dynasties; 2160–2010 B.C.)

Central authority collapsed, dynasties competed and local lords held sway in various areas. This period produced significant works of pessimistic literature.[4]

Middle Kingdom Period (Eleventh and Twelfth Dynasties; 2106–1786 B.C., overlapping the First Intermediate period)

The pharaohs reestablished central authority, and Joseph's administration brought much Egyptian land under the pharaoh's direct control (Ge 47:13–26). Some historians, in fact, suggest that Joseph played a significant role in bringing about the end of Egyptian feudal power.

Second Intermediate Period (Thirteenth through Seventeenth Dynasties; 1786–1550 B.C.)

Centralized authority again collapsed. Dynasties Fifteen and Sixteen were **Hyksos** (ruled by Semitic rulers who took control of Lower—northern—Egypt). The relationship of the Hyksos to the exodus is much debated.[5]

New Kingdom Period (Eighteenth through Twentieth Dynasties; 1550–1069 B.C.)

Established by Ahmose, who drove out the last of the Hyksos, the powerful New Kingdom became an empire reaching through **Canaan** into Syria. Each of the two greatest pharaohs of this time, Thutmose III (c. 1479–1425 B.C.) and **Rameses II** (c. 1279–1212 B.C.), has been suggested as the pharaoh of the exodus. Although Thutmose III fits reasonably well with Biblical chronology (Jdg 11:26; 1Ki 6:1), Rameses appeared too late for this scheme.[6]

Third Intermediate Period (Twenty-first through Twenty-fifth Dynasties; 1069–656 B.C.)

A considerably weakened Egypt entered this era. At times there were rival pharaohs, and in other instances outsiders ruled. Even so, vigorous rulers did come to power, including the Libyan pharaoh Sheshonk I (c. 945–924)—the Shishak in 1 Kings 14:25.[7]

Remaining ancient Egyptian historical periods include the Saite-Persian period (Twenty-sixth through Thirtieth Dynasties; 654–332 B.C.; a "Thirty-first Dynasty" is sometimes included), the Ptolemaic period (332–30 B.C.) and the Roman period (after 30 B.C.).

During the Roman period Egyptian power was briefly ascendant again under Saite rulers (who ruled from Sais, in the western delta). Hoping to curb the rising power of the **Babylonians** and the Medes, the Saite Neco II (c. 610–595 B.C.) drove his army north through Israel, defeating and killing King Josiah of Judah in the process[8] (2Ki 23:29). Nebuchadnezzar of Babylon[9] defeated Neco II at Carchemish (605 B.C.) and drove him back into Egypt. No longer a formidable power, Egypt was annexed into the **Persian Empire** by Cambyses in 525 B.C. The subsequent fall of the Persian Empire to Alexander the Great led to the Greek takeover of Egypt in 332 B.C. After Alexander's death in 323 B.C., Ptolemy I (a Greek general) seized Egypt, and his dynasty ruled until the death of the last **Ptolemaic** ruler, the famous Cleopatra VII[10] (c. 52–30 B.C.). After that, Egypt became a Roman province.

[1]See "Pottery-Making in Bible Times" on page 1223. [2]See "Memphis" on page 1270. [3]See "Ancient Near Eastern Wisdom" on page 960. [4]See "The Harper Songs From the Tomb of Neferhotep" on page 1015, "The Harper Song From the Tomb of King Intef" on page 1018 and "Calamity and Distress in Ipuwer" on page 1309. [5]See "The Hyksos and the Exodus" on page 99 and "The Hyksos and the Old Testament" on page 121. [6]See "The Pharaoh of the Exodus" on page 98. [7]See "The Campaign of Shishak" on page 635. [8]See "Josiah, Zechariah and Neco II" on page 663. [9]See "Nebuchadnezzar" on page 571. [10]See "The Ptolemies" on page 1399.

The Plague on the Firstborn

11 Now the LORD had said to Moses, "I will bring one more plague on Pharaoh and on Egypt. After
that, he will let you go from here, and when he does, he will drive you out completely. 2 Tell the peo-
11:2 [m]Ex 3:21,22 ple that men and women alike are to ask their neighbors for articles of silver and gold."[m] 3 (The LORD
11:3 [n]Dt 34:11 made the Egyptians favorably disposed toward the people, and Moses himself was highly regarded[n] in
Egypt by Pharaoh's officials and by the people.)
11:4 [o]Ex 12:29 4 So Moses said, "This is what the LORD says: 'About midnight[o] I will go throughout Egypt. 5 Every first-
11:5 [p]Ex 4:23; Ps 78:51 born[p] son in Egypt will die, from the firstborn son of Pharaoh, who sits on the throne, to the firstborn son
of the slave girl, who is at her hand mill, and all the firstborn of the cattle as well. 6 There will be loud wail-
11:6 [q]Ex 12:30 ing[q] throughout Egypt—worse than there has ever been or ever will be again. 7 But among the Israelites
11:7 [r]Ex 8:22 not a dog will bark at any man or animal.' Then you will know that the LORD makes a distinction[r] between
11:8 [s]Ex 12:31-33 Egypt and Israel. 8 All these officials of yours will come to me, bowing down before me and saying, 'Go,[s]
you and all the people who follow you!' After that I will leave." Then Moses, hot with anger, left Pharaoh.
11:9 [t]Ex 7:4 9 The LORD had said to Moses, "Pharaoh will refuse to listen[t] to you—so that my wonders may be mul-
tiplied in Egypt." 10 Moses and Aaron performed all these wonders before Pharaoh, but the LORD hardened
11:10 [u]Ex 4:21; 10:20,27 Pharaoh's heart,[u] and he would not let the Israelites go out of his country.

The Passover

12:2 [v]Ex 13:4; Dt 16:1 12 The LORD said to Moses and Aaron in Egypt, 2 "This month is to be for you the first month,[v] the
first month of your year. 3 Tell the whole community of Israel that on the tenth day of this month
each man is to take a lamb[a] for his family, one for each household. 4 If any household is too small for a
whole lamb, they must share one with their nearest neighbor, having taken into account the number of
people there are. You are to determine the amount of lamb needed in accordance with what each person
12:5 [w]Lev 22:18-21; Heb 9:14 will eat. 5 The animals you choose must be year-old males without defect,[w] and you may take them from
12:6 [x]Lev 23:5; Nu 9:1-3,5,11 the sheep or the goats. 6 Take care of them until the fourteenth day of the month,[x] when all the people of
[y]Ex 16:12; Dt 16:4,6 the community of Israel must slaughter them at twilight.[y] 7 Then they are to take some of the blood and
12:8 [z]Ex 34:25; Nu 9:12 put it on the sides and tops of the doorframes of the houses where they eat the lambs. 8 That same night[z]
[a]Dt 16:7 [b]Nu 9:11 they are to eat the meat roasted[a] over the fire, along with bitter herbs,[b] and bread made without yeast.[c]
[c]Dt 16:3-4; 1Co 5:8 9 Do not eat the meat raw or cooked in water, but roast it over the fire—head, legs and inner parts. 10 Do
12:10 [d]Ex 23:18; 34:25 not leave any of it till morning;[d] if some is left till morning, you must burn it. 11 This is how you are to eat
it: with your cloak tucked into your belt, your sandals on your feet and your staff in your hand. Eat it in
12:11 [e]Dt 16:3 [f]ver 13,21,27,43; Dt 16:1 haste;[e] it is the LORD's Passover.[f]
12 "On that same night I will pass through[g] Egypt and strike down every firstborn—both men and
12:12 [g]Ex 11:4; Am 5:17 [h]Nu 33:4 [i]Ex 6:2 animals—and I will bring judgment on all the gods[h] of Egypt. I am the LORD.[i] 13 The blood will be a sign
for you on the houses where you are; and when I see the blood, I will pass over you. No destructive plague
will touch you when I strike Egypt.
12:14 [j]Ex 13:9 [k]ver 17,24; 14 "This is a day you are to commemorate;[j] for the generations to come you shall celebrate it as a fes-
Ex 13:5,10; 2Ki 23:21 tival to the LORD—a lasting ordinance.[k] 15 For seven days you are to eat bread made without yeast.[l] On
12:15 [l]Ex 13:6-7; 23:15; 34:18; the first day remove the yeast from your houses, for whoever eats anything with yeast in it from the first
Lev 23:6; Dt 16:3 [m]Ge 17:14; Nu 9:13 day through the seventh must be cut off[m] from Israel. 16 On the first day hold a sacred assembly, and an-
other one on the seventh day. Do no work at all on these days, except to prepare food for everyone to
eat—that is all you may do.
17 "Celebrate the Feast of Unleavened Bread, because it was on this very day that I brought your
12:17 [n]ver 41; Ex 13:3 divisions out of Egypt.[n] Celebrate this day as a lasting ordinance for the generations to come. 18 In

[a] 3 The Hebrew word can mean *lamb* or *kid*; also in verse 4.

11:1—12:30 Even if these deaths were due to bubonic plague, as many suspect, the incidence on the firstborn alone remains unexplained. Bubonic plague is said to afflict the strongest individuals, but this again does not explain why only the firstborn died.

12:2 The precise geographical and chronological details of this period have been difficult to determine, but new information from vast amounts of fragmentary archaeological and inscriptional evidence has recently been discovered. Hittite cuneiform documents are similar in content to the ancient covenant formula governing Israel's "contract" with God at Mount Sinai. The Late Bronze Age (c. 1550–1200 B.C.) was a time of major social migrations. The harsh control of the Egyptians over the Semites in the eastern Nile delta is illustrated by a system of brick-making quotas imposed on the labor force, often the landless, low-class "Apiru" (see the note on Ge 14:13). Numerous Canaanite towns were violently destroyed. New populations, including the "Sea Peoples," made their presence felt in Anatolia, Egypt, Canaan, Transjordan and elsewhere in the eastern Mediterranean.

12:14–20 Yeast ("leaven" in some translations) was excluded from the Passover (12:14–20; 23:15; 34:18; Dt 16:2–4) because of Israel's haste in leaving Egypt (Ex 12:11,29; Dt 16:3). However, the Passover as a type of Christ (see note on yeast at Ex 29:2), who was wholly free of corruption, must also be taken into account here (cf. 1Co 5:7–8).

THE DATE OF THE EXODUS

EXODUS 12 According to 1 Kings 6:1 temple construction began during the fourth year of Solomon's reign (conventionally dated to c. 965 B.C.),[1] which is also specified as being 480 years after Israel's **exodus** from Egypt. Based upon this date, the exodus would have occurred around 1445 B.C. (the "early date" view).[2]

In contrast, some historians date the exodus to approximately 1260 B.C. (the "late-date" view). They believe that the number 480, above, symbolizes 12 generations, each averaging 40 years in duration. By substituting 25 years for 40 years on the grounds that this is a more realistic figure for a single generation, they reduce the interval from 480 to approximately 300 years. Various other dates for the exodus have been suggested, but most have garnered little support among scholars.

Several lines of Biblical evidence support the early date view:

- Acts 7:29–30 records that Moses spent 40 years in Midian,[3] and Exodus 2:23 and 4:19 suggest that the pharaoh of the oppression, who sought Moses' life, had died before Moses' return to Egypt. Thutmose III reigned for more than 40 years. If his son, Amenhotep II, was the pharaoh of the exodus, his rule (mid-fifteenth century B.C.) corresponds to the early date for the exodus.
- Thutmose IV followed Amenhotep II. In an inscription called the Dream Stele, Thutmose IV implied that the "firstborn" son of Amenhotep II died before ascending to the throne. Some scholars have speculated that this son may have been a victim of the tenth plague.
- As recorded in Judges 11:26, Jephthah (c. 1100 B.C.) claimed in a message to the Ammonite king that Israel had already been in the land for 300 years. This suggests that the conquest must have taken place around 1400 B.C. and that the exodus had occurred at approximately 1440 B.C.
- The "late date" would require compression of the judges' activity into 170 years, while the "early date" allows for 350 years, a more reasonable time frame in light of the number of individual judges presented in the book of Judges.
- Acts 13:19–20 assigns about 450 years to the period between Joshua's conquest of **Canaan** and the judgeship of Samuel, a time frame that does not fit the late-date view.
- Under the late-date theory, Israel entered the land between 1250 and 1220 B.C. But these dates are uncomfortably close to that of Merneptah's **Stele**.[4] This monument describes Israel as a people defeated by Merneptah (either c. 1232 or c. 1207 B.C.). It is difficult to see how this monument could match the late date for the exodus, since the stele implies that Israel was well established in the region now called Palestine by the date of Merneptah's victories. Using the late-date view, the Israelites at that time would still have been in the wilderness or just beginning their conquest of Canaan.

Opponents of the early date argue that archaeological evidence at key sites dating from the fifteenth century B.C. does not match what the Bible records about the conquest.[5] Most archaeologists would even argue that there is little evidence placing Israel in the land of Canaan prior to the twelfth century B.C. Proponents of a fifteenth-century B.C. exodus, on the other hand, argue that some reinterpretation of archaeological data is necessary. Still, archaeological evidence supporting a later date for the exodus and conquest is widely regarded as being scanty.

Unfortunately, no single theory completely harmonizes archaeological evidence with Biblical claims. Until more definitive interpretations of archaeological findings are forthcoming, it is best to hold, as most historians do, to an earlier date for the exodus on the basis of the Biblical chronology described above.

A stepped pyramid
Preserving Bible Times; © Dr. James C. Martin

[1]See "Solomon's Temple and Other Ancient Temples" on page 620. [2]See "The Pharaoh of the Exodus" on page 98. [3]See "Midian" on page 92. [4]See "The Merneptah Stele" on page 360. [5]See "The Walls of Jericho" on page 312.

12:18 [o]ver 2; Lev 23:5-8; Nu 28:16-25 the first month[o] you are to eat bread made without yeast, from the evening of the fourteenth day un-
til the evening of the twenty-first day. 19 For seven days no yeast is to be found in your houses. And
whoever eats anything with yeast in it must be cut off from the community of Israel, whether he is
an alien or native-born. 20 Eat nothing made with yeast. Wherever you live, you must eat unleavened
bread."

21 Then Moses summoned all the elders of Israel and said to them, "Go at once and select the an-
12:21 [p]ver 11; Mk 14:12-16 imals for your families and slaughter the Passover[p] lamb. 22 Take a bunch of hyssop, dip it into the
12:22 [q]ver 7; Heb 11:28 blood in the basin and put some of the blood[q] on the top and on both sides of the doorframe. Not
one of you shall go out the door of his house until morning. 23 When the LORD goes through the land
12:23 [r]Rev 7:3 [s]ver 13 [t]1Co 10:10; Heb 11:28 to strike down the Egyptians, he will see the blood[r] on the top and sides of the doorframe and will
pass over[s] that doorway, and he will not permit the destroyer[t] to enter your houses and strike you
down.

24 "Obey these instructions as a lasting ordinance for you and your descendants. 25 When you enter
12:26 [u]Ex 10:2; 13:8,14-15; Jos 4:6 the land that the LORD will give you as he promised, observe this ceremony. 26 And when your children[u]
ask you, 'What does this ceremony mean to you?' 27 then tell them, 'It is the Passover[v] sacrifice to the LORD,
12:27 [v]ver 11 [w]Ex 4:31 who passed over the houses of the Israelites in Egypt and spared our homes when he struck down the
Egyptians.' " Then the people bowed down and worshiped.[w] 28 The Israelites did just what the LORD com-
manded Moses and Aaron.

12:29 [x]Ex 11:4 [y]Ex 4:23; Ps 78:51 [z]Ex 9:6 29 At midnight[x] the LORD struck down all the firstborn[y] in Egypt, from the firstborn of Pharaoh, who
sat on the throne, to the firstborn of the prisoner, who was in the dungeon, and the firstborn of all the
livestock[z] as well. 30 Pharaoh and all his officials and all the Egyptians got up during the night, and there
12:30 [a]Ex 11:6 was loud wailing[a] in Egypt, for there was not a house without someone dead.

The Exodus

31 During the night Pharaoh summoned Moses and Aaron and said, "Up! Leave my people, you and the
12:31 [b]Ex 8:8 Israelites! Go, worship[b] the LORD as you have requested. 32 Take your flocks and herds,[c] as you have said,
12:32 [c]Ex 10:9, 26 and go. And also bless me."

12:33 [d]Ps 105:38 33 The Egyptians urged the people to hurry and leave[d] the country. "For otherwise," they said, "we
will all die!" 34 So the people took their dough before the yeast was added, and carried it on their
shoulders in kneading troughs wrapped in clothing. 35 The Israelites did as Moses instructed and
12:35 [e]Ex 3:22 asked the Egyptians for articles of silver and gold[e] and for clothing. 36 The LORD had made the Egyp-
tians favorably disposed toward the people, and they gave them what they asked for; so they plun-
12:36 [f]Ex 3:22 dered[f] the Egyptians.

12:37 [g]Nu 33:3-5 [h]Ex 38:26; Nu 1:46; 11:13,21 37 The Israelites journeyed from Rameses to Succoth.[g] There were about six hundred thousand men[h]
on foot, besides women and children. 38 Many other people[i] went up with them, as well as large droves of
12:38 [i]Nu 11:4 livestock, both flocks and herds. 39 With the dough they had brought from Egypt, they baked cakes of un-
12:39 [j]ver 31-33; Ex 6:1; 11:1 leavened bread. The dough was without yeast because they had been driven out[j] of Egypt and did not
have time to prepare food for themselves.

12:40 [k]Ge 15:13; Ac 7:6; Gal 3:17 40 Now the length of time the Israelite people lived in Egypt[a] was 430 years.[k] 41 At the end of the 430 years,
12:41 [l]ver 17; Ex 6:26 [m]Ex 3:10 to the very day, all the LORD's divisions[l] left Egypt.[m] 42 Because the LORD kept vigil that night to bring them
12:42 [n]Ex 13:10; Dt 16:1,6 out of Egypt, on this night all the Israelites are to keep vigil to honor the LORD for the generations to come.[n]

Passover Restrictions

12:43 [o]ver 11 [p]ver 48; Nu 9:14 43 The LORD said to Moses and Aaron, "These are the regulations for the Passover:[o]
12:44 [q]Ge 17:12-13 "No foreigner[p] is to eat of it. 44 Any slave you have bought may eat of it after you have circumcised[q]
12:45 [r]Lev 22:10 him, 45 but a temporary resident and a hired worker[r] may not eat of it.

46 "It must be eaten inside one house; take none of the meat outside the house. Do not break any of the
12:46 [s]Nu 9:12; Jn 19:36* bones.[s] 47 The whole community of Israel must celebrate it.

48 "An alien living among you who wants to celebrate the LORD's Passover must have all the males in
12:48 [t]Nu 9:14 his household circumcised; then he may take part like one born in the land.[t] No uncircumcised male
12:49 [u]Nu 15:15-16,29; Gal 3:28 may eat of it. 49 The same law applies to the native-born and to the alien[u] living among you."

50 All the Israelites did just what the LORD had commanded Moses and Aaron. 51 And on that very day
12:51 [v]ver 41; Ex 6:26 the LORD brought the Israelites out of Egypt by their divisions.[v]

[a] 40 Masoretic Text; Samaritan Pentateuch and Septuagint *Egypt and Canaan*

THE ROUTE OF THE EXODUS: THE NORTHERN ROUTE THEORY

The route of the exodus
Photograph courtesy of © Dr. Gary Pratico

EXODUS 13 The itinerary of Israel's travels from Egypt to Mount Sinai (Ex 14–19; Nu 33) is little more to us than a list of obscure place-names. We know that the company moved from Rameses to Succoth, then on to Etham on the edge of the desert before proceeding to Pi Hahiroth, near Baal Zephon and Migdol. From there the procession passed through the Red Sea, stopping afterward at Marah and Elim; beside the Red Sea once again; alongside the Desert of Sin; at Dophkah, Alush and Rephidim; and in the region of Mount Sinai.[1] As specific as this itinerary is, interpreting it is much more difficult because no one knows the identities of many of these ancient place-names. In addition, there is confusion about the point at which the company crossed the Red Sea, as well as about the identity of the sea itself! Numerous routes have been proposed.

One theory argues for a more northerly **exodus** route, suggesting that the "sea" the Israelites crossed was actually Lake Sirbonis on the Mediterranean coast and that Mount Sinai was located in the northern Sinai Peninsula, perhaps synonymous with one of the mountains now named Jebel Helal, Jebel Kharif or Jebel Magharah. But God had explicitly prohibited such a route (Ex. 13:17), which would have led up the Mediterranean coast into Philistia.[2] This theory is not widely held at this time. See also "The Route of the Exodus: The Southern Route Theory" and "The Route of the Exodus: The Arabian Route Theory."

[1] See "The Location of Mount Sinai" on page 123. [2] See "The Archaeology of Philistia" on page 370.

THE ROUTE OF THE EXODUS: THE SOUTHERN ROUTE THEORY

EXODUS 13 A widely accepted view of the route of the exodus holds that Israel escaped Egypt near what is now the Wadi Tumilat and headed south into the Sinai peninsula. Before considering the viability of this route, however, it helps to consider two realities about the eastern delta during the **New Kingdom** period.

◆ The Egyptians fortified their northeastern frontier (the land between the Gulf of Suez and the Mediterranean Sea) to prevent waves of **Asiatic** migrants from Syria and **Canaan** from entering Egypt. The heaviest fortification was in the north, along the Mediterranean Sea, which provided the primary means of access into Egypt. For hundreds of years the Egyptians had struggled to bar the door to these alien peoples, and their recent experience with the **Hyksos** had only increased their fear and hatred of "Asiatics" (i.e., Semites).[1]

◆ A series of water boundaries between Egypt and the Sinai extended up from the Gulf of Suez to the Bitter Lakes and Lake Timsah. North of Lake Timsah travelers encountered a series of marshy bodies of water (now dry) called the Ballah Lakes. Evidence exists that a canal system extended from Lake Timsah to the Ballah Lakes and on to the Mediterranean. This system would have created a series of water obstacles in the isthmus between Egypt and the Sinai.

These considerations aside, according to this second theory the Israelites' itinerary would have been as follows:

Sandals and other household objects from Egypt
Preserving Bible Times; © Dr. James C. Martin; permission of The British Museum

◆ Rameses is presumed to be on the site of Qantir in the eastern delta.[2]

◆ Succoth, the first stop, is near modern Tell el-Maskhuta. Located at the eastern end of the Wadi Tumilat, southeast of Rameses, Succoth reflects the Egyptian name, Tjeku. Each of these names refers both to a central fortress and to the general region around it.[3]

◆ Etham is the next proposed site, but no such place is known in this vicinity. In addition, Etham under this scenario is notoriously difficult to locate. According to this theory the Israelites arrived here *before* the crossing of the Red Sea, while we know from Numbers 33:7–8 that they passed through the "Desert of Etham" immediately *after* the Red Sea crossing.

◆ Pi Hahiroth was near Baal Zephon and Migdol. These three names are obscure, but some scholars suggest that Pi Hahiroth, because it can be translated "mouth of the canals," was located on the northern edge of Lake Timsah where it joined the canal system. Thus the name could relate to the canal system in the region north of the Gulf of Suez.

◆ After leaving Pi Hahiroth, Israel according to this paradigm crossed the Red Sea. According to Exodus 14:21 a strong east wind blew all night long, dividing the sea to allow the Israelites—but not the pursuing Egyptians—to cross. To complicate the situation, the identity of the Red Sea itself is disputed.[4]

◆ Having crossed the sea the Israelites headed to Mount Sinai. If the Red Sea was in fact Lake Timsah or the northern tip of the Gulf of Suez, Mount Sinai was probably Jebel Musa ("Mountain of Moses") in southern Sinai.

◆ The other locales leading up to the mountain (Marah, Elim, Dophkah and Rephidim) would, according to this theory, all have been in southwestern Sinai. Again, it is vital to recognize that locating any or all of these sites is at this point a highly speculative endeavor.

Of the three routes mentioned (see articles on the other two theories), this one is the most widely espoused, but it too has a number of serious difficulties.[5] For a depiction of the exodus route that is based on the "southern route" theory (with minor variations; *many* different routes have been proposed), see "Map 3" at the back of this Bible.

[1]See "The Hyksos and the Old Testament" on page 121. [2]See "The Store Cites of Pithom and Rameses" on page 86. [3]See "Succoth/Tell Deir Alla" on page 56. [4]See "The Location of the Red Sea" on page 110. [5]See, for example, the discussion in "The Location of Mount Sinai" on page 123.

THE LOCATION OF THE RED SEA

EXODUS 13 The identity of the Red Sea itself is disputed. The Hebrew name for this body of water is *yam suph*. The word *yam* means "sea" and *suph* means "reed." The Septuagint (early Greek translation of the OT), however, translates *suph* as "red." Thus it is unclear whether the reference is to the Red Sea or the Reed Sea.

Still, there is no evidence that people ever called any body of water in the Suez region the Reed Sea. The only specific use of *yam suph* in the Old Testament is found in 1 Kings 9:26, where the reference is to the Gulf of Aqaba on the eastern side of the Sinai. Some historians argue that the Israelites considered all of these bodies of water together (i.e., the Gulf of Aqaba; the modern Red Sea; the Gulf of Suez; and the string of bodies of water extending northward from the Suez, including the Bitter Lakes and Lake Timsah) to be the *yam suph*. If so, a lake between the Suez and the Mediterranean Sea could have been considered part of the greater *yam suph*. This would appear, however, to be an unwarranted assumption because no evidence exists that the Israelites considered these diverse bodies of water together to constitute the *yam suph*.

Today, many believe that the most likely candidate for the Red Sea would appear to have been Lake Timsah—although other lakes and the northern tip of the Gulf of Suez also are possibilities. There are, however, significant problems with this interpretation, and an alternative viewpoint places the *yam suph* in the same place at which 1 Kings 9:26 puts it: at the Gulf of Aqaba.[1]

[1]See "The Wind Set-Down Hypothesis" on page 111.

The shore of the modern Red Sea
Photograph courtesy of © Dr. Gary Pratico

THE WIND SET-DOWN HYPOTHESIS

EXODUS 13 The crossing of the Red Sea is a remarkable Old Testament miracle. The Biblical narrative relies on the water's having been shallow enough that a powerful east wind blowing all night could have pushed it back, yet deep enough that pursuing chariot forces would have drowned when the waters ultimately closed in. The Bible specifically records that God used nature (the east wind) to effect this miracle, and any credible explanation must factor in that natural phenomenon.

A shallow marsh (as some have proposed) would not have sufficed, because even if one night of wind could have dried it out so that chariots would have become mired in the mud, no one would have drowned in such shallow water.

Physicist Colin Humphreys suggests that a phenomenon known as "wind set-down" satisfies the Biblical account. This occurs when a strong, steady wind blows along a lengthy body of water that is fairly long relative to its width. The water level drops significantly on the windward side, while a wall of water is pushed up on the lee side. If wind continues to blow across the length of the sea, the drag of the water causes a gap to open up and expose the sea floor. The phenomenon is observed today in various bodies of water around the world when wind conditions and the layout of the water are right.

Among the candidates for the possible location of the Red Sea, only the Gulf of Aqaba[1] could have allowed such wind set-down to occur, since the body of water needed to be long and narrow relative to its length in order for this phenomenon to have taken place. The east wind the Bible describes could have been either a northeast or a southeast wind (ancient Hebrew has no specific word for either). Since the Gulf of Aqaba is oriented northeast to southwest, a northeast wind would have pushed the waters down along the Aqaba.

Humphreys also suggests that the name Red Sea could be accounted for by the red coral that grows in the Gulf of Aqaba, whereas the name Sea of Reeds could be explained by the growth of reed plants around the northern shore.

In contrast, the lakes north of the Gulf of Suez are too small for such a large wind set-down of water, and the Gulf of Suez is oriented in the wrong direction. A northwest wind would have been required for a wind set-down in the Suez.

[1]See "The Route of the Exodus: The Arabian Route Theory" on page 112.

MODELS OF RELATING SCIENCE TO THEOLOGY AND THE BIBLE

Model	Explanation
Conflict	Science and theology deal with many of the same issues but offer competing, incompatible views. For example, the Bible describes the origin of the earth in terms that are irreconcilable with modern science, and people must opt for one explanation or the other. Both evolutionists and "young earth" creationists follow this model, although they stand on opposite sides of the issue.
Complementarity	Science and theology deal with different areas. The Bible focuses on the ultimate cause of all things (God) and on the significance of creation, whereas science deals with physical processes. The Bible's purpose in relating the incident of Israel's Red Sea crossing has nothing to do with documenting scientific fact.
Concordist	Science and theology both describe the origin of the world, as well as later events, such as the Red Sea crossing, identified as either "natural" or "miraculous," depending upon perspective. But the statements found, for example, in Genesis 1 and the descriptions of the earth's origins found in science can be reconciled. People who adhere to this concept try to extract scientific information from Biblical verses and then demonstrate that modern, scientific theories are in agreement with those readings. Those who believe that each "day" of Genesis 1 represents a long period of time are following this model.

Adapted from *Old Testament Today*, p. 111

THE ROUTE OF THE EXODUS: THE ARABIAN ROUTE THEORY

EXODUS 13 The view that the Israelites traveled through Arabia is founded on two presuppositions: that Mount Sinai was not in the Sinai peninsula but rather in Arabia[1] and that the only body of water clearly identified in the Old Testament as the Red Sea or *yam suph* is the Gulf of Aqaba.[2]

This theory agrees with the "southern route" hypothesis that Rameses was Qantir and that Succoth was Tell el-Maskhuta. From that point on, however, the proposed routes are entirely different.

✣ The Arabian theory discounts the bodies of water and fortifications in the Suez area, assuming that the Egyptian pursuit did not begin until after Israel had entered the Sinai peninsula.

✣ This system postulates that Israel would have followed the Darb el-Hajj, a trade route linking Arabia to Egypt that proceeds in a nearly straight line from just north of the Gulf of Suez to the northern tip of the Gulf of Aqaba. However, since the Sinai was considered Egyptian territory, the Israelites probably would have hurried during this part of the march in order to quit the pharaoh's domain before he changed his mind. If so, their journey to Arabia would have taken them to the northern edge of the Gulf of Aqaba.

✣ The next stop on this itinerary would have been Etham. There is, in fact, a Mount Itm (also written as Ithem or Yitm) at the northeastern tip of the Gulf of Aqaba. Exodus 14:1–4 (cf. Nu 33:7) states that the Israelites "turned back" after nearing Etham to give the Egyptians the impression that they were lost. It is conceivable that the column actually rounded the northern tip of the Gulf of Aqaba, then did an about face on the western side of the gulf. Thus the Israelites would have been on the western side of the northern edge of the Gulf of Aqaba at the time they were nearly overtaken by the Egyptians. The procession would from that point have crossed the Red Sea (Gulf of Aqaba) after the parting of the waters.[3]

✣ This third theory places the Israelites, after having crossed the sea, just south of Mount Itm in what the Bible calls the "Desert of Etham" (Nu 33:8). This desert could have been the area near Mount Itm northeast of the Gulf of Aqaba. This region is also referred to as the Desert of Shur (Ex 15:22).

An ibex on a desert cliff edge
Photograph: © Todd Bolen/Bible Places.com

✣ From here Israel would have headed south, along the western edge of Arabia, on the eastern side of the Gulf of Aqaba/Red Sea. Marah could have been the oasis at modern al-Malha.

✣ Elim, where there were "twelve springs and seventy palm trees" (15:27), could have been Ainuna, an area where similar conditions existed.

✣ Israel again set up camp by the Gulf of Aqaba/Red Sea (Nu 33:10), then moved on to the Desert of Sin (Nu 33:11), where the wanderers encountered an unusually heavy dew (see Ex 16:13–14). This phenomenon would suggest that they had moved east into the higher elevation of the Arabian Hisma, where the dew would have tended to be heavier.

✣ From there the Israelites would have traveled to Dophkah before proceeding to Sinai, which according to this theory was most likely the volcanic Mount Bedr.

This third theory represents an intriguing interpretation of the exodus itinerary, though little serious work to date has been done to confirm it.

[1]See "The Location of Mount Sinai" on page 123. [2]See "The Location of the Red Sea" on page 110. [3]See "The Wind Set-Down Hypothesis" on page 111 for a discussion of some relevant details.

Consecration of the Firstborn

13 The LORD said to Moses, 2“Consecrate to me every firstborn male.[w] The first offspring of every
womb among the Israelites belongs to me, whether man or animal.”
3Then Moses said to the people, “Commemorate this day, the day you came out of Egypt, out of the
land of slavery, because the LORD brought you out of it with a mighty hand.[x] Eat nothing containing
yeast.[y] 4Today, in the month of Abib,[z] you are leaving. 5When the LORD brings you into the land of the
Canaanites, Hittites, Amorites, Hivites and Jebusites[a]—the land he swore to your forefathers to give you,
a land flowing with milk and honey—you are to observe this ceremony[b] in this month: 6For seven days
eat bread made without yeast and on the seventh day hold a festival[c] to the LORD. 7Eat unleavened bread
during those seven days; nothing with yeast in it is to be seen among you, nor shall any yeast be seen
anywhere within your borders. 8On that day tell your son,[d] ‘I do this because of what the LORD did for
me when I came out of Egypt.’ 9This observance will be for you like a sign on your hand and a remind-
er on your forehead[e] that the law of the LORD is to be on your lips. For the LORD brought you out of Egypt
with his mighty hand. 10You must keep this ordinance[f] at the appointed time year after year.
11“After the LORD brings you into the land of the Canaanites and gives it to you, as he promised on
oath to you and your forefathers, 12you are to give over to the LORD the first offspring of every womb. All
the firstborn males of your livestock belong to the LORD.[g] 13Redeem with a lamb every firstborn donkey,
but if you do not redeem it, break its neck.[h] Redeem every firstborn among your sons.[i]
14“In days to come, when your son[j] asks you, ‘What does this mean?’ say to him, ‘With a mighty hand the
LORD brought us out of Egypt, out of the land of slavery.[k] 15When Pharaoh stubbornly refused to let us go,
the LORD killed every firstborn in Egypt, both man and animal. This is why I sacrifice to the LORD the first
male offspring of every womb and redeem each of my firstborn sons.’[l] 16And it will be like a sign on your
hand and a symbol on your forehead[m] that the LORD brought us out of Egypt with his mighty hand.”

Crossing the Sea

17When Pharaoh let the people go, God did not lead them on the road through the Philistine country,
though that was shorter. For God said, “If they face war, they might change their minds and return to
Egypt.”[n] 18So God led[o] the people around by the desert road toward the Red Sea.[a] The Israelites went up
out of Egypt armed for battle.[p]
19Moses took the bones of Joseph[q] with him because Joseph had made the sons of Israel swear an
oath. He had said, “God will surely come to your aid, and then you must carry my bones up with you
from this place.”[b][r]
20After leaving Succoth they camped at Etham on the edge of the desert.[s] 21By day the LORD went
ahead of them in a pillar of cloud[t] to guide them on their way and by night in a pillar of fire to give them
light, so that they could travel by day or night. 22Neither the pillar of cloud by day nor the pillar of fire by
night left its place in front of the people.

14 Then the LORD said to Moses, 2“Tell the Israelites to turn back and encamp near Pi Hahiroth, be-
tween Migdol[u] and the sea. They are to encamp by the sea, directly opposite Baal Zephon. 3Phar-
aoh will think, ‘The Israelites are wandering around the land in confusion, hemmed in by the desert.’
4And I will harden Pharaoh’s heart,[v] and he will pursue them. But I will gain glory[w] for myself through
Pharaoh and all his army, and the Egyptians will know that I am the LORD.”[x] So the Israelites did this.

13:2 [w]ver 12,13, 15; Ex 22:29; Nu 3:13; Dt 15:19; Lk 2:23* **13:3** [x]Ex 3:20; 6:1 [y]Ex 12:19 **13:4** [z]Ex 12:2 **13:5** [a]Ex 3:8 [b]Ex 12:25-26 **13:6** [c]Ex 12:15-20 **13:8** [d]ver 14; Ex 10:2; Ps 78:5-6 **13:9** [e]ver 16; Dt 6:8; 11:18 **13:10** [f]Ex 12:24-25 **13:12** [g]Lev 27:26; Lk 2:23* **13:13** [h]Ex 34:20 [i]Nu 18:15 **13:14** [j]Ex 10:2; 12:26-27; Dt 6:20 [k]ver 3,9 **13:15** [l]Ex 12:29 **13:16** [m]ver 9 **13:17** [n]Ex 14:11; Nu 14:1-4; Dt 17:16 **13:18** [o]Ps 136:16 [p]Jos 1:14 **13:19** [q]Jos 24:32; Ac 7:16 [r]Ge 50:24-25 **13:20** [s]Nu 33:6 **13:21** [t]Ex 14:19, 24; 33:9-10; Nu 9:16; Dt 1:33; Ne 9:12,19; Ps 78:14; 99:7; 105:39; Isa 4:5; 1Co 10:1 **14:2** [u]Nu 33:7; Jer 44:1 **14:4** [v]Ex 4:21 [w]Ro 9:17,22-23 [x]Ex 7:5

[a] *18* Hebrew *Yam Suph*; that is, Sea of Reeds [b] *19* See Gen. 50:25.

13:9 Phylacteries (also called “signs,” “reminders” or “frontlets”) are small, black, cube-shaped leather boxes that Orthodox and other conservative Jewish males aged thirteen years of age and older often wear on their arms/hands and foreheads during weekday morning prayers. The purpose of phylacteries was (and still is) to remind the Israelites/Jewish people of God’s deliverance and of their duty to remain faithful to his commands.

Mentioned in three Biblical passages (see also Dt 6:4–9; 11:13–21), phylacteries contain parchments with these same Biblical passages written on them. Phylacteries before and during Jesus’ time often included the Ten Commandments as well.

Head-phylacteries are divided into four compartments, each holding a separate parchment. The oldest discovered head-phylactery was found at Qumran (see “Biblical Interpretation at Qumran and Among the Early Rabbis” on p. 1603). Arm-phylacteries have no partitions; a single parchment includes all three Biblical passages.

It is unclear whether or not the Exodus and Deuteronomy texts were meant to be taken literally, since the commands about binding found in Proverbs 6:20–21 and 7:1–3 are not considered to be literal.

13:19 Embalming was a process of Egyptian origin intended to preserve a body from decay (see the note on Ge 50:2–3). The only clear instances of it in the Bible are of Jacob and Joseph. Joseph had ordered his slaves, the physicians, to embalm his father (Ge 50:2–3), a process that required 40 days, and later Joseph himself had been embalmed (Ge 50:26). The purpose of the Egyptians in embalming was to preserve the body for the use of the soul in a future life. The purpose of the Hebrews, however, was to preserve the bodies of Jacob and Joseph for the long journey to their resting place with Abraham (Ge 50:13). In the case of Joseph, centuries elapsed before burial in the ancestral tomb (Ex 13:19; Jos 24:32).

5 When the king of Egypt was told that the people had fled, Pharaoh and his officials changed their
minds about them and said, "What have we done? We have let the Israelites go and have lost their ser-
vices!" 6 So he had his chariot made ready and took his army with him. 7 He took six hundred of the best
chariots, along with all the other chariots of Egypt, with officers over all of them. 8 The LORD hardened the
heart[y] of Pharaoh king of Egypt, so that he pursued the Israelites, who were marching out boldly.[z] 9 The
Egyptians—all Pharaoh's horses and chariots, horsemen[a] and troops—pursued the Israelites and over-
took[a] them as they camped by the sea near Pi Hahiroth, opposite Baal Zephon.
10 As Pharaoh approached, the Israelites looked up, and there were the Egyptians, marching after them.

14:8 [y]ver 4; Ex 11:10 [z]Nu 33:3; Ac 13:17 **14:9** [a]Ex 15:9

[a] 9 Or *charioteers;* also in verses 17, 18, 23, 26 and 28

Horses and Chariots in Ancient Warfare

EXODUS 14 The use of horses and chariots revolutionized warfare in the ancient Near East. Scholars generally agree that the horse was introduced into the area during the late third millennium B.C. and had become prominent in Canaan by the early second millennium.

The development of the chariot soon followed, but scholars disagree about the history of its invention. Horses and chariots are mentioned in the **Mari**[1] tablets (eighteenth century B.C.), and the **Kassites** and the people of **Mitanni**[2] (seventeenth century B.C) were renowned for both horse breeding and chariot technology. In fact, the Kassites developed specialized and precise vocabulary for chariot components, and the Mitannian *maryannu* comprised a group of chariot experts.

In all likelihood foreigners introduced horses and chariots to the Egyptians (mentioned in ch. 15) during the **Hyksos**[3] period (eighteenth to sixteenth centuries B.C.). During the subsequent **New Kingdom** period (sixteenth through eleventh centuries B.C.) horse-drawn chariots were often used in warfare and religious processions—and sometimes even served as portable thrones. **Reliefs** and paintings from Egypt portray both Seti I and Rameses III standing in chariots, drawing their bows against enemies. Chariots have also been found among relics in Eighteenth-Dynasty tombs, such as those preserved with relation to King Tutankhamen.

Ashurbanipal of Assyria in a chariot
Preserving Bible Times; © Dr. James C. Martin; permission of Musée de Louvre

The early chariot's design permitted two people standing abreast—a driver and an archer—to occupy the small platform. The axle was made of wood, and rawhide held the frame together. Wheels were fastened to the axle with linchpins of wood or bronze. The draft pole extended to the rear of the chariot, was secured with rawhide bindings and was attached to the horses' yoke with straps.

Since horses were primarily used in ancient times to pull chariots, the term *rider* mentioned in Exodus 15:1 probably refers to the chariot driver. The song's boast that the God of Israel had hurled the horse and charioteer into the sea dramatically portrays the manner in which the power of God had bested the most technologically advanced tool of warfare available during that time.[4]

[1]See "Mari" on page 54. [2]See "Mitanni" on page 257. [3]See "The Hyksos and the Old Testament" on page 121. [4]For other warfare issues, see "Technological Supremacy of the Philistines' Iron Weapons" on page 414, "Siege Warfare" on page 465 and "Warfare in the Ancient World" on page 950.

They were terrified and cried[b] out to the LORD. 11 They said to Moses, "Was it because there were no graves
in Egypt that you brought us to the desert to die?[c] What have you done to us by bringing us out of Egypt?
12 Didn't we say to you in Egypt, 'Leave us alone; let us serve the Egyptians'? It would have been better for
us to serve the Egyptians than to die in the desert!"

13 Moses answered the people, "Do not be afraid.[d] Stand firm and you will see[e] the deliverance the
LORD will bring you today. The Egyptians you see today you will never see[f] again. 14 The LORD will fight[g]
for you; you need only to be still."[h]

15 Then the LORD said to Moses, "Why are you crying out to me? Tell the Israelites to move on. 16 Raise
your staff[i] and stretch out your hand over the sea to divide the water[j] so that the Israelites can go through
the sea on dry ground. 17 I will harden the hearts of the Egyptians so that they will go in after them.[k] And
I will gain glory through Pharaoh and all his army, through his chariots and his horsemen. 18 The Egyp-
tians will know that I am the LORD when I gain glory through Pharaoh, his chariots and his horsemen."

19 Then the angel of God, who had been traveling in front of Israel's army, withdrew and went behind
them. The pillar of cloud[l] also moved from in front and stood behind them, 20 coming between the armies
of Egypt and Israel. Throughout the night the cloud brought darkness to the one side and light to the
other side; so neither went near the other all night long.

21 Then Moses stretched out his hand over the sea, and all that night the LORD drove the sea back with
a strong east wind[m] and turned it into dry land. The waters were divided,[n] 22 and the Israelites went
through the sea on dry ground,[o] with a wall of water on their right and on their left.

23 The Egyptians pursued them, and all Pharaoh's horses and chariots and horsemen followed them
into the sea. 24 During the last watch of the night the LORD looked down from the pillar of fire and cloud[p]
at the Egyptian army and threw it into confusion. 25 He made the wheels of their chariots come off[a] so
that they had difficulty driving. And the Egyptians said, "Let's get away from the Israelites! The LORD is
fighting[q] for them against Egypt."

26 Then the LORD said to Moses, "Stretch out your hand over the sea so that the waters may flow back
over the Egyptians and their chariots and horsemen." 27 Moses stretched out his hand over the sea, and
at daybreak the sea went back to its place.[r] The Egyptians were fleeing toward[b] it, and the LORD swept
them into the sea.[s] 28 The water flowed back and covered the chariots and horsemen—the entire army
of Pharaoh that had followed the Israelites into the sea. Not one of them survived.

29 But the Israelites went through the sea on dry ground,[t] with a wall of water on their right and on
their left. 30 That day the LORD saved[u] Israel from the hands of the Egyptians, and Israel saw the Egyptians
lying dead on the shore. 31 And when the Israelites saw the great power the LORD displayed against the
Egyptians, the people feared the LORD and put their trust[v] in him and in Moses his servant.

The Song of Moses and Miriam

15 Then Moses and the Israelites sang this song[w] to the LORD:

"I will sing[x] to the LORD,
  for he is highly exalted.
The horse and its rider
  he has hurled into the sea.
2 The LORD is my strength[y] and my song;
  he has become my salvation.[z]
He is my God,[a] and I will praise him,
  my father's God, and I will exalt[b] him.
3 The LORD is a warrior;[c]
  the LORD is his name.[d]

14:10 [b]Jos 24:7; Ne 9:9; Ps 34:17 **14:11** [c]Ps 106:7-8
14:13 [d]Ge 15:1 [e]2Ch 20:17; Isa 41:10,13-14 [f]ver 30 **14:14** [g]ver 25; Ex 15:3; Dt 1:30; 3:22; 2Ch 20:29 [h]Ps 37:7; 46:10; Isa 30:15 **14:16** [i]Ex 4:17; Nu 20:8-9,11 [j]Isa 10:26 **14:17** [k]ver 4
14:19 [l]Ex 13:21
14:21 [m]Ex 15:8 [n]Ps 74:13; 114:5; Isa 63:12 **14:22** [o]Ex 15:19; Ne 9:11; Ps 66:6; Heb 11:29 **14:24** [p]Ex 13:21
14:25 [q]ver 14
14:27 [r]Jos 4:18 [s]Ex 15:1,21; Ps 78:53; 106:11
14:29 [t]ver 22
14:30 [u]Ps 106:8, 10,21
14:31 [v]Ps 106:12; Jn 2:11
15:1 [w]Rev 15:3 [x]Ps 106:12
15:2 [y]Ps 59:17 [z]Ps 18:2,46; Isa 12:2; Hab 3:18 [a]Ge 28:21 [b]Ex 3:6,15-16; Isa 25:1
15:3 [c]Ex 14:14; Ps 24:8; Rev 19:11 [d]Ex 6:2-3,7-8; Ps 83:18

[a] 25 Or *He jammed the wheels of their chariots* (see Samaritan Pentateuch, Septuagint and Syriac) [b] 27 Or *from*

14:19 The Hebrew word *shekînâh* ("dwelling of God"), though not occurring in the Bible, is employed by some Jews and by Christians to describe the visible presence of the Lord. It is alluded to in such places as Isaiah 60:2 by the phrase "his glory" and in Romans 9:4 by "the divine glory." Moses called this the "pillar of cloud." Its first appearance occurred for a twofold purpose when Israel was being led by Moses out of Egypt: It hid the Israelites from the pursuing Egyptians and lighted the way at night for Israel (13:21; 14:19–20). To the Egyptians it was a cloud of darkness, but to Israel a cloud of light. It later covered Sinai when God spoke with Moses (24:15–18), filled the tabernacle (40:34–35), guided Israel (40:36–38) and filled Solomon's temple (2Ch 7:1), and it was frequently seen in connection with Christ's ministry in the New Testament (Mt 17:5; Ac 1:9).

[4] Pharaoh's chariots and his army[e]
he has hurled into the sea.
The best of Pharaoh's officers
are drowned in the Red Sea.[a]
[5] The deep waters have covered them;
they sank to the depths like a stone.[f]

[6] "Your right hand,[g] O LORD,
was majestic in power.
Your right hand, O LORD,
shattered the enemy.
[7] In the greatness of your majesty
you threw down those who opposed you.
You unleashed your burning anger;[h]
it consumed them like stubble.
[8] By the blast of your nostrils[i]
the waters piled up.[j]
The surging waters stood firm like a wall;[k]
the deep waters congealed in the heart of the sea.

[9] "The enemy boasted,
'I will pursue,[l] I will overtake them.
I will divide the spoils;[m]
I will gorge myself on them.
I will draw my sword
and my hand will destroy them.'
[10] But you blew with your breath,
and the sea covered them.
They sank like lead
in the mighty waters.[n]
[11] "Who among the gods is like you,[o] O LORD?
Who is like you—
majestic in holiness,[p]
awesome in glory,[q]
working wonders?
[12] You stretched out your right hand
and the earth swallowed them.

[13] "In your unfailing love you will lead[r]
the people you have redeemed.
In your strength you will guide them
to your holy dwelling.[s]
[14] The nations will hear and tremble;[t]
anguish will grip the people of Philistia.
[15] The chiefs[u] of Edom will be terrified,
the leaders of Moab will be seized with trembling,[v]
the people[b] of Canaan will melt[w] away;

15:4 [e]Ex 14:6-7
15:5 [f]ver 10; Ne 9:11
15:6 [g]Ps 118:15
15:7 [h]Ps 78:49-50
15:8 [i]Ex 14:21 [j]Ps 78:13 [k]Ex 14:22
15:9 [l]Ex 14:5-9 [m]Jdg 5:30; Isa 53:12
15:10 [n]ver 5; Ex 14:27-28
15:11 [o]Ex 8:10; Dt 3:24; Ps 77:13 [p]Isa 6:3; Rev 4:8 [q]Ps 8:1
15:13 [r]Ne 9:12; Ps 77:20 [s]Ps 78:54
15:14 [t]Dt 2:25
15:15 [u]Ge 36:15 [v]Nu 22:3 [w]Jos 5:1

[a] 4 Hebrew *Yam Suph*; that is, Sea of Reeds; also in verse 22 [b] 15 Or *rulers*

15:13 A theocracy may be defined as a government in which God himself is the ruler. In one sense every ancient Near Eastern nation was a theocracy in that in each one the king was regarded either as a god (e.g., Egypt) or as the chosen representative of a god (most Mesopotamian states). See "The Ancient Near Eastern King" on page 839. On the other hand, the one true theocracy in history was the Biblical state of Israel. The theocratic ideal of Israel was a loose confederation with no central authority and thus no possibility of oppressive monarchial rule—a typical trait of "theocratic" states. Faith in God, pilgrimages to the central shrine (see "Israelite Shrines and Worship Before the Temple of Solomon" on p. 398) and loyalty to the covenant were to be the unifying factors for the nation of Israel. This was the situation during the judges period, but the ideal was perverted by the apostasy of the people. The confederation proving to have been a failure, Samuel acceded to their demand, "Now appoint a king to lead us, such as all the other nations have" (1Sa 8:5).

15:16 [x]Ex 23:27; Jos 2:9 — 16 terror[x] and dread will fall upon them.
By the power of your arm
[y]1Sa 25:37 — they will be as still as a stone[y]—
until your people pass by, O LORD,
[z]Ps 74:2 — until the people you bought[a][z] pass by.
15:17 [a]Ps 44:2 [b]Ps 78:54,68 — 17 You will bring them in and plant[a] them
on the mountain[b] of your inheritance—
the place, O LORD, you made for your dwelling,
the sanctuary, O Lord, your hands established.
18 The LORD will reign
for ever and ever."

15:19 [c]Ex 14:28 [d]Ex 14:22 — 19 When Pharaoh's horses, chariots and horsemen[b] went into the sea,[c] the LORD brought the waters of
15:20 [e]Nu 26:59 — the sea back over them, but the Israelites walked through the sea on dry ground.[d] 20 Then Miriam[e] the
[f]Jdg 4:4 [g]Jdg 11:34; 1Sa 18:6; Ps 30:11; 150:4 — prophetess,[f] Aaron's sister, took a tambourine in her hand, and all the women followed her, with tam-
bourines and dancing.[g] 21 Miriam sang to them:

"Sing to the LORD,
for he is highly exalted.
The horse and its rider
15:21 [h]ver 1; Ex 14:27 — he has hurled into the sea."[h]

The Waters of Marah and Elim

22 Then Moses led Israel from the Red Sea and they went into the Desert of Shur. For three days they
traveled in the desert without finding water. 23 When they came to Marah, they could not drink its water
15:23 [i]Nu 33:8 — because it was bitter. (That is why the place is called Marah.[c][i]) 24 So the people grumbled[j] against Moses,
15:24 [j]Ex 14:12; 16:2 — saying, "What are we to drink?"
15:25 [k]Ex 14:10 [l]Jdg 3:4 — 25 Then Moses cried out[k] to the LORD, and the LORD showed him a piece of wood. He threw it into the
water, and the water became sweet.
There the LORD made a decree and a law for them, and there he tested[l] them. 26 He said, "If you listen
carefully to the voice of the LORD your God and do what is right in his eyes, if you pay attention to his com-
15:26 [m]Dt 7:12 [n]Dt 28:27,58-60 [o]Ex 23:25-26 — mands and keep all his decrees,[m] I will not bring on you any of the diseases[n] I brought on the Egyptians,
for I am the LORD, who heals[o] you."
15:27 [p]Nu 33:9 — 27 Then they came to Elim, where there were twelve springs and seventy palm trees, and they camped[p]
there near the water.

Manna and Quail

16:1 [q]Nu 33:11, 12 — 16 The whole Israelite community set out from Elim and came to the Desert of Sin,[q] which is be-
tween Elim and Sinai, on the fifteenth day of the second month after they had come out of Egypt.
16:2 [r]Ex 14:11; 15:24; 1Co 10:10 — 2 In the desert the whole community grumbled[r] against Moses and Aaron. 3 The Israelites said to them,
16:3 [s]Ex 17:3 [t]Nu 11:4,34 — "If only we had died by the LORD's hand in Egypt![s] There we sat around pots of meat and ate all the food[t]
we wanted, but you have brought us out into this desert to starve this entire assembly to death."
16:4 [u]Dt 8:3; Jn 6:31* — 4 Then the LORD said to Moses, "I will rain down bread from heaven[u] for you. The people are to go out
each day and gather enough for that day. In this way I will test them and see whether they will follow my
16:5 [v]ver 22 — instructions. 5 On the sixth day they are to prepare what they bring in, and that is to be twice[v] as much
as they gather on the other days."

[a] 16 Or *created* [b] 19 Or *charioteers* [c] 23 *Marah* means *bitter.*

15:20–21 A woman who exercised the prophetic gift in ancient Israel or in the early church was referred to as a prophetess. In general she would possess the charismatic gifts and powers characterizing the prophets themselves. There are at least five women bearing this designation in the Old Testament: Miriam (15:20), Deborah (Jdg 4:4), Huldah (2Ki 22:14), Noadiah (Ne 6:14) and the unnamed wife of Isaiah, who bore him children to whom he gave prophetic names (Isa 8:3). In the New Testament there was Anna (Lk 2:36), and Philip the evangelist is said to have had four unmarried daughters who prophesied (Ac 21:8–9). After Pentecost the differentiation between sexes regarding prophetic gifts was eliminated (Ac 2:19; cf. Joel 2:28).

Dancing was usually performed by women, with one leading. In this instance, as well as on other occasions, a form of antiphonal (responsive) singing was used, and the dancing usually took place out of doors.

16:4 The Hebrew word *mân* means "question"; prefixed to *hu* the question would be What is it? On the other hand, the word may be an adaptation of the Egyptian *mennu,* or food. Josephus and other ancient writers attributed the name to the question, Is it food? Precisely what

6So Moses and Aaron said to all the Israelites, "In the evening you will know that it was the LORD who
brought you out of Egypt,[w] 7and in the morning you will see the glory[x] of the LORD, because he has heard
your grumbling[y] against him. Who are we, that you should grumble against us?"[z] 8Moses also said, "You
will know that it was the LORD when he gives you meat to eat in the evening and all the bread you want
in the morning, because he has heard your grumbling against him. Who are we? You are not grumbling
against us, but against the LORD."[a]
9Then Moses told Aaron, "Say to the entire Israelite community, 'Come before the LORD, for he has
heard your grumbling.' "
10While Aaron was speaking to the whole Israelite community, they looked toward the desert, and
there was the glory[b] of the LORD appearing in the cloud.[c]
11The LORD said to Moses, 12"I have heard the grumbling[d] of the Israelites. Tell them, 'At twilight you
will eat meat, and in the morning you will be filled with bread. Then you will know that I am the LORD
your God.' "
13That evening quail[e] came and covered the camp, and in the morning there was a layer of dew[f] around
the camp. 14When the dew was gone, thin flakes like frost[g] on the ground appeared on the desert floor.
15When the Israelites saw it, they said to each other, "What is it?" For they did not know what it was.
Moses said to them, "It is the bread[h] the LORD has given you to eat. 16This is what the LORD has com-
manded: 'Each one is to gather as much as he needs. Take an omer[a][i] for each person you have in your
tent.' "
17The Israelites did as they were told; some gathered much, some little. 18And when they measured it
by the omer, he who gathered much did not have too much, and he who gathered little did not have too
little.[j] Each one gathered as much as he needed.
19Then Moses said to them, "No one is to keep any of it until morning."[k]
20However, some of them paid no attention to Moses; they kept part of it until morning, but it was
full of maggots and began to smell. So Moses was angry with them.
21Each morning everyone gathered as much as he needed, and when the sun grew hot, it melted away.
22On the sixth day, they gathered twice[l] as much—two omers[b] for each person—and the leaders of the
community[m] came and reported this to Moses. 23He said to them, "This is what the LORD commanded:
'Tomorrow is to be a day of rest, a holy Sabbath[n] to the LORD. So bake what you want to bake and boil what
you want to boil. Save whatever is left and keep it until morning.' "
24So they saved it until morning, as Moses commanded, and it did not stink or get maggots in it. 25"Eat
it today," Moses said, "because today is a Sabbath to the LORD. You will not find any of it on the ground
today. 26Six days you are to gather it, but on the seventh day, the Sabbath,[o] there will not be any."
27Nevertheless, some of the people went out on the seventh day to gather it, but they found none.
28Then the LORD said to Moses, "How long will you[c] refuse to keep my commands[p] and my instructions?

16:6 [w]Ex 6:6
16:7 [x]ver 10; Isa 35:2; 40:5 [y]ver 12; Nu 14:2, 27,28 [z]Nu 16:11
16:8 [a]1Sa 8:7; Ro 13:2
16:10 [b]ver 7; Nu 16:19 [c]Ex 13:21; 1Ki 8:10
16:12 [d]ver 7
16:13 [e]Nu 11:31; Ps 78:27-28; 105:40 [f]Nu 11:9
16:14 [g]ver 31; Nu 11:7-9; Ps 105:40
16:15 [h]ver 4; Jn 6:31
16:16 [i]ver 32,36
16:18 [j]2Co 8:15*
16:19 [k]ver 23; Ex 12:10; 23:18
16:22 [l]ver 5 [m]Ex 34:31
16:23 [n]Ge 2:3; Ex 20:8; 23:12; Lev 23:3
16:26 [o]Ex 20:9-10
16:28 [p]2Ki 17:14; Ps 78:10; 106:13

[a] *16* That is, probably about 2 quarts (about 2 liters); also in verses 18, 32, 33 and 36 [b] *22* That is, probably about 4 quarts (about 4.5 liters) [c] *28* The Hebrew is plural.

---

manna was has puzzled naturalists for ages. It came at night, resembling hoarfrost and dropping with the dew (Nu 11:9), and it may have collected in dewdrops (Ex 16:4). It was white, flavorful and resembled the seed of the coriander, a plant of the eastern Mediterranean area that was both tasty and nourishing (v. 31). That it came by miraculous means is shown by its nature, its time of coming and its preservation over the Sabbath (vv 10–26; Dt 8:3). Being seed-like in form, it had to be ground (Nu 11:7–8) in order to be eaten. As soon as other food became available the provision of manna ceased.

No known substance meets the description of this food. A tamarisk plant that grows along the route of the Hebrews from Sinai exudes a sweet liquid that collects at night on twigs and falls to the ground. After sunrise it disappears unless it is protected. But this plant produces the food for only a brief period each year. Other naturalists would identify manna with a peculiar, mossy plant that at maturity is round and eaten with honey. But neither is it available for the entire year.

Asaph called manna "grain of heaven" (Ps 78:24; some translations use "corn"), and it is also called "bread of heaven" (Ps 105:40). Other Hebrew writers referred to it as "angels' bread" (2Es 2:1; WS 16:20—both Apocryphal books). The apostle John called it spiritual food—a hidden agent for spiritual sustenance for the risen saints (Rev 2:17).

16:13 The quail is a small, migratory game bird that exists in some 130 species. It lives at ground level in pasture, scrubland, arable crops, etc. Able to fly short distances at a comparatively rapid speed, the quail has some similarity to the partridge but is somewhat smaller, reaching a length of about 7 inches (18 cm). Like the partridge, the quail is a dust-bather, and it shares a similar diet of fruit, leaves and insects.

In Bible times quail were seen in large flocks, traveling most often over short distances. The birds' abundance as food for the Israelites occurred as large numbers of the Coturnix quail fell exhausted to the ground following their long flight from Africa, where they had spent the winter (16:13; Ps 105:40). The profusion of the birds is graphically described in Numbers 11:31. The flesh of the quail is delicious, as are its eggs.

16:16 An omer held about two quarts (2 l).

16:21–30 The Bible makes no expressed mention of the Sabbath prior to this passage. In the Desert of Sin, before the Israelites had reached Mount Sinai, God gave them manna, a double supply being provided on the sixth day of the week in order that the seventh day might be consecrated as a day of rest from labor (v. 23). Shortly afterward, the Ten Commandments were given by the Lord at Sinai (20:1–17; 34:1–5). The fourth commandment enjoined Israel to observe the seventh day as a holy day on which no work was to be done by people or animals. It is clear that the Lord intended the day to be a blessing to people, both physically and spiritually. See "Sabbath, Sabbath Year and the Jubilee" on page 189.

ALTERNATIVE THEORIES ABOUT THE EXODUS

EXODUS 16 The Israelites' **exodus** from Egypt is a key focus in the Old Testament, as well as an early, vital component of Biblical salvation history. The significance of this historical event is confirmed again and again throughout the Biblical **canon**. Numerous passages, beginning within the **Pentateuch**, refer to this pivotal event in God's dealings with his people. For example:

- A prologue introducing both Old Testament recitations of the Ten Commandments (Ex. 20:2; Dt. 5:6) reminded Israel of God's faithful actions during the exodus.
- The exodus provided the basis for demanding proper treatment of strangers and impoverished individuals living in Israel (Ex 22:21; 23:9; Dt 24:17–18).
- Israel's annual cycle of feasts recalled events associated with the exodus (cf. Ex 12:26–27; Lev 23:42–43; Dt 16:1).[1]
- The experience afforded the Israelites the confidence they needed to wage war (Dt 20:1).

Region of the traditional Mount Sinai
Photograph courtesy of © Dr. Gary Pratico

In addition, Israel's departure from Egypt for the promised land, along with the numerous miracles associated with that event, served as the basis for the nation's call to holiness (Nu 15:40–41) and for the evaluation of her actions (Dt 6:20–25), the principal theme of many psalms (e.g. Ps 78; 80; 81; 105; 106; 136) and an inspiration underlying many of her deepest prophetic hopes (Isa 11:16; Jer 11:3–5; 23:7–8). In profound ways this event provided the very foundation for Israel's spiritual and national life.

Despite the importance of this occurrence, a number of problems remain. The exact date, as well as the precise location and route of the exodus, are disputed.[2] The silence of Egyptian literary records concerning this momentous event, as well as of the circumstances leading up to it, is perplexing, yet undeniable. Because archaeological evidence for the exodus is fragmentary and limited and contains large gaps, some scholars go so far as to question the historicity of the exodus and suggest alternative theories concerning Israel's origins. None of these hypotheses, however, can be demonstrated archaeologically or can boast the slightest Biblical basis. Theories that have been posited include the following:

- A small group of "proto-Israelites" departed from Egypt, entered **Canaan** and attracted followers from the local population. This group eventually became the nation of Israel.
- Nomads gradually emigrated from various places into Canaan and coalesced around a common (but mythical) story of an exodus, complete with accounts of miraculous elements.
- The Israelites were Canaanite peasants who banded together, revolted against their overlords and created "Israel" out of a mythical history.
- Indigenous tribal groups within Canaan formed a people during the decline of Egyptian supremacy in the region.

Despite all the conjecture, many solid facts do support the reality of the exodus account. The Biblical record accords unparalleled significance to the event, and numerous details conform well to the cultural and political situation in Egypt during the **New Kingdom** period. For example, the Bible accurately depicts known labor conditions, proper names, governmental structures, royal theology, geography, magical practices, craftsmanship and artistic conventions of Egypt during the fourteenth and thirteenth centuries B.C.[3] Although these facts cannot in and of themselves verify the reality of the exodus, they definitely support God's own ancient Biblical testimony through his servant Hosea: "When Israel was a child, I loved him, and out of Egypt I called my son" (Hos 11:1).

[1]See "The Festivals of Israel" on page 186. [2]See "The Pharaoh of the Exodus" on page 98 and "The Route of the Exodus" articles on pages 108–112. [3]See "The Date of the Exodus" on page 106.

29 Bear in mind that the LORD has given you the Sabbath; that is why on the sixth day he gives you bread
for two days. Everyone is to stay where he is on the seventh day; no one is to go out." 30 So the people rest-
ed on the seventh day.
31 The people of Israel called the bread manna.[a][q] It was white like coriander seed and tasted like wa- **16:31** [q]Nu 11:7-9
fers made with honey. 32 Moses said, "This is what the LORD has commanded: 'Take an omer of manna and
keep it for the generations to come, so they can see the bread I gave you to eat in the desert when I brought
you out of Egypt.' "
33 So Moses said to Aaron, "Take a jar and put an omer of manna[r] in it. Then place it before the LORD **16:33** [r]Heb 9:4
to be kept for the generations to come."
34 As the LORD commanded Moses, Aaron put the manna in front of the Testimony,[s] that it might be **16:34** [s]Ex 25:16,
kept. 35 The Israelites ate manna[t] forty years,[u] until they came to a land that was settled; they ate manna 21,22; 40:20; Nu 17:4,10
until they reached the border of Canaan.[v] **16:35** [t]Jn 6:31, 49 [u]Ne 9:21
36 (An omer is one tenth of an ephah.) [v]Jos 5:12

Water From the Rock

17 The whole Israelite community set out from the Desert of Sin,[w] traveling from place to place as **17:1** [w]Ex 16:1
the LORD commanded. They camped at Rephidim, but there was no water[x] for the people to drink. [x]Nu 33:14
2 So they quarreled with Moses and said, "Give us water[y] to drink." **17:2** [y]Nu 20:2
Moses replied, "Why do you quarrel with me? Why do you put the LORD to the test?"[z] [z]Dt 6:16; Ps 78:18,41; 1Co 10:9
3 But the people were thirsty for water there, and they grumbled[a] against Moses. They said, "Why did **17:3** [a]Ex 15:24;
you bring us up out of Egypt to make us and our children and livestock die of thirst?" 16:2-3
4 Then Moses cried out to the LORD, "What am I to do with these people? They are almost ready to
stone[b] me." **17:4** [b]Nu 14:10; 1Sa 30:6
5 The LORD answered Moses, "Walk on ahead of the people. Take with you some of the elders of Israel
and take in your hand the staff with which you struck the Nile,[c] and go. 6 I will stand there before you by **17:5** [c]Ex 7:20
the rock at Horeb. Strike the rock, and water[d] will come out of it for the people to drink." So Moses did **17:6** [d]Nu 20:11; Ps 114:8; 1Co 10:4

[a] 31 *Manna* means *What is it?* (see verse 15).

16:31 The word "wafers" refers to thin cakes. In this particular verse the emphasis is on the thinness, but elsewhere the reference is to the process of beating that rendered the cakes (or bread) thin (29:2; Lev 2:4; 7:12; 8:26; Nu 6:15,19).

The Amalekites

EXODUS 17 The Amalekites, whom the Israelites encountered for the first time in Canaan (Ex 17:8), are a relatively obscure people group in the Old Testament. Unlike many other groups mentioned there, no reference to this nation has been found in any extrabiblical material. All that is known of these people comes from the Bible.

According to the genealogical record (Ge 36:12), Amalek was the son of Eliphaz and the grandson of Esau. In Numbers 24:20 the seer Balaam referred to the Amalekites using the enigmatic title the "first among the nations."[1] Their geographical range was vast, extending from the Valley of Jezreel[2] to the Arabah of Arabia. This suggests that they were a migratory people.

Because of the Amalekites' cruelty to Israel, God commanded his people in Deuteronomy 25:19 to blot out the memory of Amalek from under heaven (this is the only nation so condemned in the Bible). Despite this divine ban Amalekites reappeared intermittently throughout Israel's history:

- During Gideon's day Amalekite raiders appeared in Jezreel (Jdg 6:33), later to be defeated along with the Midianites.[3]
- Saul spared Agag the Amalekite king (1Sa 15:8–9), a costly act of disobedience that led to Saul's downfall.

David, in contrast, treated the Amalekites harshly (1Sa 27:8–9). They raided his camp at Ziklag,[4] but he appears to have bested them in the exchange (1Sa 30:1–20).

[1]See "Balaam, the Son of Beor" on page 229. [2]See "The Valley of Jezreel" on page 1412. [3]See "Midian" on page 92. [4]See "Ziklag" on page 708.

17:7 [e]Nu 20:13, 24; Ps 81:7

this in the sight of the elders of Israel. 7 And he called the place Massah[a] and Meribah[b][e] because the Is-
raelites quarreled and because they tested the LORD saying, "Is the LORD among us or not?"

The Amalekites Defeated

17:8 [f]Ge 36:12; Dt 25:17-19 17:9 [g]Ex 4:17 17:10 [h]Ex 24:14 17:11 [i]Jas 5:16

8 The Amalekites[f] came and attacked the Israelites at Rephidim. 9 Moses said to Joshua, "Choose some
of our men and go out to fight the Amalekites. Tomorrow I will stand on top of the hill with the staff[g] of
God in my hands."
10 So Joshua fought the Amalekites as Moses had ordered, and Moses, Aaron and Hur[h] went to the top
of the hill. 11 As long as Moses held up his hands, the Israelites were winning,[i] but whenever he lowered
his hands, the Amalekites were winning. 12 When Moses' hands grew tired, they took a stone and put it
under him and he sat on it. Aaron and Hur held his hands up—one on one side, one on the other—so
that his hands remained steady till sunset. 13 So Joshua overcame the Amalekite army with the sword.

17:14 [j]Ex 24:4; 34:27; Nu 33:2 [k]1Sa 15:3; 30:17-18

14 Then the LORD said to Moses, "Write[j] this on a scroll as something to be remembered and make sure
that Joshua hears it, because I will completely blot out the memory of Amalek[k] from under heaven."
15 Moses built an altar and called it The LORD is my Banner. 16 He said, "For hands were lifted up to the
throne of the LORD. The[c] LORD will be at war against the Amalekites from generation to generation."

[a] 7 *Massah* means *testing.* [b] 7 *Meribah* means *quarreling.* [c] 16 Or *"Because a hand was against the throne of the LORD, the*

17:8 The Amalekites were a tribal people living in the Negev and in the Sinai peninsula (see "The Amalekites" on p. 120).
17:14 Scrolls were long strips of leather or papyrus on which scribes wrote in columns (see Jer 36:23), sometimes on both sides (see Eze 2:10; Rev 5:1). Some Egyptian scrolls were over 100 feet (30.5 m) long; Biblical scrolls, however, rarely exceeded 30 feet (9 m) in length, as in the case of a book like Isaiah (see Lk 4:17). Reading a scroll involved unrolling it with one hand while rolling it up again with the other (see Isa 34:4; Eze 2:10). To protect its contents, a scroll was rolled up and often sealed (see Isa 29:11; Da 12:4; Rev 5:1–2,5,9). The book form used today replaced the scroll shortly after the time of Christ. See "Scrolls, Seals and Codices" on page 2053.

The Hyksos and the Old Testament

EXODUS 18 The **Hyksos**, whose name means "rulers of foreign countries," filtered into Egypt during the **Middle Bronze Age** when Egyptian authority was weak and decentralizing. They entered Egypt during the latter part of the Egyptian **Middle Kingdom** period (c. 1800–1650 B.C.) and settled in the eastern delta region. Nothing is known about their origin, but their racial identity was mixed (mostly Semitic).

During the eighteenth century B.C. the Hyksos captured the Egyptian administrative capital at Memphis[1] and soon established their own capital at Avaris (identified as modern Tell ed-Dab'a. In Upper (southern) Egypt, however, Hyksos power remained limited because Egyptian princes retained control of Thebes.

According to the Egyptian priest-historian Manetho (third century B.C.), the Hyksos established the Fifteenth and Sixteenth Egyptian Dynasties. Hyksos rulers, who controlled most of Lower (northern) Egypt for about one hundred years, used Egyptian titles, and their culture reflected a blending of Egyptian and Semitic cultures. The Hyksos introduced military innovations to Egypt, perhaps including the compound bow as well as new types of daggers, swords and battle-axes. They used horses and chariots and also may have introduced the war chariot to Egypt.[3]

Pharaoh Seqenenra of the Seventeenth Egyptian Dynasty (whose capital was Thebes[4] in Upper—southern—Egypt) attempted to eliminate Hyksos rule but was mortally wounded in combat (his mummy shows that his face was struck with a battle-ax). His successor, Kamose, led a campaign into the eastern delta and attacked the Hyksos capital, Avaris, apparently failing, however, to capture it. Three years later Ahmose, the younger brother of Kamose, ascended to the throne and successfully expelled the Hyksos from Avaris. (A temple at Abydos depicted on its walls painted scenes of Ahmose's victory over the Hyksos.) Ahmose established the powerful Eighteenth Dynasty and reunited Upper and Lower Egypt.

Interestingly, the Hyksos are not mentioned in the Bible, nor is there any known connection between this people group and the Biblical **patriarchs**. Nevertheless, it is reasonable to assume that the Israelites lived in the eastern delta (i.e., Goshen) during the period of Hyksos domination. The hatred the Egyptians held for Semites after the Hyksos expulsion would have served as an appropriate context for Egyptian enslavement of the Semitic Israelites and the resulting harsh labor forced upon them.[5]

[1]See "Memphis" on page 1270. [2]See "Anatolia and the Hittites" on page 144. [3]See "Horses and Chariots in Ancient Warfare" on page 114. [4]See "Thebes" on page 1354. [5]See "Slavery and Labor Law in the Ancient Near East" on page 127 and "The Hyksos and the Exodus" on page 99.

Jethro Visits Moses

18 Now Jethro, the priest of Midian[l] and father-in-law of Moses, heard of everything God had done for
Moses and for his people Israel, and how the LORD had brought Israel out of Egypt.
2 After Moses had sent away his wife Zipporah,[m] his father-in-law Jethro received her 3 and her two sons.[n]
One son was named Gershom,[a] for Moses said, "I have become an alien in a foreign land";[o] 4 and the other
was named Eliezer,[b][p] for he said, "My father's God was my helper; he saved me from the sword of Pharaoh."
5 Jethro, Moses' father-in-law, together with Moses' sons and wife, came to him in the desert, where he
was camped near the mountain[q] of God. 6 Jethro had sent word to him, "I, your father-in-law Jethro, am
coming to you with your wife and her two sons."
7 So Moses went out to meet his father-in-law and bowed down[r] and kissed[s] him. They greeted each
other and then went into the tent. 8 Moses told his father-in-law about everything the LORD had done to
Pharaoh and the Egyptians for Israel's sake and about all the hardships they had met along the way and
how the LORD had saved[t] them.
9 Jethro was delighted to hear about all the good things the LORD had done for Israel in rescuing them
from the hand of the Egyptians. 10 He said, "Praise be to the LORD,[u] who rescued you from the hand of the
Egyptians and of Pharaoh, and who rescued the people from the hand of the Egyptians. 11 Now I know
that the LORD is greater than all other gods,[v] for he did this to those who had treated Israel arrogantly."[w]
12 Then Jethro, Moses' father-in-law, brought a burnt offering and other sacrifices to God, and Aaron came
with all the elders of Israel to eat bread with Moses' father-in-law in the presence[x] of God.
13 The next day Moses took his seat to serve as judge for the people, and they stood around him from
morning till evening. 14 When his father-in-law saw all that Moses was doing for the people, he said, "What
is this you are doing for the people? Why do you alone sit as judge, while all these people stand around
you from morning till evening?"
15 Moses answered him, "Because the people come to me to seek God's will.[y] 16 Whenever they have a
dispute, it is brought to me, and I decide between the parties and inform them of God's decrees and laws."[z]
17 Moses' father-in-law replied, "What you are doing is not good. 18 You and these people who come to
you will only wear yourselves out. The work is too heavy for you; you cannot handle it alone.[a] 19 Listen
now to me and I will give you some advice, and may God be with you.[b] You must be the people's repre-
sentative before God and bring their disputes[c] to him. 20 Teach them the decrees and laws,[d] and show
them the way to live[e] and the duties they are to perform.[f] 21 But select capable men[g] from all the peo-
ple—men who fear God, trustworthy men who hate dishonest gain[h]—and appoint them as officials[i]
over thousands, hundreds, fifties and tens. 22 Have them serve as judges for the people at all times, but
have them bring every difficult case[j] to you; the simple cases they can decide themselves. That will make
your load lighter, because they will share[k] it with you. 23 If you do this and God so commands, you will
be able to stand the strain, and all these people will go home satisfied."
24 Moses listened to his father-in-law and did everything he said. 25 He chose capable men from all Is-
rael and made them leaders of the people, officials over thousands, hundreds, fifties and tens.[l] 26 They
served as judges for the people at all times. The difficult cases they brought to Moses, but the simple ones
they decided themselves.[m]
27 Then Moses sent his father-in-law on his way, and Jethro returned to his own country.[n]

At Mount Sinai

19 In the third month after the Israelites left Egypt—on the very day—they came to the Desert of
Sinai. 2 After they set out from Rephidim,[o] they entered the Desert of Sinai, and Israel camped
there in the desert in front of the mountain.[p]
3 Then Moses went up to God, and the LORD called[q] to him from the mountain and said, "This is what
you are to say to the house of Jacob and what you are to tell the people of Israel: 4 'You yourselves have seen
what I did to Egypt,[r] and how I carried you on eagles' wings[s] and brought you to myself. 5 Now if you
obey me fully[t] and keep my covenant,[u] then out of all nations you will be my treasured possession.[v] Al-
though the whole earth[w] is mine, 6 you[c] will be for me a kingdom of priests[x] and a holy nation.'[y] These
are the words you are to speak to the Israelites."

[a] 3 *Gershom* sounds like the Hebrew for *an alien there.* [b] 4 *Eliezer* means *my God is helper.* [c] 5,6 Or *possession, for the whole earth is mine.* 6 *You*

18:1 [l]Ex 2:16; 3:1
18:2 [m]Ex 2:21; 4:25
18:3 [n]Ex 4:20; Ac 7:29 [o]Ex 2:22
18:4 [p]1Ch 23:15
18:5 [q]Ex 3:1
18:7 [r]Ge 43:28 [s]Ge 29:13
18:8 [t]Ex 15:6,16; Ps 81:7
18:10 [u]Ge 14:20; Ps 68:19-20
18:11 [v]Ex 12:12; 15:11; 2Ch 2:5 [w]Lk 1:51
18:12 [x]Dt 12:7
18:15 [y]Nu 9:6,8; Dt 17:8-13
18:16 [z]Lev 24:12
18:18 [a]Nu 11:11,14,17
18:19 [b]Ex 3:12 [c]Nu 27:5
18:20 [d]Dt 5:1 [e]Ps 143:8 [f]Dt 1:18
18:21 [g]Ac 6:3 [h]Dt 16:19; Ps 15:5; Eze 18:8 [i]Dt 1:13,15; 2Ch 19:5-10
18:22 [j]Dt 1:17-18 [k]Nu 11:17
18:25 [l]Dt 1:13-15
18:26 [m]ver 22
18:27 [n]Nu 10:29-30
19:2 [o]Ex 17:1 [p]Ex 3:1
19:3 [q]Ex 3:4; Ac 7:38
19:4 [r]Dt 29:2 [s]Isa 63:9
19:5 [t]Ex 15:26 [u]Dt 5:2 [v]Dt 14:2; Ps 135:4 [w]Ex 9:29; Dt 10:14
19:6 [x]1Pe 2:5 [y]Dt 7:6; 26:19; Isa 62:12

19:2 See "The Location of Mount Sinai" on page 123.

THE LOCATION OF MOUNT SINAI

EXODUS 19 Scholars continue to debate the location of Mount Sinai, putting forth arguments in support of the following locations:

A Southern Sinai Location

The traditionally recognized site of Mount Sinai is Jebel Musa ("Mountain of Moses") in the southern Sinai Peninsula. This identification was first made in the fourth century A.D. in the pilgrimage journal of a man named Egeria.

Nearby is a broad plain called er-Raha, the only place in southern Sinai that could have accommodated all the migrating Israelites. But this area has little water.

A Northern Sinai Location

Those who believe Mount Sinai is located in the northern Sinai Peninsula offer two principal arguments:

◆ The Israelites' movement was slowed by children and livestock (see Ex 12:37–38). According to Deuteronomy 1:2 Mount Sinai is an eleven-day journey on foot from Kadesh Barnea—probably modern Tell el-Qudeirat in northern Sinai.[1] This would place Mount Sinai in the northern Sinai Peninsula, roughly 60 miles (97 km) from Kadesh Barnea.

But Deuteronomy 1:2 reveals that the *average* traveler could complete the trip this quickly. This suggests a location considerably farther than 60 miles away. Camp locations along traditional trade routes were often more than 30 miles apart. If anything, Deuteronomy 1:2 excludes locating Mount Sinai at less than 200 miles (323 km) from Kadesh Barnea.

◆ Moses requested permission for Israel to make a three-day journey into the desert (Ex 5:3). Assuming that the Israelites intended to travel to Mount Sinai, the mountain had to be within a three-day trek of Egypt. However, Exodus 5:3 says nothing about an intention of going to Sinai.

An Arabian Location

A third possibility is that Mount Sinai is in the Arabian Peninsula. Most interpreters have long dismissed this theory, but Colin Humphreys recently revived it, and the hypothesis offers intriguing possibilities. The main arguments are:

◆ Midian, where Moses lived after his initial flight from Egypt (2:15), was in northwestern Arabia.[2] Because the Midianites ranged over a large area (Jdg 6:1–6), Moses need not have lived in Arabia per se. However, the fact that some Midianites had left their homeland is not pertinent; the text states that Moses lived "in Midian" (almost certainly northwestern Arabia), not "among Midianites."

◆ Moses first encountered God at Mount Sinai while shepherding Jethro's flock in "the far side of the desert" (Ex 3:1; some versions say "west of the desert" or "behind the desert"). Moses must have guided Jethro's flock from Midian toward the east, since the Red Sea formed Midian's western boundary. Midian was located in the low, coastal area of western Arabia called the Tihama, an extremely hot region during the summer. Just east is a desert named the Shifa, and behind that is the Hisma, with a higher terrain and numerous oases. Shepherds routinely escaped the heat by moving up into the Hisma; this may be what Exodus 3:1 describes.

◆ According to Exodus 19:16–18 and Deuteronomy 4:11, Mount Sinai blazed with fire, was enveloped by a huge plume of cloud or smoke and shook violently as in an earthquake. Flashes of lightning and sounds like trumpet blasts[3] also occurred. The description fits a volcanic eruption. The emission of hot gases from fissures can produce trumpet-like sounds, and observers have reported seeing massive electrical displays emanating from volcanic clouds. No volcanoes are known to have erupted during that period in the Sinai Peninsula, but Arabia has many volcanoes.

One volcanic mountain in the western Arabian Peninsula, Hala al Bedr (Mount Bedr), is according to this theory a particularly promising candidate for ancient Mount Sinai. It is isolated and could have been described as in Exodus 19:12. Volcanically active during that period, the mountain sits at one end of a large, table-shaped mountain (about six miles—ten km—in diameter) called Tadra.

Tadra, large enough to have accommodated the Israelite camp (v. 2), sits in a fertile basin called al-Gaw, with numerous wells and relatively lush flora. The Israelites' eleven-month stay (Nu 10:11) would have been impossible unless the area had access to water (see also Ex 19:14).

Other arguments supporting this theory are:

◆ Demetrius, a third-century B.C. Jewish historian, made this connection.

◆ The apostle Paul stated that Mount Sinai was in Arabia (Gal 4:25).

As always, caution is necessary. Archaeology is not an exact science, and archaeologists have not fully investigated the possibility of an Arabian location for Sinai.

[1]See "Kadesh Barnea" on page 214. [2]See "Midian" on page 92. [3]See "Trumpets in the Ancient World" on page 2057.

7So Moses went back and summoned the elders of the people and set before them all the words the
LORD had commanded him to speak. 8The people all responded together, "We will do everything the LORD
has said."[z] So Moses brought their answer back to the LORD. **19:8** [z]Ex 24:3,7; Dt 5:27
9The LORD said to Moses, "I am going to come to you in a dense cloud,[a] so that the people will hear **19:9** [a]ver 16; Ex 24:15-16
me speaking[b] with you and will always put their trust in you." Then Moses told the LORD what the peo- [b]Dt 4:12,36
ple had said.
10And the LORD said to Moses, "Go to the people and consecrate[c] them today and tomorrow. Have **19:10** [c]Lev 11:44;
them wash their clothes[d] 11and be ready by the third day,[e] because on that day the LORD will come down Heb 10:22 [d]Ge 35:2
on Mount Sinai in the sight of all the people. 12Put limits for the people around the mountain and tell **19:11** [e]ver 16
them, 'Be careful that you do not go up the mountain or touch the foot of it. Whoever touches the moun-
tain shall surely be put to death. 13He shall surely be stoned[f] or shot with arrows; not a hand is to be laid **19:13**
on him. Whether man or animal, he shall not be permitted to live.' Only when the ram's horn sounds a [f]Heb 12:20*
long blast may they go up to the mountain."
14After Moses had gone down the mountain to the people, he consecrated them, and they washed their
clothes. 15Then he said to the people, "Prepare yourselves for the third day. Abstain from sexual relations."
16On the morning of the third day there was thunder and lightning, with a thick cloud over the moun-
tain, and a very loud trumpet blast.[g] Everyone in the camp trembled.[h] 17Then Moses led the people out **19:16**
of the camp to meet with God, and they stood at the foot of the mountain. 18Mount Sinai was covered with [g]Heb 12:18-19; Rev 4:1
smoke,[i] because the LORD descended on it in fire.[j] The smoke billowed up from it like smoke from a fur- [h]Heb 12:21
nace,[k] the whole mountain[a] trembled[l] violently, 19and the sound of the trumpet grew louder and loud- **19:18** [i]Ps 104:32 [j]Ex 3:2; 24:17;
er. Then Moses spoke and the voice[m] of God answered[n] him.[b] Dt 4:11; 2Ch 7:1; Ps 18:8; Heb 12:18 [k]Ge 19:28
20The LORD descended to the top of Mount Sinai and called Moses to the top of the mountain. So Mo- [l]Jdg 5:5; Ps 68:8;
ses went up 21and the LORD said to him, "Go down and warn the people so they do not force their way Jer 4:24
through to see[o] the LORD and many of them perish. 22Even the priests, who approach[p] the LORD, must **19:19** [m]Ne 9:13 [n]Ps 81:7
consecrate themselves, or the LORD will break out against them."[q] **19:21** [o]Ex 3:5; 1Sa 6:19
23Moses said to the LORD, "The people cannot come up Mount Sinai, because you yourself warned us, **19:22** [p]Lev 10:3 [q]2Sa 6:7
'Put limits[r] around the mountain and set it apart as holy.' " **19:23** [r]ver 12
24The LORD replied, "Go down and bring Aaron[s] up with you. But the priests and the people must not **19:24** [s]Ex 24:1,9
force their way through to come up to the LORD, or he will break out against them."
25So Moses went down to the people and told them.

The Ten Commandments

20 And God spoke all these words:
2"I am the LORD your God, who brought you out of Egypt, out of the land of slavery.[t] **20:2** [t]Ex 13:3
3"You shall have no other gods before[c] me.[u] **20:3** [u]Dt 6:14; Jer 35:15
4"You shall not make for yourself an idol[v] in the form of anything in heaven above or on the earth **20:4** [v]Lev 26:1;
beneath or in the waters below. 5You shall not bow down to them or worship[w] them; for I, Dt 4:15-19,23; 27:15
the LORD your God, am a jealous God,[x] punishing the children for the sin of the fathers to **20:5** [w]Isa 44:15, 17,19 [x]Ex 34:14;
the third and fourth generation[y] of those who hate me, 6but showing love to a thousand[z] Dt 4:24 [y]Nu 14:18;
⌞generations⌟ of those who love me and keep my commandments. Jer 32:18 **20:6** [z]Dt 7:9

[a] 18 Most Hebrew manuscripts; a few Hebrew manuscripts and Septuagint *all the people* [b] 19 Or *and God answered him with thunder* [c] 3 Or *besides*

20:1–21 *Judaism* refers to the religious system held by the Jews. Its teachings come from the Old Testament, especially from the Law of Moses as found in Exodus 20 through Deuteronomy, but also from the traditions of the elders (Mk 7:3–13; see the note on Mt 15:2), such as are now found in the Talmud. The principal elements of Judaism include circumcision, a strict monotheism, an abhorrence of idolatry, and Sabbath-keeping.

The Old Testament is distinctly a religion of law, with creed, cult and conduct prescribed in detail by God. Its writers praised the Torah (God's law or instructions, as set forth in the Pentateuch; cf. Ps 119:97), the revealed instruction came to God's elect nation as a gift of grace, invested with divine authority and sanction. The Torah is revered because it embodies the will and wisdom of the Creator. Expressing God's own nature, it demands of the creature only what the Creator's holiness requires for fellowship with himself. The climax of Torah is the Decalogue, the Ten Commandments or the Code of the Ten Words, received by Moses on Mount Sinai. It is the special gift of God's grace given to his people, not to bring them into bondage but precisely because they have been brought out of bondage. All of its precepts, with the exception of Sabbath-keeping, are repeated in the New Testament. Hence it is the distillation of religion and morality—simply phrased, remarkably comprehensive and universally valid. Mount Sinai was the scene of an epochal event in human history, surpassed only by Mount Calvary.

20:1–17 "Words" (v. 1) was the technical term for covenant stipulations in the ancient Near East (e.g., among the Hittites; see also 24:3,8; 34:28). The Hebrew term for *Ten Commandments* means literally "Ten Words." *Decalogue*, a word of Greek origin often used as a synonym for the Ten Commandments, carries an identical meaning.

20:4 In Israel, probably because of this commandment against representational art, there were no great contributions to the arts of

CULTURAL AND HISTORICAL NOTES

Ancient Altars

EXODUS 20 In the ancient world altars played a key role in the religious practices of many people groups. Any surface consecrated for the purpose of making sacred offerings would have been considered an altar. Biblical altars are of special interest in the context of these notes (features of altars to other gods were often similar [e.g., horns were common], but discussion of such elements is beyond the scope of this brief article).

Altar in Arad
Photograph courtesy of © Dr. Gary Pratico

The Hebrew noun *mizbeah*, translated "altar," is derived from the verbal root *zbh* (meaning "to slaughter"). God's people frequently built altars on the site of a theophany or divine appearance (e.g., Ge 12:7; 35:1,7). Theologically, altars provided a meeting place between God and humanity, an intersection between heaven and Earth. They defined the spaces in which God caused his name to dwell and at which human beings might thereby call upon that name (Ge 13:3–4; 26:25; Dt 12:11; 1Ki 8:22–54).

The special sanctity of the Israelite altar is reflected in the Biblical injunction to build it of uncut stones (Ex 20:25). This sanctity is also reflected in the fact that altars to the God of Israel were ascended via a sloping ramp rather than by a series of steps in order to prevent their defilement by the exposure of human nakedness during the priestly ascent (v. 26). Note that, although Aaron and is descendants did serve at stepped altars (see Lev 9:22; Eze 43:17), these priests were instructed to wear linen undergarments (see Ex 28:42–43; Lev 6:10; 16:3–4; Eze 44:17–18).[1]

Constructed primarily of stone, dirt, wood or metal, ancient altars of all kinds ranged from the relatively simple to the elaborately complex. Prominent characters in the Biblical narratives, including Noah (Ge 8:20), Abram (Ge 13:4), Isaac (Ge 26:25), Jacob (Ge 33:18–20) and Moses (Ex 17:15), appear to have constructed simple stone altars. Complex altars were built in conjunction with more elaborate sanctuaries, whether portable (e.g., the tabernacle)[2] or fixed (e.g., the temple).[3]

During the Old Testament period the slaughter of animals in the Israelite context took place near, rather than on, the altar (note the exception of Ge 22:9). Moreover, certain Israelite altars were used to offer grain, wine, oil and incense, sometimes in addition to animal sacrifices.[4]

The tabernacle (not yet constructed at the time represented by Ex 20) would contain an altar of bronze and another of gold. The bronze altar would be built of acacia wood, overlaid with bronze. It would stand in the courtyard, would be used specifically for burnt offerings and would have the following dimensions: 7.5 feet (2.3 m) long by 7.5 feet wide by 4.5 feet (1.4 m) high (27:1–8). The altar of gold (to be built of acacia wood and overlaid with gold; see 30:1–3) would be used for offering incense within the sanctuary and would have these dimensions: approximately 1.5 feet (.5 m) long by 1.5 feet wide by 3 feet (.9 m) high.

The bronze altar was to be hollow and fitted with four rings and two poles or staves, making it lightweight and portable. Apparently both altars were to be filled temporarily with earth and stone at each Israelite encampment (cf. 20:24–25).

Four horns, protruding from the four corners of the bronze altar, were to serve as the locations on which animal blood was to be applied to effect purification from sin (cf. 29:12). Similarly, priests were to place blood on the horns of the golden incense altar to purify it (Lev 4:7). It appears from Amos 3:14 that removal of these horns would invalidate an altar. Due to their intrinsic holiness, the horns of the altars were used to provide asylum for those who sought refuge, except in the case of intentional homicide (cf. Ex 21:14; 1Ki 1:50–51; 2:28–34).[5]

A golden incense altar and a permanent bronze altar (30 ft x 30 ft x 15 ft; 9.1 m x 9.1 m x 4.6 m) were also to be prominent fixtures in Solomon's temple (1Ki 6:22).

[1]See also "The Levites and the Priests" on page 648. [2]See "The Tabernacle and the Ark" on page 153. [3]See "Solomon's Temple and Other Ancient Temples" on page 620. [4]See "Sacrifices and Offerings in the Bible and the Ancient Near East" on page 158. [5]See "The Horned Altar" on page 924.

7 “You shall not misuse the name of the LORD your God, for the LORD will not hold anyone guiltless
who misuses his name.[a]
8 “Remember the Sabbath[b] day by keeping it holy. 9 Six days you shall labor and do all your work,[c]
10 but the seventh day is a Sabbath to the LORD your God. On it you shall not do any work, nei-
ther you, nor your son or daughter, nor your manservant or maidservant, nor your animals,
nor the alien within your gates. 11 For in six days the LORD made the heavens and the earth,
the sea, and all that is in them, but he rested[d] on the seventh day. Therefore the LORD blessed
the Sabbath day and made it holy.
12 “Honor your father and your mother,[e] so that you may live long in the land the LORD your God is
giving you.
13 “You shall not murder.[f]
14 “You shall not commit adultery.[g]
15 “You shall not steal.[h]
16 “You shall not give false testimony against your neighbor.[i]
17 “You shall not covet[j] your neighbor's house. You shall not covet your neighbor's wife, or his man-
servant or maidservant, his ox or donkey, or anything that belongs to your neighbor.”

18 When the people saw the thunder and lightning and heard the trumpet[k] and saw the mountain in
smoke, they trembled with fear. They stayed at a distance 19 and said to Moses, “Speak to us yourself and
we will listen. But do not have God speak to us or we will die.”[l]
20 Moses said to the people, “Do not be afraid. God has come to test you, so that the fear[m] of God will
be with you to keep you from sinning.”[n]
21 The people remained at a distance, while Moses approached the thick darkness[o] where God was.

Idols and Altars

22 Then the LORD said to Moses, “Tell the Israelites this: ‘You have seen for yourselves that I have spo-
ken to you from heaven:[p] 23 Do not make any gods to be alongside me;[q] do not make for yourselves gods
of silver or gods of gold.[r]
24 “ ‘Make an altar of earth for me and sacrifice on it your burnt offerings and fellowship offerings,[a]
your sheep and goats and your cattle. Wherever I cause my name[s] to be honored, I will come to you and
bless[t] you. 25 If you make an altar of stones for me, do not build it with dressed stones, for you will defile
it if you use a tool[u] on it. 26 And do not go up to my altar on steps, lest your nakedness be exposed on it.’

21 “These are the laws[v] you are to set before them:

Hebrew Servants

2 “If you buy a Hebrew servant, he is to serve you for six years. But in the seventh year, he shall go free,[w]
without paying anything. 3 If he comes alone, he is to go free alone; but if he has a wife when he comes,
she is to go with him. 4 If his master gives him a wife and she bears him sons or daughters, the woman
and her children shall belong to her master, and only the man shall go free.

20:7 [a]Lev 19:12; Mt 5:33
20:8 [b]Ex 31:13-16; Lev 26:2
20:9 [c]Ex 34:21; Lk 13:14
20:11 [d]Ge 2:2
20:12 [e]Mt 15:4*; Mk 7:10*; Eph 6:2
20:13 [f]Mt 5:21*; Ro 13:9*
20:14 [g]Mt 19:18*
20:15 [h]Lev 19:11,13; Mt 19:18*
20:16 [i]Ex 23:1,7; Mt 19:18*
20:17 [j]Ro 7:7*; 13:9*; Eph 5:3
20:18 [k]Ex 19:16-19; Heb 12:18-19
20:19 [l]Dt 5:5,23-27; Gal 3:19
20:20 [m]Dt 4:10; Isa 8:13 [n]Pr 16:6
20:21 [o]Dt 5:22
20:22 [p]Ne 9:13
20:23 [q]ver 3 [r]Ex 32:4,8,31
20:24 [s]Dt 12:5; 16:6,11; 2Ch 6:6 [t]Ge 12:2
20:25 [u]Dt 27:5-6
21:1 [v]Dt 4:14
21:2 [w]Jer 34:8, 14

[a] *24* Traditionally *peace offerings*

painting or sculpting. The major architectural work in Israel—the temple—was notable, yet even that was constructed with some help from Phoenician craftsmen (see “Ancient Craftsmanship” on p. 141 and “The Building Activity of Solomon” on p. 497). References to dance in the Old Testament are limited and afford no information on form or content. The development of music in Israel, on the other hand, is noteworthy (see “Ancient Musical Instruments” on p. 797); to judge from the titles we may assume that many of the psalms were sung and accompanied by musical instruments. Literature was the most thoroughly developed art form in Israel, reaching a level unsurpassed in all of antiquity (see “Ancient Israelite Poets and Singers” on p. 869).

20:6 In the treaty language of the ancient Near East, the “love” owed to the great king was a conventional term for total allegiance and implicit trust expressing itself in obedient service.

20:8–11 For information concerning the Sabbath, see “Sabbath, Sabbath Year and the Jubilee” on page 189. See also the note on 16:21–30.

20:24–25 The excavation of ruins of a small Iron Age (tenth, or possibly eleventh, century B.C.) Israelite temple at Arad (in the southern region of modern-day Palestine) has uncovered an altar with the same dimensions as those of the altar in the tabernacle (see 27:1). In addition, many ancient altars of undressed stones (from various periods) have been found in the region. See “Ancient Altars” on page 125.

20:26 The oldest stepped altar discovered in modern-day Palestine is located at Megiddo and dates between 3000 and 2500 B.C. Men who ascended to such altars would unavoidably expose their nakedness in the presence of God. Although Aaron and his descendants served at stepped altars (see Lev 9:22; Eze 43:17), they were instructed to wear linen undergarments (see Ex 28:42–43; Lev 6:10; 16:3–4; Eze 44:17–18). See also “Ancient Altars” on page 125.

Slavery and Labor Law in the Ancient Near East

EXODUS 21 The practice of slavery extends back into the fourth millennium B.C. and is attested widely throughout virtually all documented time periods of the ancient Near East. The institution likely originated when ancient peoples took prisoners of war and was later extended in other ways, such as enslavement for debt or for having committed a crime. Slaves, like livestock, were viewed as a form of property and were used as collateral and in dowries, as well as passed on to heirs.

Laws regulating slavery have been preserved from many ancient cultures (including those of **Sumer**, **Nuzi**, **Babylonia**, **Assyria** and Israel). The Babylonian **Code of Hammurabi** (eighteenth century B.C.) reveals much about such laws. According to this code slaves received some rights but clearly held a diminished status compared to the rest of society. This code limited debt slavery to three years and permitted slavery to be imposed upon negligent landowners and even spendthrift wives! Free citizens and slaves could intermarry, according to **Old Babylonian** law. Evidence dating to the first millennium B.C. also reveals that some slaves actually owned houses and land.

When we compare slavery laws in the broader ancient Near East to those of the Bible, both similarities and differences surface. The Old Testament regulated slavery, but the institution itself was never questioned (the same applies to the NT). Even so, limitations placed on slavery often were rooted in the Israelites' personal experience as slaves in Egypt (Dt 15:15):

✣ Unlike foreign slaves in Israel, who could be retained indefinitely (see Lev 25:44–46), a Hebrew slave (male or female) was to be released during his or her seventh year of servitude.[1]

✣ The slaveholder was obligated to supply a departing Hebrew slave with ample provisions for a successful reentrance into society (Dt 15:12–15).

✣ Exodus 21:5–6 records a rule (paralleled in Dt 15:16–17) concerning slaves who opted to remain with their masters for life. Such a slave was to have an ear pierced, a marking that demonstrated his or her voluntary lifelong servitude. Such markings on the ear, along with the practice of branding the skin, were also seen in Assyria.

✣ Exodus 21:7–11 addresses the issue of a father selling his daughter into debt-slavery (presumably to become the wife of the buyer or of the buyer's son), a practice that also occurred in Assyria during the first millennium B.C. The buyer was not free to sell the girl outside of Israel should he choose not to keep her; he was obligated either to adequately provide for her needs or permit her to go free. Thus the Old Testament law protected not only the virtue of the young woman but also her socioeconomic situation.

✣ Old Testament rules governing a female captive of war (Dt 21:10–14) seem harsh to a modern reader but were actually quite humane according to ancient standards, by which such women would in most other contexts have become the slave-concubines of enemy soldiers. The Hebrew rules required a captive woman to shave off her hair and trim her nails but also permitted her a month to mourn her situation (during this time the soldier who had captured her was not allowed sexual relations with her). This provision protected the captured woman from rape and gave the Israelite soldier a month-long "cooling-off" period, during which he could decide whether or not he truly wanted her as his wife. If he opted not to marry her she was allowed to go free.

Such laws demonstrate the Bible's alignment with the broader Near-Eastern cultural idea of slavery while, in most cases, uniquely circumscribing the limits of the practice in order to ensure more humane treatment of slaves in Israel.[2]

Samaritan document, c. 350 B.C., for the sale of a Hebrew slave

Preserving Bible Times; © Dr. James C. Martin; permission of The Israel Museum

Branding iron for runaway slaves

© The Schøyen Collection; photography courtesy of Mr. Martin Schøyen

[1]See "The Sabbath, Sabbath Year and the Jubilee" on page 189. [2]For information on slavery during the New Testament period, see "Slavery in the Greco-Roman World" on page 1979.

5"But if the servant declares, 'I love my master and my wife and children and do not want to go free,'[x] **21:5** [x]Dt 15:16
6then his master must take him before the judges.[a][y] He shall take him to the door or the doorpost and **21:6** [y]Ex 22:8-9
pierce his ear with an awl. Then he will be his servant for life.[z] [z]Ne 5:5
7"If a man sells his daughter as a servant, she is not to go free as menservants do. 8If she does not
please the master who has selected her for himself,[b] he must let her be redeemed. He has no right to sell
her to foreigners, because he has broken faith with her. 9If he selects her for his son, he must grant her
the rights of a daughter. 10If he marries another woman, he must not deprive the first one of her food,
clothing and marital rights.[a] 11If he does not provide her with these three things, she is to go free, with- **21:10** [a]1Co 7:3-5
out any payment of money.

Personal Injuries

12"Anyone who strikes a man and kills him shall surely be put to death.[b] 13However, if he does not do **21:12** [b]Ge 9:6; Mt 26:52
it intentionally, but God lets it happen, he is to flee to a place[c] I will designate. 14But if a man schemes and **21:13** [c]Nu 35:10-34; Dt 19:2-13; Jos 20:9; 1Sa 24:4,10,18
kills another man deliberately,[d] take him away from my altar and put him to death.[e] **21:14** [d]Heb 10:26 [e]Dt 19:11-12; 1Ki 2:28-34
15"Anyone who attacks[c] his father or his mother must be put to death.
16"Anyone who kidnaps another and either sells[f] him or still has him when he is caught must be put **21:16** [f]Ge 37:28
to death.[g] [g]Ex 22:4; Dt 24:7
17"Anyone who curses his father or mother must be put to death.[h] **21:17** [h]Lev 20:9-10; Mt 15:4*; Mk 7:10*
18"If men quarrel and one hits the other with a stone or with his fist[d] and he does not die but is con-
fined to bed, 19the one who struck the blow will not be held responsible if the other gets up and walks
around outside with his staff; however, he must pay the injured man for the loss of his time and see that
he is completely healed.
20"If a man beats his male or female slave with a rod and the slave dies as a direct result, he must
be punished, 21but he is not to be punished if the slave gets up after a day or two, since the slave is his
property.[i] **21:21** [i]Lev 25:44-46
22"If men who are fighting hit a pregnant woman and she gives birth prematurely[e] but there is no se-
rious injury, the offender must be fined whatever the woman's husband demands[j] and the court allows. **21:22** [j]ver 30; Dt 22:18-19
23But if there is serious injury, you are to take life for life,[k] 24eye for eye, tooth for tooth,[l] hand for hand, **21:23** [k]Lev 24:19; Dt 19:21
foot for foot, 25burn for burn, wound for wound, bruise for bruise. **21:24** [l]Mt 5:38*
26"If a man hits a manservant or maidservant in the eye and destroys it, he must let the servant go free
to compensate for the eye. 27And if he knocks out the tooth of a manservant or maidservant, he must let
the servant go free to compensate for the tooth.
28"If a bull gores a man or a woman to death, the bull must be stoned to death,[m] and its meat must **21:28** [m]ver 32; Ge 9:5
not be eaten. But the owner of the bull will not be held responsible. 29If, however, the bull has had the
habit of goring and the owner has been warned but has not kept it penned up and it kills a man or wom-
an, the bull must be stoned and the owner also must be put to death. 30However, if payment is demand-
ed of him, he may redeem his life by paying whatever is demanded.[n] 31This law also applies if the bull **21:30** [n]ver 22; Nu 35:31
gores a son or daughter. 32If the bull gores a male or female slave, the owner must pay thirty shekels[f][o] of **21:32** [o]Zec 11:12-13;
silver to the master of the slave, and the bull must be stoned. Mt 26:15; 27:3,9
33"If a man uncovers a pit or digs one and fails to cover it and an ox or a donkey falls into it, 34the
owner of the pit must pay for the loss; he must pay its owner, and the dead animal will be his.
35"If a man's bull injures the bull of another and it dies, they are to sell the live one and divide both the
money and the dead animal equally. 36However, if it was known that the bull had the habit of goring, yet the
owner did not keep it penned up, the owner must pay, animal for animal, and the dead animal will be his.

Protection of Property

22 "If a man steals an ox or a sheep and slaughters it or sells it, he must pay back[p] five head of cat- **22:1** [p]2Sa 12:6; Pr 6:31; Lk 19:8
tle for the ox and four sheep for the sheep.

[a] 6 Or *before God* [b] 8 Or *master so that he does not choose her* [c] 15 Or *kills* [d] 18 Or *with a tool* [e] 22 Or *she has a miscarriage* [f] 32 That is, about 12 ounces (about 0.3 kilogram)

21:15–17 Death was the prescribed punishment for the following sins: striking or even cursing a parent (vv. 15–17), blasphemy (Lev 24:14,16,23), Sabbath-breaking (Nu 15:32–36), witchcraft (Ex 22:18), adultery (Lev 20:10), rape (Dt 22:25), incestuous or unnatural relations (Lev 20:11,14,16), kidnapping (Ex 21:16) and idolatry (Lev 20:2).

22:2 [q]Mt 6:19-20; 24:43 2“If a thief is caught breaking in[q] and is struck so that he dies, the defender is not guilty of bloodshed;[r]
[r]Nu 35:27 3but if it happens[a] after sunrise, he is guilty of bloodshed.
22:3 [s]Ex 21:2; “A thief must certainly make restitution, but if he has nothing, he must be sold[s] to pay for his theft.
Mt 18:25 4“If the stolen animal is found alive in his possession—whether ox or donkey or sheep—he must pay
22:4 [t]Ge 43:12 back double.[t]
5“If a man grazes his livestock in a field or vineyard and lets them stray and they graze in another
man’s field, he must make restitution from the best of his own field or vineyard.
6“If a fire breaks out and spreads into thornbushes so that it burns shocks of grain or standing grain
or the whole field, the one who started the fire must make restitution.
7“If a man gives his neighbor silver or goods for safekeeping and they are stolen from the neigh-
22:7 [u]ver 4 bor’s house, the thief, if he is caught, must pay back double.[u] 8But if the thief is not found, the own-
22:8 [v]Ex 21:6; Dt 17:8-9; 19:17 er of the house must appear before the judges[b][v] to determine whether he has laid his hands on the
other man’s property. 9In all cases of illegal possession of an ox, a donkey, a sheep, a garment, or
any other lost property about which somebody says, ‘This is mine,’ both parties are to bring their
22:9 [w]ver 28; Dt 25:1 cases before the judges.[w] The one whom the judges declare[c] guilty must pay back double to his
neighbor.
10“If a man gives a donkey, an ox, a sheep or any other animal to his neighbor for safekeeping and it
dies or is injured or is taken away while no one is looking, 11the issue between them will be settled by the
22:11 [x]Heb 6:16 taking of an oath[x] before the LORD that the neighbor did not lay hands on the other person’s property. The
owner is to accept this, and no restitution is required. 12But if the animal was stolen from the neighbor,
he must make restitution to the owner. 13If it was torn to pieces by a wild animal, he shall bring in the
22:13 [y]Ge 31:39 remains as evidence and he will not be required to pay for the torn animal.[y]
14“If a man borrows an animal from his neighbor and it is injured or dies while the owner is not pres-
ent, he must make restitution. 15But if the owner is with the animal, the borrower will not have to pay. If
the animal was hired, the money paid for the hire covers the loss.

Social Responsibility

22:16 [z]Dt 22:28 16“If a man seduces a virgin[z] who is not pledged to be married and sleeps with her, he must pay the
bride-price, and she shall be his wife. 17If her father absolutely refuses to give her to him, he must still
pay the bride-price for virgins.
22:18 [a]Lev 20:27; Dt 18:11; 1Sa 28:3 18“Do not allow a sorceress[a] to live.
22:19 [b]Lev 18:23; Dt 27:21 19“Anyone who has sexual relations with an animal[b] must be put to death.
22:20 [c]Dt 17:2-5 20“Whoever sacrifices to any god other than the LORD must be destroyed.[d][c]
22:21 [d]Lev 19:33 [e]Dt 10:19 21“Do not mistreat an alien[d] or oppress him, for you were aliens[e] in Egypt.
22:22 [f]Dt 24:6, 10,12,17 22“Do not take advantage of a widow or an orphan.[f] 23If you do and they cry out[g] to me, I will certain-
22:23 [g]Lk 18:7 [h]Dt 15:9; Ps 18:6 ly hear their cry.[h] 24My anger will be aroused, and I will kill you with the sword; your wives will become
22:24 [i]Ps 69:24; 109:9 widows and your children fatherless.[i]
22:25 [j]Lev 25:35-37; Dt 23:20; Ps 15:5 25“If you lend money to one of my people among you who is needy, do not be like a moneylender;
charge him no interest.[e][j] 26If you take your neighbor’s cloak as a pledge,[k] return it to him by sunset, 27be-
cause his cloak is the only covering he has for his body. What else will he sleep in? When he cries out to
22:26 [k]Dt 24:6 me, I will hear, for I am compassionate.[l]
22:27 [l]Ex 34:6 28“Do not blaspheme God[f][m] or curse the ruler of your people.[n]
22:28 [m]Lev 24:11,16 [n]Ecc 10:20; Ac 23:5* 29“Do not hold back offerings[o] from your granaries or your vats.[g]
“You must give me the firstborn of your sons.[p] 30Do the same with your cattle and your sheep.[q] Let
22:29 [o]Ex 23:15, 16,19 [p]Ex 13:2 them stay with their mothers for seven days, but give them to me on the eighth day.[r]
22:30 [q]Ex 13:12; Dt 15:19 [r]Lev 22:27 31“You are to be my holy people.[s] So do not eat the meat of an animal torn by wild beasts;[t] throw it
22:31 [s]Lev 19:2 [t]Eze 4:14 to the dogs.

[a] 3 Or *if he strikes him* [b] 8 Or *before God*; also in verse 9 [c] 9 Or *whom God declares* [d] 20 The Hebrew term refers to the irrevocable giving over of things or persons to the LORD, often by totally destroying them. [e] 25 Or *excessive interest* [f] 28 Or *Do not revile the judges* [g] 29 The meaning of the Hebrew for this phrase is uncertain.

22:16–31 This passage demonstrates the close association between “secular,” or social, concerns and matters of proper worship. For ancient Israel all of life was rooted in worship, and the quality of people’s worship was demonstrated in part by their conduct toward others. See “The Hittite Laws” on page 281.

22:19 Acts of bestiality performed by pagan gods and demigods (mythical beings with less power than a god but more than a man) are described in the ancient myths and epics of Babylon and Canaan.

Laws of Justice and Mercy

23 “Do not spread false reports.[u] Do not help a wicked man by being a malicious witness.[v] 23:1 [u]Ex 20:16; Ps 101:5
2“Do not follow the crowd in doing wrong. When you give testimony in a lawsuit, do not pervert [v]Ps 35:11; Ac 6:11
justice[w] by siding with the crowd, 3and do not show favoritism to a poor man in his lawsuit. 23:2 [w]Dt 16:19
4“If you come across your enemy’s ox or donkey wandering off, be sure to take it back to him.[x] 5If you 23:4 [x]Dt 22:1-3
see the donkey[y] of someone who hates you fallen down under its load, do not leave it there; be sure you 23:5 [y]Dt 22:4
help him with it.
6“Do not deny justice[z] to your poor people in their lawsuits. 7Have nothing to do with a false charge[a] 23:6 [z]ver 2 23:7 [a]Eph 4:25
and do not put an innocent or honest person to death, for I will not acquit the guilty.
8“Do not accept a bribe,[b] for a bribe blinds those who see and twists the words of the righteous. 23:8 [b]Dt 10:17; 16:19; Pr 15:27
9“Do not oppress an alien;[c] you yourselves know how it feels to be aliens, because you were aliens in 23:9 [c]Ex 22:21
Egypt.

Sabbath Laws

10“For six years you are to sow your fields and harvest the crops, 11but during the seventh year let the
land lie unplowed and unused. Then the poor among your people may get food from it, and the wild animals may eat what they leave. Do the same with your vineyard and your olive grove.
12“Six days do your work,[d] but on the seventh day do not work, so that your ox and your donkey may 23:12 [d]Ex 20:9
rest and the slave born in your household, and the alien as well, may be refreshed.
13“Be careful[e] to do everything I have said to you. Do not invoke the names of other gods; do not let 23:13 [e]1Ti 4:16
them be heard on your lips.

The Three Annual Festivals

14“Three times[f] a year you are to celebrate a festival to me. 23:14 [f]Ex 34:23, 24
15“Celebrate the Feast of Unleavened Bread;[g] for seven days eat bread made without yeast, as I com- 23:15 [g]Ex 12:17
manded you. Do this at the appointed time in the month of Abib, for in that month you came out of Egypt.
“No one is to appear before me empty-handed.[h] [h]Ex 34:20
16“Celebrate the Feast of Harvest with the firstfruits[i] of the crops you sow in your field. 23:16 [i]Ex 34:22
“Celebrate the Feast of Ingathering at the end of the year, when you gather in your crops from the field.[j] [j]Dt 16:13

ANCIENT TEXTS AND ARTIFACTS

The Zukru Festival

EXODUS 23 Exodus 23:14–19 describes Israel’s three primary annual festivals.[1] Advocates of the Documentary Hypothesis[2] have argued that **Late Bronze Age** Israelites would not have been sophisticated enough to have organized such elaborate celebrations as those described in the **Pentateuch**. Instead, these scholars suggest that the descriptions of these festivals come from a priestly source developed during the **post-exilic period** (sometime after 536 B.C.). However, archaeologists are now in possession of a complex literary work from the Syrian city of Emar that contradicts this theory.

A large tablet from Emar, predating the Pentateuch’s descriptions of the festivals, intricately describes that city’s zukru festival. This elaborate commemorative celebration, which was to be conducted every seven years, required a full year of preparation! This tablet gives detailed instructions concerning the specified offerings to the city’s 70 deities: which animals were to be offered to which gods, how many animals were to be sacrificed, who was to donate each animal, the precise date of each offering and the manner in which it was to be presented. Instructions for the procession of the deities’ statues are included, with particular focus on Dagan (the chief god of Emar).

Thus we know that ancient people already adhered to complicated, written instructions for cultic rituals during the Late Bronze Age.[3] The Biblical descriptions and instructions concerning Israel’s festivals fit well into this scenario.

[1]See “The Festivals of Israel” on page 186. [2]See “The Documentary Hypothesis” on page 15. [3]See “Archaeological Periods” chart on page xx in the front of this Bible.

17 “Three times[k] a year all the men are to appear before the Sovereign LORD.

18 “Do not offer the blood of a sacrifice to me along with anything containing yeast.[l]

“The fat of my festival offerings must not be kept until morning.[m]

19 “Bring the best of the firstfruits[n] of your soil to the house of the LORD your God.

“Do not cook a young goat in its mother’s milk.[o]

God’s Angel to Prepare the Way

20 “See, I am sending an angel[p] ahead of you to guard you along the way and to bring you to the place I have prepared.[q] 21 Pay attention to him and listen[r] to what he says. Do not rebel against him; he will not forgive your rebellion,[s] since my Name is in him. 22 If you listen carefully to what he says and do all that I say, I will be an enemy[t] to your enemies and will oppose those who oppose you. 23 My angel will go ahead of you and bring you into the land of the Amorites, Hittites, Perizzites, Canaanites, Hivites and Jebusites,[u] and I will wipe them out. 24 Do not bow down before their gods or worship[v] them or follow their practices.[w] You must demolish[x] them and break their sacred stones to pieces. 25 Worship the LORD your God,[y] and his blessing[z] will be on your food and water. I will take away sickness[a] from among you, 26 and none will miscarry or be barren[b] in your land. I will give you a full life span.[c]

27 “I will send my terror[d] ahead of you and throw into confusion[e] every nation you encounter. I will make all your enemies turn their backs and run. 28 I will send the hornet[f] ahead of you to drive the Hivites, Canaanites and Hittites out of your way. 29 But I will not drive them out in a single year, because the land would become desolate and the wild animals[g] too numerous for you. 30 Little by little I will drive them out before you, until you have increased enough to take possession of the land.

31 “I will establish your borders from the Red Sea[a] to the Sea of the Philistines,[b] and from the desert to the River.[c][h] I will hand over to you the people who live in the land and you will drive them out[i] before you. 32 Do not make a covenant[j] with them or with their gods. 33 Do not let them live in your land, or they will cause you to sin against me, because the worship of their gods will certainly be a snare[k] to you.”

ANCIENT VOICES

After eating and drinking they rub all the stones with oil and blood.

In front of the Battle Gate they perform a sacrificial homage for all the gods with a ewe, two pair of thick loaves made of [barley]* mash bread, and one jar from the king.

That one ewe is to be burnt for all the gods.

The breads, the beverages, and the meat go back up into the town.

*Word in brackets added by translator for clarity

—THE ZUKRU FESTIVAL

See “The Zukru Festival” article.

The Covenant Confirmed

24 Then he said to Moses, “Come up to the LORD, you and Aaron, Nadab and Abihu,[l] and seventy of the elders[m] of Israel. You are to worship at a distance, 2 but Moses alone is to approach the LORD; the others must not come near. And the people may not come up with him.”

3 When Moses went and told the people all the LORD’s words and laws, they responded with one voice, “Everything the LORD has said we will do.”[n] 4 Moses then wrote[o] down everything the LORD had said.

He got up early the next morning and built an altar at the foot of the mountain and set up twelve stone pillars[p] representing the twelve tribes of Israel. 5 Then he sent young Israelite men, and they offered burnt offerings and sacrificed young bulls as fellowship offerings[d] to the LORD. 6 Moses took half of the blood[q] and put it in bowls, and the other half he sprinkled on the altar. 7 Then he took the Book of the Covenant[r] and read it to the people. They responded, “We will do everything the LORD has said; we will obey.”

8 Moses then took the blood, sprinkled it on the people and said, “This is the blood of the covenant[s] that the LORD has made with you in accordance with all these words.”

9 Moses and Aaron, Nadab and Abihu, and the seventy elders[t] of Israel went up 10 and saw[u] the God of Israel. Under his feet was something like a pavement made of sapphire,[e][v] clear as the sky[w] itself. 11 But God did not raise his hand against these leaders of the Israelites; they saw[x] God, and they ate and drank.

23:17 [k]Dt 16:16
23:18 [l]Ex 34:25 [m]Dt 16:4
23:19 [n]Ex 22:29; Dt 26:2,10 [o]Dt 14:21
23:20 [p]Ex 14:19; 32:34 [q]Ex 15:17
23:21 [r]Nu 14:11; Dt 18:19 [s]Ps 78:8,40,56
23:22 [t]Ge 12:3; Dt 30:7
23:23 [u]ver 20; Jos 24:8,11
23:24 [v]Ex 20:5 [w]Dt 12:30-31 [x]Ex 34:13; Nu 33:52
23:25 [y]Dt 6:13; Mt 4:10 [z]Dt 7:12-15; 28:1-14 [a]Ex 15:26
23:26 [b]Dt 7:14; Mal 3:11 [c]Job 5:26
23:27 [d]Ex 15:14; Dt 2:25 [e]Dt 7:23
23:28 [f]Dt 7:20; Jos 24:12
23:29 [g]Dt 7:22
23:31 [h]Ge 15:18 [i]Jos 21:44; 24:12,18
23:32 [j]Ex 34:12; Dt 7:2
23:33 [k]Dt 7:16; Ps 106:36
24:1 [l]Ex 6:23; Lev 10:1-2 [m]Nu 11:16
24:3 [n]Ex 19:8; Dt 5:27
24:4 [o]Dt 31:9 [p]Ge 28:18
24:6 [q]Heb 9:18
24:7 [r]Heb 9:19
24:8 [s]Heb 9:20*; 1Pe 1:2
24:9 [t]ver 1
24:10 [u]Mt 17:2; Jn 1:18; 6:46 [v]Eze 1:26 [w]Rev 4:3
24:11 [x]Ge 32:30; Ex 19:21

[a] *31* Hebrew *Yam Suph*; that is, Sea of Reeds [b] *31* That is, the Mediterranean [c] *31* That is, the Euphrates [d] *5* Traditionally *peace offerings* [e] *10* Or *lapis lazuli*

24:6–8 Sprinkling of blood, water and oil formed a vital component of the act of sacrifice. In this account of the formation of the covenant between the Lord and Israel, half the blood was sprinkled on the altar and the rest on the people. When Aaron and his sons were consecrated, some blood was sprinkled on the altar and some on Aaron and his sons and on their garments. In the various offerings blood was always sprinkled. Sprinkling was sometimes done in handfuls, sometimes with the finger and sometimes with a sprinkler—a bunch of hyssop fastened to a cedar rod.

12The LORD said to Moses, "Come up to me on the mountain and stay here, and I will give you the tab-
lets of stone,[y] with the law and commands I have written for their instruction."
13Then Moses set out with Joshua[z] his aide, and Moses went up on the mountain[a] of God. 14He said
to the elders, "Wait here for us until we come back to you. Aaron and Hur are with you, and anyone in-
volved in a dispute can go to them."
15When Moses went up on the mountain, the cloud[b] covered it, 16and the glory[c] of the LORD settled
on Mount Sinai. For six days the cloud covered the mountain, and on the seventh day the LORD called to
Moses from within the cloud.[d] 17To the Israelites the glory of the LORD looked like a consuming fire[e] on
top of the mountain. 18Then Moses entered the cloud as he went on up the mountain. And he stayed on
the mountain forty[f] days and forty nights.[g]

Offerings for the Tabernacle

25 The LORD said to Moses, 2"Tell the Israelites to bring me an offering. You are to receive the offer-
ing for me from each man whose heart prompts[h] him to give. 3These are the offerings you are to
receive from them: gold, silver and bronze; 4blue, purple and scarlet yarn and fine linen; goat hair; 5ram
skins dyed red and hides of sea cows[a]; acacia wood; 6olive oil[i] for the light; spices for the anointing oil
and for the fragrant incense; 7and onyx stones and other gems to be mounted on the ephod[j] and breast-
piece.[k]
8"Then have them make a sanctuary[l] for me, and I will dwell[m] among them. 9Make this tabernacle
and all its furnishings exactly like the pattern[n] I will show you.

The Ark

10"Have them make a chest[o] of acacia wood—two and a half cubits long, a cubit and a half wide, and
a cubit and a half high.[b] 11Overlay it with pure gold, both inside and out, and make a gold molding around
it. 12Cast four gold rings for it and fasten them to its four feet, with two rings on one side and two rings
on the other. 13Then make poles of acacia wood and overlay them with gold. 14Insert the poles into the
rings on the sides of the chest to carry it. 15The poles are to remain in the rings of this ark; they are not
to be removed.[p] 16Then put in the ark the Testimony,[q] which I will give you.
17"Make an atonement cover[c][r] of pure gold—two and a half cubits long and a cubit and a half
wide.[d] 18And make two cherubim out of hammered gold at the ends of the cover. 19Make one cherub
on one end and the second cherub on the other; make the cherubim of one piece with the cover, at the
two ends. 20The cherubim are to have their wings spread upward, overshadowing[s] the cover with them.
The cherubim are to face each other, looking toward the cover. 21Place the cover on top of the ark[t] and
put in the ark the Testimony,[u] which I will give you. 22There, above the cover between the two cheru-
bim[v] that are over the ark of the Testimony, I will meet[w] with you and give you all my commands for
the Israelites.

24:12 [y]Ex 32:15-16
24:13 [z]Ex 17:9 [a]Ex 3:1
24:15 [b]Ex 19:9
24:16 [c]Ex 16:10 [d]Ps 99:7
24:17 [e]Ex 3:2; Dt 4:36; Heb 12:18,29
24:18 [f]Dt 9:9 [g]Ex 34:28
25:2 [h]Ex 35:21; 1Ch 29:5,7,9; Ezr 2:68; 2Co 8:11-12; 9:7
25:6 [i]Ex 27:20; 30:22-32
25:7 [j]Ex 28:4,6-14 [k]Ex 28:15-30
25:8 [l]Ex 36:1-5; Heb 9:1-2 [m]Ex 29:45; 1Ki 6:13; 2Co 6:16; Rev 21:3
25:9 [n]ver 40; Ac 7:44; Heb 8:5
25:10 [o]Dt 10:1-5; Heb 9:4
25:15 [p]1Ki 8:8
25:16 [q]Dt 31:26; Heb 9:4
25:17 [r]Ro 3:25
25:20 [s]1Ki 8:7; 1Ch 28:18; Heb 9:5
25:21 [t]Ex 26:34 [u]ver 16
25:22 [v]Nu 7:89; 1Sa 4:4; 2Sa 6:2; 2Ki 19:15; Ps 80:1; Isa 37:16 [w]Ex 29:42-43

[a] *5* That is, dugongs [b] *10* That is, about 3 3/4 feet (about 1.1 meters) long and 2 1/4 feet (about 0.7 meter) wide and high
[c] *17* Traditionally *a mercy seat* [d] *17* That is, about 3 3/4 feet (about 1.1 meters) long and 2 1/4 feet (about 0.7 meter) wide

---

24:15–18 Regarding God's *shekînâh* glory (his visible Presence), see the note on 14:19.

25:4 Blue, purple and scarlet were royal colors. Blue and purple dyes were derived from various shellfish (primarily the *murex*) that swarm in the waters of the northeast Mediterranean. The dyeing industry was so important for the local economy that the promised land was known as Canaan ("land of purple") and later called Phoenicia (same meaning) by the Greeks. Scarlet dye was derived from the eggs and carcasses of the worm *coccus ilicis*, which attaches itself to the leaves of the holly plant.

The term "fine linen" refers to an exceptionally high quality cloth that was often used by Egyptian royalty. It was made from thread spun from the fibers of flax straw. Excellent examples of unusually white, tightly woven linen have been found in ancient Egyptian tombs. Some are so finely woven that they cannot be distinguished from silk without the use of a magnifying glass.

Goat hair, obtained from long-haired goats, was a coarse, black (cf. SS 1:5; 6:5) material often used to weave cloth for durable tents.

25:10–22 The word for "ark" is the same as that used of the coffin (mummy case) of Joseph (Ge 59:26). The ark of the covenant was to be constructed of acacia wood, which is darker and harder than oak and is avoided by wood-eating insects. It is common in the semi-arid conditions of the Sinai peninsula.

The ark of the covenant (or testimony) compares with the roughly contemporary shrine and funerary furniture of King Tutankhamun (c. 1350 B.C.), which, along with the Nimrud and Samaria ivories from a later period, reflects the conventional way of depicting extreme reverence in the ancient Near East—with facing winged guardians shielding a sacred place. See "The Tabernacle and the Ark" on page 153.

25:18–20 The precise appearance of the cherubim is a matter of some uncertainty, but in the Old Testament they were generally represented as winged creatures having feet and hands. Some ivory panels unearthed at Samaria depict a composite figure having a human face, a four-legged animal body and two elaborate, conspicuous wings.

Similar carvings of winged sphinxes adorned the armrests of royal thrones in many parts of the ancient Near East (see "Angels and Guardian Spirits in the Bible and the Ancient Near East" on p. 1529). In the Old Testament the cherubim were symbolic attendants that guarded the "throne" of the Lord's earthly kingdom (see 1Sa 4:4; 2Sa 6:2; 2Ki 19:15; Ps 99:1). It was from the cover of the ark (God's symbolic throne) that the Lord gave directions to Moses (see Ex 25:22; Nu 7:89). The ark's presence in the later Jerusalem temple designated Jerusalem as God's earthly, royal city (see Ps 9:11; 18:10).

The Table

25:23 [x]Heb 9:2 23“Make a table[x] of acacia wood—two cubits long, a cubit wide and a cubit and a half high.[a] 24Over-
lay it with pure gold and make a gold molding around it. 25Also make around it a rim a handbreadth[b] wide
and put a gold molding on the rim. 26Make four gold rings for the table and fasten them to the four cor-
ners, where the four legs are. 27The rings are to be close to the rim to hold the poles used in carrying the
table. 28Make the poles of acacia wood, overlay them with gold and carry the table with them. 29And
25:29 [y]Nu 4:7 25:30 make its plates and dishes of pure gold, as well as its pitchers and bowls for the pouring out of offerings.[y]
[z]Lev 24:5-9 30Put the bread of the Presence[z] on this table to be before me at all times.

The Lampstand

25:31 [a]1Ki 7:49; Zec 4:2; Heb 9:2; Rev 1:12 31“Make a lampstand[a] of pure gold and hammer it out, base and shaft; its flowerlike cups, buds and
blossoms shall be of one piece with it. 32Six branches are to extend from the sides of the lampstand—
three on one side and three on the other. 33Three cups shaped like almond flowers with buds and blos-
soms are to be on one branch, three on the next branch, and the same for all six branches extending from
the lampstand. 34And on the lampstand there are to be four cups shaped like almond flowers with buds
and blossoms. 35One bud shall be under the first pair of branches extending from the lampstand, a sec-
ond bud under the second pair, and a third bud under the third pair—six branches in all. 36The buds and
branches shall all be of one piece with the lampstand, hammered out of pure gold.
25:37 [b]Ex 27:21; Lev 24:3-4; Nu 8:2 37“Then make its seven lamps[b] and set them up on it so that they light the space in front of it. 38Its
wick trimmers and trays are to be of pure gold. 39A talent[c] of pure gold is to be used for the lampstand and
25:40 [c]Ex 26:30; Nu 8:4; Ac 7:44; Heb 8:5* all these accessories. 40See that you make them according to the pattern[c] shown you on the mountain.

The Tabernacle

26 “Make the tabernacle with ten curtains of finely twisted linen and blue, purple and scarlet yarn,
with cherubim worked into them by a skilled craftsman. 2All the curtains are to be the same
size—twenty-eight cubits long and four cubits wide.[d] 3Join five of the curtains together, and do the same
with the other five. 4Make loops of blue material along the edge of the end curtain in one set, and do the
same with the end curtain in the other set. 5Make fifty loops on one curtain and fifty loops on the end
curtain of the other set, with the loops opposite each other. 6Then make fifty gold clasps and use them
to fasten the curtains together so that the tabernacle is a unit.
7“Make curtains of goat hair for the tent over the tabernacle—eleven altogether. 8All eleven curtains
are to be the same size—thirty cubits long and four cubits wide.[e] 9Join five of the curtains together into
one set and the other six into another set. Fold the sixth curtain double at the front of the tent. 10Make

[a] *23* That is, about 3 feet (about 0.9 meter) long and 1 1/2 feet (about 0.5 meter) wide and 2 1/4 feet (about 0.7 meter) high
[b] *25* That is, about 3 inches (about 8 centimeters) [c] *39* That is, about 75 pounds (about 34 kilograms) [d] *2* That is, about 42 feet (about 12.5 meters) long and 6 feet (about 1.8 meters) wide [e] *8* That is, about 45 feet (about 13.5 meters) long and 6 feet (about 1.8 meters) wide

---

25:23 Antiochus Epiphanes took the table from the second (Zerubbabel's) temple after Rome conquered Jerusalem in A.D. 70. It is depicted on the Arch of Titus as one of the items the Romans carried back to Rome. See the photograph of the Arch of Titus on page 1606.

25:37 The ancient lamp was a small clay saucer with a spout on its rim. The top of a wick protruded from the spout, and oil contained in the saucer fed the wick. The priests were to tend the lamps, which were to burn all night in the tabernacle, and the people were to supply the oil. Seven-spouted lamps from the time of Moses have been found, and examples of a metal pedestal topped by a ledge designed to carry a lamp have been discovered in the ruins of Beth Shan and Megiddo. The classic representation of the shape of the tabernacle lampstand comes from the time of Herod the Great and may be seen on the Arch of Titus in Rome (see the note on v. 23).

26:1–37 A few desert shrines have been unearthed in the region most commonly proposed as Sinai (see "the Route of the Exodus" articles on pp. 108–112), notably at Serabit el-Khadem and at Timnah in the Negev, all showing marked Egyptian influence. Specific cultural antecedents to portable shrines carried on poles and covered with thin sheets of gold have been discovered in ancient Egypt from as early as the Old Kingdom period (2700–2160 B.C.), but these were especially prominent in the Eighteenth and Nineteenth Dynasties (1570–1180). The best examples come from the fabulous tomb of Tutankhamun (c. 1350). Comparisons of construction details in the text of chapters 25–40, with the frames, shrines, poles, sheathing, draped fabric covers, gilt rosettes and winged protective figures from the shrine of Tutankhamun, are instructive. This period, the Late Bronze Age, is commonly cited as the era of Moses and the exodus (see "The Date of the Exodus" on p. 106).

Such tent-shrines were by no means otherwise unknown in the ancient world. An early writer (c. 700 B.C.) spoke of a primitive Phoenician structure that was apparently placed on a cart and pulled by oxen. In pre-Islamic times the *qubbah,* a miniature red-leather tent with a dome-shaped top, was used for carrying the idols and cultic objects of a tribe. Some qubbahs were large enough to erect on the ground, while others were mounted on the backs of camels. Such tents were credited with the power of guiding the tribe in its journeys, and in time of war they were particularly valuable for the degree of protection they afforded.

The qubbah possessed an innate sanctity that was only slightly inferior to that of the sacred cultic objects it housed. It was used as a rallying point, a place of worship and a locale for the giving of oracles. Since the majority of tents in antiquity were dark in color, the fact that the sacred shrine was a conspicuous red (cf. 25:5) indicates a religious tradition that reaches back to remote antiquity.

26:1 See "Ancient Craftsmanship" on page 141 and the note on 25:4.

fifty loops along the edge of the end curtain in one set and also along the edge of the end curtain in the
other set. 11 Then make fifty bronze clasps and put them in the loops to fasten the tent together as a unit.
12 As for the additional length of the tent curtains, the half curtain that is left over is to hang down at the
rear of the tabernacle. 13 The tent curtains will be a cubit[a] longer on both sides; what is left will hang over
the sides of the tabernacle so as to cover it. 14 Make for the tent a covering of ram skins dyed red, and over
that a covering of hides of sea cows.[b][d]
15 "Make upright frames of acacia wood for the tabernacle. 16 Each frame is to be ten cubits long and
a cubit and a half wide,[c] 17 with two projections set parallel to each other. Make all the frames of the tab-
ernacle in this way. 18 Make twenty frames for the south side of the tabernacle 19 and make forty silver
bases to go under them—two bases for each frame, one under each projection. 20 For the other side, the
north side of the tabernacle, make twenty frames 21 and forty silver bases—two under each frame.
22 Make six frames for the far end, that is, the west end of the tabernacle, 23 and make two frames for the
corners at the far end. 24 At these two corners they must be double from the bottom all the way to the top,
and fitted into a single ring; both shall be like that. 25 So there will be eight frames and sixteen silver bas-
es—two under each frame.
26 "Also make crossbars of acacia wood: five for the frames on one side of the tabernacle, 27 five for
those on the other side, and five for the frames on the west, at the far end of the tabernacle. 28 The center
crossbar is to extend from end to end at the middle of the frames. 29 Overlay the frames with gold and
make gold rings to hold the crossbars. Also overlay the crossbars with gold.
30 "Set up the tabernacle according to the plan[e] shown you on the mountain.
31 "Make a curtain[f] of blue, purple and scarlet yarn and finely twisted linen, with cherubim[g] worked
into it by a skilled craftsman. 32 Hang it with gold hooks on four posts of acacia wood overlaid with gold
and standing on four silver bases. 33 Hang the curtain from the clasps and place the ark of the Testimo-
ny behind the curtain.[h] The curtain will separate the Holy Place from the Most Holy Place.[i] 34 Put the
atonement cover[j] on the ark of the Testimony in the Most Holy Place. 35 Place the table[k] outside the cur-
tain on the north side of the tabernacle and put the lampstand[l] opposite it on the south side.
36 "For the entrance to the tent make a curtain of blue, purple and scarlet yarn and finely twisted lin-
en—the work of an embroiderer. 37 Make gold hooks for this curtain and five posts of acacia wood over-
laid with gold. And cast five bronze bases for them.

The Altar of Burnt Offering

27 "Build an altar[m] of acacia wood, three cubits[d] high; it is to be square, five cubits long and five cu-
bits wide.[e] 2 Make a horn[n] at each of the four corners, so that the horns and the altar are of one
piece, and overlay the altar with bronze. 3 Make all its utensils of bronze—its pots to remove the ashes,
and its shovels, sprinkling bowls, meat forks and firepans. 4 Make a grating for it, a bronze network, and
make a bronze ring at each of the four corners of the network. 5 Put it under the ledge of the altar so that
it is halfway up the altar. 6 Make poles of acacia wood for the altar and overlay them with bronze. 7 The
poles are to be inserted into the rings so they will be on two sides of the altar when it is carried. 8 Make
the altar hollow, out of boards. It is to be made just as you were shown[o] on the mountain.

The Courtyard

9 "Make a courtyard for the tabernacle. The south side shall be a hundred cubits[f] long and is to have
curtains of finely twisted linen, 10 with twenty posts and twenty bronze bases and with silver hooks and
bands on the posts. 11 The north side shall also be a hundred cubits long and is to have curtains, with
twenty posts and twenty bronze bases and with silver hooks and bands on the posts.
12 "The west end of the courtyard shall be fifty cubits[g] wide and have curtains, with ten posts and ten

26:14 [d]Ex 36:19; Nu 4:25
26:30 [e]Ex 25:9, 40; Ac 7:44; Heb 8:5
26:31 [f]2Ch 3:14; Mt 27:51; Heb 9:3 [g]Ex 36:35
26:33 [h]Ex 40:3, 21; Lev 16:2 [i]Heb 9:2-3
26:34 [j]Ex 25:21; 40:20; Heb 9:5
26:35 [k]Heb 9:2 [l]Ex 40:22,24
27:1 [m]Eze 43:13
27:2 [n]Ps 118:27
27:8 [o]Ex 25:9,40

[a] *13* That is, about 1 1/2 feet (about 0.5 meter) [b] *14* That is, dugongs [c] *16* That is, about 15 feet (about 4.5 meters) long and 2 1/4 feet (about 0.7 meter) wide [d] *1* That is, about 4 1/2 feet (about 1.3 meters) [e] *1* That is, about 7 1/2 feet (about 2.3 meters) long and wide [f] *9* That is, about 150 feet (about 46 meters); also in verse 11 [g] *12* That is, about 75 feet (about 23 meters); also in verse 13

26:14 The information furnished in Exodus makes it difficult to determine whether the tabernacle proper had a flat, somewhat sagging drapery roof or one that was tent-like in shape with a ridgepole and a sloping roof. Present-day models of the tabernacle vary in their interpretation of this question. Historically speaking, if the influence of the desert tent was predominant, there may well have been some peak or apex to the structure. If, however, the tabernacle had anything in common with the design of contemporary Phoenician shrines, it probably had a flat roof.

27:1 The size of the altar of burnt offering, 7.5 feet (2.3 m) square by 4.5 feet (1.3 m) high, matches that of altars discovered at Arad and Beersheba from the period of the Israelite monarchy (see "Arad" on p. 247).

bases. 13 On the east end, toward the sunrise, the courtyard shall also be fifty cubits wide. 14 Curtains fifteen cubits[a] long are to be on one side of the entrance, with three posts and three bases, 15 and curtains fifteen cubits long are to be on the other side, with three posts and three bases.

16 "For the entrance to the courtyard, provide a curtain twenty cubits[b] long, of blue, purple and scarlet yarn and finely twisted linen—the work of an embroiderer—with four posts and four bases. 17 All the posts around the courtyard are to have silver bands and hooks, and bronze bases. 18 The courtyard shall be a hundred cubits long and fifty cubits wide,[c] with curtains of finely twisted linen five cubits[d] high, and with bronze bases. 19 All the other articles used in the service of the tabernacle, whatever their function, including all the tent pegs for it and those for the courtyard, are to be of bronze.

Oil for the Lampstand

20 "Command the Israelites to bring you clear oil of pressed olives for the light so that the lamps may be kept burning. 21 In the Tent of Meeting,[p] outside the curtain that is in front of the Testimony,[q] Aaron and his sons are to keep the lamps[r] burning before the LORD from evening till morning. This is to be a lasting ordinance[s] among the Israelites for the generations to come.

The Priestly Garments

28

"Have Aaron[t] your brother brought to you from among the Israelites, along with his sons Nadab and Abihu, Eleazar and Ithamar, so they may serve me as priests.[u] 2 Make sacred garments[v] for your brother Aaron, to give him dignity and honor. 3 Tell all the skilled men[w] to whom I have given wisdom[x] in such matters that they are to make garments for Aaron, for his consecration, so he may serve me as priest. 4 These are the garments they are to make: a breastpiece,[y] an ephod, a robe,[z] a woven tunic,[a] a turban and a sash. They are to make these sacred garments for your brother Aaron and his sons, so they may serve me as priests. 5 Have them use gold, and blue, purple and scarlet yarn, and fine linen.

27:21 [p]Ex 28:43 [q]Ex 26:31,33 [r]Ex 25:37; 30:8; 1Sa 3:3; 2Ch 13:11 [s]Ex 29:9; Lev 3:17; 16:34; Nu 18:23; 19:21
28:1 [t]Heb 5:4 [u]Nu 18:1-7; Heb 5:1
28:2 [v]Ex 29:5,29; 31:10; 39:1; Lev 8:7-9,30
28:3 [w]Ex 31:6; 36:1 [x]Ex 31:3
28:4 [y]ver 15-30 [z]ver 31-35 [a]ver 39

The Ephod

6 "Make the ephod of gold, and of blue, purple and scarlet yarn, and of finely twisted linen—the work of a skilled craftsman. 7 It is to have two shoulder pieces attached to two of its corners, so it can be fastened. 8 Its skillfully woven waistband is to be like it—of one piece with the ephod and made with gold, and with blue, purple and scarlet yarn, and with finely twisted linen.

9 "Take two onyx stones and engrave on them the names of the sons of Israel 10 in the order of their birth—six names on one stone and the remaining six on the other. 11 Engrave the names of the sons of Israel on the two stones the way a gem cutter engraves a seal. Then mount the stones in gold filigree settings 12 and fasten them on the shoulder pieces of the ephod as memorial stones for the sons of Israel. Aaron is to bear the names on his shoulders as a memorial before the LORD. 13 Make gold filigree settings 14 and two braided chains of pure gold, like a rope, and attach the chains to the settings.

The Breastpiece

15 "Fashion a breastpiece for making decisions—the work of a skilled craftsman. Make it like the ephod: of gold, and of blue, purple and scarlet yarn, and of finely twisted linen. 16 It is to be square—a span[e] long and a span wide—and folded double. 17 Then mount four rows of precious stones on it. In the first row there shall be a ruby, a topaz and a beryl; 18 in the second row a turquoise, a sapphire[f] and an emerald; 19 in the third row a jacinth, an agate and an amethyst; 20 in the fourth row a chrysolite, an onyx and a jasper.[g] Mount them in gold filigree settings. 21 There are to be twelve stones, one for each of the names of the sons of Israel, each engraved like a seal with the name of one of the twelve tribes.

22 "For the breastpiece make braided chains of pure gold, like a rope. 23 Make two gold rings for it and fasten them to two corners of the breastpiece. 24 Fasten the two gold chains to the rings at the corners of the breastpiece, 25 and the other ends of the chains to the two settings, attaching them to the shoulder pieces of the ephod at the front. 26 Make two gold rings and attach them to the other two corners of the breastpiece on the inside edge next to the ephod. 27 Make two more gold rings and attach them to the bottom of the shoulder pieces on the front of the ephod, close to the seam just above the waistband of

[a] *14* That is, about 22 1/2 feet (about 6.9 meters); also in verse 15 [b] *16* That is, about 30 feet (about 9 meters) [c] *18* That is, about 150 feet (about 46 meters) long and 75 feet (about 23 meters) wide [d] *18* That is, about 7 1/2 feet (about 2.3 meters) [e] *16* That is, about 9 inches (about 22 centimeters) [f] *18* Or *lapis lazuli* [g] *20* The precise identification of some of these precious stones is uncertain.

the ephod. 28 The rings of the breastpiece are to be tied to the rings of the ephod with blue cord, connect-
ing it to the waistband, so that the breastpiece will not swing out from the ephod.
29 "Whenever Aaron enters the Holy Place,[b] he will bear the names of the sons of Israel over his heart on — **28:29** [b]ver 12
the breastpiece of decision as a continuing memorial before the LORD. 30 Also put the Urim and the Thum-
mim[c] in the breastpiece, so they may be over Aaron's heart whenever he enters the presence of the LORD. — **28:30** [c]Lev 8:8; Nu 27:21; Dt 33:8; Ezr 2:63; Ne 7:65
Thus Aaron will always bear the means of making decisions for the Israelites over his heart before the LORD.

Other Priestly Garments

31 "Make the robe of the ephod entirely of blue cloth, 32 with an opening for the head in its center. There
shall be a woven edge like a collar[a] around this opening, so that it will not tear. 33 Make pomegranates of
blue, purple and scarlet yarn around the hem of the robe, with gold bells between them. 34 The gold bells
and the pomegranates are to alternate around the hem of the robe. 35 Aaron must wear it when he min-
isters. The sound of the bells will be heard when he enters the Holy Place before the LORD and when he
comes out, so that he will not die.
36 "Make a plate of pure gold and engrave on it as on a seal: HOLY TO THE LORD.[d] 37 Fasten a blue cord to — **28:36** [d]Zec 14:20
it to attach it to the turban; it is to be on the front of the turban. 38 It will be on Aaron's forehead, and he
will bear the guilt[e] involved in the sacred gifts the Israelites consecrate, whatever their gifts may be. It will — **28:38** [e]Lev 10:17; 22:9, 16; Nu 18:1; Heb 9:28; 1Pe 2:24
be on Aaron's forehead continually so that they will be acceptable to the LORD.
39 "Weave the tunic of fine linen and make the turban of fine linen. The sash is to be the work of an
embroiderer. 40 Make tunics, sashes and headbands for Aaron's sons,[f] to give them dignity and honor. — **28:40** [f]ver 4; Ex 39:41
41 After you put these clothes on your brother Aaron and his sons, anoint[g] and ordain them. Consecrate — **28:41** [g]Ex 29:7; Lev 10:7 [h]Ex 29:7-9; 30:30; 40:15; Lev 8:1-36; Heb 7:28
them so they may serve me as priests.[h]
42 "Make linen undergarments[i] as a covering for the body, reaching from the waist to the thigh. 43 Aar- — **28:42** [i]Lev 6:10; 16:4,23; Eze 44:18
on and his sons must wear them whenever they enter the Tent of Meeting[j] or approach the altar to min- — **28:43** [j]Ex 27:21 [k]Ex 20:26
ister in the Holy Place, so that they will not incur guilt and die.[k]
"This is to be a lasting ordinance[l] for Aaron and his descendants. — [l]Lev 17:7

[a] 32 The meaning of the Hebrew for this word is uncertain.

28:30 The Urim and Thummim were sacred lots used in times of crisis to determine God's will. See "The Urim and Thummim" on page 136.

The Urim and Thummim

EXODUS 28 God used various methods to guide the ancient Israelites, including the Urim and the Thummim. The high priest carried these objects in his "breastpiece of decision" and used them in seeking God's will (Ex 28:29–30). Reliance on this unique means of revelation (Nu 27:21; Dt 33:8) seems to have ceased after David's reign, although an attempt to revive the practice occurred during the **postexilic period**, in the fifth century B.C. (see Ezr 2:63; Ne 7:65).

The Urim and Thummim may have been small metal objects or stones or sticks inscribed with symbols, possibly the 22 letters of the Hebrew alphabet based on the fact that the first letter of Urim (*aleph*) and the first letter of Thummim (*tau*) are the first and final letters of this alphabet, respectively.

Most likely, as Biblical passages imply, the Urim and Thummim were cast as lots in order to obtain yes or no answers from God. Casting of lots is widely attested in the Bible[1] (cf. Lev 16:8; Nu 33:54; Pr 16:33; Ac 1:26). But two passages suggest that asking God a series of questions and using a process of elimination to determine his answers yielded more subtle revelation, such as a person's hiding place or a complex battle strategy (see 1Sa 10:20–22; 2Sa 5:22–24). Some Biblical historians believe that the high priest would disclose an oracle and that the Urim and Thummim would be used to confirm its truth.

[1]See "Casting Lots" on page 744.

Consecration of the Priests

29 "This is what you are to do to consecrate them, so they may
serve me as priests: Take a young bull and two rams with-
out defect. 2 And from fine wheat flour, without yeast, make bread,
29:2 [m]Lev 2:1,4; 6:19-23 and cakes mixed with oil, and wafers spread with oil.[m] 3 Put them in
a basket and present them in it—along with the bull and the two
rams. 4 Then bring Aaron and his sons to the entrance to the Tent of
29:4 [n]Ex 40:12; Heb 10:22 Meeting and wash them with water.[n] 5 Take the garments[o] and dress
29:5 [o]Ex 28:2; Lev 8:7 [p]Ex 28:8 Aaron with the tunic, the robe of the ephod, the ephod itself and the
breastpiece. Fasten the ephod on him by its skillfully woven waist-
29:6 [q]Lev 8:9 band.[p] 6 Put the turban on his head and attach the sacred diadem[q]
29:7 [r]Ex 30:25, 30,31; Lev 8:12; 21:10; Nu 35:25; Ps 133:2 to the turban. 7 Take the anointing oil[r] and anoint him by pouring it
on his head. 8 Bring his sons and dress them in tunics 9 and put head-
29:9 [s]Ex 28:40 [t]Ex 40:15; Nu 3:10; 18:7; 25:13; Dt 18:5 bands on them. Then tie sashes on Aaron and his sons.[a][s] The priest-
hood is theirs by a lasting ordinance.[t] In this way you shall ordain
Aaron and his sons.

10 "Bring the bull to the front of the Tent of Meeting, and Aaron
and his sons shall lay their hands on its head. 11 Slaughter it in the
LORD's presence at the entrance to the Tent of Meeting. 12 Take some
29:12 [u]Ex 27:2 of the bull's blood and put it on the horns[u] of the altar with your fin-
29:13 [v]Lev 3:3, 5,9 ger, and pour out the rest of it at the base of the altar. 13 Then take all the fat[v] around the inner parts, the
covering of the liver, and both kidneys with the fat on them, and burn them on the altar. 14 But burn the
29:14 [w]Lev 4:11-12,21; Heb 13:11 bull's flesh and its hide and its offal outside the camp.[w] It is a sin offering.

15 "Take one of the rams, and Aaron and his sons shall lay their hands on its head. 16 Slaughter it and
take the blood and sprinkle it against the altar on all sides. 17 Cut the ram into pieces and wash the inner
parts and the legs, putting them with the head and the other pieces. 18 Then burn the entire ram on the
29:18 [x]Ge 8:21 altar. It is a burnt offering to the LORD, a pleasing aroma,[x] an offering made to the LORD by fire.

29:19 [y]ver 3 19 "Take the other ram,[y] and Aaron and his sons shall lay their hands on its head. 20 Slaughter it, take
some of its blood and put it on the lobes of the right ears of Aaron and his sons, on the thumbs of their
right hands, and on the big toes of their right feet. Then sprinkle blood against the altar on all sides. 21 And
29:21 [z]Heb 9:22 [a]Ex 30:25,31 take some of the blood[z] on the altar and some of the anointing oil[a] and sprinkle it on Aaron and his gar-
[b]ver 1 ments and on his sons and their garments. Then he and his sons and their garments will be consecrated.[b]

22 "Take from this ram the fat, the fat tail, the fat around the inner parts, the covering of the liver, both
kidneys with the fat on them, and the right thigh. (This is the ram for the ordination.) 23 From the bas-
ket of bread made without yeast, which is before the LORD, take a loaf, and a cake made with oil, and a
wafer. 24 Put all these in the hands of Aaron and his sons and wave them before the LORD as a wave offer-
29:24 [c]Lev 7:30 ing.[c] 25 Then take them from their hands and burn them on the altar along with the burnt offering for a
pleasing aroma to the LORD, an offering made to the LORD by fire. 26 After you take the breast of the ram
29:26 [d]Lev 7:31-34 for Aaron's ordination, wave it before the LORD as a wave offering, and it will be your share.[d]

29:27 [e]Lev 7:31, 34; Dt 18:3 27 "Consecrate those parts of the ordination ram that belong to Aaron and his sons:[e] the breast that
was waved and the thigh that was presented. 28 This is always to be the regular share from the Israelites
for Aaron and his sons. It is the contribution the Israelites are to make to the LORD from their fellowship
29:28 [f]Lev 10:15 offerings.[b][f]

29 "Aaron's sacred garments will belong to his descendants so that they can be anointed and ordained
29:29 [g]Nu 20:26, 28 in them.[g] 30 The son[h] who succeeds him as priest and comes to the Tent of Meeting to minister in the
29:30 [h]Nu 20:28 Holy Place is to wear them seven days.

[a] 9 Hebrew; Septuagint *on them* [b] 28 Traditionally *peace offerings*

ANCIENT VOICES

The clan head slaughters one sheep at his house. Once he cooks it, they set five tables with three standard loaves each at the gate of the storm god's temple, in the room of the high priestess.

One table is for the previous high priestess.
One table is for the high priestess of Sumi.
One table is for the war-priestess.
One table is for the king of the land of Emar.
One table is [for the king of Satappi].*

*Words in brackets added by translator where text has gaps

—RITUALS FROM EMAR

See "The Installation of Priests at Emar and in Israel" article on the next page.

29:2 Yeast ("leaven" in some translations) was rigorously excluded from meal offerings in the Sinaitic legislation (29:2,23,32; Lev 2:1–16; 6:14–23; 7:9–10; 8:2,26,31; 10:12; Nu 15:1–9,17–21; 18:9; cf Ex 23:18; 34:15). It was originally eliminated from the bread of the Passover meal because the Israelites had to prepare it in haste in order to be ready for the exodus (Ex 12). In the course of time, because of its frequent exclusion from sacrifices, yeast came to represent corruption. Still, yeast was permitted in certain offerings (23:15–16; 34:22–23; Lev 2:11; 7:13–14; 23:17–18; Nu 15:20). See also the note on Exodus 12:14–20.

29:20 In Biblical times people were said to speak to each other's ears; instead of listening they "inclined their ears." When they prayed, God in turn "bowed down his ear" to hear them. The ear had a significant part in some Jewish ceremonies. It was sanctified by blood in the consecration of Aaron and his sons to the priesthood (29:20; Lev 8:24) and at the cleansing of a leper (Lev 14:14).

31 "Take the ram for the ordination and cook the meat in a sacred place. 32 At the entrance to the Tent
of Meeting, Aaron and his sons are to eat the meat of the ram and the bread[i] that is in the basket. 33 They **29:32** [i]Mt 12:4
are to eat these offerings by which atonement was made for their ordination and consecration. But no one
else may eat[j] them, because they are sacred. 34 And if any of the meat of the ordination ram or any bread **29:33** [j]Lev 10:14; 22:10,13
is left over till morning,[k] burn it up. It must not be eaten, because it is sacred. **29:34** [k]Ex 12:10
35 "Do for Aaron and his sons everything I have commanded you, taking seven days to ordain them.
36 Sacrifice a bull each day[l] as a sin offering to make atonement. Purify the altar by making atonement for **29:36** [l]Heb 10:11 [m]Ex 40:10
it, and anoint it to consecrate[m] it. 37 For seven days make atonement for the altar and consecrate it. Then
the altar will be most holy, and whatever touches it will be holy.[n] **29:37** [n]Ex 30:28-29; 40:10; Mt 23:19

ANCIENT TEXTS AND ARTIFACTS

The Installation of Priests at Emar and in Israel

EXODUS 29 Cuneiform tablets dating to the fourteenth through thirteenth centuries B.C. detail the rituals for installing the storm god's high priestess in Emar, a **Bronze Age**[1] city in Syria.[2] When a former high priestess died, the daughter of a local family was chosen by lot to replace her. This young woman was anointed with sacred oil and, on the next day, followed festive singers and sacrificial animals to the storm god's temple. At the entrance to the temple courtyard her head was shaved and all of the city's numerous gods reconsecrated.

Following her actual installation on the third day, the newly initiated high priestess participated in a ritual procession to sacred sites throughout Emar, receiving in the process gold jewelry, a sacred headdress, aromatics and an abundance of food items. Storm god-related sacrifices and feasts continued for a total of seven days, culminating in the presentation of the high priestess as a bride to the storm god.

In a similar way, new priests of Israel were anointed with oil and received sacred garments to wear. Accompanied by multiple sacrifices,[3] the consecration ceremony for each new Israelite priest and of the altar also took place during a seven-day period.

Significant differences nevertheless existed between the two cultures' priestly installation rituals. Whereas the storm god's newly installed high priestess was shaved at the temple entrance, the novice Biblical priests were ceremonially washed at the entrance to the Tent of Meeting.[4] And, unlike the Emar rituals, the Biblical instructions expressly forbade any recognition of other deities.

A Hittite storm god
Preserving Bible Times; © Dr. James C. Martin

The most notable difference between the two traditions, however, was the hereditary nature of the Biblical priesthood. Rather than selecting successive priests by lot,[5] the God of Israel personally designated that Aaron and his male descendants were to represent him perpetually as his priests.[6] Although ancient Israel in many ways shared with surrounding nations a common cultural milieu, its unique priestly rituals and laws marked the Israelites as a distinctive, special people—the chosen, covenantal people of the Creator God!

[1]See "Archaeological Periods" chart on page xx in the front of this Bible. [2]See "The Zukru Festival" on page 130. [3]See "Sacrifices and Offerings in the Bible and the Ancient Near East" on page 158. [4]See "Ritual Purity in Israel and the Ancient Near East" on page 166. [5]See "Casting Lots" on page 744. [6]See "The Levites and the Priests" on page 648.

29:38 [o]Nu 28:3-8; 1Ch 16:40; Da 12:11 — 38 "This is what you are to offer on the altar regularly each day:[o] two lambs a year old. 39 Offer one in
29:39 [p]Eze 46:13-15 — the morning and the other at twilight.[p] 40 With the first lamb offer a tenth of an ephah[a] of fine flour mixed
with a quarter of a hin[b] of oil from pressed olives, and a quarter of a hin of wine as a drink offering.
41 Sacrifice the other lamb at twilight with the same grain offering and its drink offering as in the morn-
ing—a pleasing aroma, an offering made to the LORD by fire.

29:42 [q]Ex 30:8 [r]Ex 25:22 — 42 "For the generations to come[q] this burnt offering is to be made regularly at the entrance to the Tent
of Meeting before the LORD. There I will meet you and speak to you;[r] 43 there also I will meet with the Is-
29:43 [s]1Ki 8:11 — raelites, and the place will be consecrated by my glory.[s]

44 "So I will consecrate the Tent of Meeting and the altar and will consecrate Aaron and his sons to
29:44 [t]Lev 21:15 — serve me as priests.[t] 45 Then I will dwell[u] among the Israelites and be their God.[v] 46 They will know that
29:45 [u]Ex 25:8; Lev 26:12; Zec 2:10; Jn 14:17 [v]2Co 6:16; Rev 21:3 — I am the LORD their God, who brought them out of Egypt so that I might dwell among them. I am the
LORD their God.[w]

29:46 [w]Ex 20:2

The Altar of Incense

30:1 [x]Ex 37:25 [y]Rev 8:3 — **30** "Make an altar[x] of acacia wood for burning incense.[y] 2 It is to be square, a cubit long and a cubit
30:2 [z]Ex 27:2 — wide, and two cubits high[c]—its horns[z] of one piece with it. 3 Overlay the top and all the sides
and the horns with pure gold, and make a gold molding around it. 4 Make two gold rings for the altar be-
low the molding—two on opposite sides—to hold the poles used to carry it. 5 Make the poles of acacia
wood and overlay them with gold. 6 Put the altar in front of the curtain that is before the ark of the Tes-
30:6 [a]Ex 25:22; 26:34 — timony—before the atonement cover[a] that is over the Testimony—where I will meet with you.

30:7 [b]ver 34-35; Ex 27:21; 1Sa 2:28 — 7 "Aaron must burn fragrant incense[b] on the altar every morning when he tends the lamps. 8 He must
burn incense again when he lights the lamps at twilight so incense will burn regularly before the LORD
30:9 [c]Lev 10:1 — for the generations to come. 9 Do not offer on this altar any other incense[c] or any burnt offering or grain
30:10 [d]Lev 16:18-19,30 — offering, and do not pour a drink offering on it. 10 Once a year Aaron shall make atonement[d] on its horns.
This annual atonement must be made with the blood of the atoning sin offering for the generations to
come. It is most holy to the LORD."

Atonement Money

30:12 [e]Ex 38:25; Nu 1:2,49; 2Sa 24:1 — 11 Then the LORD said to Moses, 12 "When you take a census[e] of the Israelites to count them, each one
[f]Nu 31:50; Mt 20:28 — must pay the LORD a ransom[f] for his life at the time he is counted. Then no plague[g] will come on them
[g]2Sa 24:13 — when you number them. 13 Each one who crosses over to those already counted is to give a half shekel,[d]
30:13 [h]Nu 3:47; Mt 17:24 — according to the sanctuary shekel,[h] which weighs twenty gerahs. This half shekel is an offering to the
LORD. 14 All who cross over, those twenty years old or more, are to give an offering to the LORD. 15 The rich
30:15 [i]Pr 22:2; Eph 6:9 — are not to give more than a half shekel and the poor are not to give less[i] when you make the offering to
the LORD to atone for your lives. 16 Receive the atonement money from the Israelites and use it for the ser-
30:16 [j]Ex 38:25-28 — vice of the Tent of Meeting.[j] It will be a memorial for the Israelites before the LORD, making atonement
for your lives."

Basin for Washing

30:18 [k]Ex 38:8; 40:7,30 — 17 Then the LORD said to Moses, 18 "Make a bronze basin,[k] with its bronze stand, for washing. Place it
between the Tent of Meeting and the altar, and put water in it. 19 Aaron and his sons are to wash their
30:19 [l]Ex 40:31-32; Isa 52:11 [m]Ps 26:6 — hands and feet[l] with water[m] from it. 20 Whenever they enter the Tent of Meeting, they shall wash with wa-
ter so that they will not die. Also, when they approach the altar to minister by presenting an offering
made to the LORD by fire, 21 they shall wash their hands and feet so that they will not die. This is to be a
30:21 [n]Ex 27:21; 28:43 — lasting ordinance[n] for Aaron and his descendants for the generations to come."

Anointing Oil

30:23 [o]Ge 37:25 — 22 Then the LORD said to Moses, 23 "Take the following fine spices: 500 shekels[e] of liquid myrrh,[o] half
as much (that is, 250 shekels) of fragrant cinnamon, 250 shekels of fragrant cane, 24 500 shekels of

[a] *40* That is, probably about 2 quarts (about 2 liters) [b] *40* That is, probably about 1 quart (about 1 liter) [c] *2* That is, about 1 1/2 feet (about 0.5 meter) long and wide and about 3 feet (about 0.9 meter) high [d] *13* That is, about 1/5 ounce (about 6 grams); also in verse 15 [e] *23* That is, about 12 1/2 pounds (about 6 kilograms)

30:9 Incense, an aromatic substance made of gums and spices to be burned, especially in religious worship, was compounded according to a prescription of gum resin, onycha, galbanum and pure frankincense in equal proportions, tempered with salt (vv. 34–35). It was not to be mixed for ordinary purposes (see also Lev 10:1–7), and incense not properly compounded was rejected (Ex 30:9). See "Incense" on page 1209.

cassia[p]—all according to the sanctuary shekel—and a hin[a] of olive oil. 25 Make these into a sacred anointing oil, a fragrant blend, the work of a perfumer.[q] It will be the sacred anointing oil.[r] 26 Then use it to anoint[s] the Tent of Meeting, the ark of the Testimony, 27 the table and all its articles, the lampstand and its accessories, the altar of incense, 28 the altar of burnt offering and all its utensils, and the basin with its stand. 29 You shall consecrate them so they will be most holy, and whatever touches them will be holy.[t]

30 "Anoint Aaron and his sons and consecrate[u] them so they may serve me as priests. 31 Say to the Israelites, 'This is to be my sacred anointing oil for the generations to come. 32 Do not pour it on men's bodies and do not make any oil with the same formula. It is sacred, and you are to consider it sacred.[v] 33 Whoever makes perfume like it and whoever puts it on anyone other than a priest must be cut off[w] from his people.' "

Incense

34 Then the LORD said to Moses, "Take fragrant spices—gum resin, onycha and galbanum—and pure frankincense, all in equal amounts, 35 and make a fragrant blend of incense, the work of a perfumer.[x] It is to be salted and pure and sacred. 36 Grind some of it to powder and place it in front of the Testimony in the Tent of Meeting, where I will meet with you. It shall be most holy[y] to you. 37 Do not make any incense with this formula for yourselves; consider it holy[z] to the LORD. 38 Whoever makes any like it to enjoy its fragrance must be cut off[a] from his people."

Bezalel and Oholiab

31 Then the LORD said to Moses, 2 "See, I have chosen Bezalel[b] son of Uri, the son of Hur, of the tribe of Judah, 3 and I have filled him with the Spirit of God, with skill, ability and knowledge in all kinds of crafts[c]— 4 to make artistic designs for work in gold, silver and bronze, 5 to cut and set stones, to work in wood, and to engage in all kinds of craftsmanship. 6 Moreover, I have appointed Oholiab son of Ahisamach, of the tribe of Dan, to help him. Also I have given skill to all the craftsmen to make everything I have commanded you: 7 the Tent of Meeting,[d] the ark of the Testimony[e] with the atonement cover[f] on it, and all the other furnishings of the tent— 8 the table[g] and its articles, the pure gold lampstand[h] and all its accessories, the altar of incense, 9 the altar of burnt offering and all its utensils, the basin with its stand— 10 and also the woven garments[i], both the sacred garments for Aaron the priest and the garments for his sons when they serve as priests, 11 and the anointing oil[j] and fragrant incense for the Holy Place. They are to make them just as I commanded you."

The Sabbath

12 Then the LORD said to Moses, 13 "Say to the Israelites, 'You must observe my Sabbaths.[k] This will be a sign[l] between me and you for the generations to come, so you may know that I am the LORD, who makes you holy.[b][m]

14 " 'Observe the Sabbath, because it is holy to you. Anyone who desecrates it must be put to death;[n] whoever does any work on that day must be cut off from his people. 15 For six days, work[o] is to be done, but the seventh day is a Sabbath of rest,[p] holy to the LORD. Whoever does any work on the Sabbath day must be put to death. 16 The Israelites are to observe the Sabbath, celebrating it for the generations to come as a lasting covenant. 17 It will be a sign[q] between me and the Israelites forever, for in six days the LORD made the heavens and the earth, and on the seventh day he abstained from work and rested.[r]' "

18 When the LORD finished speaking to Moses on Mount Sinai, he gave him the two tablets of the Testimony, the tablets of stone[s] inscribed by the finger of God.[t]

30:24 [p]Ps 45:8 **30:25** [q]Ex 37:29 [r]Ex 40:9 **30:26** [s]Ex 40:9; Lev 8:10; Nu 7:1 **30:29** [t]Ex 29:37 **30:30** [u]Ex 29:7; Lev 8:2,12,30 **30:32** [v]ver 25,37 **30:33** [w]ver 38; Ge 17:14 **30:35** [x]ver 25 **30:36** [y]ver 32; Ex 29:37; Lev 2:3 **30:37** [z]ver 32 **30:38** [a]ver 33 **31:2** [b]Ex 36:1,2; 1Ch 2:20 **31:3** [c]1Ki 7:14 **31:7** [d]Ex 36:8-38 [e]Ex 37:1-5 [f]Ex 37:6 **31:8** [g]Ex 37:10-16 [h]Ex 37:17-24 **31:10** [i]Ex 28:2; 39:1,41 **31:11** [j]Ex 30:22-32 **31:13** [k]Ex 20:8; Lev 19:3,30 [l]Eze 20:12,20 [m]Lev 11:44 **31:14** [n]Nu 15:32-36 **31:15** [o]Ex 20:8-11 [p]Ge 2:3; Ex 16:23 **31:17** [q]ver 13 [r]Ge 2:2-3 **31:18** [s]Ex 24:12 [t]Ex 32:15-16; 34:1,28; Dt 4:13; 5:22

[a] *24* That is, probably about 4 quarts (about 4 liters) [b] *13* Or *who sanctifies you*; or *who sets you apart as holy*

30:34–38 The recipe for the incense was to be prepared by a skilled perfumer. This mixture was designed specifically and solely for the altar of incense in the Holy Place (cf. 30:7–9 and the note on v. 9), but such fragrances were important to ancient peoples—particularly for burials.

31:18 Ancient Near Eastern practice called for one copy of a covenant document to be given to each party. The "two tablets" referred to in this verse were therefore duplicates of the covenant document, not two sections of the Ten Commandments. Since Israel's copy was to be placed in the presence of God (according to custom), both covenant tablets (God's and Israel's) were left inside the ark (see 25:21).

Ancient Craftsmanship

EXODUS 31 Since prehistoric times artistic people have used both natural resources and materials acquired by trade to create beautiful artifacts and then passed along their techniques to others. As ancient technology advanced, the materials used included the following:

✣ *Clay*. Sun-dried or kiln-fired clay was the most common material used both in large-scale building projects and in crafting vessels for daily, household use. Mass production of mud brick (e.g., Ge 11:3; Ex 1:11–14) enabled ancient craftsmen to create monumental feats of architecture.

Dyeing agents
Preserving Bible Times; © Dr. James C. Martin

As early as **Neolithic** times (c. 8000 B.C.) potters crafted fired-clay pottery. The invention of the potter's wheel in approximately 4000 B.C. rendered pottery-making so widespread that archaeologists are able to infer dates of archaeological strata based solely upon the designs and material characteristics of pottery **sherds**.[1]

✣ *Stone*. Stonemasons and sculptors used quarried stones in monumental construction projects, as well as in statuary. They utilized iron picks for rough shaping, then hammers and chisels for the finer work of **reliefs** and inscriptions. Jerusalem's temple and royal palace were constructed of large limestone blocks "cut to size and trimmed with a saw" (1Ki 7:9). The prized "Siloam inscription" celebrates the astonishing achievement of stonecutters who carved a tunnel through rock to divert the spring waters of the Gihon into Jerusalem (cf. 2Ch 32:30).[2]

Artisans also worked with precious and semiprecious stones to create cylinder seals (stone cylinders engraved in intaglio—engraved or incised figures in stone depressed below the surface so the impression yields an image in relief—and used in ancient Mesopotamia to roll impressions on wet clay), **amulets** (charms or ornaments, often inscribed with magic incantations or symbols to protect against evil), pendants and inlays. Ornamental stones were typically finished in a rounded form, with smooth and polished sides and engravings (Ex 28:11,21).

✣ *Wood*. Used structurally for building flat roofs, doors and columns (1Ki 7:1–8), wood was also used decoratively in such building projects as the Jerusalem temple, the interior of which was paneled in carved wood and overlaid with sheet gold (1Ki 6:15–20). Wooden furniture for sacred or royal use also was frequently overlaid with gold or inlaid with ivory (Ex 25:10–11; 1Ki 10:18; Am 6:4). Carpenters used such tools as chisels (Isa 44:13), hammers (Isa 44:12; Jer 10:4), workman's hammers (or mallets; Jdg 5:26), axes (Isa 10:34) and measuring lines (2Sa 8:2).

✣ *Metal*. Ancient peoples principally used copper, silver, lead and gold prior to the introduction of iron. Naturally occurring copper, used since 3200 B.C., was later alloyed with other metals like tin and arsenic to achieve differing levels of hardness and flexibility. The Israelites learned ironworking from the Philistines (1Sa 13:20).[3] Iron was the material of choice for tools and weapons (e.g., 1Sa 17:7; 2Ki 6:5–6), bronze for large sculptures and pillars (1Ki 7:15–16) and gold for overlays and jewelry (e.g., Ge 24:22; Ex 25:17–18; 28:11–13; Jdg 8:24).

The two most common techniques in metalworking were casting and hammering. Casting was preferred for the process of crafting multiple similar objects like tools. Molten metal was poured into a mold, which took the shape of the cavity as it solidified. Hammering was used for shaping earrings, appliqués, sheet overlays—and idols (Isa 44:12).

✣ *Textiles*. Women spun wool and linen cloth by hand or spindle (Ex 35:25; Pr 31:19). Tombs discovered at Beni Hasan contain pictures both of horizontal ground looms and of vertical looms. Evidence of warp-weighted looms (looms that use weights to hold the warp tight for weaving) has been established at such sites as Beth Shan, Gezer[4] and Ekron,[4] where loom weights (weights that hold the warp threads in tension during weaving) have also been recovered.

Plants were the source of most dyes (e.g., indigo for blue and henna for red), but the most famous and expensive dye, Phoenician purple, was made of pigment from the murex snail. Fabrics like those worn by the high priests were richly embroidered (Ex 28) and sometimes finished with fringed hems (Nu 15:38; Mt 23:5). Metal needles stored in ivory boxes found at **Hazor**[5] and **Megiddo**[5] attest to the arts of sewing and needlework.

[1]See "The Potsherd: Pottery in the Bible" on page 738 and "Pottery-Making in Bible Times" on page 1223. [2]See "Hezekiah's Tunnel" on page 564. [3]See "Technological Superiority of the Philistines' Iron Weapons" on page 414. [4]See "Gezer" on page 588 and "The Ekron Inscription of Akhayus" on page 428. [5]See "Hazor" on page 322 and "Megiddo" on page 1541.

The Golden Calf

32 When the people saw that Moses was so long in coming down from the mountain,[u] they gath-
ered around Aaron and said, "Come, make us gods[a] who will go before us. As for this fellow Mo-
ses who brought us up out of Egypt, we don't know what has happened to him."[v]
2 Aaron answered them, "Take off the gold earrings[w] that your wives, your sons and your daughters
are wearing, and bring them to me." 3 So all the people took off their earrings and brought them to Aar-
on. 4 He took what they handed him and made it into an idol cast in the shape of a calf,[x] fashioning it
with a tool. Then they said, "These are your gods,[b] O Israel, who brought you up out of Egypt."
5 When Aaron saw this, he built an altar in front of the calf and announced, "Tomorrow there will be
a festival[y] to the LORD." 6 So the next day the people rose early and sacrificed burnt offerings and present-
ed fellowship offerings.[c][z] Afterward they sat down to eat and drink and got up to indulge in revelry.[a]
7 Then the LORD said to Moses, "Go down, because your people, whom you brought up out of Egypt,[b]
have become corrupt.[c] 8 They have been quick to turn away from what I commanded them and have
made themselves an idol[d] cast in the shape of a calf. They have bowed down to it and sacrificed[e] to it
and have said, 'These are your gods, O Israel, who brought you up out of Egypt.'[f]
9 "I have seen these people," the LORD said to Moses, "and they are a stiff-necked[g] people. 10 Now leave
me alone so that my anger may burn against them and that I may destroy them. Then I will make you
into a great nation."[h]
11 But Moses sought the favor[i] of the LORD his God. "O LORD," he said, "why should your anger burn
against your people, whom you brought out of Egypt with great power and a mighty hand?[j] 12 Why should
the Egyptians say, 'It was with evil intent that he brought them out, to kill them in the mountains and to
wipe them off the face of the earth'?[k] Turn from your fierce anger; relent and do not bring disaster on your
people. 13 Remember[l] your servants Abraham, Isaac and Israel, to whom you swore by your own self:[m] 'I
will make your descendants as numerous as the stars[n] in the sky and I will give your descendants all this
land[o] I promised them, and it will be their inheritance forever.' " 14 Then the LORD relented[p] and did not
bring on his people the disaster he had threatened.
15 Moses turned and went down the mountain with the two tablets of the Testimony[q] in his hands.[r]
They were inscribed on both sides, front and back. 16 The tablets were the work of God; the writing was
the writing of God, engraved on the tablets.[s]
17 When Joshua heard the noise of the people shouting, he said to Moses, "There is the sound of war
in the camp."
18 Moses replied:

"It is not the sound of victory,
it is not the sound of defeat;
it is the sound of singing that I hear."

19 When Moses approached the camp and saw the calf[t] and the dancing, his anger burned and he
threw the tablets out of his hands, breaking them to pieces[u] at the foot of the mountain. 20 And he took
the calf they had made and burned it in the fire; then he ground it to powder, scattered it on the water[v]
and made the Israelites drink it.
21 He said to Aaron, "What did these people do to you, that you led them into such great sin?"
22 "Do not be angry, my lord," Aaron answered. "You know how prone these people are to evil.[w] 23 They
said to me, 'Make us gods who will go before us. As for this fellow Moses who brought us up out of Egypt,
we don't know what has happened to him.'[x] 24 So I told them, 'Whoever has any gold jewelry, take it off.'
Then they gave me the gold, and I threw it into the fire, and out came this calf!"[y]

32:1 [u]Ex 24:18; Dt 9:9-12 [v]Ac 7:40*
32:2 [w]Ex 35:22
32:4 [x]Dt 9:16; Ne 9:18; Ps 106:19; Ac 7:41
32:5 [y]Lev 23:2, 37; 2Ki 10:20
32:6 [z]Nu 25:2; Ac 7:41 [a]ver 17-19; 1Co 10:7*
32:7 [b]ver 4,11 [c]Ge 6:11-12; Dt 9:12
32:8 [d]Ex 20:4 [e]Ex 22:20 [f]1Ki 12:28
32:9 [g]Ex 33:3,5; 34:9; Isa 48:4; Ac 7:51
32:10 [h]Nu 14:12; Dt 9:14
32:11 [i]Dt 9:18 [j]Dt 9:26
32:12 [k]Nu 14:13-16; Dt 9:28
32:13 [l]Ex 2:24 [m]Ge 22:16; Heb 6:13 [n]Ge 15:5; 26:4 [o]Ge 12:7
32:14 [p]2Sa 24:16; Ps 106:45
32:15 [q]Ex 31:18 [r]Dt 9:15
32:16 [s]Ex 31:18
32:19 [t]Dt 9:16 [u]Dt 9:17
32:20 [v]Dt 9:21
32:22 [w]Dt 9:24
32:23 [x]ver 1
32:24 [y]ver 4

[a] *1* Or *a god*; also in verses 23 and 31 [b] *4* Or *This is your god*; also in verse 8 [c] *6* Traditionally *peace offerings*

32:1–6 The ancients saw in an idol an earthly *representation* of a god—not the god itself. It was widely thought that calves or bulls functioned as pedestals for the gods. The Israelites likely viewed the calf as the place above which God was enthroned, thus ensuring his presence with them.

32:4 The idol was either constructed of gold plating over a carved wooden calf or crudely cast in solid gold and then shaped with a tool, later to be melted down in the fire. The calf was probably similar to representations of the Egyptian bull-god Apis, a symbol of fertility and strength in Egypt. Its manufacture was a flagrant violation of the second commandment (20:4–5). See "The Golden Calf" on page 143.

32:7 The Hebrew verb translated "indulge in revelry" often has sexual connotations. In ancient times immoral orgies frequently accompanied pagan worship.

32:15 Ancient tablets were often inscribed on both sides.

32:19 The sexes never intermingled in Israelite dancing, except where pagan influences crept in. Dances were usually performed by women, with one leading, as in the case of Miriam (15:20–21). See the note about anger on Genesis 27:45.

[25]Moses saw that the people were running wild and that Aaron had let them get out of control and so
become a laughingstock to their enemies. [26]So he stood at the entrance to the camp and said, "Whoev-
er is for the LORD, come to me." And all the Levites rallied to him.
[27]Then he said to them, "This is what the LORD, the God of Israel, says: 'Each man strap a sword to his
side. Go back and forth through the camp from one end to the other, each killing his brother and friend
32:27 [z]Nu 25:3, 5; Dt 33:9 and neighbor.' "[z] [28]The Levites did as Moses commanded, and that day about three thousand of the
people died. [29]Then Moses said, "You have been set apart to the LORD today, for you were against your
own sons and brothers, and he has blessed you this day."

The Golden Calf

EXODUS 32 In art and legend gods were frequently represented by animals thought to symbolize the attributes of a particular deity. In the overall religious experience of the ancient Near East, for example, bulls and bull calves were associated with strength, virility and kingship. The bull was regarded as the earthly form or representation of the heavenly god, embodying physical strength and the procreative power found in nature.

Several religious cults in Egypt (that of Apis being the most prominent) worshiped the bull and calf. Deification of a live, "sacred" bull was initiated during the First Egyptian Dynasty and continued throughout ancient Egypt's long history. Bull cults of the Nile delta, which existed at the same time and location as the Israelites' sojourn in Egypt, were dedicated to Horus, the "god of heaven."

The Canaanites also venerated bulls. El, the chief god of the Canaanite pantheon (officially recognized list of gods), was referred to as the "heavenly bull." Baal, the storm god, was likewise associated with the bull on account of that animal's fertility.[1] Artistic traditions from **Canaan** depict gods as riding on bulls, which had become living pedestals emblematic of kingship and power over nature.

The golden calf was Israel's first foray into syncretism, the combining of faith in the one true God with pagan traditions. In taking this step, God's chosen people exchanged his glory—the true, manifest Presence of God—for the image of a bull—a false representation of God's presence (Ps 106:19–20). The Israelites had tragically fallen prey to cultural influences from Egypt (from which they had departed) and Canaan (where they would settle). God's people were unwittingly associating their God with the gods of the nations.[2]

It is important to recognize, as hinted above, that the Israelites believed they were acting with piety. Everything they saw in the world around them suggested that God would find such idol-worshiping both acceptable and pleasing. His people were in their own minds attempting to honor him by representing him as the chief of the gods. But the reality was that they were compromising his uniqueness and incomparability—a trend that would continue to haunt them until after their eventual return from Babylonian captivity. God's nature cannot be represented by inanimate objects or by anything else in all creation (Dt 4:15–19; Isa 46:5–9). The cry of the exodus deliverance, "Who among the gods is like you, O LORD?" (Ex 15:11), would be belied again and again by idolatry—Israel's colossal stumbling block.

Bull statuette found at Ashkelon
Preserving Bible Times; © Dr. James C. Martin

[1]See "The Ugaritic Text of the Myth of Baal" on page 905. [2]See "Praise of the 'Bull' in the Cairo Hymn of Amon-Re" on page 911.

30 The next day Moses said to the people, "You have committed a great sin.[a] But now I will go up to the
LORD; perhaps I can make atonement[b] for your sin."
31 So Moses went back to the LORD and said, "Oh, what a great sin these people have committed![c] They
have made themselves gods of gold.[d] 32 But now, please forgive their sin—but if not, then blot me[e] out
of the book[f] you have written."
33 The LORD replied to Moses, "Whoever has sinned against me I will blot out[g] of my book. 34 Now go,
lead the people to the place[h] I spoke of, and my angel[i] will go before you. However, when the time comes
for me to punish,[j] I will punish them for their sin."
35 And the LORD struck the people with a plague because of what they did with the calf[k] Aaron had made.

32:30 [a]1Sa 12:20 [b]Lev 1:4; Nu 25:13
32:31 [c]Dt 9:18 [d]Ex 20:23
32:32 [e]Ro 9:3 [f]Ps 69:28; Da 12:1; Php 4:3; Rev 3:5; 21:27
32:33 [g]Dt 29:20; Ps 9:5
32:34 [h]Ex 3:17 [i]Ex 23:20 [j]Dt 32:35; Ps 99:8; Ro 2:5-6
32:35 [k]ver 4

Anatolia and the Hittites

EXODUS 33 Exodus 33:2 includes the **Hittites** in the listing of people groups Israel was to conquer (cf. Dt 7:1; Jos 3:10). This gives readers the impression that the Hittites comprised a local culture in **Canaan.** In fact, the term *Hittites* usually refers to a people group based in central **Anatolia** (modern Turkey) who controlled a sizable empire during the second millennium B.C. Thought to have entered Anatolia around 2300 B.C., the Hittites were Indo-Europeans (like the Greeks), not Semites (like the Israelites, **Assyrians** and most Canaanites).

Hittites lived in Canaan as early as the time of the **patriarchs** (cf. Ge 23:10) and still inhabited the region as late as the time of David, as indicated by the presence of Uriah the Hittite in David's army (2Sa 11–12). Possibly these "Palestinian" Hittites were simply dispersed members of the Anatolian Hittite populace. On the other hand, there might have been two separate "Hittite" peoples in the Old Testament: an indigenous Canaanite population in the region only much later known as Palestine and the remnants of the Hittite empire in Anatolia (cf. 2Ki 7:6). In fact, these two groups may have been unrelated and the use of the common name purely coincidental.

The capital city and center of Hittite power was in central Turkey at Boghazkoy (named Hattusa by the Hittites). A large archive containing tablets in **Akkadian**, Hittite and other languages has been discovered there.[1] This archive library includes a wide variety of materials, including letters, military instructions and laws.[2] In addition, Hittite prayer and ritual texts reveal a great deal about their religion.[3]

Hittite history may be divided into three distinct periods:

- *Old Kingdom Period* (c. 1600–1400 B.C.): The two greatest kings of this era were Hattusili I and his successor, Mursili I (mid-sixteenth century B.C.). These rulers dramatically increased the size of the Hittite kingdom, expanding in particular toward Syria and **Mesopotamia**, defeating the **Hurrians** and sacking **Babylon** around 1531 B.C. After the assassination of Mursili I, the kingdom declined into factionalism and weakness. Another Hittite king, Telipinu, attempted to put an end to palace strife by creating rules for succession.[4]
- *Middle Kingdom Period* (c. 1400–1340 B.C.): Tudhaliya II reinvigorated his people, but the Hittites continued to be troubled by their enemies, particularly those from the north.
- *New Kingdom/Empire Period* (c. 1340–1200 B.C.): The Hittite Empire returned to its former glory with the accession of Suppiluliumas I, who extended Hittite power to the south, defeating the Hurrian kingdom of **Mitanni** in Syria. Thus the Hittites became the major power in the north and a counterpoint to Egypt, the principle southern power. Around 1275 B.C. the Hittite king Muwatalli fought one of the most famous battles of antiquity at Kadesh against Pharaoh **Rameses II**—ending in a draw. Hittite power dwindled and finally died out around 1200 B.C. as a result of unknown calamities that overtook much of the world at the end of the **Bronze Age.**[5]

At the height of their power, the Hittites exercised control over a vast area extending from the Aegean coast to Damascus (cf. Jos 1:4). Although they held no direct sway over the Holy Land, the Hittite presence in Canaan would have been felt by Israel because geopolitical realities placed the region as a buffer zone between the Egyptians and the Hittites.

[1]See "Languages of the Old Testament World" on page 672. [2]See "Hittite Instructions for Border Outposts" on page 695 and "The Hittite Laws" on page 281. [3]See "The Hittite Ritual of Establishing a New Temple for the Goddess of the Night" on page 146, "A Hittite Ritual Against Plague" on page 758, "A Hittite Blessing for a House" on page 936 and "The Hittite Ritual of Passing Between the Pieces of a Sacrifice" on page 1251. [4]See "Ambitious Princes Among the Hittites" on page 469. [5]See "Archaeological Periods" chart on page xx in the front of this Bible.

33 Then the LORD said to Moses, "Leave this place, you and the people you brought up out of Egypt, and go up to the land I promised on oath to Abraham, Isaac and Jacob, saying, 'I will give it to your descendants.'[l] 2 I will send an angel[m] before you and drive out the Canaanites, Amorites, Hittites, Perizzites, Hivites and Jebusites.[n] 3 Go up to the land flowing with milk and honey.[o] But I will not go with you, because you are a stiff-necked[p] people and I might destroy[q] you on the way."

4 When the people heard these distressing words, they began to mourn[r] and no one put on any ornaments. 5 For the LORD had said to Moses, "Tell the Israelites, 'You are a stiff-necked people. If I were to go with you even for a moment, I might destroy you. Now take off your ornaments and I will decide what to do with you.' " 6 So the Israelites stripped off their ornaments at Mount Horeb.

The Tent of Meeting

7 Now Moses used to take a tent and pitch it outside the camp some distance away, calling it the "tent of meeting."[s] Anyone inquiring of the LORD would go to the tent of meeting outside the camp. 8 And whenever Moses went out to the tent, all the people rose and stood at the entrances to their tents,[t] watching Moses until he entered the tent. 9 As Moses went into the tent, the pillar of cloud[u] would come down and stay at the entrance, while the LORD spoke[v] with Moses. 10 Whenever the people saw the pillar of cloud standing at the entrance to the tent, they all stood and worshiped, each at the entrance to his tent. 11 The LORD would speak to Moses face to face,[w] as a man speaks with his friend. Then Moses would return to the camp, but his young aide Joshua son of Nun did not leave the tent.

Moses and the Glory of the LORD

12 Moses said to the LORD, "You have been telling me, 'Lead these people,'[x] but you have not let me know whom you will send with me. You have said, 'I know you by name[y] and you have found favor with me.' 13 If you are pleased with me, teach me your ways[z] so I may know you and continue to find favor with you. Remember that this nation is your people."[a]

14 The LORD replied, "My Presence[b] will go with you, and I will give you rest."[c]

15 Then Moses said to him, "If your Presence does not go with us, do not send us up from here. 16 How will anyone know that you are pleased with me and with your people unless you go with us?[d] What else will distinguish me and your people from all the other people on the face of the earth?"[e]

17 And the LORD said to Moses, "I will do the very thing you have asked, because I am pleased with you and I know you by name."

18 Then Moses said, "Now show me your glory."

19 And the LORD said, "I will cause all my goodness to pass in front of you, and I will proclaim my name, the LORD, in your presence. I will have mercy on whom I will have mercy, and I will have compassion on whom I will have compassion.[f] 20 But," he said, "you cannot see my face, for no one may see[g] me and live."

21 Then the LORD said, "There is a place near me where you may stand on a rock. 22 When my glory passes by, I will put you in a cleft in the rock and cover you with my hand[h] until I have passed by. 23 Then I will remove my hand and you will see my back; but my face must not be seen."

The New Stone Tablets

34 The LORD said to Moses, "Chisel out two stone tablets like the first ones, and I will write on them the words that were on the first tablets,[i] which you broke.[j] 2 Be ready in the morning, and then come up on Mount Sinai.[k] Present yourself to me there on top of the mountain. 3 No one is to come with you or be seen anywhere on the mountain;[l] not even the flocks and herds may graze in front of the mountain."

4 So Moses chiseled out two stone tablets like the first ones and went up Mount Sinai early in the morning, as the LORD had commanded him; and he carried the two stone tablets in his hands. 5 Then the LORD came down in the cloud and stood there with him and proclaimed his name, the LORD.[m] 6 And he passed in front of Moses, proclaiming, "The LORD, the LORD, the compassionate[n] and gracious God, slow to anger,[o] abounding in love[p] and faithfulness,[q] 7 maintaining love to thousands,[r] and forgiving wickedness, rebellion and sin.[s] Yet he does not leave the guilty unpunished;[t] he punishes the children and their children for the sin of the fathers to the third and fourth generation."

8 Moses bowed to the ground at once and worshiped. 9 "O Lord, if I have found favor in your eyes," he said, "then let the Lord go with us.[u] Although this is a stiff-necked people, forgive our wickedness and our sin, and take us as your inheritance."[v]

33:1 [l]Ge 12:7
33:2 [m]Ex 32:34 [n]Ex 23:27-31; Jos 24:11
33:3 [o]Ex 3:8 [p]Ex 32:9 [q]Ex 32:10
33:4 [r]Nu 14:39
33:7 [s]Ex 29:42-43
33:8 [t]Nu 16:27
33:9 [u]Ex 13:21 [v]Ex 31:18; Ps 99:7
33:11 [w]Nu 12:8; Dt 34:10
33:12 [x]Ex 3:10 [y]ver 17; Jn 10:14-15; 2Ti 2:19
33:13 [z]Ps 25:4; 86:11; 119:33 [a]Ex 34:9; Dt 9:26, 29
33:14 [b]Isa 63:9 [c]Jos 21:44; 22:4
33:16 [d]Nu 14:14 [e]Ex 34:10
33:19 [f]Ro 9:15*
33:20 [g]Ge 32:30; Isa 6:5
33:22 [h]Ps 91:4
34:1 [i]Dt 10:2,4 [j]Ex 32:19
34:2 [k]Ex 19:11
34:3 [l]Ex 19:12-13,21
34:5 [m]Ex 33:19
34:6 [n]Ps 86:15 [o]Nu 14:18; Ro 2:4 [p]Ne 9:17; Ps 103:8; Joel 2:13 [q]Ps 108:4
34:7 [r]Ex 20:6 [s]Ps 103:3; 130:4, 8; Da 9:9; 1Jn 1:9 [t]Job 10:14; Na 1:3
34:9 [u]Ex 33:15 [v]Ps 33:12

10Then the LORD said: "I am making a covenant[w] with you. Before all your people I will do wonders
never before done in any nation in all the world.[x] The people you live among will see how awesome is the
work that I, the LORD, will do for you. 11Obey what I command you today. I will drive out before you the
Amorites, Canaanites, Hittites, Perizzites, Hivites and Jebusites.[y] 12Be careful not to make a treaty with
those who live in the land where you are going, or they will be a snare[z] among you. 13Break down their
altars, smash their sacred stones and cut down their Asherah poles.[a][a] 14Do not worship any other god,[b]
for the LORD, whose name is Jealous, is a jealous God.[c]
15"Be careful not to make a treaty with those who live in the land; for when they prostitute[d] themselves
to their gods and sacrifice to them, they will invite you and you will eat their sacrifices.[e] 16And when you
choose some of their daughters as wives[f] for your sons and those daughters prostitute themselves to
their gods,[g] they will lead your sons to do the same.
17"Do not make cast idols.[h]
18"Celebrate the Feast of Unleavened Bread.[i] For seven days eat bread made without yeast,[j] as I com-
manded you. Do this at the appointed time in the month of Abib,[k] for in that month you came out of Egypt.
19"The first offspring[l] of every womb belongs to me, including all the firstborn males of your live-
stock, whether from herd or flock. 20Redeem the firstborn donkey with a lamb, but if you do not redeem
it, break its neck.[m] Redeem all your firstborn sons.
"No one is to appear before me empty-handed.[n]
21"Six days you shall labor, but on the seventh day you shall rest;[o] even during the plowing season
and harvest you must rest.
22"Celebrate the Feast of Weeks with the firstfruits of the wheat harvest, and the Feast of Ingathering[p]
at the turn of the year.[b] 23Three times[q] a year all your men are to appear before the Sovereign LORD, the

34:10 [w]Dt 5:2-3 [x]Ex 33:16; Dt 4:32
34:11 [y]Ex 33:2
34:12 [z]Ex 23:32-33
34:13 [a]Ex 23:24; Dt 12:3; 2Ki 18:4
34:14 [b]Ex 20:3 [c]Ex 20:5; Dt 4:24
34:15 [d]Jdg 2:17 [e]Nu 25:2; 1Co 8:4
34:16 [f]Dt 7:3 [g]1Ki 11:4
34:17 [h]Ex 32:8
34:18 [i]Ex 12:17 [j]Ex 12:15 [k]Ex 12:2
34:19 [l]Ex 13:2
34:20 [m]Ex 13:13, 15 [n]Ex 23:15; Dt 16:16
34:21 [o]Ex 20:9; Lk 13:14
34:22 [p]Ex 23:16
34:23 [q]Ex 23:14

a 13 That is, symbols of the goddess Asherah   *b 22* That is, in the fall

ANCIENT TEXTS AND ARTIFACTS

The Hittite Ritual of Establishing a New Temple for the Goddess of the Night

EXODUS 34 Ancient **cuneiform** texts attest to **Hittites** worshiping hundreds—and possibly even thousands!—of deities.[1] One of these texts, a four-columned tablet discovered in southeastern **Anatolia** and dated to the **Late Bronze Age**,[2] contains instructions for the Hittite ritual of establishing a new temple for a goddess of the night.

Interestingly, aspects of this ritual are similar to those God established concerning the tabernacle's construction (Ex 25–40).[3] For example:

- Both procedures involve adorning the place of worship with precious metals and gems.
- Both specify the use of bronze utensils, altars and washing basins.
- Both stipulate finely woven curtains to serve as doorway screens.
- Both assigned priests special clothing and required that they engage in ceremonial washing rituals.[4]
- Both had corresponding characteristics related to sacrificial rites.[5]

Despite these parallels, a number of differences illustrate unique aspects of Israelite religious practices. The Hittite text commanded workers to fashion a statue of their goddess. The priests were instructed to lure the goddess into the temple with food and gifts, and efforts were undertaken to make the idol holy. In contrast, Yahweh:

- Forbad the Israelites from fashioning images (20:4; 34:17).
- Did not need to be sanctified by human ritual; he consecrated his own tabernacle, as well as his priests (29:43–44; 40:9–15).
- Did not need to be provided with food or clothing; rather, he cared for his people's needs (Dt 29:5).
- Chose to dwell among his people (Ex 29:45–46). He did not ask or need to be enticed—he both pronounced his own coming and made his presence known in the tabernacle (25:8; 40:34–38).

Even so, it is important to recognize that the Israelites followed customs common in their day. This helps us to keep the Bible in perspective as an ancient book written within—and expressing reality as it was lived within—a historical context. It also assures us that the priestly rules in the Old Testament are truly ancient (second millennium B.C.), as opposed to relatively late (around the fourth century B.C., as some scholars argue).[6]

[1]For example, see "The Hittite Storm Gods" on page 784. [2]See "Archaeological Periods" chart on page xx in the front of this Bible. [3]See "The Tabernacle and the Ark" on page 153. [4]See "Ritual Purity in Israel and the Ancient Near East" on page 166. [5]See "Sacrifices and Offerings in the Bible and the Ancient Near East" on page 158. [6]See "Hittite Instructions for Priests" on page 208.

34:24 [r]Ex 23:28; 33:2; Ps 78:55 God of Israel. 24I will drive out nations[r] before you and enlarge your
territory, and no one will covet your land when you go up three times
each year to appear before the LORD your God.
25"Do not offer the blood of a sacrifice to me along with anything
34:25 [s]Ex 23:18 [t]Ex 12:8,10 containing yeast,[s] and do not let any of the sacrifice from the Pass-
over Feast remain until morning.[t]
26"Bring the best of the firstfruits of your soil to the house of the
LORD your God.
34:26 [u]Ex 23:19 "Do not cook a young goat in its mother's milk."[u]
34:27 [v]Ex 17:14; 24:4 27Then the LORD said to Moses, "Write[v] down these words, for in
accordance with these words I have made a covenant with you and
with Israel." 28Moses was there with the LORD forty days and forty
34:28 [w]Ge 7:4; Ex 24:18; Mt 4:2 [x]ver 1; Ex 31:18 [y]Dt 4:13; 10:4 nights[w] without eating bread or drinking water. And he wrote on the
tablets[x] the words of the covenant—the Ten Commandments.[y]

The Radiant Face of Moses

29When Moses came down from Mount Sinai with the two tab-
34:29 [z]Ex 32:15 [a]Ps 34:5; Mt 17:2; 2Co 3:7,13 lets of the Testimony in his hands,[z] he was not aware that his face
was radiant[a] because he had spoken with the LORD. 30When Aaron
and all the Israelites saw Moses, his face was radiant, and they were
afraid to come near him. 31But Moses called to them; so Aaron and
all the leaders of the community came back to him, and he spoke to
them. 32Afterward all the Israelites came near him, and he gave them
34:32 [b]Ex 24:3 all the commands[b] the LORD had given him on Mount Sinai.
34:33 [c]2Co 3:13 33When Moses finished speaking to them, he put a veil[c] over his
face. 34But whenever he entered the LORD's presence to speak with him, he removed the veil until he came
out. And when he came out and told the Israelites what he had been commanded, 35they saw that his face
was radiant. Then Moses would put the veil back over his face until he went in to speak with the LORD.

Sabbath Regulations

35:1 [d]Ex 34:32 35 Moses assembled the whole Israelite community and said to them, "These are the things the
LORD has commanded[d] you to do: 2For six days, work is to be done, but the seventh day shall be
35:2 [e]Ex 20:9-10; 34:21; Lev 23:3 35:3 [f]Ex 16:23 your holy day, a Sabbath[e] of rest to the LORD. Whoever does any work on it must be put to death. 3Do not
light a fire in any of your dwellings on the Sabbath day.[f]"

Materials for the Tabernacle

4Moses said to the whole Israelite community, "This is what the LORD has commanded: 5From what
you have, take an offering for the LORD. Everyone who is willing is to bring to the LORD an offering of gold,
silver and bronze; 6blue, purple and scarlet yarn and fine linen; goat hair; 7ram skins dyed red and hides
of sea cows[a]; acacia wood; 8olive oil for the light; spices for the anointing oil and for the fragrant incense;
9and onyx stones and other gems to be mounted on the ephod and breastpiece.
35:10 [g]Ex 31:6 10"All who are skilled among you are to come and make everything the LORD has commanded:[g] 11the
35:11 [h]Ex 26:1-37 tabernacle[h] with its tent and its covering, clasps, frames, crossbars, posts and bases; 12the ark[i] with its
35:12 [i]Ex 25:10-22 poles and the atonement cover and the curtain that shields it; 13the table[j] with its poles and all its arti-
35:13 [j]Ex 25:23-30; Lev 24:5-6 cles and the bread of the Presence; 14the lampstand[k] that is for light with its accessories, lamps and oil
35:14 [k]Ex 25:31 35:15 [l]Ex 30:1-6 for the light; 15the altar[l] of incense with its poles, the anointing oil[m] and the fragrant incense;[n] the cur-
[m]Ex 30:25 tain for the doorway at the entrance to the tabernacle; 16the altar[o] of burnt offering with its bronze grat-
[n]Ex 30:34-38 35:16 [o]Ex 27:1-8 ing, its poles and all its utensils; the bronze basin with its stand; 17the curtains of the courtyard with its
35:17 [p]Ex 27:9 posts and bases, and the curtain for the entrance to the courtyard;[p] 18the tent pegs for the tabernacle
and for the courtyard, and their ropes; 19the woven garments worn for ministering in the sanctuary—
35:19 [q]Ex 28:2; 31:10; 39:1 both the sacred garments[q] for Aaron the priest and the garments for his sons when they serve as priests."
20Then the whole Israelite community withdrew from Moses' presence, 21and everyone who was will-
ing and whose heart moved him came and brought an offering to the LORD for the work on the Tent of

ANCIENT VOICES

When on the morning of the second day the Sun God has not yet risen, they take these things of his from the house of the officiant: One skein/strand of red wool, one skein/strand of blue wool, one plain (i.e., undyed)* wool, one shekel of silver, one (bolt of [?]) *gazzarnul* fabric, a small amount of fine oil, three flat breads, one pitcher of wine. They go for drawing to the waters of purification and they draw the waters of purification. They carry them to the temple of the Deity of the Night from the temple of the Deity of the Night—(that is, from) the temple of the Deity of the Night which is being built to that (old) temple of the Deity of the Night.

*Words or punctuation in brackets or parentheses added by translator for clarity or where text has gaps

—ESTABLISHING A NEW TEMPLE FOR THE GODDESS OF THE NIGHT

See "The Hittite Ritual of Establishing a New Temple for the Goddess of the Night" article.

[a] 7 That is, dugongs; also in verse 23

Meeting, for all its service, and for the sacred garments. 22 All who were willing, men and women alike, came and brought gold jewelry of all kinds: brooches, earrings, rings and ornaments. They all presented their gold as a wave offering to the LORD. 23 Everyone who had blue, purple or scarlet yarn[r] or fine linen, or goat hair, ram skins dyed red or hides of sea cows brought them. 24 Those presenting an offering of silver or bronze brought it as an offering to the LORD, and everyone who had acacia wood for any part of the work brought it. 25 Every skilled woman[s] spun with her hands and brought what she had spun—blue, purple or scarlet yarn or fine linen. 26 And all the women who were willing and had the skill spun the goat hair. 27 The leaders[t] brought onyx stones and other gems to be mounted on the ephod and breastpiece. 28 They also brought spices and olive oil for the light and for the anointing oil and for the fragrant incense.[u] 29 All the Israelite men and women who were willing[v] brought to the LORD freewill offerings[w] for all the work the LORD through Moses had commanded them to do.

Bezalel and Oholiab

30 Then Moses said to the Israelites, "See, the LORD has chosen Bezalel son of Uri, the son of Hur, of the tribe of Judah, 31 and he has filled him with the Spirit of God, with skill, ability and knowledge in all kinds of crafts[x]— 32 to make artistic designs for work in gold, silver and bronze, 33 to cut and set stones, to work in wood and to engage in all kinds of artistic craftsmanship. 34 And he has given both him and Oholiab[y] son of Ahisamach, of the tribe of Dan, the ability to teach[z] others. 35 He has filled them with skill to do all kinds of work[a] as craftsmen, designers, embroiderers in blue, purple and scarlet yarn and fine linen, and weavers—all of them master craftsmen and designers.

36 1 So Bezalel, Oholiab and every skilled person[b] to whom the LORD has given skill and ability to know how to carry out all the work of constructing the sanctuary[c] are to do the work just as the LORD has commanded."

2 Then Moses summoned Bezalel[d] and Oholiab[e] and every skilled person to whom the LORD had given ability and who was willing[f] to come and do the work. 3 They received from Moses all the offerings[g] the Israelites had brought to carry out the work of constructing the sanctuary. And the people continued to bring freewill offerings morning after morning. 4 So all the skilled craftsmen who were doing all the work on the sanctuary left their work 5 and said to Moses, "The people are bringing more than enough[h] for doing the work the LORD commanded to be done."

6 Then Moses gave an order and they sent this word throughout the camp: "No man or woman is to make anything else as an offering for the sanctuary." And so the people were restrained from bringing more, 7 because what they already had was more[i] than enough to do all the work.

The Tabernacle

8 All the skilled men among the workmen made the tabernacle with ten curtains of finely twisted linen and blue, purple and scarlet yarn, with cherubim worked into them by a skilled craftsman. 9 All the curtains were the same size—twenty-eight cubits long and four cubits wide.[a] 10 They joined five of the curtains together and did the same with the other five. 11 Then they made loops of blue material along the edge of the end curtain in one set, and the same was done with the end curtain in the other set. 12 They also made fifty loops on one curtain and fifty loops on the end curtain of the other set, with the loops opposite each other. 13 Then they made fifty gold clasps and used them to fasten the two sets of curtains together so that the tabernacle was a unit.[j]

14 They made curtains of goat hair for the tent over the tabernacle—eleven altogether. 15 All eleven curtains were the same size—thirty cubits long and four cubits wide.[b] 16 They joined five of the curtains into one set and the other six into another set. 17 Then they made fifty loops along the edge of the end curtain in one set and also along the edge of the end curtain in the other set. 18 They made fifty bronze clasps to fasten the tent together as a unit.[k] 19 Then they made for the tent a covering of ram skins dyed red, and over that a covering of hides of sea cows.[c]

20 They made upright frames of acacia wood for the tabernacle. 21 Each frame was ten cubits long and a cubit and a half wide,[d] 22 with two projections set parallel to each other. They made all the frames of the tabernacle in this way. 23 They made twenty frames for the south side of the tabernacle 24 and made forty silver bases to go under them—two bases for each frame, one under each projection. 25 For the other side, the north side of the tabernacle, they made twenty frames 26 and forty silver bases—two under

35:23 [r] 1Ch 29:8
35:25 [s] Ex 28:3
35:27 [t] 1Ch 29:6; Ezr 2:68
35:28 [u] Ex 25:6
35:29 [v] ver 21; 1Ch 29:9 [w] ver 4-9; Ex 25:1-7; 36:3; 2Ki 12:4
35:31 [x] ver 35; 2Ch 2:7,14
35:34 [y] Ex 31:6 [z] 2Ch 2:14
35:35 [a] ver 31; Ex 31:3,6; 1Ki 7:14
36:1 [b] Ex 28:3 [c] Ex 25:8
36:2 [d] Ex 31:2 [e] Ex 31:6 [f] Ex 25:2; 35:21,26; 1Ch 29:5
36:3 [g] Ex 35:29
36:5 [h] 2Ch 24:14; 31:10; 2Co 8:2-3
36:7 [i] 1Ki 7:47
36:13 [j] ver 18
36:18 [k] ver 13

[a] *9* That is, about 42 feet (about 12.5 meters) long and 6 feet (about 1.8 meters) wide [b] *15* That is, about 45 feet (about 13.5 meters) long and 6 feet (about 1.8 meters) wide [c] *19* That is, dugongs [d] *21* That is, about 15 feet (about 4.5 meters) long and 2 1/4 feet (about 0.7 meter) wide

each frame. 27They made six frames for the far end, that is, the west end of the tabernacle, 28and two
frames were made for the corners of the tabernacle at the far end. 29At these two corners the frames were
double from the bottom all the way to the top and fitted into a single ring; both were made alike. 30So there
were eight frames and sixteen silver bases—two under each frame.

31They also made crossbars of acacia wood: five for the frames on one side of the tabernacle, 32five for
those on the other side, and five for the frames on the west, at the far end of the tabernacle. 33They made
the center crossbar so that it extended from end to end at the middle of the frames. 34They overlaid the
frames with gold and made gold rings to hold the crossbars. They also overlaid the crossbars with gold.

36:35 [l]Ex 39:38; Mt 27:51; Lk 23:45; Heb 9:3 35They made the curtain[l] of blue, purple and scarlet yarn and finely twisted linen, with cherubim
worked into it by a skilled craftsman. 36They made four posts of acacia wood for it and overlaid them with
gold. They made gold hooks for them and cast their four silver bases. 37For the entrance to the tent they
36:37 [m]Ex 27:16 made a curtain of blue, purple and scarlet yarn and finely twisted linen—the work of an embroiderer;[m]
38and they made five posts with hooks for them. They overlaid the tops of the posts and their bands with
gold and made their five bases of bronze.

The Ark

37:1 [n]Ex 31:2 [o]Ex 30:6; 39:35; Dt 10:3 **37:2** [p]ver 11,26

37 Bezalel[n] made the ark[o] of acacia wood—two and a half cubits long, a cubit and a half wide, and
a cubit and a half high.[a] 2He overlaid it with pure gold,[p] both inside and out, and made a gold
molding around it. 3He cast four gold rings for it and fastened them to its four feet, with two rings on one
side and two rings on the other. 4Then he made poles of acacia wood and overlaid them with gold. 5And
he inserted the poles into the rings on the sides of the ark to carry it.

37:6 [q]Ex 26:34; 31:7; Heb 9:5 6He made the atonement cover[q] of pure gold—two and a half cubits long and a cubit and a half wide.[b]
37:7 [r]Eze 41:18 7Then he made two cherubim[r] out of hammered gold at the ends of the cover. 8He made one cherub on
one end and the second cherub on the other; at the two ends he made them of one piece with the cover.
37:9 [s]Heb 9:5 9The cherubim had their wings spread upward, overshadowing[s] the cover with them. The cherubim faced
[t]Dt 10:3 each other, looking toward the cover.[t]

The Table

37:10 [u]Heb 9:2 10They[c] made the table[u] of acacia wood—two cubits long, a cubit wide, and a cubit and a half high.[d]
37:11 [v]ver 2 11Then they overlaid it with pure gold[v] and made a gold molding around it. 12They also made around it
a rim a handbreadth[e] wide and put a gold molding on the rim. 13They cast four gold rings for the table
37:14 [w]ver 27 and fastened them to the four corners, where the four legs were. 14The rings[w] were put close to the rim
to hold the poles used in carrying the table. 15The poles for carrying the table were made of acacia wood
and were overlaid with gold. 16And they made from pure gold the articles for the table—its plates and
dishes and bowls and its pitchers for the pouring out of drink offerings.

The Lampstand

37:17 [x]Heb 9:2; Rev 1:12 17They made the lampstand[x] of pure gold and hammered it out, base and shaft; its flowerlike cups,
buds and blossoms were of one piece with it. 18Six branches extended from the sides of the lampstand—
three on one side and three on the other. 19Three cups shaped like almond flowers with buds and blos-
soms were on one branch, three on the next branch and the same for all six branches extending from the
lampstand. 20And on the lampstand were four cups shaped like almond flowers with buds and blossoms.
21One bud was under the first pair of branches extending from the lampstand, a second bud under the
second pair, and a third bud under the third pair—six branches in all. 22The buds and the branches were
37:22 [y]ver 17; Nu 8:4 all of one piece with the lampstand, hammered out of pure gold.[y]
37:23 [z]Ex 40:4, 25 23They made its seven lamps,[z] as well as its wick trimmers and trays, of pure gold. 24They made the
lampstand and all its accessories from one talent[f] of pure gold.

The Altar of Incense

37:25 [a]Ex 30:34-36; Lk 1:11; Heb 9:4; Rev 8:3 [b]Ex 27:2; Rev 9:13 25They made the altar of incense[a] out of acacia wood. It was square, a cubit long and a cubit wide,
and two cubits high[g]—its horns[b] of one piece with it. 26They overlaid the top and all the sides and the

[a] *1* That is, about 3 3/4 feet (about 1.1 meters) long and 2 1/4 feet (about 0.7 meter) wide and high [b] *6* That is, about 3 3/4 feet (about 1.1 meters) long and 2 1/4 feet (about 0.7 meter) wide [c] *10* Or *He*; also in verses 11-29 [d] *10* That is, about 3 feet (about 0.9 meter) long, 1 1/2 feet (about 0.5 meter) wide, and 2 1/4 feet (about 0.7 meter) high [e] *12* That is, about 3 inches (about 8 centimeters) [f] *24* That is, about 75 pounds (about 34 kilograms) [g] *25* That is, about 1 1/2 feet (about 0.5 meter) long and wide, and about 3 feet (about 0.9 meter) high

horns with pure gold, and made a gold molding around it. 27 They made two gold rings[c] below the molding—two on opposite sides—to hold the poles used to carry it. 28 They made the poles of acacia wood and overlaid them with gold.[d]

29 They also made the sacred anointing oil[e] and the pure, fragrant incense[f]—the work of a perfumer.

37:27 [c]ver 14
37:28 [d]Ex 25:13
37:29 [e]Ex 31:11 [f]Ex 30:1,25; 39:38

The Altar of Burnt Offering

38 They[a] built the altar of burnt offering of acacia wood, three cubits[b] high; it was square, five cubits long and five cubits wide.[c] 2 They made a horn at each of the four corners, so that the horns and the altar were of one piece, and they overlaid the altar with bronze.[g] 3 They made all its utensils[h] of bronze—its pots, shovels, sprinkling bowls, meat forks and firepans. 4 They made a grating for the altar, a bronze network, to be under its ledge, halfway up the altar. 5 They cast bronze rings to hold the poles for the four corners of the bronze grating. 6 They made the poles of acacia wood and overlaid them with bronze. 7 They inserted the poles into the rings so they would be on the sides of the altar for carrying it. They made it hollow, out of boards.

38:2 [g]2Ch 1:5
38:3 [h]Ex 31:9

Basin for Washing

8 They made the bronze basin[i] and its bronze stand from the mirrors of the women[j] who served at the entrance to the Tent of Meeting.

38:8 [i]Ex 30:18; 40:7 [j]Dt 23:17; 1Sa 2:22; 1Ki 14:24

The Courtyard

9 Next they made the courtyard. The south side was a hundred cubits[d] long and had curtains of finely twisted linen, 10 with twenty posts and twenty bronze bases, and with silver hooks and bands on the posts. 11 The north side was also a hundred cubits long and had twenty posts and twenty bronze bases, with silver hooks and bands on the posts.

12 The west end was fifty cubits[e] wide and had curtains, with ten posts and ten bases, with silver hooks and bands on the posts. 13 The east end, toward the sunrise, was also fifty cubits wide. 14 Curtains fifteen cubits[f] long were on one side of the entrance, with three posts and three bases, 15 and curtains fifteen cubits long were on the other side of the entrance to the courtyard, with three posts and three bases. 16 All the curtains around the courtyard were of finely twisted linen. 17 The bases for the posts were bronze. The hooks and bands on the posts were silver, and their tops were overlaid with silver; so all the posts of the courtyard had silver bands.

18 The curtain for the entrance to the courtyard was of blue, purple and scarlet yarn and finely twisted linen—the work of an embroiderer. It was twenty cubits[g] long and, like the curtains of the courtyard, five cubits[h] high, 19 with four posts and four bronze bases. Their hooks and bands were silver, and their tops were overlaid with silver. 20 All the tent pegs[k] of the tabernacle and of the surrounding courtyard were bronze.

38:20 [k]Ex 35:18

The Materials Used

21 These are the amounts of the materials used for the tabernacle, the tabernacle of the Testimony,[l] which were recorded at Moses' command by the Levites under the direction of Ithamar[m] son of Aaron, the priest. 22 (Bezalel[n] son of Uri, the son of Hur, of the tribe of Judah, made everything the LORD commanded Moses; 23 with him was Oholiab[o] son of Ahisamach, of the tribe of Dan—a craftsman and designer, and an embroiderer in blue, purple and scarlet yarn and fine linen.) 24 The total amount of the

38:21 [l]Nu 1:50, 53; 8:24; 9:15; 10:11; 17:7; 1Ch 23:32; 2Ch 24:6; Ac 7:44; Rev 15:5 [m]Nu 4:28,33
38:22 [n]Ex 31:2
38:23 [o]Ex 31:6

[a] *1* Or *He*; also in verses 2-9 [b] *1* That is, about 4 1/2 feet (about 1.3 meters) [c] *1* That is, about 7 1/2 feet (about 2.3 meters) long and wide [d] *9* That is, about 150 feet (about 46 meters) [e] *12* That is, about 75 feet (about 23 meters) [f] *14* That is, about 22 1/2 feet (about 6.9 meters) [g] *18* That is, about 30 feet (about 9 meters) [h] *18* That is, about 7 1/2 feet (about 2.3 meters)

38:1–7 The worlds of Biblical study and archaeology come together with respect to altars. The Israelites' altar of burnt offering from the tabernacle has not been found, but others like it have been unearthed. An altar located in Arad not only has horns but is also five cubits square, like the one described here (see the note on 27:1). The presence of horned altars in antiquity is thus well established, suggesting the authenticity of this one. See "Ancient Altars" on page 125 and "The Horned Altar" on page 924, as well as the notes on 20:24–25, 20:26 and 27:1.

38:8 Mirrored glass was unknown in ancient times, but highly polished bronze provided adequate reflection.

38:9 Ancient Egypt was known as the center for trading linen. It came in many grades and textures, as evidenced by the different Hebrew words for this cloth (see the note on 25:4). God did not ask the Israelites to use materials that would require traveling long distances or become a hardship for them to acquire. Instead, he instructed them to donate materials for his tabernacle from the items they had received as bounty when leaving Egypt (12:35–36).

38:24 [p]Ex 30:16 [q]Ex 30:13; Lev 27:25; Nu 3:47; 18:16
38:25 [r]Ex 30:12
38:26 [s]Ex 30:12 [t]Ex 30:13 [u]Ex 30:14 [v]Ex 12:37; Nu 1:46
38:27 [w]Ex 26:19

gold from the wave offering used for all the work on the sanctuary[p] was 29 talents and 730 shekels,[a] according to the sanctuary shekel.[q]

25 The silver obtained from those of the community who were counted in the census[r] was 100 talents and 1,775 shekels,[b] according to the sanctuary shekel— 26 one beka per person,[s] that is, half a shekel,[c] according to the sanctuary shekel,[t] from everyone who had crossed over to those counted, twenty years old or more,[u] a total of 603,550 men.[v] 27 The 100 talents[d] of silver were used to cast the bases[w] for the sanctuary and for the curtain—100 bases from the 100 talents, one talent for each base. 28 They used the 1,775 shekels[e] to make the hooks for the posts, to overlay the tops of the posts, and to make their bands.

29 The bronze from the wave offering was 70 talents and 2,400 shekels.[f] 30 They used it to make the bases for the entrance to the Tent of Meeting, the bronze altar with its bronze grating and all its utensils, 31 the bases for the surrounding courtyard and those for its entrance and all the tent pegs for the tabernacle and those for the surrounding courtyard.

The Priestly Garments

39:1 [x]Ex 35:23 [y]Ex 35:19 [z]ver 41; Ex 28:2

39 From the blue, purple and scarlet yarn[x] they made woven garments for ministering in the sanctuary.[y] They also made sacred garments[z] for Aaron, as the LORD commanded Moses.

The Ephod

2 They[g] made the ephod of gold, and of blue, purple and scarlet yarn, and of finely twisted linen. 3 They hammered out thin sheets of gold and cut strands to be worked into the blue, purple and scarlet yarn and fine linen—the work of a skilled craftsman. 4 They made shoulder pieces for the ephod, which were attached to two of its corners, so it could be fastened. 5 Its skillfully woven waistband was like it—of one piece with the ephod and made with gold, and with blue, purple and scarlet yarn, and with finely twisted linen, as the LORD commanded Moses.

39:7 [a]Lev 24:7; Jos 4:7

6 They mounted the onyx stones in gold filigree settings and engraved them like a seal with the names of the sons of Israel. 7 Then they fastened them on the shoulder pieces of the ephod as memorial[a] stones for the sons of Israel, as the LORD commanded Moses.

The Breastpiece

39:8 [b]Lev 8:8
39:14 [c]Rev 21:12

8 They fashioned the breastpiece[b]—the work of a skilled craftsman. They made it like the ephod: of gold, and of blue, purple and scarlet yarn, and of finely twisted linen. 9 It was square—a span[h] long and a span wide—and folded double. 10 Then they mounted four rows of precious stones on it. In the first row there was a ruby, a topaz and a beryl; 11 in the second row a turquoise, a sapphire[i] and an emerald; 12 in the third row a jacinth, an agate and an amethyst; 13 in the fourth row a chrysolite, an onyx and a jasper.[j] They were mounted in gold filigree settings. 14 There were twelve stones, one for each of the names of the sons of Israel, each engraved like a seal with the name of one of the twelve tribes.[c]

15 For the breastpiece they made braided chains of pure gold, like a rope. 16 They made two gold filigree settings and two gold rings, and fastened the rings to two of the corners of the breastpiece. 17 They fastened the two gold chains to the rings at the corners of the breastpiece, 18 and the other ends of the chains to the two settings, attaching them to the shoulder pieces of the ephod at the front. 19 They made two gold rings and attached them to the other two corners of the breastpiece on the inside edge next to the ephod. 20 Then they made two more gold rings and attached them to the bottom of the shoulder pieces on the front of the ephod, close to the seam just above the waistband of the ephod. 21 They tied the rings of the breastpiece to the rings of the ephod with blue cord, connecting it to the waistband so that the breastpiece would not swing out from the ephod—as the LORD commanded Moses.

Other Priestly Garments

22 They made the robe of the ephod entirely of blue cloth—the work of a weaver— 23 with an opening in the center of the robe like the opening of a collar,[k] and a band around this opening, so that it would

[a] *24* The weight of the gold was a little over one ton (about 1 metric ton). [b] *25* The weight of the silver was a little over 3 3/4 tons (about 3.4 metric tons). [c] *26* That is, about 1/5 ounce (about 5.5 grams) [d] *27* That is, about 3 3/4 tons (about 3.4 metric tons) [e] *28* That is, about 45 pounds (about 20 kilograms) [f] *29* The weight of the bronze was about 2 1/2 tons (about 2.4 metric tons). [g] *2* Or *He*; also in verses 7, 8 and 22 [h] *9* That is, about 9 inches (about 22 centimeters) [i] *11* Or *lapis lazuli* [j] *13* The precise identification of some of these precious stones is uncertain. [k] *23* The meaning of the Hebrew for this word is uncertain.

not tear. 24 They made pomegranates of blue, purple and scarlet yarn and finely twisted linen around the
hem of the robe. 25 And they made bells of pure gold and attached them around the hem between the
pomegranates. 26 The bells and pomegranates alternated around the hem of the robe to be worn for min-
istering, as the LORD commanded Moses.

27 For Aaron and his sons, they made tunics of fine linen[d]—the work of a weaver— 28 and the turban[e]
of fine linen, the linen headbands and the undergarments of finely twisted linen. 29 The sash was of fine-
ly twisted linen and blue, purple and scarlet yarn—the work of an embroiderer—as the LORD com-
manded Moses.

30 They made the plate, the sacred diadem, out of pure gold and engraved on it, like an inscription on
a seal: HOLY TO THE LORD. 31 Then they fastened a blue cord to it to attach it to the turban, as the LORD com-
manded Moses.

Moses Inspects the Tabernacle

32 So all the work on the tabernacle, the Tent of Meeting, was completed. The Israelites did everything
just as the LORD commanded Moses.[f] 33 Then they brought the tabernacle to Moses: the tent and all its fur-
nishings, its clasps, frames, crossbars, posts and bases; 34 the covering of ram skins dyed red, the cover-
ing of hides of sea cows[a] and the shielding curtain; 35 the ark of the Testimony[g] with its poles and the
atonement cover; 36 the table with all its articles and the bread of the Presence; 37 the pure gold lamp-
stand[h] with its row of lamps and all its accessories, and the oil for the light; 38 the gold altar,[i] the anoint-
ing oil, the fragrant incense, and the curtain[j] for the entrance to the tent; 39 the bronze altar with its bronze
grating, its poles and all its utensils; the basin with its stand; 40 the curtains of the courtyard with its posts
and bases, and the curtain for the entrance to the courtyard;[k] the ropes and tent pegs for the courtyard;
all the furnishings for the tabernacle, the Tent of Meeting; 41 and the woven garments worn for minister-
ing in the sanctuary, both the sacred garments for Aaron the priest and the garments for his sons when
serving as priests.

42 The Israelites had done all the work just as the LORD had commanded Moses.[l] 43 Moses inspected the
work and saw that they had done it just as the LORD had commanded. So Moses blessed[m] them.

Setting Up the Tabernacle

40 Then the LORD said to Moses: 2 "Set up the tabernacle, the Tent of Meeting,[n] on the first day of the
first month.[o] 3 Place the ark[p] of the Testimony in it and shield the ark with the curtain. 4 Bring in
the table and set out what belongs on it.[q] Then bring in the lampstand[r] and set up its lamps. 5 Place the
gold altar[s] of incense in front of the ark of the Testimony and put the curtain at the entrance to the tab-
ernacle.

6 "Place the altar of burnt offering in front of the entrance to the tabernacle, the Tent of Meeting; 7 place
the basin[t] between the Tent of Meeting and the altar and put water in it. 8 Set up the courtyard around it
and put the curtain at the entrance to the courtyard.

9 "Take the anointing oil and anoint[u] the tabernacle and everything in it; consecrate it and all its fur-
nishings, and it will be holy. 10 Then anoint the altar of burnt offering and all its utensils; consecrate[v] the
altar, and it will be most holy. 11 Anoint the basin and its stand and consecrate them.

12 "Bring Aaron and his sons to the entrance to the Tent of Meeting and wash them with water.[w] 13 Then
dress Aaron in the sacred garments,[x] anoint him and consecrate[y] him so he may serve me as priest.
14 Bring his sons and dress them in tunics. 15 Anoint them just as you anointed their father, so they may
serve me as priests. Their anointing will be to a priesthood that will continue for all generations to
come.[z]" 16 Moses did everything just as the LORD commanded him.

17 So the tabernacle[a] was set up on the first day of the first month[b] in the second year. 18 When Moses
set up the tabernacle, he put the bases in place, erected the frames, inserted the crossbars and set up the
posts. 19 Then he spread the tent over the tabernacle and put the covering over the tent, as the LORD com-
manded him.

20 He took the Testimony[c] and placed it in the ark, attached the poles to the ark and put the atone-
ment cover over it. 21 Then he brought the ark into the tabernacle and hung the shielding curtain[d] and
shielded the ark of the Testimony, as the LORD commanded him.

22 Moses placed the table[e] in the Tent of Meeting on the north side of the tabernacle outside the cur-
tain 23 and set out the bread[f] on it before the LORD, as the LORD commanded him.

39:27 [d]Lev 6:10 **39:28** [e]Ex 28:4
39:32 [f]ver 42-43; Ex 25:9
39:35 [g]Ex 30:6
39:37 [h]Ex 25:31 **39:38** [i]Ex 30:1-10 [j]Ex 36:35
39:40 [k]Ex 27:9-19
39:42 [l]Ex 25:9
39:43 [m]Lev 9:22,23; Nu 6:23-27; 2Sa 6:18; 1Ki 8:14,55; 2Ch 30:27
40:2 [n]Nu 1:1 [o]ver 17; Ex 12:2
40:3 [p]ver 21; Nu 4:5; Ex 26:33
40:4 [q]Ex 25:30 [r]ver 22-25; Ex 26:35
40:5 [s]ver 26; Ex 30:1
40:7 [t]ver 30; Ex 30:18
40:9 [u]Ex 30:26; Lev 8:10
40:10 [v]Ex 29:36
40:12 [w]Lev 8:1-13
40:13 [x]Ex 28:41 [y]Lev 8:12
40:15 [z]Ex 29:9; Nu 25:13
40:17 [a]Nu 7:1 [b]ver 2
40:20 [c]Ex 16:34; 25:16; Dt 10:5; 1Ki 8:9; Heb 9:4
40:21 [d]Ex 26:33
40:22 [e]Ex 26:35
40:23 [f]ver 4

[a] 34 That is, dugongs

The Tabernacle and the Ark

EXODUS 40 The tabernacle, a portable sanctuary that served as the center for Israelite worship until the building of Solomon's temple, was known by various terms in Scripture. Each name highlighted an aspect of its function:

- It was commonly known as the "sanctuary" (some translations say "dwelling") because God had chosen to live there among his people (Ex 25:8).
- God held audience with them in the "Tent of Meeting" to accept their sacrifices and forgive their sins (28:43).[1]
- As the "tabernacle of the Testimony," it housed the tablets of God's covenant with his people (38:21).

The tabernacle's layout and construction resembled ancient Egypt's portable pavilions and military encampments. On Mount Sinai God had handed Moses an architectural blueprint for this transportable sanctuary (25:9), and craftsmen gifted by the Holy Spirit executed the work precisely as specified (31:1–11; Heb 8:5).

A rectangular enclosure of white linen curtains formed an outer court (Ex 27:9ff.) in which priests offered sacrifices on a four-horned altar of acacia wood overlaid with bronze.[2] All accompanying utensils were fashioned of bronze, as was the laver—a bowl on a base in which the priests washed their hands and feet (30:17–21).

The tent began as a wooden, latticework frame, allowing for easy assembly and disassembly (see 26:15–30), over which were draped multilayered coverings of finely woven blue, purple and scarlet cloth embroidered with representations of cherubim (angelic figures). A layer of goats' hair covered by a double layer of tanned leather skins formed a protective roof/covering (40:1–14). The completed structure was 45 feet long by 10 feet (13.7 x 3 m) wide by 10 feet high.

Inside the tent were two areas separated by a veil: the Holy Place and the Most Holy Place. Articles of furniture graced the interior of the Holy Place. All were fashioned with rings through which poles could be fitted for transport—and for elimination of the possibility of defilement of these holy objects by human touch.

A gold-overlaid table was set with 12 loaves of bread for the priests to eat once each week to commune with God and enjoy his hospitality on Israel's behalf (Lev 24:8–9). Opposite the table was a golden lampstand, the base of which branched out into seven shafts holding almond-blossom-shaped lamps. Almond blossoms, petals and calyxes (the green outer whorls of flowers) ornamented each branch. The arboreal design and floral adornment of the lampstand, which was kept perpetually burning (Ex 27:20), recalled the burning bush through which God had manifested himself to Moses (3:2–3). Marking the boundary of priestly ministration at the veil stood a gold-overlaid incense altar on which burned a perpetual sacrifice of aromatic incense (30:1–10).[3]

Separated from the Holy Place and concealed by a cherubim-embroidered veil was the Most Holy Place, the inner sanctum housing the ark of the covenant (26:31–34). The cherubim symbolized the Garden of Eden, where such angelic creatures had been stationed to guard the way to the tree of life (Ge 3:24).

The ark, a chest of acacia wood overlaid inside and out with gold, was about 3 feet long by 2 feet wide (.9 x .6 m) by 2 feet high. A golden molding adorned its cover. On either end of its lid rose two cherubim crafted of beaten gold. These figures faced each other, their wings outstretched to shelter the ark as though under a canopy. The ark represented God's footstool (1Ch 28:2) and the cherubim his throne (1Sa 4:4; Isa 37:16).

Inside the ark were placed the stone tablets of the covenant (Ex 25:21), a jar of manna (16:33) and Aaron's staff (Nu 17:10). The tablets of the Law reminded the people that God would enforce the terms of his covenant with them. On the annual Day of Atonement the blood of sacrificial animals was to be sprinkled on the ark's lid, covering the tablets defining the terms the people had transgressed (Lev 16:14–16; 30).[4]

After the craftsmen had completed work on the tabernacle, God's glory that had rested atop Mount Sinai descended to fill the sanctuary and lead Israel into the promised land (Ex 40:34–38). The tabernacle served as a "portable Sinai" from within which God continued to dwell among his people (29:45–46).

[1]See "Sacrifices and Offerings in the Bible and the Ancient Near East" on page 158. [2]See "Ancient Altars" on page 125 and "The Horned Altar" on page 924. [3]See "Incense" on page 1209. [4]See "The Day of Atonement" on page 176.

Byzantine synagogue mosaic depicting the menorah and the veil of the temple

Preserving Bible Times; © Dr. James C. Martin; permission of The Israel Museum

24 He placed the lampstand[g] in the Tent of Meeting opposite the table on the south side of the taber-
nacle 25 and set up the lamps[h] before the LORD, as the LORD commanded him.
26 Moses placed the gold altar[i] in the Tent of Meeting in front of the curtain 27 and burned fragrant in-
cense on it, as the LORD commanded[j] him. 28 Then he put up the curtain[k] at the entrance to the tabernacle.
29 He set the altar of burnt offering near the entrance to the tabernacle, the Tent of Meeting, and of-
fered on it burnt offerings and grain offerings,[l] as the LORD commanded him.
30 He placed the basin[m] between the Tent of Meeting and the altar and put water in it for washing,
31 and Moses and Aaron and his sons used it to wash their hands and feet. 32 They washed whenever they
entered the Tent of Meeting or approached the altar,[n] as the LORD commanded Moses.
33 Then Moses set up the courtyard[o] around the tabernacle and altar and put up the curtain[p] at the en-
trance to the courtyard. And so Moses finished the work.

The Glory of the LORD

34 Then the cloud[q] covered the Tent of Meeting, and the glory of the LORD filled the tabernacle. 35 Mo-
ses could not enter the Tent of Meeting because the cloud had settled upon it, and the glory of the LORD
filled the tabernacle.[r]
36 In all the travels of the Israelites, whenever the cloud lifted from above the tabernacle, they would
set out;[s] 37 but if the cloud did not lift, they did not set out—until the day it lifted. 38 So the cloud[t] of the
LORD was over the tabernacle by day, and fire was in the cloud by night, in the sight of all the house of Is-
rael during all their travels.

40:24 [g]Ex 26:35
40:25 [h]ver 4; Ex 25:37
40:26 [i]ver 5; Ex 30:6
40:27 [j]Ex 30:7
40:28 [k]Ex 26:36
40:29 [l]ver 6; Ex 29:38-42
40:30 [m]ver 7
40:32 [n]Ex 30:20
40:33 [o]Ex 27:9 [p]ver 8
40:34 [q]Nu 9:15-23; 1Ki 8:12
40:35 [r]1Ki 8:11; 2Ch 5:13-14
40:36 [s]Nu 9:17-23; 10:13; Ne 9:19
40:38 [t]Ex 13:21; Nu 9:15; 1Co 10:1

40:34–38 Regarding God's *shekînâh* glory (his visible Presence), see the note on 14:19.

INTRODUCTION TO 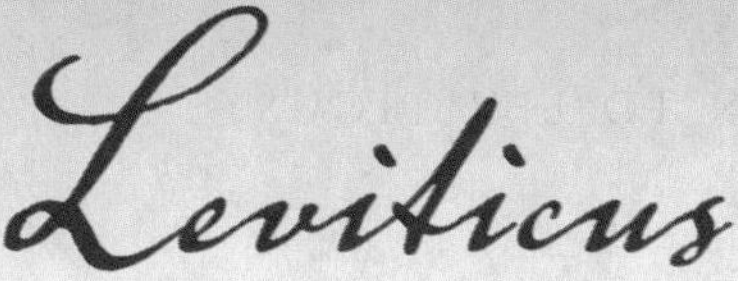

AUTHOR, PLACE AND DATE OF WRITING

God gave the contents of Leviticus to Moses (see 27:34) while the Israelites were camped at Mount Sinai, and historical Jewish tradition assigns primary authorship of the book to him. Leviticus repeatedly states that God conveyed to Moses specific laws (e.g., 1:1; 4:1; 6:1), a reality confirmed in the New Testament (e.g., Ro 10:5). But Moses most likely did not compose Leviticus in its final, edited form.

Not all scholars agree that Moses was the primary writer/compiler of this or the other books of the Pentateuch (Ge–Dt). See "The Documentary Hypothesis" on page 15.

If Moses did indeed write Leviticus, as well as the other four books of the Pentateuch, he must have done so during the exodus period, widely accepted among conservative evangelical scholars to be from approximately 1440 to 1400 B.C.

AUDIENCE

It is likely that the Israelite priests and Levites read Leviticus, as did the lay people who took part in the exodus and subsequent desert wandering. Succeeding generations of Israelites no doubt also studied the book to learn God's laws for worship and sacrificial practices and to be reminded of their calling to be his holy people in covenant relationship with him.

CULTURAL FACTS AND HIGHLIGHTS

In comparison to the books around it, Leviticus may seem difficult to the casual or first-time reader. Instead of miraculous, suspense-filled stories and narratives about prominent people, we read page after page of meticulous detail concerning regulations for offerings, the installation of priests, distinctions between what was ritually clean and unclean, principles for holy living, etc. True, this seeming minutia played a key role in the Israelites' spiritual growth and development, but what do we gain by reading about it?

Leviticus picks up where the book of Exodus left off. The tabernacle had been built, and now the priests (Aaron's sons), assisted by others from the tribe of Levi, needed to understand and follow proper, worship-related protocol. The other Israelites, who were familiar with the worship and sacrificial practices of the ancient world, needed to learn *God's* worship-related laws and regulations—what was and was not acceptable to him in terms of ritual and sacrifice. Relationships were at the heart of God's covenant with Israel—his people's relationship with him and with one another.

Leviticus reveals God's directives regarding rituals, ceremonial "cleanness" and the behavior by which the Israelites could be made holy before their holy God (e.g., 11:44–45) and worship him in a consecrated manner. It was essential that God's people understand and practice holiness—separation from sin, being set apart for the Lord's exclusive purpose and glory. The formal procedures regarding Israel's religious observance, the details of which are included in Leviticus, played a central role in the people's everyday spiritual life.

TIMELINE

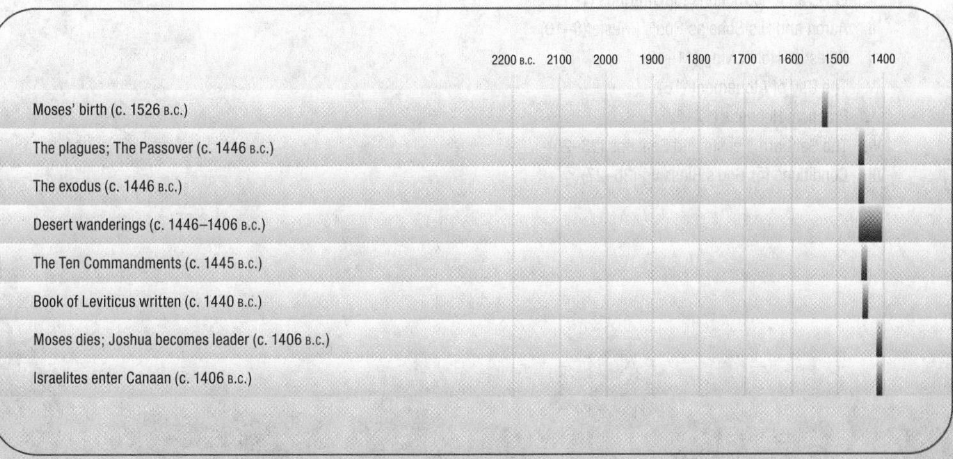

AS YOU READ

Think about how God regulated the Israelites' communal, religious and personal lives in order to establish them as his holy people and to teach them about holy living. The Lord wanted to bless them but required them first to be obedient and to maintain a holy awe of him.

Notice the numerous regulations directly related to the tabernacle (chs. 1–16), which God's Presence now occupied. He wanted his people to present their sacrifices properly (1:1—7:38), to set up and maintain the priesthood in a specified way (8:1—10:20) and to carefully differentiate between what was ritually clean and unclean in his eyes (11:1—16:34). Why? Because God wanted them to take his Presence seriously.

Pay attention to the code of holiness (17:1—25:55) that covers everything from sexual behavior to punishing serious crimes to religious observance. To reinforce the weight of these laws, God delineated near the end of this book (26:1–46) the respective consequences of disobedience and obedience.

DID YOU KNOW?

- Other ancient cultures viewed sacrifices as "food for the gods" (see Eze 16:20; cf. Ps 50:9–13), but Israel's offerings—though sometimes called "food" metaphorically (21:6,8,17,21; 22:25)—were viewed as gifts to God that he would receive with delight (3:11,16).
- The phrase "eye for eye, tooth for tooth" represents a statement of principle: The penalty was to fit the crime, not to exceed it (24:20).

THEMES

Leviticus contains the following themes:

1. *Holiness.* "Be holy because I, the Lord your God, am holy" (19:2) is the overwhelming message of this book. In Leviticus spiritual holiness is symbolized by physical perfection, or purity, as well as by separation from the world. The wall dividing Jewish and Christian worship was later removed by God's invitation to faith in Christ and in his completed work on the cross (Gal 3:28; Eph 2:11–22), so the laws of Leviticus need no longer be observed. But the moral principles they espouse still apply today (Mt 5:1—7:29; 12:11–12; Mk 2:23–28).

2. *Sin, sacrifice, atonement.* Since no human being is perfect, God provided the Old Testament sacrificial system as a means of atonement. In this system, a life was to be given for a life. This temporary arrangement is no longer necessary, for Jesus' death paid the penalty for sin once for all time and for all people (Heb 9:23–28).

3. *Worship.* Leviticus reveals God's desire to be present with his people and to enjoy fellowship with them. Through worship God's people acknowledge who he is and what he has done by expressing their love, honor, thanks and praise to him.

OUTLINE

I. Laws and Instructions for Offerings (1–7)
II. Aaron and His Sons as God's Priests (8–10)
III. Rules for Holy Living (11–15)
IV. The Day of Atonement (16)
V. Practical Holiness (17–22)
VI. The Sabbath, Feasts and Seasons (23–25)
VII. Conditions for God's Blessing (26–27)

The Burnt Offering

1 The LORD called to Moses[a] and spoke to him from the Tent of Meeting.[b] He said, 2 “Speak to the Is-
raelites and say to them: ‘When any of you brings an offering to the LORD, bring as your offering an
animal from either the herd or the flock.[c]
3 “ ‘If the offering is a burnt offering from the herd, he is to offer a male without defect.[d] He must pre-
sent it at the entrance to the Tent[e] of Meeting so that it[a] will be acceptable to the LORD. 4 He is to lay his
hand on the head[f] of the burnt offering, and it will be accepted on his behalf to make atonement[g] for
him. 5 He is to slaughter[h] the young bull before the LORD, and then Aaron’s sons the priests shall bring the
blood and sprinkle it against the altar on all sides[i] at the entrance to the Tent of Meeting. 6 He is to skin[j]
the burnt offering and cut it into pieces. 7 The sons of Aaron the priest are to put fire on the altar and ar-
range wood[k] on the fire. 8 Then Aaron’s sons the priests shall arrange the pieces, including the head and
the fat,[l] on the burning wood that is on the altar. 9 He is to wash the inner parts and the legs with water,
and the priest is to burn all of it on the altar.[m] It is a burnt offering, an offering made by fire, an aroma
pleasing to the LORD.[n]
10 “ ‘If the offering is a burnt offering from the flock, from either the sheep or the goats,[o] he is to offer
a male without defect. 11 He is to slaughter it at the north side of the altar before the LORD, and Aaron’s sons
the priests shall sprinkle its blood against the altar on all sides.[p] 12 He is to cut it into pieces, and the priest
shall arrange them, including the head and the fat, on the burning wood that is on the altar. 13 He is to
wash the inner parts and the legs with water, and the priest is to bring all of it and burn it on the altar. It
is a burnt offering, an offering made by fire, an aroma pleasing to the LORD.
14 “ ‘If the offering to the LORD is a burnt offering of birds, he is to offer a dove or a young pigeon.[q]
15 The priest shall bring it to the altar, wring off the head and burn it on the altar; its blood shall be drained
out on the side of the altar.[r] 16 He is to remove the crop with its contents[b] and throw it to the east side of
the altar, where the ashes[s] are. 17 He shall tear it open by the wings, not severing it completely,[t] and then
the priest shall burn it on the wood[u] that is on the fire on the altar. It is a burnt offering, an offering made
by fire, an aroma pleasing to the LORD.

The Grain Offering

2 “ ‘When someone brings a grain offering[v] to the LORD, his offering is to be of fine flour. He is to pour
oil[w] on it, put incense on it 2 and take it to Aaron’s sons the priests. The priest shall take a handful of
the fine flour[x] and oil, together with all the incense,[y] and burn this as a memorial portion[z] on the altar,
an offering made by fire, an aroma pleasing to the LORD. 3 The rest of the grain offering belongs to Aaron
and his sons;[a] it is a most holy part of the offerings made to the LORD by fire.
4 “ ‘If you bring a grain offering baked in an oven, it is to consist of fine flour: cakes made without
yeast and mixed with oil, or[c] wafers made without yeast and spread with oil.[b] 5 If your grain offering is
prepared on a griddle, it is to be made of fine flour mixed with oil, and without yeast. 6 Crumble it and

1:1 [a]Ex 19:3; 25:22 [b]Nu 7:89
1:2 [c]Lev 22:18-19
1:3 [d]Ex 12:5; Dt 15:21; Heb 9:14; 1Pe 1:19 [e]Lev 17:9
1:4 [f]Ex 29:10,15; Lev 3:2 [g]2Ch 29:23-24
1:5 [h]Lev 3:2,8 [i]Heb 12:24; 1Pe 1:2
1:6 [j]Lev 7:8
1:7 [k]Lev 6:12
1:8 [l]ver 12
1:9 [m]Ex 29:18 [n]ver 13; Ge 8:21; Nu 15:8-10; Eph 5:2
1:10 [o]ver 3; Ex 12:5
1:11 [p]ver 5
1:14 [q]Ge 15:9; Lev 5:7; Lk 2:24
1:15 [r]Lev 5:9
1:16 [s]Lev 6:10
1:17 [t]Ge 15:10 [u]Lev 5:8
2:1 [v]Lev 6:14-18 [w]Nu 15:4
2:2 [x]Lev 5:11 [y]Lev 6:15; Isa 66:3 [z]ver 9, 16; Lev 5:12; 6:15; 24:7; Ac 10:4
2:3 [a]ver 10; Lev 6:16; 10:12, 13
2:4 [b]Ex 29:2

[a] 3 Or *he* [b] 16 Or *crop and the feathers*; the meaning of the Hebrew for this word is uncertain. [c] 4 Or *and*

1:1–17 The distinguishing mark of the burnt offering was that it was wholly consumed on the altar, while in other animal sacrifices only the fat portions were burned. The purpose of the burnt offering was propitiation or atonement, but with this idea was united another: the entire consecration of the worshiper to the Lord. Because no part of the animal was left for human consumption, the term “whole burnt offerings” was used (Ps 51:19). The burnt offering was the normal sacrifice of the Israelite in proper covenant relationship with God—the only sacrifice regularly appointed for the sanctuary service. It was offered every day, in the morning and again in the evening. On ordinary days a yearling lamb was sacrificed, while on the Sabbath two lambs were offered both in the morning and in the evening (Nu 28:9–10). Other special feast days called for a larger number of animals. There were also burnt offerings when a Nazirite either fulfilled his vow or defiled himself (Nu 6), at the consecration of priests (Ex 29:15), at the cleansing of lepers (Lev 14:9), at the purification of women (12:6) and in response to other ceremonial uncleanness (15:15,30). This was the only kind of offering in which a non-Israelite was permitted to participate (17:8; 22:18,25).
1:2 The practice of sacrificing animals was not peculiar to Israel. Neighboring nations also had elaborate sacrificial systems (see “Sacrifices and Offerings in the Bible and the Ancient Near East” on p. 158).
1:3 Anyone could offer special burnt offerings to express devotion to God. The whole sacrifice was to be burned up, including the head, legs, fat and inner organs (v. 9).
1:4 The people laid their hands on their offering as a symbol of (1) the animal’s becoming their substitute and (2) transferring their sins to the sin-bearer.
2:1–16 Grain offerings (vv. 1–16; 6:14–18) were gifts of fine flour; unleavened bread, cakes or wafers; or toasted ears of grain, always with salt and, except in the sin offering (see note on 4:1–35), with olive oil (2:1,4,13–14; 5:11). They were sometimes accompanied by frankincense. Only a portion was consumed by fire on the altar; the rest was kept by the priests, who ate it in a holy place (6:16; 10:12–13). The grain offering accompanied the other offerings, except for the sin offering, on all important occasions (7:11ff.; Nu 15). It always followed the morning and evening burnt offerings. The idea behind the grain offering seems to have been that since people would not ordinarily eat meals consisting only of flesh, it would be wrong to offer only flesh to God.

CULTURAL AND HISTORICAL NOTES

Sacrifices and Offerings in the Bible and the Ancient Near East

LEVITICUS 1 Mosaic Law prescribed five categories of sacrifices and other offerings:

- *Burnt offerings* effected atonement and emphasized total devotion to the Lord.
- *Grain offerings* expressed an individual's petition for God's bestowal of covenantal blessings, as well as the dedication of the fruit of his or her labor to God.
- *Fellowship offerings* (sometimes referred to as "peace" offerings) accompanied expressions of thanksgiving or were offered in fulfillment of vows. As the occasion for a communal meal, such an offering emphasized covenantal fellowship.
- *Sin/purification offerings* effected expiation for unintentional sins, such as those committed from negligence, as well as for ritual impurity.[1]
- *Guilt/reparation offerings* provided atonement for unintentional sins against God's "holy things" and commandments. The aspect of restitution was intrinsic to these mandatory offerings.

In addition to the above, the Israelites were required to bring tithes and other offerings (e.g., Dt 14:22). Different types of offerings were presented in diverse combinations on various occasions, such as during the ordination of priests and the sanctifying of sacred objects (Lev 8–9; Nu 7), during the daily sacrifices (Lev 6:8–13) and annual feasts[2] and at milestone moments in the life of a family (ch. 12).

It is difficult to uncover the full significance of each offering, especially since the regulations in Leviticus 1–7 were directed to the priests (in some sense the religious "professionals") and are therefore somewhat terse, without a great deal of amplification in terms of their meaning. Leviticus 17:11 indicates clearly enough, however, that the costly blood of the animal sacrifice was God's provision to atone for the offender, whose offerings were most likely accompanied by psalm singing, confession of sin and/or special petitions. Viewed in this light, it is clear that the laws governing the presentation of Israel's offerings were not heavy burdens but rather the welcomed means by which God's people could officially recognize their sins, experience God's forgiveness and remain secure within his covenant. At the same time, portions of every offering (except for the whole burnt offering) provided food for the priests and their families.[3]

Although Leviticus 1–7 is unparalleled among ancient Near Eastern texts in its degree of detail, the sacrifice of animals (as well as offerings and libations—"poured" offerings—of other foods and drinks) was by no means peculiar to Israel. A wide range of technical, sacrificial terms (several of which are nearly identical to Israel's) is found in texts from **Late Bronze**[4,5] and Early **Iron Age** Canaanite areas, including **Ugarit**, **Phoenicia**, Syria, **Ammon** and **Moab**. They demonstrate that Israel's neighbors also had elaborate sacrificial systems.[6] In Ugarit and Phoenicia, for example, burnt offerings, fruit and grain offerings and libations were specified, but certain animals (pigs in particular) were forbidden for use as sacrifices to Baal. Ugarit practiced both whole burnt offerings (that fed a deity) and peace offerings (that nourished the people). The great religious centers of Egypt and **Mesopotamia** also stipulated highly ordered and meticulous sacrificial practices.

But despite any commonalities Israel's sacrificial system was unique by virtue of its covenantal context. Its complex sacrificial laws made sense within the bounds of the story of God's redemption of his people from Egyptian bondage. The sacrificial system was not magical. Its efficacy depended not upon the offering of a particular animal (although following the prescribed rules was essential because it taught the Israelites that they were to approach God only on his terms) but rather on God himself, who had ordained these sacrifices. Fully as important, without an attitude of repentance, perfunctory observance of sacrificial rituals was meaningless—and denounced repeatedly by God's prophets (e.g., 1Sa 15:22; Am 5:21–24; Mic 6:6–8; cf. Ps 51:14–19).

[1]See "Ritual Purity in Israel and the Ancient Near East" on page 166. [2]See "The Festivals of Israel" on page 186. [3]See "The Levites and the Priests" on page 648. [4]See "Archaeological Periods" chart on page xx in the front of this Bible. [5]See Glossary on page 2080 for definitions of bolded words. [6]For example, see "The Zukru Festival" on page 130.

The temple of Satet at Elephantine

Preserving Bible Times; © Dr. James C. Martin

pour oil on it; it is a grain offering. 7 If your grain offering is cooked in a pan,[c] it is to be made of fine
flour and oil. 8 Bring the grain offering made of these things to the LORD; present it to the priest, who shall
take it to the altar. 9 He shall take out the memorial portion[d] from the grain offering and burn it on the
altar as an offering made by fire, an aroma pleasing to the LORD.[e] 10 The rest of the grain offering belongs
to Aaron and his sons;[f] it is a most holy part of the offerings made to the LORD by fire.
11 " 'Every grain offering you bring to the LORD must be made without yeast,[g] for you are not to burn
any yeast or honey in an offering made to the LORD by fire. 12 You may bring them to the LORD as an
offering of the firstfruits,[h] but they are not to be offered on the altar as a pleasing aroma. 13 Season all
your grain offerings with salt. Do not leave the salt of the covenant[i] of your God out of your grain offer-
ings; add salt to all your offerings.
14 " 'If you bring a grain offering of firstfruits[j] to the LORD, offer crushed heads of new grain roasted
in the fire. 15 Put oil and incense on it; it is a grain offering. 16 The priest shall burn the memorial por-
tion[k] of the crushed grain and the oil, together with all the incense, as an offering made to the LORD by
fire.

The Fellowship Offering

3 " 'If someone's offering is a fellowship offering,[a][l] and he offers an animal from the herd, whether
male or female, he is to present before the LORD an animal without defect.[m] 2 He is to lay his hand on
the head[n] of his offering and slaughter it[o] at the entrance to the Tent of Meeting. Then Aaron's sons the
priests shall sprinkle the blood against the altar on all sides. 3 From the fellowship offering he is to bring
a sacrifice made to the LORD by fire: all the fat[p] that covers the inner parts or is connected to them, 4 both
kidneys with the fat on them near the loins, and the covering of the liver, which he will remove with the
kidneys. 5 Then Aaron's sons[q] are to burn it on the altar on top of the burnt offering[r] that is on the burn-
ing wood, as an offering made by fire, an aroma pleasing to the LORD.
6 " 'If he offers an animal from the flock as a fellowship offering[s] to the LORD, he is to offer a male or
female without defect. 7 If he offers a lamb, he is to present it before the LORD.[t] 8 He is to lay his hand on
the head of his offering and slaughter it[u] in front of the Tent of Meeting. Then Aaron's sons shall sprin-
kle its blood against the altar on all sides. 9 From the fellowship offering he is to bring a sacrifice made
to the LORD by fire: its fat, the entire fat tail cut off close to the backbone, all the fat that covers the inner
parts or is connected to them, 10 both kidneys with the fat on them near the loins, and the covering of
the liver, which he will remove with the kidneys. 11 The priest shall burn them on the altar[v] as food,[w] an
offering made to the LORD by fire.
12 " 'If his offering is a goat, he is to present it before the LORD. 13 He is to lay his hand on its head and
slaughter it in front of the Tent of Meeting. Then Aaron's sons shall sprinkle[x] its blood against the altar
on all sides. 14 From what he offers he is to make this offering to the LORD by fire: all the fat that covers
the inner parts or is connected to them, 15 both kidneys with the fat on them near the loins, and the cov-
ering of the liver, which he will remove with the kidneys. 16 The priest shall burn them on the altar as
food, an offering made by fire, a pleasing aroma. All the fat is the LORD's.[y]
17 " 'This is a lasting ordinance for the generations to come,[z] wherever you live: You must not eat any
fat or any blood.[a]' "

2:7 [c]Lev 7:9
2:9 [d]ver 2 [e]Ex 29:18; Lev 6:15
2:10 [f]ver 3
2:11 [g]Ex 23:18; 34:25; Lev 6:16
2:12 [h]Lev 7:13; 23:10
2:13 [i]Nu 18:19; Eze 43:24
2:14 [j]Lev 23:10
2:16 [k]ver 2
3:1 [l]Lev 7:11-34 [m]Lev 1:3; 22:21
3:2 [n]Ex 29:10,15 [o]Lev 1:5
3:3 [p]Ex 29:13
3:5 [q]Lev 7:29-34 [r]Ex 29:13,38-42
3:6 [s]ver 1
3:7 [t]Lev 17:8-9
3:8 [u]ver 2; Lev 1:5
3:11 [v]ver 5 [w]ver 16; Lev 21:6, 17
3:13 [x]Ex 24:6
3:16 [y]1Sa 2:16
3:17 [z]Lev 6:18; 17:7 [a]Ge 9:4; Lev 7:25-26; 17:10-16; Dt 12:16; Ac 15:20

[a] *1* Traditionally *peace offering*; also in verses 3, 6 and 9

2:11 For a discussion of the significance of the exclusion of yeast/leaven, see the note on Exodus 29:2.

Some suggest that honey was forbidden on the altar because of its use in Canaanite cultic practices.

2:13 Salt was often costly but was an important part of the diet in ancient times. Perhaps this is why it was used as a covenant sign and was required for sacrifices. See the note on Numbers 18:19.

3:1–17 These offerings were called fellowship offerings because they were given by those who were at peace with God in order to express their gratitude, obligation and/or fellowship with him. They were not commanded for any set time except for Pentecost (23:20) and were presented spontaneously as prompted by the feelings of the worshiper (19:5).

The ritual was the same as for the sin offering (see the note on 4:1–35), except that the blood was wholly poured on the altar, as in the guilt offering and the burnt offering. The fat was burned; the breast and thigh were retained by the priests for their own consumption; and the rest of the flesh was eaten at the sanctuary by the sacrificer and his friends/family (7:15–16,30–34; Dt 12:1,17–18). A meat and drink offering always accompanied this sacrifice. This meal denoted the fellowship that existed between the worshiper and God and was a symbol and pledge of friendship and peace with him.

There were three kinds of fellowship offerings: praise offerings, votive offerings and freewill offerings. For all three classes oxen, sheep and goats of either gender could be provided (Lev 3:1,6,12). The animals had to be without blemish, except for the freewill offerings, where animals with an unusually short or long limb were permitted (22:23). Fellowship offerings were also given upon occasions of great public solemnity or rejoicing.

3:11 Other ancient cultures viewed sacrifices as "food to the idols" (see Eze 16:20; cf. Ps 50:9–13), but Israel's offerings—though sometimes called "food" metaphorically (Lev 21:6,8,17,21; 22:25)—were viewed as gifts to God that he would receive with delight (though not consume).

The Sin Offering

4 The LORD said to Moses, 2"Say to the Israelites: 'When anyone sins unintentionally[b] and does what
is forbidden in any of the LORD's commands—
3" 'If the anointed priest sins, bringing guilt on the people, he must bring to the LORD a young bull[c]
without defect as a sin offering[d] for the sin he has committed. 4He is to present the bull at the entrance
to the Tent of Meeting before the LORD.[e] He is to lay his hand on its head and slaughter it before the LORD.
5Then the anointed priest shall take some of the bull's blood[f] and carry it into the Tent of Meeting. 6He
is to dip his finger into the blood and sprinkle some of it seven times before the LORD, in front of the cur-
tain of the sanctuary. 7The priest shall then put some of the blood on the horns of the altar of fragrant
incense that is before the LORD in the Tent of Meeting. The rest of the bull's blood he shall pour out at the
base of the altar[g] of burnt offering[h] at the entrance to the Tent of Meeting. 8He shall remove all the fat[i]
from the bull of the sin offering—the fat that covers the inner parts or is connected to them, 9both kid-
neys with the fat on them near the loins, and the covering of the liver, which he will remove with the kid-
neys[j]— 10just as the fat is removed from the ox[a] sacrificed as a fellowship offering.[b] Then the priest shall
burn them on the altar of burnt offering. 11But the hide of the bull and all its flesh, as well as the head and
legs, the inner parts and offal[k]— 12that is, all the rest of the bull—he must take outside the camp[l] to a
place ceremonially clean,[m] where the ashes are thrown, and burn it in a wood fire on the ash heap.

13" 'If the whole Israelite community sins unintentionally[n] and does what is forbidden in any of the
LORD's commands, even though the community is unaware of the matter, they are guilty. 14When they
become aware of the sin they committed, the assembly must bring a young bull[o] as a sin offering[p] and
present it before the Tent of Meeting. 15The elders of the community are to lay their hands on the bull's
head[q] before the LORD, and the bull shall be slaughtered before the LORD. 16Then the anointed priest is to
take some of the bull's blood[r] into the Tent of Meeting. 17He shall dip his finger into the blood and sprin-
kle it before the LORD[s] seven times in front of the curtain. 18He is to put some of the blood on the horns
of the altar that is before the LORD[t] in the Tent of Meeting. The rest of the blood he shall pour out at the
base of the altar of burnt offering at the entrance to the Tent of Meeting. 19He shall remove all the fat[u] from
it and burn it on the altar, 20and do with this bull just as he did with the bull for the sin offering. In this
way the priest will make atonement[v] for them, and they will be forgiven.[w] 21Then he shall take the bull
outside the camp and burn it as he burned the first bull. This is the sin offering for the community.[x]

22" 'When a leader[y] sins unintentionally[z] and does what is forbidden in any of the commands of the
LORD his God, he is guilty. 23When he is made aware of the sin he committed, he must bring as his offer-
ing a male goat without defect. 24He is to lay his hand on the goat's head and slaughter it at the place
where the burnt offering is slaughtered before the LORD. It is a sin offering. 25Then the priest shall take
some of the blood of the sin offering with his finger and put it on the horns of the altar of burnt offering
and pour out the rest of the blood at the base of the altar.[a] 26He shall burn all the fat on the altar as he
burned the fat of the fellowship offering. In this way the priest will make atonement for the man's sin, and
he will be forgiven.[b]

27" 'If a member of the community sins unintentionally[c] and does what is forbidden in any of the LORD's
commands, he is guilty. 28When he is made aware of the sin he committed, he must bring as his offering[d]
for the sin he committed a female goat[e] without defect. 29He is to lay his hand on the head[f] of the sin offer-
ing[g] and slaughter it at the place of the burnt offering. 30Then the priest is to take some of the blood with
his finger and put it on the horns of the altar of burnt offering[h] and pour out the rest of the blood at the base
of the altar. 31He shall remove all the fat, just as the fat is removed from the fellowship offering, and the
priest shall burn it on the altar as an aroma pleasing to the LORD.[i] In this way the priest will make atone-
ment for him, and he will be forgiven.

4:2 [b]Lev 5:15-18; Ps 19:12; Heb 9:7
4:3 [c]ver 14; Ps 66:15 [d]Lev 9:2-22; Heb 9:13-14
4:4 [e]Lev 1:3
4:5 [f]Lev 16:14
4:7 [g]ver 34; Lev 8:15 [h]ver 18, 30; Lev 5:9; 9:9; 16:18
4:8 [i]Lev 3:3-5
4:9 [j]Lev 3:4
4:11 [k]Ex 29:14; Lev 9:11; Nu 19:5
4:12 [l]Heb 13:11 [m]Lev 6:11
4:13 [n]ver 2; Lev 5:2-4,17; Nu 15:24-26
4:14 [o]ver 3 [p]ver 23,28
4:15 [q]Lev 1:4; 8:14,22; Nu 8:10
4:16 [r]ver 5
4:17 [s]ver 6
4:18 [t]ver 7
4:19 [u]ver 8
4:20 [v]Heb 10:10-12 [w]Nu 15:25
4:21 [x]Lev 16:5, 15
4:22 [y]Nu 31:13 [z]ver 2
4:25 [a]ver 7,18, 30,34; Lev 9:9
4:26 [b]Lev 5:10
4:27 [c]ver 2; Nu 15:27
4:28 [d]ver 23 [e]ver 3
4:29 [f]ver 4,24 [g]Lev 1:4
4:30 [h]ver 7
4:31 [i]Ge 8:21

[a] *10* The Hebrew word can include both male and female. [b] *10* Traditionally *peace offering*; also in verses 26,31 and 35

4:1–35 Sin offerings were given to cover sins unconsciously or unintentionally committed; sins committed intentionally, but with mitigating circumstances (5:2–3; 12:6–8); certain kinds of ceremonial defilements (5:2–3; 12:6–8); and sins deliberately committed but afterward voluntarily confessed. For conscious and deliberate violations of the law no atonement was possible, with some exceptions, for which provision was made in the guilt offerings. Sin offerings were made for the whole congregation on all the feast days and especially on the annual Day of Atonement (see "The Day of Atonement" on p. 176). With the exception of these important national occasions, the sin offerings were presented only for special circumstances that demanded expiation of sin.

4:31 The subcutaneous layer of fat around the animal's kidneys and other viscera, like the blood, was forbidden by the Mosaic Law to be

4:32 [j]ver 28 32“ ‘If he brings a lamb as his sin offering, he is to bring a female without defect.[j] 33He is to lay
4:33 [k]ver 29 his hand on its head and slaughter it for a sin offering at the place where the burnt offering is
slaughtered.[k] 34Then the priest shall take some of the blood of the sin offering with his finger and
4:34 [l]ver 7 put it on the horns of the altar of burnt offering and pour out the rest of the blood at the base of
the altar.[l] 35He shall remove all the fat, just as the fat is removed from the lamb of the fellowship
4:35 [m]ver 26,31 offering, and the priest shall burn it on the altar[m] on top of the offerings made to the LORD by fire.
In this way the priest will make atonement for him for the sin he has committed, and he will be
forgiven.

5:1 [n]Pr 29:24 [o]ver 17 5 “ ‘If a person sins because he does not speak up when he hears a public charge to testify[n] regarding
something he has seen or learned about, he will be held responsible.[o]
2“ ‘Or if a person touches anything ceremonially unclean—whether the carcasses of unclean wild
5:2 [p]Lev 11:11, 24-40; Dt 14:8 animals or of unclean livestock or of unclean creatures that move along the ground[p]—even though he
is unaware of it, he has become unclean and is guilty.
5:3 [q]Nu 19:11-16 3“ ‘Or if he touches human uncleanness[q]—anything that would make him unclean—even though
he is unaware of it, when he learns of it he will be guilty.
5:4 [r]Nu 30:6,8 4“ ‘Or if a person thoughtlessly takes an oath[r] to do anything, whether good or evil—in any matter
one might carelessly swear about—even though he is unaware of it, in any case when he learns of it he
will be guilty.
5:5 [s]Lev 16:21; 26:40; Nu 5:7; Pr 28:13 5“ ‘When anyone is guilty in any of these ways, he must confess[s] in what way he has sinned 6and, as
a penalty for the sin he has committed, he must bring to the LORD a female lamb or goat from the flock
5:6 [t]Lev 4:28 as a sin offering;[t] and the priest shall make atonement for him for his sin.
5:7 [u]Lev 12:8; 14:21 7“ ‘If he cannot afford[u] a lamb, he is to bring two doves or two young pigeons to the LORD as a penal-
ty for his sin—one for a sin offering and the other for a burnt offering. 8He is to bring them to the priest,
5:8 [v]Lev 1:15 [w]Lev 1:17 who shall first offer the one for the sin offering. He is to wring its head from its neck,[v] not severing it
completely,[w] 9and is to sprinkle some of the blood of the sin offering against the side of the altar; the
5:9 [x]Lev 4:7,18 rest of the blood must be drained out at the base of the altar.[x] It is a sin offering. 10The priest shall then
5:10 [y]Lev 1:14-17 [z]Lev 4:26 offer the other as a burnt offering in the prescribed way[y] and make atonement for him for the sin he has
committed, and he will be forgiven.[z]
11“ ‘If, however, he cannot afford two doves or two young pigeons, he is to bring as an offering for
5:11 [a]Lev 2:1 his sin a tenth of an ephah[a] of fine flour[a] for a sin offering. He must not put oil or incense on it, be-
cause it is a sin offering. 12He is to bring it to the priest, who shall take a handful of it as a memori-
al portion and burn it on the altar on top of the offerings made to the LORD by fire. It is a sin offer-
5:13 [b]Lev 4:26 [c]Lev 2:3 ing. 13In this way the priest will make atonement[b] for him for any of these sins he has committed,
and he will be forgiven. The rest of the offering will belong to the priest,[c] as in the case of the grain
offering.’ ”

The Guilt Offering

14The LORD said to Moses: 15“When a person commits a violation and sins unintentionally in regard
5:15 [d]Lev 22:14 [e]Nu 5:8 [f]Ex 30:13 to any of the LORD’s holy things, he is to bring to the LORD as a penalty[d] a ram[e] from the flock, one with-
out defect and of the proper value in silver, according to the sanctuary shekel.[b][f] It is a guilt offering. 16He
5:16 [g]Lev 6:4 [h]Lev 22:14; Nu 5:7 must make restitution[g] for what he has failed to do in regard to the holy things, add a fifth of the value[h]
to that and give it all to the priest, who will make atonement for him with the ram as a guilt offering, and
he will be forgiven.
17“If a person sins and does what is forbidden in any of the LORD’s commands, even though he does not

[a] *11* That is, probably about 2 quarts (about 2 liters) [b] *15* That is, about 2/5 ounce (about 11.5 grams)

---

used for food but was burned as an offering to the Lord, for a sweet aroma to him. This had to be done on the very day the animal was killed, apparently to remove the temptation to eat it (Ex 23:18). The purpose of this law was to teach the Israelites that their best belonged to God. Long before the Mosaic Law had been given, Abel had brought the fat of the firstborn of his flock to the Lord, and we read that God had looked with favor upon Abel and his offering (Ge 4:4).

5:14—6:7 The guilt offering was a special kind of sin offering for transgressions for which restitution or other legal satisfaction could be made. When the rights of God or other people had been violated, the wrong had to be righted, the broken law honored and the sin expiated by a guilt offering. The offering, which was always a lamb, with one exception (14:12), was given after the required satisfaction had been made. The ritual was the same as for the sin offering, except that the blood was not sprinkled but poured over the surface of the altar. The main purpose of this sacrifice was to make expiation for dues withheld from God, such as neglect to pay at the proper time what was due to the sanctuary; and from other people, such as robbery, failure to return a deposit, swearing falsely regarding anything lost or seduction of a betrothed slave girl. The sin offering of a lamb made atonement to God. Restitution, along with an additional one-fifth, made reparation to the other individual(s) involved.

know it,[i] he is guilty and will be held responsible. 18 He is to bring to the priest as a guilt offering a ram from 5:17 [i]ver 15; Lev 4:2
the flock, one without defect and of the proper value. In this way the priest will make atonement for him
for the wrong he has committed unintentionally, and he will be forgiven.[j] 19 It is a guilt offering; he has 5:18 [j]ver 15
been guilty of[a] wrongdoing against the LORD."

6 The LORD said to Moses: 2 "If anyone sins and is unfaithful to the LORD[k] by deceiving his neighbor[l] 6:2 [k]Nu 5:6; Ac 5:4; Col 3:9
about something entrusted to him or left in his care[m] or stolen, or if he cheats him, 3 or if he finds [l]Pr 24:28 [m]Ex 22:7
lost property and lies about it,[n] or if he swears falsely, or if he commits any such sin that people may 6:3 [n]Dt 22:1-3
do— 4 when he thus sins and becomes guilty, he must return[o] what he has stolen or taken by extortion, 6:4 [o]Lk 19:8
or what was entrusted to him, or the lost property he found, 5 or whatever it was he swore falsely about.
He must make restitution[p] in full, add a fifth of the value to it and give it all to the owner on the day he 6:5 [p]Nu 5:7
presents his guilt offering.[q] 6 And as a penalty he must bring to the priest, that is, to the LORD, his guilt [q]Lev 5:15
offering,[r] a ram from the flock, one without defect and of the proper value. 7 In this way the priest will 6:6 [r]Lev 5:15
make atonement[s] for him before the LORD, and he will be forgiven for any of these things he did that 6:7 [s]Lev 4:26
made him guilty."

The Burnt Offering

8 The LORD said to Moses: 9 "Give Aaron and his sons this command: 'These are the regulations for the
burnt offering: The burnt offering is to remain on the altar hearth throughout the night, till morning,
and the fire must be kept burning on the altar. 10 The priest shall then put on his linen clothes, with lin-
en undergarments next to his body,[t] and shall remove the ashes of the burnt offering that the fire has con- 6:10 [t]Ex 28:39-42,43; 39:28
sumed on the altar and place them beside the altar. 11 Then he is to take off these clothes and put on oth-
ers, and carry the ashes outside the camp to a place that is ceremonially clean.[u] 12 The fire on the altar
must be kept burning; it must not go out. Every morning the priest is to add firewood and arrange the 6:11 [u]Lev 4:12
burnt offering on the fire and burn the fat of the fellowship offerings[b] on it. 13 The fire must be kept burn-
ing on the altar continuously; it must not go out.

The Grain Offering

14 " 'These are the regulations for the grain offering:[v] Aaron's sons are to bring it before the LORD, in 6:14 [v]Lev 2:1; 15:4
front of the altar. 15 The priest is to take a handful of fine flour and oil, together with all the incense on
the grain offering,[w] and burn the memorial portion[x] on the altar as an aroma pleasing to the LORD. 16 Aar- 6:15 [w]Lev 2:9 [x]Lev 2:2
on and his sons[y] shall eat the rest[z] of it, but it is to be eaten without yeast[a] in a holy place;[b] they are to 6:16 [y]Lev 2:3 [z]Eze 44:29
eat it in the courtyard of the Tent of Meeting. 17 It must not be baked with yeast; I have given it as their [a]Lev 2:11
share of the offerings made to me by fire. Like the sin offering and the guilt offering, it is most holy.[c] [b]Lev 10:13 6:17 [c]ver 29; Ex 40:10;
18 Any male descendant of Aaron may eat it.[d] It is his regular share of the offerings made to the LORD by Nu 18:9,10
fire for the generations to come. Whatever touches them will become holy.[c][e]' " 6:18 [d]ver 29; Nu 18:9-10 [e]ver 27

19 The LORD also said to Moses, 20 "This is the offering Aaron and his sons are to bring to the LORD on
the day he[d] is anointed: a tenth of an ephah[e][f] of fine flour as a regular grain offering,[g] half of it in the 6:20 [f]Ex 16:36 [g]Ex 29:2
morning and half in the evening. 21 Prepare it with oil on a griddle;[h] bring it well-mixed and present the 6:21 [h]Lev 2:5
grain offering broken[f] in pieces as an aroma pleasing to the LORD. 22 The son who is to succeed him as
anointed priest shall prepare it. It is the LORD's regular share and is to be burned completely. 23 Every grain
offering of a priest shall be burned completely; it must not be eaten."

The Sin Offering

24 The LORD said to Moses, 25 "Say to Aaron and his sons: 'These are the regulations for the sin offer-
ing: The sin offering is to be slaughtered before the LORD[i] in the place[j] the burnt offering is slaugh- 6:25 [i]Lev 1:3 [j]Lev 1:5,11
tered; it is most holy. 26 The priest who offers it shall eat it; it is to be eaten in a holy place,[k] in the court- 6:26 [k]ver 16
yard[l] of the Tent of Meeting. 27 Whatever touches any of the flesh will become holy,[m] and if any of the [l]Lev 10:17-18 6:27 [m]Ex 29:37
blood is spattered on a garment, you must wash it in a holy place. 28 The clay pot[n] the meat is cooked 6:28 [n]Lev 11:33; 15:12
in must be broken; but if it is cooked in a bronze pot, the pot is to be scoured and rinsed with water.
29 Any male in a priest's family may eat it;[o] it is most holy.[p] 30 But any sin offering whose blood is 6:29 [o]ver 18 [p]ver 17
brought into the Tent of Meeting to make atonement in the Holy Place[q] must not be eaten; it must be 6:30 [q]Lev 4:18
burned.[r] [r]Lev 4:12

[a] *19* Or *has made full expiation for his* [b] *12* Traditionally *peace offerings* [c] *18* Or *Whoever touches them must be holy*; similarly in verse 27 [d] *20* Or *each* [e] *20* That is, probably about 2 quarts (about 2 liters) [f] *21* The meaning of the Hebrew for this word is uncertain.

The Guilt Offering

7 " 'These are the regulations for the guilt offering,[s] which is most holy: 2The guilt offering is to be slaughtered in the place where the burnt offering is slaughtered, and its blood is to be sprinkled against the altar on all sides. 3All its fat[t] shall be offered: the fat tail and the fat that covers the inner parts, 4both kidneys with the fat on them near the loins, and the covering of the liver, which is to be removed with the kidneys. 5The priest shall burn them on the altar as an offering made to the LORD by fire. It is a guilt offering. 6Any male in a priest's family may eat it,[u] but it must be eaten in a holy place; it is most holy.[v]

7" 'The same law applies to both the sin offering and the guilt offering: They belong to the priest[w] who makes atonement with them. 8The priest who offers a burnt offering for anyone may keep its hide for himself. 9Every grain offering baked in an oven or cooked in a pan or on a griddle[x] belongs to the priest who offers it, 10and every grain offering, whether mixed with oil or dry, belongs equally to all the sons of Aaron.

The Fellowship Offering

11" 'These are the regulations for the fellowship offering[a] a person may present to the LORD:

12" 'If he offers it as an expression of thankfulness, then along with this thank offering[y] he is to offer cakes of bread made without yeast and mixed with oil, wafers[z] made without yeast and spread with oil, and cakes of fine flour well-kneaded and mixed with oil. 13Along with his fellowship offering of thanksgiving he is to present an offering with cakes of bread made with yeast.[a] 14He is to bring one of each kind as an offering, a contribution to the LORD; it belongs to the priest who sprinkles the blood of the fellowship offerings. 15The meat of his fellowship offering of thanksgiving must be eaten on the day it is offered; he must leave none of it till morning.[b]

16" 'If, however, his offering is the result of a vow or is a freewill offering, the sacrifice shall be eaten on the day he offers it, but anything left over may be eaten on the next day.[c] 17Any meat of the sacrifice left over till the third day must be burned up. 18If any meat of the fellowship offering is eaten on the third day, it will not be accepted.[d] It will not be credited[e] to the one who offered it, for it is impure; the person who eats any of it will be held responsible.

19" 'Meat that touches anything ceremonially unclean must not be eaten; it must be burned up. As for other meat, anyone ceremonially clean may eat it. 20But if anyone who is unclean eats any meat of the fellowship offering belonging to the LORD, that person must be cut off from his people.[f] 21If anyone touches something unclean[g]—whether human uncleanness or an unclean animal or any unclean, detestable thing—and then eats any of the meat of the fellowship offering belonging to the LORD, that person must be cut off from his people.' "

Eating Fat and Blood Forbidden

22The LORD said to Moses, 23"Say to the Israelites: 'Do not eat any of the fat of cattle, sheep or goats.[h] 24The fat of an animal found dead or torn by wild animals[i] may be used for any other purpose, but you must not eat it. 25Anyone who eats the fat of an animal from which an offering by fire may be[b] made to the LORD must be cut off from his people. 26And wherever you live, you must not eat the blood[j] of any bird or animal. 27If anyone eats blood,[k] that person must be cut off from his people.' "

The Priests' Share

28The LORD said to Moses, 29"Say to the Israelites: 'Anyone who brings a fellowship offering to the LORD is to bring part of it as his sacrifice to the LORD. 30With his own hands he is to bring the offering made to the LORD by fire; he is to bring the fat, together with the breast, and wave the breast before the LORD as a wave offering.[l] 31The priest shall burn the fat on the altar, but the breast belongs to Aaron and his sons.[m] 32You are to give the right thigh of your fellowship offerings to the priest as a contribution.[n] 33The son of Aaron who offers the blood and the fat of the fellowship offering shall have the right thigh as his share. 34From the fellowship offerings of the Israelites, I have taken the breast that is waved and the thigh[o] that is presented and have given them to Aaron the priest and his sons[p] as their regular share from the Israelites.' "

7:1 [s]Lev 5:14-6:7
7:3 [t]Ex 29:13; Lev 3:4,9
7:6 [u]Lev 6:18; Nu 18:9-10 [v]Lev 2:3
7:7 [w]Lev 6:17,26; 1Co 9:13
7:9 [x]Lev 2:5
7:12 [y]ver 13,15 [z]Lev 2:4; Nu 6:15
7:13 [a]Lev 23:17; Am 4:5
7:15 [b]Lev 22:30
7:16 [c]Lev 19:5-8
7:18 [d]Lev 19:7 [e]Nu 18:27
7:20 [f]Lev 22:3-7
7:21 [g]Lev 5:2; 11:24,28
7:23 [h]Lev 3:17; 17:13-14
7:24 [i]Ex 22:31
7:26 [j]Ge 9:4
7:27 [k]Lev 17:10-24; Ac 15:20,29
7:30 [l]Ex 29:24; Nu 6:20
7:31 [m]ver 34
7:32 [n]ver 34; Lev 9:21; Nu 6:20
7:34 [o]Lev 10:15 [p]Ex 29:27; Nu 18:18-19

[a] *11* Traditionally *peace offering*; also in verses 13-37 [b] *25* Or *fire is*

7:15 All meat had to be eaten promptly. One reason may have been that in Canaan meat spoiled quickly and thus became ceremonially impure (v. 18) and was then no longer perfect (1:3).

35 This is the portion of the offerings made to the LORD by fire that were allotted to Aaron and his sons
on the day they were presented to serve the LORD as priests. 36 On the day they were anointed,[q] the LORD
commanded that the Israelites give this to them as their regular share for the generations to come.

37 These, then, are the regulations for the burnt offering,[r] the grain offering,[s] the sin offering, the guilt
offering, the ordination offering[t] and the fellowship offering, 38 which the LORD gave Moses on Mount Si-
nai on the day he commanded the Israelites to bring their offerings to the LORD,[u] in the Desert of Sinai.

The Ordination of Aaron and His Sons

8 The LORD said to Moses, 2 "Bring Aaron and his sons, their garments, the anointing oil,[v] the bull for
the sin offering, the two rams and the basket containing bread made without yeast,[w] 3 and gather
the entire assembly[x] at the entrance to the Tent of Meeting." 4 Moses did as the LORD commanded him,
and the assembly gathered at the entrance to the Tent of Meeting.

5 Moses said to the assembly, "This is what the LORD has commanded to be done." 6 Then Moses brought
Aaron and his sons forward and washed them with water.[y] 7 He put the tunic on Aaron, tied the sash
around him, clothed him with the robe and put the ephod on him. He also tied the ephod to him by its
skillfully woven waistband; so it was fastened on him.[z] 8 He placed the breastpiece on him and put the
Urim and Thummim[a] in the breastpiece. 9 Then he placed the turban on Aaron's head and set the gold
plate, the sacred diadem,[b] on the front of it, as the LORD commanded Moses.

10 Then Moses took the anointing oil[c] and anointed[d] the tabernacle and everything in it, and so con-
secrated them. 11 He sprinkled some of the oil on the altar seven times, anointing the altar and all its
utensils and the basin with its stand, to consecrate them.[e] 12 He poured some of the anointing oil on Aar-
on's head and anointed[f] him to consecrate him.[g] 13 Then he brought Aaron's sons forward, put tunics on
them, tied sashes around them and put headbands on them, as the LORD commanded Moses.

14 He then presented the bull[h] for the sin offering,[i] and Aaron and his sons laid their hands on its head.
15 Moses slaughtered the bull and took some of the blood, and with his finger he put it on all the horns
of the altar[j] to purify the altar.[k] He poured out the rest of the blood at the base of the altar. So he conse-
crated it to make atonement for it.[l] 16 Moses also took all the fat around the inner parts, the covering of
the liver, and both kidneys and their fat, and burned it on the altar. 17 But the bull with its hide and its flesh
and its offal[m] he burned up outside the camp,[n] as the LORD commanded Moses.

18 He then presented the ram[o] for the burnt offering, and Aaron and his sons laid their hands on its
head. 19 Then Moses slaughtered the ram and sprinkled the blood against the altar on all sides. 20 He cut
the ram into pieces and burned the head, the pieces and the fat. 21 He washed the inner parts and the legs
with water and burned the whole ram on the altar as a burnt offering, a pleasing aroma, an offering made
to the LORD by fire, as the LORD commanded Moses.

22 He then presented the other ram, the ram for the ordination,[p] and Aaron and his sons laid their
hands on its head. 23 Moses slaughtered the ram and took some of its blood and put it on the lobe of Aar-
on's right ear, on the thumb of his right hand and on the big toe of his right foot. 24 Moses also brought
Aaron's sons forward and put some of the blood on the lobes of their right ears, on the thumbs of their
right hands and on the big toes of their right feet. Then he sprinkled blood against the altar on all sides.[q]
25 He took the fat, the fat tail, all the fat around the inner parts, the covering of the liver, both kidneys and
their fat and the right thigh. 26 Then from the basket of bread made without yeast, which was before the
LORD, he took a cake of bread, and one made with oil, and a wafer; he put these on the fat portions and
on the right thigh. 27 He put all these in the hands of Aaron and his sons and waved them before the LORD
as a wave offering. 28 Then Moses took them from their hands and burned them on the altar on top of the
burnt offering as an ordination offering, a pleasing aroma, an offering made to the LORD by fire. 29 He also
took the breast—Moses' share of the ordination ram[r]—and waved it before the LORD as a wave offer-
ing, as the LORD commanded Moses.

30 Then Moses took some of the anointing oil and some of the blood from the altar and sprinkled
them on Aaron and his garments[s] and on his sons and their garments. So he consecrated[t] Aaron and his
garments and his sons and their garments.

31 Moses then said to Aaron and his sons, "Cook the meat at the entrance to the Tent of Meeting and
eat it there with the bread from the basket of ordination offerings, as I commanded, saying,[a] 'Aaron and

7:36 [q]Ex 40:13,15; Lev 8:12,30
7:37 [r]Lev 6:9 [s]Lev 6:14 [t]ver 1, 11
7:38 [u]Lev 1:2
8:2 [v]Ex 30:23-25, 30 [w]Ex 29:2-3
8:3 [x]Nu 8:9
8:6 [y]Ex 29:4; 30:19; Ps 26:6; Ac 22:16; 1Co 6:11; Eph 5:26
8:7 [z]Ex 28:4
8:8 [a]Ex 28:30
8:9 [b]Ex 28:36
8:10 [c]ver 2 [d]Ex 30:26
8:11 [e]Ex 30:29
8:12 [f]Lev 21:10, 12 [g]Ex 30:30
8:14 [h]Lev 4:3 [i]Ps 66:15; Eze 43:19
8:15 [j]Lev 4:7 [k]Heb 9:22 [l]Eze 43:20
8:17 [m]Lev 4:11 [n]Lev 4:12
8:18 [o]ver 2
8:22 [p]ver 2
8:24 [q]Heb 9:18-22
8:29 [r]Lev 7:31-34
8:30 [s]Ex 28:2 [t]Nu 3:3

[a] 31 Or *I was commanded:*

his sons are to eat it.' 32Then burn up the rest of the meat and the bread. 33Do not leave the entrance to
the Tent of Meeting for seven days, until the days of your ordination are completed, for your ordination
8:34 [u]Heb 7:16 will last seven days. 34What has been done today was commanded by the LORD[u] to make atonement for
you. 35You must stay at the entrance to the Tent of Meeting day and night for seven days and do what the
8:35 [v]Nu 3:7; 9:19; Dt 11:1; LORD requires,[v] so you will not die; for that is what I have been commanded." 36So Aaron and his sons did
1Ki 2:3; Eze 48:11 everything the LORD commanded through Moses.

The Priests Begin Their Ministry

9:1 [w]Eze 43:27 **9** On the eighth day[w] Moses summoned Aaron and his sons and the elders of Israel. 2He said to Aar-
on, "Take a bull calf for your sin offering and a ram for your burnt offering, both without defect, and
present them before the LORD. 3Then say to the Israelites: 'Take a male goat for a sin offering, a calf and
a lamb—both a year old and without defect—for a burnt offering, 4and an ox[a] and a ram for a fellow-
ship offering[b] to sacrifice before the LORD, together with a grain offering mixed with oil. For today the
9:4 [x]Ex 29:43 LORD will appear to you.[x]' "

5They took the things Moses commanded to the front of the Tent of Meeting, and the entire assem-
bly came near and stood before the LORD. 6Then Moses said, "This is what the LORD has commanded you
9:6 [y]ver 23; Ex 24:16 to do, so that the glory of the LORD[y] may appear to you."

7Moses said to Aaron, "Come to the altar and sacrifice your sin offering and your burnt offering and
make atonement for yourself and the people; sacrifice the offering that is for the people and make atone-
9:7 [z]Heb 5:1,3; 7:27 ment for them, as the LORD has commanded.[z]"

9:8 [a]Lev 4:1-12 8So Aaron came to the altar and slaughtered the calf as a sin offering[a] for himself. 9His sons brought
9:9 [b]ver 12,18 [c]Lev 4:7 the blood to him,[b] and he dipped his finger into the blood and put it on the horns of the altar; the rest
of the blood he poured out at the base of the altar.[c] 10On the altar he burned the fat, the kidneys and the
9:11 [d]Lev 4:11 [e]Lev 4:12; 8:17 covering of the liver from the sin offering, as the LORD commanded Moses; 11the flesh and the hide[d] he
burned up outside the camp.[e]

12Then he slaughtered the burnt offering. His sons handed him the blood, and he sprinkled it against
the altar on all sides. 13They handed him the burnt offering piece by piece, including the head, and he
9:13 [f]Lev 1:8 burned them on the altar.[f] 14He washed the inner parts and the legs and burned them on top of the burnt
offering on the altar.

9:15 [g]Lev 4:27-31 15Aaron then brought the offering that was for the people.[g] He took the goat for the people's sin offer-
ing and slaughtered it and offered it for a sin offering as he did with the first one.

9:16 [h]Lev 1:1-13 16He brought the burnt offering and offered it in the prescribed way.[h] 17He also brought the grain of-
9:17 [i]Lev 2:1-2; 3:5 fering, took a handful of it and burned it on the altar in addition to the morning's burnt offering.[i]

9:18 [j]Lev 3:1-11 18He slaughtered the ox and the ram as the fellowship offering for the people.[j] His sons handed him
the blood, and he sprinkled it against the altar on all sides. 19But the fat portions of the ox and the ram—
the fat tail, the layer of fat, the kidneys and the covering of the liver— 20these they laid on the breasts,
and then Aaron burned the fat on the altar. 21Aaron waved the breasts and the right thigh before the LORD
9:21 [k]Ex 29:24, 26; Lev 7:30-34 as a wave offering,[k] as Moses commanded.

9:22 [l]Nu 6:23; Dt 21:5; Lk 24:50 22Then Aaron lifted his hands toward the people and blessed them.[l] And having sacrificed the sin of-
fering, the burnt offering and the fellowship offering, he stepped down.

23Moses and Aaron then went into the Tent of Meeting. When they came out, they blessed the people;
9:23 [m]ver 6 and the glory of the LORD[m] appeared to all the people. 24Fire[n] came out from the presence of the LORD and
9:24 [n]Jdg 6:21; 2Ch 7:1 consumed the burnt offering and the fat portions on the altar. And when all the people saw it, they shout-
[o]1Ki 18:39 ed for joy and fell facedown.[o]

The Death of Nadab and Abihu

10:1 [p]Ex 24:1; Nu 3:2-4; 26:61 **10** Aaron's sons Nadab and Abihu[p] took their censers, put fire in them[q] and added incense; and they
[q]Lev 16:12 [r]Ex 30:9 offered unauthorized fire before the LORD, contrary to his command.[r] 2So fire came out from the

[a] 4 The Hebrew word can include both male and female; also in verses 18 and 19. [b] 4 Traditionally *peace offering*; also in verses 18 and 22

8:33 *Consecration* ("ordination" in the NIV) may be defined as an act by which a person or thing is dedicated to the service and worship of God. In the KJV translation the word "consecrate" translates several Hebrew and Greek words of differing meanings. One of these, the Hebrew *millç' yadh* (lit., "to fill the hands"), is a peculiar idiom normally used for the installation of a priest into his office or of the installation offerings placed into his hands (Ex 29:9,29; Lev 8:33).

9:1–22 For information on sacrifices, see "Sacrifices and Offerings in the Bible and the Ancient Near East" on page 158 and "Ancient Altars" on page 125.

10:1–7 See the note on incense at Exodus 30:9.

presence of the LORD and consumed them,[s] and they died before the LORD. [3]Moses then said to Aaron,
"This is what the LORD spoke of when he said:

" 'Among those who approach me[t]
I will show myself holy;[u]
in the sight of all the people
I will be honored.[v]' "

Aaron remained silent.
[4]Moses summoned Mishael and Elzaphan,[w] sons of Aaron's uncle Uzziel,[x] and said to them, "Come
here; carry your cousins outside the camp,[y] away from the front of the sanctuary." [5]So they came and
carried them, still in their tunics,[z] outside the camp, as Moses ordered.
[6]Then Moses said to Aaron and his sons Eleazar and Ithamar, "Do not let your hair become un-
kempt,[a][a] and do not tear your clothes, or you will die and the LORD will be angry with the whole com-
munity.[b] But your relatives, all the house of Israel, may mourn for those the LORD has destroyed by fire.
[7]Do not leave the entrance to the Tent of Meeting or you will die, because the LORD's anointing oil[c] is on
you." So they did as Moses said.
[8]Then the LORD said to Aaron, [9]"You and your sons are not to drink wine[d] or other fermented drink[e]
whenever you go into the Tent of Meeting, or you will die. This is a lasting ordinance for the generations

[a] 6 Or *Do not uncover your heads*

10:2 [s]Nu 3:4; 16:35; 26:61
10:3 [t]Ex 19:22 [u]Ex 30:29; Lev 21:6; Eze 28:22 [v]Isa 49:3
10:4 [w]Ex 6:22 [x]Ex 6:18 [y]Ac 5:6, 9,10
10:5 [z]Lev 8:13
10:6 [a]Lev 21:10 [b]Nu 1:53; 16:22; Jos 7:1; 22:18; 2Sa 24:1
10:7 [c]Ex 28:41; Lev 21:12
10:9 [d]Hos 4:11 [e]Pr 20:1; Isa 28:7; Eze 44:21; Lk 1:15; Eph 5:18; 1Ti 3:3; Tit 1:7

10:6 Tearing one's clothing was a sign of deep distress and grief (see "Sackcloth and Ashes: Rituals of Lamentation" on p. 820).
10:9 Although the word *asceticism* is not used in the Bible, the concept is found frequently. In the sense of self-discipline, asceticism normally occurs in the Old Testament in connection with particular circumstances such as repentance (1Sa 7:6) or religious regula-

Ritual Purity in Israel and the Ancient Near East

LEVITICUS 10 Before entering the Lord's presence priests were required to attain a state of ritual purity—they needed to be "clean." In fact, if the "holy" were to come into contact with the "unclean," the results would be devastating (Lev 10:8–11; 15:31). Uncleanness in a holy space (especially in the tabernacle, but by extension anywhere in the Holy Land) defiled that space and, if the situation were to have been left unresolved, would have constituted justification for God to withdraw his Presence (cf. Eze 8–11).

Israel's purity laws (Lev 11–15), the details of which are unparalleled in any other ancient Near Eastern literature, reminded the Israelites of the gaping divide between themselves and their holy God (cf. 10:3) and of God's burning desire for them to become like him in purity (11:44–45; 19:1–2; cf. Jesus' words in Mt 5:48). These laws also taught the Israelites that their uncleanness resulted not from demonic powers, as was widely believed in the broader world around them, but from disobedience to God's law. Even more fundamentally, uncleanness or ritual impurity (the condition that barred an individual from God's Presence in the sanctuary) was a state that occurred in all people from time to time, simply by virtue of their human nature (cf. Lev 12; 15).

The major threat, then, was not uncleanness per se but protracted, disregarded uncleanness. God prescribed regular purification rituals through which uncleanness was removed, the threat of judgment lifted and entry into the Lord's Presence once again permitted. Essential to this process was the Lord's acceptance of a blood sacrifice, especially the one offered annually by the high priest on the Day of Atonement (ch. 16; cf. 17:11).[1] Non-sacrificial regulations, such as washing with water, are also detailed in chapters 11–15. Even so, true holiness was not—and still is not—attainable without justice, love of neighbor and a heart wholly committed to the Lord and to his covenant (19:2; cf. Am 5:21–23).

[1]See "The Day of Atonement" on page 176.

to come. 10 You must distinguish between the holy and the common, between the unclean and the clean,[f]
11 and you must teach[g] the Israelites all the decrees the LORD has given them through Moses.[h]"
12 Moses said to Aaron and his remaining sons, Eleazar and Ithamar, "Take the grain offering left over
from the offerings made to the LORD by fire and eat it prepared without yeast beside the altar,[i] for it is most
holy. 13 Eat it in a holy place, because it is your share and your sons' share of the offerings made to the
LORD by fire; for so I have been commanded. 14 But you and your sons and your daughters may eat the
breast that was waved and the thigh that was presented. Eat them in a ceremonially clean place;[j] they
have been given to you and your children as your share of the Israelites' fellowship offerings.[a] 15 The thigh[k]
that was presented and the breast that was waved must be brought with the fat portions of the offerings
made by fire, to be waved before the LORD as a wave offering. This will be the regular share for you and
your children, as the LORD has commanded."
16 When Moses inquired about the goat of the sin offering[l] and found that it had been burned up, he
was angry with Eleazar and Ithamar, Aaron's remaining sons, and asked, 17 "Why didn't you eat the sin
offering[m] in the sanctuary area? It is most holy; it was given to you to take away the guilt of the commu-
nity by making atonement for them before the LORD. 18 Since its blood was not taken into the Holy Place,[n]
you should have eaten the goat in the sanctuary area, as I commanded."
19 Aaron replied to Moses, "Today they sacrificed their sin offering and their burnt offering[o] before
the LORD, but such things as this have happened to me. Would the LORD have been pleased if I had eaten
the sin offering today?" 20 When Moses heard this, he was satisfied.

Clean and Unclean Food

11 The LORD said to Moses and Aaron, 2 "Say to the Israelites: 'Of all the animals that live on land,
these are the ones you may eat:[p] 3 You may eat any animal that has a split hoof completely divid-
ed and that chews the cud.
4 " 'There are some that only chew the cud or only have a split hoof, but you must not eat them. The
camel, though it chews the cud, does not have a split hoof; it is ceremonially unclean for you. 5 The coney,[b]
though it chews the cud, does not have a split hoof; it is unclean for you. 6 The rabbit, though it chews the
cud, does not have a split hoof; it is unclean for you. 7 And the pig,[q] though it has a split hoof complete-
ly divided, does not chew the cud; it is unclean for you. 8 You must not eat their meat or touch their car-
casses; they are unclean for you.[r]
9 " 'Of all the creatures living in the water of the seas and the streams, you may eat any that have fins
and scales. 10 But all creatures in the seas or streams that do not have fins and scales—whether among
all the swarming things or among all the other living creatures in the water—you are to detest.[s] 11 And
since you are to detest them, you must not eat their meat and you must detest their carcasses. 12 Any-
thing living in the water that does not have fins and scales is to be detestable to you.
13 " 'These are the birds you are to detest and not eat because they are detestable: the eagle, the vul-
ture, the black vulture, 14 the red kite, any kind of black kite, 15 any kind of raven, 16 the horned owl, the
screech owl, the gull, any kind of hawk, 17 the little owl, the cormorant, the great owl, 18 the white owl, the
desert owl, the osprey, 19 the stork, any kind of heron, the hoopoe and the bat.[c]
20 " 'All flying insects that walk on all fours are to be detestable to you.[t] 21 There are, however, some
winged creatures that walk on all fours that you may eat: those that have jointed legs for hopping on the
ground. 22 Of these you may eat any kind of locust,[u] katydid, cricket or grasshopper. 23 But all other winged
creatures that have four legs you are to detest.
24 " 'You will make yourselves unclean by these; whoever touches their carcasses will be unclean till
evening. 25 Whoever picks up one of their carcasses must wash his clothes,[v] and he will be unclean till
evening.[w]

10:10 [f] Lev 11:47; 20:25; Eze 22:26 **10:11** [g] Mal 2:7 [h] Dt 24:8
10:12 [i] Lev 6:14-18; 21:22
10:14 [j] Ex 29:24, 26-27; Lev 7:31, 34; Nu 18:11 **10:15** [k] Lev 7:34
10:16 [l] Lev 9:3
10:17 [m] Lev 6:24-30
10:18 [n] Lev 6:26, 30
10:19 [o] Lev 9:12
11:2 [p] Ac 10:12-14
11:7 [q] Isa 65:4; 66:3,17
11:8 [r] Isa 52:11; Heb 9:10
11:10 [s] Lev 7:18
11:20 [t] Ac 10:14
11:22 [u] Mt 3:4; Mk 1:6
11:25 [v] Lev 14:8, 47; 15:5 [w] ver 40; Nu 31:24

[a] *14* Traditionally *peace offerings* [b] *5* That is, the hyrax or rock badger [c] *19* The precise identification of some of the birds, insects and animals in this chapter is uncertain.

---

tions (Lev 10:9; Nu 6:1–8). In the New Testament, however, it affects the whole lifestyle, calling for renunciation of everything that hinders discipleship (Mt 19:21–22; Mk 10:29–30). Self-control is listed as a fruit of the Spirit (Gal 5:23) and is demanded of a contestant (1Co 9:25), of church elders (Tit 1:8) and of Christians in general (2Pe 1:6), who are not to let the *good* things of this world rob them of the *best* things.

11:7 Pigs may have been considered "unclean" for a variety of reasons. See "Clean and Unclean Foods in the Bible and Ancient Near East" on page 168.

11:20 Although insects have six legs, people in ancient times may not have counted as ordinary legs the two large hind legs used for jumping.

Clean and Unclean Foods in the Bible and the Ancient Near East

LEVITICUS 11 The rationale behind the designation of certain creatures as "clean" and others as "unclean" for dietary purposes (Lev 11; cf. Dt 14:3–21) has perplexed Bible readers throughout the ages. Possible explanations include:

- *hygienic reasons* (e.g., the fact that pork, especially if not thoroughly cooked, could prove unhealthful and carry disease);
- *allegorical explanations* (the notion that the character of certain animals determined whether or not they were clean—e.g., pigs were thought to exemplify lazy, gluttonous, uncouth behavior and thus were deemed unclean);
- *arbitrary testing* (the idea that God randomly designated some animals as unclean in order to test his people's obedience);
- *pagan association* (the suggestion that animals labeled "unclean" were those used in non-Israelite rituals—e.g., certain pagan rites entailed the sacrifice of pigs);
- *conformity to an ideal* (the supposition that only those animals conforming to what was considered "normal" for their species were "clean"—e.g., sea creatures without fins and/or scales were abnormal and therefore unclean); and
- *heavenly analogy* (the notion that "clean" animals constituted God's own "diet").

Some of these explanations are plainly far-fetched; indeed, the suggestion that certain foods comprise God's diet lacks any merit. It is important to note, however, that *all* of them are hypothetical, unsupported by any specific Biblical teaching. Also, none fully accounts for the distinctions detailed in Leviticus 11. Regardless of which hypothetical rationale, if any, historians may offer for the diet of the ancient Israelites, clearly the distinction between clean and unclean foods ensured them a healthful diet and enabled them to maintain their identity as God's covenantal people (Da 1). Adherence to these food laws consecrated the Israelites, setting them apart as holy, just as **Yahweh,** their God, is holy (Lev 11:44–47).[1]

Although outside ancient Israel there is no known system as comprehensive in differentiating between permitted and prohibited foods, dietary restrictions of one kind or another are attested in the ancient Near East from Egypt to **Babylonia**. Inscriptions in Egyptian temples include lists of foods (mostly animal products) certain groups of people were not to eat. The cow, for example, was off limits in Dendera, where the goddess Hathor was said to be manifested in bovine form. In **Mesopotamia**, eating certain animals was prohibited on special occasions, such as rituals in which pigs were sacrificed (otherwise, pork was widely eaten). Numerous ancient cults also had specific taboos regarding food consumption (cf. Col 2:20–21).

[1]See also "Food and Agriculture" on page 390.

CLEAN AND UNCLEAN ANIMALS

Classes	*Clean*	*Unclean*
Mammals	Two qualifications: 1. Cloven hoofs 2. Chewing of the cud (Lev 11:3–7; Dt 14:6–8)	Carnivores and those not meeting both "clean" qualifications
Birds	Those not specifically listed as forbidden	Birds of prey or scavengers (Lev 11:13–19; Dt 14:11–20)
Reptiles	None	All (Lev 11:29–30)
Water Animals	Two qualifications: 1. Fins 2. Scales (Lev 11:9–12; Dt 14:9–10)	Those not meeting both "clean" qualifications
Insects	Those in the grasshopper family (Lev 11:20–23)	Winged quadrupeds

Chronological and Background Charts of the Old Testament, p. 23

26 " 'Every animal that has a split hoof not completely divided or that does not chew the cud is unclean
for you; whoever touches ⌊the carcass of⌋ any of them will be unclean. 27 Of all the animals that walk on
all fours, those that walk on their paws are unclean for you; whoever touches their carcasses will be un-
clean till evening. 28 Anyone who picks up their carcasses must wash his clothes, and he will be unclean
till evening. They are unclean for you.

11:29 [x]Isa 66:17 29 " 'Of the animals that move about on the ground, these are unclean for you: the weasel, the rat,[x] any
kind of great lizard, 30 the gecko, the monitor lizard, the wall lizard, the skink and the chameleon. 31 Of
all those that move along the ground, these are unclean for you. Whoever touches them when they are
dead will be unclean till evening. 32 When one of them dies and falls on something, that article, what-
11:32 [y]Lev 15:12 ever its use, will be unclean, whether it is made of wood, cloth, hide or sackcloth.[y] Put it in water; it will
be unclean till evening, and then it will be clean. 33 If one of them falls into a clay pot, everything in it
11:33 [z]Lev 6:28; 15:12 will be unclean, and you must break the pot.[z] 34 Any food that could be eaten but has water on it from
such a pot is unclean, and any liquid that could be drunk from it is unclean. 35 Anything that one of their
carcasses falls on becomes unclean; an oven or cooking pot must be broken up. They are unclean, and
you are to regard them as unclean. 36 A spring, however, or a cistern for collecting water remains clean,
but anyone who touches one of these carcasses is unclean. 37 If a carcass falls on any seeds that are to
be planted, they remain clean. 38 But if water has been put on the seed and a carcass falls on it, it is un-
clean for you.

39 " 'If an animal that you are allowed to eat dies, anyone who touches the carcass will be unclean till
evening. 40 Anyone who eats some of the carcass must wash his clothes, and he will be unclean till eve-
11:40 [a]Lev 17:15; 22:8; Eze 44:31 ning.[a] Anyone who picks up the carcass must wash his clothes, and he will be unclean till evening.

41 " 'Every creature that moves about on the ground is detestable; it is not to be eaten. 42 You are not to
eat any creature that moves about on the ground, whether it moves on its belly or walks on all fours or
11:43 [b]Lev 20:25 on many feet; it is detestable. 43 Do not defile yourselves by any of these creatures.[b] Do not make your-
11:44 [c]Ex 6:2,7; Isa 43:3; 51:15 selves unclean by means of them or be made unclean by them. 44 I am the LORD your God;[c] consecrate
[d]Lev 20:7 [e]Ex 19:6 yourselves[d] and be holy,[e] because I am holy.[f] Do not make yourselves unclean by any creature that moves
[f]Lev 19:2; Ps 99:3; Eph 1:4; 1Th 4:7; 1Pe 1:15,16* about on the ground. 45 I am the LORD who brought you up out of Egypt[g] to be your God;[h] therefore be
holy, because I am holy.[i]

11:45 [g]Lev 25:38,55; Ex 6:7; 20:2 46 " 'These are the regulations concerning animals, birds, every living thing that moves in the water
[h]Ge 17:7 [i]Ex 19:6; 1Pe 1:16* and every creature that moves about on the ground. 47 You must distinguish between the unclean and
11:47 [j]Lev 10:10 the clean, between living creatures that may be eaten and those that may not be eaten.[j] ' "

Purification After Childbirth

12 The LORD said to Moses, 2 "Say to the Israelites: 'A woman who becomes pregnant and gives
12:2 [k]Lev 15:19; 18:19 birth to a son will be ceremonially unclean for seven days, just as she is unclean during her
12:3 [l]Ge 17:12; Lk 1:59; 2:21 monthly period.[k] 3 On the eighth day the boy is to be circumcised.[l] 4 Then the woman must wait thir-
ty-three days to be purified from her bleeding. She must not touch anything sacred or go to the sanc-
tuary until the days of her purification are over. 5 If she gives birth to a daughter, for two weeks the
woman will be unclean, as during her period. Then she must wait sixty-six days to be purified from
12:6 [m]Lk 2:22 her bleeding.

[n]Ex 29:38; Lev 23:12; Nu 6:12,14; 7:15 6 " 'When the days of her purification for a son or daughter are over,[m] she is to bring to the priest at
[o]Lev 5:7 the entrance to the Tent of Meeting a year-old lamb[n] for a burnt offering and a young pigeon or a dove
for a sin offering.[o] 7 He shall offer them before the LORD to make atonement for her, and then she will be
ceremonially clean from her flow of blood.

" 'These are the regulations for the woman who gives birth to a boy or a girl. 8 If she cannot afford a
12:8 [p]Ge 15:9; Lev 14:22 lamb, she is to bring two doves or two young pigeons,[p] one for a burnt offering and the other for a sin of-
[q]Lev 5:7; Lk 2:22-24* [r]Lev 4:26 fering.[q] In this way the priest will make atonement for her, and she will be clean.[r] ' "

11:36 The use of waterproof plaster for lining cisterns dug into the ground was an important factor in helping the Israelites to settle the dry areas of Canaan after the conquest (see "Wells, Cisterns and Aqueducts in the Ancient World" on p. 1259).
11:44 Holiness is regarded in the Bible as God's central ethical character. Basic ethical principles are revealed by the will of God and derived from and based upon his character. "Be holy, because I am holy" (v. 45) is his mandate.
12:2 The uncleanness came from the bleeding (vv. 4–5,7), not from the birth. It is unclear why the period of uncleanness after the birth of a baby boy (40 days) was half that for a girl (80 days).

Regulations About Infectious Skin Diseases

13 The LORD said to Moses and Aaron, 2“When anyone has a swelling[s] or a rash or a bright spot[t] on
his skin that may become an infectious skin disease,[a][u] he must be brought to Aaron the priest[v]
or to one of his sons[b] who is a priest. 3The priest is to examine the sore on his skin, and if the hair in the
sore has turned white and the sore appears to be more than skin deep,[c] it is an infectious skin disease.
When the priest examines him, he shall pronounce him ceremonially unclean.[w] 4If the spot[x] on his skin
is white but does not appear to be more than skin deep and the hair in it has not turned white, the priest
is to put the infected person in isolation for seven days.[y] 5On the seventh day[z] the priest is to examine
him,[a] and if he sees that the sore is unchanged and has not spread in the skin, he is to keep him in iso-
lation another seven days. 6On the seventh day the priest is to examine him again, and if the sore has
faded and has not spread in the skin, the priest shall pronounce him clean;[b] it is only a rash. The man
must wash his clothes,[c] and he will be clean.[d] 7But if the rash does spread in his skin after he has shown
himself to the priest to be pronounced clean, he must appear before the priest again.[e] 8The priest is to
examine him, and if the rash has spread in the skin, he shall pronounce him unclean; it is an infectious
disease.
9“When anyone has an infectious skin disease, he must be brought to the priest. 10The priest is to ex-
amine him, and if there is a white swelling in the skin that has turned the hair white and if there is raw
flesh in the swelling, 11it is a chronic skin disease[f] and the priest shall pronounce him unclean. He is not
to put him in isolation, because he is already unclean.
12“If the disease breaks out all over his skin and, so far as the priest can see, it covers all the skin of
the infected person from head to foot, 13the priest is to examine him, and if the disease has covered his
whole body, he shall pronounce that person clean. Since it has all turned white, he is clean. 14But when-
ever raw flesh appears on him, he will be unclean. 15When the priest sees the raw flesh, he shall pro-
nounce him unclean. The raw flesh is unclean; he has an infectious disease.[g] 16Should the raw flesh
change and turn white, he must go to the priest. 17The priest is to examine him, and if the sores have
turned white, the priest shall pronounce the infected person clean;[h] then he will be clean.
18“When someone has a boil[i] on his skin and it heals, 19and in the place where the boil was, a white
swelling or reddish-white[j] spot[k] appears, he must present himself to the priest. 20The priest is to exam-
ine it, and if it appears to be more than skin deep and the hair in it has turned white, the priest shall pro-
nounce him unclean. It is an infectious skin disease[l] that has broken out where the boil was. 21But if,
when the priest examines it, there is no white hair in it and it is not more than skin deep and has faded,
then the priest is to put him in isolation for seven days. 22If it is spreading in the skin, the priest shall
pronounce him unclean; it is infectious. 23But if the spot is unchanged and has not spread, it is only a scar
from the boil, and the priest shall pronounce him clean.[m]
24“When someone has a burn on his skin and a reddish-white or white spot appears in the raw flesh
of the burn, 25the priest is to examine the spot, and if the hair in it has turned white, and it appears to be
more than skin deep, it is an infectious disease that has broken out in the burn. The priest shall pro-
nounce him unclean; it is an infectious skin disease.[n] 26But if the priest examines it and there is no white
hair in the spot and if it is not more than skin deep and has faded, then the priest is to put him in isola-
tion for seven days.[o] 27On the seventh day the priest is to examine him,[p] and if it is spreading in the skin,
the priest shall pronounce him unclean; it is an infectious skin disease. 28If, however, the spot is un-
changed and has not spread in the skin but has faded, it is a swelling from the burn, and the priest shall
pronounce him clean; it is only a scar from the burn.[q]
29“If a man or woman has a sore on the head[r] or on the chin, 30the priest is to examine the sore, and
if it appears to be more than skin deep and the hair in it is yellow and thin, the priest shall pronounce
that person unclean; it is an itch, an infectious disease of the head or chin. 31But if, when the priest ex-

13:2 [s]ver 10,19, 28,43 [t]ver 4,38, 39; Lev 14:56 [u]ver 3,9,15; Ex 4:6; Lev 14:3, 32; Nu 5:2; Dt 24:8 [v]Dt 24:8
13:3 [w]ver 8,11, 20,30; Lev 21:1; Nu 9:6
13:4 [x]ver 2 [y]ver 5,21,26,33, 46; Lev 14:38; Nu 12:14,15; Dt 24:9
13:5 [z]Lev 14:9 [a]ver 27,32,34,51
13:6 [b]ver 13,17, 23,28,34; Mt 8:3; Lk 5:12-14 [c]Lev 11:25 [d]Lev 11:25; 14:8, 9,20,48; 15:8; Nu 8:7
13:7 [e]Lk 5:14
13:11 [f]Ex 4:6; Lev 14:8; Nu 12:10; Mt 8:2
13:15 [g]ver 2
13:17 [h]ver 6
13:18 [i]Ex 9:9
13:19 [j]ver 24,42; Lev 14:37 [k]ver 2
13:20 [l]ver 2
13:23 [m]ver 6
13:25 [n]ver 11
13:26 [o]ver 4
13:27 [p]ver 5
13:28 [q]ver 2
13:29 [r]ver 43,44

[a] 2 Traditionally *leprosy*; the Hebrew word was used for various diseases affecting the skin—not necessarily leprosy; also elsewhere in this chapter. [b] 2 Or *descendants* [c] 3 Or *be lower than the rest of the skin*; also elsewhere in this chapter

---

13:1–46 The familiar but incorrect translation “leprosy” (in most versions, but not in the NIV) for the scaly skin disease referred to here arose from confusion regarding translation of a Greek word in the Septuagint (early Greek translation of the OT). *Lepra* is not leprosy (Hansen's disease).

13:2 Since it is unlikely that ancient people would have understood the concept of contagion, the rendering “infectious skin disease” is questionable; the Hebrew should probably be translated simply “skin disease.” Such diseases were visible defects that could function as symbols of defilement—as could mildew (cf. vv. 47–59). See “Skin Diseases in the Ancient World” on page 171.

amines this kind of sore, it does not seem to be more than skin deep and there is no black hair in it, then
13:31 [s]ver 4 the priest is to put the infected person in isolation for seven days.[s] 32On the seventh day the priest is to
13:32 [t]ver 5 examine the sore,[t] and if the itch has not spread and there is no yellow hair in it and it does not appear
to be more than skin deep, 33he must be shaved except for the diseased area, and the priest is to keep
13:34 [u]ver 5 him in isolation another seven days. 34On the seventh day the priest is to examine the itch,[u] and if it has
not spread in the skin and appears to be no more than skin deep, the priest shall pronounce him clean.
[v]Lev 11:25 He must wash his clothes, and he will be clean.[v] 35But if the itch does spread in the skin after he is pro-
nounced clean, 36the priest is to examine him, and if the itch has spread in the skin, the priest does not
13:36 [w]ver 30 need to look for yellow hair; the person is unclean.[w] 37If, however, in his judgment it is unchanged and
black hair has grown in it, the itch is healed. He is clean, and the priest shall pronounce him clean.

38"When a man or woman has white spots on the skin, 39the priest is to examine them, and if the
spots are dull white, it is a harmless rash that has broken out on the skin; that person is clean.

13:40 [x]Lev 21:5; 2Ki 2:23; Isa 3:24; 15:2; 22:12; Eze 27:31; 29:18; Am 8:10; Mic 1:16 40"When a man has lost his hair and is bald,[x] he is clean. 41If he has lost his hair from the front of his
scalp and has a bald forehead, he is clean. 42But if he has a reddish-white sore on his bald head or fore-
head, it is an infectious disease breaking out on his head or forehead. 43The priest is to examine him,
and if the swollen sore on his head or forehead is reddish-white like an infectious skin disease, 44the man
is diseased and is unclean. The priest shall pronounce him unclean because of the sore on his head.

13:45 [y]Lev 10:6 [z]Eze 24:17,22; Mic 3:7 [a]Lev 5:2; La 4:15; Lk 17:12 45"The person with such an infectious disease must wear torn clothes,[y] let his hair be unkempt,[a] cov-
er the lower part of his face[z] and cry out, 'Unclean! Unclean!'[a] 46As long as he has the infection he re-
13:46 [b]Nu 5:1-4; 12:14; 2Ki 7:3; 15:5; Lk 17:12 mains unclean. He must live alone; he must live outside the camp.[b]

[a] 45 *Or clothes, uncover his head*

Skin Diseases in the Ancient World

LEVITICUS 13 The Bible describes various categories of skin-related problems:

- ✢ *festering or running sores* (Lev 21:20; 22:22);
- ✢ *itches* (Dt 28:27), including those caused by fungal infestations (e.g., ringworm), eczema and parasitic diseases (e.g., scabies);
- ✢ *boils and/or inflamed swellings and rashes* (Ex 9:9–10; Lev 13:2; Job 2:7; Isa 38:21);
- ✢ *warts* (Lev 22:22); and
- ✢ *a disease traditionally rendered as "leprosy"* (Nu 12:10; 2Ch 26:19).

Although some researchers do identify this last condition with modern leprosy (Hansen's disease), this diagnosis is almost certainly incorrect for several reasons:

- ✢ The hair in the affected spots is sometimes described as turning white (Lev 13:13,25), an effect rarely seen in Hansen's disease.
- ✢ Hansen's disease causes increasing numbness as it spreads, but the Bible never mentions this characteristic.
- ✢ Biblical "leprosy" could clear up without treatment (14:3), while Hansen's disease cannot (barring a miraculous cure).

It is more likely then, that Biblical "leprosy" refers to a group of infectious conditions under the category of "scaly" skin diseases (cf. 14:54–57).

Affliction with a skin disease meant that an individual was ritually unclean,[1] but the illness was not necessarily an indication of direct punishment from God or the uncleanness a manifestation of a moral or character flaw. In certain instances, however, God did choose to inflict such diseases as consequences for specific sins (e.g., the pharaoh in Ex 9:8–12; Miriam in Nu 12:10; Uzziah in 2Ki 15:5).

[1]See "Ritual Purity in Israel and the Ancient Near East" on page 166.

Regulations About Mildew

47 "If any clothing is contaminated with mildew—any woolen or linen clothing, 48 any woven or knit-
ted material of linen or wool, any leather or anything made of leather— 49 and if the contamination in
the clothing, or leather, or woven or knitted material, or any leather article, is greenish or reddish, it is a
spreading mildew and must be shown to the priest.[c] 50 The priest is to examine the mildew[d] and isolate
the affected article for seven days. 51 On the seventh day he is to examine it,[e] and if the mildew has spread
in the clothing, or the woven or knitted material, or the leather, whatever its use, it is a destructive mil-
dew; the article is unclean.[f] 52 He must burn up the clothing, or the woven or knitted material of wool or
linen, or any leather article that has the contamination in it, because the mildew is destructive; the arti-
cle must be burned up.[g]

53 "But if, when the priest examines it, the mildew has not spread in the clothing, or the woven or knit-
ted material, or the leather article, 54 he shall order that the contaminated article be washed. Then he is
to isolate it for another seven days. 55 After the affected article has been washed, the priest is to examine
it, and if the mildew has not changed its appearance, even though it has not spread, it is unclean. Burn
it with fire, whether the mildew has affected one side or the other. 56 If, when the priest examines it, the
mildew has faded after the article has been washed, he is to tear the contaminated part out of the cloth-
ing, or the leather, or the woven or knitted material. 57 But if it reappears in the clothing, or in the woven
or knitted material, or in the leather article, it is spreading, and whatever has the mildew must be burned
with fire. 58 The clothing, or the woven or knitted material, or any leather article that has been washed and
is rid of the mildew, must be washed again, and it will be clean."

59 These are the regulations concerning contamination by mildew in woolen or linen clothing, woven
or knitted material, or any leather article, for pronouncing them clean or unclean.

Cleansing From Infectious Skin Diseases

14 The LORD said to Moses, 2 "These are the regulations for the diseased person at the time of his cer-
emonial cleansing, when he is brought to the priest:[h] 3 The priest is to go outside the camp and ex-
amine him.[i] If the person has been healed of his infectious skin disease,[a] 4 the priest shall order that two
live clean birds and some cedar wood, scarlet yarn and hyssop be brought for the one to be cleansed.[j] 5 Then
the priest shall order that one of the birds be killed over fresh water in a clay pot. 6 He is then to take the live
bird and dip it, together with the cedar wood, the scarlet yarn and the hyssop, into the blood of the bird
that was killed over the fresh water.[k] 7 Seven times he shall sprinkle[l] the one to be cleansed of the infectious
disease and pronounce him clean. Then he is to release the live bird in the open fields.

8 "The person to be cleansed must wash his clothes,[m] shave off all his hair and bathe with water;[n] then
he will be ceremonially clean.[o] After this he may come into the camp,[p] but he must stay outside his tent for
seven days. 9 On the seventh day he must shave off all his hair; he must shave his head, his beard, his eye-
brows and the rest of his hair. He must wash his clothes and bathe himself with water, and he will be clean.

10 "On the eighth day[q] he must bring two male lambs and one ewe lamb a year old, each without de-
fect, along with three-tenths of an ephah[b] of fine flour mixed with oil for a grain offering,[r] and one log[c]
of oil.[s] 11 The priest who pronounces him clean shall present both the one to be cleansed and his offer-
ings before the LORD at the entrance to the Tent of Meeting.

12 "Then the priest is to take one of the male lambs and offer it as a guilt offering,[t] along with the log
of oil; he shall wave them before the LORD as a wave offering.[u] 13 He is to slaughter the lamb in the holy
place[v] where the sin offering and the burnt offering are slaughtered. Like the sin offering, the guilt offer-
ing belongs to the priest;[w] it is most holy. 14 The priest is to take some of the blood of the guilt offering
and put it on the lobe of the right ear of the one to be cleansed, on the thumb of his right hand and on
the big toe of his right foot.[x] 15 The priest shall then take some of the log of oil, pour it in the palm of his
own left hand, 16 dip his right forefinger into the oil in his palm, and with his finger sprinkle some of it

13:49 [c]Mk 1:44 **13:50** [d]Eze 44:23 **13:51** [e]ver 5 [f]Lev 14:44 **13:52** [g]ver 55,57

14:2 [h]Mt 8:2-4; Mk 1:40-44; Lk 5:12-14; 17:14 **14:3** [i]Lev 13:46 **14:4** [j]ver 6,49, 51,52; Nu 19:6; Ps 51:7 **14:6** [k]ver 4 **14:7** [l]2Ki 5:10, 14; Isa 52:15; Eze 36:25 **14:8** [m]Lev 11:25; 13:6 [n]ver 9 [o]ver 20 [p]Nu 5:2,3; 12:14,15; 2Ch 26:21 **14:10** [q]Mt 8:4; Mk 1:44; Lk 5:14 [r]Lev 2:1 [s]ver 12, 15,21,24 **14:12** [t]Lev 5:18; 6:6-7 [u]Ex 29:24 **14:13** [v]Ex 29:11 [w]Lev 6:24-30; 7:7 **14:14** [x]Ex 29:20; Lev 8:23

[a] *3* Traditionally *leprosy*; the Hebrew word was used for various diseases affecting the skin—not necessarily leprosy; also elsewhere in this chapter. [b] *10* That is, probably about 6 quarts (about 6.5 liters) [c] *10* That is, probably about 2/3 pint (about 0.3 liter); also in verses 12, 15, 21 and 24

14:1–57 The division found in the Old Testament between clean and unclean was fundamental to the Hebrew/Israelite religion. The Lord was to be served and worshiped by a clean, pure and chaste people. They were to be physically clean (Ex 19:10ff.; 30:18–21), ritually and ceremonially clean (having offered the right sacrifices and been through the correct ceremonies (e.g., chs. 14–15) and morally clean in heart. David later prayed, "Cleanse me with hyssop, and I will be clean; wash me, and I will be whiter than snow" (Ps 51:7). See "Ritual Purity in Israel and the Ancient Near East" on page 166.

14:6 See the related note on 16:8.

before the LORD seven times. 17 The priest is to put some of the oil remaining in his palm on the lobe of the right ear of the one to be cleansed, on the thumb of his right hand and on the big toe of his right foot, on top of the blood of the guilt offering. 18 The rest of the oil in his palm the priest shall put on the head of the one to be cleansed and make atonement for him before the LORD.

19 "Then the priest is to sacrifice the sin offering and make atonement for the one to be cleansed from his uncleanness. After that, the priest shall slaughter the burnt offering 20 and offer it on the altar, together with the grain offering, and make atonement for him, and he will be clean.[y]

21 "If, however, he is poor[z] and cannot afford these,[a] he must take one male lamb as a guilt offering to be waved to make atonement for him, together with a tenth of an ephah[a] of fine flour mixed with oil for a grain offering, a log of oil, 22 and two doves or two young pigeons,[b] which he can afford, one for a sin offering and the other for a burnt offering.

23 "On the eighth day he must bring them for his cleansing to the priest at the entrance to the Tent of Meeting, before the LORD.[c] 24 The priest is to take the lamb for the guilt offering,[d] together with the log of oil,[e] and wave them before the LORD as a wave offering.[f] 25 He shall slaughter the lamb for the guilt offering and take some of its blood and put it on the lobe of the right ear of the one to be cleansed, on the thumb of his right hand and on the big toe of his right foot.[g] 26 The priest is to pour some of the oil into the palm of his own left hand,[h] 27 and with his right forefinger sprinkle some of the oil from his palm seven times before the LORD. 28 Some of the oil in his palm he is to put on the same places he put the blood of the guilt offering—on the lobe of the right ear of the one to be cleansed, on the thumb of his right hand and on the big toe of his right foot. 29 The rest of the oil in his palm the priest shall put on the head of the one to be cleansed, to make atonement for him before the LORD.[i] 30 Then he shall sacrifice the doves or the young pigeons, which the person can afford,[j] 31 one[b] as a sin offering and the other as a burnt offering,[k] together with the grain offering. In this way the priest will make atonement before the LORD on behalf of the one to be cleansed.[l]"

32 These are the regulations for anyone who has an infectious skin disease[m] and who cannot afford the regular offerings[n] for his cleansing.

Cleansing From Mildew

33 The LORD said to Moses and Aaron, 34 "When you enter the land of Canaan,[o] which I am giving you as your possession,[p] and I put a spreading mildew in a house in that land, 35 the owner of the house must go and tell the priest, 'I have seen something that looks like mildew in my house.' 36 The priest is to order the house to be emptied before he goes in to examine the mildew, so that nothing in the house will be pronounced unclean. After this the priest is to go in and inspect the house. 37 He is to examine the mildew on the walls, and if it has greenish or reddish[q] depressions that appear to be deeper than the surface of the wall, 38 the priest shall go out the doorway of the house and close it up for seven days.[r] 39 On the seventh day[s] the priest shall return to inspect the house. If the mildew has spread on the walls, 40 he is to order that the contaminated stones be torn out and thrown into an unclean place outside the town.[t] 41 He must have all the inside walls of the house scraped and the material that is scraped off dumped into an unclean place outside the town. 42 Then they are to take other stones to replace these and take new clay and plaster the house.

43 "If the mildew reappears in the house after the stones have been torn out and the house scraped and plastered, 44 the priest is to go and examine it and, if the mildew has spread in the house, it is a destructive mildew; the house is unclean.[u] 45 It must be torn down—its stones, timbers and all the plaster—and taken out of the town to an unclean place.

46 "Anyone who goes into the house while it is closed up will be unclean till evening.[v] 47 Anyone who sleeps or eats in the house must wash his clothes.[w]

48 "But if the priest comes to examine it and the mildew has not spread after the house has been plastered, he shall pronounce the house clean,[x] because the mildew is gone. 49 To purify the house he is to take two birds and some cedar wood, scarlet yarn and hyssop.[y] 50 He shall kill one of the birds over fresh water in a clay pot.[z] 51 Then he is to take the cedar wood, the hyssop,[a] the scarlet yarn and the live bird, dip them into the blood of the dead bird and the fresh water, and sprinkle the house seven times.[b] 52 He shall purify the house with the bird's blood, the fresh water, the live bird, the cedar wood, the hyssop and the scarlet yarn. 53 Then he is to release the live bird in the open fields[c] outside the town. In this way he will make atonement for the house, and it will be clean.[d]"

14:20 [y]ver 8
14:21 [z]Lev 5:7; 12:8 [a]ver 22,32
14:22 [b]Lev 5:7
14:23 [c]ver 10,11
14:24 [d]Nu 6:14 [e]ver 10 [f]ver 12
14:25 [g]ver 14; Ex 29:20
14:26 [h]ver 15
14:29 [i]ver 18
14:30 [j]Lev 5:7
14:31 [k]ver 22; Lev 5:7; 15:15,30 [l]ver 18,19
14:32 [m]Lev 13:2 [n]ver 21
14:34 [o]Ge 12:5; Ex 6:4; Nu 13:2 [p]Ge 17:8; 48:4; Nu 27:12; 32:22; Dt 3:27; 7:1; 32:49
14:37 [q]Lev 13:19
14:38 [r]Lev 13:4
14:39 [s]Lev 13:5
14:40 [t]ver 45
14:44 [u]Lev 13:51
14:46 [v]Lev 11:24
14:47 [w]Lev 11:25
14:48 [x]Lev 13:6
14:49 [y]ver 4; 1Ki 4:33; ver 4
14:50 [z]ver 5
14:51 [a]ver 6; Ps 51:7 [b]ver 4,7
14:53 [c]ver 7 [d]ver 20

[a] *21* That is, probably about 2 quarts (about 2 liters) [b] *31* Septuagint and Syriac; Hebrew *31 such as the person can afford, one*

54These are the regulations for any infectious skin disease,[e] for an itch, 55for mildew[f] in clothing or in 14:54 [e]Lev 13:2, 30
a house, 56and for a swelling, a rash or a bright spot,[g] 57to determine when something is clean or unclean. 14:55 [f]Lev 13:47-52
These are the regulations for infectious skin diseases and mildew.[h] 14:56 [g]Lev 13:2 14:57 [h]Lev 10:10

Discharges Causing Uncleanness

15 The LORD said to Moses and Aaron, 2"Speak to the Israelites and say to them: 'When any man
has a bodily discharge,[i] the discharge is unclean. 3Whether it continues flowing from his body 15:2 [i]ver 16,32; Lev 22:4; Nu 5:2; 2Sa 3:29; Mt 9:20
or is blocked, it will make him unclean. This is how his discharge will bring about uncleanness:
4" 'Any bed the man with a discharge lies on will be unclean, and anything he sits on will be unclean.
5Anyone who touches his bed must wash his clothes[j] and bathe with water,[k] and he will be unclean till 15:5 [j]Lev 11:25 [k]Lev 14:8
evening.[l] 6Whoever sits on anything that the man with a discharge sat on must wash his clothes and [l]Lev 11:24
bathe with water, and he will be unclean till evening.
7" 'Whoever touches the man[m] who has a discharge[n] must wash his clothes and bathe with water, 15:7 [m]ver 19; Lev 22:5 [n]ver 16; Lev 22:4
and he will be unclean till evening.
8" 'If the man with the discharge spits[o] on someone who is clean, that person must wash his clothes 15:8 [o]Nu 12:14
and bathe with water, and he will be unclean till evening.
9" 'Everything the man sits on when riding will be unclean, 10and whoever touches any of the things
that were under him will be unclean till evening; whoever picks up those things[p] must wash his clothes 15:10 [p]Nu 19:10
and bathe with water, and he will be unclean till evening.
11" 'Anyone the man with a discharge touches without rinsing his hands with water must wash his
clothes and bathe with water, and he will be unclean till evening.
12" 'A clay pot[q] that the man touches must be broken, and any wooden article[r] is to be rinsed with 15:12 [q]Lev 6:28 [r]Lev 11:32
water.
13" 'When a man is cleansed from his discharge, he is to count off seven days[s] for his ceremonial 15:13 [s]Lev 8:33 [t]ver 5
cleansing; he must wash his clothes and bathe himself with fresh water, and he will be clean.[t] 14On the
eighth day he must take two doves or two young pigeons[u] and come before the LORD to the entrance to 15:14 [u]Lev 14:22
the Tent of Meeting and give them to the priest. 15The priest is to sacrifice them, the one for a sin offer-
ing[v] and the other for a burnt offering.[w] In this way he will make atonement before the LORD for the man 15:15 [v]Lev 5:7 [w]Lev 14:31
because of his discharge.[x] [x]Lev 14:18,19
16" 'When a man has an emission of semen,[y] he must bathe his whole body with water, and he will 15:16 [y]ver 2; Lev 22:4;
be unclean till evening.[z] 17Any clothing or leather that has semen on it must be washed with water, and Dt 23:10 [z]ver 5; Dt 23:11
it will be unclean till evening. 18When a man lies with a woman and there is an emission of semen,[a] both 15:18 [a]1Sa 21:4
must bathe with water, and they will be unclean till evening.
19" 'When a woman has her regular flow of blood, the impurity of her monthly period[b] will last sev- 15:19 [b]ver 24; Lev 12:2
en days, and anyone who touches her will be unclean till evening.
20" 'Anything she lies on during her period will be unclean, and anything she sits on will be unclean.
21Whoever touches her bed must wash his clothes and bathe with water, and he will be unclean till eve-
ning.[c] 22Whoever touches anything she sits on must wash his clothes and bathe with water, and he will be 15:21 [c]ver 27
unclean till evening. 23Whether it is the bed or anything she was sitting on, when anyone touches it, he
will be unclean till evening.
24" 'If a man lies with her and her monthly flow[d] touches him, he will be unclean for seven days; any 15:24 [d]ver 19; Lev 12:2; 18:19; 20:18; Eze 18:6
bed he lies on will be unclean.
25" 'When a woman has a discharge of blood for many days at a time other than her monthly period[e] 15:25 [e]Mt 9:20; Mk 5:25; Lk 8:43
or has a discharge that continues beyond her period, she will be unclean as long as she has the discharge,
just as in the days of her period. 26Any bed she lies on while her discharge continues will be unclean, as
is her bed during her monthly period, and anything she sits on will be unclean, as during her period.
27Whoever touches them will be unclean; he must wash his clothes and bathe with water, and he will be
unclean till evening.
28" 'When she is cleansed from her discharge, she must count off seven days, and after that she will
be ceremonially clean. 29On the eighth day she must take two doves or two young pigeons[f] and bring 15:29 [f]Lev 14:22
them to the priest at the entrance to the Tent of Meeting. 30The priest is to sacrifice one for a sin offering

---

15:2 The "bodily discharge" probably refers to either diarrhea or urethral discharge (various kinds of infections). The contamination of anything "under" a man (v. 10) indicates that the discharge had to do with the buttocks or genitals.

15:16 Normal sexual activity and a woman's menstruation required no sacrifices but only a washing and a minimal period of uncleanness.

15:30 [g]Lev 5:10; 14:20,31; 18:19; 2Sa 11:4; Mk 5:25; Lk 8:43
15:31 [h]Lev 20:3; Nu 5:3; 19:13,20; 2Sa 15:25; 2Ki 21:7; Ps 33:14; 74:7; 76:2; Eze 5:11; 23:38
15:32 [i]ver 2
15:33 [j]ver 19,24, 25
16:1 [k]Lev 10:1
16:2 [l]Ex 30:10; Heb 9:7 [m]Heb 9:25; 10:19 [n]Ex 25:22 [o]Ex 40:34
16:3 [p]Heb 9:24, 25
16:4 [q]Ex 28:39 [r]Ex 28:42 [s]ver 24; Heb 10:22
16:5 [t]Lev 4:13-21 [u]2Ch 29:23
16:6 [v]Lev 9:7; Heb 5:3; 7:27; 9:7,12
16:10 [w]Isa 53:4-10; Ro 3:25; 1Jn 2:2
16:11 [x]Heb 7:27; 9:7
16:12 [y]Lev 10:1 [z]Ex 30:34-38
16:13 [a]Ex 28:43; Lev 22:9
16:14 [b]Lev 4:5; Heb 9:7,13,25 [c]Lev 4:6
16:15 [d]Heb 9:7, 12 [e]Heb 9:3
16:16 [f]Ex 29:36
16:18 [g]Lev 4:7 [h]Lev 4:25
16:19 [i]Eze 43:20

and the other for a burnt offering. In this way he will make atonement for her before the LORD for the un-
cleanness of her discharge.[g]
31“ ‘You must keep the Israelites separate from things that make them unclean, so they will not die in
their uncleanness for defiling my dwelling place,[a][h] which is among them.’ ”
32These are the regulations for a man with a discharge, for anyone made unclean by an emission of
semen,[i] 33for a woman in her monthly period, for a man or a woman with a discharge, and for a man
who lies with a woman who is ceremonially unclean.[j]

The Day of Atonement

16 The LORD spoke to Moses after the death of the two sons of Aaron who died when they ap-
proached the LORD.[k] 2The LORD said to Moses: “Tell your brother Aaron not to come whenever he
chooses[l] into the Most Holy Place[m] behind the curtain in front of the atonement cover on the ark, or else
he will die, because I appear[n] in the cloud[o] over the atonement cover.
3“This is how Aaron is to enter the sanctuary area:[p] with a young bull for a sin offering and a ram for
a burnt offering. 4He is to put on the sacred linen tunic, with linen undergarments next to his body; he
is to tie the linen sash around him and put on the linen turban.[q] These are sacred garments;[r] so he must
bathe himself with water[s] before he puts them on. 5From the Israelite community[t] he is to take two male
goats[u] for a sin offering and a ram for a burnt offering.
6“Aaron is to offer the bull for his own sin offering to make atonement for himself and his household.[v]
7Then he is to take the two goats and present them before the LORD at the entrance to the Tent of Meet-
ing. 8He is to cast lots for the two goats—one lot for the LORD and the other for the scapegoat.[b] 9Aaron
shall bring the goat whose lot falls to the LORD and sacrifice it for a sin offering. 10But the goat chosen by
lot as the scapegoat shall be presented alive before the LORD to be used for making atonement[w] by send-
ing it into the desert as a scapegoat.
11“Aaron shall bring the bull for his own sin offering to make atonement for himself and his house-
hold,[x] and he is to slaughter the bull for his own sin offering. 12He is to take a censer full of burning coals[y]
from the altar before the LORD and two handfuls of finely ground fragrant incense[z] and take them behind
the curtain. 13He is to put the incense on the fire before the LORD, and the smoke of the incense will con-
ceal the atonement cover above the Testimony, so that he will not die.[a] 14He is to take some of the bull’s
blood[b] and with his finger sprinkle it on the front of the atonement cover; then he shall sprinkle some
of it with his finger seven times before the atonement cover.[c]
15“He shall then slaughter the goat for the sin offering for the people[d] and take its blood behind the
curtain[e] and do with it as he did with the bull’s blood: He shall sprinkle it on the atonement cover and
in front of it. 16In this way he will make atonement[f] for the Most Holy Place because of the uncleanness
and rebellion of the Israelites, whatever their sins have been. He is to do the same for the Tent of Meet-
ing, which is among them in the midst of their uncleanness. 17No one is to be in the Tent of Meeting from
the time Aaron goes in to make atonement in the Most Holy Place until he comes out, having made atone-
ment for himself, his household and the whole community of Israel.
18“Then he shall come out to the altar[g] that is before the LORD and make atonement for it. He shall take
some of the bull’s blood and some of the goat’s blood and put it on all the horns of the altar.[h] 19He shall
sprinkle some of the blood on it with his finger seven times to cleanse it and to consecrate it from the
uncleanness of the Israelites.[i]
20“When Aaron has finished making atonement for the Most Holy Place, the Tent of Meeting and the

[a] *31* Or *my tabernacle* [b] *8* That is, the goat of removal; Hebrew *azazel*; also in verses 10 and 26

16:8 “Scapegoat,” a term that occurs in verses 8, 10 and 26, has been interpreted variously. It is used to refer to the second of two goats for which lots were cast on the annual Day of Atonement. The first was sacrificed as a sin offering (v. 9), but the second goat, the scapegoat (v. 26), had the people’s sins transferred to it by prayer and the laying on of hands before being taken into the wilderness. The Hebrew term translated “scapegoat” is thought to be related to an Arabic word meaning “remove.” Thus it is often translated “removal.” The actual meaning of the term and its use in the context of Leviticus 16 are uncertain.

Some authorities regard this word to be the name of a solitary place to which the goat was taken, although this seems unlikely. The KJV translators regarded the term as a qualifying word for goat (i.e., the goat that removed the guilt of the people). Some scholars see in the word the name of a personal being—a demon of the wilderness or a fallen angel who seduced people to evil (as in the Book of Enoch), or as an epithet applied to the devil (see Goat-Demons and Desert Satyrs” on p. 177).

A parallel to the scapegoat may be seen in Scripture. In the ritual for a recovered leper, a living bird was released in the country to carry away the evil, after which the leper was declared clean (14:6). In the Babylonian New Year’s Day festival a similar rite was practiced, in which a slain sheep was taken and thrown into the river, after which its bearers were regarded as unclean (cf. 16:26). Certainly the general idea of the scapegoat is clear: The sin of guilty Israel had been removed and “forgotten” by God.

altar, he shall bring forward the live goat. 21 He is to lay both hands on the head of the live goat and con-
fess[j] over it all the wickedness and rebellion of the Israelites—all their sins—and put them on the goat's 16:21 [j]Lev 5:5
head. He shall send the goat away into the desert in the care of a man appointed for the task. 22 The goat
will carry on itself all their sins[k] to a solitary place; and the man shall release it in the desert. 16:22 [k]Isa 53:12
23 "Then Aaron is to go into the Tent of Meeting and take off the linen garments he put on before he
entered the Most Holy Place, and he is to leave them there.[l] 24 He shall bathe himself with water in a holy 16:23 [l]Eze 42:14; 44:19
place and put on his regular garments.[m] Then he shall come out and sacrifice the burnt offering for him- 16:24 [m]ver 3-5
self and the burnt offering for the people, to make atonement for himself and for the people. 25 He shall
also burn the fat of the sin offering on the altar.

The Day of Atonement

LEVITICUS 16 Once each year, on the tenth day of the seventh month, the high priest entered the Most Holy Place to make atonement for himself, the other priests, the tabernacle and altar and the entire population of Israel (Lev 16). The purification rites enacted during this most special of days presupposed that the ordinary means of atonement (chs. 1–7; 11–15) were insufficient to purify the people completely and to make full satisfaction for all of their sins. This was in large part because of the Israelites' inevitable failure to follow perfectly all of the provisions God had made for them, but also because an innumerable accumulation of inadvertent sins had gone unrecognized and thus had not been expiated. Because God's wrath had not been appeased for these impurities and transgressions, they had contaminated the Most Holy Place (16:16).

Two key issues concerning the Day of Atonement were the order and significance of the ritual and the meaning/identity of the scapegoat.

After bathing on this central day of the Israelite religious year, the high priest donned white undergarments and a white tunic. He was not upon this occasion to wear his traditional ceremonial insignia, communicating by the absence of this "status symbol" that no one can approach God with any pretense of special authority or prestige.

The high priest began the ritual observance by offering a bull for his own sins and those of his household, after which he took a censer with burning coals and incense into the Most Holy Place and sprinkled blood from the bull onto the ark of the covenant.[1] This deliberate self-inclusion demonstrated that no one, including the high priest, could stand guiltless before God.

The high priest proceeded to cast lots over two goats; one would be sacrificed, while the other was to become the "scapegoat." The sacrificed goat represented *propitiation*, whereby the wrath of God against his people was turned aside. The scapegoat, on the other hand, represented *expiation*, whereby the guilt of the sinners was removed.

The priest sacrificed one goat for the sins of the people, sprinkling some of its blood on the ark, after which he emerged from the tent and cleansed the altar with the blood of the bull and the goat.

Placing his hands on the head of the scapegoat, the high priest confessed the people's sins over it. An individual appointed to lead the scapegoat out into the wilderness and release it was required afterward to wash his clothes and bathe before returning to the camp.[2]

The high priest left his white clothing in the Tent of Meeting, bathed again and clothed himself in his regular priestly apparel. These actions communicated that the holiness of the sanctuary had to remain there; none of it could be carried out with the priest into the camp. The sacrificed bull and goat were to be burned up entirely.

Some argue that the Israelites viewed the scapegoat as the physical embodiment of a "goat-demon" of the desert.[3] This interpretation, however, contradicts the teaching of Leviticus 17:7, which prohibited Israelites from making offerings to goat deities.

More likely, the Hebrew word translated "scapegoat" simply referred to a goat that was to be sent away. This is the interpretation suggested both in the **Septuagint** (early Greek translation of the OT) and the **Vulgate** (early Latin version of the Bible).

[1]See "The Tabernacle and the Ark" on page 153. [2]See "Ritual Purity in Israel and the Ancient Near East" on page 166. [3]See "Goat-Demons and Desert Satyrs" on page 177.

16:26 ⁿLev 11:25
16:27 ᵒLev 4:12, 21; Heb 13:11
16:29 ᵖLev 23:27,32; Nu 29:7; Isa 58:3
16:30 ᵠJer 33:8; Eph 5:26
16:31 ʳIsa 58:3,5
16:32 ˢver 4; Nu 20:26,28
16:33 ᵗver 11,16-18
16:34 ᵘHeb 9:7, 25

[26]"The man who releases the goat as a scapegoat must wash his clothes[n] and bathe himself with wa-
ter; afterward he may come into the camp. [27]The bull and the goat for the sin offerings, whose blood was
brought into the Most Holy Place to make atonement, must be taken outside the camp;[o] their hides, flesh
and offal are to be burned up. [28]The man who burns them must wash his clothes and bathe himself with
water; afterward he may come into the camp.
[29]"This is to be a lasting ordinance for you: On the tenth day of the seventh month you must deny
yourselves[a][p] and not do any work—whether native-born or an alien living among you— [30]because on
this day atonement will be made for you, to cleanse you. Then, before the LORD, you will be clean from
all your sins.[q] [31]It is a sabbath of rest, and you must deny yourselves;[r] it is a lasting ordinance. [32]The
priest who is anointed and ordained to succeed his father as high priest is to make atonement. He is to
put on the sacred linen garments[s] [33]and make atonement for the Most Holy Place, for the Tent of Meet-
ing and the altar, and for the priests and all the people of the community.[t]
[34]"This is to be a lasting ordinance for you: Atonement is to be made once a year[u] for all the sins of
the Israelites."

And it was done, as the LORD commanded Moses.

[a] *29* Or *must fast;* also in verse 31

16:26 See the note at verse 8.
16:29–34 Theologically and spiritually, the Day of Atonement is the center of Leviticus, "the book of holiness." The divinely inspired commentary on chapter 16 is found in Hebrews 9:1—10:25. Israel had two beginnings for each year, almost exactly six months apart. In the first month on the fourteenth day the people ate the Passover as a memorial of the events leading to the exodus from Egypt. Half a year later, in the seventh month on the tenth day (Lev 16:29), the priest made atonement for them. The Jews now celebrate their New Year's Day (Rosh Hashanah) on the first day of the seventh month (September) and the Day of Atonement (Yom Kippur, properly *yom hakkippurim*) on the tenth day of the same month. See "The Day of Atonement" on page 176 and "The Jewish Calendar" on page 241.

Goat-Demons and Desert Satyrs

LEVITICUS 17 God commanded that no Israelite was to sacrifice an ox, lamb or goat either within the confines of the camp or outside in the open country (Lev 17:1–9). Instead, the animals were to be brought to the door of the Tent of Meeting. This practice effectively eliminated ambiguity as to the nature of any sacrifice.[1] As a case in point, no Israelite was to offer an illicit sacrifice to a pagan deity outside the view of the Lord's priests and, when discovered, claim to be offering it to the God of Israel. This law was important because Israelites had previously offered sacrifices to goats as objects of worship.

Whether the reference in verse 7 is to live goats worshiped as manifestations of "goat spirits" or to man-made idols in the form of goats, we have no way of knowing for certain (the NIV translators chose to render the Hebrew term here as "goat idols"). It is also possible that the goats in question were thought to have been some kind of "demons" or "satyrs" (i.e., creatures that were part goat, part man). We have no certain grounds for suggesting that this is what the Biblical writer had in mind, but in light of analogies from ancient pagan religions the association is not impossible. It is true that the Hebrew word sometimes translated "goat idols" or "goat demons" more frequently refers simply to goats (e.g., Isa 34:14).

We are aware that goat images were worshiped many years later, during the reign of Jeroboam I (2Ch 11:15), who introduced a rival religious system into the northern kingdom (1Ki 12:28–31), complete with priests, high places and images of calves and goats.[2] Although the Israelites sometimes sacrificed goats (Lev 16), they were never to sacrifice *to* goats.

The goat-like god Pan, from Greece
Preserving Bible Times; © Dr. James C. Martin; permission of The British Museum

[1]See "Sacrifices and Offerings in the Bible and the Ancient Near East" on page 158. [2]See "The High Place at Dan" on page 504.

Eating Blood Forbidden

17 The LORD said to Moses, 2"Speak to Aaron and his sons and to all the Israelites and say to them: 'This
is what the LORD has commanded: 3Any Israelite who sacrifices an ox,[a] a lamb or a goat in the camp
or outside of it 4instead of bringing it to the entrance to the Tent of Meeting to present it as an offering to
the LORD in front of the tabernacle of the LORD[v]—that man shall be considered guilty of bloodshed; he has
shed blood and must be cut off from his people.[w] 5This is so the Israelites will bring to the LORD the sacri-
fices they are now making in the open fields. They must bring them to the priest, that is, to the LORD, at the
entrance to the Tent of Meeting and sacrifice them as fellowship offerings.[b] 6The priest is to sprinkle the
blood against the altar of the LORD[x] at the entrance to the Tent of Meeting and burn the fat as an aroma
pleasing to the LORD.[y] 7They must no longer offer any of their sacrifices to the goat idols[c][z] to whom they
prostitute themselves.[a] This is to be a lasting ordinance for them and for the generations to come.'

8"Say to them: 'Any Israelite or any alien living among them who offers a burnt offering or sacrifice
9and does not bring it to the entrance to the Tent of Meeting[b] to sacrifice it to the LORD—that man must
be cut off from his people.

10" 'Any Israelite or any alien living among them who eats any blood—I will set my face against that
person who eats blood[c] and will cut him off from his people. 11For the life of a creature is in the blood,[d]
and I have given it to you to make atonement for yourselves on the altar; it is the blood that makes atone-
ment for one's life.[e] 12Therefore I say to the Israelites, "None of you may eat blood, nor may an alien liv-
ing among you eat blood."

13" 'Any Israelite or any alien living among you who hunts any animal or bird that may be eaten must
drain out the blood and cover it with earth,[f] 14because the life of every creature is its blood. That is why
I have said to the Israelites, "You must not eat the blood of any creature, because the life of every crea-
ture is its blood; anyone who eats it must be cut off."[g]

15" 'Anyone, whether native-born or alien, who eats anything
found dead or torn by wild animals[h] must wash his clothes and
bathe with water, and he will be ceremonially unclean till evening;
then he will be clean. 16But if he does not wash his clothes and bathe
himself, he will be held responsible.' "

ANCIENT VOICES

If a man says to his comrade, either in private or in a public quarrel, "Everyone has sex with your wife," and further, "I can prove the charges," but he is unable to prove the charges and does not prove the charges, they shall strike that man 40 blows with rods; he shall perform the king's service for one full month; they shall cut off his hair; moreover, he shall pay 3,600 shekels of lead.

—THE MIDDLE ASSYRIAN LAWS

See "The Middle Assyrian Laws" article.

Unlawful Sexual Relations

18 The LORD said to Moses, 2"Speak to the Israelites and say to
them: 'I am the LORD your God.[i] 3You must not do as they do
in Egypt, where you used to live, and you must not do as they do in
the land of Canaan, where I am bringing you. Do not follow their
practices.[j] 4You must obey my laws and be careful to follow my de-
crees. I am the LORD your God.[k] 5Keep my decrees and laws, for the
man who obeys them will live by them.[l] I am the LORD.

6" 'No one is to approach any close relative to have sexual rela-
tions. I am the LORD.

7" 'Do not dishonor your father[m] by having sexual relations with
your mother.[n] She is your mother; do not have relations with her.

8" 'Do not have sexual relations with your father's wife;[o] that would dishonor your father.[p]

9" 'Do not have sexual relations with your sister,[q] either your father's daughter or your mother's
daughter, whether she was born in the same home or elsewhere.

10" 'Do not have sexual relations with your son's daughter or your daughter's daughter; that would
dishonor you.

11" 'Do not have sexual relations with the daughter of your father's wife, born to your father; she is your
sister.

12" 'Do not have sexual relations with your father's sister;[r] she is your father's close relative.

13" 'Do not have sexual relations with your mother's sister, because she is your mother's close relative.

17:4 [v]Dt 12:5-21 [w]Ge 17:14
17:6 [x]Lev 3:2 [y]Nu 18:17
17:7 [z]Ex 22:20; 2Ch 11:15 [a]Ex 32:8; 34:15; Dt 32:17; 1Co 10:20
17:9 [b]ver 4
17:10 [c]Ge 9:4; Lev 3:17; Dt 12:16,23; 1Sa 14:33
17:11 [d]ver 14; Ge 9:4 [e]Heb 9:22
17:13 [f]Lev 7:26; Dt 12:16
17:14 [g]ver 11; Ge 9:4
17:15 [h]Ex 22:31; Dt 14:21
18:2 [i]Ex 6:7; Lev 11:44; Eze 20:5
18:3 [j]ver 24-30; Ex 23:24; Lev 20:23
18:4 [k]ver 2
18:5 [l]Eze 20:11; Ro 10:5*; Gal 3:12*
18:7 [m]Lev 20:11 [n]Eze 22:10
18:8 [o]1Co 5:1 [p]Lev 20:11
18:9 [q]Lev 20:17
18:12 [r]Lev 20:19

[a] 3 The Hebrew word can include both male and female. [b] 5 Traditionally *peace offerings* [c] 7 Or *demons*

17:7 See "Goat-Demons and Desert Satyrs" on page 177.

14“ ‘Do not dishonor your father’s brother by approaching his wife to have sexual relations; she is your
aunt.[s]
15“ ‘Do not have sexual relations with your daughter-in-law.[t] She is your son’s wife; do not have relations with her.
16“ ‘Do not have sexual relations with your brother’s wife;[u] that would dishonor your brother.
17“ ‘Do not have sexual relations with both a woman and her daughter.[v] Do not have sexual relations
with either her son’s daughter or her daughter’s daughter; they are her close relatives. That is wickedness.
18“ ‘Do not take your wife’s sister as a rival wife and have sexual relations with her while your wife is
living.
19“ ‘Do not approach a woman to have sexual relations during the uncleanness of her monthly period.[w]
20“ ‘Do not have sexual relations with your neighbor’s wife[x] and defile yourself with her.
21“ ‘Do not give any of your children[y] to be sacrificed[a] to Molech,[z] for you must not profane the name
of your God.[a] I am the LORD.
22“ ‘Do not lie with a man as one lies with a woman;[b] that is detestable.

18:14 [s]Lev 20:20 **18:15** [t]Lev 20:12 **18:16** [u]Lev 20:21 **18:17** [v]Lev 20:14 **18:19** [w]Lev 15:24; 20:18 **18:20** [x]Ex 20:14; Lev 20:10; Mt 5:27,28; 1Co 6:9; Heb 13:4 **18:21** [y]Dt 12:31 [z]Lev 20:2-5 [a]Lev 19:12; 21:6; Eze 36:20 **18:22** Dt 23:18; Ro 1:27

[a] 21 Or *to be passed through* ⌊*the fire*⌋

18:19–30 Not surprisingly, many Middle Assyrian laws gave men greater rights than women. The Biblical commands demonstrate greater equality between the sexes and greater respect for human life and moral purity. See “The Middle Assyrian Laws” on page 179 and “The Hittite Laws” on page 281.
18:20 Due regard for one’s neighbor is expressed in the great Old Testament and New Testament precept “Love your neighbor as yourself” (19:18: Mt 10:30–37). The parable of the Good Samaritan (Lk 10:30–37) was given in answer to the question, “And who is my neighbor?” (Lk 10:29).
18:21 The detestable practice of sacrificing children to Molech, the god of the Ammonites, was common in Phoenicia and its surrounding countries. See “Human Sacrifice in the Ancient Near East” on page 182.
18:22 See “Homosexuality in the Ancient World” on page 1836.

ANCIENT TEXTS AND ARTIFACTS

The Middle Assyrian Laws

LEVITICUS 18 German excavations at ancient **Asshur** in modern Iraq between 1903 and 1914 yielded a significant number of **cuneiform** tablets containing regulations now known as the Middle **Assyrian** laws. Although this cannot be established with certainty, the widely accepted view is that they date to the reign of Assyria’s Tiglath-Pileser I (1114–1076 B.C.). It is notable, however, that these tablets are copies of even earlier laws that originated during the fourteenth or fifteenth centuries B.C.

Each tablet contains a separate law collection concerned with particular life issues such as theft, inheritance, marriage and family law, witchcraft, fornication, false accusation, irrigation, property rights, abortion, blasphemy, etc. These decrees, like many of those recorded in Leviticus and Deuteronomy, are “casuistic laws”; that is, they follow an “if . . . then” pattern. For example: “If the wife of a man should go out of her own house, and go to another man where he resides, and should he fornicate with her knowing that she is the wife of a man, the man and the wife shall be killed.” This particular law has direct Biblical parallels in Leviticus 18:20 and Deuteronomy 22:22. In other cases, however, the Middle Assyrian laws prescribed harsher punishments than Biblical commands; theft, for example, was punishable by death or mutilation of the ears and nose.

Many Middle Assyrian laws demonstrate that men had greater rights than women in that ancient society. For example, if a married man were to rape an unmarried woman, his own wife was turned over to be raped and the rapist was obligated to marry the woman he had violated. Acceptable means by which a man could punish his wife included beatings, whippings, plucking out her hair and mutilating her ears. Wherever the decrees of Leviticus and Deuteronomy differ from the Middle Assyrian laws, the Biblical commands demonstrate greater equality between the sexes and a higher level of respect for human life and moral purity.[1]

[1]For other ancient, extrabiblical laws, see “Custom and Law in Ancient Mesopotamia” on page 36, “Slavery and Labor Law in the Ancient Near East” on page 127, “The Laws of Eshnunna” on page 267 and “The Hittite Laws” on page 281.

23 " 'Do not have sexual relations with an animal and defile yourself with it. A woman must not pre-
sent herself to an animal to have sexual relations with it; that is a perversion.[c] 18:23 [c]Ex 22:19; Lev 20:15; Dt 27:21
24 " 'Do not defile yourselves in any of these ways, because this is how the nations that I am going to
drive out before you[d] became defiled.[e] 25 Even the land was defiled; so I punished it for its sin,[f] and the 18:24 [d]ver 3,27, 30 [e]Dt 18:12
land vomited out its inhabitants.[g] 26 But you must keep my decrees and my laws. The native-born and 18:25 [f]Lev 20:23; Dt 9:5; 18:12
the aliens living among you must not do any of these detestable things, 27 for all these were done [g]ver 28; Lev 20:22
by the people who lived in the land before you, and the land became defiled. 28 And if you defile the land,
it will vomit you out as it vomited out the nations that were before you.
29 " 'Everyone who does any of these detestable things—such persons must be cut off from their peo-
ple. 30 Keep my requirements[h] and do not follow any of the detestable customs that were practiced before 18:30 [h]Dt 11:1 [i]ver 2
you came and do not defile yourselves with them. I am the LORD your God.[i]' " 19:2 [j]1Pe 1:16*; Lev 11:44

Various Laws

19 The LORD said to Moses, 2 "Speak to the entire assembly of Israel and say to them: 'Be holy because
I, the LORD your God, am holy.[j]
3 " 'Each of you must respect his mother and father,[k] and you must observe my Sabbaths. I am the 19:3 [k]Ex 20:12 [l]Lev 11:44
LORD your God.[l]
4 " 'Do not turn to idols or make gods of cast metal for yourselves.[m] I am the LORD your God. 19:4 [m]Ex 20:4, 23; 34:17; Lev 26:1; Ps 96:5; 115:4-7
5 " 'When you sacrifice a fellowship offering[a] to the LORD, sacrifice it in such a way that it will be ac-
cepted on your behalf. 6 It shall be eaten on the day you sacrifice it or on the next day; anything left over
until the third day must be burned up. 7 If any of it is eaten on the third day, it is impure and will not be
accepted. 8 Whoever eats it will be held responsible because he has desecrated what is holy to the LORD;
that person must be cut off from his people.
9 " 'When you reap the harvest of your land, do not reap to the very edges of your field or gather the
gleanings of your harvest.[n] 10 Do not go over your vineyard a second time or pick up the grapes that have 19:9 [n]Lev 23:10, 22; Dt 24:19-22
fallen. Leave them for the poor and the alien. I am the LORD your God.
11 " 'Do not steal.[o] 19:11 [o]Ex 20:15 [p]Eph 4:25
" 'Do not lie.[p]
" 'Do not deceive one another.
12 " 'Do not swear falsely by my name[q] and so profane the name of your God. I am the LORD. 19:12 [q]Ex 20:7; Mt 5:33

[a] 5 Traditionally *peace offering*

Tattoos and Self-Laceration in Ancient Religion

LEVITICUS 19 In ancient pagan religions, tattooing was often thought to protect the individual so marked from harmful magic. Some tattoos also indicated that a person belonged to a certain god or cult (analogous to the fact that slaves were often branded or tattooed).

The earliest evidence of tattooing in the ancient Near East comes from **Neolithic** fertility figurines discovered in Jordan. In **Middle Kingdom** Egypt, tattoos associated with Hathor (a fertility goddess) were discovered on the mummy of a priestess, as well as on figurines. These figurines, referred to as "Brides of the Dead," linked sexuality with rebirth as a means of ensuring the resurrection of the dead. People in **New Kingdom** Egypt sported tattoos depicting Bes, a god of childbirth and the home. In **Mesopotamia**, temple slaves were often branded or tattooed with the symbol of the respective temples to which they belonged.

Like tattooing, self-laceration in the ancient Near East was associated with death. Mesopotamian women slashed themselves as a sign of grief, and in the fertility cult of Baal self-laceration was also associated with mourning for a "deceased" deity.

It seems likely that the Biblical prohibition against tattoos and self-laceration for the dead (Lev 19:28) was directed against specific idolatrous practices, particularly erotic religious rites associated with the dead. The Old Testament treats tattooing and bodily disfigurement as inherently pagan and depraved (cf. Dt 14:1; 1Ki 18:28).

19:13 [r]Ex 22:15, 25-27 [s]Dt 24:15; Jas 5:4 13“ ‘Do not defraud your neighbor or rob him.[r]
“ ‘Do not hold back the wages of a hired man overnight.[s]
19:14 [t]Dt 27:18 14“ ‘Do not curse the deaf or put a stumbling block in front of the blind,[t] but fear your God. I am the LORD.
19:15 [u]Ex 23:2,6 [v]Dt 1:17 15“ ‘Do not pervert justice;[u] do not show partiality[v] to the poor or favoritism to the great, but judge
your neighbor fairly.
19:16 [w]Ps 15:3; Eze 22:9 [x]Ex 23:7 16“ ‘Do not go about spreading slander[w] among your people.
“ ‘Do not do anything that endangers your neighbor’s life.[x] I am the LORD.
19:17 [y]1Jn 2:9; 3:15 [z]Mt 18:15; Lk 17:3 17“ ‘Do not hate your brother in your heart.[y] Rebuke your neighbor frankly[z] so you will not share in
his guilt.
19:18 [a]Ro 12:19 [b]Ps 103:9 [c]Mt 5:43*; 19:16*; 22:39*; Mk 12:31*; Lk 10:27*; Jn 13:34; Ro 13:9*; Gal 5:14*; Jas 2:8* 18“ ‘Do not seek revenge[a] or bear a grudge[b] against one of your people, but love your neighbor as
yourself.[c] I am the LORD.
19“ ‘Keep my decrees.
“ ‘Do not mate different kinds of animals.
“ ‘Do not plant your field with two kinds of seed.[d]
19:19 [d]Dt 22:9 [e]Dt 22:11 “ ‘Do not wear clothing woven of two kinds of material.[e]
20“ ‘If a man sleeps with a woman who is a slave girl promised to another man but who has not been
ransomed or given her freedom, there must be due punishment. Yet they are not to be put to death, be-
cause she had not been freed. 21 The man, however, must bring a ram to the entrance to the Tent of Meet-
19:21 [f]Lev 5:15 ing for a guilt offering to the LORD.[f] 22 With the ram of the guilt offering the priest is to make atonement
for him before the LORD for the sin he has committed, and his sin will be forgiven.
23“ ‘When you enter the land and plant any kind of fruit tree, regard its fruit as forbidden.[a] For three
19:24 [g]Pr 3:9 years you are to consider it forbidden[b]; it must not be eaten. 24 In the fourth year all its fruit will be holy,[g]
an offering of praise to the LORD. 25 But in the fifth year you may eat its fruit. In this way your harvest will
be increased. I am the LORD your God.
9:26 [h]Lev 17:10 [i]Dt 18:10 26“ ‘Do not eat any meat with the blood still in it.[h]
“ ‘Do not practice divination or sorcery.[i]
19:27 [j]Lev 21:5 27“ ‘Do not cut the hair at the sides of your head or clip off the edges of your beard.[j]
28“ ‘Do not cut your bodies for the dead or put tattoo marks on yourselves. I am the LORD.
19:29 [k]Dt 23:18 29“ ‘Do not degrade your daughter by making her a prostitute,[k] or the land will turn to prostitution
and be filled with wickedness.
19:30 [l]Lev 26:2 30“ ‘Observe my Sabbaths and have reverence for my sanctuary. I am the LORD.[l]
19:31 [m]Lev 20:6; Isa 8:19 31“ ‘Do not turn to mediums or seek out spiritists,[m] for you will be defiled by them. I am the LORD
your God.
19:32 [n]1Ti 5:1 32“ ‘Rise in the presence of the aged, show respect for the elderly[n] and revere your God. I am the LORD.
33“ ‘When an alien lives with you in your land, do not mistreat him. 34 The alien living with you must
19:34 [o]Ex 12:48 [p]Dt 10:19 be treated as one of your native-born.[o] Love him as yourself, for you were aliens in Egypt.[p] I am the LORD
your God.
35“ ‘Do not use dishonest standards when measuring length, weight or quantity. 36 Use honest scales
19:36 [q]Dt 25:13-15 and honest weights, an honest ephah[b] and an honest hin.[c][q] I am the LORD your God, who brought you out
of Egypt.
37“ ‘Keep all my decrees and all my laws and follow them. I am the LORD.’ ”

[a] *23* Hebrew *uncircumcised* [b] *36* An ephah was a dry measure. [c] *36* A hin was a liquid measure.

19:27–28 The ancient Hebrews placed a much greater emphasis on external symbolic acts than do modern Western people, and people in the Near East today still carry on this respect for symbolic actions. Ceremonies for expressing grief at the death of a relative or on some other unhappy occasion are referred to frequently in the Bible (see “Sackcloth and Ashes: Rituals of Lamentation” on p. 820). Persons raised in the modern West do well to exercise caution against viewing these public expressions as hypocritical; they were a natural and valid manifestation of grief in that culture.

The Old Testament, however, contains warnings against pagan mourning rites (vv. 27–28; Dt 14:1–2). Israelite priests were not allowed to take part in any such funeral ceremonies (Lev 21:1–4,10–11). In particular, self-laceration and tattooing were pagan practices associated with death and various fertility cults. See “Tattoos and Self-Laceration in Ancient Religion” on page 180.

19:27 A beard for Asiatics was a badge of manly dignity, in contrast to the Egyptians, who usually shaved both the head and the face. As a sign of mourning, however, it was the custom for a man to pluck out his beard or to cut it off. The Israelites were forbidden to shave off the corners of their beards, probably because that act was regarded as a sign of paganism (v. 27). To force a man to cut off his beard was to inflict upon him a shameful disgrace (2Sa 10:4–5). See “Beards and Hairstyles in the Biblical World” on page 1084.

19:29 Legal measures were in force concerning prostitutes. Parents were not to force their daughters into the practice (21:7,14), priests were not to marry harlots (19:29) and the wages of prostitution were not to be brought into the temple to pay a vow (Dt 23:18).

19:32 Old age is referred to in the Bible as the reward of filial obedience according to the commandment in Exodus 20:12. The Mosaic legislation spelled out the respect to be shown to the aged (Lev 19:32). Along this vein, younger men were trained to wait to express themselves on a subject until their elders had spoken (Job 32:4).

19:35 In ancient times cheating in business transactions by falsification of standards was common practice (see Dt 25:13–16; Pr 11:1;

Punishments for Sin

20 The LORD said to Moses, [2]"Say to the Israelites: 'Any Israelite or any alien living in Israel who gives[a] any of his children to Molech must be put to death. The people of the community are to stone him. [3]I will set my face against that man and I will cut him off from his people; for by giving his

[a] 2 Or *sacrifices*; also in verses 3 and 4

16:11; 20:10,23); there was no bureau of weights and measures. Israel's prophets condemned such deceit (Am 8:5; Mic 6:10–11). See the notes on Proverbs 11:1 and 16:11; see also "Banking and Money in the Ancient World" on page 696 and "Weights and Measures" on page 1459.

Human Sacrifice in the Ancient Near East

LEVITICUS 20 Numerous archaeological discoveries and ancient (including several OT) texts record various examples of human sacrifice that took place throughout the ancient Near East. For example,

- A **relief** on a tower in southern Spain, dating to approximately 500 B.C., gruesomely depicts a child, cradled in a bowl, about to be sacrificed as part of a banquet feast to a two-headed monster.
- Excavators have uncovered a large, sacred cemetery, dating to 400–200 B.C., in the **Phoenician** city of Carthage in North Africa. They estimate that the Carthaginians buried more than 20,000 urns here, each holding the remains of one or two children, most of them aged four years or younger. Inscriptions on the urns indicate that all of these infants and toddlers were sacrificed to a Phoenician deity.
- During times of national emergency, children were sacrificed in an attempt to placate various deities (e.g., by the king of **Moab** as recorded in 2Ki 3:26–27).
- Royal tombs excavated in Ur (**Mesopotamia**) and Egypt contained the remains of ritually slain attendants intended to accompany the deceased into the afterlife.
- Children were used in Mesopotamia as foundation sacrifices, a practice whereby a sacrificial victim was interred in the foundation of a building or gateway for the purpose of affording magical protection for the site.
- Several authors who wrote during the thousand-year period from the fifth century B.C. to the fifth century A.D. attest that child sacrifice was a Phoenician custom. Tertullian, an early church father who lived in North Africa around A.D. 160–225, decried the continuing practice of child sacrifice.

Some Israelites also are known to have made human sacrifices. Ahaz (2Ki 16:3; 2Chr 28:3) and the people of Israel and Judah (2Ki 17:17) sacrificed their children, a practice God condemned as "detestable" (Dt 12:31; Jer 32:35).

Israelites were known to sacrifice their sons or daughters "in the fire" to Molech in the Valley of Ben Hinnom (2Ki 23:10; Jer 32:35). "In the fire," rendered in the New American Standard Bible with the ambiguous phrase "passed through the fire," is clarified in Jeremiah 7:31, which records that the people "burn[ed] their sons and daughters in the fire" (both NIV and NASB) in the Valley of Ben Hinnom.

Considerable controversy surrounds the "Molech" offerings. Some scholars argue that Molech was not a deity at all but a type of sacrifice in which children were dedicated as temple prostitutes.[1] But Biblical evidence clearly indicates that Molech was an Ammonite[2] deity (1Ki 11:7).

Abraham was willing at God's command to sacrifice Isaac (Ge 22), but God at the last moment provided a substitute offering, highlighting both his own ability to provide and Abraham's faithfulness, as well as implicitly expressing his disapproval of human sacrifice.

God condemned this practice not only because it was horrible (unthinkable from our twenty-first-century perspective!) but also because it defiled his sanctuary and profaned his holy name (Lev 18:21; 20:2–5). Because of this and other sins God had expelled the majority of the original pagan inhabitants of the promised land; the Israelites were required to keep his commandments, lest the land "vomit" them out as well (20:22–23)!

[1]See "Prostitution in the Ancient World" on page 284. [2]See "Ammon" on page 364.

20:3 [r]Lev 15:31 [s]Lev 18:21 children to Molech, he has defiled my sanctuary[r] and profaned my holy name.[s] 4 If the people of the com-
munity close their eyes when that man gives one of his children to Molech and they fail to put him to
20:4 [t]Dt 17:2-5 death,[t] 5 I will set my face against that man and his family and will cut off from their people both him and
all who follow him in prostituting themselves to Molech.

6 " 'I will set my face against the person who turns to mediums and spiritists to prostitute himself by
20:6 [u]Lev 19:31 following them, and I will cut him off from his people.[u]

20:7 [v]Eph 1:4; 1Pe 1:16* 7 " 'Consecrate yourselves and be holy,[v] because I am the LORD your God. 8 Keep my decrees and fol-
20:8 [w]Ex 31:13 low them. I am the LORD, who makes you holy.[a][w]

20:9 [x]Dt 27:16 [y]Ex 21:17; Mt 15:4*; Mk 7:10* [z]ver 11; 2Sa 1:16 9 " 'If anyone curses his father or mother,[x] he must be put to death.[y] He has cursed his father or his
mother, and his blood will be on his own head.[z]

10 " 'If a man commits adultery with another man's wife[a]—with the wife of his neighbor—both the
20:10 [a]Ex 20:14; Dt 5:18; 22:22 adulterer and the adulteress must be put to death.

20:11 [b]Lev 18:7; Dt 27:23 11 " 'If a man sleeps with his father's wife, he has dishonored his father.[b] Both the man and the wom-
an must be put to death; their blood will be on their own heads.

20:12 [c]Lev 18:15 12 " 'If a man sleeps with his daughter-in-law,[c] both of them must be put to death. What they have
done is a perversion; their blood will be on their own heads.

20:13 [d]Lev 18:22 13 " 'If a man lies with a man as one lies with a woman, both of them have done what is detestable.[d]
They must be put to death; their blood will be on their own heads.

20:14 [e]Lev 18:17 [f]Dt 27:23 14 " 'If a man marries both a woman and her mother,[e] it is wicked. Both he and they must be burned
in the fire, so that no wickedness will be among you.[f]

20:15 [g]Lev 18:23 15 " 'If a man has sexual relations with an animal,[g] he must be put to death, and you must kill the animal.

16 " 'If a woman approaches an animal to have sexual relations with it, kill both the woman and the
animal. They must be put to death; their blood will be on their own heads.

20:17 [h]Lev 18:9 17 " 'If a man marries his sister[h], the daughter of either his father or his mother, and they have sexu-
al relations, it is a disgrace. They must be cut off before the eyes of their people. He has dishonored his
sister and will be held responsible.

20:18 [i]Lev 15:24; 18:19 18 " 'If a man lies with a woman during her monthly period[i] and has sexual relations with her, he has
exposed the source of her flow, and she has also uncovered it. Both of them must be cut off from their
people.

20:19 [j]Lev 18:12-13 19 " 'Do not have sexual relations with the sister of either your mother or your father,[j] for that would
dishonor a close relative; both of you would be held responsible.

20:20 [k]Lev 18:14 20 " 'If a man sleeps with his aunt,[k] he has dishonored his uncle. They will be held responsible; they
will die childless.

20:21 [l]Lev 18:16 21 " 'If a man marries his brother's wife,[l] it is an act of impurity; he has dishonored his brother. They
will be childless.

20:22 [m]Lev 18:25-28 22 " 'Keep all my decrees and laws and follow them, so that the land[m] where I am bringing you to live
20:23 [n]Lev 18:3 [o]Lev 18:24,27,30 may not vomit you out. 23 You must not live according to the customs of the nations[n] I am going to drive
out before you.[o] Because they did all these things, I abhorred them. 24 But I said to you, "You will possess
20:24 [p]Ex 3:8; 13:5; 33:3 [q]Ex 33:16 their land; I will give it to you as an inheritance, a land flowing with milk and honey."[p] I am the LORD
your God, who has set you apart from the nations.[q]

25 " 'You must therefore make a distinction between clean and unclean animals and between unclean
20:25 [r]Lev 11:1-47; Dt 14:3-21 and clean birds.[r] Do not defile yourselves by any animal or bird or anything that moves along the
ground—those which I have set apart as unclean for you. 26 You are to be holy to me[b] because I, the LORD,
20:26 [s]Lev 19:2 am holy,[s] and I have set you apart from the nations to be my own.

20:27 [t]Lev 19:31 27 " 'A man or woman who is a medium or spiritist among you must be put to death.[t] You are to stone
them; their blood will be on their own heads.' "

Rules for Priests

21 The LORD said to Moses, "Speak to the priests, the sons of Aaron, and say to them: 'A priest must
21:1 [u]Eze 44:25 not make himself ceremonially unclean for any of his people who die,[u] 2 except for a close rela-
tive, such as his mother or father, his son or daughter, his brother, 3 or an unmarried sister who is depen-
dent on him since she has no husband—for her he may make himself unclean. 4 He must not make him-
self unclean for people related to him by marriage,[c] and so defile himself.

[a] 8 Or *who sanctifies you*; or *who sets you apart as holy* [b] 26 Or *be my holy ones* [c] 4 Or *unclean as a leader among his people*

5" 'Priests must not shave their heads or shave off the edges of their beards[v] or cut their bodies.[w]
6They must be holy to their God and must not profane the name of their God.[x] Because they present the
offerings made to the LORD by fire,[y] the food of their God, they are to be holy.
7" 'They must not marry women defiled by prostitution or divorced from their husbands,[z] because
priests are holy to their God.[a] 8Regard them as holy,[b] because they offer up the food of your God. Con-
sider them holy, because I the LORD am holy—I who make you holy.[a]
9" 'If a priest's daughter defiles herself by becoming a prostitute, she disgraces her father; she must
be burned in the fire.[c]
10" 'The high priest, the one among his brothers who has had the anointing oil poured on his head and
who has been ordained to wear the priestly garments,[d] must not let his hair become unkempt[b] or tear
his clothes.[e] 11He must not enter a place where there is a dead body.[f] He must not make himself un-
clean,[g] even for his father or mother, 12nor leave the sanctuary of his God or desecrate it, because he has
been dedicated by the anointing oil[h] of his God. I am the LORD.
13" 'The woman he marries must be a virgin.[i] 14He must not marry a widow, a divorced woman, or a
woman defiled by prostitution, but only a virgin from his own people, 15so he will not defile his offspring
among his people. I am the LORD, who makes him holy.[c] ' "
16The LORD said to Moses, 17"Say to Aaron: 'For the generations to come none of your descendants
who has a defect may come near to offer the food of his God.[j] 18No man who has any defect[k] may come
near: no man who is blind or lame, disfigured or deformed; 19no man with a crippled foot or hand, 20or
who is hunchbacked or dwarfed, or who has any eye defect, or who has festering or running sores or
damaged testicles.[l] 21No descendant of Aaron the priest who has any defect is to come near to present
the offerings made to the LORD by fire. He has a defect; he must not come near to offer the food of his God.
22He may eat the most holy food of his God,[m] as well as the holy food; 23yet because of his defect, he must
not go near the curtain or approach the altar, and so desecrate my sanctuary. I am the LORD, who makes
them holy.[d] ' "
24So Moses told this to Aaron and his sons and to all the Israelites.

22 The LORD said to Moses, 2"Tell Aaron and his sons to treat with respect the sacred offerings the
Israelites consecrate to me, so they will not profane my holy name. I am the LORD.
3"Say to them: 'For the generations to come, if any of your descendants is ceremonially unclean and
yet comes near the sacred offerings that the Israelites consecrate to the LORD, that person must be cut off
from my presence.[n] I am the LORD.
4" 'If a descendant of Aaron has an infectious skin disease[e] or a bodily discharge,[o] he may not eat the
sacred offerings until he is cleansed. He will also be unclean if he touches something defiled by a corpse[p]
or by anyone who has an emission of semen, 5or if he touches any crawling thing[q] that makes him un-
clean, or any person[r] who makes him unclean, whatever the uncleanness may be. 6The one who touch-
es any such thing will be unclean till evening. He must not eat any of the sacred offerings unless he has
bathed himself with water. 7When the sun goes down, he will be clean, and after that he may eat the sa-
cred offerings, for they are his food.[s] 8He must not eat anything found dead[t] or torn by wild animals,[u]
and so become unclean[v] through it. I am the LORD.
9" 'The priests are to keep my requirements so that they do not become guilty and die[w] for treating
them with contempt. I am the LORD, who makes them holy.[f]
10" 'No one outside a priest's family may eat the sacred offering, nor may the guest of a priest or his
hired worker eat it. 11But if a priest buys a slave with money, or if a slave is born in his household, that
slave may eat his food.[x] 12If a priest's daughter marries anyone other than a priest, she may not eat any
of the sacred contributions. 13But if a priest's daughter becomes a widow or is divorced, yet has no chil-
dren, and she returns to live in her father's house as in her youth, she may eat of her father's food. No un-
authorized person, however, may eat any of it.
14" 'If anyone eats a sacred offering by mistake, he must make restitution to the priest for the offer-
ing and add a fifth of the value[y] to it. 15The priests must not desecrate the sacred offerings the Israelites
present to the LORD[z] 16by allowing them to eat the sacred offerings and so bring upon them guilt requir-
ing payment.[a] I am the LORD, who makes them holy.' "

21:5 [v]Eze 44:20 [w]Lev 19:28; Dt 14:1
21:6 [x]Lev 18:21 [y]Lev 3:11
21:7 [z]ver 13,14
21:7 [a]Eze 44:22
21:8 [b]ver 6
21:9 [c]Ge 38:24; Lev 19:29
21:10 [d]Lev 16:32 [e]Lev 10:6
21:11 [f]Nu 19:11, 13,14 [g]Lev 19:28
21:12 [h]Ex 29:6-7; Lev 10:7
21:13 [i]Eze 44:22
21:17 [j]ver 6
21:18 [k]Lev 22:19-25
21:20 [l]Dt 23:1; Isa 56:3
21:22 [m]1Co 9:13
22:3 [n]Lev 7:20, 21; Nu 19:13
22:4 [o]Lev 14:1-32; 15:2-15 [p]Lev 11:24-28,39
22:5 [q]Lev 11:24-28,43 [r]Lev 15:7
22:7 [s]Nu 18:11
22:8 [t]Lev 11:39 [u]Ex 22:31; Lev 17:15 [v]Lev 11:40
22:9 [w]ver 16; Ex 28:43
22:11 [x]Ge 17:13; Ex 12:44
22:14 [y]Lev 5:15
22:15 [z]Nu 18:32
22:16 [a]ver 9

[a] 8 Or *who sanctify you*; or *who set you apart as holy* [b] 10 Or *not uncover his head* [c] 15 Or *who sanctifies him*; or *who sets him apart as holy* [d] 23 Or *who sanctifies them*; or *who sets them apart as holy* [e] 4 Traditionally *leprosy*; the Hebrew word was used for various diseases affecting the skin—not necessarily leprosy. [f] 9 Or *who sanctifies them*; or *who sets them apart as holy*; also in verse 16

Unacceptable Sacrifices

17 The LORD said to Moses, 18 "Speak to Aaron and his sons and to all the Israelites and say to them: 'If any of you—either an Israelite or an alien living in Israel—presents a gift[b] for a burnt offering to the LORD, either to fulfill a vow or as a freewill offering, 19 you must present a male without defect[c] from the cattle, sheep or goats in order that it may be accepted on your behalf. 20 Do not bring anything with a defect,[d] because it will not be accepted on your behalf. 21 When anyone brings from the herd or flock a fellowship offering[a][e] to the LORD to fulfill a special vow or as a freewill offering, it must be without defect or blemish to be acceptable. 22 Do not offer to the LORD the blind, the injured or the maimed, or anything with warts or festering or running sores. Do not place any of these on the altar as an offering made to the LORD by fire. 23 You may, however, present as a freewill offering an ox[b] or a sheep that is deformed or stunted, but it will not be accepted in fulfillment of a vow. 24 You must not offer to the LORD an animal whose testicles are bruised, crushed, torn or cut.[f] You must not do this in your own land, 25 and you must not accept such animals from the hand of a foreigner and offer them as the food of your God.[g] They will not be accepted on your behalf, because they are deformed and have defects.' "

26 The LORD said to Moses, 27 "When a calf, a lamb or a goat is born, it is to remain with its mother for seven days.[h] From the eighth day on, it will be acceptable as an offering made to the LORD by fire. 28 Do not slaughter a cow or a sheep and its young on the same day.[i]

29 "When you sacrifice a thank offering[j] to the LORD, sacrifice it in such a way that it will be accepted on your behalf. 30 It must be eaten that same day; leave none of it till morning.[k] I am the LORD.

31 "Keep[l] my commands and follow them. I am the LORD. 32 Do not profane my holy name.[m] I must be acknowledged as holy by the Israelites.[n] I am the LORD, who makes[c] you holy[d] 33 and who brought you out of Egypt to be your God.[o] I am the LORD."

22:18 [b]Lev 1:2
22:19 [c]Lev 1:3
22:20 [d]Dt 15:21; 17:1; Mal 1:8,14; Heb 9:14; 1Pe 1:19
22:21 [e]Lev 3:6; Nu 15:3,8
22:24 [f]Lev 21:20
22:25 [g]Lev 21:6
22:27 [h]Ex 22:30
22:28 [i]Dt 22:6,7
22:29 [j]Lev 7:12; Ps 107:22
22:30 [k]Lev 7:15
22:31 [l]Dt 4:2,40; Ps 105:45
22:32 [m]Lev 18:21 [n]Lev 10:3
22:33 [o]Lev 11:45

23

The LORD said to Moses, 2 "Speak to the Israelites and say to them: 'These are my appointed feasts,[p] the appointed feasts of the LORD, which you are to proclaim as sacred assemblies.[q]

The Sabbath

3 " 'There are six days when you may work,[r] but the seventh day is a Sabbath of rest,[s] a day of sacred assembly. You are not to do any work; wherever you live, it is a Sabbath to the LORD.

The Passover and Unleavened Bread

4 " 'These are the LORD's appointed feasts, the sacred assemblies you are to proclaim at their appointed times: 5 The LORD's Passover begins at twilight on the fourteenth day of the first month.[t] 6 On the fifteenth day of that month the LORD's Feast of Unleavened Bread begins; for seven days you must eat bread made without yeast. 7 On the first day hold a sacred assembly[u] and do no regular work. 8 For seven days present an offering made to the LORD by fire. And on the seventh day hold a sacred assembly and do no regular work.' "

Firstfruits

9 The LORD said to Moses, 10 "Speak to the Israelites and say to them: 'When you enter the land I am going to give you and you reap its harvest, bring to the priest a sheaf[v] of the first grain you harvest. 11 He is to wave the sheaf before the LORD[w] so it will be accepted on your behalf; the priest is to wave it on the day after the Sabbath. 12 On the day you wave the sheaf, you must sacrifice as a burnt offering to the LORD a lamb a year old without defect, 13 together with its grain offering[x] of two-tenths of an ephah[e] of fine flour mixed with oil—an offering made to the LORD by fire, a pleasing aroma—and its drink offering of a

23:2 [p]ver 4,37, 44; Nu 29:39 [q]ver 21,27
23:3 [r]Ex 20:9 [s]Ex 20:10; 31:13-17; Lev 19:3; Dt 5:13; Heb 4:9, 10
23:5 [t]Ex 12:18-19; Nu 28:16-17; Dt 16:1-8
23:7 [u]ver 3,8
23:10 [v]Ex 23:16, 19; 34:26
23:11 [w]Ex 29:24
23:13 [x]Lev 2:14-16; 6:20

[a] *21* Traditionally *peace offering* [b] *23* The Hebrew word can include both male and female. [c] *32* Or *made* [d] *32* Or *who sanctifies you;* or *who sets you apart as holy* [e] *13* That is, probably about 4 quarts (about 4.5 liters); also in verse 17

23:3 The feast of the weekly Sabbath stood at the head of the sacred seasons. The holy meetings by which the Sabbath was distinguished were quite local. Families and other small groups assembled under the guidance of Levites or elders and engaged in common acts of devotion, the forms and manner of which were not prescribed. Little is known of where or how the people met before the captivity; afterward they assembled in synagogues and were led in worship by teachers learned in the Law.

23:10 In acknowledgment of the fact that all the products of the land came from God, and to demonstrate thankfulness for his goodness, Israelites brought as an offering a portion of their fruits that ripened first. These were looked upon as a pledge of the coming harvest. Such an offering was made both on behalf of the nation (vv. 10,17) and by individuals (Ex 23:19; Dt 26:1–11). These firstfruits went for the support of the priesthood.

23:13 Drink offerings were not independent offerings under the law but were made only in connection with the grain offering that accompanied all burnt offerings and all fellowship offerings that were Nazirite,

CULTURAL AND HISTORICAL NOTES

The Festivals of Israel

LEVITICUS 23 God summoned the Israelites to worship and to celebrate various feasts he had appointed (Lev 23:2–6). During these holy convocations the priests presented sacrifices and other offerings, while the common people rested from their daily labor, sometimes fasting and sometimes feasting, and celebrated the seasonal blessings of God and the great redemptive moments in the lives of his people. Following a sabbatical principle, pre-exilic Israel observed seven annual feasts (ch. 23; cf. Nu 28–29; Dt 16:1–17).

A booth, as would have been used for the Festival of Booths (Tabernacles)

Preserving Bible Times; © Dr. James C. Martin

✣ *Passover* was celebrated on the tenth day of the first month of the Hebrew calendar (our late March to early April). According to Exodus 12:26–27, when subsequent generations inquired about the meaning of the Passover, they were to be told that it commemorated the manner in which the Lord had spared the Israelites the night he struck down the Egyptians' firstborn sons (Ex 12:29–30). Jesus' Last Supper was a Passover meal.[1] Jesus Christ is accordingly described in the New Testament as "our Passover lamb" (1Co 5:7) and as "the Lamb, who was slain" (Rev 5:12).

✣ *The Feast of Unleavened Bread* immediately followed the Passover (Ex 12:15–20) and lasted for one week. In the context of the **exodus**, eating bread without yeast signified hasty preparation and a readiness to depart. Yeast, which was studiously avoided during this feast, became a symbol of the pervasive influence of evil (cf. Mk 8:15; 1Co 5:7–8).

✣ *The Offering of Firstfruits* took place at the beginning of the harvest and signified Israel's gratitude to and dependence upon God (Lev 23:9–14). It occurred in conjunction with the Feast of Unleavened Bread and focused on the barley harvest, but there was also an offering of firstfruits associated with the Feast of Weeks or Pentecost (see below) in celebration of the wheat harvest (Nu 28:26–31).

✣ *The Feast of Weeks* or *Pentecost* (Lev 23:15–21), occurring seven weeks after Passover, was a day of sacred assembly in which no work was allowed. Its primary focus was an expression of gratitude to God for the wheat harvest. Verses 17–20 and Numbers 28:27–30 delineate detailed lists of what the priests were to offer to God on behalf of the nation.

✣ *The Feast of Trumpets*, celebrated on the first day of the seventh Hebrew month (Lev 23:23–25; Nu 29:1–6), marked the end of the agricultural year. The seventh month was important because it also included two major holy days—the Day of Atonement[2] and the Feast of Booths. The blasting of trumpets announced the commencement of this special month.

The Israelites associated the sound of trumpets with the theophany (visible manifestation of God) on Mount Sinai (Ex 19:16–19). Priests had also sounded trumpets prior to the destruction of Jericho (Jos 6:16), and trumpets were regularly used in Israel as a military signal (2Sa 2:28). Thus, the blast of trumpets at the onset of the seventh month added to the solemnity of this sacred season.[3]

✣ *The Day of Atonement* (see Lev 16)[2] focused exclusively on atonement for the sins of the people. This ceremony took place on the tenth day of the seventh month. The high priest made atonement first for himself and his family and finally for all the people. Coming at the end of the agricultural year, this feast symbolized a final reckoning before God.

✣ *The Feast of Booths* (also called the Feast of Tabernacles or *Sukkoth*) took place five days after the Day of Atonement (Nu 29:12–40). The people "camped out" in small huts during this time in order to recall their temporary living quarters prior to taking the land of **Canaan** (Lev 23:43). This joyous week was a time of final celebration and thanksgiving for the year's harvest (Dt 16:14–15). As the seventh and last annual feast, the Feast of Booths also represented the Sabbath principle.[4]

[1]See "The Last Supper and the Passover" on page 1611. [2]See "The Day of Atonement" on page 176. [3]See "Trumpets in the Ancient World" on page 2057. [4]See "Sabbath, Sabbath Year and the Jubilee" on page 189.

quarter of a hin[a] of wine. 14You must not eat any bread, or roasted or new grain, until the very day you
23:14 [y]Ex 34:26 [z]Nu 15:21 bring this offering to your God.[y] This is to be a lasting ordinance for the generations to come,[z] wherever
you live.

Feast of Weeks

15" 'From the day after the Sabbath, the day you brought the sheaf of the wave offering, count off sev-
23:16 [a]Nu 28:26; Ac 2:1 en full weeks. 16Count off fifty days up to the day after the seventh Sabbath,[a] and then present an offering
of new grain to the LORD. 17From wherever you live, bring two loaves made of two-tenths of an ephah of
23:17 [b]Ex 34:22; Lev 2:12 fine flour, baked with yeast, as a wave offering of firstfruits[b] to the LORD. 18Present with this bread seven
male lambs, each a year old and without defect, one young bull and two rams. They will be a burnt of-
fering to the LORD, together with their grain offerings and drink offerings—an offering made by fire, an
aroma pleasing to the LORD. 19Then sacrifice one male goat for a sin offering and two lambs, each a year
old, for a fellowship offering.[b] 20The priest is to wave the two lambs before the LORD as a wave offering,
together with the bread of the firstfruits. They are a sacred offering to the LORD for the priest. 21On that
23:21 [c]ver 2 [d]ver 3 same day you are to proclaim a sacred assembly[c] and do no regular work.[d] This is to be a lasting ordi-
nance for the generations to come, wherever you live.
23:22 [e]Lev 19:9 [f]Lev 19:10; Dt 24:19-21; Ru 2:15 22" 'When you reap the harvest[e] of your land, do not reap to the very edges of your field or gather the
gleanings of your harvest.[f] Leave them for the poor and the alien. I am the LORD your God.' "

Feast of Trumpets

23The LORD said to Moses, 24"Say to the Israelites: 'On the first day of the seventh month you are to
23:24 [g]Lev 25:9; Nu 10:9,10; 29:1 have a day of rest, a sacred assembly commemorated with trumpet blasts.[g] 25Do no regular work,[h] but
23:25 [h]ver 21 present an offering made to the LORD by fire.' "

Day of Atonement

23:27 [i]Lev 16:29 [j]Ex 30:10 [k]Nu 29:7 26The LORD said to Moses, 27"The tenth day of this seventh month[i] is the Day of Atonement.[j] Hold a
sacred assembly[k] and deny yourselves,[c] and present an offering made to the LORD by fire. 28Do no work
on that day, because it is the Day of Atonement, when atonement is made for you before the LORD your
23:29 [l]Ge 17:14; Nu 5:2 God. 29Anyone who does not deny himself on that day must be cut off from his people.[l] 30I will destroy
23:30 [m]Lev 20:3 from among his people[m] anyone who does any work on that day. 31You shall do no work at all. This is to
be a lasting ordinance for the generations to come, wherever you live. 32It is a sabbath of rest for you, and
you must deny yourselves. From the evening of the ninth day of the month until the following evening
you are to observe your sabbath."

Feast of Tabernacles

33The LORD said to Moses, 34"Say to the Israelites: 'On the fifteenth day of the seventh month the LORD's
23:34 [n]Ex 23:16; Dt 16:13; Ezr 3:4; Ne 8:14; Zec 14:16; Jn 7:2 Feast of Tabernacles[n] begins, and it lasts for seven days. 35The first day is a sacred assembly; do no regu-
lar work. 36For seven days present offerings made to the LORD by fire, and on the eighth day hold a sacred
23:36 [o]2Ch 7:9; Ne 8:18; Jn 7:37 assembly[o] and present an offering made to the LORD by fire. It is the closing assembly; do no regular work.
37(" 'These are the LORD's appointed feasts, which you are to proclaim as sacred assemblies for bring-
ing offerings made to the LORD by fire—the burnt offerings and grain offerings, sacrifices and drink of-
23:37 [p]ver 2,4 ferings[p] required for each day. 38These offerings are in addition to those for the LORD's Sabbaths[q] and[d]
23:38 [q]Eze 45:17 in addition to your gifts and whatever you have vowed and all the freewill offerings you give to the LORD.)
39" 'So beginning with the fifteenth day of the seventh month, after you have gathered the crops of
23:39 [r]Ex 23:16; Dt 16:13 the land, celebrate the festival to the LORD for seven days;[r] the first day is a day of rest, and the eighth day

[a] *13* That is, probably about 1 quart (about 1 liter) [b] *19* Traditionally *peace offering* [c] *27* Or *and fast*; also in verses 29 and 32
[d] *38* Or *These feasts are in addition to the LORD's Sabbaths, and these offerings are*

---

votive or freewill (Nu 6:17; 15:1–2). Drink offerings did not accompany sin or guilt offerings. These offerings consisted of wine, which was poured out on the altar, probably on the flesh of the sacrifice.

23:15–22 See "Pentecost" on page 275.

23:22 Grain crops were reaped with sickles, after which the cut stalks were laid in bunches that were carried to the threshing floor (see "The Threshing Floor" on p. 608). Some laws governed these simple harvest operations. The corners of the fields were not to be reaped, and the scatterings of the cut grain were not to be picked up. The part of the crop thus left was for the use of the poor (v. 22). The owner of a field was required each year to present the firstfruits of his crop as an offering to God before he could take any of it for his own use (vv. 10,14; see the note on v. 10). Beyond this, stalks of grain that had grown up without having been sown were not to be harvested (25:5). With regard to a new orchard or vineyard the fruit was not to be gathered for three years, and the fourth year's crop had to be given entirely to the Lord. So the owner had to wait until the fifth year to reap any of the fruit for himself (19:23–25).

also is a day of rest. 40 On the first day you are to take choice fruit from the trees, and palm fronds, leafy branches and poplars,[s] and rejoice before the LORD your God for seven days. 41 Celebrate this as a festival to the LORD for seven days each year. This is to be a lasting ordinance for the generations to come; celebrate it in the seventh month. 42 Live in booths[t] for seven days: All native-born Israelites are to live in booths 43 so your descendants will know[u] that I had the Israelites live in booths when I brought them out of Egypt. I am the LORD your God.' "

44 So Moses announced to the Israelites the appointed feasts of the LORD.

Oil and Bread Set Before the LORD

24 The LORD said to Moses, 2 "Command the Israelites to bring you clear oil of pressed olives for the light so that the lamps may be kept burning continually. 3 Outside the curtain of the Testimony in the Tent of Meeting, Aaron is to tend the lamps before the LORD from evening till morning, continually. This is to be a lasting ordinance for the generations to come. 4 The lamps on the pure gold lampstand[v] before the LORD must be tended continually.

5 "Take fine flour and bake twelve loaves of bread,[w] using two-tenths of an ephah[a] for each loaf. 6 Set them in two rows, six in each row, on the table of pure gold[x] before the LORD. 7 Along each row put some pure incense as a memorial portion[y] to represent the bread and to be an offering made to the LORD by fire. 8 This bread is to be set out before the LORD regularly,[z] Sabbath after Sabbath,[a] on behalf of the Israelites, as a lasting covenant. 9 It belongs to Aaron and his sons,[b] who are to eat it in a holy place, because it is a most holy part of their regular share of the offerings made to the LORD by fire."

A Blasphemer Stoned

10 Now the son of an Israelite mother and an Egyptian father went out among the Israelites, and a fight broke out in the camp between him and an Israelite. 11 The son of the Israelite woman blasphemed the Name[c] with a curse; so they brought him to Moses. (His mother's name was Shelomith, the daughter of Dibri the Danite.) 12 They put him in custody until the will of the LORD should be made clear to them.[d]

13 Then the LORD said to Moses: 14 "Take the blasphemer outside the camp. All those who heard him are to lay their hands on his head, and the entire assembly is to stone him.[e] 15 Say to the Israelites: 'If anyone curses his God,[f] he will be held responsible; 16 anyone who blasphemes the name of the LORD must be put to death.[g] The entire assembly must stone him. Whether an alien or native-born, when he blasphemes the Name, he must be put to death.

17 " 'If anyone takes the life of a human being, he must be put to death.[h] 18 Anyone who takes the life of someone's animal must make restitution[i]—life for life. 19 If anyone injures his neighbor, whatever he has done must be done to him: 20 fracture for fracture, eye for eye, tooth for tooth.[j] As he has injured the other, so he is to be injured. 21 Whoever kills an animal must make restitution, but whoever kills a man must be put to death.[k] 22 You are to have the same law for the alien[l] and the native-born.[m] I am the LORD your God.' "

23 Then Moses spoke to the Israelites, and they took the blasphemer outside the camp and stoned him. The Israelites did as the LORD commanded Moses.

The Sabbath Year

25 The LORD said to Moses on Mount Sinai, 2 "Speak to the Israelites and say to them: 'When you enter the land I am going to give you, the land itself must observe a sabbath to the LORD. 3 For six years sow your fields, and for six years prune your vineyards and gather their crops.[n] 4 But in the seventh year the land is to have a sabbath of rest, a sabbath to the LORD. Do not sow your fields or prune your vineyards. 5 Do not reap what grows of itself or harvest the grapes of your untended vines. The land is to have a year of rest. 6 Whatever the land yields during the sabbath year[o] will be food for you—for

23:40 [s]Ne 8:14-17
23:42 [t]Ne 8:14-16
23:43 [u]Dt 31:13; Ps 78:5
24:4 [v]Ex 25:31; 31:8
24:5 [w]Ex 25:30
24:6 [x]Ex 25:23-30; 1Ki 7:48
24:7 [y]Lev 2:2
24:8 [z]Nu 4:7; 1Ch 9:32; 2Ch 2:4 [a]Mt 12:5
24:9 [b]Lev 8:31; Mt 12:4; Mk 2:26; Lk 6:4
24:11 [c]Ex 3:15
24:12 [d]Ex 18:16; Nu 15:34
24:14 [e]Lev 20:27; Dt 13:9; 17:5,7; 21:21
24:15 [f]Ex 22:28
24:16 [g]1Ki 21:10, 13; Mt 26:66
24:17 [h]Ge 9:6; Ex 21:12; Nu 35:30-31; Dt 27:24
24:18 [i]ver 21
24:20 [j]Ex 21:24; Mt 5:38*
24:21 [k]ver 17
24:22 [l]Ex 12:49 [m]Nu 9:14; 15:16
25:3 [n]Ex 23:10
25:6 [o]ver 20

[a] 5 That is, probably about 4 quarts (about 4.5 liters)

24:8 The bread, signifying that God sustained his people, was eaten by the priests (v. 9).

24:20 The phrase "eye for eye, tooth for tooth" represents a statement of principle: The penalty was to fit the crime, not to exceed it. A similar law of retaliation is found in the Code of Hammurabi (an ancient Babylonian law code; see "Hammurabi" on p. 271), but it also seems not to have been literally applied. Jesus objected to an extremist use of this principle to excuse private vengeance (see Mt 5:38–42). On the subject of equality of punishment, see also the note on Deuteronomy 19:15–21.

25:1–55 For information concerning the sabbath year and the Year of Jubilee, see "Sabbath, Sabbath Year and the Jubilee" on page 189.

yourself, your manservant and maidservant, and the hired worker and temporary resident who live
among you, 7 as well as for your livestock and the wild animals in your land. Whatever the land produc-
es may be eaten.

The Year of Jubilee

8" 'Count off seven sabbaths of years—seven times seven years—so that the seven sabbaths of years
25:9 [p]Lev 23:24 amount to a period of forty-nine years. 9 Then have the trumpet[p] sounded everywhere on the tenth day
of the seventh month; on the Day of Atonement sound the trumpet throughout your land. 10 Consecrate
25:10 [q]Isa 61:1; the fiftieth year and proclaim liberty[q] throughout the land to all its inhabitants. It shall be a jubilee[r] for
Jer 34:8,15,17; Lk 4:19 [r]Nu 36:4 you; each one of you is to return to his family property and each to his own clan. 11 The fiftieth year shall
be a jubilee for you; do not sow and do not reap what grows of itself or harvest the untended vines. 12 For
it is a jubilee and is to be holy for you; eat only what is taken directly from the fields.
25:13 [s]ver 10 13" 'In this Year of Jubilee[s] everyone is to return to his own property.
25:14 [t]Lev 19:13; 1Sa 12:3,4 14" 'If you sell land to one of your countrymen or buy any from him, do not take advantage of each
25:15 [u]Lev 27:18,23 other.[t] 15 You are to buy from your countryman on the basis of the number of years[u] since the Jubilee. And
25:16 [v]ver 27,51, 52 he is to sell to you on the basis of the number of years left for harvesting crops. 16 When the years are
25:17 [w]Pr 22:22; Jer 7:5,6; 1Th 4:6 many, you are to increase the price, and when the years are few, you are to decrease the price,[v] because
[x]Lev 19:14 [y]Lev 19:32 what he is really selling you is the number of crops. 17 Do not take advantage of each other,[w] but fear your
25:18 [z]Lev 26:4, 5; Dt 12:10; God.[x] I am the LORD your God.[y]
Ps 4:8; Jer 23:6 18" 'Follow my decrees and be careful to obey my laws, and you will live safely in the land.[z] 19 Then
25:19 [a]Lev 26:4 the land will yield its fruit,[a] and you will eat your fill and live there in safety. 20 You may ask, "What will

Sabbath, Sabbath Year and the Jubilee

LEVITICUS 25 The Sabbath day, a day of rest from labor, occurred every seventh day in ancient Israel. The Sabbath day was intricately connected to God's covenant with his people. According to Deuteronomy 5:12–15 the purpose of the Sabbath was to remind God's people that they had been slaves in Egypt and that he had delivered them and brought them into the promised land, their "resting place" (see Dt 12:9; Ps 95:11).

Exodus 20:11 roots the Sabbath in creation, when the Lord blessed the Sabbath and "made it holy" (Ge 2:2–3). At the end of creation God's rest and his consecration of the seventh day as a Sabbath rest for humans became the sign of God's covenant with Israel. Failure to observe the Sabbath was tantamount to rejecting the covenant and thus resulted both in excommunication and divine punishment (cf. Ex 31:14; Ne 13:17–18; Eze 20:13).

According to Leviticus 25 the principle of the Sabbath day was extended to legislation of a "sabbatical year" every seven years and a "Jubilee" every fifty years (that is, after seven times seven years). Verse 4 stipulated that every seventh year the Israelites were to give the land a "sabbath of rest" and to allow anyone, including slaves and sojourners (temporary residents), to gather the produce that had grown that year. Then, every fiftieth year, following "seven sabbaths of years," those who had acquired others' ancestral lands were obligated to return them to their original owners (vv. 8–10). Israelite slaves were also to be released and allowed to return to their families (vv. 39–41).[1] Had this been practiced (it appears that the laws regarding the sabbath and Jubilee years went largely unheeded prior to the **exile**), this sabbatical system would have helped to restore social equality by checking the mass accumulation of wealth by a few, providing less fortunate Israelites a way out of permanent servitude and offering a second chance to debtors at least once during their lifetimes.

It is significant that the Jubilee was proclaimed on the Day of Atonement (v. 9), when all people—free and slave, landowner and tenant, as well as the land itself—were purified from sin and uncleanness (16:29–30). The Day of Atonement reminded the Israelites of their own forgiveness and deliverance from the curse of sin, and the release of slaves was to be their response to the grace of God.[2] Sabbath day, sabbath year and Jubilee each reaffirmed to the Israelites that their Creator and Redeemer owned the title to their land, as well as their very lives (25:23,55).

[1]See "Slavery and Labor Law in the Ancient Near East" on page 127. [2]See "The Day of Atonement" on page 176.

we eat in the seventh year[b] if we do not plant or harvest our crops?" 21 I will send you such a blessing[c]
in the sixth year that the land will yield enough for three years. 22 While you plant during the eighth
year, you will eat from the old crop and will continue to eat from it until the harvest of the ninth year
comes in.[d]
23 " 'The land must not be sold permanently, because the land is mine[e] and you are but aliens[f] and my
tenants. 24 Throughout the country that you hold as a possession, you must provide for the redemption
of the land.
25 " 'If one of your countrymen becomes poor and sells some of his property, his nearest relative[g] is
to come and redeem[h] what his countryman has sold. 26 If, however, a man has no one to redeem it for
him but he himself prospers and acquires sufficient means to redeem it, 27 he is to determine the value
for the years since he sold it and refund the balance to the man to whom he sold it; he can then go back
to his own property. 28 But if he does not acquire the means to repay him, what he sold will remain in the
possession of the buyer until the Year of Jubilee. It will be returned in the Jubilee, and he can then go
back to his property.[i]
29 " 'If a man sells a house in a walled city, he retains the right of redemption a full year after its sale.
During that time he may redeem it. 30 If it is not redeemed before a full year has passed, the house in the
walled city shall belong permanently to the buyer and his descendants. It is not to be returned in the
Jubilee. 31 But houses in villages without walls around them are to be considered as open country. They
can be redeemed, and they are to be returned in the Jubilee.
32 " 'The Levites always have the right to redeem their houses in the Levitical towns,[j] which they possess.
33 So the property of the Levites is redeemable—that is, a house sold in any town they hold—and is to be
returned in the Jubilee, because the houses in the towns of the Levites are their property among the Isra-
elites. 34 But the pastureland belonging to their towns must not be sold; it is their permanent possession.[k]
35 " 'If one of your countrymen becomes poor[l] and is unable to support himself among you, help him[m]
as you would an alien or a temporary resident, so he can continue to live among you. 36 Do not take in-
terest[n] of any kind[a] from him, but fear your God, so that your countryman may continue to live among
you. 37 You must not lend him money at interest or sell him food at a profit. 38 I am the LORD your God, who
brought you out of Egypt to give you the land of Canaan and to be your God.[o]
39 " 'If one of your countrymen becomes poor among you and sells himself to you, do not make him
work as a slave.[p] 40 He is to be treated as a hired worker or a temporary resident among you; he is to work
for you until the Year of Jubilee. 41 Then he and his children are to be released, and he will go back to his
own clan and to the property[q] of his forefathers. 42 Because the Israelites are my servants, whom I brought
out of Egypt, they must not be sold as slaves. 43 Do not rule over them ruthlessly,[r] but fear your God.
44 " 'Your male and female slaves are to come from the nations around you; from them you may buy
slaves. 45 You may also buy some of the temporary residents living among you and members of their clans
born in your country, and they will become your property. 46 You can will them to your children as inherit-
ed property and can make them slaves for life, but you must not rule over your fellow Israelites ruthlessly.
47 " 'If an alien or a temporary resident among you becomes rich and one of your countrymen be-
comes poor and sells himself to the alien living among you or to a member of the alien's clan, 48 he re-
tains the right of redemption after he has sold himself. One of his relatives[s] may redeem him: 49 An un-
cle or a cousin or any blood relative in his clan may redeem him. Or if he prospers,[t] he may redeem
himself. 50 He and his buyer are to count the time from the year he sold himself up to the Year of Jubilee.
The price for his release is to be based on the rate paid to a hired man[u] for that number of years. 51 If
many years remain, he must pay for his redemption a larger share of the price paid for him. 52 If only a
few years remain until the Year of Jubilee, he is to compute that and pay for his redemption accordingly.
53 He is to be treated as a man hired from year to year; you must see to it that his owner does not rule
over him ruthlessly.
54 " 'Even if he is not redeemed in any of these ways, he and his children are to be released in the Year
of Jubilee, 55 for the Israelites belong to me as servants. They are my servants, whom I brought out of
Egypt. I am the LORD your God.

[a] 36 Or *take excessive interest*; similarly in verse 37

25:20 [b]ver 4
25:21 [c]Dt 28:8, 12; Hag 2:19; Mal 3:10
25:22 [d]Lev 26:10
25:23 [e]Ex 19:5 [f]Ge 23:4; 1Ch 29:15; Ps 39:12; Heb 11:13; 1Pe 2:11
25:25 [g]Ru 2:20; Jer 32:7 [h]Lev 27:13,19,31; Ru 4:4
25:28 [i]ver 10
25:32 [j]Nu 35:1-8; Jos 21:2
25:34 [k]Nu 35:2-5
25:35 [l]Dt 24:14, 15 [m]Dt 15:8; Ps 37:21,26; Lk 6:35
25:36 [n]Ex 22:25; Dt 23:19-20
25:38 [o]Ge 17:7; Lev 11:45
25:39 [p]Ex 21:2; Dt 15:12; 1Ki 9:22
25:41 [q]ver 28
25:43 [r]Ex 1:13; Eze 34:4; Col 4:1
25:48 [s]Ne 5:5
25:49 [t]ver 26
25:50 [u]Job 7:1; Isa 16:14; 21:16

25:29–30 The chief feature distinguishing a city from a village was that it had a wall. Walls 20 and 30 feet (6 to 9 m) thick were not unusual. See "The Israelites Town and Home" on page 1205.

25:44–46 For commentary concerning slavery, see "Slavery and Labor Law in the Ancient Near East" on page 127.

Reward for Obedience

26 " 'Do not make idols[v] or set up an image or a sacred stone[w] for yourselves, and do not place a carved stone[x] in your land to bow down before it. I am the LORD your God.

2 " 'Observe my Sabbaths and have reverence for my sanctuary.[y] I am the LORD.

3 " 'If you follow my decrees and are careful to obey[z] my commands, 4 I will send you rain[a] in its season, and the ground will yield its crops and the trees of the field their fruit.[b] 5 Your threshing will continue until grape harvest and the grape harvest will continue until planting, and you will eat all the food you want[c] and live in safety in your land.[d]

6 " 'I will grant peace in the land,[e] and you will lie down[f] and no one will make you afraid.[g] I will remove savage beasts[h] from the land, and the sword will not pass through your country. 7 You will pursue your enemies, and they will fall by the sword before you. 8 Five of you will chase a hundred, and a hundred of you will chase ten thousand, and your enemies will fall by the sword before you.[i]

9 " 'I will look on you with favor and make you fruitful and increase your numbers,[j] and I will keep my covenant[k] with you. 10 You will still be eating last year's harvest when you will have to move it out to make room for the new.[l] 11 I will put my dwelling place[a][m] among you, and I will not abhor you. 12 I will walk[n] among you and be your God, and you will be my people.[o] 13 I am the LORD your God, who brought you out of Egypt so that you would no longer be slaves to the Egyptians; I broke the bars of your yoke[p] and enabled you to walk with heads held high.

Punishment for Disobedience

14 " 'But if you will not listen to me and carry out all these commands,[q] 15 and if you reject my decrees and abhor my laws and fail to carry out all my commands and so violate my covenant, 16 then I will do this to you: I will bring upon you sudden terror, wasting diseases and fever[r] that will destroy your sight and drain away your life.[s] You will plant seed in vain, because your enemies will eat it.[t] 17 I will set my face[u] against you so that you will be defeated by your enemies; those who hate you will rule over you,[v] and you will flee even when no one is pursuing you.[w]

18 " 'If after all this you will not listen to me, I will punish you for your sins seven times over.[x] 19 I will break down your stubborn pride[y] and make the sky above you like iron and the ground beneath you like bronze.[z] 20 Your strength will be spent in vain,[a] because your soil will not yield its crops, nor will the trees of the land yield their fruit.[b]

21 " 'If you remain hostile toward me and refuse to listen to me, I will multiply your afflictions seven times over,[c] as your sins deserve. 22 I will send wild animals[d] against you, and they will rob you of your children, destroy your cattle and make you so few in number that your roads will be deserted.

23 " 'If in spite of these things you do not accept my correction[e] but continue to be hostile toward me, 24 I myself will be hostile toward you and will afflict you for your sins seven times over. 25 And I will bring the sword upon you to avenge the breaking of the covenant. When you withdraw into your cities, I will send a plague[f] among you, and you will be given into enemy hands. 26 When I cut off your supply of bread,[g] ten women will be able to bake your bread in one oven, and they will dole out the bread by weight. You will eat, but you will not be satisfied.

27 " 'If in spite of this you still do not listen to me but continue to be hostile toward me, 28 then in my anger I will be hostile toward you, and I myself will punish you for your sins seven times over. 29 You will eat the flesh of your sons and the flesh of your daughters.[h] 30 I will destroy your high places,[i] cut down your incense altars[j] and pile your dead bodies on the lifeless forms of your idols,[k] and I will abhor you. 31 I will turn your cities into ruins and lay waste your sanctuaries,[l] and I will take no delight in the pleasing aroma of your offerings. 32 I will lay waste the land,[m] so that your enemies who live there will be appalled. 33 I will scatter you among the nations[n] and will draw out my sword and pursue you. Your land will be laid waste, and your cities will lie in ruins. 34 Then the land will enjoy its sabbath years all the time that it lies desolate and you are in the country of your enemies;[o] then the land will rest and enjoy its sabbaths. 35 All the time that it lies desolate, the land will have the rest it did not have during the sabbaths you lived in it.

36 " 'As for those of you who are left, I will make their hearts so fearful in the lands of their enemies that the sound of a windblown leaf will put them to flight.[p] They will run as though fleeing from the sword, and they will fall, even though no one is pursuing them. 37 They will stumble over one another

26:1 [v]Ex 20:4; Lev 19:4; Dt 5:8 [w]Ex 23:24 [x]Nu 33:52
26:2 [y]Lev 19:30
26:3 [z]Dt 7:12; 11:13,22; 28:1,9
26:4 [a]Dt 11:14 [b]Ps 67:6
26:5 [c]Dt 11:15; Joel 2:19,26; Am 9:13 [d]Lev 25:18
26:6 [e]Ps 29:11; 85:8; 147:14 [f]Ps 4:8 [g]Zep 3:13 [h]ver 22
26:8 [i]Dt 32:30; Jos 23:10
26:9 [j]Ge 17:6; Ne 9:23 [k]Ge 17:7
26:10 [l]Lev 25:22
26:11 [m]Ex 25:8; Ps 76:2; Eze 37:27
26:12 [n]Ge 3:8 [o]2Co 6:16*
26:13 [p]Eze 34:27
26:14 [q]Dt 28:15-68; Mal 2:2
26:16 [r]Dt 28:22,35 [s]1Sa 2:33 [t]Job 31:8
26:17 [u]Lev 17:10 [v]Ps 106:41 [w]ver 36,37; Dt 28:7,25; Ps 53:5
26:18 [x]ver 21
26:19 [y]Isa 25:11 [z]Dt 28:23
26:20 [a]Ps 127:1; Isa 17:11 [b]Dt 11:17
26:21 [c]ver 18
26:22 [d]Dt 32:24
26:23 [e]Jer 2:30; 5:3
26:25 [f]Nu 14:12; Eze 5:17
26:26 [g]Ps 105:16; Isa 3:1; Mic 6:14
26:29 [h]Dt 28:53
26:30 [i]2Ch 34:3; Eze 6:3 [j]Eze 6:6 [k]Eze 6:13
26:31 [l]Ps 74:3-7
26:32 [m]Jer 9:11
26:33 [n]Dt 4:27; Eze 12:15; 20:23; Zec 7:14
26:34 [o]ver 43; 2Ch 36:21
26:36 [p]Eze 21:7

[a] *11* Or *my tabernacle*

as though fleeing from the sword, even though no one is pursuing them. So you will not be able to
stand before your enemies.[q] 38You will perish among the nations; the land of your enemies will devour
you.[r] 39Those of you who are left will waste away in the lands of their enemies because of their sins;
also because of their fathers' sins they will waste away.[s]
40" 'But if they will confess their sins and the sins of their fathers[t]—their treachery against me
and their hostility toward me, 41which made me hostile toward them so that I sent them into the
land of their enemies—then when their uncircumcised hearts[u] are humbled and they pay for their
sin, 42I will remember my covenant with Jacob[v] and my covenant with Isaac[w] and my covenant
with Abraham, and I will remember the land. 43For the land will be deserted by them and will en-
joy its sabbaths while it lies desolate without them. They will pay for their sins because they re-
jected my laws and abhorred my decrees. 44Yet in spite of this, when they are in the land of their
enemies, I will not reject them or abhor[x] them so as to destroy them completely,[y] breaking my cov-
enant[z] with them. I am the LORD their God. 45But for their sake I will remember[a] the covenant with
their ancestors whom I brought out of Egypt[b] in the sight of the nations to be their God. I am the
LORD.' "
46These are the decrees, the laws and the regulations that the LORD established on Mount Sinai be-
tween himself and the Israelites through Moses.[c]

Redeeming What Is the LORD's

27 The LORD said to Moses, 2"Speak to the Israelites and say to them: 'If anyone makes a special
vow[d] to dedicate persons to the LORD by giving equivalent values, 3set the value of a male be-
tween the ages of twenty and sixty at fifty shekels[a] of silver, according to the sanctuary shekel[b];[e] 4and if
it is a female, set her value at thirty shekels.[c] 5If it is a person between the ages of five and twenty, set the
value of a male at twenty shekels[d] and of a female at ten shekels.[e] 6If it is a person between one month
and five years, set the value of a male at five shekels[f][f] of silver and that of a female at three shekels[g] of sil-
ver. 7If it is a person sixty years old or more, set the value of a male at fifteen shekels[h] and of a female at
ten shekels. 8If anyone making the vow is too poor to pay[g] the specified amount, he is to present the per-
son to the priest, who will set the value[h] for him according to what the man making the vow can afford.
9" 'If what he vowed is an animal that is acceptable as an offering to the LORD, such an animal given
to the LORD becomes holy. 10He must not exchange it or substitute a good one for a bad one, or a bad one
for a good one;[i] if he should substitute one animal for another, both it and the substitute become holy.
11If what he vowed is a ceremonially unclean animal—one that is not acceptable as an offering to the
LORD—the animal must be presented to the priest, 12who will judge its quality as good or bad. Whatev-
er value the priest then sets, that is what it will be. 13If the owner wishes to redeem[j] the animal, he must
add a fifth to its value.
14" 'If a man dedicates his house as something holy to the LORD, the priest will judge its quality as
good or bad. Whatever value the priest then sets, so it will remain. 15If the man who dedicates his house
redeems it,[k] he must add a fifth to its value, and the house will again become his.
16" 'If a man dedicates to the LORD part of his family land, its value is to be set according to the amount
of seed required for it—fifty shekels of silver to a homer[i] of barley seed. 17If he dedicates his field dur-
ing the Year of Jubilee, the value that has been set remains. 18But if he dedicates his field after the Jubi-
lee, the priest will determine the value according to the number of years that remain[l] until the next Year
of Jubilee, and its set value will be reduced. 19If the man who dedicates the field wishes to redeem it, he
must add a fifth to its value, and the field will again become his. 20If, however, he does not redeem the
field, or if he has sold it to someone else, it can never be redeemed. 21When the field is released in the Ju-
bilee,[m] it will become holy, like a field devoted to the LORD;[n] it will become the property of the priests.[j]
22" 'If a man dedicates to the LORD a field he has bought, which is not part of his family land, 23the
priest will determine its value up to the Year of Jubilee, and the man must pay its value on that day as

26:37 [q]Jos 7:12
26:38 [r]Dt 4:26
26:39 [s]Eze 4:17
26:40 [t]Jer 3:12-15; Lk 15:18; 1Jn 1:9
26:41 [u]Eze 44:7, 9; Ac 7:51
26:42 [v]Ge 22:15-18; 28:15 [w]Ge 26:5
26:44 [x]Ro 11:2 [y]Dt 4:31; Jer 30:11 [z]Jer 33:26
26:45 [a]Ge 17:7 [b]Ex 6:8; Lev 25:38
26:46 [c]Lev 7:38; 27:34
27:2 [d]Nu 6:2
27:3 [e]Ex 30:13; Nu 3:47; 18:16
27:6 [f]Nu 18:16
27:8 [g]Lev 5:11 [h]ver 12,14
27:10 [i]ver 33
27:13 [j]ver 15,19; Lev 25:25
27:15 [k]ver 13,20
27:18 [l]Lev 25:15
27:21 [m]Lev 25:10 [n]ver 28; Nu 18:14; Eze 44:29

[a] *3* That is, about 1 1/4 pounds (about 0.6 kilogram); also in verse 16 [b] *3* That is, about 2/5 ounce (about 11.5 grams); also in verse 25 [c] *4* That is, about 12 ounces (about 0.3 kilogram) [d] *5* That is, about 8 ounces (about 0.2 kilogram) [e] *5* That is, about 4 ounces (about 110 grams); also in verse 7 [f] *6* That is, about 2 ounces (about 55 grams) [g] *6* That is, about 1 1/4 ounces (about 35 grams) [h] *7* That is, about 6 ounces (about 170 grams) [i] *16* That is, probably about 6 bushels (about 220 liters) [j] *21* Or *priest*

27:1–34 This final chapter concerns promises made to the Lord in kind: servants, animals, houses or lands. But provision was made for the option of giving money instead of the animal or item, in which case the addition of a fifth of its value was usually required.

something holy to the LORD. 24 In the Year of Jubilee the field will revert to the person from whom he
27:24 [o]Lev 25:28 27:25 [p]Ex 30:13; Nu 18:16 [q]Nu 3:47; Eze 45:12 bought it,[o] the one whose land it was. 25 Every value is to be set according to the sanctuary shekel,[p] twen-
ty gerahs[q] to the shekel.
26 " 'No one, however, may dedicate the firstborn of an animal, since the firstborn already belongs to the
27:26 [r]Ex 13:2, 12 LORD;[r] whether an ox[a] or a sheep, it is the LORD's. 27 If it is one of the unclean animals,[s] he may buy it back
27:27 [s]ver 11 at its set value, adding a fifth of the value to it. If he does not redeem it, it is to be sold at its set value.
27:28 [t]Nu 18:14; Jos 6:17-19 28 " 'But nothing that a man owns and devotes[b][t] to the LORD—whether man or animal or family
land—may be sold or redeemed; everything so devoted is most holy to the LORD.
29 " 'No person devoted to destruction[c] may be ransomed; he must be put to death.
27:30 [u]Ge 28:22; 2Ch 31:6; Mal 3:8 30 " 'A tithe[u] of everything from the land, whether grain from the soil or fruit from the trees, belongs
to the LORD; it is holy to the LORD. 31 If a man redeems any of his tithe, he must add a fifth of the value to
27:32 [v]Jer 33:13; Eze 20:37 it. 32 The entire tithe of the herd and flock—every tenth animal that passes under the shepherd's rod[v]—
27:33 [w]ver 10 will be holy to the LORD. 33 He must not pick out the good from the bad or make any substitution.[w] If he
does make a substitution, both the animal and its substitute become holy and cannot be redeemed.' "

27:34 [x]Lev 26:46; Dt 4:5 34 These are the commands the LORD gave Moses on Mount Sinai for the Israelites.[x]

[a] *26* The Hebrew word can include both male and female. [b] *28* The Hebrew term refers to the irrevocable giving over of things or persons to the LORD. [c] *29* The Hebrew term refers to the irrevocable giving over of things or persons to the LORD, often by totally destroying them.

INTRODUCTION TO 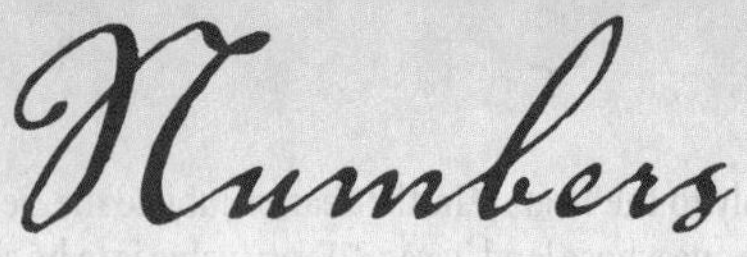

AUTHOR, PLACE AND DATE OF WRITING

Like the books of Exodus and Leviticus, Numbers repeatedly asserts that God gave specific laws and commands to Moses (e.g., 1:1; 3:44; 15:1). Combined with statements about Moses' writing (e.g., 33:1–2; cf. Ex 17:14; 24:3–4; 34:27) and the assumption that a single author composed the first five books of the Bible, Moses is traditionally considered among conservative evangelical scholars to have been the primary writer/compiler of Numbers. It is probable that scribes and/or editors later added portions of the book (see, e.g., 12:3).

Quite likely Moses wrote/compiled Numbers after the exodus period—probably around 1440 to 1400 B.C.

AUDIENCE

Israelites who survived the period of desert wandering, as well as their subsequent generations, read Numbers. No doubt they used this book to spur their memories regarding Israel's sins and failings, as well as to remember God's ongoing faithfulness toward his disobedient people.

CULTURAL FACTS AND HIGHLIGHTS

Numbers, which in Hebrew means "in the desert," records Israel's journey from Mount Sinai to the plains of Moab, on the border of the promised land. In the process we read stories, census lists, lists of offerings, a pagan prophet's oracles, more laws, a genealogy, a record of locations visited, details about the boundaries of Canaan—a truly diverse hodgepodge of topics. Yet various highlights stand out:

- God's willingness not only to live with the Israelites but also to speak directly with Moses (7:89).
- God's careful guidance as his people traveled—when to camp and when and where to travel (9:15–23).
- Israel's rebellious refusal to trust God and to enter the promised land (ch. 14).
- God's willingness to listen and even to change his mind (16:20–22).
- God's patience with his continually rebellious people, combined with various punishments.
- Moses' disobedience that prevented him from entering Canaan (ch. 20).
- God's love of holiness and hatred of such sins as idol worship and sexual immorality (ch. 25).

TIMELINE

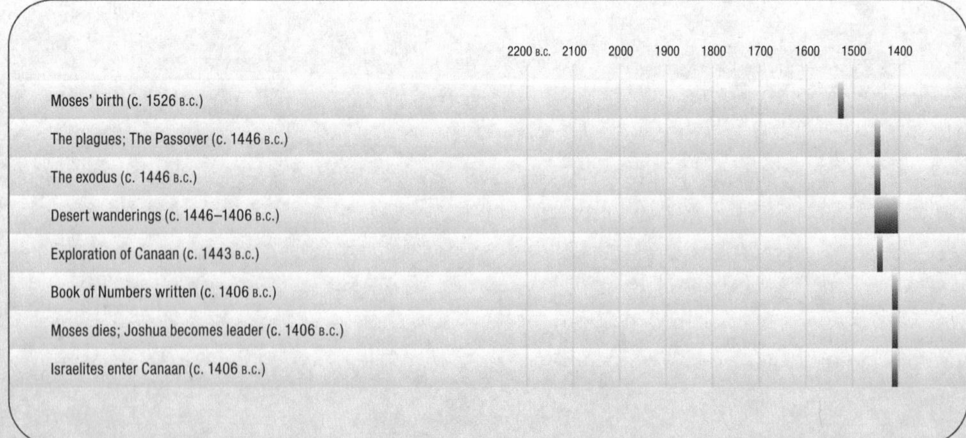

AS YOU READ

Despite the Israelites' ongoing disobedience, God had long before promised Abraham that his descendants would possess Canaan. God's commitment to keep that promise links together the narratives of Numbers. Notice his responses to the people's disobedience and his methods of preparing them for upcoming battles. Keep in mind, too, that the law-related passages continue to emphasize the people's relationship with God.

Pay close attention to all the Israelites' misadventures and try to imagine how tired Moses must have become in dealing with their complaints and rebellion. Again and again they disobeyed God, challenged Moses and gave generations of readers memorable examples of what *not* to do. Yet Numbers fills in key details about the Israelites' journey to Canaan and sets the stage for their upcoming conquest of the promised land.

DID YOU KNOW?

- The God-ordained test for an unfaithful wife was a means of protecting innocent women from false accusation by jealous husbands within a male-dominated court system (5:21–22).
- Trumpets—long, straight, slender metal tues, with flared ends—were blown for order and discipline (10:1–10).
- God waived his right to receive fulfillment of a dependent woman's vow in favor of preserving something highly valuable to him: harmony in the home (30:3–15).

THEMES

The book of Numbers includes the following themes:

1. *God's mercy and faithfulness.* Numbers shows God guiding (9:17) and comforting his people as he offers them forgiveness, reconciliation and hope. Their rebellion and unfaithfulness is contrasted with God's ever faithful love for his own (14:18).

2. *God's justice.* Numbers describes the grumbling, complaining and rebellion of the people (11:1,4–6; 13:1—14:45) and of their leaders (12:1–2; 16:1–11; 20:1–13) against God and his provisions. Although God is merciful, judgment follows repeated rebellion (11:1,33; 12:4–10; 14:11–37; 16:25–49; 20:12–13,24) and unbelief (14:1–38; Heb 3:16–19).

3. *Hope.* Disobedience brings judgment and pain (11:1,33; 14:39–45; 16:31–35), but repentance (11:2; 12:13–15; 16:22,46–48) and obedience (13:30; 14:24) result in forgiveness and hope (14:20; 15:25–26). Even after their repeated failures, God did not leave the Israelites to die in the desert. Through this and other notable events Numbers displays the truths that God is sovereign and that his plan will be accomplished.

OUTLINE

I. Israel at Sinai, Preparing to Leave for Canaan (1:1—10:10)
II. From Sinai to Kadesh (10:11—12:16)
III. Israel at Kadesh, the Delay Resulting From Rebellion (13:1—20:13)
IV. From Kadesh to the Plains of Moab (20:14—22:1)
V. Israel on the Plains of Moab, Anticipating the Taking of Canaan (22:2—32:42)
VI. Supplements Dealing With Various Matters (33–36)

The Census

1 The LORD spoke to Moses in the Tent of Meeting[a] in the Desert of Sinai[b] on the first day of the sec-
ond month[c] of the second year after the Israelites came out of Egypt. He said: 2"Take a census[d] of
the whole Israelite community by their clans and families, listing every man by name, one by one. 3You
and Aaron are to number by their divisions all the men in Israel twenty years old or more[e] who are able
to serve in the army. 4One man from each tribe, each the head of his family,[f] is to help you.[g] 5These are
the names of the men who are to assist you:

from Reuben,[h] Elizur son of Shedeur;
6from Simeon, Shelumiel son of Zurishaddai;
7from Judah,[i] Nahshon son of Amminadab;[j]
8from Issachar,[k] Nethanel son of Zuar;
9from Zebulun,[l] Eliab son of Helon;
10from the sons of Joseph:
from Ephraim,[m] Elishama son of Ammihud;
from Manasseh, Gamaliel son of Pedahzur;
11from Benjamin, Abidan son of Gideoni;
12from Dan,[n] Ahiezer son of Ammishaddai;
13from Asher,[o] Pagiel son of Ocran;
14from Gad, Eliasaph son of Deuel;[p]
15from Naphtali,[q] Ahira son of Enan."

16These were the men appointed from the community, the leaders[r] of their ancestral tribes. They were
the heads of the clans of Israel.[s]
17Moses and Aaron took these men whose names had been given, 18and they called the whole com-
munity together on the first day of the second month.[t] The people indicated their ancestry[u] by their
clans and families, and the men twenty years old or more were listed by name, one by one, 19as the LORD
commanded Moses. And so he counted them in the Desert of Sinai:

20From the descendants of Reuben[v] the firstborn son of Israel:
All the men twenty years old or more who were able to serve in the army were listed by name,
one by one, according to the records of their clans and families. 21The number from the tribe
of Reuben was 46,500.

22From the descendants of Simeon:[w]
All the men twenty years old or more who were able to serve in the army were counted and list-
ed by name, one by one, according to the records of their clans and families. 23The number
from the tribe of Simeon was 59,300.

24From the descendants of Gad:[x]
All the men twenty years old or more who were able to serve in the army were listed by name,
according to the records of their clans and families. 25The number from the tribe of Gad was
45,650.

26From the descendants of Judah:[y]
All the men twenty years old or more who were able to serve in the army were listed by name,
according to the records of their clans and families. 27The number from the tribe of Judah was
74,600.

1:1 [a]Ex 40:2 [b]Ex 19:1 [c]Ex 40:17
1:2 [d]Ex 30:11-16; Nu 26:2
1:3 [e]Ex 30:14
1:4 [f]ver 16 [g]Ex 18:21; Dt 1:15
1:5 [h]Ge 29:32; Dt 33:6; Rev 7:5
1:7 [i]Ge 29:35; Ps 78:68 [j]Ru 4:20; 1Ch 2:10; Lk 3:32
1:8 [k]Ge 30:18
1:9 [l]ver 30
1:10 [m]ver 32
1:12 [n]ver 38
1:13 [o]ver 40
1:14 [p]Nu 2:14
1:15 [q]ver 42
1:16 [r]Ex 18:25 [s]ver 4; Ex 18:21; Nu 7:2
1:18 [t]ver 1 [u]Ezr 2:59; Heb 7:3
1:20 [v]Nu 26:5-11; Rev 7:5
1:22 [w]Nu 26:12-14; Rev 7:7
1:24 [x]Ge 30:11; Nu 26:15-18; Rev 7:5
1:26 [y]Ge 29:35; Nu 26:19-22; Mt 1:2; Rev 7:5

1:1 The book of Numbers is called "In the Wilderness" by Jews. The Hebrew title is more meaningful than the English, as the book picks up the account of the wilderness wandering after the Israelites' arrival at Sinai (Ex 19) and records their Bedouin-like travels through the 40 years of wandering.

1:2–46 The name Numbers comes from the Greek translation, which gives a misleading impression of one of the features of the book. Both at the beginning (vv. 2–46) and near the end (26:2–51) of the book, the number of the Israelites is given. The procedure sounds familiar to us: We call it a census. But Israel was not merely interested in vital statistics. This was a count of the fighting forces; indeed, it probably involved an actual mustering and organizing of the army. For this reason the women, children and Levites were not included. The numbering occurs twice because the army was called up twice for battle—first at the abortive attempt to invade the land at Kadesh Barnea (see "Kadesh Barnea" on p. 214) and second at the end of the 40 years of wandering just before the conquest of Canaan.

1:2 God commanded the Israelites to take a military census (lit., "lift the head") of men twenty years old or older who could serve as soldiers. This was preliminary to conscription and organization of an army able to exert maximum force to conquer Canaan. God directed the Israelite army to be organized by family units, so that each soldier would train and fight alongside his relatives. A casualty would not simply be a fellow private, sergeant or lieutenant, but a brother, cousin or uncle!

1:28 [z]Nu 26:23-25; Rev 7:7

28 From the descendants of Issachar:[z]

All the men twenty years old or more who were able to serve in the army were listed by name,
according to the records of their clans and families. 29 The number from the tribe of Issachar
was 54,400.

1:30 [a]Nu 26:26-27; Rev 7:8

30 From the descendants of Zebulun:[a]

All the men twenty years old or more who were able to serve in the army were listed by name,
according to the records of their clans and families. 31 The number from the tribe of Zebulun
was 57,400.

CULTURAL AND HISTORICAL NOTES

Numbers and Their Meaning

NUMBERS 1 According to Numbers 1 there were in the **exodus**[1] generation 603,550 combat-ready men aged twenty years and older. This figure suggests an enormous overall population, perhaps as large as two million. The obvious question is how this many people could have survived in the desert.

What other indications does the Bible offer concerning the Israelite population at the time of the exodus?

- When all the census figures of Numbers 1 are added up, the total is indeed 603,550, suggesting that the tally be taken at face value.
- Exodus 1:7–9 states that the Israelites had multiplied so steadily that the pharaoh complained that "the Israelites have become much too numerous for us." But the pharaoh may have been describing how he perceived the Israelites, based on his fear and hatred of foreigners.
- In contrast, Deuteronomy 7:7 states that Israel was "the fewest of all peoples" (cf. Ex 23:29–30).
- It is difficult to visualize an army of over 600,000 being panic-stricken at the prospect of being pursued by only 600 chariots (Ex 14:5–12).
- It is curious that all Israel is purported to have used only two midwives (Ex 1:15). Some theorize that they were actually representative leaders of a large midwifery guild.
- Numbers 3:43 reports 22,273 firstborn males in Israel. This would suggest that only 22,273 mothers had borne sons. Taking into account the many sons under age twenty, there would have to have been at least one million males in total. The implication, absurd as it may be, is that each mother had at least 44 sons!
- Looking at the data another way, if there were 22,273 firstborn sons, each of whom had an average of five brothers, the total number of men would have been around 133,638, a figure still far too low to reconcile with the census results in Numbers 1.
- If there were 603,550 men-at-arms, the majority of whom would likely have been married, how is it that there were only 22,273 firstborn sons?

We could attempt to adjust the estimated total number of births per mother by assuming that many households were polygamous, resulting in more mothers than firstborn sons. But polygamy was not widely practiced among commoners, and few slaves could afford more than one wife.

Scholars have argued that the word translated "thousand" (*eleph*) can also mean something like "squad" and that the data represent both the number of squads and the number of men in them. The figure for Reuben, using this hypothesis, would be reduced from 46,500 to "46 squads: 500 men." If we add up all the numbers in this way, the final tally for men-at-arms in Numbers 1 is 5,550 (i.e., 5 *eleph* [here meaning "thousands"] plus 550). This could explain the 603,550 in Numbers 1:46: The final figure ("603 *eleph* 550") could equate to "598 *eleph* [squads]: 5 *eleph* [thousands] plus 550 men." If so, the total population would have been about 20,000.

But this theory, too, has difficulties:

- The numbers for the Levites (ch. 3) seem to have been computed differently. For example, Gershon is numbered at 7,500 (3:22), which would mean "7 squads: 500 men." But why would the number of men per "squad" (over 71) be so much higher here than in Numbers 1 (approximately 10)? It may be that the priestly groups had more men per "squad" because the organizational structure for priests and Levites was different from that used for soldiers.
- If the total population of Israel was only about 20,000, what are we to make of the 22,273 firstborn males alleged in 3:43? We cannot take the total number of firstborn males to be only 273, since the text says that there were 273 more firstborn than there were Levites.

Whatever we make of all the difficulties described above, it is clear that the ancient Israelites had ways of dealing with numbers that are perplexing to us. The Bible is an ancient book from an ancient culture, and we cannot assume that it handles data in the same way a modern census-taker would. It is important to realize that the Biblical account is neither erroneous nor deliberately misleading. We simply do not understand how the Israelites conducted and reported either a military or a Levitical census.

[1]See Glossary on page 2080 for definitions of bolded words.

32 From the sons of Joseph:
From the descendants of Ephraim:[b] 1:32 [b]Nu 26:35-37
All the men twenty years old or more who were able to serve in the army were listed by name, according to the records of their clans and families. 33 The number from the tribe of Ephraim was 40,500.

34 From the descendants of Manasseh:[c] 1:34 [c]Nu 26:28-34; Rev 7:6
All the men twenty years old or more who were able to serve in the army were listed by name, according to the records of their clans and families. 35 The number from the tribe of Manasseh was 32,200.

36 From the descendants of Benjamin:[d] 1:36 [d]Nu 26:38-41; 2Ch 17:17; Rev 7:8
All the men twenty years old or more who were able to serve in the army were listed by name, according to the records of their clans and families. 37 The number from the tribe of Benjamin was 35,400.

38 From the descendants of Dan:[e] 1:38 [e]Ge 30:6; Nu 26:42-43
All the men twenty years old or more who were able to serve in the army were listed by name, according to the records of their clans and families. 39 The number from the tribe of Dan was 62,700.

40 From the descendants of Asher:[f] 1:40 [f]Nu 26:44-47; Rev 7:6
All the men twenty years old or more who were able to serve in the army were listed by name, according to the records of their clans and families. 41 The number from the tribe of Asher was 41,500.

42 From the descendants of Naphtali:[g] 1:42 [g]Nu 26:48-50; Rev 7:6
All the men twenty years old or more who were able to serve in the army were listed by name, according to the records of their clans and families. 43 The number from the tribe of Naphtali was 53,400.

44 These were the men counted by Moses and Aaron[h] and the twelve leaders of Israel, each one repre- 1:44 [h]Nu 26:64
senting his family. 45 All the Israelites twenty years old or more who were able to serve in Israel's army were
counted according to their families. 46 The total number was 603,550.[i] 1:46 [i]Ex 12:37; 38:26; Nu 2:32; 26:51
47 The families of the tribe of Levi,[j] however, were not counted[k] along with the others. 48 The LORD had
said to Moses: 49 "You must not count the tribe of Levi or include them in the census of the other Israel- 1:47 [j]Nu 2:33; 26:57 [k]Nu 4:3,49
ites. 50 Instead, appoint the Levites to be in charge of the tabernacle of the Testimony[l]—over all its fur- 1:50 [l]Ex 38:21; Ac 7:44
nishings and everything belonging to it. They are to carry the tabernacle and all its furnishings; they are
to take care of it and encamp around it. 51 Whenever the tabernacle is to move, the Levites are to take it
down, and whenever the tabernacle is to be set up, the Levites shall do it.[m] Anyone else who goes near it 1:51 [m]Nu 3:38; 4:1-33
shall be put to death. 52 The Israelites are to set up their tents by divisions, each man in his own camp un-
der his own standard.[n] 53 The Levites, however, are to set up their tents around the tabernacle of the Tes- 1:52 [n]Nu 2:2; Ps 20:5
timony so that wrath will not fall[o] on the Israelite community. The Levites are to be responsible for the 1:53 [o]Lev 10:6; Nu 16:46; 18:5
care of the tabernacle of the Testimony.[p]" [p]Nu 18:2-4
54 The Israelites did all this just as the LORD commanded Moses.

The Arrangement of the Tribal Camps

2 The LORD said to Moses and Aaron: 2 "The Israelites are to camp around the Tent of Meeting some distance from it, each man under his standard[q] with the banners of his family." 2:2 [q]Nu 1:52; Ps 74:4; Isa 31:9

3 On the east, toward the sunrise, the divisions of the camp of Judah are to encamp under their standard. The leader of the people of Judah is Nahshon son of Amminadab.[r] 4 His division numbers 74,600. 2:3 [r]Nu 10:14; Ru 4:20; 1Ch 2:10

5 The tribe of Issachar will camp next to them. The leader of the people of Issachar is Nethanel son of Zuar.[s] 6 His division numbers 54,400. 2:5 [s]Nu 1:8

2:1–34 If the Israelite men were to be organized into an army, their camp would be a military camp. The tribes were to be arranged in a square like the Egyptian war camp of Pharaoh Rameses II (thirteenth century B.C.). While the similarity is striking, however, so is a crucial difference: The center of the Israelite war camp was occupied by God's sanctuary, not the tent of Pharaoh, a human god-king.

2:7 [t]Nu 1:9 7 The tribe of Zebulun will be next. The leader of the people of Zebulun is Eliab son of Helon.[t]
8 His division numbers 57,400.
9 All the men assigned to the camp of Judah, according to their divisions, number 186,400. They
2:9 [u]Nu 10:14 will set out first.[u]

10 On the south will be the divisions of the camp of Reuben under their standard. The leader of
2:10 [v]Nu 1:5 the people of Reuben is Elizur son of Shedeur.[v] 11 His division numbers 46,500.
12 The tribe of Simeon will camp next to them. The leader of the people of Simeon is Shelumi-
2:12 [w]Nu 1:6 el son of Zurishaddai.[w] 13 His division numbers 59,300.
2:14 [x]Nu 1:14 14 The tribe of Gad will be next. The leader of the people of Gad is Eliasaph son of Deuel.[a][x] 15 His
division numbers 45,650.
2:16 [y]Nu 10:18 16 All the men assigned to the camp of Reuben,[y] according to their divisions, number 151,450.
They will set out second.

2:17 [z]Nu 1:53; 10:21 17 Then the Tent of Meeting and the camp of the Levites[z] will set out in the middle of the camps.
They will set out in the same order as they encamp, each in his own place under his standard.

2:18 [a]Ge 48:20; Jer 31:18-20 18 On the west will be the divisions of the camp of Ephraim[a] under their standard. The leader
[b]Nu 1:10 of the people of Ephraim is Elishama son of Ammihud.[b] 19 His division numbers 40,500.
20 The tribe of Manasseh will be next to them. The leader of the people of Manasseh is Gama-
2:20 [c]Nu 1:10 liel son of Pedahzur.[c] 21 His division numbers 32,200.
22 The tribe of Benjamin will be next. The leader of the people of Benjamin is Abidan son of
2:22 [d]Nu 1:11; Ps 68:27 Gideoni.[d] 23 His division numbers 35,400.
2:24 [e]Nu 10:22 24 All the men assigned to the camp of Ephraim,[e] according to their divisions, number 108,100.
[f]Ps 80:2 They will set out third.[f]
25 On the north will be the divisions of the camp of Dan, under their standard. The leader of the
2:25 [g]Nu 1:12 people of Dan is Ahiezer son of Ammishaddai.[g] 26 His division numbers 62,700.
27 The tribe of Asher will camp next to them. The leader of the people of Asher is Pagiel son of
2:27 [h]Nu 1:13 Ocran.[h] 28 His division numbers 41,500.
2:29 [i]Nu 1:15 29 The tribe of Naphtali will be next. The leader of the people of Naphtali is Ahira son of Enan.[i]
30 His division numbers 53,400.
2:31 [j]Nu 10:25 31 All the men assigned to the camp of Dan number 157,600. They will set out last,[j] under their
standards.

32 These are the Israelites, counted according to their families. All those in the camps, by their
2:32 [k]Ex 38:26; Nu 1:46 divisions, number 603,550.[k] 33 The Levites, however, were not counted[l] along with the other Isra-
2:33 [l]Nu 1:47; 26:57-62 elites, as the LORD commanded Moses.

34 So the Israelites did everything the LORD commanded Moses; that is the way they encamped under
their standards, and that is the way they set out, each with his clan and family.

The Levites

3:1 [m]Ex 6:27 3 This is the account of the family of Aaron and Moses[m] at the time the LORD talked with Moses on
Mount Sinai.
3:2 [n]Ex 6:23; Nu 26:60 2 The names of the sons of Aaron were Nadab the firstborn and Abihu, Eleazar and Ithamar.[n] 3 Those
3:3 [o]Ex 28:41 were the names of Aaron's sons, the anointed priests,[o] who were ordained to serve as priests. 4 Nadab and
3:4 [p]Lev 10:2 Abihu, however, fell dead before the LORD[p] when they made an offering with unauthorized fire before
[q]Lev 10:1 him in the Desert of Sinai.[q] They had no sons; so only Eleazar and Ithamar served as priests during the
[r]1Ch 24:1 lifetime of their father Aaron.[r]
3:6 [s]Dt 10:8; 31:9; 1Ch 15:2 5 The LORD said to Moses, 6 "Bring the tribe of Levi[s] and present them to Aaron the priest to assist
[t]Nu 8:6-22; 18:1-7; 2Ch 29:11 him.[t] 7 They are to perform duties for him and for the whole community at the Tent of Meeting by doing

[a] *14* Many manuscripts of the Masoretic Text, Samaritan Pentateuch and Vulgate (see also Num. 1:14); most manuscripts of the Masoretic Text *Reuel*

3:1–37 The top echelon of the Levites was occupied by Aaron and his sons, who they alone were priests in the restricted sense of serving at the tabernacle. The priests belonged to the family of Kohath. The middle echelon included all the other Kohathites who were not of Aaron's family. To them were given certain privileges of carrying the most sacred parts of the tabernacle (vv. 27–32; 4:4–5; 7:9). The bottom level comprised all members of the families of Gershon and Merari, to whom lesser duties were prescribed (3:21–26,33–37).

the work[u] of the tabernacle. 8 They are to take care of all the furnishings of the Tent of Meeting, fulfilling
the obligations of the Israelites by doing the work of the tabernacle. 9 Give the Levites to Aaron and his
sons;[v] they are the Israelites who are to be given wholly to him.[a] 10 Appoint Aaron and his sons to serve
as priests;[w] anyone else who approaches the sanctuary must be put to death."[x]
11 The LORD also said to Moses, 12 "I have taken the Levites[y] from among the Israelites in place of the
first male offspring[z] of every Israelite woman. The Levites are mine,[a] 13 for all the firstborn are mine.[b]
When I struck down all the firstborn in Egypt, I set apart for myself every firstborn in Israel, whether
man or animal. They are to be mine. I am the LORD."
14 The LORD said to Moses in the Desert of Sinai, 15 "Count[c] the Levites by their families and clans.
Count every male a month old or more."[d] 16 So Moses counted them, as he was commanded by the word
of the LORD.
17 These were the names of the sons of Levi:[e]

Gershon, Kohath and Merari.[f]

18 These were the names of the Gershonite clans:

Libni and Shimei.[g]

19 The Kohathite clans:

Amram, Izhar, Hebron and Uzziel.[h]

20 The Merarite clans:[i]

Mahli and Mushi.[j]

These were the Levite clans, according to their families.

21 To Gershon belonged the clans of the Libnites and Shimeites;[k] these were the Gershonite clans. 22 The
number of all the males a month old or more who were counted was 7,500. 23 The Gershonite clans were
to camp on the west, behind the tabernacle. 24 The leader of the families of the Gershonites was Eliasaph
son of Lael. 25 At the Tent of Meeting the Gershonites were responsible for the care of the tabernacle[l] and
tent, its coverings,[m] the curtain at the entrance[n] to the Tent of Meeting, 26 the curtains of the courtyard[o],
the curtain at the entrance to the courtyard surrounding the tabernacle and altar, and the ropes[p]—and
everything related to their use.

27 To Kohath belonged the clans of the Amramites, Izharites, Hebronites and Uzzielites;[q] these were the
Kohathite clans. 28 The number of all the males a month old or more was 8,600.[b] The Kohathites were re-
sponsible for the care of the sanctuary. 29 The Kohathite clans were to camp on the south side[r] of the tab-
ernacle. 30 The leader of the families of the Kohathite clans was Elizaphan son of Uzziel. 31 They were re-
sponsible for the care of the ark,[s] the table,[t] the lampstand,[u] the altars,[v] the articles of the sanctuary
used in ministering, the curtain,[w] and everything related to their use.[x] 32 The chief leader of the Levites
was Eleazar son of Aaron, the priest. He was appointed over those who were responsible for the care of
the sanctuary.

33 To Merari belonged the clans of the Mahlites and the Mushites;[y] these were the Merarite clans. 34 The
number of all the males a month old or more who were counted was 6,200. 35 The leader of the families
of the Merarite clans was Zuriel son of Abihail; they were to camp on the north side of the tabernacle.[z]
36 The Merarites were appointed[a] to take care of the frames of the tabernacle, its crossbars, posts, bases,
all its equipment, and everything related to their use, 37 as well as the posts of the surrounding courtyard
with their bases, tent pegs and ropes.

38 Moses and Aaron and his sons were to camp to the east[b] of the tabernacle, toward the sunrise, in
front of the Tent of Meeting.[c] They were responsible for the care of the sanctuary[d] on behalf of the Isra-
elites. Anyone else who approached the sanctuary was to be put to death.[e]

3:7 [u]Lev 8:35; Nu 1:50
3:9 [v]Nu 8:19; 18:6
3:10 [w]Ex 29:9 [x]Nu 1:51
3:12 [y]Mal 2:4 [z]ver 41; Nu 8:16, 18 [a]Ex 13:2
3:13 [b]Ex 13:12
3:15 [c]ver 39 [d]Nu 26:62
3:17 [e]Ge 46:11 [f]Ex 6:16
3:18 [g]Ex 6:17
3:19 [h]Ex 6:18
3:20 [i]Ge 46:11 [j]Ex 6:19
3:21 [k]Ex 6:17
3:25 [l]Ex 25:9 [m]Ex 26:14 [n]Ex 26:36; Nu 4:25
3:26 [o]Ex 27:9 [p]Ex 35:18
3:27 [q]1Ch 26:23
3:29 [r]Nu 1:53
3:31 [s]Ex 25:10-22 [t]Ex 25:23 [u]Ex 25:31 [v]Ex 27:1; 30:1 [w]Ex 26:33 [x]Nu 4:15
3:33 [y]Ex 6:19
3:35 [z]Nu 1:53; 2:25
3:36 [a]Nu 4:32
3:38 [b]Nu 2:3 [c]Nu 1:53 [d]ver 7; Nu 18:5 [e]ver 10; Nu 1:51

[a] 9 Most manuscripts of the Masoretic Text; some manuscripts of the Masoretic Text, Samaritan Pentateuch and Septuagint (see also Num. 8:16) *to me* [b] 28 Hebrew; some Septuagint manuscripts *8,300*

3:10 The Mosaic legislation made a sharp distinction between the priests and the non-priests or ordinary Levites: (1) The priests had to belong to Aaron's family, while the Levites belonged to the larger family of Levi. (2) Priests were consecrated (Ex 29:1–37; Lev 8), while Levites were purified (Nu 8:5–22). (3) Levites were considered a gift to Aaron and his sons (3:5–13; 8:19; 18:1–7). (4) The fundamental difference consisted of this: Only the priest had the right to enter the sanctuary (Ex 28:1; 29:9; Nu 3:10,38; 4:15,19–20; 18:1–7; 25:10–13). See note on Korah's rebellion at 16:1–50.

39 The total number of Levites counted at the LORD's command by Moses and Aaron according to their
3:39 [f]Nu 26:62 clans, including every male a month old or more, was 22,000.[f]

3:40 [g]ver 15 40 The LORD said to Moses, "Count all the firstborn Israelite males who are a month old or more[g] and
3:41 [h]ver 12 make a list of their names. 41 Take the Levites for me in place of all the firstborn of the Israelites,[h] and the
livestock of the Levites in place of all the firstborn of the livestock of the Israelites. I am the LORD."

42 So Moses counted all the firstborn of the Israelites, as the LORD commanded him. 43 The total num-
3:43 [i]ver 39 ber of firstborn males a month old or more, listed by name, was 22,273.[i]

44 The LORD also said to Moses, 45 "Take the Levites in place of all the firstborn of Israel, and the live-
3:46 [j]Ex 13:13; Nu 18:15 stock of the Levites in place of their livestock. The Levites are to be mine. I am the LORD. 46 To redeem[j] the
3:47 [k]Lev 27:6 273 firstborn Israelites who exceed the number of the Levites, 47 collect five shekels[a][k] for each one, ac-
[l]Ex 30:13 [m]Lev 27:25 cording to the sanctuary shekel,[l] which weighs twenty gerahs.[m] 48 Give the money for the redemption of
the additional Israelites to Aaron and his sons."

49 So Moses collected the redemption money from those who exceeded the number redeemed by the
3:50 [n]ver 46-48 Levites. 50 From the firstborn of the Israelites he collected silver weighing 1,365 shekels,[b][n] according to
the sanctuary shekel. 51 Moses gave the redemption money to Aaron and his sons, as he was command-
ed by the word of the LORD.

The Kohathites

4:2 [o]Ex 30:12 4 The LORD said to Moses and Aaron: 2 "Take a census[o] of the Kohathite branch of the Levites by their
4:3 [p]ver 23; Nu 8:25; 1Ch 23:3,24,27; Ezr 3:8 clans and families. 3 Count all the men from thirty to fifty years of age[p] who come to serve in the
work in the Tent of Meeting.

4:4 [q]ver 19 4 "This is the work of the Kohathites in the Tent of Meeting: the care of the most holy things.[q] 5 When
4:5 [r]Ex 26:31,33 [s]Ex 25:10,16 the camp is to move, Aaron and his sons are to go in and take down the shielding curtain[r] and cover the
ark of the Testimony with it.[s] 6 Then they are to cover this with hides of sea cows,[c] spread a cloth of sol-
4:6 [t]Ex 25:13-15; 1Ki 8:7; 2Ch 5:8 id blue over that and put the poles[t] in place.

4:7 [u]Ex 25:23,29; Lev 24:6 7 "Over the table of the Presence[u] they are to spread a blue cloth and put on it the plates, dishes and
[v]Ex 25:30 bowls, and the jars for drink offerings; the bread that is continually there[v] is to remain on it. 8 Over these
they are to spread a scarlet cloth, cover that with hides of sea cows and put its poles in place.

9 "They are to take a blue cloth and cover the lampstand that is for light, together with its lamps, its
4:9 [w]Ex 25:31,37,38 wick trimmers and trays,[w] and all its jars for the oil used to supply it. 10 Then they are to wrap it and all
its accessories in a covering of hides of sea cows and put it on a carrying frame.

4:11 [x]Ex 30:1 11 "Over the gold altar[x] they are to spread a blue cloth and cover that with hides of sea cows and put
its poles in place.

12 "They are to take all the articles used for ministering in the sanctuary, wrap them in a blue cloth,
cover that with hides of sea cows and put them on a carrying frame.

4:13 [y]Ex 27:1-8 13 "They are to remove the ashes from the bronze altar[y] and spread a purple cloth over it. 14 Then they are
4:14 [z]2Ch 4:16 [a]Jer 52:18 to place on it all the utensils used for ministering at the altar, including the firepans, meat forks,[z] shovels
[b]Ex 27:6 and sprinkling bowls.[a] Over it they are to spread a covering of hides of sea cows and put its poles[b] in place.

15 "After Aaron and his sons have finished covering the holy furnishings and all the holy articles, and
4:15 [c]Nu 7:9 when the camp is ready to move, the Kohathites are to come to do the carrying.[c] But they must not touch
[d]Nu 1:51; 2Sa 6:6,7 the holy things or they will die.[d] The Kohathites are to carry those things that are in the Tent of Meeting.

4:16 [e]Lev 10:6 [f]Ex 25:6 16 "Eleazar[e] son of Aaron, the priest, is to have charge of the oil for the light,[f] the fragrant incense, the
[g]Ex 29:41; Lev 6:14-23 regular grain offering[g] and the anointing oil. He is to be in charge of the entire tabernacle and every-
thing in it, including its holy furnishings and articles."

17 The LORD said to Moses and Aaron, 18 "See that the Kohathite tribal clans are not cut off from the Le-
4:19 [h]ver 15 vites. 19 So that they may live and not die when they come near the most holy things,[h] do this for them:
Aaron and his sons are to go into the sanctuary and assign to each man his work and what he is to car-
4:20 [i]Ex 19:21; 1Sa 6:19 ry. 20 But the Kohathites must not go in to look[i] at the holy things, even for a moment, or they will die."

[a] *47* That is, about 2 ounces (about 55 grams) [b] *50* That is, about 35 pounds (about 15.5 kilograms) [c] *6* That is, dugongs; also in verses 8, 10, 11, 12, 14 and 25

3:47 The "sanctuary shekel" was a unit of weight, not a coin, since coinage was not invented until the seventh century B.C. The standard weights used at the tabernacle may have varied slightly from those used in the marketplace. See "Weights and Measures" on page 1459 and "Coins and Numismatics" on page 1699.

The Gershonites

[21]The LORD said to Moses, [22]"Take a census also of the Gershonites by their families and clans. [23]Count
all the men from thirty to fifty years of age[j] who come to serve in the work at the Tent of Meeting. 4:23 [j]ver 3; 1Ch 23:3,24,27
[24]"This is the service of the Gershonite clans as they work and carry burdens: [25]They are to carry the
curtains of the tabernacle,[k] the Tent of Meeting,[l] its covering[m] and the outer covering of hides of sea 4:25 [k]Ex 27:10-18; Nu 3:26
cows, the curtains for the entrance to the Tent of Meeting, [26]the curtains of the courtyard surrounding [l]Nu 3:25
the tabernacle and altar, the curtain for the entrance, the ropes and all the equipment used in its service. [m]Ex 26:14
The Gershonites are to do all that needs to be done with these things. [27]All their service, whether carrying
or doing other work, is to be done under the direction of Aaron and his sons. You shall assign to them as
their responsibility all they are to carry. [28]This is the service of the Gershonite clans[n] at the Tent of Meet- 4:28 [n]Nu 7:7
ing. Their duties are to be under the direction of Ithamar son of Aaron, the priest.

The Merarites

[29]"Count the Merarites by their clans and families.[o] [30]Count all the men from thirty to fifty years of 4:29 [o]Ge 46:11
age who come to serve in the work at the Tent of Meeting. [31]This is their duty as they perform service at
the Tent of Meeting: to carry the frames of the tabernacle, its crossbars, posts and bases,[p] [32]as well as the 4:31 [p]Nu 3:36
posts of the surrounding courtyard with their bases, tent pegs, ropes, all their equipment and everything
related to their use. Assign to each man the specific things he is to carry. [33]This is the service of the Me-
rarite clans as they work at the Tent of Meeting under the direction of Ithamar son of Aaron, the priest."

The Numbering of the Levite Clans

[34]Moses, Aaron and the leaders of the community counted the Kohathites[q] by their clans and fami- 4:34 [q]ver 2
lies. [35]All the men from thirty to fifty years of age who came to serve in the work in the Tent of Meeting,
[36]counted by clans, were 2,750. [37]This was the total of all those in the Kohathite clans[r] who served in the 4:37 [r]Nu 3:27
Tent of Meeting. Moses and Aaron counted them according to the LORD's command through Moses.
[38]The Gershonites[s] were counted by their clans and families. [39]All the men from thirty to fifty years 4:38 [s]Ge 46:11
of age who came to serve in the work at the Tent of Meeting, [40]counted by their clans and families, were
2,630. [41]This was the total of those in the Gershonite clans who served at the Tent of Meeting. Moses and
Aaron counted them according to the LORD's command.
[42]The Merarites were counted by their clans and families. [43]All the men from thirty to fifty years of
age who came to serve in the work at the Tent of Meeting, [44]counted by their clans, were 3,200. [45]This was
the total of those in the Merarite clans.[t] Moses and Aaron counted them according to the LORD's command 4:45 [t]ver 29
through Moses.
[46]So Moses, Aaron and the leaders of Israel counted all the Levites by their clans and families. [47]All
the men from thirty to fifty years of age[u] who came to do the work of serving and carrying the Tent of 4:47 [u]ver 3
Meeting [48]numbered 8,580.[v] [49]At the LORD's command through Moses, each was assigned his work and 4:48 [v]Nu 3:39
told what to carry.
Thus they were counted,[w] as the LORD commanded Moses. 4:49 [w]Nu 1:47

The Purity of the Camp

5 The LORD said to Moses, [2]"Command the Israelites to send away from the camp anyone who has an
infectious skin disease[a][x] or a discharge[y] of any kind, or who is ceremonially unclean[z] because of a 5:2 [x]Lev 13:46 [y]Lev 15:2; Mt 9:20
dead body. [3]Send away male and female alike; send them outside the camp so they will not defile their [z]Lev 13:3; Nu 9:6-10
camp, where I dwell among them.[a]" [4]The Israelites did this; they sent them outside the camp. They did 5:3 [a]Lev 26:12; Nu 35:34; 2Co 6:16
just as the LORD had instructed Moses.

Restitution for Wrongs

[5]The LORD said to Moses, [6]"Say to the Israelites: 'When a man or woman wrongs another in any way[b]
and so is unfaithful[b] to the LORD, that person is guilty[c] [7]and must confess[d] the sin he has committed. He 5:6 [b]Lev 6:2 [c]Lev 5:14-6:7
must make full restitution[e] for his wrong, add one fifth to it and give it all to the person he has wronged. 5:7 [d]Lev 5:5; 26:40; Jos 7:19; Lk 19:8 [e]Lev 6:5

[a] *2* Traditionally *leprosy*; the Hebrew word was used for various diseases affecting the skin—not necessarily leprosy.
[b] *6* Or *woman commits any wrong common to mankind*

5:1–4 See "Skin Diseases in the Ancient World" on page 171.

8 But if that person has no close relative to whom restitution can be made for the wrong, the restitution
belongs to the LORD and must be given to the priest, along with the ram with which atonement is made
for him.[f] 9 All the sacred contributions the Israelites bring to a priest will belong to him.[g] 10 Each man's
sacred gifts are his own, but what he gives to the priest will belong to the priest.[h]' "

The Test for an Unfaithful Wife

11 Then the LORD said to Moses, 12 "Speak to the Israelites and say to them: 'If a man's wife goes astray[i]
and is unfaithful to him 13 by sleeping with another man,[j] and this is hidden from her husband and her
impurity is undetected (since there is no witness against her and she has not been caught in the act),
14 and if feelings of jealousy[k] come over her husband and he suspects his wife and she is impure—or if
he is jealous and suspects her even though she is not impure— 15 then he is to take his wife to the priest.
He must also take an offering of a tenth of an ephah[a][l] of barley flour[m] on her behalf. He must not pour
oil on it or put incense on it, because it is a grain offering for jealousy, a reminder[n] offering to draw at-
tention to guilt.

16 " 'The priest shall bring her and have her stand before the LORD. 17 Then he shall take some holy wa-
ter in a clay jar and put some dust from the tabernacle floor into the water. 18 After the priest has had the
woman stand before the LORD, he shall loosen her hair[o] and place in her hands the reminder offering, the
grain offering for jealousy, while he himself holds the bitter water that brings a curse. 19 Then the priest
shall put the woman under oath and say to her, "If no other man has slept with you and you have not
gone astray[p] and become impure while married to your husband, may this bitter water that brings a
curse not harm you. 20 But if you have gone astray[q] while married to your husband and you have defiled
yourself by sleeping with a man other than your husband"— 21 here the priest is to put the woman un-
der this curse of the oath[r]—"may the LORD cause your people to curse and denounce you when he caus-
es your thigh to waste away and your abdomen to swell.[b] 22 May this water[s] that brings a curse[t] enter
your body so that your abdomen swells and your thigh wastes away.[c]"

" 'Then the woman is to say, "Amen. So be it.[u]"

23 " 'The priest is to write these curses on a scroll[v] and then wash them off into the bitter water. 24 He
shall have the woman drink the bitter water that brings a curse, and this water will enter her and cause
bitter suffering. 25 The priest is to take from her hands the grain offering for jealousy, wave it before the
LORD[w] and bring it to the altar. 26 The priest is then to take a handful of the grain offering as a memorial
offering and burn it on the altar; after that, he is to have the woman drink the water. 27 If she has defiled
herself and been unfaithful to her husband, then when she is made to drink the water that brings a curse,
it will go into her and cause bitter suffering; her abdomen will swell and her thigh waste away,[d] and she
will become accursed[x] among her people. 28 If, however, the woman has not defiled herself and is free
from impurity, she will be cleared of guilt and will be able to have children.

29 " 'This, then, is the law of jealousy when a woman goes astray[y] and defiles herself while married to
her husband, 30 or when feelings of jealousy come over a man because he suspects his wife. The priest is
to have her stand before the LORD and is to apply this entire law to her. 31 The husband will be innocent
of any wrongdoing, but the woman will bear the consequences[z] of her sin.' "

The Nazirite

6 The LORD said to Moses, 2 "Speak to the Israelites and say to them: 'If a man or woman wants to make
a special vow[a], a vow of separation to the LORD as a Nazirite,[b] 3 he must abstain from wine[c] and oth-
er fermented drink and must not drink vinegar[d] made from wine or from other fermented drink. He

5:8 [f]Lev 6:6,7; 7:7
5:9 [g]Lev 6:17; 7:6-14
5:10 [h]Lev 10:13
5:12 [i]Ex 20:14
5:13 [j]Lev 18:20; 20:10
5:14 [k]Pr 6:34; SS 8:6
5:15 [l]Ex 16:36 [m]Lev 6:20 [n]Eze 29:16
5:18 [o]Lev 10:6; 1Co 11:6
5:19 [p]ver 12,29
5:20 [q]ver 12
5:21 [r]Jos 6:26; 1Sa 14:24; Ne 10:29
5:22 [s]Ps 109:18 [t]ver 18 [u]Dt 27:15
5:23 [v]Jer 45:1
5:25 [w]Lev 8:27
5:27 [x]Isa 43:28; 65:15; Jer 26:6; 29:18; 42:18; 44:12,22; Zec 8:13
5:29 [y]ver 19
5:31 [z]Lev 5:1; 20:17
6:2 [a]Ge 28:20; Ac 21:23 [b]Jdg 13:5; 16:17; Am 2:11,12
6:3 [c]Lk 1:15 [d]Ru 2:14; Ps 69:21; Pr 10:26

[a] *15* That is, probably about 2 quarts (about 2 liters) [b] *21* Or *causes you to have a miscarrying womb and barrenness* [c] *22* Or *body and cause you to be barren and have a miscarrying womb* [d] *27* Or *suffering; she will have barrenness and a miscarrying womb*

5:11–28 *Water of Jealousy* (a phrase not mentioned in the NIV) was the name given to the holy water used to determine the guilt or innocence of a wife accused by her husband of unfaithfulness. The accuser brought his wife and made an offering, after which dust from the tabernacle floor was mixed with holy water, which the woman drank. If she were guilty, the curse pronounced would come true for her. If not, she would be cleared of guilt.

5:21–22 The language regarding the woman's thigh wasting away and abdomen swelling speaks figuratively of an inability to conceive—or of miscarriage (see the NIV text notes on vv. 21,22, 27). For a woman in the ancient Near East to be denied the ability to bear children was a personal loss of inestimable proportions. Since it was solely in the bearing of children that a woman's worth was realized, this was a grievous punishment indeed.

In clear cases of adultery, the penalty for both the man and the woman was death (Lev 20:10). But to protect innocent women from false accusation by a jealous husband within a male-dominated court system, God removed their fates from human jurisdiction.

6:1–21 A Nazirite was an Israelite who consecrated himself or herself and took a vow of separation and self-imposed abstinence for the

must not drink grape juice or eat grapes or raisins. 4 As long as he is a Nazirite, he must not eat anything
that comes from the grapevine, not even the seeds or skins.
5 " 'During the entire period of his vow of separation no razor[e] may be used on his head.[f] He must be 6:5 [e]Ps 52:2;
holy until the period of his separation to the LORD is over; he must let the hair of his head grow long. 57:4; 59:7; Isa 7:20; Eze 5:1
6 Throughout the period of his separation to the LORD he must not go near a dead body.[g] 7 Even if his own [f]1Sa 1:11 6:6 [g]Lev 21:1-3;
father or mother or brother or sister dies, he must not make himself ceremonially unclean[h] on account Nu 19:11-22 6:7 [h]Nu 9:6
of them, because the symbol of his separation to God is on his head. 8 Throughout the period of his sep-
aration he is consecrated to the LORD.
9 " 'If someone dies suddenly in his presence, thus defiling the hair he has dedicated,[i] he must shave 6:9 [i]ver 18
his head on the day of his cleansing[j]—the seventh day. 10 Then on the eighth day he must bring two doves [j]Lev 14:9
or two young pigeons[k] to the priest at the entrance to the Tent of Meeting. 11 The priest is to offer one as 6:10 [k]Lev 5:7;
a sin offering and the other as a burnt offering[l] to make atonement[m] for him because he sinned by be- 14:22 6:11 [l]Ge 8:20
ing in the presence of the dead body. That same day he is to consecrate his head. 12 He must dedicate him- [m]Ex 29:36
self to the LORD for the period of his separation and must bring a year-old male lamb as a guilt offering.
The previous days do not count, because he became defiled during his separation.
13 " 'Now this is the law for the Nazirite when the period of his separation is over.[n] He is to be 6:13 [n]Ac 21:26
brought to the entrance to the Tent of Meeting. 14 There he is to present his offerings to the LORD: a
year-old male lamb without defect for a burnt offering, a year-old ewe lamb without defect for a sin
offering,[o] a ram without defect for a fellowship offering,[a] 15 together with their grain offerings and 6:14 [o]Lev 14:10; Nu 15:27

[a] *14* Traditionally *peace offering*; also in verses 17 and 18

purpose of some special service. The question of whether the concept of the Nazirite was indigenous to Israel has often been asked. It would appear that the practice of separation for religious purposes is very ancient and is shared by a number of peoples. In Israel, however, it assumed unique proportions. Its regulatory laws are laid down in verses 1–21. There were two different types of Naziritism, the temporary and the perpetual, of which the first was far more common. In fact, we know of only three of the latter class: Samson, Samuel and John the Baptist.

The reasons for taking a Nazirite vow were numerous. Such a vow might be assumed by a parent before the birth of a child; by an individual in some sort of distress or trouble; or by a woman suspected by her husband of unfaithfulness in their marriage relationship until the suspicion could be removed. Women and slaves could take vows only if sanctioned by their husbands or masters.

The minimum period of time for a Nazirite vow was 30 days. During the Maccabean days (see "The Intertestamental Period" on p. 1551) a number of Jews became Nazirites as a matter of protest against the Hellenistic practices and demands of Antiochus Epiphanes.

ANCIENT TEXTS AND ARTIFACTS

The Ketef Hinnom Amulets

NUMBERS 6 In 1979 archaeologists unearthed a burial site at Ketef Hinnom, just south of Jerusalem, on the southwestern side of Gehenna, near the Biblical boundary between the tribes of Judah and Benjamin (Jos 18:16). Excavated from within a burial repository were two small, rolled plaques of thin, pliable silver, each about the size of a credit card. When unrolled, they revealed delicately etched inscriptions that included a shortened version of the priestly benediction recorded in Numbers 6:24–26. One section has been translated as follows:

The LORD bless and keep you;
The LORD make his face shine upon you
and give you peace.

Archaeological and **paleographic** evidence dates these plaques to the late seventh century B.C., thereby making them the earliest written citations of Scripture. They may relate to rituals of worship, during which priests would have recited this priestly benediction (cf. Lev 9:22). Perhaps worn as amulets (charms inscribed with incantations or symbols to aid the wearer or to protect him or her against evil), the plaques do reveal that this benediction was used in popular religious practice, perhaps to secure blessing for the owner. Since later Jewish traditions also quoted Numbers 6:24–26 in the context of funeral rites, the discovery of the plaques in the burial repository suggests that they served to bless the deceased person's journey to Sheol, the netherworld or abode of the dead.[1]

[1]For more on burial rites, see "Jewish Burial Practices" on page 1688.

6:15 [p]Nu 15:1-7 [q]Ex 29:2; Lev 2:4 drink offerings,[p] and a basket of bread made without yeast—cakes made of fine flour mixed with oil,
and wafers spread with oil.[q]
16" 'The priest is to present them before the LORD and make the sin offering and the burnt offering.
17 He is to present the basket of unleavened bread and is to sacrifice the ram as a fellowship offering to
the LORD, together with its grain offering and drink offering.
18" 'Then at the entrance to the Tent of Meeting, the Nazirite must shave off the hair that he dedicat-
6:18 [r]ver 9; Ac 21:24 ed.[r] He is to take the hair and put it in the fire that is under the sacrifice of the fellowship offering.
19" 'After the Nazirite has shaved off the hair of his dedication, the priest is to place in his hands a
boiled shoulder of the ram, and a cake and a wafer from the basket, both made without yeast. 20 The priest
shall then wave them before the LORD as a wave offering; they are holy and belong to the priest, together
6:20 [s]Ecc 9:7 with the breast that was waved and the thigh that was presented. After that, the Nazirite may drink wine.[s]
21" 'This is the law of the Nazirite who vows his offering to the LORD in accordance with his separa-
tion, in addition to whatever else he can afford. He must fulfill the vow he has made, according to the law
of the Nazirite.' "

The Priestly Blessing

6:23 [t]Dt 21:5; 1Ch 23:13 22 The LORD said to Moses, 23 "Tell Aaron and his sons, 'This is how you are to bless[t] the Israelites. Say
to them:

6:24 [u]Dt 28:3-6; Ps 28:9 [v]1Sa 2:9; Ps 17:8 24" ' "The LORD bless you[u]
and keep you;[v]
6:25 [w]Job 29:24; Ps 31:16; 80:3; 119:135 [x]Ge 43:29; Ps 25:16; 86:16 25 the LORD make his face shine upon you[w]
and be gracious to you;[x]
6:26 [y]Ps 4:6; 44:3 [z]Ps 29:11; 37:11,37; Jn 14:27 26 the LORD turn his face[y] toward you
and give you peace.[z]" '

6:27 [a]Dt 28:10; 2Sa 7:23; 2Ch 7:14; Ne 9:10; Jer 25:29 27 "So they will put my name[a] on the Israelites, and I will bless them."

Offerings at the Dedication of the Tabernacle

7:1 [b]Ex 40:17 [c]Ex 40:9 [d]ver 84, 88; Ex 40:10 7 When Moses finished setting up the tabernacle,[b] he anointed it and consecrated it and all its furnish-
7:2 [e]Nu 1:5-16 ings.[c] He also anointed and consecrated the altar and all its utensils.[d] 2 Then the leaders of Israel,[e]
the heads of families who were the tribal leaders in charge of those who were counted, made offerings.
3 They brought as their gifts before the LORD six covered carts and twelve oxen—an ox from each leader
and a cart from every two. These they presented before the tabernacle.
4 The LORD said to Moses, 5 "Accept these from them, that they may be used in the work at the Tent of
Meeting. Give them to the Levites as each man's work requires."
6 So Moses took the carts and oxen and gave them to the Levites. 7 He gave two carts and four oxen to
7:7 [f]Nu 4:24-26, 28 the Gershonites,[f] as their work required, 8 and he gave four carts and eight oxen to the Merarites,[g] as their
7:8 [g]Nu 4:31-33 work required. They were all under the direction of Ithamar son of Aaron, the priest. 9 But Moses did not
7:9 [h]Nu 4:15 give any to the Kohathites, because they were to carry on their shoulders[h] the holy things, for which they
were responsible.
7:10 [i]ver 1 [j]2Ch 7:9 10 When the altar was anointed,[i] the leaders brought their offerings for its dedication[j] and presented
them before the altar. 11 For the LORD had said to Moses, "Each day one leader is to bring his offering for
the dedication of the altar."

12 The one who brought his offering on the first day was Nahshon son of Amminadab of the tribe of Judah.
13 His offering was one silver plate weighing a hundred and thirty shekels,[a] and one silver sprin-
7:13 [k]Ex 30:13; Nu 3:47 [l]Lev 2:1 kling bowl weighing seventy shekels,[b] both according to the sanctuary shekel,[k] each filled with
fine flour mixed with oil as a grain offering;[l] 14 one gold dish weighing ten shekels,[c] filled with in-
7:14 [m]Ex 30:34 cense;[m] 15 one young bull,[n] one ram and one male lamb a year old, for a burnt offering;[o] 16 one male
7:15 [n]Ex 24:5; 29:3; Nu 28:11 [o]Lev 1:3 goat for a sin offering;[p] 17 and two oxen, five rams, five male goats and five male lambs a year old,
7:16 [p]Lev 4:3,23 7:17 [q]Lev 3:1 [r]Nu 1:7 to be sacrificed as a fellowship offering.[d][q] This was the offering of Nahshon son of Amminadab.[r]

[a] *13* That is, about 3 1/4 pounds (about 1.5 kilograms); also elsewhere in this chapter [b] *13* That is, about 1 3/4 pounds (about 0.8 kilogram); also elsewhere in this chapter [c] *14* That is, about 4 ounces (about 110 grams); also elsewhere in this chapter
[d] *17* Traditionally *peace offering*; also elsewhere in this chapter

---

6:22–27 See "The Ketef Hinnom Amulets" on page 204.

18 On the second day Nethanel son of Zuar,[s] the leader of Issachar, brought his offering. 7:18 [s]Nu 1:8
19 The offering he brought was one silver plate weighing a hundred and thirty shekels, and one sil-
ver sprinkling bowl weighing seventy shekels, both according to the sanctuary shekel, each filled
with fine flour mixed with oil as a grain offering; 20 one gold dish[t] weighing ten shekels, filled with 7:20 [t]ver 14
incense; 21 one young bull, one ram and one male lamb a year old, for a burnt offering; 22 one male
goat for a sin offering; 23 and two oxen, five rams, five male goats and five male lambs a year old,
to be sacrificed as a fellowship offering. This was the offering of Nethanel son of Zuar.

24 On the third day, Eliab son of Helon,[u] the leader of the people of Zebulun, brought his offering. 7:24 [u]Nu 1:9
25 His offering was one silver plate weighing a hundred and thirty shekels, and one silver sprin-
kling bowl weighing seventy shekels, both according to the sanctuary shekel, each filled with fine
flour mixed with oil as a grain offering; 26 one gold dish weighing ten shekels, filled with incense;
27 one young bull, one ram and one male lamb a year old, for a burnt offering; 28 one male goat for
a sin offering; 29 and two oxen, five rams, five male goats and five male lambs a year old, to be sac-
rificed as a fellowship offering. This was the offering of Eliab son of Helon.

30 On the fourth day Elizur son of Shedeur,[v] the leader of the people of Reuben, brought his offering. 7:30 [v]Nu 1:5
31 His offering was one silver plate weighing a hundred and thirty shekels, and one silver sprin-
kling bowl weighing seventy shekels, both according to the sanctuary shekel, each filled with fine
flour mixed with oil as a grain offering; 32 one gold dish weighing ten shekels, filled with incense;
33 one young bull, one ram and one male lamb a year old, for a burnt offering; 34 one male goat for
a sin offering; 35 and two oxen, five rams, five male goats and five male lambs a year old, to be sac-
rificed as a fellowship offering. This was the offering of Elizur son of Shedeur.

36 On the fifth day Shelumiel son of Zurishaddai,[w] the leader of the people of Simeon, brought his offering. 7:36 [w]Nu 1:6
37 His offering was one silver plate weighing a hundred and thirty shekels, and one silver sprin-
kling bowl weighing seventy shekels, both according to the sanctuary shekel, each filled with fine
flour mixed with oil as a grain offering; 38 one gold dish weighing ten shekels, filled with incense;
39 one young bull, one ram and one male lamb a year old, for a burnt offering; 40 one male goat for
a sin offering; 41 and two oxen, five rams, five male goats and five male lambs a year old, to be sac-
rificed as a fellowship offering. This was the offering of Shelumiel son of Zurishaddai.

42 On the sixth day Eliasaph son of Deuel,[x] the leader of the people of Gad, brought his offering. 7:42 [x]Nu 1:14
43 His offering was one silver plate weighing a hundred and thirty shekels, and one silver sprin-
kling bowl weighing seventy shekels, both according to the sanctuary shekel, each filled with fine
flour mixed with oil as a grain offering; 44 one gold dish weighing ten shekels, filled with incense;
45 one young bull, one ram and one male lamb a year old, for a burnt offering; 46 one male goat for
a sin offering; 47 and two oxen, five rams, five male goats and five male lambs a year old, to be sac-
rificed as a fellowship offering. This was the offering of Eliasaph son of Deuel.

48 On the seventh day Elishama son of Ammihud,[y] the leader of the people of Ephraim, brought his offering. 7:48 [y]Nu 1:10
49 His offering was one silver plate weighing a hundred and thirty shekels, and one silver sprin-
kling bowl weighing seventy shekels, both according to the sanctuary shekel, each filled with fine
flour mixed with oil as a grain offering; 50 one gold dish weighing ten shekels, filled with incense;
51 one young bull, one ram and one male lamb a year old, for a burnt offering; 52 one male goat for
a sin offering; 53 and two oxen, five rams, five male goats and five male lambs a year old, to be sac-
rificed as a fellowship offering. This was the offering of Elishama son of Ammihud.[z] 7:53 [z]Nu 1:10

54 On the eighth day Gamaliel son of Pedahzur,[a] the leader of the people of Manasseh, brought his offering. 7:54 [a]Nu 1:10; 2:20
55 His offering was one silver plate weighing a hundred and thirty shekels, and one silver sprin-
kling bowl weighing seventy shekels, both according to the sanctuary shekel, each filled with fine
flour mixed with oil as a grain offering; 56 one gold dish weighing ten shekels, filled with incense;
57 one young bull, one ram and one male lamb a year old, for a burnt offering; 58 one male goat for
a sin offering; 59 and two oxen, five rams, five male goats and five male lambs a year old, to be sac-
rificed as a fellowship offering. This was the offering of Gamaliel son of Pedahzur.

60 On the ninth day Abidan son of Gideoni,[b] the leader of the people of Benjamin, brought his offering. 7:60 [b]Nu 1:11
61 His offering was one silver plate weighing a hundred and thirty shekels, and one silver sprin-
kling bowl weighing seventy shekels, both according to the sanctuary shekel, each filled with fine

flour mixed with oil as a grain offering; 62 one gold dish weighing ten shekels, filled with incense;
63 one young bull, one ram and one male lamb a year old, for a burnt offering; 64 one male goat for
a sin offering; 65 and two oxen, five rams, five male goats and five male lambs a year old, to be sac-
rificed as a fellowship offering. This was the offering of Abidan son of Gideoni.

7:66 [c]Nu 1:12; 2:25 66 On the tenth day Ahiezer son of Ammishaddai,[c] the leader of the people of Dan, brought his offering.
67 His offering was one silver plate weighing a hundred and thirty shekels, and one silver sprin-
kling bowl weighing seventy shekels, both according to the sanctuary shekel, each filled with fine
flour mixed with oil as a grain offering; 68 one gold dish weighing ten shekels, filled with incense;
69 one young bull, one ram and one male lamb a year old, for a burnt offering; 70 one male goat for
a sin offering; 71 and two oxen, five rams, five male goats and five male lambs a year old, to be sac-
rificed as a fellowship offering. This was the offering of Ahiezer son of Ammishaddai.

7:72 [d]Nu 1:13 72 On the eleventh day Pagiel son of Ocran,[d] the leader of the people of Asher, brought his offering.
73 His offering was one silver plate weighing a hundred and thirty shekels, and one silver sprin-
kling bowl weighing seventy shekels, both according to the sanctuary shekel, each filled with fine
flour mixed with oil as a grain offering; 74 one gold dish weighing ten shekels, filled with incense;
75 one young bull, one ram and one male lamb a year old, for a burnt offering; 76 one male goat for
a sin offering; 77 and two oxen, five rams, five male goats and five male lambs a year old, to be sac-
rificed as a fellowship offering. This was the offering of Pagiel son of Ocran.

7:78 [e]Nu 1:15; 2:29 78 On the twelfth day Ahira son of Enan,[e] the leader of the people of Naphtali, brought his offering.
79 His offering was one silver plate weighing a hundred and thirty shekels, and one silver sprin-
kling bowl weighing seventy shekels, both according to the sanctuary shekel, each filled with fine
flour mixed with oil as a grain offering; 80 one gold dish weighing ten shekels, filled with incense;
81 one young bull, one ram and one male lamb a year old, for a burnt offering; 82 one male goat for
a sin offering; 83 and two oxen, five rams, five male goats and five male lambs a year old, to be sac-
rificed as a fellowship offering. This was the offering of Ahira son of Enan.

84 These were the offerings of the Israelite leaders for the dedication of the altar when it was anoint-
7:84 [f]ver 1,10 [g]Nu 4:14 [h]ver 14 ed:[f] twelve silver plates, twelve silver sprinkling bowls[g] and twelve gold dishes.[h] 85 Each silver plate
weighed a hundred and thirty shekels, and each sprinkling bowl seventy shekels. Altogether, the silver
dishes weighed two thousand four hundred shekels,[a] according to the sanctuary shekel. 86 The twelve
gold dishes filled with incense weighed ten shekels each, according to the sanctuary shekel. Altogether,
the gold dishes weighed a hundred and twenty shekels.[b] 87 The total number of animals for the burnt of-
fering came to twelve young bulls, twelve rams and twelve male lambs a year old, together with their
grain offering. Twelve male goats were used for the sin offering. 88 The total number of animals for the sac-
rifice of the fellowship offering came to twenty-four oxen, sixty rams, sixty male goats and sixty male
7:88 [i]ver 1,10 lambs a year old. These were the offerings for the dedication of the altar after it was anointed.[i]
7:89 [j]Ex 25:21, 22; 33:9,11 [k]Ps 80:1; 99:1 89 When Moses entered the Tent of Meeting to speak with the LORD,[j] he heard the voice speaking to him
from between the two cherubim above the atonement cover[k] on the ark of the Testimony. And he spoke
with him.

Setting Up the Lamps

8:2 [l]Ex 25:37; Lev 24:2,4 **8** The LORD said to Moses, 2 "Speak to Aaron and say to him, 'When you set up the seven lamps, they
are to light the area in front of the lampstand.[l]' "
3 Aaron did so; he set up the lamps so that they faced forward on the lampstand, just as the LORD com-
8:4 [m]Ex 25:18, 36; 25:18 [n]Ex 25:9 manded Moses. 4 This is how the lampstand was made: It was made of hammered gold[m]—from its base
to its blossoms. The lampstand was made exactly like the pattern[n] the LORD had shown Moses.

The Setting Apart of the Levites

5 The LORD said to Moses: 6 "Take the Levites from among the other Israelites and make them cere-
8:6 [o]Lev 22:2; Isa 1:16; 52:11 **8:7** [p]Nu 19:9,17 monially clean.[o] 7 To purify them, do this: Sprinkle the water of cleansing[p] on them; then have them shave

[a] *85* That is, about 60 pounds (about 28 kilograms) [b] *86* That is, about 3 pounds (about 1.4 kilograms)

8:1–26 See "Hittite Instructions for Priests" on page 208.

their whole bodies[q] and wash their clothes,[r] and so purify themselves. 8Have them take a young bull with 8:7 [q]Lev 14:9;
its grain offering of fine flour mixed with oil;[s] then you are to take a second young bull for a sin offer- Dt 21:12 [r]Lev 14:8
ing. 9Bring the Levites to the front of the Tent of Meeting[t] and assemble the whole Israelite community.[u] 8:8 [s]Lev 2:1; Nu 15:8-10
10You are to bring the Levites before the LORD, and the Israelites are to lay their hands on them.[v] 11Aar- 8:9 [t]Ex 40:12 [u]Lev 8:3
on is to present the Levites before the LORD as a wave offering[w] from the Israelites, so that they may be 8:10 [v]Ac 6:6
ready to do the work of the LORD. 8:11 [w]Lev 7:30

12"After the Levites lay their hands on the heads of the bulls,[x] use the one for a sin offering to the LORD 8:12 [x]Ex 29:10
and the other for a burnt offering, to make atonement[y] for the Levites. 13Have the Levites stand in front [y]Ex 29:36
of Aaron and his sons and then present them as a wave offering to the LORD. 14In this way you are to set

ANCIENT TEXTS AND ARTIFACTS

Hittite Instructions for Priests

NUMBERS 8 Several copies of a **Hittite** text outlining the instructions for priests and temple personnel are currently housed in Turkish collections. Dating prior to the time of the Hittite King Suppiluliumas I[1] (c. 1350–1325 B.C), the text details these temple officials' proper appearance and conduct during the performance of their duties. A few instructions nearly parallel the Biblical rules for priests and Levites:

✣ Hittite temple kitchen attendants were to trim their hair and fingernails and dress in clean garments. The house in which the sacred bread was baked was to be swept clean, and no pigs or dogs (animals considered filthy in antiquity) were allowed in that house. Similarly, the Biblical consecration ritual for the Levites required them to shave their entire bodies and wash their clothes to symbolize their absolute ritual purity before God (Nu 8:7).[2] Further, the Israelite high priest was to maintain clean and well-coiffed hair and to refrain from tearing his clothes in mourning because he had been dedicated with the anointing oil of the Lord (Lev 21:10–12).

✣ Although Hittite temple servants received a daily allowance of foodstuffs for themselves and their families, if a servant were to siphon extra wine or steal a portion of any item intended for sacrifice, he was to be put to death. Likewise, if such a servant were to pilfer a temple treasure or any other article designated for the gods' use, he and his entire family were to be killed.

In Israel, Levites too received daily allowances from their congregations' sacrifices (Lev 28–36; Nu 18:8–19; Dt 18:1–5).[3] Yet Eli's wicked sons selected the choicest portions of meat before the sacrifice was properly divided, thereby incurring God's wrath (1Sa 2:12–17,27–34). And, just as the Hittites were warned (under punishment of death) not to steal from the gods, Achan and his family were stoned to death because he retained some plunder that was to have been devoted to the Lord (Jos 7:1,16–26).

✣ Hittite priests were to conduct designated feasts at their appointed times, using the requisite number of animals and/or other food supplies. Similarly, God instructed Moses regarding the observance of specific feasts at particular times throughout the year (Lev 23; Nu 9:1–14; Dt 16:1–17).[4]

✣ Hittite farmers and herdsmen were to bring the firstfruits of their crops and herds to the temple. If they attempted to cheat the gods by withholding the best produce or highest-quality fatted animals for themselves, they were severely punished, often by their own deaths and those of their entire families. Likewise, the Israelites were to donate the firstfruits of their harvests to the Lord: The firstborn of man and beast were to be redeemed—in a sense "purchased back" through sacrifices—in recognition that God had provided for and sustained them (Lev 23:9–14; Nu 18:13; Dt 18:4; Ne 10:35–36).

The fact that the priestly stipulations in effect during the times of Moses, Eli and Samuel had contemporary parallels among the Hittites is important because such commonality undermines the widely accepted theory that the Biblical priestly code is a very late work that could not have originated during the time of Moses.

[1]See "Anatolia and the Hittites" on page 144.
[2]See "Ritual Purity in Israel and the Ancient Near East" on page 166. [3]See "Sacrifices and Offerings in the Bible and the Ancient Near East" on page 158.
[4]See "The Festivals of Israel" on page 186.

Hittite goblet
Preserving Bible Times; © Dr. James C. Martin; permission of Turkish Antiquities

the Levites apart from the other Israelites, and the Levites will be
8:14 zNu 3:12 mine.[z]
15"After you have purified the Levites and presented them as a
8:15 aEx 29:24 wave offering,[a] they are to come to do their work at the Tent of Meet-
ing. 16They are the Israelites who are to be given wholly to me. I have
taken them as my own in place of the firstborn, the first male off-
8:16 bNu 3:12 spring[b] from every Israelite woman. 17Every firstborn male in Isra-
8:17 cEx 4:23 dEx 13:2; Lk 2:23 el, whether man or animal,[c] is mine. When I struck down all the
firstborn in Egypt, I set them apart for myself.[d] 18And I have taken
8:18 eNu 3:12 the Levites in place of all the firstborn sons in Israel.[e] 19Of all the Is-
8:19 fNu 3:9 raelites, I have given the Levites as gifts to Aaron and his sons[f] to do
8:19 gNu 1:53 hNu 16:46 the work at the Tent of Meeting on behalf of the Israelites[g] and to
make atonement for them[h] so that no plague will strike the Israel-
ites when they go near the sanctuary."
20Moses, Aaron and the whole Israelite community did with the
Levites just as the LORD commanded Moses. 21The Levites purified
8:21 iver 7 jver 12 themselves and washed their clothes.[i] Then Aaron presented them
as a wave offering before the LORD and made atonement for them to
purify them.[j] 22After that, the Levites came to do their work at the
Tent of Meeting under the supervision of Aaron and his sons. They did with the Levites just as the LORD
commanded Moses.
8:24 k1Ch 23:3 lEx 38:21; Nu 4:3 23The LORD said to Moses, 24"This applies to the Levites: Men twenty-five years old or more[k] shall
come to take part in the work at the Tent of Meeting,[l] 25but at the age of fifty, they must retire from their
regular service and work no longer. 26They may assist their brothers in performing their duties at the
Tent of Meeting, but they themselves must not do the work. This, then, is how you are to assign the re-
sponsibilities of the Levites."

The Passover

9:1 mEx 40:2 nNu 1:1 **9** The LORD spoke to Moses in the Desert of Sinai in the first month[m] of the second year after they
came out of Egypt.[n] He said, 2"Have the Israelites celebrate the Passover at the appointed time. 3Cel-
ebrate it at the appointed time, at twilight on the fourteenth day of this month, in accordance with all its
9:3 oEx 12:2-11, 43-49; Lev 23:5-8; Dt 16:1-8 rules and regulations.[o]"
4So Moses told the Israelites to celebrate the Passover, 5and they did so in the Desert of Sinai at twilight
9:5 pEx 12:1-13; Jos 5:10 on the fourteenth day of the first month.[p] The Israelites did everything just as the LORD commanded Moses.
6But some of them could not celebrate the Passover on that day because they were ceremonially un-
9:6 qLev 5:3 rEx 18:15; Nu 27:2 clean[q] on account of a dead body. So they came to Moses and Aaron[r] that same day 7and said to Moses,
"We have become unclean because of a dead body, but why should we be kept from presenting the LORD's
offering with the other Israelites at the appointed time?"
9:8 sEx 18:15; Nu 27:5,21; Ps 85:8 8Moses answered them, "Wait until I find out what the LORD commands concerning you."[s]
9Then the LORD said to Moses, 10"Tell the Israelites: 'When any of you or your descendants are un-
9:10 t2Ch 30:2 clean because of a dead body or are away on a journey, they may still celebrate[t] the LORD's Passover. 11They
are to celebrate it on the fourteenth day of the second month at twilight. They are to eat the lamb, togeth-
9:11 uEx 12:8 er with unleavened bread and bitter herbs.[u] 12They must not leave any of it till morning[v] or break any of
9:12 vEx 12:10, 43 wEx 12:46; Jn 19:36* its bones.[w] When they celebrate the Passover, they must follow all the regulations. 13But if a man who is
ceremonially clean and not on a journey fails to celebrate the Passover, that person must be cut off from
9:13 xGe 17:14; Ex 12:15 his people[x] because he did not present the LORD's offering at the appointed time. That man will bear the
consequences of his sin.
9:14 yEx 12:48, 49 14" 'An alien[y] living among you who wants to celebrate the LORD's Passover must do so in accordance
with its rules and regulations. You must have the same regulations for the alien and the native-born.' "

ANCIENT VOICES

Further: Let those who make the daily bread be clean. Let them be washed and trimmed. Let (their)* hair(?) and finger[nails] be trimmed. Let them be clothed in clean garments. I[f] (they are) [not], let them not prepare (them). Let those who normally [propit]iate the spirit and body of the gods prepare them. The baker's house in which they bake them must be swept and sprinkled down.

*Words or syllables in brackets or parentheses added by translator for clarity or where text has gaps. Uncertainty in text indicated by question mark in parentheses.

—INSTRUCTIONS TO PRIESTS AND TEMPLE OFFICIALS

See "Hittite Instructions for Priests" article.

8:16 The appointment of Aaron and his sons as priests (Ex 28–29) had preceded the events at Sinai (Ex 32) that had led to the appointment of the tribe of Levi to officiate before the Lord—and to do so instead of the firstborn (Nu 8:16). It appears that the Lord had intended that a priestly people would exercise their priesthood through their firstborn sons under the rule of the house of Aaron but that this became, through the failure of the people, the Aaronic-Levitical system familiar throughout the Old Testament period. Yet in the background the vision of the priest-people remained, waiting to become the "priesthood of all believers" under the one and only New Testament Priest, the Lord Jesus Christ (see 1Pe 2:5,9).

9:3 Traditional Jewish practice regards twilight as the end of one day and the beginning of the next.

The Cloud Above the Tabernacle

15On the day the tabernacle, the Tent of the Testimony, was set up, the cloud[z] covered it. From evening
till morning the cloud above the tabernacle looked like fire.[a] 16That is how it continued to be; the cloud
covered it, and at night it looked like fire. 17Whenever the cloud lifted from above the Tent, the Israelites
set out; wherever the cloud settled, the Israelites encamped.[b] 18At the LORD's command the Israelites set
out, and at his command they encamped. As long as the cloud stayed over the tabernacle, they remained
in camp. 19When the cloud remained over the tabernacle a long time, the Israelites obeyed the LORD's or-
der and did not set out. 20Sometimes the cloud was over the tabernacle only a few days; at the LORD's
command they would encamp, and then at his command they would set out. 21Sometimes the cloud
stayed only from evening till morning, and when it lifted in the morning, they set out. Whether by day
or by night, whenever the cloud lifted, they set out. 22Whether the cloud stayed over the tabernacle for two
days or a month or a year, the Israelites would remain in camp and not set out; but when it lifted, they
would set out. 23At the LORD's command they encamped, and at the LORD's command they set out. They
obeyed the LORD's order, in accordance with his command through Moses.

The Silver Trumpets

10 The LORD said to Moses: 2"Make two trumpets[c] of hammered silver, and use them for calling the
community[d] together and for having the camps set out. 3When both are sounded, the whole
community is to assemble before you at the entrance to the Tent of Meeting. 4If only one is sounded, the
leaders[e]—the heads of the clans of Israel—are to assemble before you. 5When a trumpet blast is sound-
ed, the tribes camping on the east are to set out.[f] 6At the sounding of a second blast, the camps on the
south are to set out.[g] The blast will be the signal for setting out. 7To gather the assembly, blow the trum-
pets,[h] but not with the same signal.[i]
8"The sons of Aaron, the priests, are to blow the trumpets. This is to be a lasting ordinance for you and
the generations to come.[j] 9When you go into battle in your own land against an enemy who is oppress-
ing you,[k] sound a blast on the trumpets. Then you will be remembered[l] by the LORD your God and res-
cued from your enemies.[m] 10Also at your times of rejoicing—your appointed feasts and New Moon fes-
tivals[n]—you are to sound the trumpets[o] over your burnt offerings and fellowship offerings,[a] and they
will be a memorial for you before your God. I am the LORD your God."

The Israelites Leave Sinai

11On the twentieth day of the second month of the second year,[p] the cloud lifted[q] from above the tab-
ernacle of the Testimony. 12Then the Israelites set out from the Desert of Sinai and traveled from place
to place until the cloud came to rest in the Desert of Paran. 13They set out, this first time, at the LORD's
command through Moses.[r]
14The divisions of the camp of Judah went first, under their standard.[s] Nahshon son of Amminadab[t]
was in command. 15Nethanel son of Zuar was over the division of the tribe of Issachar, 16and Eliab son
of Helon was over the division of the tribe of Zebulun. 17Then the tabernacle was taken down, and the
Gershonites and Merarites, who carried it, set out.[u]
18The divisions of the camp of Reuben went next, under their standard.[v] Elizur son of Shedeur was
in command. 19Shelumiel son of Zurishaddai was over the division of the tribe of Simeon, 20and Eliasaph
son of Deuel was over the division of the tribe of Gad. 21Then the Kohathites set out, carrying the holy
things.[w] The tabernacle was to be set up before they arrived.[x]
22The divisions of the camp of Ephraim[y] went next, under their standard. Elishama son of Ammihud
was in command. 23Gamaliel son of Pedahzur was over the division of the tribe of Manasseh, 24and Abi-
dan son of Gideoni was over the division of the tribe of Benjamin.
25Finally, as the rear guard[z] for all the units, the divisions of the camp of Dan set out, under their stan-
dard. Ahiezer son of Ammishaddai was in command. 26Pagiel son of Ocran was over the division of the
tribe of Asher, 27and Ahira son of Enan was over the division of the tribe of Naphtali. 28This was the or-
der of march for the Israelites divisions as they set out.

[a] 10 Traditionally *peace offerings*

9:15 [z]Ex 40:34 [a]Ex 13:21
9:17 [b]Ex 40:36-38; Nu 10:11,12; 1Co 10:1
10:2 [c]Ne 12:35; Ps 47:5 [d]Jer 4:5, 19; 6:1; Hos 5:8; Joel 2:1,15; Am 3:6
10:4 [e]Ex 18:21; Nu 1:16; 7:2
10:5 [f]ver 14
10:6 [g]ver 18
10:7 [h]Eze 33:3; Joel 2:1 [i]1Co 14:8
10:8 [j]Nu 31:6
10:9 [k]Jdg 2:18; 6:9; 1Sa 10:18; Ps 106:42 [l]Ge 8:1 [m]Ps 106:4
10:10 [n]Ps 81:3 [o]Lev 23:24
10:11 [p]Ex 40:17 [q]Nu 9:17
10:13 [r]Dt 1:6
10:14 [s]Nu 2:3-9 [t]Nu 1:7
10:17 [u]Nu 4:21-32
10:18 [v]Nu 2:10-16
10:21 [w]Nu 4:20 [x]ver 17
10:22 [y]Nu 2:24
10:25 [z]Nu 2:31; Jos 6:9

10:1-10 Trumpets—long, straight, slender metal tubes with flared ends—were blown for order and discipline. See "Trumpets in the Ancient World" on page 2057.

10:29 [a]Jdg 4:11 29 Now Moses said to Hobab[a] son of Reuel[b] the Midianite, Moses' father-in-law,[c] "We are setting out
[b]Ex 2:18 [c]Ex 3:1 for the place about which the LORD said, 'I will give it to you.'[d] Come with us and we will treat you well,
[d]Ge 12:7 for the LORD has promised good things to Israel."
10:30 [e]Mt 21:29 30 He answered, "No, I will not go;[e] I am going back to my own land and my own people."
31 But Moses said, "Please do not leave us. You know where we should camp in the desert, and you can
10:31 [f]Job 29:15 be our eyes.[f] 32 If you come with us, we will share with you[g] whatever good things the LORD gives us.[h]"
10:32 [g]Dt 10:18 [h]Ps 22:27-31; 67:5-7 33 So they set out[i] from the mountain of the LORD and traveled for three days. The ark of the covenant
10:33 [i]ver 12; Dt 1:33 [j]Jos 3:3 of the LORD[j] went before them during those three days to find them a place to rest. 34 The cloud of the
10:34 [k]Nu 9:15-23 LORD was over them by day when they set out from the camp.[k]
35 Whenever the ark set out, Moses said,

"Rise up, O LORD!
10:35 [l]Ps 68:1 [m]Dt 7:10; 32:41; Ps 68:2; Isa 17:12-14 May your enemies be scattered;[l]
may your foes flee before you.[m]"

36 Whenever it came to rest, he said,

10:36 [n]Isa 63:17 [o]Dt 1:10 "Return,[n] O LORD,
to the countless thousands of Israel.[o]"

Fire From the LORD

11 Now the people complained about their hardships in the hearing of the LORD, and when he heard
11:1 [p]Lev 10:2 them his anger was aroused. Then fire from the LORD burned among them[p] and consumed some
11:2 [q]Nu 21:7 of the outskirts of the camp. 2 When the people cried out to Moses, he prayed to the LORD[q] and the fire
11:3 [r]Dt 9:22 died down. 3 So that place was called Taberah,[a][r] because fire from the LORD had burned among them.

Quail From the LORD

11:4 [s]Ex 12:38 4 The rabble with them began to crave other food,[s] and again the Israelites started wailing[t] and said,
[t]Ps 78:18; 1Co 10:6 "If only we had meat to eat! 5 We remember the fish we ate in Egypt at no cost—also the cucumbers,
11:5 [u]Ex 16:3 melons, leeks, onions and garlic.[u] 6 But now we have lost our appetite; we never see anything but this
manna!"
11:7 [v]Ex 16:31 7 The manna was like coriander seed[v] and looked like resin.[w] 8 The people went around gathering it,
[w]Ge 2:12 and then ground it in a handmill or crushed it in a mortar. They cooked it in a pot or made it into cakes.
11:9 [x]Ex 16:13 And it tasted like something made with olive oil. 9 When the dew[x] settled on the camp at night, the man-
na also came down.
10 Moses heard the people of every family wailing, each at the entrance to his tent. The LORD became
exceedingly angry, and Moses was troubled. 11 He asked the LORD, "Why have you brought this trouble on
11:11 [y]Ex 5:22 your servant? What have I done to displease you that you put the burden of all these people on me?[y] 12 Did
I conceive all these people? Did I give them birth? Why do you tell me to carry them in my arms, as a
11:12 [z]Isa 40:11; 49:23 [a]Ex 13:5 nurse carries an infant,[z] to the land you promised on oath to their forefathers?[a] 13 Where can I get meat
11:13 [b]Jn 6:5-9 for all these people?[b] They keep wailing to me, 'Give us meat to eat!' 14 I cannot carry all these people by
11:14 [c]Ex 18:18 myself; the burden is too heavy for me.[c] 15 If this is how you are going to treat me, put me to death[d] right
11:15 [d]Ex 32:32 [e]1Ki 19:4; Jnh 4:3 now[e]—if I have found favor in your eyes—and do not let me face my own ruin."
16 The LORD said to Moses: "Bring me seventy of Israel's elders who are known to you as leaders and
officials among the people. Have them come to the Tent of Meeting, that they may stand there with you.
17 I will come down and speak with you there, and I will take of the Spirit that is on you and put the Spir-
11:17 [f]ver 25,29; 1Sa 10:6; 2Ki 2:9, 15; Joel 2:28 [g]Ex 18:18 it on them.[f] They will help you carry the burden of the people so that you will not have to carry it alone.[g]
18 "Tell the people: 'Consecrate yourselves[h] in preparation for tomorrow, when you will eat meat. The
11:18 [h]Ex 19:10 [i]Ex 16:7 [j]ver 5; Ac 7:39 LORD heard you when you wailed,[i] "If only we had meat to eat! We were better off in Egypt!"[j] Now the LORD
will give you meat, and you will eat it. 19 You will not eat it for just one day, or two days, or five, ten or
11:20 [k]Ps 78:29; 106:14,15 twenty days, 20 but for a whole month—until it comes out of your nostrils and you loathe it[k]—because
[l]Jos 24:27; 1Sa 10:19 you have rejected the LORD,[l] who is among you, and have wailed before him, saying, "Why did we ever
leave Egypt?" ' "

[a] 3 *Taberah* means *burning.*

11:1 See the note about anger on Genesis 27:45.

11:10 See again the note on anger at Genesis 27:45.

21 But Moses said, "Here I am among six hundred thousand men[m] on foot, and you say, 'I will give
them meat to eat for a whole month!' 22 Would they have enough if flocks and herds were slaughtered for
them? Would they have enough if all the fish in the sea were caught for them?"[n]
23 The LORD answered Moses, "Is the LORD's arm too short?[o] You will now see whether or not what I say
will come true for you.[p]"
24 So Moses went out and told the people what the LORD had said. He brought together seventy of their
elders and had them stand around the Tent. 25 Then the LORD came down in the cloud[q] and spoke with
him,[r] and he took of the Spirit[s] that was on him and put the Spirit on the seventy elders.[t] When the Spir-
it rested on them, they prophesied,[u] but they did not do so again.[a]
26 However, two men, whose names were Eldad and Medad, had remained in the camp. They were list-
ed among the elders, but did not go out to the Tent. Yet the Spirit also rested on them, and they prophe-
sied in the camp. 27 A young man ran and told Moses, "Eldad and Medad are prophesying in the camp."
28 Joshua son of Nun, who had been Moses' aide[v] since youth, spoke up and said, "Moses, my lord, stop
them!"[w]
29 But Moses replied, "Are you jealous for my sake? I wish that all the LORD's people were prophets[x] and
that the LORD would put his Spirit on them!" 30 Then Moses and the elders of Israel returned to the camp.
31 Now a wind went out from the LORD and drove quail[y] in from the sea. It brought them[b] down all
around the camp to about three feet[c] above the ground, as far as a day's walk in any direction. 32 All that
day and night and all the next day the people went out and gathered quail. No one gathered less than ten
homers.[d] Then they spread them out all around the camp. 33 But while the meat was still between their
teeth[z] and before it could be consumed, the anger of the LORD burned against the people, and he struck
them with a severe plague.[a] 34 Therefore the place was named Kibroth Hattaavah,[e][b] because there they
buried the people who had craved other food.
35 From Kibroth Hattaavah the people traveled to Hazeroth[c] and stayed there.

Miriam and Aaron Oppose Moses

12 Miriam and Aaron began to talk against Moses because of his Cushite wife,[d] for he had married
a Cushite. 2 "Has the LORD spoken only through Moses?" they asked. "Hasn't he also spoken
through us?"[e] And the LORD heard this.[f]
3 (Now Moses was a very humble man,[g] more humble than anyone else on the face of the earth.)
4 At once the LORD said to Moses, Aaron and Miriam, "Come out to the Tent of Meeting, all three of
you." So the three of them came out. 5 Then the LORD came down in a pillar of cloud;[h] he stood at the en-
trance to the Tent and summoned Aaron and Miriam. When both of them stepped forward, 6 he said,
"Listen to my words:

"When a prophet of the LORD is among you,
I reveal myself to him in visions,[i]
I speak to him in dreams.[j]
7 But this is not true of my servant Moses;[k]
he is faithful in all my house.[l]
8 With him I speak face to face,
clearly and not in riddles;[m]
he sees the form of the LORD.[n]
Why then were you not afraid
to speak against my servant Moses?"

9 The anger of the LORD burned against them, and he left them.[o]
10 When the cloud lifted from above the Tent, there stood Miriam—leprous,[a] like snow.[p] Aaron turned

11:21 [m]Ex 12:37
11:22 [n]Mt 15:33
11:23 [o]Isa 50:2; 59:1 [p]Nu 23:19; Eze 12:25; 24:14
11:25 [q]Nu 12:5 [r]ver 17 [s]1Sa 10:6 [t]Ac 2:17 [u]1Sa 10:10
11:28 [v]Ex 33:11; Jos 1:1 [w]Mk 9:38-40
11:29 [x]1Co 14:5
11:31 [y]Ex 16:13; Ps 78:26-28
11:33 [z]Ps 78:30 [a]Ps 106:15
11:34 [b]Dt 9:22
11:35 [c]Nu 33:17
12:1 [d]Ex 2:21
12:2 [e]Nu 16:3 [f]Nu 11:1
12:3 [g]Mt 11:29
12:5 [h]Nu 11:25
12:6 [i]Ge 15:1; 46:2 [j]Ge 31:10; 1Ki 3:5; Heb 1:1
12:7 [k]Jos 1:1-2; Ps 105:26 [l]Heb 3:2,5
12:8 [m]Dt 34:10 [n]Ex 20:4; Ps 17:15
12:9 [o]Ge 17:22
12:10 [p]Ex 4:6; Dt 24:9

[a] 25 Or *prophesied and continued to do so* [b] 31 Or *They flew* [c] 31 Hebrew *two cubits* (about 1 meter) [d] 32 That is, probably about 60 bushels (about 2.2 kiloliters) [e] 34 *Kibroth Hattaavah* means *graves of craving.* [f] 10 The Hebrew word was used for various diseases affecting the skin—not necessarily leprosy.

11:31–32 Large numbers of quail migrate each year across the Sinai Peninsula from Africa on their way to Europe and Asia. Since these birds have heavy bodies and do not fly well, they partly depend on prevailing winds to assist their flight and become exhausted by long journeys. During the 1900s Arabs living in northern Sinai used nets to catch between one and two million low-flying quail.

12:1 Cush was the first son of Ham, the father of the southernmost peoples known to the Hebrews, living in the southern Nile valley. If Moses' "Cushite wife" refers to Zipporah, the term is a reference to her Midianite ancestry. See "Midian" on page 92.

12:10 See "Skin Diseases in the Ancient World" on page 171.

12:10 [q]2Ki 5:1,27 toward her and saw that she had leprosy;[q] 11and he said to Moses, "Please, my lord, do not hold against
12:11 [r]2Sa 19:19; 24:10 us the sin we have so foolishly committed.[r] 12Do not let her be like a stillborn infant coming from its
mother's womb with its flesh half eaten away."
12:13 [s]Isa 30:26; Jer 17:14 13So Moses cried out to the LORD, "O God, please heal her![s]"
12:14 [t]Dt 25:9; Job 17:6; 30:9-10; Isa 50:6 14The LORD replied to Moses, "If her father had spit in her face,[t] would she not have been in disgrace
[u]Lev 13:46; Nu 5:2-3 for seven days? Confine her outside the camp[u] for seven days; after that she can be brought back." 15So
Miriam was confined outside the camp for seven days, and the people did not move on till she was
brought back.
12:16 [v]Nu 11:35 16After that, the people left Hazeroth[v] and encamped in the Desert of Paran.

Exploring Canaan

13:2 [w]Dt 1:22 **13** The LORD said to Moses, 2"Send some men to explore[w] the land of Canaan, which I am giving to
the Israelites. From each ancestral tribe send one of its leaders."
3So at the LORD's command Moses sent them out from the Desert of Paran. All of them were leaders
of the Israelites. 4These are their names:

from the tribe of Reuben, Shammua son of Zaccur;
5from the tribe of Simeon, Shaphat son of Hori;
13:6 [x]ver 30; Nu 14:6,24; 34:19; Jdg 1:12-15 6from the tribe of Judah, Caleb son of Jephunneh;[x]
7from the tribe of Issachar, Igal son of Joseph;
8from the tribe of Ephraim, Hoshea son of Nun;
9from the tribe of Benjamin, Palti son of Raphu;
10from the tribe of Zebulun, Gaddiel son of Sodi;
11from the tribe of Manasseh (a tribe of Joseph), Gaddi son of Susi;
12from the tribe of Dan, Ammiel son of Gemalli;
13from the tribe of Asher, Sethur son of Michael;
14from the tribe of Naphtali, Nahbi son of Vophsi;
15from the tribe of Gad, Geuel son of Maki.

13:16 [y]ver 8 [z]Dt 32:44 16These are the names of the men Moses sent to explore the land. (Moses gave Hoshea son of Nun[y] the
name Joshua.)[z]
13:17 [a]Ge 12:9 [b]Jdg 1:9 17When Moses sent them to explore Canaan, he said, "Go up through the Negev[a] and on into the hill
country.[b] 18See what the land is like and whether the people who live there are strong or weak, few or
many. 19What kind of land do they live in? Is it good or bad? What kind of towns do they live in? Are they
unwalled or fortified? 20How is the soil? Is it fertile or poor? Are there trees on it or not? Do your best to
13:20 [c]Dt 1:25 bring back some of the fruit of the land.[c]" (It was the season for the first ripe grapes.)
13:21 [d]Nu 20:1; 27:14; 33:36; Jos 15:1 21So they went up and explored the land from the Desert of Zin[d] as far as Rehob,[e] toward Lebo[a] Ha-
[e]Jos 19:28 math.[f] 22They went up through the Negev and came to Hebron, where Ahiman, Sheshai and Talmai,[g] the
[f]Jos 13:5 descendants of Anak,[h] lived. (Hebron had been built seven years before Zoan in Egypt.)[i] 23When they
13:22 [g]Jos 15:14 [h]Jos 15:13 reached the Valley of Eshcol,[b] they cut off a branch bearing a single cluster of grapes. Two of them car-
[i]Ps 78:12,43; Isa 19:11,13 ried it on a pole between them, along with some pomegranates and figs. 24That place was called the Val-
ley of Eshcol because of the cluster of grapes the Israelites cut off there. 25At the end of forty days they
returned from exploring the land.

Report on the Exploration

26They came back to Moses and Aaron and the whole Israelite community at Kadesh in the Desert of
13:26 [j]Nu 32:8 Paran. There they reported to them[j] and to the whole assembly and showed them the fruit of the land.
27They gave Moses this account: "We went into the land to which you sent us, and it does flow with milk
13:27 [k]Ex 3:8 [l]Dt 1:25 and honey![k] Here is its fruit.[l] 28But the people who live there are powerful, and the cities are fortified and
13:28 [m]Dt 1:28; 9:1,2 very large.[m] We even saw descendants of Anak there. 29The Amalekites live in the Negev; the Hittites,
Jebusites and Amorites live in the hill country; and the Canaanites live near the sea and along the Jordan."

[a] 21 Or *toward the entrance to* [b] 23 *Eshcol* means *cluster*; also in verse 24.

13:2 The use of spies was a common practice in the ancient Near East, as it is today.

13:22 The Anakites were men of great stature; their physical size brought fear to the people. They were related to the Nephilim, giants known for their great strength (see "Who Were the Nephilim?" on p. 215).

13:29 See "Lesser Known Peoples of the Old Testament" on page 265.

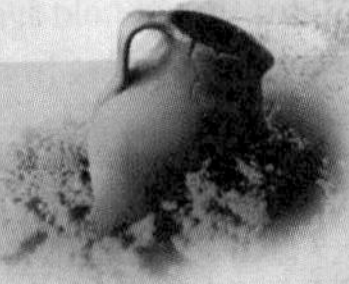

ARCHAEOLOGICAL SITES

KADESH BARNEA

NUMBERS 13 Sometimes referred to as Kadesh (Nu 13:26; 20:1) or Kedesh (Jos 15:23), the Biblical site of Kadesh Barnea is an important location in Israelite history. Miriam, Moses' sister, died there (Nu 20:1), and Moses, overcome by anger, disobediently struck the rock that brought forth water at this location (20:11). The 12 spies also returned there after their foray into the promised land (13:26). Although the name Kadesh is probably related to the Hebrew word *qadesh*, meaning "holiness," the origin of "Barnea" is unknown.

Since 1905 modern Ain el-Qudeirat in the Wadi el-Ain of the northern Sinai has been widely accepted to be the location of the Biblical Kadesh Barnea ("Map 1"). Several **Iron Age**[1] fortresses have been excavated there. The oldest, a small, elliptical structure, dates to the tenth century B.C. but was evidently abandoned for some time after the first fort's destruction. A second fort constructed during the eighth century B.C. (probably during the reign of Uzziah)[2] was destroyed during the seventh century B.C., most likely during Manasseh's[2] reign. This fort was somewhat larger and rectangular in shape, and a good amount of pottery associated with this structure has been found. Most significantly, two **ostraca** (pottery fragments containing writing) engraved in Hebrew have been recovered there, suggesting that Israelites did indeed occupy this site.

In 586 B.C. the Babylonians may have destroyed a final fortress, which appears to have been built during Josiah's[3] rule. Some ostraca containing inventories of goods have also been unearthed; their texts are in Hebrew, but the numerals are hieratic (a cursive form of Egyptian **hieroglyphics** that became common during the late Judahite monarchy).

At Ain el-Qudeirat, not a single pottery **sherd** has been discovered dating to the **Late Bronze** or **Iron** I periods. This archaeological gap has troubled historians who have sought evidence for an Israelite presence there, as indicated in Numbers. Skeptics have suggested that this interruption gives reason to question the veracity of the Biblical accounts of the **exodus** and the subsequent conquest of **Canaan**.[4]

Others have interpreted this pause differently, challenging the identification of Ain el-Qudeirat with the Biblical Kadesh Barnea and suggesting alternative sites at Ain Qedeis and Ain Qeseimeh. But problems exist with these sites, too. The Kadesh Barnea mentioned in Numbers (chs. 20 and 33) was probably a region rather than a specific site (see 33:36), and the Bible does not imply that a significant settlement existed there when the Israelites passed through.

Since the archaeological work at Ain el-Qudeirat has not been completed, the possibility remains that **Late Bronze** or **Iron Age** I evidence will in fact surface. Future excavations there and elsewhere may help to answer lingering questions concerning this Biblical location.

[1]See "Archaeological Periods" chart on page xx in the front of this Bible. [2]To learn more about these kings, see "Uzziah, King of Judah, and Jeroboam II, King of Israel" on page 650, as well as "The Seal of Manasseh" on page 565. [3]See "The Tragic Reign of King Josiah" on page 569. [4]See "The Conquest of Canaan" on page 310.

Kadesh Barnea ruins

Photograph courtesy of © Dr. Gary Pratico

30 Then Caleb silenced the people before Moses and said, "We should go up and take possession of the
land, for we can certainly do it."
31 But the men who had gone up with him said, "We can't attack those people; they are stronger than
we are."[n] 32 And they spread among the Israelites a bad report[o] about the land they had explored. They
said, "The land we explored devours[p] those living in it. All the people we saw there are of great size.[q] 33 We
saw the Nephilim[r] there (the descendants of Anak[s] come from the Nephilim). We seemed like grasshop-
pers in our own eyes, and we looked the same to them."

13:31 [n]Dt 1:28; 9:1; Jos 14:8 **13:32** [o]Nu 14:36, 37 [p]Eze 36:13,14 [q]Am 2:9 **13:33** [r]Ge 6:4 [s]Dt 1:28

Who Were the Nephilim?

NUMBERS 13 There are only two Biblical references to the Nephilim (Ge 6:4; Nu 13:33), people of "great size" (v. 32) from whom the Anakites were said to have descended. Upon glimpsing these imposing inhabitants of **Canaan**,[1] ten of the twelve spies became demoralized and terrified. The Nephilim may have been similar in appearance to the Rephaites, a race of strong, tall men with whom the Anakites are compared in Deuteronomy 2:21.

The Nephilim are described in Genesis 6:4 as having been mighty men who lived before the great flood. The author of Genesis linked them to "the sons of God" (other translations render this "sons of the gods"), either in terms of being identical to this group or of being their offspring. Three theories have been proposed regarding the parentage of these Nephilim (these hypotheses do not address the problem of how they might have survived the flood to appear in Canaan at the time of the spy expedition):

✣ Some Biblical historians argue that the "sons of God" were righteous men (descendants of Seth) who married worldly, female descendants of Cain and thus became defiled. Their progeny increased in sinfulness until God rectified the worsening situation with the flood. However, this theory does not explain why the word translated "men" in Genesis 6:1 describes all of humanity, while the same word in verse 2 designates only Cain's line.

✣ Other scholars argue that "the sons of God" (Ge 6:2) were kings who took multiple wives in order to build dynasties from their numerous descendants. In several instances ancient Near Eastern documents refer to kings as being the sons of particular gods. Also, **Akkadian** texts indicate that the Hebrew word translated "men" in Genesis 6:4 could alternatively mean "commoners" in some contexts. This would suggest that the Nephilim were kings who acquired harems, using the daughters of commoners, and sired large families through them. But no other Biblical passages refer to kings in general as "sons of God," and later kings (such as Solomon) who had many wives are not identified as being among the Nephilim.

✣ Still other scholars believe that the "sons of God" were angels who impregnated human women and sired demigods (beings with more power than humans but less than gods) who were able to do whatever they pleased on Earth (much like the mythical Greek Titans), prompting God's determination to destroy humankind to root out the growing evil.

Jesus specified, however, that angels do not marry (Mt 22:30), and from this it can be argued that they do not procreate. Yet procreation by these particular angels could be regarded as aberrant behavior (see Jude 6). It may be helpful to note that the phrase "sons of God" as used elsewhere in the Old Testament and in other ancient Semitic languages always refers to divine beings (e.g., Job 1:6, where the same Hebrew word is translated "angels").

Ancient Jewish interpreters unanimously believed the "sons of God" to have been angelic beings, a view possibly reflected in 1 Peter 3:20 and 2 Peter 2:4–5. But if the "sons of God" mentioned in Genesis 6 were indeed angels, and the Nephilim were their offspring, how do these facts relate to the Nephilim mentioned in Numbers 13? Most likely the word "Nephilim" in this later context means something like "giants" or "Titans" (i.e., the term was used literally in Ge 6 but metaphorically in Nu 13).

[1]See "Canaan" on page 324.

The People Rebel

14 That night all the people of the community raised their voices and wept aloud. 2All the Israelites
grumbled against Moses and Aaron, and the whole assembly said to them, "If only we had died
in Egypt! Or in this desert![t] 3Why is the LORD bringing us to this land only to let us fall by the sword? Our
wives and children will be taken as plunder. Wouldn't it be better for us to go back to Egypt?" 4And they
said to each other, "We should choose a leader and go back to Egypt.[u]"
5Then Moses and Aaron fell facedown[v] in front of the whole Israelite assembly gathered there. 6Joshua son
of Nun and Caleb son of Jephunneh, who were among those who had explored the land, tore their clothes 7and
said to the entire Israelite assembly, "The land we passed through and explored is exceedingly good.[w] 8If the
LORD is pleased with us,[x] he will lead us into that land, a land flowing with milk and honey,[y] and will give it
to us. 9Only do not rebel[z] against the LORD. And do not be afraid of the people of the land,[a] because we will
swallow them up. Their protection is gone, but the LORD is with us. Do not be afraid of them."
10But the whole assembly talked about stoning[b] them. Then the glory of the LORD[c] appeared at the
Tent of Meeting to all the Israelites. 11The LORD said to Moses, "How long will these people treat me with
contempt? How long will they refuse to believe in me,[d] in spite of all the miraculous signs I have
performed among them? 12I will strike them down with a plague and destroy them, but I will make you
into a nation[e] greater and stronger than they."
13Moses said to the LORD, "Then the Egyptians will hear about it! By your power you brought these
people up from among them.[f] 14And they will tell the inhabitants of this land about it. They have already
heard[g] that you, O LORD, are with these people and that you, O LORD, have been seen face to face, that your
cloud stays over them, and that you go before them in a pillar of cloud by day and a pillar of fire by night.[h]
15If you put these people to death all at one time, the nations who have heard this report about you will
say, 16'The LORD was not able to bring these people into the land he promised them on oath; so he slaugh-
tered them in the desert.'[i]
17"Now may the Lord's strength be displayed, just as you have declared: 18'The LORD is slow to anger,
abounding in love and forgiving sin and rebellion.[j] Yet he does not leave the guilty unpunished; he pun-
ishes the children for the sin of the fathers to the third and fourth generation.'[k] 19In accordance with
your great love, forgive[l] the sin of these people,[m] just as you have pardoned them from the time they left
Egypt until now."[n]
20The LORD replied, "I have forgiven them,[o] as you asked. 21Nevertheless, as surely as I live[p] and as
surely as the glory of the LORD fills the whole earth,[q] 22not one of the men who saw my glory and the mi-
raculous signs I performed in Egypt and in the desert but who disobeyed me and tested me ten times[r]—
23not one of them will ever see the land I promised on oath[s] to their forefathers. No one who has treat-
ed me with contempt will ever see it.[t] 24But because my servant Caleb has a different spirit and follows
me wholeheartedly,[u] I will bring him into the land he went to, and his descendants will inherit it.[v] 25Since
the Amalekites and Canaanites are living in the valleys, turn[w] back tomorrow and set out toward the
desert along the route to the Red Sea.[a]"
26The LORD said to Moses and Aaron: 27"How long will this wicked community grumble against me?
I have heard the complaints of these grumbling Israelites.[x] 28So tell them, 'As surely as I live,[y] declares the
LORD, I will do to you the very things I heard you say: 29In this desert your bodies will fall[z]—every one
of you twenty years old or more[a] who was counted in the census and who has grumbled against me.
30Not one of you will enter the land I swore with uplifted hand to make your home, except Caleb son of
Jephunneh and Joshua son of Nun. 31As for your children that you said would be taken as plunder, I will
bring them in to enjoy the land you have rejected.[b] 32But you—your bodies will fall[c] in this desert. 33Your
children will be shepherds here for forty years, suffering for your unfaithfulness, until the last of your
bodies lies in the desert. 34For forty years—one year for each of the forty days you explored the land[d]—
you will suffer for your sins and know what it is like to have me against you.' 35I, the LORD, have spoken,
and I will surely do these things[e] to this whole wicked community, which has banded together against
me. They will meet their end in this desert; here they will die."
36So the men Moses had sent[f] to explore the land, who returned and made the whole community
grumble against him by spreading a bad report[g] about it— 37these men responsible for spreading the
bad report[h] about the land were struck down and died of a plague[i] before the LORD. 38Of the men who
went to explore the land, only Joshua son of Nun and Caleb son of Jephunneh survived.[j]

14:2 [t]Nu 11:1
14:4 [u]Ne 9:17
14:5 [v]Nu 16:4, 22,45
14:7 [w]Nu 13:27; Dt 1:25
14:8 [x]Dt 10:15 [y]Nu 13:27
14:9 [z]Dt 1:26; 9:7,23,24 [a]Dt 1:21; 7:18; 20:1
14:10 [b]Ex 17:4 [c]Lev 9:23
14:11 [d]Ps 78:22; 106:24
14:12 [e]Ex 32:10
14:13 [f]Ex 32:11-14; Ps 106:23
14:14 [g]Ex 15:14 [h]Ex 13:21
14:16 [i]Jos 7:7
14:18 [j]Ex 34:6; Ps 145:8; Jnh 4:2 [k]Ex 20:5
14:19 [l]Ex 34:9 [m]Ps 106:45 [n]Ps 78:38
14:20 [o]Ps 106:23; Mic 7:18-20
14:21 [p]Dt 32:40; Isa 49:18 [q]Ps 72:19; Isa 6:3; Hab 2:14
14:22 [r]Ex 14:11; 32:1; 1Co 10:5
14:23 [s]Nu 32:11 [t]Heb 3:18
14:24 [u]ver 6-9; Jos 14:8,14 [v]Nu 32:12
14:25 [w]Dt 1:40
14:27 [x]Ex 16:12
14:28 [y]ver 21
14:29 [z]Nu 26:65 [a]Nu 1:45
14:31 [b]Ps 106:24
14:32 [c]1Co 10:5
14:34 [d]Nu 13:25
14:35 [e]Nu 23:19
14:36 [f]Nu 13:4-16 [g]Nu 13:32
14:37 [h]1Co 10:10 [i]Nu 16:49
14:38 [j]Jos 14:6

[a] 25 Hebrew *Yam Suph*; that is, Sea of Reeds

14:39 [k]Ex 33:4
14:40 [l]Dt 1:41
14:41 [m]2Ch 24:20
14:42 [n]Dt 1:42
14:44 [o]Dt 1:43 [p]Nu 31:6
14:45 [q]Nu 21:3; Dt 1:44; Jdg 1:17

[39]When Moses reported this to all the Israelites, they mourned[k] bitterly. [40]Early the next morning
they went up toward the high hill country. "We have sinned[l]," they said. "We will go up to the place the
LORD promised."
[41]But Moses said, "Why are you disobeying the LORD's command? This will not succeed![m] [42]Do not go
up, because the LORD is not with you. You will be defeated by your enemies,[n] [43]for the Amalekites and
Canaanites will face you there. Because you have turned away from the LORD, he will not be with you and
you will fall by the sword."
[44]Nevertheless, in their presumption they went up[o] toward the high hill country, though neither Mo-
ses nor the ark of the LORD's covenant moved from the camp.[p] [45]Then the Amalekites and Canaanites
who lived in that hill country came down and attacked them and beat them down all the way to Hormah.[q]

Supplementary Offerings

15:2 [r]Lev 23:10
15:3 [s]Lev 1:2 [t]ver 24; Ge 8:21; Ex 29:18 [u]Nu 28:19,27 [v]Lev 22:18,21; Ezr 1:4 [w]Lev 23:1-44
15:4 [x]Lev 2:1; 6:14
15:5 [y]Nu 28:7,14

15 The LORD said to Moses, [2]"Speak to the Israelites and say to them: 'After you enter the land I am
giving you[r] as a home [3]and you present to the LORD offerings made by fire, from the herd or the
flock,[s] as an aroma pleasing to the LORD[t]—whether burnt offerings[u] or sacrifices, for special vows or
freewill offerings[v] or festival offerings[w]— [4]then the one who brings his offering shall present to the LORD
a grain offering[x] of a tenth of an ephah[a] of fine flour mixed with a quarter of a hin[b] of oil. [5]With each lamb
for the burnt offering or the sacrifice, prepare a quarter of a hin of wine[y] as a drink offering.

[a] 4 That is, probably about 2 quarts (about 2 liters) [b] 4 That is, probably about 1 quart (about 1 liter); also in verse 5

15:1—21:11 This section records repeated unfaithfulness on the part of the people. Apparently during much of the 40 years, according to Amos 5:25–26 and Joshua 5:2ff., they wandered far away from God, and even their national unity may have lapsed temporarily. The 40 years are treated here very briefly.

Fringe (Tassels) on Garments

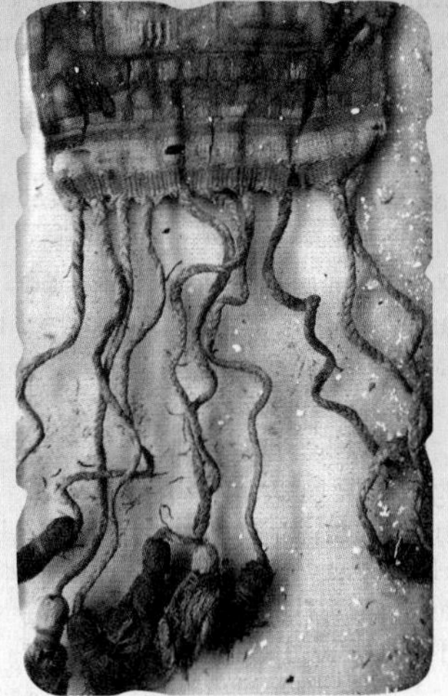

Priestly tassels
Preserving Bible Times; © Dr. James C. Martin; permission of The Cairo Museum

NUMBERS 15 God's command to affix tassels to the hems of Israelite garments carried rich symbolism in the ancient world. People perceived the hem of a garment to be an extension of the wearer's person and status (cf. Ru 3:9; 1Sa 24:11,20; Mt 9:21; 23:5; note that the connection in most of these references would have been understood by ancient Hebrews/Jews, although it may not be explicitly stated). So strongly did the hem represent the wearer's identity that legally binding agreements were sealed by impressing the hem as a "signature" onto the wet clay tablet of a recorded contract.[1]

In Israel, fringed hems with twisted cords of blue marked the wearers' community as being consecrated to the Lord (Nu 15:37–40). The prescribed blue color of the tassels was reminiscent of the "sacred" blue textiles used to make tabernacle coverings and high priestly garments (Ex 26:31; 28:31). Israelites affixed these tassels to their garments to jog their memories in terms of the commandments the keeping of which would make them holy. God's people were to be set apart by dress and observance of the law as "a kingdom of priests and a holy nation" (Ex 19:6).

[1]See "Cuneiform and Clay Tablets in the Ancient Near East" on page 1108.

6 " 'With a ram[z] prepare a grain offering[a] of two-tenths of an ephah[a] of fine flour mixed with a third 15:6 [z]Lev 5:15
of a hin[b] of oil,[b] 7 and a third of a hin of wine as a drink offering. Offer it as an aroma pleasing to the [a]Nu 28:12 [b]Eze 46:14
LORD.
8 " 'When you prepare a young bull as a burnt offering or sacrifice, for a special vow or a fellowship of-
fering[c][c] to the LORD, 9 bring with the bull a grain offering of three-tenths of an ephah[d][d] of fine flour mixed 15:8 [c]Lev 1:3; 3:1
with half a hin[e] of oil. 10 Also bring half a hin of wine as a drink offering. It will be an offering made by 15:9 [d]Lev 14:10
fire, an aroma pleasing to the LORD. 11 Each bull or ram, each lamb or young goat, is to be prepared in this
manner. 12 Do this for each one, for as many as you prepare.
13 " 'Everyone who is native-born[e] must do these things in this way when he brings an offering made 15:13 [e]Lev 16:29
by fire as an aroma pleasing to the LORD. 14 For the generations to come, whenever an alien or anyone else
living among you presents an offering made by fire as an aroma pleasing to the LORD, he must do exact-
ly as you do. 15 The community is to have the same rules for you and for the alien living among you; this
is a lasting ordinance for the generations to come.[f] You and the alien shall be the same before the LORD: 15:15 [f]ver 29; Nu 9:14
16 The same laws and regulations will apply both to you and to the alien living among you.[g]' " 15:16 [g]Nu 9:14
17 The LORD said to Moses, 18 "Speak to the Israelites and say to them: 'When you enter the land to
which I am taking you 19 and you eat the food of the land,[h] present a portion as an offering to the LORD. 15:19 [h]Jos 5:11, 12
20 Present a cake from the first of your ground meal[i] and present it as an offering from the threshing floor.[j] 15:20 [i]Ex 34:26; Lev 23:14; Dt 26:2,10
21 Throughout the generations to come you are to give this offering to the LORD from the first of your [j]Lev 2:14
ground meal.[k] 15:21 [k]Ro 11:16

Offerings for Unintentional Sins

22 " 'Now if you unintentionally fail to keep any of these commands the LORD gave Moses[l]— 23 any of 15:22 [l]Lev 4:2
the LORD's commands to you through him, from the day the LORD gave them and continuing through the
generations to come— 24 and if this is done unintentionally without the community being aware of it,[m] 15:24 [m]Lev 5:15
then the whole community is to offer a young bull for a burnt offering[n] as an aroma pleasing to the LORD, [n]Lev 4:14
along with its prescribed grain offering and drink offering, and a male goat for a sin offering.[o] 25 The [o]Lev 4:3
priest is to make atonement for the whole Israelite community, and they will be forgiven,[p] for it was not 15:25 [p]Lev 4:20;
intentional and they have brought to the LORD for their wrong an offering made by fire and a sin offer- Ro 3:25; Heb 2:17
ing. 26 The whole Israelite community and the aliens living among them will be forgiven, because all the
people were involved in the unintentional wrong.[q] 15:26 [q]ver 24
27 " 'But if just one person sins unintentionally,[r] he must bring a year-old female goat for a sin offer- 15:27 [r]Lev 4:27
ing. 28 The priest is to make atonement before the LORD for the one who erred by sinning unintentional-
ly, and when atonement has been made for him, he will be forgiven.[s] 29 One and the same law applies to 15:28 [s]Lev 4:35
everyone who sins unintentionally, whether he is a native-born Israelite or an alien.
30 " 'But anyone who sins defiantly,[t] whether native-born or alien,[u] blasphemes the LORD, and that 15:30 [t]Nu 14:40-44; Dt 1:43;
person must be cut off from his people. 31 Because he has despised the LORD's word and broken his com- 17:13; Ps 19:13
mands,[v] that person must surely be cut off; his guilt remains on him.[w]' " [u]ver 14 15:31 [v]2Sa 12:9; Ps 119:126; Pr 13:13 [w]Lev 5:1; Eze 18:20

The Sabbath-Breaker Put to Death

32 While the Israelites were in the desert, a man was found gathering wood on the Sabbath day.[x] 15:32 [x]Ex 31:14, 15; 35:2,3
33 Those who found him gathering wood brought him to Moses and Aaron and the whole assembly, 34 and
they kept him in custody, because it was not clear what should be done to him.[y] 35 Then the LORD said to 15:34 [y]Nu 9:8
Moses, "The man must die.[z] The whole assembly must stone him outside the camp.[a]" 36 So the assembly 15:35 [z]Ex 31:14, 15; Dt 21:21
took him outside the camp and stoned him to death, as the LORD commanded Moses. [a]Lev 20:2; 24:14; Ac 7:58

Tassels on Garments

37 The LORD said to Moses, 38 "Speak to the Israelites and say to them: 'Throughout the generations to
come you are to make tassels on the corners of your garments,[b] with a blue cord on each tassel. 39 You will 15:38 [b]Dt 22:12; Mt 23:5
have these tassels to look at and so you will remember[c] all the commands of the LORD, that you may obey 15:39 [c]Dt 4:23; 6:12; Ps 73:27
them and not prostitute yourselves by going after the lusts of your own hearts and eyes. 40 Then you will
remember to obey all my commands and will be consecrated to your God.[d] 41 I am the LORD your God, 15:40 [d]Lev 11:44;
who brought you out of Egypt to be your God. I am the LORD your God.' " Ro 12:1; Col 1:22; 1Pe 1:15

[a] 6 That is, probably about 4 quarts (about 4.5 liters) [b] 6 That is, probably about 1 1/4 quarts (about 1.2 liters); also in verse 7
[c] 8 Traditionally *peace offering* [d] 9 That is, probably about 6 quarts (about 6.5 liters) [e] 9 That is, probably about 2 quarts (about 2 liters); also in verse 10

Korah, Dathan and Abiram

16:1 [e]Jude 1:11 — **16** Korah[e] son of Izhar, the son of Kohath, the son of Levi, and certain Reubenites—Dathan and
[f]Nu 26:8; Dt 11:6 — Abiram, sons of Eliab,[f] and On son of Peleth—became insolent[a] 2and rose up against Moses.
With them were 250 Israelite men, well-known community leaders who had been appointed members
16:2 [g]Nu 1:16; 26:9 — of the council.[g] 3They came as a group to oppose Moses and Aaron[h] and said to them, "You have gone
16:3 [h]ver 7; Ps 106:16 — too far! The whole community is holy,[i] every one of them, and the LORD is with them.[j] Why then do you
[i]Ex 19:6 — set yourselves above the LORD's assembly?"[k]
[j]Nu 14:14 [k]Nu 12:2 — 4When Moses heard this, he fell facedown.[l] 5Then he said to Korah and all his followers: "In the morn-
16:4 [l]Nu 14:5 16:5 [m]Lev 10:3; — ing the LORD will show who belongs to him and who is holy,[m] and he will have that person come near him.
2Ti 2:19* [n]Nu 17:5; Ps 65:4 — The man he chooses[n] he will cause to come near him. 6You, Korah, and all your followers are to do this:
Take censers 7and tomorrow put fire and incense in them before the LORD. The man the LORD chooses will
be the one who is holy. You Levites have gone too far!"
8Moses also said to Korah, "Now listen, you Levites! 9Isn't it enough for you that the God of Israel has
separated you from the rest of the Israelite community and brought you near himself to do the work at
16:9 [o]Nu 3:6; Dt 10:8 — the LORD's tabernacle and to stand before the community and minister to them?[o] 10He has brought you
16:10 [p]Nu 3:10; 18:7 — and all your fellow Levites near himself, but now you are trying to get the priesthood too.[p] 11It is against
16:11 [q]1Co 10:10 [r]Ex 16:7 — the LORD that you and all your followers have banded together. Who is Aaron that you should grumble[q]
against him?[r]"
12Then Moses summoned Dathan and Abiram, the sons of Eliab. But they said, "We will not come!
13Isn't it enough that you have brought us up out of a land flowing with milk and honey to kill us in the
16:13 [s]Nu 14:2 [t]Ac 7:27,35 — desert?[s] And now you also want to lord it over us?[t] 14Moreover, you haven't brought us into a land flow-
16:14 [u]Lev 20:24 [v]Ex 22:5; 23:11; — ing with milk and honey[u] or given us an inheritance of fields and vineyards.[v] Will you gouge out the eyes
Nu 20:5 [w]Jdg 16:21; 1Sa 11:2 — of[b] these men?[w] No, we will not come!"
15Then Moses became very angry and said to the LORD, "Do not accept their offering. I have not tak-
16:15 [x]1Sa 12:3 — en so much as a donkey[x] from them, nor have I wronged any of them."
16Moses said to Korah, "You and all your followers are to appear before the LORD tomorrow—you and
16:16 [y]ver 6 — they and Aaron.[y] 17Each man is to take his censer and put incense in it—250 censers in all—and pre-
sent it before the LORD. You and Aaron are to present your censers also." 18So each man took his censer,
put fire and incense in it, and stood with Moses and Aaron at the entrance to the Tent of Meeting. 19When
16:19 [z]ver 42 [a]Ex 16:7; — Korah had gathered all his followers in opposition to them[z] at the entrance to the Tent of Meeting, the
Nu 14:10; 20:6 — glory of the LORD[a] appeared to the entire assembly. 20The LORD said to Moses and Aaron, 21"Separate
16:21 [b]Ex 32:10 — yourselves from this assembly so I can put an end to them at once."[b]
16:22 [c]Nu 14:5 [d]Nu 27:16; — 22But Moses and Aaron fell facedown[c] and cried out, "O God, God of the spirits of all mankind,[d] will
Job 12:10; Heb 12:9 — you be angry with the entire assembly when only one man sins?"[e]
[e]Ge 18:23 — 23Then the LORD said to Moses, 24"Say to the assembly, 'Move away from the tents of Korah, Dathan
and Abiram.' "
25Moses got up and went to Dathan and Abiram, and the elders of Israel followed him. 26He warned
16:26 [f]Isa 52:11 [g]Ge 19:15 — the assembly, "Move back from the tents of these wicked men![f] Do not touch anything belonging to them,
or you will be swept away[g] because of all their sins." 27So they moved away from the tents of Korah, Da-
than and Abiram. Dathan and Abiram had come out and were standing with their wives, children and
little ones at the entrances to their tents.
16:28 [h]Ex 3:12; Jn 5:36; 6:38 — 28Then Moses said, "This is how you will know that the LORD has sent me[h] to do all these things and
that it was not my idea: 29If these men die a natural death and experience only what usually happens to
16:29 [i]Ecc 3:19 — men, then the LORD has not sent me.[i] 30But if the LORD brings about something totally new, and the earth
opens its mouth and swallows them, with everything that belongs to them, and they go down alive into
16:30 [j]ver 33; Ps 55:15 — the grave,[c][j] then you will know that these men have treated the LORD with contempt."
16:31 [k]Mic 1:3-4 — 31As soon as he finished saying all this, the ground under them split apart[k] 32and the earth opened
16:32 [l]Nu 26:11; Dt 11:6; — its mouth and swallowed them,[l] with their households and all Korah's men and all their possessions.
Ps 106:17 — 33They went down alive into the grave, with everything they owned; the earth closed over them, and they

[a] 1 Or *Peleth—took ⌊men⌋* [b] 14 Or *you make slaves of;* or *you deceive* [c] 30 Hebrew *Sheol;* also in verse 33

16:1–50 The rebellion of Korah, a Kohathite illustrated, in the way it was subdued, the seriousness of attempting to enter the priesthood without the necessary prerequisites. God's choice of Aaron was further confirmed by the budding of his rod (17:1–11; Heb 9:4).

perished and were gone from the community. 34At their cries, all the Israelites around them fled, shouting, "The earth is going to swallow us too!"

35And fire came out from the LORD[m] and consumed[n] the 250 men who were offering the incense.

36The LORD said to Moses, 37"Tell Eleazar son of Aaron, the priest, to take the censers out of the smoldering remains and scatter the coals some distance away, for the censers are holy— 38the censers of the men who sinned at the cost of their lives.[o] Hammer the censers into sheets to overlay the altar, for they were presented before the LORD and have become holy. Let them be a sign[p] to the Israelites."

39So Eleazar the priest collected the bronze censers brought by those who had been burned up, and he had them hammered out to overlay the altar, 40as the LORD directed him through Moses. This was to remind the Israelites that no one except a descendant of Aaron should come to burn incense[q] before the LORD,[r] or he would become like Korah and his followers.[s]

41The next day the whole Israelite community grumbled against Moses and Aaron. "You have killed the LORD's people," they said.

42But when the assembly gathered in opposition[t] to Moses and Aaron and turned toward the Tent of Meeting, suddenly the cloud covered it and the glory of the LORD appeared. 43Then Moses and Aaron went to the front of the Tent of Meeting, 44and the LORD said to Moses, 45"Get away from this assembly so I can put an end to them at once." And they fell facedown.

46Then Moses said to Aaron, "Take your censer and put incense in it, along with fire from the altar, and hurry to the assembly[u] to make atonement[v] for them. Wrath has come out from the LORD; the plague[w] has started." 47So Aaron did as Moses said, and ran into the midst of the assembly. The plague had already started among the people,[x] but Aaron offered the incense and made atonement for them. 48He stood between the living and the dead, and the plague stopped.[y] 49But 14,700 people died from the plague, in addition to those who had died because of Korah.[z] 50Then Aaron returned to Moses at the entrance to the Tent of Meeting, for the plague had stopped.

The Budding of Aaron's Staff

17 The LORD said to Moses, 2"Speak to the Israelites and get twelve staffs from them, one from the leader of each of their ancestral tribes. Write the name of each man on his staff. 3On the staff of Levi write Aaron's name,[a] for there must be one staff for the head of each ancestral tribe. 4Place them in the Tent of Meeting in front of the Testimony,[b] where I meet with you.[c] 5The staff belonging to the man I choose[d] will sprout, and I will rid myself of this constant grumbling against you by the Israelites."

6So Moses spoke to the Israelites, and their leaders gave him twelve staffs, one for the leader of each of their ancestral tribes, and Aaron's staff was among them. 7Moses placed the staffs before the LORD in the Tent of the Testimony.[e]

8The next day Moses entered the Tent of the Testimony and saw that Aaron's staff, which represented the house of Levi, had not only sprouted but had budded, blossomed and produced almonds.[f] 9Then Moses brought out all the staffs from the LORD's presence to all the Israelites. They looked at them, and each man took his own staff.

10The LORD said to Moses, "Put back Aaron's staff in front of the Testimony, to be kept as a sign to the rebellious.[g] This will put an end to their grumbling against me, so that they will not die." 11Moses did just as the LORD commanded him.

12The Israelites said to Moses, "We will die! We are lost, we are all lost![h] 13Anyone who even comes near the tabernacle of the LORD will die.[i] Are we all going to die?"

Duties of Priests and Levites

18 The LORD said to Aaron, "You, your sons and your father's family are to bear the responsibility for offenses against the sanctuary,[j] and you and your sons alone are to bear the responsibility for offenses against the priesthood. 2Bring your fellow Levites from your ancestral tribe to join you and assist you when you and your sons minister[k] before the Tent of the Testimony. 3They are to be responsible to you and are to perform all the duties of the Tent,[l] but they must not go near the furnishings of the sanctuary or the altar, or both they and you will die.[m] 4They are to join you and be responsible for the care of the Tent of Meeting—all the work at the Tent—and no one else may come near where you are.

5"You are to be responsible for the care of the sanctuary and the altar,[n] so that wrath will not fall on the Israelites again. 6I myself have selected your fellow Levites from among the Israelites as a gift to you,[o]

16:35 [m]Nu 11:1-3; 26:10 [n]Lev 10:2
16:38 [o]Pr 20:2 [p]Nu 26:10; Eze 14:8; 2Pe 2:6
16:40 [q]Ex 30:7-10; Nu 1:51 [r]2Ch 26:18 [s]Nu 3:10
16:42 [t]ver 19; Nu 20:6
16:46 [u]Lev 10:6 [v]Nu 18:5; 25:13; Dt 9:22 [w]Nu 8:19; Ps 106:29
16:47 [x]Nu 25:6-8
16:48 [y]Nu 25:8; Ps 106:30
16:49 [z]ver 32
17:3 [a]Nu 1:3
17:4 [b]ver 7 [c]Ex 25:22
17:5 [d]Nu 16:5
17:7 [e]Ex 38:21; Ac 7:44
17:8 [f]Eze 17:24; Heb 9:4
17:10 [g]Dt 9:24
17:12 [h]Isa 6:5
17:13 [i]Nu 1:51
18:1 [j]Ex 28:38
18:2 [k]Nu 3:10
18:3 [l]Nu 1:51 [m]ver 7; Nu 4:15
18:5 [n]Nu 16:46
18:6 [o]Nu 3:9

dedicated to the LORD to do the work at the Tent of Meeting. 7But only you and your sons may serve as
18:7 [p]Heb 9:3,6 priests in connection with everything at the altar and inside the curtain.[p] I am giving you the service of
[q]ver 20; Ex 29:9 [r]Nu 3:10 the priesthood as a gift.[q] Anyone else who comes near the sanctuary must be put to death.[r]"

Offerings for Priests and Levites

8Then the LORD said to Aaron, "I myself have put you in charge of the offerings presented to me;
all the holy offerings the Israelites give me I give to you and your sons as your portion and regular
18:8 [s]Lev 6:16; 7:6,31-34,36 share.[s] 9You are to have the part of the most holy offerings that is kept from the fire. From all the gifts
18:9 [t]Lev 2:1 they bring me as most holy offerings, whether grain[t] or sin[u] or guilt offerings,[v] that part belongs to
[u]Lev 6:25 [v]Lev 5:15; 7:7 you and your sons. 10Eat it as something most holy; every male shall eat it.[w] You must regard it as
18:10 [w]Lev 6:16 holy.
18:11 [x]Ex 29:26 11"This also is yours: whatever is set aside from the gifts of all the wave offerings[x] of the Israelites. I
give this to you and your sons and daughters as your regular share. Everyone in your household who is
[y]Lev 22:1-16 ceremonially clean[y] may eat it.
12"I give you all the finest olive oil and all the finest new wine and grain they give the LORD as the first-
18:12 [z]Ex 23:19; Ne 10:35 fruits of their harvest.[z] 13All the land's firstfruits that they bring to the LORD will be yours.[a] Everyone in
18:13 [a]Ex 22:29; 23:19 your household who is ceremonially clean may eat it.
18:14 [b]Lev 27:28 14"Everything in Israel that is devoted[a] to the LORD[b] is yours. 15The first offspring of every womb, both
18:15 [c]Ex 13:2 [d]Nu 3:46 man and animal, that is offered to the LORD is yours.[c] But you must redeem[d] every firstborn son and ev-
[e]Ex 13:13 ery firstborn male of unclean animals.[e] 16When they are a month old, you must redeem them at the re-
18:16 [f]Lev 27:6 [g]Ex 30:13 demption price set at five shekels[b][f] of silver, according to the sanctuary shekel,[g] which weighs twenty
gerahs.
18:17 [h]Dt 15:19 [i]Lev 3:2 17"But you must not redeem the firstborn of an ox, a sheep or a goat; they are holy.[h] Sprinkle their
blood[i] on the altar and burn their fat as an offering made by fire, an aroma pleasing to the LORD. 18Their
18:18 [j]Lev 7:30 meat is to be yours, just as the breast of the wave offering[j] and the right thigh are yours. 19Whatever is
set aside from the holy offerings the Israelites present to the LORD I give to you and your sons and daugh-
18:19 [k]Lev 2:13; 2Ch 13:5 ters as your regular share. It is an everlasting covenant of salt[k] before the LORD for both you and your off-
spring."
20The LORD said to Aaron, "You will have no inheritance in their land, nor will you have any share
18:20 [l]Dt 12:12 [m]Dt 10:9; 14:27; 18:1-2; among them;[l] I am your share and your inheritance[m] among the Israelites.
21"I give to the Levites all the tithes[n] in Israel as their inheritance[o] in return for the work they do while
Jos 13:33; Eze 44:28 serving at the Tent of Meeting. 22From now on the Israelites must not go near the Tent of Meeting, or
18:21 [n]Dt 14:22; Mal 3:8 they will bear the consequences of their sin and will die.[p] 23It is the Levites who are to do the work at the
[o]Lev 27:30-33; Heb 7:5 Tent of Meeting and bear the responsibility for offenses against it. This is a lasting ordinance for the gen-
18:22 [p]Lev 22:9; Nu 1:51 erations to come. They will receive no inheritance[q] among the Israelites. 24Instead, I give to the Levites
18:23 [q]ver 20 as their inheritance the tithes that the Israelites present as an offering to the LORD. That is why I said con-
cerning them: 'They will have no inheritance among the Israelites.' "
25The LORD said to Moses, 26"Speak to the Levites and say to them: 'When you receive from the Isra-
18:26 [r]ver 21 [s]Ne 10:38 elites the tithe I give you[r] as your inheritance, you must present a tenth of that tithe as the LORD's offer-
ing.[s] 27Your offering will be reckoned to you as grain from the threshing floor or juice from the wine-
18:28 [t]Mal 3:8 press. 28In this way you also will present an offering to the LORD from all the tithes[t] you receive from the
Israelites. From these tithes you must give the LORD's portion to Aaron the priest. 29You must present as
the LORD's portion the best and holiest part of everything given to you.'
30"Say to the Levites: 'When you present the best part, it will be reckoned to you as the product of the
18:30 [u]ver 27 threshing floor or the winepress.[u] 31You and your households may eat the rest of it anywhere, for it is
18:32 [v]Lev 22:15 [w]Lev 19:8 your wages for your work at the Tent of Meeting. 32By presenting the best part[v] of it you will not be guilty
in this matter; then you will not defile the holy offerings[w] of the Israelites, and you will not die.' "

[a] *14* The Hebrew term refers to the irrevocable giving over of things or persons to the LORD. [b] *16* That is, about 2 ounces (about 55 grams)

18:12 Oil, wine and grain were the staples of Israelite diet (see "Food and Agriculture" on p. 390). God's people were to give the finest of their produce to the Lord. These items became the special foods of the priests and their families.

18:19 Since salt is also a necessary part of the daily diet, and salt was always used in sacrifices to the Lord (Lev 2:13), it was not long before people saw a connection between salt and covenant making. To "eat salt with" a person meant to share his or her hospitality. When covenants were made, they were usually confirmed with sacrificial meals, at which salt was always present. Numbers 18:19 specified that offerings were to be "an everlasting covenant of salt before the LORD."

The Water of Cleansing

19 The LORD said to Moses and Aaron: [2]"This is a requirement of the law that the LORD has com-
manded: Tell the Israelites to bring you a red heifer[x] without defect or blemish[y] and that has
never been under a yoke.[z] [3]Give it to Eleazar[a] the priest; it is to be taken outside the camp[b] and
slaughtered in his presence. [4]Then Eleazar the priest is to take some of its blood on his finger and
sprinkle[c] it seven times toward the front of the Tent of Meeting. [5]While he watches, the heifer is to
be burned—its hide, flesh, blood and offal.[d] [6]The priest is to take some cedar wood, hyssop[e] and
scarlet wool[f] and throw them onto the burning heifer. [7]After that, the priest must wash his clothes and
bathe himself with water.[g] He may then come into the camp, but he will be ceremonially unclean till
evening. [8]The man who burns it must also wash his clothes and bathe with water, and he too will be
unclean till evening.

[9]"A man who is clean shall gather up the ashes of the heifer[h] and put them in a ceremonially clean
place outside the camp. They shall be kept by the Israelite community for use in the water of cleansing;[i]
it is for purification from sin. [10]The man who gathers up the ashes of the heifer must also wash his
clothes, and he too will be unclean till evening. This will be a lasting ordinance both for the Israelites
and for the aliens living among them.

[11]"Whoever touches the dead body[j] of anyone will be unclean for seven days.[k] [12]He must purify him-
self with the water on the third day and on the seventh day;[l] then he will be clean. But if he does not pu-
rify himself on the third and seventh days, he will not be clean. [13]Whoever touches the dead body[m] of

19:2 [x]Ge 15:9; Heb 9:13 [y]Lev 22:19-25 [z]Dt 21:3; 1Sa 6:7
19:3 [a]Nu 3:4 [b]Lev 4:12,21; Heb 13:11
19:4 [c]Lev 4:17
19:5 [d]Ex 29:14
19:6 [e]ver 18; Ps 51:7 [f]Lev 14:4
19:7 [g]Lev 11:25; 16:26,28; 22:6
19:9 [h]Heb 9:13 [i]ver 13; Nu 8:7
19:11 [j]Lev 21:1; Nu 5:2 [k]Nu 31:19
19:12 [l]ver 19; Nu 31:19
19:13 [m]Lev 20:3

19:1–10 The ritual of the red heifer transferred impurity from the individual to the heifer. See "The Red Heifer," below.

The Red Heifer

NUMBERS 19 The ritual of the red heifer was a purification rite intended to cleanse Israelites defiled by contact with the dead.[1] Anyone who had touched a corpse became ritually impure for seven days with a contagious impurity that could defile other persons, vessels and, at worst, the Lord's sanctuary (Nu 19:20). The young red cow selected was to be without defect or blemish and never to have borne a yoke (i.e., never to have been used for secular service; see v. 2). As the heifer was being completely incinerated, the priest was to add cedar wood, hyssop and scarlet wool to the pyre (v. 6). These materials were also associated with other purification rituals (cf. Lev 14:4–7; Ps 51:7).[2]

The priest then mixed the heifer's ashes with spring water to produce a cleansing solution, with which the impure person was sprinkled on the third and seventh days, after which he or she was considered to be ritually clean (Nu 19:12).[3]

The ritual of the red heifer was unique among Israel's ceremonial traditions for the following reasons:

- The animal was burned outside the camp rather than being sacrificed on the altar (v. 3).[4] The heifer's blood and dung were burned alongside the carcass, a procedure otherwise forbidden in sacrificial law (v. 5; see Lev 4:11–12). Blood was not drained from the sacrifice because it constituted a necessary cleansing ingredient, along with the ashes.
- The officiants themselves contracted impurity while making this sacrifice and themselves had to be purified, though not using the same procedure (Nu 19:7–10).

The efficacy of this ritual lay in the transfer of impurity from the defiled person to the heifer. The corrupted animal was burned outside the camp lest it pollute the congregation in the same way it had tainted those with whom it had already come into contact. Ironically, as the heifer and its associated impurity were completely destroyed, the resulting ashes were able to purify those who had become ritually defiled.

The New Testament reinforces the significance of the red heifer in relation to the sacrificial work of Christ. Just as the heifer was slaughtered outside the camp to attain purification for the defiled, so Jesus—who bore the sins and impurities of all humanity—was crucified outside Jerusalem in order to achieve redemption through his blood for all sinners (Heb 13:11–12; cf. Heb 9:13–14).

[1]See "Ritual Purity in Israel and the Ancient Near East" on page 166. [2]See "Hyssop and the Rituals of Cleansing" on page 847. [3]See also "Bathing" on page 456.
[4]See "Sacrifices and Offerings in the Bible and the Ancient Near East" on page 158.

anyone and fails to purify himself defiles the LORD's tabernacle.[n] That person must be cut off from Israel.[o] Because the water of cleansing has not been sprinkled on him, he is unclean;[p] his uncleanness remains on him.

14"This is the law that applies when a person dies in a tent: Anyone who enters the tent and anyone who is in it will be unclean for seven days, 15and every open container without a lid fastened on it will be unclean.

16"Anyone out in the open who touches someone who has been killed with a sword or someone who has died a natural death,[q] or anyone who touches a human bone or a grave,[r] will be unclean for seven days.

17"For the unclean person, put some ashes[s] from the burned purification offering into a jar and pour fresh water over them. 18Then a man who is ceremonially clean is to take some hyssop,[t] dip it in the water and sprinkle the tent and all the furnishings and the people who were there. He must also sprinkle anyone who has touched a human bone or a grave or someone who has been killed or someone who has died a natural death. 19The man who is clean is to sprinkle the unclean person on the third and seventh days, and on the seventh day he is to purify him.[u] The person being cleansed must wash his clothes and bathe with water, and that evening he will be clean. 20But if a person who is unclean does not purify himself, he must be cut off from the community, because he has defiled the sanctuary of the LORD. The water of cleansing has not been sprinkled on him, and he is unclean. 21This is a lasting ordinance for them.

"The man who sprinkles the water of cleansing must also wash his clothes, and anyone who touches the water of cleansing will be unclean till evening. 22Anything that an unclean[v] person touches becomes unclean, and anyone who touches it becomes unclean till evening."

Water From the Rock

20 In the first month the whole Israelite community arrived at the Desert of Zin,[w] and they stayed at Kadesh.[x] There Miriam[y] died and was buried.

2Now there was no water for the community,[z] and the people gathered in opposition[a] to Moses and Aaron. 3They quarreled[b] with Moses and said, "If only we had died when our brothers fell dead before the LORD![c] 4Why did you bring the LORD's community into this desert, that we and our livestock should die here?[d] 5Why did you bring us up out of Egypt to this terrible place? It has no grain or figs, grapevines or pomegranates.[e] And there is no water to drink!"

6Moses and Aaron went from the assembly to the entrance to the Tent of Meeting and fell facedown,[f] and the glory of the LORD[g] appeared to them. 7The LORD said to Moses, 8"Take the staff,[h] and you and your brother Aaron gather the assembly together. Speak to that rock before their eyes and it will pour out its water.[i] You will bring water out of the rock for the community so they and their livestock can drink."

9So Moses took the staff from the LORD's presence,[j] just as he commanded him. 10He and Aaron gathered the assembly together in front of the rock and Moses said to them, "Listen, you rebels, must we bring you water out of this rock?"[k] 11Then Moses raised his arm and struck the rock twice with his staff. Water[l] gushed out, and the community and their livestock drank.

12But the LORD said to Moses and Aaron, "Because you did not trust in me enough to honor me as holy[m] in the sight of the Israelites, you will not bring this community into the land I give them."[n]

13These were the waters of Meribah,[a][o] where the Israelites quarreled[p] with the LORD and where he showed himself holy among them.

Edom Denies Israel Passage

14Moses sent messengers from Kadesh[q] to the king of Edom,[r] saying:

"This is what your brother Israel says: You know[s] about all the hardships that have come upon us. 15Our forefathers went down into Egypt,[t] and we lived there many years.[u] The Egyptians mistreated[v] us and our fathers, 16but when we cried out to the LORD, he heard our cry[w] and sent an angel[x] and brought us out of Egypt.

19:13 [n]Lev 15:31; 2Ch 36:14 [o]Lev 7:20; 22:3 [p]Hag 2:13
19:16 [q]Nu 31:19 [r]Mt 23:27
19:17 [s]ver 9
19:18 [t]ver 6
19:19 [u]Eze 36:25; Heb 10:22
19:22 [v]Lev 5:2; Hag 2:13,14
20:1 [w]Nu 13:21 [x]Nu 33:36 [y]Ex 15:20
20:2 [z]Ex 17:1 [a]Nu 16:19
20:3 [b]Ex 17:2 [c]Nu 14:2; 16:31-35
20:4 [d]Ex 14:11; 17:3; Nu 14:3; 16:13
20:5 [e]Nu 16:14
20:6 [f]Nu 14:5 [g]Nu 16:19
20:8 [h]Ex 4:17,20 [i]Ex 17:6; Isa 43:20
20:9 [j]Nu 17:10
20:10 [k]Ps 106:32,33
20:11 [l]Ex 17:6; Dt 8:15; Ps 78:16; Isa 48:2; 1Co 10:4
20:12 [m]Nu 27:14 [n]ver 24; Dt 1:37; 3:27
20:13 [o]Ex 17:7 [p]Dt 33:8; Ps 95:8; 106:32
20:14 [q]Jdg 11:16-17 [r]Dt 2:4 [s]Jos 2:11; 9:9
20:15 [t]Ge 46:6 [u]Ge 15:13; Ex 12:40 [v]Ex 1:11; Dt 26:6
20:16 [w]Ex 2:23; 3:7 [x]Ex 14:19

[a] 13 *Meribah* means *quarreling.*

20:1 The prophet Micah would later refer to Miriam, along with her brothers, as a leader whom the Lord had provided to bring Israel out of Egyptian bondage (Mic 6:4).

20:14 The people of Edom were descended from Esau, the brother of Jacob (see Ge 36:1). See "Edom" on page 1467.

A TIMELINE FOR THE WILDERNESS WANDERINGS

NUMBERS 20 Because they failed to trust God after having heard the ten spies' negative majority report about Canaan (Nu 13), God required the Israelites to wander for 40 years until every disbelieving person aged twenty or older had passed away (14:26–35). This forty-year period began retroactively on the day Israel had left Egypt—the fifteenth day of the first month of the first year, according to the Hebrew calendar (33:3), as well as the day after the first Passover[1]—and lasted until the first Passover in the promised land, the fourteenth day of the first month of the forty-first year (Jos 5:10).

The wilderness record preserved in Scripture covers approximately the first year and eight months of this protracted period (Ex 12:31—40:38; all of the book of Lev; Nu 1:1—19:22; 33:1–36; Dt 1:6–46), as well as the final year (Nu 20:1—32:42; 33:37—36:13; Dt 2–34; Jos 1:1—5:10; Jdg 11:14–22) of their sojourn. The intervening 37 years and four months constitutes a period of silence (between Nu 19 and 20; 33:36 and 37; and Dt 1 and 2). Dates are included for key events, so a fairly complete timeline for the beginning and the end of the wilderness wandering period has been calculated.

During the first month the Israelites traveled from Rameses to the Desert of Sin (Ex 12:31—16:1).[2] They spent one additional month trekking to Mount Sinai, where they stayed put for eleven months (Ex 16:2—Nu 10:11).[3] From there they journeyed for a little more than a month until they reached Kadesh Barnea, where they spent about six months (10:12—19:22).[4] After their departure from Kadesh Barnea (Dt 2:14), the Israelites' precise whereabouts during the next 37 years and four months is unknown. After this period of silence they returned to Kadesh Barnea and during the following year forged ahead to **Canaan** by way of the **Transjordan**.

[1]See "The Jewish Calendar" on page 241. [2]See "The Store Cities of Pithom and Rameses" on page 86 and "The Route of the Exodus" articles on pages 108–112. [3]See "The Location of Mount Sinai" on page 123. [4]See "Kadesh Barnea" on page 214.

Kadesh Barnea valley
Photograph courtesy of © Dr. Gary Pratico

"Now we are here at Kadesh, a town on the edge of your territory. [17]Please let us pass through
your country. We will not go through any field or vineyard, or drink water from any well. We will
travel along the king's highway and not turn to the right or to the left until we have passed through
20:17 [y]Nu 21:22 your territory.[y]"

[18]But Edom answered:

"You may not pass through here; if you try, we will march out and attack you with the sword."

[19]The Israelites replied:

20:19 [z]Ex 12:38 "We will go along the main road, and if we or our livestock[z] drink any of your water, we will pay
[a]Dt 2:6,28 for it.[a] We only want to pass through on foot—nothing else."

[20]Again they answered:

"You may not pass through."

Then Edom came out against them with a large and powerful army. [21]Since Edom refused to let them
20:21 [b]Dt 2:8; Jdg 11:18 go through their territory, Israel turned away from them.[b]

The Death of Aaron

20:22 [c]Nu 33:37 [22]The whole Israelite community set out from Kadesh and came to Mount Hor.[c] [23]At Mount Hor,
20:23 [d]Nu 33:37 **20:24** [e]Ge 25:8 near the border of Edom,[d] the LORD said to Moses and Aaron, [24]"Aaron will be gathered to his people.[e]
20:24 [f]ver 10 He will not enter the land I give the Israelites, because both of you rebelled against my command[f] at
20:25 [g]Nu 33:38 the waters of Meribah. [25]Get Aaron and his son Eleazar and take them up Mount Hor.[g] [26]Remove Aar-
20:26 [h]ver 24 on's garments and put them on his son Eleazar, for Aaron will be gathered to his people;[h] he will die
there."

20:28 [i]Ex 29:29 [27]Moses did as the LORD commanded: They went up Mount Hor in the sight of the whole commu-
[j]Nu 33:38; Dt 10:6; 32:50 nity. [28]Moses removed Aaron's garments and put them on his son Eleazar.[i] And Aaron died there[j]
on top of the mountain. Then Moses and Eleazar came down from the mountain, [29]and when the
20:29 [k]Dt 34:8 whole community learned that Aaron had died, the entire house of Israel mourned for him[k] thirty
days.

Arad Destroyed

21:1 [l]Nu 33:40; Jos 12:14 **21** When the Canaanite king of Arad,[l] who lived in the Negev,[m] heard that Israel was coming along
[m]Jdg 1:9,16 the road to Atharim, he attacked the Israelites and captured some of them. [2]Then Israel made this
vow to the LORD: "If you will deliver these people into our hands, we will totally destroy[a] their cities."
[3]The LORD listened to Israel's plea and gave the Canaanites over to them. They completely destroyed them
and their towns; so the place was named Hormah.[b]

The Bronze Snake

21:4 [n]Nu 20:22 [4]They traveled from Mount Hor[n] along the route to the Red Sea,[c] to go around Edom. But the people
[o]Dt 2:8; Jdg 11:18 grew impatient on the way;[o] [5]they spoke against God[p] and against Moses, and said, "Why have you
21:5 [p]Ps 78:19 [q]Nu 14:2,3 brought us up out of Egypt to die in the desert?[q] There is no bread! There is no water! And we detest this
[r]Nu 11:6 miserable food!"[r]

21:6 [s]Dt 8:15; Jer 8:17 [6]Then the LORD sent venomous snakes[s] among them; they bit the people and many Israelites died.[t]
[t]1Co 10:9 [7]The people came to Moses[u] and said, "We sinned when we spoke against the LORD and against you. Pray
21:7 [u]Ps 78:34; Hos 5:15 [v]Ex 8:8; that the LORD[v] will take the snakes away from us." So Moses prayed[w] for the people.
Ac 8:24 [w]Nu 11:2 **21:8** [x]Jn 3:14 [8]The LORD said to Moses, "Make a snake and put it up on a pole;[x] anyone who is bitten can look at it
21:9 [y]2Ki 18:4 and live." [9]So Moses made a bronze snake[y] and put it up on a pole. Then when anyone was bitten by a
[z]Jn 3:14-15 snake and looked at the bronze snake, he lived.[z]

[a] *2* The Hebrew term refers to the irrevocable giving over of things or persons to the LORD, often by totally destroying them; also in verse 3. [b] *3* *Hormah* means *destruction.* [c] *4* Hebrew *Yam Suph*; that is, Sea of Reeds

20:17 The King's Highway was the major north-south trade route in Transjordan, extending from Arabia to Damascus.

20:22–29 Other than its proximity to the border of Edom (v. 23), the location of Mount Hor remains uncertain.

21:1 See "Arad" on page 247.

The Journey to Moab

[10]The Israelites moved on and camped at Oboth.[a] [11]Then they set out from Oboth and camped in Iye 21:10 [a]Nu 33:43
Abarim, in the desert that faces Moab[b] toward the sunrise. [12]From there they moved on and camped in 21:11 [b]Nu 33:44
the Zered Valley.[c] [13]They set out from there and camped alongside the Arnon[d], which is in the desert ex- 21:12 [c]Dt 2:13, 14
tending into Amorite territory. The Arnon is the border of Moab, between Moab and the Amorites. [14]That 21:13 [d]Nu 22:36; Jdg 11:13,18
is why the Book of the Wars of the LORD says:

"...Waheb in Suphah[a] and the ravines,
the Arnon [15]and[b] the slopes of the ravines
that lead to the site of Ar[e] 21:15 [e]ver 28; Dt 2:9,18
and lie along the border of Moab."

[16]From there they continued on to Beer,[f] the well where the LORD said to Moses, "Gather the people to- 21:16 [f]Jdg 9:21
gether and I will give them water."

[a] 14 The meaning of the Hebrew for this phrase is uncertain. [b] 14,15 Or *"I have been given from Suphah and the ravines / of the Arnon [15]to*

21:11 The material from this point through the end of the book is studied by scholars with special interest because this section appears to use a very early type of Hebrew.
21:13 The Arnon River, the traditional northern boundary of the Moabites and the southern boundary of the Amorites, runs from east to west into the midpoint of the Dead Sea.
21:14 The Book of the Wars of the LORD is mentioned only here in the Old Testament. Though not known to be in existence today, it was probably an ancient collection of songs of war in praise of God. Compare the Book of Jashar (Jos 10:13; 2Sa 1:18).
21:16 The quest for water posed a constant problem during the desert wanderings.

ANCIENT TEXTS AND ARTIFACTS

Ugaritic Liturgy Against Venomous Snakes

NUMBERS 21 Poisonous snakes posed a serious and ever-present threat to people in the ancient world. Three texts from **Ugarit**, all of which address this problem, suggest that the typical pagan solution was to search for a magic formula to counter the results of the venom. One of these texts is but a fragment, another a mythical narrative and the third a magical incantation.

In the myth (second text), twelve different deities are asked for a cure for snakebite. Eleven respond with an ability to charm the serpent, but only one, Horanu, successfully neutralizes the venom. He counteracts the poison by casting trees into the Tigris River,[1] ritually enacting the manner by which he will weaken the venom as if diluting it in water.

The third text, written for the benefit of a high official, is an incantation employing a ritual similar to Horanu's to protect both against serpents and the sorcerers who used them.

The Israelites, like the inhabitants of Ugarit, feared the lethal snakes so abundant both in the wilderness and in the land of Canaan. God's snake-related punishment recorded in Numbers 21:6–9 demonstrated that only the Lord has ultimate power over serpents (and, indeed, over all evil). Not only did he send venomous snakes to punish the Israelites because of their ingratitude, but he also provided the means of cure (i.e., the bronze snake) when his people repented and sought his mercy. It is noteworthy that, although the Israelites were required to gaze up at the bronze serpent in order to receive restoration, the Biblical text mentions no magical ritual or incantation.

To learn more about the role of the snake in the Ancient Near East, see "The Serpent Motif in Other Ancient Near Eastern Literature" on page 8.

[1]See "The Tigris and Euphrates Rivers" on page 604.

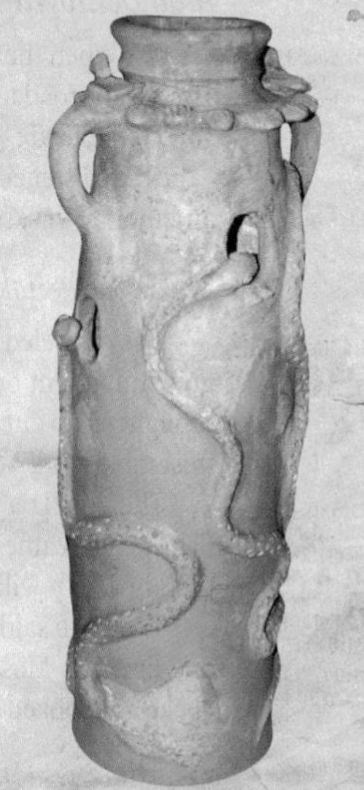

Cultic stand with snakes from Israel
Preserving Bible Times; © Dr. James C. Martin; permission of The Israel Museum

21:17 [g]Ex 15:1 17 Then Israel sang this song:[g]

"Spring up, O well!
Sing about it,
18 about the well that the princes dug,
that the nobles of the people sank—
the nobles with scepters and staffs."

Then they went from the desert to Mattanah, 19 from Mattanah to
Nahaliel, from Nahaliel to Bamoth, 20 and from Bamoth to the valley
in Moab where the top of Pisgah overlooks the wasteland.

Defeat of Sihon and Og

21:21 [h]Dt 1:4; 2:26-27; Jdg 11:19-21 21 Israel sent messengers to say to Sihon[h] king of the Amorites:

22 "Let us pass through your country. We will not turn aside
into any field or vineyard, or drink water from any well. We
will travel along the king's highway until we have passed
21:22 [i]Nu 20:17 through your territory.[i]"

21:23 [j]Nu 20:21 [k]Dt 2:32; Jdg 11:20 23 But Sihon would not let Israel pass through his territory.[j] He
mustered his entire army and marched out into the desert against
Israel. When he reached Jahaz,[k] he fought with Israel. 24 Israel, how-
21:24 [l]Dt 2:33; Ps 135:10-11; Am 2:9 [m]Dt 2:37 ever, put him to the sword[l] and took over his land from the Arnon to
the Jabbok, but only as far as the Ammonites,[m] because their border
21:25 [n]Nu 13:29; Jdg 10:11; Am 2:10 was fortified. 25 Israel captured all the cities of the Amorites[n] and occupied them, including Heshbon and
21:26 [o]Dt 29:7; Ps 135:11 all its surrounding settlements. 26 Heshbon was the city of Sihon[o] king of the Amorites, who had fought
against the former king of Moab and had taken from him all his land as far as the Arnon.
27 That is why the poets say:

"Come to Heshbon and let it be rebuilt;
let Sihon's city be restored.

28 "Fire went out from Heshbon,
21:28 [p]Jer 48:45 [q]ver 15 [r]Nu 22:41; Isa 15:2 a blaze from the city of Sihon.[p]
It consumed Ar[q] of Moab,
the citizens of Arnon's heights.[r]
21:29 [s]Isa 25:10; Jer 48:46 [t]Jdg 11:24; 1Ki 11:7,33; 2Ki 23:13; Jer 48:7,46 [u]Isa 15:5 [v]Isa 16:2 29 Woe to you, O Moab![s]
You are destroyed, O people of Chemosh![t]
He has given up his sons as fugitives[u]
and his daughters as captives[v]
to Sihon king of the Amorites.

30 "But we have overthrown them;
21:30 [w]Nu 32:3; Isa 15:2; Jer 48:18,22 Heshbon is destroyed all the way to Dibon.[w]
We have demolished them as far as Nophah,
which extends to Medeba."

Ancient Voices

My incantation for serpent bite,
for the scaly serpent's poison:
From it, O charmer, destroy,
from it cast out the venom.
Then he binds the serpent,
feeds the scaly [serpent],*
draws up a chair and sits.

*Word in brackets added by translator where text has gap

—Ugaritic Liturgy Against Venomous Snakes

See "Ugaritic Liturgy Against Venomous Snakes" article.

21:21–24 Sihon, an Amorite king, became prominent in history chiefly because of his opposition to the Israelites on their journey. His capital in the land east of the Jordan River was Heshbon (see "The Kingdoms of Sihon and Og" on p. 244). Prior to Israel's journey, the Amorites under his leadership had driven out the Moabites from this section of land and had taken over this territory. God permitted Sihon to dispossess the Moabites, but when he led his attack against Israel he was killed and his foes scattered (vv. 21–24; Dt 1:4,20,24–30). Sihon's capital was taken and the territory given to Israel. When the Moabites later came and demanded that Israel return this land (Jdg 11:12–13), Jephthah reminded them that Sihon had seized this property but that God had given it to Israel. Neither they nor the Ammonites had any intrinsic right to it.

21:25 Ancient farmers did not own their own farms. At the end of a day's work they retired to a nearby village or city. Smaller villages sought the protection of nearby cities—accounting for the expression, frequently appended to the name of a city, "and all its surrounding settlements" (cf. 32:42). In return for the protection offered against nomadic attacks, the cities received payment in services and produce. Sometimes a city was protected by a feudal lord around or near whose fortress it had been built. Often it depended entirely upon the strength of its walls and the bravery of its men. See "The Israelite Town and Home" on page 1205.

21:27–30 This third ancient poem in chapter 21 was an Amorite taunt song about this nation's earlier victory over Moab (v. 29). Perhaps the song of Heshbon was also preserved in "the Book of the Wars of the LORD" (v. 14).

31 So Israel settled in the land of the Amorites.
32 After Moses had sent spies to Jazer,[x] the Israelites captured its surrounding settlements and drove — **21:32** [x]Nu 32:1,
out the Amorites who were there. 33 Then they turned and went up along the road toward Bashan[y,z] and — 3,35; Jer 48:32 **21:33** [y]Dt 3:3
Og king of Bashan and his whole army marched out to meet them in battle at Edrei.[a] — [z]Dt 3:4 [a]Dt 1:4; 3:1,10;
34 The LORD said to Moses, "Do not be afraid of him, for I have handed him over to you, with his whole — Jos 13:12,31
army and his land. Do to him what you did to Sihon king of the Amorites, who reigned in Heshbon.[b]" — **21:34** [b]Dt 3:2
35 So they struck him down, together with his sons and his whole army, leaving them no survivors. And
they took possession of his land.

> **ANCIENT VOICES**
>
> Balaam arose on the morrow;
> He summoned the heads of the assembly
> unto him,
> And for two days he fasted, and wept
> bitterly,
> Then his intimates entered into
> his presence,
> And they said to Balaam, son of Beor:
> "Why do you fast,
> And why do you weep?"
> Then he said to them:
> "Be seated, and I will relate to you
> what the
> Shaddai-gods have planned,
> And go, see the acts of the gods!"
>
> —THE DEIR ALLA PLASTER INSCRIPTIONS
>
> See "Balaam, the Son of Beor" article.

Balak Summons Balaam

22 Then the Israelites traveled to the plains of Moab and
camped along the Jordan across from Jericho.[a][c] — **22:1** [c]Nu 33:48
2 Now Balak son of Zippor[d] saw all that Israel had done to the — **22:2** [d]Jdg 11:25
Amorites, 3 and Moab was terrified because there were so many peo-
ple. Indeed, Moab was filled with dread[e] because of the Israelites. — **22:3** [e]Ex 15:15
4 The Moabites said to the elders of Midian, "This horde is going to
lick up everything around us, as an ox licks up the grass of the field."
So Balak son of Zippor, who was king of Moab at that time, 5 sent
messengers to summon Balaam son of Beor,[f] who was at Pethor, — **22:5** [f]Dt 23:4; Jos 13:22; 24:9;
near the River,[b] in his native land. Balak said: — Ne 13:2; Mic 6:5; 2Pe 2:15

"A people has come out of Egypt; they cover the face of the
land and have settled next to me. 6 Now come and put a curse[g] — **22:6** [g]ver 12,17; Nu 23:7,11,13
on these people, because they are too powerful for me. Per-
haps then I will be able to defeat them and drive them out of
the country. For I know that those you bless are blessed, and
those you curse are cursed."

7 The elders of Moab and Midian left, taking with them the fee
for divination.[h] When they came to Balaam, they told him what Ba- — **22:7** [h]Nu 23:23; 24:1
lak had said.
8 "Spend the night here," Balaam said to them, "and I will bring
you back the answer the LORD gives me.[i]" So the Moabite princes stayed with him. — **22:8** [i]ver 19
9 God came to Balaam[j] and asked,[k] "Who are these men with you?" — **22:9** [j]Ge 20:3 [k]ver 20
10 Balaam said to God, "Balak son of Zippor, king of Moab, sent me this message: 11 'A people that has
come out of Egypt covers the face of the land. Now come and put a curse on them for me. Perhaps then
I will be able to fight them and drive them away.' "
12 But God said to Balaam, "Do not go with them. You must not put a curse on those people, because
they are blessed.[l]" — **22:12** [l]Ge 12:2; 22:17; Nu 23:20
13 The next morning Balaam got up and said to Balak's princes, "Go back to your own country, for the
LORD has refused to let me go with you."
14 So the Moabite princes returned to Balak and said, "Balaam refused to come with us."
15 Then Balak sent other princes, more numerous and more distinguished than the first. 16 They came
to Balaam and said:

"This is what Balak son of Zippor says: Do not let anything keep you from coming to me, 17 be-
cause I will reward you handsomely[m] and do whatever you say. Come and put a curse[n] on these — **22:17** [m]ver 37; Nu 24:11 [n]ver 6
people for me."

18 But Balaam answered them, "Even if Balak gave me his palace filled with silver and gold, I could not
do anything great or small to go beyond the command of the LORD my God.[o] 19 Now stay here tonight as — **22:18** [o]ver 38; Nu 23:12,26; 24:13; 1Ki 22:14; 2Ch 18:13; Jer 42:4
the others did, and I will find out what else the LORD will tell me.[p]" — **22:19** [p]ver 8

[a] *1* Hebrew *Jordan of Jericho*; possibly an ancient name for the Jordan River [b] *5* That is, the Euphrates

---

22:5 Balak tried to oppose God's people through pagan divination because he believed there was no military way to successfully withstand Israel (vv. 6–7). Balaam was a diviner with an international reputation, one of whose nonbiblical prophecies, dating to approximately 700 B.C., is preserved in an Aramaic text from Deir Alla in the Jordan Valley. See "Balaam, the Son of Beor" on page 229.

22:20 [q]Ge 20:3 [r]ver 35,38; Nu 23:5,12,16, 26; 24:13; 2Ch 18:13
22:22 [s]Ex 4:14 [t]Ge 16:7; Ex 23:20; Jdg 13:3,6,13
22:23 [u]Jos 5:13 [v]ver 25,27
22:27 [w]Nu 11:1; Jas 1:19
22:28 [x]2Pe 2:16 [y]ver 32
22:29 [z]Dt 25:4; Pr 12:10; 27:23-27; Mt 15:19
22:31 [a]Ge 21:19

20 That night God came to Balaam[q] and said, "Since these men have come to summon you, go with
them, but do only what I tell you."[r]

Balaam's Donkey

21 Balaam got up in the morning, saddled his donkey and went with the princes of Moab. 22 But God
was very angry[s] when he went, and the angel of the LORD[t] stood in the road to oppose him. Balaam was
riding on his donkey, and his two servants were with him. 23 When the donkey saw the angel of the LORD
standing in the road with a drawn sword[u] in his hand, she turned off the road into a field. Balaam beat
her[v] to get her back on the road.
24 Then the angel of the LORD stood in a narrow path between two vineyards, with walls on both sides.
25 When the donkey saw the angel of the LORD, she pressed close to the wall, crushing Balaam's foot against
it. So he beat her again.
26 Then the angel of the LORD moved on ahead and stood in a narrow place where there was no room
to turn, either to the right or to the left. 27 When the donkey saw the angel of the LORD, she lay down un-
der Balaam, and he was angry[w] and beat her with his staff. 28 Then the LORD opened the donkey's mouth,[x]
and she said to Balaam, "What have I done to you to make you beat me these three times?[y]"
29 Balaam answered the donkey, "You have made a fool of me! If I had a sword in my hand, I would kill
you right now.[z]"
30 The donkey said to Balaam, "Am I not your own donkey, which you have always ridden, to this day?
Have I been in the habit of doing this to you?"
"No," he said.
31 Then the LORD opened Balaam's eyes,[a] and he saw the angel of the LORD standing in the road with
his sword drawn. So he bowed low and fell facedown.
32 The angel of the LORD asked him, "Why have you beaten your donkey these three times? I have come
here to oppose you because your path is a reckless one before me.[a] 33 The donkey saw me and turned

[a] *32* The meaning of the Hebrew for this clause is uncertain.

22:21 While Balaam is said here to have "saddled" his donkey, donkeys were not actually ridden with saddles. Instead, a donkey carrying a heavy burden was fitted with a thick cushion on its back to relieve the pressure. The verb *habhash*, "to bind on," was used of preparing a donkey for riding (see also Ge 22:3; Jdg 19:10; 2Sa 16:1; 17:23; 19:26; 1Ki 2:40; 2Ki 4:24).

ANCIENT TEXTS AND ARTIFACTS

Balaam, the Son of Beor

NUMBERS 22 "The misfortunes of the Book of Balaam, son of Beor. A divine seer was he." These are the first words of a remarkable fragmentary inscription discovered in 1967 at Deir Alla, Jordan, about 25 miles (40 km) north of the plains of **Moab**,[1] where the Israelites camped. Written in black and red ink on a plaster wall, this fragmentary inscription dates to between 800 and 700 B.C.

The prophet Balaam was active on the eastern side of the Jordan River at the time the Israelites entered **Canaan**.[2] He was referred to hundreds of years later not only by the author of the Deir Alla inscription but also over a wide range of time by various Biblical writers (see Ne 13:2; Mic 6:5; 2Pe 2:15; Rev 2:14).

There is no doubt that this is the same Balaam mentioned in Numbers. The distinctive name "Balaam son of Beor" is rendered identically in both contexts. In addition, the inscription was found in the same general area as the events described in Numbers 22–24. Reflecting the activities of the Biblical Balaam and using language similar to that found in the Numbers account, the Deir Alla inscription speaks of divine visitations and visions, signs, admonitions, destruction and death.[3]

Yet, except for including the name Balaam and describing him as a "seer," the Deir Alla inscription does not mention any details found in the account in Numbers 22–24. Nor does it speak of **Yahweh**, although it does refer to gods as *shaddayyin*, a word similar to the Hebrew *el shaddai*, usually translated "God Almighty."[4] So it is unlikely that either author borrowed from the other. Both seem to have gone back to independent traditions.

[1]See "Moab" on page 292. [2]See "The Conquest of Canaan" on page 310. [3]See "Prophets in the Bible and Pagan Nations" on page 1457. [4]See "The Names of God" chart on page 90.

away from me these three times. If she had not turned away, I would certainly have killed you by now,[b]
but I would have spared her."
34 Balaam said to the angel of the LORD, "I have sinned.[c] I did not realize you were standing in the road
to oppose me. Now if you are displeased, I will go back."
35 The angel of the LORD said to Balaam, "Go with the men, but speak only what I tell you." So Ba-
laam went with the princes of Balak.
36 When Balak heard that Balaam was coming, he went out to meet him at the Moabite town on the
Arnon[d] border, at the edge of his territory. 37 Balak said to Balaam, "Did I not send you an urgent sum-
mons? Why didn't you come to me? Am I really not able to reward you?"
38 "Well, I have come to you now," Balaam replied. "But can I say just anything? I must speak only what
God puts in my mouth."[e]
39 Then Balaam went with Balak to Kiriath Huzoth. 40 Balak sacrificed cattle and sheep,[f] and gave some
to Balaam and the princes who were with him. 41 The next morning Balak took Balaam up to Bamoth
Baal,[g] and from there he saw part of the people.[h]

Balaam's First Oracle

23 Balaam said, "Build me seven altars here, and prepare seven bulls and seven rams[i] for me." 2 Ba-
lak did as Balaam said, and the two of them offered a bull and a ram on each altar.[j]
3 Then Balaam said to Balak, "Stay here beside your offering while I go aside. Perhaps the LORD will
come to meet with me.[k] Whatever he reveals to me I will tell you." Then he went off to a barren height.
4 God met with him,[l] and Balaam said, "I have prepared seven altars, and on each altar I have offered
a bull and a ram."
5 The LORD put a message in Balaam's mouth[m] and said, "Go back to Balak and give him this message."[n]
6 So he went back to him and found him standing beside his offering, with all the princes of Moab.[o]
7 Then Balaam[p] uttered his oracle:[q]

"Balak brought me from Aram,
 the king of Moab from the eastern mountains.
'Come,' he said, 'curse Jacob for me;
 come, denounce Israel.'[r]
8 How can I curse
 those whom God has not cursed?[s]
How can I denounce
 those whom the LORD has not denounced?
9 From the rocky peaks I see them,
 from the heights I view them.
I see a people who live apart
 and do not consider themselves one of the nations.[t]
10 Who can count the dust of Jacob[u]
 or number the fourth part of Israel?
Let me die the death of the righteous,[v]
 and may my end be like theirs![w]"

11 Balak said to Balaam, "What have you done to me? I brought you to curse my enemies, but you have
done nothing but bless them!"[x]
12 He answered, "Must I not speak what the LORD puts in my mouth?"[y]

Balaam's Second Oracle

13 Then Balak said to him, "Come with me to another place where you can see them; you will see only
a part but not all of them. And from there, curse them for me." 14 So he took him to the field of Zophim
on the top of Pisgah, and there he built seven altars and offered a bull and a ram on each altar.[z]
15 Balaam said to Balak, "Stay here beside your offering while I meet with him over there."
16 The LORD met with Balaam and put a message in his mouth[a] and said, "Go back to Balak and give
him this message."

22:33 [b]ver 29
22:34 [c]Ge 39:9; Nu 14:40; 1Sa 15:24,30; 2Sa 12:13; 24:10; Job 33:27; Ps 51:4
22:36 [d]Nu 21:13
22:38 [e]Nu 23:5, 16,26
22:40 [f]Nu 23:1, 14,29; Eze 45:23
22:41 [g]Nu 21:28 [h]Nu 23:13
23:1 [i]Nu 22:40
23:2 [j]ver 14,30
23:3 [k]ver 15
23:4 [l]ver 16
23:5 [m]Dt 18:18; Jer 1:9 [n]Nu 22:20
23:6 [o]ver 17
23:7 [p]Nu 22:5 [q]ver 18; Nu 24:3, 21
[r]Nu 22:6; Dt 23:4
23:8 [s]Nu 22:12
23:9 [t]Ex 33:16; Dt 32:8; 33:28
23:10 [u]Ge 13:16 [v]Ps 116:15; Isa 57:1 [w]Ps 37:37
23:11 [x]Nu 24:10; Ne 13:2
23:12 [y]Nu 22:20, 38
23:14 [z]ver 2
23:16 [a]Nu 22:38

23:1 The number seven (signifying completeness) was held in high regard among Semitic peoples in general, and the many animals would have provided abundant liver and organ materials for the diviner from the east. See "Akkadian Divination" on page 277.

17 So he went to him and found him standing beside his offering, with the princes of Moab. Balak asked him, "What did the LORD say?"

18 Then he uttered his oracle:

"Arise, Balak, and listen;
hear me, son of Zipper.

23:19 [b]Isa 55:9; Hos 11:9 [c]1Sa 15:29; Mal 3:6; Tit 1:2; Jas 1:17

19 God is not a man,[b] that he should lie,
nor a son of man, that he should change his mind.[c]
Does he speak and then not act?
Does he promise and not fulfill?
20 I have received a command to bless;
he has blessed,[d] and I cannot change it.[e]

23:20 [d]Ge 22:17; Nu 22:12 [e]Isa 43:13
23:21 [f]Ps 32:2,5; Ro 4:7-8 [g]Isa 40:2; Jer 50:20 [h]Ex 29:45,46; Ps 145:18 [i]Dt 33:5; Ps 89:15-18
23:22 [j]Nu 24:8 [k]Dt 33:17; Job 39:9

21 "No misfortune is seen in Jacob,[f]
no misery observed in Israel.[a][g]
The LORD their God is with them;[h]
the shout of the King[i] is among them.
22 God brought them out of Egypt;[j]
they have the strength of a wild ox.[k]

23:23 [l]Nu 24:1; Jos 13:22

23 There is no sorcery against Jacob,
no divination[l] against Israel.
It will now be said of Jacob
and of Israel, 'See what God has done!'

23:24 [m]Na 2:11 [n]Ge 49:9

24 The people rise like a lioness;[m]
they rouse themselves like a lion[n]
that does not rest till he devours his prey
and drinks the blood of his victims."

25 Then Balak said to Balaam, "Neither curse them at all nor bless them at all!"

26 Balaam answered, "Did I not tell you I must do whatever the LORD says?"

Balaam's Third Oracle

23:27 [o]ver 13
23:28 [p]Ps 106:28

27 Then Balak said to Balaam, "Come, let me take you to another place.[o] Perhaps it will please God to let
you curse them for me from there." 28 And Balak took Balaam to the top of Peor,[p] overlooking the wasteland.
29 Balaam said, "Build me seven altars here, and prepare seven bulls and seven rams for me." 30 Balak
did as Balaam had said, and offered a bull and a ram on each altar.

24:1 [q]Nu 23:23 [r]Nu 23:28
24:2 [s]Nu 11:25, 26; 1Sa 10:10; 19:20; 2Ch 15:1

24 Now when Balaam saw that it pleased the LORD to bless Israel, he did not resort to sorcery[q] as at
other times, but turned his face toward the desert.[r] 2 When Balaam looked out and saw Israel en-
camped tribe by tribe, the Spirit of God came upon him[s] 3 and he uttered his oracle:

"The oracle of Balaam son of Beor,
the oracle of one whose eye sees clearly,

24:4 [t]Nu 22:20 [u]Ge 15:1

4 the oracle of one who hears the words of God,[t]
who sees a vision from the Almighty,[b][u]
who falls prostrate, and whose eyes are opened:

5 "How beautiful are your tents, O Jacob,
your dwelling places, O Israel!

24:6 [v]Ps 45:8 [w]Ps 1:3; 104:16

6 "Like valleys they spread out,
like gardens beside a river,
like aloes[v] planted by the LORD,
like cedars beside the waters.[w]

[a] 21 Or *He has not looked on Jacob's offenses / or on the wrongs found in Israel.* [b] 4 Hebrew *Shaddai*; also in verse 16

23:22 The wild ox (*aurochs* or *oryx*) was a traditional image of power in the ancient Near East (see also 24:8).

[7] Water will flow from their buckets;
their seed will have abundant water.

"Their king will be greater than Agag;[x]
their kingdom will be exalted.[y]

24:7 [x]2Sa 15:8 [y]2Sa 5:12; 1Ch 14:2; Ps 145:11-13

[8] "God brought them out of Egypt;
they have the strength of a wild ox.
They devour hostile nations
and break their bones in pieces;[z]
with their arrows they pierce them.[a]
[9] Like a lion they crouch and lie down,
like a lioness[b]—who dares to rouse them?

"May those who bless you be blessed
and those who curse you be cursed!"[c]

24:8 [z]Ps 2:9; Jer 50:17 [a]Ps 45:5
24:9 [b]Ge 49:9; Nu 23:24 [c]Ge 12:3

[10] Then Balak's anger burned against Balaam. He struck his hands together[d] and said to him, "I sum-
moned you to curse my enemies, but you have blessed them[e] these three times.[f] [11] Now leave at once and
go home! I said I would reward you handsomely,[g] but the LORD has kept you from being rewarded."
[12] Balaam answered Balak, "Did I not tell the messengers you sent me,[h] [13] 'Even if Balak gave me his
palace filled with silver and gold, I could not do anything of my own accord, good or bad, to go beyond
the command of the LORD[i]—and I must say only what the LORD says'?[j] [14] Now I am going back to my
people, but come, let me warn you of what this people will do to your people in days to come."[k]

24:10 [d]Eze 21:14 [e]Nu 23:11 [f]Ne 13:2
24:11 [g]Nu 22:17
24:12 [h]Nu 22:18
24:13 [i]Nu 22:18 [j]Nu 22:20
24:14 [k]Ge 49:1; Nu 31:8,16; Da 2:28; Mic 6:5

Balaam's Fourth Oracle

[15] Then he uttered his oracle:

"The oracle of Balaam son of Beor,
the oracle of one whose eye sees clearly,
[16] the oracle of one who hears the words of God,
who has knowledge from the Most High,
who sees a vision from the Almighty,
who falls prostrate, and whose eyes are opened:

[17] "I see him, but not now;
I behold him, but not near.[l]
A star will come out of Jacob;[m]
a scepter will rise out of Israel.[n]
He will crush the foreheads of Moab,[o]
the skulls[a] of[b] all the sons of Sheth.[c]
[18] Edom[p] will be conquered;
Seir, his enemy, will be conquered,
but Israel will grow strong.
[19] A ruler will come out of Jacob[q]
and destroy the survivors of the city."

24:17 [l]Rev 1:7
24:17 [m]Mt 2:2 [n]Ge 49:10 [o]Nu 21:29; Isa 15:1–16:14
24:18 [p]Am 9:12
24:19 [q]Ge 49:10; Mic 5:2

Balaam's Final Oracles

[20] Then Balaam saw Amalek[r] and uttered his oracle:

"Amalek was first among the nations,
but he will come to ruin at last."

24:20 [r]Ex 17:14

[a] 17 Samaritan Pentateuch (see also Jer. 48:45); the meaning of the word in the Masoretic Text is uncertain. [b] 17 Or possibly *Moab, / batter* [c] 17 Or *all the noisy boasters*

24:17 The "sons of Sheth" may have been the early inhabitants of Moab (see "Moab" on p. 292). Ancient Egyptian documents refer to them as the Shutu people.

24:21 sGe 15:19
24:22 tGe 10:22
24:24 uGe 10:4 vGe 10:21 wver 20
24:25 xNu 31:8
25:1 yJos 2:1; Mic 6:5 z1Co 10:8; Rev 2:14 aNu 31:16
25:2 bEx 34:15 cEx 20:5; Dt 32:38; 1Co 10:20
25:3 dPs 106:28; Hos 9:10
25:4 eDt 4:3 fDt 13:17
25:5 gEx 32:27

21 Then he saw the Kenites[s] and uttered his oracle:

"Your dwelling place is secure,
your nest is set in a rock;
22 yet you Kenites will be destroyed
when Asshur[t] takes you captive."

23 Then he uttered his oracle:

"Ah, who can live when God does this?[a]
24 Ships will come from the shores of Kittim;[u]
they will subdue Asshur and Eber,[v]
but they too will come to ruin.[w]"

25 Then Balaam[x] got up and returned home and Balak went his own way.

Moab Seduces Israel

25 While Israel was staying in Shittim,[y] the men began to indulge in sexual immorality[z] with Mo-
abite women,[a] 2 who invited them to the sacrifices[b] to their gods.[c] The people ate and bowed
down before these gods. 3 So Israel joined in worshiping the Baal of Peor.[d] And the LORD's anger burned
against them.
4 The LORD said to Moses, "Take all the leaders of these people, kill them and expose them in broad day-
light before the LORD,[e] so that the LORD's fierce anger[f] may turn away from Israel."
5 So Moses said to Israel's judges, "Each of you must put to death[g] those of your men who have joined
in worshiping the Baal of Peor."
6 Then an Israelite man brought to his family a Midianite woman right before the eyes of Moses and
the whole assembly of Israel while they were weeping at the entrance to the Tent of Meeting. 7 When Phin-

[a] 23 Masoretic Text; with a different word division of the Hebrew *A people will gather from the north.*

25:1 The Israelites' engagement in the fertility rites of Baal not only involved them in the evil of sexual immorality but was also a breach of their covenant with the Lord. See "Baal and the Fertility Cults" on page 1414.

ARCHAEOLOGICAL SITES

SHITTIM

NUMBERS 25 Shittim, abbreviated from *Abel Shittim* ("brook of acacias"), was the Israelites' final wilderness encampment before they crossed the Jordan River. From this location in the plains of **Moab**[1] (see Abel Shittim on "Map 3"), Moses ascended Mount Nebo to view the promised land and Joshua sent spies to Jericho.[2] At Shittim, Israel also fell into the immorality associated with the worship of Baal of Peor,[3] suffering severe casualties as a result of God's anger (Nu 25:1–9).

Shittim can probably be identified with the present archaeological site of Tell el-Hammam, 8.5 miles (13.7 km) east of the Jordan River, opposite the ancient city of Jericho. This excavation site is covered with the ruins of houses, as well as of an **Iron I-period**[4] fortress with towers at both ends. The fortress walls were 4 feet (1.2 m) thick and surrounded by a massive **glacis** (slope running downward from a fortification). This site was strategically located 100 feet (30.5 m) above the plains of Moab, no doubt enabling its ancient inhabitants to control access from the mountains. A perennial stream nearby, the Wadi el-Kefrein, could have provided an adequate water supply for the encamped Israelites.

The meaning of the name Shittim suggests that acacia trees grew there, watered by the nearby stream—although the acacia is known to survive in arid regions. Its wood, light but hard and moisture resistant, had been used to construct both the tabernacle and its furnishings (Ex 25–38).[5]

[1]See "Moab" on page 292. [2]See "The Walls of Jericho" on page 312. [3]See "Baal and the Fertility Cults" on page 1414. [4]See "Archaeological Periods" chart on page xx in the front of this Bible. [5]See "The Tabernacle and the Ark" on page 153.

ehas son of Eleazar, the son of Aaron, the priest, saw this, he left the assembly, took a spear in his hand
8 and followed the Israelite into the tent. He drove the spear through both of them—through the Israel-
ite and into the woman's body. Then the plague against the Israelites was stopped;[h] 9 but those who died
in the plague[i] numbered 24,000.[j]

10 The LORD said to Moses, 11 "Phinehas son of Eleazar, the son of Aaron, the priest, has turned my an-
ger away from the Israelites;[k] for he was as zealous as I am for my honor[l] among them, so that in my zeal
I did not put an end to them. 12 Therefore tell him I am making my covenant of peace[m] with him. 13 He
and his descendants will have a covenant of a lasting priesthood,[n] because he was zealous for the hon-
or of his God and made atonement[o] for the Israelites."

14 The name of the Israelite who was killed with the Midianite woman was Zimri son of Salu, the lead-
er of a Simeonite family. 15 And the name of the Midianite woman who was put to death was Cozbi[p]
daughter of Zur, a tribal chief of a Midianite family.[q]

16 The LORD said to Moses, 17 "Treat the Midianites[r] as enemies and kill them, 18 because they treated
you as enemies when they deceived you in the affair of Peor[s] and their sister Cozbi, the daughter of a
Midianite leader, the woman who was killed when the plague came as a result of Peor."

The Second Census

26 After the plague the LORD said to Moses and Eleazar son of Aaron, the priest, 2 "Take a census[t] of
the whole Israelite community by families—all those twenty years old or more who are able to
serve in the army[u] of Israel." 3 So on the plains of Moab[v] by the Jordan across from Jericho,[a][w] Moses and
Eleazar the priest spoke with them and said, 4 "Take a census of the men twenty years old or more, as the
LORD commanded Moses."

These were the Israelites who came out of Egypt:

5 The descendants of Reuben, the firstborn son of Israel, were:
through Hanoch,[x] the Hanochite clan;
through Pallu,[y] the Palluite clan;
6 through Hezron, the Hezronite clan;
through Carmi, the Carmite clan.
7 These were the clans of Reuben; those numbered were 43,730.

8 The son of Pallu was Eliab, 9 and the sons of Eliab[z] were Nemuel, Dathan and Abiram. The same Da-
than and Abiram were the community[a] officials who rebelled against Moses and Aaron and were among
Korah's followers when they rebelled against the LORD.[b] 10 The earth opened its mouth and swallowed
them along with Korah, whose followers died when the fire devoured the 250 men. And they served as a
warning sign.[c] 11 The line of Korah,[d] however, did not die out.[e]

12 The descendants of Simeon by their clans were:
through Nemuel, the Nemuelite clan;
through Jamin,[f] the Jaminite clan;
through Jakin, the Jakinite clan;
13 through Zerah,[g] the Zerahite clan;
through Shaul, the Shaulite clan.
14 These were the clans of Simeon; there were 22,200 men.[h]

15 The descendants of Gad by their clans were:
through Zephon,[i] the Zephonite clan;
through Haggi, the Haggite clan;
through Shuni, the Shunite clan;
16 through Ozni, the Oznite clan;
through Eri, the Erite clan;
17 through Arodi,[b] the Arodite clan;
through Areli, the Arelite clan.
18 These were the clans of Gad;[j] those numbered were 40,500.

25:8 [h]Nu 16:46-48; Ps 106:30
25:9 [i]Nu 14:37; 1Co 10:8 [j]Nu 31:16
25:11 [k]Ps 106:30 [l]Ex 20:5; Dt 32:16,21; Ps 78:58
25:12 [m]Isa 54:10; Eze 34:25; Mal 2:4,5
25:13 [n]Ex 29:9 [o]Nu 16:46
25:15 [p]ver 18 [q]Nu 31:8; Jos 13:21
25:17 [r]Nu 31:1-3
25:18 [s]Nu 31:16
26:2 [t]Ex 30:11-16; 38:25-26; Nu 1:2 [u]Nu 1:3
26:3 [v]Nu 33:48 [w]Nu 22:1
26:5 [x]Ge 46:9 [y]1Ch 5:3
26:9 [z]Nu 16:1 [a]Nu 1:16 [b]Nu 16:2
26:10 [c]Nu 16:35,38
26:11 [d]Ex 6:24 [e]Nu 16:33; Dt 24:16
26:12 [f]1Ch 4:24
26:13 [g]Ge 46:10
26:14 [h]Nu 1:23
26:15 [i]Ge 46:16
26:18 [j]Nu 1:25; Jos 13:24-28

[a] *3* Hebrew *Jordan of Jericho*; possibly an ancient name for the Jordan River; also in verse 63 [b] *17* Samaritan Pentateuch and Syriac (see also Gen. 46:16); Masoretic Text *Arod*

26:19 [k]Ge 38:2-10; 46:12 19 Er and Onan were sons of Judah, but they died[k] in Canaan.
20 The descendants of Judah by their clans were:
26:20 [l]1Ch 2:3 [m]Jos 7:17 through Shelah,[l] the Shelanite clan;
through Perez, the Perezite clan;
through Zerah, the Zerahite clan.[m]
21 The descendants of Perez were:
26:21 [n]Ru 4:19; 1Ch 2:9 through Hezron,[n] the Hezronite clan;
through Hamul, the Hamulite clan.
26:22 [o]Nu 1:27 22 These were the clans of Judah;[o] those numbered were 76,500.

23 The descendants of Issachar by their clans were:
26:23 [p]Ge 46:13; 1Ch 7:1 through Tola,[p] the Tolaite clan;
through Puah, the Puite[a] clan;
26:24 [q]Ge 46:13 24 through Jashub,[q] the Jashubite clan;
through Shimron, the Shimronite clan.
26:25 [r]Nu 1:29 25 These were the clans of Issachar;[r] those numbered were 64,300.

26 The descendants of Zebulun by their clans were:
through Sered, the Seredite clan;
through Elon, the Elonite clan;
through Jahleel, the Jahleelite clan.
26:27 [s]Nu 1:31 27 These were the clans of Zebulun;[s] those numbered were 60,500.

28 The descendants of Joseph by their clans through Manasseh and Ephraim were:

29 The descendants of Manasseh:
26:29 [t]Jos 17:1 [u]Jdg 11:1 through Makir,[t] the Makirite clan (Makir was the father of Gilead[u]);
through Gilead, the Gileadite clan.
30 These were the descendants of Gilead:
26:30 [v]Jos 17:2; Jdg 6:11 through Iezer,[v] the Iezerite clan;
through Helek, the Helekite clan;
31 through Asriel, the Asrielite clan;
through Shechem, the Shechemite clan;
32 through Shemida, the Shemidaite clan;
through Hepher, the Hepherite clan.
26:33 [w]Nu 27:1 [x]Nu 36:11 33 (Zelophehad[w] son of Hepher had no sons; he had only daughters, whose names were Mahlah,
Noah, Hoglah, Milcah and Tirzah.)[x]
26:34 [y]Nu 1:35 34 These were the clans of Manasseh; those numbered were 52,700.[y]

35 These were the descendants of Ephraim by their clans:
through Shuthelah, the Shuthelahite clan;
through Beker, the Bekerite clan;
through Tahan, the Tahanite clan.
36 These were the descendants of Shuthelah:
through Eran, the Eranite clan.
26:37 [z]Nu 1:33 37 These were the clans of Ephraim;[z] those numbered were 32,500.

These were the descendants of Joseph by their clans.

26:38 [a]Ge 46:21; 1Ch 7:6 38 The descendants of Benjamin[a] by their clans were:
through Bela, the Belaite clan;
through Ashbel, the Ashbelite clan;
through Ahiram, the Ahiramite clan;
39 through Shupham,[b] the Shuphamite clan;
through Hupham, the Huphamite clan.

[a] 23 Samaritan Pentateuch, Septuagint, Vulgate and Syriac (see also 1 Chron. 7:1); Masoretic Text *through Puvah, the Punite*
[b] 39 A few manuscripts of the Masoretic Text, Samaritan Pentateuch, Vulgate and Syriac (see also Septuagint); most manuscripts of the Masoretic Text *Shephupham*

40 The descendants of Bela through Ard[b] and Naaman were:
through Ard,[a] the Ardite clan;
through Naaman, the Naamite clan.
41 These were the clans of Benjamin;[c] those numbered were 45,600.

42 These were the descendants of Dan by their clans:
through Shuham,[d] the Shuhamite clan.
These were the clans of Dan: 43 All of them were Shuhamite clans; and those numbered were 64,400.

44 The descendants of Asher by their clans were:
through Imnah, the Imnite clan;
through Ishvi, the Ishvite clan;
through Beriah, the Beriite clan;
45 and through the descendants of Beriah:
through Heber, the Heberite clan;
through Malkiel, the Malkielite clan.
46 (Asher had a daughter named Serah.)
47 These were the clans of Asher;[e] those numbered were 53,400.

48 The descendants of Naphtali[f] by their clans were:
through Jahzeel, the Jahzeelite clan;
through Guni, the Gunite clan;
49 through Jezer, the Jezerite clan;
through Shillem, the Shillemite clan.
50 These were the clans of Naphtali;[g] those numbered were 45,400.

51 The total number of the men of Israel was 601,730.[h]

52 The LORD said to Moses, 53 "The land is to be allotted to them as an inheritance based on the number of names.[i] 54 To a larger group give a larger inheritance, and to a smaller group a smaller one; each is to receive its inheritance according to the number[j] of those listed. 55 Be sure that the land is distributed by lot.[k] What each group inherits will be according to the names for its ancestral tribe. 56 Each inheritance is to be distributed by lot among the larger and smaller groups."

57 These were the Levites[l] who were counted by their clans:
through Gershon, the Gershonite clan;
through Kohath, the Kohathite clan;
through Merari, the Merarite clan.
58 These also were Levite clans:
the Libnite clan,
the Hebronite clan,
the Mahlite clan,
the Mushite clan,
the Korahite clan.
(Kohath was the forefather of Amram;[m] 59 the name of Amram's wife was Jochebed,[n] a descendant
of Levi, who was born to the Levites[b] in Egypt. To Amram she bore Aaron, Moses[o] and their sister Miriam. 60 Aaron was the father of Nadab and Abihu, Eleazar and Ithamar.[p] 61 But Nadab and
Abihu[q] died when they made an offering before the LORD with unauthorized fire.)[r]

62 All the male Levites a month old or more numbered 23,000.[s] They were not counted[t] along with the other Israelites because they received no inheritance[u] among them.[v]

63 These are the ones counted by Moses and Eleazar the priest when they counted the Israelites on the plains of Moab[w] by the Jordan across from Jericho. 64 Not one of them was among those counted[x] by Moses and Aaron the priest when they counted the Israelites in the Desert of Sinai. 65 For the LORD had told those Israelites they would surely die in the desert,[y] and not one of them was left except Caleb son of Jephunneh and Joshua son of Nun.[z]

[a] 40 Samaritan Pentateuch and Vulgate (see also Septuagint); Masoretic Text does not have *through Ard.* [b] 59 Or *Jochebed, a daughter of Levi, who was born to Levi*

26:40 [b]Ge 46:21; 1Ch 8:3
26:41 [c]Nu 1:37
26:42 [d]Ge 46:23
26:47 [e]Nu 1:41
26:48 [f]Ge 46:24; 1Ch 7:13
26:50 [g]Nu 1:43
26:51 [h]Ex 12:37; 38:26; Nu 1:46; 11:21
26:53 [i]Jos 11:23; 14:1; Eze 45:8
26:54 [j]Nu 33:54
26:55 [k]Nu 34:14
26:57 [l]Ge 46:11; Ex 6:16-19
26:58 [m]Ex 6:20
26:59 [n]Ex 2:1 [o]Ex 6:20
26:60 [p]Nu 3:2
26:61 [q]Lev 10:1-2 [r]Nu 3:4
26:62 [s]Nu 3:39 [t]Nu 1:47 [u]Nu 18:23 [v]Nu 2:33; Dt 10:9
26:63 [w]ver 3
26:64 [x]Nu 14:29; Dt 2:14-15; Heb 3:17
26:65 [y]Nu 14:28; 1Co 10:5 [z]Jos 14:6-10

CULTURAL AND HISTORICAL NOTES

The Itinerary in Numbers

NUMBERS 27 The Israelites' journey from Egypt to the Red Sea and then on to Mount Sinai, Kadesh Barnea and **Moab** is recorded in the book of Numbers in two forms. First, isolated references from chapters 1 to 32 form a part of the narrative (e.g., 27:14). Second, an explicit itinerary of this journey is spelled out in 33:1–49.

Traditional site of Sinai mountains

Photograph courtesy of © Dr. Gary Pratico

Numbers 33 identifies 42 sites, 16 of which appear in no other Biblical text. Many of these locations can no longer be identified, probably because they were undeveloped caravan stops, significant only based upon the availability of water.[1] Yet collaborating texts from Egypt, Moab and **Mesopotamia** shed light on both the form of the list and its interpretation, helping to confirm the Biblical account's credibility and antiquity and suggesting that the itinerary recorded in Numbers 33 should be interpreted as the account of a protracted military campaign. Such records would have been retained as a continuing reminder of the protection God had provided his people as he led them through the wilderness.[2]

Extrabiblical texts shedding light on this itinerary are as follows:

✣ Three lists from Egypt mention sites that also appear in the Numbers 33 register. One is an inscription of Thutmose III at the temple of Amon at Karnak. The other two are from Amenhotep III; both are inscribed on a temple at Soleb. Comparison of the three texts provides the series of place-names in the identical order in which they are found in the Biblical text (33:44–49): Iyyin equates to Iyim, Dibon corresponds with Gad, and Abel is a reference to both Abel-Shittim and the Jordan.

✣ The annals of Egypt's Thutmose III reveal that his campaigns were recorded on a leather scroll deposited in the temple of Amon, an attestation that military record-keeping was practiced prior to the Mosaic period (see 33:2).

✣ Although no evidence of **Late Bronze Age**[3] occupation has been discovered at Dibon (modern Dhiban), the appearance of this name in these Egyptian texts confirms its existence during this early period. The Moabite Stone, a ninth-century B.C. inscription of Mesha, king of Moab, mentions Dibon and Almon Diblathaim, both of which are also listed in the Biblical itinerary (33:46).[4]

✣ Mesopotamian texts demonstrate that the genre of the Israelite itinerary (the type of literature, not the itinerary itself) was widely attested in the ancient world. Other examples have been found in two military texts dating to the **Assyrian** kings Tukulti-Ninurta II and Ashurnasirpal II (ninth century B.C.).

Such texts follow a recurring pattern: "From [city A] I departed; in [city B] I passed the night." In this formula the name of each site is mentioned twice: first as a destination ("B") and next as a departure point ("A"). This follows closely the general format seen in Numbers 33.

The extrabiblical itineraries briefly comment on water crossings, encampment sites, military encounters, problems associated with the water supply and other events, such as those remarks we find scattered throughout Numbers 33.

[1]See "Caravan Trading and Routes in the Ancient Near East" on page 63 and "The Route of the Exodus" articles on pages 108–112. [2]See also "A Timeline for the Wilderness Wanderings" on page 224. [3]See "Archaeological Periods" chart on page xx in the front of this Bible. [4]See "The Mesha (Moabite) Stone" on page 530 and "Moab" on page 292.

Zelophehad's Daughters

27 The daughters of Zelophehad[a] son of Hepher,[b] the son of Gilead, the son of Makir,[c] the son of Ma-
nasseh, belonged to the clans of Manasseh son of Joseph. The names of the daughters were Mah-
lah, Noah, Hoglah, Milcah and Tirzah. They approached 2 the entrance to the Tent of Meeting and stood
before Moses, Eleazar the priest, the leaders and the whole assembly, and said, 3 "Our father died in the
desert.[d] He was not among Korah's followers, who banded together against the LORD,[e] but he died for his
own sin and left no sons.[f] 4 Why should our father's name disappear from his clan because he had no
son? Give us property among our father's relatives."
5 So Moses brought their case[g] before the LORD[h] 6 and the LORD said to him, 7 "What Zelophehad's
daughters are saying is right. You must certainly give them property as an inheritance[i] among their fa-
ther's relatives and turn their father's inheritance over to them.[j]
8 "Say to the Israelites, 'If a man dies and leaves no son, turn his inheritance over to his daughter. 9 If he
has no daughter, give his inheritance to his brothers. 10 If he has no brothers, give his inheritance to his fa-
ther's brothers. 11 If his father had no brothers, give his inheritance to the nearest relative in his clan, that
he may possess it. This is to be a legal requirement[k] for the Israelites, as the LORD commanded Moses.' "

Joshua to Succeed Moses

12 Then the LORD said to Moses, "Go up this mountain in the Abarim range[l] and see the land[m] I have
given the Israelites. 13 After you have seen it, you too will be gathered to your people,[n] as your brother
Aaron[o] was, 14 for when the community rebelled at the waters in the Desert of Zin, both of you disobeyed
my command to honor me as holy[p] before their eyes." (These were the waters of Meribah[q] Kadesh, in
the Desert of Zin.)
15 Moses said to the LORD, 16 "May the LORD, the God of the spirits of all mankind,[r] appoint a man over
this community 17 to go out and come in before them, one who will lead them out and bring them in, so
the LORD's people will not be like sheep without a shepherd."[s]
18 So the LORD said to Moses, "Take Joshua son of Nun, a man in whom is the spirit,[a][t] and lay your
hand on him.[u] 19 Have him stand before Eleazar the priest and the entire assembly and commission him[v]
in their presence.[w] 20 Give him some of your authority so the whole Israelite community will obey him.[x]
21 He is to stand before Eleazar the priest, who will obtain decisions for him by inquiring[y] of the Urim[z]
before the LORD. At his command he and the entire community of the Israelites will go out, and at his
command they will come in."
22 Moses did as the LORD commanded him. He took Joshua and had him stand before Eleazar the priest
and the whole assembly. 23 Then he laid his hands on him and commissioned him, as the LORD instruct-
ed through Moses.

Daily Offerings

28 The LORD said to Moses, 2 "Give this command to the Israelites and say to them: 'See that you pre-
sent to me at the appointed time the food[a] for my offerings made by fire, as an aroma pleasing
to me.' 3 Say to them: 'This is the offering made by fire that you are to present to the LORD: two lambs a
year old without defect, as a regular burnt offering each day.[b] 4 Prepare one lamb in the morning and the
other at twilight, 5 together with a grain offering of a tenth of an ephah[b] of fine flour mixed with a quar-
ter of a hin[c] of oil[c] from pressed olives. 6 This is the regular burnt offering instituted at Mount Sinai[d] as
a pleasing aroma, an offering made to the LORD by fire. 7 The accompanying drink offering[e] is to be a
quarter of a hin of fermented drink with each lamb. Pour out the drink offering to the LORD at the sanc-
tuary.[f] 8 Prepare the second lamb at twilight, along with the same kind of grain offering and drink offer-
ing that you prepare in the morning. This is an offering made by fire, an aroma pleasing to the LORD.[g]

27:1 [a]Nu 26:33 [b]Jos 17:2,3 [c]Nu 36:1
27:3 [d]Nu 26:65 [e]Nu 16:2 [f]Nu 26:33
27:5 [g]Ex 18:19 [h]Nu 9:8
27:7 [i]Job 42:15 [j]Jos 17:4
27:11 [k]Nu 35:29
27:12 [l]Nu 33:47; Jer 22:20 [m]Dt 3:23-27; 32:48-52
27:13 [n]Nu 31:2 [o]Nu 20:28
27:14 [p]Nu 20:12 [q]Ex 17:7; Dt 32:51; Ps 106:32
27:16 [r]Nu 16:22
27:17 [s]Dt 31:2; 1Ki 22:17; Eze 34:5; Zec 10:2; Mt 9:36; Mk 6:34
27:18 [t]Ge 41:38; Nu 11:25-29 [u]ver 23; Dt 34:9
27:19 [v]Dt 3:28; 31:14,23 [w]Dt 31:7
27:20 [x]Jos 1:16, 17
27:21 [y]Jos 9:14 [z]Ex 28:30
28:2 [a]Lev 3:11
28:3 [b]Ex 29:38
28:5 [c]Lev 2:1; Nu 15:4
28:6 [d]Ex 19:3
28:7 [e]Ex 29:41 [f]Lev 3:7
28:8 [g]Lev 1:9

[a] *18* Or *Spirit* [b] *5* That is, probably about 2 quarts (about 2 liters); also in verses 13, 21 and 29 [c] *5* That is, probably about 1 quart (about 1 liter); also in verses 7 and 14

27:1–11 The law held that only sons had the right to inherit, and the firstborn son was to receive a double share of the family estate (Dt 21:15–17). The daughters of Zelophehad, a man who had no sons, were concerned about their rights of inheritance and the preservation of their father's name in the land (v. 4). See "Inheritance in the Ancient Near East" on page 250.

27:7–8 The solution for Zelophehad's daughters would elevate their status to that of property owners, but this was only to bridge the gap in the male line for the sake of their father's honor. They did not need to inherit property for their own survival and prosperity, since they would be supported by the families into which they would marry (cf. ch. 36).

27:21 See "The Urim and Thummim" on page 136.

Sabbath Offerings

28:9 [h]Ex 20:10 9“ ‘On the Sabbath[h] day, make an offering of two lambs a year old without defect, together with its
[i]Lev 23:13 28:10 [j]ver 3 drink offering and a grain offering of two-tenths of an ephah[a][i] of fine flour mixed with oil. 10 This is the
burnt offering for every Sabbath, in addition to the regular burnt offering[j] and its drink offering.

Monthly Offerings

28:11 [k]Nu 10:10 11“ ‘On the first of every month,[k] present to the LORD a burnt offering of two young bulls, one ram
[l]Lev 1:3 28:12 [m]Nu 15:6 and seven male lambs a year old, all without defect.[l] 12 With each bull there is to be a grain offering[m] of
[n]Nu 15:9 three-tenths of an ephah[b][n] of fine flour mixed with oil; with the ram, a grain offering of two-tenths of
28:13 [o]Lev 6:14 an ephah of fine flour mixed with oil; 13 and with each lamb, a grain offering[o] of a tenth of an ephah of
fine flour mixed with oil. This is for a burnt offering, a pleasing aroma, an offering made to the LORD by
28:14 [p]Nu 15:7 fire. 14 With each bull there is to be a drink offering[p] of half a hin[c] of wine; with the ram, a third of a hin[d];
[q]Ezr 3:5 and with each lamb, a quarter of a hin. This is the monthly burnt offering to be made at each new moon[q]
28:15 [r]ver 3,23, during the year. 15 Besides the regular burnt offering[r] with its drink offering, one male goat is to be pre-
24 [s]Lev 4:3 sented to the LORD as a sin offering.[s]

The Passover

28:16 [t]Ex 12:6, 16“ ‘On the fourteenth day of the first month the LORD's Passover[t] is to be held. 17 On the fifteenth day
18; Lev 23:5; Dt 16:1 of this month there is to be a festival; for seven days[u] eat bread made without yeast.[v] 18 On the first day
28:17 [u]Ex 12:19 [v]Ex 23:15; 34:18; hold a sacred assembly and do no regular work.[w] 19 Present to the LORD an offering made by fire, a burnt
Lev 23:6; Dt 16:3-8 offering of two young bulls, one ram and seven male lambs a year old, all without defect. 20 With each
28:18 [w]Ex 12:16; Lev 23:7 bull prepare a grain offering of three-tenths of an ephah[x] of fine flour mixed with oil; with the ram, two-
28:20 [x]Lev 14:10 tenths; 21 and with each of the seven lambs, one-tenth. 22 Include one male goat as a sin offering[y] to make
28:22 [y]Ro 8:3 [z]Nu 15:28 atonement for you.[z] 23 Prepare these in addition to the regular morning burnt offering. 24 In this way pre-
pare the food for the offering made by fire every day for seven days as an aroma pleasing to the LORD; it
is to be prepared in addition to the regular burnt offering and its drink offering. 25 On the seventh day hold
a sacred assembly and do no regular work.

Feast of Weeks

28:26 [a]Ex 34:22 26“ ‘On the day of firstfruits,[a] when you present to the LORD an offering of new grain during the Feast
[b]Ex 23:16 [c]ver 18; Dt 16:10 of Weeks,[b] hold a sacred assembly and do no regular work.[c] 27 Present a burnt offering of two young bulls,
one ram and seven male lambs a year old as an aroma pleasing to the LORD. 28 With each bull there is to
be a grain offering of three-tenths of an ephah of fine flour mixed with oil; with the ram, two-tenths;
28:29 [d]ver 13 29 and with each of the seven lambs, one-tenth.[d] 30 Include one male goat to make atonement for you.
28:31 [e]ver 3,19 31 Prepare these together with their drink offerings, in addition to the regular burnt offering[e] and its grain
offering. Be sure the animals are without defect.

Feast of Trumpets

29:1 [f]Lev 23:24 29 “ ‘On the first day of the seventh month hold a sacred assembly and do no regular work.[f] It is a
29:2 [g]Nu 28:2 [h]Nu 28:3 day for you to sound the trumpets. 2 As an aroma pleasing to the LORD,[g] prepare a burnt offering
of one young bull, one ram and seven male lambs a year old, all without defect.[h] 3 With the bull prepare
a grain offering of three-tenths of an ephah[e] of fine flour mixed with oil; with the ram, two-tenths[f]; 4 and
29:5 [i]Nu 28:15 with each of the seven lambs, one-tenth.[g] 5 Include one male goat[i] as a sin offering to make atonement
29:6 [j]Nu 28:11 [k]Nu 28:3 for you. 6 These are in addition to the monthly[j] and daily burnt offerings[k] with their grain offerings and
drink offerings as specified. They are offerings made to the LORD by fire—a pleasing aroma.

Day of Atonement

29:7 [l]Ac 27:9 7“ ‘On the tenth day of this seventh month hold a sacred assembly. You must deny yourselves[h][l] and
[m]Ex 31:15; Lev 16:29; 23:26-32 do no work.[m] 8 Present as an aroma pleasing to the LORD a burnt offering of one young bull, one ram and
29:9 [n]ver 3,18 seven male lambs a year old, all without defect. 9 With the bull prepare a grain offering[n] of three-tenths
of an ephah of fine flour mixed with oil; with the ram, two-tenths; 10 and with each of the seven lambs,

[a] *9* That is, probably about 4 quarts (about 4.5 liters); also in verses 12, 20 and 28 [b] *12* That is, probably about 6 quarts (about 6.5 liters); also in verses 20 and 28 [c] *14* That is, probably about 2 quarts (about 2 liters) [d] *14* That is, probably about 1 1/4 quarts (about 1.2 liters) [e] *3* That is, probably about 6 quarts (about 6.5 liters); also in verses 9 and 14 [f] *3* That is, probably about 4 quarts (about 4.5 liters); also in verses 9 and 14 [g] *4* That is, probably about 2 quarts (about 2 liters); also in verses 10 and 15 [h] *7* Or *must fast*

RHYTHM OF SACRED TIMES AND SEASONS

Daily Cycle	◆ Old Testament sacrifice, morning and evening (Ex 29:39) ◆ Old Testament prayer, morning, noon, and evening (Ps 55:17) ◆ New Testament sacrifice and prayer seem to adopt the theological idea of Psalm 119:164, prayer seven times a day or continually (i.e., the Christian offers his or her life as a living sacrifice and prays always; Ro 12:1–2; 1Th 5:17)
Weekly Cycle	◆ Old Testament Sabbath (creation/rest; Ge 2:2–3; Ex 20:8–11) ◆ New Testament Sunday (Christ's resurrection; Jn 20:1; Ac 20:7)
Monthly Cycle	◆ New Moon Festival (Nu 10:10) ◆ Seasonal festivals/annual cycle ◆ Old Testament: Passover, Pentecost, Tabernacles (Ex 23:14–17) ◆ New Testament: Advent, Easter, Pentecost
Multiyear Cycle	◆ Sabbath year (every seventh year; Lev 25:1–7) ◆ Jubilee year (every fiftieth year; Lev 25:8–13)
Significance	The rhythms of time for worship, especially festival time, are a rejection of death and the impact of the fall. The rejoicing and sharing associated with the feasts asserted the quality of life and value of community and affirmed the goodness of God's original creation. The rhythms of time for worship are a return to creation principles, in that "redeeming" the time in this way conquers "chaos" and recovers "cosmos" or order in the fallen world.

Old Testament Today, p. 80

one-tenth.[o] 11 Include one male goat as a sin offering, in addition to the sin offering for atonement and
the regular burnt offering[p] with its grain offering, and their drink offerings.

Feast of Tabernacles

12 " 'On the fifteenth day of the seventh[q] month,[r] hold a sacred assembly and do no regular work. Cel-
ebrate a festival to the LORD for seven days. 13 Present an offering made by fire as an aroma pleasing to the
LORD, a burnt offering of thirteen young bulls, two rams and fourteen male lambs a year old, all without
defect. 14 With each of the thirteen bulls prepare a grain offering[s] of three-tenths of an ephah of fine flour
mixed with oil; with each of the two rams, two-tenths; 15 and with each of the fourteen lambs, one-tenth.
16 Include one male goat as a sin offering, in addition to the regular burnt offering with its grain offering
and drink offering.[t]

17 " 'On the second day[u] prepare twelve young bulls, two rams and fourteen male lambs a year old, all
without defect.[v] 18 With the bulls, rams and lambs, prepare their grain offerings[w] and drink offerings[x] ac-
cording to the number specified.[y] 19 Include one male goat as a sin offering,[z] in addition to the regular
burnt offering with its grain offering, and their drink offerings.

20 " 'On the third day prepare eleven bulls, two rams and fourteen male lambs a year old, all without
defect.[a] 21 With the bulls, rams and lambs, prepare their grain offerings and drink offerings according to
the number specified.[b] 22 Include one male goat as a sin offering, in addition to the regular burnt offer-
ing with its grain offering and drink offering.

29:10 [o]Nu 28:13
29:11 [p]Lev 16:3; Nu 28:3
29:12 [q]1Ki 8:2 [r]Lev 23:24
29:14 [s]ver 3
29:16 [t]ver 6
29:17 [u]Lev 23:36 [v]Nu 28:3
29:18 [w]ver 9 [x]Nu 28:7 [y]Nu 15:4-12
29:19 [z]Nu 28:15
29:20 [a]ver 17
29:21 [b]ver 18

23“ ‘On the fourth day prepare ten bulls, two rams and fourteen male lambs a year old, all without defect. 24 With the bulls, rams and lambs, prepare their grain offerings and drink offerings according to the number specified. 25 Include one male goat as a sin offering, in addition to the regular burnt offering with its grain offering and drink offering.

26“ ‘On the fifth day prepare nine bulls, two rams and fourteen male lambs a year old, all without defect. 27 With the bulls, rams and lambs, prepare their grain offerings and drink offerings according to the number specified. 28 Include one male goat as a sin offering, in addition to the regular burnt offering with its grain offering and drink offering.

The Jewish Calendar

NUMBERS 29 Most people groups of the ancient world calculated months by the cycles of the moon; each new moon marked the beginning of a new month. However, the moon completes one revolution around the earth in only about 29.5 days. So the lunar year of 12 lunar months is only 354 days long—somewhat shorter than the solar year of 365.25 days. During a period of a few years the months would begin to misalign with their associated seasons on a lunar calendar. This phenomenon no doubt caused great confusion and consternation in matters such as setting a schedule of annual festivals or creating an agricultural calendar.

The Babylonians periodically added intercalary days (days inserted into a calendar) to the year in order to realign the solar and lunar years. The **Assyrians**, however, allowed the lunar months to fall behind the solar year until finally adopting the Babylonian system during the reign of Tiglath-Pileser III.[1] The Egyptians did not follow a lunar year but divided the year into 12 equal months, each with 30 days, and added 5 extra days at the end of each year. The Jewish calendar, which was similar to its Babylonian counterpart, derived the names of the months from the Babylonian names.

The first month of the Jewish calendar, Nisan, corresponds to the Canaanite Abib. These names sometimes appear in the Bible (e.g., Ne 2:1; Est 8:9; Zec 1:7), although most months mentioned there are simply designated by number (e.g., the "eleventh month").

Some confusion exists about whether the Israelites began their calendar year in the spring or in the fall. The first day of the seventh month (Tishri) is designated for the Feast of Trumpets (Nu 29:1),[2] and that same date eventually became fixed as the day of the Jewish New Year (Rosh Hashanah). This suggests an autumnal new year. However, most evidence points to the spring being the season of the new year. Most significantly, Nisan, which begins in March and ends in April, is routinely called the "first month" in the Bible. Thus it appears that the Israelites began their calendar year in the spring but followed an agricultural year that went from autumn to autumn. The Gezer Calendar, for example, reflects the agricultural year.[3] To explain this difference using a modern analogy, our calendar year begins on January 1, but many institutions and nations run on a fiscal-year calendar that begins and ends on different dates.

Scholars also have differing opinions about whether the Israelites regarded evening or morning as the beginning of a new day. Most evidence implies that their day began in the evening (cf. Lev 23:32). The Israelites observed a seven-day week (Ex 34:21; cf. the creation account in Ge 1:1—2:3), and the Roman Empire officially adopted the seven-day week during the reign of Constantine in A.D. 321.[4]

The matter of enumerating years during ancient times sometimes caused great confusion because there was no universally accepted, fixed point for the beginning of "Year One." The Romans counted their years from the commonly accepted date of the founding of Rome, but ancient Israel, like most other Near Eastern nations, numbered years according to the reigns of kings (e.g., "in the second year of king X"), which, of course, overlapped and varied in terms of duration. The difficulties with such a system were aggravated by the fact that a king's "first year" could be either the year during which he became king or the first full year of his reign after "New Year's Day."[5]

[1]To learn more about this ruler, see "Menahem and Pekah of Israel, Jotham of Judah and Tiglath-Pileser III of Assyria" on page 553. [2]See "The Festivals of Israel" on page 186. [3]See "The Gezer Calendar" on page 913. [4]See "Constantine and Queen Helena's Role in Preserving Holy Sites" on page 1758. [5]See "The Problem of the Chronology of the Kings of Judah and Israel" on page 508.

29" 'On the sixth day prepare eight bulls, two rams and fourteen male lambs a year old, all without defect. 30 With the bulls, rams and lambs, prepare their grain offerings and drink offerings according to the number specified. 31 Include one male goat as a sin offering, in addition to the regular burnt offering with its grain offering and drink offering.

32" 'On the seventh day prepare seven bulls, two rams and fourteen male lambs a year old, all without defect. 33 With the bulls, rams and lambs, prepare their grain offerings and drink offerings according to the number specified. 34 Include one male goat as a sin offering, in addition to the regular burnt offering with its grain offering and drink offering.

35" 'On the eighth day hold an assembly[c] and do no regular work. 36 Present an offering made by fire as an aroma pleasing to the LORD,[d] a burnt offering of one bull, one ram and seven male lambs a year old,[e] all without defect. 37 With the bull, the ram and the lambs, prepare their grain offerings and drink offerings according to the number specified. 38 Include one male goat as a sin offering, in addition to the regular burnt offering with its grain offering and drink offering.

29:35 [c]Lev 23:36
29:36 [d]Lev 1:9 [e]ver 2

39" 'In addition to what you vow[f] and your freewill offerings, prepare these for the LORD at your appointed feasts:[g] your burnt offerings,[h] grain offerings, drink offerings and fellowship offerings.[a]' "

40 Moses told the Israelites all that the LORD commanded him.

29:39 [f]Nu 6:2 [g]Lev 23:2 [h]Lev 1:3; 1Ch 23:31; 2Ch 31:3

Vows

30 Moses said to the heads of the tribes of Israel:[i] "This is what the LORD commands: 2 When a man makes a vow to the LORD or takes an oath to obligate himself by a pledge, he must not break his word but must do everything he said.[j]

3 "When a young woman still living in her father's house makes a vow to the LORD or obligates herself by a pledge 4 and her father hears about her vow or pledge but says nothing to her, then all her vows and every pledge by which she obligated herself will stand.[k] 5 But if her father forbids her when he hears about it, none of her vows or the pledges by which she obligated herself will stand; the LORD will release her because her father has forbidden her.

30:1 [i]Nu 1:4
30:2 [j]Dt 23:21-23; Jdg 11:35; Job 22:27; Ps 22:25; 50:14; 116:14; Pr 20:25; Ecc 5:4,5; Jnh 1:16
30:4 [k]ver 7

6 "If she marries after she makes a vow[l] or after her lips utter a rash promise by which she obligates herself 7 and her husband hears about it but says nothing to her, then her vows or the pledges by which she obligated herself will stand. 8 But if her husband[m] forbids her when he hears about it, he nullifies the vow that obligates her or the rash promise by which she obligates herself, and the LORD will release her.

30:6 [l]Lev 5:4
30:8 [m]Ge 3:16

9 "Any vow or obligation taken by a widow or divorced woman will be binding on her.

10 "If a woman living with her husband makes a vow or obligates herself by a pledge under oath 11 and her husband hears about it but says nothing to her and does not forbid her, then all her vows or the pledges by which she obligated herself will stand. 12 But if her husband nullifies them when he hears about them, then none of the vows or pledges that came from her lips will stand.[n] Her husband has nullified them, and the LORD will release her. 13 Her husband may confirm or nullify any vow she makes or any sworn pledge to deny herself. 14 But if her husband says nothing to her about it from day to day, then he confirms all her vows or the pledges binding on her. He confirms them by saying nothing to her when he hears about them. 15 If, however, he nullifies them some time after he hears about them, then he is responsible for her guilt."

30:12 [n]Eph 5:22; Col 3:18

16 These are the regulations the LORD gave Moses concerning relationships between a man and his wife, and between a father and his young daughter still living in his house.

Vengeance on the Midianites

31 The LORD said to Moses, 2 "Take vengeance on the Midianites[o] for the Israelites. After that, you will be gathered to your people.[p]"

3 So Moses said to the people, "Arm some of your men to go to war against the Midianites and to carry out the LORD's vengeance[q] on them. 4 Send into battle a thousand men from each of the tribes of Israel." 5 So twelve thousand men armed for battle, a thousand from each tribe, were supplied from the clans

31:2 [o]Ge 25:2 [p]Nu 20:26; 27:13
31:3 [q]Jdg 11:36; 1Sa 24:12; 2Sa 4:8; 22:48; Ps 94:1; 149:7

[a] 39 Traditionally *peace offerings*

30:3–15 The main concern of this chapter was not the binding nature of vows and oaths taken by men but the tension that could have arisen if dependent women had bound themselves by obligations to God that conflicted with the will of their fathers or husbands—to whom they were legally subordinate if they were either still living with their parents or married. The vows and obligations of widowed or divorced women, who were independent, were binding like those of men. God waived his right to receive fulfillment of a dependent woman's vow in favor of preserving something highly valuable to him: harmony in the home.

of Israel. 6 Moses sent them into battle, a thousand from each tribe, along with Phinehas son of Eleazar,
31:6 [r]Nu 14:44 the priest, who took with him articles from the sanctuary[r] and the trumpets[s] for signaling.
[s]Nu 10:9 31:7 [t]Dt 20:13; 7 They fought against Midian, as the LORD commanded Moses, and killed every man.[t] 8 Among their
Jdg 21:11; 1Ki 11:15,16 victims were Evi, Rekem, Zur, Hur and Reba[u]—the five kings of Midian.[v] They also killed Balaam son
31:8 [u]Jos 13:21 [v]Nu 25:15 of Beor with the sword.[w] 9 The Israelites captured the Midianite women and children and took all the
[w]Jos 13:22 31:10 [x]Ge 25:16; Midianite herds, flocks and goods as plunder. 10 They burned all the towns where the Midianites had set-
1Ch 6:54; Ps 69:25; tled, as well as all their camps.[x] 11 They took all the plunder and spoils, including the people and ani-
Eze 25:4 mals,[y] 12 and brought the captives, spoils and plunder to Moses and Eleazar the priest and the Israelite
31:11 [y]Dt 20:14 31:12 [z]Nu 27:2 assembly[z] at their camp on the plains of Moab, by the Jordan across from Jericho.[a]
13 Moses, Eleazar the priest and all the leaders of the community went to meet them outside the camp.
31:14 [a]ver 48; Ex 18:21; Dt 1:15 14 Moses was angry with the officers of the army[a]—the commanders of thousands and commanders of
hundreds—who returned from the battle.
15 "Have you allowed all the women to live?" he asked them. 16 "They were the ones who followed Ba-
31:16 [b]2Pe 2:15; Rev 2:14 laam's advice[b] and were the means of turning the Israelites away from the LORD in what happened at
[c]Nu 25:1-9 Peor,[c] so that a plague struck the LORD's people. 17 Now kill all the boys. And kill every woman who has
31:17 [d]Dt 7:2; 20:16-18; slept with a man,[d] 18 but save for yourselves every girl who has never slept with a man.
Jdg 21:11 19 "All of you who have killed anyone or touched anyone who was killed[e] must stay outside the camp
31:19 [e]Nu 19:16 [f]Nu 19:12 seven days. On the third and seventh days you must purify yourselves[f] and your captives. 20 Purify every
31:20 [g]Nu 19:19 garment[g] as well as everything made of leather, goat hair or wood."
21 Then Eleazar the priest said to the soldiers who had gone into battle, "This is the requirement of
31:22 [h]Jos 6:19; 22:8 the law that the LORD gave Moses: 22 Gold, silver, bronze, iron,[h] tin, lead 23 and anything else that can with-
31:23 [i]1Co 3:13 [j]Nu 19:9,17 stand fire must be put through the fire,[i] and then it will be clean. But it must also be purified with the
water of cleansing.[j] And whatever cannot withstand fire must be put through that water. 24 On the sev-
31:24 [k]Lev 11:25 enth day wash your clothes and you will be clean.[k] Then you may come into the camp."

Dividing the Spoils

25 The LORD said to Moses, 26 "You and Eleazar the priest and the family heads of the community are
31:26 [l]Nu 1:19 to count all the people[l] and animals that were captured. 27 Divide[m] the spoils between the soldiers who
31:27 [m]Jos 22:8; 1Sa 30:24 took part in the battle and the rest of the community. 28 From the soldiers who fought in the battle, set

[a] 12 Hebrew *Jordan of Jericho*; possibly an ancient name for the Jordan River

Theophoric Names and Their Significance

NUMBERS 31 In the ancient world people and sometimes places often were given "theophoric" names—proper names that included the name of a deity. This practice occurred in pagan lands as well as in Israel, and such names can convey significant information to scholars today. For example, the name Sennacherib[1] (a well-known Assyrian king) means "(the god) Sin [the moon god] has substituted (for) the dead brothers." This suggests that Sennacherib was born into a family that worshiped the moon god Sin and that at least two brothers born before him died before reaching adulthood.

The God of Israel, as we know, was called by the name Yahweh. Not surprisingly, after God had established his covenant with Israel at Sinai, many Israelites gave their children names that included some element of Yahweh.[2] Sometimes the Yahweh part of the name came first in the form of *yeho* or *yo;* sometimes it came at the end of the name in the form of *yahu* or *ya*. For example, Jonathan may be rendered *yeho-nathan*, which means "Yahweh has given." Micah stems from *mi-k-ya* or *mi-k-yahu*, meaning "Who is like Yahweh?"

Israelite proper names given prior to the Sinai covenant typically did not contain an element of Yahweh. For example, the name Eleazar is derived from *el-azar*, meaning "God [the more generic *el*, not Yahweh] has helped."

[1]To learn more about Sennacherib, see "The Death of Sennacherib" on page 562 and "Hezekiah Against the Assyrians" on page 1118. [2]See "YHWH: The Name of God in the Old Testament" on page 89.

apart as tribute for the LORD[n] one out of every five hundred, whether persons, cattle, donkeys, sheep or 31:28 [n]Nu 18:21
goats. 29 Take this tribute from their half share and give it to Eleazar the priest as the LORD's part. 30 From
the Israelites' half, select one out of every fifty, whether persons, cattle, donkeys, sheep, goats or other
animals. Give them to the Levites, who are responsible for the care of the LORD's tabernacle.[o]" 31 So Mo- 31:30 [o]Nu 3:7; 18:3
ses and Eleazar the priest did as the LORD commanded Moses.

32 The plunder remaining from the spoils that the soldiers took was 675,000 sheep, 33 72,000 cattle,
34 61,000 donkeys 35 and 32,000 women who had never slept with a man.

36 The half share of those who fought in the battle was:

337,500 sheep, 37 of which the tribute for the LORD[p] was 675; 31:37 [p]ver 38-41
38 36,000 cattle, of which the tribute for the LORD was 72;
39 30,500 donkeys, of which the tribute for the LORD was 61;
40 16,000 people, of which the tribute for the LORD was 32.

41 Moses gave the tribute to Eleazar the priest as the LORD's part,[q] as the LORD commanded Moses. 31:41 [q]Nu 5:9; 18:8

42 The half belonging to the Israelites, which Moses set apart from that of the fighting men— 43 the
community's half—was 337,500 sheep, 44 36,000 cattle, 45 30,500 donkeys 46 and 16,000 people. 47 From the
Israelites' half, Moses selected one out of every fifty persons and animals, as the LORD commanded him,
and gave them to the Levites, who were responsible for the care of the LORD's tabernacle.

48 Then the officers who were over the units of the army—the commanders of thousands and com-
manders of hundreds—went to Moses 49 and said to him, "Your servants have counted the soldiers un-
der our command, and not one is missing.[r] 50 So we have brought as an offering to the LORD the gold ar- 31:49 [r]Jer 23:4
ticles each of us acquired—armlets, bracelets, signet rings, earrings and necklaces—to make atonement
for ourselves[s] before the LORD." 31:50 [s]Ex 30:16

51 Moses and Eleazar the priest accepted from them the gold—all the crafted articles. 52 All the gold
from the commanders of thousands and commanders of hundreds that Moses and Eleazar presented as
a gift to the LORD weighed 16,750 shekels.[a] 53 Each soldier had taken plunder[t] for himself. 54 Moses and 31:53 [t]Dt 20:14
Eleazar the priest accepted the gold from the commanders of thousands and commanders of hundreds
and brought it into the Tent of Meeting as a memorial[u] for the Israelites before the LORD. 31:54 [u]Ex 28:12

[a] 52 That is, about 420 pounds (about 190 kilograms)

The Kingdoms of Sihon and Og

NUMBERS 32 Moses gave the Gadites, Reubenites and the half-tribe of Manasseh the territories of Sihon and Og, two kings whom the Israelites had defeated prior to crossing the Jordan into the promised land (Nu 32:33). Because there is no extrabiblical reference to either of these two names, all that is known of them comes from the Old Testament.

Og is usually referenced in the Bible as "Og [king] of Bashan," the geographical region east of the Sea of Galilee (see map on p. 245). Og was also a member of the Rephaites (Dt 3:11), an unexplained designation that appears as well in **Ugaritic** texts and has often been associated with giants. According to this same verse, Og had an iron bed or couch of legendary proportions (more than 13 feet [4 m] long and 6 feet [1.8 m] wide). Joshua 12:4 also links Og with the Rephaites and further connects him to two specific cities, Edrei and Ashtaroth.

Sihon is said to have been one of the **Amorites**, a western Semitic group that was well documented throughout the Near East during the **Bronze Age**.[1] He is often associated with Heshbon, a kingdom whose borders extended north to the Jabbok River, west to the Jordan River and south to the Arnon River (Jdg 11:22).

These kingdoms of the **Transjordan** stood between the Israelites and the Jordan River, which constituted Israel's gateway into the land of Canaan.[2] The defeat of Transjordan's inhabitants at the hands of Israel precipitated the resettlement of the area by the tribes of Reuben, Gad and half of Manasseh. So foundational were these formidable victories that their memory was attested in Israel as late as the days of Nehemiah (Ne 9:22).

[1]See "Archaeological Periods" chart on page xx in the front of this Bible. [2]See "The Conquest of Canaan" on page 310 and "Canaan" on page 324.

The Transjordan Tribes

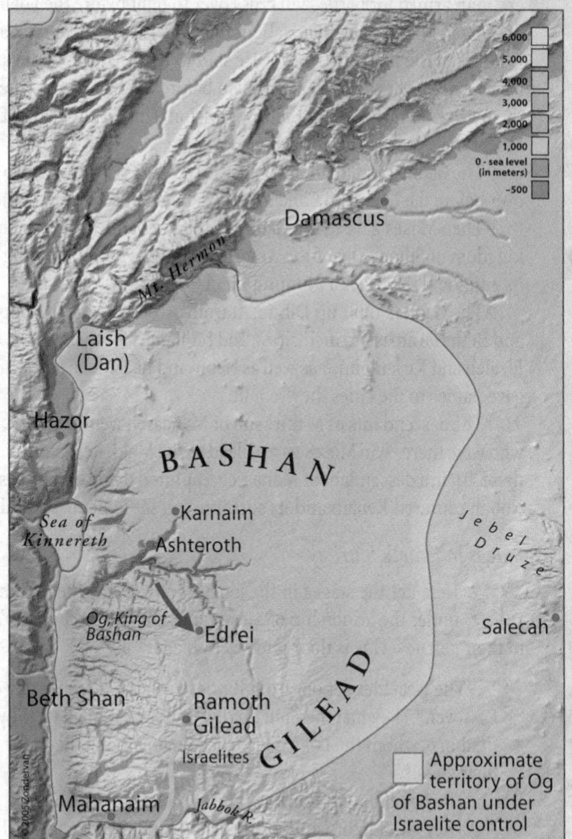

Zondervan NIV Altas of the Bible, p. 93

32 The Reubenites and Gadites,
who had very large herds
and flocks, saw that the lands of Ja-
32:1 [v]Nu 21:32 [w]Ex 12:38 zer[v] and Gilead were suitable for live-
stock.[w] 2So they came to Moses and
Eleazar the priest and to the leaders
of the community, and said, 3"Ata-
32:3 [x]ver 34 [y]ver 36 [z]ver 37; Isa 15:4; 16:9; Jer 48:34 [a]ver 38; Jos 13:17; Eze 25:9 roth,[x] Dibon, Jazer, Nimrah,[y] Hesh-
bon, Elealeh,[z] Sebam, Nebo and
Beon[a]— 4the land the LORD sub-
32:4 [b]Nu 21:34 [c]Ex 12:38 dued[b] before the people of Israel—
are suitable for livestock,[c] and your
servants have livestock. 5If we have
found favor in your eyes," they said,
"let this land be given to your ser-
vants as our possession. Do not
make us cross the Jordan."

6Moses said to the Gadites and
Reubenites, "Shall your countrymen
go to war while you sit here? 7Why do
you discourage the Israelites from go-
ing over into the land the LORD has
32:7 [d]Nu 13:27–14:4 given them?[d] 8This is what your fa-
32:8 [e]Nu 13:3, 26; Dt 1:19-25 thers did when I sent them from Ka-
desh Barnea to look over the land.[e]
9After they went up to the Valley of
32:9 [f]Nu 13:23; Dt 1:24 Eshcol[f] and viewed the land, they dis-
couraged the Israelites from entering
the land the LORD had given them.
32:10 [g]Nu 11:1 10The LORD's anger was aroused[g] that
day and he swore this oath: 11'Be-
cause they have not followed me
32:11 [h]Ex 30:14 [i]Nu 14:23 [j]Nu 14:28-30 wholeheartedly, not one of the men twenty years old or more[h] who came up out of Egypt will see the land
I promised on oath[i] to Abraham, Isaac and Jacob[j]— 12not one except Caleb son of Jephunneh the Keniz-
32:12 [k]Nu 14:24, 30; Dt 1:36; Ps 63:8 zite and Joshua son of Nun, for they followed the LORD wholeheartedly.'[k] 13The LORD's anger burned against
Israel[l] and he made them wander in the desert forty years, until the whole generation of those who had
32:13 [l]Ex 4:14 [m]Nu 14:28-35; 26:64,65 done evil in his sight was gone.[m]

14"And here you are, a brood of sinners, standing in the place of your fathers and making the LORD even
32:14 [n]ver 10; Dt 1:34; Ps 78:59 more angry with Israel.[n] 15If you turn away from following him, he will again leave all this people in the
32:15 [o]Dt 30:17-18; 2Ch 7:20 desert, and you will be the cause of their destruction.[o]"

32:16 [p]Ex 12:38; Dt 3:19 16Then they came up to him and said, "We would like to build pens here for our livestock[p] and cities
32:17 [q]Jos 4:12, 13 [r]Nu 22:4; Dt 3:20 for our women and children. 17But we are ready to arm ourselves and go ahead of the Israelites[q] until we
have brought them to their place.[r] Meanwhile our women and children will live in fortified cities, for pro-
tection from the inhabitants of the land. 18We will not return to our homes until every Israelite has re-
32:18 [s]Jos 22:1-4 ceived his inheritance.[s] 19We will not receive any inheritance with them on the other side of the Jordan,
32:19 [t]Jos 12:1 because our inheritance has come to us on the east side of the Jordan."[t]

20Then Moses said to them, "If you will do this—if you will arm yourselves before the LORD for bat-
32:20 [u]Dt 3:18 tle,[u] 21and if all of you will go armed over the Jordan before the LORD until he has driven his enemies out
32:22 [v]Jos 22:4 [w]Dt 3:18-20 before him— 22then when the land is subdued before the LORD, you may return[v] and be free from your
obligation to the LORD and to Israel. And this land will be your possession before the LORD.[w]

23"But if you fail to do this, you will be sinning against the LORD; and you may be sure that your sin
32:23 [x]Ge 4:7; 44:16; Isa 59:12 will find you out.[x] 24Build cities for your women and children, and pens for your flocks,[y] but do what
32:24 [y]ver 1,16 [z]Nu 30:2 you have promised.[z]"

25The Gadites and Reubenites said to Moses, "We your servants will do as our lord commands. 26Our

children and wives, our flocks and herds will remain here in the cities of Gilead.[a] 27 But your servants, ev- **32:26** a Jos 1:14
ery man armed for battle, will cross over to fight before the LORD, just as our lord says."

28 Then Moses gave orders about them[b] to Eleazar the priest and Joshua son of Nun and to the fami- **32:28** b Dt 3:18-20; Jos 1:13
ly heads of the Israelite tribes. 29 He said to them, "If the Gadites and Reubenites, every man armed for
battle, cross over the Jordan with you before the LORD, then when the land is subdued before you, give
them the land of Gilead as their possession. 30 But if they do not cross over with you armed, they must
accept their possession with you in Canaan."

31 The Gadites and Reubenites answered, "Your servants will do what the LORD has said.[c] 32 We will cross **32:31** c ver 29
over before the LORD into Canaan armed, but the property we inherit will be on this side of the Jordan."

33 Then Moses gave to the Gadites,[d] the Reubenites and the half-tribe of Manasseh son of Joseph the **32:33** d Jos 13:24-28;
kingdom of Sihon king of the Amorites[e] and the kingdom of Og king of Bashan—the whole land with 1Sa 13:7 e Dt 2:26
its cities and the territory around them.[f] f Nu 21:24; Jos 12:6

34 The Gadites built up Dibon, Ataroth, Aroer,[g] 35 Atroth Shophan, Jazer,[h] Jogbehah, 36 Beth Nimrah[i] **32:34** g Dt 2:36; Jdg 11:26
and Beth Haran as fortified cities, and built pens for their flocks. 37 And the Reubenites rebuilt Heshbon, **32:35** h ver 3
Elealeh and Kiriathaim, 38 as well as Nebo[j] and Baal Meon (these names were changed) and Sibmah. They **32:36** i ver 3 **32:38** j ver 3;
gave names to the cities they rebuilt. Isa 15:2; Jer 48:1, 22

39 The descendants of Makir[k] son of Manasseh went to Gilead, captured it and drove out the Amorites **32:39** k Ge 50:23
who were there. 40 So Moses gave Gilead to the Makirites,[l] the descendants of Manasseh, and they settled **32:40** l Dt 3:15; Jos 17:1
there. 41 Jair, a descendant of Manasseh, captured their settlements and called them Havvoth Jair.[a][m] 42 And **32:41** m Dt 3:14;
Nobah captured Kenath and its surrounding settlements and called it Nobah after himself.[n] Jos 13:30; Jdg 10:4; 1Ch 2:23

Stages in Israel's Journey

32:42 n 2Sa 18:18; Ps 49:11

33 Here are the stages in the journey of the Israelites when they came out of Egypt[o] by divisions **33:1** o Mic 6:4
under the leadership of Moses and Aaron.[p] 2 At the LORD's command Moses recorded the stages p Ps 77:20
in their journey. This is their journey by stages:

3 The Israelites set out from Rameses on the fifteenth day of the first month, the day after the
Passover.[q] They marched out boldly[r] in full view of all the Egyptians, 4 who were burying all their **33:3** q Ex 13:4
firstborn, whom the LORD had struck down among them; for the LORD had brought judgment on r Ex 14:8
their gods.[s] **33:4** s Ex 12:12

5 The Israelites left Rameses and camped at Succoth.[t] **33:5** t Ex 12:37

6 They left Succoth and camped at Etham, on the edge of the desert.[u] **33:6** u Ex 13:20

7 They left Etham, turned back to Pi Hahiroth, to the east of Baal Zephon,[v] and camped near **33:7** v Ex 14:9
Migdol.[w] w Ex 14:2

8 They left Pi Hahiroth[b] and passed through the sea[x] into the desert, and when they had trav- **33:8** x Ex 14:22
eled for three days in the Desert of Etham, they camped at Marah.[y] y Ex 15:23

9 They left Marah and went to Elim, where there were twelve springs and seventy palm trees, and
they camped[z] there. **33:9** z Ex 15:27

10 They left Elim and camped by the Red Sea.[c]

11 They left the Red Sea and camped in the Desert of Sin.[a] **33:11** a Ex 16:1

12 They left the Desert of Sin and camped at Dophkah.

13 They left Dophkah and camped at Alush.

14 They left Alush and camped at Rephidim, where there was no water for the people to drink.

15 They left Rephidim[b] and camped in the Desert of Sinai.[c] **33:15** b Ex 17:1 c Ex 19:1

16 They left the Desert of Sinai and camped at Kibroth Hattaavah.[d] **33:16** d Nu 11:34

17 They left Kibroth Hattaavah and camped at Hazeroth.[e] **33:17** e Nu 11:35

18 They left Hazeroth and camped at Rithmah.

19 They left Rithmah and camped at Rimmon Perez.

[a] *41* Or *them the settlements of Jair* [b] *8* Many manuscripts of the Masoretic Text, Samaritan Pentateuch and Vulgate; most manuscripts of the Masoretic Text *left from before Hahiroth* [c] *10* Hebrew *Yam Suph*; that is, Sea of Reeds; also in verse 11

33:3–49 The numerous stopovers (significantly 40 between Rameses and the plains of Moab) of Israel's desert experience are listed here. Unfortunately, most of the sites were desert encampments, not cities with lasting archaeological records, so they are difficult to locate. Many of them (e.g., in vv. 19–29) are not otherwise recorded in Exodus or Numbers. Interestingly, some other placenames that do occur elsewhere (e.g., Taberah, 11:3) are missing here. See "The Route of the Exodus: The Arabian Route Theory" on page 112 and "The Itinerary in Numbers" on page 237.

33:20 [f]Jos 10:29 20 They left Rimmon Perez and camped at Libnah.[f]
21 They left Libnah and camped at Rissah.
22 They left Rissah and camped at Kehelathah.
23 They left Kehelathah and camped at Mount Shepher.
24 They left Mount Shepher and camped at Haradah.
25 They left Haradah and camped at Makheloth.
26 They left Makheloth and camped at Tahath.
27 They left Tahath and camped at Terah.
28 They left Terah and camped at Mithcah.
29 They left Mithcah and camped at Hashmonah.
33:30 [g]Dt 10:6 30 They left Hashmonah and camped at Moseroth.[g]
31 They left Moseroth and camped at Bene Jaakan.
32 They left Bene Jaakan and camped at Hor Haggidgad.
33:33 [h]Dt 10:7 33 They left Hor Haggidgad and camped at Jotbathah.[h]
34 They left Jotbathah and camped at Abronah.
33:35 [i]Dt 2:8; 1Ki 9:26; 22:48 35 They left Abronah and camped at Ezion Geber.[i]
33:36 [j]Nu 20:1 36 They left Ezion Geber and camped at Kadesh, in the Desert of Zin.[j]
33:37 [k]Nu 20:22 [l]Nu 20:16; 21:4 37 They left Kadesh and camped at Mount Hor,[k] on the border of Edom.[l] 38 At the LORD's com-
33:38 [m]Dt 10:6 [n]Nu 20:25-28 mand Aaron the priest went up Mount Hor, where he died[m] on the first day of the fifth month of
the fortieth year after the Israelites came out of Egypt.[n] 39 Aaron was a hundred and twenty-three
years old when he died on Mount Hor.
33:40 [o]Nu 21:1 40 The Canaanite king of Arad,[o] who lived in the Negev of Canaan, heard that the Israelites were
coming.

ARCHAEOLOGICAL SITES

ARAD

NUMBERS 33 The ancient Israelite city of Arad was located at modern Tell Arad, in the Negev[1] south of Jerusalem (see "Map 7"). Archaeological excavation there has uncovered a large, well-preserved, **Early Bronze Age**[2] city that served as an important post on key trade routes. Hebrew **ostraca** (pottery fragments containing writing) bearing the name Arad have been found there, as have a large quantity of ostraca bearing other Hebrew or Aramaic inscriptions.[3]

A series of fortified occupations dating from the reign of Solomon to that of Zedekiah also have been found at Tell Arad. The site appears to have been more or less deserted during the **Middle** and **Late Bronze** Ages, but during the **Iron Age** Israelites built a fortress on the summit of Tell Arad to guard the eastern Negev basin from nomadic peoples and **Transjordan**ian enemies—especially Edom.[4] The structures belonging to the final level of Israelite occupation at Arad were destroyed during the **Babylonian** conquest of Judah in 586 B.C.[5]

An impressive Israelite temple has also been unearthed at Arad. The only Israelite temple recovered by archaeologists to date, it may have been modeled after Solomon's temple; like Solomon's it was oriented toward the east.[6] This structure had a sacrificial altar in the courtyard, as well as two incense altars and two standing stones in its "Most Holy Place."

Archaeologists have determined that this particular temple was deliberately put out of use. This probably happened during the reforms of either Hezekiah or Josiah, when local temples situated outside of the control of the king and the Jerusalem priesthood were dismantled because they tended to become focal points for the growth of pagan and/or aberrant religious movements.[7]

The location of Arad, however, poses a problem related to the conquest narrative.[8] The king of Arad attacked the Israelites, who were traveling near the southern border of Canaan. After suffering an initial loss, Israel defeated this king and destroyed his cities (Nu 21:1–3). Yet Tell Arad lacks any remains dating to the time of Moses. A possible solution exists in the campaign account of Pharaoh Shishak, whose tenth-century B.C. list mentions the conquests of two Arads: Arad the Great and Arad of Yrhm.[9] The Israelites could have destroyed the second Arad, the location of which remains uncertain. Another possibility is that the Arad mentioned in Numbers 21 actually refers to the general region and that the king of Arad (21:1) lived in the city of Hormah (21:3).

[1]See "The Negev: Its Climate and Features" on page 34. [2]See "Archaeological Periods" chart on page xx in the front of this Bible. [3]See "The Arad Ostraca" on page 1215. [4]See "Edom" on page 1467. [5]See also "The Last Days of Jerusalem" on page 1197. [6]See "Solomon's Temple and Other Ancient Temples" on page 620. [7]See "The Kuntillet Ajrûd Inscriptions: The Lord's Asherah?" on page 1220. [8]See "The Conquest of Canaan" on page 310. [9]See "The Campaign of Shishak" on page 635.

41 They left Mount Hor and camped at Zalmonah.
42 They left Zalmonah and camped at Punon.
43 They left Punon and camped at Oboth.[p] **33:43** [p]Nu 21:10
44 They left Oboth and camped at Iye Abarim, on the border of Moab.[q] **33:44** [q]Nu 21:11
45 They left Iyim[a] and camped at Dibon Gad.
46 They left Dibon Gad and camped at Almon Diblathaim.
47 They left Almon Diblathaim and camped in the mountains of Abarim,[r] near Nebo. **33:47** [r]Nu 27:12
48 They left the mountains of Abarim and camped on the plains of Moab by the Jordan across
from Jericho.[b][s] 49 There on the plains of Moab they camped along the Jordan from Beth Jeshimoth **33:48** [s]Nu 22:1
to Abel Shittim.[t] **33:49** [t]Nu 25:1

50 On the plains of Moab by the Jordan across from Jericho the LORD said to Moses, 51 "Speak to the Is-
raelites and say to them: 'When you cross the Jordan into Canaan,[u] 52 drive out all the inhabitants of the **33:51** [u]Jos 3:17
land before you. Destroy all their carved images and their cast idols, and demolish all their high places.[v] **33:52** [v]Ex 23:24; 34:13; Lev 26:1; Dt 7:2,5; 12:3; Jos 11:12; Ps 106:34-36
53 Take possession of the land and settle in it, for I have given you the land to possess.[w] 54 Distribute the
land by lot, according to your clans.[x] To a larger group give a larger inheritance, and to a smaller group
a smaller one. Whatever falls to them by lot will be theirs. Distribute it according to your ancestral tribes. **33:53** [w]Dt 11:31; Jos 21:43
55 " 'But if you do not drive out the inhabitants of the land, those you allow to remain will become **33:54** [x]Nu 26:54
barbs in your eyes and thorns[y] in your sides. They will give you trouble in the land where you will live. **33:55** [y]Jos 23:13; Jdg 2:3; Ps 106:36
56 And then I will do to you what I plan to do to them.' "

Boundaries of Canaan

34 The LORD said to Moses, 2 "Command the Israelites and say to them: 'When you enter Canaan, the
land that will be allotted to you as an inheritance[z] will have these boundaries:[a] **34:2** [z]Ge 17:8; Dt 1:7-8; Ps 78:54-55 [a]Eze 47:15

3 " 'Your southern side will include some of the Desert of Zin[b] along the border of Edom. On the east,
your southern boundary will start from the end of the Salt Sea,[c][c] 4 cross south of Scorpion[d] Pass,[d] con- **34:3** [b]Jos 15:1-3 [c]Ge 14:3
tinue on to Zin and go south of Kadesh Barnea.[e] Then it will go to Hazar Addar and over to Azmon, **34:4** [d]Jos 15:3 [e]Nu 32:8
5 where it will turn, join the Wadi of Egypt[f] and end at the Sea.[e] **34:5** [f]Ge 15:18; Jos 15:4
6 " 'Your western boundary will be the coast of the Great Sea. This will be your boundary on the west.
7 " 'For your northern boundary,[g] run a line from the Great Sea to Mount Hor 8 and from Mount Hor **34:7** [g]Eze 47:15-17
to Lebo[f] Hamath.[h] Then the boundary will go to Zedad, 9 continue to Ziphron and end at Hazar Enan. This **34:8** [h]Nu 13:21; Jos 13:5
will be your boundary on the north.
10 " 'For your eastern boundary, run a line from Hazar Enan to Shepham. 11 The boundary will go down
from Shepham to Riblah[i] on the east side of Ain and continue along the slopes east of the Sea of Kinne- **34:11** [i]2Ki 23:33; Jer 39:5 [j]Dt 3:17; Jos 11:2; 13:27
reth.[g][j] 12 Then the boundary will go down along the Jordan and end at the Salt Sea.
" 'This will be your land, with its boundaries on every side.' "
13 Moses commanded the Israelites: "Assign this land by lot as an inheritance.[k] The LORD has ordered **34:13** [k]Jos 14:1-5
that it be given to the nine and a half tribes, 14 because the families of the tribe of Reuben, the tribe of Gad
and the half-tribe of Manasseh have received their inheritance.[l] 15 These two and a half tribes have re- **34:14** [l]Nu 32:33; Jos 14:3
ceived their inheritance on the east side of the Jordan of Jericho,[h] toward the sunrise."
16 The LORD said to Moses, 17 "These are the names of the men who are to assign the land for you as an
inheritance: Eleazar the priest and Joshua[m] son of Nun. 18 And appoint one leader from each tribe to **34:17** [m]Jos 14:1
help[n] assign the land. 19 These are their names: **34:18** [n]Nu 1:4,16

Caleb[o] son of Jephunneh, **34:19** [o]Nu 26:65 [p]Ge 29:35; Dt 33:7
from the tribe of Judah;[p]
20 Shemuel son of Ammihud,
from the tribe of Simeon;[q] **34:20** [q]Ge 49:5
21 Elidad son of Kislon,
from the tribe of Benjamin;[r] **34:21** [r]Ge 49:27; Ps 68:27
22 Bukki son of Jogli,
the leader from the tribe of Dan;

[a] *45* That is, Iye Abarim [b] *48* Hebrew *Jordan of Jericho*; possibly an ancient name for the Jordan River; also in verse 50
[c] *3* That is, the Dead Sea; also in verse 12 [d] *4* Hebrew *Akrabbim* [e] *5* That is, the Mediterranean; also in verses 6 and 7
[f] *8* Or *to the entrance to* [g] *11* That is, Galilee [h] *15* *Jordan of Jericho* was possibly an ancient name for the Jordan River.

23 Hanniel son of Ephod,
the leader from the tribe of Manasseh son of Joseph;
24 Kemuel son of Shiphtan,
the leader from the tribe of Ephraim son of Joseph;
25 Elizaphan son of Parnach,
the leader from the tribe of Zebulun;
26 Paltiel son of Azzan,
the leader from the tribe of Issachar;
27 Ahihud son of Shelomi,
34:27 [s]Nu 1:40 the leader from the tribe of Asher;[s]
28 Pedahel son of Ammihud,
the leader from the tribe of Naphtali."
29 These are the men the LORD commanded to assign the inheritance to the Israelites in the land of Canaan.

Towns for the Levites

35 On the plains of Moab by the Jordan across from Jericho,[a] the LORD said to Moses, 2 "Command
35:2 [t]Lev 25:32-34; Jos 14:3,4 the Israelites to give the Levites towns to live in[t] from the inheritance the Israelites will possess.
And give them pasturelands around the towns. 3 Then they will have towns to live in and pasturelands
for their cattle, flocks and all their other livestock.
4 "The pasturelands around the towns that you give the Levites will extend out fifteen hundred feet[b]
from the town wall. 5 Outside the town, measure three thousand feet[c] on the east side, three thousand on
the south side, three thousand on the west and three thousand on the north, with the town in the center. They will have this area as pastureland for the towns.

Cities of Refuge

6 "Six of the towns you give the Levites will be cities of refuge, to which a person who has killed some-
35:6 [u]Jos 20:7-9; 21:3,13 one may flee.[u] In addition, give them forty-two other towns. 7 In all you must give the Levites forty-eight
towns, together with their pasturelands. 8 The towns you give the Levites from the land the Israelites possess are to be given in proportion to the inheritance of each tribe: Take many towns from a tribe that has
35:8 [v]Nu 26:54; 33:54; Jos 21:1-42 many, but few from one that has few."[v]
9 Then the LORD said to Moses: 10 "Speak to the Israelites and say to them: 'When you cross the Jordan
35:10 [w]Jos 20:2 into Canaan,[w] 11 select some towns to be your cities of refuge, to which a person who has killed someone[x]
35:11 [x]ver 22-25 [y]Ex 21:13; Dt 19:1-13 accidentally[y] may flee. 12 They will be places of refuge from the avenger,[z] so that a person accused of mur-
35:12 [z]Dt 19:6; Jos 20:3 der may not die before he stands trial before the assembly. 13 These six towns you give will be your cities
of refuge. 14 Give three on this side of the Jordan and three in Canaan as cities of refuge. 15 These six towns
will be a place of refuge for Israelites, aliens and any other people living among them, so that anyone
who has killed another accidentally can flee there.
16 " 'If a man strikes someone with an iron object so that he dies, he is a murderer; the murderer shall
35:16 [a]Ex 21:12; Lev 24:17 be put to death.[a] 17 Or if anyone has a stone in his hand that could kill, and he strikes someone so that he
dies, he is a murderer; the murderer shall be put to death. 18 Or if anyone has a wooden object in his hand
that could kill, and he hits someone so that he dies, he is a murderer; the murderer shall be put to death.
35:19 [b]ver 21 19 The avenger of blood shall put the murderer to death; when he meets him, he shall put him to death.[b]
35:20 [c]Ge 4:8; Ex 21:14; Dt 19:11; 2Sa 3:27; 20:10 20 If anyone with malice aforethought shoves another or throws something at him intentionally[c] so that

[a] *1* Hebrew *Jordan of Jericho*; possibly an ancient name for the Jordan River [b] *4* Hebrew *a thousand cubits* (about 450 meters)
[c] *5* Hebrew *two thousand cubits* (about 900 meters)

35:12 For a discussion of the role of the *go'el* (here translated "avenger"), see the note at Deuteronomy 19:15–21.

35:19 From the days of Noah the Biblical penalty for murder had been death (Ge 9:6). Throughout Old Testament times the ancient Semitic custom of the avenger of blood was followed: A murdered man's nearest relative (the *go'el*) had the duty to pursue the murderer and kill him (see "The Kinsman-Redeemer" on p. 391). Since in the practice of avenging blood in this fashion men failed to distinguish between murder and manslaughter, and vicious blood feuds would frequently arise, the Mosaic Law provided for cities of refuge (ch. 35) to which a person pursued by an avenger of blood could flee (see "Cities of Refuge" on p. 334). He would be admitted and tried; if judged guilty of murder, he would be turned over to the avenger, but if declared innocent he would be afforded protection in this city from the avenger. It appears likely that the advent of the monarchy began a trend away from the ancient *go'el* custom; we find the king putting one murderer to death (1Ki 2:34) and pardoning another (2Sa 14:6–8).

In a murder trial the collaborative testimony of at least two persons was necessary for conviction (Nu 35:30; Dt 17:6). The right of asylum was not granted a murderer. Instead, he was dragged away even from the horns of the altar (Ex 21:14; 1Ki 2:28–34). Nor could a ransom be accepted for a murderer (Nu 35:21).

he dies 21 or if in hostility he hits him with his fist so that he dies, that person shall be put to death; he is
a murderer. The avenger of blood shall put the murderer to death when he meets him.
22 " 'But if without hostility someone suddenly shoves another or throws something at him uninten-
tionally[d] 23 or, without seeing him, drops a stone on him that could kill him, and he dies, then since he was **35:22** [d]ver 11; Ex 21:13
not his enemy and he did not intend to harm him, 24 the assembly[e] must judge between him and the **35:24** [e]ver 12; Jos 20:6
avenger of blood according to these regulations. 25 The assembly must protect the one accused of mur-
der from the avenger of blood and send him back to the city of refuge to which he fled. He must stay
there until the death of the high priest, who was anointed with the holy oil.[f] **35:25** [f]Ex 29:7
26 " 'But if the accused ever goes outside the limits of the city of refuge to which he has fled 27 and the
avenger of blood finds him outside the city, the avenger of blood may kill the accused without being
guilty of murder. 28 The accused must stay in his city of refuge until the death of the high priest; only af-
ter the death of the high priest may he return to his own property.
29 " 'These are to be legal requirements[g] for you throughout the generations to come, wherever you **35:29** [g]Nu 27:11
live.
30 " 'Anyone who kills a person is to be put to death as a murderer only on the testimony of witness-
es. But no one is to be put to death on the testimony of only one witness.[h] **35:30** [h]ver 16; Dt 17:6; 19:15; Mt 18:16; Jn 7:51; 2Co 13:1; Heb 10:28
31 " 'Do not accept a ransom for the life of a murderer, who deserves to die. He must surely be put to death.
32 " 'Do not accept a ransom for anyone who has fled to a city of refuge and so allow him to go back
and live on his own land before the death of the high priest.
33 " 'Do not pollute the land where you are. Bloodshed pollutes the land,[i] and atonement cannot be **35:33** [i]Ge 9:6; Ps 106:38; Mic 4:11
made for the land on which blood has been shed, except by the blood of the one who shed it. 34 Do not
defile the land[j] where you live and where I dwell,[k] for I, the LORD, dwell among the Israelites.' " **35:34** [j]Lev 18:24, 25 [k]Ex 29:45

Inheritance in the Ancient Near East

NUMBERS 36 Inheritance laws in the ancient Near East played a critical role in preserving a family line and perpetuating its land holdings. Wealth and social standing were tied to landed property, and rules of kinship regulated the land's division. Customary law held that only sons had the right to inherit, and the firstborn son received a double share of the family estate (Dt 21:15–17).

In the absence of male heirs, however, daughters could inherit. The early Sumerian law code of Lipit-Ishtar (c. 1930 B.C.) explicitly stated that if a man died without leaving male offspring, his unmarried daughter would be his heir. In addition, family archives at Nuzi show that when a man had no sons he could deed his estate to his daughter as his principal heir or, more typically, as joint heir with her husband, who was said to be "adopted" into the family.

Hammurabi's law code (c. 1750 B.C.) recorded cases in which daughters were treated as coheirs with their brothers. A daughter's dowry, consisting primarily of moveable property (personal servants, household vessels, jewelry and the like), was said to be her inheritance portion.

Special inheritance privileges also were granted to temple priestesses who had no children. They were awarded a certain portion of their fathers' estates to ensure their financial security, although after their deaths the inheritance share was to revert back to their brothers.

The case of Zelophehad's five daughters explores the implications of Israelite daughters inheriting their fathers' lands. The empowerment of these particular daughters as principal heirs was an accommodation to unusual circumstances. The concern was that once they married there would be nothing to prevent their passing along their land holdings in the usual manner to their children and thus into the patrimony of another tribe (Nu 27:1–11).

The solution was straightforward: These women would be obligated to marry within their own clan so as not to disturb the balance of the tribal allotments (36:1–9; cf. 1Ch 23:22). These daughters' inheritance rights ultimately existed for the purpose of retaining the estate for their future sons. This was similar to the institution of levirate marriage that sought to produce an heir to whom a deceased husband's property could be bequeathed (Dt 25:5–6).[1]

See also "Custom and Law in Ancient Mesopotamia" on page 36 and "The Rights of the Firstborn" on page 43.

[1] See "Levirate Marriage" on page 64.

Inheritance of Zelophehad's Daughters

36:1 [l]Nu 26:29 [m]Nu 27:2 **36** The family heads of the clan of Gilead[l] son of Makir, the son of Manasseh, who were from the
clans of the descendants of Joseph, came and spoke before Moses and the leaders,[m] the heads of
the Israelite families. 2 They said, "When the LORD commanded my lord to give the land as an inheritance
36:2 [n]Nu 26:33; 27:1,7 to the Israelites by lot, he ordered you to give the inheritance of our brother Zelophehad[n] to his daugh-
ters. 3 Now suppose they marry men from other Israelite tribes; then their inheritance will be taken from
our ancestral inheritance and added to that of the tribe they marry into. And so part of the inheritance
36:4 [o]Lev 25:10 allotted to us will be taken away. 4 When the Year of Jubilee[o] for the Israelites comes, their inheritance
will be added to that of the tribe into which they marry, and their property will be taken from the trib-
al inheritance of our forefathers."

5 Then at the LORD's command Moses gave this order to the Israelites: "What the tribe of the descen-
dants of Joseph is saying is right. 6 This is what the LORD commands for Zelophehad's daughters: They may
36:7 [p]1Ki 21:3 marry anyone they please as long as they marry within the tribal clan of their father. 7 No inheritance[p]
in Israel is to pass from tribe to tribe, for every Israelite shall keep the tribal land inherited from his fore-
fathers. 8 Every daughter who inherits land in any Israelite tribe must marry someone in her father's trib-
36:8 [q]1Ch 23:22 al clan,[q] so that every Israelite will possess the inheritance of his fathers. 9 No inheritance may pass from
tribe to tribe, for each Israelite tribe is to keep the land it inherits."

10 So Zelophehad's daughters did as the LORD commanded Moses. 11 Zelophehad's daughters—Mah-
36:11 [r]Nu 26:33; 27:1 lah, Tirzah, Hoglah, Milcah and Noah[r]—married their cousins on their father's side. 12 They married
within the clans of the descendants of Manasseh son of Joseph, and their inheritance remained in their
father's clan and tribe.

36:13 [s]Lev 26:46; 27:34 13 These are the commands and regulations the LORD gave through Moses[s] to the Israelites on the
[t]Nu 22:1 plains of Moab by the Jordan across from Jericho.[a][t]

[a] *13* Hebrew *Jordan of Jericho*; possibly an ancient name for the Jordan River

---

36:1–12 Zelophehad, a Manassite who died in the wilderness, left five daughters but no sons. In the division of the land they begged for a share in the inheritance (27:1–11). This the Lord granted, and when their tribesmen feared that their property might be alienated from the tribe by marriage (36:1–12), God commanded that they should marry only within their tribe. This became a general law among Israelite heiresses. See "Inheritance in the Ancient Near East" on page 250.

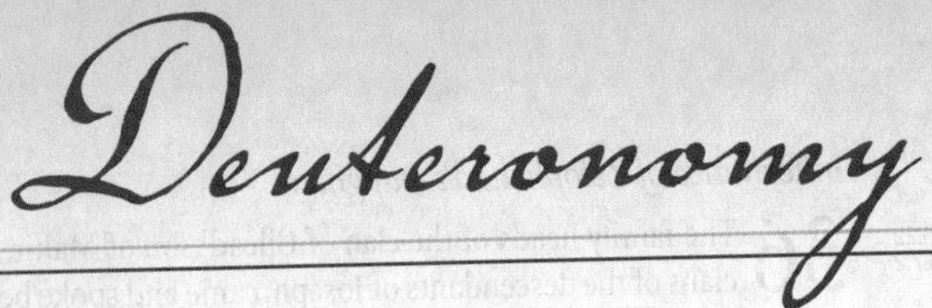

AUTHOR, PLACE AND DATE OF WRITING

Moses is attested to have written most of this book (see 1:1,5; 31:24–25), as well as most of the Pentateuch. Numerous New Testament references attribute passages of Deuteronomy to him (see, e.g., Mt 19:7–8; Mk 10:3–5; Ac 3:22–23; 7:37–38; Ro 10:19). An unknown author must have filled in the narrative framework surrounding the Mosaic material (the preamble in Dt 1–5 and the conclusion in ch. 34), as well as other, smaller passages.

According to 1:5, Moses presented his speeches as the Israelites camped in Moab, at the point where the Jordan River flows into the Dead Sea, after which he wrote them down (31:24–25). This suggests that the speeches and events recorded in Deuteronomy took place just prior to the conquest—traditionally dated by many conservative evangelical scholars to approximately 1440–1400 B.C.

AUDIENCE

The original audience for Deuteronomy was the generation of Israelites who would soon enter Canaan. Since this book summarized the law for their future generations as well, those who followed after were also to understand and obey it (see, e.g., 4:9,40). Numerous New Testament references to Moses and Deuteronomy illustrate this book's importance.

CULTURAL FACTS AND HIGHLIGHTS

After 40 years of desert wandering the Israelites were poised to enter Canaan, the promised land. God had proved his faithfulness again and again, but as soon as they crossed the Jordan River they would have numerous battles to fight—physical clashes with the Canaanites and spiritual frays in order for them to remain God's holy people. At this key time in history God gave Moses important truths to share as the former shepherd prepared to turn over his leadership to Joshua.

God and Moses knew the many challenges the Israelites would face in their new land, and this new generation needed a refresher course concerning the covenant God had made with them through their forebears. All but two members of the older generation (the faithful spies, Joshua and Caleb) that had camped by Mount Sinai when God had given Moses the law had died in the wilderness.

TIMELINE

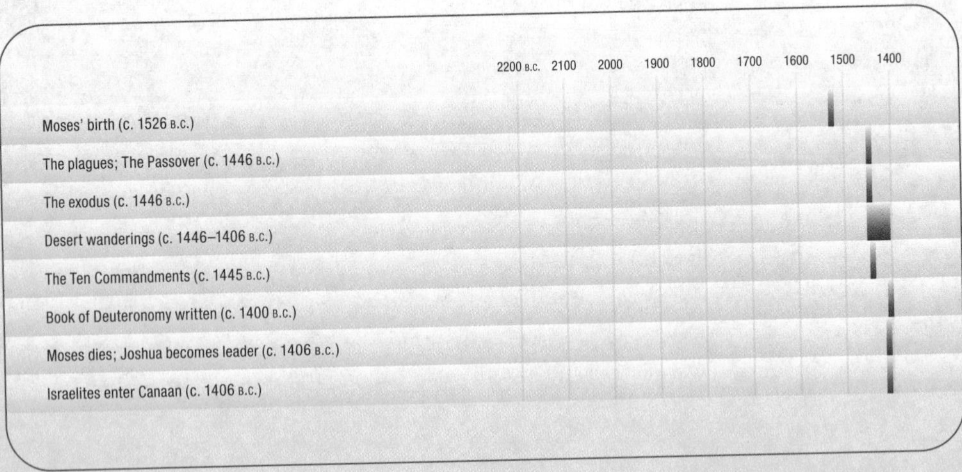

AS YOU READ

Visualize the Israelites gathered on Canaan's border, eager to hear what their elderly, faithful leader had to say. Most of them had been born or had reached adulthood in the desert. Moses knew he could not enter Canaan because of his earlier disobedience (Nu 20:12), but filled with God's Spirit he still delivered three lengthy speeches, which together restated God's covenant requirements with Israel and the need for future generations to remember and live according to them. Make an attempt to enter vicariously into the anticipation of that gathered throng who had waited so long for the events about to take place. These were truly momentous speeches at a vital time in Israel's history.

DID YOU KNOW?

- It is not unusual in the Old Testament for events to be reported out of chronological order—or for a leader to be credited with doing something actually accomplished by someone else (Dt 10:1–11).
- The reason for prohibitions against eating "unclean" animals was basically spiritual, though there may have been psychological and health considerations as well (14:1–21).
- Contempt of court—whether by a judge who for whatever reason did not want to exact the stipulated punishment or by a regular citizen—was a capital offense (17:8–13).
- Israelite military officers spelled out to potential inductees ways to be excused from service. If a man did not fit any of the specific categories of exemption, the last—"Is any man afraid or fainthearted?"—would relieve him of duty if he so desired (20:1–20).
- Mosaic Law forbade a person who found a bird's nest with the mother and her brood in it from harming the mother bird. Semite people in general viewed with extreme disfavor anyone who willfully disturbed a bird in the nest (22:6).
- "Cleanliness is next to godliness" is not an Old Testament quote, as some think, but the concept does have a Biblical basis (23:9–14).

THEMES

Deuteronomy contains the following themes:

1. *The covenant.* The major theme of Deuteronomy is the covenant relationship between God and his people. God's unmerited love (7:6–9) is the basis not only of the covenant but also of his people's trust in him. Covenants, a central focus in Scripture, take on a historical progression: the Noahic covenant (Ge 9:8–17), the Abrahamic covenant (Ge 15:9–21), the Sinaitic covenant (Ex 19:5–6); the Levitical covenant (Nu 25:10–13), the Davidic covenant (2Sa 7:5–16) and the new covenant (Jer 31:31–34).

2. *Choices.* The covenant exhorted God's people to teach, remember and obey (Dt 6:6–25). God promised that obedience would bring blessing (28:1–14) but warned that disobedience would result in harm (28:15–68).

3. *The poor.* As a reflection of God's love for society's socially vulnerable (10:18–19), Deuteronomy designated special protections and commands involving the inclusion of widows, orphans, resident foreigners, the disabled and the elderly (5:14; 14:29; 15:7–11; 16:11,14; 24:10–21; 26:12–13; 27:19).

OUTLINE

- I. Preamble (1:1–5)
- II. Historical Prologue (1:6—4:43)
- III. Stipulations of the Covenant (4:44—26:19)
  - A. Primary Demands (4:44—11:32)
  - B. Supplementary Requirements (12–26)
- IV. Ratification; Curses and Blessings (27–30)
- V. Leadership Succession Under the Covenant (31–34)

The Command to Leave Horeb

1 These are the words Moses spoke to all Israel in the desert east of the Jordan—that is, in the Ara-
bah—opposite Suph, between Paran and Tophel, Laban, Hazeroth and Dizahab. 2 (It takes eleven
days to go from Horeb[a] to Kadesh Barnea[b] by the Mount Seir road.) 1:2 [a]Ex 3:1 [b]Nu 13:26;
3 In the fortieth year,[c] on the first day of the eleventh month, Moses proclaimed[d] to the Israelites all that Dt 9:23
the LORD had commanded him concerning them. 4 This was after he had defeated Sihon[e] king of the Am- 1:3 [c]Nu 33:38 [d]Dt 4:1-2
orites, who reigned in Heshbon,[f] and at Edrei had defeated Og[g] king of Bashan, who reigned in Ashtaroth. 1:4 [e]Nu 21:21-26 [f]Nu 21:25
5 East of the Jordan in the territory of Moab, Moses began to expound this law, saying: [g]Nu 21:33-35; Jos 13:12

6 The LORD our God said to us[h] at Horeb,[i] "You have stayed long enough at this mountain. 7 Break camp 1:6 [h]Nu 10:13 [i]Ex 3:1
and advance into the hill country of the Amorites; go to all the neighboring peoples in the Arabah, in the
mountains, in the western foothills, in the Negev[j] and along the coast, to the land of the Canaanites and 1:7 [j]Jos 10:40 [k]Dt 11:24
to Lebanon,[k] as far as the great river, the Euphrates. 8 See, I have given you this land. Go in and take pos-
session of the land that the LORD swore[l] he would give to your fathers—to Abraham, Isaac and Jacob— 1:8 [l]Ge 12:7; 15:18; 17:7-8;
and to their descendants after them." 26:4; 28:13

The Appointment of Leaders

9 At that time I said to you, "You are too heavy a burden for me to carry alone.[m] 10 The LORD your God 1:9 [m]Ex 18:18
has increased your numbers so that today you are as many[n] as the stars in the sky.[o] 11 May the LORD, the 1:10 [n]Ge 15:5 [o]Dt 10:22; 28:62
God of your fathers, increase you a thousand times and bless you as he has promised![p] 12 But how can I 1:11 [p]Ge 22:17; Ex 32:13
bear your problems and your burdens and your disputes all by myself? 13 Choose some wise, understand-
ing and respected men[q] from each of your tribes, and I will set them over you." 1:13 [q]Ex 18:21
14 You answered me, "What you propose to do is good."
15 So I took[r] the leading men of your tribes, wise and respected men, and appointed them to have author- 1:15 [r]Ex 18:25
ity over you—as commanders of thousands, of hundreds, of fifties and of tens and as tribal officials. 16 And
I charged your judges at that time: Hear the disputes between your brothers and judge fairly,[s] whether the 1:16 [s]Dt 16:18; Jn 7:24
case is between brother Israelites or between one of them and an alien.[t] 17 Do not show partiality[u] in judg- [t]Lev 24:22 1:17 [u]Lev 19:15;
ing; hear both small and great alike. Do not be afraid of any man,[v] for judgment belongs to God. Bring me Dt 16:19; Pr 24:23; Jas 2:1
any case too hard for you, and I will hear it.[w] 18 And at that time I told you everything you were to do. [v]2Ch 19:6 [w]Ex 18:26

Spies Sent Out

19 Then, as the LORD our God commanded us, we set out from Horeb and went toward the hill coun-
try of the Amorites through all that vast and dreadful desert[x] that you have seen, and so we reached Ka- 1:19 [x]Dt 8:15; Jer 2:2,6 [y]ver 2;
desh Barnea.[y] 20 Then I said to you, "You have reached the hill country of the Amorites, which the LORD Nu 13:26
our God is giving us. 21 See, the LORD your God has given you the land. Go up and take possession of it as
the LORD, the God of your fathers, told you. Do not be afraid;[z] do not be discouraged." 1:21 [z]Jos 1:6,9, 18
22 Then all of you came to me and said, "Let us send men ahead to spy out the land for us and bring
back a report about the route we are to take and the towns we will come to."
23 The idea seemed good to me; so I selected[a] twelve of you, one man from each tribe. 24 They left and 1:23 [a]Nu 13:1-3
went up into the hill country, and came to the Valley of Eshcol[b] and explored it. 25 Taking with them some 1:24 [b]Nu 13:21-25
of the fruit of the land, they brought it down to us and reported,[c] "It is a good land that the LORD our God 1:25 [c]Nu 13:27
is giving us."

Rebellion Against the LORD

26 But you were unwilling to go up;[d] you rebelled against the command of the LORD your God. 27 You 1:26 [d]Nu 14:1-4
grumbled[e] in your tents and said, "The LORD hates us; so he brought us out of Egypt to deliver us into 1:27 [e]Dt 9:28; Ps 106:25
the hands of the Amorites to destroy us. 28 Where can we go? Our brothers have made us lose heart. They

---

1:1 The English title for this book is unfortunate, as it is based on the Septuagint's mistranslation of the phrase "a copy of this law" (17:18) as *deuterononomion touto*, "this second law." The Jewish name *debârîm*, "words," derives from the opening expression, "These are the words Moses spoke" (1:1). This title is well-suited because it focuses attention on a clue to the peculiar literary character of the book; the treaties imposed by ancient imperial lords on their vassals began with such an expression. Deuteronomy is the text or "words" of a suzerainty covenant made by the Lord of heaven through the mediatorship of Moses with the servant people Israel beyond the Jordan.

1:7 The Negev is the dry wasteland stretching southward from Beersheba. See "The Negev: Its Climate and Features" on page 34.
1:13 The office of judge was elective. In time judges were chosen primarily from among the Levites, although this was never a necessity. Judges were held in high regard, and the law profession continued to develop among the Hebrews, its members being called "lawyers," "scribes" or "doctors of the law" (Lk 2:46 KJV; the NIV renders this "teachers").

THE RELIABILITY OF THE BIBLE

DEUTERONOMY AND THE COVENANT TREATY FORM

DEUTERONOMY 1 International treaties drafted between **suzerains**[1] (overlords) and **vassals** (subject peoples) during the fourteenth and thirteenth centuries B.C. closely parallel the structure of the book of Deuteronomy.[2] The best-preserved examples of these treaties come from the **Hittites**, but treaties from **Mesopotamia**, Syria and Egypt demonstrate that a similar form was commonly used. The suzerain-vassal form of treaty also defined the relationship of God (suzerain) to his people (vassals), as evidenced in the overall form, as well as the content, of Deuteronomy.

The Hittite treaties of the fourteenth through thirteenth centuries B.C. differ somewhat from later **Assyrian** treaties of the eighth through seventh centuries B.C. In these later treaties the historical prologue and the blessings disappear, a greater emphasis is placed on the curses and the order of elements is more variable.

Deuteronomy's closer connection to the earlier treaties confirms that this book was written during the Mosaic period, not in Israel's late **monarchic period** (late seventh century B.C.), as many scholars contend.[3] Furthermore, Deuteronomy's close correspondence of form to these earlier treaties strongly suggests that the book should be considered an essential literary unit rather than a later composite of materials from various sources.

[1]See Glossary on page 2080 for definitions of bolded words. [2]For example, see "The Treaty of Suppiluliumas" on page 269. [3]See "The Date of Deuteronomy" on page 259.

1:28 [f]Nu 13:32 [g]Nu 13:33; Dt 9:1-3
1:30 [h]Ex 14:14; Dt 3:22; Ne 4:20
1:31 [i]Dt 32:10-12; Isa 46:3-4; 63:9; Hos 11:3; Ac 13:18
1:32 [j]Ps 106:24; Jude 1:5
1:33 [k]Ex 13:21; Ps 78:14 [l]Nu 10:33
1:34 [m]Nu 14:23, 28-30
1:35 [n]Ps 95:11
1:36 [o]Nu 14:24; Jos 14:9
1:37 [p]Dt 3:26; 4:21 [q]Nu 20:12
1:38 [r]Nu 14:30 [s]Dt 31:7 [t]Dt 3:28
1:39 [u]Nu 14:3 [v]Isa 7:15-16
1:40 [w]Nu 14:25

say, 'The people are stronger and taller[f] than we are; the cities are large, with walls up to the sky. We even
saw the Anakites[g] there.' "
29 Then I said to you, "Do not be terrified; do not be afraid of them. 30 The LORD your God, who is go-
ing before you, will fight[h] for you, as he did for you in Egypt, before your very eyes, 31 and in the desert.
There you saw how the LORD your God carried[i] you, as a father carries his son, all the way you went un-
til you reached this place."
32 In spite of this, you did not trust[j] in the LORD your God, 33 who went ahead of you on your journey,
in fire by night and in a cloud by day,[k] to search[l] out places for you to camp and to show you the way you
should go.
34 When the LORD heard what you said, he was angry and solemnly swore:[m] 35 "Not a man of this evil
generation shall see the good land[n] I swore to give your forefathers, 36 except Caleb son of Jephunneh. He
will see it, and I will give him and his descendants the land he set his feet on, because he followed the LORD
wholeheartedly.[o]"
37 Because of you the LORD became angry[p] with me also and said, "You shall not enter[q] it, either. 38 But
your assistant, Joshua[r] son of Nun, will enter it. Encourage[s] him, because he will lead[t] Israel to inherit it.
39 And the little ones that you said would be taken captive,[u] your children who do not yet know[v] good
from bad—they will enter the land. I will give it to them and they will take possession of it. 40 But as for
you, turn around and set out toward the desert along the route to the Red Sea.[a][w]"
41 Then you replied, "We have sinned against the LORD. We will go up and fight, as the LORD our God
commanded us." So every one of you put on his weapons, thinking it easy to go up into the hill country.

[a] 40 Hebrew *Yam Suph*; that is, Sea of Reeds

42 But the LORD said to me, "Tell them, 'Do not go up and fight, because I will not be with you. You will
be defeated by your enemies.' "[x] 1:42 [x]Nu 14:41-43
43 So I told you, but you would not listen. You rebelled against the LORD's command and in your arro-
gance you marched up into the hill country. 44 The Amorites who lived in those hills came out against
you; they chased you like a swarm of bees[y] and beat you down from Seir all the way to Hormah. 45 You 1:44 [y]Ps 118:12
came back and wept before the LORD, but he paid no attention to your weeping and turned a deaf ear to
you. 46 And so you stayed in Kadesh[z] many days—all the time you spent there. 1:46 [z]Nu 20:1; Jdg 11:17

Wanderings in the Desert

2 Then we turned back and set out toward the desert along the route to the Red Sea,[a][a] as the LORD had 2:1 [a]Nu 21:4
directed me. For a long time we made our way around the hill country of Seir.
2 Then the LORD said to me, 3 "You have made your way around this hill country long enough; now turn
north. 4 Give the people these orders:[b] 'You are about to pass through the territory of your brothers the de- 2:4 [b]Nu 20:14-21
scendants of Esau, who live in Seir. They will be afraid of you, but be very careful. 5 Do not provoke them to
war, for I will not give you any of their land, not even enough to put your foot on. I have given Esau the hill
country of Seir as his own.[c] 6 You are to pay them in silver for the food you eat and the water you drink.' " 2:5 [c]Ge 36:8; Jos 24:4
7 The LORD your God has blessed you in all the work of your hands. He has watched[d] over your jour- 2:7 [d]Dt 8:2-4
ney through this vast desert. These forty years the LORD your God has been with you, and you have not
lacked anything.
8 So we went on past our brothers the descendants of Esau, who live in Seir. We turned from the Ara-
bah road, which comes up from Elath and Ezion Geber,[e] and traveled along the desert road of Moab.[f] 2:8 [e]1Ki 9:26 [f]Jdg 11:18
9 Then the LORD said to me, "Do not harass the Moabites or provoke them to war, for I will not give
you any part of their land. I have given Ar[g] to the descendants of Lot[h] as a possession." 2:9 [g]Nu 21:15 [h]Ge 19:36-38
10 (The Emites[i] used to live there—a people strong and numerous, and as tall as the Anakites.[j] 11 Like 2:10 [i]Ge 14:5 [j]Nu 13:22,33
the Anakites, they too were considered Rephaites, but the Moabites called them Emites. 12 Horites used
to live in Seir, but the descendants of Esau drove them out. They destroyed the Horites from before them
and settled in their place, just as Israel did[k] in the land the LORD gave them as their possession.) 2:12 [k]ver 22
13 And the LORD said, "Now get up and cross the Zered Valley." So we crossed the valley.
14 Thirty-eight years passed from the time we left Kadesh Barnea[l] until we crossed the Zered Valley. 2:14 [l]Nu 13:26 [m]Nu 14:29-35 [n]Dt 1:34-35
By then, that entire generation[m] of fighting men had perished from the camp, as the LORD had sworn to
them.[n] 15 The LORD's hand was against them until he had completely eliminated[o] them from the camp. 2:15 [o]Ps 106:26
16 Now when the last of these fighting men among the people had died, 17 the LORD said to me, 18 "To-
day you are to pass by the region of Moab at Ar. 19 When you come to the Ammonites,[p] do not harass 2:19 [p]Ge 19:38 [q]ver 9
them or provoke them to war, for I will not give you possession of any land belonging to the Ammonites.
I have given it as a possession to the descendants of Lot.[q]"
20 (That too was considered a land of the Rephaites, who used to live there; but the Ammonites called
them Zamzummites. 21 They were a people strong and numerous, and as tall as the Anakites.[r] The LORD 2:21 [r]ver 10
destroyed them from before the Ammonites, who drove them out and settled in their place. 22 The LORD
had done the same for the descendants of Esau, who lived in Seir,[s] when he destroyed the Horites from 2:22 [s]Ge 36:8
before them. They drove them out and have lived in their place to this day. 23 And as for the Avvites[t] who 2:23 [t]Jos 13:3 [u]Ge 10:14 [v]Am 9:7
lived in villages as far as Gaza, the Caphtorites[u] coming out from Caphtor[b][v] destroyed them and settled
in their place.)

Defeat of Sihon King of Heshbon

24 "Set out now and cross the Arnon Gorge.[w] See, I have given into your hand Sihon the Amorite, king 2:24 [w]Nu 21:13-14; Jdg 11:13,18
of Heshbon, and his country. Begin to take possession of it and engage him in battle. 25 This very day I

[a] *1* Hebrew *Yam Suph*; that is, Sea of Reeds [b] *23* That is, Crete

2:1–23 The Lord instructed Moses not to engage the Edomites, Moabites and Ammonites in battle as Israel passed through or near their territories. These nations were ancient relatives of Israel—Edom through Jacob's brother, Esau; Moab and Ammon through the two sons of Abraham's nephew Lot. God had given the descendants of Esau and Lot their territory, just as he was giving the Israelites the land of Canaan.
2:8 The "Arabah road" ran from the head of the Gulf of Aqaba northward and to the east of Moab.
2:24–37 God's prohibition against Israel's disturbing the Edomites, Moabites or Ammonites did not extend to the Amorites. In this instance God allowed the Israelites to take plunder. Later he would, in certain situations, demand total destruction (cf. the stories of Achan in Jos 7 and Saul in 1Sa 15; see also "*Herem* Holy War" on p. 419). We know from other Old Testament sources that such destruction was generally the result of long-delayed judgment. The detestable idolatrous practices of these hostile peoples included religious prostitution and human sacrifice—sometimes even of their own children (see "Human Sacrifice in the Ancient Near East" on p. 182).

2:25 [x]Dt 11:25 [y]Jos 2:9,11 [z]Ex 15:14-16 will begin to put the terror[x] and fear[y] of you on all the nations under heaven. They will hear reports of
you and will tremble[z] and be in anguish because of you."
26 From the desert of Kedemoth I sent messengers to Sihon king of Heshbon offering peace and say-
ing, 27 "Let us pass through your country. We will stay on the main road; we will not turn aside to the
2:27 [a]Nu 21:21-22 right or to the left.[a] 28 Sell us food to eat and water to drink for their price in silver. Only let us pass through
2:28 [b]Nu 20:19 on foot[b]— 29 as the descendants of Esau, who live in Seir, and the Moabites, who live in Ar, did for us—
until we cross the Jordan into the land the LORD our God is giving us." 30 But Sihon king of Heshbon re-
2:30 [c]Jos 11:20 [d]Ex 4:21; Nu 21:23; Ro 9:18 fused to let us pass through. For the LORD[c] your God had made his spirit stubborn[d] and his heart obsti-
nate in order to give him into your hands, as he has now done.
31 The LORD said to me, "See, I have begun to deliver Sihon and his country over to you. Now begin to
2:31 [e]Dt 1:8 conquer and possess his land."[e]
2:32 [f]Nu 21:23 32 When Sihon and all his army came out to meet us in battle[f] at Jahaz, 33 the LORD our God delivered
2:33 [g]Dt 29:7 him over to us and we struck him down,[g] together with his sons and his whole army. 34 At that time we
2:34 [h]Dt 3:6; 7:2 took all his towns and completely destroyed[a][h] them—men, women and children. We left no survivors.
35 But the livestock and the plunder from the towns we had captured we carried off for ourselves. 36 From
2:36 [i]Dt 3:12; 4:48; Jos 13:9 Aroer[i] on the rim of the Arnon Gorge, and from the town in the gorge, even as far as Gilead, not one town
[j]Ps 44:3 was too strong for us. The LORD our God gave[j] us all of them. 37 But in accordance with the command of
2:37 [k]ver 18-19 [l]Nu 21:24 the LORD our God,[k] you did not encroach on any of the land of the Ammonites,[l] neither the land along
[m]Ge 32:22; Dt 3:16 the course of the Jabbok[m] nor that around the towns in the hills.

[a] *34* The Hebrew term refers to the irrevocable giving over of things or persons to the LORD, often by totally destroying them.

Mitanni

DEUTERONOMY 2 Centered beyond the Euphrates River in the Kharbur Valley of northern **Mesopotamia**, the kingdom of **Mitanni** encompassed a league of Indo-European **Hurrian** states.[1] It became the most powerful kingdom in Mesopotamia and Syria during much of the fifteenth through fourteenth centuries B.C., the probable time frame for the Israelite **exodus** and conquest.[2] Although Mitanni is never mentioned in the Bible, its economic and cultural influence unquestionably affected the perspectives and lifestyles of the Biblical world during the latter half of the second millennium B.C. And this kingdom's documented customs and social conditions enhance the credibility of corresponding Biblical accounts of events during this period.[3]

The details of Mitanni's history have for the most part been lost with the onrush of time, but a basic outline is clear. Tensions with Egypt to the south colored Mitanni's early years, but these stresses were eclipsed by Mitannian expansion during the latter half of the fifteenth century B.C. A dynastic marriage between Mitanni and Egypt around the turn of the ensuing century brought peace to the region, as well as thriving commerce, industry and arts.

But this harmony was shattered when northern neighbors, the **Hittites** under the leadership of King Suppiluliuma, began to subjugate a number of Mitanni's vassal states to the west.[4] Seeing Mitanni's political situation in turmoil, the eastern kingdom of **Assyria** took advantage of her deteriorating circumstances to descend upon Mitanni, capturing her capital and ending Mitannian domination. Retaining little influence or power after this defeat, Mitanni still survived as a kingdom at least into the mid-thirteenth century B.C.

[1]See "The Hurrians" on page 57. [2]See "The Date of the Exodus" on page 106 and "The Conquest of Canaan" on page 310. [3]See "Nuzi" on page 52. [4]See "Anatolia and the Hittites" on page 144.

Defeat of Og King of Bashan

3 Next we turned and went up along the road toward Bashan, and Og king of Bashan with his whole army marched out to meet us in battle at Edrei.[n] 2 The LORD said to me, "Do not be afraid[o] of him, for I have handed him over to you with his whole army and his land. Do to him what you did to Sihon king of the Amorites, who reigned in Heshbon."

3 So the LORD our God also gave into our hands Og king of Bashan and all his army. We struck them down, leaving no survivors.[p] 4 At that time we took all his cities. There was not one of the sixty cities that we did not take from them—the whole region of Argob, Og's kingdom in Bashan.[q] 5 All these cities were fortified with high walls and with gates and bars, and there were also a great many unwalled villages. 6 We completely destroyed[a] them, as we had done with Sihon king of Heshbon, destroying[a][r] every city—men, women and children. 7 But all the livestock and the plunder from their cities we carried off for ourselves.

8 So at that time we took from these two kings of the Amorites the territory east of the Jordan, from the Arnon Gorge as far as Mount Hermon. 9 (Hermon is called Sirion[s] by the Sidonians; the Amorites call it Senir.)[t] 10 We took all the towns on the plateau, and all Gilead, and all Bashan as far as Salecah[u] and Edrei, towns of Og's kingdom in Bashan. 11 (Only Og king of Bashan was left of the remnant of the Rephaites.[v] His bed[b] was made of iron and was more than thirteen feet long and six feet wide.[c] It is still in Rabbah[w] of the Ammonites.)

Division of the Land

12 Of the land that we took over at that time, I gave the Reubenites and the Gadites the territory north of Aroer[x] by the Arnon Gorge, including half the hill country of Gilead, together with its towns. 13 The rest of Gilead and also all of Bashan, the kingdom of Og, I gave to the half-tribe of Manasseh. (The whole region of Argob in Bashan used to be known as a land of the Rephaites. 14 Jair,[y] a descendant of Manasseh, took the whole region of Argob as far as the border of the Geshurites and the Maacathites; it was named after him, so that to this day Bashan is called Havvoth Jair.[d]) 15 And I gave Gilead to Makir.[z] 16 But to the Reubenites and the Gadites I gave the territory extending from Gilead down to the Arnon Gorge (the middle of the gorge being the border) and out to the Jabbok River,[a] which is the border of the Ammonites. 17 Its western border was the Jordan in the Arabah, from Kinnereth[b] to the Sea of the Arabah (the Salt Sea[e][c]), below the slopes of Pisgah.

18 I commanded you at that time: "The LORD your God has given you this land to take possession of it. But all your able-bodied men, armed for battle, must cross over ahead of your brother Israelites.[d] 19 However, your wives, your children and your livestock (I know you have much livestock) may stay in the towns I have given you, 20 until the LORD gives rest to your brothers as he has to you, and they too have taken over the land that the LORD your God is giving them, across the Jordan. After that, each of you may go back to the possession I have given you."

Moses Forbidden to Cross the Jordan

21 At that time I commanded Joshua: "You have seen with your own eyes all that the LORD your God has done to these two kings. The LORD will do the same to all the kingdoms over there where you are going. 22 Do not be afraid[e] of them; the LORD your God himself will fight[f] for you."

23 At that time I pleaded with the LORD: 24 "O Sovereign LORD, you have begun to show to your servant your greatness[g] and your strong hand. For what god[h] is there in heaven or on earth who can do the deeds and mighty works[i] you do?[j] 25 Let me go over and see the good land[k] beyond the Jordan—that fine hill country and Lebanon."

26 But because of you the LORD was angry[l] with me and would not listen to me. "That is enough," the

3:1 [n]Nu 21:33
3:2 [o]Nu 21:34
3:3 [p]Nu 21:35
3:4 [q]1Ki 4:13
3:6 [r]Dt 2:24,34
3:9 [s]Dt 4:48; Ps 29:6 [t]1Ch 5:23
3:10 [u]Jos 13:11
3:11 [v]Ge 14:5 [w]2Sa 12:26; Jer 49:2
3:12 [x]Nu 32:32-38; Dt 2:36; Jos 13:8-13
3:14 [y]Nu 32:41; 1Ch 2:22
3:15 [z]Nu 32:39-40
3:16 [a]Nu 21:24
3:17 [b]Nu 34:11; Jos 13:27 [c]Ge 14:3; Jos 12:3
3:18 [d]Nu 32:17
3:22 [e]Dt 1:29 [f]Ex 14:14; Dt 20:4
3:24 [g]Dt 11:2 [h]Ex 15:11; Ps 86:8 [i]Ps 71:16, 19 [j]2Sa 7:22
3:25 [k]Dt 4:22
3:26 [l]Dt 1:37; 31:2

[a] *6* The Hebrew term refers to the irrevocable giving over of things or persons to the LORD, often by totally destroying them.
[b] *11* Or *sarcophagus* [c] *11* Hebrew *nine cubits long and four cubits wide* (about 4 meters long and 1.8 meters wide)
[d] *14* Or *called the settlements of Jair* [e] *17* That is, the Dead Sea

---

3:1 Bashan, located east of the Sea of Galilee, was known for its rich pastureland, sleek cattle and magnificent oak trees.
3:5 Primitive locks used to fasten city gates consisted simply of heavy beams of wood, the ends of which were dropped into slots cut into the masonry of the gate (see Ne 3:3–15; cf. 1Sa 23:7).
3:9 The name Sirion for Mount Hermon has also been found in a Canaanite document contemporary with Moses. Another name, Senir, appears in Assyrian sources.
3:11 This "bed" may have been a sarcophagus (coffin). Such sarcophagi have been unearthed in Bashan, and the Hebrew words for "bed" and "iron" may reflect this. If this was an actual bed, it was probably made of wood but with certain iron fixtures, as were the "iron chariots" (see note at Jos 17:16).

Renamed Philadelphia in New Testament times, Rabbah was the capital of ancient Ammon (Am 1:13–14; see "Rabbah" on p. 606). We know the site today as Amman, the capital of Jordan.

THE DATE OF DEUTERONOMY

DEUTERONOMY 3 Until the nineteenth century most Biblical scholars simply assumed that Deuteronomy was written during the days of Moses, its Biblically acknowledged author. The book is presented as an address from Moses' mouth, so its authorship and approximate date of origin were seen as self-evident.

Certain features of Deuteronomy, however, seem incompatible with Mosaic authorship. An obvious issue is that someone other than Moses must have written the account of Moses' death and Joshua's assumption of leadership (34:5–12). On the other hand, it is important to realize that the central issue is not whether Moses wrote Deuteronomy precisely as it now reads, but whether he actually gave the speeches contained in the book. Thus it would be quite possible to accept that someone else wrote about Moses' death and still not deny that the speeches are authentically Mosaic.

Some scholars, however, have questioned the entire notion of a Mosaic origin for Deuteronomy. Many of them contend instead for a seventh-century B.C. date for its writing, associated with the reign of the reformer king Josiah. Such theologians/historians argue that the "Book of the Law" that was "found" during a renovation of the temple in Josiah's day (2Ki 22:8) was in fact Deuteronomy—but that the work itself was a pious fraud written by Josiah's officials to legitimize the king's reforms.[1]

Critical to the argument either way is the comparison of Deuteronomy to other ancient Near Eastern "suzerain-vassal treaties."[2] Because Deuteronomy is also a treaty (covenant) between a suzerain (God) and a vassal (Israel), it most likely dates to the time of the particular treaties it most closely resembles. Some scholars argue that Deuteronomy parallels fourteenth-century B.C. **Hittite** treaties (suggesting a traditional, fourteenth-century date for Dt as well), while others view it as more similar to the later, seventh-century B.C. Neo-**Assyrian** treaties. Incidental points have variously been used to support both sides of this argument:

- Scholars supporting a later date point out that the order of the curses in Deuteronomy 27 and the Neo-Assyrian treaties dating from Esarhaddon's day are similar.
- Deuteronomy and the Neo-Assyrian treaties share such phrases as "to go after" ("to follow"), "to fear" and "to listen to the voice of."
- But historians supporting an earlier date point out that Hittite treaties included a historical prologue like Deuteronomy, a feature lacking in their Neo-Assyrian counterparts.
- Deuteronomy and the Hittite treaties both use the word "love" to indicate the sovereign's fidelity to the vassal, but such usage is absent in the later, Neo-Assyrian treaties (where love is only commanded of the vassal). An identical, dual use of "love" appears among the **Amarna** letters, fourteenth-century B.C. correspondence between Egypt and its vassals and allies in Syria-Palestine.
- Most significantly, the overall structure of Deuteronomy more closely follows the structure of Hittite (fourteenth century B.C.) than Neo-Assyrian (seventh century B.C.) treaties.[2]

Another issue related to the dating of Deuteronomy is its similarity to the so-called "Deuteronomistic" texts of other Biblical books. Some scholars contend that several other Old Testament books reflect a theological perspective similar to that of Deuteronomy, citing this as the reason this particular viewpoint has been dubbed Deuteronomistic. Many of these other Biblical texts date from the eighth to sixth centuries B.C. (e.g., Jer, Hos and portions of Sa and Ki). Based on this reasoning, such scholars argue that Deuteronomy was written during this time, when "Deuteronomistic" theology was in its ascendancy. Yet a strong case can be made that books like Hosea allude to a Deuteronomistic brand of theology that already existed—in the book of Deuteronomy.

The theological problem posed by the projected "late date" for Deuteronomy is significant. If the book is indeed a "pious fraud" written during the reign of Josiah, it is difficult to imagine how it could still be regarded as authoritative Scripture. Overall, arguments for dating Deuteronomy to the second millennium B.C., as well as for believing its speeches to be authentic and written by Moses, remain strong.

[1]See "The Tragic Reign of King Josiah" on page 569. [2]See "Deuteronomy and the Covenant Treaty Form" on page 255.

LORD said. "Do not speak to me anymore about this matter. [27]Go up to the top of Pisgah and look west and north and south and east. Look at the land with your own eyes, since you are not going to cross this Jordan.[m] [28]But commission[n] Joshua, and encourage and strengthen him, for he will lead this people across[o] and will cause them to inherit the land that you will see." [29]So we stayed in the valley near Beth Peor.[p]

Obedience Commanded

4 Hear now, O Israel, the decrees and laws I am about to teach you. Follow them so that you may live[q] and may go in and take possession of the land that the LORD, the God of your fathers, is giving you. [2]Do not add[r] to what I command you and do not subtract from it, but keep the commands of the LORD your God that I give you.

[3]You saw with your own eyes what the LORD did at Baal Peor.[s] The LORD your God destroyed from among you everyone who followed the Baal of Peor, [4]but all of you who held fast to the LORD your God are still alive today.

[5]See, I have taught you decrees and laws as the LORD my God commanded me, so that you may follow them in the land you are entering to take possession of it. [6]Observe them carefully, for this will show your wisdom[t] and understanding to the nations, who will hear about all these decrees and say, "Surely this great nation is a wise and understanding people."[u] [7]What other nation is so great[v] as to have their gods near[w] them the way the LORD our God is near us whenever we pray to him? [8]And what other nation is so great as to have such righteous decrees and laws as this body of laws I am setting before you today?

[9]Only be careful,[x] and watch yourselves closely so that you do not forget the things your eyes have seen or let them slip from your heart as long as you live. Teach[y] them to your children[z] and to their children after them. [10]Remember the day you stood before the LORD your God at Horeb,[a] when he said to me, "Assemble the people before me to hear my words so that they may learn to revere me as long as they live in the land and may teach them to their children." [11]You came near and stood at the foot of the mountain while it blazed with fire[b] to the very heavens, with black clouds and deep darkness. [12]Then the LORD spoke[c] to you out of the fire. You heard the sound of words but saw no form; there was only a voice. [13]He declared to you his covenant,[d] the Ten Commandments,[e] which he commanded you to follow and then wrote them on two stone tablets. [14]And the LORD directed me at that time to teach you the decrees and laws you are to follow in the land that you are crossing the Jordan to possess.

Idolatry Forbidden

[15]You saw no form[f] of any kind the day the LORD spoke to you at Horeb out of the fire. Therefore watch yourselves very carefully,[g] [16]so that you do not become corrupt and make for yourselves an idol,[h] an image of any shape, whether formed like a man or a woman, [17]or like any animal on earth or any bird that flies in the air, [18]or like any creature that moves along the ground or any fish in the waters below. [19]And when you look up to the sky and see the sun,[i] the moon and the stars—all the heavenly array[j]—do not be enticed into bowing down to them and worshiping things the LORD your God has apportioned to all the nations under heaven. [20]But as for you, the LORD took you and brought you out of the iron-smelting furnace,[k] out of Egypt, to be the people of his inheritance,[l] as you now are.

[21]The LORD was angry with me[m] because of you, and he solemnly swore that I would not cross the Jordan and enter the good land the LORD your God is giving you as your inheritance. [22]I will die in this land; I will not cross the Jordan; but you are about to cross over and take possession of that good land.[n] [23]Be careful not to forget the covenant[o] of the LORD your God that he made with you; do not make for yourselves an idol[p] in the form of anything the LORD your God has forbidden. [24]For the LORD your God is a consuming fire,[q] a jealous God.

[25]After you have had children and grandchildren and have lived in the land a long time—if you then become corrupt and make any kind of idol, doing evil[r] in the eyes of the LORD your God and provoking him to anger, [26]I call heaven and earth as witnesses against you[s] this day that you will quickly perish from the land that you are crossing the Jordan to possess. You will not live there long but will certainly be destroyed. [27]The LORD will scatter[t] you among the peoples, and only a few of you will survive among

3:27 [m]Nu 27:12 **3:28** [n]Nu 27:18-23 [o]Dt 31:3,23
3:29 [p]Dt 4:46; 34:6
4:1 [q]Dt 5:33; 8:1; 16:20; 30:15-20; Eze 20:11; Ro 10:5
4:2 [r]Dt 12:32; Jos 1:7; Rev 22:18-19
4:3 [s]Nu 25:1-9; Ps 106:28
4:6 [t]Dt 30:19-20; Ps 19:7; Pr 1:7 [u]Job 28:28
4:7 [v]2Sa 7:23 [w]Ps 46:1; Isa 55:6
4:9 [x]Pr 4:23 [y]Ge 18:19; Eph 6:4 [z]Ps 78:5-6
4:10 [a]Ex 19:9,16
4:11 [b]Ex 19:18; Heb 12:18-19
4:12 [c]Ex 20:22; Dt 5:4,22
4:13 [d]Dt 9:9,11 [e]Ex 24:12; 31:18; 34:28
4:15 [f]Isa 40:18 [g]Jos 23:11
4:16 [h]Ex 20:4-5; 32:7; Dt 5:8; Ro 1:23
4:19 [i]Dt 17:3; Job 31:26 [j]2Ki 17:16; 21:3; Ro 1:25
4:20 [k]1Ki 8:51; Jer 11:4 [l]Ex 19:5; Dt 9:29
4:21 [m]Nu 20:12; Dt 1:37
4:22 [n]Dt 3:25
4:23 [o]ver 9,16 [p]Ex 20:4
4:24 [q]Ex 24:17; Dt 9:3; Heb 12:29
4:25 [r]2Ki 17:2,17
4:26 [s]Dt 30:18-19; Isa 1:2
4:27 [t]Lev 26:33; Dt 28:36,64; Ne 1:8

4:9 The home was the first and most effective agency for religious training. The varied commands in Deuteronomy to teach children clearly imply domestic education (v. 9; 6:7–9; 11:19; 32:46).
4:11 See "The Location of Mount Sinai" on page 123.

4:19 In the Old Testament there is no word for religion. *Fear* (Ps 2:11; Pr 1:7) and *worship* (Dt 4:19; 29:26; Ps 5:7; 29:2) of God refer primarily to attitudes of the mind and to acts of adoration—not to rituals.

4:28 [u]Dt 28:36, 64; 1Sa 26:19; Jer 16:13 [v]Ps 115:4-8; **4:29** [w]2Ch 15:4; [x]Jer 29:13 [y]Dt 30:1-3,10 **4:30** [z]Dt 31:29; Jer 23:20; **4:31** [a]2Ch 30:9; Ps 116:5; Jnh 4:2

the nations to which the LORD will drive you. 28 There you will worship man-made gods[u] of wood and
stone, which cannot see or hear or eat or smell.[v] 29 But if from there you seek[w] the LORD your God, you
will find him if you look for him with all your heart[x] and with all your soul.[y] 30 When you are in distress
and all these things have happened to you, then in later days[z] you will return to the LORD your God and
obey him. 31 For the LORD your God is a merciful[a] God; he will not abandon or destroy you or forget the
covenant with your forefathers, which he confirmed to them by oath.

4:31 In ancient times parties to a covenant were expected to confirm their commitments by invoking self-maledictory (cursing) oaths (see the note on Ge 15:17).

ARCHAEOLOGICAL SITES

RAMOTH (IN) GILEAD

DEUTERONOMY 4 Ramoth in Gilead, one of three cities of refuge set apart for the **Transjordan**ian tribes,[1] was apportioned to the tribe of Gad (Dt 4:43; Jos 20:8; 21:38; 1Ch 6:80) and later given as a Levitical city[2] to the sons of Merari (Jos 21:34–38). As a city of refuge, Ramoth was no doubt easily accessible, perhaps located along the **King's Highway** (cf. Nu 20:17; 21:22; Dt 2:27). This city became a focus of conflict between Syria and the northern kingdom of the divided Israel during the reigns of Ahab, Joram and Jehu (c. 874–814 B.C.).[3]

The Hebrew *Ramoth* means "heights" or "knolls." Gilead is an elevated region extending between Heshbon and Bashan, divided by the Jabbok River and heavily wooded during the Biblical period. The status of Ramoth in Gilead during the period of the conquest is not directly indicated, but other cities in the same region are referred to as *havvoth* ("tent-villages"; Nu 32:41; 1Ki 4:13). Perhaps Ramoth at this stage of its history was an unfortified population center.

The site of Ramoth in Gilead has not been firmly identified (but see possible location on "Map 4"), but the location most commonly accepted, Tell Ramith, seems too far north to be a part of the inheritance of the tribe of Gad. Paul Lapp's excavations of the site during the 1940s revealed **Iron Age** II[4] fortifications (1000–800 B.C.), and the bedrock level there dates from the period of Solomon. Other site suggestions include locations south of the Jabbok River. If Ramoth in Gilead was essentially a tent village during the conquest period, there is little hope that surviving archaeological remains will be sufficient to make identification certain.

[1]See "Cities of Refuge" on page 334. [2]See "Levitical Towns" on page 335. [3]See "Ben-Hadad I and II" on page 521 and "Ahab and the Battle of Qarqar" on page 524. [4]See "Archaeological Periods" chart on page xx in the front of this Bible.

The River Jabbok
Photograph courtesy of © Dr. Gary Pratico

The Lord Is God

32 Ask[b] now about the former days, long before your time, from the day God created man on the earth;[c]
ask from one end of the heavens to the other.[d] Has anything so great as this ever happened, or has any-
thing like it ever been heard of? 33 Has any other people heard the voice of God[a] speaking out of fire, as
you have, and lived?[e] 34 Has any god ever tried to take for himself one nation out of another nation,[f] by
testings, by miraculous signs[g] and wonders,[h] by war, by a mighty hand and an outstretched arm,[i] or by
great and awesome deeds,[j] like all the things the LORD your God did for you in Egypt before your very
eyes?

35 You were shown these things so that you might know that the LORD is God; besides him there is no
other.[k] 36 From heaven he made you hear his voice[l] to discipline you. On earth he showed you his great
fire, and you heard his words from out of the fire. 37 Because he loved[m] your forefathers and chose their
descendants after them, he brought you out of Egypt by his Presence and his great strength,[n] 38 to drive
out before you nations greater and stronger than you and to bring you into their land to give it to you for
your inheritance,[o] as it is today.

39 Acknowledge and take to heart this day that the LORD is God in heaven above and on the earth be-
low. There is no other.[p] 40 Keep[q] his decrees and commands, which I am giving you today, so that it may
go well[r] with you and your children after you and that you may live long[s] in the land the LORD your God
gives you for all time.

Cities of Refuge

41 Then Moses set aside three cities east of the Jordan, 42 to which anyone who had killed a person
could flee if he had unintentionally killed his neighbor without malice aforethought. He could flee into
one of these cities and save his life. 43 The cities were these: Bezer in the desert plateau, for the Reuben-
ites; Ramoth in Gilead, for the Gadites; and Golan in Bashan, for the Manassites.

Introduction to the Law

44 This is the law Moses set before the Israelites. 45 These are the stipulations, decrees and laws Moses
gave them when they came out of Egypt 46 and were in the valley near Beth Peor east of the Jordan, in the
land of Sihon[t] king of the Amorites, who reigned in Heshbon and was defeated by Moses and the Isra-
elites as they came out of Egypt. 47 They took possession of his land and the land of Og king of Bashan,
the two Amorite kings east of the Jordan. 48 This land extended from Aroer[u] on the rim of the Arnon
Gorge to Mount Siyon[b][v] (that is, Hermon), 49 and included all the Arabah east of the Jordan, as far as the
Sea of the Arabah,[c] below the slopes of Pisgah.

The Ten Commandments

5 Moses summoned all Israel and said:
Hear, O Israel, the decrees and laws I declare in your hearing today. Learn them and be sure to fol-
low them. 2 The LORD our God made a covenant[w] with us at Horeb. 3 It was not with our fathers that the
LORD made this covenant, but with us, with all of us who are alive here today.[x] 4 The LORD spoke[y] to you
face to face out of the fire on the mountain. 5 (At that time I stood between[z] the LORD and you to declare
to you the word of the LORD, because you were afraid[a] of the fire and did not go up the mountain.) And
he said:

6 "I am the LORD your God, who brought you out of Egypt, out of the land of slavery.
7 "You shall have no other gods before[d] me.
8 "You shall not make for yourself an idol in the form of anything in heaven above or on the earth
beneath or in the waters below. 9 You shall not bow down to them or worship them; for I,
the LORD your God, am a jealous God, punishing the children for the sin of the fathers to
the third and fourth generation of those who hate me,[b] 10 but showing love to a thousand
⌞generations⌟ of those who love me and keep my commandments.[c]
11 "You shall not misuse the name of the LORD your God, for the LORD will not hold anyone guiltless
who misuses his name.[d]

4:32 [b]Dt 32:7; Job 8:8 [c]Ge 1:27 [d]Mt 24:31
4:33 [e]Ex 20:22; Dt 5:24-26
4:34 [f]Ex 6:6 [g]Ex 7:3 [h]Dt 7:19; 26:8 [i]Ex 13:3 [j]Dt 34:12
4:35 [k]Dt 32:39; 1Sa 2:2; Isa 45:5, 18
4:36 [l]Ex 19:9,19
4:37 [m]Dt 10:15 [n]Ex 13:3,9,14
4:38 [o]Dt 7:1; 9:5
4:39 [p]ver 35; Jos 2:11
4:40 [q]Lev 22:31; Dt 5:33 [r]Dt 5:16 [s]Dt 6:3,18; Eph 6:2-3
4:46 [t]Nu 21:26; Dt 3:29
4:48 [u]Dt 2:36 [v]Dt 3:9
5:2 [w]Ex 19:5
5:3 [x]Heb 8:9
5:4 [y]Dt 4:12,33, 36
5:5 [z]Gal 3:19 [a]Ex 20:18,21
5:9 [b]Ex 34:7
5:10 [c]Jer 32:18
5:11 [d]Lev 19:12; Mt 5:33-37

[a] 33 Or *of a god* [b] 48 Hebrew; Syriac (see also Deut. 3:9) *Sirion* [c] 49 That is, the Dead Sea [d] 7 Or *besides*

12 “Observe the Sabbath day by keeping it holy,[e] as the LORD your God has commanded you. 13 Six
days you shall labor and do all your work, 14 but the seventh day[f] is a Sabbath to the LORD
your God. On it you shall not do any work, neither you, nor your son or daughter, nor your
manservant or maidservant, nor your ox, your donkey or any of your animals, nor the alien
within your gates, so that your manservant and maidservant may rest, as you do. 15 Remem-
ber that you were slaves in Egypt and that the LORD your God brought you out of there with
a mighty hand and an outstretched arm.[g] Therefore the LORD your God has commanded
you to observe the Sabbath day.

16 “Honor your father and your mother,[h] as the LORD your God has commanded you, so that you may
live long[i] and that it may go well with you in the land the LORD your God is giving you.

17 “You shall not murder.[j]

18 “You shall not commit adultery.[k]

19 “You shall not steal.

20 “You shall not give false testimony against your neighbor.

21 “You shall not covet your neighbor's wife. You shall not set your desire on your neighbor's house
or land, his manservant or maidservant, his ox or donkey, or anything that belongs to your
neighbor.”[l]

22 These are the commandments the LORD proclaimed in a loud voice to your whole assembly there on
the mountain from out of the fire, the cloud and the deep darkness; and he added nothing more. Then
he wrote them on two stone tablets[m] and gave them to me.

23 When you heard the voice out of the darkness, while the mountain was ablaze with fire, all the
leading men of your tribes and your elders came to me. 24 And you said, “The LORD our God has shown
us his glory and his majesty, and we have heard his voice from the fire. Today we have seen that a man
can live even if God speaks with him.[n] 25 But now, why should we die? This great fire will consume us,
and we will die if we hear the voice of the LORD our God any longer.[o] 26 For what mortal man has ever
heard the voice of the living God speaking out of fire, as we have, and survived?[p] 27 Go near and listen
to all that the LORD our God says. Then tell us whatever the LORD our God tells you. We will listen and
obey.”

28 The LORD heard you when you spoke to me and the LORD said to me, “I have heard what this people
said to you. Everything they said was good.[q] 29 Oh, that their hearts would be inclined to fear me[r] and keep
all my commands[s] always, so that it might go well with them and their children forever![t]

30 “Go, tell them to return to their tents. 31 But you stay here[u] with me so that I may give you all the
commands, decrees and laws you are to teach them to follow in the land I am giving them to possess.”

32 So be careful to do what the LORD your God has commanded you; do not turn aside to the right or
to the left.[v] 33 Walk in all the way that the LORD your God has commanded you,[w] so that you may live and
prosper and prolong your days[x] in the land that you will possess.

Love the LORD Your God

6 These are the commands, decrees and laws the LORD your God directed me to teach you to observe
in the land that you are crossing the Jordan to possess, 2 so that you, your children and their chil-
dren after them may fear[y] the LORD your God as long as you live by keeping all his decrees and com-
mands that I give you, and so that you may enjoy long life. 3 Hear, O Israel, and be careful to obey so that
it may go well with you and that you may increase greatly[z] in a land flowing with milk and honey,[a] just
as the LORD, the God of your fathers, promised you.

5:12 [e]Ex 20:8
5:14 [f]Ge 2:2; Heb 4:4
5:15 [g]Dt 4:34
5:16 [h]Ex 20:12; Lev 19:3; Dt 27:16; Eph 6:2-3*; Col 3:20 [i]Dt 4:40
5:17 [j]Mt 5:21-22*
5:18 [k]Mt 5:27-30; Lk 18:20*; Jas 2:11*
5:21 [l]Ro 7:7*; 13:9*
5:22 [m]Ex 24:12; 31:18; Dt 4:13
5:24 [n]Ex 19:19
5:25 [o]Dt 18:16
5:26 [p]Dt 4:33
5:28 [q]Dt 18:17
5:29 [r]Ps 81:8,13 [s]Dt 11:1; Isa 48:18 [t]Dt 4:1,40
5:31 [u]Ex 24:12
5:32 [v]Dt 17:11,20; 28:14; Jos 1:7; 23:6; Pr 4:27
5:33 [w]Jer 7:23 [x]Dt 4:40
6:2 [y]Ex 20:20; Dt 10:12-13
6:3 [z]Dt 5:33 [a]Ex 3:8

5:12–15 See “Sabbath, Sabbath Year and the Jubilee” on page 189.

5:26 In this verse it is made clear that when covenants were renewed the former obligations were repeated and brought up to date. Thus chapters 5–11 review the Decalogue with its primary obligation of fidelity to Yahweh, while chapters 12–26 in considerable measure renew the stipulations of the Book of the Covenant (Ex 21–33) and other Sinaitic legislation, adapting where necessary to the new conditions awaiting Israel in Canaan. In chapters 27–30 directions were first given for the future and final act in this covenant renewal to be conducted by Joshua in Canaan (ch. 27). Moses then pronounced the blessings and curses as reasons for Israel's immediate ratification of the covenant, but also as a prophecy of Israel's future down to its ultimate exile and restoration (chs. 28–30). In chapters 31–34 preparations were made for the continuity of leadership through the succession of Joshua and for the continuing confrontation of Israel with the way of the covenant by periodic reading of the covenant document, which was to be deposited in the sanctuary, as well as by a prophetic song of covenant witness (chs. 31–32). The book ends with the final blessings and the death of Moses (chs. 33–34).

4 Hear, O Israel: The LORD our God, the LORD is one.[a][b] 5 Love[c] the LORD your God with all your heart and with all your soul and with all your strength.[d] 6 These commandments that I give you today are to be upon your hearts.[e] 7 Impress them on your children. Talk about them when you sit at home and when you walk along the road, when you lie down and when you get up.[f] 8 Tie them as symbols on your hands and bind them on your foreheads.[g] 9 Write them on the doorframes of your houses and on your gates.[h]

10 When the LORD your God brings you into the land he swore to your fathers, to Abraham, Isaac and Jacob, to give you—a land with large, flourishing cities you did not build,[i] 11 houses filled with all kinds of good things you did not provide, wells you did not dig, and vineyards and olive groves you did not plant—then when you eat and are satisfied,[j] 12 be careful that you do not forget the LORD, who brought you out of Egypt, out of the land of slavery.

13 Fear the LORD[k] your God, serve him only[l] and take your oaths in his name. 14 Do not follow other gods, the gods of the peoples around you; 15 for the LORD your God[m], who is among you, is a jealous God and his anger will burn against you, and he will destroy you from the face of the land. 16 Do not test the LORD your God[n] as you did at Massah. 17 Be sure to keep the commands of the LORD your God and the stipulations and decrees he has given you.[o] 18 Do what is right and good in the LORD's sight, so that it may go well[p] with you and you may go in and take over the good land that the LORD promised on oath to your forefathers, 19 thrusting out all your enemies before you, as the LORD said.

20 In the future, when your son asks you,[q] "What is the meaning of the stipulations, decrees and laws the LORD our God has commanded you?" 21 tell him: "We were slaves of Pharaoh in Egypt, but the LORD brought us out of Egypt with a mighty hand. 22 Before our eyes the LORD sent miraculous signs and wonders—great and terrible—upon Egypt and Pharaoh and his whole household. 23 But he brought us out from there to bring us in and give us the land that he promised on oath to our forefathers. 24 The LORD commanded us to obey all these decrees and to fear the LORD our God,[r] so that we might always prosper and be kept alive, as is the case today.[s] 25 And if we are careful to obey all this law before the LORD our God, as he has commanded us, that will be our righteousness.[t]"

Driving Out the Nations

7 When the LORD your God brings you into the land you are entering to possess and drives out before you many nations[u]—the Hittites, Girgashites, Amorites, Canaanites, Perizzites, Hivites and Jebusites, seven nations larger and stronger than you— 2 and when the LORD your God has delivered them over to you and you have defeated them, then you must destroy them totally.[b] Make no treaty[v] with them, and show them no mercy.[w] 3 Do not intermarry with them.[x] Do not give your daughters to their sons or take their daughters for your sons, 4 for they will turn your sons away from following me to serve other gods, and the LORD's anger will burn against you and will quickly destroy[y] you. 5 This is what you are to do to them: Break down their altars, smash their sacred stones, cut down their Asherah poles[c] and burn their idols in the fire.[z] 6 For you are a people holy[a] to the LORD your God.[b] The LORD your God has chosen[c] you out of all the peoples on the face of the earth to be his people, his treasured possession.

7 The LORD did not set his affection on you and choose you because you were more numerous than other peoples, for you were the fewest of all peoples.[d] 8 But it was because the LORD loved[e] you and kept the oath he swore[f] to your forefathers that he brought you out with a mighty hand and redeemed you from the land of slavery,[g] from the power of Pharaoh king of Egypt. 9 Know therefore that the LORD your God is God;[h] he is the faithful God,[i] keeping his covenant of love[j] to a thousand generations of those who love him and keep his commands. 10 But

those who hate him he will repay to their face by destruction;
he will not be slow to repay to their face those who hate him.

6:4 [b]Mk 12:29*; 1Co 8:4
6:5 [c]Mt 22:37*; Mk 12:30*; Lk 10:27* [d]Dt 10:12
6:6 [e]Dt 11:18
6:7 [f]Dt 4:9; 11:19; Eph 6:4
6:8 [g]Ex 13:9,16; Dt 11:18
6:9 [h]Dt 11:20
6:10 [i]Jos 24:13
6:11 [j]Dt 8:10
6:13 [k]Dt 10:20 [l]Mt 4:10*; Lk 4:8*
6:15 [m]Dt 4:24
6:16 [n]Ex 17:7; Mt 4:7*; Lk 4:12*
6:17 [o]Dt 11:22; Ps 119:4
6:18 [p]Dt 4:40
6:20 [q]Ex 13:14
6:24 [r]Dt 10:12; Jer 32:39 [s]Ps 41:2
6:25 [t]Dt 24:13; Ro 10:3,5
7:1 [u]Dt 31:3; Ac 13:19
7:2 [v]Ex 23:32 [w]Dt 13:8
7:3 [x]Ex 34:15-16; Ezr 9:2
7:4 [y]Dt 6:15
7:5 [z]Ex 23:24; Dt 12:2-3
7:6 [a]Ex 19:5-6; 1Pe 2:9 [b]Ps 50:5; Jer 2:3 [c]Dt 14:2
7:7 [d]Dt 10:22
7:8 [e]Dt 10:15 [f]Ex 32:13 [g]Ex 13:14
7:9 [h]Dt 4:35 [i]1Co 1:9; 2Ti 2:13 [j]Ne 1:5; Da 9:4

[a] 4 Or *The LORD our God is one LORD*; or *The LORD is our God, the LORD is one*; or *The LORD is our God, the LORD alone*
[b] 2 The Hebrew term refers to the irrevocable giving over of things or persons to the LORD, often by totally destroying them; also in verse 26.
[c] 5 That is, symbols of the goddess Asherah; here and elsewhere in Deuteronomy

6:4–9 Known as the *Shema*, Hebrew for "Hear," this has become the Jewish confession of faith, still today recited daily by pious Jews (see Mt 22:37–38; Mk 12:29–30; Lk 10:27).

6:8–9 Many Jews take these verses literally and tie phylacteries to their foreheads and left arms (see the note on Ex 13:9). Some also attach *mezuzot* (small wooden or metal containers in which passages of Scripture are placed) to the doorframes of their houses.

6:11 Wells were dug into impermeable rock or built with rock and then coated with a thick layer of lime plaster, which prevented seepage. See "Wells, Cisterns and Aqueducts in the Ancient World" on page 1259.

7:1 See "Anatolia and the Hittites" on page 144 and "Lesser Known Peoples of the Old Testament" on page 265.

7:12 [k]Lev 26:3-13; Dt 28:1-14; Ps 105:8-9
7:13 [l]Jn 14:21
7:13 [m]Dt 28:4
7:14 [n]Ex 23:26
7:15 [o]Ex 15:26

[11]Therefore, take care to follow the commands, decrees and laws I give you today.
[12]If you pay attention to these laws and are careful to follow them, then the LORD your God will keep
his covenant of love with you, as he swore to your forefathers.[k] [13]He will love you and bless you[l] and
increase your numbers. He will bless the fruit of your womb, the crops of your land—your grain, new
wine and oil—the calves of your herds and the lambs of your flocks in the land that he swore to your fore-
fathers to give you.[m] [14]You will be blessed more than any other people; none of your men or women will
be childless, nor any of your livestock without young.[n] [15]The LORD will keep you free from every disease.[o]
He will not inflict on you the horrible diseases you knew in Egypt, but he will inflict them on all who

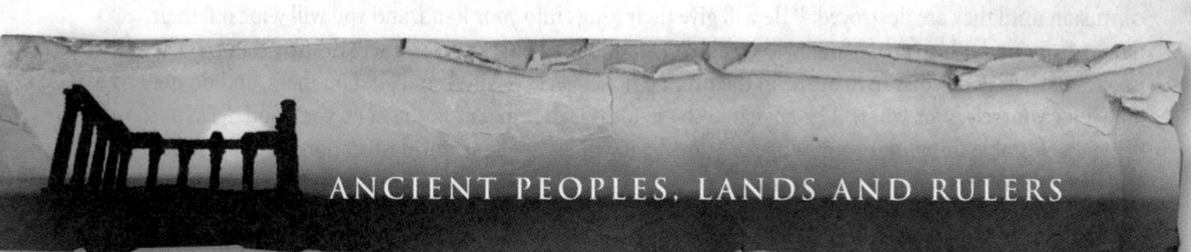

Lesser Known Peoples of the Old Testament

Modern Jerusalem: The western wall and the Dome of the Rock

Photograph courtesy of © Dr. Gary Pratico

DEUTERONOMY 7 At the time of the conquest, the population of Syria-Palestine was a mixture of various ethnic elements.[1] Seven people groups, however, are mentioned repeatedly:

✣ ***Hittites:*** The Hittite Empire, centered at Hattusus (Boghazköey, Turkey), extended to Hamath and Qadesh in Syria, but isolated groups were located in central Judah. Note the area populated by the Hittites on "Map 1." Several **patriarchs** encountered Hittites: See, for example, Genesis 23, 26–34 and 2 Samuel 11:3. Those Hittites not exterminated during Joshua's conquest maintained separate status until Solomon consigned them to forced labor (2Ch 8:7–8), and they eventually blended in with the people of Israel.

✣ *Girgashites*: Not much is known of this group, though the name *grgsh* is mentioned in **Ugaritic** texts. They probably lived east of the Sea of Galilee.

✣ ***Amorites***: A people called Amurru controlled portions of Syria and Babylon, but "Amorite" is used in the Bible as a broad ethnic label, referring to the general population of the Holy Land (e.g., Ge 15:16). As such, the term is essentially interchangeable with "Canaanite." It often refers, however, to the population of the hills (e.g., Nu 13:29) and is used specifically of two kings in the **Transjordan**, Sihon and Og,[2] who were conquered under Moses' leadership (Nu 21:21–31). Other Amorite centers were Ai, Hebron, Jarmuth, Jerusalem, Eglon and the region of Lebanon.

✣ ***Canaanites***: The term "Canaanite" is often used generically of the population of the Holy Land (e.g., Ge 10:18; Jdg 4:23–24) or "the land of Canaan." Elsewhere its usage is limited to the population of the coastal regions, including southern Syria, and specifically to inhabitants of the valleys and plains, including the Jordan Valley (e.g., Jos 5:1; 11:3). "Canaanite" later came to mean "merchant"—the principal occupation of these coastal peoples (e.g., Job 41:6; Eze 17:4).

✣ *Perizzites*: Located mainly in the hill country of Judah, Ephraim and Manasseh, the Perizzites were associated with the Jebusites (Jos 11:3). "Perizzites" may have meant "inhabitants of peasant villages."

✣ *Hivites*: These people were located in the Lebanon region "from Mount Baal-Hermon to Lebo Hamath" (Jdg 3:3). "Hivite" may mean "tent-dweller" and refer to Bedouins.

✣ *Jebusites*: This clan lived mainly in Jerusalem (called Jebus in some texts; e.g., Jdg 19:10–11) and the surrounding hills. The Jebusites maintained limited independence at least until the time of King David, who captured Jerusalem (2Sa 5:6–9) and later purchased the temple mound from a Jebusite,[3] Araunah (2Sa 24:18–25).

[1]See "The Conquest of Canaan" on page 310. [2]See "The Kingdoms of Sihon and Og" on page 244. [3]See "The Jebusites" on page 596.

hate you. 16 You must destroy all the peoples the LORD your God gives over to you. Do not look on them
with pity[p] and do not serve their gods, for that will be a snare[q] to you.
17 You may say to yourselves, "These nations are stronger than we are. How can we drive them out?[r]"
18 But do not be afraid[s] of them; remember well what the LORD your God did to Pharaoh and to all Egypt.[t]
19 You saw with your own eyes the great trials, the miraculous signs and wonders, the mighty hand and
outstretched arm, with which the LORD your God brought you out. The LORD your God will do the same
to all the peoples you now fear.[u] 20 Moreover, the LORD your God will send the hornet[v] among them until
even the survivors who hide from you have perished. 21 Do not be terrified by them, for the LORD your
God, who is among you,[w] is a great and awesome God.[x] 22 The LORD your God will drive out those na-
tions before you, little by little.[y] You will not be allowed to eliminate them all at once, or the wild animals
will multiply around you. 23 But the LORD your God will deliver them over to you, throwing them into great
confusion until they are destroyed. 24 He will give their kings into your hand, and you will wipe out their
names from under heaven. No one will be able to stand up against you;[z] you will destroy them. 25 The
images of their gods you are to burn[a] in the fire. Do not covet[b] the silver and gold on them, and do not
take it for yourselves, or you will be ensnared[c] by it, for it is detestable[d] to the LORD your God. 26 Do not
bring a detestable thing into your house or you, like it, will be set apart for destruction.[e] Utterly abhor
and detest it, for it is set apart for destruction.

Do Not Forget the LORD

8 Be careful to follow every command I am giving you today, so that you may live[f] and increase and
may enter and possess the land that the LORD promised on oath to your forefathers. 2 Remember how
the LORD your God led[g] you all the way in the desert these forty years, to humble you and to test you in
order to know what was in your heart, whether or not you would keep his commands. 3 He humbled you,
causing you to hunger and then feeding you with manna,[h] which neither you nor your fathers had known,
to teach you that man does not live on bread alone but on every word that comes from the mouth of the
LORD.[i] 4 Your clothes did not wear out and your feet did not swell during these forty years.[j] 5 Know then
in your heart that as a man disciplines his son, so the LORD your God disciplines you.[k]
6 Observe the commands of the LORD your God, walking in his ways and revering him.[l] 7 For the LORD
your God is bringing you into a good land—a land with streams and pools of water, with springs flow-
ing in the valleys and hills;[m] 8 a land with wheat and barley, vines and fig trees, pomegranates, olive oil
and honey; 9 a land where bread will not be scarce and you will lack nothing; a land where the rocks are
iron and you can dig copper out of the hills.
10 When you have eaten and are satisfied,[n] praise the LORD your God for the good land he has given you.
11 Be careful that you do not forget the LORD your God, failing to observe his commands, his laws and his
decrees that I am giving you this day. 12 Otherwise, when you eat and are satisfied, when you build fine
houses and settle down,[o] 13 and when your herds and flocks grow large and your silver and gold increase
and all you have is multiplied, 14 then your heart will become proud and you will forget[p] the LORD your
God, who brought you out of Egypt, out of the land of slavery. 15 He led you through the vast and dread-
ful desert,[q] that thirsty and waterless land, with its venomous snakes[r] and scorpions. He brought you
water out of hard rock.[s] 16 He gave you manna to eat in the desert, something your fathers had never
known,[t] to humble and to test you so that in the end it might go well with you. 17 You may say to your-
self,[u] "My power and the strength of my hands have produced this wealth for me." 18 But remember the
LORD your God, for it is he who gives you the ability to produce wealth,[v] and so confirms his covenant,
which he swore to your forefathers, as it is today.
19 If you ever forget the LORD your God and follow other gods and worship and bow down to them, I
testify against you today that you will surely be destroyed.[w] 20 Like the nations the LORD destroyed before
you, so you will be destroyed for not obeying the LORD your God.

Not Because of Israel's Righteousness

9 Hear, O Israel. You are now about to cross the Jordan to go in and dispossess nations greater and
stronger than you,[x] with large cities that have walls up to the sky.[y] 2 The people are strong and tall—

7:16 [p] ver 2; Ex 23:33 [q] Jdg 8:27 **7:17** [r] Nu 33:53 **7:18** [s] Dt 31:6 [t] Ps 105:5 **7:19** [u] Dt 4:34 **7:20** [v] Ex 23:28; Jos 24:12 **7:21** [w] Jos 3:10 [x] Dt 10:17; Ne 9:32 **7:22** [y] Ex 23:28-30 **7:24** [z] Jos 23:9 **7:25** [a] Ex 32:20; 1Ch 14:12 [b] Jos 7:21 [c] Jdg 8:27 [d] Dt 17:1 **7:26** [e] Lev 27:28-29

8:1 [f] Dt 4:1 **8:2** [g] Am 2:10 **8:3** [h] Ex 16:12,14,35 [i] Ex 16:2-3; Mt 4:4*; Lk 4:4* **8:4** [j] Dt 29:5; Ne 9:21 **8:5** [k] 2Sa 7:14; Pr 3:11-12; Heb 12:5-11; Rev 3:19 **8:6** [l] Dt 5:33 **8:7** [m] Dt 11:9-12 **8:10** [n] Dt 6:10-12 **8:12** [o] Hos 13:6 **8:14** [p] Ps 106:21 **8:15** [q] Jer 2:6 [r] Nu 21:6 [s] Nu 20:11; Ps 78:15; 114:8 **8:16** [t] Ex 16:15 **8:17** [u] Dt 9:4,7,24 **8:18** [v] Pr 10:22; Hos 2:8 **8:19** [w] Dt 4:26; 30:18

9:1 [x] Dt 4:38; 11:23,31 [y] Dt 1:28

8:9 Iron is mined in the mountains of southern Lebanon, as well as in the regions east of the Sea of Galilee and south of the Dead Sea. Both copper and iron were plentiful in the part of the Arabah south of the Dead Sea. Some of the copper mines in that region date to the time of Solomon and earlier. Some bronze objects found in Zarethan, a center for bronze works in Solomon's time (1Ki 7:45–46), precede the Solomonic period, and today there are copper works at Timnah in the Negev.

Anakites! You know about them and have heard it said: "Who can stand up against the Anakites?"[z] 3 But
be assured today that the LORD your God is the one who goes across ahead of you[a] like a devouring fire.[b]
He will destroy them; he will subdue them before you. And you will drive them out and annihilate them
quickly,[c] as the LORD has promised you.
4 After the LORD your God has driven them out before you, do not say to yourself,[d] "The LORD has brought
me here to take possession of this land because of my righteousness." No, it is on account of the wickedness
of these nations[e] that the LORD is going to drive them out before you. 5 It is not because of your righteous-
ness or your integrity[f] that you are going in to take possession of their land; but on account of the wicked-
ness of these nations, the LORD your God will drive them out before you, to accomplish what he swore[g] to
your fathers, to Abraham, Isaac and Jacob. 6 Understand, then, that it is not because of your righteousness
that the LORD your God is giving you this good land to possess, for you are a stiff-necked people.[h]

The Golden Calf

7 Remember this and never forget how you provoked the LORD your God to anger in the desert. From
the day you left Egypt until you arrived here, you have been rebellious against the LORD. 8 At Horeb you
aroused the LORD's wrath so that he was angry enough to destroy you.[i] 9 When I went up on the moun-
tain to receive the tablets of stone, the tablets of the covenant that the LORD had made with you, I stayed
on the mountain forty days and forty nights; I ate no bread and drank no water.[j] 10 The LORD gave me two
stone tablets inscribed by the finger of God.[k] On them were all the commandments the LORD proclaimed
to you on the mountain out of the fire, on the day of the assembly.
11 At the end of the forty days and forty nights, the LORD gave me the two stone tablets, the tablets of
the covenant. 12 Then the LORD told me, "Go down from here at once, because your people whom you

9:2 [z] Nu 13:22,28, 32-33 **9:3** [a] Dt 31:3; Jos 3:11 [b] Dt 4:24; Heb 12:29 [c] Ex 23:31; Dt 7:23-24 **9:4** [d] Dt 8:17 [e] Lev 18:21,24-30; Dt 18:9-14 **9:5** [f] Tit 3:5 [g] Ge 12:7; 13:15; 15:7; 17:8; 26:4 **9:6** [h] ver 13; Ex 32:9; Dt 31:27 **9:8** [i] Ex 32:7-10; Ps 106:19 **9:9** [j] Ex 24:12,15, 18; 34:28 **9:10** [k] Ex 31:18; Dt 4:13

ANCIENT TEXTS AND ARTIFACTS

The Laws of Eshnunna

DEUTERONOMY 9 Eshnunna, which lay east of **Babylon**, was for a brief period around 1800 B.C. a dominant city in **Mesopotamia**, and a code of laws has been discovered from this civilization. Judging from the fragments that remain of the laws' **superscription**, it appears that King Dadusha, successor of Naram-Sin (founder of the dynasty), issued this law code for his city. It is the earliest example of an **Akkadian** law code discovered to date and anticipates in form and content its successor, the much more famous **Code of Hammurabi** (who conquered Eshnunna in c. 1766 B.C.).

The code of Eshnunna is fairly short but covers a wide range of topics, including price controls for products like barley and wool and regulations involving theft, the status of slaves, marital relations, crimes of violence, and vicious animals. It includes, for example, laws concerning a dangerous ox and the liability of its owner, which are closely paralleled in Exodus 21:28–32.

The Eshnunna law code is significant for Biblical studies. It reconfirms that the Bible did not spring into existence in isolation from its larger cultural and political milieu, as well as reinforces that a code of laws similar to those we find in the Bible could have existed as early as the time of Moses (some historians have argued that the bulk of Israel's laws were very late, coming into existence long after Moses' day).

It is striking, however, that while the superscription to the Eshnunna code celebrates the military prowess and worthiness of King Dadusha, Deuteronomy 9 focuses on the weakness and unworthiness of Israel, thereby emphasizing God's grace.

See also "Custom and Law in Ancient Mesopotamia" on page 36.

The Code of Hammurabi (full stele)

Preserving Bible Times; © Dr. James C. Martin; permission of Musée de Louvre

brought out of Egypt have become corrupt.[l] They have turned away quickly[m] from what I commanded them and have made a cast idol for themselves."

13 And the LORD said to me, "I have seen this people[n], and they are a stiff-necked people indeed! 14 Let me alone,[o] so that I may destroy them and blot out[p] their name from under heaven. And I will make you into a nation stronger and more numerous than they."

15 So I turned and went down from the mountain while it was ablaze with fire. And the two tablets of the covenant were in my hands.[a][q] 16 When I looked, I saw that you had sinned against the LORD your God; you had made for yourselves an idol cast in the shape of a calf.[r] You had turned aside quickly from the way that the LORD had commanded you. 17 So I took the two tablets and threw them out of my hands, breaking them to pieces before your eyes.

18 Then once again I fell[s] prostrate before the LORD for forty days and forty nights; I ate no bread and drank no water, because of all the sin you had committed, doing what was evil in the LORD's sight and so provoking him to anger. 19 I feared the anger and wrath of the LORD, for he was angry enough with you to destroy you.[t] But again the LORD listened to me.[u] 20 And the LORD was angry enough with Aaron to destroy him, but at that time I prayed for Aaron too. 21 Also I took that sinful thing of yours, the calf you had made, and burned it in the fire. Then I crushed it and ground it to powder as fine as dust and threw the dust into a stream that flowed down the mountain.[v]

22 You also made the LORD angry at Taberah,[w] at Massah[x] and at Kibroth Hattaavah.[y]

23 And when the LORD sent you out from Kadesh Barnea, he said, "Go up and take possession of the land I have given you." But you rebelled against the command of the LORD your God. You did not trust[z] him or obey him. 24 You have been rebellious against the LORD ever since I have known you.[a]

25 I lay prostrate before the LORD those forty days and forty nights because the LORD had said he would destroy you.[b] 26 I prayed to the LORD and said, "O Sovereign LORD, do not destroy your people, your own inheritance that you redeemed by your great power and brought out of Egypt with a mighty hand.[c] 27 Remember your servants Abraham, Isaac and Jacob. Overlook the stubbornness of this people, their wickedness and their sin. 28 Otherwise, the country from which you brought us will say, 'Because the LORD was not able to take them into the land he had promised them, and because he hated them, he brought them out to put them to death in the desert.'[d] 29 But they are your people, your inheritance[e] that you brought out by your great power and your outstretched arm.[f]"

9:12 [l]Ex 32:7-8; Dt 31:29 [m]Jdg 2:17
9:13 [n]ver 6; Ex 32:9; Dt 10:16
9:14 [o]Ex 32:10 [p]Nu 14:12; Dt 29:20
9:15 [q]Ex 19:18; 32:15
9:16 [r]Ex 32:19
9:18 [s]Ex 34:28
9:19 [t]Ex 32:10-11,14 [u]Dt 10:10
9:21 [v]Ex 32:20
9:22 [w]Nu 11:3 [x]Ex 17:7 [y]Nu 11:34
9:23 [z]Ps 106:24
9:24 [a]ver 7; Dt 31:27
9:25 [b]ver 18
9:26 [c]Ex 32:11
9:28 [d]Ex 32:12; Nu 14:16
9:29 [e]Dt 4:20; 1Ki 8:51 [f]Dt 4:34; Ne 1:10

Tablets Like the First Ones

10 At that time the LORD said to me, "Chisel out two stone tablets[g] like the first ones and come up to me on the mountain. Also make a wooden chest.[b] 2 I will write on the tablets the words that were on the first tablets, which you broke. Then you are to put them in the chest."[h]

3 So I made the ark out of acacia wood[i] and chiseled[j] out two stone tablets like the first ones, and I went up on the mountain with the two tablets in my hands. 4 The LORD wrote on these tablets what he had written before, the Ten Commandments he had proclaimed[k] to you on the mountain, out of the fire, on the day of the assembly. And the LORD gave them to me. 5 Then I came back down the mountain[l] and put the tablets in the ark[m] I had made, as the LORD commanded me, and they are there now.[n]

6 (The Israelites traveled from the wells of the Jaakanites to Moserah.[o] There Aaron died and was buried, and Eleazar his son succeeded him as priest.[p] 7 From there they traveled to Gudgodah and on to Jotbathah, a land with streams of water.[q] 8 At that time the LORD set apart the tribe of Levi[r] to carry the ark of the covenant of the LORD, to stand before the LORD to minister[s] and to pronounce blessings[t] in his name, as they still do today. 9 That is why the Levites have no share or inheritance among their brothers; the LORD is their inheritance,[u] as the LORD your God told them.)

10 Now I had stayed on the mountain forty days and nights, as I did the first time, and the LORD listened to me at this time also. It was not his will to destroy you.[v] 11 "Go," the LORD said to me, "and lead the people on their way, so that they may enter and possess the land that I swore to their fathers to give them."

10:1 [g]Ex 25:10; 34:1-2
10:2 [h]Ex 25:16, 21; Dt 4:13
10:3 [i]Ex 25:5,10; 37:1-9 [j]Ex 34:4
10:4 [k]Ex 20:1
10:5 [l]Ex 34:29 [m]Ex 40:20 [n]1Ki 8:9
10:6 [o]Nu 33:30-31,38 [p]Nu 20:25-28
10:7 [q]Nu 33:32-34
10:8 [r]Nu 3:6 [s]Dt 18:5 [t]Dt 21:5
10:9 [u]Nu 18:20; Dt 18:1-2; Eze 44:28
10:10 [v]Ex 33:17; 34:28; Dt 9:18-19,25

[a] 15 Or *And I had the two tablets of the covenant with me, one in each hand* [b] 1 That is, an ark

---

10:1–11 The order of events recorded here does not match the initial, longer account in Exodus 34–37. The report here implies that Moses himself made the chest (or ark) before climbing Mount Sinai the second time and that he personally placed the tablets in it immediately after having descended the mountain. Yet we know from Exodus 37:1–9 that the ark was built by Bezalel after Moses' return, during the course of tabernacle construction. It is not unusual in the Old Testament for events to be reported out of chronological order—or for a leader to be credited with doing something actually accomplished by someone else.

Fear the LORD

10:12 [w]Mic 6:8 [x]Dt 5:33; 6:13; Mt 22:37 [y]Dt 6:5
10:14 [z]1Ki 8:27 [a]Ex 19:5
10:15 [b]Dt 4:37
10:16 [c]Jer 4:4 [d]Dt 9:6
10:17 [e]Jos 22:22; Da 2:47 [f]Ac 10:34; Ro 2:11; Eph 6:9
10:18 [g]Ps 68:5
10:19 [h]Lev 19:34
10:20 [i]Mt 4:10 [j]Dt 11:22 [k]Ps 63:11
10:21 [l]Ex 15:2; Jer 17:14 [m]Ps 106:21-22
10:22 [n]Ge 46:26-27 [o]Ge 15:5; Dt 1:10

12 And now, O Israel, what does the LORD your God ask of you[w] but to fear the LORD your God, to walk
in all his ways, to love him,[x] to serve the LORD your God with all your heart[y] and with all your soul, 13 and
to observe the LORD's commands and decrees that I am giving you today for your own good?
14 To the LORD your God belong the heavens, even the highest heavens,[z] the earth and everything in
it.[a] 15 Yet the LORD set his affection on your forefathers and loved[b] them, and he chose you, their descen-
dants, above all the nations, as it is today. 16 Circumcise[c] your hearts, therefore, and do not be stiff-necked[d]
any longer. 17 For the LORD your God is God of gods[e] and Lord of lords, the great God, mighty and awe-
some, who shows no partiality[f] and accepts no bribes. 18 He defends the cause of the fatherless and the
widow,[g] and loves the alien, giving him food and clothing. 19 And you are to love those who are aliens, for
you yourselves were aliens in Egypt.[h] 20 Fear the LORD your God and serve him.[i] Hold fast[j] to him and
take your oaths in his name.[k] 21 He is your praise;[l] he is your God, who performed for you those great
and awesome wonders[m] you saw with your own eyes. 22 Your forefathers who went down into Egypt were
seventy in all,[n] and now the LORD your God has made you as numerous as the stars in the sky.[o]

Love and Obey the LORD

11:1 [p]Dt 10:12 [q]Zec 3:7
11:2 [r]Dt 5:24; 8:5

11 Love[p] the LORD your God and keep his requirements, his decrees, his laws and his commands al-
ways.[q] 2 Remember today that your children were not the ones who saw and experienced the dis-
cipline of the LORD your God:[r] his majesty, his mighty hand, his outstretched arm; 3 the signs he per-
formed and the things he did in the heart of Egypt, both to Pharaoh king of Egypt and to his whole
country; 4 what he did to the Egyptian army, to its horses and chariots, how he overwhelmed them with

ANCIENT TEXTS AND ARTIFACTS

The Treaty of Suppiluliumas

DEUTERONOMY 11 For much of the second half of the second millennium B.C., the dominant power in central **Anatolia**[1] (modern Turkey) was the **Hittite**[1] Empire. Among the greatest Hittite kings was Suppiluliumas I, who reigned from approximately 1380–1346 B.C. Suppiluliumas extended Hittite power to the southeast into Syria, where he struggled for supremacy against Egypt, **Assyria** and **Mitanni**. Aziru, king of the Syrian state of Amurru, recognizing that Hittite power was on the rise, broke his treaty with Egypt and submitted to Suppiluliumas.

One Hittite and six **Akkadian** copies of a treaty between Suppiluliumas and Aziru exist; all are fragmentary, but by comparing them scholars have been able to reconstruct a fairly complete version. The treaty required that Aziru submit to and support Suppiluliumas, who in turn was to protect Aziru. This covenant is broadly similar in outline to Deuteronomy, which is also a treaty between a **suzerain** (**Yahweh**) and a **vassal** (Israel). This treaty, therefore, provides a specific point of comparison to the covenant text that we call Deuteronomy.[2]

The Suppiluliumas treaty begins with a preamble and a statement about the main objective of the treaty—that Aziru offer uncompromised devotion to Suppiluliumas (cf. Dt 1:1–5 and chs. 5–6). The historical background follows (cf. 1:6—4:49). The treaty then delineates specific stipulations relating to military and extradition obligations (cf. chs. 7–26).

At that point the Suppiluliumas treaty calls on all gods and goddesses as witnesses and pronounces both curses for disobedience and blessings for obedience. Deuteronomy 27–30 also pronounces curses and blessings, but 30:19 calls upon heaven and Earth, not on lesser gods, as witnesses.

The importance of these parallels can hardly be overstated. As pointed out in the more general article "The Date of Deuteronomy" on page 259, they indicate once again that Deuteronomy is remarkably similar in form and content to second millennium B.C. Hittite treaties and should for that reason most likely be dated early rather than late. They also help us to understand the literary context for Deuteronomy.

[1]See "Anatolia and the Hittites" on page 144. [2]For a broader outline of the issues, see "Deuteronomy and the Covenant Treaty Form" on page 255.

Ancient Voices

If a man brings the bridewealth for the daughter of a man, but another, without the consent of her father and mother, abducts her and then deflowers her, it is indeed a capital offense—he shall die.

If a man marries the daughter of another man without the consent of her father and mother, and moreover does not conclude the nuptial feast and the contract for(?)* her father and mother, should she reside in his house for even one full year, she is not a wife.

*Uncertainty in text indicated by question mark in parentheses

—The Laws of Eshnunna

See "The Treaty of Suppiluliumas" article on previous page.

the waters of the Red Sea[a][s] as they were pursuing you, and how the
LORD brought lasting ruin on them. 5 It was not your children who
saw what he did for you in the desert until you arrived at this place,
6 and what he did[t] to Dathan and Abiram, sons of Eliab the Reuben-
ite, when the earth opened its mouth right in the middle of all Isra-
el and swallowed them up with their households, their tents and ev-
ery living thing that belonged to them. 7 But it was your own eyes
that saw all these great things the LORD has done.
8 Observe therefore all the commands I am giving you today, so
that you may have the strength to go in and take over the land that
you are crossing the Jordan to possess,[u] 9 and so that you may live
long[v] in the land that the LORD swore[w] to your forefathers to give to
them and their descendants, a land flowing with milk and honey.[x]
10 The land you are entering to take over is not like the land of Egypt,
from which you have come, where you planted your seed and irrigat-
ed it by foot as in a vegetable garden. 11 But the land you are cross-
ing the Jordan to take possession of is a land of mountains and val-
leys that drinks rain from heaven.[y] 12 It is a land the LORD your God
cares for; the eyes[z] of the LORD your God are continually on it from
the beginning of the year to its end.
13 So if you faithfully obey[a] the commands I am giving you today—to love[b] the LORD your God and
to serve him with all your heart and with all your soul— 14 then I will send rain[c] on your land in its sea-
son, both autumn and spring rains,[d] so that you may gather in your grain, new wine and oil. 15 I will pro-
vide grass[e] in the fields for your cattle, and you will eat and be satisfied.[f]
16 Be careful, or you will be enticed to turn away and worship other gods and bow down to them.[g]
17 Then the LORD's anger[h] will burn against you, and he will shut[i] the heavens so that it will not rain and
the ground will yield no produce, and you will soon perish[j] from the good land the LORD is giving you.
18 Fix these words of mine in your hearts and minds; tie them as symbols on your hands and bind them
on your foreheads.[k] 19 Teach them to your children,[l] talking about them when you sit at home and when
you walk along the road, when you lie down and when you get up.[m] 20 Write them on the doorframes of
your houses and on your gates,[n] 21 so that your days and the days of your children may be many[o] in the
land that the LORD swore to give your forefathers, as many as the days that the heavens are above the earth.[p]
22 If you carefully observe[q] all these commands I am giving you to follow—to love the LORD your God,
to walk in all his ways and to hold fast[r] to him— 23 then the LORD will drive out all these nations before
you, and you will dispossess nations larger and stronger than you.[s] 24 Every place where you set your foot
will be yours:[t] Your territory will extend from the desert to Lebanon, and from the Euphrates River to the
western sea.[b] 25 No man will be able to stand against you. The LORD your God, as he promised you, will
put the terror and fear of you on the whole land, wherever you go.[u]
26 See, I am setting before you today a blessing and a curse[v]— 27 the blessing[w] if you obey the com-
mands of the LORD your God that I am giving you today; 28 the curse if you disobey[x] the commands of the
LORD your God and turn from the way that I command you today by following other gods, which you have
not known. 29 When the LORD your God has brought you into the land you are entering to possess, you are
to proclaim on Mount Gerizim the blessings, and on Mount Ebal the curses.[y] 30 As you know, these moun-
tains are across the Jordan, west of the road,[c] toward the setting sun, near the great trees of Moreh,[z] in the

11:4 [s]Ex 14:27
11:6 [t]Nu 16:1-35
11:8 [u]Jos 1:7
11:9 [v]Dt 4:40; Pr 10:27 [w]Dt 9:5 [x]Ex 3:8
11:11 [y]Dt 8:7
11:12 [z]1Ki 9:3
11:13 [a]Dt 6:17 [b]Dt 10:12
11:14 [c]Lev 26:4; Dt 28:12 [d]Joel 2:23; Jas 5:7
11:15 [e]Ps 104:14 [f]Dt 6:11
11:16 [g]Dt 8:19; 29:18; Job 31:9, 27
11:17 [h]Dt 6:15 [i]1Ki 8:35; 2Ch 6:26 [j]Dt 4:26
11:18 [k]Dt 6:6-8
11:19 [l]Dt 6:7 [m]Dt 4:9-10
11:20 [n]Dt 6:9
11:21 [o]Pr 3:2; 4:10 [p]Ps 72:5
11:22 [q]Dt 6:17 [r]Dt 10:20
11:23 [s]Dt 4:38; 9:1
11:24 [t]Ge 15:18; Ex 23:31; Jos 1:3; 14:9
11:25 [u]Ex 23:27; Dt 7:24
11:26 [v]Dt 30:1, 15,19
11:27 [w]Dt 28:1-14
11:28 [x]Dt 28:15
11:29 [y]Dt 27:12-13; Jos 8:33
11:30 [z]Ge 12:6

[a] *4* Hebrew *Yam Suph*; that is, Sea of Reeds [b] *24* That is, the Mediterranean [c] *30* Or *Jordan, westward*

11:10–12 Irrigation channels dug by foot and/or fed by devices powered by foot brought the water of the Nile to the gardens in Egypt, in contrast to the rains that watered Canaan (v. 11). The contrast between Egypt and the area today known as Palestine in rainfall is brought out in verses 10–12. The summer is extremely dry in Israel, and the rainy seasons come in the fall (the "former rains") through the spring (the "latter rains"). Virtually no rain falls between about May 1 and October 15: "The winter is past; the rains are over and gone" (SS 2:11). Still today, many people sleep on the roofs of their houses during the summer to escape the oppressive heat and to enjoy the cooling night breezes. The greatest amount of rain falls between November and February, tapering off until the coming of summer and beginning again the next autumn. The withholding of rain at its regular season, particularly in the springtime, was regarded as a most severe punishment (Dt 28:23–24; 1Ki 17:1–16; 18:18).

11:13–21 See the note on Exodus 13:9.

11:20 See the note on 6:8–9.

11:30 The "great trees of Moreh" are a landmark near Mounts Ebal and Gerizim. Sacred oaks have been known in Palestine from the earliest times. Probably believed by the Canaanites to have been the abode of ancestral spirits, they were thought to have oracular powers and may have been tended by priests, as are cedars of Lebanon today. See "Trees of Ancient Israel" on page 1357.

11:30 [a]Jos 4:19 territory of those Canaanites living in the Arabah in the vicinity of Gilgal.[a] 31 You are about to cross the Jor-
11:31 [b]Dt 9:1; dan to enter and take possession[b] of the land the LORD your God is giving you. When you have taken it
Jos 1:11 over and are living there, 32 be sure that you obey all the decrees and laws I am setting before you today.

The One Place of Worship

12 These are the decrees and laws you must be careful to follow in the land that the LORD, the God of
12:1 [c]Dt 4:9-10; 1Ki 8:40 your fathers, has given you to possess—as long as you live in the land.[c] 2 Destroy completely all
12:2 [d]2Ki 16:4; 17:10 the places on the high mountains and on the hills and under every spreading tree[d] where the nations you
12:3 [e]Nu 33:52; Dt 7:5; Jdg 2:2 are dispossessing worship their gods. 3 Break down their altars, smash[e] their sacred stones and burn their
Asherah poles in the fire; cut down the idols of their gods and wipe out their names from those places.
4 You must not worship the LORD your God in their way. 5 But you are to seek the place the LORD your
12:5 [f]ver 11,13; 2Ch 7:12,16 God will choose from among all your tribes to put his Name there for his dwelling.[f] To that place you
12:6 [g]Dt 14:22-23 must go; 6 there bring your burnt offerings and sacrifices, your tithes[g] and special gifts, what you have
vowed to give and your freewill offerings, and the firstborn of your herds and flocks. 7 There, in the pres-
12:7 [h]ver 12,18; Lev 23:40; Dt 14:26 ence of the LORD your God, you and your families shall eat and shall rejoice[h] in everything you have put
your hand to, because the LORD your God has blessed you.
8 You are not to do as we do here today, everyone as he sees fit, 9 since you have not yet reached the
resting place and the inheritance the LORD your God is giving you. 10 But you will cross the Jordan and set-
12:10 [i]Dt 11:31 tle in the land the LORD your God is giving[i] you as an inheritance, and he will give you rest from all your
enemies around you so that you will live in safety. 11 Then to the place the LORD your God will choose as
12:11 [j]ver 5; Dt 15:20; 16:2 a dwelling for his Name[j]—there you are to bring everything I command you: your burnt offerings and
sacrifices, your tithes and special gifts, and all the choice possessions you have vowed to the LORD. 12 And

Hammurabi

DEUTERONOMY 12 Hammurabi (also called Hammurapi) was the sixth king of the first dynasty of Babylon. Reigning in approximately the eighteenth century B.C., he was a vigorous and successful, but not a spectacular king. However, because of the universal fame of the Law Code of Hammurabi, and especially because of the large **stele** (inscribed stone monument) of that name now housed in the Louvre in Paris, he is without question the most recognized figure of Mesopotamian history.

Hammurabi began his royal career ruling over a city (Babylon) that was but one of many vying for power at the time in Mesopotamia. Through cunning diplomacy and force of arms, however, Hammurabi defeated first his main rival to the south, Rim-sin of Larsa, and then his challenger to the north, Zimri-lim of Mari. The empire Hammurabi put together, however, collapsed after his death.

The era of Hammurabi was in some respects quite literate. In addition to the famous law code, diplomatic and personal correspondence has survived from his court, providing us a picture of the man himself. He appears to have been somewhat harsh and arbitrary, though not altogether tyrannical. His law code was not original to him but followed a pattern that had already been set in Mesopotamian society. Some scholars have noted that the laws of Hammurabi do not appear to have been the basis for day-to-day adjudication in his time but instead were probably exemplary.

Setting up steles with the king's laws inscribed on them, moreover, served to remind the people of Hammurabi's authority over all his domain. Some have suggested that Hammurabi was in fact the Biblical Amraphel from Shinar (Ge 14:1,9), but few espouse this view today. Although Hammurabi's laws remind us that legal texts did exist in the early second millennium B.C. (contrary to those who date the Biblical books of the law to the late first millennium—a later date), there does not appear to be any direct connection between Hammurabi and the Bible.

The top of the diorite stele of the Code of Hammurabi (the sun-god Shamash, seated, gives Hammurabi the symbols of power)

Preserving Bible Times; © Dr. James C. Martin; permission of Musée de Louvre

there rejoice[k] before the LORD your God, you, your sons and daughters, your menservants and maidser- **12:12** [k]ver 7
vants, and the Levites from your towns, who have no allotment or inheritance[l] of their own. 13 Be care- [l]Dt 10:9; 14:29
ful not to sacrifice your burnt offerings anywhere you please. 14 Offer them only at the place the LORD will
choose[m] in one of your tribes, and there observe everything I command you. **12:14** [m]ver 11
15 Nevertheless, you may slaughter your animals in any of your towns and eat as much of the meat as
you want, as if it were gazelle or deer,[n] according to the blessing the LORD your God gives you. Both the **12:15** [n]ver 20-
ceremonially unclean and the clean may eat it. 16 But you must not eat the blood;[o] pour it out on the 23; Dt 14:5; 15:22 **12:16** [o]Ge 9:4;
ground like water.[p] 17 You must not eat in your own towns the tithe of your grain and new wine and oil, Lev 7:26; 17:10-12 [p]Dt 15:23
or the firstborn of your herds and flocks, or whatever you have vowed to give, or your freewill offerings
or special gifts. 18 Instead, you are to eat[q] them in the presence of the LORD your God at the place the LORD **12:18** [q]Dt 14:23
your God will choose[r]—you, your sons and daughters, your menservants and maidservants, and the [r]ver 5
Levites from your towns—and you are to rejoice[s] before the LORD your God in everything you put your [s]ver 7,12
hand to. 19 Be careful not to neglect the Levites[t] as long as you live in your land. **12:19** [t]Dt 14:27
20 When the LORD your God has enlarged your territory[u] as he promised[v] you, and you crave meat and **12:20** [u]Dt 19:8
say, "I would like some meat," then you may eat as much of it as you want. 21 If the place where the LORD [v]Ge 15:18; Dt 11:24
your God chooses to put his Name is too far away from you, you may slaughter animals from the herds
and flocks the LORD has given you, as I have commanded you, and in your own towns you may eat as
much of them as you want. 22 Eat them as you would gazelle or deer.[w] Both the ceremonially unclean and **12:22** [w]ver 15
the clean may eat. 23 But be sure you do not eat the blood,[x] because the blood is the life, and you must not **12:23** [x]ver 16;
eat the life with the meat. 24 You must not eat the blood; pour it out on the ground like water. 25 Do not eat Ge 9:4; Lev 17:11, 14
it, so that it may go well[y] with you and your children after you, because you will be doing what is right[z] **12:25** [y]Dt 4:40;
in the eyes of the LORD. Isa 3:10 [z]Ex 15:26; Dt 13:18;
26 But take your consecrated things and whatever you have vowed to give,[a] and go to the place the 1Ki 11:38
LORD will choose. 27 Present your burnt offerings[b] on the altar of the LORD your God, both the meat and **12:26** [a]ver 17; Nu 5:9-10
the blood. The blood of your sacrifices must be poured beside the altar of the LORD your God, but you may **12:27** [b]Lev 1:5,9, 13
eat the meat. 28 Be careful to obey all these regulations I am giving you, so that it may always go well[c] **12:28** [c]ver 25;
with you and your children after you, because you will be doing what is good and right in the eyes of the Dt 4:40
LORD your God.
29 The LORD your God will cut off[d] before you the nations you are about to invade and dispossess. But **12:29** [d]Jos 23:4
when you have driven them out and settled in their land, 30 and after they have been destroyed before
you, be careful not to be ensnared by inquiring about their gods, saying, "How do these nations serve
their gods? We will do the same." 31 You must not worship the LORD your God in their way, because in wor-
shiping their gods, they do all kinds of detestable things the LORD hates.[e] They even burn their sons[f] and **12:31** [e]Dt 9:5
daughters in the fire as sacrifices to their gods. [f]Dt 18:10; Jer 32:35
32 See that you do all I command you; do not add[g] to it or take away from it. **12:32** [g]Dt 4:2; Jos 1:7; Rev 22:18-19

Worshiping Other Gods

13 If a prophet,[h] or one who foretells by dreams, appears among you and announces to you a mi- **13:1** [h]Mt 24:24;
raculous sign or wonder, 2 and if the sign or wonder of which he has spoken takes place, and he Mk 13:22; 2Th 2:9
says, "Let us follow other gods"[i] (gods you have not known) "and let us worship them," 3 you must not **13:2** [i]ver 6,13
listen to the words of that prophet or dreamer. The LORD your God is testing[j] you to find out whether you **13:3** [j]Dt 8:2,16
love him with all your heart and with all your soul. 4 It is the LORD your God you must follow,[k] and him **13:4** [k]2Ki 23:3;
you must revere. Keep his commands and obey him; serve him and hold fast[l] to him. 5 That prophet or 2Ch 34:31 [l]Dt 10:20
dreamer must be put to death, because he preached rebellion against the LORD your God, who brought
you out of Egypt and redeemed you from the land of slavery; he has tried to turn you from the way the
LORD your God commanded you to follow. You must purge the evil[m] from among you. **13:5** [m]Dt 17:7,
6 If your very own brother, or your son or daughter, or the wife you love, or your closest friend secret- 12; 1Co 5:13
ly entices[n] you, saying, "Let us go and worship other gods" (gods that neither you nor your fathers have **13:6** [n]Dt 17:2-7;
known, 7 gods of the peoples around you, whether near or far, from one end of the land to the other), 8 do 29:18
not yield[o] to him or listen to him. Show him no pity. Do not spare him or shield him. 9 You must certain- **13:8** [o]Pr 1:10
ly put him to death.[p] Your hand must be the first in putting him to death, and then the hands of all the **13:9** [p]Dt 17:5,7
people. 10 Stone him to death, because he tried to turn you away from the LORD your God, who brought

12:31 See "Human Sacrifice in the Ancient Near East" on page 182.

13:11 [q]Dt 19:20 you out of Egypt, out of the land of slavery. 11 Then all Israel will hear and be afraid,[q] and no one among
you will do such an evil thing again.
12 If you hear it said about one of the towns the LORD your God is giving you to live in 13 that wicked
13:13 [r]ver 2,6; men[r] have arisen among you and have led the people of their town astray, saying, “Let us go and worship
1Jn 2:19 other gods” (gods you have not known), 14 then you must inquire, probe and investigate it thoroughly.
And if it is true and it has been proved that this detestable thing has been done among you, 15 you must
certainly put to the sword all who live in that town. Destroy it completely,[a] both its people and its
livestock. 16 Gather all the plunder of the town into the middle of the public square and completely burn
13:16 [s]Jos 6:24 [t]Jos 8:28; the town and all its plunder as a whole burnt offering to the LORD your God.[s] It is to remain a ruin[t] for-
Jer 49:2 ever, never to be rebuilt. 17 None of those condemned things[a] shall be found in your hands, so that the
13:17 [u]Nu 25:4 [v]Dt 30:3 [w]Dt 7:13 LORD will turn from his fierce anger;[u] he will show you mercy, have compassion[v] on you, and increase your
[x]Ge 22:17; 26:4, 24; 28:14 numbers,[w] as he promised[x] on oath to your forefathers, 18 because you obey the LORD your God, keeping
13:18 [y]Dt 12:25, 28 all his commands that I am giving you today and doing what is right[y] in his eyes.

Clean and Unclean Food

14:1 [z]Lev 19:28; 21:5; Jer 16:6; **14** You are the children[z] of the LORD your God. Do not cut yourselves or shave the front of your heads
41:5; Ro 8:14; 9:8; Gal 3:26 for the dead, 2 for you are a people holy to the LORD your God.[a] Out of all the peoples on the face
14:2 [a]Lev 20:26 [b]Dt 7:6; 26:18-19 of the earth, the LORD has chosen you to be his treasured possession.[b]
14:3 [c]Eze 4:14 3 Do not eat any detestable thing.[c] 4 These are the animals you may eat:[d] the ox, the sheep, the goat, 5 the
14:4 [d]Lev 11:2-45; Ac 10:14 deer, the gazelle, the roe deer, the wild goat, the ibex, the antelope and the mountain sheep.[b] 6 You may eat
any animal that has a split hoof divided in two and that chews the cud. 7 However, of those that chew the
cud or that have a split hoof completely divided you may not eat the camel, the rabbit or the coney.[c] Al-
though they chew the cud, they do not have a split hoof; they are ceremonially unclean for you. 8 The pig
is also unclean; although it has a split hoof, it does not chew the cud. You are not to eat their meat or
14:8 [e]Lev 11:26-27 touch their carcasses.[e]
9 Of all the creatures living in the water, you may eat any that has fins and scales. 10 But anything that
does not have fins and scales you may not eat; for you it is unclean.
11 You may eat any clean bird. 12 But these you may not eat: the eagle, the vulture, the black vulture,
13 the red kite, the black kite, any kind of falcon, 14 any kind of raven, 15 the horned owl, the screech owl,
the gull, any kind of hawk, 16 the little owl, the great owl, the white owl, 17 the desert owl, the osprey, the
cormorant, 18 the stork, any kind of heron, the hoopoe and the bat.
19 All flying insects that swarm are unclean to you; do not eat them. 20 But any winged creature that is
clean you may eat.
14:21 [f]Lev 17:15; 22:8 [g]ver 2 21 Do not eat anything you find already dead.[f] You may give it to an alien living in any of your towns,
[h]Ex 23:19; 34:26 and he may eat it, or you may sell it to a foreigner. But you are a people holy to the LORD your God.[g]
Do not cook a young goat in its mother’s milk.[h]

Tithes

14:22 [i]Lev 27:30; 22 Be sure to set aside a tenth[i] of all that your fields produce each year. 23 Eat the tithe of your grain, new
Dt 12:6,17; Ne 10:37 wine and oil, and the firstborn of your herds and flocks in the presence of the LORD your God at the place
14:23 [j]Dt 12:5 [k]Dt 4:10 he will choose as a dwelling for his Name,[j] so that you may learn[k] to revere the LORD your God always.

[a] *15,17* The Hebrew term refers to the irrevocable giving over of things or persons to the LORD, often by totally destroying them.
[b] *5* The precise identification of some of the birds and animals in this chapter is uncertain. [c] *7* That is, the hyrax or rock badger

---

14:1–2 See “Tattoos and Self-Laceration in Ancient Religion” on page 180. See also the note on Leviticus 19:27–28 for a discussion of mourning in the ancient Near East, as well as prohibitions against priests participating in pagan mourning rituals.

Natural baldness is seldom mentioned in the Bible, but it was believed to result from either hard work (Eze 29:18) or disease (Isa 3:17,24). Baldness produced by shaving the head, however, is frequently referred to, often as a mark of mourning for the dead (Lev 21:5; Isa 15:2; 22:12; Mic 1:16). Shaving the head as a sacrifice to a deity was customary for pagans in the land, and the Israelites were strictly forbidden to follow this practice (Lev 21:5; Dt 14:1). The custom among neighboring nations of shaving all but a small patch in the center of the head was also prohibited (Lev 19:27; 21:5). See “Beards and Hairstyles in the Biblical World: on page 1084.

14:22–23 Just when and where the idea arose of making the tenth the rate of paying tribute to rulers and of offering gifts as a religious duty cannot be determined. History reveals that it existed in Babylon in ancient times, as well as in Persia, Egypt and even China. It is quite certain that Abraham knew of it when he migrated from Ur (Ge 14:17–20).

It was a long time, however, before definite legal requirements were set on tithing, so customs regarding its payment varied. At first the tither was entitled to share his tithe with the Levites (Dt 14:22–23). After the Levitical code had been completed, however, tithes belonged exclusively to the Levities (Nu 18:21). Later on, if a Hebrew lived too far from the temple to make it practicable for him to take his tithes (in the form of animals) there, he was permitted to sell his livestock and to use the money gained to purchase substitutes at the tabernacle/temple (Dt 14:24–26). This eventually led to abuses by priests (Mt 21:12–13; Mk 11:15–17). Tithed animals were shared with the Levities (Dt 14:19–20).

24 But if that place is too distant and you have been blessed by the LORD your God and cannot carry your
tithe (because the place where the LORD will choose to put his Name is so far away), 25 then exchange your
tithe for silver, and take the silver with you and go to the place the LORD your God will choose. 26 Use the
silver to buy whatever you like: cattle, sheep, wine or other fermented drink, or anything you wish. Then
you and your household shall eat there in the presence of the LORD your God and rejoice.[l] 27 And do not 14:26 [l]Dt 12:7-8
neglect the Levites[m] living in your towns, for they have no allotment or inheritance of their own.[n] 14:27 [m]Dt 12:19 [n]Nu 18:20
28 At the end of every three years, bring all the tithes of that year's produce and store it in your towns,[o] 14:28 [o]Dt 26:12
29 so that the Levites (who have no allotment[p] or inheritance of their own) and the aliens,[q] the fatherless 14:29 [p]ver 27
and the widows who live in your towns may come and eat and be satisfied, and so that the LORD your [q]Dt 26:12 [r]Dt 15:10;
God may bless[r] you in all the work of your hands. Mal 3:10

The Year for Canceling Debts

15 At the end of every seven years you must cancel debts.[s] 2 This is how it is to be done: Every cred- 15:1 [s]Dt 31:10
itor shall cancel the loan he has made to his fellow Israelite. He shall not require payment from
his fellow Israelite or brother, because the LORD's time for canceling debts has been proclaimed. 3 You may
require payment from a foreigner,[t] but you must cancel any debt your brother owes you. 4 However, there 15:3 [t]Dt 23:20
should be no poor among you, for in the land the LORD your God is giving you to possess as your inher-
itance, he will richly bless[u] you, 5 if only you fully obey the LORD your God and are careful to follow[v] all 15:4 [u]Dt 28:8
these commands I am giving you today. 6 For the LORD your God will bless you as he has promised, and 15:5 [v]Dt 28:1
you will lend to many nations but will borrow from none. You will rule over many nations but none will
rule over you.[w] 15:6 [w]Dt 28:12-13,44
7 If there is a poor man among your brothers in any of the towns of the land that the LORD your God
is giving you, do not be hardhearted or tightfisted[x] toward your poor brother. 8 Rather be openhanded[y] 15:7 [x]1Jn 3:17
and freely lend him whatever he needs. 9 Be careful not to harbor this wicked thought: "The seventh year, 15:8 [y]Mt 5:42; Lk 6:34
the year for canceling debts,[z] is near," so that you do not show ill will[a] toward your needy brother and give 15:9 [z]ver 1 [a]Mt 20:15
him nothing. He may then appeal to the LORD against you, and you will be found guilty of sin.[b] 10 Give gen- [b]Dt 24:15
erously to him and do so without a grudging heart;[c] then because of this the LORD your God will bless[d] 15:10 [c]2Co 9:5 [d]Dt 14:29; 24:19
you in all your work and in everything you put your hand to. 11 There will always be poor people in the
land. Therefore I command you to be openhanded toward your brothers and toward the poor and needy
in your land.[e] 15:11 [e]Mt 26:11; Mk 14:7; Jn 12:8

Freeing Servants

12 If a fellow Hebrew, a man or a woman, sells himself to you and serves you six years, in the seventh
year you must let him go free.[f] 13 And when you release him, do not send him away empty-handed. 14 Sup- 15:12 [f]Ex 21:2; Lev 25:39; Jer 34:14
ply him liberally from your flock, your threshing floor and your winepress. Give to him as the LORD your
God has blessed you. 15 Remember that you were slaves[g] in Egypt and the LORD your God redeemed you.[h] 15:15 [g]Dt 5:15 [h]Dt 16:12
That is why I give you this command today.
16 But if your servant says to you, "I do not want to leave you," because he loves you and your family
and is well off with you, 17 then take an awl and push it through his ear lobe into the door, and he will be-
come your servant for life. Do the same for your maidservant.
18 Do not consider it a hardship to set your servant free, because his service to you these six years has
been worth twice as much as that of a hired hand. And the LORD your God will bless you in everything
you do.

The Firstborn Animals

19 Set apart for the LORD your God every firstborn male[i] of your herds and flocks. Do not put the first- 15:19 [i]Ex 13:2
born of your oxen to work, and do not shear the firstborn of your sheep. 20 Each year you and your fam-
ily are to eat them in the presence of the LORD your God at the place he will choose.[j] 21 If an animal has a 15:20 [j]Dt 12:5-7, 17,18; 14:23
defect, is lame or blind, or has any serious flaw, you must not sacrifice it to the LORD your God.[k] 22 You are 15:21 [k]Lev 22:19-25
to eat it in your own towns. Both the ceremonially unclean and the clean may eat it, as if it were gazelle 15:22 [l]Dt 12:15, 22
or deer.[l] 23 But you must not eat the blood; pour it out on the ground like water.[m] 15:23 [m]Dt 12:16

15:12–17 See "Slavery and Labor Law in the Ancient Near East" on page 127.
15:18 According to this translation, a Hebrew servant had to work twice as many years as required in the Code of Hammurabi (see "Hammurabi" on p. 271) for release from debt. Other ancient legal texts, however, support "equivalent to" as a possible translation of the phrase "twice as much as."

Passover

16 Observe the month of Abib[n] and celebrate the Passover of the LORD your God, because in the month of Abib he brought you out of Egypt by night. [2]Sacrifice as the Passover to the LORD your God an animal from your flock or herd at the place the LORD will choose as a dwelling for his Name.[o] [3]Do not eat it with bread made with yeast, but for seven days eat unleavened bread, the bread of affliction,[p] because you left Egypt in haste[q]—so that all the days of your life you may remember the time of your departure from Egypt.[r] [4]Let no yeast be found in your possession in all your land for seven days. Do not let any of the meat you sacrifice on the evening of the first day remain until morning.[s]

[5]You must not sacrifice the Passover in any town the LORD your God gives you [6]except in the place he will choose as a dwelling for his Name. There you must sacrifice the Passover in the evening, when the sun goes down, on the anniversary[a][t] of your departure from Egypt. [7]Roast[u] it and eat it at the place the LORD your God will choose. Then in the morning return to your tents. [8]For six days eat unleavened bread and on the seventh day hold an assembly[v] to the LORD your God and do no work.

Feast of Weeks

[9]Count off seven weeks[w] from the time you begin to put the sickle to the standing grain.[x] [10]Then celebrate the Feast of Weeks to the LORD your God by giving a freewill offering in proportion to the blessings the LORD your God has given you. [11]And rejoice[y] before the LORD your God at the place he will choose as a dwelling for his Name—you, your sons and daughters, your menservants and maidservants, the

16:1 [n]Ex 12:2; 13:4
16:2 [o]Dt 12:5,26
16:3 [p]Ex 12:8,39; 34:18 [q]Ex 12:11, 15,19 [r]Ex 13:3, 6-7
16:4 [s]Ex 12:10; 34:25
16:6 [t]Ex 12:6; Dt 12:5
16:7 [u]Ex 12:8; 2Ch 35:13
16:8 [v]Ex 12:16; 13:6; Lev 23:8
16:9 [w]Ex 34:22; Lev 23:15 [x]Ex 23:16; Nu 28:26
16:11 [y]Dt 12:7

[a] 6 Or *down, at the time of day*

Pentecost

DEUTERONOMY 16 *Pentecost,* Greek for "fiftieth," refers in the Old Testament to the Israelite Feast of Weeks—so called because it took place in the spring seven weeks, or 50 days (counting inclusively), after the beginning of the grain harvest (Lev 23:15; Dt 16:9–10).[1] The Greek name appears also in the **Apocryphal** works of Tobit (2:1) and 2 Maccabees (12:32),[2] as well as in the writings of the ancient Jewish historian Josephus (*Antiquities*, 3.10.6) and in the New Testament (Ac 2:1; 20:16; 1Co 16:8). The actual mention of 50 days comes from Leviticus 23:16.

Pentecost is one of three major Israelite festivals at which all males were required to appear before the Lord at the central sanctuary to make an offering (Dt 16:16; the other two are the Feasts of Unleavened Bread and Tabernacles). The Feast of Weeks came at the close of the period of grain harvests, ending with the wheat harvest, which took place in the spring.[3]

Although verse 12 enjoined the Israelites to reflect at the time of this feast upon their slavery in Egypt, there is no other connection made between the festival and any important events in Israel's history, in contrast to Passover[4] and Tabernacles. In all probability the Old Testament Pentecost commemoration retained thanksgiving for the harvest as its primary focus. The main stipulations of verses 10–11 were to make a freewill offering to God and to conduct communal celebration in all the villages of Israel. Both of these elements are naturally linked to harvest time, with the offering being a means of thanking God for the harvest and the celebration a common element of harvest time remembrances in ancient agrarian societies (cf. Ru 3:7; Isa 9:3).

Christians naturally question the link between Old Testament Pentecost and the gift of the Holy Spirit in Acts 2. But already in the Old Testament there was a link between the agricultural blessings of rain and a good harvest and the spiritual blessings of the outpouring of the Spirit. This is especially clear in Joel, where a promise of rain and a good harvest (Joel 2:21–27) is immediately followed by a promise of the pouring out of the Spirit (Joel 2:28–32). In light of this connection, it makes sense that the gift of the Spirit is associated for Christians with Pentecost, an agricultural thanksgiving holiday.

[1]See "The Festivals of Israel" on page 186. [2]See "The Apocrypha" on page 1973. [3]See "Food and Agriculture" on page 390. [4]See "The Passover" on page 656.

Levites[z] in your towns, and the aliens, the fatherless and the widows living among you. 12 Remember that 16:11 zDt 12:12
you were slaves in Egypt,[a] and follow carefully these decrees. 16:12 aDt 15:15

Feast of Tabernacles

13 Celebrate the Feast of Tabernacles for seven days after you have gathered the produce of your
threshing floor[b] and your winepress.[c] 14 Be joyful[d] at your Feast—you, your sons and daughters, your 16:13 bLev 23:34
menservants and maidservants, and the Levites, the aliens, the fatherless and the widows who live in cEx 23:16 16:14 dver 11
your towns. 15 For seven days celebrate the Feast to the LORD your God at the place the LORD will choose.
For the LORD your God will bless you in all your harvest and in all the work of your hands, and your joy[e] 16:15 eLev 23:39
will be complete.
16 Three times a year all your men must appear before the LORD your God at the place he will choose:
at the Feast of Unleavened Bread, the Feast of Weeks and the Feast of Tabernacles.[f] No man should ap- 16:16 fEx 23:14,
pear before the LORD empty-handed:[g] 17 Each of you must bring a gift in proportion to the way the LORD 16 gEx 34:20
your God has blessed you.

Judges

18 Appoint judges[h] and officials for each of your tribes in every town the LORD your God is giving you, 16:18 hDt 1:16
and they shall judge the people fairly. 19 Do not pervert justice[i] or show partiality.[j] Do not accept a bribe,[k] 16:19 iEx 23:2,8
for a bribe blinds the eyes of the wise and twists the words of the righteous. 20 Follow justice and justice jLev 19:15; Dt 1:17 kEcc 7:7
alone, so that you may live and possess the land the LORD your God is giving you.

Worshiping Other Gods

21 Do not set up any wooden Asherah pole[a][l] beside the altar you build to the LORD your God,[m] 22 and 16:21 lDt 7:5
do not erect a sacred stone,[n] for these the LORD your God hates. mEx 34:13; 2Ki 17:16; 21:3;
17 Do not sacrifice to the LORD your God an ox or a sheep that has any defect[o] or flaw in it, for that 2Ch 33:3 16:22 nLev 26:1
would be detestable to him.[p] 17:1 oMal 1:8,13 pDt 15:21
2 If a man or woman living among you in one of the towns the LORD gives you is found doing evil in the
eyes of the LORD your God in violation of his covenant,[q] 3 and contrary to my command[r] has worshiped oth- 17:2 qDt 13:6-11
er gods, bowing down to them or to the sun[s] or the moon or the stars of the sky, 4 and this has been brought 17:3 rJer 7:22-23 sJob 31:26
to your attention, then you must investigate it thoroughly. If it is true and it has been proved that this detest-
able thing has been done in Israel,[t] 5 take the man or woman who has done this evil deed to your city gate 17:4 tDt 13:12-14
and stone that person to death.[u] 6 On the testimony of two or three witnesses a man shall be put to death, but 17:5 uLev 24:14
no one shall be put to death on the testimony of only one witness.[v] 7 The hands of the witnesses must be the 17:6 vNu 35:30; Dt 19:15;
first in putting him to death, and then the hands of all the people. You must purge the evil[w] from among you. Jos 7:25; Mt 18:16; Jn 8:17; 2Co 13:1; 1Ti 5:19; Heb 10:28

Law Courts

8 If cases come before your courts that are too difficult for you to judge—whether bloodshed, lawsuits 17:7 wDt 13:5,9
or assaults[x]—take them to the place the LORD your God will choose.[y] 9 Go to the priests, who are Levites, 17:8 x2Ch 19:10 yDt 12:5;
and to the judge who is in office at that time. Inquire of them and they will give you the verdict.[z] 10 You must Hag 2:11
act according to the decisions they give you at the place the LORD will choose. Be careful to do everything 17:9 zDt 19:17; Eze 44:24
they direct you to do. 11 Act according to the law they teach you and the decisions they give you. Do not turn
aside from what they tell you, to the right or to the left.[a] 12 The man who shows contempt[b] for the judge or 17:11 aDt 25:1
for the priest who stands ministering there to the LORD your God must be put to death. You must purge 17:12 bNu 15:30
the evil from Israel. 13 All the people will hear and be afraid, and will not be contemptuous again.[c] 17:13 cDt 13:11; 19:20

[a] 21 Or *Do not plant any tree dedicated to Asherah*

16:21 The chosen symbol of the fertility cult of Asherah was the trunk of a tree. This explains the prohibition against the planting of trees near the altar of the Lord (v. 21; Jdg 6:25,28,31). See "The Kuntillet Ajrûd Inscriptions: The Lord's Asherah?" on page 1220 and "Trees of Ancient Israel" on page 1357.

17:2–5 The Israelites were not to worship sun, moon or stars, either as physical entities or as representations of pagan deities. In Old Testament theology the sun, moon and stars, along with other natural elements—like mountains and seas—showcased God's glory, as they do today. But they were not to be made into physical or idolatrous representations of God (Ps 8:3; 19:1–6; 148:3–6; Jer 10:10–13; see also Ro 1:20).

17:6 For a discussion of the legal provisions with regard to murder in ancient Israel, see the note on Numbers 35:19.

17:8–13 No provision was made in the Old Testament for reconsideration from a lower to a higher court of a case already tried. Exodus 18:26 shows, however, that Moses provided for lower and higher courts: In Deuteronomy 17:8–13 provision was made for a lower court under certain conditions to seek instructions as to procedure from a higher court.

17:12 Contempt of court—whether by a judge who for whatever reason did not want to exact the stipulated punishment or by a regular citizen—was a capital offense. The priest or judge deciding matters of law between people was seen as "ministering there to the LORD." Contempt of court was serious because the individual was in effect demonstrating contempt for God.

The King

14 When you enter the land the LORD your God is giving you and have taken possession of it and set-
17:14 [d]Dt 11:31; tled in it, and you say, "Let us set a king over us like all the nations around us,"[d] 15 be sure to appoint over
1Sa 8:5,19-20 17:15 [e]Jer 30:21 you the king the LORD your God chooses. He must be from among your own brothers.[e] Do not place a for-
eigner over you, one who is not a brother Israelite. 16 The king, moreover, must not acquire great numbers
17:16 [f]1Ki 4:26; of horses for himself[f] or make the people return to Egypt[g] to get more of them,[h] for the LORD has told
10:26 [g]Isa 31:1; Hos 11:5 you, "You are not to go back that way again."[i] 17 He must not take many wives,[j] or his heart will be led
[h]1Ki 10:28; Eze 17:15 astray. He must not accumulate large amounts of silver and gold.
[i]Ex 13:17 17:17 [j]1Ki 11:3 18 When he takes the throne of his kingdom, he is to write[k] for himself on a scroll a copy of this law,
17:18 [k]Dt 31:22, 24 taken from that of the priests, who are Levites. 19 It is to be with him, and he is to read it all the days of
17:19 [l]Jos 1:8 his life[l] so that he may learn to revere the LORD his God and follow carefully all the words of this law and
17:20 [m]1Ki 15:5 these decrees 20 and not consider himself better than his brothers and turn from the law[m] to the right or
[n]Dt 5:32 to the left.[n] Then he and his descendants will reign a long time over his kingdom in Israel.

Offerings for Priests and Levites

18 The priests, who are Levites—indeed the whole tribe of Levi—are to have no allotment or in-
heritance with Israel. They shall live on the offerings made to the LORD by fire, for that is their in-
18:1 [o]Dt 10:9; 1Co 9:13 heritance.[o] 2 They shall have no inheritance among their brothers; the LORD is their inheritance, as he
promised them.

17:18 Writing a copy of the law for himself would be a sign of submission on the part of Israel's future king to the Lord as *his* King; this copy was then to be used as a guide for the king's rule in obedience to his heavenly Suzerain. This was already a familiar procedure to the Israelites, as it was a requirement for vassal kings under the suzerainty treaties among the Hittites and others both before and during this period (see "Deuteronomy and the Covenant Treaty Form" on p. 255 and the note on 31:9).

ANCIENT TEXTS AND ARTIFACTS

Akkadian Divination

DEUTERONOMY 18 Deuteronomy 18:9–14 prohibited the Israelites from making use of diviners and sorcerers, who engaged in activities God regarded as detestable practices of the nations. Many ancient peoples, however, regarded divination, the attempt to find and interpret omens from the gods, as a science handed down from heaven. In fact, an enormous amount of **Akkadian** literature was devoted to cataloging particular signs and their meanings.

A few of the numerous means of divination practiced in Old Testament times were the reading of animal entrails (extispicy), the observation of patterns in oil dropped onto water (lecanomancy) and dream interpretation (oneiromancy). The extrabiblical omen texts assigned specific meanings to possible outcomes with regard to each sign. For example:

- If a drop of oil spilled on water split in two, a sick individual would die or an army would fail to return from battle.
- If a person dreamed about a dog ripping his or her clothing, that individual was in for a financial loss.
- A black cat in someone's house was a sign of good fortune.

Assyrian incantation text; Assyria, 900–600 B.C.
© The Schøyen Collection; photography courtesy of Mr. Martin Schøyen

- Magical texts also provided incantations useful in specific situations (e.g., there was an incantation to cure sick livestock).

In the Bible such natural events are never regarded as omens. There are no incantations for practicing magic or for counteracting evil portents. Although both Joseph and Daniel interpreted dreams based upon God's leading, no code for oneiromancy may be found in Scripture. Rather, interpretation comes from God (Ge 40:8) and relates only to specific situations. God did provide Israel with a mysterious form of casting lots in the Urim and Thummim[1] (Ex 28:29–30; 1Sa 14:36–41), but the lack of any Biblical description or explanation of these tools seems significant. It would appear that the texts do not intend for the reader to focus on or attempt to replicate these items.

[1]See "The Urim and Thummim" on page 136 and "Casting Lots" on page 744.

3This is the share due the priests from the people who sacrifice a bull or a sheep: the shoulder, the
jowls and the inner parts.[p] 4You are to give them the firstfruits of your grain, new wine and oil, and the 18:3 [p]Lev 7:28-34
first wool from the shearing of your sheep,[q] 5for the LORD your God has chosen them[r] and their descen- 18:4 [q]Ex 22:29; Nu 18:12
dants out of all your tribes to stand and minister[s] in the LORD's name always. 18:5 [r]Ex 28:1 [s]Dt 10:8
6If a Levite moves from one of your towns anywhere in Israel where he is living, and comes in all ear-
nestness to the place the LORD will choose,[t] 7he may minister in the name of the LORD his God like all his 18:6 [t]Nu 35:2-3
fellow Levites who serve there in the presence of the LORD. 8He is to share equally in their benefits, even
though he has received money from the sale of family possessions.[u] 18:8 [u]2Ch 31:4; Ne 12:44,47

Detestable Practices

9When you enter the land the LORD your God is giving you, do not learn to imitate[v] the detestable 18:9 [v]Dt 12:29-31
ways of the nations there. 10Let no one be found among you who sacrifices his son or daughter in[a] the
fire, who practices divination[w] or sorcery, interprets omens, engages in witchcraft,[x] 11or casts spells, or 18:10 [w]Dt 12:31 [x]Lev 19:31
who is a medium or spiritist or who consults the dead. 12Anyone who does these things is detestable to
the LORD, and because of these detestable practices the LORD your
God will drive out those nations before you.[y] 13You must be blame- 18:12 [y]Lev 18:24; Dt 9:4
less before the LORD your God.

ANCIENT VOICES

If a snake crosses from the right of a man to the left of a man—he will have a good name.

If a snake crosses from the left of a man to the right of a man—he will have a bad name.

—MESOPOTAMIAN OMENS

See "Akkadian Divination" article.

The Prophet

14The nations you will dispossess listen to those who practice
sorcery or divination. But as for you, the LORD your God has not per-
mitted you to do so. 15The LORD your God will raise up for you a
prophet like me from among your own brothers.[z] You must listen to 18:15 [z]Jn 1:21; Ac 3:22*; 7:37*
him. 16For this is what you asked of the LORD your God at Horeb on
the day of the assembly when you said, "Let us not hear the voice of
the LORD our God nor see this great fire anymore, or we will die."[a] 18:16 [a]Ex 20:19; Dt 5:23-27
17The LORD said to me: "What they say is good. 18I will raise up for
them a prophet like you from among their brothers; I will put my words[b] in his mouth, and he will tell 18:18 [b]Isa 51:16; Jn 17:8 [c]Jn 4:25-26; 8:28; 12:49-50
them everything I command him.[c] 19If anyone does not listen to my words that the prophet speaks in
my name, I myself will call him to account.[d] 20But a prophet who presumes to speak in my name any- 18:19 [d]Ac 3:23*
thing I have not commanded him to say, or a prophet who speaks in the name of other gods,[e] must be 18:20 [e]Jer 14:14 [f]Dt 13:1-5
put to death."[f]
21You may say to yourselves, "How can we know when a message has not been spoken by the LORD?"
22If what a prophet proclaims in the name of the LORD does not take place or come true, that is a mes-
sage the LORD has not spoken.[g] That prophet has spoken presumptuously.[h] Do not be afraid of him. 18:22 [g]Jer 28:9 [h]ver 20

Cities of Refuge

19 When the LORD your God has destroyed the nations whose land he is giving you, and when you
have driven them out and settled in their towns and houses,[i] 2then set aside for yourselves three 19:1 [i]Dt 12:29
cities centrally located in the land the LORD your God is giving you to possess. 3Build roads to them and
divide into three parts the land the LORD your God is giving you as an inheritance, so that anyone who
kills a man may flee there.
4This is the rule concerning the man who kills another and flees there to save his life—one who kills
his neighbor unintentionally, without malice aforethought. 5For instance, a man may go into the forest

[a] 10 *Or who makes his son or daughter pass through*

18:10–18 These verses represent the Bible's classic passage on the subject of divination, of which there were various modes: (1) reading omens; (2) interpreting dreams, both involuntary dreams and those induced by what is called "incubation" (sleeping in some sacred place where the god was said to reveal his secrets to the sleeper); (3) the use of the lot; (4) hydromancy or foretelling the future from the appearance of water; (5) astrology or the determination of the supposed influence of the heavenly bodies on the destiny of a person or nation; (6) rhabdomancy or the use of the divining rod (Hos 4:12; Eze 8:17); (7) hepatoscopy or divination by an examination of the liver of an animal; (8) necromancy or consultation of the dead; and (9) the sacrifice of children by burning. See "Human Sacrifice in the Ancient Near East" on page 182, "Akkadian Divination" on page 277, "Ancient Necromancy" on page 435, "Dream Oracles in the Ancient World" on page 741 and "Oracles of the Ancient World" on page 1507.

In warning his people against Canaanite superstition (Dt 18:10–13), Moses made no reference to astrology or to any other sort of fortune-telling by means of the stars. Although this practice later found its way into what is now western Palestine, it was essentially a Babylonian or Mesopotamian study.

with his neighbor to cut wood, and as he swings his ax to fell a tree, the head may fly off and hit his neigh-
bor and kill him. That man may flee to one of these cities and save his life. 6 Otherwise, the avenger of
19:6 [j]Nu 35:12 blood[j] might pursue him in a rage, overtake him if the distance is too great, and kill him even though he
is not deserving of death, since he did it to his neighbor without malice aforethought. 7 This is why I com-
mand you to set aside for yourselves three cities.

8 If the LORD your God enlarges your territory, as he promised on oath to your forefathers, and gives
you the whole land he promised them, 9 because you carefully follow all these laws I command you to-
19:9 [k]Jos 20:7-8 day—to love the LORD your God and to walk always in his ways[k]—then you are to set aside three more
cities. 10 Do this so that innocent blood will not be shed in your land, which the LORD your God is giving
19:10 [l]Nu 35:33; Dt 21:1-9 you as your inheritance, and so that you will not be guilty of bloodshed.[l]
19:11 [m]Nu 35:16 11 But if a man hates his neighbor and lies in wait for him, assaults and kills him,[m] and then flees to
one of these cities, 12 the elders of his town shall send for him, bring him back from the city, and hand him
19:13 [n]Dt 7:2 over to the avenger of blood to die. 13 Show him no pity.[n] You must purge from Israel the guilt of shed-
[o]1Ki 2:31 ding innocent blood,[o] so that it may go well with you.

14 Do not move your neighbor's boundary stone set up by your predecessors in the inheritance you
19:14 [p]Dt 27:17; Pr 22:28; Hos 5:10 receive in the land the LORD your God is giving you to possess.[p]

Witnesses

15 One witness is not enough to convict a man accused of any crime or offense he may have commit-
19:15 [q]Nu 35:30; Dt 17:6; Mt 18:16*; Jn 8:17; 2Co 13:1*; 1Ti 5:19; Heb 10:28 ted. A matter must be established by the testimony of two or three witnesses.[q]
16 If a malicious witness[r] takes the stand to accuse a man of a crime, 17 the two men involved in the dis-
pute must stand in the presence of the LORD before the priests and the judges[s] who are in office at the
19:16 [r]Ex 23:1; Ps 27:12 time. 18 The judges must make a thorough investigation, and if the witness proves to be a liar, giving false
19:17 [s]Dt 17:9 testimony against his brother, 19 then do to him as he intended to do to his brother.[t] You must purge the
19:19 [t]Pr 19:5,9 evil from among you. 20 The rest of the people will hear of this and be afraid,[u] and never again will such
19:20 [u]Dt 17:13; 21:21 an evil thing be done among you. 21 Show no pity:[v] life for life, eye for eye, tooth for tooth, hand for hand,
19:21 [v]ver 13 [w]Ex 21:24; Lev 24:20; Mt 5:38* foot for foot.[w]

Going to War

20 When you go to war against your enemies and see horses and chariots and an army greater than
20:1 [x]Ps 20:7; Isa 31:1 [y]Dt 31:6, 8 [z]2Ch 32:7-8 yours,[x] do not be afraid[y] of them,[z] because the LORD your God, who brought you up out of Egypt,
will be with you. 2 When you are about to go into battle, the priest shall come forward and address the
army. 3 He shall say: "Hear, O Israel, today you are going into battle against your enemies. Do not be faint-
20:3 [a]Jos 23:10 hearted[a] or afraid; do not be terrified or give way to panic before them. 4 For the LORD your God is the one
20:4 [b]Dt 1:30; 3:22; Jos 23:10 who goes with you to fight[b] for you against your enemies to give you victory."
20:5 [c]Ne 12:27 5 The officers shall say to the army: "Has anyone built a new house and not dedicated[c] it? Let him go
home, or he may die in battle and someone else may dedicate it. 6 Has anyone planted a vineyard and not
begun to enjoy it? Let him go home, or he may die in battle and someone else enjoy it. 7 Has anyone

---

19:14 Agriculture was the background for all of the legislation of Israel. At the time of the conquest every family probably received a parcel of land, marked off by stones that could not be lawfully removed (see also 27:17; Hos 5:10). Fertilizing was almost unknown; in order to maintain the soil's natural fertility the law required that farms, vineyards and olive orchards were to lie fallow during every seventh year (Ex 23:10). Terracing was necessary to make use of soil on the hillsides. Irrigation was not required, since there was usually sufficient rainfall at optimal times of the agricultural year (see the note on Dt 11:10–12).

19:15–21 Genesis 9:6 states the Biblical law of equity: The taking of a life by murder required the taking of the life of the murderer. The Old Testament recognized in this connection both the function of the courts (e.g., Ex 24:12) and the rights of the victim's family. The next of kin was permitted to exact the death penalty. The word that is questionably translated "avenger" (e.g., Nu 35:12) is properly "next of kin" or "redeemer" (*go'el*). Not only in capital cases but in all the vicissitudes of life the *go'el* was at hand to take upon himself whatever need might be oppressing his close relative. See "The Kinsman-Redeemer" on page 391.

19:20 Old Testament law was dominated by the concept of equality: an exact equivalence between crime and punishment. It expressed this in characteristically vigorous terms—as in this verse (cf. Ex 21:23–24; Lev 24:20). It is helpful to note that these passages all refer to punishments imposed by courts of law and are not rules for private conduct. In the case of murder, where life was to be taken for life, the next of kin took up the dreadful duty, carefully circumscribed in his actions by the clear Old Testament distinction between capital murder and accidental manslaughter and by limitation of vengeance to the murderer only (Dt 24:16).

20:1–4 Every phase of Israel's life, including the nation's warfare, was bound up with God. War therefore had religious significance (see "*Herem*, Holy War" on p. 419). It was customary for priests to accompany Israel's armies into battle. In addition, campaigns were begun and engagements entered into with sacrificial rites (1Sa 7:8–10; 13:9) and after consulting the Lord (Jdg 20:18ff.; 1Sa 14:37; 23:2; 28:6; 30:8). Prophets were sometimes asked for guidance before a campaign (1Ki 22:5; 1Ki 3:11).

20:5–8 Military officers spelled out to potential inductees ways in which they might be excused from service. Only the ready and willing were wanted for battle. If a man did not fit any of the other specific categories of exemption, the last—"Is any man afraid or fainthearted?" (v. 8)—would have relieved him of duty if he so desired.

become pledged to a woman and not married her? Let him go home, or he may die in battle and someone else marry her.[d]" 8 Then the officers shall add, "Is any man afraid or fainthearted? Let him go home so that his brothers will not become disheartened too."[e] 9 When the officers have finished speaking to the army, they shall appoint commanders over it.

10 When you march up to attack a city, make its people an offer of peace.[f] 11 If they accept and open their gates, all the people in it shall be subject to forced labor[g] and shall work for you. 12 If they refuse to make peace and they engage you in battle, lay siege to that city. 13 When the LORD your God delivers it into your hand, put to the sword all the men in it.[h] 14 As for the women, the children, the livestock[i] and everything else in the city, you may take these as plunder for yourselves. And you may use the plunder the LORD your God gives you from your enemies. 15 This is how you are to treat all the cities that are at a distance from you and do not belong to the nations nearby.

20:7 [d] Dt 24:5
20:8 [e] Jdg 7:3
20:10 [f] Lk 14:31-32
20:11 [g] 1Ki 9:21
20:13 [h] Nu 31:7
20:14 [i] Jos 8:2; 22:8

16 However, in the cities of the nations the LORD your God is giving you as an inheritance, do not leave alive anything that breathes.[j] 17 Completely destroy[a] them—the Hittites, Amorites, Canaanites, Perizzites, Hivites and Jebusites—as the LORD your God has commanded you. 18 Otherwise, they will teach you to follow all the detestable things they do in worshiping their gods,[k] and you will sin[l] against the LORD your God.

20:16 [j] Ex 23:31-33; Nu 21:2-3; Dt 7:2; Jos 11:14
20:18 [k] Ex 34:16; Dt 7:4; 12:30-31 [l] Ex 23:33

19 When you lay siege to a city for a long time, fighting against it to capture it, do not destroy its trees by putting an ax to them, because you can eat their fruit. Do not cut them down. Are the trees of the field people, that you should besiege them?[b] 20 However, you may cut down trees that you know are not fruit trees and use them to build siege works until the city at war with you falls.

ANCIENT VOICES

If anyone bites off the nose of a free man, he shall pay 30 minas (i.e. 1,200 shekels) of silver. He shall look to his house for it.

If anyone bites off the nose of a male or female slave, he shall pay 3 shekels of silver. He shall look to his house for it.

—HITTITE LAWS

See "The Hittite Laws" article.

Atonement for an Unsolved Murder

21 If a man is found slain, lying in a field in the land the LORD your God is giving you to possess, and it is not known who killed him, 2 your elders and judges shall go out and measure the distance from the body to the neighboring towns. 3 Then the elders of the town nearest the body shall take a heifer that has never been worked and has never worn a yoke 4 and lead her down to a valley that has not been plowed or planted and where there is a flowing stream. There in the valley they are to break the heifer's neck. 5 The priests, the sons of Levi, shall step forward, for the LORD your God has chosen them to minister and to pronounce blessings[m] in the name of the LORD and to decide all cases of dispute and assault.[n] 6 Then all the elders of the town nearest the body shall wash their hands[o] over the heifer whose neck was broken in the valley, 7 and they shall declare: "Our hands did not shed this blood, nor did our eyes see it done. 8 Accept this atonement for your people Israel, whom you have redeemed, O LORD, and do not hold your people guilty of the blood of an innocent man." And the bloodshed will be atoned for.[p] 9 So you will purge[q] from yourselves the guilt of shedding innocent blood, since you have done what is right in the eyes of the LORD.

21:5 [m] 1Ch 23:13 [n] Dt 17:8-11
21:6 [o] Mt 27:24
21:8 [p] Nu 35:33-34
21:9 [q] Dt 19:13

Marrying a Captive Woman

10 When you go to war against your enemies and the LORD your God delivers them into your hands[r] and you take captives, 11 if you notice among the captives a beautiful woman and are attracted to her, you may take her as your wife. 12 Bring her into your home and have her shave her head,[s] trim her nails 13 and put aside the clothes she was wearing when captured. After she has lived in your house and mourned

21:10 [r] Jos 21:44
21:12 [s] Lev 14:9; Nu 6:9

[a] *17* The Hebrew term refers to the irrevocable giving over of things or persons to the LORD, often by totally destroying them.
[b] *19* Or *down to use in the siege, for the fruit trees are for the benefit of man.*

21:10–14 These verses relate to the marriage of an Israelite man to an unmarried woman captured in warfare "at a distance" from Canaan (see 20:10–15). Because of the distance, the woman would not be under the ban of total destruction (see 20:16–18), and the couple would be subject to all rules pertaining to Israelite marriage. Cleansing rites (cf. Lev 14:8; Nu 8:7; 2Sa 19:24) would initiate the woman into the family, but she was to be given one month to mourn her parents. Because he had already engaged in intercourse with her, if the husband became displeased he was to let her go free rather than keep her as a slave. Although this passage might seem shocking, these rules were humane considering how ancient women and girls were generally treated during or after warfare. See "Slavery and Labor Law in the Ancient Near East" on page 127.

21:13 The list of a man's possessions included his wife, servants,

21:13 tPs 45:10 her father and mother for a full month,[t] then you may go to her and be her husband and she shall be
your wife. 14If you are not pleased with her, let her go wherever she wishes. You must not sell her or treat
21:14 uGe 34:2 her as a slave, since you have dishonored her.[u]

---

slaves, goods and animals (Ex 20:17; Dt 5:21). Even the phrase "to marry a woman" derived from one that means "to become the master of a wife" (see also 24:1). Although she would address her husband in subservient terms, the status of the wife was higher than that of the rest of the household.

The primary responsibility of the mother was to produce children, preferably sons. A large number of sons, who were to become workers from an early age, ensured the future economic prosperity and security of the family. Women typically nursed children for several years; some authorities suggest that weaning took place around age three, but ancient statuary depicts children apparently as old as five or six standing to nurse from their mothers.

ANCIENT TEXTS AND ARTIFACTS

The Hittite Laws

DEUTERONOMY 21 Many historians date Biblical law texts to fairly late in Israel's history. Explicitly or implicitly, they view regulations such as those spelled out in Exodus or Deuteronomy as too complex and advanced to stem from such a "primitive" period as that of Moses and Joshua. As already discussed in "The Middle Assyrian Laws" on page 179 and "The Laws of Eshnunna" on page 267, however, the discoveries of lengthy and detailed law codes from the ancient Near East would seem to belie this notion.

The **Hittite** laws have come to us in two versions, the first from the Old Kingdom period (c. 1600–1400 B.C.) and the second from the Middle Kingdom and Empire periods (c. 1400–1200). The second iteration parallels the first, being similar in order and content. Hittite laws deal with many of the same issues as their Biblical counterparts: quarrels resulting in maiming or unintended homicide (Ex 21:12–27); marriages and dowries (Ex 22:16–17); theft, especially of animals (Ex 22:1–15); and incest and bestiality (Lev 18).

Of course, the specific stipulations of Biblical and Hittite laws are often quite different. For example, the Hittite New Kingdom law IV states that if a murdered man was found on another's property, the owner was to forfeit his house, property and 6,040 shekels of silver. If the corpse was located in an open field, a village within 3 miles (4.8 km) of the victim was to pay the fee. In Deuteronomy 21:1–9, on the other hand, if the body of a murder victim was discovered in an open field, the elders of the nearest village were to make a sacrifice and swear that they had no knowledge of the crime's perpetrator(s). This would purge the village of any culpability, and no fee was involved.

Once again, Hittite laws reveal that lengthy, complex law codes could and did exist in the mid-second millennium B.C., the implication being that Exodus and Deuteronomy may indeed be dated to this earlier period.

ANCIENT NEAR EASTERN VERSUS ISRAELITE LAWS AND LAW COLLECTIONS

Ancient Near East	Israel
Law: Amoral and meant to insure the smooth running of society; offenses of the law were considered as offenses against civilization.	*Law:* Meant to be a guide to godlikeness; offenses of the law were considered offenses against God.
Law Collections: Propagandistic report to deity; a theoretical development of some of the forms justice might take.	*Law Collections:* Development of the forms morality or holiness would take; civil law tied to moral absolutes.

Old Testament Today, p. 63

The Right of the Firstborn

15 If a man has two wives, and he loves one but not the other, and both bear him sons but the firstborn
is the son of the wife he does not love,[v] 16 when he wills his property to his sons, he must not give the **21:15** [v]Ge 29:33
rights of the firstborn to the son of the wife he loves in preference to his actual firstborn, the son of the
wife he does not love.[w] 17 He must acknowledge the son of his unloved wife as the firstborn by giving **21:16** [w]1Ch 26:10
him a double share of all he has. That son is the first sign of his father's strength.[x] The right of the first- **21:17** [x]Ge 49:3 [y]Ge 25:31
born belongs to him.[y]

A Rebellious Son

18 If a man has a stubborn and rebellious son who does not obey his father and mother[z] and will not **21:18** [z]Pr 1:8; Isa 30:1; Eph 6:1-3
listen to them when they discipline him, 19 his father and mother shall take hold of him and bring him
to the elders at the gate of his town. 20 They shall say to the elders, "This son of ours is stubborn and re-
bellious. He will not obey us. He is a profligate and a drunkard." 21 Then all the men of his town shall
stone him to death. You must purge the evil[a] from among you. All Israel will hear of it and be afraid.[b] **21:21** [a]Dt 19:19; 1Co 5:13* [b]Dt 13:11

Various Laws

22 If a man guilty of a capital offense[c] is put to death and his body is hung on a tree, 23 you must not **21:22** [c]Dt 22:26; Mk 14:64; Ac 23:29
leave his body on the tree overnight.[d] Be sure to bury him that same day, because anyone who is hung **21:23** [d]Jos 8:29; 10:27; Jn 19:31 [e]Gal 3:13* [f]Lev 18:25; Nu 35:34
on a tree is under God's curse.[e] You must not desecrate[f] the land the LORD your God is giving you as an
inheritance.

22 If you see your brother's ox or sheep straying, do not ignore it but be sure to take it back to him.[g] **22:1** [g]Ex 23:4-5
2 If the brother does not live near you or if you do not know who he is, take it home with you and
keep it until he comes looking for it. Then give it back to him. 3 Do the same if you find your brother's don-
key or his cloak or anything he loses. Do not ignore it.
4 If you see your brother's donkey[h] or his ox fallen on the road, do not ignore it. Help him get it to its feet. **22:4** [h]Ex 23:5
5 A woman must not wear men's clothing, nor a man wear women's clothing, for the LORD your God de-
tests anyone who does this.
6 If you come across a bird's nest beside the road, either in a tree or on the ground, and the mother is
sitting on the young or on the eggs, do not take the mother with the young.[i] 7 You may take the young,
but be sure to let the mother go, so that it may go well with you and you may have a long life.[j] **22:6** [i]Lev 22:28
8 When you build a new house, make a parapet around your roof so that you may not bring the guilt **22:7** [j]Dt 4:40
of bloodshed on your house if someone falls from the roof.
9 Do not plant two kinds of seed in your vineyard;[k] if you do, not only the crops you plant but also the **22:9** [k]Lev 19:19
fruit of the vineyard will be defiled.[a]
10 Do not plow with an ox and a donkey yoked together.[l] **22:10** [l]2Co 6:14
11 Do not wear clothes of wool and linen woven together.[m] **22:11** [m]Lev 19:19
12 Make tassels on the four corners of the cloak you wear.[n] **22:12** [n]Nu 15:37-41; Mt 23:5

[a] 9 Or *be forfeited to the sanctuary*

21:15–17 Numerous Old Testament family dysfunctions can be traced directly back to polygamy. While not officially approved in ancient Biblical times, the practice was allowed. See "Inheritance in the Ancient Near East" on page 250.

From time immemorial a man's firstborn son has been given privileges above those of his younger sons. This is illustrated today by the order of succession to the throne (e.g., in Britain). Among the Israelites God had a special claim on the firstborn, at least from the time of the Exodus, when he destroyed the firstborn of Egypt and claimed those of Israel by right of redemption (Ex 13:2,12–16). The birthright included a double portion of the inheritance. In Israel God later set apart the tribe of Levi instead of the firstborn for the privilege of priesthood (Ex 13:1–2;24:5). (Note Nu 3:38–51, where the Levites were about the same in number as the firstborn of Israel).

In terms of the conditions of inheritance, the firstborn son possessed the birthright (the right to a double portion of the father's possessions), and to him belonged the duty of maintaining the females of the family. The other sons received equal shares. If there were no sons, the property went to the daughters (Nu 27:8), on the condition that they not marry outside their own tribe (Nu 36:6ff.).
(See "The Rights of the Firstborn" on p. 43 and "Inheritance in the Ancient Near East" on p. 250). Parallels to this practice come from Nuzi, Larsa in the Old Babylonian period and Assyria in the Middle Assyrian period. To receive a double portion of an estate was equivalent to succession (see 2Ki 2:9).

21:21 The punishment of being stoned to death was intended to purge the evil from among the people (13:5; 17:7,12). Fear of this fate was expected to restrain such rebellion, which was strictly forbidden by the fifth commandment (5:16; see Ex 20:12; cf. Ex 21:15).

22:5 This rule was probably intended to prohibit such perversions as transvestism and homosexuality.

22:6 Mosaic Law forbade a person who found a bird's nest with the mother and her brood in it from harming the mother bird. Semitic people in general viewed with extreme disfavor anyone who willfully disturbed a bird in the nest. Isaiah compared the despoiling of Israel by the Assyrians to the robbing of a bird's nest (Isa 10:14), and Jesus contrasted birds having nests with his own lack of a home (Mt 8:20; Lk 9:58).

22:8 Houses in the ancient Near East had flat roofs with outside staircases. The roof was a convenient place for relaxation and privacy and a good location to catch the cool evening breeze. Sometimes a small room was built on the roof. See "The Israelite Town and Home" on page 1205.

Marriage Violations

22:13 [o]Dt 24:1 13 If a man takes a wife and, after lying with her[o], dislikes her 14 and slanders her and gives her a bad
name, saying, "I married this woman, but when I approached her, I did not find proof of her virginity,"
15 then the girl's father and mother shall bring proof that she was a virgin to the town elders at the gate.
16 The girl's father will say to the elders, "I gave my daughter in marriage to this man, but he dislikes her.
17 Now he has slandered her and said, 'I did not find your daughter to be a virgin.' But here is the proof of
my daughter's virginity." Then her parents shall display the cloth before the elders of the town, 18 and the
22:18 [p]Ex 18:21 elders[p] shall take the man and punish him. 19 They shall fine him a hundred shekels of silver[a] and give
them to the girl's father, because this man has given an Israelite virgin a bad name. She shall continue to
be his wife; he must not divorce her as long as he lives.

20 If, however, the charge is true and no proof of the girl's virginity can be found, 21 she shall be brought
to the door of her father's house and there the men of her town shall stone her to death. She has done a
22:21 [q]Ge 34:7; Dt 13:5; 23:17-18; Jdg 20:6; 2Sa 13:12 disgraceful thing[q] in Israel by being promiscuous while still in her father's house. You must purge the
evil from among you.

22 If a man is found sleeping with another man's wife, both the man who slept with her and the wom-
22:22 [r]Lev 20:10; Jn 8:5 an must die.[r] You must purge the evil from Israel.

23 If a man happens to meet in a town a virgin pledged to be married and he sleeps with her, 24 you shall
take both of them to the gate of that town and stone them to death—the girl because she was in a town
and did not scream for help, and the man because he violated another man's wife. You must purge the evil
22:24 [s]ver 21-22; 1Co 5:13* from among you.[s]

25 But if out in the country a man happens to meet a girl pledged to be married and rapes her, only the
man who has done this shall die. 26 Do nothing to the girl; she has committed no sin deserving death.
This case is like that of someone who attacks and murders his neighbor, 27 for the man found the girl out
in the country, and though the betrothed girl screamed, there was no one to rescue her.

28 If a man happens to meet a virgin who is not pledged to be married and rapes her and they are dis-
22:28 [t]Ex 22:16 covered,[t] 29 he shall pay the girl's father fifty shekels of silver.[b] He must marry the girl, for he has violat-
ed her. He can never divorce her as long as he lives.

22:30 [u]Lev 18:8; 20:11; Dt 27:20; 1Co 5:1 30 A man is not to marry his father's wife; he must not dishonor his father's bed.[u]

Exclusion From the Assembly

23 No one who has been emasculated by crushing or cutting may enter the assembly of the LORD.
2 No one born of a forbidden marriage[c] nor any of his descendants may enter the assembly of
the LORD, even down to the tenth generation.

3 No Ammonite or Moabite or any of his descendants may enter the assembly of the LORD, even down to
23:3 [v]Ne 13:2 the tenth generation.[v] 4 For they did not come to meet you with bread and water on your way when you came
23:4 [w]Nu 22:5-6; 23:7; 2Pe 2:15 out of Egypt, and they hired Balaam[w] son of Beor from Pethor in Aram Naharaim[d] to pronounce a curse on
23:5 [x]Pr 26:2 you. 5 However, the LORD your God would not listen to Balaam but turned the curse[x] into a blessing for you,
23:6 [y]Ezr 9:12 because the LORD your God loves you. 6 Do not seek a treaty of friendship with them as long as you live.[y]

23:7 [z]Ge 25:26; Ob 1:10,12 7 Do not abhor an Edomite, for he is your brother.[z] Do not abhor an Egyptian, because you lived as an
[a]Ex 22:21; 23:9; Lev 19:34; Dt 10:19 alien in his country.[a] 8 The third generation of children born to them may enter the assembly of the LORD.

Uncleanness in the Camp

9 When you are encamped against your enemies, keep away from everything impure. 10 If one of your
23:10 [b]Lev 15:16 men is unclean because of a nocturnal emission, he is to go outside the camp and stay there.[b] 11 But as
evening approaches he is to wash himself, and at sunset he may return to the camp.

12 Designate a place outside the camp where you can go to relieve yourself. 13 As part of your equipment
have something to dig with, and when you relieve yourself, dig a hole and cover up your excrement. 14 For

[a] *19* That is, about 2 1/2 pounds (about 1 kilogram) [b] *29* That is, about 1 1/4 pounds (about 0.6 kilogram) [c] *2* Or *one of illegitimate birth* [d] *4* That is, Northwest Mesopotamia

---

22:17 The "proof" of virginity was probably a bloodstained bed sheet or garment, resulting from the new wife's first experience of intercourse. Though not infallible, such items were widely accepted in the ancient Near East as indications of prior virginity.
23:2 The ambiguous language "born of a forbidden marriage" probably refers to a child of incest, not to an illegitimate child.

23:9–14 "Cleanliness is next to godliness" is not an Old Testament quote, as some think, but the concept does have a Biblical basis. For the ancient Israelites, holiness was indeed identified with hygiene. Only the ritually clean person could approach the Lord in worship (Ex 19:10–11; 30:18–21; Jos 3:5; Ps 51:7,10).

the LORD your God moves[c] about in your camp to protect you and to deliver your enemies to you. Your camp must be holy,[d] so that he will not see among you anything indecent and turn away from you.

23:14 [c]Lev 26:12 [d]Ex 3:5

Miscellaneous Laws

15 If a slave has taken refuge with you, do not hand him over to his master.[e] 16 Let him live among you
wherever he likes and in whatever town he chooses. Do not oppress[f] him.
17 No Israelite man[g] or woman is to become a shrine prostitute.[h] 18 You must not bring the earnings
of a female prostitute or of a male prostitute[a] into the house of the LORD your God to pay any vow, because the LORD your God detests them both.

23:15 [e]1Sa 30:15
23:16 [f]Ex 22:21
23:17 [g]Ge 19:25; 2Ki 23:7 [h]Lev 19:29; Dt 22:21

[a] 18 Hebrew *of a dog*

Prostitution in the Ancient World

DEUTERONOMY 23 Prostitution was known throughout the ancient world. While some who practiced the trade worked independently, others (such as slaves) were forced into it. In **Mesopotamia** it was actually possible to adopt a girl and then hire her out as a prostitute.

There is considerable controversy over the so-called temple prostitute. Herodotus (*Histories*, 1.199) recorded that every **Babylonian** woman was required to prostitute herself at least once in the temple of Ishtar, but the reliability of this claim is disputed.[1] Most scholars agree that "sacred prostitution" was part of the ritual of the fertility cult, but some argue against this claim, suggesting that women sometimes prostituted themselves to obtain money to pay a vow or that temples simply used whoredom as a source of income.

In the Greco-Roman world prostitution was also associated with the temples of Aphrodite (especially at Corinth, according to the ancient Greek historian Strabo), but the nature of this prostitution is uncertain.[2] It is unlikely, however, that temples used such women only as sources of income with no religious link to the function of the temple itself; the promiscuous act was probably regarded as some kind of sacred rite, even as it catered to the lusts of the people. The weight of evidence suggests that "sacred prostitution" was real.

Biblical texts provide evidence for temple prostitution. The practice is associated with pagan worship in Hosea 4:14, a passage that condemns men who had encounters with the sacred prostitutes at the shrines and who offered sacrifices there. Prostitution is often used in the Old Testament as a metaphor for idolatry (Ex 34:15–16; Lev 17:7), which may strengthen the connection between temple prostitution and the idolatrous practices of other peoples. Prostitution or harlotry in any form was forbidden to the Israelites (Lev 19:29; Dt 23:17).

"The Woman at the Window": possibly a prostitute in the cult of Astarte
Preserving Bible Times; © Dr. James C. Martin; permission of Musée de Louvre

[1] See "Sexuality and Religion in the Sumerian Hymns to Ishtar" on page 1340. [2] See "The Role of Women in Religious Life in the Greco-Roman World" on page 1879 and "Corinth" on page 1887.

19 Do not charge your brother interest, whether on money or food or anything else that may earn in-
23:19 [i]Ex 22:25; Lev 25:35-37 terest.[i] 20 You may charge a foreigner interest, but not a brother Israelite, so that the LORD your God may
23:20 [j]Dt 15:10; 28:12 bless[j] you in everything you put your hand to in the land you are entering to possess.
21 If you make a vow to the LORD your God, do not be slow to pay it, for the LORD your God will certain-
23:21 [k]Nu 30:1-2; Ecc 5:4-5; Mt 5:33 ly demand it of you and you will be guilty of sin.[k] 22 But if you refrain from making a vow, you will not
be guilty. 23 Whatever your lips utter you must be sure to do, because you made your vow freely to the
LORD your God with your own mouth.
24 If you enter your neighbor's vineyard, you may eat all the grapes you want, but do not put any in
your basket. 25 If you enter your neighbor's grainfield, you may pick kernels with your hands, but you
23:25 [l]Mt 12:1; Mk 2:23; Lk 6:1 must not put a sickle to his standing grain.[l]
24:1 [m]Dt 22:13 [n]Mt 5:31*; 19:7-9; Mk 10:4-5 24 If a man marries a woman who becomes displeasing to him[m] because he finds something inde-
cent about her, and he writes her a certificate of divorce,[n] gives it to her and sends her from his
house, 2 and if after she leaves his house she becomes the wife of another man, 3 and her second husband
dislikes her and writes her a certificate of divorce, gives it to her and sends her from his house, or if he
dies, 4 then her first husband, who divorced her, is not allowed to marry her again after she has been de-
24:4 [o]Jer 3:1 filed. That would be detestable in the eyes of the LORD. Do not bring sin upon the land the LORD[o] your God
is giving you as an inheritance.

23:20 Foreign merchants who came into Israel for financial advantage could be charged interest, but interest-bearing loans to fellow Israelites were prohibited (Ex 22:25). See "Banking and Money in the Ancient World" on page 696.

24:1–4 Divorce in the books of Moses (here and in Lev 21:7,14; 22:13; Nu 30:9) was a fact of life—permitted under some circumstances but regulated. Its basis could not be frivolous or trivial. The phrase "something indecent" (Dt 24:1) possibly refers to an infraction less than adultery, which was punishable by death (22:22–27; cf. Lev 20:10). Childlessness was considered just cause for divorce.

The bill of divorce could be a simple repudiation, such as "She is not my wife, and I am not her husband" (Hos 2:2). Although

The Care of Widows and Orphans in the Bible and the Ancient Near East

DEUTERONOMY 24 In Old Testament laws God commanded the Israelites not to "take advantage of a widow or an orphan" (Ex 22:22). In fact, Psalm 68:5 describes God himself as "a father to the fatherless, a defender of widows." Israelite farmers were instructed to leave some grain unharvested so that Levites, widows, orphans and foreigners could glean the leftovers in their fields and eat (Dt 24:17–22). In addition, the tithes of every third year were to provide for widows, orphans, aliens and priests (26:12–13). Hebrews, who themselves had been aliens and slaves in Egypt, were never to pervert the justice due to widows, orphans or foreigners (24:17–18). In fact, one of the reasons God stipulated for allowing Israel and Judah to fall before **Assyria** and **Babylon** was his people's failure in their obligation to "defend the cause of the fatherless" and "plead the case of the widow" (Isa 1:17).

In the New Testament the widow of Zarephath[1] (Lk 4:24–26; cf. 1Ki 17:7–24) and the widowed prophetess Anna (Lk 2:36–38) are cited as examples of faith, and an impoverished widow was held up by Jesus as a model of generosity (Lk 21:2–4). In one of Jesus' parables a widow provided a clear example of the innocent being easy prey for the unjust and indifferent (Lk 18:3–5). Jesus demonstrated mercy toward the widow at Nain (Lk 7:12–13) and refused to leave his own disciples "as orphans" with relation to his own coming departure from Earth (Jn 14:18). A Jewish widow had the right to expect financial maintenance from her husband's heirs. Yet Jesus went so far as to accuse religious scribes of stealing widows' properties (Mk 12:40; Lk 20:47).

The early church continued God's concern for such otherwise destitute women. Needy widows were fed (Ac 6:1–3), and the disciple Dorcas of her own accord sewed clothing especially for them (Ac 9:39). A ministerial order of widows was begun for the purpose of prayer (1Ti 5:3–10), and James, Jesus' brother, defined true worship as that demonstrated by visitation of distressed orphans and widows (Jas 1:27).

[1]See "Zarephath" on page 514.

5 If a man has recently married, he must not be sent to war or have any other duty laid on him. For one
year he is to be free to stay at home and bring happiness to the wife he has married.[p]
6 Do not take a pair of millstones—not even the upper one—as security for a debt, because that
would be taking a man's livelihood as security.
7 If a man is caught kidnapping one of his brother Israelites and treats him as a slave or sells him, the
kidnapper must die.[q] You must purge the evil from among you.
8 In cases of leprous[a] diseases be very careful to do exactly as the priests, who are Levites, instruct
you. You must follow carefully what I have commanded them.[r] 9 Remember what the LORD your God did
to Miriam along the way after you came out of Egypt.[s]
10 When you make a loan of any kind to your neighbor, do not go into his house to get what he is of-
fering as a pledge. 11 Stay outside and let the man to whom you are making the loan bring the pledge out
to you. 12 If the man is poor, do not go to sleep with his pledge in your possession. 13 Return his cloak to
him by sunset[t] so that he may sleep in it. Then he will thank you, and it will be regarded as a righteous
act in the sight of the LORD your God.[u]
14 Do not take advantage of a hired man who is poor and needy, whether he is a brother Israelite or an
alien living in one of your towns.[v] 15 Pay him his wages each day before sunset, because he is poor[w] and
is counting on it.[x] Otherwise he may cry to the LORD against you, and you will be guilty of sin.[y]
16 Fathers shall not be put to death for their children, nor children put to death for their fathers; each
is to die for his own sin.[z]
17 Do not deprive the alien or the fatherless of justice,[a] or take the cloak of the widow as a pledge. 18 Re-
member that you were slaves in Egypt and the LORD your God redeemed you from there. That is why I
command you to do this.
19 When you are harvesting in your field and you overlook a sheaf, do not go back to get it.[b] Leave
it for the alien, the fatherless and the widow, so that the LORD your God may bless[c] you in all the
work of your hands. 20 When you beat the olives from your trees, do not go over the branches a sec-
ond time.[d] Leave what remains for the alien, the fatherless and the widow. 21 When you harvest the
grapes in your vineyard, do not go over the vines again. Leave what remains for the alien, the fa-
therless and the widow. 22 Remember that you were slaves in Egypt. That is why I command you to
do this.[e]

25 When men have a dispute, they are to take it to court and the judges will decide the case,[f] ac-
quitting the innocent and condemning the guilty.[g] 2 If the guilty man deserves to be beaten,[h] the
judge shall make him lie down and have him flogged in his presence with the number of lashes his crime
deserves, 3 but he must not give him more than forty lashes.[i] If he is flogged more than that, your broth-
er will be degraded in your eyes.[j]
4 Do not muzzle an ox while it is treading out the grain.[k]
5 If brothers are living together and one of them dies without a son, his widow must not marry out-
side the family. Her husband's brother shall take her and marry her and fulfill the duty of a brother-in-
law to her.[l] 6 The first son she bears shall carry on the name of the dead brother so that his name will not
be blotted out from Israel.[m]
7 However, if a man does not want to marry his brother's wife, she shall go to the elders at the town gate
and say, "My husband's brother refuses to carry on his brother's name in Israel. He will not fulfill the duty

24:5 [p]Dt 20:7
24:7 [q]Ex 21:16
24:8 [r]Lev 13:1-46; 14:2
24:9 [s]Nu 12:10
24:13 [t]Ex 22:26 [u]Dt 6:25; Da 4:27
24:14 [v]Lev 25:35-43; Dt 15:12-18
24:15 [w]Jer 22:13 [x]Lev 19:13 [y]Dt 15:9; Jas 5:4
24:16 [z]2Ki 14:6; 2Ch 25:4; Jer 31:29-30; Eze 18:20
24:17 [a]Dt 1:17; 10:17-18; 16:19
24:19 [b]Lev 19:9; 23:22 [c]Pr 19:17
24:20 [d]Lev 19:10
24:22 [e]ver 18
25:1 [f]Dt 19:17 [g]Dt 1:16-17
25:2 [h]Lk 12:47-48
25:3 [i]2Co 11:24 [j]Job 18:3
25:4 [k]Pr 12:10; 1Co 9:9*; 1Ti 5:18*
25:5 [l]Mt 22:24; Mk 12:19; Lk 20:28
25:6 [m]Ge 38:9; Ru 4:5,10

[a] 8 The Hebrew word was used for various diseases affecting the skin—not necessarily leprosy.

either party could begin the divorce proceedings, it was considered a Gentile custom for the wife to do so (Mk 10:11–12). Because of the strength of the family unit, divorce was in actual fact uncommon among the Hebrews.

24:8 See "Skin Diseases in the Ancient World" on page 171.

24:13 In the East, in ancient times as now, the very poor slept on the ground, their outer garments serving as both mattress and blanket. The law, therefore, did not allow such a garment to be kept in pledge after sunset, in order to prevent the man from being without covering (v. 13).

24:16 Regarding murder/manslaughter, see the note on 19:21.

To prevent the work of the "avenger" (see also the note on 19:15–21) from becoming a family vendetta, Old Testament law appointed cities of refuge to which an individual guilty of manslaughter could flee for safety and where the avenger was not permitted to enter (see "Cities of Refuge" on p. 334). Also, the Old Testament insisted that children could not be punished for their parent's crime or vice versa.

24:19 For a discussion of sheaves and threshing, see the note on Ruth 2:7. See also "The Threshing Floor" on page 608 and "Food and Agriculture" on page 390.

25:2–3 Scourging by lashing was a common form of punishment in ancient times. The Israelite (and later Jewish) law authorized it for certain religious offenses.

25:4 Mosaic Law forbade the muzzling of oxen when they were treading out the grain (threshing). This was a simple, humane command, in accordance with the kindly spirit of much of the law. Paul made an interesting use of this injunction in 1 Corinthians 9:9 and 1 Timothy 5:18, where he quoted the command in support of his thesis: "The worker deserves his wages."

For a discussion of the threshing floor, see the note on Ruth 3:4–7. See also "The Threshing Floor" on page 608.

25:7 [n]Ru 4:1-2, 5-6 of a brother-in-law to me."[n] 8Then the elders of his town shall summon him and talk to him. If he per-
sists in saying, "I do not want to marry her," 9his brother's widow shall go up to him in the presence of
25:9 [o]Ru 4:7-8, 11 the elders, take off one of his sandals,[o] spit in his face and say, "This is what is done to the man who will
not build up his brother's family line." 10That man's line shall be known in Israel as The Family of the
Unsandaled.
11If two men are fighting and the wife of one of them comes to rescue her husband from his assail-
ant, and she reaches out and seizes him by his private parts, 12you shall cut off her hand. Show her no
25:12 [p]Dt 19:13 pity.[p]
25:13 [q]Lev 19:35-37; Pr 11:1; Eze 45:10; Mic 6:11 13Do not have two differing weights in your bag—one heavy, one light.[q] 14Do not have two differing
measures in your house—one large, one small. 15You must have accurate and honest weights and mea-
sures, so that you may live long[r] in the land the LORD your God is giving you. 16For the LORD your God de-
25:15 [r]Ex 20:12 **25:16** [s]Pr 11:1 tests anyone who does these things, anyone who deals dishonestly.[s]
25:17 [t]Ex 17:8 17Remember what the Amalekites[t] did to you along the way when you came out of Egypt. 18When you
were weary and worn out, they met you on your journey and cut off all who were lagging behind; they
25:18 [u]Ps 36:1; Ro 3:18 had no fear of God.[u] 19When the LORD your God gives you rest from all the enemies around you in the
25:19 [v]1Sa 15:2-3 land he is giving you to possess as an inheritance, you shall blot out the memory of Amalek[v] from un-
der heaven. Do not forget!

Firstfruits and Tithes

26 When you have entered the land the LORD your God is giving you as an inheritance and have tak-
26:2 [w]Ex 22:29; 23:16,19; Nu 18:13; Pr 3:9 [x]Dt 12:5 en possession of it and settled in it, 2take some of the firstfruits[w] of all that you produce from
the soil of the land the LORD your God is giving you and put them in a basket. Then go to the place the
LORD your God will choose as a dwelling for his Name[x] 3and say to the priest in office at the time, "I de-
clare today to the LORD your God that I have come to the land the LORD swore to our forefathers to give
us." 4The priest shall take the basket from your hands and set it down in front of the altar of the LORD
26:5 [y]Hos 12:12 [z]Ge 43:1-2; 45:7, 11; 46:27; Dt 10:22 your God. 5Then you shall declare before the LORD your God: "My father was a wandering Aramean,[y] and
he went down into Egypt with a few people[z] and lived there and became a great nation, powerful and
26:6 [a]Ex 1:11,14 numerous. 6But the Egyptians mistreated us and made us suffer,[a] putting us to hard labor. 7Then we
26:7 [b]Ex 2:23-25 [c]Ex 3:9 cried out to the LORD, the God of our fathers, and the LORD heard our voice[b] and saw[c] our misery, toil
and oppression. 8So the LORD brought us out of Egypt with a mighty hand and an outstretched arm,
26:8 [d]Dt 4:34 with great terror and with miraculous signs and wonders.[d] 9He brought us to this place and gave us
26:9 [e]Ex 3:8 this land, a land flowing with milk and honey;[e] 10and now I bring the firstfruits of the soil that you,
O LORD, have given me." Place the basket before the LORD your God and bow down before him. 11And you
26:11 [f]Dt 12:7 [g]Dt 16:11 and the Levites[f] and the aliens among you shall rejoice[g] in all the good things the LORD your God has
given to you and your household.
26:12 [h]Lev 27:30 [i]Nu 18:24; Dt 14:28-29; Heb 7:5,9 12When you have finished setting aside a tenth[h] of all your produce in the third year, the year of the
tithe,[i] you shall give it to the Levite, the alien, the fatherless and the widow, so that they may eat in your
towns and be satisfied. 13Then say to the LORD your God: "I have removed from my house the sacred
portion and have given it to the Levite, the alien, the fatherless and the widow, according to all you com-
26:13 [j]Ps 119:141,153, 176 manded. I have not turned aside from your commands nor have I forgotten any of them.[j] 14I have not
eaten any of the sacred portion while I was in mourning, nor have I removed any of it while I was un-
26:14 [k]Lev 7:20; Hos 9:4 clean,[k] nor have I offered any of it to the dead. I have obeyed the LORD my God; I have done everything
26:15 [l]Isa 63:15; Zec 2:13 you commanded me. 15Look down from heaven,[l] your holy dwelling place, and bless your people Isra-
el and the land you have given us as you promised on oath to our forefathers, a land flowing with milk
and honey."

Follow the LORD's Commands

16The LORD your God commands you this day to follow these decrees and laws; carefully observe them
26:16 [m]Dt 4:29 with all your heart and with all your soul.[m] 17You have declared this day that the LORD is your God and
26:18 [n]Ex 6:7; 19:5; Dt 7:6; 14:2; 28:9 that you will walk in his ways, that you will keep his decrees, commands and laws, and that you will obey
him. 18And the LORD has declared this day that you are his people, his treasured possession[n] as he

---

25:19 See "The Amalekites" on page 120.
26:5 "Wandering Aramean" is a reference to Jacob, who had wandered from southern Canaan to Haran and back (Ge 27–35) and had later migrated to Egypt (Ge 46:3–7). See "Canaan" on page 324 and "Haran" on page 47.

promised, and that you are to keep all his commands. 19 He has declared that he will set you in praise, fame
and honor high above all the nations[o] he has made and that you will be a people holy[p] to the LORD your 26:19 [o]Dt 4:7-8; 28:1,13,44
God, as he promised. [p]Ex 19:6; Dt 7:6; 1Pe 2:9

The Altar on Mount Ebal

27 Moses and the elders of Israel commanded the people: "Keep all these commands that I give you
today. 2 When you have crossed the Jordan into the land the LORD your God is giving you, set up
some large stones and coat them with plaster.[q] 3 Write on them all the words of this law when you have 27:2 [q]Jos 8:31
crossed over to enter the land the LORD your God is giving you, a land flowing with milk and honey,[r] just 27:3 [r]Dt 26:9
as the LORD, the God of your fathers, promised you. 4 And when you have crossed the Jordan, set up these
stones on Mount Ebal,[s] as I command you today, and coat them with plaster. 5 Build there an altar[t] to the 27:4 [s]Dt 11:29
LORD your God, an altar of stones. Do not use any iron tool[u] upon them. 6 Build the altar of the LORD your 27:5 [t]Jos 8:31 [u]Ex 20:25
God with fieldstones and offer burnt offerings on it to the LORD your God. 7 Sacrifice fellowship offerings[a]
there, eating them and rejoicing in the presence of the LORD your God. 8 And you shall write very clearly
all the words of this law on these stones you have set up."

[a] 7 Traditionally *peace offerings*

27:1—30:20 For a breakdown of chapters 5–34, see the note on 5:26.

27:1–8 Upon entering Canaan, the Israelites were to set up on Mount Ebal inscribed stones and an altar (see "Joshua's Altar on Mount Ebal," below). Writing laws on stones (or even on mountainsides) was common practice in the ancient Near East. Large writing stones, some 8 feet (2.4 m) tall, from before Moses' time have been found. This altar would not replace the tabernacle altar but was for use on special occasions.

ANCIENT TEXTS AND ARTIFACTS

JOSHUA'S ALTAR ON MOUNT EBAL

DEUTERONOMY 27 Both Deuteronomy 27:1–18 and Joshua 8:30–35 describe the, altar the Israelites constructed on Mount Ebal ("Map 2") after entering **Canaan**.[1] A structure discovered on Mount Ebal in 1980 offers tantalizing parallels to the Biblical description of Joshua's altar. Constructed of unworked stones (in the state in which they were originally found), this rectangular structure, roughly 29 feet (9 m) long by 23 feet (7 m) wide, is filled with layers of ash, animal bones, pot**sherds** and stones. Fragments of lime plaster were discovered in the immediate vicinity (cf. Dt 27:2, 4; Jos 8:30–31). In front of the installation a sloping wall divides two stone-paved courtyards, forming a ramp that ascends to the altar (cf. Ex 20:26). A low stone wall encloses the entire site, covering an area of 11,500 square feet (1,070 sq m). Based upon the pottery and associated finds at this open-air cult site, excavators have dated it to the early **Iron Age**,[2] approximately 1200 B.C. (a date significantly later than the conquest).

While it is possible that this is Joshua's altar, a number of indicators suggest that it is not:

- The current dating of the site does not fit with Biblical chronology, which suggests an earlier, fourteenth century (c. 1400 B.C.) date for Joshua and the conquest.[3] **Late Bronze Age** pottery, possibly dating to the fourteenth century B.C., was unearthed at the site, but the main phase, during which the ramped structure was built, appears definitely to date to the later Iron I period.
- Likewise, Biblical sources mention only cattle, sheep, goats, doves and pigeons as valid sacrifices. Remains of these were found, but bones of other species were present as well, especially those of fallow deer.[4]

It is possible that the Iron I structure was constructed on the site of Joshua's earlier altar. The locations of ancient sacred sites tended to persist over time. Although the general tradition of the site's holiness may have been preserved, worship practices may have become heterodox (nontraditional or deviant) if foreign elements had at some point been introduced (such as offering animals other than those prescribed in the Biblical text).[5]

[1]See "Canaan" on page 324. [2]See "Archaeological Periods" chart on page xx in the front of this Bible. [3]See "The Conquest of Canaan" on page 310. [4]See "Sacrifices and Offerings in the Bible and the Ancient Near East" on page 158. [5]See also "Ancient Altars" on page 125.

Curses From Mount Ebal

9Then Moses and the priests, who are Levites, said to all Israel, "Be silent, O Israel, and listen! You have
now become the people of the LORD your God.[v] 10Obey the LORD your God and follow his commands and
decrees that I give you today."

11On the same day Moses commanded the people:
12When you have crossed the Jordan, these tribes shall stand on Mount Gerizim[w] to bless the people:
Simeon, Levi, Judah, Issachar, Joseph and Benjamin.[x] 13And these tribes shall stand on Mount Ebal to
pronounce curses: Reuben, Gad, Asher, Zebulun, Dan and Naphtali.
14The Levites shall recite to all the people of Israel in a loud voice:

15"Cursed is the man who carves an image or casts an idol[y]—a thing detestable to the LORD,
the work of the craftsman's hands—and sets it up in secret."

Then all the people shall say, "Amen!"

16"Cursed is the man who dishonors his father or his mother."[z]

Then all the people shall say, "Amen!"

17"Cursed is the man who moves his neighbor's boundary stone."[a]

Then all the people shall say, "Amen!"

18"Cursed is the man who leads the blind astray on the road."[b]

Then all the people shall say, "Amen!"

19"Cursed is the man who withholds justice from the alien,[c] the fatherless or the widow."[d]

Then all the people shall say, "Amen!"

20"Cursed is the man who sleeps with his father's wife, for he dishonors his father's bed."[e]

Then all the people shall say, "Amen!"

21"Cursed is the man who has sexual relations with any animal."[f]

Then all the people shall say, "Amen!"

22"Cursed is the man who sleeps with his sister, the daughter of his father or the daughter of his
mother."[g]

Then all the people shall say, "Amen!"

23"Cursed is the man who sleeps with his mother-in-law."[h]

Then all the people shall say, "Amen!"

24"Cursed is the man who kills[i] his neighbor secretly."

Then all the people shall say, "Amen!"

25"Cursed is the man who accepts a bribe to kill an innocent person."[j]

Then all the people shall say, "Amen!"

26"Cursed is the man who does not uphold the words of this law by carrying them out."[k]

Then all the people shall say, "Amen!"

Blessings for Obedience

28 If you fully obey the LORD your God and carefully follow all his commands[l] I give you today, the
LORD your God will set you high above all the nations on earth.[m] 2All these blessings will come
upon you[n] and accompany you if you obey the LORD your God:

3You will be blessed[o] in the city and blessed in the country.[p]
4The fruit of your womb will be blessed, and the crops of your land and the young of your live-
stock—the calves of your herds and the lambs of your flocks.[q]
5Your basket and your kneading trough will be blessed.
6You will be blessed when you come in and blessed when you go out.[r]

7The LORD will grant that the enemies who rise up against you will be defeated before you. They will
come at you from one direction but flee from you in seven.[s]
8The LORD will send a blessing on your barns and on everything you put your hand to. The LORD your
God will bless you in the land he is giving you.

27:9 [v]Dt 26:18
27:12 [w]Dt 11:29 [x]Jos 8:35
27:15 [y]Ex 20:4; 34:17; Lev 19:4; 26:1; Dt 4:16,23; 5:8; Isa 44:9
27:16 [z]Ex 20:12; 21:17; Lev 19:3; 20:9
27:17 [a]Dt 19:14; Pr 22:28
27:18 [b]Lev 19:14
27:19 [c]Ex 22:21; Dt 24:19 [d]Dt 10:18
27:20 [e]Lev 18:7; Dt 22:30
27:21 [f]Lev 18:23
27:22 [g]Lev 18:9; 20:17
27:23 [h]Lev 20:14
27:24 [i]Lev 24:17; Nu 35:31
27:25 [j]Ex 23:7-8; Dt 10:17; Eze 22:12
27:26 [k]Jer 11:3; Gal 3:10*
28:1 [l]Ex 15:26; Lev 26:3; Dt 7:12-26 [m]Dt 26:19
28:2 [n]Zec 1:6
28:3 [o]Ps 128:1,4 [p]Ge 39:5
28:4 [q]Ge 49:25; Pr 10:22
28:6 [r]Ps 121:8
28:7 [s]Lev 26:8,17

27:17 Regarding the removal of boundary stones, see the note on 19:14.

9 The LORD will establish you as his holy people,[t] as he promised you on oath, if you keep the com-
mands of the LORD your God and walk in his ways. 10 Then all the peoples on earth will see that you are
called by the name[u] of the LORD, and they will fear you. 11 The LORD will grant you abundant prosperity—
in the fruit of your womb, the young of your livestock and the crops of your ground—in the land he
swore to your forefathers to give you.[v]
12 The LORD will open the heavens, the storehouse of his bounty, to send rain[w] on your land in season
and to bless all the work of your hands. You will lend to many nations but will borrow from none.[x] 13 The
LORD will make you the head, not the tail. If you pay attention to the commands of the LORD your God that
I give you this day and carefully follow them, you will always be at the top, never at the bottom. 14 Do not
turn aside from any of the commands I give you today, to the right or to the left,[y] following other gods
and serving them.

Curses for Disobedience

15 However, if you do not obey[z] the LORD your God and do not carefully follow all his commands and
decrees I am giving you today, all these curses will come upon you and overtake you:[a]

16 You will be cursed in the city and cursed in the country.
17 Your basket and your kneading trough will be cursed.
18 The fruit of your womb will be cursed, and the crops of your land, and the calves of your herds
and the lambs of your flocks.
19 You will be cursed when you come in and cursed when you go out.

20 The LORD will send on you curses,[b] confusion and rebuke[c] in everything you put your hand to, un-
til you are destroyed and come to sudden ruin[d] because of the evil you have done in forsaking him.[a]
21 The LORD will plague you with diseases until he has destroyed you from the land you are entering to pos-
sess.[e] 22 The LORD will strike you with wasting disease, with fever and inflammation, with scorching heat
and drought,[f] with blight and mildew, which will plague you until you perish.[g] 23 The sky over your head
will be bronze, the ground beneath you iron.[h] 24 The LORD will turn the rain of your country into dust
and powder; it will come down from the skies until you are destroyed.
25 The LORD will cause you to be defeated before your enemies. You will come at them from one direc-
tion but flee from them in seven,[i] and you will become a thing of horror to all the kingdoms on earth.[j]
26 Your carcasses will be food for all the birds of the air and the beasts of the earth, and there will be no
one to frighten them away.[k] 27 The LORD will afflict you with the boils of Egypt[l] and with tumors, fester-
ing sores and the itch, from which you cannot be cured. 28 The LORD will afflict you with madness, blind-
ness and confusion of mind. 29 At midday you will grope[m] about like a blind man in the dark. You will be
unsuccessful in everything you do; day after day you will be oppressed and robbed, with no one to res-
cue you.
30 You will be pledged to be married to a woman, but another will take her and ravish her.[n] You will
build a house, but you will not live in it.[o] You will plant a vineyard, but you will not even begin to enjoy
its fruit.[p] 31 Your ox will be slaughtered before your eyes, but you will eat none of it. Your donkey will be
forcibly taken from you and will not be returned. Your sheep will be given to your enemies, and no one
will rescue them. 32 Your sons and daughters will be given to another nation,[q] and you will wear out your
eyes watching for them day after day, powerless to lift a hand. 33 A people that you do not know will eat
what your land and labor produce, and you will have nothing but cruel oppression all your days.[r] 34 The
sights you see will drive you mad. 35 The LORD will afflict your knees and legs with painful boils[s] that can-
not be cured, spreading from the soles of your feet to the top of your head.
36 The LORD will drive you and the king[t] you set over you to a nation unknown to you or your fathers.[u]
There you will worship other gods, gods of wood and stone.[v] 37 You will become a thing of horror and an
object of scorn and ridicule to all the nations where the LORD will drive you.[w]
38 You will sow much seed in the field but you will harvest little,[x] because locusts will devour[y] it. 39 You
will plant vineyards and cultivate them but you will not drink the wine or gather the grapes, because

28:9 [t]Ex 19:6; Dt 7:6
28:10 [u]2Ch 7:14
28:11 [v]Dt 30:9; Pr 10:22
28:12 [w]Lev 26:4 [x]Dt 15:3,6
28:14 [y]Dt 5:32
28:15 [z]Lev 26:14 [a]Jos 23:15; Da 9:11; Mal 2:2
28:20 [b]Mal 2:2 [c]Isa 51:20; 66:15 [d]Dt 4:26
28:21 [e]Lev 26:25; Jer 24:10
28:22 [f]Lev 26:16 [g]Am 4:9
28:23 [h]Lev 26:19
28:25 [i]Isa 30:17 [j]Jer 15:4; 24:9; Eze 23:46
28:26 [k]Jer 7:33; 16:4; 34:20
28:27 [l]ver 60-61; 1Sa 5:6
28:29 [m]Job 5:14; Isa 59:10
28:30 [n]Job 31:10; Jer 8:10 [o]Am 5:11 [p]Jer 12:13
28:32 [q]ver 41
28:33 [r]Jer 5:15-17
28:35 [s]ver 27
28:36 [t]2Ki 17:4, 6; 24:12,14; 25:7, 11 [u]Jer 16:13 [v]Dt 4:28
28:37 [w]Jer 24:9
28:38 [x]Mic 6:15; Hag 1:6,9 [y]Joel 1:4

[a] 20 Hebrew *me*

28:9–10 When a person gave his own name to another, it signified the joining of the two in very close unity, as when God gave his name to Israel. See "Naming of Children" on page 28.

28:23–24 See the note on 11:10–12 for a discussion of annual rainfall in the region.

28:39 [z]Isa 5:10; 17:10-11 worms will eat them.[z] 40 You will have olive trees throughout your country but you will not use the oil,
28:40 [a]Mic 6:15 because the olives will drop off.[a] 41 You will have sons and daughters but you will not keep them, because
28:41 [b]ver 32 they will go into captivity.[b] 42 Swarms of locusts will take over all your trees and the crops of your land.
43 The alien who lives among you will rise above you higher and higher, but you will sink lower and
28:43 [c]ver 13 28:44 [d]ver 12 [e]ver 13 lower.[c] 44 He will lend to you, but you will not lend to him.[d] He will be the head, but you will be the tail.[e]
28:45 [f]ver 15 45 All these curses will come upon you. They will pursue you and overtake you until you are destroyed,[f]
because you did not obey the LORD your God and observe the commands and decrees he gave you. 46 They
28:46 [g]Isa 8:18; Eze 14:8 will be a sign and a wonder to you and your descendants forever.[g] 47 Because you did not serve[h] the LORD
28:47 [h]Dt 32:15 [i]Ne 9:35 your God joyfully and gladly[i] in the time of prosperity, 48 therefore in hunger and thirst, in nakedness
28:48 [j]Jer 28:13-14 and dire poverty, you will serve the enemies the LORD sends against you. He will put an iron yoke[j] on your
neck until he has destroyed you.
28:49 [k]Jer 5:15; 6:22 [l]La 4:19; Hos 8:1 49 The LORD will bring a nation against you from far away, from the ends of the earth,[k] like an eagle[l]
swooping down, a nation whose language you will not understand, 50 a fierce-looking nation without re-
28:50 [m]Isa 47:6 spect for the old[m] or pity for the young. 51 They will devour the young of your livestock and the crops of
your land until you are destroyed. They will leave you no grain, new wine or oil, nor any calves of your
28:51 [n]ver 33 herds or lambs of your flocks until you are ruined.[n] 52 They will lay siege to all the cities throughout your
land until the high fortified walls in which you trust fall down. They will besiege all the cities through-
28:52 [o]Jer 10:18; Zep 1:14-16,17 out the land the LORD your God is giving you.[o]
53 Because of the suffering that your enemy will inflict on you during the siege, you will eat the fruit
28:53 [p]Lev 26:29; 2Ki 6:28-29; Jer 19:9; La 2:20; 4:10 of the womb, the flesh of the sons and daughters the LORD your God has given you.[p] 54 Even the most gen-
tle and sensitive man among you will have no compassion on his own brother or the wife he loves or his
surviving children, 55 and he will not give to one of them any of the flesh of his children that he is eating.
It will be all he has left because of the suffering your enemy will inflict on you during the siege of all your
28:56 [q]ver 54 cities. 56 The most gentle and sensitive[q] woman among you—so sensitive and gentle that she would not
venture to touch the ground with the sole of her foot—will begrudge the husband she loves and her own
son or daughter 57 the afterbirth from her womb and the children she bears. For she intends to eat them
secretly during the siege and in the distress that your enemy will inflict on you in your cities.
58 If you do not carefully follow all the words of this law, which are written in this book, and do not re-
28:58 [r]Mal 1:14 [s]Ex 6:3 vere[r] this glorious and awesome name[s]—the LORD your God— 59 the LORD will send fearful plagues on
you and your descendants, harsh and prolonged disasters, and severe and lingering illnesses. 60 He will
28:60 [t]ver 27 bring upon you all the diseases of Egypt[t] that you dreaded, and they will cling to you. 61 The LORD will also
bring on you every kind of sickness and disaster not recorded in this Book of the Law, until you are de-
28:61 [u]Dt 4:25-26 stroyed.[u] 62 You who were as numerous as the stars in the sky[v] will be left but few in number, because
28:62 [v]Dt 4:27; 10:22; Ne 9:23 you did not obey the LORD your God. 63 Just as it pleased[w] the LORD to make you prosper and increase in
28:63 [w]Jer 32:41 [x]Pr 1:26 [y]Jer 12:14; 45:4 number, so it will please[x] him to ruin and destroy you. You will be uprooted[y] from the land you are en-
tering to possess.
28:64 [z]Lev 26:33; Dt 4:27 [a]Ne 1:8 64 Then the LORD will scatter[z] you among all nations,[a] from one end of the earth to the other. There you
will worship other gods—gods of wood and stone, which neither you nor your fathers have known.
65 Among those nations you will find no repose, no resting place for the sole of your foot. There the LORD
28:65 [b]Lev 26:16,36 will give you an anxious mind, eyes weary with longing, and a despairing heart.[b] 66 You will live in con-
stant suspense, filled with dread both night and day, never sure of your life. 67 In the morning you will say,
"If only it were evening!" and in the evening, "If only it were morning!"—because of the terror that will
28:67 [c]ver 34; Job 7:4 fill your hearts and the sights that your eyes will see.[c] 68 The LORD will send you back in ships to Egypt
on a journey I said you should never make again. There you will offer yourselves for sale to your ene-
mies as male and female slaves, but no one will buy you.

Renewal of the Covenant

29:1 [d]Dt 5:2-3 **29** These are the terms of the covenant the LORD commanded Moses to make with the Israelites in
Moab, in addition to the covenant he had made with them at Horeb.[d]
2 Moses summoned all the Israelites and said to them:

29:2 [e]Ex 19:4 Your eyes have seen all that the LORD did in Egypt to Pharaoh, to all his officials and to all his land.[e]
29:3 [f]Dt 4:34; 7:19 3 With your own eyes you saw those great trials, those miraculous signs and great wonders.[f] 4 But to this
29:4 [g]Isa 6:10; Ac 28:26-27; Ro 11:8*; Eph 4:18 day the LORD has not given you a mind that understands or eyes that see or ears that hear.[g] 5 During the
forty years that I led you through the desert, your clothes did not wear out, nor did the sandals on your

feet.[h] 6You ate no bread and drank no wine or other fermented drink. I did this so that you might know 29:5 [h]Dt 8:4
that I am the LORD your God.[i] 29:6 [i]Dt 8:3
7When you reached this place, Sihon[j] king of Heshbon and Og king of Bashan came out to fight against 29:7 [j]Dt 2:32; 3:1 [k]Nu 21:21-24,33-35
us, but we defeated them.[k] 8We took their land and gave it as an inheritance to the Reubenites, the Gad-
ites and the half-tribe of Manasseh.[l] 29:8 [l]Nu 32:33; Dt 3:12-13
9Carefully follow[m] the terms of this covenant, so that you may prosper in everything you do.[n] 10All of 29:9 [m]Dt 4:6; Jos 1:7 [n]1Ki 2:3
you are standing today in the presence of the LORD your God—your leaders and chief men, your elders
and officials, and all the other men of Israel, 11together with your children and your wives, and the aliens
living in your camps who chop your wood and carry your water.[o] 12You are standing here in order to en- 29:11 [o]Jos 9:21, 23,27
ter into a covenant with the LORD your God, a covenant the LORD is making with you this day and sealing
with an oath, 13to confirm you this day as his people,[p] that he may be your God[q] as he promised you and 29:13 [p]Dt 28:9 [q]Ge 17:7; Ex 6:7
as he swore to your fathers, Abraham, Isaac and Jacob. 14I am making this covenant,[r] with its oath, not 29:14 [r]Jer 31:31
only with you 15who are standing here with us today in the presence of the LORD our God but also with
those who are not here today.[s] 29:15 [s]Ac 2:39
16You yourselves know how we lived in Egypt and how we passed through the countries on the way
here. 17You saw among them their detestable images and idols of wood and stone, of silver and gold.[t] 29:17 [t]Dt 28:36
18Make sure there is no man or woman, clan or tribe among you today whose heart turns away from the
LORD our God to go and worship the gods of those nations; make sure there is no root among you that
produces such bitter poison.[u] 29:18 [u]Dt 11:16; Heb 12:15
19When such a person hears the words of this oath, he invokes a blessing on himself and therefore
thinks, "I will be safe, even though I persist in going my own way." This will bring disaster on the wa-

Moab

DEUTERONOMY 29 Surprisingly little is known of **Moab**, a neighbor and frequent enemy of Israel. The information we have can be summarized succinctly:

✣ *Moabite Territory*:

Moab proper (see Ge 19:30–38 for origins of Moab) lay between the deep gorges of the Arnon River in the north (Nu 21:13) and the Zered River in the south ("Map 4"). Moabite territory also included the "plains of Moab," situated in the Jordan Valley northeast of the Dead Sea (cf. Nu 22:1; Dt 34:1).

Numerous Biblical events related to Moab are connected to yet another area, the tableland north of the Arnon. This fertile agricultural zone was highly contested and regularly changed hands (Nu 21:21–32; Jdg 11:14–27). Thus, with few exceptions (cf. Ruth), Moabites and Israelites remained in almost steady conflict over the land (Nu 22–24; Jer 48).

✣ *Moabite History and Culture*:

Moabites were closely related to the Israelites, as attested by the Biblical account linking Moab to Lot (Ge 19:37). The Moabite language was similar to Biblical Hebrew.

Moabite territory was known and recognized from the time of Moses (Nu 21:10–20; Dt 2:9–19). The Moabite king at the time of the conquest was Balak (Nu 22–24).

A Moabite ruler, Eglon, oppressed Israel during the Judges period (Jdg 3:12–30).

Moabite territory was at times under Israelite control (2Sa 8:2), but the inhabitants were known to rebel and break free of Israelite influence (2Ki 1:1; 3:4–27).

Archaeological evidence suggests that Moab was dominated by **Assyria** during the eighth century B.C. Moab was conquered by **Nebuchadnezzar** around 582 B.C., after which it ceased to exist as an identifiable entity.[1] The land was subsequently occupied by other peoples, such as the Nabatean Arabs.

The Moabite national god was Chemosh, but the people were thoroughly polytheistic.

✣ *Archaeology and Moab*:

There is evidence of an increase in Moabite settlement during the **Iron** I[2] period (1200–1000 B.C.), particularly in the form of small fortified farmsteads. However, it is difficult to make precise historical connections to the Moabites or to Israelite settlements in **Transjordan** (Nu 21:21–35; 32; Dt 2–3; Jos 13).[3]

In contrast, the Mesha Inscription from the ninth century B.C. provides clear information about the wars between Israel and Moab (cf. 2Ki 3). This inscription attests to the regional importance of Moab during Israel's monarchy and is the most significant archaeological artifact discovered to date from Moab.[4]

Assyrian, and possibly Egyptian, texts also mention Moab.

[1]See "Nebuchadnezzar" on page 571. [2]See "Archaeological Periods" chart on page xx in the front of this Bible. [3]See "Changes in Canaan" on page 358. [4]See "The Mesha (Moabite) Stone" on page 530.

tered land as well as the dry.[a] 20The LORD will never be willing to forgive him; his wrath and zeal[v] will
burn[w] against that man. All the curses written in this book will fall upon him, and the LORD will blot[x] out
his name from under heaven. 21The LORD will single him out from all the tribes of Israel for disaster, ac-
cording to all the curses of the covenant written in this Book of the Law.
22Your children who follow you in later generations and foreigners who come from distant lands will
see the calamities that have fallen on the land and the diseases with which the LORD has afflicted it.[y]
23The whole land will be a burning waste[z] of salt[a] and sulfur—nothing planted, nothing sprouting, no
vegetation growing on it. It will be like the destruction of Sodom and Gomorrah,[b] Admah and Zeboiim,
which the LORD overthrew in fierce anger. 24All the nations will ask: "Why has the LORD done this to this
land?[c] Why this fierce, burning anger?"
25And the answer will be: "It is because this people abandoned the covenant of the LORD, the God of
their fathers, the covenant he made with them when he brought them out of Egypt. 26They went off and
worshiped other gods and bowed down to them, gods they did not know, gods he had not given them.
27Therefore the LORD's anger burned against this land, so that he brought on it all the curses written in
this book.[d] 28In furious anger and in great wrath the LORD uprooted[e] them from their land and thrust
them into another land, as it is now."
29The secret things belong to the LORD our God, but the things revealed belong to us and to our chil-
dren forever, that we may follow all the words of this law.

Prosperity After Turning to the LORD

30 When all these blessings and curses[f] I have set before you come upon you and you take them to
heart wherever the LORD your God disperses you among the nations,[g] 2and when you and your
children return[h] to the LORD your God and obey him with all your heart and with all your soul accord-
ing to everything I command you today, 3then the LORD your God will restore your fortunes[b][i] and have
compassion on you and gather[j] you again from all the nations where he scattered you.[k] 4Even if you have
been banished to the most distant land under the heavens, from there the LORD your God will gather you
and bring you back.[l] 5He will bring[m] you to the land that belonged to your fathers, and you will take pos-
session of it. He will make you more prosperous and numerous than your fathers. 6The LORD your God
will circumcise your hearts and the hearts of your descendants,[n] so that you may love him with all your
heart and with all your soul, and live. 7The LORD your God will put all these curses on your enemies who
hate and persecute you.[o] 8You will again obey the LORD and follow all his commands I am giving you to-
day. 9Then the LORD your God will make you most prosperous in all the work of your hands and in the
fruit of your womb, the young of your livestock and the crops of your land.[p] The LORD will again delight
in you and make you prosperous, just as he delighted in your fathers, 10if you obey the LORD your God and
keep his commands and decrees that are written in this Book of the Law and turn to the LORD your God
with all your heart and with all your soul.[q]

The Offer of Life or Death

11Now what I am commanding you today is not too difficult for you or beyond your reach.[r] 12It is not
up in heaven, so that you have to ask, "Who will ascend into heaven to get it and proclaim it to us so we
may obey it?"[s] 13Nor is it beyond the sea, so that you have to ask, "Who will cross the sea to get it and pro-
claim it to us so we may obey it?" 14No, the word is very near you; it is in your mouth and in your heart
so you may obey it.
15See, I set before you today life and prosperity, death and destruction.[t] 16For I command you today
to love the LORD your God, to walk in his ways, and to keep his commands, decrees and laws; then you
will live and increase, and the LORD your God will bless you in the land you are entering to possess.
17But if your heart turns away and you are not obedient, and if you are drawn away to bow down to

29:20 [v]Eze 23:25 [w]Ps 74:1; 79:5 [x]Ex 32:33; Dt 9:14
29:22 [y]Jer 19:8
29:23 [z]Isa 34:9 [a]Jer 17:6 [b]Ge 19:24,25; Zep 2:9
29:24 [c]1Ki 9:8; Jer 22:8-9
29:27 [d]Da 9:11, 13,14
29:28 [e]1Ki 14:15; 2Ch 7:20; Ps 52:5; Pr 2:22
30:1 [f]ver 15,19; Dt 11:26 [g]Lev 26:40-45; Dt 28:64; 29:28; 1Ki 8:47
30:2 [h]Dt 4:30; Ne 1:9
30:3 [i]Ps 126:4 [j]Ps 147:2; Jer 32:37; Eze 34:13 [k]Jer 29:14
30:4 [l]Ne 1:8-9; Isa 43:6
30:5 [m]Jer 29:14
30:6 [n]Dt 10:16; Jer 32:39
30:7 [o]Dt 7:15
30:9 [p]Dt 28:11; Jer 31:28; 32:41
30:10 [q]Dt 4:29
30:11 [r]Isa 45:19, 23
30:12 [s]Ro 10:6*
30:15 [t]Dt 11:26

a 19 Or *way, in order to add drunkenness to thirst."* *b 3* Or *will bring you back from captivity*

30:19–20 Throughout the book of Deuteronomy, the Israelites were confronted with the demands of God's governmental omnipotence, redemptive grace and consuming jealousy. They were to show their consecration to the Lord by obeying his mandate to establish his kingdom in his land. That involved conquering the land, by which divine judgment would be visited on those who worshiped alien gods in God's land, and also establishing a community of mutual caring in common service to the Lord within the promised land. This covenant calling was not an unconditional license to national privilege and prosperity. By the covenant oath Israel came under both the curses and the blessings that were to be meted out according to God's righteous judgment. The covenant relationship called for responsible decision making.

other gods and worship them, 18 I declare to you this day that you will certainly be destroyed.[u] You will
not live long in the land you are crossing the Jordan to enter and possess.
19 This day I call heaven and earth as witnesses against you[v] that I have set before you life and death,
blessings and curses.[w] Now choose life, so that you and your children may live 20 and that you may love[x]
the LORD your God, listen to his voice, and hold fast to him. For the LORD is your life,[y] and he will give you
many years in the land he swore to give to your fathers, Abraham, Isaac and Jacob.

Joshua to Succeed Moses

31 Then Moses went out and spoke these words to all Israel: 2 "I am now a hundred and twenty years
old[z] and I am no longer able to lead you.[a] The LORD has said to me, 'You shall not cross the Jor-
dan.'[b] 3 The LORD your God himself will cross[c] over ahead of you.[d] He will destroy these nations before
you, and you will take possession of their land. Joshua also will cross[e] over ahead of you, as the LORD
said. 4 And the LORD will do to them what he did to Sihon and Og, the kings of the Amorites, whom he de-
stroyed along with their land. 5 The LORD will deliver[f] them to you, and you must do to them all that I
have commanded you. 6 Be strong and courageous.[g] Do not be afraid or terrified[h] because of them, for
the LORD your God goes with you;[i] he will never leave you[j] nor forsake[k] you."
7 Then Moses summoned Joshua and said[l] to him in the presence of all Israel, "Be strong and coura-
geous, for you must go with this people into the land that the LORD swore to their forefathers to give them,
and you must divide it among them as their inheritance. 8 The LORD himself goes before you and will be
with you;[m] he will never leave you nor forsake you. Do not be afraid; do not be discouraged."

The Reading of the Law

9 So Moses wrote down this law and gave it to the priests, the sons of Levi, who carried[n] the ark of the
covenant of the LORD, and to all the elders of Israel. 10 Then Moses commanded them: "At the end of ev-
ery seven years, in the year for canceling debts,[o] during the Feast of Tabernacles,[p] 11 when all Israel comes
to appear[q] before the LORD your God at the place he will choose, you shall read this law[r] before them in
their hearing. 12 Assemble the people—men, women and children, and the aliens living in your towns—
so they can listen and learn[s] to fear the LORD your God and follow carefully all the words of this law.
13 Their children,[t] who do not know this law, must hear it and learn to fear the LORD your God as long as
you live in the land you are crossing the Jordan to possess."

Israel's Rebellion Predicted

14 The LORD said to Moses, "Now the day of your death[u] is near. Call Joshua and present yourselves at
the Tent of Meeting, where I will commission him." So Moses and Joshua came and presented themselves
at the Tent of Meeting.
15 Then the LORD appeared at the Tent in a pillar of cloud, and the cloud stood over the entrance to
the Tent.[v] 16 And the LORD said to Moses: "You are going to rest with your fathers, and these people will
soon prostitute[w] themselves to the foreign gods of the land they are entering. They will forsake[x] me and
break the covenant I made with them. 17 On that day I will become angry[y] with them and forsake[z] them;
I will hide[a] my face from them, and they will be destroyed. Many disasters and difficulties will come
upon them, and on that day they will ask, 'Have not these disasters come upon us because our God is
not with us?'[b] 18 And I will certainly hide my face on that day because of all their wickedness in turn-
ing to other gods.
19 "Now write down for yourselves this song and teach it to the Israelites and have them sing it, so
that it may be a witness for me against them. 20 When I have brought them into the land flowing with
milk and honey, the land I promised on oath to their forefathers,[c] and when they eat their fill and
thrive, they will turn to other gods[d] and worship them, rejecting me and breaking my covenant.[e] 21 And
when many disasters and difficulties come upon them,[f] this song will testify against them, because it
will not be forgotten by their descendants. I know what they are disposed to do,[g] even before I bring
them into the land I promised them on oath." 22 So Moses wrote[h] down this song that day and taught
it to the Israelites.

30:18 [u]Dt 8:19
30:19 [v]Dt 4:26 [w]ver 1
30:20 [x]Dt 6:5; 10:20 [y]Ps 27:1; Jn 11:25
31:2 [z]Dt 34:7 [a]Nu 27:17; 1Ki 3:7 [b]Dt 3:23, 26
31:3 [c]Nu 27:18 [d]Dt 9:3 [e]Dt 3:28
31:5 [f]Dt 7:2
31:6 [g]Jos 10:25; 1Ch 22:13 [h]Dt 7:18 [i]Dt 1:29; 20:4 [j]Jos 1:5 [k]Heb 13:5*
31:7 [l]Dt 1:38; 3:28
31:8 [m]Ex 13:21; 33:14
31:9 [n]ver 25; Nu 4:15; Jos 3:3
31:10 [o]Dt 15:1 [p]Lev 23:34
31:11 [q]Dt 16:16 [r]Jos 8:34-35; 2Ki 23:2
31:12 [s]Dt 4:10
31:13 [t]Dt 11:2; Ps 78:6-7
31:14 [u]Nu 27:13; Dt 32:49-50
31:15 [v]Ex 33:9
31:16 [w]Jdg 2:12 [x]Jdg 10:6,13
31:17 [y]Jdg 2:14, 20 [z]Jdg 6:13; 2Ch 15:2 [a]Dt 32:20; Isa 1:15; 8:17 [b]Nu 14:42
31:20 [c]Dt 6:10-12 [d]Dt 32:15-17 [e]ver 16
31:21 [f]ver 17 [g]Hos 5:3
31:22 [h]ver 19

31:1—34:12 For a breakdown of chapters 5–34, see the note on 5:26.

31:9 Since ancient treaties required that a copy of the treaty be placed before the gods at the religious centers of the nations involved, Israel placed this one in the ark of the covenant (see 33:9).

23 The LORD gave this command[i] to Joshua son of Nun: "Be strong and courageous,[j] for you will bring
the Israelites into the land I promised them on oath, and I myself will be with you."
24 After Moses finished writing in a book the words of this law from beginning to end, 25 he gave this
command to the Levites who carried the ark of the covenant of the LORD: 26 "Take this Book of the Law
and place it beside the ark of the covenant of the LORD your God. There it will remain as a witness against
you.[k] 27 For I know how rebellious and stiff-necked[l] you are. If you have been rebellious against the LORD
while I am still alive and with you, how much more will you rebel after I die! 28 Assemble before me all
the elders of your tribes and all your officials, so that I can speak these words in their hearing and call
heaven and earth to testify against them.[m] 29 For I know that after my death you are sure to become utterly
corrupt[n] and to turn from the way I have commanded you. In days to come, disaster[o] will fall upon you
because you will do evil in the sight of the LORD and provoke him to anger by what your hands have
made."

The Song of Moses

30 And Moses recited the words of this song from beginning to end in the hearing of the whole assembly of Israel:

32

Listen, O heavens,[p] and I will speak;
hear, O earth, the words of my mouth.
2 Let my teaching fall like rain
and my words descend like dew,[q]
like showers[r] on new grass,
like abundant rain on tender plants.

3 I will proclaim the name of the LORD.[s]
Oh, praise the greatness[t] of our God!
4 He is the Rock,[u] his works are perfect,[v]
and all his ways are just.
A faithful God[w] who does no wrong,
upright and just is he.

5 They have acted corruptly toward him;
to their shame they are no longer his children,
but a warped and crooked generation.[a][x]
6 Is this the way you repay[y] the LORD,
O foolish and unwise people?[z]
Is he not your Father,[a] your Creator,[b]
who made you and formed you?[b]

7 Remember the days of old;
consider the generations long past.
Ask your father and he will tell you,
your elders, and they will explain to you.[c]
8 When the Most High gave the nations their inheritance,
when he divided all mankind,[d]
he set up boundaries for the peoples
according to the number of the sons of Israel.[c]
9 For the LORD's portion[e] is his people,
Jacob his allotted inheritance.[f]

10 In a desert[g] land he found him,
in a barren and howling waste.
He shielded him and cared for him;
he guarded him as the apple of his eye,[h]

31:23 [i]ver 7 [j]Jos 1:6
31:26 [k]ver 19
31:27 [l]Ex 32:9; Dt 9:6,24
31:28 [m]Dt 4:26; 30:19; 32:1
31:29 [n]Dt 32:5; Jdg 2:19 [o]Dt 28:15
32:1 [p]Isa 1:2
32:2 [q]Isa 55:11 [r]Ps 72:6
32:3 [s]Ex 33:19 [t]Dt 3:24
32:4 [u]ver 15,18, 30 [v]2Sa 22:31 [w]Dt 7:9
32:5 [x]Dt 31:29
32:6 [y]Ps 116:12 [z]Ps 74:2 [a]Dt 1:31; Isa 63:16 [b]ver 15
32:7 [c]Ex 13:14
32:8 [d]Ge 11:8; Ac 17:26
32:9 [e]Jer 10:16 [f]1Ki 8:51,53
32:10 [g]Jer 2:6 [h]Ps 17:8; Zec 2:8

[a] 5 Or *Corrupt are they and not his children, / a generation warped and twisted to their shame* [b] 6 Or *Father, who bought you*
[c] 8 Masoretic Text; Dead Sea Scrolls (see also Septuagint) *sons of God*

11 like an eagle that stirs up its nest
and hovers over its young,[i]
that spreads its wings to catch them
and carries them on its pinions.
12 The LORD alone led him;
no foreign god was with him.[j]

13 He made him ride on the heights[k] of the land
and fed him with the fruit of the fields.
He nourished him with honey from the rock,
and with oil[l] from the flinty crag,
14 with curds and milk from herd and flock
and with fattened lambs and goats,
with choice rams of Bashan
and the finest kernels of wheat.[m]
You drank the foaming blood of the grape.[n]

15 Jeshurun[a] grew fat[o] and kicked;
filled with food, he became heavy and sleek.
He abandoned[p] the God who made him
and rejected the Rock[q] his Savior.
16 They made him jealous[r] with their foreign gods
and angered[s] him with their detestable idols.
17 They sacrificed to demons, which are not God—
gods they had not known,[t]
gods that recently appeared,[u]
gods your fathers did not fear.
18 You deserted the Rock, who fathered you;
you forgot[v] the God who gave you birth.

19 The LORD saw this and rejected them[w]
because he was angered by his sons and daughters.[x]
20 "I will hide my face[y] from them," he said,
"and see what their end will be;
for they are a perverse generation,[z]
children who are unfaithful.
21 They made me jealous[a] by what is no god
and angered me with their worthless idols.[b]
I will make them envious by those who are not a people;
I will make them angry by a nation that has no understanding.[c]
22 For a fire has been kindled by my wrath,
one that burns to the realm of death[b] below.[d]
It will devour the earth and its harvests
and set afire the foundations of the mountains.

23 "I will heap calamities[e] upon them
and spend my arrows[f] against them.
24 I will send wasting famine against them,
consuming pestilence[g] and deadly plague;[h]
I will send against them the fangs of wild beasts,[i]
the venom of vipers[j] that glide in the dust.
25 In the street the sword will make them childless;
in their homes terror will reign.[k]
Young men and young women will perish,
infants and gray-haired men.[l]

32:11 [i]Ex 19:4
32:12 [j]ver 39
32:13 [k]Isa 58:14 [l]Job 29:6
32:14 [m]Ps 81:16; 147:14 [n]Ge 49:11
32:15 [o]Dt 31:20 [p]ver 6; Isa 1:4,28 [q]ver 4
32:16 [r]1Co 10:22 [s]Ps 78:58
32:17 [t]Dt 28:64 [u]Jdg 5:8
32:18 [v]Isa 17:10
32:19 [w]Jer 44:21-23 [x]Ps 106:40
32:20 [y]Dt 31:17, 29 [z]ver 5
32:21 [a]1Co 10:22 [b]1Ki 16:13,26 [c]Ro 10:19*
32:22 [d]Ps 18:7-8; Jer 15:14; La 4:11
32:23 [e]Dt 29:21 [f]Ps 7:13; Eze 5:16
32:24 [g]Dt 28:22 [h]Ps 91:6 [i]Lev 26:22 [j]Am 5:18-19
32:25 [k]Eze 7:15 [l]2Ch 36:17; La 2:21

[a] 15 *Jeshurun* means *the upright one,* that is, Israel. [b] 22 Hebrew *to Sheol*

32:26 [m]Dt 4:27 [n]Ps 34:16
32:27 [o]Isa 10:13
32:29 [p]Dt 5:29; Ps 81:13
32:30 [q]Lev 26:8 [r]Ps 44:12
32:33 [s]Ps 58:4
32:34 [t]Jer 2:22; Hos 13:12
32:35 [u]Ro 12:19*; Heb 10:30* [v]Jer 23:12 [w]Eze 7:8-9
32:36 [x]Dt 30:1-3; Ps 135:14; Joel 2:14
32:37 [y]Jdg 10:14; Jer 2:28
32:39 [z]Isa 41:4 [a]Isa 45:5 [b]1Sa 2:6; Ps 68:20 [c]Hos 6:1 [d]Ps 50:22
32:41 [e]Isa 34:6; 66:16; Eze 21:9-10 [f]Jer 50:29
32:42 [g]ver 23 [h]Jer 46:10,14

26 I said I would scatter[m] them
and blot out their memory from mankind,[n]
27 but I dreaded the taunt of the enemy,
lest the adversary misunderstand
and say, 'Our hand has triumphed;
the LORD has not done all this.' "[o]
28 They are a nation without sense,
there is no discernment in them.
29 If only they were wise and would understand this[p]
and discern what their end will be!
30 How could one man chase a thousand,
or two put ten thousand to flight,[q]
unless their Rock had sold them,
unless the LORD had given them up?[r]
31 For their rock is not like our Rock,
as even our enemies concede.
32 Their vine comes from the vine of Sodom
and from the fields of Gomorrah.
Their grapes are filled with poison,
and their clusters with bitterness.
33 Their wine is the venom of serpents,
the deadly poison of cobras.[s]

34 "Have I not kept this in reserve
and sealed it in my vaults?[t]
35 It is mine to avenge; I will repay.[u]
In due time their foot will slip;[v]
their day of disaster is near
and their doom rushes upon them."[w]

36 The LORD will judge his people
and have compassion on his servants[x]
when he sees their strength is gone
and no one is left, slave or free.
37 He will say: "Now where are their gods,
the rock they took refuge in,[y]
38 the gods who ate the fat of their sacrifices
and drank the wine of their drink offerings?
Let them rise up to help you!
Let them give you shelter!

39 "See now that I myself am He![z]
There is no god besides me.[a]
I put to death and I bring to life,[b]
I have wounded and I will heal,[c]
and no one can deliver out of my hand.[d]
40 I lift my hand to heaven and declare:
As surely as I live forever,
41 when I sharpen my flashing sword[e]
and my hand grasps it in judgment,
I will take vengeance on my adversaries
and repay those who hate me.[f]
42 I will make my arrows drunk with blood,[g]
while my sword devours flesh:[h]
the blood of the slain and the captives,
the heads of the enemy leaders."

43 Rejoice,[i] O nations, with his people,[a,b]
for he will avenge the blood of his servants;[j]
he will take vengeance on his enemies
and make atonement for his land and people.[k]

44 Moses came with Joshua[c][l] son of Nun and spoke all the words of this song in the hearing of the peo-
ple. 45 When Moses finished reciting all these words to all Israel, 46 he said to them, "Take to heart all the
words I have solemnly declared to you this day,[m] so that you may command your children to obey
carefully all the words of this law. 47 They are not just idle words for you—they are your life.[n] By them
you will live long in the land you are crossing the Jordan to possess."

Moses to Die on Mount Nebo

48 On that same day the LORD told Moses, 49 "Go up into the Abarim[o] Range to Mount Nebo in Moab,
across from Jericho, and view Canaan, the land I am giving the Israelites as their own possession. 50 There
on the mountain that you have climbed you will die[p] and be gathered to your people, just as your broth-
er Aaron died on Mount Hor and was gathered to his people. 51 This is because both of you broke faith with
me in the presence of the Israelites at the waters of Meribah Kadesh in the Desert of Zin[q] and because
you did not uphold my holiness among the Israelites.[r] 52 Therefore, you will see the land only from a dis-
tance;[s] you will not enter[t] the land I am giving to the people of Israel."

Moses Blesses the Tribes

33 This is the blessing that Moses the man of God[u] pronounced on the Israelites before his death.
2 He said:

"The LORD came from Sinai[v]
and dawned over them from Seir;[w]
he shone forth from Mount Paran.[x]
He came with[d] myriads of holy ones[y]
from the south, from his mountain slopes.[e]
3 Surely it is you who love[z] the people;
all the holy ones are in your hand.[a]
At your feet they all bow down,[b]
and from you receive instruction,
4 the law that Moses gave us,[c]
the possession of the assembly of Jacob.[d]
5 He was king over Jeshurun[f]
when the leaders of the people assembled,
along with the tribes of Israel.

6 "Let Reuben live and not die,
nor[g] his men be few."

7 And this he said about Judah:[e]

"Hear, O LORD, the cry of Judah;
bring him to his people.
With his own hands he defends his cause.
Oh, be his help against his foes!"

8 About Levi he said:

"Your Thummim and Urim[f] belong
to the man you favored.

32:43 [i]Ro 15:10* [j]2Ki 9:7 [k]Ps 65:3; 85:1; Rev 19:2
32:44 [l]Nu 13:8, 16
32:46 [m]Eze 40:4
32:47 [n]Dt 30:20
32:49 [o]Nu 27:12
32:50 [p]Ge 25:8
32:51 [q]Nu 20:11-13 [r]Nu 27:14
32:52 [s]Dt 34:1-3 [t]Dt 1:37
33:1 [u]Jos 14:6
33:2 [v]Ex 19:18; Ps 68:8 [w]Jdg 5:4 [x]Hab 3:3 [y]Da 7:10; Ac 7:53; Rev 5:11
33:3 [z]Hos 11:1 [a]Dt 14:2 [b]Lk 10:39
33:4 [c]Jn 1:17 [d]Ps 119:111
33:7 [e]Ge 49:10
33:8 [f]Ex 28:30

[a] 43 Or *Make his people rejoice, O nations* [b] 43 Masoretic Text; Dead Sea Scrolls (see also Septuagint) *people, / and let all the angels worship him /* [c] 44 Hebrew *Hoshea,* a variant of *Joshua* [d] 2 Or *from* [e] 2 The meaning of the Hebrew for this phrase is uncertain. [f] 5 *Jeshurun* means *the upright one,* that is, Israel; also in verse 26. [g] 6 Or *but let*

33:8 See "The Urim and Thummim" on page 136.

You tested him at Massah;
you contended with him at the waters of Meribah.[g]
9 He said of his father and mother,[h]
'I have no regard for them.'
He did not recognize his brothers
or acknowledge his own children,
but he watched over your word
and guarded your covenant.[i]
10 He teaches your precepts to Jacob
and your law to Israel.[j]
He offers incense before you
and whole burnt offerings on your altar.[k]
11 Bless all his skills, O LORD,
and be pleased with the work of his hands.[l]
Smite the loins of those who rise up against him;
strike his foes till they rise no more."

12 About Benjamin he said:

"Let the beloved of the LORD rest secure in him,[m]
for he shields him all day long,
and the one the LORD loves rests between his shoulders.[n]"

13 About Joseph[o] he said:

"May the LORD bless his land
with the precious dew from heaven above
and with the deep waters that lie below;[p]
14 with the best the sun brings forth
and the finest the moon can yield;
15 with the choicest gifts of the ancient mountains[q]
and the fruitfulness of the everlasting hills;
16 with the best gifts of the earth and its fullness
and the favor of him who dwelt in the burning bush.[r]
Let all these rest on the head of Joseph,
on the brow of the prince among[a] his brothers.
17 In majesty he is like a firstborn bull;
his horns are the horns of a wild ox.[s]
With them he will gore[t] the nations,
even those at the ends of the earth.
Such are the ten thousands of Ephraim;
such are the thousands of Manasseh."

18 About Zebulun[u] he said:

"Rejoice, Zebulun, in your going out,
and you, Issachar, in your tents.
19 They will summon peoples to the mountain[v]
and there offer sacrifices of righteousness;[w]
they will feast on the abundance of the seas,[x]
on the treasures hidden in the sand."

33:8 gEx 17:7
33:9 hEx 32:26-29
33:9 iMal 2:5
33:10 jLev 10:11; Dt 31:9-13 kPs 51:19
33:11 l2Sa 24:23
33:12 mDt 12:10 nEx 28:12
33:13 oGe 49:25 pGe 27:28
33:15 qHab 3:6
33:16 rEx 3:2
33:17 sNu 23:22 t1Ki 22:11; Ps 44:5
33:18 uGe 49:13-15
33:19 vEx 15:17; Isa 2:3 wPs 4:5 xIsa 60:5,11

[a] 16 Or *of the one separated from*

33:13–16 Under the Lord's blessing, Joseph's land in the central part of Canaan was to be unusually fertile and productive.
33:18–19 Although Zebulun's territory was landlocked by the tribes of Asher and Manasseh, the descendants of Zebulun were within 10 miles (16 km) of the Mediterranean Sea and acquired wealth in maritime trade.

[20]About Gad[y] he said:

"Blessed is he who enlarges Gad's domain!
Gad lives there like a lion,
tearing at arm or head.
[21]He chose the best land for himself;[z]
the leader's portion was kept for him.
When the heads of the people assembled,
he carried out the LORD's righteous will,[a]
and his judgments concerning Israel."

33:20 [y]Ge 49:19
33:21 [z]Nu 32:1-5,31-32 [a]Jos 4:12; 22:1-3

[22]About Dan[b] he said:

"Dan is a lion's cub,
springing out of Bashan."

33:22 [b]Ge 49:16

[23]About Naphtali he said:

"Naphtali is abounding with the favor of the LORD
and is full of his blessing;
he will inherit southward to the lake."

[24]About Asher[c] he said:

"Most blessed of sons is Asher;
let him be favored by his brothers,
and let him bathe his feet in oil.[d]
[25]The bolts of your gates will be iron and bronze,
and your strength will equal your days.[e]

[26]"There is no one like the God of Jeshurun,[f]
who rides on the heavens to help you[g]
and on the clouds in his majesty.
[27]The eternal God is your refuge,[h]
and underneath are the everlasting arms.
He will drive out your enemy before you,[i]
saying, 'Destroy him!'[j]
[28]So Israel will live in safety alone;[k]
Jacob's spring is secure
in a land of grain and new wine,
where the heavens drop dew.[l]
[29]Blessed are you, O Israel![m]
Who is like you,[n]
a people saved by the LORD?[o]
He is your shield and helper[p]
and your glorious sword.
Your enemies will cower before you,
and you will trample down their high places.[a][q]"

33:24 [c]Ge 49:21 [d]Ge 49:20; Job 29:6
33:25 [e]Dt 4:40; 32:47
33:26 [f]Ex 15:11 [g]Ps 104:3
33:27 [h]Ps 90:1 [i]Jos 24:18 [j]Dt 7:2
33:28 [k]Nu 23:9; Jer 23:6 [l]Ge 27:28
33:29 [m]Ps 144:15 [n]Ps 18:44 [o]2Sa 7:23 [p]Ps 115:9-11 [q]Dt 32:13

The Death of Moses

34 Then Moses climbed Mount Nebo from the plains of Moab to the top of Pisgah, across from Jer-
icho.[r] There the LORD showed[s] him the whole land—from Gilead to Dan, [2]all of Naphtali, the
territory of Ephraim and Manasseh, all the land of Judah as far as the western sea,[b][t] [3]the Negev and the
whole region from the Valley of Jericho, the City of Palms,[u] as far as Zoar. [4]Then the LORD said to him,
"This is the land I promised on oath[v] to Abraham, Isaac and Jacob when I said, 'I will give it[w] to your de-
scendants.' I have let you see it with your eyes, but you will not cross[x] over into it."
[5]And Moses the servant of the LORD[y] died[z] there in Moab, as the LORD had said. [6]He buried him[c] in
Moab, in the valley opposite Beth Peor,[a] but to this day no one knows where his grave is.[b] [7]Moses was a

34:1 [r]Dt 32:49 [s]Dt 32:52
34:2 [t]Dt 11:24
34:3 [u]Jdg 1:16; 3:13; 2Ch 28:15
34:4 [v]Ge 28:13 [w]Ge 12:7 [x]Dt 3:27
34:5 [y]Nu 12:7 [z]Dt 32:50; Jos 1:1-2
34:6 [a]Dt 3:29 [b]Jude 1:9

[a] 29 Or *will tread upon their bodies* [b] 2 That is, the Mediterranean [c] 6 Or *He buried*

34:7 [c]Dt 31:2 [d]Ge 27:1
34:8 [e]Ge 50:3,10; 2Sa 11:27
34:9 [f]Ge 41:38; Isa 11:2; Da 6:3 [g]Nu 27:18,23
34:10 [h]Dt 18:15,18 [i]Ex 33:11; Nu 12:6,8; Dt 5:4
34:11 [j]Dt 4:34 [k]Dt 7:19

hundred and twenty years old[c] when he died, yet his eyes were not weak[d] nor his strength gone. 8 The Is-
raelites grieved for Moses in the plains of Moab thirty days, until the time of weeping and mourning[e] was
over.

9 Now Joshua son of Nun was filled with the spirit[a] of wisdom[f] because Moses had laid his hands on
him.[g] So the Israelites listened to him and did what the LORD had commanded Moses.

10 Since then, no prophet has risen in Israel like Moses,[h] whom the LORD knew face to face,[i] 11 who did
all those miraculous signs and wonders[j] the LORD sent him to do in Egypt—to Pharaoh and to all his of-
ficials[k] and to his whole land. 12 For no one has ever shown the mighty power or performed the awesome
deeds that Moses did in the sight of all Israel.

[a] 9 Or *Spirit*

INTRODUCTION TO *Joshua*

AUTHOR, PLACE AND DATE OF WRITING

No one knows for certain who wrote/compiled the book of Joshua or when or where it was written. Scholars have proposed dates ranging from immediately after Joshua's lifetime to the time of Samuel to the early monarchy and even to the postexilic period.

According to early Jewish tradition, Joshua wrote the entire book, except, of course, for the passage concerning his funeral. Several verses do refer to his writing or to those whom he commanded to write (Jos 18:8; 24:25), and in 5:1 and 6 the author described details as though he were present, using the pronouns "us" and "we."

Yet evidence suggesting that the book was written years after Joshua's death includes:

- An eyewitness to the miracle of the sun standing still would not have needed to cite a source (i.e., the Book of Jashar; 10:13).
- The writer used the phrase "to this day" 12 times (e.g., 7:26; 8:29; 15:63), implying that he lived after the events had taken place. On the other hand, some verses (e.g., 6:25) imply that the book, or at least its sources, was written before the generation of Israelites involved in the conquest had died.

Scholars who date the book of Joshua after the end of the monarchy in 586 B.C. consider it to be part of a unified "Deuteronomistic history" of Israel that spans the historical books of Deuteronomy through Kings. This would place its writing about 800 years after the events it records. Some scholars suggest that Samuel may have helped to shape or compile the book.

AUDIENCE

Israelites born after the conquest were the original readers of this book.

CULTURAL FACTS AND HIGHLIGHTS

Joshua continues the story of the conquest from the point at which Deuteronomy left off. The military superpowers who had been players in the action (Hittites, Babylonians, Egyptians) no longer had a significant presence; instead, the Israelites would have to confront a number of independent city-states or groupings of states (cf. 9:1–2; 10:5–20; 11:1–8).

Canaanite culture was thriving during this period of the Late Bronze Age, as illustrated by thousands of artifacts, as well as by the excavated ruins of the ancient kingdom of Ugarit, tombs, altars and pagan temples.

TIMELINE

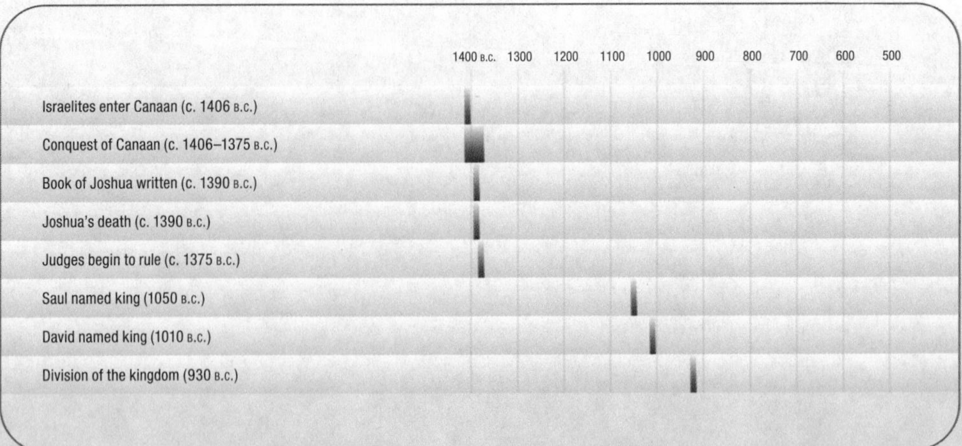

AS YOU READ

Empowered by God and commissioned to replace Moses (Dt 31:23; Jos 1:5), Joshua stood ready to complete Moses' work: to establish Israel—a second generation of former slaves—in the promised land. Be on the alert for evidence that, as God's handpicked spokesperson, Joshua would make every attempt to hold Israel accountable to fulfilling its part of its covenant with God.

Note God's unwavering resolution and intervention in helping the Israelites defeat the idolatrous Canaanites. Pay close attention to the consequences of covenant disobedience at Ai (ch. 7). Think about the significance of Israel's covenant renewal with the one true God (8:30–35; 24:1–27), who had called his people to obey him and to reflect his character. Try to enter vicariously into the joy the Israelites must have felt as they received God's promised gift of land (chs. 13–21).

DID YOU KNOW?

- In the ancient Near East a judicial verdict of the gods was commonly obtained by compelling an accused person to submit to a trial-by-water ordeal. Usually this involved casting the accused into a river. If the person drowned, the gods had found him or her guilty. Here the Israelites engaged in a different kind of trial-by-water ordeal (3:10–11).
- When Israelite officers placed their feet on the necks of great and powerful kings they had subdued, they were recognizing them as frail human beings like everyone else. This practice, widespread in ancient times, is pictured in the artwork of Egypt and Assyria (10:24).
- The use of lots in Old Testament contexts placed everything in God's hands—making it clear that chance *did not* come into the picture (14:1–5).
- Horses and chariots posed an awesome challenge to the Israelites, whose own army was made up exclusively of foot soldiers (11:1–5).
- "Defiled," a term for ritual uncleanness, did not necessarily imply something sinful (22:19).

THEMES

Joshua's themes include:

1. *God, the great warrior.* This book depicts God as a warrior who rescues his people from their enemies (1:1—12:24; cf. Ex 15:3). God's people are still at war today. Indeed, we are engaged in an infinitely more dangerous confrontation—against evil itself (Eph 6:12). But God has given us powerful spiritual weapons (Eph 6:10–18), and we enter this battle confident that Christ has already assured the final outcome by his victory (Col 2:13–15; Rev 19:11–21).

2. *God's faithfulness.* The second half of Joshua (13:1—24:33) portrays God's faithfulness to his promises (21:45; 23:14). As Israel took possession of the land, the ancient promises to Abraham (Ge 12:1–3) became concrete realities. God is a promise keeper, and Christians today have been given "great and precious promises" (2Pe 1:4), every one of which is fulfilled in Jesus (2Co 1:20).

OUTLINE

- I. Preparation and Entrance Into Canaan (1:1—5:12)
- II. Conquest of the Land (5:13—12:24)
  - A. Jericho and Ai (5:13—8:35)
  - B. Gibeonites, Amorites and Southern Cities (9–10)
  - C. Northern Kings (11)
  - D. List of Defeated Kings (12)
- III. The Division of the Land by Tribes (13–21)
- IV. Joshua's Farewell and Death (22–24)

The LORD Commands Joshua

1 After the death of Moses the servant of the LORD,[a] the LORD said to Joshua[b] son of Nun, Moses' aide:
2“Moses my servant is dead. Now then, you and all these people, get ready to cross the Jordan River[c]
into the land I am about to give to them—to the Israelites. 3I will give you every place where you set
your foot,[d] as I promised Moses. 4Your territory will extend from the desert to Lebanon, and from the
great river, the Euphrates[e]—all the Hittite country—to the Great Sea[a] on the west.[f] 5No one will be able
to stand up against you[g] all the days of your life. As I was with[h] Moses, so I will be with you; I will never
leave you nor forsake[i] you.
6“Be strong and courageous, because you will lead these people to inherit the land I swore to their
forefathers[j] to give them. 7Be strong and very courageous. Be careful to obey all the law my servant Mo-
ses gave you; do not turn from it to the right or to the left,[k] that you may be successful wherever you go.[l]
8Do not let this Book of the Law depart from your mouth; meditate on it day and night, so that you may
be careful to do everything written in it. Then you will be prosperous and successful.[m] 9Have I not com-
manded you? Be strong and courageous. Do not be terrified;[n] do not be discouraged, for the LORD your
God will be with you wherever you go.”[o]
10So Joshua ordered the officers of the people: 11“Go through the camp and tell the people, ‘Get your
supplies ready. Three days from now you will cross the Jordan here to go in and take possession[p] of the
land the LORD your God is giving you for your own.’ ”
12But to the Reubenites, the Gadites and the half-tribe of Manasseh,[q] Joshua said, 13“Remember the
command that Moses the servant of the LORD gave you: ‘The LORD your God is giving you rest[r] and has
granted you this land.’ 14Your wives, your children and your livestock may stay in the land that Moses

1:1 [a]Nu 12:7; Dt 34:5 [b]Ex 24:13; Dt 1:38
1:2 [c]ver 11
1:3 [d]Dt 11:24
1:4 [e]Ge 15:18 [f]Nu 34:2-12
1:5 [g]Dt 7:24 [h]Jos 3:7; 6:27 [i]Dt 31:6-8
1:6 [j]Dt 31:23
1:7 [k]Dt 5:32; 28:14 [l]Jos 11:15
1:8 [m]Dt 29:9; Ps 1:1-3
1:9 [n]Ps 27:1 [o]ver 7; Dt 31:7-8; Jer 1:8
1:11 [p]Joel 3:2
1:12 [q]Nu 32:20-22
1:13 [r]Dt 3:18-20

[a] *4* That is, the Mediterranean

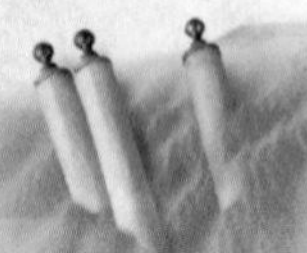

ANCIENT TEXTS AND ARTIFACTS

Tablets From Ugarit and Canaanite Religion

JOSHUA 1 The land Joshua was commanded by God to enter was that of the **Canaanites**.[1,2] Although the Old Testament provides us with some information concerning these non-Israelite people and their religion, we gain much of our knowledge from the writings of a people not far removed from the Canaanites themselves. **Ugarit**, a city in northern Syria (“Map 1”), has yielded a huge archive of tablets dating from approximately 1400 B.C.[3] Though not located in Canaan proper, Ugarit (modern Ras Shamra) shared many close cultural ties with the Canaanites, including a similar religious system and language.

The language in which the tablets from Ugarit were written is now simply called Ugaritic. It is closely related to Hebrew and is of great value in helping scholars to better understand ancient Hebrew.[4] These tablets include texts of various kinds and incorporate a great number of mythological and ritual religious elements. The deities they mention constitute the pantheon (list of officially recognized gods) of Ugarit and of the Canaanite people.

The highest deity was El, the aged father god. His consort or partner was Athirat, a sea goddess also known in the Old Testament as Asherah.[5] The principal player in the major mythological text from Ugarit is Baal (possibly El's grandson), the mighty storm god and fertility deity who figures so prominently in many of the Old Testament historical and prophetic books.[6] In the battles depicted in the Baal cycle, this notorious god defeated the deities Yam (the sea) and Mot (death).[7] His consorts were Anat, a warrior goddess who also was his wife-sister, and Astarte.[8] Other features of Canaanite religion attested at Ugarit include animal sacrifices, seasonal festivals and belief in an afterlife. Child sacrifice, a recurring motif of Canaanite religion in the Old Testament, is not mentioned in Ugaritic texts.[9]

[1]See Glossary on page 2080 for definitions of bolded words. [2]See “Canaan” on page 324. [3]See “Ugarit/Ras Shamra” on page 819. [4]See “Languages of the Old Testament World” on page 672. [5]See also “The Kuntillet Ajrûd Inscriptions: The Lord's Asherah?” on page 1220. [6]See “Baal and the Fertility Cults” on page 1414. [7]See “The Ugaritic Text of the Myth of Baal” on page 905. [8]See “The Queen of Heaven” on page 1267. [9]See “Human Sacrifice in the Ancient Near East” on page 182.

gave you east of the Jordan, but all your fighting men, fully armed, must cross over ahead of your broth-
ers. You are to help your brothers 15 until the LORD gives them rest, as he has done for you, and until they
too have taken possession of the land that the LORD your God is giving them. After that, you may go back
and occupy your own land, which Moses the servant of the LORD gave you east of the Jordan toward the
1:15 [s]Jos 22:1-4 sunrise."[s]
16 Then they answered Joshua, "Whatever you have commanded us we will do, and wherever you send
1:17 [t]ver 5,9 us we will go. 17 Just as we fully obeyed Moses, so we will obey you.[t] Only may the LORD your God be with
you as he was with Moses. 18 Whoever rebels against your word and does not obey your words, whatev-
er you may command them, will be put to death. Only be strong and courageous!"

Rahab and the Spies

2:1 [u]Jas 2:25 [v]Nu 25:1; Jos 3:1 [w]Heb 11:31 2 Then Joshua son of Nun secretly sent two spies[u] from Shittim.[v] "Go, look over the land," he said, "es-
pecially Jericho." So they went and entered the house of a prostitute[a] named Rahab[w] and stayed
there.
2 The king of Jericho was told, "Look! Some of the Israelites have come here tonight to spy out the
land." 3 So the king of Jericho sent this message to Rahab: "Bring out the men who came to you and en-
tered your house, because they have come to spy out the whole land."
2:4 [x]2Sa 17:19-20 4 But the woman had taken the two men and hidden them.[x] She said, "Yes, the men came to me, but I
did not know where they had come from. 5 At dusk, when it was time to close the city gate, the men left.
I don't know which way they went. Go after them quickly. You may catch up with them." 6 (But she had tak-
2:6 [y]Jas 2:25 [z]Ex 1:17,19; 2Sa 17:19 en them up to the roof and hidden them under the stalks of flax[y] she had laid out on the roof.)[z] 7 So the
men set out in pursuit of the spies on the road that leads to the fords of the Jordan, and as soon as the
pursuers had gone out, the gate was shut.

[a] *1* Or possibly *an innkeeper*

2:1 Jericho ("moon city"), also called the "City of Palms", was the primary focus of the spies. A fortified city, it was located just five miles (eight km) west of the Jordan River and had springs that made it an oasis. Archaeological excavations of Jericho reveal continuous occupation to this point back to at least 7000 B.C.

2:2 The Amarna letters of the fourteenth century B.C. (see "The Amarna Tablets and the Habiru" on p. 347) verify that the major cities of Canaan were in reality small kingdoms, each ruled by a local king.

ARCHAEOLOGICAL SITES

RAHAB'S HOUSE

JOSHUA 2 The Israelite spies instructed Rahab to gather her family into her house, where they would be spared from the coming calamity (Jos 2:18–19). Later, Rahab and her family members were rescued as promised (6:17,22–23). Joshua 2:15 indicates that Rahab's house was located within the fortifications of Jericho ("Maps 2–3"). Translated literally, the Hebrew reads, "Her house was against the vertical surface of the city wall, and in the city wall she lived." How was her house preserved when the wall fell? Remarkably, archaeology provides an answer.

German excavations from 1907–1909 on the northern section of the site uncovered a portion of the lower city wall that did not fall as it did everywhere else.[1] The still-standing section rose as high as 8 feet (nearly 2.5 m), with houses built against it still intact. A second wall at the crest of the embankment revealed that these particular houses were situated between the upper and lower city walls and were thus "in the city wall." Since the lower wall also formed the back wall of the houses, an opening (window) in the wall would have provided a convenient escape route for the spies. From this northerly location it was only a short distance to the hills of the Judean wilderness, where the spies hid for three days (2:16,22).

See also "New Testament Jericho" on page 1646.

[1]See "The Walls of Jericho" on page 312.

8Before the spies lay down for the night, she went up on the roof 9and said to them, "I know that the
LORD has given this land to you and that a great fear[a] of you has fallen on us, so that all who live in this 2:9 [a]Ge 35:5;
country are melting in fear because of you. 10We have heard how the LORD dried up[b] the water of the Red Ex 23:27; Dt 2:25 2:10 [b]Ex 14:21
Sea[a] for you when you came out of Egypt,[c] and what you did to Sihon and Og,[d] the two kings of the [c]Nu 23:22 [d]Nu 21:21,24,34-
Amorites east of the Jordan, whom you completely destroyed.[b] 11When we heard of it, our hearts melt- 35
ed and everyone's courage failed because of you,[e] for the LORD your God is God in heaven above and on 2:11 [e]Ex 15:14;
the earth[f] below. 12Now then, please swear to me by the LORD that you will show kindness to my fami- Jos 5:1; 7:5; Ps 22:14; Isa 13:7
ly, because I have shown kindness to you. Give me a sure sign[g] 13that you will spare the lives of my fa- [f]Dt 4:39 2:12 [g]ver 18
ther and mother, my brothers and sisters, and all who belong to them, and that you will save us from
death."
14"Our lives for your lives!" the men assured her. "If you don't tell what we are doing, we will treat you
kindly and faithfully[h] when the LORD gives us the land." 2:14 [h]Jdg 1:24; Mt 5:7
15So she let them down by a rope through the window,[i] for the house she lived in was part of the city 2:15 [i]Ac 9:25
wall. 16Now she had said to them, "Go to the hills so the pursuers will not find you. Hide yourselves there
three days[j] until they return, and then go on your way."[k] 2:16 [j]Jas 2:25 [k]Heb 11:31
17The men said to her, "This oath[l] you made us swear will not be binding on us 18unless, when we en- 2:17 [l]Ge 24:8
ter the land, you have tied this scarlet cord in the window through which you let us down, and unless

[a] *10* Hebrew *Yam Suph*; that is, Sea of Reeds [b] *10* The Hebrew term refers to the irrevocable giving over of things or persons to the LORD, often by totally destroying them.

2:15 Rahab's house was located within the fortifications of Jericho (see "Rahab's House" on p. 305).

Crossing the Jordan

JOSHUA 3 The Bible describes the miracle of the crossing of the Jordan in graphic language: "The water from upstream stopped flowing. It piled up in a heap a great distance away, at a town called Adam in the vicinity of Zarethan, while the water flowing down to the Sea of the Arabah (the Salt Sea) was completely cut off. So the people crossed over opposite Jericho" (Jos 3:16).

The town of Adam (now a site called Tell ed-Damiyeh) was approximately 16 miles (nearly 26 km) north of the point at which the Israelite procession crossed the Jordan, located at a spot were the river flowed near high banks. The Jordan Valley, part of the great Rift Valley, is an unstable region where earthquakes frequently occur. On a number of occasions throughout recorded history earthquakes have dislodged the riverbanks in the vicinity of Adam, resulting in a damming of the Jordan. The most recent occurrence was the quake of 1927, at which time a 150-foot-high (46 m) embankment on the western side of the river collapsed, completely blocking the waters for more than 21 hours. Similar cutoffs have been recorded (moving backward in time) in A.D. 1906, 1834, 1546, 1267 and 1160.

Excavations at Jericho indicate that an earthquake did in fact occur at the time that city was destroyed. This suggests the possibility of seismic activity around the time of the crossing of the Jordan. It is possible that God used one tremor to dam up the Jordan and a second a short time later to bring down the walls of Jericho.[1]

[1]See "The Walls of Jericho" on page 312.

Fragment of the book of Joshua from the Dead Sea Scrolls

© The Schøyen Collection; photography courtesy of Mr. Martin Schøyen

2:18 [m]ver 12; Jos 6:23 — you have brought your father and mother, your brothers and all your family[m] into your house. 19 If any-
2:19 [n]Eze 33:4 — one goes outside your house into the street, his blood will be on his own head;[n] we will not be responsi-
[o]Mt 27:25 — ble. As for anyone who is in the house with you, his blood will be on our head[o] if a hand is laid on him.
20 But if you tell what we are doing, we will be released from the oath you made us swear."
21 "Agreed," she replied. "Let it be as you say." So she sent them away and they departed. And she tied
the scarlet cord in the window.
22 When they left, they went into the hills and stayed there three days, until the pursuers had searched
all along the road and returned without finding them. 23 Then the two men started back. They went down
out of the hills, forded the river and came to Joshua son of Nun and told him everything that had hap-
2:24 [p]ver 9; Jos 6:2 — pened to them. 24 They said to Joshua, "The LORD has surely given the whole land into our hands;[p] all the
people are melting in fear because of us."

Crossing the Jordan

3:1 [q]Jos 2:1 — 3 Early in the morning Joshua and all the Israelites set out from Shittim[q] and went to the Jordan, where
3:2 [r]Jos 1:11 — they camped before crossing over. 2 After three days the officers went throughout the camp,[r] 3 giving
3:3 [s]Nu 10:33 [t]Dt 31:9 — orders to the people: "When you see the ark of the covenant[s] of the LORD your God, and the priests,[t] who
are Levites, carrying it, you are to move out from your positions and follow it. 4 Then you will know which
way to go, since you have never been this way before. But keep a distance of about a thousand yards[a] be-
tween you and the ark; do not go near it."
3:5 [u]Ex 19:10,14; Lev 20:7; Jos 7:13; 1Sa 16:5; Joel 2:16 — 5 Joshua told the people, "Consecrate yourselves,[u] for tomorrow the LORD will do amazing things
among you."
6 Joshua said to the priests, "Take up the ark of the covenant and pass on ahead of the people." So they
took it up and went ahead of them.
3:7 [v]Jos 4:14; 1Ch 29:25 — 7 And the LORD said to Joshua, "Today I will begin to exalt you[v] in the eyes of all Israel, so they may
[w]Jos 1:5 — know that I am with you as I was with Moses.[w] 8 Tell the priests[x] who carry the ark of the covenant: 'When
3:8 [x]ver 3 — you reach the edge of the Jordan's waters, go and stand in the river.' "
9 Joshua said to the Israelites, "Come here and listen to the words of the LORD your God. 10 This is how
3:10 [y]Dt 5:26; 1Sa 17:26,36; 2Ki 19:4,16; Hos 1:10; Mt 16:16; 1Th 1:9 — you will know that the living God[y] is among you and that he will certainly drive out before you the Ca-
naanites, Hittites, Hivites, Perizzites, Girgashites, Amorites and Jebusites.[z] 11 See, the ark of the covenant
[z]Ex 33:2; Dt 7:1 — of the Lord of all the earth[a] will go into the Jordan ahead of you. 12 Now then, choose twelve men[b] from
3:11 [a]ver 13; Job 41:11; Zec 6:5 — the tribes of Israel, one from each tribe. 13 And as soon as the priests who carry the ark of the LORD—the
Lord of all the earth[c]—set foot in the Jordan, its waters flowing downstream[d] will be cut off and stand
3:12 [b]Jos 4:2,4 — up in a heap.[e]"
3:13 [c]ver 11 [d]ver 16 [e]Ex 15:8; Ps 78:13 — 14 So when the people broke camp to cross the Jordan, the priests carrying the ark of the covenant[f]
3:14 [f]Ps 132:8 [g]Ac 7:44-45 — went ahead[g] of them. 15 Now the Jordan is at flood stage[h] all during harvest. Yet as soon as the priests
3:15 [h]Jos 4:18; 1Ch 12:15 — who carried the ark reached the Jordan and their feet touched the water's edge, 16 the water from up-
stream stopped flowing.[i] It piled up in a heap a great distance away, at a town called Adam in the vicin-
3:16 [i]Ps 66:6; 74:15 [j]1Ki 4:12; 7:46 [k]ver 13 — ity of Zarethan,[j] while the water flowing down[k] to the Sea of the Arabah[l] (the Salt Sea[b][m]) was complete-
[l]Dt 1:1 [m]Ge 14:3 — ly cut off. So the people crossed over opposite Jericho. 17 The priests who carried the ark of the covenant
of the LORD stood firm on dry ground in the middle of the Jordan, while all Israel passed by until the
3:17 [n]Ex 14:22, 29 — whole nation had completed the crossing on dry ground.[n]

[a] 4 Hebrew *about two thousand cubits* (about 900 meters) [b] 16 That is, the Dead Sea

---

2:22 The high, rugged hills of the Holy Land's central mountain ridge lay directly west of ancient Jericho. Their honeycombed caves made the concealment and escape of the two spies relatively easy.

3:10–11 Two fundamental questions needed to be addressed: (1) Was the God of Israel or the god on whom the Canaanites depended (Baal, who was believed to reign as king among the gods because he had triumphed over the sea god) the true and mighty God? By opening the way through the flooded Jordan, the Lord would show both Israel and the Canaanites that he is Lord over the waters. (2) Did the Lord of the Israelites have a rightful claim to the land? By passing safely through the Jordan at the head of his army, God demonstrated the validity of his claim.

In the ancient Near East a judicial verdict of the gods was commonly obtained by compelling an accused person to submit to a trial-by-water ordeal. Usually this involved casting the accused individual into a river (if the person drowned, the gods had found him or her guilty; if not, the gods had acquitted the individual). In Israel, however, another form of water ordeal was practiced (see Nu 5:16–28). It is significant that the Lord would enter the Jordan first and then remain there until his whole army had crossed safely over. His claim to the land was thereby vindicated before the eyes of all who heard about it. And it was his claim, not Israel's; she accompanied him through the Jordan as his army, "baptized" into his service.

3:15–16 The grain harvest took place in April and May, so it was springtime. The Jordan was at flood stage due to the spring rains and the melting of snow on Mount Hermon. Earthquakes in the region of Adam have occurred several times in recorded history, resulting in a damming of the Jordan. The most recent occurrence was the quake of 1927, at which time an embankment on the western side of the river collapsed, completely blocking the waters for over 21 hours. (See "Crossing the Jordan" on p. 306.)

4 When the whole nation had finished crossing the Jordan,[o] the LORD said to Joshua, 2"Choose twelve — 4:1 [o]Dt 27:2
men[p] from among the people, one from each tribe, 3and tell them to take up twelve stones[q] from — 4:2 [p]Jos 3:12
the middle of the Jordan from right where the priests stood and to carry them over with you and put — 4:3 [q]ver 20 [r]ver 19
them down at the place where you stay tonight.[r]"
4So Joshua called together the twelve men he had appointed from the Israelites, one from each tribe,
5and said to them, "Go over before the ark of the LORD your God into the middle of the Jordan. Each of you
is to take up a stone on his shoulder, according to the number of the tribes of the Israelites, 6to serve as a
sign among you. In the future, when your children ask you, 'What do these stones mean?'[s] 7tell them that — 4:6 [s]ver 21; Ex 12:26; 13:14
the flow of the Jordan was cut off[t] before the ark of the covenant of the LORD. When it crossed the Jordan, — 4:7 [t]Jos 3:13 [u]Ex 12:14
the waters of the Jordan were cut off. These stones are to be a memorial[u] to the people of Israel forever."
8So the Israelites did as Joshua commanded them. They took twelve stones from the middle of the
Jordan, according to the number of the tribes of the Israelites, as the LORD had told Joshua;[v] and they — 4:8 [v]ver 20
carried them over with them to their camp, where they put them down. 9Joshua set up the twelve stones[w] — 4:9 [w]Ge 28:18; Jos 24:26; 1Sa 7:12
that had been[a] in the middle of the Jordan at the spot where the priests who carried the ark of the cov-
enant had stood. And they are there to this day.
10Now the priests who carried the ark remained standing in the middle of the Jordan until everything
the LORD had commanded Joshua was done by the people, just as Moses had directed Joshua. The peo-
ple hurried over, 11and as soon as all of them had crossed, the ark of the LORD and the priests came to the
other side while the people watched. 12The men of Reuben, Gad and the half-tribe of Manasseh crossed
over, armed, in front of the Israelites,[x] as Moses had directed them. 13About forty thousand armed for bat- — 4:12 [x]Nu 32:27
tle crossed over before the LORD to the plains of Jericho for war.
14That day the LORD exalted[y] Joshua in the sight of all Israel; and they revered him all the days of his — 4:14 [y]Jos 3:7
life, just as they had revered Moses.
15Then the LORD said to Joshua, 16"Command the priests carrying the ark of the Testimony[z] to come — 4:16 [z]Ex 25:22
up out of the Jordan."

[a] 9 Or *Joshua also set up twelve stones*

4:1–9 Stone monuments were a common means in the Old Testament of inviting future generations to remember—and participate in—the great acts God had accomplished for his people (Ge 28:18–22; 31:45–46; Jos 24:26–27; 1Sa 7:12).

ARCHAEOLOGICAL SITES

THE CAMP AT GILGAL

JOSHUA 4 After the Israelites had crossed the Jordan River,[1] they established a camp at Gilgal (Jos 4:19; see "Map 3"). There Joshua set up 12 stones from the river as a memorial (vv. 20–24). All Israelite males born subsequent to the **exodus** were circumcised there (5:2–9),[2] and the first Passover in the promised land was celebrated (v. 10).[3] Gilgal became the base of operations for the ensuing six years of the conquest.[4]

Following the conquest Joshua established the primary Israelite religious center of the time at Shiloh (18:1; "Map 3"). After the Philistines had destroyed Shiloh (see Jer 7) the religious center shifted back to Gilgal (1Sa 10:8; 11:14–15; 13:15–18; 15:10–33), where it remained until David brought the ark to Jerusalem (2Sa 6).[5] Gilgal remained a prestigious religious hub in Israel, unfortunately also becoming a center for apostasy (Hos 12:11). During the **Byzantine** period a church was built at the traditional site of Gilgal. It is depicted on the **Madaba map**, a sixth-century mosaic map of the Holy Land on the floor of Saint George's church in Madaba, Jordan.

Joshua 4:19 states that Gilgal was located "on the eastern border of Jericho." The most likely location for the site is a cluster of small, ancient mounds about 1 mile (1.6 km) northeast of Jericho. This area fits the locational requirements of the Jewish historian Josephus and other ancient writers and sits on the exact spot at which the Gilgal church is depicted on the Madaba map.

[1]See "Crossing the Jordan" on page 306. [2]See "Circumcision in the Ancient World" on page 1840. [3]See "The Festivals of Israel" on page 186. [4]See "The Conquest of Canaan" on page 310. [5]See "The Tabernacle and the Ark" on page 153.

17 So Joshua commanded the priests, "Come up out of the Jordan."
18 And the priests came up out of the river carrying the ark of the covenant of the LORD. No sooner
had they set their feet on the dry ground than the waters of the Jordan returned to their place and ran at
4:18 [a]Jos 3:15 flood stage[a] as before.
4:19 [b]Jos 5:9 19 On the tenth day of the first month the people went up from the Jordan and camped at Gilgal[b] on
4:20 [c]ver 3,8 the eastern border of Jericho. 20 And Joshua set up at Gilgal the twelve stones[c] they had taken out of the
Jordan. 21 He said to the Israelites, "In the future when your descendants ask their fathers, 'What do these
4:21 [d]ver 6 stones mean?'[d] 22 tell them, 'Israel crossed the Jordan on dry ground.'[e] 23 For the LORD your God dried up
4:22 [e]Jos 3:17 the Jordan before you until you had crossed over. The LORD your God did to the Jordan just what he had
4:23 [f]Ex 14:21 done to the Red Sea[a] when he dried it up before us until we had crossed over.[f] 24 He did this so that all
4:24 [g]1Ki 8:42-43; 2Ki 19:19; Ps 106:8; Jer 10:7 [h]Ex 15:16; 1Ch 29:12; Ps 89:13 [i]Ex 14:31 the peoples of the earth might know[g] that the hand of the LORD is powerful[h] and so that you might al-
ways fear the LORD your God.[i]"

Circumcision at Gilgal

5:1 [j]Nu 13:29 [k]Jos 2:9-11 **5** Now when all the Amorite kings west of the Jordan and all the Canaanite kings along the coast[j] heard
how the LORD had dried up the Jordan before the Israelites until we had crossed over, their hearts
melted[k] and they no longer had the courage to face the Israelites.
5:2 [l]Ex 4:25 2 At that time the LORD said to Joshua, "Make flint knives[l] and circumcise the Israelites again." 3 So
Joshua made flint knives and circumcised the Israelites at Gibeath Haaraloth.[b]
4 Now this is why he did so: All those who came out of Egypt—all the men of military age—died in
5:4 [m]Dt 2:14 the desert on the way after leaving Egypt.[m] 5 All the people that came out had been circumcised, but all
the people born in the desert during the journey from Egypt had not. 6 The Israelites had moved about
5:6 [n]Dt 2:7 [o]Nu 14:23,29-35; Dt 2:14 [p]Ex 3:8 in the desert forty years[n] until all the men who were of military age when they left Egypt had died, since
they had not obeyed the LORD. For the LORD had sworn to them that they would not see the land that he
had solemnly promised their fathers to give us,[o] a land flowing with milk and honey.[p] 7 So he raised up
their sons in their place, and these were the ones Joshua circumcised. They were still uncircumcised be-
cause they had not been circumcised on the way. 8 And after the whole nation had been circumcised, they
5:8 [q]Ge 34:25 remained where they were in camp until they were healed.[q]
9 Then the LORD said to Joshua, "Today I have rolled away the reproach of Egypt from you." So the place
has been called Gilgal[c] to this day.
5:10 [r]Ex 12:6 10 On the evening of the fourteenth day of the month,[r] while camped at Gilgal on the plains of Jericho,
the Israelites celebrated the Passover. 11 The day after the Passover, that very day, they ate some of the
5:11 [s]Nu 15:19 [t]Lev 23:14 produce of the land:[s] unleavened bread and roasted grain.[t] 12 The manna stopped the day after[d] they ate
this food from the land; there was no longer any manna for the Israelites, but that year they ate of the pro-
5:12 [u]Ex 16:35 duce of Canaan.[u]

The Fall of Jericho

5:13 [v]Ge 18:2; 32:24 [w]Nu 22:23 13 Now when Joshua was near Jericho, he looked up and saw a man[v] standing in front of him with a
drawn sword[w] in his hand. Joshua went up to him and asked, "Are you for us or for our enemies?"
14 "Neither," he replied, "but as commander of the army of the LORD I have now come." Then Joshua
5:14 [x]Ge 17:3 fell facedown[x] to the ground in reverence, and asked him, "What message does my Lord[e] have for his
servant?"
15 The commander of the LORD's army replied, "Take off your sandals, for the place where you are
5:15 [y]Ex 3:5; Ac 7:33 standing is holy."[y] And Joshua did so.

[a] 23 Hebrew *Yam Suph*; that is, Sea of Reeds [b] 3 *Gibeath Haaraloth* means *hill of foreskins.* [c] 9 *Gilgal* sounds like the Hebrew for *roll.* [d] 12 Or *the day* [e] 14 Or *lord*

5:2 Metal knives were available, but flint made a more efficient surgical tool, as modern demonstrations have shown. For information on the discovery of flint at the site of Gilgal, see "The Camp at Gilgal" on page 308.
5:3–8 No uncircumcised males had been allowed to participate in the original Passover meal (Ex 12:48–49). Circumcision was practiced by other nations (e.g., as a puberty rite), but not for covenantal reasons (see the note on Ge 17:10). Of course, only males could be circumcised, but Israelites of both genders and all ages were included in the covenant community and celebrated Passover (Ex 12:3–4,24–27).

5:13–15 The appearance of "the commander of the army of the LORD" (v. 14) served not only as a dramatic sentence on Jericho but also as a visible confirmation of Joshua's divine call, similar to the appearance of the angel of the Lord to Moses at the burning bush (Ex 3:2–6).
5:15 Removing one's sandals was a sign of respect and humility in the ancient Near East (cf. Ex 3:5, where God instructed Moses to remove his sandals at the site of the burning bush). This practice is still followed by Muslims before entering a mosque.

The Conquest of Canaan

JOSHUA 5 After defeating the nations east of the Jordan, Israel turned to the promised land west of the Jordan Valley.[1] The Canaanites occupied the coastal and valley areas and the **Amorites** the highlands (Nu 13:29). Old Testament chronological data (Jdg 11:26; 1Ki 6:1) suggests that the conquest took place at the end of the fifteenth century B.C.[2] The entire process, including the taking of **Transjordan**, took about seven years, most of that time spent in conquering Canaan (Dt 2:14; Jos 14:6–10).

Archaeologists disagree about the date of the conquest, variously supporting the following possibilities:

A Late Bronze II Age Conquest

This view, placing the **exodus** during the reign of Pharaoh **Rameses II** and the conquest at the end of the thirteenth century B.C., was once almost unanimously held. Cities like Debir, Lachish,[3] Bethel[3] and **Hazor**[3] were said to have been destroyed around 1220 B.C. by the Israelite onslaught. But today many scholars have abandoned this thesis:

✣ These cities are now believed to have been overtaken at different times by various armies.

✣ The Merneptah Stele (inscribed stone slab) suggests that Israel was already settled in the land.[4]

✣ Few walled cities have been discovered from this period (cf. Dt 1:28).

✣ It is impossible to place Jericho's fall at this time.

Middle Bronze Age walls at Shechem
Preserving Bible Times; © Dr. James C. Martin

A Late Bronze I Age Conquest

This position argues for a conquest around 1400 B.C., as supported by a current understanding of the Biblical chronology. The scenario:

✣ Jericho's capture gave the Israelites a foothold. From their camp at Gilgal they launched attacks westward into the highlands.[5] After taking Ai they subjugated the southern part of the country (Jos 10).[6]

✣ Joshua did not attack Shechem, thought to be a major city at this time, instead striking a coalition of northern kings at Hazor (11:1–15). Shechem, in the central highlands near Mount Ebal and Mount Gerazim, separated the southern from the northern city-states. Joshua could not have avoided Shechem (8:30–33),[7] and some scholars even suggest Shechemite cooperation with Israel.[8]

Problems With a Late Bronze I Age Conquest

✣ Canaan was sparsely populated, lacking the great cities the Bible mentions.

✣ Most interpreters date Jericho's destruction to the end of the Middle Bronze Age, over 100 years earlier.[9]

✣ The book of Joshua nowhere cites Shechem as a powerful city.

✣ God commanded Israel to exterminate the Canaanites (Dt 7:1–2). Joshua 9 mentions the Gibeonite trick, but this only underscores Joshua's unwillingness to cooperate with Canaanite cities and contradicts the notion of Shechemite cooperation with Israel.

A Late Middle Bronze Age Conquest

✣ Cities were heavily fortified.

✣ The end of this age saw a major societal collapse and the destruction of numerous cities, including Jericho. The population may have plummeted by as much as 80 percent. Most scholars have attributed this destruction to the Egyptians—a premise now widely questioned based on lack of evidence.

Problems With a Late Middle Bronze Age Conquest

✣ This period is thought to have ended about 1550 B.C., too early for the Bible's chronology.

✣ It is difficult to relate Egyptian chronology to a 1550 B.C. conquest. No suitable pharaoh reigned then.[10]

Proposed Solutions to the Problems With a Late Middle Bronze Age Conquest

Scholars have tried to correlate the exodus with the expulsion from Egypt of the Hyksos.[10] This solution is unconvincing, and there remains the problem of the discrepancy with Biblical chronology.

Some historians suggest redating the end of the Middle Bronze period. If the date were lowered by 150 years, to around 1400 B.C., this era could have ended at the traditional date of the conquest. But this would also require a redating of Egyptian chronology. Most interpreters find this view unconvincing and eccentric.

Archaeologists routinely revise older, seemingly well-established conclusions. The interpretation of the data in Palestine is fraught with difficulties; even well-received interpretations may be built upon flimsy foundations. Given this uncertainty, it would be amazing if researchers were able to attain conclusive evidence regarding the time and circumstances of the conquest.

[1]See "Canaan" on page 324. [2]See "The Date of the Exodus" on page 106. [3]See "The Lachish Reliefs" on page 559, "Bethel" on page 59 and "Hazor" on page 322. [4]See "The Merneptah Stele" on page 360. [5]See "The Camp at Gilgal" on page 308. [6]See "Ai" on page 316. [7]See "Joshua's Altar on Mount Ebal" on page 288. [8]See "Shechem" on page 340. [9]See "The Walls of Jericho" on page 312. [10]See "The Pharaoh of the Exodus" on page 98.

6 Now Jericho[z] was tightly shut up because of the Israelites. No one went out and no one came in.
2 Then the LORD said to Joshua, "See, I have delivered[a] Jericho into your hands, along with its king and
its fighting men. 3 March around the city once with all the armed men. Do this for six days. 4 Have seven
priests carry trumpets of rams' horns in front of the ark. On the seventh day, march around the city sev-
en times, with the priests blowing the trumpets.[b] 5 When you hear them sound a long blast[c] on the trum-
pets, have all the people give a loud shout;[d] then the wall of the city will collapse and the people will go
up, every man straight in."
6 So Joshua son of Nun called the priests and said to them, "Take up the ark of the covenant of the
LORD and have seven priests carry trumpets in front of it." 7 And he ordered the people, "Advance[e]! March
around the city, with the armed guard going ahead of the ark of the LORD."
8 When Joshua had spoken to the people, the seven priests carrying the seven trumpets before the
LORD went forward, blowing their trumpets, and the ark of the LORD's covenant followed them. 9 The
armed guard marched ahead of the priests who blew the trumpets, and the rear guard[f] followed the ark.
All this time the trumpets were sounding. 10 But Joshua had commanded the people, "Do not give a war
cry, do not raise your voices, do not say a word until the day I tell you to shout. Then shout![g]" 11 So he had
the ark of the LORD carried around the city, circling it once. Then the people returned to camp and spent
the night there.
12 Joshua got up early the next morning and the priests took up the ark of the LORD. 13 The seven priests
carrying the seven trumpets went forward, marching before the ark of the LORD and blowing the trum-
pets. The armed men went ahead of them and the rear guard followed the ark of the LORD, while the
trumpets kept sounding. 14 So on the second day they marched around the city once and returned to the
camp. They did this for six days.
15 On the seventh day, they got up at daybreak and marched around the city seven times in the same
manner, except that on that day they circled the city seven times.[h] 16 The seventh time around, when
the priests sounded the trumpet blast, Joshua commanded the people, "Shout! For the LORD has giv-
en you the city! 17 The city and all that is in it are to be devoted[a][i] to the LORD. Only Rahab the prosti-
tute[b] and all who are with her in her house shall be spared, because she hid[j] the spies we sent. 18 But
keep away from the devoted things,[k] so that you will not bring about your own destruction by taking
any of them. Otherwise you will make the camp of Israel liable to destruction[l] and bring trouble[m] on
it. 19 All the silver and gold and the articles of bronze and iron[n] are sacred to the LORD and must go into
his treasury."
20 When the trumpets sounded,[o] the people shouted, and at the sound of the trumpet, when the peo-
ple gave a loud shout,[p] the wall collapsed; so every man charged straight in, and they took the city.[q]
21 They devoted the city to the LORD and destroyed[r] with the sword every living thing in it—men and
women, young and old, cattle, sheep and donkeys.

6:1 [z]Jos 24:11 **6:2** [a]Dt 7:24; Jos 2:9,24; 8:1 **6:4** [b]Lev 25:9; Nu 10:8 **6:5** [c]Ex 19:13 [d]ver 20; 1Sa 4:5; Ps 42:4; Isa 42:13 **6:7** [e]Ex 14:15 **6:9** [f]ver 13; Isa 52:12 **6:10** [g]ver 20 **6:15** [h]1Ki 18:44 **6:17** [i]Lev 27:28; Dt 20:17 [j]Jos 2:4 **6:18** [k]Jos 7:1 [l]Jos 7:12 [m]Jos 7:25,26 **6:19** [n]ver 24; Nu 31:22 **6:20** [o]Jdg 6:34; Jer 4:21; Am 2:2 [p]ver 5 [q]Heb 11:30 **6:21** [r]Dt 20:16

[a] *17* The Hebrew term refers to the irrevocable giving over of things or persons to the LORD, often by totally destroying them; also in verses 18 and 21. [b] *17* Or possibly *innkeeper*; also in verses 22 and 25

6:1—10:15 Archaeological evidence for the conquest is mixed, in part because the chronological problems are unresolved (see "The Conquest of Canaan" on p. 310 and "Jericho and the Date of the Conquest" on p. 314). On the one hand, clay tablets containing cuneiform letters to the Egyptian court have been found at Tell el-Amarna in Egypt from approximately 1375 B.C. These mention bands of *Habiru* who were threatening many of the cities of the Holy Land and creating fear among the Canaanite inhabitants (see "The Amarna Tablets and the Habiru" on p. 347). On the other hand, numerous towns were destroyed around 1230 B.C. by unknown assailants, presumably the "Sea Peoples," but possibly including the Israelites as well (see "Greece: From the Prehistoric Period Through the Mycenaean Empire" on p. 1810). The Biblical chronology based on 1 Kings 6:1 seems to demand an even earlier dating, near the end of the fifteenth century.

6:4 The "trumpets of rams' horns" were not instruments of music but instruments for signaling, used in both religious and military contexts (in this case in both).

6:5 The "loud blast" and "loud shout" signaled the onset of the attack—psychological warfare intended to create panic and confusion (see Jdg 7). In the Dead Sea Scroll of "The War of the Sons of Light Against the Sons of Darkness," the Levites were instructed to blow in unison a great battle fanfare to melt the heart of the enemy.

6:12–14 Literary repetition, which reflected repetition in action, is a common feature found in ancient Near Eastern literature.

6:17 True to the promise of protection the spies had made to Rahab and her family, Joshua and his men spared them after they had captured the city. Jewish tradition has held Rahab in high esteem, one tradition making her the wife of Joshua himself. According to Matthew's genealogy (Mt 1:5), she is not only one of the four women mentioned in the family tree of the Savior but also the mother of Boaz, the husband of Ruth, and the great-grandmother of King David (Ru 4:18–21). The author of Hebrews spoke of Rahab as an example of faith (Heb 11:31), and James showed his appreciation of her as a person in whom faith was not merely "theological" but also practical (Jas 2:5). See "The Walls of Jericho" on page 312.

6:18–19 A "devoted thing" was set apart to the Lord; thus it no longer belonged to the former owner and could not be used for sacrifice. Whereas a sacrifice or offering was a voluntary gift that could be recalled at any time prior to the ceremony, it was not a devoted thing. Achan's sin at Jericho was considered far more serious than mere stealing, for he had taken something devoted. Nations, cities or people who were "devoted" were to be utterly destroyed (e.g., the Amalekites; 1Sa 15). See "*Herem*, Holy War" on page 419.

22 Joshua said to the two men who had spied out the land, "Go into the prostitute's house and bring her
out and all who belong to her, in accordance with your oath to her.[s]" 23 So the young men who had done
the spying went in and brought out Rahab, her father and mother and brothers and all who belonged to
her.[t] They brought out her entire family and put them in a place outside the camp of Israel.
24 Then they burned the whole city and everything in it, but they put the silver and gold and the arti-
cles of bronze and iron[u] into the treasury of the LORD's house. 25 But Joshua spared Rahab the prostitute,[v]
with her family and all who belonged to her, because she hid the men Joshua had sent as spies to Jeri-
cho[w]—and she lives among the Israelites to this day.

6:22 [s]Jos 2:14; Heb 11:31
6:23 [t]Jos 2:13
6:24 [u]ver 19
6:25 [v]Heb 11:31 [w]Jos 2:6

ARCHAEOLOGICAL SITES

THE WALLS OF JERICHO

JOSHUA 6 Old Testament Jericho ("Maps 2–3") has undergone four excavations: by Charles Warren (1867–1868); Ernst Sellin and Carl Watzinger (1907–1909); John Garstang (1930–1936); and Kathleen Kenyon (1952–1958). Unfortunately, the first three digs used methods modern archaeologists consider primitive and unreliable, and the site has suffered from erosion.

Watzinger concluded that Jericho was unoccupied during the **Late Bronze Age**,[1] when it was supposed to have been destroyed by Joshua, while Garstang determined that the heavily fortified city was destroyed late in this period. But Kenyon argued that it was annihilated at the end of the **Middle Bronze Age**, around 1550 B.C., after which it boasted at best a meager settlement through the Late Bronze period—leaving no fortified city for Joshua to destroy.[2]

Dating issues aside, much of the archaeological data corresponds with the Biblical account:

Jericho's prominence (Jos 5–6) and wealth (7:21) suggest a great city. Excavations have shown that Jericho had massive defenses. Its **tell** (mound composed of remains of successive settlements) was surrounded by an earthen embankment stabilized by a 15-foot (4.6 m) stone wall. Atop the **retaining wall** stood a free-standing mud brick wall about 6 feet (1.8 m) thick and three or four times as high. A similar wall topped the embankment.

The walls of Jericho
Photograph courtesy of © Dr. Gary Pratico

Jericho's mud brick walls crumpled in a heap at the base of the retaining wall (6:20). Archaeologists suggest that an earthquake took place[3] and that the fallen bricks formed a ramp by which the Israelites surmounted the retaining wall.

A 3 foot (.9 m) high ash layer verifies a massive conflagration (v. 24).

There are indications of plague in Jericho before its fall (cf. Nu 25:8–9).

Joshua 3:15 states that Israel forded the Jordan at harvest time. Collaborating evidence includes Rahab's drying of flax on her roof (2:6)[4] and Israel's Passover celebration (a springtime festival observed just prior to harvest) immediately before the battle (5:10).[5]

Full jars of recently harvested grain confirm the brevity of the siege (6:15).

That Jericho's grain was left to burn is extraordinary, suggesting that the invaders had an unusual reason for leaving it intact (see vv. 17–19).

The details surrounding the destruction of Jericho City IV thus closely parallel what we read in the Bible. Unfortunately, the date of the fall of this city remains a problem. If, as Watzinger and Kenyon argued, Jericho fell around 1550 B.C, there would have been no significant city there when Joshua arrived around 1400 B.C. Nevertheless, however one deals with the chronological problem,[6] there is much about City IV to encourage the Christian reader about the reliability of the Joshua 6 account.

[1]See "Archaeological Periods" chart on page xx in the front of this Bible. [2]See "The Conquest of Canaan" on page 310. [3]See also "Crossing the Jordan" on page 306. [4]See "Rahab's House" on page 305. [5]See "The Festivals of Israel" on page 186. [6]See "Jericho and the Date of the Conquest" on page 314.

26 At that time Joshua pronounced this solemn oath: "Cursed before the LORD is the man who under-
takes to rebuild this city, Jericho:

> "At the cost of his firstborn son
> will he lay its foundations;
> at the cost of his youngest
> 6:26 [x]1Ki 16:34 will he set up its gates."[x]

6:27 [y]Ge 39:2; Jos 1:5 [z]Jos 9:1 27 So the LORD was with Joshua,[y] and his fame spread[z] throughout the land.

Achan's Sin

7:1 [a]Jos 6:18 **7** But the Israelites acted unfaithfully in regard to the devoted things[a];[a] Achan son of Carmi, the son
[b]Jos 22:20 of Zimri,[b] the son of Zerah,[b] of the tribe of Judah, took some of them. So the LORD's anger burned
against Israel.
7:2 [c]Jos 18:12; 1Sa 13:5; 14:23 2 Now Joshua sent men from Jericho to Ai, which is near Beth Aven[c] to the east of Bethel, and told
them, "Go up and spy out the region." So the men went up and spied out Ai.
3 When they returned to Joshua, they said, "Not all the people will have to go up against Ai. Send two
or three thousand men to take it and do not weary all the people, for only a few men are there." 4 So about
7:4 [d]Lev 26:17; Dt 28:25 three thousand men went up; but they were routed by the men of Ai,[d] 5 who killed about thirty-six of
them. They chased the Israelites from the city gate as far as the stone quarries[c] and struck them down
7:5 [e]Lev 26:36; Jos 2:9,11; Eze 21:7; Na 2:10 on the slopes. At this the hearts of the people melted[e] and became like water.
7:6 [f]Ge 37:29 [g]1Sa 4:12; 2Sa 13:19; Ne 9:1; Job 2:12; La 2:10; Rev 18:19 6 Then Joshua tore his clothes[f] and fell facedown to the ground before the ark of the LORD, remaining
there till evening. The elders of Israel did the same, and sprinkled dust[g] on their heads. 7 And Joshua
said, "Ah, Sovereign LORD, why did you ever bring this people across the Jordan to deliver us into the
hands of the Amorites to destroy us?[h] If only we had been content to stay on the other side of the Jordan!
7:7 [h]Ex 5:22 8 O Lord, what can I say, now that Israel has been routed by its enemies? 9 The Canaanites and the other
people of the country will hear about this and they will surround us and wipe out our name from the
7:9 [i]Ex 32:12; Dt 9:28 earth.[i] What then will you do for your own great name?"
10 The LORD said to Joshua, "Stand up! What are you doing down on your face? 11 Israel has sinned; they
7:11 [j]Jos 6:17-19 [k]Ac 5:1-2 have violated my covenant,[j] which I commanded them to keep. They have taken some of the devoted
things; they have stolen, they have lied,[k] they have put them with their own possessions. 12 That is why
7:12 [l]Nu 14:45; Jdg 2:14 [m]Jos 6:18 the Israelites cannot stand against their enemies;[l] they turn their backs and run because they have been
made liable to destruction.[m] I will not be with you anymore unless you destroy whatever among you is
devoted to destruction.
7:13 [n]Jos 3:5; 6:18 13 "Go, consecrate the people. Tell them, 'Consecrate yourselves[n] in preparation for tomorrow; for this
is what the LORD, the God of Israel, says: That which is devoted is among you, O Israel. You cannot stand
against your enemies until you remove it.
7:14 [o]Pr 16:33 14 " 'In the morning, present yourselves tribe by tribe. The tribe that the LORD takes[o] shall come for-
ward clan by clan; the clan that the LORD takes shall come forward family by family; and the family that
the LORD takes shall come forward man by man. 15 He who is caught with the devoted things shall be de-
7:15 [p]1Sa 14:39 [q]ver 11 [r]Ge 34:7 stroyed by fire, along with all that belongs to him.[p] He has violated the covenant[q] of the LORD and has done
a disgraceful thing in Israel!' "[r]
16 Early the next morning Joshua had Israel come forward by tribes, and Judah was taken. 17 The clans
7:17 [s]Nu 26:20 of Judah came forward, and he took the Zerahites.[s] He had the clan of the Zerahites come forward by
families, and Zimri was taken. 18 Joshua had his family come forward man by man, and Achan son of
Carmi, the son of Zimri, the son of Zerah, of the tribe of Judah, was taken.

[a] *1* The Hebrew term refers to the irrevocable giving over of things or persons to the LORD, often by totally destroying them; also in verses 11, 12, 13 and 15. [b] *1* See Septuagint and 1 Chron. 2:6; Hebrew *Zabdi*; also in verses 17 and 18. [c] *5* Or *as far as Shebarim*

6:26 Joshua's oath reflects that Jericho was to remain an object lesson of God's great victory in Israel's first battle. The city was soon resettled (18:21; Jdg 3:13; 2Sa 10:5) but remained without a wall. The curse was fulfilled during the reign of the evil king Ahab, when Hiel rebuilt the wall around Jericho (1Ki 16:34). It is unclear whether fulfillment came via a plague or accident or whether Hiel offered his son as a sacrifice.

7:6–9 When the disobedience of Achan brought defeat at Ai, Joshua's prayer, his zeal for God's glory and his enforcement of divine judgment (vv. 6–9,19,25) compared favorably with his subsequent faithfulness to God's orders and exemplary execution of Ai's king (8:2,29; cf. 10:24–27,40–41). See "Ai" on page 316.

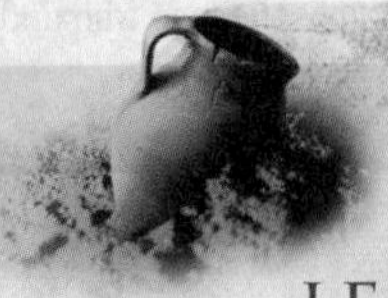

ARCHAEOLOGICAL SITES

JERICHO AND THE DATE OF THE CONQUEST

Middle Bronze Age wall at Shechem

Photograph: © Todd Bolen/Bible Places.com

JOSHUA 7 Who destroyed Jericho City IV?[1] The "early date" for the conquest places it at around 1400 B.C., while the "late date" sets it at about 1220 B.C. There are at least three different ways interpreters have tried to correlate the fall of City IV with the "early date:"

✣ A Late Bronze I[2] conquest theory asserts that Jericho was conquered by Joshua in the latter part of Late Bronze I at about 1400 B.C. This theory is based on the presence of Late Bronze I pottery at the site. Also, **scarabs** of Egyptian pharaohs Hatshepsut, Thutmose III and Amenhotep III have been found there. These scarabs indicate a habitation of the site during the Egyptian Eighteenth Dynasty, or during Late Bronze I. All of this suggests that the catastrophic destruction of Jericho City IV took place at the close of Late Bronze I, about 1400 B.C. Against this view, others have made the following arguments:

Late Bronze I does not work well with an Israelite conquest. There were very few great, walled cities in **Canaan** during this period, in contrast to the Bible's assertions that the Israelites were in awe of the high-walled cities that confronted them (Dt 1:28).

A number of scholars believe that a small-scale occupation of Jericho during the Late Bronze Age had no walls and could not have been the city Joshua encountered. The Late Bronze I pottery found there may relate to this small occupation, not to City IV, and the Late Bronze I pottery at Jericho may have no relationship to Joshua's conquest.

The scarab of Amenhotep III poses an obstacle for arguing this view. If the Late Bronze I Jericho was indeed destroyed by Joshua, then the scarab of Amenhotep III obviously had to have arrived there before the city fell. The dates of Amenhotep's reign are usually set at 1390–1352 (or 1386–1349), too late for Joshua's victory, which is generally set at around 1400 B.C.

✣ The redated Middle Bronze conquest theory agrees with the conventional wisdom that Jericho City IV fell at the end of the Middle Bronze Age. However, it redates the Middle Bronze Age and asserts that the chronology of Egypt and the Middle Bronze Age needs to be revised downward by about 150 years. Under this premise Jericho City IV actually did fall at the end of the Middle Bronze period—around 1400, not 1550 B.C. Two facts are in favor of this approach, but there is a problem as well:

Most interpreters believe that City IV fell at the end of the Middle Bronze Age, so this theory does not have the burden of having to overturn that conclusion.

A conquest of Canaan works well with what is known about the end of the Middle Bronze Age. The cities of the land were fortified with high walls at this time, but in the next period, Late Bronze I, they were for the most part meager sites with little or no fortification. It is conceivable that the Israelite conquest was instrumental in bringing Middle Bronze culture to an end.

Most interpreters, however, regard the redating of the end of the Middle Bronze Age by 150 years to be radical and unwarranted. There is currently a movement in some quarters to lower dramatically the conventional chronology for Egypt and thus also the date for the Middle Bronze/Late Bronze boundary, but mainstream Egyptology has yet to embrace this proposal.

✣ The conventional Middle Bronze conquest theory holds to both a Middle Bronze date for Jericho City IV and the conventional chronology. It argues that the **exodus** took place during the Middle Bronze Age and that Joshua came to Jericho about 1550. This approach, however, has very few supporters:

It flies in the face of the Bible's own chronology, which strongly indicates a conquest in about 1400.

It unconvincingly entangles the exodus story with the history of the Hyksos.[3]

It is extremely difficult archaeologically to account for Israel in the land as early as the year 1550. Thus, the archaeology of Jericho as we currently understand it is impossible to reconcile with a "late date" for the conquest (c. 1220 B.C.).

[1]See "The Walls of Jericho" on page 312. [2]See "Archaeological Periods" chart on page xx in the front of this Bible. [3]See "The Hyksos and the Exodus" on page 99.

7:19 [t]1Sa 6:5; Jer 13:16; 19Then Joshua said to Achan, “My son, give glory[t] to the LORD,[a] the God of Israel, and give him the
Jn 9:24* praise.[b] Tell[u] me what you have done; do not hide it from me.”
[u]1Sa 14:43 20Achan replied, “It is true! I have sinned against the LORD, the God of Israel. This is what I have done:
21When I saw in the plunder a beautiful robe from Babylonia,[c] two hundred shekels[d] of silver and a wedge
7:21 [v]Dt 7:25; of gold weighing fifty shekels,[e] I coveted[v] them and took them. They are hidden in the ground inside my
Eph 5:5; 1Ti 6:10 tent, with the silver underneath.”
22So Joshua sent messengers, and they ran to the tent, and there it was, hidden in his tent, with the sil-
ver underneath. 23They took the things from the tent, brought them to Joshua and all the Israelites and
spread them out before the LORD.
24Then Joshua, together with all Israel, took Achan son of Zerah, the silver, the robe, the gold wedge,
7:24 [w]ver 26; Jos 15:7 his sons and daughters, his cattle, donkeys and sheep, his tent and all that he had, to the Valley of Achor.[w]
7:25 [x]Jos 6:18 25Joshua said, “Why have you brought this trouble[x] on us? The LORD will bring trouble on you today.”
[y]Dt 17:5 Then all Israel stoned him,[y] and after they had stoned the rest, they burned them. 26Over Achan they
heaped up a large pile of rocks, which remains to this day. Then the LORD turned from his fierce anger.[z]
7:26 [z]Nu 25:4; Dt 13:17 [a]ver 24; Isa 65:10; Hos 2:15 Therefore that place has been called the Valley of Achor[f][a] ever since.

Ai Destroyed

8:1 [b]Dt 31:6 [c]Dt 1:21; 7:18; Jos 1:9 [d]Jos 10:7 [e]Jos 6:2 **8** Then the LORD said to Joshua, “Do not be afraid;[b] do not be discouraged.[c] Take the whole army[d] with
you, and go up and attack Ai. For I have delivered[e] into your hands the king of Ai, his people, his city
and his land. 2You shall do to Ai and its king as you did to Jericho and its king, except that you may car-
8:2 [f]ver 27; Dt 20:14 ry off their plunder and livestock for yourselves.[f] Set an ambush behind the city.”
3So Joshua and the whole army moved out to attack Ai. He chose thirty thousand of his best fighting
men and sent them out at night 4with these orders: “Listen carefully. You are to set an ambush behind the
city. Don’t go very far from it. All of you be on the alert. 5I and all those with me will advance on the city,
and when the men come out against us, as they did before, we will flee from them. 6They will pursue us
until we have lured them away from the city, for they will say, ‘They are running away from us as they did
before.’ So when we flee from them, 7you are to rise up from ambush and take the city. The LORD your
8:7 [g]Jdg 7:7; 1Sa 23:4 God will give it into your hand.[g] 8When you have taken the city, set it on fire.[h] Do what the LORD has com-
8:8 [h]Jdg 20:29-38 [i]ver 19 manded.[i] See to it; you have my orders.”
8:9 [j]2Ch 13:13 9Then Joshua sent them off, and they went to the place of ambush[j] and lay in wait between Bethel
and Ai, to the west of Ai—but Joshua spent that night with the people.
8:10 [k]Ge 22:3 [l]Jos 7:6 10Early the next morning[k] Joshua mustered his men, and he and the leaders of Israel[l] marched before
them to Ai. 11The entire force that was with him marched up and approached the city and arrived in front
of it. They set up camp north of Ai, with the valley between them and the city. 12Joshua had taken about
five thousand men and set them in ambush between Bethel and Ai, to the west of the city. 13They had the
soldiers take up their positions—all those in the camp to the north of the city and the ambush to the west
of it. That night Joshua went into the valley.
14When the king of Ai saw this, he and all the men of the city hurried out early in the morning to meet
8:14 [m]Dt 1:1 Israel in battle at a certain place overlooking the Arabah.[m] But he did not know[n] that an ambush had
[n]Jdg 20:34 8:15 [o]Jdg 20:36 been set against him behind the city. 15Joshua and all Israel let themselves be driven back[o] before them,
[p]Jos 15:61; 16:1; 18:12 and they fled toward the desert.[p] 16All the men of Ai were called to pursue them, and they pursued Josh-
8:16 [q]Jdg 20:31 ua and were lured away[q] from the city. 17Not a man remained in Ai or Bethel who did not go after Isra-
el. They left the city open and went in pursuit of Israel.
8:18 [r]Job 41:26; 18Then the LORD said to Joshua, “Hold out toward Ai the javelin[r] that is in your hand,[s] for into your
Ps 35:3 [s]Ex 4:2; 14:16; 17:9-12 hand I will deliver the city.” So Joshua held out his javelin[t] toward Ai. 19As soon as he did this, the men
[t]ver 26 8:19 [u]Jdg 20:33 in the ambush rose quickly[u] from their position and rushed forward. They entered the city and captured
[v]ver 8 it and quickly set it on fire.[v]
8:20 [w]Jdg 20:40 20The men of Ai looked back and saw the smoke of the city rising against the sky,[w] but they had no
chance to escape in any direction, for the Israelites who had been fleeing toward the desert had turned
back against their pursuers. 21For when Joshua and all Israel saw that the ambush had taken the city and

[a] 19 A solemn charge to tell the truth [b] 19 Or *and confess to him* [c] 21 Hebrew *Shinar* [d] 21 That is, about 5 pounds (about 2.3 kilograms) [e] 21 That is, about 1 1/4 pounds (about 0.6 kilogram) [f] 26 *Achor* means *trouble.*

8:9 Bethel played an important role in the lives of Abraham and Jacob. Abraham built an altar between Bethel and Ai (Ge 12:8), and Jacob, en route to Haran while fleeing from Esau, experienced a vivid dream at Bethel (Ge 28:10–17). See “Bethel” on page 59.

ARCHAEOLOGICAL SITES

AI

JOSHUA 8 Locating Bible places is one of the most vexing issues of Biblical archaeology. Professional archaeologists must debate minute points, and lay people are often bewildered by the references to so many unfamiliar sites in the Holy Land, all with modern Arabic names. Pinpointing the location of ancient Ai illustrates this dilemma, which has proven overall to be a thorny problem in Old Testament studies. Sometimes these seemingly obscure issues can have major consequences. Because of questions concerning the location of Ai (but see "Map 3" for proposed location), for example, many scholars argue that the entire story of this city's conquest is simply a legend.

Joshua 7:2 states that Ai was east of **Bethel**, near Beth Aven. Bethel is often identified as modern Beitin, but this is by no means certain. Alternatively, it may have been located at modern El-Bireh, with Beth Aven being modern Beitin.

Because of an influential article in 1924 by W.F. Albright, the "father" of Biblical archaeology, nearly all scholars have accepted the large site of et-Tell as Ai. But this poses a problem, since et-Tell was not occupied in Joshua's time. People did live there during the **Early Bronze Age** (early **patriarchal period**),[1] however, and this location is indeed probably the landmark (original) site of Ai (Ge 12:8). Since the Bible states that the Ai captured by Joshua was small (Jos 7:3, 10:2), it is possible that a fortress near modern et-Tell was called Ai during Joshua's time.

Et-Tell

Photograph: © Todd Bolen/Bible Places.com

In 1838 the English scholar Edward Robinson was informed of a tradition in the Holy Land that Ai was located at modern Khirbet el-Maqatir. This same notion was encountered in 1899 by the German scholar Ernst Sellin. Since 1995, Bryant Wood has conducted excavations at Khirbet el-Maqatir, determining that a small fortress dating to the fifteenth century B.C. was indeed there—and that it meets all the Biblical requirements for Joshua's Ai.

Geographically, Khirbet el-Maqatir fits the description in Joshua 7 and 8, though the disputed locations of other places come into play. It is located nearly 1 mile (1.6 km) southeast of Beth Aven (7:2), *if* Beitin is accepted as the site of Beth Aven.[2] It is 2 miles (3.2 km) east-northeast of Bethel (v. 2), *if* El-Bireh is accepted as the site of Bethel.[3]

In addition, Khirbet el-Maqatir fits the narrative of Joshua 8 well. Between this location and El-Bireh is a deep valley, the Wadi Sheban, which could easily have accommodated a large ambush force such as the one described in verse 9. Joshua 8:11 mentions Joshua's men ascending to the north of Ai and setting up camp. Jebel Abu Ammar, 1 mile (1.6 km) due north of Khirbet el-Maqatir, is the highest hill in the region, providing a commanding view of the battle area. A shallow valley lying north of this site, the Wadi Gayeh, is located between Khirbet el-Maqatir and Jebel Abu Ammar; from here the king of Ai could have seen Joshua and his men (v. 14).

Khirbet el-Maqatir also fits the archaeological requirements for identification as Joshua's Ai. A small fortress in the area (7:3,5; 10:2), approximately three acres in size, has yielded pottery dating from the fifteenth century B.C. Although 8:25 states that the town had 12,000 inhabitants, there is reason to believe that textual corruption has increased the number tenfold (i.e., it should read 1,200).[4] According to Joshua 7:3 the Israelites calculated that 3,000 soldiers at most would constitute a sufficient force to conquer Ai due to its small size.

The gate of the fortress is located on the north side, corresponding to the Bible's identification of a northern front for the fortress (8:11). Abundant ash at the site, along with burned pottery, stones and bedrock, evidences destruction by fire (cf. v. 28).

In conclusion, the site of et-Tell, identified as Ai by Albright, is most likely the location of Ai in the early patriarchal period. By Joshua's time, however, the fortress had evidently migrated slightly to the west—to Khirbet el-Maqatir. The significance? The taking of Ai by Joshua and his forces was a historical event—a conclusion with profound implications for the acceptance of the whole Bible as God's infallible, inspired truth.

[1]See "Archaeological Periods" chart on page xx in the front of this Bible. [2]See "Beth Aven: A Lesson in the Difficulty of Biblical Geography" on page 1417. [3]See "Bethel" on page 59. [4]See "Textual Criticism" on page 1151.

that smoke was going up from the city, they turned around and attacked the men of Ai. [22]The men of the
ambush also came out of the city against them, so that they were caught in the middle, with Israelites on
both sides. Israel cut them down, leaving them neither survivors nor fugitives.[x] [23]But they took the king
of Ai alive[y] and brought him to Joshua.

[24]When Israel had finished killing all the men of Ai in the fields and in the desert where they had chased
them, and when every one of them had been put to the sword, all the Israelites returned to Ai and killed
those who were in it. [25]Twelve thousand men and women fell that day—all the people of Ai.[z] [26]For Josh-
ua did not draw back the hand that held out his javelin until he had destroyed[a][a] all who lived in Ai.[b] [27]But
Israel did carry off for themselves the livestock and plunder of this city, as the LORD had instructed Joshua.[c]

[28]So Joshua burned[d] Ai[e] and made it a permanent heap of ruins,[f] a desolate place to this day.[g] [29]He
hung the king of Ai on a tree and left him there until evening. At sunset,[h] Joshua ordered them to take
his body from the tree and throw it down at the entrance of the city gate. And they raised a large pile of
rocks[i] over it, which remains to this day.

The Covenant Renewed at Mount Ebal

[30]Then Joshua built on Mount Ebal[j] an altar[k] to the LORD, the God of Israel, [31]as Moses the servant of
the LORD had commanded the Israelites. He built it according to what is written in the Book of the Law
of Moses—an altar of uncut stones, on which no iron tool[l] had been used. On it they offered to the LORD
burnt offerings and sacrificed fellowship offerings.[b][m] [32]There, in the presence of the Israelites, Joshua
copied on stones the law of Moses, which he had written.[n] [33]All Israel, aliens and citizens[o] alike, with
their elders, officials and judges, were standing on both sides of the ark of the covenant of the LORD, fac-
ing those who carried it—the priests, who were Levites.[p] Half of the people stood in front of Mount Ge-
rizim and half of them in front of Mount Ebal,[q] as Moses the servant of the LORD had formerly com-
manded when he gave instructions to bless the people of Israel.

[34]Afterward, Joshua read all the words of the law—the blessings and the curses—just as it is writ-
ten in the Book of the Law.[r] [35]There was not a word of all that Moses had commanded that Joshua did
not read to the whole assembly of Israel, including the women and children, and the aliens who lived
among them.[s]

The Gibeonite Deception

9 Now when all the kings west of the Jordan heard about these things—those in the hill country, in
the western foothills, and along the entire coast of the Great Sea[c][t] as far as Lebanon (the kings of the
Hittites, Amorites, Canaanites, Perizzites, Hivites and Jebusites)[u]— [2]they came together to make war
against Joshua and Israel.

[3]However, when the people of Gibeon[v] heard what Joshua had done to Jericho and Ai, [4]they resorted
to a ruse: They went as a delegation whose donkeys were loaded[d] with worn-out sacks and old wine-
skins, cracked and mended. [5]The men put worn and patched sandals on their feet and wore old clothes.
All the bread of their food supply was dry and moldy. [6]Then they went to Joshua in the camp at Gilgal[w]
and said to him and the men of Israel, "We have come from a distant country; make a treaty with us."

[7]The men of Israel said to the Hivites,[x] "But perhaps you live near us. How then can we make a trea-
ty[y] with you?"

[8]"We are your servants,[z]" they said to Joshua.

But Joshua asked, "Who are you and where do you come from?"

[9]They answered: "Your servants have come from a very distant country[a] because of the fame of the
LORD your God. For we have heard reports[b] of him: all that he did in Egypt, [10]and all that he did to the
two kings of the Amorites east of the Jordan—Sihon king of Heshbon, and Og king of Bashan,[c] who
reigned in Ashtaroth.[d] [11]And our elders and all those living in our country said to us, 'Take provisions
for your journey; go and meet them and say to them, "We are your servants; make a treaty with us." '
[12]This bread of ours was warm when we packed it at home on the day we left to come to you. But now

8:22 [x]Dt 7:2; Jos 10:1
8:23 [y]1Sa 15:8
8:25 [z]Dt 20:16-18
8:26 [a]Nu 21:2 [b]Ex 17:12
8:27 [c]ver 2
8:28 [d]Nu 31:10 [e]Jos 7:2; Jer 49:3 [f]Dt 13:16; Jos 10:1 [g]Ge 35:20
8:29 [h]Dt 21:23; Jn 19:31 [i]2Sa 18:17
8:30 [j]Dt 11:29 [k]Ex 20:24
8:31 [l]Ex 20:25 [m]Dt 27:6-7
8:32 [n]Dt 27:8
8:33 [o]Lev 16:29 [p]Dt 31:12 [q]Dt 11:29; 27:11-14
8:34 [r]Dt 28:61; 31:11; Jos 1:8
8:35 [s]Ex 12:38; Dt 31:12
9:1 [t]Nu 34:6 [u]Ex 3:17; Jos 3:10
9:3 [v]ver 17; Jos 10:2; 2Sa 2:12; 2Ch 1:3; Isa 28:21
9:6 [w]Jos 5:10
9:7 [x]ver 1; Jos 11:19 [y]Ex 23:32; Dt 7:2
9:8 [z]Dt 20:11; 2Ki 10:5
9:9 [a]Dt 20:15 [b]ver 24; Jos 2:9
9:10 [c]Nu 21:33 [d]Nu 21:24,35

[a] *26* The Hebrew term refers to the irrevocable giving over of things or persons to the LORD, often by totally destroying them. [b] *31* Traditionally *peace offerings* [c] *1* That is, the Mediterranean [d] *4* Most Hebrew manuscripts; some Hebrew manuscripts, Vulgate and Syriac (see also Septuagint) *They prepared provisions and loaded their donkeys*

9:1 See "Lesser Known Peoples of the Old Testament" on page 265.

9:9 "Fame," here translating a Hebrew word commonly rendered as "name," includes more than just the idea of renown. A person's name stood for his or her character (7:9).

see how dry and moldy it is. 13 And these wineskins that we filled were new, but see how cracked they
are. And our clothes and sandals are worn out by the very long journey."
14 The men of Israel sampled their provisions but did not inquire[e] of the LORD. 15 Then Joshua made a 9:14 [e]Nu 27:21
treaty of peace[f] with them to let them live, and the leaders of the assembly ratified it by oath. 9:15 [f]Ex 23:32;
16 Three days after they made the treaty with the Gibeonites, the Israelites heard that they were neigh- Jos 11:19;
bors, living near them. 17 So the Israelites set out and on the third day came to their cities: Gibeon, Ke- 2Sa 21:2
phirah, Beeroth[g] and Kiriath Jearim.[h] 18 But the Israelites did not attack them, because the leaders of the 9:17 [g]Jos 18:25
assembly had sworn an oath[i] to them by the LORD, the God of Israel. [h]1Sa 7:1-2 9:18 [i]Ps 15:4
The whole assembly grumbled[j] against the leaders, 19 but all the leaders answered, "We have given [j]Ex 15:24
them our oath by the LORD, the God of Israel, and we cannot touch them now. 20 This is what we will do
to them: We will let them live, so that wrath will not fall on us for breaking the oath we swore to them."
21 They continued, "Let them live,[k] but let them be woodcutters and water carriers[l] for the entire commu- 9:21 [k]ver 15
nity." So the leaders' promise to them was kept. [l]Dt 29:11
22 Then Joshua summoned the Gibeonites and said, "Why did you deceive us by saying, 'We live a long
way[m] from you,' while actually you live near[n] us? 23 You are now under a curse:[o] You will never cease to 9:22 [m]ver 6
serve as woodcutters and water carriers for the house of my God." [n]ver 16 9:23 [o]Ge 9:25
24 They answered Joshua, "Your servants were clearly told[p] how the LORD your God had commanded 9:24 [p]ver 9
his servant Moses to give you the whole land and to wipe out all its inhabitants from before you. So we
feared for our lives because of you, and that is why we did this. 25 We are now in your hands.[q] Do to us 9:25 [q]Ge 16:6
whatever seems good and right to you."
26 So Joshua saved them from the Israelites, and they did not kill them. 27 That day he made the Gibe-
onites woodcutters and water carriers for the community and for the altar of the LORD at the place the
LORD would choose.[r] And that is what they are to this day. 9:27 [r]Dt 12:5

ARCHAEOLOGICAL SITES

GIBEON

JOSHUA 9 Gibeon ("Map 3") is located at the modern village of el-Jib, 6 miles (9.6 km) northwest of Jerusalem. Pottery and two Egyptian **scarabs** (stone beetles used as talismans, ornaments or symbols of resurrection) indicate occupation at the time of the conquest,[1] but no architecture from that period has yet been unearthed. Only a small fraction of the site has been excavated, however, so there is much more to investigate.

Gibeon was "an important city, like one of the royal cities" (10:2). It ruled a small league of cities that included Kephirah, Beeroth and Kiriath Jearim (9:17). When the Gibeonites arrived at Gilgal, 16 miles (nearly 26 km) to the east,[2] they deceived the Israelites by noting the condition of their wineskins: "These wineskins that we filled were new, but see how cracked they are" (v. 13).

In the **divided monarchy** period wine-making was a major industry in Gibeon.[3] The people used both wineskins and jars as containers for wine. The handles of the jars in which the wine was exported were inscribed with the name of the city, along with that of the vintner. Some 31 jar handles have been discovered here inscribed with the name "Gibeon," making identification of the site a certainty—a welcome rarity in the archaeology of Palestine.

When Joshua discovered the Gibeonites' deception, he consigned them to servitude as "woodcutters and water carriers for the house of my God" (v. 23). The most conspicuous feature of Gibeon is in fact its abundant water supply: one major and seven minor springs. The "pool of Gibeon" is mentioned in 2 Samuel 2:13[4] and the "great pool in Gibeon" in Jeremiah 41:12.

Gibeon
Photograph courtesy of © Dr. Gary Pratico

[1]See "The Conquest of Canaan" on page 310. [2]See "The Camp at Gilgal" on page 308. [3]See "The Winepress" on page 1171. [4]See "The Pool of Gibeon" on page 444.

THE RELIABILITY OF THE **BIBLE**

STOPPING THE SUN

JOSHUA 10 The battle of "Joshua's long day" took place in the Valley of Aijalon (Jos 10:12), a strategic trade route through the northern Shephelah (an area of low-lying hills located between the coast and the higher Judean hill country). The city of Aijalon is mentioned outside the Bible in the **Amarna** Letters[1] and, centuries later, by the ancient Jewish historians Josephus and Eusebius. The precise location of Aijalon is uncertain (but see the proposed location northwest of Jerusalem on "Map 6").

There are numerous proposed explanations for the "long day" of verses 12–13. The traditional view holds that the Lord stopped the rotation of the earth, so that the sun and moon remained stationary from the perspective of the soldiers. Some proponents of this theory insist that there is astronomical evidence to support this long day, but such claims are unsubstantiated. Other, more conservative scholars read the passage in a figurative sense. Arguments in favor of a figurative reading are as follows:

- This is one of only two passages of poetry in Joshua, and the similar poetry in Judges 5:20 and Habakkuk 3:10–11 is likely figurative.
- It might be possible to translate the Hebrew word for "stood still" as "silenced," conceivably suggesting that the heat of the day was lifted to give the soldiers (on both sides) some welcome reprieve from the beating sun. Interpreting the Hebrew to mean simply that the weather became cooler, however, is a doubtful premise.
- Some argue that the sun's standing still refers to prolonged darkness rather than to prolonged daylight. The attack apparently took place at or before dawn (Jos 10:9), and verse 12 seems to indicate that sun and moon were low on the horizon when Joshua prayed. The hailstorm (v. 11) suggests dark conditions. Against this view, verse 13 appears to say that the sun was suspended in place.

The fact that a text is formatted as poetry does not necessarily imply that the event described is figurative or metaphorical. If what occurred was a pure miracle, of course, archaeological or astronomical evidence could not account for it. Regardless of the interpretation, we can agree on the crucial point of this passage: The Lord heard Joshua's request and granted Israel a miraculous defeat of the **Amorites**.

[1]See "The Amarna Tablets and the Habiru" on page 347.

The Sun Stands Still

10:1 [s]Jdg 1:7 [t]Jos 8:1 [u]Dt 20:16; Jos 8:22 [v]Jos 9:15
10 Now Adoni-Zedek king of Jerusalem[s] heard that Joshua had taken Ai[t] and totally destroyed[a][u] it,
doing to Ai and its king as he had done to Jericho and its king, and that the people of Gibeon had
made a treaty of peace[v] with Israel and were living near them. 2 He and his people were very much
alarmed at this, because Gibeon was an important city, like one of the royal cities; it was larger than Ai,
and all its men were good fighters. 3 So Adoni-Zedek king of Jerusalem appealed to Hoham king of He-
10:3 [w]Ge 13:18 [x]2Ch 11:9; 25:27; Ne 11:30; Isa 36:2; 37:8; Jer 34:7; Mic 1:13 bron,[w] Piram king of Jarmuth, Japhia king of Lachish[x] and Debir king of Eglon. 4 "Come up and help me
10:4 [y]Jos 9:15 attack Gibeon," he said, "because it has made peace[y] with Joshua and the Israelites."
10:5 [z]Nu 13:29 5 Then the five kings of the Amorites[z]—the kings of Jerusalem, Hebron, Jarmuth, Lachish and Eg-
lon—joined forces. They moved up with all their troops and took up positions against Gibeon and at-
tacked it.
6 The Gibeonites then sent word to Joshua in the camp at Gilgal: "Do not abandon your servants. Come
up to us quickly and save us! Help us, because all the Amorite kings from the hill country have joined forc-
es against us."
10:7 [a]Jos 8:1 7 So Joshua marched up from Gilgal with his entire army,[a] including all the best fighting men. 8 The
10:8 [b]Dt 3:2; Jos 1:9 LORD said to Joshua, "Do not be afraid[b] of them; I have given them into your hand. Not one of them will
be able to withstand you."
9 After an all-night march from Gilgal, Joshua took them by surprise. 10 The LORD threw them into

[a] *1* The Hebrew term refers to the irrevocable giving over of things or persons to the LORD, often by totally destroying them; also in verses 28, 35, 37, 39 and 40.

confusion before Israel,[c] who defeated them in a great victory at Gibeon. Israel pursued them along the **10:10** [c]Dt 7:23
road going up to Beth Horon[d] and cut them down all the way to Azekah[e] and Makkedah. 11As they fled [d]Jos 16:3,5 [e]Jos 15:35
before Israel on the road down from Beth Horon to Azekah, the LORD hurled large hailstones[f] down on **10:11** [f]Ps 18:12;
them from the sky, and more of them died from the hailstones than were killed by the swords of the Is- Isa 28:2,17
raelites.
12On the day the LORD gave the Amorites[g] over to Israel, Joshua said to the LORD in the presence of **10:12** [g]Am 2:9
Israel: [h]Jdg 1:35; 12:12

> "O sun, stand still over Gibeon,
> O moon, over the Valley of Aijalon.[h]"
> 13So the sun stood still,[i] **10:13** [i]Hab 3:11
> and the moon stopped, [j]2Sa 1:18
> till the nation avenged itself on[a] its enemies, [k]Isa 38:8

as it is written in the Book of Jashar.[j] **10:14** [l]ver 42;
The sun stopped[k] in the middle of the sky and delayed going down about a full day. 14There has nev- Ex 14:14; Dt 1:30;
er been a day like it before or since, a day when the LORD listened to a man. Surely the LORD was fighting[l] Ps 106:43; 136:24
for Israel!
15Then Joshua returned with all Israel to the camp at Gilgal.[m] **10:15** [m]ver 43

Five Amorite Kings Killed

16Now the five kings had fled and hidden in the cave at Makkedah. 17When Joshua was told that the
five kings had been found hiding in the cave at Makkedah, 18he said, "Roll large rocks up to the mouth
of the cave, and post some men there to guard it. 19But don't stop! Pursue your enemies, attack them from
the rear and don't let them reach their cities, for the LORD your God has given them into your hand."
20So Joshua and the Israelites destroyed them completely[n]—almost to a man—but the few who were **10:20** [n]Dt 20:16
left reached their fortified cities. 21The whole army then returned safely to Joshua in the camp at Mak-
kedah, and no one uttered a word against the Israelites.
22Joshua said, "Open the mouth of the cave and bring those five kings out to me." 23So they brought
the five kings out of the cave—the kings of Jerusalem, Hebron, Jarmuth, Lachish and Eglon. 24When
they had brought these kings to Joshua, he summoned all the men of Israel and said to the army com-
manders who had come with him, "Come here and put your feet[o] on the necks of these kings." So they **10:24** [o]Mal 4:3
came forward and placed their feet[p] on their necks. [p]Ps 110:1
25Joshua said to them, "Do not be afraid; do not be discouraged. Be strong and courageous.[q] This is **10:25** [q]Dt 31:6
what the LORD will do to all the enemies you are going to fight." 26Then Joshua struck and killed the kings
and hung them on five trees, and they were left hanging on the trees until evening.
27At sunset[r] Joshua gave the order and they took them down from the trees and threw them into the **10:27** [r]Dt 21:23;
cave where they had been hiding. At the mouth of the cave they placed large rocks, which are there to Jos 8:9,29
this day.
28That day Joshua took Makkedah. He put the city and its king to the sword and totally destroyed
everyone in it. He left no survivors.[s] And he did to the king of Makkedah as he had done to the king **10:28** [s]Dt 20:16
of Jericho.[t] [t]Jos 6:21

Southern Cities Conquered

29Then Joshua and all Israel with him moved on from Makkedah to Libnah and attacked it. 30The
LORD also gave that city and its king into Israel's hand. The city and everyone in it Joshua put to the sword.
He left no survivors there. And he did to its king as he had done to the king of Jericho.
31Then Joshua and all Israel with him moved on from Libnah to Lachish; he took up positions against

[a] 13 Or *nation triumphed over*

10:12 For a note on Aijalon, see 19:42.
10:13 The Book of Jashar, now lost, was an early account of Israel's wars (perhaps all in poetic form; see 2Sa 1:18).
10:16–43 Lachish, Debir, Libnah, Eglon and Makkedah (a town near Beth Shemesh and Azekah; its exact location is unknown) were all captured by controlling the approaches to the Judahite plateau. Several of these towns, most notably Lachish, contain destruction evidence that might possibly be correlated with the Israelite conquest, but the historical implications are not clear with regard to Jericho and Ai (see "The Walls of Jericho" on p. 312, "Jericho and the Date of the Conquest" on p. 314 and "Ai" on p. 316).
10:24 This public humiliation of defeated enemy chieftains, pictured in the artwork of Egypt and Assyria, was the usual climax of warfare in ancient times and the customary sign of total subjection.

it and attacked it. 32 The LORD handed Lachish over to Israel, and Joshua took it on the second day. The city and everyone in it he put to the sword, just as he had done to Libnah. 33 Meanwhile, Horam king of Gezer[u] had come up to help Lachish, but Joshua defeated him and his army—until no survivors were left.

34 Then Joshua and all Israel with him moved on from Lachish to Eglon; they took up positions against it and attacked it. 35 They captured it that same day and put it to the sword and totally destroyed everyone in it, just as they had done to Lachish.

36 Then Joshua and all Israel with him went up from Eglon to Hebron[v] and attacked it. 37 They took the city and put it to the sword, together with its king, its villages and everyone in it. They left no survivors. Just as at Eglon, they totally destroyed it and everyone in it.

38 Then Joshua and all Israel with him turned around and attacked Debir.[w] 39 They took the city, its king and its villages, and put them to the sword. Everyone in it they totally destroyed. They left no survivors. They did to Debir and its king as they had done to Libnah and its king and to Hebron.

40 So Joshua subdued the whole region, including the hill country, the Negev,[x] the western foothills and the mountain slopes,[y] together with all their kings.[z] He left no survivors. He totally destroyed all who breathed, just as the LORD, the God of Israel, had commanded.[a] 41 Joshua subdued them from Kadesh Barnea[b] to Gaza[c] and from the whole region of Goshen[d] to Gibeon. 42 All these kings and their lands Joshua conquered in one campaign, because the LORD, the God of Israel, fought[e] for Israel.

43 Then Joshua returned with all Israel to the camp at Gilgal.[f]

Northern Kings Defeated

11 When Jabin[g] king of Hazor[h] heard of this, he sent word to Jobab king of Madon, to the kings of Shimron[i] and Acshaph, 2 and to the northern kings who were in the mountains, in the Arabah[j] south of Kinnereth,[k] in the western foothills and in Naphoth Dor[a][l] on the west; 3 to the Canaanites in the east and west; to the Amorites, Hittites, Perizzites and Jebusites in the hill country; and to the Hivites[m] below Hermon in the region of Mizpah.[n] 4 They came out with all their troops and a large number of horses and chariots—a huge army, as numerous as the sand on the seashore.[o] 5 All these kings joined forces[p] and made camp together at the Waters of Merom, to fight against Israel.

6 The LORD said to Joshua, "Do not be afraid of them, because by this time tomorrow I will hand all of them over[q] to Israel, slain. You are to hamstring[r] their horses and burn their chariots."

7 So Joshua and his whole army came against them suddenly at the Waters of Merom and attacked them, 8 and the LORD gave them into the hand of Israel. They defeated them and pursued them all the way to Greater Sidon, to Misrephoth Maim,[s] and to the Valley of Mizpah on the east, until no survivors were left. 9 Joshua did to them as the LORD had directed: He hamstrung their horses and burned their chariots.

10 At that time Joshua turned back and captured Hazor and put its king to the sword. (Hazor had been the head of all these kingdoms.) 11 Everyone in it they put to the sword. They totally destroyed[b] them, not sparing anything that breathed,[t] and he burned up Hazor itself.

12 Joshua took all these royal cities and their kings and put them to the sword. He totally destroyed them, as Moses the servant of the LORD had commanded.[u] 13 Yet Israel did not burn any of the cities built on their mounds—except Hazor, which Joshua burned. 14 The Israelites carried off for themselves all the plunder and livestock of these cities, but all the people they put to the sword until they completely destroyed them, not sparing anyone that breathed.[v] 15 As the LORD commanded his servant Moses, so Moses commanded Joshua, and Joshua did it; he left nothing undone of all that the LORD commanded Moses.[w]

10:33 [u]Jos 16:3, 10; Jdg 1:29; 1Ki 9:15
10:36 [v]Jos 14:13; 15:13; Jdg 1:10
10:38 [w]Jos 15:15; Jdg 1:11
10:40 [x]Ge 12:9; Jos 12:8 [y]Dt 1:7 [z]Dt 7:24 [a]Dt 20:16-17
10:41 [b]Ge 14:7 [c]Ge 10:19 [d]Jos 11:16; 15:51
10:42 [e]ver 14
10:43 [f]ver 15; Jos 5:9
11:1 [g]Jdg 4:2,7, 23 [h]ver 10; 1Sa 12:9 [i]Jos 19:15
11:2 [j]Jos 12:3 [k]Nu 34:11 [l]Jos 17:11; Jdg 1:27; 1Ki 4:11
11:3 [m]Dt 7:1; Jdg 3:3,5; 1Ki 9:20 [n]Ge 31:49; Jos 15:38; 18:26
11:4 [o]Jdg 7:12; 1Sa 13:5
11:5 [p]Jdg 5:19
11:6 [q]Jos 10:8 [r]2Sa 8:4
11:8 [s]Jos 13:6
11:11 [t]Dt 20:16-17
11:12 [u]Nu 33:50-52; Dt 7:2
11:14 [v]Nu 31:11-12
11:15 [w]Ex 34:11; Jos 1:7

[a] *2* Or *in the heights of Dor* [b] *11* The Hebrew term refers to the irrevocable giving over of things or persons to the LORD, often by totally destroying them; also in verses 12, 20 and 21.

10:33 The defeat of Horam, king of Gezer, is an important detail, as he ruled the most powerful city in the area. Gezer was eventually taken over by the Egyptians and given to King Solomon as a wedding gift (see 1Ki 9:16; see also "Gezer" on p. 588).

10:38 While Debir (also known as Kiriath Sepher; 15:15) has previously been identified with Tell Beit Mirsim, it has more recently been equated with Khirbet Rabud, located about 8 miles (13 km) southwest of Hebron. (See "Tell Beit Mirsim" on p. 328 and "Hebron" on p. 446.)

10:40 The *Shephçlâh* ("lowland") is in reality not a valley but the low-lying hills that stretch from Israel's coast up the mountains.

10:41 This Goshen refers to the eastern Negev, not to be confused with the Goshen in the delta of Egypt.

11:1–5 Canaan was at this time made up of independent, generally hostile city-states, but a common enemy led them to combine forces. The northern coalition was Israel's most formidable foe to date. Horses and chariots posed an awesome challenge to the Israelites, whose army was made up of foot soldiers (see "Horses and Chariots in Ancient Warfare" on p. 114).

11:13 The Hebrew word for "mound" is *tel* (Arabic *tell*), a hill formed by the accumulated debris of multiple ancient settlements layered one upon another.

16 So Joshua took this entire land: the hill country, all the Negev, the whole region of Goshen, the west-
ern foothills,[x] the Arabah and the mountains of Israel with their foothills, 17 from Mount Halak, which 11:16 [x]Jos 10:41
rises toward Seir, to Baal Gad in the Valley of Lebanon[y] below Mount Hermon. He captured all their kings 11:17 [y]Jos 12:7
and struck them down, putting them to death.[z] 18 Joshua waged war against all these kings for a long [z]Dt 7:24
time. 19 Except for the Hivites living in Gibeon,[a] not one city made a treaty of peace with the Israelites, 11:19 [a]Jos 9:3
who took them all in battle. 20 For it was the LORD himself who hardened their hearts[b] to wage war against 11:20 [b]Ex 14:17;
Israel, so that he might destroy them totally, exterminating them without mercy, as the LORD had com- Ro 9:18 [c]Dt 7:16; Jdg 14:4
manded Moses.[c]

ARCHAEOLOGICAL SITES

HAZOR

A water system complex at Hazor
Photograph courtesy of © Dr. Gary Pratico

JOSHUA 11 **Hazor** (see "Map 3") was the largest city-state in **Canaan** at the time of the conquest, dominating the upper Galilee region.[1] This ancient site, located in the southwestern corner of the Hula Valley, approximately 8.5 miles (14 km) north-northeast of the Sea of Galilee, comprised an "upper city" (*acropolis*) of approximately 26 acres and a "lower city" of about 162 acres. It was heavily fortified with stone and mud brick walls as wide as 24 feet (7.3 m). One of the more important discoveries at Hazor was made by a tourist in 1962—a clay tablet with the name of the city on it.[2]

After the armies of the Canaanite northern coalition were defeated at Merom—most likely Tell el-Khureibeh, 9 miles (14.5 km) west of Hazor—Joshua captured Hazor and put it to the torch. Evidence of destruction by fire at the time of the conquest (late fifteenth century B.C.) has been discovered in many places at the site. Three temples from the same period have been excavated: the Long Temple in the upper city and the **Orthostat** and Square temples in the lower. All three had been violently destroyed, in keeping with God's command to "break down their altars, smash their sacred stones and cut down their Asherah poles" (Ex 34:13). Two of the temples, the Long Temple and the Square Temple, were so severely damaged that they were never rebuilt.

Soon after its destruction, however, the city as a whole was restored. The ruler of Hazor was the only leader referred to as king in the **Amarna Letters**, correspondence from the Canaanite rulers to the pharaoh of Egypt in the mid-fourteenth century B.C.[3] This special recognition demonstrates Hazor's importance in comparison to the other Canaanite city-states, as well as the accuracy of the Biblical phrase "head of all these kingdoms" (Jos 11:10). Canaanite Hazor met its end when Deborah and Barak destroyed the city in the late thirteenth century B.C.[4]

[1]See "The Conquest of Canaan" on page 310 and "Canaan" on page 324. [2]See "Cuneiform and Clay Tablets in the Ancient Near East" on page 1108 and "Writing Materials in the Ancient World" on page 2037. [3]See "The Amarna Tablets and the Habiru" on page 347. [4]See "Deborah and Barak and the Destruction of Hazor" on page 350.

11:21 [d]Nu 13:22, | 21 At that time Joshua went and destroyed the Anakites[d] from the hill country: from Hebron, Debir
33; Dt 9:2 | and Anab, from all the hill country of Judah, and from all the hill country of Israel. Joshua totally de-
11:22 [e]1Sa 17:4; 1Ki 2:39; | stroyed them and their towns. 22 No Anakites were left in Israelite territory; only in Gaza, Gath[e] and Ash-
1Ch 8:13 | dod[f] did any survive. 23 So Joshua took the entire land,[g] just as the LORD had directed Moses, and he gave
[f]1Sa 5:1; Isa 20:1 11:23 | it as an inheritance[h] to Israel according to their tribal divisions.[i]
[g]Jos 21:43-45 [h]Dt 1:38; 12:9-10; 25:19 [i]Nu 26:53 [j]Jos 14:15 | Then the land had rest from war.[j]

List of Defeated Kings

12 These are the kings of the land whom the Israelites had defeated and whose territory they took
12:1 [k]Dt 3:8 | over east of the Jordan, from the Arnon Gorge to Mount Hermon,[k] including all the eastern side
of the Arabah:

2 Sihon king of the Amorites,
who reigned in Heshbon. He ruled from Aroer on the rim of the Arnon Gorge—from the middle
of the gorge—to the Jabbok River, which is the border of the Ammonites. This included half of Gil-
12:2 [l]Dt 2:36 | ead.[l] 3 He also ruled over the eastern Arabah from the Sea of Kinnereth[a][m] to the Sea of the Arabah
12:3 [m]Jos 11:2 [n]Jos 13:20 | (the Salt Sea[b]), to Beth Jeshimoth,[n] and then southward below the slopes of Pisgah.

12:4 [o]Nu 21:21, 33; Dt 3:11 | 4 And the territory of Og king of Bashan,[o]
[p]Dt 1:4 | one of the last of the Rephaites, who reigned in Ashtaroth[p] and Edrei. 5 He ruled over Mount Her-
12:5 [q]Dt 3:10 | mon, Salecah,[q] all of Bashan to the border of the people of Geshur[r] and Maacah,[s] and half of Gil-
[r]1Sa 27:8 [s]Dt 3:14 | ead to the border of Sihon king of Heshbon.

6 Moses, the servant of the LORD, and the Israelites conquered them. And Moses the servant of the
12:6 [t]Nu 32:29, 33; Jos 13:8 | LORD gave their land to the Reubenites, the Gadites and the half-tribe of Manasseh to be their possession.[t]
7 These are the kings of the land that Joshua and the Israelites conquered on the west side of the Jor-
12:7 [u]Jos 11:17 | dan, from Baal Gad in the Valley of Lebanon[u] to Mount Halak, which rises toward Seir (their lands Josh-
ua gave as an inheritance to the tribes of Israel according to their tribal divisions— 8 the hill country, the
12:8 [v]Jos 11:16 | western foothills, the Arabah, the mountain slopes, the desert and the Negev[v]—the lands of the Hittites,
Amorites, Canaanites, Perizzites, Hivites and Jebusites):

12:9 [w]Jos 6:2	9 the king of Jericho[w]	one
[x]Jos 8:29	the king of Ai[x] (near Bethel)	one
12:10 [y]Jos 10:23	10 the king of Jerusalem[y]	one
	the king of Hebron	one
	11 the king of Jarmuth	one
	the king of Lachish	one
	12 the king of Eglon	one
12:12 [z]Jos 10:33	the king of Gezer[z]	one
	13 the king of Debir	one
	the king of Geder	one
	14 the king of Hormah	one
12:14 [a]Nu 21:1	the king of Arad[a]	one
	15 the king of Libnah	one
	the king of Adullam	one
	16 the king of Makkedah	one
12:16 [b]Jos 7:2	the king of Bethel[b]	one
	17 the king of Tappuah	one
12:17 [c]1Ki 4:10	the king of Hepher[c]	one

[a] 3 That is, Galilee [b] 3 That is, the Dead Sea

11:21–22 The Anakites, a people "of great size" (Nu 13:32), were so feared by the Israelites that they had initially refused to undertake the conquest. The Anakites were related to the Nephilim (see "Who Were the Nephilim?" on p. 215).

12:1–24 The conquest is summarized by a listing of the kings Israel defeated. East of the Jordan were only two kings, each of whom ruled a wide area with many cities. The land west of the Jordan was divided into individual city-states.

12:12 The king of Gezer had been defeated in the siege of Lachish (10:33), but the city itself was not captured by Joshua, nor were the cities of Aphek, Taanach, Megiddo or Dor (vv. 18–23; see Jdg 1:27–31; see also "Apkek" on p. 437, "Tanaach" on p. 591 and "Megiddo" on p. 1541).

Judah's prosperity was intermittent and depended in large part upon control of the trade routes to Egypt and the Red Sea. Border fortresses in the Judahite desert guarded the approaches from Edom. The "front door" of Judah was through Lachish and from there up to Hebron and Jerusalem.

Canaan

A ninth-century B.C. Israelite building at Hazor

Photograph courtesy of © Dr. Gary Pratico

JOSHUA 12 The land of **Canaan**, which the Lord had promised to give to Abraham (Ge 17:8), was recognized as a geopolitical unit in **Nuzi** texts (fifteenth century B.C.), in the **Amarna** letters of Egypt (fourteenth century B.C.) and in other ancient Near Eastern sources. Canaanite culture and religion are reflected in the **Late Bronze Age** (sixteenth to twelfth centuries. B.C.) literature of **Ugarit** (Byblos) in Syria. Worship of Baal as the god of war and of agricultural productivity is prominent in this literature.[1]

The derivation of the name Canaan is uncertain. It may stem from the Semitic root denoting "to be low" (e.g., lowlands) or relate to a purple dye produced by mollusks native to the region. It also has been suggested that the word originally meant "merchants," based on usage in some **Mari** and Egyptian texts, as well as in certain Biblical passages in which the word for "Canaanite" can also be rendered as "trader."

The Canaanite language was a mixture of various related dialects, although it appears that there was a higher, literary style all Canaanites shared in common. Ancient Hebrew is essentially a variety of the related Canaanite dialects, while standard Biblical Hebrew is probably closely related to the literary Canaanite form.[2]

The northern border of Canaan extended to Tyre and Sidon (Isa 23:11), veering inland (see especially Nu 34:2–12). The eastern border was just east of the Sea of Galilee and along the Jordan River to the Dead Sea. The southern border passed from the Dead Sea through Kadesh Barnea[3] in the northern Sinai Peninsula, and the Mediterranean Sea formed its western border.

Canaan thus occupied the middle ground between Egypt, Syria and **Anatolia**, and **Mesopotamia**, and by way of its seacoast was open to western peoples. Their main ports were Tyre, Sidon, Beirut and Byblos in modern Lebanon. Ships from these ports carried cedar wood, oil, wine and other goods to Egypt, Crete and Greece. They brought back linen from Egypt and fine pottery from Cyprus and Greece. Papyrus was carried from Egypt to Byblos; when the Greeks first saw papyrus scrolls, they called them *biblia*, "Byblos things," giving us the word "Bible." The area has a long history as a battleground among great powers, as well as of a region in which diverse peoples lived side by side.[4]

The **Transjordanian** territories of Kings Sihon and Og,[5] though captured and resettled by Israelite tribes, were neither included in God's original promise to Abraham nor considered a part of Canaan (although both the Moabites and the Ammonites were closely related to the Canaanites and spoke a Canaanite dialect).

The Israelites of the conquest encountered a mixture of people groups in Canaan,[6] most of them listed in the "table of nations" as descendants of Canaan, son of Ham, son of Noah (Ge 10:15–19). The Bible identifies more than 25 cities as Canaanite, including Gilgal, Hebron, Shiloh, Megiddo and Hazor. These "city-states," each with its own king, were only loosely organized but readily formed alliances in times of military crisis.[7]

See the "Index to Color Maps" on pages 2303–2306 in the back of this Bible for the locations of some of the places mentioned in this article.

[1]See "Tablets From Ugarit and Canaanite Religion" on page 304 and "Ugarit/Ras Shamra" on page 819. [2]See also "Languages of the Old Testament World" on page 672. [3]See "Kadesh Barnea" on page 214. [4]See "The History of the Holy Land" in the front of this Bible. [5]See "The Kingdoms of Sihon and Og" on page 244. [6]See "Lesser Known Peoples of the Old Testament" on page 265. [7]See "The Camp at Gilgal" on page 308, "Hebron" at on page 446, "The Tabernacle at Shiloh" on page 401, "The Destruction of Shiloh" on page 1200, "Megiddo" on page 1541 and "Hazor" on page 322.

18 the king of Aphek[d] — one
the king of Lasharon — one
19 the king of Madon — one
the king of Hazor — one
20 the king of Shimron Meron — one
the king of Acshaph[e] — one
21 the king of Taanach — one
the king of Megiddo — one
22 the king of Kedesh[f] — one
the king of Jokneam in Carmel[g] — one
23 the king of Dor (in Naphoth Dor[a][h]) — one
the king of Goyim in Gilgal — one
24 the king of Tirzah — one
thirty-one kings in all.[i]

Land Still to Be Taken

13 When Joshua was old and well advanced in years,[j] the LORD said to him, "You are very old, and
there are still very large areas of land to be taken over.

2 "This is the land that remains: all the regions of the Philistines and Geshurites: 3 from the Shihor
River[k] on the east of Egypt to the territory of Ekron[l] on the north, all of it counted as Canaanite
(the territory of the five Philistine rulers[m] in Gaza, Ashdod, Ashkelon, Gath and Ekron—that of
the Avvites);[n] 4 from the south, all the land of the Canaanites, from Arah of the Sidonians as far as
Aphek,[o] the region of the Amorites,[p] 5 the area of the Gebalites[b];[q] and all Lebanon[r] to the east,
from Baal Gad below Mount Hermon to Lebo[c] Hamath.

6 "As for all the inhabitants of the mountain regions from Lebanon to Misrephoth Maim,[s] that is, all
the Sidonians, I myself will drive them out before the Israelites. Be sure to allocate this land to Israel for
an inheritance, as I have instructed you,[t] 7 and divide it as an inheritance[u] among the nine tribes and
half of the tribe of Manasseh."

Division of the Land East of the Jordan

8 The other half of Manasseh,[d] the Reubenites and the Gadites had received the inheritance that Moses
had given them east of the Jordan, as he, the servant of the LORD, had assigned[v] it to them.

9 It extended from Aroer[w] on the rim of the Arnon Gorge, and from the town in the middle of the
gorge, and included the whole plateau[x] of Medeba as far as Dibon,[y] 10 and all the towns of Sihon
king of the Amorites, who ruled in Heshbon, out to the border of the Ammonites.[z] 11 It also includ-
ed Gilead, the territory of the people of Geshur and Maacah, all of Mount Hermon and all Bashan
as far as Salecah[a]— 12 that is, the whole kingdom of Og in Bashan,[b] who had reigned in Ashta-
roth[c] and Edrei and had survived as one of the last of the Rephaites.[d] Moses had defeated them
and taken over their land. 13 But the Israelites did not drive out the people of Geshur[e] and Maa-
cah,[f] so they continue to live among the Israelites to this day.

12:18 [d]Jos 13:4
12:20 [e]Jos 11:1
12:22 [f]Jos 19:37; 20:7; 21:32 [g]1Sa 15:12
12:23 [h]Jos 11:2
12:24 [i]Ps 135:11; Dt 7:24
13:1 [j]Ge 24:1; Jos 14:10
13:3 [k]Jer 2:18 [l]Jdg 1:18 [m]Jdg 3:3 [n]Dt 2:23
13:4 [o]Jos 12:18; 19:30 [p]Am 2:10
13:5 [q]1Ki 5:18; Ps 83:7; Eze 27:9 [r]Jos 12:7
13:6 [s]Jos 11:8 [t]Nu 33:54
13:7 [u]Jos 11:23; Ps 78:55
13:8 [v]Jos 12:6
13:9 [w]ver 16; Jdg 11:26 [x]Jer 48:8,21 [y]Nu 21:30
13:10 [z]Nu 21:24
13:11 [a]Jos 12:5
13:12 [b]Dt 3:11 [c]Jos 12:4 [d]Ge 14:5
13:13 [e]Jos 12:5 [f]Dt 3:14

[a] 23 Or *in the heights of Dor* [b] 5 That is, the area of Byblos [c] 5 Or *to the entrance to* [d] 8 Hebrew *With it* (that is, with the other half of Manasseh)

13:1–6 The Israelites had taken the less desirable hill country, but the fertile plains and cities were still largely in Canaanite hands. It was one thing for the Hebrew armies to sweep through the land but quite another for the individuals and tribes of the Hebrews to dispossess the Canaanites from that land and settle there. Their failure to do so meant that the Israelites lived as neighbors with pagan Canaanites, preparing the way for syncretism (combined worship of the Lord with that of idols). See "The Conquest of Canaan" on page 310.

13:1 After Moses' death, Joshua, the oldest man in Israel, must have been in his nineties (Caleb was eighty-five; see Jos 13:1; 14:7–11). Yet God assured him of victory, as he relied on the inspired Book of Moses (1:6–9). From this point onward Joshua's history is that of Israel's occupation of Canaan. Joshua's personal actions, however, included making preparations (1:10–18), sending spies against Jericho (2:1,23–24) and ordering Israel's advance across the Jordan (3:1). Joshua's esteem among the Israelites was similar to that of Moses himself (3:7; 4:14). West of the Jordan Joshua superintended Israel's rituals (5:2) and the construction of monuments for building the faith of children yet to come (4:4–7).

13:2–7 Moses had anticipated a gradual occupation of the promised land (Ex 23:28–30), and God had left in Canaan many nations, subdued but still powerful, to test his people (Jos 13:2–6; Jdg 2:21—3:4). So Joshua could not achieve Israel's final "rest" (Heb 4:8). Because of his advanced age, he divided Canaan among the tribes (Jos 13:6–7; 14:1; 19:51).

13:5 The Gebalites were inhabitants of the ancient city of Byblos (see the NIV text note and "Byblos" on p. 1349), just north of modern Beirut. The Phoenicians and the Philistines held most of the territory still to be occupied by Israel.

13:8—21:45 At Gilgal Joshua confirmed Moses' Transjordanian

14But to the tribe of Levi he gave no inheritance, since the offerings made by fire to the LORD, the God
of Israel, are their inheritance, as he promised them.[g]

15This is what Moses had given to the tribe of Reuben, clan by clan:

16The territory from Aroer[h] on the rim of the Arnon Gorge, and from the town in the middle of the
gorge, and the whole plateau past Medeba[i] 17to Heshbon and all its towns on the plateau, including
Dibon,[j] Bamoth Baal, Beth Baal Meon,[k] 18Jahaz,[l] Kedemoth, Mephaath,[m] 19Kiriathaim,[n] Sibmah,
Zereth Shahar on the hill in the valley, 20Beth Peor,[o] the slopes of Pisgah, and Beth Jeshimoth 21—
all the towns on the plateau and the entire realm of Sihon king of the Amorites, who ruled at Hesh-
bon. Moses had defeated him and the Midianite chiefs,[p] Evi, Rekem, Zur, Hur and Reba[q]—princ-
es allied with Sihon—who lived in that country. 22In addition to those slain in battle, the Israelites
had put to the sword Balaam son of Beor,[r] who practiced divination. 23The boundary of the Reu-
benites was the bank of the Jordan. These towns and their villages were the inheritance of the Reu-
benites, clan by clan.

24This is what Moses had given to the tribe of Gad, clan by clan:

25The territory of Jazer,[s] all the towns of Gilead and half the Ammonite country as far as Aroer, near
Rabbah; 26and from Heshbon[t] to Ramath Mizpah and Betonim, and from Mahanaim to the terri-
tory of Debir;[u] 27and in the valley, Beth Haram, Beth Nimrah, Succoth[v] and Zaphon with the rest
of the realm of Sihon king of Heshbon (the east side of the Jordan, the territory up to the end of
the Sea of Kinnereth[a][w]). 28These towns and their villages were the inheritance of the Gadites,[x]
clan by clan.

29This is what Moses had given to the half-tribe of Manasseh, that is, to half the family of the descendants
of Manasseh, clan by clan:

30The territory extending from Mahanaim[y] and including all of Bashan, the entire realm of Og
king of Bashan—all the settlements of Jair[z] in Bashan, sixty towns, 31half of Gilead, and Ashta-
roth and Edrei (the royal cities of Og in Bashan). This was for the descendants of Makir[a] son of Ma-
nasseh—for half of the sons of Makir, clan by clan.

32This is the inheritance Moses had given when he was in the plains of Moab across the Jordan east
of Jericho. 33But to the tribe of Levi, Moses had given no inheritance; the LORD, the God of Israel, is their
inheritance,[b] as he promised them.[c]

Division of the Land West of the Jordan

14 Now these are the areas the Israelites received as an inheritance in the land of Canaan, which Ele-
azar the priest, Joshua son of Nun and the heads of the tribal clans of Israel allotted to them.[d] 2Their
inheritances were assigned by lot[e] to the nine-and-a-half tribes, as the LORD had commanded through Mo-
ses. 3Moses had granted the two-and-a-half tribes their inheritance east of the Jordan[f] but had not grant-
ed the Levites an inheritance among the rest,[g] 4for the sons of Joseph had become two tribes—Manasseh
and Ephraim.[h] The Levites received no share of the land but only towns to live in, with pasturelands for
their flocks and herds. 5So the Israelites divided the land, just as the LORD had commanded Moses.[i]

Hebron Given to Caleb

6Now the men of Judah approached Joshua at Gilgal, and Caleb son of Jephunneh[j] the Kenizzite said
to him, "You know what the LORD said to Moses the man of God at Kadesh Barnea[k] about you and me. 7I
was forty years old when Moses the servant of the LORD sent me from Kadesh Barnea to explore the land.[l]
And I brought him back a report according to my convictions,[m] 8but my brothers who went up with me
made the hearts of the people melt with fear.[n] I, however, followed the LORD my God wholeheartedly.[o]
9So on that day Moses swore to me, 'The land on which your feet have walked will be your inheritance
and that of your children[p] forever, because you have followed the LORD my God wholeheartedly.'[b]

[a] 27 That is, Galilee [b] 9 Deut. 1:36

13:14 [g]ver 33; Dt 18:1-2
13:16 [h]ver 9; Jos 12:2 [i]Nu 21:30
13:17 [j]Nu 32:3 [k]1Ch 5:8
13:18 [l]Nu 21:23 [m]Jer 48:21
13:19 [n]Nu 32:37
13:20 [o]Dt 3:29
13:21 [p]Nu 25:15 [q]Nu 31:8
13:22 [r]Nu 22:5; 31:8
13:25 [s]Nu 21:32; Jos 21:39
13:26 [t]Nu 21:25; Jer 49:3 [u]Jos 10:3
13:27 [v]Ge 33:17 [w]Nu 34:11
13:28 [x]Nu 32:33
13:30 [y]Ge 32:2 [z]Nu 32:41
13:31 [a]Ge 50:23
13:33 [b]Nu 18:20 [c]ver 14; Jos 18:7
14:1 [d]Nu 34:17-18
14:2 [e]Nu 26:55
14:3 [f]Nu 32:33 [g]Jos 13:14
14:4 [h]Ge 41:52; 48:5
14:5 [i]Nu 34:13; 35:2; Jos 21:2
14:6 [j]Nu 13:6; 14:30 [k]Nu 13:26
14:7 [l]Nu 13:17 [m]Nu 13:30; 14:6-9
14:8 [n]Nu 13:31 [o]Nu 14:24
14:9 [p]Nu 14:24; Dt 1:36

---

settlement of the two and one-half tribes (13:8–33) and assigned territory to Judah (15:1–63), including Caleb's portion at Hebron (14:13; 15:13), and to Ephraim and Manasseh (16:1—17:13), encouraging them to more effective conquest, even while refusing to show them partiality (17:14–18). Later, at Shiloh, he exhorted the seven hesitant tribes (18:3), dispatched a commission on apportionment (18:8–10) and thus allotted the remaining lands (18:11—21:45), including cities of refuge and Levitical assignments (chs. 20–21). Joshua himself requested and built Timnath Serah in Ephraim (19:49–51).

10“Now then, just as the LORD promised,[q] he has kept me alive for forty-five years since the time he
said this to Moses, while Israel moved about in the desert. So here I am today, eighty-five years old! 11I
am still as strong[r] today as the day Moses sent me out; I’m just as vigorous to go out to battle now as I
was then. 12Now give me this hill country that the LORD promised me that day. You yourself heard then
that the Anakites[s] were there and their cities were large and fortified,[t] but, the LORD helping me, I will
drive them out just as he said.”
13Then Joshua blessed[u] Caleb son of Jephunneh and gave him Hebron[v] as his inheritance.[w] 14So He-
bron has belonged to Caleb son of Jephunneh the Kenizzite ever since, because he followed the LORD, the
God of Israel, wholeheartedly. 15(Hebron used to be called Kiriath Arba[x] after Arba,[y] who was the great-
est man among the Anakites.)
Then the land had rest[z] from war.

Allotment for Judah

15 The allotment for the tribe of Judah, clan by clan, extended down to the territory of Edom,[a] to
the Desert of Zin[b] in the extreme south.
2Their southern boundary started from the bay at the southern end of the Salt Sea,[a] 3crossed
south of Scorpion[b] Pass,[c] continued on to Zin and went over to the south of Kadesh Barnea. Then
it ran past Hezron up to Addar and curved around to Karka. 4It then passed along to Azmon[d] and
joined the Wadi of Egypt,[e] ending at the sea. This is their[c] southern boundary.
5The eastern boundary[f] is the Salt Sea as far as the mouth of the Jordan.
The northern boundary[g] started from the bay of the sea at the mouth of the Jordan, 6went up
to Beth Hoglah[h] and continued north of Beth Arabah to the Stone of Bohan[i] son of Reuben. 7The
boundary then went up to Debir from the Valley of Achor[j] and turned north to Gilgal, which fac-
es the Pass of Adummim south of the gorge. It continued along to the waters of En Shemesh and
came out at En Rogel.[k] 8Then it ran up the Valley of Ben Hinnom along the southern slope of the
Jebusite[l] city (that is, Jerusalem). From there it climbed to the top of the hill west of the Hinnom
Valley at the northern end of the Valley of Rephaim. 9From the hilltop the boundary headed toward
the spring of the waters of Nephtoah,[m] came out at the towns of Mount Ephron and went down to-
ward Baalah[n] (that is, Kiriath Jearim). 10Then it curved westward from Baalah to Mount Seir, ran
along the northern slope of Mount Jearim (that is, Kesalon), continued down to Beth Shemesh
and crossed to Timnah.[o] 11It went to the northern slope of Ekron, turned toward Shikkeron, passed
along to Mount Baalah and reached Jabneel.[p] The boundary ended at the sea.
12The western boundary is the coastline of the Great Sea.[d][q]
These are the boundaries around the people of Judah by their clans.

13In accordance with the LORD’s command to him, Joshua gave to Caleb son of Jephunneh a portion
in Judah—Kiriath Arba, that is, Hebron. (Arba was the forefather of Anak.)[r] 14From Hebron Caleb drove
out the three Anakites[s]—Sheshai, Ahiman and Talmai[t]—descendants of Anak.[u] 15From there he
marched against the people living in Debir (formerly called Kiriath Sepher). 16And Caleb said, “I will
give my daughter Acsah[v] in marriage to the man who attacks and captures Kiriath Sepher.” 17Othniel[w]
son of Kenaz, Caleb’s brother, took it; so Caleb gave his daughter Acsah to him in marriage.
18One day when she came to Othniel, she urged him[e] to ask her father for a field. When she got off her
donkey, Caleb asked her, “What can I do for you?”
19She replied, “Do me a special favor. Since you have given me land in the Negev, give me also springs
of water.” So Caleb gave her the upper and lower springs.

14:10 [q]Nu 14:30 **14:11** [r]Dt 34:7 **14:12** [s]Nu 13:33 [t]Nu 13:28 **14:13** [u]Jos 22:6, 7 [v]Jos 10:36 [w]Jdg 1:20; 1Ch 6:56 **14:15** [x]Ge 23:2 [y]Jos 15:13 [z]Jos 11:23 **15:1** [a]Nu 34:3 [b]Nu 33:36 **15:3** [c]Nu 34:4 **15:4** [d]Nu 34:5 [e]Ge 15:18 **15:5** [f]Nu 34:10 [g]Jos 18:15-19 **15:6** [h]Jos 18:19, 21 [i]Jos 18:17 **15:7** [j]Jos 7:24 [k]2Sa 17:17; 1Ki 1:9 **15:8** [l]ver 63; Jos 18:16,28; Jdg 1:21; 19:10 **15:9** [m]Jos 18:15 [n]1Ch 13:6 **15:10** [o]Ge 38:12; Jdg 14:1 **15:11** [p]Jos 19:33 **15:12** [q]Nu 34:6 **15:13** [r]Jos 14:13-15 **15:14** [s]Nu 13:33 [t]Nu 13:22 [u]Jdg 1:10,20 **15:16** [v]Jdg 1:12 **15:17** [w]Jdg 3:9, 11

[a] *2* That is, the Dead Sea; also in verse 5 [b] *3* Hebrew *Akrabbim* [c] *4* Hebrew *your* [d] *12* That is, the Mediterranean; also in verse 47 [e] *18* Hebrew and some Septuagint manuscripts; other Septuagint manuscripts (see also note at Judges 1:14) *Othniel, he urged her*

15:13–19 All Biblical references to Debir (“Map 3”) appear in the context of the conquest and distribution of Canaan. Debir, a major Canaanite city during the period of the conquest (10:38–39), was located in the Negev of the southern hill country (15:13–19,48–51) in the vicinity of Hebron (11:21). Designated a Levitical city, it possessed ample pasturelands (21:13–15). Caleb had originally received Debir as part of his inheritance in the land (15:15).

Khirbet Rabud, 8 miles (nearly 13 km) southwest of Hebron, has been suggested as the site of Biblical Debir because (1) it is located on the edge of the Negev, (2) its occupational history matches that of the Biblical record, (3) no other major Canaanite city is located in the region and (4) its water supply is like that described as having been given upon request to Acsah, Caleb’s daughter, as part of her dowry (vv. 13–19; Jdg 1:11–15). Two spring-fed, “upper” and “lower” underground chambers, each tapped by a well, were located just 2 miles (3.2 km) north of Khirbet Rabud.

ARCHAEOLOGICAL SITES

TELL BEIT MIRSIM

JOSHUA 15 Tell Beit Mirsim, located 15 miles (9.3 km) southwest of Hebron[1] ("Map 3"), was excavated in the late 1920s and the early 1930s. W. F. Albright, a principal excavator of the site, believed it to be the Biblical Debir. This identification is now widely rejected; Khirbet Rabud is now considered to be a better candidate for Debir ("Map 3"), and no one knows the name by which Tell Beit Mirsim was known in Biblical times. Even so, Albright's careful excavation of Tell Beit Mirsim has helped to define the modern science of archaeology. The story of Tell Beit Mirsim, a particularly informative site, helps us to understand the basics of archaeological methods.

✣ In digging a site, it is important to be able to distinguish the strata for that site. *Strata* refer to the layers formed by successive occupations of a location. Throughout the history of a city, newer occupation levels are built on top of older ones (i.e., earlier occupation levels are lower, with more recent levels closer to the surface). For example, a city may have existed at a particular spot in the twelfth century B.C.—until it was burned down by an enemy. Rebuilding could have occurred at some later time at the site, only for it to have been destroyed again. For example, the presence of clearly defined burn layers at Tell Beit Mirsim have helped archaeologists to distinguish the various strata of that site.

✣ Pottery helps to date the strata at a site. The use of pottery to fix a date for a stratum is referred to as "ceramic dating."[2] Pottery samples were collected from Tell Beit Mirsim and compared to finds from other sites in Palestine. Careful classification of excavated pottery at the Tell Beit Mirsim site helped to refine and establish the pottery-dating system.

✣ Tell Beit Mirsim was unusual in that it held remains from *ten* different occupation levels, spanning the **Early Bronze**, **Middle Bronze**, **Late Bronze** and **Iron** periods.[3] Also, the site yielded excellent examples of the **material culture** of a Judean town during the **monarchic period** (when Israel and Judah were ruled by kings). This evidence is useful for making comparisons to physical remains from other sites, especially those related to the archaeology of early Israel.

✣ Periodically the tools of archaeology need to be refined. As an example, Albright attributed the final destruction of Tell Beit Mirsim to the **Babylonians** in 589–587 B.C. Recent investigation, however, has indicated that its ultimate demise likely came at the hands of the **Assyrians**, as part of the campaign of Sennacherib in 701 B.C.[4] Based upon the new evidence supporting this dating adjustment, archaeologists have found it necessary to make minor adjustments in the ceramic chronology.

[1]See "Hebron" on page 446. [2]See "The Potsherd: Pottery in the Bible" on page 738. [3]See "Archaeological Periods" chart on page xx in the front of this Bible. [4]See "Hezekiah Against the Assyrians" on page 1118.

An excavation in progress
Preserving Bible Times; © Dr. James C. Martin

20 This is the inheritance of the tribe of Judah, clan by clan:

21 The southernmost towns of the tribe of Judah in the Negev toward the boundary of Edom were:
Kabzeel, Eder,[x] Jagur, 22 Kinah, Dimonah, Adadah, 23 Kedesh, Hazor, Ithnan, 24 Ziph,[y] Telem, Bealoth, 25 Hazor Hadattah, Kerioth Hezron (that is, Hazor), 26 Amam, Shema, Moladah,[z] 27 Hazar Gaddah, Heshmon, Beth Pelet, 28 Hazar Shual, Beersheba,[a] Biziothiah, 29 Baalah,[b] Iim, Ezem, 30 Eltolad,[c] Kesil, Hormah, 31 Ziklag,[d] Madmannah, Sansannah, 32 Lebaoth, Shilhim, Ain and Rimmon[e]—a total of twenty-nine towns and their villages.

33 In the western foothills:
Eshtaol,[f] Zorah, Ashnah, 34 Zanoah,[g] En Gannim, Tappuah, Enam, 35 Jarmuth,[h] Adullam,[i] Socoh, Azekah, 36 Shaaraim, Adithaim and Gederah[j] (or Gederothaim)[a]—fourteen towns and their villages.

37 Zenan, Hadashah, Migdal Gad, 38 Dilean, Mizpah, Joktheel,[k] 39 Lachish,[l] Bozkath,[m] Eglon, 40 Cabbon, Lahmas, Kitlish, 41 Gederoth, Beth Dagon, Naamah and Makkedah[n]—sixteen towns and their villages.

42 Libnah, Ether, Ashan,[o] 43 Iphtah, Ashnah, Nezib, 44 Keilah, Aczib[p] and Mareshah[q]—nine towns and their villages.

45 Ekron, with its surrounding settlements and villages; 46 west of Ekron, all that were in the vicinity of Ashdod, together with their villages; 47 Ashdod,[r] its surrounding settlements and villages; and Gaza, its settlements and villages, as far as the Wadi of Egypt[s] and the coastline of the Great Sea.[t]

48 In the hill country:
Shamir, Jattir,[u] Socoh, 49 Dannah, Kiriath Sannah (that is, Debir[v]), 50 Anab, Eshtemoh,[w] Anim, 51 Goshen,[x] Holon and Giloh—eleven towns and their villages.

52 Arab, Dumah,[y] Eshan, 53 Janim, Beth Tappuah, Aphekah, 54 Humtah, Kiriath Arba (that is, Hebron) and Zior—nine towns and their villages.

55 Maon, Carmel,[z] Ziph, Juttah, 56 Jezreel,[a] Jokdeam, Zanoah, 57 Kain, Gibeah[b] and Timnah—ten towns and their villages.

58 Halhul, Beth Zur,[c] Gedor, 59 Maarath, Beth Anoth and Eltekon—six towns and their villages.

60 Kiriath Baal (that is, Kiriath Jearim[d]) and Rabbah[e]—two towns and their villages.

61 In the desert:
Beth Arabah, Middin, Secacah, 62 Nibshan, the City of Salt and En Gedi[f]—six towns and their villages.

63 Judah could not[g] dislodge the Jebusites[h], who were living in Jerusalem; to this day the Jebusites live there with the people of Judah.

Allotment for Ephraim and Manasseh

16 The allotment for Joseph began at the Jordan of Jericho,[b] east of the waters of Jericho, and went up from there through the desert[i] into the hill country of Bethel. 2 It went on from Bethel (that is, Luz[j]),[c] crossed over to the territory of the Arkites in Ataroth, 3 descended westward to the territory of the Japhletites as far as the region of Lower Beth Horon[k] and on to Gezer,[l] ending at the sea.

[a] 36 Or *Gederah and Gederothaim* [b] 1 *Jordan of Jericho* was possibly an ancient name for the Jordan River. [c] 2 Septuagint; Hebrew *Bethel to Luz*

15:21 [x]Ge 35:21
15:24 [y]1Sa 23:14
15:26 [z]1Ch 4:28
15:28 [a]Ge 21:31
15:29 [b]ver 9
15:30 [c]Jos 19:4
15:31 [d]1Sa 27:6
15:32 [e]Jdg 20:45
15:33 [f]Jdg 13:25; 16:31
15:34 [g]1Ch 4:18; Ne 3:13
15:35 [h]Jos 10:3 [i]1Sa 22:1
15:36 [j]1Ch 12:4
15:38 [k]2Ki 14:7
15:39 [l]Jos 10:3; 2Ki 14:19 [m]2Ki 22:1
15:41 [n]Jos 10:10
15:42 [o]1Sa 30:30
15:44 [p]Jdg 1:31 [q]Mic 1:15
15:47 [r]Jos 11:22 [s]ver 4 [t]Nu 34:6
15:48 [u]1Sa 30:27
15:49 [v]Jos 10:3
15:50 [w]Jos 21:14
15:51 [x]Jos 10:41; 11:16
15:52 [y]Ge 25:14
15:55 [z]Jos 12:22
15:56 [a]Jos 17:16
15:57 [b]Jos 18:28; Jdg 19:12
15:58 [c]1Ch 2:45
15:60 [d]Jos 18:14 [e]Dt 3:11
15:62 [f]1Sa 23:29
15:63 [g]Jdg 1:21 [h]2Sa 5:6
16:1 [i]Jos 8:15; 18:12
16:2 [j]Jos 18:13
16:3 [k]2Ch 8:5 [l]Jos 10:33; 1Ki 9:15

15:41 Dagon, the chief god of the Philistines, who was originally worshiped by the Canaanites before the Philistine invasion of Canaan, is indicated in such place-names as Beth Dagon in Judah (v. 41) and in Asher (19:27). Either a fish god or the god of agriculture, he is pictured on a wall of a palace in Babylon as half a fish.
15:42 Ashan, a town in the tribe of Judah, was later given to Simeon because Judah's territory was too large—then still later given to the priests (v. 42; 19:7; 1Ch 4:32; 6:59). This was one of about a dozen towns mentioned in the lists of both Judah and Simeon, as the boundary was indistinct and the territories overlapped.
15:43 Nezib, a village mentioned only here in the Bible, belonged to Judah and lay about 10 miles (17 km) northwest of Hebron. The word means "something set"; hence, a garrison. The site still retains this name: Beit Nusib, "House of the Garrison."
15:62 In a country near the desert, springs, pools, pits, cisterns and fountains are of great importance (see "Wells, Cisterns and Aqueducts in the Ancient World" on p. 1259). Many towns and other locations are named for the springs at their sites (e.g., En Gedi, "the fountain of the kid").
16:2 Luz was located on the northern boundary of the area of the tribe of Benjamin (v. 2; 18:13). Jacob had slept there when fleeing from home, at which time God had appeared to him in a dream. To commemorate the occasion Jacob had changed the name of the town to Bethel ("house of God"; Ge 28:19). But the place continued to be called Luz down to the time of the judges. See "Bethel" on page 59.

4 So Manasseh and Ephraim, the descendants of Joseph, received their inheritance.[m] 16:4 [m]Jos 17:14

5 This was the territory of Ephraim, clan by clan:
The boundary of their inheritance went from Ataroth Addar[n] in the east to Upper Beth Horon 16:5 [n]Jos 18:13
6 and continued to the sea. From Micmethath[o] on the north it curved eastward to Taanath Shiloh, 16:6 [o]Jos 17:7
passing by it to Janoah on the east. 7 Then it went down from Janoah to Ataroth[p] and Naarah, 16:7 [p]1Ch 7:28
touched Jericho and came out at the Jordan. 8 From Tappuah the border went west to the Kanah Ra-
vine[q] and ended at the sea. This was the inheritance of the tribe of the Ephraimites, clan by clan. 16:8 [q]Jos 17:9
9 It also included all the towns and their villages that were set aside for the Ephraimites within the
inheritance of the Manassites.
10 They did not dislodge the Canaanites living in Gezer; to this day the Canaanites live among the people
of Ephraim but are required to do forced labor.[r] 16:10 [r]Jos 17:13; Jdg 1:28-29; 1Ki 9:16

17 This was the allotment for the tribe of Manasseh as Joseph's firstborn,[s] that is, for Makir,[t] Ma-
nasseh's firstborn. Makir was the ancestor of the Gileadites, who had received Gilead and Ba- 17:1 [s]Ge 41:51 [t]Ge 50:23
shan because the Makirites were great soldiers. 2 So this allotment was for the rest of the people of Ma-
nasseh—the clans of Abiezer,[u] Helek, Asriel, Shechem, Hepher and Shemida. These are the other male 17:2 [u]Nu 26:30; 1Ch 7:18
descendants of Manasseh son of Joseph by their clans.
3 Now Zelophehad son of Hepher,[v] the son of Gilead, the son of Makir, the son of Manasseh, had no 17:3 [v]Nu 27:1 [w]Nu 26:33
sons but only daughters,[w] whose names were Mahlah, Noah, Hoglah, Milcah and Tirzah. 4 They went to
Eleazar the priest, Joshua son of Nun, and the leaders and said, "The LORD commanded Moses to give us
an inheritance among our brothers." So Joshua gave them an inheritance along with the brothers of their
father, according to the LORD's command.[x] 5 Manasseh's share consisted of ten tracts of land besides Gil- 17:4 [x]Nu 27:5-7
ead and Bashan east of the Jordan, 6 because the daughters of the tribe of Manasseh received an inheri-
tance among the sons. The land of Gilead belonged to the rest of the descendants of Manasseh.

16:6 Micmethath, a landmark on the borders of Ephraim and Manasseh (see also 17:7), was east of, but quite close to, Shechem ("Map 3"; see "Shechem" on p. 340). Instead of being a town, it may have been, as its name implies, merely a "lurking place."
16:10 Surviving Canaanites were conscripted to "forced labor" (cf. 17:13; Jdg 1:28–30,33,35). The entire native population was supposed to have been put to death without pity or exception (Dt 20:10–18). As a result of their failure to follow through with this mandate, the Israelites would be corrupted by intermarrying with these pagans and by engaging in their perverse and idolatrous worship practices (see Jdg 2:1–3; 3:5–6; 10:6).
17:3–5 The daughters of Zelophehad based their claim on what "the LORD commanded Moses" (v. 4; cf. Nu 27:5–7). Whether the rights of the father or of the daughters were primarily being protected, an unusual privilege and a remarkable measure of equality were granted to these women.

ANCIENT TEXTS AND ARTIFACTS

The Taanach Cult Stands

JOSHUA 17 Occupied from the third millennium B.C. until the fourteenth century A.D. (although not continuously), the city of Taanach ("Map 4") is located a few miles southeast of Megiddo in the foothills above the Valley of Jezreel.[1] Along with several other items used in deity worship, two tenth-century B.C. cult stands have been recovered intact from this site. The first was uncovered during excavations from 1902–1904 and is about 35 inches (89 cm) tall. The second, discovered when excavations were resumed in the 1960s, is somewhat smaller, measuring about 23.5 inches (60 cm) in height.

Both stands contain panels of sculpted figures surrounding a hollow core. The larger stand boasts two decorated panels with griffin- or sphinx-like creatures on them, as well as the protruding heads of other animal and human figures. The smaller is decorated in four panels: The bottom is of a female figure holding two lions; the next a cut-out space flanked by griffins (mythical animals combining physical characteristics of eagles and lions); the third a sacred tree with an ibex (wild goat) on either side, each surrounded by lion-like creatures; and the uppermost a winged sun disk on the back of a horse or bull.

This winged sun disk may represent the **Canaanite** god Baal,[2] while the female figure with the lions may depict his consort or partner, Asherah. These were gods to whom the Israelites turned when they fell into apostasy.[3]

[1]See "Taanach" on page 591, "The Valley of Jezreel" on page 1412 and "Megiddo" on page 1541. [2]See "Baal and the Fertility Cults" on page 1414. [3]See "Devotion to Asherah in the Khirbet El-Qom Inscription" on page 638 and "The Kuntillet Ajrûd Inscriptions: The Lord's Asherah?" on page 1220.

7 The territory of Manasseh extended from Asher to Micmethath[y] east of Shechem.[z] The boundary ran southward from there to include the people living at En Tappuah. 8 (Manasseh had the land of Tappuah, but Tappuah[a] itself, on the boundary of Manasseh, belonged to the Ephraimites.) 9 Then the boundary continued south to the Kanah Ravine.[b] There were towns belonging to Ephraim lying among the towns of Manasseh, but the boundary of Manasseh was the northern side of the ravine and ended at the sea. 10 On the south the land belonged to Ephraim, on the north to Manasseh. The territory of Manasseh reached the sea and bordered Asher on the north and Issachar[c] on the east.

11 Within Issachar and Asher, Manasseh also had Beth Shan,[d] Ibleam and the people of Dor,[e] Endor,[f] Taanach and Megiddo,[g] together with their surrounding settlements (the third in the list is Naphoth[a]).

12 Yet the Manassites were not able[h] to occupy these towns, for the Canaanites were determined to live in that region. 13 However, when the Israelites grew stronger, they subjected the Canaanites to forced labor but did not drive them out completely.[i]

14 The people of Joseph said to Joshua, "Why have you given us only one allotment and one portion for an inheritance? We are a numerous people and the LORD has blessed us abundantly."[j]

15 "If you are so numerous," Joshua answered, "and if the hill country of Ephraim is too small for you, go up into the forest and clear land for yourselves there in the land of the Perizzites and Rephaites.[k]"

16 The people of Joseph replied, "The hill country is not enough for us, and all the Canaanites who live in the plain have iron chariots,[l] both those in Beth Shan and its settlements and those in the Valley of Jezreel."

17 But Joshua said to the house of Joseph—to Ephraim and Manasseh—"You are numerous and very powerful. You will have not only one allotment 18 but the forested hill country as well. Clear it, and its farthest limits will be yours; though the Canaanites have iron chariots[m] and though they are strong, you can drive them out."

Division of the Rest of the Land

18 The whole assembly of the Israelites gathered at Shiloh[n] and set up the Tent of Meeting[o] there. The country was brought under their control, 2 but there were still seven Israelite tribes who had not yet received their inheritance.

3 So Joshua said to the Israelites: "How long will you wait before you begin to take possession of the land that the LORD, the God of your fathers, has given you? 4 Appoint three men from each tribe. I will send them out to make a survey of the land and to write a description of it, according to the inheritance of each.[p] Then they will return to me. 5 You are to divide the land into seven parts. Judah is to remain in its territory on the south[q] and the house of Joseph in its territory on the north.[r] 6 After you have written descriptions of the seven parts of the land, bring them here to me and I will cast lots[s] for you in the presence of the LORD our God. 7 The Levites, however, do not get a portion among you, because the priestly service of the LORD is their inheritance.[t] And Gad, Reuben and the half-tribe of Manasseh have already received their inheritance on the east side of the Jordan. Moses the servant of the LORD gave it to them.[u]"

8 As the men started on their way to map out the land, Joshua instructed them, "Go and make a survey of the land and write a description of it. Then return to me, and I will cast lots for you here at Shiloh[v] in the presence of the LORD." 9 So the men left and went through the land. They wrote its description on a scroll, town by town, in seven parts, and returned to Joshua in the camp at Shiloh. 10 Joshua then cast lots[w] for them in Shiloh in the presence[x] of the LORD, and there he distributed the land to the Israelites according to their tribal divisions.[y]

Allotment for Benjamin

11 The lot came up for the tribe of Benjamin, clan by clan. Their allotted territory lay between the tribes of Judah and Joseph:

[a] *11* That is, Naphoth Dor

17:7 [y]Jos 16:6 [z]Ge 12:6; Jos 21:21
17:8 [a]Jos 16:8
17:9 [b]Jos 16:8
17:10 [c]Ge 30:18
17:11 [d]1Sa 31:10; 1Ki 4:12; 1Ch 7:29 [e]Jos 11:2 [f]1Sa 28:7; Ps 83:10 [g]1Ki 9:15
17:12 [h]Jdg 1:27
17:13 [i]Jos 16:10
17:14 [j]Nu 26:28-37
17:15 [k]Ge 14:5
17:16 [l]Jdg 1:19; 4:3,13
17:18 [m]ver 16
18:1 [n]Jos 19:51; 21:2; Jdg 18:31; 21:12,19; 1Sa 1:3; 4:3; Jer 7:12; 26:6 [o]Ex 27:21
18:4 [p]Mic 2:5
18:5 [q]Jos 15:1 [r]Jos 16:1-4
18:6 [s]Jos 14:2
18:7 [t]Jos 13:33 [u]Jos 13:8
18:8 [v]ver 1
18:10 [w]Nu 34:13 [x]ver 1; Jer 7:12 [y]Nu 33:54; Jos 19:51

17:16 Chariots were effective only in the plains. Certain parts of chariots—very likely the axles—were made of iron. The use of iron was a new development, and these advanced implements of war were not used by the armies of Israel until the time of Solomon (see 1Ki 9:22; 10:26–29; see also "Horses and Chariots in Ancient Warfare" on p. 114).

12 On the north side their boundary began at the Jordan, passed the northern slope of Jericho
and headed west into the hill country, coming out at the desert[z] of Beth Aven.[a] 13 From there it
crossed to the south slope of Luz[b] (that is, Bethel[c]) and went down to Ataroth Addar[d] on the hill
south of Lower Beth Horon.
14 From the hill facing Beth Horon[e] on the south the boundary turned south along the western
side and came out at Kiriath Baal (that is, Kiriath Jearim), a town of the people of Judah. This was
the western side.
15 The southern side began at the outskirts of Kiriath Jearim on the west, and the boundary came
out at the spring of the waters of Nephtoah.[f] 16 The boundary went down to the foot of the hill fac-
ing the Valley of Ben Hinnom, north of the Valley of Rephaim. It continued down the Hinnom Val-
ley[g] along the southern slope of the Jebusite city and so to En Rogel.[h] 17 It then curved north, went
to En Shemesh, continued to Geliloth, which faces the Pass of Adummim, and ran down to the Stone
of Bohan[i] son of Reuben. 18 It continued to the northern slope of Beth Arabah[a][j] and on down into
the Arabah. 19 It then went to the northern slope of Beth Hoglah and came out at the northern bay
of the Salt Sea,[b][k] at the mouth of the Jordan in the south. This was the southern boundary.
20 The Jordan formed the boundary on the eastern side.
These were the boundaries that marked out the inheritance of the clans of Benjamin on all sides.[l]
21 The tribe of Benjamin, clan by clan, had the following cities:
Jericho, Beth Hoglah, Emek Keziz, 22 Beth Arabah, Zemaraim, Bethel,[m] 23 Avvim, Parah, Oph-
rah, 24 Kephar Ammoni, Ophni and Geba[n]—twelve towns and their villages.
25 Gibeon,[o] Ramah,[p] Beeroth,[q] 26 Mizpah,[r] Kephirah, Mozah, 27 Rekem, Irpeel, Taralah, 28 Zelah,[s]
Haeleph, the Jebusite city[t] (that is, Jerusalem[u]), Gibeah[v] and Kiriath—fourteen towns and their
villages.
This was the inheritance of Benjamin for its clans.

Allotment for Simeon

19 The second lot came out for the tribe of Simeon, clan by clan. Their inheritance lay within the
territory of Judah.[w] 2 It included:
Beersheba[x] (or Sheba),[c] Moladah, 3 Hazar Shual, Balah, Ezem, 4 Eltolad, Bethul, Hormah, 5 Zik-
lag, Beth Marcaboth, Hazar Susah, 6 Beth Lebaoth and Sharuhen—thirteen towns and their vil-
lages;
7 Ain, Rimmon, Ether and Ashan[y]—four towns and their villages— 8 and all the villages around
these towns as far as Baalath Beer (Ramah in the Negev).[z]
This was the inheritance of the tribe of the Simeonites, clan by clan. 9 The inheritance of the Simeonites
was taken from the share of Judah,[a] because Judah's portion was more than they needed. So the Sime-
onites received their inheritance within the territory of Judah.[b]

Allotment for Zebulun

10 The third lot came up for Zebulun,[c] clan by clan:
The boundary of their inheritance went as far as Sarid. 11 Going west it ran to Maralah, touched
Dabbesheth, and extended to the ravine near Jokneam.[d] 12 It turned east from Sarid toward the
sunrise to the territory of Kisloth Tabor and went on to Daberath and up to Japhia. 13 Then it con-
tinued eastward to Gath Hepher and Eth Kazin; it came out at Rimmon[e] and turned toward Neah.
14 There the boundary went around on the north to Hannathon and ended at the Valley of Iphtah
El. 15 Included were Kattath, Nahalal, Shimron, Idalah and Bethlehem.[f] There were twelve towns
and their villages.
16 These towns and their villages were the inheritance of Zebulun,[g] clan by clan.[h]

Allotment for Issachar

17 The fourth lot came out for Issachar,[i] clan by clan. 18 Their territory included:

18:12 [z]Jos 16:1 [a]Jos 7:2
18:13 [b]Ge 28:19 [c]Jdg 1:23 [d]Jos 16:5
18:14 [e]Jos 10:10
18:15 [f]Jos 15:9
18:16 [g]Jos 15:8; 2Ki 23:10 [h]Jos 15:7
18:17 [i]Jos 15:6
18:18 [j]Jos 15:6
18:19 [k]Ge 14:3
18:20 [l]Jos 21:4, 17; 1Sa 9:1
18:22 [m]Jos 16:1
18:24 [n]Isa 10:29
18:25 [o]Jos 9:3 [p]Jdg 4:5 [q]Jos 9:17
18:26 [r]Jos 11:3
18:28 [s]2Sa 21:14 [t]Jos 15:8 [u]Jos 10:1 [v]Jos 15:57
19:1 [w]ver 9; Ge 49:7
19:2 [x]Ge 21:14; 1Ki 19:3
19:7 [y]Jos 15:42
19:8 [z]Jos 10:40
19:9 [a]Ge 49:7 [b]Eze 48:24
19:10 [c]Jos 21:7, 34
19:11 [d]Jos 12:22
19:13 [e]Jos 15:32
19:15 [f]Ge 35:19
19:16 [g]ver 10; Jos 21:7 [h]Eze 48:26
19:17 [i]Ge 30:18

[a] *18* Septuagint; Hebrew *slope facing the Arabah* [b] *19* That is, the Dead Sea [c] *2* Or *Beersheba, Sheba*; 1 Chron. 4:28 does not have *Sheba*.

19:15 This Bethlehem is Beth Lahm, east of Mount Carmel—not to be confused with Bethlehem in Judah.

19:18 [j]Jos 15:56 Jezreel,[j] Kesulloth, Shunem,[k] 19Hapharaim, Shion, Anaharath, 20Rabbith, Kishion, Ebez, 21Re-
[k]1Sa 28:4; 2Ki 4:8 19:22 [l]Jdg 4:6, meth, En Gannim, En Haddah and Beth Pazzez. 22The boundary touched Tabor,[l] Shahazumah and
12; Ps 89:12 [m]Jos 15:10 Beth Shemesh,[m] and ended at the Jordan. There were sixteen towns and their villages.
19:23 [n]Jos 17:10 [o]Ge 49:15; 23These towns and their villages were the inheritance of the tribe of Issachar,[n] clan by clan.[o]
Eze 48:25

Allotment for Asher

19:24 [p]Jos 17:7 24The fifth lot came out for the tribe of Asher,[p] clan by clan. 25Their territory included:
Helkath, Hali, Beten, Acshaph, 26Allammelech, Amad and Mishal. On the west the boundary
19:26 [q]Jos 12:22 touched Carmel[q] and Shihor Libnath. 27It then turned east toward Beth Dagon, touched Zebulun[r]
19:27 [r]ver 10 [s]1Ki 9:13 and the Valley of Iphtah El, and went north to Beth Emek and Neiel, passing Cabul[s] on the left. 28It
19:28 [t]Jdg 1:31 [u]1Ch 6:76 went to Abdon,[a] Rehob,[t] Hammon[u] and Kanah, as far as Greater Sidon.[v] 29The boundary then
[v]Ge 10:19; Jos 11:8 turned back toward Ramah[w] and went to the fortified city of Tyre,[x] turned toward Hosah and
19:29 [w]Jos 18:25 [x]2Sa 5:11; 24:7; came out at the sea in the region of Aczib,[y] 30Ummah, Aphek and Rehob. There were twenty-two
Isa 23:1; towns and their villages.
Jer 25:22; Eze 26:2 31These towns and their villages were the inheritance of the tribe of Asher,[z] clan by clan.
[y]Jdg 1:31 19:31 [z]Ge 30:13; Eze 48:2

Allotment for Naphtali

32The sixth lot came out for Naphtali, clan by clan:
33Their boundary went from Heleph and the large tree in Zaanannim, passing Adami Nekeb
and Jabneel to Lakkum and ending at the Jordan. 34The boundary ran west through Aznoth Tabor
and came out at Hukkok. It touched Zebulun on the south, Asher on the west and the Jordan[b] on
19:35 [a]Jos 11:2 the east. 35The fortified cities were Ziddim, Zer, Hammath, Rakkath, Kinnereth,[a] 36Adamah, Ra-
19:36 [b]Jos 18:25 [c]Jos 11:1 mah,[b] Hazor,[c] 37Kedesh, Edrei,[d] En Hazor, 38Iron, Migdal El, Horem, Beth Anath and Beth She-
19:37 [d]Nu 21:33 mesh. There were nineteen towns and their villages.
19:39 [e]Dt 33:23; Eze 48:3 39These towns and their villages were the inheritance of the tribe of Naphtali, clan by clan.[e]

Allotment for Dan

40The seventh lot came out for the tribe of Dan, clan by clan. 41The territory of their inheritance included:
19:42 [f]Jdg 1:35 Zorah, Eshtaol, Ir Shemesh, 42Shaalabbin, Aijalon,[f] Ithlah, 43Elon, Timnah,[g] Ekron, 44Eltekeh,
19:43 [g]Ge 38:12 19:45 Gibbethon, Baalath, 45Jehud, Bene Berak, Gath Rimmon,[h] 46Me Jarkon and Rakkon, with the area
[h]Jos 21:24; 1Ch 6:69 facing Joppa.[i]
19:46 [i]2Ch 2:16; Jnh 1:3 47(But the Danites had difficulty taking possession of their territory,[j] so they went up and attacked Le-
19:47 [j]Jdg 18:1 [k]Jdg 18:7,14 shem[k], took it, put it to the sword and occupied it. They settled in Leshem and named it Dan after their
[l]Jdg 18:27,29 forefather.)[l]
19:48 [m]Ge 30:6 48These towns and their villages were the inheritance of the tribe of Dan,[m] clan by clan.

Allotment for Joshua

49When they had finished dividing the land into its allotted portions, the Israelites gave Joshua son
of Nun an inheritance among them, 50as the LORD had commanded. They gave him the town he asked
19:50 [n]Jos 24:30 for—Timnath Serah[c][n] in the hill country of Ephraim. And he built up the town and settled there.
51These are the territories that Eleazar the priest, Joshua son of Nun and the heads of the tribal clans
of Israel assigned by lot at Shiloh in the presence of the LORD at the entrance to the Tent of Meeting. And
19:51 [o]Jos 14:1; 18:10; Ac 13:19 so they finished dividing the land.[o]

Cities of Refuge

20 Then the LORD said to Joshua: 2"Tell the Israelites to designate the cities of refuge, as I instruct-
20:3 [p]Lev 4:2 [q]Nu 35:12 ed you through Moses, 3so that anyone who kills a person accidentally and unintentionally[p] may
flee there and find protection from the avenger of blood.[q]

[a] 28 Some Hebrew manuscripts (see also Joshua 21:30); most Hebrew manuscripts *Ebron* [b] 34 Septuagint; Hebrew *west, and Judah, the Jordan,* [c] 50 Also known as *Timnath Heres* (see Judges 2:9)

19:35 Rakkath, one of the fortified cities assigned to the tribe of Naphthali, lay near the Sea of Galilee. There is some evidence that Tiberias was much later built on the site of its ruins (see "Tiberias" on page 1732).

19:42 Aijalon ("Map 6"), a city in Dan assigned to the Levite sons of Kohath (1 Ch 6:69), is mentioned most notably in the memorable words of Joshua: "O sun, stand still over Gibeon, O moon, over the Valley of Aijalon" (Jos 10:12). It is identified with the modern Yalo, 14 miles (22 km) from Jerusalem, north of the Jaffa road.

20:1–6 The principle of blood vengeance, an ancient custom traceable all the way back to Cain's expectation that he would be killed in revenge for murdering his brother Abel (Ge 4:13–14), was still in force

4“When he flees to one of these cities, he is to stand in the entrance of the city gate[r] and state his case
before the elders[s] of that city. Then they are to admit him into their city and give him a place to live with
them. 5If the avenger of blood pursues him, they must not surrender the one accused, because he killed
his neighbor unintentionally and without malice aforethought. 6He is to stay in that city until he has
stood trial before the assembly[t] and until the death of the high priest who is serving at that time. Then
he may go back to his own home in the town from which he fled.”
7So they set apart Kedesh[u] in Galilee in the hill country of Naphtali, Shechem[v] in the hill country of
Ephraim, and Kiriath Arba (that is, Hebron[w]) in the hill country of Judah.[x] 8On the east side of the Jor-
dan of Jericho[a] they designated Bezer[y] in the desert on the plateau in the tribe of Reuben, Ramoth in
Gilead[z] in the tribe of Gad, and Golan in Bashan in the tribe of Manasseh. 9Any of the Israelites or any
alien living among them who killed someone accidentally could flee to these designated cities and not
be killed by the avenger of blood prior to standing trial before the assembly.[a]

20:4 [r]Ru 4:1; Jer 38:7 [s]Jos 7:6
20:6 [t]Nu 35:12
20:7 [u]Jos 21:32; 1Ch 6:76 [v]Ge 12:6 [w]Jos 10:36; 21:11 [x]Lk 1:39
20:8 [y]Jos 21:36; 1Ch 6:78 [z]Jos 12:2
20:9 [a]Ex 21:13; Nu 35:15

Towns for the Levites

21 Now the family heads of the Levites approached Eleazar the priest, Joshua son of Nun, and the
heads of the other tribal families of Israel[b] 2at Shiloh[c] in Canaan and said to them, “The LORD

21:1 [b]Jos 14:1
21:2 [c]Jos 18:1

[a] 8 *Jordan of Jericho* was possibly an ancient name for the Jordan River.

during the time of the monarchy (cf. 2Sa 3:27; 14:6–7). Although the right of sanctuary was respected widely in the ancient Near East, the provision of cities of refuge was a practice without parallel. The goal was to distinguish between murder and accidental killing (manslaughter) and to grant the right of trial to suspected murderers. Asylum in the cities of refuge was offered to “any alien” living within Israel's borders (Jos 20:9; see “Cities of Refuge,” below). Although the Israelites stood against the pagan societies around them, their hearts were to be open to receive any foreigner willing to adopt their religion and customs.

22:5 Obedience to the laws of God requires love and service from the heart. In the ancient Near East *love* was also a political term indicating wholehearted loyalty to one's king.

Cities of Refuge

JOSHUA 20 The cities of refuge, six cities evenly distributed throughout the land of Israel, were designated centers of asylum for the “manslayer”—roughly the equivalent of the individual in our culture convicted of manslaughter, the person who had killed another human being without prior intent or premeditation (Jos 20:3). These cities served as sites for fair and impartial trial to determine the intentionality of a criminal/crime (v. 9). Each such city was to become a refuge for the innocent from the “avenger of blood,” the victim's next of kin, whose family obligation it was to even the score for the loss of life within his clan (Dt 19:6).[1]

Typical ancient Near Eastern law codes treated the loss of life in economic terms: The crime of murder was redressed by payment of damages to the victim's family.[2] Israelite law, however, with its high view of the sanctity of human life, strictly prohibited monetary compensation for a life (Nu 35:31). When an Israelite was murdered, a debit of blood had to be requited (offset by a “credit” of blood). If this deficit went unfulfilled, the land and community were defiled (Nu 35:33; Dt 21:9). The rule for the punishment of homicide was unambiguous: “a life for a life” (Ex 21:12,23). In the case of unintentional homicide, there was to be a vicarious payment of blood, provision for which would be made at the time of the natural death of the high priest (Jos 20:6). Thus, the manslayer who had killed without intent was to seek asylum until the death of the high priest; if he did not, he could be killed with impunity.

The city of refuge, then, was at once a safe haven and a form of exile, protecting the manslayer from blood vengeance while effectively placing him under the death penalty in the event he were to leave the city prematurely (Nu 35:26–28). Even though the manslayer was not guilty of premeditated murder, he was still held responsible for causing the loss of a human life. In a situation somewhat comparable to our house arrest, this individual served what amounted to the closest analogy to a jail term in the Old Testament.

[1]See “The Kinsman-Redeemer” on page 391. [2]See, for example, “The Hittite Laws” on page 281.

21:2 dNu 35:2-3 commanded through Moses that you give us towns to live in, with pasturelands for our livestock."[d] 3So,
as the LORD had commanded, the Israelites gave the Levites the following towns and pasturelands out of
their own inheritance:
4The first lot came out for the Kohathites, clan by clan. The Levites who were descendants of Aar-
21:4 ever 19 on the priest were allotted thirteen towns from the tribes of Judah, Simeon and Benjamin.[e] 5The rest
of Kohath's descendants were allotted ten towns from the clans of the tribes of Ephraim, Dan and half
21:5 fver 26 of Manasseh.[f]
21:6 gGe 30:18 6The descendants of Gershon were allotted thirteen towns from the clans of the tribes of Issachar,[g]
Asher, Naphtali and the half-tribe of Manasseh in Bashan.

Levitical Towns

JOSHUA 21 The tribe of Levi was not granted a self-contained territorial allotment as were all the other ancestral tribes, because the Lord himself was their lot: "I am your share and your inheritance among the Israelites" (Nu 18:20; cf. Dt 18:1–2; Jos 13:33). Not being possessed of land or encumbered by the attendant obligations, the Levites were consecrated to the Lord and free to fulfill their priestly duties.[1] According to Numbers 35:1–8, God commanded the remaining tribes to donate forty-eight walled "Levitical towns" from their various tribal allotments, six of which were to serve as cities of refuge.[2] Each Levitical town was surrounded by an area of land in which the Levites might pasture their flocks and herds (Nu 35:2–5). Together with the people's tithes and offerings (Nu 18:21), these provisions sustained the Levites economically.

The actual distribution of the Levitical towns is delineated in Joshua 21:1–42 and 1 Chronicles 6:54–81; the average number of towns coming from each of the 12 tribes was roughly four. This more or less even sprinkling of Levitical towns throughout the tribal territories would have served to provide centers of religious instruction throughout the land (2Ch 17:7–9).

Levitical land was subject to a distinctive set of laws. In ancient Israel a family in debt could sell its property to obtain cash—in effect pawning the land, since family property could later be redeemed and reclaimed by its original owners (Lev 25:32).[3] Plots of Levitical pastureland, however, were off limits for sale (Lev 25:34).

The historical existence of the Levitical towns has been the subject of academic inquiry. The Bible appears to indicate that the allotment of these cities took place during the period of the conquest,[4] but scholars have suggested a variety of other explanations for the lists of Levitical cities on the grounds that archaeologists have uncovered little evidence that all of these cities were in fact held by Levites.

✢ W.F. Albright posited that the lists of Levitical towns actually date from the period of the **united monarchy** (tenth century B.C.), since this was the only point in time in which all of the named cities were actually known to have been within Israel's territorial borders. Some argue that David settled the Levites in these cities throughout Israel in order to utilize the clergy to strengthen his hold on the people's loyalties.

✢ Other scholars date the lists to an even later time in the monarchy, some suggesting that they were composed as late as the eighth century B.C.—centuries after the conquest under Joshua.

✢ Still others reference these lists to the **postexilic period**. Many of these particular interpreters, in fact, regard them as utopian fantasies created very late in Israel's history and projected back to an idealized but nonhistorical era.

It is important to realize, however, that the list in Joshua 21 is not accompanied by an explicit statement that each of these cities was actually inhabited by Levites at this point in time. Rather, the list seems intended as a designation of (some possibly future or intended) Levitical cities. The tribe of Dan, we might recall, was initially given an allotment of land in the southwestern part of the country (19:40–46) but in reality moved north when the Danites failed to gain control of their allotted territory.[5] The mere fact that the towns were *designated* as Levitical cities does not require that all of them served that purpose in Joshua's time.

[1]See "The Levites and the Priests" on page 648. [2]See "Cities of Refuge" on page 334. [3]See "The Kinsman-Redeemer" on page 391. [4]See "The Conquest of Canaan" on page 310. [5]See "The Migration of the Danites" on page 378.

7 The descendants of Merari,[h] clan by clan, received twelve towns from the tribes of Reuben, Gad and
Zebulun.[i]
8 So the Israelites allotted to the Levites these towns and their pasturelands, as the LORD had com-
manded through Moses.

9 From the tribes of Judah and Simeon they allotted the following towns by name 10 (these towns were
assigned to the descendants of Aaron who were from the Kohathite clans of the Levites, because the first
lot fell to them):

11 They gave them Kiriath Arba (that is, Hebron[j]), with its surrounding pastureland, in the hill
country of Judah. (Arba was the forefather of Anak.) 12 But the fields and villages around the city
they had given to Caleb son of Jephunneh as his possession.

13 So to the descendants of Aaron the priest they gave Hebron (a city of refuge for one accused
of murder), Libnah,[k] 14 Jattir,[l] Eshtemoa,[m] 15 Holon,[n] Debir, 16 Ain, Juttah[o] and Beth Shemesh,[p] to-
gether with their pasturelands—nine towns from these two tribes.

17 And from the tribe of Benjamin they gave them Gibeon, Geba,[q] 18 Anathoth and Almon, to-
gether with their pasturelands—four towns.

19 All the towns for the priests, the descendants of Aaron, were thirteen, together with their pasturelands.

20 The rest of the Kohathite clans of the Levites were allotted towns from the tribe of Ephraim:

21 In the hill country of Ephraim they were given Shechem[r] (a city of refuge for one accused of
murder) and Gezer, 22 Kibzaim and Beth Horon,[s] together with their pasturelands—four towns.[t]

23 Also from the tribe of Dan they received Eltekeh, Gibbethon, 24 Aijalon and Gath Rimmon,[u]
together with their pasturelands—four towns.

25 From half the tribe of Manasseh they received Taanach and Gath Rimmon, together with their
pasturelands—two towns.

26 All these ten towns and their pasturelands were given to the rest of the Kohathite clans.

27 The Levite clans of the Gershonites were given:
from the half-tribe of Manasseh,
Golan in Bashan[v] (a city of refuge for one accused of murder[w]) and Be Eshtarah, together with
their pasturelands—two towns;
28 from the tribe of Issachar,[x]
Kishion, Daberath, 29 Jarmuth and En Gannim, together with their pasturelands—four towns;
30 from the tribe of Asher,[y]
Mishal, Abdon, 31 Helkath and Rehob, together with their pasturelands—four towns;
32 from the tribe of Naphtali,
Kedesh[z] in Galilee (a city of refuge for one accused of murder[a]), Hammoth Dor and Kartan, togeth-
er with their pasturelands—three towns.
33 All the towns of the Gershonite[b] clans were thirteen, together with their pasturelands.

34 The Merarite clans (the rest of the Levites) were given:
from the tribe of Zebulun,[c]
Jokneam, Kartah, 35 Dimnah and Nahalal, together with their pasturelands—four towns;
36 from the tribe of Reuben,
Bezer,[d] Jahaz, 37 Kedemoth and Mephaath, together with their pasturelands—four towns;
38 from the tribe of Gad,
Ramoth[e] in Gilead (a city of refuge for one accused of murder), Mahanaim,[f] 39 Heshbon and Jazer,
together with their pasturelands—four towns in all.
40 All the towns allotted to the Merarite clans, who were the rest of the Levites, were twelve.

41 The towns of the Levites in the territory held by the Israelites were forty-eight in all, together with
their pasturelands.[g] 42 Each of these towns had pasturelands surrounding it; this was true for all these
towns.

43 So the LORD gave Israel all the land he had sworn to give their forefathers,[h] and they took posses-
sion[i] of it and settled there.[j] 44 The LORD gave them rest[k] on every side, just as he had sworn to their fore-
fathers. Not one of their enemies[l] withstood them; the LORD handed all their enemies[m] over to them.[n]
45 Not one of all the LORD's good promises[o] to the house of Israel failed; every one was fulfilled.

21:7 [h]Ex 6:16 [i]Jos 19:10
21:11 [j]Jos 15:13; 1Ch 6:55
21:13 [k]Jos 15:42; 1Ch 6:57
21:14 [l]Jos 15:48 [m]Jos 15:50
21:15 [n]Jos 15:51
21:16 [o]Jos 15:55 [p]Jos 15:10
21:17 [q]Jos 18:24
21:21 [r]Jos 17:7; 20:7
21:22 [s]Jos 10:10 [t]1Sa 1:1
21:24 [u]Jos 19:45
21:27 [v]Jos 12:5 [w]Nu 35:6
21:28 [x]Ge 30:18
21:30 [y]Jos 17:7
21:32 [z]Jos 12:22 [a]Nu 35:6; Jos 20:7
21:33 [b]ver 6
21:34 [c]Jos 19:10; 1Ch 6:77
21:36 [d]Jos 20:8
21:38 [e]Dt 4:43 [f]Ge 32:2
21:41 [g]Nu 35:7
21:43 [h]Dt 34:4 [i]Dt 11:31 [j]Dt 17:14
21:44 [k]Ex 33:14; Jos 1:13 [l]Dt 6:19 [m]Ex 23:31 [n]Dt 7:24; 21:10
21:45 [o]Jos 23:14; Ne 9:8

Eastern Tribes Return Home

22 Then Joshua summoned the Reubenites, the Gadites and the half-tribe of Manasseh 2 and said to
them, "You have done all that Moses the servant of the LORD commanded,[p] and you have obeyed
me in everything I commanded. 3 For a long time now—to this very day—you have not deserted your
brothers but have carried out the mission the LORD your God gave you. 4 Now that the LORD your God has
given your brothers rest as he promised, return to your homes[q] in the land that Moses the servant of the
LORD gave you on the other side of the Jordan.[r] 5 But be very careful to keep the commandment[s] and the
law that Moses the servant of the LORD gave you: to love the LORD your God, to walk in all his ways, to obey
his commands,[t] to hold fast to him and to serve him with all your heart and all your soul.[u]"

6 Then Joshua blessed[v] them and sent them away, and they went to their homes. 7 (To the half-tribe of
Manasseh Moses had given land in Bashan,[w] and to the other half of the tribe Joshua gave land on the
west side[x] of the Jordan with their brothers.) When Joshua sent them home, he blessed them, 8 saying, "Re-
turn to your homes with your great wealth—with large herds of livestock,[y] with silver, gold, bronze and
iron, and a great quantity of clothing—and divide[z] with your brothers the plunder[a] from your enemies."

9 So the Reubenites, the Gadites and the half-tribe of Manasseh left the Israelites at Shiloh in Canaan
to return to Gilead,[b] their own land, which they had acquired in accordance with the command of the
LORD through Moses.

10 When they came to Geliloth near the Jordan in the land of Canaan, the Reubenites, the Gadites and
the half-tribe of Manasseh built an imposing altar there by the Jordan. 11 And when the Israelites heard
that they had built the altar on the border of Canaan at Geliloth near the Jordan on the Israelite side,
12 the whole assembly of Israel gathered at Shiloh[c] to go to war against them.

13 So the Israelites sent Phinehas[d] son of Eleazar,[e] the priest, to the land of Gilead—to Reuben, Gad
and the half-tribe of Manasseh. 14 With him they sent ten of the chief men, one for each of the tribes of
Israel, each the head of a family division among the Israelite clans.[f]

15 When they went to Gilead—to Reuben, Gad and the half-tribe of Manasseh—they said to them:
16 "The whole assembly of the LORD says: 'How could you break faith[g] with the God of Israel like this? How
could you turn away from the LORD and build yourselves an altar in rebellion[h] against him now? 17 Was
not the sin of Peor[i] enough for us? Up to this very day we have not cleansed ourselves from that sin, even
though a plague fell on the community of the LORD! 18 And are you now turning away from the LORD?

" 'If you rebel against the LORD today, tomorrow he will be angry with the whole community[j] of Isra-
el. 19 If the land you possess is defiled, come over to the LORD's land, where the LORD's tabernacle stands,
and share the land with us. But do not rebel against the LORD or against us by building an altar for your-
selves, other than the altar of the LORD our God. 20 When Achan son of Zerah acted unfaithfully regard-
ing the devoted things,[a][k] did not wrath[l] come upon the whole community of Israel? He was not the only
one who died for his sin.' "[m]

21 Then Reuben, Gad and the half-tribe of Manasseh replied to the heads of the clans of Israel: 22 "The
Mighty One, God, the LORD! The Mighty One, God,[n] the LORD![o] He knows![p] And let Israel know! If this has
been in rebellion or disobedience to the LORD, do not spare us this day. 23 If we have built our own altar
to turn away from the LORD and to offer burnt offerings and grain offerings,[q] or to sacrifice fellowship
offerings[b] on it, may the LORD himself call us to account.[r]

24 "No! We did it for fear that some day your descendants might say to ours, 'What do you have to do
with the LORD, the God of Israel? 25 The LORD has made the Jordan a boundary between us and you—
you Reubenites and Gadites! You have no share in the LORD.' So your descendants might cause ours to
stop fearing the LORD.

26 "That is why we said, 'Let us get ready and build an altar—but not for burnt offerings or sacrific-
es.' 27 On the contrary, it is to be a witness[s] between us and you and the generations that follow, that we
will worship the LORD at his sanctuary with our burnt offerings, sacrifices and fellowship offerings.[t] Then
in the future your descendants will not be able to say to ours, 'You have no share in the LORD.'

28 "And we said, 'If they ever say this to us, or to our descendants, we will answer: Look at the replica

22:2 pNu 32:25
22:4 qNu 32:22; Dt 3:20 rNu 32:18; Jos 1:13-15
22:5 sIsa 43:22 tDt 5:29 uDt 6:6, 17
22:6 vEx 39:43
22:7 wNu 32:33; Jos 12:5 xJos 17:2,5
22:8 yDt 20:14 zNu 31:27 aGe 49:27; 1Sa 30:16; Isa 9:3
22:9 bNu 32:26, 29
22:12 cJos 18:1
22:13 dNu 25:7 eNu 3:32; Jos 24:33
22:14 fNu 1:4
22:16 gDt 13:14 hDt 12:13-14
22:17 iNu 25:1-9
22:18 jLev 10:6; Nu 16:22
22:20 kJos 7:1 lPs 7:11 mJos 7:5
22:22 nDt 10:17 oPs 50:1 p1Ki 8:39; Job 10:7; Ps 44:21; Jer 17:10
22:23 qJer 41:5 rDt 12:11; 18:19; 1Sa 20:16
22:27 sGe 21:30; Jos 24:27 tDt 12:6

a *20* The Hebrew term refers to the irrevocable giving over of things or persons to the LORD, often by totally destroying them.
b *23* Traditionally *peace offerings*; also in verse 27

22:19 *Defiled*, a term for ritual uncleanness, did not necessarily imply something sinful.

22:34 Long, explanatory names were common in the ancient Near East.

of the LORD's altar, which our fathers built, not for burnt offerings and sacrifices, but as a witness be-
tween us and you.'

29“Far be it from us to rebel[u] against the LORD and turn away from him today by building an altar for
burnt offerings, grain offerings and sacrifices, other than the altar of the LORD our God that stands be-
fore his tabernacle.[v]”

30When Phinehas the priest and the leaders of the community—the heads of the clans of the Israel-
ites—heard what Reuben, Gad and Manasseh had to say, they were pleased. 31And Phinehas son of El-
eazar, the priest, said to Reuben, Gad and Manasseh, “Today we know that the LORD is with us,[w] because
you have not acted unfaithfully toward the LORD in this matter. Now you have rescued the Israelites from
the LORD's hand.”

32Then Phinehas son of Eleazar, the priest, and the leaders returned to Canaan from their meeting
with the Reubenites and Gadites in Gilead and reported to the Israelites. 33They were glad to hear the re-
port and praised God.[x] And they talked no more about going to war against them to devastate the coun-
try where the Reubenites and the Gadites lived.

34And the Reubenites and the Gadites gave the altar this name: A Witness[y] Between Us that the LORD
is God.

Joshua's Farewell to the Leaders

23 After a long time had passed and the LORD had given Israel rest[z] from all their enemies around
them, Joshua, by then old and well advanced in years,[a] 2summoned all Israel—their elders,[b]
leaders, judges and officials[c]—and said to them: “I am old and well advanced in years. 3You yourselves
have seen everything the LORD your God has done to all these nations for your sake; it was the LORD your
God who fought for you.[d] 4Remember how I have allotted[e] as an inheritance for your tribes all the land
of the nations that remain—the nations I conquered—between the Jordan and the Great Sea[a][f] in the
west. 5The LORD your God himself will drive them out of your way. He will push them out before you, and
you will take possession of their land, as the LORD your God promised you.[g]

6“Be very strong; be careful to obey all that is written in the Book of the Law of Moses, without turn-
ing aside to the right or to the left.[h] 7Do not associate with these nations that remain among you; do not
invoke the names of their gods or swear[i] by them. You must not serve them or bow down[j] to them. 8But
you are to hold fast to the LORD[k] your God, as you have until now.

9“The LORD has driven out before you great and powerful nations;[l] to this day no one has been able
to withstand you.[m] 10One of you routs a thousand,[n] because the LORD your God fights for you,[o] just as he
promised. 11So be very careful to love the LORD[p] your God.

12“But if you turn away and ally yourselves with the survivors of these nations that remain among
you and if you intermarry with them[q] and associate with them,[r] 13then you may be sure that the LORD
your God will no longer drive out these nations before you. Instead, they will become snares[s] and traps
for you, whips on your backs and thorns in your eyes,[t] until you perish from this good land, which the
LORD your God has given you.

14“Now I am about to go the way of all the earth.[u] You know with all your heart and soul that not one
of all the good promises the LORD your God gave you has failed. Every promise has been fulfilled; not
one has failed.[v] 15But just as every good promise of the LORD your God has come true, so the LORD will
bring on you all the evil he has threatened, until he has destroyed you from this good land he has given
you.[w] 16If you violate the covenant of the LORD your God, which he commanded you, and go and serve
other gods and bow down to them, the LORD's anger will burn against you, and you will quickly perish
from the good land he has given you.[x]”

The Covenant Renewed at Shechem

24 Then Joshua assembled all the tribes of Israel at Shechem. He summoned the elders, leaders,
judges and officials of Israel,[y] and they presented themselves before God.

[a] 4 That is, the Mediterranean

22:29 [u]Jos 24:16 [v]Dt 12:13-14
22:31 [w]Lev 26:11-12; 2Ch 15:2
22:33 [x]1Ch 29:20; Da 2:19; Lk 2:28
22:34 [y]Ge 21:30
23:1 [z]Dt 12:9; Jos 21:44 [a]Jos 13:1
23:2 [b]Jos 7:6 [c]Jos 24:1
23:3 [d]Ex 14:14
23:4 [e]Jos 19:51 [f]Nu 34:6
23:5 [g]Ex 23:30; Nu 33:53
23:6 [h]Dt 5:32; Jos 1:7
23:7 [i]Ex 23:13; Ps 16:4; Jer 5:7 [j]Ex 20:5
23:8 [k]Dt 10:20
23:9 [l]Dt 11:23 [m]Dt 7:24
23:10 [n]Lev 26:8 [o]Ex 14:14; Dt 3:22
23:11 [p]Jos 22:5
23:12 [q]Dt 7:3 [r]Ex 34:16; Ps 106:34-35
23:13 [s]Ex 23:33 [t]Nu 33:55
23:14 [u]1Ki 2:2 [v]Jos 21:45
23:15 [w]Lev 26:17; Dt 28:15
23:16 [x]Dt 4:25-26
24:1 [y]Jos 23:2

23:1—24:31 As his death approached, Joshua first summoned Israel's leaders, urging them to faithfulness in conquest (ch. 23), and then assembled the tribal heads to Shechem, charging them, “Choose for yourselves this day whom you will serve” (24:15). Having renewed their covenant with the Lord, he inserted it in the Book of the Law (24:25–26) and died at the age of one hundred ten (24:29–30; Jdg 2:8–9). Throughout his days, and even afterward, Joshua's influence caused Israel to remain faithful to her Lord (Jos 24:31; Jdg 1:1; 2:7). See “Shechem” on page 340.

24:1–27 The ceremony of covenant renewal at Shechem (see “Shechem” on p. 340) is similar to the suzerainty treaties common in the ancient Near East (a suzerain was a feudal lord or overlord).

2 Joshua said to all the people, "This is what the LORD, the God of Israel, says: 'Long ago your forefathers,
24:2 zGe 11:32 including Terah the father of Abraham and Nahor, lived beyond the River[a] and worshiped other gods.[z]
24:3 aGe 12:1 3 But I took your father Abraham from the land beyond the River and led him throughout Canaan[a] and
bGe 15:5 cGe 21:3 24:4 dGe 25:26 gave him many descendants.[b] I gave him Isaac,[c] 4 and to Isaac I gave Jacob and Esau.[d] I assigned the hill
eDt 2:5 fGe 46:5-6 country of Seir[e] to Esau, but Jacob and his sons went down to Egypt.[f]
24:5 gEx 3:10 5 " 'Then I sent Moses and Aaron,[g] and I afflicted the Egyptians by what I did there, and I brought
you out. 6 When I brought your fathers out of Egypt, you came to the sea, and the Egyptians pursued
24:6 hEx 14:9 them with chariots and horsemen[b][h] as far as the Red Sea.[c] 7 But they cried to the LORD for help, and he
24:7 iEx 14:20 put darkness[i] between you and the Egyptians; he brought the sea over them and covered them.[j] You saw
jEx 14:28 kDt 1:46 with your own eyes what I did to the Egyptians. Then you lived in the desert for a long time.[k]
8 " 'I brought you to the land of the Amorites who lived east of the Jordan. They fought against you,
but I gave them into your hands. I destroyed them from before you, and you took possession of their
24:8 lNu 21:31 land.[l] 9 When Balak son of Zippor,[m] the king of Moab, prepared to fight against Israel, he sent for Balaam
24:9 mNu 22:2 nNu 22:6 son of Beor to put a curse on you.[n] 10 But I would not listen to Balaam, so he blessed you[o] again and again,
24:10 oNu 23:11; Dt 23:5 and I delivered you out of his hand.
24:11 pJos 3:16-17 qJos 6:1 11 " 'Then you crossed the Jordan[p] and came to Jericho.[q] The citizens of Jericho fought against you, as
rEx 23:23; Dt 7:1 did also the Amorites, Perizzites, Canaanites, Hittites, Girgashites, Hivites and Jebusites, but I gave them
24:12 sEx 23:28; into your hands.[r] 12 I sent the hornet[s] ahead of you, which drove them out before you—also the two Am-
Dt 7:20; Ps 44:3, 6-7 orite kings. You did not do it with your own sword and bow. 13 So I gave you a land on which you did not
toil and cities you did not build; and you live in them and eat from vineyards and olive groves that you
24:13 tDt 6:10-11 did not plant.'[t]
24:14 uDt 10:12; 18:13; 1Sa 12:24; 14 "Now fear the LORD and serve him with all faithfulness.[u] Throw away the gods[v] your forefathers
2Co 1:12 vver 23 wEze 23:3 worshiped beyond the River and in Egypt,[w] and serve the LORD. 15 But if serving the LORD seems unde-
sirable to you, then choose for yourselves this day whom you will serve, whether the gods your forefathers
24:15 xJdg 6:10; served beyond the River, or the gods of the Amorites,[x] in whose land you are living. But as for me and
Ru 1:15 yRu 1:16; 1Ki 18:21 my household, we will serve the LORD."[y]
16 Then the people answered, "Far be it from us to forsake the LORD to serve other gods! 17 It was the
LORD our God himself who brought us and our fathers up out of Egypt, from that land of slavery, and
performed those great signs before our eyes. He protected us on our entire journey and among all the na-
tions through which we traveled. 18 And the LORD drove out before us all the nations, including the Am-
orites, who lived in the land. We too will serve the LORD, because he is our God."
24:19 zLev 19:2; 19 Joshua said to the people, "You are not able to serve the LORD. He is a holy God;[z] he is a jealous God.[a]
20:26 aEx 20:5 bEx 23:21 He will not forgive your rebellion[b] and your sins. 20 If you forsake the LORD[c] and serve foreign gods, he will
24:20 c1Ch 28:9, 20 dAc 7:42 eJos 23:15 turn[d] and bring disaster on you and make an end of you,[e] after he has been good to you."
21 But the people said to Joshua, "No! We will serve the LORD."
24:22 fPs 119:30, 173 22 Then Joshua said, "You are witnesses against yourselves that you have chosen[f] to serve the LORD."
"Yes, we are witnesses," they replied.
24:23 gver 14 h1Ki 8:58; 23 "Now then," said Joshua, "throw away the foreign gods[g] that are among you and yield your hearts[h]
Ps 119:36; 141:4 to the LORD, the God of Israel."
24:24 iEx 19:8; 24 And the people said to Joshua, "We will serve the LORD our God and obey him."[i]
24:3,7; Dt 5:27 24:25 jEx 24:8 25 On that day Joshua made a covenant[j] for the people, and there at Shechem he drew up for them de-
kEx 15:25 24:26 lDt 31:24 crees and laws.[k] 26 And Joshua recorded these things in the Book of the Law of God.[l] Then he took a large
mGe 28:18 stone[m] and set it up there under the oak near the holy place of the LORD.
24:27 nJos 22:27 27 "See!" he said to all the people. "This stone will be a witness[n] against us. It has heard all the words
the LORD has said to us. It will be a witness against you if you are untrue to your God."

[a] 2 That is, the Euphrates; also in verses 3, 14 and 15 [b] 6 Or *charioteers* [c] 6 Hebrew *Yam Suph*; that is, Sea of Reeds

---

As in those covenants, the past history of how the suzerain (God) had benefited his subjects (Israel) was recounted (vv. 2–13). After stating the stipulations demanded of the subject nation (v. 14), Joshua professed his own commitment—hoping that the people would do the same (v. 15). See "Deuteronomy and the Covenant Treaty Form" on page 255.

24:2 A brief recital of the past history of the relationship preceded the making of covenant commitments in ancient Near Eastern treaties (covenants). Similarly, Joshua focused on the separation of Abraham from his polytheistic family, the deliverance of Israel from Egypt and the Lord's establishment of his people in Canaan.

24:14 The Israelites were to put away the gods their forefathers had worshiped in Mesopotamia and Egypt. In Ur and Haran, Terah's family would have been exposed to the worship of the moon god, Nannar, or Sin. The golden calf incident of Exodus 32:4 may be an example of their worship of the gods of Egypt, for it was probably patterned after Apis, the sacred bull of Egypt. The golden calves set up by Jeroboam at Bethel and Dan, on the other hand, probably represented mounts or pedestals for a riding or standing deity (see 1Ki 12:28–29.) See also "The High Place at Dan" on p. 504.

Shechem

JOSHUA 24 The city of Shechem ("Map 3") is perhaps best remembered by Bible readers as the place at which Jacob's sons Simeon and Levi deceitfully carried out a terrible slaughter of the local population to avenge the rape of their sister Dinah (Ge 34). Shechem is located in the hill country of Ephraim, in a pass with Mount Ebal to the north and Mount Gerizim to the south. Unfortunately, there are many unanswered questions about its history, particularly as it relates to the Bible.

The earliest occupation of Shechem is known to have been during the **Chalcolithic** period, from approximately 4000–3500 B.C. No occupation levels of the site are apparent at all from the third millennium B.C., although a substantial city did arise there during the **Middle Bronze Age** (c. 1900–1550 B.C.). This city suffered a calamitous annihilation at the end of this period; a great deal of destruction debris was found at this level. Shechem was again rebuilt during the **Late Bronze Age**. A large temple found there probably was that of El-Berith, mentioned in Judges 9:46–49, the site at which Abimelech killed about a thousand people.[1] Shechem appears to have been a fairly modest city throughout much of the **Iron Age** and the **postexilic period**. First Kings 12:25 mentions that Jeroboam made it his residence for a time, and Shechem is also mentioned in Jeremiah 41:4–8.

The situation of Late Bronze-era Shechem presents the greatest challenges for archaeologists. Many believe that the city was rebuilt in approximately 1450 B.C. (after having been completely destroyed at the end of the Middle Bronze period). A commonly held view is that a people group called Labayu dominated the central hill country, using Shechem as a base during the Late Bronze II Age, from approximately 1400–1300 B.C. (also called the "Amarna Age" because of the **Amarna** Letters, diplomatic correspondence between **Canaan** and Egypt from this time period).[2]

Wall at Shechem made of rough-hewn "cyclopean" stones

Photograph courtesy of © Dr. Gary Pratico

A problem here is the Biblical reference to Joshua's gathering of Israel at Shechem for covenant ceremonies in the vicinities of Mount Ebal and Mount Gerizim (Jos 8:30–35; 24:1).[3] An encounter with the city or people of Shechem is never mentioned in this context, though it would have been unavoidable if the site had been occupied by a regional power at that time. Some historians suggest that the Shechemites cooperated with the Israelites, but this is highly unlikely, given God's stipulation that the Israelites were to exterminate the Canaanites—not to negotiate concessions from them (Dt 7:1–2).[4]

The chronology and history of Late Bronze Age Shechem are far from settled matters. The notion that Labayu dominated the hill country from Shechem is speculative. There is also uncertainty about when the first Late Bronze period city at Shechem was actually built. This may have occurred after the conquest; Joshua 8 and 24 appear by their silence to imply that there was no significant Canaanite city there in Joshua's time. Joshua 24 does mention a place by this name but never alludes to an encounter with Canaanite inhabitants of the city. The Biblical and archaeological evidence for Shechem is difficult to work into a coherent history, and this dilemma is compounded by other issues surrounding the date of the conquest.[4] Researchers are wise, as always, to exercise caution about jumping to conclusions.

[1]See "Abimelech at Shechem" on page 363. [2]See "The Amarna Tablets and the Habiru" on page 347. [3]See "Joshua's Altar on Mount Ebal" on page 288. [4]See "The Conquest of Canaan" on page 310.

Buried in the Promised Land

[28]Then Joshua sent the people away, each to his own inheritance.
24:29 oJdg 2:8 [29]After these things, Joshua son of Nun, the servant of the LORD, died at the age of a hundred and ten.[o]
24:30 pJos 19:50 [30]And they buried him in the land of his inheritance, at Timnath Serah[ap] in the hill country of Ephra-
im, north of Mount Gaash.
24:31 qJdg 2:7 [31]Israel served the LORD throughout the lifetime of Joshua and of the elders[q] who outlived him and
who had experienced everything the LORD had done for Israel.
24:32 rGe 50:25; Ex 13:19 sGe 33:19; Jn 4:5; Ac 7:16 [32]And Joseph's bones, which the Israelites had brought up from Egypt,[r] were buried at Shechem in the
tract of land[s] that Jacob bought for a hundred pieces of silver[b] from the sons of Hamor, the father of She-
chem. This became the inheritance of Joseph's descendants.
24:33 tJos 22:13 uEx 6:25 [33]And Eleazar son of Aaron[t] died and was buried at Gibeah, which had been allotted to his son Phin-
ehas[u] in the hill country of Ephraim.

[a] *30* Also known as *Timnath Heres* (see Judges 2:9) [b] *32* Hebrew *hundred kesitahs*; a kesitah was a unit of money of unknown weight and value.

DISTANCES IN MILES BETWEEN OLD TESTAMENT CITIES
(1 mi = 1.6 km)

	Ashkelon	Babylon	Beersheba	Bethel	Beth Shan	Carchemish	Damascus	Dan	Haran	Hazor	Hebron	Jericho	Jerusalem	Joppa	Lachish	Mari	Megiddo	Memphis	Nineveh	Samaria	Shechem	Sidon	Susa	Thebes	Tyre	Ur
Ashkelon		900	36	48	87	454	178	139	519	117	36	57	44	32	21	653	80	269	726	60	63	155	1118	601	133	1070
Babylon	900		930	869	823	479	724	764	442	783	901	869	880	868	907	251	824	1172	264	845	847	779	218	1504	792	170
Beersheba	36	930		58	104	484	206	166	549	147	28	61	47	62	25	679	116	259	752	80	78	190	1148	591	176	1100
Bethel	48	869	58		47	423	145	105	488	86	31	12	11	32	40	618	50	303	691	26	22	129	1087	635	115	1039
Beth Shan	87	823	104	47		377	92	59	442	40	78	45	57	59	86	572	21	349	645	27	26	82	1041	681	62	993
Carchemish	454	479	484	423	377		278	318	65	337	455	423	434	366	461	228	378	726	285	399	401	333	697	1058	346	649
Damascus	178	724	206	145	92	278		45	343	59	177	134	149	133	181	473	98	441	546	121	123	55	942	773	68	894
Dan	139	764	166	105	59	318	45		383	19	137	105	116	104	142	513	59	408	586	80	82	29	982	740	28	934
Haran	519	442	549	488	442	65	343	383		402	520	488	500	396	526	191	443	791	215	464	466	398	660	1123	411	612
Hazor	117	783	147	86	40	337	59	19	402		118	86	97	85	124	532	41	389	605	62	64	43	1001	721	29	953
Hebron	36	901	28	31	78	455	177	137	520	118		36	21	45	17	650	80	297	723	51	53	161	1119	629	147	1071
Jericho	57	869	61	12	45	423	134	105	488	86	36		15	43	44	618	54	307	691	32	26	129	1087	639	115	1039
Jerusalem	44	880	47	11	57	434	149	116	500	97	21	15		36	29	629	61	292	702	37	33	140	1098	624	126	1050
Joppa	32	868	62	32	59	366	133	104	396	85	45	43	36		37	372	53	301	548	31	36	112	1086	633	89	1038
Lachish	21	907	25	40	86	461	181	142	526	124	17	44	29	37		656	83	281	729	66	62	158	1125	613	136	1077
Mari	653	251	679	618	572	228	473	513	191	532	650	618	629	372	656		573	921	173	594	596	528	469	1253	541	421
Megiddo	80	824	116	50	21	378	98	59	443	41	80	54	61	53	83	573		348	646	25	29	75	1042	680	53	994
Memphis	269	1172	259	303	349	726	441	408	791	389	297	307	292	301	281	921	348		994	329	325	424	1390	332	402	1342
Nineveh	726	264	752	691	645	285	546	586	215	605	723	691	702	548	729	173	646	994		667	669	601	453	1326	614	434
Samaria	60	845	80	26	27	399	121	80	464	62	51	32	37	31	66	594	25	329	667		8	105	1063	661	77	1015
Shechem	63	847	78	22	26	401	123	82	466	64	53	26	33	36	62	596	29	325	669	8		107	1065	657	80	1017
Sidon	155	779	190	129	82	333	55	29	398	43	161	129	140	112	158	528	75	424	601	105	107		997	755	25	949
Susa	1118	218	1148	1087	1041	697	942	982	660	1001	1119	1087	1098	1086	1125	469	1042	1390	453	1063	1065	997		1722	1110	145
Thebes	601	1504	591	635	681	1058	773	740	1123	721	629	639	624	633	613	1253	680	332	1326	661	657	755	1722		733	1674
Tyre	133	792	176	115	62	346	68	28	411	29	147	115	126	89	136	541	53	402	614	77	80	25	1110	733		962
Ur	1070	170	1100	1039	993	649	894	934	612	953	1071	1039	1050	1038	1077	421	994	1342	434	1015	1017	949	145	1674	962	

Note: These distances are meant only as rough estimates. They do not take into account terrain obstacles, although they do, for the most part, follow ancient routes (e.g., around the Fertile Crescent rather than across the desert).

Chronological and Background Charts of the Old Testament, p. 116

INTRODUCTION TO *Judges*

AUTHOR, PLACE AND DATE OF WRITING

The author of the book of Judges is unknown. The Jewish Talmud states not only that Samuel wrote this book but also that he authored the books of Samuel—most of the events of which occurred after his death. It is conceivable that Samuel compiled some accounts from the period of the judges and that afterward such prophets as Gad and Nathan helped to edit the material (cf. 1Ch 29:29).

The frequently repeated phrase "in those days Israel had no king" (e.g., Jdg 17:6; 18:1; 19:1) does suggest a date after the monarchy had been established. Some scholars believe that this book was written before David had captured Jerusalem (c. 1000 B.C.) because the Jebusites still controlled that city (1:21). Yet Judges 17–21 alludes to a time after the Davidic dynasty had been established (tenth century B.C.).

AUDIENCE

Generations of Israelites after the time of the judges who read this book were reminded of their ancestors' rebellion against God and of their own need of his divine deliverance.

CULTURAL FACTS AND HIGHLIGHTS

During this dark time in Israel's history the nation experienced repeated periods of chaos: political disunity, infighting, invasions from other nations, spiritual and moral depravity. Repeatedly the Israelites broke their covenant with God, lost sight of their identity as his people and experienced punishment. Yet again and again God raised up deliverers when they cried out for relief.

TIMELINE

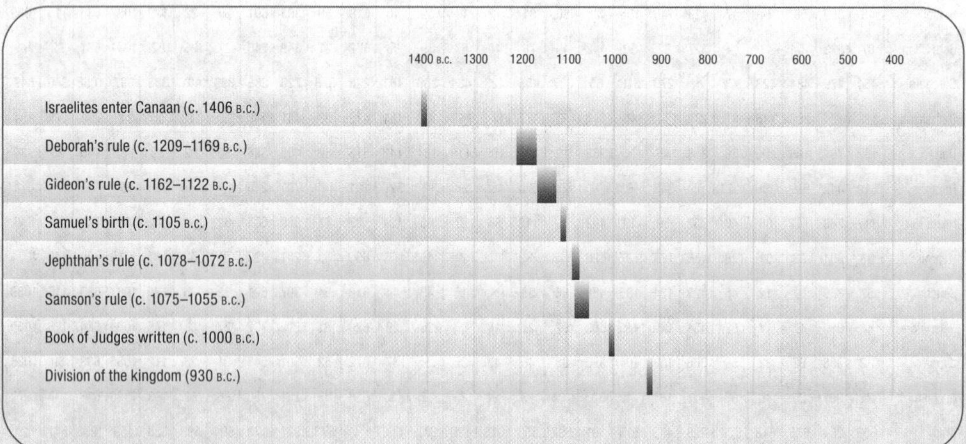

AS YOU READ

Notice how far Israel had fallen since entering Canaan. Listen as the people admitted their sins and then fell back into the old, familiar patterns. Yet God remained patient and faithful to his promises, using selected individuals to deliver Israel from foreign oppressors. Pay attention to the rhythm of these up-and-down cycles.

Explore the lives of the judges God raised up to deliver his people. Some, like Ehud, stepped into the picture for only a short time. Others, like Deborah, demonstrated that God overrides cultural norms. Listen to Gideon's fears and note his need to test God's faithfulness. Then reflect upon how deeply his idolatrous example later influenced the people. Note how God used Samson, despite his character flaws, but then allowed that mighty man to reap the consequences of his actions.

Reflect on the implications of the repeated declaration "In those days Israel had no king; everyone did as he saw fit" (21:25), both for the days of the judges and for your own culture.

DID YOU KNOW?

- It was a common practice in the ancient Near East to physically mutilate prisoners of war, thereby rendering them unfit for future military service (1:6).
- Any distinct ethnicity of the Israelites is almost impossible to determine from archaeological records from the period 1200–1000 B.C. (2:6—3:6).
- At the heart of the idolatry practiced by the ancient fertility cults was the idea that the deity magically took up residence within the man-made idol (3:7).
- Many Benjamite soldiers were left-handed or ambidextrous. Left-handedness may have been artificially induced by binding the right arms of young boys to produce superior warriors (3:15–23).
- "Curdled milk" was artificially soured by being shaken in a skin-bottle and then allowed to ferment due to bacteria that remained in the skin from previous use (5:25).
- The use of riddles at feasts and on special occasions was popular in the ancient world (14:12).

THEMES

The book of Judges includes the following themes:

1. *God's faithfulness.* Through the repeated cycle of disobedience, oppression, repentance and deliverance (e.g., 2:11–19), Judges portrays a God of both judgment and forgiveness.

2. *Compromise.* Judges illustrates that compromise with the world can only bring disaster.

3. *Need for godly leadership.* The period of the judges was a time of political fragmentation. The failures of Israel's leaders—parents (2:6–10), priests (17:1–13) and judges (8:27)—pointed out the importance of godly leadership, which came later in the form of Davidic kingship and ultimately in the kingship of Christ.

OUTLINE

- I. Introduction: Incomplete Conquest and Apostasy (1:1—3:6)
  - A. First Episode (1:1—2:5)
  - B. Second Episode (2:6—3:6)
- II. Oppression by Enemies and Deliverance by Judges (3:7—16:31)
  - A. Othniel (3:7–11)
  - B. Ehud and Shamgar (3:12–31)
  - C. Deborah (4–5)
  - D. Gideon, Tola and Jair (6:1—10:5)
  - E. Jephthah, Ibzan, Elon and Abdon (10:6—12:15)
  - F. Samson (13–16)
- III. Epilogue: Religious and Moral Disorder (17–21)
  - A. First Episode (17–18)
  - B. Second Episode (19–21)

Israel Fights the Remaining Canaanites

1 After the death[a] of Joshua, the Israelites asked the LORD, "Who will be the first[b] to go up and fight 1:1 [a]Jos 24:29 [b]Nu 27:21
for us against the Canaanites?[c]" [c]ver 27; Jdg 3:1-6
[2]The LORD answered, "Judah[d] is to go; I have given the land into their hands.[e]" 1:2 [d]Ge 49:8 [e]ver 4; Jdg 3:28
[3]Then the men of Judah said to the Simeonites their brothers, "Come up with us into the territory al-
lotted to us, to fight against the Canaanites. We in turn will go with you into yours." So the Simeonites[f] 1:3 [f]ver 17
went with them.
[4]When Judah attacked, the LORD gave the Canaanites and Perizzites[g] into their hands and they struck 1:4 [g]Ge 13:7; Jos 3:10
down ten thousand men at Bezek.[h] [5]It was there that they found Adoni-Bezek and fought against him, [h]1Sa 11:8
putting to rout the Canaanites and Perizzites. [6]Adoni-Bezek fled, but they chased him and caught him,
and cut off his thumbs and big toes.
[7]Then Adoni-Bezek said, "Seventy kings with their thumbs and big toes cut off have picked up scraps
under my table. Now God has paid me back[i] for what I did to them." They brought him to Jerusalem, and 1:7 [i]Lev 24:19
he died there.
[8]The men of Judah attacked Jerusalem[j] also and took it. They put the city to the sword and set it on fire. 1:8 [j]ver 21; Jos 15:63
[9]After that, the men of Judah went down to fight against the Canaanites living in the hill country,[k] 1:9 [k]Nu 13:17 [l]Nu 21:1
the Negev[l] and the western foothills. [10]They advanced against the Canaanites living in Hebron[m] (former- 1:10 [m]Ge 13:18
ly called Kiriath Arba[n]) and defeated Sheshai, Ahiman and Talmai.[o] [n]Ge 35:27 [o]Jos 15:14

1:1 The high priest used the Urim and Thummim to obtain yes or no answers from God (see "The Urim and Thummim" on p. 136).

1:6 It was a common practice in the ancient Near East to physically mutilate prisoners of war, thereby rendering them unfit for future military service (see the note on 16:21).

The Judges Period

JUDGES 1 The period of the judges extended from the end of the conquest, around 1400 B.C., until Saul was anointed king of Israel in approximately 1050 B.C. An Egyptian document, Papyrus Anastasi I, describes Canaan at that time as something like the American "Wild West," with roads nearly impassable by chariot and boding ever-present dangers from wild animals and robbers. During this era Israel functioned as a tribal society led by leaders called judges, and its religious center was at Shiloh (Jos 18:1; "Map 3").[1]

By the late thirteenth century B.C. the Israelites were the major political power in the region. That changed, however, with the invasion of the Philistines in the early twelfth century B.C.[2] The Israelites were almost continuously at war with the Philistines for the next two centuries, until David finally subdued this troublesome adversary once and for all.[3]

A major socioeconomic change took place in the eastern Mediterranean region during the period of the judges. The city-states that had predominated in the **Late Bronze Age**[4,5] were destroyed in the late thirteenth and early twelfth centuries B.C., ushering in the **Iron Age.**[6] Rural shepherds like the Israelites could no longer depend upon the city-states for produce and were forced to settle down and become agriculturists in order to survive. Thus, while the Israelites were pastoralists, dependent largely upon flocks and herds for their economic security (Ge 46:32–34; 47:3; Ex 12:38; Jdg 5:16) and dwelling in tents (20:8) at the beginning of the Judges period, by the time of Gideon, around 1190 B.C., at least some of them had become farmers living in villages (6:3–4,11,27–30,37).[7]

Many scholars claim that the record of the conquest in Joshua is idealistic, with a more realistic account detailed in Judges 1. However, the two books identify the same list of cities that could not be conquered (Jos 13:3–4; 15:63; 16:10; 17:11–12,16; Jdg 1:27–36). The focus in Joshua is not on those failures but rather on the victories resulting from remaining true to the Lord. Judges, on the other hand, emphasizes Israel's failings during a period when the people of God followed the pagan ways of the nations around them.

[1]See "The Tabernacle at Shiloh" on page 401. [2]See "The Archaeology of Philistia" on page 370 and "Technological Supremacy of the Philistines' Iron Weapons" on page 414. [3]See "David" on page 443. [4]See Glossary on page 2080 for definitions of bolded words. [5]See "Archaeological Periods" chart on page xx in the front of this Bible. [6]See "Changes in Canaan" on page 358. [7]See "Food and Agriculture" on page 390.

1:11 [p]Jos 15:15 11 From there they advanced against the people living in Debir[p] (formerly called Kiriath Sepher). 12 And
Caleb said, "I will give my daughter Acsah in marriage to the man who attacks and captures Kiriath Se-
pher." 13 Othniel son of Kenaz, Caleb's younger brother, took it; so Caleb gave his daughter Acsah to him
in marriage.
14 One day when she came to Othniel, she urged him[a] to ask her father for a field. When she got off her
donkey, Caleb asked her, "What can I do for you?"
15 She replied, "Do me a special favor. Since you have given me land in the Negev, give me also springs
of water." Then Caleb gave her the upper and lower springs.
1:16 [q]Nu 10:29 [r]Ge 15:19; Jdg 4:11 [s]Dt 34:3; Jdg 3:13 [t]Nu 21:1 16 The descendants of Moses' father-in-law,[q] the Kenite,[r] went up from the City of Palms[b][s] with the
men of Judah to live among the people of the Desert of Judah in the Negev near Arad.[t]
1:17 [u]ver 3 [v]Nu 21:3 17 Then the men of Judah went with the Simeonites[u] their brothers and attacked the Canaanites liv-
ing in Zephath, and they totally destroyed[c] the city. Therefore it was called Hormah.[d][v] 18 The men of Ju-
1:18 [w]Jos 11:22 dah also took[e] Gaza,[w] Ashkelon and Ekron—each city with its territory.
1:19 [x]ver 2 [y]Jos 17:16 19 The LORD was with[x] the men of Judah. They took possession of the hill country, but they were un-
able to drive the people from the plains, because they had iron chariots.[y] 20 As Moses had promised, He-
1:20 [z]Jos 14:9; 15:13-14 [a]ver 10; Jos 14:13 bron[z] was given to Caleb, who drove from it the three sons of Anak.[a] 21 The Benjamites, however, failed[b]
1:21 [b]Jos 15:63 [c]ver 8 to dislodge the Jebusites, who were living in Jerusalem;[c] to this day the Jebusites live there with the Ben-
jamites.
22 Now the house of Joseph attacked Bethel, and the LORD was with them. 23 When they sent men to
1:23 [d]Ge 28:19 spy out Bethel (formerly called Luz),[d] 24 the spies saw a man coming out of the city and they said to him,
1:24 [e]Jos 2:12, 14 "Show us how to get into the city and we will see that you are treated well.[e]" 25 So he showed them, and
1:25 [f]Jos 6:25 they put the city to the sword but spared[f] the man and his whole family. 26 He then went to the land of the
Hittites, where he built a city and called it Luz, which is its name to this day.
1:27 [g]Jos 17:11 [h]ver 1 27 But Manasseh did not drive out the people of Beth Shan or Taanach or Dor or Ibleam[g] or Megiddo
and their surrounding settlements, for the Canaanites[h] were determined to live in that land. 28 When Is-
rael became strong, they pressed the Canaanites into forced labor but never drove them out completely.
1:29 [i]1Ki 9:16 [j]Jos 16:10 29 Nor did Ephraim drive out the Canaanites living in Gezer,[i] but the Canaanites continued to live there
among them.[j] 30 Neither did Zebulun drive out the Canaanites living in Kitron or Nahalol, who remained
among them; but they did subject them to forced labor. 31 Nor did Asher drive out those living in Acco or
1:31 [k]Jdg 10:6 Sidon or Ahlab or Aczib[k] or Helbah or Aphek or Rehob, 32 and because of this the people of Asher lived
among the Canaanite inhabitants of the land. 33 Neither did Naphtali drive out those living in Beth She-
1:33 [l]Jos 19:38 mesh or Beth Anath[l]; but the Naphtalites too lived among the Canaanite inhabitants of the land, and
1:34 [m]Ex 3:17 those living in Beth Shemesh and Beth Anath became forced laborers for them. 34 The Amorites[m] confined
the Danites to the hill country, not allowing them to come down into the plain. 35 And the Amorites were
1:35 [n]Jos 19:42 determined also to hold out in Mount Heres, Aijalon[n] and Shaalbim, but when the power of the house of
Joseph increased, they too were pressed into forced labor. 36 The boundary of the Amorites was from Scor-
1:36 [o]Jos 15:3 pion[f] Pass[o] to Sela and beyond.

The Angel of the LORD at Bokim

2:1 [p]Jdg 6:11 [q]ver 5 [r]Ex 20:2 [s]Ge 17:8 2 The angel of the LORD[p] went up from Gilgal to Bokim[q] and said, "I brought you up out of Egypt[r] and
led you into the land that I swore to give to your forefathers.[s] I said, 'I will never break my covenant
[t]Lev 26:42-44; Dt 7:9 with you,[t] 2 and you shall not make a covenant with the people of this land,[u] but you shall break down
2:2 [u]Ex 23:32; 34:12; Dt 7:2 [v]Ex 34:13 their altars.[v]' Yet you have disobeyed me. Why have you done this? 3 Now therefore I tell you that I will not
2:3 [w]Jos 23:13 [x]Nu 33:55 [y]Dt 7:16; Jdg 3:6; Ps 106:36 drive them out before you;[w] they will be ⌞thorns⌟[x] in your sides and their gods will be a snare[y] to you."

[a] 14 Hebrew; Septuagint and Vulgate *Othniel, he urged her* [b] 16 That is, Jericho [c] 17 The Hebrew term refers to the irrevocable giving over of things or persons to the LORD, often by totally destroying them. [d] 17 *Hormah* means *destruction.* [e] 18 Hebrew; Septuagint *Judah did not take* [f] 36 Hebrew *Akrabbim*

1:16 The "City of Palms" was Jericho.
1:18 The five main Philistine cities (Gaza, Ashkelon, Ashdod, Ekron and Gath) were commercial trading centers with important connections reaching as far as Egypt along the coastal route, the "interstate highway" of the ancient world. The ships of Phoenicia, Cyprus, Crete and the Aegean called at Philistia's seaports, which included a site today called Tell Qasile, where a Philistine temple has been excavated, on the Yarkon River just north of modern Tel Aviv. See "The Archaeology of Philistia" on page 370.
1:19 Iron weapons proved the decisive element in the Philistines' early domination of Israel, and the Philistines guarded their technology jealously (see "Technological Supremacy of the Philistines' Iron Weapons" on p. 414). The "iron chariots" were probably wooden vehicles with iron axles (see the note on Jos 17:16).
1:22 Archaeological evidence of the destruction of Bethel ("Map 4") in the thirteenth century B.C. may reflect the battle mentioned in this verse. See "Bethel" on page 59.
2:1 Gilgal ("Map 4") was the place where Israel first became established in the land under Joshua (see Jos 4:19—5:12; see also "The Camp at Gilgal" on p. 308).

EGYPT DURING THE BRONZE AGE

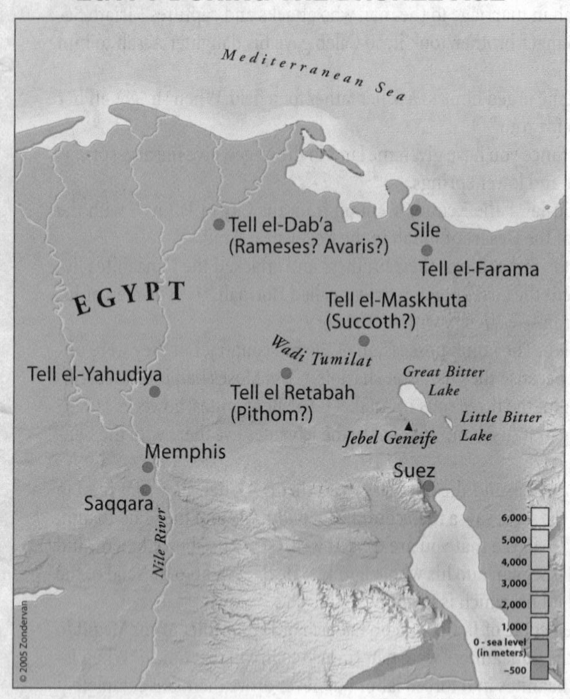

Zondervan NIV Altas of the Bible, p. 89

4 When the angel of the LORD had
spoken these things to all the Israel-
ites, the people wept aloud, 5 and they
called that place Bokim.[a] There they
offered sacrifices to the LORD.

Disobedience and Defeat

6 After Joshua had dismissed the
Israelites, they went to take posses-
sion of the land, each to his own in-
heritance. 7 The people served the
LORD throughout the lifetime of Josh-
ua and of the elders who outlived
him and who had seen all the great
things the LORD had done for Israel.
8 Joshua son of Nun, the servant
of the LORD, died at the age of a hun-
dred and ten. 9 And they buried him
in the land of his inheritance, at
Timnath Heres[b][z] in the hill country
of Ephraim, north of Mount Gaash.
10 After that whole generation had
been gathered to their fathers, an-
other generation grew up, who knew
neither the LORD nor what he had
done for Israel.[a] 11 Then the Israelites
did evil in the eyes of the LORD[b] and
served the Baals.[c] 12 They forsook the LORD, the God of their fathers, who had brought them out of Egypt.
They followed and worshiped various gods[d] of the peoples around them.[e] They provoked the LORD to
anger 13 because they forsook him and served Baal and the Ashtoreths.[f] 14 In his anger[g] against Israel the
LORD handed them over[h] to raiders who plundered them. He sold them[i] to their enemies all around,
whom they were no longer able to resist.[j] 15 Whenever Israel went out to fight, the hand of the LORD was
against them to defeat them, just as he had sworn to them. They were in great distress.
16 Then the LORD raised up judges,[c][k] who saved[l] them out of the hands of these raiders. 17 Yet they
would not listen to their judges but prostituted[m] themselves to other gods and worshiped them. Un-
like their fathers, they quickly turned from the way in which their fathers had walked, the way of obe-
dience to the LORD's commands.[n] 18 Whenever the LORD raised up a judge for them, he was with the
judge and saved them out of the hands of their enemies as long as the judge lived; for the LORD had
compassion[o] on them as they groaned[p] under those who oppressed and afflicted them. 19 But when
the judge died, the people returned to ways even more corrupt[q] than those of their fathers, following

2:9 [z]Jos 19:50
2:10 [a]Ex 5:2; 1Sa 2:12; 1Ch 28:9; Gal 4:8
2:11 [b]Jdg 3:12; 4:1; 6:1; 10:6 [c]Jdg 3:7; 8:33
2:12 [d]Ps 106:36 [e]Dt 31:16; Jdg 10:6
2:13 [f]Jdg 10:6
2:14 [g]Dt 31:17 [h]Ps 106:41 [i]Dt 32:30; Jdg 3:8 [j]Dt 28:25
2:16 [k]Ac 13:20 [l]Ps 106:43
2:17 [m]Ex 34:15 [n]ver 7
2:18 [o]Dt 32:36; Jos 1:5 [p]Ps 106:44
2:19 [q]Jdg 3:12

[a] 5 *Bokim* means *weepers.* [b] 9 Also known as *Timnath Serah* (see Joshua 19:50 and 24:30) [c] 16 Or *leaders*; similarly in verses 17-19

2:6—3:6 Any distinct ethnicity of the Israelites is almost impossible to determine from archaeological records from the period 1200–1000 B.C. They intermarried with the Canaanites and served their gods. In religious and social matters most were indistinguishable from their neighbors. See "The Amarna Tablets and the Habiru" on page 347.

2:11—3:6 The cycle of the judges is set forth in the abstract in this section. It is notable that these individuals were not principally civil magistrates but military deliverers. In fact, many of them seem to have been singularly unfitted to be what we would today call judges. See "The Judges Period" on page 344.

2:13 The Canaanites and Phoenicians worshiped the god Baal ("lord"), who was variously known as the son of Dagon and the son of El. He was called Hadad in Aram (Syria) and Adad in Babylonia. As the god of fertility—both human and agricultural—he is pictured as standing on a bull, a popular symbol of fertility and strength (see 1Ki 12:28). The storm cloud was viewed as his chariot, thunder as his voice and lightning as his spear and arrows. Ritual prostitution and sometimes even child sacrifice were characteristic of Baal worship (see Jer 19:5). See "Baal and the Fertility Cults" on page 1414, "Storm Gods, Storm Imagery and Theopany" on page 808, "The Ugaritic Text of the Myth of Baal" on page 905, "Prostitution in the Ancient World" on page 284 and "Human Sacrifice in the Ancient Near East" on page 182.

Ashtoreths, or female deities, included Ashtoreth (consort of Baal) and Asherah (consort of El, the chief god of the Canaanite pantheon). Ashtoreth was thought to be the beautiful goddess of war and fertility. Associated with the evening star, she was worshiped as Ishtar in Babylonia, Athtart in Aram, Astarte or Aphrodite by the Greeks and Venus by the Romans. Worship of the Ashtoreths involved extremely lewd practices (1Ki 14:24; 2Ki 23:7). See "The Kuntillet Ajrûd Inscriptions: The Lord's Asherah?" on page 1220.

2:16 These "judges" were the leaders of Israel from the time of the elders who outlived Joshua until the days of the monarchy. Their principal purpose was to deliver Israel from her oppressors.

2:19 [r]Jdg 4:1; 8:33
2:20 [s]ver 14; Jos 23:16
2:21 [t]Jos 23:13
2:22 [u]Dt 8:2,16; Jdg 3:1,14

other gods and serving and worshiping them.[r] They refused to give up their evil practices and stub-
born ways.
20 Therefore the LORD was very angry[s] with Israel and said, "Because this nation has violated the cov-
enant that I laid down for their forefathers and has not listened to me, 21 I will no longer drive out[t] before
them any of the nations Joshua left when he died. 22 I will use them to test[u] Israel and see whether they
will keep the way of the LORD and walk in it as their forefathers did." 23 The LORD had allowed those na-
tions to remain; he did not drive them out at once by giving them into the hands of Joshua.

The Amarna Tablets and the Habiru

JUDGES 2 A few decades after the conquest, in the mid-fourteenth century B.C., a reformer and visionary named **Amenhotep IV** came to the throne in Egypt. He instituted sweeping changes in the areas of art, politics and especially religion. Amenhotep IV rejected the traditional pantheon of Egyptian deities and worshiped only "Aten," the sun disk. Amenhotep changed his name to Akhenaten, "One who is effective on behalf of the Aten," and built a new capital which he called Akhetaten, "the horizon of Aten," in **Amarna** about 250 miles (403 km) north of the original capital of Thebes (see El Amarna and Thebes on the map of Egypt on page 346). Life in the new capital centered upon the worship of Aten. Following Akhenaten's 17-year reign, the conservative Egyptians soon reverted to their old ways, moving the capital back to Thebes[1] and reestablishing their traditional gods.

In 1887 a Bedouin woman discovered a number of clay tablets with writing on them among the ruins of Akhetaten.[2] When it was learned that the tablets were valuable, the local natives dug up several hundred of them and sold them to various museums and individuals. A few more were later found in officially sanctioned excavations. Altogether, 382 tablets have been recovered, nearly all of which are diplomatic correspondence and thus referred to in total as the Amarna Letters.

An Amarna tablet
Preserving Bible Times; © Dr. James C. Martin; permission of The Cairo Museum

The letters are written in **Akkadian** (Babylonian), the international language of the day, instead of in Egyptian **hieroglyphics**.[3] They span a period of about 20 years during the mid-fourteenth century B.C. A stamped brick identified the building where the tablets were found as the "Place of the Pharaoh's Correspondence." A few of the letters are in the form of outgoing correspondence, but the vast majority are incoming diplomatic messages from throughout the ancient Near East. Some 106 of them are from Egypt's **vassal** kings in **Canaan** and thus are of great interest to students of the Bible.

The letters from Canaan provide a rare glimpse into conditions a half century or so after the conquest.[4] This was early in the period of the judges, when individual tribes were consolidating their hold upon the land. The Biblical account is similar to the situation reflected in the Amarna Letters. The city-state rulers reported hostilities throughout Canaan. In particular, they complained about a group of people called *Habiru*. If the pharaoh did not take action, the letters warned, all of Canaan would be taken over by these people. The king of Jerusalem lamented, "The war against me is severe ... Habiru have plundered all the lands of the king." But who were these Habiru?

The Habiru are mentioned in texts from various places in the Near East between about 1750 and 1150 B.C. These texts indicate that they were nomadic tribesmen or fugitives who had penetrated urbanized areas and were proving troublesome to the metropolitan populations. It is possible that there is a linguistic connection between the term "Habiru" and the Biblical name "Hebrew." Some of the Habiru in the highlands of Canaan in the mid-fourteenth century B.C. may in fact have been the Israelites, since the Bible identifies them as having been in this area at that time. Although it is certain that not all people called Habiru were Israelites, the indigenous peoples of Canaan may well have dubbed the Israelites as such, and the name may have stuck as Hebrews.

See the study note at Genesis 10:21 for another possible origin for the name Hebrews.

[1]See "Thebes" on page 1354. [2]See "Cuneiform and Clay Tablets in the Ancient Near East" on page 1108. [3]See "Languages of the Old Testament World" on page 672. [4]See "Canaan" on page 324.

3 These are the nations the LORD left to test[v] all those Israelites who had not experienced any of the 3:1 [v]Jdg 2:21-22
wars in Canaan [2](he did this only to teach warfare to the descendants of the Israelites who had not
had previous battle experience): [3]the five[w] rulers of the Philistines, all the Canaanites, the Sidonians, 3:3 [w]Jos 13:3
and the Hivites living in the Lebanon mountains from Mount Baal Hermon to Lebo[a] Hamath. [4]They
were left to test[x] the Israelites to see whether they would obey the LORD's commands, which he had giv- 3:4 [x]Dt 8:2; Jdg 2:22
en their forefathers through Moses.
[5]The Israelites lived[y] among the Canaanites, Hittites, Amorites, Perizzites, Hivites and Jebusites. [6]They 3:5 [y]Ps 106:35
took their daughters in marriage and gave their own daughters to their sons, and served their gods.[z] 3:6 [z]Ex 34:16; Dt 7:3-4

Othniel 3:7 [a]Dt 4:9 [b]Ex 34:13; Jdg 2:11,13

[7]The Israelites did evil in the eyes of the LORD; they forgot the LORD[a] their God and served the Baals 3:8 [c]Jdg 2:14
and the Asherahs.[b] [8]The anger of the LORD burned against Israel so that he sold[c] them into the hands of 3:9 [d]ver 15;
Cushan-Rishathaim king of Aram Naharaim,[b] to whom the Israelites were subject for eight years. [9]But Jdg 6:6,7; 10:10; Ps 106:44 [e]Jdg 1:13
when they cried out[d] to the LORD, he raised up for them a deliverer, Othniel[e] son of Kenaz, Caleb's youn- 3:10 [f]Nu 11:25, 29; 24:2;
ger brother, who saved them. [10]The Spirit of the LORD came upon him,[f] so that he became Israel's judge[c] Jdg 6:34; 11:29; 13:25; 14:6,19; 1Sa 11:6

[a] 3 Or *to the entrance to* [b] 8 That is, Northwest Mesopotamia [c] 10 Or *leader*

3:3–4 Hamath ("Map 5"), located in upper Syria on the Orontes River, from which it derives its water by means of immense water wheels driven by the current, is one of the most ancient surviving cities on Earth. This area was intended to be the northern limit of Israel, but God allowed some of the Hivites to remain in the neighborhood, evidently to serve as a test of Israel's faithfulness.

3:7–11 The judges and the parts of Israel that they served (when that can be known) are listed below:

1. Othniel (3:7–11)
2. Ehud (3:12–30): Central Palestine and Transjordan
3. Shamgar (3:31): Philistine plain
4. Deborah and Barak (chs. 4–5): Central Palestine and Galilee
5. Gideon (chs 6–8): Central Palestine and Transjordan
6. Abimelech (ch 9): Central Palestine (Abimelech is considered by many as merely an outlaw and not a judge)
7. Tola (10:1–2): Central Palestine
8. Jair (10:3–5): Transjordan
9. Jephthah (10:6—12:7): Transjordan
10. Ibzan (12:8–10): Southern Palestine
11. Elon (12:11–12): Northern Palestine
12. Abdon (12:13–15): Central Palestine
13. Samson (chs. 13–16): Philistine plain

3:7 The gods Baal and Asherah were part of a fertility religion (see "Baal and the Fertility Cults" on p. 1414). Worshipers were concerned with success and materialism—securing for themselves a large family, ample flocks and herds and abundant crops. At the heart of this idolatry was the idea that the deity magically took up residence within the man-made idol. Idols were produced using precise methods and specific materials to ensure that this "magic indwelling" would take place (see "Idols and Idol-Making" on p. 1136).

ARCHAEOLOGICAL SITES

EGLON'S PALACE

JUDGES 3 Eglon, king of **Moab**,[1] led a coalition of Moabites, Ammonites and Amalekites from east of the Dead Sea and the Jordan Valley and subdued the Israelite tribes during the second half of the fourteenth century B.C. (Jdg 3:12–14). He established a headquarters at Jericho, the City of Palms (8 mi—nearly 13 km—northeast of the Dead Sea), and from there collected tribute from the Israelites. When British archaeologist John Garstang excavated Jericho in 1933 he discovered a large structure that he identified as the palace of Eglon. He dubbed it the "Middle Building," since it was sandwiched between **Iron Age**[2] structures above and the destroyed **Bronze Age** city below.[3] It had been erected sometime during the second half of the fourteenth century B.C., precisely the time of Eglon.

The building measured 39 feet (11.9 m) by 48 feet (14.6 m) and had much expensive local and imported painted pottery inside. A **cuneiform** tablet, a rare find in Palestine, attested that the owner had been involved in high-level administrative activities. No other buildings from that time period were discovered, so it is evident that there was no local community. The single structure that was excavated had been occupied for a relatively short period of time and then abandoned. This matches the situation in Judges 3. Apparently Eglon traveled to Jericho periodically to collect tribute from the Israelites. There he constructed a luxury villa, as mentioned in chapter 3. But this building was indeed abandoned after 18 years when Eglon was assassinated by Ehud and the Moabites fled back across the Jordan River.

[1]See "Moab" on page 292. [2]See "Archaeological Periods" chart on page xx in the front of this Bible. [3]See "The Walls of Jericho" on page 312.

and went to war. The LORD gave Cushan-Rishathaim king of Aram into the hands of Othniel, who over-
powered him. 11 So the land had peace for forty years, until Othniel son of Kenaz died.

Ehud

3:12 [g]Jdg 2:11, 14 [h]1Sa 12:9 12 Once again the Israelites did evil in the eyes of the LORD,[g] and because they did this evil the LORD
gave Eglon king of Moab[h] power over Israel. 13 Getting the Ammonites and Amalekites to join him, Eg-
3:13 [i]Jdg 1:16 lon came and attacked Israel, and they took possession of the City of Palms.[a][i] 14 The Israelites were sub-
ject to Eglon king of Moab for eighteen years.
3:15 [j]ver 9; Ps 78:34; 107:13 15 Again the Israelites cried out to the LORD, and he gave them a deliverer[j]—Ehud, a left-handed man,
the son of Gera the Benjamite. The Israelites sent him with tribute to Eglon king of Moab. 16 Now Ehud
had made a double-edged sword about a foot and a half[b] long, which he strapped to his right thigh un-
3:17 [k]ver 12 der his clothing. 17 He presented the tribute to Eglon king of Moab, who was a very fat man.[k] 18 After Ehud
had presented the tribute, he sent on their way the men who had carried it. 19 At the idols[c] near Gilgal he
himself turned back and said, "I have a secret message for you, O king."

The king said, "Quiet!" And all his attendants left him.

20 Ehud then approached him while he was sitting alone in the upper room of his summer palace[d]
and said, "I have a message from God for you." As the king rose from his seat, 21 Ehud reached with his
left hand, drew the sword from his right thigh and plunged it into the king's belly. 22 Even the handle sank
in after the blade, which came out his back. Ehud did not pull the sword out, and the fat closed in over
it. 23 Then Ehud went out to the porch[e]; he shut the doors of the upper room behind him and locked them.

24 After he had gone, the servants came and found the doors of the upper room locked. They said, "He
3:24 [l]1Sa 24:3 must be relieving himself[l] in the inner room of the house." 25 They waited to the point of embarrass-
3:25 [m]2Ki 2:17; 8:11 ment,[m] but when he did not open the doors of the room, they took a key and unlocked them. There they
saw their lord fallen to the floor, dead.

26 While they waited, Ehud got away. He passed by the idols and escaped to Seirah. 27 When he arrived
3:27 [n]Jdg 6:34; 1Sa 13:3 there, he blew a trumpet[n] in the hill country of Ephraim, and the Israelites went down with him from the
hills, with him leading them.

3:28 [o]Jdg 7:9,15 [p]Jos 2:7; Jdg 7:24; 12:5 28 "Follow me," he ordered, "for the LORD has given Moab, your enemy, into your hands.[o]" So they fol-
lowed him down and, taking possession of the fords of the Jordan[p] that led to Moab, they allowed no one
to cross over. 29 At that time they struck down about ten thousand Moabites, all vigorous and strong; not
3:30 [q]ver 11 a man escaped. 30 That day Moab was made subject to Israel, and the land had peace[q] for eighty years.

Shamgar

3:31 [r]Jdg 5:6 [s]Jos 23:10 31 After Ehud came Shamgar son of Anath,[r] who struck down six hundred[s] Philistines with an ox-
goad. He too saved Israel.

Deborah

4:1 [t]Jdg 2:19 4 After Ehud died, the Israelites once again did evil[t] in the eyes of the LORD. 2 So the LORD sold them
4:2 [u]Jos 11:1 into the hands of Jabin, a king of Canaan, who reigned in Hazor.[u] The commander of his army was

[a] 13 That is, Jericho [b] 16 Hebrew *a cubit* (about 0.5 meter) [c] 19 Or *the stone quarries*; also in verse 26 [d] 20 The meaning of the Hebrew for this phrase is uncertain. [e] 23 The meaning of the Hebrew for this word is uncertain.

3:11 The term "40 years" is a conventional number of years for a generation.

3:12–31 The first judge mentioned in detail is Ehud. The gory details of Ehud's deed fit well with this violent period.

3:15–23 Left-handedness was common in the tribe of Benjamin (see 20:16; cf. 1Ch 12:2) and may have been artificially induced by binding the right arms of young boys to produce superior warriors. Being left-handed, Ehud could conceal his dagger on the side where it was not expected (see 3:31).

3:19 The word *idols* literally means "carved (stone) things," a frequent Hebrew term for stone idols (see the NIV text note). But here the reference may be to carved stone statues of Eglon (see "Eglon's Palace" on p. 348) that marked the boundary of the territory he claimed as part of his expanded realm—a common practice in the ancient Near East.

3:23–24 For commentary on locking and opening house doors, see the note on Song of Songs 5:5.

3:31 An oxgoad was a long, wooden rod, sometimes having a metal tip, similar to a modern-day cattle prod. *Oxgoad* literally means "an instrument of learning." To be sure, Shamgar "taught" the Philistines a thing or two.

4:1—5:31 In this second detailed deliverance narrative in the book of Judges, the scene shifts from the lower Jordan Valley to the Valley of Jezreel and the Galilee hill country in northern Palestine. The oppressor is Jabin, the king of Canaan, who reigned in Hazor ("Map 4") and whose 900 chariots of iron must have struck terror into the Hebrew tribes, who knew no such machines of war (1Sa 13:19–22). The recent excavation of Hazor by Israeli scholars has underscored the importance of this Canaanite stronghold, probably the largest city in ancient Palestine. See "Horses and Chariots in Ancient Warfare" on page 114, "Hazor" on page 322, "Deborah and Barak and the Destruction of Hazor" on page 350 and "Technological Supremacy of the Philistines' Iron Weapons" on page 414.

4:2 The dates of Jabin's reign are unknown. Hazor was destroyed around 1220, although it had been quite powerful a century earlier. Thus, a date of around 1350 B.C. for Jabin is probably not far off. Joshua had earlier slain another king by the name of Jabin and had captured the city of Hazor (see Jos 11:1,10).

DEBORAH AND BARAK AND THE DESTRUCTION OF HAZOR

JUDGES 4 After 20 years of oppression Deborah and Barak rallied six Israelite tribes and defeated the army of Jabin, king of Canaan, at the Kishon River (Jdg 4:15). Sisera was Jabin's general. Deborah and Barak continued their offensive "until they destroyed" Jabin, who ruled at **Hazor** (v. 24; see "Map 3").[1] According to the chronological data in the Old Testament this event would have occurred during the second half of the thirteenth century B.C.

Excavations at Hazor have indeed revealed evidence of massive destruction at this time—so severe that the city was not rebuilt until the time of Solomon, during the tenth century B.C.[2] An intriguing aspect of the destruction is that the heads and hands of the statues of both deities and dignitaries were intentionally broken off (cf. 1Sa 5:4). Excavators suggest that this could have been the work of the Israelites, carrying out Moses' injunction to "cut down the idols of their gods" (Dt 12:3).

At first glance it might appear strangely coincidental that Jabin was the name both of the king of Hazor defeated by Deborah and Barak and of the king of the same city defeated by Joshua (Jos 11). However, an eighteenth- or seventeenth-century B.C. royal letter from Hazor, eighteenth-century tablets from **Mari**[3] and a thirteenth-century Egyptian text all refer to kings at Hazor with the name Jabin. Clearly, Jabin was a dynastic name at Hazor (much as individual Egyptian rulers were each called Pharaoh), and the Bible accurately reflects this historical fact.

[1]See "Hazor" on page 322. [2]See "The Building Activity of Solomon" on page 497. [3]See "Mari" on page 54.

Kishon Pass, the lower gate
Photograph: © Todd Bolen/Bible Places.com

Sisera,[v] who lived in Harosheth Haggoyim. 3 Because he had nine hundred iron chariots[w] and had cruelly oppressed[x] the Israelites for twenty years, they cried to the LORD for help.

4 Deborah, a prophetess, the wife of Lappidoth, was leading[a] Israel at that time. 5 She held court under the Palm of Deborah between Ramah and Bethel[y] in the hill country of Ephraim, and the Israelites came to her to have their disputes decided. 6 She sent for Barak son of Abinoam[z] from Kedesh in Naphtali and said to him, "The LORD, the God of Israel, commands you: 'Go, take with you ten thousand men of Naphtali and Zebulun and lead the way to Mount Tabor. 7 I will lure Sisera, the commander of Jabin's army, with his chariots and his troops to the Kishon River[a] and give him into your hands.' "

8 Barak said to her, "If you go with me, I will go; but if you don't go with me, I won't go."

9 "Very well," Deborah said, "I will go with you. But because of the way you are going about this,[b] the honor will not be yours, for the LORD will hand Sisera over to a woman." So Deborah went with Barak to Kedesh,[b] 10 where he summoned[c] Zebulun and Naphtali. Ten thousand men followed him, and Deborah also went with him.

11 Now Heber the Kenite had left the other Kenites,[d] the descendants of Hobab,[e] Moses' brother-in-law,[c] and pitched his tent by the great tree in Zaanannim[f] near Kedesh.

12 When they told Sisera that Barak son of Abinoam had gone up to Mount Tabor, 13 Sisera gathered together his nine hundred iron chariots[g] and all the men with him, from Harosheth Haggoyim to the Kishon River.

14 Then Deborah said to Barak, "Go! This is the day the LORD has given Sisera into your hands. Has not the LORD gone ahead[h] of you?" So Barak went down Mount Tabor, followed by ten thousand men. 15 At Barak's advance, the LORD routed[i] Sisera and all his chariots and army by the sword, and Sisera abandoned his chariot and fled on foot. 16 But Barak pursued the chariots and army as far as Harosheth Haggoyim. All the troops of Sisera fell by the sword; not a man was left.[j]

17 Sisera, however, fled on foot to the tent of Jael, the wife of Heber the Kenite, because there were friendly relations between Jabin king of Hazor and the clan of Heber the Kenite.

18 Jael went out to meet Sisera and said to him, "Come, my lord, come right in. Don't be afraid." So he entered her tent, and she put a covering over him.

19 "I'm thirsty," he said. "Please give me some water." She opened a skin of milk,[k] gave him a drink, and covered him up.

20 "Stand in the doorway of the tent," he told her. "If someone comes by and asks you, 'Is anyone here?' say 'No.' "

21 But Jael, Heber's wife, picked up a tent peg and a hammer and went quietly to him while he lay fast asleep, exhausted. She drove the peg through his temple into the ground, and he died.[l]

22 Barak came by in pursuit of Sisera, and Jael went out to meet him. "Come," she said, "I will show you the man you're looking for." So he went in with her, and there lay Sisera with the tent peg through his temple—dead.

23 On that day God subdued[m] Jabin, the Canaanite king, before the Israelites. 24 And the hand of the Israelites grew stronger and stronger against Jabin, the Canaanite king, until they destroyed him.

The Song of Deborah

5 On that day Deborah and Barak son of Abinoam sang this song:[n]

2 "When the princes in Israel take the lead,
when the people willingly offer[o] themselves—
praise the LORD![p]

4:2 [v]ver 13,16; 1Sa 12:9; Ps 83:9 **4:3** [w]Jdg 1:19 [x]Ps 106:42 **4:5** [y]Ge 35:8 **4:6** [z]Heb 11:32 **4:7** [a]Ps 83:9 **4:9** [b]ver 21; Jdg 2:14 **4:10** [c]ver 14; Jdg 5:15,18 **4:11** [d]Jdg 1:16 [e]Nu 10:29 [f]Jos 19:33 **4:13** [g]ver 3 **4:14** [h]Dt 9:3; 2Sa 5:24; Ps 68:7 **4:15** [i]Jos 10:10; Ps 83:9-10 **4:16** [j]Ps 83:9 **4:19** [k]Jdg 5:25 **4:21** [l]Jdg 5:26 **4:23** [m]Ne 9:24; Ps 18:47 **5:1** [n]Ex 15:1 **5:2** [o]2Ch 17:16; Ps 110:3 [p]ver 9

[a] 4 Traditionally *judging* [b] 9 Or *But on the expedition you are undertaking* [c] 11 Or *father-in-law*

4:3 The number "nine hundred" probably represents a coalition rather than the chariot force of one city. Pharaoh Thutmose III boasted of having captured 924 chariots at the battle of Megiddo in the fifteenth century B.C.

4:4 See the note on prophetesses at Exodus 15:20–21.

4:6 Mount Tabor is about 1,300 feet (296 m) high and was located northeast of the battle site.

4:11 The Kenites were descendants of Hobab, the brother-in-law of Moses. Hobab visited the Israelites as they left Sinai, and Moses invited him to come along and to act as a pathfinder (Nu 10:29–32). Hobab's descendants were friendly with Israel; they traveled with Judah from Jericho (Jdg 1:16) and amalgamated with the tribe of Judah. Later, Heber the Kenite separated from the others, moved northward to Kedesh near the Sea of Galilee and made peace with Jabin, king of Hazor. Heber's wife Jael killed Sisera, the Canaanite general, so fulfilling Deborah's prophecy to Barak that a woman would secure the honor for this victory.

4:18 Jael's assassination of Sisera would have been considered by an ancient reader a horrendous crime or even a sacrilege on two counts: Her family was formally at peace with Jabin of Hazor (v. 17), and Jael invited Sisera into her home and then violated rules of hospitality by doing violence to him under her roof.

5:1–31 Deborah's warlike song of praise is believed to be one of the oldest poems in the Bible and is noted for its rough, primitive vigor (see "The Bulletin and Poetic Accounts of the Battle of Kadesh" on p. 353).

3 "Hear this, you kings! Listen, you rulers!
I will sing to[a] the LORD, I will sing;
I will make music to[b] the LORD, the God of Israel.[q]

4 "O LORD, when you went out from Seir,[r]
when you marched from the land of Edom,
the earth shook, the heavens poured,
the clouds poured down water.[s]
5 The mountains quaked[t] before the LORD, the One of Sinai,
before the LORD, the God of Israel.

6 "In the days of Shamgar son of Anath,[u]
in the days of Jael,[v] the roads[w] were abandoned;
travelers took to winding paths.
7 Village life[c] in Israel ceased,
ceased until I,[d] Deborah, arose,
arose a mother in Israel.
8 When they chose new gods,[x]
war came to the city gates,
and not a shield or spear was seen
among forty thousand in Israel.
9 My heart is with Israel's princes,
with the willing volunteers[y] among the people.
Praise the LORD!

10 "You who ride on white donkeys,[z]
sitting on your saddle blankets,
and you who walk along the road,
consider 11 the voice of the singers[e] at the watering places.
They recite the righteous acts[a] of the LORD,
the righteous acts of his warriors[f] in Israel.

"Then the people of the LORD
went down to the city gates.[b]
12 'Wake up,[c] wake up, Deborah!
Wake up, wake up, break out in song!
Arise, O Barak!
Take captive your captives,[d] O son of Abinoam.'

13 "Then the men who were left
came down to the nobles;
the people of the LORD
came to me with the mighty.
14 Some came from Ephraim, whose roots were in Amalek;[e]
Benjamin was with the people who followed you.
From Makir captains came down,
from Zebulun those who bear a commander's staff.
15 The princes of Issachar were with Deborah;[f]
yes, Issachar was with Barak,
rushing after him into the valley.
In the districts of Reuben
there was much searching of heart.

5:3 [q]Ps 27:6
5:4 [r]Dt 33:2 [s]Ps 68:8
5:5 [t]Ex 19:18; Ps 68:8; 97:5; Isa 64:3
5:6 [u]Jdg 3:31 [v]Jdg 4:17 [w]Isa 33:8
5:8 [x]Dt 32:17
5:9 [y]ver 2
5:10 [z]Jdg 10:4; 12:14
5:11 [a]1Sa 12:7; Mic 6:5 [b]ver 8
5:12 [c]Ps 57:8 [d]Ps 68:18; Eph 4:8
5:14 [e]Jdg 3:13
5:15 [f]Jdg 4:10

[a] 3 Or *of* [b] 3 Or / *with song I will praise* [c] 7 Or *Warriors* [d] 7 Or *you* [e] 11 Or *archers*; the meaning of the Hebrew for this word is uncertain. [f] 11 Or *villagers*

5:6–8 This period coincides with the unrest that followed the Hittite colapse and the death of Egypt's Rameses II, the treaties between which had preserved order in the Holy Land for 80 years. Rameses' successor, however, was the elderly Merneptah. Despte his claim to have pacified both Canaanites and Israelites, disorder became rampant. Hence "the roads were abandoned . . . and not a shield or spear was seen."

5:16 [g]Nu 32:1
5:17 [h]Jos 19:29
5:18 [i]Jdg 4:6,10
5:19 [j]Jos 11:5; Jdg 4:13 [k]Jdg 1:27 [l]ver 30

16 Why did you stay among the campfires[a]
to hear the whistling for the flocks?[g]
In the districts of Reuben
there was much searching of heart.
17 Gilead stayed beyond the Jordan.
And Dan, why did he linger by the ships?
Asher remained on the coast[h]
and stayed in his coves.
18 The people of Zebulun risked their very lives;
so did Naphtali on the heights of the field.[i]

19 "Kings came[j], they fought;
the kings of Canaan fought
at Taanach by the waters of Megiddo,[k]
but they carried off no silver, no plunder.[l]

[a] 16 Or *saddlebags*

5:17 The Hebrews were an agricultural people, and the Phoenicians and Philistines, over long periods, separated them from a coastline that was itself harborless and difficult. In this verse there is a cryptic reference to some experience with ships in the case of the tribes of Dan and Asher, but seafaring was secondary for the Hebrews. See "Seafaring in the Ancient World" on page 1473.
5:19 The main pass that runs northeast through the hill country from the plain of Sharon to the Valley of Jezreel was dominated by Megiddo and Taanach (five mi—eight km—from Megiddo). Because of its strategic location, the "plain of Megiddo" (2Ch 35:22) has been a frequent battleground from the earliest times. According to Judges 5:19, the forces of Israel under Deborah and Barak crushed the Canaanites "by the waters of Megiddo." There Judah's good king Josiah died in battle against Pharaoh Neco II in 609 B.C. (2Ki 23:29), there Pharaoh Thutmose III defeated a Canaanite coalition in 1468 B.C., and there in A.D. 1917 the British under General Allenby ended the rule of the Turks in Palestine by vanquishing them in the Valley of Jezreel opposite Megiddo. The plain of Megiddo is also referred to in

ANCIENT TEXTS AND ARTIFACTS

The Bulletin and Poetic Accounts of the Battle of Kadesh

JUDGES 5 Judges 4 records in prose the defeat of Sisera, captain of Jabin's army, at the hand of a Kenite woman. This is followed in chapter 5 by a poetic account of the same event. Differences in style and detail between the two versions have led many scholars to discount the reliability of one or the other account. For instance, chapter 4 mentions only the tribes of Naphtali and Zebulun as having been involved in the battle (4:6,10), while chapter 5 also includes Ephraim, Benjamin, Manasseh and Issachar (4:13–18). Some argue that the two versions stem from separate sources that were later combined by the ancient editor of the book of Judges. This conclusion, however, is unnecessary, as the seeming discrepancies can be explained by other means.

That prosaic and poetic accounts of the same events occurred together in antiquity can be demonstrated by Egyptian literary carvings. In the fifth year of the reign of Egypt's **Rameses II** (1275 B.C.), the Egyptian army fought Muwatalli II of the **Hittites** at the site of Kadesh ("Map 5") near the Orontes River.[1] The Egyptian triumph is depicted in paired wall **reliefs** that were carved on several Egyptian temples, always accompanied by double inscriptions recounting the heroic role of Rameses II in the victory (although the victory was not as complete as the inscriptions suggest).

One of the two accounts appearing with the battle scenes is known as the Poem, a poetic description of the entire battle with an occasional prosaic section. A prose text (known as the Bulletin) provides supplementary information, namely an account of the pharaoh questioning two Hittite scouts. Like Judges 4 and 5, the Bulletin and Poem recount a military victory in differing forms: one prosaic, the other poetic. In addition, the two works do not repeat precisely the same information but complement one another, with the Poem being the more complete or universal account of the battle. The appearance of these two segments, together with the same two battle reliefs on several temples, indicates that they were intended to be read together and had been commissioned and composed at the same time.

Therefore, the fact that Judges 4 comprises a narrative account of the battle against Jabin and Sisera, while Judges 5 is a poetic rendering of the same event, is not a signal that one report is less reliable than the other. It was not uncommon for significant events to be memorialized in a literary, poetic form while also being recorded in more ordinary prose. As the Bulletin account gives more precise information regarding specific events at the Kadesh battle, Judges 4 most likely focuses on the two tribes that provided the most significant military force, even though other tribes assisted in the fight.

[1]See "Anatolia and the Hittites" on page 144.

[20]From the heavens[m] the stars fought,
from their courses they fought against Sisera.
[21]The river Kishon[n] swept them away,
the age-old river, the river Kishon.
March on, my soul; be strong!
[22]Then thundered the horses' hoofs—
galloping, galloping go his mighty steeds.
[23]'Curse Meroz,' said the angel of the LORD.
'Curse its people bitterly,
because they did not come to help the LORD,
to help the LORD against the mighty.'

[24]"Most blessed of women be Jael,[o]
the wife of Heber the Kenite,
most blessed of tent-dwelling women.
[25]He asked for water, and she gave him milk;[p]
in a bowl fit for nobles she brought him curdled milk.
[26]Her hand reached for the tent peg,
her right hand for the workman's hammer.
She struck Sisera, she crushed his head,
she shattered and pierced his temple.[q]
[27]At her feet he sank,
he fell; there he lay.
At her feet he sank, he fell;
where he sank, there he fell—dead.

[28]"Through the window peered Sisera's mother;
behind the lattice she cried out,[r]
'Why is his chariot so long in coming?
Why is the clatter of his chariots delayed?'
[29]The wisest of her ladies answer her;
indeed, she keeps saying to herself,
[30]'Are they not finding and dividing the spoils:[s]
a girl or two for each man,
colorful garments as plunder for Sisera,
colorful garments embroidered,
highly embroidered garments for my neck—
all this as plunder?'

[31]"So may all your enemies perish, O LORD!
But may they who love you be like the sun[t]
when it rises in its strength."

Then the land had peace[u] forty years.

5:20 [m]Jos 10:11
5:21 [n]Jdg 4:7
5:24 [o]Jdg 4:17
5:25 [p]Jdg 4:19
5:26 [q]Jdg 4:21
5:28 [r]Pr 7:6
5:30 [s]Ex 15:9; 1Sa 30:24
5:31 [t]2Sa 23:4; Ps 19:4; 89:36 [u]Jdg 3:11

Gideon

6 Again the Israelites did evil in the eyes of the LORD,[v] and for seven years he gave them into the hands
of the Midianites.[w] [2]Because the power of Midian was so oppressive,[x] the Israelites prepared shelters

6:1 [v]Jdg 2:11 [w]Nu 25:15-18; 31:1-3
6:2 [x]1Sa 13:6; Isa 8:21

Revelation 16:16 as "the place that in Hebrew is called Armageddon" (i.e., "Mount Megiddo"), the site of the "battle on the great day of God Almighty" (Rev 16:14). See "Taanach" on page 591 and "Megiddo" on page 1541.

5:21–22 For the battle site, Sisera cleverly chose the Valley of Jezreel along the Kishon River, where his chariot forces would have ample maneuvering space to range the battlefield and attack in numbers from any quarter. But God fought from heaven, using a storm and flood to defeat Sisera. Even in modern times storms have rendered the plain along the Kishon virtually impassable. In April of 1799 the flooded Kishon River aided Napoleon's victory over a Turkish army. See "The Bulletin and Poetic Accounts of the Battle of Kadesh" on page 353.

5:25 "Curdled milk" was artificially soured by being shaken in a skin-bottle and then allowed to ferment (due to bacteria that remained in the skin from previous use).

6:1—8:35 The third great judge was Gideon. He was from the village of Ophran, the location of which is uncertain. It was located somewhere west of the Jordan, probably in the region between Beth Shan and Tabor ("Map 4"). The oppressing Midianites, desert

6:2 [y]Heb 11:38 for themselves in mountain clefts, caves and strongholds.[y] [3]Whenever the Israelites planted their crops,
6:3 [z]Jdg 3:13 the Midianites, Amalekites[z] and other eastern peoples invaded the country. [4]They camped on the land
6:4 [a]Lev 26:16; Dt 28:30,51 and ruined the crops[a] all the way to Gaza and did not spare a living thing for Israel, neither sheep nor
6:5 [b]Jdg 7:12 cattle nor donkeys. [5]They came up with their livestock and their tents like swarms of locusts.[b] It was im-
[c]Jdg 8:10 possible to count the men and their camels;[c] they invaded the land to ravage it. [6]Midian so impover-
6:6 [d]Jdg 3:9 ished the Israelites that they cried out[d] to the LORD for help.
[7]When the Israelites cried to the LORD because of Midian, [8]he sent them a prophet, who said, "This is
6:8 [e]Jdg 2:1 what the LORD, the God of Israel, says: I brought you up out of Egypt,[e] out of the land of slavery. [9]I
snatched you from the power of Egypt and from the hand of all your oppressors. I drove them from be-
6:9 [f]Ps 44:2 fore you and gave you their land.[f] [10]I said to you, 'I am the LORD your God; do not worship[g] the gods of
6:10 [g]2Ki 17:35 [h]Jer 10:2 the Amorites,[h] in whose land you live.' But you have not listened to me."
6:11 [i]Ge 16:7 [j]Jos 17:2 [11]The angel of the LORD[i] came and sat down under the oak in Ophrah that belonged to Joash the Abi-
[k]Heb 11:32 ezrite,[j] where his son Gideon[k] was threshing wheat in a winepress to keep it from the Midianites. [12]When
6:12 [l]Jos 1:5; Jdg 13:3; Lk 1:11, 28 the angel of the LORD appeared to Gideon, he said, "The LORD is with you,[l] mighty warrior."
[13]"But sir," Gideon replied, "if the LORD is with us, why has all this happened to us? Where are all his
6:13 [m]Ps 44:1 [n]2Ch 15:2 wonders that our fathers told[m] us about when they said, 'Did not the LORD bring us up out of Egypt?' But
now the LORD has abandoned[n] us and put us into the hand of Midian."
6:14 [o]Heb 11:34 [14]The LORD turned to him and said, "Go in the strength you have[o] and save Israel out of Midian's hand.
Am I not sending you?"
6:15 [p]Ex 3:11; 1Sa 9:21 [15]"But Lord,[a]" Gideon asked, "how can I save Israel? My clan is the weakest in Manasseh, and I am the
least in my family.[p]"
6:16 [q]Ex 3:12; Jos 1:5 [16]The LORD answered, "I will be with you[q], and you will strike down all the Midianites together."
6:17 [r]ver 36-37; Ge 24:14; [17]Gideon replied, "If now I have found favor in your eyes, give me a sign[r] that it is really you talking
Isa 38:7-8 to me. [18]Please do not go away until I come back and bring my offering and set it before you."
And the LORD said, "I will wait until you return."
[19]Gideon went in, prepared a young goat, and from an ephah[b] of flour he made bread without yeast.
Putting the meat in a basket and its broth in a pot, he brought them out and offered them to him under
6:19 [s]Ge 18:7-8 the oak.[s]
6:20 [t]Jdg 13:19 [20]The angel of God said to him, "Take the meat and the unleavened bread, place them on this rock,[t]
and pour out the broth." And Gideon did so. [21]With the tip of the staff that was in his hand, the angel of
6:21 [u]Lev 9:24 the LORD touched the meat and the unleavened bread.[u] Fire flared from the rock, consuming the meat and
6:22 [v]Jdg 13:16, 21 [w]Ge 32:30; the bread. And the angel of the LORD disappeared. [22]When Gideon realized[v] that it was the angel of the
Ex 33:20; Jdg 13:22 LORD, he exclaimed, "Ah, Sovereign LORD! I have seen the angel of the LORD face to face!"[w]
6:23 [x]Da 10:19 [23]But the LORD said to him, "Peace! Do not be afraid.[x] You are not going to die."
6:24 [y]Ge 22:14 [z]Jdg 8:32 [24]So Gideon built an altar to the LORD there and called[y] it The LORD is Peace. To this day it stands in
Ophrah[z] of the Abiezrites.
[25]That same night the LORD said to him, "Take the second bull from your father's herd, the one seven
6:25 [a]Ex 34:13; Dt 7:5 years old.[c] Tear down your father's altar to Baal and cut down the Asherah pole[d][a] beside it. [26]Then build
a proper kind of[e] altar to the LORD your God on the top of this height. Using the wood of the Asherah pole
that you cut down, offer the second[f] bull as a burnt offering."
[27]So Gideon took ten of his servants and did as the LORD told him. But because he was afraid of his
family and the men of the town, he did it at night rather than in the daytime.
6:28 [b]1Ki 16:32 [28]In the morning when the men of the town got up, there was Baal's altar,[b] demolished, with the Ashe-
rah pole beside it cut down and the second bull sacrificed on the newly built altar!

[a] *15* Or *sir* [b] *19* That is, probably about 3/5 bushel (about 22 liters) [c] *25* Or *Take a full-grown, mature bull from your father's herd* [d] *25* That is, a symbol of the goddess Asherah; here and elsewhere in Judges [e] *26* Or *build with layers of stone an* [f] *26* Or *full-grown*; also in verse 28

Bedouin from the Transjordan region, had crossed the Jordan and were raiding in Palestine proper. Gideon's ruse, carried out by a mere 300 companions, frightened the disorganized Bedouin from the Valley of Jezreel into full retreat across the Jordan. Gideon promptly called the Ephraimites to take the Jordan fords and thereby destroyed the Midianites. Gideon appears to have established some form of regular rule over at least the region of the Jezreel Valley during his lifetime. His importance can be gauged by his rather large domestic establishment (8:30). Adhering to the ancient ideal of charismatic leadership, he rejected the idea of setting up a dynasty (8:22–23).

6:11 Rather than threshing wheat in the usual, exposed area (see note on Ru 1:22; see also "The Threshing Floor" on p. 608), Gideon felt more secure threshing in the better protected but very confining space of a winepress (see "The Winepress" on p. 1171).

6:25 The chosen symbol of the fertility cult of Asherah was the trunk of a tree (see "Devotion to Asherah in the Khirbet El-Qom Inscription" on p. 638). This explains the prohibition against the planting of trees near the altar of the Lord (see also vv. 23,31; Dt 16:21).

[29]They asked each other, "Who did this?"
When they carefully investigated, they were told, "Gideon son of Joash did it."
[30]The men of the town demanded of Joash, "Bring out your son. He must die, because he has broken
down Baal's altar and cut down the Asherah pole beside it."
[31]But Joash replied to the hostile crowd around him, "Are you going to plead Baal's cause? Are you try-
ing to save him? Whoever fights for him shall be put to death by morning! If Baal really is a god, he can
defend himself when someone breaks down his altar." [32]So that day they called Gideon "Jerub-Baal,[a][c]" **6:32** [c]Jdg 7:1; 8:29,35; 1Sa 12:11
saying, "Let Baal contend with him," because he broke down Baal's altar.

[a] 32 *Jerub-Baal* means *let Baal contend.*

ANCIENT TEXTS AND ARTIFACTS

The Descent of Ishtar

JUDGES 6 Modern Christian readers of Judges 6 may be astonished to learn how quickly—and evidently almost casually—Israelite families fell into the worship of pagan gods and set up shrines in their honor. It is helpful to see how widespread and universally accepted these myths of pagan gods were. For example, there are several versions of the Descent of the Goddess Inanna (also called Ishtar) Into the Underworld.

Hymn to Inanna (Ishtar); Babylonia, twentieth–seventeenth centuries B.C.

© The Schøyen Collection; photography courtesy of Mr. Martin Schøyen

A Sumerian version begins with the goddess Inanna determined to visit the underworld, perhaps in order to rule there. She gains admission but must pass through seven gates in order to enter the underworld. At each gate she is divested of the symbols of her prestige and divinity: her crown, jewelry and garments. The process is symbolic of death, and Inanna arrives naked, as the dead do when they enter the underworld. Inanna is then condemned for her act of entering the underworld, and her corpse is hung up.

Inanna's servant Ninshubur appeals to the gods, and Enki, the god of wisdom, fashions two creatures who enter the underworld and revive Inanna. Inanna is allowed to return to the world above but must find a substitute to take her place. She determines not to take anyone who has mourned for her but is angered to discover her former lover Dumuzi arrayed in splendid robes rather than in mourning clothes. Dumuzi's sister Geshtinanna pleads for him, and an arrangement is made whereby Dumuzi and Geshtinanna will each spend half of the year in the underworld. Their cycles of descending into death and again ascending symbolize the seasons and the apparent annual death of vegetation (in an Akkadian version, no plants on Earth would grow while Inanna/Ishtar was in the underworld).

Variants of this myth can be found throughout the ancient world. Dumuzi is mentioned in the Bible under the name Tammuz.[1] The **Canaanite** counterpart to the Sumerian Inanna or the Akkadian Ishtar is Astarte[2] (or sometimes Anat). The Egyptian goddess Isis plays a similar role. Although the details differ, there are overtones here as well of the Greek myth of Persephone. Through these myths ancient peoples attempted to come to terms with issues of fertility, the seasons, sexuality and death. Because the myths were almost universally held, and because they seemed to help people understand the most fundamental problems of life, it was difficult for the average Israelite to avoid succumbing to their allure. Despite all they had been told to the contrary, many Israelites believed that they could embrace these myths and the gods and goddesses behind them and yet remain faithful to their God, **Yahweh**, and his covenant.

[1]See "Mourning for Tammuz" on page 1320.
[2]See "The Queen of Heaven" on page 1267.

6:33 [d]ver 3 [e]Jos 17:16 33 Now all the Midianites, Amalekites and other eastern peoples[d]
joined forces and crossed over the Jordan and camped in the Valley
6:34 [f]Jdg 3:10; 1Ch 12:18; 2Ch 24:20 [g]Jdg 3:27 of Jezreel.[e] 34 Then the Spirit of the LORD came upon[f] Gideon, and he
blew a trumpet,[g] summoning the Abiezrites to follow him. 35 He sent
messengers throughout Manasseh, calling them to arms, and also
6:35 [h]Jdg 4:6 into Asher, Zebulun and Naphtali,[h] so that they too went up to meet
them.
6:36 [i]ver 14 36 Gideon said to God, "If you will save[i] Israel by my hand as you
have promised— 37 look, I will place a wool fleece on the threshing
6:37 [j]Ex 4:3-7 [k]Ge 24:14 floor.[j] If there is dew only on the fleece and all the ground is dry,
then I will know[k] that you will save Israel by my hand, as you said."
38 And that is what happened. Gideon rose early the next day; he
squeezed the fleece and wrung out the dew—a bowlful of water.
39 Then Gideon said to God, "Do not be angry with me. Let me
6:39 [l]Ge 18:32 make just one more request.[l] Allow me one more test with the fleece.
This time make the fleece dry and the ground covered with dew."
40 That night God did so. Only the fleece was dry; all the ground was
covered with dew.

Gideon Defeats the Midianites

7:1 [m]Jdg 6:32 [n]Ge 12:6 **7** Early in the morning, Jerub-Baal[m] (that is, Gideon) and all his
men camped at the spring of Harod. The camp of Midian was
north of them in the valley near the hill of Moreh.[n] 2 The LORD said
to Gideon, "You have too many men for me to deliver Midian into their hands. In order that Israel may
7:2 [o]Dt 8:17; 2Co 4:7 not boast against me that her own strength[o] has saved her, 3 announce now to the people, 'Anyone who
7:3 [p]Dt 20:8 trembles with fear may turn back and leave Mount Gilead.[p]' " So twenty-two thousand men left, while
ten thousand remained.
7:4 [q]1Sa 14:6 4 But the LORD said to Gideon, "There are still too many[q] men. Take them down to the water, and I will
sift them for you there. If I say, 'This one shall go with you,' he shall go; but if I say, 'This one shall not go
with you,' he shall not go."
5 So Gideon took the men down to the water. There the LORD told him, "Separate those who lap the
water with their tongues like a dog from those who kneel down to drink." 6 Three hundred men lapped
with their hands to their mouths. All the rest got down on their knees to drink.
7 The LORD said to Gideon, "With the three hundred men that lapped I will save you and give the Mid-
7:7 [r]1Sa 14:6 ianites into your hands. Let all the other men go, each to his own place."[r] 8 So Gideon sent the rest of the
Israelites to their tents but kept the three hundred, who took over the provisions and trumpets of the
others.
Now the camp of Midian lay below him in the valley. 9 During that night the LORD said to Gideon, "Get
7:9 [s]Jos 2:24; 10:8; 11:6 up, go down against the camp, because I am going to give it into your hands.[s] 10 If you are afraid to at-
tack, go down to the camp with your servant Purah 11 and listen to what they are saying. Afterward, you
will be encouraged to attack the camp." So he and Purah his servant went down to the outposts of the
7:12 [t]Jdg 8:10 [u]Jdg 6:5 [v]Jer 49:29 [w]Jos 11:4 camp. 12 The Midianites, the Amalekites[t] and all the other eastern peoples had settled in the valley, thick
as locusts.[u] Their camels[v] could no more be counted than the sand on the seashore.[w]
13 Gideon arrived just as a man was telling a friend his dream. "I had a dream," he was saying. "A round
loaf of barley bread came tumbling into the Midianite camp. It struck the tent with such force that the
tent overturned and collapsed."
14 His friend responded, "This can be nothing other than the sword of Gideon son of Joash, the Isra-
elite. God has given the Midianites and the whole camp into his hands."
7:15 [x]1Sa 15:31 15 When Gideon heard the dream and its interpretation, he worshiped God.[x] He returned to the camp
of Israel and called out, "Get up! The LORD has given the Midianite camp into your hands." 16 Dividing the
7:16 [y]Ge 14:15 [z]2Sa 18:2 three hundred men[y] into three companies,[z] he placed trumpets and empty jars in the hands of all of
them, with torches inside.
17 "Watch me," he told them. "Follow my lead. When I get to the edge of the camp, do exactly as I do.
7:18 [a]Jdg 3:27 18 When I and all who are with me blow our trumpets,[a] then from all around the camp blow yours and
shout, 'For the LORD and for Gideon.' "

ANCIENT VOICES

To Kurnugi, land of [no return],*
Ishtar daughter of Sin was [determined]
to go;
The daughter of Sin was determined
to go
To the dark house, dwelling of
Erkalla's god,
To the house which those who enter
cannot leave,
On the road where traveling is one-way
only,
To the house where those who enter are
deprived of light,
Where dust is their food, clay their bread.
They see no light, they dwell in
darkness. . .

*Words in brackets added by translator for clarity or where text has gaps

—THE DESCENT OF ISHTAR TO THE UNDERWORLD

See "The Descent of Ishtar" article.

Changes in Canaan

JUDGES 7 During the course of the period of the judges (c. 1400–1050 B.C.), major political, social and economic changes impacting the Israelite tribes took place throughout the Mediterranean region. When the Israelites entered **Canaan**[1] they encountered fortified city-states. On the eve of their entry Moses warned them that they were going in to face great cities fortified "to the sky" (Dt 9:1). Israel managed to subdue the highlands, leaving that area nearly devoid of any urban population. Urban centers, however, remained intact in the lowlands.

In the late thirteenth century B.C., for reasons not totally understood, urban cultures throughout the Mediterranean began to collapse. Beginning in the twelfth century B.C. a new culture appeared in Canaan—small, unwalled, agricultural villages dispersed across the landscape. Archaeologists refer to this as the **Iron Age I**[2] period.

These agricultural centers provide the first tangible archaeological evidence for Israel's presence in Canaan. Prior to the twelfth century B.C., evidence for Israel's existence in the land is virtually impossible to find. Also, we have no records in the Bible or elsewhere of God's people encountering the Egyptian forces that sometimes swept through Canaan during the **Late Bronze Age**. The first documented encounter, in fact, does not occur until the time of Merneptah at the end of the thirteenth century.[3]

A group of scholars, therefore, believes that Israel did not exist in the land until about 1200 B.C. Some maintain that the Israelite nation emerged from the indigenous Canaanite population at this time. This theory totally dismisses as nonhistorical the Biblical record of the **patriarchs**,[4] Egyptian sojourn, exodus,[5] wilderness wanderings,[6] conquest[7] and the period of the early judges.[8]

While it is true that there is sparse evidence for the Israelites in the land of Canaan during the Late Bronze Age, several identifiable factors may reasonably account for this:

✣ For the first 200 years of their existence in Canaan, the Israelites had no material culture of their own. The generation that had departed from Egypt equipped with knowledge of building techniques, crafts, etc., had died out during the 40 years of wilderness wandering. Those who entered Canaan, with the exception of Joshua and Caleb, had been born and raised as shepherds in the Sinai wilderness. Thus, during the early period of the judges (fourteenth and thirteenth centuries B.C.) the Israelites, although present, were archaeologically "invisible."

✣ The rural, pastoral existence of the early Israelites is not likely to have left much behind in the way of material evidence.

✣ The number of Israelites who entered Canaan may have been relatively small. The issue here is how we are to understand the census figures given in Numbers 1. It is possible that the total number of Israelites departing Egypt was only around 20,000; if so, their archaeological impact upon entering Canaan would have been minimal.[9]

✣ Some of the language of the book of Joshua is misleading to the modern reader, and this problem is compounded by the picture of "Israel During the Period of the Judges" typically shown on Bible maps. We get the impression that the Israelites ruled all the territory that had been allotted to them by Joshua and that they were a unified nation with fixed borders. This perception is entirely erroneous. Joshua's allotment represented the ultimate, ideal situation, but many areas were never conquered. The tribe of Dan, for example, was totally unable to secure its prearranged territory.[10]

✣ Because the Israelites tended to be rural and pastoral in their lifestyle, and because they settled in the highlands, they tended to be bypassed by major military forces sweeping through the area, such as the army of the Egyptian pharaoh **Rameses II** (c. 1279–1213). These frequently nomadic shepherds and herdsmen were much more likely to be troubled by local enemies like the Amalekites (Jdg 6–7) and the Ammonites (chs. 10–11).

There are limits to what archaeology can tell us about early Israel. However, what information this discipline does provide corresponds well with a careful reading of the Biblical account.

Fragment of the book of Judges from Qumran, first century B.C.

© The Schøyen Collection; photography courtesy of Mr. Martin Schøyen

[1]See "Canaan" on page 324. [2]See "Archaeological Periods" chart on page xx in the front of this Bible. [3]See "The Merneptah Stele" on page 360. [4]See "The Historicity of the Patriarchal Narratives" on page 73. [5]See "The Date of the Exodus" on page 106. [6]See "A Timeline for the Wilderness Wanderings" on page 224. [7]See "The Conquest of Canaan" on page 310. [8]See "The Judges Period" on page 344. [9]See "Numbers and Their Meaning" on page 197. [10]See "The Migration of the Danites" on page 378.

19 Gideon and the hundred men with him reached the edge of the camp at the beginning of the mid-
dle watch, just after they had changed the guard. They blew their trumpets and broke the jars that were
in their hands. 20 The three companies blew the trumpets and smashed the jars. Grasping the torches in
7:20 [b]ver 14 their left hands and holding in their right hands the trumpets they were to blow, they shouted, "A sword[b]
for the LORD and for Gideon!" 21 While each man held his position around the camp, all the Midianites ran,
7:21 [c]2Ki 7:7 crying out as they fled.[c]
7:22 [d]Jos 6:20 22 When the three hundred trumpets sounded,[d] the LORD caused the men throughout the camp to
[e]1Sa 14:20; 2Ch 20:23 turn on each other[e] with their swords. The army fled to Beth Shittah toward Zererah as far as the bor-
[f]1Ki 4:12; 19:16 **7:23** [g]Jdg 6:35 der of Abel Meholah[f] near Tabbath. 23 Israelites from Naphtali, Asher and all Manasseh were called out,[g]
and they pursued the Midianites. 24 Gideon sent messengers throughout the hill country of Ephraim, say-
7:24 [h]Jdg 3:28 ing, "Come down against the Midianites and seize the waters of the Jordan[h] ahead of them as far as Beth
Barah."

So all the men of Ephraim were called out and they took the waters of the Jordan as far as Beth Bar-
7:25 [i]Jdg 8:3; Ps 83:11 ah. 25 They also captured two of the Midianite leaders, Oreb and Zeeb[i]. They killed Oreb at the rock of
[j]Isa 10:26 Oreb,[j] and Zeeb at the winepress of Zeeb. They pursued the Midianites and brought the heads of Oreb
[k]Jdg 8:4 and Zeeb to Gideon, who was by the Jordan.[k]

Zebah and Zalmunna

8 Now the Ephraimites asked Gideon, "Why have you treated us like this? Why didn't you call us when
8:1 [l]Jdg 12:1 [m]2Sa 19:41 you went to fight Midian?"[l] And they criticized him sharply.[m]
2 But he answered them, "What have I accomplished compared to you? Aren't the gleanings of Ephra-
8:3 [n]Jdg 7:25; Pr 15:1 im's grapes better than the full grape harvest of Abiezer? 3 God gave Oreb and Zeeb,[n] the Midianite
leaders, into your hands. What was I able to do compared to you?" At this, their resentment against
him subsided.
8:4 [o]Jdg 7:25 4 Gideon and his three hundred men, exhausted yet keeping up the pursuit, came to the Jordan[o] and
8:5 [p]Ge 33:17 [q]Ps 83:11 crossed it. 5 He said to the men of Succoth,[p] "Give my troops some bread; they are worn out, and I am
still pursuing Zebah and Zalmunna,[q] the kings of Midian."
6 But the officials of Succoth said, "Do you already have the hands of Zebah and Zalmunna in your
8:6 [r]1Sa 25:11 [s]ver 15 possession? Why should we give bread[r] to your troops?"[s]
8:7 [t]Jdg 7:15 7 Then Gideon replied, "Just for that, when the LORD has given Zebah and Zalmunna[t] into my hand, I
will tear your flesh with desert thorns and briers."
8:8 [u]Ge 32:30; 1Ki 12:25 8 From there he went up to Peniel[a][u] and made the same request of them, but they answered as the
men of Succoth had. 9 So he said to the men of Peniel, "When I return in triumph, I will tear down this
8:9 [v]ver 17 tower."[v]
10 Now Zebah and Zalmunna were in Karkor with a force of about fifteen thousand men, all that were
8:10 [w]Jdg 6:5; 7:12; Isa 9:4 left of the armies of the eastern peoples; a hundred and twenty thousand swordsmen had fallen.[w] 11 Gid-
8:11 [x]Nu 32:42 [y]Nu 32:35 eon went up by the route of the nomads east of Nobah[x] and Jogbehah[y] and fell upon the unsuspecting
army. 12 Zebah and Zalmunna, the two kings of Midian, fled, but he pursued them and captured them,
routing their entire army.
13 Gideon son of Joash then returned from the battle by the Pass of Heres. 14 He caught a young man
of Succoth and questioned him, and the young man wrote down for him the names of the seventy-sev-
en officials of Succoth, the elders of the town. 15 Then Gideon came and said to the men of Succoth, "Here
are Zebah and Zalmunna, about whom you taunted me by saying, 'Do you already have the hands of Ze-
8:15 [z]ver 6 bah and Zalmunna in your possession? Why should we give bread to your exhausted men?[z]' " 16 He took
8:16 [a]ver 7 the elders of the town and taught the men of Succoth a lesson[a] by punishing them with desert thorns and
8:17 [b]ver 9 briers. 17 He also pulled down the tower of Peniel and killed the men of the town.[b]
8:18 [c]Jos 19:22; Jdg 4:6 18 Then he asked Zebah and Zalmunna, "What kind of men did you kill at Tabor?[c]"
"Men like you," they answered, "each one with the bearing of a prince."
19 Gideon replied, "Those were my brothers, the sons of my own mother. As surely as the LORD lives, if
you had spared their lives, I would not kill you." 20 Turning to Jether, his oldest son, he said, "Kill them!"
But Jether did not draw his sword, because he was only a boy and was afraid.

[a] 8 Hebrew *Penuel,* a variant of *Peniel;* also in verses 9 and 17

7:19 Watches of the night were the divisions into which the 12 hours of darkness were divided. The Israelites had a threefold division, while the later Romans had four watches (Mk 6:48; see the note on Mt 14:15).

ANCIENT TEXTS AND ARTIFACTS

The Merneptah Stele

JUDGES 8 The Merneptah **Stele** is an inscribed stone slab discovered in Pharaoh Merneptah's mortuary temple in Thebes, Egypt (see the map of Egypt on p. 346), in 1896 (Merneptah is sometimes spelled Merenptah). This monument is the earliest record of Israel outside the Bible and contains the *only mention* of Israel in Egyptian records. This reference occurs in a short section describing a military campaign in **Canaan** conducted by Merneptah during the first few years of his reign, around 1210 B.C. It claims that "Israel is wasted, its seed is not; and Hurru is become a widow because of Egypt."

As was often the case in ancient records, the text exaggerates Merneptah's accomplishments. He did not in fact annihilate Israel as the stele implies. Israel's mention in the list of city-states and nations supposedly defeated by this pharaoh attests that Israel was an important entity in Merneptah's day—assuming that he would not have seen fit to boast about defeating an obscure or defenseless people group.

The real importance of the Merneptah Stele, however, is difficult to exaggerate:

- It demonstrates that Israel was a recognized people in the land of Canaan in approximately 1200 B.C. This is important because some scholars today suggest that Israel did not even exist as a recognizable entity at this time. In the light of this contemporary witness to Israel's existence, such a claim makes no sense.
- It provides us with an outside boundary for fixing the date of the exodus and conquest. Some scholars postulate a very late date for the conquest—even as late as about 1150 B.C. in the **Iron Age** I.[1] However, the stele indicates that Israel was already in the land and apparently well established.[2] Although it does not totally rule it out, the stele also makes unlikely the more broadly accepted "late date" for the exodus and conquest (in the late thirteenth century).[3]

The Merneptah Stele
Preserving Bible Times; © Dr. James C. Martin; permission of The Cairo Museum

[1]See "Archaeological Periods" chart on page xx in the front of this Bible. [2]See also "The Pharaoh of the Exodus" on page 98. [3]See "The Date of the Exodus" on page 106 and "The Conquest of Canaan" on page 310.

Egyptian wall inscriptions at Karnak
Preserving Bible Times; © Dr. James C. Martin

21 Zebah and Zalmunna said, "Come, do it yourself. 'As is the man, so is his strength.' " So Gideon
8:21 [d]ver 26; Ps 83:11 stepped forward and killed them, and took the ornaments[d] off their camels' necks.

Gideon's Ephod

22 The Israelites said to Gideon, "Rule over us—you, your son and your grandson—because you have
saved us out of the hand of Midian."
8:23 [e]Ex 16:8; 1Sa 8:7; 10:19; 12:12 23 But Gideon told them, "I will not rule over you, nor will my son rule over you. The LORD will rule[e]
over you." 24 And he said, "I do have one request, that each of you give me an earring from your share of
8:24 [f]Ge 25:13 the plunder." (It was the custom of the Ishmaelites[f] to wear gold earrings.)
25 They answered, "We'll be glad to give them." So they spread out a garment, and each man threw a
ring from his plunder onto it. 26 The weight of the gold rings he asked for came to seventeen hundred
shekels,[a] not counting the ornaments, the pendants and the purple garments worn by the kings of Mid-
8:27 [g]Jdg 17:5; 18:14 [h]Dt 7:16; Ps 106:39 ian or the chains that were on their camels' necks. 27 Gideon made the gold into an ephod,[g] which he
placed in Ophrah, his town. All Israel prostituted themselves by worshiping it there, and it became a
snare[h] to Gideon and his family.

Gideon's Death

28 Thus Midian was subdued before the Israelites and did not raise its head again. During Gideon's
8:28 [i]Jdg 5:31 lifetime, the land enjoyed peace[i] forty years.
8:29 [j]Jdg 7:1 29 Jerub-Baal[j] son of Joash went back home to live. 30 He had seventy sons[k] of his own, for he had many
8:30 [k]Jdg 9:2,5, 18,24 wives. 31 His concubine, who lived in Shechem, also bore him a son, whom he named Abimelech.[l] 32 Gid-
8:31 [l]Jdg 9:1 8:32 [m]Ge 25:8 eon son of Joash died at a good old age[m] and was buried in the tomb of his father Joash in Ophrah of the
Abiezrites.
8:33 [n]Jdg 2:11, 13,19 [o]Jdg 9:4 33 No sooner had Gideon died than the Israelites again prostituted themselves to the Baals.[n] They set
[p]Jdg 9:27,46 up Baal-Berith[o] as their god[p] and 34 did not remember[q] the LORD their God, who had rescued them from
8:34 [q]Jdg 3:7; Dt 4:9; Ps 78:11, 42 the hands of all their enemies on every side. 35 They also failed to show kindness to the family of Jerub-
8:35 [r]Jdg 9:16 Baal (that is, Gideon) for all the good things he had done for them.[r]

Abimelech

9:1 [s]Jdg 8:31 **9** Abimelech[s] son of Jerub-Baal went to his mother's brothers in Shechem and said to them and to all
his mother's clan, 2 "Ask all the citizens of Shechem, 'Which is better for you: to have all seventy of
9:2 [t]Ge 29:14; Jdg 8:30 Jerub-Baal's sons rule over you, or just one man?' Remember, I am your flesh and blood.[t]"
3 When the brothers repeated all this to the citizens of Shechem, they were inclined to follow Abime-
lech, for they said, "He is our brother." 4 They gave him seventy shekels[b] of silver from the temple of Baal-
9:4 [u]Jdg 8:33 [v]Jdg 11:3; 2Ch 13:7 Berith,[u] and Abimelech used it to hire reckless adventurers,[v] who became his followers. 5 He went to his
father's home in Ophrah and on one stone murdered his seventy brothers,[w] the sons of Jerub-Baal. But
9:5 [w]ver 2; Jdg 8:30 [x]2Ki 11:2 Jotham, the youngest son of Jerub-Baal, escaped by hiding.[x] 6 Then all the citizens of Shechem and Beth
Millo gathered beside the great tree at the pillar in Shechem to crown Abimelech king.
9:7 [y]Dt 11:29; 27:12; Jn 4:20 7 When Jotham was told about this, he climbed up on the top of Mount Gerizim[y] and shouted to them,
"Listen to me, citizens of Shechem, so that God may listen to you. 8 One day the trees went out to anoint
a king for themselves. They said to the olive tree, 'Be our king.'

[a] *26* That is, about 43 pounds (about 19.5 kilograms) [b] *4* That is, about 1 3/4 pounds (about 0.8 kilogram)

8:21 These "ornaments" were crescent necklaces (as in Isa 3:18) that were probably moon-shaped, implying veneration of the popular moon god.

9:1–57 The account of Gideon's son Abimelech and his violent rule over the Shechem area is recounted in this chapter. Abimelech is not called a judge, and he appears to have been more of a brigand or political-military adventurer than a deliverer of Israel from an oppressing enemy. He died as he had lived—his skull was cracked by a millstone, and he was finally killed by his armor bearer. It is well possible that Abimelech's career was described solely to give a feeling for the violent, unsettled state of affairs during the time of the judges. If that was its purpose, it can be said to have succeeded.

9:1 Shechem ("Map 4") was an important city in central Canaan, first built and inhabited during the patriarchal period. Ruins dating from the Canaanite era give evidence of a sacred area that was probably associated with the temple of Baal-Berith or El-Berith (vv. 4,46). Archaeological evidence compatible with the destruction of Shechem by Abimelech indicates that its sacred area was never rebuilt after this time. See "Shechem" on page 340 and "Abimelech at Shechem" on page 363.

9:4 Ancient temples served as repositories for personal and civic funds. Gifts, as well as the payments of vows and penalties, were part of the temple treasury.

The phrase "reckless adventurers" probably refers to mercenaries used to accomplish political or military goals, a common practice in ancient times. Jephthah (11:3), David (1Sa 22:1–2), Absalom (2Sa 15:1), Adonijah (1Ki 1:5), Rezon (1Ki 11:23–24) and Jeroboam (2Ch 13:6–7) also used them.

9:7–15 A fable may be defined as a narrative in which animals and inanimate objects of nature are made to act and speak as though they were human beings. The word *fable* is not found in the Old Testament, but two fables appear there: this passage and 2 Kings 14:9.

9 "But the olive tree answered, 'Should I give up my oil, by which both gods and men are honored, to
hold sway over the trees?'
10 "Next, the trees said to the fig tree, 'Come and be our king.'
11 "But the fig tree replied, 'Should I give up my fruit, so good and sweet, to hold sway over the trees?'
12 "Then the trees said to the vine, 'Come and be our king.'
13 "But the vine answered, 'Should I give up my wine,[z] which cheers both gods and men, to hold sway 9:13 [z]Ecc 2:3
over the trees?'
14 "Finally all the trees said to the thornbush, 'Come and be our king.'
15 "The thornbush said to the trees, 'If you really want to anoint me king over you, come and take
refuge in my shade;[a] but if not, then let fire come out[b] of the thornbush and consume the cedars of 9:15 [a]Isa 30:2
Lebanon!'[c] [b]ver 20 [c]Isa 2:13
16 "Now if you have acted honorably and in good faith when you made Abimelech king, and if you
have been fair to Jerub-Baal and his family, and if you have treated him as he deserves— 17 and to think
that my father fought for you, risked his life to rescue you from the hand of Midian 18 (but today you have
revolted against my father's family, murdered his seventy sons[d] on a single stone, and made Abimelech, 9:18 [d]ver 5-6;
the son of his slave girl, king over the citizens of Shechem because he is your brother)— 19 if then you Jdg 8:30
have acted honorably and in good faith toward Jerub-Baal and his family today, may Abimelech be your
joy, and may you be his, too! 20 But if you have not, let fire come out[e] from Abimelech and consume you, 9:20 [e]ver 15
citizens of Shechem and Beth Millo, and let fire come out from you, citizens of Shechem and Beth Mil-
lo, and consume Abimelech!"
21 Then Jotham fled, escaping to Beer, and he lived there because he was afraid of his brother Abim-
elech.
22 After Abimelech had governed Israel three years, 23 God sent an evil spirit[f] between Abimelech and 9:23 [f]1Sa 16:14,
the citizens of Shechem, who acted treacherously against Abimelech. 24 God did this in order that the 23; 18:10;
crime against Jerub-Baal's seventy sons, the shedding[g] of their blood, might be avenged[h] on their broth- 1Ki 22:22; Isa 19:14; 33:1 9:24 [g]Nu 35:33;
er Abimelech and on the citizens of Shechem, who had helped him[i] murder his brothers. 25 In opposition 1Ki 2:32 [h]ver 56-57 [i]Dt 27:25
to him these citizens of Shechem set men on the hilltops to ambush and rob everyone who passed by, and
this was reported to Abimelech.
26 Now Gaal son of Ebed moved with his brothers into Shechem, and its citizens put their confidence
in him. 27 After they had gone out into the fields and gathered the grapes and trodden[j] them, they held a 9:27 [j]Am 9:13
festival in the temple of their god.[k] While they were eating and drinking, they cursed Abimelech. 28 Then [k]Jdg 8:33
Gaal son of Ebed said, "Who[l] is Abimelech, and who is Shechem, that we should be subject to him? Isn't 9:28 [l]1Sa 25:10;
he Jerub-Baal's son, and isn't Zebul his deputy? Serve the men of Hamor,[m] Shechem's father! Why should 1Ki 12:16 [m]Ge 34:2,6
we serve Abimelech? 29 If only this people were under my command![n] Then I would get rid of him. I would 9:29 [n]2Sa 15:4
say to Abimelech, 'Call out your whole army!' "[a]
30 When Zebul the governor of the city heard what Gaal son of Ebed said, he was very angry. 31 Under
cover he sent messengers to Abimelech, saying, "Gaal son of Ebed and his brothers have come to Shechem
and are stirring up the city against you. 32 Now then, during the night you and your men should come
and lie in wait[o] in the fields. 33 In the morning at sunrise, advance against the city. When Gaal and his 9:32 [o]Jos 8:2
men come out against you, do whatever your hand finds to do.[p]" 9:33 [p]1Sa 10:7
34 So Abimelech and all his troops set out by night and took up concealed positions near Shechem in
four companies. 35 Now Gaal son of Ebed had gone out and was standing at the entrance to the city gate
just as Abimelech and his soldiers came out from their hiding place.[q] 9:35 [q]Ps 32:7; Jer 49:10
36 When Gaal saw them, he said to Zebul, "Look, people are coming down from the tops of the moun-
tains!"
Zebul replied, "You mistake the shadows of the mountains for men."
37 But Gaal spoke up again: "Look, people are coming down from the center of the land, and a compa-
ny is coming from the direction of the soothsayers' tree."
38 Then Zebul said to him, "Where is your big talk now, you who said, 'Who is Abimelech that we should
be subject to him?' Aren't these the men you ridiculed?[r] Go out and fight them!" 9:38 [r]ver 28-29
39 So Gaal led out[b] the citizens of Shechem and fought Abimelech. 40 Abimelech chased him, and many
fell wounded in the flight—all the way to the entrance to the gate. 41 Abimelech stayed in Arumah, and
Zebul drove Gaal and his brothers out of Shechem.

[a] 29 Septuagint; Hebrew *him." Then he said to Abimelech, "Call out your whole army!"* [b] 39 Or *Gaal went out in the sight of*

[42]The next day the people of Shechem went out to the fields, and this was reported to Abimelech. [43]So
9:43 sJdg 7:16 he took his men, divided them into three companies[s] and set an ambush in the fields. When he saw the
people coming out of the city, he rose to attack them. [44]Abimelech and the companies with him rushed
forward to a position at the entrance to the city gate. Then two companies rushed upon those in the fields
and struck them down. [45]All that day Abimelech pressed his attack against the city until he had captured
9:45 tver 20; 2Ki 3:25 uDt 29:23 it and killed its people. Then he destroyed the city[t] and scattered salt[u] over it.
9:46 vJdg 8:33 [46]On hearing this, the citizens in the tower of Shechem went into the stronghold of the temple[v] of El-

ARCHAEOLOGICAL SITES

ABIMELECH AT SHECHEM

Shechem
Photograph courtesy of © Dr. Gary Pratico

JUDGES 9 Gideon's son Abimelech attempted to become king of Israel by taking control of **Shechem**[1] (see "Map 3"), an important commercial and political center. He was given funds from "the temple of Baal-Berith" (Jdg 9:4), also known as "Baal of the covenant." Baal was the **Canaanite** storm god and the god of fertility.[2] Further references to the "temple of their god" (v. 27), the "tower of Shechem" (vv. 46–47,49) and the "temple of El-Berith" (v. 46) all appear to regard the same temple. Several archaeological findings at Shechem relate directly to Judges 9:

✣ A great fortress-temple excavated there has been identified as the temple of this chapter. It was constructed in the seventeenth century B.C. and lasted until the city's destruction by Abimelech in the twelfth century B.C. The largest temple yet found in Canaan, it measures 70 feet (21 m) by 86 feet (26 m), with foundations 17 feet (5 m) thick.

✣ In front is a courtyard with a sacred stone 4.8 feet (1.5 m) wide and 16.5 inches (.4 m) thick. It was broken in antiquity but still stands 4.8 feet (1.5 m) high. This sacred stone may be the "pillar" where the coronation ceremony took place when Abimelech was declared king (v. 6).

✣ The city gate from the time of Abimelech was excavated on the eastern side of the site. It was from this point that Abimelech's rival, Gaal, observed Abimelech and his men approaching the city (vv. 35–37). Leaving the security of the walls of Shechem, Gaal engaged Abimelech in battle but was defeated (vv. 38–40). The gate is an impressive structure some 54 feet (16.5 m) wide and 44 feet (13.4 m) deep, with **orthostats** (stone slabs) lining its walls.[3]

✣ Evidence of massive destruction from the time of Abimelech has been found throughout the site, attesting to his razing of the city (v. 45).

[1]See "Shechem" on page 340. [2]See "Baal and the Fertility Cults" on page 1414. [3]See "The City Gate" on page 392.

Berith. 47When Abimelech heard that they had assembled there, 48he and all his men went up Mount
Zalmon.[w] He took an ax and cut off some branches, which he lifted to his shoulders. He ordered the men **9:48** [w]Ps 68:14
with him, "Quick! Do what you have seen me do!" 49So all the men cut branches and followed Abime-
lech. They piled them against the stronghold and set it on fire over the people inside. So all the people in
the tower of Shechem, about a thousand men and women, also died.
50Next Abimelech went to Thebez[x] and besieged it and captured it. 51Inside the city, however, was a **9:50** [x]2Sa 11:21
strong tower, to which all the men and women—all the people of the city—fled. They locked them-
selves in and climbed up on the tower roof. 52Abimelech went to the tower and stormed it. But as he ap-

Ammon

JUDGES 10 Excavations of Rabbah-Ammon ("Map 2"), the capital of ancient Ammon, indicate occupation levels going back to the **Early Bronze Age.**[1] Although it appears to have been an important city in the **Middle Bronze Age**, it experienced the population decline that was characteristic of the region's **Late Bronze** period. Fortifications appear again from the **Iron Age**, suggesting that Ammon was once again becoming a powerful state.

The Bible indicates that the Ammonites were related both to the Moabites[2] and to the Israelites (Ge 19:37–38). By the time of the exodus the Ammonites and Moabites together occupied the southern **Transjordan**. When the Israelites passed through this territory on their way to the promised land, they were specifically forbidden because of this relationship to conquer the land of the Ammonites (Dt 2:19,37).

During the period of the judges[3] the Ammonites and Amalekites aided the Moabites in regaining land lost to Israel (Jdg 3:13), but the Lord raised up Ehud to deliver his people. Later, Jephthah routed the Ammonites who were oppressing Israel, especially the Transjordanian tribes (10:6–33). That Ammon had become an impressive force by this time is evident from the eleventh-century B.C. massive stone fortifications that have been discovered there. When Nahash ascended the Ammonite throne in approximately 1020 B.C., he attempted to reestablish control over the Transjordanian tribes, attacking Jabesh Gilead (1Sa 11:1). King Saul led 33,000 soldiers to rescue the town, crushing Nahash's forces (1Sa 11:4–11).

Nahash and David were on friendly terms while David was fleeing from Saul. When Nahash died David sent his condolences to his heir, Hanun, but Hanun shamed the delegation David had sent, thereby inciting war (2Sa 10:1–6). David's army defeated Hanun's mercenaries, and Rabbah, the Ammonite capital, was eventually defeated by Joab (2Sa 11:1; 12:26–31).

The Ammonites later declared their independence from Israel after the Egyptian pharaoh Shishak invaded the region only much later called Palestine.[4] In the mid-ninth century B.C. the Ammonite king Baasha joined the league that stopped **Shalmaneser III** as he drove toward the Mediterranean Sea.[5] This league, mentioned in **Assyrian** annals, was headed by Hadadezer of Damascus and Ahab of Israel.[6] Soon afterward the Ammonites, Moabites and Meunites attacked Jehoshaphat (2Ch 20:1–30), perhaps fearing that Judah was growing too powerful under his rule. But the members of the Transjordanian league turned against each other and ceased to threaten Judah (2Ch 20:22–23).

King Uzziah of Judah was able to regain control over Ammon in the early eighth century. When the Ammonites attempted to revolt against Uzziah's successor, Jotham, they were quickly defeated and afterward sent an annual tribute to Jotham (c. 740 B.C.). The **Assyrian** king Tiglath-Pileser reduced all the states of the area to vassalhood around 732 B.C., including Israel, Judah and Ammon.[7] Several Ammonite kings are mentioned in subsequent Assyrian annals as having paid tribute to Sennacherib and Esarhaddon,[8] and it appears that Ammon enjoyed a degree of prosperity under Assyrian rule.

When the Assyrian Empire fell to the **Babylonians** in 612 B.C., Ammonites moved into territory once held by Judah. **Nebuchadnezzar II** of Babylon protected the Ammonites from invading Arab forces, while using Ammonite forces to harass the Judahites in the Transjordan (2Ki 24:2).[9] As Babylonian oppression increased, however, Ammon joined a conspiracy, led by Judah, against Babylon. When it failed, as Jeremiah had warned that it would, many survivors fled to Ammon as Nebuchadnezzar crushed Jerusalem. Ammon was later annihilated as Nebuchadnezzar attacked Rabbah (c. 581 B.C.). Although Ammonites still lived in the area at the time of the exiles' return from captivity (Ne 2:10), they never again enjoyed autonomy.

[1]See "Archaeological Periods" chart on page xx in the front of this Bible. [2]See "Moab" on page 292. [3]See "The Judges Period" on page 344. [4]See "The Campaign of Shishak" on page 635. [5]See "Jehu/The Black Obelisk of Shalmaneser III" on page 544. [6]See "Ahab and the Battle of Qarqar" on page 524. [7]See "Menahem and Pekah of Israel, Jotham of Judah and Tiglath-Pileser III of Assyria" on page 553. [8]See "The Sennacherib Prism" on page 659. [9]See "Nebuchadnezzar" on page 571.

proached the entrance to the tower to set it on fire, [53]a woman dropped an upper millstone on his head
9:53 [y]2Sa 11:21 and cracked his skull.[y]
9:54 [z]1Sa 31:4; [54]Hurriedly he called to his armor-bearer, "Draw your sword and kill me,[z] so that they can't say, 'A
2Sa 1:9 woman killed him.' " So his servant ran him through, and he died. [55]When the Israelites saw that Abim-
elech was dead, they went home.
[56]Thus God repaid the wickedness that Abimelech had done to his father by murdering his seventy
9:57 [a]ver 20 brothers. [57]God also made the men of Shechem pay for all their wickedness.[a] The curse of Jotham son
of Jerub-Baal came on them.

Tola

10:1 [b]Ge 30:18 **10** After the time of Abimelech a man of Issachar,[b] Tola son of Puah,[c] the son of Dodo, rose to save[d]
[c]Ge 46:13 [d]Jdg 2:16; 6:14 Israel. He lived in Shamir, in the hill country of Ephraim. [2]He led[a] Israel twenty-three years; then
he died, and was buried in Shamir.

Jair

[3]He was followed by Jair of Gilead, who led Israel twenty-two years. [4]He had thirty sons, who rode
10:4 [e]Nu 32:41 thirty donkeys. They controlled thirty towns in Gilead, which to this day are called Havvoth Jair.[b][e] [5]When
Jair died, he was buried in Kamon.

Jephthah

10:6 [f]Jdg 2:11 [6]Again the Israelites did evil in the eyes of the LORD.[f] They served the Baals and the Ashtoreths,[g] and
[g]Jdg 2:13 the gods of Aram, the gods of Sidon, the gods of Moab, the gods of the Ammonites and the gods of the
[h]Jdg 2:12 [i]Dt 32:15 Philistines.[h] And because the Israelites forsook the LORD[i] and no longer served him, [7]he became angry[j]
10:7 [j]Dt 31:17 [k]Dt 32:30; with them. He sold them[k] into the hands of the Philistines and the Ammonites, [8]who that year shattered
Jdg 2:14; 1Sa 12:9 and crushed them. For eighteen years they oppressed all the Israelites on the east side of the Jordan in
Gilead, the land of the Amorites. [9]The Ammonites also crossed the Jordan to fight against Judah, Benja-
min and the house of Ephraim; and Israel was in great distress. [10]Then the Israelites cried out to the
10:10 [l]1Sa 12:10 LORD, "We have sinned against you, forsaking our God and serving the Baals."[l]
10:11 [m]Ex 14:30 [11]The LORD replied, "When the Egyptians,[m] the Amorites, the Ammonites,[n] the Philistines,[o] [12]the Si-
[n]Nu 21:21; Jdg 3:13 donians, the Amalekites and the Maonites[c] oppressed you[p] and you cried to me for help, did I not save
[o]Jdg 3:31 **10:12** [p]Ps 106:42 you from their hands? [13]But you have forsaken me and served other gods, so I will no longer save you.
10:14 [q]Dt 32:37 [14]Go and cry out to the gods you have chosen. Let them save you when you are in trouble![q]"
10:15 [r]1Sa 3:18; [15]But the Israelites said to the LORD, "We have sinned. Do with us whatever you think best,[r] but please
2Sa 15:26 **10:16** rescue us now." [16]Then they got rid of the foreign gods among them and served the LORD.[s] And he could
[s]Jos 24:23; Jer 18:8 [t]Isa 63:9 bear Israel's misery[t] no longer.[u]
[u]Dt 32:36; Ps 106:44-45 [17]When the Ammonites were called to arms and camped in Gilead, the Israelites assembled and
10:17 [v]Ge 31:49; camped at Mizpah.[v] [18]The leaders of the people of Gilead said to each other, "Whoever will launch the
Jdg 11:29 **10:18** attack against the Ammonites will be the head[w] of all those living in Gilead."
[w]Jdg 11:8,9 **11** Jephthah[x] the Gileadite was a mighty warrior.[y] His father was a prosti-
11:1 [x]Heb 11:32 [y]Jdg 6:12 tute. [2]Gilead's wife also bore him sons, and when they were grown up, they drove Jephthah away.
"You are not going to get any inheritance in our family," they said, "because you are the son of another
11:3 [z]2Sa 10:6,8 woman." [3]So Jephthah fled from his brothers and settled in the land of Tob,[z] where a group of adventur-
[a]Jdg 9:4 ers[a] gathered around him and followed him.
11:4 [b]Jdg 10:9 [4]Some time later, when the Ammonites[b] made war on Israel, [5]the elders of Gilead went to get Jeph-
thah from the land of Tob. [6]"Come," they said, "be our commander, so we can fight the Ammonites."

[a] *2* Traditionally *judged*; also in verse 3 [b] *4* Or *called the settlements of Jair* [c] *12* Hebrew; some Septuagint manuscripts *Midianites*

9:53 While the men used bows, arrows and spears, women helped to defend the tower by dropping heavy stones on those who came near it. The "upper millstone" was the upper, revolving stone of a mill; it was circular, with a hole in its center. Grinding grain was women's work (see Ex 11:5), usually considered too lowly for men to perform (see Jdg 16:21). Abimelech was killed by a woman using a domestic implement (see also 4:21).

10:6—12:7 Jephthah, a Transjordanian chieftain, delivered Gilead and Manasseh (northern Transjordan) from the oppression of the Ammonites, a pastoral people who pressured Manasseh from the south. Authorities differ as to what was involved in his vow (11:30–31; see "The Virgin" on p. 367). Although some have objected that this was completely out of keeping with Hebrew religious practice, it may be argued that this only emphasized the extent of the religious degradation of the Israelites during this turbulent period.

7Jephthah said to them, "Didn't you hate me and drive me from my father's house?[c] Why do you come
to me now, when you're in trouble?"
8The elders of Gilead said to him, "Nevertheless, we are turning to you now; come with us to fight the
Ammonites, and you will be our head[d] over all who live in Gilead."
9Jephthah answered, "Suppose you take me back to fight the Ammonites and the LORD gives them to
me—will I really be your head?"
10The elders of Gilead replied, "The LORD is our witness;[e] we will certainly do as you say." 11So Jeph-
thah went with the elders of Gilead, and the people made him head and commander over them. And he
repeated all his words before the LORD in Mizpah.[f]
12Then Jephthah sent messengers to the Ammonite king with the question: "What do you have against
us that you have attacked our country?"
13The king of the Ammonites answered Jephthah's messengers, "When Israel came up out of Egypt, they
took away my land from the Arnon to the Jabbok,[g] all the way to the Jordan. Now give it back peaceably."
14Jephthah sent back messengers to the Ammonite king, 15saying:

"This is what Jephthah says: Israel did not take the land of Moab[h] or the land of the Ammonites.[i]
16But when they came up out of Egypt, Israel went through the desert to the Red Sea[a][j] and on to
Kadesh.[k] 17Then Israel sent messengers[l] to the king of Edom, saying, 'Give us permission to go
through your country,'[m] but the king of Edom would not listen. They sent also to the king of Moab,
and he refused.[n] So Israel stayed at Kadesh.

18"Next they traveled through the desert, skirted the lands of Edom[o] and Moab, passed along
the eastern side[p] of the country of Moab, and camped on the other side of the Arnon.[q] They did
not enter the territory of Moab, for the Arnon was its border.

19"Then Israel sent messengers to Sihon king of the Amorites, who ruled in Heshbon, and said to
him, 'Let us pass through your country to our own place.'[r] 20Sihon, however, did not trust Israel[b] to
pass through his territory. He mustered all his men and encamped at Jahaz and fought with Israel.[s]

21"Then the LORD, the God of Israel, gave Sihon and all his men into Israel's hands, and they
defeated them. Israel took over all the land of the Amorites who lived in that country, 22capturing
all of it from the Arnon to the Jabbok and from the desert to the Jordan.[t]

23"Now since the LORD, the God of Israel, has driven the Amorites out before his people Israel,
what right have you to take it over? 24Will you not take what your god Chemosh[u] gives you? Like-
wise, whatever the LORD our God has given us, we will possess. 25Are you better than Balak son of
Zippor,[v] king of Moab? Did he ever quarrel with Israel or fight with them?[w] 26For three hundred
years Israel occupied[x] Heshbon, Aroer, the surrounding settlements and all the towns along the Ar-
non. Why didn't you retake them during that time? 27I have not wronged you, but you are doing me
wrong by waging war against me. Let the LORD, the Judge,[c][y] decide[z] the dispute this day between
the Israelites and the Ammonites."

28The king of Ammon, however, paid no attention to the message Jephthah sent him.
29Then the Spirit[a] of the LORD came upon Jephthah. He crossed Gilead and Manasseh, passed through
Mizpah of Gilead, and from there he advanced against the Ammonites. 30And Jephthah made a vow[b] to
the LORD: "If you give the Ammonites into my hands, 31whatever comes out of the door of my house to
meet me when I return in triumph from the Ammonites will be the LORD's, and I will sacrifice it as a
burnt offering."
32Then Jephthah went over to fight the Ammonites, and the LORD gave them into his hands. 33He dev-
astated twenty towns from Aroer to the vicinity of Minnith,[c] as far as Abel Keramim. Thus Israel sub-
dued Ammon.

11:7 [c]Ge 26:27
11:8 [d]Jdg 10:18
11:10 [e]Ge 31:50; Jer 42:5
11:11 [f]Jos 11:3; Jdg 10:17; 20:1; 1Sa 10:17
11:13 [g]Ge 32:22; Nu 21:24
11:15 [h]Dt 2:9 [i]Dt 2:19
11:16 [j]Nu 14:25; Dt 1:40 [k]Nu 20:1
11:17 [l]Nu 20:14 [m]Nu 20:18,21 [n]Jos 24:9
11:18 [o]Nu 21:4 [p]Dt 2:8 [q]Nu 21:13
11:19 [r]Nu 21:21-22; Dt 2:26-27
11:20 [s]Nu 21:23; Dt 2:32
11:22 [t]Dt 2:36
11:24 [u]Nu 21:29; Jos 3:10; 1Ki 11:7
11:25 [v]Nu 22:2 [w]Jos 24:9
11:26 [x]Nu 21:25
11:27 [y]Ge 18:25 [z]Ge 16:5; 31:53; 1Sa 24:12,15
11:29 [a]Nu 11:25; Jdg 3:10; 6:34; 14:6,19; 15:14; 1Sa 11:6; 16:13; Isa 11:2
11:30 [b]Ge 28:20
11:33 [c]Eze 27:17

[a] *16* Hebrew *Yam Suph*; that is, Sea of Reeds [b] *20* Or *however, would not make an agreement for Israel* [c] *27* Or *Ruler*

11:14–27 Jephthah's response conformed to international policies of the time. His letter is a classic example of international correspondence of the period and reflects the common belief that the gods of a people established and protected their political boundaries and decided all boundary disputes.

11:24 Jephthah referred to Chemosh as god of the Ammonites either by mistake or because Ammon worshiped Chemosh, the God of Moab, in addition to Molech.

11:29–40 Leviticus 27:1–8 contemplates the possibility of someone's vowing to give himself or some other person of his household to the Lord and makes provision for the redemption of such an individual by the payment of money. We know, too, from the experience of Samuel that sometimes persons coming under a vow were handed over for the service of the sanctuary (1Sa 1:11). It is, therefore, thought by some that Jephthah redeemed his daughter with money and gave her up to the service of the Lord as a perpetual virgin. See "The Virgin" on page 367.

11:34 [d]Ex 15:20; Jer 31:4
11:35 [e]Nu 30:2; Ecc 5:2,4,5

[34]When Jephthah returned to his home in Mizpah, who should come out to meet him but his daugh-
ter, dancing to the sound of tambourines![d] She was an only child. Except for her he had neither son nor
daughter. [35]When he saw her, he tore his clothes and cried, "Oh! My daughter! You have made me miser-
able and wretched, because I have made a vow to the LORD that I cannot break.[e]"

11:34 See the note on religious dancing at Psalm 149:3.
11:35 In the Old Testament vows were never regarded as a religious duty (Dt 23:22), but once they were made they were considered sacred and binding (Dt 23:21–23; Jdg 11:35). Almost anything—people, possessions, oneself—except what was already the Lord's or was an abomination to the Lord (Dt 23:18) could be vowed; and all these things could be redeemed with money, their value to be determined by a priest. Houses, lands and unclean animals that were redeemed had to have a fifth of their value added to make up the redemption money.

The Virgin

JUDGES 11 The request of Jephthah's daughter to be allowed to go out into the hills and weep over her virginity (Jdg 11:37) strikes modern readers as almost incomprehensible. Why would a girl who was about to be put to death as a sacrifice focus attention on her virginity?[1] In order to begin to understand this, it is necessary to recognize the enormous importance attached to virginity in ancient cultures, especially in Israel. A few examples will make the point:

✣ In Aeschylus's play *Suppliant Maidens*, a father appeals to his daughters to maintain their virtue in the face of the lustful desires of men. He charges them, "Honor your chastity more than your life" (line 1013).

✣ Euripides' play *Alcestis* tells the story of a woman who gives up her life to save that of her husband. Awaiting her death, she weeps over the fate that has befallen her. In her lamentation, she looks upon her bed and declares, "O bed, where I lost my virginal maidenhood by this man for whom I die. Farewell!" (lines 177–179). Like Jephthah's daughter she thinks of her virginity as she faces death.

✣ Josephus, in *Antiquities*, 1.246, recounted the story of Rebekah from Genesis 24 and had her say, "They call me Rebekah. My father was Bethuel, but he is dead, and Laban is my brother and, together with my mother, he takes care of all our family affairs and is the guardian of my virginity." The Genesis account does not explicitly cast Laban in this role, but the idea is one that both Jewish and Gentile readers of the time would readily have comprehended.

✣ The story of the rape of Absalom's sister Tamar by Amnon (2Sa 13) illustrates both how strongly young women felt about their celibacy and its significance for their reputation. In the story Amnon deceived his half-sister Tamar and raped her by force, then despised her and sent her away. Prior to this Tamar had worn a special garment that signified her virgin status, but after the rape she tore it in her grief. Even so, she would have been willing to marry Amnon, one of the vilest characters in the Old Testament, rather than live with the disgrace of being an unmarried woman who had lost her virginity.

✣ Deuteronomy 22:13–21 describes a man who marries a woman but then begins to loathe her and to tell people that she has not come to the marriage as a virgin. It falls upon the woman's family to produce evidence of her virginity (Dt 22:17). This confirmation evidently consisted of bedclothes stained with her blood on the wedding night, at which time she had purportedly lost her virginity. The elders of the town were to punish the man for slandering her (Dt 22:19). But had the woman actually engaged in intercourse before marriage she would have been stoned to death (Dt 22:21).

✣ The Hebrew Bible regularly refers to cities or countries by the term "virgin" (e.g., Isa 47:1; Jer 31:4). This is because a virgin in ancient Israel was to be protected from outsiders. In the same way cities and countries were to be protected from invaders and kept inviolable.

Given this cultural background, it is clear that Jephthah's daughter, like most Israelite girls, would have regarded the preservation of her virginity until marriage as central to her identity. This young woman would never obtain the goal of coming to marriage as a chaste bride.

[1]For the issue of human sacrifice, see "Human Sacrifice in the Ancient Near East" on page 182.

36 "My father," she replied, "you have given your word to the LORD. Do to me just as you promised,[f] now 11:36 [f]Lk 1:38
that the LORD has avenged you of your enemies,[g] the Ammonites. 37 But grant me this one request," she [g]2Sa 18:19
said. "Give me two months to roam the hills and weep with my friends, because I will never marry."
38 "You may go," he said. And he let her go for two months. She and the girls went into the hills and wept
because she would never marry. 39 After the two months, she returned to her father and he did to her as
he had vowed. And she was a virgin.
From this comes the Israelite custom 40 that each year the young women of Israel go out for four days
to commemorate the daughter of Jephthah the Gileadite.

Jephthah and Ephraim

12 The men of Ephraim called out their forces, crossed over to Zaphon and said to Jephthah, "Why
did you go to fight the Ammonites without calling us to go with you?[h] We're going to burn down 12:1 [h]Jdg 8:1
your house over your head."
2 Jephthah answered, "I and my people were engaged in a great struggle with the Ammonites, and al-
though I called, you didn't save me out of their hands. 3 When I saw that you wouldn't help, I took my life
in my hands[i] and crossed over to fight the Ammonites, and the LORD gave me the victory over them. Now 12:3 [i]1Sa 19:5;
why have you come up today to fight me?" 28:21; Job 13:14
4 Jephthah then called together the men of Gilead and fought against Ephraim. The Gileadites struck
them down because the Ephraimites had said, "You Gileadites are renegades from Ephraim and Manas-
seh." 5 The Gileadites captured the fords of the Jordan[j] leading to Ephraim, and whenever a survivor of 12:5 [j]Jos 22:11;
Ephraim said, "Let me cross over," the men of Gilead asked him, "Are you an Ephraimite?" If he replied, Jdg 3:28
"No," 6 they said, "All right, say 'Shibboleth.' " If he said, "Sibboleth," because he could not pronounce the
word correctly, they seized him and killed him at the fords of the Jordan. Forty-two thousand Ephraim-
ites were killed at that time.
7 Jephthah led[a] Israel six years. Then Jephthah the Gileadite died, and was buried in a town in Gilead.

Ibzan, Elon and Abdon

8 After him, Ibzan of Bethlehem led Israel. 9 He had thirty sons and thirty daughters. He gave his daugh-
ters away in marriage to those outside his clan, and for his sons he brought in thirty young women as wives
from outside his clan. Ibzan led Israel seven years. 10 Then Ibzan died, and was buried in Bethlehem.
11 After him, Elon the Zebulunite led Israel ten years. 12 Then Elon died, and was buried in Aijalon in
the land of Zebulun.
13 After him, Abdon son of Hillel, from Pirathon, led Israel. 14 He had forty sons and thirty grandsons,[k] 12:14 [k]Jdg 10:4
who rode on seventy donkeys.[l] He led Israel eight years. 15 Then Abdon son of Hillel died, and was bur- [l]Jdg 5:10
ied at Pirathon in Ephraim, in the hill country of the Amalekites.[m] 12:15 [m]Jdg 5:14

The Birth of Samson

13 Again the Israelites did evil in the eyes of the LORD, so the LORD delivered them into the hands of
the Philistines[n] for forty years. 13:1 [n]Jdg 2:11; 1Sa 12:9
2 A certain man of Zorah,[o] named Manoah, from the clan of the Danites, had a wife who was sterile 13:2 [o]Jos 15:33; 19:41
and remained childless. 3 The angel of the LORD[p] appeared to her[q] and said, "You are sterile and childless, 13:3 [p]ver 6,8; Jdg 6:12 [q]ver 10

[a] 7 Traditionally *judged;* also in verses 8-14

12:5–6 The Hebrew *shĭb'bō-lĕth,* "an ear of grain" or "a stream," was pronounced differently on the two sides of the Jordan and so was used by the men of Gilead under Jephthah as a test to determine whether or not the speaker was from Ephraim. This word is still used proverbially today in an expression like "That was his Shibboleth."

13:1—16:31 The last of the great judges was Samson, with whom the scene shifts to a different part of Palestine, the Philistine plain. It is likely that Samson lived late in the judges period, at the time when a large invasion of the Palestinian seacoast was occurring. The invaders, sea peoples from the Aegean area, had been repulsed by Rameses III in their attempts to enter Egypt and had subsequently settled in what became known as the Philistine plain (see "The Archaeology of Philistia" on p. 370). Samson lived in the Shephelah area that bordered that plain. Although dedicated to a life of Nazirite obedience from his birth, his life was a tragedy of one whose great potential was negated by a lack of self-discipline.

On account of his great strength Samson became the Hebrews' champion against the Philistines, just as the Philistine Goliath would later become the Philistines' champion against Israel. Samson's failure to discipline his sensuous nature led him into three liaisons with Philistine women. Doubtless each was an instrument of the Philistine lords in their efforts to subdue their nemesis.

We do not read that Samson ever led an army against the Philistines. Rather, he made single-handed exploits into Philistine territory (e.g., 14:19; 15:4–5,8,15; 16:3). Killing in his death more Philistines than he had during his life (16:30), he became at the last a tragic figure (see "Samson and the Temple of Dagon" on p. 375).

It is notable that Eli (1Sa 1–4) and Samuel (1Sa 2:12) were also called judges. Although they did do some of the work of the judges described in this book, it would seem better to regard them as priest and prophet, respectively—transitional figures preparing the way for the monarchy.

THE RELIABILITY OF JUDGES

JUDGES 12 The book of Judges is often regarded as an amalgamation of history, legend and simple fiction. The findings of archaeology, however, have demonstrated that we have good reason to maintain the accuracy of the accounts preserved in this book. Drawing together the essential data, we can summarize evidence that supports reading Judges as a trustworthy account:

◆ Immediately after the conquest the Israelite tribes were engaged in securing their assigned allotments. It was a time of conflict and turmoil. A group of about 100 letters written by Canaanite kings to the king of Egypt indicates that there was much hostility in **Canaan** approximately 50 years after the conquest. A people called Habiru (a term from which the name Hebrew may have been derived) were attacking the cities and taking over the land.[1]

◆ Early in the period of the judges Eglon, king of **Moab**, built a palace at Jericho, where he collected tribute from the tribes (3:15–30). A palace from the time of Eglon matching the Biblical description has been excavated at Jericho.[2]

◆ Judges 4–5 documents the demise of **Hazor** (see "Map 3"), the most powerful city-state in Canaan, at the hands of a coalition of Israelite tribes. Excavations there reveal destruction at this time (second half of the thirteenth century B.C.) so severe that the city never recovered. Evidence points to the Israelites as the most likely agents.[3] This victory made Israel the strongest force in the region.

◆ An inscription of Pharaoh Merneptah, who ruled from approximately 1210–1202 B.C., states that he annihilated the Israelites. Although the boast was far from the truth, the inscription demonstrates that Israel was an important group in Canaan at that time.[4]

◆ Early in the twelfth century B.C. the tribe of Dan migrated from its original allotment west of Benjamin to the city of Laish in northern Galilee (ch. 18). The Philistines, who had taken over the southern coastal area, had most likely forced them out. At the site of Laish, renamed Dan (you can locate the city of Dan near the top of "Map 2" in the back of this Bible), excavations uncovered a burn layer dating to the early twelfth century B.C. (v. 27) and subsequent occupation by newcomers who used a new type of pottery known to be of Israelite origin.[5]

◆ In the mid twelfth century B.C. Gideon's son Abimelech attempted to become king of Israel (ch. 9). The ill-fated affair took place at **Shechem** ("Map 3"), where abundant evidence has been found to corroborate the Biblical account, including the destruction of the city as recorded in Judges 9:45.[6]

The stories of Judges are not legends or myths but gritty and often tragic accounts of the follies of God's people. Archaeological evidence strongly supports taking the stories at face value.

Outer gate at high place at Dan
Photograph: © Todd Bolen/BiblePlaces.com

[1]See "The Amarna Tablets and the Habiru" on page 347. [2]See "Eglon's Palace" on page 348. [3]See "Deborah and Barak and the Destruction of Hazor" on page 350. [4]See "The Merneptah Stele" on page 360. [5]See "The Migration of the Danites" on page 378. [6]See "Abimelech at Shechem" on page 363.

but you are going to conceive and have a son.[r] 4Now see to it that you drink no wine or other fermented
drink and that you do not eat anything unclean,[s] 5because you will conceive and give birth to a son. No
razor[t] may be used on his head, because the boy is to be a Nazirite,[u] set apart to God from birth, and he
will begin[v] the deliverance of Israel from the hands of the Philistines."
6Then the woman went to her husband and told him, "A man of God[w] came to me. He looked like an
angel of God,[x] very awesome. I didn't ask him where he came from, and he didn't tell me his name. 7But
he said to me, 'You will conceive and give birth to a son. Now then, drink no wine or other fermented
drink and do not eat anything unclean, because the boy will be a Nazirite of God from birth until the
day of his death.' "

13:3 [r]Lk 1:13
13:4 [s]ver 14; Nu 6:2-4; Lk 1:15
13:5 [t]Nu 6:5; 1Sa 1:11 [u]Nu 6:2, 13 [v]1Sa 7:13
13:6 [w]ver 8; 1Sa 2:27; 9:6 [x]ver 17-18; Mt 28:3

The Archaeology of Philistia

The temple at Medinet Habu, where the victory of Rameses III over the Sea Peoples is commemorated

Photograph: © Todd Bolen/Bible Places.com

Philistine anthropoid coffin

Preserving Bible Times; © Dr. James C. Martin; permission of The British Museum

JUDGES 13 Egyptian texts suggest that the Philistines were part of a large-scale emigration of various tribes from the Aegean, referred to as **Sea Peoples**, who attempted to enter Egypt. As they made their way by land and sea down the Mediterranean coast, they left a swath of destruction behind them. The tribes arrived at the border of Egypt around 1177 B.C. but were repulsed by Rameses III. They retreated to **Canaan**[1] and settled in previously conquered areas. The Philistines seized one of the choicest parts, the southeastern coast, which became known as Philistia.

The Philistines had five major centers: Gaza, Ashkelon, Ashdod, Ekron and Gath (1Sa 6:17; "Map 4"). Excavations at these sites have revealed a common pattern of Philistine settlement—the previous city was violently destroyed and a larger, well-planned, fortified city built in its place. The Philistines brought with them their native Aegean culture in the form of architecture, pottery, cultic items, metallurgy (1Sa 13:19–22),[2] burial customs and language.

Soon the Philistines expanded eastward and dominated the Israelites (Jdg 13:1). The tribe of Dan was directly impacted, since its allotment was in the northern sector of Philistia.[3] Samson was the first Israelite military leader to counteract the Philistine oppression, probably in the later part of the twelfth century B.C. (v. 5).[4]

[1]See "Canaan" on page 324. [2]See "Technological Supremacy of the Philistines' Iron Weapons" on page 414. [3]See "The Migration of the Danites" on page 378. [4]See "Samson and the Temple of Dagon" on page 375.

8 Then Manoah prayed to the LORD: "O Lord, I beg you, let the man of God you sent to us come again
to teach us how to bring up the boy who is to be born."

9 God heard Manoah, and the angel of God came again to the woman while she was out in the field;
but her husband Manoah was not with her. 10 The woman hurried to tell her husband, "He's here! The
man who appeared to me the other day!"

11 Manoah got up and followed his wife. When he came to the man, he said, "Are you the one who
talked to my wife?"

"I am," he said.

12 So Manoah asked him, "When your words are fulfilled, what is to be the rule for the boy's life and
work?"

13 The angel of the LORD answered, "Your wife must do all that I have told her. 14 She must not eat any-
thing that comes from the grapevine, nor drink any wine or other fermented drink[y] nor eat anything
unclean.[z] She must do everything I have commanded her."

15 Manoah said to the angel of the LORD, "We would like you to stay until we prepare a young goat[a] for
you."

16 The angel of the LORD replied, "Even though you detain me, I will not eat any of your food. But if you
prepare a burnt offering,[b] offer it to the LORD." (Manoah did not realize that it was the angel of the LORD.)

17 Then Manoah inquired of the angel of the LORD, "What is your name,[c] so that we may honor you
when your word comes true?"

18 He replied, "Why do you ask my name?[d] It is beyond understanding.[a]" 19 Then Manoah took a young
goat, together with the grain offering, and sacrificed it on a rock[e] to the LORD. And the LORD did an amaz-
ing thing while Manoah and his wife watched: 20 As the flame[f] blazed up from the altar toward heaven,
the angel of the LORD ascended in the flame. Seeing this, Manoah and his wife fell with their faces to the
ground.[g] 21 When the angel of the LORD did not show himself again to Manoah and his wife, Manoah re-
alized[h] that it was the angel of the LORD.

22 "We are doomed[i] to die!" he said to his wife. "We have seen[j] God!"

23 But his wife answered, "If the LORD had meant to kill us, he would not have accepted a burnt offer-
ing and grain offering from our hands, nor shown us all these things or now told us this."[k]

24 The woman gave birth to a boy and named him Samson.[l] He grew[m] and the LORD blessed him,[n] 25 and
the Spirit of the LORD began to stir[o] him while he was in Mahaneh Dan,[p] between Zorah and Eshtaol.

Samson's Marriage

14 Samson went down to Timnah[q] and saw there a young Philistine woman. 2 When he returned,
he said to his father and mother, "I have seen a Philistine woman in Timnah; now get her for me
as my wife."[r]

3 His father and mother replied, "Isn't there an acceptable woman among your relatives or among all
our people?[s] Must you go to the uncircumcised[t] Philistines to get a wife?[u]"

But Samson said to his father, "Get her for me. She's the right one for me." 4 (His parents did not know
that this was from the LORD, who was seeking an occasion to confront the Philistines;[v] for at that time
they were ruling over Israel.)[w] 5 Samson went down to Timnah together with his father and mother. As
they approached the vineyards of Timnah, suddenly a young lion came roaring toward him. 6 The Spirit
of the LORD came upon him in power[x] so that he tore the lion apart with his bare hands as he might have
torn a young goat. But he told neither his father nor his mother what he had done. 7 Then he went down
and talked with the woman, and he liked her.

8 Some time later, when he went back to marry her, he turned aside to look at the lion's carcass. In it
was a swarm of bees and some honey, 9 which he scooped out with his hands and ate as he went along.
When he rejoined his parents, he gave them some, and they too ate it. But he did not tell them that he had
taken the honey from the lion's carcass.

13:14 [y]Nu 6:4 [z]ver 4
13:15 [a]ver 3; Jdg 6:19
13:16 [b]Jdg 6:20
13:17 [c]Ge 32:29
13:18 [d]Isa 9:6
13:19 [e]Jdg 6:20
13:20 [f]Lev 9:24 [g]1Ch 21:16; Eze 1:28; Mt 17:6
13:21 [h]ver 16; Jdg 6:22
13:22 [i]Dt 5:26 [j]Ge 32:30; Jdg 6:22
13:23 [k]Ps 25:14
13:24 [l]Heb 11:32 [m]1Sa 3:19 [n]Lk 1:80
13:25 [o]Jdg 3:10 [p]Jdg 18:12
14:1 [q]Ge 38:12
14:2 [r]Ge 21:21; 34:4
14:3 [s]Ge 24:4 [t]Dt 7:3 [u]Ex 34:16
14:4 [v]Jos 11:20 [w]Jdg 13:1
14:6 [x]Jdg 3:10; 13:25

[a] *18* Or *is wonderful*

13:15 A young goat would have been considered a special delicacy. Hospitality of this kind was common in the ancient Near East (see Ge 18:1–8; Jdg 6:18–19).

14:1 Timnah has been identified as Tel Batash in the Sorek Valley, west of Beth Shemesh (see "Timnah" on p. 372). Archaeologists have uncovered the Philistine layer of the town.

14:3 While some of Israel's neighbors practiced varying forms of circumcision (see "Circumcision in the Ancient World" on p. 1840), Philistine males were not circumcised. The term *uncircumcised* was often used by Israelites as an expression of scorn.

14:5 It was customary in ancient Israel for parents to arrange their children's marriages (Ge 24:47–53; 38:6; 1Sa 18:17).

14:9 To eat honey taken from the carcass of a lion was a heinous violation of kosher laws. See Leviticus 11.

10 Now his father went down to see the woman. And Samson made a feast there, as was customary for
bridegrooms. 11 When he appeared, he was given thirty companions.
12 "Let me tell you a riddle,[y]" Samson said to them. "If you can give me the answer within the seven **14:12** [y]1Ki 10:1; Eze 17:2 [z]Ge 29:27 [a]Ge 45:22; 2Ki 5:5
days of the feast,[z] I will give you thirty linen garments and thirty sets of clothes.[a] 13 If you can't tell me
the answer, you must give me thirty linen garments and thirty sets of clothes."
"Tell us your riddle," they said. "Let's hear it."
14 He replied,

> "Out of the eater, something to eat;
> out of the strong, something sweet."

For three days they could not give the answer.
15 On the fourth[a] day, they said to Samson's wife, "Coax[b] your husband into explaining the riddle for **14:15** [b]Jdg 16:5; Ecc 7:26 [c]Jdg 15:6
us, or we will burn you and your father's household to death.[c] Did you invite us here to rob us?"
16 Then Samson's wife threw herself on him, sobbing, "You hate me! You don't really love me.[d] You've **14:16** [d]Jdg 16:15
given my people a riddle, but you haven't told me the answer."
"I haven't even explained it to my father or mother," he replied, "so why should I explain it to you?"
17 She cried the whole seven days[e] of the feast. So on the seventh day he finally told her, because she con- **14:17** [e]Est 1:5
tinued to press him. She in turn explained the riddle to her people.

a *15* Some Septuagint manuscripts and Syriac; Hebrew *seventh*

14:10 Prolonged wedding feasts were common in the ancient Near East (see Ge 29:22,27; see also "Weddings in Ancient Israel" on p. 1039), and this one lasted for seven days (v. 12; see Ge 29:27). Since it no doubt included drinking wine, Samson may have violated his Nazirite vow during the course of the festivities (see 13:4,7).

14:12–14 The use of riddles at feasts and special occasions was popular in the ancient world. This form of language has long been used. The queen of Sheba propounded to Solomon "hard questions," very likely riddles (1Ki 10:1; 2Ch 9:1). A classic example of the riddle is the one used here by Samson to entrap his enemies, as is his noted retort to the Philistines (Jdg 14:18). Solomon later became famous as an author of proverbs and riddles (1Ki 4:32), and Ezekiel was instructed to speak a riddle to Israel (Eze 17:2). To know dark sayings was considered a mark of wisdom (Pr 1:6).

14:17 Traditionally, feasting for a marriage lasted for seven days (vv. 12,17), although this period was sometimes doubled in length and was marked by music and entertainment of various kinds, including special poems and songs proclaiming the praises and extolling the charms of the bride and bridegroom. If some Bedouin practices are any guide as to the nature of ancient Hebrew marriage proceedings, the songs and poems would have been of a decidedly erotic character. The bride would observe the activities and might sometimes participate in the dancing with her female attendants. Then, at an approved point in the ceremonies, she would be escorted to the specially prepared bridal chamber, to the cheers, laughter and enthusiasm of the assembled guests.

ARCHAEOLOGICAL SITES

TIMNAH

JUDGES 14 Joshua 15:10–11 informs us that Timnah was situated between Beth Shemesh (Tell er-Rumeilah; "Map 4") and Ekron (Tel Miqne; also see "Map 4"). The only site of significance between these two places is Tel Batash. Philistine pottery uncovered in excavations there further confirms the identification of Tel Batash as the Biblical Timnah.[1] Tel Batash is located in the coastal plain, in the western part of the fertile Sorek Valley, 16 miles (26 km) from the Mediterranean coast and 20 miles (32 km) west of Jerusalem.

Timnah was on the eastern border of Philistine territory, with the two larger cities of the Philistine confederation, Ekron and Ashkelon, 3.5 miles (5.6 km) to the west and 30 miles (48 km) to the southwest, respectively (Jdg. 14:19; "Map 4"). Samson himself lived in Mahaneh-dan, the "camp of Dan," at the edge of the Israelite hill country 6 miles (9.6 km) east of Timnah. The Bible's statement that Samson "went down to Timnah" (v. 1) is literal; there is an 800 foot (244 m) drop in elevation between the area of Samson's home and the base of Tel Batash.

Excavations were carried out at Tel Batash between 1977 and 1989. The town of Samson's day was a fortified urban center about five acres in size, well planned and densely populated.[2] The buildings were constructed of mud brick walls on stone foundations. A storage jar with a letter incised on the handle shows that there was knowledge of writing in the town. A clay **bulla** (lump of clay with impressions on it) was found, indicating that some of the writing was done on papyrus.[3]

[1]See "The Potsherd: Pottery in the Bible" on page 738.

[2]See "The Archaeology of Philistia" on page 370.

[3]See "Writing Materials in the Ancient World" on page 2037.

18 Before sunset on the seventh day the men of the town said to him,

> "What is sweeter than honey?
> What is stronger than a lion?"[f]

Samson said to them,

> "If you had not plowed with my heifer,
> you would not have solved my riddle."

19 Then the Spirit of the LORD came upon him in power.[g] He went down to Ashkelon, struck down thirty of their men, stripped them of their belongings and gave their clothes to those who had explained the riddle. Burning with anger,[h] he went up to his father's house. 20 And Samson's wife was given to the friend[i] who had attended him at his wedding.

Samson's Vengeance on the Philistines

15 Later on, at the time of wheat harvest, Samson took a young goat[j] and went to visit his wife. He said, "I'm going to my wife's room." But her father would not let him go in.

2 "I was so sure you thoroughly hated her," he said, "that I gave her to your friend.[k] Isn't her younger sister more attractive? Take her instead."

3 Samson said to them, "This time I have a right to get even with the Philistines; I will really harm them." 4 So he went out and caught three hundred foxes and tied them tail to tail in pairs. He then fastened a torch to every pair of tails, 5 lit the torches and let the foxes loose in the standing grain of the Philistines. He burned up the shocks and standing grain, together with the vineyards and olive groves.

6 When the Philistines asked, "Who did this?" they were told, "Samson, the Timnite's son-in-law, because his wife was given to his friend."

So the Philistines went up and burned her and her father to death.[l] 7 Samson said to them, "Since you've acted like this, I won't stop until I get my revenge on you." 8 He attacked them viciously and slaughtered many of them. Then he went down and stayed in a cave in the rock of Etam.

9 The Philistines went up and camped in Judah, spreading out near Lehi.[m] 10 The men of Judah asked, "Why have you come to fight us?"

"We have come to take Samson prisoner," they answered, "to do to him as he did to us."

11 Then three thousand men from Judah went down to the cave in the rock of Etam and said to Samson, "Don't you realize that the Philistines are rulers over us?[n] What have you done to us?"

He answered, "I merely did to them what they did to me."

12 They said to him, "We've come to tie you up and hand you over to the Philistines."

Samson said, "Swear to me that you won't kill me yourselves."

13 "Agreed," they answered. "We will only tie you up and hand you over to them. We will not kill you." So they bound him with two new ropes and led him up from the rock. 14 As he approached Lehi, the Philistines came toward him shouting. The Spirit of the LORD came upon him in power.[o] The ropes on his arms became like charred flax, and the bindings dropped from his hands. 15 Finding a fresh jawbone of a donkey, he grabbed it and struck down a thousand men.[p]

16 Then Samson said,

> "With a donkey's jawbone
> I have made donkeys of them.[a]
> With a donkey's jawbone
> I have killed a thousand men."

17 When he finished speaking, he threw away the jawbone; and the place was called Ramath Lehi.[b]

18 Because he was very thirsty, he cried out to the LORD,[q] "You have given your servant this great victory. Must I now die of thirst and fall into the hands of the uncircumcised?" 19 Then God opened up the

14:18 [f] ver 14
14:19 [g] Nu 11:25; Jdg 3:10; 6:34; 11:29; 13:25; 15:14; 1Sa 11:6; 16:13; 1Ki 18:46; 2Ch 24:20; Isa 11:2 [h] 1Sa 11:6
14:20 [i] Jdg 15:2, 6; Jn 3:29
15:1 [j] Ge 38:17
15:2 [k] Jdg 14:20
15:6 [l] Jdg 14:15
15:9 [m] ver 14, 17, 19
15:11 [n] Jdg 13:1; 14:4; Ps 106:40-42
5:14 [o] Jdg 3:10; 14:19; 1Sa 11:6
15:15 [p] Lev 26:8; Jos 23:10; Jdg 3:31
15:18 [q] Jdg 16:28

[a] 16 Or *made a heap or two*; the Hebrew for *donkey* sounds like the Hebrew for *heap.* [b] 17 *Ramath Lehi* means *jawbone hill.*

15:4 The Hebrew word here translated "foxes" may refer to either foxes or jackals, both of which are still found in modern Israel.

15:7 Revenge was a common feature of life in the ancient Near East. Six cities of refuge were designated by the Lord to prevent endless killings (Jos 20:1–9). See "Cities of Refuge" on page 334.

hollow place in Lehi, and water came out of it. When Samson drank, his strength returned and he revived.[r] So the spring was called En Hakkore,[a] and it is still there in Lehi.

20 Samson led[b] Israel for twenty years[s] in the days of the Philistines.

Samson and Delilah

16 One day Samson went to Gaza, where he saw a prostitute. He went in to spend the night with her. 2 The people of Gaza were told, "Samson is here!" So they surrounded the place and lay in wait for him all night at the city gate.[t] They made no move during the night, saying, "At dawn we'll kill him."

3 But Samson lay there only until the middle of the night. Then he got up and took hold of the doors of the city gate, together with the two posts, and tore them loose, bar and all. He lifted them to his shoulders and carried them to the top of the hill that faces Hebron.[u]

4 Some time later, he fell in love[v] with a woman in the Valley of Sorek whose name was Delilah. 5 The rulers of the Philistines[w] went to her and said, "See if you can lure[x] him into showing you the secret of his great strength and how we can overpower him so we may tie him up and subdue him. Each one of us will give you eleven hundred shekels[c] of silver."[y]

6 So Delilah said to Samson, "Tell me the secret of your great strength and how you can be tied up and subdued."

7 Samson answered her, "If anyone ties me with seven fresh thongs[d] that have not been dried, I'll become as weak as any other man."

8 Then the rulers of the Philistines brought her seven fresh thongs that had not been dried, and she tied him with them. 9 With men hidden in the room,[z] she called to him, "Samson, the Philistines are upon you!" But he snapped the thongs as easily as a piece of string snaps when it comes close to a flame. So the secret of his strength was not discovered.

10 Then Delilah said to Samson, "You have made a fool of me;[a] you lied to me. Come now, tell me how you can be tied."

11 He said, "If anyone ties me securely with new ropes[b] that have never been used, I'll become as weak as any other man."

12 So Delilah took new ropes and tied him with them. Then, with men hidden in the room, she called to him, "Samson, the Philistines are upon you!" But he snapped the ropes off his arms as if they were threads.

13 Delilah then said to Samson, "Until now, you have been making a fool of me and lying to me. Tell me how you can be tied."

He replied, "If you weave the seven braids of my head into the fabric ⌞on the loom⌟ and tighten it with the pin, I'll become as weak as any other man." So while he was sleeping, Delilah took the seven braids of his head, wove them into the fabric 14 and[e] tightened it with the pin.

Again she called to him, "Samson, the Philistines are upon you!"[c] He awoke from his sleep and pulled up the pin and the loom, with the fabric.

15 Then she said to him, "How can you say, 'I love you,'[d] when you won't confide in me? This is the third time[e] you have made a fool of me and haven't told me the secret of your great strength."[f] 16 With such nagging she prodded him day after day until he was tired to death.

17 So he told her everything.[g] "No razor has ever been used on my head," he said, "because I have been a Nazirite[h] set apart to God since birth. If my head were shaved, my strength would leave me, and I would become as weak as any other man."

18 When Delilah saw that he had told her everything, she sent word to the rulers of the Philistines[i], "Come back once more; he has told me everything." So the rulers of the Philistines returned with the silver in their hands. 19 Having put him to sleep on her lap, she called a man to shave off the seven braids of his hair, and so began to subdue him.[f] And his strength left him.[j]

20 Then she called, "Samson, the Philistines are upon you!"

15:19 [r] Ge 45:27; Isa 40:29
15:20 [s] Jdg 13:1; 16:31; Heb 11:32
16:2 [t] 1Sa 23:26; Ps 118:10-12; Ac 9:24
16:3 [u] Jos 10:36
16:4 [v] Ge 24:67
16:5 [w] Jos 13:3 [x] Ex 10:7; Jdg 14:15 [y] ver 18
16:9 [z] ver 12
16:10 [a] ver 13
16:11 [b] Jdg 15:13
16:14 [c] ver 9,20
16:15 [d] Jdg 14:16 [e] Nu 24:10 [f] ver 5
16:17 [g] Mic 7:5 [h] Nu 6:2,5; Jdg 13:5
16:18 [i] Jos 13:3; 1Sa 5:8
16:19 [j] Pr 7:26-27

[a] *19 En Hakkore* means *caller's spring.* [b] *20* Traditionally *judged* [c] *5* That is, about 28 pounds (about 13 kilograms)
[d] *7* Or *bowstrings*; also in verses 8 and 9 [e] *13,14* Some Septuagint manuscripts; Hebrew *"⌞I can⌟ if you weave the seven braids of my head into the fabric ⌞on the loom⌟." 14So she* [f] *19* Hebrew; some Septuagint manuscripts *and he began to weaken*

16:17–20 For a discussion of literal and figurative references to hair in the Bible, see the note on Psalm 40:12. See also "Beards and Hairstyles in the Biblical World" on page 1084.

He awoke from his sleep and thought, "I'll go out as before and shake myself free." But he did not know
16:20 [k]Nu 14:42; Jos 7:12; 1Sa 16:14; 18:12; 28:15
that the LORD had left him.[k]
16:21 [l]Jer 47:1 [m]Nu 16:14 [n]Job 31:10; Isa 47:2
21 Then the Philistines[l] seized him, gouged out his eyes[m] and took him down to Gaza. Binding him
with bronze shackles, they set him to grinding[n] in the prison. 22 But the hair on his head began to grow
again after it had been shaved.

The Death of Samson

16:23 [o]1Sa 5:2; 1Ch 10:10
23 Now the rulers of the Philistines assembled to offer a great sacrifice to Dagon[o] their god and to celebrate, saying, "Our god has delivered Samson, our enemy, into our hands."
16:24 [p]Da 5:4 [q]1Sa 31:9; 1Ch 10:9
24 When the people saw him, they praised their god,[p] saying,

> "Our god has delivered our enemy
> into our hands,[q]
> the one who laid waste our land
> and multiplied our slain."

16:25 [r]Jdg 9:27; Ru 3:7; Est 1:10
25 While they were in high spirits,[r] they shouted, "Bring out Samson to entertain us." So they called
Samson out of the prison, and he performed for them.
When they stood him among the pillars, 26 Samson said to the servant who held his hand, "Put me
where I can feel the pillars that support the temple, so that I may lean against them." 27 Now the temple
16:27 [s]Dt 22:8; Jos 2:8
was crowded with men and women; all the rulers of the Philistines were there, and on the roof[s] were about
16:28 [t]Jdg 15:18 [u]Jer 15:15
three thousand men and women watching Samson perform. 28 Then Samson prayed to the LORD,[t] "O Sovereign LORD, remember me. O God, please strengthen me just once more, and let me with one blow get revenge[u] on the Philistines for my two eyes." 29 Then Samson reached toward the two central pillars on which
the temple stood. Bracing himself against them, his right hand on the one and his left hand on the other,

---

16:21 Physical mutilation of prisoners of war was common in the ancient Near East (see 1Sa 11:2; 2Ki 25:7; see also the note on Jdg 1:6). The Philistines gave Samson the task of grinding grain in the prison at Gaza (see "Samson and the Temple of Dagon" on p. 375).

16:23 In the ancient Near East it was common to attribute a victory to a country's national deities.

16:27 The temple complex probably surrounded an open court and had a flat roof on which a large number of people had gathered, possibly to catch a glimpse of Samson.

Samson and the Temple of Dagon

JUDGES 16 Only limited excavation has been undertaken at Gaza ("Map 4"), so we have little idea of what the city of Samson's day was like.[1] However, grinding houses (Jdg 16:21) and a temple (vv. 23–30) similar to those referred to in Judges 16 have been unearthed at other sites. Grinding houses, known both from ancient texts and excavated examples, were places where prisoners would grind grain for their masters. The tools were simple, hand grinding stones—a loaf-shaped upper stone and a larger, slightly concave, lower stone called a saddle quern. Samson spent his days kneeling in front of a quern, pushing an upper stone back and forth, grinding grain into meal.

Samson's greatest feat was the destruction of the temple of **Dagon**.[2] The only definite Philistine temples found to date are those at Tell Qasile, on the outskirts of modern Tel Aviv. Three temples, each larger than the previous, were built on the same spot over a period of 150 years. The latest, from the eleventh century B.C., approximately the time of Samson, measured 26 feet (7.8 m) by 48 feet (14.6 m). Two pillars supported the roof, just as in the temple of Dagon described in Judges 16. They were made of cedar wood approximately 1 foot (30.5 cm) in diameter and rested on stone bases set in the floor. It would have been possible to dislodge the central pillar in the Tell Qasile temple, since it was held in place on the stone base only by the weight of the roof. A large man with his arms extended could have spanned the 7 foot (2.1 m) distance between the two pillars. Also, it is conceivable that the pillars of Dagon's temple were closer together than those of the Tell Qasile temple.

[1]See "The Archaeology of Philistia" on page 370. [2]See "Dagon" on page 404.

[30]Samson said, "Let me die with the Philistines!" Then he pushed with all his might, and down came the
temple on the rulers and all the people in it. Thus he killed many more when he died than while he lived.
[31]Then his brothers and his father's whole family went down to get him. They brought him back and
buried him between Zorah and Eshtaol in the tomb of Manoah[v] his father. He had led[a w] Israel twenty
years.[x]

[a] *31* Traditionally *judged*

16:31 [v]Jdg 13:2 [w]Ru 1:1; 1Sa 4:18 [x]Jdg 15:20

16:30 Samson pushed the wooden pillars from their stone bases. Archaeologists have in fact discovered a Philistine temple with such a pair of closely spaced pillar bases (see "Samson and the Temple of Dagon" on p. 375).

CULTURAL AND HISTORICAL NOTES

Tombs in Ancient Israel

JUDGES 17 The most important feature of ancient Israelite burials is reflected in the interment of Samson in the tomb of his father. Other individuals are specified to have been buried in their father's tombs, including Gideon (Jdg 8:32), Asahel (2Sa 2:32) and Ahithophel (2Sa 17:23). The first such burial noted in Scripture is that of Abraham, interred in the tomb of Sarah, his wife, later followed by their children and grandchildren.[1] Caves were often used for such tombs. Only the wealthiest could afford a tomb that had been quarried out of rock; the prophet Isaiah condemned the royal steward Shebna for his arrogance in constructing just such a burial monument (Isa 22:15–16). The poor could not afford a rock-hewn tomb and were buried in common graves dug into the soil (cf. 2Ki 23:6; Jer 26:23).

Tomb with rolling stone near Megiddo
Photograph: © Todd Bolen/Bible Places.com

The graves of the poor have generally not been preserved for archaeologists. Excavations have unearthed many examples of family burials in caves and rock-hewn tombs from the Old Testament period, with instances of more than 100 individuals interred in a single tomb. These tombs consisted of a square chamber or, in more elaborate examples, up to nine chambers for members of the extended family. Each chamber typically contained three waist-high benches that lined the room on every side except the entrance. The deceased were laid out on these benches immediately after death, along with burial gifts, including bowls for food, perfume juglets, oil lamps, weapons and jewelry.[2] The benches included ledges to prevent the contents from falling off, and headrests were frequently carved out of the rock to hold the deceased's head. After the flesh of the corpse had decayed, the bones were collected along with the gifts and deposited into a repository hewn beneath one of the burial benches. Thus the repositories were filled with the bones and objects of generations of the family. This process of burial makes it clear that the Biblical phrase "gathered to their fathers" (e.g., Jdg 2:10) was more than metaphorical.[3]

[1]See "The Cave of Machpelah" on page 38. [2]See "The Ketef Hinnom Amulets" on page 204. [3]See also "Rachel's Tomb" on page 411 and "Jewish Burial Practices" on page 1688.

Micah's Idols

17 Now a man named Micah[y] from the hill country of Ephraim [2]said to his mother, "The eleven
hundred shekels[a] of silver that were taken from you and about which I heard you utter a curse—
I have that silver with me; I took it."
Then his mother said, "The LORD bless you,[z] my son!"
[3]When he returned the eleven hundred shekels of silver to his mother, she said, "I solemnly consecrate
my silver to the LORD for my son to make a carved image and a cast idol.[a] I will give it back to you."
[4]So he returned the silver to his mother, and she took two hundred shekels[b] of silver and gave them
to a silversmith, who made them into the image and the idol.[b] And they were put in Micah's house.
[5]Now this man Micah had a shrine,[c] and he made an ephod[d] and some idols[e] and installed[f] one of
his sons as his priest.[g] [6]In those days Israel had no king;[h] everyone did as he saw fit.[i]
[7]A young Levite from Bethlehem in Judah,[j] who had been living within the clan of Judah, [8]left that
town in search of some other place to stay. On his way[c] he came to Micah's house in the hill country of
Ephraim.
[9]Micah asked him, "Where are you from?"
"I'm a Levite from Bethlehem in Judah," he said, "and I'm looking for a place to stay."
[10]Then Micah said to him, "Live with me and be my father and priest,[k] and I'll give you ten shekels[d]
of silver a year, your clothes and your food." [11]So the Levite agreed to live with him, and the young man
was to him like one of his sons. [12]Then Micah installed[l] the Levite, and the young man became his priest
and lived in his house. [13]And Micah said, "Now I know that the LORD will be good to me, since this Le-
vite has become my priest."

Danites Settle in Laish

18 In those days Israel had no king.[m]
And in those days the tribe of the Danites was seeking a place of their own where they might
settle, because they had not yet come into an inheritance among the tribes of Israel.[n] [2]So the Danites[o]
sent five warriors from Zorah and Eshtaol to spy out the land and explore it. These men represented all
their clans. They told them, "Go, explore the land."[p]
The men entered the hill country of Ephraim and came to the house of Micah,[q] where they spent the
night. [3]When they were near Micah's house, they recognized the voice of the young Levite; so they turned
in there and asked him, "Who brought you here? What are you doing in this place? Why are you here?"
[4]He told them what Micah had done for him, and said, "He has hired me and I am his priest.[r]"
[5]Then they said to him, "Please inquire of God[s] to learn whether our journey will be successful."
[6]The priest answered them, "Go in peace[t]. Your journey has the LORD's approval."
[7]So the five men left and came to Laish,[u] where they saw that the people were living in safety, like the
Sidonians, unsuspecting and secure. And since their land lacked nothing, they were prosperous.[e] Also,
they lived a long way from the Sidonians[v] and had no relationship with anyone else.[f]
[8]When they returned to Zorah and Eshtaol, their brothers asked them, "How did you find things?"
[9]They answered, "Come on, let's attack them! We have seen that the land is very good. Aren't you going

17:1 [y]Jdg 18:2, 13
17:2 [z]Ru 2:20; 1Sa 15:13; 2Sa 2:5
17:3 [a]Ex 20:4,23; 34:17; Lev 19:4
17:4 [b]Ex 32:4; Isa 17:8
17:5 [c]Isa 44:13; Eze 8:10 [d]Jdg 8:27 [e]Ge 31:19; Jdg 18:14 [f]Nu 16:10 [g]Ex 29:9; Jdg 18:24
17:6 [h]Jdg 18:1; 19:1; 21:25 [i]Dt 12:8
17:7 [j]Jdg 19:1; Ru 1:1-2; Mic 5:2; Mt 2:1
17:10 [k]Jdg 18:19
17:12 [l]Nu 16:10
18:1 [m]Jdg 17:6; 19:1 [n]Jos 19:47
18:2 [o]Jdg 13:25 [p]Jos 2:1 [q]Jdg 17:1
18:4 [r]Jdg 17:12
18:5 [s]1Ki 22:5
18:6 [t]1Ki 22:6
18:7 [u]Jos 19:47 [v]ver 28

[a] *2* That is, about 28 pounds (about 13 kilograms) [b] *4* That is, about 5 pounds (about 2.3 kilograms) [c] *8* Or *To carry on his profession* [d] *10* That is, about 4 ounces (about 110 grams) [e] *7* The meaning of the Hebrew for this clause is uncertain. [f] *7* Hebrew; some Septuagint manuscripts *with the Arameans*

17:1—18:31 The Levite was a priest who could follow his religious practice anywhere. He was hired as a family chaplain and soothsayer, and his presence was considered to be certain to bring "good luck" (see 17:13). He evidently functioned with idols (18:20) and was quite willing to change situations if the transition involved a better salary (18:19–20). All of this is in direct contrast to the divine commands concerning the priesthood in the Mosaic Law.

17:4–5 The "silversmith" was a maker of idols (see "Idols and Idol-Making" on p. 1136). Wooden idols were often plated with precious metals to make them more attractive (see Isa 2:20; 30:22; 40:19). The idols here were household gods that were used for divining (cf. Eze 21:21; Zec 10:2).

18:1 The migration of the Danites was necessitated by their failure to capture the territory assigned to them (Jos 19:40–48; Jdg 1:34–36). They traveled to a northern valley, remote and defenseless, captured it and settled there. They conquered Laish (18:27-29) and renamed it Dan. Thus originated the northern Dan, known in the expression "from Dan to Beersheba" (e.g., 1Sa 3:20; 2Sa 3:10; 1Ki 4:25). See "The Migration of the Danites" on page 378.

18:7 Laish, about 100 miles (161 km) north of Zorah and Eshtaol (v. 2), is called Leshem in Joshua 19:47. After its capture by the Danites, Laish, renamed Dan (v. 29; see "Map 4"), became Israel's northernmost settlement (see 20:1; 1Sa 3:20; 2Sa 3:10). Excavations of the site show that the earliest Israelite occupation of Dan was in the twelfth century B.C. and that the first Israelite inhabitants apparently lived in tents or temporary huts. Although the site continued to be occupied into the Assyrian period, the town was destroyed and rebuilt numerous times. A large "high place" attached to the city had often been extensively rebuilt and refurbished and was in use into the Hellenistic period.

The Sidonians were a peaceful Phoenician people who engaged in commerce throughout the Mediterranean world. Not feeling threatened by other powers, they sought no treaties for mutual defense. See "Sidon" on page 1536.

to do something? Don't hesitate to go there and take it over.[w] 10When you get there, you will find an un-
suspecting people and a spacious land that God has put into your hands, a land that lacks nothing[x] what-
ever.[y]"
11Then six hundred men[z] from the clan of the Danites,[a] armed for battle, set out from Zorah and Esh-
taol. 12On their way they set up camp near Kiriath Jearim in Judah. This is why the place west of Kiriath

18:9 [w]Nu 13:30; 1Ki 22:3 **18:10** [x]ver 7,27; Dt 8:9 [y]1Ch 4:40
18:11 [z]ver 16,17 [a]Jdg 13:2

18:11 Members of a clan accepted a communal responsibility for assistance, protection, the sharing of work, loyalty and cooperation for the general well-being of the family. In places where the nomadic life gave way to a more settled existence, groups of villages (often interdependent and with intermarried members) formed a "family," as did the Danites at Zoreh and Eshtaol.

The Migration of the Danites

JUDGES 18 The tribe of Dan was unable to occupy its assigned allotment west of Benjamin (Jos 19:40–46; Jdg 1:34). The Danites chose to migrate to Laish, which they renamed Dan[1] (see "Map 2" for the city of Dan). This took place after the time of Deborah in the late thirteenth century B.C., around the time of the destruction of Shiloh ("Map 3") around 1100 B.C. (18:31).[2] The incursion of the Philistines into the southwestern coastal plain in approximately 1177 B.C. may have precipitated the migration.[3]

Laish/Dan has been identified as Tell el-Qadi, now called Tel Dan, at the foot of Mount Hermon, approximately 25 miles (40 km) north of the Sea of Galilee. Excavations have revealed a prosperous **Late Bronze Age**[4] city that was destroyed by fire early in the twelfth century B.C., most likely by the Danites (v. 27). Laish had a strong connection, perhaps as a partner in international trade, with coastal Sidon, approximately 28 miles (45 km) to the northwest (vv. 7,28).[5] The most impressive discovery in the destroyed city of Laish was a tomb containing imported pottery from Greece.[6]

After the destruction a nomadic or semi-nomadic culture occupied the site. This culture is distinctive for its use of pits apparently dug for storing grain. Large storage jars, well known from the highlands where they are associated with Israelite settlement, were located in the pits. The jars were fashioned from clay not native to the Tel Dan area, indicating that the new settlers had brought them from elsewhere. Archaeologists have identified this new culture as that of the Danites. This tribe soon became urbanized, however, and built a dense array of domestic and industrial structures across the site (v. 28). This stratum was destroyed in a fierce conflagration in the mid-eleventh century B.C., possibly at the hands of the Philistines at the same time Shiloh was destroyed.

[1]For a discussion of later idolatry here, see "The High Place at Dan" on page 504. [2]See "The Destruction of Shiloh" on page 1200. [3]See "The Archaeology of Philistia" on page 370 and "Technological Supremacy of the Philistines' Iron Weapons" on page 414. [4]See "Archaeological Periods" chart on page xx in the front of this Bible. [5]See "Phoenicia" on page 488 and "Sidon" on page 1536. [6]See "Tombs in Ancient Israel" on page 376.

Detail of stonework from Dan
Photograph courtesy of © Dr. Gary Pratico

18:12 [b]Jdg 13:25 Jearim is called Mahaneh Dan[a][b] to this day. 13From there they went on to the hill country of Ephraim
and came to Micah's house.
14Then the five men who had spied out the land of Laish said to their brothers, "Do you know that
18:14 [c]Ge 31:19; Jdg 17:5 one of these houses has an ephod, other household gods, a carved image and a cast idol?[c] Now you
know what to do." 15So they turned in there and went to the house of the young Levite at Micah's place
18:16 [d]ver 11 and greeted him. 16The six hundred Danites,[d] armed for battle, stood at the entrance to the gate. 17The
five men who had spied out the land went inside and took the carved image, the ephod, the other house-
18:17 [e]Ge 31:19; Mic 5:13 hold gods[e] and the cast idol while the priest and the six hundred armed men stood at the entrance to
the gate.
18:18 [f]Isa 46:2; Jer 43:11; Hos 10:5 18When these men went into Micah's house and took[f] the carved image, the ephod, the other house-
hold gods and the cast idol, the priest said to them, "What are you doing?"
18:19 [g]Job 21:5; 29:9; 40:4; Mic 7:16 [h]Jdg 17:10 19They answered him, "Be quiet![g] Don't say a word. Come with us, and be our father and priest.[h] Isn't
it better that you serve a tribe and clan in Israel as priest rather than just one man's household?" 20Then
the priest was glad. He took the ephod, the other household gods and the carved image and went along
with the people. 21Putting their little children, their livestock and their possessions in front of them, they
turned away and left.
22When they had gone some distance from Micah's house, the men who lived near Micah were called
together and overtook the Danites. 23As they shouted after them, the Danites turned and said to Micah,
"What's the matter with you that you called out your men to fight?"
24He replied, "You took the gods I made, and my priest, and went away. What else do I have? How can
you ask, 'What's the matter with you?' "
25The Danites answered, "Don't argue with us, or some hot-tempered men will attack you, and you and
your family will lose your lives." 26So the Danites went their way, and Micah, seeing that they were too
18:26 [i]Ps 18:17; 35:10 strong for him,[i] turned around and went back home.
27Then they took what Micah had made, and his priest, and went on to Laish, against a peaceful and
18:27 [j]ver 7,10 [k]Ge 49:17; Jos 19:47 unsuspecting people.[j] They attacked them with the sword and burned down their city.[k] 28There was no
18:28 [l]ver 7 [m]Nu 13:21; 2Sa 10:6 one to rescue them because they lived a long way from Sidon[l] and had no relationship with anyone else.
The city was in a valley near Beth Rehob.[m]
18:29 [n]Ge 14:14 [o]Jos 19:47; 1Ki 15:20 The Danites rebuilt the city and settled there. 29They named it Dan[n] after their forefather Dan, who
was born to Israel—though the city used to be called Laish.[o] 30There the Danites set up for themselves
18:30 [p]Ex 2:22; Jdg 17:3,5 the idols, and Jonathan son of Gershom,[p] the son of Moses,[b] and his sons were priests for the tribe of Dan
until the time of the captivity of the land. 31They continued to use the idols Micah had made, all the time
18:31 [q]Jdg 19:18 [r]Jos 18:1; Jer 7:14 the house of God[q] was in Shiloh.[r]

A Levite and His Concubine

19 In those days Israel had no king.
19:1 [s]Jdg 18:1 [t]Ru 1:1 Now a Levite who lived in a remote area in the hill country of Ephraim[s] took a concubine from
Bethlehem in Judah.[t] 2But she was unfaithful to him. She left him and went back to her father's house in
Bethlehem, Judah. After she had been there four months, 3her husband went to her to persuade her to re-
turn. He had with him his servant and two donkeys. She took him into her father's house, and when her
father saw him, he gladly welcomed him. 4His father-in-law, the girl's father, prevailed upon him to stay;
19:4 [u]Ex 32:6 so he remained with him three days, eating and drinking,[u] and sleeping there.
5On the fourth day they got up early and he prepared to leave, but the girl's father said to his son-in-
19:5 [v]ver 8; Ge 18:5 law, "Refresh yourself[v] with something to eat; then you can go." 6So the two of them sat down to eat and
19:6 [w]ver 9,22; Jdg 16:25 drink together. Afterward the girl's father said, "Please stay tonight and enjoy yourself."[w] 7And when the

[a] *12 Mahaneh Dan* means *Dan's camp.* [b] *30* An ancient Hebrew scribal tradition, some Septuagint manuscripts and Vulgate; Masoretic Text *Manasseh*

18:31 Excavations of the site indicate that Shiloh ("Map 4") was destroyed about 1050 B.C. and left uninhabited for many centuries (see "The Destruction of Shiloh" on p. 1200).

19:1—21:25 The narrative of the Levite's concubine casts a vivid light upon the brutality of the times and introduces the war of the tribes against the Benjamites (chs. 20–21). This is not the only intertribal war of the period (see 8:1–3; 12:1–6). In fact, it is clear that the loyalty of the Hebrews at this time was a merely tribal one, as is the case with the Bedouin still today. There was no real Hebrew nation; Israel was at best a loose confederation of tribes around a central sanctuary, the tabernacle at Shiloh (18:31).

The cruelty and paganism of the narratives of Judges are often a stumbling block to readers, but we do well instead to view them as a history of the tragic judgment of God on a people who failed to keep their heritage of true religious faith by assimilating far too much of their surrounding culture. The history of the judges has been called "the struggle between faith and culture." In this struggle, faith lost. And, of course, culture suffered as well.

man got up to go, his father-in-law persuaded him, so he stayed there that night. 8On the morning of the
fifth day, when he rose to go, the girl's father said, "Refresh yourself. Wait till afternoon!" So the two of
them ate together.
9Then when the man, with his concubine and his servant, got up to leave, his father-in-law, the girl's
father, said, "Now look, it's almost evening. Spend the night here; the day is nearly over. Stay and enjoy
yourself. Early tomorrow morning you can get up and be on your way home." 10But, unwilling to stay an-
other night, the man left and went toward Jebus[x] (that is, Jerusalem), with his two saddled donkeys and
his concubine.

19:10 [x]Ge 10:16; Jos 15:8; 1Ch 11:4-5

ARCHAEOLOGICAL SITES

GIBEAH

JUDGES 19 The name Gibeah ("hill") indicates several different locations in the Old Testament. The Gibeah of Judges 19–21, however, first mentioned in this passage, and then throughout the Old Testament, is specifically associated with the tribe of Benjamin. This particular Gibeah was destroyed by the rest of the Israelites during the period of the judges (20:40).[1] Gibeah was apparently inhabited again some time later; King Saul came from this city (1Sa 10:26). Saul in fact fought the Philistines in the region and seems to have made Gibeah his base of operations (1Sa 15:34; 22:6; 23:19). Later we read that David chose three of his thirty mighty men from this city (2Sa 23:29; 1Ch 12:3).

Centuries later the prophet Hosea cited ancient Gibeah as an example of wickedness (Hos 9:9; 10:9).[2] Hosea seems to have been referring to the events of Judges 19–20, illustrating the profound impact of this terrible episode on the psyche of the nation. Gibeah became known as a place of corruption and judgment, not unlike Sodom and Gomorrah.

Despite the frequency of Biblical references to Gibeah, its location has been a source of intense dispute among scholars. The debate is focused on whether Gibeah was near modern Jeba or at the impressive Tell el-Fûl, which is located on the watershed highway slightly more than 3 miles (4.8 km) north of Jerusalem.

W.F. Albright excavated at Tell el-Fûl in 1922–23 and again in 1933. He found traces of an **Iron Age**[3] village that had been destroyed, as well as the remains of a strong fortress that had been built soon after. The stronghold measured approximately 111.5 feet (34 m) by 170.6 feet (52 m) and was constructed of large, uncut stones that had been joined in a fairly crude fashion. The walls were nearly 5 feet (1.5 m) thick. Albright dated the village destruction layer to the twelfth century B.C. and the stronghold to the late eleventh century B.C. The sequence of these remains matches the Biblical chronology: destruction during the period of the judges and fortification during the life of Saul.

Paul Lapp led a salvage operation in 1964, just before King Hussein of Jordan leveled Tell el-Fûl in order to build a palace (the area was at this time under Jordan's control). Lapp concluded that the first period of habitation should be dated approximately 1200–1150 B.C., while the fortress should be assigned to the period of approximately 1025–950 B.C. These more precise dates still coincide with the Old Testament accounts. Lapp's study of the pottery record confirmed a gap in habitation between the earlier village and the fortress.[4] We would expect to see such a lull following the large-scale destruction described in Judges 20. Lapp also uncovered evidence of significant later Iron Age settlements on the site. The conclusions by Albright and Lapp in favor of the identification of Tell el-Fûl as Gibeah are still accepted by the majority of scholars.

A vocal minority, however, argues that Jeba is a better candidate for ancient Gibeah. One argument is that Tell el-Fûl is located on a hill above a large plain; it is therefore unlikely that its inhabitants would have been ambushed by hidden Israelite warriors, as 20:29 describes. This scenario is more plausible in the hilly, canyon-filled region of Jeba.

The question remains open. The destruction of Tell el-Fûl was a substantial setback, and sufficient archaeological work has not yet been done at Jeba. At this point we can confirm that the habitation pattern at Tell el-Fûl matches the Biblical chronology, while such a fit has yet to be demonstrated at Jeba.

[1]See "The Judges Period" on page 344. [2]See "Hosea's Use of the Old Testament" on page 1428. [3]See "Archaeological Periods" chart on page xx in the front of this Bible. [4]See "The Potsherd: Pottery in the Bible" on page 738.

11 When they were near Jebus and the day was almost gone, the servant said to his master, "Come, let's stop at this city of the Jebusites[y] and spend the night."

12 His master replied, "No. We won't go into an alien city, whose people are not Israelites. We will go on to Gibeah." 13 He added, "Come, let's try to reach Gibeah or Ramah[z] and spend the night in one of those places." 14 So they went on, and the sun set as they neared Gibeah in Benjamin.[a] 15 There they stopped to spend the night. They went and sat in the city square,[b] but no one took them into his home for the night.

16 That evening[c] an old man from the hill country of Ephraim,[d] who was living in Gibeah (the men of the place were Benjamites), came in from his work in the fields. 17 When he looked and saw the traveler in the city square, the old man asked, "Where are you going? Where did you come from?"[e]

18 He answered, "We are on our way from Bethlehem in Judah to a remote area in the hill country of Ephraim where I live. I have been to Bethlehem in Judah and now I am going to the house of the LORD.[f] No one has taken me into his house. 19 We have both straw and fodder[g] for our donkeys and bread and wine[h] for ourselves your servants—me, your maidservant, and the young man with us. We don't need anything."

20 "You are welcome at my house," the old man said. "Let me supply whatever you need. Only don't spend the night in the square." 21 So he took him into his house and fed his donkeys. After they had washed their feet, they had something to eat and drink.[i]

22 While they were enjoying themselves,[j] some of the wicked men[k] of the city surrounded the house. Pounding on the door, they shouted to the old man who owned the house, "Bring out the man who came to your house so we can have sex with him.[l]"

23 The owner of the house went outside[m] and said to them, "No, my friends, don't be so vile. Since this man is my guest, don't do this disgraceful thing.[n] 24 Look, here is my virgin daughter,[o] and his concubine. I will bring them out to you now, and you can use them and do to them whatever you wish. But to this man, don't do such a disgraceful thing."

25 But the men would not listen to him. So the man took his concubine and sent her outside to them, and they raped her and abused her[p] throughout the night, and at dawn they let her go. 26 At daybreak the woman went back to the house where her master was staying, fell down at the door and lay there until daylight.

27 When her master got up in the morning and opened the door of the house and stepped out to continue on his way, there lay his concubine, fallen in the doorway of the house, with her hands on the threshold. 28 He said to her, "Get up; let's go." But there was no answer. Then the man put her on his donkey and set out for home.

29 When he reached home, he took a knife[q] and cut up his concubine, limb by limb, into twelve parts and sent them into all the areas of Israel.[r] 30 Everyone who saw it said, "Such a thing has never been seen or done, not since the day the Israelites came up out of Egypt.[s] Think about it! Consider it! Tell us what to do![t]"

Israelites Fight the Benjamites

20 Then all the Israelites[u] from Dan to Beersheba[v] and from the land of Gilead came out as one man[w] and assembled[x] before the LORD in Mizpah. 2 The leaders of all the people of the tribes of Israel took their places in the assembly of the people of God, four hundred thousand soldiers[y] armed with swords. 3 (The Benjamites heard that the Israelites had gone up to Mizpah.) Then the Israelites said, "Tell us how this awful thing happened."

4 So the Levite, the husband of the murdered woman, said, "I and my concubine came to Gibeah[z] in Benjamin to spend the night.[a] 5 During the night the men of Gibeah came after me and surrounded the house, intending to kill me.[b] They raped my concubine, and she died.[c] 6 I took my concubine, cut her into pieces and sent one piece to each region of Israel's inheritance,[d] because they committed this lewd and disgraceful act[e] in Israel. 7 Now, all you Israelites, speak up and give your verdict.[f]"

8 All the people rose as one man, saying, "None of us will go home. No, not one of us will return to his house. 9 But now this is what we'll do to Gibeah: We'll go up against it as the lot directs.[g] 10 We'll take ten

19:11 [y]Jos 3:10
19:13 [z]Jos 18:25
19:14 [a]1Sa 10:26; Isa 10:29
19:15 [b]Ge 19:2
19:16 [c]Ps 104:23 [d]ver 1
19:17 [e]Ge 29:4
19:18 [f]Jdg 18:31
19:19 [g]Ge 24:25 [h]Ge 14:18
19:21 [i]Ge 24:32-33; Lk 7:44
19:22 [j]Jdg 16:25 [k]Dt 13:13 [l]Ge 19:4-5; Jdg 20:5; Ro 1:26-27
19:23 [m]Ge 19:6 [n]Ge 34:7; Lev 19:29; Dt 22:21; Jdg 20:6; 2Sa 13:12; Ro 1:27
19:24 [o]Ge 19:8; Dt 21:14
19:25 [p]1Sa 31:4
19:29 [q]Ge 22:6 [r]Jdg 20:6; 1Sa 11:7
19:30 [s]Hos 9:9 [t]Jdg 20:7; Pr 13:10
20:1 [u]Jdg 21:5 [v]1Sa 3:20; 2Sa 3:10; 1Ki 4:25 [w]1Sa 11:7 [x]1Sa 7:5
20:2 [y]Jdg 8:10
20:4 [z]Jos 15:57 [a]Jdg 19:15
20:5 [b]Jdg 19:22 [c]Jdg 19:25-26
20:6 [d]Jdg 19:29 [e]Jos 7:15; Jdg 19:23
20:7 [f]Jdg 19:30
20:9 [g]Lev 16:8

19:21 Washing a guest's feet was a common act of hospitality in the ancient Near East, where travelers usually wore sandals as they walked the dusty roads (see Ge 18:4; 24:32; 43:24; Lk 7:44; Jn 13:5–14).
19:42 Aijalon ("Map 6"), a city in Dan assigned to the Levite sons of Kohath (1Ch 6:69), is mentioned most notably in the memorable words of Joshua: "O sun, stand still over Gibeon, O moon, over the Valley of Aijalon" (Jos 10:12). It is identified with the modern Yalo, 14 miles (22 km) from Jerusalem, north of the Jaffa road.
20:1 The phrase "from Dan to Beersheba" was a conventional way of speaking of all Israel from north (Dan) to south (Beersheba).

men out of every hundred from all the tribes of Israel, and a hundred from a thousand, and a thousand
from ten thousand, to get provisions for the army. Then, when the army arrives at Gibeah[a] in Benjamin,
it can give them what they deserve for all this vileness done in Israel." 11 So all the men of Israel got to-
gether and united as one man[h] against the city. **20:11** [h]ver 1

12 The tribes of Israel sent men throughout the tribe of Benjamin, saying, "What about this awful crime
that was committed among you? 13 Now surrender those wicked men[i] of Gibeah so that we may put them **20:13** [i]Dt 13:13; Jdg 19:22
to death and purge the evil from Israel.[j]" [j]Dt 17:12

But the Benjamites would not listen to their fellow Israelites. 14 From their towns they came together
at Gibeah to fight against the Israelites. 15 At once the Benjamites mobilized twenty-six thousand swords-
men from their towns, in addition to seven hundred chosen men from those living in Gibeah. 16 Among
all these soldiers there were seven hundred chosen men who were left-handed,[k] each of whom could **20:16** [k]Jdg 3:15; 1Ch 12:2
sling a stone at a hair and not miss.

17 Israel, apart from Benjamin, mustered four hundred thousand swordsmen, all of them fighting men.

18 The Israelites went up to Bethel[b] and inquired of God.[l] They said, "Who of us shall go first to fight[m] **20:18** [l]ver 26-27; Nu 27:21 [m]ver 23, 28
against the Benjamites?"

The LORD replied, "Judah shall go first."

19 The next morning the Israelites got up and pitched camp near Gibeah. 20 The men of Israel went out
to fight the Benjamites and took up battle positions against them at Gibeah. 21 The Benjamites came out
of Gibeah and cut down twenty-two thousand Israelites[n] on the battlefield that day. 22 But the men of Is- **20:21** [n]ver 25
rael encouraged one another and again took up their positions where they had stationed themselves the
first day. 23 The Israelites went up and wept before the LORD until evening,[o] and they inquired of the LORD. **20:23** [o]Jos 7:6
They said, "Shall we go up again to battle[p] against the Benjamites, our brothers?" [p]ver 18

The LORD answered, "Go up against them."

24 Then the Israelites drew near to Benjamin the second day. 25 This time, when the Benjamites came
out from Gibeah to oppose them, they cut down another eighteen thousand Israelites,[q] all of them armed **20:25** [q]ver 21
with swords.

26 Then the Israelites, all the people, went up to Bethel, and there they sat weeping before the LORD.[r] **20:26** [r]ver 23
They fasted that day until evening and presented burnt offerings and fellowship offerings[c] to the LORD.[s] [s]Jdg 21:4
27 And the Israelites inquired of the LORD. (In those days the ark of the covenant of God[t] was there, 28 with **20:27** [t]Jos 18:1
Phinehas son of Eleazar,[u] the son of Aaron, ministering before it.)[v] They asked, "Shall we go up again to **20:28** [u]Jos 24:33
battle with Benjamin our brother, or not?" [v]Dt 18:5 [w]Jdg 7:9

The LORD responded, "Go, for tomorrow I will give them into your hands.[w]"

29 Then Israel set an ambush[x] around Gibeah. 30 They went up against the Benjamites on the third **20:29** [x]Jos 8:2,4
day and took up positions against Gibeah as they had done before. 31 The Benjamites came out to meet
them and were drawn away[y] from the city. They began to inflict casualties on the Israelites as before, **20:31** [y]Jos 8:16
so that about thirty men fell in the open field and on the roads—the one leading to Bethel and the oth-
er to Gibeah.

32 While the Benjamites were saying, "We are defeating them as before,"[z] the Israelites were saying, **20:32** [z]ver 39
"Let's retreat and draw them away from the city to the roads."

33 All the men of Israel moved from their places and took up positions at Baal Tamar, and the Israel-
ite ambush charged out of its place[a] on the west[d] of Gibeah.[e] 34 Then ten thousand of Israel's finest men **20:33** [a]Jos 8:19
made a frontal attack on Gibeah. The fighting was so heavy that the Benjamites did not realize[b] how near **20:34** [b]Jos 8:14 [c]Isa 47:11
disaster was.[c] 35 The LORD defeated Benjamin[d] before Israel, and on that day the Israelites struck down **20:35** [d]1Sa 9:21
25,100 Benjamites, all armed with swords. 36 Then the Benjamites saw that they were beaten.

Now the men of Israel had given way[e] before Benjamin, because they relied on the ambush they had **20:36** [e]Jos 8:15
set near Gibeah. 37 The men who had been in ambush made a sudden dash into Gibeah, spread out and
put the whole city to the sword.[f] 38 The men of Israel had arranged with the ambush that they should **20:37** [f]Jos 8:19
send up a great cloud of smoke[g] from the city, 39 and then the men of Israel would turn in the battle. **20:38** [g]Jos 8:20

[a] *10* One Hebrew manuscript; most Hebrew manuscripts *Geba*, a variant of *Gibeah* [b] *18* Or *to the house of God*; also in verse 26
[c] *26* Traditionally *peace offerings* [d] *33* Some Septuagint manuscripts and Vulgate; the meaning of the Hebrew for this word is uncertain. [e] *33* Hebrew *Geba*, a variant of *Gibeah*

20:18–48. For a discussion of the religious significance of Israel's wars, see the note on Deuteronomy 20:1–4.

ARCHAEOLOGICAL SITES

MIZPAH

JUDGES 20 Approximately 7 miles (11 km) northwest of Jerusalem lies Tell en-Nasbeh, a mound 853 feet (nearly 260 m) long by 426.5 feet (nearly 130 m) wide, covering a total surface area of about 7.7 acres. Most scholars identify this site with the Biblical Mizpah ("Map 4"). Little is known about Mizpah during the pre-monarchial period because the city is seldom mentioned in texts and few archaeological remains from this era have been discovered. Excavations between 1926 and 1935 unearthed three tombs, two caves and various fragments of pottery from the Late **Chalcolithic**[1] and **Early Bronze** I periods, which predate any Biblical reference.

Ruins of Mizpah
Photograph: © Todd Bolen/Bible Places.com

Judges identifies Mizpah as the assembly point for a combined Israelite military force that attacked the Benjamites at Gibeah[2] (Jdg 20:1). Mizpah's central location on the watershed highway between Ramah and Bethel would have made it a natural mustering point, even if no archaeological record of a major settlement exists from that period. The force then moved north to Bethel[3] to inquire of the Lord before launching its attack, and Mizpah played no further role in the account.

By the time of Samuel, Mizpah had become an important regional center. The prophet summoned all the Israelites there to seek forgiveness for their idolatry. While the assembled Israelites were fasting before the Lord, the Philistines launched an attack, but God intervened with thunder and scattered them (1Sa 7:5–11). After this Samuel, who was serving as Israel's judge, returned to Mizpah each year as part of a circuit that also included Bethel and Gilgal (1Sa 7:16). It was also at Mizpah that Samuel revealed Saul as Israel's first king (1Sa 10:17–21).[4] Philistine and other local pottery, along with the remains of rock-cut cisterns and houses, attests to a resurgence of population around the time of Samuel, as the Biblical text suggests.

During the **divided monarchy**, Mizpah was a border city between Israel and Judah. In approximately 895 B.C. King Baasha of Israel pushed his territory south as far as Ramah and built a fortification there (1Ki 15:17–22; 2Ch 16:1–6). This cut off Judah's primary land route to the coastal plain. King Asa of Judah responded by bribing the Arameans to attack Israel from the north. Baasha had to redirect his forces to this northern front, and Asa seized the opportunity to dismantle the Israelite fortification at Ramah. He then used the materials to construct Judahite strongholds farther north in Mizpah and Geba.

Excavations at Tell en-Nasbeh have revealed the remains of a massive defensive construction of the early ninth century B.C. A wall of roughly shaped and plastered stones reached a height of nearly 46 feet (14 m) and was reinforced by a series of ten towers. A stone **glacis** (slope at the base of the fortification wall) ended in a dry moat 16.4 feet (5 m) wide and 6.56 feet (2 m) deep, while a double gate complex protected the entrance to the city. It is the only fortification of this type in the region. Houses were built against the inside of the wall. Remains of olive oil presses and storage bins from the period have also been unearthed, along with a cemetery on a ridge just outside the city. These finds confirm that Asa expended considerable resources in the strengthening of this crucial defensive position.

Following the Babylonian destruction of Jerusalem and most of Judah in 586 B.C.,[5] Mizpah became the residence of Gedaliah,[6] the Babylonian-appointed governor of Judah (2Ki 25:23; Jer 40:1—41:16). Gedaliah's tenure was short-lived, for Ishmael, son of Nethaniah, and some other political insurgents assassinated him less than six months after his arrival in Mizpah. The city continued to serve as the regional capital until at least the time of Nehemiah. During this era of Babylonian control, larger, more elaborate private dwellings and public buildings replaced the smaller houses of Asa's time.

Subsequent Biblical references to Mizpah are few and brief. Even so, numerous examples of **Persian** seals and seal impressions, pieces of Greek and Roman pottery and other items suggest virtually continuous habitation on the mound throughout antiquity. The cemetery at Mizpah remained in use until the **Byzantine** period, when a Christian church was constructed nearby.

[1]See "Archaeological Periods" chart on page xx in the front of this Bible. [2]See "Gibeah" on page 380. [3]See "Bethel" on page 59. [4]See "Samuel and Saul" on page 410. [5]See "The Last Days of Jerusalem" on page 1197. [6]See "Gedaliah, Governor of Judah, and Baalis, King of Ammon" on page 1261.

The Benjamites had begun to inflict casualties on the men of Israel (about thirty), and they said, "We
are defeating them as in the first battle."[h] 40 But when the column of smoke began to rise from the city, **20:39** [h]ver 32
the Benjamites turned and saw the smoke of the whole city going up into the sky.[i] 41 Then the men of Is- **20:40** [i]Jos 8:20
rael turned on them, and the men of Benjamin were terrified, because they realized that disaster had
come upon them. 42 So they fled before the Israelites in the direction of the desert, but they could not es-
cape the battle. And the men of Israel who came out of the towns cut them down there. 43 They surround-
ed the Benjamites, chased them and easily[a] overran them in the vicinity of Gibeah on the east. 44 Eigh-
teen thousand Benjamites fell, all of them valiant fighters.[j] 45 As they turned and fled toward the desert **20:44** [j]Ps 76:5
to the rock of Rimmon,[k] the Israelites cut down five thousand men along the roads. They kept pressing **20:45**
after the Benjamites as far as Gidom and struck down two thousand more. [k]Jos 15:32; Jdg 21:13

46 On that day twenty-five thousand Benjamite swordsmen fell, all of them valiant fighters. 47 But six
hundred men turned and fled into the desert to the rock of Rimmon, where they stayed four months.
48 The men of Israel went back to Benjamin and put all the towns to the sword, including the animals
and everything else they found. All the towns they came across they set on fire.[l] **20:48** [l]Jdg 21:23

Wives for the Benjamites

21 The men of Israel had taken an oath[m] at Mizpah:[n] "Not one of us will give[o] his daughter in mar- **21:1** [m]Jos 9:18 [n]Jdg 20:1 [o]ver 7, 18
riage to a Benjamite."

2 The people went to Bethel,[b] where they sat before God until evening, raising their voices and weep-
ing bitterly. 3 "O LORD, the God of Israel," they cried, "why has this happened to Israel? Why should one
tribe be missing from Israel today?"

[a] *43* The meaning of the Hebrew for this word is uncertain. [b] *2* Or *to the house of God*

ARCHAEOLOGICAL SITES

JABESH GILEAD

JUDGES 21 Jabesh Gilead was located in the territory of Manasseh on the eastern side of the Jordan River ("Map 4"). However, its exact location is unknown. Judges provides no specific information regarding the city's precise location, surrounding topography or characteristics. Judges 21 states that its inhabitants were massacred by 12,000 Israelite warriors because Jabesh Gilead had not sent soldiers for the attack on the Benjamites following the atrocity at Gibeah[1] (chs. 19–20). Only 400 virgins were spared. These unfortunate young women were designated for the Benjamite men, since the other Israelites had sworn not to give them their own daughters as wives.

Jabesh Gilead is next mentioned in the context of Saul. According to 1 Samuel 11, Nahash the Ammonite besieged the city and demanded, as a condition of peace, the right to gouge out the right eye of every resident. The city sent messengers to the newly anointed Saul and begged for help. Saul quickly gathered a sizable pan-Israelite force and devastated the army of Nahash. The residents of Jabesh Gilead did not forget this deliverance. Later, when Saul and his sons died on Mount Gilboa, the Philistines hung their bodies on the wall of Beth Shan as trophies. The men of Jabesh Gilead traveled by night to Beth Shan, reclaimed the bodies and brought them back to Jabesh Gilead for cremation and burial (1Sa 31).[2] They then mourned for Saul and fasted for seven days. When David learned of this brave action, he sent special messengers to carry a blessing to the city (2Sa 2:4–7).

Scholars have attempted to approximate Jabesh Gilead's location based upon the fact that it was a night's journey from Beth Shan. Our only other clue comes from Eusebius, a Christian historian from the fourth century A.D. If Eusebius's information is correct, the modern hill Tell Maqlub must be the location of the Biblical Jabesh Gilead. Surface surveys have yielded pottery from **Iron Age** I,[3] which suggests that its habitation history matches the Biblical chronology. The site is only 10 miles (16 km) from Beth Shan, so an overnight trip to Beth Shan on foot is quite reasonable. Tell Maqlub remains unexcavated.

[1]See "Gibeah" on page 380. [2]See "The Beth Shan Temples" on page 438. [3]See "Archaeological Periods" chart on page xx in the front of this Bible.

21:4 [p]Jdg 20:26; 2Sa 24:25 — 4 Early the next day the people built an altar and presented burnt offerings and fellowship offerings.[a][p]
21:5 [q]Jdg 5:23; 20:1 — 5 Then the Israelites asked, "Who from all the tribes of Israel[q] has failed to assemble before the LORD?"
For they had taken a solemn oath that anyone who failed to assemble before the LORD at Mizpah should
certainly be put to death.
6 Now the Israelites grieved for their brothers, the Benjamites. "Today one tribe is cut off from Israel,"
21:7 [r]ver 1 — they said. 7 "How can we provide wives for those who are left, since we have taken an oath[r] by the LORD
not to give them any of our daughters in marriage?" 8 Then they asked, "Which one of the tribes of Isra-
21:8 [s]1Sa 11:1; 31:11 — el failed to assemble before the LORD at Mizpah?" They discovered that no one from Jabesh Gilead[s] had
come to the camp for the assembly. 9 For when they counted the people, they found that none of the peo-
ple of Jabesh Gilead were there.
10 So the assembly sent twelve thousand fighting men with instructions to go to Jabesh Gilead and
put to the sword those living there, including the women and children. 11 "This is what you are to do,"
21:11 [t]Nu 31:17-18 — they said. "Kill every male and every woman who is not a virgin."[t] 12 They found among the people liv-
ing in Jabesh Gilead four hundred young women who had never slept with a man, and they took them
21:12 [u]Jos 18:1 — to the camp at Shiloh[u] in Canaan.
21:13 [v]Dt 20:10 [w]Jdg 20:47 — 13 Then the whole assembly sent an offer of peace[v] to the Benjamites at the rock of Rimmon.[w] 14 So the
Benjamites returned at that time and were given the women of Jabesh Gilead who had been spared. But
there were not enough for all of them.
21:15 [x]ver 6 — 15 The people grieved for Benjamin,[x] because the LORD had made a gap in the tribes of Israel. 16 And
the elders of the assembly said, "With the women of Benjamin destroyed, how shall we provide wives for
the men who are left? 17 The Benjamite survivors must have heirs," they said, "so that a tribe of Israel will
not be wiped out. 18 We can't give them our daughters as wives, since we Israelites have taken this oath:
21:18 [y]ver 1 — 'Cursed be anyone who gives[y] a wife to a Benjamite.' 19 But look, there is the annual festival of the LORD
21:19 [z]Jos 18:1; Jdg 18:31; 1Sa 1:3 — in Shiloh,[z] to the north of Bethel, and east of the road that goes from Bethel to Shechem, and to the south
of Lebonah."
20 So they instructed the Benjamites, saying, "Go and hide in the vineyards 21 and watch. When the
21:21 [a]Ex 15:20; Jdg 11:34 — girls of Shiloh come out to join in the dancing,[a] then rush from the vineyards and each of you seize a wife
from the girls of Shiloh and go to the land of Benjamin. 22 When their fathers or brothers complain to us,
we will say to them, 'Do us a kindness by helping them, because we did not get wives for them during the
21:22 [b]ver 1,18 — war, and you are innocent, since you did not give[b] your daughters to them.' "
23 So that is what the Benjamites did. While the girls were dancing, each man caught one and carried
21:23 [c]Jdg 20:48 — her off to be his wife. Then they returned to their inheritance and rebuilt the towns and settled in them.[c]
24 At that time the Israelites left that place and went home to their tribes and clans, each to his own
inheritance.
21:25 [d]Dt 12:8; Jdg 17:6; 18:1; 19:1 — 25 In those days Israel had no king; everyone did as he saw fit.[d]

[a] 4 Traditionally *peace offerings*

INTRODUCTION TO Ruth

AUTHOR, PLACE AND DATE OF WRITING

The author of this little book is unknown. Some scholars have attributed it to Samuel, but its literary style suggests that it may date to the period of the monarchy, years after the events it describes.

AUDIENCE

Generations of Israelites after the time of the judges read Ruth. The book offered the Israelites a view of true faith and piety during a time of national disunity, foreign oppression and religious and moral degeneracy.

CULTURAL FACTS AND HIGHLIGHTS

During Ruth's day the Israelites alternated between pleading with God for help during desperate times and forgetting all about the Lord and participating in the debauchery of neighboring cultures. Yet God, working behind the scenes, continued to fulfill his plan of redemption. In a surprising way he used Ruth, a faithful, courageous—and female—foreigner, not only to impact the Jews but also to exercise a key role in changing the world through Jesus.

TIMELINE

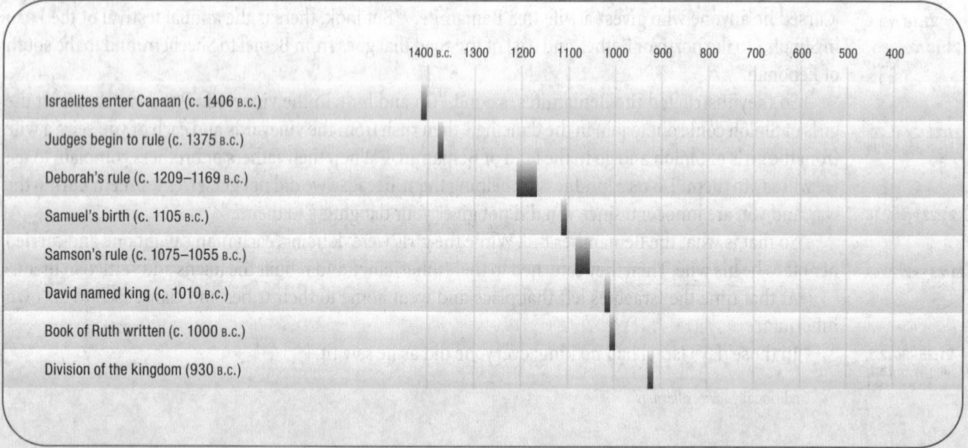

AS YOU READ

Notice the motif of faithful love among God's people—Ruth's loyalty to Naomi, the acceptance of Ruth by the citizens of Bethlehem and Boaz's kindness toward both widows (chs. 2–4). Observe how God orchestrated seemingly insignificant details to work out his overriding purpose. Follow Naomi's transformation from emptiness to fullness (3:17). Finally, discover the story's true significance at the end of the book (cf. Mt 1:5–6,16): Ruth, a foreigner whose faith touched God's heart, is listed in the lineage of Jesus, who completed God's redemptive work and fulfilled the promised blessings of God's kingdom.

DID YOU KNOW?

- Uncovering a man's feet and lying down was a customary, nonverbal means of requesting marriage (3:1–4).
- The land of a family or clan could not be sold permanently (4:1–3).
- Taking off one's sandal and giving it to another was a public way of renouncing one's property rights and transferring them to another (4:7). The Nuzi documents (Akkadian, mid-second millennium B.C.) refer to a similar custom, which no longer applied during the time of Israel's judges.

THEMES

The book of Ruth contains the following themes:

1. *Acceptance.* Ruth demonstrates the truth that participation in the family of God is not based on birth or nationality but on faith in, and obedience to, God.

2. *Kindness and faithfulness.* Naomi's transformation from a woman in despair (1:20) to a joyful person (4:14–16) through the selfless loyalty and kindness of Ruth and Boaz reflects that God's provision often comes through the love and faithfulness of his obedient people (2:20; 3:10; Lev 19:9–10; Dt 24:19–22).

3. *Redemption.* Boaz's actions to redeem the land (Lev 25:25–29), marry Ruth (Dt 25:5–10) and father a child to keep Naomi's family line alive (Dt 25:6)—all are symbolic of Christ's redemption of his bride, the church (Eph 5:25–27; Rev 19:1–8; 22:17), and of his people (Tit 2:14).

OUTLINE

I. Introduction: Naomi Emptied (1:1–5)
II. Naomi Returns From Moab (1:6–22)
III. Ruth and Boaz Meet in the Harvest Fields (2)
IV. Ruth Goes to Boaz (3)
V. Boaz Arranges to Marry Ruth (4:1–12)
VI. Conclusion: Naomi Filled (4:13–17)
VII. Epilogue: Genealogy of David (4:18–22)

Naomi and Ruth

1 In the days when the judges ruled,[a][a] there was a famine in the land,[b] and a man from Bethlehem in
Judah, together with his wife and two sons, went to live for a while in the country of Moab.[c] [2]The
man's name was Elimelech, his wife's name Naomi, and the names of his two sons were Mahlon and Kil-
ion. They were Ephrathites from Bethlehem,[d] Judah. And they went to Moab and lived there.
[3]Now Elimelech, Naomi's husband, died, and she was left with her two sons. [4]They married Moabite
women, one named Orpah and the other Ruth.[e] After they had lived there about ten years, [5]both Mah-
lon and Kilion also died, and Naomi was left without her two sons and her husband.
[6]When she heard in Moab that the LORD had come to the aid of his people[f] by providing food[g] for
them, Naomi and her daughters-in-law prepared to return home from there. [7]With her two daughters-
in-law she left the place where she had been living and set out on the road that would take them back to
the land of Judah.
[8]Then Naomi said to her two daughters-in-law, "Go back, each of you, to your mother's home. May
the LORD show kindness[h] to you, as you have shown to your dead[i] and to me. [9]May the LORD grant that
each of you will find rest[j] in the home of another husband."
Then she kissed them and they wept aloud [10]and said to her, "We will go back with you to your people."
[11]But Naomi said, "Return home, my daughters. Why would you come with me? Am I going to have
any more sons, who could become your husbands?[k] [12]Return home, my daughters; I am too old to have
another husband. Even if I thought there was still hope for me—even if I had a husband tonight and
then gave birth to sons— [13]would you wait until they grew up? Would you remain unmarried for them?
No, my daughters. It is more bitter for me than for you, because the LORD's hand has gone out against me!"[l]
[14]At this they wept again. Then Orpah kissed her mother-in-law[m] good-by, but Ruth clung to her.[n]
[15]"Look," said Naomi, "your sister-in-law is going back to her people and her gods.[o] Go back with her."
[16]But Ruth replied, "Don't urge me to leave you[p] or to turn back from you. Where you go I will go, and
where you stay I will stay. Your people will be my people and your God my God.[q] [17]Where you die I will
die, and there I will be buried. May the LORD deal with me, be it ever so severely,[r] if anything but death
separates you and me." [18]When Naomi realized that Ruth was determined to go with her, she stopped
urging her.[s]
[19]So the two women went on until they came to Bethlehem. When they arrived in Bethlehem, the
whole town was stirred[t] because of them, and the women exclaimed, "Can this be Naomi?"
[20]"Don't call me Naomi,[b]" she told them. "Call me Mara,[c] because the Almighty[d][u] has made my life
very bitter.[v] [21]I went away full, but the LORD has brought me back empty.[w] Why call me Naomi? The LORD
has afflicted[e] me; the Almighty has brought misfortune upon me."
[22]So Naomi returned from Moab accompanied by Ruth the Moabitess, her daughter-in-law, arriving
in Bethlehem as the barley harvest[x] was beginning.[y]

1:1 [a]Jdg 2:16-18 [b]Ge 12:10; Ps 105:16 [c]Jdg 3:30
1:2 [d]Ge 35:19
1:4 [e]Mt 1:5
1:6 [f]Ex 4:31; Jer 29:10; Zep 2:7 [g]Ps 132:15; Mt 6:11
1:8 [h]Ru 2:20; 2Ti 1:16 [i]ver 5
1:9 [j]Ru 3:1
1:11 [k]Ge 38:11; Dt 25:5
1:13 [l]Jdg 2:15; Job 4:5; 19:21; Ps 32:4
1:14 [m]Ru 2:11 [n]Pr 17:17; 18:24
1:15 [o]Jos 24:14; Jdg 11:24
1:16 [p]2Ki 2:2 [q]Ru 2:11,12
1:17 [r]1Sa 3:17; 25:22; 2Sa 19:13; 2Ki 6:31
1:18 [s]Ac 21:14
1:19 [t]Mt 21:10
1:20 [u]Ex 6:3 [v]ver 13; Job 6:4
1:21 [w]Job 1:21
1:22 [x]Ex 9:31; Ru 2:23 [y]2Sa 21:9

[a] *1* Traditionally *judged* [b] *20 Naomi* means *pleasant*; also in verse 21. [c] *20 Mara* means *bitter.* [d] *20* Hebrew *Shaddai*; also in verse 21 [e] *21* Or *has testified against*

1:1 In ancient times in the region now called Palestine and in Egypt, famines were not infrequent. They were produced by lack of rainfall in due season, destructive hail storms and rain out of season, destruction of crops by locusts and caterpillars and the cutting off of food supplies by a siege. Pestilence often followed, and the suffering was great. Famines that were the result of natural causes are recorded as occurring during the lives of Abraham (Ge 12:10), Joseph (Ge 41:56), the judges (Ru 1:1), David (2Sa 21:1), Ahab and Elijah (1Ki 17:1; 18:2) and Elisha (2Ki 4:38; Lk 4:25). A famine produced by a siege is mentioned in 2 Kings 6:25, and Nehemiah 5:3 tells of such conditions after the return from the Babylonian captivity. The New Testament speaks of a famine "over the entire Roman world" (Ac 11:28), and Jesus predicted famines in various places (Mt 24:7; Mk 13:8; Lk 21:11), a prophecy believed to have been partly fulfilled in the siege of Jerusalem by Titus and described with harrowing detail by Josephus, who stated that "neither did any other city ever suffer such miseries" (*Wars,* 5.10.5). See "Famine in the Ancient Near East" on page 70.

1:20 In the ancient Near East a person's name was often descriptive (see "Naming of Children" on p. 28).

1:22 In ancient Canaan the harvesting of grain took place in April and May (barley first, with wheat a few weeks later; see 2:23). It involved the following steps:

1. The ripened, standing grain was cut (usually by men) with hand sickles (Dt 16:9; 23:25; Jer 50:16; Joel 3:13).
2. The grain was bound (by men *and* women) into sheaves (Ge 37:7; Job 24:10; Ps 126:6 have masculine subjects, supporting the male role in this step).
3. The stalks of grain left behind were gathered (called "gleaning"; 2:7). The gleanings were to be left to the poor, as in Ruth's case (cf. Lev 23:22).
4. The sheaves were transported to the threshing floor (usually by donkey, sometimes by cart; Am 2:13).
5. The grain was loosened from the straw (called "threshing") by the treading of cattle (Dt 25:4; Hos 10:11), the wheels of carts (Isa 28:28) or toothed threshing sledges (Isa 41:15; Am 1:3).
6. The grain was tossed into the air with winnowing forks (called "winnowing"; Jer 15:7) so that the wind, which usually came up for a few hours in the afternoon, blew away the straw and chaff (Ps 1:4), leaving the grain at the winnower's feet.
7. The grain was sifted (Am 9:9) to remove any foreign matter, such as small stones or refuse gathered with it when it was scooped up from the ground.

Study note continues on next page.

Ruth Meets Boaz

2:1 [z]Ru 3:2,12 2 Now Naomi had a relative[z] on her husband's side, from the clan of Elimelech,[a] a man of standing,
[a]Ru 1:2 [b]Ru 4:21 whose name was Boaz.[b]
2:2 [c]ver 7; 2 And Ruth the Moabitess said to Naomi, "Let me go to the fields and pick up the leftover grain[c] be-
Lev 19:9; 23:22; Dt 24:19 hind anyone in whose eyes I find favor."
Naomi said to her, "Go ahead, my daughter." 3 So she went out and began to glean in the fields behind
the harvesters. As it turned out, she found herself working in a field belonging to Boaz, who was from the
clan of Elimelech.
2:4 [d]Jdg 6:12; Lk 1:28; 2Th 3:16 4 Just then Boaz arrived from Bethlehem and greeted the harvesters, "The LORD be with you![d]"
[e]Ps 129:7-8 "The LORD bless you![e]" they called back.
5 Boaz asked the foreman of his harvesters, "Whose young woman is that?"
2:6 [f]Ru 1:22 6 The foreman replied, "She is the Moabitess[f] who came back from Moab with Naomi. 7 She said, 'Please
let me glean and gather among the sheaves behind the harvesters.' She went into the field and has worked
steadily from morning till now, except for a short rest in the shelter."
8 So Boaz said to Ruth, "My daughter, listen to me. Don't go and glean in another field and don't go
away from here. Stay here with my servant girls. 9 Watch the field where the men are harvesting, and fol-
low along after the girls. I have told the men not to touch you. And whenever you are thirsty, go and get
a drink from the water jars the men have filled."
2:10 [g]1Sa 25:23 10 At this, she bowed down with her face to the ground.[g] She exclaimed, "Why have I found such fa-
[h]Ps 41:1 [i]Dt 15:3 vor in your eyes that you notice me[h]—a foreigner?[i]"
2:11 [j]Ru 1:14 11 Boaz replied, "I've been told all about what you have done for your mother-in-law[j] since the death
[k]Ru 1:16-17 of your husband—how you left your father and mother and your homeland and came to live with a peo-
ple you did not know before.[k] 12 May the LORD repay you for what you have done. May you be richly re-
2:12 [l]1Sa 24:19 warded by the LORD,[l] the God of Israel, under whose wings[m] you have come to take refuge.[n]"
[m]Ps 17:8; 36:7; 57:1; 61:4; 63:7; 13 "May I continue to find favor in your eyes, my lord," she said. "You have given me comfort and have
91:4 [n]Ru 1:16 spoken kindly to your servant—though I do not have the standing of one of your servant girls."
14 At mealtime Boaz said to her, "Come over here. Have some bread and dip it in the wine vinegar."
When she sat down with the harvesters, he offered her some roasted grain. She ate all she wanted and
2:14 [o]ver 18 had some left over.[o] 15 As she got up to glean, Boaz gave orders to his men, "Even if she gathers among the
sheaves, don't embarrass her. 16 Rather, pull out some stalks for her from the bundles and leave them for
her to pick up, and don't rebuke her."
17 So Ruth gleaned in the field until evening. Then she threshed the barley she had gathered, and it
amounted to about an ephah.[a] 18 She carried it back to town, and her mother-in-law saw how much she
2:18 [p]ver 14 had gathered. Ruth also brought out and gave her what she had left over[p] after she had eaten enough.
19 Her mother-in-law asked her, "Where did you glean today? Where did you work? Blessed be the man
2:19 [q]ver 10; Ps 41:1 who took notice of you![q]"
Then Ruth told her mother-in-law about the one at whose place she had been working. "The name of
the man I worked with today is Boaz," she said.

[a] *17* That is, probably about 3/5 bushel (about 22 liters)

---

8. The grain was bagged for transportation and storage (Ge 42–44).

Both threshing and winnowing occurred on the threshing floor. Threshing floors were hard, smooth, open places, prepared on either rock or clay and carefully chosen for favorable exposure to the prevailing winds—usually on the eastern side (i.e., downwind) of the village. See "Food and Agriculture" on page 390 and "The Threshing Floor" on page 608.

2:2 The law (Lev 19:9–10; 23:22; Dt 24:19–21) gave resident aliens, widows and orphans the right to glean, but permission was not guaranteed. Ruth's words here ("behind anyone in whose eyes I find favor") suggest her anxiety. Her social status in the field was tenuous without connection to a male provider.

2:4 Greetings in the Bible sometimes included acts as well as words: a profound obeisance or prostration, a kissing of the hand, kneeling, falling on the neck of another person or embracing. Nearly every situation in life called for its own salutation: the return of a friend from a journey, the birth of a son, a marriage, the wearing of new clothes, dining and the appeals of a beggar. Among the more common salutations upon meetings were the following: "God be gracious to you" (Ge 43:29); "The LORD be with you" (Ru 2:4); "Peace be with you" (Lk 24:36); "Greetings" (Mt 26:49). Because salutations could be time-consuming, when Jesus sent out the Seventy he forbade salutations along the way (Lk 10:4). Salutations were given at partings as well as at meetings: "Go in peace," or "Farewell" (1Sa 1:17; 20:42; 2Sa 15:9; Mk 5:34). The salutations in the apostle Paul's New Testament letters are usually elaborate and of rich spiritual fullness.

2:7 The sheaf was a handful of grain left behind the reaper and then gathered and bound, usually by children or women (2:7,15), who are depicted in Scripture as being in a joyous mood (Ps 126:6; 129:7–8). Thus stacked, the sheaves became dry and inflammable (Zec 12:6) but made a beautiful sight (SS 7:2). A donkey (Ne 13:15) or a heavily loaded cart (Am 2:13) bore these bundles to the threshing floor (Ru 3:6–7; Mic 4:12). Some sheaves, however, were deliberately left behind for the poor (Dt 24:19; cf. Ru 2:7,15; Job 24:10).

2:17 The ephah was a large container holding about 22 liters or .62 bushels. Ruth had gleaned an unusually large amount of barley for one day's gleaning.

Food and Agriculture

Olive press
Preserving Bible Times; © Dr. James C. Martin; permission of Eretz Israel Museum

RUTH 2 As the story of Cain and Abel indicates, the two main sources of food in ancient times were animal husbandry and the cultivation of edible plants. Apart from fishing, the only other way to obtain food was through hunting and gathering wild food; a society that had to rely exclusively on hunting and gathering was either very primitive or in a dire situation (cf. Isa 7:18–25). Farming is already attested at sites from the Egyptian **Neolithic period**.[1,2]

Ruth 2–3 reflects the annual cycle of planting and harvesting various crops in Israel.[3] The agricultural year is also reflected in Israel's annual festivals (such as Firstfruits and Pentecost),[4] as well as in the Gezer Calendar.[5] Plowing and the planting of grains (wheat and barley) began after the "early" or autumn rains in October through November. Plants would grow through the heavy winter rains and the "latter," or spring, rains. At harvest (April–May), workers would cut the grain with sickles and bind them into sheaves. After the harvest the grain would be taken to threshing floors, where threshing sledges would separate it from the chaff.[6] The time of winnowing was also a time for celebration, since the task indicated that a successful harvest had been brought in (Ru 3:7; Isa 9:3). Once the grain was winnowed it was stored in silos. Using millstones, women ground the harvested grain into flour.

Other crops had their own routines and seasons. Olive trees grow in the thin soil of Israel's hills, but they take many years to mature and bear fruit only every other year. Olives were pressed under heavy weights and the oil extruded into vats, with several pressings of a single batch yielding several different grades of olive oil. Other important crops were date palms, pomegranates, figs and apples (some scholars deny that ancient Israel had apples, but this fruit was widely known in the ancient world and frequently appears in classical artwork).

Viniculture was vitally important in ancient Israel. Vineyards were of great value and had to be protected. Both Greek and Hebrew sources describe how young people were given the task of keeping foxes away from the grapes (SS 2:15), and Isaiah 5:2 notes that a wise vintner would erect a watchtower in his vineyard. Grapes ripened in June or July, and the vintage season carried through to September. At harvest, grape bunches were cut off the vines with pruning knives, and people would press out the grapes in vats, using their bare feet.[7] Other methods of pressing out grapes are attested in the ancient world as well; there is evidence from Egypt of a method of twisting linen sheets to press out and filter grape juice. The juice was made into wine, the primary beverage of ancient Israel. Egyptians preferred beer.[8]

For the Israelite, the choice of edible meats was governed by the rules of cleanness (Lev 11; Dt 14).[9] In brief, sheep, goats, cattle, certain birds (e.g., doves and geese) and fish with fins and scales were considered ritually clean. Chickens are not mentioned in the Bible until the New Testament (e.g., Mt 23:37, although Pr 30:31 may refer to a rooster), but archaeological evidence suggests that they were in fact eaten in ancient Israel. Pigs, of course, were declared ritually unclean, but outside of Israel swine herding was common. On the basis of statements from certain classical Greek writers, some have argued that the Egyptians did not eat pork, but archaeological evidence suggests that at least some did.

[1]See Glossary on page 2080 for definitions of bolded words. [2]See "Archaeological Periods" chart on page xx in the front of this Bible. [3]See "The Jewish Calendar" on page 241. [4]See "The Festivals of Israel" on page 186. [5]See "The Gezer Calendar" on page 913. [6]See "The Threshing Floor" on page 608. [7]See "The Winepress" on page 1171. [8]See "Wine and Alcoholic Beverages in the Ancient World" on page 2015. [9]See "Clean and Unclean Foods in the Bible and the Ancient Near East" on page 168.

Basalt millstone
Preserving Bible Times; © Dr. James C. Martin; permission of Eretz Israel Museum

2:20 [r]Ru 3:10; 2Sa 2:5; Pr 17:17 [s]Ru 3:9,12; 4:1, 14

20 “The LORD bless him!” Naomi said to her daughter-in-law. “He has not stopped showing his kindness[r] to
the living and the dead.” She added, “That man is our close relative; he is one of our kinsman-redeemers.[s]”
21 Then Ruth the Moabitess said, “He even said to me, ‘Stay with my workers until they finish harvest-
ing all my grain.’ ”
22 Naomi said to Ruth her daughter-in-law, “It will be good for you, my daughter, to go with his girls,
because in someone else’s field you might be harmed.”

2:23 [t]Dt 16:9

23 So Ruth stayed close to the servant girls of Boaz to glean until the barley and wheat harvests[t] were
finished. And she lived with her mother-in-law.

Ruth and Boaz at the Threshing Floor

3:1 [u]Ru 1:9
3:2 [v]Dt 25:5-10; Ru 2:1
3:3 [w]2Sa 14:2

3 One day Naomi her mother-in-law said to her, “My daughter, should I not try to find a home[a][u] for
you, where you will be well provided for? 2 Is not Boaz, with whose servant girls you have been, a
kinsman[v] of ours? Tonight he will be winnowing barley on the threshing floor. 3 Wash and perfume your-
self,[w] and put on your best clothes. Then go down to the threshing floor, but don’t let him know you are
there until he has finished eating and drinking. 4 When he lies down, note the place where he is lying.
Then go and uncover his feet and lie down. He will tell you what to do.”

3:5 [x]Eph 6:1; Col 3:20

5 “I will do whatever you say,”[x] Ruth answered. 6 So she went down to the threshing floor and did ev-
erything her mother-in-law told her to do.

3:7 [y]Jdg 19:6,9, 22; 2Sa 13:28; 1Ki 21:7; Est 1:10

7 When Boaz had finished eating and drinking and was in good spirits,[y] he went over to lie down
at the far end of the grain pile. Ruth approached quietly, uncovered his feet and lay down. 8 In the

[a] *1* Hebrew *find rest* (see Ruth 1:9)

3:1–4 Naomi saw and seized an opportunity, counseling Ruth to take the initiative to encourage Boaz to act upon the principle of the kinsman-redeemer and to marry her (see Dt 25:5–10). The symbolic change in Ruth’s appearance would signal to Boaz both her availability and her serious intentions. Uncovering a man’s feet and lying down constituted a customary, nonverbal means of requesting marriage. But these actions were not without risk.

3:4–7 The threshing floor was typically made of clay soil packed to a hard, smooth surface. Sheaves of grain were spread on the floor and trampled by oxen, often drawing crude wooden sleds with notched rims (Dt 25:4; Isa 28:27; 1Co 9:9). A shovel and fan were used in winnowing the grain (Isa 30:24). Since robbers would sometimes visit the floor at threshing time (1Sa 23:1), the laborers slept there. Threshing floors were often located on hills where the night winds could more easily blow away the chaff. See the note on 2:7; see also “The Threshing Floor” on page 608 and “Food and Agriculture” on page 390.

The Kinsman-Redeemer

RUTH 3 In ancient Israelite society the following well-defined legal obligations fell to the next of kin, known as the *(go’el)* or “kinsman-redeemer”:

✣ *Redemption of property* (Nu 27:8–11). Family lands could not be permanently sold out of family possession. A destitute relative could sell inheritance land to pay debtors, but landless people were effectively reduced to servitude. It fell to the go’el to redeem lands and family members by payment of outstanding debts. Where no go’el existed, the land could be sold outside the family, eventually reverting back in the Jubilee year.[1]

✣ *Levirate marriage* (Dt 25:5–10). In the event of the death of a man without an heir, a surviving brother was obligated to redeem (i.e., marry) the widow and raise up an heir for the deceased. This implied a financial and emotional commitment that not all brothers were willing to undertake. The go’el could seek legal exemption from the obligation, but such exemption was considered a dereliction of duty and involved considerable disgrace.[2]

✣ *Vengeance for the wrongful death of a family member* (Nu 35:9–21). In a society lacking a standing police force, the responsibility for executing a death sentence for the murder of a family member would fall to the *go’el haddam* or “avenger of blood (guilt).” Mosaic Law prohibited indiscriminate vengeance, allowing the accused to flee to a city of refuge, where his case would be evaluated by the city elders.[3] However, no mercy was shown to those who had deliberately committed murder.

[1]See “Sabbath, Sabbath Year and the Jubilee” on page 189. [2]See “Levirate Marriage” on page 64. [3]See “Cities of Refuge” on page 334.

middle of the night something startled the man, and he turned and discovered a woman lying at his
feet.
[9]"Who are you?" he asked.
"I am your servant Ruth," she said. "Spread the corner of your garment[z] over me, since you are a kins-
man-redeemer.[a]"
[10]"The LORD bless you, my daughter," he replied. "This kindness is greater than that which you showed
earlier: You have not run after the younger men, whether rich or poor. [11]And now, my daughter, don't be
afraid. I will do for you all you ask. All my fellow townsmen know that you are a woman of noble char-
acter.[b] [12]Although it is true that I am near of kin, there is a kinsman-redeemer[c] nearer than[d] I. [13]Stay
here for the night, and in the morning if he wants to redeem,[e] good; let him redeem. But if he is not will-
ing, as surely as the LORD lives[f] I will do it. Lie here until morning."

3:9 [z]Eze 16:8 [a]ver 12; Ru 2:20
3:11 [b]Pr 12:4; 31:10
3:12 [c]ver 9 [d]Ru 4:1
3:13 [e]Dt 25:5; Ru 4:5; Mt 22:24 [f]Jdg 8:19; Jer 4:2

3:9 Levirate law required a brother-in-law to marry his widowed sister-in-law in the event that his brother had died and left her childless (see "Levirate Marriage" on p. 64). If the deceased husband had no brothers (1:10–13), or if they declined to fulfill their duty (Ge 38), other relatives might elect to assume the responsibility. Ruth's request was an appeal to Boaz's kinsman obligation (see "The Kinsman-Redeemer" on p. 391). The garment covering was symbolic of entering a marriage relationship (see Eze 16:8); a similar custom is still practiced in some parts of the Middle East today.

3:12–13 The Hebrew word *go'el* has a two-sided application of its basic meaning. At heart it is an exceedingly gracious word: It refers to the "next of kin" who possesses the right to take upon himself whatever need may have overwhelmed his kinsman or kinswoman. We see this at its human best here in the book of Ruth (3:12–13; 4:2–10) and at its highest when the Lord himself is called our *go'el* (Isa 43:14). But there is a darker side, having to do with exacting the vengeance demanded by the law for a crime (see, e.g., Ex 21:23–24; Lev 24:20; Nu 35:11–34; Dt 19:21). The dual functions of the *go'el* are epitomized in two starkly opposite and seemingly contradictory terms: *redeemer* (see "The Kinsman Redeemer" on p. 391) and *avenger.*

Boaz could marry Ruth only after the nearer kinsman had declined the privilege—or the duty. The other most likely refused because if he were to have married Ruth and had a son with her, a portion of his property would have gone to the credit of Elimelech's posterity rather than to his own by a former marriage.

CULTURAL AND HISTORICAL NOTES

The City Gate

RUTH 4 The city gate played a key role in the city's defensive structure. In fact, "to possess the gate" of a city was to possess the city itself (Ge 24:60).[1] The role of such a gate, however, also extended to the economic, legal and civic spheres of life. In **Mesopotamia**, neighborhoods based upon kin or craft may have been organized around the various city gates. Markets, as well as various legal proceedings, were held by the gates (2Ki 7:1). For example, Abraham purchased the cave of Machpelah[2] (Ge 23:3ff.) at a city gate, and Boaz was granted the right to obtain both real property and Ruth as a wife at such a location (Ru 4:1ff.). Kings frequently held public audiences there, and prophets addressed both royalty and commoners at these gates (2Sa 19:8; 1Ki 22:10; Jer 17:19). At Tel Dan, excavations inside the outer gate complex have uncovered a raised platform for the canopied seat of a king or judge, as well as a bench for the elders. This arrangement illustrates the Biblical descriptions of legal cases being brought before the elders (Dt 22:15; 25:7) and judgments being carried out (Dt 17:5; 22:24) at such a location. To sit in the city gate among the elders (Job 29:7–8; Pr 31:23) denoted honor, while the right to enter a gate indicated citizenship (Ge 23:10,18), even in the new Jerusalem (Rev 22:14).

Seat at the gate at Dan

Preserving Bible Times; © Dr. James C. Martin

[1]See "The Ancient City" on page 1790. [2]See "The Cave of Machpelah" on page 38.

14 So she lay at his feet until morning, but got up before anyone could be recognized; and he said, "Don't
3:14 [g]Ro 14:16; 2Co 8:21 let it be known that a woman came to the threshing floor."[g]
15 He also said, "Bring me the shawl you are wearing and hold it out." When she did so, he poured into
it six measures of barley and put it on her. Then he[a] went back to town.
16 When Ruth came to her mother-in-law, Naomi asked, "How did it go, my daughter?"
Then she told her everything Boaz had done for her 17 and added, "He gave me these six measures of
barley, saying, 'Don't go back to your mother-in-law empty-handed.' "
18 Then Naomi said, "Wait, my daughter, until you find out what happens. For the man will not rest
3:18 [h]Ps 37:3-5 until the matter is settled today."[h]

Boaz Marries Ruth

4 Meanwhile Boaz went up to the town gate and sat there. When the kinsman-redeemer he had men-
4:1 [i]Ru 3:12 tioned[i] came along, Boaz said, "Come over here, my friend, and sit down." So he went over and sat
down.
4:2 [j]1Ki 21:8; Pr 31:23 2 Boaz took ten of the elders[j] of the town and said, "Sit here," and they did so. 3 Then he said to the kins-
man-redeemer, "Naomi, who has come back from Moab, is selling the piece of land that belonged to our
brother Elimelech. 4 I thought I should bring the matter to your attention and suggest that you buy it in the
presence of these seated here and in the presence of the elders of my people. If you will redeem it, do so. But
4:4 [k]Lev 25:25; Jer 32:7-8 if you[b] will not, tell me, so I will know. For no one has the right to do it except you,[k] and I am next in line."
"I will redeem it," he said.
5 Then Boaz said, "On the day you buy the land from Naomi and from Ruth the Moabitess, you ac-
4:5 [l]Ge 38:8; Dt 25:5-6; Ru 3:13; Mt 22:24 quire[c] the dead man's widow, in order to maintain the name of the dead with his property."[l]
6 At this, the kinsman-redeemer said, "Then I cannot redeem[m] it because I might endanger my own
4:6 [m]Lev 25:25; Ru 3:13 estate. You redeem it yourself. I cannot do it."
7 (Now in earlier times in Israel, for the redemption and transfer of property to become final, one par-
4:7 [n]Dt 25:7-9 ty took off his sandal and gave it to the other. This was the method of legalizing transactions in Israel.)[n]
8 So the kinsman-redeemer said to Boaz, "Buy it yourself." And he removed his sandal.
9 Then Boaz announced to the elders and all the people, "Today you are witnesses that I have bought
from Naomi all the property of Elimelech, Kilion and Mahlon. 10 I have also acquired Ruth the Moabit-
ess, Mahlon's widow, as my wife, in order to maintain the name of the dead with his property, so that his
4:10 [o]Dt 25:6 name will not disappear from among his family or from the town records.[o] Today you are witnesses!"
4:11 [p]Dt 25:9 [q]Ps 127:3; 128:3 [r]Ge 35:16 11 Then the elders and all those at the gate said, "We are witnesses.[p] May the LORD make the woman
who is coming into your home like Rachel and Leah,[q] who together built up the house of Israel. May you
have standing in Ephrathah[r] and be famous in Bethlehem. 12 Through the offspring the LORD gives you
4:12 [s]ver 18; Ge 38:29 by this young woman, may your family be like that of Perez,[s] whom Tamar bore to Judah."

The Genealogy of David

13 So Boaz took Ruth and she became his wife. Then he went to her, and the LORD enabled her to con-
4:13 [t]Ge 29:31; 33:5; Ru 3:11 ceive,[t] and she gave birth to a son. 14 The women[u] said to Naomi: "Praise be to the LORD, who this day has
4:14 [u]Lk 1:58 not left you without a kinsman-redeemer. May he become famous throughout Israel! 15 He will renew
your life and sustain you in your old age. For your daughter-in-law, who loves you and who is better to
4:15 [v]Ru 1:16-17; 2:11-12; 1Sa 1:8 you than seven sons,[v] has given him birth."
16 Then Naomi took the child, laid him in her lap and cared for him. 17 The women living there said,
4:17 [w]ver 22; 1Sa 16:1,18; 1Ch 2:12,13 "Naomi has a son." And they named him Obed. He was the father of Jesse,[w] the father of David.

[a] *15* Most Hebrew manuscripts; many Hebrew manuscripts, Vulgate and Syriac *she* [b] *4* Many Hebrew manuscripts, Septuagint, Vulgate and Syriac; most Hebrew manuscripts *he* [c] *5* Hebrew; Vulgate and Syriac *Naomi, you acquire Ruth the Moabitess,*

4:1–3 There are two possible explanations for Boaz's terminology that Naomi was "selling" the field. She may have owned the land but been so poor that she had been forced to sell it. Through Boaz, Naomi was appealing for a kinsman to purchase back the land and keep it in the family. It seems more likely that Naomi's husband had sold it (to an unnamed third party) before leaving for Moab. The land of a family or clan could not be sold permanently (Lev 25:23–28), so Naomi had the right to buy it back. Unable to do so, she transferred this right or obligation to her nearest kinsman. In this case, Naomi would have been "selling" the right of redemption.

4:2 Ten elders comprised a full court for legal proceedings.

4:7 Taking off one's sandal and giving it to another was a public way of renouncing one's property rights and transferring them to another (cf. Am 2:6; 8:6). The Nuzi documents (Akkadian, mid-second millennium B.C.) refer to a similar custom.

4:12 Perez was Boaz's ancestor (vv. 18–21). His birth to Judah was from a union based on the levirate practice (Ge 38:27–30; see also "Levirate Marriage" on p. 64). Perez was therefore an appropriate model within Boaz's ancestry for the blessing the elders gave to Boaz.

[18]This, then, is the family line of Perez[x]:

Perez was the father of Hezron,
[19]Hezron the father of Ram,
Ram the father of Amminadab,[y]
[20]Amminadab the father of Nahshon,
Nahshon the father of Salmon,[a]
[21]Salmon the father of Boaz,[z]
Boaz the father of Obed,
[22]Obed the father of Jesse,
and Jesse the father of David.

[a] *20* A few Hebrew manuscripts, some Septuagint manuscripts and Vulgate (see also verse 21 and Septuagint of 1 Chron. 2:11); most Hebrew manuscripts *Salma*

4:18 [x]Mt 1:3-6
4:19 [y]Ex 6:23
4:21 [z]Ru 2:1

INTRODUCTION TO *1 Samuel*

AUTHOR, PLACE AND DATE OF WRITING

We do not know who wrote 1 and 2 Samuel, which were named after the judge and prophet God used to establish Israel's monarchy. Originally these now separated sections comprised one book, which was divided into two parts by the translators of the Septuagint (early Greek translation of the OT). Based upon the wide span of history covered in 1 and 2 Samuel—from the days of Eli (1Sa 1) to the end of David's reign (2Sa 24)—we know that no single writer or compiler could have been alive to record all of this information based upon direct knowledge.

Some features of 1 Samuel suggest that several independent, unedited sources, including firsthand accounts, were used, possibly at times verbatim, in the authors' compositions. Scholars sometimes speak of the "Succession Narrative" (2Sa 9–1Ki 2) as being a single-source document, but this viewpoint is debated. The writers/compilers certainly referenced the historical records of Samuel, Saul and David.

The book of 1 Samuel (as well as its various sources) was evidently written between the end of David's life and some point during Solomon's reign. We cannot pinpoint exact dates because the data is insufficient to build a precise chronology. David's birth and the length of his reign are certain (cf. 2Sa 5:4–5), but most other dates are not—including that of Saul's ascension to the throne and the end of his reign. Adding to these chronological challenges is the lack of dates for Samuel's birth and death. To complicate the situation still further, the editors/compilers of 1 Samuel did not always arrange their material in strict chronological sequence. The following proposed dates provide a helpful framework:

- Birth of Samuel, about 1105 B.C.
- Birth of Saul, about 1080 B.C.
- Birth of David, 1040 B.C.
- David anointed to be Saul's successor, about 1025 B.C.
- End of David's reign, 970 B.C.

AUDIENCE

The original audience of 1 Samuel consisted of the Israelites who lived during the reigns of David and Solomon, as well as of their successive generations. The stories in this book spoke most directly to Israelites who lived while the monarchy was being established, particularly in light of the fact that the account legitimized God's choice of David (16:13).

CULTURAL FACTS AND HIGHLIGHTS

During this period (c. the eleventh century B.C.) no superpower overshadowed the region now known as Palestine. Consequently, led by David, Israel used its opportunities to subdue other nations in Canaan. The Philistines, however, who lived in the coastal areas along the Mediterranean Sea, proved to be a resilient and persistent enemy. The book of 1 Samuel introduces Samuel and goes on to explore the tension between covenant loyalty to God and human kingship. King Saul generally disobeyed God, so God set plans in motion for David to become Israel's next king.

TIMELINE

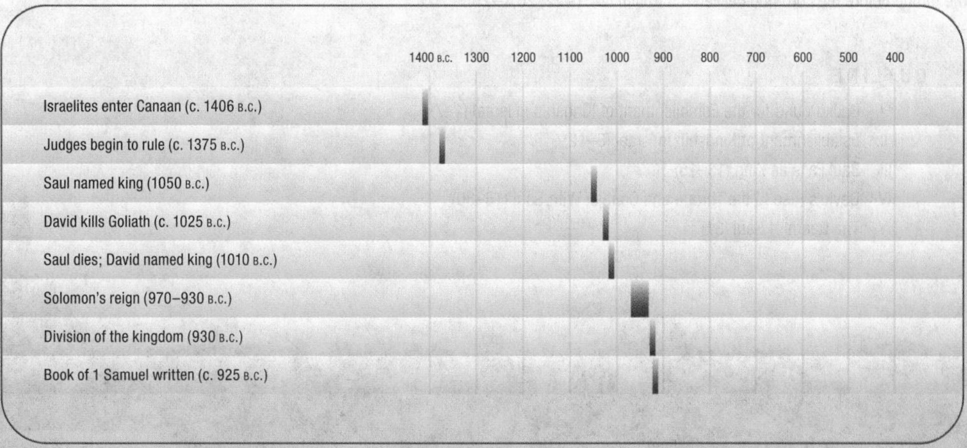

AS YOU READ

Watch events unfold as God answered Hannah's devout prayer and then used her son Samuel to facilitate Israel's transition from God's direct covenant rule to a political system led by a human king as his representative. Notice the give-and-take between God and the people, who wanted a king like other nations. Samuel—the divinely ordained leader, prophet, priest and judge—played a key role in establishing kingship, despite his warning Israel of the inevitable negative consequences of her choice. Visualize this unrelenting servant of God urging the people to keep up their covenant obligations and emphasizing that King Saul and all future kings were to be under God's direct authority and law.

Follow David's long, circuitous and difficult journey to the throne. Notice his unwavering loyalty to God; to Saul, Israel's ordained king; and to Saul's son Jonathan, David's best friend and the apparent crown prince.

DID YOU KNOW?

- The ancient Greeks, to whom the Philistines were apparently related, sometimes decided issues of war through chosen champions who met in combat between the armies. This "trial by battle ordeal" was based upon the belief that the gods of each army actually fought or decided the battle (17:4).
- Using the normal conventions of Hebrew poetry—in which 10,000 was typically used as the parallel for 1,000—the phrase "David his tens of thousands" was the women's way of saying, "Saul and David have slain thousands" (18:7).
- Priests and diviners were sometimes forced, under penalty of death, to take oaths of loyalty to the king, committing to serve as his informants (22:9–18).
- Grasping the hem of a garment symbolized loyalty, but cutting off a piece of a person's robe signified disloyalty and rebellion (24:4–5).

THEMES

First Samuel includes the following themes:

1. *Kingship.* For Israel, kingship held great promise, as well as tremendous danger. The wrong type of king might plunder the very people he was supposed to support, protect and help (8:10–18). More importantly, he might turn the people's hearts from their covenant relationship with God (8:7). First Samuel demonstrates that human leaders are not the most powerful force in the universe. God, the sovereign King, can remove his human representatives to protect the well-being of his people, as evidenced in the decline of Saul and the rise of David.

2. *Obedience.* For Israel, a king was not autonomous in authority and power but was an instrument of God's rule (12:14–15; 15:11,20). First Samuel emphasizes that obedience, not ritual or tradition, pleases God (15:22). All leaders are flawed, but wholehearted devotion to the Lord is an essential characteristic of any godly leader (13:14).

3. *Friendship and loyalty.* David and Jonathan maintained a friendship that withstood tremendous forces. Jonathan would have been king had Saul not been rejected by God for his disobedience. And David would logically have been Jonathan's rival. Yet despite Saul's campaign of terror against David, Jonathan remained true to their friendship, protecting David from his father's wrath and repeated plots on his life (18:1–4; 19:1–10; 20:1–42). David in turn remained loyal not only to Jonathan but also to King Saul, not attempting to assume the throne before the Lord had delivered it to him (24:1–22; 26:1–25).

OUTLINE

I. Background for the Establishment of Kingship in Israel (1–7)
II. Establishment of Kingship in Israel (8–12)
III. Saul Fails as King (13–15)
IV. David's Rise to the Throne and Conflict With Saul (16–30)
V. The Death of Saul (31)

The Birth of Samuel

1 There was a certain man from Ramathaim, a Zuphite[a] from the hill country[a] of Ephraim, whose name was Elkanah[b] son of Jeroham, the son of Elihu, the son of Tohu, the son of Zuph, an Ephraimite. 2 He had two wives;[c] one was called Hannah and the other Peninnah. Peninnah had children, but Hannah had none.

3 Year after year[d] this man went up from his town to worship[e] and sacrifice to the LORD Almighty at Shiloh,[f] where Hophni and Phinehas, the two sons of Eli, were priests of the LORD. 4 Whenever the day came for Elkanah to sacrifice,[g] he would give portions of the meat to his wife Peninnah and to all her sons and daughters. 5 But to Hannah he gave a double portion because he loved her, and the LORD had closed her womb.[h] 6 And because the LORD had closed her womb, her rival kept provoking her in order to irritate her.[i] 7 This went on year after year. Whenever Hannah went up to the house of the LORD, her rival provoked her till she wept and would not eat. 8 Elkanah her husband would say to her, "Hannah, why are you weeping? Why don't you eat? Why are you downhearted? Don't I mean more to you than ten sons?[j]"

9 Once when they had finished eating and drinking in Shiloh, Hannah stood up. Now Eli the priest was sitting on a chair by the doorpost of the LORD's temple.[b][k] 10 In bitterness of soul[l] Hannah wept much and prayed to the LORD. 11 And she made a vow, saying, "O LORD Almighty, if you will only look upon your servant's misery and remember[m] me, and not forget your servant but give her a son, then I will give him to the LORD for all the days of his life, and no razor[n] will ever be used on his head."

12 As she kept on praying to the LORD, Eli observed her mouth. 13 Hannah was praying in her heart, and her lips were moving but her voice was not heard. Eli thought she was drunk 14 and said to her, "How long will you keep on getting drunk? Get rid of your wine."

15 "Not so, my lord," Hannah replied, "I am a woman who is deeply troubled. I have not been drinking wine or beer; I was pouring[o] out my soul to the LORD. 16 Do not take your servant for a wicked woman; I have been praying here out of my great anguish and grief."

17 Eli answered, "Go in peace,[p] and may the God of Israel grant you what you have asked of him.[q]"

18 She said, "May your servant find favor in your eyes.[r]" Then she went her way and ate something, and her face was no longer downcast.[s]

19 Early the next morning they arose and worshiped before the LORD and then went back to their home at Ramah. Elkanah lay with Hannah his wife, and the LORD remembered[t] her. 20 So in the course of time Hannah conceived and gave birth to a son. She named[u] him Samuel,[c] saying, "Because I asked the LORD for him."

Hannah Dedicates Samuel

21 When the man Elkanah went up with all his family to offer the annual[v] sacrifice to the LORD and to fulfill his vow,[w] 22 Hannah did not go. She said to her husband, "After the boy is weaned, I will take him and present[x] him before the LORD, and he will live there always."

23 "Do what seems best to you," Elkanah her husband told her. "Stay here until you have weaned him; only may the LORD make good[y] his[d] word." So the woman stayed at home and nursed her son until she had weaned him.

24 After he was weaned, she took the boy with her, young as he was, along with a three-year-old bull,[e][z] an ephah[f] of flour and a skin of wine, and brought him to the house of the LORD at Shiloh. 25 When they had slaughtered the bull, they brought the boy to Eli, 26 and she said to him, "As surely as you live, my lord, I am the woman who stood here beside you praying to the LORD. 27 I prayed[a] for this child, and the LORD has granted me what I asked of him. 28 So now I give him to the LORD. For his whole life[b] he will be given over to the LORD." And he worshiped the LORD there.

1:1 aJos 17:17-18 b1Ch 6:27,34
1:2 cDt 21:15-17; Lk 2:36
1:3 dver 21; Ex 23:14; 34:23; Lk 2:41 eDt 12:5-7 fJos 18:1
1:4 gDt 12:17-18
1:5 hGe 16:1; 30:2
1:6 iJob 24:21
1:8 jRu 4:15
1:9 k1Sa 3:3
1:10 lJob 7:11
1:11 mGe 8:1; 28:20; 29:32 nNu 6:1-21; Jdg 13:5
1:15 oPs 42:4; 62:8; La 2:19
1:17 pJdg 18:6; 1Sa 25:35; 2Ki 5:19; Mk 5:34 qPs 20:3-5
1:18 rRu 2:13 sEcc 9:7; Ro 15:13
1:19 tGe 4:1; 30:22
1:20 uGe 41:51-52; Ex 2:10,22; Mt 1:21
1:21 vver 3 wDt 12:11
1:22 xver 11,28; Lk 2:22
1:23 yver 17; Nu 30:7
1:24 zNu 15:8-10; Dt 12:5; Jos 18:1
1:27 aver 11-13; Ps 66:19-20
1:28 bver 11,22; Ge 24:26,52

a *1* Or *from Ramathaim Zuphim* *b* *9* That is, tabernacle *c* *20* *Samuel* sounds like the Hebrew for *heard of God.*
d *23* Masoretic Text; Dead Sea Scrolls, Septuagint and Syriac *your* *e* *24* Dead Sea Scrolls, Septuagint and Syriac; Masoretic Text *with three bulls* *f* *24* That is, probably about 3/5 bushel (about 22 liters)

1:3 The tabernacle was erected at Shiloh, making Shiloh Israel's religious center for over 300 years (Jos 18:1; see "The Tabernacle at Shiloh" on p. 401). Shiloh ceased to exist after its destruction by the Philistines in the early eleventh century B.C. (see "The Destruction of Shiloh" on p. 1200).

1:17 For a discussion of salutations in the Bible, see the note on Ruth 2:4.

1:22 It was customary in the Near East to nurse children for three years or longer (2Mc 7:27, an Apocryphal book) since there was no way to keep milk sweet.

Israelite Shrines and Worship Before the Temple of Solomon

1 SAMUEL 1 Following the conquest,[1] Israelite worship was conducted at the tabernacle at Shiloh[2] ("Map 4"). This was in keeping with the laws of the sanctuary given in Deuteronomy 12:5,13–14. However, in the books of Joshua through 1 Chronicles at least 20 local shrines, altars or high places are mentioned as pre-Solomonic places of worship, with roughly one-third of these referred to in 1 Samuel.[3] The Israelites did at times follow **Canaanite**[4] cultic practices, worshiping the local Baals and Ashteroths (cf. Jdg 3:7).[5] Canaanite worship at local shrines involved the erection of sacred pillars representing the deities; the planting of sacred trees; engagement in sacrifice, feasting and ritualized prostitution (cf. Ge 38:21; 1Ki 14:24);[6] and participation in pilgrimages to cult sites. Human sacrifice was practiced as well.[7] Did worship at Israelite high places differ? It often did, and it is important to realize that not all of the outlying shrines were illicit or pagan.

After the apparent destruction of Shiloh[8] the Israelites returned to traditional custom, worshiping God at local, open-air cult sites as the **patriarchs** had done (cf., e.g., Ge 12:6–8; 26:23–25; 28:10–22). The Baals and Ashteroth were removed, God alone was worshiped (1Sa 7:3–4) and the grossly pagan features of Canaanite worship were absent. Israelite worship included pilgrimage, the offering of sacrifices and libations, feasting (cf. 9:12–24), musical praise (cf. 10:5) and prayer and fasting (cf. 7:5–6). Sites were probably chosen as places of worship on the basis of associations with the patriarchs or on their connection to great moments in Israel's history or prior appearances of the Lord. The presence of the ark of the covenant lent sanctity to some sites (cf. 2Sa 6:12ff.), as did the tabernacle to others (cf. 1Sa 21:4–6; 1Ch 16:39; 21:29).[9] Common to all Israelite high places was an altar, but some sites had other associated structures as well (cf. 1Sa 9:22).[10] Prior to the construction of the temple in Jerusalem, worship at local shrines was common practice among the Israelites.

Shrine from Hazor, c. fourteenth century B.C., showing a lion orthostat, stelae, statue and offering table
Preserving Bible Times; © Dr. James C. Martin; permission of The Israel Museum

The multiplicity of shrines in early Israel helps us to make sense of the apparently contradictory rules concerning worship that we find in the law. On the one hand, we see frequent reference to the central sanctuary as "the place the LORD your God will choose as a dwelling for his Name" (e.g., Dt 12:11). We also see clear indication that the line of Aaron was the only legitimate priestly line; all other Levites were subordinates who were entrusted with sanctuary duties but did not serve as priests (e.g., Nu 18:1–7,21–24). On the other hand, some texts seem to imply that all Levites had priestly authority (Jdg 17:13).

The solution lies in the fact that Israel did have one central shrine, the place where the ark of the covenant resided and where the priests of Aaron's line officiated. This shrine was first at Shiloh and later at Jerusalem. However, most people could not make frequent trips there, and thus there were numerous other sites throughout Israel where the people could worship routinely. Any Levite—but only a Levite—it appears, could serve as a priest at one of these outlying shrines. However, if a Levite came to the central shrine, he could perform only subordinate duties (could not wear the priestly vestments or assume the duties of the Aaronic priests).[11]

[1]See "The Conquest of Canaan" on page 310. [2]See "The Tabernacle at Shiloh" on page 401. [3]See "The High Place at Dan" on page 504 and "The High Places" on page 1318. [4]See Glossary on page 2080 for definitions of bolded words. [5]See "Baal and the Fertility Cults" on page 1414, "The Ugaritic Text of the Myth of Baal" on page 284, "Devotion to Asherah in the Khirbet El-Qom Inscription" on page 638 and "The Kuntillet Ajrûd Inscriptions: The Lord's Asherah?" on page 1220. [6]See "Prostitution in the Ancient World" on page 284. [7]See "Human Sacrifice in the Ancient Near East" on page 182. [8]See "The Destruction of Shiloh" on page 401. [9]See "The Tabernacle and the Ark" on page 153. [10]See "Ancient Altars" on page 125. [11]See "The Levites and the Priests" on page 648.

Hannah's Prayer

2:1 [c]Lk 1:46-55 [d]Ps 9:14; 13:5 [e]Ps 89:17,24; 92:10; Isa 12:2-3

2 Then Hannah prayed and said:[c]

"My heart rejoices[d] in the LORD;
in the LORD my horn[a][e] is lifted high.
My mouth boasts over my enemies,
for I delight in your deliverance.

2:2 [f]Ex 15:11; Lev 19:2 [g]Dt 32:30-31; 2Sa 22:2,32

2 "There is no one holy[b][f] like the LORD;
there is no one besides you;
there is no Rock[g] like our God.

2:3 [h]Pr 8:13 [i]1Sa 16:7; 1Ki 8:39 [j]Pr 16:2; 24:11-12

3 "Do not keep talking so proudly
or let your mouth speak such arrogance,[h]
for the LORD is a God who knows,
and by him deeds[i] are weighed.[j]

2:4 [k]Ps 37:15

4 "The bows of the warriors are broken,[k]
but those who stumbled are armed with strength.
5 Those who were full hire themselves out for food,
but those who were hungry hunger no more.

2:5 [l]Ps 113:9; Jer 15:9

She who was barren[l] has borne seven children,
but she who has had many sons pines away.

2:6 [m]Dt 32:39 [n]Isa 26:19

6 "The LORD brings death and makes alive;[m]
he brings down to the grave[c] and raises up.[n]

2:7 [o]Dt 8:18 [p]Job 5:11; Ps 75:7

7 The LORD sends poverty and wealth;[o]
he humbles and he exalts.[p]

[a] *1 Horn* here symbolizes strength; also in verse 10. [b] *2* Or *no Holy One* [c] *6* Hebrew *Sheol*

2:6 The "grave" was Sheol, believed to be the dark underworld of the dead (see "Sheol, Hades, Gehenna, the Abyss and Tartarus: Images of Hell" on p. 946).

The Ephod

1 SAMUEL 2 The ephod was a sacral garment, either a simple linen uniform worn by all priests in service to the Lord (1Sa 2:28) or the more elaborate apparel of the high priest (Ex 28:6). The ephod of ordinary priests was of white linen (1Sa 22:18), a material preferred by all priesthoods of the ancient world because of its association with ritual purity.[1] Ordination of the Israelite Old Testament priesthood involved investiture (a ceremony of installing someone to priestly office, often including the conferring of special garments; see Lev 8:30; Nu 20:26), and thus the privilege of wearing the ephod that was conferred upon the Levites carried a special significance (1Sa 2:28). When David donned a linen ephod to bring the ark to Jerusalem, he did so to emphasize his priestly role before the Lord (2Sa 6:14).

The high priestly ephod was a sleeveless garment similar to an apron, held up by the shoulders and fastened in the back by a belt. Its fabric was an intricate weave of gold, blue, purple and scarlet threads. Hammered gold leaf cords were worked into each individual colored thread so that gold was the predominant material of the ephod's fabrication (Ex 39:3). Yet it was the revelatory nature of this garment that rendered it the most important piece of priestly attire. Hanging from the ephod was the breastplate that contained the Urim and Thummim, oracle stones through which the high priest could determine the will of God.[2] In the hope of receiving an oracle from the Lord, the ephod was often carried into battle (1Sa 23:9; 30:7–8).

[1] See "Ritual Purity in Israel and the Ancient Near East" on page 166. [2] See "The Urim and Thummim" on page 136.

8 He raises[q] the poor from the dust
and lifts the needy from the ash heap;
he seats them with princes
and has them inherit a throne of honor.[r]

"For the foundations[s] of the earth are the LORD's;
upon them he has set the world.
9 He will guard the feet[t] of his saints,
but the wicked will be silenced in darkness.[u]

"It is not by strength[v] that one prevails;
10 those who oppose the LORD will be shattered.[w]
He will thunder[x] against them from heaven;
the LORD will judge[y] the ends of the earth.

"He will give strength[z] to his king
and exalt the horn[a] of his anointed."

11 Then Elkanah went home to Ramah, but the boy ministered[b] before the LORD under Eli the priest.

2:8 [q]Ps 113:7-8 [r]Job 36:7 [s]Job 38:4
2:9 [t]Ps 91:12 [u]Mt 8:12 [v]Ps 33:16-17
2:10 [w]Ps 2:9 [x]Ps 18:13 [y]Ps 96:13 [z]Ps 21:1 [a]Ps 89:24
2:11 [b]ver 18; 1Sa 3:1

Eli's Wicked Sons

12 Eli's sons were wicked men; they had no regard[c] for the LORD. 13 Now it was the practice of the priests with the people that whenever anyone offered a sacrifice and while the meat[d] was being boiled, the servant of the priest would come with a three-pronged fork in his hand. 14 He would plunge it into the pan or kettle or caldron or pot, and the priest would take for himself whatever the fork brought up. This is how they treated all the Israelites who came to Shiloh. 15 But even before the fat was burned, the servant of the priest would come and say to the man who was sacrificing, "Give the priest some meat to roast; he won't accept boiled meat from you, but only raw."

16 If the man said to him, "Let the fat be burned up first, and then take whatever you want," the servant would then answer, "No, hand it over now; if you don't, I'll take it by force."

17 This sin of the young men was very great in the LORD's sight, for they[a] were treating the LORD's offering with contempt.[e]

18 But Samuel was ministering[f] before the LORD—a boy wearing a linen ephod.[g] 19 Each year his mother made him a little robe and took it to him when she went up with her husband to offer the annual[h] sacrifice. 20 Eli would bless Elkanah and his wife, saying, "May the LORD give you children by this woman to take the place of the one she prayed[i] for and gave to the LORD." Then they would go home. 21 And the LORD was gracious to Hannah;[j] she conceived and gave birth to three sons and two daughters. Meanwhile, the boy Samuel grew[k] up in the presence of the LORD.

22 Now Eli, who was very old, heard about everything his sons were doing to all Israel and how they slept with the women[l] who served at the entrance to the Tent of Meeting. 23 So he said to them, "Why do you do such things? I hear from all the people about these wicked deeds of yours. 24 No, my sons; it is not a good report that I hear spreading among the LORD's people. 25 If a man sins against another man, God[b] may mediate for him; but if a man sins against the LORD, who will[m] intercede[n] for him?" His sons, however, did not listen to their father's rebuke, for it was the LORD's will to put them to death.

26 And the boy Samuel continued to grow[o] in stature and in favor with the LORD and with men.

2:12 [c]Jer 2:8; 9:6
2:13 [d]Lev 7:29-34
2:17 [e]Mal 2:7-9
2:18 [f]ver 11; 1Sa 3:1 [g]ver 28
2:19 [h]1Sa 1:3
2:20 [i]1Sa 1:11, 27-28; Lk 2:34
2:21 [j]Ge 21:1 [k]ver 26; Jdg 13:24; 1Sa 3:19; Lk 2:40
2:22 [l]Ex 38:8
2:25 [m]Nu 15:30; Jos 11:20 [n]Dt 1:17; 1Sa 3:14; Heb 10:26
2:26 [o]ver 21; Lk 2:52

Prophecy Against the House of Eli

27 Now a man of God[p] came to Eli and said to him, "This is what the LORD says: 'Did I not clearly reveal myself to your father's house when they were in Egypt under Pharaoh? 28 I chose[q] your father out

2:27 [p]Ex 4:14-16; 1Ki 13:1
2:28 [q]Ex 28:1

[a] 17 Or *men* [b] 25 Or *the judges*

2:9 Travel in ancient Israel was usually undertaken by foot over rocky, dangerous trails (see Ps 91:11–12; 121:3).

2:12–17 Apparently the priests' portion of the fellowship offering was determined by a random thrust of the fork *after* the fat (the Lord's portion) had been burned up (Lev 3:16; 4:10,26,31,35; 7:28,30–31) and while the meat was being boiled (Nu 6:19–20). Eli's sons arrogantly violated that custom and the law.

2:13 Bronze, three-pronged forks have been found in excavations at Gezer (see "Gezer" on p. 588).

2:18 A linen ephod (see "The Ephod" on p. 399) was a priestly garment worn by those who served before the Lord at his sanctuary (see 22:18; 2Sa 6:14). A close-fitting, sleeveless pullover, usually of hip length, it was different from the special ephod worn by the high priest.

2:28 [r]Lev 8:7-8 of all the tribes of Israel to be my priest, to go up to my altar, to burn incense, and to wear an ephod[r]
in my presence. I also gave your father's house all the offerings made with fire by the Israelites. 29 Why
2:29 [s]ver 12-17 [t]Dt 12:5; Mt 10:37 do you[f] scorn my sacrifice and offering[s] that I prescribed for my dwelling?[t] Why do you honor your
sons more than me by fattening yourselves on the choice parts of every offering made by my people
Israel?'

30 "Therefore the LORD, the God of Israel, declares: 'I promised that your house and your father's house
2:30 [u]Ex 29:9 [v]Ps 50:23; 91:15 [w]Mal 2:9 would minister before me forever.[u]' But now the LORD declares: 'Far be it from me! Those who honor me
I will honor,[v] but those who despise[w] me will be disdained. 31 The time is coming when I will cut short
your strength and the strength of your father's house, so that there will not be an old man in your fam-
2:31 [x]1Sa 4:11-18; 22:16-20 ily line[x] 32 and you will see distress in my dwelling. Although good will be done to Israel, in your family
2:32 [y]1Ki 2:26-27; Zec 8:4 line there will never be an old man.[y] 33 Every one of you that I do not cut off from my altar will be spared
only to blind your eyes with tears and to grieve your heart, and all your descendants will die in the prime
of life.

34 " 'And what happens to your two sons, Hophni and Phinehas, will be a sign to you—they will both
2:34 [z]1Sa 4:11 [a]1Ki 13:3 die[z] on the same day.[a] 35 I will raise up for myself a faithful priest,[b] who will do according to what is in
2:35 [b]1Sa 12:3; 1Ki 2:35 [c]1Sa 16:13; 2Sa 7:11,27; 1Ki 11:38 my heart and mind. I will firmly establish his house, and he will minister before my anointed[c] one al-
ways. 36 Then everyone left in your family line will come and bow down before him for a piece of silver
2:36 [d]1Ki 2:27 and a crust of bread and plead, "Appoint me to some priestly office so I can have food to eat.[d]" ' "

[f] 29 The Hebrew is plural.

2:30–36 This prediction of the decimation of Eli's priestly family line was fulfilled, successively, in the death of his sons (4:11), in the massacre of his descendants by Saul at Nob (22:18–19) and in the removal of Abiathar from his priestly office (1Ki 2:26–27).

ARCHAEOLOGICAL SITES

THE TABERNACLE AT SHILOH

1 SAMUEL 3 Shiloh is identifiable from the description in Judges 21:19 and by the name preserved in Arabic form at Khirbet Seilun, 18 miles (29 km) north of Jerusalem. It was the Israelite shrine at which the tabernacle was installed (Jos 18:1).[1] At a yearly festival there the young virgins would dance (Jdg 21:19–21). Elkanah and his family visited Shiloh annually, and Hannah placed the boy Samuel in the care of the priest Eli there (1Sa 1–3). It appears that the Philistines destroyed Shiloh after capturing the ark of the covenant in battle at Ebenezer (4:1—7:2). The city's only mention in later Biblical history is as the hometown of the prophet Ahijah during the reign of Jeroboam I (1Ki 14:4) and as an example of God's judgment on his sanctuary (Ps 78:60; Jer 7:12–14; 26:6).[2]

Archaeological findings correspond quite well to the Biblical record. Work by Danish excavators (1926–1932) and by Bar Ilan University (1981 onward) demonstrate that Shiloh was used as a cultic center by pre-Israelite occupants during the **Middle Bronze Age**.[3] Evidence suggests that its use as a sanctuary continued into the **Late Bronze Age**. This suggests some continuity between pre-Israelite and Israelite usage: A site that had been regarded as sacred prior to the Israelite arrival became the place where the tabernacle remained.

Archaeology can tell us nothing about worship at Shiloh, and no vestiges of the original tabernacle remain. We can only infer the type of worship practiced there from what we read in various Biblical texts, especially 1 Samuel 1. Verse 3 of this chapter suggests that pious Israelites were expected to make at least one annual pilgrimage to the Shiloh shrine, and verse 11 demonstrates that they commonly went there to make a vow. This chapter also indicates that lay people, including women, were able to approach fairly close to the main shrine itself (vv. 9,12). Priests and others who ministered there apparently lived in the immediate vicinity, some even sleeping within its precincts (3:1–3). Women served there, but, tragically, some priests took advantage of their authority and committed immoral acts with them (2:22).

[1]See "Israelite Shrines and Worship Before the Temple of Solomon" on page 398. [2]See "The Destruction of Shiloh" on page 1200. [3]See "Archaeological Periods" chart on page xx in the front of this Bible.

The Lord *Calls Samuel*

3 The boy Samuel ministered[e] before the LORD under Eli. In those days the word of the LORD was rare;[f] there were not many visions.[g]

2 One night Eli, whose eyes[h] were becoming so weak that he could barely see, was lying down in his usual place. 3 The lamp[i] of God had not yet gone out, and Samuel was lying down in the temple[a] of the LORD, where the ark of God was. 4 Then the LORD called Samuel.

Samuel answered, "Here I am.[j]" 5 And he ran to Eli and said, "Here I am; you called me."

But Eli said, "I did not call; go back and lie down." So he went and lay down.

6 Again the LORD called, "Samuel!" And Samuel got up and went to Eli and said, "Here I am; you called me."

"My son," Eli said, "I did not call; go back and lie down."

7 Now Samuel did not yet know the LORD: The word of the LORD had not yet been revealed[k] to him.

8 The LORD called Samuel a third time, and Samuel got up and went to Eli and said, "Here I am; you called me."

Then Eli realized that the LORD was calling the boy. 9 So Eli told Samuel, "Go and lie down, and if he calls you, say, 'Speak, LORD, for your servant is listening.' " So Samuel went and lay down in his place.

10 The LORD came and stood there, calling as at the other times, "Samuel! Samuel!"

Then Samuel said, "Speak, for your servant is listening."

11 And the LORD said to Samuel: "See, I am about to do something in Israel that will make the ears of everyone who hears of it tingle.[l] 12 At that time I will carry out against Eli everything[m] I spoke against his family—from beginning to end. 13 For I told him that I would judge his family forever because of the sin he knew about; his sons made themselves contemptible,[b] and he failed to restrain[n] them. 14 Therefore, I swore to the house of Eli, 'The guilt of Eli's house will never be atoned[o] for by sacrifice or offering.' "

15 Samuel lay down until morning and then opened the doors of the house of the LORD. He was afraid to tell Eli the vision, 16 but Eli called him and said, "Samuel, my son."

Samuel answered, "Here I am."

17 "What was it he said to you?" Eli asked. "Do not hide it from me. May God deal with you, be it ever so severely,[p] if you hide from me anything he told you." 18 So Samuel told him everything, hiding nothing from him. Then Eli said, "He is the LORD; let him do what is good in his eyes."[q]

19 The LORD was with[r] Samuel as he grew[s] up, and he let none[t] of his words fall to the ground. 20 And all Israel from Dan to Beersheba[u] recognized that Samuel was attested as a prophet of the LORD. 21 The LORD continued to appear at Shiloh, and there he revealed[v] himself to Samuel through his word.

4 And Samuel's word came to all Israel.

The Philistines Capture the Ark

Now the Israelites went out to fight against the Philistines. The Israelites camped at Ebenezer,[w] and the Philistines at Aphek.[x] 2 The Philistines deployed their forces to meet Israel, and as the battle spread, Israel was defeated by the Philistines, who killed about four thousand of them on the battlefield. 3 When the soldiers returned to camp, the elders of Israel asked, "Why[y] did the LORD bring defeat upon us today before the Philistines? Let us bring the ark[z] of the LORD's covenant from Shiloh, so that it[c] may go with us and save us from the hand of our enemies."

4 So the people sent men to Shiloh, and they brought back the ark of the covenant of the LORD Almighty, who is enthroned between the cherubim.[a] And Eli's two sons, Hophni and Phinehas, were there with the ark of the covenant of God.

5 When the ark of the LORD's covenant came into the camp, all Israel raised such a great shout[b] that the ground shook. 6 Hearing the uproar, the Philistines asked, "What's all this shouting in the Hebrew camp?"

3:1 [e] 1Sa 2:11 [f] Ps 74:9 [g] Am 8:11
3:2 [h] 1Sa 4:15
3:3 [i] Lev 24:1-4
3:4 [j] Isa 6:8
3:7 [k] Ac 19:12
3:11 [l] 2Ki 21:12; Jer 19:3
3:12 [m] 1Sa 2:27-36
3:13 [n] 1Sa 2:12, 17,22,29-31
3:14 [o] Lev 15:30-31; 1Sa 2:25; Isa 22:14
3:17 [p] Ru 1:17; 2Sa 3:35
3:18 [q] Job 2:10; Isa 39:8
3:19 [r] Ge 21:22; 39:2 [s] 1Sa 2:21 [t] 1Sa 9:6
3:20 [u] Jdg 20:1
3:21 [v] ver 10
4:1 [w] 1Sa 7:12 [x] Jos 12:18; 1Sa 29:1
4:3 [y] Jos 7:7 [z] Nu 10:35; Jos 6:7
4:4 [a] Ex 25:22; 2Sa 6:2
4:5 [b] Jos 6:5,10

[a] 3 That is, tabernacle [b] 13 Masoretic Text; an ancient Hebrew scribal tradition and Septuagint *sons blasphemed God*
[c] 3 Or *he*

3:1 Samuel was no longer a little child (see 2:21,26). While the Jewish historian Josephus placed his age at twelve years, he may in fact have been older.

3:4 Some interpreters compare Samuel's experience to the incubation ritual found in ancient Near Eastern texts, in which an individual goes to sleep in a temple and receives a message from a god (see "The Cylinders of Gudea" on p. 485). In the Greco-Roman world many sick people would sleep in a temple of Asclepius in the hope of receiving a healing dream from the god, which would cure their disease. It is important to note, however, that Samuel slept in the shrine area because it was his duty; he was not seeking a sign.

4:1 For background on the Philistines, see "The Judges Period" on page 344, "The Archaeology of Philistia" on page 370 and "The Ekron Inscription of Akhayus" on page 428.

4:7 [c]Ex 15:14 When they learned that the ark of the LORD had come into the camp, 7 the Philistines were afraid.[c] "A
god has come into the camp," they said. "We're in trouble! Nothing like this has happened before. 8 Woe
to us! Who will deliver us from the hand of these mighty gods? They are the gods who struck the Egyp-
tians with all kinds of plagues in the desert. 9 Be strong, Philistines! Be men, or you will be subject to the
4:9 [d]Jdg 13:1; 1Co 16:13 Hebrews, as they[d] have been to you. Be men, and fight!"
4:10 [e]ver 2; Dt 28:25; 2Sa 18:17; 2Ki 14:12 10 So the Philistines fought, and the Israelites were defeated[e] and every man fled to his tent. The slaugh-
ter was very great; Israel lost thirty thousand foot soldiers. 11 The ark of God was captured, and Eli's two
4:11 [f]1Sa 2:34; Ps 78:61,64 sons, Hophni and Phinehas, died.[f]

Death of Eli

4:12 [g]Jos 7:6; 2Sa 1:2; 15:32; Ne 9:1; Job 2:12 12 That same day a Benjamite ran from the battle line and went to Shiloh, his clothes torn and dust[g]
on his head. 13 When he arrived, there was Eli[h] sitting on his chair by the side of the road, watching, be-
4:13 [h]ver 18; 1Sa 1:9 cause his heart feared for the ark of God. When the man entered the town and told what had happened,
the whole town sent up a cry.
14 Eli heard the outcry and asked, "What is the meaning of this uproar?"
4:15 [i]1Sa 3:2 The man hurried over to Eli, 15 who was ninety-eight years old and whose eyes[i] were set so that he
could not see. 16 He told Eli, "I have just come from the battle line; I fled from it this very day."
Eli asked, "What happened, my son?"
17 The man who brought the news replied, "Israel fled before the Philistines, and the army has suf-
fered heavy losses. Also your two sons, Hophni and Phinehas, are dead, and the ark of God has been cap-
tured."
18 When he mentioned the ark of God, Eli fell backward off his chair by the side of the gate. His neck
4:18 [j]ver 13 was broken and he died, for he was an old man and heavy. He had led[a][j] Israel forty years.
19 His daughter-in-law, the wife of Phinehas, was pregnant and near the time of delivery. When she
heard the news that the ark of God had been captured and that her father-in-law and her husband were

[a] 18 Traditionally *judged*

4:18 The city gate was the location at which the leaders of the city met to hold court, where the marketplace was located and where official business transactions took place (see "The City Gate" on p. 392).

ANCIENT TEXTS AND ARTIFACTS

Izbet Sartah Ostracon

1 SAMUEL 4 In 1 Samuel 4 Israel is encamped at Ebenezer in order to face the Philistines at Aphek ("Map 4"), approximately 2 miles (3.2 km) to the west. Although Ebenezer's size is debated, the site has been tentatively identified by some archaeologists as a moderate hill called Izbet Sartah.

In 1977 the lead archaeologist at Izbet Sartah, Moshe Kochavi, published an **ostracon**, an inscribed pottery **sherd**, that sheds new light upon the development of the **Proto-Canaanite** script used by the ancient Israelites. The ostracon was unearthed in a storage pit in stratum II, a short-lived (aproximately 20-year) level at Izbet Sartah, probably destroyed due to Philistine encroachment. The inscription appears to have been a practice text used by someone learning the alphabet. Not all the letters are present, and those that are do not appear in a standard order. When compared with other inscriptions from roughly the same period, the shape and form of the letters place the ostracon in the early twelfth century B.C., approximately the time Israel was fighting the Philistines in this area. If indeed Izbet Sartah is the modern site for the Biblical Ebenezer, the ostracon may have been inscribed by an Israelite. If this is so, this pottery fragment provides a small but intriguing archaeological glimpse into the life of twelfth-century Israel. Additional finds like the Izbet Sartah ostracon may one day indicate the literacy rate among Israelites of the **Late Bronze Age**.[1]

[1]See "Archaeological Periods" chart on page xx in the front of this Bible.

dead, she went into labor and gave birth, but was overcome by her labor pains. [20]As she was dying, the
women attending her said, "Don't despair; you have given birth to a son." But she did not respond or pay
any attention.
[21]She named the boy Ichabod,[a][k] saying, "The glory[l] has departed from Israel"—because of the cap- **4:21** [k]Ge 35:18 [l]Ps 26:8; Jer 2:11
ture of the ark of God and the deaths of her father-in-law and her husband. [22]She said, "The glory has
departed from Israel, for the ark of God has been captured."

The Ark in Ashdod and Ekron

5 After the Philistines had captured the ark of God, they took it from Ebenezer[m] to Ashdod.[n] [2]Then **5:1** [m]1Sa 4:1; 7:12 [n]Jos 13:3
they carried the ark into Dagon's temple and set it beside Dagon.[o] [3]When the people of Ashdod rose **5:2** [o]Jdg 16:23
early the next day, there was Dagon, fallen[p] on his face on the ground before the ark of the LORD! They **5:3** [p]Isa 19:1; 46:7
took Dagon and put him back in his place. [4]But the following morning when they rose, there was Dagon,
fallen on his face on the ground before the ark of the LORD! His head and hands had been broken[q] off and **5:4** [q]Eze 6:6; Mic 1:7
were lying on the threshold; only his body remained. [5]That is why to this day neither the priests of Da-
gon nor any others who enter Dagon's temple at Ashdod step on the threshold.[r] **5:5** [r]Zep 1:9
[6]The LORD's hand[s] was heavy upon the people of Ashdod and its vicinity; he brought devastation[t] **5:6** [s]ver 7; Ex 9:3; Ps 32:4; Ac 13:11
upon them and afflicted them with tumors.[b][u] [7]When the men of Ashdod saw what was happening, they [t]ver 11; Ps 78:66
said, "The ark of the god of Israel must not stay here with us, because his hand is heavy upon us and [u]Dt 28:27; 1Sa 6:5
upon Dagon our god." [8]So they called together all the rulers of the Philistines and asked them, "What
shall we do with the ark of the god of Israel?"
They answered, "Have the ark of the god of Israel moved to Gath.[v]" So they moved the ark of the God **5:8** [v]ver 11
of Israel.
[9]But after they had moved it, the LORD's hand was against that city, throwing it into a great panic.[w] He **5:9** [w]ver 6,11; Dt 2:15; 1Sa 7:13; Ps 78:66

[a] 21 *Ichabod* means *no glory.* [b] 6 Hebrew; Septuagint and Vulgate *tumors. And rats appeared in their land, and death and destruction were throughout the city*

5:1–4 The Philistines placed the ark next to the image of Dagon (see "Dagon" on p. 404) in order to demonstrate Dagon's superiority over the God of Israel. But the symbolism was reversed when Dagon was toppled to a position of homage before the ark of the Lord.

5:1 Ashdod was about 2.5 miles (4 km) from the Mediterranean Sea and to the west of Jerusalem. It was occupied from the Middle Bronze Age through the Philistine period, being a center of Philistine power during much of Israelite history.

Dagon

1 SAMUEL 5 Dagon was one of the most widely worshiped deities in the ancient Near East:

✣ Sargon the Great (third millennium B.C.) worshiped Dagon after his military victories in **Mesopotamia**.

✣ The cities of Mari ("Map 1"), Tuttul and Teqra contained temples to Dagon, and he is well attested in the Mari[1] archives (second millennium B.C.).

✣ Although Dagon is almost absent from **Ugarit**'s ("Map 1") mythology, he possibly had a temple there since he is mentioned in Ugarit's many offering lists.[2]

✣ In the Holy Land Dagon appears as a principal Philistine god, with temples at Gaza (Jdg 16:23), **Beth Shan** (1Ch 10:10) and Ashdod ("Map 4"), where his temple has possibly been identified by archaeologists.[3]

✣ Sadly, Dagon-worship even influenced Israel (Jos 15:41 mentions Beth Dagon).

Unfortunately, the meaning of Dagon's name and his specific function are unclear. Some connect his name with *wheat*, *fish* or *cloudy*, due to similarities between the name and these words in Semitic languages. Dagon is also at times associated with military power. In 1 Samuel 5 the Philistines credited Dagon with their military victory over Israel (and thus over **Yahweh**). Ironically, it was Dagon who was subsequently forced to submit before Yahweh's ark. Worship of Dagon died out during the **intertestamental period** (a temple of Dagon is mentioned in 1Mc 10:84).[4]

[1]See "Mari" on page 54. [2]See "Tablets From Ugarit and Canaanite Religion" on page 304. [3]See "Samson and the Temple of Dagon" on page 375. [4]For more on this period, see "The Intertestamental Period" on page 1551. First Maccabees is an Apocryphal book, never accepted into the standard Protestant canon.

afflicted the people of the city, both young and old, with an outbreak of tumors.[a] 10So they sent the ark
of God to Ekron.
As the ark of God was entering Ekron, the people of Ekron cried out, "They have brought the ark of
5:11 xver 6,8-9 the god of Israel around to us to kill us and our people." 11So they called together all the rulers[x] of the Phi-
listines and said, "Send the ark of the god of Israel away; let it go back to its own place, or it[b] will kill us
and our people." For death had filled the city with panic; God's hand was very heavy upon it. 12Those
who did not die were afflicted with tumors, and the outcry of the city went up to heaven.

The Ark Returned to Israel

6 When the ark of the LORD had been in Philistine territory seven months, 2the Philistines called for
6:2 yGe 41:8; Ex 7:11; Isa 2:6 the priests and the diviners[y] and said, "What shall we do with the ark of the LORD? Tell us how we
should send it back to its place."
6:3 zEx 23:15; Dt 16:16 aLev 5:15 bver 9 3They answered, "If you return the ark of the god of Israel, do not send it away empty,[z] but by all
means send a guilt offering[a] to him. Then you will be healed, and you will know why his hand[b] has not
been lifted from you."
4The Philistines asked, "What guilt offering should we send to him?"
6:4 cver 17-18; Jos 13:3; Jdg 3:3 They replied, "Five gold tumors and five gold rats, according to the number[c] of the Philistine rulers,
6:5 d1Sa 5:6-11 because the same plague has struck both you and your rulers. 5Make models of the tumors[d] and of the
eJos 7:19; Isa 42:12; rats that are destroying the country, and pay honor[e] to Israel's god. Perhaps he will lift his hand from
Jn 9:24; Rev 14:7 6:6 fEx 7:13; you and your gods and your land. 6Why do you harden[f] your hearts as the Egyptians and Pharaoh did?
8:15; 9:34; 14:17 gEx 12:31,33 When he[c] treated them harshly, did they[g] not send the Israelites out so they could go on their way?

[a] 9 Or *with tumors in the groin* (see Septuagint) [b] 11 Or *he* [c] 6 That is, God

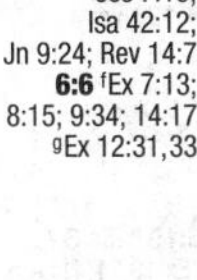

ARCHAEOLOGICAL SITES

BETH SHEMESH

1 SAMUEL 6 The city to which the Philistines returned the ark of the covenant, Beth Shemesh[1] ("Map 4"), was a prominent site in the **Shephelah** near their border with Israel. Located at the modern village of Ain Shemesh (which preserves the ancient name), there are six major occupation levels at this site. The earliest (stratum VI) is meager and dates to the **Early Bronze Age.**[2] Stratum V is a fortified **Canaanite** settlement from **Middle Bronze Age** II that was completely destroyed sometime during the second half of the sixteenth century B.C. In the centuries following Israel's conquest of the land,[3] Beth Shemesh's location along a major route as well as its proximity to the Philistine plain, made the city vulnerable to attack. Stratum IV dates roughly from the fifteenth through thirteenth centuries B.C. This would have been the city that was allotted to Judah and designated as a Levitical city (Jos 15:10; 21:16).[4] A few inscriptions in **Ugaritic cuneiform** and Hebrew-Phoenician, as well as a hoard of jewelry, were found there. This city was completely destroyed. The stratum that follows (stratum III) is a rather large but unplanned village that dates to **Iron I** (the late **judges period**). It, too, was violently destroyed, possibly by Philistines.

The next city, stratum II, lasted throughout the entire **monarchic period** until the fall of Judah in 586 B.C., although the city seems to have suffered in the invasion led by Pharaoh Sheshonk (Biblical Shishak; 1Ki 14:25)[5] in the late tenth century B.C. The city suffered major destruction in Sennacherib's campaign in 701 B.C.,[6] and little was left of it when it was finally destroyed by Nebuchadnezzar in 586 B.C.[7]

Recent excavations of stratum II have revealed a gate, a city square and a large public building. In addition, a huge underground reservoir was hewn inside the city, with a storage capacity sufficient to outlast a three-month siege. In about 800 B.C. Beth Shemesh was the scene of a battle between the armies of Israel and Judah, in which King Jehoash of Israel carried off King Amaziah as prisoner (2Ki 14:11–13; 2Ch 25:21–23). In the days of King Ahaz Judahite weakness allowed the Philistines to temporarily capture the city (2Ch 28:18). A large number of royal seal impressions from the time of King Hezekiah indicates that Beth Shemesh was an important supply center during his time.

The portrait of Beth Shemesh in 1 Samuel 6 accords well with archaeological finds. The city at that time bordered a powerful Philistine population but was itself Israelite. Excavation at stratum III, for example, reveals a city that was fundamentally Canaanite but used Philistine bichrome pottery (decorated in two colors), attesting to the influence of the neighboring Philistines.

[1]See "The Tabernacle and the Ark" on page 153. [2]See "Archaeological Periods" chart on page xx in the front of this Bible. [3]See "The Conquest of Canaan" on page 310. [4]See "Levitical Towns" on page 335. [5]See "The Campaign of Shishak" on page 635. [6]See "The Sennacherib Prism" on page 659. [7]See "Nebuchadnezzar" on page 571.

7“Now then, get a new cart[h] ready, with two cows that have calved and have never been yoked.[i] Hitch 6:7 [h]2Sa 6:3 [i]Nu 19:2
the cows to the cart, but take their calves away and pen them up. 8Take the ark of the LORD and put it on
the cart, and in a chest beside it put the gold objects you are sending back to him as a guilt offering. Send
it on its way, 9but keep watching it. If it goes up to its own territory, toward Beth Shemesh,[j] then the LORD 6:9 [j]ver 3; Jos 15:10; 21:16
has brought this great disaster on us. But if it does not, then we will know that it was not his hand that
struck us and that it happened to us by chance.”
10So they did this. They took two such cows and hitched them to the cart and penned up their calves.
11They placed the ark of the LORD on the cart and along with it the chest containing the gold rats and the
models of the tumors. 12Then the cows went straight up toward Beth Shemesh, keeping on the road and
lowing all the way; they did not turn to the right or to the left. The rulers of the Philistines followed them
as far as the border of Beth Shemesh.
13Now the people of Beth Shemesh were harvesting their wheat in the valley, and when they looked
up and saw the ark, they rejoiced at the sight. 14The cart came to the field of Joshua of Beth Shemesh, and
there it stopped beside a large rock. The people chopped up the wood of the cart and sacrificed the cows
as a burnt offering[k] to the LORD. 15The Levites[l] took down the ark of the LORD, together with the chest con- 6:14 [k]2Sa 24:22; 1Ki 19:21
taining the gold objects, and placed them on the large rock. On that day the people of Beth Shemesh of- 6:15 [l]Jos 3:3
fered burnt offerings and made sacrifices to the LORD. 16The five rulers of the Philistines saw all this and
then returned that same day to Ekron.
17These are the gold tumors the Philistines sent as a guilt offering to the LORD—one each[m] for Ashdod, 6:17 [m]ver 4
Gaza, Ashkelon, Gath and Ekron. 18And the number of the gold rats was according to the number of Phi-
listine towns belonging to the five rulers—the fortified towns with their country villages. The large rock,
on which[a] they set the ark of the LORD, is a witness to this day in the field of Joshua of Beth Shemesh.
19But God struck down[n] some of the men of Beth Shemesh, putting seventy[b] of them to death be- 6:19 [n]2Sa 6:7
cause they had looked[o] into the ark of the LORD. The people mourned because of the heavy blow the LORD [o]Ex 19:21; Nu 4:5, 15,20

[a] 18 A few Hebrew manuscripts (see also Septuagint); most Hebrew manuscripts *villages as far as Greater Abel, where*
[b] 19 A few Hebrew manuscripts; most Hebrew manuscripts and Septuagint *50,070*

6:7–9 The cows had not been trained to pull a cart and would not have willingly left their suckling calves.

6:12 Beth Shemesh was an Israelite town near the Philistine border (see “Beth Shemesh” on p. 405).

ARCHAEOLOGICAL SITES

KIRIATH JEARIM

1 SAMUEL 7 Originally Kiriath Jearim (“Map 4”) was named Baalah (Jos 15:9) or Kiriath Baal, probably indicative of its religious significance when the city belonged to Canaanites who worshiped Baal.[1] After the Israelites had entered **Canaan** under Joshua’s command, the town was allotted to the tribe of Judah, very close to the southern border of Benjamin (Jos 18:14). Kiriath Jearim, which means “city of forests,” was strategically situated along an important route leading from the coastal plain to the Benjamin plateau and on to Jerusalem.

Following the capture of the ark of the covenant by the Philistines and its subsequent return to Beth Shemesh[2] (“Map 4”), men from Kiriath Jearim retrieved the ark and brought it to the house of Abinadab. The ark remained in Kiriath Jearim for 20 years (1Sa 7:2), until the nation repented at Mizpah. David conveyed it from Abinadab’s house to Jerusalem during his reign (2Sa 6:2–4; 2Ch 1:4), and Solomon fortified the site (see 1Ki 9:18), but Pharaoh Shishak is thought to have destroyed it.[3] The final references to Kiriath Jearim in the Biblical record are as the hometown of the prophet Uriah (Jer 26:20) and the destination of some of the returnees from **exile** (Ne 7:29). Kiriath Jearim has been identified with Deir el-Azhar, a hilltop that may preserve the name of Eleazar, the son of Abinadab, who was consecrated to guard the ark. An inscription found at the site indicates that the Tenth Roman Legion was later stationed there, and excavations in the early twentieth century have revealed a **Byzantine** church constructed there during the fifth century A.D.[4]

[1]See “Tablets From Ugarit and Canaanite Religion” on page 304 and “Baal and the Fertility Cults” on page 1414. [2]See “Beth Shemesh” on page 405. [3]See “The Campaign of Shishak” on page 635. [4]For more on the ark, see “The Tabernacle and the Ark” on page 153.

had dealt them, 20and the men of Beth Shemesh asked, "Who can stand[p] in the presence of the LORD, this holy[q] God? To whom will the ark go up from here?"

21Then they sent messengers to the people of Kiriath Jearim,[r] saying, "The Philistines have returned the ark of the LORD. Come down and take it up to your place."

7 1So the men of Kiriath Jearim came and took up the ark of the LORD. They took it to Abinadab's[s] house on the hill and consecrated Eleazar his son to guard the ark of the LORD.

Samuel Subdues the Philistines at Mizpah

2It was a long time, twenty years in all, that the ark remained at Kiriath Jearim, and all the people of Israel mourned and sought after the LORD. 3And Samuel said to the whole house of Israel, "If you are returning[t] to the LORD with all your hearts, then rid[u] yourselves of the foreign gods and the Ashtoreths[v] and commit[w] yourselves to the LORD and serve him only,[x] and he will deliver you out of the hand of the Philistines." 4So the Israelites put away their Baals and Ashtoreths, and served the LORD only.

5Then Samuel said, "Assemble all Israel at Mizpah[y] and I will intercede with the LORD for you." 6When they had assembled at Mizpah, they drew water and poured[z] it out before the LORD. On that day they fasted and there they confessed, "We have sinned against the LORD." And Samuel was leader[a][a] of Israel at Mizpah.

7When the Philistines heard that Israel had assembled at Mizpah, the rulers of the Philistines came up to attack them. And when the Israelites heard of it, they were afraid[b] because of the Philistines. 8They said to Samuel, "Do not stop crying[c] out to the LORD our God for us, that he may rescue us from the hand of the Philistines." 9Then Samuel[d] took a suckling lamb and offered it up as a whole burnt offering to the LORD. He cried out to the LORD on Israel's behalf, and the LORD answered him.[e]

10While Samuel was sacrificing the burnt offering, the Philistines drew near to engage Israel in battle. But that day the LORD thundered[f] with loud thunder against the Philistines and threw them into such a panic[g] that they were routed before the Israelites. 11The men of Israel rushed out of Mizpah and pursued the Philistines, slaughtering them along the way to a point below Beth Car.

12Then Samuel took a stone[h] and set it up between Mizpah and Shen. He named it Ebenezer,[b] saying, "Thus far has the LORD helped us." 13So the Philistines were subdued[i] and did not invade Israelite territory again.

Throughout Samuel's lifetime, the hand of the LORD was against the Philistines. 14The towns from Ekron to Gath that the Philistines had captured from Israel were restored to her, and Israel delivered the neighboring territory from the power of the Philistines. And there was peace between Israel and the Amorites.

15Samuel[j] continued as judge over Israel all the days of his life. 16From year to year he went on a circuit from Bethel to Gilgal to Mizpah, judging Israel in all those places. 17But he always went back to Ramah,[k] where his home was, and there he also judged Israel. And he built an altar[l] there to the LORD.

Israel Asks for a King

8 When Samuel grew old, he appointed[m] his sons as judges for Israel. 2The name of his firstborn was Joel and the name of his second was Abijah, and they served at Beersheba.[n] 3But his sons did not walk in his ways. They turned aside after dishonest gain and accepted bribes[o] and perverted justice.

4So all the elders of Israel gathered together and came to Samuel at Ramah.[p] 5They said to him, "You are old, and your sons do not walk in your ways; now appoint a king[q] to lead[c] us, such as all the other nations have."

6But when they said, "Give us a king to lead us," this displeased[r] Samuel; so he prayed to the LORD. 7And the LORD told him: "Listen to all that the people are saying to you; it is not you they have rejected, but they have rejected me as their king.[s] 8As they have done from the day I brought them up out of Egypt until this day, forsaking me and serving other gods, so they are doing to you. 9Now listen to them; but warn them solemnly and let them know[t] what the king who will reign over them will do."

10Samuel told all the words of the LORD to the people who were asking him for a king. 11He said, "This

6:20 [p]2Sa 6:9; Mal 3:2; Rev 6:17 [q]Lev 11:45
6:21 [r]Jos 9:17; 15:9,60; 1Ch 13:5-6
7:1 [s]2Sa 6:3
7:3 [t]Dt 30:10; Isa 55:7; Hos 6:1 [u]Ge 35:2; Jos 24:14 [v]Jdg 2:12-13; 1Sa 31:10 [w]Joel 2:12 [x]Dt 6:13; Mt 4:10; Lk 4:8
7:5 [y]Jdg 20:1
7:6 [z]Ps 62:8; La 2:19 [a]Jdg 10:10; Ne 9:1; Ps 106:6
7:7 [b]1Sa 17:11
7:8 [c]1Sa 12:19, 23; Isa 37:4; Jer 15:1
7:9 [d]Ps 99:6 [e]Jer 15:1
7:10 [f]1Sa 2:10; 2Sa 22:14-15 [g]Jos 10:10
7:12 [h]Ge 35:14; Jos 4:9
7:13 [i]Jdg 13:1,5; 1Sa 13:5
7:15 [j]ver 6; 1Sa 12:11
7:17 [k]1Sa 1:19; 8:4 [l]Jdg 21:4
8:1 [m]Dt 16:18-19
8:2 [n]Ge 22:19; 1Ki 19:3; Am 5:4-5
8:3 [o]Ex 23:8; Dt 16:19; Ps 15:5
8:4 [p]1Sa 7:17
8:5 [q]Dt 17:14-20
8:6 [r]1Sa 15:11
8:7 [s]Ex 16:8; 1Sa 10:19
8:9 [t]ver 11-18; 1Sa 10:25

[a] 6 Traditionally *judge* [b] 12 *Ebenezer* means *stone of help.* [c] 5 Traditionally *judge*; also in verses 6 and 20

7:3 Ashtoreth, a goddess of love, fertility and war, was worshiped in various forms by many peoples of the ancient Near East, including the Canaanites (see note on Jdg 2:13). Worship of Ashtoreth and of Baal was frequently combined (see Jdg 2:13; 3:7; 10:6; 1Sa 7:4; see also "The Kuntillet Ajrud Inscriptions: The Lord's Asherah?" on p. 1220), for it was common practice in fertility cults to associate male and female deities.

7:6 For a discussion of asceticism in the Old Testament, see the note on Leviticus 10:9.

8:5 For comments on Israel's theocracy (government in which God himself was the ruler), see the note on Exodus 15:13.

KEY THEOLOGICAL DISTINCTIONS BETWEEN ISRAEL AND HER NEIGHBORS

Issue	Israelite Ideal	Pagan Polytheism
Ultimacy of deity	Yahweh is the ultimate power in the universe. He answers to no one and there are no limitations on his jurisdiction.	The gods have competing agendas and limited jurisdiction. Even as a corporate, body they do not exercise ultimate sovereignty.
Manifestation of deity	Yahweh cannot be represented in material form or in the form of any natural phenomena.	Deities represented iconically, anthropomorphically or in natural phenomena.
Disposition of deity	Yahweh is consistent in character and has bound himself by his attributes.	Deity is not bound by any code of conduct. Inconsistent, unpredictable and accountable only marginally to the divine assembly.
Autonomy of deity	Yahweh is not dependent on people for the provision of any needs.	People provided food and housing for deity (sacrifices and temples).
Requirements of deity	Made known in detail through the giving of the law.	Not revealed; could only be inferred from one's fortunes.
Response of deity	Yahweh expects conformity to the Law and to his holiness and justice.	Ritualistic, though maintaining an ordered society was important.
Creation of the cosmos	Yahweh undertook and sovereignly executed a cohesive plan of creation.	Accomplished by procreation of the gods, with no directing influence and was organized and established through conflict between the gods.
Human dignity	Derived from being created in the image of God and placed over creation. Yahweh created for people and with people in mind.	Since humans were a bother and an afterthought, created as slaves, dignity derived from the belief that they provided the needs of the gods.
Revelation	Yahweh's will, purposes, and nature were a matter of public record provided by Yahweh.	The will, purposes, and nature of deity could only be inferred.
Election	Israel understood herself to be the elect people of God.	Occasionally a king or dynasty was considered elect, but no sustained doctrine of election existed.
Historiography	History recorded as a means of Yahweh's revelation and therefore didactic.	History recorded as a means of propagandistic justification and certification of the current regime.
Divine intervention	Directed toward an established and consistent goal in keeping with Yahweh's intention of revealing himself and his attributes.	Directed toward maintaining a *status quo* or returning to a previous *status quo* and is primarily *ad hoc*.
Omens	Worldview of Israel rejected omen mentality.	Viewed as indicating whether the gods were bringing favorable or unfavorable circumstances.
Incantations	Worldview of Israel rejected manipulation of deity by incantations.	Incantations used as a magical means of coercing deity to respond in desired ways.

Chronological and Background Charts of the Old Testament, p. 84

is what the king who will reign over you will do: He will take[u] your sons and make them serve with his
chariots and horses, and they will run in front of his chariots.[v] 12 Some he will assign to be command-
ers[w] of thousands and commanders of fifties, and others to plow his ground and reap his harvest, and
still others to make weapons of war and equipment for his chariots. 13 He will take your daughters to be
perfumers and cooks and bakers. 14 He will take the best of your[x] fields and vineyards[y] and olive groves
and give them to his attendants. 15 He will take a tenth of your grain and of your vintage and give it to his
officials and attendants. 16 Your menservants and maidservants and the best of your cattle[a] and donkeys
he will take for his own use. 17 He will take a tenth of your flocks, and you yourselves will become his
slaves. 18 When that day comes, you will cry out for relief from the king you have chosen, and the LORD will
not answer[z] you in that day."
19 But the people refused[a] to listen to Samuel. "No!" they said. "We want a king over us. 20 Then we will
be like all the other nations,[b] with a king to lead us and to go out before us and fight our battles."
21 When Samuel heard all that the people said, he repeated[c] it before the LORD. 22 The LORD answered,
"Listen[d] to them and give them a king."
Then Samuel said to the men of Israel, "Everyone go back to his town."

Samuel Anoints Saul

9 There was a Benjamite, a man of standing, whose name was Kish[e] son of Abiel, the son of Zeror, the
son of Becorath, the son of Aphiah of Benjamin. 2 He had a son named Saul, an impressive young
man without equal[f] among the Israelites—a head taller[g] than any of the others.
3 Now the donkeys belonging to Saul's father Kish were lost, and Kish said to his son Saul, "Take one
of the servants with you and go and look for the donkeys." 4 So he passed through the hill[h] country of
Ephraim and through the area around Shalisha,[i] but they did not find them. They went on into the dis-
trict of Shaalim, but the donkeys were not there. Then he passed through the territory of Benjamin, but
they did not find them.
5 When they reached the district of Zuph,[j] Saul said to the servant who was with him, "Come, let's go
back, or my father will stop thinking about the donkeys and start worrying[k] about us."
6 But the servant replied, "Look, in this town there is a man of God;[l] he is highly respected, and every-
thing[m] he says comes true. Let's go there now. Perhaps he will tell us what way to take."
7 Saul said to his servant, "If we go, what can we give the man? The food in our sacks is gone. We have
no gift[n] to take to the man of God. What do we have?"
8 The servant answered him again. "Look," he said, "I have a quarter of a shekel[b] of silver. I will give it
to the man of God so that he will tell us what way to take." 9 (Formerly in Israel, if a man went to inquire
of God, he would say, "Come, let us go to the seer," because the prophet of today used to be called a seer.)[o]
10 "Good," Saul said to his servant. "Come, let's go." So they set out for the town where the man of God was.
11 As they were going up the hill to the town, they met some girls coming out to draw[p] water, and they
asked them, "Is the seer here?"
12 "He is," they answered. "He's ahead of you. Hurry now; he has just come to our town today, for the
people have a sacrifice[q] at the high place.[r] 13 As soon as you enter the town, you will find him before he
goes up to the high place to eat. The people will not begin eating until he comes, because he must bless
the sacrifice; afterward, those who are invited will eat. Go up now; you should find him about this time."
14 They went up to the town, and as they were entering it, there was Samuel, coming toward them on
his way up to the high place.
15 Now the day before Saul came, the LORD had revealed this to Samuel: 16 "About this time tomorrow
I will send you a man from the land of Benjamin. Anoint[s] him leader over my people Israel; he will de-
liver[t] my people from the hand of the Philistines. I have looked upon my people, for their cry has
reached me."
17 When Samuel caught sight of Saul, the LORD said to him, "This[u] is the man I spoke to you about; he
will govern my people."

8:11 [u]1Sa 10:25; 14:52 [v]Dt 17:16; 2Sa 15:1
8:12 [w]1Sa 22:7
8:14 [x]Eze 46:18 [y]1Ki 21:7,15
8:18 [z]Pr 1:28; Isa 1:15; Mic 3:4
8:19 [a]Isa 66:4; Jer 44:16
8:20 [b]ver 5
8:21 [c]Jdg 11:11
8:22 [d]ver 7
9:1 [e]1Sa 14:51; 1Ch 8:33; 9:39
9:2 [f]1Sa 10:24 [g]1Sa 10:23
9:4 [h]Jos 24:33 [i]2Ki 4:42
9:5 [j]1Sa 1:1 [k]1Sa 10:2
9:6 [l]Dt 33:1; 1Ki 13:1 [m]1Sa 3:19
9:7 [n]1Ki 14:3; 2Ki 5:5,15; 8:8
9:9 [o]2Sa 24:11; 2Ki 17:13; 1Ch 9:22; 26:28; 29:29; Isa 30:10; Am 7:12
9:11 [p]Ge 24:11, 13
9:12 [q]Nu 28:11-15; 1Sa 7:17 [r]Ge 31:54; 1Sa 10:5; 1Ki 3:2
9:16 [s]1Sa 10:1 [t]Ex 3:7-9
9:17 [u]1Sa 16:12

[a] 16 Septuagint; Hebrew *young men*   [b] 8 That is, about 1/10 ounce (about 3 grams)

9:12 After entering the promised land, the Israelites often followed the Canaanite custom of erecting local altars on hills (see "Israelite Shrines and Worship Before the Temple of Solomon" on p. 398). At this time the central sanctuary was not functioning because the ark of God was separated from the tabernacle, Shiloh had been destroyed (see "The Destruction of Shiloh" on p. 1200) and the priestly family, after the death of Eli's sons, was apparently still inactive. Worship at these "high places" was later condemned because it allowed the infiltration of pagan practices into Israel's religious observances (see "The High Places" on p. 1318).

18 Saul approached Samuel in the gateway and asked, "Would you please tell me where the seer's
house is?"
19 "I am the seer," Samuel replied. "Go up ahead of me to the high place, for today you are to eat with
me, and in the morning I will let you go and will tell you all that is in your heart. 20 As for the donkeys[v] **9:20** [v]ver 3
you lost three days ago, do not worry about them; they have been found. And to whom is all the desire[w] [w]1Sa 8:5; 12:13
of Israel turned, if not to you and all your father's family?"
21 Saul answered, "But am I not a Benjamite, from the smallest tribe[x] of Israel, and is not my clan the **9:21** [x]1Sa 15:17
least of all the clans of the tribe of Benjamin?[y] Why do you say such a thing to me?" [y]Jdg 20:35,46
22 Then Samuel brought Saul and his servant into the hall and seated them at the head of those who
were invited—about thirty in number. 23 Samuel said to the cook, "Bring the piece of meat I gave you, the
one I told you to lay aside."
24 So the cook took up the leg[z] with what was on it and set it in front of Saul. Samuel said, "Here is **9:24** [z]Lev 7:32-
what has been kept for you. Eat, because it was set aside for you for this occasion, from the time I said, 'I 34; Nu 18:18
have invited guests.' " And Saul dined with Samuel that day.
25 After they came down from the high place to the town, Samuel talked with Saul on the roof[a] of his **9:25** [a]Dt 22:8;
house. 26 They rose about daybreak and Samuel called to Saul on the roof, "Get ready, and I will send you Ac 10:9
on your way." When Saul got ready, he and Samuel went outside together. 27 As they were going down to
the edge of the town, Samuel said to Saul, "Tell the servant to go on ahead of us"—and the servant did
so—"but you stay here awhile, so that I may give you a message from God."

9:25 Houses in the ancient Near East had flat roofs with outside staircases. The roof was a convenient location for relaxation and privacy and a good place to catch the cool evening breeze. Sometimes a small room was constructed on the roof. See "The Israelite Town and Home" on page 1205.

ANCIENT PEOPLES, LANDS AND RULERS

Samuel and Saul

1 SAMUEL 9 Samuel and Saul were transitional leaders in Israel's history during the period dating from approximately 1070–1000 B.C., between the time of the judges and the **united monarchy**. "In those days the word of the LORD was rare" (1Sa 3:1), but the miraculous conception of Samuel to the barren Hannah (ch. 1), along with Samuel's unique prophetic call (3:4–14), denoted a special work of God on behalf of his people. Seemingly not of priestly stock (1Ch 6:49–53; cf. 1Sa 1:1), although his father was a Levite (1Ch 6:25–26), Samuel grew up at Shiloh ("Map 4"), Israel's primary worship center,[1] where he was trained under the high priest Eli (1:27–28; 2:11; 3:1). Samuel's ministry, however, was not that of priest but of prophet (3:20—4:1a; 9:6–11). He spoke on God's behalf and called the nation to repentance (7:3; 8:10–18; 12:6–25; 13:13–14; 15:1–2,17–23). Samuel both appointed earthly kings (10:1,24; 16:12–13) and denounced them (13:13–14; 15:22–23; 28:17–19), and he enforced God's covenant in Israel (7:15–17).

Saul was a tragic expression of Israel's waywardness. Under Philistine oppression the Israelites began to question God's presence and power among them (cf. 4:21–22) and to imagine that only a warrior-king could bring them deliverance (8:20). In so doing they rejected God as their king (8:7). Saul was tall, strong and courageous (9:2; 11:6–11), and the people chose him as king without hesitation (8:18; 9:16; 10:24; 12:13). Indeed, he embodied the human ideal of a king.[2] God commissioned Saul to fight both the Philistines (9:17; 10:7; 17:11) and the Amalekites (15:2–3), but Israel's first king often failed to follow all of God's directives (e.g., 13:13; 15:17–19; cf. Dt 17:14–20). Three confrontations with Samuel made clear **Yahweh**'s verdict: Saul's kingship was rejected, and he would be replaced by an individual hand-picked by God (13:14; 15:28; 28:17). The remaining years of Saul's reign were scarred with fear, treachery and anger, as David rose to prominence in Israel.[3] Saul's death at the hands of the Philistines ended his reign (31:1–4).

[1]See "The Tabernacle at Shiloh" on page 401. [2]See "The Ancient Near Eastern King" on page 839. [3]See "David" on page 443.

10 Then Samuel took a flask[b] of oil and poured it on Saul's head and kissed him, saying, "Has not
the LORD anointed[c] you leader over his inheritance?[a][d] 2 When you leave me today, you will meet
two men near Rachel's tomb,[e] at Zelzah on the border of Benjamin. They will say to you, 'The donkeys[f]
you set out to look for have been found. And now your father has stopped thinking about them and is
worried[g] about you. He is asking, "What shall I do about my son?" '
3 "Then you will go on from there until you reach the great tree of Tabor. Three men going up to God
at Bethel[h] will meet you there. One will be carrying three young goats, another three loaves of bread, and
another a skin of wine. 4 They will greet you and offer you two loaves of bread, which you will accept from
them.
5 "After that you will go to Gibeah of God, where there is a Philistine outpost.[i] As you approach the
town, you will meet a procession of prophets coming down from the high place[j] with lyres, tambourines,
flutes and harps[k] being played before them, and they will be prophesying.[l] 6 The Spirit[m] of the LORD will
come upon you in power, and you will prophesy with them; and you will be changed into a different per-
son. 7 Once these signs are fulfilled, do whatever[n] your hand finds to do, for God is with[o] you.
8 "Go down ahead of me to Gilgal.[p] I will surely come down to you to sacrifice burnt offerings and fel-
lowship offerings,[b] but you must wait seven days until I come to you and tell you what you are to do."

Saul Made King

9 As Saul turned to leave Samuel, God changed[q] Saul's heart, and all these signs were fulfilled that day.
10 When they arrived at Gibeah, a procession of prophets met him; the Spirit of God came upon him in
power, and he joined in their prophesying.[r] 11 When all those who had formerly known him saw him
prophesying with the prophets, they asked each other, "What is this[s] that has happened to the son of
Kish? Is Saul also among the prophets?"[t]
12 A man who lived there answered, "And who is their father?" So it became a saying: "Is Saul also
among the prophets?" 13 After Saul stopped prophesying, he went to the high place.
14 Now Saul's uncle[u] asked him and his servant, "Where have you been?"
"Looking for the donkeys," he said. "But when we saw they were not to be found, we went to Samuel."

10:1 [b]1Sa 16:13; 2Ki 9:1,3,6 [c]Ps 2:12 [d]Dt 32:9; Ps 78:62,71
10:2 [e]Ge 35:20 [f]1Sa 9:4 [g]1Sa 9:5
10:3 [h]Ge 28:22; 35:7-8
10:5 [i]1Sa 13:3 [j]1Sa 9:12 [k]2Ki 3:15 [l]1Sa 19:20; 1Co 14:1
10:6 [m]ver 10; Nu 11:25; 1Sa 19:23-24
10:7 [n]Ecc 9:10 [o]Jos 1:5; Jdg 6:12; Heb 13:5
10:8 [p]1Sa 11:14-15
10:9 [q]ver 6
10:10 [r]ver 5-6; 1Sa 19:20
10:11 [s]Mt 13:54; Jn 7:15 [t]1Sa 19:24
10:14 [u]1Sa 14:50

[a] 1 Hebrew; Septuagint and Vulgate *over his people Israel? You will reign over the LORD's people and save them from the power of their enemies round about. And this will be a sign to you that the LORD has anointed you leader over his inheritance:* [b] 8 Traditionally *peace offerings*

ARCHAEOLOGICAL SITES

RACHEL'S TOMB

1 SAMUEL 10 Rachel died near Ephrath, which is another name for Bethlehem (Ge 35:19; 48:7).[1] Traditionally, her burial place has been located at a medieval building near the town, but 1 Samuel 10:2 indicates that the site was within the tribal territory of Benjamin. Jeremiah 31:15, in which Rachel's weeping voice is heard "in Ramah," suggests that the site was actually in the vicinity of Benjamite Ramah, located a few miles north of Jerusalem. Some suggest that there was another Bethlehem nearby, a "Bethlehem of Benjamin," but evidence for this is slight, and most believe that the only Bethlehem/Ephrath of the Bible was in Judah, south of Jerusalem (according to Jos 19:15 there was another Bethlehem in Zebulun, but this has no bearing on the burial place of Rachel).

Where, then, was Rachel buried? One possible solution is that she was actually buried in Bethlehem of Judah but that her tomb in Benjamin was a cenotaph, an empty tomb intended to serve as a memorial to a deceased ancestor. Cenotaphs were common in the ancient world, and the Benjamites had a particular reason to so honor Rachel: The matriarch of the tribe, she had died giving birth to Benjamin.

Matthew 2:18 cites Jeremiah 31:15, claiming that this prophecy was fulfilled in the slaughter of the innocents. It appears that Matthew was working from two different perspectives. First, Rachel's actual burial place was in Bethlehem, where the slaughter took place. Second, Jesus' suffering and the bloodshed around him echoed the suffering of Ephraim and Benjamin that Jeremiah 31:15 bewailed.

[1]See "Bethlehem" on page 59.

15 Saul's uncle said, "Tell me what Samuel said to you."
16 Saul replied, "He assured us that the donkeys[v] had been found." But he did not tell his uncle what
Samuel had said about the kingship.
17 Samuel summoned the people of Israel to the LORD at Mizpah[w] 18 and said to them, "This is what the
LORD, the God of Israel, says: 'I brought Israel up out of Egypt, and I delivered you from the power of
Egypt and all the kingdoms that oppressed[x] you.' 19 But you have now rejected your God, who saves you
out of all your calamities and distresses. And you have said, 'No, set a king[y] over us.' So now present[z]
yourselves before the LORD by your tribes and clans."
20 When Samuel brought all the tribes of Israel near, the tribe of Benjamin was chosen. 21 Then he
brought forward the tribe of Benjamin, clan by clan, and Matri's clan was chosen. Finally Saul son of Kish
was chosen. But when they looked for him, he was not to be found. 22 So they inquired[a] further of the
LORD, "Has the man come here yet?"
And the LORD said, "Yes, he has hidden himself among the baggage."
23 They ran and brought him out, and as he stood among the people he was a head taller[b] than any of
the others. 24 Samuel said to all the people, "Do you see the man the LORD has chosen?[c] There is no one
like him among all the people."
Then the people shouted, "Long live[d] the king!"
25 Samuel explained to the people the regulations[e] of the kingship. He wrote them down on a scroll and
deposited it before the LORD. Then Samuel dismissed the people, each to his own home.
26 Saul also went to his home in Gibeah,[f] accompanied by valiant men whose hearts God had touched.
27 But some troublemakers[g] said, "How can this fellow save us?" They despised him and brought him no
gifts.[h] But Saul kept silent.

Saul Rescues the City of Jabesh

11 Nahash[i] the Ammonite went up and besieged Jabesh Gilead.[j] And all the men of Jabesh said to
him, "Make a treaty[k] with us, and we will be subject to you."
2 But Nahash the Ammonite replied, "I will make a treaty with you only on the condition that I gouge[l]
out the right eye of every one of you and so bring disgrace[m] on all Israel."
3 The elders of Jabesh said to him, "Give us seven days so we can send messengers throughout Israel;
if no one comes to rescue us, we will surrender to you."
4 When the messengers came to Gibeah[n] of Saul and reported these terms to the people, they all wept[o]
aloud. 5 Just then Saul was returning from the fields, behind his oxen, and he asked, "What is wrong with
the people? Why are they weeping?" Then they repeated to him what the men of Jabesh had said.
6 When Saul heard their words, the Spirit[p] of God came upon him in power, and he burned with an-
ger. 7 He took a pair of oxen, cut them into pieces, and sent the pieces by messengers throughout Isra-
el,[q] proclaiming, "This is what will be done to the oxen of anyone[r] who does not follow Saul and Sam-
uel." Then the terror of the LORD fell on the people, and they turned out as one man. 8 When Saul
mustered[s] them at Bezek,[t] the men of Israel numbered three hundred thousand and the men of Judah
thirty thousand.
9 They told the messengers who had come, "Say to the men of Jabesh Gilead, 'By the time the sun is hot
tomorrow, you will be delivered.' " When the messengers went and reported this to the men of Jabesh, they
were elated. 10 They said to the Ammonites, "Tomorrow we will surrender[u] to you, and you can do to us
whatever seems good to you."
11 The next day Saul separated his men into three divisions;[v] during the last watch of the night they
broke into the camp of the Ammonites and slaughtered them until the heat of the day. Those who sur-
vived were scattered, so that no two of them were left together.

Saul Confirmed as King

12 The people then said to Samuel, "Who[w] was it that asked, 'Shall Saul reign over us?' Bring these men
to us and we will put them to death."
13 But Saul said, "No one shall be put to death today,[x] for this day the LORD has rescued[y] Israel."
14 Then Samuel said to the people, "Come, let us go to Gilgal[z] and there reaffirm the kingship.[a]" 15 So
all the people went to Gilgal[b] and confirmed Saul as king in the presence of the LORD. There they sacri-
ficed fellowship offerings[a] before the LORD, and Saul and all the Israelites held a great celebration.

10:16 [v] 1Sa 9:20
10:17 [w] Jdg 20:1; 1Sa 7:5
10:18 [x] Jdg 6:8-9
10:19 [y] 1Sa 8:5-7; 12:12 [z] Jos 7:14; 24:1
10:22 [a] 1Sa 23:2, 4,9-11
10:23 [b] 1Sa 9:2
10:24 [c] Dt 17:15; 2Sa 21:6 [d] 1Ki 1:25,34,39
10:25 [e] Dt 17:14-20; 1Sa 8:11-18
10:26 [f] 1Sa 11:4
10:27 [g] Dt 13:13 [h] 1Ki 10:25; 2Ch 17:5
11:1 [i] 1Sa 12:12 [j] Jdg 21:8 [k] 1Ki 20:34; Eze 17:13
11:2 [l] Nu 16:14 [m] 1Sa 17:26
11:4 [n] 1Sa 10:5, 26; 15:34 [o] Jdg 2:4; 1Sa 30:4
11:6 [p] Jdg 3:10; 6:34; 13:25; 14:6; 1Sa 10:10; 16:13
11:7 [q] Jdg 19:29 [r] Jdg 21:5
11:8 [s] Jdg 20:2 [t] Jdg 1:4
11:10 [u] ver 3
11:11 [v] Jdg 7:16
11:12 [w] 1Sa 10:27; Lk 19:27
11:13 [x] 2Sa 19:22 [y] Ex 14:13; 1Sa 19:5
11:14 [z] 1Sa 10:8 [a] 1Sa 10:25
11:15 [b] 1Sa 10:8, 17

[a] 15 Traditionally *peace offerings*

Samuel's Farewell Speech

12 Samuel said to all Israel, "I have listened[c] to everything you said to me and have set a king[d] over
you. 2Now you have a king as your leader.[e] As for me, I am old and gray, and my sons are here with
you. I have been your leader from my youth until this day. 3Here I stand. Testify against me in the pres-
ence of the LORD and his anointed.[f] Whose ox have I taken? Whose donkey[g] have I taken? Whom have I
cheated? Whom have I oppressed? From whose hand have I accepted a bribe[h] to make me shut my eyes?
If I have done[i] any of these, I will make it right."
4"You have not cheated or oppressed us," they replied. "You have not taken anything from anyone's hand."
5Samuel said to them, "The LORD is witness against you, and also his anointed is witness this day, that
you have not found anything[j] in my hand.[k]"
"He is witness," they said.
6Then Samuel said to the people, "It is the LORD who appointed Moses and Aaron and brought[l] your
forefathers up out of Egypt. 7Now then, stand here, because I am going to confront[m] you with evidence
before the LORD as to all the righteous acts performed by the LORD for you and your fathers.
8"After Jacob entered Egypt, they cried[n] to the LORD for help, and the LORD sent[o] Moses and Aaron,
who brought your forefathers out of Egypt and settled them in this place.
9"But they forgot[p] the LORD their God; so he sold them into the hand of Sisera,[q] the commander of the
army of Hazor, and into the hands of the Philistines[r] and the king of Moab,[s] who fought against them.
10They cried out to the LORD and said, 'We have sinned; we have forsaken[t] the LORD and served the Baals
and the Ashtoreths.[u] But now deliver us from the hands of our enemies, and we will serve you.' 11Then
the LORD sent Jerub-Baal,[a][v] Barak,[b][w] Jephthah[x] and Samuel,[c] and he delivered you from the hands of
your enemies on every side, so that you lived securely.
12"But when you saw that Nahash[y] king[z] of the Ammonites was moving against you, you said to me,
'No, we want a king to rule[a] over us'—even though the LORD your God was your king. 13Now here is the
king[b] you have chosen, the one you asked[c] for; see, the LORD has set a king over you. 14If you fear[d] the LORD
and serve and obey him and do not rebel against his commands, and if both you and the king who reigns
over you follow the LORD your God—good! 15But if you do not obey the LORD, and if you rebel against[e]
his commands, his hand will be against you, as it was against your fathers.
16"Now then, stand still and see[f] this great thing the LORD is about to do before your eyes! 17Is it not
wheat harvest[g] now? I will call[h] upon the LORD to send thunder and rain.[i] And you will realize what an
evil[j] thing you did in the eyes of the LORD when you asked for a king."
18Then Samuel called upon the LORD, and that same day the LORD sent thunder and rain. So all the peo-
ple stood in awe[k] of the LORD and of Samuel.
19The people all said to Samuel, "Pray[l] to the LORD your God for your servants so that we will not die,
for we have added to all our other sins the evil of asking for a king."
20"Do not be afraid," Samuel replied. "You have done all this evil; yet do not turn away from the LORD,
but serve the LORD with all your heart. 21Do not turn away after useless[m] idols.[n] They can do you no good,
nor can they rescue you, because they are useless. 22For the sake[o] of his great name[p] the LORD will not re-
ject[q] his people, because the LORD was pleased to make[r] you his own. 23As for me, far be it from me that
I should sin against the LORD by failing to pray[s] for you. And I will teach[t] you the way that is good and
right. 24But be sure to fear[u] the LORD and serve him faithfully with all your heart; consider[v] what great[w]
things he has done for you. 25Yet if you persist[x] in doing evil, both you and your king will be swept[y] away."

Samuel Rebukes Saul

13 Saul was ⌞thirty⌟[d] years old when he became king, and he reigned over Israel ⌞forty-⌟[e] two years.
2Saul[f] chose three thousand men from Israel; two thousand were with him at Micmash and in
the hill country of Bethel, and a thousand were with Jonathan at Gibeah[z] in Benjamin. The rest of the men
he sent back to their homes.

12:1 [c]1Sa 8:7 [d]1Sa 10:24; 11:15
12:2 [e]1Sa 8:5
12:3 [f]1Sa 10:1; 24:6; 2Sa 1:14 [g]Nu 16:15 [h]Dt 16:19 [i]Ac 20:33
12:5 [j]Ac 23:9; 24:20 [k]Ex 22:4
12:6 [l]Ex 6:26; Mic 6:4
12:7 [m]Isa 1:18; Mic 6:1-5
12:8 [n]Ex 2:23 [o]Ex 3:10; 4:16
12:9 [p]Jdg 3:7 [q]Jdg 4:2 [r]Jdg 10:7; 13:1 [s]Jdg 3:12
12:10 [t]Jdg 10:10, 15 [u]Jdg 2:13
12:11 [v]Jdg 6:14, 32 [w]Jdg 4:6 [x]Jdg 11:1
12:12 [y]1Sa 11:1 [z]1Sa 8:5 [a]Jdg 8:23; 1Sa 8:6,19
12:13 [b]1Sa 8:5; Hos 13:11 [c]1Sa 10:24
12:14 [d]Jos 24:14
12:15 [e]ver 9; Jos 24:20; Isa 1:20
12:16 [f]Ex 14:13
12:17 [g]1Sa 7:9-10 [h]Jas 5:18 [i]Pr 26:1 [j]1Sa 8:6-7
12:18 [k]Ex 14:31
12:19 [l]ver 23; Ex 9:28; Jas 5:18; 1Jn 5:16
12:21 [m]Isa 41:24,29; Jer 16:19; Hab 2:18 [n]Dt 11:16
12:22 [o]Ps 106:8 [p]Jos 7:9 [q]1Ki 6:13 [r]Dt 7:7; 1Pe 2:9
12:23 [s]Ro 1:9-10; Col 1:9; 2Ti 1:3 [t]1Ki 8:36; Ps 34:11; Pr 4:11
12:24 [u]Ecc 12:13 [v]Isa 5:12 [w]Dt 10:21
12:25 [x]1Sa 31:1-5 [y]Jos 24:20
13:2 [z]1Sa 10:26

[a] *11* Also called *Gideon* [b] *11* Some Septuagint manuscripts and Syriac; Hebrew *Bedan* [c] *11* Hebrew; some Septuagint manuscripts and Syriac *Samson* [d] *1* A few late manuscripts of the Septuagint; Hebrew does not have *thirty.* [e] *1* See the round number in Acts 13:21; Hebrew does not have *forty-.* [f] *1,2* Or *and when he had reigned over Israel two years, 2he*

12:11 Jerub-Baal is another name for Gideon (see "Early Scribal Emenelation" on p. 448).

13:1 The Hebrew text actually states that Saul was one year old when he became king and that he reigned for two years. This is obviously not correct, and a scribal error is apparent (see "Textual Criticism" on p. 1151). Acts 13:21 preserves a tradition that he reigned for 40 years.

3Jonathan attacked the Philistine outpost[a] at Geba, and the Philistines heard about it. Then Saul had
the trumpet blown throughout the land and said, "Let the Hebrews hear!" 4So all Israel heard the news:
"Saul has attacked the Philistine outpost, and now Israel has become a stench[b] to the Philistines." And
the people were summoned to join Saul at Gilgal.
5The Philistines assembled to fight Israel, with three thousand[a] chariots, six thousand charioteers, and
soldiers as numerous as the sand[c] on the seashore. They went up and camped at Micmash, east of Beth
Aven. 6When the men of Israel saw that their situation was critical and that their army was hard pressed,
they hid in caves and thickets, among the rocks, and in pits and cisterns.[d] 7Some Hebrews even crossed
the Jordan to the land of Gad[e] and Gilead.
Saul remained at Gilgal, and all the troops with him were quaking with fear. 8He waited seven[f] days,
the time set by Samuel; but Samuel did not come to Gilgal, and Saul's men began to scatter. 9So he said,
"Bring me the burnt offering and the fellowship offerings.[b]" And Saul offered[g] up the burnt offering.
10Just as he finished making the offering, Samuel[h] arrived, and Saul went out to greet him.
11"What have you done?" asked Samuel.
Saul replied, "When I saw that the men were scattering, and that you did not come at the set time, and
that the Philistines were assembling at Micmash,[i] 12I thought, 'Now the Philistines will come down against
me at Gilgal, and I have not sought the LORD's favor.[j]' So I felt compelled to offer the burnt offering."
13"You acted foolishly,[k]" Samuel said. "You have not kept[l] the command the LORD your God gave you;
if you had, he would have established your kingdom over Israel for all time. 14But now your kingdom[m]
will not endure; the LORD has sought out a man after his own heart[n] and appointed[o] him leader of his peo-
ple, because you have not kept the LORD's command."

13:3 a1Sa 10:5
13:4 bGe 34:30
13:5 cJos 11:4
13:6 dJdg 6:2
13:7 eNu 32:33
13:8 f1Sa 10:8
13:9 g2Sa 24:25; 1Ki 3:4
13:10 h1Sa 15:13
13:11 iver 2,5, 16,23
13:12 jJer 26:19
13:13 k2Ch 16:9 l1Sa 15:23,24
13:14 m1Sa 15:28 nAc 7:46; 13:22 o2Sa 6:21

[a] 5 Some Septuagint manuscripts and Syriac; Hebrew *thirty thousand* [b] 9 Traditionally *peace offerings*

CULTURAL AND HISTORICAL NOTES

Technological Supremacy of the Philistines' Iron Weapons

1 SAMUEL 13 Iron weaponry placed the Philistines in a position of distinct advantage over their adversaries. Perhaps more than any other factor, iron weapons proved the decisive element in the Philistines' early domination of Israel. The Philistines were one of the **Sea Peoples** who had arrived on the **Canaanite** shores at the end of the **Bronze Age**.[1] There is evidence of ironwork from the early **Iron Age** both in Egypt to the south and in the **Hittite** Empire in **Asia Minor** to the north. But both empires guarded their technological advancement. Still, during the second half of the second millennium B.C., the Philistines defeated the Hittites and most likely took from them the technology of ironwork.

To protect this valuable commodity and their corresponding advantage, the Philistines guarded the technology from their neighbors, notably the Israelites. Within Palestine, facilities of iron smelting have been discovered in the ancient Philistine settlements at Ekron ("Map 4") and Tell Qasile. In fact, the Philistines prohibited Israelites from engaging in the trade of ironsmithing, lest the Israelites also gain iron weapons (1Sa 13:19–20). Goliath the Philistine had a spearhead made of iron. The Hebrew text describes this spear as a "weaver's beam"; it is possible that this term was used because the iron weapon was relatively new to the Israelite culture and no word had as yet been coined to describe it.

It was partially the threat of the Philistines and their superior weapons that motivated the tribes of Israel to demand a king. As the monarchy began under Saul, the Philistines continued to dominate Israel's armies in open battle, including the battle at Mount Gilboa ("Map 3") where Saul and his sons died (ch. 31). To combat the weapon superiority of the Philistines, the Israelites relied upon superior knowledge of the landscape and on guerilla warfare. But it was not until David was crowned king that the Israelites began to experience victory over their traditional foe.[2] As David's conquests expanded the borders of Israel, he was able to secure rich iron deposits to the south in Edom (2Sa 8).[3] These proved an extremely valuable asset to Israel.

[1]See "The Archaeology of Philistia" on page 370; see also "Archaeological Periods" chart on page xx in the front of this Bible. [2]See "David" on page 443. [3]See "Edom" on page 1467.

13:15 [p]1Sa 14:2 [15]Then Samuel left Gilgal[a] and went up to Gibeah[p] in Benjamin, and Saul counted the men who were
with him. They numbered about six hundred.

Israel Without Weapons

[16]Saul and his son Jonathan and the men with them were staying in Gibeah[b] in Benjamin, while the
13:17 [q]1Sa 14:15 Philistines camped at Micmash. [17]Raiding[q] parties went out from the Philistine camp in three detach-
[r]Jos 18:23 13:18 [s]Jos 18:13-14 ments. One turned toward Ophrah[r] in the vicinity of Shual, [18]another toward Beth Horon,[s] and the third
[t]Ne 11:34 toward the borderland overlooking the Valley of Zeboim[t] facing the desert.
13:19 [u]2Ki 24:14; Jer 24:1 [19]Not a blacksmith[u] could be found in the whole land of Israel, because the Philistines had said, "Oth-
erwise the Hebrews will make swords or spears!" [20]So all Israel went down to the Philistines to have their
plowshares, mattocks, axes and sickles[c] sharpened. [21]The price was two thirds of a shekel[d] for sharpening
plowshares and mattocks, and a third of a shekel[e] for sharpening forks and axes and for repointing goads.
13:22 [v]1Ch 9:39 [w]Jdg 5:8 [22]So on the day of the battle not a soldier with Saul and Jonathan[v] had a sword or spear[w] in his hand;
only Saul and his son Jonathan had them.

Jonathan Attacks the Philistines

13:23 [x]1Sa 14:4 **14** [23]Now a detachment of Philistines had gone out to the pass[x] at Micmash. [1]One day Jonathan son
of Saul said to the young man bearing his armor, "Come, let's go over to the Philistine outpost on
the other side." But he did not tell his father.
14:2 [y]1Sa 13:15 [z]Isa 10:28 [2]Saul was staying on the outskirts of Gibeah[y] under a pomegranate tree in Migron.[z] With him were
about six hundred men, [3]among whom was Ahijah, who was wearing an ephod. He was a son of Icha-
14:3 [a]1Sa 4:21 [b]1Sa 22:11,20 bod's[a] brother Ahitub[b] son of Phinehas, the son of Eli,[c] the LORD's priest in Shiloh. No one was aware
[c]1Sa 2:28 that Jonathan had left.
14:4 [d]1Sa 13:23 [4]On each side of the pass[d] that Jonathan intended to cross to reach the Philistine outpost was a cliff;
one was called Bozez, and the other Seneh. [5]One cliff stood to the north toward Micmash, the other to the
south toward Geba.
14:6 [e]1Sa 17:26, 36; Jer 9:26 [6]Jonathan said to his young armor-bearer, "Come, let's go over to the outpost of those uncircumcised[e]
[f]Heb 11:34 [g]Jdg 7:4 fellows. Perhaps the LORD will act in our behalf. Nothing[f] can hinder the LORD from saving, whether by
[h]1Sa 17:46-47 many[g] or by few.[h]"
[7]"Do all that you have in mind," his armor-bearer said. "Go ahead; I am with you heart and soul."
[8]Jonathan said, "Come, then; we will cross over toward the men and let them see us. [9]If they say to us,
'Wait there until we come to you,' we will stay where we are and not go up to them. [10]But if they say, 'Come
14:10 [i]Ge 24:14; Jdg 6:36-37 up to us,' we will climb up, because that will be our sign[i] that the LORD has given them into our hands."
[11]So both of them showed themselves to the Philistine outpost. "Look!" said the Philistines. "The He-
14:11 [j]1Sa 13:6 brews are crawling out of the holes they were hiding[j] in." [12]The men of the outpost shouted to Jonathan
14:12 [k]1Sa 17:43-44 and his armor-bearer, "Come up to us and we'll teach you a lesson.[k]"
[l]2Sa 5:24 So Jonathan said to his armor-bearer, "Climb up after me; the LORD has given them into the hand[l] of
Israel."
[13]Jonathan climbed up, using his hands and feet, with his armor-bearer right behind him. The Phi-
listines fell before Jonathan, and his armor-bearer followed and killed behind him. [14]In that first attack
Jonathan and his armor-bearer killed some twenty men in an area of about half an acre.[f]

Israel Routs the Philistines

14:15 [m]Ge 35:5; 2Ki 7:5-7 [15]Then panic[m] struck the whole army—those in the camp and field, and those in the outposts and
[n]1Sa 13:17 raiding[n] parties—and the ground shook. It was a panic sent by God.[g]

[a] 15 Hebrew; Septuagint *Gilgal and went his way; the rest of the people went after Saul to meet the army, and they went out of Gilgal*
[b] 16 Two Hebrew manuscripts; most Hebrew manuscripts *Geba,* a variant of *Gibeah* [c] 20 Septuagint; Hebrew *plowshares*
[d] 21 Hebrew *pim;* that is, about 1/4 ounce (about 8 grams) [e] 21 That is, about 1/8 ounce (about 4 grams) [f] 14 Hebrew *half a yoke;* a "yoke" was the land plowed by a yoke of oxen in one day. [g] 15 Or *a terrible panic*

13:17–18 The Philistines held decisive military superiority. They substantially outnumbered Israel's troops and could send out raiding parties in different directions to seal off Saul's forces, preventing reinforcements from arriving to help.

13:19 The Philistines had the upper hand as well in military equipment. By controlling a monopoly in metallurgical technology, they limited not only Israel's agricultural implements but also her arsenal of weapons (see "Ancient Craftsmanship" on p. 141 and "Technological Supremacy of the Philistines' Iron Weapons" on p. 414). The result: Only Saul and Jonathan were adequately armed, and the Israelite forces were in danger of annihilation.

13:23 See "The Pass at Micmash" on page 417.

14:14 In this verse, as well as in Isaiah 5:10, the area referred to by the English term *acre* is in reality the average amount of ground a yoke of oxen could plow in a day. The actual area is unknown, and the translation "acre" is merely conventional.

16Saul's lookouts[o] at Gibeah in Benjamin saw the army melting away in all directions. 17Then Saul **14:16** [o]2Sa 18:24
said to the men who were with him, "Muster the forces and see who has left us." When they did, it was
Jonathan and his armor-bearer who were not there.
18Saul said to Ahijah, "Bring[p] the ark of God." (At that time it was with the Israelites.)[a] 19While Saul **14:18** [p]1Sa 30:7
was talking to the priest, the tumult in the Philistine camp increased more and more. So Saul said to the
priest,[q] "Withdraw your hand." **14:19** [q]Nu 27:21
20Then Saul and all his men assembled and went to the battle. They found the Philistines in total con-
fusion, striking[r] each other with their swords. 21Those Hebrews who had previously been with the Phi- **14:20** [r]Jdg 7:22; 2Ch 20:23
listines and had gone up with them to their camp went[s] over to the Israelites who were with Saul and Jon- **14:21** [s]1Sa 29:4
athan. 22When all the Israelites who had hidden[t] in the hill country of Ephraim heard that the Philistines **14:22** [t]1Sa 13:6
were on the run, they joined the battle in hot pursuit. 23So the LORD rescued[u] Israel that day, and the bat- **14:23** [u]Ex 14:30; Ps 44:6-7
tle moved on beyond Beth Aven.[v] [v]1Sa 13:5

Jonathan Eats Honey

24Now the men of Israel were in distress that day, because Saul had bound the people under an oath,[w] **14:24** [w]Jos 6:26
saying, "Cursed be any man who eats food before evening comes, before I have avenged myself on my en-
emies!" So none of the troops tasted food.
25The entire army[b] entered the woods, and there was honey on the ground. 26When they went into
the woods, they saw the honey oozing out, yet no one put his hand to his mouth, because they feared the
oath. 27But Jonathan had not heard that his father had bound the people with the oath, so he reached out
the end of the staff that was in his hand and dipped it into the honeycomb.[x] He raised his hand to his **14:27** [x]ver 43; 1Sa 30:12
mouth, and his eyes brightened.[c] 28Then one of the soldiers told him, "Your father bound the army un-
der a strict oath, saying, 'Cursed be any man who eats food today!' That is why the men are faint."
29Jonathan said, "My father has made trouble[y] for the country. See how my eyes brightened[d] when I **14:29** [y]Jos 7:25; 1Ki 18:18
tasted a little of this honey. 30How much better it would have been if the men had eaten today some of
the plunder they took from their enemies. Would not the slaughter of the Philistines have been even
greater?"
31That day, after the Israelites had struck down the Philistines from Micmash to Aijalon,[z] they were **14:31** [z]Jos 10:12
exhausted. 32They pounced on the plunder[a] and, taking sheep, cattle and calves, they butchered them on **14:32** [a]1Sa 15:19
the ground and ate them, together with the blood.[b] 33Then someone said to Saul, "Look, the men are sin- [b]Ge 9:4; Lev 3:17; 7:26; 17:10-14; 19:26; Dt 12:16, 23-24
ning against the LORD by eating meat that has blood in it."
"You have broken faith," he said. "Roll a large stone over here at once." 34Then he said, "Go out among
the men and tell them, 'Each of you bring me your cattle and sheep, and slaughter them here and eat
them. Do not sin against the LORD by eating meat with blood still in it.' "
So everyone brought his ox that night and slaughtered it there. 35Then Saul built an altar[c] to the LORD; **14:35** [c]1Sa 7:17
it was the first time he had done this.
36Saul said, "Let us go down after the Philistines by night and plunder them till dawn, and let us not
leave one of them alive."
"Do whatever seems best to you," they replied.
But the priest said, "Let us inquire of God here."
37So Saul asked God, "Shall I go down after the Philistines? Will you give them into Israel's hand?" But
God did not answer[d] him that day. **14:37** [d]1Sa 10:22; 28:6, 15
38Saul therefore said, "Come here, all you who are leaders of the army, and let us find out what sin has
been committed[e] today. 39As surely as the LORD who rescues Israel lives,[f] even if it lies with my son Jon- **14:38** [e]Jos 7:11; 1Sa 10:19
athan, he must die." But not one of the men said a word. **14:39** [f]2Sa 12:5
40Saul then said to all the Israelites, "You stand over there; I and Jonathan my son will stand over here."

[a] 18 Hebrew; Septuagint *"Bring the ephod." (At that time he wore the ephod before the Israelites.)* [b] 25 Or *Now all the people of the land* [c] 27 Or *his strength was renewed* [d] 29 Or *my strength was renewed*

14:18 When Saul saw what was happening in the Philistine camp, he called for Ahijah to bring "the ark of God" (see "The Tabernacle and the Ark" on p. 153). But the Septuagint (early Greek translation of the OT) perhaps preserves the original text: Saul may instead have called for the high priest's ephod (cf. v. 3), which contained the Urim and Thummim used to discern God's will (cf. Ex 28:30; see "The Urim and Thummim" on p. 136 and "The Ephod" on p. 399). Saul at first determined to ask for God's guidance but suddenly halted the inquiry and rushed off to the battlefield.

14:33 The Israelites were not permitted to eat blood (Lev 17:11; 19:26; Dt 12:16).

14:37 For a discussion of the religious significance of Israel's wars, see the note on Deuteronomy 20:1–4.

14:41 [g]Ac 1:24 [h]Pr 16:33
14:43 [i]Jos 7:19 [j]ver 27
14:44 [k]Ru 1:17 [l]ver 39

"Do what seems best to you," the men replied.
41 Then Saul prayed to the LORD, the God of Israel, "Give[g] me the right[h] answer."[a] And Jonathan and
Saul were taken by lot, and the men were cleared. 42 Saul said, "Cast the lot between me and Jonathan my
son." And Jonathan was taken.
43 Then Saul said to Jonathan, "Tell me what you have done."[i]
So Jonathan told him, "I merely tasted a little honey[j] with the end of my staff. And now must I die?"
44 Saul said, "May God deal with me, be it ever so severely,[k] if you do not die, Jonathan.[l]"

[a] 41 Hebrew; Septuagint *"Why have you not answered your servant today? If the fault is in me or my son Jonathan, respond with Urim, but if the men of Israel are at fault, respond with Thummim."*

ARCHAEOLOGICAL SITES

THE PASS AT MICMASH

1 SAMUEL 14 Reference to a specific geographic feature is not typical in Scripture, but the geographic details of the pass near Micmash and Geba are carefully described in 1 Samuel 14:5. Most north/south traffic in the hill country follows the watershed ridge, because of the deeply cutting ravines (***wadis***) on either side. The mile-wide break in the otherwise steep cliffs of the Wadi Suwenit allowed for the existence of a secondary route in the territory of Benjamin, which paralleled the watershed ridge route and came to be known simply as "the pass."

During the time of King Saul the Philistines guarded this pass, but Jonathan and his armor-bearer surprised the enemy garrison by circumventing it and climbing the steep cliffs of Bozez and Seneh (1Sa 13:23—14:14). Isaiah prophesied of a terrifying army that would travel along this road, leaving baggage at Micmash and spending the night at Geba (Isa 10:28–29). Asa's earlier fortifications of Geba were also an apparent recognition of the importance of this route (1Ki 15:22).

Scholars routinely identify Micmash with the modern Arab village of Mukhmas, nearly 7 miles (11.2 km) northeast of Jerusalem in the West Bank. However, very few **Iron Age**[1] remains have been found there, and thus some suggest that Micmash may have been at Khirbet el-Hara el-Fawqa, less than 1 mile (1.6 km) farther north—a spot at which researchers have found both **Iron** I and II **Age sherds.**[2]

[1]See "Archaeological Periods" chart on page xx in the front of this Bible. [2]See "The Potsherd: Pottery in the Bible" on page 738.

Micmash cliffs

Photograph: © Todd Bolen/Bible Places.com

45 But the men said to Saul, "Should Jonathan die—he who has brought about this great deliverance
in Israel? Never! As surely as the LORD lives, not a hair[m] of his head will fall to the ground, for he did this
today with God's help." So the men rescued[n] Jonathan, and he was not put to death.
46 Then Saul stopped pursuing the Philistines, and they withdrew to their own land.
47 After Saul had assumed rule over Israel, he fought against their enemies on every side: Moab, the
Ammonites,[o] Edom, the kings[a] of Zobah,[p] and the Philistines. Wherever he turned, he inflicted punish-
ment on them.[b] 48 He fought valiantly and defeated the Amalekites,[q] delivering Israel from the hands of
those who had plundered them.

Saul's Family

49 Saul's sons were Jonathan, Ishvi and Malki-Shua.[r] The name of his older daughter was Merab, and
that of the younger was Michal.[s] 50 His wife's name was Ahinoam daughter of Ahimaaz. The name of the
commander of Saul's army was Abner son of Ner, and Ner was Saul's uncle. 51 Saul's father Kish[t] and Ab-
ner's father Ner were sons of Abiel.
52 All the days of Saul there was bitter war with the Philistines, and whenever Saul saw a mighty or
brave man, he took[u] him into his service.

The LORD Rejects Saul as King

15 Samuel said to Saul, "I am the one the LORD sent to anoint[v] you king over his people Israel; so lis-
ten now to the message from the LORD. 2 This is what the LORD Almighty says: 'I will punish the
Amalekites[w] for what they did to Israel when they waylaid them as they came up from Egypt. 3 Now go,
attack the Amalekites and totally[x] destroy[c] everything that belongs to them. Do not spare them; put to
death men and women, children and infants, cattle and sheep, camels and donkeys.' "
4 So Saul summoned the men and mustered them at Telaim—two hundred thousand foot soldiers
and ten thousand men from Judah. 5 Saul went to the city of Amalek and set an ambush in the ravine.
6 Then he said to the Kenites,[y] "Go away, leave the Amalekites so that I do not destroy you along with
them; for you showed kindness to all the Israelites when they came up out of Egypt." So the Kenites
moved away from the Amalekites.
7 Then Saul attacked the Amalekites[z] all the way from Havilah to Shur,[a] to the east of Egypt. 8 He took
Agag king of the Amalekites alive,[b] and all his people he totally destroyed with the sword. 9 But Saul and
the army spared[c] Agag and the best of the sheep and cattle, the fat calves[d] and lambs—everything that
was good. These they were unwilling to destroy completely, but everything that was despised and weak
they totally destroyed.
10 Then the word of the LORD came to Samuel: 11 "I am grieved[d] that I have made Saul king, because
he has turned[e] away from me and has not carried out my instructions."[f] Samuel was troubled,[g] and he
cried out to the LORD all that night.
12 Early in the morning Samuel got up and went to meet Saul, but he was told, "Saul has gone to Car-
mel.[h] There he has set up a monument in his own honor and has turned and gone on down to Gilgal."
13 When Samuel reached him, Saul said, "The LORD bless you! I have carried out the LORD's instruc-
tions."
14 But Samuel said, "What then is this bleating of sheep in my ears? What is this lowing of cattle that
I hear?"
15 Saul answered, "The soldiers brought them from the Amalekites; they spared the best of the sheep
and cattle to sacrifice to the LORD your God, but we totally destroyed the rest."
16 "Stop!" Samuel said to Saul. "Let me tell you what the LORD said to me last night."
"Tell me," Saul replied.

14:45 [m] 1Ki 1:52; Lk 21:18; Ac 27:34 [n] 2Sa 14:11
14:47 [o] 1Sa 11:1-13 [p] ver 52; 2Sa 10:6
14:48 [q] 1Sa 15:2,7
14:49 [r] 1Sa 31:2; 1Ch 8:33 [s] 1Sa 18:17-20
14:51 [t] 1Sa 9:1
14:52 [u] 1Sa 8:11
15:1 [v] 1Sa 9:16
15:2 [w] Ex 17:8-14; Nu 24:20; Dt 25:17-19
15:3 [x] Nu 24:20; Dt 20:16-18; Jos 6:17; 1Sa 22:19
15:6 [y] Ex 18:10, 19; Nu 10:29-32; 24:22; Jdg 1:16; 4:1
15:7 [z] 1Sa 14:48 [a] Ge 16:7; 25:17-18; Ex 15:22
15:8 [b] 1Sa 30:1
15:9 [c] ver 3,15
15:11 [d] Ge 6:6; 2Sa 24:16 [e] Jos 22:16 [f] 1Sa 13:13; 1Ki 9:6-7 [g] ver 35
15:12 [h] Jos 15:55

[a] *47* Masoretic Text; Dead Sea Scrolls and Septuagint *king* [b] *47* Hebrew; Septuagint *he was victorious* [c] *3* The Hebrew term refers to the irrevocable giving over of things or persons to the LORD, often by totally destroying them; also in verses 8, 9, 15, 18, 20 and 21. [d] *9* Or *the grown bulls*; the meaning of the Hebrew for this phrase is uncertain.

15:2–3 The Amalekites (see "Amalekites" on p. 120), a Bedouin people descended from Esau (see Ge 36:12,16), were generally located in the Negev and Sinai regions.

For "totally destroy," see "*Herem,* Holy War" on page 419.

15:6 The Kenites (see "The Kenites" on p. 434) were a Bedouin people closely related to the Midianites (see "Midian" on p. 92). Moses had married a Kenite woman (see Ex 2:15,21–22; Nu 10:29), and some Kenites had accompanied the Israelites when they settled in the land of Canaan (see Jdg 1:16).

Herem, *Holy War*

1 SAMUEL 15 The command given to Saul in 1 Samuel 15:3 to "totally destroy everything" that belonged to the Amalekites represents the translation of the Hebrew word *haram*. This verb, which means to "ban" or "completely destroy," has a related noun, *herem*, meaning "absolute destruction." In keeping with its frequent use within the context of Old Testament Hebrew warfare, the verb is also found in Deuteronomy 20:16–18, where the Israelites were commanded to "completely destroy" all the peoples living within the land God had given them as an inheritance. These verses in Deuteronomy indicate that this total destruction involved killing all the people and domestic animals belonging to a place. The same verb appears in the Moabite language, as attested on the ninth-century B.C. Mesha Stele, an inscribed stone monument on which King Mesha of Moab claimed to have "totally destroyed" the people of Nebo for the god Chemosh.[1] Mesha's use of this verb demonstrates a connection between Israel and her neighbors in the realm of warfare ideology.

While the phrase "holy war" may be somewhat misleading, the Biblical idea of war is rooted in the notion that God led his people into battle and that certain Old Testament battles were executed as religious acts. Although it has been suggested that *herem* was an element of every Biblical holy war, this is most unlikely, since it was not decreed in every battle.

While it is not mentioned in 1 Samuel 15, the ark of the covenant served as the palladium (a religious image or object thought to provide divine protection to a people or place) that signified **Yahweh**'s presence among the Israelite army in battle. Yahweh was often portrayed as a warrior God who was victorious over the powers of chaos. This ideology was prevalent throughout the ancient Near East, and, along with associated injunctions to purity among the warriors (Dt 23:9–10), it provided the essential elements of the holy war. In the Bible this offers a powerful metaphor for God's mighty acts in salvation history that will culminate in the absolute destruction of all who oppose him.

The *herem* in Israelite warfare strikes many readers as cruel, but it is helpful to keep three factors in mind:

- The Israelites were executing divine judgment on **Canaan** specifically; they were not called to wage holy war on the nations around them in order to create an empire.
- The *herem* was intended to remove permanently the pagan influence from the Israelite vicinity.
- The *herem* was meant to remind the Israelites that their warfare was not for the purpose of acquiring slaves and booty but was meant to secure the land as their inheritance. When the Israelites failed to carry out the *herem*, the reason was often not mercy on their part but greed (1Sa 15:9).

For other war-related issues, see "Horses and Chariots in Ancient Warfare" on page 114, "Battle by Champions" on page 422, "Siege Warfare" on page 465, "Songs of Warriors" on page 474 and "Warfare in the Ancient World" on page 950.

[1]See "The Mesha (Moabite) Stone" on page 530.

The "War Scroll" from Qumran

Preserving Bible Times; © Dr. James C. Martin; permission of The Israel Museum/Shrine of the Book

17 Samuel said, "Although you were once small[i] in your own eyes, did you not become the head of the 15:17 [i]1Sa 9:21
tribes of Israel? The LORD anointed you king over Israel. 18 And he sent you on a mission, saying, 'Go and com-
pletely destroy those wicked people, the Amalekites; make war on them until you have wiped them out.'
19 Why did you not obey the LORD? Why did you pounce on the plunder[j] and do evil in the eyes of the LORD?" 15:19 [j]1Sa 14:32
20 "But I did obey[k] the LORD," Saul said. "I went on the mission the LORD assigned me. I completely de- 15:20 [k]ver 13
stroyed the Amalekites and brought back Agag their king. 21 The soldiers took sheep and cattle from the
plunder, the best of what was devoted to God, in order to sacrifice them to the LORD your God at Gilgal."
22 But Samuel replied:

> "Does the LORD delight in burnt offerings and sacrifices
> as much as in obeying the voice of the LORD?
> To obey is better than sacrifice,[l]
> and to heed is better than the fat of rams.
> 23 For rebellion is like the sin of divination,[m]
> and arrogance like the evil of idolatry.
> Because you have rejected[n] the word of the LORD,
> he has rejected you as king."

15:22 [l]Ps 40:6-8; 51:16; Isa 1:11-15; Jer 7:22; Hos 6:6; Mic 6:6-8; Mt 12:7; Mk 12:33; Heb 10:6-9
15:23 [m]Dt 18:10 [n]1Sa 13:13

24 Then Saul said to Samuel, "I have sinned.[o] I violated the LORD's command and your instructions. I 15:24 [o]2Sa 12:13
was afraid[p] of the people and so I gave in to them. 25 Now I beg you, forgive[q] my sin and come back with [p]Pr 29:25; Isa 51:12-13
me, so that I may worship the LORD." 15:25 [q]Ex 10:17
26 But Samuel said to him, "I will not go back with you. You have rejected[r] the word of the LORD, and 15:26 [r]1Sa 13:14
the LORD has rejected you as king over Israel!"
27 As Samuel turned to leave, Saul caught hold of the hem of his robe, and it tore.[s] 28 Samuel said to him, 15:27 [s]1Ki 11:11, 31
"The LORD has torn[t] the kingdom of Israel from you today and has given it to one of your neighbors— 15:28 [t]1Sa 28:17; 1Ki 11:31
to one better than you. 29 He who is the Glory of Israel does not lie[u] or change[v] his mind; for he is not a 15:29 [u]1Ch 29:11; Tit 1:2 [v]Nu 23:19; Eze 24:14
man, that he should change his mind."
30 Saul replied, "I have sinned. But please honor[w] me before the elders of my people and before Isra- 15:30 [w]Isa 29:13; Jn 5:44; 12:43
el; come back with me, so that I may worship the LORD your God." 31 So Samuel went back with Saul, and
Saul worshiped the LORD.
32 Then Samuel said, "Bring me Agag king of the Amalekites."
Agag came to him confidently,[a] thinking, "Surely the bitterness of death is past."
33 But Samuel said,

> "As your sword has made women childless,
> so will your mother be childless among women."[x] 15:33 [x]Ge 9:6; Jdg 1:7

And Samuel put Agag to death before the LORD at Gilgal.
34 Then Samuel left for Ramah,[y] but Saul went up to his home in Gibeah[z] of Saul. 35 Until the day Sam- 15:34 [y]1Sa 7:17 [z]1Sa 11:4
uel[a] died, he did not go to see Saul again, though Samuel mourned[b] for him. And the LORD was grieved 15:35 [a]1Sa 19:24 [b]1Sa 16:1
that he had made Saul king over Israel.

Samuel Anoints David

16 The LORD said to Samuel, "How long will you mourn[c] for Saul, since I have rejected[d] him as king 16:1 [c]1Sa 15:35 [d]1Sa 15:23
over Israel? Fill your horn with oil[e] and be on your way; I am sending you to Jesse[f] of Bethle- [e]2Ki 9:1 [f]Ru 4:17; 1Sa 9:16
hem. I have chosen[g] one of his sons to be king." [g]Ps 78:70; Ac 13:22
2 But Samuel said, "How can I go? Saul will hear about it and kill me."
The LORD said, "Take a heifer with you and say, 'I have come to sacrifice to the LORD.' 3 Invite Jesse to
the sacrifice, and I will show[h] you what to do. You are to anoint[i] for me the one I indicate." 16:3 [h]Ex 4:15 [i]Dt 17:15; 1Sa 9:16
4 Samuel did what the LORD said. When he arrived at Bethlehem,[j] the elders of the town trembled when 16:4 [j]Ge 48:7; Lk 2:4
they met him. They asked, "Do you come in peace?[k]" [k]1Ki 2:13; 2Ki 9:17

[a] 32 *Or him trembling, yet*

16:1 In Israel, kings and high priests were routinely anointed with oil, and a king could be referred to simply as the "Lord's anointed." The practice of anointing kings does not appear to have been universal in the ancient Near East, but there are other analogies. Pharaohs anointed subordinate officers, suggesting that to be the "Lord's anointed" was to be his subordinate ruler. In 2 Samuel 2:4 the "men of Judah" anointed David, perhaps implying that he was their representative head. See "Perfumes and Anointing Oils" on page 1746.

16:5 [l]Ex 19:10,22 — 5 Samuel replied, "Yes, in peace; I have come to sacrifice to the LORD. Consecrate[l] yourselves and come
to the sacrifice with me." Then he consecrated Jesse and his sons and invited them to the sacrifice.
16:6 [m]1Sa 17:13 — 6 When they arrived, Samuel saw Eliab[m] and thought, "Surely the LORD's anointed stands here before
the LORD."

7 But the LORD said to Samuel, "Do not consider his appearance or his height, for I have rejected him.
16:7 [n]Ps 147:10 [o]1Ki 8:39; 1Ch 28:9; Isa 55:8 — The LORD does not look at the things man looks at. Man looks at the outward appearance,[n] but the LORD
looks at the heart."[o]
16:8 [p]1Sa 17:13 — 8 Then Jesse called Abinadab[p] and had him pass in front of Samuel. But Samuel said, "The LORD has
not chosen this one either." 9 Jesse then had Shammah pass by, but Samuel said, "Nor has the LORD cho-
sen this one." 10 Jesse had seven of his sons pass before Samuel, but Samuel said to him, "The LORD has
16:11 [q]1Sa 17:12 — not chosen these." 11 So he asked Jesse, "Are these all[q] the sons you have?"

"There is still the youngest," Jesse answered, "but he is tending the sheep."

Samuel said, "Send for him; we will not sit down[a] until he arrives."

16:12 [r]1Sa 9:17 [s]Ge 39:6; 1Sa 17:42 — 12 So he[r] sent and had him brought in. He was ruddy, with a fine appearance and handsome[s] features.
Then the LORD said, "Rise and anoint him; he is the one."

13 So Samuel took the horn of oil and anointed him in the presence of his brothers, and from that day
16:13 [t]Nu 27:18; Jdg 11:29 [u]1Sa 10:1,6,9-10; 11:6 — on the Spirit of the LORD[t] came upon David in power.[u] Samuel then went to Ramah.

David in Saul's Service

16:14 [v]Jdg 16:20 [w]Jdg 9:23; 1Sa 18:10 — 14 Now the Spirit of the LORD had departed[v] from Saul, and an evil[b] spirit[w] from the LORD tormented
him.

15 Saul's attendants said to him, "See, an evil spirit from God is tormenting you. 16 Let our lord com-
16:16 [x]ver 23; 1Sa 18:10; 19:9; 2Ki 3:15 — mand his servants here to search for someone who can play the harp.[x] He will play when the evil spirit
from God comes upon you, and you will feel better."

17 So Saul said to his attendants, "Find someone who plays well and bring him to me."

18 One of the servants answered, "I have seen a son of Jesse of Bethlehem who knows how to play the
16:18 [y]1Sa 3:19; 17:32-37 — harp. He is a brave man and a warrior. He speaks well and is a fine-looking man. And the LORD is with[y]
him."

19 Then Saul sent messengers to Jesse and said, "Send me your son David, who is with the sheep." 20 So
16:20 [z]1Sa 10:27; Pr 18:16 — Jesse took a donkey loaded with bread,[z] a skin of wine and a young goat and sent them with his son Da-
vid to Saul.
16:21 [a]Ge 41:46; Pr 22:29 — 21 David came to Saul and entered his service.[a] Saul liked him very much, and David became one of
his armor-bearers. 22 Then Saul sent word to Jesse, saying, "Allow David to remain in my service, for I am
pleased with him."

23 Whenever the spirit from God came upon Saul, David would take his harp and play. Then relief
16:23 [b]ver 14-16 — would come to Saul; he would feel better, and the evil spirit[b] would leave him.

David and Goliath

17:1 [c]1Sa 13:5 [d]Jos 15:35; 2Ch 28:18 — **17** Now the Philistines gathered their forces for war and assembled[c] at Socoh in Judah. They pitched
camp at Ephes Dammim, between Socoh[d] and Azekah. 2 Saul and the Israelites assembled and
17:2 [e]1Sa 21:9 — camped in the Valley of Elah[e] and drew up their battle line to meet the Philistines. 3 The Philistines oc-
cupied one hill and the Israelites another, with the valley between them.
17:4 [f]Jos 11:21-22; 2Sa 21:19 — 4 A champion named Goliath,[f] who was from Gath, came out of the Philistine camp. He was over nine
feet[c] tall. 5 He had a bronze helmet on his head and wore a coat of scale armor of bronze weighing five
17:6 [g]ver 45 — thousand shekels[d]; 6 on his legs he wore bronze greaves, and a bronze javelin[g] was slung on his back. 7 His
17:7 [h]2Sa 21:19 [i]ver 41 — spear shaft was like a weaver's rod,[h] and its iron point weighed six hundred shekels.[e] His shield bearer[i]
went ahead of him.

8 Goliath stood and shouted to the ranks of Israel, "Why do you come out and line up for battle? Am I

[a] 11 Some Septuagint manuscripts; Hebrew *not gather around* [b] 14 Or *injurious*; also in verses 15, 16 and 23 [c] 4 Hebrew *was six cubits and a span* (about 3 meters) [d] 5 That is, about 125 pounds (about 57 kilograms) [e] 7 That is, about 15 pounds (about 7 kilograms)

17:4 The ancient Greeks, to whom the Philistines were apparently related (see "The Ekron Inscription of Akhayus" on p. 428), sometimes decided issues of war through chosen champions who met in combat in an area between the armies (see "Battle by Champions" on p. 422). This "trial by battle ordeal" was based upon the belief that the gods of each army actually fought or decided the battle. Israel, too, may have practiced this unconventional type of warfare (see 2Sa 2:14–16).

not a Philistine, and are you not the servants of Saul? Choose[j] a man and have him come down to me. 9If
he is able to fight and kill me, we will become your subjects; but if I overcome him and kill him, you will
become our subjects and serve us." 10Then the Philistine said, "This day I defy[k] the ranks of Israel! Give
me a man and let us fight each other." 11On hearing the Philistine's words, Saul and all the Israelites were
dismayed and terrified.

12Now David was the son of an Ephrathite named Jesse,[l] who was from Bethlehem[m] in Judah. Jesse
had eight[n] sons, and in Saul's time he was old and well advanced in years. 13Jesse's three oldest sons had
followed Saul to the war: The firstborn was Eliab;[o] the second, Abinadab; and the third, Shammah.[p] 14Da-

17:8 [j]1Sa 8:17
17:10 [k]ver 26,45; 2Sa 21:21
17:12 [l]Ru 4:17; 1Ch 2:13-15 [m]Ge 35:19 [n]1Sa 16:11
17:13 [o]1Sa 16:6 [p]1Sa 16:9

Battle by Champions

1 SAMUEL 17 The story of David and Goliath stands within the tradition of "battle by champions" in the ancient Near East. Such battles differed from duels in that they had ramifications for entire armies or nations. The strongest member, or champion, of each party fought a similar representative of the opponent to the death, and the victory of one man vindicated the entire host. Similar battles are found in the Egyptian History of Sinuhe, in the encounter of Marduk and Tiamat in the Babylonian epic *Enuma Elish*[1] and in the conflict of Paris and Menelaus in Homer's *Iliad*, 3.340–82. Second Samuel 2:12–16 also contains an account of a representative battle waged by 12 selected warriors.

Assyrian slingers attack a city in an Assyrian panel dated approximately 700 B.C.

Preserving Bible Times; © Dr. James C. Martin; permission of The British Museum

Such "single combat" was practiced based upon the belief that the gods of each army actually fought or decided the battle. Therefore, only one "champion" was needed from each side. This concept is clear in 1 Samuel 17:43–45, as both David and the Philistine call upon their respective gods. David's victory over the Philistine giant indeed proves that, against either pagan armies or false gods, "the battle is the LORD's" (v. 47). Unlike those who trusted in the stature, strength and skill of their best warriors, Israel sent an untrained, ill-equipped boy into battle as its only willing champion. David himself, however, trusted in God's might rather than his own.

For other war-related issues, see "Horses and Chariots in Ancient Warfare" on page 114, "Technological Supremacy of the Philistines' Iron Weapons" on page 414, "*Herem*, Holy War" on page 419, "Siege Warfare" on page 465, "Songs of Warriors" on page 474 and "Warfare in the Ancient World" on page 950.

[1]See "The *Enuma Elish* and the Biblical Concept of Creation" on page 888.

vid was the youngest. The three oldest followed Saul, 15but David went back and forth from Saul to tend
17:15 q1Sa 16:19 his father's sheep[q] at Bethlehem.
16For forty days the Philistine came forward every morning and evening and took his stand.
17:17 r1Sa 25:18 17Now Jesse said to his son David, "Take this ephah[a] of roasted grain[r] and these ten loaves of bread
for your brothers and hurry to their camp. 18Take along these ten cheeses to the commander of their
17:18 sGe 37:14 unit.[b] See how your brothers[s] are and bring back some assurance[c] from them. 19They are with Saul and
all the men of Israel in the Valley of Elah, fighting against the Philistines."
20Early in the morning David left the flock with a shepherd, loaded up and set out, as Jesse had direct-
ed. He reached the camp as the army was going out to its battle positions, shouting the war cry. 21Israel
and the Philistines were drawing up their lines facing each other. 22David left his things with the keep-
er of supplies, ran to the battle lines and greeted his brothers. 23As he was talking with them, Goliath,
17:23 tver 8-10 the Philistine champion from Gath, stepped out from his lines and shouted his usual[t] defiance, and Da-
vid heard it. 24When the Israelites saw the man, they all ran from him in great fear.
25Now the Israelites had been saying, "Do you see how this man keeps coming out? He comes out to
17:25 uJos 15:16; 1Sa 18:17 defy Israel. The king will give great wealth to the man who kills him. He will also give him his daughter[u]
in marriage and will exempt his father's family from taxes in Israel."
26David asked the men standing near him, "What will be done for the man who kills this Philistine
17:26 v1Sa 11:2 w1Sa 14:6 xver 10 yDt 5:26 and removes this disgrace[v] from Israel? Who is this uncircumcised[w] Philistine that he should defy[x] the
armies of the living[y] God?"
27They repeated to him what they had been saying and told him, "This is what will be done for the man
who kills him."
17:28 zGe 37:4,8, 11; Pr 18:19; Mt 10:36 28When Eliab, David's oldest brother, heard him speaking with the men, he burned with anger[z] at him
and asked, "Why have you come down here? And with whom did you leave those few sheep in the desert?
I know how conceited you are and how wicked your heart is; you came down only to watch the battle."
29"Now what have I done?" said David. "Can't I even speak?" 30He then turned away to someone else
and brought up the same matter, and the men answered him as before. 31What David said was overheard
and reported to Saul, and Saul sent for him.
17:32 aDt 20:3; 1Sa 16:18 32David said to Saul, "Let no one lose heart[a] on account of this Philistine; your servant will go and
fight him."
17:33 bNu 13:31 33Saul replied,[b] "You are not able to go out against this Philistine and fight him; you are only a boy, and
he has been a fighting man from his youth."
17:34 cJer 49:19; Am 3:12 34But David said to Saul, "Your servant has been keeping his father's sheep. When a lion[c] or a bear
came and carried off a sheep from the flock, 35I went after it, struck it and rescued the sheep from its
mouth. When it turned on me, I seized it by its hair, struck it and killed it. 36Your servant has killed both
the lion and the bear; this uncircumcised Philistine will be like one of them, because he has defied the
17:37 d2Co 1:10 e2Ti 4:17 f1Sa 20:13; 1Ch 22:11,16 armies of the living God. 37The LORD who delivered[d] me from the paw of the lion[e] and the paw of the
bear will deliver me from the hand of this Philistine."
Saul said to David, "Go, and the LORD be with[f] you."
38Then Saul dressed David in his own tunic. He put a coat of armor on him and a bronze helmet on
his head. 39David fastened on his sword over the tunic and tried walking around, because he was not
used to them.
"I cannot go in these," he said to Saul, "because I am not used to them." So he took them off. 40Then
he took his staff in his hand, chose five smooth stones from the stream, put them in the pouch of his
shepherd's bag and, with his sling in his hand, approached the Philistine.
41Meanwhile, the Philistine, with his shield bearer in front of him, kept coming closer to David. 42He
17:42 g1Sa 16:12 hPs 123:3-4; Pr 16:18 looked David over and saw that he was only a boy, ruddy and handsome,[g] and he despised[h] him. 43He
17:43 i1Sa 24:14; 2Sa 3:8; 9:8; 2Ki 8:13 said to David, "Am I a dog,[i] that you come at me with sticks?" And the Philistine cursed David by his
17:44 j1Ki 20:10-11 gods. 44"Come here," he said, "and I'll give your flesh to the birds of the air and the beasts of the field![j]"

[a] *17* That is, probably about 3/5 bushel (about 22 liters) [b] *18* Hebrew *thousand* [c] *18* Or *some token*; or *some pledge of spoils*

17:23 The city of Gath predates the Philistines, who entered the area around 1200 B.C. Usually identified as Tell Zafit, Gath is prominent in the David narrative. Goliath was from Gath, and when David fled Saul he surprisingly headed there (ch. 27). Hazael of Damascus captured the city and used its location in the Valley of Elah as an avenue by which to attack Jerusalem (2Ki 12:17). After its capture by Sargon II of Assyria in approximately 712 B.C., Gath ceased to be of major importance.

17:40 See the note on stones and gravel at Isaiah 27:9.

45 David said to the Philistine, "You come against me with sword and spear and javelin, but I come
against you in the name[k] of the LORD Almighty, the God of the armies of Israel, whom you have defied.[l]
46 This day the LORD will hand you over to me, and I'll strike you down and cut off your head. Today I will
give the carcasses[m] of the Philistine army to the birds of the air and the beasts of the earth, and the whole
world[n] will know that there is a God in Israel.[o] 47 All those gathered here will know that it is not by sword[p]
or spear that the LORD saves;[q] for the battle[r] is the LORD's, and he will give all of you into our hands."
48 As the Philistine moved closer to attack him, David ran quickly toward the battle line to meet him.
49 Reaching into his bag and taking out a stone, he slung it and struck the Philistine on the forehead. The
stone sank into his forehead, and he fell facedown on the ground.
50 So David triumphed over the Philistine with a sling[s] and a stone; without a sword in his hand he
struck down the Philistine and killed him.
51 David ran and stood over him. He took hold of the Philistine's sword and drew it from the scabbard.
After he killed him, he cut[t] off his head with the sword.[u]
When the Philistines saw that their hero was dead, they turned and ran. 52 Then the men of Israel and
Judah surged forward with a shout and pursued the Philistines to the entrance of Gath[a] and to the gates
of Ekron.[v] Their dead were strewn along the Shaaraim[w] road to Gath and Ekron. 53 When the Israelites
returned from chasing the Philistines, they plundered their camp. 54 David took the Philistine's head and
brought it to Jerusalem, and he put the Philistine's weapons in his own tent.
55 As Saul watched David[x] going out to meet the Philistine, he said to Abner, commander of the army,
"Abner, whose son is that young man?"
Abner replied, "As surely as you live, O king, I don't know."
56 The king said, "Find out whose son this young man is."
57 As soon as David returned from killing the Philistine, Abner took him and brought him before Saul,
with David still holding the Philistine's head.
58 "Whose son are you, young man?" Saul asked him.
David said, "I am the son of your servant Jesse[y] of Bethlehem."

Saul's Jealousy of David

18 After David had finished talking with Saul, Jonathan became one in spirit with David, and he
loved[z] him as himself.[a] 2 From that day Saul kept David with him and did not let him return to
his father's house. 3 And Jonathan made a covenant[b] with David because he loved him as himself. 4 Jon-
athan took off the robe[c] he was wearing and gave it to David, along with his tunic, and even his sword,
his bow and his belt.
5 Whatever Saul sent him to do, David did it so successfully[b] that Saul gave him a high rank in the
army. This pleased all the people, and Saul's officers as well.
6 When the men were returning home after David had killed the Philistine, the women came out from
all the towns of Israel to meet King Saul with singing and dancing,[d] with joyful songs and with tambou-
rines[e] and lutes. 7 As they danced, they sang:[f]

> "Saul has slain his thousands,
> and David his tens[g] of thousands."

8 Saul was very angry; this refrain galled him. "They have credited David with tens of thousands," he
thought, "but me with only thousands. What more can he get but the kingdom?[h]" 9 And from that time
on Saul kept a jealous eye on David.
10 The next day an evil[c] spirit[i] from God came forcefully upon Saul. He was prophesying in his house,
while David was playing the harp, as he usually[j] did. Saul had a spear in his hand 11 and he hurled it, say-
ing to himself,[k] "I'll pin David to the wall." But David eluded[l] him twice.
12 Saul was afraid[m] of David, because the LORD[n] was with[o] David but had left Saul. 13 So he sent David
away from him and gave him command over a thousand men, and David led[p] the troops in their cam-
paigns.[q] 14 In everything he did he had great success,[d r] because the LORD was with[s] him. 15 When Saul

[a] 52 Some Septuagint manuscripts; Hebrew *a valley* [b] 5 Or *wisely* [c] 10 Or *injurious* [d] 14 Or *he was very wise*

17:45 [k]2Sa 22:33,35; 2Ch 32:8; Ps 124:8; Heb 11:32-34 [l]ver 10
17:46 [m]Dt 28:26 [n]Jos 4:24; 1Ki 8:43; Isa 52:10 [o]1Ki 18:36; 2Ki 19:19; Isa 37:20
17:47 [p]Hos 1:7; Zec 4:6 [q]1Sa 14:6; 2Ch 14:11 [r]2Ch 20:15; Ps 44:6-7
17:50 [s]2Sa 23:21
17:51 [t]Heb 11:34 [u]1Sa 21:9
17:52 [v]Jos 15:11 [w]Jos 15:36
17:55 [x]1Sa 16:21
17:58 [y]ver 12
18:1 [z]2Sa 1:26 [a]Ge 44:30
18:3 [b]1Sa 20:8, 16,17,42
18:4 [c]Ge 41:42
18:6 [d]Ex 15:20 [e]Jdg 11:34; Ps 68:25
18:7 [f]Ex 15:21 [g]1Sa 21:11; 29:5
18:8 [h]1Sa 15:8
18:10 [i]1Sa 16:14 [j]1Sa 19:7
18:11 [k]1Sa 20:7, 33 [l]1Sa 19:10
18:12 [m]ver 15,29 [n]1Sa 16:13 [o]1Sa 28:15
18:13 [p]ver 16; Nu 27:17 [q]2Sa 5:2
18:14 [r]Ge 39:3 [s]Ge 39:2,23; Jos 6:27; 1Sa 16:18

18:6 For commentary on Old Testament expressions of joy, see the note on Psalm 96:11.
18:7 Using the normal conventions of Hebrew poetry—in which 10,000 was typically used as the parallel for 1,000 (see Dt 32:30; Ps 91:7; Mic 6:7; this may also be seen in Canaanite poetry found at Ugarit)—the phrase "David his tens of thousands" was in effect the women's way of saying, "Saul and David have slain thousands."

saw how successful[a] he was, he was afraid of him. 16 But all Israel and Judah loved David, because he led
them in their campaigns.[t]
17 Saul said to David, "Here is my older daughter[u] Merab. I will give her to you in marriage; only serve
me bravely and fight the battles[v] of the LORD." For Saul said to himself,[w] "I will not raise a hand against
him. Let the Philistines do that!"
18 But David said to Saul, "Who am I,[x] and what is my family or my father's clan in Israel, that I should
become the king's son-in-law?[y]" 19 So[b] when the time came for Merab,[z] Saul's daughter, to be given to
David, she was given in marriage to Adriel of Meholah.[a]
20 Now Saul's daughter Michal[b] was in love with David, and when they told Saul about it, he was
pleased. 21 "I will give her to him," he thought, "so that she may be a snare[c] to him and so that the hand
of the Philistines may be against him." So Saul said to David, "Now you have a second opportunity to be-
come my son-in-law."
22 Then Saul ordered his attendants: "Speak to David privately and say, 'Look, the king is pleased with
you, and his attendants all like you; now become his son-in-law.' "
23 They repeated these words to David. But David said, "Do you think it is a small matter to become
the king's son-in-law? I'm only a poor man and little known."
24 When Saul's servants told him what David had said, 25 Saul replied, "Say to David, 'The king wants
no other price[d] for the bride than a hundred Philistine foreskins, to take revenge on his enemies.' " Saul's
plan[e] was to have David fall by the hands of the Philistines.
26 When the attendants told David these things, he was pleased to become the king's son-in-law. So be-
fore the allotted time elapsed, 27 David and his men went out and killed two hundred Philistines. He
brought their foreskins and presented the full number to the king so that he might become the king's
son-in-law. Then Saul gave him his daughter Michal[f] in marriage.
28 When Saul realized that the LORD was with David and that his daughter Michal loved David, 29 Saul
became still more afraid of him, and he remained his enemy the rest of his days.
30 The Philistine commanders continued to go out to battle, and as often as they did, David met with
more success[c][g] than the rest of Saul's officers, and his name became well known.

Saul Tries to Kill David

19 Saul told his son Jonathan[h] and all the attendants to kill[i] David. But Jonathan was very fond of
David 2 and warned him, "My father Saul is looking for a chance to kill you. Be on your guard to-
morrow morning; go into hiding and stay there. 3 I will go out and stand with my father in the field where
you are. I'll speak[j] to him about you and will tell you what I find out."
4 Jonathan spoke[k] well of David to Saul his father and said to him, "Let not the king do wrong[l] to his
servant David; he has not wronged you, and what he has done has benefited you greatly. 5 He took his life
in his hands when he killed the Philistine. The LORD won a great victory[m] for all Israel, and you saw it and
were glad. Why then would you do wrong to an innocent[n] man like David by killing him for no reason?"
6 Saul listened to Jonathan and took this oath: "As surely as the LORD lives, David will not be put to death."
7 So Jonathan called David and told him the whole conversation. He brought him to Saul, and David
was with Saul as before.[o]
8 Once more war broke out, and David went out and fought the Philistines. He struck them with such
force that they fled before him.
9 But an evil[d] spirit[p] from the LORD came upon Saul as he was sitting in his house with his spear in his
hand. While David was playing the harp, 10 Saul tried to pin him to the wall with his spear, but David
eluded[q] him as Saul drove the spear into the wall. That night David made good his escape.
11 Saul sent men to David's house to watch[r] it and to kill him in the morning. But Michal, David's wife,
warned him, "If you don't run for your life tonight, tomorrow you'll be killed." 12 So Michal let David down
through a window,[s] and he fled and escaped. 13 Then Michal took an idol[e] and laid it on the bed, cover-
ing it with a garment and putting some goats' hair at the head.
14 When Saul sent the men to capture David, Michal said,[t] "He is ill."

18:16 [t] ver 5
18:17 [u] 1Sa 17:25 [v] Nu 21:14; 1Sa 25:28 [w] ver 25
18:18 [x] 1Sa 9:21; 2Sa 7:18 [y] ver 23
18:19 [z] 2Sa 21:8 [a] Jdg 7:22
18:20 [b] ver 28
18:21 [c] ver 17,26
18:25 [d] Ge 34:12; Ex 22:17; 1Sa 14:24 [e] ver 17
18:27 [f] ver 13; 2Sa 3:14
18:30 [g] ver 5; 2Sa 11:1
19:1 [h] 1Sa 18:1 [i] 1Sa 18:9
19:3 [j] 1Sa 20:12
19:4 [k] 1Sa 20:32; Pr 31:8,9; Jer 18:20 [l] Ge 42:22; Pr 17:13
19:5 [m] 1Sa 11:13; 17:49-50; 1Ch 11:14 [n] Dt 19:10-13; 1Sa 20:32; Mt 27:4
19:7 [o] 1Sa 16:21; 18:2,13
19:9 [p] 1Sa 16:14; 18:10-11
19:10 [q] 1Sa 18:11
19:11 [r] Ps 59 Title
19:12 [s] Jos 2:15; Ac 9:25
19:14 [t] Jos 2:4

[a] 15 Or *wise* [b] 19 Or *However,* [c] 30 Or *David acted more wisely* [d] 9 Or *injurious* [e] 13 Hebrew *teraphim*; also in verse 16

19:13 The precise nature of the "idol" that Michal used is uncertain, although most scholars consider it to have been some kind of household god. Since we do not know what it looked like or how big it was, it is difficult to determine what role it played in deceiving David's pursuers. Some suggest that it was a life-sized human form, while others picture a kind of mask (perhaps representing ancestors).

15 Then Saul sent the men back to see David and told them, "Bring him up to me in his bed so that I
may kill him." 16 But when the men entered, there was the idol in the bed, and at the head was some goats'
hair.
17 Saul said to Michal, "Why did you deceive me like this and send my enemy away so that he escaped?"
Michal told him, "He said to me, 'Let me get away. Why should I kill you?' "
18 When David had fled and made his escape, he went to Samuel at Ramah[u] and told him all that Saul 19:18 [u]1Sa 7:17
had done to him. Then he and Samuel went to Naioth and stayed there. 19 Word came to Saul: "David is
in Naioth at Ramah"; 20 so he sent men to capture him. But when they saw a group of prophets[v] prophe- 19:20 [v]ver 11,14;
sying, with Samuel standing there as their leader, the Spirit of God came upon[w] Saul's men and they also Jn 7:32,45 [w]Nu 11:25
prophesied.[x] 21 Saul was told about it, and he sent more men, and they prophesied too. Saul sent men a [x]1Sa 10:5; Joel 2:28
third time, and they also prophesied. 22 Finally, he himself left for Ramah and went to the great cistern at
Secu. And he asked, "Where are Samuel and David?"
"Over in Naioth at Ramah," they said.
23 So Saul went to Naioth at Ramah. But the Spirit of God came even upon him, and he walked along
prophesying[y] until he came to Naioth. 24 He stripped[z] off his robes and also prophesied in Samuel's pres- 19:23 [y]1Sa 10:13
ence. He lay that way all that day and night. This is why people say, "Is Saul also among the prophets?"[a] 19:24 [z]2Sa 6:20; Isa 20:2; Mic 1:8 [a]1Sa 10:11

David and Jonathan

20 Then David fled from Naioth at Ramah and went to Jonathan and asked, "What have I done?
What is my crime? How have I wronged[b] your father, that he is trying to take my life?" 20:1 [b]1Sa 24:9
2 "Never!" Jonathan replied. "You are not going to die! Look, my father doesn't do anything, great or
small, without confiding in me. Why would he hide this from me? It's not so!"
3 But David took an oath[c] and said, "Your father knows very well that I have found favor in your eyes, 20:3 [c]Dt 6:13
and he has said to himself, 'Jonathan must not know this or he will be grieved.' Yet as surely as the LORD
lives and as you live, there is only a step between me and death."
4 Jonathan said to David, "Whatever you want me to do, I'll do for you."
5 So David said, "Look, tomorrow is the New Moon festival,[d] and I am supposed to dine with the king; 20:5 [d]Nu 10:10;
but let me go and hide[e] in the field until the evening of the day after tomorrow. 6 If your father misses me 28:11 [e]1Sa 19:2
at all, tell him, 'David earnestly asked my permission to hurry to Bethlehem,[f] his hometown, because an 20:6 [f]1Sa 17:58
annual[g] sacrifice is being made there for his whole clan.' 7 If he says, 'Very well,' then your servant is safe. [g]Dt 12:5
But if he loses his temper,[h] you can be sure that he is determined to harm me. 8 As for you, show kind- 20:7 [h]1Sa 25:17
ness to your servant, for you have brought him into a covenant[i] with you before the LORD. If I am guilty, 20:8 [i]1Sa 18:3;
then kill[j] me yourself! Why hand me over to your father?" 23:18 [j]2Sa 14:32
9 "Never!" Jonathan said. "If I had the least inkling that my father was determined to harm you,
wouldn't I tell you?"
10 David asked, "Who will tell me if your father answers you harshly?"
11 "Come," Jonathan said, "let's go out into the field." So they went there together.
12 Then Jonathan said to David: "By the LORD, the God of Israel, I will surely sound out my father by
this time the day after tomorrow! If he is favorably disposed toward you, will I not send you word and
let you know? 13 But if my father is inclined to harm you, may the LORD deal with me, be it ever so severe-
ly,[k] if I do not let you know and send you away safely. May the LORD be with[l] you as he has been with my 20:13 [k]Ru 1:17;
father. 14 But show me unfailing kindness like that of the LORD as long as I live, so that I may not be killed, 1Sa 3:17 [l]Jos 1:5; 1Sa 17:37; 18:12;
15 and do not ever cut off your kindness from my family[m]—not even when the LORD has cut off every one 1Ch 22:11,16 20:15 [m]2Sa 9:7
of David's enemies from the face of the earth."
16 So Jonathan made a covenant[n] with the house of David, saying, "May the LORD call David's enemies 20:16 [n]1Sa 25:22
to account." 17 And Jonathan had David reaffirm his oath[o] out of love for him, because he loved him as he 20:17 [o]1Sa 18:3
loved himself.
18 Then Jonathan said to David: "Tomorrow is the New Moon festival. You will be missed, because your
seat will be empty.[p] 19 The day after tomorrow, toward evening, go to the place where you hid[q] when this 20:18 [p]ver 5,25
trouble began, and wait by the stone Ezel. 20 I will shoot three arrows to the side of it, as though I were 20:19 [q]1Sa 19:2
shooting at a target. 21 Then I will send a boy and say, 'Go, find the arrows.' If I say to him, 'Look, the arrows

---

20:5 Each new month of the year (i.e., the New Moon) was consecrated to the Lord by the bringing of special sacrifices (Nu 28:11–15) and the blowing of trumpets (Nu 10:10). This observance also involved cessation from normal work.

20:14 It was common in the ancient world for the first ruler of a new dynasty to secure his position by murdering all potential claimants to the throne from the preceding dynasty (see 1Ki 15:29; 16:11; 2Ki 10:7; 11:1; see also "Ambitious Princes Among the Hitites" on p. 469).

are on this side of you; bring them here,' then come, because, as surely as the LORD lives, you are safe; there is no danger. 22 But if I say to the boy, 'Look, the arrows are beyond[r] you,' then you must go, because the LORD has sent you away. 23 And about the matter you and I discussed—remember, the LORD is witness[s] between you and me forever."

24 So David hid in the field, and when the New Moon festival came, the king sat down to eat. 25 He sat in his customary place by the wall, opposite Jonathan,[a] and Abner sat next to Saul, but David's place was empty.[t] 26 Saul said nothing that day, for he thought, "Something must have happened to David to make him ceremonially unclean—surely he is unclean.[u]" 27 But the next day, the second day of the month, David's place was empty again. Then Saul said to his son Jonathan, "Why hasn't the son of Jesse come to the meal, either yesterday or today?"

28 Jonathan answered, "David earnestly asked me for permission[v] to go to Bethlehem. 29 He said, 'Let me go, because our family is observing a sacrifice in the town and my brother has ordered me to be there. If I have found favor in your eyes, let me get away to see my brothers.' That is why he has not come to the king's table."

30 Saul's anger flared up at Jonathan and he said to him, "You son of a perverse and rebellious woman! Don't I know that you have sided with the son of Jesse to your own shame and to the shame of the mother who bore you? 31 As long as the son of Jesse lives on this earth, neither you nor your kingdom will be established. Now send and bring him to me, for he must die!"

32 "Why[w] should he be put to death? What[x] has he done?" Jonathan asked his father. 33 But Saul hurled his spear at him to kill him. Then Jonathan knew that his father intended[y] to kill David.

34 Jonathan got up from the table in fierce anger; on that second day of the month he did not eat, because he was grieved at his father's shameful treatment of David.

35 In the morning Jonathan went out to the field for his meeting with David. He had a small boy with him, 36 and he said to the boy, "Run and find the arrows I shoot." As the boy ran, he shot an arrow beyond him. 37 When the boy came to the place where Jonathan's arrow had fallen, Jonathan called out after him, "Isn't the arrow beyond[z] you?" 38 Then he shouted, "Hurry! Go quickly! Don't stop!" The boy picked up the arrow and returned to his master. 39 (The boy knew nothing of all this; only Jonathan and David knew.) 40 Then Jonathan gave his weapons to the boy and said, "Go, carry them back to town."

41 After the boy had gone, David got up from the south side ⌊of the stone⌋ and bowed down before Jonathan three times, with his face to the ground. Then they kissed each other and wept together—but David wept the most.

42 Jonathan said to David, "Go in peace,[a] for we have sworn friendship[b] with each other in the name of the LORD, saying, 'The LORD is witness between you and me, and between your descendants and my descendants forever.' " Then David left, and Jonathan went back to the town.

David at Nob

21 David went to Nob,[c] to Ahimelech the priest. Ahimelech trembled[d] when he met him, and asked, "Why are you alone? Why is no one with you?"

2 David answered Ahimelech the priest, "The king charged me with a certain matter and said to me, 'No one is to know anything about your mission and your instructions.' As for my men, I have told them to meet me at a certain place. 3 Now then, what do you have on hand? Give me five loaves of bread, or whatever you can find."

4 But the priest answered David, "I don't have any ordinary bread[e] on hand; however, there is some consecrated[f] bread here—provided the men have kept[g] themselves from women."

5 David replied, "Indeed women have been kept from us, as usual whenever[b] I set out. The men's things[c] are holy[h] even on missions that are not holy. How much more so today!" 6 So the priest gave him the consecrated bread,[i] since there was no bread there except the bread of the Presence that had been removed from before the LORD and replaced by hot bread on the day it was taken away.

20:22 [r]ver 37
20:23 [s]ver 14-15; Ge 31:50
20:25 [t]ver 18
20:26 [u]Lev 7:20-21; 15:5; 1Sa 16:5
20:28 [v]ver 6
20:32 [w]1Sa 19:4; Mt 27:23 [x]Ge 31:36; Lk 23:22
20:33 [y]ver 7; 1Sa 18:11,17
20:37 [z]ver 22
20:42 [a]ver 22; 1Sa 1:17 [b]2Sa 1:26; Pr 18:24
21:1 [c]1Sa 14:3; 22:9,19; Ne 11:32; Isa 10:32 [d]1Sa 16:4
21:4 [e]Lev 24:8-9 [f]Ex 25:30; Mt 12:4 [g]Ex 19:15
21:5 [h]1Th 4:4
21:6 [i]Lev 24:8-9; Mt 12:3-4; Mk 2:25-28; Lk 6:1-5

[a] 25 Septuagint; Hebrew *wall. Jonathan arose* [b] 5 Or *from us in the past few days since* [c] 5 Or *bodies*

20:42 For a discussion of salutations in the Bible, see the note on Ruth 2:4.

21:1 Nob, a town northeast of Jerusalem and south of Gibeah, was the location at which the tabernacle was relocated after the destruction of Shiloh (see 4:2–3; see also "The Destruction of Shiloh" on p. 1200).

21:4 The bread was placed in the Holy Place in the tabernacle (and later in the temple) as a thank offering to the Lord, symbolizing his provision of daily bread. It could be eaten only by the priests (see Lev 24:9).

7 Now one of Saul's servants was there that day, detained before the LORD; he was Doeg[j] the Edomite,[k] **21:7** [j]1Sa 22:9, 22 [k]1Sa 14:47; Ps 52 Title
Saul's head shepherd.
8 David asked Ahimelech, "Don't you have a spear or a sword here? I haven't brought my sword or any
other weapon, because the king's business was urgent."
9 The priest replied, "The sword[l] of Goliath the Philistine, whom you killed in the Valley of Elah,[m] is **21:9** [l]1Sa 17:51 [m]1Sa 17:2
here; it is wrapped in a cloth behind the ephod. If you want it, take it; there is no sword here but that one."
David said, "There is none like it; give it to me."

David at Gath

10 That day David fled from Saul and went[n] to Achish king of Gath. 11 But the servants of Achish said **21:10** [n]1Sa 27:2
to him, "Isn't this David, the king of the land? Isn't he the one they sing about in their dances:

> " 'Saul has slain his thousands,
> and David his tens of thousands'?"[o] **21:11** [o]1Sa 18:7; 29:5; Ps 56 Title

12 David took these words to heart and was very much afraid of Achish king of Gath. 13 So he pretend-
ed to be insane[p] in their presence; and while he was in their hands he acted like a madman, making **21:13** [p]Ps 34 Title
marks on the doors of the gate and letting saliva run down his beard.
14 Achish said to his servants, "Look at the man! He is insane! Why bring him to me? 15 Am I so short
of madmen that you have to bring this fellow here to carry on like this in front of me? Must this man
come into my house?"

David at Adullam and Mizpah

22 David left Gath and escaped to the cave[q] of Adullam. When his brothers and his father's house- **22:1** [q]2Sa 23:13; Ps 57 Title; 142 Title
hold heard about it, they went down to him there. 2 All those who were in distress or in debt or
discontented gathered[r] around him, and he became their leader. About four hundred men were with him. **22:2** [r]1Sa 23:13; 25:13; 2Sa 15:20
3 From there David went to Mizpah in Moab and said to the king of Moab, "Would you let my father

---

22:3–4 The king of Moab (see "Moab" on p. 292) was a natural ally for David because Saul had warred against him (see 14:47), and David's own great-grandmother, Ruth, was a Moabitess (see Ru 4:13,22).

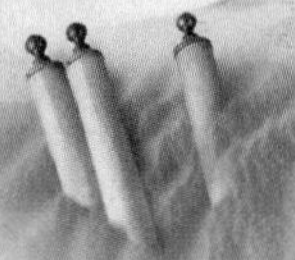

ANCIENT TEXTS AND ARTIFACTS

The Ekron Inscription of Akhayus

1 SAMUEL 21 Sometimes evidence from proper names (onomastic evidence) helps us to reconstruct the history and racial identity of a people. In 1996 a dedicatory inscription was discovered in a Philistine temple at Ekron ("Map 4"), reading in part: "The temple that Achish, son of Padi, . . . ruler of Ekron, built for PTGYH." Although PTGYH's identity is debated, Achish and Padi are known from **Assyrian** records as kings of Ekron. Achish appears by the name Ikausu in Ashurbanipal's annals from the early seventh century B.C. But both appear to derive from a previous form of the name, Akhayus, which is similar to the Greek term *Achaios* (Achaean). The Achaeans were one of the archaic Greek peoples. In short, widespread evidence suggests that the Philistines were related to the Greeks.

According to 1 Samuel 21:11–16, 27:1—29:9 and 1 Kings 2:39–40, the ruler(s) of Gath ("Map 4") were named Achish from the time of Saul to the days of Solomon (tenth–ninth centuries B.C.). Similarly, an eighth-century Philistine ruler of Ashdod used the nickname Yamani, which seems to be a corruption of the word *Ionian* (another Greek people). Thus it appears that various Philistine rulers used their Greek ethnic identity as a title for themselves. This conclusion is supported by their **material culture** in the twelfth century B.C., which is Achaean. This evidence also fits well with the assertions of Jeremiah 47:4, Amos 9:7 and Zephaniah 2:4–6 that the Philistines were Kerethites (hailing from Crete [aka Caphtor])[1] who came to **Canaan** along with the Greek **Sea Peoples**.[2]

[1]See "Greece: From the Prehistoric Period Through the Mycenaean Empire" on page 1810 and "Crete" on page 1972. [2]See "The Archaeology of Philistia" on page 370.

and mother come and stay with you until I learn what God will do for me?" 4So he left them with the
king of Moab, and they stayed with him as long as David was in the stronghold.
22:5 [s]2Sa 24:11; 1Ch 21:9; 29:29; 2Ch 29:25 5But the prophet Gad[s] said to David, "Do not stay in the stronghold. Go into the land of Judah." So Da-
vid left and went to the forest of Hereth.

Saul Kills the Priests of Nob

22:6 [t]Jdg 4:5 [u]Ge 21:33 6Now Saul heard that David and his men had been discovered. And Saul, spear in hand, was seated[t]
under the tamarisk[u] tree on the hill at Gibeah, with all his officials standing around him. 7Saul said to
them, "Listen, men of Benjamin! Will the son of Jesse give all of you fields and vineyards? Will he make
22:7 [v]1Sa 8:14 all of you commanders[v] of thousands and commanders of hundreds? 8Is that why you have all conspired
22:8 [w]1Sa 18:3; 20:16 [x]1Sa 23:21 against me? No one tells me when my son makes a covenant[w] with the son of Jesse. None of you is con-
cerned[x] about me or tells me that my son has incited my servant to lie in wait for me, as he does today."
22:9 [y]1Sa 21:7; Ps 52 Title [z]1Sa 21:1 9But Doeg[y] the Edomite, who was standing with Saul's officials, said, "I saw the son of Jesse come to
Ahimelech son of Ahitub at Nob.[z] 10Ahimelech inquired[a] of the LORD for him; he also gave him provi-
22:10 [a]Nu 27:21; 1Sa 10:22 [b]1Sa 21:6 sions[b] and the sword of Goliath the Philistine."
11Then the king sent for the priest Ahimelech son of Ahitub and his father's whole family, who were
the priests at Nob, and they all came to the king. 12Saul said, "Listen now, son of Ahitub."
"Yes, my lord," he answered.
22:13 [c]ver 8 13Saul said to him, "Why have you conspired[c] against me, you and the son of Jesse, giving him bread
and a sword and inquiring of God for him, so that he has rebelled against me and lies in wait for me, as
he does today?"
22:14 [d]1Sa 19:4 14Ahimelech answered the king, "Who[d] of all your servants is as loyal as David, the king's son-in-law,
captain of your bodyguard and highly respected in your household? 15Was that day the first time I in-
quired of God for him? Of course not! Let not the king accuse your servant or any of his father's family,
for your servant knows nothing at all about this whole affair."
16But the king said, "You will surely die, Ahimelech, you and your father's whole family."
17Then the king ordered the guards at his side: "Turn and kill the priests of the LORD, because they too
have sided with David. They knew he was fleeing, yet they did not tell me."
22:17 [e]Ex 1:17 But the king's officials were not willing[e] to raise a hand to strike the priests of the LORD.
18The king then ordered Doeg, "You turn and strike down the priests." So Doeg the Edomite turned
22:18 [f]1Sa 2:18, 31 and struck them down. That day he killed eighty-five men who wore the linen ephod.[f] 19He also put to
22:19 [g]1Sa 15:3 the sword[g] Nob, the town of the priests, with its men and women, its children and infants, and its cattle,
donkeys and sheep.
22:20 [h]1Sa 23:6, 9; 30:7; 1Ki 2:22, 26,27 [i]1Sa 2:32 20But Abiathar,[h] a son of Ahimelech son of Ahitub, escaped and fled to join David.[i] 21He told David
that Saul had killed the priests of the LORD. 22Then David said to Abiathar: "That day, when Doeg[j] the
22:22 [j]1Sa 21:7 Edomite was there, I knew he would be sure to tell Saul. I am responsible for the death of your father's
22:23 [k]1Ki 2:26 whole family. 23Stay with me; don't be afraid; the man who is seeking your life[k] is seeking mine also. You
will be safe with me."

David Saves Keilah

23:1 [l]Jos 15:44 **23** When David was told, "Look, the Philistines are fighting against Keilah[l] and are looting the
23:2 [m]ver 4,12; 1Sa 30:8; 2Sa 5:19,23 threshing floors," 2he inquired[m] of the LORD, saying, "Shall I go and attack these Philistines?"
The LORD answered him, "Go, attack the Philistines and save Keilah."
3But David's men said to him, "Here in Judah we are afraid. How much more, then, if we go to Keilah
against the Philistine forces!"
4Once again David inquired of the LORD, and the LORD answered him, "Go down to Keilah, for I am go-
23:4 [n]Jos 8:7; Jdg 7:7 ing to give the Philistines into your hand."[n] 5So David and his men went to Keilah, fought the Philistines
and carried off their livestock. He inflicted heavy losses on the Philistines and saved the people of Kei-
23:6 [o]1Sa 22:20 lah. 6(Now Abiathar[o] son of Ahimelech had brought the ephod down with him when he fled to David at
Keilah.)

22:9–18 Priests and diviners were sometimes forced, under penalty of death, to take oaths of loyalty to the king—committing to serve as his informants.

23:1 For a discussion of the threshing floor, see the note on Ruth 3:4–7. See also "The Threshing Floor" on page 608.

23:6 This was the special ephod of the high priest (see Ex 28:4–13; see also "The Ephod" on p. 399). The breastplate containing the Urim and Thummim was attached to the ephod (see "The Urim and Thummim" on p. 136).

Saul Pursues David

7 Saul was told that David had gone to Keilah, and he said, "God has handed him over to me, for David has imprisoned himself by entering a town with gates and bars." 8 And Saul called up all his forces for battle, to go down to Keilah to besiege David and his men.

9 When David learned that Saul was plotting against him, he said to Abiathar[p] the priest, "Bring the ephod." 10 David said, "O LORD, God of Israel, your servant has heard definitely that Saul plans to come to Keilah and destroy the town on account of me. 11 Will the citizens of Keilah surrender me to him? Will Saul come down, as your servant has heard? O LORD, God of Israel, tell your servant."

And the LORD said, "He will."

12 Again David asked, "Will the citizens of Keilah surrender[q] me and my men to Saul?"

And the LORD said, "They will."

13 So David and his men,[r] about six hundred in number, left Keilah and kept moving from place to place. When Saul was told that David had escaped from Keilah, he did not go there.

14 David stayed in the desert strongholds and in the hills of the Desert of Ziph.[s] Day after day Saul searched[t] for him, but God did not[u] give David into his hands.

15 While David was at Horesh in the Desert of Ziph, he learned that Saul had come out to take his life. 16 And Saul's son Jonathan went to David at Horesh and helped him find strength[v] in God. 17 "Don't be afraid," he said. "My father Saul will not lay a hand on you. You will be king[w] over Israel, and I will be second to you. Even my father Saul knows this." 18 The two of them made a covenant[x] before the LORD. Then Jonathan went home, but David remained at Horesh.

19 The Ziphites[y] went up to Saul at Gibeah and said, "Is not David hiding among us[z] in the strongholds at Horesh, on the hill of Hakilah,[a] south of Jeshimon? 20 Now, O king, come down whenever it pleases you to do so, and we will be responsible for handing[b] him over to the king."

21 Saul replied, "The LORD bless you for your concern[c] for me. 22 Go and make further preparation. Find out where David usually goes and who has seen him there. They tell me he is very crafty. 23 Find out about all the hiding places he uses and come back to me with definite information.[a] Then I will go with you; if he is in the area, I will track him down among all the clans of Judah."

24 So they set out and went to Ziph ahead of Saul. Now David and his men were in the Desert of Maon,[d] in the Arabah south of Jeshimon. 25 Saul and his men began the search, and when David was told about it, he went down to the rock and stayed in the Desert of Maon. When Saul heard this, he went into the Desert of Maon in pursuit of David.

26 Saul[e] was going along one side of the mountain, and David and his men were on the other side, hurrying to get away from Saul. As Saul and his forces were closing in on David and his men to capture them, 27 a messenger came to Saul, saying, "Come quickly! The Philistines are raiding the land." 28 Then Saul broke off his pursuit of David and went to meet the Philistines. That is why they call this place Sela Hammahlekoth.[b] 29 And David went up from there and lived in the strongholds of En Gedi.[f]

David Spares Saul's Life

24 After Saul returned from pursuing the Philistines, he was told, "David is in the Desert of En Gedi.[g]" 2 So Saul took three thousand chosen men from all Israel and set out to look[h] for David and his men near the Crags of the Wild Goats.

3 He came to the sheep pens along the way; a cave[i] was there, and Saul went in to relieve[j] himself. David and his men were far back in the cave. 4 The men said, "This is the day the LORD spoke[k] of when he said[c] to you, 'I will give your enemy into your hands for you to deal with as you wish.' "[l] Then David crept up unnoticed and cut off a corner of Saul's robe.

5 Afterward, David was conscience-stricken[m] for having cut off a corner of his robe. 6 He said to his men, "The LORD forbid that I should do such a thing to my master, the LORD's anointed,[n] or lift my hand against him; for he is the anointed of the LORD." 7 With these words David rebuked his men and did not allow them to attack Saul. And Saul left the cave and went his way.

8 Then David went out of the cave and called out to Saul, "My lord the king!" When Saul looked behind

23:9 [p] ver 6; 1Sa 22:20; 30:7
23:12 [q] ver 20
23:13 [r] 1Sa 22:2; 25:13
23:14 [s] Jos 15:24,55 [t] Ps 54:3-4 [u] Ps 32:7
23:16 [v] 1Sa 30:6
23:17 [w] 1Sa 20:31; 24:20
23:18 [x] 1Sa 18:3; 20:16,42; 2Sa 9:1; 21:7
23:19 [y] 1Sa 26:1 [z] Ps 54 Title [a] 1Sa 26:3
23:20 [b] ver 12
23:21 [c] 1Sa 22:8
23:24 [d] Jos 15:55; 1Sa 25:2
23:26 [e] Ps 17:9
23:29 [f] 2Ch 20:2
24:1 [g] 1Sa 23:28-29
24:2 [h] 1Sa 26:2
24:3 [i] Ps 57 Title; 142 Title [j] Jdg 3:24
24:4 [k] 1Sa 25:28-30 [l] 1Sa 23:17; 26:8
24:5 [m] 2Sa 24:10
24:6 [n] 1Sa 26:11

[a] 23 Or *me at Nacon* [b] 28 *Sela Hammahlekoth* means *rock of parting.* [c] 4 Or *"Today the LORD is saying*

24:4–5 David's cutting off of a corner of Saul's robe was probably more than a means of proving his goodwill toward Saul. To grasp the hem of a garment symbolized loyalty, however, while cutting off a piece of a person's robe ordinarily signified disloyalty and rebellion.

him, David bowed down and prostrated himself with his face to the ground.[o] 9He said to Saul, "Why do you listen when men say, 'David is bent on harming you'? 10This day you have seen with your own eyes how the LORD delivered you into my hands in the cave. Some urged me to kill you, but I spared you; I said, 'I will not lift my hand against my master, because he is the LORD's anointed.' 11See, my father, look at this piece of your robe in my hand! I cut off the corner of your robe but did not kill you. Now understand and recognize that I am not guilty[p] of wrongdoing or rebellion. I have not wronged you, but you are hunting[q] me down to take my life. 12May the LORD judge[r] between you and me. And may the LORD avenge[s] the wrongs you have done to me, but my hand will not touch you. 13As the old saying goes, 'From evildoers come evil deeds,'[t] so my hand will not touch you.

14"Against whom has the king of Israel come out? Whom are you pursuing? A dead dog?[u] A flea?[v] 15May the LORD be our judge[w] and decide between us. May he consider my cause and uphold[x] it; may he vindicate[y] me by delivering[z] me from your hand."

16When David finished saying this, Saul asked, "Is that your voice,[a] David my son?" And he wept aloud. 17"You are more righteous than I,"[b] he said. "You have treated me well,[c] but I have treated you badly. 18You have just now told me of the good you did to me; the LORD delivered[d] me into your hands, but you did not kill me. 19When a man finds his enemy, does he let him get away unharmed? May the LORD reward you well for the way you treated me today. 20I know that you will surely be king[e] and that the kingdom[f] of Israel will be established in your hands. 21Now swear[g] to me by the LORD that you will not cut off my descendants or wipe out my name from my father's family.[h]"

22So David gave his oath to Saul. Then Saul returned home, but David and his men went up to the stronghold.[i]

David, Nabal and Abigail

25 Now Samuel died,[j] and all Israel assembled and mourned[k] for him; and they buried him at his home in Ramah.[l]

Then David moved down into the Desert of Maon.[a] 2A certain man in Maon,[m] who had property there at Carmel, was very wealthy. He had a thousand goats and three thousand sheep, which he was shearing in Carmel. 3His name was Nabal and his wife's name was Abigail.[n] She was an intelligent and beautiful woman, but her husband, a Calebite,[o] was surly and mean in his dealings.

24:8 [o]1Sa 25:23-24
24:11 [p]Ps 7:3 [q]1Sa 23:14,23; 26:20
24:12 [r]Ge 16:5; 31:53; Job 5:8 [s]Jdg 11:27; 1Sa 26:10
24:13 [t]Mt 7:20
24:14 [u]1Sa 17:43; 2Sa 9:8 [v]1Sa 26:20
24:15 [w]ver 12 [x]Ps 35:1,23; Mic 7:9 [y]Ps 43:1 [z]Ps 119:134,154
24:16 [a]1Sa 26:17
24:17 [b]Ge 38:26; 1Sa 26:21 [c]Mt 5:44
24:18 [d]1Sa 26:23
24:20 [e]1Sa 23:17 [f]1Sa 13:14
24:21 [g]Ge 21:23; 2Sa 21:1-9 [h]1Sa 20:14-15
24:22 [i]1Sa 23:29
25:1 [j]1Sa 28:3 [k]Nu 20:29; Dt 34:8 [l]Ge 21:21; 2Ch 33:20
25:2 [m]Jos 15:55; 1Sa 23:24
25:3 [n]Pr 31:10 [o]Jos 15:13

[a] *1* Some Septuagint manuscripts; Hebrew *Paran*

Bywords and Insults in the Ancient World

1 SAMUEL 25 Nabal's answer to David's agents (1Sa 25:10–11) was a flagrant insult; David had been serving him with honor, but Nabal responded by speaking of David in scurrilous terms as an outlaw. In the ancient world men (and particularly warriors) placed an enormous premium on their personal reputations and thus took insults and perceived slights to their honor very seriously. Examples of this abound in ancient literature; perhaps the most famous is the Greek hero Achilles, who sat in his tent and refused to fight against the Trojans when he felt that his fellow Greeks had failed to show due respect for his prestige (as described in Homer's *Iliad*). When the Philistine Goliath defied the ranks of Israel (ch. 17), the young David regarded this as reason enough to go out to fight the giant.[1] David was later willing to start a war with the Ammonites to avenge their humiliating treatment of his ambassadors (2Sa 10).

Insults and slights required an appropriate response on behalf of the individual so affronted. Exodus 21:17 prescribes the death penalty for those who cursed (reviled or insulted) their parents, and the 42 young men making fun of Elisha were mauled by two bears (2Ki 2:23–25). The New Testament calls upon Christians to be forbearing toward those who insult them (1Pe 3:9), but in order to understand David and his responses to taunts we need to comprehend the warrior-culture in which he lived.[2] In addition, as in the above examples, when **Yahweh**'s people or his anointed are insulted the reputation of Yahweh himself has been affronted.

[1]See "Battle by Champions" on page 422. [2]See "Songs of Warriors" on page 474.

4While David was in the desert, he heard that Nabal was shearing sheep. 5So he sent ten young men
and said to them, "Go up to Nabal at Carmel and greet him in my name. 6Say to him: 'Long life to you!
Good health[p] to you and your household! And good health to all that is yours![q]
7" 'Now I hear that it is sheep-shearing time. When your shepherds were with us, we did not mistreat[r]
them, and the whole time they were at Carmel nothing of theirs was missing. 8Ask your own servants and
they will tell you. Therefore be favorable toward my young men, since we come at a festive time. Please
give your servants and your son David whatever[s] you can find for them.' "
9When David's men arrived, they gave Nabal this message in David's name. Then they waited.
10Nabal answered David's servants, "Who[t] is this David? Who is this son of Jesse? Many servants are
breaking away from their masters these days. 11Why should I take my bread[u] and water, and the meat I
have slaughtered for my shearers, and give it to men coming from who knows where?"
12David's men turned around and went back. When they arrived, they reported every word. 13David
said to his men, "Put on your swords!" So they put on their swords, and David put on his. About four
hundred men went[v] up with David, while two hundred stayed with the supplies.[w]
14One of the servants told Nabal's wife Abigail: "David sent messengers from the desert to give our
master his greetings,[x] but he hurled insults at them. 15Yet these men were very good to us. They did not
mistreat[y] us, and the whole time we were out in the fields near them nothing was missing.[z] 16Night and
day they were a wall[a] around us all the time we were herding our sheep near them. 17Now think it over
and see what you can do, because disaster is hanging over our master and his whole household. He is such
a wicked[b] man that no one can talk to him."
18Abigail lost no time. She took two hundred loaves of bread, two skins of wine, five dressed sheep,
five seahs[a] of roasted grain, a hundred cakes of raisins[c] and two hundred cakes of pressed figs, and load-
ed them on donkeys.[d] 19Then she told her servants, "Go on ahead;[e] I'll follow you." But she did not tell
her husband Nabal.
20As she came riding her donkey into a mountain ravine, there were David and his men descending to-
ward her, and she met them. 21David had just said, "It's been useless—all my watching over this fellow's
property in the desert so that nothing of his was missing. He has paid[f] me back evil for good. 22May God
deal with David,[b] be it ever so severely,[g] if by morning I leave alive one male[h] of all who belong to him!"
23When Abigail saw David, she quickly got off her donkey and bowed down before David with her
face to the ground.[i] 24She fell at his feet and said: "My lord, let the blame be on me alone. Please let your
servant speak to you; hear what your servant has to say. 25May my lord pay no attention to that wicked
man Nabal. He is just like his name—his name is Fool,[j] and folly goes with him. But as for me, your ser-
vant, I did not see the men my master sent.
26"Now since the LORD has kept you, my master, from bloodshed[k] and from avenging[l] yourself
with your own hands, as surely as the LORD lives and as you live, may your enemies and all who in-
tend to harm my master be like Nabal.[m] 27And let this gift,[n] which your servant has brought to my
master, be given to the men who follow you. 28Please forgive[o] your servant's offense, for the LORD
will certainly make a lasting[p] dynasty for my master, because he fights the LORD's battles.[q] Let no
wrongdoing[r] be found in you as long as you live. 29Even though someone is pursuing you to take
your life, the life of my master will be bound securely in the bundle of the living by the LORD your
God. But the lives of your enemies he will hurl[s] away as from the pocket of a sling. 30When the LORD
has done for my master every good thing he promised concerning him and has appointed him lead-
er[t] over Israel, 31my master will not have on his conscience the staggering burden of needless blood-
shed or of having avenged himself. And when the LORD has brought my master success, remember[u]
your servant."
32David said to Abigail, "Praise[v] be to the LORD, the God of Israel, who has sent you today to meet me.
33May you be blessed for your good judgment and for keeping me from bloodshed[w] this day and from
avenging myself with my own hands. 34Otherwise, as surely as the LORD, the God of Israel, lives, who has

25:6 [p]Ps 122:7; Lk 10:5 [q]1Ch 12:18
25:7 [r]ver 15
25:8 [s]Ne 8:10
25:10 [t]Jdg 9:28
25:11 [u]Jdg 8:6
25:13 [v]1Sa 23:13 [w]1Sa 30:24
25:14 [x]1Sa 13:10
25:15 [y]ver 7 [z]ver 21
25:16 [a]Ex 14:22; Job 1:10
25:17 [b]1Sa 20:7
25:18 [c]1Ch 12:40 [d]2Sa 16:1
25:19 [e]Ge 32:20
25:21 [f]Ps 109:5
25:22 [g]1Sa 3:17; 20:13 [h]1Ki 14:10; 21:21; 2Ki 9:8
25:23 [i]1Sa 20:41
25:25 [j]Pr 14:16
25:26 [k]ver 33 [l]Heb 10:30 [m]2Sa 18:32
25:27 [n]Ge 33:11; 1Sa 30:26
25:28 [o]ver 24 [p]2Sa 7:11,26 [q]1Sa 18:17 [r]1Sa 24:11
25:29 [s]Jer 10:18
25:30 [t]1Sa 13:14
25:31 [u]Ge 40:14
25:32 [v]Ge 24:27; Ex 18:10; Lk 1:68
25:33 [w]ver 26

[a] *18* That is, probably about a bushel (about 37 liters) [b] *22* Some Septuagint manuscripts; Hebrew *with David's enemies*

25:8 David and his men were asking for remuneration for their protection of Nabal's shepherds and flocks against pillage (see vv. 15–16,21).

25:13 Nabal's insult required that David defend his honor and reputation (see "Bywords and Insults in the Ancient World" on p. 431).

25:18 Grapes were an important element in the diet of Hebrews. A part of the harvest was preserved in the form of raisin cakes. Grapes were also the people's main source of sugar. The juice of the grapes was drunk both fresh and fermented.

25:25 In ancient times a person's name was believed to reflect his or her nature and character (see "Naming of Children" on p. 28). In Hebrew the name Nabal means "fool."

kept me from harming you, if you had not come quickly to meet me, not one male belonging to Nabal
would have been left alive by daybreak.”
35 Then David accepted from her hand what she had brought him and said, “Go home in peace. I have
25:35 [x]Ge 19:21; 1Sa 20:42; 2Ki 5:19 heard your words and granted[x] your request.”
36 When Abigail went to Nabal, he was in the house holding a banquet like that of a king. He was in
25:36 [y]2Sa 13:23 [z]Pr 20:1; Isa 5:11, 22; Hos 4:11 [a]ver 19 high[y] spirits and very drunk.[z] So she told[a] him nothing until daybreak. 37 Then in the morning, when
Nabal was sober, his wife told him all these things, and his heart failed him and he became like a stone.
25:38 [b]1Sa 26:10; 2Sa 6:7 38 About ten days later, the LORD struck[b] Nabal and he died.
39 When David heard that Nabal was dead, he said, “Praise be to the LORD, who has upheld my cause
against Nabal for treating me with contempt. He has kept his servant from doing wrong and has brought
Nabal’s wrongdoing down on his own head.”
Then David sent word to Abigail, asking her to become his wife. 40 His servants went to Carmel and
said to Abigail, “David has sent us to you to take you to become his wife.”
41 She bowed down with her face to the ground and said, “Here is your maidservant, ready to serve
25:42 [c]Ge 24:61-67 you and wash the feet of my master’s servants.” 42 Abigail[c] quickly got on a donkey and, attended by her
25:43 [d]Jos 15:56 [e]1Sa 27:3; 30:5 five maids, went with David’s messengers and became his wife. 43 David had also married Ahinoam[d] of
Jezreel, and they both were his wives.[e] 44 But Saul had given his daughter Michal, David’s wife, to Palti-
25:44 [f]2Sa 3:15 [g]Isa 10:30 el[a][f] son of Laish, who was from Gallim.[g]

David Again Spares Saul’s Life

26:1 [h]1Sa 23:19 [i]Ps 54 Title **26** The Ziphites[h] went to Saul at Gibeah and said, “Is not David hiding[i] on the hill of Hakilah, which
faces Jeshimon?”
26:2 [j]1Sa 13:2; 24:2 2 So Saul went down to the Desert of Ziph, with his three thousand chosen men of Israel, to search[j]
there for David. 3 Saul made his camp beside the road on the hill of Hakilah facing Jeshimon, but David
stayed in the desert. When he saw that Saul had followed him there, 4 he sent out scouts and learned that
Saul had definitely arrived.[b]
26:5 [k]1Sa 14:50; 17:55 5 Then David set out and went to the place where Saul had camped. He saw where Saul and Abner[k] son
of Ner, the commander of the army, had lain down. Saul was lying inside the camp, with the army en-
camped around him.
26:6 [l]Jdg 7:10-11; 1Ch 2:16 6 David then asked Ahimelech the Hittite and Abishai son of Zeruiah,[l] Joab’s brother, “Who will go
down into the camp with me to Saul?”
“I’ll go with you,” said Abishai.
7 So David and Abishai went to the army by night, and there was Saul, lying asleep inside the camp with
his spear stuck in the ground near his head. Abner and the soldiers were lying around him.
8 Abishai said to David, “Today God has delivered your enemy into your hands. Now let me pin him
to the ground with one thrust of my spear; I won’t strike him twice.”
26:9 [m]2Sa 1:14 [n]1Sa 24:5 9 But David said to Abishai, “Don’t destroy him! Who can lay a hand on the LORD’s anointed[m] and be
26:10 [o]1Sa 25:38; Ro 12:19 [p]Ge 47:29; Dt 31:14; Ps 37:13 [q]1Sa 31:6; 2Sa 1:1 guiltless?[n] 10 As surely as the LORD lives,” he said, “the LORD himself will strike[o] him; either his time[p] will
come and he will die,[q] or he will go into battle and perish. 11 But the LORD forbid that I should lay a hand
on the LORD’s anointed. Now get the spear and water jug that are near his head, and let’s go.”
12 So David took the spear and water jug near Saul’s head, and they left. No one saw or knew about it,
26:12 [r]Ge 2:21; 15:12 nor did anyone wake up. They were all sleeping, because the LORD had put them into a deep sleep.[r]
13 Then David crossed over to the other side and stood on top of the hill some distance away; there was
a wide space between them. 14 He called out to the army and to Abner son of Ner, “Aren’t you going to an-
swer me, Abner?”
Abner replied, “Who are you who calls to the king?”
15 David said, “You’re a man, aren’t you? And who is like you in Israel? Why didn’t you guard your lord
the king? Someone came to destroy your lord the king. 16 What you have done is not good. As surely as
the LORD lives, you and your men deserve to die, because you did not guard your master, the LORD’s anoint-
ed. Look around you. Where are the king’s spear and water jug that were near his head?”
26:17 [s]1Sa 24:16 17 Saul recognized David’s voice and said, “Is that your voice,[s] David my son?”
David replied, “Yes it is, my lord the king.” 18 And he added, “Why is my lord pursuing his servant? What
26:18 [t]1Sa 24:9, 11-14 have I done, and what wrong[t] am I guilty of? 19 Now let my lord the king listen to his servant’s words. If the
26:19 [u]2Sa 16:11 LORD has incited you against me, then may he accept an offering.[u] If, however, men have done it, may they

[a] 44 Hebrew *Palti*, a variant of *Paltiel* [b] 4 Or *had come to Nacon*

be cursed before the LORD! They have now driven me from my share in the LORD's inheritance[v] and have
said, 'Go, serve other gods.' 20 Now do not let my blood fall to the ground far from the presence of the LORD.
The king of Israel has come out to look for a flea[w]—as one hunts a partridge in the mountains."
21 Then Saul said, "I have sinned.[x] Come back, David my son. Because you considered my life precious[y]
today, I will not try to harm you again. Surely I have acted like a fool and have erred greatly."
22 "Here is the king's spear," David answered. "Let one of your young men come over and get it. 23 The
LORD rewards[z] every man for his righteousness[a] and faithfulness. The LORD delivered you into my hands
today, but I would not lay a hand on the LORD's anointed. 24 As surely as I valued your life today, so may
the LORD value my life and deliver[b] me from all trouble."
25 Then Saul said to David, "May you be blessed, my son David; you will do great things and surely triumph."

So David went on his way, and Saul returned home.

26:19 [v]2Sa 14:16
26:20 [w]1Sa 24:14
26:21 [x]Ex 9:27; 1Sa 15:24 [y]1Sa 24:17
26:23 [z]Ps 62:12 [a]Ps 7:8; 18:20,24
26:24 [b]Ps 54:7

David Among the Philistines

27 But David thought to himself, "One of these days I will be destroyed by the hand of Saul. The best
thing I can do is to escape to the land of the Philistines. Then Saul will give up searching for me
anywhere in Israel, and I will slip out of his hand."
2 So David and the six hundred men[c] with him left and went[d] over to Achish[e] son of Maoch king of
Gath. 3 David and his men settled in Gath with Achish. Each man had his family with him, and David had
his two wives:[f] Ahinoam of Jezreel and Abigail of Carmel, the widow of Nabal. 4 When Saul was told that
David had fled to Gath, he no longer searched for him.
5 Then David said to Achish, "If I have found favor in your eyes, let a place be assigned to me in one of
the country towns, that I may live there. Why should your servant live in the royal city with you?"
6 So on that day Achish gave him Ziklag,[g] and it has belonged to the kings of Judah ever since. 7 David
lived[h] in Philistine territory a year and four months.

27:2 [c]1Sa 25:13 [d]1Sa 21:10 [e]1Ki 2:39
27:3 [f]1Sa 25:43; 30:3
27:6 [g]Jos 15:31; 19:5; Ne 11:28
27:7 [h]1Sa 29:3

27:6 No one knows precisely where Ziklag was, although it appears to have been located somewhere between Beersheba and Gath in the area where the Shephelah and the Negev meet. Some identify it with a place called Tell esh-Sharia, where excavations have uncovered four-room houses typical of Israelite villages dating from the tenth to the ninth centuries B.C. This accords well with the note in the text that the village remained in Israelite hands after David's death. See "The Israelite Town and Home" on page 1205.

The Kenites

1 SAMUEL 27 The Kenites are listed among the nations of the land promised to Abraham (Ge 15:19–21; cf. Jdg 1:16). The root of "Kenite" ("smith") may indicate a connection to metalworking activities. The Kenites were generally located in the southeastern regions of Israel (Jdg 1:16; 1Sa 27:10; 30:29). However, being pastoral nomads, some Kenites could be found as far north as the Jezreel Valley[1] (Jdg 4:11,17) or as far south as the Sinai region (Ex 3:1; Jdg 1:16). A **postexilic** source indicates that several Kenite households took on the scribal profession as well (1Ch 2:55).[2]

The Kenites' kinship to Moses through his Midianite father-in-law (Jdg 1:16)[3] appears to have set a positive tone in Israelite-Kenite relations. During the **judges period**[4] Jael's loyalty and her "nailing" of Sisera were celebrated in the Song of Deborah (Jdg 5:24–27; cf. 4:17–22). The Kenites apparently avoided direct involvement in the conflicts between Israel and Midian (Nu 31; Jdg 6–7), although Balaam briefly mentioned them in a judgment oracle (Nu 24:21–22). The bond remained strong during the **united monarchy**, when both Saul and David went out of their way to spare the Kenites when attacking the Amalekites (cf. 1Sa 15:6; 30:26–31)[5]. Attesting to their fluid connections, some Kenite families were also included in the **Recabite** family tree (1Ch 2:55; cf. Ne 3:14; Jer 35:1–11).[6]

[1]See "The Valley of Jezreel" on page 1412. [2]See "The Scribe" on page 682. [3]See "Midian" on page 92. [4]See "The Judges Period" on page 344. [5]See "The Amalekites" on page 120. [6]See "Genealogies in Ancient Israel" on page 1559.

27:8 [i]Jos 13:2,13 [j]Ex 17:8; 1Sa 15:7-8 [k]Ex 15:22
27:9 [l]1Sa 15:3
27:10 [m]1Sa 30:29; 1Ch 2:9,25 [n]Jdg 1:16

8 Now David and his men went up and raided the Geshurites,[i] the Girzites and the Amalekites.[j] (From
ancient times these peoples had lived in the land extending to Shur[k] and Egypt.) 9 Whenever David at-
tacked an area, he did not leave a man or woman alive,[l] but took sheep and cattle, donkeys and camels,
and clothes. Then he returned to Achish.
10 When Achish asked, "Where did you go raiding today?" David would say, "Against the Negev of Judah"
or "Against the Negev of Jerahmeel[m]" or "Against the Negev of the Kenites.[n]" 11 He did not leave a man or
woman alive to be brought to Gath, for he thought, "They might inform on us and say, 'This is what David
did.' " And such was his practice as long as he lived in Philistine territory. 12 Achish trusted David and said
to himself, "He has become so odious to his people, the Israelites, that he will be my servant forever."

Saul and the Witch of Endor

28:1 [o]1Sa 29:1
28:3 [p]1Sa 25:1 [q]1Sa 7:17 [r]Ex 22:18; Lev 19:31; 20:27; Dt 18:10-11; 1Sa 15:23
28:4 [s]Jos 19:18; 2Ki 4:8

28 In those days the Philistines gathered[o] their forces to fight against Israel. Achish said to David,
"You must understand that you and your men will accompany me in the army."
2 David said, "Then you will see for yourself what your servant can do."
Achish replied, "Very well, I will make you my bodyguard for life."
3 Now Samuel was dead,[p] and all Israel had mourned for him and buried him in his own town of Ra-
mah.[q] Saul had expelled the mediums and spiritists[r] from the land.
4 The Philistines assembled and came and set up camp at Shunem,[s] while Saul gathered all the

28:1 In the ancient Near East, to accept sanctuary within a given country involved obligations of military service.

Ancient Necromancy

1 SAMUEL 28 Necromancy, the practice of divination through inquiring of the dead, was forbidden under Biblical law (Lev 19:31; 20:6). Saul himself had banned this activity from the land and yet, in his desperation to receive some instruction regarding the future, he himself turned to a necromancer. Such attempts to communicate with the dead are known throughout the ancient Near East. **Mesopotamia** provides a few examples of such behavior, the most famous of which is the **Sumerian** story of "Gilgamesh, Enkidu and the Netherworld," in which Nergal summons the ghost of Enkidu to rise from a hole in the ground in order that he might speak to Gilgamesh.[1] Other Mesopotamian examples attest to necromancers (both male and female) using skulls to house the spirits while they were being questioned. In Egypt, letters were written to the dead, most likely for purposes of necromancy.

In 1 Samuel 28:13, when the necromancer sees Samuel she asserts that she is seeing a "divine being" or "gods" (*elohim* in Hebrew). This use of *elohim* to refer to a ghost is unique in the Bible and has given rise to numerous historical and theological questions. Is this an indication that the dead were deified in ancient Israel and could be sought out in order to provide an oracle? Other surrounding cultures had ceremonies to honor the dead in cultic fashion; in Mesopotamia such a ceremony was called the *kispu* ritual. The cities of **Mari** and **Ugarit** (both "Map 1") also practiced food offerings and libations for the dead.[2] Laws against such activities in the Bible (Dt 26:14) suggest that a similar practice was well known, though forbidden, in Israel. Saul's willingness to contravene his own decree and engage in the heterodox practice of divining the dead demonstrates the desperation and degradation to which his unfaithfulness had brought him.

For other forms of divination, see "Akkadian Divination" on page 277.

[1]For more on Gilgamesh, see "The Serpent Motif in Other Ancient Near Eastern Literature" on page 8 and "Ecclesiastes and the Epic of Gilgamesh" on page 1027. [2]See "Mari" on page 54 and "Ugarit/Ras Shamra" on page 819.

Israelites and set up camp at Gilboa.[t] 5When Saul saw the Philistine army, he was afraid; terror filled
his heart. 6He inquired[u] of the LORD, but the LORD did not answer him by dreams[v] or Urim[w] or proph-
ets. 7Saul then said to his attendants, "Find me a woman who is a medium,[x] so I may go and inquire
of her."

"There is one in Endor,[y]" they said.

8So Saul disguised[z] himself, putting on other clothes, and at night he and two men went to the wom-
an. "Consult[a] a spirit for me," he said, "and bring up for me the one I name."

9But the woman said to him, "Surely you know what Saul has done. He has cut off[b] the mediums and
spiritists from the land. Why have you set a trap for my life to bring about my death?"

10Saul swore to her by the LORD, "As surely as the LORD lives, you will not be punished for this."

11Then the woman asked, "Whom shall I bring up for you?"

"Bring up Samuel," he said.

12When the woman saw Samuel, she cried out at the top of her voice and said to Saul, "Why have you
deceived me? You are Saul!"

13The king said to her, "Don't be afraid. What do you see?"

The woman said, "I see a spirit[a] coming up out of the ground."

14"What does he look like?" he asked.

"An old man wearing a robe[c] is coming up," she said.

Then Saul knew it was Samuel, and he bowed down and prostrated himself with his face to the
ground.

15Samuel said to Saul, "Why have you disturbed me by bringing me up?"

"I am in great distress," Saul said. "The Philistines are fighting against me, and God has turned[d] away
from me. He no longer answers me, either by prophets or by dreams. So I have called on you to tell me
what to do."

16Samuel said, "Why do you consult me, now that the LORD has turned away from you and become
your enemy? 17The LORD has done what he predicted through me. The LORD has torn[e] the kingdom out
of your hands and given it to one of your neighbors—to David. 18Because you did not obey[f] the LORD or
carry out his fierce wrath[g] against the Amalekites, the LORD has done this to you today. 19The LORD will
hand over both Israel and you to the Philistines, and tomorrow you and your sons[h] will be with me. The
LORD will also hand over the army of Israel to the Philistines."

20Immediately Saul fell full length on the ground, filled with fear because of Samuel's words. His
strength was gone, for he had eaten nothing all that day and night.

21When the woman came to Saul and saw that he was greatly shaken, she said, "Look, your maidser-
vant has obeyed you. I took my life[i] in my hands and did what you told me to do. 22Now please listen to
your servant and let me give you some food so you may eat and have the strength to go on your way."

23He refused[j] and said, "I will not eat."

But his men joined the woman in urging him, and he listened to them. He got up from the ground and
sat on the couch.

24The woman had a fattened calf at the house, which she butchered at once. She took some flour,
kneaded it and baked bread without yeast. 25Then she set it before Saul and his men, and they ate. That
same night they got up and left.

Achish Sends David Back to Ziklag

29 The Philistines gathered[k] all their forces at Aphek,[l] and Israel camped by the spring in Jezreel.[m]
2As the Philistine rulers marched with their units of hundreds and thousands, David and his
men were marching at the rear[n] with Achish. 3The commanders of the Philistines asked, "What about
these Hebrews?"

28:4 [t]1Sa 31:1,3
28:6 [u]1Sa 14:37; 1Ch 10:13-14; Pr 1:28 [v]Nu 12:6 [w]Ex 28:30; Nu 27:21
28:7 [x]Ac 16:16 [y]Jos 17:11
28:8 [z]2Ch 18:29; 35:22 [a]Dt 18:10-11; 1Ch 10:13; Isa 8:19
28:9 [b]ver 3
28:14 [c]1Sa 15:27; 24:8
28:15 [d]ver 6; 1Sa 18:12
28:17 [e]1Sa 15:28
28:18 [f]1Sa 15:20 [g]1Ki 20:42
28:19 [h]1Sa 31:2
28:21 [i]Jdg 12:3; 1Sa 19:5; Job 13:14
28:23 [j]2Ki 5:13
29:1 [k]1Sa 28:1 [l]Jos 12:18; 1Sa 4:1 [m]2Ki 9:30
29:2 [n]1Sa 28:2

[a] 13 Or *see spirits*; or *see gods*

28:8 See "Ancient Necromancy" on page 435.
28:13 This text is without parallel elsewhere in the Bible. There is no indication of what ritual the medium used to call up Samuel's ghost. In Homer's *Odyssey* Book XI, Odysseus sails to the edge of the world, to the gateway to Hades, and there makes an animal sacrifice. The disembodied spirits swarm out of the underworld to feast on the blood of the sacrifice. It is conceivable that the Biblical writer may have deliberately declined to offer any account of the ritual used here in order to avoid any implication of legitimizing necromancy.
29:1 For information on the Philistines, see "The Judges Period" on page 344, "The Archaeology of Philistia" on page 370 and "The Ekron Inscription of Akhayus" on page 428. See also "Aphek" on page 437.

Achish replied, "Is this not David, who was an officer of Saul king of Israel? He has already been with
29:3 [o]1Sa 27:7; Da 6:5 me for over a year,[o] and from the day he left Saul until now, I have found no fault in him."
29:4 [p]1Ch 12:19 [q]1Sa 14:21 4 But the Philistine commanders were angry with him and said, "Send[p] the man back, that he may re-
turn to the place you assigned him. He must not go with us into battle, or he will turn[q] against us dur-
ing the fighting. How better could he regain his master's favor than by taking the heads of our own men?
5 Isn't this the David they sang about in their dances:

" 'Saul has slain his thousands,
29:5 [r]1Sa 18:7; 21:11 and David his tens of thousands'?"[r]

6 So Achish called David and said to him, "As surely as the LORD lives, you have been reliable, and I
29:6 [s]1Sa 27:8-12 [t]ver 3 would be pleased to have you serve with me in the army. From the day[s] you came to me until now, I have
found no fault in you, but the rulers[t] don't approve of you. 7 Turn back and go in peace; do nothing to dis-
please the Philistine rulers."
8 "But what have I done?" asked David. "What have you found against your servant from the day I came
to you until now? Why can't I go and fight against the enemies of my lord the king?"
29:9 [u]2Sa 14:17, 20; 19:27 [v]ver 4 9 Achish answered, "I know that you have been as pleasing in my eyes as an angel[u] of God; neverthe-
less, the Philistine commanders[v] have said, 'He must not go up with us into battle.' 10 Now get up early,
29:10 [w]1Ch 12:19 along with your master's servants who have come with you, and leave[w] in the morning as soon as it is
light."
11 So David and his men got up early in the morning to go back to the land of the Philistines, and the
Philistines went up to Jezreel.

ARCHAEOLOGICAL SITES

APHEK

1 SAMUEL 29 In 1 Samuel 29:1 the Philistines used Aphek as a place to muster their troops against Israel. Previously they had gathered at this same location just before they had routed the army of Israel (ch. 4). The precise location of Aphek is somewhat problematic because of the numerous places that share this or a very similar name.

Aphek is mentioned eight times in the Old Testament (nine if we include the place called Aphekah in Jos 15:53), and the scholarly consensus is that there are four distinct locations so designated:

- Joshua 19:29–30 refers to a town within the tribal allotment of Asher.
- First Kings 20:26,30 and 2 Kings 13:17 speak of a town in Aram (Syria), north of Israel.
- Joshua 13:4 speaks of another Aphek that most likely served as the northern border of the land of **Canaan**.
- The fourth Aphek was located in the Sharon plain. This may be the Aphek of Joshua 12:18 and is most likely the Aphek of 1 Samuel 4 and 1 Samuel 29.

Tel Ras el-Ain, northeast of Joppa at the source of the Yarkon River, is assumed to be the modern location for the fourth Aphek. Its relative proximity to Philistine territory confirms the likelihood that this is the town intended in 1 Samuel 29. This Aphek is attested in Egyptian sources from the fifteenth century B.C. in a topographical listing of place names (possibly of the cities taken in a military campaign or in an itinerary) from Thutmose III, as well as in an account of Amenhotep II's second military campaign to the region.

In 1 Samuel 28:4 the Philistine army was encamped at Shunem, near En Dor, the Valley of Jezreel[1] ("Map 4") and Mount Gilboa (the location of Saul's death). It is most likely that the reference to Aphek in chapter 29 indicates that the events of this chapter actually preceded those of 28:3–25. Aphek would have been a natural staging area for the Philistine push northward to meet the Israelite forces at Jezreel.[2] In addition to being the most logical reconstruction of Philistine troop movements, such a reading does no violence to the Biblical portrayal of events in chapters 28–31. The author evidently used a thematic, rather than a strictly chronological, arrangement to structure this account.

[1]See "The Valley of Jezreel" on page 1412. [2]See "Technological Supremacy of the Philistines' Iron Weapons" on page 414.

David Destroys the Amalekites

30 David and his men reached Ziklag[x] on the third day. Now the Amalekites[y] had raided the Negev **30:1** [x]1Sa 29:4,
and Ziklag. They had attacked Ziklag and burned it, 2 and had taken captive the women and all who 11 [y]1Sa 15:7; 27:8
were in it, both young and old. They killed none of them, but carried them off as they went on their way.
3 When David and his men came to Ziklag, they found it destroyed by fire and their wives and sons
and daughters taken captive. 4 So David and his men wept aloud until they had no strength left to weep.
5 David's two wives[z] had been captured—Ahinoam of Jezreel and Abigail, the widow of Nabal of Car- **30:5** [z]1Sa 25:43; 2Sa 2:2
mel. 6 David was greatly distressed because the men were talking of stoning[a] him; each one was bitter in **30:6** [a]Ex 17:4; Jn 8:59
spirit because of his sons and daughters. But David found strength[b] in the LORD his God. [b]Ps 27:14; 56:3-4,11; Ro 4:20
7 Then David said to Abiathar[c] the priest, the son of Ahimelech, "Bring me the ephod.[d]" Abiathar brought **30:7** [c]1Sa 22:20 [d]1Sa 23:9
it to him, 8 and David inquired[e] of the LORD, "Shall I pursue this raiding party? Will I overtake them?" **30:8** [e]1Sa 23:2
"Pursue them," he answered. "You will certainly overtake them and succeed[f] in the rescue." [f]ver 18
9 David and the six hundred men[g] with him came to the Besor Ravine, where some stayed behind, **30:9** [g]1Sa 27:2
10 for two hundred men were too exhausted[h] to cross the ravine. But David and four hundred men con- **30:10** [h]ver 9,21
tinued the pursuit.
11 They found an Egyptian in a field and brought him to David. They gave him water to drink and food
to eat— 12 part of a cake of pressed figs and two cakes of raisins. He ate and was revived,[i] for he had not **30:12** [i]Jdg 15:19
eaten any food or drunk any water for three days and three nights.
13 David asked him, "To whom do you belong, and where do you come from?"

30:1 See "The Amalekites" on page 120.

ANCIENT TEXTS AND ARTIFACTS

The Beth Shan Temples

1 SAMUEL 31 Following their victory over the Israelites at Mount Gilboa, the Philistines cut off Saul's head and stripped his body of his weapons. First Samuel 31:10 informs us that "they put his armor in the temple of the Ashtoreths and fastened his body to the wall of Beth Shan," suggesting that this temple was in the city of Beth Shan (also spelled "Beth Shean"; see "Map 4"), about five miles (eight km) east of Mount Gilboa. The account in 1 Chronicles 10:10 states that "they put his armor in the temple of their gods and hung up his head in the temple of Dagon." It appears that there were temples of both **Dagon** and Ashtoreth in Beth Shan.[1] Second Samuel 21:12 indicates that the bodies of Saul's sons also were put on display, being hung in "the public square at Beth Shan."

Beth Shan had a long history, with occupation periods from the **Early Bronze**[2] to the **Byzantine** and Arab periods. At the beginning of the **Iron Age** (twelfth century B.C.), it was inhabited by peoples who were either heavily influenced by Egypt or were themselves Egyptian. (A large number of Egyptian style artifacts were found there. In addition, famous but grotesque "anthropoid coffins" were uncovered—see photograph accompanying the article "Deborah and Barak and the Destruction of Hazor" on page 350.)

After the decline of Egyptian influence, the site was occupied by **Canaanites** and **Sea Peoples** (primarily Philistines). Two adjacent temples have been found there at stratum V, with artifacts dating to the tenth century B.C. Oriented from west to east, the temples were unique in plan. The northernmost was 64 feet by 37 feet (19.5 x 11.3 m) in outside dimensions, with its roof supported by four pillars. The southernmost was much larger—79 feet by 60 feet (24 x 18.3 m). Inside was a central hall with six columns and auxiliary rooms on either side. Some researchers conjecture that the northern temple was that of Ashtoreth (31:10) and the southern temple that of Dagon (1Ch 10:10).[3]

[1]See "Dagon" on page 404. [2]See "Archaeological Periods" chart on page xx in the front of this Bible. [3]See also "Samson and the Temple of Dagon" on page 375.

He said, "I am an Egyptian, the slave of an Amalekite. My master abandoned me when I became ill
three days ago. 14 We raided the Negev of the Kerethites[j] and the territory belonging to Judah and the Ne-
gev of Caleb.[k] And we burned[l] Ziklag."
15 David asked him, "Can you lead me down to this raiding party?"
He answered, "Swear to me before God that you will not kill me or hand me over to my master, and I
will take you down to them."
16 He led David down, and there they were, scattered over the countryside, eating, drinking and rev-
eling[m] because of the great amount of plunder[n] they had taken from the land of the Philistines and from
Judah. 17 David fought[o] them from dusk until the evening of the next day, and none of them got away, ex-
cept four hundred young men who rode off on camels and fled.[p] 18 David recovered[q] everything the Am-
alekites had taken, including his two wives. 19 Nothing was missing: young or old, boy or girl, plunder or
anything else they had taken. David brought everything back. 20 He took all the flocks and herds, and his
men drove them ahead of the other livestock, saying, "This is David's plunder."
21 Then David came to the two hundred men who had been too exhausted[r] to follow him and who
were left behind at the Besor Ravine. They came out to meet David and the people with him. As David
and his men approached, he greeted them. 22 But all the evil men and troublemakers among David's fol-
lowers said, "Because they did not go out with us, we will not share with them the plunder we recovered.
However, each man may take his wife and children and go."
23 David replied, "No, my brothers, you must not do that with what the LORD has given us. He has pro-
tected us and handed over to us the forces that came against us. 24 Who will listen to what you say? The
share of the man who stayed with the supplies is to be the same as that of him who went down to the bat-
tle. All will share alike.[s]" 25 David made this a statute and ordinance for Israel from that day to this.
26 When David arrived in Ziklag, he sent some of the plunder to the elders of Judah, who were his
friends, saying, "Here is a present for you from the plunder of the LORD's enemies."
27 He sent it to those who were in Bethel,[t] Ramoth[u] Negev and Jattir;[v] 28 to those in Aroer,[w] Siphmoth,
Eshtemoa[x] 29 and Racal; to those in the towns of the Jerahmeelites[y] and the Kenites;[z] 30 to those in Hor-
mah,[a] Bor Ashan,[b] Athach 31 and Hebron;[c] and to those in all the other places where David and his men
had roamed.

Saul Takes His Life

31 Now the Philistines fought against Israel; the Israelites fled before them, and many fell slain on
Mount Gilboa.[d] 2 The Philistines pressed hard after Saul and his sons, and they killed his sons
Jonathan, Abinadab and Malki-Shua. 3 The fighting grew fierce around Saul, and when the archers over-
took him, they wounded[e] him critically.
4 Saul said to his armor-bearer, "Draw your sword and run me through,[f] or these uncircumcised[g] fel-
lows will come and run me through and abuse me."
But his armor-bearer was terrified and would not do it; so Saul took his own sword and fell on it.
5 When the armor-bearer saw that Saul was dead, he too fell on his sword and died with him. 6 So Saul and
his three sons and his armor-bearer and all his men died together that same day.
7 When the Israelites along the valley and those across the Jordan saw that the Israelite army had fled
and that Saul and his sons had died, they abandoned their towns and fled. And the Philistines came and
occupied them.
8 The next day, when the Philistines came to strip the dead, they found Saul and his three sons fallen
on Mount Gilboa. 9 They cut off his head and stripped off his armor, and they sent messengers through-
out the land of the Philistines to proclaim the news[h] in the temple of their idols and among their people.[i]
10 They put his armor in the temple of the Ashtoreths[j] and fastened his body to the wall of Beth Shan.[k]
11 When the people of Jabesh Gilead[l] heard of what the Philistines had done to Saul, 12 all their valiant
men journeyed through the night to Beth Shan. They took down the bodies of Saul and his sons from the
wall of Beth Shan and went to Jabesh, where they burned[m] them. 13 Then they took their bones[n] and bur-
ied them under a tamarisk[o] tree at Jabesh, and they fasted[p] seven days.[q]

30:14 j2Sa 8:18; 1Ki 1:38,44; Eze 25:16; Zep 2:5 kver 16; Jos 14:13; 15:13 lver 1
30:16 mLk 12:19 nver 14
30:17 o1Sa 11:11 p1Sa 15:3
30:18 qGe 14:16
30:21 rver 10
30:24 sNu 31:27; Jos 22:8
30:27 tJos 7:2 uJos 19:8 vJos 15:48
30:28 wJos 13:16 xJos 15:50
30:29 y1Sa 27:10 zJdg 1:16; 1Sa 15:6
30:30 aNu 14:45; Jdg 1:17 bJos 15:42
30:31 cJos 14:13; 2Sa 2:1,4
31:1 d1Sa 28:4; 1Ch 10:1-12
31:3 e2Sa 1:6
31:4 fJdg 9:54; 2Sa 1:6,10 g1Sa 14:6
31:9 h2Sa 1:20 iJdg 16:24
31:10 jJdg 2:12-13; 1Sa 7:3 kJos 17:11; 2Sa 21:12
31:11 l1Sa 11:1
31:12 m2Sa 2:4-7; 2Ch 16:14; Am 6:10
31:13 n2Sa 21:12-14 o1Sa 22:6 p2Sa 1:12 qGe 50:10

31:4–13 Saul died in battle against the very enemies he was supposed to have subdued (cf. 9:15–16).
31:9–10 Saul's body was dismembered and desecrated in a way that seemed especially appalling to ancient peoples (see "The Beth Shan Temples" on p. 438).
31:12 Cremation, while not customary in ancient Israel, appears to have been performed in this situation in order to prevent any further abuse of the bodies of Saul and his sons by the Philistines.

INTRODUCTION TO 2 *Samuel*

AUTHOR, PLACE AND DATE OF WRITING

We do not know who wrote 1 and 2 Samuel, both of which were named after Israel's last judge and one of her great prophets, whom God used to establish the nation's monarchy. Originally the two comprised one book, but the translators of the Septuagint divided it into two parts.

Some features of 2 Samuel suggest that several independent, unedited sources, including firsthand accounts, were used or even quoted in the authors' compositions. Scholars often speak of a "Succession Narrative" (2Sa 9—1Ki 2) as being a single-source document, but this viewpoint is debated. One way or the other, it is certain that the writers/compilers of 1 and 2 Samuel referenced the historical records of Samuel, Saul and David.

Second Samuel (as well as its various sources) was evidently composed between the end of David's life and some point during Solomon's reign.

AUDIENCE

The early audience of 2 Samuel included the generations of Israelites who lived during the reigns of David and Solomon, as well as their succeeding generations. The stories in this book spoke most directly to Israelites who lived during the early monarchy. They reveal David as Israel's greatest king and a man of profound faith—as well as his blatant weaknesses and failures. Readers learned about the Davidic covenant God had established (ultimately fulfilled in Jesus, the son of David) but also saw the tragic consequences David's sinful actions inflicted both upon his family and upon the entire nation.

CULTURAL FACTS AND HIGHLIGHTS

During this time period Israel subdued her enemies in Canaan under King David's leadership, and Jerusalem became David's royal city.

TIMELINE

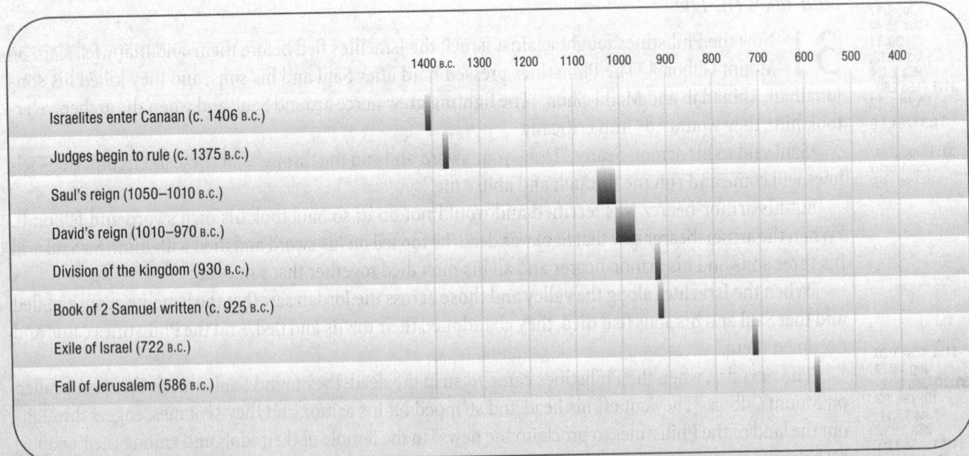

AS YOU READ

Pay close attention to the ups and downs in this book. Imagine David's ultimate elation—following his period of grief over the demise of Saul and Jonathan—when he finally became king of both Israel and Judah. David faced great hardship, but God continued to bless him and even provided battlefield strategies that brought David and his troops victory after victory. Notice how, speaking through the prophet Nathan, God pledged to make David's kingdom last forever—a promise fulfilled through Jesus of Nazareth.

Watch what happened to David after his life finally seemed to be running smoothly. After rejoicing in God's blessings and demonstrating deep compassion for other people, this man after God's heart allowed sexual temptation to take root in his own, all too human heart. The consequences of David's extramarital affair with Bathsheba and of other sins plagued him, his family and the rest of God's people during the remainder of David's life and beyond. Be prepared to read about blatant sinfulness, including murder, rape, pride, lack of parental discipline, deceit and civil war. But God still extended grace to David, whose reign became legendary, because the king did not rationalize or try to avoid his wrongdoing. Notice how, despite his glaring faults, David worked hard to maintain his covenant relationship with God.

DID YOU KNOW?

- It was customary for new kings to assume the harem of their predecessors (3:7).
- Ancient cultures viewed disability as a sign of sin or of God's disfavor (4:4).
- Royal women played a significant political role in ancient societies (16:21–22).
- Threshing floors, normally on hills, were traditional sites for receiving divine messages (24:18–25).

THEMES

Second Samuel includes the following themes:

1. *The Davidic covenant.* The apex of David's life came when God entered into a covenant relationship with him, promising to establish a dynasty through his descendants (7:5–16). This covenant had a conditional element associated with it, since it warned that unfaithful kings in David's line would receive God's punishment (v. 14).

2. *Consequences of sin.* David's sin of adultery and murder (11:1–21) was the turning point in his reign. Although his repentance was genuine and God's forgiveness immediate (12:13), his sin still had irreversible consequences (vv. 10–12). His family life was characterized by one disaster after another, with negative consequences for the kingdom, including a period of civil war. By the end of the narrative David was an elderly king whose kingdom, though intact, was diminished. Nonetheless God was gracious to him, and David's wholehearted devotion to God became his most memorable attribute (2Ki 18:3; 22:2; Ac 13:22).

3. *Abuse of power.* Several narratives in Samuel describe the terrible effects of people's abuse of power, notably Joab's murder of Abner, David's arrangements for Uriah's death in battle, Amnon's rape of Tamar, Absalom's murder of Amnon and Absalom's rebellion.

OUTLINE

I. David Becomes King Over Judah (1–4)
II. David Becomes King Over All Israel (5:1–5)
III. David's Kingship in Its Accomplishments and Glory (5:6—9:13)
IV. David's Kingship in Its Weaknesses and Failures (10–20)
V. Final Reflections on David's Reign (21–24)

David Hears of Saul's Death

1 After the death[a] of Saul, David returned from defeating[b] the Amalekites and stayed in Ziklag two
days. 2 On the third day a man[c] arrived from Saul's camp, with his clothes torn and with dust on his
head.[d] When he came to David, he fell to the ground to pay him honor.
3 "Where have you come from?" David asked him.
He answered, "I have escaped from the Israelite camp."
4 "What happened?" David asked. "Tell me."
He said, "The men fled from the battle. Many of them fell and died. And Saul and his son Jonathan are
dead."
5 Then David said to the young man who brought him the report, "How do you know that Saul and his
son Jonathan are dead?"
6 "I happened to be on Mount Gilboa,[e]" the young man said, "and there was Saul, leaning on his spear,
with the chariots and riders almost upon him. 7 When he turned around and saw me, he called out to
me, and I said, 'What can I do?'
8 "He asked me, 'Who are you?'
" 'An Amalekite,[f]' I answered.
9 "Then he said to me, 'Stand over me and kill me! I am in the throes of death, but I'm still alive.'
10 "So I stood over him and killed him, because I knew that after he had fallen he could not survive. And
I took the crown[g] that was on his head and the band on his arm and have brought them here to my lord."
11 Then David and all the men with him took hold of their clothes and tore[h] them. 12 They mourned
and wept and fasted till evening for Saul and his son Jonathan, and for the army of the LORD and the
house of Israel, because they had fallen by the sword.
13 David said to the young man who brought him the report, "Where are you from?"
"I am the son of an alien, an Amalekite,[i]" he answered.
14 David asked him, "Why were you not afraid to lift your hand to destroy the LORD's anointed?[j]"
15 Then David called one of his men and said, "Go, strike him down!"[k] So he struck him down, and he
died.[l] 16 For David had said to him, "Your blood be on your own head.[m] Your own mouth testified against
you when you said, 'I killed the LORD's anointed.' "

David's Lament for Saul and Jonathan

17 David took up this lament[n] concerning Saul and his son Jonathan, 18 and ordered that the men of Ju-
dah be taught this lament of the bow (it is written in the Book of Jashar):[o]

19 "Your glory, O Israel, lies slain on your heights.
How the mighty have fallen![p]

20 "Tell it not in Gath,[q]
proclaim it not in the streets of Ashkelon,
lest the daughters of the Philistines[r] be glad,
lest the daughters of the uncircumcised rejoice.[s]

21 "O mountains of Gilboa,[t]
may you have neither dew nor rain,
nor fields that yield offerings[u] ⌊of grain⌋.
For there the shield of the mighty was defiled,
the shield of Saul—no longer rubbed with oil.[v]
22 From the blood[w] of the slain,
from the flesh of the mighty,
the bow[x] of Jonathan did not turn back,
the sword of Saul did not return unsatisfied.

23 "Saul and Jonathan—
in life they were loved and gracious,
and in death they were not parted.

1:1 [a]1Sa 31:6 [b]1Sa 30:17
1:2 [c]2Sa 4:10 [d]1Sa 4:12
1:6 [e]1Sa 28:4; 31:2-4
1:8 [f]1Sa 15:2; 30:13,17
1:10 [g]Jdg 9:54; 2Ki 11:12
1:11 [h]Ge 37:29; 2Sa 3:31; 13:31
1:13 [i]ver 8
1:14 [j]1Sa 24:6; 26:9
1:15 [k]2Sa 4:12 [l]2Sa 4:10
1:16 [m]Lev 20:9; 2Sa 3:28-29; 1Ki 2:32; Mt 27:24-25; Ac 18:6
1:17 [n]2Ch 35:25
1:18 [o]Jos 10:13; 1Sa 31:3
1:19 [p]ver 27
1:20 [q]Mic 1:10 [r]1Sa 31:8 [s]Ex 15:20; 1Sa 18:6
1:21 [t]ver 6; 1Sa 31:1 [u]Eze 31:15 [v]Isa 21:5
1:22 [w]Isa 34:3,7 [x]Dt 32:42; 1Sa 18:4

1:17 Composing laments for fallen leaders or heroes was a common practice in the ancient Near East. See "Songs of Warriors" on page 474 and "Ancient Near Eastern Laments" on page 1305.

1:18 The Book of Jashar, now lost, was an early account of Israel's wars (perhaps all in poetic form).

1:21 Leather shields were rubbed with oil for preservation.

David

2 SAMUEL 1 David's rise from shepherd of sheep in Bethlehem[1] to shepherd of Israel in Hebron[2] (see "Map 5") and then Jerusalem (c. 1010–970 B.C.) is recounted in 1 Samuel 16—2 Samuel 5. His acts as the second of the **united kingdom**'s[3] three kings are recorded in both 2 Samuel 5—1 Kings 2 and in 1 Chronicles.

David was a shepherd from Bethlehem with an extraordinary sense of duty and courage (1Sa 17:34–35). His rise to prominence is attributed first to his slaying of Goliath[4] and then to his ability to calm the volatile King Saul with his music (1Sa 16–17). Even so, he was anointed by Samuel to replace Saul while David was still an obscure young man (1Sa 16:1–13). After rising to prominence, he provoked Saul's jealousy and was forced to flee for his life. For a number of years David lived as a mercenary in the wilderness of Judah while eluding Saul (1Sa 18–27). After Saul was killed by the Philistines in a battle at Mount Gilboa (1Sa 28; 31), David rose to power. He defeated the house of Saul under Saul's son Ish-Bosheth in a civil war and became the sole ruler of Israel (2Sa 2–5). David expanded the size and wealth of Israel, conquered Jerusalem and made it his capital city and moved the ark of the covenant there (1Sa 6–10).[5]

There was a dark side to his reign as well. David committed murder and adultery (1Sa 11–12), and troubles in his family led to civil war incited by his son Absalom (1Sa 13–18). Other troubles plagued David in his later years, as both his own heirs and others struggled for power (2Sa 19—1Ki 1).

The saga of David's rise to power in 2 Samuel serves, in part, as an apologetic for his ascent to the throne by establishing his innocence with regard to any attempt to take Saul's throne through his own machinations. Even so, the Bible portrays David honestly, with all his shortcomings, and focuses primarily on God, who chose David as king (1Sa 16; cf. 2Sa 18–19). God protected David in the face of grave danger (1Sa 17–30; cf. 2Sa 15–18) and gave him the kingdom (1Sa 31—2Sa 5; cf. ch. 19). As God orchestrated David's victory over his enemies (chs. 5–10), he also expanded the kingdom and fulfilled the promise he had long ago made to Abraham (Ge 15:18–21; 2Sa 8:3; 1Ki 4:21; 8:65).

The book of Chronicles, which was written after the **exile**, attributes to David a foundational role in the establishment and organization of temple worship (1Ch 6:31; 15:16; 16:4; 23:6; 2Ch 7:6). David's importance in Israel's worship is also reflected in the fact that 73 of the 150 psalms are attributed to him.[6] These psalms add spiritual depth to David's story in their portrayal, through David's praise, penitence and petitions, of God's transformation of his heart in the midst of personal and national crises (cf. Ps 3; 60). David even represents the ideal penitent (cf. Ps 6; 51) and model worshiper of God (cf. Ps 8; 145); he was also a righteous servant who called on the Lord in the midst of suffering (cf. Ps 3; 7). Just as Israel's emergence would have been inconceivable apart from the faith of Abraham and the **exodus** unimaginable without Moses, so also the nation's once and future kingdom would have been unthinkable apart from God's eternal covenant with David (see, e.g., 2Sa 7; 1Ch 17; Ps 89; Isa 9:1–7; Jer 33:14–26; Mic 5:2–4).

For a long time no inscription relating to David's reign could be found by archaeologists, but recently a composition from a king of Syria, referring to the "house of David," was discovered at Tel Dan. This writing provides tangible evidence that ancient rulers indeed recognized the dynasty of David in Judah.[7]

The Eastern slope of the city of David
Photograph: © Todd Bolen/Bible Places.com

[1]See "Bethlehem" on page 1487. [2]See "Hebron" on page 446. [3]See Glossary on page 2080 for definitions of bolded words. [4]See "Battle by Champions" on page 422. [5]See "The Tabernacle and the Ark" on page 153. [6]See "The Psalm Superscripts" on page 795. [7]See "The Tel Dan Stele" on page 540.

They were swifter than eagles,[y]
they were stronger than lions.[z]

24 "O daughters of Israel,
weep for Saul,
who clothed you in scarlet and finery,
who adorned your garments with ornaments of gold.

25 "How the mighty have fallen in battle!
Jonathan lies slain on your heights.
26 I grieve for you, Jonathan my brother;[a]
you were very dear to me.
Your love for me was wonderful,[b]
more wonderful than that of women.

27 "How the mighty have fallen!
The weapons of war have perished!"[c]

1:23 [y]Dt 28:49; Jer 4:13 [z]Jdg 14:18
1:26 [a]1Sa 20:42 [b]1Sa 18:1
1:27 [c]ver 19,25; 1Sa 2:4

David Anointed King Over Judah

2 In the course of time, David inquired[d] of the LORD. "Shall I go up to one of the towns of Judah?" he asked.

The LORD said, "Go up."

David asked, "Where shall I go?"

"To Hebron,"[e] the LORD answered.

2:1 [d]1Sa 23:2, 11-12 [e]Ge 13:18; 1Sa 30:31

ARCHAEOLOGICAL SITES

THE POOL OF GIBEON

2 SAMUEL 2 In 2 Samuel 2:12–17 David's forces, led by Joab, defeated Saul's army under the command of Abner at "the pool of Gibeon" (v. 13). The archaeological site identified as the Biblical Gibeon[1] (modern el-Jib; see "Map 4" for Gibeon) has a great cistern that may no doubt be identified with this pool. This cistern, cut into solid rock, is 82 feet (25 m) deep and 37 feet (11 m) in diameter. A tunnel connects the cistern to another chamber at groundwater level. The water is accessible by descending steps along the circumference of the cistern and then following a tunnel to a chamber fed by a spring outside the city wall. Constructed in the early eleventh century B.C., the pool of Gibeon had been used for over 100 years by the time of the battle recounted in 2 Samuel 2. It was still in use in the sixth century B.C., as attested by Jeremiah's report that Johanan and his men there caught up to Ishmael, the assassin who had killed the Judahite governor Gedaliah (Jer 41:12).[2]

The pool of Gibeon
Preserving Bible Times; © Dr. James C. Martin

[1]See "Gibeon" on page 318. [2]See "Gedaliah, Governor of Judah, and Baalis, King of Ammon" on page 1261.

2:2 [f]1Sa 25:43; 30:5 [g]1Sa 25:42
2:3 [h]1Sa 27:2; 30:9
2:4 [i]1Sa 30:31 [j]1Sa 2:35; 2Sa 5:3-5 [k]1Sa 31:11-13
2:5 [l]1Sa 23:21
2:6 [m]Ex 34:6; 1Ti 1:16

2 So David went up there with his two wives,[f] Ahinoam of Jezreel and Abigail,[g] the widow of Nabal of
Carmel. 3 David also took the men who were with him,[h] each with his family, and they settled in Hebron
and its towns. 4 Then the men of Judah came to Hebron[i] and there they anointed[j] David king over the
house of Judah.

When David was told that it was the men of Jabesh Gilead[k] who had buried Saul, 5 he sent messengers
to the men of Jabesh Gilead to say to them, "The LORD bless[l] you for showing this kindness to Saul your
master by burying him. 6 May the LORD now show you kindness and faithfulness,[m] and I too will show
you the same favor because you have done this. 7 Now then, be strong and brave, for Saul your master is
dead, and the house of Judah has anointed me king over them."

War Between the Houses of David and Saul

2:8 [n]1Sa 14:50 [o]Ge 32:2
2:9 [p]Nu 32:26 [q]Jdg 1:32 [r]1Ch 12:29
2:11 [s]2Sa 5:5
2:12 [t]Jos 18:25
2:13 [u]2Sa 8:16; 1Ch 2:16; 11:6

8 Meanwhile, Abner[n] son of Ner, the commander of Saul's army, had taken Ish-Bosheth son of Saul
and brought him over to Mahanaim.[o] 9 He made him king over Gilead,[p] Ashuri[a][q] and Jezreel, and also over
Ephraim, Benjamin and all Israel.[r]

10 Ish-Bosheth son of Saul was forty years old when he became king over Israel, and he reigned two
years. The house of Judah, however, followed David. 11 The length of time David was king in Hebron over
the house of Judah was seven years and six months.[s]

12 Abner son of Ner, together with the men of Ish-Bosheth son of Saul, left Mahanaim and went to
Gibeon.[t] 13 Joab[u] son of Zeruiah and David's men went out and met them at the pool of Gibeon. One
group sat down on one side of the pool and one group on the other side.

14 Then Abner said to Joab, "Let's have some of the young men get up and fight hand to hand in front
of us."

"All right, let them do it," Joab said.

15 So they stood up and were counted off—twelve men for Benjamin and Ish-Bosheth son of Saul,
and twelve for David. 16 Then each man grabbed his opponent by the head and thrust his dagger into his
opponent's side, and they fell down together. So that place in Gibeon was called Helkath Hazzurim.[b]

2:17 [v]2Sa 3:1
2:18 [w]2Sa 3:39 [x]2Sa 3:30 [y]1Sa 26:6 [z]1Ch 2:16 [a]1Ch 12:8
2:22 [b]2Sa 3:27
2:23 [c]2Sa 3:27; 4:6 [d]2Sa 20:12
2:26 [e]Dt 32:42; Jer 46:10,14
2:28 [f]2Sa 18:16 [g]Jdg 3:27
2:29 [h]ver 8

17 The battle that day was very fierce, and Abner and the men of Israel were defeated[v] by David's men.
18 The three sons of Zeruiah[w] were there: Joab,[x] Abishai[y] and Asahel.[z] Now Asahel was as fleet-foot-
ed as a wild gazelle.[a] 19 He chased Abner, turning neither to the right nor to the left as he pursued him.
20 Abner looked behind him and asked, "Is that you, Asahel?"

"It is," he answered.

21 Then Abner said to him, "Turn aside to the right or to the left; take on one of the young men and strip
him of his weapons." But Asahel would not stop chasing him.

22 Again Abner warned Asahel, "Stop chasing me! Why should I strike you down? How could I look
your brother Joab in the face?"[b]

23 But Asahel refused to give up the pursuit; so Abner thrust the butt of his spear into Asahel's stom-
ach,[c] and the spear came out through his back. He fell there and died on the spot. And every man stopped
when he came to the place where Asahel had fallen and died.[d]

24 But Joab and Abishai pursued Abner, and as the sun was setting, they came to the hill of Ammah,
near Giah on the way to the wasteland of Gibeon. 25 Then the men of Benjamin rallied behind Abner.
They formed themselves into a group and took their stand on top of a hill.

26 Abner called out to Joab, "Must the sword devour[e] forever? Don't you realize that this will end in
bitterness? How long before you order your men to stop pursuing their brothers?"

27 Joab answered, "As surely as God lives, if you had not spoken, the men would have continued the
pursuit of their brothers until morning.[c]"

28 So Joab[f] blew the trumpet,[g] and all the men came to a halt; they no longer pursued Israel, nor did
they fight anymore.

29 All that night Abner and his men marched through the Arabah. They crossed the Jordan, contin-
ued through the whole Bithron[d] and came to Mahanaim.[h]

[a] 9 Or *Asher* [b] 16 *Helkath Hazzurim* means *field of daggers* or *field of hostilities.* [c] 27 Or *spoken this morning, the men would not have taken up the pursuit of their brothers*; or *spoken, the men would have given up the pursuit of their brothers by morning*
[d] 29 Or *morning*; or *ravine*; the meaning of the Hebrew for this word is uncertain.

2:4–7 See "Jabesh Gilead" on page 384.
2:13 See "Gibeon" on page 318 and "The Pool of Gibeon" on page 444.
2:14 See "Battle by Champions" on page 422.
2:29 For information on the Arabah, see the note on Deuteronomy 1:1.

30 Then Joab returned from pursuing Abner and assembled all his men. Besides Asahel, nineteen of
David's men were found missing. 31 But David's men had killed three hundred and sixty Benjamites who
were with Abner. 32 They took Asahel and buried him in his father's tomb[i] at Bethlehem. Then Joab and 2:32 [i]Ge 49:29
his men marched all night and arrived at Hebron by daybreak.

3 The war between the house of Saul and the house of David lasted a long time.[j] David grew stronger 3:1 [j]1Ki 14:30
and stronger,[k] while the house of Saul grew weaker and weaker.[l] [k]2Sa 5:10 [l]2Sa 2:17

2 Sons were born to David in Hebron:

His firstborn was Amnon the son of Ahinoam[m] of Jezreel; 3:2 [m]1Sa 25:43; 1Ch 3:1-3
3 his second, Kileab the son of Abigail[n] the widow of Nabal of Carmel; 3:3 [n]1Sa 25:42
the third, Absalom[o] the son of Maacah daughter of Talmai king of Geshur;[p] [o]2Sa 13:1,28 [p]1Sa 27:8; 2Sa 13:37; 14:32; 15:8
4 the fourth, Adonijah[q] the son of Haggith; 3:4 [q]1Ki 1:5,11
the fifth, Shephatiah the son of Abital;
5 and the sixth, Ithream the son of David's wife Eglah.
These were born to David in Hebron.

Abner Goes Over to David

6 During the war between the house of Saul and the house of David, Abner had been strengthening his
own position in the house of Saul. 7 Now Saul had had a concubine[r] named Rizpah[s] daughter of Aiah. 3:7 [r]2Sa 16:21-22 [s]2Sa 21:8-11
And Ish-Bosheth said to Abner, "Why did you sleep with my father's concubine?"
8 Abner was very angry because of what Ish-Bosheth said and he answered, "Am I a dog's head[t]—on 3:8 [t]1Sa 24:14; 2Sa 9:8; 16:9

3:7 It was customary for new kings to assume the harem of their predecessors, so Ish-Bosheth suspected that Abner's act was part of a conspiracy to seize the kingship.

ARCHAEOLOGICAL SITES

HEBRON

2 SAMUEL 3 Hebron (meaning "confederacy") is situated on a hill about 19 miles (30 km) south-southwest of Jerusalem ("Map 5"). Numbers 13:22 states that the city was built seven years before the Egyptian city of Zoan ("Tanis" in Greek),[1] around 1735 B.C., but this must have been a rebuilding since excavations have uncovered occupation levels dating back a millennium and a half earlier. Formerly, Hebron was called Kiriath Arba (Ge 23:2). Some have suggested that this means "town of four," indicating a league of four towns in the vicinity, but Joshua 14:15 and 15:3 state that it was named after Arba, an ancestor of the Anakim.

Abraham lived at Hebron near "the great trees of Mamre" (Ge 13:18) and built an altar to **Yahweh** there. Mamre was a small site less than 2 miles (3.2 km) north of Hebron, named after Mamre the Amorite (Ge 14:13). Abraham was visited there by the Lord and two angels, who repeated the promise of a son (Ge 18:1–15). At Hebron Abraham also purchased the cave of Machpelah (Ge 23:17)[2] as a family burial site.

During the conquest Joshua defeated the ruler of Hebron (Jos 10:1–27), and the city was given to Caleb on account of his bravery (Jos 14:6–15; 15:13–14). It was later set apart as a city of refuge and a Levitical town (Jos 20:7; 21:11).[3]

During the **judges period** Samson carried the gates of Gaza ("Map 4") toward Hebron (Jdg 16:3). David and his mercenaries curried the favor of the Hebron inhabitants after defeating the Amalekites (1Sa 30:26–31), and after Saul's death David ruled Judah from this location before becoming king over all of Israel (2Sa 2:1; 5:4–5). Absalom began his conspiracy at Hebron, his birthplace (3:2–3; 15:7–12), and during the reign of Rehoboam the city was among the many that were fortified in preparation for possible attack (2Ch 11:5–12).

Excavations have uncovered a portion of a **Middle Bronze Age**[4] wall about 30 feet (9.1 m) wide and a large domicile from the **Iron** I period. **Hellenistic period** kilns and pottery were discovered there, as well as **Byzantine** period burial places. Herod the Great built an enclosure of large **ashlar** masonry around the burial cave of the **patriarchs** (the *Haram* in Arabic). A Byzantine church and a mosque were later successively built above the Haram, which remains a sacred site for Muslims. Two ancient oaks are traditionally revered as the "great trees of Mamre," but the Hebrew most likely refers to terebinth trees.

[1]See "The Store Cities of Pithom and Rameses" on page 86 [2]See "The Cave of Machpelah" on page 38. [3]See "Cities of Refuge" on page 334 and "Levitical Towns" on page 335. [4]See "Archaeological Periods" chart on page xx in the front of this Bible.

Judah's side? This very day I am loyal to the house of your father Saul and to his family and friends. I
haven't handed you over to David. Yet now you accuse me of an offense involving this woman! 9 May God
3:9 [u]1Sa 15:28; 1Ki 19:2 deal with Abner, be it ever so severely, if I do not do for David what the LORD promised[u] him on oath 10 and
transfer the kingdom from the house of Saul and establish David's throne over Israel and Judah from Dan
3:10 [v]Jdg 20:1; 1Sa 3:20 to Beersheba."[v] 11 Ish-Bosheth did not dare to say another word to Abner, because he was afraid of him.
12 Then Abner sent messengers on his behalf to say to David, "Whose land is it? Make an agreement
with me, and I will help you bring all Israel over to you."
13 "Good," said David. "I will make an agreement with you. But I demand one thing of you: Do not
3:13 [w]Ge 43:5; 1Sa 18:20 come into my presence unless you bring Michal daughter of Saul when you come to see me."[w] 14 Then Da-
3:14 [x]1Sa 18:27 vid sent messengers to Ish-Bosheth son of Saul, demanding, "Give me my wife Michal,[x] whom I betrothed
to myself for the price of a hundred Philistine foreskins."
3:15 [y]Dt 24:1-4 [z]1Sa 25:44 15 So Ish-Bosheth gave orders and had her taken away from her husband[y] Paltiel[z] son of Laish. 16 Her
3:16 [a]2Sa 16:5; 19:16 husband, however, went with her, weeping behind her all the way to Bahurim.[a] Then Abner said to him,
"Go back home!" So he went back.
3:17 [b]Jdg 11:11 17 Abner conferred with the elders[b] of Israel and said, "For some time you have wanted to make Da-
vid your king. 18 Now do it! For the LORD promised David, 'By my servant David I will rescue my people
3:18 [c]1Sa 9:16 [d]1Sa 15:28; 2Sa 8:6 Israel from the hand of the Philistines[c] and from the hand of all their enemies.[d]'"
19 Abner also spoke to the Benjamites in person. Then he went to Hebron to tell David everything that
3:19 [e]1Sa 10:20-21; 1Ch 12:2,16, 29 Israel and the whole house of Benjamin[e] wanted to do. 20 When Abner, who had twenty men with him,
came to David at Hebron, David prepared a feast for him and his men. 21 Then Abner said to David, "Let
3:21 [f]ver 10,12 [g]1Ki 11:37 me go at once and assemble all Israel for my lord the king, so that they may make a compact[f] with you,
and that you may rule over all that your heart desires."[g] So David sent Abner away, and he went in peace.

Joab Murders Abner

22 Just then David's men and Joab returned from a raid and brought with them a great deal of plun-
der. But Abner was no longer with David in Hebron, because David had sent him away, and he had gone
in peace. 23 When Joab and all the soldiers with him arrived, he was told that Abner son of Ner had come
to the king and that the king had sent him away and that he had gone in peace.
24 So Joab went to the king and said, "What have you done? Look, Abner came to you. Why did you let
him go? Now he is gone! 25 You know Abner son of Ner; he came to deceive you and observe your move-
ments and find out everything you are doing."
26 Joab then left David and sent messengers after Abner, and they brought him back from the well of
3:27 [h]2Sa 2:8 [i]2Sa 2:22; 20:9-10; 1Ki 2:5 Sirah. But David did not know it. 27 Now when Abner[h] returned to Hebron, Joab took him aside into the
gateway, as though to speak with him privately. And there, to avenge the blood of his brother Asahel, Joab
stabbed him in the stomach, and he died.[i]
3:28 [j]ver 37; Dt 21:9 28 Later, when David heard about this, he said, "I and my kingdom are forever innocent[j] before the
3:29 [k]Lev 20:9 [l]1Ki 2:31-33 [m]Lev 15:2 LORD concerning the blood of Abner son of Ner. 29 May his blood[k] fall upon the head of Joab and upon all
his father's house![l] May Joab's house never be without someone who has a running sore[m] or leprosy[a] or
who leans on a crutch or who falls by the sword or who lacks food."
30 (Joab and his brother Abishai murdered Abner because he had killed their brother Asahel in the
battle at Gibeon.)
3:31 [n]2Sa 1:2,11; Ps 30:11; Isa 20:2 [o]Ge 37:34 31 Then David said to Joab and all the people with him, "Tear your clothes and put on sackcloth[n] and
walk in mourning[o] in front of Abner." King David himself walked behind the bier. 32 They buried Abner
3:32 [p]Nu 14:1; Pr 24:17 in Hebron, and the king wept[p] aloud at Abner's tomb. All the people wept also.
3:33 [q]2Sa 1:17 33 The king sang this lament[q] for Abner:

"Should Abner have died as the lawless die?
34 Your hands were not bound,
your feet were not fettered.
You fell as one falls before wicked men."

And all the people wept over him again.

[a] *29* The Hebrew word was used for various diseases affecting the skin—not necessarily leprosy.

3:10 For commentary on the phrase "from Dan to Beersheba," see the note on Judges 20:1.

3:31 See the note on sackcloth at Job 16:15, as well as "Sackcloth and Ashes: Rituals of Lamentation" on page 820.

EARLY SCRIBAL EMENDATION

2 SAMUEL 4 Generations of scribes, working for the most part in anonymity, have faithfully rendered the Bible as the best preserved work of the ancient world.[1] Although each pen stroke was the result of a scribe's action, there are in fact very few places where a scribe appears to have intentionally altered the "received" text. Such changes in the Hebrew Bible are identified by the scribal tradition as *tiqqune sopherim* ("emendations of the scribes"). Various **midrashic** and **Masoretic** lists enumerate specific emendations, ranging in total from seven to eighteen.

Most of these early scribal emendations were introduced based on religious motives in an effort to preserve the sanctity and dignity of the Biblical text. For example, Genesis 18:22 reports that "the men turned away and went toward Sodom, but Abraham remained standing before the LORD." According to some lists, this verse reflects a *tiqqun sopherim*, a deliberate scribal change at the end of a verse that originally read "while the LORD was still standing before Abraham." This change sought to avoid depicting God as a servant awaiting Abraham's instruction. Another example occurs in Zechariah 2:8 (cf. Heb 2:12), which warns that whoever struck Israel touched "the apple of [God's] eye." Scribal lists inform the reader that the original text has a first person suffix, providing the reading "the apple of my eye." This change sought to avoid the impression that God himself was speaking anthropomorphically, as though he had a physical eye.

Scribal marks between columns of the Isaiah Scroll

© Dr. James C. Martin; permission of The Israel Museum/Shrine of the Book

Some changes in the Biblical text, including euphemistic expressions (intended, e.g., to express something less starkly), are not explicitly marked. One such example occurs with respect to the proper names that contain the element "Baal." The noun *Baal*, which originally meant simply "Lord," came later to signify almost exclusively the proper name of the **Canaanite** god.[2] Later readers were apt to be offended by the appearance of this name in the Scripture, especially when associated with an Israelite. Thus, names that included "Baal" were sometimes changed in order to refrain from speaking even indirectly of false gods. For example, in 1 Chronicles the son of Jonathan is identified as Merib-Baal (1Ch 8:34; 9:40), whereas in 2 Samuel he is called Mephibosheth (2Sa 4:4). Similarly, a son of Saul is called Esh-Baal in 1 Chronicles 8:33 and 9:39 but Ish-Bosheth in 2 Samuel 2:8. In both cases the name Baal has been substituted with "bosheth," the Hebrew noun for "shame." The change does not appear to reflect a negative judgment on the individual in question, but rather was a way of condemning the name of Baal.

The cumulative evidence of the Hebrew Bible shows that such emendations were not carried out systematically. It is also important to emphasize that most early scribal emendations are explicitly identified as such by marginal notations that preserve the text of the original reading. Viewed in this light, such changes provide insight into the religious sensibilities of various readers of the Bible rather than reflecting an attempt to alter the actual wording of the sacred text.[3]

[1]See "The Scribe" on page 682 [2]See "Baal and the Fertility Cults" on page 1414. [3]See also "Textual Criticism" on page 1151.

[35]Then they all came and urged David to eat something while it was still day; but David took an oath, saying, "May God deal with me, be it ever so severely,[r] if I taste bread[s] or anything else before the sun sets!"

[36]All the people took note and were pleased; indeed, everything the king did pleased them. [37]So on that day all the people and all Israel knew that the king had no part[t] in the murder of Abner son of Ner.

[38]Then the king said to his men, "Do you not realize that a prince and a great man has fallen[u] in Israel this day? [39]And today, though I am the anointed king, I am weak, and these sons of Zeruiah[v] are too strong for me.[w] May the LORD repay[x] the evildoer according to his evil deeds!"

Ish-Bosheth Murdered

4 When Ish-Bosheth son of Saul heard that Abner[y] had died in Hebron, he lost courage, and all Israel became alarmed. [2]Now Saul's son had two men who were leaders of raiding bands. One was named Baanah and the other Recab; they were sons of Rimmon the Beerothite from the tribe of Benjamin—Beeroth[z] is considered part of Benjamin, [3]because the people of Beeroth fled to Gittaim[a] and have lived there as aliens to this day.

[4](Jonathan[b] son of Saul had a son who was lame in both feet. He was five years old when the news[c] about Saul and Jonathan came from Jezreel. His nurse picked him up and fled, but as she hurried to leave, he fell and became crippled.[d] His name was Mephibosheth.)[e]

[5]Now Recab and Baanah, the sons of Rimmon the Beerothite, set out for the house of Ish-Bosheth,[f] and they arrived there in the heat of the day while he was taking his noonday rest. [6]They went into the inner part of the house as if to get some wheat, and they stabbed[g] him in the stomach. Then Recab and his brother Baanah slipped away.

[7]They had gone into the house while he was lying on the bed in his bedroom. After they stabbed and killed him, they cut off his head. Taking it with them, they traveled all night by way of the Arabah. [8]They brought the head of Ish-Bosheth to David at Hebron and said to the king, "Here is the head of Ish-Bosheth son of Saul,[h] your enemy, who tried to take your life. This day the LORD has avenged my lord the king against Saul and his offspring."

[9]David answered Recab and his brother Baanah, the sons of Rimmon the Beerothite, "As surely as the LORD lives, who has delivered[i] me out of all trouble, [10]when a man told me, 'Saul is dead,' and thought he was bringing good news, I seized him and put him to death in Ziklag.[j] That was the reward I gave him for his news! [11]How much more—when wicked men have killed an innocent man in his own house and on his own bed—should I not now demand his blood[k] from your hand and rid the earth of you!"

[12]So David gave an order to his men, and they killed them.[l] They cut off their hands and feet and hung the bodies by the pool in Hebron. But they took the head of Ish-Bosheth and buried it in Abner's tomb at Hebron.

David Becomes King Over Israel

5 All the tribes of Israel[m] came to David at Hebron and said, "We are your own flesh and blood.[n] [2]In the past, while Saul was king over us, you were the one who led Israel on their military campaigns.[o] And the LORD said to you, 'You will shepherd[p] my people Israel, and you will become their ruler.[q]' "

[3]When all the elders of Israel had come to King David at Hebron, the king made a compact[r] with them at Hebron before the LORD, and they anointed[s] David king over Israel.

[4]David was thirty years old[t] when he became king, and he reigned[u] forty[v] years. [5]In Hebron he reigned over Judah seven years and six months,[w] and in Jerusalem he reigned over all Israel and Judah thirty-three years.

David Conquers Jerusalem

[6]The king and his men marched to Jerusalem[x] to attack the Jebusites,[y] who lived there. The Jebusites said to David, "You will not get in here; even the blind and the lame can ward you off." They thought, "David cannot get in here." [7]Nevertheless, David captured the fortress of Zion, the City of David.[z]

3:35 [r]Ru 1:17; 1Sa 3:17 [s]1Sa 31:13; 2Sa 1:12; 12:17; Jer 16:7
3:37 [t]ver 28
3:38 [u]2Sa 1:19
3:39 [v]2Sa 2:18 [w]2Sa 19:5-7 [x]1Ki 2:5-6,33-34; Ps 41:10; 101:8
4:1 [y]2Sa 3:27; Ezr 4:4
4:2 [z]Jos 9:17; 18:25
4:3 [a]Ne 11:33
4:4 [b]1Sa 18:1 [c]1Sa 31:1-4 [d]Lev 21:18 [e]2Sa 9:3,6; 1Ch 8:34; 9:40
4:5 [f]2Sa 2:8
4:6 [g]2Sa 2:23
4:8 [h]1Sa 24:4; 25:29
4:9 [i]Ge 48:16; 1Ki 1:29
4:10 [j]2Sa 1:2-16
4:11 [k]Ge 9:5; Ps 9:12
4:12 [l]2Sa 1:15
5:1 [m]2Sa 19:43 [n]1Ch 11:1
5:2 [o]1Sa 18:5,13,16 [p]1Sa 16:1; 2Sa 7:7 [q]1Sa 25:30
5:3 [r]2Sa 3:21 [s]2Sa 2:4
5:4 [t]Lk 3:23 [u]1Ki 2:11; 1Ch 3:4 [v]1Ch 26:31; 29:27
5:5 [w]2Sa 2:11; 1Ch 3:4
5:6 [x]Jdg 1:8 [y]Jos 15:8
5:7 [z]2Sa 6:12,16; 1Ki 2:10

4:4 Just as impressive physical features confirmed the right of both Saul and David to rule (1Sa 9:2; 10:23; 16:12), so Mephibosheth's impairment rendered him an unlikely choice. Ancient cultures viewed disability as a sign either of sin or of God's disfavor.

5:6 David could not rule a newly unified nation from a southern base at Hebron. Jerusalem was ideal for its central location, natural defenses (the city was located on a rise surrounded on three sides by deep valleys) and lack of previous attachment to any of the tribes of Israel (although it was situated in the territory of Benjamin). The site was first occupied during the third millennium B.C. and was a royal city during the time of Abraham. At the time of the conquest both Judah and Benjamin had attacked the city, but it was quickly lost again to the Jebusites (Jos 15:63; see "The Jebusites" on p. 596) and was sometimes referred to by the name Jebus (see Jdg 19:10; 1Ch 11:4; see also "Jerusalem" on p. 1191). David cleverly devised a means of attack and turned the venerable old fortress into his own possession—the City of David.

[8]On that day, David said, "Anyone who conquers the Jebusites will have to use the water shaft[a] to reach
those 'lame and blind' who are David's enemies.[b]" That is why they say, "The 'blind and lame' will not
enter the palace."
[9]David then took up residence in the fortress and called it the City of David. He built up the area
around it, from the supporting terraces[c][a] inward. [10]And he became more and more powerful,[b] because 5:9 [a]ver 7; 1Ki 9:15,24
the LORD God Almighty was with him. 5:10 [b]2Sa 3:1

[a] 8 Or *use scaling hooks* [b] 8 Or *are hated by David* [c] 9 Or *the Millo*

The Tsinnor

2 SAMUEL 5 The word translated as "water shaft" in 2 Samuel 5:8 is the Hebrew *tsinnor*. Used in only one other Biblical passage (Ps 42:7), the term's interpretation has long been debated by scholars. It is apparent from the context that the *tsinnor* was a means of conquering the city. While some suggest meanings such as "dagger," "hook" or "grappling-iron," the context of Psalm 42:7 (where the NIV translates *tsinnor* as "waterfalls") implies that the word in 2 Samuel 5:8 has to do with a water system. Cognates (words related by descent from the same ancestral language) from **Aramaic** and **Ugaritic** also indicate that *tsinnor* refers to a watercourse, shaft or tunnel. This implies that Joab led the charge through an underground waterway (cf. 1Ch 11:6).

At one time archaeologists thought that the site known as "Warren's Shaft" was the *tsinnor*. From the top of Warren's Shaft a stepped tunnel leads to an above-ground entrance inside the **Canaanite** city wall. Joab was thought to have entered the water system through the Gihon spring and climbed up the once narrow shaft to conquer the city.

New discoveries made since 1995, however, have shed new light on this water system. It now appears that the stepped tunnel that leads from the entrance to Warren's Shaft did not have its present form until the eighth century B.C. In Joab's time the top of Warren's Shaft was still buried 4 feet (1.2 m) below the floor of the tunnel. Joab's entrance into the city via the *tsinnor* had to have been by some other water source or passage. As helpful as archaeology is in bringing the Bible to life, it is important to realize that old conclusions often need to be revisited in light of more recent excavation and analysis.

Warren's Shaft

Photograph: © Todd Bolen/Bible Places.com

11 Now Hiram[c] king of Tyre sent messengers to David, along with cedar logs and carpenters and stonemasons, and they built a palace for David. 12 And David knew that the LORD had established him as king over Israel and had exalted his kingdom for the sake of his people Israel.

13 After he left Hebron, David took more concubines and wives[d] in Jerusalem, and more sons and daughters were born to him. 14 These are the names of the children born to him there:[e] Shammua, Shobab, Nathan, Solomon, 15 Ibhar, Elishua, Nepheg, Japhia, 16 Elishama, Eliada and Eliphelet.

David Defeats the Philistines

17 When the Philistines heard that David had been anointed king over Israel, they went up in full force to search for him, but David heard about it and went down to the stronghold.[f] 18 Now the Philistines had come and spread out in the Valley of Rephaim;[g] 19 so David inquired[h] of the LORD, "Shall I go and attack the Philistines? Will you hand them over to me?"

The LORD answered him, "Go, for I will surely hand the Philistines over to you."

20 So David went to Baal Perazim, and there he defeated them. He said, "As waters break out, the LORD has broken out against my enemies before me." So that place was called Baal Perazim.[a][i] 21 The Philistines abandoned their idols there, and David and his men carried them off.[j]

22 Once more the Philistines came up and spread out in the Valley of Rephaim; 23 so David inquired of the LORD, and he answered, "Do not go straight up, but circle around behind them and attack them in front of the balsam trees. 24 As soon as you hear the sound[k] of marching in the tops of the balsam trees, move quickly, because that will mean the LORD has gone out in front[l] of you to strike the Philistine army." 25 So David did as the LORD commanded him, and he struck down the Philistines all the way from Gibeon[b][m] to Gezer.[n]

The Ark Brought to Jerusalem

6 David again brought together out of Israel chosen men, thirty thousand in all. 2 He and all his men set out from Baalah[o] of Judah[c] to bring up from there the ark[p] of God, which is called by the Name,[d][q] the name of the LORD Almighty, who is enthroned[r] between the cherubim[s] that are on the ark. 3 They set the ark of God on a new cart[t] and brought it from the house of Abinadab, which was on the hill. Uzzah and Ahio, sons of Abinadab, were guiding the new cart 4 with the ark of God on it,[e] and Ahio was walking in front of it. 5 David and the whole house of Israel were celebrating with all their might before the LORD, with songs[f] and with harps, lyres, tambourines, sistrums and cymbals.[u]

6 When they came to the threshing floor of Nacon, Uzzah reached out and took hold of[v] the ark of God, because the oxen stumbled. 7 The LORD's anger burned against Uzzah because of his irreverent act;[w] therefore God struck him down[x] and he died there beside the ark of God.

8 Then David was angry because the LORD's wrath[y] had broken out against Uzzah, and to this day that place is called Perez Uzzah.[g][z]

9 David was afraid of the LORD that day and said, "How[a] can the ark of the LORD ever come to me?" 10 He was not willing to take the ark of the LORD to be with him in the City of David. Instead, he took it aside to the house of Obed-Edom[b] the Gittite. 11 The ark of the LORD remained in the house of Obed-Edom the Gittite for three months, and the LORD blessed him and his entire household.[c]

12 Now King David[d] was told, "The LORD has blessed the household of Obed-Edom and everything he has, because of the ark of God." So David went down and brought up the ark of God from the house of Obed-Edom to the City of David with rejoicing. 13 When those who were carrying the ark of the LORD had taken six steps, he sacrificed[e] a bull and a fattened calf. 14 David, wearing a linen ephod,[f] danced[g] before the LORD with all his might, 15 while he and the entire house of Israel brought up the ark of the LORD with shouts and the sound of trumpets.[h]

5:11 [c]1Ki 5:1,18; 1Ch 14:1
5:13 [d]Dt 17:17; 1Ch 3:9
5:14 [e]1Ch 3:5
5:17 [f]2Sa 23:14; 1Ch 11:16
5:18 [g]Jos 15:8; 17:15; 18:16
5:19 [h]1Sa 23:2; 2Sa 2:1
5:20 [i]Isa 28:21
5:21 [j]Dt 7:5; 1Ch 14:12; Isa 46:2
5:24 [k]2Ki 7:6 [l]Jdg 4:14
5:25 [m]Isa 28:21 [n]1Ch 14:16
6:2 [o]Jos 15:9 [p]1Sa 4:4; 7:1 [q]Lev 24:16; Isa 63:14 [r]Ps 99:1 [s]Ex 25:22; 1Ch 13:5-6
6:3 [t]Nu 7:4-9; 1Sa 6:7
6:5 [u]1Sa 18:6-7; Ezr 3:10; Ps 150:5
6:6 [v]Nu 4:15,19-20; 1Ch 13:9
6:7 [w]1Ch 15:13-15 [x]Ex 19:22; 1Sa 6:19
6:8 [y]Ps 7:11 [z]Ge 38:29
6:9 [a]Ps 119:120
6:10 [b]1Ch 13:13; 26:4-5
6:11 [c]Ge 30:27; 39:5
6:12 [d]1Ki 8:1; 1Ch 15:25
6:13 [e]1Ki 8:5,62
6:14 [f]Ex 19:6; 1Sa 2:18 [g]Ex 15:20
6:15 [h]Ps 47:5; 98:6

[a] *20 Baal Perazim* means *the lord who breaks out.* [b] *25* Septuagint (see also 1 Chron. 14:16); Hebrew *Geba* [c] *2* That is, Kiriath Jearim; Hebrew *Baale Judah,* a variant of *Baalah of Judah* [d] *2* Hebrew; Septuagint and Vulgate do not have *the Name.*
[e] *3,4* Dead Sea Scrolls and some Septuagint manuscripts; Masoretic Text *cart* [4] *and they brought it with the ark of God from the house of Abinadab, which was on the hill* [f] *5* See Dead Sea Scrolls, Septuagint and 1 Chronicles 13:8; Masoretic Text *celebrating before the LORD with all kinds of instruments made of pine.* [g] *8 Perez Uzzah* means *outbreak against Uzzah.*

5:11 Hiram was the Phoenician king who was the first to accord King David international recognition. Hiram desired good relations with Israel because Israel dominated the inland trade routes to Tyre (an important Phoenician seaport on the Mediterranean coast north of Israel), which was dependent on Israelite agriculture for much of its food. A close relationship existed between the two realms until the Babylonian invasions (see "Solomon and the Israelite Empire: on p. 490).

A Near Eastern king's possession of a palace was the chief symbolic indication of his status.

6:14 See the note on religious dancing at Psalm 149:3.

16 As the ark of the LORD was entering the City of David,[i] Michal daughter of Saul watched from a win-
dow. And when she saw King David leaping and dancing before the LORD, she despised him in her heart.
17 They brought the ark of the LORD and set it in its place inside the tent that David had pitched for it,[j]
and David sacrificed burnt offerings[k] and fellowship offerings[a] before the LORD. 18 After he had finished
sacrificing[l] the burnt offerings and fellowship offerings, he blessed the people in the name of the LORD
Almighty. 19 Then he gave a loaf of bread, a cake of dates and a cake of raisins[m] to each person in the
whole crowd of Israelites, both men and women.[n] And all the people went to their homes.
20 When David returned home to bless his household, Michal daughter of Saul came out to meet him
and said, "How the king of Israel has distinguished himself today, disrobing[o] in the sight of the slave girls
of his servants as any vulgar fellow would!"
21 David said to Michal, "It was before the LORD, who chose me rather than your father or anyone from
his house when he appointed[p] me ruler over the LORD's people Israel—I will celebrate before the LORD.
22 I will become even more undignified than this, and I will be humiliated in my own eyes. But by these
slave girls you spoke of, I will be held in honor."
23 And Michal daughter of Saul had no children to the day of her death.

God's Promise to David

7 After the king was settled in his palace[q] and the LORD had given him rest from all his enemies around
him, 2 he said to Nathan the prophet, "Here I am, living in a palace[r] of cedar, while the ark of God re-
mains in a tent."[s]
3 Nathan replied to the king, "Whatever you have in mind, go ahead and do it, for the LORD is with you."
4 That night the word of the LORD came to Nathan, saying:

5 "Go and tell my servant David, 'This is what the LORD says: Are you[t] the one to build me a house
to dwell in?[u] 6 I have not dwelt in a house from the day I brought the Israelites up out of Egypt to
this day. I have been moving from place to place with a tent[v] as my dwelling.[w] 7 Wherever I have
moved with all the Israelites,[x] did I ever say to any of their rulers whom I commanded to shepherd[y]
my people Israel, "Why have you not built me a house of cedar?[z]" '
8 "Now then, tell my servant David, 'This is what the LORD Almighty says: I took you from the
pasture and from following the flock[a] to be ruler[b] over my people Israel.[c] 9 I have been with you
wherever you have gone,[d] and I have cut off all your enemies from before you.[e] Now I will make
your name great, like the names of the greatest men of the earth. 10 And I will provide a place for
my people Israel and will plant[f] them so that they can have a home of their own and no longer be
disturbed. Wicked[g] people will not oppress them anymore,[h] as they did at the beginning 11 and
have done ever since the time I appointed leaders[b][i] over my people Israel. I will also give you rest
from all your enemies.[j]
" 'The LORD declares to you that the LORD himself will establish[k] a house[l] for you: 12 When your
days are over and you rest[m] with your fathers, I will raise up your offspring to succeed you, who
will come from your own body,[n] and I will establish his kingdom. 13 He is the one who will build a
house for my Name,[o] and I will establish the throne of his kingdom forever.[p] 14 I will be his father,
and he will be my son.[q] When he does wrong, I will punish him with the rod[r] of men, with flog-
gings inflicted by men. 15 But my love will never be taken away from him, as I took it away from
Saul,[s] whom I removed from before you. 16 Your house and your kingdom will endure forever be-
fore me[c]; your throne[t] will be established forever.[u]' "

17 Nathan reported to David all the words of this entire revelation.

David's Prayer

18 Then King David went in and sat before the LORD, and he said:

"Who am I,[v] O Sovereign LORD, and what is my family, that you have brought me this far? 19 And
as if this were not enough in your sight, O Sovereign LORD, you have also spoken about the future
of the house of your servant. Is this your usual way of dealing with man,[w] O Sovereign LORD?
20 "What more can David say to you? For you know[x] your servant,[y] O Sovereign LORD. 21 For the

6:16 [i]2Sa 5:7
6:17 [j]1Ch 15:1; 2Ch 1:4 [k]Lev 1:1-17; 1Ki 8:62-64
6:18 [l]1Ki 8:22
6:19 [m]Hos 3:1 [n]Ne 8:10
6:20 [o]ver 14,16
6:21 [p]1Sa 13:14; 15:28
7:1 [q]1Ch 17:1
7:2 [r]2Sa 5:11 [s]Ex 26:1; Ac 7:45-46
7:5 [t]1Ki 8:19; 1Ch 22:8 [u]1Ki 5:3-5
7:6 [v]Ex 40:18,34 [w]1Ki 8:16
7:7 [x]Dt 23:14 [y]2Sa 5:2 [z]Lev 26:11-12
7:8 [a]1Sa 16:11 [b]2Sa 6:21 [c]Ps 78:70-72; 2Co 6:18*
7:9 [d]2Sa 5:10 [e]Ps 18:37-42
7:10 [f]Ex 15:17; Isa 5:1-7 [g]Ps 89:22-23 [h]Isa 60:18
7:11 [i]Jdg 2:16; 1Sa 12:9-11 [j]ver 1 [k]1Sa 25:28 [l]ver 27
7:12 [m]1Ki 2:1 [n]Ps 132:11-12
7:13 [o]1Ki 5:5; 8:19,29 [p]Isa 9:7
7:14 [q]Ps 89:26; Heb 1:5* [r]Ps 89:30-33
7:15 [s]1Sa 15:23, 28
7:16 [t]Ps 89:36-37 [u]ver 13
7:18 [v]Ex 3:11; 1Sa 18:18
7:19 [w]Isa 55:8-9
7:20 [x]Jn 21:17 [y]1Sa 16:7

[a] *17* Traditionally *peace offerings*; also in verse 18 [b] *11* Traditionally *judges* [c] *16* Some Hebrew manuscripts and Septuagint; most Hebrew manuscripts *you*

sake of your word and according to your will, you have done this great thing and made it known
to your servant.
22"How great[z] you are,[a] O Sovereign LORD! There is no one like you, and there is no God[b] but
you, as we have heard with our own ears.[c] 23And who is like your people Israel[d]—the one nation
on earth that God went out to redeem as a people for himself, and to make a name for himself,
and to perform great and awesome wonders[e] by driving out nations and their gods from before
your people, whom you redeemed[f] from Egypt?[a] 24You have established your people Israel as your
very own[g] forever, and you, O LORD, have become their God.[h]
25"And now, LORD God, keep forever the promise you have made concerning your servant and his
house. Do as you promised, 26so that your name will be great forever. Then men will say, 'The LORD
Almighty is God over Israel!' And the house of your servant David will be established before you.
27"O LORD Almighty, God of Israel, you have revealed this to your servant, saying, 'I will build a
house for you.' So your servant has found courage to offer you this prayer. 28O Sovereign LORD, you
are God! Your words are trustworthy,[i] and you have promised these good things to your servant.
29Now be pleased to bless the house of your servant, that it may continue forever in your sight; for
you, O Sovereign LORD, have spoken, and with your blessing[j] the house of your servant will be
blessed forever."

David's Victories

8 In the course of time, David defeated the Philistines and subdued them, and he took Metheg Ammah from the control of the Philistines.
2David also defeated the Moabites.[k] He made them lie down on the ground and measured them off
with a length of cord. Every two lengths of them were put to death, and the third length was allowed to
live. So the Moabites became subject to David and brought tribute.
3Moreover, David fought Hadadezer[l] son of Rehob, king of Zobah,[m] when he went to restore his control along the Euphrates River. 4David captured a thousand of his chariots, seven thousand charioteers[b]
and twenty thousand foot soldiers. He hamstrung[n] all but a hundred of the chariot horses.
5When the Arameans of Damascus[o] came to help Hadadezer king of Zobah, David struck down twenty-two thousand of them. 6He put garrisons in the Aramean kingdom of Damascus, and the Arameans
became subject to him and brought tribute. The LORD gave David victory wherever he went.[p]
7David took the gold shields[q] that belonged to the officers of Hadadezer and brought them to Jerusalem. 8From Tebah[c] and Berothai,[r] towns that belonged to Hadadezer, King David took a great quantity
of bronze.
9When Tou[d] king of Hamath[s] heard that David had defeated the entire army of Hadadezer, 10he sent
his son Joram[e] to King David to greet him and congratulate him on his victory in battle over Hadadezer,
who had been at war with Tou. Joram brought with him articles of silver and gold and bronze.
11King David dedicated[t] these articles to the LORD, as he had done with the silver and gold from all the
nations he had subdued: 12Edom[f] and Moab,[u] the Ammonites[v] and the Philistines,[w] and Amalek.[x] He
also dedicated the plunder taken from Hadadezer son of Rehob, king of Zobah.
13And David became famous[y] after he returned from striking down eighteen thousand Edomites[g] in
the Valley of Salt.[z]
14He put garrisons throughout Edom, and all the Edomites[a] became subject to David.[b] The LORD gave
David victory wherever he went.[c]

7:22 [z]Ps 48:1; 86:10; Jer 10:6 [a]Dt 3:24 [b]Ex 15:11 [c]Ex 10:2; Ps 44:1
7:23 [d]Dt 4:32-38 [e]Dt 10:21 [f]Dt 9:26; 15:15
7:24 [g]Dt 26:18 [h]Ex 6:6-7; Ps 48:14
7:28 [i]Ex 34:6; Jn 17:17
7:29 [j]Nu 6:23-27
8:2 [k]Ge 19:37; Nu 24:17
8:3 [l]2Sa 10:16,19 [m]1Sa 14:47
8:4 [n]Jos 11:9
8:5 [o]1Ki 11:24
8:6 [p]ver 14; 2Sa 3:18; 7:9
8:7 [q]1Ki 10:16
8:8 [r]Eze 47:16
8:9 [s]1Ki 8:65; 2Ch 8:4
8:11 [t]1Ki 7:51; 1Ch 26:26
8:12 [u]ver 2 [v]2Sa 10:14 [w]2Sa 5:25 [x]1Sa 27:8
8:13 [y]2Sa 7:9 [z]2Ki 14:7; 1Ch 18:12
8:14 [a]Nu 24:17-18 [b]Ge 27:29,37-40 [c]ver 6

[a] *23* See Septuagint and 1 Chron. 17:21; Hebrew *wonders for your land and before your people, whom you redeemed from Egypt, from the nations and their gods.* [b] *4* Septuagint (see also Dead Sea Scrolls and 1 Chron. 18:4); Masoretic Text *captured seventeen hundred of his charioteers* [c] *8* See some Septuagint manuscripts (see also 1 Chron. 18:8); Hebrew *Betah.* [d] *9* Hebrew *Toi,* a variant of *Tou;* also in verse 10 [e] *10* A variant of *Hadoram* [f] *12* Some Hebrew manuscripts, Septuagint and Syriac (see also 1 Chron. 18:11); most Hebrew manuscripts *Aram* [g] *13* A few Hebrew manuscripts, Septuagint and Syriac (see also 1 Chron. 18:12); most Hebrew manuscripts *Aram* (that is, Arameans)

8:2 The Moabites, descendants of Lot (Ge 19:37), occupied territory east of the Dead Sea (see "Moab" on p. 292).

8:3 The precise identity of Hadadezer and the exact location of Zobah are both unknown. However, the town was in Syrian territory (perhaps in the Beqa Valley of Lebanon), and Hadadezer's name, meaning "Hadad is (my) help," is certainly authentic (Hadad is the Syrian name for the god Baal). The Assyrian king at this time, Ashurrabi II, carried on warfare with an unnamed Syrian adversary, who may have been the Biblical Hadadezer. Second Samuel 10:16 mentions another battle between David and Hadadezer, although some interpreters believe that the two conflicts are one and the same.

8:9 Hamath was a kingdom centered on the Orontes River, north of Zobah.

8:13 The Valley of Salt is generally identified with the region of the Arabah, directly south of the Dead Sea.

David's Officials

15 David reigned over all Israel, doing what was just and right for all his people. 16 Joab[d] son of Zerui-
ah was over the army; Jehoshaphat[e] son of Ahilud was recorder; 17 Zadok[f] son of Ahitub and Ahimelech
son of Abiathar were priests; Seraiah was secretary;[g] 18 Benaiah[h] son of Jehoiada was over the Kereth-
ites[i] and Pelethites; and David's sons were royal advisers.[a]

David and Mephibosheth

9 David asked, "Is there anyone still left of the house of Saul to whom I can show kindness for Jona-
than's sake?"[j]
2 Now there was a servant of Saul's household named Ziba.[k] They called him to appear before David,
and the king said to him, "Are you Ziba?"
"Your servant," he replied.
3 The king asked, "Is there no one still left of the house of Saul to whom I can show God's kindness?"
Ziba answered the king, "There is still a son of Jonathan;[l] he is crippled[m] in both feet."
4 "Where is he?" the king asked.
Ziba answered, "He is at the house of Makir[n] son of Ammiel in Lo Debar."
5 So King David had him brought from Lo Debar, from the house of Makir son of Ammiel.
6 When Mephibosheth son of Jonathan, the son of Saul, came to David, he bowed down to pay him
honor.[o]
David said, "Mephibosheth!"
"Your servant," he replied.
7 "Don't be afraid," David said to him, "for I will surely show you kindness for the sake of your father
Jonathan. I will restore to you all the land that belonged to your grandfather Saul, and you will always eat
at my table.[p]"
8 Mephibosheth bowed down and said, "What is your servant, that you should notice a dead dog[q]
like me?"
9 Then the king summoned Ziba, Saul's servant, and said to him, "I have given your master's grandson
everything that belonged to Saul and his family. 10 You and your servants are to farm the land
for him and bring in the crops, so that your master's grandson[r] may be provided for. And Mephibosheth,
grandson of your master, will always eat at my table." (Now Ziba had fifteen sons and twenty servants.)
11 Then Ziba said to the king, "Your servant will do whatever my lord the king commands his servant
to do." So Mephibosheth ate at David's[b] table like one of the king's sons.[s]
12 Mephibosheth had a young son named Mica, and all the members of Ziba's household were ser-
vants of Mephibosheth.[t] 13 And Mephibosheth lived in Jerusalem, because he always ate at the king's ta-
ble, and he was crippled in both feet.

David Defeats the Ammonites

10 In the course of time, the king of the Ammonites died, and his son Hanun succeeded him as
king. 2 David thought, "I will show kindness to Hanun son of Nahash,[u] just as his father showed
kindness to me." So David sent a delegation to express his sympathy to Hanun concerning his father.
When David's men came to the land of the Ammonites, 3 the Ammonite nobles said to Hanun their
lord, "Do you think David is honoring your father by sending men to you to express sympathy? Hasn't Da-
vid sent them to you to explore the city and spy it out and overthrow it?" 4 So Hanun seized David's men,

8:16 [d]2Sa 19:13; 1Ch 11:6 [e]2Sa 20:24; 1Ki 4:3
8:17 [f]2Sa 15:24, 29; 1Ch 16:39; 24:3 [g]1Ki 4:3; 2Ki 12:10
8:18 [h]2Sa 20:23; 1Ki 1:8,38; 1Ch 18:17 [i]1Sa 30:14
9:1 [j]1Sa 20:14-17,42
9:2 [k]2Sa 16:1-4; 19:17,26,29
9:3 [l]1Sa 20:14 [m]2Sa 4:4
9:4 [n]2Sa 17:27-29
9:6 [o]2Sa 16:4; 19:24-30
9:7 [p]ver 1,3; 2Sa 12:8; 19:28; 1Ki 2:7; 2Ki 25:29
9:8 [q]2Sa 16:9
9:10 [r]ver 7,11, 13; 2Sa 19:28
9:11 [s]Job 36:7; Ps 113:8
9:12 [t]1Ch 8:34
10:2 [u]1Sa 11:1

[a] 18 Or *were priests* [b] 11 Septuagint; Hebrew *my*

8:17 Zadok, a descendant of Eleazar, the son of Aaron, remained loyal to David throughout his reign and eventually anointed Solomon as David's successor (1Ki 1:8,45; 2:35; 4:4).
8:18 The Kerethites and Pelethites were Philistine mercenaries who formed a royal guard for David (23:22–23).
9:4 Lo Debar was a town located deep within Gileadite territory in Transjordan, far from both the family estate and from David's court.
9:7–10 In ancient times the family of a king replaced by another did not expect consideration. New dynasties routinely eliminated all members of families of the old order to solidify a power base (see "Ambitious Princes Among the Hittites" on p. 469). It was risky for David to grant Saul's grandson access to the royal palace and financial freedom (see 16:3). David's kindness to Mephibosheth certainly surpassed his obligation to allow the young man merely to stay alive.
10:1 See "Ammon" on page 364.
10:4 Hanun's humiliation of David's men was, in effect, a declaration of war. The beard was the pride and joy of an Israelite male, cut only for periods of mourning or as an act of self-humiliation (see "Beards and Hairstyles in the Biblical World" on p. 1084). Since garments often reflected status, power or identity, the insult of cutting the ambassadors' clothes at their hips was a further humiliation to David's men (see "Bywords and Insults in the Ancient World" on p. 431).

10:4 [v]Lev 19:27; shaved off half of each man's beard,[v] cut off their garments in the middle at the buttocks,[w] and sent them
Isa 15:2; Jer 48:37 away.
[w]Isa 20:4 5 When David was told about this, he sent messengers to meet the men, for they were greatly humili-
ated. The king said, "Stay at Jericho till your beards have grown, and then come back."
10:6 [x]Ge 34:30 6 When the Ammonites realized that they had become a stench[x] in David's nostrils, they hired twen-
[y]2Sa 8:5 [z]Jdg 18:28 ty thousand Aramean[y] foot soldiers from Beth Rehob[z] and Zobah, as well as the king of Maacah[a] with
[a]Dt 3:14 a thousand men, and also twelve thousand men from Tob.
7 On hearing this, David sent Joab out with the entire army of fighting men. 8 The Ammonites came out
and drew up in battle formation at the entrance to their city gate, while the Arameans of Zobah and Re-
hob and the men of Tob and Maacah were by themselves in the open country.
9 Joab saw that there were battle lines in front of him and behind him; so he selected some of the best
troops in Israel and deployed them against the Arameans. 10 He put the rest of the men under the com-
mand of Abishai his brother and deployed them against the Ammonites. 11 Joab said, "If the Arameans
are too strong for me, then you are to come to my rescue; but if the Ammonites are too strong for you,
10:12 [b]Dt 31:6; then I will come to rescue you. 12 Be strong[b] and let us fight bravely for our people and the cities of our
1Co 16:13; Eph 6:10 God. The LORD will do what is good in his sight."[c]
[c]Jdg 10:15; 1Sa 3:18; Ne 4:14 13 Then Joab and the troops with him advanced to fight the Arameans, and they fled before him.
14 When the Ammonites saw that the Arameans were fleeing, they fled before Abishai and went inside
the city. So Joab returned from fighting the Ammonites and came to Jerusalem.
15 After the Arameans saw that they had been routed by Israel, they regrouped. 16 Hadadezer had Ar-
ameans brought from beyond the River[a]; they went to Helam, with Shobach the commander of Hadad-
ezer's army leading them.
17 When David was told of this, he gathered all Israel, crossed the Jordan and went to Helam. The Ar-
ameans formed their battle lines to meet David and fought against him. 18 But they fled before Israel, and
David killed seven hundred of their charioteers and forty thousand of their foot soldiers.[b] He also struck
down Shobach the commander of their army, and he died there. 19 When all the kings who were vassals
of Hadadezer saw that they had been defeated by Israel, they made peace with the Israelites and became
10:19 [d]2Sa 8:6 [e]1Ki 11:25; subject[d] to them.
2Ki 5:1 So the Arameans[e] were afraid to help the Ammonites anymore.

David and Bathsheba

11:1 [f]1Ki 20:22, 26 [g]2Sa 2:18 11 In the spring,[f] at the time when kings go off to war, David sent Joab[g] out with the king's men
[h]1Ch 20:1 [i]2Sa 12:26-28 and the whole Israelite army.[h] They destroyed the Ammonites and besieged Rabbah.[i] But David
remained in Jerusalem.
11:2 [j]Dt 22:8; 2 One evening David got up from his bed and walked around on the roof[j] of the palace. From the roof
Jos 2:8 [k]Mt 5:28 he saw[k] a woman bathing. The woman was very beautiful, 3 and David sent someone to find out about
11:3 [l]1Ch 3:5 her. The man said, "Isn't this Bathsheba,[l] the daughter of Eliam[m] and the wife of Uriah[n] the Hittite?"
[m]2Sa 23:34 [n]2Sa 23:39 4 Then David sent messengers to get her.[o] She came to him, and he slept[p] with her. (She had purified her-
11:4 [o]Lev 20:10; Ps 51 Title; self from her uncleanness.)[q] Then[c] she went back home. 5 The woman conceived and sent word to Da-
Jas 1:14-15 [p]Dt 22:22 vid, saying, "I am pregnant."
[q]Lev 15:25-30; 18:19 6 So David sent this word to Joab: "Send me Uriah[r] the Hittite." And Joab sent him to David. 7 When Uri-
11:6 [r]1Ch 11:41 ah came to him, David asked him how Joab was, how the soldiers were and how the war was going. 8 Then
11:8 [s]Ge 18:4; 43:24; Lk 7:44 David said to Uriah, "Go down to your house and wash your feet."[s] So Uriah left the palace, and a gift
from the king was sent after him. 9 But Uriah slept at the entrance to the palace with all his master's ser-
vants and did not go down to his house.
10 When David was told, "Uriah did not go home," he asked him, "Haven't you just come from a dis-
tance? Why didn't you go home?"
11:11 [t]2Sa 7:2 11 Uriah said to David, "The ark[t] and Israel and Judah are staying in tents, and my master Joab and my

[a] *16* That is, the Euphrates [b] *18* Some Septuagint manuscripts (see also 1 Chron. 19:18); Hebrew *horsemen* [c] *4* Or *with her. When she purified herself from her uncleanness,*

11:2 The roof was flat, and David had probably gone there to enjoy the cool evening air.

11:4 Bathsheba had just become ceremonially clean after the seven-day period of monthly impurity due to menstruation (Lev 15:19–30; see "Bathing" on p. 456). The purpose of this parenthetical statement is to indicate her condition at the time of her sexual relations with David. The context makes it clear that she was not already pregnant by her own husband.

lord's men are camped in the open fields. How could I go to my house to eat and drink and lie with my
wife? As surely as you live, I will not do such a thing!"
12 Then David said to him, "Stay here one more day, and tomorrow I will send you back." So Uriah re-
mained in Jerusalem that day and the next. 13 At David's invitation, he ate and drank with him, and Da-
vid made him drunk. But in the evening Uriah went out to sleep on his mat among his master's servants;
he did not go home.
14 In the morning David wrote a letter[u] to Joab and sent it with Uriah. 15 In it he wrote, "Put Uriah in the **11:14** [u]1Ki 21:8
front line where the fighting is fiercest. Then withdraw from him so he will be struck down[v] and die.[w]" **11:15** [v]2Sa 12:9 [w]2Sa 12:12

Bathing

2 SAMUEL 11 The description of Bathsheba's bathing in 2 Samuel 11:2 employs the verb *rahas*—"to wash"—which, when used alone, implies "to bathe the entire body." When limited to a portion of the body, the intended body part is stipulated. Thus, we know from the grammar (as well as from the context) that Bathsheba was bathing. The text informs us that she was purifying herself from her uncleanness, indicating that she had just completed her menstrual cycle. While no such ordinance exists in the relevant texts of Leviticus 15:19–24, it appears that Bathsheba was bathing for ritual or hygienic purposes.[1]

Ritual purity was achieved partly by bathing, as is seen in the directive given to Aaron and his sons (Lev 8:6). Such practices among the priesthood are also attested in Egypt, where the priests were instructed to bathe three times daily to remove physical pollution and to attain a spiritual life. Purification from defilement among laity and priests alike often involved the washing of the body (e.g., Lev 15:18,21). Washing the feet, attested many times in both the Old Testament (e.g., Ge 18:4; 19:2; 24:32; 43:24; Jdg 19:21) and the New Testament (most notably Jn 13:1–17), must have been a common occurrence in Israel. While Rabbinical texts that speak of the necessity of washing the hands before eating (e.g., Mt 15:2) probably have roots in an earlier era, it is uncertain how far back these traditions extend.

How widespread and frequent non-ceremonial bathing was in Israel is impossible to determine. The Old Testament accounts of such bathing undertaken by David (2Sa 12:20), Ruth (Ru 3:3), **Samarian** harlots (1Ki 22:38), Naaman (2Ki 5:10) and the allegorical Oholah and Oholibah (Eze 23:40) indicate that the practice was fairly common and not exclusive to members of the upper class. Further indication comes from the **Phoenician** town Achzib.[2] An eighth–seventh century B.C. terracotta figurine depicting a woman bathing while sitting in an oval bathtub was unearthed there. This, too, suggests that bathing was widely practiced.

[1]See "Ritual Purity in Israel and the Ancient Near East" on page 166. [2]See "Phoenicia" on page 488.

Roman era stone bath

Preserving Bible Times; © Dr. James C. Martin

16So while Joab had the city under siege, he put Uriah at a place where he knew the strongest defend-
ers were. 17When the men of the city came out and fought against Joab, some of the men in David's army
fell; moreover, Uriah the Hittite died.
18Joab sent David a full account of the battle. 19He instructed the messenger: "When you have fin-
ished giving the king this account of the battle, 20the king's anger may flare up, and he may ask you, 'Why
did you get so close to the city to fight? Didn't you know they would shoot arrows from the wall? 21Who
11:21 [x]Jdg 8:31 [y]Jdg 9:50-54 killed Abimelech[x] son of Jerub-Besheth[a]? Didn't a woman throw an upper millstone on him from the
wall,[y] so that he died in Thebez? Why did you get so close to the wall?' If he asks you this, then say to
him, 'Also, your servant Uriah the Hittite is dead.' "
22The messenger set out, and when he arrived he told David everything Joab had sent him to say.
23The messenger said to David, "The men overpowered us and came out against us in the open, but we
drove them back to the entrance to the city gate. 24Then the archers shot arrows at your servants from
the wall, and some of the king's men died. Moreover, your servant Uriah the Hittite is dead."
25David told the messenger, "Say this to Joab: 'Don't let this upset you; the sword devours one as well
as another. Press the attack against the city and destroy it.' Say this to encourage Joab."
26When Uriah's wife heard that her husband was dead, she mourned for him. 27After the time of
mourning was over, David had her brought to his house, and she became his wife and bore him a son.
11:27 [z]2Sa 12:9; Ps 51:4-5 But the thing David had done displeased[z] the LORD.

Nathan Rebukes David

12:1 [a]2Sa 7:2; 1Ki 20:35-41 [b]Ps 51 Title [c]2Sa 14:4 12 The LORD sent Nathan[a] to David.[b] When he came to him,[c] he said, "There were two men in a cer-
tain town, one rich and the other poor. 2The rich man had a very large number of sheep and cat-
tle, 3but the poor man had nothing except one little ewe lamb he had bought. He raised it, and it grew up
with him and his children. It shared his food, drank from his cup and even slept in his arms. It was like
a daughter to him.

[a] 21 Also known as *Jerub-Baal* (that is, Gideon)

11:21 Jerub-Besheth (or Jerub-Bosheth or Jerub-Baal) refers to Gideon (Jdg 6:32). The author of Samuel made other similar name changes, altering Ish-Baal to Ish-Bosheth (2:8) and Merib-Baal to Mephibosheth (4:4). See "Early Scribal Emendation" on page 448.

ANCIENT TEXTS AND ARTIFACTS

The Mountain and the Deer: A Hurrian Parable

2 SAMUEL 12 In antiquity, wisdom literature often took the form of parables.[1] The story of the mountain and the deer, found in a collection of **Hurrian** parables,[2] illustrates a particular genre of wisdom literature in which animals depicted human subjects. In this story, a deer left the mountain on which it had been born and went to graze upon another mountain. Although the deer grew fat there, it was ungrateful and began to call down curses of lightning upon the summit of the new mountain. In retaliation, the mountain summoned hunters to kill the deer. At the conclusion of the parable the interpretation is spelled out: The deer was a man who for some reason had fled his hometown and taken refuge in another. He was unappreciative, however, and began to do evil there, as a result being cursed by the gods of that town.

The prophet Nathan used a similar technique to convict David of his sin against Uriah (2Sa 12). He told a story about two men, one wealthy and the other poor, representing David and Uriah, respectively. The poor man's lamb depicted Bathsheba. Unaware that Nathan's account was a parable, the outraged King David instantly pronounced judgment against the unjust rich man. Only then did Nathan reveal that David himself was that man![3]

[1]See "Ancient Near Eastern Wisdom" on page 960. [2]See "The Hurrians" on page 57. [3]See "David" on page 443.

ANCIENT VOICES

A mountain expelled a deer from its expanse (lit., 'body'),* and the deer went to another mountain. He became fat and he sought a confrontation. He began to curse the mountain: "If only fire would burn up the mountain on which I graze! If only the Storm-god would smite it (with lightning) and fire burn it up!" When the mountain heard, it became sick at heart and in response the mountain cursed the deer: "The deer whom I fattened up now curses me in return. Let the hunters bring down the deer! Let the fowlers capture him! Let the hunters take his meat, and the fowlers take his skin!"

*Words in parentheses added by translator for clarity or where text has gaps

—EXCERPT FROM THE HURRO-HITTITE BILINGUAL WISDOM TEXT

See "The Mountain and the Deer: A Hurrian Parable" article on the previous page.

4“Now a traveler came to the rich man, but the rich man refrained from taking one of his own sheep or cattle to prepare a meal for the traveler who had come to him. Instead, he took the ewe lamb that belonged to the poor man and prepared it for the one who had come to him.”

5David[d] burned with anger against the man and said to Nathan, “As surely as the LORD lives, the man who did this deserves to die! 6He must pay for that lamb four times over,[e] because he did such a thing and had no pity.”

7Then Nathan said to David, “You are the man! This is what the LORD, the God of Israel, says: ‘I anointed[f] you[g] king over Israel, and I delivered you from the hand of Saul. 8I gave your master’s house to you,[h] and your master’s wives into your arms. I gave you the house of Israel and Judah. And if all this had been too little, I would have given you even more. 9Why did you despise[i] the word of the LORD by doing what is evil in his eyes? You struck down[j] Uriah the Hittite with the sword and took his wife to be your own. You killed him with the sword of the Ammonites. 10Now, therefore, the sword[k] will never depart from your house, because you despised me and took the wife of Uriah the Hittite to be your own.’

11“This is what the LORD says: ‘Out of your own household I am going to bring calamity upon you.[l] Before your very eyes I will take your wives and give them to one who is close to you, and he will lie with your wives in broad daylight. 12You did it in secret,[m] but I will do this thing in broad daylight[n] before all Israel.’ ”

13Then David said to Nathan, “I have sinned[o] against the LORD.”

Nathan replied, “The LORD has taken away[p] your sin.[q] You are not going to die.[r] 14But because by doing this you have made the enemies of the LORD show utter contempt,[a][s] the son born to you will die.”

15After Nathan had gone home, the LORD struck[t] the child that Uriah’s wife had borne to David, and he became ill. 16David pleaded with God for the child. He fasted and went into his house and spent the nights lying[u] on the ground. 17The elders of his household stood beside him to get him up from the ground, but he refused, and he would not eat any food with them.[v]

18On the seventh day the child died. David’s servants were afraid to tell him that the child was dead, for they thought, “While the child was still living, we spoke to David but he would not listen to us. How can we tell him the child is dead? He may do something desperate.”

19David noticed that his servants were whispering among themselves and he realized the child was dead. “Is the child dead?” he asked.

“Yes,” they replied, “he is dead.”

20Then David got up from the ground. After he had washed,[w] put on lotions and changed his clothes,[x] he went into the house of the LORD and worshiped. Then he went to his own house, and at his request they served him food, and he ate.

21His servants asked him, “Why are you acting this way? While the child was alive, you fasted and wept,[y] but now that the child is dead, you get up and eat!”

22He answered, “While the child was still alive, I fasted and wept. I thought, ‘Who knows?[z] The LORD may be gracious to me and let the child live.’[a] 23But now that he is dead, why should I fast? Can I bring him back again? I will go to him,[b] but he will not return to me.”[c]

24Then David comforted his wife Bathsheba,[d] and he went to her and lay with her. She gave birth to a son, and they named him Solomon.[e] The LORD loved him; 25and because the LORD loved him, he sent word through Nathan the prophet to name him Jedidiah.[b][f]

26Meanwhile Joab fought against Rabbah[g] of the Ammonites and captured the royal citadel. 27Joab then sent messengers to David, saying, “I have fought against Rabbah and taken its water supply. 28Now muster the rest of the troops and besiege the city and capture it. Otherwise I will take the city, and it will be named after me.”

12:5 [d]1Ki 20:40
12:6 [e]Ex 22:1; Lk 19:8
12:7 [f]1Sa 16:13 [g]1Ki 20:42
12:8 [h]2Sa 9:7
12:9 [i]Nu 15:31; 1Sa 15:19 [j]2Sa 11:15
12:10 [k]2Sa 13:28; 18:14-15; 1Ki 2:25
12:11 [l]Dt 28:30; 2Sa 16:21-22
12:12 [m]2Sa 11:4-15 [n]2Sa 16:22
12:13 [o]Ge 13:13; Nu 22:34; 1Sa 15:24; 2Sa 24:10 [p]Ps 32:1-5; 51:1, 9; 103:12; Zec 3:4,9 [q]Pr 28:13; Mic 7:18-19 [r]Lev 20:10; 24:17
12:14 [s]Isa 52:5; Ro 2:24
12:15 [t]1Sa 25:38
12:16 [u]2Sa 13:31; Ps 5:7
12:17 [v]2Sa 3:35
12:20 [w]Mt 6:17 [x]Job 1:20
12:21 [y]Jdg 20:26
12:22 [z]Jnh 3:9 [a]Isa 38:1-5
12:23 [b]Ge 37:35 [c]1Sa 31:13; 2Sa 13:39; Job 7:10; 10:21
12:24 [d]1Ki 1:11 [e]1Ki 1:10; 1Ch 22:9; 28:5; Mt 1:6
12:25 [f]Ne 13:26
12:26 [g]Dt 3:11; 1Ch 20:1-3

[a] 14 Masoretic Text; an ancient Hebrew scribal tradition *this you have shown utter contempt for the LORD* [b] 25 *Jedidiah* means *loved by the LORD.*

29 So David mustered the entire army and went to Rabbah, and attacked and captured it. 30 He took the crown[h] from the head of their king[a]—its weight was a talent[b] of gold, and it was set with precious stones—and it was placed on David's head. He took a great quantity of plunder from the city 31 and brought out the people who were there, consigning them to labor with saws and with iron picks and axes, and he made them work at brickmaking.[c] He did this to all the Ammonite[i] towns. Then David and his entire army returned to Jerusalem.

Amnon and Tamar

13 In the course of time, Amnon[j] son of David fell in love with Tamar,[k] the beautiful sister of Absalom[l] son of David.

2 Amnon became frustrated to the point of illness on account of his sister Tamar, for she was a virgin, and it seemed impossible for him to do anything to her.

3 Now Amnon had a friend named Jonadab son of Shimeah,[m] David's brother. Jonadab was a very shrewd man. 4 He asked Amnon, "Why do you, the king's son, look so haggard morning after morning? Won't you tell me?"

Amnon said to him, "I'm in love with Tamar, my brother Absalom's sister."

5 "Go to bed and pretend to be ill," Jonadab said. "When your father comes to see you, say to him, 'I would like my sister Tamar to come and give me something to eat. Let her prepare the food in my sight so I may watch her and then eat it from her hand.' "

6 So Amnon lay down and pretended to be ill. When the king came to see him, Amnon said to him, "I would like my sister Tamar to come and make some special bread in my sight, so I may eat from her hand."

7 David sent word to Tamar at the palace: "Go to the house of your brother Amnon and prepare some food for him." 8 So Tamar went to the house of her brother Amnon, who was lying down. She took some dough, kneaded it, made the bread in his sight and baked it. 9 Then she took the pan and served him the bread, but he refused to eat.

"Send everyone out of here,"[n] Amnon said. So everyone left him. 10 Then Amnon said to Tamar, "Bring the food here into my bedroom so I may eat from your hand." And Tamar took the bread she had prepared and brought it to her brother Amnon in his bedroom. 11 But when she took it to him to eat, he grabbed[o] her and said, "Come to bed with me, my sister."[p]

12 "Don't, my brother!" she said to him. "Don't force me. Such a thing should not be done in Israel![q] Don't do this wicked thing.[r] 13 What about me?[s] Where could I get rid of my disgrace? And what about you? You would be like one of the wicked fools in Israel. Please speak to the king; he will not keep me from being married to you." 14 But he refused to listen to her, and since he was stronger than she, he raped her.[t]

15 Then Amnon hated her with intense hatred. In fact, he hated her more than he had loved her. Amnon said to her, "Get up and get out!"

16 "No!" she said to him. "Sending me away would be a greater wrong than what you have already done to me."

But he refused to listen to her. 17 He called his personal servant and said, "Get this woman out of here and bolt the door after her." 18 So his servant put her out and bolted the door after her. She was wearing a richly ornamented[d] robe,[u] for this was the kind of garment the virgin daughters of the king wore. 19 Tamar put ashes[v] on her head and tore the ornamented[e] robe she was wearing. She put her hand on her head and went away, weeping aloud as she went.

20 Her brother Absalom said to her, "Has that Amnon, your brother, been with you? Be quiet now, my sister; he is your brother. Don't take this thing to heart." And Tamar lived in her brother Absalom's house, a desolate woman.

21 When King David heard all this, he was furious.[w] 22 Absalom never said a word to Amnon, either good or bad;[x] he hated[y] Amnon because he had disgraced his sister Tamar.

12:30 [h]1Ch 20:2; Est 8:15; Ps 21:3; 132:18
12:31 [i]1Sa 14:47
13:1 [j]2Sa 3:2 [k]2Sa 14:27; 1Ch 3:9 [l]2Sa 3:3
13:3 [m]1Sa 16:9
13:9 [n]Ge 45:1
13:11 [o]Ge 39:12 [p]Ge 38:16
13:12 [q]Lev 20:17; Jdg 20:6 [r]Ge 34:7; Jdg 19:23
13:13 [s]Ge 20:12; Lev 18:9; Dt 22:21,23-24
13:14 [t]Ge 34:2; Dt 22:25; Eze 22:11
13:18 [u]Ge 37:23; Jdg 5:30
13:19 [v]Jos 7:6; 1Sa 4:12; 2Sa 1:2; Est 4:1; Da 9:3
13:21 [w]Ge 34:7
13:22 [x]Ge 31:24 [y]Lev 19:17-18; 1Jn 2:9-11

[a] *30* Or *of Milcom* (that is, Molech) [b] *30* That is, about 75 pounds (about 34 kilograms) [c] *31* The meaning of the Hebrew for this clause is uncertain. [d] *18* The meaning of the Hebrew for this phrase is uncertain. [e] *19* The meaning of the Hebrew for this word is uncertain.

13:2 For information regarding the enormous importance attached to virginity in ancient cultures, see "The Virgin" on page 367.

Absalom Kills Amnon

23 Two years later, when Absalom's sheepshearers[z] were at Baal Hazor near the border of Ephraim, he 13:23 [z]1Sa 25:7
invited all the king's sons to come there. 24 Absalom went to the king and said, "Your servant has had
shearers come. Will the king and his officials please join me?"
25 "No, my son," the king replied. "All of us should not go; we would only be a burden to you." Although
Absalom urged him, he still refused to go, but gave him his blessing.
26 Then Absalom said, "If not, please let my brother Amnon come with us."
The king asked him, "Why should he go with you?" 27 But Absalom urged him, so he sent with him
Amnon and the rest of the king's sons.
28 Absalom[a] ordered his men, "Listen! When Amnon is in high[b] spirits from drinking wine and I say 13:28 [a]2Sa 3:3
to you, 'Strike Amnon down,' then kill him. Don't be afraid. Have not I given you this order? Be strong [b]Jdg 19:6,9,22; Ru 3:7; 1Sa 25:36
and brave.[c]" 29 So Absalom's men did to Amnon what Absalom had ordered. Then all the king's sons got [c]2Sa 12:10
up, mounted their mules and fled.
30 While they were on their way, the report came to David: "Absalom has struck down all the king's
sons; not one of them is left." 31 The king stood up, tore[d] his clothes and lay down on the ground; and all 13:31 [d]Nu 14:6; 2Sa 1:11; 12:16
his servants stood by with their clothes torn.
32 But Jonadab son of Shimeah, David's brother, said, "My lord should not think that they killed all the
princes; only Amnon is dead. This has been Absalom's expressed intention ever since the day Amnon
raped his sister Tamar. 33 My lord the king should not be concerned about the report that all the king's sons
are dead. Only Amnon is dead."
34 Meanwhile, Absalom had fled.
Now the man standing watch looked up and saw many people on the road west of him, coming down
the side of the hill. The watchman went and told the king, "I see men in the direction of Horonaim, on
the side of the hill."[a]
35 Jonadab said to the king, "See, the king's sons are here; it has happened just as your servant said."
36 As he finished speaking, the king's sons came in, wailing loudly. The king, too, and all his servants
wept very bitterly.
37 Absalom fled and went to Talmai[e] son of Ammihud, the king of Geshur. But King David mourned 13:37 [e]ver 34; 2Sa 3:3; 14:23,32
for his son every day.
38 After Absalom fled and went to Geshur, he stayed there three years. 39 And the spirit of the king[b]
longed to go to Absalom,[f] for he was consoled[g] concerning Amnon's death. 13:39 [f]2Sa 14:13 [g]2Sa 12:19-23

Absalom Returns to Jerusalem

14 Joab[h] son of Zeruiah knew that the king's heart longed for Absalom. 2 So Joab sent someone to 14:1 [h]2Sa 2:18
Tekoa[i] and had a wise woman[j] brought from there. He said to her, "Pretend you are in mourning. 14:2 [i]2Ch 11:6; Ne 3:5; Jer 6:1; Am 1:1
Dress in mourning clothes, and don't use any cosmetic lotions.[k] Act like a woman who has spent many [j]2Sa 20:16
days grieving for the dead. 3 Then go to the king and speak these words to him." And Joab[l] put the words [k]Ru 3:3; 2Sa 12:20; Isa 1:6
in her mouth. 14:3 [l]ver 19
4 When the woman from Tekoa went[c] to the king, she fell with her face to the ground to pay him hon-
or, and she said, "Help me, O king!"
5 The king asked her, "What is troubling you?"
She said, "I am indeed a widow; my husband is dead. 6 I your servant had two sons. They got into a
fight with each other in the field, and no one was there to separate them. One struck the other and killed
him. 7 Now the whole clan has risen up against your servant; they say, 'Hand over the one who struck his
brother down, so that we may put him to death[m] for the life of his brother whom he killed; then we will 14:7 [m]Nu 35:19
get rid of the heir[n] as well.' They would put out the only burning coal I have left,[o] leaving my husband [n]Mt 21:38 [o]Dt 19:10-13
neither name nor descendant on the face of the earth."
8 The king said to the woman, "Go home,[p] and I will issue an order in your behalf." 14:8 [p]1Sa 25:35

[a] 34 Septuagint; Hebrew does not have this sentence. [b] 39 Dead Sea Scrolls and some Septuagint manuscripts; Masoretic Text *But* ⌊*the spirit of*⌋ *David the king* [c] 4 Many Hebrew manuscripts, Septuagint, Vulgate and Syriac; most Hebrew manuscripts *spoke*

13:23–29 Absalom's two-year wait, during which he nursed his hatred and plotted his revenge, culminated in Amnon's murder. Rape was condemned in the Old Testament, but the punishment was not murder (Dt 22:28–29). Absalom's extreme action was unjustified and cold-blooded.

14:6–8 See the note on Numbers 35:19.

14:9 [q]1Sa 25:24 [r]Mt 27:25 [s]1Sa 25:28; 1Ki 2:33 — 9 But the woman from Tekoa said to him, "My lord the king, let the blame[q] rest on me and on my fa-
ther's family,[r] and let the king and his throne be without guilt.[s]"
10 The king replied, "If anyone says anything to you, bring him to me, and he will not bother you again."
14:11 [t]Nu 35:12, 21 [u]Mt 10:30 [v]1Sa 14:45 — 11 She said, "Then let the king invoke the LORD his God to prevent the avenger[t] of blood from adding
to the destruction, so that my son will not be destroyed."
"As surely as the LORD lives," he said, "not one hair[u] of your son's head will fall to the ground.[v]"
12 Then the woman said, "Let your servant speak a word to my lord the king."
"Speak," he replied.
13 The woman said, "Why then have you devised a thing like this against the people of God? When the
14:13 [w]2Sa 12:7; 1Ki 20:40 [x]2Sa 13:38-39 — king says this, does he not convict himself,[w] for the king has not brought back his banished son?[x] 14 Like
14:14 [y]Job 14:11; Ps 58:7; Isa 19:5 [z]Job 10:8; 17:13; 30:23; Ps 22:15; Heb 9:27 [a]Nu 35:15,25-28; Job 34:15 — water[y] spilled on the ground, which cannot be recovered, so we must die.[z] But God does not take away
life; instead, he devises ways so that a banished person[a] may not remain estranged from him.
15 "And now I have come to say this to my lord the king because the people have made me afraid. Your
servant thought, 'I will speak to the king; perhaps he will do what his servant asks. 16 Perhaps the king will
agree to deliver his servant from the hand of the man who is trying to cut off both me and my son from
14:16 [b]Ex 34:9; 1Sa 26:19 — the inheritance[b] God gave us.'
17 "And now your servant says, 'May the word of my lord the king bring me rest, for my lord the king
14:17 [c]ver 20; 1Sa 29:9; 2Sa 19:27 [d]1Ki 3:9; Da 2:21 — is like an angel[c] of God in discerning[d] good and evil. May the LORD your God be with you.' "
18 Then the king said to the woman, "Do not keep from me the answer to what I am going to ask you."
"Let my lord the king speak," the woman said.
14:19 [e]ver 3 — 19 The king asked, "Isn't the hand of Joab[e] with you in all this?"
The woman answered, "As surely as you live, my lord the king, no one can turn to the right or to the
left from anything my lord the king says. Yes, it was your servant Joab who instructed me to do this and
who put all these words into the mouth of your servant. 20 Your servant Joab did this to change the pres-
14:20 [f]1Ki 3:12, 28; Isa 28:6 [g]ver 17; 2Sa 18:13; 19:27 — ent situation. My lord has wisdom[f] like that of an angel of God—he knows everything that happens in
the land.[g]"
21 The king said to Joab, "Very well, I will do it. Go, bring back the young man Absalom."
14:22 [h]Ge 47:7 — 22 Joab fell with his face to the ground to pay him honor, and he blessed the king.[h] Joab said, "Today
your servant knows that he has found favor in your eyes, my lord the king, because the king has grant-
ed his servant's request."
23 Then Joab went to Geshur and brought Absalom back to Jerusalem. 24 But the king said, "He must
go to his own house; he must not see my face." So Absalom went to his own house and did not see the
face of the king.
25 In all Israel there was not a man so highly praised for his handsome appearance as Absalom. From
the top of his head to the sole of his foot there was no blemish in him. 26 Whenever he cut the hair of his
14:26 [i]2Sa 18:9; Eze 44:20 — head[i]—he used to cut his hair from time to time when it became too heavy for him—he would weigh
it, and its weight was two hundred shekels[a] by the royal standard.
14:27 [j]2Sa 18:18 [k]2Sa 13:1 — 27 Three sons[j] and a daughter were born to Absalom. The daughter's name was Tamar,[k] and she be-
came a beautiful woman.
28 Absalom lived two years in Jerusalem without seeing the king's face. 29 Then Absalom sent for Joab
in order to send him to the king, but Joab refused to come to him. So he sent a second time, but he re-
14:30 [l]Ex 9:31 — fused to come. 30 Then he said to his servants, "Look, Joab's field is next to mine, and he has barley[l] there.
Go and set it on fire." So Absalom's servants set the field on fire.
31 Then Joab did go to Absalom's house and he said to him, "Why have your servants set my field on
14:31 [m]Jdg 15:5 — fire?[m]"
32 Absalom said to Joab, "Look, I sent word to you and said, 'Come here so I can send you to the king
14:32 [n]2Sa 3:3 [o]1Sa 20:8 — to ask, "Why have I come from Geshur?[n] It would be better for me if I were still there!" ' Now then, I want
to see the king's face, and if I am guilty of anything, let him put me to death."[o]
33 So Joab went to the king and told him this. Then the king summoned Absalom, and he came in and
14:33 [p]Ge 33:4; Lk 15:20 — bowed down with his face to the ground before the king. And the king kissed[p] Absalom.

[a] *26* That is, about 5 pounds (about 2.3 kilograms)

14:26 For commentary on literal and figurative references to hair in the Bible, see the note on Psalm 40:12. See also "Beards and Hairstyles in the Biblical World" on page 1084.

Absalom's Conspiracy

15 In the course of time,[q] Absalom provided himself with a chariot[r] and horses and with fifty men 15:1 q2Sa 12:11
to run ahead of him. 2 He would get up early and stand by the side of the road leading to the city r1Sa 8:11; 1Ki 1:5
gate.[s] Whenever anyone came with a complaint to be placed before the king for a decision, Absalom would 15:2 sGe 23:10;
call out to him, "What town are you from?" He would answer, "Your servant is from one of the tribes of Is- 2Sa 19:8
rael." 3 Then Absalom would say to him, "Look, your claims are valid and proper, but there is no represen-
tative of the king to hear you."[t] 4 And Absalom would add, "If only I were appointed judge in the land![u] 15:3 tPr 12:2
Then everyone who has a complaint or case could come to me and I would see that he gets justice." 15:4 uJdg 9:29
5 Also, whenever anyone approached him to bow down before him, Absalom would reach out his hand,
take hold of him and kiss him. 6 Absalom behaved in this way toward all the Israelites who came to the
king asking for justice, and so he stole the hearts[v] of the men of Israel. 15:6 vRo 16:18
7 At the end of four[a] years, Absalom said to the king, "Let me go to Hebron and fulfill a vow I made to
the LORD. 8 While your servant was living at Geshur[w] in Aram, I made this vow:[x] 'If the LORD takes me 15:8 w2Sa 3:3;
back to Jerusalem, I will worship the LORD in Hebron.[b] '" 13:37-38 xGe 28:20
9 The king said to him, "Go in peace." So he went to Hebron.
10 Then Absalom sent secret messengers throughout the tribes of Israel to say, "As soon as you hear the
sound of the trumpets,[y] then say, 'Absalom is king in Hebron.'" 11 Two hundred men from Jerusalem had 15:10 y1Ki 1:34, 39; 2Ki 9:13
accompanied Absalom. They had been invited as guests and went quite innocently, knowing nothing
about the matter. 12 While Absalom was offering sacrifices, he also sent for Ahithophel[z] the Gilonite, Da- 15:12 zver 31,34;
vid's counselor,[a] to come from Giloh,[b] his hometown. And so the conspiracy gained strength, and Absa- 2Sa 16:15,23; 1Ch 27:33
lom's following kept on increasing.[c] aJob 19:14; Ps 41:9; 55:13; Jer 9:4 bJos 15:51 cPs 3:1

David Flees

13 A messenger came and told David, "The hearts of the men of Israel are with Absalom."
14 Then David said to all his officials who were with him in Jerusalem, "Come! We must flee,[d] or none 15:14 d2Sa 12:11;
of us will escape from Absalom.[e] We must leave immediately, or he will move quickly to overtake us and 1Ki 2:26; Ps 3
bring ruin upon us and put the city to the sword." Title; 132:1 e2Sa 19:9
15 The king's officials answered him, "Your servants are ready to do whatever our lord the king
chooses."
16 The king set out, with his entire household following him; but he left ten concubines[f] to take care 15:16
of the palace. 17 So the king set out, with all the people following him, and they halted at a place some f2Sa 16:21-22; 20:3
distance away. 18 All his men marched past him, along with all the Kerethites[g] and Pelethites; and all the 15:18
six hundred Gittites who had accompanied him from Gath marched before the king. g1Sa 30:14;
19 The king said to Ittai[h] the Gittite, "Why should you come along with us? Go back and stay with King 2Sa 8:18; 20:7, 23; 1Ki 1:38,44; 1Ch 18:17
Absalom. You are a foreigner,[i] an exile from your homeland. 20 You came only yesterday. And today shall 15:19 h2Sa 18:2 iGe 31:15
I make you wander[j] about with us, when I do not know where I am going? Go back, and take your coun- 15:20 j1Sa 23:13
trymen. May kindness and faithfulness[k] be with you." k2Sa 2:6
21 But Ittai replied to the king, "As surely as the LORD lives, and as my lord the king lives, wherever my
lord the king may be, whether it means life or death, there will your servant be."[l] 15:21 lRu 1:16-17; Pr 17:17
22 David said to Ittai, "Go ahead, march on." So Ittai the Gittite marched on with all his men and the
families that were with him.
23 The whole countryside wept aloud as all the people passed by. The king also crossed the Kidron Val-
ley,[m] and all the people moved on toward the desert. 15:23 m2Ch 29:16
24 Zadok[n] was there, too, and all the Levites who were with him were carrying the ark[o] of the covenant 15:24 n2Sa 8:17
of God. They set down the ark of God, and Abiathar[p] offered sacrifices[c] until all the people had finished oNu 4:15
leaving the city. p1Sa 22:20
25 Then the king said to Zadok, "Take the ark of God back into the city. If I find favor in the LORD's eyes,

[a] 7 Some Septuagint manuscripts, Syriac and Josephus; Hebrew *forty* [b] 8 Some Septuagint manuscripts; Hebrew does not have *in Hebron.* [c] 24 Or *Abiathar went up*

15:2 For information on the city gate, see the note on 1 Samuel 4:18. See also "The City Gate" on page 392.
15:6 The "heart" in Old Testament Hebrew referred to the seat of intellect as well as of emotion. Rather than merely winning the affections of the Israelites, Absalom "stole the hearts of the men of Israel" by duping their minds. This was clearly the situation with regard to the 200 men who accompanied him to Hebron. Once there, they would be indelibly marked as rebels.
15:9 For a discussion of salutations in the Bible, see the note on Ruth 2:4.
15:18 The Kerethites and Pelethites were Philistine mercenaries who constituted David's royal bodyguard.

he will bring me back and let me see it and his dwelling place[q] again. 26 But if he says, 'I am not pleased with you,' then I am ready; let him do to me whatever seems good to him.[r]"

27 The king also said to Zadok the priest, "Aren't you a seer?[s] Go back to the city in peace, with your son Ahimaaz and Jonathan[t] son of Abiathar. You and Abiathar take your two sons with you. 28 I will wait at the fords[u] in the desert until word comes from you to inform me." 29 So Zadok and Abiathar took the ark of God back to Jerusalem and stayed there.

30 But David continued up the Mount of Olives, weeping[v] as he went; his head[w] was covered and he was barefoot. All the people with him covered their heads too and were weeping as they went up. 31 Now David had been told, "Ahithophel[x] is among the conspirators with Absalom." So David prayed, "O LORD, turn Ahithophel's counsel into foolishness."

32 When David arrived at the summit, where people used to worship God, Hushai the Arkite[y] was there to meet him, his robe torn and dust[z] on his head. 33 David said to him, "If you go with me, you will be a burden[a] to me. 34 But if you return to the city and say to Absalom, 'I will be your servant, O king; I was your father's servant in the past, but now I will be your servant,'[b] then you can help me by frustrating Ahithophel's advice. 35 Won't the priests Zadok and Abiathar be there with you? Tell them anything you hear in the king's palace.[c] 36 Their two sons, Ahimaaz son of Zadok and Jonathan[d] son of Abiathar, are there with them. Send them to me with anything you hear."

37 So David's friend Hushai[e] arrived at Jerusalem as Absalom[f] was entering the city.

David and Ziba

16 When David had gone a short distance beyond the summit, there was Ziba,[g] the steward of Mephibosheth, waiting to meet him. He had a string of donkeys saddled and loaded with two hundred loaves of bread, a hundred cakes of raisins, a hundred cakes of figs and a skin of wine.[h]

2 The king asked Ziba, "Why have you brought these?"

Ziba answered, "The donkeys are for the king's household to ride on, the bread and fruit are for the men to eat, and the wine is to refresh[i] those who become exhausted in the desert."

3 The king then asked, "Where is your master's grandson?"[j]

Ziba said to him, "He is staying in Jerusalem, because he thinks, 'Today the house of Israel will give me back my grandfather's kingdom.' "

4 Then the king said to Ziba, "All that belonged to Mephibosheth is now yours."

"I humbly bow," Ziba said. "May I find favor in your eyes, my lord the king."

Shimei Curses David

5 As King David approached Bahurim,[k] a man from the same clan as Saul's family came out from there. His name was Shimei[l] son of Gera, and he cursed[m] as he came out. 6 He pelted David and all the king's officials with stones, though all the troops and the special guard were on David's right and left. 7 As he cursed, Shimei said, "Get out, get out, you man of blood, you scoundrel! 8 The LORD has repaid you for all the blood you shed in the household of Saul, in whose place you have reigned.[n] The LORD has handed the kingdom over to your son Absalom. You have come to ruin because you are a man of blood!"

9 Then Abishai[o] son of Zeruiah said to the king, "Why should this dead dog curse my lord the king? Let me go over and cut off his head."[p]

10 But the king said, "What do you and I have in common, you sons of Zeruiah?[q] If he is cursing because the LORD said to him, 'Curse David,' who can ask, 'Why do you do this?' "[r]

11 David then said to Abishai and all his officials, "My son,[s] who is of my own flesh, is trying to take my life. How much more, then, this Benjamite! Leave him alone; let him curse, for the LORD has told him to.[t] 12 It may be that the LORD will see my distress[u] and repay me with good[v] for the cursing I am receiving today.[w]"

13 So David and his men continued along the road while Shimei was going along the hillside opposite him, cursing as he went and throwing stones at him and showering him with dirt. 14 The king and all the people with him arrived at their destination exhausted.[x] And there he refreshed himself.

The Advice of Ahithophel and Hushai

15 Meanwhile, Absalom[y] and all the men of Israel came to Jerusalem, and Ahithophel[z] was with him. 16 Then Hushai[a] the Arkite, David's friend, went to Absalom and said to him, "Long live the king! Long live the king!"

15:25 q Ex 15:13; Ps 43:3; Jer 25:30
15:26 r 1Sa 3:18; 2Sa 22:20; 1Ki 10:9
15:27 s 1Sa 9:9 t 2Sa 17:17
15:28 u 2Sa 17:16
15:30 v 2Sa 19:4; Ps 126:6 w Est 6:12; Isa 20:2-4
15:31 x ver 12; 2Sa 16:23; 17:14, 23
15:32 y Jos 16:2 z 2Sa 1:2
15:33 a 2Sa 19:35
15:34 b 2Sa 16:19
15:35 c 2Sa 17:15-16
15:36 d ver 27; 2Sa 17:17
15:37 e 2Sa 16:16-17; 1Ch 27:33 f 2Sa 16:15
16:1 g 2Sa 9:1-13 h 1Sa 25:18
16:2 i 2Sa 17:27-29
16:3 j 2Sa 9:9-10; 19:26-27
16:5 k 2Sa 3:16 l 2Sa 19:16-23; 1Ki 2:8-9,36,44 m Ex 22:28
16:8 n 2Sa 21:9
16:9 o 2Sa 9:8 p Ex 22:28; Lk 9:54
16:10 q 2Sa 19:22 r Ro 9:20
16:11 s 2Sa 12:11 t Ge 45:5
16:12 u Ps 4:1; 25:18 v Dt 23:5; Ro 8:28 w Ps 109:28
16:14 x 2Sa 17:2
16:15 y 2Sa 15:37 z 2Sa 15:12
16:16 a 2Sa 15:37

17 Absalom asked Hushai, "Is this the love you show your friend? Why didn't you go with your friend?"[b]
18 Hushai said to Absalom, "No, the one chosen by the LORD, by these people, and by all the men of Is-
rael—his I will be, and I will remain with him. 19 Furthermore, whom should I serve? Should I not serve
the son? Just as I served your father, so I will serve you."[c]
20 Absalom said to Ahithophel, "Give us your advice. What should we do?"
21 Ahithophel answered, "Lie with your father's concubines whom he left to take care of the palace.
Then all Israel will hear that you have made yourself a stench in your father's nostrils, and the hands of
everyone with you will be strengthened." 22 So they pitched a tent for Absalom on the roof, and he lay with
his father's concubines in the sight of all Israel.[d]
23 Now in those days the advice[e] Ahithophel gave was like that of one who inquires of God. That was
how both David[f] and Absalom regarded all of Ahithophel's advice.

17 Ahithophel said to Absalom, "I would[a] choose twelve thousand men and set out tonight in pur-
suit of David. 2 I would[b] attack him while he is weary and weak.[g] I would[b] strike him with ter-
ror, and then all the people with him will flee. I would[b] strike down only the king[h] 3 and bring all the peo-
ple back to you. The death of the man you seek will mean the return of all; all the people will be
unharmed." 4 This plan seemed good to Absalom and to all the elders of Israel.
5 But Absalom said, "Summon also Hushai[i] the Arkite, so we can hear what he has to say." 6 When Hu-
shai came to him, Absalom said, "Ahithophel has given this advice. Should we do what he says? If not, give
us your opinion."
7 Hushai replied to Absalom, "The advice Ahithophel has given is not good this time. 8 You know your
father and his men; they are fighters, and as fierce as a wild bear robbed of her cubs.[j] Besides, your fa-
ther is an experienced fighter;[k] he will not spend the night with the troops. 9 Even now, he is hidden in a
cave or some other place.[l] If he should attack your troops first,[c] whoever hears about it will say, 'There
has been a slaughter among the troops who follow Absalom.' 10 Then even the bravest soldier, whose heart
is like the heart of a lion,[m] will melt[n] with fear, for all Israel knows that your father is a fighter and that
those with him are brave.[o]
11 "So I advise you: Let all Israel, from Dan to Beersheba[p]—as numerous as the sand[q] on the sea-
shore—be gathered to you, with you yourself leading them into battle. 12 Then we will attack him wher-
ever he may be found, and we will fall on him as dew settles on the ground. Neither he nor any of his
men will be left alive. 13 If he withdraws into a city, then all Israel will bring ropes to that city, and we will
drag it down to the valley[r] until not even a piece of it can be found."
14 Absalom and all the men of Israel said, "The advice[s] of Hushai the Arkite is better than that of Ahith-
ophel."[t] For the LORD had determined to frustrate[u] the good advice of Ahithophel in order to bring di-
saster[v] on Absalom.[w]
15 Hushai told Zadok and Abiathar, the priests, "Ahithophel has advised Absalom and the elders of Is-
rael to do such and such, but I have advised them to do so and so. 16 Now send a message immediately
and tell David, 'Do not spend the night at the fords in the desert;[x] cross over without fail, or the king and
all the people with him will be swallowed up.[y]' "
17 Jonathan[z] and Ahimaaz were staying at En Rogel.[a] A servant girl was to go and inform them, and
they were to go and tell King David, for they could not risk being seen entering the city. 18 But a young man
saw them and told Absalom. So the two of them left quickly and went to the house of a man in Bahurim.[b]
He had a well in his courtyard, and they climbed down into it. 19 His wife took a covering and spread it
out over the opening of the well and scattered grain over it. No one knew anything about it.[c]

16:17 [b]2Sa 19:25
16:19 [c]2Sa 15:34
16:22 [d]2Sa 12:11-12; 15:16
16:23 [e]2Sa 17:14,23 [f]2Sa 15:12
17:2 [g]2Sa 16:14 [h]1Ki 22:31; Zec 13:7
17:5 [i]2Sa 15:32
17:8 [j]Hos 13:8 [k]1Sa 16:18
17:9 [l]Jer 41:9
17:10 [m]1Ch 12:8 [n]Jos 2:9,11; Eze 21:15 [o]2Sa 23:8; 1Ch 11:11
17:11 [p]Jdg 20:1 [q]Ge 12:2; 22:17; Jos 11:4
17:13 [r]Mic 1:6
17:14 [s]2Sa 16:23 [t]2Sa 15:12 [u]2Sa 15:34; Ne 4:15 [v]Ps 9:16 [w]2Ch 10:8
17:16 [x]2Sa 15:28 [y]2Sa 15:35
17:17 [z]2Sa 15:27,36 [a]Jos 15:7; 18:16
17:18 [b]2Sa 3:16; 16:5
17:19 [c]Jos 2:6

[a] 1 Or *Let me* [b] 2 Or *will* [c] 9 Or *When some of the men fall at the first attack*

16:21–22 Royal women played a significant political role in ancient societies. Sexual relations with a king's wife or concubine constituted a claim on the throne—a common practice when a king was replaced by a new dynasty (see "Ambitious Princes Among the Hittites" on p. 469).
16:22 See the note on the nuptial tent at Song of Songs 1:16–17.
16:23 Some interpreters, on the basis of 1 Samuel 23:34 and 1 Chronicles 3:5 (equating Ammiel with Eliam), believe that Ahithophel was the grandfather of Bathsheba. If so, this could explain Ahithophel's siding with Absalom; he may have wanted revenge for David's murder of Uriah and sexual humiliation of Bathsheba. Absalom's public rape of David's concubines would have been considered an appropriate revenge. On the other hand, it is not clear that Bathsheba actually was Ahithophel's granddaughter. Had Absalom been successful, not only would Solomon never have become king, but he most likely would have been put to death. Ahithophel may have joined Absalom simply because he, like many others, was disillusioned with David's reign or because he wanted more power for himself.
17:18 The most common beverage of the Jews was water. This was procured chiefly in two ways: by means of cisterns, which were possessed by every well-appointed house (cf. Jer 38:6), and wells, which were rare and usually the possession of a clan or community (see "Wells, Cisterns and Aqueducts in the Ancient World" on p. 1259).

Wine was also widely used, both in the form of new wine, called *must*, and fermented wine. In the heat of harvest, frequent use was

CULTURAL AND HISTORICAL NOTES

Siege Warfare

2 SAMUEL 17 Siege warfare was a military strategy in which an attacking force would encircle a fortified position, generally a walled city, in order to defeat the inhabiting population. The strategy was employed either to gain control of a city (Dt 20:10–14) or to regain control of a rebellious city (2Ki 17:1–6). An attacking force would encamp near the target city, block off all roads leading in and out of the city and cut off access to supply channels, most notably those involving water. Once these preliminaries had been achieved, several strategies could be implemented. (These approaches were not mutually exclusive; often a force would combine two or more tactics during a siege.)

Masada siege ramp
Photograph: © Todd Bolen/Bible Places.com

✣ A show of force could intimidate the inhabitants to the point of surrender. This line of attack had obvious advantages in that it would prevent a prolonged and potentially costly siege. Sennacherib's representative employed this strategy—unsuccessfully—against Jerusalem during the reign of Hezekiah (2Ki 18:19—19:35).[1]

✣ Sometimes an army relied upon a ruse, such as in the story of the Trojan horse. During the siege of Ai (see "Map 3"), Joshua divided his troops as a means of enticing the defenders of Ai to leave their defensive positions in order to pursue a portion of Joshua's forces. Once this had been accomplished, Joshua and his remaining troops were able to enter and destroy the defenseless city (Jos 8:10–23).[2]

✣ All other approaches failing, a besieging army was compelled to resort to direct assault on a city's wall. The fastest but most dangerous method of taking a defensive wall was to scale it, a tactic commonly involving the use of assault ladders. An Egyptian tomb relief dating to the Fifth Dynasty of the **Early Bronze Age**[3] depicts warriors raising ladders against a besieged city wall. Depending upon the height of the walls and the tenacity of the defenders, the attackers could suffer extraordinarily high casualties.

The nineteenth century B.C. saw the development of effective battering rams, perhaps the greatest invention of siege warfare. These weapons consisted of a long pole, often metal-tipped, that hung from a covered framework (offering protection to the attackers). It would be hurled repeatedly against the wall or gate in a pendulum motion.

Many cities were surrounded by defensive fosses or dry moats, but would-be attackers would frequently surround such a city with trenches of their own. A process of two opposing armies digging trenches and counter-trenches took place at the Athenian siege of Syracuse in 414 B.C.[4]

Sometimes earthen ramps were constructed against a city's wall. Remnants of the siege mound constructed by Sennacherib during the siege of Lachish ("Map 4") in 701 B.C. are still visible,[5] as is the siege mound used by the Romans during the siege of Masada in A.D. 73[6] ("Map 9").

Sometimes attackers attempted to compromise a wall by tunneling beneath it. This was achieved by "sappers," or tunnel engineers. The annals of Sennacherib describe such a strategy during the siege of Hezekiah's Judean cities.

✣ Siege warfare was also a strategy of attrition, demanding commitment and often patience. (**Nebuchadnezzar**'s siege of Tyre, e.g., lasted for 13 years.) It sought to defeat the enemy not primarily by sword but by starvation and thirst. Defenses against a siege included the stockpiling of food and water (2Ki 25:3), the construction of tall walls and fosses and the reinforcement of city gates with strong bars (Am 1:5). The city walls themselves could be quite sophisticated in design as well. For example, one technique was to use an **offset-inset wall**, in which the surface of the city wall was not flat but protruded at intervals. Defending inhabitants would also send out sorties in counterattacks in the hope of breaking a siege (2Sa 11:17; 1Ki 20:15–21). A defending force's greatest advantage was its superior height. This allowed defenders to hurl down stones, arrows, javelins, hot oil or water and even millstones (Jdg 9:53).

For other war-related issues, see "Horses and Chariots in Ancient Warfare" on page 114, "Technological Supremacy of the Philistines' Iron Weapons" on page 414, "*Herem*, Holy War" on page 419, "Songs of Warriors" on page 474 and "Warfare in the Ancient World" on page 950.

[1]See "Hezekiah Against the Assyrians" on page 1118. [2]See "Ai" on page 316. [3]See "Archaeological Periods" chart on page xx in the front of this Bible. [4]See "Greece: From Independent City-states Through Alexander the Great" on page 1814. [5]See "The Lachish Reliefs" on page 559. [6]See "Masada" on page 1775.

20 When Absalom's men came to the woman[d] at the house, they asked, "Where are Ahimaaz and Jonathan?"

The woman answered them, "They crossed over the brook."[a] The men searched but found no one, so they returned to Jerusalem.

21 After the men had gone, the two climbed out of the well and went to inform King David. They said to him, "Set out and cross the river at once; Ahithophel has advised such and such against you." 22 So David and all the people with him set out and crossed the Jordan. By daybreak, no one was left who had not crossed the Jordan.

23 When Ahithophel saw that his advice[e] had not been followed, he saddled his donkey and set out for his house in his hometown. He put his house in order[f] and then hanged himself. So he died and was buried in his father's tomb.

24 David went to Mahanaim,[g] and Absalom crossed the Jordan with all the men of Israel. 25 Absalom had appointed Amasa[h] over the army in place of Joab. Amasa was the son of a man named Jether,[b][i] an Israelite[c] who had married Abigail,[d] the daughter of Nahash and sister of Zeruiah the mother of Joab. 26 The Israelites and Absalom camped in the land of Gilead.

27 When David came to Mahanaim, Shobi son of Nahash[j] from Rabbah[k] of the Ammonites, and Makir[l] son of Ammiel from Lo Debar, and Barzillai[m] the Gileadite[n] from Rogelim 28 brought bedding and bowls and articles of pottery. They also brought wheat and barley, flour and roasted grain, beans and lentils,[e] 29 honey and curds, sheep, and cheese from cows' milk for David and his people to eat.[o] For they said, "The people have become hungry and tired and thirsty in the desert.[p]"

17:20 [d]Ex 1:19; Jos 2:3-5; 1Sa 19:12-17
17:23 [e]2Sa 15:12; 16:23 [f]2Ki 20:1; Mt 27:5
17:24 [g]Ge 32:2; 2Sa 2:8
17:25 [h]2Sa 19:13; 20:4, 9-12; 1Ki 2:5,32; 1Ch 12:18 [i]1Ch 2:13-17
17:27 [j]1Sa 11:1 [k]Dt 3:11; 2Sa 10:1-2; 12:26,29 [l]2Sa 9:4 [m]2Sa 19:31-39; 1Ki 2:7 [n]2Sa 19:31; Ezr 2:61
17:29 [o]1Ch 12:40 [p]2Sa 16:2; Ro 12:13

Absalom's Death

18 David mustered the men who were with him and appointed over them commanders of thousands and commanders of hundreds. 2 David sent the troops out[q]—a third under the command of Joab, a third under Joab's brother Abishai[r] son of Zeruiah, and a third under Ittai[s] the Gittite. The king told the troops, "I myself will surely march out with you."

3 But the men said, "You must not go out; if we are forced to flee, they won't care about us. Even if half of us die, they won't care; but you are worth ten[t] thousand of us.[f] It would be better now for you to give us support from the city."[u]

4 The king answered, "I will do whatever seems best to you."

So the king stood beside the gate while all the men marched out in units of hundreds and of thousands. 5 The king commanded Joab, Abishai and Ittai, "Be gentle with the young man Absalom for my sake." And all the troops heard the king giving orders concerning Absalom to each of the commanders.

6 The army marched into the field to fight Israel, and the battle took place in the forest[v] of Ephraim. 7 There the army of Israel was defeated by David's men, and the casualties that day were great—twenty thousand men. 8 The battle spread out over the whole countryside, and the forest claimed more lives that day than the sword.

9 Now Absalom happened to meet David's men. He was riding his mule, and as the mule went under the thick branches of a large oak, Absalom's head[w] got caught in the tree. He was left hanging in midair, while the mule he was riding kept on going.

10 When one of the men saw this, he told Joab, "I just saw Absalom hanging in an oak tree."

11 Joab said to the man who had told him this, "What! You saw him? Why didn't you strike[x] him to the ground right there? Then I would have had to give you ten shekels[g] of silver and a warrior's belt.[y]"

18:2 [q]Jdg 7:16; 1Sa 11:11 [r]1Sa 26:6 [s]2Sa 15:19
18:3 [t]1Sa 18:7 [u]2Sa 21:17
18:6 [v]Jos 17:18
18:9 [w]2Sa 14:26
18:11 [x]2Sa 3:39 [y]1Sa 18:4

[a] 20 Or *"They passed by the sheep pen toward the water."* [b] 25 Hebrew *Ithra,* a variant of *Jether* [c] 25 Hebrew and some Septuagint manuscripts; other Septuagint manuscripts (see also 1 Chron. 2:17) *Ishmaelite* or *Jezreelite* [d] 25 Hebrew *Abigal,* a variant of *Abigail* [e] 28 Most Septuagint manuscripts and Syriac; Hebrew *lentils, and roasted grain* [f] 3 Two Hebrew manuscripts, some Septuagint manuscripts and Vulgate; most Hebrew manuscripts *care; for now there are ten thousand like us* [g] 11 That is, about 4 ounces (about 115 grams)

---

made of a sour drink mixture of water and wine, as well as of a strong drink called *shekhar.* How the latter was prepared is unknown. Wine was sometimes spiced to improve its taste. It was also made from pomegranates and possibly from ripe dates and barley. The Mishnah speaks both of honey-wine and of cider. See "Wine and Alcoholic Beverages in the Ancient World" on page 2015.

Next to bread and vegetables, the most important "food" was milk, both from larger and smaller cattle, and especially goat's milk, all of which was usually kept in skins. Because of the hot climate fresh milk soon became sour, but it was highly effective for quenching thirst.

18:9 This verse is rich in symbolism. The mule was the usual mount for princes and kings. As Absalom lost his mule from underneath him, so he lost his royal "seat." His suspension "in midair" indicates that the rebellion had left him without ground beneath his feet, powerless to defend himself, much less to lead a nation. Most interpreters feel that Absalom was caught in the tree by his luxuriant hair (cf. 14:25–26). Here was a promising young man entangled by his own pride.

For a discussion of literal and figurative references to hair in the Bible, see the note on Psalm 40:12. See also "Beards and Hairstyles in the Biblical World" on page 1084.

12 But the man replied, "Even if a thousand shekels[a] were weighed out into my hands, I would not lift
my hand against the king's son. In our hearing the king commanded you and Abishai and Ittai, 'Protect
the young man Absalom for my sake.[b]' 13 And if I had put my life in jeopardy[c]—and nothing is hidden
18:13 [z]2Sa 14:19-20 from the king[z]—you would have kept your distance from me."
18:14 [a]2Sa 2:18; 14:30 14 Joab[a] said, "I'm not going to wait like this for you." So he took three javelins in his hand and plunged
them into Absalom's heart while Absalom was still alive in the oak tree. 15 And ten of Joab's armor-bear-
18:15 [b]2Sa 12:10 ers surrounded Absalom, struck him and killed him.[b]
18:16 [c]2Sa 2:28; 20:22 16 Then Joab[c] sounded the trumpet, and the troops stopped pursuing Israel, for Joab halted them.
18:17 [d]Jos 7:26 [e]Jos 8:29 17 They took Absalom, threw him into a big pit in the forest and piled up[d] a large heap of rocks[e] over him.
Meanwhile, all the Israelites fled to their homes.
18:18 [f]Ge 14:17 [g]Ge 50:5; Nu 32:42; 1Sa 15:12 [h]2Sa 14:27 18 During his lifetime Absalom had taken a pillar and erected it in the King's Valley[f] as a monument[g]
to himself, for he thought, "I have no son[h] to carry on the memory of my name." He named the pillar af-
ter himself, and it is called Absalom's Monument to this day.

David Mourns

18:19 [i]2Sa 15:36 [j]ver 31; Jdg 11:36 19 Now Ahimaaz[i] son of Zadok said, "Let me run and take the news to the king that the LORD has de-
livered him from the hand of his enemies.[j]"
20 "You are not the one to take the news today," Joab told him. "You may take the news another time,
but you must not do so today, because the king's son is dead."
21 Then Joab said to a Cushite, "Go, tell the king what you have seen." The Cushite bowed down before
Joab and ran off.
22 Ahimaaz son of Zadok again said to Joab, "Come what may, please let me run behind the Cushite."
But Joab replied, "My son, why do you want to go? You don't have any news that will bring you a re-
ward."
23 He said, "Come what may, I want to run."
So Joab said, "Run!" Then Ahimaaz ran by way of the plain[d] and outran the Cushite.
18:24 [k]1Sa 14:16; 2Sa 19:8; 2Ki 9:17; Jer 51:12 24 While David was sitting between the inner and outer gates, the watchman[k] went up to the roof of
the gateway by the wall. As he looked out, he saw a man running alone. 25 The watchman called out to the
king and reported it.
The king said, "If he is alone, he must have good news." And the man came closer and closer.
26 Then the watchman saw another man running, and he called down to the gatekeeper, "Look, an-
other man running alone!"
18:26 [l]1Ki 1:42; Isa 52:7; 61:1 The king said, "He must be bringing good news,[l] too."
18:27 [m]2Ki 9:20 27 The watchman said, "It seems to me that the first one runs like[m] Ahimaaz son of Zadok."
"He's a good man," the king said. "He comes with good news."
28 Then Ahimaaz called out to the king, "All is well!" He bowed down before the king with his face to
the ground and said, "Praise be to the LORD your God! He has delivered up the men who lifted their hands
against my lord the king."
29 The king asked, "Is the young man Absalom safe?"
Ahimaaz answered, "I saw great confusion just as Joab was about to send the king's servant and me,
your servant, but I don't know what it was."
30 The king said, "Stand aside and wait here." So he stepped aside and stood there.
31 Then the Cushite arrived and said, "My lord the king, hear the good news! The LORD has delivered
you today from all who rose up against you."
32 The king asked the Cushite, "Is the young man Absalom safe?"
The Cushite replied, "May the enemies of my lord the king and all who rise up to harm you be like that
18:32 [n]Jdg 5:31; 1Sa 25:26 young man."[n]
33 The king was shaken. He went up to the room over the gateway and wept. As he went, he said: "O my
18:33 [o]Ex 32:32 [p]Ge 43:14; 2Sa 19:4; Ro 9:3 son Absalom! My son, my son Absalom! If only I had died[o] instead of you—O Absalom, my son, my son!"[p]

19 Joab was told, "The king is weeping and mourning for Absalom." 2 And for the whole army the
victory that day was turned into mourning, because on that day the troops heard it said, "The
king is grieving for his son." 3 The men stole into the city that day as men steal in who are ashamed when

[a] 12 That is, about 25 pounds (about 11 kilograms) [b] 12 A few Hebrew manuscripts, Septuagint, Vulgate and Syriac; most Hebrew manuscripts may be translated *Absalom, whoever you may be.* [c] 13 Or *Otherwise, if I had acted treacherously toward him* [d] 23 That is, the plain of the Jordan

they flee from battle. 4The king covered his face and cried aloud, "O my son Absalom! O Absalom, my son, my son!"

5Then Joab went into the house to the king and said, "Today you have humiliated all your men, who have just saved your life and the lives of your sons and daughters and the lives of your wives and concubines. 6You love those who hate you and hate those who love you. You have made it clear today that the commanders and their men mean nothing to you. I see that you would be pleased if Absalom were alive today and all of us were dead. 7Now go out and encourage your men. I swear by the LORD that if you don't go out, not a man will be left with you by nightfall. This will be worse for you than all the calamities that have come upon you from your youth till now."[q]

8So the king got up and took his seat in the gateway. When the men were told, "The king is sitting in the gateway,[r]" they all came before him.

David Returns to Jerusalem

Meanwhile, the Israelites had fled to their homes. 9Throughout the tribes of Israel, the people were all arguing with each other, saying, "The king delivered us from the hand of our enemies; he is the one who rescued us from the hand of the Philistines.[s] But now he has fled the country because of Absalom;[t] 10and Absalom, whom we anointed to rule over us, has died in battle. So why do you say nothing about bringing the king back?"

11King David sent this message to Zadok[u] and Abiathar, the priests: "Ask the elders of Judah, 'Why should you be the last to bring the king back to his palace, since what is being said throughout Israel has reached the king at his quarters? 12You are my brothers, my own flesh and blood. So why should you be the last to bring back the king?' 13And say to Amasa,[v] 'Are you not my own flesh and blood?[w] May God deal with me, be it ever so severely,[x] if from now on you are not the commander of my army in place of Joab.[y]' "

14He won over the hearts of all the men of Judah as though they were one man. They sent word to the king, "Return, you and all your men." 15Then the king returned and went as far as the Jordan.

Now the men of Judah had come to Gilgal[z] to go out and meet the king and bring him across the Jordan. 16Shimei[a] son of Gera, the Benjamite from Bahurim, hurried down with the men of Judah to meet King David. 17With him were a thousand Benjamites, along with Ziba,[b] the steward of Saul's household,[c] and his fifteen sons and twenty servants. They rushed to the Jordan, where the king was. 18They crossed at the ford to take the king's household over and to do whatever he wished.

When Shimei son of Gera crossed the Jordan, he fell prostrate before the king 19and said to him, "May my lord not hold me guilty. Do not remember how your servant did wrong on the day my lord the king left Jerusalem.[d] May the king put it out of his mind. 20For I your servant know that I have sinned, but today I have come here as the first of the whole house of Joseph to come down and meet my lord the king."

21Then Abishai[e] son of Zeruiah said, "Shouldn't Shimei be put to death for this? He cursed[f] the LORD's anointed."[g]

22David replied, "What do you and I have in common, you sons of Zeruiah?[h] This day you have become my adversaries! Should anyone be put to death in Israel today?[i] Do I not know that today I am king over Israel?" 23So the king said to Shimei, "You shall not die." And the king promised him on oath.[j]

24Mephibosheth,[k] Saul's grandson, also went down to meet the king. He had not taken care of his feet or trimmed his mustache or washed his clothes from the day the king left until the day he returned safely. 25When he came from Jerusalem to meet the king, the king asked him, "Why didn't you go with me,[l] Mephibosheth?"

26He said, "My lord the king, since I your servant am lame,[m] I said, 'I will have my donkey saddled and will ride on it, so I can go with the king.' But Ziba[n] my servant betrayed me. 27And he has slandered your servant to my lord the king. My lord the king is like an angel[o] of God; so do whatever pleases you. 28All my grandfather's descendants deserved nothing but death[p] from my lord the king, but you gave

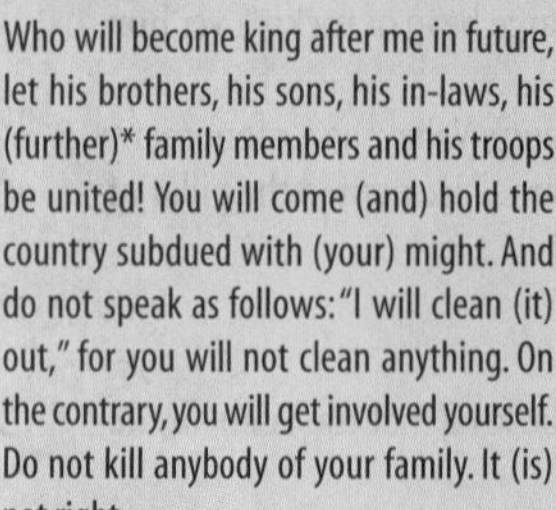

ANCIENT VOICES

Who will become king after me in future, let his brothers, his sons, his in-laws, his (further)* family members and his troops be united! You will come (and) hold the country subdued with (your) might. And do not speak as follows: "I will clean (it) out," for you will not clean anything. On the contrary, you will get involved yourself. Do not kill anybody of your family. It (is) not right.

*Words in parentheses added by translator for clarity or where text has gaps

—THE PROCLAMATION OF TELIPINU

See "Ambitious Princes Among the Hittites" article.

19:7 [q]Pr 14:28
19:8 [r]2Sa 15:2
19:9 [s]2Sa 8:1-14 [t]2Sa 15:14
19:11 [u]2Sa 15:24
19:13 [v]2Sa 17:25 [w]Ge 29:14 [x]Ru 1:17; 1Ki 19:2; 8:16 [y]2Sa 2:13
19:15 [z]Jos 5:9; 1Sa 11:15
19:16 [a]2Sa 16:5-13; 1Ki 2:8
19:17 [b]2Sa 9:2; 16:1-2 [c]Ge 43:16
19:19 [d]1Sa 22:15; 2Sa 16:6-8
19:21 [e]1Sa 26:6 [f]Ex 22:28 [g]1Sa 12:3; 26:9; 2Sa 16:7-8
19:22 [h]2Sa 2:18; 16:10 [i]1Sa 11:13
19:23 [j]1Ki 2:8,42
19:24 [k]2Sa 4:4; 9:6-10
19:25 [l]2Sa 16:17
19:26 [m]Lev 21:18 [n]2Sa 9:2
19:27 [o]1Sa 29:9; 2Sa 14:17,20
19:28 [p]2Sa 16:8; 21:6-9

19:8 See "The City Gate" on page 392.

19:28 [q]2Sa 9:7, 13 your servant a place among those who eat at your table.[q] So what right do I have to make any more ap-
peals to the king?"
29 The king said to him, "Why say more? I order you and Ziba to divide the fields."
30 Mephibosheth said to the king, "Let him take everything, now that my lord the king has arrived
home safely."
19:31 [r]2Sa 17:27-29; 1Ki 2:7 31 Barzillai[r] the Gileadite also came down from Rogelim to cross the Jordan with the king and to send
him on his way from there. 32 Now Barzillai was a very old man, eighty years of age. He had provided for
19:32 [s]1Sa 25:2; 2Sa 17:27 the king during his stay in Mahanaim, for he was a very wealthy[s] man. 33 The king said to Barzillai, "Cross
over with me and stay with me in Jerusalem, and I will provide for you."
34 But Barzillai answered the king, "How many more years will I live, that I should go up to Jerusalem
19:35 [t]Ps 90:10 [u]2Ch 35:25; Ezr 2:65; Ecc 2:8; 12:1; Isa 5:11-12 [v]2Sa 15:33 with the king? 35 I am now eighty[t] years old. Can I tell the difference between what is good and what is
not? Can your servant taste what he eats and drinks? Can I still hear the voices of men and women sing-
ers?[u] Why should your servant be an added[v] burden to my lord the king? 36 Your servant will cross over
the Jordan with the king for a short distance, but why should the king reward me in this way? 37 Let your
19:37 [w]Ge 49:29; 1Ki 2:7 [x]ver 40; Jer 41:17 servant return, that I may die in my own town near the tomb of my father[w] and mother. But here is your
servant Kimham.[x] Let him cross over with my lord the king. Do for him whatever pleases you."
38 The king said, "Kimham shall cross over with me, and I will do for him whatever pleases you. And
anything you desire from me I will do for you."
39 So all the people crossed the Jordan, and then the king crossed over. The king kissed Barzillai and
19:39 [y]Ge 31:55; 47:7 gave him his blessing,[y] and Barzillai returned to his home.
40 When the king crossed over to Gilgal, Kimham crossed with him. All the troops of Judah and half
the troops of Israel had taken the king over.

ANCIENT TEXTS AND ARTIFACTS

Ambitious Princes Among the Hittites

2 SAMUEL 19 Expunging the bloodline of one's opponent was common practice in ancient monarchies. The decree of the **Hittite** king Telipinu describes the political upheaval that often ensued as a throne changed hands. This document provides a historical account of the succession of Hittite kings from the seventeenth–fourteenth centuries B.C.[1] At the outset succession was orderly, and the land prospered. Soon, however, the princes' servants (often family members), in a lust for power, began to conspire against their lords. A series of palace intrigues ensued, during which a relative of the king would rise up, kill his master and assume control. He would exterminate all of the former king's descendants so that no threat to his rule remained. Eventually one of his family members, sometimes his own son, would rebel against him, and a new cycle of regicide would begin.

Telipinu was the first Hittite king to attempt to end such bloodshed. Having exiled the monarch who had tried to eliminate him, Telipinu himself became king, but he treated the family of his predecessor kindly. He then established rules of succession and proclaimed that future kings were to unite the royal family rather than to splinter it by murderous intent. Finally, he decreed that anyone conspiring to kill members of the royal family would be executed, even if that individual were a prince himself.

The problem of palace intrigues and dynastic succession had its parallels in Israelite society. Like Telipinu, the Biblical David demonstrated that he would not condone the murder of his rival's family. When a young man claimed to have slain King Saul (2Sa 1:1–15) and two others reported that they had killed Saul's son (4:1–12), David had them executed for their purported treacherous deeds. He went on to seek out Saul's living relatives for the purpose of showing them kindness, to the extent of providing personal care and protection to Saul's lame grandson, Mephibosheth (9:1–13). David's own family, however, was not immune from the pattern of the surrounding cultures. His son Absalom attempted to usurp the throne and to kill his father in battle. When Absalom himself was killed, David grieved so profoundly that the victory celebration was overshadowed by his mourning.[2]

[1]See "Anatolia and the Hittites" on page 144. [2]See "David" on page 443.

[41]Soon all the men of Israel were coming to the king and saying to him, "Why did our brothers, the
men of Judah, steal the king away and bring him and his household across the Jordan, together with all
his men?"[z]
[42]All the men of Judah answered the men of Israel, "We did this because the king is closely related to
us. Why are you angry about it? Have we eaten any of the king's provisions? Have we taken anything for
ourselves?"
[43]Then the men of Israel[a] answered the men of Judah, "We have ten shares in the king; and besides,
we have a greater claim on David than you have. So why do you treat us with contempt? Were we not the
first to speak of bringing back our king?"

But the men of Judah responded even more harshly than the men of Israel.

Sheba Rebels Against David

20 Now a troublemaker named Sheba son of Bicri, a Benjamite, happened to be there. He sounded
the trumpet and shouted,

"We have no share[b] in David,[c]
no part in Jesse's son![d]
Every man to his tent, O Israel!"

[2]So all the men of Israel deserted David to follow Sheba son of Bicri. But the men of Judah stayed by
their king all the way from the Jordan to Jerusalem.
[3]When David returned to his palace in Jerusalem, he took the ten concubines[e] he had left to take care
of the palace and put them in a house under guard. He provided for them, but did not lie with them. They
were kept in confinement till the day of their death, living as widows.
[4]Then the king said to Amasa,[f] "Summon the men of Judah to come to me within three days, and be
here yourself." [5]But when Amasa went to summon Judah, he took longer than the time the king had set
for him.
[6]David said to Abishai,[g] "Now Sheba son of Bicri will do us more harm than Absalom did. Take your
master's men and pursue him, or he will find fortified cities and escape from us." [7]So Joab's men and the
Kerethites[h] and Pelethites and all the mighty warriors went out under the command of Abishai. They
marched out from Jerusalem to pursue Sheba son of Bicri.
[8]While they were at the great rock in Gibeon,[i] Amasa came to meet them. Joab[j] was wearing his mil-
itary tunic, and strapped over it at his waist was a belt with a dagger in its sheath. As he stepped forward,
it dropped out of its sheath.
[9]Joab said to Amasa, "How are you, my brother?" Then Joab took Amasa by the beard with his right
hand to kiss him. [10]Amasa was not on his guard against the dagger[k] in Joab's[l] hand, and Joab plunged it
into his belly, and his intestines spilled out on the ground. Without being stabbed again, Amasa died.
Then Joab and his brother Abishai pursued Sheba son of Bicri.
[11]One of Joab's men stood beside Amasa and said, "Whoever favors Joab, and whoever is for David,
let him follow Joab!" [12]Amasa lay wallowing in his blood in the middle of the road, and the man saw that
all the troops came to a halt[m] there. When he realized that everyone who came up to Amasa stopped, he
dragged him from the road into a field and threw a garment over him. [13]After Amasa had been removed
from the road, all the men went on with Joab to pursue Sheba son of Bicri.
[14]Sheba passed through all the tribes of Israel to Abel Beth Maacah[a] and through the entire region of
the Berites,[n] who gathered together and followed him. [15]All the troops with Joab came and besieged She-
ba in Abel Beth Maacah.[o] They built a siege ramp[p] up to the city, and it stood against the outer fortifica-
tions. While they were battering the wall to bring it down, [16]a wise woman[q] called from the city, "Listen!
Listen! Tell Joab to come here so I can speak to him." [17]He went toward her, and she asked, "Are you Joab?"

"I am," he answered.

She said, "Listen to what your servant has to say."

"I'm listening," he said.

[18]She continued, "Long ago they used to say, 'Get your answer at Abel,' and that settled it. [19]We are the
peaceful[r] and faithful in Israel. You are trying to destroy a city that is a mother in Israel. Why do you want
to swallow up the LORD's inheritance?"[s]

[a] *14* Or *Abel, even Beth Maacah*; also in verse 15

19:41 [z]Jdg 8:1; 12:1
19:43 [a]2Sa 5:1
20:1 [b]Ge 31:14 [c]Ge 29:14; 1Ki 12:16 [d]1Sa 22:7-8; 2Ch 10:16
20:3 [e]2Sa 15:16; 16:21-22
20:4 [f]2Sa 17:25; 19:13
20:6 [g]2Sa 21:17
20:7 [h]1Sa 30:14; 2Sa 8:18; 15:18; 1Ki 1:38
20:8 [i]Jos 9:3 [j]2Sa 2:18
20:10 [k]Jdg 3:21; 2Sa 2:23; 3:27 [l]1Ki 2:5
20:12 [m]2Sa 2:23
20:14 [n]Nu 21:16
20:15 [o]1Ki 15:20; 2Ki 15:29 [p]2Ki 19:32; Isa 37:33; Jer 6:6; 32:24
20:16 [q]2Sa 14:2
20:19 [r]Dt 2:26 [s]1Sa 26:19; 2Sa 21:3

20“Far be it from me!” Joab replied, “Far be it from me to swallow up or destroy! 21That is not the case. A man named Sheba son of Bicri, from the hill country of Ephraim, has lifted up his hand against the king, against David. Hand over this one man, and I'll withdraw from the city.”

The woman said to Joab, “His head[t] will be thrown to you from the wall.”

22Then the woman went to all the people with her wise advice,[u] and they cut off the head of Sheba son of Bicri and threw it to Joab. So he sounded the trumpet, and his men dispersed from the city, each returning to his home. And Joab went back to the king in Jerusalem.

23Joab[v] was over Israel's entire army; Benaiah son of Jehoiada was over the Kerethites and Pelethites; 24Adoniram[a][w] was in charge of forced labor; Jehoshaphat[x] son of Ahilud was recorder; 25Sheva was secretary; Zadok[y] and Abiathar were priests; 26and Ira the Jairite was David's priest.

The Gibeonites Avenged

21 During the reign of David, there was a famine[z] for three successive years; so David sought[a] the face of the LORD. The LORD said, “It is on account of Saul and his blood-stained house; it is because he put the Gibeonites to death.”

2The king summoned the Gibeonites[b] and spoke to them. (Now the Gibeonites were not a part of Israel but were survivors of the Amorites; the Israelites had sworn to ⌞spare⌟ them, but Saul in his zeal for Israel and Judah had tried to annihilate them.) 3David asked the Gibeonites, “What shall I do for you? How shall I make amends so that you will bless the LORD's inheritance?”[c]

4The Gibeonites answered him, “We have no right to demand silver or gold from Saul or his family, nor do we have the right to put anyone in Israel to death.”[d]

“What do you want me to do for you?” David asked.

5They answered the king, “As for the man who destroyed us and plotted against us so that we have been decimated and have no place anywhere in Israel, 6let seven of his male descendants be given to us to be killed and exposed[e] before the LORD at Gibeah of Saul—the LORD's chosen[f] one.”

So the king said, “I will give them to you.”

7The king spared Mephibosheth[g] son of Jonathan, the son of Saul, because of the oath[h] before the LORD between David and Jonathan son of Saul. 8But the king took Armoni and Mephibosheth, the two sons of Aiah's daughter Rizpah,[i] whom she had borne to Saul, together with the five sons of Saul's daughter Merab,[b] whom she had borne to Adriel son of Barzillai the Meholathite.[j] 9He handed them over to the Gibeonites, who killed and exposed them on a hill before the LORD. All seven of them fell together; they were put to death[k] during the first days of the harvest, just as the barley harvest was beginning.[l]

10Rizpah daughter of Aiah took sackcloth and spread it out for herself on a rock. From the beginning of the harvest till the rain poured down from the heavens on the bodies, she did not let the birds of the air touch them by day or the wild animals by night.[m] 11When David was told what Aiah's daughter Rizpah, Saul's concubine, had done, 12he went and took the bones of Saul[n] and his son Jonathan from the citizens of Jabesh Gilead. (They had taken them secretly from the public square at Beth Shan,[o] where the Philistines had hung[p] them after they struck Saul down on Gilboa.) 13David brought the bones of Saul and his son Jonathan from there, and the bones of those who had been killed and exposed were gathered up.

14They buried the bones of Saul and his son Jonathan in the tomb of Saul's father Kish, at Zela[q] in Benjamin, and did everything the king commanded. After that,[r] God answered prayer[s] in behalf of the land.

Wars Against the Philistines

15Once again there was a battle between the Philistines[t] and Israel. David went down with his men to fight against the Philistines, and he became exhausted. 16And Ishbi-Benob, one of the descendants of Rapha, whose bronze spearhead weighed three hundred shekels[c] and who was armed with a new ⌞sword⌟, said he would kill David. 17But Abishai[u] son of Zeruiah came to David's rescue; he struck the Philistine

20:21 [t]2Sa 4:8
20:22 [u]Ecc 9:13
20:23 [v]2Sa 2:28; 8:16-18; 24:2
20:24 [w]1Ki 4:6; 5:14; 12:18; 2Ch 10:18 [x]2Sa 8:16; 1Ki 4:3
20:25 [y]1Sa 2:35; 2Sa 8:17
21:1 [z]Ge 12:10; Dt 32:24 [a]Ex 32:11
21:2 [b]Jos 9:15
21:3 [c]1Sa 26:19; 2Sa 20:19
21:4 [d]Nu 35:33-34
21:6 [e]Nu 25:4 [f]1Sa 10:24
21:7 [g]2Sa 4:4 [h]1Sa 18:3; 20:8, 15; 2Sa 9:7
21:8 [i]2Sa 3:7 [j]1Sa 18:19
21:9 [k]2Sa 16:8 [l]Ru 1:22
21:10 [m]ver 8; Dt 21:23; 1Sa 17:44
21:12 [n]1Sa 31:11-13 [o]Jos 17:11 [p]1Sa 31:10
21:14 [q]Jos 18:28 [r]Jos 7:26 [s]2Sa 24:25
21:15 [t]2Sa 5:25
21:17 [u]2Sa 20:6

[a] *24* Some Septuagint manuscripts (see also 1 Kings 4:6 and 5:14); Hebrew *Adoram* [b] *8* Two Hebrew manuscripts, some Septuagint manuscripts and Syriac (see also 1 Samuel 18:19); most Hebrew and Septuagint manuscripts *Michal* [c] *16* That is, about 7 1/2 pounds (about 3.5 kilograms)

21:1 See the note on famine at Ruth 1:1, as well as “Famine in the Ancient Near East” on page 70.

21:8 Merab, the daughter of Saul, had been promised to David, since he was the man who had killed Goliath (1Sa 18:19).

21:11–12 See “Jabesh Gilead” on page 384 and “The Beth Shan Temples” on page 438.

down and killed him. Then David's men swore to him, saying, "Never again will you go out with us to
battle, so that the lamp[v] of Israel will not be extinguished.[w]"
18 In the course of time, there was another battle with the Philistines, at Gob. At that time Sibbecai[x] the
Hushathite killed Saph, one of the descendants of Rapha.
19 In another battle with the Philistines at Gob, Elhanan son of Jaare-Oregim[a] the Bethlehemite killed
Goliath[b] the Gittite, who had a spear with a shaft like a weaver's rod.[y]
20 In still another battle, which took place at Gath, there was a huge man with six fingers on each hand
and six toes on each foot—twenty-four in all. He also was descended from Rapha. 21 When he taunted
Israel, Jonathan son of Shimeah,[z] David's brother, killed him.
22 These four were descendants of Rapha in Gath, and they fell at the hands of David and his men.

21:17 [v]1Ki 11:36 [w]2Sa 18:3
21:18 [x]1Ch 11:29; 20:4; 27:11
21:19 [y]1Sa 17:7
21:21 [z]1Sa 16:9

David's Song of Praise

22 David sang[a] to the LORD the words of this song when the LORD delivered him from the hand of
all his enemies and from the hand of Saul. 2 He said:

"The LORD is my rock,[b] my fortress[c] and my deliverer;[d]
3 my God is my rock, in whom I take refuge,[e]
my shield[f] and the horn[c][g] of my salvation.
He is my stronghold,[h] my refuge and my savior—
from violent men you save me.
4 I call to the LORD, who is worthy[i] of praise,
and I am saved from my enemies.

5 "The waves[j] of death swirled about me;
the torrents of destruction overwhelmed me.
6 The cords of the grave[d][k] coiled around me;
the snares of death confronted me.
7 In my distress[l] I called[m] to the LORD;
I called out to my God.
From his temple he heard my voice;
my cry came to his ears.

8 "The earth[n] trembled and quaked,[o]
the foundations[p] of the heavens[e] shook;
they trembled because he was angry.
9 Smoke rose from his nostrils;
consuming fire[q] came from his mouth,
burning coals blazed out of it.
10 He parted the heavens and came down;
dark clouds[r] were under his feet.
11 He mounted the cherubim and flew;
he soared[f] on the wings of the wind.[s]
12 He made darkness his canopy around him—
the dark[g] rain clouds of the sky.
13 Out of the brightness of his presence
bolts of lightning[t] blazed forth.
14 The LORD thundered[u] from heaven;
the voice of the Most High resounded.
15 He shot arrows[v] and scattered ⌊the enemies⌋,
bolts of lightning and routed them.

22:1 [a]Ex 15:1; Jdg 5:1; Ps 18:2-50
22:2 [b]Dt 32:4; Ps 71:3 [c]Ps 31:3; 91:2 [d]Ps 144:2
22:3 [e]Dt 32:37; Jer 16:19 [f]Ge 15:1 [g]Lk 1:69 [h]Ps 9:9
22:4 [i]Ps 48:1; 96:4
22:5 [j]Ps 69:14-15; 93:4; Jnh 2:3
22:6 [k]Ps 116:3
22:7 [l]Ps 120:1 [m]Ps 34:6,15; 116:4
22:8 [n]Jdg 5:4; Ps 97:4 [o]Ps 77:18 [p]Job 26:11
22:9 [q]Ps 97:3; Heb 12:29
22:10 [r]1Ki 8:12; Na 1:3
22:11 [s]Ps 104:3
22:13 [t]ver 9
22:14 [u]1Sa 2:10
22:15 [v]Dt 32:23

[a] 19 Or *son of Jair the weaver* [b] 19 Hebrew and Septuagint; 1 Chron. 20:5 *son of Jair killed Lahmi the brother of Goliath* [c] 3 *Horn* here symbolizes strength. [d] 6 Hebrew *Sheol* [e] 8 Hebrew; Vulgate and Syriac (see also Psalm 18:7) *mountains* [f] 11 Many Hebrew manuscripts (see also Psalm 18:10); most Hebrew manuscripts *appeared* [g] 12 Septuagint and Vulgate (see also Psalm 18:11); Hebrew *massed*

22:14–15 The motif of a deity shooting thunderstorm arrows from on high is characteristic of many storm-gods, such as Baal of Canaan and Zeus of the Greeks (see "Storm Gods, Storm Imagery and Theophany" on p. 808). The Hittites also worshiped a storm god (see "The Hittite Storm Gods" on p. 784). In this text David has used a literary-religious motif of his own time to communicate the power of Israel's God.

[16]The valleys of the sea were exposed
and the foundations of the earth laid bare
at the rebuke[w] of the LORD,
at the blast of breath from his nostrils.

[17]"He reached down from on high[x] and took hold of me;
he drew[y] me out of deep waters.
[18]He rescued me from my powerful enemy,
from my foes, who were too strong for me.
[19]They confronted me in the day of my disaster,
but the LORD was my support.[z]
[20]He brought me out into a spacious[a] place;
he rescued[b] me because he delighted[c] in me.[d]

[21]"The LORD has dealt with me according to my righteousness;[e]
according to the cleanness of my hands[f] he has rewarded me.
[22]For I have kept[g] the ways of the LORD;
I have not done evil by turning from my God.
[23]All his laws are before me;[h]
I have not turned[i] away from his decrees.
[24]I have been blameless[j] before him
and have kept myself from sin.
[25]The LORD has rewarded me according to my righteousness,[k]
according to my cleanness[a] in his sight.

[26]"To the faithful you show yourself faithful,
to the blameless you show yourself blameless,
[27]to the pure[l] you show yourself pure,
but to the crooked you show yourself shrewd.[m]
[28]You save the humble,[n]
but your eyes are on the haughty to bring them low.[o]
[29]You are my lamp,[p] O LORD;
the LORD turns my darkness into light.
[30]With your help I can advance against a troop[b];
with my God I can scale a wall.

[31]"As for God, his way is perfect;[q]
the word of the LORD is flawless.[r]
He is a shield
for all who take refuge in him.
[32]For who is God besides the LORD?
And who is the Rock[s] except our God?
[33]It is God who arms me with strength[c]
and makes my way perfect.
[34]He makes my feet like the feet of a deer;[t]
he enables me to stand on the heights.[u]
[35]He trains my hands[v] for battle;
my arms can bend a bow of bronze.
[36]You give me your shield[w] of victory;
you stoop down to make me great.
[37]You broaden the path[x] beneath me,
so that my ankles do not turn.

[38]"I pursued my enemies and crushed them;
I did not turn back till they were destroyed.

22:16 [w]Na 1:4
22:17 [x]Ps 144:7 [y]Ex 2:10
22:19 [z]Ps 23:4
22:20 [a]Ps 31:8 [b]Ps 118:5 [c]Ps 22:8 [d]2Sa 15:26
22:21 [e]1Sa 26:23 [f]Ps 24:4
22:22 [g]Ge 18:19; Ps 128:1; Pr 8:32
22:23 [h]Dt 6:4-9; Ps 119:30-32 [i]Ps 119:102
22:24 [j]Ge 6:9; Eph 1:4
22:25 [k]ver 21
22:27 [l]Mt 5:8 [m]Lev 26:23-24
22:28 [n]Ex 3:8; Ps 72:12-13 [o]Isa 2:12,17; 5:15
22:29 [p]Ps 27:1
22:31 [q]Dt 32:4; Mt 5:48 [r]Ps 12:6; 119:140; Pr 30:5-6
22:32 [s]1Sa 2:2
22:34 [t]Hab 3:19 [u]Dt 32:13
22:35 [v]Ps 144:1
22:36 [w]Eph 6:16
22:37 [x]Pr 4:11

[a] 25 Hebrew; Septuagint and Vulgate (see also Psalm 18:24) *to the cleanness of my hands* [b] 30 Or *can run through a barricade* [c] 33 Dead Sea Scrolls, some Septuagint manuscripts, Vulgate and Syriac (see also Psalm 18:32); Masoretic Text *who is my strong refuge*

[39] I crushed[y] them completely, and they could not rise;
they fell beneath my feet.
[40] You armed me with strength for battle;
you made my adversaries bow at my feet.[z]
[41] You made my enemies turn their backs[a] in flight,
and I destroyed my foes.
[42] They cried for help,[b] but there was no one to save them—[c]
to the LORD, but he did not answer.
[43] I beat them as fine as the dust of the earth;
I pounded and trampled[d] them like mud[e] in the streets.

[44] "You have delivered[f] me from the attacks of my people;
you have preserved[g] me as the head of nations.
People[h] I did not know are subject to me,
[45] and foreigners come cringing[i] to me;
as soon as they hear me, they obey me.
[46] They all lose heart;
they come trembling[a][j] from their strongholds.

[47] "The LORD lives! Praise be to my Rock!
Exalted be God, the Rock, my Savior![k]

22:39 [y]Mal 4:3
22:40 [z]Ps 44:5
22:41 [a]Ex 23:27
22:42 [b]Isa 1:15 [c]Ps 50:22
22:43 [d]Mic 7:10 [e]Isa 10:6; Mic 7:10
22:44 [f]2Sa 3:1 [g]Dt 28:13 [h]2Sa 8:1-14; Isa 55:3-5
22:45 [i]Ps 66:3; 81:15
22:46 [j]Mic 7:17
22:47 [k]Ps 89:26

[a] 46 Some Septuagint manuscripts and Vulgate (see also Psalm 18:45); Masoretic Text *they arm themselves.*

CULTURAL AND HISTORICAL NOTES

Songs of Warriors

2 SAMUEL 22 The Bible attests to the fact that ancient warriors often celebrated their achievements in song. Indeed, the first song recorded in the Bible is that of Lamech (Ge 4:23–24), a fighter who boasted of killing a man who had wounded him. Songs by or about warriors have surfaced in several varieties:

✣ In what may be called the "victory song," a warrior sang of his triumphs in battle. Such a song could be blatantly boastful, like Lamech's, or could give thanks to God, as did David's in 2 Samuel 22. This song praises God but is clearly military in orientation: "He trains my hands for battle; my arms can bend a bow of bronze" (v. 35). There are pagan analogies for such songs; an **Akkadian** hymn celebrating the military campaigns of the **Assyrian** king Ashurnasirpal II (r. 883–859 B.C.) begins with the king claiming that he would sing in praise of his god, Enlil, but quickly moves on to a boastful account of Ashurnasirpal's triumphs. The Greeks somewhat transformed this genre and composed songs in honor of athletes, as in the odes of Pindar (fifth century B.C.), who celebrated the victors in the Olympic and other games.

Ashurnasirpal II
Preserving Bible Times; © Dr. James C. Martin; permission of The British Museum

✣ A second type of military song was the lament over fallen heroes. A magnificent example is that of David over Jonathan and Saul (1:17–27). The Greek poet Simonides (fifth century B.C.) composed verses for the Greeks who died at the battle of Thermopylae, also commemorating the Greek victory over the Persians at Plataea.

✣ Epic poetry, which memorializes at length the deeds of great heroes, can be considered a third genre. Examples include the **Sumerian** Epic of Gilgamesh[1], the Ugaritic epic of Kirta[2] and the well-known Greek *Iliad* and *Odyssey* by Homer. The Bible, because it focuses on God and his covenant rather than on the exploits of heroic human beings, includes no epic poetry.

[1]See "Ecclesiastes and the Epic of Gilgamesh" on page 1027. [2]See "The Kirta Epic" on page 736.

22:48 [l]Ps 94:1; 144:2; 1Sa 25:39

48 He is the God who avenges me,[l]
who puts the nations under me,

22:49 [m]Ps 140:1,4

49 who sets me free from my enemies.[m]
You exalted me above my foes;
from violent men you rescued me.
50 Therefore I will praise you, O LORD, among the nations;

22:50 [n]Ro 15:9*

I will sing praises to your name.[n]

22:51 [o]Ps 144:9-10 [p]Ps 89:20 [q]2Sa 7:13 [r]Ps 89:24,29

51 He gives his king great victories;[o]
he shows unfailing kindness to his anointed,[p]
to David[q] and his descendants forever."[r]

The Last Words of David

23 These are the last words of David:

"The oracle of David son of Jesse,

23:1 [s]2Sa 7:8-9; Ps 78:70-71; 89:27 [t]1Sa 16:12-13; Ps 89:20

the oracle of the man exalted[s] by the Most High,
the man anointed[t] by the God of Jacob,
Israel's singer of songs[a]:

23:2 [u]Mt 22:43; 2Pe 1:21

2 "The Spirit[u] of the LORD spoke through me;
his word was on my tongue.
3 The God of Israel spoke,

23:3 [v]Dt 32:4; 2Sa 22:2,32 [w]Ps 72:2 [x]2Ch 19:7,9; Isa 11:1-5

the Rock[v] of Israel said to me:
'When one rules over men in righteousness,[w]
when he rules in the fear of God,[x]

23:4 [y]Jdg 5:31; Ps 89:36

4 he is like the light of morning at sunrise[y]
on a cloudless morning,
like the brightness after rain
that brings the grass from the earth.'

5 "Is not my house right with God?

23:5 [z]Ps 89:29; Isa 55:3

Has he not made with me an everlasting covenant,[z]
arranged and secured in every part?
Will he not bring to fruition my salvation
and grant me my every desire?

23:6 [a]Mt 13:40-41

6 But evil men are all to be cast aside like thorns,[a]
which are not gathered with the hand.
7 Whoever touches thorns
uses a tool of iron or the shaft of a spear;
they are burned up where they lie."

David's Mighty Men

8 These are the names of David's mighty men:
Josheb-Basshebeth,[b] a Tahkemonite,[c] was chief of the Three; he raised his spear against eight hundred men, whom he killed[d] in one encounter.

23:9 [b]1Ch 27:4 [c]1Ch 8:4

9 Next to him was Eleazar son of Dodai[b] the Ahohite.[c] As one of the three mighty men, he was with
David when they taunted the Philistines gathered ⌊at Pas Dammim⌋[e] for battle. Then the men of Israel
retreated, 10 but he stood his ground and struck down the Philistines till his hand grew tired and froze to
the sword. The LORD brought about a great victory that day. The troops returned to Eleazar, but only to
strip the dead.
11 Next to him was Shammah son of Agee the Hararite. When the Philistines banded together at a
place where there was a field full of lentils, Israel's troops fled from them. 12 But Shammah took his stand

[a] 1 Or *Israel's beloved singer* [b] 8 Hebrew; some Septuagint manuscripts suggest *Ish-Bosheth,* that is, *Esh-Baal* (see also 1 Chron. 11:11 *Jashobeam*). [c] 8 Probably a variant of *Hacmonite* (see 1 Chron. 11:11) [d] 8 Some Septuagint manuscripts (see also 1 Chron. 11:11); Hebrew and other Septuagint manuscripts *Three; it was Adino the Eznite who killed eight hundred men*
[e] 9 See 1 Chron. 11:13; Hebrew *gathered there.*

in the middle of the field. He defended it and struck the Philistines down, and the LORD brought about a
great victory.
13 During harvest time, three of the thirty chief men came down to David at the cave of Adullam,[d]
while a band of Philistines was encamped in the Valley of Rephaim.[e] 14 At that time David was in the
stronghold,[f] and the Philistine garrison was at Bethlehem.[g] 15 David longed for water and said, "Oh, that
someone would get me a drink of water from the well near the gate of Bethlehem!" 16 So the three mighty
men broke through the Philistine lines, drew water from the well near the gate of Bethlehem and carried
it back to David. But he refused to drink it; instead, he poured[h] it out before the LORD. 17 "Far be it from
me, O LORD, to do this!" he said. "Is it not the blood[i] of men who went at the risk of their lives?" And Da-
vid would not drink it.

Such were the exploits of the three mighty men.

18 Abishai[j] the brother of Joab son of Zeruiah was chief of the Three.[a] He raised his spear against three
hundred men, whom he killed, and so he became as famous as the Three. 19 Was he not held in greater
honor than the Three? He became their commander, even though he was not included among them.

20 Benaiah[k] son of Jehoiada was a valiant fighter from Kabzeel,[l] who performed great exploits. He
struck down two of Moab's best men. He also went down into a pit on a snowy day and killed a lion.
21 And he struck down a huge Egyptian. Although the Egyptian had a spear in his hand, Benaiah went
against him with a club. He snatched the spear from the Egyptian's hand and killed him with his own
spear. 22 Such were the exploits of Benaiah son of Jehoiada; he too was as famous as the three mighty
men. 23 He was held in greater honor than any of the Thirty, but he was not included among the Three.
And David put him in charge of his bodyguard.

24 Among the Thirty were:
Asahel[m] the brother of Joab,
Elhanan son of Dodo from Bethlehem,
25 Shammah the Harodite,[n]
Elika the Harodite,
26 Helez[o] the Paltite,
Ira son of Ikkesh from Tekoa,
27 Abiezer from Anathoth,[p]
Mebunnai[b] the Hushathite,
28 Zalmon the Ahohite,
Maharai[q] the Netophathite,[r]
29 Heled[c] son of Baanah the Netophathite,
Ithai son of Ribai from Gibeah[s] in Benjamin,
30 Benaiah the Pirathonite,[t]
Hiddai[d] from the ravines of Gaash,[u]
31 Abi-Albon the Arbathite,
Azmaveth the Barhumite,[v]
32 Eliahba the Shaalbonite,
the sons of Jashen,
Jonathan 33 son of[e] Shammah the Hararite,
Ahiam son of Sharar[f] the Hararite,
34 Eliphelet son of Ahasbai the Maacathite,
Eliam[w] son of Ahithophel[x] the Gilonite,
35 Hezro the Carmelite,[y]
Paarai the Arbite,
36 Igal son of Nathan from Zobah,[z]
the son of Hagri,[g]

23:13 [d]1Sa 22:1 [e]2Sa 5:18
23:14 [f]1Sa 22:4-5 [g]Ru 1:19
23:16 [h]Ge 35:14
23:17 [i]Lev 17:10-12
23:18 [j]2Sa 10:10,14; 1Ch 11:20
23:20 [k]2Sa 8:18; 20:23 [l]Jos 15:21
23:24 [m]2Sa 2:18
23:25 [n]Jdg 7:1; 1Ch 11:27
23:26 [o]1Ch 27:10
23:27 [p]Jos 21:18
23:28 [q]1Ch 27:13 [r]2Ki 25:23; Ne 7:26
23:29 [s]Jos 15:57
23:30 [t]Jdg 12:13 [u]Jos 24:30
23:31 [v]2Sa 3:16
23:34 [w]2Sa 11:3 [x]2Sa 15:12
23:35 [y]Jos 12:22
23:36 [z]1Sa 14:47

[a] *18* Most Hebrew manuscripts (see also 1 Chron. 11:20); two Hebrew manuscripts and Syriac *Thirty* [b] *27* Hebrew; some Septuagint manuscripts (see also 1 Chron. 11:29) *Sibbecai* [c] *29* Some Hebrew manuscripts and Vulgate (see also 1 Chron. 11:30); most Hebrew manuscripts *Heleb* [d] *30* Hebrew; some Septuagint manuscripts (see also 1 Chron. 11:32) *Hurai* [e] *33* Some Septuagint manuscripts (see also 1 Chron. 11:34); Hebrew does not have *son of.* [f] *33* Hebrew; some Septuagint manuscripts (see also 1 Chron. 11:35) *Sacar* [g] *36* Some Septuagint manuscripts (see also 1 Chron. 11:38); Hebrew *Haggadi*

23:29 See "Gibeah" on page 380.

[37] Zelek the Ammonite,
Naharai the Beerothite, the armor-bearer of Joab son of Zeruiah,
23:38 [a]2Sa 20:26; 1Ch 2:53 [38] Ira the Ithrite,[a]
Gareb the Ithrite
23:39 [b]2Sa 11:3 [39] and Uriah[b] the Hittite.
There were thirty-seven in all.

David Counts the Fighting Men

24:1 [c]Jos 9:15 [d]1Ch 27:23
24 Again[c] the anger of the LORD burned against Israel, and he incited David against them, saying,
"Go and take a census of[d] Israel and Judah."
24:2 [e]2Sa 20:23 [f]Jdg 20:1; 2Sa 3:10
[2] So the king said to Joab[e] and the army commanders[a] with him, "Go throughout the tribes of Israel
from Dan to Beersheba[f] and enroll the fighting men, so that I may know how many there are."
24:3 [g]Dt 1:11
[3] But Joab replied to the king, "May the LORD your God multiply the troops a hundred times over,[g] and
may the eyes of my lord the king see it. But why does my lord the king want to do such a thing?"
[4] The king's word, however, overruled Joab and the army commanders; so they left the presence of the
king to enroll the fighting men of Israel.
24:5 [h]Dt 2:36; Jos 13:9 [i]Nu 21:32
[5] After crossing the Jordan, they camped near Aroer,[h] south of the town in the gorge, and then went
through Gad and on to Jazer.[i] [6] They went to Gilead and the region of Tahtim Hodshi, and on to Dan Jaan
24:6 [j]Ge 10:19; Jos 19:28; Jdg 1:31
and around toward Sidon.[j] [7] Then they went toward the fortress of Tyre[k] and all the towns of the Hivites
24:7 [k]Jos 19:29 [l]Ge 21:22-33 [m]Dt 1:7; Jos 11:3
and Canaanites. Finally, they went on to Beersheba[l] in the Negev[m] of Judah.

[a] 2 Septuagint (see also verse 4 and 1 Chron. 21:2); Hebrew *Joab the army commander*

ANCIENT TEXTS AND ARTIFACTS

Plague Prayers of Mursilis II

2 SAMUEL 24 The story recounted in 2 Samuel 24 is unusual on several accounts. First, God is said to have been angry with Israel and to have incited David to sin in order that the Lord might thereby punish the nation (v. 1). Second, the nature of the sin itself—conducting a census—has always been difficult to explain, although many regard it as a sign of pride or of dependence upon wealth and power rather than upon God. Third, it is unusual that the plague stopped specifically at "the threshing floor of Araunah the Jebusite" (v. 16).

The prayers for deliverance from the plague (vv. 14,17) are not difficult to understand and have analogies from ancient literature. The act of addressing God in prayer in such a situation (which included confessing sins, seeking an explanation for the divine anger and asking for relief from the plague) was by no means unique to Israel.

✣ The best known plague of ancient history struck Athens during the years 430–427 B.C. and was described in detail by the Greek historian Thucydides in Book 2 of his history of the Peloponnesian War.[1] Thucydides described how supplications were lifted up and rites of divination carried out in an effort to placate the gods and halt the plague.

✣ A closer analogy to the 2 Samuel 24 story appears in tablets recording the prayers of the **Hittite** king Mursilis II (r. c. 1321–1298 B.C.). The Hittites had been struck by a widespread, devastating plague. The population of the kingdom had been severely decimated; even Mursilis's predecessors, his father Suppiluliumas I and his brother Arnuwanda II, had succumbed. In his prayers Mursilis pleaded with the Hittite gods for relief, confessed his sin and even reminded the gods that it was not in their best interest to strike down all the people who served them.[2]

It is perhaps significant, however, that the Bible variously attributes such events both to divine sovereignty and to human sin (v. 1). Even the fact that this particular plague ceased abruptly at a specific place and time is remarkable (v. 16). Perhaps most significant, however, was David's willingness in this case to suffer in the place of his people (v. 17). Whereas Mursilis of the Hittites stopped at offering to make restitution to the gods if such was needed, David offered *himself* to the Lord on his people's behalf.

[1]See "Athens" on page 1804. [2]See "Anatolia and the Hittites" on page 144.

8 After they had gone through the entire land, they came back to Jerusalem at the end of nine months
and twenty days.
9 Joab reported the number of the fighting men to the king: In Israel there were eight hundred thou-
sand able-bodied men who could handle a sword, and in Judah five hundred thousand.[n]
10 David was conscience-stricken[o] after he had counted the fighting men, and he said to the LORD, "I
have sinned[p] greatly in what I have done. Now, O LORD, I beg you, take away the guilt of your servant. I
have done a very foolish thing.[q]"
11 Before David got up the next morning, the word of the LORD had come to Gad[r] the prophet, David's
seer:[s] 12 "Go and tell David, 'This is what the LORD says: I am giving you three options. Choose one of
them for me to carry out against you.' "
13 So Gad went to David and said to him, "Shall there come upon you three[a] years of famine[t] in your
land? Or three months of fleeing from your enemies while they pursue you? Or three days of plague[u] in
your land? Now then, think it over and decide how I should answer the one who sent me."
14 David said to Gad, "I am in deep distress. Let us fall into the hands of the LORD, for his mercy[v] is
great; but do not let me fall into the hands of men."
15 So the LORD sent a plague on Israel from that morning until the end of the time designated, and sev-
enty thousand of the people from Dan to Beersheba died.[w] 16 When the angel stretched out his hand to
destroy Jerusalem, the LORD was grieved[x] because of the calamity and said to the angel who was afflict-
ing the people, "Enough! Withdraw your hand." The angel of the LORD[y] was then at the threshing floor of
Araunah the Jebusite.
17 When David saw the angel who was striking down the people, he said to the LORD, "I am the one
who has sinned and done wrong. These are but sheep.[z] What have they done? Let your hand fall upon me
and my family."[a]

David Builds an Altar

18 On that day Gad went to David and said to him, "Go up and build an altar to the LORD on the thresh-
ing floor of Araunah the Jebusite." 19 So David went up, as the LORD had commanded through Gad. 20 When
Araunah looked and saw the king and his men coming toward him, he went out and bowed down before
the king with his face to the ground.
21 Araunah said, "Why has my lord the king come to his servant?"
"To buy your threshing floor," David answered, "so I can build an altar to the LORD, that the plague on
the people may be stopped."[b]
22 Araunah said to David, "Let my lord the king take whatever pleases him and offer it up. Here are
oxen[c] for the burnt offering, and here are threshing sledges and ox yokes for the wood. 23 O king, Arau-
nah gives[d] all this to the king." Araunah also said to him, "May the LORD your God accept you."
24 But the king replied to Araunah, "No, I insist on paying you for it. I will not sacrifice to the LORD my
God burnt offerings that cost me nothing."[e]
So David bought the threshing floor and the oxen and paid fifty shekels[b] of silver for them. 25 David
built an altar[f] to the LORD there and sacrificed burnt offerings and fellowship offerings.[c] Then the LORD
answered prayer[g] in behalf of the land, and the plague on Israel was stopped.

24:9 [n]Nu 1:44-46; 1Ch 21:5 **24:10** [o]1Sa 24:5 [p]2Sa 12:13 [q]Nu 12:11; 1Sa 13:13
24:11 [r]1Sa 22:5 [s]1Sa 9:9; 1Ch 29:29
24:13 [t]Dt 28:38-42,48; Eze 14:21 [u]Lev 26:25
24:14 [v]Ne 9:28; Ps 51:1; 103:8, 13; 130:4
24:15 [w]1Ch 27:24 **24:16** [x]Ge 6:6; 1Sa 15:11 [y]Ex 12:23; Ac 12:23
24:17 [z]Ps 74:1 [a]Jnh 1:12
24:21 [b]Nu 16:44-50 **24:22** [c]1Sa 6:14; 1Ki 19:21 **24:23** [d]Eze 20:40-41
24:24 [e]Mal 1:13-14
24:25 [f]1Sa 7:17 [g]2Sa 21:14

[a] 13 Septuagint (see also 1 Chron. 21:12); Hebrew *seven* [b] 24 That is, about 1 1/4 pounds (about 0.6 kilogram)
[c] 25 Traditionally *peace offerings*

24:10 It is unclear why David was conscience-stricken or why taking a census is here presented as a sin, although 1 Chronicles 21:3 reports that Joab considered it to be an unlawful act, and verse 7 of the same chapter states that it was evil in God's sight. In contrast, Israel had conducted a census in Numbers 1 under God's direction.

24:16 The name Araunah is not Hebrew; Araunah is said to have been a Jebusite, descended from the pre-Israelite inhabitants of Jerusalem. See "The Jebusites" on page 596.

24:18–25 Threshing floors, ordinarily located on hills, were traditional sites for receiving divine messages. The text emphasizes that the plague ceased at this very spot in response to David's prayer (see "Plague Prayers of Mursilis II" on p. 477). The Chronicler (2Ch 3:1) added that this site, north of David's city, was eventually chosen for Solomon's temple (having been purchased with David's money and made sacred by his offerings).

INTRODUCTION TO 1 Kings

AUTHOR, PLACE AND DATE OF WRITING

Thought to have been written/compiled by an unknown Judahite exile, 1 and 2 Kings were originally one literary work. Translators of the Septuagint (early Greek translation of the OT) divided the original work (called simply "Kings" in the Hebrew tradition) into two books around A.D. 400. Because both have similarities to the book of Jeremiah, some scholars have attributed all three books to this renowned prophet, but this theory cannot be verified. Perhaps the author of 1 and 2 Kings used the book of Jeremiah—as well as Isaiah—as a source (Isa 36, e.g., is virtually identical to 2Ki 18:13–37, but cf. 2Ki 24:18—25:30 to Jer 52:1–34 and 39:1–10). Clearly the author used many sources, including three that are specifically named (1Ki 11:41; 14:19,29).

The ending of 2 Kings 25 suggests that 1 and 2 Kings were written/compiled during the reign of Babylon's Evil-Merodach, after Jehoiachin's release from prison (562 B.C.; 2Ki 25:27–30) but before the Babylonian exile ended in 538 B.C. Some scholars, however, suggest that earlier "editions" of both books were supplemented with material from Israel's later history. Their primary basis for believing that earlier editions existed is the presence of statements to the effect that something is "still there today" (cf. 1Ki 8:8). Much information in these two books did undoubtedly originate from earlier sources, whose authors had direct access to details of Israel's history. Perhaps these sources were the official court annals in the archives of the kings of Israel and Judah, as compiled by the succession of Israel's prophets spanning the kingdom period.

AUDIENCE

The books of Kings were originally written for the Jews living in exile in Babylon to preserve a detailed history of Israel and Judah—from the last days of King David (c. 970 B.C.) to the exile to Babylon (c. 586 B.C.). First Kings includes the history of the united kingdom under King Solomon (1:1—11:43), as well as that of the first 80 years of the divided kingdom of Israel and Judah (12:1—22:53).

Readers of 1 Kings especially were confronted with the northern kingdom's apostasy and the ways in which God tried to use the prophets Elijah and Elisha to turn the people back to covenant faithfulness.

CULTURAL FACTS AND HIGHLIGHTS

Although 1 Kings begins with Solomon's succession to the throne, his request for God's wisdom and the construction of the temple, the situation soon deteriorated from many perspectives. Solomon imposed heavy taxation, used slave labor and allowed his many pagan wives to draw him into idol worship, and his blatant disobedience sowed seeds of evil that soon sprouted. The nation of Israel split apart. Later kings also disobeyed God's covenant and decrees, further weakening the influence of God's people in their culture and setting them up for great instability and hardship.

TIMELINE

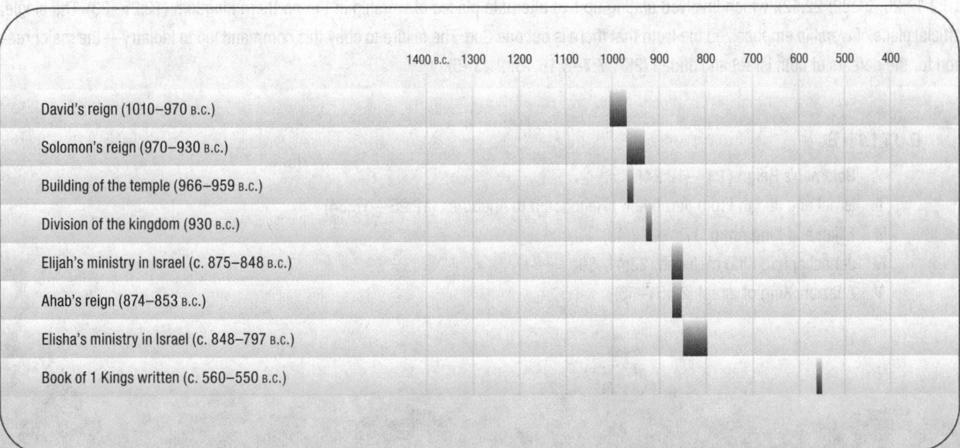

AS YOU READ

Picking up where 1 and 2 Samuel left off, 1 Kings presents the continuing story of Israel's declining monarchy. Notice what happened when God's people disobeyed their covenants with God and disregarded his prophets. Track their continuing inclination toward sinfulness and lack of repentance, a trend recorded in previous Old Testament books. Listen as an elderly David urged his son and successor, Solomon, to remain obedient to God and to pay close attention to the consequences of his actions. Learn why the nation of Israel split apart and what King Jeroboam of Israel had to say about his golden calves. Finally, note the standard by which kings were judged and the courageous faith Elijah and Elisha demonstrated as they served God during this violent, unstable time.

DID YOU KNOW?

- Most ancient prostitutes were slaves, often daughters who had been sold by their parents or poor women who had never married or had lost their husbands (3:16).
- Since Solomon had 1,400 chariots (10:26; 2Ch 1:14), his stables included stalls for 2,800 chariot horses (two for each chariot), with additional stalls for 1,200 horses (1Ki 4:26).
- Ancient wisdom included music, poetry, proverbial sayings for wise conduct and what we would now call science (4:29–34).
- It was common during Old Testament times for the people of one nation to recognize the deities of another (5:7).
- The Palace of the Forest of Lebanon was so named because its many pillars were made from the trunks of cedars of Lebanon, giving the appearance of a massive forest (7:2).
- The "Sea of cast metal" was an enormous reservoir of water, holding about 11,500 gallons—43,527 liters—and used by the priests for ritual cleansing (7:23).

THEMES

First Kings includes the following themes:

1. *The Mosaic covenant.* The history of Israel's kings is presented from a covenantal, rather than from a social, political or economic viewpoint. Assessments of the various kings are based upon their degree of obedience to the Mosaic covenant (see Dt 17:14–20). A major premise of the book is that obedience brings blessing, while disobedience results in judgment.

2. *The Davidic covenant.* The historical significance of the Davidic covenant is demonstrated by references to God's promise to David (1Ki 8:20,25; 11:36) and to the use of David's life and reign as the standard by which later kings were measured (9:4; 11:4,6; 14:8; 15:3–5,11; 2Ki 16:2; 18:3; 22:2).

3. *One true God.* There was to be one central place of worship (Dt 12:1–14), the temple in Jerusalem (1Ki 9:3; 2Ki 21:4,7). The importance of this is seen in the writer's repeated expressions of abhorrence for "the sin of the house of Jeroboam" (1Ki 13:34; see 15:34; 16:2,19,26; 21:22; 22:52), which involved setting up two alternate places of worship in the northern kingdom (12:25–33). The single, official place of worship emphasized the truth that there is but one God. The failure to obey this command led to idolatry—the major reason for the defeats of both Israel and Judah (2Ki 17:7–8,16,19; 21:3–5).

OUTLINE

I. Solomon's Reign (1:1—12:24)
II. Israel and Judah From Jeroboam I/Rehoboam to Ahab/Asa (12:25—16:34)
III. Elijah and King Ahab (17:1—22:40)
IV. Jehoshaphat, King of Judah (22:41–50)
V. Ahaziah, King of Israel (22:51–53)

Adonijah Sets Himself Up as King

1 When King David was old and well advanced in years, he could not keep warm even when they put
covers over him. 2 So his servants said to him, "Let us look for a young virgin to attend the king and
take care of him. She can lie beside him so that our lord the king may keep warm."
1:3 [a]Jos 19:18 3 Then they searched throughout Israel for a beautiful girl and found Abishag, a Shunammite,[a] and
brought her to the king. 4 The girl was very beautiful; she took care of the king and waited on him, but
the king had no intimate relations with her.
1:5 [b]2Sa 3:4 5 Now Adonijah,[b] whose mother was Haggith, put himself forward and said, "I will be king." So he
[c]2Sa 15:1 1:6 [d]2Sa 3:3-4 got chariots[c] and horses[a] ready, with fifty men to run ahead of him. 6 (His father had never interfered[d]
with him by asking, "Why do you behave as you do?" He was also very handsome and was born next
after Absalom.)
1:7 [e]1Ki 2:22,28; 7 Adonijah conferred with Joab[e] son of Zeruiah and with Abiathar[f] the priest, and they gave him their
1Ch 11:6 [f]1Sa 22:20; support. 8 But Zadok[g] the priest, Benaiah[h] son of Jehoiada, Nathan[i] the prophet, Shimei[j] and Rei[b] and
2Sa 20:25 1:8 [g]2Sa 20:25 David's special guard[k] did not join Adonijah.
[h]2Sa 8:18 [i]2Sa 12:1 9 Adonijah then sacrificed sheep, cattle and fattened calves at the Stone of Zoheleth near En Rogel.[l] He
[j]1Ki 4:18 [k]2Sa 23:8 invited all his brothers, the king's sons, and all the men of Judah who were royal officials, 10 but he did not
1:9 [l]2Sa 17:17 invite Nathan the prophet or Benaiah or the special guard or his brother Solomon.[m]
1:10 [m]2Sa 12:24 1:11 [n]2Sa 12:24 11 Then Nathan asked Bathsheba,[n] Solomon's mother, "Have you not heard that Adonijah,[o] the son of
[o]2Sa 3:4 1:12 [p]Pr 15:22 Haggith, has become king without our lord David's knowing it? 12 Now then, let me advise[p] you how you
can save your own life and the life of your son Solomon. 13 Go in to King David and say to him, 'My lord
1:13 [q]ver 30; the king, did you not swear[q] to me your servant: "Surely Solomon your son shall be king after me, and
1Ch 22:9-13 he will sit on my throne"? Why then has Adonijah become king?' 14 While you are still there talking to the
king, I will come in and confirm what you have said."
1:15 [r]ver 1 15 So Bathsheba went to see the aged king in his room, where Abishag[r] the Shunammite was attend-
ing him. 16 Bathsheba bowed low and knelt before the king.
"What is it you want?" the king asked.
1:17 [s]ver 13,30 17 She said to him, "My lord, you yourself swore[s] to me your servant by the LORD your God: 'Solomon
your son shall be king after me, and he will sit on my throne.' 18 But now Adonijah has become king, and
1:19 [t]ver 9 you, my lord the king, do not know about it. 19 He has sacrificed[t] great numbers of cattle, fattened calves,
and sheep, and has invited all the king's sons, Abiathar the priest and Joab the commander of the army,
but he has not invited Solomon your servant. 20 My lord the king, the eyes of all Israel are on you, to learn
from you who will sit on the throne of my lord the king after him. 21 Otherwise, as soon as my lord the
1:21 [u]Dt 31:16; king is laid to rest[u] with his fathers, I and my son Solomon will be treated as criminals."
1Ki 2:10 22 While she was still speaking with the king, Nathan the prophet arrived. 23 And they told the king, "Na-
than the prophet is here." So he went before the king and bowed with his face to the ground.
24 Nathan said, "Have you, my lord the king, declared that Adonijah shall be king after you, and that
he will sit on your throne? 25 Today he has gone down and sacrificed great numbers of cattle, fattened
calves, and sheep. He has invited all the king's sons, the commanders of the army and Abiathar the priest.
Right now they are eating and drinking with him and saying, 'Long live King Adonijah!' 26 But me your
servant, and Zadok the priest, and Benaiah son of Jehoiada, and your servant Solomon he did not in-
1:26 [v]ver 8,10 vite.[v] 27 Is this something my lord the king has done without letting his servants know who should sit on
the throne of my lord the king after him?"

David Makes Solomon King

28 Then King David said, "Call in Bathsheba." So she came into the king's presence and stood before
him.
29 The king then took an oath: "As surely as the LORD lives, who has delivered me out of every trou-
1:29 [w]2Sa 4:9 ble,[w] 30 I will surely carry out today what I swore[x] to you by the LORD, the God of Israel: Solomon your son
1:30 [x]ver 13,17 shall be king after me, and he will sit on my throne in my place."

[a] 5 Or *charioteers* [b] 8 Or *and his friends*

1:3 Abishag came from Shunem, located near the plain of Jezreel in the tribal territory of Issachar.

1:9 *En Rogel* means "spring of Rogel." It was located just south of Jerusalem in the Kidron Valley.

1:12 Eliminating all potential claimants to the throne was common practice in ancient monarchies (see 15:29; 2Ki 10:11; 11:1; see also "Ambitious Princes Among the Hittites" on p. 469).

31 Then Bathsheba bowed low with her face to the ground and, kneeling before the king, said, "May my
lord King David live forever!"
32 King David said, "Call in Zadok the priest, Nathan the prophet and Benaiah son of Jehoiada." When
they came before the king, 33 he said to them: "Take your lord's servants with you and set Solomon my son
on my own mule[y] and take him down to Gihon.[z] 34 There have Zadok the priest and Nathan the prophet
anoint[a] him king over Israel. Blow the trumpet[b] and shout, 'Long live King Solomon!' 35 Then you are to
go up with him, and he is to come and sit on my throne and reign in my place. I have appointed him rul-
er over Israel and Judah."
36 Benaiah son of Jehoiada answered the king, "Amen! May the LORD, the God of my lord the king, so
declare it. 37 As the LORD was with my lord the king, so may he be with[c] Solomon to make his throne even
greater[d] than the throne of my lord King David!"
38 So Zadok[e] the priest, Nathan the prophet, Benaiah son of Jehoiada, the Kerethites[f] and the Pelethites
went down and put Solomon on King David's mule and escorted him to Gihon.[g] 39 Zadok the priest took
the horn of oil[h] from the sacred tent and anointed Solomon. Then they sounded the trumpet and all the
people shouted,[i] "Long live King Solomon!" 40 And all the people went up after him, playing flutes and re-
joicing greatly, so that the ground shook with the sound.
41 Adonijah and all the guests who were with him heard it as they were finishing their feast. On hear-
ing the sound of the trumpet, Joab asked, "What's the meaning of all the noise in the city?"
42 Even as he was speaking, Jonathan[j] son of Abiathar the priest arrived. Adonijah said, "Come in. A
worthy man like you must be bringing good news."[k]
43 "Not at all!" Jonathan answered. "Our lord King David has made Solomon king. 44 The king has sent
with him Zadok the priest, Nathan the prophet, Benaiah son of Jehoiada, the Kerethites and the Pele-
thites, and they have put him on the king's mule, 45 and Zadok the priest and Nathan the prophet have
anointed him king at Gihon. From there they have gone up cheering, and the city resounds[l] with it. That's
the noise you hear. 46 Moreover, Solomon has taken his seat on the royal throne. 47 Also, the royal officials
have come to congratulate our lord King David, saying, 'May your God make Solomon's name more fa-
mous than yours and his throne greater[m] than yours!' And the king bowed in worship on his bed 48 and
said, 'Praise be to the LORD, the God of Israel, who has allowed my eyes to see a successor[n] on my throne
today.' "
49 At this, all Adonijah's guests rose in alarm and dispersed. 50 But Adonijah, in fear of Solomon, went
and took hold of the horns[o] of the altar. 51 Then Solomon was told, "Adonijah is afraid of King Solomon
and is clinging to the horns of the altar. He says, 'Let King Solomon swear to me today that he will not
put his servant to death with the sword.' "
52 Solomon replied, "If he shows himself to be a worthy man, not a hair[p] of his head will fall to the
ground; but if evil is found in him, he will die." 53 Then King Solomon sent men, and they brought him
down from the altar. And Adonijah came and bowed down to King Solomon, and Solomon said, "Go to
your home."

David's Charge to Solomon

2 When the time drew near for David to die,[q] he gave a charge to Solomon his son.
2 "I am about to go the way of all the earth,"[r] he said. "So be strong,[s] show yourself a man, 3 and ob-
serve[t] what the LORD your God requires: Walk in his ways, and keep his decrees and commands, his laws
and requirements, as written in the Law of Moses, so that you may prosper[u] in all you do and wherever
you go, 4 and that the LORD may keep his promise[v] to me: 'If your descendants watch how they live, and
if they walk faithfully[w] before me with all their heart and soul, you will never fail to have a man on the
throne of Israel.'
5 "Now you yourself know what Joab[x] son of Zeruiah did to me—what he did to the two commanders
of Israel's armies, Abner[y] son of Ner and Amasa[z] son of Jether. He killed them, shedding their blood in
peacetime as if in battle, and with that blood stained the belt around his waist and the sandals on his feet.
6 Deal with him according to your wisdom,[a] but do not let his gray head go down to the grave[a] in peace.

1:33 [y] 2Sa 20:6-7 [z] 2Ch 32:30; 33:14
1:34 [a] 1Sa 10:1; 16:3,12; 1Ki 19:16; 2Ki 9:3,13 [b] ver 25; 2Sa 5:3; 15:10
1:37 [c] Jos 1:5,17; 1Sa 20:13 [d] ver 47
1:38 [e] ver 8 [f] 2Sa 8:18 [g] ver 33
1:39 [h] Ex 30:23-32; Ps 89:20 [i] ver 34; 1Sa 10:24
1:42 [j] 2Sa 15:27,36 [k] 2Sa 18:26
1:45 [l] ver 40
1:47 [m] ver 37; Ge 47:31
1:48 [n] 2Sa 7:12; 1Ki 3:6
1:50 [o] 1Ki 2:28
1:52 [p] 1Sa 14:45; 2Sa 14:11
2:1 [q] Ge 47:29; Dt 31:14
2:2 [r] Jos 23:14 [s] Dt 31:7,23; Jos 1:6
2:3 [t] Dt 17:14-20; Jos 1:7 [u] 1Ch 22:13
2:4 [v] 2Sa 7:13,25; 1Ki 8:25 [w] 2Ki 20:3; Ps 132:12
2:5 [x] 2Sa 2:18; 18:5,12,14 [y] 2Sa 3:27 [z] 2Sa 20:10
2:6 [a] ver 9

[a] 6 Hebrew *Sheol*; also in verse 9

1:33 Gihon was the site of a spring on the eastern slope of Mount Zion.

1:38 For information on the Kerethites and Pelethites, see the note on 2 Samuel 15:18.

2:7 [b]2Sa 17:27; 7“But show kindness to the sons of Barzillai[b] of Gilead and let them be among those who eat at your
19:31-39 [c]2Sa 9:7 table.[c] They stood by me when I fled from your brother Absalom.
2:8 [d]2Sa 16:5-13 8“And remember, you have with you Shimei[d] son of Gera, the Benjamite from Bahurim, who called
[e]2Sa 19:18-23 down bitter curses on me the day I went to Mahanaim. When he came down to meet me at the Jordan, I
swore[e] to him by the LORD: ‘I will not put you to death by the sword.’ 9But now, do not consider him in-
2:9 [f]ver 6 nocent. You are a man of wisdom;[f] you will know what to do to him. Bring his gray head down to the
grave in blood.”
2:10 [g]Ac 2:29; 10Then David rested with his fathers and was buried[g] in the City of David.[h] 11He had reigned[i] forty
13:36 [h]2Sa 5:7 2:11 [i]2Sa 5:4,5 years over Israel—seven years in Hebron and thirty-three in Jerusalem. 12So Solomon sat on the throne[j]
2:12 [j]1Ch 29:23 [k]2Ch 1:1 of his father David, and his rule was firmly established.[k]

Solomon’s Throne Established

13Now Adonijah, the son of Haggith, went to Bathsheba, Solomon’s mother. Bathsheba asked him, “Do
2:13 [l]1Sa 16:4 you come peacefully?”[l]
He answered, “Yes, peacefully.” 14Then he added, “I have something to say to you.”
“You may say it,” she replied.
15“As you know,” he said, “the kingdom was mine. All Israel looked to me as their king. But things
changed, and the kingdom has gone to my brother; for it has come to him from the LORD. 16Now I have
one request to make of you. Do not refuse me.”
“You may make it,” she said.
2:17 [m]1Ki 1:3 17So he continued, “Please ask King Solomon—he will not refuse you—to give me Abishag[m] the Shu-
nammite as my wife.”
18“Very well,” Bathsheba replied, “I will speak to the king for you.”
19When Bathsheba went to King Solomon to speak to him for Adonijah, the king stood up to meet
2:19 [n]1Ki 15:13 her, bowed down to her and sat down on his throne. He had a throne brought for the king’s mother,[n] and
[o]Ps 45:9 she sat down at his right hand.[o]
20“I have one small request to make of you,” she said. “Do not refuse me.”
The king replied, “Make it, my mother; I will not refuse you.”
2:21 [p]1Ki 1:3 21So she said, “Let Abishag[p] the Shunammite be given in marriage to your brother Adonijah.”
2:22 [q]2Sa 12:8; 22King Solomon answered his mother, “Why do you request Abishag[q] the Shunammite for Adonijah?
1Ki 1:3 [r]1Ch 3:2 You might as well request the kingdom for him—after all, he is my older brother[r]—yes, for him and for
Abiathar the priest and Joab son of Zeruiah!”
2:23 [s]Ru 1:17 23Then King Solomon swore by the LORD: “May God deal with me, be it ever so severely,[s] if Adonijah
does not pay with his life for this request! 24And now, as surely as the LORD lives—he who has estab-
lished me securely on the throne of my father David and has founded a dynasty for me as he prom-
2:24 [t]2Sa 7:11; ised[t]—Adonijah shall be put to death today!” 25So King Solomon gave orders to Benaiah[u] son of Jehoi-
1Ch 22:10 2:25 [u]2Sa 8:18 ada, and he struck down Adonijah and he died.
2:26 [v]1Sa 22:20 26To Abiathar[v] the priest the king said, “Go back to your fields in Anathoth.[w] You deserve to die, but I
[w]Jos 21:18 [x]2Sa 15:24 will not put you to death now, because you carried the ark[x] of the Sovereign LORD before my father Da-
[y]1Sa 23:6 vid and shared all my father’s hardships.”[y] 27So Solomon removed Abiathar from the priesthood of the
2:27 [z]1Sa 2:27-36 LORD, fulfilling[z] the word the LORD had spoken at Shiloh about the house of Eli.
28When the news reached Joab, who had conspired with Adonijah though not with Absalom, he fled
2:28 [a]1Ki 1:7,50 to the tent of the LORD and took hold of the horns[a] of the altar. 29King Solomon was told that Joab had
2:29 [b]ver 25 fled to the tent of the LORD and was beside the altar. Then Solomon ordered Benaiah[b] son of Jehoiada, “Go,
strike him down!”
2:30 [c]Ex 21:14 30So Benaiah entered the tent of the LORD and said to Joab, “The king says, ‘Come out![c]’ ”
But he answered, “No, I will die here.”
Benaiah reported to the king, “This is how Joab answered me.”
2:31 [d]Nu 35:33; Dt 19:13; 21:8-9 31Then the king commanded Benaiah, “Do as he says. Strike him down and bury him, and so clear me
2:32 [e]Jdg 9:57; Ps 7:16 and my father’s house of the guilt of the innocent blood[d] that Joab shed. 32The LORD will repay[e] him for

---

2:17–22 Solomon understood Adonijah’s request to marry Abishag as another attempt to gain the throne. Although Abishag had remained a virgin while caring for David (1:1–4), the people would have regarded her as a member of David’s harem—meaning that Adonijah’s marriage to her would have strengthened his position.

2:28–34 For a discussion of the legal provisions with regard to murder in ancient Israel, see the note on Numbers 35:19.

the blood he shed,[f] because without the knowledge of my father David he attacked two men and killed
them with the sword. Both of them—Abner son of Ner, commander of Israel's army, and Amasa[g] son of
Jether, commander of Judah's army—were better[h] men and more upright than he. 33 May the guilt of
their blood rest on the head of Joab and his descendants forever. But
on David and his descendants, his house and his throne, may there
be the LORD's peace forever."
34 So Benaiah son of Jehoiada went up and struck down Joab and
killed him, and he was buried on his own land[a] in the desert. 35 The
king put Benaiah[i] son of Jehoiada over the army in Joab's position
and replaced Abiathar with Zadok[j] the priest.
36 Then the king sent for Shimei[k] and said to him, "Build yourself
a house in Jerusalem and live there, but do not go anywhere else.
37 The day you leave and cross the Kidron Valley,[l] you can be sure you
will die; your blood will be on your own head."[m]
38 Shimei answered the king, "What you say is good. Your servant
will do as my lord the king has said." And Shimei stayed in Jerusa-
lem for a long time.
39 But three years later, two of Shimei's slaves ran off to Achish[n]
son of Maacah, king of Gath, and Shimei was told, "Your slaves are
in Gath." 40 At this, he saddled his donkey and went to Achish at Gath
in search of his slaves. So Shimei went away and brought the slaves
back from Gath.
41 When Solomon was told that Shimei had gone from Jerusalem to Gath and had returned, 42 the king
summoned Shimei and said to him, "Did I not make you swear by the LORD and warn you, 'On the day
you leave to go anywhere else, you can be sure you will die'? At that time you said to me, 'What you say is
good. I will obey.' 43 Why then did you not keep your oath to the LORD and obey the command I gave you?"
44 The king also said to Shimei, "You know in your heart all the wrong[o] you did to my father David. Now
the LORD will repay you for your wrongdoing. 45 But King Solomon will be blessed, and David's throne
will remain secure[p] before the LORD forever."
46 Then the king gave the order to Benaiah son of Jehoiada, and he went out and struck Shimei down
and killed him.

The kingdom was now firmly established[q] in Solomon's hands.

ANCIENT VOICES

The decreed brick lifted its head toward him, stretched out its neck toward him to build the holy temple.

On that day in a night vision (he saw)*
his king, Gudea saw the lord Ningirsu,
(and) he commanded him to build his temple.
The Eninnu, its stature being the greatest,
he displayed to him.

*Words in parentheses added by translator for clarity or where text has gaps

—THE CYLINDERS OF GUDEA

See "The Cylinders of Gudea" article.

Solomon Asks for Wisdom

3 Solomon made an alliance with Pharaoh king of Egypt and married[r] his daughter.[s] He brought her
to the City of David[t] until he finished building his palace[u] and the temple of the LORD, and the wall
around Jerusalem. 2 The people, however, were still sacrificing at the high places,[v] because a temple had
not yet been built for the Name of the LORD. 3 Solomon showed his love[w] for the LORD by walking accord-
ing to the statutes[x] of his father David, except that he offered sacrifices and burned incense on the high
places.
4 The king went to Gibeon[y] to offer sacrifices, for that was the most important high place, and Solo-
mon offered a thousand burnt offerings on that altar. 5 At Gibeon the LORD appeared[z] to Solomon during
the night in a dream,[a] and God said, "Ask for whatever you want me to give you."
6 Solomon answered, "You have shown great kindness to your servant, my father David, because he
was faithful[b] to you and righteous and upright in heart. You have continued this great kindness to him
and have given him a son[c] to sit on his throne this very day.
7 "Now, O LORD my God, you have made your servant king in place of my father David. But I am only

2:32 [f]Jdg 9:24 [g]2Sa 3:27; 20:10 [h]2Ch 21:13
2:35 [i]1Ki 4:4 [j]ver 27; 1Ch 29:22
2:36 [k]ver 8; 2Sa 16:5
2:37 [l]2Sa 15:23 [m]Lev 20:9; Jos 2:19; 2Sa 1:16
2:39 [n]1Sa 27:2
2:44 [o]1Sa 25:39; 2Sa 16:5-13; Eze 17:19
2:45 [p]2Sa 7:13; Pr 25:5
2:46 [q]ver 12; 2Ch 1:1
3:1 [r]1Ki 7:8 [s]1Ki 9:24 [t]2Sa 5:7 [u]1Ki 7:1; 9:15,19
3:2 [v]Lev 17:3-5; Dt 12:2,4-5; 1Ki 22:43
3:3 [w]Dt 6:5; Ps 31:23; 1Co 8:3 [x]1Ki 2:3; 9:4; 11:4,6,38
3:4 [y]1Ch 16:39
3:5 [z]1Ki 9:2 [a]Nu 12:6; Mt 1:20
3:6 [b]1Ki 2:4; 9:4 [c]1Ki 1:48

[a] 34 *Or buried in his tomb*

2:39–40 Regarding Achish of Gath, see "The Ekron Inscriptions of Akhayus" on page 428.
3:1 The identity of this pharaoh is somewhat problematic (see "The Pharaoh Whose Daughter Solomon Married" on p. 493).
3:2 "High places" were local, open-air shrines, frequently, but not always, located on a hill. Many high places were located in spots that had originally been sacred to the Canaanites but had become venues for Israelite worship. (See "The High Places" on p. 1318.)
3:4 See "Sacrifices and Offerings in the Bible and the Ancient Near East" on page 158 and "Gibeon" on page 318.
3:5 Revelation through dreams is well attested in the ancient world, including in the Bible. See "Dream Oracles in the Ancient World" on page 741.

3:7 [d]Nu 27:17; 1Ch 29:1 **3:8** [e]Dt 7:6 [f]Ge 15:5 **3:9** [g]2Sa 14:17; Jas 1:5 [h]Pr 2:3-9; Heb 5:14 [i]Ps 72:1-2 **3:11** [j]Jas 4:3 **3:12** [k]1Jn 5:14-15 [l]1Ki 4:29,30, 31; 5:12; 10:23; Ecc 1:16 **3:13** [m]Mt 6:33; Eph 3:20 [n]1Ki 4:21-24; Pr 3:1-2,16 [o]1Ki 10:23 **3:14** [p]ver 6; Pr 3:1-2,16 [q]Ps 61:6; 91:16 **3:15** [r]Ge 41:7 [s]1Ki 8:65 [t]Mk 6:21 [u]Est 1:3, 9; Da 5:1

a little child[d] and do not know how to carry out my duties. 8 Your servant is here among the people you
have chosen,[e] a great people, too numerous to count or number.[f] 9 So give your servant a discerning[g]
heart to govern your people and to distinguish[h] between right and wrong. For who is able[i] to govern this
great people of yours?"
10 The Lord was pleased that Solomon had asked for this. 11 So God said to him, "Since you have asked[j]
for this and not for long life or wealth for yourself, nor have asked for the death of your enemies but for
discernment in administering justice, 12 I will do what you have asked.[k] I will give you a wise[l] and discern-
ing heart, so that there will never have been anyone like you, nor will there ever be. 13 Moreover, I will give
you what you have not[m] asked for—both riches and honor[n]—so that in your lifetime you will have no
equal[o] among kings. 14 And if you walk[p] in my ways and obey my statutes and commands as David your
father did, I will give you a long life."[q] 15 Then Solomon awoke[r]—and he realized it had been a dream.

He returned to Jerusalem, stood before the ark of the Lord's covenant and sacrificed burnt offerings[s]
and fellowship offerings.[a][t] Then he gave a feast[u] for all his court.

A Wise Ruling

16 Now two prostitutes came to the king and stood before him. 17 One of them said, "My lord, this wom-
an and I live in the same house. I had a baby while she was there with me. 18 The third day after my child
was born, this woman also had a baby. We were alone; there was no one in the house but the two of us.

[a] 15 Traditionally *peace offerings*

3:16 Brothels were common in ancient Near Eastern cities. Most ancient prostitutes were slaves, often daughters who had been sold by their parents or destitute women who had never married or had lost their husbands. See "Prostitution in the Ancient World" on page 284.

ANCIENT TEXTS AND ARTIFACTS

The Cylinders of Gudea

1 KINGS 3 Two large, inscribed clay cylinders were discovered at the end of the nineteenth century. After their broken pieces had been meticulously reassembled, the cylinders revealed a lengthy **Sumerian**[1] composition memorializing the building of a new temple by a Mesopotamian ruler named Gudea (r. c. 2112–2095 B.C. or shortly before.)

The cylinders claim that the deity Ningirsu appeared to Gudea in a dream, commanding him to build his new temple, the Eninnu. Gudea prayed and slept in the temple already existing on the site, waiting for a second dream; in it Ningirsu revealed the new temple's plan. The cylinders provide detailed information about the preparation and purification of the temple area and specifics about conscripting workers, the acquisition of building materials and the laying of the foundations. Next, they describe the building process, decorations and furnishings. Gudea then installed the statues of Ningirsu and his consort, Baba, offered dedicatory prayers and hosted a seven-day banquet. Upon completion of the project, Gudea recorded, he was blessed and promised long life by his personal gods.

It has been suggested that the account of Solomon's construction of the Jerusalem temple follows this same general outline. Since divine sanction for Solomon's temple building had been given to his father, David (2Sa 7:12–13), Solomon declared his intention to build **Yahweh**'s temple in fulfillment of the divine command (1Ki 5:3–5). This is followed by a description of the arrangements between Hiram of Tyre and Solomon, which provided for Hiram to contribute cedars and pine for the building project, as well as for Solomon's levy for laborers and the quarrying of stone for the foundation (5:6–18). The details of the construction process, including the layout and dimensions of the individual rooms, are included (6:1–38), as are directives regarding the furnishings (7:13–51).

Just as Gudea installed the statues of his deities to symbolize their presence in the temple, Solomon brought the ark of the covenant, which represented God's footstool (1Ch 28:2),[2] into the temple in Jerusalem (1Ki 8:1–21). He then offered his prayer of dedication and hosted a seven-day feast (8:22–66). Finally, the Lord appeared to the king to bless him and promise him an everlasting throne over Israel, provided Solomon would continue to follow his commands (9:1–9).

That the account of Solomon's temple building follows the same structure need not surprise or alarm the reader. The inspired writers worked within familiar cultural and literary structures to faithfully transmit the history of Israel and the Word of God.

[1]See Glossary on page 2080 for definitions of bolded words. [2]See "The Tabernacle and the Ark" on page 153.

[19]"During the night this woman's son died because she lay on him. [20]So she got up in the middle of
the night and took my son from my side while I your servant was asleep. She put him by her breast and
put her dead son by my breast. [21]The next morning, I got up to nurse my son—and he was dead! But
when I looked at him closely in the morning light, I saw that it wasn't the son I had borne."
[22]The other woman said, "No! The living one is my son; the dead one is yours."
But the first one insisted, "No! The dead one is yours; the living one is mine." And so they argued before the king.
[23]The king said, "This one says, 'My son is alive and your son is dead,' while that one says, 'No! Your son is dead and mine is alive.' "
[24]Then the king said, "Bring me a sword." So they brought a sword for the king. [25]He then gave an or-
der: "Cut the living child in two and give half to one and half to the other."
[26]The woman whose son was alive was filled with compassion[v] for her son and said to the king, "Please, my lord, give her the living baby! Don't kill him!"
But the other said, "Neither I nor you shall have him. Cut him in two!"
[27]Then the king gave his ruling: "Give the living baby to the first woman. Do not kill him; she is his mother."
[28]When all Israel heard the verdict the king had given, they held the king in awe, because they saw that he had wisdom[w] from God to administer justice.

3:26 [v]Ge 43:30; Isa 49:15; Jer 31:20; Hos 11:8

3:28 [w]ver 9,11-12; Col 2:3

Solomon's Officials and Governors

4 So King Solomon ruled over all Israel. [2]And these were his chief officials:

Azariah[x] son of Zadok—the priest;
[3]Elihoreph and Ahijah, sons of Shisha—secretaries;
Jehoshaphat[y] son of Ahilud—recorder;

4:2 [x]1Ch 6:10

4:3 [y]2Sa 8:16

4:1–19 The 12 district governors were responsible on a rotating basis for taxation and provision of food for Solomon's court and animals (vv. 27–28). The geographical divisions reflected social and political realities rather than traditional tribal boundaries. (See "Egyptian and Israelite Administration" on p. 486.)

Egyptian and Israelite Administration

1 KINGS 4 Archaeological investigations of ancient Israelite sites have shown that the Israelites had adopted an Egyptian script, hieratic, for recording numbers and measures. For example, several **ostraca** found at Arad (see "Map 7") in the Judean Negev employed hieratic symbols for numerals in listing commodities.[1] This demonstrates that at least in some respects Egyptian administrative models influenced Israel; scholars continue to look for other parallels.

One of the more widely discussed correspondences involves Solomon's division of Israel into 12 administrative districts (1Ki 4:7–19). The governors of these districts "supplied provisions for the king and the royal household. Each one had to provide supplies for one month in the year" (v. 7). According to a recently discovered **stele,** Solomon's contemporary, Sheshonk I of Egypt's Twenty-first Dynasty,[2] instituted a similar policy for provisioning the temple of Arsaphes in Herakleopolis. He divided the nome (administrative district) of Herakleopolis into 12 sections, with each one responsible for supporting the temple for one month per year. As with 1 Kings 4, the Egyptian stele defines each of the 12 districts, as well as designating their respective administrators. It is an open question whether the Egyptian model influenced the Israelite version or the other way around, or whether the parallel is coincidental. One thing is clear, however: The Israelites did not live in isolation; they both knew and were influenced by Egyptian (and other) models.

[1]See "The Arad Ostraca" on page 1215. [2]See "The Campaign of Shishak" on page 635.

4:4 [z]1Ki 2:35 4 Benaiah[z] son of Jehoiada—commander in chief;
[a]1Ki 2:27 Zadok[a] and Abiathar—priests;
5 Azariah son of Nathan—in charge of the district officers;
Zabud son of Nathan—a priest and personal adviser to the king;
6 Ahishar—in charge of the palace;
Adoniram son of Abda—in charge of forced labor.

7 Solomon also had twelve district governors over all Israel, who supplied provisions for the king and
the royal household. Each one had to provide supplies for one month in the year. 8 These are their names:

4:8 [b]Jos 24:33 Ben-Hur—in the hill country[b] of Ephraim;
4:9 [c]Jdg 1:35 [d]Jos 21:16 9 Ben-Deker—in Makaz, Shaalbim,[c] Beth Shemesh[d] and Elon Bethhanan;
4:10 [e]Jos 15:35 [f]Jos 12:17 10 Ben-Hesed—in Arubboth (Socoh[e] and all the land of Hepher[f] were his);
4:11 [g]Jos 11:2 11 Ben-Abinadab—in Naphoth Dor[a][g] (he was married to Taphath daughter of Solomon);
4:12 [h]Jos 17:11; Jdg 5:19 [i]Jos 3:16 [j]1Ki 19:16 [k]1Ch 6:68 12 Baana son of Ahilud—in Taanach and Megiddo, and in all of Beth Shan[h] next to Zarethan[i] below
Jezreel, from Beth Shan to Abel Meholah[j] across to Jokmeam;[k]
4:13 [l]Nu 32:41 [m]Dt 3:4 13 Ben-Geber—in Ramoth Gilead (the settlements of Jair[l] son of Manasseh in Gilead were his, as
well as the district of Argob in Bashan and its sixty large walled cities[m] with bronze gate bars);
4:14 [n]Jos 13:26 14 Ahinadab son of Iddo—in Mahanaim;[n]
4:15 [o]2Sa 15:27 15 Ahimaaz[o]—in Naphtali (he had married Basemath daughter of Solomon);
4:16 [p]2Sa 15:32 16 Baana son of Hushai[p]—in Asher and in Aloth;
17 Jehoshaphat son of Paruah—in Issachar;
4:18 [q]1Ki 1:8 18 Shimei[q] son of Ela—in Benjamin;
4:19 [r]Dt 3:8-10 19 Geber son of Uri—in Gilead (the country of Sihon king of the Amorites and the country of Og[r]
king of Bashan). He was the only governor over the district.

Solomon's Daily Provisions

4:20 [s]Ge 22:17; 32:12; 1Ki 3:8 20 The people of Judah and Israel were as numerous as the sand[s] on the seashore; they ate, they drank
4:21 [t]2Ch 9:26; Ps 72:11 and they were happy. 21 And Solomon ruled[t] over all the kingdoms from the River[b][u] to the land of the
[u]Jos 1:4; Ps 72:8 [v]Ge 15:18 Philistines, as far as the border of Egypt.[v] These countries brought tribute[w] and were Solomon's subjects
[w]Ps 68:29 all his life.

22 Solomon's daily provisions were thirty cors[c] of fine flour and sixty cors[d] of meal, 23 ten head of stall-
fed cattle, twenty of pasture-fed cattle and a hundred sheep and goats, as well as deer, gazelles, roebucks
4:24 [x]Ps 72:11 [y]1Ch 22:9 and choice fowl. 24 For he ruled over all the kingdoms west of the River, from Tiphsah[x] to Gaza, and had
4:25 [z]Jdg 20:1 [a]Jer 23:6 peace[y] on all sides. 25 During Solomon's lifetime Judah and Israel, from Dan to Beersheba,[z] lived in safe-
[b]Mic 4:4; Zec 3:10 ty,[a] each man under his own vine and fig tree.[b]
4:26 [c]1Ki 10:26; 2Ch 1:14 26 Solomon had four[e] thousand stalls for chariot horses,[c] and twelve thousand horses.[f]
4:27 [d]ver 7 27 The district officers,[d] each in his month, supplied provisions for King Solomon and all who came
to the king's table. They saw to it that nothing was lacking. 28 They also brought to the proper place their
quotas of barley and straw for the chariot horses and the other horses.

Solomon's Wisdom

4:29 [e]1Ki 3:12 29 God gave Solomon wisdom[e] and very great insight, and a breadth of understanding as measure-
less as the sand on the seashore. 30 Solomon's wisdom was greater than the wisdom of all the men of the
4:30 [f]Ge 25:6 [g]Ac 7:22 East,[f] and greater than all the wisdom of Egypt.[g] 31 He was wiser[h] than any other man, including Ethan
4:31 [h]1Ki 3:12; 1Ch 2:6; 6:33; 15:19; Ps 89 Title

[a] 11 Or *in the heights of Dor* [b] 21 That is, the Euphrates; also in verse 24 [c] 22 That is, probably about 185 bushels (about 6.6 kiloliters) [d] 22 That is, probably about 375 bushels (about 13.2 kiloliters) [e] 26 Some Septuagint manuscripts (see also 2 Chron. 9:25); Hebrew *forty* [f] 26 Or *charioteers*

4:20–21 Solomon reigned from the Euphrates River to the border of Egypt. The territory from Tiphsah (on the southern bend of the Euphrates) to Gaza (on the southeastern Mediterranean coast) included Syria and Sinai, as well as, in all likelihood, territory east of the Jordan River.

4:26 Since Solomon had 1,400 chariots (10:26; 2Ch 1:14), his stables included stalls for 2,800 chariot horses (two for each chariot), with additional stalls for 1,200 horses. By way of comparison, an Assyrian account of the battle of Qarqar in 853 B.C. (about a century after Solomon) speaks of 1,200 chariots from Damascus, 700 chariots from Hamath and 2,000 chariots from Israel (the northern kingdom). See "Horses and Chariots in Ancient Warfare" on page 114.

4:29–34 In addition to the wisdom required to govern a vast kingdom, Solomon had been endowed by God with a breadth of knowledge unrivaled in his time. Ancient wisdom included music, poetry, proverbial sayings for wise conduct and what we would now call science. Solomon's interest in nature went beyond its basis for

the Ezrahite—wiser than Heman, Calcol and Darda, the sons of Mahol. And his fame spread to all the
surrounding nations. 32 He spoke three thousand proverbs[i] and his songs[j] numbered a thousand and five. 4:32 [i]Pr 1:1;
33 He described plant life, from the cedar of Lebanon to the hyssop that grows out of walls. He also taught Ecc 12:9 [j]SS 1:1
about animals and birds, reptiles and fish. 34 Men of all nations came to listen to Solomon's wisdom, sent
by all the kings[k] of the world, who had heard of his wisdom. 4:34 [k]1Ki 10:1;
2Ch 9:23

Preparations for Building the Temple

5 When Hiram[l] king of Tyre heard that Solomon had been anointed king to succeed his father David, 5:1 [l]ver 10,18;
he sent his envoys to Solomon, because he had always been on friendly terms with David. 2 Solomon 2Sa 5:11;
sent back this message to Hiram: 1Ch 14:1

3 "You know that because of the wars[m] waged against my father David from all sides, he could 5:3 [m]1Ch 22:8;
not build a temple for the Name of the LORD his God until the LORD put his enemies under his feet. 28:3
4 But now the LORD my God has given me rest[n] on every side, and there is no adversary or disas- 5:4 [n]1Ki 4:24;
ter. 5 I intend, therefore, to build a temple[o] for the Name of the LORD my God, as the LORD told my 1Ch 22:9 5:5 [o]1Ch 17:12
father David, when he said, 'Your son whom I will put on the throne in your place will build the [p]2Sa 7:13; 1Ch 22:10
temple for my Name.'[p]

---

proverbs. Such knowledge also provided a perspective for understanding life in this world. Solomon's classification of creatures into the categories of animals, birds, reptiles and fish revealed another aspect of his comprehensive knowledge.

The phrase "men of the East" (v. 30) is a general reference to the peoples of Mesopotamia (see Ge 29:1) and Arabia (see Jer 49:28; Eze 25:4,10). Numerous examples of Mesopotamian wisdom literature have been recovered (see "Ancient Near Eastern Wisdom" on p. 960). Examples of Egyptian wisdom literature include the proverbs of Ptahhotep (c. 2450 B.C.) and Amenemope (see "The Teaching of Amenemope" on p. 994).

4:32 Solomon was famous for his proverbs and riddles. On the popularity and function of riddles in the ancient world, see the note on Judges 14:12–14.

Phoenicia

1 KINGS 5 The **Phoenicians** were descendants of the people of **Canaan** (cf. Ge 10:15). Phoenicia was never organized as a nation-state but consisted of a group of independent port cities along the northern seacoast of Israel. Phoenicia's main centers included Arwad, Byblos ("Map 5"), Sidon and Tyre[1] (both "Map 6"). Relatively few **Iron Age**[2] remains have been located at these sites.

Following the socioeconomic collapse of the **Late Bronze Age**,[3] the Phoenicians established themselves as the preeminent sea traders in the Mediterranean. Their craftsmen's need for metals and other goods led merchants to establish colonies throughout the Mediterranean, as far away as Spain and the Atlantic coast of northern Africa. Phoenician fame also spread from its lumber trade[4] and its thriving purple dye industry. A noted legacy is the Phoenician alphabet, which the Greeks borrowed, probably during the eighth century B.C.

Solomon solicited Phoenician expertise for the construction of the temple and for the maritime gold trade (1Ki 5; 9:26–28).[5] The king of Tyre provided cedar and pine in exchange for wheat and olive oil and sent experienced sailors to assist Solomon's fleet. But the Phoenicians also exported their religion to Israel. The Sidonian princess Jezebel, who was given in marriage to Omri's son Ahab, used her position to promote Baal worship in Israel (16:29–33; 18).[6] Phoenician influence also penetrated the kingdom of Judah, including, among other things, the practice of child sacrifice in the Hinnom Valley of Jerusalem (2Ki 23:10).

Excavations at Carthage in northern Africa, the most famous of the Phoenician/Punic colonies, provide grim evidence of the longstanding practice of child sacrifice (eighth–second centuries B.C.). Thousands of urns containing the charred bones of infants and children have been excavated from the ritual burial precinct of Tannit, a Phoenician goddess. These Phoenician religious practices became a stumbling block to both Israel and Judah (e.g., 2Ki 16:3; 21:6) and a recurring theme of Israelite prophetic rebuke (Jer 19:5–6; 32:35; Eze 16:20–22; Mic 6:7).[7]

[1]See "Sidon" on page 1536 and "The Downfall of Tyre" on page 1345. [2]See "Archaeological Periods" chart on page xx in the front of this Bible. [3]See "Changes in Canaan" on page 1358. [4]See "Byblos" on page 1349. [5]See "Solomon's Temple and Other Ancient Temples" on page 620. [6]See "Baal and the Fertility Cults" on page 1414. [7]See "Human Sacrifice in the Ancient Near East" on page 182.

6“So give orders that cedars of Lebanon be cut for me. My men will work with yours, and I will
pay you for your men whatever wages you set. You know that we have no one so skilled in felling
timber as the Sidonians.”

7When Hiram heard Solomon's message, he was greatly pleased and said, “Praise be to the LORD to-
day, for he has given David a wise son to rule over this great nation.”
8So Hiram sent word to Solomon:

“I have received the message you sent me and will do all you want in providing the cedar and
5:9 [q]Ezr 3:7 pine logs. 9My men will haul them down from Lebanon to the sea[q], and I will float them in rafts
[r]Eze 27:17; by sea to the place you specify. There I will separate them and you can take them away. And you
Ac 12:20 are to grant my wish by providing food[r] for my royal household.”

10In this way Hiram kept Solomon supplied with all the cedar and pine logs he wanted, 11and Solo-
mon gave Hiram twenty thousand cors[a] of wheat as food for his household, in addition to twenty thou-
sand baths[b,c] of pressed olive oil. Solomon continued to do this for Hiram year after year. 12The LORD
5:12 [s]1Ki 3:12 gave Solomon wisdom,[s] just as he had promised him. There were peaceful relations between Hiram and
[t]Am 1:9 Solomon, and the two of them made a treaty.[t]
5:13 [u]1Ki 9:15 13King Solomon conscripted laborers[u] from all Israel—thirty thousand men. 14He sent them off to
Lebanon in shifts of ten thousand a month, so that they spent one month in Lebanon and two months at
5:14 [v]1Ki 4:6; home. Adoniram[v] was in charge of the forced labor. 15Solomon had seventy thousand carriers and eighty
2Ch 10:18
5:16 [w]1Ki 9:23 thousand stonecutters in the hills, 16as well as thirty-three hundred[d] foremen[w] who supervised the proj-
5:17 [x]1Ki 6:7 ect and directed the workmen. 17At the king's command they removed from the quarry[x] large blocks of
[y]1Ch 22:2 quality stone[y] to provide a foundation of dressed stone for the temple. 18The craftsmen of Solomon and
5:18 [z]Jos 13:5 Hiram and the men of Gebal[e][z] cut and prepared the timber and stone for the building of the temple.

Solomon Builds the Temple

6 In the four hundred and eightieth[f] year after the Israelites had come out of Egypt, in the fourth year
of Solomon's reign over Israel, in the month of Ziv, the second month, he began to build the temple
6:1 [a]Ac 7:47 of the LORD.[a]
6:2 [b]Eze 41:1 2The temple[b] that King Solomon built for the LORD was sixty cubits long, twenty wide and thirty high.[g]
3The portico at the front of the main hall of the temple extended the width of the temple, that is twenty
6:4 [c]Eze 40:16; cubits,[h] and projected ten cubits[i] from the front of the temple. 4He made narrow clerestory windows[c] in
41:16 the temple. 5Against the walls of the main hall and inner sanctuary he built a structure around the build-
6:5 [d]ver 16,19- ing, in which there were side rooms.[d] 6The lowest floor was five cubits[j] wide, the middle floor six cubits[k]
21; Eze 41:5-6 and the third floor seven.[l] He made offset ledges around the outside of the temple so that nothing would
be inserted into the temple walls.
6:7 [e]Ex 20:25 7In building the temple, only blocks dressed[e] at the quarry were used, and no hammer, chisel or any
[f]Dt 27:5 other iron tool[f] was heard at the temple site while it was being built.
8The entrance to the lowest[m] floor was on the south side of the temple; a stairway led up to the mid-
dle level and from there to the third. 9So he built the temple and completed it, roofing it with beams and
6:9 [g]ver 14,38 cedar[g] planks. 10And he built the side rooms all along the temple. The height of each was five cubits, and
they were attached to the temple by beams of cedar.

[a] *11* That is, probably about 125,000 bushels (about 4,400 kiloliters) [b] *11* Septuagint (see also 2 Chron. 2:10); Hebrew *twenty cors* [c] *11* That is, about 115,000 gallons (about 440 kiloliters) [d] *16* Hebrew; some Septuagint manuscripts (see also 2 Chron. 2:2,18) *thirty-six hundred* [e] *18* That is, Byblos [f] *1* Hebrew; Septuagint *four hundred and fortieth* [g] *2* That is, about 90 feet (about 27 meters) long and 30 feet (about 9 meters) wide and 45 feet (about 13.5 meters) high [h] *3* That is, about 30 feet (about 9 meters) [i] *3* That is, about 15 feet (about 4.5 meters) [j] *6* That is, about 7 1/2 feet (about 2.3 meters); also in verses 10 and 24 [k] *6* That is, about 9 feet (about 2.7 meters) [l] *6* That is, about 10 1/2 feet (about 3.1 meters) [m] *8* Septuagint; Hebrew *middle*

5:6 Lebanon's cedars were widely used in the ancient Near East in the construction of royal houses and temples. (See “Cedars of Lebanon” on p. 1043.)

5:7 Although Hiram's statement obviously demonstrated an acknowledgment of the God of Israel, it is unlikely that he had chosen Solomon's religion over his own. It was common practice for the people of one nation to recognize the deities of another (cf. 10:9).

5:18 “Gebal” is Byblos (see the NIV text note), an important ancient city on the coast between Sidon and Arvad. Its natural harbor made it an important trade and religious center. See “Byblos” on page 1349.

6:2 The temple was patterned after the tabernacle; its dimensions in most instances seem to be double those of the tabernacle. Its architectural design reflects the long-room, tripartite temple plan typical of Syro-Phoenician construction (6:2–10; see “Solomon's Temple and Other Ancient Temples” on p. 620).

Many archaeological parallels—such as the stone and cedar beam technique (6:36)—can be drawn to the methods of construction used in the temple. Interestingly, evidence for the largest bronze-casting industry ever found in the region comes from the same locale (Zarethan in the Jordan Valley) and period (c. 1000 B.C.) as that indicated in Scripture.

11 The word of the LORD came to Solomon: 12 "As for this temple you are building, if you follow my de-
crees, carry out my regulations and keep all my commands and obey them, I will fulfill through you the
promise[h] I gave to David your father. 13 And I will live among the Israelites and will not abandon[i] my peo-
ple Israel."
14 So Solomon built the temple and completed[j] it. 15 He lined its interior walls with cedar boards, pan-
eling them from the floor of the temple to the ceiling,[k] and covered the floor of the temple with planks
of pine. 16 He partitioned off twenty cubits[a] at the rear of the temple with cedar boards from floor to ceil-
ing to form within the temple an inner sanctuary, the Most Holy Place.[l] 17 The main hall in front of this

6:12 [h]2Sa 7:12-16; 1Ki 2:4; 9:5 **6:13** [i]Ex 25:8; Lev 26:11; Dt 31:6; Heb 13:5 **6:14** [j]ver 9,38 **6:15** [k]1Ki 7:7 **6:16** [l]Ex 26:33; Lev 16:2; 1Ki 8:6

[a] 16 That is, about 30 feet (about 9 meters)

Solomon and the Israelite Empire

1 KINGS 6 Solomon inherited a vast empire, extending from the Euphrates to the Gulf of Aqaba and from Tyre to Egypt. He maintained this kingdom during a 40-year reign through diplomacy, industry and effective administration. Although Israel dominated the political scene of his day, the name Solomon is not attested in extrabiblical records discovered to date. Even so, archaeology gives us a better appreciation for the glory of Solomon's age.

Administration

✣ Efficient internal administration facilitated control of the empire. Royal administrators included a chief of staff, secretaries, a military commander, a supervisor of forced labor, royal priests, a recorder (for foreign affairs) and a chief over regional districts.

✣ Twelve regional governors each furnished a month's support for the central government. A similar administrative structure may have been in place in Egypt.[1]

Fortified Cities

✣ An older contemporary, Pharaoh Siamun, may have conquered the Philistine city of Gezer ("Map 4") and given it to his daughter, with whom Solomon is thought to have entered a marriage alliance (the identity of this pharaoh has not been authoritatively confirmed).[2] Excavations at Gezer confirm its destruction in the early tenth century B.C.[3]

✣ Archaeological finds confirm the rebuilding of Gezer, **Megiddo** ("Map 6") and **Hazor** ("Map 6"), as described in 1 Kings 9:15.[4]

✣ Fortified cities controlled the major trade arteries around and through the Holy Land. More than 40 small, tenth-century B.C. fortresses have been discovered in the southern Negev.

✣ Storehouses have been excavated at Hazor, Beth Shemesh ("Map 4") and other locations. Similar structures at Megiddo, previously identified as "Solomon's stables," have more recently been assigned archaeologically to the time of Jeroboam. However, these structures may have been built on foundations from an earlier period.[5]

Trade and Wealth

✣ Sources of revenue were foreign trade, caravan tolls, the export of refined copper and tribute from vassal nations. Solomon capitalized on a vigorous import-export trade in horses and chariots with Egypt, **Anatolia**, Syria and **Mesopotamia**.

✣ An alliance with Hiram, king of Tyre, allowed Solomon to develop trade between the Red Sea and the Mediterranean Sea. Hiram provided experienced seamen and experts in both ship and harbor construction.

✣ The visit of the queen of Sheba to Jerusalem was probably concluded with a trade agreement. Israelite sea trading ventures from Ezion Geber on the Gulf of Aqaba threatened overland trade, previously monopolized by Arabian tribes. The precise location of Ezion Geber[6] is disputed (but see proposed location on "Map 5").

✣ Subjugation of Ammon, **Moab**, Edom and Syria gave Solomon control over the major north-south land routes through the region.[7]

The Temple and the Palace

✣ Hiram furnished artisans and architects for Solomon's construction projects. Nothing remains of the Jerusalem temple, but it is described in detail in 1 Kings 6.[8]

✣ Phoenician influence in the temple's architecture and decoration has been confirmed by comparison with other temples excavated in Syria and Palestine. The Ain Dara Temple near Halab (Aleppo) in northern Syria, roughly contemporary with Solomon's temple, was remarkably similar in size and style. It featured a portico with two columns, one on each side of the entryway. Within, it was divided into three parts, with an antechamber, main hall and main shrine ("Most Holy Place"). A multi-story corridor enclosed the inner temple on three sides. Ornamentation using both cherubim and palm trees is well attested in **Canaanite** art of the **Iron Age**.[9]

✣ A twelfth-century B.C. ivory panel recovered from Megiddo depicts a throne similar to Solomon's (see 10:18–19).

[1]See "Egyptian and Israelite Administration" on page 486. [2]See "The Pharaoh Whose Daughter Solomon Married" on page 493. [3]See "Gezer" on page 588. [4]See "The Building Activity of Solomon" on page 497. [5]See also "Hazor" on page 322, "Beth Shemesh" on page 405 and "Megiddo" on page 1541. [6]See "Ezion Geber" on page 631. [7]See "Ammon" on page 364, "Moab" on page 292, "Edom" on page 1467 and "Syria/Aram" on page 534. [8]See "Solomon's Temple and Other Ancient Temples" on page 620. [9]See "Archaeological Periods" chart on page xx in the front of this Bible.

6:18 [m]1Ki 7:24; Ps 74:6 — room was forty cubits[a] long. 18 The inside of the temple was cedar,[m] carved with gourds and open flow-
ers. Everything was cedar; no stone was to be seen.
6:19 [n]1Ki 8:6 [o]1Sa 3:3 — 19 He prepared the inner sanctuary[n] within the temple to set the ark of the covenant[o] of the LORD there.
6:20 [p]Eze 41:3-4 — 20 The inner sanctuary[p] was twenty cubits long, twenty wide and twenty high.[b] He overlaid the inside
with pure gold, and he also overlaid the altar of cedar. 21 Solomon covered the inside of the temple with
pure gold, and he extended gold chains across the front of the inner sanctuary, which was overlaid with
gold. 22 So he overlaid the whole interior with gold. He also overlaid with gold the altar that belonged to
the inner sanctuary.
6:23 [q]Ex 37:1-9 — 23 In the inner sanctuary he made a pair of cherubim[q] of olive wood, each ten cubits[c] high. 24 One wing
of the first cherub was five cubits long, and the other wing five cubits—ten cubits from wing tip to wing
tip. 25 The second cherub also measured ten cubits, for the two cherubim were identical in size and shape.
6:27 [r]Ex 25:20; 37:9; 1Ki 8:7; 2Ch 5:8 — 26 The height of each cherub was ten cubits. 27 He placed the cherubim[r] inside the innermost room of the
temple, with their wings spread out. The wing of one cherub touched one wall, while the wing of the oth-
er touched the other wall, and their wings touched each other in the middle of the room. 28 He overlaid
the cherubim with gold.
6:29 [s]ver 32,35 — 29 On the walls all around the temple, in both the inner and outer rooms, he carved cherubim,[s] palm
trees and open flowers. 30 He also covered the floors of both the inner and outer rooms of the temple with
gold.
31 For the entrance of the inner sanctuary he made doors of olive wood with five-sided jambs. 32 And
on the two olive wood doors he carved cherubim, palm trees and open flowers, and overlaid the cheru-
bim and palm trees with beaten gold. 33 In the same way he made four-sided jambs of olive wood for the
entrance to the main hall. 34 He also made two pine doors, each having two leaves that turned in sockets.
35 He carved cherubim, palm trees and open flowers on them and overlaid them with gold hammered
evenly over the carvings.
6:36 [t]1Ki 7:12; Ezr 6:4 — 36 And he built the inner courtyard of three courses[t] of dressed stone and one course of trimmed ce-
dar beams.
37 The foundation of the temple of the LORD was laid in the fourth year, in the month of Ziv. 38 In the
eleventh year in the month of Bul, the eighth month, the temple was finished in all its details according
6:38 [u]Heb 8:5 — to its specifications.[u] He had spent seven years building it.

Solomon Builds His Palace

7:1 [v]1Ki 9:10; 2Ch 8:1 — 7 It took Solomon thirteen years, however, to complete the construction of his palace.[v] 2 He built the
7:2 [w]2Sa 7:2 [x]1Ki 10:17; 2Ch 9:16 — Palace[w] of the Forest of Lebanon[x] a hundred cubits long, fifty wide and thirty high,[d] with four rows
of cedar columns supporting trimmed cedar beams. 3 It was roofed with cedar above the beams that rest-
ed on the columns—forty-five beams, fifteen to a row. 4 Its windows were placed high in sets of three,
facing each other. 5 All the doorways had rectangular frames; they were in the front part in sets of three,
facing each other.[e]
6 He made a colonnade fifty cubits long and thirty wide.[f] In front of it was a portico, and in front of
that were pillars and an overhanging roof.
7:7 [y]Ps 122:5; Pr 20:8 [z]1Ki 6:15 — 7 He built the throne hall, the Hall of Justice, where he was to judge,[y] and he covered it with cedar from
floor to ceiling.[g][z] 8 And the palace in which he was to live, set farther back, was similar in design. Solo-
7:8 [a]1Ki 3:1; 2Ch 8:11 — mon also made a palace like this hall for Pharaoh's daughter, whom he had married.[a]
9 All these structures, from the outside to the great courtyard and from foundation to eaves, were made
of blocks of high-grade stone cut to size and trimmed with a saw on their inner and outer faces. 10 The
foundations were laid with large stones of good quality, some measuring ten cubits[h] and some eight.[i]

[a] *17* That is, about 60 feet (about 18 meters) [b] *20* That is, about 30 feet (about 9 meters) long, wide and high [c] *23* That is, about 15 feet (about 4.5 meters) [d] *2* That is, about 150 feet (about 46 meters) long, 75 feet (about 23 meters) wide and 45 feet (about 13.5 meters) high [e] *5* The meaning of the Hebrew for this verse is uncertain. [f] *6* That is, about 75 feet (about 23 meters) long and 45 feet (about 13.5 meters) wide [g] *7* Vulgate and Syriac; Hebrew *floor* [h] *10* That is, about 15 feet (about 4.5 meters) [i] *10* That is, about 12 feet (about 3.6 meters)

6:18 Early Jewish synagogues were adorned with similar motifs. The depiction of cherubim and beautiful trees (v. 29) and flowers is reminiscent of the Garden of Eden. Similar carvings have been found in ancient royal palaces (see note on 22:39; see also "Ancient Craftsmanship" on p. 141 and "Angels and Guardian Spirits in the Bible and the Ancient Near East" on p. 1529).

7:2 The Palace of the Forest of Lebanon was so named because its many pillars were made from the trunks of cedars of Lebanon, giving the appearance of a massive forest. It was much larger than the temple and appears to have served both as a great assembly hall and as an armory (10:16–17,21; Isa 22:8). It is unclear whether the Hall of Justice (1Ki 7:7), Solomon's personal living quarters (v. 8) and the palace for Pharaoh's daughter (v. 8) were separate buildings or separate locations within the Palace of the Forest of Lebanon.

11 Above were high-grade stones, cut to size, and cedar beams. 12 The great courtyard was surrounded by
a wall of three courses[b] of dressed stone and one course of trimmed cedar beams, as was the inner court-
yard of the temple of the LORD with its portico.

The Temple's Furnishings

13 King Solomon sent to Tyre and brought Huram,[a c] 14 whose mother was a widow from the tribe of
Naphtali and whose father was a man of Tyre and a craftsman in bronze. Huram was highly skilled[d]
and experienced in all kinds of bronze work. He came to King Solomon and did all[e] the work assigned
to him.

15 He cast two bronze pillars,[f] each eighteen cubits high and twelve cubits around,[b] by line. 16 He also
made two capitals[g] of cast bronze to set on the tops of the pillars; each capital was five cubits[c] high. 17 A
network of interwoven chains festooned the capitals on top of the pillars, seven for each capital. 18 He
made pomegranates in two rows[d] encircling each network to decorate the capitals on top of the pillars.[e]
He did the same for each capital. 19 The capitals on top of the pillars in the portico were in the shape of
lilies, four cubits[f] high. 20 On the capitals of both pillars, above the bowl-shaped part next to the network,
were the two hundred pomegranates[h] in rows all around. 21 He erected the pillars at the portico of the
temple. The pillar to the south he named Jakin[g] and the one to the north Boaz.[h i] 22 The capitals on top
were in the shape of lilies. And so the work on the pillars was completed.

23 He made the Sea[j] of cast metal, circular in shape, measuring ten cubits[i] from rim to rim and five cu-
bits high. It took a line of thirty cubits[j] to measure around it. 24 Below the rim, gourds encircled it—ten
to a cubit. The gourds were cast in two rows in one piece with the Sea.

25 The Sea stood on twelve bulls,[k] three facing north, three facing west, three facing south and three
facing east. The Sea rested on top of them, and their hindquarters were toward the center. 26 It was a hand-
breadth[k] in thickness, and its rim was like the rim of a cup, like a lily blossom. It held two thousand baths.[l]

27 He also made ten movable stands[l] of bronze; each was four cubits long, four wide and three high.[m]
28 This is how the stands were made: They had side panels attached to uprights. 29 On the panels between
the uprights were lions, bulls and cherubim—and on the uprights as well. Above and below the lions
and bulls were wreaths of hammered work. 30 Each stand[m] had four bronze wheels with bronze axles,
and each had a basin resting on four supports, cast with wreaths on each side. 31 On the inside of the
stand there was an opening that had a circular frame one cubit[n] deep. This opening was round, and with
its basework it measured a cubit and a half.[o] Around its opening there was engraving. The panels of the
stands were square, not round. 32 The four wheels were under the panels, and the axles of the wheels were
attached to the stand. The diameter of each wheel was a cubit and a half. 33 The wheels were made like
chariot wheels; the axles, rims, spokes and hubs were all of cast metal.

34 Each stand had four handles, one on each corner, projecting from the stand. 35 At the top of the stand
there was a circular band half a cubit[p] deep. The supports and panels were attached to the top of the
stand. 36 He engraved cherubim, lions and palm trees on the surfaces of the supports and on the panels,
in every available space, with wreaths all around. 37 This is the way he made the ten stands. They were all
cast in the same molds and were identical in size and shape.

38 He then made ten bronze basins,[n] each holding forty baths[q] and measuring four cubits across, one

7:12 [b]1Ki 6:36
7:13 [c]2Ch 2:13
7:14 [d]Ex 31:2-5; 35:31; 36:1; 2Ch 2:14 [e]2Ch 4:11,16
7:15 [f]2Ki 25:17; 2Ch 3:15; 4:12; 52:17,21
7:16 [g]2Ki 25:17
7:20 [h]2Ch 3:16; 4:13; Jer 52:23
7:21 [i]1Ki 6:3; 2Ch 3:17
7:23 [j]2Ki 25:13; 1Ch 18:8; Jer 52:17
7:25 [k]2Ch 4:4-5; Jer 52:20
7:27 [l]ver 38; 2Ch 4:14
7:30 [m]2Ki 16:17
7:38 [n]Ex 30:18; 2Ch 4:6

[a] *13* Hebrew *Hiram*, a variant of *Huram*; also in verses 40 and 45 [b] *15* That is, about 27 feet (about 8.1 meters) high and 18 feet (about 5.4 meters) around [c] *16* That is, about 7 1/2 feet (about 2.3 meters); also in verse 23 [d] *18* Two Hebrew manuscripts and Septuagint; most Hebrew manuscripts *made the pillars, and there were two rows* [e] *18* Many Hebrew manuscripts and Syriac; most Hebrew manuscripts *pomegranates* [f] *19* That is, about 6 feet (about 1.8 meters); also in verse 38 [g] *21* *Jakin* probably means *he establishes.* [h] *21* *Boaz* probably means *in him is strength.* [i] *23* That is, about 15 feet (about 4.5 meters) [j] *23* That is, about 45 feet (about 13.5 meters) [k] *26* That is, about 3 inches (about 8 centimeters) [l] *26* That is, probably about 11,500 gallons (about 44 kiloliters); the Septuagint does not have this sentence. [m] *27* That is, about 6 feet (about 1.8 meters) long and wide and about 4 1/2 feet (about 1.3 meters) high [n] *31* That is, about 1 1/2 feet (about 0.5 meter) [o] *31* That is, about 2 1/4 feet (about 0.7 meter); also in verse 32 [p] *35* That is, about 3/4 foot (about 0.2 meter) [q] *38* That is, about 230 gallons (about 880 liters)

7:13–14 King Hiram of Tyre supplied Solomon with materials (such as cedar, pine and gold) and craftsmen (such as Huram) for building the temple (see 9:11; see also "Ancient Craftsmanship" on p. 141 and "Solomon and the Israelite Empire" on p. 490).

7:23 The "Sea of cast metal" was an enormous reservoir of water, holding about 11,500 gallons (see the NIV text note), or 43,527 liters, and used by the priests for ritual cleansing (2Ch 4:6).

7:27 The "movable stands of bronze" were designed to hold water basins (see v. 38) much smaller than the bronze Sea (cf. notes on vv. 23,38). Water from the basins was used to wash certain prescribed parts of the animals that were slaughtered for burnt offerings (see Lev 1:9,13; 2Ch 4:6). Archaeological excavations on Cyprus have unearthed an extremely close parallel to the wheeled, portable basins used in the courtyard of the temple.

7:38 The bronze water basins each held about 230 gallons (see the NIV text note), or 871 liters.

basin to go on each of the ten stands. 39 He placed five of the stands on the south side of the temple and
five on the north. He placed the Sea on the south side, at the southeast corner of the temple. 40 He also
made the basins and shovels and sprinkling bowls.

So Huram finished all the work he had undertaken for King Solomon in the temple of the LORD:

41 the two pillars;
the two bowl-shaped capitals on top of the pillars;
the two sets of network decorating the two bowl-shaped capitals on top of the pillars;
42 the four hundred pomegranates for the two sets of network (two rows of pomegranates for each
7:42 [o]ver 20 network, decorating the bowl-shaped capitals[o] on top of the pillars);
43 the ten stands with their ten basins;
44 the Sea and the twelve bulls under it;
7:45 [p]Ex 27:3 45 the pots, shovels and sprinkling bowls.[p]

All these objects that Huram made for King Solomon for the temple of the LORD were of burnished
7:46 [q]2Ch 4:17 [r]Ge 33:17; Jos 13:27 bronze. 46 The king had them cast in clay molds in the plain[q] of the Jordan between Succoth[r] and Zare-
[s]Jos 3:16 than.[s] 47 Solomon left all these things unweighed,[t] because there were so many; the weight of the bronze
7:47 [t]1Ch 22:3 was not determined.

7:46 Succoth (see "Succoth/Tell Deir Alla" on p. 56) was located on the eastern side of the Jordan River (Ge 33:17; Jos 13:27; Jdg 8:4–5), just north of the Jabbok River. Excavations in this area have confirmed that Succoth was a center of metallurgy during the period of the monarchy.

The Pharaoh Whose Daughter Solomon Married

1 KINGS 7 Solomon acquired a number of foreign wives (1Ki 11:1) as the result of diplomatic marriages as he forged peaceful ties with surrounding nations early in his reign (3:1). The only such wife about whom we know anything specific is the daughter of an anonymous pharaoh. Solomon gave her a private palace (7:8), and she received the city of Gezer ("Map 4") as a dowry gift from her father (9:16).[1]

The identity of the pharaoh whose daughter Solomon married is somewhat problematic. The rulers of Egypt during this time (the Twenty-first Dynasty) were from Libya, so the pharaoh's daughter would have been of Libyan descent. Based upon the dates of Solomon's reign (970–930 B.C.) and Egyptian chronology, the most likely candidate is Siamun, who ruled from the capital at Tanis in northern Egypt from 979 to 960 B.C. A relief located at Tanis ("Map 1") depicts Siamun slaying a captive. Some suggest that this represents a campaign to Philistia, since the captive is pictured holding a double ax, a weapon thought to be Philistine.[2] Thus, some scholars argue that Siamun led a campaign against the Philistines and in the process captured Gezer, which he later gave to his daughter.

There are several difficulties with this explanation, however:

- The era of David and Solomon was the high point of Israelite power, and it would have been imprudent for an Israelite king to have allowed a foreign invader like a pharaoh to come so near the heart of Israelite territory.
- The pharaohs of the late Twenty-first Dynasty were ineffective, and it is questionable whether Siamun could have mounted such a campaign.
- Philistines are nowhere else represented with double-bladed battle axes, and thus the relief portraying the warrior with such an ax is of doubtful significance.

Still, there is no reason to doubt that Solomon did marry an Egyptian princess. Both Israel and Egypt engaged in diplomatic marriages, and the Biblical account seems too detailed to be a fabrication. Also, the capture of Gezer by the pharaoh's forces may have been by prior agreement with Solomon's government. Gezer was at this time a weak city, and if its capture was carried out with Israel's support it would not have required a major Egyptian expedition. Allowing Siamun the honor of capturing this city could conceivably have been a face-saving way for Solomon to enable a weak pharaoh to provide his daughter with a meaningful dowry.

[1]See "Gezer" on page 588. [2]See "The Archaeology of Philistia" on page 370.

48 Solomon also made all the furnishings that were in the LORD's temple:

the golden altar;
the golden table[u] on which was the bread of the Presence;[v]
49 the lampstands[w] of pure gold (five on the right and five on the left, in front of the inner sanctuary);
the gold floral work and lamps and tongs;
50 the pure gold basins, wick trimmers, sprinkling bowls, dishes and censers;[x]
and the gold sockets for the doors of the innermost room, the Most Holy Place, and also for the
doors of the main hall of the temple.

51 When all the work King Solomon had done for the temple of the LORD was finished, he brought in
the things his father David had dedicated[y]—the silver and gold and the furnishings—and he placed
them in the treasuries of the LORD's temple.

The Ark Brought to the Temple

8 Then King Solomon summoned into his presence at Jerusalem the elders of Israel, all the heads of
the tribes and the chiefs[z] of the Israelite families, to bring up the ark[a] of the LORD's covenant from
Zion, the City of David.[b] 2 All the men of Israel came together to King Solomon at the time of the festi-
val[c] in the month of Ethanim, the seventh month.[d]
3 When all the elders of Israel had arrived, the priests[e] took up the ark, 4 and they brought up the ark
of the LORD and the Tent of Meeting[f] and all the sacred furnishings in it. The priests and Levites carried
them up, 5 and King Solomon and the entire assembly of Israel that had gathered about him were before
the ark, sacrificing[g] so many sheep and cattle that they could not be recorded or counted.
6 The priests then brought the ark of the LORD's covenant[h] to its place in the inner sanctuary of the
temple, the Most Holy Place, and put it beneath the wings of the cherubim.[i] 7 The cherubim spread their
wings over the place of the ark and overshadowed the ark and its carrying poles. 8 These poles were so
long that their ends could be seen from the Holy Place in front of the inner sanctuary, but not from out-
side the Holy Place; and they are still there today.[j] 9 There was nothing in the ark except the two stone
tablets[k] that Moses had placed in it at Horeb, where the LORD made a covenant with the Israelites after
they came out of Egypt.
10 When the priests withdrew from the Holy Place, the cloud[l] filled the temple of the LORD. 11 And the
priests could not perform their service because of the cloud, for the glory of the LORD filled his temple.
12 Then Solomon said, "The LORD has said that he would dwell in a dark cloud;[m] 13 I have indeed built
a magnificent temple for you, a place for you to dwell[n] forever."
14 While the whole assembly of Israel was standing there, the king turned around and blessed[o] them.
15 Then he said:

"Praise be to the LORD,[p] the God of Israel, who with his own hand has fulfilled what he prom-
ised with his own mouth to my father David. For he said, 16 'Since the day I brought my people Is-
rael out of Egypt, I have not chosen a city in any tribe of Israel to have a temple built for my Name[q]
to be there, but I have chosen[r] David[s] to rule my people Israel.'
17 "My father David had it in his heart to build a temple[t] for the Name of the LORD, the God of
Israel. 18 But the LORD said to my father David, 'Because it was in your heart to build a temple for
my Name, you did well to have this in your heart. 19 Nevertheless, you[u] are not the one to build the
temple, but your son, who is your own flesh and blood—he is the one who will build the temple
for my Name.'[v]
20 "The LORD has kept the promise he made: I have succeeded David my father and now I sit on
the throne of Israel, just as the LORD promised, and I have built[w] the temple for the Name of the
LORD, the God of Israel. 21 I have provided a place there for the ark, in which is the covenant of the
LORD that he made with our fathers when he brought them out of Egypt."

7:48 [u]Ex 37:10 [v]Ex 25:30 **7:49** [w]Ex 25:31-38 **7:50** [x]2Ki 25:13 **7:51** [y]2Sa 8:11 **8:1** [z]Nu 7:2 [a]2Sa 6:17 [b]2Sa 5:7 **8:2** [c]2Ch 7:8 [d]Lev 23:34 **8:3** [e]Nu 7:9; Jos 3:3 **8:4** [f]1Ki 3:4; 2Ch 1:3 **8:5** [g]2Sa 6:13 **8:6** [h]2Sa 6:17 [i]1Ki 6:19,27 **8:8** [j]Ex 25:13-15 **8:9** [k]Ex 24:7-8; 25:21; 40:20; Dt 10:2-5; Heb 9:4 **8:10** [l]Ex 40:34-35; 2Ch 7:1-2 **8:12** [m]Ps 18:11; 97:2 **8:13** [n]Ex 15:17; 2Sa 7:13; Ps 132:13 **8:14** [o]2Sa 6:18 **8:15** [p]2Sa 7:12-13; 1Ch 29:10, 20; Ne 9:5; Lk 1:68 **8:16** [q]Dt 12:5 [r]1Sa 16:1 [s]2Sa 7:4-6,8 **8:17** [t]2Sa 7:2; 1Ch 17:1 **8:19** [u]2Sa 7:5 [v]2Sa 7:13; 1Ki 5:3,5 **8:20** [w]1Ch 28:6

7:48 A stone incense altar excavated at Megiddo has four horns on the corners and provides a clear idea of the shape of the golden incense altar in the temple. (See "The Horned Altar" on p. 924.)

The bread of the Presence was placed on the golden table (see Ex 25:23–30; 1Ch 9:32; 2Ch 13:11; 29:18). First Chronicles 28:16 and 2 Chronicles 4:8, 19 mention ten such golden tables—five each placed on the north and south sides of the temple.

7:49 The tabernacle had only one lampstand with seven arms, which was placed opposite the table for the bread of the Presence (Ex 25:31–40; 26:35). The ten lampstands in the temple, five each on the north and south sides, created a lane of light in the Holy Place. Ritual sevenfold lamps have been discovered at several locations in Palestine, including Hazor and Dothan.

Solomon's Prayer of Dedication

22 Then Solomon stood before the altar of the LORD in front of the whole assembly of Israel, spread out
his hands[x] toward heaven 23 and said:
"O LORD, God of Israel, there is no God like[y] you in heaven above or on earth below—you who
keep your covenant of love[z] with your servants who continue wholeheartedly in your way. 24 You
have kept your promise to your servant David my father; with your mouth you have promised and
with your hand you have fulfilled it—as it is today.
25 "Now LORD, God of Israel, keep for your servant David my father the promises[a] you made to
him when you said, 'You shall never fail to have a man to sit before me on the throne of Israel, if
only your sons are careful in all they do to walk before me as you have done.' 26 And now, O God of
Israel, let your word that you promised[b] your servant David my father come true.
27 "But will God really dwell[c] on earth? The heavens, even the highest heaven, cannot contain[d]
you. How much less this temple I have built! 28 Yet give attention to your servant's prayer and his
plea for mercy, O LORD my God. Hear the cry and the prayer that your servant is praying in your
presence this day. 29 May your eyes be open[e] toward[f] this temple night and day, this place of which
you said, 'My Name[g] shall be there,' so that you will hear the prayer your servant prays toward this
place. 30 Hear the supplication of your servant and of your people Israel when they pray toward
this place. Hear from heaven, your dwelling place, and when you hear, forgive.[h]
31 "When a man wrongs his neighbor and is required to take an oath and he comes and swears
the oath[i] before your altar in this temple, 32 then hear from heaven and act. Judge between your
servants, condemning the guilty and bringing down on his own head what he has done. Declare
the innocent not guilty, and so establish his innocence.[j]
33 "When your people Israel have been defeated[k] by an enemy because they have sinned[l] against
you, and when they turn back to you and confess your name, praying and making supplication to
you in this temple, 34 then hear from heaven and forgive the sin of your people Israel and bring
them back to the land you gave to their fathers.
35 "When the heavens are shut up and there is no rain[m] because your people have sinned against
you, and when they pray toward this place and confess your name and turn from their sin because
you have afflicted them, 36 then hear from heaven and forgive the sin of your servants, your peo-
ple Israel. Teach[n] them the right way[o] to live, and send rain on the land you gave your people for
an inheritance.
37 "When famine[p] or plague comes to the land, or blight[q] or mildew, locusts or grasshoppers,
or when an enemy besieges them in any of their cities, whatever disaster or disease may come,
38 and when a prayer or plea is made by any of your people Israel—each one aware of the afflic-
tions of his own heart, and spreading out his hands toward this temple— 39 then hear from heav-
en, your dwelling place. Forgive and act; deal with each man according to all he does, since you
know[r] his heart (for you alone know the hearts of all men), 40 so that they will fear[s] you all the time
they live in the land you gave our fathers.
41 "As for the foreigner who does not belong to your people Israel but has come from a distant
land because of your name— 42 for men will hear of your great name and your mighty hand[t] and
your outstretched arm—when he comes and prays toward this temple, 43 then hear from heaven,
your dwelling place, and do whatever the foreigner asks of you, so that all the peoples of the earth
may know[u] your name and fear[v] you, as do your own people Israel, and may know that this house
I have built bears your Name.
44 "When your people go to war against their enemies, wherever you send them, and when they
pray to the LORD toward the city you have chosen and the temple I have built for your Name, 45 then
hear from heaven their prayer and their plea, and uphold their cause.
46 "When they sin against you—for there is no one who does not sin[w]—and you become an-
gry with them and give them over to the enemy, who takes them captive[x] to his own land, far away
or near; 47 and if they have a change of heart in the land where they are held captive, and repent and
plead[y] with you in the land of their conquerors and say, 'We have sinned, we have done wrong, we
have acted wickedly';[z] 48 and if they turn back to you with all their heart[a] and soul in the land of
their enemies who took them captive, and pray[b] to you toward the land you gave their fathers, to-
ward the city you have chosen and the temple[c] I have built for your Name; 49 then from heaven,

8:22 [x]Ex 9:29; Ezr 9:5
8:23 [y]1Sa 2:2; 2Sa 7:22 [z]Dt 7:9, 12; Ne 1:5; 9:32; Da 9:4
8:25 [a]1Ki 2:4
8:26 [b]2Sa 7:25
8:27 [c]Ac 7:48 [d]2Ch 2:6; Ps 139:7-16; Isa 66:1; Jer 23:24
8:29 [e]2Ch 7:15; Ne 1:6 [f]Da 6:10 [g]Dt 12:11
8:30 [h]Ps 85:2
8:31 [i]Ex 22:11
8:32 [j]Dt 25:1
8:33 [k]Lev 26:17; Dt 28:25 [l]Lev 26:39
8:35 [m]Lev 26:19; Dt 28:24
8:36 [n]1Sa 12:23; Ps 25:4; 94:12 [o]Ps 5:8; 27:11; Jer 6:16
8:37 [p]Lev 26:26 [q]Dt 28:22
8:39 [r]1Sa 16:7; 1Ch 28:9; Ps 11:4; Jer 17:10; Jn 2:24; Ac 1:24
8:40 [s]Ps 130:4
8:42 [t]Dt 3:24
8:43 [u]1Sa 17:46; 2Ki 19:19 [v]Ps 102:15
8:46 [w]Pr 20:9; Ecc 7:20; Ro 3:9; 1Jn 1:8-10 [x]Lev 26:33-39; Dt 28:64
8:47 [y]Lev 26:40; Ne 1:6 [z]Ps 106:6; Da 9:5
8:48 [a]Dt 4:29; Jer 29:12-14 [b]Da 6:10 [c]Jnh 2:4

your dwelling place, hear their prayer and their plea, and uphold their cause. 50 And forgive your
people, who have sinned against you; forgive all the offenses they have committed against you,
and cause their conquerors to show them mercy;[d] 51 for they are your people and your inheritance,[e]
whom you brought out of Egypt, out of that iron-smelting furnace.[f]

52 "May your eyes be open to your servant's plea and to the plea of your people Israel, and may
you listen to them whenever they cry out to you. 53 For you singled them out from all the nations
of the world to be your own inheritance,[g] just as you declared through your servant Moses when
you, O Sovereign LORD, brought our fathers out of Egypt."

54 When Solomon had finished all these prayers and supplications to the LORD, he rose from before
the altar of the LORD, where he had been kneeling with his hands spread out toward heaven. 55 He stood
and blessed[h] the whole assembly of Israel in a loud voice, saying:

56 "Praise be to the LORD, who has given rest[i] to his people Israel just as he promised. Not one
word has failed of all the good promises[j] he gave through his servant Moses. 57 May the LORD our
God be with us as he was with our fathers; may he never leave us nor forsake[k] us. 58 May he turn
our hearts[l] to him, to walk in all his ways and to keep the commands, decrees and regulations he
gave our fathers. 59 And may these words of mine, which I have prayed before the LORD, be near to
the LORD our God day and night, that he may uphold the cause of his servant and the cause of his
people Israel according to each day's need, 60 so that all the peoples[m] of the earth may know that
the LORD is God and that there is no other.[n] 61 But your hearts must be fully committed[o] to the LORD
our God, to live by his decrees and obey his commands, as at this time."

The Dedication of the Temple

62 Then the king and all Israel with him offered sacrifices before the LORD. 63 Solomon offered a sacri-
fice of fellowship offerings[a] to the LORD: twenty-two thousand cattle and a hundred and twenty thou-
sand sheep and goats. So the king and all the Israelites dedicated the temple of the LORD.
64 On that same day the king consecrated the middle part of the courtyard in front of the temple of the
LORD, and there he offered burnt offerings, grain offerings and the fat of the fellowship offerings, because
the bronze altar[p] before the LORD was too small to hold the burnt offerings, the grain offerings and the
fat of the fellowship offerings.
65 So Solomon observed the festival[q] at that time, and all Israel with him—a vast assembly, people
from Lebo[b] Hamath[r] to the Wadi of Egypt.[s] They celebrated it before the LORD our God for seven days
and seven days more, fourteen days in all. 66 On the following day he sent the people away. They blessed
the king and then went home, joyful and glad in heart for all the good things the LORD had done for his
servant David and his people Israel.

The LORD Appears to Solomon

9 When Solomon had finished[t] building the temple of the LORD and the royal palace, and had achieved
all he had desired to do, 2 the LORD appeared[u] to him a second time, as he had appeared to him at Gib-
eon. 3 The LORD said to him:

"I have heard[v] the prayer and plea you have made before me; I have consecrated this temple,
which you have built, by putting my Name there forever. My eyes[w] and my heart will always be there.
4 "As for you, if you walk before me in integrity of heart[x] and uprightness, as David[y] your father
did, and do all I command and observe my decrees and laws, 5 I will establish[z] your royal throne
over Israel forever, as I promised David your father when I said, 'You shall never fail[a] to have a man
on the throne of Israel.'

6 "But if you[c] or your sons turn away[b] from me and do not observe the commands and decrees
I have given you[c] and go off to serve other gods and worship them, 7 then I will cut off Israel from
the land[c] I have given them and will reject this temple I have consecrated for my Name.[d] Israel
will then become a byword[e] and an object of ridicule[f] among all peoples. 8 And though this tem-
ple is now imposing, all who pass by will be appalled and will scoff and say, 'Why has the LORD
done such a thing to this land and to this temple?'[g] 9 People will answer, 'Because they have for-
saken the LORD their God, who brought their fathers out of Egypt, and have embraced other gods,
worshiping and serving them—that is why the LORD brought all this disaster on them.' "

8:50 [d]2Ch 30:9; Ps 106:46
8:51 [e]Dt 4:20; 9:29; Ne 1:10 [f]Jer 11:4
8:53 [g]Ex 19:5; Dt 9:26-29
8:55 [h]ver 14; 2Sa 6:18
8:56 [i]Dt 12:10 [j]Jos 21:45; 23:15
8:57 [k]Dt 31:6; Jos 1:5; Heb 13:5
8:58 [l]Ps 119:36
8:60 [m]Jos 4:24; 1Sa 17:46 [n]Dt 4:35; 1Ki 18:39; Jer 10:10-12
8:61 [o]1Ki 11:4; 15:3,14; 2Ki 20:3
8:64 [p]2Ch 4:1
8:65 [q]ver 2; Lev 23:34 [r]Nu 34:8; Jos 13:5; Jdg 3:3; 2Ki 14:25 [s]Ge 15:18
9:1 [t]1Ki 7:1; 2Ch 8:6
9:2 [u]1Ki 3:5
9:3 [v]2Ki 20:5; Ps 10:17 [w]Dt 11:12; 1Ki 8:29
9:4 [x]Ge 17:1 [y]1Ki 15:5
9:5 [z]1Ch 22:10 [a]2Sa 7:15; 1Ki 2:4
9:6 [b]2Sa 7:14
9:7 [c]2Ki 17:23; 25:21 [d]Jer 7:14 [e]Ps 44:14 [f]Dt 28:37
9:8 [g]Dt 29:24; Jer 22:8-9

[a] 63 Traditionally *peace offerings*; also in verse 64 [b] 65 Or *from the entrance to* [c] 6 The Hebrew is plural.

Solomon's Other Activities

10 At the end of twenty years, during which Solomon built these two buildings—the temple of the
LORD and the royal palace— 11 King Solomon gave twenty towns in Galilee to Hiram king of Tyre, because
9:11 h2Ch 8:2 Hiram had supplied him with all the cedar and pine and gold[h] he wanted. 12 But when Hiram went from
Tyre to see the towns that Solomon had given him, he was not pleased with them. 13 "What kind of towns

9:10–14 It appears that Solomon gave Hiram the 20 towns in the Phoenician-Galilee border area as a surety for repayment of gold (v. 14). Payment for building materials and wages had already been made in annual contributions of grain and oil (5:6,10–11). The weight of a talent varied in different systems and times, but at minimum Hiram had given Solomon several tons of gold (see the NIV

The Building Activity of Solomon

1 KINGS 9 Royal inscriptions throughout the ancient Near East attest to the building activities of kings who wished to consolidate their military and political gains. While his father had wielded the sword to secure land from the Philistines, Solomon built an administrative and commercial apparatus for the young kingdom.[1] Beginning with Jerusalem he authorized the construction both of the temple[2] and of his palace, as well as reinforcing the *millo*, a term meaning "supporting terraces" (1Ki 9:15). This may have been an artificial landfill of terraces between the temple mount and the eastern side of Jerusalem.

Most scholars concur that there is archaeological evidence for building activity during the tenth century B.C. at **Hazor, Megiddo** and **Gezer** (all on "Map 6"). First Kings 9:15 specifies that Solomon fortified these cities, and evidence indicates that he did so through the use of **casemate walls**, a new defensive structure employing a double wall. The work in these cities made use of **ashlar** masonry and displayed similar facades, dimensions and designs. The cities also featured six-chambered gates, with three chambers on each side of a gateway. This evidence is of enormous importance for establishing the historicity of Solomon's reign. Today, some scholars argue that the Biblical account is at best an exaggeration and at worst a complete fiction. The excavation of the cities of 1 Kings 9:15 helps to demonstrate that the age of Solomon was precisely as the Bible describes it.[3]

Whereas Hazor, Megiddo and Gezer lay along a north-south axis through Israel's northern territory, Lower Beth Horon, Baalath and Tadmor (vv. 17–18) occupied critical positions along important trade routes within the tribe of Judah. Solomon's building activity crossed traditional tribal boundaries and signaled his intention both to ensure a consolidated nation and to secure a place in international commerce. His fleet of ships at Ezion Geber[4] (v. 26), located at the head of the Gulf of Aqaba ("Map 3"), also enabled the king to expand Israelite trade. Both the Bible and archaeology suggest that Solomon's reign was a time of great prosperity and significant cultural transition. The nation progressed from being a confederation of shepherds and peasants to becoming a nation-state with international trade and urban centers that transcended traditional tribal boundaries.

[1]See "Solomon and the Israelite Empire" on page 490. [2]See "Solomon's Temple and Other Ancient Temples" on page 620. [3]See "Hazor" on page 322, "Megiddo" on page 1541 and "Gezer" on page 588. [4]See "Ezion Geber" on page 631.

Casemate wall at Hazor

Photograph: © Todd Bolen/Bible Places.com

are these you have given me, my brother?" he asked. And he called them the Land of Cabul,[a][i] a name they
have to this day. 14 Now Hiram had sent to the king 120 talents[b] of gold.
15 Here is the account of the forced labor King Solomon conscripted[j] to build the LORD's temple, his own
palace, the supporting terraces,[c][k] the wall of Jerusalem, and Hazor,[l] Megiddo and Gezer.[m] 16 (Pharaoh
king of Egypt had attacked and captured Gezer. He had set it on fire. He killed its Canaanite inhabitants
and then gave it as a wedding gift to his daughter, Solomon's wife. 17 And Solomon rebuilt Gezer.) He built
up Lower Beth Horon,[n] 18 Baalath,[o] and Tadmor[d] in the desert, within his land, 19 as well as all his store
cities[p] and the towns for his chariots[q] and for his horses[e]—whatever he desired to build in Jerusalem,
in Lebanon and throughout all the territory he ruled.
20 All the people left from the Amorites, Hittites, Perizzites, Hivites and Jebusites (these peoples were
not Israelites), 21 that is, their descendants[r] remaining in the land, whom the Israelites could not exter-
minate[f][s]—these Solomon conscripted for his slave labor force,[t] as it is to this day. 22 But Solomon did
not make slaves[u] of any of the Israelites; they were his fighting men, his government officials, his officers,
his captains, and the commanders of his chariots and charioteers. 23 They were also the chief officials[v]
in charge of Solomon's projects—550 officials supervising the men who did the work.
24 After Pharaoh's daughter[w] had come up from the City of David to the palace Solomon had built for
her, he constructed the supporting terraces.[x]
25 Three[y] times a year Solomon sacrificed burnt offerings and fellowship offerings[g] on the altar he
had built for the LORD, burning incense before the LORD along with them, and so fulfilled the temple
obligations.

9:13 [i]Jos 19:27
9:15 [j]Jos 16:10; 1Ki 5:13 [k]ver 24; 2Sa 5:9 [l]Jos 19:36 [m]Jos 17:11
9:17 [n]Jos 16:3; 2Ch 8:5
9:18 [o]Jos 19:44
9:19 [p]ver 1 [q]1Ki 4:26
9:21 [r]Ge 9:25-26 [s]Jos 15:63; 17:12; Jdg 1:21, 27,29 [t]Ezr 2:55, 58
9:22 [u]Lev 25:39
9:23 [v]1Ki 5:16
9:24 [w]1Ki 3:1; 7:8 [x]2Sa 5:9; 1Ki 11:27; 2Ch 32:5
9:25 [y]Ex 23:14; 2Ch 8:12-13,16

[a] *13* *Cabul* sounds like the Hebrew for *good-for-nothing.* [b] *14* That is, about 4 1/2 tons (about 4 metric tons) [c] *15* Or *the Millo;* also in verse 24 [d] *18* The Hebrew may also be read *Tamar.* [e] *19* Or *charioteers* [f] *21* The Hebrew term refers to the irrevocable giving over of things or persons to the LORD, often by totally destroying them. [g] *25* Traditionally *peace offerings*

text note on 9:14). Hiram thought the 20 settlements in northern Galilee a miserly return on his investment. Second Chronicles 8:1–2 indicates that at some later date when Solomon's gold reserves were increased, perhaps after the return of the expedition to Ophir (1Ki 9:26–28; 10:11) or the visit of the queen of Sheba (10:1–13), he settled his debt with Hiram and recovered the 20 towns held as collateral.

9:15 Solomon fortified the strategically located cities of Hazor, Megiddo and Gezer. Solomonic gates, probably built by the same masons, have been unearthed at all three sites. (See "The Building Activity of Solomon" on p. 497, "Hazor" on p. 322, "Megiddo" on p. 1541 and "Gezer" on p. 588.)

9:16 See "The Pharaoh Whose Daughter Solomon Married" on page 493.

ARCHAEOLOGICAL SITES

SHEBA

1 KINGS 10 Sheba, land of the queen who visited Solomon (1Ki 10:1–13), was located at the southwestern tip of the Arabian Peninsula, in modern Yemen. This location permitted the people of Sheba (Sabeans) to conduct sea trade with both Africa and India. In addition, caravan trade in gold, jewels, myrrh, frankincense and spices from the East was facilitated by the domestication of the camel.[1] No other pack animal could survive the long distances between water sources.

The Sabeans, who had a reputation as raiders (see Job 1:15), may have been descendants of Abraham through his second wife, Keturah (Ge 25:1–3). Elements in the Sabean dialect connect them linguistically with northwestern Semites. The Sabeans moved from northern Arabia before the tenth century B.C. and developed a capital at Marib, sustained by a large dam that collected seasonal rainfall. **Assyrian** inscriptions attest that several queens ruled the Sabeans during this period.

Solomon's maritime enterprises threatened the Sabean trade monopoly, and many scholars speculate that their queen visited Solomon to negotiate a trade agreement. A ninth-century B.C. stamp with a southern Arabic script, made of a reddish-brown clay indigenous to Yemen and unearthed at Bethel,[2] corroborates this theory.

[1]See "Camels" on page 41 and "Caravan Trading and Routes in the Ancient Near East" on page 63. [2]See "Bethel" on page 59.

26 King Solomon also built ships[z] at Ezion Geber,[a] which is near Elath in Edom, on the shore of the Red Sea.[a] 27 And Hiram sent his men—sailors[b] who knew the sea—to serve in the fleet with Solomon's men. 28 They sailed to Ophir[c] and brought back 420 talents[b] of gold, which they delivered to King Solomon.

The Queen of Sheba Visits Solomon

10 When the queen of Sheba[d] heard about the fame of Solomon and his relation to the name of the LORD, she came to test him with hard questions.[e] 2 Arriving at Jerusalem with a very great caravan—with camels carrying spices, large quantities of gold, and precious stones—she came to Solomon and talked with him about all that she had on her mind. 3 Solomon answered all her questions; nothing was too hard for the king to explain to her. 4 When the queen of Sheba saw all the wisdom of Solomon and the palace he had built, 5 the food on his table,[f] the seating of his officials, the attending servants in their robes, his cupbearers, and the burnt offerings he made at[c] the temple of the LORD, she was overwhelmed.

6 She said to the king, "The report I heard in my own country about your achievements and your wisdom is true. 7 But I did not believe these things until I came and saw with my own eyes. Indeed, not even half was told me; in wisdom and wealth[g] you have far exceeded the report I heard. 8 How happy your men must be! How happy your officials, who continually stand before you and hear[h] your wisdom! 9 Praise[i] be to the LORD your God, who has delighted in you and placed you on the throne of Israel. Because of the LORD's eternal love for Israel, he has made you king, to maintain justice[j] and righteousness."

10 And she gave the king 120 talents[d] of gold,[k] large quantities of spices, and precious stones. Never again were so many spices brought in as those the queen of Sheba gave to King Solomon.

11 (Hiram's ships brought gold from Ophir;[l] and from there they brought great cargoes of almugwood[e] and precious stones. 12 The king used the almugwood to make supports for the temple of the LORD and for the royal palace, and to make harps and lyres for the musicians. So much almugwood has never been imported or seen since that day.)

13 King Solomon gave the queen of Sheba all she desired and asked for, besides what he had given her out of his royal bounty. Then she left and returned with her retinue to her own country.

Solomon's Splendor

14 The weight of the gold[m] that Solomon received yearly was 666 talents,[f] 15 not including the revenues from merchants and traders and from all the Arabian kings and the governors of the land.

16 King Solomon made two hundred large shields[n] of hammered gold; six hundred bekas[g] of gold went into each shield. 17 He also made three hundred small shields of hammered gold, with three minas[h] of gold in each shield. The king put them in the Palace of the Forest of Lebanon.[o]

18 Then the king made a great throne inlaid with ivory and overlaid with fine gold. 19 The throne had six steps, and its back had a rounded top. On both sides of the seat were armrests, with a lion standing beside each of them. 20 Twelve lions stood on the six steps, one at either end of each step. Nothing like it had ever been made for any other kingdom. 21 All King Solomon's goblets were gold, and all the household articles in the Palace of the Forest of Lebanon were pure gold. Nothing was made of silver, because silver was considered of little value in Solomon's days. 22 The king had a fleet of trading ships[i][p] at sea

9:26 [z]1Ki 22:48 [a]Nu 33:35; Dt 2:8 **9:27** [b]1Ki 10:11; Eze 27:8 **9:28** [c]1Ch 29:4
10:1 [d]Ge 10:7, 28; Mt 12:42; Lk 11:31 [e]Jdg 14:12
10:5 [f]1Ch 26:16
10:7 [g]1Ch 29:25
10:8 [h]Pr 8:34 **10:9** [i]1Ki 5:7 [j]2Sa 8:15; Ps 33:5; 72:2
10:10 [k]ver 2
10:11 [l]Ge 10:29; 1Ki 9:27-28
10:14 [m]1Ki 9:28
10:16 [n]1Ki 14:26-28
10:17 [o]1Ki 7:2
10:22 [p]1Ki 9:26

[a] 26 Hebrew *Yam Suph*; that is, Sea of Reeds [b] 28 That is, about 16 tons (about 14.5 metric tons) [c] 5 Or *the ascent by which he went up to* [d] 10 That is, about 4 1/2 tons (about 4 metric tons) [e] 11 Probably a variant of *algumwood*; also in verse 12 [f] 14 That is, about 25 tons (about 23 metric tons) [g] 16 That is, about 7 1/2 pounds (about 3.5 kilograms) [h] 17 That is, about 3 3/4 pounds (about 1.7 kilograms) [i] 22 Hebrew *of ships of Tarshish*

9:26 See "The Location of the Red Sea" on page 110.
9:28 Ophir was a source for gold (2Ch 8:18; Job 28:16; Ps 45:9; Isa 13:12), almugwood and precious stones (1Ki 10:11), as well as silver, ivory, apes and baboons (10:22). Suggestions for its location include southeastern Arabia, southwestern Arabia and the northeastern African coast. If Ophir was located in Arabia, it was probably a trading center for goods from farther east, as well as from east Africa. But the three-year voyages of Solomon's merchant vessels (10:22) suggest a more distant location than the Arabian coast.
10:1 "Hard questions" may refer to riddles. On the popularity and function of riddles in the ancient world, see the note on Judges 14:12–14.

Sheba was in southwest Arabia—present-day Yemen. Although it was the best-watered and most fertile area of Arabia, its chief strength was as a center of trade. It profited from the sea trade of India and eastern Africa by transporting luxury commodities north to Damascus and Gaza on caravan routes through the Arabian Desert. Solomon's fame had reached the queen, probably through the caravan traders who regularly passed through Israel on their way to Damascus or Gaza. It is possible that Solomon's fleet of ships threatened Sheba's continued dominance of this trading business. (See "Caravan Trading and Routes in the Ancient Near East" on p. 63 and "Sheba" on p. 498.)
10:11–12 For information on Ophir, see note on 9:28.
10:14–15 "Revenues . . . from all the Arabian kings" probably refers to tribute collected from Bedouin sheiks for passage of their caravans through Israelite territory. Solomon's wealth from taxes and trade was unparalleled (vv. 22–23).

along with the ships of Hiram. Once every three years it returned, carrying gold, silver and ivory, and
apes and baboons.
23 King Solomon was greater in riches[q] and wisdom[r] than all the other kings of the earth. 24 The whole
world sought audience with Solomon to hear the wisdom[s] God had put in his heart. 25 Year after year, ev-
eryone who came brought a gift—articles of silver and gold, robes, weapons and spices, and horses and
mules.
26 Solomon accumulated chariots and horses;[t] he had fourteen hundred chariots and twelve thousand
horses,[a] which he kept in the chariot cities and also with him in Jerusalem. 27 The king made silver as
common[u] in Jerusalem as stones, and cedar as plentiful as sycamore-fig trees in the foothills. 28 Solo-
mon's horses were imported from Egypt[b] and from Kue[c]—the royal merchants purchased them from
Kue. 29 They imported a chariot from Egypt for six hundred shekels[d] of silver, and a horse for a hundred
and fifty.[e] They also exported them to all the kings of the Hittites[v] and of the Arameans.

10:23 [q] 1Ki 3:13 [r] 1Ki 4:30
10:24 [s] 1Ki 3:9, 12,28
10:26 [t] Dt 17:16; 1Ki 4:26; 9:19; 2Ch 1:14; 9:25
10:27 [u] Dt 17:17
10:29 [v] 2Ki 7:6-7

Solomon's Wives

11 King Solomon, however, loved many foreign women[w] besides Pharaoh's daughter—Moabites,
Ammonites, Edomites, Sidonians and Hittites. 2 They were from nations about which the LORD
had told the Israelites, "You must not intermarry[x] with them, because they will surely turn your hearts
after their gods." Nevertheless, Solomon held fast to them in love. 3 He had seven hundred wives of royal
birth and three hundred concubines, and his wives led him astray. 4 As Solomon grew old, his wives
turned his heart after other gods, and his heart was not fully devoted[y] to the LORD his God, as the heart
of David his father had been. 5 He followed Ashtoreth[z] the goddess of the Sidonians, and Molech[f][a] the de-
testable god of the Ammonites. 6 So Solomon did evil in the eyes of the LORD; he did not follow the LORD
completely, as David his father had done.
7 On a hill east[b] of Jerusalem, Solomon built a high place for Chemosh[c] the detestable god of Moab,
and for Molech[d] the detestable god of the Ammonites. 8 He did the same for all his foreign wives, who
burned incense and offered sacrifices to their gods.
9 The LORD became angry with Solomon because his heart had turned away from the LORD, the God
of Israel, who had appeared[e] to him twice. 10 Although he had forbidden Solomon to follow other gods,[f]
Solomon did not keep the LORD's command.[g] 11 So the LORD said to Solomon, "Since this is your attitude
and you have not kept my covenant and my decrees, which I commanded you, I will most certainly tear[h]
the kingdom away from you and give it to one of your subordinates. 12 Nevertheless, for the sake of Da-
vid your father, I will not do it during your lifetime. I will tear it out of the hand of your son. 13 Yet I will
not tear the whole kingdom from him, but will give him one tribe[i] for the sake[j] of David my servant and
for the sake of Jerusalem, which I have chosen."[k]

11:1 [w] Dt 17:17; Ne 13:26
11:2 [x] Ex 34:16; Dt 7:3-4
11:4 [y] 1Ki 8:61; 9:4
11:5 [z] ver 33; Jdg 2:13; 2Ki 23:13 [a] ver 7
11:7 [b] 2Ki 23:13 [c] Nu 21:29; Jdg 11:24 [d] Lev 20:2-5; Ac 7:43
11:9 [e] ver 2-3; 1Ki 3:5; 9:2
11:10 [f] 1Ki 9:6 [g] 1Ki 6:12
11:11 [h] ver 31; 1Ki 12:15-16; 2Ki 17:21
11:13 [i] 1Ki 12:20 [j] 2Sa 7:15 [k] Dt 12:11

Solomon's Adversaries

14 Then the LORD raised up against Solomon an adversary, Hadad the Edomite, from the royal line of
Edom. 15 Earlier when David was fighting with Edom, Joab the commander of the army, who had gone
up to bury the dead, had struck down all the men in Edom.[l] 16 Joab and all the Israelites stayed there for
six months, until they had destroyed all the men in Edom. 17 But Hadad, still only a boy, fled to Egypt
with some Edomite officials who had served his father. 18 They set out from Midian and went to Paran.[m]
Then taking men from Paran with them, they went to Egypt, to Pharaoh king of Egypt, who gave Hadad
a house and land and provided him with food.
19 Pharaoh was so pleased with Hadad that he gave him a sister of his own wife, Queen Tahpenes, in
marriage. 20 The sister of Tahpenes bore him a son named Genubath, whom Tahpenes brought up in the
royal palace. There Genubath lived with Pharaoh's own children.
21 While he was in Egypt, Hadad heard that David rested with his fathers and that Joab the commander
of the army was also dead. Then Hadad said to Pharaoh, "Let me go, that I may return to my own country."

11:15 [l] Dt 20:13; 2Sa 8:14; 1Ch 18:12
11:18 [m] Nu 10:12

[a] 26 Or *charioteers* [b] 28 Or possibly *Muzur*, a region in Cilicia; also in verse 29 [c] 28 Probably *Cilicia* [d] 29 That is, about 15 pounds (about 7 kilograms) [e] 29 That is, about 3 3/4 pounds (about 1.7 kilograms) [f] 5 Hebrew *Milcom*; also in verse 33

11:1 It was common in the ancient Near East for kings to use marriage for the purpose of cementing international relationships with various kingdoms. But this practice violated not only the prohibition against many wives (Dt 17:17) but also the ban against taking wives from among the pagan peoples among whom Israel had settled (see Ex 34:16; Dt 7:1–3; Jos 23:12–13; Ezr 9:2; 10:2–3; Ne 13:23–27).

11:13 The "one tribe" was Judah.

22 "What have you lacked here that you want to go back to your own country?" Pharaoh asked.
"Nothing," Hadad replied, "but do let me go!"
11:23 [n]ver 14 23 And God raised up against Solomon another adversary,[n] Rezon son of Eliada, who had fled from his
[o]2Sa 8:3 master, Hadadezer[o] king of Zobah. 24 He gathered men around him and became the leader of a band of
11:24 [p]2Sa 8:5; 10:8,18 rebels when David destroyed the forces[a] ⌊of Zobah⌋; the rebels went to Damascus,[p] where they settled and
took control. 25 Rezon was Israel's adversary as long as Solomon lived, adding to the trouble caused by
11:25 [q]2Sa 10:19 Hadad. So Rezon ruled in Aram[q] and was hostile toward Israel.

Jeroboam Rebels Against Solomon

11:26 [r]2Sa 20:21; 1Ki 12:2; 2Ch 13:6 26 Also, Jeroboam son of Nebat rebelled[r] against the king. He was one of Solomon's officials, an Ephra-
imite from Zeredah, and his mother was a widow named Zeruah.
27 Here is the account of how he rebelled against the king: Solomon had built the supporting terrac-
11:27 [s]1Ki 9:24 es[b][s] and had filled in the gap in the wall of the city of David his father. 28 Now Jeroboam was a man of
11:28 [t]Ru 2:1 [u]Pr 22:29 standing,[t] and when Solomon saw how well[u] the young man did his work, he put him in charge of the
whole labor force of the house of Joseph.
11:29 [v]1Ki 12:15; 14:2; 2Ch 9:29 29 About that time Jeroboam was going out of Jerusalem, and Ahijah[v] the prophet of Shiloh met him
on the way, wearing a new cloak. The two of them were alone out in the country, 30 and Ahijah took hold
11:30 [w]1Sa 15:27 of the new cloak he was wearing and tore[w] it into twelve pieces. 31 Then he said to Jeroboam, "Take ten
11:31 [x]ver 11 pieces for yourself, for this is what the LORD, the God of Israel, says: 'See, I am going to tear[x] the kingdom
out of Solomon's hand and give you ten tribes. 32 But for the sake of my servant David and the city of Je-
rusalem, which I have chosen out of all the tribes of Israel, he will have one tribe. 33 I will do this because
11:33 [y]ver 5-7 [z]1Ki 3:3 they have[c] forsaken me and worshiped[y] Ashtoreth the goddess of the Sidonians, Chemosh the god of the
Moabites, and Molech the god of the Ammonites, and have not walked in my ways, nor done what is right
in my eyes, nor kept my statutes[z] and laws as David, Solomon's father, did.
34 " 'But I will not take the whole kingdom out of Solomon's hand; I have made him ruler all the days
of his life for the sake of David my servant, whom I chose and who observed my commands and statutes.
11:36 [a]ver 13; 1Ki 12:17 35 I will take the kingdom from his son's hands and give you ten tribes. 36 I will give one tribe[a] to his son
[b]1Ki 15:4; 2Ki 8:19 so that David my servant may always have a lamp[b] before me in Jerusalem, the city where I chose to put
11:37 [c]2Sa 3:21 my Name. 37 However, as for you, I will take you, and you will rule over all that your heart desires;[c] you
will be king over Israel. 38 If you do whatever I command you and walk in my ways and do what is right
11:38 [d]Dt 17:19 in my eyes by keeping my statutes[d] and commands, as David my servant did, I will be with you. I will
[e]Jos 1:5; 2Sa 7:11,27 build you a dynasty[e] as enduring as the one I built for David and will give Israel to you. 39 I will humble
David's descendants because of this, but not forever.' "
11:40 [f]2Ch 12:2 40 Solomon tried to kill Jeroboam, but Jeroboam fled to Egypt, to Shishak[f] the king, and stayed there
until Solomon's death.

Solomon's Death

41 As for the other events of Solomon's reign—all he did and the wisdom he displayed—are they not
written in the book of the annals of Solomon? 42 Solomon reigned in Jerusalem over all Israel forty years.
11:43 [g]1Ki 14:21; Mt 1:7 43 Then he rested with his fathers and was buried in the city of David his father. And Rehoboam[g] his son
succeeded him as king.

[a] 24 Hebrew *destroyed them* [b] 27 Or *the Millo* [c] 33 Hebrew; Septuagint, Vulgate and Syriac *because he has*

11:26 Jeroboam son of Nebat, later called Jeroboam I, was the first king of the secessionist northern kingdom of Israel. Solomon's extravagances and his ambition to make Israel a world power led him to set up a tremendously expensive capital and a very elaborate harem, resulting in burdensome taxation. Ahijah the prophet revealed to Jeroboam that he was to rule ten of the tribes (11:26–40), whereupon Jeroboam fled to Egypt to escape Solomon. After Solomon's death, Jeroboam returned from Egypt, and through him an appeal was made to Rehoboam for less oppresive taxes. Rehoboam, however, refused to heed the appeal, with the result that Israel rebelled against him. When Adoram was sent to collect the tribute, he was killed, and Rehoboam fled to Jerusalem (12:16–19). Jeroboam was then made king of the ten tribes. Rehoboam raised an army from Judah and Benjamin, but was forbidden by God to attack (12:20–24). Jeroboam then fortified Shechem and Peniel, instituted pagan rites and waged a relentless struggle against Rehoboam (12:25–28; 14:29–30). In order to prevent the people from returning to Jerusalem for worship (and from thereby having their loyalty to the house of David rekindled), Jeroboam set up rival shrines at Dan and Bethel (12:29; see "The High Place at Dan" on p. 504). Although the Bible does not mention it, Shishak of Egypt ravaged the northern kingdom in the same campaign in which he sacked Jerusalem (see "The Campaign of Shishak" on p. 635).

11:41 The annals (historical records or chronicles) of Solomon refer to a written source used by the author of Kings. He would later mention the annals of the kings of Israel and of Judah (e.g., 14:19,29). These additional accounts may have been lost when Jerusalem was destroyed.

Israel Rebels Against Rehoboam

12 Rehoboam went to Shechem, for all the Israelites had gone there to make him king. [2]When Jer-
oboam son of Nebat heard this (he was still in Egypt, where he had fled[h] from King Solomon),
he returned from[a] Egypt. [3]So they sent for Jeroboam, and he and the whole assembly of Israel went to

12:2 [h]1Ki 11:40

[a] 2 Or *he remained in*

12:1 Rehoboam lost control of the ten northern tribes after he had arrogantly refused to lighten the people's tax burden (vv. 1–16). After having been dissuaded from attacking Israel, Rehoboam began to strengthen his land. He fortified Bethlehem, Gath, Lachish, Hebron

The Overseer of the Forced Labor

Stone quarry on Mount Carmel

Photograph: © Todd Bolen/Bible Places.com

1 KINGS 12 By the time Rehoboam became king, the northern tribes had grown weary of Solomon's oppressive forced labor policy (1Ki 5:13–18; 12:4).[1] They asked Rehoboam to lighten their burden; but rather than following the wise counsel of the elders who had served under Solomon, Rehoboam listened to his young peers and pledged to intensify the burden of labor (vv. 6–14). This prompted the ten northern tribes to secede (v. 16). Their new leader was Jeroboam, himself a former overseer of forced labor for the tribes of Ephraim and Manasseh (11:28).

In a final effort to resolve the crisis, Rehoboam dispatched Adoniram, the official in charge of forced labor, to broker a settlement. Adoniram was experienced in these matters, having served as national overseer of forced labor under both David (2Sa 20:24) and Solomon (1Ki 5:14). Tragically, Adoniram was stoned to death, and Rehoboam himself was compelled to flee in his chariot to avoid a similar fate (12:18).

The seal of a later overseer of forced labor has appeared on the antiquities market. One side was for personal use, while the other designated his official title. Side A reads "(Belonging) to Pelayahu (son of) Mattityahu," while Side B specifies "(Belonging) to Pelayahu over(seer of) the forced labor."

Pelayahu ("Yahweh is wondrous") is not mentioned in the Bible. His function as an administrator "over the forced labor," however, uses exactly the same terminology we find in the Old Testament with regard to Adoniram and Jeroboam. The seal therefore serves as external verification for the administrative policies of the early monarchy as described in the Bible.

[1]See "Slavery and Labor Law in the Ancient Near East" on page 127.

12:4 [i]1Sa 8:11- Rehoboam and said to him: 4“Your father put a heavy yoke[i] on us, but now lighten the harsh labor and
18; 1Ki 4:20-28 the heavy yoke he put on us, and we will serve you.”
5Rehoboam answered, “Go away for three days and then come back to me.” So the people went away.
12:6 [j]1Ki 4:2 6Then King Rehoboam consulted the elders[j] who had served his father Solomon during his lifetime.
“How would you advise me to answer these people?” he asked.
7They replied, “If today you will be a servant to these people and serve them and give them a favor-
12:7 [k]Pr 15:1 able answer,[k] they will always be your servants.”
8But Rehoboam rejected the advice the elders gave him and consulted the young men who had grown
up with him and were serving him. 9He asked them, “What is your advice? How should we answer these
people who say to me, ‘Lighten the yoke your father put on us’?”
10The young men who had grown up with him replied, “Tell these people who have said to you, ‘Your
father put a heavy yoke on us, but make our yoke lighter’—tell them, ‘My little finger is thicker than my
father’s waist. 11My father laid on you a heavy yoke; I will make it even heavier. My father scourged you
with whips; I will scourge you with scorpions.’ ”
12Three days later Jeroboam and all the people returned to Rehoboam, as the king had said, “Come
back to me in three days.” 13The king answered the people harshly. Rejecting the advice given him by the
elders, 14he followed the advice of the young men and said, “My father made your yoke heavy; I will make
12:14 [l]Ex 1:14; it even heavier. My father scourged[l] you with whips; I will scourge you with scorpions.” 15So the king did
5:5-9,16-18 **12:15** [m]ver 24; not listen to the people, for this turn of events was from the LORD,[m] to fulfill the word the LORD had spo-
Dt 2:30; Jdg 14:4; 2Ch 22:7; 25:20 [n]1Ki 11:29 ken to Jeroboam son of Nebat through Ahijah[n] the Shilonite.
16When all Israel saw that the king refused to listen to them, they answered the king:

> “What share do we have in David,
> what part in Jesse’s son?
12:16 [o]2Sa 20:1 > To your tents, O Israel![o]
> Look after your own house, O David!”

12:17 [p]1Ki 11:13, So the Israelites went home. 17But as for the Israelites who were living in the towns of Judah,[p] Rehobo-
36 am still ruled over them.
12:18 18King Rehoboam sent out Adoniram,[a][q] who was in charge of forced labor, but all Israel stoned him
[q]2Sa 20:24; 1Ki 4:6; 5:14 to death. King Rehoboam, however, managed to get into his chariot and escape to Jerusalem. 19So Isra-
12:19 [r]2Ki 17:21 el has been in rebellion against the house of David[r] to this day.
20When all the Israelites heard that Jeroboam had returned, they sent and called him to the assem-
12:20 [s]1Ki 11:13, bly and made him king over all Israel. Only the tribe of Judah remained loyal to the house of David.[s]
32 21When Rehoboam arrived in Jerusalem, he mustered the whole house of Judah and the tribe of Ben-
12:21 [t]2Ch 11:1 jamin—a hundred and eighty thousand fighting men—to make war[t] against the house of Israel and to
regain the kingdom for Rehoboam son of Solomon.
12:22 22But this word of God came to Shemaiah[u] the man of God: 23“Say to Rehoboam son of Solomon king
[u]2Ch 12:5-7 of Judah, to the whole house of Judah and Benjamin, and to the rest of the people, 24‘This is what the
LORD says: Do not go up to fight against your brothers, the Israelites. Go home, every one of you, for this
is my doing.’ ” So they obeyed the word of the LORD and went home again, as the LORD had ordered.

Golden Calves at Bethel and Dan

12:25 [v]Jdg 9:45 25Then Jeroboam fortified Shechem[v] in the hill country of Ephraim and lived there. From there he
[w]Jdg 8:8,17 went out and built up Peniel.[b][w]
26Jeroboam thought to himself, “The kingdom will now likely revert to the house of David. 27If these
12:27 [x]Dt 12:5-6 people go up to offer sacrifices at the temple of the LORD in Jerusalem,[x] they will again give their allegiance
to their lord, Rehoboam king of Judah. They will kill me and return to King Rehoboam.”

[a] 18 Some Septuagint manuscripts and Syriac (see also 1 Kings 4:6 and 5:14); Hebrew *Adoram* [b] 25 Hebrew *Penuel,* a variant of *Peniel*

---

and other cities and prepared them to endure a siege by enemy forces. He gave refuge to priests and Levites whom Jeroboam had driven from Israel, and they brought wisdom and strength to his realm (2Ch 11:5-17). Jerusalem, along with the cities of the north, was sacked by Pharaoh Shishak of Egypt (see “The Campaign of Shishak” on p. 635). Rehoboam seems to have inherited his father’s love for luxury and show, for he gathered a substantial harem and reared a large family (2Ch 11:18-23): He had 18 wives and 60 concubines. He was not content with fortifying his land but spent large sums on ornate places of worship; sadly, though, his lasting legacy was the division of Israel into two nations.

12:11 “Scorpions” is a reference to metal-spiked leather lashes.

12:18 See “The Overseer of the Forced Labor” on page 502.

[28]After seeking advice, the king made two golden calves.[y] He said to the people, "It is too much for you
to go up to Jerusalem. Here are your gods, O Israel, who brought you up out of Egypt."[z] [29]One he set up
in Bethel,[a] and the other in Dan.[b] [30]And this thing became a sin;[c] the people went even as far as Dan to
worship the one there.
[31]Jeroboam built shrines[d] on high places and appointed priests[e] from all sorts of people, even though

12:28 [y]Ex 32:4; 2Ki 10:29; 17:16
12:29 [a]Ge 28:19 [b]Jdg 18:27-31
12:30 [c]1Ki 13:34; 2Ki 17:21
12:31 [d]1Ki 13:32 [e]Nu 3:10

12:28–29 Aramean and Canaanite gods were often depicted as standing on calves or bulls as symbols of their strength and fertility (see the note on Jdg 2:13; see also "The High Place at Dan" on p. 504 and "Bethel" on p. 59). Although Jeroboam made no physical representation of the Lord—no "god" stood on the backs of his bulls—he combined the pagan calf symbol with the worship of the Lord.

ARCHAEOLOGICAL SITES

THE HIGH PLACE AT DAN

1 KINGS 12 According to 1 Kings 12 Israel's King Jeroboam I challenged Jerusalem's claim to be the only legitimate location for worshiping and offering sacrifices. Jeroboam built "shrines on high places" (v. 31) in Dan and Bethel ("Map 6") as rivals to the Jerusalem temple,[1] installed golden calves in each,[2] appointed priests and institutionalized festival days. During excavations at Tel Dan (Tell el-Qadi) beginning in 1966, archaeologist A. Biran discovered a sacred precinct that has been identified as almost certainly the one established by King Jeroboam I in the nineteenth century B.C. The shrine was renovated and expanded under Kings Ahab and Jeroboam II during the eighth and seventh centuries B.C., respectively.

In the sacred area a massive stairway (approximately 27 feet [8.2 m] long and 26 feet [7.9 m] wide) leads up to an **ashlar** block platform, which is nearly 10 feet (3 m) high. This "high place," where the golden calves would have been displayed, was either an open-air sanctuary or served as the base of a temple structure. Within the sacred precinct Biran uncovered both small and large four-horned altars (the smaller ones for incense and burnt offerings, such as birds, and the large altar for bigger animals, like sheep and goats, the remains of which were also unearthed). Iron shovels, a jar used for ash disposal, a ceremonial drinking bowl, oil lamps with seven spouts and numerous other religious objects were also found.[3]

By all archaeological and Biblical indications, Jeroboam I was successful in rerouting Israelite pilgrims from Jerusalem to Dan and other shrines (v. 30). These shrines were condemned by the prophets as spurious and as enticements to apostasy.[4]

[1]See "The Migration of the Danites" on page 378 and "Bethel" on page 59. [2]See "The Golden Calf" on page 143. [3]See "Ancient Altars" on page 125 and "The Horned Altar" on page 924. [4]See "The High Places" on page 1318.

The altar at Dan

Preserving Bible Times; © Dr. James C. Martin

12:32 [f]Lev 23:33-34; Nu 29:12 they were not Levites. 32He instituted a festival on the fifteenth day of the eighth[f] month, like the festival
held in Judah, and offered sacrifices on the altar. This he did in Bethel, sacrificing to the calves he had
made. And at Bethel he also installed priests at the high places he had made. 33On the fifteenth day of the
12:33 [g]Nu 15:39; 1Ki 13:1; Am 7:13 eighth month, a month of his own choosing, he offered sacrifices on the altar he had built at Bethel.[g] So
he instituted the festival for the Israelites and went up to the altar to make offerings.

The Man of God From Judah

13:1 [h]2Ki 23:17 [i]1Ki 12:32-33 **13** By the word of the LORD a man of God[h] came from Judah to Bethel,[i] as Jeroboam was standing
by the altar to make an offering. 2He cried out against the altar by the word of the LORD: "O altar,
13:2 [j]2Ki 23:15-16,20 altar! This is what the LORD says: 'A son named Josiah[j] will be born to the house of David. On you he will
sacrifice the priests of the high places who now make offerings here, and human bones will be burned
13:3 [k]Jdg 6:17; Isa 7:14; Jn 2:11; 1Co 1:22 on you.' " 3That same day the man of God gave a sign:[k] "This is the sign the LORD has declared: The altar
will be split apart and the ashes on it will be poured out."
4When King Jeroboam heard what the man of God cried out against the altar at Bethel, he stretched
out his hand from the altar and said, "Seize him!" But the hand he stretched out toward the man shriv-
eled up, so that he could not pull it back. 5Also, the altar was split apart and its ashes poured out accord-
ing to the sign given by the man of God by the word of the LORD.
13:6 [l]Ex 8:8; 9:28; 10:17; Lk 6:27-28; Ac 8:24; Jas 5:16 6Then the king said to the man of God, "Intercede[l] with the LORD your God and pray for me that my
hand may be restored." So the man of God interceded with the LORD, and the king's hand was restored
and became as it was before.
7The king said to the man of God, "Come home with me and have something to eat, and I will give you
13:7 [m]1Sa 9:7; 2Ki 5:15 a gift."[m]
13:8 [n]Nu 22:18; 24:13 [o]ver 16 8But the man of God answered the king, "Even if you were to give me half your possessions,[n] I would
not go with you, nor would I eat bread[o] or drink water here. 9For I was commanded by the word of the
LORD: 'You must not eat bread or drink water or return by the way you came.' " 10So he took another road
and did not return by the way he had come to Bethel.
11Now there was a certain old prophet living in Bethel, whose sons came and told him all that the man
of God had done there that day. They also told their father what he had said to the king. 12Their father
asked them, "Which way did he go?" And his sons showed him which road the man of God from Judah
had taken. 13So he said to his sons, "Saddle the donkey for me." And when they had saddled the donkey
for him, he mounted it 14and rode after the man of God. He found him sitting under an oak tree and
asked, "Are you the man of God who came from Judah?"
"I am," he replied.
15So the prophet said to him, "Come home with me and eat."
13:16 [p]ver 8 16The man of God said, "I cannot turn back and go with you, nor can I eat bread[p] or drink water with
you in this place. 17I have been told by the word of the LORD: 'You must not eat bread or drink water there
or return by the way you came.' "
18The old prophet answered, "I too am a prophet, as you are. And an angel said to me by the word of
the LORD: 'Bring him back with you to your house so that he may eat bread and drink water.' " (But he was
13:18 [q]Dt 13:3 lying[q] to him.) 19So the man of God returned with him and ate and drank in his house.
20While they were sitting at the table, the word of the LORD came to the old prophet who had brought
him back. 21He cried out to the man of God who had come from Judah, "This is what the LORD says: 'You
13:21 [r]ver 26 have defied[r] the word of the LORD and have not kept the command the LORD your God gave you. 22You
came back and ate bread and drank water in the place where he told you not to eat or drink. Therefore
your body will not be buried in the tomb of your fathers.' "
23When the man of God had finished eating and drinking, the prophet who had brought him back sad-
13:24 [s]1Ki 20:36 dled his donkey for him. 24As he went on his way, a lion[s] met him on the road and killed him, and his body
was thrown down on the road, with both the donkey and the lion standing beside it. 25Some people who
passed by saw the body thrown down there, with the lion standing beside the body, and they went and
reported it in the city where the old prophet lived.
26When the prophet who had brought him back from his journey heard of it, he said, "It is the man

13:24 Menacing carnivores—such as bears, lions, leopards, wolves and jackals—were common in Israel (see "Lions and Other Wild Beasts in Ancient Israel" on p. 813). That the donkey did not run and the lion did not attack the donkey or disturb the man's body (v. 28) clearly stamped the incident as a divine judgment.

of God who defied the word of the LORD. The LORD has given him over to the lion, which has mauled him
and killed him, as the word of the LORD had warned him."
27 The prophet said to his sons, "Saddle the donkey for me," and they did so. 28 Then he went out and
found the body thrown down on the road, with the donkey and the lion standing beside it. The lion had
neither eaten the body nor mauled the donkey. 29 So the prophet picked up the body of the man of God,
laid it on the donkey, and brought it back to his own city to mourn for him and bury him. 30 Then he laid
the body in his own tomb, and they mourned over him and said, "Oh, my brother!"[t] **13:30** [t]Jer 22:18
31 After burying him, he said to his sons, "When I die, bury me in the grave where the man of God is
buried; lay my bones[u] beside his bones. 32 For the message he declared by the word of the LORD against **13:31** [u]2Ki 23:18

The History of the Northern Kingdom

1 KINGS 13 The northern kingdom is variously called **Samaria** (after its capital), Ephraim (after its dominant tribe) or Israel. Nineteen kings, representing nine different families, reigned there for a combined period of 208 years.

After Solomon's death (930 B.C.) Jeroboam I led the northern tribes to separate from Judah (under Rehoboam) and to establish Israel as a separate kingdom. Jeroboam built a capital at Tirzah ("Map 4") and set up golden calves in Bethel and Dan (both "Map 6") to rival worship in Jerusalem.[1] But he lost territory in **Moab** and Syria,[2] and tensions smoldered between Israel and Judah for half a century. Jeroboam's son Nadab was assassinated by Baasha.

Israel fell into disorder. Baasha exacerbated tensions with King Asa of Judah by fortifying Ramah, near Jerusalem, to which Asa responded by hiring Syria's Ben-Hadad to attack Israel (1Ki 15:16–22). Baasha's dynasty ended when Zimri killed his son Elah. After a seven-day reign, Zimri burned the palace, with himself inside, at Tirzah.[3]

Israel returned to power and stability under Omri (884–873 B.C.), who bested Tibni in a four-year civil war and established a capital at Samaria ("Map 4"). He warred continually against Syria, subdued Moab, made peace with Judah and entered into a trade alliance with **Phoenicia**, resulting in the marriage of his son Ahab to Jezebel, daughter of the Sidonian king.[4] Revolts in Moab plagued the Omrides (Omri, Ahab, Ahaziah and Jehoram), and Samaria was fortified heavily against attacks from Syria-Damascus.[5] These same kingdoms, however, cooperated with one another when their personal interests were at stake. A temporary alliance of Syrian-Palestinian states pitted itself against Assyria at the battle of Qarqar (853 B.C.).[6]

The Omride dynasty was characterized by apostasy. During this time the prophets Elijah and Elisha confronted the religious policies of Israel's kings. Jezebel introduced the worship of Baal-Melqart, and this cult was promoted by Omride kings until the usurper Jehu executed Omri's descendants, along with Jezebel and the prophets of Baal (841 B.C.).

The fourth-dynasty kings (Jehu, Jehoahaz, Jehoash, Jeroboam II and Zechariah; 2Ki 10:30), despite a temporary suppression of the Baal cult (2Ki 10:18–27), maintained the worship of the golden calves of Jeroboam I. Syria and Assyria continued to menace Israel over the next 50 years. Israel was greatly reduced in territory and military resources and regularly paid tribute to Assyria. But Assyria, after considerably weakening Damascus (Syria), suffered its own period of vulnerability. With its two principal enemies in a diminished state, Israel's Jeroboam II was able to regain some territory. This period ended when Shallum assassinated Jeroboam II's successor, Zechariah.

Israel then fell rapidly into chaos and crisis. Shallum was assassinated by Menahem, and a fifth dynasty (Menahem and Pekahiah) briefly came to power around 746 B.C. Anti-Assyrian sentiment flared after Menahem exacted a head-tax to pay tribute to Tiglath-Pileser III.[7] Following a coup d'état, Pekah seized control of Israel, forming an anti-Assyrian alliance with Syria's Rezin. Pekah and Rezin pressured Ahaz of Judah to join them and attacked Jerusalem when he resisted. Ahaz sent tribute to Tiglath-Pileser III, king of a resurgent Assyria, seeking help, to which Assyria responded by sweeping down over northern Israel and Damascus. Rezin was killed and his subjects deported to Assyria.[8]

A new usurper seized Israel's throne: Hoshea assassinated Pekah and ruled in his place. Soon after the death of Tiglath-Pileser III (727 B.C.), Hoshea withheld tribute from Assyria. Shalmaneser V, successor to Tiglath-Pileser III, imprisoned Hoshea and put Samaria under siege.[9] With the fall of the city (722 B.C.) and the deportation of its population, the northern kingdom came to an end.

The northern kingdom was noteworthy in three ways:

- It was powerful relative to Judah.
- It was idolatrous.
- It was politically unstable.

[1]See "The High Place at Dan" on page 504. [2]See "Moab" on page 292 and "Damascus" on page 1087. [3]See "Tirzah" on page 509. [4]See "Sidon" on page 1536. [5]See "The Mesha (Moabite) Stone" on page 530. [6]See "Ahab and the Battle of Qarqar" on page 524. [7]See "Menahem and Pekah of Israel, Jotham of Judah and Tiglath-Pileser III of Assyria" on page 553. [8]See "Ahaz, King of Judah, and Rezin, King of Aram" on page 554. [9]See "Hoshea, King of Israel, and Shalmaneser V, King of Assyria" on page 556.

13:32 [v]ver 2; Lev 26:30 [w]1Ki 16:24,28 [x]2Ki 23:16
13:33 [y]1Ki 12:31; 2Ch 11:15; 13:9
13:34 [z]1Ki 12:30 [a]1Ki 14:10
14:2 [b]1Sa 28:8; 2Sa 14:2; 1Ki 11:29
14:3 [c]1Sa 9:7
14:7 [d]2Sa 12:7-8; 1Ki 16:2
14:8 [e]1Ki 11:31, 33,38 [f]1Ki 15:5
14:9 [g]Ex 34:17; 1Ki 12:28; 2Ch 11:15 [h]Ne 9:26; Ps 50:17; Eze 23:35
14:10 [i]Dt 32:36; 1Ki 21:21; 2Ki 9:8-9; 14:26 [j]1Ki 15:29
14:11 [k]1Ki 16:4; 21:24
14:13 [l]2Ch 12:12; 19:3
14:15 [m]Dt 29:28; 2Ki 15:29; 17:6; Ps 52:5 [n]Jos 23:15-16 [o]Ex 34:13; Dt 12:3
14:16 [p]1Ki 12:30; 13:34; 15:30,34; 16:2
14:17 [q]ver 12; 1Ki 15:33; 16:6-9
14:21 [r]ver 31; 1Ki 11:1; 2Ch 12:13

the altar in Bethel and against all the shrines on the high places[v] in the towns of Samaria[w] will certainly
come true."[x]
33 Even after this, Jeroboam did not change his evil ways, but once more appointed priests for the high
places from all sorts[y] of people. Anyone who wanted to become a priest he consecrated for the high
places. 34 This was the sin[z] of the house of Jeroboam that led to its downfall and to its destruction[a] from
the face of the earth.

Ahijah's Prophecy Against Jeroboam

14 At that time Abijah son of Jeroboam became ill, 2 and Jeroboam said to his wife, "Go, disguise
yourself, so you won't be recognized as the wife of Jeroboam. Then go to Shiloh. Ahijah[b] the
prophet is there—the one who told me I would be king over this people. 3 Take ten loaves of bread[c] with
you, some cakes and a jar of honey, and go to him. He will tell you what will happen to the boy." 4 So Jer-
oboam's wife did what he said and went to Ahijah's house in Shiloh.
Now Ahijah could not see; his sight was gone because of his age. 5 But the LORD had told Ahijah, "Jer-
oboam's wife is coming to ask you about her son, for he is ill, and you are to give her such and such an
answer. When she arrives, she will pretend to be someone else."
6 So when Ahijah heard the sound of her footsteps at the door, he said, "Come in, wife of Jeroboam.
Why this pretense? I have been sent to you with bad news. 7 Go, tell Jeroboam that this is what the LORD,
the God of Israel, says: 'I raised you up from among the people and made you a leader[d] over my people
Israel. 8 I tore[e] the kingdom away from the house of David and gave it to you, but you have not been like
my servant David, who kept my commands and followed me with all his heart, doing only what was
right[f] in my eyes. 9 You have done more evil than all who lived before you. You have made for yourself
other gods, idols[g] made of metal; you have provoked me to anger and thrust me behind your back.[h]
10 " 'Because of this, I am going to bring disaster on the house of Jeroboam. I will cut off from Jero-
boam every last male in Israel—slave or free.[i] I will burn up the house of Jeroboam as one burns dung,
until it is all gone.[j] 11 Dogs[k] will eat those belonging to Jeroboam who die in the city, and the birds of the
air will feed on those who die in the country. The LORD has spoken!'
12 "As for you, go back home. When you set foot in your city, the boy will die. 13 All Israel will mourn
for him and bury him. He is the only one belonging to Jeroboam who will be buried, because he is the
only one in the house of Jeroboam in whom the LORD, the God of Israel, has found anything good.[l]
14 "The LORD will raise up for himself a king over Israel who will cut off the family of Jeroboam. This
is the day! What? Yes, even now.[a] 15 And the LORD will strike Israel, so that it will be like a reed swaying in
the water. He will uproot[m] Israel from this good land that he gave to their forefathers and scatter them
beyond the River,[b] because they provoked[n] the LORD to anger by making Asherah[o] poles.[c] 16 And he will
give Israel up because of the sins[p] Jeroboam has committed and has caused Israel to commit."
17 Then Jeroboam's wife got up and left and went to Tirzah.[q] As soon as she stepped over the thresh-
old of the house, the boy died. 18 They buried him, and all Israel mourned for him, as the LORD had said
through his servant the prophet Ahijah.
19 The other events of Jeroboam's reign, his wars and how he ruled, are written in the book of the an-
nals of the kings of Israel. 20 He reigned for twenty-two years and then rested with his fathers. And Na-
dab his son succeeded him as king.

Rehoboam King of Judah

21 Rehoboam son of Solomon was king in Judah. He was forty-one years old when he became king, and
he reigned seventeen years in Jerusalem, the city the LORD had chosen out of all the tribes of Israel in
which to put his Name. His mother's name was Naamah; she was an Ammonite.[r]

[a] *14* The meaning of the Hebrew for this sentence is uncertain. [b] *15* That is, the Euphrates [c] *15* That is, symbols of the goddess Asherah; here and elsewhere in 1 Kings

---

14:15 Asherah was the consort of Baal (cf. Jdg 3:7; 2Ki 23:4), and Asherah poles were probably her wooden representations. (See "Devotion to Asherah in the Khirbet El-Qom Inscription" on p. 638 and "The Kuntillet Ajrûd Inscriptions: The Lord's Asherah?" on p. 1220.)
14:17 Tirzah was the royal city of the kings of Israel until Omri purchased and built up Samaria to serve as the capital of the northern kingdom (16:24; see "Omri and Samaria" on p. 512). This is also the probable location of the modern Tell el-Farah, about 7 miles (11 km) north of Shechem. (See "Tirzah" on p. 509.)

14:19 The "book of the annals of the kings of Israel" was a record of the reigns of the kings of the northern kingdom. Although some scholars have concluded that this, as well as the "annals of Solomon" (11:41) and the "annals of the kings of Judah" (14:29), are to be viewed as official court records from the royal archives in Jerusalem and Samaria, this is by no means certain. They may have been chronicles of the reigns of the kings of Israel and Judah compiled by the succession of Israel's prophets spanning the kingdom period.

THE PROBLEM OF THE CHRONOLOGY OF THE KINGS OF JUDAH AND ISRAEL

1 KINGS 14 One of the most vexing problems in the Old Testament is the chronology of the **divided monarchy**. Interpreters as early as the Greek translators of the Old Testament have struggled to understand the lengths of reigns of the Israelite and Judahite kings. In some cases the numbers simply do not seem to add up.

- First Kings 15:25 states that Nadab began to rule in Asa's second year, and verse 28 claims that he died in Asa's third year. Simple math would indicate that Nadab reigned for one year, but verse 25 states that he ruled for two.
- Second Kings 3:1 notes that Joram began to rule in Jehoshaphat's eighteenth year, but according to 1:17 Joram ascended the throne in Jehoram's second year.
- According to 9:24–27 Jehu killed King Joram of Israel and mortally wounded King Ahaziah of Judah on the same day. Thus, the total length of reigns for the kings of Israel and Judah from the division of the **united kingdom** in Rehoboam's time to Jehu's assassinations must have been equal. But adding up the numbers in the Biblical text yields a total of 98 years for Israel and only 95 for Judah.

Probably the best approach to resolving these chronological problems has been proposed by Edwin Thiele, who determined how chronological reckoning was handled by the ancient Israelites. Three important aspects of Israelite chronology are as follows:

- Different calendar years were in use in Israel and Judah. Israel began its calendar year in the month of Nisan (in the spring), while Judah's year started in Tishri (in the fall).[1]
- There were two different ways to count the first year of a king's rule. In the "accession year" system, the time from the day a king began to reign until the beginning of the new year was counted as his "accession year"—not his first year, which would begin on the first day of the official new year. "Non-accession year" reckoning, by contrast, counted the time from the king's accession until the beginning of the new year as his first year; in this system, the first day of the new year marked the start of the king's second year, no matter how long he had reigned during his "first year." In the non-accession year system, then, the "first year" was always less than one full year. Israel apparently followed the non-accession year system until the reign of Jehoash, when the nation shifted to accession year reckoning. Judah adhered to the accession year system except for a brief time when peaceful relations with the northern kingdom led to a temporary change. The northern kingdom's early use of the non-accession year system explains how Nadab's rule of one actual year was counted as two.
- Sometimes Israel was ruled by coregents (father and son reigning simultaneously). In such a situation the son would be elevated to the throne before his father's death and would begin counting his regnal years immediately. Such was the case for Jehoshaphat, who apparently installed his son Jehoram as coregent five years before his own death. Joram of Israel came to the throne during Jehoshaphat's eighteenth year (2Ki 3:1), which was also Jehoram's second year (2Ki 1:17). Because two Judahite rulers were each counting the years of overlap in their regnal totals, adding up the Biblical numbers understandably results in a figure too high for the period and unequal to the regnal totals in the northern kingdom.

Recently some scholars have proposed minor modifications to the dates set forth by Thiele for the reigns of the kings of Israel and Judah, but on the whole the principles he outlined and the chronology he established have stood the test of scholarly scrutiny. When coordinated with absolute dates known from **Assyrian** and Egyptian records, the chronological principles recognized by Thiele make excellent sense of a thorny problem and provide an accurate chronology of the kings based upon the sum total of the Scriptural data.

For more on the kingdoms of Israel and Judah, see "The History of the Northern Kingdom" on page 506 and "The History of the Southern Kingdom" on page 538.

[1]See "The Jewish Calendar" on page 241.

14:22 [s]2Ch 12:1 [t]Dt 32:21; Ps 78:58; 1Co 10:22
14:23 [u]Dt 16:22; 2Ki 17:9-10; Eze 16:24-25 [v]Dt 12:2; Isa 57:5
14:24 [w]Dt 23:17; 1Ki 15:12; 2Ki 23:7
14:25 [x]1Ki 11:40; 2Ch 12:2
14:26 [y]1Ki 15:15, 18 [z]1Ki 10:17

22 Judah[s] did evil in the eyes of the LORD. By the sins they committed they stirred up his jealous an-
ger[t] more than their fathers had done. 23 They also set up for themselves high places, sacred stones[u] and
Asherah poles on every high hill and under every spreading tree.[v] 24 There were even male shrine pros-
titutes[w] in the land; the people engaged in all the detestable practices of the nations the LORD had driv-
en out before the Israelites.

25 In the fifth year of King Rehoboam, Shishak king of Egypt attacked[x] Jerusalem. 26 He carried off the
treasures of the temple[y] of the LORD and the treasures of the royal palace. He took everything, including
all the gold shields[z] Solomon had made. 27 So King Rehoboam made bronze shields to replace them and
assigned these to the commanders of the guard on duty at the entrance to the royal palace. 28 Whenever
the king went to the LORD's temple, the guards bore the shields, and afterward they returned them to the
guardroom.

29 As for the other events of Rehoboam's reign, and all he did, are they not written in the book of the
14:30 [a]1Ki 12:21; 15:6 annals of the kings of Judah? 30 There was continual warfare[a] between Rehoboam and Jeroboam. 31 And
Rehoboam rested with his fathers and was buried with them in the City of David. His mother's name
14:31 [b]ver 21; 2Ch 12:16 was Naamah; she was an Ammonite.[b] And Abijah[a] his son succeeded him as king.

Abijah King of Judah

15 In the eighteenth year of the reign of Jeroboam son of Nebat, Abijah[b] became king of Judah, 2 and
15:2 [c]2Ch 11:20; 13:2 he reigned in Jerusalem three years. His mother's name was Maacah[c] daughter of Abishalom.[c]

[a] *31* Some Hebrew manuscripts and Septuagint (see also 2 Chron. 12:16); most Hebrew manuscripts *Abijam* [b] *1* Some Hebrew manuscripts and Septuagint (see also 2 Chron. 12:16); most Hebrew manuscripts *Abijam*; also in verses 7 and 8 [c] *2* A variant of *Absalom*; also in verse 10

14:23–24 "Sacred stones" were stone pillars with religious significance that were placed next to the altars. The use of such pillars was common among the Canaanites but was explicitly forbidden to the Israelites under the Mosaic Law (Ex 23:24; Lev 26:1; Dt 16:21–22). It is likely that the pillars were intended to be representations of the deity (2Ki 3:2; see "Israelite Shrines and Worship Before the Temple of Solomon" on p. 398). For legitimate uses of stone pillars, see Genesis 28:18, 31:45 and Exodus 24:4.

14:25–28 Egypt had been Israel's ally during the days of Solomon, with Pharaoh's daughter becoming Solomon's queen (see "The Pharaoh Whose Daughter Solomon Married" on p. 493). But only five years after Rehoboam began to reign, Shishak (also called Sheshonk) plundered the gold Solomon had amassed. Shishak's invasion is described in more detail in 2 Chronicles 12:2–4. His expedition into the Holy Land is attested in a victory inscription found on the walls of the temple of Amon in Karnak, near Thebes; the inscription lists numerous cities that Shishak plundered in both Judah and the northern kingdom. See "The Campaign of Shishak" on page 635.

15:1–2 See "The Problem of the Chronology of the Kings of Judah and Israel" on page 508.

ARCHAEOLOGICAL SITES

TIRZAH

1 KINGS 15 Tirzah ("Map 6") was the capital of the northern kingdom for about 40 years, including the 24-year reign of its third king, Baasha (1Ki 15:33). It is located at Tell el-Far'ah ("North") in the tribal area of Manasseh, approximately 36 miles (58 km) north of Jerusalem. Baasha was buried at Tirzah (16:6)—the only Israelite king whom the Bible specifically states was interred there. Baasha's son Elah, who ruled for two years (16:8), was overthrown by a chariot commander named Zimri around 885 B.C. (16:9–10). After only seven days on the throne, Zimri was supplanted by Omri, the army general (16:15–20). Recognizing his imminent defeat, Zimri "went into the citadel of the royal palace and set the palace on fire around him" (16:18).[1] Excavators at Tell el-Far'ah have found evidence of destruction by fire early in the ninth century B.C., with the debris layer as much as 3 feet (.9 m) thick in some places.

Reconstruction of Tirzah began after a short period of abandonment. The major building of this time was a solidly constructed structure of 31 feet (9.4 m) by 44 feet (13.4 m), built of well-dressed masonry. It was never completed, however, as evidenced by the presence of abandoned building materials, partly dressed stones and the absence of ruins. This fits the Biblical record, which states that Omri ruled at Tirzah for only six years, after which he established a new capital at **Samaria** (vv. 23–24; "Map 4").[2] Omri abruptly halted the rebuilding of Tirzah when he started construction on Samaria. Tirzah's significance dwindled thereafter; by the **postexilic period**[3] the city was abandoned. Song of Songs 6:4 sets Tirzah alongside Jerusalem as one of Israel's two great cities, indicating that the Song was written during Tirzah's glory days.[4]

[1]See "The History of the Northern Kingdom" on page 506. [2]See "Omri and Samaria" on page 512. [3]See "The Postexilic Period of the Old Testament: The Persian Period" on page 699. [4]See "Archaeology and the Date of Song of Songs" on page 1049.

3 He committed all the sins his father had done before him; his heart was not fully devoted[d] to the 15:3 [d]1Ki 11:4; Ps 119:80
LORD his God, as the heart of David his forefather had been. 4 Nevertheless, for David's sake the LORD his
God gave him a lamp[e] in Jerusalem by raising up a son to succeed him and by making Jerusalem strong. 15:4 [e]2Sa 21:17; 1Ki 11:36; 2Ch 21:7
5 For David had done what was right in the eyes of the LORD and had not failed to keep[f] any of the LORD's
commands all the days of his life—except in the case of Uriah[g] the Hittite. 15:5 [f]1Ki 9:4; 14:8 [g]2Sa 11:2-27; 12:9
6 There was war[h] between Rehoboam[a] and Jeroboam throughout ⌞Abijah's⌟ lifetime. 7 As for the oth- 15:6 [h]1Ki 14:30
er events of Abijah's reign, and all he did, are they not written in the book of the annals of the kings of
Judah? There was war between Abijah and Jeroboam. 8 And Abijah rested with his fathers and was bur-
ied in the City of David. And Asa his son succeeded him as king.

Asa King of Judah

9 In the twentieth year of Jeroboam king of Israel, Asa became king of Judah, 10 and he reigned in Je-
rusalem forty-one years. His grandmother's name was Maacah[i] daughter of Abishalom. 15:10 [i]ver 2
11 Asa did what was right in the eyes of the LORD, as his father David had done. 12 He expelled the male
shrine prostitutes[j] from the land and got rid of all the idols his fathers had made. 13 He even deposed his 15:12 [j]1Ki 14:24; 22:46
grandmother Maacah from her position as queen mother, because she had made a repulsive Asherah
pole. Asa cut the pole down[k] and burned it in the Kidron Valley. 14 Although he did not remove the high 15:13 [k]Ex 32:20
places, Asa's heart was fully committed[l] to the LORD all his life. 15 He brought into the temple of the LORD 15:14 [l]ver 3; 1Ki 8:61; 22:43
the silver and gold and the articles that he and his father had dedicated.[m] 15:15 [m]1Ki 7:51
16 There was war[n] between Asa and Baasha king of Israel throughout their reigns. 17 Baasha king of 15:16 [n]ver 32
Israel went up against Judah and fortified Ramah[o] to prevent anyone from leaving or entering the terri- 15:17 [o]Jos 18:25; 1Ki 12:27
tory of Asa king of Judah.
18 Asa then took all the silver and gold that was left in the treasuries of the LORD's temple[p] and of his 15:18 [p]ver 15; 1Ki 14:26 [q]2Ki 12:18 [r]1Ki 11:23-24
own palace. He entrusted it to his officials and sent[q] them to Ben-Hadad[r] son of Tabrimmon, the son of
Hezion, the king of Aram, who was ruling in Damascus. 19 "Let there be a treaty between me and you,"
he said, "as there was between my father and your father. See, I am sending you a gift of silver and gold.
Now break your treaty with Baasha king of Israel so he will withdraw from me."
20 Ben-Hadad agreed with King Asa and sent the commanders of his forces against the towns of Isra-
el. He conquered[s] Ijon, Dan, Abel Beth Maacah and all Kinnereth in addition to Naphtali. 21 When Baa- 15:20 [s]Jdg 18:29; 2Sa 20:14; 2Ki 15:29
sha heard this, he stopped building Ramah and withdrew to Tirzah. 22 Then King Asa issued an order to
all Judah—no one was exempt—and they carried away from Ramah the stones and timber Baasha had
been using there. With them King Asa built up Geba[t] in Benjamin, and also Mizpah. 15:22 [t]Jos 18:24; 21:17
23 As for all the other events of Asa's reign, all his achievements, all he did and the cities he built, are
they not written in the book of the annals of the kings of Judah? In his old age, however, his feet became
diseased. 24 Then Asa rested with his fathers and was buried with them in the city of his father David. And
Jehoshaphat[u] his son succeeded him as king. 15:24 [u]Mt 1:8

Nadab King of Israel

25 Nadab son of Jeroboam became king of Israel in the second year of Asa king of Judah, and he reigned

[a] 6 Most Hebrew manuscripts; some Hebrew manuscripts and Syriac *Abijam* (that is, Abijah)

15:3 Abijah of Judah, the son and successor of Rehoboam, made war on Jeroboam in an effort to recover the ten tribes of Israel. In a speech before a battle in which his army was greatly outnumbered by the forces of the northern kingdom, he appealed to Jeroboam not to oppose the God of Israel, for God had given the kingdom to David and his sons forever (2Ch 13:4–12). Abijah gained a decisive victory. Against this pious speech in Chronicles, 1 Kings 15:3 dismisses Abijah as a wicked king, perhaps indicating that the truth is more complex than either narrative by itself could indicate. Prosperity tempted Abijah to take multiple wives and to follow the evil ways of his father. He reigned for three years (2Ch 12:16—14:1).
15:8 Asa began his reign by deposing his grandmother, Maacah, and by destroying an image that she had set up. He then drove out the male shrine prostitutes and destroyed idols that his fathers had worshiped (15:12), commanding Judah to seek the Lord (2Ch 14:4). In the early days of his reign, he gathered into the temple the things that he and his father had dedicated to the Lord (1Ki 15:15). In about 897 B.C. Zerah the Cushite came against him with an immense force. The Lord helped Judah defeat this army because of Asa's faith (2Ch 14:9–15). Later, in approximately 895/94 B.C., Baasha of the northern kingdom made war against Judah. Instead of trusting the Lord, Asa bribed Ben-Hadad of Syria to break his league with Baasha so as to draw away the forces of Israel. Ben-Hadad did this, but the prophet Hanani rebuked Asa for trusting foreign powers rather than God (1Ki 15:16–22; 2Ch 16:1–10). Asa died from a severe disease of the feet (2Ch 16:11–14).
15:17 Although the precise location of Ramah of Benjamin is unknown, we do know that it was somewhere near Bethel. Deborah had sat as a judge in Israel somewhere between Bethel and Ramah (Jdg 4:5). The location of Ramah somewhere north of Jerusalem allowed it to control the route to that city; it was of such importance that when Baasha sought to make fortifications against Jerusalem, Asa appealed to Syria for support (1Ki 15:16–21). Later invaders also subdued Ramah. A column of Sennacherib's Assyrian army took it while heading south (Isa 10:29), and Jeremiah bewailed the coming of the Babylonians by describing Rachel weeping there for her children (Jer 31:15).
15:25 The dynasty of Jeroboam I survived him by only two years in the person of his son, Nadab. The Bible tells us nothing about Nadab's reign other than that he did evil and that he was murdered by Baasha while laying siege to the Philistine city of Gibbethon.

over Israel two years. 26 He did evil in the eyes of the LORD, walking in the ways of his father[v] and in his
sin, which he had caused Israel to commit.
27 Baasha son of Ahijah of the house of Issachar plotted against him, and he struck him down[w] at Gib-
bethon,[x] a Philistine town, while Nadab and all Israel were besieging it. 28 Baasha killed Nadab in the
third year of Asa king of Judah and succeeded him as king.
29 As soon as he began to reign, he killed Jeroboam's whole family.[y] He did not leave Jeroboam any-
one that breathed, but destroyed them all, according to the word of the LORD given through his servant
Ahijah the Shilonite— 30 because of the sins[z] Jeroboam had committed and had caused Israel to com-
mit, and because he provoked the LORD, the God of Israel, to anger.
31 As for the other events of Nadab's reign, and all he did, are they not written in the book of the annals
of the kings of Israel? 32 There was war[a] between Asa and Baasha king of Israel throughout their reigns.

Baasha King of Israel

33 In the third year of Asa king of Judah, Baasha son of Ahijah became king of all Israel in Tirzah, and
he reigned twenty-four years. 34 He did evil[b] in the eyes of the LORD, walking in the ways of Jeroboam and
in his sin, which he had caused Israel to commit.

16 Then the word of the LORD came to Jehu[c] son of Hanani[d] against Baasha: 2 "I lifted you up from the
dust[e] and made you leader[f] of my people Israel, but you walked in the ways of Jeroboam and
caused[g] my people Israel to sin and to provoke me to anger by their sins. 3 So I am about to consume Baa-
sha and his house,[h] and I will make your house like that of Jeroboam son of Nebat. 4 Dogs[i] will eat those be-
longing to Baasha who die in the city, and the birds of the air will feed on those who die in the country."
5 As for the other events of Baasha's reign, what he did and his achievements, are they not written in
the book of the annals[j] of the kings of Israel? 6 Baasha rested with his fathers and was buried in Tirzah.[k]
And Elah his son succeeded him as king.
7 Moreover, the word of the LORD came[l] through the prophet Jehu[m] son of Hanani to Baasha and his
house, because of all the evil he had done in the eyes of the LORD, provoking him to anger by the things
he did, and becoming like the house of Jeroboam—and also because he destroyed it.

Elah King of Israel

8 In the twenty-sixth year of Asa king of Judah, Elah son of Baasha became king of Israel, and he
reigned in Tirzah two years.
9 Zimri, one of his officials, who had command of half his chariots, plotted against him. Elah was in
Tirzah at the time, getting drunk[n] in the home of Arza, the man in charge[o] of the palace at Tirzah. 10 Zim-
ri came in, struck him down and killed him in the twenty-seventh year of Asa king of Judah. Then he suc-
ceeded him as king.
11 As soon as he began to reign and was seated on the throne, he killed off Baasha's whole family.[p] He
did not spare a single male, whether relative or friend. 12 So Zimri destroyed the whole family of Baasha,
in accordance with the word of the LORD spoken against Baasha through the prophet Jehu— 13 because
of all the sins Baasha and his son Elah had committed and had caused Israel to commit, so that they pro-
voked the LORD, the God of Israel, to anger by their worthless idols.[q]
14 As for the other events of Elah's reign, and all he did, are they not written in the book of the annals
of the kings of Israel?

Zimri King of Israel

15 In the twenty-seventh year of Asa king of Judah, Zimri reigned in Tirzah seven days. The army was
encamped near Gibbethon,[r] a Philistine town. 16 When the Israelites in the camp heard that Zimri had

15:26 [v] 1Ki 12:30; 14:16
15:27 [w] 1Ki 14:14 [x] Jos 19:44; 21:23
15:29 [y] 1Ki 14:10, 14
15:30 [z] 1Ki 14:9, 16
15:32 [a] ver 16
15:34 [b] ver 26; 1Ki 12:28-29; 13:33; 14:16
16:1 [c] ver 7; 2Ch 19:2; 20:34 [d] 2Ch 16:7
16:2 [e] 1Sa 2:8 [f] 1Ki 14:7-9 [g] 1Ki 15:34
16:3 [h] ver 11; 1Ki 14:10; 15:29; 21:22
16:4 [i] 1Ki 14:11
16:5 [j] 1Ki 14:19; 15:31
16:6 [k] 1Ki 14:17; 15:33
16:7 [l] 1Ki 15:27, 29 [m] ver 1
16:9 [n] 2Ki 9:30-33 [o] 1Ki 18:3
16:11 [p] ver 3
16:13 [q] Dt 32:21; 1Sa 12:21; Isa 41:29
16:15 [r] Jos 19:44; 1Ki 15:27

16:1 The prophet Jehu brought God's word of condemnation to the king. The same prophet also rebuked Jehoshaphat of Judah (2Ch 19:2–3).

16:8 All we know of Elah suggests that he was a dissolute reprobate; he died while on a drinking binge at the house of his chamberlain (officer in charge of a sovereign's personal affairs) while the army was away besieging Gibbethon. With his death, the short dynasty of Baasha ended. The Chronicler (1 and 2 Ch) did not even mention him.

16:10 Having murdered and usurped the throne from Elah, Zimri reigned for a mere seven days before Omri came with the army and besieged him in Tirzah. Zimri's suicidal death—he set the palace at Tirzah on fire around himself—did have lasting significance, however. Until this point Tirzah had been the capital city of Israel. Omri would create Samaria as his new capital, and the once great city of Tirzah would fade from history (see "Tirzah" on p. 509).

16:15 The precise location of Gibbethon is uncertain. The city was important enough, however, that it was besieged, first by Nadab and then 26 years later by Omri, at that time an officer serving under Elah (vv. 14–17). After Zimri's coup, the army withdrew from Gibbethon to besiege Tirzah. About 150 years later Sargon II of Assyria (r. 721–705 B.C.) besieged Gibbethon in his campaign in the Levant (Syria/Palestine); the city is portrayed on a panel in the Khorsabad palace (see "The Annals of Sargon II" on p. 1072).

plotted against the king and murdered him, they proclaimed Omri, the commander of the army, king
over Israel that very day there in the camp. 17 Then Omri and all the Israelites with him withdrew from
Gibbethon and laid siege to Tirzah. 18 When Zimri saw that the city was taken, he went into the citadel of
the royal palace and set the palace on fire around him. So he died, 19 because of the sins he had commit-
ted, doing evil in the eyes of the LORD and walking in the ways of Jeroboam and in the sin he had com-
mitted and had caused Israel to commit.
20 As for the other events of Zimri's reign, and the rebellion he carried out, are they not written in the
book of the annals of the kings of Israel?

Omri King of Israel

21 Then the people of Israel were split into two factions; half supported Tibni son of Ginath for king,
and the other half supported Omri. 22 But Omri's followers proved stronger than those of Tibni son of Gi-
nath. So Tibni died and Omri became king.
23 In the thirty-first year of Asa king of Judah, Omri became king of Israel, and he reigned twelve years,
six of them in Tirzah.[s] 24 He bought the hill of Samaria from Shemer for two talents[a] of silver and built
a city on the hill, calling it Samaria,[t] after Shemer, the name of the former owner of the hill.

16:23 [s] 1Ki 15:21
16:24 [t] 1Ki 13:32; Jn 4:4

[a] *24* That is, about 150 pounds (about 70 kilograms)

16:21 When Zimri died, Tibni was an unsuccessful competitor for the throne of Israel (vv. 15–21). Nothing else is known about him. The fact that the text merely states that he "died" (v. 22) rather than that he was killed may imply that his death was natural—in effect, that he had become so insignificant that killing him was unnecessary. On the other hand, behind this passing notice may have been a major civil war between Tibni and Omri.

16:24 Samaria, which lay 7 miles (11.3 km) northwest of Shechem, was ideal as the capital city of the northern kingdom, for it was nearly impregnable, rising about 300 feet (91 m) above the surrounding fer-

ARCHAEOLOGICAL SITES

OMRI AND SAMARIA

1 KINGS 16 Following his coup Omri ruled the northern kingdom for 12 years (1Ki 16:15–22). Although a failure as a spiritual leader, Omri was a powerful king (vv. 16–18,21–28). Perhaps his most significant accomplishment was the founding of the new capital at **Samaria** (v. 24; see "Map 6"). It was established around 885 B.C. and remained the capital until the demise of the northern kingdom in 722 B.C.[1]

Samaria is situated at a crossroads near the main north-south road through the highlands of Israel, 34 miles (55 km) north of Jerusalem. Situated on a high hill, the city dominates the surrounding countryside. Excavations at the site have unearthed Omri's royal citadel on the **acropolis**. It was surrounded by a 5 foot (1.5 m) thick wall enclosing a four-acre area. The wall was constructed of fine **ashlar** (cut) masonry laid in header-stretcher fashion (alternating narrow-face and wide-face placement of rectangular blocks). On the southwestern side of the enclosure was a palace constructed around a central courtyard. The preserved portion is 78 feet (24 m) by 88 feet (27 m) in size. Outside the royal quarter was a lower city built on the slope of the hill.

Omri's name appears in a number of ancient documents:

✣ The earliest known inscription to mention a king of Judah or Israel is the Mesha (or Moabite) Inscription, written approximately 846 B.C.[2] It states that "Omri had occupied the land of Medeba [northern **Moab**], and had dwelt there in his time."

✣ In a document from about five years later the Assyrian king **Shalmaneser III** referred to Jehu, a later Israelite king, as the "son of Omri."[3]

✣ Other Assyrian kings, such as Tiglath-Pileser III (c. 732 B.C.) and Sargon II (c. 721 B.C.),[4] attached such importance to the reign of Omri that they referred to Israel as "Omri-Land."

Omri was an enormously famous and successful king, yet the Bible pays him virtually no attention. Political success, in the eyes of the Biblical writers, counted for very little if an individual had turned away from God.

[1]See "The History of the Northern Kingdom" on page 506. [2]See "The Mesha (Moabite) Stone" on page 530. [3]See "Jehu/The Black Obelisk of Shalmaneser III" on page 544. [4]See "The Annals of Sargon II" on page 1072.

16:25 [u]Dt 4:25; Mic 6:16 — 25 But Omri did evil[u] in the eyes of the LORD and sinned more than all those before him. 26 He walked
16:26 [v]ver 19 — in all the ways of Jeroboam son of Nebat and in his sin, which he had caused[v] Israel to commit, so that
[w]Dt 32:21 — they provoked the LORD, the God of Israel, to anger by their worthless idols.[w]
27 As for the other events of Omri's reign, what he did and the things he achieved, are they not written
in the book of the annals of the kings of Israel? 28 Omri rested with his fathers and was buried in Samar-
ia. And Ahab his son succeeded him as king.

Ahab Becomes King of Israel

29 In the thirty-eighth year of Asa king of Judah, Ahab son of Omri became king of Israel, and he
16:30 [x]ver 25; 1Ki 14:9 — reigned in Samaria over Israel twenty-two years. 30 Ahab son of Omri did more[x] evil in the eyes of the LORD
than any of those before him. 31 He not only considered it trivial to commit the sins of Jeroboam son of
16:31 [y]Dt 7:3; 1Ki 11:2 — Nebat, but he also married[y] Jezebel daughter[z] of Ethbaal king of the Sidonians, and began to serve Baal[a]
[z]Jdg 18:7; 2Ki 9:34 — and worship him. 32 He set up an altar for Baal in the temple[b] of Baal that he built in Samaria. 33 Ahab
[a]2Ki 10:18; 17:16 — also made an Asherah pole[c] and did more[d] to provoke the LORD, the God of Israel, to anger than did all
16:32 [b]2Ki 10:21, 27; 11:18 — the kings of Israel before him.
16:33 [c]2Ki 13:6 [d]ver 29,30; 1Ki 14:9; 21:25 — 34 In Ahab's time, Hiel of Bethel rebuilt Jericho. He laid its foundations at the cost of his firstborn son
Abiram, and he set up its gates at the cost of his youngest son Segub, in accordance with the word of the
16:34 [e]Jos 6:26 — LORD spoken by Joshua son of Nun.[e]

Elijah Fed by Ravens

17:1 [f]Mal 4:5; Jas 5:17 — **17** Now Elijah[f] the Tishbite, from Tishbe[a] in Gilead,[g] said to Ahab, "As the LORD, the God of Israel,
[g]Jdg 12:4 [h]Dt 10:8; — lives, whom I serve, there will be neither dew nor rain[h] in the next few years except at my word."
1Ki 18:1; — 2 Then the word of the LORD came to Elijah: 3 "Leave here, turn eastward and hide in the Kerith Ravine,
2Ki 3:14; Lk 4:25 17:4 [i]Ge 8:7 — east of the Jordan. 4 You will drink from the brook, and I have ordered the ravens[i] to feed you there."
5 So he did what the LORD had told him. He went to the Kerith Ravine, east of the Jordan, and stayed
17:6 [j]Ex 16:8 — there. 6 The ravens brought him bread and meat in the morning[j] and bread and meat in the evening, and
he drank from the brook.

The Widow at Zarephath

7 Some time later the brook dried up because there had been no rain in the land. 8 Then the word of
17:9 [k]Ob 1:20 [l]Lk 4:26 — the LORD came to him: 9 "Go at once to Zarephath[k] of Sidon and stay there. I have commanded a widow[l]
in that place to supply you with food." 10 So he went to Zarephath. When he came to the town gate, a wid-
ow was there gathering sticks. He called to her and asked, "Would you bring me a little water in a jar so
17:10 [m]Ge 24:17; Jn 4:7 — I may have a drink?"[m] 11 As she was going to get it, he called, "And bring me, please, a piece of bread."
12 "As surely as the LORD your God lives," she replied, "I don't have any bread—only a handful of flour
17:12 [n]ver 1; 2Ki 4:2 — in a jar and a little oil[n] in a jug. I am gathering a few sticks to take home and make a meal for myself and
my son, that we may eat it—and die."
13 Elijah said to her, "Don't be afraid. Go home and do as you have said. But first make a small cake of
bread for me from what you have and bring it to me, and then make something for yourself and your
son. 14 For this is what the LORD, the God of Israel, says: 'The jar of flour will not be used up and the jug
of oil will not run dry until the day the LORD gives rain on the land.' "
15 She went away and did as Elijah had told her. So there was food every day for Elijah and for the
woman and her family. 16 For the jar of flour was not used up and the jug of oil did not run dry, in keep-
ing with the word of the LORD spoken by Elijah.

[a] *1* Or *Tishbite, of the settlers*

---

tile valleys (see 20:1–21; 2Ki 6:25; 18:9–10). Archaeologists have discovered that Omri and Ahab adorned it with magnificent structures to rival those Solomon had erected in Jerusalem. From this time on the northern kingdom could be designated by the name of the royal city, just as the southern kingdom could be identified by its capital, Jerusalem (see, e.g., 21:1; Isa 10:10; Am 6:1).

16:31 The Jewish historian Josephus referred to Ethbaal as a king-priest who ruled over Tyre and Sidon for 32 years (see "Sidon" on p. 1536). Ahab had already married Jezebel, effecting a political alliance between Israel and Phoenicia that also brought widespread Baal worship to the northern kingdom.

17:1 See the note on famine at Ruth 1:1. Also see "Famine in the Ancient Near East" on page 70.

Elijah's message to Ahab was delivered in the form of an oath. As such, it called upon God as the guarantor of the truth of the words spoken. An oath was the most solemn form of binding obligation between parties. In this case it was sanctioned by God, given as his challenge to Baal, who was represented by Ahab. If the Lord withheld the rain, rendering Baal—considered the god of fertility and lord of the rain clouds—powerless, he would be proven the true God and Elijah the true prophet of his word.

17:8 See "Zarephath" on page 514.

[17]Some time later the son of the woman who owned the house became ill. He grew worse and worse,
and finally stopped breathing. [18]She said to Elijah, "What do you have against me, man of God? Did you
come to remind me of my sin[o] and kill my son?" 17:18 [o]2Ki 3:13; Lk 5:8
[19]"Give me your son," Elijah replied. He took him from her arms, carried him to the upper room where
he was staying, and laid him on his bed. [20]Then he cried out to the LORD, "O LORD my God, have you brought
tragedy also upon this widow I am staying with, by causing her son to die?" [21]Then he stretched[p] himself 17:21 [p]2Ki 4:34; Ac 20:10
out on the boy three times and cried to the LORD, "O LORD my God, let this boy's life return to him!"
[22]The LORD heard Elijah's cry, and the boy's life returned to him, and he lived. [23]Elijah picked up the
child and carried him down from the room into the house. He gave him to his mother and said, "Look,
your son is alive!"
[24]Then the woman said to Elijah, "Now I know[q] that you are a man of God and that the word of the 17:24 [q]Jn 3:2; 16:30 [r]Ps 119:43; Jn 17:17
LORD from your mouth is the truth."[r]

Elijah and Obadiah

18 After a long time, in the third[s] year, the word of the LORD came to Elijah: "Go and present your- 18:1 [s]1Ki 17:1; Lk 4:25; Jas 5:17 [t]Dt 28:12
self to Ahab, and I will send rain[t] on the land." [2]So Elijah went to present himself to Ahab.
Now the famine was severe in Samaria, [3]and Ahab had summoned Obadiah, who was in charge[u] of 18:3 [u]1Ki 16:9 [v]Ne 7:2
his palace. (Obadiah was a devout believer[v] in the LORD. [4]While Jezebel[w] was killing off the LORD's proph- 18:4 [w]2Ki 9:7 [x]ver 13; Isa 16:3
ets, Obadiah had taken a hundred prophets and hidden[x] them in two caves, fifty in each, and had sup-
plied them with food and water.) [5]Ahab had said to Obadiah, "Go through the land to all the springs and
valleys. Maybe we can find some grass to keep the horses and mules alive so we will not have to kill any
of our animals." [6]So they divided the land they were to cover, Ahab going in one direction and Obadiah
in another.

17:19–24 Elijah's actions just prior to the child's resuscitation were similar to Babylonian practices involving magic. But the Hebrew worldview prohibited the use of magic. Elijah's prayer was not for restoration or reunification of the boy's "soul" to his body (the Hebrew word *nephesh* indicates the breath or life possessed by animals as well as by people; e.g., Ge 1:20–21,24). Life was restored to the child, demonstrating to this foreign mother that Elijah truly was a man of God and that God's word operated in him.

18:5 According to the annals of the Assyrian ruler Shalmaneser III, Ahab had a force of at least 2,000 chariots, so food and water for his horses were essential to maintain his military power. (See "Horses and Chariots in Ancient Warfare" on p. 114).

ARCHAEOLOGICAL SITES

ZAREPHATH

1 KINGS 17 A city on the Mediterranean coast 14 miles (22.5 km) north of Tyre and 8 miles (13 km) south of Sidon,[1] Zarephath ("Map 7") is mentioned in Neo-**Assyrian** records of the seventh century B.C. (when it surrendered to the Assyrian king Sennacherib), as well as in an Egyptian **papyrus** from the thirteenth century B.C. Today the small village of Sarafand lies close to the remains of the old city. Excavations have uncovered that this ancient port was not only a commercial center for the export of wine, olive oil and the purple dye extracted from murex shells but also a manufacturing hub for textiles, pottery and glassware. In the **Roman period** the city featured a shrine to the goddess Tannit, to whom child sacrifices are believed to have been made.[2] By the fourth century A.D. pilgrims were making their way to Zarephath to commemorate Elijah's miracles there, and a tower was erected to mark the site of the "upper room" in which he had lived (1Ki 17:19). Though never considered a city of great importance, Zarephath's location places it in the center of the **Phoenician** heartland.[3]

First Kings 17 demonstrates in no uncertain terms that **Yahweh**, the God of Israel, was more powerful than the **Canaanite** god Baal, who was worshiped as the god of rain and fertility and the vanquisher of death.[4] But in 1 Kings 17 the God of Israel provides sustenance during a famine and proves his power over death in the raising of a child (v. 22). The next chapter, 1 Kings 18, recounts the triumph of Yahweh and his prophet over Baal and his prophets.

God's command to Elijah to remain in the home of a pagan widow must have seemed strange. Jesus cited this story as an example of how a prophet is often unwelcome in his home country (Lk 4:26).

[1]See "Sidon" on page 1536. [2]See "Human Sacrifice in the Ancient Near East" on page 182. [3]See "Phoenicia" on page 488. [4]See "The Ugaritic Text of the Myth of Baal" on page 905 and "Baal and the Fertility Cults" on page 1414.

18:7 y2Ki 1:8 [7]As Obadiah was walking along, Elijah met him. Obadiah recognized[y] him, bowed down to the
ground, and said, "Is it really you, my lord Elijah?"
[8]"Yes," he replied. "Go tell your master, 'Elijah is here.' "
[9]"What have I done wrong," asked Obadiah, "that you are handing your servant over to Ahab to be
put to death? [10]As surely as the LORD your God lives, there is not a nation or kingdom where my master
18:10 z1Ki 17:3 has not sent someone to look[z] for you. And whenever a nation or kingdom claimed you were not there,

ANCIENT NEAR EASTERN DEITIES

Palestinian Deities in Scripture:

Deity	Country	Position	Reference
Baal	Canaan	Young storm god	1Ki 16:31; 18:18–46
Ashtoreth (Astarte)	Canaan	Mother-goddess; love; fertility	Jdg 2:13; 10:6; 1Sa 12:10; 1Ki 11:5
Chemosh	Moab	National god of war	Nu 21:29; Jdg 11:24; 1Ki 11:7,33; Jer 48:7
Molech (Malcam, Milcom)	Ammon	National god	Jer 49:1; Zep 1:5
Dagon	Philistia	National god of grain	Jdg 16:23;1Sa 5:2–7
Queen of Heaven	Canaan	Same as Ashtoreth (similar to Anat and Ishtar)	Jer 7:18; 44:17–25

Mesopotamian Deities in Scripture:

Deity	Country	Position	Reference
Marduk	Babylon	Young storm god; chief god	Jer 50:2
Bel	Babylon	Another name for Marduk	Isa 46:1; Jer 50:2; 51:44
Nebo (Nabu)	Babylon	Son of Marduk	Isa 46:1
Tammuz (Dumuzi)	Sumerian	Young storm god	Eze 8:14

Major Deities not in Scripture:

Egypt	Mesopotamia	Canaan-Syria
Osiris—death	**Anu**—head of pantheon (officially recognized gods)	**El**—head of Canaanite pantheon
Isis—life	**Enlil**—storm	**Anat**—war
Horus—sun	**Ea-Enki**—fresh water and subterranean water	**Mot**—death, sterility
Hathor—mother-goddess	**Sin (Nanna)**—moon	**Adad**—Syrian storm god
Ra (Re)—sun	**Ishtar**—sex, fertility	**Teshub**—Hittite storm god
Seth—evil storm	**Ninurta**—war	**Hannahanna**—Hittite mother-goddess
Ptah—artists; Memphite creator	**Tiamat**—salt water	**Arinna**—Hittite sun goddess

Deities of these civilizations, particularly Egypt, vary as to attributes and rank, depending upon the time period and the areas of the country. The ones listed are basic.

Chronological and Background Charts of the Old Testament, p. 83

he made them swear they could not find you. 11 But now you tell me to go to my master and say, 'Elijah is
here.' 12 I don't know where the Spirit[a] of the LORD may carry you when I leave you. If I go and tell Ahab 18:12 [a]2Ki 2:16;
and he doesn't find you, he will kill me. Yet I your servant have worshiped the LORD since my youth. Eze 3:14; Ac 8:39
13 Haven't you heard, my lord, what I did while Jezebel was killing the prophets of the LORD? I hid a hun-
dred of the LORD's prophets in two caves, fifty in each, and supplied them with food and water. 14 And
now you tell me to go to my master and say, 'Elijah is here.' He will kill me!"
15 Elijah said, "As the LORD Almighty lives, whom I serve, I will surely present[b] myself to Ahab today." 18:15 [b]1Ki 17:1

Elijah on Mount Carmel

16 So Obadiah went to meet Ahab and told him, and Ahab went to meet Elijah. 17 When he saw Elijah,
he said to him, "Is that you, you troubler[c] of Israel?" 18:17 [c]Jos 7:25;
18 "I have not made trouble for Israel," Elijah replied. "But you[d] 1Ki 21:20; Ac 16:20
and your father's family have. You have abandoned[e] the LORD's com- 18:18 [d]1Ki 16:31, 33; 21:25
mands and have followed the Baals. 19 Now summon the people from [e]2Ch 15:2
all over Israel to meet me on Mount Carmel.[f] And bring the four 18:19 [f]Jos 19:26
hundred and fifty prophets of Baal and the four hundred prophets
of Asherah, who eat at Jezebel's table."
20 So Ahab sent word throughout all Israel and assembled the
prophets on Mount Carmel. 21 Elijah went before the people and said,
"How long will you waver[g] between two opinions? If the LORD is God, 18:21
follow him; but if Baal is God, follow him." [g]Jos 24:15; 2Ki 17:41; Mt 6:24
But the people said nothing.
22 Then Elijah said to them, "I am the only one of the LORD's
prophets left,[h] but Baal has four hundred and fifty prophets.[i] 23 Get 18:22 [h]1Ki 19:10
two bulls for us. Let them choose one for themselves, and let them [i]ver 19
cut it into pieces and put it on the wood but not set fire to it. I will
prepare the other bull and put it on the wood but not set fire to it.
24 Then you call on the name of your god, and I will call on the name
of the LORD. The god who answers by fire[j]—he is God." 18:24 [j]ver 38;
Then all the people said, "What you say is good." 1Ch 21:26
25 Elijah said to the prophets of Baal, "Choose one of the bulls and
prepare it first, since there are so many of you. Call on the name of
your god, but do not light the fire." 26 So they took the bull given them
and prepared it.
Then they called on the name of Baal from morning till noon.
"O Baal, answer us!" they shouted. But there was no response;[k] no 18:26 [k]Ps 115:4-
one answered. And they danced around the altar they had made. 5; Jer 10:5; 1Co 8:4; 12:2
27 At noon Elijah began to taunt them. "Shout louder!" he said.
"Surely he is a god! Perhaps he is deep in thought, or busy, or trav-
eling. Maybe he is sleeping and must be awakened."[l] 28 So they shout- 18:27 [l]Hab 2:19
ed louder and slashed[m] themselves with swords and spears, as was 18:28
their custom, until their blood flowed. 29 Midday passed, and they [m]Lev 19:28; Dt 14:1
continued their frantic prophesying until the time for the evening
sacrifice.[n] But there was no response, no one answered, no one paid 18:29 [n]Ex 29:41
attention.[o] [o]ver 26

ANCIENT VOICES

Dead was Mighty Balu,
perished the Prince master of the earth.
Thereupon the Gracious One, the
kindly god,
descends from the throne, sits on
the footstool,
(descends)* from the footstool,
sits on the earth.
He pours dirt of mourning on his head,
dust of humiliation on his cranium,
for clothing, he is covered with a girded
garment.
With a stone he scratches incisions
on (his) skin,
with a razor he cuts cheeks and chin.
He harrows his upper arms,
plows (his) back like a (garden in a)
valley.
He raises his voice and cries aloud:
Balu is dead, what (is to become of)
the people,
the Son of Dagan (is dead), what
(is to become of)
the hordes (of the earth)?
After Balu, I also shall descend into
the earth.

*Words in parentheses added by translator for clarity or where text has gaps

—THE BALU (BAAL) MYTH

See study note 18:28, below.

18:19 Mount Carmel is a high ridge next to the Mediterranean Sea, where the effects of the drought would have been least apparent.
18:24 Both the Lord and Baal were said to ride the thunderstorm as their divine chariots (see Ps 104:3); thunder was God's voice (see Ps 29:3–9) and lightning his weapon (see Ps 18:14), and the same was purported of Baal. See "Storm Gods, Storm Imagery and Theophany" on page 808.
18:28 Self-mutilation is an indicator of spiritual decadence. In the Ugaritic Baal myth (see "The Ugaritic Text of the Myth of Baal" on p. 905) the deities 'Ilu and 'Anatu mourn the death of the divine Baal by scraping their skin with sharp stones, cutting their faces with razors and thoroughly mutilating their own bodies. Like the gods they worshiped, the Canaanites also marred their bodies in mourning rituals and other religious ceremonies in an attempt to invoke their deities. In the myth Baal later revived and received kingly authority; the Canaanites were reenacting the mourning that had preceded Baal's rise to prominence.

The Israelites, however, were expressly forbidden to tattoo or otherwise disfigure themselves while lamenting their dead (Lev 19:28; see "Tattoos and Self-Laceration in Ancient Religion" on p. 180). When the prophets of Baal cut themselves with swords and lances to arouse Baal to action, Elijah needed only to call upon the name of Yahweh for him to act on behalf of his servant and demonstrate that he is indeed the one and only true God.

18:30 [p]1Ki 19:10 30 Then Elijah said to all the people, "Come here to me." They came to him, and he repaired the altar[p]
of the LORD, which was in ruins. 31 Elijah took twelve stones, one for each of the tribes descended from
18:31 [q]Ge 32:28; Jacob, to whom the word of the LORD had come, saying, "Your name shall be Israel."[q] 32 With the stones
35:10; 2Ki 17:34 18:32 [r]Col 3:17 he built an altar in the name[r] of the LORD, and he dug a trench around it large enough to hold two seahs[a]
18:33 [s]Ge 22:9; of seed. 33 He arranged[s] the wood, cut the bull into pieces and laid it on the wood. Then he said to them,
Lev 1:6-8 "Fill four large jars with water and pour it on the offering and on the wood."
34 "Do it again," he said, and they did it again.
"Do it a third time," he ordered, and they did it the third time. 35 The water ran down around the altar
and even filled the trench.
18:36 [t]Ex 3:6; 36 At the time of sacrifice, the prophet Elijah stepped forward and prayed: "O LORD, God of Abraham,[t]
Mt 22:32 [u]1Ki 8:43; Isaac and Israel, let it be known[u] today that you are God in Israel and that I am your servant and have
2Ki 19:19 [v]Nu 16:28 done all these things at your command.[v] 37 Answer me, O LORD, answer me, so these people will know
that you, O LORD, are God, and that you are turning their hearts back again."
18:38 [w]Lev 9:24; 38 Then the fire[w] of the LORD fell and burned up the sacrifice, the wood, the stones and the soil, and
Jdg 6:21; 1Ch 21:26; also licked up the water in the trench.
2Ch 7:1; Job 1:16 39 When all the people saw this, they fell prostrate and cried, "The LORD—he is God! The LORD—he
18:39 [x]ver 24 is God!"[x]
40 Then Elijah commanded them, "Seize the prophets of Baal. Don't let anyone get away!" They seized
18:40 [y]Jdg 4:7 them, and Elijah had them brought down to the Kishon Valley[y] and slaughtered[z] there.
[z]Dt 13:5; 18:20; 2Ki 10:24-25 41 And Elijah said to Ahab, "Go, eat and drink, for there is the sound of a heavy rain." 42 So Ahab went
off to eat and drink, but Elijah climbed to the top of Carmel, bent down to the ground and put his face
18:42 [a]ver 19-20; Jas 5:18 between his knees.[a]
43 "Go and look toward the sea," he told his servant. And he went up and looked.
"There is nothing there," he said.
Seven times Elijah said, "Go back."
18:44 [b]Lk 12:54 44 The seventh time the servant reported, "A cloud[b] as small as a man's hand is rising from the sea."
So Elijah said, "Go and tell Ahab, 'Hitch up your chariot and go down before the rain stops you.' "
45 Meanwhile, the sky grew black with clouds, the wind rose, a heavy rain came on and Ahab rode off
18:46 [c]2Ki 3:15 to Jezreel. 46 The power[c] of the LORD came upon Elijah and, tucking his cloak into his belt,[d] he ran ahead
[d]2Ki 4:29; 9:1 of Ahab all the way to Jezreel.

Elijah Flees to Horeb

19:1 [e]1Ki 18:40 **19** Now Ahab told Jezebel everything Elijah had done and how he had killed[e] all the prophets with
the sword. 2 So Jezebel sent a messenger to Elijah to say, "May the gods deal with me, be it ever
19:2 [f]1Ki 20:10; 2Ki 6:31; Ru 1:17 so severely,[f] if by this time tomorrow I do not make your life like that of one of them."
19:3 [g]Ge 31:21 3 Elijah was afraid[b] and ran[g] for his life. When he came to Beersheba in Judah, he left his servant there,
4 while he himself went a day's journey into the desert. He came to a broom tree, sat down under it and
19:4 [h]Nu 11:15; prayed that he might die. "I have had enough, LORD," he said. "Take my life;[h] I am no better than my an-
Jer 20:18; Jnh 4:8 19:5 [i]Ge 28:11 cestors." 5 Then he lay down under the tree and fell asleep.[i]
All at once an angel touched him and said, "Get up and eat." 6 He looked around, and there by his
head was a cake of bread baked over hot coals, and a jar of water. He ate and drank and then lay down
again.
7 The angel of the LORD came back a second time and touched him and said, "Get up and eat, for the
journey is too much for you." 8 So he got up and ate and drank. Strengthened by that food, he traveled
19:8 [j]Ex 24:18; forty[j] days and forty nights until he reached Horeb,[k] the mountain of God. 9 There he went into a cave[l]
34:28; Dt 9:9-11, 18; Mt 4:2 [k]Ex 3:1 and spent the night.
19:9 [l]Ex 33:22

The LORD Appears to Elijah

And the word of the LORD came to him: "What are you doing here, Elijah?"
19:10 [m]Nu 25:13 10 He replied, "I have been very zealous[m] for the LORD God Almighty. The Israelites have rejected your

[a] *32* That is, probably about 13 quarts (about 15 liters) [b] *3* Or *Elijah saw*

19:3 See "Beersheba" on page 518.
19:8 Horeb is likely another name for Mount Sinai, which is located in the desert about 250 miles (403 km) south of Beersheba (but see "The Location of Mount Sinai" on p. 123; see also "Beersheba" on p. 518).

ARCHAEOLOGICAL SITES

BEERSHEBA

1 KINGS 19 Beersheba was the proverbial southern limit of Israel, as in the expression "from Dan [in the north] to Beersheba" (e.g., Jdg 20:1; see "Map 6"). Elijah, therefore, wanting to separate himself as far as possible from Queen Jezebel of the northern kingdom, fled to Beersheba. The name of the site originates from Abraham's treaty with Abimelech and means "well of the oath" or "well of the seven" (Ge 21:31). Located 50 miles (81 km) south of Jerusalem in the center of the Negev region,[1] Beersheba's general location is not in doubt, although scholars have debated which mound to identify as the city's location during the time of the monarchy.

Domestic structures at Beersheba
Photograph courtesy of © Dr. Gary Pratico

Beersheba assumed a prominent role in the administration of the southern region of the kingdom during the **united** and later the **divided monarchy**. Archaeological excavations of Tel Beersheba have revealed nine strata, or levels of occupation, dating from the **Iron Age**.[2] The earliest, strata IX through VI from the Iron Age I (late **judges period**), reveal a site no larger than a small village. Strata V through II date to the period of the monarchy, with stratum II being the best preserved and most visible today. Stratum V has been equated with the Beersheba of the united monarchy, which was violently destroyed, quite possibly during the campaign of Pharaoh Sheshonk (Biblical Shishak; 1Ki 14:25).[3] Soon afterward the city was rebuilt, but it was again destroyed at the stratum II level. This destruction is generally dated to Sennacherib's campaign against Judah in 701 B.C.,[4] although some suggest that it was leveled by **Nebuchadnezzar** in 586 B.C.[5] Stratum I (the most recent)—fairly meager and soon abandoned—was built shortly thereafter.

Beersheba occupied a three-acre site and was used largely for governmental purposes. The city was laid out in an oval shape, with a ring of typical Israelite houses abutting its **casemate wall**. Streets radiated out from the town gate and plaza, with three large government storehouses located near the gate.[6] One large structure from stratum II, dubbed the "Governor's Palace," was an impressive administrative building featuring three large reception halls. It was built of **ashlars** (cut stones), in contrast to the other buildings, which were constructed of field stones. A remarkable find at Beersheba was a dismantled, sacrificial altar. Archaeologists who located the stones of this altar—in secondary use in one of these storehouses—were able to reconstruct it. The altar may have been part of a temple complex destroyed during the reforms of King Hezekiah (2Ki 18:4). The prophet Amos spoke harshly against the religious practices that took place in this city (Am 5:5; 8:14).

The location of the Beersheba of the **patriarchs** is unknown. This earlier settlement was undoubtedly in the Beersheba Valley but not necessarily at the identical site. The Bible does not suggest a large settlement at Beersheba during patriarchal times, and it is unlikely that archaeologists will be able to pinpoint its location.

A partition wall in a storehouse at Iron Age Beersheba
Photograph courtesy of © Dr. Gary Pratico

[1]See "The Negev: Its Climate and Features" on page 34. [2]See "Archaeological Periods" chart on page xx in the beginning of this Bible. [3]See "The Campaign of Shishak" on page 635. [4]See "The Sennacherib Prism" on page 659. [5]See "Nebuchadnezzar" on page 571. [6]See "The Israelite Town and Home" on page 1205.

covenant, broken down your altars, and put your prophets to death with the sword. I am the only one
left,[n] and now they are trying to kill me too."
11 The LORD said, "Go out and stand on the mountain[o] in the presence of the LORD, for the LORD is about
to pass by."
Then a great and powerful wind[p] tore the mountains apart and shattered the rocks before the LORD,
but the LORD was not in the wind. After the wind there was an earthquake, but the LORD was not in the
earthquake. 12 After the earthquake came a fire, but the LORD was not in the fire. And after the fire came
a gentle whisper.[q] 13 When Elijah heard it, he pulled his cloak over his face[r] and went out and stood at the
mouth of the cave.
Then a voice said to him, "What are you doing here, Elijah?"
14 He replied, "I have been very zealous for the LORD God Almighty. The Israelites have rejected your
covenant, broken down your altars, and put your prophets to death with the sword. I am the only one
left,[s] and now they are trying to kill me too."
15 The LORD said to him, "Go back the way you came, and go to the Desert of Damascus. When you get
there, anoint Hazael[t] king over Aram. 16 Also, anoint[u] Jehu son of Nimshi king over Israel, and anoint Eli-
sha[v] son of Shaphat from Abel Meholah to succeed you as prophet. 17 Jehu will put to death any who es-
cape the sword of Hazael,[w] and Elisha will put to death any who escape the sword of Jehu. 18 Yet I reserve[x]
seven thousand in Israel—all whose knees have not bowed down to Baal and all whose mouths have
not kissed[y] him."

The Call of Elisha

19 So Elijah went from there and found Elisha son of Shaphat. He was plowing with twelve yoke of
oxen, and he himself was driving the twelfth pair. Elijah went up to him and threw his cloak[z] around
him. 20 Elisha then left his oxen and ran after Elijah. "Let me kiss my father and mother good-by,"[a] he
said, "and then I will come with you."
"Go back," Elijah replied. "What have I done to you?"
21 So Elisha left him and went back. He took his yoke of oxen[b] and slaughtered them. He burned the
plowing equipment to cook the meat and gave it to the people, and they ate. Then he set out to follow
Elijah and became his attendant.[c]

Ben-Hadad Attacks Samaria

20 Now Ben-Hadad[d] king of Aram mustered his entire army. Accompanied by thirty-two kings
with their horses and chariots, he went up and besieged Samaria and attacked it. 2 He sent mes-
sengers into the city to Ahab king of Israel, saying, "This is what Ben-Hadad says: 3 'Your silver and gold
are mine, and the best of your wives and children are mine.' "
4 The king of Israel answered, "Just as you say, my lord the king. I and all I have are yours."
5 The messengers came again and said, "This is what Ben-Hadad says: 'I sent to demand your silver
and gold, your wives and your children. 6 But about this time tomorrow I am going to send my officials
to search your palace and the houses of your officials. They will seize everything you value and carry it
away.' "
7 The king of Israel summoned all the elders of the land and said to them, "See how this man is looking
for trouble![e] When he sent for my wives and my children, my silver and my gold, I did not refuse him."

19:10 [n]1Ki 18:4, 22; Ro 11:3* **19:11** [o]Ex 24:12 [p]Eze 1:4; 37:7 **19:12** [q]Job 4:16; Zec 4:6 **19:13** [r]ver 9; Ex 3:6 **19:14** [s]ver 10 **19:15** [t]2Ki 8:7-15 **19:16** [u]2Ki 9:1-3, 6 [v]ver 21; 2Ki 2:9, 15 **19:17** [w]2Ki 8:12, 29; 9:14; 13:3,7, 22 **19:18** [x]Ro 11:4* [y]Hos 13:2 **19:19** [z]2Ki 2:8,14 **19:20** [a]Mt 8:21-22; Lk 9:61 **19:21** [b]2Sa 24:22 [c]ver 16 **20:1** [d]1Ki 15:18; 22:31; 2Ki 6:24 **20:7** [e]2Ki 5:7

19:17 Unraveling the chronology of Jehu's coup is difficult, especially since so many names are repeated, but the following summarizes the major events of the time. All dates are approximate.

- Shalmaneser III stated on the Black Obelisk that the battle of Qarqar, at which Ahab fought as an ally of Syria, took place during his sixth year, around 853 B.C.
- Ahab was killed at Ramoth Gilead later in the campaign season of 853 in a battle against Syria (his alliance with Syria at Qarqar was short-lived).
- Ahaziah of Israel reigned in 853 and 852.
- The first year of Joram of Israel was approximately 852, and his twelfth was around 841.
- Thus, the year Ahaziah of Judah reigned was around 841.
- Joram of Israel and Ahaziah of Judah fought Hazael of Syria in 841—and lost.
- Later in 841 Shalmaneser III attacked Damascus, devastating Syria. Therefore, Syria's defeat of Joram and Ahaziah had to have been prior to Shalmaneser III's campaign against Hazael.
- Jehu's revolt came after the Ramoth Gilead defeat in 841.
- Shalmaneser III stated that he received tribute from Jehu in his eighteenth year (c. 841, apparently later in the year).

19:19–21 The transfer of Elijah's cloak to Elisha signified a transmission both of Elijah's mission and of his ability, with God's help, to accomplish it. Elisha's sacrifice of the oxen was a thank offering for his calling—a celebration in which his neighbors were invited to join. His burning of the farm equipment signified a complete break with his past. From that time on Elisha became Elijah's protégé.

20:1 Aram, Israel's perennial enemy, was located northeast of Israel and is known today as Syria (see "Syria/Aram" on p. 534). Ben-Hadad was a common name among Aram's kings. Like Pharaoh, it may have been a throne name rather than a personal name (see "Ben-Hadad I and II" on p. 521). Ben-Hadad saw his opportunity to eliminate a famine-weakened Israel. Gathering a coalition of 32 "kings"—tribal chieftains or city-state heads—Ben-Hadad swept southward, quickly putting Samaria under siege.

8 The elders and the people all answered, "Don't listen to him or agree to his demands."
9 So he replied to Ben-Hadad's messengers, "Tell my lord the king, 'Your servant will do all you de-
manded the first time, but this demand I cannot meet.'" They left and took the answer back to Ben-
Hadad.
10 Then Ben-Hadad sent another message to Ahab: "May the gods deal with me, be it ever so severe-
ly, if enough dust[f] remains in Samaria to give each of my men a handful."
11 The king of Israel answered, "Tell him: 'One who puts on his armor should not boast[g] like one who
takes it off.'"
12 Ben-Hadad heard this message while he and the kings were drinking[h] in their tents,[a] and he or-
dered his men: "Prepare to attack." So they prepared to attack the city.

Ahab Defeats Ben-Hadad

13 Meanwhile a prophet came to Ahab king of Israel and announced, "This is what the LORD says: 'Do
you see this vast army? I will give it into your hand today, and then you will know[i] that I am the LORD.'"
14 "But who will do this?" asked Ahab.
The prophet replied, "This is what the LORD says: 'The young officers of the provincial commanders
will do it.'"
"And who will start[j] the battle?" he asked.
The prophet answered, "You will."
15 So Ahab summoned the young officers of the provincial commanders, 232 men. Then he assem-
bled the rest of the Israelites, 7,000 in all. 16 They set out at noon while Ben-Hadad and the 32 kings al-
lied with him were in their tents getting drunk.[k] 17 The young officers of the provincial commanders went
out first.
Now Ben-Hadad had dispatched scouts, who reported, "Men are advancing from Samaria."
18 He said, "If they have come out for peace, take them alive; if they have come out for war, take them
alive."
19 The young officers of the provincial commanders marched out of the city with the army behind
them 20 and each one struck down his opponent. At that, the Arameans fled, with the Israelites in pursuit.
But Ben-Hadad king of Aram escaped on horseback with some of his horsemen. 21 The king of Israel ad-
vanced and overpowered the horses and chariots and inflicted heavy losses on the Arameans.
22 Afterward, the prophet[l] came to the king of Israel and said, "Strengthen your position and see what
must be done, because next spring[m] the king of Aram will attack you again."
23 Meanwhile, the officials of the king of Aram advised him, "Their gods are gods[n] of the hills. That is
why they were too strong for us. But if we fight them on the plains, surely we will be stronger than they.
24 Do this: Remove all the kings from their commands and replace them with other officers. 25 You must
also raise an army like the one you lost—horse for horse and chariot for chariot—so we can fight Isra-
el on the plains. Then surely we will be stronger than they." He agreed with them and acted accordingly.
26 The next spring[o] Ben-Hadad mustered the Arameans and went up to Aphek[p] to fight against Israel.
27 When the Israelites were also mustered and given provisions, they marched out to meet them. The Is-
raelites camped opposite them like two small flocks of goats, while the Arameans covered the countryside.[q]
28 The man of God came up and told the king of Israel, "This is what the LORD says: 'Because the Ara-
means think the LORD is a god of the hills and not a god[r] of the valleys, I will deliver this vast army into
your hands, and you will know[s] that I am the LORD.'"
29 For seven days they camped opposite each other, and on the seventh day the battle was joined. The
Israelites inflicted a hundred thousand casualties on the Aramean foot soldiers in one day. 30 The rest of
them escaped to the city of Aphek,[t] where the wall collapsed on twenty-seven thousand of them. And
Ben-Hadad fled to the city and hid[u] in an inner room.
31 His officials said to him, "Look, we have heard that the kings of the house of Israel are merciful. Let
us go to the king of Israel with sackcloth[v] around our waists and ropes around our heads. Perhaps he
will spare your life."

20:10 [f]2Sa 22:43; 1Ki 19:2
20:11 [g]Pr 27:1; Jer 9:23
20:12 [h]ver 16; 1Ki 16:9
20:13 [i]ver 28; Ex 6:7
20:14 [j]Jdg 1:1
20:16 [k]ver 12; 1Ki 16:9
20:22 [l]ver 13 [m]ver 26; 2Sa 11:1
20:23 [n]1Ki 14:23; Ro 1:21-23
20:26 [o]ver 22 [p]2Ki 13:17
20:27 [q]Jdg 6:6; 1Sa 13:6
20:28 [r]ver 23 [s]ver 13
20:30 [t]ver 26 [u]1Ki 22:25; 2Ch 18:24
20:31 [v]Ge 37:34

[a] 12 Or *in Succoth*; also in verse 16

20:26 See "Aphek" on page 437.
20:31–32 The clothing worn by the Hebrew people of Biblical times was graceful, modest and exceedingly significant (see "Ancient Israelite Clothing and Jewelry" on p. 1059). Clothes were considered so much a part of those who wore them that they not only told who and what they were but were intended as external symbols of the

[32]Wearing sackcloth around their waists and ropes around their heads, they went to the king of Isra-
el and said, "Your servant Ben-Hadad says: 'Please let me live.' "
The king answered, "Is he still alive? He is my brother."
[33]The men took this as a good sign and were quick to pick up his word. "Yes, your brother Ben-Ha-
dad!" they said.
"Go and get him," the king said. When Ben-Hadad came out, Ahab had him come up into his chariot.
[34]"I will return the cities[w] my father took from your father," Ben-Hadad offered. "You may set up your
own market areas in Damascus,[x] as my father did in Samaria."
⌊Ahab said,⌋ "On the basis of a treaty[y] I will set you free." So he made a treaty with him, and let him go.

A Prophet Condemns Ahab

[35]By the word of the LORD one of the sons of the prophets said to his companion, "Strike me with your
weapon," but the man refused.[z]
[36]So the prophet said, "Because you have not obeyed the LORD, as soon as you leave me a lion[a] will kill
you." And after the man went away, a lion found him and killed him.

20:34 [w]1Ki 15:20 [x]Jer 49:23-27 [y]Ex 23:32
20:35 [z]1Ki 13:21; 2Ki 2:3-7
20:36 [a]1Ki 13:24

---

individual's innermost feelings and deepest woes, and of his or her moral urge to represent God aright. With certain kinds of cloth and with astonishingly vivid colors of white, purple, scarlet, blue, yellow and black, they represented the state of their minds and emotions. When joyful and ready to enter into festive occasions, they donned their garments of brightest array, and when they mourned or humbled themselves they put on sackcloth—literally cloth from which sacks were made—which was considered the very poorest kind of dress and quite indicative of their lowly feelings (20:31–32; Job 16:15; Isa 15:3; Jer 4:8; 6:26; La 2:10; Eze 7:18; Da 9:3; Joel 1:8). See also the note on sackcloth at Job 16:15, as well as "Sackcloth and Ashes: Rituals of Lamentation" on page 820.

Ben-Hadad I and II

1 KINGS 20 There are at least two, and probably three, kings named Ben-Hadad in the Old Testament. They ruled Aram from Syria's capital city, Damascus[1] (see "Map 6"). Ben-Hadad I (late tenth to early ninth centuries B.C.), the son of Tabrimmon, is known in the Bible for having entered into a treaty with Judah to attack Israel (1Ki 15).

Ben-Hadad II (also called Hadadezer; r. c. 860–841 B.C.) is prominent in 1 Kings 20 and 24 and in 2 Kings 5–8. He attacked **Samaria** ("Map 4") around 857 B.C. but was defeated by Ahab (1Ki 20:1–21). The following year he returned to engage Israel at Aphek[2] ("Map 4"), 3 miles (4.8 km) east of the southern coast of the Sea of Galilee, but once again Ahab emerged victorious (vv. 22–34). Ben-Hadad was more successful three years later when he at last overcame the joint forces of Ahab and Jehoshaphat of Judah at Ramoth Gilead[3] (ch. 22; "Map 4"). Ben-Hadad laid siege to Samaria once again during the reign of Joram (2Ki 6–7)—and once again was defeated, this time by divine intervention (2Ki 7:6).[4]

Apart from the Bible, ancient inscriptions also mention Ben-Hadad II:

✣ In the records of **Shalmaneser III**, king of Assyria from approximately 858–824 B.C., Ben-Hadad II is referred to as "Adad-idri." Along with other kings from the region (including Ahab of Israel), Ben-Hadad fought against Shalmaneser repeatedly—in 853, 849, 848 and 845 B.C. In the battle of Qarqar, Syria, in 853 B.C., Ben-Hadad commanded a force of 20,000 foot soldiers, 1,200 chariots and 1,200 cavalry.[5]

✣ Lines 3 and 4 of the Tel Dan **Stele** refer to an unnamed individual as "my father."[6] Since the author of the text appears to have been Hazael, Ben-Hadad II's successor (but not actually his son),[7] the reference to "my father" is probably to Ben-Hadad II.

An apparent third Ben-Hadad ruled during the early eighth century B.C. and fought against Jehoash (see 2Ki 13:14–19,25).[8]

[1]See "Damascus" on page 1087. [2]See "Aphek" on page 437. [3]See "Ramoth (in) Gilead" on page 261. [4]See "Dothan, Ben-Hadad and a Chronological Problem" on page 536. [5]See "Ahab and the Battle of Qarqar" on page 524. [6]See "The Tel Dan Stele" on page 540. [7]See "Hazael, the Nemesis of Israel" on page 539. [8]See also "Ben-Hadad III of Aram and Jehoash of Israel" on page 548.

37 The prophet found another man and said, "Strike me, please." So the man struck him and wound-
ed him. 38 Then the prophet went and stood by the road waiting for the king. He disguised himself with
his headband down over his eyes. 39 As the king passed by, the prophet called out to him, "Your servant
went into the thick of the battle, and someone came to me with a captive and said, 'Guard this man. If he
is missing, it will be your life for his life,[b] or you must pay a talent[a] of silver.' 40 While your servant was — **20:39** [b]2Ki 10:24
busy here and there, the man disappeared."

"That is your sentence," the king of Israel said. "You have pronounced it yourself."

41 Then the prophet quickly removed the headband from his eyes, and the king of Israel recognized
him as one of the prophets. 42 He said to the king, "This is what the LORD says: 'You have set free a man I
had determined should die.[b][c] Therefore it is your life for his life,[d] your people for his people.' " 43 Sullen — **20:42** [c]Jer 48:10 [d]ver 39; Jos 2:14;
and angry,[e] the king of Israel went to his palace in Samaria. — 1Ki 22:31-37 **20:43** [e]1Ki 21:4

Naboth's Vineyard

21 Some time later there was an incident involving a vineyard belonging to Naboth[f] the Jezreelite. — **21:1** [f]2Ki 9:21
The vineyard was in Jezreel,[g] close to the palace of Ahab king of Samaria. 2 Ahab said to Naboth, — [g]1Ki 18:45-46
"Let me have your vineyard to use for a vegetable garden, since it is close to my palace. In exchange I will
give you a better vineyard or, if you prefer, I will pay you whatever it is worth."

3 But Naboth replied, "The LORD forbid that I should give you the inheritance[h] of my fathers." — **21:3** [h]Lev 25:23; Nu 36:7;

4 So Ahab went home, sullen and angry[i] because Naboth the Jezreelite had said, "I will not give you the — Eze 46:18
inheritance of my fathers." He lay on his bed sulking and refused to eat. — **21:4** [i]1Ki 20:43

5 His wife Jezebel came in and asked him, "Why are you so sullen? Why won't you eat?"

6 He answered her, "Because I said to Naboth the Jezreelite, 'Sell me your vineyard; or if you prefer, I
will give you another vineyard in its place.' But he said, 'I will not give you my vineyard.' "

7 Jezebel his wife said, "Is this how you act as king over Israel? Get up and eat! Cheer up. I'll get you the
vineyard[j] of Naboth the Jezreelite." — **21:7** [j]1Sa 8:14

8 So she wrote letters in Ahab's name, placed his seal[k] on them, and sent them to the elders and no- — **21:8** [k]Ge 38:18;
bles who lived in Naboth's city with him. 9 In those letters she wrote: — Est 3:12; 8:8,10

> "Proclaim a day of fasting and seat Naboth in a prominent place among the people. 10 But seat
> two scoundrels[l] opposite him and have them testify that he has cursed[m] both God and the king. — **21:10** [l]Ac 6:11 [m]Ex 22:28;
> Then take him out and stone him to death." — Lev 24:15-16

11 So the elders and nobles who lived in Naboth's city did as Jezebel directed in the letters she had writ-
ten to them. 12 They proclaimed a fast[n] and seated Naboth in a prominent place among the people. 13 Then — **21:12** [n]Isa 58:4
two scoundrels came and sat opposite him and brought charges against Naboth before the people, say-
ing, "Naboth has cursed both God and the king." So they took him outside the city and stoned him to
death.[o] 14 Then they sent word to Jezebel: "Naboth has been stoned and is dead." — **21:13** [o]2Ki 9:26

15 As soon as Jezebel heard that Naboth had been stoned to death, she said to Ahab, "Get up and take
possession of the vineyard[p] of Naboth the Jezreelite that he refused to sell you. He is no longer alive, but — **21:15** [p]1Sa 8:14
dead." 16 When Ahab heard that Naboth was dead, he got up and went down to take possession of Na-
both's vineyard.

17 Then the word of the LORD came to Elijah the Tishbite: 18 "Go down to meet Ahab king of Israel, who
rules in Samaria. He is now in Naboth's vineyard, where he has gone to take possession of it. 19 Say to him,
'This is what the LORD says: Have you not murdered a man and seized his property?' Then say to him, 'This
is what the LORD says: In the place where dogs licked up Naboth's blood,[q] dogs[r] will lick up your blood— — **21:19** [q]2Ki 9:26; Ps 9:12; Isa 14:20
yes, yours!' " — [r]1Ki 22:38

20 Ahab said to Elijah, "So you have found me, my enemy!"[s] — **21:20** [s]1Ki 18:17

"I have found you," he answered, "because you have sold[t] yourself to do evil in the eyes of the LORD. — [t]ver 25; 2Ki 17:17;
21 'I am going to bring disaster on you. I will consume your descendants and cut off from Ahab every last — Ro 7:14

[a] *39* That is, about 75 pounds (about 34 kilograms) [b] *42* The Hebrew term refers to the irrevocable giving over of things or persons to the LORD, often by totally destroying them.

21:1–7 Because royal power in Israel was limited by covenantal law (Dt 17:14–20; 1Sa 10:25), Ahab was unable simply to confiscate privately held land. Naboth's refusal to give up his property was in the spirit of each family jealously preserving its allotted portion as its permanent inheritance in the promised land (Nu 36:7). As a Phoenician, Jezebel's sarcastic question to Ahab (1Ki 21:7) was based on firsthand knowledge of the despotic practices of Phoenician and Canaanite kings, who did not hesitate to exploit their power to satisfy their personal interests (cf. 1Sa 8:9–18, especially v. 14).

male[u] in Israel—slave or free. 22I will make your house[v] like that of Jeroboam son of Nebat and that of
Baasha son of Ahijah, because you have provoked me to anger and have caused Israel to sin.'[w]
23"And also concerning Jezebel the LORD says: 'Dogs[x] will devour Jezebel by the wall of[a] Jezreel.'
24"Dogs[y] will eat those belonging to Ahab who die in the city, and the birds of the air will feed on
those who die in the country."
25(There was never[z] a man like Ahab, who sold himself to do evil in the eyes of the LORD, urged on by
Jezebel his wife. 26He behaved in the vilest manner by going after idols, like the Amorites[a] the LORD drove
out before Israel.)
27When Ahab heard these words, he tore his clothes, put on sackcloth[b] and fasted. He lay in sackcloth
and went around meekly.
28Then the word of the LORD came to Elijah the Tishbite: 29"Have you noticed how Ahab has humbled
himself before me? Because he has humbled himself, I will not bring this disaster in his day, but I will
bring it on his house in the days of his son."[c]

Micaiah Prophesies Against Ahab

22 For three years there was no war between Aram and Israel. 2But in the third year Jehoshaphat
king of Judah went down to see the king of Israel. 3The king of Israel had said to his officials,
"Don't you know that Ramoth Gilead[d] belongs to us and yet we are doing nothing to retake it from the
king of Aram?"
4So he asked Jehoshaphat, "Will you go with me to fight[e] against Ramoth Gilead?"
Jehoshaphat replied to the king of Israel, "I am as you are, my people as your people, my horses as
your horses." 5But Jehoshaphat also said to the king of Israel, "First seek the counsel[f] of the LORD."
6So the king of Israel brought together the prophets—about four hundred men—and asked them,
"Shall I go to war against Ramoth Gilead, or shall I refrain?"
"Go,"[g] they answered, "for the Lord will give it into the king's hand."
7But Jehoshaphat asked, "Is there not a prophet[h] of the LORD here whom we can inquire of?"
8The king of Israel answered Jehoshaphat, "There is still one man through whom we can inquire of
the LORD, but I hate[i] him because he never prophesies anything good[j] about me, but always bad. He is Mi-
caiah son of Imlah."
"The king should not say that," Jehoshaphat replied.
9So the king of Israel called one of his officials and said, "Bring Micaiah son of Imlah at once."
10Dressed in their royal robes, the king of Israel and Jehoshaphat king of Judah were sitting on their
thrones at the threshing floor[k] by the entrance of the gate of Samaria, with all the prophets prophesying
before them. 11Now Zedekiah son of Kenaanah had made iron horns[l] and he declared, "This is what the
LORD says: 'With these you will gore the Arameans until they are destroyed.' "
12All the other prophets were prophesying the same thing. "Attack Ramoth Gilead and be victorious,"
they said, "for the LORD will give it into the king's hand."
13The messenger who had gone to summon Micaiah said to him, "Look, as one man the other proph-
ets are predicting success for the king. Let your word agree with theirs, and speak favorably."
14But Micaiah said, "As surely as the LORD lives, I can tell him only what the LORD tells me."[m]
15When he arrived, the king asked him, "Micaiah, shall we go to war against Ramoth Gilead, or shall
I refrain?"
"Attack and be victorious," he answered, "for the LORD will give it into the king's hand."
16The king said to him, "How many times must I make you swear to tell me nothing but the truth in
the name of the LORD?"
17Then Micaiah answered, "I saw all Israel scattered on the hills like sheep without a shepherd,[n] and
the LORD said, 'These people have no master. Let each one go home in peace.' "
18The king of Israel said to Jehoshaphat, "Didn't I tell you that he never prophesies anything good
about me, but only bad?"
19Micaiah continued, "Therefore hear the word of the LORD: I saw the LORD sitting on his throne[o] with

21:21 [u]1Ki 14:10; 2Ki 9:8
21:22 [v]1Ki 15:29; 16:3 [w]1Ki 12:30
21:23 [x]2Ki 9:10, 34-36
21:24 [y]1Ki 14:11; 16:4
21:25 [z]ver 20; 1Ki 16:33
21:26 [a]Ge 15:16; Lev 18:25-30; 2Ki 21:11
21:27 [b]Ge 37:34; 2Sa 3:31; 2Ki 6:30
21:29 [c]2Ki 9:26
22:3 [d]Dt 4:43; Jos 21:38
22:4 [e]2Ki 3:7
22:5 [f]Ex 33:7; 2Ki 3:11
22:6 [g]1Ki 18:19
22:7 [h]2Ki 3:11
22:8 [i]Am 5:10 [j]Isa 5:20
22:10 [k]ver 6
22:11 [l]Dt 33:17; Zec 1:18-21
22:14 [m]Nu 22:18; 24:13; 1Ki 18:10, 15
22:17 [n]ver 34-36; Nu 27:17; Mt 9:36
22:19 [o]Isa 6:1; Eze 1:26; Da 7:9

[a] 23 Most Hebrew manuscripts; a few Hebrew manuscripts, Vulgate and Syriac (see also 2 Kings 9:26) *the plot of ground at*

21:27 See the note on sackcloth at Job 16:15. See also "Sackcloth and Ashes: Rituals of Lamentation" on page 820.

22:5 For a discussion of the religious significance of Israel's wars, see the note on Deuteronomy 20:1–4.

22:10 See "The City Gate" on page 392.

all the host[p] of heaven standing around him on his right and on his left. 20 And the LORD said, 'Who will 22:19 [p]Job 1:6; 2:1; Ps 103:20-21; Mt 18:10; Heb 1:7,14
entice Ahab into attacking Ramoth Gilead and going to his death there?'
"One suggested this, and another that. 21 Finally, a spirit came forward, stood before the LORD and said,
'I will entice him.'
22 " 'By what means?' the LORD asked.
" 'I will go out and be a lying[q] spirit in the mouths of all his prophets,' he said. 22:22 [q]Jdg 9:23; 1Sa 16:14; 18:10; 19:9; Eze 14:9; 2Th 2:11
" 'You will succeed in enticing him,' said the LORD. 'Go and do it.'
23 "So now the LORD has put a lying spirit in the mouths of all these prophets[r] of yours. The LORD has 22:23 [r]Eze 14:9
decreed disaster for you."
24 Then Zedekiah[s] son of Kenaanah went up and slapped[t] Micaiah in the face. "Which way did the 22:24 [s]ver 11 [t]Ac 23:2
spirit from[a] the LORD go when he went from me to speak to you?" he asked.
25 Micaiah replied, "You will find out on the day you go to hide[u] in an inner room." 22:25 [u]1Ki 20:30
26 The king of Israel then ordered, "Take Micaiah and send him back to Amon the ruler of the city and
to Joash the king's son 27 and say, 'This is what the king says: Put this fellow in prison[v] and give him noth- 22:27 [v]2Ch 16:10
ing but bread and water until I return safely.' "
28 Micaiah declared, "If you ever return safely, the LORD has not spoken[w] through me." Then he add- 22:28 [w]Dt 18:22
ed, "Mark my words, all you people!"

Ahab Killed at Ramoth Gilead

29 So the king of Israel and Jehoshaphat king of Judah went up to Ramoth Gilead. 30 The king of Isra-
el said to Jehoshaphat, "I will enter the battle in disguise,[x] but you wear your royal robes." So the king of 22:30 [x]2Ch 35:32
Israel disguised himself and went into battle.

[a] 24 Or *Spirit of*

Ahab and the Battle of Qarqar

1 KINGS 22 Ahab, son of Omri, ruled the northern kingdom for 22 years, from approximately 874–853 B.C.—the fourth longest rule of the 20 kings of that nation.[1] Four Old Testament chapters are devoted to his reign (1Ki 18; 20–22), more than to any other king of the northern kingdom. Because Ahab promoted the worship of Baal and Asherah, he carries the ignominious distinction of having been Israel's most wicked king (16:30–33).[2] During the last four years of his reign Ahab was involved in a war with Aram to the north. In his first two encounters with the Arameans he was victorious,[3] but in the third recorded battle, at Ramoth Gilead[4] ("Map 4"), Israel was badly defeated and Ahab mortally wounded (22:29–37). Although he died a violent death, Ahab at least avoided the fate of several other kings of the north, who were assassinated by rivals (see 21:20–29).

Ahab was known as an enthusiastic and skilled "builder" (meaning that he commissioned the construction of various buildings; 16:32; 22:39), and archaeological findings have borne this out. Remains of his palace have been unearthed at Samaria, where Ahab expanded the royal quarters built by his father.[5] Inside the compound archaeologists have unearthed numerous fragments of carved ivory plaques from his palace (v. 39).[6] In the northwest corner of the citadel was a pool, quite possibly the one in which Ahab's bloodied chariot was washed (v. 38). Fortifications and elaborate constructions at **Megiddo**, **Hazor** (both "Map 6") and Tel Dan have also been attributed to this king.

In 853 B.C., just prior to his engagement with the Arameans at Ramoth Gilead ("Map 4"), Ahab participated in a coalition of 12 states that were opposed to **Assyria**'s westward expansion, an event not recorded in the Old Testament. The Assyrian king **Shalmaneser III** confronted the coalition at Qarqar, Syria, and defeated its combined forces. In the Assyrian record of the event, "Ahab the Israelite" is credited with having contributed one of the largest forces—2,000 chariots and 10,000 infantry soldiers. The Assyrian record, as well as artifactual and architectural evidence excavated in Israel, fully substantiates the tone of the Biblical record concerning Ahab. He was a powerful and prosperous, albeit idolatrous, Biblical king.

[1]See "The History of the Northern Kingdom" on page 506. [2]See "Baal and the Fertility Cults" on page 1414 and "Devotion to Asherah in the Khirbet El-Qom Inscription" on page 638. [3]See "Ben-Hadad I and II" on page 521. [4]See "Ramoth (in) Gilead" on page 261. [5]See "Omri and Samaria" on page 512. [6]See "The Samaria Ivories" on page 1449.

31 Now the king of Aram had ordered his thirty-two chariot commanders, "Do not fight with anyone,
22:31 y2Sa 17:2 small or great, except the king[y] of Israel." 32 When the chariot commanders saw Jehoshaphat, they thought,
"Surely this is the king of Israel." So they turned to attack him, but when Jehoshaphat cried out, 33 the
chariot commanders saw that he was not the king of Israel and stopped pursuing him.
22:34 z2Ch 35:23 34 But someone drew his bow[z] at random and hit the king of Israel between the sections of his armor.
The king told his chariot driver, "Wheel around and get me out of the fighting. I've been wounded." 35 All
day long the battle raged, and the king was propped up in his chariot facing the Arameans. The blood
from his wound ran onto the floor of the chariot, and that evening he died. 36 As the sun was setting, a cry
22:36 a2Ki 14:12 spread through the army: "Every man to his town; everyone to his land!"[a]
37 So the king died and was brought to Samaria, and they buried him there. 38 They washed the char-
22:38 b1Ki 21:19 iot at a pool in Samaria (where the prostitutes bathed),[a] and the dogs[b] licked up his blood, as the word
of the LORD had declared.
39 As for the other events of Ahab's reign, including all he did, the palace he built and inlaid with ivo-
22:39 c2Ch 9:17; Am 3:15 ry,[c] and the cities he fortified, are they not written in the book of the annals of the kings of Israel? 40 Ahab
rested with his fathers. And Ahaziah his son succeeded him as king.

Jehoshaphat King of Judah

41 Jehoshaphat son of Asa became king of Judah in the fourth year of Ahab king of Israel. 42 Jehosha-
phat was thirty-five years old when he became king, and he reigned in Jerusalem twenty-five years. His
22:43 d2Ch 17:3 mother's name was Azubah daughter of Shilhi. 43 In everything he walked in the ways of his father Asa[d]
e1Ki 3:2; 15:14; 2Ki 12:3 and did not stray from them; he did what was right in the eyes of the LORD. The high places,[e] however,
were not removed, and the people continued to offer sacrifices and burn incense there. 44 Jehoshaphat
was also at peace with the king of Israel.
45 As for the other events of Jehoshaphat's reign, the things he achieved and his military exploits, are
they not written in the book of the annals of the kings of Judah? 46 He rid the land of the rest of the male
22:46 fDt 23:17; 1Ki 14:24; 15:12 shrine prostitutes[f] who remained there even after the reign of his father Asa. 47 There was then no king[g]
22:47 g2Sa 8:14; 2Ki 3:9; 8:20 in Edom; a deputy ruled.
22:48 h1Ki 9:26; 10:22 48 Now Jehoshaphat built a fleet of trading ships[b][h] to go to Ophir for gold, but they never set sail—they
were wrecked at Ezion Geber. 49 At that time Ahaziah son of Ahab said to Jehoshaphat, "Let my men sail
with your men," but Jehoshaphat refused.
50 Then Jehoshaphat rested with his fathers and was buried with them in the city of David his father.
And Jehoram his son succeeded him.

Ahaziah King of Israel

51 Ahaziah son of Ahab became king of Israel in Samaria in the seventeenth year of Jehoshaphat king
22:52 i1Ki 15:26; 21:25 of Judah, and he reigned over Israel two years. 52 He did evil[i] in the eyes of the LORD, because he walked
in the ways of his father and mother and in the ways of Jeroboam son of Nebat, who caused Israel to sin.
22:53 jJdg 2:11 k1Ki 16:30-32 53 He served and worshiped Baal[j] and provoked the LORD, the God of Israel, to anger, just as his father[k]
had done.

[a] 38 Or *Samaria and cleaned the weapons* [b] 48 Hebrew *of ships of Tarshish*

22:31 They were intent on fighting "the king of Israel"; if their leader were killed or captured, ancient armies usually fell apart (cf. vv. 35–36).

22:38 See "Bathing" on page 456.

22:39 Using ivory in this way was indicative of the realm's economic prosperity during Ahab's reign. Excavators have discovered ivory inlays in some of the buildings of Samaria dating from this period of Israel's history (see "The Samaria Ivories" on p. 1449). They have also found evidence that Ahab strengthened the fortifications of Megiddo and Hazor (see "Hazor" on p. 322 and "Megiddo" on p. 1541).

22:41 Jehoshaphat was, after Asa, the second of the five godly kings of Judah, the later ones being Joash, Hezekiah and Josiah. Chronicles devotes much attention to his reign (2Ch 17–20), but Kings hardly mentions Jehoshaphat except as it pertained to his dealings with an Israelite king. Jehoshaphat did away with the high places and Asherah poles (2Ch 17:6), although he apparently was unable to prevent the people from using certain high places in worshiping the Lord (1Ki 22:43). He sent out princes, priests and Levites to teach the people the law of the Lord (2Ch 17:7–9) but made the almost fatal mistake of associating with King Ahab in a campaign to recover Ramoth Gilead (1Ki 22:1–37). Also, his son Jehoram married Ahab's daughter (or sister) Athaliah, who nearly destroyed the entire dynasty.

22:48 For information on Ophir, see the note on 9:28.

22:51–53 Our books of 1 and 2 Kings, like 1 and 2 Samuel and 1 and 2 Chronicles, were originally one literary work. The division into two books was introduced by the translators of the Septuagint and was subsequently followed in the Latin Vulgate (c. A.D. 400), as well as in most modern versions.

INTRODUCTION TO 2 Kings

AUTHOR, PLACE AND DATE OF WRITING

Thought to have been composed by an unknown Judahite in exile, 1 and 2 Kings were originally one literary work. Translators of the Septuagint divided the original work into two books around A.D. 400.

See the introduction to 1 Kings for additional detail.

AUDIENCE

The combined book of Kings was originally written for the Jews living in exile in Babylon to preserve a detailed history of Israel and Judah from the last days of King David (c. 970 B.C.) to the exile to Babylon (c. 586 B.C.). Second Kings includes the history of the divided kingdom (1:1—17:41), as well as that of the surviving kingdom of Judah (18:1—25:30).

In addition to learning more about Israel's history, readers came to understand more about Judah and such godly kings as Hezekiah and Josiah. Stories about the prophets Elijah and Elisha reinforced the people's need to obey God and repent of their sins. Throughout these pages God demonstrated his covenant faithfulness and miraculous power, as well as his stern justice when his people refused to repent.

CULTURAL FACTS AND HIGHLIGHTS

The book of 2 Kings first focuses on the prophetic ministries of Elijah and Elisha. Building upon his earlier writing, now preserved in 1 Kings, the author continued to record the history of the northern kingdom of Israel and the southern kingdom of Judah through the lives of their various kings. Unfortunately, God's people still refused to repent of their sinfulness, so God permitted Assyria to conquer Israel in 722 B.C. and Babylon to overthrow Judah in 586 B.C.

TIMELINE

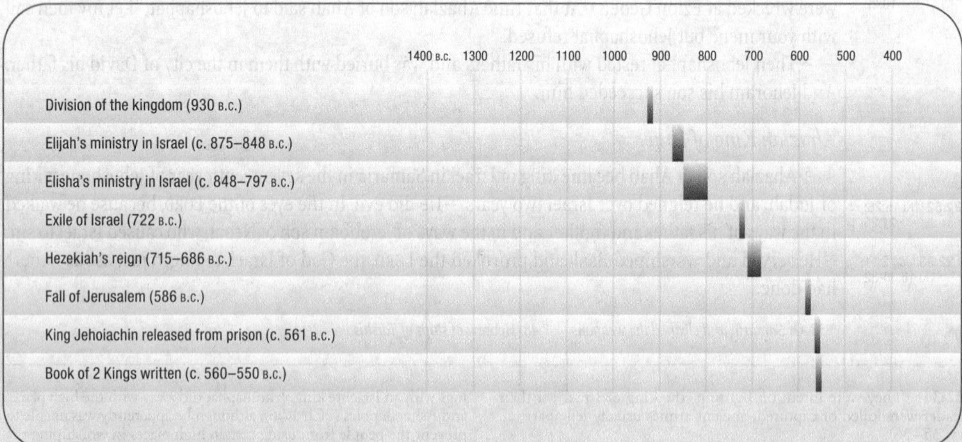

AS YOU READ

Not surprisingly, the themes of 1 Kings are also present in 2 Kings, where the author continued to record the history of Israel and Judah. Notice that God repeatedly exhibited his power and urged repentance, while remaining faithful to his people, most of whom continued in their failure to uphold their covenant promises. Place yourself in the position of Elijah (who soon left the narrative) and then of Elisha as they demonstrated God's truth and dramatic power to the people. Experience the evil arrogance of kings who defiantly challenged God by word and deed. Reflect on such kings as Hezekiah and Josiah, whose bright passion for God illuminated, albeit briefly, previously dark spiritual paths. Imagine the despair of God's chosen people when God finally allowed them to be captured by their enemies and to face exile. Finally, be alert to the hint of hope at the book's end, when Jehoiachin was released.

DID YOU KNOW?

- Ancient pagans thought that the magical power of curses could be nullified either by forcing the pronouncer of a curse to retract the statement or by killing him or her so that the curse would accompany that individual to the netherworld (1:6–15).
- Baldness, uncommon among the ancient Jews, was considered an object for mockery, while luxuriant hair seems to have been viewed as a sign of strength and vigor (2:23).
- It is still common for wadis (dry river beds) in the Arabah to become streams after a cloudburst, leaving behind pools of water. The storm may occur far enough away that no sound of wind or rain can be heard, but the water gathers and rushes down the valleys, often taking travelers by surprise (3:20).
- It was commonly assumed throughout the ancient Near East that a deity could be worshiped only on the soil of the nation to which he or she was bound (5:17).
- Women's makeup was sophisticated: black kohl to outline the eyes, blue eye shadow from lapis lazuli, crushed cochineal to serve as lipstick and scarlet henna to paint fingernails and toenails. There were also powders and an array of perfumes and ointments (9:30).
- It was common in the ancient Near East to seek omens by examining the entrails of sacrificed animals (16:15).

THEMES

Second Kings includes the following themes:

1. *Judgment.* The book explains that the destruction of Samaria and Jerusalem, the exile of the northern kingdom of Israel to Assyria (17:7–23; 18:9–12) and that of the southern kingdom of Judah to Babylon (21:1–16; 24:1–4,13–16) were all results of the people's persistent covenant breaking through idolatry. As the spiritual climate declined, so did political and economic conditions. God was patient, but eventually his ancient covenant curses were realized (Lev 26:27–43; Dt 28:64–68).

2. *Prophets.* God used prophets to call his people and their leaders back to a covenant relationship with himself (2Ki 17:13), warning them of coming judgment should they fail to repent and obey him. The two greatest prophets during this period were Elijah (1Ki 17–19; 2Ki 1–2) and Elisha (1Ki 19; 2Ki 2–13), both of whom ministered to the northern kingdom of Israel.

OUTLINE

I. Elijah and Elisha (1:1—8:15)
II. Israel and Judah From Joram/Jehoram to Israel's Exile (8:16—17:41)
III. Judah From Hezekiah to the Babylonian Exile (18–25)

The LORD's Judgment on Ahaziah

1 After Ahab's death, Moab[a] rebelled against Israel. 2 Now Ahaziah had fallen through the lattice of his
upper room in Samaria and injured himself. So he sent messengers,[b] saying to them, "Go and con-
sult Baal-Zebub,[c] the god of Ekron,[d] to see if I will recover[e] from this injury."
3 But the angel[f] of the LORD said to Elijah[g] the Tishbite, "Go up and meet the messengers of the king
of Samaria and ask them, 'Is it because there is no God in Israel[h] that you are going off to consult Baal-
Zebub, the god of Ekron?' 4 Therefore this is what the LORD says: 'You will not leave[i] the bed you are lying
on. You will certainly die!' " So Elijah went.
5 When the messengers returned to the king, he asked them, "Why have you come back?"
6 "A man came to meet us," they replied. "And he said to us, 'Go back to the king who sent you and tell
him, "This is what the LORD says: Is it because there is no God in Israel that you are sending men to con-
sult Baal-Zebub, the god of Ekron? Therefore you will not leave the bed you are lying on. You will cer-
tainly die!" ' "
7 The king asked them, "What kind of man was it who came to meet you and told you this?"
8 They replied, "He was a man with a garment of hair[j] and with a leather belt around his waist."
The king said, "That was Elijah the Tishbite."
9 Then he sent[k] to Elijah a captain[l] with his company of fifty men. The captain went up to Elijah, who
was sitting on the top of a hill, and said to him, "Man of God, the king says, 'Come down!' "
10 Elijah answered the captain, "If I am a man of God, may fire come down from heaven and consume
you and your fifty men!" Then fire[m] fell from heaven and consumed the captain and his men.
11 At this the king sent to Elijah another captain with his fifty men. The captain said to him, "Man of
God, this is what the king says, 'Come down at once!' "
12 "If I am a man of God," Elijah replied, "may fire come down from heaven and consume you and your
fifty men!" Then the fire of God fell from heaven and consumed him and his fifty men.
13 So the king sent a third captain with his fifty men. This third captain went up and fell on his knees
before Elijah. "Man of God," he begged, "please have respect for my life[n] and the lives of these fifty men,
your servants! 14 See, fire has fallen from heaven and consumed the first two captains and all their men.
But now have respect for my life!"
15 The angel[o] of the LORD said to Elijah, "Go down with him; do not be afraid[p] of him." So Elijah got
up and went down with him to the king.
16 He told the king, "This is what the LORD says: Is it because there is no God in Israel for you to con-
sult that you have sent messengers[q] to consult Baal-Zebub, the god of Ekron? Because you have done
this, you will never leave[r] the bed you are lying on. You will certainly die!" 17 So he died,[s] according to the
word of the LORD that Elijah had spoken.
Because Ahaziah had no son, Joram[a][t] succeeded him as king in the second year of Jehoram son of Je-
hoshaphat king of Judah. 18 As for all the other events of Ahaziah's reign, and what he did, are they not
written in the book of the annals of the kings of Israel?

Elijah Taken Up to Heaven

2 When the LORD was about to take[u] Elijah up to heaven in a whirlwind,[v] Elijah and Elisha[w] were on
their way from Gilgal.[x] 2 Elijah said to Elisha, "Stay here;[y] the LORD has sent me to Bethel."
But Elisha said, "As surely as the LORD lives and as you live, I will not leave you."[z] So they went down
to Bethel.
3 The company[a] of the prophets at Bethel came out to Elisha and asked, "Do you know that the LORD
is going to take your master from you today?"
"Yes, I know," Elisha replied, "but do not speak of it."
4 Then Elijah said to him, "Stay here, Elisha; the LORD has sent me to Jericho.[b]"

1:1 [a]Ge 19:37; 2Sa 8:2; 2Ki 3:5
1:2 [b]ver 16 [c]Mk 3:22 [d]1Sa 6:2; Isa 2:6; 14:29; Mt 10:25 [e]Jdg 18:5; 2Ki 8:7-10
1:3 [f]ver 15; Ge 16:7 [g]1Ki 17:1 [h]1Sa 28:8
1:4 [i]ver 6,16; Ps 41:8
1:8 [j]1Ki 18:7; Zec 13:4; Mt 3:4; Mk 1:6
1:9 [k]2Ki 6:14 [l]Ex 18:25; Isa 3:3
1:10 [m]1Ki 18:38; Lk 9:54; Rev 11:5; 13:13
1:13 [n]1Sa 26:21; Ps 72:14
1:15 [o]ver 3 [p]Isa 51:12; 57:11; Jer 1:17; Eze 2:6
1:16 [q]ver 2 [r]ver 4
1:17 [s]2Ki 8:15; Jer 20:6; 28:17 [t]2Ki 3:1; 8:16
2:1 [u]Ge 5:24; Heb 11:5 [v]ver 11; 1Ki 19:11; Isa 5:28; 66:15; Jer 4:13; Na 1:3 [w]1Ki 19:16,21 [x]Dt 11:30; 2Ki 4:38
2:2 [y]ver 6 [z]Ru 1:16; 1Sa 1:26; 2Ki 4:30
2:3 [a]1Sa 10:5; 2Ki 4:1,38
2:4 [b]Jos 3:16; 6:26

[a] 17 Hebrew *Jehoram,* a variant of *Joram*

1:2 Immersed in the Baal worship of his father, King Ahaziah sent messengers to inquire of Baal-Zebub as to whether or not he would recover from his injuries. The name "Baal-Zebub" means "lord of the flies," a deliberate change by followers of the Lord (Yahweh) to ridicule and protest the worship of Baal-Zebul ("Baal the Prince"), a name known from ancient Canaanite texts.

1:6–15 The pagan people of the time thought that the magical power of curses could be nullified either by forcing the pronouncer of the curse to retract the statement or by killing him or her so that the curse would accompany that individual to the netherworld. It appears that Ahaziah shared this view and tried to take Elijah prisoner to counteract his pronouncement of the king's death.

And he replied, "As surely as the LORD lives and as you live, I will not leave you." So they went to Jericho.
2:5 [c]ver 3 5The company[c] of the prophets at Jericho went up to Elisha and asked him, "Do you know that the
LORD is going to take your master from you today?"
"Yes, I know," he replied, "but do not speak of it."
2:6 [d]ver 2 6Then Elijah said to him, "Stay here;[d] the LORD has sent me to the Jordan."[e]
[e]Jos 3:15 [f]Ru 1:16 And he replied, "As surely as the LORD lives and as you live, I will not leave you."[f] So the two of them
walked on.
7Fifty men of the company of the prophets went and stood at a distance, facing the place where Eli-
2:8 [g]1Ki 19:19 [h]ver 14 [i]Ex 14:21 jah and Elisha had stopped at the Jordan. 8Elijah took his cloak,[g] rolled it up and struck[h] the water with
[j]Ex 14:22,29 it. The water divided[i] to the right and to the left, and the two of them crossed over on dry[j] ground.
9When they had crossed, Elijah said to Elisha, "Tell me, what can I do for you before I am taken from
you?"
2:9 [k]Dt 21:17 "Let me inherit a double[k] portion of your spirit,"[l] Elisha replied.
[l]Nu 11:17 10"You have asked a difficult thing," Elijah said, "yet if you see me when I am taken from you, it will
be yours—otherwise not."
2:11 [m]2Ki 6:17; Ps 68:17; 104:3, 11As they were walking along and talking together, suddenly a chariot of fire[m] and horses of fire ap-
4; Isa 66:15; Hab 3:8; Zec 6:1 peared and separated the two of them, and Elijah went up to heaven[n] in a whirlwind.[o] 12Elisha saw this
[n]Ge 5:24 [o]ver 1 and cried out, "My father! My father! The chariots[p] and horsemen of Israel!" And Elisha saw him no
2:12 [p]2Ki 6:17; 13:14 [q]Ge 37:29 more. Then he took hold of his own clothes and tore[q] them apart.
13He picked up the cloak that had fallen from Elijah and went back and stood on the bank of the Jor-
2:14 [r]1Ki 19:19 dan. 14Then he took the cloak[r] that had fallen from him and struck[s] the water with it. "Where now is the
[s]ver 8 LORD, the God of Elijah?" he asked. When he struck the water, it divided to the right and to the left, and
he crossed over.
2:15 [t]ver 7; 1Sa 10:5 15The company[t] of the prophets from Jericho, who were watching, said, "The spirit[u] of Elijah is rest-
[u]Nu 11:17 ing on Elisha." And they went to meet him and bowed to the ground before him. 16"Look," they said, "we
2:16 [v]1Ki 18:12 your servants have fifty able men. Let them go and look for your master. Perhaps the Spirit[v] of the LORD
[w]Ac 8:39 has picked him up[w] and set him down on some mountain or in some valley."
"No," Elisha replied, "do not send them."
2:17 [x]2Ki 8:11 17But they persisted until he was too ashamed[x] to refuse. So he said, "Send them." And they sent fif-
ty men, who searched for three days but did not find him. 18When they returned to Elisha, who was stay-
ing in Jericho, he said to them, "Didn't I tell you not to go?"

Healing of the Water

19The men of the city said to Elisha, "Look, our lord, this town is well situated, as you can see, but the
water is bad and the land is unproductive."
20"Bring me a new bowl," he said, "and put salt in it." So they brought it to him.
2:21 [y]Ex 15:25; 2Ki 4:41; 6:6 21Then he went out to the spring and threw[y] the salt into it, saying, "This is what the LORD says: 'I have
healed this water. Never again will it cause death or make the land unproductive.' " 22And the water has
2:22 [z]Ex 15:25 remained wholesome[z] to this day, according to the word Elisha had spoken.

Elisha Is Jeered

2:23 [a]Ex 22:28; 2Ch 36:16; 23From there Elisha went up to Bethel. As he was walking along the road, some youths came out of the
Job 19:18; Ps 31:18 town and jeered[a] at him. "Go on up, you baldhead!" they said. "Go on up, you baldhead!" 24He turned
2:24 [b]Ge 4:11; Ne 13:25-27 around, looked at them and called down a curse[b] on them in the name[c] of the LORD. Then two bears
[c]Dt 18:19 came out of the woods and mauled forty-two of the youths. 25And he went on to Mount Carmel[d] and
2:25 [d]1Ki 18:20; 2Ki 4:25 from there returned to Samaria.

2:9 Elisha was not expressing a desire for a ministry twice as great as Elijah's but was using terms derived from inheritance law to express his desire to carry on Elijah's ministry. Inheritance law assigned a double portion of a father's possessions to the firstborn son (see "The Rights of the Firstborn" on p. 43 and "Inheritance in the Ancient Near East" on p. 250).

2:19 Although Jericho had been rebuilt (with difficulty) during the days of Ahab (1Ki 16:34), the city had remained unproductive. Apparently the water still lay under Joshua's curse (Jos 6:26), and both people and land suffered greatly. Elisha's miracle fully removed this older judgment (2Ki 2:21). Any suggestion of a magical effect of the salt in the purification of the water is excluded by the explicit statement that the Lord himself healed, or purified, the water.

2:23 Baldness, uncommon among the ancient Jews, was considered a disgrace (Isa 3:17,24), while luxuriant hair seems to have been viewed as a sign of strength and vigor (cf. 2Sa 14:25–26). By calling Elisha "baldhead," the youths from Bethel expressed that city's utter disdain for the Lord's representative. (See "Bywords and Insults in the Ancient World" on p. 431 and "Beards and Hairstyles in the Biblical World" on p. 1084.)

Moab Revolts

3 Joram[a][e] son of Ahab became king of Israel in Samaria in the eighteenth year of Jehoshaphat king 3:1 [e]2Ki 1:17
of Judah, and he reigned twelve years. 2He did evil[f] in the eyes of the LORD, but not as his father[g] and 3:2 [f]1Ki 15:26 [g]1Ki 16:30-32
mother had done. He got rid of the sacred stone[h] of Baal that his father had made. 3Nevertheless he clung [h]Ex 23:24; 2Ki 10:18,26-28
to the sins[i] of Jeroboam son of Nebat, which he had caused Israel to commit; he did not turn away from 3:3 [i]1Ki 12:28-32; 14:9,16
them.

4Now Mesha king of Moab[j] raised sheep, and he had to supply the king of Israel with a hundred thou- 3:4 [j]Ge 19:37; 2Ki 1:1 [k]Ezr 7:17; Isa 16:1
sand lambs[k] and with the wool of a hundred thousand rams. 5But after Ahab died, the king of Moab re-
belled[l] against the king of Israel. 6So at that time King Joram set out from Samaria and mobilized all Is- 3:5 [l]2Ki 1:1
rael. 7He also sent this message to Jehoshaphat king of Judah: "The king of Moab has rebelled against
me. Will you go with me to fight[m] against Moab?" 3:7 [m]1Ki 22:4

"I will go with you," he replied. "I am as you are, my people as your people, my horses as your horses."
8"By what route shall we attack?" he asked.
"Through the Desert of Edom," he answered.
9So the king of Israel set out with the king of Judah and the king of Edom.[n] After a roundabout march 3:9 [n]1Ki 22:47
of seven days, the army had no more water for themselves or for the animals with them.
10"What!" exclaimed the king of Israel. "Has the LORD called us three kings together only to hand us
over to Moab?"

[a] 1 Hebrew *Jehoram*, a variant of *Joram*; also in verse 6

3:1 See "The Problem of the Chronology of the Kings of Judah and Israel" on page 508.

ANCIENT TEXTS AND ARTIFACTS

The Mesha (Moabite) Stone

2 KINGS 3 Mesha, king of **Moab**,[1,2] west of the Dead Sea, revolted against Israel (2Ki 3:4–5), but Israel's king Jehoram set out to reassert Israelite authority (vv. 6–9). He succeeded in defeating the Moabite army and destroying some cities but was unable to capture Moab's capital, Kir Hareseth (vv. 21–27; see "Map 6"; modern name is Kerak). It appears that Mesha retained his independence.

A unique discovery made in Dhiban, Jordan, in 1868 describes Mesha's revolt from the Moabite perspective. This document, called both the Mesha Inscription and the Moabite Stone, uses language very similar to what we see in the Old Testament. **Yahweh**,[3] the God of Israel, shows up in the inscription, as does Chemosh, the national god of Moab. Mesha describes how Omri of Israel[4] oppressed Moab and attributes Moab's suffering to the displeasure of Chemosh. He claims to have been inspired by Chemosh to rise up and deliver Moab, indicating also that he slaughtered the entire town of Nebo, which he proceeded to put under the "ban."[5]

The Old Testament assertion that Mesha raised sheep (v. 4) is corroborated by a statement by Mesha to the effect that he brought flocks to the house of Baal Meon. The **stele** notes that the tribe of Gad was living in Ataroth, as mentioned in Numbers 32:34. In addition to Ataroth, 12 other Moabite towns are mentioned in the inscription. These same towns are described in the Bible as being located in Moab. Several of them are mentioned by the prophets Isaiah (Isa 15), Jeremiah (Jer 48) and Ezekiel (Eze 25) as part of their predictions of the downfall of this ancient kingdom. Some scholars believe that the stele also has a reference to the house of David, but this interpretation has not won universal acceptance.

The Mesha (Moabite) Stone
Preserving Bible Times; © Dr. James C. Martin; permission of Musée de Louvre

[1]See Glossary on page 2080 for definitions of bolded words. [2]See "Moab" on page 292 [3]See "YHWH: The Name of God in the Old Testament" on page 89. [4]See "Omri and Samaria" on page 512. [5]See "Herem, *Holy War*" on page 419.

3:11 oGe 25:22; 1Ki 22:7 pGe 20:7 q1Ki 19:16
3:12 rNu 11:17
3:15 s1Sa 16:23 tJer 15:17; Eze 1:3
3:17 uPs 107:35; Isa 32:2; 35:6; 41:18
3:18 vGe 18:14; 2Ki 20:10; Isa 49:6; Jer 32:17,27; Mk 10:27
3:20 wEx 29:39-40 xEx 17:6
3:25 yver 19; Isa 15:1; 16:7; Jer 48:31,36
3:27 zDt 12:31; 2Ki 16:3; 21:6; 2Ch 28:3; Ps 106:38; Jer 19:4-5; Am 2:1; Mic 6:7
4:1 a1Sa 10:5; 2Ki 2:3 bEx 22:26; Lev 25:39-43; Ne 5:3-5; Job 22:6; 24:9
4:2 c1Ki 17:12

11 But Jehoshaphat asked, "Is there no prophet of the LORD here, that we may inquire[o] of the LORD through him?"

An officer of the king of Israel answered, "Elisha[p] son of Shaphat is here. He used to pour water on the hands of Elijah.[a][q]"

12 Jehoshaphat said, "The word[r] of the LORD is with him." So the king of Israel and Jehoshaphat and the king of Edom went down to him.

13 Elisha said to the king of Israel, "What do we have to do with each other? Go to the prophets of your father and the prophets of your mother."

"No," the king of Israel answered, "because it was the LORD who called us three kings together to hand us over to Moab."

14 Elisha said, "As surely as the LORD Almighty lives, whom I serve, if I did not have respect for the presence of Jehoshaphat king of Judah, I would not look at you or even notice you. 15 But now bring me a harpist."[s]

While the harpist was playing, the hand[t] of the LORD came upon Elisha 16 and he said, "This is what the LORD says: Make this valley full of ditches. 17 For this is what the LORD says: You will see neither wind nor rain, yet this valley will be filled with water,[u] and you, your cattle and your other animals will drink. 18 This is an easy[v] thing in the eyes of the LORD; he will also hand Moab over to you. 19 You will overthrow every fortified city and every major town. You will cut down every good tree, stop up all the springs, and ruin every good field with stones."

20 The next morning, about the time[w] for offering the sacrifice, there it was—water flowing from the direction of Edom! And the land was filled with water.[x]

21 Now all the Moabites had heard that the kings had come to fight against them; so every man, young and old, who could bear arms was called up and stationed on the border. 22 When they got up early in the morning, the sun was shining on the water. To the Moabites across the way, the water looked red—like blood. 23 "That's blood!" they said. "Those kings must have fought and slaughtered each other. Now to the plunder, Moab!"

24 But when the Moabites came to the camp of Israel, the Israelites rose up and fought them until they fled. And the Israelites invaded the land and slaughtered the Moabites. 25 They destroyed the towns, and each man threw a stone on every good field until it was covered. They stopped up all the springs and cut down every good tree. Only Kir Hareseth[y] was left with its stones in place, but men armed with slings surrounded it and attacked it as well.

26 When the king of Moab saw that the battle had gone against him, he took with him seven hundred swordsmen to break through to the king of Edom, but they failed. 27 Then he took his firstborn[z] son, who was to succeed him as king, and offered him as a sacrifice on the city wall. The fury against Israel was great; they withdrew and returned to their own land.

Ancient Voices

Omri was the king of Israel,
and he oppressed Moab for many days,
for Kemosh was angry with his land.
And his son succeeded him,
and he said–he too—
"I will oppress Moab!"
In my days did he say [so],*
but I looked down on him and on his house,
and Israel has gone to ruin, yes, it has gone to ruin for ever!

*Word in brackets added by translator for clarity where text has gap

—The Inscpription of King Mesha

See "The Mesha (Moabite) Stone" article.

The Widow's Oil

4 The wife of a man from the company[a] of the prophets cried out to Elisha, "Your servant my husband is dead, and you know that he revered the LORD. But now his creditor[b] is coming to take my two boys as his slaves."

2 Elisha replied to her, "How can I help you? Tell me, what do you have in your house?"

"Your servant has nothing there at all," she said, "except a little oil."[c]

[a] *11* That is, he was Elijah's personal servant.

3:11 For a discussion of the religious significance of Israel's wars, see the note on Deuteronomy 20:1–4.

3:20 It is still common for wadis (dry river beds) in the region to become streams after a cloudburst, leaving behind pools of water. The storm may occur far enough away that no sound of wind or rain can be heard, but the water gathers and rushes down the valleys, often taking travelers by surprise. Although such occurrences were not infrequent, there was nothing natural about the deliverance experienced by the three armies.

3:25 Kir Hareseth was the capital city of Moab (see "Moab" on p. 292). It is usually identified with present-day Kerak, located about 11 miles (18 km) east of the Dead Sea and 15 miles (24 km) south of the Arnon River.

3:27 King Mesha offered his oldest son, the crown prince, to the Moabite god Chemosh in an attempt to induce that deity to come to his aid (see "Human Sacrifice in the Ancient Near East" on p. 182).

3 Elisha said, "Go around and ask all your neighbors for empty jars. Don't ask for just a few. 4 Then go
inside and shut the door behind you and your sons. Pour oil into all the jars, and as each is filled, put it
to one side."

5 She left him and afterward shut the door behind her and her sons. They brought the jars to her and
she kept pouring. 6 When all the jars were full, she said to her son, "Bring me another one."

But he replied, "There is not a jar left." Then the oil stopped flowing.

7 She went and told the man of God,[d] and he said, "Go, sell the oil and pay your debts. You and your **4:7** [d]1Ki 12:22
sons can live on what is left."

The Shunammite's Son Restored to Life

8 One day Elisha went to Shunem.[e] And a well-to-do woman was there, who urged him to stay for a **4:8** [e]Jos 19:18
meal. So whenever he came by, he stopped there to eat. 9 She said to her husband, "I know that this man
who often comes our way is a holy man of God. 10 Let's make a small room on the roof and put in it a bed
and a table, a chair and a lamp for him. Then he can stay[f] there whenever he comes to us." **4:10** [f]Mt 10:41; Ro 12:13

11 One day when Elisha came, he went up to his room and lay down there. 12 He said to his servant Ge-
hazi, "Call the Shunammite."[g] So he called her, and she stood before him. 13 Elisha said to him, "Tell her, **4:12** [g]2Ki 8:1
'You have gone to all this trouble for us. Now what can be done for you? Can we speak on your behalf to
the king or the commander of the army?' "

She replied, "I have a home among my own people."

14 "What can be done for her?" Elisha asked.

Gehazi said, "Well, she has no son and her husband is old."

15 Then Elisha said, "Call her." So he called her, and she stood in the doorway. 16 "About this time[h] next **4:16** [h]Ge 18:10
year," Elisha said, "you will hold a son in your arms."

"No, my lord," she objected. "Don't mislead your servant, O man of God!"

17 But the woman became pregnant, and the next year about that same time she gave birth to a son,
just as Elisha had told her.

18 The child grew, and one day he went out to his father, who was with the reapers.[i] 19 "My head! My **4:18** [i]Ru 2:3
head!" he said to his father.

His father told a servant, "Carry him to his mother." 20 After the servant had lifted him up and carried
him to his mother, the boy sat on her lap until noon, and then he died. 21 She went up and laid him on the
bed[j] of the man of God, then shut the door and went out. **4:21** [j]ver 32

22 She called her husband and said, "Please send me one of the servants and a donkey so I can go to
the man of God quickly and return."

23 "Why go to him today?" he asked. "It's not the New Moon[k] or the Sabbath." **4:23** [k]Nu 10:10; 1Ch 23:31; Ps 81:3

"It's all right," she said.

24 She saddled the donkey and said to her servant, "Lead on; don't slow down for me unless I tell you."
25 So she set out and came to the man of God at Mount Carmel.[l] **4:25** [l]1Ki 18:20; 2Ki 2:25

When he saw her in the distance, the man of God said to his servant Gehazi, "Look! There's the Shu-
nammite! 26 Run to meet her and ask her, 'Are you all right? Is your husband all right? Is your child all
right?' "

"Everything is all right," she said.

27 When she reached the man of God at the mountain, she took hold of his feet. Gehazi came over to
push her away, but the man of God said, "Leave her alone! She is in bitter distress,[m] but the LORD has hid- **4:27** [m]1Sa 1:15
den it from me and has not told me why."

28 "Did I ask you for a son, my lord?" she said. "Didn't I tell you, 'Don't raise my hopes'?"

29 Elisha said to Gehazi, "Tuck your cloak into your belt,[n] take my staff[o] in your hand and run. If you **4:29** [n]1Ki 18:46; 2Ki 2:8,14; 9:1 [o]Ex 4:2; 7:19; 14:16
meet anyone, do not greet him, and if anyone greets you, do not answer. Lay my staff on the boy's face."

30 But the child's mother said, "As surely as the LORD lives and as you live, I will not leave you." So he
got up and followed her.

31 Gehazi went on ahead and laid the staff on the boy's face, but there was no sound or response. So
Gehazi went back to meet Elisha and told him, "The boy has not awakened."

4:14 Childlessness was a bitter disappointment because it meant that the family's name would cease and that its land and possessions would pass on to others.

4:23 The Sabbath and New Moon were observed by cessation from work (see the note on 1Sa 20:5).

4:32 [p]ver 21 — 32 When Elisha reached the house, there was the boy lying dead on his couch.[p] 33 He went in, shut the
4:33 [q]1Ki 17:20; Mt 6:6 — door on the two of them and prayed[q] to the LORD. 34 Then he got on the bed and lay upon the boy, mouth
4:34 [r]1Ki 17:21; Ac 20:10 — to mouth, eyes to eyes, hands to hands. As he stretched[r] himself out upon him, the boy's body grew warm.
35 Elisha turned away and walked back and forth in the room and then got on the bed and stretched out
4:35 [s]Jos 6:15 [t]2Ki 8:5 — upon him once more. The boy sneezed seven times[s] and opened his eyes.[t]
36 Elisha summoned Gehazi and said, "Call the Shunammite." And he did. When she came, he said, "Take
4:36 [u]Heb 11:35 — your son."[u] 37 She came in, fell at his feet and bowed to the ground. Then she took her son and went out.

Death in the Pot

4:38 [v]2Ki 2:1 [w]Lev 26:26; 2Ki 8:1 — 38 Elisha returned to Gilgal[v] and there was a famine[w] in that region. While the company of the proph-
ets was meeting with him, he said to his servant, "Put on the large pot and cook some stew for these men."
39 One of them went out into the fields to gather herbs and found a wild vine. He gathered some of its
gourds and filled the fold of his cloak. When he returned, he cut them up into the pot of stew, though no
one knew what they were. 40 The stew was poured out for the men, but as they began to eat it, they cried
out, "O man of God, there is death in the pot!" And they could not eat it.
41 Elisha said, "Get some flour." He put it into the pot and said, "Serve it to the people to eat." And there
4:41 [x]Ex 15:25; 2Ki 2:21 — was nothing harmful in the pot.[x]

Feeding of a Hundred

4:42 [y]1Sa 9:4 [z]Mt 14:17; 15:36 [a]1Sa 9:7 — 42 A man came from Baal Shalishah,[y] bringing the man of God twenty loaves[z] of barley bread[a] baked
from the first ripe grain, along with some heads of new grain. "Give it to the people to eat," Elisha said.
43 "How can I set this before a hundred men?" his servant asked.
4:43 [b]Lk 9:13 [c]Mt 14:20; Jn 6:12 — But Elisha answered, "Give it to the people to eat.[b] For this is what the LORD says: 'They will eat and
have some left over.[c]' " 44 Then he set it before them, and they ate and had some left over, according to the
word of the LORD.

Naaman Healed of Leprosy

5:1 [d]Ge 10:22; 2Sa 10:19 [e]Ex 4:6; Nu 12:10; Lk 4:27 — **5** Now Naaman was commander of the army of the king of Aram.[d] He was a great man in the sight of
his master and highly regarded, because through him the LORD had given victory to Aram. He was
a valiant soldier, but he had leprosy.[a][e]
5:2 [f]2Ki 6:23; 13:20; 24:2 — 2 Now bands[f] from Aram had gone out and had taken captive a young girl from Israel, and she served
5:3 [g]Ge 20:7 — Naaman's wife. 3 She said to her mistress, "If only my master would see the prophet[g] who is in Samaria!
He would cure him of his leprosy."
4 Naaman went to his master and told him what the girl from Israel had said. 5 "By all means, go," the
king of Aram replied. "I will send a letter to the king of Israel." So Naaman left, taking with him ten tal-
5:5 [h]ver 22; Ge 24:53; Jdg 14:12; 1Sa 9:7 — ents[b] of silver, six thousand shekels[c] of gold and ten sets of clothing.[h] 6 The letter that he took to the king
of Israel read: "With this letter I am sending my servant Naaman to you so that you may cure him of his
leprosy."
5:7 [i]2Ki 19:14 [j]Ge 30:2 [k]Dt 32:39; 1Sa 2:6 [l]1Ki 20:7 — 7 As soon as the king of Israel read the letter,[i] he tore his robes and said, "Am I God?[j] Can I kill and bring
back to life?[k] Why does this fellow send someone to me to be cured of his leprosy? See how he is trying
to pick a quarrel[l] with me!"
8 When Elisha the man of God heard that the king of Israel had torn his robes, he sent him this mes-
5:8 [m]1Ki 22:7 — sage: "Why have you torn your robes? Have the man come to me and he will know that there is a prophet[m]
in Israel." 9 So Naaman went with his horses and chariots and stopped at the door of Elisha's house. 10 Eli-
5:10 [n]Jn 9:7 [o]Ge 33:3; Lev 14:7 — sha sent a messenger to say to him, "Go, wash[n] yourself seven times[o] in the Jordan, and your flesh will
be restored and you will be cleansed."

[a] *1* The Hebrew word was used for various diseases affecting the skin—not necessarily leprosy; also in verses 3, 6, 7, 11 and 27.
[b] *5* That is, about 750 pounds (about 340 kilograms) [c] *5* That is, about 150 pounds (about 70 kilograms)

4:38 See the note on Ruth 1:1, as well as "Famine in the Ancient Near East" on page 70.
4:42 Instead of bringing the firstfruits of the new harvest (see Lev 2:14; 23:15–17; Dt 18:3–5) to the apostate priests at Bethel and Dan (see 1Ki 12:28–31), godly people in the northern kingdom may have contributed their offerings for the sustenance of Elisha and those associated with him.
5:1 See "Skin Diseases in the Ancient World" on page 171.
5:5 Silver and gold were highly valued in commercial exchange. They were measured by weight, as coinage did not come into existence until the seventh century B.C. (see "Coins and Numismatics" on p. 1699).

11 But Naaman went away angry and said, "I thought that he would surely come out to me and stand
and call on the name of the LORD his God, wave his hand[p] over the spot and cure me of my leprosy. 12 Are 5:11 [p]Ex 7:19
not Abana and Pharpar, the rivers of Damascus, better than any of the waters[q] of Israel? Couldn't I wash 5:12 [q]Isa 8:6
in them and be cleansed?" So he turned and went off in a rage.[r] [r]Pr 14:17,29; 19:11; 29:11
13 Naaman's servants went to him and said, "My father,[s] if the prophet had told you to do some great 5:13 [s]2Ki 6:21; 13:14
thing, would you not have done it? How much more, then, when he tells you, 'Wash and be cleansed'!" 14 So
he went down and dipped himself in the Jordan seven times,[t] as the man of God had told him, and his 5:14 [t]Ge 33:3; Lev 14:7; Jos 6:15 [u]Ex 4:7 [v]Job 33:25; Lk 4:27
flesh was restored[u] and became clean like that of a young boy.[v]
15 Then Naaman and all his attendants went back to the man of God[w]. He stood before him and said,
"Now I know[x] that there is no God in all the world except in Israel. Please accept now a gift[y] from your 5:15 [w]Jos 2:11 [x]Jos 4:24; 1Sa 17:46; Da 2:47 [y]1Sa 9:7; 25:27
servant."
16 The prophet answered, "As surely as the LORD lives, whom I serve, I will not accept a thing." And even
though Naaman urged him, he refused.[z] 5:16 [z]ver 20,26; Ge 14:23; Da 5:17
17 "If you will not," said Naaman, "please let me, your servant, be given as much earth[a] as a pair of 5:17 [a]Ex 20:24
mules can carry, for your servant will never again make burnt offerings and sacrifices to any other god
but the LORD. 18 But may the LORD forgive your servant for this one thing: When my master enters the
temple of Rimmon to bow down and he is leaning[b] on my arm and I bow there also—when I bow down 5:18 [b]2Ki 7:2
in the temple of Rimmon, may the LORD forgive your servant for this."

5:17 Naaman had become convinced that the Lord alone was God. Accordingly, he asked Elisha for two mule loads of Israelite soil to take back to Aram (see "Syria/Aram," below). It was commonly thought that a deity could be worshiped only on the soil of the nation to which he or she was bound.

Syria / Aram

2 KINGS 5 Israel and Aram (Syria) were ethnically related. Abraham was of Aramean stock, having come from the area of Haran[1] in southern Turkey (Ge 24:4; see "Map 1"). Jacob was called an Aramean (Dt 26:5), as was his uncle Laban (Ge 25:20) and grandfather Bethuel (Ge 25:20; 28:5). The Arameans were a tribal Semitic people located in **Mesopotamia** and Syria. Their lifestyle was that of semi-nomadic pastoralists (shepherds and herders of livestock) living in small villages. When the **Hittite** Empire collapsed at the end of the second millennium B.C.,[2] the Aramean tribes in Syria developed into powerful city-state monarchies that flourished in the eleventh–eighth centuries B.C.

In Syria the Arameans built large, well-fortified cities, including grand palaces. Each city had its own pantheon (official listing of gods) and patron deity. The most prominent was Hadad, the weather-fertility god. Naaman talked about accompanying the Aramean king into the "temple of Rimmon" in Damascus[3] (2Ki 5:18; "Map 6"). This was probably the temple of Hadad-Rimmon (Zec 12:11), meaning "Hadad the thunderer." Other deities worshiped by the Arameans included Sin, the moon god; El, the "creator" god; Shamash, the sun god; and Reshep, the god of plague. The Lord had long before called Abraham out of the paganism of the Aramean culture to establish a godly nation (Ge 12:1; Jos 24:2–3; cf. Ge 31:19,30; 35:2–4).

The Israelites came into contact with the Aramean kingdoms in Lebanon and Syria, immediately to their north. They engaged primarily in turf battles, particularly with the city-state of Damascus, called Aram in the Bible,[4] but occasionally also entered with them into trade agreements (1Ki 20:34) and alliances.

The most lasting legacy of the Arameans was their language, **Aramaic**. It was the major spoken language of upper Mesopotamia and Syria during the early part of the first millennium B.C., as well as the diplomatic language of this time. From about the third century B.C. to the end of the Jewish state, Aramaic was the common language of the Jews.[5]

[1]See "Haran" on page 47. [2]See "Anatolia and the Hittites" on page 144. [3]See "Damascus" on page 1087. [4]See "The Syro-Ephraimite War" on page 1066. [5]See "Languages of the Old Testament World" on page 672.

5:19 [c]1Sa 1:17; Ac 15:33 — 19“Go in peace,”[c] Elisha said.
After Naaman had traveled some distance, 20Gehazi, the servant of Elisha the man of God, said to
himself, “My master was too easy on Naaman, this Aramean, by not accepting from him what he brought.
5:20 [d]Ex 20:7 — As surely as the LORD[d] lives, I will run after him and get something from him.”
21So Gehazi hurried after Naaman. When Naaman saw him running toward him, he got down from
the chariot to meet him. “Is everything all right?” he asked.
22“Everything is all right,” Gehazi answered. “My master sent me to say, ‘Two young men from the
company of the prophets have just come to me from the hill country of Ephraim. Please give them a tal-
5:22 [e]ver 5; Ge 45:22 — ent[a] of silver and two sets of clothing.’ ”[e]
23“By all means, take two talents,” said Naaman. He urged Gehazi to accept them, and then tied up
the two talents of silver in two bags, with two sets of clothing. He gave them to two of his servants, and
they carried them ahead of Gehazi. 24When Gehazi came to the hill, he took the things from the servants
and put them away in the house. He sent the men away and they left. 25Then he went in and stood before
his master Elisha.
“Where have you been, Gehazi?” Elisha asked.
“Your servant didn’t go anywhere,” Gehazi answered.
26But Elisha said to him, “Was not my spirit with you when the man got down from his chariot to
5:26 [f]ver 16 [g]Jer 45:5 — meet you? Is this the time[f] to take money, or to accept clothes, olive groves, vineyards, flocks, herds, or
5:27 [h]Nu 12:10; 2Ki 15:5 [i]Col 3:5 [j]Ex 4:6 — menservants and maidservants?[g] 27Naaman’s leprosy[h] will cling to you and to your descendants forever.”
Then Gehazi[i] went from Elisha’s presence and he was leprous, as white as snow.[j]

An Axhead Floats

6:1 [k]1Sa 10:5; 2Ki 4:38 — 6 The company[k] of the prophets said to Elisha, “Look, the place where we meet with you is too small
for us. 2Let us go to the Jordan, where each of us can get a pole; and let us build a place there for us
to live.”
And he said, “Go.”
3Then one of them said, “Won’t you please come with your servants?”
“I will,” Elisha replied. 4And he went with them.
They went to the Jordan and began to cut down trees. 5As one of them was cutting down a tree, the
iron axhead fell into the water. “Oh, my lord,” he cried out, “it was borrowed!”
6The man of God asked, “Where did it fall?” When he showed him the place, Elisha cut a stick and
6:6 [l]Ex 15:25; 2Ki 2:21 — threw[l] it there, and made the iron float. 7“Lift it out,” he said. Then the man reached out his hand and
took it.

Elisha Traps Blinded Arameans

8Now the king of Aram was at war with Israel. After conferring with his officers, he said, “I will set up
my camp in such and such a place.”
6:9 [m]ver 12 — 9The man of God sent word to the king[m] of Israel: “Beware of passing that place, because the Arame-
ans are going down there.” 10So the king of Israel checked on the place indicated by the man of God. Time
6:10 [n]Jer 11:18 — and again Elisha warned[n] the king, so that he was on his guard in such places.
11This enraged the king of Aram. He summoned his officers and demanded of them, “Will you not tell
me which of us is on the side of the king of Israel?”
6:12 [o]ver 9 — 12“None of us, my lord the king[o],” said one of his officers, “but Elisha, the prophet who is in Israel,
tells the king of Israel the very words you speak in your bedroom.”
13“Go, find out where he is,” the king ordered, “so I can send men and capture him.” The report came
6:13 [p]Ge 37:17 6:14 [q]2Ki 1:9 — back: “He is in Dothan.”[p] 14Then he sent[q] horses and chariots and a strong force there. They went by
night and surrounded the city.
15When the servant of the man of God got up and went out early the next morning, an army with
horses and chariots had surrounded the city. “Oh, my lord, what shall we do?” the servant asked.

[a] 22 That is, about 75 pounds (about 34 kilograms)

6:5 An iron implement was costly—too much for a prophet to repay. This man would have been forced to work as a bondservant to pay off such a debt.

6:13 Dothan was located on a hill about halfway between Jezreel and Samaria, the site of the main royal residences (see “Dothan, Ben-Hadad and a Chronological Problem” on p. 536).

16 "Don't be afraid,"[r] the prophet answered. "Those who are with us are more[s] than those who are with
them."
17 And Elisha prayed, "O LORD, open his eyes so he may see." Then the LORD opened the servant's eyes,
and he looked and saw the hills full of horses and chariots[t] of fire all around Elisha.
18 As the enemy came down toward him, Elisha prayed to the LORD, "Strike these people with blind-
ness."[u] So he struck them with blindness, as Elisha had asked.
19 Elisha told them, "This is not the road and this is not the city. Follow me, and I will lead you to the
man you are looking for." And he led them to Samaria.

6:16 [r]Ge 15:1 [s]2Ch 32:7; Ps 55:18; Ro 8:31; 1Jn 4:4
6:17 [t]2Ki 2:11, 12; Ps 68:17; Zec 6:1-7
6:18 [u]Ge 19:11; Ac 13:11

Dothan, Ben-Hadad and a Chronological Problem

2 KINGS 6 The chronology of 2 Kings 6 is difficult to reconstruct. There were at least three Aramean (Syrian) kings at Damascus ("Map 6" in the back of this Bible) named Ben-Hadad. A plausible sequence is as follows:

- *Ben-Hadad I* (son of Tabrimmon; r. in late tenth to early ninth century B.C.; 1Ki 15:18)
- *Ben-Hadad II* (father's name never given; r. mid-ninth century B.C.)[1]
- *Hazael* (r. late ninth century B.C., c. 842–800)[2]
- *Ben-Hadad III* (the son of Hazael; r. early eighth century B.C.)[3]

In addition, it is difficult to determine the historical circumstances behind 2 Kings 6–8. Basic facts are as follows:

- According to 6:8–23, a king of Damascus tried unsuccessfully to capture Elisha at Dothan. After this episode Israel was for a time spared the depravations brought about by bands of Arameans, but neither the king of Damascus nor the king of Israel is named.
- However, 6:24—7:20 describes an invasion led by "Ben-Hadad king of Aram" that nearly brought **Samaria** to its knees (6:25). The text identifies the leader of the Arameans as Ben-Hadad; otherwise, we know only that this event occurred during Elisha's ministry.
- Second Kings 8:7–15 describes the death of "Ben-Hadad" (probably Ben-Hadad II) and the rise of Hazael. This suggests that Ben-Hadad II was the king of chapters 6–7.

The archaeology of Dothan, where Elisha resided, may have bearing on Ben-Hadad's invasion. Dothan is mentioned in the Bible only in Genesis 37:17 and 2 Kings 6:13. It was strategically located on a highway in the southern Dothan Valley in central Israel, with the Jezreel Valley to the north and Samaria to the south.[4]

Evidence of occupation levels from the **Chalcolithic** and all three **Bronze Ages**[5] was found at Dothan ("Map 1"), but most of the finds are from the **Iron Age** II, the period of the Elisha stories. Remains of private homes, storage bins, ovens and pottery vessels were unearthed, along with a large public building.

Excavations were conducted at Dothan in the 1950s. Unfortunately, the reports are unclear, and this lack of definition has made it difficult to piece together the site's history. There is evidence of a late ninth-century B.C. destruction of Dothan, possibly related to Ben-Hadad's invasion in verse 24. We might speculate that the Ben-Hadad of this verse demolished Dothan during the course of this invasion to secure supply lines for his troops around Samaria. If this Ben-Hadad was indeed Ben-Hadad II, he may also have been the anonymous Aramean king who tried to capture Elisha at Dothan (vv. 8–23).

This premise would require that both episodes took place early in Elisha's ministry. Based upon 1 Kings 19:16 and 2 Kings 3, Elisha was anointed around 855 B.C. (near the end of Ahab's reign) and began his ministry around 851 B.C. (the beginning of Joram's). Second Kings 6:31 suggests that Elisha was already a prophet of renown during the invasion of verse 24, since Israel's king was angry that Elisha had not done more to thwart the incursion. It may be that the events of verses 8–23 helped to establish Elisha's reputation. If all of this was so, these events must have occurred around 850 B.C., with verses 24 and following taking place around 845 B.C. We might speculate that the ninth-century destruction of Dothan took place around 845 if that destruction is related to this story.

Another possibility is that the Ben-Hadad of verse 24 was Ben-Hadad III and that this story was related out of sequence for thematic purposes.

Evidence suggests that Dothan was rebuilt and reoccupied in the eighth century B.C. but destroyed again by the **Assyrians**, either in the invasion of Tiglath-Pileser III in 732[6] or in the final obliteration of the northern kingdom around 721 B.C. Among the pottery finds at eighth-century Dothan were **carinated** bowls of Assyrian origin, attesting to an Assyrian presence or influence at that time. Dothan was then abandoned, although a small settlement was established there during the **Hellenistic period**.

[1]See "Ben-Hadad I and II" on page 521. [2]See "Hazael, the Nemesis of Israel" on page 539. [3]See "Ben-Hadad III of Aram and Jehoash of Israel" on page 548. [4]See "The Valley of Jezreel" on page 1412 and "Omri and Samaria" on page 512. [5]See "Archaeological Periods" chart on page xx in the front of this Bible. [6]See "Menahem and Pekah of Israel, Jotham of Judah and Tiglath-Pileser III of Assyria" on page 553.

20 After they entered the city, Elisha said, "LORD, open the eyes of these men so they can see." Then the
LORD opened their eyes and they looked, and there they were, inside Samaria.
6:21 [v]2Ki 5:13 21 When the king of Israel saw them, he asked Elisha, "Shall I kill them, my father?[v] Shall I kill them?"
6:22 [w]Dt 20:11; 2Ch 28:8-15; Ro 12:20 22 "Do not kill them," he answered. "Would you kill men you have captured[w] with your own sword
or bow? Set food and water before them so that they may eat and drink and then go back to their
master." 23 So he prepared a great feast for them, and after they had finished eating and drinking, he
6:23 [x]2Ki 5:2 sent them away, and they returned to their master. So the bands[x] from Aram stopped raiding Israel's
territory.

Famine in Besieged Samaria

6:24 [y]1Ki 15:18; 20:1; 2Ki 8:7 24 Some time later, Ben-Hadad[y] king of Aram mobilized his entire army and marched up and laid
[z]Dt 28:52 siege[z] to Samaria. 25 There was a great famine[a] in the city; the siege lasted so long that a donkey's head
6:25 [a]Lev 26:26; Ru 1:1 [b]Isa 36:12 sold for eighty shekels[a] of silver, and a quarter of a cab[b] of seed pods[c][b] for five shekels.[d]
26 As the king of Israel was passing by on the wall, a woman cried to him, "Help me, my lord the king!"
27 The king replied, "If the LORD does not help you, where can I get help for you? From the threshing
floor? From the winepress?" 28 Then he asked her, "What's the matter?"
She answered, "This woman said to me, 'Give up your son so we may eat him today, and tomorrow we'll
6:29 [c]Lev 26:29; Dt 28:53-55 eat my son.' 29 So we cooked my son and ate[c] him. The next day I said to her, 'Give up your son so we may
eat him,' but she had hidden him."
6:30 [d]2Ki 18:37; Isa 22:15 30 When the king heard the woman's words, he tore[d] his robes. As he went along the wall, the people
[e]Ge 37:34; 1Ki 21:27 looked, and there, underneath, he had sackcloth[e] on his body. 31 He said, "May God deal with me, be it ever
so severely, if the head of Elisha son of Shaphat remains on his shoulders today!"
6:32 [f]Eze 8:1; 14:1; 20:1 32 Now Elisha was sitting in his house, and the elders[f] were sitting with him. The king sent a messen-
[g]1Ki 18:4 [h]ver 31 ger ahead, but before he arrived, Elisha said to the elders, "Don't you see how this murderer[g] is sending
someone to cut off my head?[h] Look, when the messenger comes, shut the door and hold it shut against
him. Is not the sound of his master's footsteps behind him?"
33 While he was still talking to them, the messenger came down to him. And ⌊the king⌋ said, "This di-
6:33 [i]Lev 24:11; Job 2:9; 14:14; Isa 40:31 saster is from the LORD. Why should I wait[i] for the LORD any longer?"
7 Elisha said, "Hear the word of the LORD. This is what the LORD says: About this time tomorrow, a
7:1 [j]ver 16 seah[e] of flour will sell for a shekel[f] and two seahs[g] of barley for a shekel[j] at the gate of Samaria."
7:2 [k]2Ki 5:18 2 The officer on whose arm the king was leaning[k] said to the man of God, "Look, even if the LORD
[l]ver 19; Ge 7:11; Ps 78:23; Mal 3:10 [m]ver 17 should open the floodgates[l] of the heavens, could this happen?"
"You will see it with your own eyes," answered Elisha, "but you will not eat[m] any of it!"

The Siege Lifted

7:3 [n]Lev 13:45-46; Nu 5:1-4 3 Now there were four men with leprosy[h][n] at the entrance of the city gate. They said to each other,
"Why stay here until we die? 4 If we say, 'We'll go into the city'—the famine is there, and we will die. And
if we stay here, we will die. So let's go over to the camp of the Arameans and surrender. If they spare us,
we live; if they kill us, then we die."
5 At dusk they got up and went to the camp of the Arameans. When they reached the edge of the camp,
7:6 [o]Ex 14:24; 2Sa 5:24; Eze 1:24 not a man was there, 6 for the Lord had caused the Arameans to hear the sound[o] of chariots and horses
[p]2Sa 10:6; Jer 46:21 and a great army, so that they said to one another, "Look, the king of Israel has hired[p] the Hittite[q] and
[q]Nu 13:29 Egyptian kings to attack us!" 7 So they got up and fled[r] in the dusk and abandoned their tents and their
7:7 [r]Jdg 7:21; Ps 48:4-6; Pr 28:1; Isa 30:17 horses and donkeys. They left the camp as it was and ran for their lives.
7:8 [s]Isa 33:23; 35:6 8 The men who had leprosy[s] reached the edge of the camp and entered one of the tents. They ate and

[a] *25* That is, about 2 pounds (about 1 kilogram) [b] *25* That is, probably about 1/2 pint (about 0.3 liter) [c] *25* Or *of doves' dung* [d] *25* That is, about 2 ounces (about 55 grams) [e] *1* That is, probably about 7 quarts (about 7.3 liters); also in verses 16 and 18 [f] *1* That is, about 2/5 ounce (about 11 grams); also in verses 16 and 18 [g] *1* That is, probably about 13 quarts (about 15 liters); also in verses 16 and 18 [h] *3* The Hebrew word is used for various diseases affecting the skin—not necessarily leprosy; also in verse 8.

6:25 See the note on Ruth 1:1. See also "Famine in the Ancient Near East" on page 70.

The donkey was an "unclean" animal; that is, forbidden to the Israelites as food (Lev 11:2–7; Dt 14:4–8). The severity of the famine caused the people of Samaria not only to disregard the laws of uncleanness but to place a high value on the least edible part of the donkey.

6:30 Sackcloth was a coarse cloth worn as a sign of mourning (see the note on Job 16:15, as well as "Sackcloth and Ashes: Rituals of Lamentation" on p. 820).

7:1 See "The City Gate" on page 392.

7:3 According to ritual law, lepers were quarantined outside the community (Lev 13:46).

drank, and carried away silver, gold and clothes, and went off and hid them. They returned and entered
another tent and took some things from it and hid them also.
[9]Then they said to each other, "We're not doing right. This is a day of good news and we are keeping
it to ourselves. If we wait until daylight, punishment will overtake us. Let's go at once and report this to
the royal palace."
[10]So they went and called out to the city gatekeepers and told them, "We went into the Aramean camp
and not a man was there—not a sound of anyone—only tethered horses and donkeys, and the tents
left just as they were." [11]The gatekeepers shouted the news, and it was reported within the palace.

The History of the Southern Kingdom

2 KINGS 7 The southern kingdom of Judah came into being when the northern ten tribes broke away from the **united monarchy** in approximately 930 B.C. (1Ki 12:1–24). The remaining kingdom, consisting of the tribes of Judah and Benjamin, retained Jerusalem, the capital of the united monarchy, as its capital.

Twenty kings ruled the southern kingdom throughout its 345-year span. All were from the line of David, with one exception—Athaliah, daughter of Ahab, king of the northern kingdom (2Ki 8:18). She married into the royal Judean family and became queen for six years, from 841–835 B.C. (ch. 11). Of those twenty kings, seven are attested in records outside the Bible.[1] In addition, seals or seal impressions have been discovered for fifteen Judean officials and priests named in the Bible.[2]

In the fifth year of Rehoboam, the first king of the southern kingdom after the division of the land, Egypt's Pharaoh Shishak campaigned against Judah, plundering the temple and the royal palace (2Ch 12:1–9). Inscribed on a wall of the temple of Amon in Thebes, Egypt (see the map of Egypt on p. 346), is a list of places Shishak conquered.[3] Rehoboam was compelled to buy off Shishak with a large payment of tribute.

While the ninth century B.C. saw skirmishes with the small kingdoms bordering Judah, the eighth century was largely one of peace—the most prosperous era of Judean history. It is estimated that the population of the southern kingdom was 120,000–150,000 at this time, with the majority of people living in Jerusalem and its environs. All of this changed, however, with the coming of the **Assyrians** during the last quarter of the century.

In 701 B.C. Sennacherib ravaged Judah (2Ki 18:13),[4] and for the next half century Judah was dominated by Assyria. When this world power grew weak, Josiah (641–609 B.C.) was able to focus again on internal matters and to lead a religious revival (2Ch 34:3—35:19).[5] From 609–605 B.C. the southern kingdom was subject to Egypt (2Ki 23:31–35). With the defeat of Pharaoh Neco at Carchemish by Nebuchadnezzar in 605 B.C.,[6] Jerusalem fell under Babylonian domination. Nebuchadnezzar crushed one rebellion at Jerusalem in 597 B.C. (24:10–16)[7] and 11 years later destroyed the city, bringing the southern kingdom to an end (25:1–21).[8]

The "House of David" inscription from Tel Dan
Preserving Bible Times; © Dr. James C. Martin; permission of The Israel Museum

[1]See, for example, "The Tel Dan Stele" on page 540, "Menahem and Pekah of Israel, Jotham of Judah and Tiglath-Pileser III of Assyria" on page 553, "Ahaz, King of Judah, and Rezin, King of Aram" on page 554, "The Seal of Manasseh" on page 565 and "Uzziah, King of Judah, and Jeroboam II, King of Israel" on page 650. [2]See, for example, "The Huldah Delegation and Nathan-Melech, the Official" on page 567, "The Seals of Jaazaniah, Ishmael and Elishama" on page 573, "Baruch, Scribe of Jeremiah" on page 1248, "Gemariah, the Official, and Jerahmeel, the King's Son" on page 1255, "Gedaliah, Governor of Judah, and Baalis, King of Ammon" on page 1261 and "Seraiah the Quartermaster" on page 1290. [3]See "The Campaign of Shishak" on page 635. [4]See "Hezekiah Against the Assyrians" on page 1118. [5]See "The Tragic Reign of King Josiah" on page 569. [6]See "Josiah, Zechariah and Neco II" on page 663. [7]See "Nebuchadnezzar" on page 571. [8]See "The Last Days of Jerusalem" on page 1197.

12 The king got up in the night and said to his officers, "I will tell you what the Arameans have done
7:12 [t]Jos 8:4; 2Ki 6:25-29 to us. They know we are starving; so they have left the camp to hide[t] in the countryside, thinking, 'They
will surely come out, and then we will take them alive and get into the city.' "
13 One of his officers answered, "Have some men take five of the horses that are left in the city. Their
plight will be like that of all the Israelites left here—yes, they will only be like all these Israelites who are
doomed. So let us send them to find out what happened."
14 So they selected two chariots with their horses, and the king sent them after the Aramean army. He
commanded the drivers, "Go and find out what has happened." 15 They followed them as far as the Jor-
dan, and they found the whole road strewn with the clothing and equipment the Arameans had thrown
away in their headlong flight. So the messengers returned and reported to the king. 16 Then the people
7:16 [u]Isa 33:4,23 [v]ver 1 went out and plundered[u] the camp of the Arameans. So a seah of flour sold for a shekel, and two seahs
of barley sold for a shekel,[v] as the LORD had said.
17 Now the king had put the officer on whose arm he leaned in charge of the gate, and the people tram-
7:17 [w]ver 2; 2Ki 6:32 pled him in the gateway, and he died,[w] just as the man of God had foretold when the king came down to
his house. 18 It happened as the man of God had said to the king: "About this time tomorrow, a seah of
flour will sell for a shekel and two seahs of barley for a shekel at the gate of Samaria."
7:19 [x]ver 2 19 The officer had said to the man of God, "Look, even if the LORD should open the floodgates[x] of the
heavens, could this happen?" The man of God had replied, "You will see it with your own eyes, but you
will not eat any of it!" 20 And that is exactly what happened to him, for the people trampled him in the
gateway, and he died.

ANCIENT PEOPLES, LANDS AND RULERS

Hazael, the Nemesis of Israel

2 KINGS 8 Hazael's usurpation of the throne of Damascus ("Map 6") is described in 2 Kings 8:7–15, but the Biblical writers were not the only ones who recognized that he had no rightful claim to the throne. In 1903 German excavators unearthed the Basalt Statue of **Shalmaneser III**, which contains a short inscription boasting of this Assyrian king's victories over the kings of Damascus (Syria). After briefly describing how he had defeated a coalition led by one "Adad-idri" of Damascus (probably Ben-Hadad II),[1] Shalmaneser III recounted how "Hazael the son of a nobody" (i.e., a usurper) had taken the throne. Shalmaneser then claimed to have defeated Hazael in battle, to have pursued him back to Damascus and to have laid waste his orchards.

Hazael himself seems to have sought to shake off the label of usurper. In some texts known as the "booty inscriptions," Hazael claimed that the god Hadad had given him military victories and the booty that went with them. If the Tel Dan inscription[2] is from Hazael, as seems probable, he did the same there. Hazael was perhaps suggesting that the god Hadad had endorsed his seizure of the throne. More significantly, in the Tel Dan inscription he referred to Ben-Hadad, whom he had murdered, as "my father." This was a bold claim to legitimacy indeed!

Hazael reigned from approximately 842 to 800 B.C. Almost immediately after seizing power he went to war against Joram of Israel, whom he defeated at Ramoth Gilead[3] ("Map 6"). This action, in which Joram was wounded, led to Jehu's coup in Israel and to the fall of the house of Omri (2Ki 9). From 841 to 836 Hazael was involved in wars against Shalmaneser III, as described in the Basalt Statue. Once the pressure from Assyria in the east had abated, Hazael was free to turn his attention south against Israel (10:32–33), Judah and Philistia (12:17–18). Hazael apparently died near the end of the reign of Jehoahaz of Israel (c. 805–802 B.C.), but he remained Israel's nemesis to the end (13:22). Indeed, Hazael nearly succeeded in eliminating Israel entirely as a military power (13:7).

[1]See "Ben-Hadad I and II" on page 521. [2]See "The Tel Dan Stele" on page 540. [3]See "Ramoth (in) Gilead" on page 261.

The Shunammite's Land Restored

8 Now Elisha had said to the woman[y] whose son he had restored to life, "Go away with your family 8:1 [y]2Ki 4:8-37
and stay for a while wherever you can, because the LORD has decreed a famine[z] in the land that will [z]Lev 26:26; Dt 28:22; Ru 1:1
last seven years."[a] 2The woman proceeded to do as the man of God said. She and her family went away [a]Ge 12:10; Ps 105:16;
and stayed in the land of the Philistines seven years. Hag 1:11
3At the end of the seven years she came back from the land of the Philistines and went to the king to
beg for her house and land. 4The king was talking to Gehazi, the servant of the man of God, and had said,
"Tell me about all the great things Elisha has done." 5Just as Gehazi was telling the king how Elisha had
restored[b] the dead to life, the woman whose son Elisha had brought back to life came to beg the king for 8:5 [b]2Ki 4:35
her house and land.
Gehazi said, "This is the woman, my lord the king, and this is her son whom Elisha restored to life."
6The king asked the woman about it, and she told him.
Then he assigned an official to her case and said to him, "Give back everything that belonged to her,
including all the income from her land from the day she left the country until now."

Hazael Murders Ben-Hadad

7Elisha went to Damascus,[c] and Ben-Hadad[d] king of Aram was ill. When the king was told, "The man 8:7 [c]2Sa 8:5; 1Ki 11:24 [d]2Ki 6:24
of God has come all the way up here," 8he said to Hazael,[e] "Take a gift[f] with you and go to meet the man 8:8 [e]1Ki 19:15 [f]Ge 32:20; 1Sa 9:7; 2Ki 1:2
of God. Consult[g] the LORD through him; ask him, 'Will I recover from this illness?' " [g]Jdg 18:5

8:7 The annals of the Assyrian ruler Shalmaneser III record Assyrian victories over Ben-Hadad of Damascus in 846 B.C. and over Hazael of Damascus in 842. Elisha's visit to Damascus dates to about 843. (See "Ben-Hadad I and II" on p. 521 and "Dothan, Ben-Hadad and a Chronological Problem" on p. 536.)

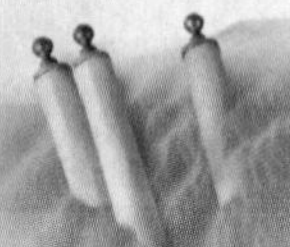

ANCIENT TEXTS AND ARTIFACTS

The Tel Dan Stele

2 KINGS 8 In 1993 and 1994 fragments of an **Aramaic** monumental inscription were discovered in Tel Dan, Israel. Although only a fraction of the original inscription was recovered, the preserved portion alludes to eight Biblical kings. Based on the names recorded in the document, it can be dated to around 841 B.C. Even though his name is missing, it appears that Hazael,[1] king of Aram from approximately 842–800 B.C., commissioned the stela (or **stele**) to commemorate his defeat of Joram and Ahaziah at Ramoth Gilead (2Ki 8:28–29; see "Map 6" at the back of this Bible). Hazael is mentioned in the records of **Shalmaneser III**, king of **Assyria** from approximately 858–824 B.C., and his name is inscribed on objects taken as booty by the Assyrians.

The initial lines of the inscription mention "my father," possibly a reference to Ben-Hadad II,[2] Hazael's predecessor. The names of Joram and Ahab can be restored in the phrase "[I killed Jo]ram son of [Ahab] king of Israel," where the brackets indicate **lacunae** in the original text. Joram was king of Israel from approximately 852 to 841 B.C., while Ahab ruled from approximately 874 to 853 B.C. This is followed by the statement "and [I] killed [Ahaz]iahu son of [Jehoram kin]g of the House of David." Ahaziah/Ahaziahu ruled Judah in 841 B.C. The name of Jehoram, who reigned from 848 to 841 B.C., can be supplied where the text is missing.[3]

The most remarkable aspect of the Tel Dan Stele is the phrase "House of David," providing extrabiblical evidence for the existence of David.[4] This is important because some recent scholars have denied the existence of the **united kingdom** under David and Solomon, treating David as a character more of legend than of reality. This inscription demonstrates that ancient kings recognized the Davidic dynasty over Jerusalem and by implication validates the historicity of David himself. Some scholars have tried to avoid this implication by arguing for an alternative translation for "House of David," claiming that the words refer to some place or to a god rather than to King David. Few are persuaded by these protests, and the inscription is widely recognized to be an extrabiblical witness to the dynasty of David.

[1]See "Hazael, the Nemesis of Israel" on page 539. [2]See "Ben-Hadad I and II" on page 521. [3]See "The History of the Southern Kingdom" on page 538.
[4]See "David" on page 443.

9 Hazael went to meet Elisha, taking with him as a gift forty camel-loads of all the finest wares of Da-
mascus. He went in and stood before him, and said, "Your son Ben-Hadad king of Aram has sent me to
ask, 'Will I recover from this illness?' "
8:10 [h]Isa 38:1 10 Elisha answered, "Go and say to him, 'You will certainly recover';[h] but[a] the LORD has revealed to me
8:11 [i]Jdg 3:25 that he will in fact die." 11 He stared at him with a fixed gaze until Hazael felt ashamed.[i] Then the man of
[j]Lk 19:41 God began to weep.[j]
12 "Why is my lord weeping?" asked Hazael.
8:12 [k]1Ki 19:17; 2Ki 10:32; 12:17; "Because I know the harm[k] you will do to the Israelites," he answered. "You will set fire to their forti-
13:3,7 [l]Ps 137:9; Isa 13:16; fied places, kill their young men with the sword, dash[l] their little children[m] to the ground, and rip open[n]
Hos 13:16; Na 3:10; Lk 19:44 their pregnant women."
[m]Ge 34:29 [n]2Ki 15:16; 13 Hazael said, "How could your servant, a mere dog,[o] accomplish such a feat?"
Am 1:13 8:13 [o]1Sa 17:43; "The LORD has shown me that you will become king[p] of Aram," answered Elisha.
2Sa 3:8 [p]1Ki 19:15 14 Then Hazael left Elisha and returned to his master. When Ben-Hadad asked, "What did Elisha say
to you?" Hazael replied, "He told me that you would certainly recover." 15 But the next day he took a thick
8:15 [q]2Ki 1:17 cloth, soaked it in water and spread it over the king's face, so that he died.[q] Then Hazael succeeded him
as king.

Jehoram King of Judah

8:16 [r]2Ki 1:17; 16 In the fifth year of Joram[r] son of Ahab king of Israel, when Jehoshaphat was king of Judah, Jehoram[s]
3:1 [s]2Ch 21:1-4 son of Jehoshaphat began his reign as king of Judah. 17 He was thirty-two years old when he became king,
and he reigned in Jerusalem eight years. 18 He walked in the ways of the kings of Israel, as the house of
8:18 [t]ver 26; 2Ki 11:1 Ahab had done, for he married a daughter[t] of Ahab. He did evil in the eyes of the LORD. 19 Nevertheless,
8:19 [u]Ge 6:13 [v]2Sa 21:17; 7:13; for the sake of his servant David, the LORD was not willing to destroy[u] Judah. He had promised to main-
1Ki 11:36; Rev 21:23 tain a lamp[v] for David and his descendants forever.
8:20 [w]1Ki 22:47 20 In the time of Jehoram, Edom rebelled against Judah and set up its own king.[w] 21 So Jehoram[b] went
to Zair with all his chariots. The Edomites surrounded him and his chariot commanders, but he rose up
and broke through by night; his army, however, fled back home. 22 To this day Edom has been in rebel-
8:22 [x]Ge 27:40 [y]Nu 33:20; lion[x] against Judah. Libnah[y] revolted at the same time.
Jos 21:13; 2Ki 19:8 23 As for the other events of Jehoram's reign, and all he did, are they not written in the book of the an-
nals of the kings of Judah? 24 Jehoram rested with his fathers and was buried with them in the City of Da-
vid. And Ahaziah his son succeeded him as king.

Ahaziah King of Judah

8:25 [z]2Ki 9:29 25 In the twelfth[z] year of Joram son of Ahab king of Israel, Ahaziah son of Jehoram king of Judah be-
gan to reign. 26 Ahaziah was twenty-two years old when he became king, and he reigned in Jerusalem
8:26 [a]ver 18 [b]1Ki 16:23 one year. His mother's name was Athaliah,[a] a granddaughter of Omri[b] king of Israel. 27 He walked in the
8:27 [c]1Ki 16:30 [d]1Ki 15:26 ways of the house of Ahab[c] and did evil[d] in the eyes of the LORD, as the house of Ahab had done, for he
was related by marriage to Ahab's family.
8:28 [e]Dt 4:43; 1Ki 22:3,29 28 Ahaziah went with Joram son of Ahab to war against Hazael king of Aram at Ramoth Gilead.[e] The

[a] *10* The Hebrew may also be read *Go and say, 'You will certainly not recover,' for.* [b] *21* Hebrew *Joram,* a variant of *Jehoram;* also in verses 23 and 24

8:13 The "feat," as Hazael called it, of smashing children and slashing pregnant women spelled victory for a conquering king.

Elisha's prophecy suggests that Hazael was not a legitimate successor to Ben-Hadad (see "Ben-Hadad I and II" on p. 521). The Basalt Statue of Shalmaneser III designates Hazael as "the son of a nobody" (i.e., a commoner) who usurped the throne. (See "Hazael, the Nemesis of Israel" on p. 539 and "The Tel Dan Stele" on p. 540.)

8:16 Jehoram of Judah was coregent with his father Jehoshaphat for the last four or five years of Jehoshaphat's reign. He took complete charge at his father's death in about 848. Jehoshaphat, who had seven sons, tried to eliminate the possibility of rivalry for the throne by meting out a degree of power to each son (2Ch 21:2–3), but Jehoram murdered all of his brothers. During his reign, Edom revolted from under the rule of Judah. Libnah in Judah, a Levitical city far enough from Jerusalem to be somewhat independent, also rejected Jehoram's authority (2Ki 8:22). Jehoram himself died, unlamented, from some kind of bowel disease, perhaps dysentery (2Ch 21:18–20), in about 841. Various raiders, including Philistines and Arabs, plundered Judah and killed all of Jehoram's sons except Ahaziah, the youngest, who succeeded his father at his death (2Ch 21:17).

8:26 Athaliah is regularly understood to be the daughter of Ahab and Jezebel (v. 18). However, verse 26 (with 2Ch 22:2) actually states that she was the daughter of Omri, the father of Ahab, although the NIV and some other translations render this as "granddaughter of Omri." While this later translation is possible, it entails certain chronological and interpretive problems; some authorities believe that she was actually Omri's daughter and Ahab's sister.

The queen mother could exercise considerable influence in the affairs of court (e.g., Maacah, who was removed from her position by her grandson Asa because of her idolatry; 1Ki 15:13). Jezebel's influence in fostering foreign cults in Jerusalem was continued through the equally wicked Athaliah, the mother of Ahaziah.

Arameans wounded Joram; 29so King Joram returned to Jezreel[f] to recover from the wounds the Arame-
ans had inflicted on him at Ramoth[a] in his battle with Hazael[g] king of Aram.
Then Ahaziah son of Jehoram king of Judah went down to Jezreel to see Joram son of Ahab, because
he had been wounded.

Jehu Anointed King of Israel

9 The prophet Elisha summoned a man from the company[h] of the prophets and said to him, "Tuck
your cloak into your belt,[i] take this flask of oil[j] with you and go to Ramoth Gilead.[k] 2When you get
there, look for Jehu son of Jehoshaphat, the son of Nimshi. Go to him, get him away from his companions
and take him into an inner room. 3Then take the flask and pour the oil[l] on his head and declare, 'This is
what the LORD says: I anoint you king over Israel.' Then open the door and run; don't delay!"
4So the young man, the prophet, went to Ramoth Gilead. 5When he arrived, he found the army offi-
cers sitting together. "I have a message for you, commander," he said.
"For which of us?" asked Jehu.
"For you, commander," he replied.
6Jehu got up and went into the house. Then the prophet poured the oil[m] on Jehu's head and declared,
"This is what the LORD, the God of Israel, says: 'I anoint you king over the LORD's people Israel. 7You are
to destroy the house of Ahab your master, and I will avenge[n] the blood of my servants[o] the prophets and
the blood of all the LORD's servants shed by Jezebel.[p] 8The whole house[q] of Ahab will perish. I will cut off
from Ahab every last male[r] in Israel—slave or free. 9I will make the house of Ahab like the house of Jer-
oboam[s] son of Nebat and like the house of Baasha[t] son of Ahijah. 10As for Jezebel, dogs[u] will devour her
on the plot of ground at Jezreel, and no one will bury her.' " Then he opened the door and ran.
11When Jehu went out to his fellow officers, one of them asked him, "Is everything all right? Why did
this madman[v] come to you?"
"You know the man and the sort of things he says," Jehu replied.
12"That's not true!" they said. "Tell us."
Jehu said, "Here is what he told me: 'This is what the LORD says: I anoint you king over Israel.' "
13They hurried and took their cloaks and spread[w] them under him on the bare steps. Then they blew
the trumpet[x] and shouted, "Jehu is king!"

Jehu Kills Joram and Ahaziah

14So Jehu son of Jehoshaphat, the son of Nimshi, conspired against Joram. (Now Joram and all Israel
had been defending Ramoth Gilead[y] against Hazael king of Aram, 15but King Joram[b] had returned to
Jezreel to recover[z] from the wounds the Arameans had inflicted on him in the battle with Hazael king of
Aram.) Jehu said, "If this is the way you feel, don't let anyone slip out of the city to go and tell the news
in Jezreel." 16Then he got into his chariot and rode to Jezreel, because Joram was resting there and Aha-
ziah[a] king of Judah had gone down to see him.
17When the lookout[b] standing on the tower in Jezreel saw Jehu's troops approaching, he called out, "I
see some troops coming."
"Get a horseman," Joram ordered. "Send him to meet them and ask, 'Do you come in peace?[c]' "
18The horseman rode off to meet Jehu and said, "This is what the king says: 'Do you come in peace?' "
"What do you have to do with peace?" Jehu replied. "Fall in behind me."
The lookout reported, "The messenger has reached them, but he isn't coming back."
19So the king sent out a second horseman. When he came to them he said, "This is what the king says:
'Do you come in peace?' "
Jehu replied, "What do you have to do with peace? Fall in behind me."
20The lookout reported, "He has reached them, but he isn't coming back either. The driving is like[d]
that of Jehu son of Nimshi—he drives like a madman."
21"Hitch up my chariot," Joram ordered. And when it was hitched up, Joram king of Israel and Ahazi-
ah king of Judah rode out, each in his own chariot, to meet Jehu. They met him at the plot of ground that
had belonged to Naboth[e] the Jezreelite. 22When Joram saw Jehu he asked, "Have you come in peace, Jehu?"

8:29 [f]2Ki 9:15 [g]1Ki 19:15,17
9:1 [h]1Sa 10:5 [i]2Ki 4:29 [j]1Sa 10:1 [k]2Ki 8:28
9:3 [l]1Ki 19:16
9:6 [m]1Ki 19:16; 2Ch 22:7
9:7 [n]Ge 4:24; Rev 6:10 [o]Dt 32:43 [p]1Ki 18:4; 21:15
9:8 [q]2Ki 10:17 [r]Dt 32:36; 1Sa 25:22; 1Ki 21:21; 2Ki 14:26
9:9 [s]1Ki 14:10; 15:29; 16:3,11 [t]1Ki 16:3
9:10 [u]ver 35-36; 1Ki 21:23
9:11 [v]Jer 29:26; Jn 10:20; Ac 26:24
9:13 [w]Mt 21:8; Lk 19:36 [x]2Sa 15:10; 1Ki 1:34,39
9:14 [y]Dt 4:43; 2Ki 8:28
9:15 [z]2Ki 8:29
9:16 [a]2Ch 22:7
9:17 [b]Isa 21:6 [c]1Sa 16:4
9:20 [d]2Sa 18:27
9:21 [e]ver 26; 1Ki 21:1-7,15-19

[a]29 Hebrew *Ramah,* a variant of *Ramoth* [b]15 Hebrew *Jehoram,* a variant of *Joram*; also in verses 17 and 21-24

9:30 Women "painted" their eyes by daubing them with kohl, a soot-like compound, to draw attention to them.

"How can there be peace," Jehu replied, "as long as all the idolatry and witchcraft of your mother Jez-
9:22 [f]1Ki 16:30-33; 18:19; ebel[f] abound?"
2Ch 21:13; 23 Joram turned about and fled, calling out to Ahaziah, "Treachery,[g] Ahaziah!"
Rev 2:20 9:23 [g]2Ki 11:14 24 Then Jehu drew his bow[h] and shot Joram between the shoulders. The arrow pierced his heart and
9:24 [h]1Ki 22:34 he slumped down in his chariot. 25 Jehu said to Bidkar, his chariot officer, "Pick him up and throw him on
the field that belonged to Naboth the Jezreelite. Remember how you and I were riding together in char-
9:25 [i]1Ki 21:19-22,24-29 iots behind Ahab his father when the LORD made this prophecy[i] about him: 26 'Yesterday I saw the blood
9:26 [j]1Ki 21:19 of Naboth[j] and the blood of his sons, declares the LORD, and I will surely make you pay for it on this plot
[k]1Ki 21:29 of ground, declares the LORD.'[a] Now then, pick him up and throw him on that plot, in accordance with the
word of the LORD."[k]

27 When Ahaziah king of Judah saw what had happened, he fled up the road to Beth Haggan.[b] Jehu
chased him, shouting, "Kill him too!" They wounded him in his chariot on the way up to Gur near Ible-
9:27 [l]Jdg 1:27 [m]2Ki 23:29 am,[l] but he escaped to Megiddo[m] and died there. 28 His servants took him by chariot[n] to Jerusalem and
9:28 [n]2Ki 14:20; 23:30 buried him with his fathers in his tomb in the City of David. 29 (In the eleventh[o] year of Joram son of
9:29 [o]2Ki 8:25 Ahab, Ahaziah had become king of Judah.)

Jezebel Killed

9:30 [p]Jer 4:30; Eze 23:40 30 Then Jehu went to Jezreel. When Jezebel heard about it, she painted[p] her eyes, arranged her hair and
9:31 [q]1Ki 16:9-10 looked out of a window. 31 As Jehu entered the gate, she asked, "Have you come in peace, Zimri,[q] you mur-
derer of your master?"[c]

32 He looked up at the window and called out, "Who is on my side? Who?" Two or three eunuchs looked
down at him. 33 "Throw her down!" Jehu said. So they threw her down, and some of her blood spattered
9:33 [r]Ps 7:5 the wall and the horses as they trampled her underfoot.[r]

34 Jehu went in and ate and drank. "Take care of that cursed woman," he said, "and bury her, for she was
9:34 [s]1Ki 16:31; 21:25 a king's daughter."[s] 35 But when they went out to bury her, they found nothing except her skull, her feet
and her hands. 36 They went back and told Jehu, who said, "This is the word of the LORD that he spoke
9:36 [t]Ps 68:23; Jer 15:3 through his servant Elijah the Tishbite: On the plot of ground at Jezreel dogs[t] will devour Jezebel's flesh.[d][u]
[u]1Ki 21:23 37 Jezebel's body will be like refuse[v] on the ground in the plot at Jezreel, so that no one will be able to say,
9:37 [v]Ps 83:10; Isa 5:25; Jer 8:2; 9:22; 16:4; 25:33; Zep 1:17 'This is Jezebel.' "

Ahab's Family Killed

10:1 [w]1Ki 13:32 [x]Jdg 8:30 **10** Now there were in Samaria[w] seventy sons[x] of the house of Ahab. So Jehu wrote letters and sent
[y]1Ki 21:1 [z]ver 5 them to Samaria: to the officials of Jezreel,[e][y] to the elders and to the guardians[z] of Ahab's chil-
dren. He said, 2 "As soon as this letter reaches you, since your master's sons are with you and you have
chariots and horses, a fortified city and weapons, 3 choose the best and most worthy of your master's
sons and set him on his father's throne. Then fight for your master's house."

4 But they were terrified and said, "If two kings could not resist him, how can we?"

5 So the palace administrator, the city governor, the elders and the guardians sent this message to Jehu:
10:5 [a]Jos 9:8; 1Ki 20:4,32 "We are your servants[a] and we will do anything you say. We will not appoint anyone as king; you do what-
ever you think best."

6 Then Jehu wrote them a second letter, saying, "If you are on my side and will obey me, take the heads
of your master's sons and come to me in Jezreel by this time tomorrow."

Now the royal princes, seventy of them, were with the leading men of the city, who were rearing them.
10:7 [b]1Ki 21:21 [c]2Sa 4:8 7 When the letter arrived, these men took the princes and slaughtered all seventy[b] of them. They put their
heads[c] in baskets and sent them to Jehu in Jezreel. 8 When the messenger arrived, he told Jehu, "They
have brought the heads of the princes."

Then Jehu ordered, "Put them in two piles at the entrance of the city gate until morning."

9 The next morning Jehu went out. He stood before all the people and said, "You are innocent. It was I
who conspired against my master and killed him, but who killed all these? 10 Know then, that not a word

[a] 26 See 1 Kings 21:19. [b] 27 Or *fled by way of the garden house* [c] 31 Or *"Did Zimri have peace, who murdered his master?"*
[d] 36 See 1 Kings 21:23. [e] 1 Hebrew; some Septuagint manuscripts and Vulgate *of the city*

10:6–7 The "heads of your master's sons" (v. 6) could be understood as a reference to the leading figures among the 70 descendants of Ahab, such as the crown prince and several other sons of special ability and standing. Eliminating potential claimants to the throne was common practice in ancient monarchies. (See "Ambitious Princes Among the Hittites" on p. 469.)

the LORD has spoken against the house of Ahab will fail. The LORD has done what he promised[d] through
his servant Elijah."[e] 11 So Jehu[f] killed everyone in Jezreel who remained of the house of Ahab, as well as
all his chief men, his close friends and his priests, leaving him no survivor.[g]
12 Jehu then set out and went toward Samaria. At Beth Eked of the Shepherds, 13 he met some relatives
of Ahaziah king of Judah and asked, "Who are you?"
They said, "We are relatives of Ahaziah,[h] and we have come down to greet the families of the king and
of the queen mother.[i]"
14 "Take them alive!" he ordered. So they took them alive and slaughtered them by the well of Beth
Eked—forty-two men. He left no survivor.

10:10 [d]2Ki 9:7-10 [e]1Ki 21:29
10:11 [f]Hos 1:4 [g]ver 14; Job 18:19
10:13 [h]2Ki 8:24, 29; 2Ch 22:8 [i]1Ki 2:19

ANCIENT TEXTS AND ARTIFACTS

Jehu / The Black Obelisk of Shalmaneser III

Processions of people bearing tribute

Preserving Bible Times; © Dr. James C. Martin; permission of The British Museum

Black Obelisk: Shalmaneser III, standing beneath parasol, receives homage from King Jehu

Preserving Bible Times; © Dr. James C. Martin; permission of The British Museum

2 KINGS 10 In 841 B.C. Jehu became king of the northern kingdom by means of a bloody coup (2Ki 9–10). He moved to rid Israel of Baal worship (10:18–28), but this did not end idolatry, for Jehu continued to worship the golden calves at Bethel and Dan[1] (v. 29; both "Map 6").

No sooner had Jehu established his rule than he found himself forced to pay homage to **Shalmaneser III**, king of **Assyria** (an event not mentioned in the Bible but recorded in several inscriptions by Shalmaneser). The most interesting record is the Black Obelisk of Shalmaneser, discovered by Englishman Sir Henry Layard in Calah, Iraq, in 1846. This obelisk provides both a written and a pictorial record of the kings who paid tribute to Assyria.

It depicts Jehu, on his hands and knees with his nose and chin toward the ground, before Shalmaneser. Behind Jehu (on the other three sides of the obelisk) are 13 Israelite emissaries bearing tribute. The inscription reads, "I received the tribute of Jehu of the House of Omri (i.e., Israel): silver, gold, a golden bowl, a golden goblet, golden cups, golden buckets, tin, a staff of the king's hand, (and) javelins (?)." All 14 of the Israelites pictured are bearded, with long hair and pointed caps. Each wears a belted tunic with fringe at the bottom. In addition, each of the 13 porters wears a mantle or cloak over the tunic, which extends over the shoulders and is fringed or tasseled down the front on both sides.[2] Jehu is not wearing the outer garment, possibly as a sign of humiliation before Shalmaneser. The Obelisk of Shalmaneser provides the only known surviving likeness of a king of Israel or Judah.

[1]See "The Golden Calf" on page 143 and "The High Place at Dan" on page 504. [2]See "Ancient Israelite Clothing and Jewelry" on page 1059.

10:15 [j]Jer 35:6, 14-19 [k]1Ch 2:55; Jer 35:2 [l]Ezr 10:19; Eze 17:18 15 After he left there, he came upon Jehonadab[j] son of Recab,[k]
who was on his way to meet him. Jehu greeted him and said, "Are
you in accord with me, as I am with you?"
"I am," Jehonadab answered.
"If so," said Jehu, "give me your hand."[l] So he did, and Jehu helped
him up into the chariot. 16 Jehu said, "Come with me and see my
10:16 [m]Nu 25:13; 1Ki 19:10 zeal[m] for the LORD." Then he had him ride along in his chariot.
17 When Jehu came to Samaria, he killed all who were left there
10:17 [n]2Ki 9:8 of Ahab's family;[n] he destroyed them, according to the word of the
LORD spoken to Elijah.

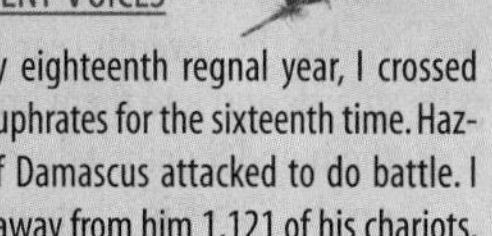

ANCIENT VOICES

In my eighteenth regnal year, I crossed the Euphrates for the sixteenth time. Hazael of Damascus attacked to do battle. I took away from him 1,121 of his chariots, 470 of his cavalry together with his camp.

—THE BLACK OBELISK

See "Jehu/The Black Obelisk of Shalmaneser III" article.

Ministers of Baal Killed

10:18 [o]Jdg 2:11; 1Ki 16:31-32 18 Then Jehu brought all the people together and said to them, "Ahab served[o] Baal a little; Jehu will
10:19 [p]1Ki 18:19; 22:6 serve him much. 19 Now summon[p] all the prophets of Baal, all his ministers and all his priests. See that
no one is missing, because I am going to hold a great sacrifice for Baal. Anyone who fails to come will no
longer live." But Jehu was acting deceptively in order to destroy the ministers of Baal.
10:20 [q]Ex 32:5; Joel 1:14 20 Jehu said, "Call an assembly[q] in honor of Baal." So they proclaimed it. 21 Then he sent word through-
out Israel, and all the ministers of Baal came; not one stayed away. They crowded into the temple of Baal
until it was full from one end to the other. 22 And Jehu said to the keeper of the wardrobe, "Bring robes
for all the ministers of Baal." So he brought out robes for them.
23 Then Jehu and Jehonadab son of Recab went into the temple of Baal. Jehu said to the ministers of Baal,
"Look around and see that no servants of the LORD are here with you—only ministers of Baal." 24 So they
went in to make sacrifices and burnt offerings. Now Jehu had posted eighty men outside with this warn-
10:24 [r]1Ki 20:39 ing: "If one of you lets any of the men I am placing in your hands escape, it will be your life for his life."[r]
25 As soon as Jehu had finished making the burnt offering, he ordered the guards and officers: "Go in
10:25 [s]Ex 22:20; 2Ki 11:18 [t]1Ki 18:40 and kill[s] them; let no one escape."[t] So they cut them down with the sword. The guards and officers threw
the bodies out and then entered the inner shrine of the temple of Baal. 26 They brought the sacred stone[u]
10:26 [u]1Ki 14:23 out of the temple of Baal and burned it. 27 They demolished the sacred stone of Baal and tore down the
10:27 [v]1Ki 16:32 temple[v] of Baal, and people have used it for a latrine to this day.
10:28 [w]1Ki 19:17 28 So Jehu[w] destroyed Baal worship in Israel. 29 However, he did not turn away from the sins[x] of Jero-
10:29 [x]1Ki 12:30 [y]1Ki 12:28-29 boam son of Nebat, which he had caused Israel to commit—the worship of the golden calves[y] at Bethel[z]
[z]1Ki 12:32 and Dan.
30 The LORD said to Jehu, "Because you have done well in accomplishing what is right in my eyes and
have done to the house of Ahab all I had in mind to do, your descendants will sit on the throne of Israel
10:30 [a]ver 35; 2Ki 15:12 to the fourth generation."[a] 31 Yet Jehu was not careful[b] to keep the law of the LORD, the God of Israel, with
10:31 [b]Pr 4:23 [c]1Ki 12:30 all his heart. He did not turn away from the sins[c] of Jeroboam, which he had caused Israel to commit.
10:32 [d]2Ki 13:25 32 In those days the LORD began to reduce[d] the size of Israel. Hazael[e] overpowered the Israelites
[e]1Ki 19:17; 2Ki 8:12 throughout their territory 33 east of the Jordan in all the land of Gilead (the region of Gad, Reuben and
10:33 [f]Nu 32:34; Dt 2:36; Jdg 11:26; Isa 17:2 Manasseh), from Aroer[f] by the Arnon Gorge through Gilead to Bashan.
34 As for the other events of Jehu's reign, all he did, and all his achievements, are they not written in
10:34 [g]1Ki 15:31 the book of the annals[g] of the kings of Israel?
35 Jehu rested with his fathers and was buried in Samaria. And Jehoahaz his son succeeded him as
king. 36 The time that Jehu reigned over Israel in Samaria was twenty-eight years.

Athaliah and Joash

11:1 [h]2Ki 8:18 11 When Athaliah[h] the mother of Ahaziah saw that her son was dead, she proceeded to destroy the
whole royal family. 2 But Jehosheba, the daughter of King Jehoram[a] and sister of Ahaziah, took Jo-
11:2 [i]ver 21; 2Ki 12:1 ash[i] son of Ahaziah and stole him away from among the royal princes, who were about to be murdered.

[a] 2 Hebrew *Joram,* a variant of *Jehoram*

10:29 For information on the "sins of Jeroboam," see 1 Kings 12:25–33; see also "The High Place at Dan" on page 504 and "Bethel" on page 59.
10:34 The Black Obelisk of the Assyrian ruler Shalmaneser III informs us that Jehu paid tribute to the Assyrians shortly after ascending to the throne of the northern kingdom in 841 B.C. (see "Jehu/The Black Obelisk of Shalmaneser III" on p. 544). There is no reference to this payment of tribute in the Biblical narratives of Jehu's reign.
11:1 It is difficult to comprehend Athaliah's slaughter of her own grandchildren (vv. 1–2). Second Chronicles 24:7 refers to "sons of … Athaliah" who were as devoted to Baal as she was, making it unlikely

She put him and his nurse in a bedroom to hide him from Athaliah; so he was not killed.[j] 3He remained
hidden with his nurse at the temple of the LORD for six years while Athaliah ruled the land.
4In the seventh year Jehoiada sent for the commanders of units of a hundred, the Carites[k] and the
guards and had them brought to him at the temple of the LORD. He made a covenant with them and put
them under oath at the temple of the LORD. Then he showed them the king's son. 5He commanded them,
saying, "This is what you are to do: You who are in the three companies that are going on duty on the
Sabbath[l]—a third of you guarding the royal palace,[m] 6a third at the Sur Gate, and a third at the gate be-
hind the guard, who take turns guarding the temple— 7and you who are in the other two companies
that normally go off Sabbath duty are all to guard the temple for the king. 8Station yourselves around
the king, each man with his weapon in his hand. Anyone who approaches your ranks[a] must be put to
death. Stay close to the king wherever he goes."
9The commanders of units of a hundred did just as Jehoiada the priest ordered. Each one took his men—
those who were going on duty on the Sabbath and those who were going off duty—and came to Jehoiada
the priest. 10Then he gave the commanders the spears and shields[n] that had belonged to King David and
that were in the temple of the LORD. 11The guards, each with his weapon in his hand, stationed themselves
around the king—near the altar and the temple, from the south side to the north side of the temple.
12Jehoiada brought out the king's son and put the crown on him; he presented him with a copy of the
covenant[o] and proclaimed him king. They anointed[p] him, and the people clapped their hands[q] and shout-
ed, "Long live the king!"[r]
13When Athaliah heard the noise made by the guards and the people, she went to the people at the
temple of the LORD. 14She looked and there was the king, standing by the pillar,[s] as the custom was. The
officers and the trumpeters were beside the king, and all the people of the land were rejoicing and blow-
ing trumpets.[t] Then Athaliah tore[u] her robes and called out, "Treason! Treason!"[v]
15Jehoiada the priest ordered the commanders of units of a hundred, who were in charge of the troops:
"Bring her out between the ranks[b] and put to the sword anyone who follows her." For the priest had said,
"She must not be put to death in the temple[w] of the LORD." 16So they seized her as she reached the place
where the horses enter[x] the palace grounds, and there she was put to death.[y]
17Jehoiada then made a covenant[z] between the LORD and the king and people that they would be the
LORD's people. He also made a covenant between the king and the people.[a] 18All the people of the land
went to the temple[b] of Baal and tore it down. They smashed[c] the altars and idols to pieces and killed
Mattan the priest[d] of Baal in front of the altars.
Then Jehoiada the priest posted guards at the temple of the LORD. 19He took with him the command-
ers of hundreds, the Carites,[e] the guards and all the people of the land, and together they brought the king
down from the temple of the LORD and went into the palace, entering by way of the gate of the guards.
The king then took his place on the royal throne, 20and all the people of the land rejoiced.[f] And the city
was quiet, because Athaliah had been slain with the sword at the palace.
21Joash[c] was seven years old when he began to reign.

Joash Repairs the Temple

12 In the seventh year of Jehu, Joash[d][g] became king, and he reigned in Jerusalem forty years. His
mother's name was Zibiah; she was from Beersheba. 2Joash did what was right in the eyes of the
LORD all the years Jehoiada the priest instructed him. 3The high places,[h] however, were not removed; the
people continued to offer sacrifices and burn incense there.
4Joash said to the priests, "Collect[i] all the money that is brought as sacred offerings[j] to the temple of
the LORD—the money collected in the census,[k] the money received from personal vows and the money
brought voluntarily[l] to the temple. 5Let every priest receive the money from one of the treasurers, and let
it be used to repair whatever damage is found in the temple."

11:2 [j]Jdg 9:5
11:4 [k]ver 19
11:5 [l]1Ch 9:25 [m]1Ki 14:27
11:10 [n]2Sa 8:7; 1Ch 18:7
11:12 [o]Ex 25:16; 2Ki 23:3 [p]1Sa 9:16; 1Ki 1:39 [q]Ps 47:1; 98:8; Isa 55:12 [r]1Sa 10:24
11:14 [s]1Ki 7:15; 2Ki 23:3; 2Ch 34:31 [t]1Ki 1:39 [u]Ge 37:29 [v]2Ki 9:23
11:15 [w]1Ki 2:30
11:16 [x]Ne 3:28; Jer 31:40 [y]Ge 4:14
11:17 [z]Ex 24:8; 2Sa 5:3; 2Ch 15:12; 23:3; 29:10; 34:31; Ezr 10:3 [a]2Ki 23:3; Jer 34:8
11:18 [b]1Ki 16:32 [c]Dt 12:3 [d]1Ki 18:40; 2Ki 10:25; 23:20
11:19 [e]ver 4
11:20 [f]Pr 11:10; 28:12; 29:2
12:1 [g]2Ki 11:2
12:3 [h]1Ki 3:3; 2Ki 14:4; 15:35; 18:4
12:4 [i]2Ki 22:4 [j]Ex 35:5 [k]Ex 30:12 [l]Ex 35:29; 1Ch 29:3-9

[a] 8 Or *approaches the precincts* [b] 15 Or *out from the precincts* [c] 21 Hebrew *Jehoash,* a variant of *Joash* [d] 1 Hebrew *Jehoash,* a variant of *Joash*; also in verses 2, 4, 6, 7 and 18

that she would have eliminated them for religious or political reasons. We can only assume that her desire for power was so strong that she could endure no rivals, but obviously the details of the court history are lost to us.

11:21 Joash reigned from 835 to 796, although he was a child for much of this time, having been crowned at age seven. Second Chronicles 24 presents his reign in two phases: The first, while he was under the influence of Jehoiada the priest, was marked by a cleansing of the temple and reorganization of its finances. The second, after Jehoiada's death, was characterized by apostasy and violence, including the murder of Zechariah, the son of Jehoiada. Joash's reign ended miserably; after having been defeated and personally injured by an inferior Syrian force, he was assassinated by his own (non-Israelite) bodyguard as he lay recuperating (or an invalid) in Jerusalem.

6But by the twenty-third year of King Joash the priests still had not repaired the temple. 7Therefore
King Joash summoned Jehoiada the priest and the other priests and asked them, "Why aren't you repair-
ing the damage done to the temple? Take no more money from your treasurers, but hand it over for re-
pairing the temple." 8The priests agreed that they would not collect any more money from the people
and that they would not repair the temple themselves.
9Jehoiada the priest took a chest and bored a hole in its lid. He placed it beside the altar, on the right
12:9 [m]Jer 35:4 side as one enters the temple of the LORD. The priests who guarded the entrance[m] put into the chest all
[n]2Ch 24:8; Mk 12:41; Lk 21:1 the money[n] that was brought to the temple of the LORD. 10Whenever they saw that there was a large
12:10 [o]2Sa 8:17 amount of money in the chest, the royal secretary[o] and the high priest came, counted the money that
had been brought into the temple of the LORD and put it into bags. 11When the amount had been deter-
mined, they gave the money to the men appointed to supervise the work on the temple. With it they paid
those who worked on the temple of the LORD—the carpenters and builders, 12the masons and stonecut-
12:12 [p]2Ki 22:5-6 ters.[p] They purchased timber and dressed stone for the repair of the temple of the LORD, and met all the
other expenses of restoring the temple.
13The money brought into the temple was not spent for making silver basins, wick trimmers, sprinkling
12:13 [q]1Ki 7:48-51; 2Ch 24:14 bowls, trumpets or any other articles of gold[q] or silver for the temple of the LORD; 14it was paid to the work-
men, who used it to repair the temple. 15They did not require an accounting from those to whom they
12:15 [r]2Ki 22:7; 1Co 4:2 gave the money to pay the workers, because they acted with complete honesty.[r] 16The money from the
12:16 [s]Lev 5:14-19; Nu 18:9 [t]Lev 4:1-35 [u]Lev 7:7 guilt offerings[s] and sin offerings[t] was not brought into the temple of the LORD; it belonged[u] to the priests.
17About this time Hazael[v] king of Aram went up and attacked Gath and captured it. Then he turned
12:17 [v]2Ki 8:12 to attack Jerusalem. 18But Joash king of Judah took all the sacred objects dedicated by his fathers—Je-
hoshaphat, Jehoram and Ahaziah, the kings of Judah—and the gifts he himself had dedicated and all the
12:18 [w]1Ki 15:18; 2Ch 21:16-17 [x]1Ki 15:21 gold found in the treasuries of the temple of the LORD and of the royal palace, and he sent[w] them to Haz-
ael king of Aram, who then withdrew[x] from Jerusalem.
19As for the other events of the reign of Joash, and all he did, are they not written in the book of the
12:20 [y]2Ki 14:5 [z]2Ch 24:25 [a]Jdg 9:6 annals of the kings of Judah? 20His officials[y] conspired against him and assassinated[z] him at Beth Mil-
lo,[a] on the road down to Silla. 21The officials who murdered him were Jozabad son of Shimeath and Je-
hozabad son of Shomer. He died and was buried with his fathers in the City of David. And Amaziah his
son succeeded him as king.

Jehoahaz King of Israel

13 In the twenty-third year of Joash son of Ahaziah king of Judah, Jehoahaz son of Jehu became
13:2 [b]1Ki 12:26-33 king of Israel in Samaria, and he reigned seventeen years. 2He did evil[b] in the eyes of the LORD
by following the sins of Jeroboam son of Nebat, which he had caused Israel to commit, and he did not
13:3 [c]Dt 31:17; Jdg 2:14 turn away from them. 3So the LORD's anger[c] burned against Israel, and for a long time he kept them un-
[d]1Ki 8:12; 12:17; 19:17 [e]ver 24 der the power[d] of Hazael king of Aram and Ben-Hadad[e] his son.
13:4 [f]Dt 4:29; Ps 78:34 [g]Ex 3:7; Dt 26:7 4Then Jehoahaz sought[f] the LORD's favor, and the LORD listened to him, for he saw[g] how severely the
[h]2Ki 14:26 king of Aram was oppressing[h] Israel. 5The LORD provided a deliverer[i] for Israel, and they escaped from
13:5 [i]ver 25; 2Ki 14:25,27 the power of Aram. So the Israelites lived in their own homes as they had before. 6But they did not turn
13:6 [j]1Ki 12:30 away from the sins[j] of the house of Jeroboam, which he had caused Israel to commit; they continued in
[k]1Ki 16:33 them. Also, the Asherah pole[a][k] remained standing in Samaria.

[a] 6 That is, a symbol of the goddess Asherah; here and elsewhere in 2 Kings

---

12:21 Amaziah of Judah (r. 796–767) was for about one year a co-regent with his father, Joash, who had been wounded by Syrian troops (2Ch 24:23–25). Amaziah's first act was to execute his father's murderers, although he spared their children. He then assembled an army of Judah, which he supplemented with Israelite mercenaries. However, warned by "a man of God" that God was not with these Israelite troops (2Ch 25:7), Amaziah dismissed them. He proceeded to go up against Edom and took Sela (2Ki 14:7), possibly the city now identified as Petra. Amaziah then challenged Jehoash of Israel to war, refusing to heed Jehoash's warning against letting his ambitions lead him into folly. Judah was routed, Amaziah captured and Jerusalem sacked. Fifteen years later a conspiracy compelled Amaziah to flee to Lachish, but he was pursued and killed.

13:1 Jehoahaz of Israel reigned from approximately 814–798 B.C. At this time Syria, under King Hazael, controlled almost the whole of Israel (see "Hazael, The Nemesis of Israel" on p. 539). Jehoahaz was allowed to maintain only 10 chariots and 50 horsemen with 10,000 footmen. He is noted for having called on Yahweh for deliverance, and his prayer was answered. This does not imply that Jehoahaz abandoned the apostasy of the earlier kings, but neither should his action be dismissed as sham devotion. In 805 the Assyrian king Adadnirari III began to apply pressure against Syria. He may be the "deliverer" of verse 5.

13:2 Jeroboam had set up golden calves at Bethel and Dan for the people to worship (1Ki 12:26–30; see "Bethel" on p. 59 and "The High Place at Dan" on p. 504). The phrase "the sins of Jeroboam," or "the ways of Jeroboam," became a catchall to refer to the sins of Israel in general—appearing 17 times in 1 and 2 Kings.

13:5 Various suggestions have been made for this "deliverer": (1) the Assyrian ruler Adadnirari III (810–783 B.C.); (2) Jehoash, son of Jehoahaz; or (3) Jeroboam II. (See "Ben-Hadad III of Aram and Jehoash of Israel" on p. 548.)

Ben-Hadad III of Aram and Jehoash of Israel

2 KINGS 13 During the second half of the ninth century B.C., the northern kingdom suffered a great deal in wars with Hazael,[1] king of Aram (2Ki 8:28–29; 13:3,22). During the reign of Jehoash (c. 798–782 B.C.), however, the tide turned. Elisha predicted that Jehoash would be victorious over the Arameans three times (v. 17). In about 800 B.C. Hazael was succeeded by his son Ben-Hadad. (Being the third king with that name in the Old Testament, he is usually referred to as Ben-Hadad III.[2] Elisha's prophecy came true as Jehoash defeated Ben-Hadad III three times and recovered all of the cities Hazael had captured from Israel (vv. 24–25). This most likely occurred after Ben-Hadad's subjugation by the **Assyrians**, when the Aramean kingdom was considerably weakened.

The Tell al-Rimah Stele, an inscription that comes from Adadnirari III (king of Assyria from 810 to 783 B.C.), mentions Jehoash and apparently Ben-Hadad III. Discovered in 1967 at the site of Tell al-Rimah in modern Iraq, some 40 miles (64.5 km) west of Nineveh, it is a record of Adadnirari's campaign to the west in about 796 B.C. According to the **stele** Adadnirari received tribute payments from "Mari of Damascus," "Joash the Samarian" and unnamed rulers of Tyre and Sidon. Mari of Damascus is probably Ben-Hadad III; the inscription states that he sent vast amounts of silver, copper, iron and clothing to Adadnirari. Joash the Samarian is Jehoash of Israel (see vv. 9–14,25).[3] The amount of tribute paid by Jehoash and the rulers of Tyre and Sidon is not mentioned, but in another stele, the "Sabaa Stele," Adadnirari gives another account of a triumph over "Mari of Damascus," whom he confined to Damascus and from whom he exacted an enormous amount of gold and silver.[4]

[1]See "Hazael, the Nemesis of Israel" on page 539 and "The Tel Dan Stele" on page 540. [2]For information on the others, see "Ben-Hadad I and II" on page 521. [3]See "Omri and Samaria" on page 512. [4]See "Damascus" on page 1087.

Iron Age ruins of Samaria at the city's acropolis

Photograph: © Todd Bolen/Bible Places.com

7 Nothing had been left[l] of the army of Jehoahaz except fifty horsemen, ten chariots and ten thousand foot soldiers, for the king of Aram had destroyed the rest and made them like the dust[m] at threshing time.

8 As for the other events of the reign of Jehoahaz, all he did and his achievements, are they not written in the book of the annals of the kings of Israel? 9 Jehoahaz rested with his fathers and was buried in Samaria. And Jehoash[a] his son succeeded him as king.

Jehoash King of Israel

10 In the thirty-seventh year of Joash king of Judah, Jehoash son of Jehoahaz became king of Israel in Samaria, and he reigned sixteen years. 11 He did evil in the eyes of the LORD and did not turn away from any of the sins of Jeroboam son of Nebat, which he had caused Israel to commit; he continued in them.

12 As for the other events of the reign of Jehoash, all he did and his achievements, including his war against Amaziah[n] king of Judah, are they not written in the book of the annals[o] of the kings of Israel? 13 Jehoash rested with his fathers, and Jeroboam[p] succeeded him on the throne. Jehoash was buried in Samaria with the kings of Israel.

14 Now Elisha was suffering from the illness from which he died. Jehoash king of Israel went down to see him and wept over him. "My father! My father!" he cried. "The chariots[q] and horsemen of Israel!"

15 Elisha said, "Get a bow and some arrows," [r] and he did so. 16 "Take the bow in your hands," he said to the king of Israel. When he had taken it, Elisha put his hands on the king's hands.

17 "Open the east window," he said, and he opened it. "Shoot!"[s] Elisha said, and he shot. "The LORD's arrow of victory, the arrow of victory over Aram!" Elisha declared. "You will completely destroy the Arameans at Aphek."[t]

18 Then he said, "Take the arrows," and the king took them. Elisha told him, "Strike the ground." He struck it three times and stopped. 19 The man of God was angry with him and said, "You should have struck the ground five or six times; then you would have defeated Aram and completely destroyed it. But now you will defeat it only three times."[u]

20 Elisha died and was buried.

Now Moabite raiders[v] used to enter the country every spring. 21 Once while some Israelites were burying a man, suddenly they saw a band of raiders; so they threw the man's body into Elisha's tomb. When the body touched Elisha's bones, the man came to life[w] and stood up on his feet.

22 Hazael king of Aram oppressed[x] Israel throughout the reign of Jehoahaz. 23 But the LORD was gracious to them and had compassion and showed concern for them because of his covenant[y] with Abraham, Isaac and Jacob. To this day he has been unwilling to destroy[z] them or banish them from his presence.[a]

24 Hazael king of Aram died, and Ben-Hadad[b] his son succeeded him as king. 25 Then Jehoash son of Jehoahaz recaptured from Ben-Hadad son of Hazael the towns he had taken in battle from his father Jehoahaz. Three times[c] Jehoash defeated him, and so he recovered[d] the Israelite towns.

Amaziah King of Judah

14 In the second year of Jehoash[b] son of Jehoahaz king of Israel, Amaziah son of Joash king of Judah began to reign. 2 He was twenty-five years old when he became king, and he reigned in Jerusalem twenty-nine years. His mother's name was Jehoaddin; she was from Jerusalem. 3 He did what was right in the eyes of the LORD, but not as his father David had done. In everything he followed the example of his father Joash. 4 The high places,[e] however, were not removed; the people continued to offer sacrifices and burn incense there.

5 After the kingdom was firmly in his grasp, he executed[f] the officials[g] who had murdered his father

[a] *9* Hebrew *Joash,* a variant of *Jehoash;* also in verses 12-14 and 25 [b] *1* Hebrew *Joash,* a variant of *Jehoash;* also in verses 13, 23 and 27

13:7 [l]2Ki 10:32-33 [m]2Sa 22:43
13:12 [n]2Ki 14:15 [o]1Ki 15:31
13:13 [p]2Ki 14:23; Hos 1:1
13:14 [q]2Ki 2:12
13:15 [r]1Sa 20:20
13:17 [s]Jos 8:18 [t]1Ki 20:26
13:19 [u]ver 25
13:20 [v]2Ki 3:7; 24:2
13:21 [w]Mt 27:52
13:22 [x]1Ki 19:17; 2Ki 8:12
13:23 [y]Ge 13:16-17; Ex 2:24 [z]Dt 29:20 [a]Ex 33:15; 2Ki 14:27; 17:18; 24:3,20
13:24 [b]ver 3
13:25 [c]ver 18,19 [d]2Ki 10:32
14:4 [e]2Ki 12:3; 16:4
14:5 [f]2Ki 21:24 [g]2Ki 12:20

13:7 Ten chariots constituted a dismally meager force. According to the Assyrian annals of Shalmaneser III, Ahab had contributed 2,000 chariots and 10,000 foot soldiers to the coalition of forces that had opposed the Assyrians at the battle of Qarqar in 853 B.C. (see Horses and Chariots in Ancient Warfare" on p. 114 and "Ahab and the Battle of Qarqar" on p. 524). At that time this would have represented only a contingent of Israel's army, while here it constituted the entire Israelite infantry.

13:9 Jehoash of Israel reigned from approximately 798–782 B.C. The situation during his reign was better than that which had confronted his father, Jehoahaz. Adadnirari III of Assyria (c. 810–782) had already forced the Syrians to pay heavy tribute. Hazael of Damascus died and was followed by a weaker Ben-Hadad III, whom Jehoash defeated three times. With the collapse of power in Damascus and the full weight of Assyria yet to fall upon Israel, the stage was set for a resurgence of Israelite power under Jeroboam II, the son of Jehoash.

13:24 See "Ben-Hadad I and II" on page 521.

the king. 6 Yet he did not put the sons of the assassins to death, in accordance with what is written in the
Book of the Law[h] of Moses where the LORD commanded: "Fathers shall not be put to death for their chil- 14:6 [h]Dt 28:61
dren, nor children put to death for their fathers; each is to die for his own sins."[a][i] [i]Nu 26:11; Job 21:20; Jer 31:30; 44:3; Eze 18:4,20
7 He was the one who defeated ten thousand Edomites in the Valley of Salt[j] and captured Sela[k] in bat-
tle, calling it Joktheel, the name it has to this day. 14:7 [j]2Sa 8:13; 2Ch 25:11
8 Then Amaziah sent messengers to Jehoash son of Jehoahaz, the son of Jehu, king of Israel, with the [k]Jdg 1:36
challenge: "Come, meet me face to face."
9 But Jehoash king of Israel replied to Amaziah king of Judah: "A thistle[l] in Lebanon sent a message to 14:9 [l]Jdg 9:8-15
a cedar in Lebanon, 'Give your daughter to my son in marriage.' Then a wild beast in Lebanon came along
and trampled the thistle underfoot. 10 You have indeed defeated Edom and now you are arrogant.[m] Glo- 14:10 [m]Dt 8:14; 2Ch 26:16; 32:25
ry in your victory, but stay at home! Why ask for trouble and cause your own downfall and that of Judah
also?"
11 Amaziah, however, would not listen, so Jehoash king of Israel attacked. He and Amaziah king of Ju-
dah faced each other at Beth Shemesh[n] in Judah. 12 Judah was routed by Israel, and every man fled to his 14:11 [n]Jos 15:10
home.[o] 13 Jehoash king of Israel captured Amaziah king of Judah, the son of Joash, the son of Ahaziah, at 14:12 [o]2Sa 18:17
Beth Shemesh. Then Jehoash went to Jerusalem and broke down the wall[p] of Jerusalem from the Ephra- 14:13 [p]1Ki 3:1; 2Ch 33:14; 36:19; Jer 39:2
im Gate[q] to the Corner Gate[r]—a section about six hundred feet long.[b] 14 He took all the gold and silver
and all the articles found in the temple of the LORD and in the treasuries of the royal palace. He also took [q]Ne 8:16; 12:39
hostages and returned to Samaria. [r]2Ch 25:23; Jer 31:38; Zec 14:10
15 As for the other events of the reign of Jehoash, what he did and his achievements, including his war[s] 14:15 [s]2Ki 13:12
against Amaziah king of Judah, are they not written in the book of the annals of the kings of Israel? 16 Je-
hoash rested with his fathers and was buried in Samaria with the kings of Israel. And Jeroboam his son
succeeded him as king.

[a] 6 Deut. 24:16 [b] 13 Hebrew *four hundred cubits* (about 180 meters)

14:7 The Valley of Salt is generally identified with the Arabah, directly south of the Dead Sea.
14:9 A fable may be defined as a narrative in which animals and inanimate objects of nature are made to act and speak as though they were human beings. The word *fable* is not found in the Old Testament, but two fables do appear here and in Judges 9:7–15.

ANCIENT TEXTS AND ARTIFACTS

The Samaria Ostraca

2 KINGS 14 A collection of inscriptions written with ink on pottery fragments or ostraca (singular **ostracon**)[1] was discovered during excavations at **Samaria**[2] ("Map 6") in 1910. They record shipments of wine and oil received in Samaria from locations in its vicinity, apparently during the ninth, tenth and fifteenth years of Jeroboam II (c. 786–746 B.C.), although the dating of the ostraca is disputed. The texts include some or all of the following elements: date (year of a king), place, clan name, sender, recipient and commodity (wine or oil).

The ostraca provide samples of Israelite script, showing us how Hebrew was written at this time. They also illustrate the record-keeping of the time and provide valuable geographic information on towns in the area.

The most interesting aspect of the ostraca is the clan names. Samaria is located in the tribal area of Manasseh. Ten clans of Manasseh settled in **Canaan** and received tracts of land (Jos 17:1–13). Those clans were Abiezer, Asriel, Helek, Shechem and Shemida, sons of Gilead (Jos 17:1–2); and Hoglah, Mahlah, Milcah, Noah and Tirzah, the daughters of Zelophehad, son of Hepher (Jos 17:3–4).[3] All of the clans named after Gilead's sons are represented in the ostraca, along with two of the five clans named after Zelophehad's daughters (those of Hoglah and Noah). The clan names preserved on the Samaria Ostraca provide an extrabiblical link between the clans of Manasseh and the territory in which the Bible claims they settled.

[1]See "Writing Materials in the Ancient World" on page 2037. [2]See "Omri and Samaria" on page 512. [3]For the inheritance rights of these five women, see "Inheritance in the Ancient Near East" on page 250.

14:19 [t]2Ki 12:20 [u]Jos 10:3; 2Ki 18:14,17
14:20 [v]2Ki 9:28
14:21 [w]2Ki 15:1; 2Ch 26:23
14:22 [x]1Ki 9:26; 2Ki 16:6

17 Amaziah son of Joash king of Judah lived for fifteen years after the death of Jehoash son of Jehoa-
haz king of Israel. 18 As for the other events of Amaziah's reign, are they not written in the book of the an-
nals of the kings of Judah?
19 They conspired[t] against him in Jerusalem, and he fled to Lachish,[u] but they sent men after him to
Lachish and killed him there. 20 He was brought back by horse[v] and was buried in Jerusalem with his fa-
thers, in the City of David.
21 Then all the people of Judah took Azariah,[a][w] who was sixteen years old, and made him king in place
of his father Amaziah. 22 He was the one who rebuilt Elath[x] and restored it to Judah after Amaziah rest-
ed with his fathers.

Jeroboam II King of Israel

14:23 [y]2Ki 13:13
14:24 [z]1Ki 15:30
14:25 [a]Nu 13:21; 1Ki 8:65 [b]Dt 3:17 [c]Jnh 1:1; Mt 12:39
14:26 [d]Dt 32:36 [e]2Ki 13:4 [f]Ps 18:41; 22:11; 72:12; 107:12; Isa 63:5; La 1:7
14:27 [g]2Ki 13:23 [h]Jdg 6:14
14:28 [i]2Sa 8:5; 1Ki 11:24 [j]2Ch 8:3 [k]1Ki 15:31

23 In the fifteenth year of Amaziah son of Joash king of Judah, Jeroboam[y] son of Jehoash king of Isra-
el became king in Samaria, and he reigned forty-one years. 24 He did evil in the eyes of the LORD and did
not turn away from any of the sins of Jeroboam son of Nebat, which he had caused Israel to commit.[z] 25 He
was the one who restored the boundaries of Israel from Lebo[b] Hamath[a] to the Sea of the Arabah,[c][b] in ac-
cordance with the word of the LORD, the God of Israel, spoken through his servant Jonah[c] son of Amit-
tai, the prophet from Gath Hepher.
26 The LORD had seen how bitterly everyone in Israel, whether slave or free,[d] was suffering;[e] there was
no one to help them.[f] 27 And since the LORD had not said he would blot out[g] the name of Israel from un-
der heaven, he saved[h] them by the hand of Jeroboam son of Jehoash.
28 As for the other events of Jeroboam's reign, all he did, and his military achievements, including how
he recovered for Israel both Damascus[i] and Hamath,[j] which had belonged to Yaudi,[d] are they not writ-
ten in the book of the annals[k] of the kings of Israel? 29 Jeroboam rested with his fathers, the kings of Is-
rael. And Zechariah his son succeeded him as king.

Azariah King of Judah

15:1 [l]ver 32; 2Ki 14:21
15:5 [m]Ge 12:17 [n]Lev 13:46 [o]2Ch 27:1 [p]Ge 41:40
15:7 [q]Isa 6:1; 14:28 [r]ver 5

15 In the twenty-seventh year of Jeroboam king of Israel, Azariah[l] son of Amaziah king of Judah
began to reign. 2 He was sixteen years old when he became king, and he reigned in Jerusalem fif-
ty-two years. His mother's name was Jecoliah; she was from Jerusalem. 3 He did what was right in the
eyes of the LORD, just as his father Amaziah had done. 4 The high places, however, were not removed; the
people continued to offer sacrifices and burn incense there.
5 The LORD afflicted[m] the king with leprosy[e] until the day he died, and he lived in a separate house.[f][n]
Jotham[o] the king's son had charge of the palace[p] and governed the people of the land.
6 As for the other events of Azariah's reign, and all he did, are they not written in the book of the an-
nals of the kings of Judah? 7 Azariah rested[q] with his fathers and was buried near them in the City of Da-
vid. And Jotham[r] his son succeeded him as king.

[a] 21 Also called *Uzziah* [b] 25 Or *from the entrance to* [c] 25 That is, the Dead Sea [d] 28 Or *Judah* [e] 5 The Hebrew word was used for various diseases affecting the skin—not necessarily leprosy. [f] 5 Or *in a house where he was relieved of responsibility*

14:22 Elath was located near Ezion Geber; these towns were at the head of the Gulf of Aqaba, in the land of Edom. Solomon had developed Ezion Geber as a major seaport and maintained a fleet there (see "Ezion Geber" on p. 631).
14:23 Jeroboam II (r. c. 793–753) governed when the other powers of the day, notably Syria and Assyria, were not a presence in the land. He continued and brought to a successful conclusion the wars that his father had undertaken against Syria, taking their chief cities, Damascus and Hamath, which had once been subject to David, and restoring to Israel territory east of the Jordan from Lebanon to the Dead Sea (v. 25; Am 6:14). Moab and Ammon were also brought back under Israelite control (Am 1:13; 2:1–3). During the reign of Jeroboam the prophets Hosea, Joel and Amos ministered, and Jonah belatedly embarked on his reluctant mission to a weakened Nineveh.
14:25 Jeroboam II's successful wars brought much tribute to Israel, and the noble class enjoyed enormous prosperity. The prophet Amos, a contemporary of Jeroboam in his later years, provided a graphic description of a banqueting scene of the time (Am 6:4–6). But alongside this luxury there was much poverty in the land. Worship of a syncretistic sort went on at Dan and Bethel, as well as at shrines at Gilgal and Beersheba (Am 4:4; 5:5; 8:14).
14:28 Some equate Yaudi with a site in northern Aram (see "Syria/Aram" on p. 534) referred to in a few Assyrian inscriptions. Others believe it to be a reference to Judah (see the NIV text note), in the sense that Damascus and Hamath were once included in territory ruled by David and Solomon (see 2Sa 8:6; 2Ch 8:3).
15:1 Azariah was also known as Uzziah (v. 13), likely the name he took when he became king.
15:5 Jotham of Judah, son and successor to Uzziah, was for some time co-regent with his father (v. 5). The chronology of his reign is difficult to sort out, as the Biblical synchronisms are not coherent. For example, verse 32 states that Jotham reigned 16 years, whereas verse 30 states that Hoshea of Israel began to reign during Jotham's twentieth year. It may be that the sixteenth year of Jotham's reign began in 750 B.C., when he was coregent with Uzziah, and extended to about 735. He may have remained alive for another few years while his son Ahaz was effectively king, thus allowing the Bible to speak of Jotham's "twentieth year." Second Chronicles 27:1–9 praises Jotham as a godly man and notes his military success against Ammon.
15:6 The annals of Tiglath-Pileser (745–723) state that during his third regnal year he assaulted and brought into subjection the city of Azriyau of Ya-u-da. This name would seem to be Azariah (Uzziah) of Judah. On the other hand, the context for Tiglath-

Zechariah King of Israel

8 In the thirty-eighth year of Azariah king of Judah, Zechariah son of Jeroboam became king of Isra-
el in Samaria, and he reigned six months. 9 He did evil[s] in the eyes of the LORD, as his fathers had done. **15:9** [s]1Ki 15:26
He did not turn away from the sins of Jeroboam son of Nebat, which he had caused Israel to commit.
10 Shallum son of Jabesh conspired against Zechariah. He attacked him in front of the people,[a] assas-
sinated[t] him and succeeded him as king. 11 The other events of Zechariah's reign are written in the book **15:10** [t]2Ki 12:20
of the annals[u] of the kings of Israel. 12 So the word of the LORD spoken to Jehu was fulfilled:[v] "Your descen- **15:11** [u]1Ki 15:31
dants will sit on the throne of Israel to the fourth generation."[b] **15:12** [v]2Ki 10:30

Shallum King of Israel

13 Shallum son of Jabesh became king in the thirty-ninth year of Uzziah king of Judah, and he reigned
in Samaria[w] one month. 14 Then Menahem son of Gadi went from Tirzah[x] up to Samaria. He attacked **15:13** [w]ver 1,8
Shallum son of Jabesh in Samaria, assassinated[y] him and succeeded him as king. **15:14** [x]1Ki 14:17 [y]2Ki 12:20
15 The other events of Shallum's reign, and the conspiracy he led, are written in the book of the annals[z] **15:15** [z]1Ki 15:31
of the kings of Israel.
16 At that time Menahem, starting out from Tirzah, attacked Tiphsah[a] and everyone in the city and its **15:16** [a]1Ki 4:24
vicinity, because they refused to open[b] their gates. He sacked Tiphsah and ripped open all the pregnant [b]2Ki 8:12; Hos 13:16
women.

Menahem King of Israel

17 In the thirty-ninth year of Azariah king of Judah, Menahem son of Gadi became king of Israel, and
he reigned in Samaria ten years. 18 He did evil in the eyes of the LORD. During his entire reign he did not
turn away from the sins of Jeroboam son of Nebat, which he had caused Israel to commit.
19 Then Pul[c][c] king of Assyria invaded the land, and Menahem gave him a thousand talents[d] of silver **15:19** [c]1Ch 5:6, 26
to gain his support and strengthen his own hold on the kingdom. 20 Menahem exacted this money from
Israel. Every wealthy man had to contribute fifty shekels[e] of silver to be given to the king of Assyria. So
the king of Assyria withdrew[d] and stayed in the land no longer. **15:20** [d]2Ki 12:18
21 As for the other events of Menahem's reign, and all he did, are they not written in the book of the
annals of the kings of Israel? 22 Menahem rested with his fathers. And Pekahiah his son succeeded him
as king.

Pekahiah King of Israel

23 In the fiftieth year of Azariah king of Judah, Pekahiah son of Menahem became king of Israel in Sa-
maria, and he reigned two years. 24 Pekahiah did evil in the eyes of the LORD. He did not turn away from
the sins of Jeroboam son of Nebat, which he had caused Israel to commit. 25 One of his chief officers, Pe-
kah[e] son of Remaliah, conspired against him. Taking fifty men of Gilead with him, he assassinated[f] **15:25** [e]2Ch 28:6; Isa 7:1 [f]2Ki 12:20

[a] *10* Hebrew; some Septuagint manuscripts *in Ibleam* [b] *12* 2 Kings 10:30 [c] *19* Also called *Tiglath-Pileser* [d] *19* That is, about 37 tons (about 34 metric tons) [e] *20* That is, about 1 1/4 pounds (about 0.6 kilogram)

Pileser's inscription suggests that the place was in Syria, leading some to propose that the inscription refers to a northern Syrian state known as Y'di. Other scholars reject the equation of "Ya-u-da" with Y'di and seek to harmonize this encounter with Tiglath-Pileser with what is known of the career of Uzziah. Today most scholars reject equating Azriyau with Uzziah of Judah and assert that the identity of Azriyau remains unknown.

15:8 Zechariah of Israel reigned in about 753 B.C. In fulfillment of 10:30 he was the last king of the house of Jehu. After reigning six months, Zechariah was killed by Shallum, his successor (15:8–10).

15:13 Shallum of Israel reigned for one month in about 752 B.C. He murdered Zechariah, king of Israel, usurped the throne, and then was himself assassinated. Nothing else is known of his reign.

15:14 Menahem of Israel (r. 752–742 B.C.; see vv. 13–22) began his ten-year reign by killing his predecessor, Shallum. Through gifts collected from his subjects, he bribed the Assyrian king Pul (Tiglath-Pileser III) and was thereby able to retain his throne (1Ki 15:20). A passage in the Annals of Tiglath-Pileser records tribute paid by "Menihimmu of Samarina." This event may be dated to 743, but some date it to 738 and adjust the years of Menahem's reign accordingly. During this restless period of the northern kingdom, with ambitious men usurping the throne through assassination of their predecessors, Menahem was the only king who died a natural death. His son Pekahiah inherited the kingdom.

15:19 Pul is the Babylonian name of the Assyrian ruler Tiglath-Pileser III (745–727 B.C.). His record lists Menahem, king of Israel, as one of many who paid tribute to him (see "Menahem and Pekah of Israel, Jotham of Judah and Tiglath-Pileser III of Assyria" on p. 553).

Menahem's tribute to Tiglath-Pileser III was 1,000 talents, amounting to a tax of 50 shekels from each of 60,000 men of middle- and upper-class status. The data give us some idea of the population of Israel at the time. Fifty shekels, the price of a slave in Assyria, indicates the status of Israel before Assyria. A similar tribute was exacted by Tiglath-Pileser from Pekah and by Sennacherib from Hezekiah (see "Hezekiah Against the Assyrians" on p. 1118).

15:22 Pekahiah was noteworthy only for the fact that he was the last Israelite king to succeed his own father. He appears to have reigned from approximately 742–740 B.C. Pekahiah was murdered by a usurper, Pekah.

Pekahiah, along with Argob and Arieh, in the citadel of the royal palace at Samaria. So Pekah killed Pek-
ahiah and succeeded him as king.
26 The other events of Pekahiah's reign, and all he did, are written in the book of the annals of the kings
of Israel.

Pekah King of Israel

27 In the fifty-second year of Azariah king of Judah, Pekah[g] son of Remaliah[h] became king of Israel in
Samaria, and he reigned twenty years. 28 He did evil in the eyes of the LORD. He did not turn away from
the sins of Jeroboam son of Nebat, which he had caused Israel to commit.
29 In the time of Pekah king of Israel, Tiglath-Pileser[i] king of Assyria came and took Ijon,[j] Abel Beth
Maacah, Janoah, Kedesh and Hazor. He took Gilead and Galilee, including all the land of Naphtali,[k] and

15:27 [g]2Ch 28:6; Isa 7:1 [h]Isa 7:4 **15:29** [i]2Ki 16:7; 17:6; 1Ch 5:26; 2Ch 28:20; Jer 50:17 [j]1Ki 15:20 [k]2Ki 16:9; 17:24; 2Ch 16:4; Isa 9:1

15:27 Pekah of Israel is said to have ruled for 20 years and to have begun his reign during the fifty-second year of Azariah (Uzziah) of Judah. Since Uzziah's fifty-second year was 740 B.C., and Pekah's governance was followed by the nine-year reign of Hoshea (after which the kingdom fell in 722), the chronology for Pekah's reign is obviously a problem. The most probable solution is that Pekah was from approximately 752 to 740 a rival king based in Gilead (v. 25) but that he was Israel's sole king from approximately 740 to 732. If this is the case, around the time that Shallum murdered Zechariah and so ended the dynasty of Jehu, Pekah set up a power base (probably on the eastern side of the Jordan) and was a rival at various times to Shallum, Menahem and Pekahiah, although he was most likely nominally subordinate to Menahem. Israel at this time was no longer a unified monarchy but a domain of war lords. By 740 Pekah finally had sufficient power to murder Pekahiah and become sole ruler.

15:29 Pekah's power was destined to remain limited as long as Assyria was a presence in the Levant (Syria/Palestine). For this reason he allied himself with Rezin of Damascus in an anti-Assyrian coalition. Rezin and Pekah sought to shore up their power by removing Ahaz from the throne in Jerusalem and placing a puppet, the "son of Tabeel," on the throne (Isa 7:6). In 734 B.C. Tiglath-Pileser invaded Israel in an attempt to eliminate resistance to Assyria. He also captured Damascus and put Rezin to death (2Ki 16:9). According to 15:30 Pekah was assassinated by Hoshea, who then seized the throne. See "Menahem and Pekah of Israel, Jotham of Judah and Tiglah-Pileser III of Assyria" on page 553.

Menahem and Pekah of Israel, Jotham of Judah and Tiglath-Pileser III of Assyria

2 KINGS 15 Fifteen kings are named in 2 Kings 15, covering a span of about 35 years, from approximately 767 to 732 B.C. Nine are kings of Israel (Jeroboam I, Jeroboam II, Zechariah, Shallum, Jehu, Menahem, Pekahiah, Pekah and Hoshea), four of Judah (Amaziah, Azariah/Uzziah, Jotham and Ahaz), one of **Assyria** (Pul/Tiglath-Pileser III) and one of Aram/Syria (Rezin).[1] Ten of the fifteen are named in contemporary sources outside the Bible. A few examples are as follows:

✣ Menahem, king of Israel (c. 747–737 B.C.), paid tribute to Tiglath-Pileser III, king of Assyria, from approximately 745 to 727 B.C. (vv. 19–20). Scholars believe this tribute was paid at the time of the first campaign of Tiglath-Pileser III into the region in approximately 740 B.C. Menahem is mentioned twice in Tiglath-Pileser's records. Both the Iran **Stele**, purchased from an antiquities dealer in western Iran, and Tiglath-Pileser's annals, excavated in his palace in Calah, Iraq, state that "Menahem of **Samaria**" paid tribute to the king in his eighth year, approximately 738 B.C.

✣ Pekah, king of Israel (c. 735–732 B.C.), joined forces with Rezin, king of Aram, in a revolt against Tiglath-Pileser III.[2] The two attempted to force Judah to join them (v. 37; 16:5; 2Ch 28:5–8; Isa 7:1–9). This provoked the wrath of the Assyrian king, who defeated Damascus,[3] the capital of Aram, and devastated Israel in 732 B.C. (2Ki 15:29; 16:7–9; 1Ch 5:26). The records of Tiglath-Pileser III twice refer to this campaign and to the demise of Pekah. An ancient seal depicts a figure facing left, with the name Pekah written behind him. This was most likely Pekah's seal when he was an officer under Pekahiah prior to his becoming king (2Ki 15:25).

✣ The names of Jotham and Ahaz, kings of Judah (c. 759–743 B.C.), appear on a clay seal impression or **bulla**. This bulla, from the reign of Jotham's son Ahaz, once sealed an official papyrus document. The full name of a man in ancient Israel was rendered as "X, son of Y"; thus the impression reads, "Belonging to Ahaz, (son of) Jotham, king of Judah."

✣ Tiglath-Pileser III, king of Assyria (c. 745–727 B.C.),[4] is named nine times in the Bible. Many records from his reign, including sculptured **reliefs** depicting the king himself, were found in his palace at Calah, Iraq.

[1]See "Syria/Aram" on page 534. [2]See "The Syro-Ephraimite War" on page 1066. [3]See "Damascus" on page 1087. [4]See "Assyria From the Neo-Assyrian Period Forward" on page 1502.

deported[l] the people to Assyria. 30 Then Hoshea[m] son of Elah conspired against Pekah son of Remaliah.
He attacked and assassinated[n] him, and then succeeded him as king in the twentieth year of Jotham son
of Uzziah.
31 As for the other events of Pekah's reign, and all he did, are they not written in the book of the an-
nals of the kings of Israel?

15:29 [l]2Ki 24:14-16; 1Ch 5:22; Isa 14:6,17; 36:17; 45:13
15:30 [m]2Ki 17:1 [n]2Ki 12:20

Jotham King of Judah

32 In the second year of Pekah son of Remaliah king of Israel, Jotham[o] son of Uzziah king of Judah be-
gan to reign. 33 He was twenty-five years old when he became king, and he reigned in Jerusalem sixteen
years. His mother's name was Jerusha daughter of Zadok. 34 He did what was right[p] in the eyes of the LORD,
just as his father Uzziah had done. 35 The high places,[q] however, were not removed; the people continued
to offer sacrifices and burn incense there. Jotham rebuilt the Upper Gate[r] of the temple of the LORD.
36 As for the other events of Jotham's reign, and what he did, are they not written in the book of the an-
nals of the kings of Judah? 37 (In those days the LORD began to send Rezin[s] king of Aram and Pekah son
of Remaliah against Judah.) 38 Jotham rested with his fathers and was buried with them in the City of
David, the city of his father. And Ahaz his son succeeded him as king.

15:32 [o]1Ch 5:17
15:34 [p]ver 3; 1Ki 14:8; 2Ch 26:4-5
15:35 [q]2Ki 12:3 [r]2Ch 23:20
15:37 [s]2Ki 16:5; Isa 7:1

15:30 In his annals Tiglath-Pileser III claimed to have placed Hoshea on the throne of the northern kingdom and to have taken tribute from him. Hoshea, the last king of Israel, later conspired with Egypt and withheld the annual tribute to the Assyrians. A protracted three-year siege, conducted by Shalmaneser and concluded by Sargon II, saw the end of the Israelite kingdom in 722 B.C. (see "Hoshea, King of Israel, and Shalmaneser V, King of Assyria" on page 556). The following was found in Assyrian annals of the time: "I (Sargon) besieged and conquered Samaria, led away as booty 27,290 inhabitants . . . I installed over (those remaining) an officer of mine and imposed upon them the tribute of the former king."

Ahaz, King of Judah, and Rezin, King of Aram

2 KINGS 16 Ahaz ruled Judah for 16 years, from approximately 743 to 727 B.C. He is remembered most for his war against Israel (under Pekah) and Aram (under Rezin).[1] Ahaz sought the aid of the **Assyrian** king Tiglath-Pileser III when Pekah and Rezin sought to force him to join a coalition against Assyria (2Ki 16:5).[2] A number of inscriptions from the ancient world refer to kings of this time:

- Among the records of Tiglath-Pileser III is an entry claiming that he received tribute from "Jehoahaz of Judah" in 734 B.C. Jehoahaz, Ahaz's full name, means "**Yahweh** has possessed."
- Ahaz's name also appears on a seal and three **bullae** from Israel, all acquired from antiquities dealers:

The seal of an official during the reign of Ahaz carries the inscription "Belonging to Ushna, servant of Ahaz."

Two of the seal impressions, made from the same seal, read, "Belonging to Hezekiah (son of) Ahaz, king of Judah."

Ahaz's personal seal, on the other hand, was used to impress the third bulla with the legend "Belonging to Ahaz (son of) Yehotam (Jotham), king of Judah."

- Rezin, king of Aram, is named nine times in the Old Testament and six times in the surviving records of Tiglath-Pileser III. He paid tribute to the Assyrian king in 738 B.C. Sometime after that Rezin formed the anti-Assyrian coalition. Ahaz's appeal to Tiglath-Pileser III for help (vv. 7–8) was heeded. According to Assyrian records Tiglath-Pileser III responded by laying siege to Damascus[3] ("Map 6"), capital of Aram, in 733 B.C. In 732 B.C. Damascus was crushed, its citizens taken into captivity and Rezin killed, as recorded in verse 16:9, thus bringing the kingdom of Aram to an end.

See also "Menahem and Pekah of Israel, Jotham of Judah and Tiglath-Pileser III of Assyria" on page 553.

[1]See "Syria/Aram" on page 534. [2]See "The Syro-Ephraimite War" on page 1066. [3]See "Damascus" on page 1087.

Ahaz King of Judah

16:1 [t]Isa 1:1; 14:28 16 In the seventeenth year of Pekah son of Remaliah, Ahaz[t] son of Jotham king of Judah began to
reign. 2 Ahaz was twenty years old when he became king, and he reigned in Jerusalem sixteen
16:2 [u]1Ki 14:8 years. Unlike David his father, he did not do what was right[u] in the eyes of the LORD his God. 3 He walked
16:3 [v]Lev 18:21; 2Ki 21:6 in the ways of the kings of Israel and even sacrificed his son[v] in[a] the fire, following the detestable[w] ways
[w]Lev 18:3; Dt 9:4; 12:31 of the nations the LORD had driven out before the Israelites. 4 He offered sacrifices and burned incense at
16:4 [x]Dt 12:2; Eze 6:13 the high places, on the hilltops and under every spreading tree.[x]
16:5 [y]2Ki 15:37; Isa 7:1,4 5 Then Rezin[y] king of Aram and Pekah son of Remaliah king of Israel marched up to fight against Je-
16:6 [z]Isa 9:12 rusalem and besieged Ahaz, but they could not overpower him. 6 At that time, Rezin[z] king of Aram recov-
[a]2Ki 14:22; 2Ch 26:2 ered Elath[a] for Aram by driving out the men of Judah. Edomites then moved into Elath and have lived
there to this day.
16:7 [b]2Ki 15:29 7 Ahaz sent messengers to say to Tiglath-Pileser[b] king of Assyria, "I am your servant and vassal. Come
[c]Isa 2:6; Jer 2:18; Eze 16:28; Hos 10:6 up and save[c] me out of the hand of the king of Aram and of the king of Israel, who are attacking me." 8 And
Ahaz took the silver and gold found in the temple of the LORD and in the treasuries of the royal palace
16:8 [d]2Ki 12:18 and sent it as a gift[d] to the king of Assyria. 9 The king of Assyria complied by attacking Damascus[e] and
16:9 [e]2Ki 15:29 [f]Isa 22:6; Am 1:5; 9:7 capturing it. He deported its inhabitants to Kir[f] and put Rezin to death.
10 Then King Ahaz went to Damascus to meet Tiglath-Pileser king of Assyria. He saw an altar in Da-
16:10 [g]Isa 8:2 mascus and sent to Uriah[g] the priest a sketch of the altar, with detailed plans for its construction. 11 So
Uriah the priest built an altar in accordance with all the plans that King Ahaz had sent from Damascus
and finished it before King Ahaz returned. 12 When the king came back from Damascus and saw the al-
16:12 [h]2Ch 26:16 tar, he approached it and presented offerings[b][h] on it. 13 He offered up his burnt offering[i] and grain offer-
16:13 [i]Lev 6:8-13 [j]Lev 7:11-21 ing, poured out his drink offering, and sprinkled the blood of his fellowship offerings[c][j] on the altar. 14 The
16:14 [k]2Ch 4:1 bronze altar[k] that stood before the LORD he brought from the front of the temple—from between the
new altar and the temple of the LORD—and put it on the north side of the new altar.
16:15 [l]Ex 29:38-41 [m]1Sa 9:9 15 King Ahaz then gave these orders to Uriah the priest: "On the large new altar, offer the morning[l]
burnt offering and the evening grain offering, the king's burnt offering and his grain offering, and the
burnt offering of all the people of the land, and their grain offering and their drink offering. Sprinkle on
the altar all the blood of the burnt offerings and sacrifices. But I will use the bronze altar for seeking
guidance."[m] 16 And Uriah the priest did just as King Ahaz had ordered.
17 King Ahaz took away the side panels and removed the basins from the movable stands. He removed
16:17 [n]1Ki 7:27 the Sea from the bronze bulls that supported it and set it on a stone base.[n] 18 He took away the Sabbath
canopy[d] that had been built at the temple and removed the royal entryway outside the temple of the LORD,
16:18 [o]Eze 16:28 in deference to the king of Assyria.[o]
19 As for the other events of the reign of Ahaz, and what he did, are they not written in the book of the
annals of the kings of Judah? 20 Ahaz rested with his fathers and was buried with them in the City of Da-
vid. And Hezekiah his son succeeded him as king.

Hoshea Last King of Israel

17:1 [p]2Ki 15:30 17 In the twelfth year of Ahaz king of Judah, Hoshea[p] son of Elah became king of Israel in Samar-
ia, and he reigned nine years. 2 He did evil in the eyes of the LORD, but not like the kings of Isra-
el who preceded him.
17:3 [q]2Ki 18:9-12; Hos 10:14 3 Shalmaneser[q] king of Assyria came up to attack Hoshea, who had been Shalmaneser's vassal and

[a] 3 Or *even made his son pass through* [b] 12 Or *and went up* [c] 13 Traditionally *peace offerings* [d] 18 Or *the dais of his throne* (see Septuagint)

16:3 See "Human Sacrifice in the Ancient Near East" on page 182.
16:8 The name Jehoahaz of Judah (Ahaz) appears on a listing of rulers (including those of the Philistines, Ammonites, Moabites and Edomites) who brought tribute to Tiglath-Pileser (see "Ahaz, King of Judah, and Rezin, King of Aram" on p. 554).
16:15 It was common in the Near East to seek omens by examining the entrails of sacrificed animals. Ahaz intended to follow this Assyrian divination technique in an attempt to secure the Lord's guidance.
17:3–6 Much mythology has developed around the theme of the so-called ten lost tribes of Israel. A close examination of Assyrian records reveals that the deportations approximated only a limited percentage of the population, generally consisting of noble families. Agricultural workers, no doubt the majority, were deliberately left behind to care for the crops (cf. the Babylonian practice; 24:14; 25:12).
17:3 Hoshea, the last king of Israel, reigned from approximately 732–722 B.C. By the time he assassinated Pekah, Israel had been reduced to little more than the Ephraimite region immediately surrounding Samaria. Tiglath-Pileser III had annexed virtually everything else, including the Gileadite territory east of the Jordan, to Assyria. Tiglath-Pileser died in 727 and was succeeded by Shalmaneser V. Hoshea, seizing what he saw as an opportunity, ceased paying tribute and sought help from Egypt (v. 4). Shalmaneser marched against Samaria and captured Hoshea, after which either he or his successor, Sargon II, destroyed the city and ended the northern kingdom. See "Hoshea, King of Israel, and Shalmaneser V, King of Assyria" on page 556.

had paid him tribute. 4But the king of Assyria discovered that Hoshea was a traitor, for he had sent en-
voys to So[a] king of Egypt, and he no longer paid tribute to the king of Assyria, as he had done year by
year. Therefore Shalmaneser seized him and put him in prison. 5The king of Assyria invaded the entire
land, marched against Samaria and laid siege[r] to it for three years. 6In the ninth year of Hoshea, the king
of Assyria captured Samaria[s] and deported[t] the Israelites to Assyria. He settled them in Halah, in Gozan[u]
on the Habor River and in the towns of the Medes.

Israel Exiled Because of Sin

7All this took place because the Israelites had sinned[v] against the LORD their God, who had brought
them up out of Egypt[w] from under the power of Pharaoh king of Egypt. They worshiped other gods
8and followed the practices of the nations[x] the LORD had driven out before them, as well as the practic-
es that the kings of Israel had introduced. 9The Israelites secretly did things against the LORD their God
that were not right. From watchtower to fortified city[y] they built themselves high places in all their
towns. 10They set up sacred stones and Asherah poles[z] on every high hill and under every spreading
tree.[a] 11At every high place they burned incense, as the nations whom the LORD had driven out before
them had done. They did wicked things that provoked the LORD to anger. 12They worshiped idols,[b]
though the LORD had said, "You shall not do this."[b] 13The LORD warned Israel and Judah through all his
prophets and seers:[c] "Turn from your evil ways.[d] Observe my commands and decrees, in accordance
with the entire Law that I commanded your fathers to obey and that I delivered to you through my ser-
vants the prophets."

14But they would not listen and were as stiff-necked[e] as their fathers, who did not trust in the LORD
their God. 15They rejected his decrees and the covenant[f] he had made with their fathers and the warn-
ings he had given them. They followed worthless idols[g] and themselves became worthless. They imitat-

17:5 [r]Hos 13:16
17:6 [s]Hos 13:16 [t]Dt 28:36,64; 2Ki 18:10-11 [u]1Ch 5:26
17:7 [v]Jos 23:16; Jdg 6:10 [w]Ex 14:15-31
17:8 [x]Lev 18:3; Dt 18:9; 2Ki 16:3
17:9 [y]2Ki 18:8
17:10 [z]Ex 34:13; Mic 5:14 [a]1Ki 14:23
17:12 [b]Ex 20:4
17:13 [c]1Sa 9:9 [d]Jer 18:11; 25:5; 35:15
17:14 [e]Ex 32:9; Dt 31:27; Ac 7:51
17:15 [f]Dt 29:25 [g]Dt 32:21; Ro 1:21-23

[a] 4 Or *to Sais, to the*; *So* is possibly an abbreviation for *Osorkon*. [b] *12* Exodus 20:4,5

17:4 The identity of "So," the king of Egypt to whom Hoshea appealed for help, is uncertain. The pharaoh contemporary with Hoshea was Tefnakht I (c. 727–720 B.C.). It may be that "So" actually refers to Sais, the capital city of Egypt at this time.

17:6 Gozan was an Assyrian provincial capital located on a tributary of the Euphrates River. The "towns of the Medes" were situated in the area south of the Caspian Sea and northeast of the Tigris River.

Hoshea, King of Israel, and Shalmaneser V, King of Assyria

2 KINGS 17 Hoshea was the nineteenth and last king of the northern kingdom, ruling for nine years, from approximately 731 to 722 B.C.[1] In his annals the **Assyrian** king Tiglath-Pileser III claims to have killed Pekah, king of Israel, and installed Hoshea in his place (2Ki 15:30).[2] The Bible and Assyrian records agree that Hoshea initially paid tribute to his Assyrian overlords (17:3–4). The annals of Tiglath-Pileser III state that he received from Israel ten talents of gold, as well as silver and other booty. Under the next Assyrian king, Shalmaneser V, Hoshea stopped paying tribute and sought help from Egypt. This proved to be his undoing, as Shalmaneser V imprisoned Hoshea and invaded Israel (vv. 4–5). After a three-year siege, Israel's capital, **Samaria** ("Map 6"), fell and its inhabitants were taken into captivity, bringing an end to the nation (v. 6; 18:9–11).

Shalmaneser V, son of Tiglath-Pileser III, ruled Assyria[3] for five years, from approximately 727 to 722 B.C. Few records survive from his reign. The most important are two entries from the Babylonian Chronicles, a series of **cuneiform** tablets recording important events from 745 B.C. to the second century B.C. For the year 727 B.C. the Chronicle states that on the twenty-seventh of the month Tebet (December–January) Shalmaneser ascended the throne in Assyria and destroyed Samaria. The next entry, for 722 B.C., records that Shalmaneser died five years later, again in the month Tebet.

[1]See "The History of the Northern Kingdom" on page 506. [2]See "Menahem and Pekah of Israel, Jotham of Judah and Tiglath-Pileser III of Assyria" on page 553. [3]See "Assyria From the Neo-Assyrian Period Forward" on page 1502.

17:15 [h]Dt 12:30-31 ed the nations[h] around them although the LORD had ordered them, "Do not do as they do," and they did
the things the LORD had forbidden them to do.
[16]They forsook all the commands of the LORD their God and made for themselves two idols cast in
17:16 [i]1Ki 12:28 [j]1Ki 14:15,23 [k]2Ki 21:3 [l]1Ki 16:31 the shape of calves,[i] and an Asherah[j] pole. They bowed down to all the starry hosts,[k] and they worshiped
Baal.[l] [17]They sacrificed[m] their sons and daughters in[a] the fire. They practiced divination and sorcery[n] and
17:17 [m]Dt 18:10-12; 2Ki 16:3 [n]Lev 19:26 [o]1Ki 21:20 sold[o] themselves to do evil in the eyes of the LORD, provoking him to anger.
[18]So the LORD was very angry with Israel and removed them from his presence. Only the tribe of Ju-
dah was left, [19]and even Judah did not keep the commands of the LORD their God. They followed the prac-
17:19 [p]1Ki 14:22-23; 2Ki 16:3 tices Israel had introduced.[p] [20]Therefore the LORD rejected all the people of Israel; he afflicted them and
17:20 [q]2Ki 15:29 gave them into the hands of plunderers,[q] until he thrust them from his presence.
17:21 [r]1Ki 11:11 [s]1Ki 12:20 [21]When he tore[r] Israel away from the house of David, they made Jeroboam son of Nebat their king.[s]
Jeroboam enticed Israel away from following the LORD and caused them to commit a great sin. [22]The Is-
raelites persisted in all the sins of Jeroboam and did not turn away from them [23]until the LORD removed
them from his presence, as he had warned through all his servants the prophets. So the people of Israel
were taken from their homeland into exile in Assyria, and they are still there.

Samaria Resettled

17:24 [t]Ezr 4:2,10 [u]2Ki 18:34 [24]The king of Assyria[t] brought people from Babylon, Cuthah, Avva, Hamath and Sepharvaim[u] and
settled them in the towns of Samaria to replace the Israelites. They took over Samaria and lived in its
17:25 [v]Ge 37:20 towns. [25]When they first lived there, they did not worship the LORD; so he sent lions[v] among them and
they killed some of the people. [26]It was reported to the king of Assyria: "The people you deported and re-
settled in the towns of Samaria do not know what the god of that country requires. He has sent lions
among them, which are killing them off, because the people do not know what he requires."
[27]Then the king of Assyria gave this order: "Have one of the priests you took captive from Samaria go
back to live there and teach the people what the god of the land requires." [28]So one of the priests who
had been exiled from Samaria came to live in Bethel and taught them how to worship the LORD.
17:29 [w]Jer 2:28 [x]1Ki 12:31 [y]Mic 4:5 [29]Nevertheless, each national group made its own gods in the several towns[w] where they settled, and
set them up in the shrines[x] the people of Samaria had made at the high places.[y] [30]The men from Bab-
ylon made Succoth Benoth, the men from Cuthah made Nergal, and the men from Hamath made Ashi-
ma; [31]the Avvites made Nibhaz and Tartak, and the Sepharvites burned their children in the fire as sac-
17:31 [z]2Ki 19:37 [a]ver 24 rifices to Adrammelech[z] and Anammelech, the gods of Sepharvaim.[a] [32]They worshiped the LORD, but
17:32 [b]1Ki 12:31 they also appointed all sorts[b] of their own people to officiate for them as priests in the shrines at the
high places. [33]They worshiped the LORD, but they also served their own gods in accordance with the cus-
toms of the nations from which they had been brought.
[34]To this day they persist in their former practices. They neither worship the LORD nor adhere to the
decrees and ordinances, the laws and commands that the LORD gave the descendants of Jacob, whom he
17:34 [c]Ge 32:28; 35:10; 1Ki 18:31 named Israel.[c] [35]When the LORD made a covenant with the Israelites, he commanded them: "Do not wor-
17:35 [d]Ex 20:5; Jdg 6:10 ship[d] any other gods or bow down to them, serve them or sacrifice to them. [36]But the LORD, who brought
17:36 [e]Ex 3:20; 6:6; Ps 136:12 you up out of Egypt with mighty power and outstretched arm,[e] is the one you must worship. To him you
17:37 [f]Dt 5:32 shall bow down and to him offer sacrifices. [37]You must always be careful[f] to keep the decrees and ordi-
17:38 [g]Dt 4:23; 6:12 nances, the laws and commands he wrote for you. Do not worship other gods. [38]Do not forget[g] the cov-
enant I have made with you, and do not worship other gods. [39]Rather, worship the LORD your God; it is
he who will deliver you from the hand of all your enemies."
[40]They would not listen, however, but persisted in their former practices. [41]Even while these people
17:41 [h]ver 32-33; 1Ki 18:21; Mt 6:24 were worshiping the LORD,[h] they were serving their idols. To this day their children and grandchildren
continue to do as their fathers did.

[a] 17 Or *They made their sons and daughters pass through*

17:24–41 In accordance with the deportation system used so successfully by Tiglath-Pileser III and followed by his successors, a vast transplantation of populaces occurred. Israelites were sent to Assyria, while Babylonians and Arameans were transferred to Israel. One of Israel's exiled priests returned and reinstituted the worship of God at Bethel, the traditional cult center of the northern kingdom. The religion this priest taught, however, was likely the false worship established by Jeroboam I (cf. 1Ki 12:31–32). The result was a mixture of truth combined with the corrupted experience of Israel and the pagan rites brought in by the deportees.

Such confusion continued until the writing of Kings (2Ki 17:34), following the fall of Judah in 586 B.C. Later the Samaritans—a mixed race made up of a combination of Israelites who remained in the land and these non-Israelites settlers—came to follow the teachings of Moses, including monotheism (cf. Jn 4:4–26).

Hezekiah King of Judah

18 In the third year of Hoshea son of Elah king of Israel, Hezekiah[i] son of Ahaz king of Judah be- **18:1** [i]Isa 1:1;
gan to reign. 2 He was twenty-five years old when he became king, and he reigned in Jerusalem 2Ch 28:27
twenty-nine years.[j] His mother's name was Abijah[a] daughter of Zechariah. 3 He did what was right in the **18:2** [j]Isa 38:5
eyes of the LORD, just as his father David[k] had done. 4 He removed[l] the high places, smashed the sacred **18:3** [k]Isa 38:5 **18:4** [l]2Ch 31:1
stones[m] and cut down the Asherah poles. He broke into pieces the bronze snake[n] Moses had made, for [m]Ex 23:24
up to that time the Israelites had been burning incense to it. (It was called[b] Nehushtan.[c]) [n]Nu 21:9
5 Hezekiah trusted[o] in the LORD, the God of Israel. There was no one like him among all the kings of **18:5** [o]2Ki 19:10;
Judah, either before him or after him. 6 He held fast[p] to the LORD and did not cease to follow him; he kept 23:25 **18:6** [p]Dt 10:20;
the commands the LORD had given Moses. 7 And the LORD was with him; he was successful[q] in whatever Jos 23:8 **18:7** [q]Ge 39:3;
he undertook. He rebelled[r] against the king of Assyria and did not serve him. 8 From watchtower to for- 1Sa 18:14 [r]2Ki 16:7
tified city,[s] he defeated the Philistines, as far as Gaza and its territory. **18:8** [s]2Ki 17:9;
9 In King Hezekiah's fourth year,[t] which was the seventh year of Hoshea son of Elah king of Israel, Isa 14:29 **18:9** [t]Isa 1:1
Shalmaneser king of Assyria marched against Samaria and laid siege to it. 10 At the end of three years the
Assyrians took it. So Samaria was captured in Hezekiah's sixth year, which was the ninth year of Hoshea
king of Israel. 11 The king[u] of Assyria deported Israel to Assyria and settled them in Halah, in Gozan on **18:11** [u]Isa 37:12
the Habor River and in towns of the Medes. 12 This happened because they had not obeyed the LORD their
God, but had violated his covenant[v]—all that Moses the servant of the LORD commanded.[w] They neither **18:12** [v]2Ki 17:15
listened to the commands[x] nor carried them out. [w]Da 9:6,10 [x]1Ki 9:6
13 In the fourteenth year of King Hezekiah's reign, Sennacherib king of Assyria attacked all the forti-
fied cities of Judah[y] and captured them. 14 So Hezekiah king of Judah sent this message to the king of As- **18:13** [y]2Ch 32:1;
syria at Lachish: "I have done wrong.[z] Withdraw from me, and I will pay whatever you demand of me." Isa 1:7; Mic 1:9 **18:14** [z]Isa 24:5
The king of Assyria exacted from Hezekiah king of Judah three hundred talents[d] of silver and thirty tal-
ents[e] of gold. 15 So Hezekiah gave[a] him all the silver that was found in the temple of the LORD and in the **18:15** [a]1Ki 15:18;
treasuries of the royal palace. 2Ki 16:8
16 At this time Hezekiah king of Judah stripped off the gold with which he had covered the doors and
doorposts of the temple of the LORD, and gave it to the king of Assyria.

Sennacherib Threatens Jerusalem

17 The king of Assyria sent his supreme commander,[b] his chief officer and his field commander with **18:17** [b]Isa 20:1
a large army, from Lachish to King Hezekiah at Jerusalem. They came up to Jerusalem and stopped at the

[a] *2* Hebrew *Abi,* a variant of *Abijah* [b] *4* Or *He called it* [c] *4 Nehushtan* sounds like the Hebrew for *bronze* and *snake* and *unclean thing.* [d] *14* That is, about 11 tons (about 10 metric tons) [e] *14* That is, about 1 ton (about 1 metric ton)

18:1 Hezekiah of Judah ruled from approximately 715–686 B.C. When he ascended to the throne Samaria had already been destroyed, Judah was severely weakened and Assyria under Sargon II was the dominant power in the region. Egypt would soon be resurgent under the Twenty-fifth Dynasty. Hezekiah energetically dealt with the situation by beginning a series of religious and military reforms. Jerusalem's fortifications were repaired, arms were manufactured and the Siloam Tunnel dug to ensure a water supply for the city (see "Hezekiah's Tunnel" on p. 564). Major crises of his reign included the Sennacherib invasion(s) (18:13—19:8; Isa 36:1—37:8; see "Hezekiah Against the Assyrians" on p. 1118) and Hezekiah's near fatal illness (2Ki 20:1–11). The one significant spiritual failure in his life was his openness to an alliance with the Babylonian Merodach-Baladan, as described in Isaiah 39 (see "Sennacharib's Campaign Against Merodach-Baladin" on p. 1124).

18:4 Just when the bronze snake became an object of worship is not known, but perhaps this had occurred during the reign of Hezekiah's father, Ahaz (see ch. 16). Snake worship of various types was common in the ancient Near East (see "The Serpent Motif in Other Ancient Near Eastern Literature" on p. 8).

18:7 Hezekiah rebelled against Assyria, to which his father, Ahaz, had submitted as a vassal (16:7–9). He likely refused to pay the annual tribute sometime shortly after 705 B.C., when Sennacherib became Assyria's king. Sennacherib, occupied with affairs close to home, was not immediately free to deal with Hezekiah. But he soon swooped down from the north, capturing key territory that would effectively separate Judah from Egyptian help. Sensing impending doom, Hezekiah sent a letter of concession to Sennacherib, but in the end he was delivered from Sennacherib's retribution by trusting God rather than by handing over silver and gold (cf. 18:28–30; 19:32–37; see "Hezekiah Against the Assyrians" on p. 1118).

18:13–14 During the fourteenth year of Hezekiah's reign the Assyrians finally attacked Judah. The Sennacherib Prism (see "The Sennacherib Prism" on p. 659) calls Hezekiah "overbearing and proud," indicating that he was a part of Philistia and Egypt's joint effort to rebel against Assyria.

A battle in the plain of Eltekeh was won by Assyria, and the Egyptian and Cushite charioteers fled. Lachish, a fortress city in southern Judah, was besieged and taken (see "Siege Warfare" on p. 465 and "The Lachish Reliefs" on p. 559). The Assyrian annals note: "As for Hezekiah the Jew, he did not submit to my yoke. I laid siege to 46 of his strong cities, walled forts and to the countless small villages in their vicinity, and conquered them by means of well-stamped earth ramps and battering-rams brought near to the walls combined with the attack by foot-soldiers, using mines, breaches as well as sapper work. I drove out 200,150 people, young and old, male and female, horses, mules, donkeys, camels, big and small cattle beyond counting, and considered them booty. Himself I made a prisoner in Jerusalem, his royal residence, like a bird in a cage."

The Assyrian and Biblical reports of the amount of tribute paid by Hezekiah to Sennacherib agree with respect to the 30 talents of gold, but Sennacherib claimed to have received 800 talents of silver rather than the 300 specified in the Biblical text. This discrepancy may be the result of differences in the weight of Assyrian and Israelite silver talents, or it may simply be due to the Assyrian propensity for exaggeration. Nowhere, however, did the boastful Assyrian king record the disaster mentioned in 19:35–36 and Isaiah 37:36–37.

18:17 [c]2Ki 20:20; 2Ch 32:4,30; Isa 7:3
18:18 [d]2Ki 19:2; Isa 22:20
[e]Isa 22:15

aqueduct of the Upper Pool,[c] on the road to the Washerman's Field. 18They called for the king; and Elia-
kim[d] son of Hilkiah the palace administrator, Shebna[e] the secretary, and Joah son of Asaph the record-
er went out to them.
19The field commander said to them, "Tell Hezekiah:

" 'This is what the great king, the king of Assyria, says: On what are you basing this confidence
of yours? 20You say you have strategy and military strength—but you speak only empty words. On
whom are you depending, that you rebel against me? 21Look now, you are depending on Egypt,[f]

18:21 [f]Isa 20:5; Eze 29:6

ANCIENT TEXTS AND ARTIFACTS

The Lachish Reliefs

2 KINGS 18 In 1850 12 stone slabs were discovered in Sennacherib's palace in Nineveh[1] ("Map 8a"). The **reliefs** on these slabs originally formed a single, continuous work, measuring 8 feet (2.4 m) tall by 80 feet (24.4 m) long, which wrapped around the room. They vividly depict Sennacherib's victory over the fortified Judahite town of Lachish ("Map 4") in 701 B.C. (2Ki 18:13–15).

Assyrian soldiers move up the siege ramp at Lachish
Preserving Bible Times; © Dr. James C. Martin; permission of The British Museum

The "story" begins on the far left, with the **Assyrian** vanguard carrying spears and shielding screens to protect the archers and sling-throwers behind them. The viewer gets the impression of a large body of troops moving in a dense wave over the terrain. Next we see the storming of the citadel, with siege engines climbing ramps to the city gate. The defending Judahites hurl down stones and firebrands, while the Assyrians dowse their battering rams with water.[2] Captives are led out of the first captured tower with three Judahites impaled on stakes. Two more rows of captives (men, women and children) are led out of the defeated city. They are brought before Sennacherib to acknowledge him as their new sovereign before being deported to Assyria.

When these reliefs were originally displayed in the palace room, foreign emissaries and dignitaries awaiting an audience with the king would have been impressed not only by the magnitude of the artwork itself but also by the magnificent strength of the Assyrian war machine. Having viewed the fate of Lachish, visitors from other vassal states would presumably have been reluctant themselves to rebel.

For more on Sennacherib, see "The Death of Sennacherib" on page 562, "The Sennacherib Prism" on page 659 and "Sennacherib's Campaign Against Merodach-Baladan" on page 1124. For information on Lachish during Nebuchadnezzar's attack, see "The Lachish Ostraca" on page 1252.

[1]See "Nineveh" on page 1497. [2]See "Siege Warfare" on page 465.

Impaled Judahites at Lachish
Preserving Bible Times; © Dr. James C. Martin; permission of The British Museum

that splintered reed of a staff,[g] which pierces a man's hand and wounds him if he leans on it! Such 18:21 [g]Isa 30:5,7
is Pharaoh king of Egypt to all who depend on him. 22 And if you say to me, "We are depending on
the LORD our God"—isn't he the one whose high places and altars Hezekiah removed, saying to
Judah and Jerusalem, "You must worship before this altar in Jerusalem"?
23 " 'Come now, make a bargain with my master, the king of Assyria: I will give you two thou-
sand horses—if you can put riders on them! 24 How can you repulse one officer[h] of the least of my 18:24 [h]Isa 10:8
master's officials, even though you are depending on Egypt for chariots and horsemen[a]? 25 Fur-
thermore, have I come to attack and destroy this place without word from the LORD?[i] The LORD 18:25 [i]2Ki 19:6, 22
himself told me to march against this country and destroy it.' "

26 Then Eliakim son of Hilkiah, and Shebna and Joah said to the field commander, "Please speak to
your servants in Aramaic,[j] since we understand it. Don't speak to us in Hebrew in the hearing of the peo- 18:26 [j]Ezr 4:7
ple on the wall."
27 But the commander replied, "Was it only to your master and you that my master sent me to say
these things, and not to the men sitting on the wall—who, like you, will have to eat their own filth and
drink their own urine?"
28 Then the commander stood and called out in Hebrew: "Hear the word of the great king, the king of
Assyria! 29 This is what the king says: Do not let Hezekiah deceive[k] you. He cannot deliver you from my 18:29 [k]2Ki 19:10
hand. 30 Do not let Hezekiah persuade you to trust in the LORD when he says, 'The LORD will surely deliv-
er us; this city will not be given into the hand of the king of Assyria.'
31 "Do not listen to Hezekiah. This is what the king of Assyria says: Make peace with me and come out
to me. Then every one of you will eat from his own vine and fig tree[l] and drink water from his own cis- 18:31 [l]Nu 13:23; 1Ki 4:25
tern,[m] 32 until I come and take you to a land like your own, a land of grain and new wine, a land of bread [m]Jer 14:3; La 4:4
and vineyards, a land of olive trees and honey. Choose life[n] and not death! 18:32 [n]Dt 8:7-9; 30:19
"Do not listen to Hezekiah, for he is misleading you when he says, 'The LORD will deliver us.' 33 Has the
god[o] of any nation ever delivered his land from the hand of the king of Assyria? 34 Where are the gods of 18:33 [o]2Ki 19:12; Isa 10:10-11
Hamath[p] and Arpad?[q] Where are the gods of Sepharvaim, Hena and Ivvah? Have they rescued Samaria 18:34 [p]2Ki 17:24; 19:13 [q]Isa 10:9
from my hand? 35 Who of all the gods of these countries has been able to save his land from me? How
then can the LORD deliver Jerusalem from my hand?"[r] 18:35 [r]Ps 2:1-2
36 But the people remained silent and said nothing in reply, because the king had commanded, "Do not
answer him."
37 Then Eliakim son of Hilkiah the palace administrator, Shebna the secretary and Joah son of Asaph
the recorder went to Hezekiah, with their clothes torn,[s] and told him what the field commander had said. 18:37 [s]2Ki 6:30

Jerusalem's Deliverance Foretold

19 When King Hezekiah heard this, he tore[t] his clothes and put on sackcloth and went into the 19:1 [t]Ge 37:34; 1Ki 21:27; 2Ch 32:20-22
temple of the LORD. 2 He sent Eliakim the palace administrator, Shebna the secretary and the
leading priests, all wearing sackcloth, to the prophet Isaiah[u] son of Amoz. 3 They told him, "This is what 19:2 [u]Isa 1:1
Hezekiah says: This day is a day of distress and rebuke and disgrace, as when children come to the point
of birth and there is no strength to deliver them. 4 It may be that the LORD your God will hear all the
words of the field commander, whom his master, the king of Assyria, has sent to ridicule[v] the living 19:4 [v]2Ki 18:35
God, and that he will rebuke[w] him for the words the LORD your God has heard. Therefore pray for the [w]2Sa 16:12
remnant that still survives."
5 When King Hezekiah's officials came to Isaiah, 6 Isaiah said to them, "Tell your master, 'This is what
the LORD says: Do not be afraid of what you have heard—those words with which the underlings of
the king of Assyria have blasphemed[x] me. 7 Listen! I am going to put such a spirit in him that when he 19:6 [x]2Ki 18:25
hears a certain report, he will return to his own country, and there I will have him cut down with the
sword.[y]' " 19:7 [y]ver 37

[a] 24 Or *charioteers*

18:26 Aramaic had become the international language of the Near East, known and used by those experienced in diplomacy and commerce. It is surprising that the Assyrian officials were able to speak the Hebrew dialect of the common people of Judah. The Assyrian strategy was to negotiate in the hearing of the people in order to demoralize them and turn them against Hezekiah.

19:1–2 See the note on sackcloth at Job 16:15. See also "Sackcloth and Ashes: Rituals of Lamentation" on page 820.

19:4 Archaeological evidence reveals that many Israelites fled the northern kingdom during the Assyrian assaults and settled in Judah. As such, the nation of Judah was already then becoming the "remnant" of all Israel.

19:8 [z]2Ki 18:14 [8]When the field commander heard that the king of Assyria had left Lachish,[z] he withdrew and found
the king fighting against Libnah.
[9]Now Sennacherib received a report that Tirhakah, the Cushite[a] king ⌊of Egypt⌋, was marching out to
fight against him. So he again sent messengers to Hezekiah with this word: [10]"Say to Hezekiah king of Ju-
19:10 [a]2Ki 18:5 dah: Do not let the god you depend[a] on deceive[b] you when he says, 'Jerusalem will not be handed over
[b]2Ki 18:29 to the king of Assyria.' [11]Surely you have heard what the kings of Assyria have done to all the countries,
destroying them completely. And will you be delivered? [12]Did the gods of the nations that were destroyed
19:12 [c]2Ki 18:33 by my forefathers deliver[c] them: the gods of Gozan,[d] Haran,[e] Rezeph and the people of Eden who were
[d]2Ki 17:6 [e]Ge 11:31 in Tel Assar? [13]Where is the king of Hamath, the king of Arpad, the king of the city of Sepharvaim, or of
19:13 [f]2Ki 18:34 Hena or Ivvah?"[f]

Hezekiah's Prayer

[14]Hezekiah received the letter from the messengers and read it. Then he went up to the temple of the
LORD and spread it out before the LORD. [15]And Hezekiah prayed to the LORD: "O LORD, God of Israel, en-
19:15 [g]Ex 25:22 throned between the cherubim,[g] you alone are God over all the kingdoms of the earth. You have made
19:16 [h]Ps 31:2 heaven and earth. [16]Give ear,[h] O LORD, and hear;[i] open your eyes,[j] O LORD, and see; listen to the words Sen-
[i]1Ki 8:29 [j]ver 4; 2Ch 6:40 nacherib has sent to insult the living God.
[17]"It is true, O LORD, that the Assyrian kings have laid waste these nations and their lands. [18]They have
19:18 [k]Isa 44:9-11; Jer 10:3-10 thrown their gods into the fire and destroyed them, for they were not gods[k] but only wood and stone, fash-
[l]Ps 115:4; Ac 17:29 ioned by men's hands.[l] [19]Now, O LORD our God, deliver us from his hand, so that all kingdoms[m] on earth
19:19 [m]1Ki 8:43 [n]Ps 83:18 may know[n] that you alone, O LORD, are God."

Isaiah Prophesies Sennacherib's Fall

[20]Then Isaiah son of Amoz sent a message to Hezekiah: "This is what the LORD, the God of Israel, says:
19:20 [o]2Ki 20:5 I have heard[o] your prayer concerning Sennacherib king of Assyria. [21]This is the word that the LORD has
spoken against him:

19:21 [p]Jer 14:17; La 2:13 [q]Ps 22:7-8 [r]Job 16:4; Ps 109:25
" 'The Virgin Daughter[p] of Zion
despises you and mocks[q] you.
The Daughter of Jerusalem
tosses her head[r] as you flee.
[22]Who is it you have insulted and blasphemed?
Against whom have you raised your voice
and lifted your eyes in pride?
19:22 [s]Ps 71:22; Isa 5:24 Against the Holy One[s] of Israel!
[23]By your messengers
you have heaped insults on the Lord.
19:23 [t]Isa 10:18 [u]Ps 20:7 And you have said,[t]
"With my many chariots[u]
I have ascended the heights of the mountains,
the utmost heights of Lebanon.
I have cut down its tallest cedars,
the choicest of its pines.
I have reached its remotest parts,
the finest of its forests.
[24]I have dug wells in foreign lands
and drunk the water there.
With the soles of my feet
I have dried up all the streams of Egypt."

[a] 9 That is, from the upper Nile region

19:8 Libnah appears to have been located close to the Philistine border near Lachish.

19:9 In 701 B.C. Tirhakah (also called Tarhaqa) was actually a prince (the brother of the new pharaoh Shebitku, who sent him with an army to help Hezekiah withstand the Assyrian invasion). He did not become king until 690 B.C. See "Cush" on page 1519.

19:12 Gozan was an Assyrian provincial capital located on a tributary of the Euphrates River.

25 " 'Have you not heard?[v]
Long ago I ordained it.
In days of old I planned[w] it;
now I have brought it to pass,
that you have turned fortified cities
into piles of stone.[x]
26 Their people, drained of power,
are dismayed[y] and put to shame.

19:25 [v]Isa 40:21, 28 [w]Isa 10:5; 45:7 [x]Mic 1:6

19:26 [y]Ps 6:10

The Death of Sennacherib

2 KINGS 19 In 2 Kings 19:5–7 the prophet Isaiah foretold that the Lord would deliver Jerusalem from the hand of the **Assyrian** king Sennacherib (r. 704–681 B.C.), who was besieging the Judahite capital. Isaiah stated that Sennacherib would return to his own land after having heard a particular report and that there the Lord would "have him cut down with the sword" (v. 7). This prophecy was fulfilled in verses 35–37. After God had struck the Assyrian camp with a plague, Sennacherib withdrew to Assyria.[1] The "report" Sennacherib heard was that Tirhakah of Egypt was marching out against him. With 185,000 of his soldiers felled by the plague, Sennacherib's forces were so significantly depleted that he was compelled to pull back rather than face this powerful Egyptian enemy. The Biblical record informs us that, once back in Assyria, Sennacherib was killed by his sons Adrammelech and Sharezer while he was worshiping in the temple of Nisroch (v. 37). These two men escaped to Ararat, and another son, Esarhaddon, became king.

Although the identity of Sharezer is unknown from extrabiblical material, we do know of a son of Sennacherib named Arda-Mulishi. A **Neo-Babylonian** letter describes an event just prior to Sennacherib's assassination. In this account several Babylonian men hear of a conspiracy to kill Sennacherib, and one of them seeks an audience with the king to warn him. Rather than taking him to the king, however, two Assyrian officials blindfold the man and lead him before the king's son, Arda-Mulishi (also called "Arda-Ninlil"; Ninlil and Mulishi are two names for the same deity). Thinking that he is standing before Sennacherib, the man shouts that Sennacherib's son, Arda-Mulishi, is plotting to kill him. Arda-Mulishi orders that he, along with other Babylonians who know of the plot, be put to death.

Account of Sennacherib's campaigns and the rebuilding of Nineveh

Preserving Bible Times; © Dr. James C. Martin; permission of The British Museum

Assyriologists have reconstructed the events surrounding Sennacherib's murder. His oldest son had been taken captive to Elam in 694 B.C., and Arda-Mulishi, probably the next oldest, expected to succeed his father. Sennacherib, however, chose Esarhaddon over his older brothers to be the crown prince. While Esarhaddon was away from the capital, Arda-Mulishi murdered his father, probably hoping to take the throne by force. Esarhaddon returned to Nineveh[2] ("Map 8a") to contest Arda-Mulishi's claim. Many of Arda-Mulishi's soldiers and allies sided with Esarhaddon, and Arda-Mulishi fled.

The Biblical Adrammelech was most likely Arda-Mulishi. That Sennacherib's murder occurred 20 years after the siege of Jerusalem should not trouble us. Scripture does not state that Sennacherib would die *immediately* upon his return to Assyria. In fact, verse 37 begins with the words "one day," suggesting that time had passed between the previous verses and what was about to be reported. The author was simply telescoping the events in order to demonstrate that the word of the Lord in verse 7 had indeed been fulfilled.

[1]See "Assyria From the Neo-Assyrian Period Forward" on page 1502. [2]See "Nineveh" on page 1497.

They are like plants in the field,
19:26 zIsa 4:2 like tender green shoots,[z]
aPs 129:6 like grass sprouting on the roof,
scorched[a] before it grows up.

19:27 [27] " 'But I know[b] where you stay
bPs 139:1-4 and when you come and go
and how you rage against me.
[28] Because you rage against me
and your insolence has reached my ears,
19:28 cEze 19:9; I will put my hook[c] in your nose
29:4 dIsa 30:28 and my bit[d] in your mouth,
eVer 33 and I will make you return[e]
by the way you came.'

19:29 f2Ki 20:8-9; Lk 2:12 [29] "This will be the sign[f] for you, O Hezekiah:

gLev 25:5 "This year you will eat what grows by itself,[g]
hPs 107:37 and the second year what springs from that.
But in the third year sow and reap,
plant vineyards[h] and eat their fruit.
[30] Once more a remnant of the house of Judah
19:30 will take root[i] below and bear fruit above.
i2Ch 32:22-23 [31] For out of Jerusalem will come a remnant,
and out of Mount Zion a band of survivors.

19:31 jIsa 9:7 The zeal[j] of the LORD Almighty will accomplish this.

[32] "Therefore this is what the LORD says concerning the king of Assyria:

"He will not enter this city
or shoot an arrow here.
He will not come before it with shield
or build a siege ramp against it.
19:33 kver 28 [33] By the way that he came he will return;[k]
he will not enter this city,

declares the LORD.

19:34 l2Ki 20:6 [34] I will defend[l] this city and save it,
m1Ki 11:12-13 for my sake and for the sake of David[m] my servant."

19:35 nEx 12:23 [35] That night the angel of the LORD[n] went out and put to death a hundred and eighty-five thousand
oJob 24:24 men in the Assyrian camp. When the people got up the next morning—there were all the dead bodies![o]
19:36 pGe 10:11; [36] So Sennacherib king of Assyria broke camp and withdrew. He returned to Nineveh[p] and stayed there.
Jnh 1:2 [37] One day, while he was worshiping in the temple of his god Nisroch, his sons Adrammelech and Sha-
19:37 qver 7 rezer cut him down with the sword,[q] and they escaped to the land of Ararat.[r] And Esarhaddon[s] his son
rGe 8:4 sEzr 4:2 succeeded him as king.

Hezekiah's Illness

20 In those days Hezekiah became ill and was at the point of death. The prophet Isaiah son of Amoz
went to him and said, "This is what the LORD says: Put your house in order, because you are go-
ing to die; you will not recover."
20:3 tNe 13:22 [2] Hezekiah turned his face to the wall and prayed to the LORD, [3] "Remember,[t] O LORD, how I have walked
u2Ki 18:3-6 before you faithfully[u] and with wholehearted devotion and have done what is good in your eyes." And
Hezekiah wept bitterly.
[4] Before Isaiah had left the middle court, the word of the LORD came to him: [5] "Go back and tell Hezekiah,

---

19:28 The Assyrians often led captives away with a rope fastened to a hook that pierced the nose or lower lip. At the top of an Assyrian obelisk an Assyrian king (probably Esarhaddon, 681–669 B.C.) is depicted holding ropes attached to rings in the noses of four of his enemies.
19:37 See "The Death of Sennacherib" on page 562.

the leader of my people, 'This is what the LORD, the God of your father David, says: I have heard[v] your
prayer and seen your tears;[w] I will heal you. On the third day from now you will go up to the temple of
the LORD. 6 I will add fifteen years to your life. And I will deliver you and this city from the hand of the king
of Assyria. I will defend[x] this city for my sake and for the sake of my servant David.' "
7 Then Isaiah said, "Prepare a poultice of figs." They did so and applied it to the boil,[y] and he recovered.
8 Hezekiah had asked Isaiah, "What will be the sign that the LORD will heal me and that I will go up to
the temple of the LORD on the third day from now?"
9 Isaiah answered, "This is the LORD's sign[z] to you that the LORD will do what he has promised: Shall
the shadow go forward ten steps, or shall it go back ten steps?"
10 "It is a simple matter for the shadow to go forward ten steps," said Hezekiah. "Rather, have it go back
ten steps."
11 Then the prophet Isaiah called upon the LORD, and the LORD made the shadow go back[a] the ten steps
it had gone down on the stairway of Ahaz.

20:5 [v]1Sa 9:16; 1Ki 9:3; 2Ki 19:20 [w]Ps 39:12; 56:8
20:6 [x]2Ki 19:34
20:7 [y]Isa 38:21
20:9 [z]Dt 13:2; Jer 44:29
20:11 [a]Jos 10:13

Envoys From Babylon

12 At that time Merodach-Baladan son of Baladan king of Babylon sent Hezekiah letters and a gift, be-
cause he had heard of Hezekiah's illness. 13 Hezekiah received the messengers and showed them all that

---

20:12 The stated purpose for Merodach-Baladan's embassy to Hezekiah was delivery of a congratulatory message and gift. But the Babylonian king's motives were political; he hoped to find in Hezekiah a new ally in his struggles against Assyria. Hezekiah received the messengers warmly and, to impress his guests, showed them all the vast treasures of the kingdom. The presence of these riches indicates that this event took place before Hezekiah's payment of tribute to Sennacherib in 701 B.C. (18:13–16).

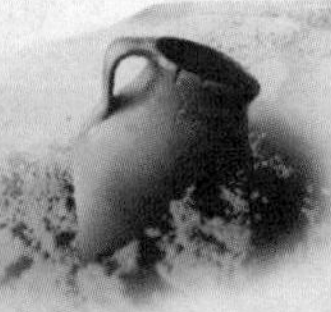

ARCHAEOLOGICAL SITES

HEZEKIAH'S TUNNEL

2 KINGS 20 One of King Hezekiah's major accomplishments was the construction of the tunnel, or conduit, that still bears his name (2Ki 20:20). He was able to ensure a steady supply of water into Jerusalem through this tunnel when the city was under siege by the **Assyrian** ruler Sennacherib in approximately 701 B.C., thus saving the city from almost certain destruction.[1] Water was redirected into Jerusalem from the Gihon spring through this underground tunnel, cut through solid rock for 1,750 feet (533 m). The tunnel followed a winding route, starting most likely at the point of a natural fissure. The pool at the end of the tunnel was located strategically inside the city wall.[2]

Siloam inscription in Hezekiah's tunnel

Photograph: © Todd Bolen/Bible Places.com

Edward Robinson was the first to explore the tunnel in modern times (1837). Much later, in 1880, children discovered the famous Siloam Inscription carved in the wall of the tunnel about 20 feet (6 m) from the Siloam end. The inscription commemorates the dramatic moment when the two original teams of tunnelers, digging with picks from opposite ends of the tunnel, met each other. One of the most important ancient Hebrew inscriptions ever discovered, it now resides in the Istanbul Archaeological Museum. Hezekiah's Tunnel, which today still brings water into Jerusalem, was a remarkable achievement in ancient engineering that also, with its inscription, provides an important link to Biblical history.

[1]See "The Sennacherib Prism" on page 659 and "Hezekiah Against the Assyrians" on page 1118. [2]See "The Pool of Siloam" on page 1739.

was in his storehouses—the silver, the gold, the spices and the fine oil—his armory and everything found among his treasures. There was nothing in his palace or in all his kingdom that Hezekiah did not show them.

[14]Then Isaiah the prophet went to King Hezekiah and asked, "What did those men say, and where did they come from?"

"From a distant land," Hezekiah replied. "They came from Babylon."

[15]The prophet asked, "What did they see in your palace?"

"They saw everything in my palace," Hezekiah said. "There is nothing among my treasures that I did not show them."

[16]Then Isaiah said to Hezekiah, "Hear the word of the LORD: [17]The time will surely come when ev-
erything in your palace, and all that your fathers have stored up until this day, will be carried off to Bab-
ylon.[b] Nothing will be left, says the LORD. [18]And some of your descendants,[c] your own flesh and blood,
that will be born to you, will be taken away, and they will become eunuchs in the palace of the king of
Babylon."

[19]"The word of the LORD you have spoken is good," Hezekiah replied. For he thought, "Will there not be peace and security in my lifetime?"

[20]As for the other events of Hezekiah's reign, all his achievements and how he made the pool[d] and the
tunnel by which he brought water into the city, are they not written in the book of the annals of the kings
of Judah? [21]Hezekiah rested with his fathers. And Manasseh his son succeeded him as king.

20:17 [b]2Ki 24:13; 25:13; 2Ch 36:10; Jer 27:22; 52:17-23
20:18 [c]2Ki 24:15; 2Ch 33:11; Da 1:3
20:20 [d]Ne 3:16

20:20 See "Hezekiah's Tunnel" on page 564.

ANCIENT TEXTS AND ARTIFACTS

The Seal of Manasseh

2 KINGS 21 Manasseh became king when he was 12 years old and ruled for 55 years (2Ki 21:1; c. 697–642 B.C.), during which time Judah was subject to **Assyria**.[1] His reign, the longest of any king of Judah or Israel, was marred by idolatry, child sacrifice and witchcraft. The Chronicler revealed that God punished Manasseh by allowing the Assyrians to imprison him in **Babylon**.[2] When he repented, Manasseh was released and permitted to return to Jerusalem, after which he initiated a building program and religious reforms (see 2Ch 33:11–17).

Manasseh's name has been found in three contemporary documents: a seal and two Assyrian inscriptions. The seal, purchased from an antiquities dealer in Jerusalem in 1974, reads, "Belonging to Manasseh Son of the King." Manasseh was probably coregent with his father Hezekiah for about ten years, and this was most likely the seal he used during that time.

Inscription describing the conquests of Ashurbanipal
Preserving Bible Times; © Dr. James C. Martin; permission of The British Museum

Because of his unusually long tenure as king, Manasseh was on the throne during the reigns of two of the strongest kings of Assyria,[3] Esarhaddon (680–669 B.C.) and Ashurbanipal (668–627 B.C.). No record has been found of Manasseh's imprisonment, but both kings mention him in their records. Manasseh was among 22 kings who, "under terrible difficulties," were obliged to transport building materials to Nineveh[4] ("Map 8a") for Esarhaddon's palace. His name also appears in a list of kings conscripted by Ashurbanipal in 667 B.C. to help repress an Egyptian revolt.

[1]See "The History of the Southern Kingdom" on page 538. [2]See "Babylon" on page 1077. [3]See "Assyria From the Neo-Assyrian Period Forward" on page 1502. [4]See "Nineveh" on page 1497.

Manasseh King of Judah

21 Manasseh was twelve years old when he became king, and he reigned in Jerusalem fifty-five
years. His mother's name was Hephzibah.[e] 2 He did evil[f] in the eyes of the LORD, following the
detestable practices[g] of the nations the LORD had driven out before the Israelites. 3 He rebuilt the high
places[h] his father Hezekiah had destroyed; he also erected altars to Baal[i] and made an Asherah pole, as
Ahab king of Israel had done. He bowed down to all the starry hosts[j] and worshiped them. 4 He built al-
tars[k] in the temple of the LORD, of which the LORD had said, "In Jerusalem I will put my Name."[l] 5 In both
courts[m] of the temple of the LORD, he built altars to all the starry hosts. 6 He sacrificed his own son[n] in[a]
the fire, practiced sorcery and divination, and consulted mediums and spiritists.[o] He did much evil in
the eyes of the LORD, provoking him to anger.

7 He took the carved Asherah pole[p] he had made and put it in the temple, of which the LORD had said
to David and to his son Solomon, "In this temple and in Jerusalem, which I have chosen out of all the
tribes of Israel, I will put my Name[q] forever. 8 I will not again[r] make the feet of the Israelites wander
from the land I gave their forefathers, if only they will be careful to do everything I commanded them
and will keep the whole Law that my servant Moses[s] gave them." 9 But the people did not listen. Manas-
seh led them astray, so that they did more evil[t] than the nations[u] the LORD had destroyed before the
Israelites.

10 The LORD said through his servants the prophets: 11 "Manasseh king of Judah has committed these
detestable sins. He has done more evil[v] than the Amorites[w] who preceded him and has led Judah into sin
with his idols. 12 Therefore this is what the LORD, the God of Israel, says: I am going to bring such disas-
ter[x] on Jerusalem and Judah that the ears of everyone who hears of it will tingle.[y] 13 I will stretch out over
Jerusalem the measuring line used against Samaria and the plumb line[z] used against the house of Ahab.
I will wipe[a] out Jerusalem as one wipes a dish, wiping it and turning it upside down. 14 I will forsake[b] the
remnant[c] of my inheritance and hand them over to their enemies. They will be looted and plundered by
all their foes, 15 because they have done evil[d] in my eyes and have provoked[e] me to anger from the day
their forefathers came out of Egypt until this day."

16 Moreover, Manasseh also shed so much innocent blood[f] that he filled Jerusalem from end to end—
besides the sin that he had caused Judah to commit, so that they did evil in the eyes of the LORD.

17 As for the other events of Manasseh's reign, and all he did, including the sin he committed, are they
not written in the book of the annals of the kings of Judah? 18 Manasseh rested with his fathers and was
buried in his palace garden,[g] the garden of Uzza. And Amon his son succeeded him as king.

Amon King of Judah

19 Amon was twenty-two years old when he became king, and he reigned in Jerusalem two years. His
mother's name was Meshullemeth daughter of Haruz; she was from Jotbah. 20 He did evil[h] in the eyes of
the LORD, as his father Manasseh had done. 21 He walked in all the ways of his father; he worshiped the
idols his father had worshiped, and bowed down to them. 22 He forsook the LORD, the God of his fathers,
and did not walk[i] in the way of the LORD.

23 Amon's officials conspired against him and assassinated[j] the king in his palace. 24 Then the people
of the land killed[k] all who had plotted against King Amon, and they made Josiah his son king in his place.

25 As for the other events of Amon's reign, and what he did, are they not written in the book of the an-
nals of the kings of Judah? 26 He was buried in his grave in the garden[l] of Uzza. And Josiah his son suc-
ceeded him as king.

The Book of the Law Found

22 Josiah was eight years old when he became king, and he reigned in Jerusalem thirty-one years.
His mother's name was Jedidah daughter of Adaiah; she was from Bozkath.[m] 2 He did what was
right[n] in the eyes of the LORD and walked in all the ways of his father David, not turning aside to the
right[o] or to the left.

21:1 [e]Isa 62:4
21:2 [f]Jer 15:4 [g]2Ki 16:3
21:3 [h]2Ki 18:4 [i]Jdg 6:28; 1Ki 16:32 [j]Dt 17:3; 2Ki 17:16
21:4 [k]Jer 32:34 [l]2Sa 7:13; 1Ki 8:29
21:5 [m]1Ki 7:12; 2Ki 23:12
21:6 [n]Lev 18:21; Dt 18:10; 2Ki 16:3; 17:17 [o]Lev 19:31
21:7 [p]Dt 16:21; 2Ki 23:4 [q]2Sa 7:13; 1Ki 8:29; 9:3; 2Ki 23:27; Jer 32:34
21:8 [r]2Sa 7:10 [s]2Ki 18:12
21:9 [t]Pr 29:12 [u]Dt 9:4
21:11 [v]2Ki 24:3-4 [w]Ge 15:16; 1Ki 21:26
21:12 [x]2Ki 23:26; 24:3; Jer 15:4 [y]1Sa 3:11; Jer 19:3
21:13 [z]Isa 34:11; La 2:8; Am 7:7-9 [a]2Ki 23:27
21:14 [b]Ps 78:58-60 [c]2Ki 19:4; Mic 2:12
21:15 [d]Ex 32:22 [e]Jer 25:7
21:16 [f]2Ki 24:4
21:18 [g]ver 26
21:20 [h]ver 2-6
21:22 [i]1Ki 11:33
21:23 [j]2Ki 12:20; 2Ch 33:24-25
21:24 [k]2Ki 14:5
21:26 [l]ver 18
22:1 [m]Jos 15:39
22:2 [n]Dt 17:19 [o]Dt 5:32

[a] 6 Or *He made his own son pass through*

21:16 Manasseh's shedding of "innocent blood" refers not only to human sacrifice but probably also to the martyrdom of God's prophets. Josephus affirmed that Manasseh not only murdered all the righteous men of Judah but killed prophets daily until Jerusalem "was overflowing with blood." Uniform Jewish and Christian tradition holds that Manasseh arranged to have Isaiah sawed in two (cf. Heb 11:37).

3 In the eighteenth year of his reign, King Josiah sent the secretary, Shaphan[p] son of Azaliah, the son
of Meshullam, to the temple of the LORD. He said: 4 "Go up to Hilkiah the high priest and have him get
ready the money that has been brought into the temple of the LORD, which the doorkeepers have collect-
ed[q] from the people. 5 Have them entrust it to the men appointed to supervise the work on the temple.
And have these men pay the workers who repair[r] the temple of the LORD— 6 the carpenters, the build-
ers and the masons. Also have them purchase timber and dressed stone to repair the temple.[s] 7 But they
need not account for the money entrusted to them, because they are acting faithfully."[t]
8 Hilkiah the high priest said to Shaphan the secretary, "I have found the Book of the Law[u] in the tem-
ple of the LORD." He gave it to Shaphan, who read it. 9 Then Shaphan the secretary went to the king and
reported to him: "Your officials have paid out the money that was in the temple of the LORD and have en-
trusted it to the workers and supervisors at the temple." 10 Then Shaphan the secretary informed the king,
"Hilkiah the priest has given me a book." And Shaphan read from it in the presence of the king.[v]
11 When the king heard the words of the Book of the Law, he tore his robes. 12 He gave these orders to
Hilkiah the priest, Ahikam[w] son of Shaphan, Acbor son of Micaiah, Shaphan the secretary and Asaiah the
king's attendant: 13 "Go and inquire of the LORD for me and for the people and for all Judah about what is
written in this book that has been found. Great is the LORD's anger[x] that burns against us because our fa-
thers have not obeyed the words of this book; they have not acted in accordance with all that is written
there concerning us."
14 Hilkiah the priest, Ahikam, Acbor, Shaphan and Asaiah went to speak to the prophetess Huldah,
who was the wife of Shallum son of Tikvah, the son of Harhas, keeper of the wardrobe. She lived in Je-
rusalem, in the Second District.
15 She said to them, "This is what the LORD, the God of Israel, says: Tell the man who sent you to me,
16 'This is what the LORD says: I am going to bring disaster[y] on this place and its people, according to ev-
erything written in the book[z] the king of Judah has read. 17 Because they have forsaken[a] me and burned

22:3 [p]2Ch 34:20; Jer 39:14
22:4 [q]2Ki 12:4-5
22:5 [r]2Ki 12:5, 11-14
22:6 [s]2Ki 12:11-12
22:7 [t]2Ki 12:15
22:8 [u]Dt 31:24
22:10 [v]Jer 36:21
22:12 [w]2Ki 25:22; Jer 26:24
22:13 [x]Dt 29:24-28; 31:17
22:16 [y]Dt 31:29; Jos 23:15 [z]Dt 29:27; Da 9:11
22:17 [a]Dt 29:25-27

22:8 The Book of the Law, also called the Book of the Covenant (23:2), was probably either the entire Pentateuch or all or part of the book of Deuteronomy.
22:14 Why the delegation sought out Huldah rather than Jeremiah or Zephaniah is not known. Perhaps it was merely a matter of her accessibility in Jerusalem. (See "The Huldah Delegation and Nathan-Melech, the Official" on p. 567.)
See also the note on prophetesses at Exodus 15:20–21.

ANCIENT TEXTS AND ARTIFACTS

The Huldah Delegation and Nathan-Melech, the Official

2 KINGS 22 The discovery of the Book of the Law caused great consternation on the part of King Josiah,[1] who sent a delegation of five officials to Huldah the prophetess to "inquire of the LORD" (2Ki 22:13): Hilkiah, Ahikam, Acbor, Shaphan and Asaiah. The names of four of the delegation members have been found on four seals and three **bullae** discovered in Israel:

✣ Hilkiah was the high priest who discovered the scroll of the law (v. 8). His name appears on a seal and a **bulla** of his son Azariah, who was also a priest and the grandfather of Ezra (1Ch 6:13–14; 9:11; Ezr 7:1). Hilkiah's name also appears on a seal of another son named Hanan.

✣ Another bulla reads "Ahikam son of Shaphan," as in 2 Kings 22:12. No doubt Ahikam was a scribe like his father, who read the scroll of the law to Josiah (v. 10). It was Ahikam who later saved Jeremiah from death at the hands of the priests, prophets and people following the prophet's temple sermon (Jer 26:24). The **Babylonian** king **Nebuchadnezzar** appointed Ahikam's son Gedaliah[2] governor of Judah after the fall of Jerusalem (2Ki 25:22). Fingerprints visible on the edge of the bulla are almost certainly those of Ahikam himself.

✣ Shaphan's name also appears on a bulla of a son named Gemariah.[3] A seal of Shaphan's father bears the inscription "Azaliah son of Meshullam" (22:3).

✣ Another official in Josiah's court was Nathan-Melech (23:11). A bulla with the inscription "Belonging to Nathan-Melech, Servant of the King," is probably that of Nathan-Melech.

[1]See "The Tragic Reign of Josiah" on page 569. [2]See "Gedaliah, Governor of Judah, and Baalis, King of Ammon" on page 1261. [3]See "Gemariah, the Official, and Jerahmeel, the King's Son" on page 1255.

incense to other gods and provoked me to anger by all the idols their hands have made,[a] my anger will
burn against this place and will not be quenched.' 18 Tell the king of Judah, who sent you to inquire[b] of the
LORD, 'This is what the LORD, the God of Israel, says concerning the words you heard: 19 Because your heart
was responsive and you humbled[c] yourself before the LORD when you heard what I have spoken against
this place and its people, that they would become accursed[d] and laid waste,[e] and because you tore your
robes and wept in my presence, I have heard you, declares the LORD. 20 Therefore I will gather you to your
fathers, and you will be buried in peace.[f] Your eyes will not see all the disaster I am going to bring on
this place.' "

So they took her answer back to the king.

Josiah Renews the Covenant

23 Then the king called together all the elders of Judah and Jerusalem. 2 He went up to the temple
of the LORD with the men of Judah, the people of Jerusalem, the priests and the prophets—all
the people from the least to the greatest. He read[g] in their hearing all the words of the Book of the Cov-
enant, which had been found in the temple of the LORD. 3 The king stood by the pillar and renewed the
covenant[h] in the presence of the LORD—to follow[i] the LORD and keep his commands, regulations and
decrees with all his heart and all his soul, thus confirming the words of the covenant written in this book.
Then all the people pledged themselves to the covenant.

4 The king ordered Hilkiah the high priest, the priests next in rank and the doorkeepers[j] to remove[k]
from the temple of the LORD all the articles made for Baal and Asherah and all the starry hosts. He burned
them outside Jerusalem in the fields of the Kidron Valley and took the ashes to Bethel. 5 He did away with
the pagan priests appointed by the kings of Judah to burn incense on the high places of the towns of Ju-
dah and on those around Jerusalem—those who burned incense to Baal, to the sun and moon, to the
constellations and to all the starry hosts.[l] 6 He took the Asherah pole from the temple of the LORD to the
Kidron Valley outside Jerusalem and burned it there. He ground it to powder and scattered the dust over
the graves of the common people.[m] 7 He also tore down the quarters of the male shrine prostitutes,[n]
which were in the temple of the LORD and where women did weaving for Asherah.

8 Josiah brought all the priests from the towns of Judah and desecrated the high places, from Geba[o]
to Beersheba, where the priests had burned incense. He broke down the shrines[b] at the gates—at the
entrance to the Gate of Joshua, the city governor, which is on the left of the city gate. 9 Although the priests
of the high places did not serve[p] at the altar of the LORD in Jerusalem, they ate unleavened bread with their
fellow priests.

10 He desecrated Topheth,[q] which was in the Valley of Ben Hinnom,[r] so no one could use it to sacri-
fice his son[s] or daughter in[c] the fire to Molech. 11 He removed from the entrance to the temple of the LORD
the horses that the kings of Judah had dedicated to the sun. They were in the court near the room of an
official named Nathan-Melech. Josiah then burned the chariots dedicated to the sun.[t]

12 He pulled down the altars the kings of Judah had erected on the roof[u] near the upper room of Ahaz,
and the altars Manasseh had built in the two courts[v] of the temple of the LORD. He removed them from
there, smashed them to pieces and threw the rubble into the Kidron Valley. 13 The king also desecrated
the high places that were east of Jerusalem on the south of the Hill of Corruption—the ones Solomon[w]
king of Israel had built for Ashtoreth the vile goddess of the Sidonians, for Chemosh the vile god of Moab,
and for Molech[d] the detestable god of the people of Ammon. 14 Josiah smashed[x] the sacred stones and cut
down the Asherah poles and covered the sites with human bones.

15 Even the altar[y] at Bethel, the high place made by Jeroboam[z] son of Nebat, who had caused Israel to
sin—even that altar and high place he demolished. He burned the high place and ground it to powder,
and burned the Asherah pole also. 16 Then Josiah[a] looked around, and when he saw the tombs that were
there on the hillside, he had the bones removed from them and burned on the altar to defile it, in accor-
dance with the word of the LORD proclaimed by the man of God who foretold these things.

22:18 [b]2Ch 34:26; Jer 21:2
22:19 [c]Ex 10:3; 1Ki 21:29; Ps 51:17; Isa 57:15; Mic 6:8 [d]Jer 26:6 [e]Lev 26:31
22:20 [f]Isa 57:1
23:2 [g]Dt 31:11; 2Ki 22:8
23:3 [h]2Ki 11:14, 17 [i]Dt 13:4
23:4 [j]2Ki 25:18 [k]2Ki 21:7
23:5 [l]2Ki 21:3; Jer 8:2
23:6 [m]Jer 26:23
23:7 [n]1Ki 14:24; 15:12; Eze 16:16
23:8 [o]1Ki 15:22
23:9 [p]Eze 44:10-14
23:10 [q]Isa 30:33; Jer 7:31,32; 19:6 [r]Jos 15:8 [s]Lev 18:21; Dt 18:10
23:11 [t]Dt 4:19
23:12 [u]Jer 19:13; Zep 1:5 [v]2Ki 21:5
23:13 [w]1Ki 11:7
23:14 [x]Ex 23:24; Dt 7:5,25
23:15 [y]1Ki 13:1-3 [z]1Ki 12:33
23:16 [a]1Ki 13:2

[a] 17 Or *by everything they have done* [b] 8 Or *high places* [c] 10 Or *to make his son or daughter pass through* [d] 13 Hebrew *Milcom*

23:6 See "Tombs in Ancient Israel" on page 376.

23:10 See "Human Sacrifice in the Ancient Near East" on page 182.

23:11 If this is a reference to live horses, they may have been used to pull chariots bearing images of a sun god in religious processions. Small images of horses have recently been discovered in a cultic area just outside one of the ancient walls of Jerusalem.

23:12 These altars, dedicated to the worship of all the starry hosts (see Jer 19:13; Zep 1:5), had been erected by Ahaz (1Ki 16:3–4,10–16), Manasseh (21:3) and Amon (21:21–22).

17 The king asked, "What is that tombstone I see?"
The men of the city said, "It marks the tomb of the man of God who came from Judah and pronounced
against the altar of Bethel the very things you have done to it."
23:18 [b]1Ki 13:31
18 "Leave it alone," he said. "Don't let anyone disturb his bones[b]." So they spared his bones and those
of the prophet who had come from Samaria.
19 Just as he had done at Bethel, Josiah removed and defiled all the shrines at the high places that the
kings of Israel had built in the towns of Samaria that had provoked the LORD to anger. 20 Josiah slaugh-
23:20 [c]Ex 22:20; 2Ki 10:25; 11:18 [d]1Ki 13:2
tered[c] all the priests of those high places on the altars and burned human bones[d] on them. Then he went
back to Jerusalem.
23:21 [e]Ex 12:11; Nu 9:2; Dt 16:1-8
21 The king gave this order to all the people: "Celebrate the Passover[e] to the LORD your God, as it is
written in this Book of the Covenant." 22 Not since the days of the judges who led Israel, nor throughout
the days of the kings of Israel and the kings of Judah, had any such Passover been observed. 23 But in the
eighteenth year of King Josiah, this Passover was celebrated to the LORD in Jerusalem.
23:24 [f]Lev 19:31; Dt 18:11; 2Ki 21:6 [g]Ge 31:19
24 Furthermore, Josiah got rid of the mediums and spiritists,[f] the household gods,[g] the idols and all
the other detestable things seen in Judah and Jerusalem. This he did to fulfill the requirements of the
law written in the book that Hilkiah the priest had discovered in the temple of the LORD. 25 Neither be-
23:25 [h]2Ki 18:5
fore nor after Josiah was there a king like him who turned[h] to the LORD as he did—with all his heart and
with all his soul and with all his strength, in accordance with all the Law of Moses.
26 Nevertheless, the LORD did not turn away from the heat of his fierce anger, which burned against Ju-
23:26 [i]2Ki 21:12; Jer 15:4 **23:27** [j]2Ki 21:13
dah because of all that Manasseh[i] had done to provoke him to anger. 27 So the LORD said, "I will remove[j]

The Tragic Reign of King Josiah

2 KINGS 23 Josiah's reign (640–609 B.C.) began during difficult times. His father, Manasseh, had been an Assyrian **vassal** for the majority of his reign, all the while undoing Hezekiah's reforms and introducing new forms of idolatry to Jerusalem.[1] At age sixteen (632 B.C.) Josiah began to seek the Lord and to rid Judah of **Canaanite** and **Assyrian** cultic practices. Assyrian power declined rapidly, as did the health of its king, Ashurbanipal. During the same period the **Neo-Babylonian** Empire arose under Nabopolassar, who united with the Medes against Assyria. Egypt, seeking to maintain a balance of power in **Mesopotamia**, allied with Assyria.

Against this political backdrop Josiah began a religious reformation in Judah. During repairs to the temple the Book of the Law was found. The prophetess Huldah[2] predicted judgment on Judah, but not during Josiah's reign. Josiah humbled himself before the Lord and increased his efforts at reformation by destroying pagan altars throughout his kingdom and centralizing sacrificial worship in Jerusalem.[3] His efforts extended to the former northern kingdom; perhaps he was attempting to reunite all Israel within boundaries once held by King David. A covenant renewal ceremony and a Passover unlike any since the days of the judges were observed.

Josiah's faithfulness seemed to be rewarded as Assyrian cities fell in quick succession: Asshur to the Medes (614 B.C.), Nineveh to the Babylonians (612 B.C.) and Harran to the Babylonians and Medes (610 B.C.). Egypt's Pharaoh Neco, however, advanced to assist the Assyrians at Carchemish (609 B.C.).[4] Josiah opposed him at **Megiddo**[5] ("Map 6") but was mortally wounded. The failure of Josiah was, according to 2 Kings 23:26–27, not the result of shortcomings on his own part but due to the apostasy of the people and of his predecessor, Manasseh.[6]

[1]See "The History of the Southern Kingdom" on page 538. [2]See "The Huldah Delegation and Nathan-Melech, the Official" on page 567. [3]See "The High Places" on page 1318. [4]See "Josiah, Zechariah and Neco II" on page 663. [5]See "Megiddo" on page 1541. [6]See "The Seal of Manasseh" on page 565.

Judah also from my presence[k] as I removed Israel, and I will reject Jerusalem, the city I chose, and this 23:27 [k]2Ki 18:11
temple, about which I said, 'There shall my Name be.'[a]"
28 As for the other events of Josiah's reign, and all he did, are they not written in the book of the an-
nals of the kings of Judah?
29 While Josiah was king, Pharaoh Neco[l] king of Egypt went up to the Euphrates River to help the king 23:29 [l]Jer 46:2
of Assyria. King Josiah marched out to meet him in battle, but Neco faced him and killed him at Megid- [m]Zec 12:11
do.[m] 30 Josiah's servants brought his body in a chariot[n] from Megiddo to Jerusalem and buried him in 23:30 [n]2Ki 9:28
his own tomb. And the people of the land took Jehoahaz son of Josiah and anointed him and made him
king in place of his father.

Jehoahaz King of Judah

31 Jehoahaz[o] was twenty-three years old when he became king, and he reigned in Jerusalem three 23:31 [o]1Ch 3:15;
months. His mother's name was Hamutal[p] daughter of Jeremiah; she was from Libnah. 32 He did evil in Jer 22:11 [p]2Ki 24:18
the eyes of the LORD, just as his fathers had done. 33 Pharaoh Neco put him in chains at Riblah[q] in the 23:33 [q]2Ki 25:6
land of Hamath[b][r] so that he might not reign in Jerusalem, and he imposed on Judah a levy of a hundred [r]1Ki 8:65
talents[c] of silver and a talent[d] of gold. 34 Pharaoh Neco made Eliakim[s] son of Josiah king in place of his 23:34 [s]1Ch 3:15;
father Josiah and changed Eliakim's name to Jehoiakim. But he took Jehoahaz and carried him off to 2Ch 36:5-8 [t]Jer 22:12;
Egypt, and there he died.[t] 35 Jehoiakim paid Pharaoh Neco the silver and gold he demanded. In order to Eze 19:3-4
do so, he taxed the land and exacted the silver and gold from the people of the land according to their as-
sessments.[u] 23:35 [u]ver 33

Jehoiakim King of Judah

36 Jehoiakim[v] was twenty-five years old when he became king, and he reigned in Jerusalem eleven 23:36 [v]Jer 26:1
years. His mother's name was Zebidah daughter of Pedaiah; she was from Rumah. 37 And he did evil in
the eyes of the LORD, just as his fathers had done.

24 During Jehoiakim's reign, Nebuchadnezzar[w] king of Babylon invaded the land, and Jehoiakim 24:1 [w]Jer 25:1,9;
became his vassal for three years. But then he changed his mind and rebelled against Nebuchad- Da 1:1
nezzar. 2 The LORD sent Babylonian,[e] Aramean,[x] Moabite and Ammonite raiders against him. He sent 24:2 [x]Jer 35:11
them to destroy[y] Judah, in accordance with the word of the LORD proclaimed by his servants the proph- [y]Jer 25:9
ets. 3 Surely these things happened to Judah according to the LORD's command,[z] in order to remove them 24:3 [z]2Ki 18:25
from his presence because of the sins of Manasseh[a] and all he had done, 4 including the shedding of in- [a]2Ki 21:12; 23:26
nocent blood.[b] For he had filled Jerusalem with innocent blood, and the LORD was not willing to forgive. 24:4 [b]2Ki 21:16
5 As for the other events of Jehoiakim's reign, and all he did, are they not written in the book of the an-
nals of the kings of Judah? 6 Jehoiakim rested[c] with his fathers. And Jehoiachin his son succeeded him as 24:6 [c]Jer 22:19
king.
7 The king of Egypt[d] did not march out from his own country again, because the king of Babylon[e] had 24:7 [d]Ge 15:18
taken all his territory, from the Wadi of Egypt to the Euphrates River. [e]Jer 37:5-7; 46:2

Jehoiachin King of Judah

8 Jehoiachin[f] was eighteen years old when he became king, and he reigned in Jerusalem three months. 24:8 [f]1Ch 3:16
His mother's name was Nehushta daughter of Elnathan; she was from Jerusalem. 9 He did evil in the eyes
of the LORD, just as his father had done.
10 At that time the officers of Nebuchadnezzar[g] king of Babylon advanced on Jerusalem and laid siege 24:10 [g]Da 1:1
to it, 11 and Nebuchadnezzar himself came up to the city while his officers were besieging it. 12 Jehoiachin
king of Judah, his mother, his attendants, his nobles and his officials all surrendered[h] to him. 24:12 [h]2Ki 25:27;
In the eighth year of the reign of the king of Babylon, he took Jehoiachin prisoner. 13 As the LORD had Jer 22:24-30; 24:1; 25:1; 29:2; 52:28

a 27 1 Kings 8:29 *b 33* Hebrew; Septuagint (see also 2 Chron. 36:3) *Neco at Riblah in Hamath removed him* *c 33* That is, about 3 3/4 tons (about 3.4 metric tons) *d 33* That is, about 75 pounds (about 34 kilograms) *e 2* Or *Chaldean*

23:31 This particular Jeremiah was not the prophet by the same name.

23:34 The change of name indicated that Jehoiakim was subject to Neco's authority.

24:10–12 Young Jehoiachin could expect no help from Egypt; Pharaoh Neco was in no position to challenge Nebuchadnezzar again (cf. v. 7). Babylonian records state that Nebuchadnezzar "encamped against the city of Judah, and on the second day of the month of Addaru [March 16, 597 B.C.] he seized the city and captured the king." He proceeded to strip the palace and temple of their treasures as spoils of war (v. 13). The Babylonian king then utilized the deportation system made famous by the Assyrians (cf. 17:24), seizing 10,000 of Jerusalem's leaders from every walk of life (24:14). With only the poorest, least skilled people of the land remaining, he could assume that Jerusalem would cause no further trouble.

24:13 [i]2Ki 20:17 [j]2Ki 25:15; Isa 39:6 [k]2Ki 25:14; Jer 20:5 [l]1Ki 7:51
24:14 [m]Jer 24:1; 52:28 [n]2Ki 25:12; Jer 40:7; 52:16
24:15 [o]Jer 22:24-28 [p]Est 2:6; Eze 17:12-14
24:16 [q]Jer 52:28
24:17 [r]1Ch 3:15; 2Ch 36:11; Jer 37:1

declared,[i] Nebuchadnezzar removed all the treasures[j] from the temple of the LORD and from the royal
palace, and took away all the gold articles[k] that Solomon[l] king of Israel had made for the temple of the
LORD. 14 He carried into exile[m] all Jerusalem: all the officers and fighting men, and all the craftsmen and
artisans—a total of ten thousand. Only the poorest[n] people of the land were left.
15 Nebuchadnezzar took Jehoiachin captive to Babylon. He also took from Jerusalem to Babylon the
king's mother,[o] his wives, his officials and the leading men[p] of the land. 16 The king of Babylon also de-
ported to Babylon the entire force of seven thousand fighting men, strong and fit for war, and a thou-
sand craftsmen and artisans.[q] 17 He made Mattaniah, Jehoiachin's uncle, king in his place and changed
his name to Zedekiah.[r]

Nebuchadnezzar

2 KINGS 24 Nebuchadnezzar II, one of the greatest and longest-reigning monarchs of **Mesopotamia**, ruled **Babylon** from 605 to 562 B.C.[1] He is mentioned some 90 times in the Old Testament, more than any other foreign king. The Bible records his campaigns against Jerusalem in 604, 597 and 586 B.C., culminating in the captivity of Judah.

The first four chapters of Daniel detail events in Babylon during Nebuchadnezzar's reign.[2] Outside the Bible we have many contemporary records from Babylon, as well as later writings extolling Nebuchadnezzar's accomplishments: hundreds of contracts, several inscriptions, detail from classical historians and the Babylonian Chronicle, which documents Nebuchadnezzar's accomplishments from his first through his eleventh year. However, there are still large gaps in our knowledge about his reign.

Nebuchadnezzar distinguished himself while still crown prince by defeating the Egyptians at Carchemish (southern Turkey) in 605 B.C. (Jer 46:2). He boasted that he had conquered all of Syria-Palestine at approximately the same time, significantly reducing the Egyptian sphere of influence. After returning briefly to Babylon to claim the throne upon receiving news of his father's death, Nebuchadnezzar resumed the consolidation of his control over Syria-Palestine. Jehoiakim of Judah served as his vassal for the next three years (2Ki 24:1), and Ashkelon ("Map 6"), which would not submit to the Babylonian king, was attacked and left in ruins (cf. Jer 47:5–7). Over the next few years Nebuchadnezzar also invaded Arabia, forcing its people to pay him yearly tribute.

In 601 B.C. Nebuchadnezzar once again routed the Egyptian forces. Pharaoh Neco II, however, imposed such heavy casualties on the Babylonian army that Jehoiakim took the opportunity to revolt against the weakened empire.[3] Babylon and her allies retaliated against rebellious Judah during the following year (2Ki 24:1–2). Jerusalem was conquered; the temple was looted; Jehoiakim's son and successor, Jehoiachin, was deported to Babylon, along with over 3,000 other captives; and Zedekiah was appointed king (vv. 10–17). These events are mentioned in Nebuchadnezzar's own records.

When Zedekiah himself rebelled in 589 B.C. the Babylonian army devastated the land of Judah. Jerusalem was ransacked and the temple destroyed in 586 B.C. (25:1–17).[4] Another massive deportation was carried out at this time, with yet another in 582 (Jer 52:29–30). We lack records for years 11–43 of Nebuchadnezzar's reign, but later historians describe a siege of Tyre that lasted for 13 years, as well as another campaign against Egypt.[5]

Apart from his military campaigns, during the course of which he consolidated control of virtually the entire ancient Near East, Nebuchadnezzar set about to transform Babylon into the greatest city in the world. Desiring to leave a lasting legacy, he erected his structures with kiln-fired bricks, as opposed to the sun-dried bricks normally used. The "blazing furnace" of Daniel 3 was undoubtedly one of the many brick kilns in Babylon that were needed for Nebuchadnezzar's aggressive building program. Many of the bricks were stamped with the king's name and titles. He constructed fortification walls, gates, palaces, temples, roads, bridges and a ziggurat (temple-tower) and is said to have designed the famous "hanging gardens" for his wife, Amytis, daughter of the Median king Astyages, to remind her of her mountainous homeland. The story of the hanging gardens is now widely regarded as a legend, however.

Through his military might and building enterprises, Nebuchadnezzar established Babylon as the most powerful empire of its day. Nebuchadnezzar died in 562 B.C. and was succeeded by his son Awil-Marduk (*Evil-Merodach* in the Hebrew), who released Jehoiachin from prison and provided him with a regular allowance (2Ki 25:27–30).[6]

[1]See "Babylon" on page 1077. [2]See "Nebuchadnezzar's Madness" on page 1391. [3]See "Josiah, Zechariah and Neco II" on page 663. [4]See "The Last Days of Jerusalem" on page 1197. [5]See "The Downfall Of Tyre" on page 1345. [6]See "Jehoiachin in Captivity and Evil-Merodach" on page 1292.

Zedekiah King of Judah

18 Zedekiah[s] was twenty-one years old when he became king, and he reigned in Jerusalem eleven 24:18 [s]Jer 52:1
years. His mother's name was Hamutal[t] daughter of Jeremiah; she was from Libnah. 19 He did evil in the [t]2Ki 23:31
eyes of the LORD, just as Jehoiakim had done. 20 It was because of the LORD's anger that all this happened
to Jerusalem and Judah, and in the end he thrust[u] them from his presence. 24:20 [u]Dt 4:26; 29:27

The Fall of Jerusalem

Now Zedekiah rebelled against the king of Babylon.

25 So in the ninth year of Zedekiah's reign, on the tenth day of the tenth month, Nebuchadnezzar[v] 25:1 [v]Jer 34:1-7
king of Babylon marched against Jerusalem with his whole army. He encamped outside the city [w]Eze 24:2
and built siege works[w] all around it. 2 The city was kept under siege until the eleventh year of King Zed-
ekiah. 3 By the ninth day of the ⌞fourth⌟[a] month the famine[x] in the city had become so severe that there 25:3 [x]Jer 14:18; La 4:9
was no food for the people to eat. 4 Then the city wall was broken through,[y] and the whole army fled at 25:4 [y]Eze 33:21
night through the gate between the two walls near the king's garden, though the Babylonians[b] were sur- [z]Jer 4:17
rounding[z] the city. They fled toward the Arabah,[c] 5 but the Babylonian[d] army pursued the king and over-
took him in the plains of Jericho. All his soldiers were separated from him and scattered,[a] 6 and he was 25:5 [a]Eze 12:14
captured.[b] He was taken to the king of Babylon at Riblah,[c] where sentence was pronounced on him. 25:6 [b]Jer 34:21-22 [c]2Ki 23:33
7 They killed the sons of Zedekiah before his eyes. Then they put out his eyes, bound him with bronze
shackles and took him to Babylon.[d] 25:7 [d]Jer 21:7; 32:4-5; Eze 12:11
8 On the seventh day of the fifth month, in the nineteenth year of Nebuchadnezzar king of Babylon,
Nebuzaradan commander of the imperial guard, an official of the king of Babylon, came to Jerusalem.
9 He set fire[e] to the temple of the LORD, the royal palace and all the houses of Jerusalem. Every important 25:9 [e]Isa 60:7
building he burned down.[f] 10 The whole Babylonian army, under the commander of the imperial guard, [f]Ps 74:3-8; Jer 2:15; Am 2:5; Mic 3:12
broke down the walls[g] around Jerusalem. 11 Nebuzaradan the commander of the guard carried into ex- 25:10 [g]Ne 1:3
ile[h] the people who remained in the city, along with the rest of the populace and those who had gone 25:11 [h]2Ki 24:14 [i]2Ki 24:1
over to the king of Babylon.[i] 12 But the commander left behind some of the poorest people[j] of the land to 25:12 [j]2Ki 24:14
work the vineyards and fields.
13 The Babylonians broke up the bronze pillars, the movable stands and the bronze Sea that were at the
temple of the LORD and they carried the bronze to Babylon. 14 They also took away the pots, shovels, wick
trimmers, dishes and all the bronze articles[k] used in the temple service. 15 The commander of the impe- 25:14 [k]Ex 27:3; 1Ki 7:47-50
rial guard took away the censers and sprinkling bowls—all that were made of pure gold or silver.
16 The bronze from the two pillars, the Sea and the movable stands, which Solomon had made for the
temple of the LORD, was more than could be weighed. 17 Each pillar[l] was twenty-seven feet[e] high. The 25:17 [l]1Ki 7:15-22
bronze capital on top of one pillar was four and a half feet[f] high and was decorated with a network and
pomegranates of bronze all around. The other pillar, with its network, was similar.
18 The commander of the guard took as prisoners Seraiah[m] the chief priest, Zephaniah[n] the priest 25:18 [m]1Ch 6:14; Ezr 7:1; Ne 11:11
next in rank and the three doorkeepers. 19 Of those still in the city, he took the officer in charge of the [n]Jer 21:1; 29:25
fighting men and five royal advisers. He also took the secretary who was chief officer in charge of con-
scripting the people of the land and sixty of his men who were found in the city. 20 Nebuzaradan the com-

[a] 3 See Jer. 52:6. [b] 4 Or *Chaldeans*; also in verses 13, 25 and 26 [c] 4 Or *the Jordan Valley* [d] 5 Or *Chaldean*; also in verses 10 and 24 [e] 17 Hebrew *eighteen cubits* (about 8.1 meters) [f] 17 Hebrew *three cubits* (about 1.3 meters)

25:1–7 After Zedekiah had rebelled against Babylon, Nebuchadnezzar responded, this time sending the full weight of his army. After setting up a headquarters in Riblah, he placed Jerusalem under total siege (see "Siege Warfare" on p. 465 and "The Lachish Ostraca" on p. 1252). Two and a half years later, on July 18, 586 B.C., the city fell (see "The Last Days of Jerusalem" on p. 1197).

Zedekiah and his remaining army were captured as they attempted to slip through a secluded gate. Before having his eyes gouged out, the king was forced to witness the executions of his sons. Judah's last king was led captive to Babylon, where he remained a prisoner until his death (cf. Jer 52:11).

25:11 Knowledge about the destiny of the captives from Israel and Judah is sparse for the period following the capture of Samaria and the later destruction of Jerusalem. Assyrians and Babylonians treated their subject peoples essentially the same: overwhelming military force used in a manner inspiring psychological terror, along with mass deportations and heavy tribute. Three deportations are mentioned in Jeremiah 52:28–30, the largest one consisting of 3,023 Jews who were taken to Babylon along with King Jehoiachin in 597 B.C.

After the destruction of Jerusalem by Nebuzaradan, the commander of the Babylonian army, hundreds of exiles were taken to Riblah "in the land of Hamath," where, in addition to Zedekiah's sons, at least 61 were executed. Jehoiachin and his family were kept in Babylon, where clay ration receipts bearing his name have been discovered in a dramatic archaeological confirmation of Biblical history.

Ezekiel 1:1–3 and 3:15 indicate that other captives were placed at Tel Abib and at the Kebar River, both probably in the locale of Nippur, as were other villages mentioned in Ezra 2:59, 8:15, 17 and Nehemiah 7:61.

Clay tablets called the Murashu archives from the fifth century B.C. have been located at Nippur. They document commercial transactions with Jewish families who remained in Mesopotamia following Ezra's return to Jerusalem.

mander took them all and brought them to the king of Babylon at Riblah. 21 There at Riblah, in the land
of Hamath, the king had them executed.
25:21 [o]Ge 12:7; So Judah went into captivity, away from her land.[o]
Dt 28:64; Jos 23:13; 22 Nebuchadnezzar king of Babylon appointed Gedaliah[p] son of Ahikam, the son of Shaphan, to be
2Ki 23:27 25:22 [p]Jer 39:14; over the people he had left behind in Judah. 23 When all the army officers and their men heard that the
40:5,7 king of Babylon had appointed Gedaliah as governor, they came to Gedaliah at Mizpah—Ishmael son
of Nethaniah, Johanan son of Kareah, Seraiah son of Tanhumeth the Netophathite, Jaazaniah the son of
the Maacathite, and their men. 24 Gedaliah took an oath to reassure them and their men. "Do not be afraid
of the Babylonian officials," he said. "Settle down in the land and serve the king of Babylon, and it will go
well with you."
25 In the seventh month, however, Ishmael son of Nethaniah, the son of Elishama, who was of royal
blood, came with ten men and assassinated Gedaliah and also the men of Judah and the Babylonians
who were with him at Mizpah. 26 At this, all the people from the least to the greatest, together with the
25:26 [q]Isa 30:2; Jer 43:7 army officers, fled to Egypt[q] for fear of the Babylonians.

Jehoiachin Released

27 In the thirty-seventh year of the exile of Jehoiachin king of Judah, in the year Evil-Merodach[a] be-
25:27 [r]2Ki 24:12; Jer 52:31-34 came king of Babylon, he released Jehoiachin[r] from prison on the twenty-seventh day of the twelfth
25:28 [s]Ezr 5:5; Ne 2:1; Da 2:48 month. 28 He spoke kindly to him and gave him a seat of honor[s] higher than those of the other kings who
were with him in Babylon. 29 So Jehoiachin put aside his prison clothes and for the rest of his life ate reg-
25:29 [t]2Sa 9:7 25:30 [u]Est 2:9; Jer 28:4 ularly at the king's table.[t] 30 Day by day the king gave Jehoiachin a regular allowance as long as he lived.[u]

[a] 27 Also called *Amel-Marduk*

25:23 Mizpah had been a town of political significance during the period just prior to the establishment of the monarchy (see "Mizpah" on p. 383), and it was there that Gedaliah set up an administrative center. In 1932 an agate seal was discovered at Tell en-Nasbeh (Mizpah), bearing the name of Jaazaniah (perhaps the man mentioned here). See "The Seals of Jaazaniah, Ishmael and Elishama" on page 573.

25:27 Babylonian administrative tablets, recording the payment of rations in oil and barley to prisoners held in Babylon, mention Yaukin (Jehoiachin) king of Iahudu (Judah) and five of his sons (cf. 24:15; see "Jehoichin in Captivity and Evil-Merodach" on p. 1292). No reason is given for Jehoiachin's release. Perhaps this was part of a general amnesty proclaimed at the beginning of Evil-Merodach's reign.

ANCIENT TEXTS AND ARTIFACTS

The Seals of Jaazaniah, Ishmael and Elishama

2 KINGS 25 Following the destruction of Jerusalem in 586 B.C., Nebuchadnezzar appointed Gedaliah governor of Judah (2Ki 25:22). Gedaliah established an administrative center at Mizpah ("Map 7"), identified as Tell en-Nasbeh, approximately 7.5 miles (12 km) north of Jerusalem. A number of army commanders rallied around him, including Jaazaniah (v. 23). The army commanders warned Gedaliah of a plot to take his life, but he dismissed their cautions (Jer 40:13–14). Gedaliah was subsequently assassinated, along with "the men of Judah and the Babylonians who were with him at Mizpah" (2Ki 25:25).

A high-quality, onyx seal with the inscription "Belonging to Jaazaniah, servant of the king," was discovered in a sixth-century B.C. tomb at Tell en-Nasbeh. It appears that Jaazaniah was among those killed defending Gedaliah at Mizpah and that he was buried there, along with his seal.

The man responsible for his assassination was Ishmael, of the royal family of David and "one of the king's officers" (Jer 41:1). Ishmael was evidently trying to reestablish the Davidic line of kingship. A **bulla** (clay seal impression) purchased from an antiquities dealer in Jerusalem bears the inscription "Belonging to Ishmael the king's son." The style of the script is from the late seventh or early sixth century B.C., and the bulla had been baked in a fire, possibly the one set by the Babylonians. It is likely that the bulla is that of Ishmael the assassin. Another bulla, purchased in Jaffa and bearing the inscription "Belonging to Elishama the king's son," may have been made by Ishmael's grandfather (2Ki 25:25).

INTRODUCTION TO 1 Chronicles

AUTHOR, PLACE AND DATE OF WRITING

According to the Jewish Talmud Ezra the scribe wrote Chronicles. Its division into two books, 1 Chronicles and 2 Chronicles, first appears in the Septuagint. Because the book of Ezra begins where 2 Chronicles leaves off (cf. 2Ch 36:22–23; Ezr 1:1–3a), many scholars believe that the same person authored/compiled 1 and 2 Chronicles, Ezra and Nehemiah. All of these books emphasize genealogies, the centrality of Jerusalem, God's temple and sacrifice. However, other scholars discount the single-author theory, arguing that the differences between Chronicles and Ezra outweigh the similarities.

The original book of Chronicles, written in Jerusalem during the fifth century B.C., describes events that happened much earlier. Clearly, the Chronicler made use of earlier Biblical sources, such as the Pentateuch, Joshua, Judges, Ruth, 1 and 2 Samuel, 1 and 2 Kings, Psalms, Isaiah, Jeremiah and Lamentations. Other, nonbiblical sources are also cited (cf. 1Ch 29:29; 2Ch 9:29; 24:27).

AUDIENCE

The primary audience of 1 and 2 Chronicles was made up of the exiled Jews who had returned to Israel after the Babylonian captivity. The house of David had been dethroned and the nation, Jerusalem and the temple destroyed. The Jews needed to reestablish a sense of the continuity of the past with the present: God was still interested in them, his covenants with them remained in force, and his promises to King David still held meaning for them. Subsequent generations that read 1 and 2 Chronicles were reminded that, as God is faithful to his covenant promises, they also needed to remain faithful.

CULTURAL FACTS AND HIGHLIGHTS

God's chosen people had experienced great hardship as a result of their sinfulness and resulting exile. Now, having returned to their home territory, they had the opportunity to start over—to obey God's covenant and to receive his blessings.

TIMELINE

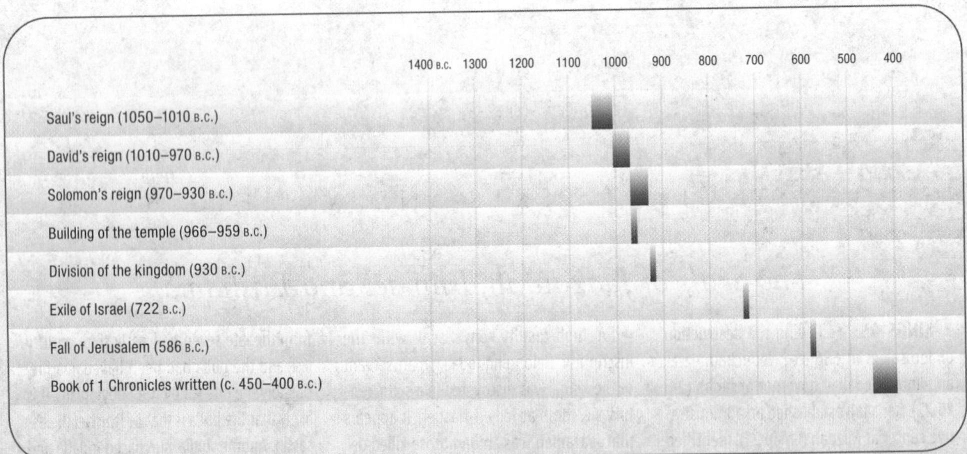

AS YOU READ

It may seem as though the author of 1 Chronicles simply repeated historical facts recorded previously in Samuel and Kings concerning such people as David and Solomon. Remember, though, that the author of 1 Chronicles wanted to emphasize God's covenant faithfulness and to encourage his readers to obey God. Yes, the long genealogies and details concerning the army, Levitical priesthood and temple service preparations can seem tedious, but allow yourself to look more deeply, paying particular attention to the manner in which the author traced God's working throughout sacred history. Note in particular how consistently he presented the line of David as the chosen lineage of Messianic kings (cf. ch. 17).

Israel had serious planning to do now that the temple of God—the center of her worship—was about to be built. The author took this seriously: It is as though he were proclaiming, "The Jerusalem temple is the true house of God, and the Levitical priesthood is the only legitimate temple ministry." In that light, notice how much attention David, Solomon and others paid to the details of the temple's construction and the joy they experienced in the renewed opportunity to make sacrifices to God (cf. chs. 28–29).

DID YOU KNOW?

- Names are often spelled differently in Chronicles than in the earlier books, but these variations are only "problems" to our modern way of thinking. The ancient world was not concerned about exact statistics and standard spellings (1:1–27).
- In ancient Egypt and Mesopotamia kings erected monuments and constructed great temples as an act of homage to the deity they considered responsible for establishing them upon their thrones (17:1–4).
- Levitical gatekeepers in a broad sense were a paramilitary security force (26:1).
- Lot-casting had nothing to do with "chance." Quite the opposite, it prevented partiality and emphasized the divine nature of the decision, since the outcome of a lot was from the Lord (26:1).
- Rather than a standing army, David's military divisions represented a militia or citizen army, something like the U.S. National Guard (27:1–15).
- There is no evidence of direct taxation during the reign of David; his court appears to have been financed by extensive landholdings, commerce, plunder from his many wars and tribute from subjugated kingdoms (27:25–31).

THEMES

First Chronicles includes the following themes:

1. *The Davidic covenant.* The genealogies in 1:1—9:44 emphasize the tribes of Judah and Benjamin because Chronicles is primarily concerned with the Davidic dynasty. God promised David that one day his descendant would rule an everlasting kingdom (17:7–14), and Chronicles demonstrates God's continuing faithfulness to that promise.

2. *Preparations for temple worship.* Meticulous emphasis is placed upon the detailed preparations David made for construction of the temple by his son Solomon. David brought the ark back to Jerusalem (15:1—16:3) and appointed Levites to attend it (16:4–38). After discovering the temple site (21:18—22:1) he began gathering and stockpiling building materials (22:2–5) and organized the priests and Levites for future temple service (23:2—26:32). David then charged his son Solomon with the building of the temple (22:6–16; 28:9–10) and ordered Israel's leaders to help with its construction (22:17–19; 28:1–8). Near the end of his life David passed on to Solomon the detailed blueprints for the temple that he had received from God (28:11–19) and called the people to bring voluntary offerings for its construction (29:1–9). The temple building project was David's dream, and he provided "all [his] resources" (29:2) for its construction.

OUTLINE

I. Genealogies: From Creation to Restoration (1–9)
II. The Reign of David (10–26)
  A. Saul's Death and David's Rise to Power (10–12)
  B. Return of the Ark (13)
  C. David's Reign Established (14–17)
  D. David's Victories and Census (18–21)
  E. Plans for Temple Construction and Organization (22–26)
III. Kingdom Organization and Staffing (27)
IV. Preparations for the Temple; Solomon's Coronation; David's Death (28–29)

Historical Records From Adam to Abraham

To Noah's Sons

1 Adam,[a] Seth, Enosh, 2 Kenan,[b] Mahalalel,[c] Jared,[d] 3 Enoch,[e] Methuselah,[f] Lamech,[g] Noah.[h]

4 The sons of Noah:[a][i]
Shem, Ham and Japheth.[j]

1:1 [a]Ge 5:1-32; Lk 3:36-38
1:2 [b]Ge 5:9 [c]Ge 5:12 [d]Ge 5:15
1:3 [e]Ge 5:18; Jude 1:14 [f]Ge 5:21 [g]Ge 5:25 [h]Ge 5:29
1:4 [i]Ge 6:10; 10:1 [j]Ge 5:32

The Japhethites

5 The sons[b] of Japheth:
Gomer, Magog, Madai, Javan, Tubal, Meshech and Tiras.
6 The sons of Gomer:
Ashkenaz, Riphath[c] and Togarmah.
7 The sons of Javan:
Elishah, Tarshish, the Kittim and the Rodanim.

The Hamites

8 The sons of Ham:
Cush, Mizraim,[d] Put and Canaan.
9 The sons of Cush:
Seba, Havilah, Sabta, Raamah and Sabteca.

[a] 4 Septuagint; Hebrew does not have this line. [b] 5 *Sons* may mean *descendants* or *successors* or *nations*; also in verses 6-10, 17 and 20. [c] 6 Many Hebrew manuscripts and Vulgate (see also Septuagint and Gen. 10:3); most Hebrew manuscripts *Diphath*
[d] 8 That is, Egypt; also in verse 11

1:1—2:2 The structure of this genealogy suggests that the Chronicler was following a known literary pattern, identical to the structure found in a copy of the Assyrian King List: There is no introduction, and the scribe had drawn lines across the tablet dividing it into four sections, two of which are lists of names without kinship terms, alternating with two lists in which relationships are specified. See "The Assyrian King Lists" on page 652.

1:4 The phrase "the sons of Noah" is not found in the Hebrew text (see the NIV text note), and this omission parallels the Assyrian King List (see the note on 1:1—2:2). The original readers would not have needed the kinship notice; they would have known that these were the sons of Noah. The Septuagint and most modern translations have inserted the phrase to clarify the relationship.

ANCIENT TEXTS AND ARTIFACTS

The Sumerian Eridu Genesis

1 CHRONICLES 1 First Chronicles opens with historical genealogies that provided needed continuity for the royal and priestly lines. Many of the individuals included had been prominent in their time, looked up to as rulers of specific areas and as builders of early cities (1:43; cf. Ge 10:8–12).

The *Eridu Genesis*, reconstructed from various fragmented texts dating from as early as the sixteenth century B.C., likewise deals with ancient rulers and cities. This important ancient Near Eastern writing constitutes the **Sumerian**[1] version of creation, the first rulers, the first cities and the great flood.

According to this unique perspective on ancient history, after the gods had fashioned humankind the mother-goddess Nintur somehow sent down intact from heaven the institution of kingship (in the form of scepter, crown and throne).[2] Each king was entrusted with advising people, overseeing their labor and leading them as a cowherd does his cattle. He was expected to perform services for the gods and to found cities, for which endeavors he was to be economically rewarded. Each city was assigned its own patron deity to protect it.

The *Eridu Genesis* cuts off at this point, but other versions indicate that what originally followed was an account of the rulers who had lived before the flood and the story of how the clamor of their people had so irritated the gods that they had decided to destroy humanity in a great deluge. The text resumes when Enki, the god of waters, revealed the gods' intent to the mortal king Ziusudra, instructing him to construct a large boat and to load it with pairs of animals. When the waters subsided, Ziusudra disembarked from his ship and offered lavish sacrifices to the gods, who in turn bestowed upon him eternal life for having safeguarded the future of humanity and the animal kingdom.[3]

[1]See Glossary on page 2080 for definitions of bolded words. [2]See "The Sumerian King List" on page 12. [3]For a comparison of this account with the Biblical flood narrative, see "Ancient Flood Narratives" on page 13.

The sons of Raamah:
Sheba and Dedan.
[10] Cush was the father[a] of
Nimrod, who grew to be a mighty warrior on earth.
[11] Mizraim was the father of
the Ludites, Anamites, Lehabites, Naphtuhites, [12] Pathrusites,
Casluhites (from whom the Philistines came) and Caphtorites.
[13] Canaan was the father of
Sidon his firstborn,[b] and of the Hittites, [14] Jebusites, Amorites,
Girgashites, [15] Hivites, Arkites, Sinites, [16] Arvadites, Zemarites
and Hamathites.

The Semites

[17] The sons of Shem:
Elam, Asshur, Arphaxad, Lud and Aram.
The sons of Aram:[c]
Uz, Hul, Gether and Meshech.
[18] Arphaxad was the father of Shelah,
and Shelah the father of Eber.
[19] Two sons were born to Eber:
One was named Peleg,[d] because in his time the earth was divided; his brother was named
Joktan.
[20] Joktan was the father of
Almodad, Sheleph, Hazarmaveth, Jerah, [21] Hadoram, Uzal, Diklah, [22] Obal,[e] Abimael, Sheba,
[23] Ophir, Havilah and Jobab. All these were sons of Joktan.

1:24 [k]Ge 10:21-25; Lk 3:34-36

[24] Shem,[k] Arphaxad,[f] Shelah,
[25] Eber, Peleg, Reu,
[26] Serug, Nahor, Terah
[27] and Abram (that is, Abraham).

The Family of Abraham

[28] The sons of Abraham:
Isaac and Ishmael.

Descendants of Hagar

[29] These were their descendants:
Nebaioth the firstborn of Ishmael, Kedar, Adbeel, Mibsam, [30] Mishma, Dumah, Massa, Hadad,
Tema, [31] Jetur, Naphish and Kedemah. These were the sons of Ishmael.

Descendants of Keturah

1:32 [l]Ge 22:24 [m]Ge 10:7

[32] The sons born to Keturah, Abraham's concubine:[l]
Zimran, Jokshan, Medan, Midian, Ishbak and Shuah.
The sons of Jokshan:
Sheba and Dedan.[m]
[33] The sons of Midian:
Ephah, Epher, Hanoch, Abida and Eldaah.
All these were descendants of Keturah.

Descendants of Sarah

1:34 [n]Lk 3:34 [o]Ge 21:2-3; Mt 1:2; Ac 7:8 [p]Ge 17:5; 25:25-26

[34] Abraham[n] was the father of Isaac.[o]
The sons of Isaac:
Esau and Israel.[p]

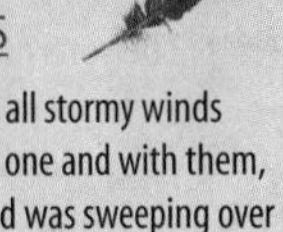

Ancient Voices

All the evil winds, all stormy winds
gathered into one and with them,
then, the Flood was sweeping over
(the cities of)* the half-bushel
baskets
for seven days and seven nights.
After the flood had swept over the
country,
after the evil wind had tossed the big
boat about on the great waters,
the sun came out spreading light over
heaven and earth.

*Words in parentheses added by translator for clarity where text has gap

—The Eridu Genesis

See "The Sumerian *Erudu Genesis*" article.

[a] *10* *Father* may mean *ancestor* or *predecessor* or *founder*; also in verses 11, 13, 18 and 20. [b] *13* Or *of the Sidonians, the foremost* [c] *17* One Hebrew manuscript and some Septuagint manuscripts (see also Gen. 10:23); most Hebrew manuscripts do not have this line. [d] *19* *Peleg* means *division.* [e] *22* Some Hebrew manuscripts and Syriac (see also Gen. 10:28); most Hebrew manuscripts *Ebal* [f] *24* Hebrew; some Septuagint manuscripts *Arphaxad, Cainan* (see also note at Gen. 11:10)

Esau's Sons

35 The sons of Esau:[q]
Eliphaz, Reuel,[r] Jeush, Jalam and Korah.
36 The sons of Eliphaz:
Teman, Omar, Zepho,[a] Gatam and Kenaz;
by Timna: Amalek.[b][s]
37 The sons of Reuel:[t]
Nahath, Zerah, Shammah and Mizzah.

1:35 [q]Ge 36:19 [r]Ge 36:4
1:36 [s]Ex 17:14
1:37 [t]Ge 36:17

The People of Seir in Edom

38 The sons of Seir:
Lotan, Shobal, Zibeon, Anah, Dishon, Ezer and Dishan.
39 The sons of Lotan:
Hori and Homam. Timna was Lotan's sister.
40 The sons of Shobal:
Alvan,[c] Manahath, Ebal, Shepho and Onam.
The sons of Zibeon:
Aiah and Anah.[u]
41 The son of Anah:
Dishon.
The sons of Dishon:
Hemdan,[d] Eshban, Ithran and Keran.
42 The sons of Ezer:
Bilhan, Zaavan and Akan.[e]
The sons of Dishan[f]:
Uz and Aran.

1:40 [u]Ge 36:2

The Rulers of Edom

43 These were the kings who reigned in Edom before any Israelite king reigned[g]:
Bela son of Beor, whose city was named Dinhabah.
44 When Bela died, Jobab son of Zerah from Bozrah succeeded him as king.
45 When Jobab died, Husham from the land of the Temanites[v] succeeded him as king.
46 When Husham died, Hadad son of Bedad, who defeated Midian in the country of Moab, succeeded him as king. His city was named Avith.
47 When Hadad died, Samlah from Masrekah succeeded him as king.
48 When Samlah died, Shaul from Rehoboth on the river[h] succeeded him as king.
49 When Shaul died, Baal-Hanan son of Acbor succeeded him as king.
50 When Baal-Hanan died, Hadad succeeded him as king. His city was named Pau,[i] and his wife's
name was Mehetabel daughter of Matred, the daughter of Me-Zahab. 51 Hadad also died.

1:45 [v]Ge 36:11

The chiefs of Edom were:
Timna, Alvah, Jetheth, 52 Oholibamah, Elah, Pinon, 53 Kenaz, Teman, Mibzar, 54 Magdiel and Iram.
These were the chiefs of Edom.

Israel's Sons

2 These were the sons of Israel:
Reuben, Simeon, Levi, Judah, Issachar, Zebulun, 2 Dan, Joseph, Benjamin, Naphtali, Gad and Asher.

[a] 36 Many Hebrew manuscripts, some Septuagint manuscripts and Syriac (see also Gen. 36:11); most Hebrew manuscripts *Zephi* [b] 36 Some Septuagint manuscripts (see also Gen. 36:12); Hebrew *Gatam, Kenaz, Timna and Amalek* [c] 40 Many Hebrew manuscripts and some Septuagint manuscripts (see also Gen. 36:23); most Hebrew manuscripts *Alian* [d] 41 Many Hebrew manuscripts and some Septuagint manuscripts (see also Gen. 36:26); most Hebrew manuscripts *Hamran* [e] 42 Many Hebrew and Septuagint manuscripts (see also Gen. 36:27); most Hebrew manuscripts *Zaavan, Jaakan* [f] 42 Hebrew *Dishon,* a variant of *Dishan* [g] 43 Or *before an Israelite king reigned over them* [h] 48 Possibly the Euphrates [i] 50 Many Hebrew manuscripts, some Septuagint manuscripts, Vulgate and Syriac (see also Gen. 36:39); most Hebrew manuscripts *Pai*

2:1 An obvious distinction between Chronicles and Kings is that Kings focuses heavily on the rulers of the northern kingdom, whereas Chronicles is almost exclusively concerned with the kings of Judah, often eliminating mention of kings of the north. Also, Chronicles is

Judah

To Hezron's Sons

2:3 [w]Ge 29:35; 38:2-10 [x]Ge 38:5 [y]Ge 38:2 [z]Nu 26:19

2:4 [a]Ge 38:11-30 [b]Ge 11:31 [c]Ge 38:29

2:5 [d]Ge 46:12 [e]Nu 26:21

2:7 [f]Jos 7:1 [g]Jos 6:18

3 The sons of Judah:[w]
Er, Onan and Shelah.[x] These three were born to him by a Canaanite woman, the daughter of
Shua.[y] Er, Judah's firstborn, was wicked in the LORD's sight; so the LORD put him to death.[z] 4 Ta-
mar,[a] Judah's daughter-in-law,[b] bore him Perez[c] and Zerah. Judah had five sons in all.

5 The sons of Perez:[d]
Hezron[e] and Hamul.
6 The sons of Zerah:
Zimri, Ethan, Heman, Calcol and Darda[a]—five in all.
7 The son of Carmi:
Achar,[b][f] who brought trouble on Israel by violating the ban on taking devoted things.[c][g]

[a] 6 Many Hebrew manuscripts, some Septuagint manuscripts and Syriac (see also 1 Kings 4:31); most Hebrew manuscripts *Dara*
[b] 7 *Achar* means *trouble*; *Achar* is called *Achan* in Joshua. [c] 7 The Hebrew term refers to the irrevocable giving over of things or persons to the LORD, often by totally destroying them.

far more concerned than Kings with the Jerusalem temple and its priesthood. Both of these distinctive traits are evident in the genealogies in Chronicles. After the patriarchal genealogies (ch. 1), the text immediately turns to southern genealogies: of Judah and in particular of David (2:1—4:23), of Simeon (4:24–43), of Benjamin (ch. 8) and of the inhabitants of Jerusalem (ch. 9). Chronicles also shows its concern about the priests and Levites with a lengthy Levitical genealogy (ch. 6). Far less attention is given to the genealogical records of the northern tribes (ch. 7). See "Genealogies in Ancient Israel" on page 1559.

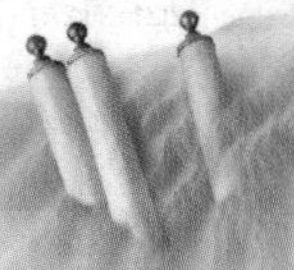

ANCIENT TEXTS AND ARTIFACTS

Sumerian Scribal Education

1 CHRONICLES 2 In the ancient world scribes held a position of high prestige, and select young men attended scribal schools to learn the trade. Several pieces of **Old Babylonian** literature tell us about **Mesopotamian** scribal schools. From at least two sources we learn that older, more advanced students, called "big brothers," supervised younger pupils and assisted them with their lessons. Students were taught not only how to read and write **cuneiform** signs[1] but also to speak **Sumerian**, the scholarly language of the day (the people's first language was **Akkadian**).[2] Students repeatedly copied works of literature and "lexical lists" (bilingual dictionaries covering both Akkadian and Sumerian words, similar to today's English-Spanish dictionaries) until they had mastered signs and their meanings. Mathematics, weights and measures, budgeting and business management were all included in the curriculum. Such an education taught the aspiring scribe how to prepare contracts (for adoptions, sales, marriages, wage agreements, etc.).

No parallel literature outlining Israel's educational system is known. We are aware that specific clans of Kenites were closely associated with the Israelites and trained in scribal art (1Ch 2:55).[3] The Levites, as keepers of the Biblical texts, appear to have served a scribal function as well. Regardless of the lack of texts related specifically to scribal training, we know from Biblical references to scribes, as well as from abundant evidence of their work, that the scribes of ancient Israel were highly trained and took pride in their work, as was the tradition throughout the ancient Near East.[4]

An Akkadian lexical tablet showing synonyms
Preserving Bible Times; © Dr. James C. Martin; permission of The British Museum

[1]See "Cuneiform and Clay Tablets in the Ancient Near East" on page 1108. [2]See "Languages of the Old Testament World" on page 672.
[3]See "The Kenites" on page 434. [4]See "The Scribe" on page 682.

Ancient Voices

If you set the task, I am not your "big brother"!
Why do you encroach on my status of "big brother"?
I have become excellent in the scribal art; I have fulfilled the function of "big brother" to perfection!
You are slow of understanding and hard of hearing; you are but a novice in the school!
You are deaf to the scribal art, and silent in Sumerian!
Your hand is crippled; it is unfit for the writing reed
And unfit for the clay; (your)* hand cannot keep up with the mouth.
And you would be a scribe like me?

*Word in parentheses added by translator for clarity where text has gap

—The Dialogue between Two Scribes

See "Sumerian Scribal Education" article on the previous page.

8 The son of Ethan:
Azariah.
9 The sons born to Hezron[h] were: 2:9 [h]Nu 26:21
Jerahmeel, Ram and Caleb.[a]

From Ram Son of Hezron

10 Ram[i] was the father of 2:10 [i]Lk 3:32-33 [j]Ex 6:23 [k]Nu 1:7
Amminadab[j], and Amminadab the father of Nahshon,[k]
the leader of the people of Judah. 11 Nahshon was the fa-
ther of Salmon,[b] Salmon the father of Boaz, 12 Boaz[l] the fa- 2:12 [l]Ru 2:1 [m]Ru 4:17
ther of Obed and Obed the father of Jesse.[m]
13 Jesse[n] was the father of 2:13 [n]Ru 4:17 [o]1Sa 16:6
Eliab[o] his firstborn; the second son was Abinadab, the
third Shimea, 14 the fourth Nethanel, the fifth Raddai, 15 the
sixth Ozem and the seventh David. 16 Their sisters were
Zeruiah[p] and Abigail. Zeruiah's[q] three sons were Abishai, 2:16 [p]1Sa 26:6 [q]2Sa 2:18 [r]2Sa 2:13
Joab[r] and Asahel. 17 Abigail was the mother of Amasa,[s] 2:17 [s]2Sa 17:25
whose father was Jether the Ishmaelite.

Caleb Son of Hezron

18 Caleb son of Hezron had children by his wife Azubah (and by
Jerioth). These were her sons: Jesher, Shobab and Ardon.
19 When Azubah died, Caleb[t] married Ephrath, who bore 2:19 [t]ver 42,50
him Hur. 20 Hur was the father of Uri, and Uri the father of
Bezalel.[u] 2:20 [u]Ex 31:2
21 Later, Hezron lay with the daughter of Makir the father of Gilead[v] (he had married her when he 2:21 [v]Nu 27:1
was sixty years old), and she bore him Segub. 22 Segub was the father of Jair, who controlled
twenty-three towns in Gilead. 23 (But Geshur and Aram captured Havvoth Jair,[c][w] as well as Ke- 2:23 [w]Nu 32:41; Dt 3:14; Jos 13:30 [x]Nu 32:42
nath[x] with its surrounding settlements—sixty towns.) All these were descendants of Makir
the father of Gilead.

24 After Hezron died in Caleb Ephrathah, Abijah the wife of Hezron bore him Ashhur[y] the father[d] of 2:24 [y]1Ch 4:5
Tekoa.

Jerahmeel Son of Hezron

25 The sons of Jerahmeel the firstborn of Hezron:
Ram his firstborn, Bunah, Oren, Ozem and[e] Ahijah. 26 Jerahmeel had another wife, whose name
was Atarah; she was the mother of Onam.
27 The sons of Ram the firstborn of Jerahmeel:
Maaz, Jamin and Eker.
28 The sons of Onam:
Shammai and Jada.
The sons of Shammai:
Nadab and Abishur.
29 Abishur's wife was named Abihail, who bore him Ahban and Molid.
30 The sons of Nadab:
Seled and Appaim. Seled died without children.
31 The son of Appaim:
Ishi, who was the father of Sheshan.
Sheshan was the father of Ahlai.
32 The sons of Jada, Shammai's brother:
Jether and Jonathan. Jether died without children.

[a] 9 Hebrew *Kelubai,* a variant of *Caleb* [b] 11 Septuagint (see also Ruth 4:21); Hebrew *Salma* [c] 23 Or *captured the settlements of Jair* [d] 24 *Father* may mean *civic leader* or *military leader*; also in verses 42, 45, 49-52 and possibly elsewhere. [e] 25 Or *Oren and Ozem, by*

33 The sons of Jonathan:
Peleth and Zaza.
These were the descendants of Jerahmeel.
34 Sheshan had no sons—only daughters.
He had an Egyptian servant named Jarha. 35 Sheshan gave his daughter in marriage to his ser-
vant Jarha, and she bore him Attai.
36 Attai was the father of Nathan,
2:36 [z]1Ch 11:41 Nathan the father of Zabad,[z]
37 Zabad the father of Ephlal,
Ephlal the father of Obed,
38 Obed the father of Jehu,
Jehu the father of Azariah,
39 Azariah the father of Helez,
Helez the father of Eleasah,
40 Eleasah the father of Sismai,
Sismai the father of Shallum,
41 Shallum the father of Jekamiah,
and Jekamiah the father of Elishama.

The Clans of Caleb

2:42 [a]ver 19 42 The sons of Caleb[a] the brother of Jerahmeel:
Mesha his firstborn, who was the father of Ziph, and his son Mareshah,[a] who was the father of
Hebron.
43 The sons of Hebron:
Korah, Tappuah, Rekem and Shema. 44 Shema was the father of Raham, and Raham the father
2:45 [b]Jos 15:55 of Jorkeam. Rekem was the father of Shammai. 45 The son of Shammai was Maon[b], and Maon
[c]Jos 15:58 was the father of Beth Zur.[c]
46 Caleb's concubine Ephah was the mother of Haran, Moza and Gazez. Haran was the father of Gazez.
47 The sons of Jahdai:
Regem, Jotham, Geshan, Pelet, Ephah and Shaaph.
48 Caleb's concubine Maacah was the mother of Sheber and Tirhanah. 49 She also gave birth to Sha-
2:49 [d]Jos 15:31 aph the father of Madmannah[d] and to Sheva the father of Macbenah and Gibea. Caleb's daugh-
[e]Jos 15:16 ter was Acsah.[e] 50 These were the descendants of Caleb.

2:50 [f]1Ch 4:4 The sons of Hur[f] the firstborn of Ephrathah:
[g]ver 19 Shobal the father of Kiriath Jearim,[g] 51 Salma the father of Bethlehem, and Hareph the father
of Beth Gader.
52 The descendants of Shobal the father of Kiriath Jearim were:
2:53 [h]2Sa 23:38 Haroeh, half the Manahathites, 53 and the clans of Kiriath Jearim: the Ithrites,[h] Puthites, Shu-
mathites and Mishraites. From these descended the Zorathites and Eshtaolites.
54 The descendants of Salma:
2:54 [i]Ezr 2:22; Ne 7:26; 12:28 Bethlehem, the Netophathites,[i] Atroth Beth Joab, half the Manahathites, the Zorites, 55 and the
clans of scribes[b] who lived at Jabez: the Tirathites, Shimeathites and Sucathites. These are the
2:55 [j]Ge 15:19; Jdg 1:16; Jdg 4:11 [k]Jos 19:35 [l]2Ki 10:15,23; Jer 35:2-19 Kenites[j] who came from Hammath,[k] the father of the house of Recab.[c][l]

The Sons of David

3:1 [m]1Ch 14:3; 28:5 [n]Jos 15:56 [o]1Sa 25:42 3 These were the sons of David[m] born to him in Hebron:
The firstborn was Amnon the son of Ahinoam of Jezreel;[n]
the second, Daniel the son of Abigail[o] of Carmel;
2 the third, Absalom the son of Maacah daughter of Talmai king of Geshur;
3:2 [p]1Ki 2:22 the fourth, Adonijah[p] the son of Haggith;

[a] 42 The meaning of the Hebrew for this phrase is uncertain. [b] 55 Or *of the Sopherites* [c] 55 Or *father of Beth Recab*

2:55 See "The Kenites" on page 434.

[3]the fifth, Shephatiah the son of Abital;
and the sixth, Ithream, by his wife Eglah.
[4]These six were born to David in Hebron,[q] where he reigned seven years and six months.[r]
David reigned in Jerusalem thirty-three years, [5]and these were the children born to him there:
Shammua,[a] Shobab, Nathan and Solomon. These four were by Bathsheba[b][s] daughter of Ammi-
el. [6]There were also Ibhar, Elishua,[c] Eliphelet, [7]Nogah, Nepheg, Japhia, [8]Elishama, Eliada and
Eliphelet—nine in all. [9]All these were the sons of David, besides his sons by his concubines.
And Tamar[t] was their sister.[u]

The Kings of Judah

[10]Solomon's son was Rehoboam,[v]
Abijah his son,
Asa his son,
Jehoshaphat[w] his son,
[11]Jehoram[d][x] his son,
Ahaziah[y] his son,
Joash[z] his son,
[12]Amaziah[a] his son,
Azariah his son,
Jotham[b] his son,
[13]Ahaz[c] his son,
Hezekiah[d] his son,
Manasseh[e] his son,
[14]Amon[f] his son,
Josiah[g] his son.
[15]The sons of Josiah:
Johanan the firstborn,
Jehoiakim[h] the second son,
Zedekiah[i] the third,
Shallum[j] the fourth.
[16]The successors of Jehoiakim:
Jehoiachin[e][k] his son,
and Zedekiah.[l]

The Royal Line After the Exile

[17]The descendants of Jehoiachin the captive:
Shealtiel[m] his son, [18]Malkiram, Pedaiah, Shenazzar,[n] Jekamiah, Hoshama and Nedabiah.[o]
[19]The sons of Pedaiah:
Zerubbabel[p] and Shimei.
The sons of Zerubbabel:
Meshullam and Hananiah.
Shelomith was their sister.
[20]There were also five others:
Hashubah, Ohel, Berekiah, Hasadiah and Jushab-Hesed.
[21]The descendants of Hananiah:
Pelatiah and Jeshaiah, and the sons of Rephaiah, of Arnan, of Obadiah and of Shecaniah.
[22]The descendants of Shecaniah:
Shemaiah and his sons:
Hattush,[q] Igal, Bariah, Neariah and Shaphat—six in all.

3:4 [q]2Sa 5:4; 1Ch 29:27 [r]2Sa 2:11; 5:5
3:5 [s]2Sa 11:3; 12:24
3:9 [t]2Sa 13:1 [u]1Ch 14:4
3:10 [v]1Ki 11:43; 14:21-31; 2Ch 12:16 [w]2Ch 17:1–21:3
3:11 [x]2Ki 8:16-24; 2Ch 21:1 [y]2Ch 22:1-10 [z]2Ki 11:1–12:21
3:12 [a]2Ki 14:1-22; 2Ch 25:1-28 [b]Isa 1:1; Hos 1:1; Mic 1:1
3:13 [c]2Ki 16:1-20; 2Ch 28:1; Isa 7:1 [d]2Ki 18:1–20:21; 2Ch 29:1; Jer 26:19 [e]2Ch 33:1
3:14 [f]2Ki 21:19-26; 2Ch 33:21; Zep 1:1 [g]2Ch 34:1; Jer 1:2; 3:6; 25:3
3:15 [h]2Ki 23:34 [i]Jer 37:1 [j]2Ki 23:31
3:16 [k]2Ki 24:6,8; Mt 1:11 [l]2Ki 24:18
3:17 [m]Ezr 3:2
3:18 [n]Ezr 1:8; 5:14 [o]Jer 22:30
3:19 [p]Ezr 2:2; 3:2; 5:2; Ne 7:7; 12:1; Hag 1:1; 2:2; Zec 4:6
3:22 [q]Ezr 8:2-3

[a] 5 Hebrew *Shimea,* a variant of *Shammua* [b] 5 One Hebrew manuscript and Vulgate (see also Septuagint and 2 Samuel 11:3); most Hebrew manuscripts *Bathshua* [c] 6 Two Hebrew manuscripts (see also 2 Samuel 5:15 and 1 Chron. 14:5); most Hebrew manuscripts *Elishama* [d] 11 Hebrew *Joram,* a variant of *Jehoram* [e] 16 Hebrew *Jeconiah,* a variant of *Jehoiachin*; also in verse 17

3:17–20 Although seven sons are attributed to Jehoiachin, not one of them succeeded him. Tablets discovered in Babylon, dating from 595 to 570 B.C. and listing deliveries of rations, mention Jehoiachin and five sons, as well as other Judahites, all held captive in Babylon. See "Jehoiachin in Captivity and Evil-Merodach" on page 1292.

23 The sons of Neariah:
Elioenai, Hizkiah and Azrikam—three in all.
24 The sons of Elioenai:
Hodaviah, Eliashib, Pelaiah, Akkub, Johanan, Delaiah and Anani—seven in all.

Other Clans of Judah

4:1 [r]Ge 29:35; 46:12; 1Ch 2:3 [s]Nu 26:21

4 The descendants of Judah:[r]
Perez, Hezron,[s] Carmi, Hur and Shobal.
2 Reaiah son of Shobal was the father of Jahath, and Jahath the father of Ahumai and Lahad. These
were the clans of the Zorathites.
3 These were the sons[a] of Etam:
Jezreel, Ishma and Idbash. Their sister was named Hazzelelponi. 4 Penuel was the father of Ge-
dor, and Ezer the father of Hushah.

4:4 [t]1Ch 2:50 [u]Ru 1:19
4:5 [v]1Ch 2:24

These were the descendants of Hur,[t] the firstborn of Ephrathah and father[b] of Bethlehem.[u]
5 Ashhur[v] the father of Tekoa had two wives, Helah and Naarah.
6 Naarah bore him Ahuzzam, Hepher, Temeni and Haahashtari. These were the descendants of
Naarah.
7 The sons of Helah:
Zereth, Zohar, Ethnan, 8 and Koz, who was the father of Anub and Hazzobebah and of the clans
of Aharhel son of Harum.

9 Jabez was more honorable than his brothers. His mother had named him Jabez,[c] saying, "I gave birth
to him in pain." 10 Jabez cried out to the God of Israel, "Oh, that you would bless me and enlarge my ter-
ritory! Let your hand be with me, and keep me from harm so that I will be free from pain." And God
granted his request.
11 Kelub, Shuhah's brother, was the father of Mehir, who was the father of Eshton. 12 Eshton was the
father of Beth Rapha, Paseah and Tehinnah the father of Ir Nahash.[d] These were the men of
Recah.

4:13 [w]Jos 15:17

13 The sons of Kenaz:
Othniel[w] and Seraiah.
The sons of Othniel:
Hathath and Meonothai.[e] 14 Meonothai was the father of Ophrah.
Seraiah was the father of Joab,
the father of Ge Harashim.[f] It was called this because its people were craftsmen.
15 The sons of Caleb son of Jephunneh:
Iru, Elah and Naam.
The son of Elah:
Kenaz.
16 The sons of Jehallelel:
Ziph, Ziphah, Tiria and Asarel.
17 The sons of Ezrah:

4:17 [x]Ex 15:20
4:18 [y]Jos 15:34

Jether, Mered, Epher and Jalon. One of Mered's wives gave birth to Miriam,[x] Shammai and Ish-
bah the father of Eshtemoa. 18 (His Judean wife gave birth to Jered the father of Gedor, Heber the
father of Soco, and Jekuthiel the father of Zanoah.[y]) These were the children of Pharaoh's
daughter Bithiah, whom Mered had married.
19 The sons of Hodiah's wife, the sister of Naham:

4:19 [z]Jos 15:44 [a]Dt 3:14

the father of Keilah[z] the Garmite, and Eshtemoa the Maacathite.[a]
20 The sons of Shimon:
Amnon, Rinnah, Ben-Hanan and Tilon.

[a] *3* Some Septuagint manuscripts (see also Vulgate); Hebrew *father* [b] *4* *Father* may mean *civic leader* or *military leader*; also in verses 12, 14, 17, 18 and possibly elsewhere. [c] *9* *Jabez* sounds like the Hebrew for *pain.* [d] *12* Or *of the city of Nahash* [e] *13* Some Septuagint manuscripts and Vulgate; Hebrew does not have *and Meonothai.* [f] *14* *Ge Harashim* means *valley of craftsmen.*

4:9–10 Inserting short historical notes into genealogical records was common practice in the ancient Near East (cf. Ge 4:19–24; 10:8–12). See "Genealogies in Ancient Israel" on page 1559.

The descendants of Ishi:
Zoheth and Ben-Zoheth.
21 The sons of Shelah[b] son of Judah:
Er the father of Lecah, Laadah the father of Mareshah and the clans of the linen workers at Beth
Ashbea, 22 Jokim, the men of Cozeba, and Joash and Saraph, who ruled in Moab and Jashubi
Lehem. (These records are from ancient times.) 23 They were the potters who lived at Netaim
and Gederah; they stayed there and worked for the king.

Simeon

24 The descendants of Simeon:[c]
Nemuel, Jamin, Jarib,[d] Zerah and Shaul;
25 Shallum was Shaul's son, Mibsam his son and Mishma his son.
26 The descendants of Mishma:
Hammuel his son, Zaccur his son and Shimei his son.

27 Shimei had sixteen sons and six daughters, but his brothers did not have many children; so their en-
tire clan did not become as numerous as the people of Judah. 28 They lived in Beersheba,[e] Moladah,[f] Ha-
zar Shual, 29 Bilhah, Ezem,[g] Tolad, 30 Bethuel, Hormah,[h] Ziklag, 31 Beth Marcaboth, Hazar Susim, Beth Biri
and Shaaraim.[i] These were their towns until the reign of David. 32 Their surrounding villages were Etam,
Ain,[j] Rimmon, Token and Ashan[k]—five towns— 33 and all the villages around these towns as far as Ba-
alath.[a] These were their settlements. And they kept a genealogical record.

34 Meshobab, Jamlech, Joshah son of Amaziah, 35 Joel, Jehu son of Joshibiah, the son of Seraiah, the
son of Asiel, 36 also Elioenai, Jaakobah, Jeshohaiah, Asaiah, Adiel, Jesimiel, Benaiah, 37 and Ziza son
of Shiphi, the son of Allon, the son of Jedaiah, the son of Shimri, the son of Shemaiah.

38 The men listed above by name were leaders of their clans. Their families increased greatly, 39 and
they went to the outskirts of Gedor[l] to the east of the valley in search of pasture for their flocks. 40 They
found rich, good pasture, and the land was spacious, peaceful and quiet.[m] Some Hamites had lived there
formerly.

41 The men whose names were listed came in the days of Hezekiah king of Judah. They attacked the
Hamites in their dwellings and also the Meunites[n] who were there and completely destroyed[b] them, as
is evident to this day. Then they settled in their place, because there was pasture for their flocks. 42 And
five hundred of these Simeonites, led by Pelatiah, Neariah, Rephaiah and Uzziel, the sons of Ishi, invad-
ed the hill country of Seir.[o] 43 They killed the remaining Amalekites[p] who had escaped, and they have
lived there to this day.

Reuben

5 The sons of Reuben[q] the firstborn of Israel (he was the firstborn, but when he defiled his father's
marriage bed,[r] his rights as firstborn were given to the sons of Joseph[s] son of Israel;[t] so he could not
be listed in the genealogical record in accordance with his birthright,[u] 2 and though Judah[v] was the stron-
gest of his brothers and a ruler[w] came from him, the rights of the firstborn[x] belonged to Joseph)— 3 the
sons of Reuben[y] the firstborn of Israel:
Hanoch, Pallu,[z] Hezron and Carmi.
4 The descendants of Joel:
Shemaiah his son, Gog his son,
Shimei his son, 5 Micah his son,
Reaiah his son, Baal his son,
6 and Beerah his son, whom Tiglath-Pileser[c][a] king of Assyria took into exile. Beerah was a lead-
er of the Reubenites.

4:21 [b]Ge 38:5
4:24 [c]Ge 29:33 [d]Nu 26:12
4:28 [e]Ge 21:14 [f]Jos 15:26
4:29 [g]Jos 15:29
4:30 [h]Nu 14:45
4:31 [i]Jos 15:36
4:32 [j]Nu 34:11 [k]Jos 15:42
4:39 [l]Jos 15:58
4:40 [m]Jdg 18:7-10
4:41 [n]2Ch 20:1; 26:7
4:42 [o]Ge 14:6
4:43 [p]1Sa 15:8; 30:17; 2Sa 8:12; Est 3:1; 9:16
5:1 [q]Ge 29:32 [r]Ge 35:22; 49:4 [s]Ge 48:16,22; 49:26 [t]Ge 48:5 [u]1Ch 26:10
5:2 [v]Ge 49:10,12 [w]1Sa 9:16; 12:12; 2Sa 6:21; 1Ch 11:2; 2Ch 7:18; Ps 60:7; Mic 5:2; Mt 2:6 [x]Ge 25:31
5:3 [y]Ge 29:32; 46:9; Ex 6:14; Nu 26:5-11 [z]Nu 26:5
5:6 [a]ver 26; 2Ki 15:19; 16:10; 2Ch 28:20

[a] 33 Some Septuagint manuscripts (see also Joshua 19:8); Hebrew *Baal* also in verse 26

[b] 41 The Hebrew term refers to the irrevocable giving over of things or persons to the LORD, often by totally destroying them.

[c] 6 Hebrew *Tilgath-Pilneser*, a variant of *Tiglath-Pileser*;

4:21 In ancient Near Eastern society clans were often associated not only with particular localities but also with special trades or guilds, such as linen workers (v. 21), potters (v. 23), royal patronage (v. 23) and scribes (2:55).

4:41 For an explanation of "completely destroyed," see "*Herem*, Holy War" on page 419.

5:7 [b]ver 17 — 7 Their relatives by clans,[b] listed according to their genealogical records:
Jeiel the chief, Zechariah, 8 and Bela son of Azaz, the son of Shema, the son of Joel. They settled
5:8 [c]Nu 32:34 — in the area from Aroer[c] to Nebo and Baal Meon. 9 To the east they occupied the land up to the
edge of the desert that extends to the Euphrates River, because their livestock had increased in
5:9 [d]Nu 32:26; Jos 22:9 — Gilead.[d]
5:10 [e]ver 18-21 — 10 During Saul's reign they waged war against the Hagrites[e], who were defeated at their hands;
they occupied the dwellings of the Hagrites throughout the entire region east of Gilead.

Gad

5:11 [f]Jos 13:24-28 [g]Dt 3:10; Jos 13:11 — 11 The Gadites[f] lived next to them in Bashan, as far as Salecah:[g]
12 Joel was the chief, Shapham the second, then Janai and Shaphat, in Bashan.
13 Their relatives, by families, were:
Michael, Meshullam, Sheba, Jorai, Jacan, Zia and Eber—seven in all.
14 These were the sons of Abihail son of Huri, the son of Jaroah, the son of Gilead, the son of Michael, the son of Jeshishai, the son of Jahdo, the son of Buz.
15 Ahi son of Abdiel, the son of Guni, was head of their family.
16 The Gadites lived in Gilead, in Bashan and its outlying villages, and on all the pasturelands of Sharon as far as they extended.
5:17 [h]2Ki 15:32 [i]2Ki 14:16,28 — 17 All these were entered in the genealogical records during the reigns of Jotham[h] king of Judah and
Jeroboam[i] king of Israel.

18 The Reubenites, the Gadites and the half-tribe of Manasseh had 44,760 men ready for military ser-
5:18 [j]Nu 1:3 — vice[j]—able-bodied men who could handle shield and sword, who could use a bow, and who were trained
5:19 [k]ver 10; Ge 25:15; 1Ch 1:31 — for battle. 19 They waged war against the Hagrites, Jetur,[k] Naphish and Nodab. 20 They were helped[l] in
fighting them, and God handed the Hagrites and all their allies over to them, because they cried[m] out to
5:20 [l]Ps 37:40 [m]1Ki 8:44; 2Ch 13:14; 14:11; Ps 20:7-9; 22:5 [n]Ps 26:1; Da 6:23 — him during the battle. He answered their prayers, because they trusted[n] in him. 21 They seized the live-
stock of the Hagrites—fifty thousand camels, two hundred fifty thousand sheep and two thousand don-
keys. They also took one hundred thousand people captive, 22 and many others fell slain, because the bat-
5:22 [o]2Ch 32:8 [p]2Ki 15:29; 17:6 — tle[o] was God's. And they occupied the land until the exile.[p]

The Half-Tribe of Manasseh

23 The people of the half-tribe of Manasseh were numerous; they settled in the land from Bashan to
5:23 [q]Dt 3:8,9; SS 4:8 — Baal Hermon, that is, to Senir (Mount Hermon).[q]
24 These were the heads of their families: Epher, Ishi, Eliel, Azriel, Jeremiah, Hodaviah and Jahdi-
5:25 [r]Dt 32:15-18; 2Ki 17:7; 1Ch 9:1; 2Ch 26:16 [s]Ex 34:15 — el. They were brave warriors, famous men, and heads of their families. 25 But they were unfaithful[r] to
the God of their fathers and prostituted[s] themselves to the gods of the peoples of the land, whom
God had destroyed before them. 26 So the God of Israel stirred up the spirit of Pul[t] king of Assyria
5:26 [t]2Ki 15:19 [u]2Ki 15:29 [v]2Ki 17:6; 18:11 — (that is, Tiglath-Pileser[u] king of Assyria), who took the Reubenites, the Gadites and the half-tribe of
Manasseh into exile. He took them to Halah,[v] Habor, Hara and the river of Gozan, where they are to
this day.

Levi

6:1 [w]Ge 46:11; Ex 6:16; Nu 26:57; 1Ch 23:6 — **6** The sons of Levi:[w]
Gershon, Kohath and Merari.
2 The sons of Kohath:
Amram, Izhar, Hebron and Uzziel.
3 The children of Amram:
Aaron, Moses and Miriam.
The sons of Aaron:
6:3 [x]Lev 10:1 — Nadab, Abihu,[x] Eleazar and Ithamar.
4 Eleazar was the father of Phinehas,
Phinehas the father of Abishua,

5:26 For information on Pul, see the note on 2 Kings 15:19–20. See also "Menahem and Pekah of Israel, Jotham of Judah and Tiglath-Pileser III of Assyria" on page 553.

[5] Abishua the father of Bukki,
Bukki the father of Uzzi,
[6] Uzzi the father of Zerahiah,
Zerahiah the father of Meraioth,
[7] Meraioth the father of Amariah,
Amariah the father of Ahitub,
[8] Ahitub the father of Zadok,[y]
Zadok the father of Ahimaaz,
[9] Ahimaaz the father of Azariah,
Azariah the father of Johanan,
[10] Johanan the father of Azariah[z] (it was he who served as priest in the temple Solomon built in Jerusalem),
[11] Azariah the father of Amariah,
Amariah the father of Ahitub,
[12] Ahitub the father of Zadok,
Zadok the father of Shallum,
[13] Shallum the father of Hilkiah,[a]
Hilkiah the father of Azariah,
[14] Azariah the father of Seraiah,[b]
and Seraiah the father of Jehozadak.

[15] Jehozadak[c] was deported when the LORD sent Judah and Jerusalem into exile by the hand of Nebuchadnezzar.

[16] The sons of Levi:[d]
Gershon,[a] Kohath and Merari.[e]
[17] These are the names of the sons of Gershon:
Libni and Shimei.
[18] The sons of Kohath:
Amram, Izhar, Hebron and Uzziel.
[19] The sons of Merari:[f]
Mahli and Mushi.
These are the clans of the Levites listed according to their fathers:
[20] Of Gershon:
Libni his son, Jehath his son,
Zimmah his son, [21] Joah his son,
Iddo his son, Zerah his son
and Jeatherai his son.
[22] The descendants of Kohath:
Amminadab his son, Korah[g] his son,
Assir his son, [23] Elkanah his son,
Ebiasaph his son, Assir his son,
[24] Tahath his son, Uriel[h] his son,
Uzziah his son and Shaul his son.
[25] The descendants of Elkanah:
Amasai, Ahimoth,
[26] Elkanah his son,[b] Zophai his son,
Nahath his son, [27] Eliab his son,
Jeroham his son, Elkanah[i] his son
and Samuel[j] his son.[c]
[28] The sons of Samuel:
Joel[d][k] the firstborn
and Abijah the second son.

6:8 [y]2Sa 8:17; 15:27; Ezr 7:2
6:10 [z]1Ki 4:2; 6:1; 2Ch 3:1; 26:17-18
6:13 [a]2Ki 22:1-20; 2Ch 34:9; 35:8
6:14 [b]2Ki 25:18; Ezr 2:2; Ne 11:11
6:15 [c]2Ki 25:18; Ne 12:1; Hag 1:1, 14; 2:2,4; Zec 6:11
6:16 [d]Ge 29:34; Ex 6:16; Nu 3:17-20 [e]Nu 26:57
6:19 [f]Ge 46:11; 1Ch 23:21; 24:26
6:22 [g]Ex 6:24
6:24 [h]1Ch 15:5
6:27 [i]1Sa 1:1 [j]1Sa 1:20
6:28 [k]ver 33; 1Sa 8:2

[a] *16* Hebrew *Gershom,* a variant of *Gershon;* also in verses 17, 20, 43, 62 and 71 [b] *26* Some Hebrew manuscripts, Septuagint and Syriac; most Hebrew manuscripts *Ahimoth* [26] *and Elkanah. The sons of Elkanah:* [c] *27* Some Septuagint manuscripts (see also 1 Samuel 1:19,20 and 1 Chron. 6:33,34); Hebrew does not have *and Samuel his son.* [d] *28* Some Septuagint manuscripts and Syriac (see also 1 Samuel 8:2 and 1 Chron. 6:33); Hebrew does not have *Joel.*

29 The descendants of Merari:
Mahli, Libni his son,
Shimei his son, Uzzah his son,
30 Shimea his son, Haggiah his son
and Asaiah his son.

The Temple Musicians

6:31 [l]1Ch 25:1; 2Ch 29:25-26; Ne 12:45 [m]1Ch 9:33; 15:19; Ezr 3:10; Ps 68:25

31 These are the men[l] David put in charge of the music[m] in the house of the LORD after the ark came
to rest there. 32 They ministered with music before the tabernacle, the Tent of Meeting, until Solomon
built the temple of the LORD in Jerusalem. They performed their duties according to the regulations laid
down for them.

33 Here are the men who served, together with their sons:
From the Kohathites:

6:33 [n]1Ki 4:31; 1Ch 15:17; 25:1 [o]ver 28
6:34 [p]1Sa 1:1
6:37 [q]Ex 6:24
6:38 [r]Ex 6:21

Heman,[n] the musician,
the son of Joel,[o] the son of Samuel,
34 the son of Elkanah,[p] the son of Jeroham,
the son of Eliel, the son of Toah,
35 the son of Zuph, the son of Elkanah,
the son of Mahath, the son of Amasai,
36 the son of Elkanah, the son of Joel,
the son of Azariah, the son of Zephaniah,
37 the son of Tahath, the son of Assir,
the son of Ebiasaph, the son of Korah,[q]
38 the son of Izhar,[r] the son of Kohath,
the son of Levi, the son of Israel;

6:39 [s]1Ch 25:1,9; 2Ch 29:13; Ne 11:17 [t]1Ch 15:17

39 and Heman's associate Asaph,[s] who served at his right hand:
Asaph son of Berekiah, the son of Shimea,[t]
40 the son of Michael, the son of Baaseiah,[a]
the son of Malkijah, 41 the son of Ethni,
the son of Zerah, the son of Adaiah,
42 the son of Ethan, the son of Zimmah,
the son of Shimei, 43 the son of Jahath,
the son of Gershon, the son of Levi;
44 and from their associates, the Merarites, at his left hand:
Ethan son of Kishi, the son of Abdi,
the son of Malluch, 45 the son of Hashabiah,
the son of Amaziah, the son of Hilkiah,
46 the son of Amzi, the son of Bani,
the son of Shemer, 47 the son of Mahli,
the son of Mushi, the son of Merari,
the son of Levi.

6:48 [u]1Ch 23:32
6:49 [v]Ex 27:1-8 [w]Ex 30:1-7,10; 2Ch 26:18

48 Their fellow Levites[u] were assigned to all the other duties of the tabernacle, the house of God. 49 But
Aaron and his descendants were the ones who presented offerings on the altar[v] of burnt offering and on
the altar of incense[w] in connection with all that was done in the Most Holy Place, making atonement for
Israel, in accordance with all that Moses the servant of God had commanded.

50 These were the descendants of Aaron:
Eleazar his son, Phinehas his son,
Abishua his son, 51 Bukki his son,
Uzzi his son, Zerahiah his son,

[a] 40 Most Hebrew manuscripts; some Hebrew manuscripts, one Septuagint manuscript and Syriac *Maaseiah*

6:31 Guilds of singers and musicians were common in Canaanite temples.

ARCHAEOLOGICAL SITES

GEZER

1 CHRONICLES 6 A Levitical city on the southern border of Ephraim's territory (Jos 21:21),[1] Gezer's strategic position (see "Map 5") made it a difficult city for either the Israelites or any other nation to hold for any length of time.[2] Adjacent to the all-important coastal route and astride the main road leading eastward into the hill country, Gezer was the scene of important events and battles both before and after the arrival of the Israelites.

Although Gezer was occupied during the **Chalcolithic**[3] and **Early Bronze Ages**, the city grew significantly during the **Middle Bronze Age** (c. 1900–1500 B.C.). It was at this time surrounded by a massive wall of roughly dressed stones.

Egypt's Thutmose III, on an inscription at Karnak, claims to have captured Gezer (c. 1482 B.C.), and the demise of the Middle Bronze city may be correlated to that event. During the first part of the **Late Bronze Age**, Gezer was thus subservient to Egypt. Indeed, during the time of **Amenhotep IV** (aka Akhenaten; c. 1352–1336 B.C.), the kings of Gezer sought Egypt's assistance in dealing with Canaanite conflicts. The **Amarna** Letters[4] contain their correspondence with Egypt and demonstrate that, although Egypt was nominally the overlord of the Canaanite cities, it was losing its grip on **Canaan**. However, Gezer was destroyed around 1210 B.C. by a later pharaoh, Merneptah. In his victory **stele** he claims to have captured Gezer, and indeed a **cartouche** of Merneptah was discovered at this level.[5]

Panel of Merneptah's cartouche regarding his campaign in Canaan

Photograph: © Todd Bolen/Bible Places.com

At the beginning of the **Iron Age** Gezer was occupied by the Philistines. Examples of the distinctive "Bichrome ware" Philistine pottery (decorated in two colors) have been found there, and the city at this time (corresponding to the late **judges period** and the reign of Saul) appears to have been relatively prosperous. By the time of Solomon, however, it had declined considerably, as indicated by a poorer material culture in terms of architecture and pottery. First Kings 9:16 states that an unnamed pharaoh captured the city, burned it and presented it to Solomon as his daughter's dowry on the occasion of their marriage.[6]

Solomon strongly fortified Gezer, together with **Hazor**[7] and **Megiddo**[7] (both on "Map 5"), in order to guard the main entry points into his kingdom (1Ki 9:15). These cities all provide examples of the fortification style developed by Solomon's engineers.[8] Notable features include an elaborate, four-entryway gate with guard chambers and a kind of double wall known as a **casemate wall**. The workmanship at Gezer during this era attests to the prosperity and sophistication of the Solomonic era. There were relatively few private homes, however, suggesting that in Solomon's day Gezer was primarily a governmental center.

This city was violently destroyed near the end of the tenth century B.C. in an event that was probably the work of Pharaoh Sheshonk I (the Shishak[9] of 1Ki 14:25). Important archaeological discoveries at Gezer, encompassing various time periods, include a series of ten large, standing stones from the Middle Bronze Canaanite settlement, the city gate that Solomon constructed and the Gezer Calendar,[10] a text inscribed on limestone describing the yearly agricultural cycle.

[1]See "Levitical Towns" on page 335. [2]See "Caravan Trading and Routes in the Ancient Near East" on page 63. [3]See "Archaeological Periods" chart on page xx in the front of this Bible. [4]See "The Amarna Tablets and the Habiru" on page 347. [5]See "The Merneptah Stele" on page 360. [6]See "The Pharaoh Whose Daughter Solomon Married" on page 493. [7]See "Hazor" on page 322 and "Megiddo" on page 1541. [8]See "The Building Activity of Solomon" on page 497. [9]See "The Campaign of Shishak" on page 635. [10]See "The Gezer Calendar" on page 913.

52 Meraioth his son, Amariah his son,
6:53 x2Sa 8:17 Ahitub his son, 53 Zadok[x] his son
and Ahimaaz his son.

6:54 yNu 31:10 54 These were the locations of their settlements[y] allotted as their territory (they were assigned to the
descendants of Aaron who were from the Kohathite clan, because the first lot was for them):
55 They were given Hebron in Judah with its surrounding pasturelands. 56 But the fields and vil-
6:56 zJos 14:13; 15:13 lages around the city were given to Caleb son of Jephunneh.[z]
6:57 aNu 33:20 bJos 15:48 57 So the descendants of Aaron were given Hebron (a city of refuge), and Libnah,[a][a] Jattir,[b] Esh-
6:58 cJos 10:3 temoa, 58 Hilen, Debir,[c] 59 Ashan,[d] Juttah[b] and Beth Shemesh, together with their pasturelands.
6:59 dJos 15:42 6:60 eJer 1:1 60 And from the tribe of Benjamin they were given Gibeon,[c] Geba, Alemeth and Anathoth,[e] togeth-
er with their pasturelands.
These towns, which were distributed among the Kohathite clans, were thirteen in all.
61 The rest of Kohath's descendants were allotted ten towns from the clans of half the tribe of Manasseh.
62 The descendants of Gershon, clan by clan, were allotted thirteen towns from the tribes of Issachar,
Asher and Naphtali, and from the part of the tribe of Manasseh that is in Bashan.
63 The descendants of Merari, clan by clan, were allotted twelve towns from the tribes of Reuben, Gad
and Zebulun.
6:64 fNu 35:1-8; Jos 21:3,41-42 64 So the Israelites gave the Levites these towns[f] and their pasturelands. 65 From the tribes of Judah,
Simeon and Benjamin they allotted the previously named towns.
66 Some of the Kohathite clans were given as their territory towns from the tribe of Ephraim.
6:67 gJos 10:33 67 In the hill country of Ephraim they were given Shechem (a city of refuge), and Gezer,[d][g] 68 Jok-
6:68 h1Ki 4:12 iJos 10:10 meam,[h] Beth Horon,[i] 69 Aijalon[j] and Gath Rimmon,[k] together with their pasturelands.
6:69 jJos 10:12 kJos 19:45 70 And from half the tribe of Manasseh the Israelites gave Aner and Bileam, together with their
pasturelands, to the rest of the Kohathite clans.

6:71 l1Ch 23:7 mJos 20:8 71 The Gershonites[l] received the following:
From the clan of the half-tribe of Manasseh
they received Golan in Bashan[m] and also Ashtaroth, together with their pasturelands;
72 from the tribe of Issachar
6:72 nJos 19:12 they received Kedesh, Daberath,[n] 73 Ramoth and Anem, together with their pasturelands;
74 from the tribe of Asher
6:74 oJos 19:28 they received Mashal, Abdon,[o] 75 Hukok[p] and Rehob,[q] together with their pasturelands;
6:75 pJos 19:34 qNu 13:21 76 and from the tribe of Naphtali
6:76 rJos 19:28 sNu 32:37 they received Kedesh in Galilee, Hammon[r] and Kiriathaim,[s] together with their pasturelands.
77 The Merarites (the rest of the Levites) received the following:
From the tribe of Zebulun
they received Jokneam, Kartah,[e] Rimmono and Tabor, together with their pasturelands;
78 from the tribe of Reuben across the Jordan east of Jericho
6:78 tJos 20:8 6:79 uDt 2:26 they received Bezer[t] in the desert, Jahzah, 79 Kedemoth[u] and Mephaath, together with their pas-
turelands;
80 and from the tribe of Gad
6:80 vJos 20:8 wGe 32:2 they received Ramoth in Gilead,[v] Mahanaim,[w] 81 Heshbon and Jazer,[x] together with their pas-
6:81 xNu 21:32 y2Ch 11:14 turelands.[y]

Issachar

7:1 zGe 30:18; Nu 26:23 aGe 46:13 **7** The sons of Issachar:[z]
Tola, Puah,[a] Jashub and Shimron—four in all.
2 The sons of Tola:
Uzzi, Rephaiah, Jeriel, Jahmai, Ibsam and Samuel—heads of their families. During the reign of
David, the descendants of Tola listed as fighting men in their genealogy numbered 22,600.

[a] *57* See Joshua 21:13; Hebrew *given the cities of refuge: Hebron, Libnah.* [b] *59* Syriac (see also Septuagint and Joshua 21:16); Hebrew does not have *Juttah.* [c] *60* See Joshua 21:17; Hebrew does not have *Gibeon.* [d] *67* See Joshua 21:21; Hebrew *given the cities of refuge: Shechem, Gezer.* [e] *77* See Septuagint and Joshua 21:34; Hebrew does not have *Jokneam, Kartah.*

6:54–81 See "Levitical Towns" on page 335.

[3] The son of Uzzi:
Izrahiah.
The sons of Izrahiah:
Michael, Obadiah, Joel and Isshiah. All five of them were chiefs. [4] According to their family ge-
nealogy, they had 36,000 men ready for battle, for they had many wives and children.
[5] The relatives who were fighting men belonging to all the clans of Issachar, as listed in their gene-
alogy, were 87,000 in all.

Benjamin

[6] Three sons of Benjamin:[b]
Bela, Beker and Jediael.
[7] The sons of Bela:
Ezbon, Uzzi, Uzziel, Jerimoth and Iri, heads of families—five in all. Their genealogical record
listed 22,034 fighting men.
[8] The sons of Beker:
Zemirah, Joash, Eliezer, Elioenai, Omri, Jeremoth, Abijah, Anathoth and Alemeth. All these were
the sons of Beker. [9] Their genealogical record listed the heads of families and 20,200 fighting
men.
[10] The son of Jediael:
Bilhan.
The sons of Bilhan:
Jeush, Benjamin, Ehud, Kenaanah, Zethan, Tarshish and Ahishahar. [11] All these sons of Jediael
were heads of families. There were 17,200 fighting men ready to go out to war.
[12] The Shuppites and Huppites were the descendants of Ir, and the Hushites the descendants of Aher.

Naphtali

[13] The sons of Naphtali:[c]
Jahziel, Guni, Jezer and Shillem[a]—the descendants of Bilhah.

Manasseh

[14] The descendants of Manasseh:[d]
Asriel was his descendant through his Aramean concubine. She gave birth to Makir the father
of Gilead.[e] [15] Makir took a wife from among the Huppites and Shuppites. His sister's name was
Maacah.
Another descendant was named Zelophehad,[f] who had only daughters.
[16] Makir's wife Maacah gave birth to a son and named him Peresh. His brother was named She-
resh, and his sons were Ulam and Rakem.
[17] The son of Ulam:
Bedan.
These were the sons of Gilead[g] son of Makir, the son of Manasseh. [18] His sister Hammoleketh gave
birth to Ishhod, Abiezer[h] and Mahlah.
[19] The sons of Shemida were:
Ahian, Shechem, Likhi and Aniam.

7:6 [b]Ge 46:21; Nu 26:38; 1Ch 8:1-40
7:13 [c]Ge 30:8; 46:24
7:14 [d]Ge 41:51; Jos 17:1; 1Ch 5:23 [e]Nu 26:30
7:15 [f]Nu 26:33; 36:1-12
7:17 [g]Nu 26:30; 1Sa 12:11
7:18 [h]Jos 17:2

[a] 13 Some Hebrew and Septuagint manuscripts (see also Gen. 46:24 and Num. 26:49); most Hebrew manuscripts *Shallum*

7:16–19 Seven of the thirteen clans of the tribe of Manasseh listed here are mentioned in the Samaria Ostraca (see "The Samaria Ostraca" on p. 550). The prominence of women in this genealogy is unusual, suggesting that it may have functioned in the domestic sphere, perhaps as a statement of the social status of the various clans of Manasseh.

It seems odd that Maacah, the "sister" of Makir (v. 15), is mentioned, and that Makir is then said to have had a wife called Maacah (v. 16). It would not appear that both refer to the same Maacah, since verse 15 states that Makir's wife was from the otherwise unknown "Huppites and Shuppites." Most interpreters suspect that the text has been corrupted (see "Textual Criticism" on p. 1151). An unrelated question is why either Maacah is mentioned at all. It may be that the Chronicler was concerned about evil associations carried by the name Maacah: Another Maacah had been the mother of David's usurping son Absalom, and the most famous Maacah (who lived later than this account in ch. 7, but most likely before Chronicles was written) was the grandmother of Asa, whom he deposed from her position as queen mother for her promotion of idolatry (2Ch 15:16). Hence, by drawing attention to the name Maacah in the genealogical records of the northern tribes, the Chronicler may have been alluding to the secessionist and idolatrous history of those tribes—an association many of his readers would likely have caught.

The daughters of Zelophehad (v. 15) had prompted the rulings on the inheritance rights of women (see Nu 26:29–34; 27:1–11; 36:1–12; Jos 17:3–4; see also "Inheritance in the Ancient Near East" on p. 250).

Ephraim

7:20 [i]Ge 41:52; Nu 1:33; 26:35
[20] The descendants of Ephraim:[i]
Shuthelah, Bered his son,
Tahath his son, Eleadah his son,
Tahath his son, [21] Zabad his son
and Shuthelah his son.
Ezer and Elead were killed by the native-born men of Gath, when they went down to seize their
livestock. [22] Their father Ephraim mourned for them many days, and his relatives came to com-
fort him. [23] Then he lay with his wife again, and she became pregnant and gave birth to a son. He
named him Beriah,[a] because there had been misfortune in his family. [24] His daughter was Shee-
7:24 [j]Jos 10:10; 16:3,5
rah, who built Lower and Upper Beth Horon[j] as well as Uzzen Sheerah.
[25] Rephah was his son, Resheph his son,[b]
Telah his son, Tahan his son,
[26] Ladan his son, Ammihud his son,
Elishama his son, [27] Nun his son
and Joshua his son.

[a] 23 *Beriah* sounds like the Hebrew for *misfortune.* [b] 25 Some Septuagint manuscripts; Hebrew does not have *his son.*

7:21 From Genesis 41:52 we know that Ephraim had been born in Egypt and presumably lived there for his entire life, along with the children of Israel. This text indicates that two sons of Ephraim, Ezer and Elead, were killed while on a raiding expedition to Gath, a city that would later be associated with the Philistines. Many interpreters take this as a reference to raiding carried out by later Ephraimites from the central hill country on the cities of the coastal plains. In the text itself, however, if this incident is interpreted consistently with what we know of Ephraim from Genesis, it would appear that this raid was carried out from the Israelite enclave in Goshen in Egypt.

ARCHAEOLOGICAL SITES

TAANACH

1 CHRONICLES 7 The city of Taanach ("Map 5") is located about 5 miles (8 km) southeast of **Megiddo**[1] (also "Map 5") in the foothills above the Valley of Jezreel.[1] It guarded one of the major passes inland from the coastal trade route known as the **Via Maris**. The king of Taanach was one of the many **Canaanites** whom Joshua defeated during the conquest (Jos 12:21).[2] The city was assigned to the tribe of Manasseh, although its members found themselves unable to dislodge the Canaanite inhabitants (Jos 17:11–12; Jdg 1:27; 1Ch 7:29).

First Chronicles 6:61 tells us that the Levites were given ten cities;[3] Joshua 21:25 identifies one of them as Taanach from the territory of Manasseh. Deborah and Barak led the Israelites against Sisera "at Taanach by the waters of Megiddo" (Jdg 5:19). That the city lay in a swampy area of the valley assisted in the Israelite defeat of Sisera's army, since his chariots could not have traveled efficiently in the swamp. Taanach is again mentioned in Solomon's delegation of administrative centers (1Ki 4:12).

This city also appears in extrabiblical texts. The Egyptian Thutmose III cited Taanach in his description of the battle against Megiddo and the surrounding area in the mid-fifteenth century B.C. It is listed on a temple at Karnak with the names of other nearby towns that Pharaoh Shishak conquered in the tenth century B.C., during the reign of Rehoboam.[4] The church historian Eusebius recorded a large population there in the fourth century A.D., but by the fourteenth century Taanach had been reduced in size to a small village.

Archaeological investigations have revealed occupation layers at Taanach dating back to the **Early Bronze Age**.[5] At that time (mid-third millennium B.C.) the city already had a protective wall and **glacis**. Later the wall was widened and larger stones incorporated into it. Because there is evidence of metal-working, as well as of the presence of scribes, scholars have suggested that Taanach served as a production center during the **Iron Age**. Others have posited that it may have been a chariot garrison. Several dwellings and a tower (all dating from the twelfth to ninth centuries B.C.) have yielded loomweights, tools, pottery and an earlier **Akkadian** archive, as well as two cult stands.[6] After this period the site seems to have been inhabited only intermittently until the third century B.C., when it once again became a thriving city.

[1]See "Megiddo" on page 1541 and "The Valley of Jezreel" on page 1412. [2]See "The Conquest of Canaan" on page 310 and "Canaan" on page 324. [3]See "Levitical Towns" on page 335. [4]See "The Campaign of Shishak" on page 635. [5]See "Archaeological Periods" chart on page xx in the front of this Bible. [6]See "The Taanach Cult Stands" on page 330.

28 Their lands and settlements included Bethel and its surrounding villages, Naaran to the east, Ge-
zer[k] and its villages to the west, and Shechem and its villages all the way to Ayyah and its villages. 29 Along 7:28 [k]Jos 10:33; 16:7
the borders of Manasseh were Beth Shan,[l] Taanach, Megiddo and Dor,[m] together with their villages. The 7:29 [l]Jos 17:11 [m]Jos 11:2
descendants of Joseph son of Israel lived in these towns.

Asher

30 The sons of Asher:[n] 7:30 [n]Ge 46:17; Nu 1:40; 26:44
Imnah, Ishvah, Ishvi and Beriah. Their sister was Serah.
31 The sons of Beriah:
Heber and Malkiel, who was the father of Birzaith.
32 Heber was the father of Japhlet, Shomer and Hotham and of their sister Shua.
33 The sons of Japhlet:
Pasach, Bimhal and Ashvath.
These were Japhlet's sons.
34 The sons of Shomer:
Ahi, Rohgah,[a] Hubbah and Aram.
35 The sons of his brother Helem:
Zophah, Imna, Shelesh and Amal.
36 The sons of Zophah:
Suah, Harnepher, Shual, Beri, Imrah, 37 Bezer, Hod, Shamma, Shilshah, Ithran[b] and Beera.
38 The sons of Jether:
Jephunneh, Pispah and Ara.
39 The sons of Ulla:
Arah, Hanniel and Rizia.
40 All these were descendants of Asher—heads of families, choice men, brave warriors and outstand-
ing leaders. The number of men ready for battle, as listed in their genealogy, was 26,000.

The Genealogy of Saul the Benjamite

8 Benjamin[o] was the father of Bela his firstborn, 8:1 [o]Ge 46:21; 1Ch 7:6
Ashbel the second son, Aharah the third,
2 Nohah the fourth and Rapha the fifth.
3 The sons of Bela were:
Addar,[p] Gera, Abihud,[c] 4 Abishua, Naaman, Ahoah,[q] 5 Gera, Shephuphan and Huram. 8:3 [p]Ge 46:21 8:4 [q]2Sa 23:9
6 These were the descendants of Ehud,[r] who were heads of families of those living in Geba and were 8:6 [r]Jdg 3:12-30; 1Ch 2:52
deported to Manahath:
7 Naaman, Ahijah, and Gera, who deported them and who was the father of Uzza and Ahihud.
8 Sons were born to Shaharaim in Moab after he had divorced his wives Hushim and Baara. 9 By his
wife Hodesh he had Jobab, Zibia, Mesha, Malcam, 10 Jeuz, Sakia and Mirmah. These were his
sons, heads of families. 11 By Hushim he had Abitub and Elpaal.
12 The sons of Elpaal:
Eber, Misham, Shemed (who built Ono[s] and Lod with its surrounding villages), 13 and Beriah 8:12 [s]Ezr 2:33; Ne 6:2; 7:37; 11:35
and Shema, who were heads of families of those living in Aijalon[t] and who drove out the inhab- 8:13 [t]Jos 10:12 [u]Jos 11:22
itants of Gath.[u]
14 Ahio, Shashak, Jeremoth, 15 Zebadiah, Arad, Eder, 16 Michael, Ishpah and Joha were the sons of Be-
riah.
17 Zebadiah, Meshullam, Hizki, Heber, 18 Ishmerai, Izliah and Jobab were the sons of Elpaal.
19 Jakim, Zicri, Zabdi, 20 Elienai, Zillethai, Eliel, 21 Adaiah, Beraiah and Shimrath were the sons of
Shimei.
22 Ishpan, Eber, Eliel, 23 Abdon, Zicri, Hanan, 24 Hananiah, Elam, Anthothijah, 25 Iphdeiah and Penuel
were the sons of Shashak.
26 Shamsherai, Shehariah, Athaliah, 27 Jaareshiah, Elijah and Zicri were the sons of Jeroham.
28 All these were heads of families, chiefs as listed in their genealogy, and they lived in Jerusalem.

29 Jeiel[d] the father[e] of Gibeon lived in Gibeon.[v] 8:29 [v]Jos 9:3

[a] 34 Or *of his brother Shomer: Rohgah* [b] 37 Possibly a variant of *Jether* [c] 3 Or *Gera the father of Ehud* [d] 29 Some Septuagint manuscripts (see also 1 Chron. 9:35); Hebrew does not have *Jeiel.* [e] 29 *Father* may mean *civic leader* or *military leader.*

His wife's name was Maacah, 30 and his firstborn son was Abdon, followed by Zur, Kish, Baal,
Ner,[a] Nadab, 31 Gedor, Ahio, Zeker 32 and Mikloth, who was the father of Shimeah. They too lived
near their relatives in Jerusalem.

33 Ner[w] was the father of Kish,[x] Kish the father of Saul[y], and Saul the father of Jonathan, Malki-Shua,
Abinadab and Esh-Baal.[b z]

34 The son of Jonathan:[a]
Merib-Baal,[c b] who was the father of Micah.

35 The sons of Micah:
Pithon, Melech, Tarea and Ahaz.

36 Ahaz was the father of Jehoaddah, Jehoaddah was the father of Alemeth, Azmaveth and Zim-
ri, and Zimri was the father of Moza. 37 Moza was the father of Binea; Raphah was his son, Ele-
asah his son and Azel his son.

38 Azel had six sons, and these were their names:
Azrikam, Bokeru, Ishmael, Sheariah, Obadiah and Hanan. All these were the sons of Azel.

39 The sons of his brother Eshek:
Ulam his firstborn, Jeush the second son and Eliphelet the third. 40 The sons of Ulam were brave
warriors who could handle the bow. They had many sons and grandsons—150 in all.

All these were the descendants of Benjamin.[c]

8:33 [w]1Sa 28:19 [x]1Sa 9:1 [y]1Sa 14:49 [z]2Sa 2:8
8:34 [a]2Sa 9:12 [b]2Sa 4:4
8:40 [c]Nu 26:38

9 All Israel was listed in the genealogies recorded in the book of the kings of Israel.

The People in Jerusalem

The people of Judah were taken captive to Babylon because of their unfaithfulness.[d] 2 Now the first to re-
settle on their own property in their own towns[e] were some Israelites, priests, Levites and temple servants.[f]

3 Those from Judah, from Benjamin, and from Ephraim and Manasseh who lived in Jerusalem were:

4 Uthai son of Ammihud, the son of Omri, the son of Imri, the son of Bani, a descendant of Perez son
of Judah.[g]

5 Of the Shilonites:
Asaiah the firstborn and his sons.

6 Of the Zerahites:
Jeuel.
The people from Judah numbered 690.

7 Of the Benjamites:
Sallu son of Meshullam, the son of Hodaviah, the son of Hassenuah;

8 Ibneiah son of Jeroham; Elah son of Uzzi, the son of Micri; and Meshullam son of Shephatiah,
the son of Reuel, the son of Ibnijah.

9 The people from Benjamin, as listed in their genealogy, numbered 956. All these men were
heads of their families.

10 Of the priests:
Jedaiah; Jehoiarib; Jakin;

11 Azariah son of Hilkiah, the son of Meshullam, the son of Zadok, the son of Meraioth, the son
of Ahitub, the official in charge of the house of God;

12 Adaiah son of Jeroham, the son of Pashhur,[h] the son of Malkijah; and Maasai son of Adiel, the
son of Jahzerah, the son of Meshullam, the son of Meshillemith, the son of Immer.

13 The priests, who were heads of families, numbered 1,760. They were able men, responsible for
ministering in the house of God.

14 Of the Levites:
Shemaiah son of Hasshub, the son of Azrikam, the son of Hashabiah, a Merarite; 15 Bakbakkar,

9:1 [d]1Ch 5:25
9:2 [e]Jos 9:27; Ezr 2:70 [f]Ezr 2:43,58; 8:20; Ne 7:60
9:4 [g]Ge 38:29; 46:12
9:12 [h]Ezr 2:38; 10:22; Ne 10:3; Jer 21:1; 38:1

[a] *30* Some Septuagint manuscripts (see also 1 Chron. 9:36); Hebrew does not have *Ner.* [b] *33* Also known as *Ish-Bosheth*
[c] *34* Also known as *Mephibosheth*

8:33–34 Esh-Baal (v. 33) is Ish-Bosheth, and Merib-Baal (v. 34) is Mephibosheth (see "Early Scribal Emendation" on p. 448).

9:2 The list of officeholders—described in greater detail in verses 3–34—includes Israelites (i.e., laity), priests, Levites and temple servants. The temple servants may originally have been foreigners who were incorporated into the Levites (Jos 9:23; Ezr 8:20) and so were not listed apart from that tribe. A similar office is known in the temple at ancient Ugarit (see "Ugarit/Ras Shamra" on p. 819).

Heresh, Galal and Mattaniah[i] son of Mica, the son of Zicri, the son of Asaph; 16 Obadiah son of
Shemaiah, the son of Galal, the son of Jeduthun; and Berekiah son of Asa, the son of Elkanah,
who lived in the villages of the Netophathites.[j]
17 The gatekeepers:[k]
Shallum, Akkub, Talmon, Ahiman and their brothers, Shallum their chief 18 being stationed at
the King's Gate[l] on the east, up to the present time. These were the gatekeepers belonging to
the camp of the Levites. 19 Shallum[m] son of Kore, the son of Ebiasaph, the son of Korah, and his
fellow gatekeepers from his family (the Korahites) were responsible for guarding the thresholds
of the Tent[a] just as their fathers had been responsible for guarding the entrance to the dwell-
ing of the LORD. 20 In earlier times Phinehas[n] son of Eleazar was in charge of the gatekeepers,
and the LORD was with him. 21 Zechariah[o] son of Meshelemiah was the gatekeeper at the en-
trance to the Tent of Meeting.
22 Altogether, those chosen to be gatekeepers[p] at the thresholds numbered 212. They were registered by
genealogy in their villages. The gatekeepers had been assigned to their positions of trust by David and
Samuel the seer.[q] 23 They and their descendants were in charge of guarding the gates of the house of the
LORD—the house called the Tent. 24 The gatekeepers were on the four sides: east, west, north and south.
25 Their brothers in their villages had to come from time to time and share their duties for seven-day[r] pe-
riods. 26 But the four principal gatekeepers, who were Levites, were entrusted with the responsibility for the
rooms and treasuries[s] in the house of God. 27 They would spend the night stationed around the house of
God,[t] because they had to guard it; and they had charge of the key[u] for opening it each morning.
28 Some of them were in charge of the articles used in the temple service; they counted them when they
were brought in and when they were taken out. 29 Others were assigned to take care of the furnishings and
all the other articles of the sanctuary,[v] as well as the flour and wine, and the oil, incense and spices. 30 But
some[w] of the priests took care of mixing the spices. 31 A Levite named Mattithiah, the firstborn son of
Shallum the Korahite, was entrusted with the responsibility for baking the offering bread. 32 Some of their
Kohathite brothers were in charge of preparing for every Sabbath the bread set out on the table.[x]
33 Those who were musicians,[y] heads of Levite families, stayed in the rooms of the temple and were
exempt from other duties because they were responsible for the work day and night.[z]
34 All these were heads of Levite families, chiefs as listed in their genealogy, and they lived in Jerusalem.

The Genealogy of Saul

35 Jeiel[a] the father[b] of Gibeon lived in Gibeon.
His wife's name was Maacah, 36 and his firstborn son was Abdon, followed by Zur, Kish, Baal,
Ner, Nadab, 37 Gedor, Ahio, Zechariah and Mikloth. 38 Mikloth was the father of Shimeam. They
too lived near their relatives in Jerusalem.
39 Ner[b] was the father of Kish,[c] Kish the father of Saul, and Saul the father of Jonathan,[d] Malki-Shua,
Abinadab and Esh-Baal.[c][e]
40 The son of Jonathan:
Merib-Baal,[d][f] who was the father of Micah.
41 The sons of Micah:
Pithon, Melech, Tahrea and Ahaz.[e]
42 Ahaz was the father of Jadah, Jadah[f] was the father of Alemeth, Azmaveth and Zimri, and Zim-
ri was the father of Moza. 43 Moza was the father of Binea; Rephaiah was his son, Eleasah his son
and Azel his son.
44 Azel had six sons, and these were their names:
Azrikam, Bokeru, Ishmael, Sheariah, Obadiah and Hanan. These were the sons of Azel.

9:15 [i]2Ch 20:14; Ne 11:22
9:16 [j]Ne 12:28
9:17 [k]ver 22; 1Ch 26:1; 2Ch 8:14; 31:14; Ezr 2:42; Ne 7:45
9:18 [l]1Ch 26:14; Eze 43:1; 46:1
9:19 [m]Jer 35:4
9:20 [n]Nu 25:7-13
9:21 [o]1Ch 26:2, 14
9:22 [p]ver 17; 1Ch 26:1-2; 2Ch 31:15,18 [q]1Sa 9:9
9:25 [r]2Ki 11:5; 2Ch 23:8
9:26 [s]1Ch 26:22
9:27 [t]Nu 3:38; 1Ch 23:30-32 [u]Isa 22:22
9:29 [v]Nu 3:28; 1Ch 23:29
9:30 [w]Ex 30:23-25
9:32 [x]Lev 24:5-8; 1Ch 23:29; 2Ch 13:11
9:33 [y]1Ch 6:31; 25:1-31 [z]Ps 134:1
9:35 [a]1Ch 8:29
9:39 [b]1Ch 8:33 [c]1Sa 9:1 [d]1Sa 13:22 [e]2Sa 2:8
9:40 [f]2Sa 4:4

[a] *19* That is, the temple; also in verses 21 and 23 [b] *35* *Father* may mean *civic leader* or *military leader.* [c] *39* Also known as *Ish-Bosheth* [d] *40* Also known as *Mephibosheth* [e] *41* Vulgate and Syriac (see also Septuagint and 1 Chron. 8:35); Hebrew does not have *and Ahaz.* [f] *42* Some Hebrew manuscripts and Septuagint (see also 1 Chron. 8:36); most Hebrew manuscripts *Jarah, Jarah*

9:32 For information on this special bread, see the note on 1 Samuel 21:4.
9:35–44 This genealogy repeats the register of Saul's family tree (with minor variations) found in 8:29–38 as one segment of the genealogy of Benjamin. Two names included here, Jeiel and Ner, are found in the previous passage only in some Septuagint manuscripts (see the NIV text notes for 8:29,30). And there are variations in the spellings of five other names recorded in the two genealogies. These minor differences may have been the result of scribal errors or of the ongoing process of language changing over time (see "Early Scribal Emendation" on p. 448 and "Textual Criticism" on p. 1151).

Saul Takes His Life

10 Now the Philistines fought against Israel; the Israelites fled before them, and many fell slain on
Mount Gilboa. 2 The Philistines pressed hard after Saul and his sons, and they killed his sons Jon-
athan, Abinadab and Malki-Shua. 3 The fighting grew fierce around Saul, and when the archers overtook
him, they wounded him.
4 Saul said to his armor-bearer, "Draw your sword and run me through, or these uncircumcised fel-
lows will come and abuse me."
But his armor-bearer was terrified and would not do it; so Saul took his own sword and fell on it.
5 When the armor-bearer saw that Saul was dead, he too fell on his sword and died. 6 So Saul and his three
sons died, and all his house died together.
7 When all the Israelites in the valley saw that the army had fled and that Saul and his sons had died,
they abandoned their towns and fled. And the Philistines came and occupied them.
8 The next day, when the Philistines came to strip the dead, they found Saul and his sons fallen on
Mount Gilboa. 9 They stripped him and took his head and his armor, and sent messengers throughout the
land of the Philistines to proclaim the news among their idols and their people. 10 They put his armor in
10:10 [g]Jdg 16:23 — the temple of their gods and hung up his head in the temple of Dagon.[g]
10:11 [h]Jdg 21:8 — 11 When all the inhabitants of Jabesh Gilead[h] heard of everything the Philistines had done to Saul,
12 all their valiant men went and took the bodies of Saul and his sons and brought them to Jabesh. Then
they buried their bones under the great tree in Jabesh, and they fasted seven days.
10:13 [i]2Sa 1:1 — 13 Saul died[i] because he was unfaithful[j] to the LORD; he did not keep[k] the word of the LORD and even
[j]1Sa 15:23; 1Ch 5:25 — consulted a medium[l] for guidance, 14 and did not inquire of the LORD. So the LORD put him to death and
[k]1Sa 13:13 [l]Lev 19:31; 20:6; Dt 18:9-14; 1Sa 28:7 — turned[m] the kingdom[n] over to David son of Jesse.
10:14 [m]1Ch 12:23 [n]1Sa 13:14; 15:28

David Becomes King Over Israel

11:1 [o]1Ch 9:1 [p]Ge 13:18; 23:19 — 11 All Israel[o] came together to David at Hebron[p] and said, "We are your own flesh and blood. 2 In the
11:2 [q]1Sa 18:5, 16 [r]Ps 78:71; Mt 2:6 [s]1Ch 5:2 — past, even while Saul was king, you were the one who led Israel on their military campaigns.[q]
And the LORD your God said to you, 'You will shepherd[r] my people Israel, and you will become their
ruler.[s]' "
3 When all the elders of Israel had come to King David at Hebron, he made a compact with them at He-
11:3 [t]1Sa 16:1-13 — bron before the LORD, and they anointed[t] David king over Israel, as the LORD had promised through
Samuel.

David Conquers Jerusalem

11:4 [u]Ge 10:16; 15:18-21; Jos 3:10; 15:8; Jdg 1:21; 19:10 — 4 David and all the Israelites marched to Jerusalem (that is, Jebus). The Jebusites[u] who lived there 5 said
to David, "You will not get in here." Nevertheless, David captured the fortress of Zion, the City of David.
11:6 [v]2Sa 2:13; 8:16 — 6 David had said, "Whoever leads the attack on the Jebusites will become commander-in-chief." Joab[v]
son of Zeruiah went up first, and so he received the command.
7 David then took up residence in the fortress, and so it was called the City of David. 8 He built up the
11:8 [w]2Sa 5:9; 2Ch 32:5 — city around it, from the supporting terraces[a][w] to the surrounding wall, while Joab restored the rest of the
11:9 [x]2Sa 3:1; Est 9:4 — city. 9 And David became more and more powerful,[x] because the LORD Almighty was with him.

David's Mighty Men

11:10 [y]ver 1 [z]ver 3; 1Ch 12:23 — 10 These were the chiefs of David's mighty men—they, together with all Israel,[y] gave his kingship
strong support to extend it over the whole land, as the LORD had promised[z]— 11 this is the list of David's
11:11 [a]2Sa 17:10 — mighty men:[a]
Jashobeam,[b] a Hacmonite, was chief of the officers[c]; he raised his spear against three hundred men,
whom he killed in one encounter.
12 Next to him was Eleazar son of Dodai the Ahohite, one of the three mighty men. 13 He was with Da-
vid at Pas Dammim when the Philistines gathered there for battle. At a place where there was a field full

[a] 8 Or *the Millo* [b] 11 Possibly a variant of *Jashob-Baal* [c] 11 Or *Thirty*; some Septuagint manuscripts *Three* (see also 2 Samuel 23:8)

10:10 See "The Beth Shan Temples" on page 438.
10:11 See "Jabesh Gilead" on page 384.
11:4–6 For a possible explanation of their entrance into the city, see "The *Tsinnor*" on page 450.

of barley, the troops fled from the Philistines. 14 But they took their stand in the middle of the field. They
defended it and struck the Philistines down, and the LORD brought about a great victory.[b] 11:14 [b]Ex 14:30; 1Sa 11:13
15 Three of the thirty chiefs came down to David to the rock at the cave of Adullam, while a band of
Philistines was encamped in the Valley[c] of Rephaim. 16 At that time David was in the stronghold,[d] and the 11:15 [c]1Ch 14:9; Isa 17:5
Philistine garrison was at Bethlehem. 17 David longed for water and said, "Oh, that someone would get me 11:16 [d]2Sa 5:17
a drink of water from the well near the gate of Bethlehem!" 18 So the Three broke through the Philistine
lines, drew water from the well near the gate of Bethlehem and carried it back to David. But he refused
to drink it; instead, he poured[e] it out before the LORD. 19 "God forbid that I should do this!" he said. "Should 11:18 [e]Dt 12:16
I drink the blood of these men who went at the risk of their lives?" Because they risked their lives to bring
it back, David would not drink it.
Such were the exploits of the three mighty men.
20 Abishai[f] the brother of Joab was chief of the Three. He raised his spear against three hundred men, 11:20 [f]1Sa 26:6
whom he killed, and so he became as famous as the Three. 21 He was doubly honored above the Three and
became their commander, even though he was not included among them.
22 Benaiah son of Jehoiada was a valiant fighter from Kabzeel,[g] who performed great exploits. He 11:22 [g]Jos 15:21 [h]1Sa 17:36
struck down two of Moab's best men. He also went down into a pit on a snowy day and killed a lion.[h]
23 And he struck down an Egyptian who was seven and a half feet[a] tall. Although the Egyptian had a
spear like a weaver's rod[i] in his hand, Benaiah went against him with a club. He snatched the spear from 11:23 [i]1Sa 17:7
the Egyptian's hand and killed him with his own spear. 24 Such were the exploits of Benaiah son of Jehoi-
ada; he too was as famous as the three mighty men. 25 He was held in greater honor than any of the Thir-
ty, but he was not included among the Three. And David put him in charge of his bodyguard.

26 The mighty men were:
Asahel[j] the brother of Joab, 11:26 [j]2Sa 2:18
Elhanan son of Dodo from Bethlehem,

[a] 23 Hebrew *five cubits* (about 2.3 meters)

11:16 Bethlehem, located five miles (eight km) south of Jerusalem, was formerly known as Ephrath (Ge 48:7). It was David's hometown (1Sa 20:6) and later became the birthplace of Jesus Christ (Mt 2:1). See "Bethlehem" on page 1487.

11:20 "The Three" probably functioned as generals, while the term "the Thirty" (v. 25) designated the complete unit of "mighty men," regardless of their exact number at any given time.

The Jebusites

1 CHRONICLES 11 The Jebusites were a **Canaanite**[1] people (Ge 10:15–16), many of whom lived in the hills in the vicinity of their city, Jebus, better known as Jerusalem. Jerusalem is mentioned in the Egyptian Execration Texts (as *Uru-shalim*), the **Amarna** correspondence (as *Urusalim*) and **Assyrian** texts (as *Urusillimmu*). We know the names of two of the city's kings: The Amarna texts mention Abdi-Hepa, and 2 Samuel 24:18 speaks of Araunah.

The Jebusites led the southern confederation of city-states within the region against Joshua and the Israelites (Jos 9:1–2) and also participated in the northern confederation of city-states under Jabin, king of **Hazor**[2] (Jos 11:1–5; "Map 5"). Jerusalem fell between the tribal allotments of Judah and Benjamin. Although Judah set the citadel on fire, Jebusites continued to inhabit Jerusalem into the period of the judges, since neither tribe succeeded in driving them out (Jdg 1:8,21). David was able to wrest the city from Jebusite control and use it as his religious and political capital. However, some Jebusites remained there until the days of Solomon, who conscripted them to forced labor along with other Canaanites (1Ki 9:20–21).[3] They were eventually absorbed into the Israelite population.

Some excavated remains from Jerusalem are attributable to the Jebusite period. These include a fortification wall, bastions, gates and a water tunnel from the Gihon spring with a deep cistern to collect the water.[4]

[1]See "Canaan" on page 324. [2]See "Hazor" on page 322. [3]See "Slavery and Labor Law in the Ancient Near East" on page 127. [4]See "The *Tsinnor*" on page 450.

11:27 [k]1Ch 27:8
27 Shammoth[k] the Harorite,
Helez the Pelonite,
28 Ira son of Ikkesh from Tekoa,
11:28 [l]1Ch 27:12
Abiezer[l] from Anathoth,
11:29 [m]2Sa 21:18
29 Sibbecai[m] the Hushathite,
Ilai the Ahohite,
30 Maharai the Netophathite,
Heled son of Baanah the Netophathite,
31 Ithai son of Ribai from Gibeah in Benjamin,
11:31 [n]1Ch 27:14 [o]Jdg 12:13
Benaiah[n] the Pirathonite,[o]
32 Hurai from the ravines of Gaash,
Abiel the Arbathite,
33 Azmaveth the Baharumite,
Eliahba the Shaalbonite,
34 the sons of Hashem the Gizonite,
Jonathan son of Shagee the Hararite,
35 Ahiam son of Sacar the Hararite,
Eliphal son of Ur,
36 Hepher the Mekerathite,
Ahijah the Pelonite,
37 Hezro the Carmelite,
Naarai son of Ezbai,
38 Joel the brother of Nathan,
Mibhar son of Hagri,
39 Zelek the Ammonite,
Naharai the Berothite, the armor-bearer of Joab son of Zeruiah,
40 Ira the Ithrite,
Gareb the Ithrite,
11:41 [p]2Sa 11:6 [q]1Ch 2:36
41 Uriah[p] the Hittite,
Zabad[q] son of Ahlai,
42 Adina son of Shiza the Reubenite, who was chief of the Reubenites, and the thirty with him,
43 Hanan son of Maacah,
Joshaphat the Mithnite,
11:44 [r]Dt 1:4
44 Uzzia the Ashterathite,[r]
Shama and Jeiel the sons of Hotham the Aroerite,
45 Jediael son of Shimri,
his brother Joha the Tizite,
46 Eliel the Mahavite,
Jeribai and Joshaviah the sons of Elnaam,
Ithmah the Moabite,
47 Eliel, Obed and Jaasiel the Mezobaite.

Warriors Join David

12:1 [s]Jos 15:31; 1Sa 27:2-6
12 These were the men who came to David at Ziklag,[s] while he was banished from the presence of
Saul son of Kish (they were among the warriors who helped him in battle; 2 they were armed
12:2 [t]Jdg 3:15; 20:16 [u]2Sa 3:19
with bows and were able to shoot arrows or to sling stones right-handed or left-handed;[t] they were kins-
men of Saul[u] from the tribe of Benjamin):

3 Ahiezer their chief and Joash the sons of Shemaah the Gibeathite; Jeziel and Pelet the sons of
Azmaveth; Beracah, Jehu the Anathothite, 4 and Ishmaiah the Gibeonite, a mighty man among
12:4 [v]Jos 15:36
the Thirty, who was a leader of the Thirty; Jeremiah, Jahaziel, Johanan, Jozabad the Gederathite,[v]
5 Eluzai, Jerimoth, Bealiah, Shemariah and Shephatiah the Haruphite; 6 Elkanah, Isshiah, Azarel,
Joezer and Jashobeam the Korahites; 7 and Joelah and Zebadiah the sons of Jeroham from
12:7 [w]Jos 15:58
Gedor.[w]

12:8 [x]Ge 30:11
8 Some Gadites[x] defected to David at his stronghold in the desert. They were brave warriors, ready for

battle and able to handle the shield and spear. Their faces were the faces of lions,[y] and they were as swift as gazelles[z] in the mountains.

9 Ezer was the chief,
Obadiah the second in command, Eliab the third,
10 Mishmannah the fourth, Jeremiah the fifth,
11 Attai the sixth, Eliel the seventh,
12 Johanan the eighth, Elzabad the ninth,
13 Jeremiah the tenth and Macbannai the eleventh.

14 These Gadites were army commanders; the least was a match for a hundred,[a] and the greatest for a thousand.[b] 15 It was they who crossed the Jordan in the first month when it was overflowing all its banks,[c] and they put to flight everyone living in the valleys, to the east and to the west.

16 Other Benjamites[d] and some men from Judah also came to David in his stronghold. 17 David went out to meet them and said to them, "If you have come to me in peace, to help me, I am ready to have you unite with me. But if you have come to betray me to my enemies when my hands are free from violence, may the God of our fathers see it and judge you."

18 Then the Spirit[e] came upon Amasai,[f] chief of the Thirty, and he said:

"We are yours, O David!
We are with you, O son of Jesse!
Success,[g] success to you,
and success to those who help you,
for your God will help you."

So David received them and made them leaders of his raiding bands.

19 Some of the men of Manasseh defected to David when he went with the Philistines to fight against Saul. (He and his men did not help the Philistines because, after consultation, their rulers sent him away. They said, "It will cost us our heads if he deserts to his master Saul.")[h] 20 When David went to Ziklag,[i] these were the men of Manasseh who defected to him: Adnah, Jozabad, Jediael, Michael, Jozabad, Elihu and Zillethai, leaders of units of a thousand in Manasseh. 21 They helped David against raiding bands, for all of them were brave warriors, and they were commanders in his army. 22 Day after day men came to help David, until he had a great army, like the army of God.[a]

Others Join David at Hebron

23 These are the numbers of the men armed for battle who came to David at Hebron[j] to turn[k] Saul's kingdom over to him, as the LORD had said:[l]

24 men of Judah, carrying shield and spear—6,800 armed for battle;
25 men of Simeon, warriors ready for battle—7,100;
26 men of Levi—4,600, 27 including Jehoiada, leader of the family of Aaron, with 3,700 men, 28 and Zadok,[m] a brave young warrior, with 22 officers from his family;
29 men of Benjamin,[n] Saul's kinsmen—3,000, most[o] of whom had remained loyal to Saul's house until then;
30 men of Ephraim, brave warriors, famous in their own clans—20,800;
31 men of half the tribe of Manasseh, designated by name to come and make David king—18,000;
32 men of Issachar, who understood the times and knew what Israel should do[p]—200 chiefs, with all their relatives under their command;
33 men of Zebulun, experienced soldiers prepared for battle with every type of weapon, to help David with undivided loyalty—50,000;
34 men of Naphtali—1,000 officers, together with 37,000 men carrying shields and spears;
35 men of Dan, ready for battle—28,600;
36 men of Asher, experienced soldiers prepared for battle—40,000;
37 and from east of the Jordan, men of Reuben, Gad and the half-tribe of Manasseh, armed with every type of weapon—120,000.

38 All these were fighting men who volunteered to serve in the ranks. They came to Hebron fully determined to make David king over all Israel.[q] All the rest of the Israelites were also of one mind to make David king. 39 The men spent three days there with David, eating and drinking,[r] for their families had

[a] 22 Or *a great and mighty army*

12:8 [y] 2Sa 17:10 [z] 2Sa 2:18
12:14 [a] Lev 26:8 [b] Dt 32:30
12:15 [c] Jos 3:15
12:16 [d] 2Sa 3:19
12:18 [e] Jdg 3:10; 6:34; 1Ch 28:12; 2Ch 15:1; 20:14; 24:20 [f] 2Sa 17:25 [g] 1Sa 25:5-6
12:19 [h] 1Sa 29:2-11
12:20 [i] 1Sa 27:6
12:23 [j] 2Sa 2:3-4 [k] 1Ch 10:14 [l] 1Sa 16:1; 1Ch 11:10
12:28 [m] 2Sa 8:17; 1Ch 6:8; 15:11; 16:39; 27:17
12:29 [n] 2Sa 3:19 [o] 2Sa 2:8-9
12:32 [p] Est 1:13
12:38 [q] 2Sa 5:1-3; 1Ch 9:1
12:39 [r] 2Sa 3:20; Isa 25:6-8

supplied provisions for them. 40 Also, their neighbors from as far away as Issachar, Zebulun and Naphta-
12:40 [s]2Sa 16:1; 17:29 [t]1Sa 25:18 [u]1Ch 29:22 li came bringing food on donkeys, camels, mules and oxen. There were plentiful supplies[s] of flour, fig
cakes, raisin[t] cakes, wine, oil, cattle and sheep, for there was joy[u] in Israel.

Bringing Back the Ark

13 David conferred with each of his officers, the commanders of thousands and commanders of
hundreds. 2 He then said to the whole assembly of Israel, "If it seems good to you and if it is the
will of the LORD our God, let us send word far and wide to the rest of our brothers throughout the terri-
tories of Israel, and also to the priests and Levites who are with them in their towns and pasturelands,
13:3 [v]1Sa 7:1-2 [w]2Ch 1:5 to come and join us. 3 Let us bring the ark of our God back to us,[v] for we did not inquire[w] of[a] it[b] during
the reign of Saul." 4 The whole assembly agreed to do this, because it seemed right to all the people.
13:5 [x]1Ch 11:1; 15:3 [y]Jos 13:3 5 So David assembled all the Israelites,[x] from the Shihor River[y] in Egypt to Lebo[c] Hamath,[z] to bring
[z]Nu 13:21 [a]1Sa 6:21; 7:2 the ark of God from Kiriath Jearim.[a] 6 David and all the Israelites with him went to Baalah[b] of Judah (Kir-
13:6 [b]Jos 15:9; 2Sa 6:2 iath Jearim) to bring up from there the ark of God the LORD, who is enthroned between the cherubim[c]—
[c]Ex 25:22; 2Ki 19:15 the ark that is called by the Name.
13:7 [d]Nu 4:15; 1Sa 7:1 7 They moved the ark of God from Abinadab's[d] house on a new cart, with Uzzah and Ahio guiding it.
13:8 [e]2Sa 6:5; 1Ch 15:16,19,24; 2Ch 5:12; Ps 92:3 8 David and all the Israelites were celebrating with all their might before God, with songs and with harps,
lyres, tambourines, cymbals and trumpets.[e]
9 When they came to the threshing floor of Kidon, Uzzah reached out his hand to steady the ark, be-
13:10 [f]1Ch 15:13,15 [g]Lev 10:2 cause the oxen stumbled. 10 The LORD's anger[f] burned against Uzzah, and he struck him down[g] because
he had put his hand on the ark. So he died there before God.
13:11 [h]1Ch 15:13; Ps 7:11 11 Then David was angry because the LORD's wrath had broken out against Uzzah, and to this day that
place is called Perez Uzzah.[d][h]
12 David was afraid of God that day and asked, "How can I ever bring the ark of God to me?" 13 He did
13:13 [i]1Ch 15:18,24; 16:38; 26:4-5,15 not take the ark to be with him in the City of David. Instead, he took it aside to the house of Obed-Edom[i]
the Gittite. 14 The ark of God remained with the family of Obed-Edom in his house for three months, and
13:14 [j]2Sa 6:11; 1Ch 26:4-5 the LORD blessed his household[j] and everything he had.

David's House and Family

14:1 [k]2Ch 2:3; Ezr 3:7 14 Now Hiram king of Tyre sent messengers to David, along with cedar logs,[k] stonemasons and
carpenters to build a palace for him. 2 And David knew that the LORD had established him as king
14:2 [l]Nu 24:7; Dt 26:19 over Israel and that his kingdom had been highly exalted[l] for the sake of his people Israel.
14:3 [m]1Ch 3:1 3 In Jerusalem David took more wives and became the father of more sons[m] and daughters. 4 These are
14:4 [n]1Ch 3:9 the names of the children born to him there:[n] Shammua, Shobab, Nathan, Solomon, 5 Ibhar, Elishua, El-
pelet, 6 Nogah, Nepheg, Japhia, 7 Elishama, Beeliada[e] and Eliphelet.

David Defeats the Philistines

14:8 [o]1Ch 11:1 8 When the Philistines heard that David had been anointed king over all Israel,[o] they went up in full
force to search for him, but David heard about it and went out to meet them. 9 Now the Philistines had
14:9 [p]ver 13; Jos 15:8; 1Ch 11:15 come and raided the Valley[p] of Rephaim; 10 so David inquired of God: "Shall I go and attack the Philis-
tines? Will you hand them over to me?"
The LORD answered him, "Go, I will hand them over to you."
14:11 [q]Isa 28:21 11 So David and his men went up to Baal Perazim,[q] and there he defeated them. He said, "As waters
break out, God has broken out against my enemies by my hand." So that place was called Baal Pera-
14:12 [r]Ex 32:20 [s]Jos 7:15 zim.[f] 12 The Philistines had abandoned their gods there, and David gave orders to burn[r] them in the fire.[s]
14:13 [t]ver 9 13 Once more the Philistines raided the valley;[t] 14 so David inquired of God again, and God answered
him, "Do not go straight up, but circle around them and attack them in front of the balsam trees. 15 As soon
as you hear the sound of marching in the tops of the balsam trees, move out to battle, because that will
mean God has gone out in front of you to strike the Philistine army." 16 So David did as God command-
14:16 [u]Jos 9:3 [v]Jos 10:33 ed him, and they struck down the Philistine army, all the way from Gibeon[u] to Gezer.[v]
14:17 [w]Jos 6:27; 2Ch 26:8 [x]Ex 15:14-16; Dt 2:25 17 So David's fame[w] spread throughout every land, and the LORD made all the nations fear[x] him.

[a] 3 Or *we neglected* [b] 3 Or *him* [c] 5 Or *to the entrance to* [d] 11 *Perez Uzzah* means *outbreak against Uzzah.*
[e] 7 A variant of *Eliada* [f] 11 *Baal Perazim* means *the lord who breaks out.*

14:16 See "Gibeon" on page 318 and "Gezer" on page 588.

The Ark Brought to Jerusalem

15 After David had constructed buildings for himself in the City of David, he prepared[y] a place for
the ark of God and pitched[z] a tent for it. 2 Then David said, "No one but the Levites[a] may carry[b]
the ark of God, because the LORD chose them to carry the ark of the LORD and to minister[c] before him
forever."
3 David assembled all Israel[d] in Jerusalem to bring up the ark of the LORD to the place he had prepared
for it. 4 He called together the descendants of Aaron and the Levites:

5 From the descendants of Kohath,
Uriel the leader and 120 relatives;
6 from the descendants of Merari,
Asaiah the leader and 220 relatives;
7 from the descendants of Gershon,*[a]*
Joel the leader and 130 relatives;
8 from the descendants of Elizaphan,[e]
Shemaiah the leader and 200 relatives;
9 from the descendants of Hebron,[f]
Eliel the leader and 80 relatives;
10 from the descendants of Uzziel,
Amminadab the leader and 112 relatives.

11 Then David summoned Zadok[g] and Abiathar[h] the priests, and Uriel, Asaiah, Joel, Shemaiah, Eliel
and Amminadab the Levites. 12 He said to them, "You are the heads of the Levitical families; you and your
fellow Levites are to consecrate[i] yourselves and bring up the ark of the LORD, the God of Israel, to the
place I have prepared for it. 13 It was because you, the Levites,[j] did not bring it up the first time that the
LORD our God broke out in anger against us.[k] We did not inquire of him about how to do it in the pre-
scribed way." 14 So the priests and Levites consecrated themselves in order to bring up the ark of the LORD,
the God of Israel. 15 And the Levites carried the ark of God with the poles on their shoulders, as Moses
had commanded[l] in accordance with the word of the LORD.
16 David told the leaders of the Levites to appoint their brothers as singers[m] to sing joyful songs, ac-
companied by musical instruments: lyres, harps and cymbals.[n]
17 So the Levites appointed Heman[o] son of Joel; from his brothers, Asaph[p] son of Berekiah; and from
their brothers the Merarites,[q] Ethan son of Kushaiah; 18 and with them their brothers next in rank: Zech-
ariah,*[b]* Jaaziel, Shemiramoth, Jehiel, Unni, Eliab, Benaiah, Maaseiah, Mattithiah, Eliphelehu, Mikneiah,
Obed-Edom[r] and Jeiel,*[c]* the gatekeepers.
19 The musicians Heman,[s] Asaph and Ethan were to sound the bronze cymbals; 20 Zechariah, Aziel,
Shemiramoth, Jehiel, Unni, Eliab, Maaseiah and Benaiah were to play the lyres according to *alamoth*,*[d]*
21 and Mattithiah, Eliphelehu, Mikneiah, Obed-Edom, Jeiel and Azaziah were to play the harps, directing
according to *sheminith*.*[d]* 22 Kenaniah the head Levite was in charge of the singing; that was his respon-
sibility because he was skillful at it.
23 Berekiah and Elkanah were to be doorkeepers for the ark. 24 Shebaniah, Joshaphat, Nethanel, Amas-
ai, Zechariah, Benaiah and Eliezer the priests were to blow trumpets[t] before the ark of God. Obed-Edom
and Jehiah were also to be doorkeepers for the ark.
25 So David and the elders of Israel and the commanders of units of a thousand went to bring up the
ark[u] of the covenant of the LORD from the house of Obed-Edom, with rejoicing. 26 Because God had
helped the Levites who were carrying the ark of the covenant of the LORD, seven bulls and seven rams[v]
were sacrificed. 27 Now David was clothed in a robe of fine linen, as were all the Levites who were car-
rying the ark, and as were the singers, and Kenaniah, who was in charge of the singing of the choirs.
David also wore a linen ephod. 28 So all Israel brought up the ark of the covenant of the LORD with
shouts, with the sounding of rams' horns[w] and trumpets, and of cymbals, and the playing of lyres and
harps.
29 As the ark of the covenant of the LORD was entering the City of David, Michal daughter of Saul
watched from a window. And when she saw King David dancing and celebrating, she despised him in
her heart.

15:1 [y]Ps 132:1-18 [z]1Ch 16:1; 17:1
15:2 [a]Nu 4:15; Dt 10:8; 2Ch 5:5 [b]Dt 31:9 [c]1Ch 23:13
15:3 [d]1Ki 8:1; 1Ch 13:5
15:8 [e]Ex 6:22
15:9 [f]Ex 6:18
15:11 [g]1Ch 12:28 [h]1Sa 22:20
15:12 [i]Ex 19:14-15; Lev 11:44; 2Ch 35:6
15:13 [j]1Ki 8:4 [k]2Sa 6:3; 1Ch 13:7-10
15:15 [l]Ex 25:14; Nu 4:5,15
15:16 [m]Ps 68:25 [n]1Ch 13:8; 25:1; Ne 12:27,36
15:17 [o]1Ch 6:33 [p]1Ch 6:39 [q]1Ch 6:44
15:18 [r]1Ch 26:4-5
15:19 [s]1Ch 25:6
15:24 [t]ver 28; 1Ch 16:6; 2Ch 7:6
15:25 [u]1Ch 13:13; 2Ch 1:4
15:26 [v]Nu 23:1-4,29
15:28 [w]1Ch 13:8

a 7 Hebrew *Gershom,* a variant of *Gershon* *b* 18 Three Hebrew manuscripts and most Septuagint manuscripts (see also verse 20 and 1 Chron. 16:5); most Hebrew manuscripts *Zechariah son and* or *Zechariah, Ben and* *c* 18 Hebrew; Septuagint (see also verse 21) *Jeiel and Azaziah* *d* 20, 21 Probably a musical term

16:1 [x]1Ch 15:1 **16** They brought the ark of God and set it inside the tent that David had pitched[x] for it, and they
presented burnt offerings and fellowship offerings[a] before God. 2 After David had finished sac-
16:2 [y]Ex 39:43 rificing the burnt offerings and fellowship offerings, he blessed[y] the people in the name of the LORD.
3 Then he gave a loaf of bread, a cake of dates and a cake of raisins to each Israelite man and woman.
16:4 [z]1Ch 15:2 4 He appointed some of the Levites to minister[z] before the ark of the LORD, to make petition, to give
thanks, and to praise the LORD, the God of Israel: 5 Asaph was the chief, Zechariah second, then Jeiel, She-
miramoth, Jehiel, Mattithiah, Eliab, Benaiah, Obed-Edom and Jeiel. They were to play the lyres and harps,
Asaph was to sound the cymbals, 6 and Benaiah and Jahaziel the priests were to blow the trumpets reg-
ularly before the ark of the covenant of God.

David's Psalm of Thanks

16:7 [a]2Sa 23:1 7 That day David first committed to Asaph and his associates this psalm[a] of thanks to the LORD:

16:8 [b]ver 34; Ps 136:1 [c]2Ki 19:19
8 Give thanks[b] to the LORD, call on his name;
make known among the nations[c] what he has done.
16:9 [d]Ex 15:1
9 Sing to him, sing praise[d] to him;
tell of all his wonderful acts.
10 Glory in his holy name;
let the hearts of those who seek the LORD rejoice.
11 Look to the LORD and his strength;
16:11 [e]1Ch 28:9; 2Ch 7:14; Ps 24:6; 119:2,58
seek[e] his face always.
16:12 [f]Ps 77:11 [g]Ps 78:43
12 Remember[f] the wonders he has done,
his miracles,[g] and the judgments he pronounced,
13 O descendants of Israel his servant,
O sons of Jacob, his chosen ones.

14 He is the LORD our God;
16:14 [h]Isa 26:9
his judgments[h] are in all the earth.
15 He remembers[b] his covenant forever,
the word he commanded, for a thousand generations,
16:16 [i]Ge 12:7; 15:18; 17:2; 22:16-18; 26:3; 28:13; 35:11
16 the covenant[i] he made with Abraham,
the oath he swore to Isaac.
16:17 [j]Ge 35:9-12
17 He confirmed it to Jacob[j] as a decree,
to Israel as an everlasting covenant:
16:18 [k]Ge 13:14-17
18 "To you I will give the land of Canaan[k]
as the portion you will inherit."
16:19 [l]Ge 34:30; Dt 7:7
19 When they were but few in number,[l]
few indeed, and strangers in it,
20 they[c] wandered from nation to nation,
from one kingdom to another.
21 He allowed no man to oppress them;
16:21 [m]Ge 12:17; 20:3; Ex 7:15-18
for their sake he rebuked kings:[m]
22 "Do not touch my anointed ones;
16:22 [n]Ge 20:7
do my prophets[n] no harm."
23 Sing to the LORD, all the earth;
proclaim his salvation day after day.
24 Declare his glory among the nations,
his marvelous deeds among all peoples.
16:25 [o]Ps 48:1 [p]Ps 76:7; 89:7 [q]Dt 32:39
25 For great is the LORD and most worthy of praise;[o]
he is to be feared[p] above all gods.[q]

[a] *1* Traditionally *peace offerings*; also in verse 2 [b] *15* Some Septuagint manuscripts (see also Psalm 105:8); Hebrew *Remember* [c] *18-20* One Hebrew manuscript, Septuagint and Vulgate (see also Psalm 105:12); most Hebrew manuscripts *inherit, / 19 though you are but few in number, / few indeed, and strangers in it." / 20 They*

16:5 See the note on Psalms 73:1—83:18 for commentary on Asaph.

[26] For all the gods of the nations are idols,
but the LORD made the heavens.[r]
[27] Splendor and majesty are before him;
strength and joy in his dwelling place.
[28] Ascribe to the LORD, O families of nations,
ascribe to the LORD glory and strength,[s]
[29] ascribe to the LORD the glory due his name.
Bring an offering and come before him;
worship the LORD in the splendor of his[a] holiness.[t]
[30] Tremble[u] before him, all the earth!
The world is firmly established; it cannot be moved.
[31] Let the heavens rejoice, let the earth be glad;[v]
let them say among the nations, "The LORD reigns![w]"
[32] Let the sea resound, and all that is in it;[x]
let the fields be jubilant, and everything in them!
[33] Then the trees[y] of the forest will sing,
they will sing for joy before the LORD,
for he comes to judge[z] the earth.

[34] Give thanks[a] to the LORD, for he is good;[b]
his love endures forever.[c]
[35] Cry out, "Save us, O God our Savior;[d]
gather us and deliver us from the nations,
that we may give thanks to your holy name,
that we may glory in your praise."
[36] Praise be to the LORD, the God of Israel,[e]
from everlasting to everlasting.

Then all the people said "Amen" and "Praise the LORD."

[37] David left Asaph and his associates before the ark of the covenant of the LORD to minister there reg-
ularly, according to each day's requirements.[f] [38] He also left Obed-Edom[g] and his sixty-eight associates
to minister with them. Obed-Edom son of Jeduthun, and also Hosah,[h] were gatekeepers.
[39] David left Zadok[i] the priest and his fellow priests before the tabernacle of the LORD at the high place
in Gibeon[j] [40] to present burnt offerings to the LORD on the altar of burnt offering regularly, morning and
evening, in accordance with everything written in the Law[k] of the LORD, which he had given Israel. [41] With
them were Heman[l] and Jeduthun and the rest of those chosen and designated by name to give thanks to
the LORD, "for his love endures forever." [42] Heman and Jeduthun were responsible for the sounding of the
trumpets and cymbals and for the playing of the other instruments for sacred song.[m] The sons of Jedu-
thun were stationed at the gate.
[43] Then all the people left, each for his own home, and David returned home to bless his family.

God's Promise to David

17 After David was settled in his palace, he said to Nathan the prophet, "Here I am, living in a pal-
ace of cedar, while the ark of the covenant of the LORD is under a tent.[n]"
[2] Nathan replied to David, "Whatever you have in mind,[o] do it, for God is with you."
[3] That night the word of God came to Nathan, saying:

[4] "Go and tell my servant David, 'This is what the LORD says: You[p] are not the one to build me a
house to dwell in. [5] I have not dwelt in a house from the day I brought Israel up out of Egypt to this

16:26 [r]Lev 19:4; Ps 102:25
16:28 [s]Ps 29:1-2
16:29 [t]Ps 29:1-2
16:30 [u]Ps 114:7
16:31 [v]Isa 44:23; 49:13 [w]Ps 93:1
16:32 [x]Ps 98:7
16:33 [y]Isa 55:12 [z]Ps 96:10; 98:9
16:34 [a]ver 8 [b]Na 1:7 [c]2Ch 5:13; 7:3; Ezr 3:11; Ps 136:1-26; Jer 33:11
16:35 [d]Mic 7:7
16:36 [e]Dt 27:15; 1Ki 8:15; Ps 72:18-19
16:37 [f]2Ch 8:14
16:38 [g]1Ch 13:13 [h]1Ch 26:10
16:39 [i]2Sa 8:17; 1Ch 15:11 [j]1Ki 3:4; 2Ch 1:3
16:40 [k]Ex 29:38; Nu 28:1-8
16:41 [l]1Ch 6:33; 25:1-6; 2Ch 5:13
16:42 [m]2Ch 7:6
17:1 [n]1Ch 15:1
17:2 [o]2Ch 6:7
17:4 [p]1Ch 28:3

[a] 29 Or *LORD with the splendor of*

16:39 Only Chronicles mentions that the Tent of Meeting resided at Gibeon during the reign of David (see also 21:29 and 2Ch 1:3). It is noteworthy that Gibeon was the city whose citizens were, according to Joshua 9:23, consigned the task of being menial servants for the Israelite shrine. See "Gibeon" on page 318.

17:1–4 David's desire to build a temple for God was typical of royal behavior in the Biblical world. In ancient Egypt and Mesopotamia kings erected monuments and constructed great temples as acts of homage to the deities they considered responsible for establishing them on the throne. (See "David" on p. 443 and "Solomon's Temple and Other Ancient Temples" on p. 620.)

day. I have moved from one tent site to another, from one dwelling place to another. 6Wherever I
have moved with all the Israelites, did I ever say to any of their leaders[a] whom I commanded to
shepherd my people, "Why have you not built me a house of cedar?" '

7"Now then, tell my servant David, 'This is what the LORD Almighty says: I took you from the
17:7 [q]2Sa 6:21 pasture and from following the flock, to be ruler[q] over my people Israel. 8I have been with you
wherever you have gone, and I have cut off all your enemies from before you. Now I will make your
name like the names of the greatest men of the earth. 9And I will provide a place for my people Is-
rael and will plant them so that they can have a home of their own and no longer be disturbed.
Wicked people will not oppress them anymore, as they did at the beginning 10and have done ever
17:10 [r]Jdg 2:16 since the time I appointed leaders[r] over my people Israel. I will also subdue all your enemies.

" 'I declare to you that the LORD will build a house for you: 11When your days are over and you
go to be with your fathers, I will raise up your offspring to succeed you, one of your own sons, and
17:12 [s]1Ki 5:5 I will establish his kingdom. 12He is the one who will build[s] a house for me, and I will establish his
[t]2Ch 7:18 17:13 [u]2Co 6:18 throne forever.[t] 13I will be his father,[u] and he will be my son.[v] I will never take my love away from
[v]Lk 1:32; Heb 1:5* him, as I took it away from your predecessor. 14I will set him over my house and my kingdom for-
17:14 [w]1Ki 2:12; 1Ch 28:5 ever; his throne[w] will be established forever.[x]' "

[x]Ps 132:11; Jer 33:17 15Nathan reported to David all the words of this entire revelation.

David's Prayer

16Then King David went in and sat before the LORD, and he said:

"Who am I, O LORD God, and what is my family, that you have brought me this far? 17And as if
this were not enough in your sight, O God, you have spoken about the future of the house of your
servant. You have looked on me as though I were the most exalted of men, O LORD God.

18"What more can David say to you for honoring your servant? For you know your servant,
17:19 [y]2Sa 7:16-17; 2Ki 20:6; 19O LORD. For the sake[y] of your servant and according to your will, you have done this great thing
Isa 9:7; 37:35; 55:3 [z]2Sa 7:25 and made known all these great promises.[z]

17:20 [a]Ex 8:10; 9:14; 15:11; 20"There is no one like you, O LORD, and there is no God but you,[a] as we have heard with our
Isa 44:6; 46:9 own ears. 21And who is like your people Israel—the one nation on earth whose God went out to
17:21 [b]Ex 6:6 redeem[b] a people for himself, and to make a name for yourself, and to perform great and awesome
wonders by driving out nations from before your people, whom you redeemed from Egypt? 22You
17:22 [c]Ex 19:5-6 made your people Israel your very own forever,[c] and you, O LORD, have become their God.

17:23 [d]1Ki 8:25 23"And now, LORD, let the promise[d] you have made concerning your servant and his house be
established forever. Do as you promised, 24so that it will be established and that your name will be
great forever. Then men will say, 'The LORD Almighty, the God over Israel, is Israel's God!' And the
house of your servant David will be established before you.

25"You, my God, have revealed to your servant that you will build a house for him. So your ser-
vant has found courage to pray to you. 26O LORD, you are God! You have promised these good things
to your servant. 27Now you have been pleased to bless the house of your servant, that it may con-
17:27 [e]Ps 16:11; 21:6 tinue forever in your sight;[e] for you, O LORD, have blessed it, and it will be blessed forever."

David's Victories

18 In the course of time, David defeated the Philistines and subdued them, and he took Gath and
its surrounding villages from the control of the Philistines.

18:2 [f]Nu 21:29 2David also defeated the Moabites,[f] and they became subject to him and brought tribute.

18:3 [g]1Ch 19:6 [h]Ge 2:14 3Moreover, David fought Hadadezer king of Zobah,[g] as far as Hamath, when he went to establish his
control along the Euphrates River.[h] 4David captured a thousand of his chariots, seven thousand chari-
18:4 [i]Ge 49:6 oteers and twenty thousand foot soldiers. He hamstrung[i] all but a hundred of the chariot horses.

18:5 [j]2Ki 16:9; 1Ch 19:6 5When the Arameans of Damascus[j] came to help Hadadezer king of Zobah, David struck down twen-
ty-two thousand of them. 6He put garrisons in the Aramean kingdom of Damascus, and the Arameans
became subject to him and brought tribute. The LORD gave David victory everywhere he went.

7David took the gold shields carried by the officers of Hadadezer and brought them to Jerusalem.
8From Tebah[b] and Cun, towns that belonged to Hadadezer, David took a great quantity of bronze, which
18:8 [k]1Ki 7:23; 2Ch 4:12,15-16 Solomon used to make the bronze Sea,[k] the pillars and various bronze articles.

[a] 6 Traditionally *judges*; also in verse 10 [b] 8 Hebrew *Tibhath*, a variant of *Tebah*

[9]When Tou king of Hamath heard that David had defeated the entire army of Hadadezer king of Zo-
bah, [10]he sent his son Hadoram to King David to greet him and congratulate him on his victory in bat-
tle over Hadadezer, who had been at war with Tou. Hadoram brought all kinds of articles of gold and sil-
ver and bronze.
[11]King David dedicated these articles to the LORD, as he had done with the silver and gold he had tak-
en from all these nations: Edom[l] and Moab, the Ammonites and the Philistines, and Amalek.[m]
[12]Abishai son of Zeruiah struck down eighteen thousand Edomites[n] in the Valley of Salt. [13]He put gar-
risons in Edom, and all the Edomites became subject to David. The LORD gave David victory everywhere
he went.

18:11 [l]Nu 24:18 [m]Nu 24:20
18:12 [n]1Ki 11:15

The Tigris and Euphrates Rivers

The Euphrates River
Preserving Bible Times; © Dr. James C. Martin

1 CHRONICLES 18 The Tigris and Euphrates are the two principal rivers flowing through ancient **Mesopotamia** (modern Iraq), and it is to them that the region owes its viability. In fact, the name Mesopotamia means the "land between the rivers." The Tigris and Euphrates cradle a fertile plain bordered by mountains to the east and north, desert to the west and southwest and the Persian Gulf to the south. This alluvial plain (its soil consists of clay, silt, sand, gravel or similar material deposited there by the running water) provided the necessary environment for the emergence of humanity's first civilization, **Sumer**,[1] and for the subsequent rise and flourishing of the **Assyrian** and **Babylonian** Empires.

The Tigris and Euphrates trace their sources to the mountain ranges of Armenia and Turkey. The Tigris, to the east, runs 1,146 miles (1,848 km) before it joins the Euphrates from the west for 68 miles (nearly 110 km) before emptying into the Persian Gulf. Capital cities of the ancient Assyrian Empire, such as Nineveh,[2] Calah ("Map 8a") and **Asshur**, once dotted the shores of the Tigris. The modern capital of Iraq, Baghdad, stands today on this river. The Euphrates, the largest river in the region, often referred to as simply "the River" in the Old Testament (e.g., Dt 11:24; the Hebrew does not contain the name "Euphrates"), runs for 1,780 miles (2,871 km); most of its course is navigable by boats and ideal for trade and transport. The ancient cities of Carchemish, **Mari**,[3] Babylon[4] and Ur (see "Map 1" for all of these sites) were situated on its banks.

The great rivers of Mesopotamia intersect with Biblical history as early as Genesis 2:14, which cites the Tigris and Euphrates as two branches of the river flowing from the Garden of Eden.[5] The Euphrates additionally marks the eastern boundary of the territorial allotment promised to Abraham and his descendants (Ge 15:18; cf. Jos 1:4). Yet it appears that for most of Israel's history this border was unrealized. Only for a brief period during the reigns of David and Solomon did Israelite control ever extend to the Euphrates (1Ch 18:3).

[1]See "Sumer" on page 10. [2]See "Nineveh" on page 1497. [3]See "Mari" on page 54. [4]See "Babylon" on page 1077. [5]See "The Location of Eden" on page 6.

David's Officials

18:14 [o]1Ch 29:26 [p]1Ch 11:1 18:15 [q]2Sa 5:6-8; 1Ch 11:6 18:16 [r]2Sa 8:17; 1Ch 6:8 [s]1Ch 24:6 18:17 [t]1Sa 30:14; 2Sa 8:18; 15:18

[14]David reigned[o] over all Israel,[p] doing what was just and right for all his people. [15]Joab[q] son of Zer-
uiah was over the army; Jehoshaphat son of Ahilud was recorder; [16]Zadok[r] son of Ahitub and Ahime-
lech[a][s] son of Abiathar were priests; Shavsha was secretary; [17]Benaiah son of Jehoiada was over the Ker-
ethites and Pelethites;[t] and David's sons were chief officials at the king's side.

The Battle Against the Ammonites

19:1 [u]Ge 19:38; Jdg 10:17–11:33; 2Ch 20:1-2; Zep 2:8-11

19 In the course of time, Nahash king of the Ammonites[u] died, and his son succeeded him as
king. [2]David thought, "I will show kindness to Hanun son of Nahash, because his father
showed kindness to me." So David sent a delegation to express his sympathy to Hanun concerning his
father.

When David's men came to Hanun in the land of the Ammonites to express sympathy to him, [3]the
Ammonite nobles said to Hanun, "Do you think David is honoring your father by sending men to you to
19:3 [v]Nu 21:32 express sympathy? Haven't his men come to you to explore and spy out[v] the country and overthrow it?"
[4]So Hanun seized David's men, shaved them, cut off their garments in the middle at the buttocks, and
sent them away.

[5]When someone came and told David about the men, he sent messengers to meet them, for they
were greatly humiliated. The king said, "Stay at Jericho till your beards have grown, and then come
back."

19:6 [w]Ge 34:30 [x]1Ch 18:3,5,9 [6]When the Ammonites realized that they had become a stench[w] in David's nostrils, Hanun and the
Ammonites sent a thousand talents[b] of silver to hire chariots and charioteers from Aram Naharaim,[c]
Aram Maacah and Zobah.[x] [7]They hired thirty-two thousand chariots and charioteers, as well as the king
19:7 [y]Nu 21:30; Jos 13:9,16 of Maacah with his troops, who came and camped near Medeba,[y] while the Ammonites were mustered
from their towns and moved out for battle.

[8]On hearing this, David sent Joab out with the entire army of fighting men. [9]The Ammonites came out
and drew up in battle formation at the entrance to their city, while the kings who had come were by them-
selves in the open country.

[10]Joab saw that there were battle lines in front of him and behind him; so he selected some of the best
troops in Israel and deployed them against the Arameans. [11]He put the rest of the men under the com-
19:11 [z]1Sa 26:6 mand of Abishai[z] his brother, and they were deployed against the Ammonites. [12]Joab said, "If the Arame-
ans are too strong for me, then you are to rescue me; but if the Ammonites are too strong for you, then I
will rescue you. [13]Be strong and let us fight bravely for our people and the cities of our God. The LORD will
do what is good in his sight."

[14]Then Joab and the troops with him advanced to fight the Arameans, and they fled before him.
[15]When the Ammonites saw that the Arameans were fleeing, they too fled before his brother Abishai and
went inside the city. So Joab went back to Jerusalem.

[16]After the Arameans saw that they had been routed by Israel, they sent messengers and had Ara-
means brought from beyond the River,[d] with Shophach the commander of Hadadezer's army leading
them.

19:17 [a]1Ch 9:1 [17]When David was told of this, he gathered all Israel[a] and crossed the Jordan; he advanced against
them and formed his battle lines opposite them. David formed his lines to meet the Arameans in bat-
tle, and they fought against him. [18]But they fled before Israel, and David killed seven thousand of their
charioteers and forty thousand of their foot soldiers. He also killed Shophach the commander of their
army.

[19]When the vassals of Hadadezer saw that they had been defeated by Israel, they made peace with
David and became subject to him.

So the Arameans were not willing to help the Ammonites anymore.

[a] *16* Some Hebrew manuscripts, Vulgate and Syriac (see also 2 Samuel 8:17); most Hebrew manuscripts *Abimelech* [b] *6* That is, about 37 tons (about 34 metric tons) [c] *6* That is, Northwest Mesopotamia [d] *16* That is, the Euphrates

---

18:17 The Kerethites and Pelethites were foreign mercenaries who constituted part of the royal bodyguard (2Sa 8:18; 20:23). They remained loyal to David during the rebellions of Absalom (2Sa 15:18) and Sheba (2Sa 20:7) and supported the succession of Solomon against his rival Adonijah (1Ki 1:38,44).

19:19 Hadadezer was the king of Zobah (18:3), an Aramean state, and the leader of the Aramean coalition. His vassals (though not Hadadezer himself) entered into a peace treaty with Israel, the terms of which apparently included a clause prohibiting the Arameans from partnering with the Ammonites in future campaigns. (See "Ammon" on p. 364 and "Syria/Aram" on p. 534.)

The Capture of Rabbah

20 In the spring, at the time when kings go off to war, Joab led out the armed forces. He laid waste
the land of the Ammonites and went to Rabbah[b] and besieged it, but David remained in 20:1 [b]Dt 3:11; 2Sa 12:26
Jerusalem. Joab attacked Rabbah and left it in ruins.[c] 2 David took the crown from the head of their [c]Am 1:13-15
king[a]—its weight was found to be a talent[b] of gold, and it was set with precious stones—and it was
placed on David's head. He took a great quantity of plunder from the city 3 and brought out the people
who were there, consigning them to labor with saws and with iron picks and axes.[d] David did this to all 20:3 [d]Dt 29:11
the Ammonite towns. Then David and his entire army returned to Jerusalem.

[a] 2 Or *of Milcom,* that is, Molech [b] 2 That is, about 75 pounds (about 34 kilograms)

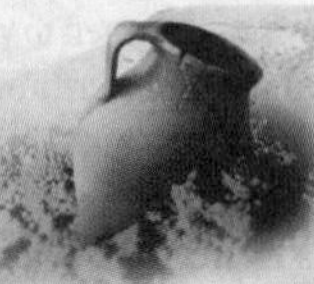

ARCHAEOLOGICAL SITES

RABBAH

Barrel cylinder from Nebuchadnezzar II

Preserving Bible Times; © Dr. James C. Martin; permission of The Israel Museum

1 CHRONICLES 20 Rabbah (see "Map 5"), the Ammonite[1] capital, situated along the **King's Highway** at the desert's edge, controlled north-south commerce in ancient times.[2] Its plentiful water supply, fertile surroundings and defensible position afforded the city security, and a thriving caravan trade maintained its prosperity. Artifacts excavated from tombs demonstrate contact with Egypt, Greece, Cyprus, **Phoenicia**, Midian and **Babylon** from the **Middle Bronze Age**[3] to the fifth century B.C. A crematorium (or possibly a temple) discovered on the current site of the Amman airport suggests the presence of **Hittites**[4] there during the fourteenth–thirteenth centuries B.C.

The iron bed of Og[5] of Bashan was located at Rabbah (Dt 3:11). Centuries later David conquered the city after its king had humiliated his ambassadors (1Ch 19–20), and it was during the siege of Rabbah that he arranged to have Uriah the Hittite killed in battle (2Sa 11). David literally took the crown of the Ammonite king (thereby figuratively subduing him) and consigned the inhabitants to forced labor. Archaeological evidence of defensive wall reconstruction in the tenth century B.C. may be attributed to David's campaign.

After the fall of Israel (722 B.C.), Ammonites annexed Gilead (the region where Rabbah was located). The site prospered, as evidenced by a seventh-century B.C. residence excavated in the center of Amman. It included four rooms, a courtyard and numerous costly artifacts. Recently discovered inscriptions and seals specify the names of 11 Ammonite kings from 1000 to 581 B.C., when Rabbah was conquered by **Nebuchadnezzar II**[6] of Babylon. Though uninhabited during the **Persian period**, the city was restored and renamed Philadelphia during the **Hellenistic period**. It then became one of the cities of the **Decapolis** under the Romans.

[1]See "Ammon" on page 364. [2]See "Caravan Trading and Routes in the Ancient Near East" on page 63. [3]See "Archaeological Periods" chart on page xx in the front of this Bible. [4]See "Anatolia and the Hittites" on page 144. [5]See "The Kingdoms of Sihon and Og" on page 244. [6]See "Nebuchadnezzar" on page 571.

War With the Philistines

20:4 [e]Jos 10:33 4 In the course of time, war broke out with the Philistines, at Gezer.[e] At that time Sibbecai the Hu-
[f]Ge 14:5 shathite killed Sippai, one of the descendants of the Rephaites,[f] and the Philistines were subjugated.
5 In another battle with the Philistines, Elhanan son of Jair killed Lahmi the brother of Goliath the
20:5 [g]1Sa 17:7 Gittite, who had a spear with a shaft like a weaver's rod.[g]
6 In still another battle, which took place at Gath, there was a huge man with six fingers on each hand
and six toes on each foot—twenty-four in all. He also was descended from Rapha. 7 When he taunted
Israel, Jonathan son of Shimea, David's brother, killed him.
8 These were descendants of Rapha in Gath, and they fell at the hands of David and his men.

David Numbers the Fighting Men

21:1 [h]2Ch 18:21; Ps 109:6 **21** Satan[h] rose up against Israel and incited David to take a census[i] of Israel. 2 So David said to Joab
[i]2Ch 14:8; 25:5 and the commanders of the troops, "Go and count[j] the Israelites from Beersheba to Dan. Then
21:2 [j]1Ch 27:23-24 report back to me so that I may know how many there are."
21:3 [k]Dt 1:11 3 But Joab replied, "May the LORD multiply his troops a hundred times over.[k] My lord the king, are
they not all my lord's subjects? Why does my lord want to do this? Why should he bring guilt on
Israel?"
4 The king's word, however, overruled Joab; so Joab left and went throughout Israel and then came
21:5 [l]1Ch 9:1 back to Jerusalem. 5 Joab reported the number of the fighting men to David: In all Israel[l] there were one
million one hundred thousand men who could handle a sword, including four hundred and seventy thou-
sand in Judah.
6 But Joab did not include Levi and Benjamin in the numbering, because the king's command was re-
pulsive to him. 7 This command was also evil in the sight of God; so he punished Israel.
8 Then David said to God, "I have sinned greatly by doing this. Now, I beg you, take away the guilt of
your servant. I have done a very foolish thing."
21:9 [m]1Sa 22:5 9 The LORD said to Gad,[m] David's seer,[n] 10 "Go and tell David, 'This is what the LORD says: I am giving
[n]1Sa 9:9 you three options. Choose one of them for me to carry out against you.' "
11 So Gad went to David and said to him, "This is what the LORD says: 'Take your choice: 12 three years
21:12 [o]Dt 32:24 of famine,[o] three months of being swept away[a] before your enemies, with their swords overtaking you,
[p]Eze 30:25 or three days of the sword[p] of the LORD[q]—days of plague in the land, with the angel of the LORD ravag-
[q]Ge 19:13 ing every part of Israel.' Now then, decide how I should answer the one who sent me."
21:13 [r]Ps 6:4; 86:15; 130:4,7 13 David said to Gad, "I am in deep distress. Let me fall into the hands of the LORD, for his mercy[r] is
very great; but do not let me fall into the hands of men."
21:14 [s]1Ch 27:24 14 So the LORD sent a plague on Israel, and seventy thousand men of Israel fell dead.[s] 15 And God sent
21:15 [t]Ge 32:1 an angel[t] to destroy Jerusalem.[u] But as the angel was doing so, the LORD saw it and was grieved[v] because
[u]Ps 125:2 [v]Ge 6:6; Ex 32:14 of the calamity and said to the angel who was destroying[w] the people, "Enough! Withdraw your hand."
[w]Ge 19:13 The angel of the LORD was then standing at the threshing floor of Araunah[b] the Jebusite.
16 David looked up and saw the angel of the LORD standing between heaven and earth, with a drawn
sword in his hand extended over Jerusalem. Then David and the elders, clothed in sackcloth, fell face-
21:16 [x]Nu 14:5; Jos 7:6 down.[x]
17 David said to God, "Was it not I who ordered the fighting men to be counted? I am the one who has
21:17 [y]2Sa 7:8; Ps 74:1 [z]Jnh 1:12 sinned and done wrong. These are but sheep.[y] What have they done? O LORD my God, let your hand fall
upon me and my family,[z] but do not let this plague remain on your people."
18 Then the angel of the LORD ordered Gad to tell David to go up and build an altar to the LORD on the
21:18 [a]2Ch 3:1 threshing floor[a] of Araunah the Jebusite. 19 So David went up in obedience to the word that Gad had spo-
ken in the name of the LORD.

[a] *12* Hebrew; Septuagint and Vulgate (see also 2 Samuel 24:13) *of fleeing* [b] *15* Hebrew *Ornan,* a variant of *Araunah*; also in verses 18-28

20:4 Rephaites were an ancient people known for their unusual stature (see Ge 14:5; Dt 2:11).

21:16 The traditional Hebrew text of 2 Samuel 24 does not include this information, so some scholars have regarded it as an addition by the Chronicler that reflects the more developed doctrine of angels in the postexilic period. However, a fragmentary Hebrew text of Samuel from the third century B.C., discovered at Qumran, does contain the verse. It now appears that the Chronicler was carefully copying the Samuel material, which differed in some respects from the Masoretic (traditional Hebrew) text. The ancient Jewish historian Josephus, who also appears to have been following the text of Samuel, reported the same information.

21:18 See "The Threshing Floor" on page 608.

The Threshing Floor

1 CHRONICLES 21 The threshing floor was an essential part of agriculture in the ancient Near East.[1] Typically round, with a diameter of 25–40 feet (7.6–12.2 m), it was usually located near a village in an area exposed to wind. Once the farmer had selected the location, he cleared the ground of stones and compressed the soil until a firm surface resulted. When the "floor" was ready, he laid recently harvested sheaves of grain on it for threshing. The farmer then used large animals, such as oxen or donkeys, to pull heavy threshing sleds over the grain, separating the kernels from the stalks and husks. When the threshing was complete, a winnowing fork was used to toss the grain into the air. The wind blew away the lighter stalks and husks (chaff), as the heavier kernels fell back to the floor. The farmer sifted the kernels through trays to remove any dirt gathered in the process and then temporarily stored the grain in heaps on the floor or sealed it in jars for later use.

While the primary focus of the threshing floor was agricultural, the separation of the wheat and chaff became a natural and fitting symbol of judgment in the Old Testament (1Ch 21:15; cf. Mt 3:12). Because the floor was often the largest open area within a village, town elders were typically present to oversee the threshing of the year's crops. The threshing floor was a suitable locale for legal transactions, criminal trials and public decisions. Alternatively, public proceedings were often carried out at the city gate.[2]

[1]See "Food and Agriculture" on page 390. [2]See "The City Gate" on page 392.

Grain silo at Tel Qasile, Israel
Preserving Bible Times; © Dr. James C. Martin; permission of Eretz Israel Museum

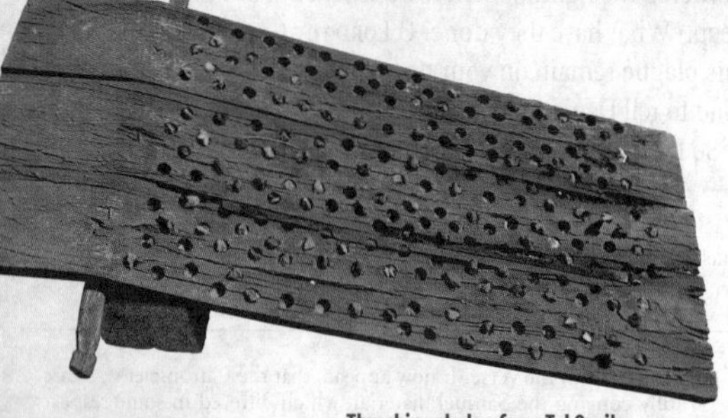

Threshing sledge from Tel Qasile
Preserving Bible Times; © Dr. James C. Martin; permission of Eretz Israel Museum

Rotary hand mill
Preserving Bible Times; © Dr. James C. Martin; permission of Eretz Israel Museum

21:20 [b]Jdg 6:11 20While Araunah was threshing wheat,[b] he turned and saw the angel; his four sons who were with
him hid themselves. 21Then David approached, and when Araunah looked and saw him, he left the
threshing floor and bowed down before David with his face to the ground.
22David said to him, "Let me have the site of your threshing floor so I can build an altar to the LORD,
that the plague on the people may be stopped. Sell it to me at the full price."
23Araunah said to David, "Take it! Let my lord the king do whatever pleases him. Look, I will give the
oxen for the burnt offerings, the threshing sledges for the wood, and the wheat for the grain offering. I
will give all this."
24But King David replied to Araunah, "No, I insist on paying the full price. I will not take for the LORD
what is yours, or sacrifice a burnt offering that costs me nothing."
25So David paid Araunah six hundred shekels[a] of gold for the site. 26David built an altar to the LORD
there and sacrificed burnt offerings and fellowship offerings.[b] He called on the LORD, and the LORD an-
21:26 [c]Lev 9:24; Jdg 6:21 swered him with fire[c] from heaven on the altar of burnt offering.
27Then the LORD spoke to the angel, and he put his sword back into its sheath. 28At that time, when Da-
vid saw that the LORD had answered him on the threshing floor of Araunah the Jebusite, he offered sac-
rifices there. 29The tabernacle of the LORD, which Moses had made in the desert, and the altar of burnt
21:29 [d]1Ki 3:4; 1Ch 16:39 offering were at that time on the high place at Gibeon.[d] 30But David could not go before it to inquire of
God, because he was afraid of the sword of the angel of the LORD.

22:1 [e]Ge 28:17; 1Ch 21:18-29; 2Ch 3:1 22 Then David said, "The house of the LORD God[e] is to be here, and also the altar of burnt offering
for Israel."

Preparations for the Temple

22:2 [f]1Ki 9:21; Isa 56:6 [g]1Ki 5:17-18 2So David gave orders to assemble the aliens[f] living in Israel, and from among them he appointed
stonecutters[g] to prepare dressed stone for building the house of God. 3He provided a large amount of
iron to make nails for the doors of the gateways and for the fittings, and more bronze than could be
22:3 [h]ver 14; 1Ki 7:47; 1Ch 29:2-5 weighed.[h] 4He also provided more cedar logs[i] than could be counted, for the Sidonians and Tyrians had
22:4 [i]1Ki 5:6 brought large numbers of them to David.
22:5 [j]1Ki 3:7; 1Ch 29:1 5David said, "My son Solomon is young[j] and inexperienced, and the house to be built for the LORD
should be of great magnificence and fame and splendor in the sight of all the nations. Therefore I will
make preparations for it." So David made extensive preparations before his death.
22:6 [k]Ac 7:47 6Then he called for his son Solomon and charged him to build[k] a house for the LORD, the God of Is-
22:7 [l]1Ch 17:2 [m]2Sa 7:2; 1Ki 8:17 [n]Dt 12:5, 11 rael. 7David said to Solomon: "My son, I had it in my heart[l] to build[m] a house for the Name[n] of the LORD
my God. 8But this word of the LORD came to me: 'You have shed much blood and have fought many wars.[o]
22:8 [o]1Ki 5:3 [p]1Ch 28:3 You are not to build a house for my Name,[p] because you have shed much blood on the earth in my sight.
22:9 [q]1Ki 5:4 [r]2Sa 12:24 [s]1Ki 4:20 9But you will have a son who will be a man of peace[q] and rest, and I will give him rest from all his ene-
mies on every side. His name will be Solomon,[c][r] and I will grant Israel peace and quiet[s] during his reign.
22:10 [t]1Ch 17:12 [u]2Sa 7:13 [v]2Sa 7:14; 2Ch 6:15 10He is the one who will build a house for my Name.[t] He will be my son,[u] and I will be his father. And I
will establish the throne of his kingdom over Israel forever.'[v]
22:11 [w]ver 16 11"Now, my son, the LORD be with[w] you, and may you have success and build the house of the LORD
22:12 [x]1Ki 3:9-12; 2Ch 1:10 your God, as he said you would. 12May the LORD give you discretion and understanding[x] when he puts
you in command over Israel, so that you may keep the law of the LORD your God. 13Then you will have suc-
22:13 [y]1Ch 28:7 [z]Dt 31:6; Jos 1:6-9; 1Ch 28:20 cess if you are careful to observe the decrees and laws[y] that the LORD gave Moses for Israel. Be strong and
courageous.[z] Do not be afraid or discouraged.
14"I have taken great pains to provide for the temple of the LORD a hundred thousand talents[d] of gold,
a million talents[e] of silver, quantities of bronze and iron too great to be weighed, and wood and stone.
22:14 [a]ver 3; 1Ch 29:2-5,19 And you may add to them.[a] 15You have many workmen: stonecutters, masons and carpenters, as well as

[a] *25* That is, about 15 pounds (about 7 kilograms) [b] *26* Traditionally *peace offerings* [c] *9* *Solomon* sounds like and may be derived from the Hebrew for *peace.* [d] *14* That is, about 3,750 tons (about 3,450 metric tons) [e] *14* That is, about 37,500 tons (about 34,500 metric tons)

21:20–21 Second Samuel 24:20 does not report that Araunah was threshing wheat as the king approached. However, Josephus and the fragmentary text of Samuel from Qumran both mention this information (see the note on v. 16).

21:25 Second Samuel 24:24 states that 50 shekels of silver were paid for the threshing floor and the oxen. This apparent discrepancy may likely be explained by the Chronicler's statement that this (600 shekels of gold) was the price for the "site," that is, for a much larger area than the threshing floor alone.

22:2 Although "aliens" were personally free, they were without political rights and could be easily exploited (see "Slavery and Labor Law in the Ancient Near East" on p. 127).

22:14 The figures for the gold and silver are, to say the least, extraordinarily large. A talent weighed at least 66 pounds (30 kg), indicating

men skilled in every kind of work 16in gold and silver, bronze and iron—craftsmen[b] beyond number. 22:16 [b]ver 11; 2Ch 2:7
Now begin the work, and the LORD be with you."
17Then David ordered[c] all the leaders of Israel to help his son Solomon. 18He said to them, "Is not the 22:17 [c]1Ch 28:1-6
LORD your God with you? And has he not granted you rest[d] on every side?[e] For he has handed the inhab- 22:18 [d]ver 9; 1Ch 23:25 [e]2Sa 7:1
itants of the land over to me, and the land is subject to the LORD and to his people. 19Now devote your heart
and soul to seeking the LORD your God.[f] Begin to build the sanctuary of the LORD God, so that you may 22:19 [f]ver 7; 1Ki 8:6; 1Ch 28:9; 2Ch 5:7; 7:14
bring the ark of the covenant of the LORD and the sacred articles belonging to God into the temple that
will be built for the Name of the LORD."

The Levites

23 When David was old and full of years, he made his son Solomon[g] king over Israel.[h] 23:1 [g]1Ki 1:33-39; 1Ch 28:5 [h]1Ki 1:30; 1Ch 29:28
2He also gathered together all the leaders of Israel, as well as the priests and Levites. 3The Levites
thirty years old or more[i] were counted, and the total number of men was thirty-eight thousand.[j] 4David 23:3 [i]ver 24; Nu 8:24 [j]Nu 4:3-49
said, "Of these, twenty-four thousand are to supervise[k] the work of the temple of the LORD and six thou-
sand are to be officials and judges.[l] 5Four thousand are to be gatekeepers and four thousand are to praise 23:4 [k]Ezr 3:8 [l]1Ch 26:29; 2Ch 19:8
the LORD with the musical instruments[m] I have provided for that purpose."[n] 23:5 [m]1Ch 15:16 [n]Ne 12:45
6David divided[o] the Levites into groups corresponding to the sons of Levi: Gershon, Kohath and
Merari. 23:6 [o]2Ch 8:14; 29:25

Gershonites

7Belonging to the Gershonites:
Ladan and Shimei.
8The sons of Ladan:
Jehiel the first, Zetham and Joel—three in all.
9The sons of Shimei:
Shelomoth, Haziel and Haran—three in all.
These were the heads of the families of Ladan.
10And the sons of Shimei:
Jahath, Ziza,[a] Jeush and Beriah.
These were the sons of Shimei—four in all.
11Jahath was the first and Ziza the second, but Jeush and Beriah did not have many sons; so they
were counted as one family with one assignment.

Kohathites

12The sons of Kohath:[p] 23:12 [p]Ex 6:18
Amram, Izhar, Hebron and Uzziel—four in all.
13The sons of Amram:[q] 23:13 [q]Ex 6:20; 28:1 [r]Ex 30:7-10; Dt 21:5 [s]Nu 6:23
Aaron and Moses.
Aaron was set apart,[r] he and his descendants forever, to consecrate the most holy things,
to offer sacrifices before the LORD, to minister before him and to pronounce blessings[s] in
his name forever. 14The sons of Moses the man[t] of God were counted as part of the tribe 23:14 [t]Dt 33:1
of Levi.
15The sons of Moses:
Gershom and Eliezer.[u] 23:15 [u]Ex 18:4
16The descendants of Gershom:[v] 23:16 [v]1Ch 26:24-28
Shubael was the first.

[a] 10 One Hebrew manuscript, Septuagint and Vulgate (see also verse 11); most Hebrew manuscripts *Zina*

---

that 100,000 talents of gold would have weighed about 6.6 million pounds (3 million kg). When Pharaoh Shishak (or Sheshonk) made an offering to the Egyptian gods after having plundered Jerusalem, he is said to have donated about 200 tons (400,000 lbs or 181,600 kg) of gold, an immense figure and the largest temple donation ever recorded to have been made by an Egyptian pharaoh. This confirms the extraordinary wealth of Solomon's Jerusalem, but it is still far short of the tonnage of gold mentioned in this verse, to say nothing of the one million talents of silver. According to 1 Kings 10:14, the annual revenue for Solomon's kingdom was the equivalent of 666 talents of gold. It is difficult to imagine that Solomon paid the equivalent of 150 years of his kingdom's income in gold, plus an enormous amount of silver, for the temple complex. It is helpful to bear in mind that numbers in the Bible are often difficult to interpret, prone to textual errors and sometimes never intended to be taken literally (see "Numbers and Their Meaning" on p. 197).

17 The descendants of Eliezer:
Rehabiah was the first.
Eliezer had no other sons, but the sons of Rehabiah were very numerous.
18 The sons of Izhar:
Shelomith was the first.
23:19 [w]1Ch 24:23 — 19 The sons of Hebron:[w]
Jeriah the first, Amariah the second, Jahaziel the third and Jekameam the fourth.
20 The sons of Uzziel:
Micah the first and Isshiah the second.

Merarites

23:21 [x]1Ch 24:26 — 21 The sons of Merari:[x]
Mahli and Mushi.
The sons of Mahli:
Eleazar and Kish.
22 Eleazar died without having sons: he had only daughters. Their cousins, the sons of Kish, mar-
ried them.
23 The sons of Mushi:
Mahli, Eder and Jerimoth—three in all.

24 These were the descendants of Levi by their families—the heads of families as they were registered
23:24 [y]Nu 4:3; 10:17,21 — under their names and counted individually, that is, the workers twenty years old or more[y] who served
23:25 [z]1Ch 22:9 — in the temple of the LORD. 25 For David had said, "Since the LORD, the God of Israel, has granted rest[z] to
his people and has come to dwell in Jerusalem forever, 26 the Levites no longer need to carry the taber-
23:26 [a]Nu 4:5, 15; 7:9; Dt 10:8 — nacle or any of the articles used in its service."[a] 27 According to the last instructions of David, the Levites
were counted from those twenty years old or more.
28 The duty of the Levites was to help Aaron's descendants in the service of the temple of the LORD: to
23:28 [b]2Ch 29:15; Ne 13:9; Mal 3:3 — be in charge of the courtyards, the side rooms, the purification[b] of all sacred things and the performance
of other duties at the house of God. 29 They were in charge of the bread set out on the table,[c] the flour for
23:29 [c]Ex 25:30 [d]Lev 2:4-7; 6:20-23 [e]Lev 19:35-36; 1Ch 9:29,32 — the grain offerings,[d] the unleavened wafers, the baking and the mixing, and all measurements of quan-
tity and size.[e] 30 They were also to stand every morning to thank and praise the LORD. They were to do
23:30 [f]1Ch 9:33; Ps 134:1 — the same in the evening[f] 31 and whenever burnt offerings were presented to the LORD on Sabbaths and at
23:31 [g]2Ki 4:23 [h]Lev 23:4; Nu 28:9–29:39; Isa 1:13-14; Col 2:16 — New Moon[g] festivals and at appointed feasts.[h] They were to serve before the LORD regularly in the prop-
er number and in the way prescribed for them.
32 And so the Levites[i] carried out their responsibilities for the Tent of Meeting,[j] for the Holy Place and,
23:32 [i]Nu 1:53; 1Ch 6:48 [j]Nu 3:6-8,38 [k]2Ch 23:18; 31:2; Eze 44:14 — under their brothers the descendants of Aaron, for the service of the temple of the LORD.[k]

The Divisions of Priests

24:1 [l]1Ch 23:6; 28:13; 2Ch 5:11; 8:14; 23:8; 31:2; 35:4,5; Ezr 6:18 [m]Nu 3:2-4 [n]Ex 6:23 — 24 These were the divisions[l] of the sons of Aaron:[m]
The sons of Aaron were Nadab, Abihu, Eleazar and Ithamar.[n] 2 But Nadab and Abihu died before
24:2 [o]Lev 10:1-2; Nu 3:4 — their father did,[o] and they had no sons; so Eleazar and Ithamar served as the priests. 3 With the help of
24:3 [p]2Sa 8:17 — Zadok[p] a descendant of Eleazar and Ahimelech a descendant of Ithamar, David separated them into di-
visions for their appointed order of ministering. 4 A larger number of leaders were found among Eleazar's
descendants than among Ithamar's, and they were divided accordingly: sixteen heads of families from
Eleazar's descendants and eight heads of families from Ithamar's descendants. 5 They divided them im-
24:5 [q]ver 31; 1Ch 25:8 — partially by drawing lots,[q] for there were officials of the sanctuary and officials of God among the descen-
dants of both Eleazar and Ithamar.
6 The scribe Shemaiah son of Nethanel, a Levite, recorded their names in the presence of the king and
24:6 [r]1Ch 18:16 — of the officials: Zadok the priest, Ahimelech[r] son of Abiathar and the heads of families of the priests and
of the Levites—one family being taken from Eleazar and then one from Ithamar.

23:24 The expression "heads of families" refers to clan leaders or family elders (cf. 27:1). The census age of twenty follows the standard practice, established by Moses (cf. Nu 1:3), of the numbering of all Israelites. The age of thirty cited in verse 3 may have applied to Levites assigned to specific tasks or to those in their twenties who may have served apprenticeships.

24:5 A total of 24 divisions was selected by lot (see "Casting Lots" on p. 744). This would have allowed for service either in monthly shifts, as with the priests in Egyptian mortuary temples, or in two-week shifts once each year, the practice followed during New Testament times. The names of the first, second, fourth, ninth and twenty-fourth divisions have been found in a Dead Sea scroll from the fourth cave at Qumran.

[7]The first lot fell to Jehoiarib,
the second to Jedaiah,[s]
[8]the third to Harim,[t]
the fourth to Seorim,
[9]the fifth to Malkijah,
the sixth to Mijamin,
[10]the seventh to Hakkoz,
the eighth to Abijah,[u]
[11]the ninth to Jeshua,
the tenth to Shecaniah,
[12]the eleventh to Eliashib,
the twelfth to Jakim,
[13]the thirteenth to Huppah,
the fourteenth to Jeshebeab,
[14]the fifteenth to Bilgah,
the sixteenth to Immer,[v]
[15]the seventeenth to Hezir,[w]
the eighteenth to Happizzez,
[16]the nineteenth to Pethahiah,
the twentieth to Jehezkel,
[17]the twenty-first to Jakin,
the twenty-second to Gamul,
[18]the twenty-third to Delaiah
and the twenty-fourth to Maaziah.

[19]This was their appointed order of ministering when they entered the temple of the LORD, according to the regulations prescribed for them by their forefather Aaron, as the LORD, the God of Israel, had commanded him.

The Rest of the Levites

[20]As for the rest of the descendants of Levi:[x]
from the sons of Amram: Shubael;
from the sons of Shubael: Jehdeiah.
[21]As for Rehabiah,[y] from his sons:
Isshiah was the first.
[22]From the Izharites: Shelomoth;
from the sons of Shelomoth: Jahath.
[23]The sons of Hebron:[z] Jeriah the first,[a] Amariah the second, Jahaziel the third and Jekameam the fourth.
[24]The son of Uzziel: Micah;
from the sons of Micah: Shamir.
[25]The brother of Micah: Isshiah;
from the sons of Isshiah: Zechariah.
[26]The sons of Merari:[a] Mahli and Mushi.
The son of Jaaziah: Beno.
[27]The sons of Merari:
from Jaaziah: Beno, Shoham, Zaccur and Ibri.
[28]From Mahli: Eleazar, who had no sons.
[29]From Kish: the son of Kish:
Jerahmeel.
[30]And the sons of Mushi: Mahli, Eder and Jerimoth.

24:7 [s]Ezr 2:36; Ne 12:6
24:8 [t]Ezr 2:39; Ne 10:5
24:10 [u]Ne 12:4, 17; Lk 1:5
24:14 [v]Jer 20:1
24:15 [w]Ne 10:20
24:20 [x]1Ch 23:6
24:21 [y]1Ch 23:17
24:23 [z]1Ch 23:19
24:26 [a]1Ch 6:19; 23:21

[a] *23* Two Hebrew manuscripts and some Septuagint manuscripts (see also 1 Chron. 23:19); most Hebrew manuscripts *The sons of Jeriah:*

24:15 The family of Hezir was prominent in intertestamental times (see "The Intertestamental Period" on p. 1551). A large tomb in the Kidron Valley, east of Jerusalem, bears the name.

24:31 [b]ver 5

These were the Levites, according to their families. [31]They also cast lots,[b] just as their brothers the descendants of Aaron did, in the presence of King David and of Zadok, Ahimelech, and the heads of families of the priests and of the Levites. The families of the oldest brother were treated the same as those of the youngest.

The Singers

25:1 [c]1Ch 6:39 [d]1Ch 6:33 [e]1Ch 16:41,42; Ne 11:17 [f]1Sa 10:5; 2Ki 3:15 [g]1Ch 15:16 [h]1Ch 6:31 [i]2Ch 5:12; 8:14; 34:12; 35:15; Ezr 3:10
25:3 [j]1Ch 16:41-42 [k]Ge 4:21; Ps 33:2

25 David, together with the commanders of the army, set apart some of the sons of Asaph,[c] Heman[d] and Jeduthun[e] for the ministry of prophesying,[f] accompanied by harps, lyres and cymbals.[g] Here is the list of the men[h] who performed this service:[i]

[2]From the sons of Asaph:

Zaccur, Joseph, Nethaniah and Asarelah. The sons of Asaph were under the supervision of Asaph, who prophesied under the king's supervision.

[3]As for Jeduthun, from his sons:[j]

Gedaliah, Zeri, Jeshaiah, Shimei,[a] Hashabiah and Mattithiah, six in all, under the supervision of their father Jeduthun, who prophesied, using the harp[k] in thanking and praising the LORD.

[4]As for Heman, from his sons:

Bukkiah, Mattaniah, Uzziel, Shubael and Jerimoth; Hananiah, Hanani, Eliathah, Giddalti and Romamti-Ezer; Joshbekashah, Mallothi, Hothir and Mahazioth. [5]All these were sons of Heman the king's seer. They were given him through the promises of God to exalt him.[b] God gave Heman fourteen sons and three daughters.

25:6 [l]1Ch 15:16 [m]1Ch 15:19 [n]2Ch 23:18; 29:25
25:8 [o]1Ch 26:13

[6]All these men were under the supervision of their fathers[l] for the music of the temple of the LORD, with cymbals, lyres and harps, for the ministry at the house of God. Asaph, Jeduthun and Heman[m] were under the supervision of the king.[n] [7]Along with their relatives—all of them trained and skilled in music for the LORD—they numbered 288. [8]Young and old alike, teacher as well as student, cast lots[o] for their duties.

25:9 [p]1Ch 6:39

[9]The first lot, which was for Asaph,[p] fell to Joseph,	
his sons and relatives,[c]	12[d]
the second to Gedaliah,	
he and his relatives and sons,	12
[10]the third to Zaccur,	
his sons and relatives,	12
[11]the fourth to Izri,[e]	
his sons and relatives,	12
[12]the fifth to Nethaniah,	
his sons and relatives,	12
[13]the sixth to Bukkiah,	
his sons and relatives,	12
[14]the seventh to Jesarelah,[f]	
his sons and relatives,	12
[15]the eighth to Jeshaiah,	
his sons and relatives,	12
[16]the ninth to Mattaniah,	
his sons and relatives,	12
[17]the tenth to Shimei,	
his sons and relatives,	12
[18]the eleventh to Azarel,[g]	
his sons and relatives,	12

[a] *3* One Hebrew manuscript and some Septuagint manuscripts (see also verse 17); most Hebrew manuscripts do not have *Shimei.* [b] *5* Hebrew *exalt the horn* [c] *9* See Septuagint; Hebrew does not have *his sons and relatives.* [d] *9* See the total in verse 7; Hebrew does not have *twelve.* [e] *11* A variant of *Zeri* [f] *14* A variant of *Asarelah* [g] *18* A variant of *Uzziel*

25:1 Instrumental music and hymns of praise were closely linked in Israelite worship. See "Ancient Musical Instruments" on page 797.

[19] the twelfth to Hashabiah,
his sons and relatives, 12
[20] the thirteenth to Shubael,
his sons and relatives, 12
[21] the fourteenth to Mattithiah,
his sons and relatives, 12
[22] the fifteenth to Jerimoth,
his sons and relatives, 12
[23] the sixteenth to Hananiah,
his sons and relatives, 12
[24] the seventeenth to Joshbekashah,
his sons and relatives, 12
[25] the eighteenth to Hanani,
his sons and relatives, 12
[26] the nineteenth to Mallothi,
his sons and relatives, 12
[27] the twentieth to Eliathah,
his sons and relatives, 12
[28] the twenty-first to Hothir,
his sons and relatives, 12
[29] the twenty-second to Giddalti,
his sons and relatives, 12
[30] the twenty-third to Mahazioth,
his sons and relatives, 12
[31] the twenty-fourth to Romamti-Ezer,
his sons and relatives, 12[q] **25:31** [q] 1Ch 9:33

The Gatekeepers

26 The divisions of the gatekeepers:[r] **26:1** [r] 1Ch 9:17

From the Korahites: Meshelemiah son of Kore, one of the sons of Asaph.
[2] Meshelemiah had sons:
Zechariah[s] the firstborn, **26:2** [s] 1Ch 9:21
Jediael the second,
Zebadiah the third,
Jathniel the fourth,
[3] Elam the fifth,
Jehohanan the sixth
and Eliehoenai the seventh.
[4] Obed-Edom also had sons:
Shemaiah the firstborn,
Jehozabad the second,
Joah the third,
Sacar the fourth,
Nethanel the fifth,
[5] Ammiel the sixth,
Issachar the seventh
and Peullethai the eighth.
(For God had blessed Obed-Edom.[t]) **26:5** [t] 2Sa 6:10; 1Ch 13:13; 16:38

[6] His son Shemaiah also had sons, who were leaders in their father's family because they were very

---

26:1 Levitical gatekeepers in a broad sense functioned as a paramilitary security force. They oversaw the temple precinct (see v. 16), were responsible for the administration of temple revenues and were in charge of maintaining the temple. Lot-casting was used to determine gate assignments, as with the previous duty rosters for priests and musicians. This method of selection prevented partiality and emphasized the divine nature of the decision, since the outcome of a lot was from the Lord (Pr 16:33; see "Casting Lots" on p. 744).

capable men. 7 The sons of Shemaiah: Othni, Rephael, Obed and Elzabad; his relatives Elihu
and Semakiah were also able men. 8 All these were descendants of Obed-Edom; they and their
sons and their relatives were capable men with the strength to do the work—descendants of
Obed-Edom, 62 in all.
9 Meshelemiah had sons and relatives, who were able men—18 in all.

10 Hosah the Merarite had sons: Shimri the first (although he was not the firstborn, his father had ap-
26:10 [u]Dt 21:16; 1Ch 5:1 — pointed him the first),[u] 11 Hilkiah the second, Tabaliah the third and Zechariah the fourth. The
sons and relatives of Hosah were 13 in all.
26:12 [v]1Ch 9:22 — 12 These divisions of the gatekeepers, through their chief men, had duties for ministering[v] in the tem-
26:13 [w]1Ch 24:5, 31; 25:8 — ple of the LORD, just as their relatives had. 13 Lots[w] were cast for each gate, according to their families,
young and old alike.
26:14 [x]1Ch 9:18 [y]1Ch 9:21 — 14 The lot for the East Gate[x] fell to Shelemiah.[a] Then lots were cast for his son Zechariah,[y] a wise coun-
26:15 [z]1Ch 13:13; 2Ch 25:24 — selor, and the lot for the North Gate fell to him. 15 The lot for the South Gate fell to Obed-Edom,[z] and the
lot for the storehouse fell to his sons. 16 The lots for the West Gate and the Shalleketh Gate on the upper
road fell to Shuppim and Hosah.
Guard was alongside of guard: 17 There were six Levites a day on the east, four a day on the north, four
a day on the south and two at a time at the storehouse. 18 As for the court to the west, there were four at
the road and two at the court itself.
26:19 [a]2Ch 35:15; Ne 7:1; Eze 44:11 — 19 These were the divisions of the gatekeepers who were descendants of Korah and Merari.[a]

The Treasurers and Other Officials

26:20 [b]2Ch 24:5 [c]1Ch 28:12 — 20 Their fellow Levites[b] were[b] in charge of the treasuries of the house of God and the treasuries for the
dedicated things.[c]
21 The descendants of Ladan, who were Gershonites through Ladan and who were heads of families
26:21 [d]1Ch 23:7; 29:8 — belonging to Ladan the Gershonite,[d] were Jehieli, 22 the sons of Jehieli, Zetham and his brother Joel. They
26:22 [e]1Ch 9:26 — were in charge of the treasuries[e] of the temple of the LORD.
26:23 [f]Nu 3:27 — 23 From the Amramites, the Izharites, the Hebronites and the Uzzielites:[f]

26:24 [g]1Ch 23:16 — 24 Shubael,[g] a descendant of Gershom son of Moses, was the officer in charge of the treasuries. 25 His
relatives through Eliezer: Rehabiah his son, Jeshaiah his son, Joram his son, Zicri his son and
26:25 [h]1Ch 23:18 — Shelomith[h] his son. 26 Shelomith and his relatives were in charge of all the treasuries for the
26:26 [i]2Sa 8:11 — things dedicated[i] by King David, by the heads of families who were the commanders of thou-
sands and commanders of hundreds, and by the other army commanders. 27 Some of the plun-
der taken in battle they dedicated for the repair of the temple of the LORD. 28 And everything
26:28 [j]1Sa 9:9 — dedicated by Samuel the seer[j] and by Saul son of Kish, Abner son of Ner and Joab son of Zer-
uiah, and all the other dedicated things were in the care of Shelomith and his relatives.
29 From the Izharites: Kenaniah and his sons were assigned duties away from the temple, as officials
26:29 [k]Dt 17:8-13; 1Ch 23:4; Ne 11:16 — and judges[k] over Israel.
26:30 [l]1Ch 27:17 — 30 From the Hebronites: Hashabiah[l] and his relatives—seventeen hundred able men—were respon-
sible in Israel west of the Jordan for all the work of the LORD and for the king's service. 31 As for
26:31 [m]1Ch 23:19 [n]2Sa 5:4 — the Hebronites,[m] Jeriah was their chief according to the genealogical records of their families.
In the fortieth[n] year of David's reign a search was made in the records, and capable men among
the Hebronites were found at Jazer in Gilead. 32 Jeriah had twenty-seven hundred relatives, who
were able men and heads of families, and King David put them in charge of the Reubenites,
the Gadites and the half-tribe of Manasseh for every matter pertaining to God and for the af-
fairs of the king.

Army Divisions

27 This is the list of the Israelites—heads of families, commanders of thousands and command-
ers of hundreds, and their officers, who served the king in all that concerned the army divisions
that were on duty month by month throughout the year. Each division consisted of 24,000 men.

[a] 14 A variant of *Meshelemiah* [b] 20 Septuagint; Hebrew *As for the Levites, Ahijah was*

26:20 The presence of temple officers who served as assayers to handle and refine the precious metals received as revenue and offerings is attested in texts from Mesopotamian temples.

27:1–15 Rather than a standing army, the military divisions described here represent a militia or citizen army, something like the U.S. National Guard. David organized his army into 12 divisions,

2 In charge of the first division, for the first month, was Jashobeam[o] son of Zabdiel. There were 24,000 men 27:2 [o]2Sa 23:8; 1Ch 11:11
in his division. 3 He was a descendant of Perez and chief of all the army officers for the first month.
4 In charge of the division for the second month was Dodai[p] the Ahohite; Mikloth was the leader of his 27:4 [p]2Sa 23:9
division. There were 24,000 men in his division.
5 The third army commander, for the third month, was Benaiah[q] son of Jehoiada the priest. He was chief 27:5 [q]2Sa 23:20
and there were 24,000 men in his division. 6 This was the Benaiah who was a mighty man among
the Thirty and was over the Thirty. His son Ammizabad was in charge of his division.
7 The fourth, for the fourth month, was Asahel[r] the brother of Joab; his son Zebadiah was his successor. 27:7 [r]2Sa 2:18; 1Ch 11:26
There were 24,000 men in his division.
8 The fifth, for the fifth month, was the commander Shamhuth[s] the Izrahite. There were 24,000 men in 27:8 [s]1Ch 11:27
his division.
9 The sixth, for the sixth month, was Ira[t] the son of Ikkesh the Tekoite. There were 24,000 men in his 27:9 [t]2Sa 23:26; 1Ch 11:28
division.
10 The seventh, for the seventh month, was Helez[u] the Pelonite, an Ephraimite. There were 24,000 men in 27:10 [u]2Sa 23:26; 1Ch 11:27
his division.
11 The eighth, for the eighth month, was Sibbecai[v] the Hushathite, a Zerahite. There were 24,000 men in 27:11 [v]2Sa 21:18
his division.
12 The ninth, for the ninth month, was Abiezer[w] the Anathothite, a Benjamite. There were 24,000 men in 27:12 [w]2Sa 23:27; 1Ch 11:28
his division.
13 The tenth, for the tenth month, was Maharai[x] the Netophathite, a Zerahite. There were 24,000 men in 27:13 [x]2Sa 23:28; 1Ch 11:30
his division.
14 The eleventh, for the eleventh month, was Benaiah[y] the Pirathonite, an Ephraimite. There were 24,000 27:14 [y]1Ch 11:31
men in his division.
15 The twelfth, for the twelfth month, was Heldai[z] the Netophathite, from the family of Othniel.[a] There 27:15 [z]2Sa 23:29 [a]Jos 15:17
were 24,000 men in his division.

Officers of the Tribes

16 The officers over the tribes of Israel:
over the Reubenites: Eliezer son of Zicri;
over the Simeonites: Shephatiah son of Maacah;
17 over Levi: Hashabiah[b] son of Kemuel; 27:17 [b]1Ch 26:30 [c]2Sa 8:17; 1Ch 12:28
over Aaron: Zadok;[c]
18 over Judah: Elihu, a brother of David;
over Issachar: Omri son of Michael;
19 over Zebulun: Ishmaiah son of Obadiah;
over Naphtali: Jerimoth son of Azriel;
20 over the Ephraimites: Hoshea son of Azaziah;
over half the tribe of Manasseh: Joel son of Pedaiah;
21 over the half-tribe of Manasseh in Gilead: Iddo son of Zechariah;
over Benjamin: Jaasiel son of Abner;
22 over Dan: Azarel son of Jeroham.
These were the officers over the tribes of Israel.

23 David did not take the number of the men twenty years old or less,[d] because the LORD had prom- 27:23 [d]1Ch 21:2-5 [e]Ge 15:5
ised to make Israel as numerous as the stars[e] in the sky. 24 Joab son of Zeruiah began to count the men
but did not finish. Wrath came on Israel on account of this numbering,[f] and the number was not entered 27:24 [f]2Sa 24:15; 1Ch 21:7
in the book[a] of the annals of King David.

The King's Overseers

25 Azmaveth son of Adiel was in charge of the royal storehouses.

[a] 24 Septuagint; Hebrew *number*

---

each commanded by a seasoned soldier from his choice corps of "mighty men" (cf. 11:10–47). Each division served the king's army for one month in a twelve-month relay. The permanent or professional army was comprised of the Three and the Thirty (see the note on 11:20), along with the Kerethites, Pelethites and Gittites (cf. 2Sa 15:18; 23:23; see the note on 18:17).

27:25–31 These verses contain a list of the administrators of David's property (v. 31). The large cities of the ancient Near East

Jonathan son of Uzziah was in charge of the storehouses in the outlying districts, in the towns, the
villages and the watchtowers.
26 Ezri son of Kelub was in charge of the field workers who farmed the land.
27 Shimei the Ramathite was in charge of the vineyards.
Zabdi the Shiphmite was in charge of the produce of the vineyards for the wine vats.
27:28 [g]1Ki 10:27; 2Ch 1:15 28 Baal-Hanan the Gederite was in charge of the olive and sycamore-fig[g] trees in the western foothills.
Joash was in charge of the supplies of olive oil.
29 Shitrai the Sharonite was in charge of the herds grazing in Sharon.
Shaphat son of Adlai was in charge of the herds in the valleys.
30 Obil the Ishmaelite was in charge of the camels.
Jehdeiah the Meronothite was in charge of the donkeys.
27:31 [h]1Ch 5:10 31 Jaziz the Hagrite[h] was in charge of the flocks.
All these were the officials in charge of King David's property.

32 Jonathan, David's uncle, was a counselor, a man of insight and a scribe. Jehiel son of Hacmoni took
care of the king's sons.
27:33 [i]2Sa 15:12 [j]2Sa 15:37 33 Ahithophel[i] was the king's counselor.
Hushai[j] the Arkite was the king's friend. 34 Ahithophel was succeeded by Jehoiada son of Benaiah and
27:34 [k]1Ki 1:7 [l]1Ch 11:6 by Abiathar.[k]
Joab[l] was the commander of the royal army.

David's Plans for the Temple

28:1 [m]1Ch 11:10; 27:1-31 **28** David summoned all the officials[m] of Israel to assemble at Jerusalem: the officers over the tribes,
the commanders of the divisions in the service of the king, the commanders of thousands and
commanders of hundreds, and the officials in charge of all the property and livestock belonging to the
king and his sons, together with the palace officials, the mighty men and all the brave warriors.
28:2 [n]1Ch 17:2 [o]Ps 99:5; 132:7 2 King David rose to his feet and said: "Listen to me, my brothers and my people. I had it in my heart[n]
to build a house as a place of rest for the ark of the covenant of the LORD, for the footstool[o] of our God,
28:3 [p]2Sa 7:5 [q]1Ch 22:8 [r]1Ki 5:3; 1Ch 17:4 and I made plans to build it. 3 But God said to me,[p] 'You are not to build a house for my Name,[q] because
you are a warrior and have shed blood.'[r]
28:4 [s]1Ch 17:23, 27; 2Ch 6:6 [t]1Sa 16:1-13 [u]Ge 49:10; 1Ch 5:2 4 "Yet the LORD, the God of Israel, chose me[s] from my whole family[t] to be king over Israel forever. He
chose Judah[u] as leader, and from the house of Judah he chose my family, and from my father's sons he
was pleased to make me king over all Israel. 5 Of all my sons—and the LORD has given me many[v]—he
28:5 [v]1Ch 3:1 [w]1Ch 22:9; 23:1 has chosen my son Solomon[w] to sit on the throne of the kingdom of the LORD over Israel. 6 He said to me:
'Solomon your son is the one who will build my house and my courts, for I have chosen him to be my
28:6 [x]2Sa 7:13; 1Ch 22:9-10 son,[x] and I will be his father. 7 I will establish his kingdom forever if he is unswerving in carrying out my
28:7 [y]1Ch 22:13 commands and laws,[y] as is being done at this time.'
8 "So now I charge you in the sight of all Israel and of the assembly of the LORD, and in the hearing of
28:8 [z]Dt 6:1 [a]Dt 4:1 our God: Be careful to follow all the commands[z] of the LORD your God, that you may possess this good
land and pass it on as an inheritance to your descendants forever.[a]
9 "And you, my son Solomon, acknowledge the God of your father, and serve him with wholehearted
28:9 [b]1Ch 29:19 [c]1Sa 16:7; Ps 7:9 [d]Ps 40:16; Jer 29:13 [e]Jos 24:20; 2Ch 15:2 [f]Ps 44:23 devotion[b] and with a willing mind, for the LORD searches every heart[c] and understands every motive be-
hind the thoughts. If you seek him,[d] he will be found by you; but if you forsake[e] him, he will reject[f] you
forever. 10 Consider now, for the LORD has chosen you to build a temple as a sanctuary. Be strong and do
the work."
28:11 [g]Ex 25:9 11 Then David gave his son Solomon the plans[g] for the portico of the temple, its buildings, its store-
rooms, its upper parts, its inner rooms and the place of atonement. 12 He gave him the plans of all that
28:12 [h]1Ch 12:18 [i]1Ch 26:20 the Spirit[h] had put in his mind for the courts of the temple of the LORD and all the surrounding rooms,
for the treasuries of the temple of God and for the treasuries for the dedicated things.[i] 13 He gave him in-
28:13 [j]1Ch 24:1 structions for the divisions[j] of the priests and Levites, and for all the work of serving in the temple of the
LORD, as well as for all the articles to be used in its service. 14 He designated the weight of gold for all the
gold articles to be used in various kinds of service, and the weight of silver for all the silver articles to be

---

had three basic economic sectors: (1) royal, (2) temple and (3) private. There is no evidence of direct taxation during the reign of David; his court appears to have been financed by extensive landholdings, commerce, plunder from his many wars and tribute from subjugated kingdoms.

used in various kinds of service: [15]the weight of gold for the gold lampstands[k] and their lamps, with the 28:15 [k]Ex 25:31
weight for each lampstand and its lamps; and the weight of silver for each silver lampstand and its lamps,
according to the use of each lampstand; [16]the weight of gold for each table[l] for consecrated bread; the 28:16 [l]Ex 25:23
weight of silver for the silver tables; [17]the weight of pure gold for the forks, sprinkling bowls[m] and pitch- 28:17 [m]Ex 27:3
ers; the weight of gold for each gold dish; the weight of silver for each silver dish; [18]and the weight of the
refined gold for the altar of incense.[n] He also gave him the plan for the chariot,[o] that is, the cherubim of 28:18 [n]Ex 30:1-10 [o]Ex 25:18-22
gold that spread their wings and shelter[p] the ark of the covenant of the LORD. [p]Ex 25:20
[19]"All this," David said, "I have in writing from the hand of the LORD upon me, and he gave me under-
standing in all the details[q] of the plan.[r]" 28:19 [q]1Ki 6:38 [r]Ex 25:9
[20]David also said to Solomon his son, "Be strong and courageous,[s] and do the work. Do not be afraid 28:20 [s]Dt 31:6; 1Ch 22:13;
or discouraged, for the LORD God, my God, is with you. He will not fail you or forsake[t] you until all the 2Ch 19:11;
work for the service of the temple of the LORD is finished.[u] [21]The divisions of the priests and Levites are Hag 2:4 [t]Dt 4:31; Jos 24:20
ready for all the work on the temple of God, and every willing man skilled[v] in any craft will help you in [u]1Ki 6:14; 2Ch 7:11
all the work. The officials and all the people will obey your every command." 28:21 [v]Ex 35:25-36:5

SOURCE BOOKS MENTIONED IN SCRIPTURE

Category	Source Book	Reference
Poetic	the Book of the Wars of the Lord	Nu 21:14
	the Book of Yashar	Jos 10:13; 2Sa 1:18
Royal Court Records	the book of the annals of King David	1Ch 27:24
	the book of the kings of Israel and Judah	2Ch 27:7; 35:27; 36:8
	the book of the kings of Judah and Israel	2Ch 16:11; 25:26; 28:26; 32:32
	the book of the kings of Israel	1Ch 9:1; 2Ch 20:34
	the annotations on the book of the kings	2Ch 24:27
	the annals of the kings of Israel	2Ch 33:18
	the directions written by David king of Israel and by his son Solomon	2Ch 35:4
Records by Prophets	the records of Samuel the seer	1Ch 29:29
	the records of Nathan the prophet	1Ch 29:29; 2Ch 9:29
	the records of Gad the seer	1Ch 29:29
	the prophecy of Ahijah the Shilonite	2Ch 9:29
	the visions of Iddo the seer	2Ch 9:29; 12:15; 13:22
	the records of Shemaiah the prophet	2Ch 12:15
	the annals of Jehu son of Hanani	2Ch 20:34
	the vision of the prophet Isaiah son of Amoz in the book of the kings of Judah and Israel	2Ch 26:22; 32:32
	the records of the seers	2Ch 33:19

Adapted from *Chronological and Background Charts of the Old Testament*, p. 34

Gifts for Building the Temple

29 Then King David said to the whole assembly: "My son Solomon, the one whom God has chosen,
is young and inexperienced.[w] The task is great, because this palatial structure is not for man but
for the LORD God. 2With all my resources I have provided for the temple of my God—gold[x] for the gold
work, silver for the silver, bronze for the bronze, iron for the iron and wood for the wood, as well as onyx
for the settings, turquoise,[a][y] stones of various colors, and all kinds of fine stone and marble—all of these
in large quantities.[z] 3Besides, in my devotion to the temple of my God I now give my personal treasures
of gold and silver for the temple of my God, over and above everything I have provided[a] for this holy
temple: 4three thousand talents[b] of gold (gold of Ophir)[b] and seven thousand talents[c] of refined silver,[c]
for the overlaying of the walls of the buildings, 5for the gold work and the silver work, and for all the work
to be done by the craftsmen. Now, who is willing to consecrate himself today to the LORD?"
6Then the leaders of families, the officers of the tribes of Israel, the commanders of thousands and
commanders of hundreds, and the officials[d] in charge of the king's work gave willingly.[e] 7They[f] gave to-
ward the work on the temple of God five thousand talents[d] and ten thousand darics[e] of gold, ten thou-
sand talents[f] of silver, eighteen thousand talents[g] of bronze and a hundred thousand talents[h] of iron.
8Any who had precious stones[g] gave them to the treasury of the temple of the LORD in the custody of Je-
hiel the Gershonite.[h] 9The people rejoiced at the willing response of their leaders, for they had given free-
ly and wholeheartedly[i] to the LORD. David the king also rejoiced greatly.

David's Prayer

10David praised the LORD in the presence of the whole assembly, saying,

"Praise be to you, O LORD,
God of our father Israel,
from everlasting to everlasting.
11 Yours, O LORD, is the greatness and the power[j]
and the glory and the majesty and the splendor,
for everything in heaven and earth is yours.[k]
Yours, O LORD, is the kingdom;
you are exalted as head over all.[l]
12 Wealth and honor[m] come from you;
you are the ruler[n] of all things.
In your hands are strength and power
to exalt and give strength to all.
13 Now, our God, we give you thanks,
and praise your glorious name.

14"But who am I, and who are my people, that we should be able to give as generously as this? Every-
thing comes from you, and we have given you only what comes from your hand. 15We are aliens and strang-
ers[o] in your sight, as were all our forefathers. Our days on earth are like a shadow,[p] without hope. 16O LORD
our God, as for all this abundance that we have provided for building you a temple for your Holy Name, it
comes from your hand, and all of it belongs to you. 17I know, my God, that you test the heart[q] and are
pleased with integrity. All these things have I given willingly and with honest intent. And now I have seen
with joy how willingly your people who are here have given to you.[r] 18O LORD, God of our fathers Abraham,
Isaac and Israel, keep this desire in the hearts of your people forever, and keep their hearts loyal to you.
19And give my son Solomon the wholehearted devotion[s] to keep your commands, requirements and de-
crees[t] and to do everything to build the palatial structure for which I have provided."[u]
20Then David said to the whole assembly, "Praise the LORD your God." So they all praised the LORD,
the God of their fathers; they bowed low and fell prostrate before the LORD and the king.

29:1 [w]1Ki 3:7; 1Ch 22:5; 2Ch 13:7 **29:2** [x]ver 7,14,16; Ezr 1:4; 6:5; Hag 2:8 [y]Isa 54:11 [z]1Ch 22:2-5 **29:3** [a]2Ch 24:10; 31:3; 35:8 **29:4** [b]Ge 10:29 [c]1Ch 22:14 **29:6** [d]1Ch 27:1; 28:1 [e]ver 9; Ex 25:1-8; 35:20-29; 36:2; 2Ch 24:10; Ezr 7:15 **29:7** [f]Ex 25:2; Ne 7:70-71 **29:8** [g]Ex 35:27 [h]1Ch 26:21 **29:9** [i]1Ki 8:61; 2Co 9:7 **29:11** [j]Ps 24:8; 59:17; 62:11 [k]Ps 89:11 [l]Rev 5:12-13 **29:12** [m]2Ch 1:12 [n]2Ch 20:6; Ro 11:36 **29:15** [o]Ps 39:12; Heb 11:13 [p]Job 14:2 **29:17** [q]Ps 139:23; Pr 15:11; 17:3; Jer 11:20; 17:10 [r]1Ch 28:9; Ps 15:1-5 **29:19** [s]1Ch 28:9 [t]Ps 72:1 [u]1Ch 22:14

[a] *2* The meaning of the Hebrew for this word is uncertain. [b] *4* That is, about 110 tons (about 100 metric tons) [c] *4* That is, about 260 tons (about 240 metric tons) [d] *7* That is, about 190 tons (about 170 metric tons) [e] *7* That is, about 185 pounds (about 84 kilograms) [f] *7* That is, about 375 tons (about 345 metric tons) [g] *7* That is, about 675 tons (about 610 metric tons) [h] *7* That is, about 3,750 tons (about 3,450 metric tons)

29:7 The daric was a Persian coin, apparently named after Darius I (522–486 B.C.), during whose reign it first appeared (see Ezr 8:27). Since the Chronicler's readers were familiar with this coin, he could use it as an up-to-date standard of value for an earlier treasure of gold.

Solomon's Temple and Other Ancient Temples

1 CHRONICLES 29 Temples were the first monumental structures ever erected in the ancient world. Viewed as the abode of deity and, frequently, as in Israel's case, called "the house of God" (cf. 1Ki 9:1), a temple was designed to function as a royal palace for the gods. No other institution of ancient Israel enjoyed the prominence of the Jerusalem temple. It was the heart of the nation's religious life, as well as the emblem of dynastic rule under **Yahweh** (2Sa 7:13–14). This temple might be described symbolically as architecture in the service of declaring God's kingship on Earth.

Cylinder of Dur Sharrukin (Khorsabad), honoring the building of the temples of the city of Dur Sharrukin by Sargon II of Assyria

Preserving Bible Times; © Dr. James C. Martin; permission of Musée de Louvre

Most temples were constructed on heights, to be accorded physical prominence in accordance with their social eminence. Accordingly, Solomon's temple was erected on the highest point of Jerusalem (Ps 121:1; 122:4). Originally the site of a threshing floor[1] (2Sa 24:18–25), the mount was identified as Moriah, thought by many to have been the place at which Abraham had been called to offer up his only son (2Ch 3:1).[2]

Since there are no archaeological remains of Solomon's temple following the **Babylonian** destruction of 586 B.C. and Herod's extensive building projects on the site of the temple mount in the first century A.D.,[3] its figurative reconstruction is dependent upon the testimony of the Bible (1Ki 6–7; 2Ch 2–4) and the analogy of other temples contemporary to it. Solomon hired **Phoenician** artisans to engineer and build the Jerusalem temple (2Ch 2:11–14). Its architectural design reflects the long-room, tripartite temple plan typical of Syro-Phoenician construction (1Ki 6:2–10), the closest parallels of which are the temples of Ain Dara (tenth–ninth centuries B.C.) and Tell Tayinat (eighth century B.C.) in northern Syria.

The tripartite plan consisted of three courts representing an inward movement from least sacred to most sacred space. The outer court served as the site of the sacrificial altar. The temple was entered from the east through a porch supported by two pillars. Tell Tayinat's monumental columns featured a pair of lions for their bases, while Israel's 270-foot (82.3-m) bronze pillars bore names: Jakin and Boaz (1Ki 7:21). The forecourt opened into a main hall, at the back of which stood the innermost sanctuary. Multistoried side chambers, used as storerooms for offerings and tribute, sometimes surrounded the structure (1Ki 6:5–10). The Jerusalem temple complex was about 165 feet (50.3 m) long by 84.5 feet (26 m) wide.

Quarried rock, hewn in rectangular blocks, or **ashlars**, was dressed off site. Every stone was cut in advance so as to fit together perfectly: "No hammer, chisel or any other iron tool was heard at the temple site while it was being built" (1Ki 6:7). The interior was paneled in cedar wood from Lebanon (1Ki 6:18)[4] and the inner sanctuary overlaid with gold from ceiling to floor and adorned with two 15-foot (4.6-m) tall, freestanding cherubim carved of olive wood and overlaid with gold (1Ki 6:20–28). Their outstretched wings spanned the room, creating the seat of a colossal throne (Ps 99:1; Eze 10:1–19).

The decorative motifs of Solomon's temple were symbols of fertility and abundance: Palmettes and blooming flowers were carved into the cedar paneling and embellished with gold; pomegranate and gourd wreaths were fashioned onto the bronze column capitals (top, ornamental pieces of the columns; cf. the leafed structure of a Corinthian column);[5] and buds and calyxes formed the cups of the ten golden lampstands. These were designed to recall the paradisiacal garden of God's first dwelling place with humanity (Ge 2:8–9), as were the gold and precious stones adorning the temple's interior (Ge 2:12; 2Ch 3:6). The furniture was modeled after that of the tabernacle, only on a grander scale (1Ki 7:23–50).[6]

The inner sanctuary ("Most Holy Place") is the point at which Solomon's temple departs from its ancient Near Eastern counterparts. Whereas other sanctuary niches housed the god's idol in order to represent the deity's presence, the Israelite temple contained no image of God.[7] The ark of the covenant alone served as a symbol of Yahweh's enthronement over his people. The temple was Yahweh's palace on Earth, the Holy Place his audience hall and the Most Holy Place his throne room.

[1]See "The Threshing Floor" on page 608. [2]See "Mount Moriah" on page 37. [3]See "Herod's Temple" on page 1648. [4]See "Cedars of Lebanon" on page 1043. [5]See "The Jerusalem Pomegranate" on page 627. [6]See "The Tabernacle and the Ark" on page 153. [7]See, for example, "The Hittite Ritual of Establishing a New Temple for the Goddess of the Night" on page 146.

Solomon Acknowledged as King

29:21 [v]1Ki 8:62 — 21 The next day they made sacrifices to the LORD and presented burnt offerings to him:[v] a thousand
bulls, a thousand rams and a thousand male lambs, together with their drink offerings, and other sac-
29:22 [w]1Ch 23:1 — rifices in abundance for all Israel. 22 They ate and drank with great joy[w] in the presence of the LORD that
[x]1Ki 1:33-39 — day.
Then they acknowledged Solomon son of David as king a second time, anointing him before the LORD
29:23 [y]1Ki 2:12 — to be ruler and Zadok[x] to be priest. 23 So Solomon sat on the throne[y] of the LORD as king in place of his
father David. He prospered and all Israel obeyed him. 24 All the officers and mighty men, as well as all of
King David's sons, pledged their submission to King Solomon.
29:25 [z]2Ch 1:1, — 25 The LORD highly exalted Solomon in the sight of all Israel and bestowed on him royal splendor[z] such
12 [a]1Ki 3:13; Ecc 2:9 — as no king over Israel ever had before.[a]

The Death of David

29:26 [b]1Ch 18:14 — 26 David son of Jesse was king[b] over all Israel. 27 He ruled over Israel forty years—seven in Hebron
29:27 [c]2Sa 5:4-5; 1Ki 2:11; — and thirty-three in Jerusalem.[c] 28 He died[d] at a good old age, having enjoyed long life, wealth and honor.
1Ch 3:4 — His son Solomon succeeded him as king.[e]
29:28 [d]Ge 15:15; Ac 13:36 — 29 As for the events of King David's reign, from beginning to end, they are written in the records of
[e]1Ch 23:1 29:29 [f]1Sa 9:9 — Samuel the seer,[f] the records of Nathan[g] the prophet and the records of Gad[h] the seer, 30 together with the
[g]2Sa 7:2 — details of his reign and power, and the circumstances that surrounded him and Israel and the kingdoms
[h]1Sa 22:5 — of all the other lands.

29:22 Although the Chronicler did not record Solomon's first anointing, the incident is recounted in 1 Kings 1:32–36. However, the phrase "second time" is missing in the Septuagint, suggesting that these words may have been an addition to the Hebrew text of this passage by an ancient scribe after the Septuagint had already been translated, in an attempt to harmonize the Chronicles account with Kings (see "Early Scribal Emendation" on p. 448.) Both Saul (1Sa 10:1,24; 11:14–15) and David (1Sa 16:13; 2Sa 2:4; 5:3) experienced multiple anointings.

INTRODUCTION TO 2 *Chronicles*

AUTHOR, PLACE AND DATE OF WRITING

See introduction to 1 Chronicles for detail.

AUDIENCE

The books of Chronicles (1 and 2 Chronicles) were originally one book written to the postexilic Jews to provide them with an accurate historical record and to help them recognize their heritage and calling.

CULTURAL FACTS AND HIGHLIGHTS

Like 1 Chronicles, 2 Chronicles records the history of David's royal line. After describing the building of the temple (chs. 1–9), the author/compiler traced the history of Judah—the southern kingdom—until Jerusalem's final destruction and the exile to Babylon of many of her people.

TIMELINE

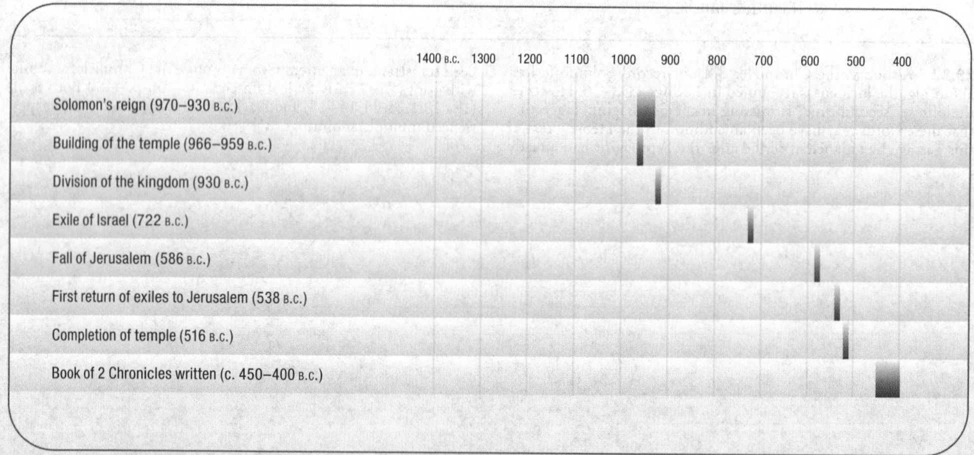

AS YOU READ

Although some parts of 2 Chronicles are similar to Samuel and Kings, bear in mind that the Chronicler wanted in particular to emphasize God's covenant faithfulness and to encourage his readers to obey the covenant. It is not surprising that in this second half of his work he continued to emphasize themes found in 1 Chronicles, such as the united monarchy under the rule of David and Solomon and the important role of God's temple. Another theme also surfaces repeatedly. Notice that the inspired author measured every king in the history of David's royal line by whether or not that king remained faithful to God.

Note also the numerous statements that God, David and the prophets made concerning sin and repentance. They repeatedly warned that if the people were to turn from God, judgment would inevitably result. On the other hand, if they were to repent, obey God's law and trust in him, they would be blessed with victory, peace and prosperity.

DID YOU KNOW?

- Stonecutters and carriers at the quarries in the hills near Jerusalem were to be drawn from among the alien population in Israel (2:1–18)
- The 666 talents of gold Solomon received annually equated to approximately 25 tons. The unspecified sum of Solomon's gross yearly income included both money from tributes and tariffs and profits from his own capital ventures, which primarily involved international trade (9:13–14).
- Salt had a ceremonial use in the ratification of treaties, standing for faith, loyalty and longevity (13:5).
- Cyrus allowed captive peoples to return to their lands. His efforts to win the favor of peoples who had been treated harshly by the Babylonians were used by God to inaugurate the restoration period (36:22–23).

THEMES

Second Chronicles includes the following themes:

1. *Blessing or judgment.* The Chronicler emphasized that God's blessings resulted from obedience to the Mosaic covenant (7:17–18; 15:12–15; 17:3–6; 30:15–20; 31:20–21) but that his judgment followed disobedience (12:1–2; 34:19–21). If the people would humbly repent, God promised to restore them (7:13–14; 12:5–12; 33:10–13).

2. *Worship.* The building and dedication of the temple (2:1—7:22) was the greatest achievement in Solomon's 40-year rule, taking 20 years to complete (8:1). The temple was the central place of worship, symbolizing God's presence among his people (7:12,16; 33:7).

OUTLINE

- I. The Reign of Solomon (1–8)
  - A. Request for Wisdom (1)
  - B. Temple Construction and Dedication (2–7)
  - C. Solomon's Activities (8)
- II. Visit of the Queen of Sheba and Solomon's Splendor (9:1–28)
- III. Solomon's Death (9:29–31)
- IV. The Kings of Judah (10:1—36:14)
- V. The Destruction of Jerusalem (36:15–23)

Solomon Asks for Wisdom

1 Solomon son of David established[a] himself firmly over his kingdom, for the LORD his God was with[b] him and made him exceedingly great.[c]

[2]Then Solomon spoke to all Israel[d]—to the commanders of thousands and commanders of hundreds, to the judges and to all the leaders in Israel, the heads of families— [3]and Solomon and the whole assembly went to the high place at Gibeon, for God's Tent of Meeting[e] was there, which Moses[f] the LORD's servant had made in the desert. [4]Now David had brought up the ark[g] of God from Kiriath Jearim to the place he had prepared for it, because he had pitched a tent[h] for it in Jerusalem. [5]But the bronze altar[i] that Bezalel[j] son of Uri, the son of Hur, had made was in Gibeon in front of the tabernacle of the LORD; so Solomon and the assembly inquired[k] of him there. [6]Solomon went up to the bronze altar before the LORD in the Tent of Meeting and offered a thousand burnt offerings on it.

[7]That night God appeared[l] to Solomon and said to him, "Ask for whatever you want me to give you."

[8]Solomon answered God, "You have shown great kindness to David my father and have made me[m] king in his place. [9]Now, LORD God, let your promise[n] to my father David be confirmed, for you have made me king over a people who are as numerous as the dust of the earth.[o] [10]Give me wisdom and knowledge, that I may lead[p] this people, for who is able to govern this great people of yours?"

[11]God said to Solomon, "Since this is your heart's desire and you have not asked for wealth,[q] riches or honor, nor for the death of your enemies, and since you have not asked for a long life but for wisdom and knowledge to govern my people over whom I have made you king, [12]therefore wisdom and knowledge will be given you. And I will also give you wealth, riches and honor,[r] such as no king who was before you ever had and none after you will have.[s]"

[13]Then Solomon went to Jerusalem from the high place at Gibeon, from before the Tent of Meeting. And he reigned over Israel.

[14]Solomon accumulated chariots[t] and horses; he had fourteen hundred chariots and twelve thousand horses,[a] which he kept in the chariot cities and also with him in Jerusalem. [15]The king made silver and gold[u] as common in Jerusalem as stones, and cedar as plentiful as sycamore-fig trees in the foothills. [16]Solomon's horses were imported from Egypt[b] and from Kue[c]—the royal merchants purchased them from Kue. [17]They imported a chariot[v] from Egypt for six hundred shekels[d] of silver, and a horse for a hundred and fifty.[e] They also exported them to all the kings of the Hittites and of the Arameans.

1:1 [a]1Ki 2:12,26; 2Ch 12:1 [b]Ge 21:22; 39:2; Nu 14:43 [c]1Ch 29:25
1:2 [d]1Ch 9:1; 28:1
1:3 [e]Ex 36:8 [f]Ex 40:18
1:4 [g]2Sa 6:2; 1Ch 15:25 [h]2Sa 6:17; 1Ch 15:1
1:5 [i]Ex 38:2 [j]Ex 31:2 [k]1Ch 13:3
1:7 [l]2Ch 7:12
1:8 [m]1Ch 23:1; 28:5
1:9 [n]2Sa 7:25; 1Ki 8:25 [o]Ge 12:2
1:10 [p]Nu 27:17; 2Sa 5:2; Pr 8:15-16
1:11 [q]Dt 17:17
1:12 [r]1Ch 29:12 [s]1Ch 29:25; 2Ch 9:22; Ne 13:26
1:14 [t]1Sa 8:11; 1Ki 4:26; 9:19
1:15 [u]1Ki 9:28; Isa 60:5
1:17 [v]SS 1:9

Preparations for Building the Temple

2 Solomon gave orders to build a temple[w] for the Name of the LORD and a royal palace for himself.[x] [2]He conscripted seventy thousand men as carriers and eighty thousand as stonecutters in the hills and thirty-six hundred as foremen over them.[y]

[3]Solomon sent this message to Hiram[f][z] king of Tyre:

"Send me cedar logs[a] as you did for my father David when you sent him cedar to build a palace to live in. [4]Now I am about to build a temple[b] for the Name of the LORD my God and to dedicate it to him for burning fragrant incense[c] before him, for setting out the consecrated bread[d] regularly, and for making burnt offerings[e] every morning and evening and on Sabbaths[f] and New Moons and at the appointed feasts of the LORD our God. This is a lasting ordinance for Israel.

[5]"The temple I am going to build will be great,[g] because our God is greater than all other gods.[h] [6]But who is able to build a temple for him, since the heavens, even the highest heavens, cannot

2:1 [w]Dt 12:5 [x]Ecc 2:4
2:2 [y]ver 18; 2Ch 10:4
2:3 [z]2Sa 5:11 [a]1Ch 14:1
2:4 [b]ver 1; Dt 12:5 [c]Ex 30:7 [d]Ex 25:30 [e]Ex 29:42; 2Ch 13:11 [f]Nu 28:9-10
2:5 [g]1Ch 22:5; Ps 135:5 [h]1Ch 16:25

[a] 14 Or *charioteers* [b] 16 Or possibly *Muzur,* a region in Cilicia; also in verse 17 [c] 16 Probably Cilicia [d] 17 That is, about 15 pounds (about 7 kilograms) [e] 17 That is, about 3 3/4 pounds (about 1.7 kilograms) [f] 3 Hebrew *Huram,* a variant of *Hiram*; also in verses 11 and 12

1:4 See "Kiriath Jearim" on page 406.

1:14 Solomon's large chariot corps may reflect love of extravagance more than military expertise. It appears that the chariot by this time was already largely obsolete and had become more a matter of prestige than of tactical value. In the hill country of Israel it had very little use, although of course a chariot force could rapidly move along major highways.

1:17 This verse suggests that a substantial portion of Solomon's income was derived from his holding of the land-bridge between Egypt and the rest of the civilized world. He was able to control and profit from all the trade that moved through his territory.

2:1–18 Solomon requested of Hiram a skilled craftsman, along with Tyre's famous lumber. In return he would provide Hiram with wheat, barley, wine and olive oil. The foodstuffs were to be sent overland to Tyre, while the timber would be floated to Joppa on rafts (vv. 15–16). The Chronicler specified that the stonecutters and carriers at the quarries in the hills near Jerusalem were to be drawn from among the alien population (vv. 2,17–18; cf. 1Ki 5:15–17). The parallel account in Kings also mentions the formation of temporary labor gangs of 30,000 Israelites conscripted to cut and dress timber in Lebanon on a rotating basis (1Ki 5:13–14; see "The Overseer of the Forced Labor" on p. 502).

2:6 [i]1Ki 8:27; 2Ch 6:18; Jer 23:24 [j]Ex 3:11 contain him?[i] Who then am I[j] to build a temple for him, except as a place to burn sacrifices before
him?

[7]"Send me, therefore, a man skilled to work in gold and silver, bronze and iron, and in purple,
crimson and blue yarn, and experienced in the art of engraving, to work in Judah and Jerusalem
2:7 [k]ver 13-14; Ex 35:31; 1Ch 22:16 with my skilled craftsmen,[k] whom my father David provided.

[8]"Send me also cedar, pine and algum[a] logs from Lebanon, for I know that your men are skilled
in cutting timber there. My men will work with yours [9]to provide me with plenty of lumber, be-
cause the temple I build must be large and magnificent. [10]I will give your servants, the woodsmen
who cut the timber, twenty thousand cors[b] of ground wheat, twenty thousand cors of barley, twenty
2:10 [l]Ezr 3:7 thousand baths[c] of wine and twenty thousand baths of olive oil.[l]"

[11]Hiram king of Tyre replied by letter to Solomon:

2:11 [m]1Ki 10:9; 2Ch 9:8 "Because the LORD loves[m] his people, he has made you their king."

[12]And Hiram added:

2:12 [n]Ne 9:6; Ps 8:3; 33:6; 102:25 "Praise be to the LORD, the God of Israel, who made heaven and earth![n] He has given King Da-
vid a wise son, endowed with intelligence and discernment, who will build a temple for the LORD
and a palace for himself.

2:13 [o]1Ki 7:13 [13]"I am sending you Huram-Abi,[o] a man of great skill, [14]whose mother was from Dan[p] and
2:14 [p]Ex 31:6 [q]Ex 35:31 [r]Ex 35:35 whose father was from Tyre. He is trained[q] to work in gold and silver, bronze and iron, stone and
wood, and with purple and blue[r] and crimson yarn and fine linen. He is experienced in all kinds
of engraving and can execute any design given to him. He will work with your craftsmen and with
those of my lord, David your father.

2:15 [s]ver 10; Ezr 3:7 [15]"Now let my lord send his servants the wheat and barley and the olive oil[s] and wine he prom-
ised, [16]and we will cut all the logs from Lebanon that you need and will float them in rafts by sea
2:16 [t]Jos 19:46; Jnh 1:3 down to Joppa.[t] You can then take them up to Jerusalem."

2:17 [u]1Ch 22:2 [v]2Sa 24:2 [17]Solomon took a census of all the aliens[u] who were in Israel, after the census[v] his father David had
2:18 [w]ver 2; 1Ch 22:2; 2Ch 8:8 taken; and they were found to be 153,600. [18]He assigned[w] 70,000 of them to be carriers and 80,000 to be
stonecutters in the hills, with 3,600 foremen over them to keep the people working.

Solomon Builds the Temple

3:1 [x]Ac 7:47 [y]Ge 28:17 [z]2Sa 24:18; 1Ch 21:18 **3** Then Solomon began to build[x] the temple of the LORD[y] in Jerusalem on Mount Moriah, where the
LORD had appeared to his father David. It was on the threshing floor of Araunah[d][z] the Jebusite, the
place provided by David. [2]He began building on the second day of the second month in the fourth year
3:2 [a]Ezr 5:11 of his reign.[a]

[3]The foundation Solomon laid for building the temple of God was sixty cubits long and twenty cubits
3:3 [b]Eze 41:2 wide[e][b] (using the cubit of the old standard). [4]The portico at the front of the temple was twenty cubits[f]
long across the width of the building and twenty cubits[g] high.

He overlaid the inside with pure gold. [5]He paneled the main hall with pine and covered it with fine
3:5 [c]Eze 40:16 gold and decorated it with palm tree[c] and chain designs. [6]He adorned the temple with precious stones.
And the gold he used was gold of Parvaim. [7]He overlaid the ceiling beams, doorframes, walls and doors
3:7 [d]Ge 3:24; 1Ki 6:29-35; Eze 41:18 of the temple with gold, and he carved cherubim[d] on the walls.

3:8 [e]Ex 26:33 [8]He built the Most Holy Place,[e] its length corresponding to the width of the temple—twenty cubits
3:9 [f]Ex 26:32 long and twenty cubits wide. He overlaid the inside with six hundred talents[h] of fine gold. [9]The gold nails[f]
weighed fifty shekels.[i] He also overlaid the upper parts with gold.

[a] *8* Probably a variant of *almug;* possibly juniper [b] *10* That is, probably about 125,000 bushels (about 4,400 kiloliters)
[c] *10* That is, probably about 115,000 gallons (about 440 kiloliters) [d] *1* Hebrew *Ornan,* a variant of *Araunah* [e] *3* That is, about 90 feet (about 27 meters) long and 30 feet (about 9 meters) wide [f] *4* That is, about 30 feet (about 9 meters); also in verses 8, 11 and 13 [g] *4* Some Septuagint and Syriac manuscripts; Hebrew *and a hundred and twenty* [h] *8* That is, about 23 tons (about 21 metric tons) [i] *9* That is, about 1 1/4 pounds (about 0.6 kilogram)

3:1 The temple was built on Mount Moriah (see "Mount Moriah" on p. 37), on the site of Araunah's threshing floor (see "The Threshing Floor" on p. 608). Pagan people groups worshiped at holy sites, often called "high places" (cf. Nu 33:52; Dt 33:29; see "The High Places" on p. 1318). Those shrines that were located in mountainous or elevated regions, as many of them were, were seen as being above ordinary life and nearer the gods' dwellings.

3:4–9 The extravagant use of gold overlay extended into the Most Holy Place.

10In the Most Holy Place he made a pair[g] of sculptured cherubim and overlaid them with gold. 11The
total wingspan of the cherubim was twenty cubits. One wing of the first cherub was five cubits[a] long and
touched the temple wall, while its other wing, also five cubits long, touched the wing of the other cher-
ub. 12Similarly one wing of the second cherub was five cubits long and touched the other temple wall, and
its other wing, also five cubits long, touched the wing of the first cherub. 13The wings of these cherubim[h]
extended twenty cubits. They stood on their feet, facing the main hall.[b]
14He made the curtain[i] of blue, purple and crimson yarn and fine linen, with cherubim[j] worked into it.
15In the front of the temple he made two pillars,[k] which ⌞together⌟ were thirty-five cubits[c] long, each
with a capital[l] on top measuring five cubits. 16He made interwoven chains[d][m] and put them on top of the
pillars. He also made a hundred pomegranates[n] and attached them to the chains. 17He erected the pil-
lars in the front of the temple, one to the south and one to the north. The one to the south he named Ja-
kin[e] and the one to the north Boaz.[f]

The Temple's Furnishings

4 He made a bronze altar[o] twenty cubits long, twenty cubits wide and ten cubits high.[g] 2He made the
Sea[p] of cast metal, circular in shape, measuring ten cubits from rim to rim and five cubits[h] high. It
took a line of thirty cubits[i] to measure around it. 3Below the rim, figures of bulls encircled it—ten to a
cubit.[j] The bulls were cast in two rows in one piece with the Sea.
4The Sea stood on twelve bulls, three facing north, three facing west, three facing south and three fac-
ing east.[q] The Sea rested on top of them, and their hindquarters were toward the center. 5It was a hand-
breadth[k] in thickness, and its rim was like the rim of a cup, like a lily blossom. It held three thousand
baths.[l]
6He then made ten basins[r] for washing and placed five on the south side and five on the north. In
them the things to be used for the burnt offerings[s] were rinsed, but the Sea was to be used by the priests
for washing.
7He made ten gold lampstands[t] according to the specifications[u] for them and placed them in the tem-
ple, five on the south side and five on the north.
8He made ten tables[v] and placed them in the temple, five on the south side and five on the north. He
also made a hundred gold sprinkling bowls.[w]
9He made the courtyard[x] of the priests, and the large court and the doors for the court, and overlaid
the doors with bronze. 10He placed the Sea on the south side, at the southeast corner.
11He also made the pots and shovels and sprinkling bowls.
So Huram finished[y] the work he had undertaken for King Solomon in the temple of God:

12the two pillars;
the two bowl-shaped capitals on top of the pillars;
the two sets of network decorating the two bowl-shaped capitals on top of the pillars;
13the four hundred pomegranates for the two sets of network (two rows of pomegranates for each network, decorating the bowl-shaped capitals on top of the pillars);
14the stands[z] with their basins;
15the Sea and the twelve bulls under it;
16the pots, shovels, meat forks and all related articles.

All the objects that Huram-Abi[a] made for King Solomon for the temple of the LORD were of polished
bronze. 17The king had them cast in clay molds in the plain of the Jordan between Succoth[b] and Zare-

3:10 [g]Ex 25:18
3:13 [h]Ex 25:18
3:14 [i]Ex 26:31, 33; Heb 9:3 [j]Ge 3:24
3:15 [k]1Ki 7:15; Rev 3:12 [l]1Ki 7:22
3:16 [m]1Ki 7:17 [n]1Ki 7:20
4:1 [o]Ex 20:24; 27:1-2; 40:6; 1Ki 8:64; 2Ki 16:14
4:2 [p]Rev 4:6; 15:2
4:4 [q]Nu 2:3-25; Eze 48:30-34; Rev 21:13
4:6 [r]Ex 30:18 [s]Ne 13:5,9; Eze 40:38
4:7 [t]Ex 25:31 [u]Ex 25:40
4:8 [v]Ex 25:23 [w]Nu 4:14
4:9 [x]1Ki 6:36; 2Ki 21:5; 2Ch 33:5
4:11 [y]1Ki 7:14
4:14 [z]1Ki 7:27-30
4:16 [a]1Ki 7:13
4:17 [b]Ge 33:17

[a] *11* That is, about 7 1/2 feet (about 2.3 meters); also in verse 15 [b] *13* Or *facing inward* [c] *15* That is, about 52 feet (about 16 meters) [d] *16* Or possibly *made chains in the inner sanctuary*; the meaning of the Hebrew for this phrase is uncertain. [e] *17 Jakin* probably means *he establishes.* [f] *17 Boaz* probably means *in him is strength.* [g] *1* That is, about 30 feet (about 9 meters) long and wide, and about 15 feet (about 4.5 meters) high [h] *2* That is, about 7 1/2 feet (about 2.3 meters) [i] *2* That is, about 45 feet (about 13.5 meters) [j] *3* That is, about 1 1/2 feet (about 0.5 meter) [k] *5* That is, about 3 inches (about 8 centimeters) [l] *5* That is, about 17,500 gallons (about 66 kiloliters)

3:10–13 Like the cherubim guarding the entrance to Eden after the fall (Ge 3:24), massive sculptures of cherubim guarded the ark of the covenant eventually installed in the Most Holy Place (5:7–8). (See also the note on Ex 25:18–20.)

3:17 Excavations of numerous temples in Palestine have uncovered remains of similar pillars (see "Solomon's Temple and Other Ancient Temples" on p. 620).

4:17 The Hebrew text here is somewhat difficult. The words translated as "in clay molds in the plain of the Jordan" are literally "in the thickness of the ground of the Jordan." But it is a reasonable surmise that this was a local metalworking operation where local clay was utilized to form molds.

4:18 [c]1Ki 7:23 than.[a] 18 All these things that Solomon made amounted to so much that the weight of the bronze[c] was not
determined.
19 Solomon also made all the furnishings that were in God's temple:

the golden altar;
4:19 [d]Ex 25:23, 30 the tables[d] on which was the bread of the Presence;
4:20 [e]Ex 25:31 20 the lampstands[e] of pure gold with their lamps, to burn in front of the inner sanctuary as prescribed;
21 the gold floral work and lamps and tongs (they were solid gold);
4:22 [f]Nu 7:14 [g]Lev 10:1 22 the pure gold wick trimmers, sprinkling bowls, dishes[f] and censers;[g] and the gold doors of the
temple: the inner doors to the Most Holy Place and the doors of the main hall.

5:1 [h]1Ki 6:14 [i]2Sa 8:11 5 When all the work Solomon had done for the temple of the LORD was finished,[h] he brought in the
things his father David had dedicated[i]—the silver and gold and all the furnishings—and he placed
them in the treasuries of God's temple.

The Ark Brought to the Temple

2 Then Solomon summoned to Jerusalem the elders of Israel, all the heads of the tribes and the chiefs
5:2 [j]Nu 3:31; 2Sa 6:12; 1Ch 15:25 of the Israelite families, to bring up the ark[j] of the LORD's covenant from Zion, the City of David. 3 And all
the men of Israel[k] came together to the king at the time of the festival in the seventh month.
5:3 [k]1Ch 9:1; 2Ch 7:8-10 4 When all the elders of Israel had arrived, the Levites took up the ark, 5 and they brought up the ark
5:5 [l]Nu 3:31; 1Ch 15:2 and the Tent of Meeting and all the sacred furnishings in it. The priests, who were Levites,[l] carried them

[a] 17 Hebrew *Zeredatha*, a variant of *Zarethan*

ANCIENT TEXTS AND ARTIFACTS

The Jerusalem Pomegranate

2 CHRONICLES 4 A thumb-sized chunk of ivory in the shape of a pomegranate may be the only archaeological find recovered from Solomon's temple.[1] This graceful, six-petaled blossom is engraved with the words "Belonging to the temple of the LORD, holy to the priests." Based upon the shape of the Hebrew letters in the inscription, the artifact was initially dated to the eighth century B.C., although that date is now in dispute. Investigators for the Israel Antiquities Authority have reassessed the artifact and concluded that although the object itself dates to about 1400 B.C. (considerably earlier than the age of Solomon), the inscription is a recent forgery. The body of the pomegranate has a hole on the bottom in which a rod might have been inserted to form a scepter.

Two ivory scepters dating to the thirteenth century B.C. have been excavated in a **Canaanite**[2] temple in Lachish ("Map 4"), each topped with a miniature pomegranate. This implies that the pomegranate was a ritual object used regularly by priests in the ancient Near East, although its use specifically by priests in the Jerusalem temple is now open to question.

Ancient art made rich use of the pomegranate as a decorative motif. In a religious vein, this fruit was used by the Israelites as a sign of the fertility of the promised land under the blessing of God (Nu 13:23; Dt 8:8). Chains of pomegranates graced the capitals of the twin bronze pillars flanking the entrance of Israel's temple (2Ch 4:13). They also adorned the hem of the high priestly robes as embroidered blossoms of blue, purple and scarlet alternating with golden bells (Ex 28:33).

Ivory pomegranate from Jerusalem
Preserving Bible Times; © Dr. James C. Martin; permission of The Israel Museum

[1]See "Solomon's Temple and Other Ancient Temples" on page 620. [2]See Glossary on page 2080 for definitions of bolded words.

up; 6 and King Solomon and the entire assembly of Israel that had gathered about him were before the ark, sacrificing so many sheep and cattle that they could not be recorded or counted.

7 The priests then brought the ark[m] of the LORD's covenant to its place in the inner sanctuary of the temple, the Most Holy Place, and put it beneath the wings of the cherubim. 8 The cherubim[n] spread their wings over the place of the ark and covered the ark and its carrying poles. 9 These poles were so long that their ends, extending from the ark, could be seen from in front of the inner sanctuary, but not from outside the Holy Place; and they are still there today. 10 There was nothing in the ark except[o] the two tablets[p] that Moses had placed in it at Horeb, where the LORD made a covenant with the Israelites after they came out of Egypt.

11 The priests then withdrew from the Holy Place. All the priests who were there had consecrated themselves, regardless of their divisions.[q] 12 All the Levites who were musicians[r]—Asaph, Heman, Jeduthun and their sons and relatives—stood on the east side of the altar, dressed in fine linen and playing cymbals, harps and lyres. They were accompanied by 120 priests sounding trumpets.[s] 13 The trumpeters and singers joined in unison, as with one voice, to give praise and thanks to the LORD. Accompanied by trumpets, cymbals and other instruments, they raised their voices in praise to the LORD and sang:

> "He is good;
> his love endures forever."[t]

Then the temple of the LORD was filled with a cloud, 14 and the priests could not perform[u] their service because of the cloud,[v] for the glory[w] of the LORD filled the temple of God.

6 Then Solomon said, "The LORD has said that he would dwell in a dark cloud;[x] 2 I have built a magnificent temple for you, a place for you to dwell forever.[y]"

3 While the whole assembly of Israel was standing there, the king turned around and blessed them. 4 Then he said:

> "Praise be to the LORD, the God of Israel, who with his hands has fulfilled what he promised with his mouth to my father David. For he said, 5 'Since the day I brought my people out of Egypt, I have not chosen a city in any tribe of Israel to have a temple built for my Name to be there, nor have I chosen anyone to be the leader over my people Israel. 6 But now I have chosen Jerusalem[z] for my Name[a] to be there, and I have chosen David[b] to rule my people Israel.'
>
> 7 "My father David had it in his heart[c] to build a temple for the Name of the LORD, the God of Israel. 8 But the LORD said to my father David, 'Because it was in your heart to build a temple for my Name, you did well to have this in your heart. 9 Nevertheless, you are not the one to build the temple, but your son, who is your own flesh and blood—he is the one who will build the temple for my Name.'
>
> 10 "The LORD has kept the promise he made. I have succeeded David my father and now I sit on the throne of Israel, just as the LORD promised, and I have built the temple for the Name of the LORD, the God of Israel. 11 There I have placed the ark, in which is the covenant[d] of the LORD that he made with the people of Israel."

Solomon's Prayer of Dedication

12 Then Solomon stood before the altar of the LORD in front of the whole assembly of Israel and spread out his hands. 13 Now he had made a bronze platform,[e] five cubits[a] long, five cubits wide and three cubits[b] high, and had placed it in the center of the outer court. He stood on the platform and then knelt down[f] before the whole assembly of Israel and spread out his hands toward heaven. 14 He said:

> "O LORD, God of Israel, there is no God like you[g] in heaven or on earth—you who keep your covenant of love[h] with your servants who continue wholeheartedly in your way. 15 You have kept your promise to your servant David my father; with your mouth you have promised[i] and with your hand you have fulfilled it—as it is today.
>
> 16 "Now LORD, God of Israel, keep for your servant David my father the promises you made to him when you said, 'You shall never fail[j] to have a man to sit before me on the throne of Israel, if

5:7 [m]Rev 11:19
5:8 [n]Ge 3:24
5:10 [o]Heb 9:4 [p]Ex 16:34; Dt 10:2
5:11 [q]1Ch 24:1
5:12 [r]1Ki 10:12; 1Ch 25:1; Ps 68:25 [s]1Ch 13:8; 15:24
5:13 [t]1Ch 16:34, 41; 2Ch 7:3; 20:21; Ezr 3:11; Ps 100:5; 136:1; Jer 33:11
5:14 [u]Ex 40:35; Rev 15:8 [v]Ex 19:16 [w]Ex 29:43; 2Ch 7:2
6:1 [x]Ex 19:9; 1Ki 8:12-50
6:2 [y]Ezr 6:12; 7:15; Ps 135:21
6:6 [z]Dt 12:5; Isa 14:1 [a]Ex 20:24; 2Ch 12:13 [b]1Ch 28:4
6:7 [c]1Sa 10:7; 1Ch 17:2; 28:2; Ac 7:46
6:11 [d]Dt 10:2; 2Ch 5:10; Ps 25:10; 50:5
6:13 [e]Ne 8:4 [f]Ps 95:6
6:14 [g]Ex 8:10; 15:11 [h]Dt 7:9
6:15 [i]1Ch 22:10
6:16 [j]2Sa 7:13, 15; 1Ki 2:4; 2Ch 7:18; 23:3

[a] 13 That is, about 7 1/2 feet (about 2.3 meters) [b] 13 That is, about 4 1/2 feet (about 1.3 meters)

5:12 See the note on Psalms 73:1—83:18 for commentary on Asaph.

only your sons are careful in all they do to walk before me according to my law,[k] as you have done.'
17 And now, O LORD, God of Israel, let your word that you promised your servant David come true.
18 "But will God really dwell[l] on earth with men? The heavens,[m] even the highest heavens,
cannot contain you. How much less this temple I have built! 19 Yet give attention to your ser-
vant's prayer and his plea for mercy, O LORD my God. Hear the cry and the prayer that your ser-
vant is praying in your presence. 20 May your eyes[n] be open toward this temple day and night,
this place of which you said you would put your Name[o] there. May you hear[p] the prayer your
servant prays toward this place. 21 Hear the supplications of your servant and of your people
Israel when they pray toward this place. Hear from heaven, your dwelling place; and when you
hear, forgive.[q]
22 "When a man wrongs his neighbor and is required to take an oath[r] and he comes and swears
the oath before your altar in this temple, 23 then hear from heaven and act. Judge between your ser-
vants, repaying[s] the guilty by bringing down on his own head what he has done. Declare the in-
nocent not guilty and so establish his innocence.
24 "When your people Israel have been defeated[t] by an enemy because they have sinned against
you and when they turn back and confess your name, praying and making supplication before
you in this temple, 25 then hear from heaven and forgive the sin of your people Israel and bring
them back to the land you gave to them and their fathers.
26 "When the heavens are shut up and there is no rain[u] because your people have sinned against
you, and when they pray toward this place and confess your name and turn from their sin because
you have afflicted them, 27 then hear from heaven and forgive[v] the sin of your servants, your peo-
ple Israel. Teach them the right way to live, and send rain on the land you gave your people for an
inheritance.
28 "When famine[w] or plague comes to the land, or blight or mildew, locusts or grasshoppers, or
when enemies besiege them in any of their cities, whatever disaster or disease may come, 29 and
when a prayer or plea is made by any of your people Israel—each one aware of his afflictions and
pains, and spreading out his hands toward this temple— 30 then hear from heaven, your dwelling
place. Forgive,[x] and deal with each man according to all he does, since you know his heart (for you
alone know the hearts of men),[y] 31 so that they will fear you[z] and walk in your ways all the time they
live in the land you gave our fathers.
32 "As for the foreigner who does not belong to your people Israel but has come[a] from a dis-
tant land because of your great name and your mighty hand[b] and your outstretched arm—
when he comes and prays toward this temple, 33 then hear from heaven, your dwelling place, and
do whatever the foreigner[c] asks of you, so that all the peoples of the earth may know your name
and fear you, as do your own people Israel, and may know that this house I have built bears your
Name.
34 "When your people go to war against their enemies,[d] wherever you send them, and when
they pray[e] to you toward this city you have chosen and the temple I have built for your Name,
35 then hear from heaven their prayer and their plea, and uphold their cause.
36 "When they sin against you—for there is no one who does not sin[f]—and you become an-
gry with them and give them over to the enemy, who takes them captive[g] to a land far away or
near; 37 and if they have a change of heart[h] in the land where they are held captive, and repent and
plead with you in the land of their captivity and say, 'We have sinned, we have done wrong and
acted wickedly'; 38 and if they turn back to you with all their heart and soul in the land of their
captivity where they were taken, and pray toward the land you gave their fathers, toward the city
you have chosen and toward the temple I have built for your Name; 39 then from heaven, your dwell-
ing place, hear their prayer and their pleas, and uphold their cause. And forgive your people, who
have sinned against you.
40 "Now, my God, may your eyes be open and your ears attentive[i] to the prayers offered in this
place.

6:16 [k]Ps 132:12
6:18 [l]Rev 21:3 [m]2Ch 2:6; Ps 11:4; Isa 40:22; 66:1; Ac 7:49
6:20 [n]Ex 3:16; Ps 34:15 [o]Dt 12:11 [p]2Ch 7:14; 30:20
6:21 [q]Ps 51:1; Isa 33:24; 40:2; 43:25; 44:22; 55:7; Mic 7:18
6:22 [r]Ex 22:11
6:23 [s]Isa 3:11; 65:6; Mt 16:27
6:24 [t]Lev 26:17
6:26 [u]Lev 26:19; Dt 11:17; 28:24; 2Sa 1:21; 1Ki 17:1
6:27 [v]ver 30,39; 2Ch 7:14
6:28 [w]2Ch 20:9
6:30 [x]ver 27 [y]1Sa 16:7; 1Ch 28:9; Ps 7:9; 44:21; Pr 16:2; 17:3
6:31 [z]Ps 103:11, 13; Pr 8:13
6:32 [a]2Ch 9:6; Jn 12:20; Ac 8:27 [b]Ex 3:19,20
6:33 [c]2Ch 7:14
6:34 [d]Dt 28:7 [e]1Ch 5:20
6:36 [f]Job 15:14; Ps 143:2; Ecc 7:20; Jer 17:9; Jas 3:1; 1Jn 1:8-10 [g]Lev 26:44
6:37 [h]2Ch 7:14; 33:12,19,23; Jer 29:13
6:40 [i]2Ch 7:15; Ne 1:6,11; Ps 17:1,6

6:19–21 Solomon's temple became the symbolic focal point of God's interest in and care for humanity. It was here that his "eyes" and "ears" were continually open to the supplications of both Israelites and foreigners (e.g., vv. 20–21,32–33). These qualities differentiated God from the idols of Israel's neighbors, who, though they possessed eyes and ears, were sightless and unhearing (cf. Ps 115:4–8; Isa 44:17–18).

6:28–30 Life in Bible times was lived on the "ragged edge" of survival. Famines and invasions were common; childbirth was often fatal to child, mother or both; and a simple infection was potentially lethal.

41 "Now arise,[j] O LORD God, and come to your resting place,[k]
you and the ark of your might.
May your priests,[l] O LORD God, be clothed with salvation,
may your saints rejoice in your goodness.[m]
42 O LORD God, do not reject your anointed one.
Remember the great love[n] promised to David your servant."

The Dedication of the Temple

7 When Solomon finished praying, fire[o] came down from heaven and consumed the burnt offering and the sacrifices, and the glory of the LORD filled[p] the temple.[q] 2 The priests could not enter[r] the temple of the LORD because the glory[s] of the LORD filled it. 3 When all the Israelites saw the fire coming down and the glory of the LORD above the temple, they knelt on the pavement with their faces to the ground, and they worshiped and gave thanks to the LORD, saying,

"He is good;
his love endures forever."[t]

4 Then the king and all the people offered sacrifices before the LORD. 5 And King Solomon offered a sacrifice of twenty-two thousand head of cattle and a hundred and twenty thousand sheep and goats. So the king and all the people dedicated the temple of God. 6 The priests took their positions, as did the Levites[u] with the LORD's musical instruments,[v] which King David had made for praising the LORD and which were used when he gave thanks, saying, "His love endures forever." Opposite the Levites, the priests blew their trumpets, and all the Israelites were standing.

7 Solomon consecrated the middle part of the courtyard in front of the temple of the LORD, and there he offered burnt offerings and the fat of the fellowship offerings,[a] because the bronze altar he had made could not hold the burnt offerings, the grain offerings and the fat portions.

8 So Solomon observed the festival[w] at that time for seven days, and all Israel with him—a vast assembly, people from Lebo[b] Hamath to the Wadi of Egypt.[x] 9 On the eighth day they held an assembly, for they had celebrated the dedication of the altar for seven days and the festival[y] for seven days more. 10 On the twenty-third day of the seventh month he sent the people to their homes, joyful and glad in heart for the good things the LORD had done for David and Solomon and for his people Israel.

The LORD Appears to Solomon

11 When Solomon had finished the temple of the LORD and the royal palace, and had succeeded in carrying out all he had in mind to do in the temple of the LORD and in his own palace, 12 the LORD appeared to him at night and said:

"I have heard your prayer and have chosen this place for myself[z] as a temple for sacrifices.

13 "When I shut up the heavens so that there is no rain,[a] or command locusts to devour the land or send a plague among my people, 14 if my people, who are called by my name, will humble[b] themselves and pray and seek my face[c] and turn[d] from their wicked ways, then will I hear from heaven and will forgive[e] their sin and will heal[f] their land. 15 Now my eyes will be open and my ears attentive to the prayers offered in this place.[g] 16 I have chosen[h] and consecrated this temple so that my Name may be there forever. My eyes and my heart will always be there.

17 "As for you, if you walk before me[i] as David your father did, and do all I command, and observe my decrees and laws, 18 I will establish your royal throne, as I covenanted with David your father when I said, 'You shall never fail to have a man[j] to rule over Israel.'[k]

19 "But if you[c] turn away[l] and forsake[m] the decrees and commands I have given you[c] and go off to serve other gods and worship them, 20 then I will uproot[n] Israel from my land,[o] which I have given them, and will reject this temple I have consecrated for my Name. I will make it a byword and an object of ridicule[p] among all peoples. 21 And though this temple is now so imposing, all who pass by will be appalled and say,[q] 'Why has the LORD done such a thing to this land and to this

6:41 [j]Isa 33:10 [k]1Ch 28:2 [l]Ps 132:16 [m]Ps 116:12
6:42 [n]Ps 89:24, 28; Isa 55:3
7:1 [o]Lev 9:24; 1Ki 18:38 [p]Ex 16:10 [q]Ps 26:8
7:2 [r]1Ki 8:11 [s]Ex 29:43; 40:35; 2Ch 5:14
7:3 [t]1Ch 16:34; 2Ch 5:13; 20:21
7:6 [u]1Ch 15:16 [v]2Ch 5:12
7:8 [w]2Ch 30:26 [x]Ge 15:18
7:9 [y]Lev 23:36
7:12 [z]Dt 12:5
7:13 [a]2Ch 6:26-28; Am 4:7
7:14 [b]Lev 26:41; 2Ch 6:37; Jas 4:10 [c]1Ch 16:11 [d]Isa 55:7; Zec 1:4 [e]2Ch 6:27 [f]2Ch 30:20; Isa 30:26; 57:18
7:15 [g]2Ch 6:40
7:16 [h]ver 12; 2Ch 6:6
7:17 [i]1Ki 9:4
7:18 [j]2Ch 6:16 [k]2Sa 7:13; 2Ch 13:5
7:19 [l]Dt 28:15 [m]Lev 26:14,33
7:20 [n]Dt 29:28 [o]1Ki 14:15 [p]Dt 28:37
7:21 [q]Dt 29:24

[a] 7 Traditionally *peace offerings* [b] 8 Or *from the entrance to* [c] 19 The Hebrew is plural.

7:1 On God's *shekînâh* glory (his visible presence), see the note on Exodus 14:19.

temple?' 22 People will answer, 'Because they have forsaken the LORD, the God of their fathers, who
brought them out of Egypt, and have embraced other gods, worshiping and serving them—that
is why he brought all this disaster on them.' "

Solomon's Other Activities

8 At the end of twenty years, during which Solomon built the temple of the LORD and his own palace,
2 Solomon rebuilt the villages that Hiram[a] had given him, and settled Israelites in them. 3 Solomon
then went to Hamath Zobah and captured it. 4 He also built up Tadmor in the desert and all the store cit-
8:5 [r]1Ch 7:24; 2Ch 14:7 ies he had built in Hamath. 5 He rebuilt Upper Beth Horon[r] and Lower Beth Horon as fortified cities, with
walls and with gates and bars, 6 as well as Baalath and all his store cities, and all the cities for his chari-
ots and for his horses[b]—whatever he desired to build in Jerusalem, in Lebanon and throughout all the
territory he ruled.
8:7 [s]Ge 10:16 7 All the people left from the Hittites, Amorites, Perizzites, Hivites and Jebusites[s] (these peoples were
not Israelites), 8 that is, their descendants remaining in the land, whom the Israelites had not destroyed—
8:8 [t]1Ki 4:6; 9:21 these Solomon conscripted[t] for his slave labor force, as it is to this day. 9 But Solomon did not make slaves
of the Israelites for his work; they were his fighting men, commanders of his captains, and command-
ers of his chariots and charioteers. 10 They were also King Solomon's chief officials—two hundred and
fifty officials supervising the men.
8:11 [u]1Ki 3:1; 7:8 11 Solomon brought Pharaoh's daughter[u] up from the City of David to the palace he had built for her,
for he said, "My wife must not live in the palace of David king of Israel, because the places the ark of the
LORD has entered are holy."
8:12 [v]1Ki 8:64; 2Ch 4:1; 15:8 12 On the altar[v] of the LORD that he had built in front of the portico, Solomon sacrificed burnt offerings

[a] 2 Hebrew *Huram,* a variant of *Hiram;* also in verse 18 [b] 6 Or *charioteers*

8:2 In contrast to this verse, 1 Kings 9:11 refers to a transfer of towns from Solomon to Hiram. It is evident that we do not have a complete picture of the financial arrangements between the two kings. In Kings, however, Hiram is reported to have complained about the low quality of the towns, whereas in Chronicles Solomon is said to have chosen to rebuild the cities he had received from Hiram. For a possible explanation, see the note on 1 Kings 9:10–14.

8:7 See "Lesser Known Peoples of the Old Testament" on page 265 and "The Jebusites" on page 596.

ARCHAEOLOGICAL SITES

EZION GEBER

2 CHRONICLES 8 Biblical mention of Ezion Geber ("Map 5") is limited to Israel's wilderness wanderings (Nu 33:35–36; Dt 2:8),[1] the Solomonic era (1Ki 9:26–28; 2Ch 8:17–18) and the time of King Jehoshaphat of Judah (1Ki 22:47–49; 2Ch 20:35–37). Ezion Geber was located near Elath on the Red Sea (i.e., the Gulf of Aqaba) in the land of Edom.[2] Solomon, in collaboration with King Hiram of Tyre, developed it as a major seaport where he maintained a fleet and imported luxury commodities from Africa and India.[3] Later, Jehoshaphat unsuccessfully attempted to duplicate Solomon's venture.

Tell el-Kheleifeh, on the northern tip of the Gulf of Aqaba, was once widely identified with Ezion Geber on the grounds that archaeological remains suggested it had been a seaport and a site for smelting minerals. These conclusions have been challenged, and this connection is now regarded as unlikely.[4]

If Tell el-Kheleifeh is not Ezion Geber, the only other adequate anchorage in the northern gulf is located on an island called Jezirat Faraun ("Pharaoh's Island"; also called Coral Island), approximately 7.5 miles (12 km) south of modern Eilat. A natural harbor was improved in antiquity by the addition of a breakwater, mooring piers and defensive towers. The structure of the port is typical of **Phoenician** improved harbors, and **Iron Age** I[5] pottery found there confirms habitation of the site during the Solomonic period.

[1]See "A Timeline for the Wilderness Wanderings" on page 224. [2]See "Edom" on page 1467. [3]See "Solomon and the Israelite Empire" on page 490. [4]See "Tell el-Kheleifeh" on page 1017. [5]See "Archaeological Periods" chart on page xx in the front of this Bible.

to the LORD, [13]according to the daily requirement[w] for offerings commanded by Moses for Sabbaths,[x] New Moons and the three[y] annual feasts—the Feast of Unleavened Bread, the Feast of Weeks[z] and the Feast of Tabernacles. [14]In keeping with the ordinance of his father David, he appointed the divisions[a] of the priests for their duties, and the Levites[b] to lead the praise and to assist the priests according to each day's requirement. He also appointed the gatekeepers[c] by divisions for the various gates, because this was what David the man of God[d] had ordered.[e] [15]They did not deviate from the king's commands to the priests or to the Levites in any matter, including that of the treasuries.

[16]All Solomon's work was carried out, from the day the foundation of the temple of the LORD was laid until its completion. So the temple of the LORD was finished.

[17]Then Solomon went to Ezion Geber and Elath on the coast of Edom. [18]And Hiram sent him ships commanded by his own officers, men who knew the sea. These, with Solomon's men, sailed to Ophir and brought back four hundred and fifty talents[a] of gold,[f] which they delivered to King Solomon.

The Queen of Sheba Visits Solomon

9 When the queen of Sheba[g] heard of Solomon's fame, she came to Jerusalem to test him with hard questions. Arriving with a very great caravan—with camels carrying spices, large quantities of gold, and precious stones—she came to Solomon and talked with him about all she had on her mind. [2]Solomon answered all her questions; nothing was too hard for him to explain to her. [3]When the queen of Sheba saw the wisdom of Solomon,[h] as well as the palace he had built, [4]the food on his table, the seating of his officials, the attending servants in their robes, the cupbearers in their robes and the burnt offerings he made at[b] the temple of the LORD, she was overwhelmed.

[5]She said to the king, "The report I heard in my own country about your achievements and your wisdom is true. [6]But I did not believe what they said until I came[i] and saw with my own eyes. Indeed, not even half the greatness of your wisdom was told me; you have far exceeded the report I heard. [7]How happy your men must be! How happy your officials, who continually stand before you and hear your wisdom! [8]Praise be to the LORD your God, who has delighted in you and placed you on his throne[j] as king to rule for the LORD your God. Because of the love of your God for Israel and his desire to uphold them forever, he has made you king[k] over them, to maintain justice and righteousness."

[9]Then she gave the king 120 talents[c] of gold,[l] large quantities of spices, and precious stones. There had never been such spices as those the queen of Sheba gave to King Solomon.

[10](The men of Hiram and the men of Solomon brought gold from Ophir;[m] they also brought algumwood[d] and precious stones. [11]The king used the algumwood to make steps for the temple of the LORD and for the royal palace, and to make harps and lyres for the musicians. Nothing like them had ever been seen in Judah.)

[12]King Solomon gave the queen of Sheba all she desired and asked for; he gave her more than she had brought to him. Then she left and returned with her retinue to her own country.

Solomon's Splendor

[13]The weight of the gold that Solomon received yearly was 666 talents,[e] [14]not including the revenues brought in by merchants and traders. Also all the kings of Arabia[n] and the governors of the land brought gold and silver to Solomon.

[15]King Solomon made two hundred large shields of hammered gold; six hundred bekas[f] of hammered gold went into each shield. [16]He also made three hundred small shields[o] of hammered gold, with three hundred bekas[g] of gold in each shield. The king put them in the Palace of the Forest of Lebanon.[p]

[17]Then the king made a great throne inlaid with ivory[q] and overlaid with pure gold. [18]The throne had six steps, and a footstool of gold was attached to it. On both sides of the seat were armrests, with a lion

8:13 [w]Ex 29:38; Nu 28:3 [x]Nu 28:9 [y]Ex 23:14; Dt 16:16 [z]Ex 23:16
8:14 [a]1Ch 24:1 [b]1Ch 25:1 [c]1Ch 9:17; 26:1 [d]Ne 12:24,36 [e]1Ch 23:6; Ne 12:45
8:18 [f]2Ch 9:9
9:1 [g]Ge 10:7; Eze 23:42; Mt 12:42; Lk 11:31
9:3 [h]1Ki 5:12
9:6 [i]2Ch 6:32
9:8 [j]1Ki 2:12; 1Ch 17:14; 28:5; 29:23; 2Ch 13:8 [k]2Ch 2:11
9:9 [l]2Ch 8:18
9:10 [m]2Ch 8:18
9:14 [n]2Ch 17:11; Isa 21:13; Jer 25:24; Eze 27:21; 30:5
9:16 [o]2Ch 12:9 [p]1Ki 7:2
9:17 [q]1Ki 22:39

[a] *18* That is, about 17 tons (about 16 metric tons) [b] *4* Or *the ascent by which he went up to* [c] *9* That is, about 4 1/2 tons (about 4 metric tons) [d] *10* Probably a variant of *almugwood* [e] *13* That is, about 25 tons (about 23 metric tons) [f] *15* That is, about 7 1/2 pounds (about 3.5 kilograms) [g] *16* That is, about 3 3/4 pounds (about 1.7 kilograms)

8:13 See "The Festivals of Israel" on page 186.
9:1 "Hard questions" may refer to riddles. On the popularity and function of riddles in the ancient world, see the note on Judges 14:12–14.
9:10 For Ophir, see the note on 1 Kings 9:28. "Algumwood" is probably a variant of "almugwood."
9:13–14 Israel's strategic location connecting the continents of Africa and Asia, along with Solomon's control of the trade routes, generated enormous wealth for him. The 666 talents of gold he received annually equated to approximately 25 tons (see the NIV text note on v. 13). The unspecified sum of Solomon's gross yearly income included both money from tributes and tariffs and profits from his own capital ventures (primarily international trade).

standing beside each of them. 19 Twelve lions stood on the six steps, one at either end of each step. Noth-
ing like it had ever been made for any other kingdom. 20 All King Solomon's goblets were gold, and all the
household articles in the Palace of the Forest of Lebanon were pure gold. Nothing was made of silver, be-
cause silver was considered of little value in Solomon's day. 21 The king had a fleet of trading ships[a]
manned by Hiram's[b] men. Once every three years it returned, carrying gold, silver and ivory, and apes and
baboons.
9:22 [r]1Ki 3:13; 2Ch 1:12 — 22 King Solomon was greater in riches and wisdom than all the other kings of the earth.[r] 23 All the
9:23 [s]1Ki 4:34 — kings[s] of the earth sought audience with Solomon to hear the wisdom God had put in his heart. 24 Year
9:24 [t]2Ch 32:23; Ps 45:12; 68:29; 72:10; Isa 18:7 — after year, everyone who came brought a gift[t]—articles of silver and gold, and robes, weapons and spic-
es, and horses and mules.
9:25 [u]1Sa 8:11; 1Ki 4:26 — 25 Solomon had four thousand stalls for horses and chariots,[u] and twelve thousand horses,[c] which he
9:26 [v]1Ki 4:21 [w]Ps 72:8-9 [x]Ge 15:18-21 — kept in the chariot cities and also with him in Jerusalem. 26 He ruled[v] over all the kings from the River[d][w]
to the land of the Philistines, as far as the border of Egypt.[x] 27 The king made silver as common in Jeru-
salem as stones, and cedar as plentiful as sycamore-fig trees in the foothills. 28 Solomon's horses were im-
ported from Egypt[e] and from all other countries.

Solomon's Death

29 As for the other events of Solomon's reign, from beginning to end, are they not written in the rec-
9:29 [y]2Sa 7:2; 1Ch 29:29 [z]1Ki 11:29 [a]2Ch 10:2 — ords of Nathan[y] the prophet, in the prophecy of Ahijah[z] the Shilonite and in the visions of Iddo the seer
concerning Jeroboam[a] son of Nebat? 30 Solomon reigned in Jerusalem over all Israel forty years. 31 Then
9:31 [b]1Ki 2:10 — he rested with his fathers and was buried in the city of David[b] his father. And Rehoboam his son succeed-
ed him as king.

Israel Rebels Against Rehoboam

10 Rehoboam went to Shechem, for all the Israelites had gone there to make him king. 2 When Jer-
10:2 [c]2Ch 9:29 [d]1Ki 11:40 — oboam[c] son of Nebat heard this (he was in Egypt, where he had fled[d] from King Solomon), he
10:3 [e]1Ch 9:1 — returned from Egypt. 3 So they sent for Jeroboam, and he and all Israel[e] went to Rehoboam and said to
10:4 [f]2Ch 2:2 — him: 4 "Your father put a heavy yoke on us,[f] but now lighten the harsh labor and the heavy yoke he put
on us, and we will serve you."
5 Rehoboam answered, "Come back to me in three days." So the people went away.
10:6 [g]Job 8:8-9; 12:12; 15:10; 32:7 — 6 Then King Rehoboam consulted the elders[g] who had served his father Solomon during his lifetime.
"How would you advise me to answer these people?" he asked.
10:7 [h]Pr 15:1 — 7 They replied, "If you will be kind to these people and please them and give them a favorable answer,[h]
they will always be your servants."
10:8 [i]2Sa 17:14 [j]Pr 13:20 — 8 But Rehoboam rejected[i] the advice the elders[j] gave him and consulted the young men who had grown
up with him and were serving him. 9 He asked them, "What is your advice? How should we answer these
people who say to me, 'Lighten the yoke your father put on us'?"
10 The young men who had grown up with him replied, "Tell the people who have said to you, 'Your fa-
ther put a heavy yoke on us, but make our yoke lighter'—tell them, 'My little finger is thicker than my
father's waist. 11 My father laid on you a heavy yoke; I will make it even heavier. My father scourged you
with whips; I will scourge you with scorpions.' "
12 Three days later Jeroboam and all the people returned to Rehoboam, as the king had said, "Come
back to me in three days." 13 The king answered them harshly. Rejecting the advice of the elders, 14 he fol-
lowed the advice of the young men and said, "My father made your yoke heavy; I will make it even heavi-
er. My father scourged you with whips; I will scourge you with scorpions." 15 So the king did not listen to
10:15 [k]2Ch 11:4; 25:16-20 [l]1Ki 11:29 — the people, for this turn of events was from God,[k] to fulfill the word the LORD had spoken to Jeroboam
son of Nebat through Ahijah the Shilonite.[l]
10:16 [m]1Ch 9:1 [n]ver 19; 2Sa 20:1 — 16 When all Israel[m] saw that the king refused to listen to them, they answered the king:

> "What share do we have in David,[n]
> what part in Jesse's son?
> To your tents, O Israel!
> Look after your own house, O David!"

[a] *21* Hebrew *of ships that could go to Tarshish* [b] *21* Hebrew *Huram,* a variant of *Hiram* [c] *25* Or *charioteers* [d] *26* That is, the Euphrates [e] *28* Or possibly *Muzur,* a region in Cilicia

So all the Israelites went home. 17But as for the Israelites who were living in the towns of Judah, Rehoboam still ruled over them.

18King Rehoboam sent out Adoniram,[a][o] who was in charge of forced labor, but the Israelites stoned him to death. King Rehoboam, however, managed to get into his chariot and escape to Jerusalem. 19So Israel has been in rebellion against the house of David to this day.

11 When Rehoboam arrived in Jerusalem,[p] he mustered the house of Judah and Benjamin—a hundred and eighty thousand fighting men—to make war against Israel and to regain the kingdom for Rehoboam.

2But this word of the LORD came to Shemaiah[q] the man of God: 3"Say to Rehoboam son of Solomon king of Judah and to all the Israelites in Judah and Benjamin, 4'This is what the LORD says: Do not go up to fight against your brothers.[r] Go home, every one of you, for this is my doing.' " So they obeyed the words of the LORD and turned back from marching against Jeroboam.

Rehoboam Fortifies Judah

5Rehoboam lived in Jerusalem and built up towns for defense in Judah: 6Bethlehem, Etam, Tekoa, 7Beth Zur, Soco, Adullam, 8Gath, Mareshah, Ziph, 9Adoraim, Lachish, Azekah, 10Zorah, Aijalon and Hebron. These were fortified cities in Judah and Benjamin. 11He strengthened their defenses and put commanders in them, with supplies of food, olive oil and wine. 12He put shields and spears in all the cities, and made them very strong. So Judah and Benjamin were his.

13The priests and Levites from all their districts throughout Israel sided with him. 14The Levites[s] even abandoned their pasturelands and property,[t] and came to Judah and Jerusalem because Jeroboam and his sons had rejected them as priests of the LORD. 15And he appointed[u] his own priests[v] for the high places and for the goat[w] and calf[x] idols he had made. 16Those from every tribe of Israel[y] who set their hearts on seeking the LORD, the God of Israel, followed the Levites to Jerusalem to offer sacrifices to the LORD, the God of their fathers. 17They strengthened[z] the kingdom of Judah and supported Rehoboam son of Solomon three years, walking in the ways of David and Solomon during this time.

Rehoboam's Family

18Rehoboam married Mahalath, who was the daughter of David's son Jerimoth and of Abihail, the daughter of Jesse's son Eliab. 19She bore him sons: Jeush, Shemariah and Zaham. 20Then he married Maacah[a] daughter of Absalom, who bore him Abijah,[b] Attai, Ziza and Shelomith. 21Rehoboam loved Maacah daughter of Absalom more than any of his other wives and concubines. In all, he had eighteen wives[c] and sixty concubines, twenty-eight sons and sixty daughters.

22Rehoboam appointed Abijah[d] son of Maacah to be the chief prince among his brothers, in order to make him king. 23He acted wisely, dispersing some of his sons throughout the districts of Judah and Benjamin, and to all the fortified cities. He gave them abundant provisions and took many wives for them.

Shishak Attacks Jerusalem

12 After Rehoboam's position as king was established[e] and he had become strong,[f] he and all Israel[b] with him abandoned the law of the LORD. 2Because they had been unfaithful[g] to the LORD, Shishak[h] king of Egypt attacked Jerusalem in the fifth year of King Rehoboam. 3With twelve hundred chariots and sixty thousand horsemen and the innumerable troops of Libyans, Sukkites and Cushites[c][i] that came with him from Egypt, 4he captured the fortified cities[j] of Judah and came as far as Jerusalem.

5Then the prophet Shemaiah[k] came to Rehoboam and to the leaders of Judah who had assembled in Jerusalem for fear of Shishak, and he said to them, "This is what the LORD says, 'You have abandoned me; therefore, I now abandon[l] you to Shishak.' "

10:18 [o]1Ki 5:14
11:1 [p]1Ki 12:21
11:2 [q]2Ch 12:5-7,15
11:4 [r]2Ch 28:8-11
11:14 [s]Nu 35:2-5 [t]2Ch 13:9
11:15 [u]1Ki 13:33 [v]1Ki 12:31 [w]Lev 17:7 [x]1Ki 12:28; 2Ch 13:8
11:16 [y]2Ch 15:9
11:17 [z]2Ch 12:1
11:20 [a]1Ki 15:2 [b]2Ch 13:2
11:21 [c]Dt 17:17
11:22 [d]Dt 21:15-17
12:1 [e]ver 13 [f]2Ch 11:17
12:2 [g]1Ki 14:22-24 [h]1Ki 11:40
12:3 [i]2Ch 16:8; Na 3:9
12:4 [j]2Ch 11:10
12:5 [k]2Ch 11:2 [l]Dt 28:15; 2Ch 15:2

[a] *18* Hebrew *Hadoram*, a variant of *Adoniram* [b] *1* That is, Judah, as frequently in 2 Chronicles [c] *3* That is, people from the upper Nile region

11:15 See "Goat-Demons and Desert Satyrs" on page 177.
11:22–23 Rehoboam imitated his father's practice of delegation of royal authority by means of district governors (cf. 1Ki 4:7–19) but made these appointments from among his own sons. This policy prevented infighting among prospective successors to the throne, solidified the king's position, guarded against coup attempts, ensured an heir for the continuation of the dynasty (since housing the princes in one location would have made it easier for a usurper to execute all rivals) and extended the influence of the royal family to outlying districts.
12:2 Shishak (r. c. 945–924 B.C.) was the founder of the Twenty-second Dynasty of Egypt. He is also called Sheshonk I (see "The Campaign of Shishak" on p. 635 and "The History of the Southern Kingdom" on p. 538).
12:3 The Sukkites were probably a group of mercenary soldiers of Libyan origin who are known from Egyptian texts.

The Campaign of Shishak

2 CHRONICLES 12 Pharaoh Sheshonk I, who ruled Egypt from around 945–924 B.C. (931–910 B.C. on an alternative chronology), is probably the Shishak of the Bible. First Kings 11:40 states that Shishak provided refuge for Jeroboam when he was fleeing from Solomon. Five years after the division of the **united monarchy**, Shishak invaded Judah (2Ch 12:1–9).[1]

At Karnak in Egypt, near Thebes (see the map of Egypt on p. 346), at the great temple of Amun, stands an entryway known as the Bubastite Portal. This imposing entrance was probably constructed or renovated by Sheshonk I (the temple complex had existed for hundreds of years prior to Sheshonk and had been built up by numerous pharaohs). On one of the walls of the Bubastite Portal is featured a commemorative **relief** of Sheshonk's expedition into the region now known as Palestine. Although it is now badly damaged, enough remains to indicate that this pharaoh not only attacked Judah, as the Bible records, but campaigned against the northern kingdom as well. Sheshonk, depicted on the right-hand side of the scene, is about to club a group of foreigners. On the left side is pictured the Egyptian god Amun leading off captive cities with ropes. Each city is represented by an oval **cartouche** containing the name of the city, with a bound prisoner on top. The list primarily contains place-names in the northern kingdom of Israel.

Megiddo[2] (see "Map 6") is one of the towns listed in the Bubastite Portal. Sheshonk's claim to have sacked Megiddo seems to be confirmed by a portion of a commemorative **stele** found there in 1926. Sheshonk's name can be clearly read, and the stele is probably from his campaign. Many other destruction layers found at Palestinian sites from this period are also attributed to Sheshonk. When his son Osorkon I took the throne, he donated huge amounts of gold and silver to the temples in Egypt, much of it very likely plunder from Sheshonk's raids on Israel and Judah.

The equation of Shishak with Sheshonk is not without its problems. Most notable is the fact that Sheshonk's invasion involved a direct attack on the cities of the northern kingdom of Israel under Jeroboam I, even though 1 Kings 11:40 suggests that Shishak was Jeroboam's patron. Also, Jerusalem is missing from Sheshonk's list of subjugated sites, although 1 Kings 14 and 2 Chronicles 12 both record Shishak's plundering of the temple and palace. However, it is certainly possible that relations between Jeroboam I and Sheshonk/Shishak had deteriorated after Jeroboam had seized control of northern Israel. The Bible does not provide us with a detailed political history of these times. Also, only about 15 percent of the writing on the Bubastite Portal is legible, and the absence of Jerusalem from the (readable) names does not prove that it was never there.

It is possible that the inscription also mentions the "highlands of David" in its reference to Israel. If so, it is the earliest extrabiblical reference to David in existence and as such affords powerful evidence that he was in fact the great king the Bible portrays him to be.[3] The interpretation of the relevant line of this text, however, is disputed.

[1]See "The History of the Southern Kingdom" on page 538. [2]See "Megiddo" on page 1541. [3]For mention of another extrabiblical reference to David, see "The Tel Dan Stele" on page 540.

The Bubastite Portal, showing bound captives, each with the name of a captured city, beneath an oversized image of Shishak

Photograph: © Todd Bolen/Bible Places.com

6 The leaders of Israel and the king humbled themselves and said, "The LORD is just."[m] 12:6 [m]Ex 9:27;
7 When the LORD saw that they humbled themselves, this word of the LORD came to Shemaiah: "Since Da 9:14
they have humbled themselves, I will not destroy them but will soon give them deliverance.[n] My wrath 12:7 [n]1Ki 21:29; Ps 78:38
will not be poured out on Jerusalem through Shishak. 8 They will, however, become subject[o] to him, so 12:8 [o]Dt 28:48
that they may learn the difference between serving me and serving the kings of other lands."
9 When Shishak king of Egypt attacked Jerusalem, he carried off the treasures of the temple of the
LORD and the treasures of the royal palace. He took everything, including the gold shields[p] Solomon 12:9 [p]2Ch 9:16
had made. 10 So King Rehoboam made bronze shields to replace them and assigned these to the com-
manders of the guard on duty at the entrance to the royal palace. 11 Whenever the king went to the
LORD's temple, the guards went with him, bearing the shields, and afterward they returned them to
the guardroom.
12 Because Rehoboam humbled himself, the LORD's anger turned from him, and he was not totally de-
stroyed. Indeed, there was some good[q] in Judah. 12:12 [q]1Ki 14:13;
13 King Rehoboam established himself firmly in Jerusalem and continued as king. He was forty-one 2Ch 19:3
years old when he became king, and he reigned seventeen years in Jerusalem, the city the LORD had cho-
sen out of all the tribes of Israel in which to put his Name.[r] His mother's name was Naamah; she was an 12:13 [r]Dt 12:5;
Ammonite. 14 He did evil because he had not set his heart on seeking the LORD. 2Ch 6:6
15 As for the events of Rehoboam's reign, from beginning to end, are they not written in the records of
Shemaiah[s] the prophet and of Iddo the seer that deal with genealogies? There was continual warfare be- 12:15 [s]2Ch 9:29;
tween Rehoboam and Jeroboam. 16 Rehoboam rested with his fathers and was buried in the City of Da- 11:2
vid. And Abijah[t] his son succeeded him as king. 12:16 [t]2Ch 11:20

Abijah King of Judah

13 In the eighteenth year of the reign of Jeroboam, Abijah became king of Judah, 2 and he reigned
in Jerusalem three years. His mother's name was Maacah,[a] a daughter[b] of Uriel of Gibeah.
There was war between Abijah[u] and Jeroboam.[v] 3 Abijah went into battle with a force of four hundred 13:2 [u]2Ch 11:20
thousand able fighting men, and Jeroboam drew up a battle line against him with eight hundred thou- [v]1Ki 15:6
sand able troops.
4 Abijah stood on Mount Zemaraim,[w] in the hill country of Ephraim, and said, "Jeroboam and all Is- 13:4 [w]Jos 18:22
rael,[x] listen to me! 5 Don't you know that the LORD, the God of Israel, has given the kingship of Israel to [x]1Ch 11:1
David and his descendants forever[y] by a covenant of salt?[z] 6 Yet Jeroboam son of Nebat, an official of Sol- 13:5 [y]2Sa 7:13
omon son of David, rebelled[a] against his master. 7 Some worthless scoundrels[b] gathered around him and [z]Lev 2:13; Nu 18:19
opposed Rehoboam son of Solomon when he was young and indecisive and not strong enough to resist 13:6 [a]1Ki 11:26 13:7 [b]Jdg 9:4
them.
8 "And now you plan to resist the kingdom of the LORD, which is in the hands of David's descendants.
You are indeed a vast army and have with you the golden calves[c] that Jeroboam made to be your gods. 13:8 [c]1Ki 12:28;
9 But didn't you drive out the priests of the LORD,[d] the sons of Aaron, and the Levites, and make priests of 2Ch 11:15 13:9 [d]2Ch 11:14-
your own as the peoples of other lands do? Whoever comes to consecrate himself with a young bull[e] and 15 [e]Ex 29:35-36
seven rams may become a priest of what are not gods.[f] [f]Jer 2:11
10 "As for us, the LORD is our God, and we have not forsaken him. The priests who serve the LORD are
sons of Aaron, and the Levites assist them. 11 Every morning and evening[g] they present burnt offerings 13:11 [g]Ex 29:39;
and fragrant incense to the LORD. They set out the bread on the ceremonially clean table[h] and light the 2Ch 2:4 [h]Lev 24:5-9
lamps on the gold lampstand every evening. We are observing the requirements of the LORD our God.
But you have forsaken him. 12 God is with us; he is our leader. His priests with their trumpets will sound
the battle cry against you.[i] Men of Israel, do not fight against the LORD,[j] the God of your fathers, for you 13:12 [i]Nu 10:8-9
will not succeed." [j]Ac 5:39
13 Now Jeroboam had sent troops around to the rear, so that while he was in front of Judah the ambush[k] 13:13 [k]Jos 8:9
was behind them. 14 Judah turned and saw that they were being attacked at both front and rear. Then they
cried out[l] to the LORD. The priests blew their trumpets 15 and the men of Judah raised the battle cry. At 13:14 [l]2Ch 14:11
the sound of their battle cry, God routed Jeroboam and all Israel[m] before Abijah and Judah. 16 The Isra- 13:15 [m]2Ch 14:12

[a] 2 Most Septuagint manuscripts and Syriac (see also 2 Chron. 11:20 and 1 Kings 15:2); Hebrew *Micaiah* [b] 2 Or *granddaughter*

13:5 A "covenant of salt" may be an allusion to the salt used in the sacrificial meal that commonly accompanied the making of a covenant (see Ge 31:54; Ex 24:5–11; Ps 50:5).

elites fled before Judah, and God delivered[n] them into their hands. 17 Abijah and his men inflicted heavy losses on them, so that there were five hundred thousand casualties among Israel's able men. 18 The men of Israel were subdued on that occasion, and the men of Judah were victorious because they relied[o] on the LORD, the God of their fathers.

19 Abijah pursued Jeroboam and took from him the towns of Bethel, Jeshanah and Ephron, with their surrounding villages. 20 Jeroboam did not regain power during the time of Abijah. And the LORD struck him down and he died.

21 But Abijah grew in strength. He married fourteen wives and had twenty-two sons and sixteen daughters.

22 The other events of Abijah's reign, what he did and what he said, are written in the annotations of the prophet Iddo.

14 And Abijah rested with his fathers and was buried in the City of David. Asa his son succeeded him as king, and in his days the country was at peace for ten years.

Asa King of Judah

2 Asa did what was good and right in the eyes of the LORD his God. 3 He removed the foreign altars and the high places, smashed the sacred stones and cut down the Asherah poles.[a][p] 4 He commanded Judah to seek the LORD, the God of their fathers, and to obey his laws and commands. 5 He removed the high places and incense altars[q] in every town in Judah, and the kingdom was at peace under him. 6 He built up the fortified cities of Judah, since the land was at peace. No one was at war with him during those years, for the LORD gave him rest.[r]

7 "Let us build up these towns," he said to Judah, "and put walls around them, with towers, gates and bars. The land is still ours, because we have sought the LORD our God; we sought him and he has given us rest on every side." So they built and prospered.

8 Asa had an army of three hundred thousand men from Judah, equipped with large shields and with spears, and two hundred and eighty thousand from Benjamin, armed with small shields and with bows. All these were brave fighting men.

9 Zerah the Cushite[s] marched out against them with a vast army[b] and three hundred chariots, and came as far as Mareshah.[t] 10 Asa went out to meet him, and they took up battle positions in the Valley of Zephathah near Mareshah.

11 Then Asa called[u] to the LORD his God and said, "LORD, there is no one like you to help the powerless against the mighty. Help us, O LORD our God, for we rely[v] on you, and in your name[w] we have come against this vast army. O LORD, you are our God; do not let man prevail[x] against you."

12 The LORD struck down[y] the Cushites before Asa and Judah. The Cushites fled, 13 and Asa and his army pursued them as far as Gerar.[z] Such a great number of Cushites fell that they could not recover; they were crushed before the LORD and his forces. The men of Judah carried off a large amount of plunder. 14 They destroyed all the villages around Gerar, for the terror[a] of the LORD had fallen upon them. They plundered all these villages, since there was much booty there. 15 They also attacked the camps of the herdsmen and carried off droves of sheep and goats and camels. Then they returned to Jerusalem.

Asa's Reform

15 The Spirit of God came upon[b] Azariah son of Oded. 2 He went out to meet Asa and said to him, "Listen to me, Asa and all Judah and Benjamin. The LORD is with you[c] when you are with him.[d] If you seek[e] him, he will be found by you, but if you forsake him, he will forsake you.[f] 3 For a long time Israel was without the true God, without a priest to teach[g] and without the law.[h] 4 But in their distress they turned to the LORD, the God of Israel, and sought him,[i] and he was found by them. 5 In those days it was

[a] 3 That is, symbols of the goddess Asherah; here and elsewhere in 2 Chronicles [b] 9 Hebrew *with an army of a thousand thousands* or *with an army of thousands upon thousands*

13:16 [n]2Ch 16:8
13:18 [o]1Ch 5:20; 2Ch 14:11; Ps 22:5
14:3 [p]Ex 34:13; Dt 7:5; 1Ki 15:12-14
14:5 [q]2Ch 34:4,7
14:6 [r]1Ch 22:9; 2Ch 15:15
14:9 [s]2Ch 12:3; 16:8 [t]2Ch 11:8
14:11 [u]2Ch 13:14 [v]2Ch 13:18 [w]1Sa 17:45 [x]1Sa 14:6; Ps 9:19
14:12 [y]2Ch 13:15
14:13 [z]Ge 10:19
14:14 [a]Ge 35:5; 2Ch 17:10
15:1 [b]Nu 11:25, 26; 24:2; 2Ch 20:14; 24:20
15:2 [c]ver 4,15; 2Ch 20:17 [d]Jas 4:8 [e]Jer 29:13 [f]1Ch 28:9; 2Ch 24:20
15:3 [g]Lev 10:11 [h]2Ch 17:9; La 2:9
15:4 [i]Dt 4:29

14:9 Zerah the Cushite is unknown from ancient records outside the Bible and appears to have been a fairly minor figure. He may have been a general leading Egyptian forces in the service of Pharaoh Osorkon I. The Cushites were natives of Nubia, the region that borders Egypt on the south—not to be confused with modern Ethiopia (see "Cush" on p. 1519). The NIV translation "a vast army" is literally "a thousand thousands" (i.e., a million). However, this may simply be hyperbole (exaggeration for rhetorical effect), or it is possible that the Hebrew actually represents a much smaller number, possibly 10,000. The numbers for the army of Judah and Benjamin are also very large (v. 8). Indeed, the Hebrew text may actually imply a combined force of approximately 5,800 men instead of 580,000 men (see "Numbers and Their Meaning" on p. 197).

not safe to travel about,[j] for all the inhabitants of the lands were in great turmoil. 6One nation was being 15:5 [j]Jdg 5:6
crushed by another and one city by another,[k] because God was troubling them with every kind of dis- 15:6 [k]Mt 24:7
tress. 7But as for you, be strong[l] and do not give up, for your work will be rewarded."[m] 15:7 [l]Jos 1:7,9 [m]Ps 58:11
8When Asa heard these words and the prophecy of Azariah son of[a] Oded the prophet, he took cour-
age. He removed the detestable idols from the whole land of Judah and Benjamin and from the towns he
had captured[n] in the hills of Ephraim. He repaired the altar[o] of the LORD that was in front of the portico 15:8 [n]2Ch 13:19 [o]2Ch 8:12
of the LORD's temple.
9Then he assembled all Judah and Benjamin and the people from Ephraim, Manasseh and Simeon
who had settled among them, for large numbers[p] had come over to him from Israel when they saw that 15:9 [p]2Ch 11:16-17
the LORD his God was with him.
10They assembled at Jerusalem in the third month of the fifteenth year of Asa's reign. 11At that time
they sacrificed to the LORD seven hundred head of cattle and seven thousand sheep and goats from the
plunder[q] they had brought back. 12They entered into a covenant[r] to seek the LORD,[s] the God of their fa- 15:11 [q]2Ch 14:13 15:12 [r]2Ki 11:17;
thers, with all their heart and soul. 13All who would not seek the LORD, the God of Israel, were to be put 2Ch 23:16; 34:31
to death,[t] whether small or great, man or woman. 14They took an oath to the LORD with loud acclama- [s]1Ch 16:11 15:13 [t]Ex 22:20;
tion, with shouting and with trumpets and horns. 15All Judah rejoiced about the oath because they had Dt 13:9-16
sworn it wholeheartedly. They sought God[u] eagerly, and he was found by them. So the LORD gave them 15:15 [u]Dt 4:29 [v]1Ch 22:9;
rest[v] on every side. 2Ch 14:7
16King Asa also deposed his grandmother Maacah from her position as queen mother, because she
had made a repulsive Asherah pole.[w] Asa cut the pole down, broke it up and burned it in the Kidron Val- 15:16 [w]Ex 34:13; 2Ch 14:2-5
ley. 17Although he did not remove the high places from Israel, Asa's heart was fully committed ⌞to the
LORD⌟ all his life. 18He brought into the temple of God the silver and gold and the articles that he and his
father had dedicated.
19There was no more war until the thirty-fifth year of Asa's reign.

[a] 8 Vulgate and Syriac (see also Septuagint and verse 1); Hebrew does not have *Azariah son of.*

15:16 See "Devotion to Asherah in the Khirbet El-Qom Inscription" on page 638.

ANCIENT TEXTS AND ARTIFACTS

Devotion to Asherah in the Khirbet El-Qom Inscription

2 CHRONICLES 15 Religious syncretism (simultaneous worship of various gods) was widespread in ancient Israel. From the time of the judges many Israelites included the **Canaanite** gods in their worship. Because the god El was in some respects considered to be analogous with the Lord, many also adopted worship of El's consort, Asherah, assuming her to be **Yahweh**'s partner as well. Frequently wooden cult objects representing Asherah were erected in sacred spots. Gideon destroyed such a cult object (Jdg 6:25–28), as did Asa (2Ch 15:16), Hezekiah (31:1) and Josiah (34:3–7).

An inscription from Khirbet el-Qom, approximately 8 miles (13 km) west of Hebron[1] ("Map 6") demonstrates why it was necessary for Hezekiah and Josiah to continue to demolish Asherah poles even after the religious reforms of Asa. This inscription, dating to the late eighth century B.C. (at least 100 years after Asa), originally appeared on a pillar of the burial chamber for an otherwise unknown man by the name of Uriyahu. His eulogy claims that the Lord had blessed him and delivered him from his enemies "by his Asherah." Similar inscriptions from Kuntillet Ajrud in the northern Sinai suggest that many Israelites continued their devotion to the goddess Asherah, worshiping her as the Lord's spouse.[2] It is just such religious syncretism and idolatry that Asa attacked in 2 Chronicles 15:8–17.

[1]See "Hebron" on page 446. [2]See "The Kuntillet Ajrûd Inscriptions: The LORD's Asherah?" on page 1220.

Asa's Last Years

16:1 [x]Jer 41:9 **16** In the thirty-sixth year of Asa's reign Baasha[x] king of Israel went up against Judah and fortified
Ramah to prevent anyone from leaving or entering the territory of Asa king of Judah.
2 Asa then took the silver and gold out of the treasuries of the LORD's temple and of his own palace
16:3 [y]2Ch 20:35 and sent it to Ben-Hadad king of Aram, who was ruling in Damascus. 3 "Let there be a treaty[y] between
me and you," he said, "as there was between my father and your father. See, I am sending you silver and
gold. Now break your treaty with Baasha king of Israel so he will withdraw from me."
4 Ben-Hadad agreed with King Asa and sent the commanders of his forces against the towns of Isra-
el. They conquered Ijon, Dan, Abel Maim[a] and all the store cities of Naphtali. 5 When Baasha heard this,
he stopped building Ramah and abandoned his work. 6 Then King Asa brought all the men of Judah, and
they carried away from Ramah the stones and timber Baasha had been using. With them he built up
Geba and Mizpah.
16:7 [z]1Ki 16:1 7 At that time Hanani[z] the seer came to Asa king of Judah and said to him: "Because you relied on the
king of Aram and not on the LORD your God, the army of the king of Aram has escaped from your hand.
16:8 [a]2Ch 12:3; 14:9 [b]2Ch 13:16 8 Were not the Cushites[b][a] and Libyans a mighty army with great numbers of chariots and horsemen[c]?
16:9 [c]Pr 15:3; Yet when you relied on the LORD, he delivered[b] them into your hand. 9 For the eyes[c] of the LORD range
Jer 16:17; Zec 4:10 throughout the earth to strengthen those whose hearts are fully committed to him. You have done a fool-
[d]1Sa 13:13 ish[d] thing, and from now on you will be at war."
10 Asa was angry with the seer because of this; he was so enraged that he put him in prison. At the
same time Asa brutally oppressed some of the people.
11 The events of Asa's reign, from beginning to end, are written in the book of the kings of Judah and
16:12 Israel. 12 In the thirty-ninth year of his reign Asa was afflicted with a disease in his feet. Though his dis-
[e]Jer 17:5-6 ease was severe, even in his illness he did not seek help from the LORD,[e] but only from the physicians.
13 Then in the forty-first year of his reign Asa died and rested with his fathers. 14 They buried him in the
tomb that he had cut out for himself in the City of David. They laid him on a bier covered with spices and
16:14 [f]Ge 50:2; Jn 19:39-40 [g]2Ch 21:19; Jer 34:5 various blended perfumes,[f] and they made a huge fire[g] in his honor.

Jehoshaphat King of Judah

17 Jehoshaphat his son succeeded him as king and strengthened himself against Israel. 2 He sta-
tioned troops in all the fortified cities of Judah and put garrisons in Judah and in the towns of
17:2 [h]2Ch 15:8 Ephraim that his father Asa had captured.[h]
17:3 [i]1Ki 22:43 3 The LORD was with Jehoshaphat because in his early years he walked in the ways his father David[i] had
17:4 [j]1Ki 12:28; 2Ch 22:9 followed. He did not consult the Baals 4 but sought[j] the God of his father and followed his commands
rather than the practices of Israel. 5 The LORD established the kingdom under his control; and all Judah
17:5 [k]1Sa 10:27 brought gifts[k] to Jehoshaphat, so that he had great wealth and honor.[l] 6 His heart was devoted[m] to the
[l]2Ch 18:1 17:6 [m]1Ki 8:61; ways of the LORD; furthermore, he removed the high places[n] and the Asherah poles[o] from Judah.[p]
2Ch 15:17 [n]1Ki 15:14; 7 In the third year of his reign he sent his officials Ben-Hail, Obadiah, Zechariah, Nethanel and Mica-
2Ch 19:3; 20:33 [o]Ex 34:13 iah to teach[q] in the towns of Judah. 8 With them were certain Levites[r]—Shemaiah, Nethaniah, Zebadi-
[p]2Ch 21:12 17:7 [q]Lev 10:11; ah, Asahel, Shemiramoth, Jehonathan, Adonijah, Tobijah and Tob-Adonijah—and the priests Elishama
Dt 6:4-9; 2Ch 15:3; 35:3 and Jehoram. 9 They taught throughout Judah, taking with them the Book of the Law[s] of the LORD; they
17:8 [r]2Ch 19:8; Ne 8:7-8 went around to all the towns of Judah and taught the people.
17:9 [s]Dt 6:4-9; 28:61 10 The fear[t] of the LORD fell on all the kingdoms of the lands surrounding Judah, so that they did not
17:10 [t]Ge 35:5; Dt 2:25 make war with Jehoshaphat. 11 Some Philistines brought Jehoshaphat gifts and silver as tribute, and the
2Ch 14:14 17:11 [u]2Ch 9:14; Arabs[u] brought him flocks:[v] seven thousand seven hundred rams and seven thousand seven hundred
26:8 [v]2Ch 21:16 goats.
12 Jehoshaphat became more and more powerful; he built forts and store cities in Judah 13 and had

a 4 Also known as *Abel Beth Maacah* *b* 8 That is, people from the upper Nile region *c* 8 Or *charioteers*

16:1 Baasha exterminated the house of Jeroboam and made Tirzah his capital. He ascended the throne in the third year of Asa, king of Judah (1Ki 15:33—16:7), and carried on a prolonged war with him. Baasha continued the calf worship begun by Jeroboam (see "The High Place at Dan" on p. 504). He attempted to fortify Ramah, a city located south of Bethel about 5 miles (8 km) north of Jerusalem, against Jerusalem but abandoned the project after Asa of Judah sent tribute to Ben-Hadad, son of Tabrimmon of Damascus, who in turn attacked Baasha from the north (1Ki 15:16–21). After a reign of 24 years he died a natural death and was succeeded by his son Elah, who, along with every other member of the house of Baasha, was killed by Zimri.

16:6 Geba and Mizpah were two cities on Judah's northern border. Geba was located to the east and Mizpah to the southwest of Ramah (see "Mizpah" on p. 383).

large supplies in the towns of Judah. He also kept experienced fighting men in Jerusalem. 14Their enroll-
ment[w] by families was as follows: 17:14 [w]2Sa 24:2

From Judah, commanders of units of 1,000:
Adnah the commander, with 300,000 fighting men;
15next, Jehohanan the commander, with 280,000;
16next, Amasiah son of Zicri, who volunteered[x] himself for the service of the LORD, with 200,000. 17:16 [x]Jdg 5:9; 1Ch 29:9
17From Benjamin:[y] 17:17 [y]Nu 1:36
Eliada, a valiant soldier, with 200,000 men armed with bows and shields;
18next, Jehozabad, with 180,000 men armed for battle.

19These were the men who served the king, besides those he stationed in the fortified cities[z] throughout 17:19 [z]2Ch 11:10
Judah.[a] [a]2Ch 25:5

Micaiah Prophesies Against Ahab

18 Now Jehoshaphat had great wealth and honor,[b] and he allied[c] himself with Ahab[d] by marriage. 18:1 [b]2Ch 17:5 [c]2Ch 19:1-3; 22:3 [d]2Ch 21:6
2Some years later he went down to visit Ahab in Samaria. Ahab slaughtered many sheep and cat-
tle for him and the people with him and urged him to attack Ramoth Gilead. 3Ahab king of Israel asked
Jehoshaphat king of Judah, "Will you go with me against Ramoth Gilead?"
Jehoshaphat replied, "I am as you are, and my people as your people; we will join you in the war." 4But
Jehoshaphat also said to the king of Israel, "First seek the counsel of the LORD."
5So the king of Israel brought together the prophets—four hundred men—and asked them, "Shall
we go to war against Ramoth Gilead, or shall I refrain?"
"Go," they answered, "for God will give it into the king's hand."
6But Jehoshaphat asked, "Is there not a prophet of the LORD here whom we can inquire of?"
7The king of Israel answered Jehoshaphat, "There is still one man through whom we can inquire of
the LORD, but I hate him because he never prophesies anything good about me, but always bad. He is Mi-
caiah son of Imlah."
"The king should not say that," Jehoshaphat replied.
8So the king of Israel called one of his officials and said, "Bring Micaiah son of Imlah at once."
9Dressed in their royal robes, the king of Israel and Jehoshaphat king of Judah were sitting on their
thrones at the threshing floor by the entrance to the gate of Samaria, with all the prophets prophesying
before them. 10Now Zedekiah son of Kenaanah had made iron horns, and he declared, "This is what the
LORD says: 'With these you will gore the Arameans until they are destroyed.' "
11All the other prophets were prophesying the same thing. "Attack Ramoth Gilead[e] and be victori- 18:11 [e]2Ch 22:5
ous," they said, "for the LORD will give it into the king's hand."
12The messenger who had gone to summon Micaiah said to him, "Look, as one man the other proph-
ets are predicting success for the king. Let your word agree with theirs, and speak favorably."
13But Micaiah said, "As surely as the LORD lives, I can tell him only what my God says."[f] 18:13 [f]Nu 22:18, 20,35
14When he arrived, the king asked him, "Micaiah, shall we go to war against Ramoth Gilead, or shall
I refrain?"
"Attack and be victorious," he answered, "for they will be given into your hand."
15The king said to him, "How many times must I make you swear to tell me nothing but the truth in
the name of the LORD?"
16Then Micaiah answered, "I saw all Israel[g] scattered on the hills like sheep without a shepherd,[h] and 18:16 [g]1Ch 9:1 [h]Nu 27:17; Eze 34:5-8
the LORD said, 'These people have no master. Let each one go home in peace.' "

18:2 Ahab, who reigned from approximately 873–851 B.C., was politically one of Israel's strongest kings. In his day Israel was at peace with Judah and maintained her dominion over Moab, which paid her a considerable tribute (2Ki 3:4). Ahab joined in battle on three different occasions in his later years against Ben-Hadad, king of Syria. While he enjoyed great success in the first two campaigns, he was defeated and mortally wounded in the third (see the final sentence of the next paragraph). Not mentioned in the Bible is Ahab's participation in the Battle of Qarqar in 854 B.C. (see "Ahab and The Battle of Qarqar" on p. 524). The "Monolith Inscription" of the Assyrian king Shalmaneser III contains a description of this battle that the Assyrians fought against a Syrian coalition of 12 kings.

Ahab's marriage to Jezebel was politically advantageous but religiously disastrous. Jezebel introduced the worship of Baal into Israel and instituted a persecution against the prophets of Yahweh. The narrative in Kings is taken up with the struggle between Ahab and the prophet Elijah. An especially egregious offense of Ahab and Jezebel was the murder of Naboth in order to gain his patrimony (1Ki 21). The prediction of Ahab's death (1Ki 20:42) was fulfilled when he was killed in battle at Ramoth Gilead (1Ki 22:34).

18:9 See "The Threshing Floor" on page 608 and "The City Gate" on page 392.

17 The king of Israel said to Jehoshaphat, "Didn't I tell you that he never prophesies anything good about me, but only bad?"

18 Micaiah continued, "Therefore hear the word of the LORD: I saw the LORD sitting on his throne[i] with all the host of heaven standing on his right and on his left. 19 And the LORD said, 'Who will entice Ahab king of Israel into attacking Ramoth Gilead and going to his death there?'

"One suggested this, and another that. 20 Finally, a spirit came forward, stood before the LORD and said, 'I will entice him.'

" 'By what means?' the LORD asked.

21 " 'I will go and be a lying spirit[j] in the mouths of all his prophets,' he said.

" 'You will succeed in enticing him,' said the LORD. 'Go and do it.'

22 "So now the LORD has put a lying spirit in the mouths of these prophets of yours.[k] The LORD has decreed disaster for you."

23 Then Zedekiah son of Kenaanah went up and slapped[l] Micaiah in the face. "Which way did the spirit from[a] the LORD go when he went from me to speak to you?" he asked.

24 Micaiah replied, "You will find out on the day you go to hide in an inner room."

25 The king of Israel then ordered, "Take Micaiah and send him back to Amon the ruler of the city and to Joash the king's son, 26 and say, 'This is what the king says: Put this fellow in prison[m] and give him nothing but bread and water until I return safely.' "

27 Micaiah declared, "If you ever return safely, the LORD has not spoken through me." Then he added, "Mark my words, all you people!"

Ahab Killed at Ramoth Gilead

28 So the king of Israel and Jehoshaphat king of Judah went up to Ramoth Gilead. 29 The king of Israel said to Jehoshaphat, "I will enter the battle in disguise, but you wear your royal robes." So the king of Israel disguised[n] himself and went into battle.

30 Now the king of Aram had ordered his chariot commanders, "Do not fight with anyone, small or great, except the king of Israel." 31 When the chariot commanders saw Jehoshaphat, they thought, "This is the king of Israel." So they turned to attack him, but Jehoshaphat cried out,[o] and the LORD helped him. God drew them away from him, 32 for when the chariot commanders saw that he was not the king of Israel, they stopped pursuing him.

33 But someone drew his bow at random and hit the king of Israel between the sections of his armor. The king told the chariot driver, "Wheel around and get me out of the fighting. I've been wounded." 34 All day long the battle raged, and the king of Israel propped himself up in his chariot facing the Arameans until evening. Then at sunset he died.[p]

19 When Jehoshaphat king of Judah returned safely to his palace in Jerusalem, 2 Jehu[q] the seer, the son of Hanani, went out to meet him and said to the king, "Should you help the wicked[r] and love[b] those who hate the LORD?[s] Because of this, the wrath[t] of the LORD is upon you. 3 There is, however, some good[u] in you, for you have rid the land of the Asherah poles[v] and have set your heart on seeking God.[w]"

Jehoshaphat Appoints Judges

4 Jehoshaphat lived in Jerusalem, and he went out again among the people from Beersheba to the hill country of Ephraim and turned them back to the LORD, the God of their fathers. 5 He appointed judges[x] in the land, in each of the fortified cities of Judah. 6 He told them, "Consider carefully what you do,[y] because you are not judging for man[z] but for the LORD, who is with you whenever you give a verdict. 7 Now let the fear of the LORD be upon you. Judge carefully, for with the LORD our God there is no injustice[a] or partiality[b] or bribery."

8 In Jerusalem also, Jehoshaphat appointed some of the Levites, priests and heads of Israelite families to administer[c] the law of the LORD and to settle disputes. And they lived in Jerusalem. 9 He gave them these orders: "You must serve faithfully and wholeheartedly in the fear of the LORD. 10 In every case that comes before you from your fellow countrymen who live in the cities—whether bloodshed or other

18:18 [i]Da 7:9
18:21 [j]1Ch 21:1; Job 1:6; Zec 3:1; Jn 8:44
18:22 [k]Job 12:16; Isa 19:14; Eze 14:9
18:23 [l]Jer 20:2; Mk 14:65; Ac 23:2
18:26 [m]2Ch 16:10; Heb 11:36
18:29 [n]1Sa 28:8
18:31 [o]2Ch 13:14
18:34 [p]2Ch 22:5
19:2 [q]1Ki 16:1 [r]2Ch 16:2-9 [s]Ps 139:21-22 [t]2Ch 24:18; 32:25; Ps 7:11
19:3 [u]1Ki 14:13; 2Ch 12:12 [v]2Ch 17:6 [w]2Ch 18:1; 20:35; 25:7; Ezr 7:10
19:5 [x]Ge 47:6; Ex 18:26
19:6 [y]Lev 19:15 [z]Dt 1:17; 16:18-20; 17:8-13
19:7 [a]Ge 18:25; Dt 32:4 [b]Dt 10:17; Job 34:19; Ro 2:11; Col 3:25
19:8 [c]2Ch 17:8-9

[a] 23 Or *Spirit of* [b] 2 Or *and make alliances with*

19:7 The injunction against showing favoritism or accepting bribes was foundational to the Mosaic legal tradition (Dt 1:16–17; 16:19–20) and is still a basic tenet of justice today.

concerns of the law, commands, decrees or ordinances—you are to warn them not to sin against the
LORD;[d] otherwise his wrath will come on you and your brothers. Do this, and you will not sin. **19:10** [d]Dt 17:8-13
11 "Amariah the chief priest will be over you in any matter concerning the LORD, and Zebadiah son of
Ishmael, the leader of the tribe of Judah, will be over you in any matter concerning the king, and the Le-
vites will serve as officials before you. Act with courage,[e] and may the LORD be with those who do well." **19:11** [e]1Ch 28:20

Jehoshaphat Defeats Moab and Ammon

20 After this, the Moabites and Ammonites with some of the Meunites[a][f] came to make war on Je- **20:1** [f]1Ch 4:41
hoshaphat.
2 Some men came and told Jehoshaphat, "A vast army is coming against you from Edom,[b] from the oth-
er side of the Sea.[c] It is already in Hazazon Tamar[g]" (that is, En Gedi). 3 Alarmed, Jehoshaphat resolved **20:2** [g]Ge 14:7
to inquire of the LORD, and he proclaimed a fast[h] for all Judah. 4 The people of Judah came together to **20:3** [h]1Sa 7:6; 2Ch 19:3; Ezr 8:21; Jer 36:9; Jnh 3:5,7
seek help from the LORD; indeed, they came from every town in Judah to seek him.
5 Then Jehoshaphat stood up in the assembly of Judah and Jerusalem at the temple of the LORD in the
front of the new courtyard 6 and said:

"O LORD, God of our fathers,[i] are you not the God who is in heaven?[j] You rule over all the king- **20:6** [i]Mt 6:9 [j]Dt 4:39 [k]1Ch 29:11-12
doms[k] of the nations. Power and might are in your hand, and no one can withstand you. 7 O our
God, did you not drive out the inhabitants of this land before your people Israel and give it forev-
er to the descendants of Abraham your friend?[l] 8 They have lived in it and have built in it a sanc- **20:7** [l]Isa 41:8; Jas 2:23
tuary[m] for your Name, saying, 9 'If calamity comes upon us, whether the sword of judgment, or **20:8** [m]2Ch 6:20
plague or famine,[n] we will stand in your presence before this temple that bears your Name and **20:9** [n]2Ch 6:28
will cry out to you in our distress, and you will hear us and save us.'
10 "But now here are men from Ammon, Moab and Mount Seir, whose territory you would not
allow Israel to invade when they came from Egypt;[o] so they turned away from them and did not **20:10** [o]Nu 20:14-21; Dt 2:4-6,9, 18-19
destroy them. 11 See how they are repaying us by coming to drive us out of the possession[p] you
gave us as an inheritance. 12 O our God, will you not judge them?[q] For we have no power to face **20:11** [p]Ps 83:1-12
this vast army that is attacking us. We do not know what to do, but our eyes are upon you.[r]" **20:12** [q]Jdg 11:27 [r]Ps 25:15; 121:1-2

13 All the men of Judah, with their wives and children and little ones, stood there before the LORD.
14 Then the Spirit[s] of the LORD came upon Jahaziel son of Zechariah, the son of Benaiah, the son of Je- **20:14** [s]2Ch 15:1
iel, the son of Mattaniah, a Levite and descendant of Asaph, as he stood in the assembly.
15 He said: "Listen, King Jehoshaphat and all who live in Judah and Jerusalem! This is what the LORD
says to you: 'Do not be afraid or discouraged[t] because of this vast army. For the battle[u] is not yours, but **20:15** [t]2Ch 32:7 [u]Ex 14:13-14; 1Sa 17:47
God's. 16 Tomorrow march down against them. They will be climbing up by the Pass of Ziz, and you will
find them at the end of the gorge in the Desert of Jeruel. 17 You will not have to fight this battle. Take up
your positions; stand firm and see[v] the deliverance the LORD will give you, O Judah and Jerusalem. Do not **20:17** [v]Ex 14:13; 2Ch 15:2
be afraid; do not be discouraged. Go out to face them tomorrow, and the LORD will be with you.' "
18 Jehoshaphat bowed[w] with his face to the ground, and all the people of Judah and Jerusalem fell **20:18** [w]Ex 4:31
down in worship before the LORD. 19 Then some Levites from the Kohathites and Korahites stood up and
praised the LORD, the God of Israel, with a very loud voice.
20 Early in the morning they left for the Desert of Tekoa. As they set out, Jehoshaphat stood and said,
"Listen to me, Judah and people of Jerusalem! Have faith[x] in the LORD your God and you will be upheld; **20:20** [x]Isa 7:9 [y]Ge 39:3; Pr 16:3
have faith in his prophets and you will be successful.[y]" 21 After consulting the people, Jehoshaphat ap-
pointed men to sing to the LORD and to praise him for the splendor of his[d] holiness[z] as they went out at **20:21** [z]1Ch 16:29; Ps 29:2 [a]2Ch 5:13; Ps 136:1
the head of the army, saying:

"Give thanks to the LORD,
for his love endures forever."[a]

22 As they began to sing and praise, the LORD set ambushes[b] against the men of Ammon and Moab **20:22** [b]Jdg 7:22; 2Ch 13:13
and Mount Seir who were invading Judah, and they were defeated. 23 The men of Ammon[c] and Moab **20:23** [c]Ge 19:38

[a] *1* Some Septuagint manuscripts; Hebrew *Ammonites* [b] *2* One Hebrew manuscript; most Hebrew manuscripts, Septuagint and Vulgate *Aram* [c] *2* That is, the Dead Sea [d] *21* Or *him with the splendor of*

20:2 See "En Gedi" on page 643.

20:20 Tekoa, the town from which the shepherd-prophet Amos came, was located 10 miles (16 km) south of Jerusalem.

20:23 [d]2Ch 21:8 [e]Jdg 7:22; 1Sa 14:20; Eze 38:21

rose up against the men from Mount Seir[d] to destroy and annihilate them. After they finished slaughter-
ing the men from Seir, they helped to destroy one another.[e]
24 When the men of Judah came to the place that overlooks the desert and looked toward the vast
army, they saw only dead bodies lying on the ground; no one had escaped. 25 So Jehoshaphat and his men
went to carry off their plunder, and they found among them a great amount of equipment and clothing[a]
and also articles of value—more than they could take away. There was so much plunder that it took

[a] 25 Some Hebrew manuscripts and Vulgate; most Hebrew manuscripts *corpses*

ARCHAEOLOGICAL SITES

EN GEDI

2 CHRONICLES 20 En Gedi ("spring of the goats"; see "Map 4") is located on the western side of the Dead Sea. The site was inhabited as far back as the fourth millennium B.C., the period from which the remains of a temple have been discovered. A cave several miles south of En Gedi has yielded ivory carvings and other objects that were probably temple items hidden by the inhabitants before an Egyptian campaign in the area. To the north of the area, occupation levels dating from the seventh century B.C. to the fifth century A.D. have been uncovered. Today a kibbutz (Israeli communal farm or settlement) and nature park are located at En Gedi.

While under Israelite occupation the city belonged to the territory of Judah (Jos 15:62). David sought refuge from Saul at En Gedi (1Sa 23:29) and hid in a cave in close reach of the king. (Still today numerous caves pockmark the hillsides above the waterfall there.) In 2 Chronicles 20:2 the site is given the name Hazazon Tamar, which in Hebrew suggests a grove of palm trees, and Song of Songs 1:14 informs us that there were beautiful vineyards there. It was from this location that the Moabites, **Amorites** and Edomites attempted to invade Judah (2Ch 20), possibly because the terrain was so difficult that an attack from this direction would have been unexpected. Nevertheless Jehoshaphat was warned of their plan, and the Lord answered his prayer by turning the invading armies upon one another, so that the Judahite army found only dead bodies and plunder (vv. 5–26).

En Gedi was destroyed by **Nebuchadnezzar** in 582 B.C. in the aftermath of his destruction of Jerusalem.[1] When the Israelites returned from captivity they rebuilt the site, which was later occupied by the **Hasmoneans**. Herod the Great[2] destroyed this town and then rebuilt and fortified it, but this settlement too was destroyed during the Jewish War. In the nearby caves several letters were found that had been written by Bar Kokhba, leader of the Jewish uprising that was defeated in A.D. 135, indicating that Bar Kokhba and his men had used En Gedi as a hideout.

[1]See "Nebuchadnezzar" on page 571 and "The Last Days of Jerusalem" on page 1197. [2]See "Herod the Great" on page 1627.

En Gedi structure from the Chalcolithic Age
Photograph: © Todd Bolen/Bible Places.com

three days to collect it. 26 On the fourth day they assembled in the Valley of Beracah, where they praised the LORD. This is why it is called the Valley of Beracah[a] to this day.

27 Then, led by Jehoshaphat, all the men of Judah and Jerusalem returned joyfully to Jerusalem, for the LORD had given them cause to rejoice over their enemies. 28 They entered Jerusalem and went to the temple of the LORD with harps and lutes and trumpets.

29 The fear[f] of God came upon all the kingdoms of the countries when they heard how the LORD had fought[g] against the enemies of Israel. 30 And the kingdom of Jehoshaphat was at peace, for his God had given him rest[h] on every side.

The End of Jehoshaphat's Reign

31 So Jehoshaphat reigned over Judah. He was thirty-five years old when he became king of Judah, and he reigned in Jerusalem twenty-five years. His mother's name was Azubah daughter of Shilhi. 32 He walked in the ways of his father Asa and did not stray from them; he did what was right in the eyes of the LORD. 33 The high places,[i] however, were not removed, and the people still had not set their hearts on the God of their fathers.

34 The other events of Jehoshaphat's reign, from beginning to end, are written in the annals of Jehu[j] son of Hanani, which are recorded in the book of the kings of Israel.

35 Later, Jehoshaphat king of Judah made an alliance[k] with Ahaziah king of Israel, who was guilty of wickedness.[l] 36 He agreed with him to construct a fleet of trading ships.[b] After these were built at Ezion Geber, 37 Eliezer son of Dodavahu of Mareshah prophesied against Jehoshaphat, saying, "Because you have made an alliance with Ahaziah, the LORD will destroy what you have made." The ships[m] were wrecked and were not able to set sail to trade.[c]

21 Then Jehoshaphat rested with his fathers and was buried with them in the City of David. And Jehoram[n] his son succeeded him as king. 2 Jehoram's brothers, the sons of Jehoshaphat, were Azariah, Jehiel, Zechariah, Azariahu, Michael and Shephatiah. All these were sons of Jehoshaphat king of Israel.[d] 3 Their father had given them many gifts[o] of silver and gold and articles of value, as well as fortified cities[p] in Judah, but he had given the kingdom to Jehoram because he was his firstborn son.

Jehoram King of Judah

4 When Jehoram established[q] himself firmly over his father's kingdom, he put all his brothers[r] to the sword along with some of the princes of Israel. 5 Jehoram was thirty-two years old when he became king, and he reigned in Jerusalem eight years. 6 He walked in the ways of the kings of Israel,[s] as the house of Ahab had done, for he married a daughter of Ahab.[t] He did evil in the eyes of the LORD. 7 Nevertheless, because of the covenant the LORD had made with David,[u] the LORD was not willing to destroy the house of David.[v] He had promised to maintain a lamp[w] for him and his descendants forever.

8 In the time of Jehoram, Edom[x] rebelled against Judah and set up its own king. 9 So Jehoram went there with his officers and all his chariots. The Edomites surrounded him and his chariot commanders, but he rose up and broke through by night. 10 To this day Edom has been in rebellion against Judah.

Libnah[y] revolted at the same time, because Jehoram had forsaken the LORD, the God of his fathers. 11 He had also built high places on the hills of Judah and had caused the people of Jerusalem to prostitute themselves and had led Judah astray.

12 Jehoram received a letter from Elijah[z] the prophet, which said:

"This is what the LORD, the God of your father[a] David, says: 'You have not walked in the ways of your father Jehoshaphat or of Asa[b] king of Judah. 13 But you have walked in the ways of the kings of

20:29 [f]Ge 35:5; Dt 2:25; 2Ch 14:14; 17:10 [g]Ex 14:14
20:30 [h]1Ch 22:9; 2Ch 14:6-7; 15:15
20:33 [i]2Ch 17:6; 19:3
20:34 [j]1Ki 16:1
20:35 [k]2Ch 16:3 [l]2Ch 19:1-3
20:37 [m]1Ki 9:26; 2Ch 9:21
21:1 [n]1Ch 3:11
21:3 [o]2Ch 11:23 [p]2Ch 11:10
21:4 [q]1Ki 2:12 [r]Jdg 9:5
21:6 [s]1Ki 12:28-30 [t]2Ch 18:1; 22:3
21:7 [u]2Sa 7:13 [v]2Sa 7:15; 2Ch 23:3 [w]2Sa 21:17; 1Ki 11:36
21:8 [x]2Ch 20:22-23
21:10 [y]Nu 33:20
21:12 [z]2Ki 1:16-17 [a]2Ch 17:3-6 [b]2Ch 14:2

[a] *26 Beracah* means *praise.* [b] *36* Hebrew *of ships that could go to Tarshish* [c] *37* Hebrew *sail for Tarshish* [d] *2* That is, Judah, as frequently in 2 Chronicles

20:33 See "The High Places" on page 1318.
20:35 Ahaziah, the son of Ahab and Jezebel, was the eighth king of Israel. He reigned from 851–850 B.C. and worshiped both Jeroboam's calves (see "The High Place at Dan" on p. 504) and his mother's idols, Baal and Ashtoreth (see "Baal and the Fertility Cults" on p. 1414). The most notable event of his reign was the revolt of the Moabites, who had been paying tribute (2Ki 1:1; 3:4–5; see "The Mesha (Moabite) Stone" on p. 530). Ahaziah was unable to put down the revolt because he was severely injured in a fall and died shortly thereafter. The Moabite rebellion continued against his brother and successor, Joram. An apparent discrepancy in the accounts concerns Ahaziah's dealings with Jehoshaphat of Judah. Second Chronicles 20:35–37 asserts that Ahaziah and Jehoshaphat of Judah collaborated in building ships at Ezion Geber (see "Ezion Geber" on p. 631) but that these were destroyed after Eliezer, son of Dodavahu, condemned the alliance with Ahaziah as displeasing to God. According to 1 Kings 22:48–49, however, Jehoshaphat built ships at Ezion Geber but refused to allow men from Ahaziah to sail with them; 1 Kings mentions that the ships were wrecked but does not allude to a partnership with Ahaziah or to this prophecy. It may be that the two kings collaborated in the shipbuilding effort but that Jehoshaphat, alarmed by Eliezer's prophecy, terminated the agreement with Ahaziah.

Israel, and you have led Judah and the people of Jerusalem to prostitute themselves, just as the
21:13 [c]ver 6,11; 1Ki 16:29-33 house of Ahab did.[c] You have also murdered your own brothers, members of your father's house,
[d]ver 4; 1Ki 2:32 men who were better[d] than you. 14 So now the LORD is about to strike your people, your sons, your
wives and everything that is yours, with a heavy blow. 15 You yourself will be very ill with a linger-
21:15 [e]ver 18-19; Nu 12:10 ing disease[e] of the bowels, until the disease causes your bowels to come out.' "
21:16 [f]2Ch 17:10-11; 22:1; 26:7 16 The LORD aroused against Jehoram the hostility of the Philistines and of the Arabs[f] who lived near
the Cushites. 17 They attacked Judah, invaded it and carried off all the goods found in the king's palace,
21:17 [g]2Ki 12:18; 2Ch 22:1; 25:23; Joel 3:5 together with his sons and wives. Not a son was left to him except Ahaziah,[a] the youngest.[g]
18 After all this, the LORD afflicted Jehoram with an incurable disease of the bowels. 19 In the course of
time, at the end of the second year, his bowels came out because of the disease, and he died in great pain.
21:19 [h]2Ch 16:14 His people made no fire in his honor,[h] as they had for his fathers.
20 Jehoram was thirty-two years old when he became king, and he reigned in Jerusalem eight years.
21:20 [i]2Ch 24:25; 28:27; 33:20; Jer 22:18,28 He passed away, to no one's regret, and was buried[i] in the City of David, but not in the tombs of the kings.

Ahaziah King of Judah

22:1 [j]2Ch 33:25; 36:1 [k]2Ch 23:20-21; 26:1 [l]2Ch 21:16-17 **22** The people[j] of Jerusalem[k] made Ahaziah, Jehoram's youngest son, king in his place, since the
raiders,[l] who came with the Arabs into the camp, had killed all the older sons. So Ahaziah son
of Jehoram king of Judah began to reign.
2 Ahaziah was twenty-two[b] years old when he became king, and he reigned in Jerusalem one year. His
mother's name was Athaliah, a granddaughter of Omri.
22:3 [m]2Ch 18:1 [n]2Ch 21:6 3 He too walked[m] in the ways of the house of Ahab,[n] for his mother encouraged him in doing wrong.
4 He did evil in the eyes of the LORD, as the house of Ahab had done, for after his father's death they be-
came his advisers, to his undoing. 5 He also followed their counsel when he went with Joram[c] son of Ahab
22:5 [o]2Ch 18:11, 34 king of Israel to war against Hazael king of Aram at Ramoth Gilead.[o] The Arameans wounded Joram; 6 so
he returned to Jezreel to recover from the wounds they had inflicted on him at Ramoth[d] in his battle with
22:6 [p]1Ki 19:15; 2Ki 8:13-15; 9:15 Hazael[p] king of Aram.
Then Ahaziah[e] son of Jehoram king of Judah went down to Jezreel to see Joram son of Ahab because
he had been wounded.
22:7 [q]2Ki 9:16; 2Ch 10:15 7 Through Ahaziah's[q] visit to Joram, God brought about Ahaziah's downfall. When Ahaziah arrived,
he went out with Joram to meet Jehu son of Nimshi, whom the LORD had anointed to destroy the house
22:8 [r]2Ki 10:13 of Ahab. 8 While Jehu was executing judgment on the house of Ahab,[r] he found the princes of Judah and
the sons of Ahaziah's relatives, who had been attending Ahaziah, and he killed them. 9 He then went in
22:9 [s]Jdg 9:5 [t]2Ch 17:4 search of Ahaziah, and his men captured him while he was hiding[s] in Samaria. He was brought to Jehu
and put to death. They buried him, for they said, "He was a son of Jehoshaphat, who sought[t] the LORD
with all his heart." So there was no one in the house of Ahaziah powerful enough to retain the kingdom.

[a] 17 Hebrew *Jehoahaz,* a variant of *Ahaziah* [b] 2 Some Septuagint manuscripts and Syriac (see also 2 Kings 8:26); Hebrew *forty-two* [c] 5 Hebrew *Jehoram,* a variant of *Joram;* also in verses 6 and 7 [d] 6 Hebrew *Ramah,* a variant of *Ramoth* [e] 6 Some Hebrew manuscripts, Septuagint, Vulgate and Syriac (see also 2 Kings 8:29); most Hebrew manuscripts *Azariah*

21:20 Only the Chronicler mentioned the refusal of the people to accord Jehoram the customary burial honors of a tomb with the other kings of Judah. Other kings not buried there include Joash (24:25), Uzziah (26:23), Ahaz (28:27) and Manasseh (33:20). (See also "Tombs in Ancient Israel" on p. 376.)

22:2 Ahaziah of Judah reigned for only one year (c. 841 B.C.). In some Bible versions (not the NIV), his name appears as Jehoahaz in 21:17 and 25:23 and as Azariah in 22:6. According to 2 Kings 8:26, Ahaziah was twenty-two years old when he began to reign. However, in some versions (again, not the NIV), 2 Chronicles 22:2 states that he was forty-two years of age when he ascended the throne. The latter may be a scribal error (see "Textual Criticism" on p. 1151), but it may alternatively indicate a coregency. Following the way of his mother, Athaliah, Ahaziah supported Canaanite idolatry (v. 3). He allied himself with Joram of Israel against Hazael of Syria, going into battle at Ramoth Gilead (v. 5). Joram was wounded, and Ahaziah went to see him at Jezreel, where Jehu assassinated Joram. Ahaziah fled but was wounded and died at Megiddo (2Ki 9:27). The Chronicler, however, indicated that Jehu found Ahaziah hiding in Samaria and killed him there (2Ch 22:6–9). Various attempts to harmonize these two accounts are not persuasive. It may be that the Chronicler here used "Samaria" to refer to the larger region, including Megiddo, and not to Samaria proper. If so, no harmonization is required.

22:5 Joram of Israel (c. 853–840 B.C.) succeeded his brother Ahaziah as king of Israel and continued the war against Mesha of Moab (2Ki 3:4). Joram asked Jehoshaphat of Judah to assist him in the war (2Ki 3:7), but while Israel and Judah, with the help of Edom, where going against Mesha, their armies ran out of water and were in despair. Elisha, in deference to Jehoshaphat (2Ki 3:14–16), instructed the kings to dig ditches. Water appeared, and the Moabites, seeing the reflection of the rising sun in the water, took it for blood and hastened to the prey, only to be badly defeated. Joram met his end, with all of his family, at the hand of Jehu (2Ki 9).

22:7 Jehu was a commander in the Israelite army who accepted a charge from Elijah to seize the throne and eliminate Baal worship from Israel (2Ki 9:1–10). Apparently there was widespread discontent with Joram's rule, since Israelite troops readily took Jehu's side (2Ki 9:11–20). At Jezreel he killed Joram (2Ki 9:21–29) and then went on to consolidate his power by killing Jezebel, the entire family of Joram, the ministers of Baal and 42 relatives of Ahaziah of Judah (2Ki 9:30—10:28). No supporter of Joram or of the house of Omri, whether in the family of Joram, among his religious supporters from Phoenicia or among his allies in Judah, was left to oppose Jehu. Now bereft of allies, however, Jehu submitted to Assyria. He paid tribute to Shalmaneser III, as is recorded in the Black Obelisk from Nimrud (see "Jehu/The Black Obelisk of Shalmaneser III" on p. 544). Jehu reigned from approximately 841 to 814 B.C.

Athaliah and Joash

[10]When Athaliah the mother of Ahaziah saw that her son was dead, she proceeded to destroy the whole
royal family of the house of Judah. [11]But Jehosheba,[a] the daughter of King Jehoram, took Joash son of
Ahaziah and stole him away from among the royal princes who were about to be murdered and put him
and his nurse in a bedroom. Because Jehosheba,[a] the daughter of King Jehoram and wife of the priest Je-
hoiada, was Ahaziah's sister, she hid the child from Athaliah so she could not kill him. [12]He remained
hidden with them at the temple of God for six years while Athaliah ruled the land.

23 In the seventh year Jehoiada showed his strength. He made a covenant with the commanders of
units of a hundred: Azariah son of Jeroham, Ishmael son of Jehohanan, Azariah son of Obed,
Maaseiah son of Adaiah, and Elishaphat son of Zicri. [2]They went throughout Judah and gathered the Le-
vites[u] and the heads of Israelite families from all the towns. When they came to Jerusalem, [3]the whole
assembly made a covenant[v] with the king at the temple of God.

Jehoiada said to them, "The king's son shall reign, as the LORD promised concerning the descendants
of David.[w] [4]Now this is what you are to do: A third of you priests and Levites who are going on duty on
the Sabbath are to keep watch at the doors, [5]a third of you at the royal palace and a third at the Founda-
tion Gate, and all the other men are to be in the courtyards of the temple of the LORD. [6]No one is to en-
ter the temple of the LORD except the priests and Levites on duty; they may enter because they are con-
secrated, but all the other men are to guard[x] what the LORD has assigned to them.[b] [7]The Levites are to
station themselves around the king, each man with his weapons in his hand. Anyone who enters the tem-
ple must be put to death. Stay close to the king wherever he goes."

[8]The Levites and all the men of Judah did just as Jehoiada the priest ordered.[y] Each one took his
men—those who were going on duty on the Sabbath and those who were going off duty—for Jehoiada
the priest had not released any of the divisions.[z] [9]Then he gave the commanders of units of a hundred
the spears and the large and small shields that had belonged to King David and that were in the temple
of God. [10]He stationed all the men, each with his weapon in his hand, around the king—near the altar
and the temple, from the south side to the north side of the temple.

[11]Jehoiada and his sons brought out the king's son and put the crown on him; they presented him
with a copy[a] of the covenant and proclaimed him king. They anointed him and shouted, "Long live the
king!"

[12]When Athaliah heard the noise of the people running and cheering the king, she went to them at the
temple of the LORD. [13]She looked, and there was the king,[b] standing by his pillar[c] at the entrance. The of-
ficers and the trumpeters were beside the king, and all the people of the land were rejoicing and blow-
ing trumpets, and singers with musical instruments were leading the praises. Then Athaliah tore her
robes and shouted, "Treason! Treason!"

[14]Jehoiada the priest sent out the commanders of units of a hundred, who were in charge of the troops,
and said to them: "Bring her out between the ranks[c] and put to the sword anyone who follows her." For
the priest had said, "Do not put her to death at the temple of the LORD." [15]So they seized her as she reached
the entrance of the Horse Gate[d] on the palace grounds, and there they put her to death.

[16]Jehoiada then made a covenant[e] that he and the people and the king[d] would be the LORD's people.
[17]All the people went to the temple of Baal and tore it down. They smashed the altars and idols and killed[f]
Mattan the priest of Baal in front of the altars.

[18]Then Jehoiada placed the oversight of the temple of the LORD in the hands of the priests, who were
Levites,[g] to whom David had made assignments in the temple,[h] to present the burnt offerings of the LORD
as written in the Law of Moses, with rejoicing and singing, as David had ordered. [19]He also stationed door-
keepers[i] at the gates of the LORD's temple so that no one who was in any way unclean might enter.

[20]He took with him the commanders of hundreds, the nobles, the rulers of the people and all the peo-
ple of the land and brought the king down from the temple of the LORD. They went into the palace through

23:2 [u]Nu 35:2-5
23:3 [v]2Ki 11:17 [w]2Sa 7:12; 1Ki 2:4; 2Ch 6:16; 7:18; 21:7
23:6 [x]1Ch 23:28-29; Zec 3:7
23:8 [y]2Ki 11:9 [z]1Ch 24:1
23:11 [a]Ex 25:16; Dt 17:18; 1Sa 10:24
23:13 [b]1Ki 1:41 [c]1Ki 7:15
23:15 [d]Ne 3:28; Jer 31:40
23:16 [e]2Ch 29:10; 34:31; Ne 9:38
23:17 [f]Dt 13:6-9
23:18 [g]1Ch 23:28-32; 2Ch 5:5 [h]1Ch 23:6; 25:6
23:19 [i]1Ch 9:22

[a] *11* Hebrew *Jehoshabeath,* a variant of *Jehosheba* [b] *6* Or *to observe the LORD's command ⌞not to enter⌟* [c] *14* Or *out from the precincts* [d] *16* Or *covenant between ⌞the LORD⌟ and the people and the king that they* (see 2 Kings 11:17)

22:10 New dynasties routinely annihilated the families of the old order in an attempt to solidify a power base (see "Ambitious Princes Among the Hittites" on p. 469).

22:12 Athaliah was the only woman who reigned over Judah (2Ki 8:18,25–28; 11:1–20; 2Ch 22:1—23:21; 24:7). Jehoram of Judah, her husband, preceded her in death. After Jehu killed her son Ahaziah, Athaliah herself reigned for six years. She ruthlessly put to death all of Ahaziah's sons except Joash, who was hidden by Jehosheba, sister of Ahaziah and wife of Jehoiada the priest. In Joash's seventh year Jehoiada conspired to put Joash on the throne. Athaliah apparently had no support in the court or among the people and was quickly put to death.

23:20 [j]2Ki 15:35 the Upper Gate[j] and seated the king on the royal throne, 21 and all the people of the land rejoiced. And the
23:21 [k]2Ch 22:1 city was quiet, because Athaliah had been slain with the sword.[k]

Joash Repairs the Temple

24 Joash was seven years old when he became king, and he reigned in Jerusalem forty years. His
mother's name was Zibiah; she was from Beersheba. 2 Joash did what was right in the eyes of the
24:2 [l]2Ch 25:2; LORD[l] all the years of Jehoiada the priest. 3 Jehoiada chose two wives for him, and he had sons and
26:5 daughters.
4 Some time later Joash decided to restore the temple of the LORD. 5 He called together the priests and
24:5 [m]Ex 30:16; Levites and said to them, "Go to the towns of Judah and collect the money[m] due annually from all Isra-
Ne 10:32-33; Mt 17:24 el,[n] to repair the temple of your God. Do it now." But the Levites[o] did not act at once.
[n]1Ch 11:1 [o]1Ch 26:20 6 Therefore the king summoned Jehoiada the chief priest and said to him, "Why haven't you required
the Levites to bring in from Judah and Jerusalem the tax imposed by Moses the servant of the LORD and
24:6 [p]Ex 30:12- by the assembly of Israel for the Tent of the Testimony?"[p]
16; Nu 1:50 7 Now the sons of that wicked woman Athaliah had broken into the temple of God and had used even
its sacred objects for the Baals.
8 At the king's command, a chest was made and placed outside, at the gate of the temple of the LORD.
9 A proclamation was then issued in Judah and Jerusalem that they should bring to the LORD the tax that
Moses the servant of God had required of Israel in the desert. 10 All the officials and all the people brought
24:10 [q]Ex 25:2; their contributions gladly,[q] dropping them into the chest until it was full. 11 Whenever the chest was
1Ch 29:3,6,9 brought in by the Levites to the king's officials and they saw that there was a large amount of money, the
royal secretary and the officer of the chief priest would come and empty the chest and carry it back to
its place. They did this regularly and collected a great amount of money. 12 The king and Jehoiada gave it
24:12 [r]2Ch 34:11 to the men who carried out the work required for the temple of the LORD. They hired[r] masons and car-
penters to restore the LORD's temple, and also workers in iron and bronze to repair the temple.
13 The men in charge of the work were diligent, and the repairs progressed under them. They rebuilt
the temple of God according to its original design and reinforced it. 14 When they had finished, they
brought the rest of the money to the king and Jehoiada, and with it were made articles for the LORD's tem-
ple: articles for the service and for the burnt offerings, and also dishes and other objects of gold and sil-
ver. As long as Jehoiada lived, burnt offerings were presented continually in the temple of the LORD.
15 Now Jehoiada was old and full of years, and he died at the age of a hundred and thirty. 16 He was
24:18 [s]ver 4; buried with the kings in the City of David, because of the good he had done in Israel for God and his
Jos 24:20; 2Ch 7:19 [t]Ex 34:13; temple.

1Ki 14:23; 2Ch 33:3;

The Wickedness of Joash

Jer 17:2 [u]Jos 22:20; 17 After the death of Jehoiada, the officials of Judah came and paid homage to the king, and he lis-
2Ch 19:2 **24:19** [v]Nu 11:29; tened to them. 18 They abandoned[s] the temple of the LORD, the God of their fathers, and worshiped Ashe-
Jer 7:25; Zec 1:4 **24:20** [w]Jdg 3:10; rah poles and idols.[t] Because of their guilt, God's anger[u] came upon Judah and Jerusalem. 19 Although the
1Ch 12:18; 2Ch 20:14 LORD sent prophets to the people to bring them back to him, and though they testified against them, they
[x]Mt 23:35; would not listen.[v]
Lk 11:51 [y]Nu 14:41 20 Then the Spirit[w] of God came upon Zechariah[x] son of Jehoiada the priest. He stood before the peo-
[z]Dt 31:17; 2Ch 15:2 ple and said, "This is what God says: 'Why do you disobey the LORD's commands? You will not prosper.[y]
24:21 [a]Jos 7:25; Ac 7:58-59 Because you have forsaken the LORD, he has forsaken[z] you.' "
[b]Ne 9:26; Jer 26:21 21 But they plotted against him, and by order of the king they stoned[a] him to death[b] in the courtyard
[c]Jer 20:2; Mt 23:35 of the LORD's temple.[c] 22 King Joash did not remember the kindness Zechariah's father Jehoiada had
24:22 [d]Ge 9:5 shown him but killed his son, who said as he lay dying, "May the LORD see this and call you to account."[d]

24:8 Offering boxes were common in Near Eastern temples. The temple revenues were administered by representatives of both the king and the temple officials (vv. 11–12).

24:21 Joash had Zechariah, the son of Jehoiada, killed in the courtyard of the temple. It is surprising that Chronicles mentions this sin of Joash, while the Kings account does not. Chronicles usually gives positive accounts of the Davidic kings, as over against the parallel accounts in 1–2 Kings. Another question pertaining to this text relates to Matthew 23:35, which speaks of "the blood of Zechariah son of Berekiah, whom you murdered between the temple and the altar." Zechariah, son of Berekiah, was the prophet and author of the book of Zechariah, and there is no Old Testament indication that he was martyred. The Lukan parallel (Lk 11:51) leaves out "son of Berekiah" and appears to have Zechariah, the son of Jehoiada, in mind. Some attribute this to a textual error in Matthew (see "Textual Criticism" on p. 1151), while others assert that Zechariah, the son of Berekiah, must actually have been martyred in the temple court, just as Zechariah, the son of Jehoiada, was, even though the Old Testament does not mention this incident.

The Levites and the Priests

2 CHRONICLES 24 The descendants of Simeon and Levi appear to have lost their right to a separate inheritance because of their treachery at Shechem (Ge 34:30; 49:5–7; see "Map 1").[1] The Simeonites, absorbed into Judah, all but disappeared from history, but Levi emerged as the priestly tribe. The Levites did not receive an allotment of the promised land but were said to have the Lord as their inheritance (Dt 18:1–2).

The elevation of Levi to the status of priestly tribe is often explained by the golden calf incident. God had claimed all of Israel's firstborn to serve as priests (Ex 12:29–30). But in the aftermath of the golden calf episode[2] the Levites' faithfulness and zeal for the purity of the priesthood led to their divine election to service in place of Israel's firstborn (Ex 32:26–29; Nu 3:11–13,41).

Yet 1 Samuel 2:27–28 indicates that the Levites had functioned in a priestly role already in Egypt. This premise appears to be supported by other texts:

- In Exodus 4:14 Aaron is called "the Levite"—a more official designation than the more typical "son of Levi."
- Exodus 28–29 describes the priestly vestments and the consecration of Aaron and his sons with no explanation as to why they were to hold this office, suggesting that everyone already knew Aaron as priest.
- At the beginning of the golden calf episode (Ex 32:1–3) the people turned to Aaron to perform a priestly act—the creation and consecration of an image.
- In the rebellion against the authority of Moses and Aaron led by Korah (a Levite), Dathan and Abiram, both sides acknowledged that the sanctuary prerogatives belonged to the Levites (Nu 16–17).

Incense shovels
Preserving Bible Times; © Dr. James C. Martin; permission of The Israel Museum/Shrine of the Book

The Bible distinguishes between priests and Levites in terms of function. The duties of the Levites were theoretically apportioned according to the descendants of Levi's three sons (Nu 3:15–17):

- The Gershonites were entrusted with the tabernacle curtains, coverings and cords (Nu 3:21–26).
- The Kohathites were to care for the sanctuary vessels, including the ark, table, lampstand and altars once they had been prepared by the priests (Nu 3:27–32).
- The Merarites were responsible for the outer structures of the tabernacle enclosure (Nu 3:33–37).

The Levites in general, then, were commissioned with the care, transportation and protection of the sanctuary. They were specifically commanded to encamp around the tabernacle, guarding it from ritual pollution and defending it from those who might have approached the sacred precinct while ritually unclean (Nu 1:50–53).[3]

The duties of the priestly descendants of Aaron consisted of the actual performance of the temple liturgy:

- Only Aaron's sons could minister at the altar of the Lord, offering incense and sacrifices there (Dt 33:10).[4]
- The priests represented Israel before the Lord (Lev 1:1–9) and were alone empowered to bless the people (Nu 6:23–27).[5]
- Priests accompanied the people during war, sounding trumpets and bearing sacred vessels (Nu 10:9; 31:6).[6]
- Priests were entrusted with teaching and interpreting the laws given by Moses (Lev 10:11; cf. Mal 2:7).
- A further distinction of holiness was made with regard to the high priest. He alone could enter the Most Holy Place to make atonement for the nation once each year, symbolically bearing the sins of Israel (Lev 16).[7]

Deuteronomy, in using the term "the priests, who are Levites" (lit., "the priests, the Levites," e.g., Dt 17:9,18), appears to regard all Levites as priests. In contrast, in much of Exodus–Numbers only Aaronites are referred to as priests, with other Levites viewed as minor clergy. The most plausible solution is that Exodus–Numbers are primarily concerned with the central sanctuary. By contrast, Deuteronomy envisioned the dispersal of the Levites to shrines scattered across Israel, where all would serve as priests. Only when the Levites came to the central shrine did they serve in a subordinate role.[8]

[1]See "Shechem" on page 340. [2]See "The Golden Calf" on page 143. [3]See "The Tabernacle and the Ark" on page 153 and "Ritual Purity in Israel and the Ancient Near East" on page 166. [4]See "Sacrifices and Offerings in the Bible and the Ancient Near East" on page 158. [5]See "The Ketef Hinnom Amulets" on page 204. [6]See "The Shofar" on page 898 and "Trumpets in the Ancient World" on page 2057. [7]See "The Day of Atonement" on page 176. [8]See "Israelite Shrines and Worship Before the Temple of Solomon" on page 398.

23 At the turn of the year,[a] the army of Aram marched against Joash; it invaded Judah and Jerusalem
24:23 [e]2Ki 12:17-18 and killed all the leaders of the people.[e] They sent all the plunder to their king in Damascus. 24 Although
24:24 [f]2Ch 14:9; 16:8; 20:2,12 [g]Lev 26:23-25; Dt 28:25 the Aramean army had come with only a few men,[f] the LORD delivered into their hands a much larger
army.[g] Because Judah had forsaken the LORD, the God of their fathers, judgment was executed on Joash.
25 When the Arameans withdrew, they left Joash severely wounded. His officials conspired against him for
24:25 [h]2Ch 21:20 murdering the son of Jehoiada the priest, and they killed him in his bed. So he died and was buried[h] in
the City of David, but not in the tombs of the kings.

26 Those who conspired against him were Zabad,[b] son of Shimeath an Ammonite woman, and Jehoz-
24:26 [i]2Ki 12:21 [j]Ru 1:4 abad, son of Shimrith[c][i] a Moabite woman.[j] 27 The account of his sons, the many prophecies about him,
and the record of the restoration of the temple of God are written in the annotations on the book of the
kings. And Amaziah his son succeeded him as king.

Amaziah King of Judah

25 Amaziah was twenty-five years old when he became king, and he reigned in Jerusalem twenty-
nine years. His mother's name was Jehoaddin[d]; she was from Jerusalem. 2 He did what was right
25:2 [k]ver 14; 1Ki 8:61; 2Ch 24:2 in the eyes of the LORD, but not wholeheartedly.[k] 3 After the kingdom was firmly in his control, he execut-
ed the officials who had murdered his father the king. 4 Yet he did not put their sons to death, but acted
25:4 [l]Dt 28:61 [m]Nu 26:11; Dt 24:16 in accordance with what is written in the Law, in the Book of Moses,[l] where the LORD commanded: "Fa-
thers shall not be put to death for their children, nor children put to death for their fathers; each is to die
for his own sins."[e][m]

5 Amaziah called the people of Judah together and assigned them according to their families to com-
25:5 [n]2Sa 24:2 [o]Ex 30:14 [p]Nu 1:3; 1Ch 21:1; 2Ch 17:14-19 manders of thousands and commanders of hundreds for all Judah and Benjamin. He then mustered[n]
those twenty years old[o] or more and found that there were three hundred thousand men ready for mil-
itary service,[p] able to handle the spear and shield. 6 He also hired a hundred thousand fighting men from
Israel for a hundred talents[f] of silver.

25:7 [q]2Ch 16:2-9; 19:1-3 7 But a man of God came to him and said, "O king, these troops from Israel[q] must not march with you,
for the LORD is not with Israel—not with any of the people of Ephraim. 8 Even if you go and fight coura-
geously in battle, God will overthrow you before the enemy, for God has the power to help or to over-
25:8 [r]2Ch 14:11; 20:6 throw."[r]

9 Amaziah asked the man of God, "But what about the hundred talents I paid for these Israelite
troops?"

25:9 [s]Dt 8:18; Pr 10:22 The man of God replied, "The LORD can give you much more than that."[s]

10 So Amaziah dismissed the troops who had come to him from Ephraim and sent them home. They
25:10 [t]ver 13 were furious with Judah and left for home in a great rage.[t]

11 Amaziah then marshaled his strength and led his army to the Valley of Salt, where he killed ten
thousand men of Seir. 12 The army of Judah also captured ten thousand men alive, took them to the top
25:12 [u]Ps 141:6; Ob 1:3 of a cliff and threw them down so that all were dashed to pieces.[u]

13 Meanwhile the troops that Amaziah had sent back and had not allowed to take part in the war raid-
ed Judean towns from Samaria to Beth Horon. They killed three thousand people and carried off great
quantities of plunder.

14 When Amaziah returned from slaughtering the Edomites, he brought back the gods of the people
25:14 [v]Ex 20:3; 2Ch 28:23; Isa 44:15 of Seir. He set them up as his own gods,[v] bowed down to them and burned sacrifices to them. 15 The an-
ger of the LORD burned against Amaziah, and he sent a prophet to him, who said, "Why do you consult
25:15 [w]Ps 96:5; Isa 36:20 this people's gods, which could not save[w] their own people from your hand?"

16 While he was still speaking, the king said to him, "Have we appointed you an adviser to the king?
Stop! Why be struck down?"

So the prophet stopped but said, "I know that God has determined to destroy you, because you have
done this and have not listened to my counsel."

17 After Amaziah king of Judah consulted his advisers, he sent this challenge to Jehoash[g] son of Jeho-
ahaz, the son of Jehu, king of Israel: "Come, meet me face to face."

25:18 [x]Jdg 9:8-15 18 But Jehoash king of Israel replied to Amaziah king of Judah: "A thistle[x] in Lebanon sent a message
to a cedar in Lebanon, 'Give your daughter to my son in marriage.' Then a wild beast in Lebanon came

[a] 23 Probably in the spring [b] 26 A variant of *Jozabad* [c] 26 A variant of *Shomer* [d] 1 Hebrew *Jehoaddan,* a variant of *Jehoaddin* [e] 4 Deut. 24:16 [f] 6 That is, about 3 3/4 tons (about 3.4 metric tons); also in verse 9 [g] 17 Hebrew *Joash,* a variant of *Jehoash*; also in verses 18, 21, 23 and 25

along and trampled the thistle underfoot. 19 You say to yourself that you have defeated Edom, and now
you are arrogant and proud. But stay at home! Why ask for trouble and cause your own downfall and
that of Judah also?"

20 Amaziah, however, would not listen, for God so worked that he might hand them over to ⌊Jehoash⌋,
because they sought the gods of Edom.[y] 21 So Jehoash king of Israel attacked. He and Amaziah king of Ju- 25:20 [y]1Ki 12:15; 2Ch 10:15; 22:7
dah faced each other at Beth Shemesh in Judah. 22 Judah was routed by Israel, and every man fled to his
home. 23 Jehoash king of Israel captured Amaziah king of Judah, the son of Joash, the son of Ahaziah,[a] at
Beth Shemesh. Then Jehoash brought him to Jerusalem and broke down the wall of Jerusalem from the
Ephraim Gate[z] to the Corner Gate[a]—a section about six hundred feet[b] long. 24 He took all the gold and 25:23 [z]2Ki 14:13; Ne 8:16; 12:39 [a]2Ch 26:9; Jer 31:38
silver and all the articles found in the temple of God that had been in the care of Obed-Edom,[b] togeth-
er with the palace treasures and the hostages, and returned to Samaria. 25:24 [b]1Ch 26:15

25 Amaziah son of Joash king of Judah lived for fifteen years after the death of Jehoash son of Jehoa-
haz king of Israel. 26 As for the other events of Amaziah's reign, from beginning to end, are they not writ-
ten in the book of the kings of Judah and Israel? 27 From the time that Amaziah turned away from follow-
ing the LORD, they conspired against him in Jerusalem and he fled to Lachish[c], but they sent men after 25:27 [c]Jos 10:3
him to Lachish and killed him there. 28 He was brought back by horse and was buried with his fathers in
the City of Judah.

Uzziah King of Judah

26 Then all the people of Judah[d] took Uzziah,[c] who was sixteen years old, and made him king in 26:1 [d]2Ch 22:1
place of his father Amaziah. 2 He was the one who rebuilt Elath and restored it to Judah after Am-
aziah rested with his fathers.

[a] 23 Hebrew *Jehoahaz,* a variant of *Ahaziah* [b] 23 Hebrew *four hundred cubits* (about 180 meters) [c] 1 Also called *Azariah*

25:21 See "Beth Shemesh" on page 405.
26:1 Uzziah (Azariah) of Judah (r. 792–740 B.C.) came to the throne at a difficult time. His father, Amaziah, was a military failure and had been assassinated (2Ki 14:19); Uzziah in fact probably served as Amaziah's coregent for some years. After Amaziah's death Uzziah promptly undertook an expedition against his father's enemies; was victorious in battles against the Edomites, Philistines, Arabians and Meunites (2Ki 14:22; 2Ch 26:1–7); and soon gained the

Uzziah, King of Judah, and Jeroboam II, King of Israel

2 CHRONICLES 26 Uzziah, called Azariah in 2 Kings 14:21 and 15:1–7, ruled Judah for 52 years, from approximately 792 to 740 B.C.[1] He "did what was right in the eyes of the LORD" (2Ki 15:3), and God blessed him both militarily and economically. Uzziah's name appears on two seals of unknown origin and in a later inscription. The seals read, respectively, "Belonging to Abiah Servant of Uzziah" and "Belonging to Shebaniah Servant of Uzziah." The inscription, also of unknown origin, states, "Hither were brought the bones of Uzziah king of Judah—do not open!"

Jeroboam II was a contemporary of Uzziah, ruling the northern kingdom for some 41 years, from around 793 to 753 B.C.[2] His career is summarized in just seven verses in 2 Kings 14:23–29. There is only one known reference to Jeroboam II outside the Bible—the famous "Shema Seal," found in excavations at **Megiddo**[3] (see "Map 6") in 1904. It was sent to the Turkish Sultan in Istanbul and unfortunately lost. Before it was sent, however, a bronze cast was made. Now on display at the Rockefeller Museum in Jerusalem, it depicts a roaring lion along with the owner's name, "Belonging to Shema," and title, "Servant of Jeroboam." The style of the lettering dates the seal to the early eighth century B.C. This is the earliest of a number of seals and seal impressions bearing the names of Biblical figures.

[1]See "The History of the Southern Kingdom" on page 538. [2]See "The History of the Northern Kingdom" on page 506. [3]See "Megiddo" on page 1541.

3Uzziah was sixteen years old when he became king, and he
reigned in Jerusalem fifty-two years. His mother's name was Jecoli-
ah; she was from Jerusalem. 4He did what was right in the eyes of
the LORD, just as his father Amaziah had done. 5He sought God dur-
ing the days of Zechariah, who instructed him in the fear[a] of God.[e]
As long as he sought the LORD, God gave him success.[f]
6He went to war against the Philistines[g] and broke down the
walls of Gath, Jabneh and Ashdod.[h] He then rebuilt towns near Ash-
dod and elsewhere among the Philistines. 7God helped him against
the Philistines and against the Arabs[i] who lived in Gur Baal and
against the Meunites.[j] 8The Ammonites[k] brought tribute to Uzziah,
and his fame spread as far as the border of Egypt, because he had
become very powerful.
9Uzziah built towers in Jerusalem at the Corner Gate,[l] at the Val-
ley Gate[m] and at the angle of the wall, and he fortified them. 10He
also built towers in the desert and dug many cisterns, because he
had much livestock in the foothills and in the plain. He had people
working his fields and vineyards in the hills and in the fertile lands,
for he loved the soil.
11Uzziah had a well-trained army, ready to go out by divisions ac-
cording to their numbers as mustered by Jeiel the secretary and Ma-
aseiah the officer under the direction of Hananiah, one of the royal
officials. 12The total number of family leaders over the fighting men
was 2,600. 13Under their command was an army of 307,500 men
trained for war, a powerful force to support the king against his enemies. 14Uzziah provided shields,
spears, helmets, coats of armor, bows and slingstones for the entire army.[n] 15In Jerusalem he made ma-
chines designed by skillful men for use on the towers and on the corner defenses to shoot arrows and hurl
large stones. His fame spread far and wide, for he was greatly helped until he became powerful.
16But after Uzziah became powerful, his pride[o] led to his downfall.[p] He was unfaithful[q] to the LORD
his God, and entered the temple of the LORD to burn incense[r] on the altar of incense. 17Azariah[s] the priest
with eighty other courageous priests of the LORD followed him in. 18They confronted him and said, "It is
not right for you, Uzziah, to burn incense to the LORD. That is for the priests,[t] the descendants[u] of Aar-
on,[v] who have been consecrated to burn incense.[w] Leave the sanctuary, for you have been unfaithful;
and you will not be honored by the LORD God."
19Uzziah, who had a censer in his hand ready to burn incense, became angry. While he was raging at
the priests in their presence before the incense altar in the LORD's temple, leprosy[b][x] broke out on his fore-
head. 20When Azariah the chief priest and all the other priests looked at him, they saw that he had lep-
rosy on his forehead, so they hurried him out. Indeed, he himself was eager to leave, because the LORD
had afflicted him.
21King Uzziah had leprosy until the day he died. He lived in a separate house[c][y]—leprous, and exclud-
ed from the temple of the LORD. Jotham his son had charge of the palace and governed the people of the
land.
22The other events of Uzziah's reign, from beginning to end, are recorded by the prophet Isaiah[z] son

26:5 [e]2Ch 15:2; 24:2; Da 1:17 [f]2Ch 27:6
26:6 [g]Isa 2:6; 11:14; 14:29; Jer 25:20 [h]Am 1:8; 3:9
26:7 [i]2Ch 21:16 [j]2Ch 20:1
26:8 [k]Ge 19:38; 2Ch 17:11
26:9 [l]2Ki 14:13; 2Ch 25:23 [m]Ne 2:13; 3:13
26:14 [n]Jer 46:4
26:16 [o]2Ch 14:10 [p]Dt 32:15; 2Ch 25:19 [q]1Ch 5:25 [r]2Ki 16:12
26:17 [s]1Ki 4:2; 1Ch 6:10
26:18 [t]Nu 16:39 [u]Nu 18:1-7 [v]Ex 30:7 [w]1Ch 6:49
26:19 [x]Nu 12:10; 2Ki 5:25-27
26:21 [y]Ex 4:6; Lev 13:46; 14:8; Nu 5:2; 19:12
26:22 [z]2Ki 15:1; Isa 1:1; 6:1

[a] 5 Many Hebrew manuscripts, Septuagint and Syriac; other Hebrew manuscripts *vision* [b] 19 The Hebrew word was used for various diseases affecting the skin—not necessarily leprosy; also in verses 20, 21 and 23. [c] 21 Or *in a house where he was relieved of responsibilities*

ANCIENT VOICES

Ashurnasirpal (II),* son of Tukulti-Ninurta, ruled for 25 years.
Shalmaneser (III), son of Ashurnasirpal, ruled for 35 years.
Shamshi-Adad (V), son of Shalmaneser, ruled for 13 years.
Adad-nerari (III), son of Shamshi-Adad, ruled for 28 years.
Shalmameser (IV), son of Adad-nerari, ruled for 10 years.
Ashur-dan (III), brother of Shalmaneser, ruled for 18 years.
Ashur-nerari (V), son of Adad-nerari, ruled for 10 years.
Tiglath-pileser (III), son of Ashur-nerari, ruled for 18 years.

*Numerals in parentheses added by translator for clarity

—ASSYRIAN KING LISTS

See "The Assyrian King Lists" article on the next page.

international reputation as a capable king (v. 8). He rebuilt the port town of Elath (Ezion Geber) at the head of the Gulf of Aqaba (see "Ezion Geber" on p. 631. All of this suggests that Uzziah undertook a policy of developing his base in the south, as opposed to repeating his father's mistake of pressing north against the larger state of Israel. Uzziah modernized the military (Assyrian reliefs indicate that Jerusalem's walls were rebuilt using a technique that made them easier to defend) and devoted a great deal of attention to expanding Judah's agricultural base (v. 10). In the Bible, however, this king is chiefly known for his impious attempt to seize the prerogatives of the priests, for which he was struck with a skin disease on account of which he lived out the end of his reign in isolation (vv. 16–21).

26:10 Excavations at Qumran, Gibeah and Beersheba have uncovered such towers and cisterns. A seal bearing Uzziah's name has been found in a cistern at Tell Beit Mirsim (see "Uzziah, King of Judah, and Jeroboam II, King of Israel" on p. 650).

26:11 Tiglath-Pileser III of Assyria stated that he was opposed in his advance toward the west (743 B.C.) by a coalition headed by "Azriau of Yaudi," perhaps Azariah (Uzziah) of Judah.

26:21 Canaanite texts from Ugarit suggest that the phrase "separate house" indicates a quarantine or separation. For commentary on "leprosy," see "Skin Diseases in the Ancient World" on page 171.

of Amoz. 23 Uzziah[a] rested with his fathers and was buried near them in a field for burial that belonged
to the kings, for people said, "He had leprosy." And Jotham his son succeeded him as king.[b]

26:23 [a]Isa 1:1; 6:1 [b]2Ki 14:21; 15:7; Am 1:1

Jotham King of Judah

27 Jotham[c] was twenty-five years old when he became king, and he reigned in Jerusalem sixteen
years. His mother's name was Jerusha daughter of Zadok. 2 He did what was right in the eyes of
the LORD, just as his father Uzziah had done, but unlike him he did not enter the temple of the LORD. The
people, however, continued their corrupt practices. 3 Jotham rebuilt the Upper Gate of the temple of the
LORD and did extensive work on the wall at the hill of Ophel.[d] 4 He built towns in the Judean hills and
forts and towers in the wooded areas.

5 Jotham made war on the king of the Ammonites[e] and conquered them. That year the Ammonites
paid him a hundred talents[a] of silver, ten thousand cors[b] of wheat and ten thousand cors of barley. The
Ammonites brought him the same amount also in the second and third years.

6 Jotham grew powerful[f] because he walked steadfastly before the LORD his God.

7 The other events in Jotham's reign, including all his wars and the other things he did, are written in
the book of the kings of Israel and Judah. 8 He was twenty-five years old when he became king, and he
reigned in Jerusalem sixteen years. 9 Jotham rested with his fathers and was buried in the City of David.
And Ahaz his son succeeded him as king.

27:1 [c]2Ki 15:5, 32; 1Ch 3:12
27:3 [d]2Ch 33:14; Ne 3:26
27:5 [e]Ge 19:38
27:6 [f]2Ch 26:5

Ahaz King of Judah

28 Ahaz[g] was twenty years old when he became king, and he reigned in Jerusalem sixteen years. Un-
like David his father, he did not do what was right in the eyes of the LORD. 2 He walked in the ways

28:1 [g]1Ch 3:13; Isa 1:1

[a] 5 That is, about 3 3/4 tons (about 3.4 metric tons) [b] 5 That is, probably about 62,000 bushels (about 2,200 kiloliters)

27:5 A seal with the name Jotham was discovered at Elath (Ezion Geber, on the Gulf of Aqaba). It was mounted in copper and thus probably belonged to an important person, possibly to King Jotham himself. The seal may have been used by a local official serving as Jotham's representative.

For information on the Ammonites, see "Ammon" on page 364.

28:1 Ahaz of Judah succeeded his father, Jotham. A chronological problem arises in comparing 28:1 and 2 Kings 16:2, both of which indicate that Ahaz died at the age of thirty-six, with 2 Chronicles 29:1, which states that Ahaz's son Hezekiah took the throne at the age twenty-five—upon the death of his father (28:27). This implies that Ahaz was only eleven years old at the birth of his son Hezekiah.

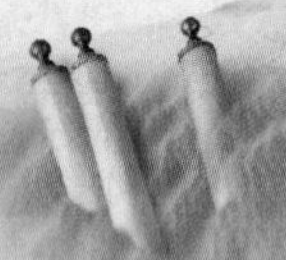

ANCIENT TEXTS AND ARTIFACTS

The Assyrian King Lists

2 CHRONICLES 27 Several first-millennium copies of **Assyrian** king lists have been discovered at the ancient Assyrian capitals of Calah, Nineveh[1] and **Asshur** (all on "Map 8a"). Although there are slight differences among the lists, they help scholars reconstruct a general, though incomplete, chronology of Assyrian rulers. The texts begin by naming 17 nomadic, tribal chieftains, followed by the 10 ancestors of a certain Aminu, whose descendants ruled Asshur. The lengths of reign of the first six descendants of Aminu are unknown, but beyond that point the texts specify the name of each king, his father and the number of years he ruled (cf. the Biblical practice spelled out in 2Ch 27:1,8–9). Occasionally an accomplishment of the king or the means by which he gained control of the throne is also mentioned.

Some Assyrian kings included in the lists are also known from the Bible, among them Tiglath-Pileser III (aka Pul; 2Ki 15:19,29; 16:7–10; 1Ch 5:26)[2] and Shalmaneser V, who laid siege to Samaria and deported Israel to Assyria (2Ki 17:1—18:12).[3] The lists are of enormous importance in reconstructing the history of the Old Testament world.

[1]See "Nineveh" on page 1497. [2]See "Menahem and Pekah of Israel, Jotham of Judah and Tiglath-Pileser III of Assyria" on page 553. [3]See "Hoshea, King of Israel, and Shalmaneser V, King of Assyria" on page 556.

of the kings of Israel and also made cast idols[h] for worshiping the Baals. 3 He burned sacrifices in the
Valley of Ben Hinnom[i] and sacrificed his sons[j] in the fire, following the detestable[k] ways of the nations
the LORD had driven out before the Israelites. 4 He offered sacrifices and burned incense at the high plac-
es, on the hilltops and under every spreading tree.
5 Therefore the LORD his God handed him over to the king of Aram.[l] The Arameans defeated him and
took many of his people as prisoners and brought them to Damascus.
He was also given into the hands of the king of Israel, who inflicted heavy casualties on him. 6 In one
day Pekah[m] son of Remaliah killed a hundred and twenty thousand soldiers in Judah[n]—because Judah
had forsaken the LORD, the God of their fathers. 7 Zicri, an Ephraimite warrior, killed Maaseiah the king's
son, Azrikam the officer in charge of the palace, and Elkanah, second to the king. 8 The Israelites took
captive from their kinsmen[o] two hundred thousand wives, sons and daughters. They also took a great
deal of plunder, which they carried back to Samaria.[p]
9 But a prophet of the LORD named Oded was there, and he went out to meet the army when it returned
to Samaria. He said to them, "Because the LORD, the God of your fathers, was angry[q] with Judah, he gave
them into your hand. But you have slaughtered them in a rage that reaches to heaven.[r] 10 And now you
intend to make the men and women of Judah and Jerusalem your slaves.[s] But aren't you also guilty of sins
against the LORD your God? 11 Now listen to me! Send back your fellow countrymen you have taken as
prisoners, for the LORD's fierce anger rests on you.[t]"
12 Then some of the leaders in Ephraim—Azariah son of Jehohanan, Berekiah son of Meshillemoth,
Jehizkiah son of Shallum, and Amasa son of Hadlai—confronted those who were arriving from the war.
13 "You must not bring those prisoners here," they said, "or we will be guilty before the LORD. Do you in-
tend to add to our sin and guilt? For our guilt is already great, and his fierce anger rests on Israel."
14 So the soldiers gave up the prisoners and plunder in the presence of the officials and all the assem-
bly. 15 The men designated by name took the prisoners, and from the plunder they clothed all who were
naked. They provided them with clothes and sandals, food and drink,[u] and healing balm. All those who
were weak they put on donkeys. So they took them back to their fellow countrymen at Jericho, the City
of Palms,[v] and returned to Samaria.
16 At that time King Ahaz sent to the king[a] of Assyria[w] for help. 17 The Edomites[x] had again come and
attacked Judah and carried away prisoners,[y] 18 while the Philistines[z] had raided towns in the foothills
and in the Negev of Judah. They captured and occupied Beth Shemesh, Aijalon[a] and Gederoth, as well as
Soco, Timnah and Gimzo, with their surrounding villages. 19 The LORD had humbled Judah because of
Ahaz king of Israel,[b] for he had promoted wickedness in Judah and had been most unfaithful[b] to the
LORD. 20 Tiglath-Pileser[c][c] king of Assyria came to him, but he gave him trouble instead of help.[d] 21 Ahaz
took some of the things from the temple of the LORD and from the royal palace and from the princes and
presented them to the king of Assyria, but that did not help him.
22 In his time of trouble King Ahaz became even more unfaithful[e] to the LORD. 23 He offered sacrifices
to the gods[f] of Damascus, who had defeated him; for he thought, "Since the gods of the kings of Aram
have helped them, I will sacrifice to them so they will help me."[g] But they were his downfall and the down-
fall of all Israel.
24 Ahaz gathered together the furnishings from the temple of God[h] and took them away.[d] He shut the
doors[i] of the LORD's temple and set up altars[j] at every street corner in Jerusalem. 25 In every town in Judah
he built high places to burn sacrifices to other gods and provoked the LORD, the God of his fathers, to anger.
26 The other events of his reign and all his ways, from beginning to end, are written in the book of the
kings of Judah and Israel. 27 Ahaz rested[k] with his fathers and was buried[l] in the city of Jerusalem, but
he was not placed in the tombs of the kings of Israel. And Hezekiah his son succeeded him as king.

28:2 [h]Ex 34:17; 2Ch 22:3 **28:3** [i]Jos 15:8; 2Ki 23:10 [j]Lev 18:21; 2Ki 3:27; 2Ch 33:6; Eze 20:26 [k]Dt 18:9; 2Ch 33:2 **28:5** [l]Isa 7:1 **28:6** [m]2Ki 15:25, 27 [n]ver 8; Isa 9:21; 11:13 **28:8** [o]Dt 28:25-41; 2Ch 11:4 [p]2Ch 29:9 **28:9** [q]2Ch 25:15; Isa 10:6; 47:6; Zec 1:15 [r]Ezr 9:6; Rev 18:5 **28:10** [s]Lev 25:39-46 **28:11** [t]2Ch 11:4; Jas 2:13 **28:15** [u]2Ki 6:22; Pr 25:21-22 [v]Dt 34:3; Jdg 1:16 **28:16** [w]2Ki 16:7 **28:17** [x]Ps 137:7; Isa 34:5 [y]2Ch 29:9 **28:18** [z]Eze 16:27,57 [a]Jos 10:12 **28:19** [b]2Ch 21:2 **28:20** [c]2Ki 15:29; 1Ch 5:6 [d]2Ki 16:7 **28:22** [e]Jer 5:3 **28:23** [f]2Ch 25:14 [g]Jer 44:17-18 **28:24** [h]2Ki 16:18 [i]2Ch 29:7 [j]2Ch 30:14 **28:27** [k]Isa 14:28-32 [l]2Ch 21:20; 24:25

[a] *16* One Hebrew manuscript, Septuagint and Vulgate (see also 2 Kings 16:7); most Hebrew manuscripts *kings* [b] *19* That is, Judah, as frequently in 2 Chronicles [c] *20* Hebrew *Tilgath-Pilneser,* a variant of *Tiglath-Pileser* [d] *24* Or *and cut them up*

Even allowing for early marriage in royal families, this hardly seems possible. The Septuagint rendering of 28:1 indicates that Ahaz died at the age of forty-one, allowing for him to have been a more reasonable sixteen years old at Hezekiah's birth. (See "The Problem of the Chronology of the Kings of Judah and Israel" on p. 508.)

The major event of Ahaz's reign was the attack by Rezin of Damascus and Pekah of Israel, as narrated in Isaiah 7. This resulted in the collapse of Judah's power in the south over Edom and Elath (2Ki 16:6). Ahaz rejected the sign of salvation that Isaiah offered and appealed to Assyria for help. Assyria not only defeated Rezin and Pekah but also denuded Judah. See "Ahaz, King of Judah, and Rezin, King of Aram" on page 554.

28:3 The Valley of Ben Hinnom was used as a trash dump and also as a site for sacrificing children to pagan gods. (See "Human Sacrifice in the Ancient Near East" on p. 182.)

28:5 Rezin, the king of Aram, and Pekah, king of Israel, acted together against Judah. See "Ahaz, King of Judah, and Rezin, King of Aram" on page 554 and "Syria/Aram" on page 534.

28:20 See "Menahem and Pekah of Israel, Jotham of Judah and Tiglath-Pileser III of Assyria" on page 553.

Hezekiah Purifies the Temple

29 Hezekiah[m] was twenty-five years old when he became king, and he reigned in Jerusalem twenty-nine years. His mother's name was Abijah daughter of Zechariah. 2 He did what was right in the eyes of the LORD, just as his father David[n] had done.

3 In the first month of the first year of his reign, he opened the doors of the temple of the LORD and repaired[o] them. 4 He brought in the priests and the Levites, assembled them in the square on the east side 5 and said: "Listen to me, Levites! Consecrate[p] yourselves now and consecrate the temple of the LORD, the God of your fathers. Remove all defilement from the sanctuary. 6 Our fathers[q] were unfaithful;[r] they did evil in the eyes of the LORD our God and forsook him. They turned their faces away from the LORD's dwelling place and turned their backs on him. 7 They also shut the doors of the portico and put out the lamps. They did not burn incense or present any burnt offerings at the sanctuary to the God of Israel. 8 Therefore, the anger of the LORD has fallen on Judah and Jerusalem; he has made them an object of dread and horror[s] and scorn,[t] as you can see with your own eyes. 9 This is why our fathers have fallen by the sword and why our sons and daughters and our wives are in captivity.[u] 10 Now I intend to make a covenant[v] with the LORD, the God of Israel, so that his fierce anger will turn away from us. 11 My sons, do not be negligent now, for the LORD has chosen you to stand before him and serve him,[w] to minister[x] before him and to burn incense."

12 Then these Levites[y] set to work:

from the Kohathites,
 Mahath son of Amasai and Joel son of Azariah;
from the Merarites,
 Kish son of Abdi and Azariah son of Jehallelel;
from the Gershonites,
 Joah son of Zimmah and Eden[z] son of Joah;
13 from the descendants of Elizaphan,
 Shimri and Jeiel;
from the descendants of Asaph,[a]
 Zechariah and Mattaniah;
14 from the descendants of Heman,
 Jehiel and Shimei;
from the descendants of Jeduthun,
 Shemaiah and Uzziel.

15 When they had assembled their brothers and consecrated themselves, they went in to purify[b] the temple of the LORD, as the king had ordered, following the word of the LORD. 16 The priests went into the sanctuary of the LORD to purify it. They brought out to the courtyard of the LORD's temple everything unclean that they found in the temple of the LORD. The Levites took it and carried it out to the Kidron Valley.[c] 17 They began the consecration on the first day of the first month, and by the eighth day of the month they reached the portico of the LORD. For eight more days they consecrated the temple of the LORD itself, finishing on the sixteenth day of the first month.

18 Then they went in to King Hezekiah and reported: "We have purified the entire temple of the LORD, the altar of burnt offering with all its utensils, and the table for setting out the consecrated bread, with all its articles. 19 We have prepared and consecrated all the articles[d] that King Ahaz removed in his unfaithfulness while he was king. They are now in front of the LORD's altar."

20 Early the next morning King Hezekiah gathered the city officials together and went up to the temple of the LORD. 21 They brought seven bulls, seven rams, seven male lambs and seven male goats as a sin offering[e] for the kingdom, for the sanctuary and for Judah. The king commanded the priests, the descendants of Aaron, to offer these on the altar of the LORD. 22 So they slaughtered the bulls, and the priests took the blood and sprinkled it on the altar; next they slaughtered the rams and sprinkled their blood on the altar; then they slaughtered the lambs and sprinkled their blood[f] on the altar. 23 The goats for the sin offering were brought before the king and the assembly, and they laid their hands[g] on them. 24 The priests then slaughtered the goats and presented their blood on the altar for a sin offering to atone[h] for all Israel, because the king had ordered the burnt offering and the sin offering for all Israel.

25 He stationed the Levites in the temple of the LORD with cymbals, harps and lyres in the way prescribed by David[i] and Gad[j] the king's seer and Nathan the prophet; this was commanded by the LORD

29:1 [m]1Ch 3:13
29:2 [n]2Ch 28:1; 34:2
29:3 [o]2Ch 28:24
29:5 [p]2Ch 35:6
29:6 [q]Ps 106:6-47; Jer 2:27 [r]1Ch 5:25; Eze 8:16
29:8 [s]Dt 28:25; 2Ch 24:18 [t]Jer 18:16; 19:8; 25:9,18
29:9 [u]2Ch 28:5-8,17
29:10 [v]2Ch 15:12; 23:16
29:11 [w]Nu 3:6; 8:6,14 [x]1Ch 15:2
29:12 [y]Nu 3:17-20 [z]2Ch 31:15
29:13 [a]1Ch 6:39
29:15 [b]ver 5; 1Ch 23:28; 2Ch 30:12
29:16 [c]2Sa 15:23
29:19 [d]2Ch 28:24
29:21 [e]Lev 4:13-14
29:22 [f]Lev 4:18
29:23 [g]Lev 4:15
29:24 [h]Ex 29:36; Lev 4:26
29:25 [i]1Ch 25:6; 2Ch 8:14 [j]1Sa 22:5; 2Sa 24:11

29:26 [k]1Ch 15:16; [l]1Ch 15:24; 23:5; 2Ch 5:12 through his prophets. 26So the Levites stood ready with David's instruments,[k] and the priests with their
trumpets.[l]
27Hezekiah gave the order to sacrifice the burnt offering on the altar. As the offering began, singing
29:27 [m]2Ch 23:18 to the LORD began also, accompanied by trumpets and the instruments[m] of David king of Israel. 28The
whole assembly bowed in worship, while the singers sang and the trumpeters played. All this continued
until the sacrifice of the burnt offering was completed.
29When the offerings were finished, the king and everyone present with him knelt down and wor-
29:29 [n]2Ch 20:18 shiped.[n] 30King Hezekiah and his officials ordered the Levites to praise the LORD with the words of Da-
vid and of Asaph the seer. So they sang praises with gladness and bowed their heads and worshiped.
31Then Hezekiah said, "You have now dedicated yourselves to the LORD. Come and bring sacrifices[o] and
thank offerings to the temple of the LORD." So the assembly brought sacrifices and thank offerings, and
29:31 [o]Heb 13:15-16 [p]Ex 25:2; 35:22 all whose hearts were willing[p] brought burnt offerings.
32The number of burnt offerings the assembly brought was seventy bulls, a hundred rams and two
hundred male lambs—all of them for burnt offerings to the LORD. 33The animals consecrated as sacri-
fices amounted to six hundred bulls and three thousand sheep and goats. 34The priests, however, were
29:34 [q]2Ch 35:11 [r]2Ch 30:3,15 too few to skin all the burnt offerings;[q] so their kinsmen the Levites helped them until the task was fin-
ished and until other priests had been consecrated,[r] for the Levites had been more conscientious in con-
secrating themselves than the priests had been. 35There were burnt offerings in abundance, together with
29:35 [s]Ex 29:13; Lev 3:16 [t]Lev 7:11-21 [u]Nu 15:5-10 the fat[s] of the fellowship offerings[a][t] and the drink offerings[u] that accompanied the burnt offerings.
So the service of the temple of the LORD was reestablished. 36Hezekiah and all the people rejoiced at
what God had brought about for his people, because it was done so quickly.

Hezekiah Celebrates the Passover

30:1 [v]Ge 41:52 [w]Ex 12:11; Nu 28:16 30 Hezekiah sent word to all Israel and Judah and also wrote letters to Ephraim and Manasseh,[v] in-
viting them to come to the temple of the LORD in Jerusalem and celebrate the Passover[w] to the
LORD, the God of Israel. 2The king and his officials and the whole assembly in Jerusalem decided to cel-
30:2 [x]Nu 9:10 ebrate[x] the Passover in the second month. 3They had not been able to celebrate it at the regular time be-
30:3 [y]2Ch 29:34 cause not enough priests had consecrated[y] themselves and the people had not assembled in Jerusalem.
4The plan seemed right both to the king and to the whole assembly. 5They decided to send a proclama-
30:5 [z]Jdg 20:1 tion throughout Israel, from Beersheba to Dan,[z] calling the people to come to Jerusalem and celebrate
the Passover to the LORD, the God of Israel. It had not been celebrated in large numbers according to what
was written.
6At the king's command, couriers went throughout Israel and Judah with letters from the king and
from his officials, which read:

> "People of Israel, return to the LORD, the God of Abraham, Isaac and Israel, that he may return
> to you who are left, who have escaped from the hand of the kings of Assyria. 7Do not be like your
> 30:7 [a]Ps 78:8,57; 106:6; Eze 20:18 [b]2Ch 29:8 30:8 [c]Ex 32:9 [d]Nu 25:4; 2Ch 29:10 30:9 [e]Dt 30:2-5; Isa 1:16; 55:7 [f]1Ki 8:50; Ps 106:46 [g]Ex 34:6-7; Dt 4:31; Mic 7:18 fathers[a] and brothers, who were unfaithful to the LORD, the God of their fathers, so that he made
> them an object of horror,[b] as you see. 8Do not be stiff-necked,[c] as your fathers were; submit to the
> LORD. Come to the sanctuary, which he has consecrated forever. Serve the LORD your God, so that
> his fierce anger[d] will turn away from you. 9If you return[e] to the LORD, then your brothers and your
> children will be shown compassion[f] by their captors and will come back to this land, for the LORD
> your God is gracious and compassionate.[g] He will not turn his face from you if you return to him."

10The couriers went from town to town in Ephraim and Manasseh, as far as Zebulun, but the people
30:10 [h]2Ch 36:16 scorned and ridiculed[h] them. 11Nevertheless, some men of Asher, Manasseh and Zebulun humbled them-
30:11 [i]ver 25 30:12 [j]Jer 32:39; Eze 11:19; Php 2:13 selves and went to Jerusalem.[i] 12Also in Judah the hand of God was on the people to give them unity[j] of
mind to carry out what the king and his officials had ordered, following the word of the LORD.
30:13 [k]Nu 28:16 13A very large crowd of people assembled in Jerusalem to celebrate the Feast of Unleavened Bread[k]
30:14 [l]2Ch 28:24 [m]2Sa 15:23 in the second month. 14They removed the altars[l] in Jerusalem and cleared away the incense altars and
threw them into the Kidron Valley.[m]
15They slaughtered the Passover lamb on the fourteenth day of the second month. The priests and the
30:15 [n]2Ch 29:34 Levites were ashamed and consecrated[n] themselves and brought burnt offerings to the temple of the
30:16 [o]2Ch 35:10 LORD. 16Then they took up their regular positions[o] as prescribed in the Law of Moses the man of God.
The priests sprinkled the blood handed to them by the Levites. 17Since many in the crowd had not

[a] *35* Traditionally *peace offerings*

consecrated themselves, the Levites had to kill[p] the Passover lambs for all those who were not ceremoni- 30:17 [p]2Ch 29:34
ally clean and could not consecrate ⌞their lambs⌟ to the LORD. [18]Although most of the many people who
came from Ephraim, Manasseh, Issachar and Zebulun had not purified themselves,[q] yet they ate the Pass- 30:18 [q]Ex 12:43-
over, contrary to what was written. But Hezekiah prayed for them, saying, "May the LORD, who is good, par- 49; Nu 9:6-10
don everyone [19]who sets his heart on seeking God—the LORD, the God of his fathers—even if he is not
clean according to the rules of the sanctuary." [20]And the LORD heard[r] Hezekiah and healed[s] the people.[t] 30:20 [r]2Ch 6:20
[21]The Israelites who were present in Jerusalem celebrated the Feast of Unleavened Bread[u] for seven [s]2Ch 7:14; Mal 4:2 [t]Jas 5:16
days with great rejoicing, while the Levites and priests sang to the LORD every day, accompanied by the 30:21 [u]Ex 12:15, 17; 13:6
LORD's instruments of praise.[a]

[22]Hezekiah spoke encouragingly to all the Levites, who showed good understanding of the service of
the LORD. For the seven days they ate their assigned portion and offered fellowship offerings[b] and praised
the LORD, the God of their fathers.

[23]The whole assembly then agreed to celebrate[v] the festival seven more days; so for another seven 30:23 [v]1Ki 8:65; 2Ch 7:9
days they celebrated joyfully. [24]Hezekiah king of Judah provided[w] a thousand bulls and seven thousand 30:24 [w]1Ki 8:5; 2Ch 29:34; 35:7; Ezr 6:17; 8:35
sheep and goats for the assembly, and the officials provided them with a thousand bulls and ten thou-
sand sheep and goats. A great number of priests consecrated themselves. [25]The entire assembly of Judah
rejoiced, along with the priests and Levites and all who had assembled from Israel[x], including the aliens 30:25 [x]ver 11
who had come from Israel and those who lived in Judah. [26]There was great joy in Jerusalem, for since
the days of Solomon[y] son of David king of Israel there had been nothing like this in Jerusalem. [27]The 30:26 [y]2Ch 7:8
priests and the Levites stood to bless[z] the people, and God heard them, for their prayer reached heaven, 30:27 [z]Ex 39:43; Nu 6:23; Dt 26:15; 2Ch 23:18; Ps 68:5
his holy dwelling place.

[a] 21 Or *priests praised the LORD every day with resounding instruments belonging to the LORD* [b] 22 Traditionally *peace offerings*

The Passover

2 CHRONICLES 30 Observance of Passover is tied to the deliverance of God's people from the plague on the Egyptian firstborn and the Israelites' subsequent **exodus** from Egypt. The feast was to be celebrated on the fourteenth day of the first month (called Abib and later Nisan, spanning late March and early April; Ex 12:2; 13:4)[1] and was combined with the Feast of Unleavened Bread observed from the fourteenth to the twenty-first day (Ex 12:18). An alternate date, one month later, was provided for anyone who had been unclean or otherwise unavailable to celebrate on the primary date (Nu 9:11).[2]

Passover was one of three annual pilgrim feasts that required attendance at the central sanctuary (Dt 16:5–6).[3] Every circumcised male was to observe the feast, including resident aliens and purchased slaves but excluding foreigners, temporary residents and hired servants. National sacrifices were offered on the fourteenth and twenty-first days of the month, and no labor could be performed on those two days.

The original celebrants—still in Egypt—were to be clothed for travel, with shoes on their feet and staffs in their hands, demonstrating that they were ready to depart from the land of their slavery. A first-year lamb, selected on the tenth day, was to be guarded by each household until its slaughter on the evening of the fourteenth day. Its blood was to be sprinkled on the door frame with a hyssop branch, signaling to the "destroyer" to "pass over" that home.[4] The lamb was eaten roasted (not raw or boiled) within a single home in one night; leftovers were burned on the following morning. The meal included bitter herbs and unleavened bread, symbolizing affliction and haste.

Passover observance is recorded only a few times in the Bible: in the days of Moses, Joshua, Hezekiah, Josiah and Zerubbabel. This does not imply that the feast was not celebrated at other times, although the commemoration does seem to have been neglected during periods of apathy and apostasy, especially during the preexilic period. Passover is mentioned in the Elephantine papyri (fifth century B.C.) and in the Temple Scroll of **Qumran**.[5]

[1]See "The Jewish Calendar" on page 241. [2]See "Ritual Purity in Israel and the Ancient Near East" on page 166. [3]See "The Festivals of Israel" on page 186.
[4]See "Hyssop and The Rituals of Cleansing" on page 847. [5]See "The Elephantine Community" on page 1264, "The Temple Scroll" on page 1371 and "The Last Supper and the Passover" on page 1611.

31 When all this had ended, the Israelites who were there went out to the towns of Judah, smashed the sacred stones and cut down[a] the Asherah poles. They destroyed the high places and the altars throughout Judah and Benjamin and in Ephraim and Manasseh. After they had destroyed all of them, the Israelites returned to their own towns and to their own property.

Contributions for Worship

2 Hezekiah[b] assigned the priests and Levites to divisions[c]—each of them according to their duties as priests or Levites—to offer burnt offerings and fellowship offerings,[a] to minister,[d] to give thanks and to sing praises[e] at the gates of the LORD's dwelling.[f] 3 The king contributed[g] from his own possessions for the morning and evening burnt offerings and for the burnt offerings on the Sabbaths, New Moons and appointed feasts as written in the Law of the LORD.[h] 4 He ordered the people living in Jerusalem to give the portion[i] due the priests and Levites so they could devote themselves to the Law of the LORD. 5 As soon as the order went out, the Israelites generously gave the firstfruits[j] of their grain, new wine,[k] oil and honey and all that the fields produced. They brought a great amount, a tithe of everything. 6 The men of Israel and Judah who lived in the towns of Judah also brought a tithe[l] of their herds and flocks and a tithe of the holy things dedicated to the LORD their God, and they piled them in heaps.[m] 7 They began doing this in the third month and finished in the seventh month.[n] 8 When Hezekiah and his officials came and saw the heaps, they praised the LORD and blessed[o] his people Israel.

9 Hezekiah asked the priests and Levites about the heaps; 10 and Azariah the chief priest, from the family of Zadok,[p] answered, "Since the people began to bring their contributions to the temple of the LORD, we have had enough to eat and plenty to spare, because the LORD has blessed his people, and this great amount is left over."[q]

11 Hezekiah gave orders to prepare storerooms in the temple of the LORD, and this was done. 12 Then they faithfully brought in the contributions, tithes and dedicated gifts. Conaniah,[r] a Levite, was in charge of these things, and his brother Shimei was next in rank. 13 Jehiel, Azaziah, Nahath, Asahel, Jerimoth, Jozabad,[s] Eliel, Ismakiah, Mahath and Benaiah were supervisors under Conaniah and Shimei his brother, by appointment of King Hezekiah and Azariah the official in charge of the temple of God.

14 Kore son of Imnah the Levite, keeper of the East Gate, was in charge of the freewill offerings given to God, distributing the contributions made to the LORD and also the consecrated gifts. 15 Eden,[t] Miniamin, Jeshua, Shemaiah, Amariah and Shecaniah assisted him faithfully in the towns[u] of the priests, distributing to their fellow priests according to their divisions, old and young alike.

16 In addition, they distributed to the males three years old or more whose names were in the genealogical records[v]—all who would enter the temple of the LORD to perform the daily duties of their various tasks, according to their responsibilities and their divisions. 17 And they distributed to the priests enrolled by their families in the genealogical records and likewise to the Levites twenty years old or more, according to their responsibilities and their divisions. 18 They included all the little ones, the wives, and the sons and daughters of the whole community listed in these genealogical records. For they were faithful in consecrating themselves.

19 As for the priests, the descendants of Aaron, who lived on the farm lands around their towns or in any other towns,[w] men were designated by name to distribute portions to every male among them and to all who were recorded in the genealogies of the Levites.

20 This is what Hezekiah did throughout Judah, doing what was good and right and faithful[x] before the LORD his God. 21 In everything that he undertook in the service of God's temple and in obedience to the law and the commands, he sought his God and worked wholeheartedly. And so he prospered.[y]

31:1 [a]2Ki 18:4; 2Ch 32:12; Isa 36:7
31:2 [b]2Ch 29:9 [c]1Ch 24:1 [d]1Ch 15:2 [e]Ps 7:17; 9:2; 47:6; 71:22 [f]1Ch 23:28-32
31:3 [g]1Ch 29:3; 2Ch 35:7; Eze 45:17 [h]Nu 28:1–29:40
31:4 [i]Nu 18:8; Dt 18:8; Ne 13:10; Mal 2:7
31:5 [j]Nu 18:12, 24; Ne 13:12; Eze 44:30 [k]Dt 12:17
31:6 [l]Lev 27:30; Ne 13:10-12 [m]Dt 14:28; Ru 3:7
31:7 [n]Ex 23:16
31:8 [o]Ps 144:13-15
31:10 [p]2Sa 8:17 [q]Ex 36:5; Eze 44:30; Mal 3:10-12
31:12 [r]2Ch 35:9
31:13 [s]2Ch 35:9
31:15 [t]2Ch 29:12 [u]Jos 21:9-19
31:16 [v]1Ch 23:3; Ezr 3:4
31:19 [w]ver 12-15; Lev 25:34; Nu 35:2-5
31:20 [x]2Ki 20:3; 22:2
31:21 [y]Dt 29:9

[a] 2 Traditionally *peace offerings*

31:4–7 Hezekiah ordered the Israelites to bring tithes and offerings to the temple in accordance with Old Testament law (Dt 12:5–19; 14:22–27; 2Ch 31:4–7; see "Sacrifices and Offerings in the Bible and the Ancient Near East" on p. 158). The offerings were needed for the subsistence of the priests and Levites, so they could "devote themselves to the Law of the LORD" (v. 4; see "The Levites and the Priests" on p. 648). The response was so great that Hezekiah found it necessary to order the preparation of storerooms in the temple to accommodate the surplus (vv. 5–11). He then appointed Levites to care for and distribute the excess to all eligible priests and Levites throughout Judah (vv. 12–19).

Among those designated to distribute the surplus was Amariah (v. 15). A clay bulla (seal impression), acquired on the antiquities market and now in the hands of a private collector, bears his personal stamp. It reads, "Belonging to Amariah [the son of] Hananiah, servant of Hezekiah." Although the Bible does not include Amariah's father's name, it is highly unlikely that two people with the name Amariah would have held high positions in Hezekiah's administration.

31:7 People began to give in May/June, the time of the Feast of Pentecost and the grain harvest. They finished in September/October, the time of the Feast of Tabernacles and the fruit and vine harvest.

31:16 Although no ancient versions or manuscripts disagree with the figure "three years old," it may represent a copyist's mistake for "thirty years," the age at which duties were assigned in the temple (1Ch 23:3).

Sennacherib Threatens Jerusalem

32 After all that Hezekiah had so faithfully done, Sennacherib[z] king of Assyria came and invaded
Judah. He laid siege to the fortified cities, thinking to conquer them for himself. 2 When Hezeki-
ah saw that Sennacherib had come and that he intended to make war on Jerusalem,[a] 3 he consulted with
his officials and military staff about blocking off the water from the springs outside the city, and they
helped him. 4 A large force of men assembled, and they blocked all the springs[b] and the stream that flowed
through the land. "Why should the kings[*a*] of Assyria come and find plenty of water?" they said. 5 Then he
worked hard repairing all the broken sections of the wall[c] and building towers on it. He built another
wall outside that one and reinforced the supporting terraces[*b*][d] of the City of David. He also made large
numbers of weapons[e] and shields.

6 He appointed military officers over the people and assembled them before him in the square at the
city gate and encouraged them with these words: 7 "Be strong and courageous.[f] Do not be afraid or dis-
couraged[g] because of the king of Assyria and the vast army with him, for there is a greater power with
us than with him.[h] 8 With him is only the arm of flesh,[i] but with us[j] is the LORD our God to help us and
to fight our battles."[k] And the people gained confidence from what Hezekiah the king of Judah said.

9 Later, when Sennacherib king of Assyria and all his forces were laying siege to Lachish,[l] he sent his
officers to Jerusalem with this message for Hezekiah king of Judah and for all the people of Judah who
were there:

10 "This is what Sennacherib king of Assyria says: On what are you basing your confidence,[m]
that you remain in Jerusalem under siege? 11 When Hezekiah says, 'The LORD our God will save us
from the hand of the king of Assyria,' he is misleading[n] you, to let you die of hunger and thirst.
12 Did not Hezekiah himself remove this god's high places and altars, saying to Judah and Jerusa-
lem, 'You must worship before one altar[o] and burn sacrifices on it'?

13 "Do you not know what I and my fathers have done to all the peoples of the other lands? Were
the gods of those nations ever able to deliver their land from my hand?[p] 14 Who of all the gods of
these nations that my fathers destroyed has been able to save his people from me? How then can
your god deliver you from my hand? 15 Now do not let Hezekiah deceive[q] you and mislead you like
this. Do not believe him, for no god of any nation or kingdom has been able to deliver[r] his people
from my hand or the hand of my fathers.[s] How much less will your god deliver you from my hand!"

16 Sennacherib's officers spoke further against the LORD God and against his servant Hezekiah. 17 The
king also wrote letters[t] insulting[u] the LORD, the God of Israel, and saying this against him: "Just as the gods[v]
of the peoples of the other lands did not rescue their people from my hand, so the god of Hezekiah will not
rescue his people from my hand." 18 Then they called out in Hebrew to the people of Jerusalem who were
on the wall, to terrify them and make them afraid in order to capture the city. 19 They spoke about the God
of Jerusalem as they did about the gods of the other peoples of the world—the work of men's hands.[w]
20 King Hezekiah and the prophet Isaiah son of Amoz cried out in prayer to heaven about this. 21 And
the LORD sent an angel,[x] who annihilated all the fighting men and the leaders and officers in the camp
of the Assyrian king. So he withdrew to his own land in disgrace. And when he went into the temple of
his god, some of his sons cut him down with the sword.[y]
22 So the LORD saved Hezekiah and the people of Jerusalem from the hand of Sennacherib king of As-
syria and from the hand of all others. He took care of them[*c*] on every side. 23 Many brought offerings to
Jerusalem for the LORD and valuable gifts[z] for Hezekiah king of Judah. From then on he was highly re-
garded by all the nations.

32:1 [z]2Ki 18:13-19; Isa 36:1; 37:9, 17,37
32:2 [a]Isa 22:7; Jer 1:15
32:4 [b]2Ki 18:17; 20:20; Isa 22:9, 11; Na 3:14
32:5 [c]2Ch 25:23; Isa 22:10 [d]1Ki 9:24; 1Ch 11:8 [e]Isa 22:8
32:7 [f]Dt 31:6; 1Ch 22:13 [g]2Ch 20:15 [h]Nu 14:9; 2Ki 6:16
32:8 [i]Job 40:9; Isa 52:10; Jer 17:5; 32:21 [j]Dt 3:22; 1Sa 17:45; 2Ch 13:12 [k]1Ch 5:22; 2Ch 20:17; Ps 20:7; Isa 28:6
32:9 [l]Jos 10:3,31
32:10 [m]Eze 29:16
32:11 [n]Isa 37:10
32:12 [o]2Ch 31:1
32:13 [p]ver 15
32:15 [q]Isa 37:10 [r]Da 3:15 [s]Ex 5:2
32:17 [t]Isa 37:14 [u]Ps 74:22; Isa 37:4,17 [v]2Ki 19:12
32:19 [w]2Ki 19:18; Ps 115:4-8; Isa 2:8; 17:8
32:21 [x]Ge 19:13 [y]2Ki 19:7
32:23 [z]2Ch 9:24; 17:5; Isa 45:14; Zec 14:16-17

[*a*] 4 Hebrew; Septuagint and Syriac *king* [*b*] 5 Or *the Millo* [*c*] 22 Hebrew; Septuagint and Vulgate *He gave them rest*

32:1 The chronology of Sennacherib's attack on Jerusalem is uncertain, but the following is a reasonable reconstruction: In 705 B.C. Sennacherib became king in Assyria and soon began a campaign in the west, subjugating 46 walled cities along the coast. He captured numerous cities of Judah, including Lachish, and received tribute from Hezekiah (2Ki 18:13—19:8). In 701 he returned east to deal with a rebellion in Babylon, giving Jerusalem and Hezekiah a respite. About this time Hezekiah became ill, recovered and received envoys from Merodach-Baladan of Babylon, seeking support for his war against Sennacherib (Isa 39). In about 689 Sennacherib destroyed Babylon and then returned west to deal with Tirhakah, the Ethiopian pharaoh of Egypt. Sennacherib began to subjugate Jerusalem but broke off to deal with Tirhakah. After that he returned to besiege Jerusalem, but his army suffered a plague from the "angel of the LORD" (2Ki 19:9–36). Nothing in the Sennacherib Prism contradicts this, and it may be regarded as supporting the Biblical account. See "The Sennacherib Prism" on page 659; "Hezekiah Against the Assyrians" on page 1118 and "Sennacherib's Campaign Against Merodach-Baladan" on page 1124.
32:9 Lachish was one of the largest towns in Judah. Sennacherib was so proud of capturing it that he decorated his palace at Nineveh with a relief picturing his exploits there (see "The Lachish Reliefs" on p. 559).

Hezekiah's Pride, Success and Death

24In those days Hezekiah became ill and was at the point of death. He prayed to the LORD, who an-
swered him and gave him a miraculous sign. 25But Hezekiah's heart was proud[a] and he did not respond
to the kindness shown him; therefore the LORD's wrath[b] was on him and on Judah and Jerusalem. 26Then
Hezekiah repented[c] of the pride of his heart, as did the people of Jerusalem; therefore the LORD's wrath
did not come upon them during the days of Hezekiah.[d]
27Hezekiah had very great riches and honor,[e] and he made treasuries for his silver and gold and for
his precious stones, spices, shields and all kinds of valuables. 28He also made buildings to store the harvest

32:25 [a]2Ki 14:10; 2Ch 26:16 [b]2Ch 19:2; 24:18 **32:26** [c]Jer 26:18-19 [d]2Ch 34:27,28; Isa 39:8 **32:27** [e]1Ch 29:12

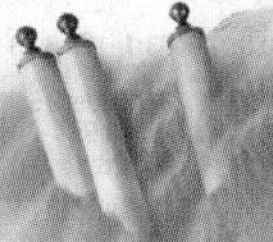

ANCIENT TEXTS AND ARTIFACTS

The Sennacherib Prism

Senracharib watches the capture of Lachish

Preserving Bible Times; © Dr. James C. Martin; permission of The British Museum

2 CHRONICLES 32 Upon his ascension to the **Assyrian** throne, Sennacherib (705–681 B.C.) had to quell numerous revolts throughout his domain. The Sennacherib Prism, a monumental text recorded in **Akkadian**, recounts his campaign to the region now known as Palestine in 701 B.C. Comparing Biblical accounts (2Ki 18:13—19:37; 2Ch 32:1–22; Isa 36–37) to Assyrian annals and other archaeological data helps us to make sense of the sequence of events:

✣ Second Chronicles records a massive invasion against the cities in Judah (32:1,9), and Sennacherib, in his prism, claims to have laid siege to 46 of Hezekiah's fortified, walled cities and surrounding towns.[1]

✣ Archaeological data supports these accounts, with evidence of widespread destruction throughout Judah (e.g., at Beersheba ["Map 6"] and Lachish ["Map 4"]).[2]

✣ The prism describes, in general terms, Sennacherib's advance through the coastal cities of Phoenicia and Philistia toward Jerusalem. This ferocious assault, in which he "slew . . . nobles who had provoked rebellion and hung their bodies on watchtowers," vividly illustrated the threats made by the Assyrian messengers (vv. 13–19). Even so, Sennacherib never claimed to have captured Jerusalem but rather to have "shut up Hezekiah in Jerusalem like a bird in a cage." This boast tacitly admits his failure to capture Jerusalem and agrees with the Biblical account.[3]

[1]See "Hezekiah Against the Assyrians" on page 1118. [2]See "Beersheba" on page 518 and "The Lachish Reliefs" on page 559. [3]See "The Death of Sennacherib" on page 562.

of grain, new wine and oil; and he made stalls for various kinds of cattle, and pens for the flocks. 29 He
built villages and acquired great numbers of flocks and herds, for God had given him very great riches.[f] **32:29** [f]1Ch 29:12
30 It was Hezekiah who blocked[g] the upper outlet of the Gihon[h] spring and channeled the water down **32:30** [g]2Ki 18:17 [h]1Ki 1:33
to the west side of the City of David. He succeeded in everything he undertook. 31 But when envoys were
sent by the rulers of Babylon[i] to ask him about the miraculous sign[j] that had occurred in the land, God **32:31** [i]Isa 39:1 [j]ver 24; Isa 38:7
left him to test[k] him and to know everything that was in his heart. [k]Ge 22:1; Dt 8:16
32 The other events of Hezekiah's reign and his acts of devotion are written in the vision of the proph-
et Isaiah son of Amoz in the book of the kings of Judah and Israel. 33 Hezekiah rested with his fathers and
was buried on the hill where the tombs of David's descendants are. All Judah and the people of Jerusa-
lem honored him when he died. And Manasseh his son succeeded him as king.

Manasseh King of Judah

33 Manasseh[l] was twelve years old when he became king, and he reigned in Jerusalem fifty-five years. **33:1** [l]1Ch 3:13
2 He did evil in the eyes of the LORD,[m] following the detestable[n] practices of the nations the LORD had **33:2** [m]Jer 15:4 [n]Dt 18:9;
driven out before the Israelites. 3 He rebuilt the high places his father Hezekiah had demolished; he also 2Ch 28:3
erected altars to the Baals and made Asherah poles.[o] He bowed down[p] to all the starry hosts and worshiped **33:3** [o]Dt 16:21-22 [p]Dt 17:3;
them. 4 He built altars in the temple of the LORD, of which the LORD had said, "My Name[q] will remain in Je- 2Ch 31:1
rusalem forever." 5 In both courts of the temple of the LORD,[r] he built altars to all the starry hosts. 6 He sac- **33:4** [q]2Ch 7:16 **33:5** [r]2Ch 4:9
rificed his sons[s] in[a] the fire in the Valley of Ben Hinnom, practiced sorcery, divination and witchcraft, and **33:6** [s]Lev 18:21;
consulted mediums[t] and spiritists.[u] He did much evil in the eyes of the LORD, provoking him to anger. Dt 18:10; 2Ch 28:3
7 He took the carved image he had made and put it in God's temple,[v] of which God had said to David [t]Lev 19:31 [u]1Sa 28:13
and to his son Solomon, "In this temple and in Jerusalem, which I have chosen out of all the tribes of Is- **33:7** [v]2Ch 7:16
rael, I will put my Name forever. 8 I will not again make the feet of the Israelites leave the land[w] I assigned **33:8** [w]2Sa 7:10
to your forefathers, if only they will be careful to do everything I commanded them concerning all the
laws, decrees and ordinances given through Moses." 9 But Manasseh led Judah and the people of Jerusa-
lem astray, so that they did more evil than the nations the LORD had destroyed before the Israelites.[x] **33:9** [x]Jer 15:4
10 The LORD spoke to Manasseh and his people, but they paid no attention. 11 So the LORD brought
against them the army commanders of the king of Assyria, who took Manasseh prisoner,[y] put a hook in **33:11** [y]Dt 28:36
his nose, bound him with bronze shackles[z] and took him to Babylon. 12 In his distress he sought the fa- [z]Ps 149:8
vor of the LORD his God and humbled[a] himself greatly before the God of his fathers. 13 And when he prayed **33:12** [a]2Ch 6:37;
to him, the LORD was moved by his entreaty and listened to his plea; so he brought him back to Jerusa- 32:26; 1Pe 5:6
lem and to his kingdom. Then Manasseh knew that the LORD is God.
14 Afterward he rebuilt the outer wall of the City of David, west of the Gihon[b] spring in the valley, as **33:14** [b]1Ki 1:33
far as the entrance of the Fish Gate[c] and encircling the hill of Ophel;[d] he also made it much higher. He [c]Ne 3:3; 12:39; Zep 1:10
stationed military commanders in all the fortified cities in Judah. [d]2Ch 27:3; Ne 3:26
15 He got rid of the foreign gods and removed[e] the image from the temple of the LORD, as well as all the **33:15** [e]ver 3-7;
altars he had built on the temple hill and in Jerusalem; and he threw them out of the city. 16 Then he re- 2Ki 23:12
stored the altar of the LORD and sacrificed fellowship offerings[b] and thank offerings[f] on it, and told Ju- **33:16** [f]Lev 7:11-
dah to serve the LORD, the God of Israel. 17 The people, however, continued to sacrifice at the high places, 18
but only to the LORD their God.
18 The other events of Manasseh's reign, including his prayer to his God and the words the seers spoke
to him in the name of the LORD, the God of Israel, are written in the annals of the kings of Israel.[c] 19 His
prayer and how God was moved by his entreaty, as well as all his sins and unfaithfulness, and the sites
where he built high places and set up Asherah poles and idols before he humbled[g] himself—all are writ- **33:19** [g]2Ch 6:37
ten in the records of the seers.[d][h] 20 Manasseh rested with his fathers and was buried[i] in his palace. And [h]2Ki 21:17 **33:20** [i]2Ki 21:18;
Amon his son succeeded him as king. 2Ch 21:20

Amon King of Judah

21 Amon[j] was twenty-two years old when he became king, and he reigned in Jerusalem two years. 22 He **33:21** [j]1Ch 3:14
did evil in the eyes of the LORD, as his father Manasseh had done. Amon worshiped and offered sacrifices

[a] 6 Or *He made his sons pass through* [b] 16 Traditionally *peace offerings* [c] 18 That is, Judah, as frequently in 2 Chronicles
[d] 19 One Hebrew manuscript and Septuagint; most Hebrew manuscripts *of Hozai*

33:1 See "The Seal of Manasseh" on page 565.
33:6 For "the Valley of Ben Hinnom," see the note on 28:3. For information on human sacrifice, see "Human Sacrifice in the Ancient Near East" on page 182.

33:23 [k]ver 12; Ex 10:3; 2Ch 7:14; Ps 18:27; 147:6; Pr 3:34
33:25 [l]2Ch 22:1

to all the idols Manasseh had made. 23But unlike his father Manasseh, he did not humble[k] himself before the LORD; Amon increased his guilt.

24Amon's officials conspired against him and assassinated him in his palace. 25Then the people[l] of the land killed all who had plotted against King Amon, and they made Josiah his son king in his place.

Josiah's Reforms

34:1 [m]1Ch 3:14 [n]Zep 1:1
34:2 [o]2Ch 29:2

34 Josiah[m] was eight years old when he became king,[n] and he reigned in Jerusalem thirty-one years. 2He did what was right in the eyes of the LORD and walked in the ways of his father David,[o] not turning aside to the right or to the left.

34:3 [p]1Ki 13:2; 1Ch 16:11; 2Ch 15:2; 33:17, 22
34:4 [q]Ex 34:13 [r]Ex 32:20; Lev 26:30; 2Ki 23:11; Mic 1:5
34:5 [s]1Ki 13:2
34:7 [t]Ex 32:20; 2Ch 31:1

3In the eighth year of his reign, while he was still young, he began to seek the God[p] of his father David. In his twelfth year he began to purge Judah and Jerusalem of high places, Asherah poles, carved idols and cast images. 4Under his direction the altars of the Baals were torn down; he cut to pieces the incense altars that were above them, and smashed the Asherah poles,[q] the idols and the images. These he broke to pieces and scattered over the graves of those who had sacrificed to them.[r] 5He burned[s] the bones of the priests on their altars, and so he purged Judah and Jerusalem. 6In the towns of Manasseh, Ephraim and Simeon, as far as Naphtali, and in the ruins around them, 7he tore down the altars and the Asherah poles and crushed the idols to powder[t] and cut to pieces all the incense altars throughout Israel. Then he went back to Jerusalem.

8In the eighteenth year of Josiah's reign, to purify the land and the temple, he sent Shaphan son of Azaliah and Maaseiah the ruler of the city, with Joah son of Joahaz, the recorder, to repair the temple of the LORD his God.

34:9 [u]1Ch 6:13; 2Ch 35:8
34:11 [v]2Ch 24:12 [w]2Ch 33:4-7

9They went to Hilkiah[u] the high priest and gave him the money that had been brought into the temple of God, which the Levites who were the doorkeepers had collected from the people of Manasseh, Ephraim and the entire remnant of Israel and from all the people of Judah and Benjamin and the inhabitants of Jerusalem. 10Then they entrusted it to the men appointed to supervise the work on the LORD's temple. These men paid the workers who repaired and restored the temple. 11They also gave money[v] to the carpenters and builders to purchase dressed stone, and timber for joists and beams for the buildings that the kings of Judah had allowed to fall into ruin.[w]

34:12 [x]2Ki 12:15 [y]1Ch 25:1
34:13 [z]1Ch 23:4

12The men did the work faithfully.[x] Over them to direct them were Jahath and Obadiah, Levites descended from Merari, and Zechariah and Meshullam, descended from Kohath. The Levites—all who were skilled in playing musical instruments—[y] 13had charge of the laborers[z] and supervised all the workers from job to job. Some of the Levites were secretaries, scribes and doorkeepers.

The Book of the Law Found

34:15 [a]2Ki 22:8; Ezr 7:6; Ne 8:1

14While they were bringing out the money that had been taken into the temple of the LORD, Hilkiah the priest found the Book of the Law of the LORD that had been given through Moses. 15Hilkiah said to Shaphan the secretary, "I have found the Book of the Law[a] in the temple of the LORD." He gave it to Shaphan.

16Then Shaphan took the book to the king and reported to him: "Your officials are doing everything that has been committed to them. 17They have paid out the money that was in the temple of the LORD and have entrusted it to the supervisors and workers." 18Then Shaphan the secretary informed the king, "Hilkiah the priest has given me a book." And Shaphan read from it in the presence of the king.

34:3 Josiah's reformation was one of the pivotal events of Old Testament history, but it was also ultimately a failure since the people did not really change their ways. Josiah wanted to consolidate worship in the Jerusalem temple so that the paganism that had flourished around the "high places" would be shut down and the religious life of the people would be easier to control. Images and altars were destroyed not only in Jerusalem and Judah but also in the cities of Manasseh, Ephraim, Simeon and as far north as Naphtali. Ultimately, however, this movement was "top-down" and had little effect on popular religious practices.

34:14 In the year 622 B.C., while the temple was being repaired, Hilkiah the priest "found the Book of the Law of the LORD that had been given through Moses" (probably the book of Dt). He handed it over to Shaphan the scribe, who read it aloud to King Josiah (see "The Tragic Reign of King Josiah" on p. 569).

When Josiah heard the book read, he tore his clothes because the Israelites had for generations disregarded God's laws. Josiah then sent a delegation to Huldah the prophetess to inquire of the Lord (see "The Huldah Delegation and Nathan-Melech, the Official" on p. 567).

34:15 While many interpreters today agree that the "Book of the Law" was probably either the whole or part of Deuteronomy, they posit that it was not actually recovered but *created* at this time. These "reformers" who are said to be behind the book of Deuteronomy, as well as of much of the material in Joshua, Judges, Samuel and Kings, are often called the "Deuteronomists," and their work in Joshua through Kings is referred to as the "Deuteronomistic History." This understanding of the origin of Deuteronomy, however, contradicts the repeated Biblical assertion that Moses is the source of that book. (See "The Date of Deuteronomy" on p. 259 and "The Documentary Hypothesis" on p. 15.)

19 When the king heard the words of the Law,[b] he tore[c] his robes. 20 He gave these orders to Hilkiah, **34:19** [b]Dt 28:3-68 [c]Jos 7:6;
Ahikam son of Shaphan[d], Abdon son of Micah,[a] Shaphan the secretary and Asaiah the king's attendant: Isa 36:22; 37:1
21 "Go and inquire of the LORD for me and for the remnant in Israel and Judah about what is written in **34:20** [d]2Ki 22:3
this book that has been found. Great is the LORD's anger that is poured out[e] on us because our fathers have **34:21** [e]2Ch 29:8;
not kept the word of the LORD; they have not acted in accordance with all that is written in this book." La 2:4; 4:11; Eze 36:18
22 Hilkiah and those the king had sent with him[b] went to speak to the prophetess[f] Huldah, who was **34:22** [f]Ex 15:20;
the wife of Shallum son of Tokhath,[c] the son of Hasrah,[d] keeper of the wardrobe. She lived in Jerusalem, Ne 6:14
in the Second District.
23 She said to them, "This is what the LORD, the God of Israel, says: Tell the man who sent you to me,
24 'This is what the LORD says: I am going to bring disaster[g] on this place and its people[h]—all the curs- **34:24** [g]Pr 16:4;
es[i] written in the book that has been read in the presence of the king of Judah. 25 Because they have for- Isa 3:9; Jer 40:2; 42:10; 44:2,11
saken me[j] and burned incense to other gods and provoked me to anger by all that their hands have made,[e] [h]2Ch 36:14-20 [i]Dt 28:15-68
my anger will be poured out on this place and will not be quenched.' 26 Tell the king of Judah, who sent **34:25** [j]2Ch 33:3-6; Jer 22:9
you to inquire of the LORD, 'This is what the LORD, the God of Israel, says concerning the words you heard:
27 Because your heart was responsive[k] and you humbled[l] yourself before God when you heard what he **34:27** [k]2Ch 12:7;
spoke against this place and its people, and because you humbled yourself before me and tore your robes 32:26 [l]Ex 10:3; 2Ch 6:37
and wept in my presence, I have heard you, declares the LORD. 28 Now I will gather you to your fathers,[m] **34:28**
and you will be buried in peace. Your eyes will not see all the disaster I am going to bring on this place [m]2Ch 35:20-25 [n]2Ch 32:26
and on those who live here.' "[n]
So they took her answer back to the king.
29 Then the king called together all the elders of Judah and Jerusalem. 30 He went up to the temple of
the LORD[o] with the men of Judah, the people of Jerusalem, the priests and the Levites—all the people **34:30** [o]2Ki 23:2;
from the least to the greatest. He read in their hearing all the words of the Book of the Covenant, which Ne 8:1-3
had been found in the temple of the LORD. 31 The king stood by his pillar[p] and renewed the covenant[q] in **34:31** [p]1Ki 7:15;
the presence of the LORD—to follow[r] the LORD and keep his commands, regulations and decrees with all 2Ki 11:14 [q]2Ki 11:17;
his heart and all his soul, and to obey the words of the covenant written in this book. 2Ch 23:16; 29:10 [r]Dt 13:4
32 Then he had everyone in Jerusalem and Benjamin pledge themselves to it; the people of Jerusalem
did this in accordance with the covenant of God, the God of their fathers.
33 Josiah removed all the detestable[s] idols from all the territory belonging to the Israelites, and he had **34:33** [s]ver 3-7;
all who were present in Israel serve the LORD their God. As long as he lived, they did not fail to follow the Dt 18:9
LORD, the God of their fathers.

Josiah Celebrates the Passover

35 Josiah celebrated the Passover[t] to the LORD in Jerusalem, and the Passover lamb was slaughtered **35:1** [t]Ex 12:1-30;
on the fourteenth day of the first month. 2 He appointed the priests to their duties and encour- Nu 9:3; 28:16
aged them in the service of the LORD's temple. 3 He said to the Levites, who instructed[u] all Israel and who **35:3** [u]Dt 33:10;
had been consecrated to the LORD: "Put the sacred ark in the temple that Solomon son of David king of 1Ch 23:26;
Israel built. It is not to be carried about on your shoulders. Now serve the LORD your God and his people 2Ch 5:7; 17:7
Israel. 4 Prepare yourselves by families in your divisions,[v] according to the directions written by David **35:4** [v]ver 10;
king of Israel and by his son Solomon. 1Ch 9:10-13; 24:1; 2Ch 8:14; Ezr 6:18
5 "Stand in the holy place with a group of Levites for each subdivision of the families of your fellow
countrymen, the lay people. 6 Slaughter the Passover lambs, consecrate yourselves[w] and prepare ⌞the **35:6** [w]Lev 11:44;
lambs⌟ for your fellow countrymen, doing what the LORD commanded through Moses." 2Ch 29:5,15
7 Josiah provided for all the lay people who were there a total of thirty thousand sheep and goats for
the Passover offerings,[x] and also three thousand cattle—all from the king's own possessions.[y] **35:7** [x]2Ch 30:24 [y]2Ch 31:3
8 His officials also contributed[z] voluntarily to the people and the priests and Levites. Hilkiah,[a] Zech- **35:8** [z]1Ch 29:3; 2Ch 29:31-36
ariah and Jehiel, the administrators of God's temple, gave the priests twenty-six hundred Passover offer- [a]1Ch 6:13

[a] 20 Also called *Acbor son of Micaiah* [b] 22 One Hebrew manuscript, Vulgate and Syriac; most Hebrew manuscripts do not have *had sent with him.* [c] 22 Also called *Tikvah* [d] 22 Also called *Harhas* [e] 25 Or *by everything they have done*

34:20 A seal has been discovered that reads, "(Belonging) to Asayahu servant of the king." By studying the style and graphics of the lettering, scholars have been able to date the seal to the seventh century B.C., the period of Josiah's reign. It is probable that this seal did in fact belong to Asaiah, a minister of King Josiah and a member of this task force. (The suffix "-iah" is simply the shortened form of "-yahu," both of which mean "the LORD.")

34:22 See "The Huldah Delegation and Nathan-Melech, the Official" on page 567.

35:1–24 See "Josiah, Zechariah and Neco II" on page 663 and "The Tragic Reign of King Josiah" on page 569.

35:9 [b]2Ch 31:12 ings and three hundred cattle. 9 Also Conaniah[b] along with Shemaiah and Nethanel, his brothers, and
[c]2Ch 31:13 Hashabiah, Jeiel and Jozabad,[c] the leaders of the Levites, provided five thousand Passover offerings and
five hundred head of cattle for the Levites.
35:10 [d]ver 4; 10 The service was arranged and the priests stood in their places with the Levites in their divisions[d]
Ezr 6:18 [e]2Ch 30:16 as the king had ordered.[e] 11 The Passover lambs were slaughtered,[f] and the priests sprinkled the blood
35:11 [f]2Ch 29:22,34; handed to them, while the Levites skinned the animals. 12 They set aside the burnt offerings to give them
30:17 to the subdivisions of the families of the people to offer to the LORD, as is written in the Book of Moses.
35:13 [g]Ex 12:2-11; They did the same with the cattle. 13 They roasted the Passover animals over the fire as prescribed,[g] and
Lev 6:25; 1Sa 2:13-15 boiled the holy offerings in pots, caldrons and pans and served them quickly to all the people. 14 After this,
they made preparations for themselves and for the priests, because the priests, the descendants of Aar-
35:14 [h]Ex 29:13 on, were sacrificing the burnt offerings and the fat portions[h] until nightfall. So the Levites made prepa-
rations for themselves and for the Aaronic priests.
35:15 [i]1Ch 25:1; 15 The musicians,[i] the descendants of Asaph, were in the places prescribed by David, Asaph, Heman
26:12-19; 2Ch 29:30; and Jeduthun the king's seer. The gatekeepers at each gate did not need to leave their posts, because their
Ne 12:46; Ps 68:25 fellow Levites made the preparations for them.
16 So at that time the entire service of the LORD was carried out for the celebration of the Passover and
the offering of burnt offerings on the altar of the LORD, as King Josiah had ordered. 17 The Israelites who
were present celebrated the Passover at that time and observed the Feast of Unleavened Bread for seven
days. 18 The Passover had not been observed like this in Israel since the days of the prophet Samuel; and
none of the kings of Israel had ever celebrated such a Passover as did Josiah, with the priests, the Levites
and all Judah and Israel who were there with the people of Jerusalem. 19 This Passover was celebrated in
the eighteenth year of Josiah's reign.

Josiah, Zechariah and Neco II

2 CHRONICLES 35 When Josiah, king of Judah (c. 640–609 B.C.), made arrangements for celebrating the Passover,[1] he and his administrators donated vast numbers of animals to be sacrificed (2Ch 35:7–9). One of the administrators was Zechariah, a temple official (v. 8). An **ostracon** (broken piece of pottery with writing on it), purchased on the antiquities market and now in a private collection, includes the names of both Josiah and Zechariah. Apparently an order for a royal temple offering, it reads, "As Ashyahu the king has commanded you to give in the hand of Zakaryahu silver of Tarshish for the House of **Yahweh**: three shekels." The name Josiah is the English equivalent of Ashyahu in the inscription, and Zechariah is the equivalent of Zakaryahu.

In 609 B.C., when Josiah was in his thirty-first year of rule and still a young man of thirty-nine (2Ki 22:1), the Egyptian army under Pharaoh Neco II (r. 610–595 B.C.) marched north to aid the **Assyrians** in their attempt to stave off the **Babylonians**. Neco II, known from both Egyptian and Babylonian records, was among the stronger of ancient Egypt's later rulers. The Assyrians were holding out at Carchemish ("Map 8a"), a prominent city on the Euphrates River (2Ch 35:20). Josiah, in an effort to undermine this force, who were dominant in the region, tried to head off Neco at **Megiddo**[2] ("Map 8a"). Tragically, the Judahite army was defeated and Josiah lost his life (vv. 21–24).[3]

Judah then became subject to Neco until 605 B.C., when the Babylonians defeated the Egyptians at Carchemish (Jer 46:2). Following Josiah's demise, his son Jehoahaz was made king. After three months Neco removed Jehoahaz and imposed a hefty tribute on Judah (2Ch 36:1–3). The Egyptian king placed Josiah's eldest son, Jehoiakim, on the throne and banished Jehoahaz to Egypt, where he lived out the rest of his days (36:4).

[1]See "The Passover" on page 656. [2]See "Megiddo" on page 1541. [3]See "The Tragic Reign of King Josiah" on page 569.

The Death of Josiah

[20]After all this, when Josiah had set the temple in order, Neco king of Egypt went up to fight at Car-
chemish[j] on the Euphrates,[k] and Josiah marched out to meet him in battle. [21]But Neco sent messengers
to him, saying, "What quarrel is there between you and me, O king of Judah? It is not you I am attacking
at this time, but the house with which I am at war. God has told[l] me to hurry; so stop opposing God, who
is with me, or he will destroy you."

[22]Josiah, however, would not turn away from him, but disguised[m] himself to engage him in battle. He
would not listen to what Neco had said at God's command but went to fight him on the plain of Megiddo.

35:20 [j]Isa 10:9; Jer 46:2 [k]Ge 2:14
35:21 [l]1Ki 13:18; 2Ki 18:25
35:22 [m]Jdg 5:19; 1Sa 28:8; 2Ch 18:29

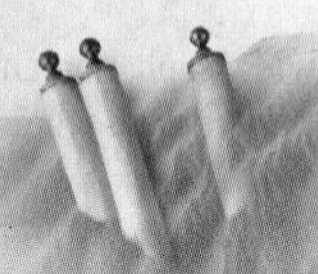

ANCIENT TEXTS AND ARTIFACTS

The Sippar Cylinder of Nabonidus

2 CHRONICLES 36 The conclusion to Chronicles describes the destruction of Jerusalem and the **exile** of the Judahites under the Babylonian King **Nebuchadnezzar** in 586 B.C.[1] The exiles served Nebuchadnezzar and his successors "until the kingdom of Persia came to power" (2Ch 36:20), at which time Cyrus conquered **Babylon** and subsequently declared that the Jewish exiles could return to their native land and rebuild their temple (vv. 22–23).[2]

An inscription discovered in the Ebabbar temple in Sippar (a Babylonian city) briefly mentions the rise of the **Persian** Empire and its king, Cyrus. It consists of several copies on clay cylinders, celebrating the rebuilding of three temples by Nabonidus (r. 556–539 B.C.), the last king of the **Neo-Babylonian** Empire. In the account Nabonidus receives a dream from the gods Sin and Marduk, requesting that he rebuild Sin's temple in the city of Harran. When Nabonidus protests that Harran is still under the control of the powerful Medes and therefore beyond his reach, the deities assure him that the Median Empire will fall to a subordinate king named Cyrus. Cyrus proceeds to defeat the great Median army and take captive the Median king. Thus Nabonidus is able to complete his rebuilding project through divine intervention, with his gods using Cyrus to remove the Median obstacle.

Although the Sippar Cylinder recounts nothing beyond the rebuilding of the three temples during the latter part of Nabonidus's reign, other historical records complete the picture. The Babylonian Chronicle states that Cyrus's army took control of Babylon itself in 539 B.C., thereby ending the reign of Nabonidus and the ascendancy of the Neo-Babylonian Empire. Later Persian sources attribute the fall of Nabonidus to his neglect of the supreme Babylonian deity, Marduk, in favor of the foreign god Sin.[3]

[1]See "The Last Days of Jerusalem" on page 1197. [2]See "Cyrus the Great" on page 669. [3]See also "Nabonidus and Belshazzar" on page 1394 and "The Prayer of Nabonidus" on page 1400.

The Sippar Cylinder

Preserving Bible Times; © Dr. James C. Martin; permission of The British Museum

35:23 [n]1Ki 22:34
[23]Archers[n] shot King Josiah, and he told his officers, "Take me
away; I am badly wounded." [24]So they took him out of his chariot,
put him in the other chariot he had and brought him to Jerusalem,
where he died. He was buried in the tombs of his fathers, and all Ju-
dah and Jerusalem mourned for him.
[25]Jeremiah composed laments for Josiah, and to this day all the
35:25 [o]Jer 22:10, 15-16
men and women singers commemorate Josiah in the laments.[o]
These became a tradition in Israel and are written in the Laments.
[26]The other events of Josiah's reign and his acts of devotion, ac-
cording to what is written in the Law of the LORD— [27]all the events,
from beginning to end, are written in the book of the kings of Israel
36 and Judah. [1]And the people of the land took Jehoahaz son of
Josiah and made him king in Jerusalem in place of his father.

Ancient Voices

Whoever you are whom Sin and Shamash will call to kingship and in whose reign that temple will fall into disrepair and who will build anew, may he find the inscription written in my name and not alter (it).* May he anoint (it) with oil, perform a sacrifice, place it with the inscription written in his own name and return it to its (original) place. Maybe Shamash and Anunitu hear his supplication, receive his utterance, march at his side, annihilate his enemy (and) daily speak good recommendations on his behalf to Sin, the father their creator.

*Words in parentheses added by translator for clarity or where text has gaps

—The Sippar Cylinder of Nabonidus

See "The Sippar Cylinder of Nabonidus" article.

Jehoahaz King of Judah

[2]Jehoahaz[a] was twenty-three years old when he became king,
and he reigned in Jerusalem three months. [3]The king of Egypt de-
throned him in Jerusalem and imposed on Judah a levy of a hun-
dred talents[b] of silver and a talent[c] of gold. [4]The king of Egypt made
Eliakim, a brother of Jehoahaz, king over Judah and Jerusalem and
36:4 [p]Jer 22:10-12
changed Eliakim's name to Jehoiakim. But Neco[p] took Eliakim's brother Jehoahaz and carried him off to
Egypt.

Jehoiakim King of Judah

36:5 [q]Jer 22:18; 26:1; 35:1
[5]Jehoiakim[q] was twenty-five years old when he became king, and he reigned in Jerusalem eleven
36:6 [r]Jer 25:9; 27:6; Eze 29:18 [s]2Ch 33:11; Eze 19:9; Da 1:1
years. He did evil in the eyes of the LORD his God. [6]Nebuchadnezzar[r] king of Babylon attacked him and
bound him with bronze shackles to take him to Babylon.[s] [7]Nebuchadnezzar also took to Babylon arti-
36:7 [t]2Ki 24:13; Ezr 1:7; Da 1:2
cles from the temple of the LORD and put them in his temple[d] there.[t]
[8]The other events of Jehoiakim's reign, the detestable things he did and all that was found against him,
are written in the book of the kings of Israel and Judah. And Jehoiachin his son succeeded him as king.

Jehoiachin King of Judah

36:9 [u]Jer 22:24-28; 52:31
[9]Jehoiachin[u] was eighteen[e] years old when he became king, and he reigned in Jerusalem three months
and ten days. He did evil in the eyes of the LORD. [10]In the spring, King Nebuchadnezzar sent for him and
36:10 [v]ver 18; 2Ki 20:17; Ezr 1:7; Jer 22:25; 24:1; 29:1; 37:1; Eze 17:12
brought him to Babylon,[v] together with articles of value from the temple of the LORD, and he made Je-
hoiachin's uncle,[f] Zedekiah, king over Judah and Jerusalem.

Zedekiah King of Judah

36:11 [w]2Ki 24:17; Jer 27:1; 28:1
[11]Zedekiah[w] was twenty-one years old when he became king, and he reigned in Jerusalem eleven
36:12 [x]Jer 37:1-39:18 [y]Dt 8:3; 2Ch 7:14; 33:23; Jer 21:3-7
years. [12]He did evil in the eyes of the LORD[x] his God and did not humble[y] himself before Jeremiah the

[a] *2* Hebrew *Joahaz,* a variant of *Jehoahaz;* also in verse 4 [b] *3* That is, about 3 3/4 tons (about 3.4 metric tons) [c] *3* That is, about 75 pounds (about 34 kilograms) [d] *7* Or *palace* [e] *9* One Hebrew manuscript, some Septuagint manuscripts and Syriac (see also 2 Kings 24:8); most Hebrew manuscripts *eight* [f] *10* Hebrew *brother,* that is, relative (see 2 Kings 24:17)

36:2–4 An alliance between Egypt and Assyria failed to save the disintegrating Assyrian Empire, but Pharaoh Neco's campaign (cf. 35:20–21) did result in Egyptian control of Judah. It is unclear whether Josiah had been obligated to oppose Neco as a vassal of Babylon or whether he had acted independently. Either way, his death marked the end of Judah's autonomy. Josiah's successor, his son Jehoahaz, was dethroned by Neco and deported to Egypt. Neco placed Eliakim (Jehoiakim) on the throne, and Judah became a vassal state to Egypt. (See "Josiah, Zechariah and Neco II" on p. 663.)
36:5–8 When Babylon emerged as a new superpower in the region, Jehoiakim shifted his allegiance from Egypt, and Judah became a vassal of Babylon. A subsequent stalemate between Babylon and Egypt afforded Jehoiakim the opportunity to throw off the yoke of vassalage and to rebel against Nebuchadnezzar (see 2Ki 24:1). Nebuchadnezzar (see "Nebuchadnezzar" on p. 571) retaliated and captured Jehoiakim, but it is uncertain whether he was actually able to take him to Babylon before Jehoiakim died (2Ch 36:6; cf. 2Ki 24:6).
36:9–10 Jehoiachin succeeded his father, Jehoiakim, as king of Judah, but in 597 B.C. he surrendered to Nebuchadnezzar's siege after reigning for only three months (v. 9; cf. 2Ki 24:8–12). Jehoiachin was deported to Babylon along with the queen mother, other high-ranking officials and numerous soldiers, craftsmen and artisans (cf. 2Ki 24:14–16). Nebuchadnezzar installed Jehoiachin's uncle, Mattaniah (changing his name to Zedekiah), as a puppet king (2Ch 36:10; cf. 2Ki 24:17).
36:11–14 After a series of political missteps, Zedekiah finally rebelled against the king of Babylon (v. 13). The response was swift and thorough. King Nebuchadnezzar laid siege to Jerusalem early in 588 B.C. The end came in July of 586 B.C., with the carnage so

prophet, who spoke the word of the LORD. 13He also rebelled against King Nebuchadnezzar, who had made
him take an oath[z] in God's name. He became stiff-necked[a] and hardened his heart and would not turn
to the LORD, the God of Israel. 14Furthermore, all the leaders of the priests and the people became more
and more unfaithful,[b] following all the detestable practices of the nations and defiling the temple of the
LORD, which he had consecrated in Jerusalem.

The Fall of Jerusalem

15The LORD, the God of their fathers, sent word to them through his messengers[c] again and again,[d] be-
cause he had pity on his people and on his dwelling place. 16But they mocked God's messengers, despised
his words and scoffed[e] at his prophets until the wrath[f] of the LORD was aroused against his people and
there was no remedy.[g] 17He brought up against them the king of the Babylonians,[a] who killed their young
men with the sword in the sanctuary, and spared neither young man[h] nor young woman, old man or
aged. God handed all of them over to Nebuchadnezzar.[i] 18He carried to Babylon all the articles[j] from the
temple of God, both large and small, and the treasures of the LORD's temple and the treasures of the king
and his officials. 19They set fire[k] to God's temple[l] and broke down the wall[m] of Jerusalem; they burned
all the palaces and destroyed[n] everything of value there.[o]

20He carried into exile[p] to Babylon the remnant, who escaped from the sword, and they became ser-
vants[q] to him and his sons until the kingdom of Persia came to power. 21The land enjoyed its sabbath
rests;[r] all the time of its desolation it rested,[s] until the seventy years[t] were completed in fulfillment of
the word of the LORD spoken by Jeremiah.

22In the first year of Cyrus[u] king of Persia, in order to fulfill the word of the LORD spoken by Jeremi-
ah, the LORD moved the heart of Cyrus king of Persia to make a proclamation throughout his realm and
to put it in writing:

23"This is what Cyrus king of Persia says:

" 'The LORD, the God of heaven, has given me all the kingdoms of the earth and he has appoint-
ed[v] me to build a temple for him at Jerusalem in Judah. Anyone of his people among you—may
the LORD his God be with him, and let him go up.' "

36:13 [z]Eze 17:13 [a]2Ki 17:14; 2Ch 30:8
36:14 [b]1Ch 5:25
36:15 [c]Isa 5:4; 44:26; Jer 7:25; Hag 1:13; Zec 1:4; Mal 2:7; 3:1 [d]Jer 7:13,25; 25:3-4; 35:14,15; 44:4-6
36:16 [e]2Ki 2:23; Pr 1:25; Jer 5:13 [f]Ezr 5:12; Pr 1:30-31 [g]2Ch 30:10; Pr 29:1; Zec 1:2
36:17 [h]Jer 6:11 [i]Ezr 5:12; Jer 32:28
36:18 [j]ver 7,10
36:19 [k]Jer 11:16; 17:27; 21:10,14; 22:7; 32:29; 39:8; La 4:11; Eze 20:47; Am 2:5; Zec 11:1 [l]1Ki 9:8-9 [m]2Ki 14:13 [n]La 2:6 [o]Ps 79:1-3
36:20 [p]Lev 26:44; 2Ki 24:14; Ezr 2:1; Ne 7:6 [q]Jer 27:7
36:21 [r]Lev 25:4; 26:34 [s]1Ch 22:9 [t]Jer 1:1; 25:11; 27:22; 29:10; 40:1; Da 9:2; Zec 1:12; 7:5
36:22 [u]Isa 44:28; 45:1,13; Jer 25:12; 29:10
36:23 [v]Jdg 4:10

[a] 17 Or *Chaldeans*

appalling and the devastation so sweeping that survivors could only sit aghast in silence as they mourned "the Daughter of Zion" (La 2:1). See "The Last Days of Jerusalem" on page 1197.

36:22–23 The information in these verses is not found in the Kings account because the writer of Kings concluded his history before the restoration. It is repeated, however, at the beginning of Ezra (Ezr 1:1–4), which resumes the history at the point where Chronicles ends—indicating that Chronicles and Ezra may have been written by the same author. See the prophecy of Jeremiah (Jer 25:1–14; cf. Da 9).

Cyrus allowed captive peoples to return to their lands. His efforts to win the favor of peoples treated harshly by the Babylonians were used by God to inaugurate the restoration period.

INTRODUCTION TO Ezra

AUTHOR, PLACE AND DATE OF WRITING

Ezra, the priest who returned to Jerusalem with a group of Babylonian exiles in 458 B.C., is assumed to have authored this book, presumably from Jerusalem, around 440 B.C. He is also thought to have written the book of Nehemiah, around 430 B.C. Originally two separate compositions, the two were combined into one book, titled Ezra, prior to A.D. 100. The oldest manuscripts of the Septuagint also treated Nehemiah and Ezra as one book. Origen (c. A.D. 185–253) was the first writer to make a distinction between the two, which he called 1 Ezra and 2 Ezra. Wycliffe's English translation (1382) also separated the books, as did Coverdale's (1535).

AUDIENCE

Generations of Israelites after the return of the exiles from Babylon read this book. Ezra clearly wanted his readers to recognize, in various historical events, the power and love God demonstrated toward his chosen people and, in turn, their covenant responsibilities toward him.

CULTURAL FACTS AND HIGHLIGHTS

In 539 B.C. Cyrus, king of Persia, decreed that Jewish exiles could return to Jerusalem under Zerubbabel's leadership. Many did undertake the journey and began rebuilding the temple and offering sacrifices to God. By the time Ezra returned with a second group of exiles, God's people had experienced many blessings:

- The temple had been rebuilt.
- The Persians had gifted the returning exiles with silver, gold, supplies, livestock and even offerings for God's temple.
- King Cyrus had returned 5,400 articles of gold and silver that King Nebuchadnezzar had removed from God's temple.
- Many of the exiles had returned to the towns from which their ancestors had come.
- Priests once again offered sacrifices to God in the temple.

TIMELINE

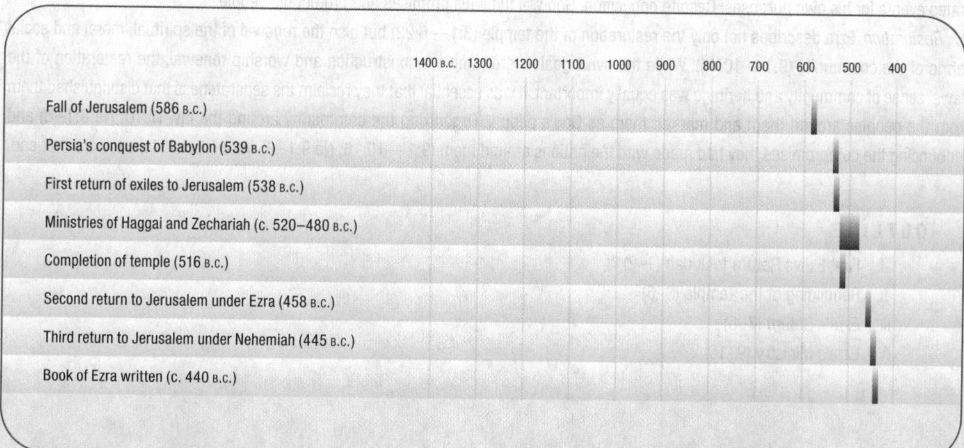

AS YOU READ

Try to imagine the joy that Ezra and his fellow returnees must have experienced as they set foot upon their home soil. God had been working miracles on their behalf: mellowing the hearts of kings, protecting the vulnerable returnees from fierce neighbors, enabling the temple to be rebuilt after initial work had been forcibly halted and overseeing every aspect of the restoration. Some of the returning Jews no doubt even reconnected with friends and relatives. Ezra, whose every wish had been granted by Artaxerxes, began teaching Moses' Law to the people, reestablishing it as the only authoritative guide for living, and temple services began in earnest. All things considered, life for the Jewish remnant was going along pretty well. Or was it?

Watch how unfalteringly Ezra, a committed follower and teacher of Moses' Law, focused upon temple worship. Imagine the people's shock as they discovered, many perhaps for the first time, the reality of their sin and their need to become God's holy people, who would once again be set apart from neighboring idol-worshipers. Experience vicariously Ezra's anger and sorrow after learning that certain Jewish men had married Canaanite women and were practicing other religions. Pay close attention to the far-reaching consequences of the priest's response to the people's sinfulness.

DID YOU KNOW?

- A shekel (about .4 oz—11.34 g—of silver) was the average wage for a month's work. Thus a mina would have been the equivalent of five years' wages and a talent of 300 years' wages (2:69)!
- Tattenai and his associates were part of the elaborate system of informers and spies used by Near Eastern kings. Two officials who reported to the Persian monarch were known as "the king's eye" and "the king's ear." (5:3–5).
- Persian kings consistently helped to restore sanctuaries in their empire (6:3–5).
- The returning exiles were not uncompromising separatists but were willing to accept any who would disconnect themselves from the paganism of the foreigners introduced into the area by the Assyrians (6:19–21).
- The story of Esther, the queen who saved the Jewish people from massacre, fits into the interval of nearly 60 years that separates Ezra 7:1 from 6:22.
- In ancient societies mothers were given custody of their children when marriages were dissolved. In Babylon divorced women were granted their children and had to wait for them to grow up before remarrying (10:3).

THEMES

The book of Ezra includes the following themes:

1. *God's sovereignty.* God is sovereign over all peoples and rulers, even pagan kings (1:1; 6:22; 7:6,27). He controls history and orchestrates events for his own purposes. Despite opposition, God will fulfill his promises and protect his people.

2. *Restoration.* Ezra describes not only the restoration of the temple (3:1—6:22) but also the renewal of the spiritual, moral and social fabric of the community (9:1—10:44). While the overt goals were temple reconstruction and worship renewal, the restoration of the Jews' sense of community and heritage was equally important. It was essential that they reclaim the separateness that distinguished them from the peoples around them and marked them as God's people. Organizing the community around the law (7:10; Ne 8:1–8) and renouncing the compromises they had made with the nations around them (9:1—10:16; Ne 9:1–3) were crucial steps toward that end.

OUTLINE

I. First Exiles Return to Judah (1–2)
II. Rebuilding of the Temple (3–6)
III. Ezra's Return (7–8)
IV. Ezra's Ministry (9–10)

Cyrus Helps the Exiles to Return

1:1 [a]Jer 25:11-12; 29:10-14 [b]2Ch 36:22,23

1 In the first year of Cyrus king of Persia, in order to fulfill the word of the LORD spoken by Jeremiah,[a]
the LORD moved the heart[b] of Cyrus king of Persia to make a proclamation throughout his realm
and to put it in writing:

2"This is what Cyrus king of Persia says:
" 'The LORD, the God of heaven, has given me all the kingdoms of the earth and he has appoint-
ed[c] me to build[d] a temple for him at Jerusalem in Judah. 3Anyone of his people among you—may
his God be with him, and let him go up to Jerusalem in Judah and build the temple of the LORD,
the God of Israel, the God who is in Jerusalem. 4And the people of any place where survivors[e] may
now be living are to provide him with silver and gold, with goods and livestock, and with freewill
offerings[f] for the temple of God in Jerusalem.' "[g]

1:2 [c]Isa 44:28; 45:13 [d]Ezr 5:13
1:4 [e]Isa 10:20-22 [f]Nu 15:3; Ps 50:14; 54:6; 116:17 [g]Ezr 4:3; 5:13; 6:3,14

5Then the family heads of Judah and Benjamin,[h] and the priests and Levites—everyone whose heart
God had moved[i]—prepared to go up and build the house[j] of the LORD in Jerusalem. 6All their neighbors
assisted them with articles of silver and gold, with goods and livestock, and with valuable gifts, in addition
to all the freewill offerings. 7Moreover, King Cyrus brought out the articles belonging to the temple of the
LORD, which Nebuchadnezzar had carried away from Jerusalem and had placed in the temple of his god.[a][k]

1:5 [h]Ezr 4:1; Ne 11:4 [i]ver 1; Ex 35:20-22; 2Ch 36:22; Hag 1:14; Php 2:13 [j]Ps 127:1
1:7 [k]2Ki 24:13; 2Ch 36:7,10; Ezr 5:14; 6:5

[a] 7 Or *gods*

1:1 Cyrus, the founder of the Persian Empire, ruled the Persians from 559 to 530 B.C. The reference to the "first year" of his reign is connected to Cyrus's expanded rule following his capture of Babylon in 539 B.C. (See "Cyrus the Great" on p. 669 and "The Sippar Cylinder of Nabonidus" on p. 664.)

1:2 The religion of the Persian rulers was Zoroastrianism, which focused on the worship of a god named Ahura Mazda. This religion is based upon the teachings of Zoroaster, but very little of his life or teachings is known with certainty (the dates of his life are set at somewhere between 1400 and 1000 B.C.). It is not clear that the Zoroastrianism of the Persian Empire was as yet monotheistic. The Persian kings regularly affirmed the gods of the other nations; their religion was at least very inclusive in nature. Zoroastrianism never became a religious force outside of Persian culture. After the Muslim conquest of Persia it was almost exterminated, although it still survives to this day.

1:3 Cyrus instituted the policy of placating the gods of his subject peoples instead of carrying off their cult images as the Assyrians and the Babylonians had done earlier. His generosity to the Jews was paralleled by his benevolence to the Babylonians.

1:5 In ancient times the social structure was made up of extended family units—more like clans than modern nuclear families. Each unit consisted of a patriarch—the adult male authority figure, who was the "family head"—along with his wife, his sons and their wives, his grandchildren and various other dependents. (See "The Role of the Patriarch in Family Life" on p. 30.)

Cyrus the Great

EZRA 1 Cyrus II (Cyrus the Great, 559–530 B.C.) was a renowned conqueror and statesman who founded the **Persian**[1] Empire. Our knowledge of him comes from Herodotus's *History*, as well as from other Greek historians, Persian texts and **Babylonian** records. Cyrus inherited the rule of a small territory called Pars in southern Iran, north of the Persian Gulf. Between 553 and 540 B.C. he subdued Media in central Iran, the kingdom of Lydia in western Anatolia (modern Turkey) and territories to the east, until he reigned from the Aegean Sea to the Indus River. Isaiah prophesied of Cyrus's deliverance of the Jews from captivity, calling him the Lord's "anointed" (Isa 45:1).

Isaiah's predictions, as well as those of Jeremiah (Jer 25:12; 29:10), were fulfilled in 539 B.C. when Cyrus captured Babylon.[2] According to the Babylonian Chronicle, Cyrus's army entered Babylon without a battle on October 12, 539 B.C. Cyrus himself entered the city 17 days later, on October 29. With the addition of the **Neo-Babylonian** Empire, he now controlled the entirety of **Mesopotamia**, **Anatolia** and the Levant (Syria-Palestine).

Cyrus was a beneficent king who allowed captive peoples to return to their homelands and restore their places of worship; this applied as well to the Jews residing in Babylon. Cyrus was not devoted to the God of Israel—in the Cyrus Cylinder he showed great reverence for Marduk of Babylon—but his policy of toleration for the religions of local populations worked to the Jews' advantage.[3]

[1]See Glossary on page 2080 for definitions of bolded words. [2]See "Herodotus and the Fall of Babylon" on page 1283. [3]See "The Cyrus Cylinder" on page 679.

[8]Cyrus king of Persia had them brought by Mithredath the treasurer, who counted them out to Sheshbazzar[l] the prince of Judah.

[9]This was the inventory:

gold dishes	30
silver dishes	1,000
silver pans[a]	29
[10]gold bowls	30
matching silver bowls	410
other articles	1,000

[11]In all, there were 5,400 articles of gold and of silver. Sheshbazzar brought all these along when the exiles came up from Babylon to Jerusalem.

1:8 [l]Ezr 5:14

The List of the Exiles Who Returned

2 Now these are the people of the province who came up from the captivity of the exiles,[m] whom Neb-
uchadnezzar king of Babylon[n] had taken captive to Babylon (they returned to Jerusalem and Judah,
each to his own town,[o] [2]in company with Zerubbabel,[p] Jeshua,[q] Nehemiah, Seraiah,[r] Reelaiah, Morde-
cai, Bilshan, Mispar, Bigvai, Rehum and Baanah):

2:1 [m]2Ch 36:20; Ne 7:6 [n]2Ki 24:16; 25:12 [o]Ne 7:73
2:2 [p]1Ch 3:19 [q]Ezr 3:2 [r]Ne 10:2

The list of the men of the people of Israel:

[3]the descendants of Parosh[s]	2,172
[4]of Shephatiah	372
[5]of Arah	775
[6]of Pahath-Moab (through the line of Jeshua and Joab)	2,812
[7]of Elam	1,254
[8]of Zattu	945
[9]of Zaccai	760
[10]of Bani	642
[11]of Bebai	623
[12]of Azgad	1,222
[13]of Adonikam[t]	666
[14]of Bigvai	2,056
[15]of Adin	454
[16]of Ater (through Hezekiah)	98
[17]of Bezai	323
[18]of Jorah	112
[19]of Hashum	223
[20]of Gibbar	95
[21]the men of Bethlehem[u]	123
[22]of Netophah	56
[23]of Anathoth	128
[24]of Azmaveth	42
[25]of Kiriath Jearim,[b] Kephirah and Beeroth	743

2:3 [s]Ezr 8:3
2:13 [t]Ezr 8:13
2:21 [u]Mic 5:2

[a] 9 The meaning of the Hebrew for this word is uncertain. [b] 25 See Septuagint (see also Neh. 7:29); Hebrew *Kiriath Arim*.

1:8 Sheshbazzar's name is Babylonian, but he was probably a Jewish official acting as a deputy governor of Judah under the satrap in Samaria (see 5:14). It was common for Jews in Babylon to receive "official" Babylonian names (cf. Da 1:7), and some scholars believe that Sheshbazzar and Zerubbabel were in fact the same person. Both were governors (Ezr 5:14; Hag 1:1; 2:2), both are said to have laid the foundation of the temple (Ezr 3:2–8; 5:16; Hag 1:14–15; Zec 4:6–10) and Josephus (*Antiquities*, 11.1.3) seems to have identified Sheshbazzar with Zerubbabel.

2:1 The caravan probably followed the Euphrates River up to a point east of Aleppo, crossed west to the Orontes River valley and then moved south. It would have passed either through the Beqa'a Valley in Lebanon or through Damascus en route to the promised land.

2:2 Zerubbabel was the son of Shealtiel and the grandson of Jehoiachin (1Ch 3:17), the next-to-last king of Judah. The last of the Davidic line to be entrusted with political authority by the occupying powers, Zerubbabel was also an ancestor of Jesus.

Jeshua is the same as the Joshua of Haggai 1:1. He was the son of the high priest Jehozadak, who was taken into exile (1Ch 6:15).

The Nehemiah here is not the Nehemiah of the book by that name.

2:26 [v]Jos 18:25	26 of Ramah[v] and Geba	621
	27 of Micmash	122
2:28 [w]Ge 12:8	28 of Bethel and Ai[w]	223
	29 of Nebo	52
	30 of Magbish	156
	31 of the other Elam	1,254
	32 of Harim	320
	33 of Lod, Hadid and Ono	725
2:34 [x]1Ki 16:34; 2Ch 28:15	34 of Jericho[x]	345
	35 of Senaah	3,630
	36 The priests:	
2:36 [y]1Ch 24:7	the descendants of Jedaiah[y] (through the family of Jeshua)	973
2:37 [z]1Ch 24:14	37 of Immer[z]	1,052
2:38 [a]1Ch 9:12	38 of Pashhur[a]	1,247
2:39 [b]1Ch 24:8	39 of Harim[b]	1,017
2:40 [c]Ge 29:34; Nu 3:9; Dt 18:6-7; 1Ch 16:4; Ezr 7:7; 8:15; Ne 12:24 [d]Ezr 3:9	40 The Levites:[c]	
	the descendants of Jeshua[d] and Kadmiel (through the line of Hodaviah)	74
2:41 [e]1Ch 15:16	41 The singers:[e]	
	the descendants of Asaph	128
2:42 [f]1Sa 3:15; 1Ch 9:17	42 The gatekeepers[f] of the temple:	
	the descendants of Shallum, Ater, Talmon, Akkub, Hatita and Shobai	139
2:43 [g]1Ch 9:2; Ne 11:21	43 The temple servants:[g]	
	the descendants of Ziha, Hasupha, Tabbaoth, 44 Keros, Siaha, Padon, 45 Lebanah, Hagabah, Akkub, 46 Hagab, Shalmai, Hanan, 47 Giddel, Gahar, Reaiah, 48 Rezin, Nekoda, Gazzam, 49 Uzza, Paseah, Besai, 50 Asnah, Meunim, Nephusim, 51 Bakbuk, Hakupha, Harhur, 52 Bazluth, Mehida, Harsha, 53 Barkos, Sisera, Temah, 54 Neziah and Hatipha	
	55 The descendants of the servants of Solomon:	
	the descendants of Sotai, Hassophereth, Peruda, 56 Jaala, Darkon, Giddel, 57 Shephatiah, Hattil, Pokereth-Hazzebaim and Ami	
2:58 [h]1Ki 9:21; 1Ch 9:2	58 The temple servants[h] and the descendants of the servants of Solomon	392

2:28 Although the towns of Bethel, Mizpah, Gibeon and Gibeah seem to have escaped the Babylonian assault, Bethel was destroyed during the transition between the Babylonian and Persian periods. Archaeological excavations reveal that there was a small town on Bethel's site in Ezra's day. (See "Bethel" on p. 59, "Mizpah" on p. 383, "Gibeon" on p. 318 and "Gibeah" on p. 380.)

Languages of the Old Testament World

Administrative letter addressed to Hammurabi
Preserving Bible Times; © Dr. James C. Martin; permission of The British Museum

EZRA 2 The ancient Near East encompassed a large number of different languages, the most significant of which were **Sumerian**, Egyptian, **Akkadian**, **Ugaritic**, **Aramaic** and Hebrew. Understanding these languages has considerably aided our knowledge of Israel's social, economic, political and linguistic environment.

✣ *Sumerian*: History's first written language (c. 3100 B.C.), Sumerian used pictures (called pictographs) to represent words or ideas. Thousands of pictographs were needed to write in Sumerian, but these eventually came to be written abstractly as **cuneiform**, wedge-shaped characters incised into clay with a pointed, reed stylus. Although Sumerian was unrelated to the ancient Semitic languages of the Near East (such as Hebrew), many Semitic languages adopted the use of cuneiform writing.[1]

✣ *Egyptian*: As history's second written language (also c. 3100 B.C.), Egyptian produced a unique pictographic script called **hieroglyphics**, which is found in pyramid inscriptions. Though not Semitic, Egyptian was related to Semitic languages and shared some features with them.

✣ *Akkadian*: A Semitic language, Akkadian falls into the same language group as Hebrew. Used from at least the seventeenth century B.C. to the first century A.D., it was a northeastern, **Mesopotamian** Semitic language that borrowed some Sumerian vocabulary. Akkadian was spoken in both **Babylonia** and **Assyria**,[2] and thousands of Akkadian tablets preserve records of the economic, religious, royal and legal life of these societies. The Babylonian dialect became the international language of communication during the **Late Bronze Age**.[3] Knowledge of the Akkadian language often helps to clarify the meaning of an obscure word in Biblical Hebrew.

✣ *Ugaritic*: This language has significantly improved our understanding of Hebrew grammar and vocabulary. It too was a northwestern Semitic language closely related to Hebrew and similar to the language of the Canaanites (by comparison, Akkadian was a northeastern Semitic language and somewhat more distant from Hebrew). Ugaritic employed an alphabetic cuneiform (i.e., used cuneiform signs to represent individual letters) and is preserved in approximately 1,300 administrative, economic and religious documents from the fourteenth to the thirteenth centuries B.C.[4]

✣ *Aramaic*: This language spans at least the last 3,000 years of the Old Testament period. Like Hebrew and Ugaritic, it was a northwestern Semitic language. Aramaic utilized a 22-letter alphabet borrowed from the **Phoenician**[5] language. It became the international language of communication for the Assyrians, Babylonians and **Persians** during the first millennium B.C. The Persian Empire's "standardized" Aramaic has been dubbed Imperial Aramaic—the dialect of the governmental communiqué in Ezra 4. The books of Ezra and Daniel were partially written in Aramaic, and traces of Aramaic are scattered throughout the Old Testament.

Hieroglyphic writing from Karnak, Egypt
Preserving Bible Times; © Dr. James C. Martin

✣ *Hebrew*: Hebrew uses the same alphabet as Aramaic. Attested outside the Bible from the tenth century B.C., it was the language of the Israelites and of most of the Old Testament. Although the present Old Testament is primarily rendered in a standard Biblical Hebrew, traces of ancient Hebrew dialects are apparent in the text (e.g., Jdg 12:6). During the **intertestamental period** Aramaic gradually replaced Hebrew as the spoken language of the Jews[6] (Jesus spoke Aramaic; e.g., Mt 27:46). A modern version of Hebrew is spoken by Israelis today, but it has a number of substantial differences from the classical form.

Early pictographic writing from Upper Egypt, c. 2950 B.C.
© The Schøyen Collection; photography courtesy of Mr. Martin Schøyen

[1]See "Cuneiform and Clay Tablets in the Ancient Near East" on page 1108 and "Writing Materials in the Ancient World" on page 2037. [2]See "Babylon" on page 1077 and "Assyria Through the Middle Assyrian Period" on page 1501. [3]See "Archaeological Periods" chart on page xx in the front of this Bible. [4]See "Tablets From Ugarit and Canaanite Religion" on page 304 and "Ugarit/Ras Shamra" on page 819. [5]See "Phoenicia" on page 488. [6]See "The Intertestamental Period" on page 1551.

59 The following came up from the towns of Tel Melah, Tel Harsha, Kerub, Addon and Immer,
2:59 [i]Nu 1:18 but they could not show that their families were descended[i] from Israel:

60 The descendants of
Delaiah, Tobiah and Nekoda 652

61 And from among the priests:

The descendants of
Hobaiah, Hakkoz and Barzillai (a man who had married a daughter of Barzillai the
2:61 [j]2Sa 17:27 Gileadite[j] and was called by that name).

62 These searched for their family records, but they could not find them and so were excluded
2:62 [k]Nu 3:10; 16:39-40 from the priesthood[k] as unclean. 63 The governor ordered them not to eat any of the most sacred
2:63 [l]Lev 2:3,10 [m]Ex 28:30; Nu 27:21 food[l] until there was a priest ministering with the Urim and Thummim.[m]

64 The whole company numbered 42,360, 65 besides their 7,337 menservants and maidservants;
2:65 [n]2Sa 19:35 and they also had 200 men and women singers.[n] 66 They had 736 horses,[o] 245 mules, 67 435 cam-
2:66 [o]Isa 66:20 els and 6,720 donkeys.

2:68 [p]Ex 25:2 68 When they arrived at the house of the LORD in Jerusalem, some of the heads of the families[p] gave
freewill offerings toward the rebuilding of the house of God on its site. 69 According to their ability they
gave to the treasury for this work 61,000 drachmas[a] of gold, 5,000 minas[b] of silver and 100 priestly gar-
ments.

70 The priests, the Levites, the singers, the gatekeepers and the temple servants settled in their own
2:70 [q]ver 1; 1Ch 9:2; Ne 11:3-4 towns, along with some of the other people, and the rest of the Israelites settled in their towns.[q]

Rebuilding the Altar

3:1 [r]Ne 7:73; 8:1 [s]Lev 23:24 3 When the seventh month came and the Israelites had settled in their towns,[r] the people assembled[s]
3:2 [t]Ezr 2:2; Ne 12:1,8; Hag 2:2 [u]Hag 1:1; Zec 6:11 as one man in Jerusalem. 2 Then Jeshua[t] son of Jozadak[u] and his fellow priests and Zerubbabel son
of Shealtiel[v] and his associates began to build the altar of the God of Israel to sacrifice burnt offerings
[v]1Ch 3:17 on it, in accordance with what is written in the Law of Moses[w] the man of God. 3 Despite their fear[x] of the
[w]Ex 20:24; Dt 12:5-6 peoples around them, they built the altar on its foundation and sacrificed burnt offerings on it to the
3:3 [x]Ezr 4:4; Da 9:25 LORD, both the morning and evening sacrifices.[y] 4 Then in accordance with what is written, they celebrat-
[y]Ex 29:39; Nu 28:1-8 ed the Feast of Tabernacles[z] with the required number of burnt offerings prescribed for each day. 5 After
3:4 [z]Ex 23:16; Nu 29:12-38; Ne 8:14-18; Zec 14:16-19 that, they presented the regular burnt offerings, the New Moon[a] sacrifices and the sacrifices for all the
appointed sacred feasts of the LORD,[b] as well as those brought as freewill offerings to the LORD. 6 On the
3:5 [a]Nu 28:3,11, 14; Col 2:16 [b]Lev 23:1-44; Nu 29:39 first day of the seventh month they began to offer burnt offerings to the LORD, though the foundation of
the LORD's temple had not yet been laid.

Rebuilding the Temple

7 Then they gave money to the masons and carpenters, and gave food and drink and oil to the people
3:7 [c]1Ch 14:1 [d]Isa 35:2 [e]Ezr 1:2-4; 6:3 of Sidon and Tyre, so that they would bring cedar logs[c] by sea from Lebanon[d] to Joppa, as authorized by
Cyrus[e] king of Persia.

8 In the second month of the second year after their arrival at the house of God in Jerusalem, Zerub-
3:8 [f]Zec 4:9 [g]1Ch 23:24 babel[f] son of Shealtiel, Jeshua son of Jozadak and the rest of their brothers (the priests and the Levites
and all who had returned from the captivity to Jerusalem) began the work, appointing Levites twenty[g]

[a] *69* That is, about 1,100 pounds (about 500 kilograms) [b] *69* That is, about 3 tons (about 2.9 metric tons)

2:59 Ezekiel 1:1 records that Jewish exiles had settled along the Kebar River, perhaps near Nippur, a city in southern Mesopotamia. Clay tablets from the Murashu archives at Nippur reveal the presence of Jews remaining there a century after Ezra.

2:63 See "The Urim and Thummim" on page 136.

2:69 The drachma was a Greek silver coin. Some believe, however, that the coin intended here was the Persian daric, a gold coin.

According to the Mesopotamian system there were 60 shekels in a mina and 60 minas in a talent. A shekel (about .4 oz—11.34 g—of silver) was the average wage for a month's work. Thus a mina would have been the equivalent of five years' wages; a talent, 300 years' wages!

3:1 The "seventh month" was Tishri (September–October), about three months after the arrival of the exiles in Judah (in 537 B.C.). Tishri was one of the most sacred months of the Jewish year (see Lev 23:23–43; see also "The Festivals of Israel" on p. 186).

3:2 Jeshua the high priest was the grandson of Seraiah, who had been put to death by Nebuchadnezzar's forces. There being no king in Jerusalem after the exile, the high priest's office took on great prestige and political power. By the time of the New Testament, priestly involvement in politics had led to great corruption in the priesthood and discontent among the Jews.

years of age and older to supervise the building of the house of the LORD. 9 Jeshua[h] and his sons and broth- 3:9 [h]Ezr 2:40
ers and Kadmiel and his sons (descendants of Hodaviah[a]) and the sons of Henadad and their sons and
brothers—all Levites—joined together in supervising those working on the house of God.
10 When the builders laid[i] the foundation of the temple of the LORD, the priests in their vestments and 3:10 [i]Ezr 5:16 [j]Nu 10:2; 1Ch 16:6 [k]1Ch 25:1 [l]1Ch 6:31 [m]Zec 6:12
with trumpets,[j] and the Levites (the sons of Asaph) with cymbals, took their places to praise[k] the LORD,
as prescribed by David[l] king of Israel.[m] 11 With praise and thanks-
giving they sang to the LORD:

> "He is good;
> his love to Israel endures forever."[n] 3:11 [n]1Ch 16:34, 41; 2Ch 7:3; Ps 107:1; 118:1 [o]Ne 12:24

And all the people gave a great shout[o] of praise to the LORD, because
the foundation of the house of the LORD was laid. 12 But many of the
older priests and Levites and family heads, who had seen the for-
mer temple,[p] wept aloud when they saw the foundation of this tem- 3:12 [p]Hag 2:3,9
ple being laid, while many others shouted for joy. 13 No one could dis-
tinguish the sound of the shouts of joy[q] from the sound of weeping, 3:13 [q]Job 8:21; Ps 27:6; Isa 16:9
because the people made so much noise. And the sound was heard
far away.

Opposition to the Rebuilding

4 When the enemies of Judah and Benjamin heard that the exiles
were building a temple for the LORD, the God of Israel, 2 they
came to Zerubbabel and to the heads of the families and said, "Let
us help you build because, like you, we seek your God and have been
sacrificing to him since the time of Esarhaddon[r] king of Assyria, 4:2 [r]2Ki 17:24; 19:37 [s]2Ki 17:41
who brought us here."[s]
3 But Zerubbabel, Jeshua and the rest of the heads of the families of Israel answered, "You have no part
with us in building a temple to our God. We alone will build it for the LORD, the God of Israel, as King Cy-
rus, the king of Persia, commanded us."[t] 4:3 [t]Ezr 1:1-4; Ne 2:20
4 Then the peoples around them set out to discourage the people of Judah and make them afraid to
go on building.[b][u] 5 They hired counselors to work against them and frustrate their plans during the en- 4:4 [u]Ezr 3:3
tire reign of Cyrus king of Persia and down to the reign of Darius king of Persia.

Later Opposition Under Xerxes and Artaxerxes

6 At the beginning of the reign of Xerxes,[c][v] they lodged an accusation against the people of Judah and 4:6 [v]Est 1:1; Da 9:1 [w]Est 3:13; 9:5
Jerusalem.[w]

ANCIENT VOICES

After (the death of)* [Pit]hana, my father, in the first year I suppressed a revolt. [Whate]ver land arose (in revolt) from the direction of the east, I de[feated] them all. I devoted (them) to the Stormgod of Nesa. We [all]otted (them) to the Stormgod [of Nesa(?)] (as) a de[voted thing]. Whoever after me becomes king, whoever resettles [the cities of Ullamma, Tenend]a, and Harkiuna, [the enemies of] Nesa, let him be enemy to [the Stormgod] of Nesa.

*Words or syllables in brackets or in parentheses added by translator for clarity or where text has gaps. Uncertainty in translation indicated by question mark within parentheses

—PROCLAMATION OF ANITTA OF KUSSAR

See "A Curse on Resettling a City From the Hittite Empire" article.

[a] 9 Hebrew *Yehudah,* probably a variant of *Hodaviah* [b] 4 Or *and troubled them as they built* [c] 6 Hebrew *Ahasuerus,* a variant of Xerxes' Persian name

3:10–11 For commentary on Old Testament expressions of joy, see the note on Psalm 96:11.
3:10 Trumpets were made of hammered silver. According to Josephus (*Antiquities*, 3.12.6, written c. A.D. 93), the trumpet was "in length a little short of a cubit [18 in. or 45.7 cm]; it is a narrow tube, slightly thicker than a flute." Trumpets were nearly always blown by priests and were most often used on joyous occasions. (See the note on Nu 10:1–10.)
3:11–13 Loud shouting expressed great jubilation or intense purpose (cf. 10:12; Jos 6:5,20; 1Sa 4:5; Ps 95:1–2). Traditionally Israelites revealed their emotions by weeping aloud (cf. Ezr 10:1; Ne 1:4; 8:9). In more recent history the Israelis reacted similarly when they reached the Wailing Wall in their war against the Arabs in 1967. For commentary on Old Testament expressions of joy, see the note on Psalm 96:11.
4:1–5 Construction of the second temple was begun in 536 B.C. on the Solomonic foundations leveled a half century earlier by the Babylonians. People who remembered the richness of the earlier temple wept at the negative comparison (3:12). Not until 516 B.C., the sixth year of the Persian emperor Darius I (see "Darius I" on p. 676), was the construction finally completed at the urging of Haggai and Zechariah (6:13–15).

Archaeological evidence confirms that the Persian period in the Holy Land was a comparatively impoverished time in terms of material culture. Later Aramaic documents from Elephantine in Upper Egypt illustrate the official process of gaining permission to construct a Jewish place of worship, as well as the opposition engendered by the presence of various foes during the period.

Of the temple and its construction little is known. Among the few contemporary buildings, the Persian palace at Lachish and the Tobiad monument at Iraq-el-Amir may be compared in terms of technique.

Unlike the more famous structures razed in 586 B.C. and A.D. 70, respectively, the temple begun by Zerubbabel suffered no major hostile destruction but was gradually repaired and reconstructed over a long period. Eventually it was replaced entirely by Herod's magnificent but short-lived edifice.
4:1–2 The people offering "help" were evidently from Samaria, the area of the former northern kingdom of Israel. After the northern kingdom's fall in 722 B.C., Assyrian kings had imported new inhabitants from Mesopotamia and Aram (see "Syria/Aram" on p. 534), who continued to worship their own gods but who also tried to worship the Lord as the god of the land (2Ki 17:24–41).
4:6–24 Ezra 4 summarizes various attempts to thwart the Jews' efforts. In verses 1–5 the author continued to describe events under

4:7 [x]Ezr 7:1; Ne 2:1 [y]2Ki 18:26; Isa 36:11; Da 2:4

[7] And in the days of Artaxerxes[x] king of Persia, Bishlam, Mithredath, Tabeel and the rest of his asso-
ciates wrote a letter to Artaxerxes. The letter was written in Aramaic script and in the Aramaic[y] lan-
guage.[a,b]

[8] Rehum the commanding officer and Shimshai the secretary wrote a letter against Jerusalem to Ar-
taxerxes the king as follows:

4:9 [z]Ezr 5:6; 6:6, 13

4:10 [a]ver 17; Ne 4:2

[9] Rehum the commanding officer and Shimshai the secretary, together with the rest of their asso-
ciates[z]—the judges and officials over the men from Tripolis, Persia,[c] Erech and Babylon, the Elam-
ites of Susa, [10] and the other people whom the great and honorable Ashurbanipal[d] deported and
settled in the city of Samaria and elsewhere in Trans-Euphrates.[a]

[11] (This is a copy of the letter they sent him.)

To King Artaxerxes,

From your servants, the men of Trans-Euphrates:

4:12 [b]Ezr 5:3,9

[12] The king should know that the Jews who came up to us from you have gone to Jerusalem and
are rebuilding that rebellious and wicked city. They are restoring the walls and repairing the foun-
dations.[b]

[a] 7 Or *written in Aramaic and translated* [b] 7 The text of Ezra 4:8–6:18 is in Aramaic. [c] 9 Or *officials, magistrates and governors over the men from* [d] 10 Aramaic *Osnappar,* a variant of *Ashurbanipal*

Cyrus (c. 536–530 B.C.), but in verse 6 he fast-forwarded to those under Xerxes (485–465 B.C.) and in verses 7–23 to occurrences under Artaxerxes I (464–424 B.C.). The situation involving Artaxerxes, which took place many years after the completion of the temple rebuilding project in 516, pertained to the rebuilding of the walls of Jerusalem—a primary setting for the book of Nehemiah. The author then reverted in verse 24 to the second year of Darius (520 B.C.), when work on the temple was renewed.

4:7 Aramaic had become the international language of the Near East, known and used by those experienced in diplomacy and commerce. (See "Languages of the Old Testament World" on p. 672.)

4:10 Ashurbanipal is not named elsewhere in the Bible, but he was probably the Assyrian king who freed Manasseh from exile (2Ch 33:11–13) and may also have been the unnamed Assyrian ruler who brought people to Samaria (2Ki 17:24). He was famous for his library at Nineveh.

"Trans-Euphrates" literally means "beyond the [Euphrates] River." From the "Palestinian" point of view the land "beyond the River" was Mesopotamia (Jos 24:2–3,14–15; 2Sa 10:16), but from the Mesopotamian perspective it included the areas of Aram, Phoenicia and the region only much later known as Palestine (1Ki 4:24). The Persians also called this area Athura. (See "Syria/Aram" on p. 534 and "Phoenicia" on p. 488.)

ANCIENT TEXTS AND ARTIFACTS

A Curse on Resettling a City From the Hittite Empire

EZRA 4 A **Hittite** document demonstrates the lasting results insurrection against one's sovereign might have brought about in the ancient Near East. In the wake of the death of the Hittite king Pithana, numerous cities revolted as Anitta, Pithana's heir, attempted to consolidate his control. King Anitta, however, proved to be a powerful ruler who was able to defeat the rebellious cities during his first regnal year (first partial year of his reign). He completely decimated the insubordinate towns and annihilated their inhabitants, proclaiming a curse upon any future king who might attempt to resettle the ruins. The remains would stand as a reminder of what had befallen those who had defied the Hittite king.[1]

A similar concern existed in the later **Persian** Empire. When the returning Jewish exiles began to rebuild the Jerusalem temple, their enemies drafted a libelous letter to King Artaxerxes,[2] reminding him of the previous rebellions of Jerusalem and suggesting that if the city were rebuilt it would exist as a seedbed of resistance to Persian rule. Their tactics were successful; the Israelites were forced to desist from work on the temple until the reign of Darius.[3]

In the ancient world kings were ever on the lookout for signs of rebellion. Reports that a city was about to revolt could prove disastrous for that city. The false accusation against the Jews was more than a nuisance: It could have provoked a holocaust.[4]

[1]See "Anatolia and the Hittites" on page 144. [2]See "Artaxerxes I, King of Persia" on page 681. [3]See "Darius I" on page 676. [4]See also "The Postexilic Period of the Old Testament: The Persian Period" on page 699.

13 Furthermore, the king should know that if this city is built and its walls are restored, no more
taxes, tribute or duty[c] will be paid, and the royal revenues will suffer. 14 Now since we are under ob- 4:13 [c]Ezr 7:24; Ne 5:4
ligation to the palace and it is not proper for us to see the king dishonored, we are sending this mes-
sage to inform the king, 15 so that a search may be made in the archives[d] of your predecessors. In 4:15 [d]Ezr 5:17; 6:1 [e]Est 3:8
these records you will find that this city is a rebellious city, troublesome to kings and provinces, a
place of rebellion from ancient times. That is why this city was destroyed.[e] 16 We inform the king that
if this city is built and its walls are restored, you will be left with nothing in Trans-Euphrates.

17 The king sent this reply:

To Rehum the commanding officer, Shimshai the secretary and the rest of their associates living
in Samaria and elsewhere in Trans-Euphrates:[f] 4:17 [f]ver 10

Greetings.

18 The letter you sent us has been read and translated in my presence. 19 I issued an order and a
search was made, and it was found that this city has a long history of revolt[g] against kings and has 4:19 [g]2Ki 18:7
been a place of rebellion and sedition. 20 Jerusalem has had powerful kings ruling over the whole
of Trans-Euphrates,[h] and taxes, tribute and duty were paid to them. 21 Now issue an order to these 4:20 [h]Ge 15:18-21; Ex 23:31; Jos 1:4; 1Ki 4:21; 1Ch 18:3; Ps 72:8-11
men to stop work, so that this city will not be rebuilt until I so order. 22 Be careful not to neglect this
matter. Why let this threat grow, to the detriment of the royal interests?[i] 4:22 [i]Da 6:2

23 As soon as the copy of the letter of King Artaxerxes was read to Rehum and Shimshai the secretary
and their associates,[j] they went immediately to the Jews in Jerusalem and compelled them by force to stop. 4:23 [j]ver 9

24 Thus the work on the house of God in Jerusalem came to a standstill until the second year of the 4:24 [k]Ne 2:1-8; Da 9:25; Hag 1:1, 15; Zec 1:1
reign of Darius[k] king of Persia.

4:24 The prophet Haggai (Hag 1:1–5) exhorted Zerubbabel to begin rebuilding the temple on August 29, 519 B.C., and work actually began on September 21 (Hag 1:15). During his first two years Darius had to establish his right to the throne by fighting numerous rebels, as recounted in his famous Behistun Inscription (see "Darius I," below). It was only after the stabilization of the Persian Empire that efforts to rebuild the temple could be permitted.

Darius I

EZRA 5 The Jews who had returned from the **Babylonian captivity** began rebuilding the temple in 536 B.C.[1] Construction was halted, however, because of opposition from local adversaries of Judah.[2] Sixteen years later, on September 21, 520 B.C., work resumed with the encouragement of the prophets Haggai and Zechariah (Ezr 4:24; 5:1–2; Hag 1:4–15). The Jews were again challenged, this time by Tattenai, governor of the **Persian** province of Trans-Euphrates (Ezr 5:3–5). He is described as a local governor under the satrap of **Babylon** and Trans-Euphrates. Tattenai expressed concern about the rebuilding to the Persian king Darius I. However, after locating a copy of a decree made by Cyrus, Darius ordered Tattenai to fully support the reconstruction and even to provide government funding (6:1–12).[3] The temple was completed on March 12, 515 B.C.

Darius I ("the Great") ruled the Persian Empire from 521 to 486 B.C. He was an accomplished military commander, monumental builder and shrewd administrator[4] who is known both from classical sources and from records contemporary to his rule. The most famous document from Darius's reign is the Behistun Inscription, emblazoned high on a cliff face in western Iran. This declaration describes Darius's rise to power in three languages and has provided the key for deciphering the **Akkadian** language of **Mesopotamia**.[5] The palace of Darius I has been excavated at the royal center of Persepolis in southern Iran;[6] his tomb, carved into a rock face, is located 3 miles (4.8 km) north of the city.

[1]See "The 70 Years of Captivity" on page 1234. [2]See "A Curse on Resettling a City From the Hittite Empire" on page 675. [3]See "The Cyrus Cylinder" on page 679. [4]See "Ancient Persian History Through Daries" on page 717. [5]See "Languages of the Old Testament World" on page 672. [6]See "Persepolis" on page 1404.

Tattenai's Letter to Darius

5:1 [l]Ezr 6:14; Hag 1:1,3,12; 2:1,10,20 [m]Zec 1:1; 7:1 [n]Hag 1:14–2:9; Zec 4:9-10; 8:9 5:2 [o]1Ch 3:19; Hag 1:14; 2:21; Zec 4:6-10 [p]Ezr 2:2; 3:2 [q]ver 8; Hag 2:2-5 5:3 [r]Ezr 6:6 [s]Ezr 6:6 [t]ver 9; Ezr 1:3; 4:12 5:5 [u]2Ki 25:28; Ezr 7:6,9,28; 8:18,22,31; Ne 2:8,18; Ps 33:18; Isa 66:14

5 Now Haggai[l] the prophet and Zechariah[m] the prophet, a descendant of Iddo, prophesied[n] to the Jews in Judah and Jerusalem in the name of the God of Israel, who was over them. 2 Then Zerubbabel[o] son of Shealtiel and Jeshua[p] son of Jozadak set to work[q] to rebuild the house of God in Jerusalem. And the prophets of God were with them, helping them.

3 At that time Tattenai,[r] governor of Trans-Euphrates, and Shethar-Bozenai[s] and their associates went to them and asked, "Who authorized you to rebuild this temple and restore this structure?"[t] 4 They also asked, "What are the names of the men constructing this building?"[a] 5 But the eye of their God[u] was watching over the elders of the Jews, and they were not stopped until a report could go to Darius and his written reply be received.

6 This is a copy of the letter that Tattenai, governor of Trans-Euphrates, and Shethar-Bozenai and their associates, the officials of Trans-Euphrates, sent to King Darius. 7 The report they sent him read as follows:

To King Darius:

Cordial greetings.

5:8 [v]ver 2

8 The king should know that we went to the district of Judah, to the temple of the great God. The people are building it with large stones and placing the timbers in the walls. The work[v] is being carried on with diligence and is making rapid progress under their direction.

5:9 [w]Ezr 4:12

9 We questioned the elders and asked them, "Who authorized you to rebuild this temple and restore this structure?"[w] 10 We also asked them their names, so that we could write down the names of their leaders for your information.

11 This is the answer they gave us:

5:11 [x]1Ki 6:1; 2Ch 3:1-2 5:12 [y]2Ch 36:16 [z]Dt 21:10; 28:36; 2Ki 24:1; 25:8,9,11; Jer 1:3 5:13 [a]Ezr 1:1

"We are the servants of the God of heaven and earth, and we are rebuilding the temple[x] that was built many years ago, one that a great king of Israel built and finished. 12 But because our fathers angered[y] the God of heaven, he handed them over to Nebuchadnezzar the Chaldean, king of Babylon, who destroyed this temple and deported the people to Babylon.[z]

13 "However, in the first year of Cyrus king of Babylon, King Cyrus issued a decree[a] to rebuild this house of God. 14 He even removed from the temple[b] of Babylon the gold and silver articles of the house of God, which Nebuchadnezzar had taken from the temple in Jerusalem and brought to the temple[b] in Babylon.[b]

5:14 [b]Ezr 1:7; 6:5; Da 5:2 [c]1Ch 3:18 5:16 [d]Ezr 3:10; 6:15

"Then King Cyrus gave them to a man named Sheshbazzar,[c] whom he had appointed governor, 15 and he told him, 'Take these articles and go and deposit them in the temple in Jerusalem. And rebuild the house of God on its site.' 16 So this Sheshbazzar came and laid the foundations of the house of God[d] in Jerusalem. From that day to the present it has been under construction but is not yet finished."

5:17 [e]Ezr 4:15; 6:1,2

17 Now if it pleases the king, let a search be made in the royal archives[e] of Babylon to see if King Cyrus did in fact issue a decree to rebuild this house of God in Jerusalem. Then let the king send us his decision in this matter.

The Decree of Darius

6:1 [f]Ezr 4:15; 5:17

6 King Darius then issued an order, and they searched in the archives[f] stored in the treasury at Babylon. 2 A scroll was found in the citadel of Ecbatana in the province of Media, and this was written on it:

Memorandum:

3 In the first year of King Cyrus, the king issued a decree concerning the temple of God in Jerusalem:

[a] 4 See Septuagint; Aramaic *4 We told them the names of the men constructing this building.* [b] 14 Or *palace*

5:3–5 Near Eastern kings were masters at using informants and spies. Egyptian sources refer to the "ears and eyes" of the pharaoh, and Sargon II of Assyria had agents in Urartu whom he instructed, "Write me whatever you see and hear." Two officials who reported to the Persian monarch were known as "the king's eye" and "the king's ear." Tattenai and his associates were part of King Darius's elaborate spying system (see "A Curse on Resettling a City From the Hittite Empire" on p. 675), and texts found in the royal city of Persepolis confirm that inquiries/reports were sent directly to the king himself for review and action. But "the eye of their God" was watching over the Jews (v. 5).

6:1–2 There were several repositories of well-preserved royal archives at the major capitals. The Babylonian priest Berossus (third century B.C.) made use in his history of Babylon of the Babylonian Chronicles, which covered events from the Assyrian to the Hellenistic eras (beginning with Alexander's conquest of Babylon in 330 B.C.).

6:3–5 A similar memorandum dealing with permission to rebuild the Jewish temple at Elephantine in Egypt was found among fifth-

Let the temple be rebuilt as a place to present sacrifices, and let its foundations be laid.[g] It is
to be ninety feet[a] high and ninety feet wide, 4with three courses[h] of large stones and one of tim-
bers. The costs are to be paid by the royal treasury.[i] 5Also, the gold[j] and silver articles of the house
of God, which Nebuchadnezzar took from the temple in Jerusalem and brought to Babylon, are
to be returned to their places in the temple in Jerusalem; they are to be deposited in the house of
God.[k]

6Now then, Tattenai,[l] governor of Trans-Euphrates, and Shethar-Bozenai[m] and you, their fel-
low officials of that province, stay away from there. 7Do not interfere with the work on this temple
of God. Let the governor of the Jews and the Jewish elders rebuild this house of God on its site.

8Moreover, I hereby decree what you are to do for these elders of the Jews in the construction
of this house of God:

The expenses of these men are to be fully paid out of the royal treasury,[n] from the revenues[o] of
Trans-Euphrates, so that the work will not stop. 9Whatever is needed—young bulls, rams, male
lambs for burnt offerings[p] to the God of heaven, and wheat, salt, wine and oil, as requested by the
priests in Jerusalem—must be given them daily without fail, 10so that they may offer sacrifices
pleasing to the God of heaven and pray for the well-being of the king and his sons.[q]

11Furthermore, I decree that if anyone changes this edict, a beam is to be pulled from his house
and he is to be lifted up and impaled[r] on it. And for this crime his house is to be made a pile of rub-
ble.[s] 12May God, who has caused his Name to dwell there,[t] overthrow any king or people who lifts
a hand to change this decree or to destroy this temple in Jerusalem.

I Darius[u] have decreed it. Let it be carried out with diligence.

Completion and Dedication of the Temple

13Then, because of the decree King Darius had sent, Tattenai, governor of Trans-Euphrates, and She-
thar-Bozenai and their associates[v] carried it out with diligence. 14So the elders of the Jews continued to
build and prosper under the preaching[w] of Haggai the prophet and Zechariah, a descendant of Iddo.
They finished building the temple according to the command of the God of Israel and the decrees of Cy-
rus,[x] Darius[y] and Artaxerxes,[z] kings of Persia. 15The temple was completed on the third day of the month
Adar, in the sixth year of the reign of King Darius.[a]

16Then the people of Israel—the priests, the Levites and the rest of the exiles—celebrated the ded-
ication[b] of the house of God with joy. 17For the dedication of this house of God they offered[c] a hun-
dred bulls, two hundred rams, four hundred male lambs and, as a sin offering for all Israel, twelve male
goats, one for each of the tribes of Israel. 18And they installed the priests in their divisions[d] and the
Levites in their groups[e] for the service of God at Jerusalem, according to what is written in the Book
of Moses.[f]

6:3 [g]Ezr 3:10; Hag 2:3
6:4 [h]1Ki 6:36 [i]ver 8; Ezr 7:20
6:5 [j]1Ch 29:2 [k]Ezr 1:7; 5:14
6:6 [l]Ezr 5:3 [m]Ezr 5:3
6:8 [n]ver 4 [o]1Sa 9:20
6:9 [p]Lev 1:3,10
6:10 [q]Ezr 7:23; 1Ti 2:1-2
6:11 [r]Dt 21:22-23; Est 2:23; 5:14; 9:14 [s]Ezr 7:26; Da 2:5; 3:29
6:12 [t]Ex 20:24; Dt 12:5; 1Ki 9:3; 2Ch 6:2 [u]ver 14
6:13 [v]Ezr 4:9
6:14 [w]Ezr 5:1 [x]Ezr 1:1-4 [y]ver 12 [z]Ezr 7:1; Ne 2:1
6:15 [a]Zec 1:1; 4:9
6:16 [b]1Ki 8:63; 2Ch 7:5
6:17 [c]2Sa 6:13; 2Ch 29:21; 30:24; Ezr 8:35
6:18 [d]1Ch 23:6; 2Ch 35:4; Lk 1:5 [e]1Ch 24:1 [f]Nu 3:6-9; 8:9-11; 18:1-32

[a] 3 Aramaic *sixty cubits* (about 27 meters)

century B.C. Aramaic papyri recovered at that site. (See "Languages of the Old Testament World" on p. 672 and "The Cyrus Cylinder" on p. 679.)

Since the accounts in Haggai and Zechariah do not refer to support from the Persian treasury, some have questioned the promises made in verses 4 and 8 (see also 7:20). Extrabiblical evidence, however, makes it clear that Persian kings consistently helped to restore sanctuaries in their empire. Cyrus repaired temples at Uruk (Erech) and Ur, and Cambyses, his successor, gave funds for the temple at Sais in Egypt. The temple of Amon in the Khargah Oasis was rebuilt by order of Darius. Texts from the treasury at Persepolis also record the disbursement of supplies and funds from the royal purse.

6:9–10 In 1973 archaeologists discovered at Xanthos in southwestern Turkey a cult foundation charter from the late Persian period that provides some striking parallels to this decree of Cyrus. As in Ezra, amounts of sacrifices, names of priests and the responsibility for the upkeep of the cult are specified. That the Persian monarchs were interested in the details of foreign cults is shown clearly by the ordinances of Cambyses and Darius I, regulating the temples and priests in Egypt. On the authority of Darius II (423–404 B.C.) a letter was written to the Jews at Elephantine concerning the keeping of the Feast of Unleavened Bread. (See the note on 7:22.)

6:11 Impalement was a common form of execution among the Persians, as is confirmed in pictures and statues from the ancient Near East. According to Herodotus (3.159), Darius I impaled 3,000 Babylonians when he took the city of Babylon, a fact Darius himself recorded in his Behistun Inscription (see "Darius I" on p. 676).

6:12 At the end of his famous Behistun Inscription, Darius I warned: "If you see this inscription or these sculptures, and destroy them and do not protect them as long as you have strength, may Ahuramazda strike you, and may you not have a family, and what you do . . . may Ahuramazda utterly destroy." (For information on Darius I and his Behistun Inscription, see "Darius I" on p. 676.)

6:14 The reference to Artaxerxes seems out of place because this king (see "Artaxerxes I, King of Persia" on p. 681) did not contribute to the rebuilding process. His name may have been inserted here because he did contribute to the work of the temple at a later date under Ezra (7:21–24).

6:15 The temple restoration was completed on March 12, 516 B.C., almost 70 years after its destruction. The renewed work had begun on September 21, 520 B.C. (Hag 1:15), and sustained effort had continued for about three and a half years. The second temple, though not as grand as Solomon's, lasted much longer. The general plan of the second temple resembled that of the first. But the Most Holy Place was left empty, for the ark of the covenant had been lost through the Babylonian conquest.

6:18 The priests were separated into 24 divisions (1Ch 24:1–19), each serving at the temple for a week at a time (cf. Lk 1:5,8). In 1962 fragments of a synagogue inscription listing the 24 divisions were discovered at Caesarea.

The Passover

6:19 [g]Ex 12:11; Nu 28:16 6:20 [h]2Ch 30:15, 17; 35:11

[19]On the fourteenth day of the first month, the exiles celebrated the Passover.[g] [20]The priests and Le-
vites had purified themselves and were all ceremonially clean. The Levites slaughtered[h] the Passover
lamb for all the exiles, for their brothers the priests and for themselves. [21]So the Israelites who had

6:19–21 The returning exiles began celebrating Passover and the Feast of Unleavened Bread on April 21, 516 B.C. They were not uncompromising separatists but were willing to accept any who would disconnect themselves from the paganism of the foreigners introduced into the area by the Assyrians. "All who had separated themsleves" likely refers to Gentile converts but could also mean Israelites from the former northern kingdom or Judahites who had remained in Judah rather than being taken into exile.

ANCIENT TEXTS AND ARTIFACTS

The Cyrus Cylinder

EZRA 6 When work on the temple resumed in 520 B.C., the **Persian** governor Tattenai requested a search for the decree Cyrus had issued in 538 B.C. authorizing the Jews to rebuild their temple (Ezr 5:6—6:1).[1] A memorandum related to the decree was discovered in the royal archive at Ecbatana, one of the three imperial capitals. This memo, the treasury record of a grant made by Cyrus for rebuilding the temple, is quoted in 6:3–5 in **Aramaic**, the official language of the Persian Empire.[2] Cyrus's decree, recorded in full in 1:2–4, along with an abridged version in 2 Chronicles 36:23, both in Hebrew, was a proclamation to the Jewish people, allowing them to return to their homeland and rebuild their temple. Such generosity on the part of Cyrus stands in sharp contrast to usual practice in antiquity. Even so, it is clear from archaeological discoveries that this was indeed the official policy of Cyrus.[3]

The Cyrus Cylinder, an inscription on a clay barrel discovered in **Babylon** in 1879,[4] documents Cyrus's policy of religious tolerance and liberation. Like most inscriptions from ancient kings, the Cyrus Cylinder is boastful (Cyrus declared himself to be the great king of Babylon, **Sumer**, **Akkad** and of the four corners of the earth) and pagan (he proclaimed himself to be beloved of the gods Bel, Nebo and Marduk). On the other hand, Cyrus was determined to be a benevolent, rather than a heavy-handed, ruler: He pointed out that after his conquest of Babylon he did not allow his troops to terrorize the city.[5] Cyrus's record fully substantiates this generous and tolerant stance. He returned stolen images to their sanctuaries and, in his own words, "gathered all their inhabitants and returned (to them) their dwellings."

[1]See "Darius I" on page 676. [2]See "Languages of the Old Testament World" on page 672. [3]See "Cyrus the Great" on page 669. [4]See "Babylon" on page 1077. [5]See "Herodotus and the Fall of Babylon" on page 1283.

The Cyrus Cylinder

Preserving Bible Times; © Dr. James C. Martin; permission of The British Museum

returned from the exile ate it, together with all who had separated themselves[i] from the unclean prac-
tices[j] of their Gentile neighbors in order to seek the LORD,[k] the God of Israel. 22 For seven days they cele-
brated with joy the Feast of Unleavened Bread,[l] because the LORD had filled them with joy by changing
the attitude[m] of the king of Assyria, so that he assisted them in the work on the house of God, the God
of Israel.

6:21 [i]Ezr 9:1; Ne 9:2 [j]Dt 18:9; Ezr 9:11; Eze 36:25 [k]1Ch 22:19; Ps 14:2 **6:22** [l]Ex 12:17 [m]Ezr 1:1

Ezra Comes to Jerusalem

7 After these things, during the reign of Artaxerxes[n] king of Persia, Ezra son of Seraiah, the son of Az-
ariah, the son of Hilkiah,[o] 2 the son of Shallum, the son of Zadok,[p] the son of Ahitub,[q] 3 the son of Am-
ariah, the son of Azariah, the son of Meraioth, 4 the son of Zerahiah, the son of Uzzi, the son of Bukki, 5 the
son of Abishua, the son of Phinehas, the son of Eleazar, the son of Aaron the chief priest— 6 this Ezra[r]
came up from Babylon. He was a teacher well versed in the Law of Moses, which the LORD, the God of Is-
rael, had given. The king had granted him everything he asked, for the hand of the LORD his God was on
him.[s] 7 Some of the Israelites, including priests, Levites, singers, gatekeepers and temple servants, also
came up to Jerusalem in the seventh year of King Artaxerxes.[t]

8 Ezra arrived in Jerusalem in the fifth month of the seventh year of the king. 9 He had begun his jour-
ney from Babylon on the first day of the first month, and he arrived in Jerusalem on the first day of the
fifth month, for the gracious hand of his God was on him.[u] 10 For Ezra had devoted himself to the study
and observance of the Law of the LORD, and to teaching[v] its decrees and laws in Israel.

7:1 [n]Ezr 4:7; 6:14; Ne 2:1 [o]2Ki 22:4 **7:2** [p]1Ki 1:8; 1Ch 6:8 [q]Ne 11:11 **7:6** [r]Ne 12:36 [s]Ezr 5:5; Isa 41:20 **7:7** [t]Ezr 8:1 **7:9** [u]ver 6 **7:10** [v]ver 25; Dt 33:10; Ne 8:1-8

King Artaxerxes' Letter to Ezra

11 This is a copy of the letter King Artaxerxes had given to Ezra the priest and teacher, a man learned
in matters concerning the commands and decrees of the LORD for Israel:

12 [a] Artaxerxes, king of kings,[w]

To Ezra the priest, a teacher of the Law of the God of heaven:

Greetings.

13 Now I decree that any of the Israelites in my kingdom, including priests and Levites, who
wish to go to Jerusalem with you, may go. 14 You are sent by the king and his seven advisers[x] to in-
quire about Judah and Jerusalem with regard to the Law of your God, which is in your hand.
15 Moreover, you are to take with you the silver and gold that the king and his advisers have freely
given[y] to the God of Israel, whose dwelling[z] is in Jerusalem, 16 together with all the silver and gold[a]
you may obtain from the province of Babylon, as well as the freewill offerings of the people and
priests for the temple of their God in Jerusalem.[b] 17 With this money be sure to buy bulls, rams
and male lambs,[c] together with their grain offerings and drink offerings,[d] and sacrifice[e] them on
the altar of the temple of your God in Jerusalem.

18 You and your brother Jews may then do whatever seems best with the rest of the silver and
gold, in accordance with the will of your God. 19 Deliver[f] to the God of Jerusalem all the articles en-

7:12 [w]Eze 26:7; Da 2:37 **7:14** [x]Est 1:14 **7:15** [y]1Ch 29:6 [z]1Ch 29:6,9; 2Ch 6:2 **7:16** [a]Ezr 8:25 [b]Zec 6:10 **7:17** [c]2Ki 3:4 [d]Nu 15:5-12 [e]Dt 12:5-11 **7:19** [f]Ezr 5:14; Jer 27:22

[a] *12* The text of Ezra 7:12-26 is in Aramaic.

6:22 "The king of Assyria" is a surprising description of Darius, the king of Persia. But even after the fall of Assyria in 612 B.C. the term "Assyria" was used for territories formerly occupied by the Assyrians. Persian kings adopted a variety of titles (much as they accumulated gods), including "king of Babylon" (cf. 5:13; Ne 13:6).

The Persians assimilated the "best" ideas (gods and titles) from the cultures under their domination, adopting what seemed to fit and discarding what did not.

7:1 For information on Artaxerxes, see "Artaxerxes I, King of Persia" on page 681.

7:2 Zadok was a priest under David (2Sa 8:17). Solomon appointed Zadok as high priest in place of Abiathar, who supported the rebel Adonijah (1Ki 1:7–8; 2:35). The Zadokites, who were regarded as free from idolatry (Eze 44:15), held the office of high priest until 171 B.C. The Sadducees may have been named after Zadok, and the Qumran community looked for the restoration of the Zadokite priesthood.

7:6 Ezra was a scribe (see "The Scribe" on p. 682). For more information on scribal education and writing materials, see "Sumerian Scribal Education" on page 579 and "Writing Materials in the Ancient World" on page 2037.

7:9 The travelers had to cover a total of about 900 miles (1,450 km), turning to the northwest along the Euphrates River and then south. The journey required four months; their relatively slow pace was caused by the presence of the elderly and children.

7:15–26 The extensive powers given to Ezra by King Artaxerxes are striking. Ezra received an enormous "blank check" (see vv. 18–22; see the NIV text note on v. 22 regarding the amount of silver), and his authority extended to secular fields—with grave consequences for disobedience (vv. 25–26).

7:16 It was customary for Jews living outside the Holy Land to send gifts to Jerusalem. This practice ended after the Jewish-Roman War, when the Romans forced the Jews to send such contributions to the temple of Jupiter instead (Josephus, *Antiquities*, 18.9.1). Such directives are evidenced in the contemporary letters from the Jewish garrison at Elephantine in Egypt, including a papyrus in which Darius II ordered: "Let grain offering, incense and burnt offering be offered" on the altar of the god Yahu "in your name."

7:20 gEzr 6:4

trusted to you for worship in the temple of your God. 20 And anything else needed for the temple
of your God that you may have occasion to supply, you may provide from the royal treasury.[g]
21 Now I, King Artaxerxes, order all the treasurers of Trans-Euphrates to provide with diligence
whatever Ezra the priest, a teacher of the Law of the God of heaven, may ask of you— 22 up to a
hundred talents[a] of silver, a hundred cors[b] of wheat, a hundred baths[c] of wine, a hundred baths[c]
of olive oil, and salt without limit. 23 Whatever the God of heaven has prescribed, let it be done with
diligence for the temple of the God of heaven. Why should there be wrath against the realm of the
king and of his sons?[h] 24 You are also to know that you have no authority to impose taxes, tribute
or duty[i] on any of the priests, Levites, singers, gatekeepers, temple servants or other workers at
this house of God.[j]
25 And you, Ezra, in accordance with the wisdom of your God, which you possess, appoint[k] magistrates and judges to administer justice to all the people of Trans-Euphrates—all who know the

7:23 hEzr 6:10
7:24 iEzr 4:13 jEzr 8:36
7:25 kEx 18:21, 26; Dt 16:18

a 22 That is, about 3 3/4 tons (about 3.4 metric tons) b 22 That is, probably about 600 bushels (about 22 kiloliters) c 22 That is, probably about 600 gallons (about 2.2 kiloliters)

7:20 See the note on 6:3–5.
7:22 Similarly, Josephus (*Antiquities*, 12.3.3) described the benefaction of Antiochus III: "In the first place we have decided, on account of their piety, to furnish for their sacrifices an allowance of sacrificial animals, wine, oil and frankincense to the value of 20,000 pieces of silver, and sacred artabae of fine flour in accordance with their native law, and 1,460 medimni of wheat and 375 medimni of salt." (See the note on 6:9–10.)
7:24 Priests and other temple personnel were often exempt from enforced labor or taxes. Darius I (see "Darius I" on p. 676) granted similar exemptions to the priests of Apollo, and Antiochus III granted such exemptions to the Jews: "The priests, the scribes of the temple and the temple singers shall be relieved from the poll tax, the crown tax and the salt tax that they pay" (Josephus, *Antiquities*, 12.3.3).
7:25–26 Ezra was given extensive powers. Implementation of these provisions probably involved a great deal of traveling, which would explain the silence about Ezra's activities between his arrival and that of Nehemiah 13 years later.

Artaxerxes I, King of Persia

EZRA 7 Artaxerxes I (also called "Longimanus"), son of Xerxes I and Amestris and grandson of Darius I, ruled the **Persian** Empire from 464 to 424 B.C.[1] His domain included most of the civilized world, extending from Egypt to the western edge of India. According to Diodorus Siculus in *Library*, 11.69, Artaxerxes came to power after Artabanus, a courtier, had assassinated Xerxes. Artaxerxes then killed his older brother, Darius, and defeated his other brother, Hystaspes, satrap of Bactria. Artaxerxes is then said to have slain Artabanus in hand-to-hand combat.

Like most Persian rulers Artaxerxes had to struggle to maintain the empire. The most significant war during his reign involved an Egyptian rebellion against Persian authority that was complicated by Athenian support for the Egyptians. The war lasted from 460 to 454 B.C., but Persian armies under the command of Megabyzus, satrap of Syria, ultimately prevailed.

Artaxerxes played a prominent role in the **postexilic** Jewish community,[2] but the chronology of events is somewhat difficult to unravel. Sometime prior to 445 B.C. Jews in Jerusalem began rebuilding the city's defenses, but adversaries informed the king and the work was halted (Ezr 4:7–23). Yet in 458 B.C. Artaxerxes I allowed Ezra, in **exile** in **Babylon**, to return to Judah as spiritual leader of the Jewish people (ch. 7). Meanwhile, Nehemiah served as cupbearer to Artaxerxes I in Susa,[3] the administrative capital of the empire (Ne 1:1,11). In 445 B.C. Artaxerxes commissioned Nehemiah as governor of Judah, a position he held for 12 years (Ne 2:1–6; 5:14). The king gave Nehemiah permission to rebuild the walls of Jerusalem, a feat the Jewish people accomplished in only 52 days (Ne 6:15). Fragmentary remains of Nehemiah's wall have been discovered on the eastern edge of the City of David, south of the temple mount. Archaeological findings indicate that Ezra and Nehemiah established Judah as an economically viable province. Prior to their arrival Judah had been in a poor and ruinous state as a continuing result of the Babylonian conquest of 586 B.C.[4]

Artaxerxes I was buried in an elaborate tomb cut into the face of a cliff 3 miles (4.8 km) north of Persepolis, the religious capital of the Persian Empire.[5]

1See "Ancient Persian History Through Darius" on page 717. 2See "The Postexilic Period of the Old Testament: The Persian Period" on page 699. 3See "Susa" on page 729. 4See "The Last Days of Jerusalem" on page 1197. 5See "Persepolis" on page 1404.

laws of your God. And you are to teach[l] any who do not know them. 26 Whoever does not obey the law of your God and the law of the king must surely be punished by death, banishment, confiscation of property, or imprisonment.[m]

27 Praise be to the LORD, the God of our fathers, who has put it into the king's heart[n] to bring honor[o]
to the house of the LORD in Jerusalem in this way 28 and who has extended his good favor[p] to me before
the king and his advisers and all the king's powerful officials. Because the hand of the LORD my God was on me,[q] I took courage and gathered leading men from Israel to go up with me.

7:25 [l]ver 10; Lev 10:11
7:26 [m]Ezr 6:11
7:27 [n]Ezr 1:1; 6:22 [o]1Ch 29:12
7:28 [p]2Ki 25:28 [q]Ezr 5:5; 9:9

The Scribe

EZRA 8 Scribes occupied an important position as a professional class in the society of the ancient world.[1] The scribal arts of reading, writing and interpreting written documents assured them a vital role in the affairs of person, state and sanctuary. Writing was typically performed as dictation (Jer 36:32), using a stylus reed pen sharpened frequently with a "scribe's knife" (Jer 36:23).[2] Scribal training was acquired in schools and was at times viewed as a family trade (1Ch 2:55). Several important personages in the Bible were scribes: Shaphan, who read the Book of the Law to King Josiah (2Ki 22:10);[3] Baruch, who recorded the words of the prophet Jeremiah (Jer 36:4);[4] Ezra, who copied and read the decrees of **Persian** kings and the Law of Moses (Ezr 7:6–11); and the evangelist Matthew, who applied his scribal training toward the composition of the first canonical Gospel (Mt 8:19; 13:52).

The Bible presents scribes accurately as royal recorders who preserved the will of kings (1Ch 24:6; Est 3:12). They occupied important posts within the military (2Ki 25:19; Jer 52:25) and are often depicted with the high priest as close advisors of kings (2Ki 12:10; 18:18, 37; Mt 2:4). Many scribes were themselves priests and were entrusted with the preservation, interpretation and exposition of Scripture (Ne 8:9; Mt 17:10; 23:2). It is, therefore, understandable that scribes became widely regarded as men of great wisdom and learning. David's uncle Jonathan is said to have been "a counselor, a man of insight and a scribe" (1Ch 27:32).

A lexical list of temples; Nineveh, c. 700 B.C.
© The Schøyen Collection; photography courtesy of Mr. Martin Schøyen

These various ideals became focused in the person of Ezra. He was an important figure in traditional Judaism who represented the ideal model for the rabbinic sage as a faithful man of learning, scholarship, counsel and service. Due to their importance and responsibility as preservers of tradition, scribes were also subjected to the scrutiny of prophetic critique. Jeremiah indicted the "lying pen of the scribes" who had forsaken the law of the Lord (Jer 8:8), and Jesus himself pronounced an extensive list of negative judgments against the scribes and Pharisees (Mt 23).

An Egyptian scribe
Preserving Bible Times; © Dr. James C. Martin; permission of The Cairo Museum

[1]See "Sumerian Scribal Education" on page 579. [2]See "Writing Materials in the Ancient World" on page 2037. [3]See "The Huldah Delegation and Nathan-Melech, the Official" on page 567. [4]See "Baruch, Scribe of Jeremiah" on page 1248.

List of the Family Heads Returning With Ezra

8 These are the family heads and those registered with them who came up with me from Babylon dur-
8:1 [r]Ezr 7:7 ing the reign of King Artaxerxes:[r]

2 of the descendants of Phinehas, Gershom;
of the descendants of Ithamar, Daniel;
8:3 [s]1Ch 3:22 of the descendants of David, Hattush 3 of the descendants of Shecaniah;[s]
[t]Ezr 2:3 of the descendants of Parosh,[t] Zechariah, and with him were registered 150 men;
8:4 [u]Ezr 2:6 4 of the descendants of Pahath-Moab,[u] Eliehoenai son of Zerahiah, and with him 200 men;
5 of the descendants of Zattu,[a] Shecaniah son of Jahaziel, and with him 300 men;
8:6 [v]Ezr 2:15; Ne 7:20; 10:16 6 of the descendants of Adin,[v] Ebed son of Jonathan, and with him 50 men;
7 of the descendants of Elam, Jeshaiah son of Athaliah, and with him 70 men;
8 of the descendants of Shephatiah, Zebadiah son of Michael, and with him 80 men;
9 of the descendants of Joab, Obadiah son of Jehiel, and with him 218 men;
10 of the descendants of Bani,[b] Shelomith son of Josiphiah, and with him 160 men;
11 of the descendants of Bebai, Zechariah son of Bebai, and with him 28 men;
12 of the descendants of Azgad, Johanan son of Hakkatan, and with him 110 men;
8:13 [w]Ezr 2:13 13 of the descendants of Adonikam,[w] the last ones, whose names were Eliphelet, Jeuel and Shemaiah,
and with them 60 men;
14 of the descendants of Bigvai, Uthai and Zaccur, and with them 70 men.

The Return to Jerusalem

8:15 [x]ver 21,31 15 I assembled them at the canal that flows toward Ahava,[x] and we camped there three days. When I
[y]Ezr 2:40; 7:7 checked among the people and the priests, I found no Levites[y] there. 16 So I summoned Eliezer, Ariel,
Shemaiah, Elnathan, Jarib, Elnathan, Nathan, Zechariah and Meshullam, who were leaders, and Joiarib
and Elnathan, who were men of learning, 17 and I sent them to Iddo, the leader in Casiphia. I told them
8:17 [z]Ezr 2:43 what to say to Iddo and his kinsmen, the temple servants[z] in Casiphia, so that they might bring atten-
8:18 [a]Ezr 5:5 dants to us for the house of our God. 18 Because the gracious hand of our God was on us,[a] they brought
us Sherebiah, a capable man, from the descendants of Mahli son of Levi, the son of Israel, and Sherebi-
ah's sons and brothers, 18 men; 19 and Hashabiah, together with Jeshaiah from the descendants of Mera-
8:20 [b]1Ch 9:2; Ezr 2:43 ri, and his brothers and nephews, 20 men. 20 They also brought 220 of the temple servants[b]—a body that
David and the officials had established to assist the Levites. All were registered by name.
8:21 [c]ver 15; 2Ch 20:3 [d]Ps 5:8; 107:7 21 There, by the Ahava Canal,[c] I proclaimed a fast, so that we might humble ourselves before our God
and ask him for a safe journey[d] for us and our children, with all our possessions. 22 I was ashamed to ask
8:22 [e]Ne 2:9; Ezr 7:6,9,28 the king for soldiers[e] and horsemen to protect us from enemies on the road, because we had told the
[f]Ezr 5:5 king, "The gracious hand of our God is on everyone[f] who looks to him, but his great anger is against all
[g]Dt 31:17; 2Ch 15:2 who forsake him.[g]" 23 So we fasted[h] and petitioned our God about this, and he answered our prayer.
8:23 [h]2Ch 20:3; 33:13 24 Then I set apart twelve of the leading priests, together with Sherebiah,[i] Hashabiah and ten of their
8:24 [i]ver 18
8:25 [j]ver 33; Ezr 7:15,16 brothers, 25 and I weighed out[j] to them the offering of silver and gold and the articles that the king, his
advisers, his officials and all Israel present there had donated for the house of our God. 26 I weighed out
to them 650 talents[c] of silver, silver articles weighing 100 talents,[d] 100 talents[d] of gold, 27 20 bowls of gold
valued at 1,000 darics,[e] and two fine articles of polished bronze, as precious as gold.
8:28 [k]Lev 21:6; 22:2-3 28 I said to them, "You as well as these articles are consecrated to the LORD.[k] The silver and gold are a
freewill offering to the LORD, the God of your fathers. 29 Guard them carefully until you weigh them out
in the chambers of the house of the LORD in Jerusalem before the leading priests and the Levites and the
family heads of Israel." 30 Then the priests and Levites received the silver and gold and sacred articles
that had been weighed out to be taken to the house of our God in Jerusalem.
8:31 [l]ver 15 31 On the twelfth day of the first month we set out from the Ahava Canal[l] to go to Jerusalem. The hand

[a] *5* Some Septuagint manuscripts (also 1 Esdras 8:32); Hebrew does not have *Zattu.* [b] *10* Some Septuagint manuscripts (also 1 Esdras 8:36); Hebrew does not have *Bani.* [c] *26* That is, about 25 tons (about 22 metric tons) [d] *26* That is, about 3 3/4 tons (about 3.4 metric tons) [e] *27* That is, about 19 pounds (about 8.5 kilograms)

8:21 "Children" designated those younger than twenty, with a stress on the younger ages. Such "little ones" (as the Hebrew word is translated in Dt 1:39) are most vulnerable in times of war or danger.

8:27 This "polished bronze" may have been orichalc, a bright yellow alloy of copper that resembles gold and was highly prized in ancient times.

of our God was on us, and he protected us from enemies and bandits along the way. 32So we arrived in
Jerusalem, where we rested three days.[m]
33On the fourth day, in the house of our God, we weighed out the silver and gold and the sacred arti-
cles into the hands of Meremoth[n] son of Uriah, the priest. Eleazar son of Phinehas was with him, and so
were the Levites Jozabad son of Jeshua and Noadiah son of Binnui.[o] 34Everything was accounted for by
number and weight, and the entire weight was recorded at that time.
35Then the exiles who had returned from captivity sacrificed burnt offerings to the God of Israel:
twelve bulls for all Israel, ninety-six rams, seventy-seven male lambs and, as a sin offering, twelve male
goats.[p] All this was a burnt offering to the LORD. 36They also delivered the king's orders[q] to the royal sa-
traps and to the governors of Trans-Euphrates, who then gave assistance to the people and to the house
of God.[r]

Ezra's Prayer About Intermarriage

9 After these things had been done, the leaders came to me and said, "The people of Israel, including
the priests and the Levites, have not kept themselves separate[s] from the neighboring peoples with
their detestable practices, like those of the Canaanites, Hittites, Perizzites, Jebusites, Ammonites,[t] Moab-
ites, Egyptians and Amorites.[u] 2They have taken some of their daughters[v] as wives for themselves and
their sons, and have mingled the holy race[w] with the peoples around them. And the leaders and officials
have led the way in this unfaithfulness."[x]
3When I heard this, I tore my tunic and cloak, pulled hair from my head and beard and sat down ap-
palled. 4Then everyone who trembled[y] at the words of the God of Israel gathered around me because of
this unfaithfulness of the exiles. And I sat there appalled until the evening sacrifice.
5Then, at the evening sacrifice,[z] I rose from my self-abasement, with my tunic and cloak torn, and
fell on my knees with my hands spread out to the LORD my God 6and prayed:

"O my God, I am too ashamed and disgraced to lift up my face to you, my God, because our
sins are higher than our heads and our guilt has reached to the heavens.[a] 7From the days of our
forefathers[b] until now, our guilt has been great. Because of our sins, we and our kings and our
priests have been subjected to the sword[c] and captivity,[d] to pillage and humiliation[e] at the hand
of foreign kings, as it is today.
8"But now, for a brief moment, the LORD our God has been gracious[f] in leaving us a remnant[g] and
giving us a firm place[h] in his sanctuary, and so our God gives light to our eyes[i] and a little relief in
our bondage. 9Though we are slaves,[j] our God has not deserted us in our bondage. He has shown
us kindness[k] in the sight of the kings of Persia: He has granted us new life to rebuild the house of
our God and repair its ruins,[l] and he has given us a wall of protection in Judah and Jerusalem.
10"But now, O our God, what can we say after this? For we have disregarded the commands[m]
11you gave through your servants the prophets when you said: 'The land you are entering to pos-
sess is a land polluted[n] by the corruption of its peoples. By their detestable practices[o] they have
filled it with their impurity from one end to the other. 12Therefore, do not give your daughters in
marriage to their sons or take their daughters for your sons. Do not seek a treaty of friendship
with them[p] at any time, that you may be strong and eat the good things of the land and leave it to
your children as an everlasting inheritance.'
13"What has happened to us is a result of our evil deeds and our great guilt, and yet, our God,
you have punished us less than our sins have deserved[q] and have given us a remnant like this.
14Shall we again break your commands and intermarry[r] with the peoples who commit such detest-

8:32 [m]Ge 40:13; Ne 2:11
8:33 [n]Ne 3:4,21 [o]Ne 3:24
8:35 [p]2Ch 29:21; Ezr 6:17
8:36 [q]Ezr 7:21-24 [r]Est 9:3
9:1 [s]Ezr 6:21; Ne 9:2 [t]Ge 19:38 [u]Ex 13:5
9:2 [v]Ex 34:16 [w]Ex 22:31 [x]Ezr 10:2
9:4 [y]Ezr 10:3
9:5 [z]Ex 29:41
9:6 [a]2Ch 28:9; Job 42:6; Ps 38:4; Rev 18:5
9:7 [b]2Ch 29:6 [c]Eze 21:1-32 [d]Dt 28:64 [e]Dt 28:37
9:8 [f]Ps 25:16; Isa 33:2 [g]Ge 45:7 [h]Ecc 12:11; Isa 22:23 [i]Ps 13:3
9:9 [j]Ex 1:14; Ne 9:36 [k]Ezr 7:28 [l]Ps 69:35; Isa 43:1; Jer 32:44
9:10 [m]Dt 11:8; Isa 1:19-20
9:11 [n]Lev 18:25-28 [o]Dt 9:4
9:12 [p]Ex 34:15; Dt 7:3; 23:6
9:13 [q]Job 11:6; Ps 103:10
9:14 [r]Ne 13:27

8:34 Ezra may have been required to send to Artaxerxes (see "Artaxerxes I, King of Persia" on p. 681) a signed certification of the items delivered. According to Babylonian practice (e.g., in the Code of Hammurabi) almost every transaction, including sales and marriages, had to be recorded in writing.

9:1 The eight groups mentioned (see "Lesser Known Peoples of the Old Testament" on p. 265 and "The Jebusites" on p. 596) are representative of the original inhabitants of Canaan (see "Canaan" on p. 324) before the Israelite conquest. Only the Ammonites, Moabites and Egyptians were still living there during the postexilic period (cf. 2Ch 8:7–8).

9:3 Although shaving one's head and/or beard was common practice (Job 1:20; Jer 41:5; 47:5; Eze 7:18; Am 8:10), Ezra's act of pulling out his hair from his head and beard is unique in the Bible. Nehemiah demonstrated a markedly different response: When confronted with the same problem of intermarriage, he pulled out the hair of the offenders (Ne 13:25)!

9:9 Cyrus (539–530 B.C.), Cambyses (530–522), Darius I (522–486), Xerxes (486–465) and Artaxerxes (465–424) were Persian kings, all of whom were favorably disposed toward the Jews. See "Ancient Persian History Through Darius" on page 717 and "Ancient Persian History From Xerses Forward" on page 718.

9:11 Texts from ancient Ugarit vividly describe the degrading practices and beliefs of the Canaanites.

able practices? Would you not be angry enough with us to destroy us,[s] leaving us no remnant[t] or survivor? 15 O LORD, God of Israel, you are righteous![u] We are left this day as a remnant. Here we are before you in our guilt, though because of it not one of us can stand[v] in your presence.[w]"

The People's Confession of Sin

10 While Ezra was praying and confessing,[x] weeping and throwing himself down before the house of God, a large crowd of Israelites—men, women and children—gathered around him. They too wept bitterly. 2 Then Shecaniah son of Jehiel, one of the descendants of Elam, said to Ezra, "We have been unfaithful[y] to our God by marrying foreign women from the peoples around us. But in spite of this, there is still hope for Israel.[z] 3 Now let us make a covenant[a] before our God to send away[b] all these women and their children, in accordance with the counsel of my lord and of those who fear the commands of our God. Let it be done according to the Law. 4 Rise up; this matter is in your hands. We will support you, so take courage and do it."

5 So Ezra rose up and put the leading priests and Levites and all Israel under oath[c] to do what had been suggested. And they took the oath. 6 Then Ezra withdrew from before the house of God and went to the room of Jehohanan son of Eliashib. While he was there, he ate no food and drank no water,[d] because he continued to mourn over the unfaithfulness of the exiles.

7 A proclamation was then issued throughout Judah and Jerusalem for all the exiles to assemble in Jerusalem. 8 Anyone who failed to appear within three days would forfeit all his property, in accordance with the decision of the officials and elders, and would himself be expelled from the assembly of the exiles.

9 Within the three days, all the men of Judah and Benjamin[e] had gathered in Jerusalem. And on the twentieth day of the ninth month, all the people were sitting in the square before the house of God, greatly distressed by the occasion and because of the rain. 10 Then Ezra the priest stood up and said to them, "You have been unfaithful; you have married foreign women, adding to Israel's guilt. 11 Now make confession to the LORD, the God of your fathers, and do his will. Separate yourselves from the peoples around you and from your foreign wives."[f]

12 The whole assembly responded with a loud voice:[g] "You are right! We must do as you say. 13 But there are many people here and it is the rainy season; so we cannot stand outside. Besides, this matter cannot be taken care of in a day or two, because we have sinned greatly in this thing. 14 Let our officials act for the whole assembly. Then let everyone in our towns who has married a foreign woman come at a set time, along with the elders and judges[h] of each town, until the fierce anger[i] of our God in this matter is turned away from us." 15 Only Jonathan son of Asahel and Jahzeiah son of Tikvah, supported by Meshullam and Shabbethai[j] the Levite, opposed this.

16 So the exiles did as was proposed. Ezra the priest selected men who were family heads, one from each family division, and all of them designated by name. On the first day of the tenth month they sat down to investigate the cases, 17 and by the first day of the first month they finished dealing with all the men who had married foreign women.

Those Guilty of Intermarriage

18 Among the descendants of the priests, the following had married foreign women:[k]

From the descendants of Jeshua[l] son of Jozadak, and his brothers: Maaseiah, Eliezer, Jarib and Gedaliah. 19 (They all gave their hands[m] in pledge to put away their wives, and for their guilt they each presented a ram from the flock as a guilt offering.)[n]

20 From the descendants of Immer:[o]
Hanani and Zebadiah.

21 From the descendants of Harim:[p]
Maaseiah, Elijah, Shemaiah, Jehiel and Uzziah.

22 From the descendants of Pashhur:[q]
Elioenai, Maaseiah, Ishmael, Nethanel, Jozabad and Elasah.

9:14 [s]Dt 9:8 [t]Dt 9:14
9:15 [u]Ge 18:25; Ps 51:4; Jer 12:1; Da 9:7 [v]Ne 9:33; Ps 130:3; Mal 3:2 [w]1Ki 8:47
10:1 [x]2Ch 20:9; Da 9:20
10:2 [y]Ezr 9:2; Ne 13:27 [z]Dt 30:8-10
10:3 [a]2Ch 34:31 [b]Ex 34:16; Dt 7:2-3; Ezr 9:4
10:5 [c]Ne 5:12; 13:25
10:6 [d]Ex 34:28; Dt 9:18
10:9 [e]Ezr 1:5
10:11 [f]ver 3; Dt 24:1; Ne 9:2; Mal 2:10-16
10:12 [g]Jos 6:5
10:14 [h]Dt 16:18 [i]Nu 25:4; 2Ch 29:10; 30:8
10:15 [j]Ne 11:16
10:18 [k]Jdg 3:6 [l]Ezr 2:2
10:19 [m]2Ki 10:15 [n]Lev 5:15; 6:6
10:20 [o]1Ch 24:14
10:21 [p]1Ch 24:8
10:22 [q]1Ch 9:12

10:3 In most ancient societies mothers were given custody of their children when marriages were dissolved (cf. Ge 21:14). In Babylonia, divorced women were granted their children but had to wait for them to grow up before remarrying. In Greece, however, the children remained with their fathers.

10:16–17 Although the guilty may not have fully realized the gravity of their offense, they had no excuse. The Scriptures plainly set forth God's standards on marriage. Some of the marriages had produced children (v. 44), but this was not accepted as a reason for halting the proceedings.

[23] Among the Levites:[r]

Jozabad, Shimei, Kelaiah (that is, Kelita), Pethahiah, Judah and Eliezer.

[24] From the singers:

Eliashib.[s]

From the gatekeepers:

Shallum, Telem and Uri.

[25] And among the other Israelites:

From the descendants of Parosh:[t]

Ramiah, Izziah, Malkijah, Mijamin, Eleazar, Malkijah and Benaiah.

[26] From the descendants of Elam:[u]

Mattaniah, Zechariah, Jehiel, Abdi, Jeremoth and Elijah.

[27] From the descendants of Zattu:

Elioenai, Eliashib, Mattaniah, Jeremoth, Zabad and Aziza.

[28] From the descendants of Bebai:

Jehohanan, Hananiah, Zabbai and Athlai.

[29] From the descendants of Bani:

Meshullam, Malluch, Adaiah, Jashub, Sheal and Jeremoth.

[30] From the descendants of Pahath-Moab:

Adna, Kelal, Benaiah, Maaseiah, Mattaniah, Bezalel, Binnui and Manasseh.

[31] From the descendants of Harim:

Eliezer, Ishijah, Malkijah, Shemaiah, Shimeon, [32] Benjamin, Malluch and Shemariah.

[33] From the descendants of Hashum:

Mattenai, Mattattah, Zabad, Eliphelet, Jeremai, Manasseh and Shimei.

[34] From the descendants of Bani:

Maadai, Amram, Uel, [35] Benaiah, Bedeiah, Keluhi, [36] Vaniah, Meremoth, Eliashib, [37] Mattaniah,
Mattenai and Jaasu.

[38] From the descendants of Binnui:[a]

Shimei, [39] Shelemiah, Nathan, Adaiah, [40] Macnadebai, Shashai, Sharai, [41] Azarel, Shelemiah,
Shemariah, [42] Shallum, Amariah and Joseph.

[43] From the descendants of Nebo:

Jeiel, Mattithiah, Zabad, Zebina, Jaddai, Joel and Benaiah.

[44] All these had married foreign women, and some of them had children by these wives.[b]

[a] 37,38 See Septuagint (also 1 Esdras 9:34); Hebrew *Jaasu* [38] *and Bani and Binnui,* [b] 44 Or *and they sent them away with their children*

10:23 [r] Ne 8:7; 9:4
10:24 [s] Ne 3:1; 12:10; 13:7,28
10:25 [t] Ezr 2:3
10:26 [u] ver 2

INTRODUCTION TO 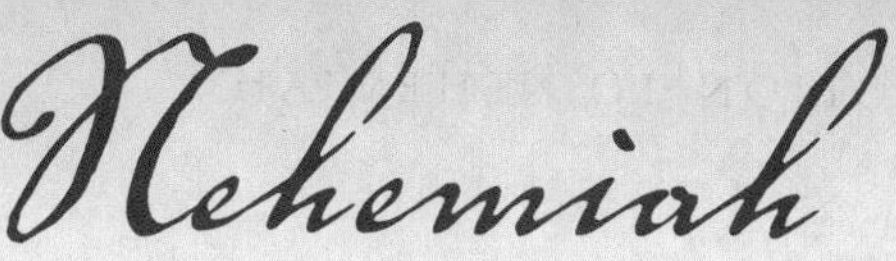

AUTHOR, PLACE AND DATE OF WRITING

Ezra the priest, who is presumed to have written this book around 430 B.C., after having returned to Jerusalem with a group of Babylonian exiles in 458 B.C., also authored the book of Ezra in about 440 B.C. Originally two separate compositions, they were combined into one book, titled Ezra, prior to A.D. 100. The oldest manuscripts of the Septuagint treated Nehemiah and Ezra as one book. Origen (c. A.D. 185–253) was the first writer to make a distinction between the two, which he called 1 Ezra and 2 Ezra. Wycliffe's (1382) and Coverdale's (1535) English translations also separated the two.

AUDIENCE

Generations of Israelites after the exiles had returned from Babylon read the book of Nehemiah. Ezra clearly wanted his readers to understand what had happened in Jerusalem as the exiles returned, as well as the issues they faced and overcame in order to reestablish their covenant relationship with God. The national identity of God's people was at stake: The community of God had to be rebuilt upon the foundation of God's covenants with his people established many years earlier.

CULTURAL FACTS AND HIGHLIGHTS

Continuing the historical record found in the book of Ezra, Nehemiah describes the Jews' return from exile in Babylon and God's continued faithfulness to his covenant people. The book's narrative is communicated through the life of Nehemiah, who left his position as cupbearer of Artaxerxes to become governor of Jerusalem when Ezra was leading the people.

TIMELINE

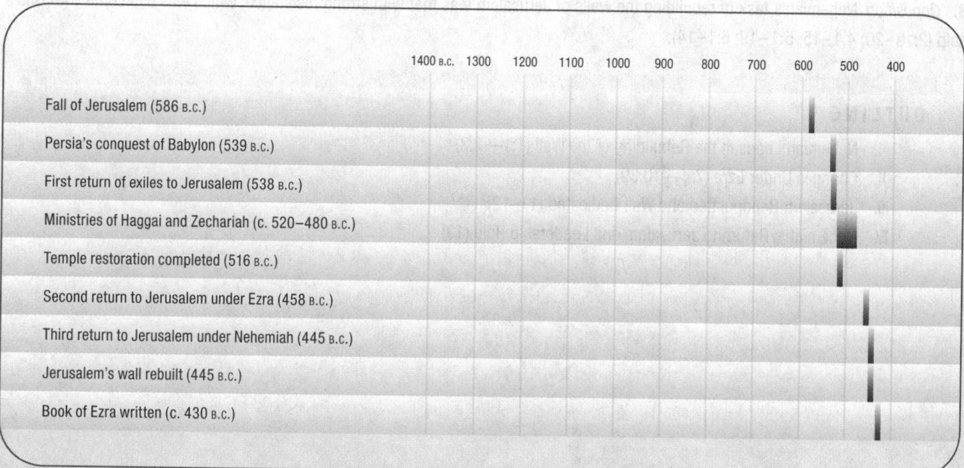

AS YOU READ

Notice the key role of prayer in Nehemiah's life, and evaluate its importance in your own life today. Imagine how the Jewish exiles must have felt as they rebuilt the walls of Jerusalem under threats from powerful neighbors and even opposition from some fellow Jews. Reflect on why—despite what they were learning about God and Moses' Law, as well as their participation in the covenant-renewal ceremony (chs. 8–10)—the members of the Jewish remnant seemed unable or unwilling to honor fully their covenant with Yahweh or to maintain purity of faith.

Carefully note the challenges Nehemiah faced. Imagine his disappointment after having returned from his visit with Artaxerxes only to discover that more problems had surfaced while he had been away: neglect of the temple, Levites not being supplied with food and supplies, God's people working on the Sabbath, men of Judah once again marrying pagan women. Follow along as he and Ezra worked to overcome these crises of national identity.

DID YOU KNOW?

- One of the cupbearer's duties was to choose and taste the king's wine to make certain it was not poisoned. The need for trustworthy court attendants is underscored by the intrigues that characterized the Persian court. Xerxes, the father of Artaxerxes I, was killed in his own bedchamber by a courtier (1:11).
- The Sheep Gate was known in New Testament times as having been located near the Bethesda Pool (in the northeastern corner of Jerusalem). Even today this area is periodically used as a sheep market (3:1).
- Women did not participate in ordinary meetings but were included, together with children, on sacred occasions. In one memorable instance the people stood for five or six hours, attentively listening to the reading and explanation of the Scriptures (8:2–3).
- The practice of forcibly redistributing populations was also used to establish Greek and Hellenistic cities (11:1–2).

THEMES

Nehemiah contains the following themes:

1. *Renewal.* While rebuilding the walls of Jerusalem was the obvious material challenge facing Nehemiah, reestablishing the Jews' commitment to God and to the Mosaic Law was his primary spiritual concern. Nehemiah 9:1—12:47 captures the people's dramatic response to the reading of the law by Ezra (8:1–18): They confessed their sins (9:1–37) and voluntarily recommitted themselves to God's covenant (9:38—10:39). Later, during a second visit from Nehemiah, they agreed to support the temple (13:4–14), keep the Sabbath (13:15–22) and divorce their foreign wives (13:23–31).

2. *Prayer.* Prayer is essential to any work of God, and Nehemiah was a model leader who initiated his plans only after consultation with God. A man of prayer (1:4; 2:4; 4:4; 5:19; 6:9,14; 13:14,22,29,31), his efforts were richly blessed by God.

3. *Opposition.* Nehemiah's task of rebuilding the walls of Jerusalem was met with strong resistance, which was overcome with God's help (2:19–20; 4:1–15; 5:1–19; 6:1–14).

OUTLINE

I. Nehemiah Leads in the Rebuilding of the Wall (1:1—7:3)
II. Changes Under Ezra (7:4—10:39)
III. Jerusalem Repopulated and Wall Dedicated (11–12)
IV. Nehemiah's Return to Jerusalem and Leadership Role (13)

Nehemiah's Prayer

1 The words of Nehemiah son of Hacaliah:

1:1 [a]Ne 10:1; In the month of Kislev[a] in the twentieth year, while I was in the citadel of Susa, 2Hanani,[b] one of my
Zec 7:1 1:2 [b]Ne 7:2 brothers, came from Judah with some other men, and I questioned them about the Jewish remnant[c] that
[c]Jer 52:28 survived the exile, and also about Jerusalem.
3They said to me, "Those who survived the exile and are back in the province are in great trouble and
1:3 [d]2Ki 25:10; disgrace. The wall of Jerusalem is broken down, and its gates have been burned with fire.[d]"
Ne 2:3,13,17 1:4 [e]Ps 137:1 4When I heard these things, I sat down and wept.[e] For some days I mourned and fasted[f] and prayed
[f]Ezr 9:4 before the God of heaven. 5Then I said:

1:5 [g]Dt 7:21; "O LORD, God of heaven, the great and awesome God,[g] who keeps his covenant of love[h] with
Ne 4:14 [h]Ex 20:6; Da 9:4 those who love him and obey his commands, 6let your ear be attentive and your eyes open to hear[i]
1:6 [i]1Ki 8:29 [j]Da 9:17 the prayer[j] your servant is praying before you day and night for your servants, the people of Isra-
el. I confess the sins we Israelites, including myself and my father's house, have committed against
1:7 [k]Dt 28:14-15; you. 7We have acted very wickedly[k] toward you. We have not obeyed the commands, decrees and
Ps 106:6 laws you gave your servant Moses.
1:8 [l]2Ki 20:3 8"Remember[l] the instruction you gave your servant Moses, saying, 'If you are unfaithful, I will
[m]Lev 26:33 scatter[m] you among the nations, 9but if you return to me and obey my commands, then even if
1:9 [n]Dt 30:4 your exiled people are at the farthest horizon, I will gather[n] them from there and bring them to the
[o]1Ki 8:48; Jer 29:14 place I have chosen as a dwelling for my Name.'[o]
10"They are your servants and your people, whom you redeemed by your great strength and
1:10 [p]Ex 32:11; your mighty hand.[p] 11O Lord, let your ear be attentive[q] to the prayer of this your servant and to the
Dt 9:29 1:11 [q]ver 6 prayer of your servants who delight in revering your name. Give your servant success today by
[r]Ge 40:1 granting him favor in the presence of this man."

I was cupbearer[r] to the king.

Artaxerxes Sends Nehemiah to Jerusalem

2:1 [s]Ezr 7:1 2 In the month of Nisan in the twentieth year of King Artaxerxes,[s] when wine was brought for him, I
took the wine and gave it to the king. I had not been sad in his presence before; 2so the king asked
me, "Why does your face look so sad when you are not ill? This can be nothing but sadness of heart."
2:3 [t]1Ki 1:31; I was very much afraid, 3but I said to the king, "May the king live forever![t] Why should my face not
Da 2:4; 5:10; 6:6, 21 [u]Ps 137:6 look sad when the city[u] where my fathers are buried lies in ruins, and its gates have been destroyed by
[v]Ne 1:3 fire?[v]"
4The king said to me, "What is it you want?"
Then I prayed to the God of heaven, 5and I answered the king, "If it pleases the king and if your ser-
vant has found favor in his sight, let him send me to the city in Judah where my fathers are buried so
that I can rebuild it."
2:6 [w]Ne 5:14; 6Then the king[w], with the queen sitting beside him, asked me, "How long will your journey take, and
13:6 when will you get back?" It pleased the king to send me; so I set a time.
2:7 [x]Ezr 8:36 7I also said to him, "If it pleases the king, may I have letters to the governors of Trans-Euphrates,[x] so

---

1:1 The "twentieth year" refers to the twentieth year of the reign of the Persian king Artaxerxes I (see "Artaxerxes I, King of Persia" on p. 681 and "The Chronology of Ezra and Nehemiah" on p. 690).
1:2 Hanani is probably a shortened form of Hananiah. The Elephantine papyri mention a Hananiah who was the head of Jewish affairs in Jerusalem. Many believe that he was Nehemiah's brother and that he may have governed between Nehemiah's first and second terms (see the NIV text note on 7:2).
1:3 Despite abortive attempts to rebuild them (Ezr 4:7–23), Jerusalem's walls, which had been destroyed by the Babylonians in 586 B.C., remained in ruins. Without protective walls Jerusalem was vulnerable to her numerous enemies. Excavations have revealed that the lack of a wall on the eastern slopes also led to the disintegration of the terraces there.
1:11 One of the cupbearer's duties was to choose and taste the king's wine to make certain that it was not poisoned (see 2:1). Thus Nehemiah was undoubtedly a man who enjoyed the king's unreserved confidence. The need for trustworthy court attendants is underscored by the intrigues that characterized the Persian court. Xerxes, the father of Artaxerxes I, was killed in his own bedchamber by a courtier. See "Counselors and Concubines: Life in an Ancient Royal Palace" on page 719.
2:1–3 The king's servants were expected to keep their feelings to themselves and to display a cheerful disposition at all times before him. Yet anxiety gripped Nehemiah, likely not so much because of the king's question but in anticipation of the request he was to make. Nehemiah knew full well that Artaxerxes himself had earlier stopped the Jews from rebuilding the wall (Ezr 4:17–23).
2:6 Nehemiah probably asked for a brief leave of absence, which was subsequently extended. His first term as governor in Jerusalem lasted 12 years (5:14), after which he returned to report to the king; he then went back to Judah for a second term (13:6–7).
2:7 Nehemiah's request for "letters" would provide him with safe passage and provisions during the course of his journey. A contemporary document from Arsames, the satrap of Egypt who was at the Persian court, to one of his officers who was returning to Egypt ordered Persian officials to provide him with food and drink on the various stages of his journey.

THE CHRONOLOGY OF EZRA AND NEHEMIAH

NEHEMIAH 1 The chronology of Ezra and Nehemiah is a complex issue, especially as the events these books recount took place during a relatively obscure period of Biblical history. According to the Bible, Ezra arrived in Jerusalem during the seventh year of the reign of Artaxerxes I, in 458 B.C. (Ezr 7:8), and Nehemiah in the twentieth year of the same king, 445 B.C. (Ne 2:1).[1] Two other passages suggest that the two leaders were present in the city at the same time (8:9; 12:36). This data suggests the priority of Ezra's mission, while acknowledging the close relationship of the respective activities of the two leaders.

Modern research has raised a number of objections against the traditional sequence, however, and some scholars suggest that Nehemiah's mission occurred prior to Ezra's. The most significant argument is based on the succession of high priests recorded in the Bible in comparison to the extrabiblical evidence. The book of Nehemiah records Eliashib as the high priest with whom Nehemiah dealt (3:1,20; 13:28). Nehemiah 12:10–11 presents the succession of high priests as follows: "Jeshua was the father of Joiakim, Joiakim the father of Eliashib, Eliashib the father of Joiada, Joiada the father of Jonathan, and Jonathan the father of Jaddua." Chapter 12:22 lists names from the same progression as "Eliashib, Joiada, Johanan [a variation of Jonathan] and Jaddua." Furthermore, 12:23 refers to Johanan as the son (i.e., grandson) of Eliashib.

The difficulty arises in the comparison of this sequence with that found in Ezra. According to Ezra 10:6 "Ezra withdrew from before the house of God and went to the room of Jehohanan [another variation of Jonathan] son of Eliashib." This passage seems at first glance to suggest that Ezra dealt with the grandson of the man whom Nehemiah knew—necessitating the conclusion that Nehemiah's ministry must have preceded Ezra's. This deduction appears to receive confirmation from the Elephantine papyri (documents from the Jewish colony at Elephantine[2] in Egypt), which clearly identify a Johanan as high priest around 410 B.C.

Scholars who espouse this theory accept the 445 B.C. date for Nehemiah's arrival in Jerusalem but place the ministry of Ezra as beginning in 398 B.C., the seventh year of Artaxerxes II (not Artaxerxes I). A minority opinion conjectures that Ezra 7:8 originally read as the thirty-seventh year of Artaxerxes I, or 428 B.C. However, no textual evidence suggests a scribal error in Ezra 7:8.

Temple of the god Khnum at Elephantine
Preserving Bible Times; © Dr. James C. Martin

Further, at least three important points render this conclusion unnecessary:

◆ The names of Eliashib and Jonathan were extremely common (there are three different men named Eliashib in Ezr 10 alone). Therefore, it is not at all certain that the Jonathan of Nehemiah 12 and the one of Ezra 10 were the same person.

◆ Ezra 10:6 indicates that Ezra entered the chamber of Jehohanan (Jonathan) but does not identify Jehohanan as the reigning high priest. It is entirely possible to maintain the traditional sequence on the assumption that Jonathan was a young man from a high priestly family with access to the temple at the time of his meeting with Ezra.

◆ There was indeed a high priest named Johanan at the beginning of the fourth century B.C., but the ancient Jewish historian Josephus described how this Johanan killed his own brother Jesus in the year 398 B.C. within the temple itself (*Antiquities*, 11.297–301). On the basis of this scandalous crime, the **Persian**[3] governor Bagoas, a supporter of this Jesus, placed the Jews under a seven-year period of punishment. It is most unlikely that Ezra could have received the judicial and financial support of the Persian crown for doing his work at this very time (Ezr 7:6,11–28). The Biblical data, as well as historical information described by Josephus, suggests the priority of Ezra's mission and so should be maintained.

[1]See "Artaxerxes I, King of Persia" on page 681. [2]For more information on Elephantine, see "The Elephantine Community" on page 1264. [3]See Glossary on page 2080 for definitions of bolded words.

that they will provide me safe-conduct until I arrive in Judah? 8And may I have a letter to Asaph, keep-
2:8 [y]Ne 7:2 [z]ver 18; Ezr 5:5; 7:6 er of the king's forest, so he will give me timber to make beams for the gates of the citadel[y] by the tem-
ple and for the city wall and for the residence I will occupy?" And because the gracious hand of my God
was upon me,[z] the king granted my requests. 9So I went to the governors of Trans-Euphrates and gave
2:9 [a]Ezr 8:22 them the king's letters. The king had also sent army officers and cavalry[a] with me.
2:10 [b]ver 19; Ne 4:1,7 [c]Ne 4:3; 13:4-7 [d]Est 10:3 10When Sanballat[b] the Horonite and Tobiah[c] the Ammonite official heard about this, they were very
much disturbed that someone had come to promote the welfare of the Israelites.[d]

Nehemiah Inspects Jerusalem's Walls

2:11 [e]Ge 40:13 11I went to Jerusalem, and after staying there three days[e] 12I set out during the night with a few men.
I had not told anyone what my God had put in my heart to do for Jerusalem. There were no mounts with
me except the one I was riding on.
2:13 [f]2Ch 26:9 [g]Ne 3:13 [h]Ne 1:3 13By night I went out through the Valley Gate[f] toward the Jackal[a] Well and the Dung Gate,[g] examining
the walls[h] of Jerusalem, which had been broken down, and its gates, which had been destroyed by fire.

[a] 13 Or *Serpent* or *Fig*

2:8 The name Asaph is Jewish, naturally implying that this "keeper of the king's forest" was a Jew. The location of the forest is uncertain. Some argue that it is the cedars of Lebanon; from ancient times kings and pharaohs were anxious to maintain access to the trees of Lebanon (see "Cedars of Lebanon" on p. 1043). On the other hand, the fact that the official in question had a Jewish name suggests a more local forest. Some posit that the forest in question was the garden of Etham, a few miles south of Jerusalem, or that it was located somewhere else in the region of Jerusalem.

2:13 Nehemiah did not make a complete circuit of the walls, but only of the southern area. Jerusalem had always been attacked from the north, where it was most vulnerable, so Nehemiah likely assumed that the northern walls had been completely destroyed. Jerusalem's walls and gates had lain in ruins since their destruction by Neb-

Sanballat, Tobiah and Geshem

NEHEMIAH 2 When Nehemiah began rebuilding the walls of Jerusalem in 445 B.C., he met with strong resistance from three individuals named Sanballat, Tobiah and Geshem. Although Nehemiah did not record their titles, we know from extrabiblical evidence that they were rulers of adjoining areas (cf. Ne 2:9–10):

✣ *Sanballat*: Sanballat was the governor of Samaria, the province north of Judah. We know, in fact, of three men by this name who ruled Samaria at different times. A 407 B.C. **papyrus** letter from Elephantine[1] in Egypt mentions the Sanballat of Nehemiah's time. Written to the governor of Judah, requesting permission to rebuild the ruined temple at Elephantine, it states: "All these things in a letter we sent in our name to Delaiah and Shelemiah sons of Sanballat governor of Samaria." It appears that at this time, 38 years after Sanballat's confrontation with Nehemiah, Sanballat's sons were acting on behalf of their aged father.

A coin and a **bulla** (seal impression) from the mid-fourth century B.C., inscribed with the name of Sanballat, governor of Samaria, were discovered in a cave in the wilderness of Judah. This particular Sanballat was likely the grandson of Nehemiah's Sanballat. The ancient Jewish historian Josephus mentions a third Sanballat, who was ruling Samaria in 332 B.C. and was perhaps the great-grandson of the Sanballat who opposed Nehemiah.

✣ *Tobiah*: The Tobiah family was well known in the third century B.C. as powerful Jewish aristocrats living in the **Transjordan**. Papyrus letters of an Egyptian official named Zenon, dating from around 260 B.C., mention a wealthy landowner, businessman and tax collector named Tobias (an alternative spelling of Tobiah) in the province of Ammonitis. Ruins of the Tobiah family's palatial estate from the second century B.C., mentioned by Josephus, have been excavated 11 miles (18 km) west of modern Amman, Jordan. The family name is inscribed above two entrances to rock-cut halls on the estate. The Tobiah of Nehemiah's acquaintance appears to have been governor of the province of Ammon, east of Judah in Transjordan.

✣ *Geshem*: An inscription found in northwestern Arabia from the time of Nehemiah reads, "Geshem son of Sahr and Abd, governor of Dedan." A silver offering bowl uncovered in the eastern delta region of Egypt from the late fifth century B.C. bears the same name, stating, "That which Kainu son of Geshem king of Kedar offered to Hanilat." Since Dedan and Kedar were tribal nations occupying the eastern desert, including Syria, northern Arabia, Sinai and northern Egypt, Geshem must have been a powerful ruler who controlled a vast area.

[1] See "The Elephantine Community" on page 1264.

14 Then I moved on toward the Fountain Gate[i] and the King's Pool,[j] but there was not enough room for **2:14** [i]Ne 3:15 [j]2Ki 18:17
my mount to get through; 15 so I went up the valley by night, examining the wall. Finally, I turned back
and reentered through the Valley Gate. 16 The officials did not know where I had gone or what I was do-
ing, because as yet I had said nothing to the Jews or the priests or nobles or officials or any others who
would be doing the work.
17 Then I said to them, "You see the trouble we are in: Jerusalem lies in ruins, and its gates have been
burned with fire.[k] Come, let us rebuild the wall[l] of Jerusalem, and we will no longer be in disgrace.[m]" 18 I **2:17** [k]Ne 1:3 [l]Ps 102:16; Isa 30:13; 58:12 [m]Eze 5:14
also told them about the gracious hand of my God upon me[n] and what the king had said to me.
They replied, "Let us start rebuilding." So they began this good work. **2:18** [n]2Sa 2:7
19 But when Sanballat the Horonite, Tobiah the Ammonite official and Geshem[o] the Arab heard about **2:19** [o]Ne 6:1,2,6 [p]Ps 44:13-16
it, they mocked and ridiculed us.[p] "What is this you are doing?" they asked. "Are you rebelling against
the king?"
20 I answered them by saying, "The God of heaven will give us success. We his servants will start re-
building, but as for you, you have no share[q] in Jerusalem or any claim or historic right to it." **2:20** [q]Ezr 4:3

Builders of the Wall

3 Eliashib[r] the high priest and his fellow priests went to work and rebuilt[s] the Sheep Gate.[t] They ded- **3:1** [r]Ezr 10:24 [s]Isa 58:12 [t]ver 32; Ne 12:39 [u]Ne 12:39; Jer 31:38; Zec 14:10
icated it and set its doors in place, building as far as the Tower of the Hundred, which they dedicat-
ed, and as far as the Tower of Hananel.[u] 2 The men of Jericho[v] built the adjoining section, and Zaccur son **3:2** [v]Ne 7:36
of Imri built next to them.

3 The Fish Gate[w] was rebuilt by the sons of Hassenaah. They laid its beams and put its doors and bolts **3:3** [w]2Ch 33:14; Ne 12:39
and bars in place. 4 Meremoth son of Uriah, the son of Hakkoz, repaired the next section. Next to him
Meshullam son of Berekiah, the son of Meshezabel, made repairs, and next to him Zadok son of Baana
also made repairs. 5 The next section was repaired by the men of Tekoa,[x] but their nobles would not put **3:5** [x]2Sa 14:2
their shoulders to the work under their supervisors.[a]

6 The Jeshanah[b] Gate[y] was repaired by Joiada son of Paseah and Meshullam son of Besodeiah. They **3:6** [y]Ne 12:39
laid its beams and put its doors and bolts and bars in place. 7 Next to them, repairs were made by men
from Gibeon[z] and Mizpah—Melatiah of Gibeon and Jadon of Meronoth—places under the authority **3:7** [z]Jos 9:3; Ne 2:7
of the governor of Trans-Euphrates. 8 Uzziel son of Harhaiah, one of the goldsmiths, repaired the next
section; and Hananiah, one of the perfume-makers, made repairs next to that. They restored[c] Jerusalem
as far as the Broad Wall.[a] 9 Rephaiah son of Hur, ruler of a half-district of Jerusalem, repaired the next sec- **3:8** [a]Ne 12:38
tion. 10 Adjoining this, Jedaiah son of Harumaph made repairs opposite his house, and Hattush son of
Hashabneiah made repairs next to him. 11 Malkijah son of Harim and Hasshub son of Pahath-Moab re-
paired another section and the Tower of the Ovens.[b] 12 Shallum son of Hallohesh, ruler of a half-district **3:11** [b]Ne 12:38
of Jerusalem, repaired the next section with the help of his daughters.

[a] 5 Or *their Lord* or *the governor*   [b] 6 Or *Old*   [c] 8 Or *They left out part of*

---

uchadnezzar some 140 years earlier, despite aborted attempts to rebuild them.

Uzziah had fortified towers in the western wall (2Ch 26:9), overlooking the central valley between the Hinnom and Kidron Valleys. Excavations in 1927–1928 uncovered the remains of a gate from the Persian period that has been identified as the Valley Gate. Many scholars suggest that the Jackal Well was En Rogel (Jos 15:7–8; 18:16; 2Sa 17:17; 1Ki 1:9), a well situated at the junction of the Hinnom and Kidron Valleys, 250 yards (229 m) south of the southeastern ridge of Jerusalem. Others suggest that it was the Pool of Siloam. The Dung Gate, situated about 500 yards (457 m) south of the Valley Gate (3:13), may have been the gate leading to the rubbish dump in the Hinnom Valley (cf. vv. 13–14; 12:31; 2Ki 23:10).

2:14 The Fountain Gate was possibly in the southeastern wall facing toward En Rogel (see 3:15; 12:37). The King's Pool was probably the Pool of Siloam (3:15; see "The Pool of Siloam" on p. 1739) or the adjacent Birket el-Hamra. It may have been created by diverting the overflow from Hezekiah's Siloam tunnel (cf. 2Ki 20:20; 2Ch 32:30; see "Hezekiah's Tunnel" on p. 564) to irrigate the royal gardens (2Ki 25:4) located outside the city walls at the junction of the Kidron and Hinnom Valleys.

2:19 Arabs became dominant in Transjordan from the Assyrian to the Persian periods. Sargon II of Assyria resettled some Arabs in Samaria in 715 B.C. Classical sources reveal that the Arabs enjoyed a favored status under the Persians.

3:1–32 This chapter describes the reconstruction of about 45 sections of wall, from a starting point on the northern side and moving counterclockwise. The account suggests that most of the rebuilding was concerned with the gates, as enemy assaults would have focused on those structures.

3:1 It was appropriate that the high priest should be part of the rebuilding process and set an example for the people. Ancient Sumerian kings would themselves carry bricks for the building of a temple.

The Sheep Gate was known in New Testament times (Jn 5:2) as having been located near the Bethesda Pool (in the northeastern corner of Jerusalem; see "The Pool of Bethseda in Jerusalem" on p. 1728). Even today this area is periodically used as a sheep market. The Sheep Gate may have replaced the earlier Benjamin Gate (Jer 37:13; 38:7; Zec 14:10).

Regarding the Tower of the Hundred, "Hundred" may have referred to (1) its height (100 cubits), (2) the number of its steps or (3) a military unit (cf. Dt 1:15). The Tower of the Hundred and the Tower of Hananel were associated with the "citadel by the temple" (Ne 2:8) in protecting the vulnerable northern approaches to the city.

3:8 Archaeological excavations in Jerusalem have uncovered a wall west of the temple area dated to the early seventh century B.C. and probably built under the direction of Hezekiah (2Ch 32:5). The expansion to and beyond the Broad Wall may have become necessary because of the influx of refugees fleeing from the fall of Samaria in 722–721 B.C.

3:13 c2Ch 26:9 13 The Valley Gate[c] was repaired by Hanun and the residents of Zanoah.[d] They rebuilt it and put its
dJos 15:34 eNe 2:13 doors and bolts and bars in place. They also repaired five hundred yards[a] of the wall as far as the Dung
Gate.[e]

3:14 fJer 6:1 14 The Dung Gate was repaired by Malkijah son of Recab, ruler of the district of Beth Hakkerem.[f] He
rebuilt it and put its doors and bolts and bars in place.

15 The Fountain Gate was repaired by Shallun son of Col-Hozeh, ruler of the district of Mizpah. He re-
built it, roofing it over and putting its doors and bolts and bars in place. He also repaired the wall of the
3:15 gIsa 8:6; Jn 9:7 Pool of Siloam,[b][g] by the King's Garden, as far as the steps going down from the City of David. 16 Beyond
3:16 hJos 15:58 him, Nehemiah son of Azbuk, ruler of a half-district of Beth Zur,[h] made repairs up to a point opposite
iAc 2:29 the tombs[c][i] of David, as far as the artificial pool and the House of the Heroes.
17 Next to him, the repairs were made by the Levites under Rehum son of Bani. Beside him, Hasha-
3:17 jJos 15:44 biah, ruler of half the district of Keilah,[j] carried out repairs for his district. 18 Next to him, the repairs
were made by their countrymen under Binnui[d] son of Henadad, ruler of the other half-district of Kei-
lah. 19 Next to him, Ezer son of Jeshua, ruler of Mizpah, repaired another section, from a point facing
the ascent to the armory as far as the angle. 20 Next to him, Baruch son of Zabbai zealously repaired an-
other section, from the angle to the entrance of the house of Eliashib the high priest. 21 Next to him,
3:21 kEzr 8:33 Meremoth[k] son of Uriah, the son of Hakkoz, repaired another section, from the entrance of Eliashib's
house to the end of it.
22 The repairs next to him were made by the priests from the surrounding region. 23 Beyond them,
Benjamin and Hasshub made repairs in front of their house; and next to them, Azariah son of Maase-
3:24 lEzr 8:33 iah, the son of Ananiah, made repairs beside his house. 24 Next to him, Binnui[l] son of Henadad repaired
another section, from Azariah's house to the angle and the corner, 25 and Palal son of Uzai worked oppo-
3:25 mJer 32:2; 37:21; 39:14 site the angle and the tower projecting from the upper palace near the court of the guard.[m] Next to him,
nEzr 2:3 Pedaiah son of Parosh[n] 26 and the temple servants[o] living on the hill of Ophel[p] made repairs up to a point
3:26 oNe 7:46; 11:21 p2Ch 33:14 opposite the Water Gate[q] toward the east and the projecting tower. 27 Next to them, the men of Tekoa[r] re-
qNe 8:1,3,16; 12:37 paired another section, from the great projecting tower[s] to the wall of Ophel.
3:27 rver 5 sPs 48:12
3:28 t2Ki 11:16; 2Ch 23:15; Jer 31:40 28 Above the Horse Gate,[t] the priests made repairs, each in front of his own house. 29 Next to them, Za-
dok son of Immer made repairs opposite his house. Next to him, Shemaiah son of Shecaniah, the guard
at the East Gate, made repairs. 30 Next to him, Hananiah son of Shelemiah, and Hanun, the sixth son of
Zalaph, repaired another section. Next to them, Meshullam son of Berekiah made repairs opposite his liv-
ing quarters. 31 Next to him, Malkijah, one of the goldsmiths, made repairs as far as the house of the tem-
ple servants and the merchants, opposite the Inspection Gate, and as far as the room above the corner;
3:32 uver 1; Jn 5:2 32 and between the room above the corner and the Sheep Gate[u] the goldsmiths and merchants made re-
pairs.

Opposition to the Rebuilding

4:1 vNe 2:10 4 When Sanballat[v] heard that we were rebuilding the wall, he became angry and was greatly incensed.
4:2 wEzr 4:9-10 He ridiculed the Jews, 2 and in the presence of his associates[w] and the army of Samaria, he said,
xPs 79:1; Jer 26:18 "What are those feeble Jews doing? Will they restore their wall? Will they offer sacrifices? Will they fin-
ish in a day? Can they bring the stones back to life from those heaps of rubble[x]—burned as they are?"
4:3 yNe 2:10 3 Tobiah[y] the Ammonite, who was at his side, said, "What they are building—if even a fox climbed
zJob 13:12; 15:3 up on it, he would break down their wall of stones!"[z]

[a] *13* Hebrew *a thousand cubits* (about 450 meters) [b] *15* Hebrew *Shelah,* a variant of *Shiloah,* that is, Siloam [c] *16* Hebrew; Septuagint, some Vulgate manuscripts and Syriac *tomb* [d] *18* Two Hebrew manuscripts and Syriac (see also Septuagint and verse 24); most Hebrew manuscripts *Bavvai*

3:16 Beth Zur was a district capital 13 miles (21 km) south of Jerusalem. Excavations in 1931 and 1957 revealed that occupation was sparse during the early Persian period but was resumed in the fifth century B.C.

David had been buried in the city area of Jerusalem (1Ki 2:10; 2Ch 21:20; 32:33; Ac 2:29). The so-called Tomb of David on Mount Zion, venerated today by Jewish pilgrims, is located in the Coenaculum building, erected in the fourteenth century A.D. Such a site for David's tomb is mentioned no earlier than the ninth century A.D.

The House of the Heroes may have been the housing unit for David's "mighty men" (see 2Sa 23:8–39), which perhaps served later as the barracks or armory.

3:26 The Water Gate led to the Gihon spring, the main source of Jerusalem's water. It must have opened onto a large area, for the reading of the law took place there (8:1,3,16; 12:37).

The "projecting tower" may have been the large tower whose ruins were discovered by archaeologists on the crest of the Ophel hill in 1923–1925. Excavations at the base of the tower in 1978 revealed a level dating to the Persian era.

4:2 Fire had damaged the stones, which were probably limestone, and had caused many of them to crack and crumble.

4 Hear us, O our God, for we are despised.[a] Turn their insults back on their own heads. Give them over
as plunder in a land of captivity. 5 Do not cover up their guilt[b] or blot out their sins from your sight,[c] for
they have thrown insults in the face of[a] the builders.

6 So we rebuilt the wall till all of it reached half its height, for the people worked with all their heart.
7 But when Sanballat, Tobiah,[d] the Arabs, the Ammonites and the men of Ashdod heard that the re-
pairs to Jerusalem's walls had gone ahead and that the gaps were being closed, they were very angry.
8 They all plotted together[e] to come and fight against Jerusalem and stir up trouble against it. 9 But we
prayed to our God and posted a guard day and night to meet this threat.
10 Meanwhile, the people in Judah said, "The strength of the laborers[f] is giving out, and there is so
much rubble that we cannot rebuild the wall."
11 Also our enemies said, "Before they know it or see us, we will be right there among them and will
kill them and put an end to the work."
12 Then the Jews who lived near them came and told us ten times over, "Wherever you turn, they will
attack us."
13 Therefore I stationed some of the people behind the lowest points of the wall at the exposed plac-
es, posting them by families, with their swords, spears and bows. 14 After I looked things over, I stood up
and said to the nobles, the officials and the rest of the people, "Don't be afraid[g] of them. Remember[h] the
Lord, who is great and awesome,[i] and fight[j] for your brothers, your sons and your daughters, your wives
and your homes."
15 When our enemies heard that we were aware of their plot and that God had frustrated it,[k] we all re-
turned to the wall, each to his own work.
16 From that day on, half of my men did the work, while the other half were equipped with spears,
shields, bows and armor. The officers posted themselves behind all the people of Judah 17 who were build-
ing the wall. Those who carried materials did their work with one hand and held a weapon[l] in the oth-
er, 18 and each of the builders wore his sword at his side as he worked. But the man who sounded the
trumpet[m] stayed with me.
19 Then I said to the nobles, the officials and the rest of the people, "The work is extensive and spread
out, and we are widely separated from each other along the wall. 20 Wherever you hear the sound of the
trumpet,[n] join us there. Our God will fight[o] for us!"
21 So we continued the work with half the men holding spears, from the first light of dawn till the
stars came out. 22 At that time I also said to the people, "Have every man and his helper stay inside Je-
rusalem at night, so they can serve us as guards by night and workmen by day." 23 Neither I nor my
brothers nor my men nor the guards with me took off our clothes; each had his weapon, even when he
went for water.[b]

Nehemiah Helps the Poor

5 Now the men and their wives raised a great outcry against their Jewish brothers. 2 Some were say-
ing, "We and our sons and daughters are numerous; in order for us to eat and stay alive, we must get
grain."
3 Others were saying, "We are mortgaging our fields,[p] our vineyards and our homes to get grain dur-
ing the famine."[q]
4 Still others were saying, "We have had to borrow money to pay the king's tax[r] on our fields and vine-
yards. 5 Although we are of the same flesh and blood[s] as our countrymen and though our sons are as
good as theirs, yet we have to subject our sons and daughters to slavery.[t] Some of our daughters have al-
ready been enslaved, but we are powerless, because our fields and our vineyards belong to others."[u]

4:4 [a]Ps 44:13; 79:12; 123:3-4; Jer 33:24
4:5 [b]Isa 2:9; La 1:22 [c]2Ki 14:27; Ps 51:1; 69:27-28; 109:14; Jer 18:23
4:7 [d]Ne 2:10
4:8 [e]Ps 2:2; 83:1-18
4:10 [f]1Ch 23:4
4:14 [g]Ge 28:15; Nu 14:9; Dt 1:29 [h]Ne 1:8 [i]Ne 1:5 [j]2Sa 10:12
4:15 [k]2Sa 17:14; Job 5:12
4:17 [l]Ps 149:6
4:18 [m]Nu 10:2
4:20 [n]Eze 33:3 [o]Ex 14:14; Dt 1:30; 20:4; Jos 10:14
5:3 [p]Ps 109:11 [q]Ge 47:23
5:4 [r]Ezr 4:13
5:5 [s]Ge 29:14 [t]Lev 25:39-43,47; 2Ki 4:1; Isa 50:1 [u]Dt 15:7-11; 2Ki 4:1

[a] 5 Or *have provoked you to anger before* [b] 23 The meaning of the Hebrew for this clause is uncertain.

4:7–8 The reasons that Sanballat and Tobiah opposed Nehemiah were not basically religious but political. The authority of the Samaritan governor in particular was threatened by the arrival of Nehemiah, the new governor of Judah (cf. 5:14). The Arabs (4:7), led by Geshem (2:19), were probably afraid that Judah's strengthening under Nehemiah would cut into their lucrative trade enterprise.

4:23 Constant preparedness was the rule. According to Josephus (*Antiquities*, 11.5.8), Nehemiah "himself made the rounds of the city by night, never tiring either through work or lack of food and sleep, neither of which he took for pleasure but as a necessity."

5:3 See the note on famine at Ruth 1:1. Also see "Famine in the Ancient Near East" on page 70.

5:4 It is estimated that the Persian king collected the equivalent of 20 million darics (100 million dollars) each year in taxes. Little was ever returned to benefit the provinces, because most of it was melted down and stored as bullion. For information on the daric, see the note on 1 Chronicles 29:7.

5:7 [v]Ex 22:25-27; Lev 25:35-37; Dt 23:19-20; 24:10-13 5:8 [w]Lev 25:47 [x]Jer 34:8

6When I heard their outcry and these charges, I was very angry. 7I pondered them in my mind and
then accused the nobles and officials. I told them, "You are exacting usury[v] from your own countrymen!"
So I called together a large meeting to deal with them 8and said: "As far as possible, we have bought[w]
back our Jewish brothers who were sold to the Gentiles. Now you are selling your brothers, only for them
to be sold back to us!" They kept quiet, because they could find nothing to say.[x]

5:7 Josephus (*Antiquities*, 4.8.25) explained the prohibition of usury: "Let it not be permitted to lend upon usury to any Hebrew either meat or drink; for it is not just to draw a revenue from the misfortunes of a fellow countryman. Rather, in consoling him in his distress, you should reckon as gain the gratitude of such persons and the recompense that God has in store for an act of generosity."

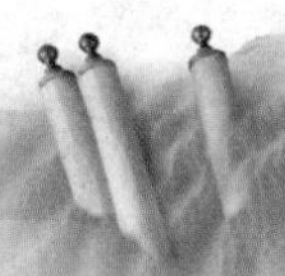

ANCIENT TEXTS AND ARTIFACTS

Hittite Instructions for Border Outposts

NEHEMIAH 4 Nehemiah 3–4 describes Nehemiah's attempt to rebuild Jerusalem in the face of violent opposition. Nehemiah had to inspire the people under his command to rebuild the walls and towers of the city, while simultaneously maintaining discipline for the Jewish militia defending it. This was not unusual; throughout the ancient Near East kings established military procedures for the commanders who manned their watchtowers and outposts.

A group of **Hittite** administrative texts describes the guidelines a "lord of a watchtower" (a garrison commander) was to follow. These included fixed procedures for the changing of the guard, for opening the gates of a city, for patrolling access routes and for maintaining a roster of troops. The Hittites also had specific procedures for the building and fortification of walls, to ensure that they would be resistant to burning and tunneling by sappers (men whose specialty it was to tunnel under a city wall). Interestingly, Hittite regulations also required that commanders oversee the maintenance of the priesthood, temples and rituals for the Hittite storm god (cf. chs. 7; 10).[1] They also had to ensure that deportees could recover from their destitute situation (cf. ch. 5). Chronologically, these Hittite texts are distant from the time of Nehemiah, but they do attest to the duties any governor of an ancient garrison city would presumably have been expected to fulfill.

[1]See "The Hittite Storm Gods" on page 784.

A watchtower in Judah
Preserving Bible Times; © Dr. James C. Martin

9 So I continued, "What you are doing is not right. Shouldn't you walk in the fear of our God to avoid
the reproach[y] of our Gentile enemies? 10 I and my brothers and my men are also lending the people mon- 5:9 [y]Isa 52:5
ey and grain. But let the exacting of usury stop![z] 11 Give back to them immediately their fields, vineyards, 5:10 [z]Ex 22:25
olive groves and houses, and also the usury[a] you are charging them—the hundredth part of the mon- 5:11 [a]Isa 58:6
ey, grain, new wine and oil."
12 "We will give it back," they said. "And we will not demand anything more from them. We will do as
you say."

Banking and Money in the Ancient World

NEHEMIAH 5 The earliest monetary exchanges were made on the basis of a barter system. In **Mesopotamia** barley and dates were often standards of trade, since they could be stored for a relatively long period of time without loss. Tithes, taxes and tribute could be paid in agricultural produce. Coins were introduced in Lydia during the seventh century B.C. but were not common until the time of Alexander the Great (c. 330 B.C.).[1] Barter was used even in Roman times. Precious metals (e.g., silver, gold and electrum) formed into vessels (cups, bowls, dishes) or jewelry (rings, earrings, bracelets) often were used as items of exchange.[2]

An item's weight (e.g., a silver plate of 130 shekels; Nu 7:13) was the primary indication of its monetary value, although other factors, such as the quality of the craftsmanship, were important as well. Common units of weight were the gerah (.02 ou or .6 g), the shekel (.4 ou or 11.5 g), the mina (1.5 lbs or .6 kg) and the talent (74 lbs or 34 kg). All of these weight equivalents are approximate and to a degree conjectural, however, and weights were not fixed for all places throughout the entire Biblical period. This does not mean that ancient people were casual about weights and exchanges; the condemnation of fraudulent weights and scales, in fact, shows how seriously they treated precision in such matters (cf. Lev 19:36; Pr 16:11).[3]

Prices naturally fluctuated through the centuries, and it is difficult to ascertain how much a particular commodity may have cost at a given time and place—and equally difficult to communicate prices in a manner meaningful to a modern reader. The laws of supply and demand operated then as now. Second Kings 7:1 indicates that in the ninth century B.C. the price of one silver shekel for two seahs (about 24 qts or 14.6 l) of barley was regarded as so inexpensive that it would only occur when grain was overly abundant. The prophet Hosea, in approximately 740 B.C., seems to have redeemed his wife, Gomer, from slavery for a price of 15 shekels of silver and "about a homer and a lethek of barley" (Hos 3:2). A homer[4] seems to have been approximately 6 bushels or 220 liters and a lethek half that, indicating a total price of about 4.46 ounces (127.5 g) of silver and 8.53 bushels (330 l) of barley for redemption of a slave woman in eighth-century Israel. Hosea's contemporaries would have been able to determine whether this represented a typical or an exorbitant price.

With regard to the Israelites/Jews, money was safeguarded in temples and palaces or buried in underground hoards. Loans were documented and witnessed. Six-month agricultural loans were common, as were promissory notes and letters of credit. Laws regulated abuse of collateral: Outer garments had to be returned that night (Ex 22:26–27), the taking of millstones was prohibited (Dt 24:6) and creditors could not enter debtors' homes to collect collateral (Dt 24:10). Interest-carrying loans to fellow Israelites were prohibited (Ex 22:25) and real estate transactions highly restricted. As in modern business ventures, risk and profit were often directly proportional. International trade was highly risky but could also be quite profitable; local trading offered lower risks but also smaller returns on investment.

Roman coins from the first century A.D.
Preserving Bible Times; © Dr. James C. Martin

[1]See "Coins and Numismatics" on page 1699. [2]See "Precious Stones of the Biblical World" on page 1156. [3]See "Weights and Measures" on page 1459, as well as the standard NIV list of Weights and Measures on page 2079 in the back of this Bible. [4]Not included in the standard NIV list of Weights and Measures.

5:12 [b]Ezr 10:5 Then I summoned the priests and made the nobles and officials take an oath[b] to do what they had
5:13 [c]Mt 10:14; Ac 18:6 promised. 13I also shook[c] out the folds of my robe and said, "In this way may God shake out of his house
and possessions every man who does not keep this promise. So may such a man be shaken out and
emptied!"
[d]Dt 27:15-26 At this the whole assembly said, "Amen,"[d] and praised the LORD. And the people did as they had
promised.
5:14 [e]Ne 2:6; 13:6 [f]Ge 42:6; Ezr 6:7; Jer 40:7; Hag 1:1 14Moreover, from the twentieth year of King Artaxerxes,[e] when I was appointed to be their governor[f]
in the land of Judah, until his thirty-second year—twelve years—neither I nor my brothers ate the food
allotted to the governor. 15But the earlier governors—those preceding me—placed a heavy burden on
the people and took forty shekels[a] of silver from them in addition to food and wine. Their assistants also
5:15 [g]Ge 20:11 5:16 [h]2Th 3:7-10 lorded it over the people. But out of reverence for God[g] I did not act like that. 16Instead,[h] I devoted my-
self to the work on this wall. All my men were assembled there for the work; we[b] did not acquire any
land.
17Furthermore, a hundred and fifty Jews and officials ate at my table, as well as those who came to us
5:18 [i]1Ki 4:23 from the surrounding nations. 18Each day one ox, six choice sheep and some poultry[i] were prepared for
me, and every ten days an abundant supply of wine of all kinds. In spite of all this, I never demanded the
food allotted to the governor, because the demands were heavy on these people.
5:19 [j]Ge 8:1; 2Ki 20:3; Ne 1:8; 13:14,22,31 19Remember[j] me with favor, O my God, for all I have done for these people.

Further Opposition to the Rebuilding

6:1 [k]Ne 2:10 [l]Ne 2:19 6 When word came to Sanballat, Tobiah,[k] Geshem[l] the Arab and the rest of our enemies that I had re-
built the wall and not a gap was left in it—though up to that time I had not set the doors in the
gates—2Sanballat and Geshem sent me this message: "Come, let us meet together in one of the villages[c]
6:2 [m]1Ch 8:12 on the plain of Ono.[m]"
But they were scheming to harm me; 3so I sent messengers to them with this reply: "I am carrying on
a great project and cannot go down. Why should the work stop while I leave it and go down to you?"
4Four times they sent me the same message, and each time I gave them the same answer.
6:5 [n]Ne 2:10 5Then, the fifth time, Sanballat[n] sent his aide to me with the same message, and in his hand was an
unsealed letter 6in which was written:

6:6 [o]Ne 2:19 "It is reported among the nations—and Geshem[d][o] says it is true—that you and the Jews are
plotting to revolt, and therefore you are building the wall. Moreover, according to these reports you
are about to become their king 7and have even appointed prophets to make this proclamation
about you in Jerusalem: 'There is a king in Judah!' Now this report will get back to the king; so
come, let us confer together."

8I sent him this reply: "Nothing like what you are saying is happening; you are just making it up out
of your head."
9They were all trying to frighten us, thinking, "Their hands will get too weak for the work, and it will
not be completed."
⌞But I prayed,⌟ "Now strengthen my hands."

[a] *15* That is, about 1 pound (about 0.5 kilogram) [b] *16* Most Hebrew manuscripts; some Hebrew manuscripts, Septuagint, Vulgate and Syriac *I* [c] *2* Or *in Kephirim* [d] *6* Hebrew *Gashmu,* a variant of *Geshem*

5:15 The Hebrew for "governor" is used of Sheshbazzar (Ezr 5:14) and Zerubbabel (Hag 1:1,14; 2:2), as well as of various Persian officials (Ezr 5:3,6; 6:6–7,13; 8:36; Ne 2:7,9; 3:7). While some believe that Judah did not have governors before Nehemiah and that the reference here is to governors of Samaria, recent archaeological evidence, in the form of seals and seal impressions, confirms the reference to the previous governors of Judah.

Since it was customary Persian practice to exempt temple personnel from taxation (see the note on Ezr 7:24), the tax burden fell even more heavily upon lay people. Governors who employed extortion often cultivated assistants who were even more oppressive (cf. Mt 18:21–35; 20:25–28).

6:2 Ono was located about 7 miles (11 km) southeast of Joppa near Lod (Lydda), in the westernmost area settled by the returning Jews.

6:5 During this period a letter was ordinarily written on a papyrus or leather sheet, which was rolled up, tied with a string and sealed with a clay bulla (seal impression) to guarantee its authenticity (see "Writing Materials in the Ancient World" on p. 2037). Sanballat apparently wanted the content of his letter to be made known to the public at large.

6:6 The Behistun Inscription of Darius I (see "Darius I" on p. 676) makes it clear that Persian kings did not tolerate rebellion or illegitimate claims to kingship. Later, in New Testament times, the Roman emperor was similarly suspicious of any unauthorized claims to royalty (Jn 19:12; cf. Mt 2:1–13).

6:9 The phrase "hands will get too weak" expresses the idea of discouragement. The Hebrew for this phrase is also used in Ezra 4:4 and Jeremiah 38:4, as well as on an ostracon from Lachish dated about 588 B.C. (see "The Lachish Ostraca" on p. 1252).

10 One day I went to the house of Shemaiah son of Delaiah, the son of Mehetabel, who was shut in at
his home. He said, "Let us meet in the house of God, inside the temple[p], and let us close the temple doors, **6:10** [p]Nu 18:7
because men are coming to kill you—by night they are coming to kill you."
11 But I said, "Should a man like me run away? Or should one like me go into the temple to save his life?
I will not go!" 12 I realized that God had not sent him, but that he had prophesied against me[q] because To- **6:12** [q]Eze 13:22-
biah and Sanballat[r] had hired him. 13 He had been hired to intimidate me so that I would commit a sin 23 [r]Ne 2:10
by doing this, and then they would give me a bad name to discredit me.[s] **6:13** [s]Jer 20:10

14 Remember[t] Tobiah and Sanballat,[u] O my God, because of what they have done; remember also the **6:14** [t]Ne 1:8 [u]Ne 2:10
prophetess[v] Noadiah and the rest of the prophets[w] who have been trying to intimidate me. [v]Ex 15:20; Eze 13:17-23; Ac 21:9; Rev 2:20 [w]Ne 13:29; Jer 23:9-40; Zec 13:2-3

The Completion of the Wall

15 So the wall was completed on the twenty-fifth of Elul, in fifty-two days. 16 When all our enemies
heard about this, all the surrounding nations were afraid and lost their self-confidence, because they re-
alized that this work had been done with the help of our God.
17 Also, in those days the nobles of Judah were sending many letters to Tobiah, and replies from Tobi-
ah kept coming to them. 18 For many in Judah were under oath to him, since he was son-in-law to Shec-
aniah son of Arah, and his son Jehohanan had married the daughter of Meshullam son of Berekiah.
19 Moreover, they kept reporting to me his good deeds and then telling him what I said. And Tobiah sent
letters to intimidate me.

7 After the wall had been rebuilt and I had set the doors in place, the gatekeepers[x] and the singers[y] and **7:1** [x]1Ch 9:27; 26:12-19; Ne 6:1,
the Levites[z] were appointed. 2 I put in charge of Jerusalem my brother Hanani,[a] along with[a] Hana- 15 [y]Ps 68:25 [z]Ne 8:9
niah[b] the commander of the citadel,[c] because he was a man of integrity and feared[d] God more than most **7:2** [a]Ne 1:2 [b]Ne 10:23 [c]Ne 2:8
men do. 3 I said to them, "The gates of Jerusalem are not to be opened until the sun is hot. While the gate- [d]1Ki 18:3
keepers are still on duty, have them shut the doors and bar them. Also appoint residents of Jerusalem as
guards, some at their posts and some near their own houses."

The List of the Exiles Who Returned

4 Now the city was large and spacious, but there were few people in it,[e] and the houses had not yet **7:4** [e]Ne 11:1
been rebuilt. 5 So my God put it into my heart to assemble the nobles, the officials and the common peo-
ple for registration by families. I found the genealogical record of those who had been the first to return.
This is what I found written there:

6 These are the people of the province who came up from the captivity of the exiles[f] whom Neb- **7:6** [f]2Ch 36:20; Ezr 2:1-70; Ne 1:2
uchadnezzar king of Babylon had taken captive (they returned to Jerusalem and Judah, each to
his own town, 7 in company with Zerubbabel,[g] Jeshua, Nehemiah, Azariah, Raamiah, Nahamani, **7:7** [g]1Ch 3:19; Ezr 2:2
Mordecai, Bilshan, Mispereth, Bigvai, Nehum and Baanah):

The list of the men of Israel:

8 the descendants of Parosh	2,172
9 of Shephatiah	372
10 of Arah	652
11 of Pahath-Moab (through the line of Jeshua and Joab)	2,818
12 of Elam	1,254
13 of Zattu	845
14 of Zaccai	760

[a] 2 Or *Hanani, that is,*

6:10–13 Since Shemaiah had access to the temple, he was probably a priest. He could have legitimately proposed that Nehemiah take refuge in the temple area at the altar of asylum (cf. Ex 21:13–14; 1Ki 1:50–53), but not in "the house of God" (Ne 6:10), the temple building itself, since as a layman Nehemiah was not permitted to enter the sanctuary (Nu 18:7).
6:14 See the note on prophetesses at Exodus 15:20–21.
6:15 The walls that lay in ruins for nearly a century and a half were rebuilt in less than two months once the people had been galvanized into action by Nehemiah's leadership. Archaeological investigations have shown that the circumference of the wall in Nehemiah's day was much reduced. Josephus stated (*Antiquities*, 11.5.8) that the rebuilding of the wall required two years and four months, but he was doubtless including such additional tasks as further strengthening its various sections, embellishing and beautifying.
7:3 Ordinarily a city's gates would have been opened each day at dawn, but Nehemiah delayed unlocking the gates to prevent an enemy attack before Jerusalem's residents were fully awake and alert. (See "The City Gate" on p. 392.)

The Postexilic Period of the Old Testament

The Persian Period

NEHEMIAH 7 The **postexilic period**, which covers over 500 years, can be conveniently divided into five periods: Persian, Greek, **Hasmonean**, Roman and Herodian.

In 539–538 B.C. Cyrus the Persian defeated the Babylonians and reversed the policy of depopulating areas and scattering people into foreign lands.[1] Almost immediately thereafter he allowed the exiled Israelites to return to their homeland under the leadership of Sheshbazzar (cf. Ezr 1–2; 5:13–16; Ne 7). The Cyrus Cylinder provides important extrabiblical confirmation.[2]

Many Jews opted to remain in the lands to which they had been exiled, though maintaining their religious and ethnic identity. This phenomenon, known as the dispersion of the Jews, had become an irreversible social reality. However, the Old Testament exilic and postexilic narratives, with the exception of the book of Esther, focus on the challenges and crises facing the returnees.

The first major challenge was the rebuilding of the temple in the face of external opposition (Ezr 4:1–5, 24; 5:1—6:18) and internal neglect (Hag 1:2–11). Its restoration was a prerequisite for the reinstatement of God's presence and blessings, and a strong priesthood was necessary to reinstitute local worship according to prescribed norms (Hag 2:11–19; Zec 3). Stirred into action by the prophets Haggai and Zechariah, and with Persian sponsorship, the Persian-appointed governor Zerubbabel and the high priest Joshua successfully completed the project, dedicating the temple in 516/515 B.C. (cf. Ezr 6:15–16).

Another challenge was the threat of assimilation and idolatry (Ezr 9). With Persian endorsement Ezra returned to Jerusalem in 458 B.C. (Ezr 7:6–10). He confronted the people, led them in confession of their unfaithfulness to God (Ezr 10) and later fulfilled his commission to teach the Book of the Law of Moses to the people (Ne 8–9).

A third significant challenge was the fortification of Jerusalem. In 445 B.C. Nehemiah, royal cupbearer to the Persian monarch, appealed to Artaxerxes I on Jerusalem's behalf.[3] Artaxerxes appointed Nehemiah governor of Judea, funded his return to Jerusalem and provided building materials (2:1–9; 5:14). Despite considerable opposition,[4] Nehemiah and the returnees succeeded in their mission (6:15).

The dedication of the wall was accompanied by extensive reading from the law and a call for covenant renewal. This period of revival was apparently short-lived, however. When Nehemiah returned to Jerusalem, perhaps in 433/432 B.C, he discovered that the priests and people alike had become negligent in their worship.

The Persian kings' endorsement and support of religious activity in "Yehud" (Judea) is consistent with their interest in temple communities in Babylonia, Syria, **Asia Minor**, Armenia, **Phoenicia** and elsewhere:

✣ Temples served as regional power centers and helped maintain civil obedience and political loyalty. It is hardly coincidental that the Persians authorized the second temple's completion shortly after their subjugation of Egypt in 526–525 B.C. They willingly commissioned Ezra and Nehemiah a few years after quelling Egypt's revolt in 460 B.C. The Egyptian threat to the south highlighted Persia's reliance upon a productive and loyal "Yehud."

✣ Priestly governmental systems were less threatening to Persian kings than were local monarchies. Judea was ruled by both a high priest and a governor (cf. Hag 1:1,14; Zec 4), and the balance of power between the two fluctuated throughout the postexilic period. Nehemiah played a crucial role as governor in the mid-fifth century B.C., yet in Judea overall this period saw an increasing role of the priesthood and a decreasing role of the Davidic royal family. By the end of the Persian period (c. 330 B.C.) the priests had risen to a prominent position.

✣ The Persians hoped to curry the favor and support of local deities and their priestly servants, who might intercede for the prosperity of the empire (cf. Ezr 6:9–10; 7:23).

✣ Religious endorsement was essential to the legitimization of Persian rule in the eyes of various peoples. The Persians were so successful in this that in Babylonia their rule was not regarded as foreign domination.

Israel's leaders and prophets recognized the constraints of their situation under Persian rule but welcomed Persian support to carry out God's commands in their homeland. Nevertheless, they consistently testified that God was the source of all blessing and success (Ezr 1:1; 7:6; Ne 2:8,20) and continued to look forward to a day when the Davidic branch would take root and all peoples would flock to Mount Zion to seek the Lord of hosts (Zec 3:8–10; 8:20–23).

[1]See "Cyrus the Great" on page 669. [2]See "The Cyrus Cylinder" on page 679. [3]See "Artaxerxes I, King of Persia" on page 681. [4]See "Sanballat, Tobiah and Geshem" on page 691.

The Postexilic Period of the Old Testament

The Greek and Hasmonean Periods

NEHEMIAH 7 *The Greeks.* Historical sources are virtually silent about the history of Judea from the later Persian period (see previous article) until the time of Alexander the Great. In 332 B.C. this Macedonian king conquered the region and ended centuries of Persian control. Alexander brought with him Hellenism, a popular form of Greek culture that left a lasting impression on all societies with which it came into contact.

Following his death in 323 B.C. Alexander's most powerful generals waged war among themselves in an effort to claim portions of the empire. By 301 the **Ptolemaic** dynasty, a Greek family that ruled Egypt, had gained control of Judea.[1] Sources for this period are scant at best, but this may suggest that the Jews existed quite peacefully under the Ptolemies.

In 200 B.C. the **Seleucid** king Antiochus III conquered Judea (the Seleucids were a Greek dynasty that ruled Syria).[2] He established favorable relations by guaranteeing religious liberty to his subjects. Antiochus IV Epiphanes, however, reversed this policy and engaged in extreme religious persecution of the Jews. He is most likely the "contemptible person" who rose to power in Daniel 11:21. Historians believe that Antiochus's desperate need for money to fight the Romans contributed to this state of affairs. It also appears that quarreling factions within the Jerusalem priestly class attempted to strengthen their own positions by cooperating with the Greek-speaking leadership, even to the point of suppressing their own people.

Antiochus used Judea as a staging ground for a campaign against Egypt, but in 168 B.C. this effort was thwarted. The repressed people of Jerusalem seized the opportunity to rebel against Antiochus, who crushed the uprising and punished the citizens by installing pagan cults in the city and forbidding the observance of Jewish religious practices. The author of 1 Maccabees (an Apocryphal book not found in the traditional Protestant canon) records that the worst insult of all occurred in 167 B.C. when Antiochus defiled the temple by sacrificing swine, an "unclean" meat, on the altar. Daniel 11:31 probably also refers to this incident, which it calls the "abomination that causes desolation."[3] The Jews reacted violently with a revolt led by the priest Mattathias of the Hasmonean family and his five sons. Within a few years the Jews had won back their religious freedom, and the temple was cleansed and rededicated in 164 B.C.

The Hasmoneans. The Maccabees, because of their victory over their Seleucid enemies, established themselves as the ruling dynasty in Judea. The most famous member of this family was Judas Maccabeus, son of Mattathias. His name provided the common title for this uprising, the Maccabean Revolt.

Judas led successful military campaigns in 163 and 162 B.C. to protect Jews who were being attacked in other areas of the Holy Land. The Hasmoneans soon gained a reputation as national leaders and defenders. The Seleucids attempted unsuccessfully to quell the growing tide of Jewish nationalism, and in 161 B.C. the Hasmoneans increased their advantage by signing a mutual defense treaty with the Roman Republic.

Meanwhile, the Seleucid Empire was crumbling from within. Ironically, the contenders for the throne now sought help from the Hasmoneans to secure their positions. In return, they promised autonomy to the Jews. The Hasmoneans profited from this period of Seleucid weakness by taking control of large areas of the Holy Land. Finally, in 141 B.C. the last Greek garrison was removed from Jerusalem, and the city no longer bore any burden of taxation by the Seleucids.

The Hasmonean dynasty achieved significant territorial expansion. John Hyrcanus I (135–104 B.C.) was particularly notable for his military campaigns against the Samaritans and **Idumeans**.[4] He destroyed the Samaritan temple on Mount Gerizim and conquered the capital at Shechem.[5] The Idumeans were allowed to stay in their lands on the condition that all their males be circumcised. Galilee fell to Hyrcanus's son, Aristobulus (104–103 B.C.). The subsequent ruler, Alexander Jannaeus (103–76 B.C.) extended the Hasmonean reach to the Greek cities along the coast of the Holy Land and to the region of the **Transjordan**. However, Jannaeus gained a reputation for severe cruelty. Internal dissension increased and threatened to tear apart this increasingly fragile state. Jannaeus bequeathed the sizable Hasmonean kingdom to his wife, Salome, whose nine-year rule was marked by a civil war between her two sons, Aristobolus II and Hyrcanus II.

Another important development of this period was the rise of the Sadducees and Pharisees. The Sadducees represented the Jewish priestly upper class and their aristocratic associates. They sought prominence in both the religious and political spheres and were seen by some as being too friendly toward **Hellenistic** cultural influences.[6] The Pharisees, or "separatists," developed as a reaction against such Hellenism. This group was characterized by its strict, uncompromising observance of the Mosaic Law. Over time its members gained a lofty status in the eyes of many Jews, who viewed them as defenders of pure religion.[7]

[1]See "The Ptolemies" on page 1399. [2]See "The Seleucids" on page 1408. [3]See "Antiochus IV Epiphanes" on page 1406. [4]See "The Samaritans" on page 1737. [5]See "The Samaritan Temple on Mount Gerizim" on page 1727. [6]See "The Sadducees" on page 1600. [7]See "The Pharisees" on page 1566.

	15 of Binnui	648
	16 of Bebai	628
	17 of Azgad	2,322
	18 of Adonikam	667
	19 of Bigvai	2,067
7:20 [h]Ezr 8:6	20 of Adin[h]	655
	21 of Ater (through Hezekiah)	98
	22 of Hashum	328
	23 of Bezai	324
	24 of Hariph	112
	25 of Gibeon	95
7:26 [i]2Sa 23:28; 1Ch 2:54	26 the men of Bethlehem and Netophah[i]	188
7:27 [j]Jos 21:18	27 of Anathoth[j]	128
	28 of Beth Azmaveth	42
7:29 [k]Jos 18:26 [l]Jos 18:25	29 of Kiriath Jearim, Kephirah[k] and Beeroth[l]	743
	30 of Ramah and Geba	621
	31 of Micmash	122
7:32 [m]Ge 12:8	32 of Bethel and Ai[m]	123
	33 of the other Nebo	52
	34 of the other Elam	1,254
	35 of Harim	320

The Postexilic Period of the Old Testament
The Roman and Herodian Periods

NEHEMIAH 7 The period of Hasmonean rule marked the last time that Jews would be under the governance of their own people until the modern state of Israel was established in 1948. Indeed, when the Hasmoneans were at the height of their power, Roman power was already growing in the region and would soon encroach upon the Hasmonean state. By the time the Roman Pompey arrived at Jerusalem with his legions in 63 B.C., Roman conquest was virtually a foregone conclusion.[1] The Romans were quite merciful and did not destroy Jerusalem or punish the people of the region. They respected the antiquity of the Jewish faith and permitted its observance to continue unabated, so long as the Jews did not threaten the Roman state.

Pompey's successor, Gabinius, governor of Syria from 57 to 55 B.C., attempted to divide the Jewish territory into five administrative units. When the people reacted violently, Gabinius abandoned his plan. From this experience the Romans learned that Judea had the potential to be a powder keg. Indeed, rebellion would prove to be the norm, not the exception, throughout the period of Roman rule.

In 37 B.C. Herod the Great was appointed vassal king over Judea by Julius Caesar and the Roman Senate.[2] He quickly granted the high priesthood to members of the Jewish **Diaspora**, men who shared his Hellenistic tendencies (in contrast to the more conservative Jewish priests)—an act that angered many Judeans. He also ruled the region with a heavy hand, believing that rebellion was best discouraged by making examples of those who challenged the peace. Matthew 2, in the account of the slaughter of the innocents, illustrates Herod's cruelty.

On the other hand, Herod could be quite sympathetic to the Jewish people. On one occasion he lobbied the imperial court in Rome on behalf of certain Jews who had revolted. He also undertook the restoration of the temple in 20 B.C. Following Herod's death in 4 B.C. Archelaus became king but proved unable to maintain order. After ten years of uprisings, Rome designated Judea a Roman province and placed it under the direct oversight of the imperial capital. Nothing, however, could coerce the Jews into being satisfied under foreign rule. It was precisely in this difficult environment that Jesus embarked upon his public ministry.

[1]See "The Roman Army and the Occupation of the Holy Land" on page 1829. [2]See "Herod the Great" on page 1627.

[36]of Jericho[n] 345 7:36 [n]Ne 3:2
[37]of Lod, Hadid and Ono[o] 721 7:37 [o]1Ch 8:12
[38]of Senaah 3,930

[39]The priests:

the descendants of Jedaiah (through the family of Jeshua) 973
[40]of Immer 1,052
[41]of Pashhur 1,247
[42]of Harim 1,017

[43]The Levites:

the descendants of Jeshua (through Kadmiel through the line of Hodaviah) 74

[44]The singers:[p] 7:44 [p]Ne 11:23

the descendants of Asaph 148

[45]The gatekeepers:[q] 7:45 [q]1Ch 9:17

the descendants of
Shallum, Ater, Talmon, Akkub, Hatita and Shobai 138

[46]The temple servants:[r] 7:46 [r]Ne 3:26

the descendants of
Ziha, Hasupha, Tabbaoth,
[47]Keros, Sia, Padon,
[48]Lebana, Hagaba, Shalmai,
[49]Hanan, Giddel, Gahar,
[50]Reaiah, Rezin, Nekoda,
[51]Gazzam, Uzza, Paseah,
[52]Besai, Meunim, Nephusim,
[53]Bakbuk, Hakupha, Harhur,
[54]Bazluth, Mehida, Harsha,
[55]Barkos, Sisera, Temah,
[56]Neziah and Hatipha

[57]The descendants of the servants of Solomon:

the descendants of
Sotai, Sophereth, Perida,
[58]Jaala, Darkon, Giddel,
[59]Shephatiah, Hattil,
Pokereth-Hazzebaim and Amon

[60]The temple servants and the descendants of the servants of Solomon[s] 392 7:60 [s]1Ch 9:2

[61]The following came up from the towns of Tel Melah, Tel Harsha, Kerub, Addon and Immer, but they could not show that their families were descended from Israel:

[62]the descendants of
Delaiah, Tobiah and Nekoda 642

[63]And from among the priests:

the descendants of
Hobaiah, Hakkoz and Barzillai (a man who had married a daughter of Barzillai the Gileadite and was called by that name).

[64]These searched for their family records, but they could not find them and so were excluded

7:44 See the note on Psalms 73:1—83:18 for commentary on Asaph.

from the priesthood as unclean. [65]The governor, therefore, ordered them not to eat any of the most sacred food until there should be a priest ministering with the Urim and Thummim.[t]

[66]The whole company numbered 42,360, [67]besides their 7,337 menservants and maidservants; and they also had 245 men and women singers. [68]There were 736 horses, 245 mules,[a] [69]435 camels and 6,720 donkeys.

[70]Some of the heads of the families contributed to the work. The governor gave to the treasury 1,000 drachmas[b] of gold, 50 bowls and 530 garments for priests. [71]Some of the heads of the families[u] gave to the treasury for the work 20,000 drachmas[c] of gold and 2,200 minas[d] of silver. [72]The total given by the rest of the people was 20,000 drachmas of gold, 2,000 minas[e] of silver and 67 garments for priests.[v]

[73]The priests, the Levites, the gatekeepers, the singers and the temple servants,[w] along with certain of the people and the rest of the Israelites, settled in their own towns.[x]

Ezra Reads the Law

8 When the seventh month came and the Israelites had settled in their towns,[y] [1]all the people assembled as one man in the square before the Water Gate.[z] They told Ezra the scribe to bring out the Book of the Law of Moses,[a] which the LORD had commanded for Israel.

[2]So on the first day of the seventh month[b] Ezra the priest brought the Law[c] before the assembly, which was made up of men and women and all who were able to understand. [3]He read it aloud from daybreak till noon as he faced the square before the Water Gate[d] in the presence of the men, women and others who could understand. And all the people listened attentively to the Book of the Law.

[4]Ezra the scribe stood on a high wooden platform[e] built for the occasion. Beside him on his right stood Mattithiah, Shema, Anaiah, Uriah, Hilkiah and Maaseiah; and on his left were Pedaiah, Mishael, Malkijah, Hashum, Hashbaddanah, Zechariah and Meshullam.

[5]Ezra opened the book. All the people could see him because he was standing[f] above them; and as he opened it, the people all stood up. [6]Ezra praised the LORD, the great God; and all the people lifted their hands[g] and responded, "Amen! Amen!" Then they bowed down and worshiped the LORD with their faces to the ground.

[7]The Levites[h]—Jeshua, Bani, Sherebiah, Jamin, Akkub, Shabbethai, Hodiah, Maaseiah, Kelita, Azariah, Jozabad, Hanan and Pelaiah—instructed[i] the people in the Law while the people were standing there. [8]They read from the Book of the Law of God, making it clear[f] and giving the meaning so that the people could understand what was being read.

[9]Then Nehemiah the governor, Ezra the priest and scribe, and the Levites[j] who were instructing the people said to them all, "This day is sacred to the LORD your God. Do not mourn or weep."[k] For all the people had been weeping as they listened to the words of the Law.

[10]Nehemiah said, "Go and enjoy choice food and sweet drinks, and send some to those who have nothing[l] prepared. This day is sacred to our Lord. Do not grieve, for the joy[m] of the LORD is your strength."

[11]The Levites calmed all the people, saying, "Be still, for this is a sacred day. Do not grieve."

[12]Then all the people went away to eat and drink, to send portions of food and to celebrate with great joy,[n] because they now understood the words that had been made known to them.

[13]On the second day of the month, the heads of all the families, along with the priests and the Levites, gathered around Ezra the scribe to give attention to the words of the Law. [14]They found written in the Law, which the LORD had commanded through Moses, that the Israelites were to live in booths during the feast of the seventh month [15]and that they should proclaim this word and spread it throughout their towns and in Jerusalem: "Go out into the hill country and bring back branches from olive and wild olive trees, and from myrtles, palms and shade trees, to make booths"—as it is written.[g]

7:65 [t]Ex 28:30; Ne 8:9
7:71 [u]1Ch 29:7
7:72 [v]Ex 25:2
7:73 [w]Ne 1:10; Ps 34:22; 103:21; 113:1; 135:1 [x]Ezr 3:1; Ne 11:1
[y]Ezr 3:1
8:1 [z]Ne 3:26 [a]Dt 28:61; 2Ch 34:15; Ezr 7:6
8:2 [b]Lev 23:23-25; Nu 29:1-6 [c]Dt 31:11
8:3 [d]Ne 3:26
8:4 [e]2Ch 6:13
8:5 [f]Jdg 3:20
8:6 [g]Ex 4:31; Ezr 9:5; 1Ti 2:8
8:7 [h]Ezr 10:23 [i]Lev 10:11; 2Ch 17:7
8:9 [j]Ne 7:1,65,70 [k]Dt 12:7,12; 16:14-15
8:10 [l]1Sa 25:8; Lk 14:12-14 [m]Lev 23:40; Dt 12:18; 16:11, 14-15
8:12 [n]Est 9:22

[a] *68* Some Hebrew manuscripts (see also Ezra 2:66); most Hebrew manuscripts do not have this verse. [b] *70* That is, about 19 pounds (about 8.5 kilograms) [c] *71* That is, about 375 pounds (about 170 kilograms); also in verse 72 [d] *71* That is, about 1 1/3 tons (about 1.2 metric tons) [e] *72* That is, about 1 1/4 tons (about 1.1 metric tons) [f] *8* Or *God, translating it* [g] *15* See Lev. 23:37-40.

7:65 See "The Urim and Thummim" on page 136.
8:2–3 Women did not participate in ordinary meetings but were included, together with children, on such sacred occasions (cf. Dt 31:12–13; Jos 8:35; Ne 10:28; 12:43). The people evidently stood for five or six hours attentively listening to the reading and explanation of the Scriptures.
8:8 The phrase "making it clear" may mean that the Levites translated the words from Hebrew into Aramaic (see the NIV text note).
8:15 Olives are widespread in Mediterranean countries and were growing in Canaan already before the conquest (Dt 8:8). Because it takes an olive tree 30 years to mature, its cultivation requires peaceful conditions (see "Food and Agriculture" on p. 390).

16 So the people went out and brought back branches and built themselves booths on their own roofs,
in their courtyards, in the courts of the house of God and in the square by the Water Gate and the one by
the Gate of Ephraim.[o] 17 The whole company that had returned from exile built booths and lived in them.
From the days of Joshua son of Nun until that day, the Israelites had not celebrated[p] it like this. And their
joy was very great.
18 Day after day, from the first day to the last, Ezra read[q] from the Book of the Law of God. They cele-
brated the feast for seven days, and on the eighth day, in accordance with the regulation,[r] there was an
assembly.

The Israelites Confess Their Sins

9 On the twenty-fourth day of the same month, the Israelites gathered together, fasting and wearing
sackcloth and having dust on their heads.[s] 2 Those of Israelite descent had separated themselves
from all foreigners.[t] They stood in their places and confessed their sins and the wickedness of their fa-
thers.[u] 3 They stood where they were and read from the Book of the Law of the LORD their God for a quar-
ter of the day, and spent another quarter in confession and in worshiping the LORD their God. 4 Standing
on the stairs were the Levites[v]—Jeshua, Bani, Kadmiel, Shebaniah, Bunni, Sherebiah, Bani and Kena-
ni—who called with loud voices to the LORD their God. 5 And the Levites—Jeshua, Kadmiel, Bani, Hash-
abneiah, Sherebiah, Hodiah, Shebaniah and Pethahiah—said: "Stand up and praise the LORD your God,[w]
who is from everlasting to everlasting.[a]"

"Blessed be your glorious name, and may it be exalted above all blessing and praise. 6 You alone
are the LORD.[x] You made the heavens,[y] even the highest heavens, and all their starry host, the earth[z]
and all that is on it, the seas[a] and all that is in them.[b] You give life to everything, and the multitudes
of heaven worship you.
7 "You are the LORD God, who chose Abram and brought him out of Ur of the Chaldeans[c] and
named him Abraham.[d] 8 You found his heart faithful to you, and you made a covenant with him to
give to his descendants the land of the Canaanites, Hittites, Amorites, Perizzites, Jebusites and Gir-
gashites.[e] You have kept your promise[f] because you are righteous.[g]
9 "You saw the suffering of our forefathers in Egypt;[h] you heard their cry at the Red Sea.[b i] 10 You
sent miraculous signs[j] and wonders against Pharaoh, against all his officials and all the people of
his land, for you knew how arrogantly the Egyptians treated them. You made a name[k] for your-
self, which remains to this day. 11 You divided the sea before them,[l] so that they passed through it
on dry ground, but you hurled their pursuers into the depths, like a stone into mighty waters.[m]
12 By day you led[n] them with a pillar of cloud,[o] and by night with a pillar of fire to give them light
on the way they were to take.
13 "You came down on Mount Sinai;[p] you spoke[q] to them from heaven. You gave them regula-
tions and laws that are just[r] and right, and decrees and commands that are good.[s] 14 You made
known to them your holy Sabbath[t] and gave them commands, decrees and laws through your ser-
vant Moses. 15 In their hunger you gave them bread from heaven[u] and in their thirst you brought
them water from the rock;[v] you told them to go in and take possession of the land you had sworn
with uplifted hand to give them.[w]
16 "But they, our forefathers, became arrogant and stiff-necked, and did not obey your com-
mands.[x] 17 They refused to listen and failed to remember[y] the miracles you performed among
them. They became stiff-necked and in their rebellion appointed a leader in order to return to
their slavery.[z] But you are a forgiving God, gracious and compassionate, slow to anger[a] and
abounding in love.[b] Therefore you did not desert them,[c] 18 even when they cast for themselves an
image of a calf[d] and said, 'This is your god, who brought you up out of Egypt,' or when they com-
mitted awful blasphemies.
19 "Because of your great compassion you did not abandon them in the desert. By day the pil-
lar of cloud did not cease to guide them on their path, nor the pillar of fire by night to shine on the
way they were to take. 20 You gave your good Spirit[e] to instruct them. You did not withhold your

8:16 [o]2Ki 14:13; Ne 12:39
8:17 [p]2Ch 7:8; 8:13; 30:21
8:18 [q]Dt 31:11 [r]Lev 23:36,40; Nu 29:35
9:1 [s]Jos 7:6; 1Sa 4:12
9:2 [t]Ne 13:3,30 [u]Ezr 10:11; Ps 106:6
9:4 [v]Ezr 10:23
9:5 [w]Ps 78:4
9:6 [x]Dt 6:4 [y]2Ki 19:15 [z]Ge 1:1; Isa 37:16 [a]Ps 95:5 [b]Dt 10:14
9:7 [c]Ge 11:31 [d]Ge 17:5
9:8 [e]Ge 15:18-21 [f]Jos 21:45 [g]Ge 15:6; Ezr 9:15
9:9 [h]Ex 3:7 [i]Ex 14:10-30
9:10 [j]Ex 10:1 [k]Jer 32:20; Da 9:15
9:11 [l]Ex 14:21; Ps 78:13 [m]Ex 15:4-5,10; Heb 11:29
9:12 [n]Ex 15:13 [o]Ex 13:21
9:13 [p]Ex 19:11 [q]Ex 19:19 [r]Ps 119:137 [s]Ex 20:1
9:14 [t]Ge 2:3; Ex 20:8-11
9:15 [u]Ex 16:4; Jn 6:31 [v]Ex 17:6; Nu 20:7-13 [w]Dt 1:8,21
9:16 [x]Dt 1:26-33; 31:29
9:17 [y]Ps 78:42 [z]Nu 14:1-4 [a]Ex 34:6 [b]Nu 14:17-19 [c]Ps 78:11
9:18 [d]Ex 32:4
9:20 [e]Nu 11:17; Isa 63:11,14

[a] 5 Or *God for ever and ever* [b] 9 Hebrew *Yam Suph*; that is, Sea of Reeds

9:1 For information on sackcloth, see the note on 2 Kings 6:30.
9:7 See "Ur" on page 705.
9:8 See "Lesser Known Peoples of the Old Testament" on page 265 and "The Jebusites" on page 596.

9:20 [f]Ex 16:15 [g]Ex 17:6 manna[f] from their mouths, and you gave them water[g] for their thirst. 21 For forty years you sus-
9:21 [h]Dt 2:7 tained them in the desert; they lacked nothing,[h] their clothes did not wear out nor did their feet
[i]Dt 8:4 become swollen.[i]

22 "You gave them kingdoms and nations, allotting to them even the remotest frontiers. They
9:22 [j]Nu 21:21 [k]Nu 21:33 took over the country of Sihon[a][j] king of Heshbon and the country of Og king of Bashan.[k] 23 You
made their sons as numerous as the stars in the sky, and you brought them into the land that you
9:24 [l]Jos 11:23 told their fathers to enter and possess. 24 Their sons went in and took possession of the land.[l] You

[a] *22* One Hebrew manuscript and Septuagint; most Hebrew manuscripts *Sihon, that is, the country of the*

ARCHAEOLOGICAL SITES

UR

NEHEMIAH 9 References to the Biblical Ur usually point to the ancient city located at modern Tell el-Muqqayyar in southern **Mesopotamia**. This was one of the great cities of the Sumerians[1] that flourished in the third millennium B.C. Founded perhaps as early as the fifth millennium, it grew during the fourth millennium and became prominent around 2600–2500 B.C., during the city's Early Dynastic period. Excavations of this phase have revealed a number of possibly royal tombs containing jewelry, ceremonial weapons and musical instruments.

After a period during which this particular Ur was under **Akkadian** domination, it achieved its greatest glory during the Third Dynasty of Ur (c. 2100–2000 B.C.), when it governed an empire that covered much of Mesopotamia. A massive ziggurat and temple complex, as well as thousands of **cuneiform** tablets, have been excavated from this period. However, the city was sacked by the **Elamites** and, although rebuilt, was never again to become the power center it had been. Even so, the city continued to exist and was periodically rebuilt by various Akkadian and **Babylonian** rulers. As late as the reign of Nabonidus of Babylon (555–539 B.C.), restoration work was carried out there. The site was finally abandoned during the **Persian period**.

Since the name Ur was identified on an inscribed brick in 1855 at Tell el-Muqqayyar, this site has been thought to be the Biblical Ur. The excavations of C.L. Woolley (1922–1934) were based on that assumption, but more recently scholars have come to question this theory for the following reasons:

An ancient Mesopotamian deity
Preserving Bible Times; © Dr. James C. Martin; permission of Musée de Louvre

✣ Although several cities named Ur existed in antiquity, the Biblical Ur is always referred to as "Ur of the Chaldeans," most likely to distinguish it from a famous city of the same name (i.e., the southern Mesopotamian Ur discussed above).

The designation Chaldean applies to southern Mesopotamia only after about 1000 B.C., long after Abraham's lifetime. Previous to that time the Chaldeans lived in northern Mesopotamia. Another city named Ur, located in the north, is in fact probably intended by the Biblical references.

✣ On a trip from the southern Mesopotamian Ur to **Canaan**, Haran is far out of the way, and yet the patriarchs stopped there (see Ge 11:31).[2] Crossing the Euphrates at **Mari**, south of Haran, would have been more direct had they begun their journey from the south. This suggests that their starting point was actually in the north.

✣ When Abraham sent his servant to his "own relatives" to procure a bride for Isaac (Ge 24:4), he went to Paddan-Aram in northern Mesopotamia (as did Jacob; see Ge 28:2).[3] The patriarchs apparently did not regard southern Mesopotamia as their ancestral home.

✣ Cultural influences (customs, laws, etc.) seen in the patriarchal narratives follow the northern Mesopotamian models of **Nuzi** and Mari rather than the southern Mesopotamian model.[4]

Based on this evidence, it appears that "Ur of the Chaldeans" is located near Haran in the north. At least two sites have been suggested: Ura (200 mi [322 km] north of Haran) and Urfa (modern Edessa), but a definite identification of Abraham's Ur is currently impossible. The archaeological artifacts of the more famous Ur, magnificent as they are, most likely have no relationship to Abraham.

[1]See "Sumer" on page 10. [2]See "Haran" on page 47. [3]See "Paddan Aram" on page 45. [4]See "The Patriarchal Period: Mesopotamia During the Time of Abraham" on page 26, "Custom and Law in Ancient Mesopotamia" on page 36, "Nuzi" on page 52 and "Mari" on page 54.

subdued before them the Canaanites, who lived in the land; you handed the Canaanites over to
them, along with their kings and the peoples of the land, to deal with them as they pleased. 25 They
captured fortified cities and fertile land; they took possession of houses filled with all kinds of
good things, wells already dug, vineyards, olive groves and fruit trees in abundance. They ate to the
full and were well-nourished;[m] they reveled in your great goodness.[n]
26 "But they were disobedient and rebelled against you; they put your law behind their backs.[o]
They killed your prophets,[p] who had admonished them in order to turn them back to you; they
committed awful blasphemies.[q] 27 So you handed them over to their enemies,[r] who oppressed them.
But when they were oppressed they cried out to you. From heaven you heard them, and in your great
compassion[s] you gave them deliverers, who rescued them from the hand of their enemies.
28 "But as soon as they were at rest, they again did what was evil in your sight. Then you aban-
doned them to the hand of their enemies so that they ruled over them. And when they cried out
to you again, you heard from heaven, and in your compassion you delivered them[t] time after time.
29 "You warned them to return to your law, but they became arrogant[u] and disobeyed your com-
mands. They sinned against your ordinances, by which a man will live if he obeys them.[v] Stub-
bornly they turned their backs on you, became stiff-necked and refused to listen.[w] 30 For many
years you were patient with them. By your Spirit you admonished them through your prophets.[x]
Yet they paid no attention, so you handed them over to the neighboring peoples. 31 But in your great
mercy you did not put an end[y] to them or abandon them, for you are a gracious and merciful God.
32 "Now therefore, O our God, the great, mighty[z] and awesome God, who keeps his covenant of
love,[a] do not let all this hardship seem trifling in your eyes—the hardship that has come upon us,
upon our kings and leaders, upon our priests and prophets, upon our fathers and all your people,
from the days of the kings of Assyria until today. 33 In all that has happened to us, you have been
just;[b] you have acted faithfully, while we did wrong.[c] 34 Our kings,[d] our leaders, our priests and our
fathers[e] did not follow your law; they did not pay attention to your commands or the warnings you
gave them. 35 Even while they were in their kingdom, enjoying your great goodness[f] to them in the
spacious and fertile land you gave them, they did not serve you[g] or turn from their evil ways.
36 "But see, we are slaves[h] today, slaves in the land you gave our forefathers so they could eat its
fruit and the other good things it produces. 37 Because of our sins, its abundant harvest goes to the
kings you have placed over us. They rule over our bodies and our cattle as they please. We are in
great distress.[i]

The Agreement of the People

38 "In view of all this, we are making a binding agreement,[j] putting it in writing,[k] and our leaders, our
Levites and our priests are affixing their seals to it."

10

Those who sealed it were:

Nehemiah the governor, the son of Hacaliah.

Zedekiah, 2 Seraiah,[l] Azariah, Jeremiah,
3 Pashhur,[m] Amariah, Malkijah,
4 Hattush, Shebaniah, Malluch,
5 Harim,[n] Meremoth, Obadiah,
6 Daniel, Ginnethon, Baruch,
7 Meshullam, Abijah, Mijamin,
8 Maaziah, Bilgai and Shemaiah.
These were the priests.

9 The Levites:[o]

Jeshua son of Azaniah, Binnui of the sons of Henadad, Kadmiel,
10 and their associates: Shebaniah,
Hodiah, Kelita, Pelaiah, Hanan,

9:25 [m]Dt 6:10-12 [n]Nu 13:27; Dt 32:12-15
9:26 [o]1Ki 14:9 [p]Mt 21:35-36 [q]Jdg 2:12-13
9:27 [r]Jdg 2:14 [s]Ps 106:45
9:28 [t]Ps 106:43
9:29 [u]Ps 5:5; Isa 2:11; Jer 43:2 [v]Dt 30:16 [w]Zec 7:11-12
9:30 [x]2Ki 17:13-18; 2Ch 36:16
9:31 [y]Isa 48:9; Jer 4:27
9:32 [z]Ps 24:8 [a]Dt 7:9
9:33 [b]Ge 18:25 [c]Jer 44:3; Da 9:7-8,14
9:34 [d]2Ki 23:11 [e]Jer 44:17
9:35 [f]Isa 63:7 [g]Dt 28:45-48
9:36 [h]Dt 28:48; Ezr 9:9
9:37 [i]Dt 28:33; La 5:5
9:38 [j]2Ch 23:16 [k]Isa 44:5
10:2 [l]Ezr 2:2
10:3 [m]1Ch 9:12
10:5 [n]1Ch 24:8
10:9 [o]Ne 12:1

9:25 Almost every house had its own well or cistern in which to preserve water from the rainy season (2Ki 18:31; Pr 5:15). Once the technique of waterproofing cisterns was developed (c. 1200 B.C.), the central hills of Judah became more heavily populated.

Still, Canaan was a land of plenty. The Egyptian story of Sinuhe (c. 2000 B.C.) describes it as follows: "Figs were in it, and grapes. It had more wine than water. Plentiful was its honey, abundant its olives. Every (kind of) fruit was on its trees."

11 Mica, Rehob, Hashabiah,
12 Zaccur, Sherebiah, Shebaniah,
13 Hodiah, Bani and Beninu.

14 The leaders of the people:

Parosh, Pahath-Moab, Elam, Zattu, Bani,
15 Bunni, Azgad, Bebai,
16 Adonijah, Bigvai, Adin,[p]
17 Ater, Hezekiah, Azzur,
18 Hodiah, Hashum, Bezai,
19 Hariph, Anathoth, Nebai,
20 Magpiash, Meshullam, Hezir,[q]
21 Meshezabel, Zadok, Jaddua,
22 Pelatiah, Hanan, Anaiah,
23 Hoshea, Hananiah,[r] Hasshub,
24 Hallohesh, Pilha, Shobek,
25 Rehum, Hashabnah, Maaseiah,
26 Ahiah, Hanan, Anan,
27 Malluch, Harim and Baanah.

28 "The rest of the people—priests, Levites, gatekeepers, singers, temple servants[s] and all who
separated themselves from the neighboring peoples[t] for the sake of the Law of God, together with
their wives and all their sons and daughters who are able to understand— 29 all these now join
their brothers the nobles, and bind themselves with a curse and an oath[u] to follow the Law of God
given through Moses the servant of God and to obey carefully all the commands, regulations and
decrees of the LORD our Lord.

30 "We promise not to give our daughters in marriage to the peoples around us or take their
daughters for our sons.[v]

31 "When the neighboring peoples bring merchandise or grain to sell on the Sabbath,[w] we will
not buy from them on the Sabbath or on any holy day. Every seventh year we will forgo working
the land[x] and will cancel all debts.[y]

32 "We assume the responsibility for carrying out the commands to give a third of a shekel[a] each
year for the service of the house of our God: 33 for the bread set out on the table;[z] for the regular
grain offerings and burnt offerings; for the offerings on the Sabbaths, New Moon[a] festivals and
appointed feasts; for the holy offerings; for sin offerings to make atonement for Israel; and for all
the duties of the house of our God.[b]

34 "We—the priests, the Levites and the people—have cast lots[c] to determine when each of
our families is to bring to the house of our God at set times each year a contribution of wood[d] to
burn on the altar of the LORD our God, as it is written in the Law.

35 "We also assume responsibility for bringing to the house of the LORD each year the firstfruits[e]
of our crops and of every fruit tree.[f]

36 "As it is also written in the Law, we will bring the firstborn[g] of our sons and of our cattle, of
our herds and of our flocks to the house of our God, to the priests ministering there.[h]

10:16 [p]Ezr 8:6
10:20 [q]1Ch 24:15
10:23 [r]Ne 7:2
10:28 [s]Ps 135:1 [t]2Ch 6:26; Ne 9:2
10:29 [u]Nu 5:21; Ps 119:106
10:30 [v]Ex 34:16; Dt 7:3; Ne 13:23
10:31 [w]Ne 13:16, 18; Jer 17:27; Eze 23:38; Am 8:5 [x]Ex 23:11; Lev 25:1-7 [y]Dt 15:1
10:33 [z]Lev 24:6 [a]Nu 10:10; Ps 81:3; Isa 1:14 [b]2Ch 24:5
10:34 [c]Lev 16:8 [d]Ne 13:31
10:35 [e]Ex 22:29; 23:19; Nu 18:12 [f]Dt 26:1-11
10:36 [g]Ex 13:2; Nu 18:14-16 [h]Ne 13:31

[a] *32* That is, about 1/8 ounce (about 4 grams)

10:31 The Romans attributed the Jewish observance of the Sabbath and the Sabbath year to laziness. According to Tacitus, the Jews "were led by the charms of indolence to give over the seventh year as well to inactivity."

10:32 Elsewhere the Old Testament speaks of a "half shekel" as the amount required as "an offering to the LORD" (Ex 30:13–14), to be given by each man who was twenty years old or older as a symbolic ransom. This amount later became that of the annual temple tax (2Ch 24:9), also called "the two-drachma tax" (Mt 17:24). (Two drachmas were equal to half a shekel.) The pledge of a third of a shekel in Nehemiah's time may have been due to the poor economic circumstances. (See "Banking and Money in the Ancient World" on p. 696.)

10:34 The perpetual burning of fire on the sanctuary altar (Lev 6:12–13) would have required a continual supply of wood. Although the Bible does not make specific reference to a wood offering, Josephus mentioned "the festival of wood offering" on the fourteenth day of the fifth month (Ab). The Jewish Mishnah (rabbinic interpretations and applications of Pentateuchal laws) lists nine instances in which certain families brought wood and stipulates that all kinds of wood were suitable except for that from the vine and the olive. The Temple Scroll from Qumran describes the celebration of a wood offering festival for six days following a new oil festival.

37 "Moreover, we will bring to the storerooms of the house of our God, to the priests, the first
of our ground meal, of our ⌞grain⌟ offerings, of the fruit of all our trees and of our new wine and
oil.[i] And we will bring a tithe[j] of our crops to the Levites,[k] for it is the Levites who collect the
tithes in all the towns where we work.[l] 38 A priest descended from Aaron is to accompany the
Levites when they receive the tithes, and the Levites are to bring a tenth of the tithes[m] up to the
house of our God, to the storerooms of the treasury. 39 The people of Israel, including the Le-
vites, are to bring their contributions of grain, new wine and oil to the storerooms where the ar-
ticles for the sanctuary are kept and where the ministering priests, the gatekeepers and the sing-
ers stay.
"We will not neglect the house of our God."[n]

10:37 [i]Lev 23:17; Nu 18:12 [j]Lev 27:30; Nu 18:21 [k]Dt 14:22-29 [l]Eze 44:30
10:38 [m]Nu 18:26
10:39 [n]Dt 12:6; Ne 13:11,12

The New Residents of Jerusalem

11 Now the leaders of the people settled in Jerusalem, and the rest of the people cast lots to bring
one out of every ten to live in Jerusalem,[o] the holy city,[p] while the remaining nine were to
stay in their own towns.[q] 2 The people commended all the men who volunteered to live in Jerusalem.
3 These are the provincial leaders who settled in Jerusalem (now some Israelites, priests, Levites,
temple servants and descendants of Solomon's servants lived in the towns of Judah, each on his own
property in the various towns,[r] 4 while other people from both Judah and Benjamin[s] lived in
Jerusalem):[t]

11:1 [o]Ne 7:4 [p]ver 18; Isa 48:2; 52:1; 64:10; Zec 14:20-21 [q]Ne 7:73
11:3 [r]1Ch 9:2-3; Ezr 2:1
11:4 [s]Ezr 1:5 [t]Ezr 2:70

10:37 The practice of giving a tenth was ancient (see Ge 14:20; 28:22). While the Law of Moses decreed that a tenth portion of plant crops was holy to the Lord (Lev 27:30), there is no reference to a tithe of cattle (cf. Lev 27:32–33). Tithes were intended for the support of the Levites (Ne 10:37; cf. Nu 18:21–24; Ne 13:10–12), who in turn were to offer the Lord "a tenth of the tithes" (Ne 10:38; cf. Nu 18:25–32).

Chambers in the outer temple courts were used as "storerooms" for silver, gold and other objects (Ne 10:38–39; 12:44; 13:4–5,9). See "Banking and Money in the Ancient World" on page 696.

11:1–2 The practice of redistributing populations was also used to establish Greek and Hellenistic cities. Known as *synoikismos,* this policy involved forcible transfer from rural settlements to urban centers. Some of the affected inhabitants were chosen by lot (v. 1), while others volunteered to live in Jerusalem (v. 2). But evidently most opted to stay in their hometowns. The first-century A.D. Jewish historian Josephus asserted: "Nehemiah, seeing that the city had a small population, urged the priests and Levites to leave the countryside and move to the city and remain there, for he had prepared houses for them at his own expense" (*Antiquities,* 11.5.8).

ARCHAEOLOGICAL SITES

ZIKLAG

NEHEMIAH 11 Nehemiah 11:28 mentions in passing that Jews settled in the town of Ziklag (see "Map 5"). This site was in fact the scene of some major conflicts because of its location as a border town.

Ziklag was apportioned to the tribe of Simeon within Judah (Jos 15:31; 19:5) but may not have been taken by Israelites before the time of David. First Samuel 27:2–6 indicates that David received the town from the Philistine king Achish, after which it served as his base of operations. Later, an Egyptian servant reported that marauding Amalekites had razed Ziklag by fire (1Sa 30:13–14).[1] The city remained in Israelite possession until the end of the monarchy and was reinhabited by Jews after the **exile** (Ne 11:25–31).

Although unconfirmed by **epigraphic** (written) evidence, the cultural remains unearthed at Tell esh-Sharia (15.5 mi [25 km] southeast of Gaza) correspond well with what is known of Biblical Ziklag. Excavation Level IX (from the early twelfth century B.C.) revealed an incinerated "governor's residence." The destruction may be attributable to nomads, such as the Amalekites, or to the **Sea Peoples**. Also found at this level were Egyptian **ostraca** in the script of the **New Kingdom** period (early twelfth century B.C.). Philistine ware was uncovered at Level VIII (twelfth–eleventh centuries B.C.), while Hebrew ostraca and a pottery vessel inscribed with "belonging to Yaram," as well as **Assyrian** palace ware and architecture, were unearthed at the seventh-century B.C. level (V). Thus, the archaeological picture is one of a border town in constant flux between Philistine, Israelite, Egyptian and Assyrian control. This is exactly what archaeologists would have expected from the city's location and from the Biblical record.

[1]See "The Amalekites" on page 120.

From the descendants of Judah:

Athaiah son of Uzziah, the son of Zechariah, the son of Amariah, the son of Shephatiah, the son of
Mahalalel, a descendant of Perez; 5 and Maaseiah son of Baruch, the son of Col-Hozeh, the son of
Hazaiah, the son of Adaiah, the son of Joiarib, the son of Zechariah, a descendant of Shelah. 6 The
descendants of Perez who lived in Jerusalem totaled 468 able men.

7 From the descendants of Benjamin:

Sallu son of Meshullam, the son of Joed, the son of Pedaiah, the son of Kolaiah, the son of Maase-
iah, the son of Ithiel, the son of Jeshaiah, 8 and his followers, Gabbai and Sallai—928 men. 9 Joel son
of Zicri was their chief officer, and Judah son of Hassenuah was over the Second District of the city.

10 From the priests:

Jedaiah; the son of Joiarib; Jakin; 11 Seraiah[u] son of Hilkiah, the son of Meshullam, the son of Za-
dok, the son of Meraioth, the son of Ahitub,[v] supervisor in the house of God, 12 and their associ-
ates, who carried on work for the temple—822 men; Adaiah son of Jeroham, the son of Pelaliah,
the son of Amzi, the son of Zechariah, the son of Pashhur, the son of Malkijah, 13 and his associ-
ates, who were heads of families—242 men; Amashsai son of Azarel, the son of Ahzai, the son of
Meshillemoth, the son of Immer, 14 and his[a] associates, who were able men—128. Their chief of-
ficer was Zabdiel son of Haggedolim.

15 From the Levites:

Shemaiah son of Hasshub, the son of Azrikam, the son of Hashabiah, the son of Bunni; 16 Shabbe-
thai[w] and Jozabad,[x] two of the heads of the Levites, who had charge of the outside work of the
house of God; 17 Mattaniah[y] son of Mica, the son of Zabdi, the son of Asaph,[z] the director who led
in thanksgiving and prayer; Bakbukiah, second among his associates; and Abda son of Shammua,
the son of Galal, the son of Jeduthun.[a] 18 The Levites in the holy city[b] totaled 284.

19 The gatekeepers:

Akkub, Talmon and their associates, who kept watch at the gates—172 men.

20 The rest of the Israelites, with the priests and Levites, were in all the towns of Judah, each on his
ancestral property.
21 The temple servants[c] lived on the hill of Ophel, and Ziha and Gishpa were in charge of them.
22 The chief officer of the Levites in Jerusalem was Uzzi son of Bani, the son of Hashabiah, the son of
Mattaniah,[d] the son of Mica. Uzzi was one of Asaph's descendants, who were the singers responsible for
the service of the house of God. 23 The singers[e] were under the king's orders, which regulated their dai-
ly activity.
24 Pethahiah son of Meshezabel, one of the descendants of Zerah[f] son of Judah, was the king's agent
in all affairs relating to the people.
25 As for the villages with their fields, some of the people of Judah lived in Kiriath Arba[g] and its sur-
rounding settlements, in Dibon[h] and its settlements, in Jekabzeel and its villages, 26 in Jeshua, in Mola-
dah, in Beth Pelet,[i] 27 in Hazar Shual, in Beersheba[j] and its settlements, 28 in Ziklag,[k] in Meconah and its
settlements, 29 in En Rimmon, in Zorah,[l] in Jarmuth,[m] 30 Zanoah, Adullam[n] and their villages, in Lachish[o]
and its fields, and in Azekah[p] and its settlements. So they were living all the way from Beersheba[q] to the
Valley of Hinnom.
31 The descendants of the Benjamites from Geba[r] lived in Micmash,[s] Aija, Bethel and its settlements,
32 in Anathoth,[t] Nob[u] and Ananiah, 33 in Hazor,[v] Ramah and Gittaim,[w] 34 in Hadid, Zeboim[x] and Nebal-
lat, 35 in Lod and Ono,[y] and in the Valley of the Craftsmen.
36 Some of the divisions of the Levites of Judah settled in Benjamin.

11:11 [u]2Ki 25:18; Ezr 2:2 [v]Ezr 7:2
11:16 [w]Ezr 10:15 [x]Ezr 8:33
11:17 [y]1Ch 9:15; Ne 12:8 [z]2Ch 5:12 [a]1Ch 25:1
11:18 [b]Rev 21:2
11:21 [c]Ezr 2:43; Ne 3:26
11:22 [d]1Ch 9:15
11:23 [e]Ne 7:44
11:24 [f]Ge 38:30
11:25 [g]Ge 35:27; Jos 14:15 [h]Nu 21:30
11:26 [i]Jos 15:27
11:27 [j]Ge 21:14
11:28 [k]1Sa 27:6
11:29 [l]Jos 15:33 [m]Jos 10:3
11:30 [n]Jos 15:35 [o]Jos 10:3 [p]Jos 10:10 [q]Jos 15:28
11:31 [r]Jos 21:17; Isa 10:29 [s]1Sa 13:2
11:32 [t]Jos 21:18; Isa 10:30 [u]1Sa 21:1
11:33 [v]Jos 11:1 [w]2Sa 4:3
11:34 [x]1Sa 13:18
11:35 [y]1Ch 8:12

[a] *14* Most Septuagint manuscripts; Hebrew *their*

11:9 Like the "market district" (Zep 1:11)—probably the Tyropoeon Valley area just south of Mount Moriah—the Second District was a new suburb west of the temple area. Archaeological excavations indicate that the city had spread outside the walls in this direction by the late eighth century B.C., before the so-called Broad Wall had been built (c. 700 B.C.) by Hezekiah.

11:27 Excavations reveal that the city of Beersheba was likely destroyed by Sennacherib in 701 B.C. and only resettled during the Persian period (see "Beersheba" on p. 518).

11:28 See "Ziklag" on page 708.

Priests and Levites

12 These were the priests[z] and Levites who returned with Zerubbabel[a] son of Shealtiel and with Jeshua:[b] 12:1 [z]Ne 10:1-8 [a]1Ch 3:19 [b]Ezr 2:2 [c]Ezr 2:2

Seraiah,[c] Jeremiah, Ezra,
2 Amariah, Malluch, Hattush,
3 Shecaniah, Rehum, Meremoth,
4 Iddo,[d] Ginnethon,[a] Abijah,[e] 12:4 [d]Zec 1:1 [e]Lk 1:5
5 Mijamin,[b] Moadiah, Bilgah,
6 Shemaiah, Joiarib, Jedaiah,[f] 12:6 [f]1Ch 24:7
7 Sallu, Amok, Hilkiah and Jedaiah.

These were the leaders of the priests and their associates in the days of Jeshua.
8 The Levites were Jeshua, Binnui, Kadmiel, Sherebiah, Judah, and also Mattaniah,[g] who, together with 12:8 [g]Ne 11:17
his associates, was in charge of the songs of thanksgiving. 9 Bakbukiah and Unni, their associates, stood
opposite them in the services.
10 Jeshua was the father of Joiakim, Joiakim the father of Eliashib,[h] Eliashib the father of Joiada, 11 Joi- 12:10 [h]Ezr 10:24
ada the father of Jonathan, and Jonathan the father of Jaddua.
12 In the days of Joiakim, these were the heads of the priestly families:

of Seraiah's family, Meraiah;
of Jeremiah's, Hananiah;
13 of Ezra's, Meshullam;
of Amariah's, Jehohanan;
14 of Malluch's, Jonathan;
of Shecaniah's,[c] Joseph;
15 of Harim's, Adna;
of Meremoth's,[d] Helkai;
16 of Iddo's,[i] Zechariah; 12:16 [i]ver 4
of Ginnethon's, Meshullam;
17 of Abijah's, Zicri;
of Miniamin's and of Moadiah's, Piltai;
18 of Bilgah's, Shammua;
of Shemaiah's, Jehonathan;
19 of Joiarib's, Mattenai;
of Jedaiah's, Uzzi;
20 of Sallu's, Kallai;
of Amok's, Eber;
21 of Hilkiah's, Hashabiah;
of Jedaiah's, Nethanel.

22 The family heads of the Levites in the days of Eliashib, Joiada, Johanan and Jaddua, as well as those
of the priests, were recorded in the reign of Darius the Persian. 23 The family heads among the descen-
dants of Levi up to the time of Johanan son of Eliashib were recorded in the book of the annals. 24 And
the leaders of the Levites[j] were Hashabiah, Sherebiah, Jeshua son of Kadmiel, and their associates, who 12:24 [j]Ezr 2:40
stood opposite them to give praise and thanksgiving, one section responding to the other, as prescribed
by David the man of God.
25 Mattaniah, Bakbukiah, Obadiah, Meshullam, Talmon and Akkub were gatekeepers who guarded the
storerooms at the gates. 26 They served in the days of Joiakim son of Jeshua, the son of Jozadak, and in the
days of Nehemiah the governor and of Ezra the priest and scribe.

[a] *4* Many Hebrew manuscripts and Vulgate (see also Neh. 12:16); most Hebrew manuscripts *Ginnethoi* [b] *5* A variant of *Miniamin* [c] *14* Very many Hebrew manuscripts, some Septuagint manuscripts and Syriac (see also Neh. 12:3); most Hebrew manuscripts *Shebaniah's* [d] *15* Some Septuagint manuscripts (see also Neh. 12:3); Hebrew *Meraioth's*

12:7 See the note on Ezra 6:18.
12:9 The singing was antiphonal, with two sections of the choir standing opposite each other.
12:11 Since verse 22 mentions a Johanan after Joiada and before Jaddua, and verse 23 identifies Johanan as "son" of Eliashib, some believe that "Jonathan" is an error for "Johanan" (see "Textual Criticism" on p. 1151). Further complicating the identification are attempts to identify this high priest with a "Johanan" mentioned both in the Elephantine papyri and in Josephus (*Antiquities*, 11.7.1).

Dedication of the Wall of Jerusalem

27 At the dedication[k] of the wall of Jerusalem, the Levites were sought out from where they lived and were brought to Jerusalem to celebrate joyfully the dedication with songs of thanksgiving and with the music of cymbals,[l] harps and lyres.[m] 28 The singers also were brought together from the region around Jerusalem—from the villages of the Netophathites,[n] 29 from Beth Gilgal, and from the area of Geba and Azmaveth, for the singers had built villages for themselves around Jerusalem. 30 When the priests and Levites had purified themselves ceremonially, they purified the people,[o] the gates and the wall.

31 I had the leaders of Judah go up on top[a] of the wall. I also assigned two large choirs to give thanks. One was to proceed on top[b] of the wall to the right, toward the Dung Gate.[p] 32 Hoshaiah and half the leaders of Judah followed them, 33 along with Azariah, Ezra, Meshullam, 34 Judah, Benjamin,[q] Shemaiah, Jeremiah, 35 as well as some priests with trumpets,[r] and also Zechariah son of Jonathan, the son of Shemaiah, the son of Mattaniah, the son of Micaiah, the son of Zaccur, the son of Asaph, 36 and his associates—Shemaiah, Azarel, Milalai, Gilalai, Maai, Nethanel, Judah and Hanani—with musical instruments[s] ⌊prescribed by⌋ David the man of God.[t] Ezra[u] the scribe led the procession. 37 At the Fountain Gate[v] they continued directly up the steps of the City of David on the ascent to the wall and passed above the house of David to the Water Gate[w] on the east.

38 The second choir proceeded in the opposite direction. I followed them on top[c] of the wall, together with half the people—past the Tower of the Ovens[x] to the Broad Wall,[y] 39 over the Gate of Ephraim,[z] the Jeshanah[d] Gate,[a] the Fish Gate,[b] the Tower of Hananel[c] and the Tower of the Hundred,[d] as far as the Sheep Gate.[e] At the Gate of the Guard they stopped.

40 The two choirs that gave thanks then took their places in the house of God; so did I, together with half the officials, 41 as well as the priests—Eliakim, Maaseiah, Miniamin, Micaiah, Elioenai, Zechariah and Hananiah with their trumpets— 42 and also Maaseiah, Shemaiah, Eleazar, Uzzi, Jehohanan, Malkijah, Elam and Ezer. The choirs sang under the direction of Jezrahiah. 43 And on that day they offered great sacrifices, rejoicing because God had given them great joy. The women and children also rejoiced. The sound of rejoicing in Jerusalem could be heard far away.

44 At that time men were appointed to be in charge of the storerooms[f] for the contributions, firstfruits and tithes.[g] From the fields around the towns they were to bring into the storerooms the portions required by the Law for the priests and the Levites, for Judah was pleased with the ministering priests and Levites.[h] 45 They performed the service of their God and the service of purification, as did also the singers and gatekeepers, according to the commands of David[i] and his son Solomon.[j] 46 For long ago, in the days of David and Asaph,[k] there had been directors for the singers and for the songs of praise[l] and thanksgiving to God. 47 So in the days of Zerubbabel and of Nehemiah, all Israel contributed the daily portions for the singers and gatekeepers. They also set aside the portion for the other Levites, and the Levites set aside the portion for the descendants of Aaron.[m]

Nehemiah's Final Reforms

13 On that day the Book of Moses was read aloud in the hearing of the people and there it was found written that no Ammonite or Moabite should ever be admitted into the assembly of God,[n] 2 because they had not met the Israelites with food and water but had hired Balaam[o] to call a curse down on them.[p] (Our God, however, turned the curse into a blessing.)[q] 3 When the people heard this law, they excluded from Israel all who were of foreign descent.[r]

4 Before this, Eliashib the priest had been put in charge of the storerooms[s] of the house of our God. He was closely associated with Tobiah,[t] 5 and he had provided him with a large room formerly used to store the grain offerings and incense and temple articles, and also the tithes[u] of grain, new wine and oil prescribed for the Levites, singers and gatekeepers, as well as the contributions for the priests.

12:27 [k]Dt 20:5 [l]2Sa 6:5 [m]1Ch 15:16,28; 25:6; Ps 92:3
12:28 [n]1Ch 2:54; 9:16
12:30 [o]Ex 19:10; Job 1:5
12:31 [p]Ne 2:13
12:34 [q]Ezr 1:5
12:35 [r]Ezr 3:10
12:36 [s]1Ch 15:16 [t]2Ch 8:14 [u]Ezr 7:6
12:37 [v]Ne 2:14; 3:15 [w]Ne 3:26
12:38 [x]Ne 3:11 [y]Ne 3:8
12:39 [z]2Ki 14:13; Ne 8:16 [a]Ne 3:6 [b]2Ch 33:14; Ne 3:3 [c]Ne 3:1 [d]Ne 3:1 [e]Ne 3:1
12:44 [f]Ne 13:4, 13 [g]Lev 27:30 [h]Dt 18:8
12:45 [i]1Ch 25:1; 2Ch 8:14 [j]1Ch 6:31; 23:5
12:46 [k]2Ch 35:15 [l]2Ch 29:27; Ps 137:4
12:47 [m]Nu 18:21; Dt 18:8
13:1 [n]ver 23; Dt 23:3
13:2 [o]Nu 22:3-11 [p]Nu 23:7; Dt 23:3 [q]Nu 23:11; Dt 23:4-5
13:3 [r]ver 23; Ne 9:2
13:4 [s]Ne 12:44 [t]Ne 2:10
13:5 [u]Lev 27:30; Nu 18:21

[a] 31 Or *go alongside* [b] 31 Or *proceed alongside* [c] 38 Or *them alongside* [d] 39 Or *Old*

12:27 The word "dedication" translates the Aramaic word *hanukkah*. The Jewish holiday in December that celebrates the recapture of the temple from the Seleucids and its rededication (165 B.C.) is formally known as Hanukkah.

Cymbals were used in religious ceremonies (1Ch 16:42; 25:1; 2Ch 5:12; 29:25), as were harps (1Sa 10:5; 2Sa 6:5; Ps 150:3). Ancient examples of cymbals have been found at Beth Shemesh and Tell Abu Hawam, and ancient harps have been reconstructed from information derived from the remains of harps at Ur, pictures of harps and cuneiform texts describing in detail their tuning. Lyres had strings of the same length but of different diameters and tensions (see 1Ch 15:16; Da 3:5). (See "Ancient Musical Instruments" on page 797.)

13:2 See "Balaam, the Son of Beor" on page 229.

6 But while all this was going on, I was not in Jerusalem, for in the thirty-second year of Artaxerxes[v] king of Babylon I had returned to the king. Some time later I asked his permission 7 and came back to Jerusalem. Here I learned about the evil thing Eliashib[w] had done in providing Tobiah a room in the courts of the house of God. 8 I was greatly displeased and threw all Tobiah's household goods out of the room.[x] 9 I gave orders to purify the rooms,[y] and then I put back into them the equipment of the house of God, with the grain offerings and the incense.

10 I also learned that the portions assigned to the Levites had not been given to them,[z] and that all the Levites and singers responsible for the service had gone back to their own fields. 11 So I rebuked the officials and asked them, "Why is the house of God neglected?"[a] Then I called them together and stationed them at their posts.

12 All Judah brought the tithes[b] of grain, new wine and oil into the storerooms.[c] 13 I put Shelemiah the priest, Zadok the scribe, and a Levite named Pedaiah in charge of the storerooms and made Hanan son of Zaccur, the son of Mattaniah, their assistant, because these men were considered trustworthy. They were made responsible for distributing the supplies to their brothers.[d]

14 Remember[e] me for this, O my God, and do not blot out what I have so faithfully done for the house of my God and its services.

15 In those days I saw men in Judah treading winepresses on the Sabbath and bringing in grain and loading it on donkeys, together with wine, grapes, figs and all other kinds of loads. And they were bringing all this into Jerusalem on the Sabbath.[f] Therefore I warned them against selling food on that day.

13:6 [v] Ne 2:6; 5:14
13:7 [w] Ezr 10:24
13:8 [x] Mt 21:12-13; Jn 2:13-16
13:9 [y] 1Ch 23:28; 2Ch 29:5
13:10 [z] Dt 12:19
13:11 [a] Ne 10:37-39; Hag 1:1-9
13:12 [b] 2Ch 31:6 [c] 1Ki 7:51; Ne 10:37-39; Mal 3:10
13:13 [d] Ne 12:44; Ac 6:1-5
13:14 [e] Ge 8:1
13:15 [f] Ex 20:8-11; 34:21; Dt 5:12-15; Ne 10:31

13:7 Nehemiah's second term must have ended before 407 B.C., when, according to the Elephantine papyri, Bagohi (Bigvai) was governor of Judah. Some have suggested that after Nehemiah's first term he was succeeded by his brother Hanani (see the note on 1:2).

13:12 Temples in Mesopotamia also levied tithes for the support of their personnel.

13:15 For a discussion of sheaves and threshing, see the note on Ruth 2:7. See also "The Threshing Floor" on page 608 and "Food and Agriculture" on page 390.

13:19 Like the Babylonians, the Israelites counted their days from sunset to sunset, while the Egyptians used a dawn-to-dawn system. The blowing of a trumpet by a priest heralded the precise moment when the Sabbath began. Josephus (*Jewish Wars*, 4.9.12) spoke of the location on the parapet of the temple where the priests "gave a signal beforehand, with a trumpet, at the beginning of every seventh day, in the evening twilight, and also at the onset of evening when that day was finished, announcing to the people the respective hours for ceasing work and for resuming their labors." Archaeological excavations at the temple mount have uncovered a stone from the southwestern corner of the parapet that had fallen to the ground during Titus's siege; it includes the inscription "for the place of the blowing (of the trumpet)."

ANCIENT TEXTS AND ARTIFACTS

The Autobiography of Idrimi

NEHEMIAH 13 In 1939 Sir Leonard Woolley, while excavating at Tell Atshana (ancient Alalakh), found a stone statue of King Idrimi seated on his throne. The statue, dating from approximately 1500 B.C., carries a lengthy inscription positioned as though it were issuing from the king's mouth. Idrimi recounts in this manner how his family fled from their ancestral city of Aleppo (see "Map 8a") during a hostile insurrection against his father. Hoping to regain his family's lost prestige, Idrimi claims to have initiated treaties with mighty warriors and kings around him, amassing an army and strengthening his power while in exile. He wiped out his enemies and reestablished his family's dominance, setting himself up as king, after which he constructed a palace and instituted reforms throughout his land, including the reestablishment of sacrifices to his patron gods. The inscription ends with a curse and blessing formula: curses on anyone who would dare to destroy the statue or alter its writings, and blessings on Idrimi and his scribe.

One thousand years later, when the Jews returned from their **exile**, Nehemiah closed his writing in a similar way. Having detailed the final religious reforms he had instituted in Jerusalem, he asked the Lord to remember him favorably for those efforts. He called down curses upon any who had defiled the priesthood, as well as upon those who had married outside the covenant, asking the Lord to remember them for their evil deeds. Unlike Idrimi, however, Nehemiah acted not for his own advancement or glory but out of zeal for God and the purity of his temple.

16 Men from Tyre who lived in Jerusalem were bringing in fish and all kinds of merchandise and selling
13:16 [g]Ne 10:31 them in Jerusalem on the Sabbath[g] to the people of Judah. 17 I rebuked the nobles of Judah and said to
them, "What is this wicked thing you are doing—desecrating the Sabbath day? 18 Didn't your forefathers
do the same things, so that our God brought all this calamity upon us and upon this city? Now you are
13:18 [h]Ne 10:31; Jer 17:21-23 stirring up more wrath against Israel by desecrating the Sabbath."[h]
13:19 [i]Lev 23:32 19 When evening shadows fell on the gates of Jerusalem before the Sabbath,[i] I ordered the doors to be
shut and not opened until the Sabbath was over. I stationed some of my own men at the gates so that no
load could be brought in on the Sabbath day. 20 Once or twice the merchants and sellers of all kinds of
goods spent the night outside Jerusalem. 21 But I warned them and said, "Why do you spend the night by
the wall? If you do this again, I will lay hands on you." From that time on they no longer came on the Sab-
bath. 22 Then I commanded the Levites to purify themselves and go and guard the gates in order to keep
the Sabbath day holy.

13:22 [j]Ge 8:1; Ne 12:30 Remember[j] me for this also, O my God, and show mercy to me according to your great love.

13:23 [k]Ezr 9:1-2; Mal 2:11 [l]ver 1; Ne 10:30 23 Moreover, in those days I saw men of Judah who had married[k] women from Ashdod, Ammon and
Moab.[l] 24 Half of their children spoke the language of Ashdod or the language of one of the other peoples,
and did not know how to speak the language of Judah. 25 I rebuked them and called curses down on them.
13:25 [m]Ezr 10:5 I beat some of the men and pulled out their hair. I made them take an oath[m] in God's name and said: "You
are not to give your daughters in marriage to their sons, nor are you to take their daughters in marriage
for your sons or for yourselves. 26 Was it not because of marriages like these that Solomon king of Israel
13:26 [n]1Ki 3:13; 2Ch 1:12 [o]2Sa 12:25 [p]1Ki 11:3 sinned? Among the many nations there was no king like him.[n] He was loved by his God,[o] and God made
him king over all Israel, but even he was led into sin by foreign women.[p] 27 Must we hear now that you
13:27 [q]Ezr 9:14; 10:2 too are doing all this terrible wickedness and are being unfaithful to our God by marrying[q] foreign
women?"

13:28 [r]Ezr 10:24 [s]Ne 2:10 28 One of the sons of Joiada son of Eliashib[r] the high priest was son-in-law to Sanballat[s] the Horonite.
And I drove him away from me.

13:29 [t]Ne 6:14 29 Remember[t] them, O my God, because they defiled the priestly office and the covenant of the priest-
hood and of the Levites.

13:30 [u]Ne 10:30 30 So I purified the priests and the Levites of everything foreign,[u] and assigned them duties, each to
13:31 [v]Ne 10:34 [w]ver 14,22; Ge 8:1 his own task. 31 I also made provision for contributions of wood[v] at designated times, and for the first-
fruits.

Remember[w] me with favor, O my God.

13:28 The high priest was not allowed to marry a foreigner (Lev 21:14). The expulsion of Joiada's son followed either this special ban or the general prohibition against intermarriage. Josephus (*Antiquities*, 11.7.2) recorded that an almost identical episode, involving a marriage between the daughter of a Sanballat of Samaria and the brother of the Jewish high priest, took place a little over a century later during the time of Alexander the Great.

INTRODUCTION TO *Esther*

AUTHOR, PLACE AND DATE OF WRITING

The unknown author of Esther appears to have been a Jew, based upon the book's emphasis on Jewish nationalism and on the origin, observance and perpetual commemoration of the Jewish festival of Purim. Scholars infer that the author lived in a Persian city because of his knowledge of Persian customs and the book's setting in the Persian capital of Susa. Scholars also consider the earliest date of authorship to be around 460 B.C., shortly after the narrated events occurred and before Ezra returned to Jerusalem. The latest date suggested for composition is around 350 B.C., just before Greece conquered the Persian Empire in 331 B.C.

AUDIENCE

Certainly Israelites familiar with the events described in this book read it, as did contemporary Jews living in other regions and subsequent generations of Jews.

CULTURAL FACTS AND HIGHLIGHTS

Throughout Israel's history God protected his chosen people from all kinds of dangers. Yes, he punished them when they refused to confess their sins and honor their covenant with him, but he was invariably also working behind the scenes, offering forgiveness and unfolding bigger plans for Israel and for all of humankind. During the reign of the Persian king Xerxes (486–465 B.C.), a generation before Ezra authored the books of Ezra and Nehemiah, God used this powerful king and several obedient believers to save the Jews from extermination and to preserve the Davidic line through which the Messiah would descend.

TIMELINE

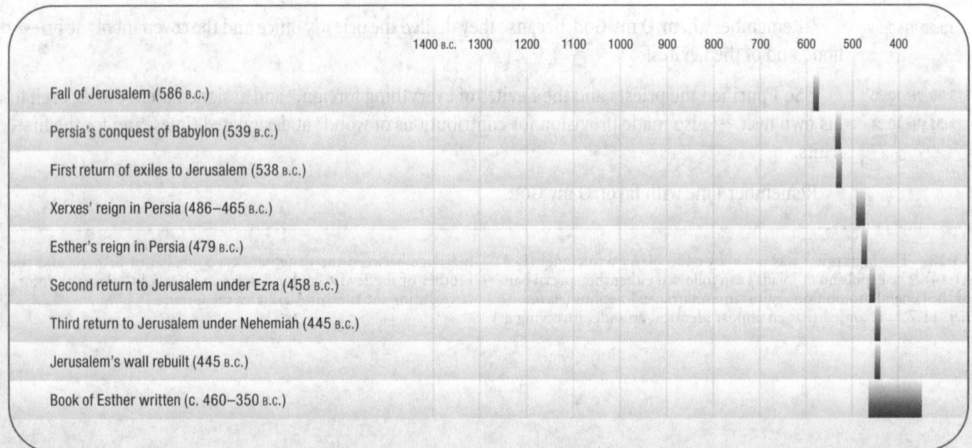

AS YOU READ

In many respects the book of Esther reads like a fast-paced novella. As the exciting plot unfolds, godly people trust the Lord and step out in faith. As you read, try to imagine what would have happened if Haman's plot had succeeded—to the Jews, to the line of David, to God's promises concerning the coming Messiah. Haman's edict constituted the last major effort during the Old Testament period to destroy God's people. Notice the multiple ironies in this story, including that of Haman's ultimate fate. Think about the influence that two particular godly people made because they trusted and obeyed God and were sensitive to his leading. Ask yourself why the author might have deliberately refrained from making any explicit reference to God, prayer, worship or sacrifice in this book, even though God worked so mightily throughout this story.

DID YOU KNOW?

- The Greek historian Herodotus explained that the Persians drank as they deliberated matters of state, believing that intoxication put them in closer touch with the spiritual world (1:10–12).
- The Persian practice of "hanging" was actually impalement for the purpose of public exhibition of a corpse (2:23).
- Among the Persians the only thing prized more highly than a large number of sons was valor in battle (5:11).
- Persian protocol dictated that no one but the king could be left alone with a woman of the royal harem (7:7–8).
- Purim is still celebrated today. The entire book of Esther is read in the synagogue on the holiday, during which noisemakers are used. People cheer at the sound of Mordecai's name and boo and hiss at the mention of Haman (9:29–32).

THEMES

The book of Esther includes the following themes:

1. *God's sovereignty.* Who is the real hero in Esther? While both Mordecai and Esther performed admirable, self-sacrificing acts of courage, the book clearly implies an unnamed force orchestrating events from behind the scenes. The "coincidences" are just too perfect to be ascribed to chance. The book of Esther demonstrates that God is indeed in control of history; he is the hero who saves and protects his own, often using ordinary people and events.

2. *Service.* Esther and Mordecai were unspectacular people whom God used in a wonderful way at a particular time and place to accomplish his purposes (4:14). Confidence in God's providential care and ability to work behind the scenes is essential for anyone called to accomplish his work and purposes.

3. *Obedience.* Conflicting demands for obedience and contrary loyalties sometimes force believers to make difficult choices. Esther opted to obey Mordecai (2:10,20; 4:8–16), but in so doing she stood up against Persian law (4:11,16; 5:1–2). Mordecai refused to obey the king's command (3:2–8) but carried out Esther's instructions (4:17). Obeying God always takes precedence over obeying humans (Ac 4:19–20; 5:29).

4. *Pride.* Haman is the prototype of the arrogant individual (3:5; 5:9–14; 7:8–10), illustrating the truth of Proverbs 16:18: "Pride goes before destruction, a haughty spirit before a fall." He is contrasted with Mordecai, who, while not seeking status for himself, allowed the Lord to elevate him in the king's eyes (6:1–13; 8:9–15; cf. Jas 4:10).

OUTLINE

I. The Feasts of Xerxes (1:1—2:18)
II. The Feasts of Esther (2:19—7:10)
III. The Feast of Purim (8–10)

Queen Vashti Deposed

1 This is what happened during the time of Xerxes,[a][a] the Xerxes who ruled over 127 provinces[b]
stretching from India to Cush[b];[c] 2 At that time King Xerxes reigned from his royal throne in the cit-
adel of Susa,[d] 3 and in the third year of his reign he gave a banquet[e] for all his nobles and officials. The
military leaders of Persia and Media, the princes, and the nobles of the provinces were present.
4 For a full 180 days he displayed the vast wealth of his kingdom and the splendor and glory of his
majesty. 5 When these days were over, the king gave a banquet, lasting seven days,[f] in the enclosed gar-
den[g] of the king's palace, for all the people from the least to the greatest, who were in the citadel of Susa.
6 The garden had hangings of white and blue linen, fastened with cords of white linen and purple materi-
al to silver rings on marble pillars. There were couches[h] of gold and silver on a mosaic pavement of por-
phyry, marble, mother-of-pearl and other costly stones. 7 Wine was served in goblets of gold, each one dif-
ferent from the other, and the royal wine was abundant, in keeping with the king's liberality.[i] 8 By the
king's command each guest was allowed to drink in his own way, for the king instructed all the wine
stewards to serve each man what he wished.
9 Queen Vashti also gave a banquet[j] for the women in the royal palace of King Xerxes.
10 On the seventh day, when King Xerxes was in high spirits[k] from wine,[l] he commanded the seven eu-
nuchs who served him—Mehuman, Biztha, Harbona,[m] Bigtha, Abagtha, Zethar and Carcas— 11 to bring[n]
before him Queen Vashti, wearing her royal crown, in order to dis-
play her beauty[o] to the people and nobles, for she was lovely to look
at. 12 But when the attendants delivered the king's command, Queen
Vashti refused to come. Then the king became furious and burned
with anger.[p]
13 Since it was customary for the king to consult experts in mat-
ters of law and justice, he spoke with the wise men who understood
the times[q] 14 and were closest to the king—Carshena, Shethar, Ad-
matha, Tarshish, Meres, Marsena and Memucan, the seven nobles[r] of
Persia and Media who had special access to the king and were high-
est in the kingdom.
15 "According to law, what must be done to Queen Vashti?" he
asked. "She has not obeyed the command of King Xerxes that the
eunuchs have taken to her."
16 Then Memucan replied in the presence of the king and the no-
bles, "Queen Vashti has done wrong, not only against the king but
also against all the nobles and the peoples of all the provinces of
King Xerxes. 17 For the queen's conduct will become known to all the
women, and so they will despise their husbands and say, 'King Xer-
xes commanded Queen Vashti to be brought before him, but she
would not come.' 18 This very day the Persian and Median women of
the nobility who have heard about the queen's conduct will respond
to all the king's nobles in the same way. There will be no end of dis-
respect and discord.[s]
19 "Therefore, if it pleases the king,[t] let him issue a royal decree
and let it be written in the laws of Persia and Media, which cannot
be repealed,[u] that Vashti is never again to enter the presence of King

1:1 [a]Ezr 4:6; Da 9:1 [b]Est 9:30; Da 3:2; 6:1 [c]Est 8:9
1:2 [d]Ezr 4:9; Ne 1:1; Est 2:8
1:3 [e]1Ki 3:15; Est 2:18
1:5 [f]Jdg 14:17 [g]2Ki 21:18; Est 7:7-8
1:6 [h]Est 7:8; Eze 23:41; Am 3:12; 6:4
1:7 [i]Est 2:18; Da 5:2
1:9 [j]1Ki 3:15
1:10 [k]Jdg 16:25; Ru 3:7 [l]Ge 14:18; Est 3:15; 5:6; 7:2; Pr 31:4-7; Da 5:1-4 [m]Est 7:9
1:11 [n]SS 2:4 [o]Ps 45:11; Eze 16:14
1:12 [p]Ge 39:19; Est 2:21; 7:7; Pr 19:12
1:13 [q]1Ch 12:32; Jer 10:7; Da 2:12
1:14 [r]2Ki 25:19; Ezr 7:14
1:18 [s]Pr 19:13; 27:15
1:19 [t]Ecc 8:4 [u]Est 8:8; Da 6:8, 12

ANCIENT VOICES

Then the king cut off the head and right hand of Cyrus, and in his pursuit, he burst into Cyrus's camp. Those who were with Ariaeus no longer stood their ground but fled through their camp to the position from which they had set out. This was said to be about a half-mile away by road. So the king and his men took many kinds of plunder and in particular took Cyrus's Phocaean concubine, who was said to be intelligent and beautiful. The young Milesian woman, however, after she had been captured by some of the king's men, fled naked toward the Greeks who happened to have been guarding the baggage train. They had formed for battle and killed many plunderers, although some of the Greeks died as well. These Greeks did not run away, but saved this young woman and everything else, whether property or persons, that came among them.

—XENOPHON DESCRIBES THE HEROISM OF THE GREEK TROOPS AFTER THE DEFEAT OF CYRUS THE YOUNGER AT CUNAXA
From Xenophon, *Anabasis*, 1.10, trans. by Duane Garrett

See "Ancient Persian History Through Darius" article.

[a] *1* Hebrew *Ahasuerus,* a variant of Xerxes' Persian name; here and throughout Esther [b] *1* That is, the upper Nile region

---

1:1 Xerxes ruled the Persian Empire from 486 to 465 B.C. (see "Ancient Persian History From Xerxes Forward" on p. 718 and "Xerxes, Vashti and Esther" on p. 726). He is best known for his failed invasion of Greece.
1:2 Susa (see "Susa" on p. 729), located in Elam (southwestern Iran), was the Persian winter capital. The three other capitals were Ecbatana (Ezr 6:2), Babylon and Persepolis. One of Daniel's visions was set in Susa (Da 8:2), and Nehemiah also served there (Ne 1:1).
1:10–12 The beautiful Vashti was a trophy of Xerxes' power and glory. He evidently desired her dramatic entrance before the men being asked to go to war for the empire. Perhaps the sight of the queen was intended to inspire patriotism, but Xerxes' drunken state may have been a factor as well. The Greek historian Herodotus explained that the Persians drank as they deliberated matters of state (cf. 3:15), believing that intoxication put them in closer touch with the spiritual world.
1:13–14 Ezra 7:14 and the Greek historian Herodotus both indicate that seven men functioned as the immediate advisers to the king. (See "Counselors and Concubines: Life in an Ancient Royal Palace" on p. 719.)

Ancient Persian History Through Darius

ESTHER 1 Persia (modern Iran) is first attested in **Assyrian**[1] documents from the ninth century B.C. The Persian Empire reached its height under the **Achaemenid** kings of the sixth–fifth centuries B.C. The events of the latter books of the Hebrew Bible (Ezra, Nehemiah, Esther, Haggai, Zechariah and Malachi) took place against the background of Persian dominance.[2]

Persian archers from the reign of Darius I
Preserving Bible Times; © Dr. James C. Martin; permission of Musée de Louvre

We know virtually nothing of the early Persians, except that they, along with the Medes, were Indo-Europeans who entered eastern Mesopotamia from the north around 1000 B.C. During the seventh century B.C. the Medes became a unified power, ruling over the Persians. Finally, in 612 B.C., in an alliance with the Chaldeans,[3] the Medes captured Nineveh and brought the Assyrian Empire to an end.[4] The Persians ultimately became the dominant partner in their alliance with the Medes, with the rise of a king now called Cyrus the Great (r. 559–530 B.C.).[5]

Cyrus began to expand Persian power. Moving westward, he defeated Croesus, king of Sardis in **Asia Minor**. But his most significant campaign was against the **Babylonian** king Nabonidus.[6] He routed the Babylonian army at Opis, and Babylon fell without a contest on October 12, 539 B.C. (Herodotus's *History*, 1.189–91).[7] After securing his empire, Cyrus sought to establish himself as a benevolent ruler. He protected existing temples from looting and rebuilt others. As part of this policy he issued a decree in 539 B.C. authorizing the return of Judean exiles and the rebuilding of the Jerusalem temple (2Ch 36:22–23; Ezr 1:1–4; Isa 44:28).[8] Cyrus died during a military campaign in Central Asia and was succeeded by his son Cambyses (530–522 B.C.).

Cambyses conquered territory as far away as Egypt but died without an heir in 522 B.C. He was succeeded by Darius I Hystaspes (522–486 B.C.; Ezr 4:24; Hag 1:1; Zec 1:1). According to Darius's official account (recorded in an inscription on the rock face of a cliff at Behistun), a priest named Gaumata, falsely claiming to be Bardiya, Cambyses' brother, seized power while Cambyses was in Egypt. Cambyses died en route back to Persia, but Darius took control of at least some of his returning forces and continued on to Persia. With the aid of six other ranking men, he killed Gaumata. The six proclaimed Darius the new king. Though not in line to inherit the throne, he was from another Achaemenid family.[9]

Historians debate the credibility of Darius's account of his rise to power. Some say he was himself no more than a usurper who killed the true heir. Others consider his story convincing.

Darius proved an able ruler and capable administrator. He established a new legal system, introduced coinage and constructed imperial palaces at Susa (see "Map 8a"), Persepolis and Babylon.[10] Early in his reign he quelled rebellions throughout the empire, in time extending its boundaries eastward to the Indus River and westward to the Aegean Sea. Darius organized this vast realm into 20 administrative districts, or satrapies, which allowed local peoples to enjoy a degree of autonomy.

Judea was part of the satrapy called "Beyond the River" (see Ezr 4:10; Ne 2:7). According to Ezra 6 Darius reconfirmed a decree of Cyrus allowing the Jews to rebuild their temple in Jerusalem and actually underwrote the costs. We should not suppose, however, that Darius was devoted to Israel's God. He viewed religion as a political tool for gaining support from subject peoples.

Darius overreached himself when he invaded Greece.[11] Greek city-states on the western coast of Asia Minor (Turkey) were under Persian control, but with the support of the city of Athens they resisted Persian authority. Darius concluded that he had to subdue mainland Greece and proceeded to invade with a massive army in 490 B.C. Persian forces were routed at the battle of Marathon. Darius died in 486 B.C. and was succeeded by his son Xerxes (r. 485–465 B.C.).

[1]See Glossary on page 2080 for definitions of bolded words. [2]See "The Postexilic Period of the Old Testament: The Persian Period" on page 699. [3]See "The Chaldeans" on page 1402. [4]See "Nineveh" on page 1497. [5]See "Cyrus the Great" on page 669. [6]See "The Sippar Cylinder of Nabonidus" on page 664. [7]See "Herodotus and the Fall of Babylon" on page 1283. [8]See "The Cyrus Cylinder" on page 679. [9]See "Darius I" on page 676. [10]For more on these cities, see "Susa" on page 729, "Persepolis" on page 1404 and "Babylon" on page 1077. [11]See "Greece: From Independent City-states Through Alexander the Great" on page 1814.

Xerxes. Also let the king give her royal position to someone else who is better than she. 20 Then when the
king's edict is proclaimed throughout all his vast realm, all the women will respect their husbands, from
the least to the greatest."
21 The king and his nobles were pleased with this advice, so the king did as Memucan proposed.
22 He sent dispatches to all parts of the kingdom, to each province in its own script and to each people
in its own language,[v] proclaiming in each people's tongue that every man should be ruler over his own
household.

1:22 [v]Ne 13:24; Est 8:9; Eph 5:22-24; 1Ti 2:12

Ancient Persian History From Xerxes Forward

ESTHER 1 Xerxes, called Ahasuerus in some translations, is the Persian king at the center of the book of Esther. After taking the throne he first had to deal with rebellions in Egypt and Babylon, but he soon turned his attention to Greece. Planning a new invasion, he put together perhaps the largest army of ancient history and, with the resources provided by his city-states on the Mediterranean, also built up a formidable navy. Intending to overwhelm the Greeks by sheer force of numbers, he began the invasion.

The campaign proved a disaster. The Persians managed to overwhelm a tiny contingent of Spartan defenders at the Thermopylae Pass, but at the cost both of high casualties and of leaving the Greeks with a legacy of fallen heroes around whom they could rally. Xerxes proceeded to take most of the land of Greece, but his fleet was crushed by a smaller Greek fleet in the bay of Salamis, near Athens, in 480 B.C. The Persian forces were driven from Greece after they were decisively beaten at Plataea in 479 B.C.

The story of Esther spans much of Xerxes' reign.[1] Although the details of Esther's story are not confirmed from external sources, the Biblical account matches well with the chronology of Xerxes' time in power, and many details of the book suggest that the author was thoroughly acquainted with Persian court life.

Xerxes was succeeded by his son, Artaxerxes I (r. 464–424 B.C.).[2] The war with Greece had not ended; it had simply shifted from the Greek mainland to the eastern Mediterranean. Soon after taking the throne, Artaxerxes was confronted with a major rebellion in Egypt; the Athenians gave military support to the Egyptian cause. The war was brutal and protracted, lasting from 460 to 450 B.C., but the Persians ultimately managed to crush the rebellion and drive out the Greeks. Exhausted, the Greeks and Persians concluded a peace treaty (the Peace of Callias). It was during Artaxerxes' reign that Ezra and Nehemiah did their work in Jerusalem, with Ezra arriving during the seventh year of Artaxerxes I and Nehemiah in the king's twentieth year.[3]

In the years that followed, dynastic succession frequently involved conflicts between rival claimants to the throne of Persia. Darius II ruled from 423 to 404 and spent much of his time putting down revolts. He was followed by Artaxerxes II (r. 404–358), who began his reign with a civil war between himself and Cyrus the Younger. When Cyrus was killed at the battle of Cunaxa (401 B.C.), the 10,000 Greek mercenaries whom Cyrus had hired had to fight their way back home through Persian territory. (This story is recounted in the famous *Anabasis* of the ancient Greek historian Xenophon.)

Artaxerxes II was succeeded by Artaxerxes III (r. 358–338), who retained the throne by massacres and a campaign of terror. Responding to revolts in the western provinces, he destroyed the **Phoenician**[4] city of Sidon and waged a brutal war in Egypt. He himself was assassinated and replaced by Darius III, who had the misfortune of having to defend his empire against a Greek army led by one of the ablest generals of ancient history: Alexander the Great. In successive battles Alexander routed the Persian armies and brought the Persian Empire to an end.

[1]See "Xerxes, Vashti and Esther" on page 726. [2]See "Artaxerxes I, King of Persia" on page 681. [3]See "The Chronology of Ezra and Nehemiah" on page 690. [3]See Glossary on page 2080 for definitions of bolded words.

Counselors and Concubines: Life in an Ancient Royal Palace

ESTHER 2 Piecing together the nature of palace life in the ancient world is fraught with difficulties, since what was true for one place and time may not have been so for another. Not all ancient courts, for instance, followed the same rules. Nevertheless, it is possible to draw together some general tendencies about ancient Near Eastern palace life from various examples from the Biblical world.

Counselors and High Officials

As advisors to the king, counselors and courtiers were held in high esteem. Their advice influenced the king and the court in many matters; this influence could be either for evil (2Ch 22:3ff.) or for good (e.g., Baruch used his influence to read Jeremiah's prophecies not only to the people but to his fellow officials as well; Jer 36:5ff.). High officials were expected to be "wise," but in the ancient Near East wisdom involved not only education or good judgment but also an ability to read omens and practice divination (as was the case in the examples of Joseph's and Daniel's ability to interpret dreams or solve riddles).[1]

The fundamental duty of royal counselors was to give the king advice that would enable him to retain his power and prestige. Thus a wise counselor could make or unmake a king, and the counselor's prestige (and sometimes his life!) depended upon whether or not the king regarded his advice as sound (see 2Sa 15:32—17:14). King Xerxes' officials advised him to remove Vashti from her position as queen and to replace her with another queen, lest other women hear of her actions and treat their husbands with contempt and the king himself become an object of scorn (Est 1:13ff.).

The Royal Wives and Concubines

The king maintained separate quarters from the women; at **Mari**, the queen was also housed separately from the concubines and other women. The concepts of "harems" and "concubines" have derogatory connotations in modern times, but this was not the case in the ancient Near East. "Harem" simply referred to the palace women (including concubines and slaves) or to the area where they lived. Persian royal women not only could attend banquets (2:10–11) but also accompanied the king on hunts and even on military campaigns.

Hunting scene from the Assyrian palace at Khorsabad
Preserving Bible Times; © Dr. James C. Martin; permission of The British Museum

Concubines in the Persian period included foreigners—daughters of other kings with whom alliances had been made. The fact that they had their own attendants indicates that they were not of low social station, though within the royal family they possessed only the rights of secondary wives. In some contexts access to the palace concubines was equated with the right to the kingship (cf. 2Sa 3:7; 16:21–22; 1Ki 2:22ff.), so the harem was guarded by a eunuch or other official. While the access of the concubines to the king was limited (Est 2:14; 4:11), this was not a function of their status; no one of any position could approach a Persian king without having been summoned (4:11). Officials, however, could not meet with royal women alone (e.g., Mordecai sent word to Esther about Haman's plot via the eunuch Hathach; 4:5–9). In the **Assyrian** court the penalty for a courtier attempting to meet alone with a royal woman was death.

Royal women could use their influence to intercede with the king, particularly on behalf of or for the benefit of family members. In this way Esther was able to reveal a plot against the king that was discovered by Mordecai (2:21–23), as well as to intercede on behalf of her people when Haman tried to destroy them (7:1ff.). Queens, in addition to supervising household management and overseeing the harem, also owned and managed estates and oversaw work details.

[1]See "Akkadian Divination" on page 277 and "Dream Oracles in the Ancient World" on page 741.

Esther Made Queen

2 Later when the anger of King Xerxes had subsided,[w] he remembered Vashti and what she had done 2:1 [w]Est 1:19-20;
and what he had decreed about her. 2Then the king's personal attendants proposed, "Let a search be 7:10
made for beautiful young virgins for the king. 3Let the king appoint commissioners in every province of
his realm to bring all these beautiful girls into the harem at the citadel of Susa. Let them be placed un-
der the care of Hegai, the king's eunuch, who is in charge of the women; and let beauty treatments be
given to them. 4Then let the girl who pleases the king be queen instead of Vashti." This advice appealed
to the king, and he followed it.
5Now there was in the citadel of Susa a Jew of the tribe of Benjamin, named Mordecai son of Jair, the
son of Shimei, the son of Kish,[x] 6who had been carried into exile from Jerusalem by Nebuchadnezzar 2:5 [x]1Sa 9:1; Est 3:2
king of Babylon, among those taken captive with Jehoiachin[a][y] king of Judah.[z] 7Mordecai had a cousin 2:6 [y]2Ki 24:6,15; 2Ch 36:10,20
named Hadassah, whom he had brought up because she had neither father nor mother. This girl, who was [z]Da 1:1-5; 5:13
also known as Esther,[a] was lovely[b] in form and features, and Mordecai had taken her as his own daugh- 2:7 [a]Ge 41:45
ter when her father and mother died. [b]Ge 39:6
8When the king's order and edict had been proclaimed, many girls were brought to the citadel of Susa[c] 2:8 [c]ver 3,15;
and put under the care of Hegai. Esther also was taken to the king's palace and entrusted to Hegai, who Ne 1:1; Est 1:2; Da 8:2
had charge of the harem. 9The girl pleased him and won his favor.[d] Immediately he provided her with 2:9 [d]Ge 39:21
her beauty treatments and special food.[e] He assigned to her seven maids selected from the king's pal- [e]ver 3,12; Ge 37:3;
ace and moved her and her maids into the best place in the harem. 1Sa 9:22-24; 2Ki 25:30;
10Esther had not revealed her nationality and family background, because Mordecai had forbidden Eze 16:9-13; Da 1:5
her to do so.[f] 11Every day he walked back and forth near the courtyard of the harem to find out how Es- 2:10 [f]ver 20
ther was and what was happening to her.
12Before a girl's turn came to go in to King Xerxes, she had to complete twelve months of beauty
treatments prescribed for the women, six months with oil of myrrh and six with perfumes[g] and cos- 2:12 [g]Pr 27:9;
metics. 13And this is how she would go to the king: Anything she wanted was given her to take with SS 1:3; Isa 3:24
her from the harem to the king's palace. 14In the evening she would go there and in the morning re-
turn to another part of the harem to the care of Shaashgaz, the king's eunuch who was in charge of the
concubines.[h] She would not return to the king unless he was pleased with her and summoned her by 2:14 [h]1Ki 11:3;
name.[i] SS 6:8; Da 5:2 [i]Est 4:11
15When the turn came for Esther (the girl Mordecai had adopted, the daughter of his uncle Abihail[j]) 2:15 [j]Est 9:29
to go to the king,[k] she asked for nothing other than what Hegai, the king's eunuch who was in charge of [k]Ps 45:14
the harem, suggested. And Esther won the favor[l] of everyone who saw her. 16She was taken to King Xer- [l]Ge 18:3; 30:27; Est 5:8
xes in the royal residence in the tenth month, the month of Tebeth, in the seventh year of his reign.
17Now the king was attracted to Esther more than to any of the other women, and she won his fa-
vor and approval more than any of the other virgins. So he set a royal crown on her head and made
her queen[m] instead of Vashti. 18And the king gave a great banquet,[n] Esther's banquet, for all his no- 2:17 [m]Est 1:11;
bles and officials.[o] He proclaimed a holiday throughout the provinces and distributed gifts with roy- Eze 16:9-13
al liberality.[p] 2:18 [n]1Ki 3:15; Est 1:3 [o]Ge 40:20 [p]Est 1:7

Mordecai Uncovers a Conspiracy

19When the virgins were assembled a second time, Mordecai was sitting at the king's gate.[q] 20But Es- 2:19 [q]ver 21;
ther had kept secret her family background and nationality just as Mordecai had told her to do, for she Est 3:2; 4:2; 5:13
continued to follow Mordecai's instructions as she had done when he was bringing her up.[r] 2:20 [r]ver 10
21During the time Mordecai was sitting at the king's gate, Bigthana[b] and Teresh, two of the king's of-
ficers[s] who guarded the doorway, became angry[t] and conspired to assassinate King Xerxes. 22But Mor- 2:21 [s]Ge 40:2;
decai found out about the plot and told Queen Esther, who in turn reported it to the king, giving credit Est 6:2 [t]Est 1:12; 3:5; 5:9; 7:7

[a] 6 Hebrew *Jeconiah,* a variant of *Jehoiachin* [b] 21 Hebrew *Bigthan,* a variant of *Bigthana*

2:1 The Greek wars intervened before a new queen was sought.

2:5 The presence of a large Jewish population in Medo-Persia has been confirmed by the discovery of an archive of texts in Nippur (southern Mesopotamia) from the period of Artaxerxes I (465–424 B.C.) and Darius II (424–405). This archive contains the names of about 100 Jews who lived in that city, some of whom had attained positions of importance and wealth. Similar Jewish populations were probable in other Medo-Persian cities.

2:12 For commentary on perfume, see the note on 7:17. See also "Perfumes and Anointing Oils" on page 1746.

2:21–23 Herodotus referred to an official listing of the king's "benefactors," recorded in the Persian archives. Acts of loyalty were ordinarily rewarded immediately and generously by Persian kings, but Mordecai's reward was initially overlooked, even though his action had been noted.

THE RELIABILITY OF THE

BIBLE

MORDECAI AND MARDUKA

ESTHER 3 The book of Esther is unique within the Old Testament in a number of respects. There is no explicit mention of God in the story, the main character is a female and the scene is set within the royal courts of **Persia**.[1] As with other Biblical accounts, archaeologists have often puzzled over the historicity of the story and its main characters. In particular, the figure of Mordecai has been questioned: Is it plausible that a Jewish man could have achieved such a prominent position within the Persian government? The name Mordecai does represent an authentic personal name from this period, occurring in **Aramaic** documents as *Mrdk* and in **cuneiform** tablets as *Mar-du-uk-ka* or *Mar-duk-ka*.

The historicity of Mordecai receives possible confirmation from a cuneiform text dating from the last years of Darius I[2] or the early years of Xerxes I. The tablet mentions a certain government official or scribe named Marduka in the context of a list of payments made to Persian officials and their retainers. The tablet was formerly part of a collection belonging to an Englishman named Lord Amherst of Hackney. At his death the collection was sold to the Vorderasiatische Museum in Berlin. The German Assyriologist Arthur Ungnad first noted the reference to Marduka and suggested a possible connection to the Biblical Mordecai in a short article published in 1941. The complete text of the tablet was later published in 1960.

At the very least this text confirms the existence of a Persian royal official named Marduka/Mordecai. This agrees in principle with the Biblical portrait of Mordecai, who is depicted as a royal official "sitting at the king's gate" (Est 2:19; 5:13; 6:10)[3] and later invested with broad administrative authority (8:2). The fragmentary nature of the evidence and the common usage of this name, however, make the identification of Marduka with the Biblical Mordecai a matter of conjecture.[4]

[1]See "Ancient Persian History From Xerxes Forward" on page 718. [2]See "Darius I" on page 676. [3]See "The King's Gate" on page 722. [4]See "Is Esther Religious Fiction?" on page 724.

2:23 [u]Ge 40:19; Ps 7:14-16; Pr 26:27 [v]Est 6:1; 10:2

to Mordecai. 23 And when the report was investigated and found to be true, the two officials were hanged[u]
on a gallows.[a] All this was recorded in the book of the annals[v] in the presence of the king.

Haman's Plot to Destroy the Jews

3:1 [w]ver 10; Ex 17:8-16; Nu 24:7; Dt 25:17-19; 1Sa 14:48; Est 5:11

3 After these events, King Xerxes honored Haman son of Hammedatha, the Agagite,[w] elevating him
and giving him a seat of honor higher than that of all the other nobles. 2 All the royal officials at the
king's gate knelt down and paid honor to Haman, for the king had commanded this concerning him. But
Mordecai would not kneel down or pay him honor.
3 Then the royal officials at the king's gate asked Mordecai, "Why do you disobey the king's com-
mand?"[x] 4 Day after day they spoke to him but he refused to comply.[y] Therefore they told Haman about
it to see whether Mordecai's behavior would be tolerated, for he had told them he was a Jew.
5 When Haman saw that Mordecai would not kneel down or pay him honor, he was enraged.[z] 6 Yet
having learned who Mordecai's people were, he scorned the idea of killing only Mordecai. Instead Haman
looked for a way[a] to destroy[b] all Mordecai's people, the Jews,[c] throughout the whole kingdom of Xerxes.

3:3 [x]Est 5:9; Da 3:12
3:4 [y]Ge 39:10
3:5 [z]Est 2:21; 5:9
3:6 [a]Pr 16:25 [b]Ps 74:8; 83:4 [c]Est 9:24

[a] 23 Or *were hung* (or *impaled*) *on poles*; similarly elsewhere in Esther

2:23 Pictures and statues from the ancient Near East and the comments of the historian Herodotus (3.125,129; 4.43) confirm that the Persian practice of "hanging" was actually impalement. According to Herodotus (3.159), Darius I impaled 3,000 Babylonians when he took Babylon, an act that Darius himself recorded in his Behistun Inscription (see "Darius I" on p. 676). In Israelite and Canaanite practice, hanging was an exhibition of the corpse and not the means of execution itself (Dt 21:22–23; Jos 8:29; 10:26; 1Sa 31:8–10; 2Sa 4:12; 21:9–10). The sons of Haman were killed by the sword, after which their corpses were displayed in this way (Est 9:5–14).

7 In the twelfth year of King Xerxes, in the first month, the month of Nisan, they cast the *pur*[d] (that is, 3:7 [d]Est 9:24,26
the lot[e]) in the presence of Haman to select a day and month. And the lot fell on[a] the twelfth month, the [e]Lev 16:8; 1Sa 10:21
month of Adar.[f] [f]ver 13; Ezr 6:15; Est 9:19
8 Then Haman said to King Xerxes, "There is a certain people dispersed and scattered among the peo-
ples in all the provinces of your kingdom whose customs[g] are different from those of all other people 3:8 [g]Ac 16:20-21
and who do not obey[h] the king's laws; it is not in the king's best interest to tolerate them.[i] 9 If it pleases [h]Jer 29:7; Da 6:13 [i]Ezr 4:15
the king, let a decree be issued to destroy them, and I will put ten thousand talents[b] of silver into the roy-
al treasury for the men who carry out this business."[j] 3:9 [j]Est 7:4
10 So the king took his signet ring[k] from his finger and gave it to Haman son of Hammedatha, the Ag- 3:10 [k]Ge 41:42; Est 7:6; 8:2
agite, the enemy of the Jews. 11 "Keep the money," the king said to Haman, "and do with the people as you
please."
12 Then on the thirteenth day of the first month the royal secretaries were summoned. They wrote out
in the script of each province and in the language[l] of each people all Haman's orders to the king's sa- 3:12 [l]Ne 13:24

[a] 7 Septuagint; Hebrew does not have *And the lot fell on.* [b] 9 That is, about 375 tons (about 345 metric tons)

3:7 The word *pur* is found in Akkadian texts with the meaning "lot" (as here). It introduces the element of destiny into the story (cf. Pr 16:33; Ac 1:26). Haman cast the lot (in essence, rolled the dice) to determine the date of death for the Jews. But God determined how the dice fell (see "Casting Lots" on p. 744). The outcome was a date 11 months off. The edict was sent out on the thirteenth day of the first month—ironically, on the eve of Passover.

3:9 Haman was offering a huge sum, almost two-thirds of the annual income of the empire. Presumably the money would have come from the plundered wealth of the victims of the decree. The "men who carry out this business" could refer either to the revenue officers who would bring the money to the treasury or to those who would carry out the decree.

3:10 See "Signet Rings" on page 728.

ARCHAEOLOGICAL SITES

THE KING'S GATE

ESTHER 4 Susa (see "Map 8a"), the city of the summer palace of the Persian rulers, is the setting for Esther. Archaeological research conducted during the 1970s by a French team has uncovered some locations mentioned in the book.[1] A particularly interesting find is the gatehouse mentioned in Esther 2:19–21, 3:2–3, 4:2 and elsewhere. This gatehouse, approximately 87.5 yards (80 m) east of the palace, was an imposing structure. It was about 43.8 yards (40 m) across and had a central room that was roughly 23 yards (21 m) square. Massive columns flanked the structure. A trilingual inscription from Xerxes himself celebrates the building of the gatehouse by his predecessor, Darius, and honors the Persian god Ahuramazda.[2] A monumental statue of Darius also once stood at the western end of the gate.[3] The historian Herodotus spoke of suppliants who wailed before the Persian king's gate (*History*, 3.117), and it may have been that the rule mentioned in 4:2—that no one could enter the gate wearing sackcloth—was intended to make the point that petitioners could come as far as, but no farther than, this gate.

[1]See "Susa" on page 729. [2]See "Xerxes, Vashti and Esther" on page 726. [3]See "Darius I" on page 676.

Restoration of the gates from the palace of Shalmaneser III of Assyria, illustrating the grandeur of an ancient royal gateway

Preserving Bible Times; © Dr. James C. Martin; permission of The British Museum

3:12 [m]Ge 38:18; 1Ki 21:8; Est 8:8-10
3:13 [n]1Sa 15:3; Ezr 4:6; Est 8:10-14 [o]ver 7 [p]Est 8:11; 9:10
3:14 [q]Est 8:8; 9:1

traps, the governors of the various provinces and the nobles of the various peoples. These were written in the name of King Xerxes himself and sealed[m] with his own ring. 13Dispatches were sent by couriers to all the king's provinces with the order to destroy, kill and annihilate all the Jews[n]—young and old, women and little children—on a single day, the thirteenth day of the twelfth month, the month of Adar,[o] and to plunder[p] their goods. 14A copy of the text of the edict was to be issued as law in every province and made known to the people of every nationality so they would be ready for that day.[q]

3:15 [r]Est 8:14 [s]Est 1:10 [t]Est 8:15

15Spurred on by the king's command, the couriers went out, and the edict was issued in the citadel of Susa.[r] The king and Haman sat down to drink,[s] but the city of Susa was bewildered.[t]

Mordecai Persuades Esther to Help

4:1 [u]Nu 14:6 [v]2Sa 13:19; Eze 27:30-31; Jnh 3:5-6 [w]Ex 11:6; Ps 30:11
4:2 [x]Est 2:19

4 When Mordecai learned of all that had been done, he tore his clothes,[u] put on sackcloth and ashes,[v] and went out into the city, wailing[w] loudly and bitterly. 2But he went only as far as the king's gate,[x] because no one clothed in sackcloth was allowed to enter it. 3In every province to which the edict and order of the king came, there was great mourning among the Jews, with fasting, weeping and wailing. Many lay in sackcloth and ashes.

4When Esther's maids and eunuchs came and told her about Mordecai, she was in great distress. She sent clothes for him to put on instead of his sackcloth, but he would not accept them. 5Then Esther summoned Hathach, one of the king's eunuchs assigned to attend her, and ordered him to find out what was troubling Mordecai and why.

4:7 [y]Est 3:9; 7:4

6So Hathach went out to Mordecai in the open square of the city in front of the king's gate. 7Mordecai told him everything that had happened to him, including the exact amount of money Haman had promised to pay into the royal treasury for the destruction of the Jews.[y] 8He also gave him a copy of the text of the edict for their annihilation, which had been published in Susa, to show to Esther and explain it to her, and he told him to urge her to go into the king's presence to beg for mercy and plead with him for her people.

4:11 [z]Est 2:14 [a]Da 2:9 [b]Est 5:1, 2; 8:4

9Hathach went back and reported to Esther what Mordecai had said. 10Then she instructed him to say to Mordecai, 11"All the king's officials and the people of the royal provinces know that for any man or woman who approaches the king in the inner court without being summoned[z] the king has but one law:[a] that he be put to death. The only exception to this is for the king to extend the gold scepter[b] to him and spare his life. But thirty days have passed since I was called to go to the king."

4:14 [c]Ecc 3:7; Isa 62:1; Am 5:13 [d]Est 9:16,22 [e]Ge 45:7; Dt 28:29 [f]Ge 50:20

12When Esther's words were reported to Mordecai, 13he sent back this answer: "Do not think that because you are in the king's house you alone of all the Jews will escape. 14For if you remain silent[c] at this time, relief[d] and deliverance[e] for the Jews will arise from another place, but you and your father's family will perish. And who knows but that you have come to royal position for such a time as this?"[f]

4:16 [g]2Ch 20:3; Est 9:31 [h]Ge 43:14

15Then Esther sent this reply to Mordecai: 16"Go, gather together all the Jews who are in Susa, and fast[g] for me. Do not eat or drink for three days, night or day. I and my maids will fast as you do. When this is done, I will go to the king, even though it is against the law. And if I perish, I perish."[h]

17So Mordecai went away and carried out all of Esther's instructions.

Esther's Request to the King

5:1 [i]Est 4:16; Eze 16:13 [j]Est 6:4; Pr 21:1

5 On the third day Esther put on her royal robes[i] and stood in the inner court of the palace, in front of the king's[j] hall. The king was sitting on his royal throne in the hall, facing the entrance. 2When he saw Queen Esther standing in the court, he was pleased with her and held out to her the gold scepter that was in his hand. So Esther approached and touched the tip of the scepter.[k]

5:2 [k]Est 4:11; 8:4; Pr 21:1
5:3 [l]Est 7:2; Da 5:16; Mk 6:23

3Then the king asked, "What is it, Queen Esther? What is your request? Even up to half the kingdom,[l] it will be given you."

4"If it pleases the king," replied Esther, "let the king, together with Haman, come today to a banquet I have prepared for him."

5"Bring Haman at once," the king said, "so that we may do what Esther asks."

5:6 [m]Est 1:10 [n]Mk 6:23 [o]Est 7:2; 9:12

So the king and Haman went to the banquet Esther had prepared. 6As they were drinking wine,[m] the king again asked Esther, "Now what is your petition? It will be given you. And what is your request? Even up to half the kingdom,[n] it will be granted."[o]

5:8 [p]Est 2:15; 7:3; 8:5 [q]1Ki 3:15; Est 6:14

7Esther replied, "My petition and my request is this: 8If the king regards me with favor[p] and if it pleases the king to grant my petition and fulfill my request, let the king and Haman come tomorrow to the banquet[q] I will prepare for them. Then I will answer the king's question."

IS ESTHER RELIGIOUS FICTION?

ESTHER 5 The book of Esther is viewed today by a majority of scholars as nonhistorical. Yet the story itself is recounted candidly, and there is nothing within it to suggest that it is fictional. Miracles or other "impossible" occurrences are totally absent. Critical scholars are bothered, however, by apparent exaggerations or suspected inaccuracies:

- The length of the 180-day feast (1:1–4) seems excessive.
- The six months of perfuming with oil and the additional six months of beautifying with spices (2:12) seem extreme.[1]
- The book claims that there were 127 Persian provinces (1:1), while the historian Herodotus speaks of only 20.
- The notion of a Persian decree being irrevocable (1:19; 8:9) is regarded as doubtful—but see Daniel 6.
- Planning for a massacre of Jews a year in advance (Est 3:8–15) strikes scholars as unlikely.
- It seems too coincidental that Haman would turn out to be a descendant of Agag the Amalekite, the enemy of Israel who cost Saul his crown (3:1; see 1Sa 15).
- Contrary to the Biblical account, Herodotus identified Xerxes' queen as Amestris,[2] not Vashti.
- Although the name Mordecai and that of Haman's son Parshandatha (Est 9:7) are attested elsewhere during the **Persian period**, Xerxes is the only indisputable historical figure in the book.
- Archaeological data from the Persian period has not specifically confirmed the story's historicity.

Thus, Esther is often read as a satire addressing the needs of Jews outside of the Holy Land. Yet these challenges, though not insignificant, are not in fact as overwhelming as they might first appear:

- The apparent exaggerations may be a result of narrative technique. The 180-day banquet may have been primarily a gathering of leaders to strategize the Greek invasion.[2] Similarly, the six-month preparation periods for the women were probably also intended for training in court decorum and protocol. The author apparently wished to highlight the splendor of the Persian court, but this does not signify that the events were manufactured.
- The discrepancy in the number of provinces in the empire is founded on the notion that the Greek *satrapeia* (in Herodotus) and the Hebrew *medinah* (in Esther) mean the same thing, but this has not been established. The higher figure in Esther may refer to smaller subdivisions.
- The idea that a royal decree was irrevocable is not documented outside the Bible, but this is probably best understood as a matter of royal etiquette and/or tradition—not as formal law.
- Regarding the length of time needed to plan a pogrom, two facts stand out. First, such a matter would require time and planning, given the size and makeup of the empire. Second, it is entirely credible that a man of the ancient world would cast lots to determine an auspicious day for following through with such a plan.[3]
- The text does not state that Haman was descended from the Agag of 1 Samuel 15. The meaning of "Agagite" in Esther is actually unknown.
- It is possible that the queen Herodotus called Amestris was in fact Esther, since the two names appear to be linguistically related (others suggest that Amestris is to be equated with Vashti).
- There are remarkable similarities between the book's statements about fifth-century Persia and what is known about that country and society from archaeology.[4] That the author had more than a casual knowledge of Persian life during this period is displayed in his references to Persian vocabulary and customs as well as in his awareness that the king had seven advisors (Est 1:14), that eating was undertaken while reclining on couches (7:8) and that royal horses could wear crowns (6:8).

It is rare for archaeology to provide direct evidence for a historical event. More often, reconstructing ancient history is a matter of combining the stories found in texts with the artifacts discovered in archaeology, though such work always requires a measure of confidence in the reliability of the texts. If every narrative from the ancient world had to be specifically confirmed by archaeology, we would have no ancient history at all.

The book of Esther makes strong implicit claims to being historical. It is precisely as *history* that Esther is most significant; it marks the beginning of the long, sad saga of pogroms and holocausts against the Jews.

[1]See "Perfumes and Anointing Oils" on page 1746. [2]See "Xerxes, Vashti and Esther" on page 726. [3]See "Casting Lots" on page 744. [4]See "Mordecai and Marduka" on page 721 and "The King's Gate" on page 722.

Haman's Rage Against Mordecai

9 Haman went out that day happy and in high spirits. But when he saw Mordecai at the king's gate and
5:9 [r]Est 2:21; Pr 14:17 [s]Est 3:3,5 observed that he neither rose nor showed fear in his presence, he was filled with rage[r] against Mordecai.[s]
10 Nevertheless, Haman restrained himself and went home.
5:10 [t]Est 6:13 Calling together his friends and Zeresh,[t] his wife, 11 Haman boasted[u] to them about his vast wealth,
5:11 [u]Pr 13:16 [v]Est 9:7-10,13 his many sons,[v] and all the ways the king had honored him and how he had elevated him above the oth-
5:12 [w]Job 22:29; Pr 16:18; 29:23 er nobles and officials. 12 "And that's not all," Haman added. "I'm the only person[w] Queen Esther invited
to accompany the king to the banquet she gave. And she has invited me along with the king tomorrow.
5:13 [x]Est 2:19 13 But all this gives me no satisfaction as long as I see that Jew Mordecai sitting at the king's gate."[x]
5:14 [y]Est 7:9 [z]Ezr 6:11; Est 6:4 14 His wife Zeresh and all his friends said to him, "Have a gallows built, seventy-five feet[a] high,[y] and
ask the king in the morning to have Mordecai hanged[z] on it. Then go with the king to the dinner and be
happy." This suggestion delighted Haman, and he had the gallows built.

Mordecai Honored

6:1 [a]Da 2:1; 6:18 [b]Est 2:23; 10:2 6 That night the king could not sleep;[a] so he ordered the book of the chronicles,[b] the record of his
reign, to be brought in and read to him. 2 It was found recorded there that Mordecai had exposed
Bigthana and Teresh, two of the king's officers who guarded the doorway, who had conspired to assassi-
nate King Xerxes.
3 "What honor and recognition has Mordecai received for this?" the king asked.
6:3 [c]Ecc 9:13-16 "Nothing has been done for him,"[c] his attendants answered.
4 The king said, "Who is in the court?" Now Haman had just entered the outer court of the palace to
speak to the king about hanging Mordecai on the gallows he had erected for him.
5 His attendants answered, "Haman is standing in the court."
"Bring him in," the king ordered.
6 When Haman entered, the king asked him, "What should be done for the man the king delights to
honor?"
Now Haman thought to himself, "Who is there that the king would rather honor than me?" 7 So he an-
6:8 [d]Ge 41:42; Isa 52:1 [e]1Ki 1:33 swered the king, "For the man the king delights to honor, 8 have them bring a royal robe[d] the king has
worn and a horse[e] the king has ridden, one with a royal crest placed on its head. 9 Then let the robe and
horse be entrusted to one of the king's most noble princes. Let them robe the man the king delights to
honor, and lead him on the horse through the city streets, proclaiming before him, 'This is what is done
6:9 [f]Ge 41:43 for the man the king delights to honor![f]' "
10 "Go at once," the king commanded Haman. "Get the robe and the horse and do just as you have sug-
gested for Mordecai the Jew, who sits at the king's gate. Do not neglect anything you have recommended."
6:11 [g]Ge 41:42 11 So Haman got[g] the robe and the horse. He robed Mordecai, and led him on horseback through the
city streets, proclaiming before him, "This is what is done for the man the king delights to honor!"
6:12 [h]2Sa 15:30; Jer 14:3,4; Mic 3:7 12 Afterward Mordecai returned to the king's gate. But Haman rushed home, with his head covered[h]
in grief, 13 and told Zeresh[i] his wife and all his friends everything that had happened to him.
6:13 [i]Est 5:10 [j]Ps 57:6; Pr 26:27; 28:18 His advisers and his wife Zeresh said to him, "Since Mordecai, before whom your downfall[j] has start-
ed, is of Jewish origin, you cannot stand against him — you will surely come to ruin!" 14 While they were
6:14 [k]1Ki 3:15; Est 5:8 still talking with him, the king's eunuchs arrived and hurried Haman away to the banquet[k] Esther had
prepared.

Haman Hanged

7:1 [l]Ge 40:20-22; Mt 22:1-14 7 So the king and Haman went to dine[l] with Queen Esther, 2 and as they were drinking wine[m] on that
7:2 [m]Est 1:10 [n]Est 5:3 [o]Est 9:12 second day, the king again asked, "Queen Esther, what is your petition? It will be given you. What is
your request? Even up to half the kingdom,[n] it will be granted."[o]

[a] 14 Hebrew *fifty cubits* (about 23 meters)

5:11 Haman had ten sons (9:7–10). Herodotus (1.136) reported that among the Persians the only thing prized more highly than a large number of sons was valor in battle.

5:14 Zeresh's advice reminds us of Jezebel's when her husband, King Ahab, was sulking like a spoiled child (1Ki 21:1–16). Jezebel's solution was to arrange a "legal" murder (the death penalty for a trumped-up charge of blasphemy) so that Ahab could have what he wanted. Here Zeresh counseled Haman simply to kill Mordecai outright. In the pagan world of ancient Persia the satisfaction of human pride in its demand for honor and respect outweighed the value of human life.

6:8 In ancient times great significance was attached to a king's garments. Wearing the king's garment was a sign of unique favor (1Sa 18:4) that represented a sharing of his power, stature, honor or sanctity (2Ki 2:13–14; Isa 61:3,10; Zec 3; Mk 5:27).

6:14 Guests were usually escorted to feasts (see Ge 43:15–26; cf. Mt 22:1–14).

THE RELIABILITY OF THE BIBLE

XERXES, VASHTI AND ESTHER

ESTHER 7 Xerxes I, who ruled the **Persian Empire** from 486 to 465 B.C.,[1] is best known for his failed invasion of Greece. Xerxes' palace at Susa ("Map 8a") has been excavated and some administrative records from his reign recovered.[2] The historian Herodotus (c. 484–425 B.C.), in his history of the war between the Greeks and the Persians, provides a great deal of information about Xerxes. However, while Herodotus's record of the major events of the war is basically trustworthy, his anecdotes about Persian court life are dismissed today by many historians as being little more than gossip (Herodotus, a Greek, they submit, wanted to portray Xerxes as a weak womanizer). Our only other major source of information about Xerxes is the Bible.

◆ Ezra recorded that at the beginning of Xerxes' reign enemies of the Jews "lodged an accusation against the people of Judah and Jerusalem" (Ezr 4:6). Egypt revolted in 486 B.C., and the allegation may have been that the Jews were planning to do the same. Thus, the book of Ezra was written against the backdrop of a Persian Empire that was likely to be alarmed by slanderous accusations of sedition.

◆ After suppressing the Egyptian revolt in 485 B.C., Xerxes invaded Greece in 481–480 B.C. The 180-day banquet Xerxes hosted during his third year (483 B.C.; Est 1:3), may have been an extended planning session for the Greek campaign.

◆ The banquet for the elite was followed by a shorter, seven-day version for all the residents of Susa (1:5–9). During this banquet Vashti embarrassed the king by disobeying his order (1:10–22). Xerxes did not take action to replace Vashti until his sixth year (480 B.C.; 2:1–4), probably because he was away for three years putting down a revolt in **Babylon** (482 B.C.)[3] and leading the unsuccessful invasion of Greece (481–480 B.C.).

◆ Esther was selected as a potential candidate for queen and, following a year of preparation (2:12) was chosen as the new queen during Xerxes' seventh year (479 B.C.; v. 16). Fourteen years later Xerxes was assassinated in a palace intrigue.

◆ Herodotus specified that Xerxes' queen was named Amestris, and some scholars have equated Amestris with Vashti and others with Esther. However, as stated earlier, Herodotus's information about Persian court life should not be used as a basis for evaluating the book of Esther.[4]

[1]See "Darius I" on page 676 and "Ancient Persian History From Xerxes Forward" on page 718. [2]See "The King's Gate" on page 722 and "Susa" on page 729. [3]See "Babylon" on page 1077. [4]See "Counselors and Concubines: Life in an Ancient Royal Palace" on page 719.

3Then Queen Esther answered, "If I have found favor[p] with you, O king, and if it pleases your majes- 7:3 pEst 2:15
ty, grant me my life — this is my petition. And spare my people — this is my request. 4For I and my peo-
ple have been sold for destruction and slaughter and annihilation.[q] If we had merely been sold as male 7:4 qEst 3:9
and female slaves, I would have kept quiet, because no such distress would justify disturbing the king.[a]"
5King Xerxes asked Queen Esther, "Who is he? Where is the man who has dared to do such a thing?"
6Esther said, "The adversary and enemy is this vile Haman."
Then Haman was terrified before the king and queen. 7The king got up in a rage,[r] left his wine and 7:7 rGe 34:7; Est 1:12; Pr 19:12; 20:1-2
went out into the palace garden.[s] But Haman, realizing that the king had already decided his fate,[t] stayed s2Ki 21:18
behind to beg Queen Esther for his life. tEst 6:13
8Just as the king returned from the palace garden to the banquet hall, Haman was falling on the couch[u] 7:8 uEst 1:6 vGe 39:14
where Esther was reclining.[v] wGe 34:7
The king exclaimed, "Will he even molest the queen while she is with me in the house?"[w] xEst 6:12
As soon as the word left the king's mouth, they covered Haman's face.[x] 9Then Harbona,[y] one of the 7:9 yEst 1:10
eunuchs attending the king, said, "A gallows seventy-five feet[b] high[z] stands by Haman's house. He had it zEst 5:14
made for Mordecai, who spoke up to help the king."

[a] 4 Or *quiet, but the compensation our adversary offers cannot be compared with the loss the king would suffer* [b] 9 Hebrew *fifty cubits* (about 23 meters)

7:7–8 Protocol dictated that no one but the king could be left alone with a woman of the royal harem (see "Counselors and Concubines: Life in an Ancient Royal Palace" on p. 719). Once the king had exited, Haman should have left Esther's presence. That he moved onto her couch was unthinkable!

The king said, "Hang him on it!"[a] 10So they hanged Haman[b] on the gallows[c] he had prepared for Mor-
decai.[d] Then the king's fury subsided.[e]

The King's Edict in Behalf of the Jews

8 That same day King Xerxes gave Queen Esther the estate of Haman,[f] the enemy of the Jews. And
Mordecai came into the presence of the king, for Esther had told how he was related to her. 2The
king took off his signet ring,[g] which he had reclaimed from Haman, and presented it to Mordecai. And
Esther appointed him over Haman's estate.[h]

3Esther again pleaded with the king, falling at his feet and weeping. She begged him to put an end to
the evil plan of Haman the Agagite, which he had devised against the Jews. 4Then the king extended the
gold scepter[i] to Esther and she arose and stood before him.

5"If it pleases the king," she said, "and if he regards me with favor and thinks it the right thing to do,
and if he is pleased with me, let an order be written overruling the dispatches that Haman son of Ham-
medatha, the Agagite, devised and wrote to destroy the Jews in all the king's provinces. 6For how can I
bear to see disaster fall on my people? How can I bear to see the destruction of my family?"[j]

7King Xerxes replied to Queen Esther and to Mordecai the Jew, "Because Haman attacked the Jews, I
have given his estate to Esther, and they have hanged him on the gallows. 8Now write another decree[k] in
the king's name in behalf of the Jews as seems best to you, and seal it with the king's signet ring[l]—for
no document written in the king's name and sealed with his ring can be revoked."[m]

9At once the royal secretaries were summoned—on the twenty-third day of the third month, the
month of Sivan. They wrote out all Mordecai's orders to the Jews, and to the satraps, governors and no-
bles of the 127 provinces stretching from India to Cush.[a][n] These orders were written in the script of each
province and the language of each people and also to the Jews in their own script and language.[o] 10Mor-
decai wrote in the name of King Xerxes, sealed the dispatches with the king's signet ring, and sent them
by mounted couriers, who rode fast horses especially bred for the king.

11The king's edict granted the Jews in every city the right to assemble and protect themselves; to de-
stroy, kill and annihilate any armed force of any nationality or province that might attack them and their
women and children; and to plunder[p] the property of their enemies. 12The day appointed for the Jews to
do this in all the provinces of King Xerxes was the thirteenth day of the twelfth month, the month of
Adar.[q] 13A copy of the text of the edict was to be issued as law in every province and made known to the
people of every nationality so that the Jews would be ready on that day[r] to avenge themselves on their
enemies.

14The couriers, riding the royal horses, raced out, spurred on by the king's command. And the edict
was also issued in the citadel of Susa.

15Mordecai[s] left the king's presence wearing royal garments of blue and white, a large crown of
gold and a purple robe of fine linen.[t] And the city of Susa held a joyous celebration.[u] 16For the Jews
it was a time of happiness and joy,[v] gladness and honor.[w] 17In every province and in every city, wher-
ever the edict of the king went, there was joy[x] and gladness among the Jews, with feasting and cele-
brating. And many people of other nationalities became Jews because fear[y] of the Jews had seized
them.[z]

Triumph of the Jews

9 On the thirteenth day of the twelfth month, the month of Adar,[a] the edict commanded by the king
was to be carried out. On this day the enemies of the Jews had hoped to overpower them, but now
the tables were turned and the Jews got the upper hand[b] over those who hated them.[c] 2The Jews assem-
bled in their cities[d] in all the provinces of King Xerxes to attack those seeking their destruction. No one
could stand against them,[e] because the people of all the other nationalities were afraid of them. 3And all
the nobles of the provinces, the satraps, the governors and the king's administrators helped the Jews,[f]
because fear of Mordecai had seized them. 4Mordecai was prominent[g] in the palace; his reputation spread
throughout the provinces, and he became more and more powerful.[h]

[a] 9 That is, the upper Nile region

7:9 [a]Ps 7:14-16; 9:16; Pr 11:5-6; 26:27; Mt 7:2 **7:10** [b]Pr 10:28 [c]Est 9:25 [d]Da 6:24 [e]Est 2:1
8:1 [f]Est 2:7; 7:6; Pr 22:22-23
8:2 [g]Ge 41:42; Est 3:10 [h]Pr 13:22; Da 2:48
8:4 [i]Est 4:11; 5:2
8:6 [j]Est 7:4; 9:1
8:8 [k]Est 3:12-14 [l]Ge 41:42 [m]Est 1:19; Da 6:15
8:9 [n]Est 1:1 [o]Est 1:22
8:11 [p]Est 9:10, 15,16
8:12 [q]Est 3:13; 9:1
8:13 [r]Est 3:14
8:15 [s]Est 9:4 [t]Ge 41:42 [u]Est 3:15
8:16 [v]Ps 97:10-12 [w]Ps 112:4
8:17 [x]Est 9:19, 27; Ps 35:27; Pr 11:10 [y]Ex 15:14,16; Dt 11:25 [z]Est 9:3
9:1 [a]Est 8:12 [b]Jer 29:4-7 [c]Est 3:12-14; Pr 22:22-23
9:2 [d]ver 15-18 [e]Est 8:11,17; Ps 71:13,24
9:3 [f]Ezr 8:36
9:4 [g]Ex 11:3 [h]2Sa 3:1; 1Ch 11:9

8:1 Herodotus (3.128–129) and Josephus (*Antiquities*, 11.17) confirmed that the property of a traitor reverted to the crown. Xerxes presented Haman's wealth (5:11) to Esther.

5 The Jews struck down all their enemies with the sword, killing and destroying them,[i] and they did what they pleased to those who hated them. 6 In the citadel of Susa, the Jews killed and destroyed five
hundred men. 7 They also killed Parshandatha, Dalphon, Aspatha, 8 Poratha, Adalia, Aridatha, 9 Parmash-
ta, Arisai, Aridai and Vaizatha, 10 the ten sons[j] of Haman son of Hammedatha, the enemy of the Jews. But they did not lay their hands on the plunder.[k]

9:5 [i]Ezr 4:6
9:10 [j]Est 5:11 [k]Ge 14:23; 1Sa 14:32; Est 3:13; 8:11

9:10 The author repeated three times that the Jews "did not lay their hands on the plunder" (vv. 10,15,16), even though Mordecai's decree would have allowed it (8:11). Mordecai included this permission because he was reversing the exact terms of Haman's decree (3:13), but a rule of ancient Jewish holy war was that plunder was not to be taken (see "*Herem*, Holy War" on p. 419). Abram (Ge 14) had refused to accept any material reward from the king of Sodom, not wanting that wicked city to be the source of his prosperity. This had set the precedent for God's people.

Signet Rings

ESTHER 8 Signets were a type of seal, worn either as a ring or on a cord around the neck and used to leave impressions in clay or wax. The impression functioned as a signature to authorize or authenticate a document, or to indicate that something had been sealed shut by the signet's owner.[1] Although the use of signet rings is attested from early times (Ge 41:42), in the ancient Near East cylinder seals[2] and scarabs (stone beetles used as talismans, ornaments or symbols of resurrection) were also common.

Impressions from a cylinder seal
Preserving Bible Times; © Dr. James C. Martin; permission of The British Museum

Seals on finger rings became more popular from the fifth century B.C. onward, and most Biblical examples come from the late preexilic (Jer 22:24) or **Persian period**. King Darius used his signet ring to seal the stone over the lions' den (Da 6:17),[3] and rulers gave signet rings to individuals as signs of high office and to enable them to implement official business. King Xerxes first presented his signet ring to Haman, authorizing him to dispose of the Jews (Est 3:10ff.). Later, Xerxes reclaimed the ring and bestowed it instead upon Mordecai, who issued an edict permitting the Jews to defend themselves against any attackers (8:2,8).[4] In Haggai 2:23 God selected Zerubbabel as his representative, likening him to God's own signet ring, as though God's name were stamped upon his representative as a verification of his office.

The signet ring of Pharaoh Tutankhamen
© The Schøyen Collection; photography courtesy of Mr. Martin Schøyen

[1]For a discussion of the use of seals during the New Testament era, see "Scrolls, Seals and Codices" on page 2053. [2]Cylinders (usually stone) engraved in intaglio—an incised figure depressed below the surface so that the impression yields an image in relief—and used to roll an impression on wet clay. [3]See "Darius the Mede" on page 1396. [4]See "Mordecai and Marduka" on page 721.

[11]The number of those slain in the citadel of Susa was reported to the king that same day. [12]The king
said to Queen Esther, "The Jews have killed and destroyed five hundred men and the ten sons of Haman
in the citadel of Susa. What have they done in the rest of the king's provinces? Now what is your petition?
It will be given you. What is your request? It will also be granted."[l]
[13]"If it pleases the king," Esther answered, "give the Jews in Susa permission to carry out this day's
edict tomorrow also, and let Haman's ten sons[m] be hanged[n] on gallows."

9:12 [l]Est 5:6; 7:2
9:13 [m]Est 5:11 [n]Dt 21:22-23

9:13 The reference here to hanging was for the purpose of displaying the corpses—not the means of the execution (see vv. 7–10 and the note on 2:23).

Susa

ESTHER 9 Susa ("Map 8a"; modern Shush, Iran) was inhabited from the fourth millennium B.C. to the thirteenth century A.D. Early on, the city became a religious center, with temples to Inshushinak ("lord of Susa") and other deities. During the third millennium B.C. Susa, along with another city called Anshan, was a center of **Elamite** civilization. It eventually came to have a large and prosperous population. Through the second and early first millenniums B.C. the city was either an independent Elamite capital or controlled by foreign powers, such as the **Babylonians** and **Assyrians**. It also became an important commercial hub, with contacts in India, Egypt, Arabia and Greece.

Susa came to the height of its power during the thirteenth and twelfth centuries B.C. One of its kings, Shutruk-Nahunte, conquered Babylon and brought fabulous spoils to Susa, including the **Code of Hammurabi** (which was discovered at the Susa acropolis in 1900). In 646 B.C. the city was destroyed by the Assyrians under Assurbanipal. Susa was rebuilt shortly afterward but again was conquered by Cyrus of Persia in 539 B.C.[1]

Darius I (522–486 B.C.) made Susa the winter palace for the **Persian Empire**, and in this capacity its prestige and prosperity greatly increased. The city grew to 625 acres. Its remains correspond to what we see described in Esther. During the reign of Darius a canal separated the unfortified, lower city on the eastern bank (i.e., "Susa"; 9:13–15) from the fortified, upper city on the western bank (i.e., "the citadel of Susa" in 1:5; cf. Da 8:2). An artisans' village was located east of the citadel. Citadel remains include a monumental gate (cf. Est 2:19,21) with trilingual inscriptions (cf. 1:22) and a large palace with two divisions: a three-acre audience hall and a ten-acre residential area with four successive inner courts (cf. 4:11; 5:1–2; 6:4).[2]

The palace of Darius burned during the reign of Artaxerxes I[3] but was restored under Artaxerxes II, who built a provisional palace in the lower city. Alexander the Great took Susa without a fight, and the city continued to flourish as a center of trade and textile production, with a large population of Jews, until it was finally abandoned during the thirteenth century A.D.

Column capitals from the audience hall of the palace of Darius I in Susa
Preserving Bible Times; © Dr. James C. Martin; permission of Musée de Louvre

[1]See "Cyrus the Great" on page 669. [2]See "The King's Gate" on page 722. [3]See "Artaxerxes I, King of Perisa" on page 681.

THE CANONICITY OF ESTHER

ESTHER 10 During its early history the book of Esther had a controversial status within the **canon** of the Hebrew Bible.[1] Esther is the only book of the Old Testament not represented in the **Dead Sea Scrolls**, suggesting that the **Qumran** community may not have viewed it as Scripture. Although the celebration of Purim (the holiday initiated in 8:16–17 to commemorate the deliverance of the Jews) was inaugurated in the book of Esther, the rabbis of the second century A.D. cited a text called *Megillat Taanit*—not Esther—to defend its celebration. This suggests that the book of Esther was not held in as high esteem as this late (first-century A.D.) work.

The status of Esther has been debated in Christian circles as well. Esther is not listed in the oldest Christian canonical catalog, that of Bishop Melito of Sardis (c. A.D. 167). Neither was it recognized by other Christian leaders, including Athanasius (A.D. 295–373) and Martin Luther, who proposed that Esther be removed from the canon of Scripture. On the other hand, early church fathers such as Origen (c. 185–254), Augustine (354–430), Innocent I (401–417) and John of Damascus (675–745) did count Esther among the accepted books of the Old Testament. And the councils of Hippo and Carthage officially recognized Esther's canonical status in the Christian Scriptures in A.D. 393 and 397, respectively.

Later, the canonicity of the Greek version of Esther (containing 107 verses not found in the Hebrew text) was debated. The additions were designated by the Protestant church as **Apocryphal** and omitted from the Protestant Bible during the Reformation. However, the Roman Catholic Council of Trent (1546) labeled the additions to Esther as **Deuterocanonical**, and the Roman Catholic Church continues to include them after the book of Esther proper.[2]

Jewish and Christian objections to the canonicity of Esther have been many and varied. Some readers have objected to the omission of any reference to God. Within the book there are nearly 200 allusions to the king of **Persia** but not a single direct reference to God! There is likewise no mention of prayer, the law, the covenant, Jerusalem or any of several other themes we would expect to find in a canonical work. Other scholars identify the book either as a parable or as a composite of two or more Persian and Palestinian myths. In addition, early Jews and Christians may have objected to the canonicity of Esther because of the prevalent drunkenness that often accompanied early celebrations of Purim.

Despite these objections, there are solid reasons for accepting the canonicity of Esther:

- The book is driven by implicit accounts of God's faithfulness and sovereignty, even though his name is unmentioned. From beginning to end the reader understands God's hand to be at work to deliver his people from the threats of foreign enemies. The events are not "miraculous" in a supernatural sense, but they suggest divine intervention.
- The omission of themes like the observance of the law, sacrifice, the temple in Jerusalem, etc., do not create an insurmountable objection when it is remembered that the book's events occurred during the **exile**. The Jews were living in Persia, far from the altar in Jerusalem, which, since the reformations of King Josiah, had been the only acceptable site for sacrifices to **Yahweh**. That these themes would go unmentioned, therefore, is understandable. The Jews' familiarity with their sacred traditions, however, is clear from their evident knowledge of the efficacy of communal fasting (4:16; cf. 2Ch 20:3; Jer 36:9)[3] and from the theme of providence that underlies the entire book.
- To Jews living under foreign oppression until the time of Christ, or to Christians living in the present age, the book of Esther demonstrates God's care for and action on behalf of his people. It affirms, in fact, that all human affairs are ultimately under his dominion.

With the exceptions noted above, the majority of Jews and Christians have accepted the book of Esther as Scripture for over 2,000 years. Its transmission and message demand that it remain a fundamental portion of God's message to his people.

Inscribed bowl of Artaxerxes I

Preserving Bible Times; © Dr. James C. Martin; permission of The British Museum

[1]See "The Old Testament Canon" on page 1552. [2]See "The Apocrypha" on page 1973. [3]See "Fasting in the Bible and Ancient Near East" on page 1569.

9:14 [o]Ezr 6:11 — [14]So the king commanded that this be done. An edict was issued in Susa, and they hanged[o] the ten
sons of Haman. [15]The Jews in Susa came together on the fourteenth day of the month of Adar, and they
9:15 [p]Ge 14:23; Est 8:11 — put to death in Susa three hundred men, but they did not lay their hands on the plunder.[p]
[16]Meanwhile, the remainder of the Jews who were in the king's provinces also assembled to protect
9:16 [q]Est 4:14 [r]Dt 25:19 [s]1Ch 4:43 — themselves and get relief[q] from their enemies.[r] They killed seventy-five thousand of them[s] but did not
lay their hands on the plunder. [17]This happened on the thirteenth day of the month of Adar, and on the
9:17 [t]1Ki 3:15 — fourteenth they rested and made it a day of feasting[t] and joy.

Purim Celebrated

[18]The Jews in Susa, however, had assembled on the thirteenth and fourteenth, and then on the fif-
teenth they rested and made it a day of feasting and joy.
9:19 [u]Est 3:7 [v]ver 22; Dt 16:11, 14; Ne 8:10,12; Est 2:9; Rev 11:10 — [19]That is why rural Jews—those living in villages—observe the fourteenth of the month of Adar[u] as
a day of joy and feasting, a day for giving presents to each other.[v]
[20]Mordecai recorded these events, and he sent letters to all the Jews throughout the provinces of King
Xerxes, near and far, [21]to have them celebrate annually the fourteenth and fifteenth days of the month of
9:22 [w]Est 4:14 [x]Ne 8:12; Ps 30:11-12 [y]2Ki 25:30 — Adar [22]as the time when the Jews got relief[w] from their enemies, and as the month when their sorrow was
turned into joy and their mourning into a day of celebration.[x] He wrote them to observe the days as days
of feasting and joy and giving presents of food[y] to one another and gifts to the poor.
[23]So the Jews agreed to continue the celebration they had begun, doing what Mordecai had written to
9:24 [z]Ex 17:8-16 [a]Est 3:7 [b]Lev 16:8 — them. [24]For Haman son of Hammedatha, the Agagite,[z] the enemy of all the Jews, had plotted against the
Jews to destroy them and had cast the *pur*[a] (that is, the lot[b]) for their ruin and destruction. [25]But when
the plot came to the king's attention,[a] he issued written orders that the evil scheme Haman had devised
9:25 [c]Ps 7:16 [d]Dt 21:22-23 [e]Est 7:10 — against the Jews should come back onto his own head,[c] and that he and his sons should be hanged[d] on
the gallows.[e] [26](Therefore these days were called Purim, from the word *pur.*[f]) Because of everything writ-
9:26 [f]ver 20; Est 3:7 — ten in this letter and because of what they had seen and what had happened to them, [27]the Jews took it
upon themselves to establish the custom that they and their descendants and all who join them should
without fail observe these two days every year, in the way prescribed and at the time appointed. [28]These
days should be remembered and observed in every generation by every family, and in every province
and in every city. And these days of Purim should never cease to be celebrated by the Jews, nor should
the memory of them die out among their descendants.
9:29 [g]Est 2:15 — [29]So Queen Esther, daughter of Abihail,[g] along with Mordecai the Jew, wrote with full authority to
confirm this second letter concerning Purim. [30]And Mordecai sent letters to all the Jews in the 127
9:30 [h]Est 1:1 — provinces[h] of the kingdom of Xerxes—words of goodwill and assurance— [31]to establish these days
of Purim at their designated times, as Mordecai the Jew and Queen Esther had decreed for them, and
9:31 [i]Est 4:16 [j]Est 4:1-3 — as they had established for themselves and their descendants in regard to their times of fasting[i] and
lamentation.[j] [32]Esther's decree confirmed these regulations about Purim, and it was written down in
the records.

The Greatness of Mordecai

10:1 [k]Ps 72:10; 97:1; Isa 24:15 — **10** King Xerxes imposed tribute throughout the empire, to its distant shores.[k] [2]And all his acts of
10:2 [l]Est 8:15; 9:4 [m]Ge 41:44 [n]Est 2:23 — power and might, together with a full account of the greatness of Mordecai[l] to which the king had
raised him,[m] are they not written in the book of the annals[n] of the kings of Media and Persia? [3]Morde-
10:3 [o]Da 5:7 [p]Ge 41:43 [q]Ge 41:40 [r]Ne 2:10; Jer 29:4-7; Da 6:3 — cai the Jew was second[o] in rank[p] to King Xerxes,[q] preeminent among the Jews, and held in high esteem
by his many fellow Jews, because he worked for the good of his people and spoke up for the welfare of all
the Jews.[r]

[a] 25 Or *when Esther came before the king*

9:18–19 This explains the tradition of observing Purim on two different days: The celebration was observed on the fourteenth day of the month in most towns, but the Jews of Susa commemorated it on the fifteenth. Today it is observed on the fourteenth—except in Jerusalem, where it is celebrated on the fifteenth.

9:20 While some take this verse as an indication that Mordecai wrote the book of Esther, the more natural understanding is that he recorded the events in the letters he sent.

9:29–32 Purim joined the existing five Jewish feasts that had been commanded by Moses in the Torah. Rather than having been prescribed by God's command, this celebration began as a spontaneous response to his covenant faithfulness.

Purim is still celebrated today. The entire book of Esther is read in the synagogue on the holiday, during which noisemakers are used. People cheer at the sound of Mordecai's name and boo and hiss at the mention of Haman. (See "The Canonicity of Esther" on p. 730.) Other important holy days from the postexilic period are Hanukkah, celebrating the Jewish victory over Antiochus IV of Syria (see "Antiochus IV Epiphanes" on p. 1406), and the Ninth of Ab, mourning the destruction of Jerusalem.

INTRODUCTION TO *Job*

AUTHOR, PLACE AND DATE OF WRITING

The book of Job is anonymous. Jewish tradition states that it was written by Moses, but there is nothing in the book itself to suggest Mosaic authorship. Many scholars today wonder whether the work is unified or the product of multiple authors. It has a prose framework (Job 1–2; 42:7–17), within which is incorporated a series of lengthy, poetic speeches. The frame tells how Job's sufferings began and how God finally vindicated him. However, many believe this outside "envelope" to be artificial and/or the Elihu speeches (chs. 32–37) to have been added at a later time.

On the other hand, Job makes little sense without the opening and closing sections. The idea that a single ancient text could not mix prose and poetry is false (see "The Bulletin and Poetic Accounts of the Battle of Kadesh" on p. 353). In addition, there is nothing about the Elihu texts that requires us to consider them to be by a later writer. We have no compelling reason to doubt that Job was the work of a single author.

Further, we have every reason to believe that the author—though not Job or his friends—was Israelite, based upon his use of the covenant name, Yahweh, for God. The story itself, however, is of much more ancient origin, most likely passed along by oral or written tradition. The author evidently made a deliberate effort to preserve the archaic, non-Israelite flavor of the language of Job and his friends.

Most interpreters consider the tenth century B.C.—the age of Solomon—to be the earliest possible date for Job. Indeed, the majority of scholars today consider the work to be postexilic. However, a postexilic date seems unlikely in light of other ancient Near Eastern texts of the same genre. A large number of "pessimistic" texts from the ancient world to one degree or another parallel the book of Job in that they engage the problem of suffering and the apparent indifference of heaven. These include texts from Mesopotamia ("A Man and His God" on p. 771 and "The Babylonian Theodicy" on p. 776) and Egypt ("The Desire for Justice in the Eloquent Peasant" on p. 1226). These are very ancient documents; "A Man and His God" comes from the Old Babylonian period (early second millennium B.C.) and the "Eloquent Peasant" from the New Kingdom period (middle to late second millennium B.C.).

The period of Solomon was a high-water mark for Israel's international contacts, wealth and concern for wisdom—a time when the intellectuals of Jerusalem would have had contact with ancient wisdom texts, including material focusing on the sufferer.

AUDIENCE

If the book was indeed written during the Solomonic period, Job's earliest readers would have been both Israelite thinkers and righteous sufferers living in the united kingdom at that time.

CULTURAL FACTS AND HIGHLIGHTS

Job sets up the problem of the righteous sufferer. The conventional answer people of Solomon's day gave to the question of why people suffer is that they were being punished for their own sins or those of their forebears (cf. Jn 9), and this is the very answer Job's friends proposed. But the reader knows from the outset that Job is suffering because he is *righteous* (Job 1). Thus, when Job rails against his pain and contends that he has not deserved it (e.g., ch. 31), the early reader—who had insider knowledge from the prelude—recognized that he spoke the truth. Unable to fall back on the pat answers that were almost universally accepted at the time, readers were forced to wrestle with the question along with Job as they worked their way through the text to God's final answer. The resultant new understanding of the meaning of suffering and the justice of God, contrary as it was to the conventional wisdom of the day, must have astonished them.

TIMELINE

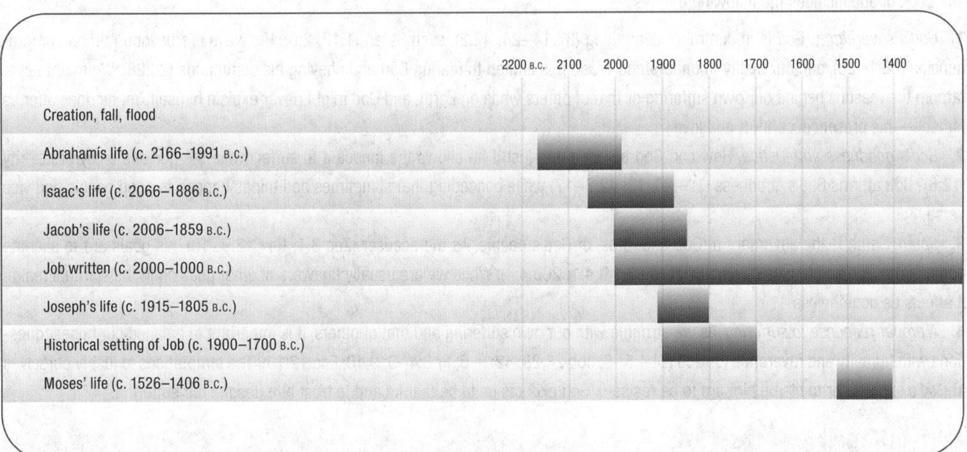

AS YOU READ

Imagine yourself in the sandals of Job, lying prostrate on the ground in agony while your entire world rocks around you. Then envision your own believing friends approaching you, not with words of Biblical comfort but with ominous warnings and pleas for you to examine your life for some terrible, encroaching sin. Would you, like Job, dare to protest, whether mildly or with vehemence? Bringing the issue closer to home, has anyone in your experience raised the question of sin or lack of faith when illness or reversal came your way?

Try to envision yourself in direct conversation with your Maker. How would you have responded to God's challenging words?

DID YOU KNOW?

- The Hebrew for the word "donkeys" is feminine in form. Donkeys that produced offspring were highly valued (1:3).
- Job, like the patriarchs Abraham, Isaac and Jacob, functioned as a priest for his family. He took his sacrificial obligation seriously, making atonement even for sins of the heart (1:5).
- Job's friends adopted a drastic form of mourning, usually reserved for death or total disaster. They tore their robes of nobility, wailed and threw dust into the air—then sat in silence before Job for seven days and nights. To speak before the individual in mourning did so was considered bad taste (2:12–13).
- The ancient Israelites, despite their limited knowledge of astronomy, were awed by the fact that God had created the constellations (9:9).
- Most people of the ancient Near East believed that at death everyone went down to the netherworld, a dark, dreary place under the earth, ruled by various gods. People there were thought to endure a shadowy, sleepy existence from which there was no escape (10:21).
- The Canaanite deity Mot ("Death") was portrayed as having a devouring throat that reached from earth to sky (18:13–14). The prophet Isaiah (Isa 25:18) reversed the figure, picturing God swallowing up death forever.
- Although Job was not an Israelite, he worshiped the one true God (23:13).
- The Hebrew word *behemoth* means "beast par excellence." It refers to a large land animal, possibly the hippopotamus or the elephant (40:15).

THEMES

The book of Job includes the following themes:

1. *God's sovereignty.* God is in control of everything (37:14–24; 42:2), even Satan (1:12; 2:6). His ways are beyond human comprehension (28:1–28), and our ability to understand wisdom is limited to fearing God and obeying his commands (28:28). We might never fathom the reasons behind our own suffering or that of others while on Earth, and God might never explain himself. Yet he does offer us himself—his presence, comfort and love.

2. *God's goodness and justice.* How can God be good and just if he allows the innocent to suffer while the godless enjoy prosperity (12:6)? Job affirms God's goodness (1:1—2:13; 42:7–17) while conceding that sometimes bad things happen to good people and vice versa.

3. *Satan.* Satan is the adversary of God and, thus, of God's people. As the accuser (Zec 3:1; Rev 12:9–10), his goals are to alienate people from God and to generate unbelief (Ge 3; Mt 4:1; 2Co 4:4). While we are usually unaware of what goes on in the spiritual realm, it affects us nonetheless.

4. *A proper response to suffering.* As we struggle with our own suffering and that of others, it is important to balance our honest questions with humility and reverence for God (Dt 4:5–6; Job 28:28; 42:1–6; Pr 8:4–9; 9:10; Ecc 12:13). The temptations to justify ourselves at God's expense or to blame him are to be resisted. God expects us to be faithful and to trust him despite our suffering.

OUTLINE

- I. Prologue: Job's Happiness; Job's Testing (1–2)
- II. Dialogue–Dispute: Job and His Friends (3–27)
  - A. Job's Opening Lament (3)
  - B. Round 1: Eliphaz, Bildad, Zophar Speak; Job Answers (4–14)
  - C. Round 2: Three Friends Speak; Job Answers (15–21)
  - D. Round 3: Two Friends Speak; Job Answers (22–26)
  - E. Job's Closing Speech (27)
- III. Interlude on Wisdom (28)
- IV. Monologues (29:1—42:6)
  - A. Job (29–31)
  - B. Elihu (32–37)
  - C. God (38:1—42:6)
- V. Epilogue: God Judges Three Friends; Job Restored (42:7–17)

Prologue

1:1 [a]Jer 25:20 [b]Eze 14:14,20; Jas 5:11 [c]Ge 6:9; 17:1 [d]Ge 22:12; Ex 18:21 1:2 [e]Job 42:13
1 In the land of Uz[a] there lived a man whose name was Job.[b] This
man was blameless[c] and upright; he feared God[d] and shunned
evil. 2 He had seven sons and three daughters,[e] 3 and he owned sev-
en thousand sheep, three thousand camels, five hundred yoke of
oxen and five hundred donkeys, and had a large number of servants.
1:3 [f]Job 29:25 He was the greatest man[f] among all the people of the East.
4 His sons used to take turns holding feasts in their homes, and
they would invite their three sisters to eat and drink with them. 5 When
a period of feasting had run its course, Job would send and have them
1:5 [g]Ge 8:20; Job 42:8 [h]Job 8:4 [i]1Ki 21:10,13 purified. Early in the morning he would sacrifice a burnt offering[g] for
each of them, thinking, "Perhaps my children have sinned[h] and cursed
God[i] in their hearts." This was Job's regular custom.

Job's First Test

1:6 [j]Job 38:7 [k]Job 2:1 6 One day the angels[a][j] came to present themselves before the
LORD, and Satan[b] also came with them.[k] 7 The LORD said to Satan,
"Where have you come from?"
Satan answered the LORD, "From roaming through the earth and
1:7 [l]1Pe 5:8 going back and forth in it."[l]
8 Then the LORD said to Satan, "Have you considered my servant
1:8 [m]Jos 1:7; Job 42:7-8 [n]ver 1 Job?[m] There is no one on earth like him; he is blameless and upright,
a man who fears God and shuns evil."[n]
1:9 [o]1Ti 6:5 9 "Does Job fear God for nothing?"[o] Satan replied. 10 "Have you not
1:10 [p]Ps 34:7 [q]ver 3; Job 29:6; 31:25; Ps 128:1-2 put a hedge around him and his household and everything he has?[p]
You have blessed the work of his hands, so that his flocks and herds
are spread throughout the land.[q] 11 But stretch out your hand and
1:11 [r]Job 19:21 [s]Job 2:5 strike everything he has,[r] and he will surely curse you to your face."[s]
12 The LORD said to Satan, "Very well, then, everything he has is in your hands, but on the man him-
self do not lay a finger."
Then Satan went out from the presence of the LORD.
13 One day when Job's sons and daughters were feasting and drinking wine at the oldest brother's
house, 14 a messenger came to Job and said, "The oxen were plowing and the donkeys were grazing nearby,
1:15 [t]Ge 10:7; Job 6:19 15 and the Sabeans[t] attacked and carried them off. They put the servants to the sword, and I am the only
one who has escaped to tell you!"

ANCIENT VOICES

The house of the king perished,
who had seven brothers,
eight siblings.
Kirta—(his)* family was crushed,
Kirta—(his) home was destroyed.
His rightful wife he never obtained,
even his legitimate spouse.
A(nother) woman he married and
she disappeared,
even the kinswoman who had
become his.
A third spouse died in good health,
a fourth in illness.
A fifth Rasap gathered in,
a sixth the lad(s) of Yammu,
the seventh of them fell by the sword.
Kirta saw his family,
he saw his family crushed,
his dwelling utterly destroyed.
Completely did the family perish,
in their entirety the heirs.

*Words or partial words in parentheses added by translator for clarity

—THE KIRTA EPIC

See "The Kirta Epic" article on the next page.

[a] 6 Hebrew *the sons of God* [b] 6 *Satan* means *accuser.*

1:1—2:13 A figure like Job, standing outside the Abrahamic and Mosaic covenants, was an ideal vehicle for Biblical Wisdom Literature, concerned as it was with the common ways and demands of God rather than with his peculiarly theocratic government of Israel. There are only a few direct references to the Mosaic Law in Biblical Wisdom Literature.

Job in some ways appears to have been like one of the patriarchs of old, as is evident from his longevity and God's revelation to him by theophany (God visibly manifesting himself). On the other hand, there are very few social or economic customs in Job that tie the book to the patriarchal period or, for that matter, to any other period. The Chaldeans were actually a late people, not appearing in the historical record until about 1000 B.C. Still, Job's patriarch-like status allows him to stand as an archetype for the suffering human being.

The particular purpose of the book of Job as Wisdom Literature is to articulate and point the direction for a true apologetic for the faith. The doctrine of God as incomprehensible Creator and sovereign Lord is offered in this book as the fundamental reality with which humans must reckon as religious beings serving God amid the historical tensions of life. It is also the presupposition with which a philosophical inquirer must begin. This enterprise is illustrated by the continuing debate to come between Job and his friends over the problem of theodicy (God's goodness versus evil). The folly of depending for answers on human observation and speculation is portrayed by the eventual silencing of the trio who represented it. The book of Job identifies the way of the covenant with the way of wisdom (cf. 28:28) and so brings philosophy under the authority of divine revelation.

1:1 Uz was a large territory east of the Jordan River (see v. 3). It included Edom in the south (see Ge 36:28; La 4:21) and the Aramean lands in the north (see Ge 10:23; 22:21). The story of Job is set in the second millennium B.C., although the book itself was written much later.

In the Bible God alone, who lacks nothing in terms of goodness or excellence, is presented as truly perfect. Everything he is, thinks and does has the character of perfection (Dt 32:4; 2Sa 22:31; Job 37:16; Ps 18:30; 19:7; Mt 5:48). When human beings are called perfect in the Old Testament, the implication is that they were "upright" or "blameless" (this latter word was chosen by the NIV translators to describe Job in this verse; cf. Ge 6:9; Ps 37:37).

1:3 The Hebrew for the word "donkeys" is feminine in form. Donkeys that produced offspring were highly valued.

1:5 On special occasions feasts might last for a week (see Ge 29:27; Jdg 14:12).

Job, like the patriarchs Abraham, Isaac and Jacob, functioned as a priest for his family. He took his sacrificial obligation seriously, making atonement even for sins of the heart. The matter of cursing or declining to curse God is key in the development of this ancient drama.

1:15 The Sabeans were nomads from Sheba living in southwestern Arabia (see the note on 1Ki 10:1). Their descendants became wealthy

16 While he was still speaking, another messenger came and said, "The fire of God fell from the sky[u] **1:16** [u]Ge 19:24
and burned up the sheep and the servants,[v] and I am the only one who has escaped to tell you!" [v]Lev 10:2; Nu 11:1-3
17 While he was still speaking, another messenger came and said, "The Chaldeans[w] formed three raid- **1:17** [w]Ge 11:28, 31
ing parties and swept down on your camels and carried them off. They put the servants to the sword, and
I am the only one who has escaped to tell you!"
18 While he was still speaking, yet another messenger came and said, "Your sons and daughters were
feasting and drinking wine at the oldest brother's house, 19 when suddenly a mighty wind[x] swept in from **1:19** [x]Jer 4:11; 13:24
the desert and struck the four corners of the house. It collapsed on them and they are dead, and I am the
only one who has escaped to tell you!"
20 At this, Job got up and tore his robe[y] and shaved his head. Then he fell to the ground in worship[z] **1:20** [y]Ge 37:29 [z]1Pe 5:6
21 and said:

> "Naked I came from my mother's womb,
> and naked I will depart.[a][a] **1:21** [a]Ecc 5:15; 1Ti 6:7 [b]1Sa 2:7 [c]Job 2:10; Eph 5:20; 1Th 5:18
> The LORD gave and the LORD has taken away;[b]
> may the name of the LORD be praised."[c]

22 In all this, Job did not sin by charging God with wrongdoing.[d] **1:22** [d]Job 2:10

[a] 21 Or *will return there*

---

traders in spices, gold and precious stones (see 1Ki 10:1–13; Ps 72:10,15; Isa 60:6; Jer 6:20; Eze 27:22; Joel 3:8). Job 6:19 refers to the Sabeans as "traveling merchants" and associates them with Tema (about 350 miles [565 km] southeast of Jerusalem).

ANCIENT TEXTS AND ARTIFACTS

The Kirta Epic

JOB 1 In 1930 excavators at Ras Shamra[1] discovered the fragments of an epic poem among the writings of **Ugarit**.[2,3] The text, called Kirta (or Keret) after the name of its hero, is sometimes compared to the story of Job or to that of David. There are similarities, but we are wise to exercise caution not to make too much of these correlations.

The poem depicts Kirta as a king who loses all of his wives and children to various disasters. He weeps bitterly, but in a dream the god El tells him what to do: He must make a sacrifice to El and then lead his army in an assault on the city of Udmu. He complies, with the result that Pabil, king of Udmu, submits to Kirta and allows him to take his daughter Hurraya as his wife. Hurraya bears Kirta many children, after which he falls seriously ill, apparently because of a failure to keep a vow to the goddess Ashera. Hurraya proceeds to prepare a banquet to mourn her husband's grave condition, and his son Iluhau and daughter Thitmanatu especially grieve the prospect of his death. El then fashions a female healer, who restores Kirta's health. After this, however, another of Kirta's sons, Yassubu, declares that Kirta is no longer fit to reign and asks him to abdicate so that he, Yassubu, may take his place. The tale ends somewhat inconclusively, with Kirta cursing Yassubu.

The Epic of Kirta at least superficially recalls the story of Job: It portrays a hero who loses his children (Job 1) and his health (ch. 2) but who also moves toward restoration (ch. 42). And the rebellion of Yassubu recalls Absalom's attempt to usurp the throne (2Sa 15–18) in the story of David. Even so, the differences between Kirta and the Biblical narratives are enormous, and we can hardly suggest that either Scriptural account may have been derived from Kirta. Even the similarities are apparently coincidental: The account of Absalom's rebellion, for example, has nothing in common with that of Yassubu beyond the fact that both concern a son who desires to overthrow his father (hardly an unusual theme in ancient monarchical societies). While Kirta is a pagan tale of myth and magic that follows the ups and downs in the career of its hero, the Biblical texts focus on the repercussions of human behavior and the theological problem of evil. Job in particular wrestles with the questions of justice, suffering and divine involvement in the world on a profound level, while Kirta does none of this.

[1]For another epic found at Ras Sharma with at least one element of similarity to Job, see "The Tale of Aqhat" on page 761. [2]See Glossary on page 2080 for definitions of bolded words. [3]See "Ugarit/Ras Shamra" on page 819.

THE HOLY SCRIPTURES

<table>
<tr><th>Hebrew Names for the Books</th><th colspan="2">Hebrew Arrangement and Classification</th><th colspan="2">English Arrangement and Classification</th></tr>
<tr><td>In the beginning
These are the names
And he called
In the wilderness
These are the words</td><td>TORAH</td><td>Genesis
Exodus
Leviticus
Numbers
Deuteronomy</td><td>Genesis
Exodus
Leviticus
Numbers
Deuteronomy</td><td>LAW
(Pentateuch)</td></tr>
<tr><td>Joshua
Judges
1 Samuel
2 Samuel
1 Kings
2 Kings</td><td>FORMER PROPHETS</td><td>Joshua
Judges
1 Samuel
2 Samuel
1 Kings
2 Kings</td><td rowspan="2">Joshua
Judges
Ruth
1 Samuel
2 Samuel
1 Kings
2 Kings
Ezra
Nehemiah
Esther</td><td rowspan="2">HISTORY</td></tr>
<tr><td rowspan="4">Isaiah
Jeremiah
Ezekiel
Hosea
Joel
Amos
Obadiah
Jonah
Micah
Nahum
Habakkuk
Zephaniah
Haggai
Zechariah
Malachi</td><td rowspan="4">LATTER PROPHETS</td><td rowspan="4">Isaiah
Jeremiah
Ezekiel
Hosea
Joel
Amos
Obadiah
Jonah
Micah
Nahum
Habakkuk
Zephaniah
Haggai
Zechariah
Malachi</td></tr>
<tr><td>Job
Psalms
Proverbs
Ecclesiastes
Song of Songs</td><td>POETRY and WISDOM</td></tr>
<tr><td>Isaiah
Jeremiah
Lamentations
Ezekiel
Daniel</td><td>MAJOR PROPHETS</td></tr>
<tr><td rowspan="2">Hosea
Joel
Amos
Obadiah
Jonah
Micah
Nahum
Habakkuk
Zephaniah
Haggai
Zechariah
Malachi</td><td rowspan="2">MINOR PROPHETS</td></tr>
<tr><td>Praises
Job
Proverbs
Ruth
Song of Songs
The Preacher
How!
Esther
Daniel
Ezra
Nehemiah
1 The words of the days
2 The words of the days</td><td>THE WRITINGS
(Hagiographa)</td><td>Psalms
Job
Proverbs
Ruth
Song of Songs
Ecclesiastes
Lamentations
Esther
Daniel
Ezra
Nehemiah
1 Chronicles
2 Chronicles</td></tr>
</table>

Chronological and Background Charts of the Old Testament, p. 12

The Potsherd: Pottery in the Bible

JOB 2 Job, his body covered with boils, sat in an ash heap seeking to relieve his pain through a counterirritant—scraping himself with a broken piece of pottery (Job 2:7–8). Earthenware vessels, used for storing, cooking and serving food and for shipping commodities, were the common containers during antiquity. Most lamps and artistic and cult objects were earthenware as well. Since pottery is brittle, vessels often broke into pieces called **potsherd**s. Isaiah alluded to sherds (i.e., fragments) being used for carrying burning coals and for scooping water from a cistern (Isa 30:14). Notes and letters were often written on potsherds.[1]

Sir Flinders Petrie, in his excavations at Tell el-Hesi in 1890, recognized the archaeological significance of pottery and began classifying pottery and potsherds. His work was carried forward by others, including William Albright, Kathleen Kenyon and Ruth Amiran. The nature of pottery makes it indispensable for archaeology. Clay vessels were fired rock-hard in a kiln, allowing the pieces to survive the ages. Changes through time in the shape, decoration and manufacturing methods of pots can be documented and used for dating purposes. In fact, pottery is the primary means of dating in Palestinian archaeology. Through knowledge of regional and national variations, pottery can also tell the archaeologist something about trade, cultural connections and the movements of people groups. Ancient habitation sites are littered with potsherds, and simply by examining this surface pottery an archaeologist can form a historical picture.

Complete vessels are often recovered from tombs,[2] and sometimes a broken pot can be reconstructed. A trained archaeologist can take pieces of the rim, handle or base ("indicator" or "diagnostic" sherds) and identify the type of vessel from which they came. In recording data about pottery at a dig, precision is critical. It is important to know, for example, exactly where a piece was found. Specialists analyze pottery finds and painstakingly sketch or photograph each piece. Color is significant too, and a sherd's hue and chroma (color saturation) are precisely recorded.

Even though its type may be known, the archaeologist may still be hard pressed to explain a vessel's use. But tomb paintings from ancient Egypt depict vessels in everyday use. Ethnoarchaeology, which examines the links between a society's material culture and its social and economic customs, can help, and the Bible itself offers clues. When Rebekah met Abraham's servant at the well in Nahor, she was carrying a water jar on her shoulder (not, as in many cultures, on her head; Ge 24:15). First Kings 17:14 indicates that flour was kept in a jar but oil in a flask (a *tsappahath*). Jars were also used to preserve documents (Jer 32:14), a practice well attested at **Qumran**.

Bichrome jug; an example of Philistine type pottery
Preserving Bible Times; © Dr. James C. Martin

Scholars have developed an extensive inventory of the jars, bowls, cups, decanters, figurines, flasks, urns and lamps discovered from antiquity. Types of pottery from different cultures and eras have distinguishing features, including type of rim or base; presence, absence or type of handles; coloration; and presence of incised or painted decorations. Some vessels have a ribbed texture, while some bowls are carinated (keel-shaped). A container's mouth may be straight or flared, and pottery may have been burnished by rubbing or polishing.

By observing the evolution of styles and techniques, archaeologists can date a piece and from this evidence proceed to date an entire excavation stratum or layer. Carefully documenting stylistic changes, scholars have assembled a fairly complete typology of pottery for the ancient Holy Land. Types and styles have been documented through the **Neolithic** and **Chalcolithic** periods, the **Bronze Age**, the **Iron Age**, the **exilic period**, the **Persian** and **Hellenistic period**s and the **Roman** and **Byzantine period**s.

Pottery analysis is also critically important in Greco-Roman studies. Early Greek pottery (c. 1050–700 B.C.) featured painted decorations in the form of geometric shapes. Such decoration eventually developed into pottery with highly naturalistic, painted scenes involving people, animals and various objects. Around 720 B.C. black-figure decoration was invented, with silhouettes incised onto vessels and black, red and white paint applied. Around 525 B.C. the red-figure technique was invented, in which the decoration was left in the natural red color of the clay, with thin painted lines in various colors providing highlighting; the background was painted black. Scholars have learned the names of some of the craftsmen and can describe the distinctive characteristics of their work. For example, Greek artisans often painted small inscriptions, such as "Psiax made me," on their pottery.

[1]For example, see "The Lachish Ostraca" on page 1252.

[2]See "Tombs in Ancient Israel" on page 376.

Job's Second Test

2 On another day the angels[a] came to present themselves before the LORD, and Satan also came with
them[e] to present himself before him. 2 And the LORD said to Satan, "Where have you come from?"
Satan answered the LORD, "From roaming through the earth and going back and forth in it."
3 Then the LORD said to Satan, "Have you considered my servant Job? There is no one on earth like
him; he is blameless and upright, a man who fears God and shuns evil.[f] And he still maintains his integ-
rity,[g] though you incited me against him to ruin him without any reason."[h]
4 "Skin for skin!" Satan replied. "A man will give all he has for his own life. 5 But stretch out your hand
and strike his flesh and bones,[i] and he will surely curse you to your face."[j]
6 The LORD said to Satan, "Very well, then, he is in your hands; but you must spare his life."[k]
7 So Satan went out from the presence of the LORD and afflicted Job with painful sores from the soles
of his feet to the top of his head.[l] 8 Then Job took a piece of broken pottery and scraped himself with it
as he sat among the ashes.[m]
9 His wife said to him, "Are you still holding on to your integrity? Curse God and die!"
10 He replied, "You are talking like a foolish[b] woman. Shall we accept good from God, and not
trouble?"[n]
In all this, Job did not sin in what he said.[o]

Job's Three Friends

11 When Job's three friends, Eliphaz the Temanite,[p] Bildad the Shuhite[q] and Zophar the Naamathite,
heard about all the troubles that had come upon him, they set out from their homes and met together
by agreement to go and sympathize with him and comfort him.[r] 12 When they saw him from a distance,
they could hardly recognize him; they began to weep aloud, and they tore their robes and sprinkled dust
on their heads.[s] 13 Then they sat on the ground with him for seven days and seven nights.[t] No one said
a word to him, because they saw how great his suffering was.

Job Speaks

3 After this, Job opened his mouth and cursed the day of his birth. 2 He said:

3 "May the day of my birth perish,
and the night it was said, 'A boy is born!'[u]

2:1 [e]Job 1:6
2:3 [f]Job 1:1,8 [g]Job 27:6 [h]Job 9:17
2:5 [i]Job 19:20 [j]Job 1:11
2:6 [k]Job 1:12
2:7 [l]Dt 28:35; Job 7:5
2:8 [m]Job 42:6; Jer 6:26; Eze 27:30; Mt 11:21
2:10 [n]Job 1:21 [o]Job 1:22; Ps 39:1; Jas 1:12; 5:11
2:11 [p]Ge 36:11; Jer 49:7 [q]Ge 25:2 [r]Job 42:11; Ro 12:15
2:12 [s]Jos 7:6; Ne 9:1; La 2:10; Eze 27:30
2:13 [t]Ge 50:10; Eze 3:15
3:3 [u]Job 10:18-19; Jer 20:14-18

[a] 1 Hebrew *the sons of God* [b] 10 The Hebrew word rendered *foolish* denotes moral deficiency.

2:4 "Skin for skin!" was most likely a proverb that originally expressed a willingness to barter one animal skin for another of equal value.

2:7 Job's illness included painful, festering sores and scabs covering his whole body (7:5); nightmares (7:14); skin that peeled and became black (30:28,30); disfigurement and a hideous appearance (2:12; 19:19); bad breath (19:17); emaciation (17:7; 19:20); fever (30:30); and unremitting pain (30:17). The Hebrew for "sores" (2:7) is translated "boil(s)" in Exodus 9:9, Leviticus 13:18 and 2 Kings 20:7.

2:8 The familiar Biblical expression "dust and ashes" (e.g., Ge 18:27) is a play on words (*aphar* and *epher*), signifying the origin of the human body from the ordinary chemical elements. It contrasts the lowliness of humankind with the dignity of God. Ashes were sprinkled over a person, or an individual sat among ashes, as a sign of mourning (2Sa 13:19; Job 2:8). The word is often united with "sackcloth" to express mourning (Jer 6:26; see "Sackcloth and Ashes: Rituals of Lamentation" on p. 820). For information on broken pottery, see "The Potsherd: Pottery in the Bible" on page 738.

2:11–13 Stylistic comparison of other ancient wisdom writings with Job reveals similarities (see "The Poor and the Afflicted in Ancient Wisdom Literature" on p. 981), but also highlights Job's uniqueness. The dialogue form of the book is paralleled to an extent in Egyptian and Babylonian wisdom poetry, and the various individual literary forms employed in Job (psalms of lament and thanksgiving, proverbs, covenant oaths, etc.) are not novelties. Nevertheless, as a masterful blend of a remarkably rich variety of forms within a narrative framework, with exquisite lyric and dramatic qualities, all devoted to didactic purpose, the book of Job creates its own literary species. Of particular significance is the bracketing of the poetic dialogue (to begin at ch. 3) with the prose (or better, semipoetic) prologue and epilogue. This A-B-A structure is found elsewhere in the ancient Near East (e.g., in the Code of Hammurabi [see "Hammurabi" on p. 271) and in the Eloquent Peasant [see "The Desire for Justice in the Eloquent Peasant" on p. 1226) and thus supports the book's integrity.

2:11 Eliphaz, the chief of Job's three friends, came from Teman, traditionally famous for its wise men (Jer 49:7). His speeches showed clearer reasoning than those of the other two friends. In his first speech (Job 4–5) Eliphaz traced back all affliction to sin, through the natural operation of cause and effect, and admonished Job to make peace with God. In his second address (ch. 15) Eliphaz expressed irritation at Job's sarcasm, reiterated his earlier arguments and depicted strongly the fate of the wicked. In his third monologue (ch. 22) Eliphaz definitely charged Job with sin and pointed out to him the path of restoration. In 42:7–9 God addressed Eliphaz as the chief of Job's friends, commanding him to make a sacrifice in expiation for having wrongly accused Job.

Bildad was evidently a descendant of Shuah (Ge 25:2), a son of Abraham by Keturah, and one who had become the patriarch of an Arab tribe. Bildad made three speeches (Job 8; 18; 25), and his distinctive character as a "traditionalist" can best be seen in 8:8–10.

Zophar, the Naamathite, had probably come from Naamah in northern Arabia (2:11; 11:1; 20:1; 42:9).

2:12–13 Job's friends adopted a drastic form of mourning, usually reserved for death or total disaster. They tore their robes of nobility, wailed and threw dust into the air—then sat in silence before Job for seven days and nights (cf. Ge 50:10; Jos 7:6; 2Sa 13:19; Eze 3:15). To speak before the sufferer did would have been considered bad taste.

[4]That day—may it turn to darkness;
may God above not care about it;
may no light shine upon it.
[5]May darkness and deep shadow[a][v] claim it once more;
may a cloud settle over it;
may blackness overwhelm its light.
[6]That night—may thick darkness[w] seize it;
may it not be included among the days of the year
nor be entered in any of the months.
[7]May that night be barren;
may no shout of joy be heard in it.
[8]May those who curse days[b] curse that day,
those who are ready to rouse Leviathan.[x]
[9]May its morning stars become dark;
may it wait for daylight in vain
and not see the first rays of dawn,[y]
[10]for it did not shut the doors of the womb on me
to hide trouble from my eyes.

[11]"Why did I not perish at birth,
and die as I came from the womb?[z]
[12]Why were there knees to receive me[a]
and breasts that I might be nursed?
[13]For now I would be lying down[b] in peace;
I would be asleep and at rest[c]
[14]with kings and counselors of the earth,[d]
who built for themselves places now lying in ruins,[e]
[15]with rulers[f] who had gold,
who filled their houses with silver.[g]
[16]Or why was I not hidden in the ground like a stillborn child,[h]
like an infant who never saw the light of day?
[17]There the wicked cease from turmoil,
and there the weary are at rest.[i]
[18]Captives also enjoy their ease;
they no longer hear the slave driver's shout.[j]
[19]The small and the great are there,
and the slave is freed from his master.

[20]"Why is light given to those in misery,
and life to the bitter of soul,[k]
[21]to those who long for death that does not come,[l]
who search for it more than for hidden treasure,[m]
[22]who are filled with gladness
and rejoice when they reach the grave?
[23]Why is life given to a man
whose way is hidden,
whom God has hedged in?[n]
[24]For sighing comes to me instead of food;[o]
my groans pour out like water.[p]
[25]What I feared has come upon me;
what I dreaded[q] has happened to me.
[26]I have no peace, no quietness;
I have no rest,[r] but only turmoil."

[a] 5 *Or and the shadow of death* [b] 8 *Or the sea*

3:5 [v]Job 10:21, 22; Ps 23:4; Jer 2:6; 13:16
3:6 [w]Job 23:17
3:8 [x]Job 41:1,8, 10,25
3:9 [y]Job 41:18
3:11 [z]Job 10:18
3:12 [a]Ge 30:3; Isa 66:12
3:13 [b]Job 17:13 [c]Job 7:8-10,21; 10:22; 14:10-12; 19:27; 21:13,23
3:14 [d]Job 12:17 [e]Job 15:28
3:15 [f]Job 12:21 [g]Job 27:17
3:16 [h]Ps 58:8; Ecc 6:3
3:17 [i]Job 17:16
3:18 [j]Job 39:7
3:20 [k]1Sa 1:10; Jer 20:18; Eze 27:30-31
3:21 [l]Rev 9:6 [m]Pr 2:4
3:23 [n]Job 19:6,8, 12; Ps 88:8; La 3:7
3:24 [o]Job 6:7; 33:20 [p]Ps 42:3,4
3:25 [q]Job 30:15
3:26 [r]Job 7:4,14

Eliphaz

4 Then Eliphaz the Temanite replied:

4:2 [s]Job 32:20
4:3 [t]Isa 35:3; Heb 12:12

2 "If someone ventures a word with you, will you be impatient?
But who can keep from speaking?[s]
3 Think how you have instructed many,
how you have strengthened feeble hands.[t]

4:1—5:27 See the note on Eliphaz at 2:11.

4:1 Teman, an Edomite town south of the Dead Sea, was renowned for its wisdom (see Jer 49:7).

ANCIENT TEXTS AND ARTIFACTS

Dream Oracles in the Ancient World

JOB 4 The belief in dream oracles is well attested in the ancient world, including in the Bible. Job's friend Eliphaz stated that he had received in a dream a divine message relating to Job's misery (Job 4:12–21). Elihu also expressed his knowledge that dreams are one means by which God communicates with people (33:14–18). The Lord visited the **patriarch** Jacob in a nocturnal vision (Ge 28:11–19). His son Joseph also received prophetic dreams (Ge 37:5–11), as did Solomon (1Ki 3:5–15), prophets in general (Nu 12:6), Daniel (Da 7) and Joseph the carpenter (Mt 1:20–24; 2:13).

Dream oracles were not exclusive to Israel, however. Joseph, the son of Jacob, interpreted the dreams of the pharaoh and his servants (Ge 40:5–22; 41:15–32), Daniel interpreted Nebuchadnezzar's dream (Da 4:4–27), and the Magi were warned in a dream not to return to King Herod (Mt 2:12).

Of course, not all dream oracles can be considered legitimate. If the omen portended in the dream encouraged the worship of anyone besides the one true God, or if the apparent implication of the dream did not come to pass, that message did not issue from the Lord (Dt 18:20–22).

Numerous texts from outside of Israel attest to the importance placed upon dreams throughout the ancient Near East:

- Prophetic dreams are attested at **Mari** (eighteenth century B.C.).[1] One text describes a dream that was repeated, as was the pharaoh's in Genesis 41.
- When seeking instructions on temple building, King Gudea of Lagash invited the deity Nirgirsu to visit him by offering sacrifices and lying down in the temple to sleep.[2]
- When venturing forth to battle a great monster, the legendary hero Gilgamesh and his companion Enkidu encouraged the gods to give them dream oracles.[3]
- **Ugaritic** texts provide examples of such dreams. In the Epic of Kirta the god El speaks to the hero in his sleep.[4]
- Handbooks for dream interpretation have been uncovered in New Kingdom Egypt (sixteenth–eleventh centuries B.C.). For example, if a man saw himself in a dream submerged in the Nile, that was a good omen, signifying that he had been purified of all evil. But seeing a dwarf in a dream portended tragedy: The dreamer's life would be shortened by half.

Dreams were one of the many ways people of the ancient world believed that humans received divine messages. It is important to observe, however, that the Bible contains no guidebook for interpreting dreams. There is no magical code we can follow. If God communicates by a dream, only God can give the interpretation (Ge 40:8).

The dream of Gilgamesh from the Epic of Gilgamesh; Babylonia, nineteenth–eighteenth centuries B.C.

© The Schøyen Collection; photography courtesy of Mr. Martin Schøyen

[1]See also "Prophets in the Bible and Pagan Nations" on page 1457. [2]See "The Cylinders of Gudea" on page 485. [3]For more information on Gilgamesh, see "Ecclesiastes and the Epic of Gilgamesh" on page 1027. [4]See "The Kirta Epic" on page 736.

4 Your words have supported those who stumbled;
you have strengthened faltering knees.[u]
5 But now trouble comes to you, and you are discouraged;
it strikes[v] you, and you are dismayed.[w]
6 Should not your piety be your confidence[x]
and your blameless[y] ways your hope?

7 "Consider now: Who, being innocent, has ever perished?[z]
Where were the upright ever destroyed?[a]
8 As I have observed, those who plow evil[b]
and those who sow trouble reap it.[c]
9 At the breath of God[d] they are destroyed;
at the blast of his anger they perish.[e]
10 The lions may roar and growl,
yet the teeth of the great lions are broken.[f]
11 The lion perishes for lack of prey,[g]
and the cubs of the lioness are scattered.

12 "A word was secretly brought to me,
my ears caught a whisper[h] of it.[i]
13 Amid disquieting dreams in the night,
when deep sleep falls on men,[j]
14 fear and trembling seized me
and made all my bones shake.[k]
15 A spirit glided past my face,
and the hair on my body stood on end.
16 It stopped,
but I could not tell what it was.
A form stood before my eyes,
and I heard a hushed voice:
17 'Can a mortal be more righteous than God?[l]
Can a man be more pure than his Maker?[m]
18 If God places no trust in his servants,
if he charges his angels with error,[n]
19 how much more those who live in houses of clay,[o]
whose foundations[p] are in the dust,[q]
who are crushed more readily than a moth!
20 Between dawn and dusk they are broken to pieces;
unnoticed, they perish forever.[r]
21 Are not the cords of their tent pulled up,[s]
so that they die without wisdom?'[a][t]

5

"Call if you will, but who will answer you?
To which of the holy ones[u] will you turn?
2 Resentment kills a fool,
and envy slays the simple.[v]
3 I myself have seen a fool taking root,[w]
but suddenly his house was cursed.[x]
4 His children are far from safety,[y]
crushed in court[z] without a defender.

4:4 [u]Isa 35:3; Heb 12:12
4:5 [v]Job 19:21 [w]Job 6:14
4:6 [x]Pr 3:26 [y]Job 1:1
4:7 [z]Job 36:7 [a]Job 8:20; Ps 37:25
4:8 [b]Job 15:35 [c]Pr 22:8; Hos 10:13; Gal 6:7-8
4:9 [d]Job 15:30; Isa 30:33; 2Th 2:8 [e]Job 40:13
4:10 [f]Job 5:15; Ps 58:6
4:11 [g]Job 27:14; Ps 34:10
4:12 [h]Job 26:14 [i]Job 33:14
4:13 [j]Job 33:15
4:14 [k]Jer 23:9; Hab 3:16
4:17 [l]Job 9:2 [m]Job 35:10
4:18 [n]Job 15:15
4:19 [o]Job 10:9 [p]Job 22:16 [q]Ge 2:7
4:20 [r]Job 14:2, 20; 20:7; Ps 90:5-6
4:21 [s]Job 8:22 [t]Job 18:21; 36:12
5:1 [u]Job 15:15
5:2 [v]Pr 12:16
5:3 [w]Ps 37:35; Jer 12:2 [x]Job 24:18
5:4 [y]Job 4:11 [z]Am 5:12

[a] 21 Some interpreters end the quotation after verse 17.

4:12–21 Eliphaz claimed to have received a divine revelation through a dream. His advice to Job was based upon this hair-raising mystical experience (see v. 15; see also "Dream Oracles in the Ancient World" on p. 741.)

5:4 The city gate was the traditional place for trials; there the elders sat to hold court (see "The City Gate" on p. 392).

5:5 [a]Job 18:8-10
5:7 [b]Job 14:1
5:8 [c]Ps 35:23; 50:15
5:9 [d]Job 42:3; Ps 40:5
5:10 [e]Job 36:28
5:11 [f]Ps 113:7-8
5:12 [g]Ne 4:15; Ps 33:10
5:13 [h]1Co 3:19*
5:14 [i]Job 12:25 [j]Dt 28:29
5:15 [k]Ps 35:10 [l]Job 4:10
5:16 [m]Ps 107:42
5:17 [n]Jas 1:12 [o]Ps 94:12; Pr 3:11 [p]Heb 12:5-11
5:18 [q]Isa 30:26 [r]1Sa 2:6
5:19 [s]Ps 34:19; 91:10
5:20 [t]Ps 33:19 [u]Ps 144:10
5:21 [v]Ps 31:20 [w]Ps 91:5
5:22 [x]Ps 91:13; Eze 34:25
5:23 [y]Ps 91:12 [z]Isa 11:6-9
5:24 [a]Job 8:6
5:25 [b]Ps 112:2 [c]Ps 72:16; Isa 44:3-4
5:26 [d]Ge 15:15

5 The hungry consume his harvest,[a]
taking it even from among thorns,
and the thirsty pant after his wealth.
6 For hardship does not spring from the soil,
nor does trouble sprout from the ground.
7 Yet man is born to trouble[b]
as surely as sparks fly upward.

8 "But if it were I, I would appeal to God;
I would lay my cause before him.[c]
9 He performs wonders that cannot be fathomed,[d]
miracles that cannot be counted.
10 He bestows rain on the earth;
he sends water upon the countryside.[e]
11 The lowly he sets on high,[f]
and those who mourn are lifted to safety.
12 He thwarts the plans[g] of the crafty,
so that their hands achieve no success.
13 He catches the wise in their craftiness,[h]
and the schemes of the wily are swept away.
14 Darkness[i] comes upon them in the daytime;
at noon they grope as in the night.[j]
15 He saves the needy[k] from the sword in their mouth;
he saves them from the clutches of the powerful.[l]
16 So the poor have hope,
and injustice shuts its mouth.[m]

17 "Blessed is the man whom God corrects;[n]
so do not despise the discipline[o] of the Almighty.[a][p]
18 For he wounds, but he also binds up;[q]
he injures, but his hands also heal.[r]
19 From six calamities he will rescue you;
in seven no harm will befall you.[s]
20 In famine[t] he will ransom you from death,
and in battle from the stroke of the sword.[u]
21 You will be protected from the lash of the tongue,[v]
and need not fear[w] when destruction comes.
22 You will laugh at destruction and famine,
and need not fear the beasts of the earth.[x]
23 For you will have a covenant with the stones[y] of the field,
and the wild animals will be at peace with you.[z]
24 You will know that your tent is secure;
you will take stock of your property and find nothing missing.[a]
25 You will know that your children will be many,[b]
and your descendants like the grass of the earth.[c]
26 You will come to the grave in full vigor,[d]
like sheaves gathered in season.

27 "We have examined this, and it is true.
So hear it and apply it to yourself."

[a] 17 Hebrew *Shaddai*; here and throughout Job

5:7 The word "sparks" is literally "sons of Resheph." In Canaanite mythology Resheph was a god of plague and destruction. "(Sons of) Resheph" is the idea behind several poetic images in the Old Testament for fire (SS 8:6), bolts of lightning (Ps 78:48) and pestilence (Dt 32:24; Hab 3:5).

Job

6 Then Job replied:

2 "If only my anguish could be weighed
and all my misery be placed on the scales![e]
3 It would surely outweigh the sand[f] of the seas—
no wonder my words have been impetuous.[g]
4 The arrows[h] of the Almighty are in me,[i]
my spirit drinks[j] in their poison;
God's terrors[k] are marshaled against me.[l]
5 Does a wild donkey bray when it has grass,
or an ox bellow when it has fodder?
6 Is tasteless food eaten without salt,
or is there flavor in the white of an egg[a]?
7 I refuse to touch it;
such food makes me ill.[m]

8 "Oh, that I might have my request,
that God would grant what I hope for,[n]
9 that God would be willing to crush me,
to let loose his hand and cut me off![o]
10 Then I would still have this consolation—
my joy in unrelenting pain—
that I had not denied the words[p] of the Holy One.[q]

11 "What strength do I have, that I should still hope?
What prospects, that I should be patient?[r]
12 Do I have the strength of stone?
Is my flesh bronze?

6:2 [e]Job 31:6
6:3 [f]Pr 27:3 [g]Job 23:2
6:4 [h]Ps 38:2 [i]Job 16:12,13 [j]Job 21:20 [k]Job 30:15 [l]Ps 88:15-18
6:7 [m]Job 3:24
6:8 [n]Job 14:13
6:9 [o]Nu 11:15; 1Ki 19:4
6:10 [p]Job 22:22; 23:12 [q]Lev 19:2; Isa 57:15
6:11 [r]Job 21:4

[a] 6 The meaning of the Hebrew for this phrase is uncertain.

Casting Lots

JOB 6 A clay cube inscribed in **Akkadian**[1] provides archaeological evidence for the use of lots in the ancient Near East. This "lot," a cube approximately 1 inch (2.5 cm) in diameter, commemorates the selection by lot of Iahali to serve as the minister of the **Assyrian** king **Shalmaneser III** (c. 828 B.C.). Though other forms of divination were prohibited in Israel (Dt 18:9–14), the casting of lots was permitted. Proverbs 16:33 makes this clear: "The lot is cast into the lap, but its every decision is from the LORD." Lots were cast for various purposes:

✣ They settled the apportionment of land, guaranteeing that it was divinely inherited (Nu 26:55).

✣ They narrowed a field of candidates in determining a selection (Saul in 1Sa 10:20ff.; Matthias in Ac 1:26), order of service (temple personnel in 1Ch 24:5ff.; Zechariah in Lk 1:8ff.) or guilt (Achan in Jos 7:14ff.; Jonathan in 1Sa 14:41ff.).

✣ They were used for dividing or distributing people (orphans in Job 6:27; prisoners of war in Joel 3:3 and Na 3:10).

✣ The sacred lots called the "Urim and Thummin" were used to determine the will of the Lord in a particular matter (Nu 27:21).[2]

[1]See "Languages of the Old Testament World" on page 672. [2]See "The Urim and Thummin" on page 136.

6:13 [s]Job 26:2
6:14 [t]Job 4:5 [u]Job 15:4
6:15 [v]Ps 38:11; Jer 15:18
6:17 [w]Job 24:19
6:19 [x]Ge 25:15; Isa 21:14
6:20 [y]Jer 14:3
6:21 [z]Ps 38:11
6:24 [a]Ps 39:1
6:25 [b]Ecc 12:11
6:26 [c]Job 8:2; 15:3
6:27 [d]Joel 3:3; Na 3:10; 2Pe 2:3
6:28 [e]Job 27:4; 33:1,3; 36:3,4
6:29 [f]Job 23:7, 10; 34:5,36; 42:6
6:30 [g]Job 27:4 [h]Job 12:11
7:1 [i]Job 14:14; Isa 40:2 [j]Job 5:7 [k]Job 14:6
7:2 [l]Lev 19:13
7:3 [m]Job 16:7; Ps 6:6
7:4 [n]Dt 28:67
7:5 [o]Job 17:14; Isa 14:11
7:6 [p]Job 9:25 [q]Job 13:15; 17:11,15
7:7 [r]Ps 78:39; Jas 4:14 [s]Job 9:25

13 Do I have any power to help myself,[s]
now that success has been driven from me?

14 "A despairing man[t] should have the devotion[u] of his friends,
even though he forsakes the fear of the Almighty.
15 But my brothers are as undependable as intermittent streams,[v]
as the streams that overflow
16 when darkened by thawing ice
and swollen with melting snow,
17 but that cease to flow in the dry season,
and in the heat[w] vanish from their channels.
18 Caravans turn aside from their routes;
they go up into the wasteland and perish.
19 The caravans of Tema[x] look for water,
the traveling merchants of Sheba look in hope.
20 They are distressed, because they had been confident;
they arrive there, only to be disappointed.[y]
21 Now you too have proved to be of no help;
you see something dreadful and are afraid.[z]
22 Have I ever said, 'Give something on my behalf,
pay a ransom for me from your wealth,
23 deliver me from the hand of the enemy,
ransom me from the clutches of the ruthless'?

24 "Teach me, and I will be quiet;[a]
show me where I have been wrong.
25 How painful are honest words![b]
But what do your arguments prove?
26 Do you mean to correct what I say,
and treat the words of a despairing man as wind?[c]
27 You would even cast lots[d] for the fatherless
and barter away your friend.

28 "But now be so kind as to look at me.
Would I lie to your face?[e]
29 Relent, do not be unjust;
reconsider, for my integrity is at stake.[a][f]
30 Is there any wickedness on my lips?[g]
Can my mouth not discern[h] malice?

7 "Does not man have hard service[i] on earth?[j]
Are not his days like those of a hired man?[k]
2 Like a slave longing for the evening shadows,
or a hired man waiting eagerly for his wages,[l]
3 so I have been allotted months of futility,
and nights of misery have been assigned to me.[m]
4 When I lie down I think, 'How long before I get up?'[n]
The night drags on, and I toss till dawn.
5 My body is clothed with worms[o] and scabs,
my skin is broken and festering.

6 "My days are swifter than a weaver's shuttle,[p]
and they come to an end without hope.[q]
7 Remember, O God, that my life is but a breath;[r]
my eyes will never see happiness again.[s]

[a] 29 Or *my righteousness still stands*

[8] The eye that now sees me will see me no longer;
you will look for me, but I will be no more.[t]
[9] As a cloud vanishes and is gone,
so he who goes down to the grave[a][u] does not return.[v]
[10] He will never come to his house again;
his place[w] will know him no more.[x]

[11] "Therefore I will not keep silent;[y]
I will speak out in the anguish of my spirit,
I will complain in the bitterness of my soul.[z]
[12] Am I the sea, or the monster of the deep,[a]
that you put me under guard?
[13] When I think my bed will comfort me
and my couch will ease my complaint,[b]
[14] even then you frighten me with dreams
and terrify[c] me with visions,
[15] so that I prefer strangling and death,[d]
rather than this body of mine.
[16] I despise my life;[e] I would not live forever.
Let me alone; my days have no meaning.

[17] "What is man that you make so much of him,
that you give him so much attention,[f]
[18] that you examine him every morning
and test him every moment?[g]
[19] Will you never look away from me,
or let me alone even for an instant?[h]
[20] If I have sinned, what have I done to you,[i]
O watcher of men?
Why have you made me your target?[j]
Have I become a burden to you?[b]
[21] Why do you not pardon my offenses
and forgive my sins?[k]
For I will soon lie down in the dust;[l]
you will search for me, but I will be no more."

7:8 [t]Job 20:7,9,21
7:9 [u]Job 11:8 [v]2Sa 12:23; Job 30:15
7:10 [w]Job 27:21,23 [x]Job 8:18
7:11 [y]Ps 40:9 [z]1Sa 1:10
7:12 [a]Eze 32:2-3
7:13 [b]Job 9:27
7:14 [c]Job 9:34
7:15 [d]1Ki 19:4
7:16 [e]Job 9:21; 10:1
7:17 [f]Ps 8:4; 144:3; Heb 2:6
7:18 [g]Job 14:3
7:19 [h]Job 9:18
7:20 [i]Job 35:6 [j]Job 16:12
7:21 [k]Job 10:14 [l]Job 10:9; Ps 104:29

Bildad

8 Then Bildad the Shuhite replied:

[2] "How long will you say such things?
Your words are a blustering wind.[m]
[3] Does God pervert justice?[n]
Does the Almighty pervert what is right?[o]
[4] When your children sinned against him,
he gave them over to the penalty of their sin.[p]
[5] But if you will look to God
and plead[q] with the Almighty,
[6] if you are pure and upright,
even now he will rouse himself on your behalf[r]
and restore you to your rightful place.[s]
[7] Your beginnings will seem humble,
so prosperous[t] will your future be.

8:2 [m]Job 6:26
8:3 [n]Dt 32:4; 2Ch 19:7; Ro 3:5 [o]Ge 18:25
8:4 [p]Job 1:19
8:5 [q]Job 11:13
8:6 [r]Ps 7:6 [s]Job 5:24
8:7 [t]Job 42:12

[a] 9 Hebrew *Sheol* [b] 20 A few manuscripts of the Masoretic Text, an ancient Hebrew scribal tradition and Septuagint; most manuscripts of the Masoretic Text *I have become a burden to myself.*

7:9 Mesopotamian descriptions of the netherworld refer to it similarly as the "land of no return." (See the note on 10:21.)

8:8 [u]Dt 4:32; 32:7; Job 15:18
8:9 [v]Ge 47:9 [w]1Ch 29:15; Job 7:6
8:12 [x]Ps 129:6; Jer 17:6
8:13 [y]Ps 9:17 [z]Job 11:20; 13:16; 15:34; Pr 10:28
8:14 [a]Isa 59:5
8:15 [b]Job 27:18 [c]Ps 49:11
8:16 [d]Ps 80:11 [e]Ps 37:35; Jer 11:16
8:18 [f]Job 7:8; Ps 37:36
8:19 [g]Job 20:5 [h]Ecc 1:4
8:20 [i]Job 1:1 [j]Job 21:30
8:21 [k]Job 5:22 [l]Ps 126:2; 132:16
8:22 [m]Ps 35:26; 109:29; 132:18 [n]Job 18:6,14,21

8 "Ask the former generations[u]
and find out what their fathers learned,
9 for we were born only yesterday and know nothing,[v]
and our days on earth are but a shadow.[w]
10 Will they not instruct you and tell you?
Will they not bring forth words from their understanding?
11 Can papyrus grow tall where there is no marsh?
Can reeds thrive without water?
12 While still growing and uncut,
they wither more quickly than grass.[x]
13 Such is the destiny of all who forget God;[y]
so perishes the hope of the godless.[z]
14 What he trusts in is fragile[a];
what he relies on is a spider's web.[a]
15 He leans on his web,[b] but it gives way;
he clings to it, but it does not hold.[c]
16 He is like a well-watered plant in the sunshine,
spreading its shoots[d] over the garden;[e]
17 it entwines its roots around a pile of rocks
and looks for a place among the stones.
18 But when it is torn from its spot,
that place disowns it and says, 'I never saw you.'[f]
19 Surely its life withers[g] away,
and[b] from the soil other plants grow.[h]

20 "Surely God does not reject a blameless[i] man
or strengthen the hands of evildoers.[j]
21 He will yet fill your mouth with laughter[k]
and your lips with shouts of joy.[l]
22 Your enemies will be clothed in shame,[m]
and the tents of the wicked will be no more."[n]

Job

9 Then Job replied:

9:2 [o]Job 4:17; Ps 143:2; Ro 3:20
9:3 [p]Job 10:2; 40:2
9:4 [q]Job 11:6 [r]Job 36:5 [s]2Ch 13:12
9:5 [t]Mic 1:4
9:6 [u]Isa 2:21; Hag 2:6; Heb 12:26 [v]Job 26:11
9:7 [w]Isa 13:10; Eze 32:8
9:8 [x]Ge 1:6; Ps 104:2-3 [y]Job 38:16; Ps 77:19
9:9 [z]Ge 1:16; Job 38:31; Am 5:8

2 "Indeed, I know that this is true.
But how can a mortal be righteous before God?[o]
3 Though one wished to dispute with him,
he could not answer him one time out of a thousand.[p]
4 His wisdom[q] is profound, his power is vast.[r]
Who has resisted him and come out unscathed?[s]
5 He moves mountains without their knowing it
and overturns them in his anger.[t]
6 He shakes the earth[u] from its place
and makes its pillars tremble.[v]
7 He speaks to the sun and it does not shine;
he seals off the light of the stars.[w]
8 He alone stretches out the heavens[x]
and treads on the waves of the sea.[y]
9 He is the Maker of the Bear and Orion,
the Pleiades and the constellations of the south.[z]

[a] 14 The meaning of the Hebrew for this word is uncertain. [b] 19 Or *Surely all the joy it has / is that*

9:8 Canaanite texts describe the goddess Asherah as walking on the sea in order to subdue it. Similarly, God "treads on the waves" to control the boisterous deep.

9:9 These three constellations are mentioned again in 38:31–32. The ancient Israelites, despite their limited knowledge of astronomy, were awed by the fact that God had created the constellations.

10 He performs wonders[a] that cannot be fathomed,
miracles that cannot be counted.[b]
11 When he passes me, I cannot see him;
when he goes by, I cannot perceive him.[c]
12 If he snatches away, who can stop him?[d]
Who can say to him, 'What are you doing?'[e]
13 God does not restrain his anger;
even the cohorts of Rahab[f] cowered at his feet.

14 "How then can I dispute with him?
How can I find words to argue with him?
15 Though I were innocent, I could not answer him;[g]
I could only plead[h] with my Judge for mercy.
16 Even if I summoned him and he responded,
I do not believe he would give me a hearing.
17 He would crush me[i] with a storm[j]
and multiply[k] my wounds for no reason.[l]
18 He would not let me regain my breath
but would overwhelm me with misery.[m]
19 If it is a matter of strength, he is mighty!
And if it is a matter of justice, who will summon him[*a*]?
20 Even if I were innocent, my mouth would condemn me;
if I were blameless, it would pronounce me guilty.

21 "Although I am blameless,[n]
I have no concern for myself;
I despise my own life.[o]
22 It is all the same; that is why I say,
'He destroys both the blameless and the wicked.'[p]
23 When a scourge[q] brings sudden death,
he mocks the despair of the innocent.[r]
24 When a land falls into the hands of the wicked,[s]
he blindfolds its judges.[t]
If it is not he, then who is it?

25 "My days are swifter than a runner;[u]
they fly away without a glimpse of joy.
26 They skim past like boats of papyrus,[v]
like eagles swooping down on their prey.[w]
27 If I say, 'I will forget my complaint,[x]
I will change my expression, and smile,'
28 I still dread[y] all my sufferings,
for I know you will not hold me innocent.[z]
29 Since I am already found guilty,
why should I struggle in vain?[a]
30 Even if I washed myself with soap[*b*]
and my hands[b] with washing soda,[c]
31 you would plunge me into a slime pit
so that even my clothes would detest me.

9:10 [a]Ps 71:15 [b]Job 5:9
9:11 [c]Job 23:8-9; 35:14
9:12 [d]Job 11:10 [e]Isa 45:9; Ro 9:20
9:13 [f]Job 26:12; Ps 89:10; Isa 30:7; 51:9
9:15 [g]Job 10:15 [h]Job 8:5
9:17 [i]Job 16:12 [j]Job 30:22 [k]Job 16:14 [l]Job 2:3
9:18 [m]Job 7:19; 27:2
9:21 [n]Job 1:1 [o]Job 7:16
9:22 [p]Job 10:8; Ecc 9:2,3; Eze 21:3
9:23 [q]Heb 11:36 [r]Job 24:1,12
9:24 [s]Job 10:3; 16:11 [t]Job 12:6
9:25 [u]Job 7:6
9:26 [v]Isa 18:2 [w]Hab 1:8
9:27 [x]Job 7:11
9:28 [y]Job 3:25; Ps 119:120 [z]Job 7:21
9:29 [a]Ps 37:33
9:30 [b]Job 31:7 [c]Jer 2:22

a 19 See Septuagint; Hebrew *me.* *b* 30 Or *snow*

9:13 Rahab refers to the mythical sea monster of the deep (see 26:12; see also "The *Enuma Elish* and the Biblical Concept of Creation" on p. 888), elsewhere cited in the Bible as symbolic of Egypt (see Isa 30:7). In this passage, as well as in others (e.g., Ps 89:10), the motif of the slaying of the dragon appears. In Isaiah 51:9 the Lord's victory is declared to be complete because he has cut Rahab, the monster, to ribbons. This poetic symbolism has much in common with the Ras Shamra literature (see "Ugarit/Ras Shamra" on p. 819) and has been the prototype of legends like "Saint George and the Dragon." The *Rahab Yashab* ("Rahab the Do-Nothing") of Isaiah 30:7 portrays the impotency of the monster of Egypt (symbolized by the crocodile) in the day of invasion.

9:30 "Soda" refers to a vegetable alkali used as a cleansing agent. The Hebrew underlying this word is translated "soap" in Jeremiah 2:22 and Malachi 3:2.

9:32 [d]Ro 9:20 [e]Ps 143:2; Ecc 6:10
9:33 [f]1Sa 2:25
9:34 [g]Job 13:21; Ps 39:10
9:35 [h]Job 13:21
10:1 [i]1Ki 19:4 [j]Job 7:11
10:2 [k]Job 9:29
10:3 [l]Job 9:22 [m]Job 14:15; Ps 138:8; Isa 64:8 [n]Job 21:16; 22:18
10:4 [o]1Sa 16:7
10:5 [p]Ps 90:2,4; 2Pe 3:8
10:6 [q]Job 14:16
10:8 [r]Ps 119:73
10:9 [s]Isa 64:8 [t]Ge 2:7
10:11 [u]Ps 139:13,15
10:12 [v]Job 33:4
10:13 [w]Job 23:13
10:14 [x]Job 7:21
10:15 [y]Job 9:13; Isa 3:11 [z]Job 9:15
10:16 [a]Isa 38:13; La 3:10 [b]Job 5:9
10:17 [c]Job 16:8 [d]Ru 1:21

32 "He is not a man like me that I might answer him,[d]
that we might confront each other in court.[e]
33 If only there were someone to arbitrate between us,[f]
to lay his hand upon us both,
34 someone to remove God's rod from me,[g]
so that his terror would frighten me no more.
35 Then I would speak up without fear of him,
but as it now stands with me, I cannot.[h]

10

"I loathe my very life;[i]
therefore I will give free rein to my complaint
and speak out in the bitterness of my soul.[j]
2 I will say to God: Do not condemn me,
but tell me what charges[k] you have against me.
3 Does it please you to oppress me,[l]
to spurn the work of your hands,[m]
while you smile on the schemes of the wicked?[n]
4 Do you have eyes of flesh?
Do you see as a mortal sees?[o]
5 Are your days like those of a mortal
or your years like those of a man,[p]
6 that you must search out my faults
and probe after my sin[q]—
7 though you know that I am not guilty
and that no one can rescue me from your hand?

8 "Your hands shaped[r] me and made me.
Will you now turn and destroy me?
9 Remember that you molded me like clay.[s]
Will you now turn me to dust again?[t]
10 Did you not pour me out like milk
and curdle me like cheese,
11 clothe me with skin and flesh
and knit me together[u] with bones and sinews?
12 You gave me life[v] and showed me kindness,
and in your providence watched over my spirit.

13 "But this is what you concealed in your heart,
and I know that this was in your mind:[w]
14 If I sinned, you would be watching me
and would not let my offense go unpunished.[x]
15 If I am guilty—woe to me![y]
Even if I am innocent, I cannot lift my head,[z]
for I am full of shame
and drowned in[a] my affliction.
16 If I hold my head high, you stalk me like a lion[a]
and again display your awesome power against me.[b]
17 You bring new witnesses against me[c]
and increase your anger toward me;[d]
your forces come against me wave upon wave.

[a] *15* Or *and aware of*

9:33 In eastern lands it was customary for a judge to place his hands upon the heads of the two parties in a dispute as a demonstration of his authority and desire to render an unbiased verdict. Job's statement implies that no human being is worthy of acting as the judge of God.

10:10 Three different Hebrew words, each appearing only once in the Old Testament, are translated "cheese." In this verse *gevînâh*, "curd" or "cheese," is from a root meaning "coagulate." In 2 Samuel 17:29 the word *shaphah* is more properly translated "cream," because it is skimmed off. In 1 Samuel 17:18 *hārītsî hehâlâv* denotes "cuts of milk"—that is, cheese. Milk of cows, goats and sheep was stored in skins, but in a warm climate without refrigeration it soon curdled. The process used to make cheese can only be guessed from the practices current in the Near East today.

18 "Why then did you bring me out of the womb?[e]
I wish I had died before any eye saw me.
19 If only I had never come into being,
or had been carried straight from the womb to the grave!
20 Are not my few days[f] almost over?[g]
Turn away from me[h] so I can have a moment's joy
21 before I go to the place of no return,[i]
to the land of gloom and deep shadow,[a][j]
22 to the land of deepest night,
of deep shadow and disorder,
where even the light is like darkness."

Zophar

11 Then Zophar the Naamathite replied:

2 "Are all these words to go unanswered?[k]
Is this talker to be vindicated?
3 Will your idle talk reduce men to silence?
Will no one rebuke you when you mock?[l]
4 You say to God, 'My beliefs are flawless[m]
and I am pure[n] in your sight.'
5 Oh, how I wish that God would speak,
that he would open his lips against you
6 and disclose to you the secrets of wisdom,[o]
for true wisdom has two sides.
Know this: God has even forgotten some of your sin.[p]

7 "Can you fathom[q] the mysteries of God?
Can you probe the limits of the Almighty?
8 They are higher than the heavens[r]—what can you do?
They are deeper than the depths of the grave[b]—what can you know?
9 Their measure is longer than the earth
and wider than the sea.

10 "If he comes along and confines you in prison
and convenes a court, who can oppose him?[s]
11 Surely he recognizes deceitful men;
and when he sees evil, does he not take note?[t]
12 But a witless man can no more become wise
than a wild donkey's colt can be born a man.[c]

13 "Yet if you devote your heart[u] to him
and stretch out your hands to him,[v]
14 if you put away the sin that is in your hand
and allow no evil[w] to dwell in your tent,[x]
15 then you will lift up your face[y] without shame;
you will stand firm and without fear.
16 You will surely forget your trouble,[z]
recalling it only as waters gone by.[a]
17 Life will be brighter than noonday,[b]
and darkness will become like morning.

10:18 [e]Job 3:11
10:20 [f]Job 14:1 [g]Job 7:19 [h]Job 7:16
10:21 [i]2Sa 12:23; Job 3:13; 16:22 [j]Ps 23:4; 88:12
11:2 [k]Job 8:2
11:3 [l]Job 17:2; 21:3
11:4 [m]Job 6:10 [n]Job 10:7
11:6 [o]Job 9:4 [p]Ezr 9:13; Job 15:5
11:7 [q]Ecc 3:11; Ro 11:33
11:8 [r]Job 22:12
11:10 [s]Job 9:12; Rev 3:7
11:11 [t]Job 34:21-25; Ps 10:14
11:13 [u]1Sa 7:3; Ps 78:8 [v]Ps 88:9
11:14 [w]Ps 101:4 [x]Job 22:23
11:15 [y]Job 22:26; 1Jn 3:21
11:16 [z]Isa 65:16 [a]Job 22:11
11:17 [b]Job 22:28; Ps 37:6; Isa 58:8, 10

[a] 21 Or *and the shadow of death*; also in verse 22 [b] 8 Hebrew *than Sheol* [c] 12 Or *wild donkey can be born tame*

10:21 Ancient Mesopotamian documents refer to the netherworld as the "house of darkness" (see "Sheol, Hades, Gehenna, the Abyss and Tartarus: Images of Hell" on p. 949).

11:18 [c]Ps 3:5 [d]Lev 26:6; Pr 3:24
11:19 [e]Lev 26:6 [f]Isa 45:14
11:20 [g]Dt 28:65; Job 17:5 [h]Job 27:22; 34:22 [i]Job 8:13

18 You will be secure, because there is hope;
you will look about you and take your rest[c] in safety.[d]
19 You will lie down, with no one to make you afraid,[e]
and many will court your favor.[f]
20 But the eyes of the wicked will fail,[g]
and escape will elude them;[h]
their hope will become a dying gasp."[i]

Job

12 Then Job replied:

12:2 [j]Job 17:10
12:3 [k]Job 13:2
12:4 [l]Job 21:3 [m]Ps 91:15 [n]Job 6:29
12:6 [o]Job 22:18 [p]Job 9:24; 21:9

2 "Doubtless you are the people,
and wisdom will die with you![j]
3 But I have a mind as well as you;
I am not inferior to you.
Who does not know all these things?[k]

4 "I have become a laughingstock[l] to my friends,
though I called upon God and he answered[m]—
a mere laughingstock, though righteous and blameless![n]
5 Men at ease have contempt for misfortune
as the fate of those whose feet are slipping.
6 The tents of marauders are undisturbed,[o]
and those who provoke God are secure[p]—
those who carry their god in their hands.[a]

7 "But ask the animals, and they will teach you,
or the birds of the air, and they will tell you;

[a] 6 Or *secure / in what God's hand brings them*

ANCIENT TEXTS AND ARTIFACTS

"I Will Praise the Lord of Wisdom"

JOB 12 From the Kassite period of **Babylon** (the second half of the second millennium B.C.) comes an **Akkadian** poem titled "I will praise the Lord of Wisdom." Because it concerns a pious sufferer, it is often compared to Job, although it is formally more similar to certain Biblical psalms in which an individual describes some illness or calamity he has suffered but praises God for having delivered him (e.g., Ps 30; 116). In this Akkadian text the poet (named Shubshi-meshre-Shakkan) says much that is similar to Job's lamentation:[1]

✣ Shubshi-meshre-Shakkan considers himself helpless before his god, Marduk, who is merciful but whose anger is like a raging storm (see Job 12:13–25).[2]

✣ Shubshi-meshre-Shakkan laments about friends and family having abandoned him (see v. 4; 19:13–20).

✣ Like Job, he exhaustively describes his physical afflictions (see 7:5) prior to his healing.

✣ Shubshi-meshre-Shakkan was delivered after having seen three godlike persons—two men and a woman—in his dreams (chs. 38–42).

In other respects, however, the Akkadian psalm is very different from Job. It focuses on omens, magical spells and dreams,[3] as well as listing rituals of healing at the gates of the temple of Marduk. In contrast, the book of Job contains no ritual or magical elements. Instead, its protagonist is a righteous sufferer, and it wrestles with fundamental issues of God's governance of the world.[4] Job is not healed by magic but by God himself after he has heard and understood God's answers to the questions he has raised.

[1]See "Ancient Near Eastern Laments" on page 1305. [2]See also "A Prayer of Confession to Marduk" on page 831. [3]See "Dream Oracles in the Ancient World" on page 741. [4]See also "A Man and His God" on page 771.

[8] or speak to the earth, and it will teach you,
or let the fish of the sea inform you.
[9] Which of all these does not know
that the hand of the LORD has done this?[q]
[10] In his hand is the life of every creature
and the breath of all mankind.[r]
[11] Does not the ear test words
as the tongue tastes food?[s]
[12] Is not wisdom found among the aged?[t]
Does not long life bring understanding?[u]

[13] "To God belong wisdom[v] and power;[w]
counsel and understanding are his.[x]
[14] What he tears down[y] cannot be rebuilt;[z]
the man he imprisons cannot be released.
[15] If he holds back the waters,[a] there is drought;[b]
if he lets them loose, they devastate the land.[c]
[16] To him belong strength and victory;
both deceived and deceiver are his.[d]
[17] He leads counselors away stripped[e]
and makes fools of judges.[f]
[18] He takes off the shackles[g] put on by kings
and ties a loincloth[a] around their waist.
[19] He leads priests away stripped
and overthrows men long established.[h]
[20] He silences the lips of trusted advisers
and takes away the discernment of elders.[i]
[21] He pours contempt on nobles
and disarms the mighty.
[22] He reveals the deep things of darkness[j]
and brings deep shadows[k] into the light.[l]
[23] He makes nations great, and destroys them;[m]
he enlarges nations,[n] and disperses them.
[24] He deprives the leaders of the earth of their reason;
he sends them wandering through a trackless waste.[o]
[25] They grope in darkness with no light;[p]
he makes them stagger like drunkards.[q]

13

"My eyes have seen all this,
my ears have heard and understood it.
[2] What you know, I also know;
I am not inferior to you.[r]
[3] But I desire to speak to the Almighty
and to argue my case with God.[s]
[4] You, however, smear me with lies;[t]
you are worthless physicians, all of you!
[5] If only you would be altogether silent!
For you, that would be wisdom.[u]
[6] Hear now my argument;
listen to the plea of my lips.
[7] Will you speak wickedly on God's behalf?
Will you speak deceitfully for him?[v]
[8] Will you show him partiality?[w]
Will you argue the case for God?

12:9 [q]Isa 41:20
12:10 [r]Job 27:3; 33:4; Ac 17:28
12:11 [s]Job 34:3
12:12 [t]Job 15:10 [u]Job 32:7,9
12:13 [v]Job 11:6 [w]Job 9:4 [x]Job 32:8; 38:36
12:14 [y]Job 19:10 [z]Job 37:7; Isa 25:2
12:15 [a]1Ki 8:35 [b]1Ki 17:1 [c]Ge 7:11
12:16 [d]Job 13:7,9
12:17 [e]Job 19:9 [f]Job 3:14
12:18 [g]Ps 116:16
12:19 [h]Job 24:12,22; 34:20,28; 35:9
12:20 [i]Job 32:9
12:22 [j]1Co 4:5 [k]Job 3:5 [l]Da 2:22
12:23 [m]Jer 25:9 [n]Ps 107:38; Isa 9:3; 26:15
12:24 [o]Ps 107:40
12:25 [p]Job 5:14 [q]Ps 107:27; Isa 24:20
13:2 [r]Job 12:3
13:3 [s]Job 23:3-4
13:4 [t]Ps 119:69; Jer 23:32
13:5 [u]Pr 17:28
13:7 [v]Job 36:4
13:8 [w]Lev 19:15

[a] 18 Or *shackles of kings / and ties a belt*

[9] Would it turn out well if he examined you?
Could you deceive him as you might deceive men?[x]
[10] He would surely rebuke you
if you secretly showed partiality.
[11] Would not his splendor[y] terrify you?
Would not the dread of him fall on you?
[12] Your maxims are proverbs of ashes;
your defenses are defenses of clay.

[13] "Keep silent and let me speak;
then let come to me what may.
[14] Why do I put myself in jeopardy
and take my life in my hands?
[15] Though he slay me, yet will I hope[z] in him;[a]
I will surely[a] defend my ways to his face.[b]
[16] Indeed, this will turn out for my deliverance,[c]
for no godless man would dare come before him!
[17] Listen carefully to my words;[d]
let your ears take in what I say.
[18] Now that I have prepared my case,[e]
I know I will be vindicated.
[19] Can anyone bring charges against me?[f]
If so, I will be silent and die.[g]

[20] "Only grant me these two things, O God,
and then I will not hide from you:
[21] Withdraw your hand[h] far from me,
and stop frightening me with your terrors.
[22] Then summon me and I will answer,[i]
or let me speak, and you reply.[j]
[23] How many wrongs and sins have I committed?[k]
Show me my offense and my sin.
[24] Why do you hide your face[l]
and consider me your enemy?[m]
[25] Will you torment a windblown leaf?[n]
Will you chase after dry chaff?[o]
[26] For you write down bitter things against me
and make me inherit the sins of my youth.[p]
[27] You fasten my feet in shackles;[q]
you keep close watch on all my paths
by putting marks on the soles of my feet.

[28] "So man wastes away like something rotten,
like a garment eaten by moths.[r]

14

"Man born of woman
is of few days and full of trouble.[s]
[2] He springs up like a flower[t] and withers away;[u]
like a fleeting shadow,[v] he does not endure.
[3] Do you fix your eye on such a one?[w]
Will you bring him[b] before you for judgment?[x]
[4] Who can bring what is pure[y] from the impure?[z]
No one![a]

13:9 [x]Job 12:16; Gal 6:7
13:11 [y]Job 31:23
13:15 [z]Job 7:6 [a]Ps 23:4; Pr 14:32 [b]Job 27:5
13:16 [c]Isa 12:1
13:17 [d]Job 21:2
13:18 [e]Job 23:4
13:19 [f]Job 40:4; Isa 50:8 [g]Job 10:8
13:21 [h]Ps 39:10
13:22 [i]Job 14:15 [j]Job 9:16
13:23 [k]1Sa 26:18
13:24 [l]Dt 32:20; Ps 13:1; Isa 8:17 [m]Job 19:11; La 2:5
13:25 [n]Lev 26:36 [o]Job 21:18; Isa 42:3
13:26 [p]Ps 25:7
13:27 [q]Job 33:11
13:28 [r]Isa 50:9; Jas 5:2
14:1 [s]Job 5:7; Ecc 2:23
14:2 [t]Jas 1:10 [u]Ps 90:5-6 [v]Job 8:9
14:3 [w]Ps 8:4; 144:3 [x]Ps 143:2
14:4 [y]Ps 51:10 [z]Eph 2:1-3 [a]Jn 3:6; Ro 5:12

[a] 15 Or *He will surely slay me; I have no hope — / yet I will* [b] 3 Septuagint, Vulgate and Syriac; Hebrew *me*

13:25 See "The Threshing Floor" on page 608.

13:27 The practice of marking slaves is attested in the Babylonian Code of Hammurabi (eighteenth century B.C.).

[5] Man's days are determined;
you have decreed the number of his months[b]
and have set limits he cannot exceed.
[6] So look away from him and let him alone,[c]
till he has put in his time like a hired man.[d]

[7] "At least there is hope for a tree:
If it is cut down, it will sprout again,
and its new shoots will not fail.
[8] Its roots may grow old in the ground
and its stump die in the soil,
[9] yet at the scent of water it will bud
and put forth shoots like a plant.
[10] But man dies and is laid low;
he breathes his last and is no more.[e]
[11] As water disappears from the sea
or a riverbed becomes parched and dry,[f]
[12] so man lies down and does not rise;
till the heavens are no more,[g] men will not awake
or be roused from their sleep.[h]

[13] "If only you would hide me in the grave[a]
and conceal me till your anger has passed![i]
If only you would set me a time
and then remember me!
[14] If a man dies, will he live again?
All the days of my hard service
I will wait for my renewal[b] to come.
[15] You will call and I will answer you;[j]
you will long for the creature your hands have made.
[16] Surely then you will count my steps[k]
but not keep track of my sin.[l]
[17] My offenses will be sealed up in a bag;[m]
you will cover over my sin.[n]

[18] "But as a mountain erodes and crumbles
and as a rock is moved from its place,
[19] as water wears away stones
and torrents wash away the soil,
so you destroy man's hope.[o]
[20] You overpower him once for all, and he is gone;
you change his countenance and send him away.
[21] If his sons are honored, he does not know it;
if they are brought low, he does not see it.[p]
[22] He feels but the pain of his own body
and mourns only for himself."

Eliphaz

15 Then Eliphaz the Temanite replied:

[2] "Would a wise man answer with empty notions
or fill his belly with the hot east wind?[q]
[3] Would he argue with useless words,
with speeches that have no value?

14:5 [b]Job 21:21
14:6 [c]Job 7:19 [d]Job 7:1,2; Ps 39:13
14:10 [e]Job 13:19
14:11 [f]Isa 19:5
14:12 [g]Rev 20:11; 21:1 [h]Ac 3:21
14:13 [i]Isa 26:20
14:15 [j]Job 13:22
14:16 [k]Ps 139:1-3; Pr 5:21; Jer 32:19 [l]Job 10:6
14:17 [m]Dt 32:34 [n]Hos 13:12
14:19 [o]Job 7:6
14:21 [p]Ecc 9:5; Isa 63:16
15:2 [q]Job 6:26

[a] *13* Hebrew *Sheol* [b] *14* Or *release*

14:19 See the note on stones and gravel at Isaiah 27:9. **15:1–35** See the note on Eliphaz at 2:11.

[4] But you even undermine piety
and hinder devotion to God.
[5] Your sin prompts your mouth;
you adopt the tongue of the crafty.[r]
[6] Your own mouth condemns you, not mine;
your own lips testify against you.[s]

[7] "Are you the first man ever born?[t]
Were you brought forth before the hills?[u]
[8] Do you listen in on God's council?[v]
Do you limit wisdom to yourself?
[9] What do you know that we do not know?
What insights do you have that we do not have?[w]
[10] The gray-haired and the aged[x] are on our side,
men even older than your father.
[11] Are God's consolations[y] not enough for you,
words[z] spoken gently to you?[a]
[12] Why has your heart[b] carried you away,
and why do your eyes flash,
[13] so that you vent your rage against God
and pour out such words from your mouth?

[14] "What is man, that he could be pure,
or one born of woman,[c] that he could be righteous?[d]
[15] If God places no trust in his holy ones,
if even the heavens are not pure in his eyes,[e]
[16] how much less man, who is vile and corrupt,[f]
who drinks up evil like water![g]

[17] "Listen to me and I will explain to you;
let me tell you what I have seen,
[18] what wise men have declared,
hiding nothing received from their fathers[h]
[19] (to whom alone the land was given
when no alien passed among them):
[20] All his days the wicked man suffers torment,
the ruthless through all the years stored up for him.[i]
[21] Terrifying sounds fill his ears;[j]
when all seems well, marauders attack him.[k]
[22] He despairs of escaping the darkness;
he is marked for the sword.[l]
[23] He wanders about[m]—food for vultures[a];
he knows the day of darkness is at hand.[n]
[24] Distress and anguish fill him with terror;
they overwhelm him, like a king poised to attack,
[25] because he shakes his fist at God
and vaunts himself against the Almighty,[o]
[26] defiantly charging against him
with a thick, strong shield.

[27] "Though his face is covered with fat
and his waist bulges with flesh,[p]

15:5 [r]Job 5:13
15:6 [s]Lk 19:22
15:7 [t]Job 38:21 [u]Ps 90:2; Pr 8:25
15:8 [v]Ro 11:34; 1Co 2:11
15:9 [w]Job 13:2
15:10 [x]Job 32:6-7
15:11 [y]2Co 1:3-4 [z]Zec 1:13 [a]Job 36:16
15:12 [b]Job 11:13
15:14 [c]Job 14:4; 25:4 [d]Pr 20:9; Ecc 7:20
15:15 [e]Job 4:18; 25:5
15:16 [f]Ps 14:1 [g]Job 34:7; Pr 19:28
15:18 [h]Job 8:8
15:20 [i]Job 24:1; 27:13-23
15:21 [j]Job 18:11; 20:25 [k]Job 27:20; 1Th 5:3
15:22 [l]Job 19:29; 27:14
15:23 [m]Ps 59:15; 109:10 [n]Job 18:12
15:25 [o]Job 36:9
15:27 [p]Ps 17:10

[a] 23 Or *about, looking for food*

15:10 Age, with its tested experience, was equated in ancient times with wisdom.

28 he will inhabit ruined towns
and houses where no one lives,[q]
houses crumbling to rubble.[r]
29 He will no longer be rich and his wealth will not endure,[s]
nor will his possessions spread over the land.
30 He will not escape the darkness;[t]
a flame[u] will wither his shoots,
and the breath of God's mouth[v] will carry him away.
31 Let him not deceive himself by trusting what is worthless,[w]
for he will get nothing in return.
32 Before his time[x] he will be paid in full,[y]
and his branches will not flourish.[z]
33 He will be like a vine stripped of its unripe grapes,[a]
like an olive tree shedding its blossoms.
34 For the company of the godless will be barren,
and fire will consume the tents of those who love bribes.[b]
35 They conceive trouble and give birth to evil;[c]
their womb fashions deceit."

Job

16 Then Job replied:

2 "I have heard many things like these;
miserable comforters are you all![d]
3 Will your long-winded speeches never end?
What ails you that you keep on arguing?[e]
4 I also could speak like you,
if you were in my place;
I could make fine speeches against you
and shake my head[f] at you.
5 But my mouth would encourage you;
comfort from my lips would bring you relief.

6 "Yet if I speak, my pain is not relieved;
and if I refrain, it does not go away.
7 Surely, O God, you have worn me out;[g]
you have devastated my entire household.
8 You have bound me—and it has become a witness;
my gauntness[h] rises up and testifies against me.[i]
9 God assails me and tears[j] me in his anger
and gnashes his teeth at me;[k]
my opponent fastens on me his piercing eyes.[l]
10 Men open their mouths[m] to jeer at me;
they strike my cheek[n] in scorn
and unite together against me.[o]
11 God has turned me over to evil men
and thrown me into the clutches of the wicked.[p]
12 All was well with me, but he shattered me;
he seized me by the neck and crushed me.[q]
He has made me his target;[r]
13 his archers surround me.
Without pity, he pierces[s] my kidneys
and spills my gall on the ground.
14 Again and again[t] he bursts upon me;
he rushes at me like a warrior.[u]

15:28 [q]Isa 5:9 [r]Job 3:14
15:29 [s]Job 27:16-17
15:30 [t]Job 5:14 [u]Job 22:20 [v]Job 4:9
15:31 [w]Isa 59:4
15:32 [x]Ecc 7:17 [y]Job 22:16; Ps 55:23 [z]Job 18:16
15:33 [a]Hab 3:17
15:34 [b]Job 8:22
15:35 [c]Ps 7:14; Isa 59:4; Hos 10:13
16:2 [d]Job 13:4
16:3 [e]Job 6:26
16:4 [f]Ps 22:7; 109:25; La 2:15; Zep 2:15; Mt 27:39
16:7 [g]Job 7:3
16:8 [h]Job 19:20 [i]Job 10:17
16:9 [j]Hos 6:1 [k]Ps 35:16; La 2:16; Ac 7:54 [l]Job 13:24
16:10 [m]Ps 22:13 [n]Isa 50:6; La 3:30; Mic 5:1; Ac 23:2 [o]Ps 35:15
16:11 [p]Job 1:15, 17
16:12 [q]Job 9:17 [r]La 3:12
16:13 [s]Job 20:24
16:14 [t]Job 9:17 [u]Joel 2:7

16:15 [v]Ge 37:34
16:17 [w]Isa 59:6; Jnh 3:8
16:18 [x]Isa 26:21 [y]Ps 66:18-19
16:19 [z]Ge 31:50; Ro 1:9; 1Th 2:5
16:20 [a]La 2:19
16:21 [b]Ps 9:4
16:22 [c]Ecc 12:5
17:1 [d]Ps 88:3-4
17:2 [e]1Sa 1:6-7
17:3 [f]Ps 119:122 [g]Pr 6:1 [h]Isa 38:14
17:5 [i]Job 11:20
17:6 [j]Job 30:9
17:7 [k]Job 16:8
17:8 [l]Job 22:19
17:9 [m]Pr 4:18 [n]Job 22:30
17:10 [o]Job 12:2
17:11 [p]Job 7:6
17:13 [q]Job 3:13

15 "I have sewed sackcloth[v] over my skin
and buried my brow in the dust.
16 My face is red with weeping,
deep shadows ring my eyes;
17 yet my hands have been free of violence[w]
and my prayer is pure.

18 "O earth, do not cover my blood;[x]
may my cry never be laid to rest![y]
19 Even now my witness[z] is in heaven;
my advocate is on high.
20 My intercessor is my friend[a]
as my eyes pour out[a] tears to God;
21 on behalf of a man he pleads[b] with God
as a man pleads for his friend.

22 "Only a few years will pass
before I go on the journey of no return.[c]

17

1 My spirit is broken,
my days are cut short,
the grave awaits me.[d]
2 Surely mockers[e] surround me;
my eyes must dwell on their hostility.

3 "Give me, O God, the pledge you demand.[f]
Who else will put up security[g] for me?[h]
4 You have closed their minds to understanding;
therefore you will not let them triumph.
5 If a man denounces his friends for reward,
the eyes of his children will fail.[i]

6 "God has made me a byword[j] to everyone,
a man in whose face people spit.
7 My eyes have grown dim with grief;[k]
my whole frame is but a shadow.
8 Upright men are appalled at this;
the innocent are aroused[l] against the ungodly.
9 Nevertheless, the righteous[m] will hold to their ways,
and those with clean hands[n] will grow stronger.

10 "But come on, all of you, try again!
I will not find a wise man among you.[o]
11 My days have passed, my plans are shattered,
and so are the desires of my heart.[p]
12 These men turn night into day;
in the face of darkness they say, 'Light is near.'
13 If the only home I hope for is the grave,[b][q]
if I spread out my bed in darkness,

[a] 20 Or *My friends treat me with scorn* [b] 13 Hebrew *Sheol*

16:15 The English word *sackcloth* is derived from the Hebrew *sak*, referring to a coarse cloth, dark in color, usually made of goat's hair. It was worn by mourners (2Sa 3:31; 2Ki 19:1–2), often by prophets (Isa 20:2; Rev 11:3) and by captives (1Ki 20:31). Its exact shape as a garment is unknown. Some surmise that it was originally a loincloth that was the only article of clothing worn by Israel's ancestors and that it was later donned only as a religious duty. Others think it resembled a corn sack, with openings for the neck and arms. Sackcloth was usually worn with another garment but sometimes next to the skin (1Ki 21:27; 2Ki 6:30; Job 16:15; Isa 32:11; Jnh 3:6). See also the note on 1 Kings 20:31–32 and "Sackcloth and Ashes: Rituals of Lamentation" on page 820.

17:6 See "Bywords and Insults in the Ancient World" on page 431.

17:13–16 The Old Testament makes three main points about Sheol: (1) All the dead alike go there (e.g., Ge 37:35; Isa 14:9ff). (2) Sheol is in some unspecified sense the lot of the wicked. References such as Psalms 6:5; 30:3, 9; and 88:3–6 (cf. Job 17:13–16; Isa 38:18) are often quoted as allegedly showing that the Old

[14] if I say to corruption, [r] 'You are my father,'
and to the worm, [s] 'My mother' or 'My sister,'
[15] where then is my hope? [t]
Who can see any hope for me?
[16] Will it go down to the gates of death[a]? [u]
Will we descend together into the dust?"

17:14 [r] Job 13:28; 30:28,30; Ps 16:10 [s] Job 21:26 17:15 [t] Job 7:6
17:16 [u] Job 3:17-19; Jnh 2:6

Bildad

18

Then Bildad the Shuhite replied:

[2] "When will you end these speeches?
Be sensible, and then we can talk.
[3] Why are we regarded as cattle
and considered stupid in your sight? [v]

18:3 [v] Ps 73:22

[a] 16 Hebrew *Sheol*

Testament knew of no hope after death, that the dead were thought to have been cut off from the Lord and he from them. In all of these references, however, the speakers believed themselves to be facing death under the wrath of God, estranged from him, with no indication of his favor. The Old Testament takes the matter no further; there is some undefined sense in which Sheol was assumed to have involved those who died under wrath in separation from God—the God their wickedness had offended. (3) On the other hand, there were those who could confidently look forward to glory (Ps 73:23–24)—which they perceived as redemption from Sheol (Ps 49:14–15). See "Sheol, Hades, Gehenna, Abyss and Tartarus: Images of Hell" on page 946.

ANCIENT TEXTS AND ARTIFACTS

A Hittite Ritual Against Plague

JOB 18 Throughout the book of Job the problem of evil is debated in terms of sin, judgment and divine sovereignty. Bildad's speech in Job 18 presents a simplistic, black-and-white perspective—that God punishes the evil and delivers the righteous. But Job himself contends that he is undeserving of what has befallen him, taking the reader to a new level in understanding the place of suffering under the hand of God. Although issues of guilt and divine justice were not unknown to pagans in the ancient Near East,[1] what is most striking in their texts is how often their religious framework for dealing with calamity is all about magic and ritual, not justice and divine purpose.[2] A **Hittite** text by Uhhamuwa of Arzawa illustrates the same philosophy, although it deals with national rather than personal disaster.

Uhhamuwa advises that if plague from an enemy god should strike a land, one should entwine wool of blue, red, yellow, black and white into a wreath and place it on a castrated ram. Then the people should drive the animal down the road while reciting a liturgy imploring the enemy god to accept the gift and be pacified (see 1Sa 6:2–9). Uhhamuwa goes on to suggest specific offerings and sacrifices to be made to the Hittite gods.

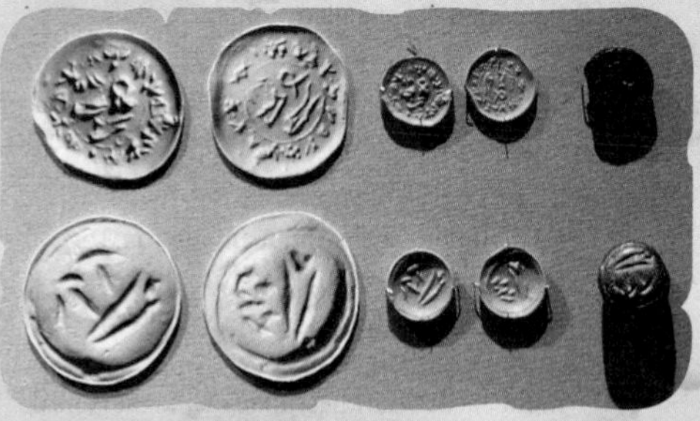

Hittite two-sided seals with enlarged images of their impressions, showing Hittite hieroglyphs and good-luck signs
Preserving Bible Times; © Dr. James C. Martin; permission of The British Museum

The basic approach of paganism is to attempt to manipulate divine powers through finding efficacious rituals and incantations.[3] In contrast to the ancient Near Eastern perspective, the complete absence of these elements in Job's confrontation with suffering is astonishing. The book of Job wrestles with real issues about God and his governance of the world and does not deal with the problem of evil through magic and superstition.

[1] See "The Babylonian Theodicy" on page 776. [2] See "'I Will Praise the Lord of Wisdom'" on page 751. [3] See "A Pagan's Prayer of Thanks" on page 922.

18:4 [w]Job 13:14

[4] You who tear yourself[w] to pieces in
your anger,
is the earth to be abandoned for
your sake?
Or must the rocks be moved from their
place?

18:5 [x]Job 21:17; Pr 13:9; 20:20; 24:20

[5] "The lamp of the wicked is snuffed out;[x]
the flame of his fire stops burning.
[6] The light in his tent becomes dark;
the lamp beside him goes out.

18:7 [y]Pr 4:12 [z]Job 5:13 [a]Job 15:6

[7] The vigor of his step is weakened;[y]
his own schemes[z] throw him down.[a]

18:8 [b]Job 22:10; Ps 9:15; 35:7

[8] His feet thrust him into a net[b]
and he wanders into its mesh.
[9] A trap seizes him by the heel;
a snare holds him fast.
[10] A noose is hidden for him on the ground;
a trap lies in his path.

18:11 [c]Job 15:21; Jer 6:25; 20:3 [d]Job 20:8

[11] Terrors startle him on every side[c]
and dog[d] his every step.

18:12 [e]Isa 8:21

[12] Calamity is hungry[e] for him;
disaster is ready for him when he falls.
[13] It eats away parts of his skin;
death's firstborn devours his limbs.[f]

18:13 [f]Zec 14:12

18:14 [g]Job 8:22

[14] He is torn from the security of his tent[g]
and marched off to the king of terrors.
[15] Fire resides[a] in his tent;
burning sulfur[h] is scattered over his
dwelling.

18:15 [h]Ps 11:6

18:16 [i]Isa 5:24; Hos 9:1-16; Am 2:9 [j]Job 15:30; Mal 4:1

[16] His roots dry up below[i]
and his branches wither above.[j]

18:17 [k]Ps 34:16; Pr 2:22; 10:7

[17] The memory of him perishes from the earth;
he has no name in the land.[k]

18:18 [l]Job 5:14

[18] He is driven from light into darkness[l]
and is banished from the world.

18:19 [m]Jer 22:30 [n]Isa 14:22 [o]Job 27:14-15

[19] He has no offspring[m] or descendants[n] among his people,
no survivor where once he lived.[o]

18:20 [p]Ps 37:13; Jer 50:27,31

[20] Men of the west are appalled at his fate;[p]
men of the east are seized with horror.

18:21 [q]Job 21:28 [r]Jer 9:3; 1Th 4:5

[21] Surely such is the dwelling[q] of an evil man;
such is the place of one who knows not God."[r]

Job

19

Then Job replied:

[2] "How long will you torment me
and crush me with words?
[3] Ten times now you have reproached me;
shamelessly you attack me.

[a] 15 Or *Nothing he had remains*

Ancient Voices

From the day the Lord punished me,
And the warrior Marduk became furious
with me,
My own god threw me over(?) and
disap[peared]*,
My goddess broke rank and vanished.
He cut off the benevolent angel who
(walked) beside [me].
My protecting spirit was frightened off,
to seek out someone else.
My vigor was taken away, my manly
appearance became gloomy,
My dignity escaped and lit on the roof.
Terrifying signs beset me:
I was forced out of my house, I wandered
outside.
My omens were confused, they were
contradictory every day,
The prognostication of diviner and dream
interpreter could not explain what I
was undergoing.
What was said in the street portended ill
for me,
When I lay down at night, my dream was
terrifying.

*Words or syllables in brackets or parentheses added by translator for clarity or where text has gaps. Uncertainty in translation indicated by question mark in parentheses

—The Poem of the Righteous Sufferer

See "A Hittite Ritual Against Plague" article.

18:13–14 This "king of terrors"—a personification of death—is reminiscent of the Canaanite deity Mot ("Death"), whose devouring throat supposedly reached from earth to sky. The prophet Isaiah reversed the figure, picturing God swallowing up death forever (Isa 25:8; cf. 1Co 15:54).

Ancient Voices

[Outwardly]* Anatu laughs,
but within she hatches [a plot].
Reconsider, valiant Aqhatu,
reconsider for your own sake [. . .].
(Otherwise) I'll meet you on the path
of rebellion.
[. . .] on the path of pride.
I'll personally bring you down and
[trample] you,
(however) good and strong (you may be)
among men.

*Words in brackets or parentheses added by translator for clarity or where text has gaps

—The Aqhatu Legend

See "The Tale of Aqhat" article.

4 If it is true that I have gone astray,
my error[s] remains my concern alone.
5 If indeed you would exalt yourselves above me[t]
and use my humiliation against me,
6 then know that God has wronged me[u]
and drawn his net[v] around me.

7 "Though I cry, 'I've been wronged!' I get no response;[w]
though I call for help, there is no justice.[x]
8 He has blocked my way so I cannot pass;[y]
he has shrouded my paths in darkness.[z]
9 He has stripped[a] me of my honor
and removed the crown from my head.[b]
10 He tears me down[c] on every side till I am gone;
he uproots my hope[d] like a tree.[e]
11 His anger[f] burns against me;
he counts me among his enemies.[g]
12 His troops advance in force;[h]
they build a siege ramp[i] against me
and encamp around my tent.

13 "He has alienated my brothers[j] from me;
my acquaintances are completely estranged from me.[k]
14 My kinsmen have gone away;
my friends have forgotten me.
15 My guests and my maidservants count me a stranger;
they look upon me as an alien.
16 I summon my servant, but he does not answer,
though I beg him with my own mouth.
17 My breath is offensive to my wife;
I am loathsome to my own brothers.
18 Even the little boys[l] scorn me;
when I appear, they ridicule me.
19 All my intimate friends[m] detest me;[n]
those I love have turned against me.
20 I am nothing but skin and bones;[o]
I have escaped with only the skin of my teeth.[a]

21 "Have pity on me, my friends, have pity,
for the hand of God has struck me.
22 Why do you pursue[p] me as God does?
Will you never get enough of my flesh?[q]

23 "Oh, that my words were recorded,
that they were written on a scroll,[r]
24 that they were inscribed with an iron tool on[b] lead,
or engraved in rock forever!
25 I know that my Redeemer[c][s] lives,[t]
and that in the end he will stand upon the earth.[d]
26 And after my skin has been destroyed,
yet[e] in[f] my flesh I will see God;[u]

19:4 [s]Job 6:24
19:5 [t]Ps 35:26; 38:16; 55:12
19:6 [u]Job 27:2 [v]Job 18:8
19:7 [w]Job 30:20 [x]Job 9:24; Hab 1:2-4
19:8 [y]Job 3:23; La 3:7 [z]Job 30:26
19:9 [a]Job 12:17 [b]Ps 89:39,44; La 5:16
19:10 [c]Job 12:14 [d]Job 7:6 [e]Job 24:20
19:11 [f]Job 16:9 [g]Job 13:24
19:12 [h]Job 16:13 [i]Job 30:12
19:13 [j]Ps 69:8 [k]Job 16:7; Ps 88:8
19:18 [l]2Ki 2:23
19:19 [m]Ps 55:12-13 [n]Ps 38:11
19:20 [o]Job 33:21; Ps 102:5
19:22 [p]Job 13:25; 16:11 [q]Ps 69:26
19:23 [r]Isa 30:8
19:25 [s]Ps 78:35; Pr 23:11; Isa 43:14; Jer 50:34 [t]Job 16:19
19:26 [u]Ps 17:15; Mt 5:8; 1Co 13:12; 1Jn 3:2

[a] 20 Or *only my gums* [b] 24 Or *and* [c] 25 Or *defender* [d] 25 Or *upon my grave* [e] 26 Or *And after I awake, / though this ⌞body⌟ has been destroyed, / then* [f] 26 Or */ apart from*

19:24 Iron did not come into common use in the ancient Near East until the twelfth century B.C.

[27] I myself will see him
with my own eyes—I, and not another.
How my heart yearns[v] within me!

19:27 [v]Ps 73:26

[28] "If you say, 'How we will hound him,
since the root of the trouble lies in him,[a]'
[29] you should fear the sword yourselves;
for wrath will bring punishment by the sword,[w]
and then you will know that there is judgment.[b]"[x]

19:29 [w]Job 15:22 [x]Job 22:4; Ps 1:5; 9:7

Zophar

20 Then Zophar the Naamathite replied:

[2] "My troubled thoughts prompt me to answer
because I am greatly disturbed.
[3] I hear a rebuke[y] that dishonors me,
and my understanding inspires me to reply.

20:3 [y]Job 19:3

[4] "Surely you know how it has been from of old,
ever since man[c] was placed on the earth,

[a] *28* Many Hebrew manuscripts, Septuagint and Vulgate; most Hebrew manuscripts *me* [b] *29* Or / *that you may come to know the Almighty* [c] *4* Or *Adam*

ANCIENT TEXTS AND ARTIFACTS

The Tale of Aqhat

JOB 20 In Job 20 Zophar asserted that God punishes all evildoers. Although his comprehension was inadequate, Zophar correctly understood that God is fundamentally just and does not capriciously inflict pain upon people. While this may seem self-evident to the modern Christian reader, it is not a viewpoint an ancient pagan would have shared or even considered. The **Ugaritic** tale of Aqhat (also called Aqhatu), located at Ras Shamra[1] in 1930, illustrates this.

The tale begins with the hero Dani-El, who makes sacrifices and prays for a son. At last his desire is granted: He is given a son, Aqhat, to whom the god Kothar-wa-Hasis bequeaths a powerful warrior's bow. But the goddess Anat (also called Anatu) covets the bow and seeks to barter with Aqhat for it. Aqhat is unwilling to part with it but offers to give her all she needs in order to have Kothar-wa-Hasis fashion a similar bow for her. Still, she wants only Aqhat's bow—and offers him eternal life for it. Aqhat, recognizing this as a fraudulent offer, tactlessly refuses. Infuriated, Anat demands permission from the high god, El, to avenge herself upon Aqhat, threatening violence against El himself if he refuses. When El accedes, Anat murders Aqhat with the aid of her henchman and gloats over her deed. What follows is incomplete and somewhat confused, but it seems that a drought ensues, Dani-El mourns his son, and Aqhat's sister Pugat seeks to avenge his death.

Readers of the *Iliad* and the *Odyssey* are familiar with pagan tales of jealous, violent and petty gods. This understanding prevailed in the ancient Near East. Israel's belief in a righteous God was truly distinctive.

A stele from Beth Shan depicting the worship of the Canaanite goddess Anat, but using Egyptian motifs
Preserving Bible Times; © Dr. James C. Martin

[1]For other tales discovered at Ras Shamra, see "The Kirta Epic" on page 736 and "The Ugaritic Text of the Myth of Baal" on page 905.

5 that the mirth of the wicked is brief,
the joy of the godless lasts but a moment.[z]
6 Though his pride reaches to the heavens
and his head touches the clouds,[a]
7 he will perish forever,[b] like his own dung;
those who have seen him will say, 'Where is he?'[c]
8 Like a dream[d] he flies away,[e] no more to be found,
banished[f] like a vision of the night.[g]
9 The eye that saw him will not see him again;
his place will look on him no more.[h]
10 His children[i] must make amends to the poor;
his own hands must give back his wealth.[j]
11 The youthful vigor[k] that fills his bones
will lie with him in the dust.[l]

12 "Though evil is sweet in his mouth
and he hides it under his tongue,
13 though he cannot bear to let it go
and keeps it in his mouth,[m]
14 yet his food will turn sour in his stomach;
it will become the venom of serpents within him.
15 He will spit out the riches he swallowed;
God will make his stomach vomit them up.
16 He will suck the poison[n] of serpents;
the fangs of an adder will kill him.[o]
17 He will not enjoy the streams,
the rivers flowing with honey[p] and cream.[q]
18 What he toiled for he must give back uneaten;
he will not enjoy the profit from his trading.
19 For he has oppressed the poor and left them destitute;[r]
he has seized houses he did not build.

20 "Surely he will have no respite from his craving;[s]
he cannot save himself by his treasure.
21 Nothing is left for him to devour;
his prosperity will not endure.[t]
22 In the midst of his plenty, distress will overtake him;
the full force of misery will come upon him.
23 When he has filled his belly,
God will vent his burning anger against him
and rain down his blows upon him.[u]
24 Though he flees[v] from an iron weapon,
a bronze-tipped arrow pierces him.
25 He pulls it out of his back,
the gleaming point out of his liver.
Terrors[w] will come over him;[x]
26 total darkness[y] lies in wait for his treasures.
A fire unfanned will consume him[z]
and devour what is left in his tent.
27 The heavens will expose his guilt;
the earth will rise up against him.[a]
28 A flood will carry off his house,[b]
rushing waters[a] on the day of God's wrath.[c]
29 Such is the fate God allots the wicked,
the heritage appointed for them by God."[d]

20:5 [z] Job 8:12; Ps 37:35-36; 73:19
20:6 [a] Isa 14:13-14; Ob 1:3-4
20:7 [b] Job 4:20 [c] Job 7:10; 8:18
20:8 [d] Ps 73:20 [e] Job 27:21-23 [f] Job 18:18 [g] Ps 90:5
20:9 [h] Job 7:8
20:10 [i] Job 5:4 [j] Job 27:16-17
20:11 [k] Job 13:26 [l] Job 21:26
20:13 [m] Nu 11:18-20
20:16 [n] Dt 32:32 [o] Dt 32:24
20:17 [p] Dt 32:13 [q] Job 29:6
20:19 [r] Job 24:4, 14; 35:9
20:20 [s] Ecc 5:12-14
20:21 [t] Job 15:29
20:23 [u] Ps 78:30-31
20:24 [v] Isa 24:18; Am 5:19
20:25 [w] Job 18:11 [x] Job 16:13
20:26 [y] Job 18:18 [z] Ps 21:9
20:27 [a] Dt 31:28
20:28 [b] Dt 28:31 [c] Job 21:17,20,30
20:29 [d] Job 27:13

[a] 28 Or *The possessions in his house will be carried off, / washed away*

Job

21 Then Job replied:

[2]"Listen carefully to my words;
let this be the consolation you give me.
[3]Bear with me while I speak,
and after I have spoken, mock on.[e]

[4]"Is my complaint directed to man?
Why should I not be impatient?[f]
[5]Look at me and be astonished;
clap your hand over your mouth.[g]
[6]When I think about this, I am terrified;
trembling seizes my body.
[7]Why do the wicked live on,
growing old and increasing in power?[h]
[8]They see their children established around them,
their offspring before their eyes.[i]
[9]Their homes are safe and free from fear;[j]
the rod of God is not upon them.
[10]Their bulls never fail to breed;
their cows calve and do not miscarry.[k]
[11]They send forth their children as a flock;
their little ones dance about.
[12]They sing to the music of tambourine and harp;
they make merry to the sound of the flute.[l]
[13]They spend their years in prosperity[m]
and go down to the grave[a] in peace.[b]
[14]Yet they say to God, 'Leave us alone![n]
We have no desire to know your ways.[o]
[15]Who is the Almighty, that we should serve him?
What would we gain by praying to him?'[p]
[16]But their prosperity is not in their own hands,
so I stand aloof from the counsel of the wicked.

[17]"Yet how often is the lamp of the wicked snuffed out?[q]
How often does calamity come upon them,
the fate God allots in his anger?
[18]How often are they like straw before the wind,
like chaff[r] swept away by a gale?
[19]⌊It is said,⌋ 'God stores up a man's punishment for his sons.'[s]
Let him repay the man himself, so that he will know it!
[20]Let his own eyes see his destruction;
let him drink[t] of the wrath of the Almighty.[c][u]
[21]For what does he care about the family he leaves behind
when his allotted months[v] come to an end?

[22]"Can anyone teach knowledge to God,[w]
since he judges even the highest?[x]
[23]One man dies in full vigor,
completely secure and at ease,
[24]his body[d] well nourished,
his bones rich with marrow.[y]

21:3 [e]Job 16:10
21:4 [f]Job 6:11
21:5 [g]Jdg 18:19; Job 29:9; 40:4
21:7 [h]Job 12:6; Ps 73:3; Jer 12:1; Hab 1:13
21:8 [i]Ps 17:14
21:9 [j]Ps 73:5
21:10 [k]Ex 23:26
21:12 [l]Ps 81:2
21:13 [m]Job 36:11
21:14 [n]Job 22:17 [o]Pr 1:29
21:15 [p]Ex 5:2; Job 34:9; Mal 3:14
21:17 [q]Job 18:5
21:18 [r]Job 13:25; Ps 1:4
21:19 [s]Ex 20:5; Jer 31:29; Eze 18:2
21:20 [t]Ps 75:8; Isa 51:17 [u]Jer 25:15; Rev 14:10
21:21 [v]Job 14:5
21:22 [w]Job 35:11; 36:22; Isa 40:13-14; Ro 11:34 [x]Ps 82:1
21:24 [y]Pr 3:8

[a] *13* Hebrew *Sheol* [b] *13* Or *in an instant* [c] *17-20* Verses 17 and 18 may be taken as exclamations and 19 and 20 as declarations. [d] *24* The meaning of the Hebrew for this word is uncertain.

[25] Another man dies in bitterness of soul,
never having enjoyed anything good.
[26] Side by side they lie in the dust,
and worms cover them both.[z]
[27] "I know full well what you are thinking,
the schemes by which you would wrong me.
[28] You say, 'Where now is the great man's[a] house,
the tents where wicked men lived?'[b]
[29] Have you never questioned those who travel?
Have you paid no regard to their accounts—
[30] that the evil man is spared from the day of calamity,[c]
that he is delivered from[a] the day of wrath?[d]
[31] Who denounces his conduct to his face?
Who repays him for what he has done?
[32] He is carried to the grave,
and watch is kept over his tomb.
[33] The soil in the valley is sweet to him;[e]
all men follow after him,
and a countless throng goes[b] before him.[f]

[34] "So how can you console me[g] with your nonsense?
Nothing is left of your answers but falsehood!"

Eliphaz

22

Then Eliphaz the Temanite replied:

[2] "Can a man be of benefit to God?[h]
Can even a wise man benefit him?
[3] What pleasure would it give the Almighty if you were righteous?
What would he gain if your ways were blameless?

[4] "Is it for your piety that he rebukes you
and brings charges against you?[i]
[5] Is not your wickedness great?
Are not your sins[j] endless?
[6] You demanded security[k] from your brothers for no reason;
you stripped men of their clothing, leaving them naked.
[7] You gave no water to the weary
and you withheld food from the hungry,[l]
[8] though you were a powerful man, owning land—
an honored man,[m] living on it.
[9] And you sent widows away empty-handed[n]
and broke the strength of the fatherless.
[10] That is why snares are all around you,
why sudden peril terrifies you,
[11] why it is so dark[o] you cannot see,
and why a flood of water covers you.[p]

[12] "Is not God in the heights of heaven?[q]
And see how lofty are the highest stars!

21:26 [z]Job 24:20; Ecc 9:2-3; Isa 14:11
21:28 [a]Job 1:3; 12:21; 31:37 [b]Job 8:22
21:30 [c]Pr 16:4 [d]Job 20:22,28; 2Pe 2:9
21:33 [e]Job 3:22; 17:16; 24:24 [f]Job 3:19
21:34 [g]Job 16:2
22:2 [h]Lk 17:10
22:4 [i]Job 14:3; 19:29; Ps 143:2
22:5 [j]Job 11:6; 15:5
22:6 [k]Ex 22:26; Dt 24:6,17; Eze 18:12,16
22:7 [l]Job 31:17, 21,31
22:8 [m]Isa 3:3; 9:15
22:9 [n]Job 24:3, 21
22:11 [o]Job 5:14 [p]Ps 69:1-2; 124:4-5; La 3:54
22:12 [q]Job 11:8

[a] 30 Or *man is reserved for the day of calamity, / that he is brought forth to* [b] 33 Or */ as a countless throng went*

22:1–30 See the note on Eliphaz at 2:11.
22:12 The Bible refers in a most striking manner to the height of the stars—that is, to their distance from the earth (cf. Isa 14:13). Note that our galaxy alone is approximately 100,000 light years across!

22:13 [r]Ps 10:11; Isa 29:15 [s]Eze 8:12
22:14 [t]Job 26:9
22:16 [u]Job 15:32 [v]Job 14:19; Mt 7:26-27
22:17 [w]Job 21:15
22:18 [x]Job 12:6 [y]Job 21:16
22:19 [z]Ps 58:10; 107:42 [a]Ps 52:6
22:20 [b]Job 15:30
22:21 [c]Ps 34:8-10
22:23 [d]Job 8:5; Isa 31:6; Zec 1:3 [e]Isa 19:22; Ac 20:32 [f]Job 11:14
22:24 [g]Job 31:25
22:25 [h]Isa 33:6
22:26 [i]Job 27:10; Isa 58:14
22:27 [j]Job 33:26; 34:28; Isa 58:9
22:29 [k]Mt 23:12; 1Pe 5:5
22:30 [l]Job 42:7-8

13 Yet you say, 'What does God know?[r]
Does he judge through such darkness?[s]
14 Thick clouds[t] veil him, so he does not see us
as he goes about in the vaulted heavens.'
15 Will you keep to the old path
that evil men have trod?
16 They were carried off before their time,[u]
their foundations washed away by a flood.[v]
17 They said to God, 'Leave us alone!
What can the Almighty do to us?'[w]
18 Yet it was he who filled their houses with good things,[x]
so I stand aloof from the counsel of the wicked.[y]

19 "The righteous see their ruin and rejoice;[z]
the innocent mock[a] them, saying,
20 'Surely our foes are destroyed,
and fire[b] devours their wealth.'

21 "Submit to God and be at peace with him;
in this way prosperity will come to you.[c]
22 Accept instruction from his mouth
and lay up his words in your heart.
23 If you return[d] to the Almighty, you will be restored:[e]
If you remove wickedness far from your tent[f]
24 and assign your nuggets to the dust,
your gold of Ophir to the rocks in the ravines,[g]
25 then the Almighty will be your gold,
the choicest silver for you.[h]
26 Surely then you will find delight in the Almighty[i]
and will lift up your face to God.
27 You will pray to him,[j] and he will hear you,
and you will fulfill your vows.
28 What you decide on will be done,
and light will shine on your ways.
29 When men are brought low and you say, 'Lift them up!'
then he will save the downcast.[k]
30 He will deliver even one who is not innocent,
who will be delivered through the cleanness of your hands."[l]

Job

23:2 [m]Job 7:11 [n]Job 6:3
23:4 [o]Job 13:18
23:6 [p]Job 9:4

23 Then Job replied:

2 "Even today my complaint[m] is bitter;[n]
his hand[a] is heavy in spite of[b] my groaning.
3 If only I knew where to find him;
if only I could go to his dwelling!
4 I would state my case[o] before him
and fill my mouth with arguments.
5 I would find out what he would answer me,
and consider what he would say.
6 Would he oppose me with great power?[p]
No, he would not press charges against me.

[a] 2 Septuagint and Syriac; Hebrew / *the hand on me* [b] 2 Or *heavy on me in*

22:24 For information on Ophir, see the note on 1 Kings 9:28.

[7] There an upright man could present his case before him,[q]
and I would be delivered forever from my judge.

[8] "But if I go to the east, he is not there;
if I go to the west, I do not find him.
[9] When he is at work in the north, I do not see him;
when he turns to the south, I catch no glimpse of him.[r]
[10] But he knows the way that I take;
when he has tested me,[s] I will come forth as gold.[t]
[11] My feet have closely followed his steps;[u]
I have kept to his way without turning aside.[v]
[12] I have not departed from the commands of his lips;[w]
I have treasured the words of his mouth more than my daily bread.[x]

[13] "But he stands alone, and who can oppose him?
He does whatever he pleases.[y]
[14] He carries out his decree against me,
and many such plans he still has in store.[z]
[15] That is why I am terrified before him;
when I think of all this, I fear him.
[16] God has made my heart faint;[a]
the Almighty[b] has terrified me.
[17] Yet I am not silenced by the darkness,[c]
by the thick darkness that covers my face.

24 "Why does the Almighty not set times for judgment?[d]
Why must those who know him look in vain for such days?[e]
[2] Men move boundary stones;[f]
they pasture flocks they have stolen.
[3] They drive away the orphan's donkey
and take the widow's ox in pledge.[g]
[4] They thrust the needy from the path
and force all the poor[h] of the land into hiding.[i]
[5] Like wild donkeys in the desert,
the poor go about their labor[j] of foraging food;
the wasteland provides food for their children.
[6] They gather fodder in the fields
and glean in the vineyards of the wicked.
[7] Lacking clothes, they spend the night naked;
they have nothing to cover themselves in the cold.[k]
[8] They are drenched by mountain rains
and hug[l] the rocks for lack of shelter.
[9] The fatherless[m] child is snatched from the breast;
the infant of the poor is seized for a debt.
[10] Lacking clothes, they go about naked;
they carry the sheaves, but still go hungry.
[11] They crush olives among the terraces[a];
they tread the winepresses, yet suffer thirst.
[12] The groans of the dying rise from the city,
and the souls of the wounded cry out for help.[n]
But God charges no one with wrongdoing.[o]

23:7 [q]Job 13:3
23:9 [r]Job 9:11
23:10 [s]Ps 66:10; 139:1-3 [t]1Pe 1:7
23:11 [u]Ps 17:5 [v]Ps 44:18
23:12 [w]Job 6:10 [x]Jn 4:32,34
23:13 [y]Ps 115:3
23:14 [z]1Th 3:3
23:16 [a]Dt 20:3; Ps 22:14; Jer 51:46 [b]Job 27:2
23:17 [c]Job 19:8
24:1 [d]Jer 46:10 [e]Ac 1:7
24:2 [f]Dt 19:14; 27:17; Pr 23:10
24:3 [g]Dt 24:6,10, 12,17; Job 22:6
24:4 [h]Job 29:12; 30:25; Ps 41:1 [i]Pr 28:28
24:5 [j]Ps 104:23
24:7 [k]Ex 22:27; Job 22:6
24:8 [l]La 4:5
24:9 [m]Dt 24:17
24:12 [n]Eze 26:15 [o]Job 9:23

[a] *11 Or olives between the millstones*; the meaning of the Hebrew for this word is uncertain.

23:13 Although Job was not an Israelite, he worshiped the one true God.
24:2 For information on boundary stones, see the note on Deuteronomy 19:14.
24:10 For a discussion of sheaves and threshing, see the note on Ruth 2:7. See also "The Threshing Floor" on page 608 and "Food and Agriculture" on page 390.

24:13 [p]Jn 3:19-20 [q]Isa 5:20

13 “There are those who rebel against the light,[p]
who do not know its ways
or stay in its paths.[q]
14 When daylight is gone, the murderer rises up
and kills the poor and needy;
in the night he steals forth like a thief.[r]

24:14 [r]Ps 10:9

15 The eye of the adulterer watches for dusk;[s]
he thinks, ‘No eye will see me,’[t]
and he keeps his face concealed.

24:15 [s]Pr 7:8-9 [t]Ps 10:11

16 In the dark, men break into houses,[u]
but by day they shut themselves in;
they want nothing to do with the light.[v]

24:16 [u]Ex 22:2; Mt 6:19 [v]Jn 3:20

17 For all of them, deep darkness is their morning[a];
they make friends with the terrors of darkness.[b]

18 “Yet they are foam[w] on the surface of the water;[x]
their portion of the land is cursed,
so that no one goes to the vineyards.

24:18 [w]Job 9:26 [x]Job 22:16

19 As heat and drought snatch away the melted snow,[y]
so the grave[c][z] snatches away those who have sinned.

24:19 [y]Job 6:17 [z]Job 21:13

20 The womb forgets them,
the worm feasts on them;
evil men are no longer remembered[a]
but are broken like a tree.[b]

24:20 [a]Job 18:17; Pr 10:7 [b]Ps 31:12; Da 4:14

21 They prey on the barren and childless woman,
and to the widow show no kindness.[c]

24:21 [c]Job 22:9

22 But God drags away the mighty by his power;
though they become established, they have no assurance of life.[d]

24:22 [d]Dt 28:66

23 He may let them rest in a feeling of security,[e]
but his eyes are on their ways.[f]

24:23 [e]Job 12:6 [f]Job 11:11

24 For a little while they are exalted, and then they are gone;[g]
they are brought low and gathered up like all others;
they are cut off like heads of grain.[h]

24:24 [g]Job 14:21; Ps 37:10 [h]Isa 17:5

25 “If this is not so, who can prove me false
and reduce my words to nothing?”[i]

24:25 [i]Job 6:28; 27:4

Bildad

25

Then Bildad the Shuhite replied:

2 “Dominion and awe belong to God;[j]
he establishes order in the heights of heaven.

25:2 [j]Job 9:4; Rev 1:6

3 Can his forces be numbered?
Upon whom does his light not rise?[k]

25:3 [k]Jas 1:17

4 How then can a man be righteous before God?
How can one born of woman be pure?[l]

25:4 [l]Job 4:17; 14:4

5 If even the moon[m] is not bright
and the stars are not pure in his eyes,[n]

25:5 [m]Job 31:26 [n]Job 15:15

6 how much less man, who is but a maggot—
a son of man,[o] who is only a worm!”[p]

25:6 [o]Job 7:17 [p]Ps 22:6

Job

26

Then Job replied:

2 “How you have helped the powerless![q]
How you have saved the arm that is feeble![r]

26:2 [q]Job 6:12 [r]Ps 71:9

[a] 17 Or *them, their morning is like the shadow of death* [b] 17 Or *of the shadow of death* [c] 19 Hebrew *Sheol*

[3] What advice you have offered to one without wisdom!
And what great insight you have displayed!
[4] Who has helped you utter these words?
And whose spirit spoke from your mouth?

[5] "The dead are in deep anguish,[s]
those beneath the waters and all that live in them.
[6] Death[a][t] is naked before God;
Destruction[b] lies uncovered.[u]
[7] He spreads out the northern ⌞skies⌟[v] over empty space;
he suspends the earth over nothing.
[8] He wraps up the waters[w] in his clouds,[x]
yet the clouds do not burst under their weight.
[9] He covers the face of the full moon,
spreading his clouds[y] over it.
[10] He marks out the horizon on the face of the waters[z]
for a boundary between light and darkness.[a]
[11] The pillars of the heavens quake,
aghast at his rebuke.
[12] By his power he churned up the sea;[b]
by his wisdom[c] he cut Rahab to pieces.
[13] By his breath the skies became fair;
his hand pierced the gliding serpent.[d]
[14] And these are but the outer fringe of his works;
how faint the whisper we hear of him!
Who then can understand the thunder of his power?"[e]

27 And Job continued his discourse:[f]

[2] "As surely as God lives, who has denied me justice,[g]
the Almighty, who has made me taste bitterness of soul,[h]
[3] as long as I have life within me,
the breath of God[i] in my nostrils,
[4] my lips will not speak wickedness,
and my tongue will utter no deceit.[j]
[5] I will never admit you are in the right;
till I die, I will not deny my integrity.[k]
[6] I will maintain my righteousness and never let go of it;
my conscience will not reproach me as long as I live.[l]

[7] "May my enemies be like the wicked,
my adversaries like the unjust!
[8] For what hope has the godless[m] when he is cut off,
when God takes away his life?[n]
[9] Does God listen to his cry
when distress comes upon him?[o]
[10] Will he find delight in the Almighty?[p]
Will he call upon God at all times?

[11] "I will teach you about the power of God;
the ways of the Almighty I will not conceal.

26:5 [s]Ps 88:10
26:6 [t]Ps 139:8 [u]Job 41:11; Pr 15:11; Heb 4:13
26:7 [v]Job 9:8
26:8 [w]Pr 30:4 [x]Job 37:11
26:9 [y]Job 22:14; Ps 97:2
26:10 [z]Pr 8:27, 29 [a]Job 38:8-11
26:12 [b]Ex 14:21; Isa 51:15; Jer 31:35 [c]Job 12:13
26:13 [d]Isa 27:1
26:14 [e]Job 36:29
27:1 [f]Job 29:1
27:2 [g]Job 34:5 [h]Job 9:18
27:3 [i]Job 32:8; 33:4
27:4 [j]Job 6:28
27:5 [k]Job 2:9; 13:15
27:6 [l]Job 2:3
27:8 [m]Job 8:13 [n]Job 11:20; Lk 12:20
27:9 [o]Job 35:12; Pr 1:28; Isa 1:15; Jer 14:12; Mic 3:4
27:10 [p]Job 22:26

[a] 6 Hebrew *Sheol* [b] 6 Hebrew *Abaddon*

26:5 The Hebrew rendered here as "the dead" is translated "spirits of the dead" in Proverbs 2:18, "spirits of the departed" in Isaiah 14:9 and "departed spirits" in Isaiah 26:14. The term is used figuratively of the deceased who supposedly inhabited the netherworld (see Job 3:13–15,17–19). The "waters" were considered part of the world inhabited by living beings and therefore above the netherworld.
26:12 See the note on 9:13.

[12]You have all seen this yourselves.
Why then this meaningless talk?

[13]"Here is the fate God allots to the wicked,
the heritage a ruthless man receives from the Almighty:[q]
[14]However many his children, their fate is the sword;[r]
his offspring will never have enough to eat.[s]
[15]The plague will bury those who survive him,
and their widows will not weep for them.[t]
[16]Though he heaps up silver like dust
and clothes like piles of clay,[u]
[17]what he lays up the righteous will wear,[v]
and the innocent will divide his silver.
[18]The house he builds is like a moth's cocoon,[w]
like a hut[x] made by a watchman.
[19]He lies down wealthy, but will do so no more;[y]
when he opens his eyes, all is gone.
[20]Terrors overtake him like a flood;[z]
a tempest snatches him away in the night.[a]
[21]The east wind carries him off, and he is gone;
it sweeps him out of his place.[b]
[22]It hurls itself against him without mercy[c]
as he flees headlong from its power.[d]
[23]It claps its hands in derision
and hisses him out of his place.[e]

28

"There is a mine for silver
and a place where gold is refined.
[2]Iron is taken from the earth,
and copper is smelted from ore.[f]
[3]Man puts an end to the darkness;[g]
he searches the farthest recesses
for ore in the blackest darkness.
[4]Far from where people dwell he cuts a shaft,
in places forgotten by the foot of man;
far from men he dangles and sways.
[5]The earth, from which food comes,[h]
is transformed below as by fire;
[6]sapphires[a] come from its rocks,
and its dust contains nuggets of gold.
[7]No bird of prey knows that hidden path,
no falcon's eye has seen it.
[8]Proud beasts do not set foot on it,
and no lion prowls there.
[9]Man's hand assaults the flinty rock
and lays bare the roots of the mountains.
[10]He tunnels through the rock;
his eyes see all its treasures.
[11]He searches[b] the sources of the rivers
and brings hidden things to light.

27:13 [q]Job 15:20; 20:29
27:14 [r]Dt 28:41; Job 15:22; Hos 9:13 [s]Job 20:10
27:15 [t]Ps 78:64
27:16 [u]Zec 9:3
27:17 [v]Pr 28:8; Ecc 2:26
27:18 [w]Job 8:14 [x]Isa 1:8
27:19 [y]Job 7:8
27:20 [z]Job 15:21 [a]Job 20:8
27:21 [b]Job 7:10; 21:18
27:22 [c]Jer 13:14; Eze 5:11; 24:14 [d]Job 11:20
27:23 [e]Job 18:18
28:2 [f]Dt 8:9
28:3 [g]Ecc 1:13
28:5 [h]Ps 104:14

[a] 6 Or *lapis lazuli*; also in verse 16 [b] 11 Septuagint, Aquila and Vulgate; Hebrew *He dams up*

28:1–11 These verses provide a fascinating, lyrical description of ancient mining techniques.
28:2 See the note on 19:24.
28:10 An eighth-century B.C. inscription found at Jerusalem's Pool of Siloam testifies to the sophistication of ancient tunneling technology. (See "Hezekiah's Tunnel" on p. 564 and "The Pool of Siloam" on p. 1739.)

ANCIENT VOICES

"Your disease is under control, let your
heart not be despondent!
The years and days you were filled with
misery are over.
Were you not ordered to live,
How could you have lasted the whole of
this grievous illness?
You have seen distress, . . . is (now)*
held back.
You have borne its massive load to
the end."

*Word in parentheses added by translator for clarity

—DIALOGUE BETWEEN A MAN AND HIS GOD

See "A Man and His God" article.

12 "But where can wisdom be found?[i]
Where does understanding dwell?
13 Man does not comprehend its worth;[j]
it cannot be found in the land of the living.
14 The deep says, 'It is not in me';
the sea says, 'It is not with me.'
15 It cannot be bought with the finest gold,
nor can its price be weighed in silver.[k]
16 It cannot be bought with the gold of Ophir,
with precious onyx or sapphires.
17 Neither gold nor crystal can compare with it,
nor can it be had for jewels of gold.[l]
18 Coral and jasper are not worthy of mention;
the price of wisdom is beyond rubies.[m]
19 The topaz of Cush cannot compare with it;
it cannot be bought with pure gold.[n]

20 "Where then does wisdom come from?
Where does understanding dwell?[o]
21 It is hidden from the eyes of every living thing,
concealed even from the birds of the air.
22 Destruction[a][p] and Death say,
'Only a rumor of it has reached our ears.'
23 God understands the way to it
and he alone knows where it dwells,[q]
24 for he views the ends of the earth[r]
and sees everything under the heavens.[s]
25 When he established the force of the wind
and measured out the waters,[t]
26 when he made a decree for the rain
and a path for the thunderstorm,[u]
27 then he looked at wisdom and appraised it;
he confirmed it and tested it.
28 And he said to man,
'The fear of the Lord—that is wisdom,
and to shun evil is understanding.[v]' "

29 Job continued his discourse:[w]

2 "How I long for the months gone by,
for the days when God watched over me,[x]
3 when his lamp shone upon my head
and by his light I walked through darkness![y]
4 Oh, for the days when I was in my prime,
when God's intimate friendship blessed my house,[z]
5 when the Almighty was still with me
and my children were around me,
6 when my path was drenched with cream[a]
and the rock[b] poured out for me streams of
olive oil.[c]

28:12 [i]Ecc 7:24
28:13 [j]Pr 3:15; Mt 13:44-46
28:15 [k]Pr 3:13-14; 8:10-11; 16:16
28:17 [l]Pr 16:16
28:18 [m]Pr 3:15
28:19 [n]Pr 8:19
28:20 [o]ver 23,28
28:22 [p]Job 26:6
28:23 [q]Pr 8:22-31
28:24 [r]Ps 33:13-14 [s]Pr 15:3
28:25 [t]Job 12:15; Ps 135:7
28:26 [u]Job 37:3, 8,11; 38:25,27
28:28 [v]Dt 4:6; Ps 111:10; Pr 1:7; 9:10
29:1 [w]Job 13:12; 27:1
29:2 [x]Jer 31:28
29:3 [y]Job 11:17
29:4 [z]Ps 25:14; Pr 3:32
29:6 [a]Job 20:17 [b]Ps 81:16 [c]Dt 32:13

[a] 22 Hebrew *Abaddon*

28:16 For information on Ophir, see the note on 1 Kings 9:28.
28:17 Both the Hebrew and Greek terms for "crystal" can also be translated "ice." Most likely the reference here is to rock crystal or to crystallized quartz. The reason for the possible rendering "ice" is the ancient belief that crystal was formed by intense cold (see also Rev 4:6; 21:11; 22:1).
28:19 Cush was located in the Upper Nile region, south of Egypt.
29:6 Cream and olive oil were symbols of wealth and luxury (see 20:17; Eze 16:19).

29:7 [d]Job 31:21
29:9 [e]Job 21:5
29:10 [f]Ps 137:6
29:12 [g]Job 24:4 [h]Job 31:17,21 [i]Ps 72:12; Pr 21:13
29:13 [j]Job 31:20 [k]Job 22:9
29:14 [l]Job 27:6; Ps 132:9; Isa 59:17; 61:10; Eph 6:14
29:15 [m]Nu 10:31
29:16 [n]Job 24:4; Pr 29:7
29:17 [o]Ps 3:7
29:18 [p]Ps 30:6

7 "When I went to the gate[d] of the city
and took my seat in the public square,
8 the young men saw me and stepped aside
and the old men rose to their feet;
9 the chief men refrained from speaking
and covered their mouths with their hands;[e]
10 the voices of the nobles were hushed,
and their tongues stuck to the roof of their mouths.[f]
11 Whoever heard me spoke well of me,
and those who saw me commended me,
12 because I rescued the poor[g] who cried for help,
and the fatherless[h] who had none to assist him.[i]
13 The man who was dying blessed me;[j]
I made the widow's[k] heart sing.
14 I put on righteousness[l] as my clothing;
justice was my robe and my turban.
15 I was eyes[m] to the blind
and feet to the lame.
16 I was a father to the needy;[n]
I took up the case of the stranger.
17 I broke the fangs of the wicked
and snatched the victims from their teeth.[o]

18 "I thought, 'I will die in my own house,
my days as numerous as the grains of sand.[p]

29:7 The most important business was conducted, and the most significant legal cases tried, at the city gate (see "The City Gate" on p. 392). Job was a city elder, a member of the ruling council.

29:12–13 See "The Care of Widows and Orphans in the Bible and the Ancient Near East" on page 285.

ANCIENT TEXTS AND ARTIFACTS

A Man and His God

JOB 29 A broken **Akkadian** tablet from the **Old Babylonian** period, sometimes called A Man and His God, describes the lament of a young man who is suffering from some dreadful but unspecified disease. He groans, weeps and cries out to his god for help. Although the text is fragmentary, it is clear that the man wrestles with the question of how he may have sinned against his god and concludes that he has committed blasphemy. In the end, his god pronounces a blessing on him, promises that he will prosper and encourages him to donate food to the poor.

At first glance the tablet may strike many readers as being similar to Job, with its pitiable account of the sufferer's lamentation, his struggle with the problem of sin and divine justice and his final deliverance by divine intervention. An important difference between the two texts, however, is that the young man of the Akkadian text finally recognized and confessed his sin, whereas Job expressly declared himself to be a righteous man who was suffering because of his virtue and not because of some sin. The Akkadian text thus lacks the profundity of the problem posed by Job: that of the righteous sufferer.[1]

[1]See also "'I Will Praise the Lord of Wisdom'" on page 751 and "The Babylonian Theodicy" on page 776.

[19] My roots will reach to the water,[q]
and the dew will lie all night on my branches.
[20] My glory will remain fresh in me,
the bow[r] ever new in my hand.'[s]

[21] "Men listened to me expectantly,
waiting in silence for my counsel.
[22] After I had spoken, they spoke no more;
my words fell gently on their ears.[t]
[23] They waited for me as for showers
and drank in my words as the spring rain.
[24] When I smiled at them, they scarcely believed it;
the light of my face was precious to them.[a]
[25] I chose the way for them and sat as their chief;
I dwelt as a king[u] among his troops;
I was like one who comforts mourners.[v]

30

"But now they mock me,[w]
men younger than I,
whose fathers I would have disdained
to put with my sheep dogs.
[2] Of what use was the strength of their hands to me,
since their vigor had gone from them?
[3] Haggard from want and hunger,
they roamed[b] the parched land
in desolate wastelands at night.
[4] In the brush they gathered salt herbs,
and their food[c] was the root of the broom tree.
[5] They were banished from their fellow men,
shouted at as if they were thieves.
[6] They were forced to live in the dry stream beds,
among the rocks and in holes in the ground.
[7] They brayed among the bushes
and huddled in the undergrowth.
[8] A base and nameless brood,
they were driven out of the land.

[9] "And now their sons mock me[x] in song;[y]
I have become a byword[z] among them.
[10] They detest me and keep their distance;
they do not hesitate to spit in my face.[a]
[11] Now that God has unstrung my bow and afflicted me,[b]
they throw off restraint[c] in my presence.
[12] On my right the tribe[d] attacks;
they lay snares for my feet,[d]
they build their siege ramps against me.[e]
[13] They break up my road;[f]
they succeed in destroying me—
without anyone's helping them.[e]

29:19 [q]Job 18:16; Jer 17:8
29:20 [r]Ps 18:34 [s]Ge 49:24
29:22 [t]Dt 32:2
29:25 [u]Job 1:3; 31:37 [v]Job 4:4
30:1 [w]Job 12:4
30:9 [x]Ps 69:11 [y]Job 12:4; La 3:14,63 [z]Job 17:6
30:10 [a]Nu 12:14; Dt 25:9; Isa 50:6; Mt 26:67
30:11 [b]Ru 1:21 [c]Ps 32:9
30:12 [d]Ps 140:4-5 [e]Job 19:12
30:13 [f]Isa 3:12

[a] 24 The meaning of the Hebrew for this clause is uncertain. [b] 3 Or *gnawed* [c] 4 Or *fuel* [d] 12 The meaning of the Hebrew for this word is uncertain. [e] 13 Or *me. / 'No one can help him,' they say.*

30:4 The term "salt herbs" probably refers to saltwort, which grows in otherwise infertile areas, including the regions east of Sinai where Job and his friends lived. The broom tree was a large bush found in the deserts of Canaan and Arabia (see 1Ki 19:4; Ps 120:4).

30:9 See "Bywords and Insults in the Ancient World" on page 431.
30:12 See "Siege Warfare" on page 465.

14 They advance as through a gaping breach;
amid the ruins they come rolling in.
15 Terrors overwhelm me;[g]
my dignity is driven away as by the wind,
my safety vanishes like a cloud.[h]

16 "And now my life ebbs away;[i]
days of suffering grip me.
17 Night pierces my bones;
my gnawing pains never rest.
18 In his great power ⌞God⌟ becomes like clothing to me[a];
he binds me like the neck of my garment.
19 He throws me into the mud,[j]
and I am reduced to dust and ashes.

20 "I cry out to you, O God, but you do not answer;[k]
I stand up, but you merely look at me.
21 You turn on me ruthlessly;[l]
with the might of your hand[m] you attack me.[n]
22 You snatch me up and drive me before the wind;[o]
you toss me about in the storm.[p]
23 I know you will bring me down to death,[q]
to the place appointed for all the living.[r]

24 "Surely no one lays a hand on a broken man
when he cries for help in his distress.[s]
25 Have I not wept for those in trouble?
Has not my soul grieved for the poor?[t]
26 Yet when I hoped for good, evil came;
when I looked for light, then came darkness.[u]
27 The churning inside me never stops;[v]
days of suffering confront me.
28 I go about blackened,[w] but not by the sun;
I stand up in the assembly and cry for help.[x]
29 I have become a brother of jackals,[y]
a companion of owls.[z]
30 My skin grows black and peels;[a]
my body burns with fever.[b]
31 My harp is tuned to mourning,[c]
and my flute to the sound of wailing.

31 "I made a covenant with my eyes
not to look lustfully at a girl.[d]
2 For what is man's lot from God above,
his heritage from the Almighty on high?[e]
3 Is it not ruin[f] for the wicked,
disaster for those who do wrong?[g]
4 Does he not see my ways[h]
and count my every step?[i]

5 "If I have walked in falsehood
or my foot has hurried after deceit[j]—

30:15 [g]Job 31:23; Ps 55:4-5 [h]Job 3:25; Hos 13:3
30:16 [i]Job 3:24; Ps 22:14; 42:4
30:19 [j]Ps 69:2, 14
30:20 [k]Job 19:7
30:21 [l]Job 19:6, **22** [m]Job 16:9,14 [n]Job 10:3
30:22 [o]Job 27:21 [p]Job 9:17
30:23 [q]Job 9:22; 10:8 [r]Job 3:19
30:24 [s]Job 19:7
30:25 [t]Job 24:4; Ps 35:13-14; Ro 12:15
30:26 [u]Job 3:25-26; 19:8; Jer 8:15
30:27 [v]La 2:11
30:28 [w]Ps 38:6; 42:9; 43:2 [x]Job 19:7
30:29 [y]Ps 44:19 [z]Ps 102:6; Mic 1:8
30:30 [a]La 4:8 [b]Ps 102:3
30:31 [c]Isa 24:8
31:1 [d]Mt 5:28
31:2 [e]Job 20:29
31:3 [f]Job 21:30 [g]Job 34:22
31:4 [h]2Ch 16:9 [i]Pr 5:21
31:5 [j]Mic 2:11

[a] 18 Hebrew; Septuagint ⌞*God*⌟ *grasps my clothing*

30:19 Dust and ashes were symbolic of humiliation and insignificance. Job would later use this combination to symbolize repentance (42:6).

[6]let God weigh me in honest scales[k]
and he will know that I am blameless—
[7]if my steps have turned from the path,[l]
if my heart has been led by my eyes,
or if my hands[m] have been defiled,
[8]then may others eat what I have sown,[n]
and may my crops be uprooted.[o]

[9]"If my heart has been enticed[p] by a woman,
or if I have lurked at my neighbor's door,
[10]then may my wife grind another man's grain,
and may other men sleep with her.[q]
[11]For that would have been shameful,
a sin to be judged.[r]
[12]It is a fire[s] that burns to Destruction[a];[t]
it would have uprooted my harvest.[u]

[13]"If I have denied justice to my menservants and
maidservants
when they had a grievance against me,[v]
[14]what will I do when God confronts me?
What will I answer when called to account?
[15]Did not he who made me in the womb make them?
Did not the same one form us both within our mothers?[w]

[16]"If I have denied the desires of the poor[x]
or let the eyes of the widow[y] grow weary,
[17]if I have kept my bread to myself,
not sharing it with the fatherless[z]—
[18]but from my youth I reared him as would a father,
and from my birth I guided the widow—
[19]if I have seen anyone perishing for lack of clothing,[a]
or a needy[b] man without a garment,
[20]and his heart did not bless me
for warming him with the fleece from my sheep,
[21]if I have raised my hand against the fatherless,[c]
knowing that I had influence in court,
[22]then let my arm fall from the shoulder,
let it be broken off at the joint.[d]
[23]For I dreaded destruction from God,
and for fear of his splendor[e] I could not do such things.

[24]"If I have put my trust in gold[f]
or said to pure gold, 'You are my security,'[g]
[25]if I have rejoiced over my great wealth,[h]
the fortune my hands had gained,
[26]if I have regarded the sun[i] in its radiance
or the moon moving in splendor,
[27]so that my heart was secretly enticed
and my hand offered them a kiss of homage,
[28]then these also would be sins to be judged,[j]
for I would have been unfaithful to God on high.

31:6 [k]Job 6:2; 27:5-6
31:7 [l]Job 23:11 [m]Job 9:30
31:8 [n]Lev 26:16; Job 20:18 [o]Mic 6:15
31:9 [p]Job 24:15
31:10 [q]Dt 28:30; Jer 8:10
31:11 [r]Ge 38:24; Lev 20:10; Dt 22:22-24
31:12 [s]Job 15:30 [t]Job 26:6 [u]Job 20:28
31:13 [v]Dt 24:14-15
31:15 [w]Job 10:3
31:16 [x]Job 5:16; 20:19 [y]Job 22:9
31:17 [z]Job 22:7; 29:12
31:19 [a]Job 22:6 [b]Job 24:4
31:21 [c]Job 22:9
31:22 [d]Job 38:15
31:23 [e]Job 13:11
31:24 [f]Job 22:25 [g]Mt 6:24; Mk 10:24
31:25 [h]Ps 62:10
31:26 [i]Eze 8:16
31:28 [j]Dt 17:2-7

[a] 12 Hebrew *Abaddon*

31:26 The sun and moon are not to be objects of worship (see Dt 4:19; 17:3; Eze 8:16–17), although worship of these heavenly bodies was widespread in the ancient Near East.

31:27 A kiss was an ancient gesture of worship (see 1Ki 19:18; Hos 13:2; see also "The Jewish Custom of Kissing" on p. 1682).

31:29 [k]Ob 1:12 [l]Pr 17:5; 24:17-18

29 "If I have rejoiced at my enemy's misfortune[k]
or gloated over the trouble that came to him[l]—
30 I have not allowed my mouth to sin
by invoking a curse against his life—
31 if the men of my household have never said,
'Who has not had his fill of Job's meat?'[m]—
32 but no stranger had to spend the night in the street,
for my door was always open to the traveler[n]—
33 if I have concealed[o] my sin as men do,[a]
by hiding[p] my guilt in my heart
34 because I so feared the crowd[q]
and so dreaded the contempt of the clans
that I kept silent and would not go outside—

31:31 [m]Job 22:7
31:32 [n]Ge 19:2-3; Ro 12:13
31:33 [o]Pr 28:13 [p]Ge 3:8
31:34 [q]Ex 23:2

35 ("Oh, that I had someone to hear me![r]
I sign now my defense—let the Almighty answer me;
let my accuser[s] put his indictment in writing.
36 Surely I would wear it on my shoulder,
I would put it on like a crown.
37 I would give him an account of my every step;
like a prince[t] I would approach him.)—

31:35 [r]Job 19:7; 30:28 [s]Job 27:7; 35:14
31:37 [t]Job 1:3; 29:25

38 "if my land cries out against me[u]
and all its furrows are wet with tears,
39 if I have devoured its yield without payment[v]
or broken the spirit of its tenants,[w]
40 then let briers[x] come up instead of wheat
and weeds instead of barley."

31:38 [u]Ge 4:10
31:39 [v]1Ki 21:19 [w]Lev 19:13; Jas 5:4
31:40 [x]Ge 3:18

The words of Job are ended.

Elihu

32:1 [y]Job 10:7; 33:9
32:2 [z]Ge 22:21 [a]Job 27:5; 30:21

32 So these three men stopped answering Job, because he was righteous in his own eyes.[y] 2 But Eli-
hu son of Barakel the Buzite,[z] of the family of Ram, became very angry with Job for justifying
himself rather than God.[a] 3 He was also angry with the three friends, because they had found no way to
refute Job, and yet had condemned him.[b] 4 Now Elihu had waited before speaking to Job because they
were older than he. 5 But when he saw that the three men had nothing more to say, his anger was aroused.
6 So Elihu son of Barakel the Buzite said:

"I am young in years,
and you are old;[b]
that is why I was fearful,
not daring to tell you what I know.
7 I thought, 'Age should speak;
advanced years should teach wisdom.'
8 But it is the spirit[c] in a man,
the breath of the Almighty,[c] that gives him understanding.[d]
9 It is not only the old[d] who are wise,[e]
not only the aged who understand what is right.

32:6 [b]Job 15:10
32:8 [c]Job 27:3; 33:4 [d]Pr 2:6
32:9 [e]1Co 1:26

10 "Therefore I say: Listen to me;
I too will tell you what I know.

[a] 33 Or *as Adam did* [b] 3 Masoretic Text; an ancient Hebrew scribal tradition *Job, and so had condemned God* [c] 8 Or *Spirit*; also in verse 18 [d] 9 Or *many*; or *great*

31:36 Inscriptions were sometimes worn on the shoulder as a perpetual reminder of their importance (see Ex 28:12).

32:2 A Buzite was an Aramean, an inhabitant of Buz, a desert region in the east (see Jer 25:23).

[11] I waited while you spoke,
I listened to your reasoning;
while you were searching for words,
[12] I gave you my full attention.
But not one of you has proved Job wrong;
none of you has answered his arguments.
[13] Do not say, 'We have found wisdom;[f]
let God refute him, not man.'
[14] But Job has not marshaled his words against me,
and I will not answer him with your arguments.

[15] "They are dismayed and have no more to say;
words have failed them.
[16] Must I wait, now that they are silent,
now that they stand there with no reply?
[17] I too will have my say;
I too will tell what I know.
[18] For I am full of words,
and the spirit within me compels me;
[19] inside I am like bottled-up wine,
like new wineskins ready to burst.
[20] I must speak and find relief;
I must open my lips and reply.
[21] I will show partiality[g] to no one,[h]
nor will I flatter any man;
[22] for if I were skilled in flattery,
my Maker would soon take me away.

32:13 [f]Jer 9:23

32:21 [g]Lev 19:15; Job 13:10 [h]Mt 22:16

32:19 Old wineskins, unlike new ones, might be expected to crack or break (see Mt 9:17). Elihu was obviously eager to speak.

ANCIENT TEXTS AND ARTIFACTS

The Babylonian Theodicy

JOB 33 An **Akkadian** text from approximately 1000 B.C. has striking similarities to the book of Job. Commonly called the "Babylonian Theodicy," it is a dialogue between a sufferer and his friend. In this text a hurting individual bemoans his fate and the treatment he has received at the hands of the gods. Like Job, he has been generous and devout, but now he is driven about in destitution, like a beggar (see Job 30:1–11). He complains that the wicked strut around, secure in their wealth (see 21:1–21). A friend responds that the sufferer does not fully understand the ways of the gods. He does not accuse the man of grievous sin in the manner of Job's friends Eliphaz, Bildad and Zophar (e.g., 22:4–5). However, in much the same vein as Elihu in Job 33, he concedes that the ways of the gods are mysterious.

The Babylonian Theodicy does not wrestle with questions of God and evil as profoundly as does the book of Job, but it does demonstrate again that this kind of literature had parallels elsewhere in the ancient Near East.[1] The date of the Babylonian Theodicy is not far removed from the golden age of wisdom under Solomon (latter tenth century B.C.), and the similarities in genre suggest that Job may have been written at about the same time.

[1]See, for example, "A Man and His God" on page 771.

33:1 [i]Job 13:6
33:3 [j]Job 6:28; 27:4; 36:4
33:4 [k]Ge 2:7; Job 10:3 [l]Job 27:3
33:5 [m]ver 32 [n]Job 13:18
33:6 [o]Job 4:19
33:7 [p]Job 9:34; 13:21; 2Co 2:4
33:9 [q]Job 10:7 [r]Job 13:23; 16:17
33:10 [s]Job 13:24
33:11 [t]Job 13:27 [u]Job 14:16
33:12 [v]Ecc 7:20
33:13 [w]Job 40:2; Isa 45:9
33:14 [x]Ps 62:11
33:15 [y]Job 4:13
33:16 [z]Job 36:10,15
33:18 [a]ver 22,24, 28,30 [b]Job 15:22
33:19 [c]Job 30:17
33:20 [d]Ps 107:18 [e]Job 3:24; 6:6
33:21 [f]Job 16:8; 19:20
33:22 [g]Ps 88:3
33:23 [h]Mic 6:8

33

"But now, Job, listen to my words;
pay attention to everything I say.[i]
2 I am about to open my mouth;
my words are on the tip of my tongue.
3 My words come from an upright heart;
my lips sincerely speak what I know.[j]
4 The Spirit of God has made me;[k]
the breath of the Almighty[l] gives me life.
5 Answer me[m] then, if you can;
prepare[n] yourself and confront me.
6 I am just like you before God;
I too have been taken from clay.[o]
7 No fear of me should alarm you,
nor should my hand be heavy upon you.[p]

8 "But you have said in my hearing—
I heard the very words—
9 'I am pure[q] and without sin;[r]
I am clean and free from guilt.
10 Yet God has found fault with me;
he considers me his enemy.[s]
11 He fastens my feet in shackles;[t]
he keeps close watch on all my paths.'[u]

12 "But I tell you, in this you are not right,
for God is greater than man.[v]
13 Why do you complain to him[w]
that he answers none of man's words[a]?
14 For God does speak[x]—now one way, now another—
though man may not perceive it.
15 In a dream,[y] in a vision of the night,
when deep sleep falls on men
as they slumber in their beds,
16 he may speak[z] in their ears
and terrify them with warnings,
17 to turn man from wrongdoing
and keep him from pride,
18 to preserve his soul from the pit,[b][a]
his life from perishing by the sword.[c][b]
19 Or a man may be chastened on a bed of pain
with constant distress in his bones,[c]
20 so that his very being finds food[d] repulsive
and his soul loathes the choicest meal.[e]
21 His flesh wastes away to nothing,
and his bones, once hidden, now stick out.[f]
22 His soul draws near to the pit,[d]
and his life to the messengers of death.[e][g]

23 "Yet if there is an angel on his side
as a mediator, one out of a thousand,
to tell a man what is right for him,[h]

[a] 13 *Or that he does not answer for any of his actions* [b] 18 *Or preserve him from the grave* [c] 18 *Or from crossing the River*
[d] 22 *Or He draws near to the grave* [e] 22 *Or to the dead*

33:18 The rendering of this verse in the NIV text note refers to the figurative waterway that was said to be the means of passage from the land of the living to the realm of the dead.

[24] to be gracious to him and say,
'Spare him from going down to the pit[a];[i]
I have found a ransom for him'—
[25] then his flesh is renewed like a child's;
it is restored as in the days of his youth.[j]
[26] He prays to God and finds favor with him,[k]
he sees God's face and shouts for joy;[l]
he is restored by God to his righteous state.[m]
[27] Then he comes to men and says,
'I sinned,[n] and perverted what was right,[o]
but I did not get what I deserved.[p]
[28] He redeemed my soul from going down to the pit,[b]
and I will live to enjoy the light.'[q]

[29] "God does all these things to a man[r]—
twice, even three times—
[30] to turn back his soul from the pit,[c]
that the light of life[s] may shine on him.

[31] "Pay attention, Job, and listen to me;
be silent, and I will speak.
[32] If you have anything to say, answer me;
speak up, for I want you to be cleared.
[33] But if not, then listen to me;
be silent, and I will teach you wisdom.[t]"

34

Then Elihu said:

[2] "Hear my words, you wise men;
listen to me, you men of learning.
[3] For the ear tests words
as the tongue tastes food.[u]
[4] Let us discern for ourselves what is right;
let us learn together what is good.[v]

[5] "Job says, 'I am innocent,[w]
but God denies me justice.[x]
[6] Although I am right,
I am considered a liar;
although I am guiltless,
his arrow inflicts an incurable wound.'[y]
[7] What man is like Job,
who drinks scorn like water?[z]
[8] He keeps company with evildoers;
he associates with wicked men.[a]
[9] For he says, 'It profits a man nothing
when he tries to please God.'[b]

[10] "So listen to me, you men of understanding.
Far be it from God to do evil,[c]
from the Almighty to do wrong.[d]
[11] He repays a man for what he has done;[e]
he brings upon him what his conduct deserves.[f]

[a] 24 Or *grave* [b] 28 Or *redeemed me from going down to the grave* [c] 30 Or *turn him back from the grave*

33:24 [i]Isa 38:17
33:25 [j]2Ki 5:14
33:26 [k]Job 34:28 [l]Job 22:26 [m]Ps 50:15; 51:12
33:27 [n]2Sa 12:13 [o]Lk 15:21 [p]Ro 6:21
33:28 [q]Job 22:28
33:29 [r]1Co 12:6; Eph 1:11; Php 2:13
33:30 [s]Ps 56:13
33:33 [t]Ps 34:11
34:3 [u]Job 12:11
34:4 [v]1Th 5:21
34:5 [w]Job 33:9 [x]Job 27:2
34:6 [y]Job 6:4
34:7 [z]Job 15:16
34:8 [a]Job 22:15; Ps 50:18
34:9 [b]Job 21:15; 35:3
34:10 [c]Ge 18:25 [d]Dt 32:4; Job 8:3; Ro 9:14
34:11 [e]Ps 62:12; Mt 16:27; Ro 2:6; 2Co 5:10 [f]Jer 32:19; Eze 33:20

33:25 Similar phrases are used in 2 Kings 5:14 with reference to healing from leprosy.

12 It is unthinkable that God would do wrong,
that the Almighty would pervert justice.[g]
13 Who appointed him over the earth?
Who put him in charge of the whole world?[h]
14 If it were his intention
and he withdrew his spirit[a] and breath,[i]
15 all mankind would perish together
and man would return to the dust.[j]

16 "If you have understanding, hear this;
listen to what I say.
17 Can he who hates justice govern?[k]
Will you condemn the just and mighty One?[l]
18 Is he not the One who says to kings, 'You are worthless,'
and to nobles, 'You are wicked,'[m]
19 who shows no partiality[n] to princes
and does not favor the rich over the poor,[o]
for they are all the work of his hands?[p]
20 They die in an instant, in the middle of the night;[q]
the people are shaken and they pass away;
the mighty are removed without human hand.[r]

21 "His eyes are on the ways of men;
he sees their every step.[s]
22 There is no dark place,[t] no deep shadow,[u]
where evildoers can hide.
23 God has no need to examine men further,
that they should come before him for judgment.[v]
24 Without inquiry he shatters the mighty[w]
and sets up others in their place.[x]
25 Because he takes note of their deeds,
he overthrows them in the night and they are crushed.
26 He punishes them for their wickedness
where everyone can see them,
27 because they turned from following him[y]
and had no regard for any of his ways.[z]
28 They caused the cry of the poor to come before him,
so that he heard the cry of the needy.[a]
29 But if he remains silent, who can condemn him?
If he hides his face, who can see him?
Yet he is over man and nation alike,
30 to keep a godless man from ruling,
from laying snares for the people.[b]

31 "Suppose a man says to God,
'I am guilty but will offend no more.
32 Teach me what I cannot see;[c]
if I have done wrong, I will not do so again.'[d]
33 Should God then reward you on your terms,
when you refuse to repent?[e]
You must decide, not I;
so tell me what you know.

34 "Men of understanding declare,
wise men who hear me say to me,

34:12 [g]Job 8:3
34:13 [h]Job 38:4,6
34:14 [i]Ps 104:29
34:15 [j]Ge 3:19; Job 9:22
34:17 [k]2Sa 23:3-4 [l]Job 40:8
34:18 [m]Ex 22:28
34:19 [n]Dt 10:17; Ac 10:34 [o]Lev 19:15 [p]Job 10:3
34:20 [q]Ex 12:29 [r]Job 12:19
34:21 [s]Job 31:4; Pr 15:3
34:22 [t]Ps 139:12 [u]Am 9:2-3
34:23 [v]Job 11:11
34:24 [w]Job 12:19 [x]Da 2:21
34:27 [y]Ps 28:5; Isa 5:12 [z]1Sa 15:11
34:28 [a]Ex 22:23; Job 35:9; Jas 5:4
34:30 [b]Pr 29:2-12
34:32 [c]Job 35:11; Ps 25:4 [d]Job 33:27
34:33 [e]Job 41:11

[a] 14 Or *Spirit*

35 'Job speaks without knowledge;[f]
his words lack insight.'
36 Oh, that Job might be tested to the utmost
for answering like a wicked man![g]
37 To his sin he adds rebellion;
scornfully he claps his hands[h] among us
and multiplies his words against God."[i]

35

Then Elihu said:

2 "Do you think this is just?
You say, 'I will be cleared by God.[a]'
3 Yet you ask him, 'What profit is it to me,[b]
and what do I gain by not sinning?'[j]

4 "I would like to reply to you
and to your friends with you.
5 Look up at the heavens[k] and see;
gaze at the clouds so high above you.[l]
6 If you sin, how does that affect him?
If your sins are many, what does that do to him?[m]
7 If you are righteous, what do you give to him,[n]
or what does he receive[o] from your hand?[p]
8 Your wickedness affects only a man like yourself,
and your righteousness only the sons of men.

9 "Men cry out[q] under a load of oppression;
they plead for relief from the arm of the powerful.[r]
10 But no one says, 'Where is God my Maker,[s]
who gives songs in the night,[t]
11 who teaches[u] more to us than to[c] the beasts of the earth
and makes us wiser than[d] the birds of the air?'
12 He does not answer[v] when men cry out
because of the arrogance of the wicked.
13 Indeed, God does not listen to their empty plea;
the Almighty pays no attention to it.[w]
14 How much less, then, will he listen
when you say that you do not see him,[x]
that your case[y] is before him
and you must wait for him,
15 and further, that his anger never punishes
and he does not take the least notice of wickedness.[e]
16 So Job opens his mouth with empty talk;
without knowledge he multiplies words."[z]

36

Elihu continued:

2 "Bear with me a little longer and I will show you
that there is more to be said in God's behalf.
3 I get my knowledge from afar;
I will ascribe justice to my Maker.[a]
4 Be assured that my words are not false;[b]
one perfect in knowledge[c] is with you.

5 "God is mighty, but does not despise men;[d]
he is mighty, and firm in his purpose.[e]

34:35 [f]Job 35:16; 38:2
34:36 [g]Job 22:15
34:37 [h]Job 27:23 [i]Job 23:2
35:3 [j]Job 9:29-31; 34:9
35:5 [k]Ge 15:5 [l]Job 22:12
35:6 [m]Pr 8:36
35:7 [n]Ro 11:35 [o]Pr 9:12 [p]Job 22:2-3; Lk 17:10
35:9 [q]Ex 2:23 [r]Job 12:19
35:10 [s]Job 27:10; Isa 51:13 [t]Ps 42:8; 149:5; Ac 16:25
35:11 [u]Ps 94:12
35:12 [v]Pr 1:28
35:13 [w]Job 27:9; Pr 15:29; Isa 1:15; Jer 11:11
35:14 [x]Job 9:11 [y]Ps 37:6
35:16 [z]Job 34:35,37
36:3 [a]Job 8:3; 37:23
36:4 [b]Job 33:3 [c]Job 37:5,16,23
36:5 [d]Ps 22:24 [e]Job 12:13

[a] 2 Or *My righteousness is more than God's* [b] 3 Or *you* [c] 11 Or *teaches us by* [d] 11 Or *us wise by* [e] 15 Symmachus, Theodotion and Vulgate; the meaning of the Hebrew for this word is uncertain.

36:6 [f]Job 8:22 [g]Job 5:15

6 He does not keep the wicked alive[f]
but gives the afflicted their rights.[g]

36:7 [h]Ps 33:18 [i]Ps 113:8

7 He does not take his eyes off the righteous;[h]
he enthrones them with kings[i]
and exalts them forever.

36:8 [j]Ps 107:10, 14

8 But if men are bound in chains,[j]
held fast by cords of affliction,
9 he tells them what they have done—

36:9 [k]Job 15:25

that they have sinned arrogantly.[k]

36:10 [l]Job 33:16 [m]2Ki 17:13

10 He makes them listen[l] to correction
and commands them to repent of their evil.[m]

36:11 [n]Isa 1:19

11 If they obey and serve him,[n]
they will spend the rest of their days in prosperity
and their years in contentment.
12 But if they do not listen,

36:12 [o]Job 15:22 [p]Job 4:21

they will perish by the sword[a][o]
and die without knowledge.[p]

36:13 [q]Ro 2:5

13 "The godless in heart[q] harbor resentment;
even when he fetters them, they do not cry for help.
14 They die in their youth,

36:14 [r]Dt 23:17

among male prostitutes of the shrines.[r]
15 But those who suffer he delivers in their suffering;
he speaks to them in their affliction.

36:16 [s]Hos 2:14 [t]Ps 23:5

16 "He is wooing[s] you from the jaws of distress
to a spacious place free from restriction,
to the comfort of your table[t] laden with choice food.
17 But now you are laden with the judgment due the wicked;

36:17 [u]Job 22:11

judgment and justice have taken hold of you.[u]
18 Be careful that no one entices you by riches;

36:18 [v]Job 34:33

do not let a large bribe turn you aside.[v]
19 Would your wealth
or even all your mighty efforts
sustain you so you would not be in distress?

36:20 [w]Job 34:20,25

20 Do not long for the night,[w]
to drag people away from their homes.[b]

36:21 [x]Ps 66:18 [y]Heb 11:25

21 Beware of turning to evil,[x]
which you seem to prefer to affliction.[y]

22 "God is exalted in his power.

36:22 [z]Isa 40:13; 1Co 2:16

Who is a teacher like him?[z]

36:23 [a]Job 34:13 [b]Job 8:3

23 Who has prescribed his ways for him,[a]
or said to him, 'You have done wrong'?[b]

36:24 [c]Ps 92:5; 138:5 [d]Ps 59:16; Rev 15:3

24 Remember to extol his work,[c]
which men have praised in song.[d]
25 All mankind has seen it;
men gaze on it from afar.

36:26 [e]1Co 13:12 [f]Job 10:5; Ps 90:2; 102:24; Heb 1:12

26 How great is God—beyond our understanding![e]
The number of his years is past finding out.[f]

27 "He draws up the drops of water,

36:27 [g]Job 38:28; Ps 147:8

which distill as rain to the streams[c];[g]
28 the clouds pour down their moisture

36:28 [h]Job 5:10

and abundant showers fall on mankind.[h]

[a] 12 Or *will cross the River* [b] 20 The meaning of the Hebrew for verses 18-20 is uncertain. [c] 27 Or *distill from the mist as rain*

[29] Who can understand how he spreads out
the clouds,
how he thunders from his pavilion?[i]
[30] See how he scatters his lightning about him,
bathing the depths of the sea.
[31] This is the way he governs[a] the nations[j]
and provides food in abundance.[k]
[32] He fills his hands with lightning
and commands it to strike its mark.[l]
[33] His thunder announces the coming storm;
even the cattle make known its approach.[b]

37

"At this my heart pounds
and leaps from its place.
[2] Listen! Listen to the roar of his voice,
to the rumbling that comes from his mouth.[m]
[3] He unleashes his lightning beneath the whole
heaven
and sends it to the ends of the earth.
[4] After that comes the sound of his roar;
he thunders with his majestic voice.
When his voice resounds,
he holds nothing back.
[5] God's voice thunders in marvelous ways;
he does great things beyond our understanding.[n]
[6] He says to the snow,[o] 'Fall on the earth,'
and to the rain shower, 'Be a mighty downpour.'[p]
[7] So that all men he has made may know his work,
he stops every man from his labor.[c][q]
[8] The animals take cover;
they remain in their dens.[r]
[9] The tempest comes out from its chamber,
the cold from the driving winds.
[10] The breath of God produces ice,
and the broad waters become frozen.[s]
[11] He loads the clouds with moisture;
he scatters his lightning through them.[t]
[12] At his direction they swirl around
over the face of the whole earth
to do whatever he commands them.[u]
[13] He brings the clouds to punish men,[v]
or to water his earth[d] and show his love.[w]

[14] "Listen to this, Job;
stop and consider God's wonders.
[15] Do you know how God controls the clouds
and makes his lightning flash?
[16] Do you know how the clouds hang poised,
those wonders of him who is perfect in
knowledge?[x]

36:29 [i]Job 26:14; 37:16
36:31 [j]Job 37:13 [k]Ps 136:25; Ac 14:17
36:32 [l]Job 37:12, 15
37:2 [m]Ps 29:3-9
37:5 [n]Job 5:9
37:6 [o]Job 38:22 [p]Job 36:27
37:7 [q]Job 12:14
37:8 [r]Job 38:40; Ps 104:22
37:10 [s]Job 38:29-30; Ps 147:17
37:11 [t]Job 36:27, 29
37:12 [u]Ps 148:8
37:13 [v]1Sa 12:17 [w]Ex 9:18; 1Ki 18:45; Job 38:27
37:16 [x]Job 36:4

[a] 31 Or *nourishes* [b] 33 Or *announces his coming— / the One zealous against evil* [c] 7 Or */ he fills all men with fear by his power*
[d] 13 Or *to favor them*

37:1–13 This passage reveals a sophisticated observation of atmospheric conditions and their effects: the evaporation and distillation of water for rain (see 36:27 and the NIV text note), the clouds as holders of moisture (see 36:28; 37:11) and the cyclonic behavior of clouds (see v. 12).

[17] You who swelter in your clothes
when the land lies hushed under the south wind,
[18] can you join him in spreading out the skies,[y]
hard as a mirror of cast bronze?

[19] "Tell us what we should say to him;
we cannot draw up our case because of our darkness.
[20] Should he be told that I want to speak?
Would any man ask to be swallowed up?
[21] Now no one can look at the sun,
bright as it is in the skies
after the wind has swept them clean.
[22] Out of the north he comes in golden splendor;
God comes in awesome majesty.
[23] The Almighty is beyond our reach and exalted in power;[z]
in his justice[a] and great righteousness, he does not oppress.[b]
[24] Therefore, men revere him,[c]
for does he not have regard for all the wise[d] in heart?[a]"

37:18 [y]Job 9:8; Ps 104:2; Isa 44:24
37:23 [z]Job 9:4; 36:4; 1Ti 6:16 [a]Job 8:3 [b]Isa 63:9; Eze 18:23,32
37:24 [c]Mt 10:28 [d]Mt 11:25

The LORD Speaks

38 Then the LORD answered Job out of the storm.[e] He said:

[2] "Who is this that darkens my counsel
with words without knowledge?[f]
[3] Brace yourself like a man;
I will question you,
and you shall answer me.[g]

[4] "Where were you when I laid the earth's foundation?[h]
Tell me, if you understand.
[5] Who marked off its dimensions?[i] Surely you know!
Who stretched a measuring line across it?
[6] On what were its footings set,
or who laid its cornerstone[j]—
[7] while the morning stars sang together
and all the angels[b] shouted for joy?

[8] "Who shut up the sea behind doors[k]
when it burst forth from the womb,[l]
[9] when I made the clouds its garment
and wrapped it in thick darkness,
[10] when I fixed limits for it[m]
and set its doors and bars in place,[n]
[11] when I said, 'This far you may come and no farther;
here is where your proud waves halt'?[o]

[12] "Have you ever given orders to the morning,
or shown the dawn its place,
[13] that it might take the earth by the edges
and shake the wicked[p] out of it?
[14] The earth takes shape like clay under a seal;
its features stand out like those of a garment.

38:1 [e]Job 40:6
38:2 [f]Job 35:16; 42:3; 1Ti 1:7
38:3 [g]Job 40:7
38:4 [h]Ps 104:5; Pr 8:29
38:5 [i]Pr 8:29; Isa 40:12
38:6 [j]Job 26:7
38:8 [k]Jer 5:22 [l]Ge 1:9-10
38:10 [m]Ps 33:7; 104:9 [n]Job 26:10
38:11 [o]Ps 89:9
38:13 [p]Ps 104:35

[a] 24 Or *for he does not have regard for any who think they are wise.* [b] 7 Hebrew *the sons of God*

37:18 In Deuteronomy 28:23 a bronze sky symbolizes unremitting heat and drought.
38:14 The phrase "like clay under a seal" refers to either a cylinder seal or a stamp seal. Small cylinder seals were used to sign clay documents by rolling them over the clay. The owner wore the seal around his neck on a cord. (See "Scrolls, Seals and Codices" on p. 2053.)

[15]The wicked are denied their light,[q]
and their upraised arm is broken.[r]

[16]"Have you journeyed to the springs of the sea
or walked in the recesses of the deep?[s]
[17]Have the gates of death[t] been shown to you?
Have you seen the gates of the shadow of death[a]?

[a] 17 Or *gates of deep shadows*

38:15 [q]Job 18:5 [r]Ps 10:15
38:16 [s]Ps 77:19
38:17 [t]Ps 9:13

ANCIENT TEXTS AND ARTIFACTS

The Hittite Storm Gods

A Hittite storm god from Karatepe
Preserving Bible Times; © Dr. James C. Martin

JOB 38 The speeches of God in Job 38–41 present him as absolute and unrivaled in his power over nature. The stars, storms, seasons and wild animals all submit to and depend upon him. He even controls Leviathan, the dragon that symbolizes chaos and evil (ch. 4). In polytheism, on the other hand, the gods are often depicted as weak and dependent.

Hittite texts of myth and ritual illustrate this. For example, the Telepinu myth recounts an incident in which the storm god Telepinu was reported to have become angry and deserted his post. In his absence the crops ceased to grow and the livestock to calve. Even the other gods began to panic at the prospect of starvation. Although the gods were unable to locate Telepinu, a bee found him asleep under a tree and wakened him with a sting. A goddess of magic and a human priest then performed expiatory rituals that assuaged Telepinu's anger.

Other Hittite myths têll of the storm god's conflict with the dragon Illuyanka. Unlike **Yahweh**'s domination of Leviathan in Job 41, however, the storm god can scarcely handle Illuyanka. In one version the storm god is at first defeated by the dragon, but the tables turn after the goddess Inara enlists the aid of a mortal, Hupashiya, by sleeping with him. She then hosts a feast; after Illuyanka gorges himself on food, Hupashiya binds the dragon with ropes so that the storm god can manage to slay him. In another version the storm god loses his heart and eyes to the dragon in their first battle, but the god's son marries Illuyanka's daughter and persuades Illuyanka to return his father's eyes and heart. The storm god resumes the battle, slaying both the dragon and his son.[1]

The profound moral and theological debate of Job could not have arisen from such pagan myths. The gods, as depicted in these tales, were simply too weak to control events in a meaningful way; they needed the assistance of other gods and even of humans and animals. There would also be no problem of evil if God were too weak to control the world; such a theological dilemma can only exist in a setting in which God is understood to be omniscient and omnipotent.

[1]See also "The Serpent Motif in Other Ancient Near Eastern Literature" on page 8.

18 Have you comprehended the vast expanses of the earth?[u]
Tell me, if you know all this.

19 "What is the way to the abode of light?
And where does darkness reside?
20 Can you take them to their places?
Do you know the paths[v] to their dwellings?
21 Surely you know, for you were already born![w]
You have lived so many years!

22 "Have you entered the storehouses of the snow[x]
or seen the storehouses of the hail,
23 which I reserve for times of trouble,[y]
for days of war and battle?[z]
24 What is the way to the place where the lightning is dispersed,
or the place where the east winds are scattered over the earth?
25 Who cuts a channel for the torrents of rain,
and a path for the thunderstorm,[a]
26 to water[b] a land where no man lives,
a desert with no one in it,
27 to satisfy a desolate wasteland
and make it sprout with grass?[c]
28 Does the rain have a father?[d]
Who fathers the drops of dew?
29 From whose womb comes the ice?
Who gives birth to the frost from the heavens[e]
30 when the waters become hard as stone,
when the surface of the deep is frozen?[f]

31 "Can you bind the beautiful[a] Pleiades?
Can you loose the cords of Orion?[g]
32 Can you bring forth the constellations in their seasons[b]
or lead out the Bear[c] with its cubs?
33 Do you know the laws[h] of the heavens?
Can you set up ⌞God's[d]⌟ dominion over the earth?

34 "Can you raise your voice to the clouds
and cover yourself with a flood of water?[i]
35 Do you send the lightning bolts on their way?[j]
Do they report to you, 'Here we are'?
36 Who endowed the heart[e] with wisdom[k]
or gave understanding[l] to the mind[e]?
37 Who has the wisdom to count the clouds?
Who can tip over the water jars of the heavens
38 when the dust becomes hard
and the clods of earth stick together?

39 "Do you hunt the prey for the lioness
and satisfy the hunger of the lions[m]
40 when they crouch in their dens[n]
or lie in wait in a thicket?
41 Who provides food for the raven[o]
when its young cry out to God
and wander about for lack of food?[p]

38:18 [u]Job 28:24
38:20 [v]Job 26:10
38:21 [w]Job 15:7
38:22 [x]Job 37:6
38:23 [y]Isa 30:30; Eze 13:11 [z]Ex 9:18; Jos 10:11; Rev 16:21
38:25 [a]Job 28:26
38:26 [b]Job 36:27
38:27 [c]Ps 104:14; 107:35
38:28 [d]Ps 147:8; Jer 14:22
38:29 [e]Ps 147:16-17
38:30 [f]Job 37:10
38:31 [g]Job 9:9; Am 5:8
38:33 [h]Ps 148:6; Jer 31:36
38:34 [i]Job 22:11; 36:27-28
38:35 [j]Job 36:32; 37:3
38:36 [k]Job 9:4 [l]Job 32:8; Ps 51:6; Ecc 2:26
38:39 [m]Ps 104:21
38:40 [n]Job 37:8
38:41 [o]Lk 12:24 [p]Ps 147:9; Mt 6:26

[a] 31 Or *the twinkling*; or *the chains of the* [b] 32 Or *the morning star in its season* [c] 32 Or *out Leo* [d] 33 Or *his*; or *their*
[e] 36 The meaning of the Hebrew for this word is uncertain.

39 "Do you know when the mountain goats[q] give birth?
Do you watch when the doe bears her fawn?
2 Do you count the months till they bear?
Do you know the time they give birth?
3 They crouch down and bring forth their young;
their labor pains are ended.
4 Their young thrive and grow strong in the wilds;
they leave and do not return.

5 "Who let the wild donkey[r] go free?
Who untied his ropes?
6 I gave him the wasteland[s] as his home,
the salt flats as his habitat.[t]
7 He laughs at the commotion in the town;
he does not hear a driver's shout.[u]
8 He ranges the hills for his pasture
and searches for any green thing.

9 "Will the wild ox[v] consent to serve you?
Will he stay by your manger at night?
10 Can you hold him to the furrow with a harness?
Will he till the valleys behind you?
11 Will you rely on him for his great strength?
Will you leave your heavy work to him?
12 Can you trust him to bring in your grain
and gather it to your threshing floor?

13 "The wings of the ostrich flap joyfully,
but they cannot compare with the pinions and feathers of the stork.
14 She lays her eggs on the ground
and lets them warm in the sand,
15 unmindful that a foot may crush them,
that some wild animal may trample them.
16 She treats her young harshly,[w] as if they were not hers;
she cares not that her labor was in vain,
17 for God did not endow her with wisdom
or give her a share of good sense.[x]
18 Yet when she spreads her feathers to run,
she laughs at horse and rider.

19 "Do you give the horse his strength
or clothe his neck with a flowing mane?
20 Do you make him leap like a locust,[y]
striking terror with his proud snorting?[z]
21 He paws fiercely, rejoicing in his strength,
and charges into the fray.[a]
22 He laughs at fear, afraid of nothing;
he does not shy away from the sword.
23 The quiver rattles against his side,
along with the flashing spear and lance.
24 In frenzied excitement he eats up the ground;
he cannot stand still when the trumpet sounds.[b]

39:1 [q]Dt 14:5
39:5 [r]Job 6:5; 11:12; 24:5
39:6 [s]Job 24:5; Ps 107:34; Jer 2:24 [t]Hos 8:9
39:7 [u]Job 3:18
39:9 [v]Nu 23:22; Dt 33:17
39:16 [w]La 4:3
39:17 [x]Job 35:11
39:20 [y]Joel 2:4-5 [z]Jer 8:16
39:21 [a]Jer 8:6
39:24 [b]Jer 4:5, 19; Eze 7:14; Am 3:6

39:9–11 In the Old Testament the wild ox (the now virtually extinct aurochs) often symbolized strength (see, e.g., Nu 23:22; 24:8; Dt 33:17; Ps 29:6). Next to the elephant and rhinoceros, the wild ox was the largest and most powerful land animal of the Old Testament world.
39:12 See "The Threshing Floor" on page 608.

39:25 [c]Jos 6:5 [d]Am 1:14; 2:2

25 At the blast of the trumpet[c] he snorts, 'Aha!'
He catches the scent of battle from afar,
the shout of commanders and the battle cry.[d]

26 "Does the hawk take flight by your wisdom
and spread his wings toward the south?
27 Does the eagle soar at your command
and build his nest on high?[e]
28 He dwells on a cliff and stays there at night;
a rocky crag is his stronghold.
29 From there he seeks out his food;[f]
his eyes detect it from afar.
30 His young ones feast on blood,
and where the slain are, there is he."[g]

39:27 [e]Jer 49:16; Ob 1:4
39:29 [f]Job 9:26
39:30 [g]Mt 24:28; Lk 17:37

40

The LORD said to Job:[h]

2 "Will the one who contends with the Almighty correct him?
Let him who accuses God answer him!"

3 Then Job answered the LORD:

4 "I am unworthy[i]—how can I reply to you?
I put my hand over my mouth.[j]
5 I spoke once, but I have no answer[k]—
twice, but I will say no more."[l]

6 Then the LORD spoke to Job out of the storm:[m]

7 "Brace yourself like a man;
I will question you,
and you shall answer me.[n]
8 "Would you discredit my justice?[o]
Would you condemn me to justify yourself?
9 Do you have an arm like God's,[p]
and can your voice thunder like his?[q]
10 Then adorn yourself with glory and splendor,
and clothe yourself in honor and majesty.[r]
11 Unleash the fury of your wrath,[s]
look at every proud man and bring him low,[t]
12 look at every proud man and humble him,[u]
crush[v] the wicked where they stand.
13 Bury them all in the dust together;
shroud their faces in the grave.
14 Then I myself will admit to you
that your own right hand can save you.[w]

15 "Look at the behemoth,[a]
which I made along with you
and which feeds on grass like an ox.
16 What strength he has in his loins,
what power in the muscles of his belly!

40:1 [h]Job 10:2; 13:3; 23:4; 31:35; 33:13
40:4 [i]Job 42:6 [j]Job 29:9
40:5 [k]Job 9:3 [l]Job 9:15
40:6 [m]Job 38:1
40:7 [n]Job 38:3; 42:4
40:8 [o]Job 27:2; Ro 3:3
40:9 [p]2Ch 32:8 [q]Job 37:5; Ps 29:3-4
40:10 [r]Ps 93:1; 104:1
40:11 [s]Isa 42:25; Na 1:6 [t]Isa 2:11, 12,17; Da 4:37
40:12 [u]1Sa 2:7 [v]Isa 13:11; 63:2-3,6
40:14 [w]Ps 20:6; 60:5; 108:6

[a] *15* Possibly the hippopotamus or the elephant

39:26 "Hawk" refers to the sparrow hawk, which is not resident to the Levant (today's Syria/Palestine) but stops there in its migration south for the winter.

40:15 The Hebrew word *behemoth* means "beast par excellence." It refers to a large land animal, possibly the hippopotamus or the elephant. It was an actual creature ("which [God] made"), not a mythical being.

17 His tail[a] sways like a cedar;
the sinews of his thighs are close-knit.
18 His bones are tubes of bronze,
his limbs like rods of iron.
19 His ranks first among the works of God,[x]
yet his Maker can approach him with his sword.
20 The hills bring him their produce,[y]
and all the wild animals play[z] nearby.
21 Under the lotus plants he lies,
hidden among the reeds in the marsh.
22 The lotuses conceal him in their shadow;
the poplars by the stream[a] surround him.
23 When the river rages, he is not alarmed;
he is secure, though the Jordan should surge against his mouth.
24 Can anyone capture him by the eyes,[b]
or trap him and pierce his nose?[b]

41

"Can you pull in the leviathan[c][c] with a fishhook
or tie down his tongue with a rope?
2 Can you put a cord through his nose
or pierce his jaw with a hook?[d]
3 Will he keep begging you for mercy?
Will he speak to you with gentle words?
4 Will he make an agreement with you
for you to take him as your slave for life?[e]
5 Can you make a pet of him like a bird
or put him on a leash for your girls?
6 Will traders barter for him?
Will they divide him up among the merchants?
7 Can you fill his hide with harpoons
or his head with fishing spears?
8 If you lay a hand on him,
you will remember the struggle and never do it again!
9 Any hope of subduing him is false;
the mere sight of him is overpowering.
10 No one is fierce enough to rouse him.[f]
Who then is able to stand against me?[g]
11 Who has a claim against me that I must pay?[h]
Everything under heaven belongs to me.[i]
12 "I will not fail to speak of his limbs,
his strength and his graceful form.
13 Who can strip off his outer coat?
Who would approach him with a bridle?
14 Who dares open the doors of his mouth,
ringed about with his fearsome teeth?
15 His back has[d] rows of shields
tightly sealed together;
16 each is so close to the next
that no air can pass between.
17 They are joined fast to one another;
they cling together and cannot be parted.

40:19 [x]Job 41:33
40:20 [y]Ps 104:14 [z]Ps 104:26
40:22 [a]Isa 44:4
40:24 [b]Job 41:2, 7,26
41:1 [c]Job 3:8; Ps 104:26; Isa 27:1
41:2 [d]Isa 37:29
41:4 [e]Ex 21:6
41:10 [f]Job 3:8 [g]Jer 50:44
41:11 [h]Ro 11:35 [i]Ex 19:5; Dt 10:14; Ps 24:1; 50:12; 1Co 10:26

[a] *17* Possibly trunk [b] *24* Or *by a water hole* [c] *1* Possibly the crocodile [d] *15* Or *His pride is his*

40:18 See the note on 19:24.

40:21–23 The area described here is probably the Huleh region, north of the Sea of Galilee.

[18] His snorting throws out flashes of light;
his eyes are like the rays of dawn.[j]
[19] Firebrands stream from his mouth;
sparks of fire shoot out.
[20] Smoke pours from his nostrils
as from a boiling pot over a fire of reeds.
[21] His breath[k] sets coals ablaze,
and flames dart from his mouth.[l]
[22] Strength resides in his neck;
dismay goes before him.
[23] The folds of his flesh are tightly joined;
they are firm and immovable.
[24] His chest is hard as rock,
hard as a lower millstone.
[25] When he rises up, the mighty are terrified;
they retreat before his thrashing.
[26] The sword that reaches him has no effect,
nor does the spear or the dart or the javelin.
[27] Iron he treats like straw
and bronze like rotten wood.
[28] Arrows do not make him flee;
slingstones are like chaff to him.
[29] A club seems to him but a piece of straw;
he laughs at the rattling of the lance.
[30] His undersides are jagged potsherds,
leaving a trail in the mud like a threshing sledge.[m]
[31] He makes the depths churn like a boiling caldron
and stirs up the sea like a pot of ointment.
[32] Behind him he leaves a glistening wake;
one would think the deep had white hair.
[33] Nothing on earth is his equal[n]—
a creature without fear.
[34] He looks down on all that are haughty;
he is king over all that are proud.[o]"

41:18 [j]Job 3:9
41:21 [k]Isa 40:7 [l]Ps 18:8
41:30 [m]Isa 41:15
41:33 [n]Job 40:19
41:34 [o]Job 28:8

Job

42

Then Job replied to the LORD:

[2] "I know that you can do all things;[p]
no plan of yours can be thwarted.[q]
[3] ⌞You asked,⌟ 'Who is this that obscures my counsel without knowledge?'[r]
Surely I spoke of things I did not understand,
things too wonderful for me to know.[s]

[4] ⌞"You said,⌟ 'Listen now, and I will speak;
I will question you,
and you shall answer me.'[t]
[5] My ears had heard of you[u]
but now my eyes have seen you.[v]
[6] Therefore I despise myself[w]
and repent in dust and ashes."[x]

42:2 [p]Ge 18:14; Mt 19:26 [q]2Ch 20:6
42:3 [r]Job 38:2 [s]Ps 40:5; 131:1; 139:6
42:4 [t]Job 38:3; 40:7
42:5 [u]Job 26:14; Ro 10:17 [v]Jdg 13:22; Isa 6:5; Eph 1:17-18
42:6 [w]Job 40:4 [x]Ezr 9:6

41:27 See the note on 19:24.

41:30 "Jagged potsherds" refers to broken pottery fragments (see "The Potsherd: Pottery in the Bible" on p. 738).

Epilogue

7 After the LORD had said these things to Job, he said to Eliphaz the Temanite, "I am angry with you and your two friends,[y] because you have not spoken of me what is right, as my servant Job has. 8 So now take seven bulls and seven rams[z] and go to my servant Job and sacrifice a burnt offering[a] for yourselves. My servant Job will pray for you, and I will accept his prayer[b] and not deal with you according to your folly.[c] You have not spoken of me what is right, as my servant Job has." 9 So Eliphaz the Temanite, Bildad the Shuhite and Zophar the Naamathite did what the LORD told them; and the LORD accepted Job's prayer.

10 After Job had prayed for his friends, the LORD made him prosperous again[d] and gave him twice as much as he had before.[e] 11 All his brothers and sisters and everyone who had known him before[f] came and ate with him in his house. They comforted and consoled him over all the trouble the LORD had brought upon him, and each one gave him a piece of silver[a] and a gold ring.

12 The LORD blessed the latter part of Job's life more than the first. He had fourteen thousand sheep, six thousand camels, a thousand yoke of oxen and a thousand donkeys. 13 And he also had seven sons and three daughters. 14 The first daughter he named Jemimah, the second Keziah and the third Keren-Happuch. 15 Nowhere in all the land were there found women as beautiful as Job's daughters, and their father granted them an inheritance along with their brothers.

16 After this, Job lived a hundred and forty years; he saw his children and their children to the fourth generation. 17 And so he died, old and full of years.[g]

42:7 [y]Job 32:3
42:8 [z]Nu 23:1,29 [a]Job 1:5 [b]Ge 20:17; Jas 5:15-16; 1Jn 5:16 [c]Job 22:30
42:10 [d]Dt 30:3; Ps 14:7 [e]Job 1:3; Ps 85:1-3; 126:5-6
42:11 [f]Job 19:13
42:17 [g]Ge 15:15; 25:8

[a] 11 Hebrew *him a kesitah*; a kesitah was a unit of money of unknown weight and value.

42:11 For information on earrings or nose rings, see the note on Ezekiel 16:12.

INTRODUCTION TO 

INTRODUCTION TO Psalms

AUTHOR, PLACE AND DATE OF WRITING

The book of Psalms is a collection—or, more precisely, a series of five collections—and as such does not reflect a single author or a concise time span. Each individual psalm had its own composer, though some appear to have been edited from their original version during postexilic times. Many psalms are anonymous, although all but 34 are prefaced by superscripts that tell us something about the psalm and its origin. Of these, at least 73 are attributed to David (either by, about or for—as in possibly dedicated to—David) and others to Asaph (Ps 50; 73–83), the sons of Korah (42–49; 84–85; 87–88), Moses (90), Solomon (127), Heman (88) and Ethan (89). Many scholars consider the superscripts to have been appended at a later time and therefore to be of limited historical value, but there are valid reasons for believing them to have been written soon after the psalms to which they are attached (see "The Psalm Superscripts" on p. 795).

The psalms were composed over a period of almost 1,000 years, dating from the time of Moses (c. 1400 B.C.) to the Babylonian captivity (586 B.C.). Most were written during Israel's wilderness wanderings or in Israel, Judah or Babylon.

The traditional Hebrew title was *tehillim* ("praises"), although many of the psalms are actually *tephillot* ("prayers"). The title "Psalms" was first used in the Septuagint.

AUDIENCE

The original audience varied, due to the eclectic nature of the book as a whole, but most early readers were Israelites or Judahites. Many of the psalms were used in corporate (group) worship settings, as they are today.

CULTURAL FACTS AND HIGHLIGHTS

Psalms is a collection of liturgical pieces for temple worship and personal devotion. There is a wide variety of psalms, and the different types served various purposes in the religious life of Israel, including praise, prayer, lament and instruction (see "Form Criticism and the Psalms" on p. 891).

Understanding how the individual psalms were collected into the current book of 150 is complicated by the fact that there are five individual books of psalm collections (see outline on p. 792). The first books tend to contain earlier psalms, whereas Book V includes many of the most recent. This suggests that there may have been a series of psalm collections through much of Israel's history prior to the completion of the final compilation.

The suggestion that there were already collections of psalms in circulation early in the period of Israel's monarchy makes sense. First Chronicles 22–26 mentions that David reorganized the worship system of the shrine in Jerusalem, and it can hardly be doubted that the temple staff maintained collections of psalms for worship. Thus the present book, which took shape during the postexilic era (most likely compiled by temple personnel in the third century B.C.), can be thought of as a final edition in a long series of temple "hymnbooks."

TIMELINE

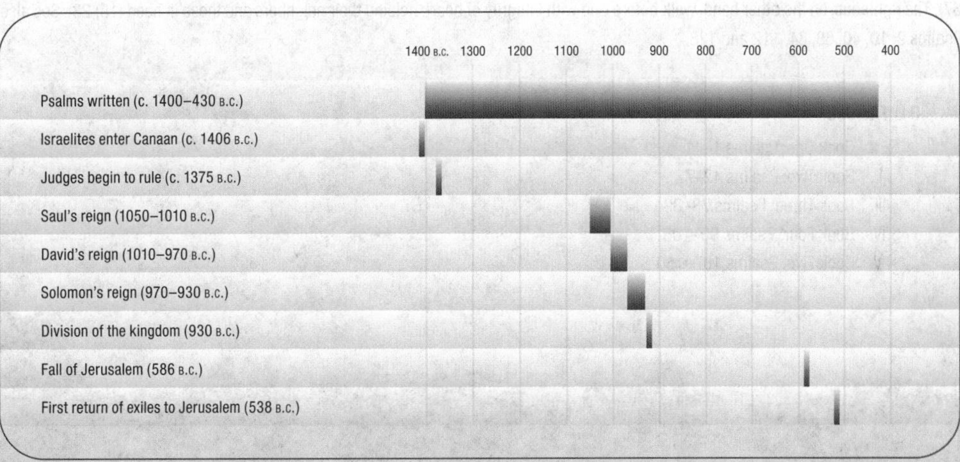

AS YOU READ

There are many different ways to approach this diverse collection of praises and prayers—and as many different schemes for grouping the psalms, with categories frequently overlapping. Although use of a commentary or study Bible with comprehensive notes can be instructive in studying the psalms, it is most effective from a purely worshipful standpoint to set aside organizational schemes and take these poetic gems at face value.

Some readers find it helpful from a devotional standpoint to "pray" through the psalms, which are replete with praises, confessions and petitions—all key elements of a well-rounded prayer life. Pay attention as well to the instructive elements, to the principles set forth in these compositions for living an effectual, God-honoring life.

DID YOU KNOW?

- Forgetting God in the Hebrew mind was a willful act of "unlearning," whereby rebellious humans rejected what they had known and sought to create a world in which God did not act or exist (42:3–4).
- Though there is evidence that ancient Israel was far more forested than it is today, the presence of flourishing trees was still a sign of divine blessing for former nomads living on the fringes of a settled, agricultural society (52:8).
- The picture of splashing joyfully about in an enemy's blood—though utterly incomprehensible to us—is a traditional Biblical image borrowed from ancient Near Eastern literature. It symbolizes victory over an enemy (58:10).
- Incense and prayer were associated. The sweet smoke of incense arose as a pleasing offering to God (141).
- It was not uncommon in the ancient world for temple columns to be shaped in the form of women (144:12).

THEMES

The book of Psalms includes the following themes:

1. *A portrait of God.* The psalms portray God as our shepherd (23; 95; 100) and the warrior who saves us from our oppressors (18). He is our King (45; 47; 97), our refuge (46; 91) and our judge (50; 52; 75–76), who is great (48; 135), eternal (90), perfect (92), powerful (76; 104; 145; 147), patient (78), just (82; 101), forgiving (103), loving (136; 145), and good (86; 104; 116). As the champion of the poor and downtrodden (72; 113), he offers hope to the struggling righteous by giving them a glimpse of their glorious future (37; 73).

2. *A model of a personal relationship with God.* The psalms openly express the range of emotions experienced in life—for example, fear (56), love (91; 116), distress (31; 42; 120; 142), dismay (10), joy (98; 100; 117), impatience (13), gratitude (107; 118; 136), shame (25; 38; 44; 69), guilt (32; 38; 51), forgiveness (32; 103) and depression that turns to hope (31; 42–43; 130). This openness inspires us to authentic communication with our loving, compassionate and understanding God.

3. *A contrast of the ways of the righteous with those of the wicked.* Psalm 1 sets the stage: The righteous are blessed and watched over by God, but the way of the wicked will perish. The wicked are those who selfishly use and abuse others without thinking about God (26; 37). The righteous, on the other hand, walk before God with integrity of heart, helping their neighbors and those in need (15; 28). See also Psalms 9, 10, 40, 68, 84, 112 and 128.

OUTLINE

I. Book One: Psalms 1–41
II. Book Two: Psalms 42–72
III. Book Three: Psalms 73–89
IV. Book Four: Psalms 90–106
V. Book Five: Psalms 107–150

BOOK I

Psalms 1–41

Psalm 1

1 Blessed is the man
who does not walk[a] in the counsel of the wicked
or stand in the way of sinners
or sit[b] in the seat of mockers.
2 But his delight[c] is in the law of the LORD,[d]
and on his law he meditates[e] day and night.
3 He is like a tree[f] planted by streams of water,[g]
which yields its fruit[h] in season
and whose leaf does not wither.
Whatever he does prospers.[i]

4 Not so the wicked!
They are like chaff[j]
that the wind blows away.
5 Therefore the wicked will not stand[k] in the judgment,[l]
nor sinners in the assembly of the righteous.

6 For the LORD watches over[m] the way of the righteous,
but the way of the wicked will perish.[n]

1:1 [a]Pr 4:14 [b]Ps 26:4; Jer 15:17
1:2 [c]Ps 119:16, 35 [d]Ps 119:1 [e]Jos 1:8
1:3 [f]Ps 128:3 [g]Jer 17:8 [h]Eze 47:12 [i]Ge 39:3
1:4 [j]Job 21:18; Isa 17:13
1:5 [k]Ps 5:5 [l]Ps 9:7-8,16
1:6 [m]Ps 37:18; 2Ti 2:19 [n]Ps 9:6

Psalm 2

1 Why do the nations conspire[a]
and the peoples plot[o] in vain?
2 The kings[p] of the earth take their stand
and the rulers gather together
against the LORD
and against his Anointed[q] One.[b][r]
3 "Let us break their chains," they say,
"and throw off their fetters."[s]

4 The One enthroned in heaven laughs;[t]
the Lord scoffs at them.
5 Then he rebukes them in his anger
and terrifies them in his wrath,[u] saying,
6 "I have installed my King[c]
on Zion, my holy hill."

7 I will proclaim the decree of the LORD:

He said to me, "You are my Son[d];
today I have become your Father.[e][v]

2:1 [o]Ps 21:11
2:2 [p]Ps 48:4 [q]Jn 1:41 [r]Ps 74:18,23; Ac 4:25-26*
2:3 [s]Jer 5:5
2:4 [t]Ps 37:13; 59:8; Pr 1:26
2:5 [u]Ps 21:9; 78:49-50
2:7 [v]Ac 13:33*; Heb 1:5*

[a] 1 Hebrew; Septuagint *rage* [b] 2 Or *anointed one* [c] 6 Or *king* [d] 7 Or *son*; also in verse 12 [e] 7 Or *have begotten you*

1:1–6 The Hebrew designation of Psalms is *Tehillîm,* meaning "praises," a term that reflects much of the book's content (cf. Ps 145, title). Its name in Latin and English Bibles, however, comes from the Greek *Psalmoi,* which literally means "twangings [of harp strings]," and then, as a result, songs sung to the accompaniment of harps. This latter name originated in the Septuagint (cf. its New Testament authentication in Lk 20:42) and reflects the form of the book's poetry. The same is true of its alternate title, *Psalterion,* meaning "psaltery," a collection of harp songs, from which comes the English term "Psalter."

1:4 The chaff blowing away is a simile of the wicked (see the note on Isa 5:24). One of the steps in the process of harvesting grain (see the note on Ru 1:22) involved throwing it into the air so that the wind would blow away the straw and chaff (the useless matter), leaving only the grain (see "The Threshing Floor" on p. 608).

2:1–12 For commentary on expressions of vengeful attitudes toward enemies, see the note on 69:22–28. See also "Curses and Imprecations" on page 883.

2:1–3 This psalm, likely written for the coronation of a Davidic king, offers insight into how the kings understood themselves—their authority, roles and hopes. In the ancient Near East the coronation of a new king was often the occasion for the revolt of peoples and other kings who had been subject to the crown.

2:7 The relationship between a great Near Eastern king and one of his subject kings, who ruled by his authority and owed him allegiance, was expressed not only by the words "lord" and "servant"

[8] Ask of me,
and I will make the nations your inheritance,
the ends of the earth[w] your possession.
[9] You will rule them with an iron scepter[a];[x]
you will dash them to pieces[y] like pottery.[z]"

[10] Therefore, you kings, be wise;
be warned, you rulers of the earth.
[11] Serve the LORD with fear
and rejoice[a] with trembling.[b]
[12] Kiss the Son,[c] lest he be angry
and you be destroyed in your way,
for his wrath[d] can flare up in a moment.
Blessed are all who take refuge[e] in him.

2:8 [w]Ps 22:27
2:9 [x]Rev 12:5 [y]Ps 89:23 [z]Rev 2:27*
2:11 [a]Heb 12:28 [b]Ps 119:119-120
2:12 [c]Jn 5:23 [d]Rev 6:16 [e]Ps 34:8; Ro 9:33

Psalm 3

A psalm of David. When he fled from his son Absalom.[f]

[1] O LORD, how many are my foes!
How many rise up against me!
[2] Many are saying of me,
"God will not deliver him.[g]" *Selah*[b]

[3] But you are a shield[h] around me, O LORD;
you bestow glory on me and lift[c] up my head.[i]
[4] To the LORD I cry aloud,
and he answers me from his holy hill.[j] *Selah*

[5] I lie down and sleep;[k]
I wake again, because the LORD sustains me.
[6] I will not fear[l] the tens of thousands
drawn up against me on every side.

[7] Arise,[m] O LORD!
Deliver me,[n] O my God!
Strike[o] all my enemies on the jaw;
break the teeth[p] of the wicked.

[8] From the LORD comes deliverance.[q]
May your blessing be on your people. *Selah*

3:1 [f]2Sa 15:14
3:2 [g]Ps 71:11
3:3 [h]Ge 15:1; Ps 28:7 [i]Ps 27:6
3:4 [j]Ps 2:6
3:5 [k]Lev 26:6; Pr 3:24
3:6 [l]Ps 27:3
3:7 [m]Ps 7:6 [n]Ps 6:4 [o]Job 16:10 [p]Ps 58:6
3:8 [q]Isa 43:3,11

Psalm 4

For the director of music. With stringed instruments. A psalm of David.

[1] Answer me when I call to you,
O my righteous God.
Give me relief from my distress;
be merciful[r] to me and hear my prayer.[s]

[2] How long, O men, will you turn my glory into shame[d]?
How long will you love delusions and seek false gods[e]?[t] *Selah*

4:1 [r]Ps 25:16 [s]Ps 17:6
4:2 [t]Ps 31:6

[a] 9 Or *will break them with a rod of iron* [b] 2 A word of uncertain meaning, occurring frequently in the Psalms; possibly a musical term [c] 3 Or *LORD, / my Glorious One, who lifts* [d] 2 Or *you dishonor my Glorious One* [e] 2 Or *seek lies*

---

but also by "father" and "son." The Davidic king was at once the Lord's "servant" and his "son" (2Sa 7:5,14).
2:9 See "The Potsherd: Pottery in the Bible" on page 738.
2:12 In the ancient Near East a kiss was a sign of submission (see 1Sa 10:1; 1Ki 19:18; Hos 13:2; see also "The Jewish Custom of Kissing" on p. 1682). Submission to an Assyrian king was expressed by kissing his feet.
3:3 That the king was the shield (protector) of his people was a common concept in ancient Israel.
4:1 Psalm 4 is an individual lament, perhaps following a crop failure due to some natural calamity, like a drought. Such distress, not uncommon in Israel, raised questions about God's ability to provide agriculturally for his people and drove many to worship foreign fertility gods (see "Baal and the Fertility Cults" on p. 1414).

THE PSALM SUPERSCRIPTS

PSALM 3 A psalm **superscript**[1] is the brief informational note that precedes many psalms. In Psalm 3, for example, the superscript is: "A psalm of David. When he fled from his son Absalom." Today many scholars disregard the superscripts, considering them untrustworthy, but two factors suggest that we do well to pay attention to them:

◆ Some superscripts refer to incidents about which the books of Samuel and Chronicles say nothing. For example, the superscript of Psalm 60 mentions otherwise unknown battles with Aram Naharaim, Aram Zobah and Edom. If a scribe had been inventing superscripts to tie the psalms artificially to historical events, he would probably have linked them to known episodes from the **canonical** text (such as David's flight from Absalom, as in Ps 3). But references to unknown events or persons imply that the superscripts were written by people with specific knowledge of events, many of which are now lost to us.

◆ The superscripts use technical, musical terms. Examples include song titles (like "The Doe of the Morning" in Ps 22), references to instruments (such as "stringed instruments" in Ps 4)[2] and special instructions (such as "For the director of music" in Ps 58). Significantly, however, as early as the third century B.C. the true meanings of many superscripts were lost. For example, the translators of the **Septuagint** evidently did not always know what to make of the Hebrew words of the superscripts and at times resorted to guesswork in translating these terms into Greek.[3] This implies that the superscripts themselves are quite old—perhaps as ancient as the psalms themselves.

[1]See Glossary on page 2080 for definitions of bolded words. [2]See "Ancient Musical Instruments" on page 797. [3]For more on the Septuagint, see "Texts of the Old Testament" on page 1491.

Edom
Photograph courtesy of © Dr. Gary Pratico

[3] Know that the LORD has set apart the godly[u] for himself;
the LORD will hear[v] when I call to him.

[4] In your anger do not sin;[w]
when you are on your beds,[x]
search your hearts and be silent. *Selah*
[5] Offer right sacrifices
and trust in the LORD.[y]

[6] Many are asking, "Who can show us any good?"
Let the light of your face shine upon us,[z] O LORD.
[7] You have filled my heart[a] with greater joy[b]
than when their grain and new wine abound.
[8] I will lie down and sleep[c] in peace,
for you alone, O LORD,
make me dwell in safety.[d]

4:3 [u]Ps 31:23 [v]Ps 6:8
4:4 [w]Eph 4:26* [x]Ps 77:6
4:5 [y]Dt 33:19; Ps 37:3
4:6 [z]Nu 6:25
4:7 [a]Ac 14:17 [b]Isa 9:3
4:8 [c]Ps 3:5 [d]Lev 25:18

Psalm 5

For the director of music. For flutes. A psalm of David.

[1] Give ear to my words, O LORD,
consider my sighing.
[2] Listen to my cry for help,[e]
my King and my God,[f]
for to you I pray.
[3] In the morning,[g] O LORD, you hear my voice;
in the morning I lay my requests before you
and wait in expectation.

[4] You are not a God who takes pleasure in evil;
with you the wicked[h] cannot dwell.
[5] The arrogant[i] cannot stand[j] in your presence;
you hate[k] all who do wrong.
[6] You destroy those who tell lies;[l]
bloodthirsty and deceitful men
the LORD abhors.

[7] But I, by your great mercy,
will come into your house;
in reverence will I bow down[m]
toward your holy temple.
[8] Lead me, O LORD, in your righteousness[n]
because of my enemies—
make straight your way[o] before me.

[9] Not a word from their mouth can be trusted;
their heart is filled with destruction.
Their throat is an open grave;[p]
with their tongue they speak deceit.[q]
[10] Declare them guilty, O God!
Let their intrigues be their downfall.
Banish them for their many sins,[r]
for they have rebelled[s] against you.

5:2 [e]Ps 3:4 [f]Ps 84:3
5:3 [g]Ps 88:13
5:4 [h]Ps 11:5; 92:15
5:5 [i]Ps 73:3 [j]Ps 1:5 [k]Ps 11:5
5:6 [l]Ps 55:23; Rev 21:8
5:7 [m]Ps 138:2
5:8 [n]Ps 31:1 [o]Ps 27:11
5:9 [p]Lk 11:44 [q]Ro 3:13*
5:10 [r]Ps 9:16 [s]Ps 107:11

4:7 In Biblical language the heart is the center of the human spirit, from which spring emotions, thoughts, motivations, courage and actions. (See "Heart, Breath, Throat and Intestines: Ancient Hebrew Anthropology" on p. 968.)

5:10 For commentary on expressions of vengeful attitudes toward enemies, see the note on 69:22–28. See also "Curses and Imprecations" on page 883.

Ancient Musical Instruments

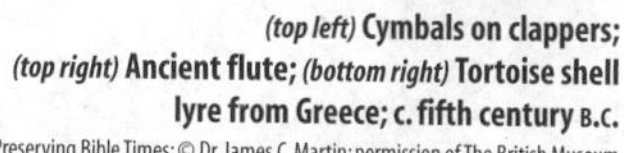

(top left) **Cymbals on clappers;** *(top right)* **Ancient flute;** *(bottom right)* **Tortoise shell lyre from Greece; c. fifth century B.C.**

Preserving Bible Times; © Dr. James C. Martin; permission of The British Museum

PSALM 5 A modest number of remains of musical instruments have been recovered by archaeologists. We do, however, have abundant evidence in ancient texts (such as the Psalms) and art (such as Egyptian tomb paintings) that attest to the varied use ancient peoples made of instruments to create music. Thus, the paucity of relics of ancient instruments is a matter of their fragility, not their scarcity. Indeed, a few of the more durable ancient instruments that have been found, such as cymbals, can still produce sound. Also, the vocabulary of musical instruments in Biblical Hebrew is fairly extensive. There can be no doubt that such instruments were widely employed in the ancient world, including Israel.

Precise translation of many Hebrew words for instruments is made difficult by the lack of Biblical descriptions. Even ancient translators, such as those working on the Greek **Septuagint**, often had little understanding of the meanings of the Hebrew musical terms. Also, modern associations with certain names can be misleading. For example, *shofar* is often translated "trumpet," calling to mind a brass instrument rather than what it actually was: a ram's horn.[1] The English "tambourine" suggests a hand drum with metal rings that jingle when shaken, but ancient Israelite hand drums probably lacked the rings. On the other hand, ancient artwork from Egypt and **Mesopotamia** provides us with clear images of what many instruments looked like. The Israelites, like their neighbors, used three basic types of instrumentation:

- *Stringed instruments*, like the lyre and harp. The lyre is well attested from ancient Israel, but the harp is more problematic. Some authorities argue that the word translated "harp" may actually refer to a kind of bass lyre or even to a lute. On the other hand, an instrument that is obviously a harp is attested from ancient Egypt and thus may have existed in Israel as well.
- Percussion instruments of two kinds:

  Drums and tambourines were constructed from animal skin stretched over a frame.

  "Idiophones" produce sound by vibrating but have neither strings nor skin membranes. Examples are objects such as bells, gongs, rattles, clappers and cymbals. These may have been made of various materials, including metal, wood, hardened clay or bone. Second Samuel 6:5 and Nehemiah 12:27 both refer to their use.
- *Wind instruments*, like pipes, trumpets or the shofar (ram's horn), are well-attested in the Bible (flute-like instruments at 1Ki 1:40; silver trumpets at Nu 10:2; the shofar at Joel 2:1).

Such instruments were widely used for entertainment and boisterous parties (Isa 5:12), but also for celebratory worship (Ps 81:2; 150:1–5). The first reference to musical instruments in the Bible is in Genesis 4:21, where Jubal, one of Cain's descendants, is described as "the father of all who play the harp and flute." Musical instruments were used at celebrations of various kinds (Ge 31:27; Job 21:11–12), including military victories (Ex 15:20). The shofar was employed primarily for signaling, especially during war (Jdg 3:27; 1Sa 13:3; Jer 6:1). Starting with the period of the monarchy, instruments were used at court (1Sa 19:9), as well as at the temple. Religious lyrics (such as those preserved in the Psalms) often called for instrumental accompaniment (Ps 150:3–5; Am 5:23).[2]

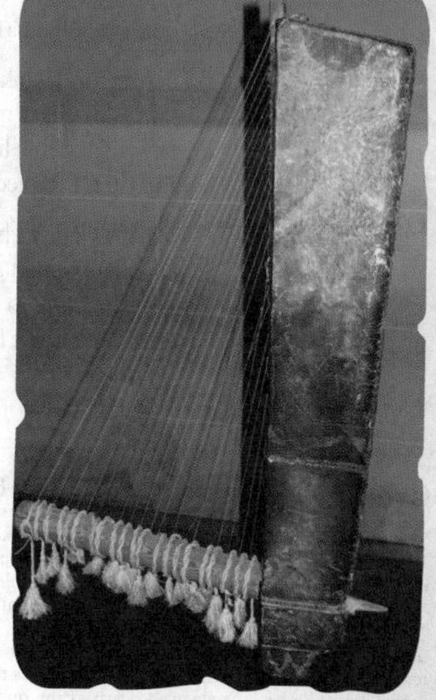

Harp from Egypt

Preserving Bible Times; © Dr. James C. Martin; permission of Musée de Louvre

[1]See "The Shofar" on page 898. [2]See "Ancient Israelite Poets and Singers" on page 869.

[11] But let all who take refuge in you be glad;
let them ever sing for joy.[t]
Spread your protection over them,
that those who love your name[u] may rejoice in you.[v]
[12] For surely, O LORD, you bless the righteous;
you surround them[w] with your favor as with a shield.

5:11 [t]Ps 2:12 [u]Ps 69:36 [v]Isa 65:13
5:12 [w]Ps 32:7

Psalm 6

For the director of music. With stringed instruments. According to *sheminith.*[a] A psalm of David.

[1] O LORD, do not rebuke me in your anger[x]
or discipline me in your wrath.
[2] Be merciful to me, LORD, for I am faint;
O LORD, heal me,[y] for my bones are in agony.[z]
[3] My soul is in anguish.[a]
How long,[b] O LORD, how long?

[4] Turn, O LORD, and deliver me;
save me because of your unfailing love.[c]
[5] No one remembers you when he is dead.
Who praises you from the grave[b]?[d]
[6] I am worn out[e] from groaning;
all night long I flood my bed with weeping
and drench my couch with tears.[f]
[7] My eyes grow weak[g] with sorrow;
they fail because of all my foes.
[8] Away from me,[h] all you who do evil,[i]
for the LORD has heard my weeping.
[9] The LORD has heard my cry for mercy;[j]
the LORD accepts my prayer.
[10] All my enemies will be ashamed and dismayed;
they will turn back in sudden disgrace.[k]

6:1 [x]Ps 38:1
6:2 [y]Hos 6:1 [z]Ps 22:14; 31:10
6:3 [a]Jn 12:27 [b]Ps 90:13
6:4 [c]Ps 17:13
6:5 [d]Ps 30:9; 88:10-12; Ecc 9:10; Isa 38:18
6:6 [e]Ps 69:3 [f]Ps 42:3
6:7 [g]Ps 31:9
6:8 [h]Ps 119:115 [i]Mt 7:23; Lk 13:27
6:9 [j]Ps 116:1
6:10 [k]Ps 71:24; 73:19

Psalm 7

A *shiggaion*[c] of David, which he sang to the LORD concerning Cush, a Benjamite.

[1] O LORD my God, I take refuge in you;
save and deliver me from all who pursue me,[l]
[2] or they will tear me like a lion[m]
and rip me to pieces with no one to rescue[n] me.
[3] O LORD my God, if I have done this
and there is guilt on my hands[o]—
[4] if I have done evil to him who is at peace with me
or without cause have robbed my foe—

7:1 [l]Ps 31:15
7:2 [m]Isa 38:13 [n]Ps 50:22
7:3 [o]1Sa 24:11; Isa 59:3

[a] Title: Probably a musical term [b] 5 Hebrew *Sheol* [c] Title: Probably a literary or musical term

6:3 The "soul" is not a spiritual aspect distinct from the physical but an individual's very self as a living, conscious, personal being. When the Hebrew writer used "soul" with "bones" (v. 2; cf. 35:9–10), he was not referencing two distinct entities but was referring to himself as a whole, as is the case also in the combination "soul" and "body" (31:9; 63:1). Compare the combination of "heart" and "bones" in 102:4 (see also its note).

6:5 The "grave" (Hebrew *Sheol*) refers in a general way to the realm of the dead, the netherworld, where, it was thought, departed spirits live. The Israelites viewed death as the opposite of life, and resurrection was not yet a part of their communal experience with God. The grave in their view brought no escape from God (see 139:8), but just how the ancient Israelites viewed the condition of the godly dead is unclear. Nonbiblical documents from the ancient Near East indicate a general conception that immortality was reserved for the gods but that the dead continued to experience some kind of shadowy existence in the dismal netherworld. (See "Sheol, Hades, Gehenna, the Abyss and Tartarus: Images of Hell" on p. 946. See also the note on Job 17:13–16).

[5] then let my enemy pursue and overtake me;
let him trample my life to the ground
and make me sleep in the dust. *Selah*

7:6 [p]Ps 94:2 [q]Ps 138:7 [r]Ps 44:23

[6] Arise,[p] O LORD, in your anger;
rise up against the rage of my enemies.[q]
Awake,[r] my God; decree justice.
[7] Let the assembled peoples gather around you.
Rule over them from on high;
[8] let the LORD judge the peoples.
Judge me, O LORD, according to my righteousness,[s]
according to my integrity, O Most High.
[9] O righteous God,[t]
who searches minds and hearts,[u]
bring to an end the violence of the wicked
and make the righteous secure.[v]

7:8 [s]Ps 18:20; 96:13
7:9 [t]Jer 11:20 [u]1Ch 28:9; Ps 26:2; Rev 2:23 [v]Ps 37:23

[10] My shield[a] is God Most High,
who saves the upright in heart.[w]
[11] God is a righteous judge,[x]
a God who expresses his wrath every day.
[12] If he does not relent,
he[b] will sharpen his sword;[y]
he will bend and string his bow.
[13] He has prepared his deadly weapons;
he makes ready his flaming arrows.

7:10 [w]Ps 125:4
7:11 [x]Ps 50:6
7:12 [y]Dt 32:41

[14] He who is pregnant with evil
and conceives trouble gives birth[z] to
disillusionment.
[15] He who digs a hole and scoops it out
falls into the pit he has made.[a]
[16] The trouble he causes recoils on himself;
his violence comes down on his own
head.
[17] I will give thanks to the LORD because of his
righteousness[b]
and will sing praise[c] to the name of the
LORD Most High.

7:14 [z]Job 15:35; Isa 59:4; Jas 1:15
7:15 [a]Job 4:8
7:17 [b]Ps 71:15-16 [c]Ps 9:2

Psalm 8

For the director of music. According to *gittith*.[c] A psalm of David.

[1] O LORD, our Lord,
how majestic is your name in all the
earth!

You have set your glory
above the heavens.[d]
[2] From the lips of children and infants
you have ordained praise[d][e]

8:1 [d]Ps 57:5; 113:4; 148:13
8:2 [e]Mt 21:16*

ANCIENT VOICES

Enki and Ninmah were drinking beer, and their heart became elated.

Ninmah said to Enki:

"What(ever)* makes the form of man good or bad—it is within my power; As my heart prompts me, I can make (its)* fate good or bad!"

Enki answered Ninmah:

"Let me counterbalance the 'fate' desired by your heart—good or bad!"

*Word and partial word in parentheses added by translator for clarity

—ENKI AND NINMAH

See "The Creation of Humans in the Sumerian Myth of Enki" article on the next page.

[a] *10* Or *sovereign* [b] *12* Or *If a man does not repent, / God* [c] Title: Probably a musical term [d] *2* Or *strength*

7:9 The Israelites used the words "minds" and "hearts" (lit., "hearts" and "kidneys") as virtual synonyms (but "heart" most often) to refer to a person's innermost center of conscious life (see the note on 4:7; see also "Heart, Breath, Throat and Intestines: Ancient Hebrew Anthropology" on p. 968). To "search mind and heart" was a conventional expression for God's examination of an individual's hidden character and motives (see Jer 11:20; 17:10; 20:12).

because of your enemies,
to silence the foe[f] and the avenger.

[3] When I consider your heavens,[g]
the work of your fingers,
the moon and the stars,[h]
which you have set in place,
[4] what is man that you are mindful of him,
the son of man that you care for him?[i]
[5] You made him a little lower than the heavenly beings[a]
and crowned him with glory and honor.[j]

[6] You made him ruler[k] over the works of your hands;
you put everything under his feet:[l m]
[7] all flocks and herds,
and the beasts of the field,
[8] the birds of the air,
and the fish of the sea,
all that swim the paths of the seas.

[9] O LORD, our Lord,
how majestic is your name in all the earth![n]

8:2 [f]Ps 44:16; 1Co 1:27
8:3 [g]Ps 89:11 [h]Ps 136:9
8:4 [i]Job 7:17; Ps 144:3; Heb 2:6
8:5 [j]Ps 21:5; 103:4
8:6 [k]Ge 1:28 [l]Heb 2:6-8* [m]1Co 15:25,27*; Eph 1:22
8:9 [n]ver 1

[a] 5 Or *than God*

ANCIENT TEXTS AND ARTIFACTS

The Creation of Humans in the Sumerian Myth of Enki

PSALM 8 The **Sumerian** myth of Enki and Ninmah describes the creation of humankind and a subsequent contest between these two deities regarding the value and occupation of disabled individuals. The myth begins when the earth was newly created and the lesser gods were charged with drudge work in service to the greater gods. Consigned to digging irrigation canals and providing their superiors with food, their toil became so wearisome that they rebelled against the high god Enki. The mother goddess, Nammu, encouraged Enki to relieve the gods' labor by forming a creature who could do the work for them. Enki accordingly devised the form of humanity and commissioned Nammu to create man and woman, using a pinch of clay (cf. Ge 2:7).

Afterward Nammu boasted that she could make a person in any form she wished, and Enki replied that he could find compensation for any deformity. Nammu deliberately fashioned a series of individuals with various disabilities, including a blind man, a cripple, a barren woman and a eunuch. Enki proceeded to find an honorable occupation for each of these persons in which their handicaps proved no obstacle. The text ends by praising the superiority of Enki.

The Biblical presentation of humanity's creation is quite different from the Sumerian myth. In the Bible men and women are not an afterthought but the pinnacle of God's creation, crowned with glory (Ps 8:5). Work itself (tending God's creation and caring for his creatures) is a God-given vocation (Ge 1:26,28; 2:15), not a form of drudgery to relieve God's burden but a means for participation in his creative work and an opportunity to act as his representatives on Earth. Human sickness and malformation, far from being the result of some divine game, are a product of humanity's fallen condition and, in God's sovereign plan, vehicles through which God can display his greatness in the lives of individuals (Jn 9:2–3).

A Babylonian text describing the creation of the world, man and the hoe; c. 1900–1700 B.C.

© The Schøyen Collection; photography courtesy of Mr. Martin Schøyen

Psalm 9[a]

For the director of music. To ˛the tune of˛ "The Death of the Son." A psalm of David.

9:1 oPs 86:12 pPs 26:7

1 I will praise you, O LORD, with all my heart;[o]
I will tell of all your wonders.[p]

9:2 qPs 5:11 rPs 92:1; 83:18

2 I will be glad and rejoice[q] in you;
I will sing praise to your name,[r] O Most High.

3 My enemies turn back;
they stumble and perish before you.

9:4 sPs 140:12 t1Pe 2:23

4 For you have upheld my right and my cause;[s]
you have sat on your throne, judging righteously.[t]
5 You have rebuked the nations and destroyed the wicked;

9:5 uPr 10:7

you have blotted out their name[u] for ever and ever.
6 Endless ruin has overtaken the enemy,
you have uprooted their cities;

9:6 vPs 34:16

even the memory of them[v] has perished.

7 The LORD reigns forever;

9:7 wPs 89:14

he has established his throne[w] for judgment.

9:8 xPs 96:13

8 He will judge the world in righteousness;[x]
he will govern the peoples with justice.
9 The LORD is a refuge for the oppressed,

9:9 yPs 32:7

a stronghold in times of trouble.[y]

9:10 zPs 91:14 aPs 37:28

10 Those who know your name[z] will trust in you,
for you, LORD, have never forsaken[a] those who seek you.

9:11 bPs 76:2 cPs 107:22 dPs 105:1

11 Sing praises to the LORD, enthroned in Zion;[b]
proclaim among the nations[c] what he has done.[d]

9:12 eGe 9:5

12 For he who avenges blood[e] remembers;
he does not ignore the cry of the afflicted.

9:13 fPs 38:19

13 O LORD, see how my enemies[f] persecute me!
Have mercy and lift me up from the gates of death,

9:14 gPs 106:2 hPs 13:5; 51:12

14 that I may declare your praises[g]
in the gates of the Daughter of Zion
and there rejoice in your salvation.[h]

9:15 iPs 7:15-16 jPs 35:8; 57:6

15 The nations have fallen into the pit they have dug;[i]
their feet are caught in the net they have hidden.[j]
16 The LORD is known by his justice;
the wicked are ensnared by the work of their hands. *Higgaion.[b] Selah*

9:17 kPs 49:14 lJob 8:13; Ps 50:22

17 The wicked return to the grave,[c][k]
all the nations that forget God.[l]
18 But the needy will not always be forgotten,

9:18 mPs 71:5; Pr 23:18 nPs 12:5

nor the hope[m] of the afflicted[n] ever perish.

19 Arise, O LORD, let not man triumph;
let the nations be judged in your presence.
20 Strike them with terror, O LORD;

9:20 oPs 62:9; Isa 31:3

let the nations know they are but men.[o] *Selah*

Psalm 10[a]

10:1 pPs 22:1,11 qPs 13:1

1 Why, O LORD, do you stand far off?[p]
Why do you hide yourself[q] in times of trouble?

[a] Psalms 9 and 10 may have been originally a single acrostic poem, the stanzas of which begin with the successive letters of the Hebrew alphabet. In the Septuagint they constitute one psalm. [b] *16* Or *Meditation*; possibly a musical notation [c] *17* Hebrew *Sheol*

[2] In his arrogance the wicked man hunts down the weak,
who are caught in the schemes he devises.
[3] He boasts[r] of the cravings of his heart;
he blesses the greedy and reviles the LORD.
[4] In his pride the wicked does not seek him;
in all his thoughts there is no room for God.[s]
[5] His ways are always prosperous;
he is haughty and your laws are far from him;
he sneers at all his enemies.
[6] He says to himself, "Nothing will shake me;
I'll always be happy[t] and never have trouble."
[7] His mouth is full of curses[u] and lies and threats;[v]
trouble and evil are under his tongue.[w]
[8] He lies in wait near the villages;
from ambush he murders the innocent,[x]
watching in secret for his victims.
[9] He lies in wait like a lion in cover;
he lies in wait to catch the helpless;[y]
he catches the helpless and drags them off in his net.
[10] His victims are crushed, they collapse;
they fall under his strength.
[11] He says to himself, "God has forgotten;[z]
he covers his face and never sees."

[12] Arise, LORD! Lift up your hand,[a] O God.
Do not forget the helpless.[b]
[13] Why does the wicked man revile God?
Why does he say to himself,
"He won't call me to account"?
[14] But you, O God, do see trouble[c] and grief;
you consider it to take it in hand.
The victim commits himself to you;[d]
you are the helper[e] of the fatherless.
[15] Break the arm of the wicked and evil man;[f]
call him to account for his wickedness
that would not be found out.

[16] The LORD is King for ever and ever;[g]
the nations[h] will perish from his land.
[17] You hear, O LORD, the desire of the afflicted;[i]
you encourage them, and you listen to their cry,
[18] defending the fatherless[j] and the oppressed,[k]
in order that man, who is of the earth, may terrify no more.

10:3 [r]Ps 94:4
10:4 [s]Ps 14:1; 36:1
10:6 [t]Rev 18:7
10:7 [u]Ro 3:14* [v]Ps 73:8 [w]Ps 140:3
10:8 [x]Ps 94:6
10:9 [y]Ps 17:12; 59:3; 140:5
10:11 [z]Job 22:13
10:12 [a]Ps 17:7; Mic 5:9 [b]Ps 9:12
10:14 [c]Ps 22:11 [d]Ps 37:5 [e]Ps 68:5
10:15 [f]Ps 37:17
10:16 [g]Ps 29:10 [h]Dt 8:20
10:17 [i]1Ch 29:18; Ps 34:15
10:18 [j]Ps 82:3 [k]Ps 9:9

Psalm 11

For the director of music. Of David.

[1] In the LORD I take refuge.[l]
How then can you say to me:
"Flee like a bird to your mountain.
[2] For look, the wicked bend their bows;
they set their arrows[m] against the strings

11:1 [l]Ps 56:11
11:2 [m]Ps 7:13

10:7 Curses, lies and threats were the three most common weapons of the tongue employed by ancient Near Eastern peoples. They thought they could manipulate supernatural powers with ritual words and actions in order to achieve the destruction of their enemies and they maintained a large conventional stock of such magic curses (see "Curses and Imprecations" on p. 883). "Lies" refers to slander and false testimony for malicious purposes (see, e.g., 1Ki 21:8–15).

11:2 For "heart," see the note on 4:7.

11:2 nPs 64:3-4
11:3 oPs 82:5

to shoot from the shadows
at the upright in heart.[n]
3 When the foundations[o] are being destroyed,
what can the righteous do[a]?"

11:4 pPs 18:6 qPs 103:19 rPs 33:13 sPs 34:15-16

4 The LORD is in his holy temple;[p]
the LORD is on his heavenly throne.[q]
He observes the sons of men;[r]
his eyes examine[s] them.

11:5 tGe 22:1; Jas 1:12 uPs 5:5

5 The LORD examines the righteous,[t]
but the wicked[b] and those who love violence
his soul hates.[u]
6 On the wicked he will rain

11:6 vEze 38:22 wJer 4:11-12

fiery coals and burning sulfur;[v]
a scorching wind[w] will be their lot.

11:7 xPs 7:9,11; 45:7 yPs 33:5 zPs 17:15

7 For the LORD is righteous,[x]
he loves justice;[y]
upright men will see his face.[z]

Psalm 12

For the director of music. According to *sheminith*.[c] A psalm of David.

12:1 aIsa 57:1

1 Help, LORD, for the godly are no more;[a]
the faithful have vanished from among men.
2 Everyone lies to his neighbor;

12:2 bPs 10:7; 41:6; 55:21; Ro 16:18

their flattering lips speak with deception.[b]
3 May the LORD cut off all flattering lips

12:3 cDa 7:8; Rev 13:5

and every boastful tongue[c]
4 that says, "We will triumph with our tongues;
we own our lips[d]—who is our master?"
5 "Because of the oppression of the weak
and the groaning of the needy,
I will now arise," says the LORD.

12:5 dPs 10:18; 34:6
12:6 e2Sa 22:31; Ps 18:30; Pr 30:5

"I will protect them[d] from those who malign them."
6 And the words of the LORD are flawless,[e]
like silver refined in a furnace of clay,
purified seven times.
7 O LORD, you will keep us safe

12:7 fPs 37:28
12:8 gPs 55:10-11

and protect us from such people forever.[f]
8 The wicked freely strut[g] about
when what is vile is honored among men.

Psalm 13

For the director of music. A psalm of David.

13:1 hJob 13:24; Ps 44:24

1 How long, O LORD? Will you forget me forever?
How long will you hide your face[h] from me?

[a] 3 Or *what is the Righteous One doing* [b] 5 Or *The LORD, the Righteous One, examines the wicked, /* [c] Title: Probably a musical term [d] 4 Or */ our lips are our plowshares*

11:7 The Hebrew for "see [the king's] face" was an expression denoting access to the king. Sometimes it referred to those who served before him (see 2Ki 25:19, where it is translated "royal advisers"; see also Est 1:14, where it is translated "[those] who had special access to the king"). Here David was speaking of special freedom of access before the heavenly King.

12:3 To "cut off" means to put an end to. Physical mutilation was not in view.

[2] How long must I wrestle with my thoughts[i]
and every day have sorrow in my heart?
How long will my enemy triumph over me?[j]

[3] Look on me and answer,[k] O LORD my God.
Give light to my eyes,[l] or I will sleep in death;[m]
[4] my enemy will say, "I have overcome him,[n]"
and my foes will rejoice when I fall.

[5] But I trust in your unfailing love;[o]
my heart rejoices in your salvation.[p]
[6] I will sing[q] to the LORD,
for he has been good to me.

13:2 [i]Ps 42:4 [j]Ps 42:9
13:3 [k]Ps 5:1 [l]Ezr 9:8 [m]Jer 51:39
13:4 [n]Ps 25:2
13:5 [o]Ps 52:8 [p]Ps 9:14
13:6 [q]Ps 116:7

Psalm 14

For the director of music. Of David.

[1] The fool[a] says in his heart,
"There is no God."[r]
They are corrupt, their deeds are vile;
there is no one who does good.

[2] The LORD looks down from heaven[s]
on the sons of men
to see if there are any who understand,[t]
any who seek God.
[3] All have turned aside,
they have together become corrupt;[u]
there is no one who does good,[v]
not even one.[w]

[4] Will evildoers never learn—[x]
those who devour my people[y] as men eat bread
and who do not call on the LORD?[z]
[5] There they are, overwhelmed with dread,
for God is present in the company of the righteous.
[6] You evildoers frustrate the plans of the poor,
but the LORD is their refuge.[a]

[7] Oh, that salvation for Israel would come out of Zion!
When the LORD restores the fortunes[b] of his people,
let Jacob rejoice and Israel be glad!

14:1 [r]Ps 10:4
14:2 [s]Ps 33:13 [t]Ps 92:6
14:3 [u]Ps 58:3 [v]Ps 143:2 [w]Ro 3:10-12*
14:4 [x]Ps 82:5 [y]Ps 27:2 [z]Ps 79:6; Isa 64:7
14:6 [a]Ps 9:9; 40:17
14:7 [b]Ps 53:6

Psalm 15

A psalm of David.

[1] LORD, who may dwell in your sanctuary?[c]
Who may live on your holy hill?[d]

[2] He whose walk is blameless
and who does what is righteous,
who speaks the truth[e] from his heart

15:1 [c]Ps 27:5-6 [d]Ps 24:3-5
15:2 [e]Ps 24:4; Zec 8:3,16; Eph 4:25

[a] *1* The Hebrew words rendered *fool* in Psalms denote one who is morally deficient.

15:1–5 For commentary on Old Testament Israel's evangelistic attitude toward the Gentiles, see the note on Zephaniah 3:10.

This brief psalm instructed those desiring to enter God's presence in his sanctuary. It may represent a type of priestly teaching presented to those approaching the temple mount in Jerusalem, encouraging them to prepare physically and spiritually for their access to the holy place for worship. Moral righteousness—not sacrifices or ritual purity as seen among the other religions of the ancient Near East—opens the way for access to the Lord.

15:3 [f]Ex 23:1

3 and has no slander[f] on his tongue,
who does his neighbor no wrong
and casts no slur on his fellowman,
4 who despises a vile man

15:4 [g]Ac 28:10 [h]Jdg 11:35

but honors[g] those who fear the LORD,
who keeps his oath[h]
even when it hurts,

15:5 [i]Ex 22:25 [j]Ex 23:8; Dt 16:19 [k]2Pe 1:10

5 who lends his money without usury[i]
and does not accept a bribe[j] against the innocent.

He who does these things
will never be shaken.[k]

Psalm 16

A *miktam*[a] of David.

16:1 [l]Ps 17:8 [m]Ps 7:1

1 Keep me safe,[l] O God,
for in you I take refuge.[m]

2 I said to the LORD, "You are my Lord;

16:2 [n]Ps 73:25

apart from you I have no good thing."[n]

16:3 [o]Ps 101:6

3 As for the saints who are in the land,[o]
they are the glorious ones in whom is all my delight.[b]

16:4 [p]Ps 32:10 [q]Ps 106:37-38 [r]Ex 23:13

4 The sorrows[p] of those will increase
who run after other gods.[q]
I will not pour out their libations of blood
or take up their names[r] on my lips.

16:5 [s]Ps 73:26 [t]Ps 23:5

5 LORD, you have assigned me my portion[s] and my cup;[t]
you have made my lot secure.
6 The boundary lines have fallen for me in pleasant places;

16:6 [u]Ps 78:55; Jer 3:19

surely I have a delightful inheritance.[u]

16:7 [v]Ps 73:24 [w]Ps 77:6

7 I will praise the LORD, who counsels me;[v]
even at night[w] my heart instructs me.
8 I have set the LORD always before me.

16:8 [x]Ps 73:23

Because he is at my right hand,[x]
I will not be shaken.

16:9 [y]Ps 4:7; 30:11 [z]Ps 4:8

9 Therefore my heart is glad[y] and my tongue rejoices;
my body also will rest secure,[z]
10 because you will not abandon me to the grave,[c]

16:10 [a]Ac 13:35*

nor will you let your Holy One[d] see decay.[a]

16:11 [b]Mt 7:14 [c]Ac 2:25-28* [d]Ps 36:7-8

11 You have made[e] known to me the path of life;[b]
you will fill me with joy in your presence,[c]
with eternal pleasures[d] at your right hand.

Psalm 17

A prayer of David.

1 Hear, O LORD, my righteous plea;

17:1 [e]Ps 61:1

listen to my cry.[e]

[a] Title: Probably a literary or musical term [b] 3 Or *As for the pagan priests who are in the land / and the nobles in whom all delight, I said:* [c] 10 Hebrew *Sheol* [d] 10 Or *your faithful one* [e] 11 Or *You will make*

16:4 "Libations of blood" refers to the blood of sacrifices poured onto altars.

16:7 For "heart" (lit., "kidneys"), see the note on 7:9.

16:9 For "heart," see also the note on 4:7.

Give ear to my prayer—
it does not rise from deceitful lips.[f]
2 May my vindication come from you;
may your eyes see what is right.

3 Though you probe my heart and examine me at night,
though you test me,[g] you will find nothing;[h]
I have resolved that my mouth will not sin.[i]
4 As for the deeds of men—
by the word of your lips
I have kept myself
from the ways of the violent.
5 My steps have held to your paths;[j]
my feet have not slipped.[k]

6 I call on you, O God, for you will answer me;[l]
give ear to me[m] and hear my prayer.[n]
7 Show the wonder of your great love,[o]
you who save by your right hand[p]
those who take refuge in you from their foes.
8 Keep me as the apple of your eye;[q]
hide me in the shadow of your wings
9 from the wicked who assail me,
from my mortal enemies who surround me.[r]

10 They close up their callous hearts,[s]
and their mouths speak with arrogance.[t]
11 They have tracked me down, they now surround me,[u]
with eyes alert, to throw me to the ground.
12 They are like a lion[v] hungry for prey,
like a great lion crouching in cover.

13 Rise up, O LORD, confront them, bring them down;[w]
rescue me from the wicked by your sword.
14 O LORD, by your hand save me from such men,
from men of this world[x] whose reward is in this life.

You still the hunger of those you cherish;
their sons have plenty,
and they store up wealth[y] for their children.
15 And I—in righteousness I will see your face;
when I awake, I will be satisfied with seeing your
likeness.[z]

17:1 [f]Isa 29:13
17:3 [g]Ps 26:2; 66:10 [h]Job 23:10; Jer 50:20 [i]Ps 39:1
17:5 [j]Ps 44:18; 119:133 [k]Ps 18:36
17:6 [l]Ps 86:7 [m]Ps 116:2 [n]Ps 88:2
17:7 [o]Ps 31:21 [p]Ps 20:6
17:8 [q]Dt 32:10
17:9 [r]Ps 31:20; 109:3
17:10 [s]Ps 73:7 [t]1Sa 2:3
17:11 [u]Ps 37:14; 88:17
17:12 [v]Ps 7:2; 10:9
17:13 [w]Ps 7:12; 22:20; 73:18
17:14 [x]Lk 16:8 [y]Ps 73:3-7
17:15 [z]Nu 12:8; Ps 4:6-7; 16:11; 1Jn 3:2

Psalm 18

For the director of music. Of David the servant of the LORD. He sang to the LORD the words of this song when the LORD delivered him from the hand of all his enemies and from the hand of Saul. He said:

1 I love you, O LORD, my strength.

2 The LORD is my rock,[a] my fortress and my deliverer;

18:2 [a]Ps 19:14

17:8 The "apple" refers to the pupil, a delicate part of the eye that is precious and in need of protection (cf. Dt 32:10; Pr 7:2). The term "shadow" is a conventional Hebrew metaphor for defense against oppression—as shade protects from the oppressive heat of the searing desert sun. The term "wings" is a metaphor for the protective outreach of God's power.

17:15 To "seek" or "see" God's face was viewed in the Old Testament as an appropriate goal of the righteous (2Ch 7:14; Ps 105:4), but numerous other passages point to fearful consequences (e.g., Ge 32:30; Ex 33:20–23; Isa 6:5). The solution may perhaps be found in Numbers 12:8, where God said of Moses, "With him I speak face to face . . . he sees the form of the LORD." Moses was in God's presence but physically saw the "form" of God rather than his very person. Similarly, David would have been satisfied being in God's presence and seeing his "likeness" (Ps 17:15; cf. the note on 11:7).

my God is my rock, in whom I take refuge.
18:2 [b]Ps 59:11 [c]Ps 75:10 He is my shield[b] and the horn[a] of my salvation,[c] my stronghold.
18:3 [d]Ps 48:1 3 I call to the LORD, who is worthy of praise,[d]
and I am saved from my enemies.

18:4 [e]Ps 116:3 4 The cords of death[e] entangled me;
[f]Ps 124:4 the torrents[f] of destruction overwhelmed me.
5 The cords of the grave[b] coiled around me;
18:5 [g]Ps 116:3 the snares of death[g] confronted me.
6 In my distress I called to the LORD;
I cried to my God for help.
18:6 [h]Ps 34:15 From his temple he heard my voice;[h]
my cry came before him, into his ears.

18:7 [i]Jdg 5:4 7 The earth trembled and quaked,[i]
[j]Ps 68:7-8 and the foundations of the mountains shook;
they trembled because he was angry.[j]
8 Smoke rose from his nostrils;
18:8 [k]Ps 50:3 consuming fire[k] came from his mouth,
burning coals blazed out of it.
18:9 [l]Ps 144:5 9 He parted the heavens and came down;[l]
dark clouds were under his feet.
18:10 [m]Ps 80:1 10 He mounted the cherubim[m] and flew;
[n]Ps 104:3 he soared on the wings of the wind.[n]
18:11 [o]Dt 4:11; 11 He made darkness his covering,[o] his canopy around him—
Ps 97:2 the dark rain clouds of the sky.
18:12 [p]Ps 104:2 12 Out of the brightness of his presence[p] clouds advanced,
[q]Ps 97:3 with hailstones and bolts of lightning.[q]
18:13 [r]Ps 29:3; 13 The LORD thundered[r] from heaven;
104:7 the voice of the Most High resounded.[c]
14 He shot his arrows and scattered ⌊the enemies⌋,
18:14 [s]Ps 144:6 great bolts of lightning and routed them.[s]
15 The valleys of the sea were exposed
and the foundations of the earth laid bare
18:15 [t]Ps 76:6; at your rebuke,[t] O LORD,
106:9 at the blast of breath from your nostrils.

16 He reached down from on high and took hold of me;
18:16 [u]Ps 144:7 he drew me out of deep waters.[u]
17 He rescued me from my powerful enemy,
18:17 [v]Ps 35:10 from my foes, who were too strong for me.[v]
18 They confronted me in the day of my disaster,
18:18 [w]Ps 59:16 but the LORD was my support.[w]
18:19 [x]Ps 31:8 19 He brought me out into a spacious place;[x]
[y]Ps 118:5 he rescued me because he delighted in me.[y]

20 The LORD has dealt with me according to my righteousness;
18:20 [z]Ps 24:4 according to the cleanness of my hands[z] he has rewarded me.
18:21 [a]2Ch 34:33 21 For I have kept the ways of the LORD;[a]
[b]Ps 119:102 I have not done evil by turning[b] from my God.
18:22 [c]Ps 119:30 22 All his laws are before me;[c]
I have not turned away from his decrees.

[a] 2 *Horn* here symbolizes strength. [b] 5 Hebrew *Sheol* [c] 13 Some Hebrew manuscripts and Septuagint (see also 2 Samuel 22:14); most Hebrew manuscripts *resounded, / amid hailstones and bolts of lightning*

18:5 For "the grave," see the note on 6:5.

23 I have been blameless before him
and have kept myself from sin.
24 The LORD has rewarded me according to my righteousness,[d] — 18:24 [d]1Sa 26:23
according to the cleanness of my hands in his sight.

25 To the faithful[e] you show yourself faithful, — 18:25 [e]1Ki 8:32; Ps 62:12; Mt 5:7
to the blameless you show yourself blameless,
26 to the pure you show yourself pure,
but to the crooked you show yourself shrewd.[f] — 18:26 [f]Pr 3:34
27 You save the humble
but bring low those whose eyes are haughty.[g] — 18:27 [g]Pr 6:17
28 You, O LORD, keep my lamp burning;
my God turns my darkness into light.[h] — 18:28 [h]Job 18:6; 29:3
29 With your help[i] I can advance against a troop[a]; — 18:29 [i]Heb 11:34
with my God I can scale a wall.

30 As for God, his way is perfect;[j] — 18:30 [j]Dt 32:4; Rev 15:3 [k]Ps 12:6 [l]Ps 17:7
the word of the LORD is flawless.[k]
He is a shield
for all who take refuge[l] in him.
31 For who is God besides the LORD?[m] — 18:31 [m]Dt 32:39; 86:8; Isa 45:5,6, 14,18,21 [n]Dt 32:31; 1Sa 2:2
And who is the Rock[n] except our God?

[a] 29 Or *can run through a barricade*

Storm Gods, Storm Imagery and Theophany

PSALM 18 It was common practice for peoples in the ancient world to identify their deities with observable, awe-inspiring natural phenomena. As **Canaan** was a land of tempests, the high-ranking deities of the Canaanite pantheons were storm gods: Teshub of the **Hittites**,[1] Hadad of the Arameans and Baal of **Ugarit**.[2] Storm gods were conceived of as vigorous warriors, revered for their ability to usher in the rains needed for fertility and feared for their destructive power unleashed in the storm. Religious iconography frequently portrays storm gods as riding on beasts while wielding weapons in their hands.

Israel's God also appears in the storm. Indeed, the Old Testament fully fleshes out the concept that God controls the storms.

✣ Although **Yahweh** is omnipresent and fills the earth (Ps 139:7–8; Jer 23:23–24), he appears in the world as a physical, divine presence at specific times and locations. This is the meaning of "theophany"—an appearance of God.

✣ The creation, which is ordered by Yahweh and submits to his will (Lk 8:22–25), at times becomes the vehicle of his manifestation (Ps 18:7–15). The raging wind is depicted as his chariot (Eze 1:4–28; Hab 3:8), peals of thunder his voice (Job 37:1–5; Ps 29:3–9; Jn 12:28–29; Rev 10:3–4) and lightning bolts his weapons (Ps 18:14; Hab 3:11).

✣ The appearance of God in the storm may be either to save (Dt 4:33–35) or to judge (Mic 1:3–5; Hab 3:3–15).

✣ Theophany is only temporary because a full revelation of God's terrifying glory cannot be endured by humans (Ex 20:18–19; 33:18–23).

✣ God appeared in the storm to make a covenant at Sinai by which Israel became his own possession (Ex 19:16–19).

✣ At the end of time God will return to the earth in the person of Jesus Christ, riding on the clouds with the sound of the trumpet to judge the living and the dead (Mt 24:30–31; 1Th 4:16–17; Rev 1:7).[3]

[1]See also "The Hittite Storm Gods" on page 784. [2]See also "The Ugaritic Text of the Myth of Baal" on page 905 and "Baal and the Fertility Cults" on page 1414. [3]See "Trumpets in the Ancient World" on page 2057.

18:32 [o]Isa 45:5

32 It is God who arms me with strength[o]
and makes my way perfect.

18:33 [p]Hab 3:19 [q]Dt 32:13

33 He makes my feet like the feet of a deer;[p]
he enables me to stand on the heights.[q]

18:34 [r]Ps 144:1

34 He trains my hands for battle;[r]
my arms can bend a bow of bronze.

18:35 [s]Ps 119:116

35 You give me your shield of victory,
and your right hand sustains[s] me;
you stoop down to make me great.
36 You broaden the path beneath me,
so that my ankles do not turn.

18:37 [t]Ps 37:20; 44:5

37 I pursued my enemies[t] and overtook them;
I did not turn back till they were destroyed.

18:38 [u]Ps 36:12 [v]Ps 47:3

38 I crushed them so that they could not rise;[u]
they fell beneath my feet.[v]
39 You armed me with strength for battle;
you made my adversaries bow at my feet.

18:40 [w]Ps 21:12 [x]Ps 94:23

40 You made my enemies turn their backs[w] in flight,
and I destroyed[x] my foes.

18:41 [y]Ps 50:22 [z]Job 27:9; Pr 1:28

41 They cried for help, but there was no one to save them[y]—
to the LORD, but he did not answer.[z]
42 I beat them as fine as dust borne on the wind;
I poured them out like mud in the streets.

18:43 [a]2Sa 8:1-14 [b]Isa 52:15; 55:5

43 You have delivered me from the attacks of the people;
you have made me the head of nations;[a]
people I did not know[b] are subject to me.

18:44 [c]Ps 66:3

44 As soon as they hear me, they obey me;
foreigners[c] cringe before me.

18:45 [d]Mic 7:17

45 They all lose heart;
they come trembling from their strongholds.[d]

18:46 [e]Ps 51:14

46 The LORD lives! Praise be to my Rock!
Exalted be God my Savior![e]

18:47 [f]Ps 47:3

47 He is the God who avenges me,
who subdues nations[f] under me,

18:48 [g]Ps 59:1

48 who saves[g] me from my enemies.
You exalted me above my foes;
from violent men you rescued me.

18:49 [h]Ps 108:1 [i]Ro 15:9*

49 Therefore I will praise you among the nations, O LORD;
I will sing[h] praises to your name.[i]

18:50 [j]Ps 144:10 [k]Ps 89:4

50 He gives his king great victories;
he shows unfailing kindness to his anointed,
to David[j] and his descendants forever.[k]

Psalm 19

For the director of music. A psalm of David.

19:1 [l]Isa 40:22 [m]Ps 50:6; Ro 1:19

1 The heavens[l] declare[m] the glory of God;
the skies proclaim the work of his hands.

19:2 [n]Ps 74:16

2 Day after day they pour forth speech;
night after night they display knowledge.[n]
3 There is no speech or language
where their voice is not heard.[a]

[a] 3 Or *They have no speech, there are no words; / no sound is heard from them*

[4] Their voice[a] goes out into all the earth,
their words to the ends of the world.[o]

In the heavens he has pitched a tent[p] for the sun,
[5] which is like a bridegroom coming forth from his pavilion,
like a champion rejoicing to run his course.
[6] It rises at one end of the heavens
and makes its circuit to the other;[q]
nothing is hidden from its heat.

[7] The law of the LORD is perfect,
reviving the soul.[r]
The statutes of the LORD are trustworthy,[s]
making wise the simple.[t]
[8] The precepts of the LORD are right,[u]
giving joy to the heart.
The commands of the LORD are radiant,
giving light to the eyes.
[9] The fear of the LORD is pure,
enduring forever.
The ordinances of the LORD are sure
and altogether righteous.[v]
[10] They are more precious than gold,[w]
than much pure gold;
they are sweeter than honey,
than honey from the comb.
[11] By them is your servant warned;
in keeping them there is great reward.

[12] Who can discern his errors?
Forgive my hidden faults.[x]
[13] Keep your servant also from willful sins;
may they not rule over me.
Then will I be blameless,
innocent of great transgression.

[14] May the words of my mouth and the meditation of my heart
be pleasing[y] in your sight,
O LORD, my Rock[z] and my Redeemer.[a]

19:4 [o] Ro 10:18* [p] Ps 104:2
19:6 [q] Ps 113:3; Ecc 1:5
19:7 [r] Ps 23:3 [s] Ps 93:5; 111:7 [t] Ps 119:98-100
19:8 [u] Ps 12:6; 119:128
19:9 [v] Ps 119:138,142
19:10 [w] Pr 8:10
19:12 [x] Ps 51:2; 90:8; 139:6
19:14 [y] Ps 104:34 [z] Ps 18:2 [a] Isa 47:4

Psalm 20

For the director of music. A psalm of David.

[1] May the LORD answer you when you are in distress;
may the name of the God of Jacob[b] protect you.[c]
[2] May he send you help from the sanctuary[d]
and grant you support from Zion.
[3] May he remember[e] all your sacrifices
and accept your burnt offerings.[f] *Selah*

20:1 [b] Ps 46:7,11 [c] Ps 91:14
20:2 [d] Ps 3:4
20:3 [e] Ac 10:4 [f] Ps 51:19

[a] 4 Septuagint, Jerome and Syriac; Hebrew *line*

19:4–6 The heavens are the "tent" for the sun—widely worshiped in the ancient Near East (cf. Dt 4:19; 17:3; 2Ki 23:5,11; Jer 8:2; Eze 8:16) but here, as in Psalm 136:7–8 and Genesis 1:16, merely a part of God's creation. Of the created realm, the sun is the supreme metaphor of the glory of God (see Ps 84:11; Isa 60:19–20), as it makes its daily, triumphant sweep across the whole extent of the heavens and pours out its heat (felt presence) upon every creature.

See the note on the nuptial tent at Song of Songs 1:16–17.

20:1–9 This psalm was concerned with the king's military activities and most likely functioned as a pledge of loyalty by the army to its ruler before a military campaign.

20:4 gPs 21:2; 145:16,19
20:5 hPs 9:14; 60:4 i1Sa 1:17
20:6 jPs 28:8; 41:11; Isa 58:9
20:7 kPs 33:17; Isa 31:1 l2Ch 32:8
20:8 mMic 7:8 nPs 37:23
20:9 oPs 3:7; 17:6

4 May he give you the desire of your heart[g]
and make all your plans succeed.
5 We will shout for joy when you are victorious
and will lift up our banners[h] in the name of our God.
May the LORD grant all your requests.[i]

6 Now I know that the LORD saves his anointed;[j]
he answers him from his holy heaven
with the saving power of his right hand.
7 Some trust in chariots and some in horses,[k]
but we trust in the name of the LORD our God.[l]
8 They are brought to their knees and fall,
but we rise up[m] and stand firm.[n]

9 O LORD, save the king!
Answer[a] us[o] when we call!

Psalm 21

For the director of music. A psalm of David.

21:1 pPs 59:16-17
21:2 qPs 37:4
21:3 r2Sa 12:30
21:4 sPs 61:5-6; 91:16; 133:3
21:5 tPs 18:50
21:6 uPs 43:4 v1Ch 17:27

1 O LORD, the king rejoices in your strength.
How great is his joy in the victories you give![p]
2 You have granted him the desire of his heart[q]
and have not withheld the request of his lips. *Selah*
3 You welcomed him with rich blessings
and placed a crown of pure gold[r] on his head.
4 He asked you for life, and you gave it to him—
length of days, for ever and ever.[s]
5 Through the victories[t] you gave, his glory is great;
you have bestowed on him splendor and majesty.
6 Surely you have granted him eternal blessings
and made him glad with the joy[u] of your presence.[v]
7 For the king trusts in the LORD;
through the unfailing love of the Most High
he will not be shaken.

21:8 wIsa 10:10
21:9 xPs 50:3; La 2:2; Mal 4:1
21:10 yDt 28:18; Ps 37:28
21:11 zPs 2:1 aPs 10:2
21:12 bPs 7:12-13; 18:40

8 Your hand will lay hold[w] on all your enemies;
your right hand will seize your foes.
9 At the time of your appearing
you will make them like a fiery furnace.
In his wrath the LORD will swallow them up,
and his fire will consume them.[x]
10 You will destroy their descendants from the earth,
their posterity from mankind.[y]
11 Though they plot evil[z] against you
and devise wicked schemes,[a] they cannot succeed;
12 for you will make them turn their backs[b]
when you aim at them with drawn bow.

13 Be exalted, O LORD, in your strength;
we will sing and praise your might.

[a] 9 Or *save! / O King, answer*

20:4 The Hebrew does not contain a word equivalent to "desire"; a literal translation might be, "May he give to you according to your heart." God's gifts to us depend in part upon the condition of our hearts. For "heart," see the note on 4:7.

21:3 The "crown of pure gold" was the ceremonial emblem of royalty—possibly the captured crown of the defeated king (see 2Sa 12:30).

Psalm 22

For the director of music. To ˻the tune of˼ "The Doe of the Morning." A psalm of David.

[1] My God, my God, why have you forsaken me?[c]
Why are you so far[d] from saving me,
so far from the words of my groaning?
[2] O my God, I cry out by day, but you do not answer,
by night,[e] and am not silent.

[3] Yet you are enthroned as the Holy One;[f]
you are the praise[g] of Israel.[a]
[4] In you our fathers put their trust;
they trusted and you delivered them.
[5] They cried to you and were saved;
in you they trusted and were not disappointed.[h]

[6] But I am a worm[i] and not a man,
scorned by men[j] and despised[k] by the people.
[7] All who see me mock me;
they hurl insults,[l] shaking their heads:[m]
[8] "He trusts in the LORD;
let the LORD rescue him.[n]
Let him deliver him,
since he delights[o] in him."

[9] Yet you brought me out of the womb;[p]
you made me trust in you
even at my mother's breast.
[10] From birth[q] I was cast upon you;
from my mother's womb you have been my God.
[11] Do not be far from me,
for trouble is near
and there is no one to help.[r]

[12] Many bulls[s] surround me;
strong bulls of Bashan[t] encircle me.
[13] Roaring lions[u] tearing their prey
open their mouths wide[v] against me.
[14] I am poured out like water,
and all my bones are out of joint.[w]
My heart has turned to wax;
it has melted away[x] within me.
[15] My strength is dried up like a potsherd,
and my tongue sticks to the roof of my mouth;[y]
you lay me[b] in the dust[z] of death.
[16] Dogs[a] have surrounded me;
a band of evil men has encircled me,
they have pierced[c][b] my hands and my feet.
[17] I can count all my bones;
people stare[c] and gloat over me.[d]

22:1 [c]Mt 27:46*; Mk 15:34* [d]Ps 10:1
22:2 [e]Ps 42:3
22:3 [f]Ps 99:9 [g]Dt 10:21
22:5 [h]Isa 49:23
22:6 [i]Job 25:6; Isa 41:14 [j]Ps 31:11 [k]Isa 49:7; 53:3
22:7 [l]Mt 27:39, 44 [m]Mk 15:29
22:8 [n]Ps 91:14 [o]Mt 27:43
22:9 [p]Ps 71:6
22:10 [q]Isa 46:3
22:11 [r]Ps 72:12
22:12 [s]Ps 68:30 [t]Dt 32:14
22:13 [u]Ps 17:12 [v]Ps 35:21
22:14 [w]Ps 31:10 [x]Job 30:16; Da 5:6
22:15 [y]Ps 38:10; Jn 19:28 [z]Ps 104:29
22:16 [a]Ps 59:6 [b]Isa 53:5; Zec 12:10; Jn 19:34
22:17 [c]Lk 23:35 [d]Lk 23:27

[a] 3 Or *Yet you are holy, / enthroned on the praises of Israel* [b] 15 Or */ I am laid* [c] 16 Some Hebrew manuscripts, Septuagint and Syriac; most Hebrew manuscripts */ like the lion,*

22:12–13 Bulls, lions and dogs (see v. 16) are all used in the Bible as metaphors for enemies (see "Lions and Other Wild Beasts in Ancient Israel" on p. 813).

Bashan lay east of the Sea of Galilee. It was known for its rich pastureland, sleek cattle and magnificent oak trees (see Dt 32:14; Eze 39:18; cf. Am 4:1).

22:14 For "heart," see the note on 4:7. For the use of "bones" with "heart," see the note on 102:4.

[18] They divide my garments among them
22:18 [e]Mt 27:35*; Lk 23:34; Jn 19:24* — and cast lots[e] for my clothing.

[19] But you, O LORD, be not far off;
22:19 [f]Ps 70:5 — O my Strength, come quickly[f] to help me.
[20] Deliver my life from the sword,
22:20 [g]Ps 35:17 — my precious life[g] from the power of the dogs.
[21] Rescue me from the mouth of the lions;
save[a] me from the horns of the wild oxen.

[22] I will declare your name to my brothers;
22:22 [h]Heb 2:12* — in the congregation I will praise you.[h]
22:23 [i]Ps 86:12; 135:19 [j]Ps 33:8 — [23] You who fear the LORD, praise him![i]
All you descendants of Jacob, honor him!
Revere him,[j] all you descendants of Israel!
[24] For he has not despised or disdained
the suffering of the afflicted one;
22:24 [k]Ps 69:17 [l]Heb 5:7 — he has not hidden his face[k] from him
but has listened to his cry for help.[l]

22:25 [m]Ps 35:18 [n]Ecc 5:4 — [25] From you comes the theme of my praise in the great assembly;[m]
before those who fear you[b] will I fulfill my vows.[n]
22:26 [o]Ps 107:9 [p]Ps 40:16 — [26] The poor will eat[o] and be satisfied;
they who seek the LORD will praise him—[p]
may your hearts live forever!
22:27 [q]Ps 2:8 — [27] All the ends of the earth[q]
will remember and turn to the LORD,

[a] 21 Or *I you have heard* [b] 25 Hebrew *him*

22:21 "Wild oxen" refers either to aurochs, wild ancestors of domestic cattle or possibly to oryx, large, straight-horned antelope.

Lions and Other Wild Beasts in Ancient Israel

PSALM 22 For the modern reader the ferocity of wild beasts is something of a cliché; we can mouth the analogy "as bold as a lion" without having had any firsthand experience with the terror these animals can inspire. In ancient Israel, though, such creatures were an all too real danger and a pervasive source of fear. Menacing carnivores included bears, lions, leopards, wolves and jackals. The situation of the ancient Israelite herdsman was all the more acute in that he had to defend his livestock from these beasts or face personal ruin. The shepherd literally stood between the predator and its prey (1Sa 17:36–37).[1]

Archaeologists have unearthed the remains of lions and bears from the **Iron Age**,[2] and many carnivores continued in the region until the fairly recent past. Leopards still survive in parts of the Negev.[3] **Relief** sculptures from Nineveh (c. 650 B.C.)[4] depict the **Assyrian** king Ashurbanipal hunting lions from the relative safety of his war chariot, indicating that these animals were neither rare nor exotic in the ancient Near East. In Psalm 22:13–14 David likened his enemies to a roaring lion that made his heart melt; no doubt many Israelites knew what it was to be paralyzed with fear by the roars, growls, howls and snarls of wild beasts.

[1]See "Shepherding in the Ancient World" on page 1363. [2]See "Archaeological Periods" chart on page xx in the front of this Bible. [3]See "The Negev: Its Climate and Features" on page 34. [4]See "Nineveh" on page 1497.

and all the families of the nations
will bow down before him,[r]
28 for dominion belongs to the LORD[s]
and he rules over the nations.

29 All the rich[t] of the earth will feast and worship;
all who go down to the dust[u] will kneel before him—
those who cannot keep themselves alive.
30 Posterity[v] will serve him;
future generations will be told about the Lord.
31 They will proclaim his righteousness
to a people yet unborn[w]—
for he has done it.

22:27 [r]Ps 86:9
22:28 [s]Ps 47:7-8
22:29 [t]Ps 45:12 [u]Isa 26:19
22:30 [v]Ps 102:28
22:31 [w]Ps 78:6

Psalm 23

A psalm of David.

1 The LORD is my shepherd,[x] I shall not be in want.[y]
2 He makes me lie down in green pastures,
he leads me beside quiet waters,[z]
3 he restores my soul.[a]
He guides me in paths of righteousness[b]
for his name's sake.
4 Even though I walk
through the valley of the shadow of death,[a][c]
I will fear no evil,[d]
for you are with me;[e]
your rod and your staff,
they comfort me.

5 You prepare a table before me
in the presence of my enemies.
You anoint my head with oil;[f]
my cup[g] overflows.
6 Surely goodness and love will follow me
all the days of my life,
and I will dwell in the house of the LORD
forever.

23:1 [x]Isa 40:11; Jn 10:11; 1Pe 2:25 [y]Php 4:19
23:2 [z]Eze 34:14; Rev 7:17
23:3 [a]Ps 19:7 [b]Ps 5:8; 85:13
23:4 [c]Job 10:21-22 [d]Ps 3:6; 27:1 [e]Isa 43:2
23:5 [f]Ps 92:10 [g]Ps 16:5

Psalm 24

Of David. A psalm.

1 The earth is the LORD's,[h] and everything in it,
the world, and all who live in it;[i]
2 for he founded it upon the seas
and established it upon the waters.

3 Who may ascend the hill[j] of the LORD?
Who may stand in his holy place?[k]

24:1 [h]Ex 9:29; Job 41:11; Ps 89:11 [i]1Co 10:26*
24:3 [j]Ps 2:6 [k]Ps 15:1; 65:4

[a] 4 Or *through the darkest valley*

23:1 "Shepherd" was a widely used metaphor for kings both in Israel and elsewhere in the ancient Near East. The Lord is often called the shepherd of Israel (see Ge 48:15; Ps 28:9; 79:13; 80:1; 95:7; 100:3; Isa 40:11; Jer 17:16; 31:10; 50:19; Eze 34:11–16). Here David the king acknowledged God as his Shepherd-King.
23:4 The rod was an instrument of authority that was also used by shepherds for counting, guiding, rescuing and protecting sheep. The staff was an instrument of support.
23:5 In the ancient Near East covenants were often concluded with a meal expressive of the bond of friendship. In the case of vassal treaties or covenants, the vassal was present as the guest of the overlord. It was customary at a banquet for an honored guest to have his head anointed with oil.

24:4 [l]Job 17:9 [m]Mt 5:8

4 He who has clean hands[l] and a pure heart,[m]
who does not lift up his soul to an idol
or swear by what is false.[a]
5 He will receive blessing from the LORD
and vindication from God his Savior.
6 Such is the generation of those who seek him,

24:6 [n]Ps 27:8

who seek your face,[n] O God of Jacob.[b] *Selah*

24:7 [o]Isa 26:2 [p]Ps 97:6; 1Co 2:8

7 Lift up your heads, O you gates;[o]
be lifted up, you ancient doors,
that the King of glory[p] may come in.
8 Who is this King of glory?
The LORD strong and mighty,

24:8 [q]Ps 76:3-6

the LORD mighty in battle.[q]
9 Lift up your heads, O you gates;
lift them up, you ancient doors,
that the King of glory may come in.
10 Who is he, this King of glory?
The LORD Almighty—
he is the King of glory. *Selah*

Psalm 25[c]

Of David.

25:1 [r]Ps 86:4

1 To you, O LORD, I lift up my soul;[r]

25:2 [s]Ps 41:11

2 in you I trust,[s] O my God.
Do not let me be put to shame,
nor let my enemies triumph over me.
3 No one whose hope is in you

25:3 [t]Isa 49:23

will ever be put to shame,[t]
but they will be put to shame
who are treacherous without excuse.

4 Show me your ways, O LORD,

25:4 [u]Ex 33:13

teach me your paths;[u]
5 guide me in your truth and teach me,
for you are God my Savior,
and my hope is in you all day long.

25:6 [v]Ps 103:17; Isa 63:7,15

6 Remember, O LORD, your great mercy and love,[v]
for they are from of old.

25:7 [w]Job 13:26; Jer 3:25 [x]Ps 51:1

7 Remember not the sins of my youth[w]
and my rebellious ways;
according to your love[x] remember me,
for you are good, O LORD.

25:8 [y]Ps 92:15 [z]Ps 32:8

8 Good and upright[y] is the LORD;
therefore he instructs[z] sinners in his ways.

25:9 [a]Ps 23:3 [b]Ps 27:11

9 He guides[a] the humble in what is right
and teaches them[b] his way.

25:10 [c]Ps 40:11 [d]Ps 103:18

10 All the ways of the LORD are loving and faithful[c]
for those who keep the demands of his
covenant.[d]

25:11 [e]Ps 31:3; 79:9

11 For the sake of your name,[e] O LORD,
forgive my iniquity, though it is great.

[a] 4 Or *swear falsely* [b] 6 Two Hebrew manuscripts and Syriac (see also Septuagint); most Hebrew manuscripts *face, Jacob*
[c] This psalm is an acrostic poem, the verses of which begin with the successive letters of the Hebrew alphabet.

[12] Who, then, is the man that fears the LORD?
He will instruct him in the way[f] chosen for him.
[13] He will spend his days in prosperity,[g]
and his descendants will inherit the land.[h]
[14] The LORD confides[i] in those who fear him;
he makes his covenant known[j] to them.
[15] My eyes are ever on the LORD,[k]
for only he will release my feet from the snare.

[16] Turn to me[l] and be gracious to me,
for I am lonely and afflicted.
[17] The troubles of my heart have multiplied;
free me from my anguish.[m]
[18] Look upon my affliction and my distress[n]
and take away all my sins.
[19] See how my enemies[o] have increased
and how fiercely they hate me!
[20] Guard my life[p] and rescue me;
let me not be put to shame,
for I take refuge in you.
[21] May integrity[q] and uprightness protect me,
because my hope is in you.

[22] Redeem Israel,[r] O God,
from all their troubles!

Psalm 26

Of David.

[1] Vindicate me, O LORD,
for I have led a blameless life;[s]
I have trusted[t] in the LORD
without wavering.[u]
[2] Test me,[v] O LORD, and try me,
examine my heart and my mind;[w]
[3] for your love is ever before me,
and I walk continually[x] in your truth.
[4] I do not sit[y] with deceitful men,
nor do I consort with hypocrites;
[5] I abhor[z] the assembly of evildoers
and refuse to sit with the wicked.
[6] I wash my hands in innocence,[a]
and go about your altar, O LORD,
[7] proclaiming aloud your praise
and telling of all your wonderful deeds.[b]
[8] I love[c] the house where you live, O LORD,
the place where your glory dwells.

[9] Do not take away my soul along with sinners,
my life with bloodthirsty men,[d]
[10] in whose hands are wicked schemes,
whose right hands are full of bribes.[e]
[11] But I lead a blameless life;
redeem me[f] and be merciful to me.

[12] My feet stand on level ground;[g]
in the great assembly[h] I will praise the LORD.

25:12 [f]Ps 37:23
25:13 [g]Pr 19:23 [h]Ps 37:11
25:14 [i]Pr 3:32 [j]Jn 7:17
25:15 [k]Ps 141:8
25:16 [l]Ps 69:16
25:17 [m]Ps 107:6
25:18 [n]2Sa 16:12
25:19 [o]Ps 3:1
25:20 [p]Ps 86:2
25:21 [q]Ps 41:12
25:22 [r]Ps 130:8
26:1 [s]Ps 7:8; Pr 20:7 [t]Ps 28:7 [u]2Ki 20:3; Heb 10:23
26:2 [v]Ps 17:3 [w]Ps 7:9
26:3 [x]2Ki 20:3
26:4 [y]Ps 1:1
26:5 [z]Ps 31:6; 139:21
26:6 [a]Ps 73:13
26:7 [b]Ps 9:1
26:8 [c]Ps 27:4
26:9 [d]Ps 28:3
26:10 [e]1Sa 8:3
26:11 [f]Ps 69:18
26:12 [g]Ps 27:11; 40:2 [h]Ps 22:22

Psalm 27

Of David.

27:1 [i]Isa 60:19 [j]Ex 15:2 [k]Ps 118:6

1 The LORD is my light[i] and my salvation[j]—
whom shall I fear?
The LORD is the stronghold of my life—
of whom shall I be afraid?[k]
2 When evil men advance against me
to devour my flesh,[a]
when my enemies and my foes attack me,
they will stumble and fall.[l]

27:2 [l]Ps 9:3; 14:4

3 Though an army besiege me,
my heart will not fear;[m]
though war break out against me,
even then will I be confident.[n]

27:3 [m]Ps 3:6 [n]Job 4:6

4 One thing[o] I ask of the LORD,
this is what I seek:
that I may dwell in the house of the LORD
all the days of my life,[p]
to gaze upon the beauty of the LORD
and to seek him in his temple.

27:4 [o]Ps 90:17 [p]Ps 23:6; 26:8

5 For in the day of trouble
he will keep me safe in his dwelling;
he will hide me[q] in the shelter of his tabernacle
and set me high upon a rock.[r]

27:5 [q]Ps 17:8; 31:20 [r]Ps 40:2

6 Then my head will be exalted[s]
above the enemies who surround me;
at his tabernacle will I sacrifice[t] with shouts of joy;
I will sing and make music to the LORD.

27:6 [s]Ps 3:3 [t]Ps 107:22

7 Hear my voice when I call, O LORD;
be merciful to me and answer me.[u]

27:7 [u]Ps 13:3

8 My heart says of you, "Seek his[b] face!"
Your face, LORD, I will seek.
9 Do not hide your face[v] from me,
do not turn your servant away in anger;
you have been my helper.
Do not reject me or forsake me,
O God my Savior.

27:9 [v]Ps 69:17

10 Though my father and mother forsake me,
the LORD will receive me.
11 Teach me your way, O LORD;
lead me in a straight path[w]
because of my oppressors.

27:11 [w]Ps 5:8; 25:4; 86:11

12 Do not turn me over to the desire of my foes,
for false witnesses[x] rise up against me,
breathing out violence.

27:12 [x]Mt 26:60; Ac 9:1

13 I am still confident of this:
I will see the goodness of the LORD[y]
in the land of the living.[z]

27:13 [y]Ps 31:19 [z]Jer 11:19; Eze 26:20

14 Wait[a] for the LORD;
be strong and take heart
and wait for the LORD.

27:14 [a]Ps 40:1

[a] 2 Or *to slander me* [b] 8 Or *To you, O my heart, he has said, "Seek my*

Psalm 28

Of David.

[1] To you I call, O LORD my Rock;
do not turn a deaf ear to me.
For if you remain silent,[b]
I will be like those who have gone down to the pit.[c]
[2] Hear my cry for mercy[d]
as I call to you for help,
as I lift up my hands
toward your Most Holy Place.[e]

[3] Do not drag me away with the wicked,
with those who do evil,
who speak cordially with their neighbors
but harbor malice in their hearts.[f]
[4] Repay them for their deeds
and for their evil work;
repay them for what their hands have done[g]
and bring back upon them what they deserve.[h]
[5] Since they show no regard for the works of the LORD
and what his hands have done,[i]
he will tear them down
and never build them up again.

[6] Praise be to the LORD,
for he has heard my cry for mercy.
[7] The LORD is my strength[j] and my shield;
my heart trusts[k] in him, and I am helped.
My heart leaps for joy
and I will give thanks to him in song.[l]

[8] The LORD is the strength of his people,
a fortress of salvation for his anointed one.[m]
[9] Save your people and bless your inheritance;[n]
be their shepherd[o] and carry them[p] forever.

28:1 [b]Ps 83:1 [c]Ps 88:4
28:2 [d]Ps 138:2; 140:6 [e]Ps 5:7
28:3 [f]Ps 12:2; Ps 26:9; Jer 9:8
28:4 [g]2Ti 4:14; Rev 22:12 [h]Rev 18:6
28:5 [i]Isa 5:12
28:7 [j]Ps 18:1 [k]Ps 13:5 [l]Ps 40:3; 69:30
28:8 [m]Ps 20:6
28:9 [n]Dt 9:29; Ezr 1:4 [o]Isa 40:11 [p]Dt 1:31; 32:11

Psalm 29

A psalm of David.

[1] Ascribe to the LORD,[q] O mighty ones,
ascribe to the LORD glory[r] and strength.
[2] Ascribe to the LORD the glory due his name;
worship the LORD in the splendor of his[a] holiness.[s]

[3] The voice[t] of the LORD is over the waters;
the God of glory thunders,[u]
the LORD thunders over the mighty waters.
[4] The voice of the LORD is powerful;[v]
the voice of the LORD is majestic.
[5] The voice of the LORD breaks the cedars;
the LORD breaks in pieces the cedars of Lebanon.[w]

29:1 [q]1Ch 16:28 [r]Ps 96:7-9
29:2 [s]2Ch 20:21
29:3 [t]Job 37:5 [u]Ps 18:13
29:4 [v]Ps 68:33
29:5 [w]Jdg 9:15

[a] 2 Or *LORD with the splendor of*

29:1–11 This hymn to Yahweh ("the LORD") served as a testimony and protest against the worship of the Canaanite god Baal, who was thought to have been the divine power present in the thunderstorm. See "Storm Gods, Storm Imagery and Theophany" on page 808.
29:5 The cedars of Lebanon (see "Cedars of Lebanon" on p. 1043) were the largest, most spectacular stands of trees in the region,

29:6 [x]Ps 114:4 [y]Dt 3:9
6 He makes Lebanon skip[x] like a calf,
Sirion[a][y] like a young wild ox.
7 The voice of the LORD strikes
with flashes of lightning.
8 The voice of the LORD shakes the desert;
29:8 [z]Nu 13:26
the LORD shakes the Desert of Kadesh.[z]
9 The voice of the LORD twists the oaks[b]
and strips the forests bare.
29:9 [a]Ps 26:8
And in his temple all cry, "Glory!"[a]

29:10 [b]Ge 6:17 [c]Ps 10:16
10 The LORD sits[c] enthroned over the flood;[b]
the LORD is enthroned as King forever.[c]
29:11 [d]Ps 28:8 [e]Ps 37:11
11 The LORD gives strength to his people;[d]
the LORD blesses his people with peace.[e]

[a] 6 That is, Mount Hermon [b] 9 Or *LORD makes the deer give birth* [c] 10 Or *sat*

---

supplying building materials for structures throughout the Mediterranean and considered sacred by locals (see also "Trees of Ancient Israel" on p. 1357). Solomon imported these trees for use in constructing his palace and the temple (1Ki 5:6–10; 7:1–12), yet God's power was displayed in his ability to break these symbols of strength and majesty.

29:6 "Sirion" is another name for Mount Hermon (see the note on Eze 27:5).

ARCHAEOLOGICAL SITES

UGARIT/RAS SHAMRA

PSALM 29 Ugarit ("Map 1") was a prominent city-state that flourished during the second millennium B.C. Its capital of the same name (modern Ras Shamra) was discovered in 1929 on the coast of Syria. The site has yielded a wealth of finds, allowing for a reconstruction of its history and an understanding of its influence in the region.

The history of the site's occupation can be traced to as early as **Neolithic**[1] times (fifth millennium B.C.), the period of the first appearance of humans in Syria. The **Middle Bronze Age** (c. 2000 B.C.) saw the migration of **Amorites** and Semitic Canaanites to Ugarit; these peoples settled there, bringing with them a knowledge of metallurgy and an instinct for commerce. The city developed as an important trade center on the Mediterranean coast, mediating contact between the great Aegean and **Mesopotamian** civilizations. At the height of its prosperity, during the fifteenth and fourteenth centuries B.C., Ugarit was a crossroads where culture and learning converged:

- Wine, oil, cosmetics and pottery from Crete, Egypt, **Asia Minor** and Cyprus were traded in the city.
- Texts in **Akkadian**, the lingua franca of the period, as well as in Egyptian, Cypriot, **Hittite** and **Hurrian** attest to Ugarit's cosmopolitan character.[2]
- The excavated areas of the site have yielded temples dedicated to Baal and **Dagon** (or possibly El), the latter dominating the highest point of the mound.
- A spacious royal palace covered nearly three acres. This and the residences of the high priest and government officials also housed official archives.
- The city was densely populated, with roomy houses arranged around individual courtyards, as well as numerous sanctuaries.
- Examples of the first indigenous Canaanite metalwork and glyptic art (art of carving or engraving, especially on gems) abound among the artifacts.

Among the most significant finds are some 1,300 inscriptions from the fourteenth century B.C. in a western Semitic language (called Ugaritic) similar to Biblical Hebrew. Ugaritic employed an innovative cuneiform alphabet. Compositions such as the Kirta (or Keret) Epic and the Legend of Aqhat bring to light the religion of the people of this land. Some scholars, in fact, have used Ugaritic poetry to try to decipher some of the more difficult passages in Biblical poetry. The literature of Ugarit will continue to contribute to our understanding of the cultural environment of ancient Israel.[3]

At the end of the **Bronze Age**, around 1200 B.C., a great upheaval of unknown origin evidently convulsed the ancient world, causing the collapse of numerous older civilizations. Ugarit was sacked around this time and the site ultimately abandoned.

[1]See "Archaeological Periods" chart on page xx in the front of this Bible. [2]See "Languages of the Old Testament World" on page 672. [3]See "Tablets From Ugarit and Canaanite Religion" on page 304, "The Ugaritic Text of the Myth of Baal" on page 905, "The Kirta Epic" on page 736 and "The Tale of Aqhat" on page 761.

Psalm 30

A psalm. A song. For the dedication of the temple.[a] Of David.

1 I will exalt you, O LORD,
for you lifted me out of the depths
and did not let my enemies gloat over me.[f]
2 O LORD my God, I called to you for help[g]
and you healed me.[h]
3 O LORD, you brought me up from the grave[b];
you spared me from going down into the pit.[i]

4 Sing to the LORD, you saints[j] of his;
praise his holy name.[k]
5 For his anger[l] lasts only a moment,
but his favor lasts a lifetime;
weeping may remain for a night,
but rejoicing comes in the morning.[m]

30:1 [f]Ps 25:2; 28:9
30:2 [g]Ps 88:13 [h]Ps 6:2
30:3 [i]Ps 28:1; 86:13
30:4 [j]Ps 149:1 [k]Ps 97:12
30:5 [l]Ps 103:9 [m]2Co 4:17

[a] Title: Or *palace* [b] 3 Hebrew *Sheol*

30:3–9 For a discussion of Sheol, see the note on Job 17:13–16. See also "Sheol, Hades, Gehenna, the Abyss and Tartarus: Images of Hell" on page 946.

Sackcloth and Ashes: Rituals of Lamentation

PSALM 30 Abject grief was poignantly expressed in the ancient world through rituals of lamentation. Upon news of a calamity the afflicted tore their clothes and donned the garments of mourning (Ge 37:34). These coarse, sack-like coverings, woven from goat hair and typically black (Isa 50:3; Rev 6:12), could be as small as a loincloth or large enough to cover the entire body. The mourner (assuming him in this case to be a man) would prostrate himself on the ground (Jer 6:26), heap ashes upon his head (La 2:10) and sit in the dust (Job 2:8).

The violent gesture of tearing one's clothes communicated deep distress, as well as the personal loss and/or ruin the grieving individual had suffered (Job 1:20–21). The custom of languishing in dust and ashes pointed to the fragility of human life and to the inexorable end of all life—a return to dust (Ge 3:19; Ps 103:14). Acts that otherwise would have been considered undignified, such as shaving one's head and tearing out one's beard (cf. 2Sa 10:4–5), became appropriate expressions of grief (Ezr 9:3; Isa 22:12). Mourners removed their shoes and fineries and refrained from anointing or perfuming themselves (2Sa 14:2; Mic 1:8). Laments were composed and chanted at a funeral (2Sa 1:17–27),[1] and professional wailing women joined family members in expressing their grief (Jer 9:17–20). The period of mourning typically lasted seven days (Ge 50:10; 1Sa 31:13).[2]

Rituals of mourning were also enacted in Israel in times of national crisis and/or repentance (2Ki 19:1; Ne 9:1–2). At such times kings and their subjects alike would humble themselves before the Lord in a posture of humility with fasting, sackcloth and ashes to repent and seek the visitation of his favor (Da 9:3; Jnh 3:5–9). The book of Lamentations is a ritual text of mourning over the fall of Jerusalem.

As anguish and despair were given vivid expression through the donning of sackcloth and ashes, so also the reversal of mourning is vividly portrayed as a joyful celebration in which the redeemed donned festal garments of salvation and robes of righteousness (Isa 61:10). Such would be the ministry of the Messiah: "to comfort all who mourn, and provide for those who grieve in Zion—to bestow on them a crown of beauty instead of ashes, the oil of gladness instead of mourning, and a garment of praise instead of a spirit of despair" (Isa 61:2b–3; cf. Lk 4:18–19).

[1]See "Ancient Near Eastern Laments" on page 1305. [2]See "Jewish Burial Practices" on page 1688.

6 When I felt secure, I said,
"I will never be shaken."
7 O LORD, when you favored me,
you made my mountain[a] stand firm;
30:7 [n]Dt 31:17; Ps 104:29
but when you hid your face,[n]
I was dismayed.

8 To you, O LORD, I called;
to the Lord I cried for mercy:
9 "What gain is there in my destruction,[b]
in my going down into the pit?
Will the dust praise you?
30:9 [o]Ps 6:5
Will it proclaim your faithfulness?[o]
10 Hear, O LORD, and be merciful to me;
O LORD, be my help."

11 You turned my wailing into dancing;
you removed my sackcloth and clothed me
30:11 [p]Ps 4:7; Jer 31:4,13
with joy,[p]
12 that my heart may sing to you and not be silent.
30:12 [q]Ps 16:9 [r]Ps 44:8
O LORD my God, I will give you thanks[q]
forever.[r]

Psalm 31

For the director of music. A psalm of David.

1 In you, O LORD, I have taken refuge;
let me never be put to shame;
deliver me in your righteousness.
2 Turn your ear to me,
come quickly to my rescue;
31:2 [s]Ps 18:2
be my rock of refuge,[s]
a strong fortress to save me.
31:3 [t]Ps 18:2 [u]Ps 23:3
3 Since you are my rock and my fortress,[t]
for the sake of your name[u] lead and guide me.
4 Free me from the trap that is set for me,
31:4 [v]Ps 25:15
for you are my refuge.[v]
31:5 [w]Lk 23:46; Ac 7:59
5 Into your hands I commit my spirit;[w]
redeem me, O LORD, the God of truth.

6 I hate those who cling to worthless idols;
31:6 [x]Jnh 2:8
I trust in the LORD.[x]
7 I will be glad and rejoice in your love,
31:7 [y]Ps 90:14 [z]Ps 10:14; Jn 10:27
for you saw my affliction[y]
and knew the anguish[z] of my soul.
31:8 [a]Dt 32:30
8 You have not handed me over[a] to the enemy
but have set my feet in a spacious place.

9 Be merciful to me, O LORD, for I am in distress;
31:9 [b]Ps 6:7
my eyes grow weak with sorrow,[b]
my soul and my body with grief.

[a] 7 Or *hill country* [b] 9 Or *there if I am silenced*

30:11 Sackcloth was a symbol of mourning (see Ge 37:34; Ps 35:13; see also "Sackcloth and Ashes: Rituals of Lamentation" on p. 820).

31:7 For commentary on Old Testament expressions of joy, see the note on 96:11.

[10] My life is consumed by anguish
and my years by groaning;[c]
my strength fails because of my affliction,[a]
and my bones grow weak.[d]
[11] Because of all my enemies,
I am the utter contempt of my neighbors;[e]
I am a dread to my friends—
those who see me on the street flee from me.
[12] I am forgotten by them as though I were dead;[f]
I have become like broken pottery.
[13] For I hear the slander of many;
there is terror on every side;[g]
they conspire against me
and plot to take my life.[h]

[14] But I trust[i] in you, O LORD;
I say, "You are my God."
[15] My times[j] are in your hands;
deliver me from my enemies
and from those who pursue me.
[16] Let your face shine[k] on your servant;
save me in your unfailing love.
[17] Let me not be put to shame,[l] O LORD,
for I have cried out to you;
but let the wicked be put to shame
and lie silent[m] in the grave.[b]
[18] Let their lying lips[n] be silenced,
for with pride and contempt
they speak arrogantly[o] against the righteous.

[19] How great is your goodness,[p]
which you have stored up for those who
fear you,
which you bestow in the sight of men[q]
on those who take refuge in you.
[20] In the shelter of your presence you hide[r] them
from the intrigues of men;[s]
in your dwelling you keep them safe
from accusing tongues.
[21] Praise be to the LORD,
for he showed his wonderful love[t] to me
when I was in a besieged city.[u]
[22] In my alarm[v] I said,
"I am cut off from your sight!"
Yet you heard my cry[w] for mercy
when I called to you for help.
[23] Love the LORD, all his saints![x]
The LORD preserves the faithful,[y]
but the proud he pays back[z] in full.
[24] Be strong and take heart,[a]
all you who hope in the LORD.

31:10 [c]Ps 13:2 [d]Ps 38:3; 39:11
31:11 [e]Job 19:13; Ps 38:11; 64:8; Isa 53:4
31:12 [f]Ps 88:4
31:13 [g]Jer 20:3, 10; La 2:22 [h]Mt 27:1
31:14 [i]Ps 140:6
31:15 [j]Job 24:1; Ps 143:9
31:16 [k]Nu 6:25; Ps 4:6
31:17 [l]Ps 25:2-3 [m]Ps 115:17
31:18 [n]Ps 120:2 [o]Ps 94:4
31:19 [p]Ro 11:22 [q]Isa 64:4
31:20 [r]Ps 27:5 [s]Job 5:21
31:21 [t]Ps 17:7 [u]1Sa 23:7
31:22 [v]Ps 116:11 [w]La 3:54
31:23 [x]Ps 34:9 [y]Ps 145:20 [z]Ps 94:2
31:24 [a]Ps 27:14

[a] *10* Or *guilt* [b] *17* Hebrew *Sheol*

31:12 See "The Potsherd: Pottery in the Bible" on page 738.

31:21 The psalmist used the picture of a besieged city to describe the threat he had experienced (see "Siege Warfare" on p. 465).

Psalm 32

Of David. A *maskil.*[a]

[1] Blessed is he
whose transgressions are forgiven,
whose sins are covered.[b]
[2] Blessed is the man
whose sin the LORD does not count against him[c]
and in whose spirit is no deceit.[d]

[3] When I kept silent,
my bones wasted away[e]
through my groaning all day long.
[4] For day and night
your hand was heavy[f] upon me;
my strength was sapped
as in the heat of summer. *Selah*
[5] Then I acknowledged my sin to you
and did not cover up my iniquity.
I said, "I will confess[g]
my transgressions[h] to the LORD"—
and you forgave
the guilt of my sin.[i] *Selah*

[6] Therefore let everyone who is godly pray to you
while you may be found;[j]
surely when the mighty waters rise,
they will not reach him.[k]
[7] You are my hiding place;
you will protect me from trouble[l]
and surround me with songs of deliverance.[m] *Selah*

[8] I will instruct[n] you and teach you in the way you should go;
I will counsel you and watch over[o] you.
[9] Do not be like the horse or the mule,
which have no understanding
but must be controlled by bit and bridle[p]
or they will not come to you.
[10] Many are the woes of the wicked,[q]
but the LORD's unfailing love
surrounds the man who trusts[r] in him.

[11] Rejoice in the LORD[s] and be glad, you righteous;
sing, all you who are upright in heart!

32:1 [b]Ps 85:2
32:2 [c]Ro 4:7-8*; 2Co 5:19 [d]Jn 1:47
32:3 [e]Ps 31:10
32:4 [f]Job 33:7
32:5 [g]Pr 28:13 [h]Ps 103:12 [i]Lev 26:40
32:6 [j]Ps 69:13; Isa 55:6 [k]Isa 43:2
32:7 [l]Ps 9:9 [m]Ex 15:1
32:8 [n]Ps 25:8 [o]Ps 33:18
32:9 [p]Pr 26:3
32:10 [q]Ro 2:9 [r]Pr 16:20
32:11 [s]Ps 64:10

Psalm 33

[1] Sing joyfully to the LORD, you righteous;
it is fitting[t] for the upright[u] to praise him.

33:1 [t]Ps 147:1 [u]Ps 32:11

[a] Title: Probably a literary or musical term

32:6 This powerful imagery of "mighty waters" was borrowed from ancient Near Eastern creation myths, in many of which a primal mass of chaotic waters (often depicted as a many-headed monster of the deep; see 74:13–15 and its note; see also "Ancient Creation Narratives" on p. 5 and "The *Enuma Elish* and the Biblical Concept of Creation" on p. 888) had to be subdued by the creator-god before he could fashion the world and/or rule over the earth. Even after the chaotic waters had been subdued when the present world was created, they remained a constant threat to the security and well-being of the world. Hence they were linked to anything in human experience that endangered or disrupted the precarious order of life. Since in Canaanite mythology Sea and Death were the two great enemies of Baal ("lord" of earth), imagery drawn from both realms was used by Old Testament poets, sometimes side by side, to depict threats and distress (see, e.g., Job 7:12; 26:12; Ps 18:4–5,16; 74:12–14; 89:9–10; 124:4–5; Isa 8:7–8; 17:12–14; 51:9–10; Jer 51:55; Hab 3:8–10).

[2] Praise the LORD with the harp;
make music to him on the ten-stringed lyre.[v]
[3] Sing to him a new song;[w]
play skillfully, and shout for joy.

[4] For the word of the LORD is right[x] and true;
he is faithful in all he does.
[5] The LORD loves righteousness and justice;[y]
the earth is full of his unfailing love.[z]

[6] By the word[a] of the LORD were the heavens made,
their starry host by the breath of his mouth.
[7] He gathers the waters of the sea into jars[a];
he puts the deep into storehouses.
[8] Let all the earth fear the LORD;
let all the people of the world revere him.[b]
[9] For he spoke, and it came to be;
he commanded,[c] and it stood firm.
[10] The LORD foils the plans of the nations;[d]
he thwarts the purposes of the peoples.
[11] But the plans of the LORD stand firm forever,
the purposes[e] of his heart through all generations.

[12] Blessed is the nation whose God is the LORD,[f]
the people he chose[g] for his inheritance.
[13] From heaven the LORD looks down
and sees all mankind;[h]
[14] from his dwelling place[i] he watches
all who live on earth—
[15] he who forms[j] the hearts of all,
who considers everything they do.[k]
[16] No king is saved by the size of his army;[l]
no warrior escapes by his great strength.
[17] A horse[m] is a vain hope for deliverance;
despite all its great strength it cannot save.
[18] But the eyes[n] of the LORD are on those who fear him,
on those whose hope is in his unfailing love,[o]
[19] to deliver them from death
and keep them alive in famine.[p]

[20] We wait[q] in hope for the LORD;
he is our help and our shield.
[21] In him our hearts rejoice,[r]
for we trust in his holy name.
[22] May your unfailing love rest upon us, O LORD,
even as we put our hope in you.

Psalm 34[b]

Of David. When he pretended to be insane before Abimelech, who drove him away, and he left.

[1] I will extol the LORD at all times;[s]
his praise will always be on my lips.
[2] My soul will boast[t] in the LORD;
let the afflicted hear and rejoice.[u]

33:2 [v]Ps 92:3
33:3 [w]Ps 96:1
33:4 [x]Ps 19:8
33:5 [y]Ps 11:7 [z]Ps 119:64
33:6 [a]Heb 11:3
33:8 [b]Ps 67:7; 96:9
33:9 [c]Ge 1:3; Ps 148:5
33:10 [d]Isa 8:10
33:11 [e]Job 23:13
33:12 [f]Ps 144:15 [g]Ex 19:5; Dt 7:6
33:13 [h]Job 28:24; Ps 11:4
33:14 [i]1Ki 8:39
33:15 [j]Job 10:8 [k]Jer 32:19
33:16 [l]Ps 44:6
33:17 [m]Ps 20:7; Pr 21:31
33:18 [n]Job 36:7; Ps 34:15 [o]Ps 147:11
33:19 [p]Job 5:20
33:20 [q]Ps 130:6
33:21 [r]Zec 10:7; Jn 16:22
34:1 [s]Ps 71:6; Eph 5:20
34:2 [t]Jer 9:24; 1Co 1:31 [u]Ps 119:74

[a] 7 Or *sea as into a heap* [b] This psalm is an acrostic poem, the verses of which begin with the successive letters of the Hebrew alphabet.

3 Glorify the LORD with me;
34:3 [v]Lk 1:46 — let us exalt[v] his name together.

34:4 [w]Mt 7:7 — 4 I sought the LORD,[w] and he answered me;
he delivered me from all my fears.
34:5 [x]Ps 36:9 — 5 Those who look to him are radiant;[x]
[y]Ps 25:3 — their faces are never covered with shame.[y]
6 This poor man called, and the LORD heard him;
he saved him out of all his troubles.
34:7 [z]2Ki 6:17; Da 6:22 — 7 The angel of the LORD[z] encamps around those who fear him,
and he delivers them.

34:8 [a]1Pe 2:3 — 8 Taste and see that the LORD is good;[a]
[b]Ps 2:12 — blessed is the man who takes refuge[b] in him.
9 Fear the LORD, you his saints,
34:9 [c]Ps 23:1 — for those who fear him lack nothing.[c]
10 The lions may grow weak and hungry,
34:10 [d]Ps 84:11 — but those who seek the LORD lack no good thing.[d]

11 Come, my children, listen to me;
34:11 [e]Ps 32:8 — I will teach you[e] the fear of the LORD.
34:12 [f]1Pe 3:10 — 12 Whoever of you loves life[f]
and desires to see many good days,
13 keep your tongue from evil
34:13 [g]1Pe 2:22 — and your lips from speaking lies.[g]
34:14 [h]Ps 37:27 — 14 Turn from evil and do good;[h]
[i]Heb 12:14 — seek peace[i] and pursue it.

34:15 [j]Ps 33:18 — 15 The eyes of the LORD[j] are on the righteous[k]
[k]Job 36:7 — and his ears are attentive to their cry;
34:16 [l]Lev 17:10; Jer 44:11 — 16 the face of the LORD is against[l] those who do evil,[m]
[m]1Pe 3:10-12* [n]Pr 10:7 — to cut off the memory[n] of them from the earth.

34:17 [o]Ps 145:19 — 17 The righteous cry out, and the LORD hears[o] them;
he delivers them from all their troubles.
34:18 [p]Ps 145:18 — 18 The LORD is close[p] to the brokenhearted[q]
[q]Isa 57:15 — and saves those who are crushed in spirit.

34:19 [r]ver 17 — 19 A righteous man may have many troubles,[r]
[s]ver 4,6; Pr 24:16 — but the LORD delivers him from them all;[s]
20 he protects all his bones,
34:20 [t]Jn 19:36* — not one of them will be broken.[t]

34:21 [u]Ps 94:23 — 21 Evil will slay the wicked;[u]
the foes of the righteous will be condemned.
34:22 [v]1Ki 1:29; Ps 71:23 — 22 The LORD redeems[v] his servants;
no one will be condemned who takes refuge in him.

Psalm 35

Of David.

1 Contend, O LORD, with those who contend with me;
35:1 [w]Ps 43:1 — fight[w] against those who fight against me.
2 Take up shield and buckler;
35:2 [x]Ps 62:2 — arise[x] and come to my aid.
3 Brandish spear and javelin[a]
against those who pursue me.

[a] 3 Or *and block the way*

Say to my soul,
"I am your salvation."

[4] May those who seek my life
be disgraced[y] and put to shame; 35:4 [y]Ps 70:2
may those who plot my ruin
be turned back in dismay.
[5] May they be like chaff[z] before the wind, 35:5 [z]Job 21:18; Ps 1:4; Isa 29:5
with the angel of the LORD driving them away;
[6] may their path be dark and slippery,
with the angel of the LORD pursuing them.
[7] Since they hid their net for me without cause
and without cause dug a pit for me,
[8] may ruin overtake them by surprise—[a] 35:8 [a]1Th 5:3 [b]Ps 9:15
may the net they hid entangle them,
may they fall into the pit,[b] to their ruin.
[9] Then my soul will rejoice[c] in the LORD 35:9 [c]Lk 1:47 [d]Isa 61:10
and delight in his salvation.[d]
[10] My whole being will exclaim,
"Who is like you,[e] O LORD? 35:10 [e]Ex 15:11 [f]Ps 18:17 [g]Ps 37:14
You rescue the poor from those too strong[f] for them,
the poor and needy[g] from those who rob them."

[11] Ruthless witnesses[h] come forward; 35:11 [h]Ps 27:12
they question me on things I know nothing about.
[12] They repay me evil for good[i] 35:12 [i]Jn 10:32
and leave my soul forlorn.
[13] Yet when they were ill, I put on sackcloth
and humbled myself with fasting.[j] 35:13 [j]Job 30:25; Ps 69:10

ANCIENT TEXTS AND ARTIFACTS

The Warrior Creed in the Akkadian Epic of Erra and Ishum

PSALM 35 Peoples of the ancient Near East understood the brutality of war from firsthand experience. In the Bible and elsewhere we see reflections of the dread of its destructiveness, but we also see examples of a "warrior creed" that glorified war and conquest.

The **Akkadian** epic of Erra and Ishum focuses on Erra (also called Nergal), a god of war, plague and the underworld. In the myth, Erra has been lethargic but threatens to arouse himself and massacre the "black-headed people" (i.e., the **Mesopotamians**). Erra is urged on by a group of seven warrior gods, but in the end the situation is defused by the counsel of the god Ishum.

Of particular interest is the manner in which the seven warrior gods urge Erra to rouse himself for battle. They inform him that staying home is effeminate and childish; the battlefield is the province in which a man gains honor. The fancy cuisine of the city, they claim, cannot begin to compare with food roasted over embers out in the field or to water drunk from a skin. Furthermore, it is a disgrace to allow weapons to rust or to become covered with cobwebs. They also exhort Erra to slaughter his opponents and thus to terrify the world. Their words probably reflect the militaristic ideology of actual **Assyrian** soldiers—a perfect example of a warrior creed.[1]

Psalm 35 is strikingly different: a prayer by David for God's help in battle. Nevertheless, the psalm offers a helpful point of comparison because it illustrates the ideology of David, who was also a warrior. There is no glorification of brutality here; to the contrary, David condemns those who declare war without just cause (vv. 19–21). As elsewhere in the Psalms, David appealed to God's justice. Most significantly, by pleading for God to intervene on his behalf, David repudiated the notion of gaining glory for himself by his own belligerence or aggression.

[1]See "Songs of Warriors" on page 474.

When my prayers returned to me
unanswered,
14 I went about mourning
as though for my friend or brother.
I bowed my head in grief
as though weeping for my mother.
15 But when I stumbled, they gathered
in glee;
attackers gathered against me when I
was unaware.
They slandered[k] me without ceasing.
16 Like the ungodly they maliciously mocked[a];
they gnashed their teeth[l] at me.
17 O Lord, how long[m] will you look on?
Rescue my life from their ravages,
my precious life[n] from these lions.
18 I will give you thanks in the great
assembly;[o]
among throngs of people I will praise
you.[p]

19 Let not those gloat over me
who are my enemies without cause;
let not those who hate me without reason[q]
maliciously wink the eye.[r]
20 They do not speak peaceably,
but devise false accusations
against those who live quietly in the
land.
21 They gape[s] at me and say, "Aha! Aha![t]
With our own eyes we have seen it."

22 O LORD, you have seen[u] this; be not silent.
Do not be far[v] from me, O Lord.
23 Awake,[w] and rise to my defense!
Contend for me, my God and Lord.
24 Vindicate me in your righteousness, O LORD my God;
do not let them gloat over me.
25 Do not let them think, "Aha, just what we wanted!"
or say, "We have swallowed him up."[x]

26 May all who gloat over my distress
be put to shame[y] and confusion;
may all who exalt themselves over me[z]
be clothed with shame and disgrace.
27 May those who delight in my vindication[a]
shout for joy[b] and gladness;
may they always say, "The LORD be exalted,
who delights[c] in the well-being of his servant."
28 My tongue will speak of your righteousness[d]
and of your praises all day long.

35:15 [k]Job 30:1,8
35:16 [l]Job 16:9; La 2:16
35:17 [m]Hab 1:13 [n]Ps 22:20
35:18 [o]Ps 22:25 [p]Ps 22:22
35:19 [q]Ps 38:19; 69:4; Jn 15:25* [r]Ps 13:4; Pr 6:13
35:21 [s]Ps 22:13 [t]Ps 40:15
35:22 [u]Ex 3:7 [v]Ps 10:1; 28:1
35:23 [w]Ps 44:23
35:25 [x]La 2:16
35:26 [y]Ps 40:14; 109:29 [z]Ps 38:16
35:27 [a]Ps 9:4 [b]Ps 32:11 [c]Ps 40:16; 147:11
35:28 [d]Ps 51:14

ANCIENT VOICES

Why do you stay in town like a feeble old man?
How can you stay at home like a lisping child?
Are we to eat women's bread, like one who has never marched on to the battlefield?
Are we to be fearful and nervous as if we had no experience of war?
To go on to the battlefield is as good as a festival for young men!
Anyone who stays in town, be he a prince, will not be satisfied with bread alone;
He will be vilified in the mouths of his own people, and dishonored.
How can he raise his hand against one who goes to the battlefield?
However great the strength of one who stays in town,
How can he prevail over one who has been on the battlefield?
City food, however fancy, cannot compare with what is cooked on the embers.

—ERRA AND ISHUM

See "The Warrior Creed in the Akkadian Epic of Erra and Ishum" article.

[a] *16* Septuagint; Hebrew may mean *ungodly circle of mockers.*

35:16 In the Old Testament the expression "to gnash with the teeth" most often represents rage, anger or hatred (see also Job 16:9; Ps 37:12; 112:10). In the New Testament this idiom expresses disappointment and agony of spirit rather than anger (Mt 8:12; 13:42,50; 22:13; 24:51; 25:30; Lk 13:28).

Psalm 36

For the director of music. Of David the servant of the LORD.

[1] An oracle is within my heart
concerning the sinfulness of the wicked:[a]
There is no fear of God
before his eyes.[e]
[2] For in his own eyes he flatters himself
too much to detect or hate his sin.
[3] The words of his mouth[f] are wicked and deceitful;
he has ceased to be wise[g] and to do good.[h]
[4] Even on his bed he plots evil;[i]
he commits himself to a sinful course[j]
and does not reject what is wrong.[k]

[5] Your love, O LORD, reaches to the heavens,
your faithfulness to the skies.
[6] Your righteousness is like the mighty mountains,
your justice like the great deep.[l]
O LORD, you preserve both man and beast.
[7] How priceless is your unfailing love!
Both high and low among men
find[b] refuge in the shadow of your wings.[m]
[8] They feast on the abundance of your house;[n]
you give them drink from your river[o] of delights.
[9] For with you is the fountain of life;[p]
in your light[q] we see light.

[10] Continue your love to those who know you,
your righteousness to the upright in heart.
[11] May the foot of the proud not come against me,
nor the hand of the wicked drive me away.
[12] See how the evildoers lie fallen—
thrown down, not able to rise![r]

Psalm 37[c]

Of David.

[1] Do not fret because of evil men
or be envious[s] of those who do wrong;[t]
[2] for like the grass they will soon wither,
like green plants they will soon die away.[u]

[3] Trust in the LORD and do good;
dwell in the land[v] and enjoy safe pasture.[w]
[4] Delight[x] yourself in the LORD
and he will give you the desires of your heart.

[5] Commit your way to the LORD;
trust in him[y] and he will do this:

36:1 [e]Ro 3:18*
36:3 [f]Ps 10:7 [g]Ps 94:8 [h]Jer 4:22
36:4 [i]Pr 4:16; Mic 2:1 [j]Isa 65:2 [k]Ps 52:3; Ro 12:9
36:6 [l]Job 11:8; Ps 77:19; Ro 11:33
36:7 [m]Ru 2:12; Ps 17:8
36:8 [n]Ps 65:4 [o]Job 20:17; Rev 22:1
36:9 [p]Jer 2:13 [q]1Pe 2:9
36:12 [r]Ps 140:10
37:1 [s]Pr 23:17-18 [t]Ps 73:3
37:2 [u]Ps 90:6
37:3 [v]Dt 30:20 [w]Isa 40:11; Jn 10:9
37:4 [x]Isa 58:14
37:5 [y]Ps 4:5; Ps 55:22; Pr 16:3; 1Pe 5:7

[a] *1* Or *heart: / Sin proceeds from the wicked.* [b] *7* Or *love, O God! / Men find*; or *love! / Both heavenly beings and men / find* [c] This psalm is an acrostic poem, the stanzas of which begin with the successive letters of the Hebrew alphabet.

36:1 "Oracle" is a technical term meaning "prophetic utterance," referring to divine revelation or insight. Rather than the usual oracle of judgment or deliverance, as seen in the prophetic books, Psalm 36 might better be called "insight" into the fate of the arrogant, self-motivated and self-focused wicked, who exhibit no "fear of God" but who often seem to prosper nonetheless.

37:1–40 For commentary on vengeful attitudes toward enemies, see the note on 69:22–28. See also "Curses and Imprecations" on page 883.

6 He will make your righteousness[z] shine like the dawn,[a]
the justice of your cause like the noonday sun.

7 Be still[b] before the LORD and wait patiently[c] for him;
do not fret when men succeed in their ways,
when they carry out their wicked schemes.

8 Refrain from anger[d] and turn from wrath;
do not fret—it leads only to evil.
9 For evil men will be cut off,
but those who hope in the LORD will inherit the land.[e]

10 A little while, and the wicked will be no more;[f]
though you look for them, they will not be found.
11 But the meek will inherit the land[g]
and enjoy great peace.

12 The wicked plot against the righteous
and gnash their teeth[h] at them;
13 but the Lord laughs at the wicked,
for he knows their day is coming.[i]

14 The wicked draw the sword
and bend the bow[j]
to bring down the poor and needy,[k]
to slay those whose ways are upright.
15 But their swords will pierce their own hearts,[l]
and their bows will be broken.

16 Better the little that the righteous have
than the wealth[m] of many wicked;
17 for the power of the wicked will be broken,[n]
but the LORD upholds the righteous.

18 The days of the blameless are known to the LORD,[o]
and their inheritance will endure forever.
19 In times of disaster they will not wither;
in days of famine they will enjoy plenty.

20 But the wicked will perish:
The LORD's enemies will be like the beauty of the fields,
they will vanish—vanish like smoke.[p]

21 The wicked borrow and do not repay,
but the righteous give generously;[q]
22 those the LORD blesses will inherit the land,
but those he curses[r] will be cut off.

23 If the LORD delights[s] in a man's way,
he makes his steps firm;[t]
24 though he stumble, he will not fall,[u]
for the LORD upholds[v] him with his hand.

25 I was young and now I am old,
yet I have never seen the righteous forsaken[w]
or their children begging bread.
26 They are always generous and lend freely;
their children will be blessed.[x]

37:6 [z]Mic 7:9 [a]Job 11:17
37:7 [b]Ps 62:5; La 3:26 [c]Ps 40:1
37:8 [d]Eph 4:31; Col 3:8
37:9 [e]Isa 57:13; 60:21
37:10 [f]Job 7:10; 24:24
37:11 [g]Mt 5:5
37:12 [h]Ps 35:16
37:13 [i]1Sa 26:10; Ps 2:4
37:14 [j]Ps 11:2 [k]Ps 35:10
37:15 [l]Ps 9:16
37:16 [m]Pr 15:16
37:17 [n]Job 38:15; Ps 10:15
37:18 [o]Ps 1:6
37:20 [p]Ps 102:3
37:21 [q]Ps 112:5
37:22 [r]Job 5:3; Pr 3:33
37:23 [s]Ps 147:11 [t]1Sa 2:9
37:24 [u]Pr 24:16 [v]Ps 145:14; 147:6
37:25 [w]Heb 13:5
37:26 [x]Ps 147:13

37:12 For the meaning of gnashing with one's teeth, see the note on 35:16.

Ancient Voices

Who has not been negligent, which one
has committed no sin?
Who can understand a god's behavior?
I would fain be obedient and incur no sin,
Yes, I would frequent the haunts of
health!
Men are commanded by the gods to act
under curse,
Divine affliction is for mankind to bear.
I am surely responsible for some neglect
of you,
I have surely trespassed the limits set by
the god.
Forget what I did in my youth, whatever
it was,
Let your heart not well up against me!
Absolve my guilt, remit my
punishment . . .

—Prayer to Marduk

See "A Prayer of Confession to Marduk" article.

27 Turn from evil and do good;[y]
then you will dwell in the land forever.
28 For the LORD loves the just
and will not forsake his faithful ones.

They will be protected forever,
but the offspring of the wicked will be cut off;[z]
29 the righteous will inherit the land[a]
and dwell in it forever.

30 The mouth of the righteous man utters wisdom,
and his tongue speaks what is just.
31 The law of his God is in his heart;[b]
his feet do not slip.[c]

32 The wicked lie in wait[d] for the righteous,
seeking their very lives;
33 but the LORD will not leave them in their power
or let them be condemned when brought to trial.[e]

34 Wait for the LORD[f]
and keep his way.
He will exalt you to inherit the land;
when the wicked are cut off, you will see[g] it.

35 I have seen a wicked and ruthless man
flourishing[h] like a green tree in its native soil,
36 but he soon passed away and was no more;
though I looked for him, he could not be found.[i]

37 Consider the blameless, observe the upright;
there is a future[a] for the man of peace.[j]
38 But all sinners will be destroyed;
the future[b] of the wicked will be cut off.[k]

39 The salvation[l] of the righteous comes from the LORD;
he is their stronghold in time of trouble.[m]
40 The LORD helps[n] them and delivers[o] them;
he delivers them from the wicked and saves them,
because they take refuge in him.

Psalm 38

A psalm of David. A petition.

1 O LORD, do not rebuke me in your anger
or discipline me in your wrath.[p]
2 For your arrows[q] have pierced me,
and your hand has come down upon me.
3 Because of your wrath there is no health in my body;
my bones[r] have no soundness because of my sin.
4 My guilt has overwhelmed me
like a burden too heavy to bear.[s]

5 My wounds fester and are loathsome
because of my sinful folly.[t]
6 I am bowed down and brought very low;
all day long I go about mourning.[u]

37:27 [y]Ps 34:14
37:28 [z]Ps 21:10; Isa 14:20
37:29 [a]ver 9; Pr 2:21
37:31 [b]Dt 6:6; Ps 40:8; Isa 51:7 [c]ver 23
37:32 [d]Ps 10:8
37:33 [e]Ps 109:31; 2Pe 2:9
37:34 [f]Ps 27:14 [g]Ps 52:6
37:35 [h]Job 5:3
37:36 [i]Job 20:5
37:37 [j]Isa 57:1-2
37:38 [k]Ps 1:4
37:39 [l]Ps 3:8 [m]Ps 9:9
37:40 [n]1Ch 5:20 [o]Isa 31:5
38:1 [p]Ps 6:1
38:2 [q]Job 6:4; Ps 32:4
38:3 [r]Ps 6:2; Isa 1:6
38:4 [s]Ezr 9:6
38:5 [t]Ps 69:5
38:6 [u]Job 30:28; Ps 35:14; 42:9

[a] 37 Or *there will be posterity* [b] 38 Or *posterity*

38:7 [v]Ps 102:3
38:8 [w]Ps 22:1
38:9 [x]Job 3:24; Ps 6:6; 10:17
38:10 [y]Ps 31:10 [z]Ps 6:7
38:11 [a]Ps 31:11
38:12 [b]Ps 140:5 [c]Ps 35:4; 54:3 [d]Ps 35:20
38:15 [e]Ps 39:7 [f]Ps 17:6
38:16 [g]Ps 35:26 [h]Ps 13:4
38:18 [i]Ps 32:5

7 My back is filled with searing pain;[v]
there is no health in my body.
8 I am feeble and utterly crushed;
I groan[w] in anguish of heart.

9 All my longings lie open before you, O Lord;
my sighing[x] is not hidden from you.
10 My heart pounds, my strength fails[y] me;
even the light has gone from my eyes.[z]
11 My friends and companions avoid me because of
my wounds;[a]
my neighbors stay far away.
12 Those who seek my life set their traps,[b]
those who would harm me talk of my ruin;[c]
all day long they plot deception.[d]

13 I am like a deaf man, who cannot hear,
like a mute, who cannot open his mouth;
14 I have become like a man who does not hear,
whose mouth can offer no reply.
15 I wait[e] for you, O LORD;
you will answer,[f] O Lord my God.
16 For I said, "Do not let them gloat[g]
or exalt themselves over me when my foot slips."[h]

17 For I am about to fall,
and my pain is ever with me.
18 I confess my iniquity;[i]
I am troubled by my sin.

ANCIENT TEXTS AND ARTIFACTS

A Prayer of Confession to Marduk

PSALM 38 Since the Psalms originated from the same cultural milieu as other ancient Near Eastern hymns and prayers, Bible readers need not be surprised to find that Israelite and pagan texts can be similar. In Psalm 38 David lamented that God was against him. God, he alleged, came at him like a warrior (v. 2), and David felt sick and feeble (vv. 3–6,10,13–14). He recognized that he had sinned against God (vv. 3,18) and concluded the psalm with a plea for the Lord's help (vv. 21–22).

From **Akkadian** literature comes a similar prayer to Marduk, the chief god of **Babylon** (date of composition unknown). In it the poet bemoaned Marduk's anger. He confessed that he had sinned against Marduk and lamented that he was so afflicted that he was bent over like an old man. He pled for forgiveness and concluded, "O warrior Marduk, let me sound your praises!" Unlike the psalmist, however, this supplicant was fatalistic about Marduk's actions ("Who can understand a god's behavior?" he bemoaned) and also sought the aid of lesser gods and goddesses.

Just as we can cite similarities between Christian and non-Christian worship in contemporary society, so also we can find correlations in the Old Testament world. The similarities between an Old Testament and a **Mesopotamian** prayer help us to see what was common to the world of that day in terms of prayer language. The differences, on the other hand, enable us to recognize the distinctive faith of Israel.[1]

[1]For further examples, see "'I Will Praise the Lord of Wisdom'" on page 751 and "A Man and His God" on page 771.

[19] Many are those who are my vigorous enemies;[j]
those who hate me without reason[k] are numerous.
[20] Those who repay my good with evil[l]
slander me when I pursue what is good.

[21] O LORD, do not forsake me;
be not far[m] from me, O my God.
[22] Come quickly to help me,[n]
O Lord my Savior.[o]

Psalm 39

For the director of music. For Jeduthun. A psalm of David.

[1] I said, "I will watch my ways[p]
and keep my tongue from sin;[q]
I will put a muzzle on my mouth
as long as the wicked are in my presence."
[2] But when I was silent[r] and still,
not even saying anything good,
my anguish increased.
[3] My heart grew hot within me,
and as I meditated, the fire burned;
then I spoke with my tongue:

[4] "Show me, O LORD, my life's end
and the number of my days;[s]
let me know how fleeting is my life.[t]
[5] You have made my days[u] a mere handbreadth;
the span of my years is as nothing before you.
Each man's life is but a breath.[v] *Selah*
[6] Man is a mere phantom[w] as he goes to and fro:
He bustles about, but only in vain;[x]
he heaps up wealth, not knowing who will get it.[y]

[7] "But now, Lord, what do I look for?
My hope is in you.[z]
[8] Save me[a] from all my transgressions;[b]
do not make me the scorn of fools.
[9] I was silent; I would not open my mouth,[c]
for you are the one who has done this.
[10] Remove your scourge from me;
I am overcome by the blow of your hand.[d]
[11] You rebuke[e] and discipline men for their sin;
you consume their wealth like a moth[f]—
each man is but a breath. *Selah*

[12] "Hear my prayer, O LORD,
listen to my cry for help;
be not deaf to my weeping.
For I dwell with you as an alien,[g]
a stranger,[h] as all my fathers were.
[13] Look away from me, that I may rejoice again
before I depart and am no more."[i]

38:19 [j]Ps 18:17 [k]Ps 35:19
38:20 [l]Ps 35:12; 1Jn 3:12
38:21 [m]Ps 35:22
38:22 [n]Ps 40:13 [o]Ps 27:1
39:1 [p]1Ki 2:4 [q]Job 2:10; Jas 3:2
39:2 [r]Ps 38:13
39:4 [s]Ps 90:12 [t]Ps 103:14
39:5 [u]Ps 89:45 [v]Ps 62:9
39:6 [w]1Pe 1:24 [x]Ps 127:2 [y]Lk 12:20
39:7 [z]Ps 38:15
39:8 [a]Ps 51:9 [b]Ps 44:13
39:9 [c]Job 2:10
39:10 [d]Job 9:34; Ps 32:4
39:11 [e]2Pe 2:16 [f]Job 13:28
39:12 [g]1Pe 2:11 [h]Heb 11:13
39:13 [i]Job 10:21; 14:10

39:12 The terms "alien" and "stranger" indicate a class of non-Israelites who were permitted to reside among God's people within the promised land but who had no inheritance there. These resident aliens could experience a degree of social interaction with the native inhabitants but enjoyed few rights. David drew upon their experience as an analogy to the kind of painful barriers sin had erected between himself and God.

Psalm 40

For the director of music. Of David. A psalm.

40:1 [j]Ps 27:14 [k]Ps 34:15
40:2 [l]Ps 69:14 [m]Ps 27:5
40:3 [n]Ps 33:3
40:4 [o]Ps 34:8 [p]Ps 84:12
40:5 [q]Ps 136:4 [r]Ps 139:18; Isa 55:8
40:6 [s]1Sa 15:22; Am 5:22 [t]Isa 1:11
40:8 [u]Jn 4:34 [v]Ps 37:31
40:9 [w]Ps 22:25 [x]Jos 22:22; Ps 119:13
40:10 [y]Ps 89:1 [z]Ac 20:20
40:11 [a]Pr 20:28 [b]Ps 43:3
40:12 [c]Ps 116:3 [d]Ps 38:4 [e]Ps 69:4 [f]Ps 73:26

1 I waited patiently[j] for the LORD;
he turned to me and heard my cry.[k]
2 He lifted me out of the slimy pit,
out of the mud and mire;[l]
he set my feet on a rock[m]
and gave me a firm place to stand.
3 He put a new song[n] in my mouth,
a hymn of praise to our God.
Many will see and fear
and put their trust in the LORD.

4 Blessed is the man[o]
who makes the LORD his trust,[p]
who does not look to the proud,
to those who turn aside to false gods.[a]
5 Many, O LORD my God,
are the wonders[q] you have done.
The things you planned for us
no one can recount[r] to you;
were I to speak and tell of them,
they would be too many to declare.

6 Sacrifice and offering you did not desire,[s]
but my ears you have pierced[b,c];
burnt offerings[t] and sin offerings
you did not require.
7 Then I said, "Here I am, I have come—
it is written about me in the scroll.[d]
8 I desire to do your will,[u] O my God;
your law is within my heart."[v]

9 I proclaim righteousness in the great assembly;[w]
I do not seal my lips,
as you know,[x] O LORD.
10 I do not hide your righteousness in my heart;
I speak of your faithfulness[y] and salvation.
I do not conceal your love and your truth
from the great assembly.[z]

11 Do not withhold your mercy from me, O LORD;
may your love[a] and your truth[b] always protect me.
12 For troubles[c] without number surround me;
my sins have overtaken me, and I cannot see.[d]
They are more than the hairs of my head,[e]
and my heart fails[f] within me.

[a] 4 Or *to falsehood* [b] 6 Hebrew; Septuagint *but a body you have prepared for me* (see also Symmachus and Theodotion) [c] 6 Or *opened* [d] 7 Or *come / with the scroll written for me*

40:7 The "scroll" probably refers to the personal copy of the law the king was to take as his covenant charter at the time of his ascension to the throne (see Dt 17:18–20; 2Ki 11:12; cf. 1Ki 2:3).
40:12 Hair varies in length, color and structure among the different races and seems to be intended by God for protection, for beauty and for identification. The peoples of the Bible lands were generally black-haired, although red-headed individuals were fairly common among the people of Israel. Hebrews and Arabs (cf. Rev 9:8) wore their beards long as a mark of dignity, but the Egyptians were clean-shaven (Ge 41:14). The men of Israel were not to clip off the edges of their beards (Lev 19:27); this prohibition explains the "prayer-locks" in front of the ears of Orthodox Jewish men today.

The word "hair" is used in the Bible in several figurative senses: for example, to signify keen marksmanship—some Benjamites could

[13] Be pleased, O LORD, to save me;
O LORD, come quickly to help me.[g] 40:13 [g]Ps 70:1
[14] May all who seek to take my life
be put to shame and confusion;
may all who desire my ruin[h] 40:14 [h]Ps 35:4
be turned back in disgrace.
[15] May those who say to me, "Aha! Aha!"
be appalled at their own shame.
[16] But may all who seek you
rejoice and be glad in you;
may those who love your salvation always say,
"The LORD be exalted!"[i] 40:16 [i]Ps 35:27

[17] Yet I am poor and needy;
may the Lord think of me.
You are my help and my deliverer;
O my God, do not delay.[j] 40:17 [j]Ps 70:5

Psalm 41

For the director of music. A psalm of David.

[1] Blessed is he who has regard for the weak;[k] 41:1 [k]Ps 82:3-4; Pr 14:21
the LORD delivers him in times of trouble.
[2] The LORD will protect him and preserve his life;
he will bless him in the land[l] 41:2 [l]Ps 37:22
and not surrender him to the desire of his foes.[m] [m]Ps 27:12
[3] The LORD will sustain him on his sickbed
and restore him from his bed of illness.

[4] I said, "O LORD, have mercy[n] on me; 41:4 [n]Ps 6:2
heal me, for I have sinned[o] against you." [o]Ps 51:4
[5] My enemies say of me in malice,
"When will he die and his name perish?[p]" 41:5 [p]Ps 38:12
[6] Whenever one comes to see me,
he speaks falsely,[q] while his heart gathers slander;[r] 41:6 [q]Ps 12:2 [r]Pr 26:24
then he goes out and spreads it abroad.

[7] All my enemies whisper together[s] against me; 41:7 [s]Ps 56:5; 71:10-11
they imagine the worst for me, saying,
[8] "A vile disease has beset him;
he will never get up from the place where he lies."
[9] Even my close friend,[t] whom I trusted, 41:9 [t]2Sa 15:12; Ps 55:12
he who shared my bread, [u]Job 19:19; Ps 55:20; Mt 26:23; Jn 13:18*
has lifted up his heel against me.[u]
[10] But you, O LORD, have mercy on me;
raise me up,[v] that I may repay them. 41:10 [v]Ps 3:3
[11] I know that you are pleased with me,[w] 41:11 [w]Ps 147:11
for my enemy does not triumph over me.[x] [x]Ps 25:2

"sling a stone at a hair and not miss" (Jdg 20:16); to connote complete safety—"Not a hair of his head will fall to the ground" (1Sa 14:45); to indicate multiplicity—"My sins . . . are more than the hairs of my head" (Ps 40:12); or to demonstrate age or dignity—"The hair of his head was white like wool" (Da 7:9).

Hair was a mark of beauty and sometimes of pride. Absalom's hair (2Sa 14:26; 18:9), of which he was inordinately proud, caused his death. Samson's uncut hair was a symbol of his Naziritic dedication, so that when he lost it his strength went with it (Jdg 13:7; 16:17–20). In New Testament times the length of the hair was one mark of distinction between the sexes, and Paul declared that, within his cultural context, this distinction should continue (1Co 11:14–16). See also "Beards and Hairstyles in the Biblical World" on page 1084.

41:12 [y]Ps 37:17 [z]Job 36:7

[12] In my integrity you uphold me[y]
and set me in your presence forever.[z]

41:13 [a]Ps 72:18 [b]Ps 89:52; 106:48

[13] Praise be to the LORD, the God of Israel,[a]
from everlasting to everlasting.
Amen and Amen.[b]

BOOK II

Psalms 42–72

Psalm 42[a]

For the director of music. A *maskil*[b] of the Sons of Korah.

42:1 [c]Ps 119:131
42:2 [d]Ps 63:1 [e]Jer 10:10 [f]Ps 43:4
42:3 [g]Ps 80:5 [h]Ps 79:10

[1] As the deer pants for streams of water,
so my soul pants[c] for you, O God.
[2] My soul thirsts[d] for God, for the living God.[e]
When can I go[f] and meet with God?
[3] My tears[g] have been my food
day and night,
while men say to me all day long,
"Where is your God?"[h]
[4] These things I remember
as I pour out my soul:
how I used to go with the multitude,
leading the procession to the house
of God,[i]
with shouts of joy and thanksgiving[j]
among the festive throng.

42:4 [i]Isa 30:29 [j]Ps 100:4
42:5 [k]Ps 38:6; 77:3 [l]La 3:24 [m]Ps 44:3

[5] Why are you downcast,[k] O my soul?
Why so disturbed within me?
Put your hope in God,[l]
for I will yet praise him,
my Savior[m] and [6]my God.

My[c] soul is downcast within me;
therefore I will remember you
from the land of the Jordan,
the heights of Hermon—from Mount Mizar.
[7] Deep calls to deep
in the roar of your waterfalls;
all your waves and breakers
have swept over me.[n]

42:7 [n]Ps 88:7; Jnh 2:3
42:8 [o]Ps 57:3 [p]Job 35:10 [q]Ps 63:6; 149:5

[8] By day the LORD directs his love,[o]
at night[p] his song[q] is with me—
a prayer to the God of my life.

[a] In many Hebrew manuscripts Psalms 42 and 43 constitute one psalm. [b] Title: Probably a literary or musical term
[c] 5,6 A few Hebrew manuscripts, Septuagint and Syriac; most Hebrew manuscripts *praise him for his saving help. / [6]O my God, my*

42:3–4 Hebrew Scripture reflects the need to preserve ("remember," v. 4) the works of God and so to proclaim his faithfulness to future generations. Forgetting God in the Hebrew mind was a willful act of "unlearning," whereby rebellious humans rejected what they had known and sought to create a world in which God did not act or exist. Such people might cry, "Where is your God?" (vv. 3,10).

42:6 Some think that the author here located himself at Mount Mizar (a small peak or village, not otherwise known) on the flanks of Mount Hermon, somewhere near the headwaters of the Jordan River.

THE ELOHISTIC PSALTER

PSALM 42 The Old Testament generally uses one of two different Hebrew words to refer to God:

◆ *Elohim*: This term, translated simply as God, is a generic Hebrew word, comparable to the English *God*, the French *Dieu* or the German *Gott*.

◆ *Yahweh*: This word is the *proper name* of God, but it is usually translated in English as "the LORD." In older translations it is sometimes written as "Jehovah."

An enigma in the Psalms is the so-called Elohistic Psalter, encompassing Psalms 42–83. This collection of psalms has been so designated because in them God is generally referred to as Elohim instead of Yahweh (230 versus 43 occurrences, respectively). We can verify this even in the English by simply comparing how often the word "God" appears in these psalms in comparison to "the LORD." Elsewhere in the Psalms, however, Yahweh is used more frequently than Elohim. How can we explain this peculiarity in Psalms 42–83?

The Rebdorf Psalter; Germany, twelfth century A.D.

© The Schøyen Collection; photography courtesy of Mr. Martin Schøyen

◆ A second possibility is that Psalms 42–83 use Elohim instead of Yahweh in order to communicate that the God whom Israel worshiped was not merely a local, national god but the One true deity over heaven and Earth: God. A problem with this explanation is that even when speaking to Gentiles about God as the universal deity, Israelites did not avoid the name *Yahweh*. Jonah, in Jonah 1:9, asserted to pagan sailors, "I worship the LORD, the God of heaven, who made the sea and the land." (See also Ps 89:6; 113:5; Jer 51:19.)

◆ A third possibility is that the Elohistic Psalter reflects a shift in attitude about speaking the divine name, Yahweh.

We know that in later Judaism the name Yahweh was never pronounced for fear of committing blasphemy.[2] Instead of pronouncing God's proper name the Israelite would say Adonai ("my Lord") or *hashem* ("the name"). When a reader in the synagogue came to the name Yahweh in a text, he would simply substitute Adonai.

◆ A hypothesis that is almost certainly incorrect relates the Elohistic Psalter to the "Documentary Hypothesis."[1] This theory states that three major documents, referred to as J, E and P, are the sources of Genesis (a fourth theoretical source, D, contributed very little to Genesis).

According to this theory J refers to God as Yahweh in Genesis because J believed that the patriarchs knew the divine name Yahweh. Thus, so-called "J" texts always refer to God as Yahweh. However, E and P call him Elohim because they believed that the name Yahweh was not revealed until the time of Moses. Thus, E and P do not use Yahweh in Genesis.

There are good reasons to believe that this theory is groundless. More than that, this hypothesis has no bearing on the divine name as it appears in the Psalms.

It may be that the Elohistic Psalter represents a specific stage in the history of the compilation of the book of Psalms. Psalm 14 is almost identical to Psalm 53, except that where Psalm 14 uses Yahweh Psalm 53 substitutes Elohim. If Psalm 14 is the original version, it may be that a later editor replaced Yahweh with Elohim in Psalm 53 (a similar relationship exists between Ps 40 and 70).

Thus, the collection and editing of the Elohistic Psalter may reflect a time when people had begun to feel uncomfortable about pronouncing the name Yahweh but had not yet developed the practice of substituting Adonai or *hashem*.

We do not know with certainty, however, why the Elohistic Psalter prefers Elohim over Yahweh. See also "The Names of God" chart on page 90.

[1]See "The Documentary Hypothesis" on page 15. [2]See "YHWH: The Name of God in the Old Testament" on page 89.

[9] I say to God my Rock,
"Why have you forgotten me?
Why must I go about mourning,[r]
oppressed by the enemy?"
[10] My bones suffer mortal agony
as my foes taunt me,
saying to me all day long,
"Where is your God?"

[11] Why are you downcast, O my soul?
Why so disturbed within me?
Put your hope in God,
for I will yet praise him,
my Savior and my God.[s]

42:9 [r]Ps 38:6
42:11 [s]Ps 43:5

Psalm 43[a]

[1] Vindicate me, O God,
and plead my cause[t] against an ungodly nation;
rescue me from deceitful and wicked men.[u]
[2] You are God my stronghold.
Why have you rejected[v] me?
Why must I go about mourning,
oppressed by the enemy?[w]
[3] Send forth your light[x] and your truth,
let them guide me;
let them bring me to your holy mountain,[y]
to the place where you dwell.[z]
[4] Then will I go to the altar[a] of God,
to God, my joy and my delight.
I will praise you with the harp,[b]
O God, my God.

[5] Why are you downcast, O my soul?
Why so disturbed within me?
Put your hope in God,
for I will yet praise him,
my Savior and my God.[c]

43:1 [t]1Sa 24:15; Ps 26:1; 35:1 [u]Ps 5:6
43:2 [v]Ps 44:9 [w]Ps 42:9
43:3 [x]Ps 36:9 [y]Ps 42:4 [z]Ps 84:1
43:4 [a]Ps 26:6 [b]Ps 33:2
43:5 [c]Ps 42:6

Psalm 44

For the director of music. Of the Sons of Korah. A *maskil*.[b]

[1] We have heard with our ears, O God;
our fathers have told us[d]
what you did in their days,
in days long ago.
[2] With your hand you drove out[e] the nations
and planted[f] our fathers;
you crushed the peoples
and made our fathers flourish.[g]
[3] It was not by their sword[h] that they won the land,
nor did their arm bring them victory;

44:1 [d]Ex 12:26; Ps 78:3
44:2 [e]Ps 78:55 [f]Ex 15:17 [g]Ps 80:9
44:3 [h]Dt 8:17; Jos 24:12

[a] In many Hebrew manuscripts Psalms 42 and 43 constitute one psalm. [b] Title: Probably a literary or musical term

43:1 The "ungodly nation" referred to here may have been the Arameans of Damascus. Perhaps the author had been taken captive by the Arameans during one of their incursions into Judah (see 2Ki 12:17–18).

it was your right hand, your arm,[i]
and the light of your face, for you loved[j] them.

[4] You are my King[k] and my God,
who decrees[a] victories for Jacob.
[5] Through you we push back our enemies;
through your name we trample[l] our foes.
[6] I do not trust in my bow,[m]
my sword does not bring me victory;
[7] but you give us victory[n] over our enemies,
you put our adversaries to shame.[o]
[8] In God we make our boast[p] all day long,
and we will praise your name forever.[q] *Selah*

[9] But now you have rejected[r] and humbled us;
you no longer go out with our armies.[s]
[10] You made us retreat[t] before the enemy,
and our adversaries have plundered us.
[11] You gave us up to be devoured like sheep[u]
and have scattered us among the nations.[v]
[12] You sold your people for a pittance,[w]
gaining nothing from their sale.

[13] You have made us a reproach to our neighbors,[x]
the scorn[y] and derision of those around us.
[14] You have made us a byword among the nations;
the peoples shake their heads[z] at us.
[15] My disgrace is before me all day long,
and my face is covered with shame
[16] at the taunts of those who reproach and revile[a] me,
because of the enemy, who is bent on revenge.

[17] All this happened to us,
though we had not forgotten[b] you
or been false to your covenant.
[18] Our hearts had not turned[c] back;
our feet had not strayed from your path.
[19] But you crushed[d] us and made us a haunt for jackals
and covered us over with deep darkness.[e]

[20] If we had forgotten[f] the name of our God
or spread out our hands to a foreign god,[g]
[21] would not God have discovered it,
since he knows the secrets of the heart?[h]
[22] Yet for your sake we face death all day long;
we are considered as sheep to be slaughtered.[i]
[23] Awake,[j] O Lord! Why do you sleep?[k]
Rouse yourself! Do not reject us forever.[l]
[24] Why do you hide your face[m]
and forget our misery and oppression?[n]

[25] We are brought down to the dust;[o]
our bodies cling to the ground.
[26] Rise up[p] and help us;
redeem[q] us because of your unfailing love.

44:3 [i]Ps 77:15 [j]Dt 4:37; 7:7-8
44:4 [k]Ps 74:12
44:5 [l]Ps 108:13
44:6 [m]Ps 33:16
44:7 [n]Ps 136:24 [o]Ps 53:5
44:8 [p]Ps 34:2 [q]Ps 30:12
44:9 [r]Ps 74:1 [s]Ps 60:1,10
44:10 [t]Lev 26:17; Jos 7:8; Ps 89:41
44:11 [u]Ro 8:36 [v]Dt 4:27; 28:64; Ps 106:27
44:12 [w]Isa 52:3; Jer 15:13
44:13 [x]Ps 79:4; 80:6 [y]Dt 28:37
44:14 [z]Ps 109:25; Jer 24:9
44:16 [a]Ps 74:10
44:17 [b]Ps 78:7, 57; Da 9:13
44:18 [c]Job 23:11
44:19 [d]Ps 51:8 [e]Job 3:5
44:20 [f]Ps 78:11 [g]Dt 6:14; Ps 81:9
44:21 [h]Ps 139:1-2; Jer 17:10
44:22 [i]Isa 53:7; Ro 8:36*
44:23 [j]Ps 7:6 [k]Ps 78:65 [l]Ps 77:7
44:24 [m]Job 13:24 [n]Ps 42:9
44:25 [o]Ps 119:25
44:26 [p]Ps 35:2 [q]Ps 25:22

[a] *4* Septuagint, Aquila and Syriac; Hebrew *King, O God; / command*

44:18 For "hearts," see the note on 4:7.

The Ancient Near Eastern King

PSALM 45 Israel's plea for a king "such as all the other nations have" (1Sa 8:5) testifies to how common this form of government was in the ancient Near East. Discharging judicial, military and sacral responsibilities along with political obligations, the king was the fulcrum of state administration and ideology. Psalm 45, a royal wedding song, alludes to several aspects of kingship. First, the Israelite king modeled and guaranteed justice and righteousness (vv. 4,7). In comparison, the Babylonian **Code of Hammurabi** proclaimed the king's divinely ordained role as legal authority. Moreover, verses 3–5 describe the king's role as the military commander-in-chief, a theme amply and ferociously demonstrated by **Assyrian** rulers who recounted military exploits in artistic **reliefs** and written annals.[1]

In antiquity religion permeated royal ideology. Rulers were expected to provide offerings, build and maintain temples and participate in ritual feasts.[2] Yet the institution of kingship was not necessarily identical from one nation to another; the nature of the king's sacred duties differed from nation to nation. According to the Egyptian Tale of Sinuhe, when king Amenemhet I died he became united with the sun god. This notion of the deification of the king and the divine nature of his office are reflected in many Egyptian texts. On the other hand, although **Mesopotamians** occasionally depicted their king as a deity, they tended to construe him as a divine representative. The king played such a critical role in the Mesopotamians' annual New Year's festival that, during the **Neo-Babylonian** period, the feast was not celebrated due to his absence.

Divine rule and human kingship were also intertwined in Israel (v. 6). The Davidic covenant (2Sa 7) and several psalms (e.g., Ps 2; 89) describe a unique father-son relationship between **Yahweh** and his anointed. Yahweh, however, placed numerous constraints and moral requirements upon the king, and this is quite different from what we see elsewhere in the ancient Near East. Prophets like Elijah and Nathan openly criticized the king when he engaged in wrong practices; Deuteronomy 17:16 severely limited his military procurements, and even his sacral duties were carefully defined (2Ch 26:16–20).

Hawara, Egypt: the site of the pyramid of Middle Kingdom pharaoh Amenemhet
Preserving Bible Times; © Dr. James C. Martin

[1]See "The Lachish Reliefs" on page 559 and "The Annals of Sargon II" on page 1072. [2]See "The Cylinders of Gudea" on page 485.

Psalm 45

For the director of music. To ⌞the tune of⌟ "Lilies."
Of the Sons of Korah. A *maskil.*[a] A wedding song.

1 My heart is stirred by a noble theme
as I recite my verses for the king;
my tongue is the pen of a skillful writer.

2 You are the most excellent of men
and your lips have been anointed with grace,[r]
since God has blessed you forever.
3 Gird your sword[s] upon your side, O mighty one;[t]
clothe yourself with splendor and majesty.
4 In your majesty ride forth victoriously[u]
in behalf of truth, humility and righteousness;
let your right hand display awesome deeds.
5 Let your sharp arrows pierce the hearts of the king's
enemies;
let the nations fall beneath your feet.
6 Your throne, O God, will last for ever and ever;[v]
a scepter of justice will be the scepter of your kingdom.
7 You love righteousness[w] and hate wickedness;
therefore God, your God, has set you above your
companions
by anointing[x] you with the oil of joy.[y]
8 All your robes are fragrant[z] with myrrh and aloes and
cassia;
from palaces adorned with ivory
the music of the strings makes you glad.
9 Daughters of kings[a] are among your honored women;
at your right hand[b] is the royal bride in gold of Ophir.

10 Listen, O daughter, consider and give ear:
Forget your people[c] and your father's house.
11 The king is enthralled by your beauty;
honor[d] him, for he is your lord.[e]
12 The Daughter of Tyre will come with a gift,[b][f]
men of wealth will seek your favor.

13 All glorious[g] is the princess within ⌞her chamber⌟;
her gown is interwoven with gold.
14 In embroidered garments she is led to the king;[h]
her virgin companions follow her
and are brought to you.

45:2 [r] Lk 4:22
45:3 [s] Heb 4:12; Rev 1:16 [t] Isa 9:6
45:4 [u] Rev 6:2
45:6 [v] Ps 93:2; 98:9
45:7 [w] Ps 33:5 [x] Isa 61:1 [y] Ps 21:6; Heb 1:8-9*
45:8 [z] SS 1:3
45:9 [a] SS 6:8 [b] 1Ki 2:19
45:10 [c] Dt 21:13
45:11 [d] Ps 95:6 [e] Isa 54:5
45:12 [f] Ps 22:29; Isa 49:23
45:13 [g] Isa 61:10
45:14 [h] SS 1:4

[a] Title: Probably a literary or musical term [b] 12 Or *A Tyrian robe is among the gifts*

45:1 This song was composed and presumably sung in praise of the king on his wedding day. He undoubtedly belonged to David's dynasty, and the song was probably used at more than one royal wedding. Since the bride was a foreign princess (see vv. 10,12), the wedding reflected the king's standing as a figure of international significance.

45:6 The king's throne may have been called God's throne because the king was God's appointed representative. Alternatively, it is possible that the king himself was called "god" as a title of honor. The pharaohs of Egypt were sometimes addressed as "my god" by their vassal kings in the region much later known as Palestine, as evidenced by the Amarna letters (see "The Amarna Tablets and the Habiru" on p. 347).

For "scepter," see the note on Zechariah 10:11.

45:8 Excavators of Samaria have unearthed ivory inlays in a building associated with the Israelite king Ahab (see "The Samaria Ivories" on p. 1449).

45:9 Gold of Ophir was a rare commodity (Isa 13:12) imported into Israel by ships that sailed from Ezion Geber in Edom (1Ki 9:26–28; 22:48) to a destination conjectured to be India, Africa, the Arabian peninsula or even South America (see "Ezion Geber" on p. 631, and see the note on 1Ki 9:28). It came to be the standard for gold of purity and quality.

45:12 The term "Daughter of Tyre" was a personification of Tyre and its inhabitants. Tyre was an important Phoenician seaport on the Mediterranean coast north of Israel. The king of Tyre was the first foreign ruler to recognize the Davidic dynasty (see 2Sa 5:11), and Solomon maintained close relations with Tyre (see 1Ki 5; 9:10–14,26–28). As a great trading center on the Mediterranean coast, Tyre was world-renowned for its wealth (see Isa 23; Eze 26:1—28:19).

15 They are led in with joy and gladness;
they enter the palace of the king.

16 Your sons will take the place of your fathers;
you will make them princes throughout the land.
17 I will perpetuate your memory through all generations;[i]
therefore the nations will praise you[j] for ever and ever.

45:17 [i]Mal 1:11 [j]Ps 138:4

Psalm 46

For the director of music. Of the Sons of Korah. According to *alamoth.*[a] A song.

1 God is our refuge[k] and strength,
an ever-present[l] help in trouble.
2 Therefore we will not fear,[m] though the earth give way[n]
and the mountains fall[o] into the heart of the sea,
3 though its waters roar[p] and foam
and the mountains quake with their surging. *Selah*

4 There is a river whose streams make glad the city of God,[q]
the holy place where the Most High dwells.
5 God is within her,[r] she will not fall;
God will help[s] her at break of day.
6 Nations[t] are in uproar, kingdoms[u] fall;
he lifts his voice, the earth melts.[v]

7 The LORD Almighty is with us;[w]
the God of Jacob is our fortress.[x] *Selah*

8 Come and see the works of the LORD,[y]
the desolations[z] he has brought on the earth.
9 He makes wars[a] cease to the ends of the earth;
he breaks the bow[b] and shatters the spear,
he burns the shields[b] with fire.[c]
10 "Be still, and know that I am God;[d]
I will be exalted[e] among the nations,
I will be exalted in the earth."

11 The LORD Almighty is with us;
the God of Jacob is our fortress. *Selah*

46:1 [k]Ps 9:9; 14:6 [l]Dt 4:7
46:2 [m]Ps 23:4 [n]Ps 82:5 [o]Ps 18:7
46:3 [p]Ps 93:3
46:4 [q]Ps 48:1,8; Isa 60:14
46:5 [r]Isa 12:6; Eze 43:7 [s]Ps 37:40
46:6 [t]Ps 2:1 [u]Ps 68:32 [v]Mic 1:4
46:7 [w]2Ch 13:12 [x]Ps 9:9
46:8 [y]Ps 66:5 [z]Isa 61:4
46:9 [a]Isa 2:4 [b]Ps 76:3 [c]Eze 39:9
46:10 [d]Ps 100:3 [e]Isa 2:11

Psalm 47

For the director of music. Of the Sons of Korah. A psalm.

1 Clap your hands,[f] all you nations;
shout to God with cries of joy.[g]
2 How awesome[h] is the LORD Most High,
the great King[i] over all the earth!
3 He subdued[j] nations under us,
peoples under our feet.
4 He chose our inheritance[k] for us,
the pride of Jacob, whom he loved. *Selah*

47:1 [f]Ps 98:8; Isa 55:12 [g]Ps 106:47
47:2 [h]Dt 7:21 [i]Mal 1:14
47:3 [j]Ps 18:39,47
47:4 [k]1Pe 1:4

[a] Title: Probably a musical term   [b] 9 Or *chariots*

46:4 Jerusalem has no river. Here "river" serves as a metaphor for the continual outpouring of the sustaining and refreshing blessings of God, which make the City of God like the Garden of Eden.
46:5 The "break of day" was the time when attacks against cities were most likely to be launched. God's help brought on the dawn of deliverance, dispelling the night of danger.
47:2 The title "great King" was often used by the imperial rulers of Assyria.

5 God has ascended amid shouts of joy,
the LORD amid the sounding of trumpets.[l] **47:5** [l]Ps 68:33; 98:6
6 Sing praises[m] to God, sing praises; **47:6** [m]Ps 68:4; 89:18
sing praises to our King, sing praises.
7 For God is the King of all the earth;[n] **47:7** [n]Zec 14:9 [o]Col 3:16
sing to him a psalm[a][o] of praise.
8 God reigns[p] over the nations; **47:8** [p]1Ch 16:31
God is seated on his holy throne.
9 The nobles of the nations assemble
as the people of the God of Abraham,
for the kings[b] of the earth belong to God;[q] **47:9** [q]Ps 72:11; 89:18 [r]Ps 97:9
he is greatly exalted.[r]

Psalm 48

A song. A psalm of the Sons of Korah.

1 Great is the LORD,[s] and most worthy of praise, **48:1** [s]Ps 96:4 [t]Ps 46:4 [u]Isa 2:2-3; Mic 4:1; Zec 8:3
in the city of our God,[t] his holy mountain.[u]
2 It is beautiful[v] in its loftiness, **48:2** [v]Ps 50:2; La 2:15 [w]Mt 5:35
the joy of the whole earth.
Like the utmost heights of Zaphon[c] is Mount Zion,
the[d] city of the Great King.[w]
3 God is in her citadels;
he has shown himself to be her fortress.[x] **48:3** [x]Ps 46:7

4 When the kings joined forces,
when they advanced together,[y] **48:4** [y]2Sa 10:1-19
5 they saw ⌊her⌋ and were astounded;
they fled in terror.[z] **48:5** [z]Ex 15:16
6 Trembling seized them there,
pain like that of a woman in labor.
7 You destroyed them like ships of Tarshish
shattered by an east wind.[a] **48:7** [a]Jer 18:17; Eze 27:26

8 As we have heard,
so have we seen
in the city of the LORD Almighty,
in the city of our God:
God makes her secure forever.[b] *Selah* **48:8** [b]Ps 87:5

9 Within your temple, O God,
we meditate on your unfailing love.[c] **48:9** [c]Ps 26:3
10 Like your name,[d] O God, **48:10** [d]Dt 28:58; Jos 7:9 [e]Isa 41:10
your praise reaches to the ends of the earth;[e]
your right hand is filled with righteousness.
11 Mount Zion rejoices,
the villages of Judah are glad
because of your judgments.[f] **48:11** [f]Ps 97:8

12 Walk about Zion, go around her,
count her towers,

[a] 7 Or *a maskil* (probably a literary or musical term) [b] 9 Or *shields* [c] 2 *Zaphon* can refer to a sacred mountain or the direction north. [d] 2 Or *earth, / Mount Zion, on the northern side / of the*

48:7 The "ships of Tarshish" were the great merchant ships of the Mediterranean (see 1Ki 10:22; see also "Seafaring in the Ancient World" on p. 1473 and "Where Was Tarshish?" on p. 1475). For a discussion of the east wind in Palestine, see the note on Hosea 13:15.

Zaphon, Olympus, Sinai and Zion: The Mountain of God

PSALM 48 Most people today are aware that the gods of the Greek myths had their palace on Mount Olympus; less well known is Zaphon, the sacred mountain of the **Canaanite** god Baal-Hadad. The actual Mount Olympus (9,573 ft [2,918 m] in height) is in northern Greece at the border of Thessaly and Macedonia; the actual Zaphon (5,807 ft [1,770 m] high) is in northern Syria on the Orontes River. In both cases the mystery and grandeur of a high mountain in the far north seemed appropriate to ancient peoples as the abodes of their gods.

The Israelites also had sacred mountains. The first of these was Mount Sinai, located far to the south.[1] Mount Sinai was not recognized as the home of God but as the mountain to which he had descended in order to meet Moses and give Israel his law. Despite the fact that a pivotal event in Israel's history had taken place there, later texts, such as the Psalms, pay relatively little attention to Sinai. It does not appear to have been a place of pilgrimage either, although on one occasion Elijah did journey to Sinai in order to encounter God (see 1Ki 19:8, where Sinai is called Horeb).

Both the psalmists and the Old Testament prophets paid far more attention to Mount Zion. This is somewhat surprising, for, unlike the other mountains mentioned above, Zion is neither remote nor particularly impressive. It constitutes the hilly area of Jerusalem—more specifically, the temple mount. The claim of Psalm 48:2 ("It is beautiful in its loftiness, the joy of the whole earth. Like the utmost heights of Zaphon is Mount Zion") would hardly seem accurate with reference to its literal height. This area of Jerusalem sits about 2,000 feet (610 m) above sea level, and although the views are impressive Zion hardly dominates the area of Judah in the same way Olympus overshadows Greece. Also, unlike the other mountains, it had a large human population and thus none of the remoteness or mystery typically associated with the mountains of the gods.

The term "Zion" in the Old Testament is used as a kind of code word for the coming kingdom of God. Zion was a symbol of God's dominion over the whole earth, as well as the promise of a great future, when the Gentiles would come and submit to Israel's God (Isa 2:2–4). The worship at the temple was a foretaste of that future, when David's kingdom would extend over all humanity forever. The very presence of Zion in a human city, Jerusalem, was proof that God's covenant was with people and that, unlike the gods of the nations, he would indeed dwell among us.

[1]But see "The Location of Mount Sinai" on page 123.

Mount Olympus

Photograph: © Todd Bolen/Bible Places.com

[13] consider well her ramparts,
view her citadels,[g]
that you may tell of them to the next generation.[h]
[14] For this God is our God for ever and ever;
he will be our guide[i] even to the end.

48:13 [g]ver 3; Ps 122:7 [h]Ps 78:6
48:14 [i]Ps 23:4

Psalm 49

For the director of music. Of the Sons of Korah. A psalm.

[1] Hear this, all you peoples;[j]
listen, all who live in this world,[k]
[2] both low and high,
rich and poor alike:
[3] My mouth will speak words of wisdom;[l]
the utterance from my heart will give understanding.[m]
[4] I will turn my ear to a proverb;[n]
with the harp I will expound my riddle:[o]

[5] Why should I fear[p] when evil days come,
when wicked deceivers surround me—
[6] those who trust in their wealth[q]
and boast of their great riches?
[7] No man can redeem the life of another
or give to God a ransom for him—
[8] the ransom for a life is costly,
no payment is ever enough—[r]
[9] that he should live on[s] forever
and not see decay.

[10] For all can see that wise men die;[t]
the foolish and the senseless alike perish
and leave their wealth to others.[u]
[11] Their tombs will remain their houses[a] forever,
their dwellings for endless generations,
though they had[b] named[v] lands after themselves.

[12] But man, despite his riches, does not endure;
he is[c] like the beasts that perish.

[13] This is the fate of those who trust in themselves,[w]
and of their followers, who approve their sayings. *Selah*
[14] Like sheep they are destined for the grave,[d][x]
and death will feed on them.
The upright will rule[y] over them in the morning;
their forms will decay in the grave,[d]
far from their princely mansions.
[15] But God will redeem my life[e] from the grave;[z]
he will surely take me to himself.[a] *Selah*

49:1 [j]Ps 78:1 [k]Ps 33:8
49:3 [l]Ps 37:30 [m]Ps 119:130
49:4 [n]Ps 78:2 [o]Nu 12:8
49:5 [p]Ps 23:4
49:6 [q]Job 31:24
49:8 [r]Mt 16:26
49:9 [s]Ps 22:29; 89:48
49:10 [t]Ecc 2:16 [u]Ecc 2:18,21
49:11 [v]Ge 4:17; Dt 3:14
49:13 [w]Lk 12:20
49:14 [x]Job 24:19; Ps 9:17 [y]Da 7:18; Mal 4:3; 1Co 6:2; Rev 2:26
49:15 [z]Ps 56:13; Hos 13:14 [a]Ps 73:24

[a] *11* Septuagint and Syriac; Hebrew *In their thoughts their houses will remain* [b] *11* Or */ for they have* [c] *12* Hebrew; Septuagint and Syriac read verse 12 the same as verse 20. [d] *14* Hebrew *Sheol*; also in verse 15 [e] *15* Or *soul*

49:14–15 For a discussion of Sheol, see the note on Job 17:13–16. See also "Sheol, Hades, Gehenna, the Abyss and Tartarus: Images of Hell" on page 946.

The psalmist portrayed death (or the grave) as an insatiable monster feeding upon its victims. This imagery was probably borrowed from Canaanite mythology, which so depicts the god Mot (see the note on Job 18:13–14). As one Canaanite document reads, "Do not approach divine Mot, lest he put you like a lamb into his mouth."

49:15 For information on the psalmists' concept of the afterlife, see the note on 6:5.

[16]Do not be overawed when a man grows rich,
when the splendor of his house increases;
[17]for he will take nothing with him when he dies,
his splendor will not descend with him.[b]
[18]Though while he lived he counted himself blessed—[c]
and men praise you when you prosper—
[19]he will join the generation of his fathers,[d]
who will never see the light[e] ⌞of life⌟.

[20]A man who has riches without understanding
is like the beasts that perish.[f]

49:17 [b]Ps 17:14; 1Ti 6:7
49:18 [c]Dt 29:19; Lk 12:19
49:19 [d]Ge 15:15 [e]Job 33:30
49:20 [f]Ecc 3:19

Psalm 50

A psalm of Asaph.

[1]The Mighty One, God, the LORD,[g]
speaks and summons the earth
from the rising of the sun to the place where it sets.[h]
[2]From Zion, perfect in beauty,[i]
God shines forth.[j]
[3]Our God comes[k] and will not be silent;
a fire devours before him,[l]
and around him a tempest rages.
[4]He summons the heavens above,
and the earth,[m] that he may judge his people:
[5]"Gather to me my consecrated ones,[n]
who made a covenant[o] with me by sacrifice."
[6]And the heavens proclaim[p] his righteousness,
for God himself is judge.[q] *Selah*

[7]"Hear, O my people, and I will speak,
O Israel, and I will testify[r] against you:
I am God, your God.[s]
[8]I do not rebuke you for your sacrifices
or your burnt offerings,[t] which are ever before me.
[9]I have no need of a bull[u] from your stall
or of goats from your pens,
[10]for every animal of the forest is mine,
and the cattle on a thousand hills.[v]
[11]I know every bird in the mountains,
and the creatures of the field are mine.
[12]If I were hungry I would not tell you,
for the world[w] is mine, and all that is in it.
[13]Do I eat the flesh of bulls
or drink the blood of goats?
[14]Sacrifice thank offerings[x] to God,
fulfill your vows[y] to the Most High,
[15]and call[z] upon me in the day of trouble;
I will deliver you, and you will honor[a] me."

[16]But to the wicked, God says:

"What right have you to recite my laws
or take my covenant on your lips?[b]

50:1 [g]Jos 22:22 [h]Ps 113:3
50:2 [i]Ps 48:2 [j]Dt 33:2; Ps 80:1
50:3 [k]Ps 96:13 [l]Ps 97:3; Da 7:10
50:4 [m]Dt 4:26; Isa 1:2
50:5 [n]Ps 30:4 [o]Ex 24:7
50:6 [p]Ps 89:5 [q]Ps 75:7
50:7 [r]Ps 81:8 [s]Ex 20:2
50:8 [t]Ps 40:6; Hos 6:6
50:9 [u]Ps 69:31
50:10 [v]Ps 104:24
50:12 [w]Ex 19:5
50:14 [x]Heb 13:15 [y]Dt 23:21
50:15 [z]Ps 81:7 [a]Ps 22:23
50:16 [b]Isa 29:13

50:1–23 See the note on 73:1—83:18 for commentary on Asaph.
50:5 Psalm 50 is a "covenant lawsuit" brought by God against his "consecrated ones, who made a covenant with [him] by sacrifice." This sort of legal proceeding was common in the Old Testament as a means by which God aired Israel's shortcomings and justified his judgment upon the nation.

[17]You hate my instruction
and cast my words behind[c] you.
[18]When you see a thief, you join[d] with him;
you throw in your lot with adulterers.
[19]You use your mouth for evil
and harness your tongue to deceit.[e]
[20]You speak continually against your brother[f]
and slander your own mother's son.
[21]These things you have done and I kept silent;[g]
you thought I was altogether[a] like you.
But I will rebuke you
and accuse[h] you to your face.

[22]"Consider this, you who forget God,[i]
or I will tear you to pieces, with none to rescue:[j]
[23]He who sacrifices thank offerings honors me,
and he prepares the way[k]
so that I may show him[b] the salvation of God.[l]"

50:17 [c]Ne 9:26; Ro 2:21-22
50:18 [d]Ro 1:32; 1Ti 5:22
50:19 [e]Ps 10:7; 52:2
50:20 [f]Mt 10:21
50:21 [g]Ecc 8:11; Isa 42:14 [h]Ps 90:8
50:22 [i]Job 8:13; Ps 9:17 [j]Ps 7:2
50:23 [k]Ps 85:13 [l]Ps 91:16

Psalm 51

For the director of music. A psalm of David. When the prophet Nathan came to him after David had committed adultery with Bathsheba.

[1]Have mercy on me, O God,
according to your unfailing love;
according to your great compassion
blot out[m] my transgressions.[n]
[2]Wash away[o] all my iniquity
and cleanse[p] me from my sin.

[3]For I know my transgressions,
and my sin is always before me.[q]
[4]Against you, you only, have I sinned
and done what is evil in your sight,[r]
so that you are proved right when you speak
and justified when you judge.[s]
[5]Surely I was sinful[t] at birth,
sinful from the time my mother conceived me.
[6]Surely you desire truth in the inner parts[a];
you teach[b] me wisdom[u] in the inmost place.[v]
[7]Cleanse me with hyssop,[w] and I will be clean;
wash me, and I will be whiter than snow.[x]
[8]Let me hear joy and gladness;[y]
let the bones you have crushed rejoice.
[9]Hide your face from my sins[z]
and blot out all my iniquity.

[10]Create in me a pure heart,[a] O God,
and renew a steadfast spirit within me.[b]

51:1 [m]Ac 3:19 [n]Isa 43:25; Col 2:14
51:2 [o]1Jn 1:9 [p]Heb 9:14
51:3 [q]Isa 59:12
51:4 [r]Ge 20:6; Lk 15:21 [s]Ro 3:4*
51:5 [t]Job 14:4
51:6 [u]Pr 2:6 [v]Ps 15:2
51:7 [w]Lev 14:4; Heb 9:19 [x]Isa 1:18
51:8 [y]Isa 35:10
51:9 [z]Jer 16:17
51:10 [a]Ps 78:37; Ac 15:9 [b]Eze 18:31

[a] 21 Or *thought the 'I AM' was* [b] 23 Or *and to him who considers his way / I will show* [a] 6 The meaning of the Hebrew for this phrase is uncertain. [b] 6 Or *you desired . . . ; / you taught*

51:1 The image is that of a papyrus scroll on which God had recorded David's deeds (see "Scrolls, Seals, and Codices" on p. 2053). The "blotting out" of sins pictures forgiveness (Jer 18:23; see also Isa 43:25).
51:7 For a discussion of cleanness and uncleanness as perceived in the Old Testament, see the note on Leviticus 14:1–57.

Hyssop was an aromatic plant (*Origanum maru*) of the mint family with a straight stalk (see Jn 19:29) and white flowers. The hairy surface of its leaves and branches held liquids well and made it suitable as a sprinkling device for use in purification rituals (see Lev 14:4–6,49–52; Nu 19:6,18; Heb 9:19).

51:11 [c]Eph 4:30
51:12 [d]Ps 13:5
51:13 [e]Ac 9:21-22 [f]Ps 22:27
51:14 [g]2Sa 12:9 [h]Ps 25:5 [i]Ps 35:28
51:15 [j]Ps 9:14
51:16 [k]1Sa 15:22; Ps 40:6
51:17 [l]Ps 34:18
51:18 [m]Ps 102:16; Isa 51:3
51:19 [n]Ps 4:5 [o]Ps 66:13 [p]Ps 66:15
52:1 [q]1Sa 22:9 [r]Ps 94:4

11 Do not cast me from your presence
or take your Holy Spirit[c] from me.
12 Restore to me the joy of your salvation[d]
and grant me a willing spirit, to sustain me.

13 Then I will teach transgressors your ways,[e]
and sinners will turn back to you.[f]
14 Save me from bloodguilt,[g] O God,
the God who saves me,[h]
and my tongue will sing of your righteousness.[i]
15 O Lord, open my lips,[j]
and my mouth will declare your praise.
16 You do not delight in sacrifice,[k] or I would bring it;
you do not take pleasure in burnt offerings.
17 The sacrifices of God are[a] a broken spirit;
a broken and contrite heart,[l]
O God, you will not despise.

18 In your good pleasure make Zion[m] prosper;
build up the walls of Jerusalem.
19 Then there will be righteous sacrifices,[n]
whole burnt offerings[o] to delight you;
then bulls[p] will be offered on your altar.

Psalm 52

For the director of music. A *maskil*[b] of David. When Doeg the Edomite[q] had gone to Saul and told him: "David has gone to the house of Ahimelech."

1 Why do you boast of evil, you mighty man?
Why do you boast[r] all day long,
you who are a disgrace in the eyes of God?

[a] 17 Or *My sacrifice, O God, is* [b] Title: Probably a literary or musical term

Hyssop and the Rituals of Cleansing

PSALM 51 The hyssop of the Bible is not the European *Hyssop officinalis* but *Origanum syriacum*, sometimes referred to as "Bible hyssop" or "Syrian oregano." A variety of oregano or marjoram that grows in rocky soil in Israel, it has hairy, gray leaves that absorb liquid well—probably accounting for its use in rituals involving cleansing.

In Leviticus 14 a person with a skin disease was to be ritually cleansed by means of two clean birds, hyssop, a piece of scarlet cloth and some cedarwood.[1] Under a priest's direction one bird was to be slaughtered and the other, along with the hyssop, yarn and cedar, dipped into the blood. The individual would be sprinkled with the blood (apparently using the hyssop) and the living bird released.

Hyssop was also used for wiping sacrificial blood on the lintel and doorposts of Israelite houses in Egypt at the time of the first Passover (Ex 12:21–22),[2] as well as in a cleansing ritual involving a red heifer (Nu 19:6).[3] Because of its association with purification rites,[4] David in Psalm 51:7 asked in his prayer for forgiveness to be cleansed with hyssop.

[1]See "Skin Diseases in the Ancient World" on page 171. [2]See "The Passover" on page 656. [3]See "The Red Heifer" on page 222. [4]See "Ritual Purity in Israel and the Ancient Near East" on page 166.

[2]Your tongue plots destruction;
it is like a sharpened razor,[s]
you who practice deceit.[t]
[3]You love evil rather than good,
falsehood[u] rather than speaking the truth. *Selah*
[4]You love every harmful word,
O you deceitful tongue![v]

[5]Surely God will bring you down to everlasting ruin:
He will snatch you up and tear[w] you from your tent;
he will uproot[x] you from the land of the living.[y] *Selah*
[6]The righteous will see and fear;
they will laugh[z] at him, saying,
[7]"Here now is the man
who did not make God his stronghold
but trusted in his great wealth[a]
and grew strong by destroying others!"

[8]But I am like an olive tree[b]
flourishing in the house of God;
I trust[c] in God's unfailing love
for ever and ever.
[9]I will praise you forever[d] for what you have done;
in your name I will hope, for your name is good.[e]
I will praise you in the presence of your saints.

52:2 [s]Ps 57:4 [t]Ps 50:19
52:3 [u]Jer 9:5
52:4 [v]Ps 120:2,3
52:5 [w]Isa 22:19 [x]Pr 2:22 [y]Ps 27:13
52:6 [z]Job 22:19; Ps 37:34; 40:3
52:7 [a]Ps 49:6
52:8 [b]Jer 11:16 [c]Ps 13:5
52:9 [d]Ps 30:12 [e]Ps 54:6

Psalm 53

For the director of music. According to *mahalath.*[a]
A *maskil*[b] of David.

[1]The fool[f] says in his heart,
"There is no God."[g]
They are corrupt, and their ways are vile;
there is no one who does good.

[2]God looks down from heaven[h]
on the sons of men
to see if there are any who understand,
any who seek God.[i]
[3]Everyone has turned away,
they have together become corrupt;
there is no one who does good,
not even one.[j]

[4]Will the evildoers never learn—
those who devour my people as men eat bread
and who do not call on God?
[5]There they were, overwhelmed with dread,
where there was nothing to dread.[k]
God scattered the bones[l] of those who attacked you;
you put them to shame, for God despised them.

53:1 [f]Ps 14:1-7; Ro 3:10 [g]Ps 10:4
53:2 [h]Ps 33:13 [i]2Ch 15:2
53:3 [j]Ro 3:10-12*
53:5 [k]Lev 26:17 [l]Eze 6:5

[a] Title: Probably a musical term [b] Title: Probably a literary or musical term

52:8 Although there is evidence that ancient Israel was far more forested than it is today, the presence of flourishing trees was still a sign of divine blessing for former nomads living on the fringes of a settled, agricultural society. The Old Testament presents a thriving tree as symbolic of the blessing of the righteous (see 1:3; Isa 61:3; Jer 17:8). This blessing is frequently contrasted with the sad state of the wicked, depicted in terms of nonproductive dryness. Olive trees, which live for hundreds of years, were not actually planted in the temple courts.

[6] Oh, that salvation for Israel would come out of Zion!
When God restores the fortunes of his people,
let Jacob rejoice and Israel be glad!

Psalm 54

For the director of music. With stringed instruments.
A *maskil*[a] of David. When the Ziphites had gone to Saul and said,
"Is not David hiding among us?"

54:1 mPs 20:1 nn2Ch 20:6
[1] Save me, O God, by your name;[m]
vindicate me by your might.[n]
54:2 oPs 5:1; 55:1
[2] Hear my prayer, O God;[o]
listen to the words of my mouth.

54:3 pPs 86:14 qPs 40:14 rPs 36:1
[3] Strangers are attacking me;[p]
ruthless men seek my life[q]—
men without regard for God.[r] *Selah*

54:4 sPs 118:7 tPs 41:12
[4] Surely God is my help;[s]
the Lord is the one who sustains me.[t]

54:5 uPs 94:23 vPs 89:49; 143:12
[5] Let evil recoil[u] on those who slander me;
in your faithfulness[v] destroy them.

54:6 wPs 50:14 xPs 52:9
[6] I will sacrifice a freewill offering[w] to you;
I will praise your name, O LORD,
for it is good.[x]
54:7 yPs 34:6 zPs 59:10
[7] For he has delivered me[y] from all my troubles,
and my eyes have looked in triumph on my foes.[z]

Psalm 55

For the director of music. With stringed instruments.
A *maskil*[a] of David.

[1] Listen to my prayer, O God,
55:1 aPs 27:9; 61:1
do not ignore my plea;[a]
55:2 bPs 66:19 cPs 77:3; Isa 38:14
[2] hear me and answer me.[b]
My thoughts trouble me and I am distraught[c]
[3] at the voice of the enemy,
at the stares of the wicked;
55:3 d2Sa 16:6-8; Ps 17:9 ePs 71:11
for they bring down suffering upon me[d]
and revile me in their anger.[e]

[4] My heart is in anguish within me;
55:4 fPs 116:3
the terrors[f] of death assail me.
55:5 gJob 21:6; Ps 119:120
[5] Fear and trembling[g] have beset me;
horror has overwhelmed me.
[6] I said, "Oh, that I had the wings of a dove!
I would fly away and be at rest—
[7] I would flee far away
and stay in the desert; *Selah*
[8] I would hurry to my place of shelter,
55:8 hIsa 4:6
far from the tempest and storm.[h]"

[a] Title: Probably a literary or musical term

54:5 For commentary on expressions of vengeful attitudes toward enemies, see the note on 69:22–28. See also "Curses and Imprecations" on page 883 and "Trees of Ancient Israel" on page 1357.

[9]Confuse the wicked, O Lord, confound their
speech,
for I see violence and strife[i] in the city.
[10]Day and night they prowl about on its walls;
malice and abuse are within it.
[11]Destructive forces[j] are at work in the city;
threats and lies[k] never leave its streets.

[12]If an enemy were insulting me,
I could endure it;
if a foe were raising himself against me,
I could hide from him.
[13]But it is you, a man like myself,
my companion, my close friend,[l]
[14]with whom I once enjoyed sweet fellowship
as we walked with the throng at the house
of God.[m]

[15]Let death take my enemies by surprise;[n]
let them go down alive to the grave,[a][o]
for evil finds lodging among them.

[16]But I call to God,
and the LORD saves me.
[17]Evening,[p] morning[q] and noon
I cry out in distress,
and he hears my voice.
[18]He ransoms me unharmed
from the battle waged against me,
even though many oppose me.
[19]God, who is enthroned forever,[r]
will hear[s] them and afflict them— *Selah*
men who never change their ways
and have no fear of God.

[20]My companion attacks his friends;[t]
he violates his covenant.[u]
[21]His speech is smooth as butter,
yet war is in his heart;
his words are more soothing than oil,[v]
yet they are drawn swords.[w]

[22]Cast your cares on the LORD
and he will sustain you;[x]
he will never let the righteous fall.[y]
[23]But you, O God, will bring down the wicked
into the pit[z] of corruption;
bloodthirsty and deceitful men[a]
will not live out half their days.[b]

But as for me, I trust in you.[c]

55:9 [i]Jer 6:7
55:11 [j]Ps 5:9 [k]Ps 10:7
55:13 [l]2Sa 15:12; Ps 41:9
55:14 [m]Ps 42:4
55:15 [n]Ps 64:7 [o]Nu 16:30,33
55:17 [p]Ps 141:2; Ac 3:1 [q]Ps 5:3
55:19 [r]Dt 33:27 [s]Ps 78:59
55:20 [t]Ps 7:4 [u]Ps 89:34
55:21 [v]Pr 5:3 [w]Ps 28:3; 57:4; 59:7
55:22 [x]Ps 37:5; Mt 6:25-34; 1Pe 5:7 [y]Ps 37:24
55:23 [z]Ps 73:18 [a]Ps 5:6 [b]Job 15:32; Pr 10:27 [c]Ps 25:2

[a] 15 Hebrew *Sheol*

55:21 Still today, after milk has been churned and butter produced, the butter is boiled and the curds separated from the almost pure oil. This is then poured into a goatskin and kept until slightly rancid (to Western taste). It is used with food but more generally for frying eggs or vegetables.

Psalm 56

For the director of music. To ⌞the tune of⌟ "A Dove on Distant Oaks." Of David. A *miktam*.[a] When the Philistines had seized him in Gath.

56:1 [d]Ps 57:1-3 — 1 Be merciful to me, O God, for men hotly pursue me;[d]
all day long they press their attack.
56:2 [e]Ps 57:3 [f]Ps 35:1 — 2 My slanderers pursue me all day long;[e]
many are attacking me in their pride.[f]

56:3 [g]Ps 55:4-5 — 3 When I am afraid,[g]
I will trust in you.
4 In God, whose word I praise,
in God I trust; I will not be afraid.
56:4 [h]Ps 118:6; Heb 13:6 — What can mortal man do to me?[h]

56:5 [i]Ps 41:7 — 5 All day long they twist my words;[i]
they are always plotting to harm me.
56:6 [j]Ps 59:3 [k]Ps 71:10 — 6 They conspire,[j] they lurk,
they watch my steps,
eager to take my life.[k]

7 On no account let them escape;
56:7 [l]Ps 36:12; 55:23 — in your anger, O God, bring down the nations.[l]
8 Record my lament;
list my tears on your scroll[b]—
56:8 [m]Mal 3:16 — are they not in your record?[m]

56:9 [n]Ps 9:3 [o]Ps 102:2 [p]Ro 8:31 — 9 Then my enemies will turn back[n]
when I call for help.[o]
By this I will know that God is for me.[p]
10 In God, whose word I praise,
in the LORD, whose word I praise—
11 in God I trust; I will not be afraid.
What can man do to me?

56:12 [q]Ps 50:14 — 12 I am under vows[q] to you, O God;
I will present my thank offerings to you.
56:13 [r]Ps 116:8 [s]Job 33:30 — 13 For you have delivered me[c] from death[r]
and my feet from stumbling,
that I may walk before God
in the light of life.[d][s]

Psalm 57

For the director of music. ⌞To the tune of⌟ "Do Not Destroy." Of David. A *miktam*.[a] When he had fled from Saul into the cave.

1 Have mercy on me, O God, have mercy on me,
57:1 [t]Ps 2:12 [u]Ps 17:8 [v]Isa 26:20 — for in you my soul takes refuge.[t]
I will take refuge in the shadow of your wings[u]
until the disaster has passed.[v]

2 I cry out to God Most High,
57:2 [w]Ps 138:8 — to God, who fulfills ⌞his purpose⌟ for me.[w]

[a] Title: Probably a literary or musical term [b] 8 Or *I put my tears in your wineskin* [c] 13 Or *my soul* [d] 13 Or *the land of the living*

56:8 "Scroll" interpretively translates a Hebrew word ordinarily meaning "wineskin." The literal meaning of the Hebrew clause is "put my tears in your wineskin" (see the NIV text note). This image seems to reflect the practice in the arid climate of Israel of preserving precious liquids in a leak-proof, leather bag. The image of saving tears is powerful; David's tears of lament were precious to God.

[3] He sends from heaven and saves me,[x]
rebuking those who hotly pursue me;[y] *Selah*
God sends his love and his faithfulness.[z]

[4] I am in the midst of lions;[a]
I lie among ravenous beasts—
men whose teeth are spears and arrows,
whose tongues are sharp swords.[b]

[5] Be exalted, O God, above the heavens;
let your glory be over all the earth.[c]

[6] They spread a net for my feet—
I was bowed down[d] in distress.
They dug a pit[e] in my path—
but they have fallen into it themselves.[f] *Selah*

[7] My heart is steadfast, O God,
my heart is steadfast;[g]
I will sing and make music.
[8] Awake, my soul!
Awake, harp and lyre![h]
I will awaken the dawn.

[9] I will praise you, O Lord, among the nations;
I will sing of you among the peoples.
[10] For great is your love, reaching to the heavens;
your faithfulness reaches to the skies.[i]

[11] Be exalted, O God, above the heavens;
let your glory be over all the earth.[j]

57:3 [x]Ps 18:9,16 [y]Ps 56:1 [z]Ps 40:11
57:4 [a]Ps 35:17 [b]Ps 55:21; Pr 30:14
57:5 [c]Ps 108:5
57:6 [d]Ps 145:14 [e]Ps 35:7 [f]Ps 7:15; Pr 28:10
57:7 [g]Ps 108:1
57:8 [h]Ps 16:9; 30:12; 150:3
57:10 [i]Ps 36:5; 103:11
57:11 [j]ver 5

Psalm 58

For the director of music. ⌊To the tune of⌋ "Do Not Destroy." Of David. A *miktam.*[a]

[1] Do you rulers indeed speak justly?[k]
Do you judge uprightly among men?
[2] No, in your heart you devise injustice,
and your hands mete out violence on the earth.[l]
[3] Even from birth the wicked go astray;
from the womb they are wayward and speak lies.
[4] Their venom is like the venom of a snake,[m]
like that of a cobra that has stopped its ears,
[5] that will not heed the tune of the charmer,
however skillful the enchanter may be.

[6] Break the teeth in their mouths, O God;[n]
tear out, O LORD, the fangs of the lions![o]
[7] Let them vanish like water that flows away;[p]
when they draw the bow, let their arrows be blunted.[q]

58:1 [k]Ps 82:2
58:2 [l]Ps 94:20; Mal 3:15
58:4 [m]Ps 140:3; Ecc 10:11
58:6 [n]Ps 3:7 [o]Job 4:10
58:7 [p]Jos 7:5; Ps 112:10 [q]Ps 64:3

[a] Title: Probably a literary or musical term

57:7 For "heart," see the note on 4:7.
57:8 The harp and lyre (here personified) were instruments used to praise the Lord at his temple in celebration of deliverance (see "Ancient Musical Instruments" on p. 797). Dawn, too, is here personified—the Canaanites even deified it.
58:1 Concern for the just use of judicial power is pervasive throughout the Old Testament. This was the primary agency in the administrative structures of the ancient Near East for the protection of the innocent, usually the poor and powerless, against the assaults of the unscrupulous, usually the rich and powerful. Israelite society was troubled with the corruption of this judicial power from the days of Samuel until the end of the monarchy. Even in David's time all was not well.
58:6–8 The author used imagery drawn from conventional curses of the ancient Near East (see the note on 10:7; see also "Curses and Imprecations" on p. 883).

8 Like a slug melting away as it moves along,
58:8 [r]Job 3:16
like a stillborn child,[r] may they not see the sun.
58:9 [s]Ps 118:12 [t]Pr 10:25
9 Before your pots can feel ⌞the heat of⌟ the thorns[s]—
whether they be green or dry—the wicked will be swept away.[a][t]
58:10 [u]Ps 64:10; 91:8 [v]Ps 68:23
10 The righteous will be glad when they are avenged,[u]
when they bathe their feet in the blood of the wicked.[v]
11 Then men will say,
"Surely the righteous still are rewarded;
58:11 [w]Ps 9:8; 18:20
surely there is a God who judges the earth."[w]

Psalm 59

For the director of music. ⌞To the tune of⌟ "Do Not Destroy." Of David. A *miktam.*[b]
When Saul had sent men to watch David's house in order to kill him.

59:1 [x]Ps 143:9
1 Deliver me from my enemies, O God;[x]
protect me from those who rise up against me.
2 Deliver me from evildoers
59:2 [y]Ps 139:19
and save me from bloodthirsty men.[y]
3 See how they lie in wait for me!
59:3 [z]Ps 56:6
Fierce men conspire[z] against me
for no offense or sin of mine, O LORD.
59:4 [a]Ps 35:19, 23
4 I have done no wrong, yet they are ready to attack me.[a]
Arise to help me; look on my plight!
5 O LORD God Almighty, the God of Israel,
rouse yourself to punish all the nations;
59:5 [b]Jer 18:23
show no mercy to wicked traitors.[b] *Selah*

6 They return at evening,
59:6 [c]ver 14
snarling like dogs,[c]
and prowl about the city.
7 See what they spew from their mouths—
59:7 [d]Ps 57:4 [e]Ps 10:11
they spew out swords[d] from their lips,
and they say, "Who can hear us?"[e]
59:8 [f]Ps 37:13; Pr 1:26 [g]Ps 2:4
8 But you, O LORD, laugh at them;[f]
you scoff at all those nations.[g]

9 O my Strength, I watch for you;
59:9 [h]Ps 9:9; 62:2
you, O God, are my fortress,[h] 10 my loving God.

God will go before me
and will let me gloat over those who slander me.
59:11 [i]Ps 84:9 [j]Dt 4:9 [k]Ps 106:27
11 But do not kill them, O Lord our shield,[c][i]
or my people will forget.[j]
In your might make them wander about,
and bring them down.[k]
59:12 [l]Ps 10:7 [m]Pr 12:13 [n]Zep 3:11
12 For the sins of their mouths,[l]
for the words of their lips,[m]
let them be caught in their pride.[n]
For the curses and lies they utter,
13 consume them in wrath,
59:13 [o]Ps 104:35
consume them till they are no more.[o]

[a] 9 The meaning of the Hebrew for this verse is uncertain. [b] Title: Probably a literary or musical term [c] 11 Or *sovereign*

58:9 Twigs from wild thornbushes were used as fuel for quick heat (see 118:12; Ecc 7:6).
58:10 The picture of splashing joyfully about in an enemy's blood (v. 10) is a traditional Biblical image—borrowed from ancient Near Eastern literature—for victory over an enemy (see 68:21–23; Isa 63:2–3; Eze 28:23; Rev 14:19–20).

Then it will be known to the ends of the earth
that God rules over Jacob.[p] *Selah* 59:13 [p]Ps 83:18

14 They return at evening,
snarling like dogs,
and prowl about the city.
15 They wander about for food[q] 59:15 [q]Job 15:23
and howl if not satisfied.
16 But I will sing of your strength,[r] 59:16 [r]Ps 21:13
in the morning[s] I will sing of your love;[t] [s]Ps 88:13 [t]Ps 101:1 [u]Ps 46:1
for you are my fortress,
my refuge in times of trouble.[u]

17 O my Strength, I sing praise to you;
you, O God, are my fortress, my loving God.

Psalm 60

For the director of music. To ⌞the tune of⌟ "The Lily of the Covenant."
A *miktam*[a] of David. For teaching. When he fought Aram Naharaim[b] and Aram Zobah,[c]
and when Joab returned and struck down twelve thousand Edomites in the Valley of Salt.

1 You have rejected us,[v] O God, and burst forth upon us; 60:1 [v]2Sa 5:20; Ps 44:9 [w]Ps 79:5 [x]Ps 80:3
you have been angry[w]—now restore us![x]
2 You have shaken the land[y] and torn it open; 60:2 [y]Ps 18:7 [z]2Ch 7:14
mend its fractures,[z] for it is quaking.
3 You have shown your people desperate times;[a] 60:3 [a]Ps 71:20 [b]Isa 51:17; Jer 25:16
you have given us wine that makes us stagger.[b]

4 But for those who fear you, you have raised a banner
to be unfurled against the bow. *Selah*

5 Save us and help us with your right hand,[c] 60:5 [c]Ps 17:7; 108:6 [d]Ps 127:2
that those you love[d] may be delivered.
6 God has spoken from his sanctuary:
"In triumph I will parcel out Shechem[e] 60:6 [e]Ge 12:6
and measure off the Valley of Succoth.
7 Gilead[f] is mine, and Manasseh is mine; 60:7 [f]Jos 13:31 [g]Dt 33:17 [h]Ge 49:10
Ephraim is my helmet,
Judah[g] my scepter.[h]
8 Moab is my washbasin,
upon Edom I toss my sandal;
over Philistia I shout in triumph.[i]" 60:8 [i]2Sa 8:1

9 Who will bring me to the fortified city?
Who will lead me to Edom?
10 Is it not you, O God, you who have rejected us
and no longer go out with our armies?[j] 60:10 [j]Jos 7:12; Ps 44:9; 108:11

[a] Title: Probably a literary or musical term [b] Title: That is, Arameans of Northwest Mesopotamia [c] Title: That is, Arameans of central Syria

60:6 Shechem and Succoth are representative of the territory west and east of the Jordan taken over by the Lord and Israel. (See "Succoth/Tell Deir Alla" on p. 56 and "Shechem" on p. 340.)

60:7 Half of Manasseh was established in Gilead, east of the Jordan, and half of it west of the Jordan, just north of Ephraim (see Jos 13:29–31; 17:5–11). This once again evidenced that the Lord's kingdom included territory on both sides of the river. Ephraim and Judah were the two leading tribes of Israel, the one representative of the Rachel tribes (Ephraim) in the north and the other of the Leah tribes (Judah) in the south. Together they represented all Israel (Isa 11:13; Zec 9:13).

60:8 Moab, Edom and Philistia were perpetual enemies situated on Israel's eastern, southern and western borders, respectively. The metaphor "Moab is my washbasin" reduced Moab to a household vessel in which the Lord washed his feet (Ge 18:4). This imagery may have been suggested by the fact that Moab lay along the eastern shore of the Dead Sea.

Tossing one's sandal perhaps refers to the conventional, symbolic act by which an individual claimed possession of land (see Ru 4:7 and its note).

60:11 [k]Ps 146:3
11 Give us aid against the enemy,
for the help of man is worthless.[k]

60:12 [l]Nu 24:18; Ps 44:5
12 With God we will gain the victory,
and he will trample down our enemies.[l]

Psalm 61

For the director of music. With stringed instruments. Of David.

61:1 [m]Ps 64:1 [n]Ps 86:6
1 Hear my cry, O God;[m]
listen to my prayer.[n]

61:2 [o]Ps 77:3 [p]Ps 18:2
2 From the ends of the earth I call to you,
I call as my heart grows faint;[o]
lead me to the rock[p] that is higher than I.

61:3 [q]Ps 62:7 [r]Pr 18:10
3 For you have been my refuge,[q]
a strong tower against the foe.[r]

61:4 [s]Ps 23:6 [t]Ps 91:4
4 I long to dwell[s] in your tent forever
and take refuge in the shelter of your wings.[t] *Selah*

61:5 [u]Ps 56:12 [v]Ps 86:11
5 For you have heard my vows,[u] O God;
you have given me the heritage of those who fear your name.[v]

61:6 [w]Ps 21:4
6 Increase the days of the king's life,
his years for many generations.[w]

61:7 [x]Ps 41:12 [y]Ps 40:11
7 May he be enthroned in God's presence forever;[x]
appoint your love and faithfulness to protect him.[y]

61:8 [z]Ps 65:1; 71:22
8 Then will I ever sing praise to your name[z]
and fulfill my vows day after day.

Psalm 62

For the director of music. For Jeduthun. A psalm of David.

62:1 [a]Ps 33:20
1 My soul finds rest[a] in God alone;
my salvation comes from him.

62:2 [b]Ps 89:26
2 He alone is my rock[b] and my salvation;
he is my fortress, I will never be shaken.

62:3 [c]Isa 30:13
3 How long will you assault a man?
Would all of you throw him down—
this leaning wall,[c] this tottering fence?

62:4 [d]Ps 28:3
4 They fully intend to topple him
from his lofty place;
they take delight in lies.
With their mouths they bless,
but in their hearts they curse.[d] *Selah*

5 Find rest, O my soul, in God alone;
my hope comes from him.
6 He alone is my rock and my salvation;
he is my fortress, I will not be shaken.

62:7 [e]Ps 46:1; 85:9; Jer 3:23
7 My salvation and my honor depend on God[a];
he is my mighty rock, my refuge.[e]

[a] 7 Or / *God Most High is my salvation and my honor*

61:2 The phrase "ends of the earth" as used here may refer to the brink of the netherworld—the grave. For "heart," see the note on 4:7.
61:6–7 This prayer for the king's long life may have been made by the king himself—such transitions to the third person are known from the literature of the ancient Near East—or it may have been the prayer of the people, perhaps voiced by a priest or Levite.

8 Trust in him at all times, O people;
pour out your hearts to him,[f]
for God is our refuge. *Selah*

9 Lowborn men are but a breath,[g]
the highborn are but a lie;
if weighed on a balance,[h] they are nothing;
together they are only a breath.
10 Do not trust in extortion
or take pride in stolen goods;[i]
though your riches increase,
do not set your heart on them.[j]

11 One thing God has spoken,
two things have I heard:
that you, O God, are strong,
12 and that you, O Lord, are loving.
Surely you will reward each person
according to what he has done.[k]

62:8 [f]1Sa 1:15; Ps 42:4; La 2:19
62:9 [g]Ps 39:5,11 [h]Isa 40:15
62:10 [i]Isa 61:8 [j]Job 31:25; 1Ti 6:6-10
62:12 [k]Job 34:11; Mt 16:27

Psalm 63

A psalm of David. When he was in the Desert of Judah.

1 O God, you are my God,
earnestly I seek you;
my soul thirsts for you,[l]
my body longs for you,
in a dry and weary land
where there is no water.

2 I have seen you in the sanctuary[m]
and beheld your power and your glory.
3 Because your love is better than life,[n]
my lips will glorify you.
4 I will praise you as long as I live,[o]
and in your name I will lift up my hands.[p]
5 My soul will be satisfied as with the richest of foods;[q]
with singing lips my mouth will praise you.

6 On my bed I remember you;
I think of you through the watches of the night.[r]
7 Because you are my help,[s]
I sing in the shadow of your wings.
8 My soul clings to you;
your right hand upholds me.[t]

9 They who seek my life will be destroyed;[u]
they will go down to the depths of the earth.[v]
10 They will be given over to the sword
and become food for jackals.

11 But the king will rejoice in God;
all who swear by God's name will praise him,[w]
while the mouths of liars will be silenced.

63:1 [l]Ps 42:2; 84:2
63:2 [m]Ps 27:4
63:3 [n]Ps 69:16
63:4 [o]Ps 104:33 [p]Ps 28:2
63:5 [q]Ps 36:8
63:6 [r]Ps 42:8
63:7 [s]Ps 27:9
63:8 [t]Ps 18:35
63:9 [u]Ps 40:14 [v]Ps 55:15
63:11 [w]Dt 6:13; Ps 21:1; Isa 45:23

62:10 For "heart," see the note on 4:7.
63:9 Here "earth" refers to the netherworld (i.e., the grave).
63:10 A proper burial was considered important, and to have one's body simply discarded was a terrible fate that brought scorn and disgrace.

Psalm 64

For the director of music.
A psalm of David.

64:1 [x]Ps 55:2 [y]Ps 140:1
1 Hear me, O God, as I voice my complaint;[x]
protect my life from the threat of the enemy.[y]
64:2 [z]Ps 56:6; 59:2
2 Hide me from the conspiracy of the wicked,[z]
from that noisy crowd of evildoers.

3 They sharpen their tongues like swords
64:3 [a]Ps 58:7
and aim their words like deadly arrows.[a]
64:4 [b]Ps 11:2 [c]Ps 55:19
4 They shoot from ambush at the innocent man;[b]
they shoot at him suddenly, without fear.[c]

5 They encourage each other in evil plans,
they talk about hiding their snares;
64:5 [d]Ps 10:11
they say, "Who will see them[a]?"[d]
6 They plot injustice and say,
"We have devised a perfect plan!"
Surely the mind and heart of man are cunning.

7 But God will shoot them with arrows;
suddenly they will be struck down.
64:8 [e]Ps 9:3; Pr 18:7 [f]Ps 22:7
8 He will turn their own tongues against them[e]
and bring them to ruin;
all who see them will shake their heads[f] in scorn.

9 All mankind will fear;
they will proclaim the works of God
64:9 [g]Jer 51:10
and ponder what he has done.[g]
10 Let the righteous rejoice in the LORD
64:10 [h]Ps 25:20 [i]Ps 32:11
and take refuge in him;[h]
let all the upright in heart praise him![i]

Psalm 65

For the director of music.
A psalm of David. A song.

1 Praise awaits[b] you, O God, in Zion;
65:1 [j]Ps 116:18
to you our vows will be fulfilled.[j]
2 O you who hear prayer,
65:2 [k]Isa 66:23
to you all men will come.[k]
65:3 [l]Ps 38:4 [m]Heb 9:14
3 When we were overwhelmed by sins,[l]
you forgave[c] our transgressions.[m]
65:4 [n]Ps 4:3; 33:12 [o]Ps 36:8
4 Blessed are those you choose[n]
and bring near to live in your courts!
We are filled with the good things of your house,[o]
of your holy temple.

5 You answer us with awesome deeds of
righteousness,
65:5 [p]Ps 85:4 [q]Ps 107:23
O God our Savior,[p]
the hope of all the ends of the earth
and of the farthest seas,[q]
6 who formed the mountains by your power,
65:6 [r]Ps 93:1
having armed yourself with strength,[r]

[a] 5 Or *us* [b] 1 Or *befits*; the meaning of the Hebrew for this word is uncertain. [c] 3 Or *made atonement for*

ANCIENT TEXTS AND ARTIFACTS

A Ugaritic Prayer for a City Under Siege

PSALM 65 In the ancient Near East warfare was frequent and often came close to home. Thus it is not surprising that religious texts from the ancient world often include prayers for victory over enemies.[1] Psalms such as Psalm 65 reflect this tendency: David either prayed for victory for himself or for Jerusalem.

A **Ugaritic** text gives us insight into how followers of Baal sought the aid of their god in times of war. This text is known as RS 24.266 ("RS" stands for "Ras Shamra," the place at which the Ugaritic tablets were discovered).[2]

The Nature of the Ugaritic Prayer Text

This text has two parts:

- *A prose portion* describes how the rituals for seeking Baal's help against enemies were to be conducted. Among other stipulations, the instructions include directions about the appropriate dates for such ritual prayers, as well as about which animals were to be offered on those dates.
- *A poetic portion* provides the prayer that was to be recited. It appeals for Baal to protect the walls of the city and devotes considerable attention to promises by the people to make various sacrifices to Baal if he would defend the city during a time of war. Some scholars suggest that the prayer includes a promise to make a human sacrifice to Baal,[3] but the text is unclear and more likely denotes an animal sacrifice.

The Value of the Ugaritic Prayer Text

This text is helpful for Biblical readers for several reasons:

- It illustrates the fact that ancient texts could be quite complex, containing both prose ritual instruction and poetic liturgy. Biblical scholars sometimes argue that a passage containing both prose and poetry must have been written by at least two authors. This wrongly assumes that ancient writers never produced complex texts: We see clear evidence in the Ugaritic texts that they did.[4]
- The content of the Ugaritic prayer, calling for help from one's god, is paralleled in David's prayer for Zion in Psalm 65. The Ugaritic text is older than the Biblical psalm, indicating that there is no reason to suppose that the psalms and prayers should be treated as late compositions (many reject the idea of Davidic authorship for the psalms and argue that these sophisticated prayers and liturgies must have come from a very late date). If such prayer-texts existed prior to David's time, there is no reason to think they could not have existed during this period.
- The Ugaritic text reminds us that the enemies the psalmist faced were not metaphors for spiritual struggles but flesh and blood foes who sought to kill the Israelites and destroy their cities. The Ugaritic prayer is clearly about real warfare.
- The theological content of the Ugaritic prayer over against the Biblical psalms is illuminating. In the Ugaritic text Baal is to some extent bribed with promises of bounteous sacrifices. Such an approach is explicitly rejected in the Bible (e.g., 51:16–19). Instead, the psalmists appeal to God's righteousness and covenant faithfulness, as in 65:4–5. No one can buy off the God of the Bible!

Slings and slingstones from Lachish

Preserving Bible Times; © Dr. James C. Martin; permission of The British Museum

[1]See also "Songs of Warriors" on page 474. [2]See "Ugarit/Ras Shamra" on page 819. [3]See "Human Sacrifice in the Ancient Near East" on page 182. [4]See also "The Bulletin and Poetic Accounts of the Battle of Kadesh" on page 353.

65:7 [s]Mt 8:26 [t]Isa 17:12-13

7 who stilled the roaring of the seas,[s]
the roaring of their waves,
and the turmoil of the nations.[t]
8 Those living far away fear your wonders;
where morning dawns and evening fades
you call forth songs of joy.

65:9 [u]Ps 68:9-10 [v]Ps 46:4; 104:14

9 You care for the land and water it;[u]
you enrich it abundantly.
The streams of God are filled with water
to provide the people with grain,[v]
for so you have ordained it.[a]
10 You drench its furrows
and level its ridges;
you soften it with showers
and bless its crops.
11 You crown the year with your bounty,
and your carts overflow with abundance.

65:12 [w]Job 28:26

12 The grasslands of the desert overflow;[w]
the hills are clothed with gladness.

65:13 [x]Ps 144:13 [y]Ps 72:16 [z]Ps 98:8; Isa 55:12

13 The meadows are covered with flocks[x]
and the valleys are mantled with grain;[y]
they shout for joy and sing.[z]

Psalm 66

For the director of music.
A song. A psalm.

66:1 [a]Ps 100:1

1 Shout with joy to God, all the earth![a]

66:2 [b]Ps 79:9

2 Sing the glory of his name;[b]
make his praise glorious!

66:3 [c]Ps 65:5 [d]Ps 18:44

3 Say to God, "How awesome are your deeds![c]
So great is your power
that your enemies cringe[d] before you.

66:4 [e]Ps 22:27 [f]Ps 67:3

4 All the earth bows down[e] to you;
they sing praise[f] to you,
they sing praise to your name." *Selah*

5 Come and see what God has done,

66:5 [g]Ps 106:22

how awesome his works[g] in man's behalf!

66:6 [h]Ex 14:22

6 He turned the sea into dry land,[h]
they passed through the waters on foot—
come, let us rejoice in him.

66:7 [i]Ps 145:13 [j]Ps 11:4 [k]Ps 140:8

7 He rules forever[i] by his power,
his eyes watch[j] the nations—
let not the rebellious[k] rise up against him. *Selah*

66:8 [l]Ps 98:4

8 Praise[l] our God, O peoples,
let the sound of his praise be heard;
9 he has preserved our lives

66:9 [m]Ps 121:3

and kept our feet from slipping.[m]

[a] 9 Or *for that is how you prepare the land*

65:7 God's stilling the turmoil of the nations is compared to his taming the turbulence of the primeval waters of chaos (see the note on 32:6).

10 For you, O God, tested us;
you refined us like silver.[n]
11 You brought us into prison
and laid burdens[o] on our backs.
12 You let men ride over our heads;[p]
we went through fire and water,
but you brought us to a place of abundance.[q]

13 I will come to your temple with burnt offerings
and fulfill my vows[r] to you—
14 vows my lips promised and my mouth spoke
when I was in trouble.
15 I will sacrifice fat animals to you
and an offering of rams;
I will offer bulls and goats.[s] *Selah*

16 Come and listen,[t] all you who fear God;
let me tell[u] you what he has done for me.
17 I cried out to him with my mouth;
his praise was on my tongue.
18 If I had cherished sin in my heart,
the Lord would not have listened;[v]
19 but God has surely listened
and heard my voice[w] in prayer.
20 Praise be to God,
who has not rejected[x] my prayer
or withheld his love from me!

66:10 [n]Ps 17:3; Isa 48:10; Zec 13:9; 1Pe 1:6-7
66:11 [o]La 1:13
66:12 [p]Isa 51:23 [q]Isa 43:2
66:13 [r]Ecc 5:4
66:15 [s]Nu 6:14; Ps 51:19
66:16 [t]Ps 34:11 [u]Ps 71:15,24
66:18 [v]Job 36:21; Isa 1:15; Jas 4:3
66:19 [w]Ps 116:1-2
66:20 [x]Ps 22:24; 68:35

66:11–12 "Prison," "burdens" and "ride over" all describe Israel's suffering: captives thrown into prison, prisoners of war turned into slaves and defeated troops overrun by a chariot force.

Selah

PSALM 66 The Hebrew word *Selah* occurs 74 times in the Old Testament, often at the ends of stanzas within psalms or at the ends of entire psalms. Three of these occurrences appear in the prayer song of Habakkuk 3. While scholars concur that this is a musical term, there is little agreement as to its precise meaning.

✣ Some suggest that *Selah* is derived from *salal*, which means "to lift up." If this is correct, *Selah* could be an instruction either to raise the voice or to increase the instrumental volume during an interlude.

✣ Some take it to indicate a pause or breath in singing, perhaps reflecting an understanding of the instrumental interlude above.

✣ Some posit that *Selah* marks an affirmation of what has just been sung—much like *Amen* in later Judaism and Christianity.

The presence of musical directions within the Psalms reminds modern readers that these compositions were not intended simply to be read but were for Israel a part of a total, vibrant worship experience.[1]

[1]See also "Ancient Musical Instruments" on page 797.

Psalm 67

For the director of music. With stringed instruments. A psalm. A song.

[1] May God be gracious to us and bless us
67:1 [y]Nu 6:24-26; Ps 4:6 — and make his face shine upon us,[y] *Selah*
[2] that your ways may be known on earth,
67:2 [z]Isa 52:10 [a]Tit 2:11 — your salvation[z] among all nations.[a]

[3] May the peoples praise you, O God;
may all the peoples praise you.
[4] May the nations be glad and sing for joy,
67:4 [b]Ps 96:10-13 — for you rule the peoples justly[b]
and guide the nations of the earth. *Selah*
[5] May the peoples praise you, O God;
may all the peoples praise you.

67:6 [c]Lev 26:4; Ps 85:12; Eze 34:27 — [6] Then the land will yield its harvest,[c]
and God, our God, will bless us.
[7] God will bless us,
67:7 [d]Ps 33:8 — and all the ends of the earth will fear him.[d]

Psalm 68

For the director of music. Of David. A psalm. A song.

[1] May God arise, may his enemies be scattered;
68:1 [e]Nu 10:35; Isa 33:3 — may his foes flee[e] before him.
68:2 [f]Hos 13:3 [g]Isa 9:18; Mic 1:4 — [2] As smoke[f] is blown away by the wind,
may you blow them away;
as wax melts[g] before the fire,
may the wicked perish before God.
[3] But may the righteous be glad
68:3 [h]Ps 32:11 — and rejoice[h] before God;
may they be happy and joyful.

68:4 [i]Ps 66:2 [j]Dt 33:26 [k]Ex 6:3; Ps 83:18 — [4] Sing to God, sing praise to his name,[i]
extol him who rides on the clouds[a][j]—
his name is the LORD[k]—
and rejoice before him.
68:5 [l]Ps 10:14 [m]Dt 10:18 [n]Dt 26:15 — [5] A father to the fatherless,[l] a defender of widows,[m]
is God in his holy dwelling.[n]
68:6 [o]Ps 113:9 [p]Ac 12:6 [q]Ps 107:34 — [6] God sets the lonely in families,[b][o]
he leads forth the prisoners[p] with singing;
but the rebellious live in a sun-scorched land.[q]

68:7 [r]Ex 13:21; Jdg 4:14 — [7] When you went out[r] before your people, O God,
when you marched through the wasteland, *Selah*
[8] the earth shook,
68:8 [s]Jdg 5:4 [t]Ex 19:16,18 — the heavens poured down rain,[s]
before God, the One of Sinai,[t]
before God, the God of Israel.

[a] 4 Or *I prepare the way for him who rides through the deserts* [b] 6 Or *the desolate in a homeland*

68:4 Canaanite literature describes Baal (the Canaanite weather god) as riding on the clouds. Here the point is made that the Lord (Yahweh, not Baal) is the exalted One who truly makes the storm clouds his chariot (see v. 33; 18:9; 104:3; Isa 19:1; Mt 26:64; see also "The Ugaritic Text of the Myth of Baal" on p. 905).
68:5–6 In ancient times adult males represented their families and provided access to the resources society provided. Unattached widows and orphans were at an extreme disadvantage, having no one to secure their rights or basic needs. They were dependent either upon their own abilities to scratch out a meager existence or on acts of charity by compassionate individuals. See "The Care of Widows and Orphans in the Bible and the Ancient Near East" on page 285.

[9] You gave abundant showers,[u] O God;
you refreshed your weary inheritance.
[10] Your people settled in it,
and from your bounty, O God, you provided[v] for the poor.

[11] The Lord announced the word,
and great was the company of those who proclaimed it:
[12] "Kings and armies flee[w] in haste;
in the camps men divide the plunder.
[13] Even while you sleep among the campfires,[a] [x]
the wings of ⌊my⌋ dove are sheathed with silver,
its feathers with shining gold."
[14] When the Almighty[b] scattered[y] the kings in the land,
it was like snow fallen on Zalmon.

[15] The mountains of Bashan are majestic mountains;
rugged are the mountains of Bashan.
[16] Why gaze in envy, O rugged mountains,
at the mountain where God chooses[z] to reign,
where the LORD himself will dwell forever?
[17] The chariots of God are tens of thousands
and thousands of thousands;[a]
the Lord ⌊has come⌋ from Sinai into his sanctuary.
[18] When you ascended on high,
you led captives[b] in your train;
you received gifts from men,[c]
even from[c] the rebellious—
that you,[d] O LORD God, might dwell there.

[19] Praise be to the Lord, to God our Savior,[d]
who daily bears our burdens.[e] *Selah*
[20] Our God is a God who saves;
from the Sovereign LORD comes escape from death.[f]

[21] Surely God will crush the heads[g] of his enemies,
the hairy crowns of those who go on in their sins.
[22] The Lord says, "I will bring them from Bashan;
I will bring them from the depths of the sea,[h]
[23] that you may plunge your feet in the blood of your foes,[i]
while the tongues of your dogs[j] have their share."

[24] Your procession has come into view, O God,
the procession of my God and King into the sanctuary.[k]
[25] In front are the singers, after them the musicians;
with them are the maidens playing tambourines.[l]
[26] Praise God in the great congregation;
praise the LORD in the assembly of Israel.[m]
[27] There is the little tribe[n] of Benjamin, leading them,
there the great throng of Judah's princes,
and there the princes of Zebulun and of Naphtali.

68:9 [u]Dt 11:11
68:10 [v]Ps 74:19
68:12 [w]Jos 10:16
68:13 [x]Ge 49:14
68:14 [y]Jos 10:10
68:16 [z]Dt 12:5
68:17 [a]Dt 33:2; Da 7:10
68:18 [b]Jdg 5:12 [c]Eph 4:8*
68:19 [d]Ps 65:5 [e]Ps 55:22
68:20 [f]Ps 56:13
68:21 [g]Ps 110:5; Hab 3:13
68:22 [h]Nu 21:33
68:23 [i]Ps 58:10 [j]1Ki 21:19
68:24 [k]Ps 63:2
68:25 [l]Jdg 11:34; 1Ch 13:8
68:26 [m]Ps 26:12; Isa 48:1
68:27 [n]1Sa 9:21

[a] 13 Or *saddlebags* [b] 14 Hebrew *Shaddai* [c] 18 Or *gifts for men, / even* [d] 18 Or *they*

68:14 Zalmon was a mountain near Shechem (see Jdg 9:46–48), but some identify it here as Jebel Druze, a dark, volcanic peak east of Bashan.
68:16 The mountains surrounding Bashan (v. 15), including the towering Mount Hermon, are portrayed as being jealous because God has chosen Mount Zion as the seat of his rule, rendering it, symbolically if not literally, the "highest" of mountains (see "Zaphon, Olympus, Sinai and Zion: The Mountain of God" on p. 843).
68:17 God's heavenly host is here likened to a vast chariot force. During the time of the Roman Empire Jesus referred to God's host in terms of "legions" (Mt 26:53).
68:22 For "Bashan," see the note on 22:12. The "depths of the sea" refers to the Mediterranean Sea.

28 Summon your power, O God[a];
show us your strength, O God, as you have done
before.
29 Because of your temple at Jerusalem
kings will bring you gifts.[o]
30 Rebuke the beast among the reeds,
the herd of bulls[p] among the calves of the nations.
Humbled, may it bring bars of silver.
Scatter the nations[q] who delight in war.
31 Envoys will come from Egypt;[r]
Cush[b] will submit herself to God.

32 Sing to God, O kingdoms of the earth,
sing praise to the Lord, *Selah*
33 to him who rides[s] the ancient skies above,
who thunders with mighty voice.[t]
34 Proclaim the power[u] of God,
whose majesty is over Israel,
whose power is in the skies.
35 You are awesome, O God, in your sanctuary;
the God of Israel gives power and strength to
his people.[v]

Praise be to God![w]

68:29 [o]Ps 72:10
68:30 [p]Ps 22:12 [q]Ps 89:10
68:31 [r]Isa 19:19; 45:14
68:33 [s]Ps 18:10 [t]Ps 29:4
68:34 [u]Ps 29:1
68:35 [v]Ps 29:11 [w]Ps 66:20

Psalm 69

For the director of music. To ⌞the tune of⌟ "Lilies." Of David.

1 Save me, O God,
for the waters have come up to my neck.[x]
2 I sink in the miry depths,[y]
where there is no foothold.
I have come into the deep waters;
the floods engulf me.
3 I am worn out calling for help;[z]
my throat is parched.
My eyes fail,[a]
looking for my God.
4 Those who hate me without reason[b]
outnumber the hairs of my head;
many are my enemies without cause,[c]
those who seek to destroy me.
I am forced to restore
what I did not steal.

5 You know my folly,[d] O God;
my guilt is not hidden from you.[e]

6 May those who hope in you
not be disgraced because of me,
O Lord, the LORD Almighty;

69:1 [x]Jnh 2:5
69:2 [y]Ps 40:2
69:3 [z]Ps 6:6 [a]Ps 119:82; Isa 38:14
69:4 [b]Jn 15:25* [c]Ps 35:19; 38:19
69:5 [d]Ps 38:5 [e]Ps 44:21

[a] 28 Many Hebrew manuscripts, Septuagint and Syriac; most Hebrew manuscripts *Your God has summoned power for you*
[b] 31 That is, the upper Nile region

68:29 In ancient times defeated kings brought tribute to their conquerors (see 2Sa 8:2,6,10; 2Ki 3:4).
68:30 The phrase "herd of bulls among the calves" refers to powerful princes who supported the pharaoh, as well as to the lesser princes of other nations. Egypt was representative of the hostile nations because of Israel's past experiences with that world power and because at the time the psalm was composed it was the one great empire on Israel's immediate horizon.

may those who seek you
not be put to shame because of me,
O God of Israel.
7 For I endure scorn for your sake,[f]
and shame covers my face.[g]
8 I am a stranger to my brothers,
an alien to my own mother's sons;[h]
9 for zeal for your house consumes me,[i]
and the insults of those who insult you fall on me.[j]
10 When I weep and fast,[k]
I must endure scorn;
11 when I put on sackcloth,[l]
people make sport of me.
12 Those who sit at the gate mock me,
and I am the song of the drunkards.[m]

13 But I pray to you, O LORD,
in the time of your favor;[n]
in your great love,[o] O God,
answer me with your sure salvation.
14 Rescue me from the mire,
do not let me sink;
deliver me from those who hate me,
from the deep waters.[p]
15 Do not let the floodwaters[q] engulf me
or the depths swallow me up[r]
or the pit close its mouth over me.
16 Answer me, O LORD, out of the goodness of your love;[s]
in your great mercy turn to me.
17 Do not hide your face[t] from your servant;
answer me quickly, for I am in trouble.[u]
18 Come near and rescue me;
redeem[v] me because of my foes.

19 You know how I am scorned,[w] disgraced and shamed;
all my enemies are before you.
20 Scorn has broken my heart
and has left me helpless;
I looked for sympathy, but there was none,
for comforters,[x] but I found none.[y]
21 They put gall in my food
and gave me vinegar for my thirst.[z]

22 May the table set before them become a snare;
may it become retribution and[a] a trap.
23 May their eyes be darkened so they cannot see,
and their backs be bent forever.[a]

69:7 [f]Jer 15:15 [g]Ps 44:15
69:8 [h]Ps 31:11; Isa 53:3
69:9 [i]Jn 2:17* [j]Ps 89:50-51; Ro 15:3*
69:10 [k]Ps 35:13
69:11 [l]Ps 35:13
69:12 [m]Job 30:9
69:13 [n]Isa 49:8; 2Co 6:2 [o]Ps 51:1
69:14 [p]ver 2; Ps 144:7
69:15 [q]Ps 124:4-5 [r]Nu 16:33
69:16 [s]Ps 63:3
69:17 [t]Ps 27:9 [u]Ps 66:14
69:18 [v]Ps 49:15
69:19 [w]Ps 22:6
69:20 [x]Job 16:2 [y]Isa 63:5
69:21 [z]Mt 27:34; Mk 15:23; Jn 19:28-30
69:23 [a]Isa 6:9-10; Ro 11:9-10*

[a] 22 Or *snare / and their fellowship become*

69:20 For "heart," see the note on 4:7.
69:22–28 A number of Old Testament psalms, particularly 2, 37, 69, 79, 109, 139 and 143, contain expressions of an apparent vengeful attitude toward enemies. For some people these expressions constitute one of the "moral difficulties" of the Old Testament. It is helpful to note, however, that: (1) Imprecations are not confined to the Old Testament; therefore, insofar as they constitute a moral problem, that problem pervades the Bible as a whole (cf. Lk 11:37–52; Gal 1:8ff.; Rev 6:10; 18:20; 19:1–6). What we find here is not a reprehensibly low morality but an aspect of the Biblical view of the conflict between good and evil. (2) Many if not all of the imprecatory psalms contain (as well as the imprecation) theological and moral sentiments that we also desire to attain (e.g., 139). We can hardly, then, dismiss these psalms under some blanket condemnation as "Old Testament morality." (3) Old Testament ethics stoutly opposed a hostile and vindictive response to opponents (e.g., Lev 19:14–18). (4) All of the imprecatory psalms except Psalm 137 are prayers. They are addressed to God about opponents, and there

69:24 [b]Ps 79:6
69:25 [c]Mt 23:38 [d]Ac 1:20*
69:26 [e]Isa 53:4; Zec 1:15
69:27 [f]Ne 4:5 [g]Ps 109:14; Isa 26:10
69:28 [h]Ex 32:32-33; Lk 10:20; Php 4:3 [i]Eze 13:9
69:29 [j]Ps 59:1; 70:5
69:30 [k]Ps 28:7 [l]Ps 34:3
69:31 [m]Ps 50:9-13
69:32 [n]Ps 34:2 [o]Ps 22:26
69:33 [p]Ps 12:5; 68:6
69:34 [q]Ps 96:11; 148:1; Isa 44:23; 49:13; 55:12
69:35 [r]Ob 1:17 [s]Ps 51:18; Isa 44:26
69:36 [t]Ps 37:29; 102:28

24 Pour out your wrath[b] on them;
let your fierce anger overtake them.
25 May their place be deserted;[c]
let there be no one to dwell in their tents.[d]
26 For they persecute those you wound
and talk about the pain of those you hurt.[e]
27 Charge them with crime upon crime;[f]
do not let them share in your salvation.[g]
28 May they be blotted out of the book of life[h]
and not be listed with the righteous.[i]

29 I am in pain and distress;
may your salvation, O God, protect me.[j]

30 I will praise God's name in song[k]
and glorify him[l] with thanksgiving.
31 This will please the LORD more than an ox,
more than a bull with its horns and hoofs.[m]
32 The poor will see and be glad[n]—
you who seek God, may your hearts live![o]
33 The LORD hears the needy[p]
and does not despise his captive people.

34 Let heaven and earth praise him,
the seas and all that move in them,[q]
35 for God will save Zion[r]
and rebuild the cities of Judah.[s]
Then people will settle there and possess it;
36 the children of his servants will inherit it,
and those who love his name will dwell there.[t]

Psalm 70

For the director of music. Of David. A petition.

70:1 [u]Ps 40:13
70:2 [v]Ps 35:4 [w]Ps 35:26
70:5 [x]Ps 40:17 [y]Ps 141:1

1 Hasten, O God, to save me;
O LORD, come quickly to help me.[u]
2 May those who seek my life[v]
be put to shame and confusion;
may all who desire my ruin
be turned back in disgrace.[w]
3 May those who say to me, "Aha! Aha!"
turn back because of their shame.
4 But may all who seek you
rejoice and be glad in you;
may those who love your salvation always say,
"Let God be exalted!"

5 Yet I am poor and needy;[x]
come quickly to me,[y] O God.
You are my help and my deliverer;
O LORD, do not delay.

---

is no suggestion in any of them that the psalmist either said any of these things to his adversary or ever intended to take vengeance into his own hands. (5) The imprecatory psalms are full of longing for the vindication of the Lord's good name. Over and over the psalmist's desire was not personal relief but that the Lord should be seen in his goodness and holiness (e.g., 58:11; 83:16–18). (6) Many of the actual imprecations do no more than ask God to do what he has already stated he would do in such situations (e.g., 5:10; 54:5; 79:6–7). (7) There is such a thing as righteous indignation, an attitude which at the least is morally preferable to indifference about evil and human suffering. See also "Curses and Imprecations" on page 883.

Psalm 71

1 In you, O LORD, I have taken refuge;
let me never be put to shame.[z]
2 Rescue me and deliver me in your righteousness;
turn your ear[a] to me and save me.
3 Be my rock of refuge,
to which I can always go;
give the command to save me,
for you are my rock and my fortress.[b]
4 Deliver me, O my God, from the hand of the wicked,[c]
from the grasp of evil and cruel men.

5 For you have been my hope, O Sovereign LORD,
my confidence[d] since my youth.
6 From birth[e] I have relied on you;
you brought me forth from my mother's womb.[f]
I will ever praise[g] you.
7 I have become like a portent[h] to many,
but you are my strong refuge.[i]
8 My mouth[j] is filled with your praise,
declaring your splendor[k] all day long.

9 Do not cast[l] me away when I am old;[m]
do not forsake me when my strength is gone.
10 For my enemies speak against me;
those who wait to kill[n] me conspire[o] together.
11 They say, "God has forsaken him;
pursue him and seize him,
for no one will rescue[p] him."
12 Be not far[q] from me, O God;
come quickly, O my God, to help[r] me.
13 May my accusers perish in shame;
may those who want to harm me
be covered with scorn and disgrace.[s]

14 But as for me, I will always have hope;[t]
I will praise you more and more.
15 My mouth will tell[u] of your righteousness,
of your salvation all day long,
though I know not its measure.
16 I will come and proclaim your mighty acts,[v] O Sovereign LORD;
I will proclaim your righteousness, yours alone.
17 Since my youth, O God, you have taught[w] me,
and to this day I declare your marvelous deeds.[x]
18 Even when I am old and gray,[y]
do not forsake me, O God,
till I declare your power to the next generation,
your might to all who are to come.[z]

19 Your righteousness reaches to the skies,[a] O God,
you who have done great things.[b]
Who, O God, is like you?[c]
20 Though you have made me see troubles,[d] many and bitter,
you will restore[e] my life again;
from the depths of the earth
you will again bring me up.

71:1 [z]Ps 25:2-3; 31:1
71:2 [a]Ps 17:6
71:3 [b]Ps 18:2; 31:2-3; 44:4
71:4 [c]Ps 140:4
71:5 [d]Job 4:6; Jer 17:7
71:6 [e]Ps 22:10 [f]Ps 22:9; Isa 46:3 [g]Ps 9:1; 34:1; 52:9; 119:164; 145:2
71:7 [h]Isa 8:18; 1Co 4:9 [i]2Sa 22:3; Ps 61:3
71:8 [j]Ps 51:15; 63:5 [k]Ps 35:28; 96:6; 104:1
71:9 [l]Ps 51:11 [m]ver 18; Ps 92:14; Isa 46:4
71:10 [n]Ps 10:8; 59:3; Pr 1:18 [o]Ps 31:13; 56:6; Mt 12:14
71:11 [p]Ps 7:2
71:12 [q]Ps 35:22; 38:21 [r]Ps 38:22; 70:1
71:13 [s]ver 24
71:14 [t]Ps 130:7
71:15 [u]Ps 35:28; 40:5
71:16 [v]Ps 106:2
71:17 [w]Dt 4:5 [x]Ps 26:7
71:18 [y]ver 9 [z]Ps 22:30,31; 78:4
71:19 [a]Ps 36:5; 57:10 [b]Ps 126:2; Lk 1:49 [c]Ps 35:10
71:20 [d]Ps 60:3 [e]Hos 6:2

71:21 [f]Ps 18:35 [g]Ps 23:4; 86:17; Isa 12:1; 49:13

[21] You will increase my honor[f]
and comfort[g] me once again.

71:22 [h]Ps 33:2 [i]Ps 92:3; 144:9 [j]2Ki 19:22

[22] I will praise you with the harp[h]
for your faithfulness, O my God;
I will sing praise to you with the lyre,[i]
O Holy One of Israel.[j]
[23] My lips will shout for joy
when I sing praise to you—
I, whom you have redeemed.[k]
[24] My tongue will tell of your righteous acts
all day long,[l]
for those who wanted to harm me[m]
have been put to shame and confusion.

71:23 [k]Ps 103:4

71:24 [l]Ps 35:28 [m]ver 13

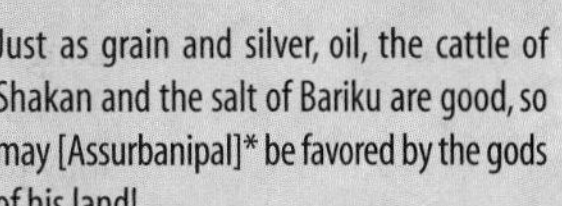

Ancient Voices

Just as grain and silver, oil, the cattle of Shakan and the salt of Bariku are good, so may [Assurbanipal]* be favored by the gods of his land!

May eloquence, understanding, truth and justice be granted him as a gift!

May the [population]** of Assur buy thirty kor of grain for one shekel of silver! May the [population] of Assur buy three seah of oil for one shekel of silver! May the [population] of Assur buy thirty minas of wool for one shekel of silver!

*Alternative spelling of name

**Words in brackets added by translator for clarity or where text has gaps

—Ashurbanipal's Coronation Hymn

See "The Coronation of Ashurbanipal" article on the next page.

Psalm 72

Of Solomon.

[1] Endow the king with your justice, O God,
the royal son with your righteousness.
[2] He will[a] judge your people in
righteousness,[n]
your afflicted ones with justice.
[3] The mountains will bring prosperity to the people,
the hills the fruit of righteousness.
[4] He will defend the afflicted among the people
and save the children of the needy;[o]
he will crush the oppressor.

72:2 [n]Isa 9:7; 11:4-5; 32:1

72:4 [o]Isa 11:4

[5] He will endure[b] as long as the sun,
as long as the moon, through all generations.
[6] He will be like rain[p] falling on a mown field,
like showers watering the earth.
[7] In his days the righteous will flourish;[q]
prosperity will abound till the moon is no more.

72:6 [p]Dt 32:2; Hos 6:3

72:7 [q]Ps 92:12; Isa 2:4

[8] He will rule from sea to sea
and from the River[c][r] to the ends of the earth.[d][s]
[9] The desert tribes will bow before him
and his enemies will lick the dust.
[10] The kings of Tarshish and of distant shores
will bring tribute to him;
the kings of Sheba[t] and Seba
will present him gifts.[u]
[11] All kings will bow down to him
and all nations will serve him.

72:8 [r]Ex 23:31 [s]Zec 9:10

72:10 [t]Ge 10:7 [u]2Ch 9:24

[12] For he will deliver the needy who cry out,
the afflicted who have no one to help.
[13] He will take pity on the weak and the needy
and save the needy from death.

[a] *2* Or *May he*; similarly in verses 3-11 and 17 [b] *5* Septuagint; Hebrew *You will be feared* [c] *8* That is, the Euphrates
[d] *8* Or *the end of the land*

71:22 For "harp" and "lyre," see the note on 57:8.
72:10 Tarshish was a distant Mediterranean seaport, possibly Tartessus in Spain (see "Where Was Tarshish?" on p. 1475). For Sheba, see the note on 1 Kings 10:1. Seba is elsewhere associated with Cush (Ge 10:7; Isa 43:3) and may refer to a region in modern Sudan, south of Egypt.

[14] He will rescue[v] them from oppression and violence,
for precious[w] is their blood in his sight.

[15] Long may he live!
May gold from Sheba[x] be given him.
May people ever pray for him
and bless him all day long.
[16] Let grain abound throughout the land;
on the tops of the hills may it sway.
Let its fruit flourish like Lebanon;[y]
let it thrive like the grass of the field.
[17] May his name endure forever;[z]
may it continue as long as the sun.[a]

All nations will be blessed through him,
and they will call him blessed.[b]

[18] Praise be to the LORD God, the God of Israel,[c]
who alone does marvelous deeds.[d]
[19] Praise be to his glorious name forever;
may the whole earth be filled with his glory.[e]
Amen and Amen.[f]

[20] This concludes the prayers of David son of Jesse.

72:14 [v]Ps 69:18 [w]1Sa 26:21; Ps 116:15
72:15 [x]Isa 60:6
72:16 [y]Ps 104:16
72:17 [z]Ex 3:15 [a]Ps 89:36 [b]Ge 12:3; Lk 1:48
72:18 [c]1Ch 29:10; Ps 41:13; 106:48 [d]Job 5:9
72:19 [e]Nu 14:21; Ne 9:5 [f]Ps 41:13

ANCIENT TEXTS AND ARTIFACTS

The Coronation of Ashurbanipal

PSALM 72 Who wrote Psalm 72, David or Solomon? This particular psalm is distinctive in that it contains both the **superscript** "Of Solomon" (which could be taken to mean "for Solomon," "about Solomon" or "by Solomon") and the **colophon** "This concludes the prayers of David son of Jesse." The colophon suggests that the superscript here means "for Solomon" and that the author of the piece was David. The psalm appears to be a prayer written by David for the occasion of the coronation of his son and successor, Solomon.[1]

Hymns and prayers composed for the coronation of kings of other nations are also found among ancient Near Eastern texts. For example, one text contains a prayer or liturgy for the coronation of Ashurbanipal, an **Assyrian** king (r. 668–627 B.C.). The liturgy invokes a variety of blessings from the Assyrian gods, including the following:

- That Ashurbanipal be granted a long life and reign,
- That he be given great eloquence and understanding,
- That the scope of his rule might expand,
- That the people of **Asshur** ("Map 1") might be so prosperous that grain and oil could be purchased inexpensively, and
- That the gods would provide abundant rain for the land.

Psalm 72 includes striking parallels to the Ashurbanipal coronation liturgy. The psalmist prayed for the Israelite king's domain to be extended (vv. 8–11) and for the land to prosper (vv. 15–16). In addition, verse 1 appeals to God to grant the king wisdom, as does the Ashurbanipal text.

At the same time, Psalm 72 is distinctive for its concern that the Israelite king should rule with righteousness and compassion (vv. 2–7). In addition, the Biblical text sought for God's name to be glorified through the king's reign (v. 5). Indeed, Psalm 72 was not seeking expanded political and military domination for Israel so much as it was looking for a fulfillment of the Messianic promises. Behind this psalm stood the assurances that the Gentiles would be blessed in Abraham (Ge 12:3) and that the reign of God would be established through the son of David (2Sa 7). Formally, then, Psalm 72 is similar to the coronation prayer for Ashurbanipal, but the message and hope of the Old Testament have invested the Biblical text with a distinctive purpose and outlook.

[1]See "The Psalm Superscripts" on page 795.

BOOK III

Psalms 73–89

Psalm 73

A psalm of Asaph.

[1] Surely God is good to Israel,
to those who are pure in heart.[g]

[2] But as for me, my feet had almost slipped;
I had nearly lost my foothold.
[3] For I envied[h] the arrogant
when I saw the prosperity of the wicked.[i]

[4] They have no struggles;
their bodies are healthy and strong.[a]
[5] They are free[j] from the burdens common to man;
they are not plagued by human ills.
[6] Therefore pride is their necklace;[k]
they clothe themselves with violence.[l]
[7] From their callous hearts[m] comes iniquity[b];
the evil conceits of their minds know no limits.

73:1 [g]Mt 5:8
73:3 [h]Ps 37:1; Pr 23:17 [i]Job 21:7; Jer 12:1
73:5 [j]Job 21:9
73:6 [k]Ge 41:42 [l]Ps 109:18
73:7 [m]Ps 17:10

[a] 4 With a different word division of the Hebrew; Masoretic Text *struggles at their death; / their bodies are healthy* [b] 7 Syriac (see also Septuagint); Hebrew *Their eyes bulge with fat*

73:1—83:18 Asaph, a Levite of the Gershonite family, was appointed over the service of praise during the time of David and Solomon (1Ch 16:5; 2Ch 5:12). He led the singing, sounded cymbals before the ark and apparently set up a school of music (Ne 7:44). Twelve psalms are credited to Asaph (Ps 50; 73–83), but this accreditation does not necessarily imply authorship and may mean no more than that these psalms constituted an Asaphic collection, begun by the great man and then prolonged over the years by the Asaph singers. The psalms themselves cover a long span of time, psalms like 74 being best understood in an exilic context. These psalms have a deep and contemplative nature.

Ancient Israelite Poets and Singers

PSALM 73 Throughout the ancient world music and hymnody played an important role in temple worship, and many temples had musical guilds that composed and sang hymns to the gods. (Examples of such liturgy are available from as far back as the **Sumerian** period.) The situation was similar for ancient Israel.

Unlike David, who was a renowned and yet amateur musician, Asaph, Heman, Ethan and the sons of Korah were in effect professional singers who created and sang psalms as part of their Levitical service in the temple.[1]

✣ Asaph, a Levitical choir leader during the time of David (1Ch 6:39), is mentioned alongside David in 2 Chronicles 29:30 as a composer of psalms and as "seer." He is credited with Psalms 50 and 73–83.

✣ Heman the Ezrahite and Ethan the Ezrahite are linked to the composition of Psalms 88 and 89. First Kings 4:31 indicates that both were highly esteemed for their wisdom.

✣ Numbers 16 describes Korah's attempt to usurp the priestly position from Aaron and of Korah's consequent death. Nevertheless, the "sons of Korah" served as gatekeepers at the sanctuary (1Ch 9:19) and rose to prominence as temple musicians. Psalms 42, 44–49, 84–85 and 87–88 are all attributed to the Korahites.

Evidently these psalmists, beyond being talented vocalists and songwriters, were highly respected as prophets and sages.[2]

[1]See "The Levites and the Priests" on page 648. [2]See "Ancient Near Eastern Wisdom" on page 960 and "The Sage" on page 1025.

[8]They scoff, and speak with malice;
in their arrogance[n] they threaten oppression.
[9]Their mouths lay claim to heaven,
and their tongues take possession of the earth.
[10]Therefore their people turn to them
and drink up waters in abundance.[a]
[11]They say, "How can God know?
Does the Most High have knowledge?"

[12]This is what the wicked are like—
always carefree, they increase in wealth.[o]

[13]Surely in vain[p] have I kept my heart pure;
in vain have I washed my hands in innocence.[q]
[14]All day long I have been plagued;
I have been punished every morning.

[15]If I had said, "I will speak thus,"
I would have betrayed your children.
[16]When I tried to understand[r] all this,
it was oppressive to me
[17]till I entered the sanctuary[s] of God;
then I understood their final destiny.[t]

[18]Surely you place them on slippery ground;[u]
you cast them down to ruin.
[19]How suddenly[v] are they destroyed,
completely swept away by terrors!
[20]As a dream[w] when one awakes,[x]
so when you arise, O Lord,
you will despise them as fantasies.

[21]When my heart was grieved
and my spirit embittered,
[22]I was senseless[y] and ignorant;
I was a brute beast[z] before you.

[23]Yet I am always with you;
you hold me by my right hand.
[24]You guide[a] me with your counsel,[b]
and afterward you will take me into glory.
[25]Whom have I in heaven but you?
And earth has nothing I desire besides you.[c]
[26]My flesh and my heart[d] may fail,[e]
but God is the strength of my heart
and my portion forever.

[27]Those who are far from you will perish;[f]
you destroy all who are unfaithful to you.
[28]But as for me, it is good to be near God.[g]
I have made the Sovereign LORD my refuge;
I will tell of all your deeds.[h]

73:8 [n]Ps 17:10; Jude 16
73:12 [o]Ps 49:6
73:13 [p]Job 21:15; 34:9 [q]Ps 26:6
73:16 [r]Ecc 8:17
73:17 [s]Ps 77:13 [t]Ps 37:38
73:18 [u]Ps 35:6
73:19 [v]Isa 47:11
73:20 [w]Job 20:8 [x]Ps 78:65
73:22 [y]Ps 49:10; 92:6 [z]Ecc 3:18
73:24 [a]Ps 48:14 [b]Ps 32:8
73:25 [c]Php 3:8
73:26 [d]Ps 84:2 [e]Ps 40:12
73:27 [f]Ps 119:155
73:28 [g]Heb 10:22; Jas 4:8 [h]Ps 40:5

[a] *10* The meaning of the Hebrew for this verse is uncertain.

73:21 For "heart," see the notes on 4:7 and 7:9.
73:23–24 For a discussion of Sheol, see the note on Job 17:13–16. See also "Sheol, Hades, Gehenna, the Abyss and Tartarus: Images of Hell" on page 946.

Psalm 74

A *maskil*[a] of Asaph.

1 Why have you rejected us forever,[i] O God?
Why does your anger smolder against the sheep of your pasture?[j]
2 Remember the people you purchased[k] of old,[l]
the tribe of your inheritance, whom you redeemed[m]—
Mount Zion, where you dwelt.[n]
3 Turn your steps toward these everlasting ruins,
all this destruction the enemy has brought on the sanctuary.

4 Your foes roared[o] in the place where you met with us;
they set up their standards[p] as signs.
5 They behaved like men wielding axes
to cut through a thicket of trees.[q]
6 They smashed all the carved[r] paneling
with their axes and hatchets.
7 They burned your sanctuary to the ground;
they defiled the dwelling place of your Name.
8 They said in their hearts, "We will crush[s] them completely!"
They burned every place where God was worshiped in the land.
9 We are given no miraculous signs;
no prophets[t] are left,
and none of us knows how long this will be.

10 How long will the enemy mock you, O God?
Will the foe revile[u] your name forever?
11 Why do you hold back your hand, your right hand?[v]
Take it from the folds of your garment and destroy them!

12 But you, O God, are my king[w] from of old;
you bring salvation upon the earth.
13 It was you who split open the sea[x] by your power;
you broke the heads of the monster[y] in the waters.
14 It was you who crushed the heads of Leviathan
and gave him as food to the creatures of the desert.
15 It was you who opened up springs[z] and streams;
you dried up[a] the ever flowing rivers.
16 The day is yours, and yours also the night;
you established the sun and moon.[b]
17 It was you who set all the boundaries[c] of the earth;
you made both summer and winter.[d]

18 Remember how the enemy has mocked you, O LORD,
how foolish people[e] have reviled your name.
19 Do not hand over the life of your dove to wild beasts;
do not forget the lives of your afflicted[f] people forever.
20 Have regard for your covenant,[g]
because haunts of violence fill the dark places of the land.

74:1 [i]Dt 29:20; Ps 44:23 [j]Ps 79:13; 95:7; 100:3
74:2 [k]Ex 15:16 [l]Dt 32:7 [m]Ex 15:13 [n]Ps 68:16
74:4 [o]La 2:7 [p]Nu 2:2
74:5 [q]Jer 46:22
74:6 [r]1Ki 6:18
74:8 [s]Ps 83:4
74:9 [t]1Sa 3:1
74:10 [u]Ps 44:16
74:11 [v]La 2:3
74:12 [w]Ps 44:4
74:13 [x]Ex 14:21 [y]Isa 51:9; Eze 29:3
74:15 [z]Ex 17:6; Nu 20:11 [a]Jos 2:10; 3:13
74:16 [b]Ge 1:16; Ps 136:7-9
74:17 [c]Dt 32:8; Ac 17:26 [d]Ge 8:22
74:18 [e]Dt 32:6; Ps 39:8
74:19 [f]Ps 9:18
74:20 [g]Ge 17:7; Ps 106:45

[a] Title: Probably a literary or musical term

74:3–8 These verses describe the Babylonians' destruction of the Lord's temple.
74:4 The term "standards" probably refers to troop standards (see Nu 1:52; Isa 31:9; Jer 4:21) used to signal victory.
74:8 The reference for "every place where God was worshiped" is uncertain. At the time of the Babylonian attacks there may have been a number of (illegitimate) locations in Judah where people went to worship God (see the note on 1Ki 3:2; and "The High Places" on p. 1318).
74:13–15 The imagery here is borrowed from ancient Near Eastern creation myths, in which the primeval chaotic waters were depicted as a many-headed monster that the creator-god overcame, after which he established the world order. (See "Ancient Creation Narratives" on p. 5.)
74:16 For commentary on Biblical use of the word "day," see the note on Obadiah 12.

[21] Do not let the oppressed[h] retreat in disgrace;
may the poor and needy[i] praise your name.

[22] Rise up, O God, and defend your cause;
remember how fools[j] mock you all day long.
[23] Do not ignore the clamor of your adversaries,[k]
the uproar of your enemies, which rises continually.

74:21 [h]Ps 103:6 [i]Ps 35:10
74:22 [j]Ps 53:1
74:23 [k]Ps 65:7

Psalm 75

For the director of music. ⌊To the tune of⌋ "Do Not Destroy." A psalm of Asaph. A song.

[1] We give thanks to you, O God,
we give thanks, for your Name is near;[l]
men tell of your wonderful deeds.[m]

[2] You say, "I choose the appointed time;
it is I who judge uprightly.
[3] When the earth and all its people quake,[n]
it is I who hold its pillars[o] firm. *Selah*
[4] To the arrogant I say, 'Boast no more,'
and to the wicked, 'Do not lift up your horns.[p]
[5] Do not lift your horns against heaven;
do not speak with outstretched neck.' "

[6] No one from the east or the west
or from the desert can exalt a man.
[7] But it is God who judges:[q]
He brings one down, he exalts another.[r]
[8] In the hand of the LORD is a cup
full of foaming wine mixed[s] with spices;
he pours it out, and all the wicked of the earth
drink it down to its very dregs.[t]

[9] As for me, I will declare[u] this forever;
I will sing praise to the God of Jacob.
[10] I will cut off the horns of all the wicked,
but the horns of the righteous will be lifted up.[v]

75:1 [l]Ps 145:18 [m]Ps 44:1; 71:16
75:3 [n]Isa 24:19 [o]1Sa 2:8
75:4 [p]Zec 1:21
75:7 [q]Ps 50:6 [r]1Sa 2:7; Ps 147:6; Da 2:21
75:8 [s]Pr 23:30 [t]Job 21:20; Jer 25:15
75:9 [u]Ps 40:10
75:10 [v]Ps 89:17; 92:10; 148:14

Psalm 76

For the director of music. With stringed instruments. A psalm of Asaph. A song.

[1] In Judah God is known;
his name is great in Israel.
[2] His tent is in Salem,[w]
his dwelling place in Zion.
[3] There he broke the flashing arrows,
the shields and the swords, the weapons of war.[x] *Selah*

[4] You are resplendent with light,
more majestic than mountains rich with game.
[5] Valiant men lie plundered,
they sleep their last sleep;[y]

76:2 [w]Ge 14:18
76:3 [x]Ps 46:9
76:5 [y]Ps 13:3

75:4 The phrase "lift up your horns" is a picture of defiant opposition, based upon the action of attacking bulls. "Horn" (see also v. 10) is a common Biblical metaphor for vigor or strength (see the NIV text note on 18:2).
75:5 An "outstretched neck" was a sign of defiance. (See "Heart, Breath, Throat and Intestines: Ancient Hebrew Anthropology" on p. 968.)
76:1–12 This psalm is in the form of a victory hymn. According to an ancient tradition it was written after God had destroyed Sennacherib's army when the Assyrians threatened Jerusalem (see 2Ki 19:35–36).

not one of the warriors
can lift his hands.
6 At your rebuke, O God of Jacob,
both horse and chariot[z] lie still.

76:6 [z]Ex 15:1

7 You alone are to be feared.[a]
Who can stand[b] before you when you are angry?[c]

76:7 [a]1Ch 16:25 [b]Ezr 9:15; Rev 6:17 [c]Ps 2:5; Na 1:6

8 From heaven you pronounced judgment,
and the land feared[d] and was quiet—
9 when you, O God, rose up to judge,[e]
to save all the afflicted of the land. *Selah*

76:8 [d]1Ch 16:30; 2Ch 20:29-30
76:9 [e]Ps 9:8

10 Surely your wrath against men brings you praise,[f]
and the survivors of your wrath are restrained.[a]

76:10 [f]Ex 9:16; Ro 9:17

11 Make vows to the LORD your God and fulfill them;[g]
let all the neighboring lands
bring gifts[h] to the One to be feared.
12 He breaks the spirit of rulers;
he is feared by the kings of the earth.

76:11 [g]Ps 50:14; Ecc 5:4-5 [h]2Ch 32:23; Ps 68:29

Psalm 77

For the director of music. For Jeduthun. Of Asaph. A psalm.

1 I cried out to God[i] for help;
I cried out to God to hear me.

77:1 [i]Ps 3:4

2 When I was in distress,[j] I sought the Lord;
at night I stretched out untiring hands[k]
and my soul refused to be comforted.[l]

77:2 [j]Ps 50:15; Isa 26:9,16 [k]Job 11:13 [l]Ge 37:35

3 I remembered you, O God, and I groaned;
I mused, and my spirit grew faint.[m] *Selah*

77:3 [m]Ps 143:4

4 You kept my eyes from closing;
I was too troubled to speak.
5 I thought about the former days,[n]
the years of long ago;
6 I remembered my songs in the night.
My heart mused and my spirit inquired:

77:5 [n]Dt 32:7; Ps 44:1; 143:5; Isa 51:9

7 "Will the Lord reject forever?
Will he never show his favor[o] again?

77:7 [o]Ps 85:1

8 Has his unfailing love vanished forever?
Has his promise[p] failed for all time?

77:8 [p]2Pe 3:9

9 Has God forgotten to be merciful?[q]
Has he in anger withheld his compassion?[r]" *Selah*

77:9 [q]Ps 25:6; 40:11; 51:1 [r]Isa 49:15

10 Then I thought, "To this I will appeal:
the years of the right hand[s] of the Most High."

77:10 [s]Ps 31:22

11 I will remember the deeds of the LORD;
yes, I will remember your miracles[t] of long ago.

77:11 [t]Ps 143:5

12 I will meditate on all your works
and consider all your mighty deeds.

13 Your ways, O God, are holy.
What god is so great as our God?[u]

77:13 [u]Ex 15:11; Ps 71:19; 86:8

[a] 10 Or *Surely the wrath of men brings you praise, / and with the remainder of wrath you arm yourself*

77:6 For "heart," see the note on 4:7.

[14] You are the God who performs miracles;
you display your power among the peoples.
[15] With your mighty arm you redeemed your people,[v]
the descendants of Jacob and Joseph. *Selah*

[16] The waters[w] saw you, O God,
the waters saw you and writhed;[x]
the very depths were convulsed.
[17] The clouds poured down water,[y]
the skies resounded with thunder;
your arrows flashed back and forth.
[18] Your thunder was heard in the whirlwind,
your lightning lit up the world;
the earth trembled and quaked.[z]
[19] Your path led through the sea,[a]
your way through the mighty waters,
though your footprints were not seen.

[20] You led your people[b] like a flock[c]
by the hand of Moses and Aaron.

77:15 [v]Ex 6:6; Dt 9:29
77:16 [w]Ex 14:21, 28; Hab 3:8 [x]Ps 114:4; Hab 3:10
77:17 [y]Jdg 5:4
77:18 [z]Jdg 5:4
77:19 [a]Hab 3:15
77:20 [b]Ex 13:21 [c]Ps 78:52; Isa 63:11

Psalm 78

A *maskil*[a] of Asaph.

[1] O my people, hear my teaching;[d]
listen to the words of my mouth.
[2] I will open my mouth in parables,[e]
I will utter hidden things, things from of old—
[3] what we have heard and known,
what our fathers have told us.[f]
[4] We will not hide them from their children;[g]
we will tell the next generation
the praiseworthy deeds[h] of the LORD,
his power, and the wonders he has done.
[5] He decreed statutes[i] for Jacob[j]
and established the law in Israel,
which he commanded our forefathers
to teach their children,
[6] so the next generation would know them,
even the children yet to be born,[k]
and they in turn would tell their children.
[7] Then they would put their trust in God
and would not forget[l] his deeds
but would keep his commands.[m]
[8] They would not be like their forefathers[n]—
a stubborn[o] and rebellious[p] generation,
whose hearts were not loyal to God,
whose spirits were not faithful to him.

[9] The men of Ephraim, though armed with bows,[q]
turned back on the day of battle;[r]

78:1 [d]Isa 51:4; 55:3
78:2 [e]Ps 49:4; Mt 13:35*
78:3 [f]Ps 44:1
78:4 [g]Dt 11:19 [h]Ps 26:7; 71:17
78:5 [i]Ps 19:7; 81:5 [j]Ps 147:19
78:6 [k]Ps 22:31; 102:18
78:7 [l]Dt 6:12 [m]Dt 5:29
78:8 [n]2Ch 30:7 [o]Ex 32:9 [p]ver 37; Isa 30:9
78:9 [q]ver 57; 1Ch 12:2 [r]Jdg 20:39

[a] Title: Probably a literary or musical term

77:15 Old Testament authors sometimes referred to the northern kingdom as "Joseph" (or "Ephraim," Joseph's son), in distinction from the southern kingdom of Judah. Here, however, Joseph represents the whole of his generation and thus also all of the descendants of Jacob.

78:9 The phrase "men of Ephraim" refers to the northern kingdom, dominated by the tribe of Ephraim. Neither the tribe of Ephraim nor the northern kingdom had a reputation for cowardice or ineffectiveness in battle. This verse is best understood as a metaphor for Israel's betrayal of God's covenant (see v. 10).

10 they did not keep God's covenant[s]
and refused to live by his law.
11 They forgot what he had done,[t]
the wonders he had shown them.
12 He did miracles[u] in the sight of their fathers
in the land of Egypt,[v] in the region of Zoan.[w]
13 He divided the sea[x] and led them through;
he made the water stand firm like a wall.[y]
14 He guided them with the cloud by day
and with light from the fire all night.[z]
15 He split the rocks[a] in the desert
and gave them water as abundant as the seas;
16 he brought streams out of a rocky crag
and made water flow down like rivers.

17 But they continued to sin[b] against him,
rebelling in the desert against the Most High.
18 They willfully put God to the test[c]
by demanding the food they craved.[d]
19 They spoke against God,[e] saying,
"Can God spread a table in the desert?
20 When he struck the rock, water gushed out,[f]
and streams flowed abundantly.
But can he also give us food?
Can he supply meat[g] for his people?"
21 When the LORD heard them, he was very angry;
his fire broke out[h] against Jacob,
and his wrath rose against Israel,
22 for they did not believe in God
or trust[i] in his deliverance.
23 Yet he gave a command to the skies above
and opened the doors of the heavens;[j]
24 he rained down manna[k] for the people to eat,
he gave them the grain of heaven.
25 Men ate the bread of angels;
he sent them all the food they could eat.
26 He let loose the east wind[l] from the heavens
and led forth the south wind by his power.
27 He rained meat down on them like dust,
flying birds like sand on the seashore.
28 He made them come down inside their camp,
all around their tents.
29 They ate till they had more than enough,[m]
for he had given them what they craved.
30 But before they turned from the food they craved,
even while it was still in their mouths,[n]
31 God's anger rose against them;
he put to death the sturdiest[o] among them,
cutting down the young men of Israel.

32 In spite of all this, they kept on sinning;
in spite of his wonders,[p] they did not believe.[q]

78:10 [s]2Ki 17:15
78:11 [t]Ps 106:13
78:12 [u]Ps 106:22 [v]Ex 7-12 [w]Nu 13:22
78:13 [x]Ex 14:21; Ps 136:13 [y]Ex 15:8
78:14 [z]Ex 13:21; Ps 105:39
78:15 [a]Nu 20:11; 1Co 10:4
78:17 [b]Dt 9:22; Isa 63:10; Heb 3:16
78:18 [c]1Co 10:9 [d]Ex 16:2; Nu 11:4
78:19 [e]Nu 21:5
78:20 [f]Nu 20:11 [g]Nu 11:18
78:21 [h]Nu 11:1
78:22 [i]Dt 1:32; Heb 3:19
78:23 [j]Ge 7:11; Mal 3:10
78:24 [k]Ex 16:4; Jn 6:31*
78:26 [l]Nu 11:31
78:29 [m]Nu 11:20
78:30 [n]Nu 11:33
78:31 [o]Isa 10:16
78:32 [p]ver 11 [q]ver 22

78:12 Zoan was a city (possibly Tanis) in the northeastern part of the Nile delta.
78:26–27 Since the quail were migrating from Egypt at this time, the south wind may have carried them north and the east wind may then have diverted them to the desert area occupied by the Israelites (see the note on Nu 11:31–32).

33 So he ended their days in futility[r]
and their years in terror.
34 Whenever God slew them, they would seek[s] him;
they eagerly turned to him again.
35 They remembered that God was their Rock,[t]
that God Most High was their Redeemer.[u]
36 But then they would flatter him with their mouths,[v]
lying to him with their tongues;
37 their hearts were not loyal[w] to him,
they were not faithful to his covenant.
38 Yet he was merciful;[x]
he forgave[y] their iniquities[z]
and did not destroy them.
Time after time he restrained his anger
and did not stir up his full wrath.
39 He remembered that they were but flesh,[a]
a passing breeze[b] that does not return.

40 How often they rebelled[c] against him in the desert[d]
and grieved him[e] in the wasteland!
41 Again and again they put God to the test;[f]
they vexed the Holy One of Israel.[g]
42 They did not remember his power—
the day he redeemed them from the oppressor,
43 the day he displayed his miraculous signs in
Egypt,
his wonders in the region of Zoan.
44 He turned their rivers to blood;[h]
they could not drink from their streams.
45 He sent swarms of flies[i] that devoured them,
and frogs[j] that devastated them.
46 He gave their crops to the grasshopper,
their produce to the locust.[k]
47 He destroyed their vines with hail[l]
and their sycamore-figs with sleet.
48 He gave over their cattle to the hail,
their livestock[m] to bolts of lightning.
49 He unleashed against them his hot anger,[n]
his wrath, indignation and hostility—
a band of destroying angels.
50 He prepared a path for his anger;
he did not spare them from death
but gave them over to the plague.
51 He struck down all the firstborn of Egypt,[o]
the firstfruits of manhood in the tents
of Ham.[p]
52 But he brought his people out like a flock;[q]
he led them like sheep through the desert.
53 He guided them safely, so they were unafraid;
but the sea engulfed[r] their enemies.[s]
54 Thus he brought them to the border of his holy land,
to the hill country his right hand[t] had taken.

78:33 [r]Nu 14:29, 35
78:34 [s]Hos 5:15
78:35 [t]Dt 32:4 [u]Dt 9:26
78:36 [v]Eze 33:31
78:37 [w]ver 8; Ac 8:21
78:38 [x]Ex 34:6 [y]Isa 48:10 [z]Nu 14:18,20
78:39 [a]Ge 6:3; Ps 103:14 [b]Job 7:7; Jas 4:14
78:40 [c]Heb 3:16 [d]Ps 95:8; 106:14 [e]Eph 4:30
78:41 [f]Nu 14:22 [g]2Ki 19:22; Ps 89:18
78:44 [h]Ex 7:20-21; Ps 105:29
78:45 [i]Ex 8:24; Ps 105:31 [j]Ex 8:2,6
78:46 [k]Ex 10:13
78:47 [l]Ex 9:23; Ps 105:32
78:48 [m]Ex 9:25
78:49 [n]Ex 15:7
78:51 [o]Ex 12:29; Ps 135:8 [p]Ps 105:23; 106:22
78:52 [q]Ps 77:20
78:53 [r]Ex 14:28 [s]Ps 106:10
78:54 [t]Ex 15:17; Ps 44:3

78:37 For "hearts," see the note on 4:7.
78:47 Sycamore-fig trees are large trees that yield fig-like fruit, as well as useful timber.
78:53 The "sea" here is the Red Sea.

78:55 [u]Ps 44:2
[v]Jos 13:7

55 He drove out nations[u] before them
and allotted their lands to them as an inheritance;[v]
he settled the tribes of Israel in their homes.

56 But they put God to the test
and rebelled against the Most High;
they did not keep his statutes.

ANCIENT TEXTS AND ARTIFACTS

Power Over Egypt in the Hymn to Osiris

PSALM 78 Frequently we find similarities between the Bible and ancient texts from Egypt or **Mesopotamia**. As significant as those commonalities are, it is at least equally important to recognize differences among the texts so that we can discern the ways in which the beliefs of Israel were truly unique. Psalm 78 is a recitation of the history of God's rule over Israel from the time of the **exodus** to that of David. The story is not fully chronological but selectively demonstrates that the Lord was sovereign over the Israelites, punishing them when they sinned but delivering them from oppression and slavery.

From the Eighteenth Dynasty of Egypt has come a **stele** that contains a hymn celebrating the rule of Osiris over Egypt. In the myth Osiris was slain by his brother, the god Seth, but was restored by his sister/consort, the goddess Isis. Osiris then became lord over the realm of the dead, as well as over Egypt, both through his son Horus and through the earthly representative of Horus, the pharaoh. The hymn proclaims how the "Two Lands" (i.e., Upper and Lower Egypt), the Nile and all the beasts of Egypt honor Osiris, Isis and Horus.[1]

As the Egyptian text does for Osiris, Psalm 78 proclaims the reign of the Lord over all Israel. And as the Egyptian text does for the pharaoh, the psalm depicts a human viceroy to the reign of God in the person of David (vv. 70–72). However, unlike the Egyptian song the psalm is focused entirely upon events in human history. The Egyptian hymn builds upon the mythical slaying and rising of Osiris, while the psalm focuses on God's dealings with his people in specific events in history. This, above everything else, separates Biblical theology from paganism.

[1]For later use of the Osiris myth, see "The Mystery Religions" on page 1939.

Images of Osiris at Karnak, Egypt
Preserving Bible Times; © Dr. James C. Martin

57 Like their fathers[w] they were disloyal and faithless,
as unreliable as a faulty bow.[x]
58 They angered him[y] with their high places;[z]
they aroused his jealousy with their idols.[a]
59 When God heard them, he was very angry;
he rejected Israel[b] completely.
60 He abandoned the tabernacle of Shiloh,[c]
the tent he had set up among men.
61 He sent ⌊the ark of⌋ his might[d] into captivity,[e]
his splendor into the hands of the enemy.
62 He gave his people over to the sword;
he was very angry with his inheritance.
63 Fire consumed[f] their young men,
and their maidens had no wedding songs;[g]
64 their priests were put to the sword,[h]
and their widows could not weep.

65 Then the Lord awoke as from sleep,[i]
as a man wakes from the stupor of wine.
66 He beat back his enemies;
he put them to everlasting shame.[j]
67 Then he rejected the tents of Joseph,
he did not choose the tribe of Ephraim;
68 but he chose the tribe of Judah,
Mount Zion,[k] which he loved.
69 He built his sanctuary like the heights,
like the earth that he established forever.
70 He chose David[l] his servant
and took him from the sheep pens;
71 from tending the sheep he brought him
to be the shepherd[m] of his people Jacob,
of Israel his inheritance.
72 And David shepherded them with integrity of heart;[n]
with skillful hands he led them.

78:57 [w]Eze 20:27 [x]Hos 7:16
78:58 [y]Jdg 2:12 [z]Lev 26:30 [a]Ex 20:4; Dt 32:21
78:59 [b]Dt 32:19
78:60 [c]Jos 18:1
78:61 [d]Ps 132:8 [e]1Sa 4:17
78:63 [f]Nu 11:1 [g]Jer 7:34; 16:9
78:64 [h]1Sa 4:17; 22:18
78:65 [i]Ps 44:23
78:66 [j]1Sa 5:6
78:68 [k]Ps 87:2
78:70 [l]1Sa 16:1
78:71 [m]2Sa 5:2; Ps 28:9
78:72 [n]1Ki 9:4

Psalm 79

A psalm of Asaph.

1 O God, the nations have invaded your inheritance;[o]
they have defiled your holy temple,
they have reduced Jerusalem to rubble.[p]
2 They have given the dead bodies of your servants
as food to the birds of the air,
the flesh of your saints to the beasts of the earth.[q]
3 They have poured out blood like water
all around Jerusalem,
and there is no one to bury the dead.[r]
4 We are objects of reproach to our neighbors,
of scorn and derision to those around us.[s]

79:1 [o]Ps 74:2 [p]2Ki 25:9
79:2 [q]Dt 28:26; Jer 7:33
79:3 [r]Jer 16:4
79:4 [s]Ps 44:13; 80:6

78:58 See "The High Places" on page 1318.
78:60 Shiloh had been the center of worship since the time of Joshua (see Jos 18:1,8; 21:1–2; Jdg 18:31; 1Sa 1:3; Jer 7:12). It was located in Ephraim between Bethel and Shechem (see "Bethel" on p. 59 and "Shechem" on p. 340). Apparently it was destroyed by the Philistines when they captured the ark or shortly afterward. See "The Tabernacle at Shiloh" on page 401 and "The Destruction of Shiloh" on page 1200.
78:62–64 In ancient warfare fire and the sword were the two primary instruments of destruction. The catastrophe here was so great that both the wedding songs of the brides and the wailing of the widows (see v. 64) were silenced.
78:67 The phrase "tents of Joseph" is a figure for the tribe of Ephraim
78:71 For "shepherd," see the note on 23:1.
79:2 See the note on 63:10.

5 How long,[t] O LORD? Will you be angry[u] forever?
How long will your jealousy burn like fire?[v]
6 Pour out your wrath[w] on the nations
that do not acknowledge[x] you,
on the kingdoms
that do not call on your name;[y]
7 for they have devoured Jacob
and destroyed his homeland.
8 Do not hold against us the sins of the fathers;[z]
may your mercy come quickly to meet us,
for we are in desperate need.[a]

9 Help us,[b] O God our Savior,
for the glory of your name;
deliver us and forgive our sins
for your name's sake.[c]
10 Why should the nations say,
"Where is their God?"[d]
Before our eyes, make known among the nations
that you avenge[e] the outpoured blood of your servants.
11 May the groans of the prisoners come before you;
by the strength of your arm
preserve those condemned to die.

12 Pay back into the laps[f] of our neighbors seven times[g]
the reproach they have hurled at you, O Lord.
13 Then we your people, the sheep of your pasture,[h]
will praise you forever;[i]
from generation to generation
we will recount your praise.

Psalm 80

For the director of music. To ⌞the tune of⌟ "The Lilies of the Covenant." Of Asaph. A psalm.

1 Hear us, O Shepherd of Israel,
you who lead Joseph like a flock;[j]
you who sit enthroned between the cherubim,[k] shine forth
2 before Ephraim, Benjamin and Manasseh.[l]
Awaken[m] your might;
come and save us.

3 Restore[n] us,[o] O God;
make your face shine upon us,
that we may be saved.

4 O LORD God Almighty,
how long will your anger smolder
against the prayers of your people?

79:5 [t]Ps 74:10 [u]Ps 74:1; 85:5 [v]Dt 29:20; Ps 89:46; Zep 3:8
79:6 [w]Ps 69:24; Rev 16:1 [x]Jer 10:25; 2Th 1:8 [y]Ps 14:4
79:8 [z]Isa 64:9 [a]Ps 116:6; 142:6
79:9 [b]2Ch 14:11 [c]Ps 25:11; 31:3; Jer 14:7
79:10 [d]Ps 42:10 [e]Ps 94:1
79:12 [f]Isa 65:6; Jer 32:18 [g]Ge 4:15
79:13 [h]Ps 74:1; 95:7 [i]Ps 44:8
80:1 [j]Ps 77:20 [k]Ex 25:22
80:2 [l]Nu 2:18-24 [m]Ps 35:23
80:3 [n]Ps 85:4; La 5:21 [o]Nu 6:25

79:6–12 For commentary on expressions of vengeful attitudes toward enemies, see the note on 69:22–28. See also "Curses and Imprecations" on page 883.
79:7 "Jacob" is a synonym for Israel (see Ge 32:28).
79:11 "Prisoners" describes the exiles in Babylon. They were not actually interred in prisons but were under threat of death should they seek to return to their homeland.
79:12 The number seven symbolized completeness.
80:1 For "shepherd," see the note on 23:1. For "Joseph," see the note on 77:15.
80:2 "Ephraim, Benjamin and Manasseh" here likely represent the northern kingdom. Although Benjamin literally belonged to the northern kingdom, part of the tribe must have remained with the southern kingdom since its territory bordered Jerusalem itself, and the southern kingdom continued to control the region around Jerusalem (see 1Ki 12:21). This suggests that the disaster suffered was the Assyrian campaign that destroyed the northern kingdom (see 2Ki 17:1–6). Archaeological surveys of the region show that Jerusalem and the surrounding area experienced a dramatic population increase at this time, probably the result of a massive influx of displaced persons from the north fleeing the Assyrians. This would explain the presence of "Ephraim, Benjamin and Manasseh" at the Jerusalem sanctuary and the national prayer for restoration with special focus on these tribes.

5 You have fed them with the bread of tears;
you have made them drink tears by the bowlful.[p] **80:5** [p]Ps 42:3; Isa 30:20
6 You have made us a source of contention to our neighbors,
and our enemies mock us.[q] **80:6** [q]Ps 79:4

7 Restore us, O God Almighty;
make your face shine upon us,
that we may be saved.

8 You brought a vine[r] out of Egypt;
you drove out[s] the nations and planted it. **80:8** [r]Isa 5:1-2; Jer 2:21 [s]Jos 13:6; Ac 7:45
9 You cleared the ground for it,
and it took root and filled the land.
10 The mountains were covered with its shade,
the mighty cedars with its branches.
11 It sent out its boughs to the Sea,[a]
its shoots as far as the River.[b][t] **80:11** [t]Ps 72:8

12 Why have you broken down its walls[u]
so that all who pass by pick its grapes? **80:12** [u]Ps 89:40; Isa 5:5
13 Boars from the forest ravage[v] it
and the creatures of the field feed on it. **80:13** [v]Jer 5:6
14 Return to us, O God Almighty!
Look down from heaven and see![w] **80:14** [w]Isa 63:15
Watch over this vine,
15 the root your right hand has planted,
the son[c] you have raised up for yourself.

16 Your vine is cut down, it is burned with fire;
at your rebuke[x] your people perish. **80:16** [x]Ps 39:11; 76:6
17 Let your hand rest on the man at your right hand,
the son of man you have raised up for yourself.
18 Then we will not turn away from you;
revive us, and we will call on your name.

19 Restore us, O LORD God Almighty;
make your face shine upon us,
that we may be saved.

Psalm 81

For the director of music. According to *gittith.*[d] Of Asaph.

1 Sing for joy to God our strength;
shout aloud to the God of Jacob![y] **81:1** [y]Ps 66:1
2 Begin the music, strike the tambourine,[z]
play the melodious harp[a] and lyre. **81:2** [z]Ex 15:20 [a]Ps 92:3

3 Sound the ram's horn at the New Moon,
and when the moon is full, on the day of our Feast;
4 this is a decree for Israel,
an ordinance of the God of Jacob.

[a] *11* Probably the Mediterranean [b] *11* That is, the Euphrates [c] *15* Or *branch* [d] Title: Probably a musical term

80:8–16 This use of the vine-vineyard metaphor is found also in the Prophets (see, e.g., Isa 3:14; 5:1–7; Jer 2:21; Eze 17:6–8; Hos 10:1).

81:3 For information on the ram's horn, see "The Shofar" on page 898. "Our Feast" was probably the Feast of Tabernacles, often called simply "the feast/festival" (see "The Festivals of Israel" on p. 186).

5 He established it as a statute for Joseph
81:5 [b]Ex 11:4 [c]Ps 114:1 — when he went out against Egypt,[b]
where we heard a language we did not understand.[a][c]

81:6 [d]Isa 9:4 — 6 He says, "I removed the burden from their shoulders;[d]
their hands were set free from the basket.
81:7 [e]Ex 2:23; Ps 50:15 [f]Ex 19:19 [g]Ex 17:7 — 7 In your distress you called[e] and I rescued you,
I answered[f] you out of a thundercloud;
I tested you at the waters of Meribah.[g] *Selah*

81:8 [h]Ps 50:7 — 8 "Hear, O my people,[h] and I will warn you—
if you would but listen to me, O Israel!
81:9 [i]Ex 20:3; Dt 32:12; Isa 43:12 — 9 You shall have no foreign god[i] among you;
you shall not bow down to an alien god.
10 I am the LORD your God,
81:10 [j]Ex 20:2 [k]Ps 107:9 — who brought you up out of Egypt.[j]
Open wide your mouth and I will fill[k] it.

11 "But my people would not listen to me;
81:11 [l]Ex 32:1-6 — Israel would not submit to me.[l]
81:12 [m]Ac 7:42; Ro 1:24 — 12 So I gave them over[m] to their stubborn hearts
to follow their own devices.

81:13 [n]Dt 5:29; Isa 48:18 — 13 "If my people would but listen to me,[n]
if Israel would follow my ways,
81:14 [o]Ps 47:3 [p]Am 1:8 — 14 how quickly would I subdue[o] their enemies
and turn my hand against[p] their foes!
15 Those who hate the LORD would cringe before him,
and their punishment would last forever.
81:16 [q]Dt 32:14 — 16 But you would be fed with the finest of wheat;[q]
with honey from the rock I would satisfy you."

Psalm 82

A psalm of Asaph.

1 God presides in the great assembly;
82:1 [r]Ps 58:11; Isa 3:13 — he gives judgment[r] among the "gods":

2 "How long will you[b] defend the unjust
82:2 [s]Dt 1:17 [t]Ps 58:1-2; Pr 18:5 — and show partiality[s] to the wicked?[t] *Selah*
82:3 [u]Dt 24:17 [v]Jer 22:16 — 3 Defend the cause of the weak and fatherless;[u]
maintain the rights of the poor[v] and oppressed.
4 Rescue the weak and needy;
deliver them from the hand of the wicked.

82:5 [w]Ps 14:4; Mic 3:1 [x]Isa 59:9 [y]Ps 11:3 — 5 "They know nothing, they understand nothing.[w]
They walk about in darkness;[x]
all the foundations[y] of the earth are shaken.

82:6 [z]Jn 10:34* — 6 "I said, 'You are "gods";[z]
you are all sons of the Most High.'

[a] 5 Or / *and we heard a voice we had not known* [b] 2 The Hebrew is plural.

81:5 For "Joseph," see the note on 77:15. The phrase "when he went out against Egypt" likely refers to the exodus period, highlighting especially God's triumph over Egypt, by which he had set his people free (see vv. 6–7).

82:1 Early Rabbinic tradition saw the "gods" (vv. 1,6) as unjust rulers and judges in Israel (see the note on 45:6). Today many identify them as kings of surrounding nations, who ruled with lofty disregard for justice. Others view them as the supposedly divine beings in whose names these kings claimed to rule.

[7] But you will die[a] like mere men;
you will fall like every other ruler."

[8] Rise up,[b] O God, judge the earth,
for all the nations are your inheritance.[c]

82:7 [a]Ps 49:12; Eze 31:14
82:8 [b]Ps 12:5 [c]Ps 2:8; Rev 11:15

Psalm 83

A song. A psalm of Asaph.

[1] O God, do not keep silent;[d]
be not quiet, O God, be not still.
[2] See how your enemies are astir,[e]
how your foes rear their heads.[f]
[3] With cunning they conspire[g] against your people;
they plot against those you cherish.
[4] "Come," they say, "let us destroy[h] them as a nation,
that the name of Israel be remembered[i]
no more."

[5] With one mind they plot together;[j]
they form an alliance against you—
[6] the tents of Edom[k] and the Ishmaelites,
of Moab[l] and the Hagrites,[m]
[7] Gebal,[a][n] Ammon and Amalek,
Philistia, with the people of Tyre.[o]
[8] Even Assyria has joined them
to lend strength to the descendants of Lot.[p] *Selah*

[9] Do to them as you did to Midian,[q]
as you did to Sisera and Jabin at the river Kishon,[r]
[10] who perished at Endor
and became like refuse[s] on the ground.
[11] Make their nobles like Oreb and Zeeb,[t]
all their princes like Zebah and Zalmunna,[u]
[12] who said, "Let us take possession[v]
of the pasturelands of God."

[13] Make them like tumbleweed, O my God,
like chaff[w] before the wind.
[14] As fire consumes the forest
or a flame sets the mountains ablaze,[x]
[15] so pursue them with your tempest
and terrify them with your storm.[y]
[16] Cover their faces with shame[z]
so that men will seek your name, O LORD.

[17] May they ever be ashamed and dismayed;
may they perish in disgrace.[a]
[18] Let them know that you, whose name is the LORD—
that you alone are the Most High over all the earth.[b]

83:1 [d]Ps 28:1; 35:22
83:2 [e]Ps 2:1; Isa 17:12 [f]Jdg 8:28; Ps 81:15
83:3 [g]Ps 31:13
83:4 [h]Est 3:6 [i]Jer 11:19
83:5 [j]Ps 2:2
83:6 [k]Ps 137:7 [l]2Ch 20:1 [m]Ge 25:16
83:7 [n]Jos 13:5 [o]Eze 27:3
83:8 [p]Dt 2:9
83:9 [q]Jdg 7:1-23 [r]Jdg 4:23-24
83:10 [s]Zep 1:17
83:11 [t]Jdg 7:25 [u]Jdg 8:12,21
83:12 [v]2Ch 20:11
83:13 [w]Ps 35:5; Isa 17:13
83:14 [x]Dt 32:22; Isa 9:18
83:15 [y]Job 9:17
83:16 [z]Ps 109:29; 132:18
83:17 [a]Ps 35:4
83:18 [b]Ps 59:13

[a] *7* That is, Byblos

83:6 Hagrites were either Ishmaelites (descendants of Hagar) or a group mentioned in Assyrian inscriptions as an Aramean confederacy (see 1Ch 5:10,18–22; 27:31).
83:7 Gebal, also called Byblos (see the NIV text note), was an important Phoenician city (see "Byblos" on p. 1349).
83:9 This refers to Gideon's defeat of Midian (Jdg 7) and Barak's victory over Sisera and Jabin (Jdg 4).
83:10 Apparently much of the retreating army was overtaken and killed at Endor, northeast of where the main battle was fought.
83:11 Oreb and Zeeb, Zebah and Zalmunna were leaders of the Midianite host destroyed by Gideon (see Jdg 7–8).
83:16–18 For commentary on expressions of vengeful attitudes toward enemies, see the note on 69:22–28. See also "Curses and Imprecations" on page 883.

Psalm 84

For the director of music. According to *gittith.*[a] Of the Sons of Korah. A psalm.

84:1 [c]Ps 27:4; 43:3; 132:5
84:2 [d]Ps 42:1-2

[1] How lovely is your dwelling place,[c]
O LORD Almighty!
[2] My soul yearns,[d] even faints,
for the courts of the LORD;

[a] Title: Probably a musical term

Curses and Imprecations

PSALM 83 To pray for someone else's well-being is to make intercession for that person, but to pray for someone's destruction is to make an imprecation. The Bible contains a number of examples of imprecations; one of the clearest is Psalm 83. Here the psalmist called on God to take action against his enemies (vv. 1–2), the Gentile nations all around (vv. 6–8) who were plotting harm against Israel (vv. 3–5). The prayer minces no words; the psalmist asked God to destroy them (vv. 9–18).

Prayers and rituals meant to bring about the destruction of enemies (whether personal or national) were common in the ancient world:

✣ Egyptians practiced an execration rite whereby they would inscribe names or figures of their adversaries on terra-cotta or pottery, after which they would pronounce a curse upon the enemy and ritually smash the pottery. **Execration texts** with lists of names of cities in Syria-Palestine have been located; the Egyptians who created these texts wished to call down destruction upon such places as Ashkelon, Byblos and Damascus.[1]

✣ **Mesopotamian** tablets contain rituals meant to call down destruction upon enemies.

✣ From the Greco-Roman world archaeologists have discovered magical **papyri** that called down curses upon all kinds of enemies. For example, there are texts that invoke curses against adversarial parties in lawsuits, as well as those that curse business competitors.[2]

Are the imprecations in the Bible any different from these curses from pagan sources? Obviously there are similarities. Psalm 83, like the execration texts, delineates a list of the foes the psalmist wanted God to punish. Several factors, however, set Biblical imprecations apart:

✣ Biblical imprecations have no tie to magic. In magic, a person seeks to manipulate supernatural powers with ritual words and actions in order to achieve his or her desire. The Bible provides no rituals to bring about the destruction of enemies. God's people could only call upon the Lord to punish the enemy and then leave it to him to decide whether or not to act.

✣ Biblical imprecations were based upon belief in the righteousness of God. When making an imprecation, a psalmist appealed to God's justice in a tacit acknowledgment that God punishes only because it is the right thing to do—not simply in response to a psalmist's anger. By contrast, in magic-based rituals justice was not an issue.

✣ Biblical imprecations were never used for personal jealousies and ambitions.

✣ Biblical imprecations ultimately sought to give glory to God. Verse 16 prays for the destruction of the wicked "so that men will seek your name, O LORD." God's honor—not Israel's—was to be maintained.

Protective spirit charm from the late Assyrian Empire
Preserving Bible Times; © Dr. James C. Martin; permission of The British Museum

[1]For more on these cities, see "Byblos" on page 1349 and "Damascus" on page 1087. [2]See "Magic in the Greco-Roman World" on page 1911.

my heart and my flesh cry out
for the living God.
3 Even the sparrow has found a home,
and the swallow a nest for herself,
where she may have her young—
a place near your altar,[e] 84:3 [e]Ps 43:4 [f]Ps 5:2
O LORD Almighty, my King and my God.[f]
4 Blessed are those who dwell in your house;
they are ever praising you. *Selah*

5 Blessed are those whose strength[g] is in you, 84:5 [g]Ps 81:1 [h]Jer 31:6
who have set their hearts on pilgrimage.[h]
6 As they pass through the Valley of Baca,
they make it a place of springs;
the autumn[i] rains also cover it with pools.[a] 84:6 [i]Joel 2:23
7 They go from strength to strength,[j] 84:7 [j]Pr 4:18 [k]Dt 16:16
till each appears[k] before God in Zion.

8 Hear my prayer, O LORD God Almighty;
listen to me, O God of Jacob. *Selah*
9 Look upon our shield,[b][l] O God; 84:9 [l]Ps 59:11 [m]1Sa 16:6; Ps 2:2; 132:17
look with favor on your anointed one.[m]

10 Better is one day in your courts
than a thousand elsewhere;
I would rather be a doorkeeper[n] in the house of my God 84:10 [n]1Ch 23:5
than dwell in the tents of the wicked.
11 For the LORD God is a sun[o] and shield;[p] 84:11 [o]Isa 60:19; Rev 21:23 [p]Ge 15:1 [q]Ps 34:10
the LORD bestows favor and honor;
no good thing does he withhold[q]
from those whose walk is blameless.

12 O LORD Almighty,
blessed[r] is the man who trusts in you. 84:12 [r]Ps 2:12

Psalm 85

For the director of music. Of the Sons of Korah. A psalm.

1 You showed favor to your land, O LORD; 85:1 [s]Ps 14:7; Jer 30:18; Eze 39:25
you restored the fortunes[s] of Jacob.
2 You forgave[t] the iniquity[u] of your people 85:2 [t]Nu 14:19 [u]Ps 78:38
and covered all their sins. *Selah*
3 You set aside all your wrath[v] 85:3 [v]Ps 106:23 [w]Ex 32:12; Dt 13:17; Ps 78:38; Jnh 3:9
and turned from your fierce anger.[w]

4 Restore[x] us again, O God our Savior, 85:4 [x]Ps 80:3,7
and put away your displeasure toward us.
5 Will you be angry with us forever?[y] 85:5 [y]Ps 79:5
Will you prolong your anger through all generations?

[a] 6 Or *blessings* [b] 9 Or *sovereign*

84:5 The phrase "who have set their hearts on pilgrimage" may be literally translated "in whose hearts are (the) highways," that is, the highways used by the Israelites as they traveled to Jerusalem to observe the religious festivals. For "hearts," see the note on 4:7.
84:6 The "autumn rains" were the gentle, early showers that preceded the later spring rains.

85:1–3 These verses may refer to the returning exiles and the hardships they experienced. Verse 12 suggests that a drought had ravaged the land, a possible reflection on the drought with which the Lord chastened his people during the time of Haggai (see Hag 1:5–11).
85:1 "Jacob" is a synonym for Israel (see Ge 32:28).

6 Will you not revive[z] us again,
that your people may rejoice in you?
7 Show us your unfailing love, O LORD,
and grant us your salvation.

8 I will listen to what God the LORD will say;
he promises peace[a] to his people, his saints—
but let them not return to folly.
9 Surely his salvation[b] is near those who fear him,
that his glory[c] may dwell in our land.

10 Love and faithfulness[d] meet together;
righteousness[e] and peace kiss each other.
11 Faithfulness springs forth from the earth,
and righteousness[f] looks down from heaven.
12 The LORD will indeed give what is good,[g]
and our land will yield[h] its harvest.
13 Righteousness goes before him
and prepares the way for his steps.

Psalm 86

A prayer of David.

1 Hear, O LORD, and answer[i] me,
for I am poor and needy.
2 Guard my life, for I am devoted to you.
You are my God; save your servant
who trusts in you.[j]
3 Have mercy[k] on me, O Lord,
for I call[l] to you all day long.
4 Bring joy to your servant,
for to you, O Lord,
I lift[m] up my soul.

5 You are forgiving and good, O Lord,
abounding in love[n] to all who call to you.
6 Hear my prayer, O LORD;
listen to my cry for mercy.
7 In the day of my trouble[o] I will call to you,
for you will answer me.

8 Among the gods there is none like you,[p] O Lord;
no deeds can compare with yours.
9 All the nations you have made
will come and worship[q] before you, O Lord;
they will bring glory[r] to your name.
10 For you are great and do marvelous deeds;[s]
you alone[t] are God.

11 Teach me your way,[u] O LORD,
and I will walk in your truth;
give me an undivided[v] heart,
that I may fear your name.
12 I will praise you, O Lord my God, with all my heart;
I will glorify your name forever.
13 For great is your love toward me;
you have delivered me from the depths of the grave.[a]

85:6 [z]Ps 80:18; Hab 3:2
85:8 [a]Zec 9:10
85:9 [b]Isa 46:13 [c]Zec 2:5
85:10 [d]Ps 89:14; Pr 3:3 [e]Ps 72:2-3; Isa 32:17
85:11 [f]Isa 45:8
85:12 [g]Ps 84:11; Jas 1:17 [h]Lev 26:4; Ps 67:6; Zec 8:12
86:1 [i]Ps 17:6
86:2 [j]Ps 25:2; 31:14
86:3 [k]Ps 4:1; 57:1 [l]Ps 88:9
86:4 [m]Ps 25:1; 143:8
86:5 [n]Ex 34:6; Ne 9:17; Ps 103:8; 145:8; Joel 2:13; Jnh 4:2
86:7 [o]Ps 50:15
86:8 [p]Ex 15:11; Dt 3:24; Ps 89:6
86:9 [q]Ps 66:4; Rev 15:4 [r]Isa 43:7
86:10 [s]Ps 72:18 [t]Dt 6:4; Mk 12:29; 1Co 8:4
86:11 [u]Ps 25:5 [v]Jer 32:39

[a] 13 Hebrew *Sheol*

[14]The arrogant are attacking me, O God;
a band of ruthless men seeks my life—
men without regard for you.[w]
[15]But you, O Lord, are a compassionate and gracious[x] God,
slow to anger, abounding in love and faithfulness.[y]
[16]Turn to me and have mercy on me;
grant your strength to your servant
and save the son of your maidservant.[a z]
[17]Give me a sign of your goodness,
that my enemies may see it and be put to shame,
for you, O LORD, have helped me and comforted me.

86:14 [w]Ps 54:3
86:15 [x]Ps 103:8 [y]Ex 34:6; Ne 9:17; Joel 2:13
86:16 [z]Ps 116:16

Psalm 87

Of the Sons of Korah. A psalm. A song.

1 He has set his foundation on the holy mountain;
2 the LORD loves the gates of Zion[a]
more than all the dwellings of Jacob.
3 Glorious things are said of you,
O city of God:[b] *Selah*
4 "I will record Rahab[b c] and Babylon
among those who acknowledge me—
Philistia too, and Tyre[d], along with Cush[c]—
and will say, 'This[d] one was born in Zion.[e]' "

5 Indeed, of Zion it will be said,
"This one and that one were born in her,
and the Most High himself will establish her."
6 The LORD will write in the register[f] of the peoples:
"This one was born in Zion." *Selah*
7 As they make music[g] they will sing,
"All my fountains[h] are in you."

87:2 [a]Ps 78:68
87:3 [b]Ps 46:4; Isa 60:1
87:4 [c]Job 9:13 [d]Ps 45:12 [e]Isa 19:25
87:6 [f]Ps 69:28; Isa 4:3; Eze 13:9
87:7 [g]Ps 149:3 [h]Ps 36:9

Psalm 88

A song. A psalm of the Sons of Korah. For the director of music.
According to *mahalath leannoth.*[e] A *maskil*[f] of Heman the Ezrahite.

1 O LORD, the God who saves me,[i]
day and night I cry out[j] before you.
2 May my prayer come before you;
turn your ear to my cry.

3 For my soul is full of trouble
and my life draws near the grave.[g k]
4 I am counted among those who go down to the pit;[l]
I am like a man without strength.
5 I am set apart with the dead,
like the slain who lie in the grave,

88:1 [i]Ps 51:14 [j]Ps 22:2; 27:9; Lk 18:7
88:3 [k]Ps 107:18, 26
88:4 [l]Ps 28:1

[a] 16 Or *save your faithful son* [b] 4 A poetic name for Egypt [c] 4 That is, the upper Nile region [d] 4 Or *"O Rahab and Babylon, / Philistia, Tyre and Cush, / I will record concerning those who acknowledge me: / 'This* [e] Title: Possibly a tune, "The Suffering of Affliction" [f] Title: Probably a literary or musical term [g] 3 Hebrew *Sheol*

87:4 "Rahab" here is a reference to Egypt; elsewhere it applies to the mythical monster of the deep (see Job 9:13; Ps 89:9–10 and their notes; see also the note on 32:6 and "The *Enuma Elish* and the Biblical Concept of Creation" on p. 888).

88:3–6 For a discussion of Sheol, see the note on Job 17:13–16. See also "Sheol, Hades, Gehenna, the Abyss and Tartarus: Images of Hell" on page 946.

whom you remember no more,
who are cut off[m] from your care.

6 You have put me in the lowest pit,
in the darkest depths.[n]
7 Your wrath lies heavily upon me;
you have overwhelmed me with all your waves.[o] *Selah*
8 You have taken from me my closest friends[p]
and have made me repulsive to them.
I am confined[q] and cannot escape;
9 my eyes[r] are dim with grief.

I call[s] to you, O LORD, every day;
I spread out my hands[t] to you.
10 Do you show your wonders to the dead?
Do those who are dead rise up and praise you?[u] *Selah*
11 Is your love declared in the grave,
your faithfulness[v] in Destruction[a]?
12 Are your wonders known in the place of darkness,
or your righteous deeds in the land of oblivion?

13 But I cry to you for help,[w] O LORD;
in the morning[x] my prayer comes before you.[y]
14 Why, O LORD, do you reject[z] me
and hide your face[a] from me?
15 From my youth I have been afflicted and close to death;
I have suffered your terrors[b] and am in despair.
16 Your wrath has swept over me;
your terrors have destroyed me.
17 All day long they surround me like a flood;[c]
they have completely engulfed me.
18 You have taken my companions[d] and loved ones from me;
the darkness is my closest friend.

Psalm 89

A *maskil*[b] of Ethan the Ezrahite.

1 I will sing[e] of the LORD's great love forever;
with my mouth I will make your faithfulness known[f] through all generations.
2 I will declare that your love stands firm forever,
that you established your faithfulness in heaven itself.[g]
3 You said, "I have made a covenant with my chosen one,
I have sworn to David my servant,
4 'I will establish your line forever
and make your throne firm through all generations.' "[h] *Selah*

5 The heavens[i] praise your wonders, O LORD,
your faithfulness too, in the assembly of the holy ones.
6 For who in the skies above can compare with the LORD?
Who is like the LORD among the heavenly beings?[j]

88:5 [m]Ps 31:22; Isa 53:8
88:6 [n]Ps 69:15; La 3:55
88:7 [o]Ps 42:7
88:8 [p]Job 19:13; Ps 31:11 [q]Jer 32:2
88:9 [r]Ps 38:10 [s]Ps 86:3 [t]Job 11:13; Ps 143:6
88:10 [u]Ps 6:5
88:11 [v]Ps 30:9
88:13 [w]Ps 30:2 [x]Ps 5:3 [y]Ps 119:147
88:14 [z]Ps 43:2 [a]Job 13:24; Ps 13:1
88:15 [b]Job 6:4
88:17 [c]Ps 22:16; 124:4
88:18 [d]ver 8; Job 19:13; Ps 38:11
89:1 [e]Ps 59:16; Ps 101:1 [f]Ps 36:5; 40:10
89:2 [g]Ps 36:5
89:4 [h]2Sa 7:12-16; 1Ki 8:16; Ps 132:11-12; Isa 9:7; Lk 1:33
89:5 [i]Ps 19:1
89:6 [j]Ps 113:5

[a] *11* Hebrew *Abaddon* [b] Title: Probably a literary or musical term

89:1-52 This psalm is a prayer mourning the downfall of the Davidic dynasty and pleading for its restoration. The historical context may have been the attack on Jerusalem by Nebuchadnezzar and the exile of King Jehoiachin in 597 B.C. (2Ki 24:8–17).

THE ENUMA ELISH AND THE BIBLICAL CONCEPT OF CREATION

PSALM 89 In the Bible we read of creation primarily in Genesis 1, but other texts enlighten us as to how the Israelites viewed the creative process (cf. Ps 89). With the discovery and decipherment of ancient texts in **Akkadian**, as well as of **hieroglyphics**, scholars have come to realize that many cultures from the ancient world had creation myths that could be compared to the Biblical creation account.[1] The most famous Akkadian creation story is called the *Enuma Elish*, a poem of about 1,100 lines.

Copies of the *Enuma Elish* exist in the form of **cuneiform** tablets dating from about 750 to 200 B.C., but the poem was no doubt composed earlier than that. The creation story contained in these tablets exalts Marduk, god of Babylon, as the greatest of the gods. Because the main purpose of the text was to glorify Marduk, some scholars resist referring to the *Enuma Elish* as a "creation" story. This reluctance is misplaced, however; many creation myths from the ancient world serve to glorify a particular god or shrine.

Enuma Elish begins with a pair of high gods, Apsu (male) and Tiamat (female), as well as a number of lower gods. Apsu threatens to kill the lower gods because of the noise they make, but he himself is slain by the god Ea. Ea in turn fathers Marduk, whose birth is attended by great celebration. Tiamat, who is alternatively pictured as an ocean or a dragon (i.e., sea monster),[2] deploys against the gods a gruesome army of monsters (lion-men, scorpion-men and the like) under the command of her second consort (partner), Kingu. Ea and the other gods are paralyzed with fear, but Marduk agrees to fight the monsters on condition that he be named king of the gods. Marduk defeats Tiamat and splits her body like a fish for drying. From one half he fashions the heavens and from the other he forms the earth. From the blood of Kingu, according to the myth, Marduk created men, after which he was indeed lauded as ruler of the gods.

At one time many scholars believed that the **Babylonian** creation story provided the source material for its Biblical counterpart. Today, however, few hold that position. Indeed, the differences between the Babylonian and Biblical accounts are more significant than their similarities:

◆ The Biblical record does not present the creative act as that of slaying a monster and making use of its body.

Some have argued that the Hebrew word for the "deep" (*tehom*) in Genesis 1:2 is related to the name Tiamat. In fact, the words are unrelated, and there is no hint in Genesis of **Yahweh** slaying a dragon.

A monster called Rahab is mentioned in Psalm 89:10. This Biblical Rahab represents forces that oppose God; even Egypt can be identified as Rahab (Isa 30:7). Whatever we make of Rahab in the Bible, it is unrelated to creation.

◆ The Biblical account describes the act of creation as proceeding simply from God's word: God *spoke* the cosmos and everything related to it into existence (Ge 1).

◆ The Biblical account leaves no room for polytheism. Even though Psalm 89:7 mentions other heavenly beings who are under God's authority, there is no multitude of gods who marry, have offspring, fight each other for supremacy and the like.

◆ The Biblical record does not promote one shrine above all others. Genesis 1 never mentions Jerusalem or any other site sacred to Israel in connection with creation. Indeed, the Bible's initial chapter never mentions Yahweh, describing the creator simply as "God." The Biblical concept of creation is truly monotheistic; there is no elevation of one god above others, for, indeed, there is only one God.

Cuneiform tablet containing an ancient version of the flood story

Preserving Bible Times; © Dr. James C. Martin; permission of The British Museum

[1]See "Ancient Creation Narratives" on page 5. [2]See "The Serpent Motif in Other Ancient Near Eastern Literature" on page 8.

89:7 [k]Ps 47:2
89:8 [l]Ps 71:19
89:9 [m]Ps 65:7
89:10 [n]Ps 87:4 [o]Ps 68:1
89:11 [p]1Ch 29:11; Ps 24:1 [q]Ge 1:1
89:12 [r]Jos 19:22 [s]Dt 3:8; Jos 12:1 [t]Ps 98:8
89:14 [u]Ps 97:2
89:15 [v]Ps 44:3
89:16 [w]Ps 105:3
89:17 [x]Ps 75:10; 92:10; 148:14
89:18 [y]Ps 47:9
89:20 [z]Ac 13:22 [a]Ps 78:70 [b]1Sa 16:1,12
89:21 [c]Ps 18:35
89:22 [d]2Sa 7:10
89:23 [e]Ps 18:40 [f]2Sa 7:9
89:24 [g]2Sa 7:15
89:25 [h]Ps 72:8
89:26 [i]2Sa 7:14 [j]2Sa 22:47
89:27 [k]Col 1:18 [l]Nu 24:7 [m]Rev 1:5; 19:16

7 In the council of the holy ones God is greatly feared;
he is more awesome than all who surround him.[k]
8 O LORD God Almighty, who is like you?[l]
You are mighty, O LORD, and your faithfulness surrounds you.

9 You rule over the surging sea;
when its waves mount up, you still them.[m]
10 You crushed Rahab[n] like one of the slain;
with your strong arm you scattered[o] your enemies.
11 The heavens are yours, and yours also the earth;[p]
you founded the world and all that is in it.[q]
12 You created the north and the south;
Tabor[r] and Hermon[s] sing for joy[t] at your name.
13 Your arm is endued with power;
your hand is strong, your right hand exalted.

14 Righteousness and justice are the foundation of your throne;[u]
love and faithfulness go before you.
15 Blessed are those who have learned to acclaim you,
who walk in the light[v] of your presence, O LORD.
16 They rejoice in your name[w] all day long;
they exult in your righteousness.
17 For you are their glory and strength,
and by your favor you exalt our horn.[a][x]
18 Indeed, our shield[b] belongs to the LORD,
our king[y] to the Holy One of Israel.

19 Once you spoke in a vision,
to your faithful people you said:
"I have bestowed strength on a warrior;
I have exalted a young man from among
the people.
20 I have found David[z] my servant;[a]
with my sacred oil I have anointed[b] him.
21 My hand will sustain him;
surely my arm will strengthen him.[c]
22 No enemy will subject him to tribute;
no wicked man will oppress[d] him.
23 I will crush his foes before him[e]
and strike down his adversaries.[f]
24 My faithful love will be with him,[g]
and through my name his horn[c] will be
exalted.
25 I will set his hand over the sea,
his right hand over the rivers.[h]
26 He will call out to me, 'You are my Father,[i]
my God, the Rock my Savior.'[j]
27 I will also appoint him my firstborn,[k]
the most exalted[l] of the kings[m] of the earth.

ANCIENT VOICES

When Tiamat [heard]* these words, they pleased her,
"[As y]ou have counseled, we will make a tempest...
(For) they have been adopting [wicked ways] against the gods [thei]r parents."
[They clo]sed ranks and drew up at Tiamat's side,
Angry, scheming, never lying down night and day,
[Ma]king warfare, rumbling, raging,
Convening in assembly, that they might start hostilities.

*Words or partial words in brackets and parentheses added by translator for clarity or where text has gaps

—EPIC OF CREATION

See "The *Enuma Elish* and the Biblical Concept of Creation" article.

[a] 17 *Horn* here symbolizes strong one. [b] 18 Or *sovereign* [c] 24 *Horn* here symbolizes strength.

89:9–10 The imagery in these verses was borrowed from ancient Near Eastern myths of creation. Rahab was the mythical monster of the deep (see the notes on Job 9:13; Ps 32:6; 87:4; see also "Ancient Creation Narratives" on p. 5 and "The *Enuma Elish* and the Biblical Concept of Creation" on p. 888), probably another name for Leviathan (see 74:14; 104:26).

89:12 Mount Tabor, a mountain about 1,300 feet (396 m) high, is located at the southeastern edge of the Jezreel Valley. Mount Hermon, snowcapped throughout the year and rising to a height of over 9,200 feet (2,804 m), is one of the most prominent and beautiful mountains in Lebanon.

[28] I will maintain my love to him forever,
and my covenant with him will never fail.[n]
[29] I will establish his line forever,
his throne as long as the heavens endure.[o]

[30] "If his sons forsake my law
and do not follow my statutes,
[31] if they violate my decrees
and fail to keep my commands,
[32] I will punish their sin with the rod,
their iniquity with flogging;[p]
[33] but I will not take my love from him,[q]
nor will I ever betray my faithfulness.
[34] I will not violate my covenant
or alter what my lips have uttered.[r]
[35] Once for all, I have sworn by my holiness—
and I will not lie to David—
[36] that his line will continue forever
and his throne endure before me like the sun;
[37] it will be established forever like the moon,
the faithful witness in the sky." *Selah*

[38] But you have rejected,[s] you have spurned,
you have been very angry with your anointed one.
[39] You have renounced the covenant with your servant
and have defiled his crown in the dust.[t]
[40] You have broken through all his walls[u]
and reduced his strongholds[v] to ruins.
[41] All who pass by have plundered him;
he has become the scorn of his neighbors.[w]
[42] You have exalted the right hand of his foes;
you have made all his enemies rejoice.[x]
[43] You have turned back the edge of his sword
and have not supported him in battle.[y]
[44] You have put an end to his splendor
and cast his throne to the ground.
[45] You have cut short the days of his youth;
you have covered him with a mantle of shame.[z] *Selah*

[46] How long, O LORD? Will you hide yourself forever?
How long will your wrath burn like fire?[a]
[47] Remember how fleeting is my life.[b]
For what futility you have created all men!
[48] What man can live and not see death,
or save himself from the power of the grave[a]?[c] *Selah*
[49] O Lord, where is your former great love,
which in your faithfulness you swore to David?
[50] Remember, Lord, how your servant has[b] been mocked,[d]
how I bear in my heart the taunts of all the nations,
[51] the taunts with which your enemies have mocked, O LORD,
with which they have mocked every step of your anointed one.[e]

[52] Praise be to the LORD forever!
Amen and Amen.[f]

89:28 [n] ver 33-34; Isa 55:3
89:29 [o] ver 4,36; Dt 11:21; Jer 33:17
89:32 [p] 2Sa 7:14
89:33 [q] 2Sa 7:15
89:34 [r] Nu 23:19
89:38 [s] Dt 32:19; 1Ch 28:9; Ps 44:9
89:39 [t] La 5:16
89:40 [u] Ps 80:12 [v] La 2:2
89:41 [w] Ps 44:13
89:42 [x] Ps 13:2; 80:6
89:43 [y] Ps 44:10
89:45 [z] Ps 44:15; 109:29
89:46 [a] Ps 79:5
89:47 [b] Job 7:7; Ps 39:5
89:48 [c] Ps 22:29; 49:9
89:50 [d] Ps 69:19
89:51 [e] Ps 74:10
89:52 [f] Ps 41:13; 72:19

[a] 48 Hebrew *Sheol* [b] 50 Or *your servants have*

FORM CRITICISM AND THE PSALMS

PSALM 90 "Form criticism" is a relatively new method of Biblical study, pioneered by the twentieth-century German scholar Herman Gunkel. This method originally had three purposes:

- *To discover the original setting of a psalm*. Was it sung by an individual or as part of congregational worship? Was it a lamentation or a song of praise? Was the psalm used in a temple setting or engaged by an individual in private?
- *To discover oral traditions behind the text*. Are there vestiges of oral tradition the psalmist incorporated into the composition?
- *To discover the structure of a psalm*. What is the psalm's basic outline? Do other psalms of the same genre have a similar structure?

Some of this slicing and dicing is of dubious value. For example, it is difficult to prove that an oral tradition lies behind a particular portion of a psalm. Also, some scholars have made claims about the original setting of certain psalms that are impossible to verify. For example, some have suggested that specific psalms were part of a New Year's festival, but there is little evidence to support this premise. In reality, we can frequently only infer the circumstances behind individual psalms.

Still, some psalms do present fairly clear life settings (e.g., an individual is calling on God for deliverance from his enemies). Also, psalms of the same type often do have features in common (e.g., psalms in which someone is calling out for help from his enemies often use similar vocabulary and have a similar structure).

Even though form criticism as originally developed by Gunkel has only limited value, the method is important in that it has forced us to reckon with the fact that the Bible contains a variety of different types of psalms. To begin with, it is helpful to ask certain basic questions of a psalm. For example,

- Is it a prayer that addresses God or an instruction for the reader?
- Does it thank and praise God or call upon him for help?
- Does it focus on special themes, such as Zion, the king or the law?

By asking these and other questions and carefully reading the psalms, we can quickly discern that there are a number of types and subtypes, a few of which follow:

- Hymns are congregational songs that praise God.
  - Praise psalms extol God for his character (Ex 15:1–18; Ps 100; 145).
  - Thanksgiving psalms express gratitude to God for his actions (Ps 32; 107; Jnh 2:2–9).
- Songs of Zion celebrate Zion as the "type," or representation, of the kingdom of God (Ps 48).
- Royal psalms focus on some aspect of Israelite kingship.
  - The coronation psalm is a prayer for the success of the king's reign (Ps 72).
  - The royal wedding song celebrates the king's wedding and anticipates the Messianic kingdom (Ps 45).
  - The royal votive psalm records the king's vow to execute justice (Ps 101).
- Wisdom and Torah psalms contrast a life lived wisely under the law with one lived foolishly. These psalms are often contemplative or address the reader directly, as though a teacher were speaking to a disciple (e.g., Ps 1; 19; 37; 119).
- Lament psalms, the most abundant psalm-type, express the anguish of worshipers due to sin, famine, enemies, etc. In these psalms a petitioner pleads with God to remove the source of his distress, often accompanied by a vow to praise God (e.g., 1Sa 2:1–10; Ps 3; 12; 22; 77; 90; La 5). Psalms of lament may be sung by the individual (Ps 13) or an entire congregation (Ps 74).[1]
- Songs of trust express confidence in God (e.g., Ps 11; 23; 121), not cries for help.

Psalm 90 illustrates the pattern of a lament. It is congregational in nature in that it speaks to the situation of all people, not to that of any one individual.

- This psalm opens with an assertion that God is Israel's refuge as the basis for an appeal for mercy (vv. 1–2).
- It laments the mortality and sinfulness of humans (vv. 3–11).
- It includes a short appeal for wisdom (v. 12), recalling the wisdom psalms.
- It closes with an appeal for God's compassion (vv. 13–17).

By understanding the type of psalm we are engaging, we are in a better position to interpret and use it appropriately.

[1]See also "Ancient Near Eastern Laments" on page 1305.

BOOK IV

Psalms 90–106

Psalm 90

A prayer of Moses the man of God.

[1] Lord, you have been our dwelling place[g]
throughout all generations.
[2] Before the mountains were born[h]
or you brought forth the earth and the world,
from everlasting to everlasting you are God.[i]

[3] You turn men back to dust,
saying, "Return to dust, O sons of men."[j]
[4] For a thousand years in your sight
are like a day that has just gone by,
or like a watch in the night.[k]
[5] You sweep men away[l] in the sleep of death;
they are like the new grass of the morning—
[6] though in the morning it springs up new,
by evening it is dry and withered.[m]

[7] We are consumed by your anger
and terrified by your indignation.
[8] You have set our iniquities before you,
our secret sins[n] in the light of your presence.
[9] All our days pass away under your wrath;
we finish our years with a moan.[o]
[10] The length of our days is seventy years—
or eighty, if we have the strength;
yet their span[a] is but trouble and sorrow,
for they quickly pass, and we fly away.[p]

[11] Who knows the power of your anger?
For your wrath is as great as the fear that is
due you.[q]
[12] Teach us to number our days[r] aright,
that we may gain a heart of wisdom.[s]

[13] Relent, O LORD! How long[t] will it be?
Have compassion on your servants.[u]
[14] Satisfy[v] us in the morning with your unfailing love,
that we may sing for joy[w] and be glad all our days.[x]
[15] Make us glad for as many days as you have afflicted us,
for as many years as we have seen trouble.
[16] May your deeds be shown to your servants,
your splendor to their children.[y]

[17] May the favor[b] of the Lord our God rest upon us;
establish the work of our hands for us—
yes, establish the work of our hands.[z]

Psalm 91

[1] He who dwells in the shelter[a] of the Most High
will rest in the shadow[b] of the Almighty.[c]

90:1 [g]Dt 33:27; Eze 11:16
90:2 [h]Job 15:7; Pr 8:25 [i]Ps 102:24-27
90:3 [j]Ge 3:19; Job 34:15
90:4 [k]2Pe 3:8
90:5 [l]Ps 73:20; Isa 40:6
90:6 [m]Mt 6:30; Jas 1:10
90:8 [n]Ps 19:12
90:9 [o]Ps 78:33
90:10 [p]Job 20:8
90:11 [q]Ps 76:7
90:12 [r]Ps 39:4 [s]Dt 32:29
90:13 [t]Ps 6:3 [u]Dt 32:36; Ps 135:14
90:14 [v]Ps 103:5 [w]Ps 85:6 [x]Ps 31:7
90:16 [y]Ps 44:1; Hab 3:2
90:17 [z]Isa 26:12
91:1 [a]Ps 31:20 [b]Ps 17:8

[a] 10 Or *yet the best of them* [b] 17 Or *beauty* [c] 1 Hebrew *Shaddai*

91:2 [c]Ps 142:5
91:3 [d]Ps 124:7; Pr 6:5 [e]1Ki 8:37
91:4 [f]Ps 17:8 [g]Ps 35:2
91:5 [h]Job 5:21
91:8 [i]Ps 37:34; 58:10; Mal 1:5
91:10 [j]Pr 12:21
91:11 [k]Heb 1:14 [l]Ps 34:7
91:12 [m]Mt 4:6*; Lk 4:10-11*
91:13 [n]Da 6:22; Lk 10:19
91:15 [o]1Sa 2:30; Ps 50:15; Jn 12:26
91:16 [p]Dt 6:2; Ps 21:4 [q]Ps 50:23
92:1 [r]Ps 147:1 [s]Ps 135:3
92:2 [t]Ps 89:1
92:3 [u]1Sa 10:5; Ne 12:27; Ps 33:2
92:4 [v]Ps 8:6; 143:5
92:5 [w]Rev 15:3 [x]Ps 40:5; 139:17; Isa 28:29; Ro 11:33
92:6 [y]Ps 73:22

2 I will say[a] of the LORD, "He is my refuge[c] and my fortress,
my God, in whom I trust."

3 Surely he will save you from the fowler's snare[d]
and from the deadly pestilence.[e]
4 He will cover you with his feathers,
and under his wings you will find refuge;[f]
his faithfulness will be your shield[g] and rampart.
5 You will not fear[h] the terror of night,
nor the arrow that flies by day,
6 nor the pestilence that stalks in the darkness,
nor the plague that destroys at midday.
7 A thousand may fall at your side,
ten thousand at your right hand,
but it will not come near you.
8 You will only observe with your eyes
and see the punishment of the wicked.[i]

9 If you make the Most High your dwelling—
even the LORD, who is my refuge—
10 then no harm[j] will befall you,
no disaster will come near your tent.
11 For he will command his angels[k] concerning you
to guard you in all your ways;[l]
12 they will lift you up in their hands,
so that you will not strike your foot against a stone.[m]
13 You will tread upon the lion and the cobra;
you will trample the great lion and the serpent.[n]

14 "Because he loves me," says the LORD, "I will rescue him;
I will protect him, for he acknowledges my name.
15 He will call upon me, and I will answer him;
I will be with him in trouble,
I will deliver him and honor him.[o]
16 With long life[p] will I satisfy him
and show him my salvation.[q]"

Psalm 92

A psalm. A song. For the Sabbath day.

1 It is good to praise the LORD
and make music to your name,[r] O Most High,[s]
2 to proclaim your love in the morning[t]
and your faithfulness at night,
3 to the music of the ten-stringed lyre
and the melody of the harp.[u]

4 For you make me glad by your deeds, O LORD;
I sing for joy at the works of your hands.[v]
5 How great are your works,[w] O LORD,
how profound your thoughts![x]
6 The senseless man[y] does not know,
fools do not understand,

[a] 2 Or *He says*

91:3 "Fowler's snare" is a metaphor for danger from an enemy.

91:6 "Pestilence" and "plague" are references to mortal diseases that often reached epidemic proportions in the ancient Near East.

[7] that though the wicked spring up like grass
and all evildoers flourish,
they will be forever destroyed.

[8] But you, O LORD, are exalted forever.

[9] For surely your enemies, O LORD,
surely your enemies will perish;
all evildoers will be scattered.[z]
[10] You have exalted my horn[a][a] like that of a wild ox;
fine oils[b] have been poured upon me.
[11] My eyes have seen the defeat of my adversaries;
my ears have heard the rout of my wicked foes.[c]

[12] The righteous will flourish like a palm tree,
they will grow like a cedar of Lebanon;[d]
[13] planted in the house of the LORD,
they will flourish in the courts of our God.[e]
[14] They will still bear fruit[f] in old age,
they will stay fresh and green,
[15] proclaiming, "The LORD is upright;
he is my Rock, and there is no wickedness
in him.[g]"

92:9 [z]Ps 68:1; 89:10
92:10 [a]Ps 89:17 [b]Ps 23:5
92:11 [c]Ps 54:7; 91:8
92:12 [d]Ps 1:3; 52:8; Jer 17:8; Hos 14:6
92:13 [e]Ps 100:4
92:14 [f]Jn 15:2
92:15 [g]Job 34:10

Psalm 93

[1] The LORD reigns,[h] he is robed in majesty;[i]
the LORD is robed in majesty
and is armed with strength.[j]
The world is firmly established;
it cannot be moved.[k]
[2] Your throne was established long ago;
you are from all eternity.[l]

[3] The seas[m] have lifted up, O LORD,
the seas have lifted up their voice;
the seas have lifted up their pounding waves.
[4] Mightier than the thunder[n] of the great waters,
mightier than the breakers of the sea—
the LORD on high is mighty.

[5] Your statutes stand firm;
holiness[o] adorns your house
for endless days, O LORD.

93:1 [h]Ps 97:1 [i]Ps 104:1 [j]Ps 65:6 [k]Ps 96:10
93:2 [l]Ps 45:6
93:3 [m]Ps 96:11
93:4 [n]Ps 65:7
93:5 [o]Ps 29:2

Psalm 94

[1] O LORD, the God who avenges,[p]
O God who avenges, shine forth.[q]
[2] Rise up, O Judge[r] of the earth;
pay back[s] to the proud what they deserve.

94:1 [p]Na 1:2; Ro 12:19 [q]Ps 80:1
94:2 [r]Ge 18:25 [s]Ps 31:23

[a] 10 *Horn* here symbolizes strength.

93:1-5 The assertion of God as universal Creator stands in stark contrast to pagan teachings of chaos, primordial forces and random happenings. God's reign is evident in his creation and acts of redemption. The rule of God is visible, as his glorious mantle spreads out over his kingdom.

93:3 "Seas" is a reference to the primeval, chaotic waters, tamed and assigned a place by the Lord's creative word (see the notes on 32:6; 89:9–10).

3 How long will the wicked, O LORD,
how long will the wicked be jubilant?

4 They pour out arrogant[t] words;
all the evildoers are full of boasting.[u]
5 They crush your people,[v] O LORD;
they oppress your inheritance.
6 They slay the widow and the alien;
they murder the fatherless.
7 They say, "The LORD does not see;[w]
the God of Jacob pays no heed."

8 Take heed, you senseless ones[x] among the people;
you fools, when will you become wise?
9 Does he who implanted the ear not hear?
Does he who formed the eye not see?[y]
10 Does he who disciplines nations not punish?
Does he who teaches[z] man lack knowledge?
11 The LORD knows the thoughts of man;
he knows that they are futile.[a]

12 Blessed is the man you discipline,[b] O LORD,
the man you teach[c] from your law;
13 you grant him relief from days of trouble,
till a pit[d] is dug for the wicked.
14 For the LORD will not reject his people;[e]
he will never forsake his inheritance.
15 Judgment will again be founded on righteousness,[f]
and all the upright in heart will follow it.

16 Who will rise up[g] for me against the wicked?
Who will take a stand for me against evildoers?[h]
17 Unless the LORD had given me help,[i]
I would soon have dwelt in the silence of death.
18 When I said, "My foot is slipping,[j]"
your love, O LORD, supported me.
19 When anxiety was great within me,
your consolation brought joy to my soul.

20 Can a corrupt throne be allied with you—
one that brings on misery by its decrees?[k]
21 They band together[l] against the righteous
and condemn the innocent[m] to death.
22 But the LORD has become my fortress,
and my God the rock in whom I take refuge.[n]
23 He will repay[o] them for their sins
and destroy them for their wickedness;
the LORD our God will destroy them.

Psalm 95

1 Come, let us sing for joy to the LORD;
let us shout aloud[p] to the Rock[q] of our salvation.
2 Let us come before him[r] with thanksgiving
and extol him with music[s] and song.

94:4 [t]Ps 31:18 [u]Ps 52:1
94:5 [v]Isa 3:15
94:7 [w]Job 22:14; Ps 10:11
94:8 [x]Ps 92:6
94:9 [y]Ex 4:11; Pr 20:12
94:10 [z]Job 35:11; Isa 28:26
94:11 [a]1Co 3:20*
94:12 [b]Job 5:17; Heb 12:5 [c]Dt 8:3
94:13 [d]Ps 55:23
94:14 [e]1Sa 12:22; Ps 37:28; Ro 11:2
94:15 [f]Ps 97:2
94:16 [g]Nu 10:35; Ps 17:13 [h]Ps 59:2
94:17 [i]Ps 124:2
94:18 [j]Ps 38:16
94:20 [k]Ps 58:2
94:21 [l]Ps 56:6 [m]Ps 106:38; Pr 17:15,26
94:22 [n]Ps 18:2; 59:9
94:23 [o]Ps 7:16
95:1 [p]Ps 81:1 [q]2Sa 22:47
95:2 [r]Mic 6:6 [s]Ps 81:2; Eph 5:19

94:7 "Jacob" is a synonym for Israel (see Ge 32:28).

³For the LORD is the great God,[t]
the great King above all gods.[u]
⁴In his hand are the depths of the earth,
and the mountain peaks belong to him.
⁵The sea is his, for he made it,
and his hands formed the dry land.[v]

⁶Come, let us bow down[w] in worship,
let us kneel[x] before the LORD our Maker;[y]
⁷for he is our God
and we are the people of his pasture,[z]
the flock under his care.

Today, if you hear his voice,
8 do not harden your hearts as you did at Meribah,[a][a]
as you did that day at Massah[b] in the desert,
⁹where your fathers tested[b] and tried me,
though they had seen what I did.
¹⁰For forty years[c] I was angry with that generation;
I said, "They are a people whose hearts go astray,
and they have not known my ways."
¹¹So I declared on oath[d] in my anger,
"They shall never enter my rest."[e]

Psalm 96

¹Sing to the LORD[f] a new song;
sing to the LORD, all the earth.
²Sing to the LORD, praise his name;
proclaim his salvation[g] day after day.
³Declare his glory among the nations,
his marvelous deeds among all peoples.

⁴For great is the LORD and most worthy of praise;[h]
he is to be feared[i] above all gods.[j]
⁵For all the gods of the nations are idols,
but the LORD made the heavens.[k]
⁶Splendor and majesty are before him;
strength and glory[l] are in his sanctuary.

⁷Ascribe to the LORD,[m] O families of nations,[n]
ascribe to the LORD glory and strength.
⁸Ascribe to the LORD the glory due his name;
bring an offering[o] and come into his courts.
⁹Worship the LORD in the splendor of his[c] holiness;[p]
tremble[q] before him, all the earth.[r]

¹⁰Say among the nations, "The LORD reigns.[s]"
The world is firmly established, it cannot be moved;[t]
he will judge the peoples with equity.[u]

95:3 [t]Ps 48:1; 145:3 [u]Ps 96:4; 97:9
95:5 [v]Ge 1:9; Ps 146:6
95:6 [w]Php 2:10 [x]2Ch 6:13 [y]Ps 100:3; 149:2; Isa 17:7; Da 6:10-11; Hos 8:14
95:7 [z]Ps 74:1; 79:13
95:8 [a]Ex 17:7
95:9 [b]Nu 14:22; Ps 78:18; 1Co 10:9
95:10 [c]Ac 7:36; Heb 3:17
95:11 [d]Nu 14:23 [e]Dt 1:35; Heb 4:3*
96:1 [f]1Ch 16:23
96:2 [g]Ps 71:15
96:4 [h]Ps 18:3; 145:3 [i]Ps 89:7 [j]Ps 95:3
96:5 [k]Ps 115:15
96:6 [l]Ps 29:1
96:7 [m]Ps 29:1 [n]Ps 22:27
96:8 [o]Ps 45:12; 72:10
96:9 [p]Ps 29:2 [q]Ps 114:7 [r]Ps 33:8
96:10 [s]Ps 97:1 [t]Ps 93:1 [u]Ps 67:4

[a] 8 *Meribah* means *quarreling.* [b] 8 *Massah* means *testing.* [c] 9 Or *LORD with the splendor of*

95:3–5 The ancient Near Eastern world had different gods for different peoples, different geographical areas, different cosmic regions (heaven, Earth, the netherworld) and different aspects of life (e.g., war, fertility, crafts). But Israel was to praise the Lord because he is above all other gods; there is no corner of the universe that is beyond the scope of his control.
95:7 A king was commonly called the "shepherd" of his people (see the note on 23:1), and his realm could be referred to as his "pasture" (see Jer 25:36; 49:20; 50:45).
95:10 For "hearts," see the note on 4:7.
96:10 The Old Testament writers viewed the world order as one, embracing both its physical and moral aspects because both were established by God as components of his one kingdom, and both are upheld by his one rule. Therefore God's rule over creation and over the affairs of humankind is often spoken of in one breath.

96:11 [v]Ps 97:1; 98:7; Isa 49:13
96:12 [w]Isa 44:23 [x]Ps 65:13
96:13 [y]Rev 19:11

11 Let the heavens rejoice, let the earth be glad;[v]
let the sea resound, and all that is in it;
12 let the fields be jubilant, and everything in them.
Then all the trees of the forest[w] will sing for joy;[x]
13 they will sing before the LORD, for he comes,
he comes to judge[y] the earth.
He will judge the world in righteousness
and the peoples in his truth.

Psalm 97

97:1 [z]Ps 96:10 [a]Ps 96:11
97:2 [b]Ex 19:9; Ps 18:11 [c]Ps 89:14
97:3 [d]Da 7:10 [e]Hab 3:5 [f]Ps 18:8
97:4 [g]Ps 104:32
97:5 [h]Ps 46:2,6; Mic 1:4 [i]Jos 3:11
97:6 [j]Ps 50:6 [k]Ps 19:1
97:7 [l]Lev 26:1 [m]Jer 10:14 [n]Heb 1:6
97:8 [o]Ps 48:11
97:9 [p]Ps 83:18; 95:3 [q]Ex 18:11
97:10 [r]Ps 34:14; Am 5:15; Ro 12:9 [s]Pr 2:8 [t]Da 3:28 [u]Ps 37:40; Jer 15:21
97:11 [v]Job 22:28
97:12 [w]Ps 30:4

1 The LORD reigns,[z] let the earth be glad;[a]
let the distant shores rejoice.

2 Clouds and thick darkness[b] surround him;
righteousness and justice are the foundation of
his throne.[c]
3 Fire[d] goes before[e] him
and consumes[f] his foes on every side.
4 His lightning lights up the world;
the earth sees and trembles.[g]
5 The mountains melt[h] like wax before the LORD,
before the Lord of all the earth.[i]
6 The heavens proclaim his righteousness,[j]
and all the peoples see his glory.[k]

7 All who worship images[l] are put to shame,[m]
those who boast in idols—
worship him,[n] all you gods!

8 Zion hears and rejoices
and the villages of Judah are glad
because of your judgments,[o] O LORD.
9 For you, O LORD, are the Most High over all the earth;[p]
you are exalted[q] far above all gods.

10 Let those who love the LORD hate evil,[r]
for he guards the lives of his faithful ones[s]
and delivers[t] them from the hand of the wicked.[u]
11 Light is shed[v] upon the righteous
and joy on the upright in heart.
12 Rejoice in the LORD, you who are righteous,
and praise his holy name.[w]

Psalm 98

A psalm.

98:1 [x]Ps 96:1 [y]Ps 96:3 [z]Ex 15:6 [a]Isa 52:10
98:2 [b]Isa 52:10

1 Sing to the LORD a new song,[x]
for he has done marvelous things;[y]
his right hand[z] and his holy arm[a]
have worked salvation for him.
2 The LORD has made his salvation known[b]
and revealed his righteousness to the nations.

96:11 In the Old Testament joy is commonly a group expression, often associated with dancing or the blessings of prosperity (Isa 60:15). God's praise is shouted or sung even in more formal public worship (Ezr 3:10–11; Ps 100:1–2). Linked with this concept also are musical instruments, clapping, leaping or foot-stamping. Feasting or offering sacrifices (Dt 12:12; Isa 56:7), celebration of harvest or victory (1Sa 18:6; Joel 1:16) and enjoying prosperity or personal triumph (Ps 31:7; Isa 61:3ff.) are all occasions for joy.

[3] He has remembered[c] his love
and his faithfulness to the house of Israel;
all the ends of the earth have seen
the salvation of our God.

[4] Shout for joy[d] to the LORD, all the earth,
burst into jubilant song with music;
[5] make music to the LORD with the harp,[e]
with the harp and the sound of singing,[f]
[6] with trumpets[g] and the blast of the ram's horn—
shout for joy before the LORD, the King.[h]

[7] Let the sea resound, and everything in it,
the world, and all who live in it.[i]
[8] Let the rivers clap their hands,
let the mountains[j] sing together for joy;
[9] let them sing before the LORD,
for he comes to judge the earth.
He will judge the world in righteousness
and the peoples with equity.[k]

Psalm 99

[1] The LORD reigns,[l]
let the nations tremble;
he sits enthroned between the cherubim,[m]
let the earth shake.

98:3 [c]Lk 1:54
98:4 [d]Isa 44:23
98:5 [e]Ps 92:3 [f]Isa 51:3
98:6 [g]Nu 10:10 [h]Ps 47:7
98:7 [i]Ps 24:1
98:8 [j]Isa 55:12
98:9 [k]Ps 96:10
99:1 [l]Ps 97:1 [m]Ex 25:22

98:6 These "trumpets" were the special long, straight trumpets used in the temple (see the note on Nu 10:1–10). The "ram's horn" was the more common trumpet.

The Shofar

PSALM 98 Psalm 98:4–6 instructs worshipers to offer joyful praise music to the Lord, using not only their voices but also various instruments. The Hebrew word translated "ram's horn" here (v. 6) is *shofar*. This instrument belongs to a class known as aerophones, which produce a sound when air is passed through them.[1] The shofar was blown in several contexts:

✣ The blast of the horn summoned warriors to battle and signaled the beginning of an attack (Jdg 3:27; 7:20; Job 39:25; Jer 4:19–21). When the Israelites marched around Jericho for the seventh time, they were instructed to blow rams' horns (Jos 6:4–5).

✣ The shofar summoned worshipers to Jerusalem (Isa 27:13).

✣ It was blown by watchmen to announce important news, whether celebratory or disastrous (1Sa 13:3; Eze 33:3–6; Joel 2:1,17; Am 2:2).

✣ It was used during coronation ceremonies, such as Solomon's (1Ki 1:34) and Jehu's (2Ki 9:13).

✣ The shofar was sounded on holy occasions such as:

The Day of Atonement during the year of Jubilee (Lev 25:9),[2]

David's return of the ark to Jerusalem (2Sa 6:15),

The covenant renewal ceremony during Asa's religious reforms (2Ch 15:14) and

Regular temple worship (Ps 47:5; 81:3; 98:6; 150:3).

See also "Trumpets in the Ancient World" on page 2057.

[1]See "Ancient Musical Instruments" on page 797. [2]See "The Day of Atonement" on page 176 and "Sabbath, Sabbath Year and the Jubilee" on page 189.

99:2 [n]Ps 48:1 [o]Ps 97:9; 113:4
99:3 [p]Ps 76:1
99:4 [q]Ps 11:7 [r]Ps 98:9
99:5 [s]Ps 132:7
99:6 [t]Ex 24:6 [u]Jer 15:1 [v]1Sa 7:9
99:7 [w]Ex 33:9

2 Great is the LORD[n] in Zion;
he is exalted[o] over all the nations.
3 Let them praise your great and awesome name[p]—
he is holy.

4 The King is mighty, he loves justice[q]—
you have established equity;[r]
in Jacob you have done
what is just and right.
5 Exalt[s] the LORD our God
and worship at his footstool;
he is holy.

6 Moses[t] and Aaron were among his priests,
Samuel[u] was among those who called on his name;
they called on the LORD
and he answered[v] them.
7 He spoke to them from the pillar of cloud;[w]
they kept his statutes and the decrees he gave them.

8 O LORD our God,
you answered them;

Thrones in the Ancient World

PSALM 99 Royal and ritual thrones of the ancient world were typically constructed of wood frames overlaid with precious metals and inlaid with gems.[1] Popular ornamentation included engravings of lions, winged sphinxes and composite mythological creatures. According to artistic tradition throughout the ancient world, these served as images of power and authority. Solomon's throne was inlaid with ivory and overlaid with gold. It featured a rounded top and a pair of standing lions for armrests. Six steps led up to the royal dais, and each step was flanked by two lions, one on each end (1Ki 10:19–20).

Aspects of the throne's design recall other royal furniture of that time and region. For example, an ivory engraving from **Megiddo** and a **sarcophagus** (coffin) from Byblos, both dating roughly to the thirteenth century B.C., picture rulers seated upon thrones with curved-top backs supported by sphinxes, their feet resting on footstools.[2] Footstools typically accompanied thrones and were occasionally engraved with scenes of vanquished foes, an image communicating triumph over one's enemies (Ps 110:1). An ancient king literally sought to make his enemies his footstool.[3]

The gods of the ancient Near East are depicted seated either upon thrones or atop animals or mythical beings (e.g., a goddess might be seated astride a lion). The creatures themselves become the seat of divinity. Images of gods carved into the hills along the Tigris River portray deities mounted upon such composite creatures.

The divine throne of **Yahweh** is envisioned as a living entity composed of fiery creatures whose outspread wings form the chariot upon which he transverses the heavens (2Sa 22:11; Ps 18:10; Eze 10:1). His throne is a spectacle of light, shining with a radiance of jewels (Eze 1:26; Rev 4:3) and issuing flames of fire (Ps 104:3–4; Da 7:9). Although heaven is God's throne and Earth his footstool (Isa 66:1), the temple and Jerusalem (i.e., the temple city) are often referred to as the throne and footstool of God, respectively (1Ch 28:2; Ps 132:7).[4] This imagery evokes the divine presence of Yahweh and his kingship over his covenant people.

[1]See "Precious Stones of the Biblical World" on page 1156. [2]For more on these cities, see "Megiddo" on page 1541 and "Byblos" on page 1349. [3]See "The Ancient Near Eastern King" on page 839. [4]See also "Solomon's Temple and Other Ancient Temples" on page 620.

you were to Israel[a] a forgiving God,[x]
though you punished their misdeeds.[b]
9 Exalt the LORD our God
and worship at his holy mountain,
for the LORD our God is holy.

99:8 [x]Nu 14:20

Psalm 100

A psalm. For giving thanks.

1 Shout for joy[y] to the LORD, all the earth.
2 Worship the LORD with gladness;
come before him[z] with joyful songs.
3 Know that the LORD is God.[a]
It is he who made us,[b] and we are his[c];
we are his people, the sheep of his pasture.[c]

4 Enter his gates with thanksgiving
and his courts with praise;
give thanks to him and praise his name.[d]
5 For the LORD is good[e] and his love endures forever;[f]
his faithfulness[g] continues through all generations.

100:1 [y]Ps 98:4
100:2 [z]Ps 95:2
100:3 [a]Ps 46:10 [b]Job 10:3 [c]Ps 74:1; Eze 34:31
100:4 [d]Ps 116:17
100:5 [e]1Ch 16:34; Ps 25:8 [f]Ezr 3:11; Ps 106:1 [g]Ps 119:90

Psalm 101

Of David. A psalm.

1 I will sing of your love[h] and justice;
to you, O LORD, I will sing praise.
2 I will be careful to lead a blameless life—
when will you come to me?

I will walk in my house
with blameless heart.
3 I will set before my eyes
no vile thing.[i]

The deeds of faithless men I hate;[j]
they will not cling to me.
4 Men of perverse heart[k] shall be far from me;
I will have nothing to do with evil.
5 Whoever slanders his neighbor[l] in secret,
him will I put to silence;
whoever has haughty eyes[m] and a proud heart,
him will I not endure.
6 My eyes will be on the faithful in the land,
that they may dwell with me;
he whose walk is blameless[n]
will minister to me.

101:1 [h]Ps 51:14; 89:1; 145:7
101:3 [i]Dt 15:9 [j]Ps 40:4
101:4 [k]Pr 11:20
101:5 [l]Ps 50:20 [m]Ps 10:5; Pr 6:17
101:6 [n]Ps 119:1

[a] 8 Hebrew *them* [b] 8 Or *I an avenger of the wrongs done to them* [c] 3 Or *and not we ourselves*

100:1–5 Scripture commonly compares God's people to sheep (see the note on 23:1). They are totally dependent upon him, as sheep upon their shepherd. To put the metaphor in perspective, sheep, despite their helplessness and weakness, represented the wealth of Israel, and shepherds dedicated a lifetime to their care.
100:1–2 For commentary on Old Testament expressions of joy, see the note on 96:11.
101:1–8 This psalm was written by one of Israel's kings, either David or one of his descendants (see heading). It is similar in form to ancient treaties. The king solemnly vowed to administer justice and to live up to the theocratic (God-governed) ideal in Israel. God had instructed the king to prepare a personal copy of the law so that he would learn to live rightly and to manage well the affairs of state as Israel's chief executive (Dt 17:14–20). The king was God's servant, appointed to carry out the wishes of his master, or overlord.

TWENTY-FIVE OF THE MOST FAMILIAR PSALM LINES

1	O LORD, our Lord, how majestic is your name in all the earth! (8:1).
2	The fool says in his heart, "There is no God" (14:1).
3	The heavens declare the glory of God (19:1).
4	My God, my God, why have you forsaken me? (22:1).
5	The LORD is my shepherd, I shall not be in want (23:1).
6	The LORD is my light and my salvation—whom shall I fear? (27:1).
7	Delight yourself in the LORD and he will give you the desires of your heart (37:4).
8	As the deer pants for streams of water, so my soul pants for you, O God (42:1).
9	God is our refuge and strength, an ever-present help in trouble (46:1).
10	Be still, and know that I am God (46:10).
11	Great is the LORD, and most worthy of praise (48:1).
12	Create in me a pure heart, O God (51:10).
13	May God be gracious to us and bless us and make his face shine upon us (67:1).
14	How lovely is your dwelling place, O LORD Almighty! (84:1).
15	Sing to the LORD a new song, for he has done marvelous things (98:1).
16	Shout for joy to the LORD, all the earth (100:1).
17	For the LORD is good and his love endures forever; his faithfulness continues through all generations (100:5).
18	As far as the east is from the west, so far has he removed our transgressions from us (103:12).
19	Give thanks to the LORD, for he is good; his love endures forever (107:1).
20	Your word is a lamp to my feet and a light for my path (119:105).
21	I lift up my eyes to the hills—where does my help come from? (121:1).
22	Unless the LORD builds the house, its builders labor in vain (127:1).
23	How good and pleasant it is when brothers live together in unity! (133:1).
24	I praise you because I am fearfully and wonderfully made (139:14).
25	Search me, O God, and know my heart (139:23).

Old Testament Today, p. 344

7 No one who practices deceit
will dwell in my house;
no one who speaks falsely
will stand in my presence.

8 Every morning[o] I will put to silence
all the wicked[p] in the land;
I will cut off every evildoer[q]
from the city of the LORD.[r]

101:8 [o]Jer 21:12 [p]Ps 75:10 [q]Ps 118:10-12 [r]Ps 46:4

Psalm 102

A prayer of an afflicted man. When he is faint and pours out his lament before the LORD.

1 Hear my prayer, O LORD;
let my cry for help[s] come to you.
2 Do not hide your face[t] from me
when I am in distress.
Turn your ear to me;
when I call, answer me quickly.

3 For my days vanish like smoke;[u]
my bones burn like glowing embers.
4 My heart is blighted and withered like grass;[v]
I forget to eat my food.
5 Because of my loud groaning
I am reduced to skin and bones.
6 I am like a desert owl,[w]
like an owl among the ruins.
7 I lie awake;[x] I have become
like a bird alone[y] on a roof.
8 All day long my enemies taunt me;
those who rail against me use my name as a curse.
9 For I eat ashes as my food
and mingle my drink with tears[z]
10 because of your great wrath,[a]
for you have taken me up and thrown me aside.
11 My days are like the evening shadow;[b]
I wither away like grass.

12 But you, O LORD, sit enthroned forever;[c]
your renown endures[d] through all generations.
13 You will arise and have compassion[e] on Zion,
for it is time to show favor to her;
the appointed time has come.
14 For her stones are dear to your servants;
her very dust moves them to pity.
15 The nations will fear[f] the name of the LORD,
all the kings[g] of the earth will revere your glory.

102:1 [s]Ex 2:23
102:2 [t]Ps 69:17
102:3 [u]Jas 4:14
102:4 [v]Ps 37:2
102:6 [w]Job 30:29; Isa 34:11
102:7 [x]Ps 77:4 [y]Ps 38:11
102:9 [z]Ps 42:3
102:10 [a]Ps 38:3
102:11 [b]Job 14:2
102:12 [c]Ps 9:7 [d]Ps 135:13
102:13 [e]Isa 60:10
102:15 [f]1Ki 8:43 [g]Ps 138:4

101:8 "Every morning" implies diligence and persistence (see Jer 21:12; Zep 3:5). It may have been traditional for kings to hear cases in the morning.
102:3 In ancient times homes were heated very differently from today. In the houses of the poorer people, the hearth consisted of a depression in the floor of a room in which a fire was kindled for cooking or for warmth. Chimneys were unknown; smoke escaped from the house as it could, or through a latticed opening for the purpose. The better houses were heated by means of a brazier of burning coals. The brazier was a wide, shallow pan that could also be used for cooking. (See Ge 18:6; Isa 30:14; Jer 36:22–23; Hos 13:3; Zec 12:6.)
102:4 For "heart," see the note on 4:7. Here "heart" is used in combination with "bones" (v. 3) to refer to the whole person (body and spirit). Compare the combination of "soul" and "bones" in 6:2–3 (see also the note on 6:3).
102:6 The owl was associated with desert areas and with ruins (see Isa 34:11,15; Jer 50:39; Zep 2:14).

102:16 [h]Isa 60:1-2
102:17 [i]Ne 1:6
102:18 [j]Ro 15:4 [k]Ps 22:31
102:19 [l]Dt 26:15
102:20 [m]Ps 79:11
102:21 [n]Ps 22:22
102:24 [o]Ps 90:2; Isa 38:10
102:25 [p]Ge 1:1; Heb 1:10-12*
102:26 [q]Isa 34:4; Mt 24:35; 2Pe 3:7-10; Rev 20:11
102:27 [r]Mal 3:6; Heb 13:8; Jas 1:17
102:28 [s]Ps 69:36 [t]Ps 89:4
103:1 [u]Ps 104:1
103:3 [v]Ps 130:8 [w]Ex 15:26
103:5 [x]Isa 40:31
103:7 [y]Ps 99:7; 147:19 [z]Ex 33:13 [a]Ps 106:22

16 For the LORD will rebuild Zion
and appear in his glory.[h]
17 He will respond to the prayer[i] of the destitute;
he will not despise their plea.

18 Let this be written[j] for a future generation,
that a people not yet created[k] may praise the LORD:
19 "The LORD looked down[l] from his sanctuary on high,
from heaven he viewed the earth,
20 to hear the groans of the prisoners[m]
and release those condemned to death."
21 So the name of the LORD will be declared[n] in Zion
and his praise in Jerusalem
22 when the peoples and the kingdoms
assemble to worship the LORD.

23 In the course of my life[a] he broke my strength;
he cut short my days.
24 So I said:
"Do not take me away, O my God, in the midst of my days;
your years go on[o] through all generations.
25 In the beginning[p] you laid the foundations of the earth,
and the heavens are the work of your hands.
26 They will perish,[q] but you remain;
they will all wear out like a garment.
Like clothing you will change them
and they will be discarded.
27 But you remain the same,[r]
and your years will never end.
28 The children of your servants[s] will live in your presence;
their descendants[t] will be established before you."

Psalm 103

Of David.

1 Praise the LORD, O my soul;[u]
all my inmost being, praise his holy name.
2 Praise the LORD, O my soul,
and forget not all his benefits—
3 who forgives all your sins[v]
and heals[w] all your diseases,
4 who redeems your life from the pit
and crowns you with love and compassion,
5 who satisfies your desires with good things
so that your youth is renewed like the eagle's.[x]

6 The LORD works righteousness
and justice for all the oppressed.

7 He made known[y] his ways[z] to Moses,
his deeds[a] to the people of Israel:

[a] 23 Or *By his power*

103:1–2 The phrase "O my soul" was a conventional Hebrew way of addressing oneself (see v. 22; 104:1,35; 116:7). For "soul," see the note on 6:3.

[8]The LORD is compassionate and gracious,[b]
slow to anger, abounding in love.
[9]He will not always accuse,
nor will he harbor his anger forever;[c]
[10]he does not treat us as our sins deserve[d]
or repay us according to our iniquities.
[11]For as high as the heavens are above the earth,
so great is his love[e] for those who fear him;
[12]as far as the east is from the west,
so far has he removed our transgressions[f] from us.
[13]As a father has compassion[g] on his children,
so the LORD has compassion on those who fear him;
[14]for he knows how we are formed,[h]
he remembers that we are dust.
[15]As for man, his days are like grass,[i]
he flourishes like a flower[j] of the field;
[16]the wind blows[k] over it and it is gone,
and its place[l] remembers it no more.
[17]But from everlasting to everlasting
the LORD's love is with those who fear him,
and his righteousness with their children's children—
[18]with those who keep his covenant
and remember to obey his precepts.[m]

[19]The LORD has established his throne in heaven,
and his kingdom rules[n] over all.

[20]Praise the LORD, you his angels,[o]
you mighty ones[p] who do his bidding,
who obey his word.
[21]Praise the LORD, all his heavenly hosts,[q]
you his servants who do his will.
[22]Praise the LORD, all his works[r]
everywhere in his dominion.

Praise the LORD, O my soul.

Psalm 104

[1]Praise the LORD, O my soul.[s]

O LORD my God, you are very great;
you are clothed with splendor and majesty.
[2]He wraps[t] himself in light as with a garment;
he stretches out the heavens[u] like a tent
[3]and lays the beams[v] of his upper chambers on their waters.
He makes the clouds[w] his chariot
and rides on the wings of the wind.[x]
[4]He makes winds his messengers,[a][y]
flames of fire[z] his servants.

[5]He set the earth[a] on its foundations;
it can never be moved.

103:8 [b]Ex 34:6; Ps 86:15; Jas 5:11
103:9 [c]Ps 30:5; Isa 57:16; Jer 3:5, 12; Mic 7:18
103:10 [d]Ezr 9:13
103:11 [e]Ps 57:10
103:12 [f]2Sa 12:13
103:13 [g]Mal 3:17
103:14 [h]Isa 29:16
103:15 [i]Ps 90:5 [j]Job 14:2; Jas 1:10; 1Pe 1:24
103:16 [k]Isa 40:7 [l]Job 7:10
103:18 [m]Dt 7:9
103:19 [n]Ps 47:2
103:20 [o]Ps 148:2; Heb 1:14 [p]Ps 29:1
103:21 [q]1Ki 22:19
103:22 [r]Ps 145:10
104:1 [s]Ps 103:22
104:2 [t]Da 7:9 [u]Isa 40:22
104:3 [v]Am 9:6 [w]Isa 19:1 [x]Ps 18:10
104:4 [y]Ps 148:8; Heb 1:7* [z]2Ki 2:11
104:5 [a]Job 26:7; Ps 24:1-2

[a] 4 Or *angels*

103:12 *Yâm,* "sea," is the Hebrew word usually used for "west," because the Mediterranean Sea lies to the west of the area known today as Palestine. The word was sometimes used figuratively with "east" to denote great distance.

104:6 [b]Ge 7:19 [c]Ge 1:2
104:7 [d]Ps 18:15
104:8 [e]Ps 33:7
104:10 [f]Ps 107:33; Isa 41:18
104:12 [g]Mt 8:20
104:13 [h]Ps 147:8; Jer 10:13
104:14 [i]Job 38:27; Ps 147:8 [j]Ge 1:30; Job 28:5

6 You covered it[b] with the deep[c] as with a garment;
the waters stood above the mountains.
7 But at your rebuke[d] the waters fled,
at the sound of your thunder they took to flight;
8 they flowed over the mountains,
they went down into the valleys,
to the place you assigned[e] for them.
9 You set a boundary they cannot cross;
never again will they cover the earth.

10 He makes springs[f] pour water into the ravines;
it flows between the mountains.
11 They give water to all the beasts of the field;
the wild donkeys quench their thirst.
12 The birds of the air[g] nest by the waters;
they sing among the branches.
13 He waters the mountains[h] from his upper chambers;
the earth is satisfied by the fruit of his work.
14 He makes grass grow[i] for the cattle,
and plants for man to cultivate—
bringing forth food[j] from the earth:

ANCIENT TEXTS AND ARTIFACTS

The Ugaritic Text of the Myth of Baal

PSALM 104 Discovered at the site of Ras Shamra (ancient **Ugarit**; see "Map 1"),[1] the Myth of Baal is one of the longest literary works of the western Semitic peoples in the second millennium B.C. It begins with a conflict over kingship between Baal, the storm god, and Yam, the sea god. Although Baal is victorious in this battle, he is later defeated and killed by Mot, the god of grain and death. After Baal's sister, Anat, mourns and buries him, she kills Mot in revenge for her brother's death. She then grinds up his body and sows it as seed. Subsequently, Baal and Mot come back to life and vie for power once again, with the result that Mot eventually capitulates to Baal. The incident with Yam is interpreted as Baal's victory over the sea, while the struggle between Baal and Mot is equated to the fertility cycle, with Baal seasonally "disappearing" from the earth.[2]

Psalm 104, a creation psalm, uses some of the imagery known from the Myth of Baal. The Lord's power over the sea in creation is described (v. 6ff.). While Baal is the "cloud-rider," the Lord "makes the clouds his chariot" (v. 3). Unlike Baal, however, the Lord is neither killed nor needs help in making the earth produce food (v. 13ff.). The attribution of aspects of Baal to the Lord, along with a demonstration of his superiority to Baal, served to exalt and praise the Lord as the true King and God of creation in an environment in which the temptation to worship Baal was rampant.

[1]See "Ugarit/Ras Shamra" on page 819. [2]See "Baal and the Fertility Cults" on page 1414.

Ugaritic tablet describing the conflict between Baal and Mot (Death)

Preserving Bible Times; © Dr. James C. Martin; permission of Musée de Louvre

Ancient Voices

The gods see them,
see Yammu's messengers,
the embassy of Ruler [Naharu]*.
The gods lower their heads
onto their knees,
onto their princely thrones.
Balu rebukes them:
Why, gods, have you lowered (your) heads
even to your knees,
even to your princely thrones?
As one must the gods answer,
the tablet of Yammu's messengers,
the embassy of Ruler Naharu!
Lift, O gods, your heads
off your knees,
off your princely thrones.
And let me answer Yammu's messengers,
the embassy of Ruler Naharu.
The gods then raise their heads
off their knees,
off their princely thrones.

*Words in brackets and parentheses added by translator for clarity or where text has gaps

—The Balu Myth

See "The Ugaritic Text of the Myth of Baal" article on the previous page.

15 wine[k] that gladdens the heart of man,
oil[l] to make his face shine,
and bread that sustains his heart.
16 The trees of the LORD are well watered,
the cedars of Lebanon that he planted.
17 There the birds[m] make their nests;
the stork has its home in the pine trees.
18 The high mountains belong to the wild goats;
the crags are a refuge for the coneys.[a][n]

19 The moon marks off the seasons,[o]
and the sun[p] knows when to go down.
20 You bring darkness,[q] it becomes night,[r]
and all the beasts of the forest[s] prowl.
21 The lions roar for their prey
and seek their food from God.[t]
22 The sun rises, and they steal away;
they return and lie down in their dens.[u]
23 Then man goes out to his work,[v]
to his labor until evening.

24 How many are your works,[w] O LORD!
In wisdom you made[x] them all;
the earth is full of your creatures.
25 There is the sea,[y] vast and spacious,
teeming with creatures beyond number—
living things both large and small.
26 There the ships[z] go to and fro,
and the leviathan,[a] which you formed to frolic there.

27 These all look to you
to give them their food[b] at the proper time.
28 When you give it to them,
they gather it up;
when you open your hand,
they are satisfied[c] with good things.
29 When you hide your face,[d]
they are terrified;
when you take away their breath,
they die and return to the dust.[e]
30 When you send your Spirit,
they are created,
and you renew the face of the earth.

31 May the glory of the LORD endure forever;
may the LORD rejoice in his works[f]—
32 he who looks at the earth, and it trembles,[g]
who touches the mountains,[h] and they smoke.[i]

33 I will sing[j] to the LORD all my life;
I will sing praise to my God as long as I live.

104:15 [k]Jdg 9:13 [l]Ps 23:5; 92:10; Lk 7:46
104:17 [m]ver 12
104:18 [n]Pr 30:26
104:19 [o]Ge 1:14 [p]Ps 19:6
104:20 [q]Isa 45:7 [r]Ps 74:16 [s]Ps 50:10
104:21 [t]Job 38:39; Ps 145:15; Joel 1:20
104:22 [u]Job 37:8
104:23 [v]Ge 3:19
104:24 [w]Ps 40:5 [x]Pr 3:19
104:25 [y]Ps 69:34
104:26 [z]Ps 107:23; Eze 27:9 [a]Job 41:1
104:27 [b]Job 36:31; Ps 136:25; 145:15; 147:9
104:28 [c]Ps 145:16
104:29 [d]Dt 31:17 [e]Job 34:14; Ecc 12:7
104:31 [f]Ge 1:31
104:32 [g]Ps 97:4 [h]Ex 19:18 [i]Ps 144:5
104:33 [j]Ps 63:4

[a] *18* That is, the hyrax or rock badger

104:16–18 Lebanon was a well-watered region. Its great trees, hordes of birds and plentiful alpine animals provided a picture of God's earthly parkland (see "Cedars of Lebanon" on p. 1043).

The word "coneys" probably refers to the Syrian rock hyrax, a shy animal about the size of a rabbit, living among the rocks.

104:26 "Leviathan" refers to the fearsome mythological monster of the deep (see the notes on Job 41:30; Ps 89:9–10). Here this frightening creature is portrayed merely as God's harmless pet cavorting in the ocean.

34 May my meditation be pleasing to him,
as I rejoice[k] in the LORD.
35 But may sinners vanish[l] from the earth
and the wicked be no more.

Praise the LORD, O my soul.

Praise the LORD.[a][m]

Psalm 105

1 Give thanks to the LORD,[n] call on his name;[o]
make known among the nations what he has done.
2 Sing to him,[p] sing praise to him;
tell of all his wonderful acts.
3 Glory in his holy name;
let the hearts of those who seek the LORD rejoice.
4 Look to the LORD and his strength;
seek his face[q] always.

5 Remember the wonders[r] he has done,
his miracles, and the judgments he pronounced,[s]
6 O descendants of Abraham his servant,[t]
O sons of Jacob, his chosen[u] ones.
7 He is the LORD our God;
his judgments are in all the earth.

8 He remembers his covenant[v] forever,
the word he commanded, for a thousand generations,
9 the covenant he made with Abraham,[w]
the oath he swore to Isaac.
10 He confirmed it[x] to Jacob as a decree,
to Israel as an everlasting covenant:
11 "To you I will give the land of Canaan[y]
as the portion you will inherit."

12 When they were but few in number,[z]
few indeed, and strangers in it,[a]
13 they wandered from nation to nation,
from one kingdom to another.
14 He allowed no one to oppress[b] them;
for their sake he rebuked kings:[c]
15 "Do not touch[d] my anointed ones;
do my prophets no harm."

16 He called down famine[e] on the land
and destroyed all their supplies of food;
17 and he sent a man before them—
Joseph, sold as a slave.[f]
18 They bruised his feet with shackles,[g]
his neck was put in irons,
19 till what he foretold[h] came to pass,
till the word of the LORD proved him true.

104:34 [k]Ps 9:2
104:35 [l]Ps 37:38 [m]Ps 105:45; 106:48
105:1 [n]1Ch 16:34 [o]Ps 99:6
105:2 [p]Ps 96:1
105:4 [q]Ps 27:8
105:5 [r]Ps 40:5 [s]Ps 77:11
105:6 [t]ver 42 [u]Ps 106:5
105:8 [v]Ps 106:45; Lk 1:72
105:9 [w]Ge 12:7; 17:2; 22:16-18; Gal 3:15-18
105:10 [x]Ge 28:13-15
105:11 [y]Ge 13:15; 15:18
105:12 [z]Ge 34:30; Dt 7:7 [a]Ge 23:4; Heb 11:9
105:14 [b]Ge 35:5 [c]Ge 12:17-20
105:15 [d]Ge 26:11
105:16 [e]Ge 41:54; Lev 26:26; Isa 3:1; Eze 4:16
105:17 [f]Ge 37:28; 45:5; Ac 7:9
105:18 [g]Ge 40:15
105:19 [h]Ge 40:20-22

[a] *35* Hebrew *Hallelu Yah*; in the Septuagint this line stands at the beginning of Psalm 105.

105:18 Iron did not come into common use in the ancient Near East until the twelfth century B.C. Earlier shackles were made of bronze (see Jdg 16:21).

[20] The king sent and released him,
the ruler of peoples set him free.[i]
[21] He made him master of his household,
ruler over all he possessed,
[22] to instruct his princes[j] as he pleased
and teach his elders wisdom.

[23] Then Israel entered Egypt;[k]
Jacob lived as an alien in the land of Ham.
[24] The LORD made his people very fruitful;
he made them too numerous[l] for their foes,
[25] whose hearts he turned[m] to hate his people,
to conspire[n] against his servants.
[26] He sent Moses[o] his servant,
and Aaron, whom he had chosen.[p]
[27] They performed[q] his miraculous signs among them,
his wonders in the land of Ham.
[28] He sent darkness[r] and made the land dark—
for had they not rebelled against his words?
[29] He turned their waters into blood,[s]
causing their fish to die.[t]
[30] Their land teemed with frogs,[u]
which went up into the bedrooms of their rulers.
[31] He spoke, and there came swarms of flies,[v]
and gnats[w] throughout their country.
[32] He turned their rain into hail,[x]
with lightning throughout their land;

105:20 [i]Ge 41:14
105:22 [j]Ge 41:43-44
105:23 [k]Ge 46:6; Ac 13:17
105:24 [l]Ex 1:7,9
105:25 [m]Ex 4:21 [n]Ex 1:6-10; Ac 7:19
105:26 [o]Ex 3:10 [p]Nu 16:5; 17:5-8
105:27 [q]Ex 7:8-12:51
105:28 [r]Ex 10:22
105:29 [s]Ps 78:44 [t]Ex 7:21
105:30 [u]Ex 8:2,6
105:31 [v]Ex 8:21-24 [w]Ex 8:16-18
105:32 [x]Ex 9:22-25

105:22 "Elders" refers to the pharaoh's counselors—typically older men of wide experience and learning.

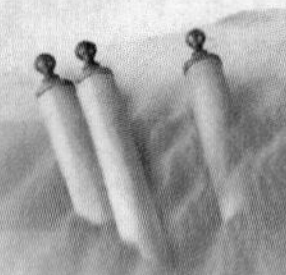

ANCIENT TEXTS AND ARTIFACTS

"The River Is Blood" in The Admonitions of Ipuwer

PSALM 105 The text called The Admonitions of Ipuwer is a lament over the breakdown of society in Egypt, and some compare it to the laments over upheavals found in the Biblical prophets.[1] Ipuwer is most famous in Biblical studies because it contains a line stating that the Nile is blood—and yet people drink from it anyway. This has an obvious historical parallel in the turning of the Nile to blood during the period of the plagues prior to the **exodus** (Ex 7:14–25). Psalm 105:29 expresses it this way: "He turned their waters into blood, causing their fish to die."

Although the date of the composition of Ipuwer is unknown, this lament was probably written long before the exodus and thus is not describing the Biblical event. The expression that the Nile "turned to blood" in Ipuwer may help us to understand what the term would have meant to ancient readers. The implication does not appear to have been that the river was literally full of blood but more likely that the water was so polluted as to have been barely usable.

[1]See "Ancient Near Eastern Laments" on page 1305 and "Calamity and Distress in Ipuwer" on page 1309.

33 he struck down their vines[y] and fig trees
and shattered the trees of their country.
34 He spoke, and the locusts came,[z]
grasshoppers without number;
35 they ate up every green thing in their land,
ate up the produce of their soil.
36 Then he struck down all the firstborn[a] in their land,
the firstfruits of all their manhood.

37 He brought out Israel, laden with silver and gold,[b]
and from among their tribes no one faltered.
38 Egypt was glad when they left,
because dread of Israel[c] had fallen on them.
39 He spread out a cloud[d] as a covering,
and a fire to give light at night.[e]
40 They asked,[f] and he brought them quail[g]
and satisfied them with the bread of heaven.[h]
41 He opened the rock,[i] and water gushed out;
like a river it flowed in the desert.

42 For he remembered his holy promise[j]
given to his servant Abraham.
43 He brought out his people with rejoicing,[k]
his chosen ones with shouts of joy;
44 he gave them the lands of the nations,[l]
and they fell heir to what others had toiled for—
45 that they might keep his precepts
and observe his laws.[m]

Praise the LORD.[a]

Psalm 106

1 Praise the LORD.[b]

Give thanks to the LORD, for he is good;[n]
his love endures forever.
2 Who can proclaim the mighty acts[o] of the LORD
or fully declare his praise?
3 Blessed are they who maintain justice,
who constantly do what is right.[p]
4 Remember me,[q] O LORD, when you show favor to
your people,
come to my aid when you save them,
5 that I may enjoy the prosperity[r] of your chosen ones,
that I may share in the joy[s] of your nation
and join your inheritance in giving praise.

6 We have sinned,[t] even as our fathers did;
we have done wrong and acted wickedly.
7 When our fathers were in Egypt,
they gave no thought to your miracles;
they did not remember[u] your many kindnesses,
and they rebelled by the sea,[v] the Red Sea.[c]
8 Yet he saved them for his name's sake,[w]
to make his mighty power known.

105:33 [y]Ps 78:47
105:34 [z]Ex 10:4, 12-15
105:36 [a]Ex 12:29
105:37 [b]Ex 12:35
105:38 [c]Ex 12:33; 15:16
105:39 [d]Ex 13:21 [e]Ne 9:12; Ps 78:14
105:40 [f]Ps 78:18,24 [g]Ex 16:13 [h]Jn 6:31
105:41 [i]Ex 17:6; Nu 20:11; Ps 78:15-16; 1Co 10:4
105:42 [j]Ge 15:13-16
105:43 [k]Ex 15:1-18; Ps 106:12
105:44 [l]Jos 13:6-7
105:45 [m]Dt 4:40; 6:21-24
106:1 [n]Ps 100:5; 105:1
106:2 [o]Ps 145:4, 12
106:3 [p]Ps 15:2
106:4 [q]Ps 119:132
106:5 [r]Ps 1:3 [s]Ps 118:15
106:6 [t]Da 9:5
106:7 [u]Ps 78:11, 42 [v]Ex 14:11-12
106:8 [w]Ex 9:16

[a] 45 Hebrew *Hallelu Yah* [b] 1 Hebrew *Hallelu Yah*; also in verse 48 [c] 7 Hebrew *Yam Suph*; that is, Sea of Reeds; also in verses 9 and 22

[9] He rebuked[x] the Red Sea, and it dried up;[y]
he led them through[z] the depths as through a desert.
[10] He saved them[a] from the hand of the foe;
from the hand of the enemy he redeemed them.[b]
[11] The waters covered[c] their adversaries;
not one of them survived.
[12] Then they believed his promises
and sang his praise.[d]

[13] But they soon forgot[e] what he had done
and did not wait for his counsel.
[14] In the desert they gave in to their craving;
in the wasteland they put God to the test.[f]
[15] So he gave them[g] what they asked for,
but sent a wasting disease[h] upon them.

[16] In the camp they grew envious[i] of Moses
and of Aaron, who was consecrated to the LORD.
[17] The earth opened[j] up and swallowed Dathan;
it buried the company of Abiram.
[18] Fire blazed[k] among their followers;
a flame consumed the wicked.

[19] At Horeb they made a calf[l]
and worshiped an idol cast from metal.
[20] They exchanged their Glory[m]
for an image of a bull, which eats grass.
[21] They forgot the God[n] who saved them,
who had done great things[o] in Egypt,
[22] miracles in the land of Ham[p]
and awesome deeds by the Red Sea.
[23] So he said he would destroy[q] them—
had not Moses, his chosen one,
stood in the breach[r] before him
to keep his wrath from destroying them.

[24] Then they despised the pleasant land;[s]
they did not believe[t] his promise.
[25] They grumbled[u] in their tents
and did not obey the LORD.
[26] So he swore[v] to them with uplifted hand
that he would make them fall in the desert,[w]
[27] make their descendants fall among the nations
and scatter[x] them throughout the lands.

[28] They yoked themselves to the Baal of Peor[y]
and ate sacrifices offered to lifeless gods;
[29] they provoked the LORD to anger by their wicked deeds,
and a plague broke out among them.
[30] But Phinehas stood up and intervened,
and the plague was checked.[z]
[31] This was credited to him[a] as righteousness
for endless generations to come.

[32] By the waters of Meribah[b] they angered the LORD,
and trouble came to Moses because of them;

106:9 [x]Ps 18:15 [y]Ex 14:21; Na 1:4 [z]Isa 63:11-14
106:10 [a]Ex 14:30 [b]Ps 107:2
106:11 [c]Ex 14:28; 15:5
106:12 [d]Ex 15:1-21
106:13 [e]Ex 15:24
106:14 [f]1Co 10:9
106:15 [g]Nu 11:31 [h]Isa 10:16
106:16 [i]Nu 16:1-3
106:17 [j]Dt 11:6
106:18 [k]Nu 16:35
106:19 [l]Ex 32:4
106:20 [m]Jer 2:11; Ro 1:23
106:21 [n]Ps 78:11 [o]Dt 10:21
106:22 [p]Ps 105:27
106:23 [q]Ex 32:10 [r]Ex 32:11-14
106:24 [s]Dt 8:7; Eze 20:6 [t]Heb 3:18-19
106:25 [u]Nu 14:2
106:26 [v]Eze 20:15; Heb 3:11 [w]Nu 14:28-35
106:27 [x]Lev 26:33; Ps 44:11
106:28 [y]Nu 25:2-3; Hos 9:10
106:30 [z]Nu 25:8
106:31 [a]Nu 25:11-13
106:32 [b]Nu 20:2-13; Ps 81:7

106:22 "The land of Ham" is Egypt.

106:33 [c]Nu 20:8-12
106:34 [d]Jdg 1:21 [e]Dt 7:16
106:35 [f]Jdg 3:5-6
106:36 [g]Jdg 2:12
106:37 [h]2Ki 16:3; 17:17
106:38 [i]Nu 35:33
106:39 [j]Eze 20:18 [k]Lev 17:7; Nu 15:39
106:40 [l]Jdg 2:14; Ps 78:59 [m]Dt 9:29
106:41 [n]Jdg 2:14; Ne 9:27

33 for they rebelled against the Spirit of God,
and rash words came from Moses' lips.[a] [c]
34 They did not destroy[d] the peoples
as the LORD had commanded[e] them,
35 but they mingled[f] with the nations
and adopted their customs.
36 They worshiped their idols,[g]
which became a snare to them.
37 They sacrificed their sons[h]
and their daughters to demons.
38 They shed innocent blood,
the blood of their sons[i] and daughters,
whom they sacrificed to the idols of Canaan,
and the land was desecrated by their blood.
39 They defiled themselves[j] by what they did;
by their deeds they prostituted[k] themselves.
40 Therefore the LORD was angry[l] with his people
and abhorred his inheritance.[m]
41 He handed them over[n] to the nations,
and their foes ruled over them.
42 Their enemies oppressed them
and subjected them to their power.

[a] 33 Or *against his spirit, / and rash words came from his lips*

106:37–38 The Hebrew word translated "demons" (v. 37) is related to a Babylonian term referring to (pagan) protective spirits. It occurs elsewhere in the Old Testament only in Deuteronomy 32:17, where it refers to false gods. See "Human Sacrifice in the Ancient Near East" on page 182.

106:39 They committed prostitution by joining themselves with false gods (see Eze 23:3,5–8; Hos 5:3; 6:10).

ANCIENT TEXTS AND ARTIFACTS

Praise of the "Bull" in the Cairo Hymn of Amon-Re

PSALM 106 When the Israelites were encamped at Mount Horeb they worshiped the image of a calf cast in gold (Ex 32; Ps 106:19–20), a practice they had no doubt learned in Egypt. The Cairo Hymn of Praise to Amon-Re describes the chief Egyptian god variously as the Goodly Bull, the bull of Heliopolis and the bull of his mother. The bull's two eyes were the sun and the moon; both bovine and solar images were incorporated into the cult of Amon-Re. He was worshiped as the creator god who generated heaven, Earth, humankind and animal life[1] and was believed to have been the father of all other gods and the sustainer of the Egyptian kings. Although Amon-Re rescued the poor and downtrodden, he nevertheless kept his name a secret from his children (Amon means "hidden").

When the Israelites formed the golden calf, they insulted God by depicting him using the same image employed to portray Egyptian and **Canaanite** gods, possibly even attributing his saving acts to one of these false gods. Unlike the "hidden" god Amon-Re, however, the one true God revealed himself to his people both in his name (Ex 3:13–14) and in his miraculous deeds. It is important to recognize that the worship of the bull god was in keeping with everything the Israelites had learned in Egypt and that it was, in their view, entirely appropriate. Although their sin was an obvious violation of God's commands, the culture of their day no doubt convinced them that what they were doing was proper and acceptable.[2]

[1]See "Cosmology in the Ancient Near East" on page 1139. [2]See "The Golden Calf" on page 143.

[43] Many times he delivered them,
but they were bent on rebellion[o]
and they wasted away in their sin.

[44] But he took note of their distress
when he heard their cry;[p]
[45] for their sake he remembered his covenant[q]
and out of his great love[r] he relented.
[46] He caused them to be pitied[s]
by all who held them captive.

[47] Save us, O LORD our God,
and gather us[t] from the nations,
that we may give thanks to your holy name
and glory in your praise.

[48] Praise be to the LORD, the God of Israel,
from everlasting to everlasting.
Let all the people say, "Amen!"[u]

Praise the LORD.

BOOK V

Psalms 107–150

Psalm 107

[1] Give thanks to the LORD,[v] for he is good;
his love endures forever.
[2] Let the redeemed[w] of the LORD say this—
those he redeemed from the hand of the foe,
[3] those he gathered[x] from the lands,
from east and west, from north and south.[a]

[4] Some wandered in desert[y] wastelands,
finding no way to a city where they could settle.
[5] They were hungry and thirsty,
and their lives ebbed away.
[6] Then they cried out[z] to the LORD in their trouble,
and he delivered them from their distress.
[7] He led them by a straight way[a]
to a city where they could settle.
[8] Let them give thanks to the LORD for his unfailing love
and his wonderful deeds for men,
[9] for he satisfies[b] the thirsty
and fills the hungry with good things.[c]

[10] Some sat in darkness[d] and the deepest gloom,
prisoners suffering in iron chains,[e]
[11] for they had rebelled[f] against the words of God
and despised the counsel[g] of the Most High.
[12] So he subjected them to bitter labor;
they stumbled, and there was no one to help.[h]
[13] Then they cried to the LORD in their trouble,
and he saved them from their distress.

106:43 [o]Jdg 2:16-19
106:44 [p]Jdg 3:9; 10:10
106:45 [q]Lev 26:42; Ps 105:8 [r]Jdg 2:18
106:46 [s]Ezr 9:9; Jer 42:12
106:47 [t]Ps 147:2
106:48 [u]Ps 41:13
107:1 [v]Ps 106:1
107:2 [w]Ps 106:10
107:3 [x]Ps 106:47; Isa 43:5-6
107:4 [y]Nu 14:33; 32:13
107:6 [z]Ps 50:15
107:7 [a]Ezr 8:21
107:9 [b]Ps 22:26; Lk 1:53 [c]Ps 34:10
107:10 [d]Lk 1:79 [e]Job 36:8
107:11 [f]Ps 106:7; La 3:42 [g]2Ch 36:16
107:12 [h]Ps 22:11

[a] 3 Hebrew *north and the sea*

107:14 [i]Ps 116:16; Lk 13:16; Ac 12:7

14 He brought them out of darkness and the deepest gloom
and broke away their chains.[i]
15 Let them give thanks to the LORD for his unfailing love
and his wonderful deeds for men,
16 for he breaks down gates of bronze
and cuts through bars of iron.

107:17 [j]Isa 65:6-7; La 3:39
107:18 [k]Job 33:20 [l]Job 33:22; Ps 9:13; 88:3

17 Some became fools through their rebellious ways
and suffered affliction[j] because of their iniquities.
18 They loathed all food[k]
and drew near the gates of death.[l]
19 Then they cried to the LORD in their trouble,
and he saved them from their distress.

107:20 [m]Mt 8:8 [n]Ps 103:3 [o]Job 33:28 [p]Ps 30:3; 49:15

20 He sent forth his word[m] and healed them;[n]
he rescued[o] them from the grave.[p]
21 Let them give thanks to the LORD for his unfailing love
and his wonderful deeds for men.

107:16 City gates (see "The City Gate" on p. 392) were normally made of wood, although here they were of bronze, the strongest gates then imaginable (see Jer 1:18). Bars that secured city gates (see Dt 3:5; Jer 51:30) were usually constructed of wood (see Na 3:13) but sometimes formed of bronze as well (see 1Ki 4:13). "Can a man break iron . . . or bronze?" was a proverb of the time (see Jer 15:12).

107:18 The realm of the dead (see "Sheol, Hades, Gehenna, the Abyss and Tartarus: Images of Hell" on p. 946) was sometimes depicted as a netherworld city with a series of concentric walls and gates (seven, each inside the next largest, according to ancient Near Eastern mythology) to keep those descending there from returning to the land of the living.

ANCIENT TEXTS AND ARTIFACTS

The Gezer Calendar

The Gezer Calendar
Preserving Bible Times; © Dr. James C. Martin; permission of Musée de Louvre

PSALM 107 Gezer (modern Tell Jezer; find "Gezer" on "Maps 4–6" in the back of this Bible) lies in the low hills that separated Philistia from Judah. It had a strategic location, guarding access to the coastal trade route, known as the **Via Maris** ("Way of the Sea"), as well as to the overland route into the hill country. The city was at various times under Egyptian, Philistine or Israelite control.[1]

In 1908 a stone was found inscribed with what appears to be an agricultural calendar. It dates to the tenth century B.C. and was probably written as a schoolboy's exercise. Rather than beginning in the spring, as does the festival calendar,[2] the "Gezer calendar" commences in the fall, suggesting that the Israelite agricultural calendar began in the autumn.[3]

Scholars have used this brief text to try to better understand Israelite agricultural practices. It suggests that the planting of grains began in October, after the rains had softened the soil to allow for plowing. Grain sowing lasted for two months, followed by two months of vegetable sowing. After a month of hoeing, the harvest began in the spring with first the barley, then the wheat, then the grapes and finally the summer fruit.[4] The text of the calendar has also proved important in the study of early Hebrew spelling and the development of the shapes of letters.

[1]See "Gezer" on page 588. [2]See "The Festivals of Israel" on page 186. [3]See "The Jewish Calendar" on page 241. [4]See "Food and Agriculture" on page 390.

[22] Let them sacrifice thank offerings[q]
and tell of his works[r] with songs of joy.
[23] Others went out on the sea in ships;
they were merchants on the mighty waters.
[24] They saw the works of the LORD,
his wonderful deeds in the deep.
[25] For he spoke[s] and stirred up a tempest[t]
that lifted high the waves.[u]
[26] They mounted up to the heavens and went down to the depths;
in their peril their courage melted[v] away.
[27] They reeled and staggered like drunken men;
they were at their wits' end.
[28] Then they cried out to the LORD in their trouble,
and he brought them out of their distress.
[29] He stilled the storm[w] to a whisper;
the waves[x] of the sea were hushed.
[30] They were glad when it grew calm,
and he guided them to their desired haven.
[31] Let them give thanks to the LORD for his unfailing love
and his wonderful deeds for men.
[32] Let them exalt him in the assembly[y] of the people
and praise him in the council of the elders.

[33] He turned rivers into a desert,[z]
flowing springs into thirsty ground,
[34] and fruitful land into a salt waste,[a]
because of the wickedness of those who lived there.
[35] He turned the desert into pools of water[b]
and the parched ground into flowing springs;
[36] there he brought the hungry to live,
and they founded a city where they could settle.
[37] They sowed fields and planted vineyards[c]
that yielded a fruitful harvest;
[38] he blessed them, and their numbers greatly increased,[d]
and he did not let their herds diminish.

[39] Then their numbers decreased,[e] and they were humbled
by oppression, calamity and sorrow;
[40] he who pours contempt on nobles[f]
made them wander in a trackless waste.[g]
[41] But he lifted the needy[h] out of their affliction
and increased their families like flocks.
[42] The upright see and rejoice,[i]
but all the wicked shut their mouths.[j]

[43] Whoever is wise,[k] let him heed these things
and consider the great love[l] of the LORD.

107:22 [q]Lev 7:12; Ps 50:14; 116:17 [r]Ps 9:11; 73:28; 118:17
107:25 [s]Ps 105:31 [t]Jnh 1:4 [u]Ps 93:3
107:26 [v]Ps 22:14
107:29 [w]Mt 8:26 [x]Ps 89:9
107:32 [y]Ps 22:22,25; 35:18
107:33 [z]1Ki 17:1; Ps 74:15
107:34 [a]Ge 13:10; 14:3; 19:25
107:35 [b]Ps 114:8; Isa 41:18
107:37 [c]Isa 65:21
107:38 [d]Ge 12:2; 17:16,20; Ex 1:7
107:39 [e]2Ki 10:32; Eze 5:12
107:40 [f]Job 12:21 [g]Job 12:24
107:41 [h]1Sa 2:8; Ps 113:7-9
107:42 [i]Job 22:19 [j]Job 5:16; Ps 63:11; Ro 3:19
107:43 [k]Jer 9:12; Hos 14:9 [l]Ps 64:9

Psalm 108

A song. A psalm of David.

[1] My heart is steadfast, O God;
I will sing and make music with all my soul.

107:23–24 The peoples of the eastern Mediterranean coastlands associated the "mighty waters" (v. 23) of the sea with the primeval, chaotic waters (see the note on 32:6). The Lord's total control of the terrifying storms that often swept through the Mediterranean gave the Israelites a sense of wonder and security.

[2] Awake, harp and lyre!
I will awaken the dawn.
[3] I will praise you, O LORD, among the nations;
I will sing of you among the peoples.
[4] For great is your love, higher than the heavens;
your faithfulness reaches to the skies.
[5] Be exalted, O God, above the heavens,
and let your glory be over all the earth.[m]

[6] Save us and help us with your right hand,
that those you love may be delivered.
[7] God has spoken from his sanctuary:
"In triumph I will parcel out Shechem
and measure off the Valley of Succoth.
[8] Gilead is mine, Manasseh is mine;
Ephraim is my helmet,
Judah[n] my scepter.
[9] Moab is my washbasin,
upon Edom I toss my sandal;
over Philistia I shout in triumph."

[10] Who will bring me to the fortified city?
Who will lead me to Edom?
[11] Is it not you, O God, you who have rejected us
and no longer go out with our armies?[o]
[12] Give us aid against the enemy,
for the help of man is worthless.
[13] With God we will gain the victory,
and he will trample down our enemies.

Psalm 109

For the director of music. Of David. A psalm.

[1] O God, whom I praise,
do not remain silent,[p]
[2] for wicked and deceitful men
have opened their mouths against me;
they have spoken against me with lying tongues.[q]
[3] With words of hatred[r] they surround me;
they attack me without cause.[s]
[4] In return for my friendship they accuse me,
but I am a man of prayer.[t]
[5] They repay me evil for good,[u]
and hatred for my friendship.

[6] Appoint[a] an evil man[b] to oppose him;
let an accuser[c][v] stand at his right hand.
[7] When he is tried, let him be found guilty,
and may his prayers condemn[w] him.
[8] May his days be few;
may another take his place[x] of leadership.

108:5 [m]Ps 57:5
108:8 [n]Ge 49:10
108:11 [o]Ps 44:9
109:1 [p]Ps 83:1
109:2 [q]Ps 52:4; 120:2
109:3 [r]Ps 69:4 [s]Ps 35:7; Jn 15:25
109:4 [t]Ps 69:13
109:5 [u]Ps 35:12; 38:20
109:6 [v]Zec 3:1
109:7 [w]Pr 28:9
109:8 [x]Ac 1:20*

[a] 6 Or ⌞*They say:*⌟ "*Appoint* (with quotation marks at the end of verse 19) [b] 6 Or *the Evil One* [c] 6 Or *let Satan*

109:1–29 For commentary on expressions of vengeful attitudes toward enemies, see the note on 69:22–28. See also "Curses and Imprecations" on page 883.

[9] May his children be fatherless
and his wife a widow.[y]
[10] May his children be wandering beggars;
may they be driven[a] from their ruined homes.
[11] May a creditor seize all he has;
may strangers plunder the fruits of his labor.[z]
[12] May no one extend kindness to him
or take pity[a] on his fatherless children.
[13] May his descendants be cut off,[b]
their names blotted out[c] from the next generation.
[14] May the iniquity of his fathers[d] be remembered before
the LORD;
may the sin of his mother never be blotted out.
[15] May their sins always remain before the LORD,
that he may cut off the memory[e] of them from
the earth.

[16] For he never thought of doing a kindness,
but hounded to death the poor
and the needy[f] and the brokenhearted.[g]
[17] He loved to pronounce a curse—
may it[b] come on him;[h]
he found no pleasure in blessing—
may it be[c] far from him.
[18] He wore cursing[i] as his garment;
it entered into his body like water,[j]
into his bones like oil.
[19] May it be like a cloak wrapped about him,
like a belt tied forever around him.
[20] May this be the LORD's payment[k] to my accusers,
to those who speak evil[l] of me.

[21] But you, O Sovereign LORD,
deal well with me for your name's sake;[m]
out of the goodness of your love,[n] deliver me.
[22] For I am poor and needy,
and my heart is wounded within me.
[23] I fade away like an evening shadow;[o]
I am shaken off like a locust.
[24] My knees give[p] way from fasting;
my body is thin and gaunt.
[25] I am an object of scorn[q] to my accusers;
when they see me, they shake their heads.[r]

[26] Help me,[s] O LORD my God;
save me in accordance with your love.
[27] Let them know[t] that it is your hand,
that you, O LORD, have done it.
[28] They may curse,[u] but you will bless;
when they attack they will be put to shame,
but your servant will rejoice.[v]

109:9 [y]Ex 22:24
109:11 [z]Job 5:5
109:12 [a]Isa 9:17
109:13 [b]Job 18:19; Ps 37:28 [c]Pr 10:7
109:14 [d]Ex 20:5; Ne 4:5; Jer 18:23
109:15 [e]Job 18:17; Ps 34:16
109:16 [f]Ps 37:14,32 [g]Ps 34:18
109:17 [h]Pr 14:14; Eze 35:6
109:18 [i]Ps 73:6 [j]Nu 5:22
109:20 [k]Ps 94:23; 2Ti 4:14 [l]Ps 71:10
109:21 [m]Ps 79:9 [n]Ps 69:16
109:23 [o]Ps 102:11
109:24 [p]Heb 12:12
109:25 [q]Ps 22:6 [r]Mt 27:39; Mk 15:29
109:26 [s]Ps 119:86
109:27 [t]Job 37:7
109:28 [u]2Sa 16:12 [v]Isa 65:14

[a] 10 Septuagint; Hebrew *sought* [b] 17 Or *curse, / and it has* [c] 17 Or *blessing, / and it is*

109:12 Ancient Near Eastern society was made up of three- or four-generation households. There was a close bond between a man and his children and between children and their parents. That deep intimacy accounts for the ancient legal principle of "punishing the children for the sin of the fathers to the third and fourth generation" (see Ex 20:5; see also Ge 18:19; Ps 103:17).
109:17 For "curse," see the note on 10:7.

109:29 [w]Ps 35:26; 132:18
109:30 [x]Ps 35:18; 111:1
109:31 [y]Ps 16:8; 73:23; 121:5

[29] My accusers will be clothed with disgrace
and wrapped in shame[w] as in a cloak.

[30] With my mouth I will greatly extol the LORD;
in the great throng[x] I will praise him.
[31] For he stands at the right hand[y] of the needy one,
to save his life from those who condemn him.

ANCIENT TEXTS AND ARTIFACTS

The Exaltation of a Holy City in the Psalms and in the Myths

PSALM 110 An ancient city would often have its own local myth that exalted that city and its patron god above all other cities and gods. These myths served to reassure the inhabitants that their city and its shrine were somehow superior to all others. One such myth comes from **Sumerian** civilization and was meant to glorify the city of **Uruk** ("Map 1") and its goddess, Inanna.

View of Dormition Abbey on modern Mount Zion
Photograph: © Todd Bolen/Bible Places.com

In the myth the god Enki possesses all the qualities of civilization in his city, Eridu. These qualities include, among others, kingship, priestly orders, crafts (carpentry, metal-working, etc.), jurisprudence and truth. Curiously, negative elements such as prostitution and deceit are also included among the qualities of civilization.[1] Inanna ventures to Eridu and is welcomed by Enki. While in a drunken state Enki confers upon Inanna the qualities of civilization, described in the story as physical objects. She proceeds to load them onto her boat and sails away. Too late, Enki realizes what he has done and tries to retrieve them, but Inanna has already conveyed them to Uruk. Thus Uruk is exalted as the favored city of Inanna.

In the Bible, and especially in the Psalms, Zion is exalted as the chosen city of God. The difference between the exaltation of Zion and the story of Inanna and Enki is profound. The Sumerian story is pure myth: Abstract qualities are described as physical objects, and gods seek to outwit or overpower one another. In contrast, Zion was exalted because of God's covenant with David and the promise of a Messiah, a greater son of David who was yet to come. The Messiah would be a king (Ps 110:1–2) but also a priest (v. 4) and warrior (vv. 5–6). We see a similar exaltation of Zion and its Messiah in Psalm 2. In short, the exaltation of Zion is not grounded in a myth but in a historical event (God's choice of David) and in a hope for the future (the advent of the Messiah).

[1]See "Prostitution in the Ancient World" on page284.

Psalm 110

Of David. A psalm.

1 The LORD says[z] to my Lord:
"Sit at my right hand
until I make your enemies
a footstool for your feet."[a]

2 The LORD will extend your mighty scepter[b]
from Zion;
you will rule in the midst of your enemies.
3 Your troops will be willing
on your day of battle.
Arrayed in holy majesty,[c]
from the womb of the dawn
you will receive the dew of your youth.[a]

4 The LORD has sworn
and will not change his mind:[d]
"You are a priest forever,[e]
in the order of Melchizedek.[f]"

5 The Lord is at your right hand;[g]
he will crush kings[h] on the day of his wrath.[i]
6 He will judge the nations,[j] heaping up the dead[k]
and crushing the rulers[l] of the whole earth.
7 He will drink from a brook beside the way[b];
therefore he will lift up his head.[m]

Psalm 111[c]

1 Praise the LORD.[d]

I will extol the LORD with all my heart
in the council of the upright and in the assembly.

2 Great are the works[n] of the LORD;
they are pondered by all who delight in them.
3 Glorious and majestic are his deeds,
and his righteousness endures forever.
4 He has caused his wonders to be remembered;
the LORD is gracious and compassionate.[o]
5 He provides food[p] for those who fear him;
he remembers his covenant forever.
6 He has shown his people the power of his works,
giving them the lands of other nations.
7 The works of his hands are faithful and just;
all his precepts are trustworthy.[q]
8 They are steadfast for ever[r] and ever,
done in faithfulness and uprightness.

110:1 [z]Mt 22:44*; Mk 12:36*; Lk 20:42*; Ac 2:34* [a]1Co 15:25
110:2 [b]Ps 45:6
110:3 [c]Jdg 5:2; Ps 96:9
110:4 [d]Nu 23:19 [e]Heb 5:6*; 7:21* [f]Heb 7:15-17*
110:5 [g]Ps 16:8 [h]Ps 2:12 [i]Ps 2:5; Ro 2:5
110:6 [j]Isa 2:4 [k]Isa 66:24 [l]Ps 68:21
110:7 [m]Ps 27:6
111:2 [n]Ps 92:5; 143:5
111:4 [o]Ps 103:8
111:5 [p]Mt 6:26, 31-33
111:7 [q]Ps 19:7; Rev 15:3
111:8 [r]Isa 40:8; Mt 5:18

[a] 3 Or / *your young men will come to you like the dew* [b] 7 Or / *The One who grants succession will set him in authority* [c] This psalm is an acrostic poem, the lines of which begin with the successive letters of the Hebrew alphabet. [d] 1 Hebrew *Hallelu Yah*

110:1 Ancient kings often had themselves portrayed as placing their feet upon their vanquished enemies (see Jos 10:24).
110:2 To "extend your mighty scepter" meant for a king to expand his reign in ever widening circles until no foe remained to oppose his rule.
110:4 For information on Melchizedek, see the note on Genesis 14:19. Hebrews 7 applies this concept to Christ's priesthood.

111:9 [s]Lk 1:68 [t]Ps 99:3; Lk 1:49

[9] He provided redemption[s] for his people;
he ordained his covenant forever—
holy and awesome[t] is his name.

111:10 [u]Pr 9:10 [v]Ecc 12:13 [w]Ps 145:2

[10] The fear of the LORD is the beginning of wisdom;[u]
all who follow his precepts have good understanding.[v]
To him belongs eternal praise.[w]

Psalm 112[a]

[1] Praise the LORD.[b]

112:1 [x]Ps 128:1 [y]Ps 119:14,16, 47,92

Blessed is the man who fears the LORD,[x]
who finds great delight[y] in his commands.

[2] His children will be mighty in the land;
the generation of the upright will be blessed.
[3] Wealth and riches are in his house,
and his righteousness endures forever.

112:4 [z]Job 11:17 [a]Ps 97:11

[4] Even in darkness light dawns[z] for the upright,
for the gracious and compassionate and righteous[a]
man.[c]

112:5 [b]Ps 37:21, 26

[5] Good will come to him who is generous and lends freely,[b]
who conducts his affairs with justice.
[6] Surely he will never be shaken;

112:6 [c]Pr 10:7

a righteous man will be remembered[c] forever.
[7] He will have no fear of bad news;

112:7 [d]Ps 57:7; Pr 1:33

his heart is steadfast,[d] trusting in the LORD.
[8] His heart is secure, he will have no fear;

112:8 [e]Ps 59:10

in the end he will look in triumph on his foes.[e]

112:9 [f]2Co 9:9* [g]Ps 75:10

[9] He has scattered abroad his gifts to the poor,[f]
his righteousness endures forever;
his horn[d] will be lifted[g] high in honor.

112:10 [h]Ps 86:17 [i]Ps 37:12 [j]Ps 58:7-8 [k]Pr 11:7

[10] The wicked man will see[h] and be vexed,
he will gnash his teeth[i] and waste away;[j]
the longings of the wicked will come to nothing.[k]

Psalm 113

[1] Praise the LORD.[e]

113:1 [l]Ps 135:1

Praise, O servants of the LORD,[l]
praise the name of the LORD.
[2] Let the name of the LORD be praised,

113:2 [m]Da 2:20

both now and forevermore.[m]

113:3 [n]Isa 59:19; Mal 1:11

[3] From the rising of the sun[n] to the place where it sets,
the name of the LORD is to be praised.

113:4 [o]Ps 99:2 [p]Ps 8:1; 97:9

[4] The LORD is exalted[o] over all the nations,
his glory above the heavens.[p]

[a] This psalm is an acrostic poem, the lines of which begin with the successive letters of the Hebrew alphabet. [b] *1* Hebrew *Hallelu Yah* [c] *4* Or */ for ⌊the LORD⌋ is gracious and compassionate and righteous* [d] *9* *Horn* here symbolizes dignity. [e] *1* Hebrew *Hallelu Yah*; also in verse 9

112:10 For the meaning of gnashing with one's teeth, see the note on 35:16.

113:1—118:29 Psalms 113–118, which were read on Passover Day, were called the "Egyptian Hallel"; Psalm 136 is an antiphonal psalm of praise that is sometimes called simply "The Hallel," and Psalms 120–136 are often referred to as "The Great Hallel."

[5] Who is like the LORD our God,[q]
the One who sits enthroned[r] on high,
[6] who stoops down to look[s]
on the heavens and the earth?

[7] He raises the poor[t] from the dust
and lifts the needy[u] from the ash heap;
[8] he seats them[v] with princes,
with the princes of their people.
[9] He settles the barren[w] woman in her home
as a happy mother of children.

Praise the LORD.

Psalm 114

[1] When Israel came out of Egypt,[x]
the house of Jacob from a people of foreign tongue,
[2] Judah became God's sanctuary,
Israel his dominion.

[3] The sea looked and fled,[y]
the Jordan turned back;[z]
[4] the mountains skipped like rams,
the hills like lambs.

[5] Why was it, O sea, that you fled,
O Jordan, that you turned back,
[6] you mountains, that you skipped like rams,
you hills, like lambs?

[7] Tremble, O earth,[a] at the presence of the Lord,
at the presence of the God of Jacob,
[8] who turned the rock into a pool,
the hard rock into springs of water.[b]

Psalm 115

[1] Not to us, O LORD, not to us
but to your name be the glory,[c]
because of your love and faithfulness.

[2] Why do the nations say,
"Where is their God?"[d]
[3] Our God is in heaven;[e]
he does whatever pleases him.[f]
[4] But their idols are silver and gold,
made by the hands of men.[g]
[5] They have mouths, but cannot speak,[h]
eyes, but they cannot see;
[6] they have ears, but cannot hear,
noses, but they cannot smell;
[7] they have hands, but cannot feel,
feet, but they cannot walk;
nor can they utter a sound with their throats.

113:5 [q]Ps 89:6 [r]Ps 103:19
113:6 [s]Ps 11:4; 138:6; Isa 57:15
113:7 [t]1Sa 2:8 [u]Ps 107:41
113:8 [v]Job 36:7
113:9 [w]1Sa 2:5; Ps 68:6; Isa 54:1
114:1 [x]Ex 13:3
114:3 [y]Ex 14:21; Ps 77:16 [z]Jos 3:16
114:7 [a]Ps 96:9
114:8 [b]Ex 17:6; Nu 20:11; Ps 107:35
115:1 [c]Ps 96:8; Isa 48:11; Eze 36:32
115:2 [d]Ps 42:3; 79:10
115:3 [e]Ps 103:19 [f]Ps 135:6; Da 4:35
115:4 [g]Dt 4:28; Jer 10:3-5
115:5 [h]Jer 10:5

113:7 The "ash heap" was symbolic of a humble status (Ge 18:27; 1Ki 16:2), but here it probably also refers to extreme distress and need (see Job 30:19; 42:6; Isa 47:1; Jer 25:34).

113:9 In that ancient society childlessness was for a woman the greatest disgrace and deepest tragedy.

[8]Those who make them will be like them,
and so will all who trust in them.

[9]O house of Israel, trust in the LORD—
he is their help and shield.
115:10 [i]Ps 118:3 [10]O house of Aaron,[i] trust in the LORD—
he is their help and shield.
[11]You who fear him, trust in the LORD—
he is their help and shield.

[12]The LORD remembers us and will bless us:
He will bless the house of Israel,
he will bless the house of Aaron,
115:13 [j]Ps 128:1,4 [13]he will bless those who fear[j] the LORD—
small and great alike.

115:14 [k]Dt 1:11 [14]May the LORD make you increase,[k]
both you and your children.
[15]May you be blessed by the LORD,
115:15 [l]Ge 1:1; 14:19; Ps 96:5 the Maker of heaven[l] and earth.

115:16 [m]Ps 89:11 [n]Ps 8:6-8 [16]The highest heavens belong to the LORD,[m]
but the earth he has given[n] to man.
115:17 [o]Ps 6:5; 88:10-12; Isa 38:18 [17]It is not the dead[o] who praise the LORD,
those who go down to silence;
[18]it is we who extol the LORD,
115:18 [p]Ps 113:2; Da 2:20 both now and forevermore.[p]

Praise the LORD.[a]

Psalm 116

116:1 [q]Ps 18:1 [r]Ps 66:19 [1]I love the LORD,[q] for he heard my voice;
he heard my cry[r] for mercy.
116:2 [s]Ps 40:1 [2]Because he turned his ear[s] to me,
I will call on him as long as I live.

116:3 [t]Ps 18:4-5 [3]The cords of death[t] entangled me,
the anguish of the grave[b] came upon me;
I was overcome by trouble and sorrow.
116:4 [u]Ps 118:5 [v]Ps 22:20 [4]Then I called on the name[u] of the LORD:
"O LORD, save me![v]"

116:5 [w]Ezr 9:15; Ne 9:8; Ps 103:8; 145:17 [5]The LORD is gracious and righteous;[w]
our God is full of compassion.
[6]The LORD protects the simplehearted;
116:6 [x]Ps 19:7; 79:8 when I was in great need,[x] he saved me.

116:7 [y]Jer 6:16; Mt 11:29 [z]Ps 13:6 [7]Be at rest[y] once more, O my soul,
for the LORD has been good[z] to you.

116:8 [a]Ps 56:13 [8]For you, O LORD, have delivered my soul[a] from death,
my eyes from tears,
my feet from stumbling,
[9]that I may walk before the LORD
116:9 [b]Ps 27:13 in the land of the living.[b]

[a] 18 Hebrew *Hallelu Yah* [b] 3 Hebrew *Sheol*

115:17 For the ancient Near Eastern view of death, see the notes on Job 10:21 and Psalm 6:5.

116:7 For "O my soul," see the note on 103:1–2.

[10] I believed;[c] therefore[a] I said,
"I am greatly afflicted."
[11] And in my dismay I said,
"All men are liars."[d]

[12] How can I repay the LORD
for all his goodness to me?
[13] I will lift up the cup of salvation
and call on the name[e] of the LORD.
[14] I will fulfill my vows[f] to the LORD
in the presence of all his people.

[15] Precious in the sight[g] of the LORD
is the death of his saints.
[16] O LORD, truly I am your servant;[h]
I am your servant, the son of your maidservant[b];[i]
you have freed me from my chains.

[17] I will sacrifice a thank offering[j] to you
and call on the name of the LORD.
[18] I will fulfill my vows to the LORD
in the presence of all his people,
[19] in the courts[k] of the house of the LORD—
in your midst, O Jerusalem.

Praise the LORD.[c]

116:10 [c]2Co 4:13*
116:11 [d]Ro 3:4
116:13 [e]Ps 16:5; 80:18
116:14 [f]Ps 22:25; Jnh 2:9
116:15 [g]Ps 72:14
116:16 [h]Ps 119:125; 143:12 [i]Ps 86:16
116:17 [j]Lev 7:12; Ps 50:14
116:19 [k]Ps 96:8; 135:2

[a] 10 Or *believed even when* [b] 16 Or *servant, your faithful son* [c] 19 Hebrew *Hallelu Yah*

116:13 The "cup of salvation" probably refers to the cup of wine drunk at the festal meal that climaxed a thank offering—called the "cup of salvation" because the thank offering and its meal celebrated deliverance by the Lord.

ANCIENT TEXTS AND ARTIFACTS

A Pagan's Prayer of Thanks

PSALM 116 Many Biblical passages are in form similar to pagan texts, but the formal similarity only makes the differences in content more apparent. An **Akkadian** psalm from **Ugarit** (referred to by scholars as Ugartica 5.162)[1] is outwardly similar to Biblical psalms of thanksgiving, such as Psalm 86 or 116. Like the writer of Psalm 116:3, the Akkadian psalmist described himself as being at death's door (probably due to illness) and vividly portrayed how he was wasting away, unable to eat anything but his own tears (see 42:3). Like Psalm 116:8 or Jonah 2, the Akkadian poet ultimately celebrated the fact that his god had snatched him from the grave.

What is distinctive, however, is the manner in which the Akkadian psalmist sought help from his god via magic and ritual.[2] He had surrounded himself by omen takers, who looked for favorable signs from incense clouds and the entrails of lambs. He depicted his brothers as having been drenched in blood and described them as being like possessed men (they practiced self-mutilation in an attempt to compel their god to act; see 1Ki 18:28–29). In contrast, although the Biblical psalmist spoke of making a sacrifice of thanksgiving (Ps 116:17), there is no implication of manipulation of divine power through magic, nor is there the sense of frantic desperation that pervades the Akkadian text. The Biblical psalmist could even make the astonishing and profound statement, "Precious in the sight of the LORD is the death of his saints" (v. 15).

[1]See "Ugarit/Ras Shamra" on page 819. [2]For similar uses of magic, see "'I Will Praise the Lord of Wisdom'" on page 751 and "A Hittite Ritual Against Plague" on page 758.

Psalm 117

117:1 [l]Ro 15:11*
117:2 [m]Ps 100:5

[1] Praise the LORD, all you nations;[l]
extol him, all you peoples.
[2] For great is his love toward us,
and the faithfulness of the LORD[m]
endures forever.

Praise the LORD.[a]

Psalm 118

118:1 [n]1Ch 16:8 [o]Ps 106:1; 136:1
118:2 [p]Ps 115:9
118:5 [q]Ps 120:1 [r]Ps 18:19
118:6 [s]Heb 13:6* [t]Ps 27:1; 56:4
118:7 [u]Ps 54:4 [v]Ps 59:10
118:8 [w]Ps 40:4 [x]Jer 17:5
118:9 [y]Ps 146:3
118:10 [z]Ps 18:40
118:11 [a]Ps 88:17 [b]Ps 3:6
118:12 [c]Dt 1:44 [d]Ps 58:9
118:13 [e]Ps 86:17; 140:4
118:14 [f]Ex 15:2 [g]Isa 12:2
118:15 [h]Ps 68:3 [i]Ps 89:13
118:17 [j]Ps 6:5; Hab 1:12 [k]Ex 15:6; Ps 73:28
118:18 [l]2Co 6:9

[1] Give thanks to the LORD,[n] for he is good;
his love endures forever.[o]

[2] Let Israel say:[p]
"His love endures forever."
[3] Let the house of Aaron say:
"His love endures forever."
[4] Let those who fear the LORD say:
"His love endures forever."

[5] In my anguish[q] I cried to the LORD,
and he answered[r] by setting me free.
[6] The LORD is with me;[s] I will not be afraid.
What can man do to me?[t]
[7] The LORD is with me; he is my helper.[u]
I will look in triumph on my enemies.[v]

[8] It is better to take refuge in the LORD[w]
than to trust in man.[x]
[9] It is better to take refuge in the LORD
than to trust in princes.[y]

[10] All the nations surrounded me,
but in the name of the LORD I cut them off.[z]
[11] They surrounded me[a] on every side,[b]
but in the name of the LORD I cut them off.
[12] They swarmed around me like bees,[c]
but they died out as quickly as burning thorns;[d]
in the name of the LORD I cut them off.

[13] I was pushed back and about to fall,
but the LORD helped me.[e]
[14] The LORD is my strength[f] and my song;
he has become my salvation.[g]

[15] Shouts of joy[h] and victory
resound in the tents of the righteous:
"The LORD's right hand[i] has done mighty things!
[16] The LORD's right hand is lifted high;
the LORD's right hand has done mighty things!"

[17] I will not die[j] but live,
and will proclaim[k] what the LORD has done.
[18] The LORD has chastened me severely,
but he has not given me over to death.[l]

[a] 2 Hebrew *Hallelu Yah*

ANCIENT VOICES

He dashed me down, then grabbed me
(as I fell),*
He scattered me wide, then garnered me,
He thrust me away, then gathered me in,
He threw me down, then lifted me high.
He snatched the jaw of death,
He raised me from hell.
He smashed my smiter's weapon,
He wrested the shovel from the digger of
my grave.

*Words in parentheses added by translator for clarity

—A SUFFERER'S SALVATION

See "A Pagan's Prayer of Thanks" article.

[19]Open for me the gates[m] of righteousness;
I will enter and give thanks to the LORD.
[20]This is the gate of the LORD
through which the righteous may enter.[n]
[21]I will give you thanks, for you answered me;[o]
you have become my salvation.

118:19 [m]Isa 26:2
118:20 [n]Ps 24:7; Isa 35:8; Rev 22:14
118:21 [o]Ps 116:1

118:19 Although some think the phrase "gates of righteousness" refers to the name of a particular gateway, the term is more likely only descriptive here of the gate "through which the righteous may enter" (v. 20). It is possible that the procession began outside the city and that "the gates of righteousness" is a reference to the gates of Jerusalem.

The Horned Altar

PSALM 118 The two most important ritual altars of Israel's religious life were the bronze altar of sacrifice and the golden altar of incense. A conspicuous feature of their design was four "horns" rising from each of the four corners, which were to be of one piece with the altar itself rather than attached separately (Ex 27:2; 30:2). Archaeological excavations have provided examples of this construction in an incense altar discovered at Megiddo and a sacrificial altar from an Israelite sanctuary at Beersheba.[1]

The precise function of the horns remains uncertain. Since the Hebrew term for altar, *mizbeah*, literally means "place of ritual slaughter," it has been suggested that the horns functioned as pegs to secure the animal about to be offered (Ps 118:27). This seems unlikely, however, since the animal was ritually slaughtered before being placed on the altar and would require no restraint (Lev 1:5–9). Perhaps the horns on the altar, and especially those of the altar of incense, which was not used for sacrifice, may be explained by the broader role of the altar within temple liturgy. Priests were commanded to daub these horns with sacrificial blood to symbolically effect purification from sin and thus to remove ritual impurity from the entire altar and sanctuary (Lev 4:7; 16:18).[2]

In addition to their role in sacrificial offerings, altars served to memorialize a theophany or physical appearance of the Lord (Ge 12:7; 35:1–7) and were intimately associated with the divine presence (Ex 20:24). It is possible that altars were constructed so as to imitate mountains upon which sacrifices were offered and with which God's presence was associated. This would explain the law prescribing that free-standing altars in Israel be constructed of packed earth or a mound of unhewn stones (Ex 20:24–26). The horns on the elaborate altars of the temple could suggest a more "stylized" mountain. Whatever the case, the special sanctity of the altar, and of the horns in particular, is evidenced by the asylum granted to anyone who seized them (1Ki 1:50–51; 2:28–34).

See also "Ancient Altars" on page 125.

[1]See "Megiddo" on page 1541 and "Beersheba" on page 518. [2]See also "Sacrifices and Offerings in the Bible and the Ancient Near East" on page 158 and "Ritual Purity in Israel and the Ancient Near East" on page 166.

Altars from Megiddo

Preserving Bible Times; © Dr. James C. Martin; permission of The Israel Museum

22 The stone the builders rejected
has become the capstone;[p]
23 the LORD has done this,
and it is marvelous in our eyes.
24 This is the day the LORD has made;
let us rejoice and be glad in it.

25 O LORD, save us;
O LORD, grant us success.
26 Blessed is he who comes[q] in the name of the LORD.
From the house of the LORD we bless you.[a]
27 The LORD is God,
and he has made his light shine[r] upon us.
With boughs in hand, join in the festal procession
up[b] to the horns of the altar.

28 You are my God, and I will give you thanks;
you are my God,[s] and I will exalt[t] you.

29 Give thanks to the LORD, for he is good;
his love endures forever.

118:22 [p]Mt 21:42; Mk 12:10; Lk 20:17*; Ac 4:11*; 1Pe 2:7*
118:26 [q]Mt 21:9*; Mk 11:9*; Lk 13:35*; 19:38*; Jn 12:13*
118:27 [r]1Pe 2:9
118:28 [s]Isa 25:1 [t]Ex 15:2

Psalm 119[c]

א Aleph

1 Blessed are they whose ways are blameless,
who walk[u] according to the law of the LORD.
2 Blessed are they who keep his statutes
and seek him with all their heart.[v]
3 They do nothing wrong;[w]
they walk in his ways.
4 You have laid down precepts
that are to be fully obeyed.
5 Oh, that my ways were steadfast
in obeying your decrees!
6 Then I would not be put to shame
when I consider all your commands.
7 I will praise you with an upright heart
as I learn your righteous laws.
8 I will obey your decrees;
do not utterly forsake me.

ב Beth

9 How can a young man keep his way pure?
By living according to your word.[x]
10 I seek you with all my heart;[y]
do not let me stray from your commands.[z]
11 I have hidden your word in my heart[a]
that I might not sin against you.

119:1 [u]Ps 128:1
119:2 [v]Dt 6:5
119:3 [w]1Jn 3:9; 5:18
119:9 [x]2Ch 6:16
119:10 [y]2Ch 15:15 [z]ver 21,118
119:11 [a]Ps 37:31; Lk 2:19,51

[a] *26* The Hebrew is plural. [b] *27* Or *Bind the festal sacrifice with ropes / and take it* [c] This psalm is an acrostic poem; the verses of each stanza begin with the same letter of the Hebrew alphabet.

118:22 A "capstone" (lit., "head of the corner") was either a large stone used as a lintel over a door or a rock used to anchor and align the corner of a wall or the keystone of an arch (see Zec 4:7; 10:4).

[12] Praise be to you, O LORD;
teach me your decrees.[b]
[13] With my lips I recount
all the laws that come from your mouth.[c]
[14] I rejoice in following your statutes
as one rejoices in great riches.
[15] I meditate on your precepts[d]
and consider your ways.
[16] I delight[e] in your decrees;
I will not neglect your word.

ג Gimel

[17] Do good to your servant,[f] and I will live;
I will obey your word.
[18] Open my eyes that I may see
wonderful things in your law.
[19] I am a stranger on earth;[g]
do not hide your commands from me.
[20] My soul is consumed[h] with longing
for your laws[i] at all times.
[21] You rebuke the arrogant, who are cursed
and who stray[j] from your commands.
[22] Remove from me scorn[k] and contempt,
for I keep your statutes.
[23] Though rulers sit together and slander me,
your servant will meditate on your decrees.
[24] Your statutes are my delight;
they are my counselors.

ד Daleth

[25] I am laid low in the dust;[l]
preserve my life[m] according to your word.
[26] I recounted my ways and you answered me;
teach me your decrees.[n]
[27] Let me understand the teaching of your precepts;
then I will meditate on your wonders.[o]
[28] My soul is weary with sorrow;[p]
strengthen me[q] according to your word.
[29] Keep me from deceitful ways;
be gracious to me through your law.
[30] I have chosen the way of truth;
I have set my heart on your laws.
[31] I hold fast[r] to your statutes, O LORD;
do not let me be put to shame.
[32] I run in the path of your commands,
for you have set my heart free.

ה He

[33] Teach me,[s] O LORD, to follow your decrees;
then I will keep them to the end.
[34] Give me understanding, and I will keep your law
and obey it with all my heart.
[35] Direct me in the path of your commands,
for there I find delight.

119:12 [b]ver 26
119:13 [c]Ps 40:9
119:15 [d]Ps 1:2
119:16 [e]Ps 1:2
119:17 [f]Ps 13:6; 116:7
119:19 [g]1Ch 29:15; Ps 39:12; 2Co 5:6; Heb 11:13
119:20 [h]Ps 42:2; 84:2 [i]Ps 63:1
119:21 [j]ver 10
119:22 [k]Ps 39:8
119:25 [l]Ps 44:25 [m]Ps 143:11
119:26 [n]Ps 25:4; 27:11; 86:11
119:27 [o]Ps 145:5
119:28 [p]Ps 107:26 [q]Ps 20:2; 1Pe 5:10
119:31 [r]Dt 11:22
119:33 [s]ver 12

119:36 [t]1Ki 8:58 [u]Eze 33:31; Mk 7:21-22; Lk 12:15; Heb 13:5
119:37 [v]Ps 71:20; Isa 33:15
119:38 [w]2Sa 7:25
119:40 [x]ver 20
119:42 [y]Pr 27:11
119:46 [z]Mt 10:18; Ac 26:1-2
119:50 [a]Ro 15:4
119:51 [b]Jer 20:7 [c]ver 157; Job 23:11; Ps 44:18
119:52 [d]Ps 103:18
119:53 [e]Ezr 9:3 [f]Ps 89:30
119:55 [g]Ps 63:6
119:57 [h]Ps 16:5; La 3:24
119:58 [i]1Ki 13:6 [j]ver 41

36 Turn my heart[t] toward your statutes
and not toward selfish gain.[u]
37 Turn my eyes away from worthless things;
preserve my life[v] according to your word.[a]
38 Fulfill your promise[w] to your servant,
so that you may be feared.
39 Take away the disgrace I dread,
for your laws are good.
40 How I long[x] for your precepts!
Preserve my life in your righteousness.

ו Waw

41 May your unfailing love come to me, O LORD,
your salvation according to your promise;
42 then I will answer[y] the one who taunts me,
for I trust in your word.
43 Do not snatch the word of truth from my mouth,
for I have put my hope in your laws.
44 I will always obey your law,
for ever and ever.
45 I will walk about in freedom,
for I have sought out your precepts.
46 I will speak of your statutes before kings[z]
and will not be put to shame,
47 for I delight in your commands
because I love them.
48 I lift up my hands to[b] your commands, which I love,
and I meditate on your decrees.

ז Zayin

49 Remember your word to your servant,
for you have given me hope.
50 My comfort in my suffering is this:
Your promise preserves my life.[a]
51 The arrogant mock me[b] without restraint,
but I do not turn[c] from your law.
52 I remember[d] your ancient laws, O LORD,
and I find comfort in them.
53 Indignation grips me[e] because of the wicked,
who have forsaken your law.[f]
54 Your decrees are the theme of my song
wherever I lodge.
55 In the night I remember[g] your name, O LORD,
and I will keep your law.
56 This has been my practice:
I obey your precepts.

ח Heth

57 You are my portion,[h] O LORD;
I have promised to obey your words.
58 I have sought your face with all my heart;
be gracious to me[i] according to your promise.[j]

[a] 37 Two manuscripts of the Masoretic Text and Dead Sea Scrolls; most manuscripts of the Masoretic Text *life in your way*
[b] 48 Or *for*

[59] I have considered my ways[k]
and have turned my steps to your statutes.
[60] I will hasten and not delay
to obey your commands.
[61] Though the wicked bind me with ropes,
I will not forget[l] your law.
[62] At midnight[m] I rise to give you thanks
for your righteous laws.
[63] I am a friend to all who fear you,[n]
to all who follow your precepts.
[64] The earth is filled with your love,[o] O LORD;
teach me your decrees.

ט Teth

[65] Do good to your servant
according to your word, O LORD.
[66] Teach me knowledge and good judgment,
for I believe in your commands.
[67] Before I was afflicted I went astray,[p]
but now I obey your word.
[68] You are good,[q] and what you do is good;
teach me your decrees.[r]
[69] Though the arrogant have smeared me with lies,[s]
I keep your precepts with all my heart.
[70] Their hearts are callous[t] and unfeeling,
but I delight in your law.
[71] It was good for me to be afflicted
so that I might learn your decrees.
[72] The law from your mouth is more precious to me
than thousands of pieces of silver and gold.[u]

י Yodh

[73] Your hands made me[v] and formed me;
give me understanding to learn your commands.
[74] May those who fear you rejoice[w] when they see me,
for I have put my hope in your word.
[75] I know, O LORD, that your laws are righteous,
and in faithfulness[x] you have afflicted me.
[76] May your unfailing love be my comfort,
according to your promise to your servant.
[77] Let your compassion[y] come to me that I may live,
for your law is my delight.
[78] May the arrogant[z] be put to shame for wronging me without cause;[a]
but I will meditate on your precepts.
[79] May those who fear you turn to me,
those who understand your statutes.
[80] May my heart be blameless toward your decrees,
that I may not be put to shame.

כ Kaph

[81] My soul faints[b] with longing for your salvation,
but I have put my hope in your word.

119:59 [k]Lk 15:17-18
119:61 [l]Ps 140:5
119:62 [m]Ac 16:25
119:63 [n]Ps 101:6-7
119:64 [o]Ps 33:5
119:67 [p]Jer 31:18-19; Heb 12:11
119:68 [q]Ps 106:1; 107:1; Mt 19:17 [r]ver 12
119:69 [s]Job 13:4; Ps 109:2
119:70 [t]Ps 17:10; Isa 6:10; Ac 28:27
119:72 [u]Ps 19:10; Pr 8:10-11,19
119:73 [v]Job 10:8; Ps 100:3; 138:8; 139:13-16
119:74 [w]Ps 34:2
119:75 [x]Heb 12:5-11
119:77 [y]ver 41
119:78 [z]Jer 50:32 [a]ver 86,161
119:81 [b]Ps 84:2

119:81 For "soul," see the note on 6:3.

119:82 [c]Ps 69:3; La 2:11
119:84 [d]Ps 39:4; Rev 6:10
119:85 [e]Ps 35:7; Jer 18:20,22
119:86 [f]Ps 35:19 [g]Ps 109:26 [h]ver 78
119:87 [i]Isa 58:2
119:89 [j]Mt 24:34-35; 1Pe 1:25
119:90 [k]Ps 36:5 [l]Ps 148:6; Ecc 1:4
119:91 [m]Jer 33:25
119:97 [n]Ps 1:2
119:98 [o]Dt 4:6
119:100 [p]Job 32:7-9
119:101 [q]Pr 1:15
119:103 [r]Ps 19:10; Pr 8:11 [s]Pr 24:13-14
119:104 [t]ver 128

82 My eyes fail,[c] looking for your promise;
I say, "When will you comfort me?"
83 Though I am like a wineskin in the smoke,
I do not forget your decrees.
84 How long[d] must your servant wait?
When will you punish my persecutors?
85 The arrogant dig pitfalls[e] for me,
contrary to your law.
86 All your commands are trustworthy;[f]
help me,[g] for men persecute me without cause.[h]
87 They almost wiped me from the earth,
but I have not forsaken[i] your precepts.
88 Preserve my life according to your love,
and I will obey the statutes of your mouth.

ל Lamedh

89 Your word, O LORD, is eternal;[j]
it stands firm in the heavens.
90 Your faithfulness[k] continues through all
generations;
you established the earth, and it endures.[l]
91 Your laws endure[m] to this day,
for all things serve you.
92 If your law had not been my delight,
I would have perished in my affliction.
93 I will never forget your precepts,
for by them you have preserved my life.
94 Save me, for I am yours;
I have sought out your precepts.
95 The wicked are waiting to destroy me,
but I will ponder your statutes.
96 To all perfection I see a limit;
but your commands are boundless.

מ Mem

97 Oh, how I love your law!
I meditate[n] on it all day long.
98 Your commands make me wiser[o] than my enemies,
for they are ever with me.
99 I have more insight than all my teachers,
for I meditate on your statutes.
100 I have more understanding than the elders,
for I obey your precepts.[p]
101 I have kept my feet[q] from every evil path
so that I might obey your word.
102 I have not departed from your laws,
for you yourself have taught me.
103 How sweet are your words to my taste,
sweeter than honey[r] to my mouth![s]
104 I gain understanding from your precepts;
therefore I hate every wrong path.[t]

119:83 A wineskin that hung in the smoke and heat above a fire would become soiled and shriveled.

נ Nun

105 Your word is a lamp to my feet
and a light[u] for my path.
106 I have taken an oath[v] and confirmed it,
that I will follow your righteous laws.
107 I have suffered much;
preserve my life, O LORD, according to your word.
108 Accept, O LORD, the willing praise of my mouth,[w]
and teach me your laws.
109 Though I constantly take my life in my hands,[x]
I will not forget your law.
110 The wicked have set a snare[y] for me,
but I have not strayed[z] from your precepts.
111 Your statutes are my heritage forever;
they are the joy of my heart.
112 My heart is set on keeping your decrees
to the very end.[a]

ס Samekh

113 I hate double-minded men,[b]
but I love your law.
114 You are my refuge and my shield;[c]
I have put my hope[d] in your word.
115 Away from me,[e] you evildoers,
that I may keep the commands of my God!
116 Sustain me[f] according to your promise, and I will live;
do not let my hopes be dashed.[g]
117 Uphold me, and I will be delivered;
I will always have regard for your decrees.
118 You reject all who stray from your decrees,
for their deceitfulness is in vain.
119 All the wicked of the earth you discard like dross;[h]
therefore I love your statutes.
120 My flesh trembles[i] in fear of you;
I stand in awe of your laws.

ע Ayin

121 I have done what is righteous and just;
do not leave me to my oppressors.
122 Ensure your servant's well-being;[j]
let not the arrogant oppress me.
123 My eyes fail, looking for your salvation,
looking for your righteous promise.[k]
124 Deal with your servant according to your love
and teach me your decrees.[l]
125 I am your servant;[m] give me discernment
that I may understand your statutes.
126 It is time for you to act, O LORD;
your law is being broken.
127 Because I love your commands
more than gold,[n] more than pure gold,

119:105 [u]Pr 6:23
119:106 [v]Ne 10:29
119:108 [w]Hos 14:2; Heb 13:15
119:109 [x]Jdg 12:3; Job 13:14
119:110 [y]Ps 140:5; 141:9 [z]ver 10
119:112 [a]ver 33
119:113 [b]Jas 1:8
119:114 [c]Ps 32:7; 91:1 [d]ver 74
119:115 [e]Ps 6:8; 139:19; Mt 7:23
119:116 [f]Ps 54:4 [g]Ps 25:2; Ro 5:5; 9:33
119:119 [h]Eze 22:18,19
119:120 [i]Hab 3:16
119:122 [j]Job 17:3
119:123 [k]ver 82
119:124 [l]ver 12
119:125 [m]Ps 116:16
119:127 [n]Ps 19:10

119:111–112 For "heart," see the note on 4:7.

119:119 "Dross" is the scum that is removed from molten ore or metal.

128 and because I consider all your precepts right,
I hate every wrong path.[o]

פ Pe

129 Your statutes are wonderful;
therefore I obey them.
130 The unfolding of your words gives light;[p]
it gives understanding to the simple.[q]
131 I open my mouth and pant,[r]
longing for your commands.[s]
132 Turn to me and have mercy[t] on me,
as you always do to those who love your name.
133 Direct my footsteps according to your word;[u]
let no sin rule[v] over me.
134 Redeem me from the oppression of men,[w]
that I may obey your precepts.
135 Make your face shine[x] upon your servant
and teach me your decrees.
136 Streams of tears[y] flow from my eyes,
for your law is not obeyed.[z]

צ Tsadhe

137 Righteous are you,[a] O LORD,
and your laws are right.[b]
138 The statutes you have laid down are righteous;[c]
they are fully trustworthy.
139 My zeal wears me out,[d]
for my enemies ignore your words.
140 Your promises have been thoroughly tested,[e]
and your servant loves them.
141 Though I am lowly and despised,[f]
I do not forget your precepts.
142 Your righteousness is everlasting
and your law is true.[g]
143 Trouble and distress have come upon me,
but your commands are my delight.
144 Your statutes are forever right;
give me understanding[h] that I may live.

ק Qoph

145 I call with all my heart; answer me, O LORD,
and I will obey your decrees.
146 I call out to you; save me
and I will keep your statutes.
147 I rise before dawn[i] and cry for help;
I have put my hope in your word.
148 My eyes stay open through the watches of the night,[j]
that I may meditate on your promises.
149 Hear my voice in accordance with your love;
preserve my life, O LORD, according to your laws.
150 Those who devise wicked schemes are near,
but they are far from your law.
151 Yet you are near,[k] O LORD,
and all your commands are true.[l]

119:128 [o]ver 104,163
119:130 [p]Pr 6:23 [q]Ps 19:7
119:131 [r]Ps 42:1 [s]ver 20
119:132 [t]Ps 25:16; 106:4
119:133 [u]Ps 17:5 [v]Ps 19:13; Ro 6:12
119:134 [w]Ps 142:6; Lk 1:74
119:135 [x]Nu 6:25; Ps 4:6
119:136 [y]Jer 9:1, 18 [z]Eze 9:4
119:137 [a]Ezr 9:15; Jer 12:1 [b]Ne 9:13
119:138 [c]Ps 19:7
119:139 [d]Ps 69:9; Jn 2:17
119:140 [e]Ps 12:6
119:141 [f]Ps 22:6
119:142 [g]Ps 19:7
119:144 [h]Ps 19:9
119:147 [i]Ps 5:3; 57:8; 108:2
119:148 [j]Ps 63:6
119:151 [k]Ps 34:18; 145:18 [l]ver 142

152 Long ago I learned from your statutes
that you established them to last forever.[m]

ר Resh

153 Look upon my suffering[n] and deliver me,
for I have not forgotten[o] your law.
154 Defend my cause[p] and redeem me;[q]
preserve my life according to your promise.
155 Salvation is far from the wicked,
for they do not seek out[r] your decrees.
156 Your compassion is great, O LORD;
preserve my life[s] according to your laws.
157 Many are the foes who persecute me,[t]
but I have not turned from your statutes.
158 I look on the faithless with loathing,[u]
for they do not obey your word.
159 See how I love your precepts;
preserve my life, O LORD, according to your love.
160 All your words are true;
all your righteous laws are eternal.

ש Sin and Shin

161 Rulers persecute me[v] without cause,
but my heart trembles at your word.
162 I rejoice in your promise
like one who finds great spoil.[w]
163 I hate and abhor falsehood
but I love your law.
164 Seven times a day I praise you
for your righteous laws.
165 Great peace[x] have they who love your law,
and nothing can make them stumble.
166 I wait for your salvation,[y] O LORD,
and I follow your commands.
167 I obey your statutes,
for I love them greatly.
168 I obey your precepts and your statutes,
for all my ways are known[z] to you.

ת Taw

169 May my cry come[a] before you, O LORD;
give me understanding according to your word.
170 May my supplication come[b] before you;
deliver me[c] according to your promise.
171 May my lips overflow with praise,[d]
for you teach me[e] your decrees.
172 May my tongue sing of your word,
for all your commands are righteous.
173 May your hand be ready to help[f] me,
for I have chosen[g] your precepts.
174 I long for your salvation,[h] O LORD,
and your law is my delight.
175 Let me live[i] that I may praise you,
and may your laws sustain me.

119:152 [m]Lk 21:33
119:153 [n]La 5:1 [o]Pr 3:1
119:154 [p]Mic 7:9 [q]1Sa 24:15
119:155 [r]Job 5:4
119:156 [s]2Sa 24:14
119:157 [t]Ps 7:1
119:158 [u]Ps 139:21
119:161 [v]1Sa 24:11
119:162 [w]1Sa 30:16
119:165 [x]Pr 3:2; Isa 26:3,12; 32:17
119:166 [y]Ge 49:18
119:168 [z]Pr 5:21
119:169 [a]Ps 18:6
119:170 [b]Ps 28:2 [c]Ps 31:2
119:171 [d]Ps 51:15 [e]Ps 94:12
119:173 [f]Ps 37:24 [g]Jos 24:22
119:174 [h]ver 166
119:175 [i]Isa 55:3

119:176 [j]Isa 53:6

176 I have strayed like a lost sheep.[j]
Seek your servant,
for I have not forgotten your commands.

Psalm 120

A song of ascents.

120:1 [k]Ps 102:2; Jnh 2:2
120:2 [l]Pr 12:22 [m]Ps 52:4
120:4 [n]Ps 45:5
120:5 [o]Ge 25:13; Jer 49:28

1 I call on the LORD in my distress,[k]
and he answers me.
2 Save me, O LORD, from lying lips[l]
and from deceitful tongues.[m]

3 What will he do to you,
and what more besides, O deceitful tongue?
4 He will punish you with a warrior's sharp arrows,[n]
with burning coals of the broom tree.

5 Woe to me that I dwell in Meshech,
that I live among the tents of Kedar![o]
6 Too long have I lived
among those who hate peace.
7 I am a man of peace;
but when I speak, they are for war.

Psalm 121

A song of ascents.

121:2 [p]Ps 115:15; 124:8
121:5 [q]Isa 25:4
121:6 [r]Ps 91:5; Isa 49:10; Rev 7:16
121:7 [s]Ps 41:2; 91:10-12
121:8 [t]Dt 28:6

1 I lift up my eyes to the hills—
where does my help come from?
2 My help comes from the LORD,
the Maker of heaven and earth.[p]

3 He will not let your foot slip—
he who watches over you will not slumber;
4 indeed, he who watches over Israel
will neither slumber nor sleep.

5 The LORD watches over[q] you—
the LORD is your shade at your right hand;
6 the sun[r] will not harm you by day,
nor the moon by night.

7 The LORD will keep you from all harm[s]—
he will watch over your life;
8 the LORD will watch over your coming and going
both now and forevermore.[t]

120:1—136:26 See the note on Psalm 113:1—118:29 regarding the "Hallel" psalms.

120:1–7 Some have thought that the Hebrew for the word "ascents" (see superscript) refers to stairs leading to the temple, hence "a song of the stairs," to be used in the temple liturgy (probably at the Feast of Tabernacles). Most believe that it refers to the annual religious pilgrimages to Jerusalem, which brought the worshipers singing to Mount Zion.

120:4 Often found in the English Bible, the word "coal" never refers to true mineral coal, which has not been found in Palestine proper, where the geological formation as a whole is recent. Coal of a poor quality has been discovered in Sidon, and for a time some was mined in Lebanon. The half dozen Hebrew and Greek words rendered "coal" refer either to charcoal or to live embers of any kind. Charcoal was used by the Hebrews to provide warmth in winter (Isa 47:14; Jn 18:18), for cooking (Isa 44:19; Jn 21:9) and for blacksmith work (Isa 44:12; 54:15). It was made by covering a carefully stacked pile of wood with leaves and earth and then setting fire to it. After several days of burning and smoldering, the wood was converted into charcoal and the pile was opened.

The broom tree, a large bush that grows in the deserts of Palestine and Arabia (see 1Ki 19:4; Job 30:4), is sometimes large enough to provide shade.

120:5 Meshech was located in central Asia Minor and Kedar in Arabia.

121:3 Pagans "permitted" their gods to sleep (see 1Ki 18:27), but the God of Israel is not like any other god—he has no need to recreate, rest or eat.

Psalm 122

A song of ascents. Of David.

1 I rejoiced with those who said to me,
"Let us go to the house of the LORD."
2 Our feet are standing
in your gates, O Jerusalem.

3 Jerusalem is built like a city
that is closely compacted together.
4 That is where the tribes go up,
the tribes of the LORD,
to praise the name of the LORD
according to the statute given to Israel.
5 There the thrones for judgment stand,
the thrones of the house of David.

6 Pray for the peace of Jerusalem:
"May those who love[u] you be secure.
7 May there be peace within your walls
and security within your citadels."
8 For the sake of my brothers and friends,
I will say, "Peace be within you."
9 For the sake of the house of the LORD our God,
I will seek your prosperity.[v]

122:6 [u]Ps 51:18
122:9 [v]Ne 2:10

Psalm 123

A song of ascents.

1 I lift up my eyes to you,
to you whose throne[w] is in heaven.
2 As the eyes of slaves look to the hand of their master,
as the eyes of a maid look to the hand of her mistress,
so our eyes look to the LORD[x] our God,
till he shows us his mercy.

3 Have mercy on us, O LORD, have mercy on us,
for we have endured much contempt.
4 We have endured much ridicule from the proud,
much contempt from the arrogant.

123:1 [w]Ps 11:4; 121:1; 141:8
123:2 [x]Ps 25:15

Psalm 124

A song of ascents. Of David.

1 If the LORD had not been on our side—
let Israel say[y]—
2 if the LORD had not been on our side
when men attacked us,
3 when their anger flared against us,
they would have swallowed us alive;
4 the flood would have engulfed us,
the torrent would have swept over us,
5 the raging waters
would have swept us away.

124:1 [y]Ps 129:1

122:1 This psalm expresses the joy of Zion from the perspective of a pilgrim who had traveled there to worship. Pilgrimages were held three times annually, during the Feasts of Passover, Firstfruits and Tabernacles. As the psalmist looked at Jerusalem and stood within her gates (v. 2), he rejoiced.

[6] Praise be to the LORD,
who has not let us be torn by their teeth.
[7] We have escaped like a bird
124:7 [z]Ps 91:3; Pr 6:5 — out of the fowler's snare;[z]
the snare has been broken,
and we have escaped.
[8] Our help is in the name of the LORD,
124:8 [a]Ge 1:1; Ps 121:2; 134:3 — the Maker of heaven[a] and earth.

Psalm 125

A song of ascents.

[1] Those who trust in the LORD are like Mount Zion,
125:1 [b]Ps 46:5 — which cannot be shaken[b] but endures forever.
[2] As the mountains surround Jerusalem,
125:2 [c]Ps 121:8; Zec 2:4-5 — so the LORD surrounds[c] his people
both now and forevermore.

125:3 [d]Ps 89:22; Pr 22:8; Isa 14:5 [e]1Sa 24:10; Ps 55:20 — [3] The scepter of the wicked will not remain[d]
over the land allotted to the righteous,
for then the righteous might use
their hands to do evil.[e]

125:4 [f]Ps 119:68 [g]Ps 7:10; 36:10; 94:15 — [4] Do good, O LORD,[f] to those who are good,
to those who are upright in heart.[g]
125:5 [h]Job 23:11 [i]Pr 2:15; Isa 59:8 [j]Ps 128:6 — [5] But those who turn[h] to crooked ways[i]
the LORD will banish with the evildoers.

Peace be upon Israel.[j]

Psalm 126

A song of ascents.

126:1 [k]Ps 85:1; Hos 6:11 — [1] When the LORD brought back[k] the captives to[a] Zion,
we were like men who dreamed.[b]
[2] Our mouths were filled with laughter,
126:2 [l]Job 8:21; Ps 51:14 [m]Ps 71:19 — our tongues with songs of joy.[l]
Then it was said among the nations,
"The LORD has done great things[m] for them."
[3] The LORD has done great things for us,
126:3 [n]Isa 25:9 — and we are filled with joy.[n]

[4] Restore our fortunes,[c] O LORD,
126:4 [o]Isa 35:6; 43:19 — like streams in the Negev.[o]
[5] Those who sow in tears
126:5 [p]Isa 35:10 — will reap with songs of joy.[p]
[6] He who goes out weeping,
carrying seed to sow,
will return with songs of joy,
carrying sheaves with him.

[a] *1* Or *LORD restored the fortunes of* [b] *1* Or *men restored to health* [c] *4* Or *Bring back our captives*

125:2 Although Jerusalem is not surrounded by a ring of peaks, the city is located in what Old Testament writers would have considered a mountainous region.
126:4 The wadis, or gullies, in the southern desert (Negev) are bone-dry in the summer, but when the winter rains come the water rushes down them with great force, a sudden and powerful unleashing of blessing.
126:6 For a discussion of sheaves and threshing, see the note on Ruth 2:7. See also "The Threshing Floor" on page 608 and "Food and Agriculture" on page 390.

Psalm 127

A song of ascents. Of Solomon.

[1] Unless the LORD builds[q] the house,
its builders labor in vain.
Unless the LORD watches[r] over the city,
the watchmen stand guard in vain.
[2] In vain you rise early
and stay up late,
toiling for food[s] to eat—
for he grants sleep[t] to[a] those he loves.

[3] Sons are a heritage from the LORD,
children a reward[u] from him.
[4] Like arrows in the hands of a warrior
are sons born in one's youth.
[5] Blessed is the man
whose quiver is full of them.
They will not be put to shame
when they contend with their enemies[v] in the gate.

127:1 [q]Ps 78:69 [r]Ps 121:4
127:2 [s]Ge 3:17 [t]Job 11:18
127:3 [u]Ge 33:5
127:5 [v]Pr 27:11

[a] 2 Or *eat— / for while they sleep he provides for*

127:5 Legal proceedings and business transactions were conducted at the city gate (see "The City Gate" on p. 392).

ANCIENT TEXTS AND ARTIFACTS

A Hittite Blessing for a House

PSALM 127 Virtually all people are concerned for the well-being of their own home and household. Frequently people will invoke divine help for the protection of their families, but often the differences we see among such invocations are far greater than what they have in common.

A **Hittite** text has been discovered that describes ritual purification of a house deemed to have become ritually polluted. The reason for the alleged defilement is unclear; perhaps its inhabitants had suffered from misfortune or infertility or the house itself had manifested problems such as mildew. The text explains that an exorcist came and ritually recited various possible explanations for the defilement, suggesting that perhaps a perjurer, murderer or witch had entered the house. The exorcist proceeded with an elaborate ritual involving the recitation of myths and magic formulas, while making animal sacrifices and pouring out libations at various locations. All of this was meant to encourage primordial deities to carry off the uncleanness of the house to the underworld.

Although the Old Testament specifies a number of rituals that concern uncleanness, none involves magic formulas, recitation of myths or the invocation of infernal deities. In fact, the Old Testament is extremely practical in its outlook regarding household defilement (see Lev 14:33–57). Psalm 127 vividly illustrates the Old Testament attitude toward the welfare of a household. First, security comes from God, not from personal diligence (vv. 1–2). Second, children, as a gift from God, constitute the true wealth of a home (vv. 3–5). Reverence for God and devotion to family are at the heart of the Bible's teaching on the well-being of a home, in contrast to the superstition of pagan teaching.

Hittite child's toy
Preserving Bible Times; © Dr. James C. Martin; permission of Turkish Antiquities

Psalm 128

A song of ascents.

128:1 [w]Ps 112:1 [x]Ps 119:1-3
128:2 [y]Isa 3:10 [z]Ecc 8:12
128:3 [a]Eze 19:10 [b]Ps 52:8; 144:12
128:5 [c]Ps 20:2; 134:3
128:6 [d]Ge 50:23; Job 42:16 [e]Ps 125:5

1 Blessed are all who fear the LORD,[w]
who walk in his ways.[x]
2 You will eat the fruit of your labor;[y]
blessings and prosperity[z] will be yours.
3 Your wife will be like a fruitful vine[a]
within your house;
your sons will be like olive shoots[b]
around your table.
4 Thus is the man blessed
who fears the LORD.

5 May the LORD bless you from Zion[c]
all the days of your life;
may you see the prosperity of Jerusalem,
6 and may you live to see your children's children.[d]

Peace be upon Israel.[e]

Psalm 129

A song of ascents.

129:1 [f]Ps 88:15; Hos 2:15 [g]Ps 124:1
129:2 [h]Mt 16:18
129:4 [i]Ps 119:137
129:5 [j]Mic 4:11 [k]Ps 71:13
129:6 [l]Ps 37:2
129:8 [m]Ru 2:4; Ps 118:26

1 They have greatly oppressed me from my youth[f]—
let Israel say[g]—
2 they have greatly oppressed me from my youth,
but they have not gained the victory[h] over me.
3 Plowmen have plowed my back
and made their furrows long.
4 But the LORD is righteous;[i]
he has cut me free from the cords of the wicked.

5 May all who hate Zion[j]
be turned back in shame.[k]
6 May they be like grass on the roof,
which withers[l] before it can grow;
7 with it the reaper cannot fill his hands,
nor the one who gathers fill his arms.
8 May those who pass by not say,
"The blessing of the LORD be upon you;
we bless you[m] in the name of the LORD."

Psalm 130

A song of ascents.

130:1 [n]Ps 42:7; 69:2; La 3:55
130:2 [o]Ps 28:2 [p]2Ch 6:40; Ps 64:1

1 Out of the depths[n] I cry to you, O LORD;
2 O Lord, hear my voice.[o]
Let your ears be attentive[p]
to my cry for mercy.

128:3 Although an olive tree might not bear fruit for 40 years, it is a symbol of long life and productivity—as are children in a household of faith. They are not like grass—here today, gone tomorrow.

The occurrence of no fewer than 250 botanical terms in the Old Testament demonstrates the Israelite fondness for flowers, fruits and pleasant grounds. These are still a delight to people living in this hot, dry country. Virtually every house court or yard had its shade tree, and the vine that grew around the trellis or outside staircase was the emblem of the loving and fruitful wife and the happy home within.

129:6 Grass that sprouted on the flat, sunbaked housetops would wither, since no plow could prepare a nurturing soil to sustain the young shoots—and so there would be no harvest. This verse expresses the hope that the same would happen to those who "plowed" the backs of Israel (v. 3). See "The Flowers of Ancient Israel" on page 1037 and "Trees of Ancient Israel" on page 1357.

129:7–8 For a discussion of sheaves and threshing, see the note on Ruth 2:7. See also "The Threshing Floor" on page 608 and "Food and Agriculture" on page 390.

[3]If you, O LORD, kept a record of sins,
O Lord, who could stand?[q]
[4]But with you there is forgiveness;[r]
therefore you are feared.[s]

[5]I wait for the LORD,[t] my soul waits,
and in his word[u] I put my hope.
[6]My soul waits for the Lord
more than watchmen[v] wait for the morning,
more than watchmen wait for the morning.[w]

[7]O Israel, put your hope[x] in the LORD,
for with the LORD is unfailing love
and with him is full redemption.
[8]He himself will redeem[y] Israel
from all their sins.

130:3 [q]Ps 76:7; 143:2
130:4 [r]Ex 34:7; Isa 55:7; Jer 33:8 [s]1Ki 8:40
130:5 [t]Ps 27:14; 33:20; Isa 8:17 [u]Ps 119:81
130:6 [v]Ps 63:6 [w]Ps 119:147
130:7 [x]Ps 131:3
130:8 [y]Lk 1:68

Psalm 131

A song of ascents. Of David.

[1]My heart is not proud,[z] O LORD,
my eyes are not haughty;
I do not concern myself with great matters
or things too wonderful for me.
[2]But I have stilled and quieted my soul;
like a weaned child with its mother,
like a weaned child is my soul[a] within me.

[3]O Israel, put your hope[b] in the LORD
both now and forevermore.

131:1 [z]Ps 101:5; Ro 12:16
131:2 [a]Mt 18:3; 1Co 14:20
131:3 [b]Ps 130:7

Psalm 132

A song of ascents.

[1]O LORD, remember David
and all the hardships he endured.

[2]He swore an oath to the LORD
and made a vow to the Mighty One of Jacob:[c]
[3]"I will not enter my house
or go to my bed—
[4]I will allow no sleep to my eyes,
no slumber to my eyelids,
[5]till I find a place[d] for the LORD,
a dwelling for the Mighty One of Jacob."

[6]We heard it in Ephrathah,[e]
we came upon it in the fields of Jaar[a]:[b][f]
[7]"Let us go to his dwelling place;[g]
let us worship at his footstool[h]—
[8]arise, O LORD,[i] and come to your resting place,
you and the ark of your might.

132:2 [c]Ge 49:24
132:5 [d]Ac 7:46
132:6 [e]1Sa 17:12 [f]1Sa 7:2
132:7 [g]Ps 5:7 [h]Ps 99:5
132:8 [i]Nu 10:35; Ps 78:61

[a] 6 That is, Kiriath Jearim [b] 6 Or *heard of it in Ephrathah, / we found it in the fields of Jaar.* (And no quotes around verses 7-9)

131:1 For "heart," see the note on 4:7.
131:2 For "soul," see the note on 6:3. A "weaned child" refers to a child of four or five years of age who walks trustingly beside his or her mother.

132:6 Ephrathah is the region around Bethlehem, David's hometown (see "Bethlehem" on p. 1487). Jaar is another name for Kiriath-Jearim, where the ark was kept after its return by the Philistines (see "Kiriath Jearim" on p. 406).

Historians in the Ancient World

PSALM 132 The poet of Psalm 132 looked back to the covenant with David and to the history of the ark of the covenant as the basis for his prayer[1]—a reflection that the Bible is rooted in history, not theology divorced from human events and cultures.

The works of ancient historians, because they provide context, are of great value in Biblical studies. Important historians include:

✣ *Herodotus of Halicarnassus*[2] (c. 484–425 B.C.): His great work is called the *Historia* ("investigation"). An account of the wars between the Greeks and Persians, his work includes other stories as well, including an interesting, if not fully credible, account of ancient Egyptian culture.

✣ *Thucydides* (c. 460–400 B.C.): Perhaps the greatest ancient historian, this Greek general wrote a lucid and gripping account of the Peloponnesian War (431–404 B.C.) between the Athenians and the Spartan alliance.[3] His work, which models scrupulous research and careful writing, has survived intact but ends abruptly.

✣ *Manetho*: Manetho, an Egyptian priest who lived during the reign of **Ptolemy** I (305–282 B.C.), compiled a history of Egypt. Unfortunately, his work has survived only in fragments, as quoted by other ancient writers (e.g., Josephus and Eusebius). His division of Egyptian history into 30 dynasties is still followed.[4]

✣ *Berosus*: The first true historian of the Mesopotamian region was this Babylonian priest. In about 290 B.C. he authored three books in Greek on Babylonian history. Berosus's history also survives only in pieces, as cited by Josephus and Eusebius. His original work covered the history of the region from the mythological past to the **Assyrians**, Babylonians and **Persians**.

✣ *Demetrius the Chronographer* (third century B.C.): Demetrius, a Jewish historian, recorded the history of his people, focusing on Biblical Israel and using the **Septuagint** as his primary source. He desired to illuminate the Bible's historical background and to resolve exegetical difficulties. His work too survives only in fragments.

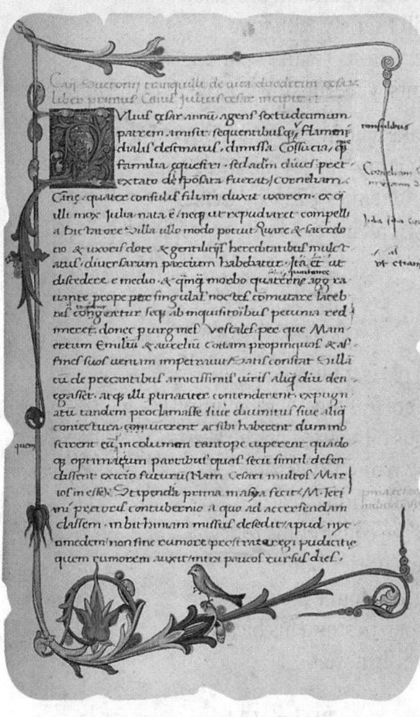

Suetonius's Lives of the Twelve Caesars; Austria, c. 1470

© The Schøyen Collection; photography courtesy of Mr. Martin Schøyen

✣ *Flavius Josephus* (c. A.D. 37–100): Josephus was the most famous Jewish historian. His *History of the Jewish War*, describing the A.D. 66–70 war between Judea and Rome,[5] ranks with Thucydides' history as one of the greatest ancient historical works. Josephus, of a priestly background (a Pharisee),[6] began the war as a combatant for the losing side. He also wrote a chronology of the Jewish people from earliest times to nearly A.D. 100 (Antiquities of the Jews). Josephus used the **Septuagint** as his primary source for the Biblical period but was also influenced by **Hellenistic** culture. He is our chief source of information regarding Herod the Great,[7] and he referred to John the Baptist, Jesus and James, the brother of Jesus, although the authenticity of his description of Jesus is disputed.[8]

✣ *Polybius* (c. 200–118 B.C.): Although a Greek, Polybius was the greatest historian of early Rome. His history is a major source for the study of the Punic Wars (Rome vs. Carthage).[9]

✣ *Appian of Alexandria* (second century A.D.): Another Greek historian, he focused on the rise of the Roman Republic.

✣ *Publius Cornelius Tacitus* (c. A.D. 56–120): Tacitus was the primary historian of the Roman Empire. His Histories and Annals focus on the imperial history of the first century A.D.

✣ *Dio Cassius* (died c. A.D. 229): His work described the history of Rome from its founding to the time of Alexander Severus (A.D. 222–235). Unfortunately, much of it has been lost.

✣ *Suetonius* (c. A.D. 69–112): Suetonius (The Lives of the Caesars)[10] wrote a biography of the early Roman emperors.

✣ *Plutarch* (c. A.D. 46–119): Another biographer, he authored the Parallel Lives of Famous Greeks and Romans, a valuable resource for Greek and Roman history.

✣ *Eusebius of Caesarea* (c. A.D. 263–339): Eusebius was the church's first great historian. His Ecclesiastical History, sometimes criticized for being more a defense of Christianity than a history, details chronologically the story of the rise of Christianity and is of enormous value.

[1]See "The Tabernacle and the Ark" on page 153. [2]See, for example, "Herodotus and the Fall of Babylon" on page 1283. [3]See "Athens" on page 1804 and "Greece: From Independent City-states Through Alexander the Great" on page 1814. [4]See "A Breakdown of Ancient Egyptian History" on page 104. [5]See "Josephus and the Fall of Jerusalem" on page 1606. [6]See "The Pharisees" on page 1566. [7]See "Herod the Great" on page 1627. [8]See "Nonbiblical Sources for the Historical Jesus" on page 1751. [9]See "The Roman Empire" on page 1566. [10]See, for example, "Claudius, Emperor of Rome" on page 1788.

[9] May your priests be clothed with righteousness;[j]
may your saints sing for joy."

[10] For the sake of David your servant,
do not reject your anointed one.

[11] The LORD swore an oath to David,[k]
a sure oath that he will not revoke:
"One of your own descendants[l]
I will place on your throne—
[12] if your sons keep my covenant
and the statutes I teach them,
then their sons will sit
on your throne[m] for ever and ever."
[13] For the LORD has chosen Zion,[n]
he has desired it for his dwelling:
[14] "This is my resting place for ever and ever;[o]
here I will sit enthroned, for I have desired it—
[15] I will bless her with abundant provisions;
her poor will I satisfy with food.[p]
[16] I will clothe her priests[q] with salvation,
and her saints will ever sing for joy.

[17] "Here I will make a horn[a] grow[r] for David
and set up a lamp[s] for my anointed one.
[18] I will clothe his enemies with shame,[t]
but the crown on his head will be resplendent."

132:9 [j]Job 29:14; Isa 61:3,10
132:11 [k]Ps 89:3-4,35 [l]2Sa 7:12
132:12 [m]Lk 1:32; Ac 2:30
132:13 [n]Ps 48:1-2
132:14 [o]Ps 68:16
132:15 [p]Ps 107:9; 147:14
132:16 [q]2Ch 6:41
132:17 [r]Eze 29:21; Lk 1:69 [s]1Ki 11:36; 2Ch 21:7
132:18 [t]Ps 35:26; 109:29

Psalm 133

A song of ascents. Of David.

[1] How good and pleasant it is
when brothers live together[u] in unity!
[2] It is like precious oil poured on the head,[v]
running down on the beard,
running down on Aaron's beard,
down upon the collar of his robes.
[3] It is as if the dew of Hermon[w]
were falling on Mount Zion.
For there the LORD bestows his blessing,[x]
even life forevermore.[y]

133:1 [u]Ge 13:8; Heb 13:1
133:2 [v]Ex 30:25
133:3 [w]Dt 4:48 [x]Lev 25:21; Dt 28:8 [y]Ps 42:8

Psalm 134

A song of ascents.

[1] Praise the LORD, all you servants[z] of the LORD
who minister by night[a] in the house of the LORD.
[2] Lift up your hands[b] in the sanctuary
and praise the LORD.

[3] May the LORD, the Maker of heaven[c] and earth,
bless you from Zion.[d]

134:1 [z]Ps 135:1-2 [a]1Ch 9:33
134:2 [b]Ps 28:2; 1Ti 2:8
134:3 [c]Ps 124:8 [d]Ps 128:5

[a] 17 *Horn* here symbolizes strong one, that is, king.

133:2 The oil of Aaron's anointing (Ex 29:7; Lev 21:10) saturated all the hair of his beard and ran down on his priestly robes, signifying his total consecration to holy service.
133:3 With its high altitude, regular precipitation and heavy dew, Mount Hermon is known for its lush greenery even during the summer. The experience of the pilgrims was like Hermon's refreshing dew. From May to October virtually no rain—or even dew—falls on Jerusalem. During these months at least two pilgrimages were held. Regardless of the harsh conditions of life in general, or of the pilgrimage in particular, the unity of God's people was refreshing.

Psalm 135

[1] Praise the LORD.[a]

Praise the name of the LORD;
praise him, you servants[e] of the LORD,
[2] you who minister in the house[f] of the LORD,
in the courts[g] of the house of our God.

[3] Praise the LORD, for the LORD is good;[h]
sing praise to his name, for that is pleasant.[i]
[4] For the LORD has chosen Jacob[j] to be his own,
Israel to be his treasured possession.[k]

[5] I know that the LORD is great,[l]
that our Lord is greater than all gods.[m]
[6] The LORD does whatever pleases him,[n]
in the heavens and on the earth,
in the seas and all their depths.
[7] He makes clouds rise from the ends of the earth;
he sends lightning with the rain[o]
and brings out the wind[p] from his storehouses.[q]

[8] He struck down the firstborn[r] of Egypt,
the firstborn of men and animals.

135:1 [e]Ps 113:1; 134:1 **135:2** [f]Lk 2:37 [g]Ps 116:19 **135:3** [h]Ps 119:68 [i]Ps 147:1 **135:4** [j]Dt 10:15; 1Pe 2:9 [k]Ex 19:5; Dt 7:6 **135:5** [l]Ps 48:1 [m]Ps 97:9 **135:6** [n]Ps 115:3 **135:7** [o]Jer 10:13; Zec 10:1 [p]Job 28:25 [q]Job 38:22 **135:8** [r]Ex 12:12; Ps 78:51

[a] *1* Hebrew *Hallelu Yah*; also in verses 3 and 21

135:4 "Jacob" is a synonym for Israel (see Ge 32:28).
135:6 The ancients viewed the heavens, earth and seas as the three great domains of the visible creation.
135:7 Baal, the Canaanite god of weather and fertility, was the "cloud-rider" (see "The Ugaritic Text of the Myth of Baal" on p. 905 and "Baal and the Fertility Cults" on p. 1414). But the Lord, the God of Israel, brings the life-giving rains and "makes the clouds his chariot" (104:3).

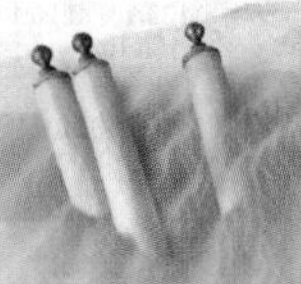

ANCIENT TEXTS AND ARTIFACTS

An Akkadian Prayer to the Gods of the Night

PSALM 134 There are several short **Akkadian** liturgies known as Prayers to the Gods of the Night. These poems, which are prayers to the celestial stars, were recited at night. One example describes the silence of the city when doors were bolted, the palace was quiet and the people were asleep. Even the major deities (e.g., the sun god) had retreated into the lap of heaven, meaning that they were not visible at that time. The petitioner addressed the night gods, represented by the various constellations, asking for a favorable omen. He then performed a ritual of extispicy (seeking an answer to his inquiry through an interpretation of the form of the animal organs).[1]

It may be that Psalm 134 is also an evening liturgy, but it is vastly different from the Akkadian poems. Psalm 134 may be a dialogue of praise sung between **Yahweh**'s worshipers as they left the temple in the evening and the Levites who would guard it by night.[2] The worshipers exhorted the Levites to continue to praise the Lord throughout the night, while the Levites in turn pronounced a benediction upon the congregants. Yahweh does not cease to work simply because it is nighttime; indeed, the Protector of Israel neither slumbers nor sleeps (121:4). The Israelites were not to worship the heavenly bodies as the surrounding nations did, for they are not divine beings but simply part of God's creation that also glorify him (Ge 1:14–18; Ps 8:3; 136:7–9; 148:3). Worship of the Lord is to continue uninterrupted by day and night.

[1]See also "Akkadian Divination" on page 277. [2]See "The Levites and the Priests" on page 648.

[9] He sent his signs[s] and wonders into your midst, O Egypt,
against Pharaoh and all his servants.[t]
[10] He struck down many[u] nations
and killed mighty kings—
[11] Sihon[v] king of the Amorites,
Og king of Bashan
and all the kings of Canaan[w]—
[12] and he gave their land as an inheritance,[x]
an inheritance to his people Israel.

[13] Your name, O LORD, endures forever,[y]
your renown,[z] O LORD, through all generations.
[14] For the LORD will vindicate his people
and have compassion on his servants.[a]

[15] The idols of the nations are silver and gold,
made by the hands of men.
[16] They have mouths, but cannot speak,
eyes, but they cannot see;
[17] they have ears, but cannot hear,
nor is there breath in their mouths.
[18] Those who make them will be like them,
and so will all who trust in them.

[19] O house of Israel, praise the LORD;
O house of Aaron, praise the LORD;
[20] O house of Levi, praise the LORD;
you who fear him, praise the LORD.
[21] Praise be to the LORD from Zion,[b]
to him who dwells in Jerusalem.

Praise the LORD.

135:9 [s]Dt 6:22 [t]Ps 136:10-15
135:10 [u]Nu 21:21-25; Ps 136:17-21
135:11 [v]Nu 21:21 [w]Jos 12:7-24
135:12 [x]Ps 78:55
135:13 [y]Ex 3:15 [z]Ps 102:12
135:14 [a]Dt 32:36
135:21 [b]Ps 134:3

Psalm 136

[1] Give thanks to the LORD, for he is good.[c]
His love endures forever.[d]
[2] Give thanks to the God of gods.[e]
His love endures forever.
[3] Give thanks to the Lord of lords:
His love endures forever.

[4] to him who alone does great wonders,[f]
His love endures forever.
[5] who by his understanding[g] made the heavens,[h]
His love endures forever.
[6] who spread out the earth[i] upon the waters,[j]
His love endures forever.
[7] who made the great lights[k]—
His love endures forever.
[8] the sun to govern[l] the day,
His love endures forever.
[9] the moon and stars to govern the night;
His love endures forever.

136:1 [c]Ps 106:1 [d]1Ch 16:34; 2Ch 20:21
136:2 [e]Dt 10:17
136:4 [f]Ps 72:18
136:5 [g]Pr 3:19; Jer 51:15 [h]Ge 1:1
136:6 [i]Ge 1:9; Jer 10:12 [j]Ps 24:2
136:7 [k]Ge 1:14, 16
136:8 [l]Ge 1:16

136:1–26 See the note on Psalm 113:1—118:29 regarding the "Hallel" psalms.

136:10 [m]Ex 12:29; Ps 135:8
136:11 [n]Ex 6:6; 12:51
136:12 [o]Dt 4:34; Ps 44:3
136:13 [p]Ex 14:21; Ps 78:13
136:14 [q]Ex 14:22
136:15 [r]Ex 14:27; Ps 135:9
136:16 [s]Ex 13:18
136:17 [t]Ps 135:9-12
136:18 [u]Dt 29:7
136:19 [v]Nu 21:21-25
136:21 [w]Jos 12:1
136:23 [x]Ps 113:7
136:24 [y]Ps 107:2
136:25 [z]Ps 104:27; 145:15

10 to him who struck down the firstborn[m] of Egypt
His love endures forever.
11 and brought Israel out[n] from among them
His love endures forever.
12 with a mighty hand and outstretched arm;[o]
His love endures forever.

13 to him who divided the Red Sea[a][p] asunder
His love endures forever.
14 and brought Israel through[q] the midst of it,
His love endures forever.
15 but swept Pharaoh and his army into the Red Sea;[r]
His love endures forever.

16 to him who led his people through the desert,[s]
His love endures forever.

17 who struck down great kings,[t]
His love endures forever.
18 and killed mighty kings[u]—
His love endures forever.
19 Sihon king of the Amorites[v]
His love endures forever.
20 and Og king of Bashan—
His love endures forever.
21 and gave their land[w] as an inheritance,
His love endures forever.
22 an inheritance to his servant Israel;
His love endures forever.

23 to the One who remembered us[x] in our low estate
His love endures forever.
24 and freed us from our enemies,[y]
His love endures forever.
25 and who gives food[z] to every creature.
His love endures forever.

26 Give thanks to the God of heaven.
His love endures forever.

Psalm 137

137:1 [a]Eze 1:1,3 [b]Ne 1:4
137:3 [c]Ps 80:6

1 By the rivers of Babylon[a] we sat and wept[b]
when we remembered Zion.
2 There on the poplars
we hung our harps,
3 for there our captors asked us for songs,
our tormentors demanded[c] songs of joy;
they said, "Sing us one of the songs of Zion!"

4 How can we sing the songs of the LORD
while in a foreign land?

[a] *13* Hebrew *Yam Suph*; that is, Sea of Reeds; also in verse 15

136:26 "The God of heaven" was a Persian title for God frequently found in the books of Ezra, Nehemiah and Daniel.
137:1 "Rivers" is a reference to the Tigris and Euphrates and to the many canals associated with them.
137:2 They "hung [their] harps" because the callous Babylonians demanded exotic entertainment, while the exiles' instruments were only "tuned to mourning" (Job 30:31). See "Ancient Musical Instruments" on page 797.

[5]If I forget you, O Jerusalem,
may my right hand forget ⌞its skill⌟.
[6]May my tongue cling to the roof[d] of my mouth
if I do not remember you,
if I do not consider Jerusalem
my highest joy.

[7]Remember, O LORD, what the Edomites[e] did
on the day Jerusalem fell.[f]
"Tear it down," they cried,
"tear it down to its foundations!"

[8]O Daughter of Babylon, doomed to destruction,[g]
happy is he who repays you
for what you have done to us—
[9]he who seizes your infants
and dashes them[h] against the rocks.

137:6 [d]Eze 3:26
137:7 [e]Jer 49:7; La 4:21-22; Eze 25:12 [f]Ob 1:11
137:8 [g]Isa 13:1, 19; Jer 25:12,26; Jer 50:15; Rev 18:6
137:9 [h]2Ki 8:12; Isa 13:16

Psalm 138

Of David.

[1]I will praise you, O LORD, with all my heart;
before the "gods"[i] I will sing your praise.
[2]I will bow down toward your holy temple[j]
and will praise your name
for your love and your faithfulness,
for you have exalted above all things
your name and your word.[k]
[3]When I called, you answered me;
you made me bold and stouthearted.[l]

[4]May all the kings of the earth[m] praise you, O LORD,
when they hear the words of your mouth.
[5]May they sing of the ways of the LORD,
for the glory of the LORD is great.

[6]Though the LORD is on high, he looks upon the lowly,[n]
but the proud[o] he knows from afar.
[7]Though I walk[p] in the midst of trouble,
you preserve my life;
you stretch out your hand against the anger of my foes,[q]
with your right hand[r] you save me.[s]
[8]The LORD will fulfill ⌞his purpose⌟[t] for me;
your love, O LORD, endures forever—
do not abandon the works of your hands.[u]

138:1 [i]Ps 95:3; 96:4
138:2 [j]1Ki 8:29; Ps 5:7; 28:2 [k]Isa 42:21
138:3 [l]Ps 28:7
138:4 [m]Ps 102:15
138:6 [n]Ps 113:6; Isa 57:15 [o]Pr 3:34; Jas 4:6
138:7 [p]Ps 23:4 [q]Jer 51:25 [r]Ps 20:6 [s]Ps 71:20
138:8 [t]Ps 57:2; Php 1:6 [u]Job 10:3,8; 14:15

Psalm 139

For the director of music. Of David. A psalm.

[1]O LORD, you have searched me[v]
and you know[w] me.

139:1 [v]Ps 17:3 [w]Jer 12:3

137:7 The enduring animosity of the Edomites—descendants of Esau, Jacob's brother—showed its most dastardly face in Jerusalem's darkest hour (Ob 8–14).

137:8 "Daughter" is here a personification of Babylon and its inhabitants.

For commentary on expressions of vengeful attitudes toward enemies, see the note on 69:22–28. See also "Curses and Imprecations" on page 883.

137:9 War was as cruel then as now, and women and children were not spared its horrors (see 2Ki 8:12; 15:16; Isa 13:16,18; Hos 10:14; 13:16; Am 1:13; Na 3:10).

138:1 For "heart," see the note on 4:7. The word "gods" refers either to pagan kings (see 138:4–5) or to the gods they claimed to represent (see the note on 82:1).

139:2 [x]2Ki 19:27 [y]Mt 9:4; Jn 2:24

[2] You know when I sit and when I rise;[x]
you perceive my thoughts[y] from afar.
[3] You discern my going out and my lying down;
you are familiar with all my ways.[z]

139:3 [z]Job 31:4

[4] Before a word is on my tongue
you know it completely,[a] O LORD.

139:4 [a]Heb 4:13

[5] You hem me in[b]—behind and before;
you have laid your hand upon me.

139:5 [b]Ps 34:7

[6] Such knowledge is too wonderful for me,
too lofty[c] for me to attain.

139:6 [c]Job 42:3; Ro 11:33

[7] Where can I go from your Spirit?
Where can I flee[d] from your presence?
[8] If I go up to the heavens,[e] you are there;
if I make my bed[f] in the depths,[a] you are there.

139:7 [d]Jer 23:24; Jnh 1:3
139:8 [e]Am 9:2-3 [f]Pr 15:11

[9] If I rise on the wings of the dawn,
if I settle on the far side of the sea,
[10] even there your hand will guide me,[g]
your right hand will hold me fast.

139:10 [g]Ps 23:3

[11] If I say, "Surely the darkness will hide me
and the light become night around me,"
[12] even the darkness will not be dark[h] to you;
the night will shine like the day,
for darkness is as light to you.

139:12 [h]Job 34:22; Da 2:22

[13] For you created my inmost being;[i]
you knit me together[j] in my mother's womb.
[14] I praise you because I am fearfully and wonderfully made;
your works are wonderful,[k]
I know that full well.

139:13 [i]Ps 119:73 [j]Job 10:11
139:14 [k]Ps 40:5

[15] My frame was not hidden from you
when I was made in the secret place.
When I was woven together[l] in the depths of the earth,[m]
[16] your eyes saw my unformed body.
All the days ordained for me
were written in your book
before one of them came to be.

139:15 [l]Job 10:11 [m]Ps 63:9

[17] How precious to[b] me are your thoughts, O God![n]
How vast is the sum of them!
[18] Were I to count them,
they would outnumber the grains of sand.
When I awake,
I am still with you.

139:17 [n]Ps 40:5

[19] If only you would slay the wicked,[o] O God!
Away from me,[p] you bloodthirsty men!
[20] They speak of you with evil intent;
your adversaries misuse your name.[q]

139:19 [o]Isa 11:4 [p]Ps 119:115
139:20 [q]Jude 15

[a] 8 Hebrew *Sheol* [b] 17 Or *concerning*

139:9 The "wings of the dawn" and the "far side of the sea" represent the two horizontal extremes: east and west. The "sea" is the Mediterranean.

139:13 The term "inmost being" (lit., "kidneys") is a Hebrew idiom referring to an individual's most intimate center of emotions and of moral sensitivity—that which God tests and examines when he "searches" a person (see the note on 7:9). (See "Heart, Breath, Throat and Intestines: Ancient Hebrew Anthropology" on p. 968.)

139:15 This verse describes the womb, called "the secret place" because it conceals (see 2Sa 12:12). It is like the "depths of the earth" in that it is dark, damp and separated from the visible realm of life.

139:19–22 For commentary on expressions of vengeful attitudes toward enemies, see the note on 69:22–28. See also "Curses and Imprecations" on page 883.

Sheol, Hades, Gehenna, the Abyss and Tartarus: Images of Hell

PSALM 139 The Psalmist declared to God, "If I make my bed in the depths, you are there" (Ps 139:8). The Hebrew word for "depths" is *Sheol*, and many translations simply leave the word untranslated. Sheol in the Old Testament view was essentially the place beneath the earth to which the dead were thought to go. Thus, Sheol can refer both to the literal grave and to the netherworld. As the netherworld, it is similar to the Greek *Hades*, the dark and sorrowful domain of the dead (as seen in Homer's *Odyssey*, book 11); in fact, it is usually translated as "Hades" in the **Septuagint**. In a single verse, however, Sheol can refer both to the gated kingdom of the netherworld and to the dusty grave (Job 17:16). In Greek mythology Hades was also a god, unlike what we see in the Hebrew Bible. On the other hand, the Bible sometimes portrays Sheol as a beast with gaping jaws (Isa 5:14; 14:9; Hab 2:5; NIV in each case, "the grave").

Visions of Sheol as a fearsome site sometimes appear in prophetic judgments and warnings. Ezekiel 31–32 includes elaborate depictions of the hordes now confined to Sheol, and this vision serves as a warning to Egypt. Similarly, in Luke 16:19–31 Jesus recounted the parable of the rich man in Hades (NIV, "hell") as a warning to his audience to repent.

The range of meanings the word *Sheol* carries explains what seem to be inconsistencies in the text. On the one hand, no one praises God in Sheol (Ps 6:5); one who is in the grave cannot testify to God's glory before the assembly of Israel at the temple (cf. Ps 51:14). On the other hand, God is present even in Sheol (139:8; NIV, "the depths"); even the dead in the netherworld are not beyond his power. It is significant to note that Sheol in the Old Testament refers simply to the habitation of the dead—not specifically to hell, the location for punishment of the wicked dead.

In the New Testament, especially when the reference is citing the Old Testament, *Hades* refers again either to the grave or to the netherworld of the dead (e.g., Ac 2:27,31, which states that Jesus was not left in Hades; NIV, "the grave"). In Revelation 20:13 Hades is the netherworld, which yields up the dead to God's judgment. Another New Testament term, *abyss*, can also refer simply to the place of the dead (Ro 10:7, citing the Old Testament; NIV, "the deep"). But the word usually describes a locale for the imprisoned demonic powers (Lk 8:31; Rev 9:1–2; 20:1). In classical Greek *abyss* connotes unfathomable depths, such as the sources of a spring.

A New Testament term with Jewish roots is *Gehenna*, named for the Hinnom Valley south of Jerusalem. Because child sacrifice was carried out in this valley (2Ki 16:3),[1] it was desecrated by King Josiah (2Ki 23:10). Jeremiah 7:32 declared that God would judge Judah there, and thus, during the **intertestamental period**, the term came to be used for the domain where the wicked would receive eternal punishment. Jesus often spoke of Gehenna as a place of fiery punishment (Mt 5:22; 10:28; 18:9; NIV in each case, "hell"), also indicating that Gehenna's original purpose was as the site of punishment for demons, although wicked humans would also be consigned there (Mt 25:41; NIV, "eternal fire"). A similar word, a verb that means "to cast into Tartarus," appears in 2 Peter 2:4 (NIV, "sent . . . to hell") to describe the place where wicked angels are punished. Tartarus in Greek literature is the deepest part of Hades and a locale of eternal punishment.

We are wise not to make too much of the origins of these words. *Gehenna* has little to do with the historical Valley of Hinnom. Similarly, the Greek words the New Testament incorporates did not, for the apostles, imply that the Greek myths were credible. The word *Sheol*, we do well to note, is pure Hebrew with no known origin or parallels in any other language.

[1]See "Human Sacrifice in the Ancient Near East" on page 182.

Neo-Assyrian invocation plaque against the demon Lamashtu

Preserving Bible Times; © Dr. James C. Martin; permission of Musée de Louvre

139:21 [r]2Ch 19:2; Ps 31:6; 119:113; 119:158

21 Do I not hate those[r] who hate you, O LORD,
and abhor those who rise up against you?
22 I have nothing but hatred for them;
I count them my enemies.

139:23 [s]Job 31:6; Ps 26:2 [t]Jer 11:20

23 Search me,[s] O God, and know my heart;[t]
test me and know my anxious thoughts.

139:24 [u]Ps 5:8; 143:10; Pr 15:9

24 See if there is any offensive way in me,
and lead me[u] in the way everlasting.

Psalm 140

For the director of music. A psalm of David.

140:1 [v]Ps 17:13 [w]Ps 18:48

1 Rescue me,[v] O LORD, from evil men;
protect me from men of violence,[w]

140:2 [x]Ps 36:4; 56:6

2 who devise evil plans[x] in their hearts
and stir up war every day.

140:3 [y]Ps 57:4 [z]Ps 58:4; Jas 3:8

3 They make their tongues as sharp as[y] a serpent's;
the poison of vipers[z] is on their lips. *Selah*

140:4 [a]Ps 141:9 [b]Ps 71:4

4 Keep me,[a] O LORD, from the hands of the wicked;[b]
protect me from men of violence
who plan to trip my feet.

140:5 [c]Ps 31:4; 35:7

5 Proud men have hidden a snare for me;
they have spread out the cords of their net
and have set traps[c] for me along my path. *Selah*

140:6 [d]Ps 16:2 [e]Ps 116:1; 143:1

6 O LORD, I say to you, "You are my God."[d]
Hear, O LORD, my cry for mercy.[e]

140:7 [f]Ps 28:8

7 O Sovereign LORD,[f] my strong deliverer,
who shields my head in the day of battle—

140:8 [g]Ps 10:2-3

8 do not grant the wicked[g] their desires, O LORD;
do not let their plans succeed,
or they will become proud. *Selah*

140:9 [h]Ps 7:16

9 Let the heads of those who surround me
be covered with the trouble their lips have caused.[h]

140:10 [i]Ps 11:6; 21:9

10 Let burning coals fall upon them;
may they be thrown into the fire,[i]
into miry pits, never to rise.

140:11 [j]Ps 34:21

11 Let slanderers not be established in the land;
may disaster hunt down men of violence.[j]

140:12 [k]Ps 9:4 [l]Ps 35:10 **140:13** [m]Ps 97:12 [n]Ps 11:7

12 I know that the LORD secures justice for the poor
and upholds the cause[k] of the needy.[l]
13 Surely the righteous will praise your name[m]
and the upright will live[n] before you.

Psalm 141

A psalm of David.

141:1 [o]Ps 22:19; 70:5 [p]Ps 143:1

1 O LORD, I call to you; come quickly[o] to me.
Hear my voice[p] when I call to you.

139:21–22 These verses echo the pledge of loyalty that ancient Near Eastern kings required of their vassals. A fourteenth-century B.C. treaty between Mursilis II, a Hittite king, and Tette of Nuhassi states, "With my friend you shall be friend, and with my enemy you shall be enemy."
139:23 For "heart," see the note on 4:7.

[2] May my prayer be set before you like incense;[q]
may the lifting up of my hands[r] be like the evening sacrifice.[s]

[3] Set a guard over my mouth, O LORD;
keep watch over the door of my lips.
[4] Let not my heart be drawn to what is evil,
to take part in wicked deeds
with men who are evildoers;
let me not eat of their delicacies.[t]

[5] Let a righteous man[a] strike me—it is a kindness;
let him rebuke me[u]—it is oil on my head.[v]
My head will not refuse it.

Yet my prayer is ever against the deeds of evildoers;
[6] their rulers will be thrown down from the cliffs,
and the wicked will learn that my words were well spoken.
[7] ⌞They will say,⌟ "As one plows and breaks up the earth,
so our bones have been scattered at the mouth[w] of the grave.[b]"
[8] But my eyes are fixed[x] on you, O Sovereign LORD;
in you I take refuge[y]—do not give me over to death.
[9] Keep me[z] from the snares they have laid for me,
from the traps set[a] by evildoers.
[10] Let the wicked fall[b] into their own nets,
while I pass by in safety.

Psalm 142

A *maskil*[c] of David. When he was in the cave. A prayer.

[1] I cry aloud to the LORD;
I lift up my voice to the LORD for mercy.[c]
[2] I pour out my complaint[d] before him;
before him I tell my trouble.

[3] When my spirit grows faint[e] within me,
it is you who know my way.
In the path where I walk
men have hidden a snare for me.
[4] Look to my right and see;
no one is concerned for me.
I have no refuge;
no one cares[f] for my life.
[5] I cry to you, O LORD;
I say, "You are my refuge,[g]
my portion[h] in the land of the living."[i]
[6] Listen to my cry,[j]
for I am in desperate need;[k]
rescue me from those who pursue me,
for they are too strong for me.
[7] Set me free from my prison,[l]
that I may praise your name.

Then the righteous will gather about me
because of your goodness to me.[m]

141:2 [q]Rev 5:8; 8:3 [r]1Ti 2:8 [s]Ex 29:39,41
141:4 [t]Pr 23:6
141:5 [u]Pr 9:8 [v]Ps 23:5
141:7 [w]Ps 53:5
141:8 [x]Ps 25:15 [y]Ps 2:12
141:9 [z]Ps 140:4 [a]Ps 38:12
141:10 [b]Ps 35:8
142:1 [c]Ps 30:8
142:2 [d]Isa 26:16
142:3 [e]Ps 140:5; 143:4,7
142:4 [f]Ps 31:11; Jer 30:17
142:5 [g]Ps 46:1 [h]Ps 16:5 [i]Ps 27:13
142:6 [j]Ps 17:1 [k]Ps 79:8; 116:6
142:7 [l]Ps 146:7 [m]Ps 13:6

[a] 5 Or *Let the Righteous One* [b] 7 Hebrew *Sheol* [c] Title: Probably a literary or musical term

141:4 For "heart," see the note on 4:7.

Psalm 143

A psalm of David.

[1] O LORD, hear my prayer,
listen to my cry for mercy;[n]
in your faithfulness[o] and righteousness[p]
come to my relief.
[2] Do not bring your servant into judgment,
for no one living is righteous[q] before you.

[3] The enemy pursues me,
he crushes me to the ground;
he makes me dwell in darkness
like those long dead.
[4] So my spirit grows faint within me;
my heart within me is dismayed.[r]

[5] I remember[s] the days of long ago;
I meditate on all your works
and consider what your hands have done.
[6] I spread out my hands[t] to you;
my soul thirsts for you like a parched land. *Selah*

[7] Answer me quickly,[u] O LORD;
my spirit fails.
Do not hide your face[v] from me
or I will be like those who go down to the pit.
[8] Let the morning bring me word of your unfailing
love,[w]
for I have put my trust in you.
Show me the way[x] I should go,
for to you I lift up my soul.[y]
[9] Rescue me from my enemies,[z] O LORD,
for I hide myself in you.
[10] Teach me to do your will,
for you are my God;
may your good Spirit
lead[a] me on level ground.

[11] For your name's sake, O LORD, preserve my life;[b]
in your righteousness,[c] bring me out of trouble.
[12] In your unfailing love, silence my enemies;
destroy all my foes,[d]
for I am your servant.[e]

Psalm 144

Of David.

[1] Praise be to the LORD my Rock,[f]
who trains my hands for war,
my fingers for battle.
[2] He is my loving God and my fortress,[g]
my stronghold and my deliverer,

143:1 [n]Ps 140:6 [o]Ps 89:1-2 [p]Ps 71:2
143:2 [q]Ps 14:3; Ecc 7:20; Ro 3:20
143:4 [r]Ps 142:3
143:5 [s]Ps 77:6
143:6 [t]Ps 63:1; 88:9
143:7 [u]Ps 69:17 [v]Ps 27:9; 28:1
143:8 [w]Ps 46:5; 90:14 [x]Ps 27:11 [y]Ps 25:1-2
143:9 [z]Ps 31:15
143:10 [a]Ne 9:20; Ps 23:3; 25:4-5
143:11 [b]Ps 119:25 [c]Ps 31:1
143:12 [d]Ps 52:5; 54:5 [e]Ps 116:16
144:1 [f]Ps 18:2, 34
144:2 [g]Ps 59:9; 91:2

143:1–12 For commentary on expressions of vengeful attitudes toward enemies, see the note on 69:22–28. See also "Curses and Imprecations" on page 883.

my shield,[h] in whom I take refuge,
who subdues peoples[a] under me. 144:2 [h]Ps 84:9

3 O LORD, what is man[i] that you care for him,
the son of man that you think of him? 144:3 [i]Ps 8:4; Heb 2:6
4 Man is like a breath;
his days are like a fleeting shadow.[j] 144:4 [j]Ps 39:11; 102:11

[a] 2 Many manuscripts of the Masoretic Text, Dead Sea Scrolls, Aquila, Jerome and Syriac; most manuscripts of the Masoretic Text *subdues my people*

Warfare in the Ancient World

PSALM 144 Modern readers may be shocked at the opening verse of Psalm 144, but warfare is a prominent theme in the Psalms. The earliest wars were conducted with crude weapons of wood and stone. Horses were of limited value during heavy combat because the stirrup had not yet been invented and a rider could easily fall.

Chariots were not used extensively until the **Late Bronze Age.**[1] An Egyptian chariot conveyed two men, a driver and an archer (chariots from the Levant [Syria] also accommodated a shield-bearer). Massed chariots used shock value and speed to demoralize and scatter an enemy. Chariots were prominent in **New Kingdom** Egypt.[2]

A revolution in military technology occurred at the beginning of the **Iron Age**. Massed armies of heavy infantry with the discipline to hold their ranks appeared on the scene. They could withstand and rout a chariot charge, making the chariot obsolete except as a prestigious vehicle for commanders.

Battles were often short, lasting only as long as one side or the other had the stamina to maintain face-to-face combat. Frequently one side would break ranks and flee. Panic was common, exacerbated by the commanders' poor control, having to rely as they did on shouted voice commands or signals.

In keeping with the hilly terrain they inhabited, the Israelites relied primarily on infantry. Light infantry soldiers wore little or no armor and typically used projectile weapons, like stones and arrows. They moved in loose formations, relying on speed (see Jdg 20:15–16; 2Ch 14:8).

Heavy infantrymen wore full armor and often carried heavy swords and long spears. They moved in large, close formations, with spears lowered to form a wall of pikes, in effect creating an ancient version of a tank. The Greek hoplite (heavily armored infantry soldier) marching in his phalanx was a classic example of heavy infantry in action. Normally a heavy infantry unit would rout a light infantry corps, but out in the open a single heavy infantryman could be at a disadvantage when pitted against a light infantryman, due to the latter's mobility and ability to strike at a distance.

The greatest armies combined heavy and light infantry with cavalry. Alexander the Great and Hannibal were masters at using their heavy infantry as a solid center for their armies, employing cavalry to flank an opponent. The Roman legions rejected the long pike in favor of a short sword. These legions had the weight and impact of heavy infantry but were much more mobile.

In addition to fighting pitched battles in the open field, armies sometimes laid siege to walled cities that were often situated atop hills.[3] How long a city could hold out depended on how much food it had in storage and upon whether it had direct access to underground springs. Plague could strike a besieged city, as happened to Athens during the Peloponnesian War in 430 B.C. Often the besieging army would seek to bring down a city by building a siege ramp and attacking the walls with siege towers.

Ancient armies were often made up of citizen soldiers called up in times of emergency. These citizens could fight with dedication but were poorly trained and armed and often needed to return home on short order to tend their crops. Citizen-soldier armies served Israel during the judges period.

Ancient societies tried to give their armies a core of professional soldiers with long-term enlistments. Kings would also hire mercenaries. The Spartans had a novel solution to the recruitment problem: Every man served in the army full-time and lived in the barracks through most of his adult life (farming was handled by slaves called *helots*).

Ancient city-states often fought each other in "wars" that lasted a single day. Casualties could be light, and frequently nothing more was at stake than settling a property claim. Other wars could be catastrophic. The Peloponnesian War lasted 27 years, destroyed the Athenian Empire and devastated the Greek world.[4] Victorious armies might slaughter cities and take survivors as slaves, effectively destroying peoples and cultures with deliberate genocide.

Armed conflict was indeed a fact of life for the peoples of ancient times. Against this reality David had ample reason to thank God, who trained his hands for war.

[1]See "Historical Periods" chart on page xx in the front of this Bible. [2]See "Horses and Chariots in Ancient Warfare" on page 114. [3]See "Siege Warfare" on page 465. [4]See "Athens" on page 1804 and "Greece: From Independent City-states Through Alexander the Great" on page 1814.

144:5 [k]Ps 18:9; Isa 64:1 [l]Ps 104:32
144:6 [m]Ps 7:12-13; 18:14
144:7 [n]Ps 69:2 [o]Ps 18:44
144:8 [p]Ps 12:2
144:9 [q]Ps 33:2-3
144:10 [r]Ps 18:50
144:11 [s]Ps 12:2; Isa 44:20
144:12 [t]Ps 128:3
144:15 [u]Ps 33:12
145:1 [v]Ps 30:1; 34:1 [w]Ps 5:2
145:2 [x]Ps 71:6
145:3 [y]Job 5:9; Ps 147:5; Ro 11:33
145:4 [z]Isa 38:19
145:5 [a]Ps 119:27

5 Part your heavens,[k] O LORD, and come down;
touch the mountains, so that they smoke.[l]
6 Send forth lightning and scatter ⌊the enemies⌋;
shoot your arrows[m] and rout them.
7 Reach down your hand from on high;
deliver me and rescue me
from the mighty waters,[n]
from the hands of foreigners[o]
8 whose mouths are full of lies,[p]
whose right hands are deceitful.

9 I will sing a new song to you, O God;
on the ten-stringed lyre[q] I will make music to you,
10 to the One who gives victory to kings,
who delivers his servant David[r] from the deadly sword.

11 Deliver me and rescue me
from the hands of foreigners
whose mouths are full of lies,
whose right hands are deceitful.[s]

12 Then our sons in their youth
will be like well-nurtured plants,[t]
and our daughters will be like pillars
carved to adorn a palace.
13 Our barns will be filled
with every kind of provision.
Our sheep will increase by thousands,
by tens of thousands in our fields;
14 our oxen will draw heavy loads.[a]
There will be no breaching of walls,
no going into captivity,
no cry of distress in our streets.

15 Blessed are the people[u] of whom this is true;
blessed are the people whose God is the LORD.

Psalm 145[b]

A psalm of praise. Of David.

1 I will exalt you,[v] my God the King;[w]
I will praise your name for ever and ever.
2 Every day I will praise[x] you
and extol your name for ever and ever.

3 Great is the LORD and most worthy of praise;
his greatness no one can fathom.[y]
4 One generation[z] will commend your works to another;
they will tell of your mighty acts.
5 They will speak of the glorious splendor of your majesty,
and I will meditate on your wonderful works.[c][a]

[a] 14 Or *our chieftains will be firmly established* [b] This psalm is an acrostic poem, the verses of which (including verse 13b) begin with the successive letters of the Hebrew alphabet. [c] 5 Dead Sea Scrolls and Syriac (see also Septuagint); Masoretic Text *On the glorious splendor of your majesty / and on your wonderful works I will meditate*

144:12 It was not uncommon in the ancient world for temple columns to be shaped in the form of women (e.g., on the Acropolis in Athens).

145:1–2 In Jewish practice this psalm was recited twice each morning and once each evening.

[6] They will tell of the power of your awesome works,[b]
and I will proclaim[c] your great deeds.
[7] They will celebrate your abundant goodness[d]
and joyfully sing of your righteousness.[e]

[8] The LORD is gracious and compassionate,[f]
slow to anger and rich in love.[g]
[9] The LORD is good[h] to all;
he has compassion on all he has made.
[10] All you have made will praise you,[i] O LORD;
your saints will extol you.[j]
[11] They will tell of the glory of your kingdom
and speak of your might,
[12] so that all men may know of your mighty acts[k]
and the glorious splendor of your kingdom.
[13] Your kingdom is an everlasting kingdom,[l]
and your dominion endures through all
generations.

The LORD is faithful to all his promises
and loving toward all he has made.[a]
[14] The LORD upholds[m] all those who fall
and lifts up all[n] who are bowed down.
[15] The eyes of all look to you,
and you give them their food[o] at the proper time.
[16] You open your hand
and satisfy the desires[p] of every living thing.

[17] The LORD is righteous in all his ways
and loving toward all he has made.
[18] The LORD is near[q] to all who call on him,[r]
to all who call on him in truth.
[19] He fulfills the desires[s] of those who fear him;
he hears their cry[t] and saves them.
[20] The LORD watches over all who love him,[u]
but all the wicked he will destroy.[v]

[21] My mouth will speak[w] in praise of the LORD.
Let every creature[x] praise his holy name
for ever and ever.

145:6 [b]Ps 66:3 [c]Dt 32:3
145:7 [d]Isa 63:7 [e]Ps 51:14
145:8 [f]Ps 86:15 [g]Ex 34:6; Nu 14:18
145:9 [h]Ps 100:5
145:10 [i]Ps 19:1 [j]Ps 68:26
145:12 [k]Ps 105:1
145:13 [l]1Ti 1:17; 2Pe 1:11
145:14 [m]Ps 37:24 [n]Ps 146:8
145:15 [o]Ps 104:27; 136:25
145:16 [p]Ps 104:28
145:18 [q]Dt 4:7 [r]Jn 4:24
145:19 [s]Ps 37:4 [t]Pr 15:29
145:20 [u]Ps 31:23; 97:10 [v]Ps 9:5
145:21 [w]Ps 71:8 [x]Ps 65:2

Psalm 146

[1] Praise the LORD.[b]

Praise the LORD,[y] O my soul.
[2] I will praise the LORD all my life;[z]
I will sing praise to my God as long as I live.

[3] Do not put your trust in princes,[a]
in mortal men,[b] who cannot save.
[4] When their spirit departs, they return to the
ground;[c]
on that very day their plans come to nothing.[d]
[5] Blessed is he[e] whose help[f] is the God of Jacob,
whose hope is in the LORD his God,

146:1 [y]Ps 103:1
146:2 [z]Ps 104:33
146:3 [a]Ps 118:9 [b]Isa 2:22
146:4 [c]Ps 104:29; Ecc 12:7 [d]Ps 33:10; 1Co 2:6
146:5 [e]Ps 144:15; Jer 17:7 [f]Ps 71:5

[a] *13* One manuscript of the Masoretic Text, Dead Sea Scrolls and Syriac (see also Septuagint); most manuscripts of the Masoretic Text do not have the last two lines of verse 13. [b] *1* Hebrew *Hallelu Yah*; also in verse 10

146:6 gPs 115:15; Ac 14:15; Rev 14:7 hPs 117:2

6 the Maker of heaven[g] and earth,
the sea, and everything in them—
the LORD, who remains faithful[h] forever.

146:7 iPs 103:6 jPs 107:9 kPs 68:6

7 He upholds the cause of the oppressed[i]
and gives food to the hungry.[j]
The LORD sets prisoners free,[k]

146:8 lMt 9:30

8 the LORD gives sight to the blind,[l]
the LORD lifts up those who are bowed down,
the LORD loves the righteous.
9 The LORD watches over the alien

146:9 mEx 22:22; Dt 10:18; Ps 68:5

and sustains the fatherless and the widow,[m]
but he frustrates the ways of the wicked.

146:10 nEx 15:18; Ps 10:16

10 The LORD reigns[n] forever,
your God, O Zion, for all generations.

Praise the LORD.

Psalm 147

1 Praise the LORD.[a]

How good it is to sing praises to our God,

147:1 oPs 135:3 pPs 33:1

how pleasant[o] and fitting to praise him![p]

147:2 qPs 102:16 rDt 30:3

2 The LORD builds up Jerusalem;[q]
he gathers the exiles[r] of Israel.
3 He heals the brokenhearted
and binds up their wounds.

147:4 sIsa 40:26

4 He determines the number of the stars[s]
and calls them each by name.

147:5 tPs 48:1 uIsa 40:28

5 Great is our Lord[t] and mighty in power;
his understanding has no limit.[u]

147:6 vPs 146:8-9

6 The LORD sustains the humble[v]
but casts the wicked to the ground.

147:7 wPs 33:3

7 Sing to the LORD[w] with thanksgiving;
make music to our God on the harp.
8 He covers the sky with clouds;

147:8 xJob 38:26 yPs 104:14

he supplies the earth with rain[x]
and makes grass grow[y] on the hills.

147:9 zPs 104:27-28; Mt 6:26 aJob 38:41

9 He provides food[z] for the cattle
and for the young ravens[a] when they call.

147:10 b1Sa 16:7 cPs 33:16-17

10 His pleasure is not in the strength[b] of the horse,[c]
nor his delight in the legs of a man;
11 the LORD delights in those who fear him,
who put their hope in his unfailing love.

12 Extol the LORD, O Jerusalem;
praise your God, O Zion,
13 for he strengthens the bars of your gates
and blesses your people within you.

147:14 dIsa 60:17-18 ePs 132:15

14 He grants peace[d] to your borders
and satisfies you[e] with the finest of wheat.

147:15 fJob 37:12

15 He sends his command[f] to the earth;
his word runs swiftly.

[a] *1* Hebrew *Hallelu Yah*; also in verse 20

16 He spreads the snow[g] like wool
and scatters the frost[h] like ashes.
17 He hurls down his hail like pebbles.
Who can withstand his icy blast?
18 He sends his word[i] and melts them;
he stirs up his breezes, and the waters flow.

19 He has revealed his word to Jacob,
his laws and decrees[j] to Israel.
20 He has done this for no other nation;[k]
they do not know his laws.

Praise the LORD.

Psalm 148

1 Praise the LORD.[a]

Praise the LORD from the heavens,
praise him in the heights above.
2 Praise him, all his angels,[l]
praise him, all his heavenly hosts.
3 Praise him, sun and moon,
praise him, all you shining stars.
4 Praise him, you highest heavens
and you waters above the skies.[m]
5 Let them praise the name of the LORD,
for he commanded[n] and they were created.
6 He set them in place for ever and ever;
he gave a decree[o] that will never pass away.

7 Praise the LORD from the earth,
you great sea creatures[p] and all ocean depths,
8 lightning and hail, snow and clouds,
stormy winds that do his bidding,[q]
9 you mountains and all hills,[r]
fruit trees and all cedars,
10 wild animals and all cattle,
small creatures and flying birds,
11 kings of the earth and all nations,
you princes and all rulers on earth,
12 young men and maidens,
old men and children.

13 Let them praise the name of the LORD,[s]
for his name alone is exalted;
his splendor is above the earth and the heavens.[t]
14 He has raised up for his people a horn,[b][u]
the praise of all his saints,
of Israel, the people close to his heart.

Praise the LORD.

Psalm 149

1 Praise the LORD.[c][v]

Sing to the LORD a new song,
his praise in the assembly[w] of the saints.

147:16 [g]Job 37:6 [h]Job 38:29
147:18 [i]Ps 33:9
147:19 [j]Dt 33:4; Mal 4:4
147:20 [k]Dt 4:7-8, 32-34
148:2 [l]Ps 103:20
148:4 [m]Ge 1:7; 1Ki 8:27
148:5 [n]Ge 1:1,6; Ps 33:6,9
148:6 [o]Job 38:33; Ps 89:37; Jer 33:25
148:7 [p]Ps 74:13-14
148:8 [q]Ps 147:15-18
148:9 [r]Isa 44:23; 49:13; 55:12
148:13 [s]Isa 12:4 [t]Ps 8:1; 113:4
148:14 [u]Ps 75:10
149:1 [v]Ps 33:2 [w]Ps 35:18

[a] *1* Hebrew *Hallelu Yah*; also in verse 14 [b] *14* *Horn* here symbolizes strong one, that is, king. [c] *1* Hebrew *Hallelu Yah*; also in verse 9

NON-CANONICAL PSALMS

The watchtower at Qumran
Preserving Bible Times; © Dr. James C. Martin

PSALM 150 Among the ancient texts of the Bible scholars sometimes encounter psalms not found in the Hebrew Bible. A **Syriac** medieval Psalter includes five **Apocryphal** psalms numbered 151 to 155. Psalm 151 also appears in numerous ancient versions (Greek, Latin, Ethiopic and others). Cave 11 of **Qumran** contained Hebrew versions of Psalms 151, 154 and 155, and several other **noncanonical** psalms were discovered in caves 4 and 11. This gives rise to the obvious question of whether these psalms were overlooked and should have been included in the Scriptures.

Psalm 151 is a pseudo-autobiographical account of the early life of David drawn from 1 Samuel,[1] although the Hebrew version also includes some material not found in the Greek. The Hebrew of Psalm 151 includes, "The mountains do not testify to him [the LORD], and the hills do not tell [of him]. The trees praise my words and the flocks [praise] my deeds." Perhaps those lines were edited out of the Greek version on the grounds that they were unorthodox or simply made no sense. Some of the noncanonical psalms have borrowed from the Biblical psalms and maintain their poetic conventions. For example, Psalms 154 and 155 are pleas to God for help and are analogous to the Biblical Psalms 61, 62 and 63. Psalm 155 opens with the words: "LORD, I have called to you; hear me," in the tradition of Psalm 61:1 and 63:1.

The reason these psalms were not included in the Bible is simply that they were written too late. Their presence at Qumran and elsewhere indicates that liturgists continued to create songs of praise in imitation of the psalms after the **canon** had closed.[2] In fact, we even see psalm-like songs of praise in the New Testament (e.g., Lk 1:46–55).

[1]See "David" on page 443. [2]See "The Old Testament Canon" on page 1552.

[2]Let Israel rejoice in their Maker;[x]
let the people of Zion be glad in their King.[y]
[3]Let them praise his name with dancing
and make music to him with tambourine and harp.[z]
[4]For the LORD takes delight[a] in his people;
he crowns the humble with salvation.[b]
[5]Let the saints rejoice[c] in this honor
and sing for joy on their beds.[d]

[6]May the praise of God be in their mouths[e]
and a double-edged[f] sword in their hands,
[7]to inflict vengeance on the nations
and punishment on the peoples,
[8]to bind their kings with fetters,
their nobles with shackles of iron,
[9]to carry out the sentence written against them.[g]
This is the glory of all his saints.[h]

Praise the LORD.

Psalm 150

[1]Praise the LORD.[a]

Praise God in his sanctuary;[i]
praise him in his mighty heavens.[j]
[2]Praise him for his acts of power;[k]
praise him for his surpassing greatness.[l]
[3]Praise him with the sounding of the trumpet,
praise him with the harp and lyre,[m]
[4]praise him with tambourine and dancing,[n]
praise him with the strings[o] and flute,
[5]praise him with the clash of cymbals,[p]
praise him with resounding cymbals.

[6]Let everything[q] that has breath praise the LORD.

Praise the LORD.

[a] *1* Hebrew *Hallelu Yah*; also in verse 6

149:2 [x]Ps 95:6 [y]Ps 47:6; Zec 9:9
149:3 [z]Ps 81:2; 150:4
149:4 [a]Ps 35:27 [b]Ps 132:16
149:5 [c]Ps 132:16 [d]Job 35:10
149:6 [e]Ps 66:17 [f]Heb 4:12; Rev 1:16
149:9 [g]Dt 7:1; Eze 28:26 [h]Ps 148:14
150:1 [i]Ps 102:19 [j]Ps 19:1
150:2 [k]Dt 3:24 [l]Ps 145:5-6
150:3 [m]Ps 149:3
150:4 [n]Ex 15:20 [o]Isa 38:20
150:5 [p]1Ch 13:8; 15:16
150:6 [q]Ps 145:21

149:3 Dance (*mâchôl*) was considered an integral part of the religious ceremonies in ancient Israel. This Hebrew word is found in Scripture associated with the word *tôph* or timbrel (see Ex 15:20 and Jdg 11:34, where "tambourine" is used). We are told also that "David, wearing a linen ephod, danced before the LORD with all his might" (2Sa 6:14). Religious dancing fell into disuse in the Jerusalem temple and is mentioned only twice in the Psalms (here and in 150:4). On the Feast of Tabernacles, at the celebration of "water libation," prominent men would dance, displaying their artistic skill in throwing and catching burning torches. The custom of a procession around the sanctuary or around the altar on the Feast of Tabernacles was retained in the temple, accompanied by singing.
150:4 See the note on dancing at 149:3.
150:6 All God's creation that "has breath"—particularly humanity—is called to praise the Lord (cf. 148:7–12). The Hebrew word used here applies to all living creatures endowed with life by the Creator.

INTRODUCTION TO

AUTHOR, PLACE AND DATE OF WRITING

The book of Proverbs is a collection of collections, all on the subject of wisdom. There are several major compilations in the book, including "the proverbs of Solomon son of David, king of Israel" (Pr 1–24), "more proverbs of Solomon, copied by the men of Hezekiah king of Judah" (chs. 25–29), "the sayings of Agur son of Jakeh" (ch. 30) and "the sayings of King Lemuel—an oracle his mother taught him" (ch. 31). In addition, there are several groupings that may be regarded as minor or sub-collections, including "Sayings of the Wise" (22:17—24:22) and "Further Sayings of the Wise" (24:23–34). The prologue (1:1–7) and epilogue (31:10–31) may well have been added at a later time.

Solomon's proverbs were written between 970 and 930 B.C., while Hezekiah's scribes compiled additional, "unpublished" Solomonic proverbs between 729 and 686 B.C. Nothing is known of Agur and King Lemuel, so the dates of composition of their contributions are unknown.

The fact that Proverbs is an anthology—almost a scrapbook—of collections implies that it was not compiled at any one given point. Even so, it is clear that according to the Biblical text Solomon was the primary source for Proverbs (whether he is thought of as a writer or a collector of these pithy nuggets of wisdom). First Kings 4:32 tells us that Solomon "spoke three thousand proverbs."

AUDIENCE

These proverbs were written to the people of Israel to show them how wisdom can be practically applied to everyday life, but the implied reader of Proverbs is primarily the young man. Thus the book routinely addresses the reader as "my son," and the major temptations described in the book—to join a gang and enter a life of crime or to run after the immoral woman—relate especially to the young man as he approaches adulthood.

CULTURAL FACTS AND HIGHLIGHTS

Many modern scholars consider the notion that Solomon had anything to do with the writing of Proverbs to be implausible and treat the book as entirely a product of the postexilic era. In fact, however, there is no good reason to dismiss Solomon's association with Proverbs. Similar compilations from the ancient Near East date from Solomon's time (tenth century B.C.) or much earlier (see "Ancient Near Eastern Wisdom" on p. 960). Solomon's era was the most prosperous and sophisticated in Israelite history. If any period was likely to have produced works of wisdom literature, it was precisely this one.

TIMELINE

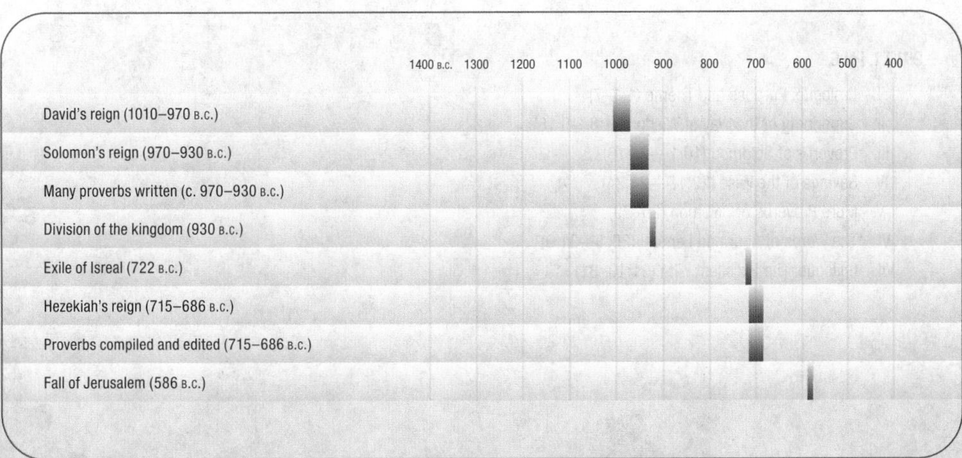

AS YOU READ

It is helpful to recognize that the pat statements so plentiful in Proverbs are not promises from God but general principles—similar to the reference to long life as the result of honoring one's parents found in the Ten Commandments (Ex 20:12). Try to dismiss from your mind the many exceptions that might otherwise cause you to read these assertions with a skeptical mindset. You might even want to identify cases in which an individual exemplifying a particular God-honoring trait has indeed enjoyed the blessings made more likely by his or her good judgment in a particular area of life.

Allow yourself to delight in the visual imagery and to chuckle at the humorous images that convey universal truths (e.g., "Better to live on a corner of the roof than share a house with a quarrelsome wife"; Pr 21:9). Enjoy the comparisons and contrasts, and don't be surprised by the lack of continuity that is often evident from one saying to the next. By way of comparison, recall some of Benjamin Franklin's proverbial maxims from the eighteenth century, such as "A penny saved is a penny earned."

Jot down a listing of some character traits that are endorsed or warned against in this book. How well does this list fit with the conventional, godly wisdom that guides your life today?

DID YOU KNOW?

- The 30 sayings of Proverbs 22:17—24:22 are similar to the 30 units of the Egyptian "Wisdom of Amenemope," written prior to Solomon's time.
- Agur was likely a non-Israelite wise man like Job and his friends (30:1).
- Total abstinence from alcohol was rare in the ancient world, even while the problems of addiction to drink were recognized (31:4–7).
- In Jewish tradition Proverbs 31:10–31 is recited by a husband to his wife on Sabbath evenings.

THEMES

The book of Proverbs includes the following themes:

1. *Wisdom.* The predominant motif of the extended discourse in 1:1—9:18 is that of two women: Wisdom and Folly. Wisdom is a personification of God's attribute of wisdom and ultimately stands for God himself, while Folly represents false gods vying for Israel's devotion. The truth expressed is that there can be no real wisdom apart from God. To fear God is to begin on the path of "knowledge"—understanding or insight (1:7).

2. *Practical living.* Proverbs presents principles for godly living and has much to say about wealth, work, giving and matters of the heart. The range and scope of its subject matter encompass nearly every aspect of life.

OUTLINE

I. Prologue: Purpose and Theme (1:1–7)
II. Superiority of the Way of Wisdom (1:8—9:18)
III. Proverbs of Solomon (10:1—22:16)
IV. Sayings of the Wise (22:17—24:34)
V. More Proverbs of Solomon (25–29)
VI. The Words of Agur and Lemuel (30:1—31:9)
VII. Epilogue: The Excellent Wife (31:10–31)

Prologue: Purpose and Theme

1:1 [a]1Ki 4:29-34 [b]Pr 10:1; 25:1; Ecc 1:1

1 The proverbs of Solomon[a] son of David, king of Israel:[b]

2 for attaining wisdom and discipline;
for understanding words of insight;
3 for acquiring a disciplined and prudent life,
doing what is right and just and fair;

1:4 [c]Pr 8:5 [d]Pr 2:10-11; 8:12

4 for giving prudence to the simple,[c]
knowledge and discretion[d] to the young—

1:5 [e]Pr 9:9

5 let the wise listen and add to their learning,[e]
and let the discerning get guidance—

1:6 [f]Ps 49:4; 78:2 [g]Nu 12:8

6 for understanding proverbs and parables,[f]
the sayings and riddles[g] of the wise.

1:7 [h]Job 28:28; Ps 111:10; Pr 9:10; 15:33; Ecc 12:13

7 The fear of the LORD[h] is the beginning of knowledge,
but fools[a] despise wisdom and discipline.

Exhortations to Embrace Wisdom

Warning Against Enticement

1:8 [i]Pr 4:1 [j]Pr 6:20

8 Listen, my son,[i] to your father's instruction
and do not forsake your mother's teaching.[j]
9 They will be a garland to grace your head

1:9 [k]Pr 4:1-9

and a chain to adorn your neck.[k]

1:10 [l]Ge 39:7 [m]Dt 13:8 [n]Pr 16:29; Eph 5:11

10 My son, if sinners entice[l] you,
do not give in[m] to them.[n]
11 If they say, "Come along with us;

1:11 [o]Ps 10:8

let's lie in wait[o] for someone's blood,
let's waylay some harmless soul;
12 let's swallow them alive, like the grave,[b]

1:12 [p]Ps 28:1

and whole, like those who go down to the pit;[p]

[a] 7 The Hebrew words rendered *fool* in Proverbs, and often elsewhere in the Old Testament, denote one who is morally deficient.
[b] 12 Hebrew *Sheol*

1:1–9 Damage has been done by some who find in the book of Proverbs merely a collection of ancient maxims for success—a kind of *Poor Richard's Almanac*. Actually, the book is a compendium of moral instruction. It deals with sin and holiness, and the vehicle of instruction is a favorite Semitic device: teaching by contrast. The style of Proverbs with its trenchant contrasts or more extended climactic poems can be paralleled in ancient literature in Egypt and Mesopotamia (see "Ancient Near Eastern Wisdom" on p. 960). The Hebrew authors, however, have given instruction on life and holiness in proverbial form. The case is similar in Christian hymnody. There are countless examples of secular poetry and melody combined in ordinary song. But Christian hymns use the vehicles of poetry and song to express distinctively Christian thought and experience.
1:1–7 The prologue connects the book of Proverbs with Solomon, who was renowned for his wisdom in general and for his prolific composition of proverbs in particular (cf. 1Ki 4:29–34). Although some compiling and editing were involved, it is likely that Solomon was the source of most of Proverbs (but see the NIV sectional headings regarding authorship). The prologue also states the book's purpose: to pass along wisdom. Such an introductory statement was not unusual in the ancient world. Egyptian instructions in wisdom often named the speaker and recipient as part of their purpose statement: to pass along wisdom for successful living from one generation to the next.
1:1 The Hebrew word translated "proverb" is also rendered "oracle" (Nu 23:7,18), "taunt" (Isa 14:4) and "parable" (Eze 17:2), so its meaning is considerably broader than the one English term. This may help to explain the presence of the longer discourse sections in Proverbs 1–9. Most proverbs are short, pithy statements that express universal truths about human behavior.
1:4 "Prudence" means good judgment or good sense (see 15:5; 19:25). Elsewhere in the Old Testament the Hebrew word is used in the negative sense of "crafty" (Ge 3:1; Job 5:13). "Simple" is used to describe an individual who lacks judgment or who is easily persuaded, immature, inexperienced or naive (cf. Ps 19:7). The Hebrew word generally refers to someone lacking moral direction and inclined to evil.
1:6 The Hebrew for "riddles" can sometimes refer to allegories (cf. Eze 17:2). On the popularity and function of riddles in the ancient world, see the note on Judges 14:12–14.
1:7—9:10 The first section of the book (note the slight variation in this alternative outline scheme to the outline in the introduction to this book) both begins and ends with the statement that "the fear of the LORD is the beginning of knowledge [wisdom]." Thus the wisdom extolled in Proverbs is not just a high degree of intelligence but a moral virtue. This is made plain by the contrasts involved. Wisdom is personified as a righteous woman (8:1). This is natural because *wisdom* in the Hebrew is a feminine noun. The foolish woman is depicted as using words similar to those of wisdom—to invite men into her house (9:4,16), but she invites them to sin. The harlot, who is given prominence in this section, represents all sin. Murder and theft are the opposite of wisdom in chapter 1, but usually the harlot, also called the strange woman, the simple woman or the foolish woman, is held up as the opposite of personified righteousness.
1:8 Proverbs was written to instruct the young and to guide them into a happy and prosperous life. This verse depicts a father preparing his son for life in the world. Here and in 6:20 the mother is also depicted as a teacher. See "The Israelite Family" on page 997.
1:12 For information on the "grave," see the note on Psalm 6:5; see also "Sheol, Hades, Gehenna, the Abyss and Tartarus: Images of Hell" on page 946.

Ancient Near Eastern Wisdom

PROVERBS 1 The ancient Near East has yielded a great deal of what scholars call "wisdom literature"—texts that instruct the reader about life, virtue and social interaction or reflect upon profound issues.

✣ *The instructive, or didactic, texts*, like Proverbs, were typically written with a boy or young man ("my son") as the implied reader. These straightforward texts, exhorting the reader to right behavior, concern issues like personal morality, work ethics, career choice or peer respect.

✣ *The reflective texts*, like Job, are addressed to a more mature reader—one who acknowledges that the world is not always as it should be. They lament societal ills and wrestle with complex issues.

✣ These categories are not mutually exclusive. Ecclesiastes wrestles with life's unfairness and perversity but also instructs the reader. We could classify Proverbs as the workbook for a beginning or "undergraduate" course, with Ecclesiastes being an advanced or "graduate school" text.

✣ Wisdom texts may address the reader directly, as do Proverbs and Ecclesiastes, or have a narrative structure, like Job.

✣ Wisdom texts may be presented as prose (like most of Ecc) or poetry (like most of Job).

✣ Didactic texts often employ simple, two-line maxims and parallelism (as in Pr), while reflective texts are typically more complex in structure (as in Job's more problematical poetic discourses).

Other nations also had wisdom literature. A few examples from the ancient Near East:

✣ Egypt

The Instruction of Vizier Ptah-hotep (Fifth Dynasty, c. 2500–2350 B.C.): An aged counselor instructs his son in how he should conduct his life.

The Instruction for Merikare (Tenth Dynasty, c. 2106–2010 B.C.): A pharaoh (apparently Khety III) initiates his son in the principles of proper and effective ruling. This text, reflecting the social turmoil of the First Intermediate period, asserts that Merikare must earn the respect of the nobles through just governance in order to maintain his hold on the throne.

The Protests of the Eloquent Peasant (oldest copy dates to the Twelfth Dynasty, c. 1963–1786 B.C.): A peasant who has been defrauded of his goods pleads for justice from high officials, eventually winning his case and gaining a high position for himself. The text reflects upon the nature of justice and the importance of eloquent speech.[1]

The Instruction of Amenemope[2] (oldest copy dates to between the tenth and sixth centuries B.C.): This text, which is remarkably similar to Proverbs 22:17—24:22, includes an introduction and 30 sections of teaching on wise behavior.

✣ Mesopotamia

Akkadian[3] *Proverb Texts*: These writings contain pithy adages and maxims of the sort found all over the world. For example, one proverb states that an enemy army never departs from a city whose weapons are weak (similar to the Roman proverb, "If you want peace, prepare for war").

Counsels of Wisdom: This Akkadian book of practical advice also addresses the reader as "my son." Examples of advice include a warning not to marry a prostitute and an admonition that the steward of a ruler's property should not give in to covetousness.

The Babylonian Theodicy (c. 1100–1000 B.C.): A cynical sufferer enters into a dispute with a man who defends traditional notions of wisdom. The text originally included 27 stanzas, each with 11 lines, but not all remain intact. This writing is often compared to Job; there are in fact both clear similarities and sharp differences between the two.[4]

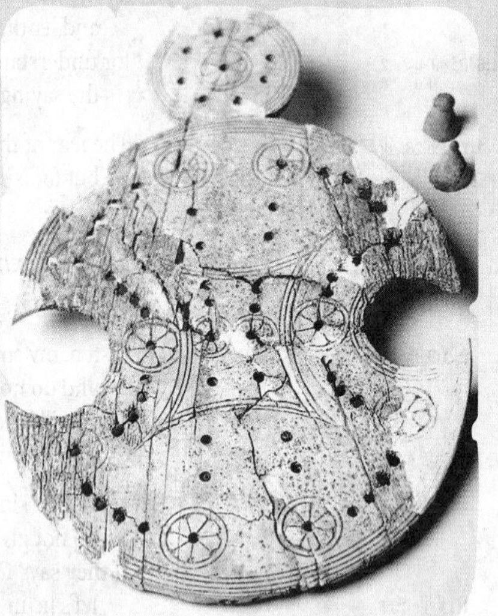
Ivory Board Game From Megiddo
Preserving Bible Times; © Dr. James C. Martin; permission of The British Museum

The Book of Ahiqar (found on a fifth-century B.C. **Aramaic papyrus** but set in **Assyria** and possibly composed originally in Akkadian): This text describes how Ahiqar overcame the adversity of a scheming and ungrateful nephew, avoided execution on false charges and proved himself to be the wisest man of his age. The story was translated into Armenian and Arabic, and the **Apocryphal** book of Tobit alludes to it. The motif of the wise man who triumphs over adversity appears repeatedly in the Bible as well.

We cannot deny that such similarities exist; the Israelites did not live in cultural isolation. At the same time, it would be a mistake to treat the Biblical texts as just another version of ancient wisdom. In grandeur of scope, internal complexity and theological profundity, the Biblical texts of Proverbs, Job and Ecclesiastes are in a class by themselves.

[1]See "The Desire for Justice in the 'Eloquent Peasant'" on page 1226. [2]See "The Teaching of Amenemope" on page 994. [3]See Glossary on page 2080 for definitions of bolded words. [4]See "The Babylonian Theodicy" on page 776.

[13]we will get all sorts of valuable things
and fill our houses with plunder;
[14]throw in your lot with us,
and we will share a common purse"—
[15]my son, do not go along with them,
do not set foot[q] on their paths;[r]
[16]for their feet rush into sin,
they are swift to shed blood.[s]
[17]How useless to spread a net
in full view of all the birds!
[18]These men lie in wait for their own blood;
they waylay only themselves!
[19]Such is the end of all who go after ill-gotten gain;
it takes away the lives of those who get it.[t]

1:15 [q]Ps 119:101 [r]Ps 1:1; Pr 4:14
1:16 [s]Pr 6:18; Isa 59:7
1:19 [t]Pr 15:27

Warning Against Rejecting Wisdom

[20]Wisdom calls aloud[u] in the street,
she raises her voice in the public squares;
[21]at the head of the noisy streets[a] she cries out,
in the gateways of the city she makes her speech:

[22]"How long will you simple ones[b][v] love your simple
ways?
How long will mockers delight in mockery
and fools hate knowledge?
[23]If you had responded to my rebuke,
I would have poured out my heart to you
and made my thoughts known to you.
[24]But since you rejected me when I called[w]
and no one gave heed when I stretched out
my hand,
[25]since you ignored all my advice
and would not accept my rebuke,
[26]I in turn will laugh[x] at your disaster;
I will mock when calamity overtakes you[y]—
[27]when calamity overtakes you like a storm,
when disaster sweeps over you like a whirlwind,
when distress and trouble overwhelm you.

[28]"Then they will call to me but I will not answer;[z]
they will look for me but will not find me.[a]
[29]Since they hated knowledge
and did not choose to fear the LORD,[b]
[30]since they would not accept my advice
and spurned my rebuke,[c]
[31]they will eat the fruit of their ways
and be filled with the fruit of their schemes.[d]

1:20 [u]Pr 8:1; 9:1-3,13-15
1:22 [v]Pr 8:5; 9:4,16
1:24 [w]Isa 65:12; 66:4; Jer 7:13; Zec 7:11
1:26 [x]Ps 2:4 [y]Pr 6:15; 10:24
1:28 [z]1Sa 8:18; Isa 1:15; Jer 11:11; Mic 3:4 [a]Job 27:9; Pr 8:17; Eze 8:18; Zec 7:13
1:29 [b]Job 21:14
1:30 [c]ver 25; Ps 81:11
1:31 [d]Job 4:8; Pr 14:14; Isa 3:11; Jer 6:19

[a] *21* Hebrew; Septuagint / *on the tops of the walls* [b] *22* The Hebrew word rendered *simple* in Proverbs generally denotes one without moral direction and inclined to evil.

1:17 Nets were used to catch both birds and land animals (see 6:5; 7:23; Ecc 9:12; Isa 51:20; Jer 5:26).

1:20–21 Mesopotamian and Egyptian writings of the second millennium B.C. often embodied abstract ideas. In Proverbs, Wisdom and Folly are personified as women, each of whom seeks to persuade "simple" youths to follow her ways. Wisdom employs appeals and warnings, whereas Folly relies upon enticements. In these discourses the young man is depicted as being enticed to folly by men who exploited others (1:10–19) and by women who sought sexual pleasure outside the bond of marriage (ch. 5; 6:20–35; ch. 7). In the culture of that day these were the two most alluring temptations for young men.

A public square was an open area inside the gate of a fortified city (see 8:3). The city gate was the place where the leaders of the city met to hold court, where the marketplace was located and where official business transactions took place (see "The City Gate" on p. 392).

[32] For the waywardness of the simple will kill them,
and the complacency of fools will destroy them;[e]
[33] but whoever listens to me will live in safety[f]
and be at ease, without fear of harm."[g]

1:32 [e] Jer 2:19
1:33 [f] Ps 25:12; Pr 3:23 [g] Ps 112:8

Moral Benefits of Wisdom

2 My son, if you accept my words
and store up my commands within you,
[2] turning your ear to wisdom
and applying your heart to understanding,[h]
[3] and if you call out for insight
and cry aloud for understanding,
[4] and if you look for it as for silver
and search for it as for hidden treasure,[i]
[5] then you will understand the fear of the LORD
and find the knowledge of God.[j]
[6] For the LORD gives wisdom,[k]
and from his mouth come knowledge and understanding.
[7] He holds victory in store for the upright,
he is a shield[l] to those whose walk is blameless,[m]
[8] for he guards the course of the just
and protects the way of his faithful ones.[n]

[9] Then you will understand what is right and just
and fair—every good path.
[10] For wisdom will enter your heart,[o]
and knowledge will be pleasant to your soul.
[11] Discretion will protect you,
and understanding will guard you.[p]

[12] Wisdom will save you from the ways of wicked men,
from men whose words are perverse,
[13] who leave the straight paths
to walk in dark ways,[q]
[14] who delight in doing wrong
and rejoice in the perverseness of evil,[r]
[15] whose paths are crooked[s]
and who are devious in their ways.[t]

[16] It will save you also from the adulteress,[u]
from the wayward wife with her seductive words,
[17] who has left the partner of her youth
and ignored the covenant she made before God.[a][v]
[18] For her house leads down to death
and her paths to the spirits of the dead.[w]
[19] None who go to her return
or attain the paths of life.[x]

[20] Thus you will walk in the ways of good men
and keep to the paths of the righteous.

2:2 [h] Pr 22:17
2:4 [i] Job 3:21; Pr 3:14; Mt 13:44
2:5 [j] Pr 1:7
2:6 [k] 1Ki 3:9,12; Jas 1:5
2:7 [l] Pr 30:5-6 [m] Ps 84:11
2:8 [n] 1Sa 2:9; Ps 66:9
2:10 [o] Pr 14:33
2:11 [p] Pr 4:6; 6:22
2:13 [q] Pr 4:19; Jn 3:19
2:14 [r] Pr 10:23; Jer 11:15
2:15 [s] Ps 125:5 [t] Pr 21:8
2:16 [u] Pr 5:1-6; 6:20-29; 7:5-27
2:17 [v] Mal 2:14
2:18 [w] Pr 7:27
2:19 [x] Ecc 7:26

[a] 17 Or *covenant of her God*

2:1–5 As was common in the ancient Near East, each section of teaching follows a predictable pattern or form. An address ("My son," v. 1) is followed by a charge or condition ("if you accept my words"), which is followed in turn by a series of motivations or rewards ("then you will understand the fear of the LORD," v. 5).
2:4 Job 28:1–11 describes ancient mining techniques, comparing this activity with the search for wisdom.
2:7 "Blameless" refers to those who are spiritually and morally upright. It does not imply sinlessness (see 19:1).
2:18 For "spirits of the dead," see Job 10:21, 26:5 and their notes. The deceased are in the grave (or Sheol), "the chambers of death" (Pr 7:27). See the note on Psalm 6:5, as well as "Sheol, Hades, Gehenna, the Abyss and Tartarus: Images of Hell" on page 946.

2:21 [y]Ps 37:29
2:22 [z]Job 18:17; Ps 37:38 [a]Dt 28:63; Pr 10:30

21 For the upright will live in the land,[y]
and the blameless will remain in it;
22 but the wicked will be cut off from the land,[z]
and the unfaithful will be torn from it.[a]

Further Benefits of Wisdom

3:1 [b]Pr 4:5
3:2 [c]Pr 4:10

3 My son, do not forget my teaching,[b]
but keep my commands in your heart,
2 for they will prolong your life many years[c]
and bring you prosperity.

3:3 [d]Ex 13:9; Pr 6:21; 7:3; 2Co 3:3
3:4 [e]1Sa 2:26; Lk 2:52
3:5 [f]Ps 37:3,5
3:6 [g]1Ch 28:9 [h]Pr 16:3; Isa 45:13
3:7 [i]Ro 12:16 [j]Job 1:1; Pr 16:6
3:8 [k]Pr 4:22 [l]Job 21:24

3 Let love and faithfulness never leave you;
bind them around your neck,
write them on the tablet of your heart.[d]
4 Then you will win favor and a good name
in the sight of God and man.[e]

5 Trust in the LORD[f] with all your heart
and lean not on your own understanding;
6 in all your ways acknowledge him,
and he will make your paths[g] straight.[a][h]

7 Do not be wise in your own eyes;[i]
fear the LORD and shun evil.[j]
8 This will bring health to your body[k]
and nourishment to your bones.[l]

3:9 [m]Ex 22:29; 23:19; Dt 26:1-15
3:10 [n]Dt 28:8 [o]Joel 2:24
3:11 [p]Job 5:17
3:12 [q]Pr 13:24; Rev 3:19 [r]Dt 8:5; Heb 12:5-6*

9 Honor the LORD with your wealth,
with the firstfruits[m] of all your crops;
10 then your barns will be filled[n] to overflowing,
and your vats will brim over with new wine.[o]

11 My son, do not despise the LORD's discipline[p]
and do not resent his rebuke,
12 because the LORD disciplines those he loves,[q]
as a father[b] the son he delights in.[r]

3:14 [s]Job 28:15; Pr 8:19; 16:16
3:15 [t]Job 28:18 [u]Pr 8:11
3:16 [v]Pr 8:18
3:17 [w]Pr 16:7; Mt 11:28-30
3:18 [x]Ge 2:9; Pr 11:30; Rev 2:7
3:19 [y]Ps 104:24 [z]Pr 8:27-29

13 Blessed is the man who finds wisdom,
the man who gains understanding,
14 for she is more profitable than silver
and yields better returns than gold.[s]
15 She is more precious than rubies;[t]
nothing you desire can compare with her.[u]
16 Long life is in her right hand;
in her left hand are riches and honor.[v]
17 Her ways are pleasant ways,
and all her paths are peace.[w]
18 She is a tree of life[x] to those who embrace her;
those who lay hold of her will be blessed.

19 By wisdom the LORD laid the earth's foundations,[y]
by understanding he set the heavens[z] in place;
20 by his knowledge the deeps were divided,
and the clouds let drop the dew.

[a] 6 Or *will direct your paths* [b] 12 Hebrew; Septuagint / *and he punishes*

2:21 See the note on verse 7.

[21] My son, preserve sound judgment and discernment,
do not let them out of your sight;[a]
[22] they will be life for you,
an ornament to grace your neck.[b]
[23] Then you will go on your way in safety,
and your foot will not stumble;[c]
[24] when you lie down,[d] you will not be afraid;
when you lie down, your sleep[e] will be sweet.
[25] Have no fear of sudden disaster
or of the ruin that overtakes the wicked,
[26] for the LORD will be your confidence
and will keep your foot[f] from being snared.

[27] Do not withhold good from those who deserve it,
when it is in your power to act.
[28] Do not say to your neighbor,
"Come back later; I'll give it tomorrow"—
when you now have it with you.[g]
[29] Do not plot harm against your neighbor,
who lives trustfully near you.
[30] Do not accuse a man for no reason—
when he has done you no harm.

[31] Do not envy[h] a violent man
or choose any of his ways,
[32] for the LORD detests a perverse man[i]
but takes the upright into his confidence.[j]

[33] The LORD's curse[k] is on the house of the wicked,[l]
but he blesses the home of the righteous.[m]
[34] He mocks proud mockers
but gives grace to the humble.[n]
[35] The wise inherit honor,
but fools he holds up to shame.

Wisdom Is Supreme

4 Listen, my sons,[o] to a father's instruction;
pay attention and gain understanding.
[2] I give you sound learning,
so do not forsake my teaching.
[3] When I was a boy in my father's house,
still tender, and an only child of my mother,
[4] he taught me and said,
"Lay hold of my words with all your heart;
keep my commands and you will live.[p]
[5] Get wisdom,[q] get understanding;
do not forget my words or swerve from them.
[6] Do not forsake wisdom, and she will protect you;[r]
love her, and she will watch over you.
[7] Wisdom is supreme; therefore get wisdom.
Though it cost all[s] you have,[a] get understanding.[t]
[8] Esteem her, and she will exalt you;
embrace her, and she will honor you.[u]

3:21 [a]Pr 4:20-22
3:22 [b]Pr 1:8-9
3:23 [c]Ps 37:24; Pr 4:12
3:24 [d]Lev 26:6; Ps 3:5 [e]Job 11:18
3:26 [f]1Sa 2:9
3:28 [g]Lev 19:13; Dt 24:15
3:31 [h]Ps 37:1; Pr 24:1-2
3:32 [i]Pr 11:20 [j]Job 29:4; Ps 25:14
3:33 [k]Dt 11:28; Mal 2:2 [l]Zec 5:4 [m]Ps 1:3
3:34 [n]Jas 4:6*; 1Pe 5:5*
4:1 [o]Pr 1:8
4:4 [p]Pr 7:2
4:5 [q]Pr 16:16
4:6 [r]2Th 2:10
4:7 [s]Mt 13:44-46 [t]Pr 23:23
4:8 [u]1Sa 2:30; Pr 3:18

[a] 7 Or *Whatever else you get*

[9] She will set a garland of grace on your head
and present you with a crown of splendor.[v]"

[10] Listen, my son, accept what I say,
and the years of your life will be many.[w]
[11] I guide[x] you in the way of wisdom
and lead you along straight paths.
[12] When you walk, your steps will not be hampered;
when you run, you will not stumble.[y]
[13] Hold on to instruction, do not let it go;
guard it well, for it is your life.[z]
[14] Do not set foot on the path of the wicked
or walk in the way of evil men.[a]
[15] Avoid it, do not travel on it;
turn from it and go on your way.
[16] For they cannot sleep till they do evil;[b]
they are robbed of slumber till they make someone fall.
[17] They eat the bread of wickedness
and drink the wine of violence.

[18] The path of the righteous[c] is like the first gleam of dawn,
shining ever brighter till the full light of day.[d]
[19] But the way of the wicked is like deep darkness;[e]
they do not know what makes them stumble.

[20] My son, pay attention to what I say;
listen closely to my words.[f]
[21] Do not let them out of your sight,[g]
keep them within your heart;
[22] for they are life to those who find them
and health to a man's whole body.[h]
[23] Above all else, guard your heart,
for it is the wellspring of life.[i]
[24] Put away perversity from your mouth;
keep corrupt talk far from your lips.
[25] Let your eyes look straight ahead,
fix your gaze directly before you.
[26] Make level[a] paths for your feet[j]
and take only ways that are firm.
[27] Do not swerve to the right or the left;[k]
keep your foot from evil.

Warning Against Adultery

5 My son, pay attention to my wisdom,
listen well to my words[l] of insight,
[2] that you may maintain discretion
and your lips may preserve knowledge.
[3] For the lips of an adulteress drip honey,
and her speech is smoother than oil;[m]
[4] but in the end she is bitter as gall,[n]
sharp as a double-edged sword.

4:9 [v]Pr 1:8-9
4:10 [w]Pr 3:2
4:11 [x]1Sa 12:23
4:12 [y]Job 18:7; Pr 3:23
4:13 [z]Pr 3:22
4:14 [a]Ps 1:1; Pr 1:15
4:16 [b]Ps 36:4; Mic 2:1
4:18 [c]Isa 26:7 [d]2Sa 23:4; Da 12:3; Mt 5:14; Php 2:15
4:19 [e]Job 18:5; Pr 2:13; Isa 59:9-10; Jn 12:35
4:20 [f]Pr 5:1
4:21 [g]Pr 3:21; 7:1-2
4:22 [h]Pr 3:8; 12:18
4:23 [i]Mt 12:34; Lk 6:45
4:26 [j]Heb 12:13*
4:27 [k]Dt 5:32; 28:14
5:1 [l]Pr 4:20; 22:17
5:3 [m]Ps 55:21; Pr 2:16; 7:5
5:4 [n]Ecc 7:26

[a] 26 Or *Consider the*

4:9 Wreaths or crowns were worn on joyous occasions, such as weddings or feasts (see SS 3:11; Eze 16:12; 23:42; cf. 1Pe 5:4).

5:4 Gall is a bitter herb (see Dt 29:18; La 3:15,19; Am 6:12), and a "double-edged sword" was a lethal weapon (see Jdg 3:16; Ps 55:21; 149:6; Heb 4:12; cf. Rev 1:16).

[5]Her feet go down to death;
her steps lead straight to the grave.[a][o] 5:5 [o]Pr 7:26-27
[6]She gives no thought to the way of life;
her paths are crooked, but she knows it not.[p] 5:6 [p]Pr 30:20

[7]Now then, my sons, listen[q] to me; 5:7 [q]Pr 7:24
do not turn aside from what I say.
[8]Keep to a path far from her,[r] 5:8 [r]Pr 7:1-27
do not go near the door of her house,
[9]lest you give your best strength to others
and your years to one who is cruel,
[10]lest strangers feast on your wealth
and your toil enrich another man's house.
[11]At the end of your life you will groan,
when your flesh and body are spent.
[12]You will say, "How I hated discipline!
How my heart spurned correction![s] 5:12 [s]Pr 1:29; 12:1
[13]I would not obey my teachers
or listen to my instructors.
[14]I have come to the brink of utter ruin
in the midst of the whole assembly."

[15]Drink water from your own cistern,
running water from your own well.
[16]Should your springs overflow in the streets,
your streams of water in the public squares?
[17]Let them be yours alone,
never to be shared with strangers.
[18]May your fountain[t] be blessed, 5:18 [t]SS 4:12-15 [u]Ecc 9:9; Mal 2:14
and may you rejoice in the wife of your youth.[u]
[19]A loving doe, a graceful deer[v]— 5:19 [v]SS 2:9; 4:5
may her breasts satisfy you always,
may you ever be captivated by her love.
[20]Why be captivated, my son, by an adulteress?
Why embrace the bosom of another man's wife?

[21]For a man's ways are in full view[w] of the LORD, 5:21 [w]Ps 119:168; Hos 7:2 [x]Job 14:16; Job 31:4; 34:21; Pr 15:3; Jer 16:17; 32:19; Heb 4:13
and he examines all his paths.[x]
[22]The evil deeds of a wicked man ensnare him;[y] 5:22 [y]Ps 9:16 [z]Nu 32:23; Ps 7:15-16; Pr 1:31-32
the cords of his sin hold him fast.[z]
[23]He will die for lack of discipline,[a] 5:23 [a]Job 4:21; 36:12
led astray by his own great folly.

Warnings Against Folly

6 My son, if you have put up security for your neighbor,[b] 6:1 [b]Pr 17:18 [c]Pr 11:15; 22:26-27
if you have struck hands in pledge[c] for another,
[2]if you have been trapped by what you said,
ensnared by the words of your mouth,
[3]then do this, my son, to free yourself,
since you have fallen into your neighbor's hands:

[a] 5 Hebrew *Sheol*

5:15 "Your own cistern ... your own well" implies "your own wife" (see SS 4:12,15)—the only legitimate source of sexual pleasure. In the Near East wells and cisterns were privately owned (Jer 38:6) and of great value (2Ki 18:31). See "Wells, Cisterns and Aqueducts in the Ancient World" on page 1259.
6:1 Taking on responsibility for someone else's debt (cf. 22:26) or obligation could result in poverty (cf. 22:27) or even slavery. For example, Judah offered himself to Joseph as a slave (Ge 44:32–33) in order to fulfill his personal guarantee of Benjamin's safe return to Jacob. Such an arrangement was sealed by "striking hands," equivalent to the modern-day handshake (see Pr 11:15; 17:18; 20:16; 22:26; cf. Job 17:3).

Go and humble yourself;
press your plea with your neighbor!
4 Allow no sleep to your eyes,
no slumber to your eyelids.[d]
5 Free yourself, like a gazelle from the hand of the hunter,
like a bird from the snare of the fowler.[e]

6 Go to the ant, you sluggard;[f]
consider its ways and be wise!
7 It has no commander,
no overseer or ruler,
8 yet it stores its provisions in summer
and gathers its food at harvest.[g]

9 How long will you lie there, you sluggard?[h]
When will you get up from your sleep?
10 A little sleep, a little slumber,
a little folding of the hands to rest[i]—
11 and poverty[j] will come on you like a bandit
and scarcity like an armed man.[a]

12 A scoundrel and villain,
who goes about with a corrupt mouth,
13 who winks with his eye,[k]
signals with his feet
and motions with his fingers,
14 who plots evil[l] with deceit in his heart—
he always stirs up dissension.[m]
15 Therefore disaster will overtake him in an instant;
he will suddenly be destroyed—without remedy.[n]

16 There are six things the LORD hates,
seven that are detestable to him:
17 haughty eyes,
a lying tongue,[o]
hands that shed innocent blood,[p]
18 a heart that devises wicked schemes,
feet that are quick to rush into evil,[q]
19 a false witness[r] who pours out lies
and a man who stirs up dissension among brothers.[s]

Warning Against Adultery

20 My son, keep your father's commands
and do not forsake your mother's teaching.[t]
21 Bind them upon your heart forever;
fasten them around your neck.[u]
22 When you walk, they will guide you;
when you sleep, they will watch over you;
when you awake, they will speak to you.
23 For these commands are a lamp,
this teaching is a light,[v]
and the corrections of discipline
are the way to life,
24 keeping you from the immoral woman,
from the smooth tongue of the wayward wife.[w]

6:4 [d]Ps 132:4
6:5 [e]Ps 91:3
6:6 [f]Pr 20:4
6:8 [g]Pr 10:4
6:9 [h]Pr 24:30-34
6:10 [i]Pr 24:33
6:11 [j]Pr 24:30-34
6:13 [k]Ps 35:19
6:14 [l]Mic 2:1 [m]ver 16-19
6:15 [n]2Ch 36:16
6:17 [o]Ps 120:2; Pr 12:22 [p]Dt 19:10; Isa 1:15; 59:7
6:18 [q]Ge 6:5
6:19 [r]Ps 27:12 [s]ver 12-15
6:20 [t]Pr 1:8
6:21 [u]Pr 3:3; 7:1-3
6:23 [v]Ps 19:8; 119:105
6:24 [w]Pr 2:16; 7:5

[a] 11 Or *like a vagrant / and scarcity like a beggar*

[25] Do not lust in your heart after her beauty
or let her captivate you with her eyes,
[26] for the prostitute reduces you to a loaf of bread,
and the adulteress preys upon your very life.[x]
[27] Can a man scoop fire into his lap
without his clothes being burned?
[28] Can a man walk on hot coals
without his feet being scorched?

6:26 [x]Pr 7:22-23; 29:3

Heart, Breath, Throat and Intestines: Ancient Hebrew Anthropology

PROVERBS 6 Biblical Hebrew, like English, uses parts of the body metaphorically to express personality, emotion or thought processes. Hebrew, however, does not always allude to the same organs as English to express these functions. A verbatim translation of these terms would often be unintelligible in English, and thus even the most "literal" of translations must resort to paraphrase in order to communicate the intended point. The English reader might have difficulty spotting where the Hebrew word for a body part occurs in the examples below:

✣ The word *leb* (usually translated "heart") can be used literally of the physical heart (e.g., Ex 28:29) or metaphorically for several aspects of the personality. Often *leb* indicates the seat of particular emotions, such as fear, lament, regret, joy, comfort, love, anger, etc. (e.g., Ps 27:3; Pr 19:3). It can also refer to thought functions, as the equivalent of "mind" in English (4:10).

✣ Hebrew words for "breath" (*ruah*, *neshamah*) can refer to a person's inner being (e.g., Job 32:8; Pr 20:27). Thus, they are often translated into English as "spirit" or "soul." But an individual's *ruah* may also experience emotional reactions (Ge 26:35) and consequently exhibit a particular behavior, such as stubbornness (Dt 2:30).

✣ There are several Hebrew words for neck or throat (e.g., *garon* or *nephesh*). The throat is the means by which a person breathes, eats and thus, so to speak, takes in life. Therefore, the word *nephesh*, although it concretely means "throat," is generally translated "life," "soul" or even "person." These words are often used to express the inner character of an individual. As such, the neck or throat can be deceitful (Ps 5:9), display arrogance (Isa 3:16), express determination or stubbornness (Ps 75:5) and praise God (Ps 149:6). The *nephesh* can be bitter or hot-tempered (Jdg 18:25; the NIV's "hot-tempered men" is actually "men of bitter *nephesh*"). Literally, necks displayed precious metals and jewels (SS 1:10) as well as the yoke of slavery (Isa 10:27). Figuratively, then, the neck or throat could be said to display what a person deemed valuable (Pr 6:21), as well as the consequences of an individual's sins (La 1:14).

✣ The words for stomach or womb (e.g., *beten*) can indicate the seat of the emotions, such as titillation (Pr 18:8) and sexual desire (SS 5:4). Other organs that Biblical Hebrew uses in this way are the liver, intestines and kidneys.

Proverbs 6 illustrates the usage described above. Verse 16 states literally that there are seven things that are detestable to the Lord's *nephesh* (his very being). Verse 30 notes that men do not despise a thief who steals to fill his *nephesh* (throat or hunger), while verse 32 claims that the adulterer destroys his own *nephesh* (life or soul). Verse 14 points out that the individual who plots evil has perversity in his *leb* (heart or mind), while verse 32 asserts that the adulterer lacks *leb* (good sense).

The teachings of the Hebrew sages are couched in terms that are sometimes alien to the modern English reader, but when understood on their own terms they create a compelling picture of a human being as a bundle of physical, emotional and spiritual capacities and needs. A man, woman, boy or girl is an integral combination of body and soul; the emotional or intellectual aspects of life simply cannot be separated from the nature of the whole person.

6:29 [y]Ex 20:14 [z]Pr 2:16-19; 5:8

[29] So is he who sleeps[y] with another man's wife;[z]
no one who touches her will go unpunished.

[30] Men do not despise a thief if he steals
to satisfy his hunger when he is starving.
[31] Yet if he is caught, he must pay sevenfold,[a]
though it costs him all the wealth of his house.
[32] But a man who commits adultery[b] lacks judgment;[c]
whoever does so destroys himself.
[33] Blows and disgrace are his lot,
and his shame will never[d] be wiped away;
[34] for jealousy[e] arouses a husband's fury,[f]
and he will show no mercy when he takes revenge.
[35] He will not accept any compensation;
he will refuse the bribe, however great it is.[g]

6:31 [a]Ex 22:1-14
6:32 [b]Ex 20:14 [c]Pr 7:7; 9:4,16
6:33 [d]Pr 5:9-14
6:34 [e]Nu 5:14 [f]Ge 34:7
6:35 [g]Job 31:9-11; SS 8:7

Warning Against the Adulteress

7 My son,[h] keep my words
and store up my commands within you.
[2] Keep my commands and you will live;[i]
guard my teachings as the apple of your eye.
[3] Bind them on your fingers;
write them on the tablet of your heart.[j]
[4] Say to wisdom, "You are my sister,"
and call understanding your kinsman;
[5] they will keep you from the adulteress,
from the wayward wife with her seductive words.[k]

[6] At the window of my house
I looked out through the lattice.
[7] I saw among the simple,
I noticed among the young men,
a youth who lacked judgment.[l]
[8] He was going down the street near her corner,
walking along in the direction of her house
[9] at twilight,[m] as the day was fading,
as the dark of night set in.

[10] Then out came a woman to meet him,
dressed like a prostitute and with crafty intent.
[11] (She is loud[n] and defiant,
her feet never stay at home;
[12] now in the street, now in the squares,
at every corner she lurks.)[o]
[13] She took hold of him[p] and kissed him
and with a brazen face she said:[q]

[14] "I have fellowship offerings[a][r] at home;
today I fulfilled my vows.
[15] So I came out to meet you;
I looked for you and have found you!

7:1 [h]Pr 1:8; 2:1
7:2 [i]Pr 4:4
7:3 [j]Dt 6:8; Pr 3:3
7:5 [k]ver 21; Job 31:9; Pr 2:16; 6:24
7:7 [l]Pr 1:22; 6:32
7:9 [m]Job 24:15
7:11 [n]Pr 9:13; 1Ti 5:13
7:12 [o]Pr 8:1-36; 23:26-28
7:13 [p]Ge 39:12 [q]Pr 1:20
7:14 [r]Lev 7:11-18

[a] 14 Traditionally *peace offerings*

6:31 Hebrew law demanded no more than fivefold payment as a penalty for any theft (Ex 22:1–9). The number seven is symbolic; the thief would pay in full.
7:2 For "apple of your eye," see the note on Psalm 17:8.
7:10 The phrase "dressed like a prostitute" may mean dressed in a gaudy manner (see Eze 16:16).
7:13 A kiss was a bold form of greeting. See "The Jewish Custom of Kissing" on page 1682.

16 I have covered my bed
with colored linens from Egypt.
17 I have perfumed my bed[s]
with myrrh,[t] aloes and cinnamon.
18 Come, let's drink deep of love till morning;
let's enjoy ourselves with love![u]
19 My husband is not at home;
he has gone on a long journey.
20 He took his purse filled with money
and will not be home till full moon."

21 With persuasive words she led him astray;
she seduced him with her smooth talk.[v]
22 All at once he followed her
like an ox going to the slaughter,
like a deer[a] stepping into a noose[b][w]
23 till an arrow pierces[x] his liver,
like a bird darting into a snare,
little knowing it will cost him his life.[y]

24 Now then, my sons, listen[z] to me;
pay attention to what I say.
25 Do not let your heart turn to her ways
or stray into her paths.[a]
26 Many are the victims she has brought down;
her slain are a mighty throng.
27 Her house is a highway to the grave,[c]
leading down to the chambers of death.[b]

7:17 [s]Est 1:6; Isa 57:7; Eze 23:41; Am 6:4 [t]Ge 37:25
7:18 [u]Ge 39:7
7:21 [v]Pr 5:3
7:22 [w]Job 18:10
7:23 [x]Job 15:22; 16:13 [y]Pr 6:26; Ecc 7:26; 9:12
7:24 [z]Pr 1:8-9; 5:7; 8:32
7:25 [a]Pr 5:7-8
7:27 [b]Pr 2:18; 5:5; 9:18; Rev 22:15

Wisdom's Call

8 Does not wisdom call out?[c]
Does not understanding raise her voice?
2 On the heights along the way,
where the paths meet, she takes her stand;
3 beside the gates leading into the city,
at the entrances, she cries aloud:[d]
4 "To you, O men, I call out;
I raise my voice to all mankind.
5 You who are simple,[e] gain prudence;[f]
you who are foolish, gain understanding.
6 Listen, for I have worthy things to say;
I open my lips to speak what is right.
7 My mouth speaks what is true,[g]
for my lips detest wickedness.
8 All the words of my mouth are just;
none of them is crooked or perverse.

8:1 [c]Pr 1:20; 9:3
8:3 [d]Job 29:7
8:5 [e]Pr 1:22 [f]Pr 1:4
8:7 [g]Ps 37:30; Jn 8:14

[a] 22 Syriac (see also Septuagint); Hebrew *fool* [b] 22 The meaning of the Hebrew for this line is uncertain. [c] 27 Hebrew *Sheol*

7:16 Linen was associated with the wealthy. Egyptian linen in particular was of great value (see Isa 19:9; Eze 27:7).
7:17 The use of perfume in the form of ointment or impregnated oil was a Middle Eastern practice long before it spread to the Mediterranean world. In all probability such ointment was originally used for ceremonial purposes, first religious and then secular, and eventually became a personal habit with the growing sophistication of society and the need for deodorants in hot lands (see also Est 2:12; Pr 27:9; Isa 57:9). So universal was the practice that its suspension was an accepted sign of mourning (Dt 28:40; Ru 3:3; 2Sa 14:2; Da 10:3; Am 6:6; Mic 6:15). The skin as well as the hair was perfumed and anointed (Ps 104:15), and especially on high occasions a scented unguent was used with profusion (Ps 133:2). See "Perfumes and Anointing Oils" on page 1746.
7:20 Pieces of silver of various weights were a common medium of exchange; coinage was not invented until a later period.
7:27 See the note on 2:18.
8:1 For commentary on Wisdom's portrayal as a righteous woman, see the note on 1:7—9:10.

9 To the discerning all of them are right;
they are faultless to those who have knowledge.
10 Choose my instruction instead of silver,
8:10 [h]Pr 3:14-15 knowledge rather than choice gold,[h]
8:11 [i]Job 28:17-19 [j]Pr 3:13-15 11 for wisdom is more precious[i] than rubies,
and nothing you desire can compare with her.[j]

12 "I, wisdom, dwell together with prudence;
8:12 [k]Pr 1:4 I possess knowledge and discretion.[k]
8:13 [l]Pr 16:6 [m]Jer 44:4 13 To fear the LORD is to hate evil;[l]
I hate[m] pride and arrogance,
evil behavior and perverse speech.
14 Counsel and sound judgment are mine;
8:14 [n]Pr 21:22; Ecc 7:19 I have understanding and power.[n]
15 By me kings reign
8:15 [o]Da 2:21; Ro 13:1 and rulers[o] make laws that are just;
16 by me princes govern,
and all nobles who rule on earth.[a]
8:17 [p]1Sa 2:30; Ps 91:14; Jn 14:21-24 [q]Pr 1:28; Jas 1:5 17 I love those who love me,[p]
and those who seek me find me.[q]

[a] *16* Many Hebrew manuscripts and Septuagint; most Hebrew manuscripts *and nobles—all righteous rulers*

Maat and Lady Wisdom

PROVERBS 8 In ancient Egypt[1] Maat was the abstract principle of truth, order, justice and harmony—as well as the name of the goddess who personified those virtues. Kings were enjoined to practice Maat in order to ensure a long reign (cf. Pr 8:15–16). When Maat held sway in the land, Egyptians believed, the Nile flooded properly to ensure good crops, there was justice for all and the classes of society coexisted in harmony. When Maat was ignored, the land fell into chaos, crime and ruin. Some funerary paintings depict a balance scale on one side of which is placed the heart of a recently deceased man and on the other side a feather, representing Maat. If the balance is in equilibrium, the soul of the deceased enters the paradise of the realm of Osiris. Should the individual's heart fail the test, a monster called the Eater stands ready to devour his soul.

Scholars naturally wonder to what degree the Egyptian concept of Maat influenced Israelite thinking on justice and order in society. Specifically, the feminine personification of Wisdom in Proverbs 8 has been suggested to have been derived from the Egyptian goddess Maat. It is, of course, important to realize that Israel did not exist in isolation; to the contrary, the Bible speaks a great deal about the Egyptian influences on Israel. The sojourn in Egypt was obviously a time when Israel would have been exposed to Egyptian culture and religion, and Solomon's era was also a period of close cultural exchange between these two societies.

Nevertheless, it is difficult to posit a direct line of influence from Egypt to Israel on the subjects of order, justice or Maat. Both Israel and Egypt understood that justice and harmony are necessary for life to function smoothly. But Wisdom, in Proverbs 8, is a personification—not a goddess. She exemplifies the order and justice God has built into creation. Lady Wisdom appears elsewhere in Proverbs; for example, in 1:20–33 she calls upon people to heed her teachings and so to find life. The embodiment of wisdom as a lady who invites people to follow her is a distinctively Israelite idea, with no analogy in Egyptian teaching.

[1]See "A Breakdown of Ancient Egyptian History" on page 104.

18 With me are riches and honor,[r]
enduring wealth and prosperity.[s]
19 My fruit is better than fine gold;
what I yield surpasses choice silver.[t]
20 I walk in the way of righteousness,
along the paths of justice,
21 bestowing wealth on those who love me
and making their treasuries full.[u]

22 "The LORD brought me forth as the first of his works,[a,b]
before his deeds of old;
23 I was appointed[c] from eternity,
from the beginning, before the world began.
24 When there were no oceans, I was given birth,
when there were no springs abounding with water;[v]
25 before the mountains were settled in place,
before the hills, I was given birth,[w]
26 before he made the earth or its fields
or any of the dust of the world.[x]
27 I was there when he set the heavens in place,[y]
when he marked out the horizon on the face of the deep,
28 when he established the clouds above
and fixed securely the fountains of the deep,
29 when he gave the sea its boundary[z]
so the waters would not overstep his command,[a]
and when he marked out the foundations of the earth.[b]
30 Then I was the craftsman at his side.[c]
I was filled with delight day after day,
rejoicing always in his presence,
31 rejoicing in his whole world
and delighting in mankind.[d]

32 "Now then, my sons, listen to me;
blessed are[e] those who keep my ways.[f]
33 Listen to my instruction and be wise;
do not ignore it.
34 Blessed is the man who listens[g] to me,
watching daily at my doors,
waiting at my doorway.
35 For whoever finds me[h] finds life
and receives favor from the LORD.[i]
36 But whoever fails to find me harms himself;[j]
all who hate me love death."

8:18 [r]Pr 3:16 [s]Dt 8:18; Mt 6:33
8:19 [t]Pr 3:13-14; 10:20
8:21 [u]Pr 24:4
8:24 [v]Ge 7:11
8:25 [w]Job 15:7
8:26 [x]Ps 90:2
8:27 [y]Pr 3:19
8:29 [z]Ge 1:9; Job 38:10; Ps 16:6 [a]Ps 104:9 [b]Job 38:5
8:30 [c]Jn 1:1-3
8:31 [d]Ps 16:3; 104:1-30
8:32 [e]Lk 11:28 [f]Ps 119:1-2
8:34 [g]Pr 3:13,18
8:35 [h]Pr 3:13-18 [i]Pr 12:2
8:36 [j]Pr 15:32

Invitations of Wisdom and of Folly

9 Wisdom has built[k] her house;
she has hewn out its seven pillars.
2 She has prepared her meat and mixed her wine;
she has also set her table.[l]
3 She has sent out her maids, and she calls[m]
from the highest point of the city.[n]

9:1 [k]Eph 2:20-22; 1Pe 2:5
9:2 [l]Lk 14:16-23
9:3 [m]Pr 8:1-3 [n]ver 14

[a] 22 Or *way*; or *dominion* [b] 22 Or *The LORD possessed me at the beginning of his work*; or *The LORD brought me forth at the beginning of his work* [c] 23 Or *fashioned*

8:30 Those skilled in various crafts were sometimes called "wise." Here, however, the term refers to the skill demonstrated in creation.

PARALLELS BETWEEN THE LAW AND WISDOM

Law and wisdom both had secular functions outside of Israel, but are transformed into spiritual concepts in Israel by God's revealed relationship to them.		
SPIRITUAL FOUNDATION: God is source	**LAW** "Be holy because I, the LORD your God, am holy" (Lev 19:2).	**WISDOM** "The fear of the LORD is the beginning of wisdom" (Pr 9:10).
MOTIVATION: Only a God-centered perspective gives ultimate value.	Not just so that society runs smoothly, but so that we will do what is right.	Not pursued for personal fulfillment, but so that we become people of faith.
FOCUS OF GOD'S SELF-REVELATION	God is characterized by absolute morality.	God is characterized by unfathomable wisdom.

Chronological and Background Charts of the Old Testament, p. 25

[4] "Let all who are simple come in here!"
she says to those who lack judgment.[o]
[5] "Come, eat my food
and drink the wine I have mixed.[p]
[6] Leave your simple ways and you will live;[q]
walk in the way of understanding.

[7] "Whoever corrects a mocker invites insult;
whoever rebukes a wicked man incurs abuse.[r]
[8] Do not rebuke a mocker[s] or he will hate you;
rebuke a wise man and he will love you.[t]
[9] Instruct a wise man and he will be wiser still;
teach a righteous man and he will add to his learning.[u]

[10] "The fear of the LORD[v] is the beginning of wisdom,
and knowledge of the Holy One is understanding.
[11] For through me your days will be many,
and years will be added to your life.[w]
[12] If you are wise, your wisdom will reward you;
if you are a mocker, you alone will suffer."

[13] The woman Folly is loud;[x]
she is undisciplined and without knowledge.[y]

9:4 [o]Pr 6:32
9:5 [p]Isa 55:1
9:6 [q]Pr 8:35
9:7 [r]Pr 23:9
9:8 [s]Pr 15:12 [t]Ps 141:5
9:9 [u]Pr 1:5,7
9:10 [v]Job 28:28; Pr 1:7
9:11 [w]Pr 3:16; 10:27
9:13 [x]Pr 7:11 [y]Pr 5:6

9:4 For commentary on the foolish woman, see the note on 1:7—9:10.

9:13 For further commentary on the woman Folly, see the notes on 1:7—9:10 and 10:1—22:16.

14 She sits at the door of her house,
on a seat at the highest point of the city,[z]
15 calling out to those who pass by,
who go straight on their way.
16 "Let all who are simple come in here!"
she says to those who lack judgment.
17 "Stolen water is sweet;
food eaten in secret is delicious![a]"
18 But little do they know that the dead are there,
that her guests are in the depths of the grave.[a][b]

9:14 [z]ver 3
9:17 [a]Pr 20:17
9:18 [b]Pr 2:18; 7:26-27

Proverbs of Solomon

10 The proverbs of Solomon:[c]

A wise son brings joy to his father,[d]
but a foolish son grief to his mother.

2 Ill-gotten treasures are of no value,[e]
but righteousness delivers from death.[f]

3 The LORD does not let the righteous go hungry[g]
but he thwarts the craving of the wicked.

4 Lazy hands make a man poor,[h]
but diligent hands bring wealth.[i]

5 He who gathers crops in summer is a wise son,
but he who sleeps during harvest is a disgraceful son.

6 Blessings crown the head of the righteous,
but violence overwhelms the mouth of the wicked.[b][j]

7 The memory of the righteous[k] will be a blessing,
but the name of the wicked[l] will rot.[m]

8 The wise in heart accept commands,
but a chattering fool comes to ruin.[n]

9 The man of integrity[o] walks securely,[p]
but he who takes crooked paths will be found out.[q]

10 He who winks maliciously[r] causes grief,
and a chattering fool comes to ruin.

11 The mouth of the righteous is a fountain of life,[s]
but violence overwhelms the mouth of the wicked.[t]

12 Hatred stirs up dissension,
but love covers over all wrongs.[u]

10:1 [c]Pr 1:1 [d]Pr 15:20; 29:3
10:2 [e]Pr 21:6 [f]Pr 11:4,19
10:3 [g]Mt 6:25-34
10:4 [h]Pr 19:15 [i]Pr 12:24; 13:4; 21:5
10:6 [j]ver 8,11,14
10:7 [k]Ps 112:6 [l]Ps 109:13 [m]Ps 9:6
10:8 [n]Mt 7:24-27
10:9 [o]Isa 33:15 [p]Ps 23:4 [q]Pr 28:18
10:10 [r]Ps 35:19
10:11 [s]Ps 37:30; Pr 13:12,14,19 [t]ver 6
10:12 [u]Pr 17:9; 1Co 13:4-7; 1Pe 4:8

[a] 18 Hebrew *Sheol* [b] 6 Or *but the mouth of the wicked conceals violence*; also in verse 11

9:18 See the note on 2:18.
10:1—22:16 In the major section of Proverbs, the same contrast between wisdom and folly (see the note on 1:7—9:10) appears in single-verse aphorisms. Here the personification of sin and righteousness does not appear, but the same synonyms for virtue and vice are repeatedly used and should be understood as such. Perhaps the greatest error in interpreting the book comes from the tendency to quote these proverbs as mere secular maxims instead of godly instruction. "Folly" here does not mean stupidity, just as "the woman Folly" (9:13) does not refer to an ignoramus. Both terms relate to sin. Throughout this whole section the terms *wisdom, understanding, integrity* and *knowledge* are synonymous references to holiness. Their opposites—*fool, folly, simple, mocker, quarrelsome,* etc.—refer to wickedness. In short, a "foolish son" is not a dullard but a scoundrel. A "mocker" is not just disdainful but a rebel against wisdom. The lack of context sometimes clouds the interpretation. But occasionally a verse is partially repeated elsewhere, where the variant form clarifies the meaning (cf. 27:15 with 21:19).

10:13 [v]ver 31 [w]Pr 26:3

[13] Wisdom is found on the lips of the discerning,[v]
but a rod is for the back of him who lacks judgment.[w]

[14] Wise men store up knowledge,
but the mouth of a fool invites ruin.[x]

10:14 [x]Pr 18:6,7

[15] The wealth of the rich is their fortified city,[y]
but poverty is the ruin of the poor.[z]

10:15 [y]Pr 18:11 [z]Pr 19:7

[16] The wages of the righteous bring them life,
but the income of the wicked brings them punishment.[a]

10:16 [a]Pr 11:18-19

[17] He who heeds discipline shows the way to life,[b]
but whoever ignores correction leads others astray.

10:17 [b]Pr 6:23

[18] He who conceals his hatred has lying lips,
and whoever spreads slander is a fool.

[19] When words are many, sin is not absent,
but he who holds his tongue is wise.[c]

10:19 [c]Pr 17:28; Ecc 5:3; Jas 1:19; 3:2-12

[20] The tongue of the righteous is choice silver,
but the heart of the wicked is of little value.

[21] The lips of the righteous nourish many,
but fools die for lack of judgment.[d]

10:21 [d]Pr 5:22-23; Hos 4:1,6,14

[22] The blessing of the LORD brings wealth,[e]
and he adds no trouble to it.

10:22 [e]Ge 24:35; Ps 37:22

[23] A fool finds pleasure in evil conduct,[f]
but a man of understanding delights in wisdom.

10:23 [f]Pr 2:14; 15:21

[24] What the wicked dreads[g] will overtake him;
what the righteous desire will be granted.[h]

10:24 [g]Isa 66:4 [h]Ps 145:17-19; Mt 5:6; 1Jn 5:14-15

[25] When the storm has swept by, the wicked are gone,
but the righteous stand firm[i] forever.[j]

10:25 [i]Ps 15:5 [j]Pr 12:3,7; Mt 7:24-27

[26] As vinegar to the teeth and smoke to the eyes,
so is a sluggard to those who send him.[k]

10:26 [k]Pr 26:6

[27] The fear of the LORD adds length to life,[l]
but the years of the wicked are cut short.[m]

10:27 [l]Pr 9:10-11 [m]Job 15:32

[28] The prospect of the righteous is joy,
but the hopes of the wicked come to nothing.[n]

10:28 [n]Job 8:13; Pr 11:7

[29] The way of the LORD is a refuge for the righteous,
but it is the ruin of those who do evil.[o]

10:29 [o]Pr 21:15

[30] The righteous will never be uprooted,
but the wicked will not remain in the land.[p]

10:30 [p]Ps 37:9, 28-29; Pr 2:20-22

[31] The mouth of the righteous brings forth wisdom,[q]
but a perverse tongue will be cut out.

10:31 [q]Ps 37:30

[32] The lips of the righteous know what is fitting,[r]
but the mouth of the wicked only what is perverse.

10:32 [r]Ecc 10:12

11

The LORD abhors dishonest scales,[s]
but accurate weights are his delight.[t]

11:1 [s]Lev 19:36; Dt 25:13-16; Pr 20:10,23 [t]Pr 16:11

11:1 Dishonest scales are denounced in the law (see Lev 19:35) and the Prophets (Am 8:5; Mic 6:11). Silver was weighed on scales balanced against a stone weight, and weights with dishonest labels were used by cheaters. For "accurate weights," see the note on Proverbs 16:11.

[2] When pride comes, then comes disgrace,[u]
but with humility comes wisdom.[v]

[3] The integrity of the upright guides them,
but the unfaithful are destroyed by their duplicity.[w]

[4] Wealth is worthless in the day of wrath,[x]
but righteousness delivers from death.[y]

[5] The righteousness of the blameless makes a straight way for them,
but the wicked are brought down by their own wickedness.[z]

[6] The righteousness of the upright delivers them,
but the unfaithful are trapped by evil desires.

[7] When a wicked man dies, his hope perishes;
all he expected from his power comes to nothing.[a]

[8] The righteous man is rescued from trouble,
and it comes on the wicked instead.[b]

[9] With his mouth the godless destroys his neighbor,
but through knowledge the righteous escape.

[10] When the righteous prosper, the city rejoices;[c]
when the wicked perish, there are shouts of joy.

[11] Through the blessing of the upright a city is exalted,
but by the mouth of the wicked it is destroyed.[d]

[12] A man who lacks judgment derides his neighbor,[e]
but a man of understanding holds his tongue.

[13] A gossip betrays a confidence,[f]
but a trustworthy man keeps a secret.

[14] For lack of guidance a nation falls,[g]
but many advisers make victory sure.[h]

[15] He who puts up security[i] for another will surely suffer,
but whoever refuses to strike hands in pledge is safe.

[16] A kindhearted woman gains respect,[j]
but ruthless men gain only wealth.

[17] A kind man benefits himself,
but a cruel man brings trouble on himself.

[18] The wicked man earns deceptive wages,
but he who sows righteousness reaps a sure reward.[k]

[19] The truly righteous man attains life,
but he who pursues evil goes to his death.

[20] The LORD detests men of perverse heart
but he delights in those whose ways are blameless.[l]

[21] Be sure of this: The wicked will not go unpunished,
but those who are righteous will go free.[m]

[22] Like a gold ring in a pig's snout
is a beautiful woman who shows no discretion.

ANCIENT VOICES

He who takes the fee but does not carry through, you make him bear the punishment.
The one who receives no fee but takes up the case of the weak,
Is pleasing to Shamash, he will make long his life.
The careful judge who gives just verdicts,
Controls the government, lives like a prince.
What return is there for the investor in dishonest dealings?
His profits are illusory, and he loses his capital.

—THE SHAMASH HYMN

See "Justice and Fraud in the Hymn to Shamash" article.

11:2 [u]Pr 16:18 [v]Pr 18:12; 29:23
11:3 [w]Pr 13:6
11:4 [x]Eze 7:19; Zep 1:18 [y]Ge 7:1; Pr 10:2
11:5 [z]Pr 5:21-23
11:7 [a]Pr 10:28
11:8 [b]Pr 21:18
11:10 [c]Pr 28:12
11:11 [d]Pr 29:8
11:12 [e]Pr 14:21
11:13 [f]Lev 19:16; Pr 20:19; 1Ti 5:13
11:14 [g]Pr 20:18 [h]Pr 15:22; 24:6
11:15 [i]Pr 6:1
11:16 [j]Pr 31:31
11:18 [k]Hos 10:12-13
11:20 [l]1Ch 29:17; Ps 119:1; Pr 12:2, 22
11:21 [m]Pr 16:5

11:22 It was common practice throughout the ancient Near East for women to wear gold rings in their noses (see Ge 24:47; Eze 16:12 and its note).

[23] The desire of the righteous ends only in good,
but the hope of the wicked only in wrath.

[24] One man gives freely, yet gains even more;
another withholds unduly, but comes to poverty.

[25] A generous man will prosper;
he who refreshes others will himself be refreshed.[n]

[26] People curse the man who hoards grain,
but blessing crowns him who is willing to sell.

[27] He who seeks good finds goodwill,
but evil comes to him who searches for it.[o]

[28] Whoever trusts in his riches will fall,[p]
but the righteous will thrive like a green leaf.[q]

[29] He who brings trouble on his family will inherit only wind,
and the fool will be servant to the wise.[r]

[30] The fruit of the righteous is a tree of life,[s]
and he who wins souls is wise.

[31] If the righteous receive their due[t] on earth,
how much more the ungodly and the sinner!

11:25 [n]Mt 5:7; 2Co 9:6-9
11:27 [o]Est 7:10; Ps 7:15-16
11:28 [p]Job 31:24-28; Ps 49:6; 52:7; Mk 10:25; 1Ti 6:17 [q]Ps 1:3; 92:12-14; Jer 17:8
11:29 [r]Pr 14:19
11:30 [s]Jas 5:20
11:31 [t]Pr 13:21; Jer 25:29; 1Pe 4:18

ANCIENT TEXTS AND ARTIFACTS

Justice and Fraud in the Hymn to Shamash

Ancient scales

Preserving Bible Times; © Dr. James C. Martin; permission of The British Museum

PROVERBS 11 Desire for justice and fairness is a universal human trait. No society can function efficiently where injustice and fraud prevail. Indeed, people the world over have long believed that justice is not merely a human institution but the will of heaven. In the ancient Near East virtually all people believed that moral obligations were imposed upon them from above. Even though only Israel had the law of God, it would be a mistake to say that the other ancient religions lacked or ignored moral teachings.

A particularly clear example appears in an **Akkadian** hymn to Shamash, the sun god. Since the sun was thought to have been an all-seeing eye that looked down from above upon the affairs of humankind, it is not surprising that Shamash in particular would be associated with justice. In the hymn Shamash is praised for bringing to light the deeds of humanity. In particular, the hymn declares that the god sees and judges anyone who invests in a shady business scheme, commits fraud using inaccurate scales, avoids by some hoax full repayment of a debt or launches groundless lawsuits. Such people, the hymn insists, will see all of their profits disappear.

Proverbs 11:1 declares, "The LORD abhors dishonest scales, but accurate weights are his delight." The fact that the Bible is not the only ancient text that speaks in such terms concerning justice does not diminish the place of Scripture as God's special revelation. Indeed, it is precisely at this point that Biblical teaching meets the wisdom of the Gentiles: The Bible affirms what is best in the teachings of the sages of the other nations, while avoiding the superstition and degradation that accompany paganism. Thus, 1:7 can recommend to all its readers that the fear of the Lord is the only valid launching pad in the quest for wisdom. Its words affirm the Gentile desire for justice but assert that this longing is best fulfilled by turning to the God of Israel.

12 Whoever loves discipline loves knowledge,
but he who hates correction is stupid.[u]

[2] A good man obtains favor from the LORD,
but the LORD condemns a crafty man.

[3] A man cannot be established through wickedness,
but the righteous cannot be uprooted.[v]

[4] A wife of noble character is her husband's crown,
but a disgraceful wife is like decay in his bones.[w]

[5] The plans of the righteous are just,
but the advice of the wicked is deceitful.

[6] The words of the wicked lie in wait for blood,
but the speech of the upright rescues them.[x]

[7] Wicked men are overthrown and are no more,[y]
but the house of the righteous stands firm.[z]

[8] A man is praised according to his wisdom,
but men with warped minds are despised.

[9] Better to be a nobody and yet have a servant
than pretend to be somebody and have no food.

[10] A righteous man cares for the needs of his animal,
but the kindest acts of the wicked are cruel.

[11] He who works his land will have abundant food,
but he who chases fantasies lacks judgment.[a]

[12] The wicked desire the plunder of evil men,
but the root of the righteous flourishes.

[13] An evil man is trapped by his sinful talk,[b]
but a righteous man escapes trouble.[c]

[14] From the fruit of his lips a man is filled with good things[d]
as surely as the work of his hands rewards him.[e]

[15] The way of a fool seems right to him,[f]
but a wise man listens to advice.

[16] A fool shows his annoyance at once,
but a prudent man overlooks an insult.[g]

[17] A truthful witness gives honest testimony,
but a false witness tells lies.[h]

[18] Reckless words pierce like a sword,[i]
but the tongue of the wise brings healing.[j]

[19] Truthful lips endure forever,
but a lying tongue lasts only a moment.

[20] There is deceit in the hearts of those who plot evil,
but joy for those who promote peace.

[21] No harm befalls the righteous,[k]
but the wicked have their fill of trouble.

12:1 [u]Pr 9:7-9; 15:5,10,12,32
12:3 [v]Pr 10:25
12:4 [w]Pr 14:30
12:6 [x]Pr 14:3
12:7 [y]Ps 37:36 [z]Pr 10:25
12:11 [a]Pr 28:19
12:13 [b]Pr 18:7 [c]Pr 21:23; 2Pe 2:9
12:14 [d]Pr 13:2; 15:23; 18:20 [e]Isa 3:10-11
12:15 [f]Pr 14:12; 16:2,25; Lk 18:11
12:16 [g]Pr 29:11
12:17 [h]Pr 14:5, 25
12:18 [i]Ps 57:4 [j]Pr 15:4
12:21 [k]Ps 91:10

12:9 Even people of moderate means commonly had servants (see Jdg 6:15,27).

12:22 [l]Pr 6:17; Rev 22:15 [m]Pr 11:20

[22] The LORD detests lying lips,[l]
but he delights in men who are truthful.[m]

12:23 [n]Pr 10:14; 13:16

[23] A prudent man keeps his knowledge to himself,[n]
but the heart of fools blurts out folly.

12:24 [o]Pr 10:4

[24] Diligent hands will rule,
but laziness ends in slave labor.[o]

12:25 [p]Pr 15:13; Isa 50:4

[25] An anxious heart weighs a man down,[p]
but a kind word cheers him up.

[26] A righteous man is cautious in friendship,[a]
but the way of the wicked leads them astray.

[27] The lazy man does not roast[b] his game,
but the diligent man prizes his possessions.

12:28 [q]Dt 30:15

[28] In the way of righteousness there is life;[q]
along that path is immortality.

13:1 [r]Pr 10:1

13 A wise son heeds his father's instruction,
but a mocker does not listen to rebuke.[r]

13:2 [s]Pr 12:14

[2] From the fruit of his lips a man enjoys good things,[s]
but the unfaithful have a craving for violence.

13:3 [t]Jas 3:2 [u]Pr 21:23 [v]Pr 18:7,20-21

[3] He who guards his lips[t] guards his life,[u]
but he who speaks rashly will come to ruin.[v]

[4] The sluggard craves and gets nothing,
but the desires of the diligent are fully satisfied.

[5] The righteous hate what is false,
but the wicked bring shame and disgrace.

13:6 [w]Pr 11:3,5

[6] Righteousness guards the man of integrity,
but wickedness overthrows the sinner.[w]

13:7 [x]2Co 6:10

[7] One man pretends to be rich, yet has nothing;
another pretends to be poor, yet has great wealth.[x]

[8] A man's riches may ransom his life,
but a poor man hears no threat.

13:9 [y]Job 18:5; Pr 4:18-19; 24:20

[9] The light of the righteous shines brightly,
but the lamp of the wicked is snuffed out.[y]

[10] Pride only breeds quarrels,
but wisdom is found in those who take advice.

13:11 [z]Pr 10:2

[11] Dishonest money dwindles away,[z]
but he who gathers money little by little makes it grow.

[12] Hope deferred makes the heart sick,
but a longing fulfilled is a tree of life.

13:13 [a]Nu 15:31; 2Ch 36:16

[13] He who scorns instruction will pay for it,[a]
but he who respects a command is rewarded.

13:14 [b]Pr 10:11 [c]Pr 14:27

[14] The teaching of the wise is a fountain of life,[b]
turning a man from the snares of death.[c]

[15] Good understanding wins favor,
but the way of the unfaithful is hard.[c]

[a] 26 Or *man is a guide to his neighbor* [b] 27 The meaning of the Hebrew for this word is uncertain. [c] 15 Or *unfaithful does not endure*

[16] Every prudent man acts out of knowledge,
but a fool exposes his folly.[d] **13:16** [d]Pr 12:23

[17] A wicked messenger falls into trouble,
but a trustworthy envoy brings healing.[e] **13:17** [e]Pr 25:13

[18] He who ignores discipline comes to poverty and shame,
but whoever heeds correction is honored.[f] **13:18** [f]Pr 15:5, 31-32

[19] A longing fulfilled is sweet to the soul,
but fools detest turning from evil.

[20] He who walks with the wise grows wise,
but a companion of fools suffers harm.[g] **13:20** [g]Pr 15:31

[21] Misfortune pursues the sinner,
but prosperity is the reward of the righteous.[h] **13:21** [h]Ps 32:10

[22] A good man leaves an inheritance for his children's children,
but a sinner's wealth is stored up for the righteous.[i] **13:22** [i]Job 27:17; Ecc 2:26

[23] A poor man's field may produce abundant food,
but injustice sweeps it away.

[24] He who spares the rod hates his son,
but he who loves him is careful to discipline him.[j] **13:24** [j]Pr 19:18; 22:15; 23:13-14; 29:15,17; Heb 12:7

[25] The righteous eat to their hearts' content,
but the stomach of the wicked goes hungry.[k] **13:25** [k]Ps 34:10; Pr 10:3

14

The wise woman builds her house,[l] **14:1** [l]Pr 24:3
but with her own hands the foolish one tears hers down.

[2] He whose walk is upright fears the LORD,
but he whose ways are devious despises him.

[3] A fool's talk brings a rod to his back,
but the lips of the wise protect them.[m] **14:3** [m]Pr 12:6

[4] Where there are no oxen, the manger is empty,
but from the strength of an ox comes an abundant harvest.

[5] A truthful witness does not deceive,
but a false witness pours out lies.[n] **14:5** [n]Pr 6:19; 12:17

[6] The mocker seeks wisdom and finds none,
but knowledge comes easily to the discerning.

[7] Stay away from a foolish man,
for you will not find knowledge on his lips.

[8] The wisdom of the prudent is to give thought to their ways,
but the folly of fools is deception.[o] **14:8** [o]ver 24

[9] Fools mock at making amends for sin,
but goodwill is found among the upright.

[10] Each heart knows its own bitterness,
and no one else can share its joy.

[11] The house of the wicked will be destroyed,
but the tent of the upright will flourish.[p] **14:11** [p]Pr 3:33; 12:7

14:4 Taking good care of one's oxen (the means of production) was a prerequisite for a good harvest.

14:12 [q]Pr 12:15 [r]Pr 16:25
14:13 [s]Ecc 2:2
14:14 [t]Pr 1:31 [u]Pr 12:14
14:16 [v]Pr 22:3
14:17 [w]ver 29
14:19 [x]Pr 11:29
14:20 [y]Pr 19:4,7

12 There is a way that seems right to a man,[q]
but in the end it leads to death.[r]

13 Even in laughter[s] the heart may ache,
and joy may end in grief.

14 The faithless will be fully repaid for their ways,[t]
and the good man rewarded for his.[u]

15 A simple man believes anything,
but a prudent man gives thought to his steps.

16 A wise man fears the LORD and shuns evil,[v]
but a fool is hotheaded and reckless.

17 A quick-tempered man does foolish things,[w]
and a crafty man is hated.

18 The simple inherit folly,
but the prudent are crowned with knowledge.

19 Evil men will bow down in the presence of the good,
and the wicked at the gates of the righteous.[x]

20 The poor are shunned even by their neighbors,
but the rich have many friends.[y]

The Poor and the Afflicted in Ancient Wisdom Literature

PROVERBS 14 The Wisdom Literature of the Old Testament has a great deal to say about the poor and afflicted. The source of poverty is variously attributed in its passages. In many proverbs, for instance, it is represented as a state one brings upon oneself through laziness, haste, lack of discipline or excessive or undisciplined consumption. However, other texts in both Proverbs and Job assert that scarcity can be attributed to injustice at the hands of greedy or corrupt people (cf. Job 24).[1] Poverty may cause sorrow (Pr 31:7), abandonment or vulnerability (18:23) and can lead to crime.

Those who are privileged to be in positions of affluence are continually exhorted to support the poor and to avoid exacerbating their affliction by oppression. Oppressors of the needy in effect taunt God their Maker, while those who are gracious to the less fortunate honor him (14:31). A mark of the righteous is their concern for the underprivileged (Job 29:12–17; Pr 29:7), and rulers in particular are exhorted to demonstrate compassion toward the needy (28:3). It is remarkable that the persons in positions of power who wrote most of Israel's Wisdom Literature did not present the poor as immoral or second-class, but as neighbors in need of mercy. On the other hand, there is never an indication that the needy are necessarily more pious; after all, poverty was never presented as an ideal of Israelite society (Dt 15:4).

The poor are not the only victims of oppression—even the king of Israel suffered affliction at the hands of his enemies (Ps 94:2,16–17; cf. Ecc 10:7). In the face of such adversity, whether one is a privileged king or an impoverished beggar, Scripture indicates that the proper response is faith in the Lord, the righteous Judge over all iniquity and injustice. Above all else, a righteous individual is to be dedicated to the Lord, knowing that it is better to be a penniless person of integrity than a prosperous individual of proud or oppressive ways (Pr 28:6,11).

[1]See also "The Desire for Justice in the Eloquent Peasant" on page 1226.

[21] He who despises his neighbor sins,[z]
but blessed is he who is kind to the needy.[a]

[22] Do not those who plot evil go astray?
But those who plan what is good find[a] love and faithfulness.

[23] All hard work brings a profit,
but mere talk leads only to poverty.

[24] The wealth of the wise is their crown,
but the folly of fools yields folly.

[25] A truthful witness saves lives,
but a false witness is deceitful.[b]

[26] He who fears the LORD has a secure fortress,[c]
and for his children it will be a refuge.

[27] The fear of the LORD is a fountain of life,
turning a man from the snares of death.[d]

[28] A large population is a king's glory,
but without subjects a prince is ruined.

[29] A patient man has great understanding,
but a quick-tempered man displays folly.[e]

[30] A heart at peace gives life to the body,
but envy rots the bones.[f]

[31] He who oppresses the poor shows contempt for their Maker,[g]
but whoever is kind to the needy honors God.

[32] When calamity comes, the wicked are brought down,[h]
but even in death the righteous have a refuge.[i]

[33] Wisdom reposes in the heart of the discerning[j]
and even among fools she lets herself be known.[b]

[34] Righteousness exalts a nation,[k]
but sin is a disgrace to any people.

[35] A king delights in a wise servant,
but a shameful servant incurs his wrath.[l]

14:21 zPr 11:12 aPs 41:1; Pr 19:17
14:25 bver 5
14:26 cPr 18:10; 19:23; Isa 33:6
14:27 dPr 13:14
14:29 eEcc 7:8-9; Jas 1:19
14:30 fPr 12:4
14:31 gPr 17:5
14:32 hPr 6:15 iJob 13:15; 2Ti 4:18
14:33 jPr 2:6-10
14:34 kPr 11:11
14:35 lMt 24:45-51; 25:14-30

15

A gentle answer turns away wrath,[m]
but a harsh word stirs up anger.

[2] The tongue of the wise commends knowledge,
but the mouth of the fool gushes folly.[n]

[3] The eyes[o] of the LORD are everywhere,[p]
keeping watch on the wicked and the good.[q]

[4] The tongue that brings healing is a tree of life,
but a deceitful tongue crushes the spirit.

[5] A fool spurns his father's discipline,
but whoever heeds correction shows prudence.[r]

15:1 mPr 25:15
15:2 nPr 12:23
15:3 o2Ch 16:9 pJob 31:4; Heb 4:13 qJob 34:21; Jer 16:17
15:5 rPr 13:1

[a] 22 Or *show* [b] 33 Hebrew; Septuagint and Syriac / *but in the heart of fools she is not known*

14:21 The book of Proverbs is replete with admonitions concerning one's neighbor, of which this verse is the epitome. Due regard for one's neighbor is expressed in the great Old and New Testament precept, "Love your neighbor as yourself" (Lev 19:18; Mt 19:19). The parable of the Good Samaritan (Lk 10:30–37) was given to answer the question, "And who is my neighbor?" (Lk 10:29).

15:1 The truth that "a harsh word stirs up anger" is exemplified in Nabal's sarcastic response that put David in a fighting mood (1Sa 25:10–13). See "Bywords and Insults in the Ancient World" on page 431.

15:6 [s]Pr 8:21
15:8 [t]Pr 21:27; Isa 1:11; Jer 6:20 [u]ver 29
15:9 [v]Pr 21:21; 1Ti 6:11
15:10 [w]Pr 1:31-32; 5:12
15:11 [x]Job 26:6; Ps 139:8 [y]2Ch 6:30; Ps 44:21
15:12 [z]Am 5:10
15:13 [a]Pr 12:25; 17:22; 18:14
15:14 [b]Pr 18:15
15:15 [c]ver 13
15:16 [d]Ps 37:16-17; Pr 16:8; 1Ti 6:6
15:17 [e]Pr 17:1
15:18 [f]Pr 26:21 [g]Ge 13:8
15:19 [h]Pr 22:5
15:20 [i]Pr 10:1
15:21 [j]Pr 10:23
15:22 [k]Pr 11:14
15:23 [l]Pr 12:14 [m]Pr 25:11
15:25 [n]Pr 12:7 [o]Dt 19:14; Ps 68:5-6; Pr 23:10-11
15:26 [p]Pr 6:16

6 The house of the righteous contains great treasure,[s]
but the income of the wicked brings them trouble.

7 The lips of the wise spread knowledge;
not so the hearts of fools.

8 The LORD detests the sacrifice of the wicked,[t]
but the prayer of the upright pleases him.[u]

9 The LORD detests the way of the wicked
but he loves those who pursue righteousness.[v]

10 Stern discipline awaits him who leaves the path;
he who hates correction will die.[w]

11 Death and Destruction[a] lie open before the LORD[x]—
how much more the hearts of men![y]

12 A mocker resents correction;[z]
he will not consult the wise.

13 A happy heart makes the face cheerful,
but heartache crushes the spirit.[a]

14 The discerning heart seeks knowledge,[b]
but the mouth of a fool feeds on folly.

15 All the days of the oppressed are wretched,
but the cheerful heart has a continual feast.[c]

16 Better a little with the fear of the LORD
than great wealth with turmoil.[d]

17 Better a meal of vegetables where there is love
than a fattened calf with hatred.[e]

18 A hot-tempered man stirs up dissension,[f]
but a patient man calms a quarrel.[g]

19 The way of the sluggard is blocked with thorns,[h]
but the path of the upright is a highway.

20 A wise son brings joy to his father,[i]
but a foolish man despises his mother.

21 Folly delights a man who lacks judgment,[j]
but a man of understanding keeps a straight course.

22 Plans fail for lack of counsel,
but with many advisers they succeed.[k]

23 A man finds joy in giving an apt reply[l]—
and how good is a timely word![m]

24 The path of life leads upward for the wise
to keep him from going down to the grave.[b]

25 The LORD tears down the proud man's house[n]
but he keeps the widow's boundaries intact.[o]

26 The LORD detests the thoughts of the wicked,[p]
but those of the pure are pleasing to him.

[a] 11 Hebrew *Sheol and Abaddon* [b] 24 Hebrew *Sheol*

15:11 See "Sheol, Hades, Gehenna, the Abyss and Tartarus: Images of Hell" on page 946.
15:25 In ancient times boundary stones marked the periphery of a person's property. Anyone who moved such a stone was, in effect, stealing land (see Job 24:2; Ps 68:5; Pr 22:28; see also Dt 19:14 and its note).

[27] A greedy man brings trouble to his family,
but he who hates bribes will live.[q]

[28] The heart of the righteous weighs its answers,[r]
but the mouth of the wicked gushes evil.

[29] The LORD is far from the wicked
but he hears the prayer of the righteous.[s]

[30] A cheerful look brings joy to the heart,
and good news gives health to the bones.

[31] He who listens to a life-giving rebuke
will be at home among the wise.[t]

[32] He who ignores discipline despises himself,[u]
but whoever heeds correction gains understanding.

[33] The fear of the LORD[v] teaches a man wisdom,[a]
and humility comes before honor.[w]

16 To man belong the plans of the heart,
but from the LORD comes the reply of the tongue.[x]

[2] All a man's ways seem innocent to him,
but motives are weighed by the LORD.[y]

[3] Commit to the LORD whatever you do,
and your plans will succeed.[z]

[4] The LORD works out everything for his own ends[a]—
even the wicked for a day of disaster.[b]

[5] The LORD detests all the proud of heart.[c]
Be sure of this: They will not go unpunished.[d]

[6] Through love and faithfulness sin is atoned for;
through the fear of the LORD a man avoids evil.[e]

[7] When a man's ways are pleasing to the LORD,
he makes even his enemies live at peace with him.

[8] Better a little with righteousness
than much gain[f] with injustice.

[9] In his heart a man plans his course,
but the LORD determines his steps.[g]

[10] The lips of a king speak as an oracle,
and his mouth should not betray justice.

[11] Honest scales and balances are from the LORD;
all the weights in the bag are of his making.[h]

[12] Kings detest wrongdoing,
for a throne is established through righteousness.[i]

[13] Kings take pleasure in honest lips;
they value a man who speaks the truth.[j]

15:27 [q]Ex 23:8; Isa 33:15
15:28 [r]1Pe 3:15
15:29 [s]Ps 145:18-19
15:31 [t]ver 5
15:32 [u]Pr 1:7
15:33 [v]Pr 1:7 [w]Pr 18:12
16:1 [x]Pr 19:21
16:2 [y]Pr 21:2
16:3 [z]Ps 37:5-6; Pr 3:5-6
16:4 [a]Isa 43:7 [b]Ro 9:22
16:5 [c]Pr 6:16 [d]Pr 11:20-21
16:6 [e]Pr 14:16
16:8 [f]Ps 37:16
16:9 [g]Jer 10:23
16:11 [h]Pr 11:1
16:12 [i]Pr 25:5
16:13 [j]Pr 14:35

[a] 33 Or *Wisdom teaches the fear of the LORD*

16:10 As God's representative, a king acted as judge, discerning between right and wrong (see 1Ki 3:9). His judgments were like divine oracles for the people (see 2Sa 14:17; 1Ki 3:28).

16:11 Stones of different sizes were used by merchants to weigh and measure quantities of silver for payment (cf. Mic 6:11). Weights with dishonest labels allowed for cheating.

16:14 [k]Pr 19:12

[14] A king's wrath is a messenger of death,[k]
but a wise man will appease it.

16:15 [l]Job 29:24

[15] When a king's face brightens, it means life;[l]
his favor is like a rain cloud in spring.

16:16 [m]Pr 8:10, 19

[16] How much better to get wisdom than gold,
to choose understanding rather than silver![m]

[17] The highway of the upright avoids evil;
he who guards his way guards his life.

16:18 [n]Pr 11:2; 18:12

[18] Pride goes before destruction,
a haughty spirit before a fall.[n]

[19] Better to be lowly in spirit and among the oppressed
than to share plunder with the proud.

16:20 [o]Ps 2:12; 34:8; Pr 19:8; Jer 17:7

[20] Whoever gives heed to instruction prospers,
and blessed is he who trusts in the LORD.[o]

16:21 [p]ver 23

[21] The wise in heart are called discerning,
and pleasant words promote instruction.[a][p]

16:22 [q]Pr 13:14

[22] Understanding is a fountain of life to those who have it,[q]
but folly brings punishment to fools.

[23] A wise man's heart guides his mouth,
and his lips promote instruction.[b]

16:24 [r]Pr 24:13-14

[24] Pleasant words are a honeycomb,
sweet to the soul and healing to the bones.[r]

16:25 [s]Pr 12:15 [t]Pr 14:12

[25] There is a way that seems right to a man,[s]
but in the end it leads to death.[t]

[26] The laborer's appetite works for him;
his hunger drives him on.

16:27 [u]Jas 3:6

[27] A scoundrel plots evil,
and his speech is like a scorching fire.[u]

16:28 [v]Pr 15:18 [w]Pr 17:9

[28] A perverse man stirs up dissension,[v]
and a gossip separates close friends.[w]

16:29 [x]Pr 1:10; 12:26

[29] A violent man entices his neighbor
and leads him down a path that is not good.[x]

[30] He who winks with his eye is plotting perversity;
he who purses his lips is bent on evil.

16:31 [y]Pr 20:29

[31] Gray hair is a crown of splendor;[y]
it is attained by a righteous life.

[32] Better a patient man than a warrior,
a man who controls his temper than one who takes a city.

[a] *21* Or *words make a man persuasive* [b] *23* Or *mouth / and makes his lips persuasive*

16:14 An angry king could quickly and effectively bring about someone's death (see 19:12; Est 7:7–10; Mt 22:7; Lk 19:27). Compare Daniel's response to the rage of Nebuchadnezzar (Da 2:12–16).
16:15 Spring rain was a sign of good things to come, a precursor to abundant barley and wheat harvests (from mid-April to mid-June). See "Food and Agriculture" on page 390.
16:17 There are about 25 Hebrew and Greek words translated "way" in the Bible. The term is often used metaphorically in the Old Testament to describe conduct or manner of life, whether of God or of human beings (see also Dt 5:33; Ps 1:6).
16:31 Deep respect was considered the due of the elderly (see Lev 19:32).

33 The lot is cast into the lap,
but its every decision is from the LORD.[z]

16:33 [z]Pr 18:18; 29:26

17 Better a dry crust with peace and quiet
than a house full of feasting,[a] with strife.[a]

17:1 [a]Pr 15:16, 17

2 A wise servant will rule over a disgraceful son,
and will share the inheritance as one of the brothers.

3 The crucible for silver and the furnace for gold,[b]
but the LORD tests the heart.[c]

17:3 [b]Pr 27:21 [c]1Ch 29:17; Ps 26:2; Jer 17:10

4 A wicked man listens to evil lips;
a liar pays attention to a malicious tongue.

5 He who mocks the poor shows contempt for their Maker;[d]
whoever gloats over disaster[e] will not go unpunished.[f]

17:5 [d]Pr 14:31 [e]Job 31:29 [f]Ob 1:12

6 Children's children[g] are a crown to the aged,
and parents are the pride of their children.

17:6 [g]Pr 13:22

7 Arrogant[b] lips are unsuited to a fool—
how much worse lying lips to a ruler!

8 A bribe is a charm to the one who gives it;
wherever he turns, he succeeds.

9 He who covers over an offense promotes love,[h]
but whoever repeats the matter separates close friends.[i]

17:9 [h]Pr 10:12 [i]Pr 16:28

10 A rebuke impresses a man of discernment
more than a hundred lashes a fool.

11 An evil man is bent only on rebellion;
a merciless official will be sent against him.

12 Better to meet a bear robbed of her cubs
than a fool in his folly.

13 If a man pays back evil[j] for good,
evil will never leave his house.

17:13 [j]Ps 109:4-5; Jer 18:20

14 Starting a quarrel is like breaching a dam;
so drop the matter before a dispute breaks out.[k]

17:14 [k]Pr 20:3

15 Acquitting the guilty and condemning the innocent[l]—
the LORD detests them both.[m]

17:15 [l]Pr 18:5 [m]Ex 23:6-7; Isa 5:23

16 Of what use is money in the hand of a fool,
since he has no desire to get wisdom?[n]

17:16 [n]Pr 23:23

17 A friend loves at all times,
and a brother is born for adversity.

18 A man lacking in judgment strikes hands in pledge
and puts up security for his neighbor.[o]

17:18 [o]Pr 6:1-5; 11:15; 22:26-27

[a] *1* Hebrew *sacrifices* [b] *7* Or *Eloquent*

16:33 Casting lots was a commonly used method for making decisions or for determining God's will (see Ex 28:30; Nu 26:53; Ne 11:1; Ps 22:18; Jnh 1:7; Ac 1:26). There were various methods of casting lots; here the lot may have involved several pebbles placed in the fold of a garment and then drawn out or shaken to the ground. God, not chance, was in control of the outcome (see 16:1,3–4,9). See "Casting Lots" on page 744.

17:3 Silver and gold were refined to remove their impurities (see Ps 12:6).

17:6 To live to see one's grandchildren was considered a great blessing (see Ge 48:11; Ps 109:12 and its note; 128:5–6; "The Israelite Family" on p. 997; and "The Role of the Patriarch in Family Life" on p. 30).

[19] He who loves a quarrel loves sin;
he who builds a high gate invites destruction.

[20] A man of perverse heart does not prosper;
he whose tongue is deceitful falls into trouble.

[21] To have a fool for a son brings grief;
there is no joy for the father of a fool.[p]

[22] A cheerful heart is good medicine,
but a crushed spirit dries up the bones.[q]

[23] A wicked man accepts a bribe[r] in secret
to pervert the course of justice.

[24] A discerning man keeps wisdom in view,
but a fool's eyes[s] wander to the ends of the earth.

[25] A foolish son brings grief to his father
and bitterness to the one who bore him.[t]

[26] It is not good to punish an innocent man,[u]
or to flog officials for their integrity.

[27] A man of knowledge uses words with restraint,
and a man of understanding is even-tempered.[v]

[28] Even a fool is thought wise if he keeps silent,
and discerning if he holds his tongue.[w]

18 An unfriendly man pursues selfish ends;
he defies all sound judgment.

[2] A fool finds no pleasure in understanding
but delights in airing his own opinions.[x]

[3] When wickedness comes, so does contempt,
and with shame comes disgrace.

[4] The words of a man's mouth are deep waters,
but the fountain of wisdom is a bubbling brook.

[5] It is not good to be partial to the wicked[y]
or to deprive the innocent of justice.[z]

[6] A fool's lips bring him strife,
and his mouth invites a beating.

[7] A fool's mouth is his undoing,
and his lips are a snare[a] to his soul.[b]

[8] The words of a gossip are like choice morsels;
they go down to a man's inmost parts.[c]

[9] One who is slack in his work
is brother to one who destroys.[d]

[10] The name of the LORD is a strong tower;[e]
the righteous run to it and are safe.

[11] The wealth of the rich is their fortified city;[f]
they imagine it an unscalable wall.

[12] Before his downfall a man's heart is proud,
but humility comes before honor.[g]

17:21 [p]Pr 10:1
17:22 [q]Ps 22:15; Pr 15:13
17:23 [r]Ex 23:8
17:24 [s]Ecc 2:14
17:25 [t]Pr 10:1
17:26 [u]Pr 18:5
17:27 [v]Pr 14:29; Jas 1:19
17:28 [w]Job 13:5
18:2 [x]Pr 12:23
18:5 [y]Lev 19:15; Pr 24:23-25; 28:21 [z]Ps 82:2; Pr 17:15
18:7 [a]Ps 140:9 [b]Ps 64:8; Pr 10:14; 12:13; 13:3; Ecc 10:12
18:8 [c]Pr 26:22
18:9 [d]Pr 28:24
18:10 [e]2Sa 22:3; Ps 61:3
18:11 [f]Pr 10:15
18:12 [g]Pr 11:2; 15:33; 16:18

13 He who answers before listening—
that is his folly and his shame.[h]

14 A man's spirit sustains him in sickness,
but a crushed spirit who can bear?[i]

15 The heart of the discerning acquires knowledge;[j]
the ears of the wise seek it out.

16 A gift[k] opens the way for the giver
and ushers him into the presence of the great.

17 The first to present his case seems right,
till another comes forward and questions him.

18 Casting the lot settles disputes[l]
and keeps strong opponents apart.

19 An offended brother is more unyielding than a fortified city,
and disputes are like the barred gates of a citadel.

20 From the fruit of his mouth a man's stomach is filled;
with the harvest from his lips he is satisfied.[m]

21 The tongue has the power of life and death,
and those who love it will eat its fruit.[n]

22 He who finds a wife finds what is good[o]
and receives favor from the LORD.[p]

23 A poor man pleads for mercy,
but a rich man answers harshly.

24 A man of many companions may come to ruin,
but there is a friend who sticks closer than a brother.[q]

19

Better a poor man whose walk is blameless
than a fool whose lips are perverse.[r]

2 It is not good to have zeal without knowledge,
nor to be hasty and miss the way.[s]

3 A man's own folly ruins his life,
yet his heart rages against the LORD.

4 Wealth brings many friends,
but a poor man's friend deserts him.[t]

5 A false witness[u] will not go unpunished,
and he who pours out lies will not go free.[v]

6 Many curry favor with a ruler,[w]
and everyone is the friend of a man who gives gifts.[x]

7 A poor man is shunned by all his relatives—
how much more do his friends avoid him!
Though he pursues them with pleading,
they are nowhere to be found.[a][y]

8 He who gets wisdom loves his own soul;
he who cherishes understanding prospers.[z]

18:13 [h]Pr 20:25; Jn 7:51
18:14 [i]Pr 15:13; 17:22
18:15 [j]Pr 15:14
18:16 [k]Ge 32:20
18:18 [l]Pr 16:33
18:20 [m]Pr 12:14
18:21 [n]Pr 13:2-3; Mt 12:37
18:22 [o]Pr 12:4 [p]Pr 19:14; 31:10
18:24 [q]Pr 17:17; Jn 15:13-15
19:1 [r]Pr 28:6
19:2 [s]Pr 29:20
19:4 [t]Pr 14:20
19:5 [u]Ex 23:1 [v]Dt 19:19; Pr 21:28
19:6 [w]Pr 29:26 [x]Pr 17:8; 18:16
19:7 [y]ver 4; Ps 38:11
19:8 [z]Pr 16:20

[a] 7 The meaning of the Hebrew for this sentence is uncertain.

18:18 See the note on 16:33.

[9]A false witness will not go unpunished,
and he who pours out lies will perish.[a]

[10]It is not fitting for a fool[b] to live in luxury—
how much worse for a slave to rule over princes![c]

[11]A man's wisdom gives him patience;[d]
it is to his glory to overlook an offense.

[12]A king's rage is like the roar of a lion,
but his favor is like dew[e] on the grass.[f]

[13]A foolish son is his father's ruin,[g]
and a quarrelsome wife is like a constant dripping.[h]

[14]Houses and wealth are inherited from parents,[i]
but a prudent wife is from the LORD.[j]

[15]Laziness brings on deep sleep,
and the shiftless man goes hungry.[k]

[16]He who obeys instructions guards his life,
but he who is contemptuous of his ways will die.[l]

[17]He who is kind to the poor lends to the LORD,
and he will reward him for what he has done.[m]

[18]Discipline your son, for in that there is hope;
do not be a willing party to his death.[n]

[19]A hot-tempered man must pay the penalty;
if you rescue him, you will have to do it again.

[20]Listen to advice and accept instruction,[o]
and in the end you will be wise.[p]

[21]Many are the plans in a man's heart,
but it is the LORD's purpose that prevails.[q]

[22]What a man desires is unfailing love[a];
better to be poor than a liar.

[23]The fear of the LORD leads to life:
Then one rests content, untouched by trouble.[r]

[24]The sluggard buries his hand in the dish;
he will not even bring it back to his mouth![s]

[25]Flog a mocker, and the simple will learn prudence;
rebuke a discerning man, and he will gain knowledge.[t]

[26]He who robs his father and drives out his mother[u]
is a son who brings shame and disgrace.

[27]Stop listening to instruction, my son,
and you will stray from the words of knowledge.

[28]A corrupt witness mocks at justice,
and the mouth of the wicked gulps down evil.[v]

[29]Penalties are prepared for mockers,
and beatings for the backs of fools.[w]

19:9 [a]ver 5
19:10 [b]Pr 26:1 [c]Pr 30:21-23; Ecc 10:5-7
19:11 [d]Pr 16:32
19:12 [e]Ps 133:3 [f]Pr 16:14-15
19:13 [g]Pr 10:1 [h]Pr 21:9
19:14 [i]2Co 12:14 [j]Pr 18:22
19:15 [k]Pr 6:9; 10:4
19:16 [l]Pr 16:17; Lk 10:28
19:17 [m]Mt 10:42; 2Co 9:6-8
19:18 [n]Pr 13:24; 23:13-14
19:20 [o]Pr 4:1 [p]Pr 12:15
19:21 [q]Ps 33:11; Pr 16:9; Isa 14:24,27
19:23 [r]Ps 25:13; Pr 12:21; 1Ti 4:8
19:24 [s]Pr 26:15
19:25 [t]Pr 9:9; 21:11
19:26 [u]Pr 28:24
19:28 [v]Job 15:16
19:29 [w]Pr 26:3

[a] 22 Or *A man's greed is his shame*

19:26 Children were expected to care for their sick or elderly parents (cf. Isa 51:18; see the note on Ps 109:12; "The Israelite Family" on p. 997; and "The Role of the Patriarch in Family Life" on p. 30). Robbing one's parents (cf. Jdg 17:1–2), attacking them or calling down curses on them (Ex 21:15,17) were all viewed as serious crimes.

20

Wine is a mocker and beer a brawler;
whoever is led astray by them is not wise.[x]

2 A king's wrath is like the roar of a lion;[y]
he who angers him forfeits his life.[z]

3 It is to a man's honor to avoid strife,
but every fool is quick to quarrel.[a]

4 A sluggard does not plow in season;
so at harvest time he looks but finds nothing.

5 The purposes of a man's heart are deep waters,
but a man of understanding draws them out.

6 Many a man claims to have unfailing love,
but a faithful man who can find?[b]

7 The righteous man leads a blameless life;
blessed are his children after him.[c]

8 When a king sits on his throne to judge,
he winnows out all evil with his eyes.[d]

9 Who can say, "I have kept my heart pure;
I am clean and without sin"?[e]

10 Differing weights and differing measures—
the LORD detests them both.[f]

11 Even a child is known by his actions,
by whether his conduct is pure[g] and right.

20:1 [x]Pr 31:4
20:2 [y]Pr 19:12 [z]Pr 8:36
20:3 [a]Pr 17:14
20:6 [b]Ps 12:1
20:7 [c]Ps 37:25-26; 112:2
20:8 [d]ver 26; Pr 25:4-5
20:9 [e]1Ki 8:46; Ecc 7:20; 1Jn 1:8
20:10 [f]ver 23; Pr 11:1
20:11 [g]Mt 7:16

20:10 See the notes on 11:1 and 16:11.

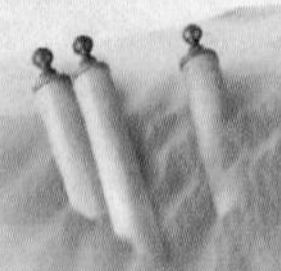

ANCIENT TEXTS AND ARTIFACTS

The Instructions of Anii

PROVERBS 20 A number of ancient texts are described as "wisdom literature" in that they give the reader advice on how to live a prudent life.[1] Some have similarities to Proverbs, illustrating that the quest for virtue was a widespread phenomenon in the ancient Near East. These include the Instructions of Anii (also spelled "Any"), a writing that dates to Egypt's Eighteenth Dynasty. The text purports to have been written by the scribe Anii and is set in the context of the Egyptian middle class. Like the book of Proverbs, Anii:

- exhorts the reader to avoid beer drinking and warns about the disgrace of public drunkenness (see Pr 20:1).
- asserts that an individual should avoid the company of brawlers and violent men (see v. 3).
- advises against taking vengeance, urging the reader instead to seek divine help (cf. v. 22).
- warns the reader to stay away from the "strange woman," the prostitute or adulteress (vv. 23–35).

Not surprisingly, many of the other admonitions in Anii are unlike those in Proverbs. For example, Anii exhorts the reader to maintain the external, formal devotion the gods demand (making sacrifices, showing obeisance before idols, etc.), but in a perfunctory manner that is totally unlike the heartfelt piety of Proverbs. Anii also has some pleasant advice on domestic life, such as a warning for husbands not to fail to show appreciation for their wives' management of household affairs.

A curiosity of Anii is that it ends with a debate between Anii and his son Khonshotep, who complains that few people are able to maintain the virtuous life Anii prescribes. Anii counters that even a beast can be taught; Khonshotep's excuse will not stand.

[1]See "Ancient Near Eastern Wisdom" on page 960.

20:12 [h]Ps 94:9
20:13 [i]Pr 6:11; 19:15
20:16 [j]Ex 22:26 [k]Pr 27:13
20:17 [l]Pr 9:17
20:18 [m]Pr 11:14; 24:6
20:19 [n]Pr 11:13
20:20 [o]Pr 30:11 [p]Ex 21:17; Job 18:5
20:22 [q]Pr 24:29 [r]Ro 12:19
20:23 [s]ver 10
20:24 [t]Jer 10:23
20:25 [u]Ecc 5:2, 4-5
20:26 [v]ver 8
20:28 [w]Pr 29:14
20:29 [x]Pr 16:31

12 Ears that hear and eyes that see—
the LORD has made them both.[h]

13 Do not love sleep or you will grow poor;[i]
stay awake and you will have food
to spare.

14 "It's no good, it's no good!" says the buyer;
then off he goes and boasts about his
purchase.

15 Gold there is, and rubies in abundance,
but lips that speak knowledge are a
rare jewel.

16 Take the garment of one who puts up
security for a stranger;
hold it in pledge[j] if he does it for a
wayward woman.[k]

17 Food gained by fraud tastes sweet to a man,[l]
but he ends up with a mouth full of gravel.

18 Make plans by seeking advice;
if you wage war, obtain guidance.[m]

19 A gossip betrays a confidence;[n]
so avoid a man who talks too much.

20 If a man curses his father or mother,[o]
his lamp will be snuffed out in pitch darkness.[p]

21 An inheritance quickly gained at the beginning
will not be blessed at the end.

22 Do not say, "I'll pay you back for this wrong!"[q]
Wait for the LORD, and he will deliver you.[r]

23 The LORD detests differing weights,
and dishonest scales do not please him.[s]

24 A man's steps are directed by the LORD.
How then can anyone understand his own way?[t]

25 It is a trap for a man to dedicate something rashly
and only later to consider his vows.[u]

26 A wise king winnows out the wicked;
he drives the threshing wheel over them.[v]

27 The lamp of the LORD searches the spirit of a man[a];
it searches out his inmost being.

28 Love and faithfulness keep a king safe;
through love his throne is made secure.[w]

29 The glory of young men is their strength,
gray hair the splendor of the old.[x]

ANCIENT VOICES

Beware of a woman who is a stranger,
One not known in her town;
Don't stare at her when she goes by,
Do not know her carnally.
A deep water whose course is unknown,
Such is a woman away from her
husband.
"I am pretty," she tells you daily,
When she has no witnesses;
She is ready to ensnare you.

—INSTRUCTION OF ANII

See "The instructions of Anii."

[a] 27 Or *The spirit of man is the LORD's lamp*

20:14 Prices were often finalized through a bargaining process. Here the buyer was discrediting the quality of the article in order to purchase it more cheaply.
20:16 A garment could be taken as security for a debt (Dt 24:10–13). Accepting responsibility for someone else's debt was a serious and risky business (see the note on Pr 6:1).
20:26 For a description of the threshing process, see the note on Ruth 1:22 and "The Threshing Floor" on page 608.

30 Blows and wounds cleanse[y] away evil,
and beatings purge the inmost being.

21 The king's heart is in the hand of the LORD;
he directs it like a watercourse wherever he pleases.

2 All a man's ways seem right to him,
but the LORD weighs the heart.[z]

3 To do what is right and just
is more acceptable to the LORD than sacrifice.[a]

4 Haughty eyes[b] and a proud heart,
the lamp of the wicked, are sin!

5 The plans of the diligent lead to profit[c]
as surely as haste leads to poverty.

6 A fortune made by a lying tongue
is a fleeting vapor and a deadly snare.[a][d]

7 The violence of the wicked will drag them away,
for they refuse to do what is right.

8 The way of the guilty is devious,[e]
but the conduct of the innocent is upright.

9 Better to live on a corner of the roof
than share a house with a quarrelsome wife.[f]

10 The wicked man craves evil;
his neighbor gets no mercy from him.

11 When a mocker is punished, the simple gain wisdom;
when a wise man is instructed, he gets knowledge.[g]

12 The Righteous One[b] takes note of the house of the wicked
and brings the wicked to ruin.[h]

13 If a man shuts his ears to the cry of the poor,
he too will cry out and not be answered.[i]

14 A gift given in secret soothes anger,
and a bribe concealed in the cloak pacifies great wrath.[j]

15 When justice is done, it brings joy to the righteous
but terror to evildoers.[k]

16 A man who strays from the path of understanding
comes to rest in the company of the dead.[l]

17 He who loves pleasure will become poor;
whoever loves wine and oil will never be rich.[m]

18 The wicked become a ransom[n] for the righteous,
and the unfaithful for the upright.

19 Better to live in a desert
than with a quarrelsome and ill-tempered wife.[o]

20:30 [y]Pr 22:15
21:2 [z]Pr 16:2; 24:12; Lk 16:15
21:3 [a]1Sa 15:22; Pr 15:8; Isa 1:11; Hos 6:6; Mic 6:6-8
21:4 [b]Pr 6:17
21:5 [c]Pr 10:4; 28:22
21:6 [d]2Pe 2:3
21:8 [e]Pr 2:15
21:9 [f]Pr 25:24
21:11 [g]Pr 19:25
21:12 [h]Pr 14:11
21:13 [i]Mt 18:30-34; Jas 2:13
21:14 [j]Pr 18:16; 19:6
21:15 [k]Pr 10:29
21:16 [l]Ps 49:14
21:17 [m]Pr 23:20-21,29-35
21:18 [n]Pr 11:8; Isa 43:3
21:19 [o]ver 9

[a] 6 Some Hebrew manuscripts, Septuagint and Vulgate; most Hebrew manuscripts *vapor for those who seek death* [b] 12 Or *The righteous man*

21:9 Houses had flat roofs on which produce could be spread out to dry (see Jos 2:6). Small rooms could also be constructed there (see 2Ki 4:10; see also "The Israelite Town and Home" on p. 1205).
21:17 Wine and oil were common components of a lavish ancient Near Eastern lifestyle (see 23:20–21; Am 6:6). Oil was used in various lotions or perfumes, some of which were extremely expensive (Jn 12:5; see "Perfumes and Anointing Oils" on p. 1746).

20 In the house of the wise are stores of choice food and oil,
but a foolish man devours all he has.

21 He who pursues righteousness and love
finds life, prosperity[a] and honor.[p]

21:21 [p]Mt 5:6

22 A wise man attacks the city of the mighty[q]
and pulls down the stronghold in which they trust.

21:22 [q]Ecc 9:15-16

23 He who guards his mouth[r] and his tongue
keeps himself from calamity.[s]

21:23 [r]Jas 3:2 [s]Pr 12:13; 13:3

24 The proud and arrogant[t] man—"Mocker" is his name;
he behaves with overweening pride.

21:24 [t]Ps 1:1; Pr 1:22; Isa 16:6; Jer 48:29

25 The sluggard's craving will be the death of him,[u]
because his hands refuse to work.

21:25 [u]Pr 13:4

26 All day long he craves for more,
but the righteous give without sparing.[v]

21:26 [v]Ps 37:26; Mt 5:42; Eph 4:28

27 The sacrifice of the wicked is detestable[w]—
how much more so when brought with evil intent![x]

21:27 [w]Isa 66:3; Jer 6:20; Am 5:22 [x]Pr 15:8

28 A false witness will perish,[y]
and whoever listens to him will be destroyed forever.[b]

21:28 [y]Pr 19:5

29 A wicked man puts up a bold front,
but an upright man gives thought to his ways.

30 There is no wisdom,[z] no insight, no plan
that can succeed against the LORD.[a]

21:30 [z]Jer 9:23 [a]Isa 8:10; Ac 5:39

31 The horse is made ready for the day of battle,
but victory rests with the LORD.[b]

21:31 [b]Ps 3:8; 33:12-19; Isa 31:1

22

A good name is more desirable than great riches;
to be esteemed is better than silver or gold.[c]

22:1 [c]Ecc 7:1

2 Rich and poor have this in common:
The LORD is the Maker of them all.[d]

22:2 [d]Job 31:15

3 A prudent man sees danger and takes refuge,[e]
but the simple keep going and suffer for it.[f]

22:3 [e]Pr 14:16 [f]Pr 27:12

4 Humility and the fear of the LORD
bring wealth and honor and life.

5 In the paths of the wicked lie thorns and snares,[g]
but he who guards his soul stays far from them.

22:5 [g]Pr 15:19

6 Train[c] a child in the way he should go,[h]
and when he is old he will not turn from it.

22:6 [h]Eph 6:4

7 The rich rule over the poor,
and the borrower is servant to the lender.

8 He who sows wickedness reaps trouble,[i]
and the rod of his fury will be destroyed.[j]

22:8 [i]Job 4:8 [j]Ps 125:3

[a] 21 Or *righteousness* [b] 28 Or / *but the words of an obedient man will live on* [c] 6 Or *Start*

22:6 This verse is an exhortation extolling the importance of parental instruction (see "The Israelite Family" on p. 997). The training was imparted primarily through conversation, example and imitation; it utilized effectively the interest aroused by actual life situations, such as the Passover, the redemption of the firstborn and family rites (Ex 12:26–27; 13:14–16). The well-known penchant of the East for storytelling was also used in the vital transmission of religious truth and faith to the children. The command to the Israelites to write the precepts of the law on their doorposts and gates (Dt 6:9; 11:20) and on great plastered stones in the land (Dt 27:2–8) implies a general ability among the people of the time to read and write.

[9] A generous man will himself be blessed,[k]
for he shares his food with the poor.[l]

[10] Drive out the mocker, and out goes strife;
quarrels and insults are ended.[m]

[11] He who loves a pure heart and whose speech is gracious
will have the king for his friend.[n]

[12] The eyes of the LORD keep watch over knowledge,
but he frustrates the words of the unfaithful.

22:9 [k]2Co 9:6 [l]Pr 19:17
22:10 [m]Pr 18:6; 26:20
22:11 [n]Pr 16:13; Mt 5:8

ANCIENT TEXTS AND ARTIFACTS

The Teaching of Amenemope

PROVERBS 22 Arranged into 30 chapters of varying lengths, the Teaching of Amenemope is an Egyptian text probably dating to the time of **Rameses.** It is preserved complete on one **papyrus** housed in the British Museum, as well as in several fragments appearing in other collections. In this text Amenemope instructs his young son in the proper conduct and mindset of the ideal man. He is to be generous, contented, confidential, self-controlled, conciliatory toward his superiors and honoring to his god.

Scholars have found striking parallels to the Teaching of Amenemope in the book of Proverbs, especially in chapters 22 and 23. Chapter 1 of Amenemope begins with an injunction similar to that in Proverbs 2:2 to give one's ears to wisdom and one's heart to understanding (cf. 22:17). Both works warn against illegally expanding one's property by moving the boundary stones demarcating the border of a field (Amenemope, VII.11–14; Pr 22:28; 23:10). Both warn against robbing the poor (Amenemope, IV.4–5; Pr 22:22), associating with hot-tempered persons (Amenemope, XI.12–14; XV.13–14; Pr 22:24–25), being gluttonous at the table of an official (Amenemope, XXIII.13–20; Pr 23:1–3) and eating the food of a hoarder (Amenemope, XV.9–12; Pr 23:6–8). Both point out the propensity of riches to sprout wings and fly away like birds (Amenemope, X.4–5; Pr 23:4–5) and note that a person's reputation is more valuable than wealth (Amenemope, XVI.11–12; Pr 22:1), that the skilled will serve rulers (Amenemope, XXVII.15–17; Pr 22:29) and that generosity is the proper response toward the poor (Amenemope, XVI.5–10; Pr 22:9). In fact, many scholars propose that Amenemope's division into 30 chapters is referred to in the original Hebrew version of verse 20.

It is quite possible that the writer of these proverbs incorporated wisdom material from other sources, such as Amenemope, when compiling his work. This does not negate the inspired nature of the Biblical text, however. The compiler of Proverbs was able to make use of those elements of foreign wisdom literature that demonstrated proper morality and justice, while maintaining that true wisdom always begins with the "fear of the LORD" (1:7).

Boundary stone from Babylon, c. 1100 B.C.
Preserving Bible Times; © Dr. James C. Martin; permission of The British Museum

22:13 [o]Pr 26:13

[13] The sluggard says, "There is a lion
outside!"[o]
or, "I will be murdered in the streets!"

22:14 [p]Pr 2:16; 5:3-5; 7:5; 23:27 [q]Ecc 7:26

[14] The mouth of an adulteress is a deep pit;[p]
he who is under the LORD's wrath will
fall into it.[q]

22:15 [r]Pr 13:24; 23:14

[15] Folly is bound up in the heart of a child,
but the rod of discipline will drive it far
from him.[r]

[16] He who oppresses the poor to increase his
wealth
and he who gives gifts to the rich—both
come to poverty.

Ancient Voices

Beware of robbing a wretch,
Or attacking a cripple;
Don't stretch out your hand to touch
an old man,
Nor open your mouth to an elder.
Don't let yourself be sent on a
mischievous errand,
Nor be friends with him who
does it.

—The Instruction of Amenemope

See "The Teaching of Amenemope" article.

Sayings of the Wise

22:17 [s]Pr 5:1

[17] Pay attention and listen to the sayings of the wise;[s]
apply your heart to what I teach,
[18] for it is pleasing when you keep them in your heart
and have all of them ready on your lips.
[19] So that your trust may be in the LORD,
I teach you today, even you.
[20] Have I not written thirty[a] sayings for you,
sayings of counsel and knowledge,

22:21 [t]Lk 1:3-4; 1Pe 3:15

[21] teaching you true and reliable words,[t]
so that you can give sound answers
to him who sent you?

22:22 [u]Zec 7:10 [v]Ex 23:6; Mal 3:5

22:23 [w]Ps 12:5 [x]1Sa 25:39; Pr 23:10-11

[22] Do not exploit the poor[u] because they are poor
and do not crush the needy in court,[v]
[23] for the LORD will take up their case[w]
and will plunder those who plunder them.[x]

[24] Do not make friends with a hot-tempered man,
do not associate with one easily angered,
[25] or you may learn his ways
and get yourself ensnared.[y]

22:25 [y]1Co 15:33

22:26 [z]Pr 11:15

[26] Do not be a man who strikes hands in pledge[z]
or puts up security for debts;
[27] if you lack the means to pay,
your very bed will be snatched from under you.[a]

22:27 [a]Pr 17:18

22:28 [b]Dt 19:14; Pr 23:10

[28] Do not move an ancient boundary stone[b]
set up by your forefathers.

22:29 [c]Ge 41:46

[29] Do you see a man skilled in his work?
He will serve[c] before kings;
he will not serve before obscure men.

[a] 20 Or *not formerly written*; or *not written excellent*

22:14 The "deep pit" may refer to a well or to a hunter's trap.
22:19—29:27 This section (again, this outline scheme differs somewhat from that found on page 958 in the introduction to this book) is more general (see the notes on 1:7—9:10 and 10:1–22:16) but uses the same vocabulary of morality. In this part of the book are some special parallels with an Egyptian work titled The Wisdom of Amenemope (see "The Teaching of Amenemope" on p. 994). The correspondence, however, does not invalidate the claim that the author(s) of Proverbs gave distinctive treatment to this theme.
22:28 See the notes on Deuteronomy 19:14 and Proverbs 15:25.
22:29 Craftsmen were considered wise, and some, such as the following, did indeed serve before kings: Joseph, an administrator (Ge 41:46); David, a musician (1Sa 16:21–23); and Huram, a worker in bronze (1Ki 7:13–14).

23

When you sit to dine with a ruler,
note well what[a] is before you,
2 and put a knife to your throat
if you are given to gluttony.
3 Do not crave his delicacies,[d]
for that food is deceptive.

4 Do not wear yourself out to get rich;
have the wisdom to show restraint.
5 Cast but a glance at riches, and they are gone,
for they will surely sprout wings
and fly off to the sky like an eagle.[e]

6 Do not eat the food of a stingy man,
do not crave his delicacies;[f]
7 for he is the kind of man
who is always thinking about the cost.[b]
"Eat and drink," he says to you,
but his heart is not with you.
8 You will vomit up the little you have eaten
and will have wasted your compliments.

9 Do not speak to a fool,
for he will scorn the wisdom of your words.[g]

10 Do not move an ancient boundary stone[h]
or encroach on the fields of the fatherless,
11 for their Defender[i] is strong;
he will take up their case against you.[j]

12 Apply your heart to instruction
and your ears to words of knowledge.

13 Do not withhold discipline from a child;
if you punish him with the rod, he will not die.
14 Punish him with the rod
and save his soul from death.[c]

15 My son, if your heart is wise,
then my heart will be glad;
16 my inmost being will rejoice
when your lips speak what is right.[k]

17 Do not let your heart envy[l] sinners,
but always be zealous for the fear of the LORD.
18 There is surely a future hope for you,
and your hope will not be cut off.[m]

19 Listen, my son, and be wise,
and keep your heart on the right path.
20 Do not join those who drink too much wine[n]
or gorge themselves on meat,
21 for drunkards and gluttons become poor,[o]
and drowsiness clothes them in rags.

23:3 [d]ver 6-8
23:5 [e]Pr 27:24
23:6 [f]Ps 141:4
23:9 [g]Pr 1:7; 9:7; Mt 7:6
23:10 [h]Dt 19:14; Pr 22:28
23:11 [i]Job 19:25 [j]Pr 22:22-23
23:16 [k]ver 24; Pr 27:11
23:17 [l]Ps 37:1; Pr 28:14
23:18 [m]Ps 9:18; Pr 24:14,19-20
23:20 [n]Isa 5:11, 22; Ro 13:13; Eph 5:18
23:21 [o]Pr 21:17

[a] *1* Or *who* [b] *7* Or *for as he thinks within himself, / so he is*; or *for as he puts on a feast, / so he is* [c] *14* Hebrew *Sheol*

23:10 See the notes on Deuteronomy 19:14 and Proverbs 15:25.
23:11 "Defender" refers to a kinsman-redeemer, someone who helped close relatives regain their land (see "The Kinsman-Redeemer" on p. 391) or avenged their deaths (Nu 35:12,19).

23:22 [p]Lev 19:32; Pr 1:8; 30:17; Eph 6:1-2
23:23 [q]Pr 4:7
23:24 [r]ver 15-16; Pr 10:1; 15:20
23:26 [s]Pr 3:1; 5:1-6 [t]Ps 18:21; Pr 4:4
23:27 [u]Pr 22:14
23:28 [v]Pr 7:11-12; Ecc 7:26
23:30 [w]Ps 75:8; Isa 5:11; Eph 5:18

22 Listen to your father, who gave you life,
and do not despise your mother when she is old.[p]
23 Buy the truth and do not sell it;
get wisdom, discipline and understanding.[q]
24 The father of a righteous man has great joy;
he who has a wise son delights in him.[r]
25 May your father and mother be glad;
may she who gave you birth rejoice!

26 My son,[s] give me your heart
and let your eyes keep to my ways,[t]
27 for a prostitute is a deep pit[u]
and a wayward wife is a narrow well.
28 Like a bandit she lies in wait,[v]
and multiplies the unfaithful among men.

29 Who has woe? Who has sorrow?
Who has strife? Who has complaints?
Who has needless bruises? Who has bloodshot eyes?
30 Those who linger over wine,[w]
who go to sample bowls of mixed wine.

The Israelite Family

PROVERBS 23 Domestic issues abound in the book of Proverbs, an indication that the family played an essential role in the development of wisdom literature, both in the Biblical and nonbiblical sense. Although the wise man had an institutional function on par with that of the priest and prophet (Jer 18:18), Proverbs illustrates the familial context of religious and ethical instruction. The concept of the family was probably more broadly defined in ancient Israel than in modern Western terms. The fundamental unit was the household (Hebrew *bet av*; lit., "father's house"), which included a patriarch with his wife, his sons and their wives, his grandsons and any other dependents.[1]

Parental exhortations to the son provide the literary shape for Proverbs 23:13–28. This very ancient form of father-son instruction occurred widely in the ancient Near East, as in the **Mesopotamian** Instructions of Shuruppak (mid-third millennium B.C.), in which the hero, Shuruppak, begins his teachings by declaring, "My son, I will instruct you." Moreover, the use of physical chastisement for a child's moral training advocated in verses 13–14 has an analogue in the **Aramaic** story of Ahiqar (seventh–sixth centuries B.C.), which similarly exhorts the reader to discipline his son with the rod.

These similarities reflect the international flavor of wisdom literature and familial responsibility for religious and ethical education (cf. Dt 6:6–7; Pr 4:1–4). Even so, Biblical wisdom, especially that presented in Proverbs, has distinctive features:

✣ Education in Proverbs is centered in the family and has the good of the individual in view. By contrast, Greek education was centered in the gymnasium and had the good of the city-state (*polis*) in view.

✣ Education in Proverbs is primarily directed at moral and spiritual virtue rather than toward vocational training. By contrast, some wisdom texts from Egypt are principally concerned with preparing a young man for work in the government or as a scribe.

✣ Education in Proverbs does not focus upon any particular social class. Egyptian wisdom literature, on the other hand, was to a large extent directed to the elite.

✣ Education in Proverbs begins with the fear of God as the source and goal of all wisdom. This focus has no parallel in other ancient texts.

[1]See "The Role of the Patriarch in Family Life" on page 30.

31 Do not gaze at wine when it is red,
when it sparkles in the cup,
when it goes down smoothly!
32 In the end it bites like a snake
and poisons like a viper.
33 Your eyes will see strange sights
and your mind imagine confusing things.
34 You will be like one sleeping on the high seas,
lying on top of the rigging.
35 "They hit me," you will say, "but I'm not hurt!
They beat me, but I don't feel it!
When will I wake up
so I can find another drink?"

24

Do not envy[x] wicked men,
do not desire their company;
2 for their hearts plot violence,
and their lips talk about making trouble.[y]

3 By wisdom a house is built,[z]
and through understanding it is established;
4 through knowledge its rooms are filled
with rare and beautiful treasures.[a]

5 A wise man has great power,
and a man of knowledge increases strength;
6 for waging war you need guidance,
and for victory many advisers.[b]

7 Wisdom is too high for a fool;
in the assembly at the gate he has nothing to say.

8 He who plots evil
will be known as a schemer.
9 The schemes of folly are sin,
and men detest a mocker.

10 If you falter in times of trouble,
how small is your strength![c]

11 Rescue those being led away to death;
hold back those staggering toward slaughter.[d]
12 If you say, "But we knew nothing about this,"
does not he who weighs[e] the heart perceive it?
Does not he who guards your life know it?
Will he not repay each person according to what he has done?[f]

13 Eat honey, my son, for it is good;
honey from the comb is sweet to your taste.
14 Know also that wisdom is sweet to your soul;
if you find it, there is a future hope for you,
and your hope will not be cut off.[g h]

15 Do not lie in wait like an outlaw against a righteous man's house,
do not raid his dwelling place;

24:1 [x]Ps 37:1; 73:3; Pr 3:31-32; 23:17-18
24:2 [y]Ps 10:7
24:3 [z]Pr 14:1
24:4 [a]Pr 8:21
24:6 [b]Pr 11:14; 20:18; Lk 14:31
24:10 [c]Job 4:5; Jer 51:46; Heb 12:3
24:11 [d]Ps 82:4; Isa 58:6-7
24:12 [e]Pr 21:2 [f]Job 34:11; Ps 62:12; Ro 2:6*
24:14 [g]Ps 119:103; Pr 16:24 [h]Pr 23:18

24:7 The city gate was the place where the leaders of the city met to hold court, where the marketplace was located and where official business transactions took place (see "The City Gate" on p. 392).

[16] for though a righteous man falls seven times,
he rises again,
but the wicked are brought down by calamity.[i]

[17] Do not gloat[j] when your enemy falls;
when he stumbles, do not let your heart rejoice,[k]
[18] or the LORD will see and disapprove
and turn his wrath away from him.

[19] Do not fret[l] because of evil men
or be envious of the wicked,
[20] for the evil man has no future hope,
and the lamp of the wicked will be snuffed out.[m]

[21] Fear the LORD and the king,[n] my son,
and do not join with the rebellious,
[22] for those two will send sudden destruction upon
them,
and who knows what calamities they can bring?

Further Sayings of the Wise

[23] These also are sayings of the wise:[o]

To show partiality[p] in judging is not good:[q]
[24] Whoever says to the guilty, "You are innocent"[r]—
peoples will curse him and nations denounce him.
[25] But it will go well with those who convict the guilty,
and rich blessing will come upon them.

[26] An honest answer
is like a kiss on the lips.

[27] Finish your outdoor work
and get your fields ready;
after that, build your house.

[28] Do not testify against your neighbor without cause,[s]
or use your lips to deceive.
[29] Do not say, "I'll do to him as he has done to me;
I'll pay that man back for what he did."[t]

[30] I went past the field of the sluggard,[u]
past the vineyard of the man who lacks judgment;
[31] thorns had come up everywhere,
the ground was covered with weeds,
and the stone wall was in ruins.
[32] I applied my heart to what I observed
and learned a lesson from what I saw:
[33] A little sleep, a little slumber,
a little folding of the hands to rest[v]—
[34] and poverty will come on you like a bandit
and scarcity like an armed man.[a][w]

24:16 [i]Job 5:19; Ps 34:19; Mic 7:8
24:17 [j]Ob 1:12 [k]Job 31:29
24:19 [l]Ps 37:1
24:20 [m]Job 18:5; Pr 13:9; 23:17-18
24:21 [n]Ro 13:1-5; 1Pe 2:17
24:23 [o]Pr 1:6 [p]Lev 19:15 [q]Pr 28:21
24:24 [r]Pr 17:15
24:28 [s]Ps 7:4; Pr 25:18; Eph 4:25
24:29 [t]Pr 20:22; Mt 5:38-41; Ro 12:17
24:30 [u]Pr 6:6-11; 26:13-16
24:33 [v]Pr 6:10
24:34 [w]Pr 10:4; Ecc 10:18

[a] 34 *Or like a vagrant / and scarcity like a beggar*

24:17–18 Edom was destroyed because she gloated over Israel's destruction (see Ps 137:7 and its note; see also Eze 35:15).

More Proverbs of Solomon

25 These are more proverbs[x] of Solomon, copied by the men of Hezekiah king of Judah:[y]

25:1 [x]1Ki 4:32 [y]Pr 1:1

[2] It is the glory of God to conceal a matter;
to search out a matter is the glory of kings.[z]

25:2 [z]Pr 16:10-15

[3] As the heavens are high and the earth is deep,
so the hearts of kings are unsearchable.

[4] Remove the dross from the silver,
and out comes material for[a] the silversmith;
[5] remove the wicked from the king's presence,[a]
and his throne will be established[b] through righteousness.[c]

25:5 [a]Pr 20:8 [b]2Sa 7:13 [c]Pr 16:12; 29:14

[6] Do not exalt yourself in the king's presence,
and do not claim a place among great men;
[7] it is better for him to say to you, "Come up here,"[d]
than for him to humiliate you before a nobleman.

25:7 [d]Lk 14:7-10

What you have seen with your eyes
8 do not bring[b] hastily to court,
for what will you do in the end
if your neighbor puts you to shame?[e]

25:8 [e]Mt 5:25-26

[9] If you argue your case with a neighbor,
do not betray another man's confidence,
[10] or he who hears it may shame you
and you will never lose your bad reputation.

[11] A word aptly spoken
is like apples of gold in settings of silver.[f]

25:11 [f]ver 12; Pr 15:23

[12] Like an earring of gold or an ornament of fine gold
is a wise man's rebuke to a listening ear.[g]

25:12 [g]ver 11; Ps 141:5; Pr 13:18; 15:31

[13] Like the coolness of snow at harvest time
is a trustworthy messenger to those who send him;
he refreshes the spirit of his masters.[h]

25:13 [h]Pr 10:26; 13:17

[14] Like clouds and wind without rain
is a man who boasts of gifts he does not give.

[15] Through patience a ruler can be persuaded,[i]
and a gentle tongue can break a bone.[j]

25:15 [i]Ecc 10:4 [j]Pr 15:1

[16] If you find honey, eat just enough—
too much of it, and you will vomit.[k]
[17] Seldom set foot in your neighbor's house—
too much of you, and he will hate you.

25:16 [k]ver 27

[18] Like a club or a sword or a sharp arrow
is the man who gives false testimony against his neighbor.[l]

25:18 [l]Ps 57:4; Pr 12:18

[19] Like a bad tooth or a lame foot
is reliance on the unfaithful in times of trouble.

[a] 4 Or *comes a vessel from* [b] 7,8 Or *nobleman / on whom you had set your eyes. / [8]Do not go*

25:1 The book of Proverbs returns here to the proverbs of Solomon, noting that these were "copied by the men of Hezekiah king of Judah." Hezekiah's reign, more than 200 years after Solomon's, saw a great revival—which explains his interest in a compilation of Solomon's proverbs. Many of the sayings in this section (25:1—29:27) were intended to be read and interpreted as pairs, one shedding more light upon the other.
25:4 The process of removing the dross from the silver is a picture of purification.
25:12 For earrings or nose rings, see the note on Ezekiel 16:12.

20 Like one who takes away a garment on a cold day,
or like vinegar poured on soda,
is one who sings songs to a heavy heart.

21 If your enemy is hungry, give him food to eat;
if he is thirsty, give him water to drink.
22 In doing this, you will heap burning coals[m] on his head,
and the LORD will reward you.[n]

23 As a north wind brings rain,
so a sly tongue brings angry looks.

24 Better to live on a corner of the roof
than share a house with a quarrelsome wife.[o]

25 Like cold water to a weary soul
is good news from a distant land.[p]

26 Like a muddied spring or a polluted well
is a righteous man who gives way to the wicked.

27 It is not good to eat too much honey,[q]
nor is it honorable to seek one's own honor.[r]

28 Like a city whose walls are broken down
is a man who lacks self-control.

25:22 [m]Ps 18:8 [n]2Sa 16:12; 2Ch 28:15; Mt 5:44; Ro 12:20*
25:24 [o]Pr 21:9
25:25 [p]Pr 15:30
25:27 [q]ver 16 [r]Pr 27:2; Mt 23:12

26

Like snow in summer or rain[s] in harvest,
honor is not fitting for a fool.[t]

2 Like a fluttering sparrow or a darting swallow,
an undeserved curse does not come to rest.[u]

3 A whip for the horse, a halter for the donkey,[v]
and a rod for the backs of fools![w]

4 Do not answer a fool according to his folly,
or you will be like him yourself.[x]

5 Answer a fool according to his folly,
or he will be wise in his own eyes.[y]

6 Like cutting off one's feet or drinking violence
is the sending of a message by the hand of a fool.[z]

7 Like a lame man's legs that hang limp
is a proverb in the mouth of a fool.[a]

8 Like tying a stone in a sling
is the giving of honor to a fool.[b]

9 Like a thornbush in a drunkard's hand
is a proverb in the mouth of a fool.[c]

10 Like an archer who wounds at random
is he who hires a fool or any passer-by.

26:1 [s]1Sa 12:17 [t]ver 8; Pr 19:10
26:2 [u]Nu 23:8; Dt 23:5
26:3 [v]Ps 32:9 [w]Pr 10:13
26:4 [x]ver 5; Isa 36:21
26:5 [y]ver 4; Pr 3:7
26:6 [z]Pr 10:26
26:7 [a]ver 9
26:8 [b]ver 1
26:9 [c]ver 7

25:22 Heaping burning coals upon a person's head was a horrible punishment reserved for the wicked. Here, however, the picture could have been one of kindness; though painful, the consequence might have served to win the individual over. Alternatively, the practice may reflect an Egyptian expiation ritual in which a guilty person, as a sign of his repentance, carried a basin of glowing coals on his head. The meaning here, then, would be that in returning good for evil—and so expressing kindness to an enemy (see Ro 12:20)—a person might motivate that adversary to repent or change.

25:28 A city whose walls were broken down was considered defenseless and disgraced (cf. Ne 1:3 and its note).

26:1 Grain was harvested from mid-April until mid-June (barley first; wheat a few weeks later). It rarely rains in Palestine from June through September.

26:8 A sling was useless as a weapon if the stone was tied into it.

11 As a dog returns to its vomit,[d]
so a fool repeats his folly.[e]

12 Do you see a man wise in his own eyes?[f]
There is more hope for a fool than for him.[g]

13 The sluggard says,[h] "There is a lion in the road,
a fierce lion roaming the streets!"[i]

26:11 [d]2Pe 2:22* [e]Ex 8:15; Ps 85:8
26:12 [f]Pr 3:7 [g]Pr 29:20
26:13 [h]Pr 6:6-11; 24:30-34 [i]Pr 22:13

CULTURAL AND HISTORICAL NOTES

Dogs in the Ancient World

PROVERBS 26 In Proverbs 26:11 a fool is said to return to his folly as surely as a dog to its vomit, and in verse 17 Solomon pointed out—possibly from childhood experience!—that it is dangerous to grab a dog by the ears. These statements would be equally true of both wild and domesticated dogs. But the question is often asked: Did the Israelites keep dogs as pets?

Dogs were first domesticated in prehistoric times. A site called Ein Mallaha in northern Israel yields the earliest uncontested archaeological evidence for domesticated dogs (c. 9600 B.C.), though there may be an earlier site at the Palegawra Cave in Iraq. Even so, most dogs in the early Biblical period were wild, and ancient people naturally regarded them with fear and disdain. The portrayal of dogs in the Bible is especially negative (e.g., 1Sa 17:42–43). They are depicted as roaming carnivores that hunted in packs, even inside cities (1Ki 14:11; Ps 22:16). To have one's corpse devoured by dogs was a dreadful fate (1Ki 21:19), and the epithet "dog" was insulting (2Ki 8:13), if not humiliating (2Sa 3:8), implying that an individual was either worthless (1Sa 24:14) or evil (Ps 22:16). In fact, the reference to a dog in Deuteronomy 23:18 probably refers to a male prostitute.

Other ancient cultures viewed dogs more positively. In **Mesopotamia** puppies were used in purification and healing rites.[1] In **Persia** dogs were revered. Similarly, in Egypt some dogs were considered sacred, and many were mummified. The Philistine city of Ashkelon, during the Persian period, maintained a cemetery of over 1,000 pits filled with carefully buried puppies, though the significance and function of this burial ground is difficult to interpret. In the Greco-Roman world dogs were frequently domesticated, as is attested in a conversation between Jesus and a Phoenician woman (Mt 15:26–27), as well as by Greek vases depicting hunters with their dogs at their sides. A Latin sign found in Pompeii reads *cave canem* ("beware of dog").[2]

Roman era statue of the goddess Artemis the Huntress with one of her hunting dogs

Preserving Bible Times; © Dr. James C. Martin; permission of The Istanbul Archaeological Museum

Whether the ancient Israelites disliked dogs more than did other peoples is unknown. Most Biblical references to dogs are negative, but that may be more an accident than a reflection of how the Israelites felt overall about this species. There are occasional positive references to dogs (Job 30:1). For the sake of comparison, we might observe that there is no word for "cat" in Biblical Hebrew, although cats were domesticated in Egypt and must have been known in Israel. It may be coincidental that cats are never mentioned in the Old Testament (although there is one reference to cats in the **Apocrypha** at Bar 6:22). The reality is that we cannot say with certainty how the ancient Israelites viewed dogs (or cats) in general or how common it was to have such animals in the home.

[1]See "The Hittite Ritual of Passing Between the Pieces of a Sacrifice" on page 1251. [2]See "Pompeii" on page 1857.

[14] As a door turns on its hinges,
so a sluggard turns on his bed.[j]

[15] The sluggard buries his hand in the dish;
he is too lazy to bring it back to his mouth.[k]

[16] The sluggard is wiser in his own eyes
than seven men who answer discreetly.

[17] Like one who seizes a dog by the ears
is a passer-by who meddles in a quarrel not his own.

[18] Like a madman shooting
firebrands or deadly arrows
[19] is a man who deceives his neighbor
and says, "I was only joking!"

[20] Without wood a fire goes out;
without gossip a quarrel dies down.[l]

[21] As charcoal to embers and as wood to fire,
so is a quarrelsome man for kindling strife.[m]

[22] The words of a gossip are like choice morsels;
they go down to a man's inmost parts.[n]

[23] Like a coating of glaze[a] over earthenware
are fervent lips with an evil heart.

[24] A malicious man disguises himself with his lips,[o]
but in his heart he harbors deceit.[p]
[25] Though his speech is charming,[q] do not believe him,
for seven abominations fill his heart.[r]
[26] His malice may be concealed by deception,
but his wickedness will be exposed in the assembly.

[27] If a man digs a pit,[s] he will fall into it;[t]
if a man rolls a stone, it will roll back on him.[u]

[28] A lying tongue hates those it hurts,
and a flattering mouth[v] works ruin.

27

Do not boast[w] about tomorrow,
for you do not know what a day may bring forth.[x]

[2] Let another praise you, and not your own mouth;
someone else, and not your own lips.[y]

[3] Stone is heavy and sand[z] a burden,
but provocation by a fool is heavier than both.

[4] Anger is cruel and fury overwhelming,
but who can stand before jealousy?[a]

[5] Better is open rebuke
than hidden love.

[6] Wounds from a friend can be trusted,
but an enemy multiplies kisses.[b]

26:14 [j]Pr 6:9
26:15 [k]Pr 19:24
26:20 [l]Pr 22:10
26:21 [m]Pr 14:17; 15:18
26:22 [n]Pr 18:8
26:24 [o]Ps 31:18 [p]Ps 41:6; Pr 10:18; 12:20
26:25 [q]Ps 28:3 [r]Jer 9:4-8
26:27 [s]Ps 7:15 [t]Est 6:13 [u]Est 2:23; 7:9; Ps 35:8; 141:10; Pr 28:10; 29:6; Isa 50:11
26:28 [v]Ps 12:3; Pr 29:5
27:1 [w]1Ki 20:11 [x]Mt 6:34; Lk 12:19-20; Jas 4:13-16
27:2 [y]Pr 25:27
27:3 [z]Job 6:3
27:4 [a]Nu 5:14
27:6 [b]Ps 141:5; Pr 28:23

[a] 23 With a different word division of the Hebrew; Masoretic Text *of silver dross*

26:18 Firebrands would easily have ignited sheaves of grain (cf. Zec 12:6).

[7] He who is full loathes honey,
but to the hungry even what is bitter tastes sweet.

[8] Like a bird that strays from its nest[c]
is a man who strays from his home.

[9] Perfume[d] and incense bring joy to the heart,
and the pleasantness of one's friend springs from his earnest counsel.

[10] Do not forsake your friend and the friend of your father,
and do not go to your brother's house when disaster[e] strikes you—
better a neighbor nearby than a brother far away.

[11] Be wise, my son, and bring joy to my heart;[f]
then I can answer anyone who treats me with contempt.[g]

[12] The prudent see danger and take refuge,
but the simple keep going and suffer for it.[h]

[13] Take the garment of one who puts up security for a stranger;
hold it in pledge if he does it for a wayward woman.[i]

[14] If a man loudly blesses his neighbor early in the morning,
it will be taken as a curse.

[15] A quarrelsome wife is like
a constant dripping[j] on a rainy day;
[16] restraining her is like restraining the wind
or grasping oil with the hand.

[17] As iron sharpens iron,
so one man sharpens another.

[18] He who tends a fig tree will eat its fruit,[k]
and he who looks after his master will be honored.[l]

[19] As water reflects a face,
so a man's heart reflects the man.

[20] Death and Destruction[a] are never satisfied,[m]
and neither are the eyes of man.[n]

[21] The crucible for silver and the furnace for gold,[o]
but man is tested by the praise he receives.

[22] Though you grind a fool in a mortar,
grinding him like grain with a pestle,
you will not remove his folly from him.

[23] Be sure you know the condition of your flocks,[p]
give careful attention to your herds;
[24] for riches do not endure forever,[q]
and a crown is not secure for all generations.
[25] When the hay is removed and new growth appears
and the grass from the hills is gathered in,
[26] the lambs will provide you with clothing,
and the goats with the price of a field.

27:8 [c]Isa 16:2
27:9 [d]Est 2:12; Ps 45:8
27:10 [e]Pr 17:17; 18:24
27:11 [f]Pr 10:1; 23:15-16 [g]Ge 24:60
27:12 [h]Pr 22:3
27:13 [i]Pr 20:16
27:15 [j]Est 1:18; Pr 19:13
27:18 [k]1Co 9:7 [l]Lk 19:12-27
27:20 [m]Pr 30:15-16; Hab 2:5 [n]Ecc 1:8; 6:7
27:21 [o]Pr 17:3
27:23 [p]Pr 12:10
27:24 [q]Pr 23:5

[a] 20 Hebrew *Sheol and Abaddon*

27:9 For commentary on perfume, see the note on 7:17. See also "Perfumes and Anointing Oils" on page 1746.
27:22 A mortar was a bowl (see Nu 11:8) and a pestle a club-like tool for pounding grain in a mortar.
27:25 Removal of hay began in March or April.
27:26 Sheep and goats sometimes served as tribute payments (see 2Ki 3:4).

[27] You will have plenty of goats' milk
to feed you and your family
and to nourish your servant girls.

28:1 [r]2Ki 7:7 [s]Lev 26:17; Ps 53:5 [t]Ps 138:3

28

The wicked man flees[r] though no one pursues,[s]
but the righteous are as bold as a lion.[t]

[2] When a country is rebellious, it has many rulers,
but a man of understanding and knowledge maintains order.

[3] A ruler[a] who oppresses the poor
is like a driving rain that leaves no crops.

[4] Those who forsake the law praise the wicked,
but those who keep the law resist them.

[5] Evil men do not understand justice,
but those who seek the LORD understand it fully.

28:6 [u]Pr 19:1

[6] Better a poor man whose walk is blameless
than a rich man whose ways are perverse.[u]

28:7 [v]Pr 23:19-21

[7] He who keeps the law is a discerning son,
but a companion of gluttons disgraces his father.[v]

28:8 [w]Ex 18:21 [x]Job 27:17; Pr 13:22 [y]Ps 112:9; Pr 14:31; Lk 14:12-14

[8] He who increases his wealth by exorbitant interest[w]
amasses it for another,[x] who will be kind to the poor.[y]

28:9 [z]Ps 66:18; 109:7; Pr 15:8; Isa 1:13

[9] If anyone turns a deaf ear to the law,
even his prayers are detestable.[z]

28:10 [a]Pr 26:27

[10] He who leads the upright along an evil path
will fall into his own trap,[a]
but the blameless will receive a good inheritance.

[11] A rich man may be wise in his own eyes,
but a poor man who has discernment sees through him.

28:12 [b]2Ki 11:20 [c]Pr 11:10; 29:2

[12] When the righteous triumph, there is great elation;[b]
but when the wicked rise to power, men go into hiding.[c]

28:13 [d]Job 31:33 [e]Ps 32:1-5; 1Jn 1:9

[13] He who conceals his sins[d] does not prosper,
but whoever confesses and renounces them finds mercy.[e]

[14] Blessed is the man who always fears the LORD,
but he who hardens his heart falls into trouble.

[15] Like a roaring lion or a charging bear
is a wicked man ruling over a helpless people.

[16] A tyrannical ruler lacks judgment,
but he who hates ill-gotten gain will enjoy a long life.

28:17 [f]Ge 9:6

[17] A man tormented by the guilt of murder
will be a fugitive[f] till death;
let no one support him.

28:18 [g]Pr 10:9

[18] He whose walk is blameless is kept safe,
but he whose ways are perverse will suddenly fall.[g]

[a] 3 Or *A poor man*

27:27 Goats' milk was commonly drunk along with cows' milk (see Dt 32:13–14; Isa 7:21–22).
28:6 For "blameless," see the note on 2:7.
28:15 See "Lions and Other Wild Beasts in Ancient Israel" on page 813.

[19] He who works his land will have abundant food,
but the one who chases fantasies will have his fill of poverty.[h] 28:19 [h]Pr 12:11

[20] A faithful man will be richly blessed,
but one eager to get rich will not go unpunished.[i] 28:20 [i]ver 22; Pr 10:6; 1Ti 6:9

[21] To show partiality is not good[j]—
yet a man will do wrong for a piece of bread.[k] 28:21 [j]Pr 18:5 [k]Eze 13:19

[22] A stingy man is eager to get rich
and is unaware that poverty awaits him.[l] 28:22 [l]ver 20; Pr 23:6

[23] He who rebukes a man will in the end gain more favor
than he who has a flattering tongue.[m] 28:23 [m]Pr 27:5-6

[24] He who robs his father or mother[n]
and says, "It's not wrong"—
he is partner to him who destroys.[o] 28:24 [n]Pr 19:26 [o]Pr 18:9

[25] A greedy man stirs up dissension,
but he who trusts in the LORD[p] will prosper. 28:25 [p]Pr 29:25

[26] He who trusts in himself is a fool,[q]
but he who walks in wisdom is kept safe. 28:26 [q]Ps 4:5; Pr 3:5

[27] He who gives to the poor will lack nothing,[r]
but he who closes his eyes to them receives many curses. 28:27 [r]Dt 15:7; 24:19; Pr 19:17; 22:9

[28] When the wicked rise to power, people go into hiding;[s]
but when the wicked perish, the righteous thrive. 28:28 [s]ver 12

29

A man who remains stiff-necked after many rebukes
will suddenly be destroyed—without remedy.[t] 29:1 [t]2Ch 36:16; Pr 6:15

[2] When the righteous thrive, the people rejoice;[u]
when the wicked rule, the people groan.[v] 29:2 [u]Est 8:15 [v]Pr 28:12

[3] A man who loves wisdom brings joy to his father,[w]
but a companion of prostitutes squanders his wealth.[x] 29:3 [w]Pr 10:1 [x]Pr 5:8-10; Lk 15:11-32

[4] By justice a king gives a country stability,[y]
but one who is greedy for bribes tears it down. 29:4 [y]Pr 8:15-16

[5] Whoever flatters his neighbor
is spreading a net for his feet.

[6] An evil man is snared by his own sin,[z]
but a righteous one can sing and be glad. 29:6 [z]Ecc 9:12

[7] The righteous care about justice for the poor,[a]
but the wicked have no such concern. 29:7 [a]Job 29:16; Ps 41:1; Pr 31:8-9

[8] Mockers stir up a city,
but wise men turn away anger.[b] 29:8 [b]Pr 11:11; 16:14

[9] If a wise man goes to court with a fool,
the fool rages and scoffs, and there is no peace.

[10] Bloodthirsty men hate a man of integrity
and seek to kill the upright.[c] 29:10 [c]1Jn 3:12

[11] A fool gives full vent to his anger,
but a wise man keeps himself under control.[d] 29:11 [d]Pr 12:16; 19:11

[12] If a ruler listens to lies,
all his officials become wicked.

[13] The poor man and the oppressor have this in common:
The LORD gives sight to the eyes of both.[e]

[14] If a king judges the poor with fairness,
his throne will always be secure.[f]

[15] The rod of correction imparts wisdom,
but a child left to himself disgraces his mother.[g]

[16] When the wicked thrive, so does sin,
but the righteous will see their downfall.[h]

[17] Discipline your son, and he will give you peace;
he will bring delight to your soul.[i]

[18] Where there is no revelation, the people cast off restraint;
but blessed is he who keeps the law.[j]

[19] A servant cannot be corrected by mere words;
though he understands, he will not respond.

[20] Do you see a man who speaks in haste?
There is more hope for a fool than for him.[k]

[21] If a man pampers his servant from youth,
he will bring grief[a] in the end.

[22] An angry man stirs up dissension,
and a hot-tempered one commits many sins.[l]

[23] A man's pride brings him low,
but a man of lowly spirit gains honor.[m]

[24] The accomplice of a thief is his own enemy;
he is put under oath and dare not testify.[n]

[25] Fear of man will prove to be a snare,
but whoever trusts in the LORD[o] is kept safe.

[26] Many seek an audience with a ruler,[p]
but it is from the LORD that man gets justice.

[27] The righteous detest the dishonest;
the wicked detest the upright.[q]

29:13 [e]Pr 22:2; Mt 5:45
29:14 [f]Ps 72:1-5; Pr 16:12
29:15 [g]Pr 10:1; 13:24; 17:21,25
29:16 [h]Ps 37:35-36; 58:10; 91:8; 92:11
29:17 [i]ver 15; Pr 10:1
29:18 [j]Ps 1:1-2; 119:1-2; Jn 13:17
29:20 [k]Pr 26:12; Jas 1:19
29:22 [l]Pr 14:17; 15:18; 26:21
29:23 [m]Pr 11:2; 15:33; 16:18; Isa 66:2; Mt 23:12
29:24 [n]Lev 5:1
29:25 [o]Pr 28:25
29:26 [p]Pr 19:6
29:27 [q]ver 10

Sayings of Agur

30 The sayings of Agur son of Jakeh—an oracle[b]:

This man declared to Ithiel,
to Ithiel and to Ucal:[c]

[2] "I am the most ignorant of men;
I do not have a man's understanding.
[3] I have not learned wisdom,
nor have I knowledge of the Holy One.[r]

30:3 [r]Pr 9:10

[a] *21* The meaning of the Hebrew for this word is uncertain. [b] *1* Or *Jakeh of Massa* [c] *1* Masoretic Text; with a different word division of the Hebrew *declared, "I am weary, O God; / I am weary, O God, and faint.*

30:1–33 Agur is the otherwise unknown author of Proverbs 30. His words are described in verse 1 as "an oracle," thus claiming divine inspiration. Many scholars, however, believe that the Hebrew indicates instead the place name Massa (cf. the NIV text note on v. 1, and see also Ge 25:14,16).

30:1 Agur was likely a non-Israelite wise man like Job and his friends.

4 Who has gone up[s] to heaven and come down?
Who has gathered up the wind in the hollow[t] of his hands?
Who has wrapped up the waters[u] in his cloak?[v]
Who has established all the ends of the earth?
What is his name,[w] and the name of his son?
Tell me if you know!

5 "Every word of God is flawless;[x]
he is a shield[y] to those who take refuge in him.
6 Do not add[z] to his words,
or he will rebuke you and prove you a liar.

7 "Two things I ask of you, O LORD;
do not refuse me before I die:
8 Keep falsehood and lies far from me;
give me neither poverty nor riches,
but give me only my daily bread.[a]
9 Otherwise, I may have too much and disown[b] you
and say, 'Who is the LORD?'[c]
Or I may become poor and steal,
and so dishonor the name of my God.[d]

10 "Do not slander a servant to his master,
or he will curse you, and you will pay for it.

11 "There are those who curse their fathers
and do not bless their mothers;[e]
12 those who are pure in their own eyes[f]
and yet are not cleansed of their filth;[g]
13 those whose eyes are ever so haughty,[h]
whose glances are so disdainful;
14 those whose teeth[i] are swords
and whose jaws are set with knives[j]
to devour[k] the poor[l] from the earth,
the needy from among mankind.[m]

15 "The leech has two daughters.
'Give! Give!' they cry.

"There are three things that are never satisfied,[n]
four that never say, 'Enough!':
16 the grave,[a][o] the barren womb,
land, which is never satisfied with water,
and fire, which never says, 'Enough!'

17 "The eye that mocks[p] a father,
that scorns obedience to a mother,
will be pecked out by the ravens of the valley,
will be eaten by the vultures.[q]

18 "There are three things that are too amazing for me,
four that I do not understand:
19 the way of an eagle in the sky,
the way of a snake on a rock,

30:4 [s]Ps 24:1-2; Jn 3:13; Eph 4:7-10 [t]Ps 104:3; Isa 40:12 [u]Job 26:8; 38:8-9 [v]Ge 1:2 [w]Rev 19:12
30:5 [x]Ps 12:6; 18:30 [y]Ge 15:1; Ps 84:11
30:6 [z]Dt 4:2; 12:32; Rev 22:18
30:8 [a]Mt 6:11
30:9 [b]Jos 24:27; Isa 1:4; 59:13 [c]Dt 6:12; 8:10-14; Hos 13:6 [d]Dt 8:12
30:11 [e]Pr 20:20
30:12 [f]Pr 16:2; Lk 18:11 [g]Jer 2:23,35
30:13 [h]2Sa 22:28; Job 41:34; Ps 131:1; Pr 6:17
30:14 [i]Job 4:11; 29:17; Ps 3:7 [j]Ps 57:4 [k]Job 24:9; Ps 14:4 [l]Am 8:4; Mic 2:2 [m]Job 19:22
30:15 [n]Pr 27:20
30:16 [o]Pr 27:20; Isa 5:14; 14:9,11; Hab 2:5
30:17 [p]Dt 21:18-21; Pr 23:22 [q]Job 15:23

[a] 16 Hebrew *Sheol*

30:11 See 19:26 and its note.
30:16 In the ancient Near East a wife without children was considered disgraced and desperate (see Ge 16:1–2; 2Ki 4:14; Ps 113:9 and their notes).
30:17 The loss of an eye was considered a terrible curse (see Jdg 16:21). Since vultures typically devoured the dead (see Jer 7:33; Mt 24:28), the meaning may be that the body of a disgraceful son would lie unburied and exposed.

the way of a ship on the high seas,
and the way of a man with a maiden.

20 "This is the way of an adulteress:
She eats and wipes her mouth
and says, 'I've done nothing wrong.'[r]

30:20 [r]Pr 5:6

21 "Under three things the earth trembles,
under four it cannot bear up:
22 a servant who becomes king,[s]
a fool who is full of food,
23 an unloved woman who is married,
and a maidservant who displaces her mistress.

30:22 [s]Pr 19:10; 29:2

24 "Four things on earth are small,
yet they are extremely wise:
25 Ants are creatures of little strength,
yet they store up their food in the summer;[t]
26 coneys[a][u] are creatures of little power,
yet they make their home in the crags;
27 locusts[v] have no king,
yet they advance together in ranks;
28 a lizard can be caught with the hand,
yet it is found in kings' palaces.

30:25 [t]Pr 6:6-8
30:26 [u]Ps 104:18
30:27 [v]Ex 10:4

29 "There are three things that are stately in their stride,
four that move with stately bearing:
30 a lion, mighty among beasts,
who retreats before nothing;
31 a strutting rooster, a he-goat,
and a king with his army around him.[b]

32 "If you have played the fool and exalted yourself,
or if you have planned evil,
clap your hand over your mouth![w]
33 For as churning the milk produces butter,
and as twisting the nose produces blood,
so stirring up anger produces strife."

30:32 [w]Job 21:5; 29:9

Sayings of King Lemuel

31 The sayings[x] of King Lemuel—an oracle[c] his mother taught him:

2 "O my son, O son of my womb,
O son of my vows,[d][y]
3 do not spend your strength on women,
your vigor on those who ruin kings.[z]

4 "It is not for kings, O Lemuel—
not for kings to drink wine,[a]
not for rulers to crave beer,

31:1 [x]Pr 22:17
31:2 [y]Jdg 11:30; Isa 49:15
31:3 [z]Dt 17:17; 1Ki 11:3; Ne 13:26; Pr 5:1-14
31:4 [a]Pr 20:1; Ecc 10:16-17; Isa 5:22

[a] *26* That is, the hyrax or rock badger [b] *31* Or *king secure against revolt* [c] *1* Or *of Lemuel king of Massa, which* [d] *2* Or */ the answer to my prayers*

30:23 An "unloved woman who is married" probably refers to an unloved woman whose husband had several wives (cf. Leah in Ge 29:31–32). If she were barren, she could be replaced by a maidservant who was able to bear children (cf. Hagar and Sarah in Ge 16:1–6; see the note on Ge 16:1–2).

31:1 King Lemuel was a non-Israelite; otherwise he is unknown.

31:4–7 Total abstinence from alcohol was rare in the ancient world, even while the problems of addiction to drink were recognized (see "The Instructions of Anii" on p. 990). Behind the recommendation to offer alcohol (vv. 6–7) lay a concern for the least powerful members of the kingdom. The king was to offer wine (instead of storing it) to comfort those who were hurting.

[5]lest they drink[b] and forget what the law decrees,[c]
and deprive all the oppressed of their rights.
[6]Give beer to those who are perishing,
wine[d] to those who are in anguish;
[7]let them drink[e] and forget their poverty
and remember their misery no more.

[8]"Speak[f] up for those who cannot speak for themselves,
for the rights of all who are destitute.
[9]Speak up and judge fairly;
defend the rights of the poor and needy."[g]

31:5 [b]1Ki 16:9 [c]Pr 16:12; Hos 4:11
31:6 [d]Ge 14:18
31:7 [e]Est 1:10
31:8 [f]1Sa 19:4; Job 29:12-17
31:9 [g]Lev 19:15; Dt 1:16; Pr 24:23; 29:7; Isa 1:17; Jer 22:16

Epilogue: The Wife of Noble Character

[10][a] A wife of noble character[h] who can find?[i]
She is worth far more than rubies.
[11]Her husband[j] has full confidence in her
and lacks nothing of value.[k]
[12]She brings him good, not harm,
all the days of her life.
[13]She selects wool and flax
and works with eager hands.[l]
[14]She is like the merchant ships,
bringing her food from afar.
[15]She gets up while it is still dark;
she provides food for her family
and portions for her servant girls.
[16]She considers a field and buys it;
out of her earnings she plants a vineyard.
[17]She sets about her work vigorously;
her arms are strong for her tasks.
[18]She sees that her trading is profitable,
and her lamp does not go out at night.
[19]In her hand she holds the distaff
and grasps the spindle with her fingers.
[20]She opens her arms to the poor
and extends her hands to the needy.[m]
[21]When it snows, she has no fear for her household;
for all of them are clothed in scarlet.
[22]She makes coverings for her bed;
she is clothed in fine linen and purple.
[23]Her husband is respected at the city gate,
where he takes his seat among the elders[n] of the land.
[24]She makes linen garments and sells them,
and supplies the merchants with sashes.
[25]She is clothed with strength and dignity;
she can laugh at the days to come.
[26]She speaks with wisdom,
and faithful instruction is on her tongue.[o]

31:10 [h]Ru 3:11; Pr 12:4; 18:22 [i]Pr 8:35; 19:14
31:11 [j]Ge 2:18 [k]Pr 12:4
31:13 [l]1Ti 2:9-10
31:20 [m]Dt 15:11; Eph 4:28; Heb 13:16
31:23 [n]Ex 3:16; Ru 4:1,11; Pr 12:4
31:26 [o]Pr 10:31

[a] *10* Verses 10-31 are an acrostic, each verse beginning with a successive letter of the Hebrew alphabet.

31:10–31 Over the centuries this poem has taken on a life of its own. In Jewish tradition it is recited by a husband to his wife on Sabbath evenings, and many Christians read it on Mother's Day.

31:21 Scarlet clothing was associated with high quality and was probably made of wool (cf. 2Sa 1:24; Rev 18:16).

31:23 See the note on 24:7.

[27] She watches over the affairs of her household
and does not eat the bread of idleness.
[28] Her children arise and call her blessed;
her husband also, and he praises her:
[29] "Many women do noble things,
but you surpass them all."
[30] Charm is deceptive, and beauty is fleeting;
but a woman who fears the LORD is to be praised.
[31] Give her the reward she has earned,
and let her works bring her praise[p] at the city gate.

31:31 [p] Pr 11:16

INTRODUCTION TO *Ecclesiastes*

AUTHOR, PLACE AND DATE OF WRITING

Although the author of Ecclesiastes referred to himself only as "the Teacher," he also claims to have been a son of David and a king over Israel in Jerusalem (Ecc 1:1,12). Allowing for the fact that "son" can mean "descendant," the only other person besides Solomon himself to fit both these descriptors would have been Solomon's son Rehoboam. No one, however, considers Rehoboam's authorship to be even a remote possibility.

Despite these claims, the traditional assumption that Solomon wrote Ecclesiastes has come under question. Many interpreters treat the Teacher's claims as a literary device, proposing that the author of Ecclesiastes took on the identity of Solomon in order to give his words a certain weightiness. It is wise, however, not to embrace this option too readily. The canonical authority of the books of the Bible is closely related to their authors. By way of comparison, Protestant believers treat the Apocryphal book titled Wisdom of Solomon as noncanonical precisely because it is a late, pseudonymous work—one that Solomon did not actually write (see "The Apocrypha" on p. 1973).

The assumption that Solomon wrote the book late in his life would place its composition at about 940 B.C. Today the vast majority of scholars treat Ecclesiastes as a late, postexilic text, many proposing a date as late as 200 B.C. Yet there are solid reasons for believing the late-date theory for Ecclesiastes to be misguided (see "The Authorship of Ecclesiastes and Song of Songs" on p. 1021). Especially significant is the fact that the author demonstrated such familiarity with ancient texts from prior to the time of Solomon (works such as the Epic of Gilgamesh and the Egyptian Harper Songs; see "Ecclesiastes and the Epic of Gilgamesh" on p. 1027). This is what we would expect from the highly literate age of Solomon, but it is hard to imagine that a writer living during the late postexilic era would have known these writings or incorporated them into his book. By contrast, Ecclesiastes shows no familiarity at all with Greek literature—which is precisely what an educated Jew of 200 B.C. would have known.

AUDIENCE

Ecclesiastes is an advanced and reflective wisdom text. Unlike Proverbs, it was not included in the canon to educate young readers in the basic principles of wisdom. Rather, it was intended for those mature and experienced enough to deal with dark and difficult questions (see "Ancient Near Eastern Wisdom" on p. 960). In addition, it is clear that Ecclesiastes was written primarily for the elite in Israelite society—people both familiar with the ancient world of wisdom and comfortable within the corridors of power.

CULTURAL FACTS AND HIGHLIGHTS

The author of Ecclesiastes clearly expected that his readers would from time to time have access to the king (8:2–5). Speaking to privileged, cultured people with money, power and intelligence, he warned this vulnerable audience that all the grandeur, brilliance and laurels this world has to offer are in the final analysis only fleeting.

TIMELINE

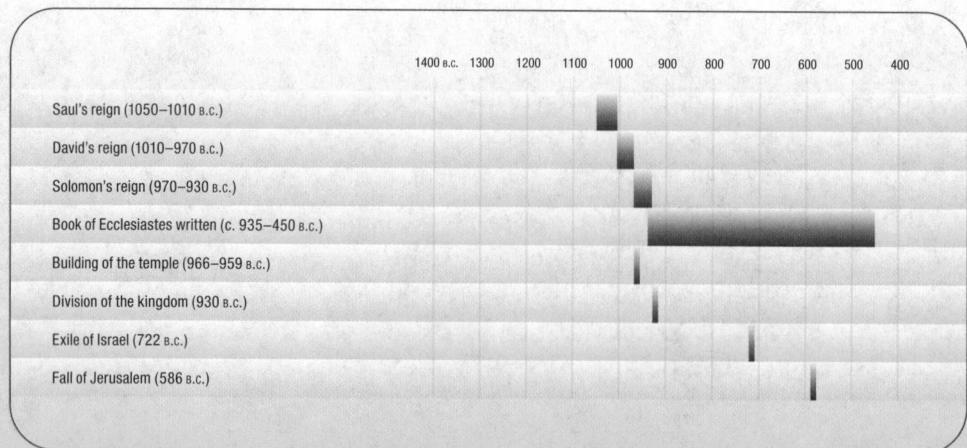

AS YOU READ

The Teacher claimed unequivocally that "there is nothing new under the sun" (1:9), but he was making this claim well over two thousand years ago. In view of the exponential advances in all areas of knowledge over the past century or so, study his arguments with a critical eye, deliberately overlooking the language and details that date the manuscript and attempting to reduce his premises to their most basic components. Do you feel the work still represents universal truth? Has the Teacher covered all basic areas? If you think there may indeed be something "new under the sun" since its writing, either in terms of God's continuing self-revelation through his Son or from the "enlightened" perspective of our own age, what might it be?

Does the author strike you as a gloom-and-doom pessimist, an at-times-"incurable" optimist or a modern-style realist? How well do you relate to his style and drastic shifts in tone?

DID YOU KNOW?

- The Babylonian Epic of Gilgamesh contains a section remarkably similar to 9:7–9, illustrating the international flavor of ancient wisdom literature.
- "Words" are a common theme in wisdom literature (10:12).
- The Teacher advocated being adventurous, for those who accept risks will reap returns (11:1).
- The Teacher encouraged diversification of investments; people can never know in advance which ventures may fail (11:2).

THEMES

The book of Ecclesiastes includes the following themes:

1. *Wisdom and pleasure alone are worthless.* Ecclesiastes points out the truth that work, pleasure, status, wealth and even wisdom in and of themselves have no lasting significance (1:12—2:16), because death renders all earthly achievements futile.

2. *God confers meaning upon work.* Ecclesiastes describes the pointlessness of human toil (2:17—3:8), comparing it negatively to God's enduring work (3:9—6:7). The author concluded that people do well to enjoy their labor (3:22), trusting that God has a purpose in it (3:1).

3. *The injustice of oppression.* The Teacher displayed concern for the oppression of the weak by the powerful (4:1–3) and expressed dismay that, from his viewpoint, the wicked often thrive while the godly suffer (7:15–18). The perspective that little, if anything, can be done about injustice is later refuted by an authoritative reminder that God himself will one day bring justice to all (12:14).

4. *Human wisdom versus God's wisdom.* Ecclesiastes demonstrates the futility of humans contending with God (6:10). His ways are mysterious—far beyond our finite comprehension (6:8—12:7).

5. *God gives meaning to life.* The ultimate conclusion of the book is that life is meaningless without God. Because humans cannot fathom God's purposes or understand his ways, submission to him is the best course of action (12:1–14), especially in view of God's final judgment of "every hidden thing" (12:14).

OUTLINE

I. Author (1:1)
II. Theme: The Efforts of People Are Meaningless Apart From God (1:2)
III. Introduction: Accumulating Things Will Fail to Bring Happiness (1:3–11)
IV. Life Is to Be Enjoyed As a Gift From God (1:12—11:6)
V. Begin Enjoying Life in Your Youth Because God Will Judge (11:7—12:8)
VI. Conclusion: Reverently Trust In and Obey God (12:9–14)

Everything Is Meaningless

1 The words of the Teacher,[a][a] son of David, king in Jerusalem:[b]

2 "Meaningless! Meaningless!"
says the Teacher.
"Utterly meaningless!
Everything is meaningless."[c]
3 What does man gain from all his labor
at which he toils under the sun?[d]
4 Generations come and generations go,
but the earth remains forever.[e]
5 The sun rises and the sun sets,
and hurries back to where it rises.[f]
6 The wind blows to the south
and turns to the north;
round and round it goes,
ever returning on its course.
7 All streams flow into the sea,
yet the sea is never full.
To the place the streams come from,
there they return again.[g]
8 All things are wearisome,
more than one can say.
The eye never has enough of seeing,[h]
nor the ear its fill of hearing.
9 What has been will be again,
what has been done will be done again;[i]
there is nothing new under the sun.
10 Is there anything of which one can say,
"Look! This is something new"?
It was here already, long ago;
it was here before our time.
11 There is no remembrance of men of old,
and even those who are yet to come
will not be remembered
by those who follow.[j]

Wisdom Is Meaningless

12 I, the Teacher,[k] was king over Israel in Jerusalem. 13 I devoted myself to study and to explore by wis-
dom all that is done under heaven. What a heavy burden God has laid on men![l] 14 I have seen all the things
that are done under the sun; all of them are meaningless, a chasing after the wind.[m]

15 What is twisted cannot be straightened;[n]
what is lacking cannot be counted.

1:1 [a]ver 12; Ecc 7:27; 12:10 [b]Pr 1:1
1:2 [c]Ps 39:5-6; 62:9; 144:4; Ecc 12:8; Ro 8:20-21
1:3 [d]Ecc 2:11,22; 3:9; 5:15-16
1:4 [e]Ps 104:5; 119:90
1:5 [f]Ps 19:5-6
1:7 [g]Job 36:28
1:8 [h]Pr 27:20
1:9 [i]Ecc 2:12; 3:15
1:11 [j]Ecc 2:16
1:12 [k]ver 1
1:13 [l]Ge 3:17; Ecc 3:10
1:14 [m]Ecc 2:11, 17
1:15 [n]Ecc 7:13

[a] *1* Or *leader of the assembly*; also in verses 2 and 12

1:1—2:23 This book presents a pessimistic view of life apart from God. The writer's observation of nature and human experience led him to conclude that they, in and of themselves, do not impart purpose and meaning to life. He observed the endless cycles of nature (1:2–11) and found in them only tedium. They do not offer satisfaction, for "the eye never has enough of seeing" (1:8). Even wisdom (1:16–18; 2:12–17), pleasure (1:1–8) and toil (1:9–11; 2:18–23) are meaningless. There is no substance or satisfaction in them. They are "a chasing after the wind" (2:17).

1:1 "Ecclesiastes" (Greek, *ekklesiastes*) comes from the Hebrew *Qoheleth*, which can be translated "teacher" or "speaker in an assembly" (see the NIV text note; see also Ex 16:3; Nu 16:3). The Teacher, an instructor of wisdom whose work is described in Ecc 12:9–10, may also have held an office in the assembly.

The Hebrew word for "son" can refer to a descendant (even many generations removed)—or even to someone who follows in the footsteps of another (see Ge 4:21; see also the introduction to this book, as well as "The Authorship of Ecclesiastes and Song of Songs" on p. 1021).

1:13 The writer consistently referred to God by the name Elohim (almost 30 instances), which emphasizes God's absolute sovereignty. In no instance did he use the covenant name Yahweh (translated "LORD"; see "The Elohistic Psalter" on p. 836 and "YHWH: The Name of God in the Old Testament" on p. 89).

1:16 °1Ki 3:12; 4:30; Ecc 2:9
1:17 pEcc 7:23
qEcc 2:3,12; 7:25
1:18 rEcc 2:23; 12:12
2:1 sEcc 7:4; 8:15; Lk 12:19
2:2 tPr 14:13; Ecc 7:6
2:3 uver 24-25; Ecc 3:12-13
vEcc 1:17
2:4 w1Ki 7:1-12
xSS 8:11

16 I thought to myself, "Look, I have grown and increased in wisdom more than anyone who has ruled
over Jerusalem before me;[o] I have experienced much of wisdom and knowledge." 17 Then I applied my-
self to the understanding of wisdom,[p] and also of madness and folly,[q] but I learned that this, too, is a
chasing after the wind.

> 18 For with much wisdom comes much sorrow;
> the more knowledge, the more grief.[r]

Pleasures Are Meaningless

2 I thought in my heart, "Come now, I will test you with pleasure[s] to find out what is good." But that
also proved to be meaningless. 2 "Laughter,"[t] I said, "is foolish. And what does pleasure accomplish?"
3 I tried cheering myself with wine,[u] and embracing folly[v]—my mind still guiding me with wisdom. I
wanted to see what was worthwhile for men to do under heaven during the few days of their lives.
4 I undertook great projects: I built houses for myself[w] and planted vineyards.[x] 5 I made gardens and

---

1:16 The phrase "anyone who has ruled over Jerusalem before me" does not necessarily exclude Solomon as the Teacher. The reference could include kings prior to David, such as Melchizedek (Ge 14:18), Adoni-Zedek (Jos 10:1) and Abdi-Khepa (mentioned in the Amarna Letters from Egypt). See "The Authorship of Ecclesiastes and Song of Songs" on page 1021.

2:4–11 Ancient kings tended to grasp after god-likeness, attempting to burst through the confines of human life and achieve some real "gain." Biblical examples include Sennacherib (2Ki 18–19; see "The Death of Sennacherib" on p. 562 and "The Sennacherib Prism"on p. 659) and Nebuchadnezzar (Da 1–4; see "Nebuchadnezzar" on p. 571). Such individuals had resources at their disposal to make what they saw to be a credible attempt at equivalence with "the gods."

For a description of Solomon's splendor and commentary on his many wives, see 1 Kings 10:14—11:3.

2:4–6 Solomon's gardens and fruit orchards with pools of water for irrigation very likely suggested the imagery of Song of Songs 4:12–15.

There is no Hebrew or Greek equivalent to the word *irrigation*, although its use for watering plants and trees is frequently implied in the Bible (cf. Isa 58:11). There was less need of irrigation in the region later known as Palestine and in Syria than in Egypt and Babylonia. In Palestine irrigation was necessary only in the summer.

ANCIENT TEXTS AND ARTIFACTS

The Harper Songs From the Tomb of Neferhotep

ECCLESIASTES 1 Dating from the late fourteenth through the early thirteenth centuries B.C., three funerary banquet songs have been discovered on the walls of a tomb near Thebes, Egypt. The tomb belonged to a certain Neferhotep, the deceased whom the songs honor. Two of them offer somewhat contradictory attitudes regarding death and the afterlife. In Song I the harpist sings of the passing generations in which children are born, breathe life and begin moving inexorably toward the grave. The sun deity rises and sets continuously, but death is inevitable. The singer urges Neferhotep to forget the evil past and to remember only joyous occasions, for death is the great equalizer—indiscriminately claiming those with full granaries and those with nothing.

Song III has a more positive tone. Although it, too, declares that death is inescapable, it asserts that people are not equal after this event. Neferhotep's devotion to the Egyptian gods will be rewarded in the afterlife; he will be remembered both by his god and by people for his religiosity. Because of his piety, Neferhotep's enemies will be eternally defeated and his soul declared justified. In fact, he will be happier in the afterlife than he ever was on Earth.

Parallels for both songs can be found in Ecclesiastes. Ecclesiastes 1:4–5 speaks of generations coming and going and of the continual cycle of the rising and setting of the sun. Surely death is inevitable and overtakes us all (2:14,16; 9:2–3). Indeed, it equalizes humanity, since no one can take his or her achievements into the afterlife, but must leave them to the next generation (cf. 2:18–19). In his summary statement, however, the Teacher concludes that a person should honor God and obey his commandments, because every action will be judged by him (12:13–14). Unlike Neferhotep's Song III, the Teacher does not suggest that outward religiosity and cultic piety will be rewarded: God sees the hidden things as well as the obvious, and living a life of true wisdom begins with a proper understanding and fear of the Lord (cf. Pr 1:7).[1]

[1] See also "The Harper Song From the Tomb of King Intef" on page 1018.

parks and planted all kinds of fruit trees in them. 6 I made reservoirs to water groves of flourishing trees.
7 I bought male and female slaves and had other slaves who were born in my house. I also owned more
herds and flocks than anyone in Jerusalem before me. 8 I amassed silver and gold[y] for myself, and the **2:8** [y]1Ki 9:28;
treasure of kings and provinces. I acquired men and women singers,[z] and a harem[a] as well—the de- 10:10,14,21 [z]2Sa 19:35
lights of the heart of man. 9 I became greater by far than anyone in Jerusalem before me.[a] In all this my **2:9** [a]1Ch 29:25; Ecc 1:16
wisdom stayed with me.

> 10 I denied myself nothing my eyes desired;
> I refused my heart no pleasure.
> My heart took delight in all my work,
> and this was the reward for all my labor.
> 11 Yet when I surveyed all that my hands had done
> and what I had toiled to achieve,
> everything was meaningless, a chasing after the wind;[b] **2:11** [b]Ecc 1:14
> nothing was gained under the sun.[c] [c]Ecc 1:3

Wisdom and Folly Are Meaningless

> 12 Then I turned my thoughts to consider wisdom,
> and also madness and folly.[d] **2:12** [d]Ecc 1:17 [e]Ecc 1:9; 7:25
> What more can the king's successor do
> than what has already been done?[e]
> 13 I saw that wisdom[f] is better than folly,[g] **2:13** [f]Ecc 7:19; 9:18 [g]Ecc 7:11-12
> just as light is better than darkness.
> 14 The wise man has eyes in his head,
> while the fool walks in the darkness;
> but I came to realize
> that the same fate overtakes them both.[h] **2:14** [h]Ps 49:10; Pr 17:24; Ecc 3:19; 6:6; 7:2; 9:3,11-12

15 Then I thought in my heart,

> "The fate of the fool will overtake me also.
> What then do I gain by being wise?"[i] **2:15** [i]Ecc 6:8
> I said in my heart,
> "This too is meaningless."
> 16 For the wise man, like the fool, will not be long remembered;
> in days to come both will be forgotten.[j] **2:16** [j]Ecc 1:11; 9:5
> Like the fool, the wise man too must die!

Toil Is Meaningless

17 So I hated life, because the work that is done under the sun was grievous to me. All of it is mean-
ingless, a chasing after the wind.[k] 18 I hated all the things I had toiled for under the sun, because I must **2:17** [k]Ecc 4:2
leave them to the one who comes after me.[l] 19 And who knows whether he will be a wise man or a fool? **2:18** [l]Ps 39:6; 49:10
Yet he will have control over all the work into which I have poured my effort and skill under the sun. This
too is meaningless. 20 So my heart began to despair over all my toilsome labor under the sun. 21 For a man
may do his work with wisdom, knowledge and skill, and then he must leave all he owns to someone who

[a] *8* The meaning of the Hebrew for this phrase is uncertain.

2:6 Among the most famous reservoirs of the region now known as Palestine were the pools of Solomon, 13 miles (22 km) from Jerusalem. Three in number, they were fed by two chief sources: surface water and springs. Cleverly engineered aqueducts carried water from the desired spring to the pools. From these pools the water was conveyed by the same means to the wells under the temple area.

In the summer of 1962 Solomon's Pools were in the news, when a severe drought made necessary an emergency pipeline from a large new well at Hebron to alleviate Jerusalem's water shortage. The 18 miles (30 km) of pipe, furnished by the United States Agency for International Development, was laid within days, and the water was pumped into the ancient reservoirs. See *Time* magazine, August 18, 1962.

2:8 "Provinces" probably refers to the administrative divisions from which provisions were collected (see "Egyptian and Israelite Administration" on p. 486).

The Hebrew for "harem" occurs only here in Scripture (see the NIV text note). An early Egyptian letter uses a similar Canaanite term for concubines. It fits the situation of Solomon, who had 300 concubines in addition to 700 wives (1Ki 11:3).

2:17 In general, life throughout Bible times was simple, work arduous, hours long and wages minimal. "Then man goes out to his work, to his labor until evening" (Ps 104:23).

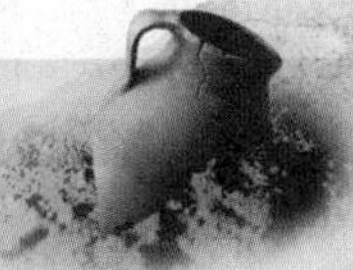

ARCHAEOLOGICAL SITES

TELL EL-KHELEIFEH

Remains of Tell el-Kheleifeh
Photograph courtesy of © Dr. Gary Pratico

ECCLESIASTES 2 Tell el-Kheleifeh was once thought to have been the site of Ezion Geber, a port city of Solomon. The site is located atop a small hillock in Jordan, approximately 547 yards (500 m) from the northern shore of the Gulf of Aqaba in the Red Sea. But scholars now recognize a lack of conclusive evidence for identifying Tell el-Kheleifeh with Ezion Geber. Early assumptions that a large-scale smelting operation took place there during Solomon's reign can no longer be sustained. If Tell el-Kheleifeh was unoccupied during Solomon's time it could not have been Ezion Geber. Although some pottery fragments at the site attest to occupation as far back as the eighth century B.C., little evidence exists for an earlier occupation.[1]

The earliest level at Tell el-Kheleifeh includes a four-room house measuring 40 square feet (12 sq m), surrounded by a mudbrick **casemate wall**[2] measuring 135 square feet (41 sq m). The structure may have served a variety of functions, possibly including use as a storehouse and as a citadel. A later phase expanded the site; it included a wall spanning 180 feet (54.9 m) on all sides, along with a four-chambered gate in the southern wall. While further excavation at this site may uncover a clearer picture of its age, identity and function, the current dearth of archaeological evidence severely limits firm conclusions. It is important to recognize that the identification of Tell el-Kheleifeh with Ezion Geber has not been disproved; in fact, some archaeologists believe that such an equation is still possible. But there is no extant evidence that Tell el-Kheleifeh was occupied in Solomon's time.

Although Solomon was a capable builder,[3] many of his works seem nowhere to be found. Some sites once thought to be Solomonic have proved not to be so. The grand works alluded to in Ecclesiastes 2 have, for the most part, simply been lost. Perhaps we do well to look on this as a metaphor reflecting that they were indeed—at least in some sense—"meaningless"!

[1]See also "Ezion Geber" on page 631. [2]See Glossary on page 2080 for definitions of bolded words. [3]See "The Building Activity of Solomon" on page 497.

has not worked for it. This too is meaningless and a great misfortune. 22 What does a man get for all the
toil and anxious striving with which he labors under the sun?[m] 23 All his days his work is pain and grief;[n]
even at night his mind does not rest. This too is meaningless.
24 A man can do nothing better than to eat and drink[o] and find satisfaction in his work.[p] This too, I
see, is from the hand of God,[q] 25 for without him, who can eat or find enjoyment? 26 To the man who pleas-
es him, God gives wisdom, knowledge and happiness, but to the sinner he gives the task of gathering
and storing up wealth[r] to hand it over to the one who pleases God.[s] This too is meaningless, a chasing
after the wind.

2:22 [m]Ecc 1:3; 3:9
2:23 [n]Job 5:7; 14:1; Ecc 1:18
2:24 [o]Ecc 8:15; 1Co 15:32 [p]Ecc 3:22 [q]Ecc 3:12-13; 5:17-19; 9:7-10
2:26 [r]Job 27:17 [s]Pr 13:22

A Time for Everything

3 There is a time[t] for everything,
and a season for every activity under heaven:

2 a time to be born and a time to die,
a time to plant and a time to uproot,
3 a time to kill and a time to heal,
a time to tear down and a time to build,
4 a time to weep and a time to laugh,
a time to mourn and a time to dance,
5 a time to scatter stones and a time to gather them,
a time to embrace and a time to refrain,
6 a time to search and a time to give up,
a time to keep and a time to throw away,

3:1 [t]ver 11,17; Ecc 8:6

2:24–26 In the history of its interpretation this book has been characterized as hedonistic because of the conclusion in verse 24. But this characterization of Ecclesiastes is rendered difficult by the fact that the writer concluded that pleasure does not lead to satisfaction either (v. 1). The book is also understood by some to be fatalistic in its approach to life. This perception is based on 3:16–22, which seems to conclude that a human being is no better off than an animal. This conclusion, however, is true only when people are viewed in and of themselves, apart from God.

Still, a positive view—a theology of contentment—emerges from the book. In view of the lack of substance and meaning in life, the Teacher urged his readers to enjoy life, for it is God who gives us that privilege (2:24–25). This satisfaction does not belong to all of humankind, for the work of the sinner ends in futility (v. 26). See also the note on 12:13–14.

ANCIENT TEXTS AND ARTIFACTS

The Harper Song From the Tomb of King Intef

ECCLESIASTES 3 A song carved on the tomb of Intef, an Egyptian pharaoh of the **Middle Kingdom** (c. 2106–1963 B.C.), has been preserved in two later copies: a **papyrus** manuscript and an inscription on a tomb contemporary with **Amenhotep IV**. Harper Songs[1] were most likely sung at funerary banquets honoring the dead and praising the afterlife, but the Intef Song is notable for its skeptical attitude toward seeking immortality. It begins by lamenting the cycle of passing generations and grieving over the silence of the graves of long-dead nobles (cf. Ecc 1:4,11).[2] The song recommends rejoicing while one is still alive, wearing fine linen and anointing oneself with oil (cf. 9:7–10). Since no one can escape death or take along earthly possessions into the afterlife, the author advocates that a person can do no better than to follow his or her heart's inclinations while here on Earth.

It is conceivable that the author of Ecclesiastes was familiar with the Intef Song. The kingdom of Solomon had strong contacts with Egypt, and the wise men of that day would have known and studied the masterpieces of Egyptian literature. If anything, this similarity reinforces the credibility of the Solomonic authorship of Ecclesiastes (see 1:1), since no other time in Israelite history was so notable for its strong interest in wisdom and close ties to Egypt. At the same time, although certain phrases and concepts of this song reflect sentiments similar to those found in Ecclesiastes, the overall effect is different. Whereas the Intef Song endorses pleasure for its own sake, the author of Ecclesiastes approved of enjoying life as an expression of gratitude for God's gifts (3:13; 9:7). Also, in Ecclesiastes, the manner in which his people celebrate is subject to God's judgment (11:7—12:1,13–14).

[1]See "The Harper Songs From the Tomb of Neferhotep" on page 1015. [2]See "Ancient Near Eastern Laments" on page 1305.

7 a time to tear and a time to mend,
a time to be silent[u] and a time to speak,
8 a time to love and a time to hate,
a time for war and a time for peace.

9 What does the worker gain from his toil?[v] 10 I have seen the burden God has laid on men.[w] 11 He has
made everything beautiful in its time.[x] He has also set eternity in the hearts of men; yet they cannot
fathom[y] what God has done from beginning to end.[z] 12 I know that there is nothing better for men than
to be happy and do good while they live. 13 That everyone may eat and drink,[a] and find satisfaction[b] in
all his toil—this is the gift of God.[c] 14 I know that everything God does will endure forever; nothing can
be added to it and nothing taken from it. God does it so that men will revere him.[d]

15 Whatever is has already been,[e]
and what will be has been before;[f]
and God will call the past to account.[a]

16 And I saw something else under the sun:

In the place of judgment—wickedness was there,
in the place of justice—wickedness was there.

17 I thought in my heart,

"God will bring to judgment[g]
both the righteous and the wicked,
for there will be a time for every activity,
a time for every deed."[h]

18 I also thought, "As for men, God tests them so that they may see
that they are like the animals.[i] 19 Man's fate[j] is like that of the animals;
the same fate awaits them both: As one dies, so dies the other. All have
the same breath[b]; man has no advantage over the animal. Everything
is meaningless. 20 All go to the same place; all come from dust, and to
dust all return.[k] 21 Who knows if the spirit of man rises upward[l] and
if the spirit of the animal[c] goes down into the earth?"
22 So I saw that there is nothing better for a man than to enjoy his
work,[m] because that is his lot.[n] For who can bring him to see what
will happen after him?

Oppression, Toil, Friendlessness

4 Again I looked and saw all the oppression[o] that was taking place
under the sun:

I saw the tears of the oppressed—
and they have no comforter;
power was on the side of their oppressors—
and they have no comforter.[p]
2 And I declared that the dead,[q]
who had already died,
are happier than the living,
who are still alive.[r]
3 But better than both
is he who has not yet been,[s]
who has not seen the evil
that is done under the sun.[t]

3:7 [u]Am 5:13
3:9 [v]Ecc 1:3
3:10 [w]Ecc 1:13
3:11 [x]ver 1 [y]Job 11:7; Ecc 8:17 [z]Job 28:23; Ro 11:33
3:13 [a]Ecc 2:3 [b]Ps 34:12 [c]Dt 12:7,18; Ecc 2:24; 5:19
3:14 [d]Job 23:15; Ecc 5:7; 7:18; 8:12-13; Jas 1:17
3:15 [e]Ecc 6:10 [f]Ecc 1:9
3:17 [g]Job 19:29; Ecc 11:9; Mt 16:27; Ro 2:6-8; 2Th 1:6-7 [h]ver 1
3:18 [i]Ps 73:22
3:19 [j]Ecc 2:14
3:20 [k]Ge 2:7; 3:19; Job 34:15
3:21 [l]Ecc 12:7
3:22 [m]Ecc 2:24; 5:18 [n]Job 31:2
4:1 [o]Ps 12:5; Ecc 3:16 [p]La 1:16
4:2 [q]Jer 20:17-18; 22:10 [r]Job 3:17; 10:18
4:3 [s]Job 3:16; Ecc 6:3 [t]Job 3:22

Ancient Voices

A generation passes,
Another stays,
Since the time of the ancestors.
The gods who were before rest in their tombs,
Blessed nobles too are buried in their tombs.
(Yet)* those who built tombs,
Their places are gone,
What has become of them?
I have heard the words of Imhotep and Harde def,
Whose sayings are recited whole.
What of their places?
Their walls have crumbled,
Their places are gone,
As though they had never been!

*Word in parentheses added by translator where text has gap

—The Song from the Tomb of King Intef

See "The Harper Song From the Tomb of King Intef" article.

[a] 15 Or *God calls back the past* [b] 19 Or *spirit* [c] 21 Or *Who knows the spirit of man, which rises upward, or the spirit of the animal, which*

3:20 "The same place" refers not to heaven or hell but to humankind's observable destination: a return to dust, just like the animals. Death is the great leveler of all living things (see Ge 3:19; Ps 103:14).

4 And I saw that all labor and all achievement spring from man's envy of his neighbor. This too is
meaningless, a chasing after the wind.[u]

5 The fool folds his hands[v]
and ruins himself.
6 Better one handful with tranquillity
than two handfuls with toil[w]
and chasing after the wind.

7 Again I saw something meaningless under the sun:

8 There was a man all alone;
he had neither son nor brother.
There was no end to his toil,
yet his eyes were not content[x] with his wealth.
"For whom am I toiling," he asked,
"and why am I depriving myself of enjoyment?"
This too is meaningless—
a miserable business!

9 Two are better than one,
because they have a good return for their work:
10 If one falls down,
his friend can help him up.
But pity the man who falls
and has no one to help him up!
11 Also, if two lie down together, they will keep warm.
But how can one keep warm alone?
12 Though one may be overpowered,
two can defend themselves.
A cord of three strands is not quickly broken.

Advancement Is Meaningless

13 Better a poor but wise youth than an old but foolish king who no longer knows how to take warn-
ing. 14 The youth may have come from prison to the kingship, or he may have been born in poverty with-
in his kingdom. 15 I saw that all who lived and walked under the sun followed the youth, the king's suc-
cessor. 16 There was no end to all the people who were before them. But those who came later were not
pleased with the successor. This too is meaningless, a chasing after the wind.

Stand in Awe of God

5 Guard your steps when you go to the house of God. Go near to listen rather than to offer the sacri-
fice of fools, who do not know that they do wrong.

2 Do not be quick with your mouth,
do not be hasty in your heart
to utter anything before God.[y]
God is in heaven
and you are on earth,
so let your words be few.[z]
3 As a dream[a] comes when there are many cares,
so the speech of a fool when there are many words.[b]

4 When you make a vow to God, do not delay in fulfilling it.[c] He has no pleasure in fools; fulfill your
vow.[d] 5 It is better not to vow than to make a vow and not fulfill it.[e] 6 Do not let your mouth lead you into
sin. And do not protest to the ⌞temple⌟ messenger, "My vow was a mistake." Why should God be angry at
what you say and destroy the work of your hands? 7 Much dreaming and many words are meaningless.
Therefore stand in awe of God.[f]

4:4 [u]Ecc 1:14
4:5 [v]Pr 6:10
4:6 [w]Pr 15:16-17; 16:8
4:8 [x]Pr 27:20
5:2 [y]Jdg 11:35 [z]Job 6:24; Pr 10:19; 20:25
5:3 [a]Job 20:8 [b]Ecc 10:14
5:4 [c]Dt 23:21; Jdg 11:35; Ps 119:60 [d]Nu 30:2; Ps 66:13-14; 76:11
5:5 [e]Nu 30:2-4; Pr 20:25; Jnh 2:9; Ac 5:4
5:7 [f]Ecc 3:14; 12:13

THE AUTHORSHIP OF ECCLESIASTES AND SONG OF SONGS

ECCLESIASTES 5 Few topics related to Biblical archaeology have generated more scholarly debate than that of the authorship of Ecclesiastes and Song of Songs. This is largely due to the unusual nature of the Hebrew used in these books. The two employ similar vocabulary, suggesting a common author. Further, a number of Biblical Hebrew words occur only in these two books, and others appear in higher frequency in these books than in others. Neither uses God's personal name, **Yahweh**, as is so common in other books.[1]

Although Ecclesiastes does not name Solomon, its description of the author as "a son of David, king in Jerusalem" (1:1; cf. 1:12) leaves little room for other conclusions. The association with Solomon is strengthened by 12:9, which describes the author as a wise man who "pondered and searched out and set in order many proverbs" (cf. 1Ki 4:32).

Ironically, the claim in Ecclesiastes 1:12, "I, the Teacher, was king over Israel," has been taken as evidence *against* Solomonic authorship due to the verb's past tense. But this can be regarded as a retrospective statement and translated as "I *have been* king over Israel." The declaration in 1:16, "I have grown and increased in wisdom more than anyone who has ruled over Jerusalem before me," is meaningful when we remember that Jebusite kings had ruled over Jerusalem since ancient times.[2]

Other objections to Solomonic authorship have been raised on the basis of language. The high number of **Aramaic** words in Ecclesiastes has been considered evidence of a **postexilic** date of writing. It is now recognized, however, that Aramaic influence on Hebrew began very early. Moreover, the vocabulary identified as Aramaic may actually have represented a northern dialect of Hebrew or a nonstandard, colloquial dialect.

Some words in both books were once alleged to have been borrowed long after Solomon's death from Persian or Greek. Examples include *pardes* ("park" or "orchard" in 2:5 and SS 4:13, respectively) and *appiryon* ("carriage" in SS 3:9). In reality, such words are of very ancient origin, some going back to Sanskrit originals. Solomon's commercial projects (see 1Ki 5; 9:26–28; 10:22) involved numerous international contacts, a possible explanation for the international vocabulary.[3]

The mention of numerous varieties of flora and fauna is consistent with Solomon's interest in natural history (1Ki 4:33). The Song's spectacular vocabulary for exotic spices and other vegetation, as well as for gold, alabaster and jewels, suggests that the book was written by someone familiar with these things. It is improbable that both Ecclesiastes and Song of Songs were written during the postexilic period, when Jerusalem was a poor, backwater town among the nations of the world, by no means awash in exotic spices and precious stones.[4]

The mention of Tirzah in parallel with Jerusalem in Song of Songs 6:4 reflects a period before Tirzah's selection as the early capital of the northern kingdom (c. 930 B.C.). In the tenth century B.C. Tirzah was beautiful and could easily have stood alongside Jerusalem as one of Israel's two grand cities. In the postexilic period, when many claim the Song was written, Tirzah no longer existed.[5] Also, mention of localities in both the north and south (e.g., Jerusalem, En Gedi, Heshbon, Carmel, Hermon and Leba non) suggests that the Song preceded the divided kingdom.

Finally, literary parallels and allusions in both Ecclesiastes and the Song suggest an earlier rather than a later date for their composition. Ecclesiastes 9:7–9, for example, strongly resembles Tablet 10, section 3, of the Epic of Gilgamesh,[6] where the hero is urged to enjoy life, wear clean clothing and enjoy his wife's love. In addition, the love poetry of the Song is similar to Egyptian poetry of this genre that flourished in the late second millennium B.C.[7] It is likely that Solomon, at the height of Israel's power, would have known this literature, but quite unlikely that obscure postexilic writers would have been familiar with it or expected their readers to appreciate it.

Given the internal indicators that point to Solomonic authorship and the lack of satisfactory evidence to the contrary, it is appropriate to read Ecclesiastes and Song of Songs as literary products of the last king of the **united monarchy**.

[1]See "YHWH: The Name of God in the Old Testament" on page 89. [2]See "The Jebusites" on page 596. [3]See "Solomon and the Israelite Empire" on page 490. [4]See "Precious Stones of the Biblical World" on page 1156. [5]See "Tirzah" on page 509. [6]See "Ecclesiastes and the Epic of Gilgamesh" on page 1027. [7]See "Ancient Love Poetry" on page 1035.

Riches Are Meaningless

8 If you see the poor oppressed[g] in a district, and justice and rights denied, do not be surprised at such **5:8** [g]Ps 12:5; Ecc 4:1
things; for one official is eyed by a higher one, and over them both are others higher still. 9 The increase
from the land is taken by all; the king himself profits from the fields.

10 Whoever loves money never has money enough;
whoever loves wealth is never satisfied with his income.
This too is meaningless.

11 As goods increase,
so do those who consume them.
And what benefit are they to the owner
except to feast his eyes on them?

12 The sleep of a laborer is sweet,
whether he eats little or much,
but the abundance of a rich man
permits him no sleep.[h] **5:12** [h]Job 20:20

13 I have seen a grievous evil under the sun:[i] **5:13** [i]Ecc 6:1-2

wealth hoarded to the harm of its owner,
14 or wealth lost through some misfortune,
so that when he has a son
there is nothing left for him.
15 Naked a man comes from his mother's womb,
and as he comes, so he departs.[j] **5:15** [j]Job 1:21 [k]Ps 49:17; 1Ti 6:7 [l]Ecc 1:3
He takes nothing from his labor[k]
that he can carry in his hand.[l]

16 This too is a grievous evil:

As a man comes, so he departs,
and what does he gain,
since he toils for the wind?[m] **5:16** [m]Pr 11:29; Ecc 1:3
17 All his days he eats in darkness,
with great frustration, affliction and anger.

18 Then I realized that it is good and proper for a man to eat and drink,[n] and to find satisfaction in his **5:18** [n]Ecc 2:3 [o]Ecc 2:10,24
toilsome labor[o] under the sun during the few days of life God has given him—for this is his lot. 19 More-
over, when God gives any man wealth and possessions,[p] and enables him to enjoy them,[q] to accept his **5:19** [p]1Ch 29:12; 2Ch 1:12 [q]Ecc 6:2 [r]Job 31:2 [s]Ecc 2:24; 3:13
lot[r] and be happy in his work—this is a gift of God.[s] 20 He seldom reflects on the days of his life, because
God keeps him occupied with gladness of heart.[t] **5:20** [t]Dt 12:7,18

6 I have seen another evil under the sun, and it weighs heavily on men: 2 God gives a man wealth, pos-
sessions and honor, so that he lacks nothing his heart desires, but God does not enable him to en-
joy them,[u] and a stranger enjoys them instead. This is meaningless, a grievous evil.[v] **6:2** [u]Ps 17:14; Ecc 5:19 [v]Ecc 5:13
3 A man may have a hundred children and live many years; yet no matter how long he lives, if he can-
not enjoy his prosperity and does not receive proper burial, I say that a stillborn[w] child is better off than **6:3** [w]Job 3:16; Ecc 4:3 [x]Job 3:3
he.[x] 4 It comes without meaning, it departs in darkness, and in darkness its name is shrouded. 5 Though
it never saw the sun or knew anything, it has more rest than does that man— 6 even if he lives a thou-
sand years twice over but fails to enjoy his prosperity. Do not all go to the same place?

7 All man's efforts are for his mouth,
yet his appetite is never satisfied.[y] **6:7** [y]Pr 16:26; 27:20
8 What advantage has a wise man
over a fool?[z] **6:8** [z]Ecc 2:15

6:3 The phrase "not receive proper burial" probably refers to dying unlamented or dishonored, like King Jehoiakim (Jer 22:18–19).

What does a poor man gain
by knowing how to conduct himself before others?
9 Better what the eye sees
than the roving of the appetite.
This too is meaningless,
a chasing after the wind.[a]

6:9 [a]Ecc 1:14

10 Whatever exists has already been named,
and what man is has been known;
no man can contend
with one who is stronger than he.
11 The more the words,
the less the meaning,
and how does that profit anyone?

12 For who knows what is good for a man in life, during the few and meaningless days[b] he passes
through like a shadow?[c] Who can tell him what will happen under the sun after he is gone?

6:12 [b]Job 10:20 [c]Job 14:2; Ps 39:6; Jas 4:14

Wisdom

7 A good name is better than fine perfume,[d]
and the day of death better than the day of birth.
2 It is better to go to a house of mourning
than to go to a house of feasting,
for death[e] is the destiny[f] of every man;
the living should take this to heart.
3 Sorrow is better than laughter,[g]
because a sad face is good for the heart.
4 The heart of the wise is in the house of mourning,
but the heart of fools is in the house of pleasure.[h]
5 It is better to heed a wise man's rebuke[i]
than to listen to the song of fools.
6 Like the crackling of thorns[j] under the pot,
so is the laughter[k] of fools.
This too is meaningless.

7:1 [d]Pr 22:1; SS 1:3
7:2 [e]Pr 11:19 [f]Ps 90:12
7:3 [g]Pr 14:13
7:4 [h]Ecc 2:1; Jer 16:8
7:5 [i]Ps 141:5; Pr 13:18; 15:31-32
7:6 [j]Ps 58:9; 118:12 [k]Ecc 2:2

7 Extortion turns a wise man into a fool,
and a bribe[l] corrupts the heart.

7:7 [l]Ex 18:21; 23:8; Dt 16:19

8 The end of a matter is better than its beginning,
and patience[m] is better than pride.
9 Do not be quickly provoked[n] in your spirit,
for anger resides in the lap of fools.

7:8 [m]Pr 14:29; Gal 5:22; Eph 4:2
7:9 [n]Mt 5:22; Pr 14:17; Jas 1:19

10 Do not say, "Why were the old days better than these?"
For it is not wise to ask such questions.

11 Wisdom, like an inheritance, is a good thing[o]
and benefits those who see the sun.[p]
12 Wisdom is a shelter
as money is a shelter,
but the advantage of knowledge is this:
that wisdom preserves the life of its possessor.

7:11 [o]Pr 8:10-11; Ecc 2:13 [p]Ecc 11:7

13 Consider what God has done:[q]

Who can straighten
what he has made crooked?[r]
14 When times are good, be happy;
but when times are bad, consider:

7:13 [q]Ecc 2:24 [r]Ecc 1:15

God has made the one
as well as the other.
Therefore, a man cannot discover
anything about his future.

15 In this meaningless life[s] of mine I have seen both of these:

7:15 [s]Job 7:7 [t]Ecc 8:12-14; Jer 12:1

a righteous man perishing in his righteousness,
and a wicked man living long in his wickedness.[t]
16 Do not be overrighteous,
neither be overwise—
why destroy yourself?
17 Do not be overwicked,
and do not be a fool—
why die before your time?[u]

7:17 [u]Job 15:32; Ps 55:23

18 It is good to grasp the one
and not let go of the other.
The man who fears God[v] will avoid all ⌞extremes⌟.[a]

7:18 [v]Ecc 3:14

19 Wisdom[w] makes one wise man more powerful[x]
than ten rulers in a city.

7:19 [w]Ecc 2:13 [x]Ecc 9:13-18

20 There is not a righteous man[y] on earth
who does what is right and never sins.[z]

7:20 [y]Ps 14:3 [z]1Ki 8:46; 2Ch 6:36; Pr 20:9; Ro 3:23

21 Do not pay attention to every word people say,
or you[a] may hear your servant cursing you—

7:21 [a]Pr 30:10

22 for you know in your heart
that many times you yourself have cursed others.

23 All this I tested by wisdom and I said,

"I am determined to be wise"[b]—
but this was beyond me.

7:23 [b]Ecc 1:17; Ro 1:22

24 Whatever wisdom may be,
it is far off and most profound—
who can discover it?[c]

7:24 [c]Job 28:12

25 So I turned my mind to understand,
to investigate and to search out wisdom and the scheme of things[d]
and to understand the stupidity of wickedness
and the madness of folly.[e]

7:25 [d]Job 28:3 [e]Ecc 1:17

26 I find more bitter than death
the woman who is a snare,[f]
whose heart is a trap
and whose hands are chains.
The man who pleases God will escape her,
but the sinner she will ensnare.[g]

7:26 [f]Ex 10:7; Jdg 14:15 [g]Pr 2:16-19; 5:3-5; 7:23; 22:14

27 "Look," says the Teacher,[b][h] "this is what I have discovered:

7:27 [h]Ecc 1:1

"Adding one thing to another to discover the scheme of things—
28 while I was still searching
but not finding—
I found one ⌞upright⌟ man among a thousand,
but not one ⌞upright⌟ woman[i] among them all.

7:28 [i]1Ki 11:3

29 This only have I found:
God made mankind upright,
but men have gone in search of many schemes."

[a] 18 Or *will follow them both* [b] 27 Or *leader of the assembly*

8

Who is like the wise man?
Who knows the explanation of things?
Wisdom brightens a man's face
and changes its hard appearance.

Obey the King

[2]Obey the king's command, I say, because you took an oath before God. [3]Do not be in a hurry to leave
the king's presence.[j] Do not stand up for a bad cause, for he will do whatever he pleases. [4]Since a king's
word is supreme, who can say to him, "What are you doing?[k]"

8:3 [j]Ecc 10:4
8:4 [k]Job 9:12; Est 1:19; Da 4:35

CULTURAL AND HISTORICAL NOTES

The Sage

ECCLESIASTES 7 The epilogue of Ecclesiastes identifies the writer as a sage or wise man (12:9). His teachings are viewed as part of "the words of the wise," which are like goads. Those who master these teachings are said to be firmly embedded nails (12:11). Such ideas represent the outlook of Biblical Wisdom Literature. Although the theme of wisdom is present throughout the Bible, most scholars consider Job, Proverbs and Ecclesiastes to be Biblical Wisdom Literature in the strictest sense. Outside the Bible, in both Jewish and pagan writings, there are many other texts that could be called wisdom literature, a genre that can be recognized both by how it speaks and by what it says.[1]

✣ Wisdom texts frequently assume the posture of a parent addressing a child. The reader is thus often addressed as "my son" (cf. Pr 1:8,10,15; 2:1; 3:1; 5:1; Ecc 12:12).

✣ Wisdom literature uses proverbial sayings and parables, as well as mnemonic (intended or arranged to assist the memory) or numerical lists (e.g., Pr 1:1; 10:1; 30:15–16,18–19,21–23,29–31; Ecc 12:9).

✣ Wisdom literature concentrates on ethical themes within wisdom texts, even to the extent of addressing the conduct of God himself (as is done several times in Job).

✣ The figure of the sage is at the center of the wisdom tradition.

Sometimes "wise" is simply an adjective to connote that an individual was thoughtful, intelligent, skilled or devout (Dt 1:13; 1Ki 2:9). In other instances, however, a wise person was assumed to have been a member of a social class of sages, whose functions included those of teacher, government counselor or scribe.

The sage was the embodiment of wisdom, the master of tradition and the teacher of all who craved instruction. The sage was the opposite of the fool (Pr 3:35; 10:1; 14:1; Ecc 10:12).

The Bible attests to the presence of sages in a technical sense in Egypt (Ge 41:8), **Babylon** (Da 2:12–18), **Persia** (Est 1:13) and Israel itself (Pr 1:6; 13:20; Ecc 12:11).

Significant examples of wisdom literature have been discovered throughout the ancient Near East. Egyptian examples can be seen in The Instruction of Ptahhotep and The Instruction of Anii.[2] **Mesopotamian** examples are found in texts such as The Wisdom of Ahiqar, The Babylonian Theodicy[3] and even aspects of The Epic of Gilgamesh.[4] Many of these texts contain ideas and terms that are similar to what is seen in Biblical wisdom traditions.[5] For some scholars the contact between the Bible and other ancient Near Eastern literature seems closest in this area.

Wisdom literature continued in the Jewish literature of the post-Biblical period. Texts in the **Apocrypha** such as The Wisdom of Sirach (or Ecclesiasticus) and The Wisdom of Solomon attest to the vibrancy of the tradition.[6] After the destruction of Herod's temple in A.D. 70, the Judaism of the rabbinic sages was constructed around wisdom's central call that "the fear of the LORD is the beginning of knowledge" (Pr 1:7; 22:4; Ecc 12:13). The voluminous Jewish literary production of **Mishnah**, **Midrash** and **Talmud** has been affectionately deemed the "literature of the sages."

[1]See "Ancient Near Eastern Wisdom" on page 960. [2]See "The Instructions of Anii" on page 990. [3]See "The Babylonian Theodicy" on page 776. [4]See "Ecclesiastes and the Epic of Gilgamesh" on page 1027. [5]See, for example, "Maat and Lady Wisdom" on page 971. [6]See "The Apocrypha" on page 1973.

5 Whoever obeys his command will come to no harm,
and the wise heart will know the proper time and procedure.
6 For there is a proper time and procedure for every matter,[l]
though a man's misery weighs heavily upon him.

7 Since no man knows the future,
who can tell him what is to come?
8 No man has power over the wind to contain it[a];
so no one has power over the day of his death.
As no one is discharged in time of war,
so wickedness will not release those who practice it.

9 All this I saw, as I applied my mind to everything done under the sun. There is a time when a man
lords it over others to his own[b] hurt. 10 Then too, I saw the wicked buried[m]—those who used to come and
go from the holy place and receive praise[c] in the city where they did this. This too is meaningless.
11 When the sentence for a crime is not quickly carried out, the hearts of the people are filled with
schemes to do wrong. 12 Although a wicked man commits a hundred crimes and still lives a long
time, I know that it will go better[n] with God-fearing men,[o] who are reverent before God.[p] 13 Yet be-
cause the wicked do not fear God,[q] it will not go well with them, and their days[r] will not lengthen
like a shadow.
14 There is something else meaningless that occurs on earth: righteous men who get what the wicked
deserve, and wicked men who get what the righteous deserve.[s] This too, I say, is meaningless.[t] 15 So I
commend the enjoyment of life[u], because nothing is better for a man under the sun than to eat and
drink[v] and be glad.[w] Then joy will accompany him in his work all the days of the life God has given him
under the sun.
16 When I applied my mind to know wisdom[x] and to observe man's labor on earth[y]—his eyes not
seeing sleep day or night— 17 then I saw all that God has done.[z] No one can comprehend what goes on
under the sun. Despite all his efforts to search it out, man cannot discover its meaning. Even if a wise
man claims he knows, he cannot really comprehend it.[a]

A Common Destiny for All

9 So I reflected on all this and concluded that the righteous and the wise and what they do are in God's
hands, but no man knows whether love or hate awaits him.[b] 2 All share a common destiny—the
righteous and the wicked, the good and the bad,[d] the clean and the unclean, those who offer sacrifices
and those who do not.

As it is with the good man,
so with the sinner;
as it is with those who take oaths,
so with those who are afraid to take them.[c]

3 This is the evil in everything that happens under the sun: The same destiny overtakes all.[d] The hearts
of men, moreover, are full of evil and there is madness in their hearts while they live,[e] and afterward
they join the dead.[f] 4 Anyone who is among the living has hope[e]—even a live dog is better off than a
dead lion!

5 For the living know that they will die,
but the dead know nothing;[g]
they have no further reward,
and even the memory of them[h] is forgotten.[i]
6 Their love, their hate
and their jealousy have long since vanished;
never again will they have a part
in anything that happens under the sun.[j]

8:6 [l]Ecc 3:1
8:10 [m]Ecc 1:11
8:12 [n]Dt 12:28; Ps 37:11,18-19; Pr 1:32-33; Isa 3:10-11 [o]Ex 1:20 [p]Ecc 3:14
8:13 [q]Ecc 3:14; Isa 3:11 [r]Dt 4:40; Job 5:26; Ps 34:12; Isa 65:20
8:14 [s]Job 21:7; Ps 73:14; Mal 3:15 [t]Ecc 7:15
8:15 [u]Ps 42:8 [v]Ex 32:6; Ecc 2:3 [w]Ecc 2:24; 3:12-13; 5:18; 9:7
8:16 [x]Ecc 1:17 [y]Ecc 1:13
8:17 [z]Job 28:3 [a]Job 5:9; 28:23; Ecc 3:11; Ro 11:33
9:1 [b]Dt 33:3; Job 12:10; Ecc 10:14
9:2 [c]Job 9:22; Ecc 2:14; 6:6; 7:2
9:3 [d]Job 9:22; Ecc 2:14 [e]Jer 11:8; 13:10; 16:12; 17:9 [f]Job 21:26
9:5 [g]Job 14:21 [h]Ps 9:6 [i]Ecc 1:11; 2:16; Isa 26:14
9:6 [j]Job 21:21

[a] 8 Or *over his spirit to retain it* [b] 9 Or *to their* [c] 10 Some Hebrew manuscripts and Septuagint (Aquila); most Hebrew manuscripts *and are forgotten* [d] 2 Septuagint (Aquila), Vulgate and Syriac; Hebrew does not have *and the bad.* [e] 4 Or *What then is to be chosen? With all who live, there is hope*

ECCLESIASTES AND THE EPIC OF GILGAMESH

ECCLESIASTES 9 The longest literary composition known from **Mesopotamia** is the Epic of Gilgamesh, the tale of an ancient king's failed quest for immortality. It is a very ancient work, dating to at least 2000 B.C., that follows the trials and adventures of Gilgamesh, king of **Uruk** ("Map 1"). The Gilgamesh Epic has come to us in more than one version (there is an **Old Babylonian** and a standard Assyrian version), but the message is essentially the same. A tavern-keeper's advice to the hero, Gilgamesh, summarizes its message: In view of the impending death of all humankind, the task of mortals is to make the most of life—to eat, drink, be merry, be clean, dress radiantly, delight in one's children and provide joy for one's spouse (Old Babylonian version, 10.3).

Scholars have long noted the similarity of this admonition to that of the "Teacher" in Ecclesiastes, whose personal wrestling with life's meaning, transience and enigmas led him to conclude that people do well to seize the day, finding satisfaction in all that God gives (see 9:3,7–10; 11:7—12:1). The Teacher also concluded that the accumulated works that have been accomplished under the sun are essentially "meaningless, a chasing after the wind" (1:14; 2:11,17,26; 5:10,16; 6:9). This outlook corresponds closely to one of Gilgamesh's statements: "Only the gods [live] forever under the sun. As for mankind, their days are numbered; whatever they achieve is but wind!" Other parallels to Ecclesiastes found in Gilgamesh include the mention of a three-stranded cord when commenting on friendship (cf. 4:9–12) and the point that no aspect of life is permanent (1:4,11; 2:16; 3:18–19; 9:5–6).

Gilgamesh and the Bull of Heaven; Sumer, c. 2600 B.C.

© The Schøyen Collection; photography courtesy of Mr. Martin Schøyen

In view of these similarities, it appears that the author of Ecclesiastes, writing from Israel during the first millennium B.C.,[1] knew and appreciated the Gilgamesh Epic, a Mesopotamian work completed early in the second millennium B.C. Because a copied fragment of the Epic, dating to the fourteenth century B.C., was discovered in northern Israel, we know that the story of Gilgamesh was at least known in the region at an early time. It is important, however, to keep the following in mind:

- The "Teacher's" apparent use of Gilgamesh does not diminish his book's **canonical** status. It is not uncommon for Biblical texts to follow the pattern of nonbiblical counterparts, even to the point of citing them directly. For example, Deuteronomy follows the pattern of an ancient Near Eastern treaty,[2] and Paul cited a poet's description of Crete (Tit 1:12).[3]
- There is no suggestion that Ecclesiastes as a whole was modeled after Gilgamesh. There are enormous differences between the two. Ecclesiastes, for example, is not an epic poem and does not tell a story.
- Although the call to joy in 9:7–10 finds its closest ancient parallel in the Gilgamesh Epic, the wording is not exact. No scholars suggest that Ecclesiastes simply lifted lines from Gilgamesh.

The probability that the author of Ecclesiastes was familiar with Gilgamesh actually supports the traditional view of the book's Solomonic authorship. It is doubtful that an anonymous, postexilic Jew, living in an impoverished cultural environment (the Jerusalem of this time) would have demonstrated intimate familiarity with this very ancient **Akkadian** text. On the other hand, the age of Solomon constituted the high-water mark of Israel's history, as well as its literary golden age. Akkadian was still widely spoken, and **cuneiform** was still in use in Solomon's day.

Some of the concepts found in Ecclesiastes also have strong parallels in Egyptian literature.[4] This suggests that Ecclesiastes was not simply borrowing from Gilgamesh but making use of wisdom literature from the great centers of learning in the ancient world.

Ecclesiastes and the Gilgamesh Epic wrestle with the same human question: How is one to live when life appears to make no sense? Despite the literary link between the two, they are worlds apart theologically. The Epic challenges people to enjoy life but holds out no lasting source of hope. Within Ecclesiastes, on the other hand, life's enigmas and sorrows are tempered by the hope that endures when an individual remembers and fears God (see 5:7; 8:12; 12:1,13–14).

[1]See "The Authorship of Ecclesiastes and Song of Songs" on page 1021. [2]See "Deuteronomy and the Covenant Treaty Form" on page 255. [3]See "Crete" on page 1972. [4]See "The Harper Songs From the Tomb of Neferhotep" on page 1015 and "The Harper Song From the Tomb of King Intef" on page 1018.

7 Go, eat your food with gladness, and drink your wine[k] with a joyful heart,[l] for it is now that God fa-
vors what you do. 8 Always be clothed in white,[m] and always anoint your head with oil. 9 Enjoy life with
your wife,[n] whom you love, all the days of this meaningless life that God has given you under the sun—
all your meaningless days. For this is your lot[o] in life and in your toilsome labor under the sun. 10 What-
ever[p] your hand finds to do, do it with all your might,[q] for in the grave,[a][r] where you are going, there is
neither working nor planning nor knowledge nor wisdom.[s]

11 I have seen something else under the sun:

The race is not to the swift
or the battle to the strong,[t]
nor does food come to the wise[u]
or wealth to the brilliant
or favor to the learned;
but time and chance[v] happen to them all.[w]

12 Moreover, no man knows when his hour will come:

As fish are caught in a cruel net,
or birds are taken in a snare,
so men are trapped by evil times[x]
that fall unexpectedly upon them.[y]

Wisdom Better Than Folly

13 I also saw under the sun this example of wisdom[z] that greatly impressed me: 14 There was once a
small city with only a few people in it. And a powerful king came against it, surrounded it and built huge
siegeworks against it. 15 Now there lived in that city a man poor but wise, and he saved the city by his
wisdom. But nobody remembered that poor man.[a] 16 So I said, "Wisdom is better than strength." But the
poor man's wisdom is despised, and his words are no longer heeded.[b]

17 The quiet words of the wise are more to be heeded
than the shouts of a ruler of fools.
18 Wisdom[c] is better than weapons of war,
but one sinner destroys much good.

10

As dead flies give perfume a bad smell,
so a little folly[d] outweighs wisdom and honor.
2 The heart of the wise inclines to the right,
but the heart of the fool to the left.
3 Even as he walks along the road,
the fool lacks sense
and shows everyone[e] how stupid he is.
4 If a ruler's anger rises against you,
do not leave your post;[f]
calmness can lay great errors to rest.[g]
5 There is an evil I have seen under the sun,
the sort of error that arises from a ruler:
6 Fools are put in many high positions,[h]
while the rich occupy the low ones.
7 I have seen slaves on horseback,
while princes go on foot like slaves.[i]
8 Whoever digs a pit may fall into it;[j]
whoever breaks through a wall may be bitten by a snake.[k]

[a] 10 Hebrew *Sheol*

9:7 [k]Nu 6:20 [l]Ecc 2:24; 8:15 **9:8** [m]Ps 23:5; Rev 3:4 **9:9** [n]Pr 5:18 [o]Job 31:2
9:10 [p]1Sa 10:7 [q]Ecc 11:6; Ro 12:11; Col 3:23 [r]Nu 16:33 [s]Ecc 2:24
9:11 [t]Am 2:14-15 [u]Job 32:13; Isa 47:10; Jer 9:23 [v]Ecc 2:14 [w]Dt 8:18
9:12 [x]Pr 29:6 [y]Ps 73:22; Ecc 2:14; 8:7
9:13 [z]2Sa 20:22
9:15 [a]Ge 40:14; Ecc 1:11; 2:16; 4:13 **9:16** [b]Pr 21:22; Ecc 7:19
9:18 [c]ver 16
10:1 [d]Pr 13:16; 18:2
10:3 [e]Pr 13:16; 18:2
10:4 [f]Ecc 8:3 [g]Pr 16:14; 25:15
10:6 [h]Pr 29:2
10:7 [i]Pr 19:10
10:8 [j]Ps 7:15; 57:6; Pr 26:27 [k]Est 2:23; Ps 9:16; Am 5:19

9:7–9 The Babylonian Epic of Gilgamesh (see "Ecclesiastes and the Epic of Gilgamesh" on p. 1027) contains a section (10.3.6–14) remarkably similar to this passage, illustrating the international flavor of ancient wisdom literature (see "Ancient Near Eastern Wisdom" on p. 960).

10:9 [l]Pr 26:27

9 Whoever quarries stones may be injured by them;
whoever splits logs may be endangered by them.[l]

10 If the ax is dull
and its edge unsharpened,
more strength is needed
but skill will bring success.

10:11 [m]Ps 58:5; Isa 3:3

11 If a snake bites before it is charmed,
there is no profit for the charmer.[m]

10:12 [n]Pr 10:32 [o]Pr 10:14; 14:3; 15:2; 18:7

12 Words from a wise man's mouth are gracious,[n]
but a fool is consumed by his own lips.[o]
13 At the beginning his words are folly;
at the end they are wicked madness—

10:14 [p]Pr 15:2; Ecc 5:3; 6:12; 8:7 [q]Ecc 9:1

14 and the fool multiplies words.[p]

No one knows what is coming—
who can tell him what will happen after him?[q]

15 A fool's work wearies him;
he does not know the way to town.

10:16 [r]Isa 3:4-5, 12

16 Woe to you, O land whose king was a servant[a][r]
and whose princes feast in the morning.
17 Blessed are you, O land whose king is of noble birth
and whose princes eat at a proper time—
for strength and not for drunkenness.[s]

10:17 [s]Dt 14:26; 1Sa 25:36; Pr 31:4

10:18 [t]Pr 20:4; 24:30-34

18 If a man is lazy, the rafters sag;
if his hands are idle, the house leaks.[t]

10:19 [u]Ge 14:18; Jdg 9:13

19 A feast is made for laughter,
and wine[u] makes life merry,
but money is the answer for everything.

10:20 [v]Ex 22:28

20 Do not revile the king[v] even in your thoughts,
or curse the rich in your bedroom,
because a bird of the air may carry your words,
and a bird on the wing may report what you say.

Bread Upon the Waters

11:1 [w]ver 6; Isa 32:20; Hos 10:12 [x]Dt 24:19; Pr 19:17; Mt 10:42

11

Cast[w] your bread upon the waters,
for after many days you will find it again.[x]
2 Give portions to seven, yes to eight,
for you do not know what disaster may come upon the land.

3 If clouds are full of water,
they pour rain upon the earth.
Whether a tree falls to the south or to the north,
in the place where it falls, there will it lie.
4 Whoever watches the wind will not plant;
whoever looks at the clouds will not reap.

[a] 16 Or *king is a child*

10:12 "Words" are a common theme in wisdom literature (see, e.g., Pr 15; Jas 3:2–12).

11:1 This verse probably refers to the benefits of sea trade (see "Seafaring in the Ancient World" on p. 1473). The Teacher advocated being adventurous, for those who accept the risks will reap the returns.

11:2 The Teacher encouraged diversification of investments, because an individual can never know in advance which ventures may succeed or fail.

5 As you do not know the path of the wind,[y]
or how the body is formed[a] in a mother's womb,[z]
so you cannot understand the work of God,
the Maker of all things.

6 Sow your seed in the morning,
and at evening let not your hands be idle,[a]
for you do not know which will succeed,
whether this or that,
or whether both will do equally well.

Remember Your Creator While Young

7 Light is sweet,
and it pleases the eyes to see the sun.[b]
8 However many years a man may live,
let him enjoy them all.
But let him remember[c] the days of darkness,
for they will be many.
Everything to come is meaningless.

9 Be happy, young man, while you are young,
and let your heart give you joy in the days of your youth.
Follow the ways of your heart
and whatever your eyes see,
but know that for all these things
God will bring you to judgment.[d]
10 So then, banish anxiety[e] from your heart
and cast off the troubles of your body,
for youth and vigor are meaningless.[f]

12 Remember[g] your Creator
in the days of your youth,
before the days of trouble[h] come
and the years approach when you will say,
"I find no pleasure in them"—
2 before the sun and the light
and the moon and the stars grow dark,
and the clouds return after the rain;
3 when the keepers of the house tremble,
and the strong men stoop,
when the grinders cease because they are few,
and those looking through the windows grow dim;
4 when the doors to the street are closed
and the sound of grinding fades;
when men rise up at the sound of birds,
but all their songs grow faint;[i]
5 when men are afraid of heights
and of dangers in the streets;
when the almond tree blossoms
and the grasshopper drags himself along
and desire no longer is stirred.

11:5 [y]Jn 3:8-10 [z]Ps 139:14-16
11:6 [a]Ecc 9:10
11:7 [b]Ecc 7:11
11:8 [c]Ecc 12:1
11:9 [d]Job 19:29; Ecc 2:24; 3:17; 12:14; Ro 14:10
11:10 [e]Ps 94:19 [f]Ecc 2:24
12:1 [g]Ecc 11:8 [h]2Sa 19:35
12:4 [i]Jer 25:10

[a] 5 Or *know how life* (or *the spirit*) */ enters the body being formed*

12:5 This verse describes the aging process. The almond tree's pale blossom possibly suggests the white hair of old age. A grasshopper, which is normally agile, slows its movements on a cold morning (cf. Na 3:17)—a depiction of the stiffness of age. In context, "eternal home" probably points simply *to* the grave, not beyond it (see Job 10:21 and its note).

12:5 [j]Job 17:13; 10:21 [k]Jer 9:17; Am 5:16

Then man goes to his eternal home[j]
and mourners[k] go about the streets.

6 Remember him—before the silver cord is severed,
or the golden bowl is broken;
before the pitcher is shattered at the spring,
or the wheel broken at the well,

12:7 [l]Ge 3:19; Job 34:15; Ps 146:4 [m]Ecc 3:21 [n]Job 20:8; Zec 12:1
12:8 [o]Ecc 1:2

7 and the dust returns[l] to the ground it came from,
and the spirit returns to God[m] who gave it.[n]

8 "Meaningless! Meaningless!" says the Teacher.[a]
"Everything is meaningless![o]"

The Conclusion of the Matter

9 Not only was the Teacher wise, but also he imparted knowledge to the people. He pondered and
12:9 [p]1Ki 4:32 searched out and set in order many proverbs.[p] 10 The Teacher searched to find just the right words, and
12:10 [q]Pr 22:20-21 what he wrote was upright and true.[q]
12:11 [r]Ezr 9:8 11 The words of the wise are like goads, their collected sayings like firmly embedded nails[r]—given
by one Shepherd. 12 Be warned, my son, of anything in addition to them.
12:12 [s]Ecc 1:18 Of making many books there is no end, and much study wearies the body.[s]

12:13 [t]Dt 4:2; 10:12 [u]Mic 6:8
12:14 [v]Ecc 3:17 [w]Mt 10:26; 1Co 4:5

13 Now all has been heard;
here is the conclusion of the matter:
Fear God and keep his commandments,[t]
for this is the whole ⌞duty⌟ of man.[u]
14 For God will bring every deed into judgment,[v]
including every hidden thing,[w]
whether it is good or evil.

[a] 8 Or *the leader of the assembly*; also in verses 9 and 10

12:6 This verse illustrates the fragility of life. The "silver cord" and "golden bowl" picture a hanging lamp suspended by a silver chain. If only one link snaps, its light is extinguished and its beauty perishes.

12:13–14 See the note on 2:24–26. Godly contentment is not the ultimate good for humanity. The Teacher reminds us of a future time when God will bring all things into judgment. This is the ultimate conclusion of his search for meaning in life (cf. Ro 8:20,22–25). The Teacher urges us to fear God and to obey him. Only when God is taken into account (Ecc 12:1) and his will observed (v. 13) does life impart purpose and satisfaction.

INTRODUCTION TO *Song of Songs*

AUTHOR, PLACE AND DATE OF WRITING

Song of Songs 1:1 tells us that the Song was written by, compiled by or belonged to Solomon. This indicates either that Solomon wrote it or that it was composed for his court and that he was the patron behind its composition. Today most scholars reject this premise, considering the Song to be a postexilic work from the Persian period. There is actually nothing in the Song itself, however, suggesting such a late date, except for a few words of debated origin. This is weak evidence, whereas internal indications in favor of composition during the Solomonic era are strong (see "The Authorship of Ecclesiastes and Song of Songs" on p. 1021).

If Song of Songs is indeed from the age of Solomon, it dates to approximately 950 B.C.

AUDIENCE

Song of Songs is a love poem or compilation of love poems written to God's people to honor and celebrate his gift of romantic, sexual love within the context of a marital relationship.

CULTURAL FACTS AND HIGHLIGHTS

The Song's purpose has been debated. For most of the history of its interpretation, it was treated as an allegory. Jewish reviewers, for the most part, saw it as a symbolic recounting of the history of Israel, with the male singer representing God and the female singer symbolizing Israel. Some medieval Jewish interpreters saw it as an allegory of philosophy, while Christians have taken it as an analogy of the love of Christ for the church or as symbolic of the love relationship between the human soul and God. Some Roman Catholic interpreters claimed that Mary was the central figure of the allegory. Since each of these conjectures was guided only by the theological presuppositions and imagination of the interpreter (and no two allegorical interpretations were alike), and since nothing in the text suggests that it is to be understood as an allegory, very few hold to this explanation today.

More recently, some have claimed that the Song is a drama about the mutual love between Solomon and a young woman, a variation being that it concerns Solomon's failed attempt to woo a woman who was in love with a shepherd. These interpretations, however, are now widely viewed to be forced upon the text. For such explanations to work, readers must supply an enormous amount of detail not included in the Song. Also, there is no analogy for such literature in the ancient Near East.

Today, many view the Song as simple love poetry. This work in fact has close analogies with Egyptian love poetry written during the centuries prior to the age of Solomon (see "Ancient Love Poetry" on p. 1035). It seems clear that the Song was meant specifically to celebrate the love between a husband and a wife. It is "love poetry," but it has a far more sublime message than that of Egypt or of any other particular land or era.

TIMELINE

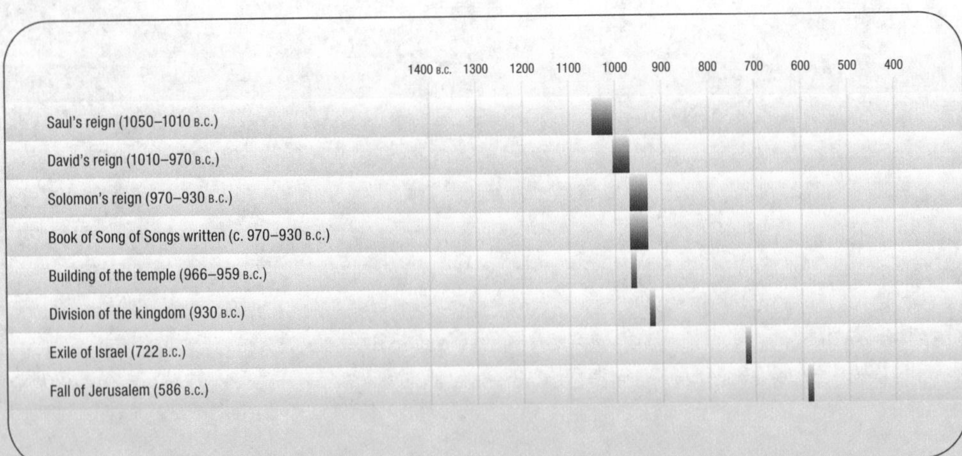

AS YOU READ

Try not to dwell on the interpretation of the book's story line or on possible, beneath-the-surface meanings. Taking as a given that the Song celebrates marital love, glean what you can from its passages—avoiding the temptation to read too much into the sometimes awkward imagery, at least from our twenty-first-century perspective. If you are married or contemplating marriage, what principles from the Song are applicable to your own situation?

DID YOU KNOW?

- Dark skin was considered unattractive by privileged women of the time (1:5).
- "Sister" was a common term of endearment in the love poetry of the ancient Near East (4:9).
- The mandrake plant was associated with the ability to arouse sexual desire and increase fertility (7:13).

THEMES

The themes of Song of Songs include:

1. *Love is a beautiful gift from God.* Song of Songs is love poetry that articulates a beautiful relationship between a husband and a wife. Its lyrics remind God's people that the intimate sexual relationship in marriage is a divine gift to be valued and enjoyed. Love is portrayed as precious (8:7b), spontaneous (2:7) and powerful (8:6–7a).

2. *Marital contentment.* Song of Songs demonstrates that contentment and fulfillment are found in the exclusivity (2:16) of the marriage relationship. The erotic love expressed in the Song is tender, delightful and natural—not shameful or debasing. The lovers are equals, praising each other and sharing the role of initiator.

3. *Love is both pleasurable and painful.* Joy is the dominant note of the Song, but the reader also is warned that love is a powerful emotion that may bring disappointments (5:2—6:3). The Song's young woman repeatedly warned her female friends not to hurry love (2:7; 3:5; 8:4). Love has a dangerous side (8:6), and it deserves to be treated with caution.

OUTLINE

I. First Meeting (1:1—2:7)
II. Second Meeting (2:8—3:5)
III. Third Meeting (3:6—5:1)
IV. Fourth Meeting (5:2—6:3)
V. Fifth Meeting (6:4—8:4)
VI. Literary Climax (8:5–7)
VII. Conclusion (8:8–14)

1

Solomon's Song of Songs.[a]

1:1 [a]1Ki 4:32

Beloved[a]

[2] Let him kiss me with the kisses of his mouth—
for your love[b] is more delightful than wine.
[3] Pleasing is the fragrance of your perfumes;[c]
your name[d] is like perfume poured out.
No wonder the maidens[e] love you!
[4] Take me away with you—let us hurry!
Let the king bring me into his chambers.[f]

1:2 [b]SS 4:10
1:3 [c]SS 4:10 [d]Ecc 7:1 [e]Ps 45:14
1:4 [f]Ps 45:15

Friends

We rejoice and delight in you[b];
we will praise your love more than wine.

Beloved

How right they are to adore you!

[5] Dark am I, yet lovely,[g]
O daughters of Jerusalem,[h]
dark like the tents of Kedar,
like the tent curtains of Solomon.[c]
[6] Do not stare at me because I am dark,
because I am darkened by the sun.
My mother's sons were angry with me
and made me take care of the vineyards;[i]
my own vineyard I have neglected.
[7] Tell me, you whom I love, where you graze your flock
and where you rest your sheep[j] at midday.
Why should I be like a veiled woman
beside the flocks of your friends?

1:5 [g]SS 2:14; 4:3 [h]SS 2:7; 5:8; 5:16
1:6 [i]Ps 69:8; SS 8:12
1:7 [j]SS 3:1-4; Isa 13:20

Friends

[8] If you do not know, most beautiful of women,[k]
follow the tracks of the sheep
and graze your young goats
by the tents of the shepherds.

1:8 [k]SS 5:9; 6:1

[a] Primarily on the basis of the gender of the Hebrew pronouns used, male and female speakers are indicated in the margins by the captions *Lover* and *Beloved* respectively. The words of others are marked *Friends*. In some instances the divisions and their captions are debatable. [b] *4* The Hebrew is masculine singular. [c] *5* Or *Salma*

1:1 The Hebrew name for this book, "Song of Songs," is taken from 1:1 and introduces the book as "the song of songs which is Solomon's." This use of the Hebrew superlative declares that the book is the best of the 1,005 songs of Solomon (1Ki 4:32), or perhaps the greatest of all songs. It also provides the basis for the older title of the book in English versions, "Song of Solomon," as well as for the title in the NIV, "Song of Songs." But see "The Authorship of Ecclesiastes and Song of Songs" on page 1021.

1:3 Perfumes were made by blending aromatic spices and gums in cosmetic oil (see "Perfumes and Anointing Oils" on p. 1746).

"Maidens" probably refers to young women of the court or of the royal city (see 6:8–9). The Old Testament has two words that English versions translate "virgin" (or, as here, "maiden"). The word *bethûlâh* is widely supposed to be the Hebrew technical word for an unmarried and therefore virgin girl, while *'almâh* presupposes a young woman of marriageable age and, if the context requires, married. These words are used in the Old Testament as follows: Nine times *'almâh* is found—four singular (Ge 24:43; Ex 2:8; Pr 30:19; Isa 7:14) and five plural (1Ch 15:20; Ps 46 superscript; 68:25; SS 1:3; 6:8). In 1 Chronicles 15 and in the superscript of Psalm 46 the word occurs in a way no longer understood and can therefore tell us nothing of its meaning.

1:5 Although the beloved was "lovely," she was self-conscious about her dark skin—considered undesirable by privileged women of the time.

The phrase "daughters of Jerusalem" probably refers to the maidens of verse 3 and usually to the "friends" in the sectional headings.

Kedar, a territory in the Arabian Desert where the Bedouin roamed, was known for its flocks; tents and tent curtains were woven by hand from black goat hair. This woman was obviously from a family in which the females were expected to contribute to the work of caring for the livestock. She was compelled to devote herself to the family concerns at the expense of her own body (see v. 6 and its note, below).

1:6 The phrase "my own vineyard" refers to her body, as in 8:12 (see also 2:15). "Vineyard" is an apt metaphor since a vineyard yields wine, and the delights of love are compared with those produced by wine (see v. 2). The beloved is also compared to a garden, yielding precious fruits for the lover (see the note on 4:12).

Lover

1:9 [l]2Ch 1:17
1:10 [m]SS 5:13 [n]Isa 61:10

[9] I liken you, my darling, to a mare
harnessed to one of the chariots[l] of Pharaoh.
[10] Your cheeks[m] are beautiful with earrings,
your neck with strings of jewels.[n]
[11] We will make you earrings of gold,
studded with silver.

ANCIENT TEXTS AND ARTIFACTS

Ancient Love Poetry

SONG OF SONGS 1 The ancient Near East produced many examples of what can broadly be called "love poetry." Some of it is overtly religious in nature, describing the love affairs of gods and goddesses. Other songs provide examples of "secular" love poems that explore both the excitement and the heartbreak so prevalent among young lovers. Examples of ancient love poetry are as follows:

✣ **Mesopotamia**[1] has produced primarily "religious" love poetry:

Nebo and Tashmetu: an **Akkadian** poem about the love between Nebo, the god of scribes, and his consort (partner), Tashmetu.

The Bridal Sheets: a **Sumerian** song featuring a playful dialogue between the god Utu and his sister Inanna, in which he gradually divulges that he has arranged for her to marry Ama-ushumgal-anna.

Songs of Ishtar and Tammuz: a compilation of songs dealing with the love affair between the goddess Ishtar and the god Tammuz.[2]

✣ Egypt has produced a number of love songs that are more "secular" in outlook in that they concern people rather than gods (c. 1300–1150 B.C.). They do, however, sometimes have fantastic or mythological motifs. These poems astutely but sometimes comically portray the emotional turmoil of young love, with striking similarities to Song of Songs.

Papyrus Harris 500: A young man and woman sing of their passionate love for each other. The dialogue-like parts for the male and female singers are similar to what we see in the Song. In some of these texts the female sings a soliloquy about her love; this too has parallels in the Song.

Cairo Love Songs: Recorded on a vase, they include the songs of a young woman, who declares her devotion to her lover, and those of a young man, who yearns to be with her—to be the ring on her finger or her laundryman so he can handle her clothing.

The Turin Love Song: a fanciful text in which various trees talk to a pair of young lovers.

Chester Beatty Papyrus I Love Songs: again include parts for male and female singers, in which they describe the intensity of their passion and their frustration at being kept apart. One compilation, the Nakhtsobek Songs, explores a man's becoming enamored of a prostitute.

The Egyptian poetry displays several parallels to the Song of Songs. Structurally they are similar in that both have parts for male and female singers. They also share similar metaphors and imagery. A few examples of common elements include:

✣ The beloved is called "brother" or "sister" as a term of endearment (SS 4:9).

✣ In the Egyptian texts the woman asserts that her man's love is better than beer (the favorite Egyptian beverage). In the Song, his love is preferable to wine (1:2).

✣ In the Egyptian poems the woman calls for her lover to come like a horse dashing to a battlefield; in the Song she summons him to hasten to her like a young stag (e.g., 8:14).

✣ In both cases the woman is said to be a flower (2:1).

✣ In each instance either the man or the woman is likened to a tree (2:3).

✣ The door image is important to both (5:2–7).

At the same time, Egyptian poetry and the Song have significant differences:

✣ Egyptian lovers often invoke Hathor, the goddess of love, in their quest to win over their beloved. The Biblical texts never suggest that God can be persuaded by a lovestruck youth to manipulate someone to fall in love with him or her.

✣ The Egyptian songs, but not the Song of Songs, often focus on youthful infatuation and thus include some frivolous elements.

✣ The Egyptian poems are generally lighthearted, intended as humorous entertainment. Song of Songs takes a much more serious look at the significance of sexual love.

It is impossible and unnecessary to deny that the Egyptian texts influenced the poetry of Song of Songs. In fact, this poetry gives us a strong reason to date Song of Songs to the age of Solomon, who not only lived near the time the Egyptian songs were being written but also maintained good relations with Egypt. Even so, the content, complexity and theological significance of Song of Songs require us to regard it not as an imitation but as an original, **canonical** text.

[1]See Glossary on page 2080 for definitions of bolded words. [2]See "Mourning for Tammuz" on page 1320.

Beloved

[12] While the king was at his table,
my perfume spread its fragrance.[o]
[13] My lover is to me a sachet of myrrh
resting between my breasts.
[14] My lover is to me a cluster of henna[p] blossoms
from the vineyards of En Gedi.[q]

Lover

[15] How beautiful[r] you are, my darling!
Oh, how beautiful!
Your eyes are doves.[s]

Beloved

[16] How handsome you are, my lover!
Oh, how charming!
And our bed is verdant.

Lover

[17] The beams of our house are cedars;[t]
our rafters are firs.

1:12 [o]SS 4:11-14
1:14 [p]SS 4:13 [q]1Sa 23:29
1:15 [r]SS 4:7 [s]SS 2:14; 4:1; 5:2,12; 6:9
1:17 [t]1Ki 6:9

Ancient Voices

I will lie down inside,
and then I will feign illness.
Then my neighbors will enter to see,
and then my sister
will come with them.
She'll put the doctors to shame
for she (alone)* will understand my illness.

*Word in parentheses added by translator for clarity

— Papyrus Harris

See "Ancient Love Poetry" article on the previous page.

Beloved[a]

2

I am a rose[b][u] of Sharon,[v]
a lily[w] of the valleys.

Lover

[2] Like a lily among thorns
is my darling among the maidens.

Beloved

[3] Like an apple tree among the trees of the forest
is my lover[x] among the young men.
I delight[y] to sit in his shade,
and his fruit is sweet to my taste.[z]
[4] He has taken me to the banquet hall,[a]
and his banner[b] over me is love.
[5] Strengthen me with raisins,
refresh me with apples,[c]
for I am faint with love.[d]
[6] His left arm is under my head,
and his right arm embraces me.[e]

2:1 [u]Isa 35:1 [v]1Ch 27:29 [w]SS 5:13; Hos 14:5
2:3 [x]SS 1:14 [y]SS 1:4 [z]SS 4:16
2:4 [a]Est 1:11 [b]Nu 1:52
2:5 [c]SS 7:8 [d]SS 5:8
2:6 [e]SS 8:3

[a] Or *Lover* [b] *1* Possibly a member of the crocus family

1:12–13 Myrrh—an aromatic resin secreted in the bark of balsam trees that grow in Arabia, Ethiopia and India—was commonly used as an alluring, feminine perfume (Est 2:12; Pr 7:17). It was also used to perfume royal nuptial robes (Ps 45:8) and as an ingredient in holy anointing oil (Ex 30:23). The Magi brought myrrh to the young Jesus as a gift fit for a king (Mt 2:2,11).
1:14 "Henna" refers to a shrub of Palestine (perhaps the cypress) with tightly clustered, aromatic blossoms. En Gedi was an oasis watered by a spring, located on the western side of the Dead Sea (see "En Gedi" on p. 643).
1:15 "Doves" is probably a reference to the shape and cosmetic highlighting of the woman's eyes (see 4:1).
1:16–17 The wedding of patriarchal times (see also the note on Jdg 14:17) was a festive affair. Often a separate small tent or hut was erected to be used by the bride and groom for the wedding night (2Sa 16:22; Ps 19:4–5; SS 1:16–17). The tent was typically round in shape and was pitched in the early evening by the women. To the accompaniment of considerable merriment, they also made ready a bed for the bridal pair. For the very poor, who could not afford this privacy, a small section of the groom's parents' tent was partitioned off for the use of the young couple. At sunset certain female relatives of the groom would enter the tent of the bride's parents and escort the young bride back to the nuptial chamber, to be joined subsequently by the bridegroom.
2:4 The king's love for her was displayed for all to see, like a large military banner.
2:5 "Raisins" and "apples" are probably metaphors for love's caresses and embraces (see v. 3).

2:7 [f]SS 5:8 [g]SS 3:5; 8:4

7 Daughters of Jerusalem, I charge you[f]
by the gazelles and by the does of the field:
Do not arouse or awaken love
until it so desires.[g]

8 Listen! My lover!
Look! Here he comes,

2:7 For "daughters of Jerusalem," see the note on 1:5.

The Flowers of Ancient Israel

SONG OF SONGS 2 Floral imagery was widely used in ancient Israel, in the decoration of the temple and the lampstands (Ex 25;37;1Ki 6;7) as well as in the prophetic and poetic writings.[1] The identification of various flowers in ancient Israel has been complicated by the following factors:

- Many newer plant species have been introduced into the region during the last few centuries.
- From the time of the church fathers, the practice of naming plants after Biblical names has served as a way of keeping Scripture alive in everyday life. Thus, flowers that did not exist in ancient Israel might still bear Biblical names. For example, *Hibiscus syriacus* has been called "the rose of Sharon," even though it is native to eastern Asia and was more recently introduced into the region now known as Palestine.
- Information is scanty. Frequently a plant's only identification might be its Biblical name, with no accompanying description. Oral tradition might provide the only clue in identifying a particular flower.

The rose of Sharon (SS 2:1) has been variously identified as narcissus, anemone or even red tulip. The lily of the valley (v. 1) has been equated to chamomile, crowfoot, various species of lily, narcissus, sea daffodil and lotus. Flowers in ancient Israel served mainly ornamental purposes, and it is likely that their beauty was the primary focus of the Song's writer. Although precise identification of the various flowers would be helpful, it is not essential for interpreting the text.

[1]See "Imagery and Metaphor in Ancient Love Poetry" on page 1046.

Flowers blooming in the wilderness
Photograph: © Todd Bolen/Bible Places.com

leaping across the mountains,
bounding over the hills.[h]
9 My lover is like a gazelle[i] or a young stag.[j]
Look! There he stands behind our wall,
gazing through the windows,
peering through the lattice.
10 My lover spoke and said to me,
"Arise, my darling,
my beautiful one, and come with me.
11 See! The winter is past;
the rains are over and gone.
12 Flowers appear on the earth;
the season of singing has come,
the cooing of doves
is heard in our land.
13 The fig tree forms its early fruit;[k]
the blossoming[l] vines spread their fragrance.
Arise, come, my darling;
my beautiful one, come with me."

Lover

14 My dove[m] in the clefts of the rock,
in the hiding places on the mountainside,
show me your face,
let me hear your voice;
for your voice is sweet,
and your face is lovely.[n]
15 Catch for us the foxes,[o]
the little foxes
that ruin the vineyards,[p]
our vineyards that are in bloom.[q]

Beloved

16 My lover is mine and I am his;[r]
he browses among the lilies.[s]
17 Until the day breaks
and the shadows flee,[t]
turn, my lover,[u]
and be like a gazelle
or like a young stag[v]
on the rugged hills.[a][w]

3 All night long on my bed
I looked[x] for the one my heart loves;
I looked for him but did not find him.
2 I will get up now and go about the city,
through its streets and squares;
I will search for the one my heart loves.
So I looked for him but did not find him.

[a] 17 Or *the hills of Bether*

2:8 [h]ver 17; SS 8:14
2:9 [i]2Sa 2:18 [j]ver 17; SS 8:14
2:13 [k]Isa 28:4; Jer 24:2; Hos 9:10; Mic 7:1; Na 3:12 [l]SS 7:12
2:14 [m]Ge 8:8; SS 1:15 [n]SS 1:5; 8:13
2:15 [o]Jdg 15:4 [p]SS 1:6 [q]SS 7:12
2:16 [r]SS 7:10 [s]SS 4:5; 6:3
2:17 [t]SS 4:6 [u]SS 1:14 [v]ver 9 [w]ver 8
3:1 [x]SS 5:6; Isa 26:9

2:9 The gazelle is known for its form and beauty. "Young stag" is an apt simile for youthful vigor (cf. Isa 35:6).
2:15 For "vineyards," see the note on 1:6. Foxes are mentioned in ancient texts as a nuisance to vintners, since they ate the young grapes (see "Food and Agriculture" on p. 390).
2:16 The two belonged to each other in an exclusive relationship. *Browsing* is a metaphor for the lover's intimate enjoyment of her charms (see 6:2–3).
2:17 The lover is again compared to a gazelle or to a young stag (see the note on v. 9).

3:3 ^y^SS 5:7

³The watchmen found me
as they made their rounds in the city.[y]
"Have you seen the one my heart loves?"
⁴Scarcely had I passed them
when I found the one my heart loves.

3:3 Watchmen were stationed at the city gates (see Ne 11:19) and on the walls (see 2Sa 18:24–27; 2Ki 9:17–20; Isa 62:6). They also patrolled the streets at night (see SS 5:7).

Weddings in Ancient Israel

SONG OF SONGS 3 A wedding, as the public solemnization of an agreement made at the time of an engagement, was an occasion for great joy.[1] The ceremony itself most likely consisted of the recitation of a simple formula, such as the one alluded to at the time of the first union between a husband and a wife (Ge 2:23). Marriage contracts from the Jewish community of Elephantine of the fifth century B.C. record a vow common to the ancient world: The groom would declare that the woman was his wife and that he was her husband for eternity. The wedding ceremony also may have involved the symbolic act of the man covering his bride with the corner of his garment to indicate that she was now under his protection and that it was his responsibility to provide for her (Ru 3:9; Eze 16:8). Blessings of fruitfulness were bestowed upon the couple by family and friends (Ge 24:60; Ru 4:11–12).

A passage from the **Babylonian Talmud** tells us that at a Jewish wedding in the early Christian era a groom would wear a ceremonial crown and receive his bride, who would make her entrance at the wedding party in a sedan chair. This event may explain the description in Song of Songs 3:6–11; it would appear that the bride was riding in such a sedan chair (NIV, "carriage"), accompanied by an honor guard. (In the phrase "Who is this?" in v. 6 the word "this" is feminine, referring to a woman.) The bride's entourage also included a musical procession (Ps 45:14; 1Mc 9:37–39).[2] The groom was attired in festive headdress (SS 3:11; Isa 61:10), and the bride was adorned in embroidered garments and jewelry (Ps 45:13–14; Isa 49:18; 61:10). A veil completed the virgin bride's costume, which may partly explain the success of Laban's ruse of substituting Leah for Rachel on Jacob's wedding night (Ge 29:23; SS 4:1).

Jesus' parable of the wise and foolish virgins (Mt 25:1–13) describes the arrival of the groom during the night prior to a wedding. He was attended by male companions, one of whom would serve as his best man (Jdg 14:20; Jn 3:29). Upon his arrival the groom's family would host a feast (Mt 22:2; Jn 2:9). Putting the evidence together, it appears that the groom with his companions would traditionally arrive at the ceremonial house first, during the night, to be received by a group of young women. Early the next day the friends of the groom would go out to bring back the bride, who would arrive in a sedan chair with the groom's friends as her symbolic honor guard.

The marriage would be consummated on the first night of a banquet celebration typically lasting for seven days (Ge 29:27; Jdg 14:12). The bridal couple would seal their union in a bridal chamber (Ps 19:5; Joel 2:16), and the blood-stained nuptial sheet would be saved by the bride's parents as proof of her prior virginity (Dt 22:17).

A wedding celebration in any time or culture typically brims with emotion, including the culmination of joy and the realization of an anticipated promise, thereby aptly expressing a believer's union with Christ at the end of time: "Let us rejoice and be glad and give him glory! For the wedding of the Lamb has come, and his bride has made herself ready. Fine linen, bright and clean, was given her to wear" (Rev 19:7–8).

[1]See "Marriage and Divorce in Ancient Israel" on page 1548. [2]First Maccabees is an Apocryphal book, not included in the traditional Protestant canon.

I held him and would not let him go
 till I had brought him to my mother's house,[z]
 to the room of the one who conceived me.[a]
5 Daughters of Jerusalem, I charge you[b]
 by the gazelles and by the does of the field:
Do not arouse or awaken love
 until it so desires.[c]

6 Who is this coming up from the desert[d]
 like a column of smoke,
perfumed with myrrh[e] and incense
 made from all the spices[f] of the merchant?
7 Look! It is Solomon's carriage,
 escorted by sixty warriors,[g]
 the noblest of Israel,
8 all of them wearing the sword,
 all experienced in battle,
each with his sword at his side,
 prepared for the terrors of the night.[h]
9 King Solomon made for himself the carriage;
 he made it of wood from Lebanon.
10 Its posts he made of silver,
 its base of gold.
Its seat was upholstered with purple,
 its interior lovingly inlaid
 by[a] the daughters of Jerusalem.
11 Come out, you daughters of Zion,[i]
 and look at King Solomon wearing the crown,
 the crown with which his mother crowned him
on the day of his wedding,
 the day his heart rejoiced.[j]

Lover

4 How beautiful you are, my darling!
 Oh, how beautiful!
 Your eyes behind your veil are doves.[k]
Your hair is like a flock of goats
 descending from Mount Gilead.[l]
2 Your teeth are like a flock of sheep just shorn,
 coming up from the washing.
Each has its twin;
 not one of them is alone.[m]

3:4 [z]SS 8:2 [a]SS 6:9
3:5 [b]SS 2:7 [c]SS 8:4
3:6 [d]SS 8:5 [e]SS 1:13; 4:6,14 [f]Ex 30:34
3:7 [g]1Sa 8:11
3:8 [h]Job 15:22; Ps 91:5
3:11 [i]Isa 4:4 [j]Isa 62:5
4:1 [k]SS 1:15; 5:12 [l]SS 6:5; Mic 7:14
4:2 [m]SS 6:6

[a] *10* Or *its inlaid interior a gift of love / from*

3:6–11 This section is perhaps spoken by the friends (see 8:5). If so, it probably portrays the wedding procession of Solomon and his bride as they approached the city.

Following the example of King Solomon, the bridegroom in a traditional Old Testament Jewish wedding was crowned king of the festival. (For additional wedding traditions, see the notes on 1:16–17 and Jdg 14:12; see also "Weddings in Ancient Israel" on p. 1039.) As a tradition evidently from about the same period (900 B.C.), the bride also submitted to a ceremonial crowning, which in effect made her queen for the duration of the celebration (Eze 16:8–13). There seem to have been some occasions when, upon the arrival at the house of the groom, the men participated in the banquet (Ge 29:22) while the women, including the bride, enjoyed a separate feast at the home of the bride's parents.

3:6 "Desert" refers to uncultivated seasonal grasslands. The spices used to make the incense were imported (see the note on 4:10, as well as "Incense" on p. 1209).

3:7 The "carriage" was a richly adorned, curtained sedan chair, carried on the shoulders of men by means of poles.

3:9 The "wood from Lebanon" refers to the famous cedars of Lebanon (see "Cedars of Lebanon" on p. 1043).

3:10 The posts supporting the canopy were probably made from cedar overlaid with silver and gold.

3:11 The "daughters of Zion" are elsewhere called "daughters of Jerusalem" (see the note on 1:5). The "crown" refers to a wedding wreath (see Isa 61:10).

4:1 For "doves," see the note on 1:15. The goats of Canaan were usually black (see the note on 1:5). The beloved's black tresses flowing from her head evidently reminded the lover of a flock of sleek black goats streaming down the hills of Gilead (noted for its good pasturage). The lover's hair was also black (5:11).

4:2 Sheep "just shorn" and "coming up from the washing" were clean, white and wet.

3 Your lips are like a scarlet ribbon;
your mouth[n] is lovely.
Your temples behind your veil
are like the halves of a pomegranate.[o]
4 Your neck is like the tower[p] of David,
built with elegance[a];
on it hang a thousand shields,[q]
all of them shields of warriors.
5 Your two breasts[r] are like two fawns,
like twin fawns of a gazelle[s]
that browse among the lilies.[t]
6 Until the day breaks
and the shadows flee,[u]
I will go to the mountain of myrrh[v]
and to the hill of incense.
7 All beautiful[w] you are, my darling;
there is no flaw in you.

8 Come with me from Lebanon, my bride,[x]
come with me from Lebanon.
Descend from the crest of Amana,
from the top of Senir,[y] the summit of Hermon,[z]
from the lions' dens
and the mountain haunts of the leopards.
9 You have stolen my heart, my sister, my bride;
you have stolen my heart
with one glance of your eyes,
with one jewel of your necklace.[a]
10 How delightful[b] is your love[c], my sister, my bride!
How much more pleasing is your love than wine,
and the fragrance of your perfume than any spice!
11 Your lips drop sweetness as the honeycomb, my bride;
milk and honey are under your tongue.[d]
The fragrance of your garments is like that of Lebanon.[e]
12 You are a garden locked up, my sister, my bride;
you are a spring enclosed, a sealed fountain.[f]
13 Your plants are an orchard of pomegranates[g]
with choice fruits,
with henna[h] and nard,

4:3 [n]SS 5:16 [o]SS 6:7
4:4 [p]SS 7:4 [q]Eze 27:10
4:5 [r]SS 7:3 [s]Pr 5:19 [t]SS 2:16; 6:2-3
4:6 [u]SS 2:17 [v]ver 14
4:7 [w]SS 1:15
4:8 [x]SS 5:1 [y]Dt 3:9 [z]1Ch 5:23
4:9 [a]Ge 41:42
4:10 [b]SS 7:6 [c]SS 1:2
4:11 [d]Ps 19:10; SS 5:1 [e]Hos 14:6
4:12 [f]Pr 5:15-18
4:13 [g]SS 6:11; 7:12 [h]SS 1:14

[a] *4* The meaning of the Hebrew for this word is uncertain.

4:3 The beloved's lips were red, perhaps painted like those of Egyptian women. Her temples were round and blushed with red, like a pomegranate.
4:4 The beloved's long, elegant, ornamented neck was like a tower on the city wall adorned with warriors' shields (cf. 7:4).
4:5 Fawns represent tender, delicate beauty and promise, rather than full growth (cf. 8:8). For "gazelle," see the note on 2:9. For a different use of "browse among the lilies," see 2:16 and its note.
4:8 Lebanon, Amana and Hermon are mountain peaks on the northern horizon. "Senir," the Amorite name for Mount Hermon, is also found in Assyrian sources. It rises 9,200 feet (2,804 m) and is snowcapped all year round.
4:9 The man called the woman his "sister," a common term of endearment in the love poetry of the ancient Near East.
4:10 Spices were imported luxury items (see 1Ki 10:2; Eze 27:22) used in the making of anointing oil (Ex 25:6; 30:23–25), incense (Ex 25:6; see "Incense" on p. 1209) and perfume (see "Perfumes and Anointing Oils" on p. 1746).
4:11 People in the ancient Near East associated sweetness with the delights of love.
4:12–15 Solomon's gardens and fruit orchards with pools of water for irrigation (Ecc 2:4–6) very likely suggested the imagery in these verses.
4:12 "Garden" refers to a place of sensual delights and is an apt metaphor for the beloved's body (see v. 16; 5:1; 6:2,11; 8:13; see also the note on 1:6). Being "locked up," "enclosed" and "sealed" are metaphors for the beloved's virginity—or perhaps for the fact that she has kept herself exclusively for her husband. Springs and fountains are sources of refreshment, metaphors for the beloved as a sexual partner (see Pr 5:15–20).
4:13 "Your plants" is a reference to all of the beloved's features that have delighted the lover. "Orchard" comes from the Hebrew *pardes* (the root of the English "paradise"), a loanword from the Old Persian language meaning "enclosure" or "park." Elsewhere in Scripture it refers to forests (Ne 2:8) and royal parks (Ecc 2:5). For "henna," see the note on Song of Songs 1:14. "Nard" is an aromatic oil extracted from the roots of a perennial herb that grows in India.

14 nard and saffron,
calamus and cinnamon,[i]
with every kind of incense tree,
with myrrh[j] and aloes
and all the finest spices.[k]
15 You are[a] a garden fountain,
a well of flowing water
streaming down from Lebanon.

4:14 [i]Ex 30:23 [j]SS 3:6 [k]SS 1:12

Beloved

16 Awake, north wind,
and come, south wind!
Blow on my garden,
that its fragrance may spread abroad.
Let my lover come into his garden
and taste its choice fruits.[l]

4:16 [l]SS 2:3; 5:1

Lover

5 I have come into my garden, my sister, my bride;[m]
I have gathered my myrrh with my spice.
I have eaten my honeycomb and my honey;
I have drunk my wine and my milk.[n]

5:1 [m]SS 4:8 [n]SS 4:11; Isa 55:1

Friends

Eat, O friends, and drink;
drink your fill, O lovers.

Beloved

2 I slept but my heart was awake.
Listen! My lover is knocking:
"Open to me, my sister, my darling,
my dove, my flawless[o] one.[p]
My head is drenched with dew,
my hair with the dampness of the night."
3 I have taken off my robe—
must I put it on again?
I have washed my feet—
must I soil them again?
4 My lover thrust his hand through the latch-opening;
my heart began to pound for him.
5 I arose to open for my lover,
and my hands dripped with myrrh,[q]

5:2 [o]SS 4:7 [p]SS 6:9

5:5 [q]ver 13

[a] 15 Or *I am* (spoken by the *Beloved*)

4:14 Saffron, a plant of the crocus family, bears purple or white flowers, parts of which, when dried, are used as a cooking spice. Calamus (the Hebrew word is translated "cane" in Ex 30:23) refers to an aromatic spice probably imported from India. It was used in the holy anointing oil (Ex 30:23,25) and in incense (Isa 43:23–24; see "Incense" on p. 1209). Cinnamon was also used in the holy anointing oil (Ex 30:23,25) and as an alluring fragrance (Pr 7:17). For "myrrh," see the note on Song of Songs 1:12–13. Aromatic aloes were used to perfume royal nuptial robes (Ps 45:8).

4:15 Fresh, cool, sparkling water flowed from the snowfields on the mountains of Lebanon.

4:16 This verse expresses the beloved's desire that her fragrance be blown about to draw her lover to her so that they can enjoy love's intimacies.

5:1 The lover claimed the beloved as his garden and enjoyed all of her delights (see the note on 4:12). For "my sister," see the note on 4:9.

5:3 There are a number of Hebrew and Greek words that in general mean "to profane, pollute, render unclean." In the Old Testament defilement was physical (this verse), sexual (Lev 18:20), ethical (Isa 59:3; Eze 37:23), ceremonial (Lev 11:24; 17:15) and religious (Nu 35:33; Jer 3:1). In the New Testament it was exclusively ethical or religious (Mk 7:19; Ac 10:15; Ro 14:20). The *teaching* of the New Testament does not include the idea of ceremonial defilement, but the *culture* of that day certainly still held it as important.

5:5 The primitive locks used to fasten city gates consisted simply of heavy beams of wood, the ends of which were dropped into slots cut into the masonry of the gate (Ne 3:3–15; cf Dt 3:5; 1Sa 23:7). To strengthen them, iron bars were used (1Ki 4:13; Isa 45:2). When used to lock house doors (Jdg 3:23–24), they were smaller and the

my fingers with flowing myrrh,
on the handles of the lock.
5:6 [r]SS 6:1 [s]SS 6:2 [t]SS 3:1
[6] I opened for my lover,[r]
but my lover had left; he was gone.[s]
My heart sank at his departure.[a]
I looked[t] for him but did not find him.
I called him but he did not answer.
[7] The watchmen found me
5:7 [u]SS 3:3
as they made their rounds in the city.[u]
They beat me, they bruised me;
they took away my cloak,
those watchmen of the walls!
5:8 [v]SS 2:7; 3:5 [w]SS 2:5
[8] O daughters of Jerusalem, I charge you[v]—
if you find my lover,
what will you tell him?
Tell him I am faint with love.[w]

Friends

[9] How is your beloved better than others,
5:9 [x]SS 1:8; 6:1
most beautiful of women?[x]
How is your beloved better than others,
that you charge us so?

[a] 6 Or *heart had gone out to him when he spoke*

bolts flat. Usually several sliding pins dropped into corresponding holes in the bar, requiring a key to release them. Keys varied in size but were often large enough to be carried on the shoulder (Isa 22:22). To open the door from the outside, the key was inserted through the hole in the door, which might be large enough to admit the hand with it (SS 5:5).

Cedars of Lebanon

SONG OF SONGS 5 A tall (averaging 120 ft [37 m] in its maturity) and majestic evergreen tree, the cedar of Lebanon was highly valued in antiquity.[1] Its durability and dimensions provided building materials for palaces, temples, ships and furnishings, and Egyptians prized its resin for mummification. **Nebuchadnezzar** wrote of hauling felled cedars to **Babylon** from Mount Lebanon, an abundant source of timber in the ancient Near East (cf. Isa 37:24). The temple and palace complex in Jerusalem were lavishly adorned with cedar (1Ki 7:2; 1Ch 22:4), and cedar wood was used for purification rituals (Lev 14:4).[2] Attesting to the use of cedar in monumental architecture, remnants of charred cedar beams were found in a **Middle Bronze Age**[3] palace (sixteenth century B.C.), as well as in a **Late Bronze Age** temple (thirteenth century B.C.) at Lachish.[4]

The height and commanding presence of the species yields vivid Biblical images. **Yahweh**'s majesty stands above all cedars (Ps 148:9,13), and his voice is so powerful that it shatters them (Ps 29:5). The development of a righteous person is compared to the cedar's steady maturing process (Ps 92:12). In the Song of Songs the lover's appearance evokes the tree's exquisite worth (SS 5:15). Yet the cedar's height can also be a visual picture of human pride and arrogance (Isa 2:12–13; Eze 31:3,10–12).

[1]See "Byblos" on page 1349. [2]See "Ritual Purity in Israel and the Ancient Near East" on page 166. [3]See "Archaeological Periods" chart on page xx in the beginning of this Bible. [4]See also "Trees of Ancient Israel" on page 1357.

Beloved

[10]My lover is radiant and ruddy,
outstanding among ten thousand.[y]
[11]His head is purest gold;
his hair is wavy
and black as a raven.
[12]His eyes are like doves[z]
by the water streams,
washed in milk,[a]
mounted like jewels.
[13]His cheeks[b] are like beds of spice[c]
yielding perfume.
His lips are like lilies[d]
dripping with myrrh.
[14]His arms are rods of gold
set with chrysolite.
His body is like polished ivory
decorated with sapphires.[a][e]
[15]His legs are pillars of marble
set on bases of pure gold.
His appearance is like Lebanon,[f]
choice as its cedars.
[16]His mouth[g] is sweetness itself;
he is altogether lovely.
This is my lover,[h] this my friend,
O daughters of Jerusalem.[i]

5:10 [y]Ps 45:2
5:12 [z]SS 1:15; 4:1 [a]Ge 49:12
5:13 [b]SS 1:10 [c]SS 6:2 [d]SS 2:1
5:14 [e]Job 28:6
5:15 [f]1Ki 4:33; SS 7:4
5:16 [g]SS 4:3 [h]SS 7:9 [i]SS 1:5

Friends

6

Where has your lover[j] gone,
most beautiful of women?[k]
Which way did your lover turn,
that we may look for him with you?

6:1 [j]SS 5:6 [k]SS 1:8

Beloved

[2]My lover has gone[l] down to his garden,[m]
to the beds of spices,[n]
to browse in the gardens
and to gather lilies.
[3]I am my lover's and my lover is mine;[o]
he browses among the lilies.[p]

6:2 [l]SS 5:6 [m]SS 4:12 [n]SS 5:13
6:3 [o]SS 7:10 [p]SS 2:16

Lover

[4]You are beautiful, my darling, as Tirzah,[q]
lovely as Jerusalem,[r]
majestic as troops with banners.[s]

6:4 [q]Jos 12:24 [r]Ps 48:2; 50:2 [s]ver 10

[a] 14 Or *lapis lazuli*

5:10–16 This is one of only a few poems that have come down to us from the ancient world in which the female gives an inventory of the male's features.
5:12 For "doves," see the note on 1:15. The lover's eyes sparkled: Their whites were clear and bright, setting off his irises like sparkling jewels.
5:13 These similes probably compare sensuous effects rather than appearances, as do the following similes and metaphors, at least in part.
5:14 The precise identification of "chrysolite" is uncertain.
5:15 For "cedars," see the note on 3:9.
5:16 For "daughters of Jerusalem," see the note on 1:5.
6:2 For "his garden," see the note on 4:12. "Beds of spices" is a reference to the beloved's sensuous attractions (cf. 5:13). To "browse" means to enjoy (see the note on 2:16). The lover, enjoying intimacies with the beloved, is compared to a graceful gazelle (see the note on 2:9) nibbling from lily to lily in undisturbed enjoyment of exotic delicacies.
6:4 Tirzah was chosen by Jeroboam I as the first capital of the northern kingdom (see "Tirzah" on p. 509). Its name, which means "pleasure" or "beauty," suggests that—like Jerusalem—it was a beautiful city. Comparing the beloved's beauty to that of a city was not surprising, since cities of the day were regularly depicted as women.

[5]Turn your eyes from me;
they overwhelm me.
Your hair is like a flock of goats
descending from Gilead.[t]
[6]Your teeth are like a flock of sheep
coming up from the washing.
Each has its twin,
not one of them is alone.[u]
[7]Your temples behind your veil[v]
are like the halves of a pomegranate.[w]
[8]Sixty queens[x] there may be,
and eighty concubines,[y]
and virgins beyond number;
[9]but my dove,[z] my perfect one,[a] is unique,
the only daughter of her mother,
the favorite of the one who bore her.[b]
The maidens saw her and called her blessed;
the queens and concubines praised her.

6:5 [t]SS 4:1
6:6 [u]SS 4:2
6:7 [v]Ge 24:65 [w]SS 4:3
6:8 [x]Ps 45:9 [y]Ge 22:24
6:9 [z]SS 1:15 [a]SS 5:2 [b]SS 3:4

Friends

[10]Who is this that appears like the dawn,
fair as the moon, bright as the sun,
majestic as the stars in procession?

Lover

[11]I went down to the grove of nut trees
to look at the new growth in the valley,
to see if the vines had budded
or the pomegranates were in bloom.[c]
[12]Before I realized it,
my desire set me among the royal chariots of
my people.[a]

6:11 [c]SS 7:12

Friends

[13]Come back, come back, O Shulammite;
come back, come back, that we may gaze
on you!

Lover

Why would you gaze on the Shulammite
as on the dance[d] of Mahanaim?

6:13 [d]Ex 15:20

7

How beautiful your sandaled feet,
O prince's[e] daughter!
Your graceful legs are like jewels,
the work of a craftsman's hands.

7:1 [e]Ps 45:13

[a] 12 Or *among the chariots of Amminadab*; or *among the chariots of the people of the prince*

6:8 If Solomon wrote this poem (see "The Authorship of Ecclesiastes and Song of Songs" on p. 1021), this verse may indicate that he did so when he was relatively young—before he had acquired 700 wives and 300 concubines (1Ki 11:3). But if the "lover" was a commoner, he was simply boasting that his bride was more impressive than a royal harem and virgins without number.

See the note on 1:3 for a discussion of the term "virgins" (or "maidens").

6:9 The woman was not literally an "only daughter" but the one uniquely loved.

6:13 There is some difference of opinion as to the origin of the term Shulammite (Hebrew *shûlammîth,* meaning "peaceful"). It is not unlikely that this is a feminine form of Solomon. If the word is the same as "Shunammite," however, as the Septuagint rendering would imply, it could have been derived from the town of Shunem.

[2]Your navel is a rounded goblet
that never lacks blended wine.
Your waist is a mound of wheat
encircled by lilies.
[3]Your breasts[f] are like two fawns,
twins of a gazelle.

7:3 [f]SS 4:5

7:2 For a discussion of sheaves and threshing, see the note on Ruth 2:7. See also "The Threshing Floor" on page 608 and "Food and Agriculture" on page 390.

Imagery and Metaphor in Ancient Love Poetry

SONG OF SONGS 7 The modern reader of Song of Songs is struck by the poem's powerful and yet eccentric images and metaphors. Why, for example, would a man tell the woman he adores that her nose is like a tower (7:4)? Unless the Israelites believed that an enormous nose was attractive, wouldn't she be insulted? Some have dealt with this problem by simply assuming that the ancients had a different way of expressing themselves and that metaphors that sound ridiculous to us were not only acceptable but pleasing to them. It turns out, however, that while many of the more easily understood metaphors of the Song do have parallels in other ancient Near Eastern texts, some of the more bizarre similes have no known correlations in other ancient love poetry.

For example, when the woman is said to be a flower (2:1) or the man exhorted to come running like a gazelle (8:14), the former obviously refers to her youthful beauty and the latter to his strength and speed—images that have fairly clear parallels in Egyptian poetry.[1] On the other hand, it is hard to find a parallel in ancient literature to a text like 4:1–5, where the woman's eyes are doves, her hair a flock of goats coming down a hill, her neck a tower covered in shields and her breasts twin fawns. Although we might find some visual correspondence between the feature represented and the chosen image, the language is shocking and at times difficult to understand. There are various ways interpreters have tried to deal with this aspect of the Song:

- Some posit that the words suggest how the singer felt about the woman, not how she looked. Thus, a tower-like nose or neck might suggest that he was in awe of her and not imply anything about the appearance of these physical features.
- Another possibility is that the metaphors really do suggest how this woman looked, but not in a crudely literal way. Her hair might in some sense have resembled a flock of goats on a hillside, with the slope of the hill and the hair of the goats somewhat similar to the appearance of her tresses cascading down over her shoulders.
- A third possibility is that the poetry is deliberately comic or ironic. This seems highly unlikely, in that the Song never suggests a humorous purpose.

The first and second suggestions no doubt have some validity, but it is difficult to avoid the fact that the Song consistently uses extravagant and unlikely metaphorical language.

Actually, some of the closest parallels to what we see in the Song may be found in prophetic and apocalyptic Bible texts. The vision of God's glory in Ezekiel 1, with wheels within wheels and wheels covered with eyes, is also startling. The book of Revelation is replete with this kind of language, as when the risen Christ is described as having a sword protruding from his mouth (see Rev 1:13–16). Thus the language of Song of Songs may be deliberately extravagant, suggesting that the man and woman are larger-than-life, representing not just two individual people but the profound mystery and power of love.

[1]See "Ancient Love Poetry" on page 1035.

7:4 [g]Ps 144:12; SS 4:4 [h]Nu 21:26 [i]SS 5:15

4 Your neck is like an ivory tower.[g]
Your eyes are the pools of Heshbon[h]
by the gate of Bath Rabbim.
Your nose is like the tower of Lebanon[i]
looking toward Damascus.

7:5 [j]Isa 35:2

5 Your head crowns you like Mount Carmel.[j]
Your hair is like royal tapestry;
the king is held captive by its tresses.

7:6 [k]SS 1:15 [l]SS 4:10

6 How beautiful[k] you are and how pleasing,
O love, with your delights![l]
7 Your stature is like that of the palm,

7:7 [m]SS 4:5

and your breasts[m] like clusters of fruit.
8 I said, "I will climb the palm tree;
I will take hold of its fruit."
May your breasts be like the clusters of the vine,

7:8 [n]SS 2:5

the fragrance of your breath like apples,[n]
9 and your mouth like the best wine.

Beloved

7:9 [o]SS 5:16

May the wine go straight to my lover,[o]
flowing gently over lips and teeth.[a]
10 I belong to my lover,

7:10 [p]Ps 45:11 [q]SS 2:16; 6:3

and his desire[p] is for me.[q]
11 Come, my lover, let us go to the countryside,
let us spend the night in the villages.[b]

7:12 [r]SS 1:6 [s]SS 2:15 [t]SS 2:13 [u]SS 4:13 [v]SS 6:11

12 Let us go early to the vineyards[r]
to see if the vines have budded,[s]
if their blossoms[t] have opened,
and if the pomegranates[u] are in bloom[v]—
there I will give you my love.

7:13 [w]Ge 30:14 [x]SS 4:16

13 The mandrakes[w] send out their fragrance,
and at our door is every delicacy,
both new and old,
that I have stored up for you, my lover.[x]

8 If only you were to me like a brother,
who was nursed at my mother's breasts!
Then, if I found you outside,
I would kiss you,
and no one would despise me.
2 I would lead you

8:2 [y]SS 3:4

and bring you to my mother's house[y]—
she who has taught me.
I would give you spiced wine to drink,
the nectar of my pomegranates.

[a] 9 Septuagint, Aquila, Vulgate and Syriac; Hebrew *lips of sleepers* [b] 11 Or *henna bushes*

7:4 Heshbon, once the royal city of King Sihon (Nu 21:26), was blessed with an abundant supply of spring water. Bath Rabbim ("daughter of many") may have been a popular name for Heshbon. The "tower of Lebanon" likely refers to the towering Lebanon mountain range.
7:5 Mount Carmel, a high ridge next to the Mediterranean Sea, was known for its beauty and wooded peak and still today is an impressive backdrop to the port of Haifa.
7:7 The "palm" here refers to the stately date palm.
7:13 The mandrake plant, with its pungent blossoms and forked roots resembling the lower part of a human body, was associated with the ability to arouse sexual desire and to increase fertility (cf. Ge 30:9–18).
8:1 The beloved was frustrated by the cultural standard that allowed family members to show public affection but forbade married couples from doing so.
8:2 The Hebrew for "nectar" refers to intoxicating juices.

[3]His left arm is under my head
and his right arm embraces me.[z]
[4]Daughters of Jerusalem, I charge you:
Do not arouse or awaken love
until it so desires.[a]

8:3 [z]SS 2:6
8:4 [a]SS 2:7; 3:5

Friends

[5]Who is this coming up from the desert[b]
leaning on her lover?

8:5 [b]SS 3:6

Beloved

Under the apple tree I roused you;
there your mother conceived[c] you,
there she who was in labor gave you birth.
[6]Place me like a seal over your heart,
like a seal on your arm;
for love[d] is as strong as death,
its jealousy[a][e] unyielding as the grave.[b]
It burns like blazing fire,
like a mighty flame.[c]
[7]Many waters cannot quench love;
rivers cannot wash it away.
If one were to give
all the wealth of his house for love,
it[d] would be utterly scorned.[f]

[c]SS 3:4
8:6 [d]SS 1:2
[e]Nu 5:14
8:7 [f]Pr 6:35

Friends

[8]We have a young sister,
and her breasts are not yet grown.
What shall we do for our sister
for the day she is spoken for?
[9]If she is a wall,
we will build towers of silver on her.
If she is a door,
we will enclose her with panels of cedar.

Beloved

[10]I am a wall,
and my breasts are like towers.
Thus I have become in his eyes
like one bringing contentment.
[11]Solomon had a vineyard[g] in Baal Hamon;
he let out his vineyard to tenants.
Each was to bring for its fruit
a thousand shekels[e][h] of silver.

8:11 [g]Ecc 2:4
[h]Isa 7:23

[a] 6 Or *ardor* [b] 6 Hebrew *Sheol* [c] 6 Or / *like the very flame of the LORD* [d] 7 Or *he* [e] 11 That is, about 25 pounds (about 11.5 kilograms); also in verse 12

8:5 In the ancient world sexual union and birth were often associated with fruit trees.
8:6–7 The "grave," a "blazing fire" and "many waters" characterize marital love as the strongest, most unyielding and invincible force in human experience.
8:6 Seals were precious to their owners, as personal as their names (see the note on Ge 38:17–18; see also "Scrolls, Seals and Codices" on p. 2053).
8:7 The phrase "many waters" suggests not only the ocean depths (see Ps 107:23) but also the primeval waters that the people of the ancient Near East regarded as a permanent threat to the world (see the note on Ps 32:6). The waters were also associated with the realm of the dead.
8:11 The location of Baal Hamon is unknown.

ARCHAEOLOGY AND THE DATE OF SONG OF SONGS

SONG OF SONGS 8 Today many scholars consider the Song of Songs to have been written during the **postexilic** era, in spite of the fact that the "official" title of the book, "Solomon's Song of Songs" (1:1),[1] associates it with the time of Solomon. Archaeology, however, has provided several good reasons for believing that the Song was indeed written early, in or around the tenth century B.C.[2]

✣ Archaeological data from this period indicates that this was a time during which Israel was under strong central authority, as the Bible suggests. Many scholars deny that there ever was a great kingdom of David and Solomon; indeed, some go so far as to theorize that these men were legendary rather than historical. Obviously, if there were no Solomonic kingdom, we could not posit that the Song was written during the Solomonic period. However, archaeology does support the Biblical portrait of Solomon's times. According to 1 Kings 9:15 Solomon did indeed build the temple, his own palace, a structure called the Millo and the wall of Jerusalem, as well as the cities of **Hazor**, **Megiddo** and Gezer ("Map 5").[3]

The temple and palace of Solomon are lost, and the location of his Millo is subject to debate, but archaeology confirms that every aspect of Solomon's temple, as described in the Bible, conforms to what we know of other temples from this time and region.[4]

The cities of Hazor, Megiddo and Gezer have been excavated and found to have similar systems of fortification and gateways that date from the time of Solomon, suggesting that they were constructed by royal engineers who worked from a common blueprint.[5]

◆ Oftentimes great literature flourishes during a period of national power and prosperity (e.g., Virgil wrote the *Aeneid* at one of the high points of Roman history, the Augustan Age). Thus the association of the Song of Songs with Solomon's era makes sense.

◆ During the latter part of the second millennium B.C. a distinctive style of love poetry flourished in Egypt, in some ways strikingly similar to the Song of Songs. Although the message of the Song is different from that of the Egyptian material, it is clear that the Hebrew poetry uses some of the same literary conventions as that of the Egyptian poetry. First Kings 9:16 indicates that Solomon, having married an Egyptian princess, had good relations with Egypt. It is reasonable to assume that this was a time of close communication and commerce between the two nations. Thus the Solomonic era is the very time at which we could most plausibly suggest that Egyptian love poetry came to be read and appreciated in the royal court of Israel.[6]

Early Bronze Age round altar area at Megiddo

Photograph courtesy of © Dr. Gary Pratico

◆ Song of Songs 6:4 indicates that at the time this poem was written Jerusalem and Tirzah were the two most magnificent cities in Israel. Tirzah (located in the north at Tell el-Farah)[7] was a great city in the northern part of Israel during Solomon's day. After the kingdom split in two it became the capital of the northern kingdom under Jeroboam I and remained so until Omri (r. c. 885–874 B.C.) built **Samaria**. Thereafter it declined, and by the postexilic period it had ceased to exist. It is unreasonable to argue that a poet of the postexilic world would have paired Jerusalem with Tirzah, which at that time was nothing more than an abandoned mound. However, it is entirely reasonable that a poet from the tenth century B.C. would have treated Tirzah as Jerusalem's counterpart and equal.

[1]Some Bible translations, such as the King James Version, use the title "Song of Solomon." [2]See also "The Authorship of Ecclesiastes and Song of Songs" on page 1021. [3]See "The Building Activity of Solomon" on page 497. [4]See "Solomon's Temple and Other Ancient Temples" on page 620. [5]See "Hazor" on page 322, "Megiddo" on page 1541 and "Gezer" on page 588. [6]See the discussion in "Ancient Love Poetry" on page 1035. [7]See "Tirzah" on page 509.

[12] But my own vineyard[i] is mine to give;
the thousand shekels are for you, O Solomon,
and two hundred[a] are for those who tend its fruit.

8:12 [i]SS 1:6

Lover

[13] You who dwell in the gardens
with friends in attendance,
let me hear your voice!

Beloved

[14] Come away, my lover,
and be like a gazelle[j]
or like a young stag[k]
on the spice-laden mountains.[l]

8:14 [j]Pr 5:19 [k]SS 2:9 [l]SS 2:8, 17

[a] *12* That is, about 5 pounds (about 2.3 kilograms)

8:12 For "my own vineyard," see the note on 1:6.

8:13 For "gardens," see the note on 4:12. "Friends" is male; perhaps they were the companions of the lover (see 1:7).

INTRODUCTION TO 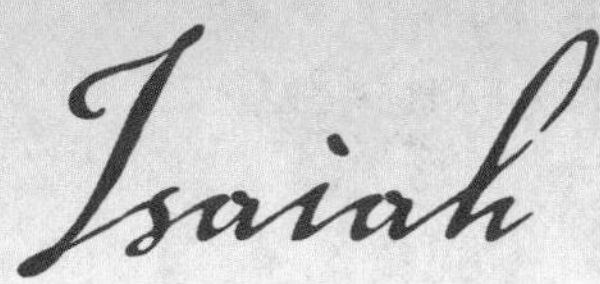

AUTHOR, PLACE AND DATE OF WRITING

Isaiah 1:1 specifies that the book was written by the eighth-century B.C. prophet Isaiah, son of Amoz, and other Scripture passages concur (Mt 12:17–21; Jn 12:38–41; Ro 10:16,20–21). Today, however, many scholars believe that only a part of the book came from this individual. Many assert that Isaiah 40–55 were added by a prophet who lived during the Babylonian exile and who is referred to as "Deutero-Isaiah" and that chapters 56–66 were composed later still by a postexilic prophet referred to as "Trito-Isaiah." This leaves only chapters 1–39 purported to be the work of "Isaiah son of Amoz" (1:1). In reality, however, most critical scholars hold to schemes for explaining the authorship of Isaiah that are much more complex than this simplified explanation would indicate. Indeed, some scholars suggest that Isaiah, son of Amoz, wrote very little of the book that bears his name.

The critical issue here is the matter of whether or not Isaiah 40–55 was written after the exile had begun. Critical scholars point to verses such as 44:26 as proof that at the time this section was being written Jerusalem was already uninhabited (having been destroyed by the Babylonians). Yet the entire book of Isaiah was written under the presupposition that Judah was doomed. This conviction was indeed the very foundation of Isaiah's ministry; he had learned of Jerusalem's imminent destruction from God in what appears to have been his prophetic calling (ch. 6). There are in fact valid reasons for believing that the prophet Isaiah wrote the entire book (see also "The Authorship of Isaiah" on p. 1055).

Isaiah dated his prophecy to the reigns of Uzziah, Jotham, Ahaz and Hezekiah (1:1). This indicates a prophetic ministry encompassing the period from roughly 740 to 700 B.C.

AUDIENCE

Isaiah's primary ministry was to the people of Judah, who were failing to live according to the requirements of God's law. But he prophesied judgment not only upon Judah but also upon Israel and the surrounding nations. On the other hand, Isaiah delivered a stirring message of repentance and salvation for any who would turn to God.

CULTURAL FACTS AND HIGHLIGHTS

Isaiah wrote during a period of upheaval and general unrest, as the Assyrian Empire was expanding and the northern kingdom of Israel facing decline and imminent disaster. Judah was also vulnerable, although her destruction was ultimately to come at the hands of a later power, Babylonia.

Taking the call of Isaiah (ch. 6) as the starting point for his ministry and message, it appears that the prophet labored under the conviction—in his mind a foregone conclusion—that the people would reject his message and the nation of Judah would be destroyed (vv. 9–13). Nevertheless, the prophet still followed through with his duty to warn the people and exhort them to repent. But beyond that Isaiah offered words of comfort: The Gentile nations would also face judgment (e.g., chs. 13–19), a remnant of Israel as a whole would be healed and restored (e.g., ch. 40) and ultimately the Gentiles would themselves turn to Israel's God (2:2–4; 42:6).

TIMELINE

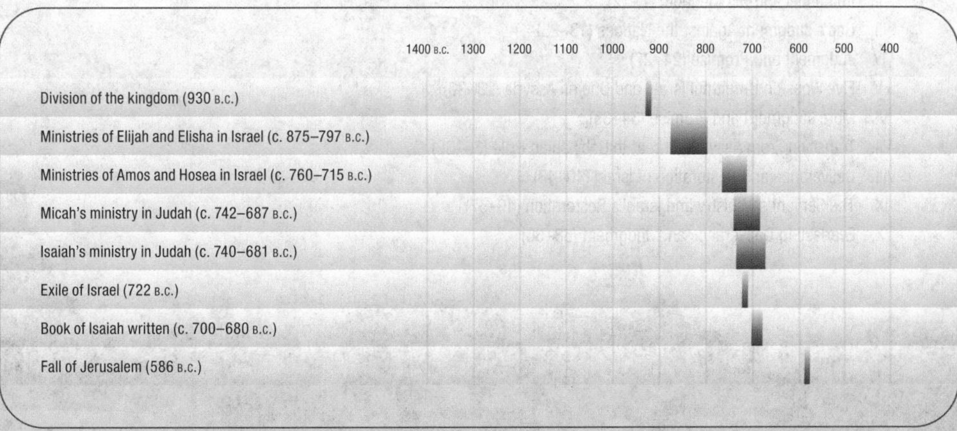

AS YOU READ

Notice Isaiah's polished literary style; rich vocabulary; beautiful and varied use of poetic imagery; and distinctive phraseology, such as "the Holy One of Israel" and "my servant." Of particular interest in this book are the following:

- Isaiah's use of fire imagery to represent punishment (e.g., 1:31; 10:17; 26:11; 33:11–14; 34:9–10; 66:24).
- The prophet's repeated symbolism of the vineyard, the winepress and the cup of God's wrath (e.g., 5:7, 63:3 and 51:17, respectively).
- The apocalyptic section of the book (chs. 24–27), focusing on the last days.
- Examples of personification, one of Isaiah's favorite literary devices (e.g., 24:23; 35:1; 44:23; 55:12).
- Development of the "servant" theme in chapters 41–54. A Bible commentary would be a helpful companion for this detailed study.

DID YOU KNOW?

- Recent archaeological discoveries confirm that some Israelites worshiped Asherah as *the Lord's* consort or partner (17:8).
- The Assyrians were notorious for leading away their captives by ropes tied to rings in their noses (37:29).
- Throughout the Old Testament we see instances of God dispatching angelic agents as carriers of plague (37:36).
- The Hebrew phrase for "a memorial and a name" (*yad vashem*) was many centuries later chosen as the name of the principal Holocaust monument in Jerusalem in modern Israel (56:5).
- During the Jerusalem siege Hebrew slaves were released—only to be reclaimed by their masters after further consideration (58:6).

THEMES

The book of Isaiah includes the following themes:

1. *Judgment and salvation.* God is "the Holy One of Israel" (1:4), who is obligated by his very nature to punish his rebellious (1:2) and sinful (v. 4) people. But after judgment he will have compassion on them (14:1–2) and redeem them (41:14; 43:3; 49:8). His rescue of his own is compared to the exodus (43:2,16–19; 52:10–12). The theme of a highway for the returning exiles also is prominent (11:16; 40:3).

2. *God as King.* Isaiah pictures God as the sovereign King, the divine ruler who is characterized by justice, righteousness and holiness (5:16). He calls his people to do right and to seek justice (1:17) and stands against those who take advantage of the poor (5:8–10).

3. *The suffering servant.* Isaiah contains four "servant songs" (42:1–9; 49:1–7; 50:4–9; 52:13—53:12) that describe the coming King. This Messianic King is called "my servant" in chapters 42–53, a term also applied to Cyrus (45:1–4), God's prophets (44:26) and Israel as a nation (41:8–9; 42:19; 44:1–2,21; 45:4; 48:20). The suffering servant would bring justice (42:1–4; 51:4) and salvation—not just for Israel (42:1–17; 43:1–7,14–21; 44:21–23) but for the Gentiles as well (42:6; 55:4–5; 53:5–12; 61:1–2). The New Testament identifies this servant as Jesus Christ (Mt 12:18–21; Lk 4:20–21).

OUTLINE

I. Messages of Rebuke and Promise (1–6)
II. Immanuel and His Kingdom (7–12)
III. God's Judgment Against the Nations (13–23)
IV. Judgment and Promise (24–27)
V. Five Woes on Unfaithful Israel and One on Assyria (28–33)
VI. More Judgment and Promise (34–35)
VII. Transition From Assyrian Threat to Babylonian Exile (36–39)
VIII. Deliverance and Restoration of Israel (40–48)
IX. The Servant's Ministry and Israel's Restoration (49–57)
X. Everlasting Deliverance and Judgment (58–66)

1:1 [a]Nu 12:6 [b]Isa 40:9 [c]Isa 2:1 [d]2Ch 26:22 [e]2Ki 16:1

1 The vision[a] concerning Judah and Jerusalem[b] that Isaiah son of Amoz saw[c] during the reigns of Uzziah,[d] Jotham, Ahaz[e] and Hezekiah, kings of Judah.

A Rebellious Nation

1:2 [f]Mic 1:2 [g]Isa 30:1,9; 65:2

[2] Hear, O heavens! Listen, O earth!
For the LORD has spoken:[f]
"I reared children and brought them up,
but they have rebelled[g] against me.
[3] The ox knows his master,
the donkey his owner's manger,
1:3 [h]Jer 8:7; 9:3,6
but Israel does not know,[h]
my people do not understand."

[4] Ah, sinful nation,
a people loaded with guilt,
1:4 [i]Isa 14:20 [j]Isa 5:19,24
a brood of evildoers,[i]
children given to corruption!
They have forsaken the LORD;
they have spurned the Holy One[j] of Israel
and turned their backs on him.

[5] Why should you be beaten anymore?
1:5 [k]Isa 31:6 [l]Isa 33:6,24
Why do you persist in rebellion?[k]
Your whole head is injured,
your whole heart afflicted.[l]
[6] From the sole of your foot to the top of your head
1:6 [m]Ps 38:3 [n]Isa 30:26; Jer 8:22 [o]Lk 10:34
there is no soundness[m]—
only wounds and welts
and open sores,
not cleansed or bandaged[n]
or soothed with oil.[o]

1:7 [p]Lev 26:34
[7] Your country is desolate,[p]
your cities burned with fire;
your fields are being stripped by foreigners
right before you,
laid waste as when overthrown by strangers.
[8] The Daughter of Zion is left
like a shelter in a vineyard,
1:8 [q]Job 27:18
like a hut[q] in a field of melons,
like a city under siege.
[9] Unless the LORD Almighty
1:9 [r]Isa 10:20-22; 37:4,31-32 [s]Ge 19:24; Ro 9:29*
had left us some survivors,[r]
we would have become like Sodom,
we would have been like Gomorrah.[s]

1:1—5:30 These introductory chapters of Isaiah contain the "great arraignment." Like so many of Isaiah's utterances, the section combines dire threatenings with urgent calls to repentance and gracious offers of forgiveness and blessing. This is followed by the promise of world redemption (2:1–5). Then comes a series of threatening passages, including a detailed description of the finery of the women of Jerusalem that serves as an illustration of the sinful frivolity of the people as a whole. The land is likened to an unfruitful vineyard, which will soon become desolate. The section concludes with a series of six woes that end in gloom: "Even the light will be darkened by the clouds" (5:30). For a synopsis of the entire book, see the notes on 6:1–13, 7:1—12:6, 13:1—23:18, 24:1—35:10, 36:1—39:8 and 40:1—66:24. Note that these divisions roughly follow the brief outline of Isaiah found on page 1052.

1:1 Uzziah, Jotham, Ahaz and Hezekiah were kings of Judah who reigned from 792 to 686 B.C. None of the kings of Israel is mentioned, since Isaiah ministered primarily to the southern kingdom of Judah.

1:7–8 The desolation of the land of Judah was the result of the Assyrian invasion (see "The Sennacherib Prism" on p. 659).

1:8 The terms "shelter" and "hut" both refer to the temporary structures used by watchmen (e.g., Job 27:18) on the lookout for thieves and intruders.

The Hebrew word here translated "melons" may actually refer to cucumbers.

1:9 Sodom and Gomorrah were classic examples of sinful cities that were completely destroyed (see Ge 19; see also "The Destruction of Sodom and Gomorrah" on p. 32).

10 Hear the word of the LORD,[t]
you rulers of Sodom;[u]
listen to the law[v] of our God,
you people of Gomorrah!
11 "The multitude of your sacrifices—
what are they to me?" says the LORD.
"I have more than enough of burnt offerings,
of rams and the fat of fattened animals;[w]
I have no pleasure
in the blood of bulls[x] and lambs and goats.[y]
12 When you come to appear before me,
who has asked this of you,[z]
this trampling of my courts?
13 Stop bringing meaningless offerings![a]
Your incense[b] is detestable to me.
New Moons, Sabbaths and convocations[c]—
I cannot bear your evil assemblies.
14 Your New Moon festivals and your appointed feasts[d]
my soul hates.
They have become a burden to me;
I am weary[e] of bearing them.
15 When you spread out your hands in prayer,
I will hide[f] my eyes from you;
even if you offer many prayers,
I will not listen.
Your hands are full of blood;[g]
16 wash and make yourselves clean.
Take your evil deeds
out of my sight![h]
Stop doing wrong,[i]
17 learn to do right!
Seek justice,[j]
encourage the oppressed.[a]
Defend the cause of the fatherless,[k]
plead the case of the widow.

18 "Come now, let us reason together,"[l]
says the LORD.
"Though your sins are like scarlet,
they shall be as white as snow;[m]
though they are red as crimson,
they shall be like wool.
19 If you are willing and obedient,
you will eat the best from the land;[n]
20 but if you resist and rebel,
you will be devoured by the sword."[o]
For the mouth of the LORD has spoken.[p]

1:10 [t]Isa 28:14 [u]Isa 3:9; Eze 16:49; Ro 9:29; Rev 11:8 [v]Isa 8:20
1:11 [w]Ps 50:8 [x]Jer 6:20 [y]1Sa 15:22; Mal 1:10
1:12 [z]Ex 23:17
1:13 [a]Isa 66:3 [b]Jer 7:9 [c]1Ch 23:31
1:14 [d]Lev 23:1-44; Nu 28:11-29:39; Isa 29:1 [e]Isa 7:13; 43:22, 24
1:15 [f]Isa 8:17; 59:2; Mic 3:4 [g]Isa 59:3
1:16 [h]Isa 52:11 [i]Isa 55:7; Jer 25:5
1:17 [j]Zep 2:3 [k]Ps 82:3
1:18 [l]Isa 41:1; 43:9,26 [m]Ps 51:7; Rev 7:14
1:19 [n]Dt 30:15-16; Isa 55:2
1:20 [o]Isa 3:25; 65:12 [p]Isa 34:16; 40:5; 58:14; Mic 4:4

[a] 17 Or / *rebuke the oppressor*

1:14 The observance of New Moon festivals, which were celebrated on the first day of every Hebrew month, included special sacrifices and feasts (see Nu 28:11–15). "Appointed feasts" refers to the more significant annual celebrations, such as Passover, Weeks (Pentecost) and Tabernacles (Ex 23:14–17; 34:18–25; Lev 23; Dt 16:1–17). See "The Festivals of Israel" on page 186.

1:17 City life had tended to fragment the family, and the size of the houses excavated during this period indicates that by this time the family unit consisted only of father, mother and children. During the kingdom period, as family/clan ties loosened, the absolute authority and responsibility of the father was transferred to the king. By the eighth century B.C. the individual, instead of working primarily for the good of the larger group, labored for his immediate family and for the ultimate benefit of the king or nation. Not surprisingly, as the focus of the family unit sharpened, the sense of communal responsibility lessened, and Biblical reminders concerning obligations toward widows and orphans, who had little power and were particularly vulnerable to oppression, became more frequent (cf. Jer 7:6; 22:3; see also "The Care of Widows and Orphans in the Bible and the Ancient Near East" on p. 285).

THE AUTHORSHIP OF ISAIAH

ISAIAH 1 Although once universally accepted as the work of one man, Isaiah son of Amoz, the book of Isaiah is now widely believed to have been written by various authors over the course of several centuries. The standard multiple-author theory claims that Isaiah had at least three authors:

- The first was Isaiah (1:1), the eighth-century B.C. prophet. Called "First Isaiah" or "Proto-Isaiah," he is thought to have produced the core of chapters 1–39.
- "Second" or "Deutero-Isaiah" is assumed to have been an anonymous prophet of the sixth century B.C., to whom are attributed chapters 40–55.
- Another **postexilic**[1] prophet, "Third" or "Trito-Isaiah," is posited to have composed most of chapters 56–66, perhaps around 400 B.C.

Advocates of this theory attempt to demonstrate that the style, theology and background of Isaiah 1–39 are unlike those of either 40–55 or 56–66. Second Isaiah—but not First—they argue, depicts God in purely monotheistic terms. Also, First Isaiah is seen as a prophet of judgment, who placed his hopes on the Davidic king, and Second Isaiah a prophet of comfort who pinned his expectations on the Lord's suffering servant.

More substantial are the arguments focusing on the backgrounds of the respective chapters. The Old Testament prophets in general are widely understood to have written from their own unique historical situations. Even if one acknowledges that Isaiah could have predicted the **Babylonian captivity**, it is argued, it is unlikely that he wrote chapters 40–55, since those texts were written from within the context of captivity. Also, the **Persian** king Cyrus (c. 539 B.C.)[2] is mentioned by name in 44:28 and 45:1, 13, suggesting that Cyrus was a contemporary of the author of chapters 40–55. The background of Third Isaiah is posited to be different again. By this point Jerusalem had been rebuilt, its citizens no longer under threat from either **Assyria** or Babylon.

Against this, proponents of the single-author stance first assert that arguments based upon style and theology are weak:

- An author's style depends upon a variety of factors (age, purpose, subject matter, audience, etc.), and stylistic factors like vocabulary are apt to change.
- The three "Isaiahs" do share many phrases and words, suggesting stylistic unity. For example, God is called the "Holy One of Israel" throughout (e.g., 10:17; 41:14; 60:9).
- The alleged theological differences are artificial. Isaiah is a lengthy book, but it does not incorporate any real internal tension or overt contradiction.
- All of Isaiah is concerned with **Canaanite** idolatry. While scholars would expect such a focus from First Isaiah, they would not anticipate it in Second or Third Isaiah (e.g., 57:13); it was not a significant issue to postexilic prophets such as Zechariah, Haggai and Malachi.
- From early on Isaiah promised that the Gentiles would submit to the God of Israel (e.g., 2:2–4), an expectation developed throughout the book (e.g., 42:4; 49:6) and a unifying theological motif for the whole of Isaiah.

Regarding the historical perspective and predictions of Isaiah, the following points are pertinent:

- Isaiah did project himself into the future to describe events as though they had already occurred (e.g., 5:13–17; 9:1–7; 23:1,14). In fact, Isaiah 6, a foundational chapter, presents the exile as inevitable. Isaiah assumed that exile was certain and wrote chapters 40–55 with that in mind.
- Isaiah's mention of Cyrus's name has a parallel in the prediction of Josiah's name in 1 Kings 13:2. It is true that predictions of this kind are fairly rare in the Old Testament, but they do occur.
- In contrast to Ezekiel, who lived in Babylon, "Second Isaiah" gave no indication at all that he was familiar with life in Babylon. This suggests that the author of Isaiah 40–55 did not in fact experience Babylonian exile—which is just what we would expect if the chapters were written by Isaiah of Jerusalem.

The only related archaeological evidence comes from a **Dead Sea Scroll** designated 1QIsa[a].[3] This nearly complete text of Isaiah confirms the conservative position in that there is no break between chapters 39 and 40.

Matthew 3:3, 4:16 and Romans 9:27, 10:20 all quote portions of Isaiah, ascribing each quotation to the prophet Isaiah. There is no tradition anywhere in ancient Jewish literature of an exilic prophet having written Isaiah 40–55. Considering that Isaiah is supposed to have been one of the greatest prophets Israel produced, this silence would indeed seem strange.

[1]See Glossary on page 2080 for definitions of bolded words. [2]See "Cyrus the Great" on page 669. [3]See "The Great Isaiah Scroll" on page 1115.

21 See how the faithful city
has become a harlot![q]
She once was full of justice;
righteousness used to dwell in her—
but now murderers!
22 Your silver has become dross,
your choice wine is diluted with water.
23 Your rulers are rebels,
companions of thieves;
they all love bribes[r]
and chase after gifts.
They do not defend the cause of the fatherless;
the widow's case does not come before them.[s]
24 Therefore the Lord, the LORD Almighty,
the Mighty One of Israel, declares:
"Ah, I will get relief from my foes
and avenge[t] myself on my enemies.
25 I will turn my hand against you;
I will thoroughly purge away your dross
and remove all your impurities.[u]
26 I will restore your judges as in days of old,[v]
your counselors as at the beginning.
Afterward you will be called
the City of Righteousness,[w]
the Faithful City.[x]"

27 Zion will be redeemed with justice,
her penitent ones with righteousness.[y]
28 But rebels and sinners will both be broken,
and those who forsake the LORD will perish.[z]

29 "You will be ashamed because of the sacred oaks[a]
in which you have delighted;
you will be disgraced because of the gardens[b]
that you have chosen.
30 You will be like an oak with fading leaves,
like a garden without water.
31 The mighty man will become tinder
and his work a spark;
both will burn together,
with no one to quench the fire.[c]"

The Mountain of the LORD

2 This is what Isaiah son of Amoz saw concerning Judah and Jerusalem:[d]

2 In the last days

the mountain[e] of the LORD's temple will be established
as chief among the mountains;
it will be raised above the hills,
and all nations will stream to it.

1:21 [q]Isa 57:3-9; Jer 2:20
1:23 [r]Ex 23:8 [s]Isa 10:2; Jer 5:28; Eze 22:6-7; Zec 7:10
1:24 [t]Isa 35:4; 59:17; 61:2; 63:4
1:25 [u]Eze 22:22; Mal 3:3
1:26 [v]Jer 33:7,11 [w]Isa 33:5; 62:1; Zec 8:3 [x]Isa 60:14; 62:2
1:27 [y]Isa 35:10; 62:12; 63:4
1:28 [z]Ps 9:5; Isa 24:20; 66:24; 2Th 1:8-9
1:29 [a]Isa 57:5 [b]Isa 65:3; 66:17
1:31 [c]Isa 5:24; 9:18-19; 26:11; 33:14; 66:15-16, 24
2:1 [d]Isa 1:1
2:2 [e]Isa 27:13; 56:7; 66:20; Mic 4:7

1:25 The process of removing dross from silver is a picture of purification.
1:29 A widely held notion throughout the ancient Near East was that oak trees were sacred. It was typical for both pagan sacrifices and sexual immorality to occur beneath oak trees and in garden settings (see 65:3; 66:17).
2:1–4 For similarity between this passage and Micah 4:1–8, see the note on this section of Micah.
2:2–3 See "Zaphon, Olympus, Sinai and Zion: The Mountain of God" on page 843.

3 Many peoples will come and say,

"Come, let us go up to the mountain of the LORD,
to the house of the God of Jacob.
He will teach us his ways,
so that we may walk in his paths."
2:3 [f]Isa 51:4,7 [g]Lk 24:47
The law[f] will go out from Zion,
the word of the LORD from Jerusalem.[g]
4 He will judge between the nations
and will settle disputes for many peoples.
They will beat their swords into plowshares
2:4 [h]Joel 3:10 [i]Ps 46:9; Isa 9:5; 11:6-9; 32:18; Hos 2:18; Zec 9:10
and their spears into pruning hooks.[h]
Nation will not take up sword against nation,[i]
nor will they train for war anymore.

2:5 [j]Isa 58:1 [k]Isa 60:1,19-20; 1Jn 1:5,7
5 Come, O house of Jacob,[j]
let us walk in the light[k] of the LORD.

The Day of the LORD

2:6 [l]Dt 31:17 [m]2Ki 1:2 [n]Pr 6:1 [o]2Ki 16:7
6 You have abandoned[l] your people,
the house of Jacob.
They are full of superstitions from the East;
they practice divination like the Philistines[m]
and clasp hands[n] with pagans.[o]
7 Their land is full of silver and gold;
there is no end to their treasures.
2:7 [p]Dt 17:16 [q]Isa 31:1; Mic 5:10
Their land is full of horses;[p]
there is no end to their chariots.[q]
2:8 [r]Isa 10:9-11 [s]Isa 17:8
8 Their land is full of idols;[r]
they bow down to the work of their hands,
to what their fingers[s] have made.
2:9 [t]Ps 62:9 [u]Isa 5:15 [v]Ne 4:5
9 So man will be brought low[t]
and mankind humbled[u]—
do not forgive them.[a][v]

10 Go into the rocks,
hide in the ground
from dread of the LORD
2:10 [w]2Th 1:9; Rev 6:15-16
and the splendor of his majesty![w]
11 The eyes of the arrogant man will be humbled
2:11 [x]Isa 5:15; 37:23
and the pride[x] of men brought low;
the LORD alone will be exalted in that day.

12 The LORD Almighty has a day in store
for all the proud and lofty,
2:12 [y]Isa 24:4,21; Mal 4:1 [z]Job 40:11
for all that is exalted[y]
(and they will be humbled),[z]
13 for all the cedars of Lebanon, tall and lofty,
2:13 [a]Zec 11:2
and all the oaks of Bashan,[a]

[a] 9 Or *not raise them up*

2:4 The object described here as a plowshare was in reality an iron point mounted on a wooden beam (ancient plows did not include what we know as a plowshare).

The pruning hook, an agricultural tool used in the cultivation of the vine, had a sharp, knifelike end for pruning (see also Joel 3:10; Mic 4:3).

2:6 "East" probably signifies Aram (Syria) and Mesopotamia. (See "Syria/Aram" on p. 534.)

2:10 When faced with relentless oppression, the beleaguered Israelites were known to find shelter in caves and holes in the ground (see Jdg 6:1–2; 1Sa 13:6).

2:13 Lebanon was famous for its luxuriant stands of cedar trees (see "Cedars of Lebanon" on p. 1043).

"Bashan," a region east of the Jordan River and north of Gilead, was known for its oaks (Eze 27:6) and animals (Eze 39:18).

14 for all the towering mountains
and all the high hills,[b]
15 for every lofty tower
and every fortified wall,[c]
16 for every trading ship[a][d]
and every stately vessel.
17 The arrogance of man will be brought low
and the pride of men humbled;
the LORD alone will be exalted in that day,[e]
18 and the idols will totally disappear.[f]

19 Men will flee to caves in the rocks
and to holes in the ground
from dread of the LORD
and the splendor of his majesty,
when he rises to shake the earth.[g]
20 In that day men will throw away
to the rodents and bats[h]
their idols of silver and idols of gold,
which they made to worship.
21 They will flee to caverns in the rocks
and to the overhanging crags
from dread of the LORD
and the splendor of his majesty,
when he rises to shake the earth.[i]

22 Stop trusting in man,[j]
who has but a breath in his nostrils.
Of what account is he?[k]

2:14 [b]Isa 30:25; 40:4
2:15 [c]Isa 25:2,12
2:16 [d]1Ki 10:22
2:17 [e]ver 11
2:18 [f]Isa 21:9
2:19 [g]Heb 12:26
2:20 [h]Lev 11:19
2:21 [i]ver 19
2:22 [j]Ps 146:3; Jer 17:5 [k]Ps 8:4; 144:3; Isa 40:15; Jas 4:14

Judgment on Jerusalem and Judah

3 See now, the Lord,
the LORD Almighty,
is about to take from Jerusalem and Judah
both supply and support:
all supplies of food[l] and all supplies of water,[m]
2 the hero and warrior,[n]
the judge and prophet,
the soothsayer and elder,[o]
3 the captain of fifty and man of rank,
the counselor, skilled craftsman and clever enchanter.

4 I will make boys their officials;
mere children will govern them.[p]
5 People will oppress each other—
man against man, neighbor against neighbor.[q]
The young will rise up against the old,
the base against the honorable.

3:1 [l]Lev 26:26 [m]Isa 5:13; Eze 4:16
3:2 [n]Eze 17:13 [o]2Ki 24:14; Isa 9:14-15
3:4 [p]Ecc 10:16 *fn*
3:5 [q]Isa 9:19; Jer 9:8; Mic 7:2,6

[a] 16 Hebrew *every ship of Tarshish*

2:16 "Trading ship" refers to one of the ships of Tarshish (see the NIV text note)—large, maritime vessels used by Solomon (1Ki 10:22) and the Phoenicians (Isa 23:1,14) to ply the seas in ambitious commercial ventures to remote locations (see "Seafaring in the Ancient World" on p. 1473). For the location of Tarshish, see "Where Was Tarshish?" on page 1475.

3:2–3 The terms "soothsayer" (v. 2) and "enchanter" (v. 3) refer to occult practitioners and snake charmers, whose activities were condemned (see Dt 18:10; see also "Akkadian Divination" on p. 277).

3:3 Fifty was a common number for either a military unit (see 2Ki 1:9) or a civil grouping (Ex 18:25).

Ancient Israelite Clothing and Jewelry

ISAIAH 3 Since the climatic conditions of Israel have made it difficult for ancient textile fragments to survive, knowledge of ancient dress comes primarily from textual and iconographic sources (i.e., from ancient documents and pictures). Egyptian funerary wall paintings at Beni-Hasan, dating to patriarchal times, picture a caravan of Semitic peoples dressed in brightly colored, woven garments. These appear to have been made of a single cloth wrapped around the body and fastened over one shoulder, leaving the other bare. Toggle pins of bone, ivory or bronze, which held the cloth in place like modern safety pins, have been located at various sites.

Tunics, with or without sleeves, are mentioned in Scripture as the principal garments of both men and women (Ge 37:3; 2Sa 13:18). These were typically ankle length and drawn up when working (2Ki 4:29). The rare textile remains are mostly of linen, with some of wool, but very few are comprised of both wool and linen threads (cf. Lev 19:19). The Black Obelisk[1] (ninth century B.C.), which visually records the **Assyrian** king **Shalmaneser III** receiving tribute from Israel, pictures King Jehu in such a short-sleeved, ankle-length robe with fringes along the bottom. The sash wrapped around his waist was of special significance for high ranking officials (Isa 22:21). Israelite tribute-bearers are shown garbed in tasseled mantles, a type of garment pictured regularly in Assyrian **reliefs** depicting Semitic peoples. Their shoes were upturned at the toes and appear to have covered the entire foot, although the Bible mentions leather sandals as the more common footwear (Ge 14:23; Dt 25:9).

As inner garments, men wore a linen waistcloth with a leather belt from which valuables could be hung, such as a knife or a signet seal (2Ki 1:8; Jer 13:1).[2] The Lachish reliefs[3] (701 B.C.) picture Israelite captives in such loincloths, with a wide fabric belt around their waist whose fringed, vertical edge was passed over the belt to hang between the knees. Undergarments, mentioned only in association with the priesthood, were designed to cover the body from the loins to the thighs when the priests were engaged in sanctuary ministry (Ex 28:42–43; Eze 44:18). Cloaks with hoods, which could be pulled over the head or used to carry loads, were the typical outer garments of both men and women (Ru 3:15; 1Ki 19:13). Linen headdresses, twisted as turbans, were common for men, wealthy women, bridegrooms and priests (Ex 28:40; Isa 3:20; 61:10).

Egyptian comb

Preserving Bible Times; © Dr. James C. Martin; permission of The Cairo Museum

At least for the wealthy, women's clothing was typically made of finer materials and perhaps richer colors than that of men (2Sa 1:24; Pr 31:22). Featured with the attire of the upper class were gauze garments, long veils, headbands and gold embroidery (Isa 3:18–23; 47:2). Women wore their hair long, with a head covering that reached down their back. An ivory from **Megiddo** pictures a woman with a long, fringed dress and shoulder-length head veil. In terms of jewelry items, hammered gold or silver was fashioned into arm bracelets, necklaces, earrings, nose rings and finger rings (Ge 24:22, 30; Est 3:10; Isa 3:18–21; Eze 16:11–12).[4] The most common earring design of ancient Israel was the "lunate," an ovoid loop resembling a crescent moon. Along with other ornaments, two sets of five solid gold bangles each, dating to the **Middle Bronze Age**, have been recovered from Tell el-Ajjul, comparable to the ten-shekel weight of Rebekah's bridal bracelets (Ge 24:22).

Clothing and jewelry distinguished between ethnic groups (Nu 15:38–40) and signaled social status within the community itself. Mourners (2Sa 14:2),[5] lepers (Lev 13:45) and prisoners (2Ki 25:29) also were sometimes identified by their dress. The garb of royalty and the affluent was most likely distinguished by profuse ornamentation (Ps 45:8–9; Eze 26:16). Since jewelry served to confer dignity and authority, in addition to its use as personal adornment, the articles mentioned in the catalog of Isaiah 3:18–23 may reflect the finery of wealth.

For a discussion of clothing in the New Testament era, see "Dress and Fashion in the Greco-Roman World" on page 2004.

[1]See "Jehu/The Black Obelisk of Shalmaneser III" on page 544. [2]See "Signet Rings" on page 728. [3]See "The Lachish Reliefs" on page 559. [4]See "Precious Stones of the Biblical World" on page 1156. [5]See "Sackcloth and Ashes: Rituals of Lamentation" on page 820.

6 A man will seize one of his brothers
at his father's home, and say,
"You have a cloak, you be our leader;
take charge of this heap of ruins!"
7 But in that day he will cry out,
"I have no remedy.[r] **3:7** [r]Eze 34:4;
I have no food or clothing in my house; Hos 5:13
do not make me the leader of the people."

8 Jerusalem staggers,
Judah is falling;[s] **3:8** [s]Isa 1:7
their words[t] and deeds are against the LORD, [t]Isa 9:15,17
defying[u] his glorious presence. [u]Ps 73:9,11
9 The look on their faces testifies against them;
they parade their sin like Sodom;[v] **3:9** [v]Ge 13:13
they do not hide it. [w]Pr 8:36; Ro 6:23
Woe to them!
They have brought disaster[w] upon themselves.
10 Tell the righteous it will be well[x] with them, **3:10** [x]Dt 28:1-14
for they will enjoy the fruit of their deeds.[y] [y]Ps 128:2
11 Woe to the wicked! Disaster[z] is upon them! **3:11** [z]Dt 28:15-68
They will be paid back for what their hands have done.

12 Youths[a] oppress my people, **3:12** [a]ver 4
women rule over them. [b]Isa 9:16
O my people, your guides lead you astray;[b]
they turn you from the path.

13 The LORD takes his place in court;
he rises to judge[c] the people. **3:13** [c]Mic 6:2
14 The LORD enters into judgment[d] **3:14** [d]Job 22:4
against the elders and leaders of his people: [e]Job 24:9; Jas 2:6
"It is you who have ruined my vineyard;
the plunder[e] from the poor is in your houses.
15 What do you mean by crushing my people[f] **3:15** [f]Ps 94:5
and grinding the faces of the poor?"
declares the Lord, the LORD Almighty.

16 The LORD says,
"The women of Zion[g] are haughty, **3:16** [g]SS 3:11
walking along with outstretched necks,
flirting with their eyes,
tripping along with mincing steps,
with ornaments jingling on their ankles.
17 Therefore the Lord will bring sores on the heads of the women of Zion;
the LORD will make their scalps bald."

18 In that day the Lord will snatch away their finery: the bangles and headbands and crescent neck- **3:18** [h]Jdg 8:21
laces,[h] 19 the earrings and bracelets and veils, 20 the headdresses[i] and ankle chains and sashes, the perfume **3:20** [i]Ex 39:28

3:9 For "Sodom," see the note on 1:9.
3:12 It was atypical, and generally frowned upon, in the ancient Near East for young men—or women of any age—to hold leadership positions.
3:15 In this graphic image, much as women would grind grain between two millstones (see the note on Jdg 9:53), Israel's leaders were systematically grinding the poor.
3:16 Ankle ornaments prohibited long, striding steps (see "Ancient Israelite Clothing and Jewelry" on p. 1059).
3:17 Baldness, an unnatural condition for most Israelite males, was commonly associated with mourning over some disaster. See "Beards and Hairstyles in the Biblical World" on page 1084.
3:18–23 In this interesting inventory of 21 items of feminine adornment, the word for "bracelets" could be rendered "twisted chains." Bracelets and other showy adornments (necklaces, anklets, nose rings, armlets, etc.) were much admired in ancient days. See "Ancient Israelite Clothing and Jewelry" on page 1059.
3:18 For information on crescent necklaces, see the note on Judges 8:21.
3:20 "Headdresses" may have been turbans (see Eze 24:17,23).
Anklets, consisting of metal or glass spangles, were sometimes linked together by ankle chains.
Isaiah spoke of the women of his day wearing charms. The Hebrew word, *lâhash,* is used in Ecclesiastes 10:11 and Jeremiah 8:17

bottles and charms, 21 the signet rings and nose rings, 22 the fine robes and the capes and cloaks, the purs-
es 23 and mirrors, and the linen garments and tiaras and shawls.

3:24 [j]Est 2:12 [k]Pr 31:24 [l]Isa 22:12 [m]La 2:10; Eze 27:30-31 [n]1Pe 3:3
3:25 [o]Isa 1:20
3:26 [p]Jer 14:2 [q]La 2:10

24 Instead of fragrance[j] there will be a stench;
  instead of a sash,[k] a rope;
instead of well-dressed hair, baldness;[l]
  instead of fine clothing, sackcloth;[m]
  instead of beauty,[n] branding.
25 Your men will fall by the sword,[o]
  your warriors in battle.
26 The gates of Zion will lament and mourn;[p]
  destitute, she will sit on the ground.[q]

4:1 [r]Isa 13:12 [s]2Th 3:12 [t]Ge 30:23

4

1 In that day seven women
  will take hold of one man[r]
and say, "We will eat our own food[s]
  and provide our own clothes;
only let us be called by your name.
  Take away our disgrace!"[t]

The Branch of the LORD

4:2 [u]Isa 11:1-5; 53:2; Jer 23:5-6; Zec 3:8; 6:12 [v]Ps 72:16
4:3 [w]Ro 11:5 [x]Isa 52:1; 60:21 [y]Lk 10:20
4:4 [z]Isa 3:24 [a]Isa 1:15 [b]Isa 28:6 [c]Isa 1:31; Mt 3:11
4:5 [d]Ex 13:21 [e]Isa 60:1
4:6 [f]Ps 27:5 [g]Isa 25:4

2 In that day the Branch of the LORD[u] will be beautiful and glorious, and the fruit[v] of the land will be
the pride and glory of the survivors in Israel. 3 Those who are left in Zion, who remain[w] in Jerusalem,
will be called holy,[x] all who are recorded[y] among the living in Jerusalem. 4 The Lord will wash away the
filth[z] of the women of Zion; he will cleanse the bloodstains[a] from Jerusalem by a spirit[a] of judgment[b]
and a spirit[a] of fire.[c] 5 Then the LORD will create over all of Mount Zion and over those who assemble
there a cloud of smoke by day and a glow of flaming fire by night;[d] over all the glory[e] will be a canopy.
6 It will be a shelter[f] and shade from the heat of the day, and a refuge[g] and hiding place from the storm
and rain.

The Song of the Vineyard

5:1 [h]Ps 80:8-9
5:2 [i]Jer 2:21 [j]Mt 21:19; Mk 11:13; Lk 13:6

5

I will sing for the one I love
  a song about his vineyard:[h]
My loved one had a vineyard
  on a fertile hillside.
2 He dug it up and cleared it of stones
  and planted it with the choicest vines.[i]
He built a watchtower in it
  and cut out a winepress as well.
Then he looked for a crop of good grapes,
  but it yielded only bad fruit.[j]

[a] 4 Or *the Spirit*

---

specifically of snake-charming (cf. the related verb in Ps 58:4–5). At root it means "a whisper." Isaiah saw the existence of those "instructed in whispering" (i.e., holding whispered communication with the dead or with spirits or making whispered communication purporting to come from "the other side") as evidence that society was about to collapse. The same word also refers to objects, such as personal ornaments, into which some magic charm has been whispered, supposed therefore to afford protection or some other "lucky" benefit to the wearer. Archaeology has revealed such practices all over the ancient world. The same Hebrew word is used in Isaiah 26:16 without any overtones of superstition or magic to mean "whisper a prayer."

3:21 A signet ring, which carried the wearer's seal, signified authority (see "Signet Rings" on p. 728), whereas nose rings, cast of gold, were often part of the apparel of Israelite brides (but see the paragraph below; see also Ge 24:22,53 and "Ancient Israelite Clothing and Jewelry" on p. 1059).

The ancient Hebrews had no specific word for earrings; these jewels were just rings or hoops, ordinarily made of gold (although sometimes the metal is not specified). They were worn by both men and women, either on the nose or on the ears: a nose ring in some passages (Ge 24:47; Isa 3:21; Eze 16:12) and an earring in others (Ge 35:4; Ex 32:2–3; Eze 16:12). In the rest of the passages where such rings or hoops are mentioned, they may be either nose rings or earrings (Ex 35:22; Nu 31:50; Jdg 8:24–26; Job 42:11; Pr 11:22; 25:12; Hos 2:13). When worn as earrings the ring was passed, as it is today, through a hole pierced in the ear lobe. It is probable that pendants were suspended from them.

3:24 Captives were often led away by ropes and were sometimes branded. A shaved head was viewed as a sign of disgrace, devastation or intense mourning.

4:1 War decimated the male population, leaving many women with the double disgrace of being both widowed and childless.

5:1–7 The common grapevine is mentioned throughout Scripture, often in a figurative sense. Grapes were grown in ancient Egypt and in Canaan prior to the time of Abraham (Ge 14:18; Nu 13:20,24). The mountain regions of Judea and Samaria, largely unsuited for grain, were well adapted for vine growing. A vineyard

[3]"Now you dwellers in Jerusalem and men of Judah,
judge between me and my vineyard.[k]
[4]What more could have been done for my vineyard
than I have done for it?[l]
When I looked for good grapes,
why did it yield only bad?
[5]Now I will tell you
what I am going to do to my vineyard:
I will take away its hedge,
and it will be destroyed;
I will break down its wall,[m]
and it will be trampled.[n]
[6]I will make it a wasteland,
neither pruned nor cultivated,
and briers and thorns[o] will grow there.
I will command the clouds
not to rain on it."

[7]The vineyard[p] of the LORD Almighty
is the house of Israel,
and the men of Judah
are the garden of his delight.
And he looked for justice,[q] but saw bloodshed;
for righteousness, but heard cries of distress.

Woes and Judgments

[8]Woe[r] to you who add house to house
and join field to fields[s]
till no space is left
and you live alone in the land.

[9]The LORD Almighty has declared in my hearing:[t]

"Surely the great houses will become desolate,[u]
the fine mansions left without occupants.
[10]A ten-acre[a] vineyard will produce only a bath[b] of wine,
a homer[c] of seed only an ephah[d] of grain."[v]

[11]Woe to those who rise early in the morning
to run after their drinks,

5:3 [k]Mt 21:40
5:4 [l]2Ch 36:15; Jer 2:5-7; Mic 6:3-4; Mt 23:37
5:5 [m]Ps 80:12 [n]Isa 28:3,18; La 1:15; Lk 21:24
5:6 [o]Isa 7:23,24; Heb 6:8
5:7 [p]Ps 80:8 [q]Isa 59:15
5:8 [r]Jer 22:13 [s]Mic 2:2; Hab 2:9-12
5:9 [t]Isa 22:14 [u]Isa 6:11-12; Mt 23:38
5:10 [v]Lev 26:26

[a] *10* Hebrew *ten-yoke,* that is, the land plowed by 10 yoke of oxen in one day [b] *10* That is, probably about 6 gallons (about 22 liters) [c] *10* That is, probably about 6 bushels (about 220 liters) [d] *10* That is, probably about 3/5 bushel (about 22 liters)

---

was usually surrounded with a protecting wall of stones or thorny hedges to keep out destructive animals (Nu 22:24; Ps 80:8–13; Pr 24:30–31; Isa 5:5). In every vineyard was a tower for the watchman, a winepress hollowed out of a flat rock and a vat into which the juice flowed from the winepress (1:8; 5:1–7; Mt 21:33–41). The vine branches were usually allowed to lie along the ground or to fall over the terraces, but sometimes they were raised above the ground with sticks or supported on poles to form a bower.

Tending a vineyard required preparation and constant care. The first year was dedicated to clearing the land of its foliage and abundant rocks. The second year the farmer purchased and carefully planted the finest vines he could afford, then piled up the cleared rocks into fences and watchtowers (see above) to keep out intruders. Finally, in the third year, the fruit of all that labor was ready for harvesting.

Vines were pruned every spring, and the ground was plowed and kept free of weeds. Pruned branches were gathered and burned (Jn 15:6). During the harvest season watchmen were stationed in the towers, and sometimes the whole family of the owner took up residence in booths as a protection against thieves. The harvest season was invariably one of special happiness. The treaders of the winepress shouted and sang as they trod the grapes (Jdg 9:27; Isa 16:10; Jer 25:30; 48:33). The gleanings were left to the poor (Lev 19:10; Dt 24:21; Jdg 8:2), and the wine was stored in new goatskin bags (Mt 9:17) or in large pottery containers. Every seventh year the vines were to be allowed to lie fallow (Ex 23:11; Lev 25:3)—although it is not clear that the Israelites were at all consistent at keeping this command.

See also "Food and Agriculture" on page 390 and "The Winepress" on page 1171.

5:6 In a region so dependent upon rain for agricultural success and ultimate survival, its absence was viewed as a curse upon the land (see Dt 28:23–24; 2Sa 1:21; 1Ki 17:1).

5:10 In this verse, as well as in 1 Samuel 14:14, the area referred to by the English term "acre" is actually the average amount of ground a yoke of oxen could plow in a day. The actual area is unknown, and the translation "acre" is merely conventional.

An ephah was a tenth of a homer (see Eze 45:11). The scanty amount of wine and grain here specified amounted to the smallest fraction of what a "ten-acre vineyard" and a "homer of seed" would ordinarily have been expected to produce.

who stay up late at night
till they are inflamed with wine.[w]
12 They have harps and lyres at their banquets,
tambourines and flutes and wine,
but they have no regard[x] for the deeds of the LORD,
no respect for the work of his hands.[y]
13 Therefore my people will go into exile[z]
for lack of understanding;[a]
their men of rank will die of hunger
and their masses will be parched with thirst.
14 Therefore the grave[a][b] enlarges its appetite
and opens its mouth[c] without limit;
into it will descend their nobles and masses
with all their brawlers and revelers.
15 So man will be brought low[d]
and mankind humbled,[e]
the eyes of the arrogant[f] humbled.
16 But the LORD Almighty will be exalted by his justice,[g]
and the holy God will show himself holy[h] by his righteousness.
17 Then sheep will graze as in their own pasture;[i]
lambs will feed[b] among the ruins of the rich.

18 Woe to those who draw sin along with cords of deceit,
and wickedness[j] as with cart ropes,
19 to those who say, "Let God hurry,
let him hasten his work
so we may see it.
Let it approach,
let the plan of the Holy One of Israel come,
so we may know it."[k]

20 Woe to those who call evil good
and good evil,
who put darkness for light
and light for darkness,[l]
who put bitter for sweet
and sweet for bitter.[m]
21 Woe to those who are wise in their own eyes[n]
and clever in their own sight.

22 Woe to those who are heroes at drinking wine[o]
and champions at mixing drinks,
23 who acquit the guilty for a bribe,[p]
but deny justice[q] to the innocent.[r]
24 Therefore, as tongues of fire lick up straw
and as dry grass sinks down in the flames,

5:11 [w]Pr 23:29-30
5:12 [x]Job 34:27 [y]Ps 28:5; Am 6:5-6
5:13 [z]Hos 4:6 [a]Isa 1:3; Hos 4:6
5:14 [b]Pr 30:16 [c]Nu 16:30
5:15 [d]Isa 10:33 [e]Isa 2:9 [f]Isa 2:11
5:16 [g]Isa 28:17; 30:18; 33:5; 61:8 [h]Isa 29:23
5:17 [i]Isa 7:25; Zep 2:6,14
5:18 [j]Isa 59:4-8; Jer 23:14
5:19 [k]Jer 17:15; Eze 12:22; 2Pe 3:4
5:20 [l]Mt 6:22-23; Lk 11:34-35 [m]Am 5:7
5:21 [n]Pr 3:7; Ro 12:16; 1Co 3:18-20
5:22 [o]Pr 23:20
5:23 [p]Ex 23:8 [q]Isa 10:2 [r]Ps 94:21; Jas 5:6

[a] *14* Hebrew *Sheol* [b] *17* Septuagint; Hebrew / *strangers will eat*

5:12 See "Ancient Musical Instruments" on page 797.
5:14 For information on the "grave" and its insatiable appetite, see the notes on Job 18:13–14, Psalm 6:5, 49:14; see also "Sheol, Hades, Gehenna, the Abyss and Tartarus: Images of Hell" on page 946.
5:22 The quality of the beer and wine was enhanced by the addition of spices (see "Wine and Alcoholic Beverages in the Ancient World" on p. 2015).
5:24 The word *chaff* ("dry grass" in this v. in the NIV) generally refers to the refuse of the grain that has been threshed and winnowed. This is partly dust and dirt, but the real chaff is the hard and inedible coating of the grain. By threshing, most of this is separated; then on a windy day the grain is tossed into the air and the chaff and the shorter pieces of grain are blown away. In this verse and in 33:11, the Hebrew word properly means "dry hay" fit for burning. The more common Hebrew word is generally used as a figure for worthless or godless men (e.g., Ps 1:4) or nations (Isa 17:13). The brevity of the human existence of the wicked is likened in Hosea 13:3 to the morning mist, the early dew, "chaff swirling from a threshing floor" and "smoke escaping through a window." In Daniel 2:35 the Aramaic word rendered "chaff" signifies the small irritants that can get into the eye. The word in Jeremiah 23:28 refers to broken straw. In Matthew 3:12 and Luke 3:17 John the Baptist proclaimed God's intention to destroy the wicked (burning "up the chaff with unquenchable fire").

so their roots will decay[s]
and their flowers blow away like dust;
for they have rejected the law of the LORD Almighty
and spurned the word[t] of the Holy One of Israel.

5:24 [s]Job 18:16 [t]Isa 8:6; 30:9,12

25 Therefore the LORD's anger[u] burns against his people;
his hand is raised and he strikes them down.
The mountains shake,
and the dead bodies are like refuse[v] in the streets.

Yet for all this, his anger is not turned away,[w]
his hand is still upraised.[x]

5:25 [u]2Ki 22:13 [v]2Ki 9:37 [w]Jer 4:8; Da 9:16 [x]Isa 9:12,17,21; 10:4

26 He lifts up a banner for the distant nations,
he whistles[y] for those at the ends of the earth.[z]
Here they come,
swiftly and speedily!

5:26 [y]Isa 7:18; Zec 10:8 [z]Dt 28:49; Isa 13:5; 18:3

27 Not one of them grows tired or stumbles,
not one slumbers or sleeps;
not a belt is loosened at the waist,[a]
not a sandal thong is broken.[b]

5:27 [a]Job 12:18 [b]Joel 2:7-8

28 Their arrows are sharp,[c]
all their bows[d] are strung;
their horses' hoofs seem like flint,
their chariot wheels like a whirlwind.

5:28 [c]Ps 45:5 [d]Ps 7:12

29 Their roar is like that of the lion,[e]
they roar like young lions;
they growl as they seize[f] their prey
and carry it off with no one to rescue.[g]

5:29 [e]Jer 51:38; Zep 3:3; Zec 11:3 [f]Isa 10:6; 49:24-25 [g]Isa 42:22; Mic 5:8

30 In that day they will roar over it
like the roaring of the sea.[h]
And if one looks at the land,
he will see darkness and distress;[i]
even the light will be darkened[j] by the clouds.

5:30 [h]Lk 21:25 [i]Isa 8:22; Jer 4:23-28 [j]Joel 2:10

Isaiah's Commission

6 In the year that King Uzziah[k] died,[l] I saw the Lord[m] seated on a throne,[n] high and exalted, and the
train of his robe filled the temple. 2 Above him were seraphs,[o] each with six wings: With two wings
they covered their faces, with two they covered their feet,[p] and with two they were flying. 3 And they were
calling to one another:

6:1 [k]2Ch 26:22,23 [l]2Ki 15:7 [m]Jn 12:41 [n]Rev 4:2
6:2 [o]Rev 4:8 [p]Eze 1:11

"Holy, holy, holy is the LORD Almighty;
the whole earth is full of his glory."[q]

6:3 [q]Ps 72:19; Rev 4:8

4 At the sound of their voices the doorposts and thresholds shook and the temple was filled with smoke.
5 "Woe to me!" I cried. "I am ruined! For I am a man of unclean lips, and I live among a people of un-
clean lips,[r] and my eyes have seen the King,[s] the LORD Almighty."

6:5 [r]Jer 9:3-8 [s]Jer 51:57

6 Then one of the seraphs flew to me with a live coal in his hand, which he had taken with tongs from
the altar. 7 With it he touched my mouth and said, "See, this has touched your lips;[t] your guilt is taken
away and your sin atoned for.[u]"

6:7 [t]Jer 1:9 [u]1Jn 1:7

5:26 A banner attached to a pole was often erected on a hilltop as a signal for gathering troops (13:2). In Isaiah it was a symbol for summoning the nations and bringing Israel back home (11:10,12; 49:22; 62:10).

6:1–13 Whether this chapter, dealing with the temple vision, represents the initial call of Isaiah has been much debated. The "Holy One of Israel" was to become one of Isaiah's favorite titles for the deity in whose name he spoke.

6:1 Uzziah, who was also known as Azariah (2Ki 14:21; 2Ch 26:1) and reigned from 792 to 740 B.C., was a godly and powerful king. When he burned incense without authorization in the temple, however, he was struck with "leprosy," a condition from which he suffered until his death (see 2Ch 26:16–21 and the NIV text note on 2Ch 26:19). See "Uzziah, King of Judah, and Jeroboam II, King of Israel" on page 650.

See "Thrones in the Ancient World" on page 899.

6:6 On the annual Day of Atonement coals of fire were conveyed by the high priest into the Most Holy Place (Lev 16:12), where sacrifice was made to atone for his own sin and that of the people. See "Ritual Purity in Israel and the Ancient Near East" on page 166 and "The Day of Atonement" on page 176.

6:8 [v]Ac 9:4 8 Then I heard the voice[v] of the Lord saying, "Whom shall I send? And who will go for us?"
And I said, "Here am I. Send me!"
6:9 [w]Eze 3:11 [x]Mt 13:15*; Lk 8:10* 9 He said, "Go[w] and tell this people:

" 'Be ever hearing, but never understanding;
be ever seeing, but never perceiving.'[x]
6:10 [y]Dt 32:15; Ps 119:70 [z]Jer 5:21 [a]Mt 13:13-15; Mk 4:12*; Ac 28:26-27* 10 Make the heart of this people calloused;[y]
make their ears dull
and close their eyes.[a]
Otherwise they might see with their eyes,
hear with their ears,[z]
understand with their hearts,
and turn and be healed."[a]

6:11 [b]Ps 79:5 [c]Lev 26:31 11 Then I said, "For how long, O Lord?"[b]
And he answered:

"Until the cities lie ruined[c]
and without inhabitant,
until the houses are left deserted
and the fields ruined and ravaged,
6:12 [d]Dt 28:64 [e]Jer 4:29 12 until the LORD has sent everyone far away[d]
and the land is utterly forsaken.[e]
6:13 [f]Isa 1:9 [g]Job 14:7 13 And though a tenth remains[f] in the land,
it will again be laid waste.
But as the terebinth and oak
leave stumps when they are cut down,
so the holy seed will be the stump in the land."[g]

The Sign of Immanuel

7:1 [h]2Ki 15:37 [i]2Ch 28:5 [j]2Ki 15:25 7 When Ahaz son of Jotham, the son of Uzziah, was king of Judah, King Rezin[h] of Aram[i] and Pekah[j]
son of Remaliah king of Israel marched up to fight against Jerusalem, but they could not over-
power it.
7:2 [k]ver 13; Isa 22:22 [l]Isa 9:9 2 Now the house of David[k] was told, "Aram has allied itself with[b] Ephraim[l]"; so the hearts of Ahaz and
his people were shaken, as the trees of the forest are shaken by the wind.
3 Then the LORD said to Isaiah, "Go out, you and your son Shear-Jashub,[c] to meet Ahaz at the end of the
7:3 [m]2Ki 18:17; Isa 36:2 aqueduct of the Upper Pool, on the road to the Washerman's Field.[m] 4 Say to him, 'Be careful, keep calm[n]
7:4 [n]Isa 30:15 [o]Isa 35:4 [p]Dt 20:3 [q]Zec 3:2 [r]Isa 10:24 and don't be afraid.[o] Do not lose heart[p] because of these two smoldering stubs[q] of firewood—because
of the fierce anger[r] of Rezin and Aram and of the son of Remaliah. 5 Aram, Ephraim and Remaliah's son
have plotted your ruin, saying, 6 "Let us invade Judah; let us tear it apart and divide it among ourselves,
and make the son of Tabeel king over it." 7 Yet this is what the Sovereign LORD says:

" 'It will not take place,
7:7 [s]Isa 8:10; Ac 4:25 it will not happen,[s]

[a] 9,10 Hebrew; Septuagint *'You will be ever hearing, but never understanding; / you will be ever seeing, but never perceiving.' / 10 This people's heart has become calloused; / they hardly hear with their ears, / and they have closed their eyes* [b] 2 Or *has set up camp in* [c] 3 *Shear-Jashub* means *a remnant will return.*

7:1—12:6 This group of chapters, the Book of Immanuel, belongs to the period of the Syro-Ephraimite War (2Ki 16:1–20; 1Ch 28). In the midst of this time of peril, Isaiah uttered his great prophecies regarding Immanuel (Isa 7:14–16; 9:6–7; 11:1–10), concluding with a song of triumphant faith that ends with the assurance, "Great is the Holy One of Israel among you" (12:6). Here again, woe (10:1–4) and threats (10:5–19) stand in vivid contrast to Messianic blessings (11:1–16).

7:1 The invasion of Rezin and Pekah (the Syro-Ephraimite War on p. 1066) probably took place in 735/734 B.C. Aram (Syria) and Israel (Ephraim) were attempting to convince Ahaz to join them in a coalition against Assyria, while Isaiah was exerting pressure on Ahaz from the other side to prevent him from entering into a counter-alliance with Assyria (see 2Ki 16:5–18; 2Ch 28:16–21). See "The Syro-Ephraimite War" on page 1066, "Syria/Aram" on page 534, "Ahaz, King of Judah, and Rezin, King of Aram" on page 554 and "Menahem and Pekah of Israel, Jotham of Judah and Tiglath-Pileser III of Assyria" on page 553.

7:2 "Ephraim" is synonymous with Israel, the northern kingdom.

7:3 The process of laundering clothes in Isaiah's day involved trampling on them in cold water. A soap (soda) or bleach was used as a cleaning agent.

7:4 Damascus, the capital of Aram (see v. 8), was demolished by Tiglath-Pileser III in 732 B.C.—the same year that Israel was thoroughly defeated (see "Damascus" on p. 1087).

7:6 "Tabeel," an Aramaic name, may be associated with the "land of Tob" east of the Jordan River.

[8]for the head of Aram is Damascus,[t]
and the head of Damascus is only Rezin.
Within sixty-five years
Ephraim will be too shattered[u] to be a people.

7:8 [t]Ge 14:15 [u]Isa 17:1-3

7:8 Beginning in about 670 B.C., Esarhaddon and later Ashurbanipal, both kings of Assyria, settled dispossessed foreign captives from other areas into Israel. The "Samaritan" race resulted from intermarriage between these newcomers and the few remaining Israelites who had not been included in the exile (see the note on 2Ki 17:24–41; see also "The Samaritans" on p. 1737). Israel never again existed as a separate nation, although the returnees following Judah's later deportation included many descendants of Israelite exiles as well.

The Syro-Ephraimite War

ISAIAH 7 The great promise of Isaiah 7:14, that a virgin would give birth to a son and call him Immanuel, did not arise in a vacuum but from within a specific historical context. In approximately 734 B.C. Israel (the northern kingdom, also called Ephraim) and Syria (also called Aram) formed a military alliance in defiance of the growing power of **Assyria**. The king of Israel was Pekah, who had apparently assassinated his predecessor, Pekahiah, son of Menahem, seized power and instituted an anti-Assyrian policy in Israel.[1] The king of Syria was Rezin.[2] Syria had for a long time been a major opponent of the Assyrian Empire, which was at that time under the control of Tiglath-Pileser III.

Assyria (located in what is now Iraq) was strategizing an approach from the east against Damascus, the capital of Syria,[3] and then **Samaria**, the capital of Israel.[4] Pekah and Rezin realized that their position would be that much more difficult if Judah, to the south of Samaria, was against them. In such a situation, they would have had to fight a two-front war against Ahaz of Judah to the south and the Assyrians to the northeast. They decided to launch a preemptive strike against Jerusalem and to replace Ahaz with a puppet king, an individual referred to simply as the "son of Tabeel" (v. 6).[5]

A historical problem in this story is that 2 Kings 15:30 reports that Hoshea, the last king of Israel, assassinated his predecessor, Pekah, in the twentieth year of Jotham, father of Ahaz. If so, how could Pekah have led a war against Ahaz? The probable solution is that Ahaz was at the time of the war a coregent with his father, Jotham.

At the opening of Isaiah 7 the prophet found Ahaz at the conduit of the Upper Pool, perhaps inspecting the city's water supply in anticipation of a siege.[6] The coalition of Syria and Israel had already devastated the territory of Judah. Isaiah offered Ahaz assurance from God that the city would not fall and urged him to ask for a sign from God, but Ahaz curtly refused. It appears that Ahaz did not want to be bothered with religious talk because he had already sent an appeal to Tiglath-Pileser for help. The Assyrian king did indeed respond and moved swiftly against the Syro-Ephraimite coalition.

But Isaiah was furious that Ahaz was placing his hope in Assyria rather than in God. He informed the king that Jerusalem would indeed survive but that Assyrian troops would pass through the land like a flood, decimating everything in their path. The Assyrians would sweep the land clean, like a razor that shaves all the hair from a man's body (v. 20). The people of Judah would be reduced to near starvation. Since farming would be impossible under these conditions, the land would revert to pasture and wilderness (v. 23). People would have to live off whatever they could hunt or gather in the wild, as well as the dairy products of whatever cattle they could manage to retain (vv. 21–25).

Just as Isaiah had predicted, the coalition of Syria and Israel came to nothing. Pekah was assassinated by Hoshea, and Damascus fell to the Assyrians in 732 B.C. Hoshea would ultimately lead Israel to resist Assyria again, and in 722 B.C. Samaria would be destroyed and the northern kingdom would come to an end.[7] But Assyrian power nearly brought down Jerusalem as well. Ahaz's rejection of the sign had nearly cost Judah everything, but it did lead to God's giving a much greater sign in verse 14.

[1]See "Menahem and Pekah of Israel, Jotham of Judah and Tiglath-Pileser III of Assyria" on page 553. [2]See "Ahaz, King of Judah, and Rezin, King of Aram" on page 554. [3]See "Damascus" on page 1087. [4]See "Omri and Samaria" on page 512. [5]Tabeel may have been Tubail, the king of Tyre. [6]See "Siege Warfare" on page 465. [7]See "Hoshea, King of Israel, and Shalmaneser V, King of Assyria" on page 556.

> 9 The head of Ephraim is Samaria,
> and the head of Samaria is only Remaliah's son.
> If you do not stand firm in your faith,[v]
> you will not stand at all.' "[w]

10 Again the LORD spoke to Ahaz, 11 "Ask the LORD your God for a sign, whether in the deepest depths
or in the highest heights."
12 But Ahaz said, "I will not ask; I will not put the LORD to the test."
13 Then Isaiah said, "Hear now, you house of David! Is it not enough to try the patience of men? Will
you try the patience of my God[x] also? 14 Therefore the Lord himself will give you[a] a sign: The virgin will
be with child and will give birth to a son,[y] and[b] will call him Immanuel.[c][z] 15 He will eat curds and hon-
ey[a] when he knows enough to reject the wrong and choose the right. 16 But before the boy knows[b] enough
to reject the wrong and choose the right, the land of the two kings you dread will be laid waste.[c] 17 The
LORD will bring on you and on your people and on the house of your father a time unlike any since Ephra-
im broke away[d] from Judah—he will bring the king of Assyria.[e]"
18 In that day the LORD will whistle[f] for flies from the distant streams of Egypt and for bees from the
land of Assyria.[g] 19 They will all come and settle in the steep ravines and in the crevices[h] in the rocks, on
all the thornbushes and at all the water holes. 20 In that day the Lord will use[i] a razor hired from beyond
the River[d]—the king of Assyria[j]—to shave your head and the hair of your legs, and to take off your
beards also. 21 In that day, a man will keep alive a young cow and two goats. 22 And because of the abun-
dance of the milk they give, he will have curds to eat. All who remain in the land will eat curds and hon-
ey. 23 In that day, in every place where there were a thousand vines worth a thousand silver shekels,[e] there
will be only briers and thorns.[k] 24 Men will go there with bow and arrow, for the land will be covered with
briers and thorns. 25 As for all the hills once cultivated by the hoe, you will no longer go there for fear of
the briers and thorns; they will become places where cattle are turned loose and where sheep run.[l]

Assyria, the LORD's Instrument

8 The LORD said to me, "Take a large scroll[m] and write on it with an ordinary pen: Maher-Shalal-Hash-
Baz.[f][n] 2 And I will call in Uriah[o] the priest and Zechariah son of Jeberekiah as reliable witnesses
for me."
3 Then I went to the prophetess, and she conceived and gave birth to a son. And the LORD said to me,
"Name him Maher-Shalal-Hash-Baz. 4 Before the boy knows[p] how to say 'My father' or 'My mother,' the
wealth of Damascus and the plunder of Samaria will be carried off by the king of Assyria.[q]"
5 The LORD spoke to me again:

> 6 "Because this people has rejected[r]
> the gently flowing waters of Shiloah[s]
> and rejoices over Rezin
> and the son of Remaliah,[t]

7:9 [v]2Ch 20:20 [w]Isa 8:6-8; 30:12-14
7:13 [x]Isa 25:1
7:14 [y]Lk 1:31 [z]Isa 8:8,10; Mt 1:23*
7:15 [a]ver 22
7:16 [b]Isa 8:4 [c]Isa 17:3; Hos 5:9,13; Am 1:3-5
7:17 [d]1Ki 12:16 [e]2Ch 28:20
7:18 [f]Isa 5:26 [g]Isa 13:5
7:19 [h]Isa 2:19
7:20 [i]Isa 10:15 [j]Isa 8:7; 10:5
7:23 [k]Isa 5:6
7:25 [l]Isa 5:17
8:1 [m]Isa 30:8; Hab 2:2 [n]ver 3; Hab 2:2
8:2 [o]2Ki 16:10
8:4 [p]Isa 7:16 [q]Isa 7:8
8:6 [r]Isa 5:24 [s]Jn 9:7 [t]Isa 7:1

[a] *14* The Hebrew is plural. [b] *14* Masoretic Text; Dead Sea Scrolls *and he* or *and they* [c] *14 Immanuel* means *God with us.* [d] *20* That is, the Euphrates [e] *23* That is, about 25 pounds (about 11.5 kilograms) [f] *1 Maher-Shalal-Hash-Baz* means *quick to the plunder, swift to the spoil*; also in verse 3.

7:9 Pekah, a usurper, hardly merited attention in a challenge against Ahaz, a "son" (descendant) of David. See "Menahem and Pekah of Israel, Jotham of Judah and Tiglath-Pileser III of Assyria" on page 553.

7:15 The phrase "when he knows . . . wrong . . . right" suggests the age of twelve or thirteen years, the time of moral determination and responsibility under the law. Thus, "when" this young boy was twelve or thirteen years of age (722/721 B.C.), he would be eating curds (a kind of yogurt) and honey instead of agricultural products—due to the devastation of Israel by Assyria. Some believe that this expression involved a shorter period of time, identical to that in verse 16 and in 8:4.

7:16 Both Aram and Israel would be plundered before this lad had reached adolescence. As events transpired, this actually happened when he was only about two years old, in 732 B.C.

7:20 For an Israelite male to be shaved, particularly against his will, was considered the height of insult (see 2Sa 10:4 and its note; see also "Beards and Hairstyles in the Biblical World" on p. 1084). "Hair of your legs" is a euphemistic reference for pubic hair.

7:21–22 See "Food and Agriculture" on page 390.

8:2 Uriah the priest served during the time of King Ahaz (see 2Ki 16:10–11).

8:3 See the note on prophetesses at Exodus 15:20–21.

Isaiah's own name ("Salvation of Yahweh") is almost identical in meaning with Joshua ("Yahweh is Salvation"), which appears in the New Testament as Jesus, the name of the Messiah whom Isaiah heralded. That the prophet's name played a formative role in his life is not improbable, since it expresses the great theme of his prophetic ministry. His father, Amoz, may have been a person of prominence, since the prophet is in 13 different instances called "the son of Amoz," but nothing is known about him. Isaiah was married and had two children, to each of whom he gave a significant name (Isa 7:3; 8:3).

8:4 At about the age of two the boy would have been able to pronounce the simple phrases "my father" or "my mother." The time period here matches that in 7:16. The destruction of the northern kingdom was prefaced by this carrying off of plunder, although Samaria's complete annihilation did not occur until 722/721 B.C.

8:6 Shiloah may refer to the water flowing from the Gihon spring (see 2Ch 32:30) to the Pool of Siloam (see Jn 9:7; see also "The Pool of Siloam" on p. 1739).

[7] therefore the Lord is about to bring against them
the mighty floodwaters[u] of the River[a]— 8:7 [u]Isa 17:12-13 [v]Isa 7:20
the king of Assyria[v] with all his pomp.
It will overflow all its channels,
run over all its banks
[8] and sweep on into Judah, swirling over it,
passing through it and reaching up to the neck.
Its outspread wings will cover the breadth of your land,
O Immanuel[b]!"[w] 8:8 [w]Isa 7:14

[9] Raise the war cry,[c][x] you nations, and be shattered! 8:9 [x]Isa 17:12-13 [y]Joel 3:9
Listen, all you distant lands.
Prepare[y] for battle, and be shattered!
Prepare for battle, and be shattered!
[10] Devise your strategy, but it will be thwarted;[z] 8:10 [z]Job 5:12 [a]Isa 7:7 [b]Isa 7:14; Ro 8:31
propose your plan, but it will not stand,[a]
for God is with us.[d][b]

Fear God

[11] The LORD spoke to me with his strong hand upon me,[c] warning me not to follow[d] the way of this peo- 8:11 [c]Eze 3:14 [d]Eze 2:8
ple. He said:

[12] "Do not call conspiracy[e] 8:12 [e]Isa 7:2; 30:1 [f]1Pe 3:14*
everything that these people call conspiracy[e];
do not fear what they fear,
and do not dread it.[f]
[13] The LORD Almighty is the one you are to regard as holy,[g] 8:13 [g]Nu 20:12 [h]Isa 29:23
he is the one you are to fear,
he is the one you are to dread,[h]
[14] and he will be a sanctuary;[i] 8:14 [i]Isa 4:6; Eze 11:16 [j]Lk 2:34; Ro 9:33*; 1Pe 2:8* [k]Isa 24:17-18
but for both houses of Israel he will be
a stone that causes men to stumble
and a rock that makes them fall.[j]
And for the people of Jerusalem he will be
a trap and a snare.[k]
[15] Many of them will stumble;[l] 8:15 [l]Isa 28:13; 59:10; Lk 20:18; Ro 9:32
they will fall and be broken,
they will be snared and captured."

[16] Bind up the testimony
and seal[m] up the law among my disciples. 8:16 [m]Isa 29:11-12
[17] I will wait[n] for the LORD, 8:17 [n]Hab 2:3 [o]Dt 31:17; Isa 54:8
who is hiding[o] his face from the house of Jacob.
I will put my trust in him.

[18] Here am I, and the children the LORD has given me.[p] We are signs[q] and symbols in Israel from the 8:18 [p]Heb 2:13* [q]Lk 2:34 [r]Ps 9:11
LORD Almighty, who dwells on Mount Zion.[r]
[19] When men tell you to consult[s] mediums and spiritists, who whisper and mutter,[t] should not a peo- 8:19 [s]1Sa 28:8 [t]Isa 29:4
ple inquire of their God? Why consult the dead on behalf of the living? [20] To the law[u] and to the testimo- 8:20 [u]Isa 1:10; Lk 16:29

[a] 7 That is, the Euphrates [b] 8 *Immanuel* means *God with us.* [c] 9 Or *Do your worst* [d] 10 Hebrew *Immanuel* [e] 12 Or *Do not call for a treaty / every time these people call for a treaty*

8:7 The image of mighty floodwaters was often employed in antiquity to symbolize a powerful, invading army.
8:8 See 30:28 and its note. Of all the cities in Judah, only Jerusalem, the "head" of the southern kingdom, was spared in Sennacherib's invasion in 701 B.C.
8:14 Israel and Judah, the northern and southern kingdoms, respectively, were intended by the term "both houses."

8:19 For "mediums and spiritists," see "Akkadian Divination" on page 277. Desperate for answers about an uncertain future, people were attempting to contact the spirits of the dead, as Saul had done when he had succeeded through a medium, the Witch of Endor, in calling up the spirit of Samuel (1Sa 28:8–11; see "Ancient Necromancy" on p. 435).

8:20 [v]Mic 3:6 ny! If they do not speak according to this word, they have no light[v] of dawn. 21 Distressed and hungry, they
will roam through the land; when they are famished, they will become enraged and, looking upward,
8:21 [w]Rev 16:11 will curse[w] their king and their God. 22 Then they will look toward the earth and see only distress and
8:22 [x]ver 20; Isa 5:30 darkness and fearful gloom, and they will be thrust into utter darkness.[x]

To Us a Child Is Born

9 Nevertheless, there will be no more gloom for those who were in distress. In the past he humbled the
9:1 [y]2Ki 15:29 land of Zebulun and the land of Naphtali,[y] but in the future he will honor Galilee of the Gentiles, by
the way of the sea, along the Jordan—

2 The people walking in darkness
9:2 [z]Eph 5:8 [a]Lk 1:79 [b]Mt 4:15-16* have seen a great light;[z]
on those living in the land of the shadow of death[a][a]
a light has dawned.[b]
3 You have enlarged the nation
and increased their joy;
they rejoice before you
as people rejoice at the harvest,
as men rejoice
when dividing the plunder.
9:4 [c]Jdg 7:25 [d]Isa 14:25 [e]Isa 10:27 [f]Isa 14:4; 49:26; 51:13; 54:14 4 For as in the day of Midian's defeat,[c]
you have shattered
the yoke[d] that burdens them,
the bar across their shoulders,[e]
the rod of their oppressor.[f]
5 Every warrior's boot used in battle
and every garment rolled in blood
9:5 [g]Isa 2:4 will be destined for burning,[g]
will be fuel for the fire.
9:6 [h]Isa 53:2; Lk 2:11 [i]Jn 3:16 [j]Mt 28:18 [k]Isa 28:29 [l]Isa 10:21; 11:2 [m]Isa 26:3,12; 66:12 6 For to us a child is born,[h]
to us a son is given,[i]
and the government[j] will be on his shoulders.
And he will be called
Wonderful Counselor,[b][k] Mighty God,[l]
Everlasting Father, Prince of Peace.[m]
7 Of the increase of his government and peace
9:7 [n]Da 2:44; Lk 1:33 [o]Isa 11:4; 16:5; 32:1,16 [p]Isa 37:32; 59:17 there will be no end.[n]
He will reign on David's throne
and over his kingdom,
establishing and upholding it
with justice[o] and righteousness
from that time on and forever.
The zeal[p] of the LORD Almighty
will accomplish this.

The LORD's Anger Against Israel

8 The Lord has sent a message against Jacob;
it will fall on Israel.
9 All the people will know it—
9:9 [q]Isa 7:9 Ephraim and the inhabitants of Samaria[q]—

[a] 2 Or *land of darkness* [b] 6 Or *Wonderful, Counselor*

9:4 The "day of Midian's defeat" refers to Gideon's victory over the hordes of Midian, who had dominated Israel (Jdg 7:22–25).
9:5 In ancient times wood, charcoal and various kinds of thorn bushes, dried grass and the dung of camels and cattle were used as fuel. There is no evidence that coal was used by the Hebrews as fuel; their houses had no chimneys (9:5,19; Eze 4:12; 15:4,6; 21:32).
9:9 For "Ephraim," see the note on 7:2.

who say with pride
and arrogance[r] of heart,
10 "The bricks have fallen down,
but we will rebuild with dressed stone;
the fig trees have been felled,
but we will replace them with cedars."
11 But the LORD has strengthened Rezin's[s] foes against them
and has spurred their enemies on.
12 Arameans[t] from the east and Philistines[u] from the west
have devoured[v] Israel with open mouth.

Yet for all this, his anger is not turned away,
his hand is still upraised.[w]

13 But the people have not returned to him who struck[x] them,
nor have they sought[y] the LORD Almighty.
14 So the LORD will cut off from Israel both head and tail,
both palm branch and reed[z] in a single day;[a]
15 the elders[b] and prominent men are the head,
the prophets who teach lies are the tail.
16 Those who guide[c] this people mislead them,
and those who are guided are led astray.[d]
17 Therefore the Lord will take no pleasure in the young men,[e]
nor will he pity[f] the fatherless and widows,
for everyone is ungodly[g] and wicked,[h]
every mouth speaks vileness.[i]

Yet for all this, his anger is not turned away,
his hand is still upraised.[j]

18 Surely wickedness burns like a fire;[k]
it consumes briers and thorns,
it sets the forest thickets ablaze,[l]
so that it rolls upward in a column of smoke.
19 By the wrath[m] of the LORD Almighty
the land will be scorched
and the people will be fuel for the fire;[n]
no one will spare his brother.[o]
20 On the right they will devour,
but still be hungry;[p]
on the left they will eat,[q]
but not be satisfied.
Each will feed on the flesh of his own offspring[a]:
21 Manasseh will feed on Ephraim, and Ephraim on Manasseh;
together they will turn against Judah.[r]

Yet for all this, his anger is not turned away,
his hand is still upraised.[s]

[a] 20 Or *arm*

9:9 [r]Isa 46:12
9:11 [s]Isa 7:8
9:12 [t]2Ki 16:6 [u]2Ch 28:18 [v]Ps 79:7 [w]Isa 5:25
9:13 [x]Jer 5:3 [y]Isa 31:1; Hos 7:7,10
9:14 [z]Isa 19:15 [a]Rev 18:8
9:15 [b]Isa 3:2-3
9:16 [c]Mt 15:14; 23:16,24 [d]Isa 3:12
9:17 [e]Jer 18:21 [f]Isa 27:11 [g]Isa 10:6 [h]Isa 1:4 [i]Mt 12:34 [j]Isa 5:25
9:18 [k]Mal 4:1 [l]Ps 83:14
9:19 [m]Isa 13:9,13 [n]Isa 1:31 [o]Mic 7:2,6
9:20 [p]Lev 26:26 [q]Isa 49:26
9:21 [r]2Ch 28:6 [s]Isa 5:25

9:10 Simple, sun-dried clay bricks tended to crack and deteriorate. Accordingly, God had instructed the Israelites to construct their altars from undressed (uncut) stones (see Ex 20:25; see also "Ancient Altars" on p. 125).

The costliest wood in the ancient Near East came from the cedars of Lebanon (see 1Ki 7:2–3; see also "Cedars of Lebanon" on p. 1043).

9:14 Both contrasting sets—"head and tail" and "palm branch and reed"—here refer to Israel's leaders, although the same two pairings refer in 19:15 to the Egyptian rulers.

9:17 Even the orphans and widows, who frequently suffered oppression and were typically presented in the Prophets as innocent victims (see the note on 1:17), are here depicted as depraved and evil.

9:19 See the note on verse 5 regarding fuel.

9:21 Manasseh and Ephraim, the northern kingdom's most prominent tribes, were descended not directly from Judah but from Joseph's two sons (see Ge 46:20; 48:5 and its note). Centuries earlier Judah and Ephraim had vied with one another (Jdg 12:4).

10:1 [t]Ps 58:2
10:2 [u]Isa 3:14 [v]Isa 5:23
10:3 [w]Job 31:14; Hos 9:7 [x]Lk 19:44 [y]Isa 20:6
10:4 [z]Isa 24:22 [a]Isa 22:2; 34:3; 66:16 [b]Isa 5:25
10:5 [c]Isa 14:25; Zep 2:13 [d]Jer 51:20 [e]Isa 13:3,5,13; 30:30; 66:14
10:6 [f]Isa 9:17 [g]Isa 9:19 [h]Isa 5:29
10:7 [i]Ge 50:20; Ac 4:23-28
10:8 [j]2Ki 18:24
10:9 [k]Ge 10:10 [l]2Ch 35:20 [m]2Ki 17:6 [n]2Ki 16:9
10:10 [o]2Ki 19:18
10:12 [p]Isa 28:21-22; 65:7 [q]2Ki 19:31 [r]Jer 50:18
10:13 [s]Isa 37:24; Da 4:30 [t]Eze 28:4
10:14 [u]Jer 49:16; Ob 1:4 [v]Job 31:25

10

Woe to those who make unjust laws,
to those who issue oppressive decrees,[t]
2 to deprive[u] the poor of their rights
and withhold justice from the oppressed of
my people,[v]
making widows their prey
and robbing the fatherless.
3 What will you do on the day of reckoning,[w]
when disaster[x] comes from afar?
To whom will you run for help?[y]
Where will you leave your riches?
4 Nothing will remain but to cringe among the captives[z]
or fall among the slain.[a]

Yet for all this, his anger is not turned away,[b]
his hand is still upraised.

God's Judgment on Assyria

5 "Woe to the Assyrian,[c] the rod of my anger,
in whose hand is the club[d] of my wrath![e]
6 I send him against a godless[f] nation,
I dispatch him against a people who anger me,[g]
to seize loot and snatch plunder,[h]
and to trample them down like mud in the streets.
7 But this is not what he intends,[i]
this is not what he has in mind;
his purpose is to destroy,
to put an end to many nations.
8 'Are not my commanders[j] all kings?' he says.
9 'Has not Calno[k] fared like Carchemish?[l]
Is not Hamath like Arpad,
and Samaria[m] like Damascus?[n]
10 As my hand seized the kingdoms of the idols,[o]
kingdoms whose images excelled those of Jerusalem
and Samaria—
11 shall I not deal with Jerusalem and her images
as I dealt with Samaria and her idols?' "

12 When the Lord has finished all his work[p] against Mount Zion[q] and Jerusalem, he will say, "I will
punish the king of Assyria[r] for the willful pride of his heart and the haughty look in his eyes. 13 For he says:

" 'By the strength of my hand I have done this,[s]
and by my wisdom, because I have understanding.
I removed the boundaries of nations,
I plundered their treasures;[t]
like a mighty one I subdued[a] their kings.
14 As one reaches into a nest,[u]
so my hand reached for the wealth[v] of the nations;

[a] 13 Or / *I subdued the mighty,*

10:2 See the notes on 1:17 and 9:17.
10:9 Calno ("Calneh" in Am 6:2) was a region in northern Aram (Syria); Carchemish a great fortress on the Euphrates River east of Calno; Hamath a city on the Orontes River that marked the northern extent of Solomon's rule (2Ch 8:4); and Arpad a city near Hamath and just south of Calno.
10:12–19 Wise men, unlike prophets, claimed no special inspiration. They exercised no priestly functions and were not, like the scribes, devoted exclusively to the study of the sacred writings. Eventually wise men and scribes coalesced into one class. With worsening political conditions and a deepening sense of moral problems during the period of the prophets and later kings, people came to despise worldly wisdom as irreligious and as characteristic of pagans, who might be superior in secular culture but who were inferior from a moral and religious point of view.

The Annals of Sargon II

ISAIAH 10 The siege and destruction of **Samaria** are attributed in the Bible to Shalmaneser V (r. 726–722 B.C.; 2Ki 17:1–6). Since the **Assyrian** king died in the same year as Samaria's capitulation, however, the deportation of the city's inhabitants and its resettlement with foreigners were most likely carried out by Shalmaneser's successor, Sargon II (r. 722–705 B.C.).

Prior to 1847, "Sargon king of Assyria" was known only from Isaiah 20:1. Since his name did not appear in classical sources, scholars concluded that the Sargon of the Bible was not a bona fide king but rather an alias for some other Assyrian ruler. Ironically, however, Sargon was the first name of an Assyrian king to be deciphered from Assyrian inscriptions when, in 1847, his vast palace of more than 200 rooms and 30 courtyards was excavated at Khorsabad in northern Iraq. The excavations also revealed **reliefs** and inscriptions on the walls comprising the annals of this Assyrian king. Now, thanks to the discoveries of archaeology, we know much about Sargon and the other kings of the Assyrian Empire.

Sargon II ruled from 721 to 705 B.C. He was probably a usurper without rightful claim to the throne; thus he dubbed himself "Sargon," which literally means "The king is legitimate," a name recalling Sargon I, a great Assyrian king of antiquity. His usurpation of the throne led to such intense internal discord that outlying regions took the opportunity to reassert their independence from their overlords. The king of Hamath led a rebellion in the west that included the cities of Arpad, Damascus and Samaria. Sargon II quickly responded, conquering the insurgents at the Battle of Qarqar in 720 B.C. He then proceeded south to Egypt, marching through the territories of Israel and Judah along the way.

Sargon II campaigned in the region of Canaan three times (in 720, 716/715 and 712/711 B.C.), in the process turning Israel into an Assyrian province and Judah into a vassal state. In 720 B.C., following the defeat of Samaria by Shalmaneser V,[1] Sargon boasted about having deported 27,280 Israelites to Assyria. In 712/711 B.C. he turned his attention to the area of Philistia. According to 20:1 he sent his commander-in-chief to capture the city of Ashdod. Assyrian records verify that Sargon remained in his capital at Khorsabad: He stayed "in the land," ostensibly to supervise the construction of his palace. Not only is the Ashdod campaign documented in the Assyrian annals, but fragments of an Assyrian victory inscription were discovered in excavations at Ashdod itself. Moreover, a mass grave from the time of the Assyrian conquest yielded the remains of approximately 3,000 individuals, many of them decapitated.

The Bible, as indicated earlier, mentions Sargon II by name only in 20:1 a passage in which his capture of Ashdod is highlighted. It seems, however, that Isaiah also had Sargon's campaigns in mind when he composed chapter 10. In describing the pride of the Assyrian monarch, the prophet wrote about previous Assyrian victories over Carchemish, Hamath, Arpad, Samaria and Damascus (10:9). In prophesying God's future punishment of Assyria, Isaiah cited the recent abuses of Assyrian power to emphasize the Lord's justice.

Winged "androcephalus" (human-headed) bull from the Palace of Sargon II, Khorsabad
Preserving Bible Times; © Dr. James C. Martin; permission of The British Museum

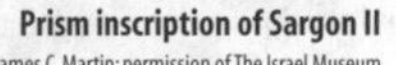
Prism inscription of Sargon II
Preserving Bible Times; © Dr. James C. Martin; permission of The Israel Museum

[1]See "Hoshea, King of Israel, and Shalmaneser V, King of Assyria" on page 556.

as men gather abandoned eggs,
so I gathered all the countries;
not one flapped a wing,
or opened its mouth to chirp.' "

15 Does the ax raise itself above him who swings it,
10:15 [w]Isa 45:9; Ro 9:20-21 [x]ver 5 — or the saw boast against him who uses it?[w]
As if a rod were to wield him who lifts it up,
or a club[x] brandish him who is not wood!

16 Therefore, the Lord, the LORD Almighty,
10:16 [y]ver 18; Isa 17:4 [z]Isa 8:7 — will send a wasting disease[y] upon his sturdy warriors;
under his pomp[z] a fire will be kindled
like a blazing flame.

10:17 [a]Isa 31:9 [b]Isa 37:23 [c]Nu 11:1-3 [d]Isa 9:18 — 17 The Light of Israel will become a fire,[a]
their Holy One[b] a flame;
in a single day it will burn and consume
his thorns[c] and his briers.[d]

10:18 [e]2Ki 19:23 — 18 The splendor of his forests[e] and fertile fields
it will completely destroy,
as when a sick man wastes away.

10:19 [f]Isa 21:17 — 19 And the remaining trees of his forests will be so few[f]
that a child could write them down.

The Remnant of Israel

10:20 [g]Isa 11:10, 11 [h]2Ki 16:7 [i]2Ch 28:20 [j]Isa 17:7 — 20 In that day[g] the remnant of Israel,
the survivors of the house of Jacob,
will no longer rely[h] on him
who struck them down[i]
but will truly rely[j] on the LORD,
the Holy One of Israel.

10:21 [k]Isa 6:13 [l]Isa 9:6 — 21 A remnant[k] will return,[a] a remnant of Jacob
will return to the Mighty God.[l]

22 Though your people, O Israel, be like the sand by the sea,
10:22 [m]Ro 9:27-28 [n]Isa 28:22; Da 9:27 — only a remnant will return.[m]
Destruction has been decreed,[n]
overwhelming and righteous.

23 The Lord, the LORD Almighty, will carry out
the destruction decreed upon the whole
10:23 [o]Isa 28:22; Ro 9:27-28* — land.[o]

24 Therefore, this is what the Lord, the LORD Almighty, says:

10:24 [p]Ps 87:5-6 [q]Ex 5:14 — "O my people who live in Zion,[p]
do not be afraid of the Assyrians,
who beat[q] you with a rod
and lift up a club against you, as
Egypt did.

10:25 [r]Isa 17:14 [s]ver 5; Da 11:36 — 25 Very soon[r] my anger against you will end
and my wrath[s] will be directed to their
destruction."

[a] 21 Hebrew *shear-jashub*; also in verse 22

ANCIENT VOICES

The Tamudi, Ibadidi, Marsima[ni]* and Hayappa, who live in distant Arabia, in the desert, who knew neither overseer nor commander, who never brought tribute to any king—with the help of Assur, my lord, I defeated them. I deported the rest of them. I settled them in Samaria/Samerina.

*Partial word in brackets added by translator for clarity

—SARGON II: THE ANNALS

See "The Annals of Sargon II" article.

10:16 The angel may have employed a particularly virulent and contagious plague in putting to death 185,000 of Sennacherib's soldiers in 701 B.C. (see the note on 37:36; cf. 2Sa 24:15–16; 1Ch 21:22,27).
10:18–19 "Forests" here depict the Assyrian army. This prophecy was most likely fulfilled between 612 B.C. (Nineveh's fall) and 605 (the battle of Carchemish).
10:20–21 A faithful remnant led by Hezekiah survived the Assyrian invasion of 701 B.C. (see 37:4). Later, a vestige (small group of people) returned from Babylonian exile.

[26]The LORD Almighty will lash[t] them with a whip,
as when he struck down Midian[u] at the rock of Oreb;
and he will raise his staff over the waters,[v]
as he did in Egypt.
[27]In that day their burden will be lifted from your shoulders,
their yoke[w] from your neck;[x]
the yoke will be broken
because you have grown so fat.[a]

[28]They enter Aiath;
they pass through Migron;[y]
they store supplies at Micmash.[z]
[29]They go over the pass, and say,
"We will camp overnight at Geba."
Ramah[a] trembles;
Gibeah of Saul flees.
[30]Cry out, O Daughter of Gallim![b]
Listen, O Laishah!
Poor Anathoth![c]
[31]Madmenah is in flight;
the people of Gebim take cover.
[32]This day they will halt at Nob;[d]
they will shake their fist
at the mount of the Daughter of Zion,[e]
at the hill of Jerusalem.

[33]See, the Lord, the LORD Almighty,
will lop off the boughs with great power.
The lofty trees will be felled,
the tall[f] ones will be brought low.
[34]He will cut down the forest thickets with an ax;
Lebanon will fall before the Mighty One.

10:26 [t]Isa 37:36-38 [u]Isa 9:4 [v]Ex 14:16
10:27 [w]Isa 9:4 [x]Isa 14:25
10:28 [y]1Sa 14:2 [z]1Sa 13:2
10:29 [a]Jos 18:25
10:30 [b]1Sa 25:44 [c]Ne 11:32
10:32 [d]1Sa 21:1 [e]Jer 6:23
10:33 [f]Am 2:9

The Branch From Jesse

11 A shoot will come up from the stump of Jesse;[g]
from his roots a Branch[h] will bear fruit.
[2]The Spirit[i] of the LORD will rest on him—
the Spirit of wisdom[j] and of understanding,
the Spirit of counsel and of power,[k]
the Spirit of knowledge and of the fear of the LORD—
[3]and he will delight in the fear of the LORD.

He will not judge by what he sees with his eyes,[l]
or decide by what he hears with his ears;[m]
[4]but with righteousness[n] he will judge the needy,
with justice[o] he will give decisions for the poor[p] of the earth.
He will strike[q] the earth with the rod of his mouth;
with the breath[r] of his lips he will slay the wicked.

11:1 [g]ver 10; Isa 9:7; Rev 5:5 [h]Isa 4:2
11:2 [i]Isa 42:1; 48:16; 61:1; Mt 3:16; Jn 1:32-33 [j]Eph 1:17 [k]2Ti 1:7
11:3 [l]Jn 7:24 [m]Jn 2:25
11:4 [n]Ps 72:2 [o]Isa 9:7 [p]Isa 3:14 [q]Mal 4:6 [r]Job 4:9; 2Th 2:8

[a] 27 Hebrew; Septuagint *broken / from your shoulders*

10:26–27 These verses predict that God would destroy the Assyrian army and break Assyria's oppressive yoke. This prophecy was fulfilled in 701 B.C.
10:26 Oreb was a Midianite leader (Jdg 7:25).
10:28 For "Micmash," see "The Pass at Micmash" on page 417.
10:29–30 Ramah, about 5 miles (8 km) north of Jerusalem, was the hometown of Samuel; Gibeah, about 3 miles (4.8 km) north of Jerusalem, was Saul's capital (see "Gibeah" on p. 380); Gallim, about 4 miles (6.4 km) north of Jerusalem, was a Benjamite town associated with Saul (see 1Sa 25:44); and Anathoth, about 2.5 miles (4 km) northeast of Jerusalem, was the hometown of Jeremiah (Jer 1:1).
10:32 Nob may have been associated with Mount Scopus, which rose near the outskirts of Jerusalem. "Daughter of Zion" embodied Jerusalem itself.
10:34 The reference to Lebanon is shorthand for its renowned cedar forests (see "Cedars of Lebanon" on p. 1043).

11:5 [s]Isa 25:1 [t]Eph 6:14

5 Righteousness will be his belt
    and faithfulness[s] the sash around his waist.[t]

11:6 [u]Isa 65:25

6 The wolf will live with the lamb,[u]
    the leopard will lie down with the goat,
the calf and the lion and the yearling[a] together;
    and a little child will lead them.
7 The cow will feed with the bear,
    their young will lie down together,
    and the lion will eat straw like the ox.
8 The infant will play near the hole of the cobra,
    and the young child put his hand into the
        viper's nest.

11:9 [v]Job 5:23 [w]Ps 98:2-3; Isa 52:10 [x]Isa 45:6,14; Hab 2:14

9 They will neither harm nor destroy[v]
    on all my holy mountain,
for the earth[w] will be full of the knowledge[x] of the LORD
    as the waters cover the sea.

11:10 [y]Jn 12:32 [z]Isa 49:23; Lk 2:32 [a]Ro 15:12* [b]Isa 14:3; 28:12; 32:17-18
11:11 [c]Isa 10:20 [d]Isa 19:24; Hos 11:11; Mic 7:12; Zec 10:10 [e]Ge 10:22 [f]Isa 42:4,10,12; 66:19
11:12 [g]Zep 3:10

10 In that day the Root of Jesse will stand as a banner[y] for the peoples; the nations[z] will rally to him,[a]
and his place of rest[b] will be glorious. 11 In that day[c] the Lord will reach out his hand a second time to re-
claim the remnant that is left of his people from Assyria,[d] from Lower Egypt, from Upper Egypt,[b] from
Cush,[c] from Elam,[e] from Babylonia,[d] from Hamath and from the islands[f] of the sea.

12 He will raise a banner for the nations
    and gather the exiles of Israel;
he will assemble the scattered people[g] of Judah
    from the four quarters of the earth.
13 Ephraim's jealousy will vanish,
    and Judah's enemies[e] will be cut off;
Ephraim will not be jealous of Judah,
    nor Judah hostile toward Ephraim.[h]

11:13 [h]Jer 3:18; Eze 37:16-17,22; Hos 1:11

14 They will swoop down on the slopes of Philistia to the west;
    together they will plunder the people to the east.
They will lay hands on Edom[i] and Moab,[j]
    and the Ammonites will be subject to them.

11:14 [i]Da 11:41; Joel 3:19 [j]Isa 16:14; 25:10

15 The LORD will dry up
    the gulf of the Egyptian sea;
with a scorching wind he will sweep his hand[k]
    over the Euphrates River.[f][l]
He will break it up into seven streams
    so that men can cross over in sandals.

11:15 [k]Isa 19:16 [l]Isa 7:20

16 There will be a highway[m] for the remnant of his people
    that is left from Assyria,
as there was for Israel
    when they came up from Egypt.[n]

11:16 [m]Isa 19:23; 62:10 [n]Ex 14:26-31

[a] *6* Hebrew; Septuagint *lion will feed* [b] *11* Hebrew *from Pathros* [c] *11* That is, the upper Nile region [d] *11* Hebrew *Shinar* [e] *13* Or *hostility* [f] *15* Hebrew *the River*

11:5 Not wanting to be encumbered by his flowing garments, a man anticipating vigorous action would have tied them up with a belt (see 5:27).
11:10 For "banner," see the note on 5:26.
11:11 "Lower Egypt" was actually the northern delta region of the Nile, while "Upper Egypt" was the southern part of the country, upstream from the delta. Elam lay northeast of the lower Tigris Valley, and Hamath, on the Orontes River, marked the northern boundary of Solomon's territory (2Ch 8:4). The "islands of the sea" were most likely the Mediterranean coastlands and islands.
11:13 See the note on 7:2 for a discussion of "Ephraim." Prior to the exile Ephraim and Judah were frequently in conflict (see 9:21 and its note).
11:14 The "people to the east" probably included, among others, the Midianites, who had frequently raided and pillaged Israel (see 9:4; see also "Midian" on p. 92). After the exodus Israel had refrained from attacking Edom, Moab and Ammon (see Jdg 11:14–18; see also "Edom" on p. 1467, "Moab" on p. 292 and "Ammon" on p. 364).
11:16 Isaiah 57:14 and 62:10 also describe the removal of obstacles and the construction of a highway to Jerusalem (cf. 35:8–10; 40:3–4 and the note on 40:3).

Songs of Praise

12 In that day you will say:

"I will praise[o] you, O LORD.
Although you were angry with me,
your anger has turned away
and you have comforted me.
2 Surely God is my salvation;
I will trust[p] and not be afraid.
The LORD, the LORD, is my strength and my song;
he has become my salvation.[q]"
3 With joy you will draw water[r]
from the wells of salvation.

4 In that day you will say:

"Give thanks to the LORD, call on his name;[s]
make known among the nations what he has done,
and proclaim that his name is exalted.
5 Sing[t] to the LORD, for he has done glorious things;[u]
let this be known to all the world.
6 Shout aloud and sing for joy, people of Zion,
for great is the Holy One of Israel[v] among you.[w]"

A Prophecy Against Babylon

13 An oracle concerning Babylon that Isaiah son of Amoz saw:

2 Raise a banner[x] on a bare hilltop,
shout to them;
beckon to them
to enter the gates of the nobles.
3 I have commanded my holy ones;
I have summoned my warriors[y] to carry out my wrath—
those who rejoice[z] in my triumph.
4 Listen, a noise on the mountains,
like that of a great multitude![a]
Listen, an uproar among the kingdoms,
like nations massing together!
The LORD Almighty is mustering
an army for war.
5 They come from faraway lands,
from the ends of the heavens[b]—
the LORD and the weapons of his wrath—
to destroy[c] the whole country.

12:1 [o]Isa 25:1
12:2 [p]Isa 26:3 [q]Ex 15:2; Ps 118:14
12:3 [r]Jn 4:10,14
12:4 [s]Ps 105:1; Isa 24:15
12:5 [t]Ex 15:1 [u]Ps 98:1
12:6 [v]Isa 49:26 [w]Zep 3:14-17
13:2 [x]Jer 50:2; 51:27
13:3 [y]Joel 3:11 [z]Ps 149:2
13:4 [a]Joel 3:14
13:5 [b]Isa 5:26 [c]Isa 24:1

13:1—23:18 These prophesies against the nations are composed of ten "oracles" (weighty, solemn and grievous utterances; see Jer 23:33 and the NIV text note there) against nations that either were or would be a menace to God's people: Babylon (Isa 13:1—14:27), Philistia (14:28–32), Moab (15:1—16:14), Damascus (17:1—18:7, Egypt (19:1—20:6), Babylon a second time (21:1–10), Dumah (21:11–12), Arabia (21:13–17), Jerusalem (22:1–25) and Tyre (23:1–18). Here prophecies regarding the near future (16:14; 21:16; cf. 22:20 with 37:2) appear along with others that refer to a more distant (23:17) or quite remote time. The fall of Babylon was so certain that Israel was apprised of the taunt that would be sung on the day of that city's fall. Compare 21:6–20, which describes this event as having already taken place, with 39:6, which speaks of the Babylonian captivity as still future—a method of prophetic description frequently employed in Isaiah. This group of prophecies was chiefly threatening, but it also contains wonderful promises of blessing. Israel's mightiest foes would share with her in this future blessedness (19:23–25).

13:1 The Hebrew for "oracle" is related to a Hebrew verb meaning "to lift up, carry." The term may, therefore, include a nuance of meaning related to lifting up one's voice or carrying a burden. Such an oracle often contained a message of doom (see "Oracles of the Ancient World" on p. 1507).

The judgment on Babylon is mentioned first because of the present Assyrian threat and because Babylon would later bring about the downfall of Judah and Jerusalem (between 605 and 586 B.C.).

13:2 For "banner," see the note on 5:26.

13:3 See "*Herem*, Holy War" on page 419.

13:6 [d]Eze 30:2 [e]Isa 2:12; Joel 1:15
13:7 [f]Eze 21:7
13:8 [g]Isa 21:4

6 Wail,[d] for the day[e] of the LORD is near;
it will come like destruction from the Almighty.[a]
7 Because of this, all hands will go limp,
every man's heart will melt.[f]
8 Terror[g] will seize them,
pain and anguish will grip them;
they will writhe like a woman in labor.

[a] 6 Hebrew *Shaddai*

Babylon

ISAIAH 13 Babylon ("Map 8a") was one of the greatest cities of ancient **Mesopotamia**. Already a fairly important city by 2100 B.C., it became the hub of the **Old Babylonian Empire** under **Hammurabi** (1792–1750 B.C.). Babylon soon declined after Hammurabi's death, however, and was sacked by the **Hittites** around 1531 B.C. But it became powerful again under Nabopolassar, who founded the **Neo-Babylonian** Empire. This was Babylon's most glorious period; it dominated the ancient Near East from 625 to 539 B.C. The most famous king of this period was **Nebuchadnezzar II** (604–562 B.C.), who, using the vast riches he had accumulated from his conquests, transformed Babylon into perhaps the most magnificent capital in antiquity.[1]

The ruins of ancient Babylon, 53 miles (83 km) south of Baghdad in modern Iraq, encompass approximately 2,100 acres. Excavations have revealed the glory of the city constructed by Nebuchadnezzar II, particularly that of its fortification system. An inner city of around 1,140 acres was built up along both sides of the Euphrates River. This was surrounded by a wall 5.5 miles (8.9 km) long, incorporating an inner wall 21 feet (6.5 m) wide and an outer wall 12 feet (3.7 km) wide, with a 24-foot (7.3-km) space between them filled with earth—resulting in a total defense depth of 57 feet (17.4 km). Outside the outer wall was a moat, fed by the Euphrates, ranging in width from 60 to 250 feet (1.5 to 76.2 m). To the east of the inner city were two more double walls totaling 4.5 miles (7.3 km) in length. To provide additional protection against invasion from the north, Nebuchadnezzar constructed an enormous wall 20 miles (32 km) north of Babylon. It was 16 feet (4.9 m) thick and extended from the Euphrates to the Tigris River, a distance of approximately 25 miles (40 km).[2] Within the city Nebuchadnezzar's magnificent palace occupied an area of about 50 acres. Along with this were over 50 temples, as well as numerous shrines and other buildings.

Babylon held a prominent place in the minds of the prophets. Isaiah and Jeremiah both predicted its downfall (Isa 13–14; Jer 50–51). Jeremiah also prophesied that the city's famous walls would be torn down (Jer 50:15; 51:44,58). In 539 B.C., after defeating the Babylonians at the northern defense wall, Cyrus the Great and his Medo-Persian army entered Babylon without a contest.[3] The Babylonian Chronicle describes the fall of Babylon to Cyrus. In 482 B.C. Babylon's revolt against the Persian king Xerxes led to the razing of its fortifications.

Thereafter Babylon experienced a slow decline. Alexander the Great died there, and long after the **exile** the city was still home to a sizable Jewish population. In Revelation 18 Babylon represents godless human culture. Today little remains of the city's former grandeur (see Isa 13:20–22; Jer 50:3,39–40; 51:29,37,43).

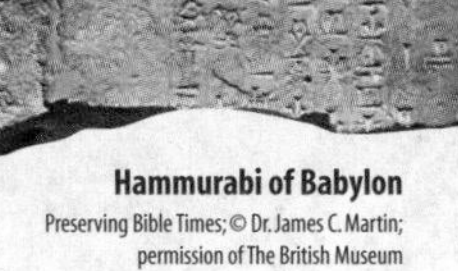

Hammurabi of Babylon
Preserving Bible Times; © Dr. James C. Martin; permission of The British Museum

[1]See "Nebuchadnezzar" on page 571. [2]See "The Tigris and Euphrates Rivers" on page 604. [3]See "Cyrus the Great" on page 669 and "Herodotus and the Fall of Babylon" on page 1283.

THE NATIONS IN PROPHECY

(prophets listed in chronological order)

	Amos	Isaiah	Jeremiah	Ezekiel	Miscellaneous
Babylon		13:1—14:23 Destruction: like Sodom and Gomorrah; no survivors	50–51 Captivity; destruction; humiliation; desolation; ruin		Habakkuk 2:6–17: Destruction; disgrace
Philistia	1:6–8 Remnant will perish; destruction	14:29–32 Helpless; famine; defeated from north	47 Conquered from north; destruction; mourning remnant	25:15–17 Destruction; remnant cut off	
Moab	2:1–3 Fire; death	15–16 Devastation; ruin; mourning; some remnant	48 Desolation; shame; exile; laughingstock; future restoration	25:8–11 Captivity	
Damascus	1:3–5 Cut off; exile	17:1–3 Ruin, but a remnant left	49:23–27 Helpless; destruction		
Egypt		19 Civil war; economic decline; military defeat; conquered by Assyria	46:1–26 To be conquered by Nebuchadnezzar	29–32 Overcome by Babylon	
Edom	1:11–12 Fire	21:11–12 Devastation, but possibility of survival	49:7–22 Flight; ruin; object of horror; like Sodom and Gomorrah; desolation	25:12–14 Laid waste	Obadiah: Destruction; no survivors
Tyre	1:9–10 Burning of citadels	23 Destruction; conquest; restoration after 70 years		26–28 Overthrown; mourning; destruction	
Ammon	1:13–15 Exile		49:1–6 Desolate heap possessed by Israel; exile; future restoration	25:1–7 Destruction	
Nineveh					Nahum: Control of Judah ended; besieged; destroyed; plundered

Chronological and Background Charts of the Old Testament, p. 74

They will look aghast at each other,
their faces aflame.[h]

9 See, the day of the LORD is coming
—a cruel day, with wrath and fierce anger—
to make the land desolate
and destroy the sinners within it.
10 The stars of heaven and their constellations
will not show their light.
The rising sun[i] will be darkened[j]
and the moon will not give its light.[k]
11 I will punish[l] the world for its evil,
the wicked for their sins.
I will put an end to the arrogance of the haughty
and will humble the pride of the ruthless.
12 I will make man[m] scarcer than pure gold,
more rare than the gold of Ophir.
13 Therefore I will make the heavens tremble;[n]
and the earth will shake from its place
at the wrath of the LORD Almighty,
in the day of his burning anger.

14 Like a hunted gazelle,
like sheep without a shepherd,[o]
each will return to his own people,
each will flee to his native land.[p]
15 Whoever is captured will be thrust through;
all who are caught will fall[q] by the sword.[r]
16 Their infants[s] will be dashed to pieces before their eyes;
their houses will be looted and their wives ravished.

17 See, I will stir up[t] against them the Medes,
who do not care for silver
and have no delight in gold.[u]
18 Their bows will strike down the young men;
they will have no mercy on infants
nor will they look with compassion on children.
19 Babylon, the jewel of kingdoms,
the glory[v] of the Babylonians'[a] pride,
will be overthrown[w] by God
like Sodom and Gomorrah.[x]
20 She will never be inhabited[y]
or lived in through all generations;
no Arab[z] will pitch his tent there,
no shepherd will rest his flocks there.
21 But desert creatures[a] will lie there,
jackals will fill her houses;

13:8 [h]Na 2:10
13:10 [i]Isa 24:23 [j]Isa 5:30; Rev 8:12 [k]Eze 32:7; Mt 24:29*; Mk 13:24*
13:11 [l]Isa 3:11; 11:4; 26:21
13:12 [m]Isa 4:1
13:13 [n]Isa 34:4; 51:6; Hag 2:6
13:14 [o]1Ki 22:17 [p]Jer 50:16
13:15 [q]Jer 51:4 [r]Isa 14:19; Jer 50:25
13:16 [s]Ps 137:9
13:17 [t]Jer 51:1 [u]Pr 6:34-35
13:19 [v]Da 4:30 [w]Rev 14:8 [x]Ge 19:24
13:20 [y]Isa 14:23; 34:10-15 [z]2Ch 17:11
13:21 [a]Rev 18:2

[a] 19 Or *Chaldeans'*

13:10 For a discussion of solar and lunar eclipses, see the note on Joel 2:31.
13:12 Solomon imported significant quantities of gold from Ophir (see 1Ki 9:28; 10:11; see also the note on Ps 45:9).
13:16 The wholesale slaughter of infants and children by invading armies appears to us as senseless violence. But the motivation was actually far-thinking; the enemy would be unable to produce a future generation of warriors or to revive its vigor as a city (or country or people). Women also suffered excruciatingly in wartime, so much so that war widows were often reduced to prostitution in order to survive.
13:17 The Medes resided in the northwestern portion of modern Iran. The eighth century B.C. did see conflict between Assyria and Media, but some scholars relate the fulfillment of this verse to the period when the Medes allied themselves with the Babylonians in defeating Assyria in 612–609 B.C.—only to join forces later with Cyrus to conquer Babylon in 539.
13:21 In both Leviticus 17:7 and 2 Chronicles 11:15 "wild goats" are associated with demons ("goat idols"), and in Revelation 18:2 fallen Babylon is described as a home for demons and evil spirits. (See "Goat-Demons and Desert Satyrs" on p. 177.)

there the owls will dwell,
and there the wild goats will leap about.
22 Hyenas will howl in her strongholds,[b]
jackals[c] in her luxurious palaces.
Her time is at hand,[d]
and her days will not be prolonged.

13:22 [b]Isa 25:2 [c]Isa 34:13 [d]Jer 51:33

14

The LORD will have compassion[e] on Jacob;
once again he will choose[f] Israel
and will settle them in their own land.
Aliens[g] will join them
and unite with the house of Jacob.
2 Nations will take them
and bring[h] them to their own place.
And the house of Israel will possess the nations[i]
as menservants and maidservants in the LORD's land.
They will make captives of their captors
and rule over their oppressors.[j]

14:1 [e]Ps 102:13; Isa 49:10,13; 54:7-8,10 [f]Isa 41:8; 44:1; 49:7; Zec 1:17; 2:12 [g]Eph 2:12-19
14:2 [h]Isa 60:9 [i]Isa 49:7,23 [j]Isa 60:14; 61:5

3On the day the LORD gives you relief[k] from suffering and turmoil and cruel bondage, 4you will take
up this taunt[l] against the king of Babylon:

14:3 [k]Isa 11:10
14:4 [l]Hab 2:6 [m]Isa 9:4

How the oppressor[m] has come to an end!
How his fury[a] has ended!
5 The LORD has broken the rod of the wicked,[n]
the scepter of the rulers,
6 which in anger struck down peoples[o]
with unceasing blows,
and in fury subdued nations
with relentless aggression.[p]
7 All the lands are at rest and at peace;
they break into singing.[q]
8 Even the pine trees[r] and the cedars of Lebanon
exult over you and say,
"Now that you have been laid low,
no woodsman comes to cut us down."

14:5 [n]Ps 125:3
14:6 [o]Isa 10:14 [p]Isa 47:6
14:7 [q]Ps 98:1; 126:1-3
14:8 [r]Eze 31:16

9 The grave[b][s] below is all astir
to meet you at your coming;
it rouses the spirits of the departed to greet you—
all those who were leaders in the world;
it makes them rise from their thrones—
all those who were kings over the nations.
10 They will all respond,
they will say to you,
"You also have become weak, as we are;
you have become like us."[t]

14:9 [s]Eze 32:21
14:10 [t]Eze 32:21

[a] 4 Dead Sea Scrolls, Septuagint and Syriac; the meaning of the word in the Masoretic Text is uncertain. [b] 9 Hebrew *Sheol*; also in verses 11 and 15

14:5 For "scepter," see the note on Zechariah 10:11.
14:8 The timbers of the highly prized cedars of Lebanon were hauled away for centuries, often as tribute payment, by the kings of Assyria and Babylon (see "Cedars of Lebanon" on p. 1043).
14:9 A little known fact of ancient shepherding is that a goat would often lead a flock of sheep (see Jer 50:8). The word here translated "leaders" is literally "goats"—synonymous with shepherds in Zechariah 10:3. These leaders are spoken of as rising from their thrones because conditions among the dead were described by the ancients in terms of their respective roles while on Earth. (For the ancient Near Eastern view of the afterlife, see the note on Ps 6:5 and "Sheol, Hades, Gehenna, the Abyss and Tartarus: Images of Hell" on p. 946.)
14:11 Music is treated here as a mark of luxury and pleasure (see Am 6:5–6; see also "Ancient Musical Instruments" on p. 797).

14:11 [u]Isa 51:8
14:12 [v]Isa 34:4; Lk 10:18 [w]2Pe 1:19; Rev 2:28; 8:10; 9:1
14:13 [x]Da 5:23; 8:10; Mt 11:23 [y]Eze 28:2; 2Th 2:4
14:14 [z]Isa 47:8; 2Th 2:4
14:15 [a]Mt 11:23; Lk 10:15
14:16 [b]Jer 50:23
14:17 [c]Joel 2:3
14:19 [d]Isa 22:16-18 [e]Jer 41:7-9
14:20 [f]Job 18:19 [g]Isa 1:4 [h]Ps 21:10
14:21 [i]Ex 20:5; Lev 26:39

11 All your pomp has been brought down to
the grave,
along with the noise of your harps;
maggots are spread out beneath you
and worms[u] cover you.

12 How you have fallen[v] from heaven,
O morning star,[w] son of the dawn!
You have been cast down to the earth,
you who once laid low the nations!
13 You said in your heart,
"I will ascend[x] to heaven;
I will raise my throne[y]
above the stars of God;
I will sit enthroned on the mount of assembly,
on the utmost heights of the sacred mountain.[a]
14 I will ascend above the tops of the clouds;
I will make myself like the Most High."[z]
15 But you are brought down to the grave,
to the depths[a] of the pit.

16 Those who see you stare at you,
they ponder your fate:[b]
"Is this the man who shook the earth
and made kingdoms tremble,
17 the man who made the world a desert,[c]
who overthrew its cities
and would not let his captives go home?"

18 All the kings of the nations lie in state,
each in his own tomb.
19 But you are cast out[d] of your tomb
like a rejected branch;
you are covered with the slain,
with those pierced by the sword,
those who descend to the stones of the pit.[e]
Like a corpse trampled underfoot,
20 you will not join them in burial,
for you have destroyed your land
and killed your people.

The offspring[f] of the wicked[g]
will never be mentioned[h] again.
21 Prepare a place to slaughter his sons
for the sins of their forefathers;[i]
they are not to rise to inherit the land
and cover the earth with their cities.

[a] 13 Or *the north*; Hebrew *Zaphon*

14:13 The "sacred mountain," Mount Zaphon (also called Mount Casius), rose about 25 miles (40 km) northeast of Ugarit in Syria (see "Ugarit/Ras Shamra" on p. 819). Much like Mount Olympus for the Greeks (see Ps 48:2), the Canaanites considered this "holy" mountain to be the dwelling and meeting place of the gods. (See "Zaphon, Olympus, Sinai and Zion: The Mountain of God" on p. 843.)
14:17 Babylon followed the Assyrian practice of deporting large segments of defeated populations. The logic was that this preventative measure would subdue any latent rebelliousness among these populations and ensure their continued subservience (see 2Ki 24:14–16; see also the notes on 2Ki 17:24–41; 24:10–12 and "Exile and Genocide in the Ancient Near East" on p. 1337).
14:19 A proper burial was of critical importance to the ancients. The discarding of an individual's body was considered a dreadful and humiliating fate.
14:20–22 A man's offspring—not simply his tombstone—were considered to be his memorial (cf. 2Sa 18:18). Babylon's king would have neither (cf. 47:9).

[22] "I will rise up against them,"
declares the LORD Almighty.
"I will cut off from Babylon her name and survivors,
her offspring and descendants,[j]"
declares the LORD.
[23] "I will turn her into a place for owls[k]
and into swampland;
I will sweep her with the broom of destruction,"
declares the LORD Almighty.

14:22 [j]1Ki 14:10; Job 18:19
14:23 [k]Isa 34:11-15; Zep 2:14

A Prophecy Against Assyria

[24] The LORD Almighty has sworn,[l]

"Surely, as I have planned, so it will be,
and as I have purposed, so it will stand.[m]
[25] I will crush the Assyrian[n] in my land;
on my mountains I will trample him down.
His yoke[o] will be taken from my people,
and his burden removed from their shoulders.[p]"

[26] This is the plan[q] determined for the whole world;
this is the hand[r] stretched out over all nations.
[27] For the LORD Almighty has purposed, and who can
thwart him?
His hand is stretched out, and who can turn
it back?[s]

14:24 [l]Isa 45:23 [m]Ac 4:28
14:25 [n]Isa 10:5, 12 [o]Isa 9:4 [p]Isa 10:27
14:26 [q]Isa 23:9 [r]Ex 15:12
14:27 [s]2Ch 20:6; Isa 43:13; Da 4:35

A Prophecy Against the Philistines

[28] This oracle[t] came in the year King Ahaz[u] died:

[29] Do not rejoice, all you Philistines,[v]
that the rod that struck you is broken;
from the root of that snake will spring up a viper,[w]
its fruit will be a darting, venomous serpent.
[30] The poorest of the poor will find pasture,
and the needy[x] will lie down in safety.[y]
But your root I will destroy by famine;[z]
it will slay[a] your survivors.

[31] Wail, O gate![b] Howl, O city!
Melt away, all you Philistines!
A cloud of smoke comes from the north,[c]
and there is not a straggler in its ranks.
[32] What answer shall be given
to the envoys[d] of that nation?
"The LORD has established Zion,[e]
and in her his afflicted people will find refuge.[f]"

14:28 [t]Isa 13:1 [u]2Ki 16:20
14:29 [v]2Ch 26:6 [w]Isa 11:8
14:30 [x]Isa 3:15 [y]Isa 7:21-22 [z]Isa 8:21; 9:20; 51:19 [a]Jer 25:16
14:31 [b]Isa 3:26 [c]Jer 1:14
14:32 [d]Isa 37:9 [e]Ps 87:2,5; Isa 44:28; 54:11 [f]Isa 4:6; Jas 2:5

14:23 Southern Babylonia, where the Chaldeans had once resided, was a territory of marshlands.

14:24 The lack of an introductory "oracle" formula here (cf. 13:1; 14:28; 15:1) clues us that this was not a separate oracle against Assyria but a conclusion to the "Babylon" oracle (see 13:1—14:27). Assyria likely represented all of the Mesopotamian powers included in the term "Babylon."

14:28 See the note on 13:1 for a discussion of "oracle."

King Ahaz likely died in 715 B.C., apparently on the occasion of the Philistine revolt against Assyria, while Sargon (see 20:1) was too preoccupied elsewhere to devote much attention to Canaan.

14:29 See "The Archaeology of Philistia" on page 370. Philistine territory, which lay along the primary route from Egypt to Mesopotamia, was particularly vulnerable to attack by the great empires (Egypt and Assyria).

"The rod" most likely represented Sargon of Assyria (see "The Annals of Sargon II" on p. 1072). If this was the intention, the reference was to the threats to his empire by a series of revolts in Babylonia and Asia Minor.

The combination of the terms "root" and "fruit" exemplifies a figure of speech referring to the whole (tree) by mentioning its opposite extremes. Sargon would be followed by his later Assyrian counterparts, Sennacherib, Esarhaddon and Ashurbanipal.

A Prophecy Against Moab

15:1 [g]Isa 11:14 [h]Jer 48:24,41

15 An oracle concerning Moab:[g]

Ar in Moab is ruined,[h]
destroyed in a night!
Kir in Moab is ruined,
destroyed in a night!
[2] Dibon goes up to its temple,
to its high places[i] to weep;
Moab wails over Nebo and Medeba.
Every head is shaved[j]
and every beard cut off.
[3] In the streets they wear sackcloth;
on the roofs and in the public squares[k]
they all wail,
prostrate with weeping.[l]
[4] Heshbon and Elealeh[m] cry out,
their voices are heard all the way to
Jahaz.
Therefore the armed men of Moab cry out,
and their hearts are faint.

[5] My heart cries out over Moab;[n]
her fugitives flee as far as Zoar,
as far as Eglath Shelishiyah.
They go up the way to Luhith,
weeping as they go;
on the road to Horonaim[o]
they lament their destruction.[p]
[6] The waters of Nimrim are dried up[q]
and the grass is withered;[r]
the vegetation is gone
and nothing green is left.
[7] So the wealth they have acquired[s] and stored up
they carry away over the Ravine of the
Poplars.
[8] Their outcry echoes along the border of Moab;
their wailing reaches as far as Eglaim,
their lamentation as far as Beer Elim.

15:2 [i]Jer 48:35 [j]Lev 21:5
15:3 [k]Jer 48:38 [l]Isa 22:4
15:4 [m]Nu 32:3
15:5 [n]Jer 48:31 [o]Jer 48:3,34 [p]Jer 4:20; 48:5
15:6 [q]Isa 19:5-7; Jer 48:34 [r]Joel 1:12
15:7 [s]Isa 30:6; Jer 48:36

15:1—16:13 Although several of the sites mentioned in chapter 15 are uncertain, many of them are also listed on the Mesha (Moabite) Stone (see "The Mesha [Moabite] Stone" on p. 530). There seems to be a north-to-south progression in this listing, which would have been characteristic of the flight of the Moabites southward before a marauding army heading south along the King's Highway. The Ravine of the Poplars (15:7) was probably at Moab's southern border with Edom. It would have been natural for the fugitives to seek refuge in Edom, but that was not the case. Instead, they begged permission for asylum in Judah (16:1–4a).

15:1 The location of Ar is unknown. "Kir," which means "city," probably refers to Kir Hareseth, the capital city of Moab, usually identified with modern-day Kerak, located about 11 miles (18 km) east of the Dead Sea and 15 miles (24 km) south of the Arnon River.

15:2 Dibon, located 4 miles (6.5 km) north of the Arnon River, had been given to the tribe of Gad (see Nu 32:34).

Nebo, north of the Arnon River, may have been in the vicinity of Mount Nebo (Dt 34:1). Medeba, about 6 miles (9.7 km) south of Heshbon (see v. 4), was at one point captured by Israel from Sihon (see Nu 21:26,30).

For a discussion of the phrase "every head is shaved," see the note on Isaiah 3:24.

15:3 Sackcloth was the coarse garb of mourners (see the notes on 1Ki 20:31–32 and Job 16:15, as well as "Sackcloth and Ashes: Rituals of Lamentation" on p. 820).

Incense to pagan deities was often burned on rooftops (see Jer 19:13 and its note; see also "Incense" on p. 1209).

15:4 Heshbon, situated approximately 18 miles (29 km) east of the northern tip of the Dead Sea, was King Sihon's capital before Israel captured the city (see Nu 21:23–26). Elealeh, about a mile (1.6 km) north of Heshbon, is always mentioned in the Bible in conjunction with it. Jahaz, just north of the Arnon River, lay about 20 miles (32 km) from Heshbon (Nu 21:23; Jer 48:34).

15:5 Zoar was probably located near the southern end of the Dead Sea. Lot fled there from Sodom (see Ge 14:2; 19:23,30).

15:6 The "waters of Nimrim" may be a reference to the Wadi en-Numeirah, 10 miles (16 km) from the southern edge of the Dead Sea (cf. Jer 48:34).

15:7 The "Ravine of the Poplars" was probably at the border between Moab and Edom (see the note on 15:1—16:13).

15:8 Eglaim may have been in the vicinity of Moab's northern border, while Beer Elim ("Beer" means "well") may have been close to its southern boundary.

9 Dimon's[a] waters are full of blood,
but I will bring still more upon
Dimon[a]—
a lion[t] upon the fugitives of Moab
and upon those who remain in
the land.

15:9 [t]2Ki 17:25

[a] 9 Masoretic Text; Dead Sea Scrolls, some Septuagint manuscripts and Vulgate *Dibon*

Beards and Hairstyles in the Biblical World

ISAIAH 15 In Isaiah 15:2 the prophet declared that every head was shaved and every beard cut off. In context, it is clear that this was a sign of mourning;[1] shaving the head and face was evidently not ordinary fashion but a way of expressing overwhelming grief. Baldness was subjected to mockery (2Ki 2:23–25; we find the same attitude in the Greek comedies of Aristophanes in the late fifth century B.C.), while luxuriant hair seems to have been viewed as a sign of strength and vigor. But how did people in the ancient world typically wear their hair?

Fashions in hairstyles and beards varied in different times and places in the Biblical world. Paul stated that, in his cultural context, it was a disgrace for men to wear their hair long or for women to have theirs shorn (1Co 11:6,14–15). Samson and Absalom both had long hair (Jdg 16:13–19; 2Sa 14:26), but the very fact that the Bible draws attention to this may indicate that this practice was outside the norm. Israelite men typically wore their beards long, although during the **intertestamental period** and the New Testament period, under the influence of Greek culture, some Jewish men were clean shaven. It is possible that some professions called for distinctive hairstyles. For example, **Mesopotamian** physicians may have shaved their heads, and Mesopotamian slaves were required to wear a particular hairstyle, with dire consequences for unlawfully altering it.

The god Hermes (note beard and hairstyle)

Preserving Bible Times; © Dr. James C. Martin; permission of The Istanbul Archaeological Museum

The Israelites, however, had some distinctive customs. Men were forbidden to trim their hair along the sides or the edges of their beards (Lev 19:27). A Nazirite who had made a vow did not allow a razor to touch his hair until that vow had been completed; at that time his hair was shaved and cast into the fire under the sacrifice of the fellowship offering he had presented to God (Nu 6:5–21). Hair and beards could have symbolic significance as well. While cutting off another man's beard was considered an insult (2Sa 10:4–5), cutting one's own hair or beard was a sign of mourning (Isa 15:2). Ezekiel, for example, shaved off his hair and beard as a symbol of the coming destruction of Jerusalem (Eze 5:1ff.).

[1]See "Sackcloth and Ashes: Rituals of Lamentation" on page 820.

16:1 [u]2Ki 3:4 [v]2Ki 14:7 [w]Isa 10:32

16

Send lambs[u] as tribute
to the ruler of the land,
from Sela,[v] across the desert,
to the mount of the Daughter of Zion.[w]
2 Like fluttering birds
pushed from the nest,[x]
so are the women of Moab
at the fords of the Arnon.[y]

16:2 [x]Pr 27:8 [y]Nu 21:13-14; Jer 48:20

3 "Give us counsel,
render a decision.
Make your shadow like night—
at high noon.
Hide the fugitives,[z]
do not betray the refugees.
4 Let the Moabite fugitives stay with you;
be their shelter from the destroyer."

16:3 [z]1Ki 18:4

The oppressor[a] will come to an end,
and destruction will cease;
the aggressor will vanish from the land.
5 In love a throne[b] will be established;
in faithfulness a man will sit on it—
one from the house[a] of David[c]—
one who in judging seeks justice[d]
and speeds the cause of righteousness.

16:4 [a]Isa 9:4
16:5 [b]Da 7:14; Mic 4:7 [c]Lk 1:32 [d]Isa 9:7

6 We have heard of Moab's[e] pride[f]—
her overweening pride and conceit,
her pride and her insolence—
but her boasts are empty.
7 Therefore the Moabites wail,[g]
they wail together for Moab.
Lament and grieve
for the men[b][h] of Kir Hareseth.[i]
8 The fields of Heshbon wither,
the vines of Sibmah also.
The rulers of the nations
have trampled down the choicest vines,
which once reached Jazer
and spread toward the desert.
Their shoots spread out
and went as far as the sea.
9 So I weep,[j] as Jazer weeps,
for the vines of Sibmah.
O Heshbon, O Elealeh,
I drench you with tears!
The shouts of joy over your ripened fruit
and over your harvests[k] have been stilled.

16:6 [e]Am 2:1; Zep 2:8 [f]Ob 1:3; Zep 2:10
16:7 [g]Jer 48:20 [h]1Ch 16:3 [i]2Ki 3:25
16:9 [j]Isa 15:3 [k]Jer 40:12

[a] 5 Hebrew *tent* [b] 7 Or "*raisin cakes*," a wordplay

16:1 Sela ("cliff") was the naturally fortified capital of the Edomites south of the Dead Sea, situated on a rocky plateau that towers 1,000 feet (305 m) above nearby Petra.

"Daughter of Zion" is a personification of Jerusalem.

16:2 The Arnon, flowing west into the midpoint of the Dead Sea, served as the border between Moab and the region of the Amorites. The women were fleeing south, away from the northern invader.

16:8 For "Heshbon," see the note on 15:4. Sibmah lay about 3 miles (4.8 km) west of Heshbon, while Jazer was possibly situated about 15 miles (24 km) north of the Dead Sea. The "desert" refers to the eastern edge of Moab, and the "sea" may be the Dead Sea.

[10]Joy and gladness are taken away from the orchards;[l]
no one sings or shouts in the vineyards;
no one treads[m] out wine at the presses,[n]
for I have put an end to the shouting.
[11]My heart laments for Moab[o] like a harp,
my inmost being[p] for Kir Hareseth.
[12]When Moab appears at her high place,
she only wears herself out;
when she goes to her shrine[q] to pray,
it is to no avail.[r]

16:10 [l]Isa 24:7-8 [m]Jdg 9:27 [n]Job 24:11
16:11 [o]Isa 15:5 [p]Isa 63:15; Hos 11:8; Php 2:1
16:12 [q]Isa 15:2 [r]1Ki 18:29

[13]This is the word the LORD has already spoken concerning Moab. [14]But now the LORD says: "Within
three years, as a servant bound by contract would count them, Moab's splendor and all her many people
will be despised,[s] and her survivors will be very few and feeble."[t]

16:14 [s]Isa 25:10; Jer 48:42 [t]Isa 21:17

An Oracle Against Damascus

17 An oracle concerning Damascus:[u]

"See, Damascus will no longer be a city
but will become a heap of ruins.[v]
[2]The cities of Aroer will be deserted
and left to flocks,[w] which will lie down,
with no one to make them afraid.[x]
[3]The fortified city will disappear from Ephraim,
and royal power from Damascus;
the remnant of Aram will be
like the glory[y] of the Israelites,"[z]
declares the LORD Almighty.

17:1 [u]Ge 14:15; Jer 49:23; Ac 9:2 [v]Isa 25:2; Am 1:3; Zec 9:1
17:2 [w]Isa 7:21; Eze 25:5 [x]Jer 7:33; Mic 4:4
17:3 [y]ver 4; Hos 9:11 [z]Isa 7:8, 16; 8:4

[4]"In that day the glory of Jacob will fade;
the fat of his body will waste[a] away.
[5]It will be as when a reaper gathers the standing grain
and harvests[b] the grain with his arm—
as when a man gleans heads of grain
in the Valley of Rephaim.
[6]Yet some gleanings will remain,[c]
as when an olive tree is beaten,[d]
leaving two or three olives on the topmost branches,
four or five on the fruitful boughs,"
declares the LORD, the God of Israel.

17:4 [a]Isa 10:16
17:5 [b]ver 11; Jer 51:33; Joel 3:13; Mt 13:30
17:6 [c]Dt 4:27; Isa 24:13 [d]Isa 27:12

[7]In that day men will look[e] to their Maker
and turn their eyes to the Holy One[f] of Israel.
[8]They will not look to the altars,
the work of their hands,[g]

17:7 [e]Isa 10:20 [f]Mic 7:7
17:8 [g]Isa 2:18, 20; 30:22

16:10 See "The Winepress" on page 1171.
16:12 See "The High Places" on page 1318.
17:1 See the note on 13:1 for a discussion of "oracle."
Damascus (see "Damascus" on p. 1087), the capital of Aram (Syria), was situated northeast of Mount Hermon at the junction of strategic trade routes joining Mesopotamia, Egypt and Arabia. Since the days of the Davidic kingdom, Israel and Aram had been engaged in regular conflict (see 2Sa 8:5; 1Ki 22:31).
17:2 Aroer, which lay approximately 14 miles (22.5 km) east of the Dead Sea along the banks of the Arnon River, marked the southern boundary of Aram's sphere of control (see 2Ki 10:32–33).
17:3 Ephraim, the northern kingdom (see the note on 7:2), is mentioned here because of its alliance with Damascus, the capital of Aram (modern Syria), against Assyria (see the note on 7:1). Aram, northeast of the Sea of Galilee (see "Syria/Aram" on p. 534) is here represented by its capital city, Damascus (see "Damascus" on p. 1087), and by Aroer (v. 2), east of the Dead Sea at the farthest southern point of Aram's control. In 732 B.C. Tiglath-Pileser III captured Damascus and made it an Assyrian province. Like Israel, Aram would be reduced to a remnant.
17:5 The Valley of Rephaim, a fertile area west and southwest of Jerusalem (Jos 15:8), was frequently the site of Philistine raids (1Ch 14:9).
17:8 The word "altars" probably refers here to altars to Baal (cf. 1Ki 16:32). Incense altars were associated with high places (see Lev 26:30; see also "The High Places" on p. 1318) and with altars for Baal (2Ch 34:4).
Asherah poles were sacred trees or wooden poles dedicated to the worship of the fertility goddess Asherah, the "consort" (partner or companion) of El, the chief Canaanite god. Recent archaeological

and they will have no regard for the Asherah poles[a]
and the incense altars their fingers have made.

9 In that day their strong cities, which they left because of the Israelites, will be like places abandoned
to thickets and undergrowth. And all will be desolation.

17:10 [h]Isa 51:13 [i]Ps 68:19; Isa 12:2

10 You have forgotten[h] God your Savior;[i]
you have not remembered the Rock, your fortress.
Therefore, though you set out the finest plants
and plant imported vines,
11 though on the day you set them out, you make them grow,
and on the morning[j] when you plant them, you bring them to bud,
yet the harvest will be as nothing[k]
in the day of disease and incurable pain.[l]

17:11 [j]Ps 90:6 [k]Hos 8:7 [l]Job 4:8

12 Oh, the raging of many nations—
they rage like the raging sea![m]
Oh, the uproar of the peoples—
they roar like the roaring of great waters!

17:12 [m]Ps 18:4; Jer 6:23; Lk 21:25

[a] 8 That is, symbols of the goddess Asherah

discoveries confirm that some Israelites worshiped Asherah as *the Lord's* consort. (See "Devotion to Asherah in the Khirbet El-Qom Inscription" on p. 638 and "The Kuntillet Ajrûd Inscriptions: The Lord's Asherah?" on p. 1220.)

ARCHAEOLOGICAL SITES

DAMASCUS

ISAIAH 17 Damascus was, and still is, the capital city of Syria. As is the case today, ancient Damascus was often set against ancient Israel.

Continuous occupation of Damascus since antiquity makes excavation of ancient remains there virtually impossible. Nevertheless **Assyrian**, Syrian and Egyptian sources all shed light on the Biblical data. The city's location along the fertile Barada River at the crossroads of major trade routes (the **Via Maris** and the **King's Highway**) ensured continued prosperity. Damascus is mentioned in a number of ancient writings. In a text at the temple of Amon at Karnak, for example, Thutmose III of Egypt claims to have forced Damascus to submit to him (c. 1482 B.C.). Damascus was the dominant city of Aram (Syria) from the eleventh century B.C. to its annexation by Assyria in 732 B.C.[1]

The city and its kings had numerous dealings with the kings of Israel:

- David subjugated the Aramean kingdom of Syria, but King Rezin of Damascus (r. c. 955–925 B.C.) regained independence during Solomon's reign.
- Ben-hadad I (r. c. 900–860 B.C.) entered an alliance with Asa of Judah to attack Baasha of Israel (1Kgs 15:16–22), and Ben-hadad II (r. c. 860–843 B.C.) began an expansion that took most of Israel's **Transjordanian** territories.[2] This project was interrupted in 853 B.C. when Damascus, Israel and other nations combined to check Assyrian expansion under **Shalmaneser III** at the Battle of Qarqar.[3]
- Under Hazael (r. c. 843–796 B.C.) Syria's expansion into Israel and Judah continued, despite losses Damascus suffered against Assyria.[4]
- Ben-Hadad III (r. c. 796–770 B.C.) was successful against Israel early in his reign and later headed a coalition against Zakur, king of Hamath.[5] Under Jeroboam II Israel recovered territory previously lost to Damascus.
- Rezin (r. c. 750–732 B.C.) and Pekah of Israel tried to force Ahaz of Judah to join an anti-Assyrian coalition, but Ahaz paid Tiglath-Pileser III to attack Damascus, resulting in its annexation into Assyria and in the death of Rezin.[6]

Damascus continued as an influential provincial city under Assyria, **Babylon**, **Persia**, Greece and Rome. It was a major cosmopolitan center during the New Testament era, when it was home to a large Jewish community. Thus Saul of Tarsus traveled there searching for early Christians. "Straight Street" of Acts 9:11 may have been a major thoroughfare from the **Roman period**, called in Latin the *cardo maximus*.

[1]See "Syria/Aram" on page 534. [2]See "Ben-Hadad I and II" on page 521. [3]See "Ahab and the Battle of Qarqar" on page 524. [4]See "Hazael, the Nemesis of Israel" on page 539. [5]See "Ben Hadad III of Aram and Jehoash of Israel" on page 548. [6]See "Ahaz, King of Judah, and Rezin, King of Aram" on page 554 and "The Syro-Ephraimite War" on page 1066.

13 Although the peoples roar like the roar of surging waters,
when he rebukes[n] them they flee[o] far away,
driven before the wind like chaff[p] on the hills,
like tumbleweed before a gale.[q]
14 In the evening, sudden terror!
Before the morning, they are gone![r]
This is the portion of those who loot us,
the lot of those who plunder us.

17:13 nPs 9:5 oIsa 13:14 pIsa 41:2,15-16 qJob 21:18
17:14 r2Ki 19:35

A Prophecy Against Cush

18 Woe to the land of whirring wings[a]
along the rivers of Cush,[b][s]
2 which sends envoys by sea
in papyrus[t] boats over the water.

Go, swift messengers,
to a people tall and smooth-skinned,
to a people feared far and wide,
an aggressive[u] nation of strange speech,
whose land is divided by rivers.[v]

3 All you people of the world,
you who live on the earth,
when a banner[w] is raised on the mountains,
you will see it,
and when a trumpet sounds,
you will hear it.
4 This is what the LORD says to me:
"I will remain quiet and will look on from my dwelling place,[x]
like shimmering heat in the sunshine,
like a cloud of dew[y] in the heat of harvest."
5 For, before the harvest, when the blossom is gone
and the flower becomes a ripening grape,
he will cut off the shoots with pruning knives,
and cut down and take away the spreading branches.[z]
6 They will all be left to the mountain birds of prey
and to the wild animals;[a]
the birds will feed on them all summer,
the wild animals all winter.
7 At that time gifts will be brought to the LORD Almighty

from a people tall and smooth-skinned,
from a people feared far and wide,

18:1 sIsa 20:3-5; Eze 30:4-5,9; Zep 2:12; 3:10
18:2 tEx 2:3 uGe 10:8-9; 2Ch 12:3 vver 7
18:3 wIsa 5:26
18:4 xIsa 26:21; Hos 5:15 yIsa 26:19; Hos 14:5
18:5 zIsa 17:10-11; Eze 17:6
18:6 aIsa 56:9; Jer 7:33; Eze 32:4; 39:17

[a] *1* Or *of locusts* [b] *1* That is, the upper Nile region

17:13 Chaff and tumbleweed were representative of the enemy (29:5; 41:15–16; cf. Ps 83:13). For further commentary on "chaff" ("dry grass" at this v. in the NIV), see the note on 5:24.
18:1 Cush (see "Cush" on p. 1519) or Nubia, located south of Egypt, was also known as Ethiopia (not to be confused with modern Ethiopia, farther to the south). In about 740 B.C. (Isaiah's day), the Cushite (Sudanese) Piankhy took over Egypt. He and his successor, Shabako, instilled new energy into Egyptian affairs. Most likely both attempted to cement alliances with various surrounding countries in order to counter the Assyrian threat.
18:2 "Sea" may here be a reference to Egypt's Nile River (cf. 19:5; Na 3:8, where the same Hebrew word is translated "river"). The plural "rivers" (later in the verse) in this context refers to the Nile and its tributaries.

Boats or rafts constructed of bound bundles of papyrus are sometimes pictured in Egyptian murals.

The "tall and smooth-skinned" people were most likely the Cushites and the Egyptians. Unlike the Semites (including the Israelites), these men were clean-shaven (see Ge 41:14 and its note).
18:3 See the note on 5:26 for a discussion of "banner."

Trumpets in the ancient Near East were often used to summon troops.
18:6 See "Lions and Other Wild Beasts in Ancient Israel" on page 813.
18:7 Second Chronicles 32:23 reports that gifts were brought to Hezekiah after Sennacherib's death (see "The Death of Sennacherib" on p. 562). In Isaiah 16:1 the Moabites were asked to send tribute to Mount Zion (cf. 45:14; Zep 3:10).

an aggressive nation of strange speech,
whose land is divided by rivers—

18:7 [b]Ps 68:31

the gifts will be brought to Mount Zion, the place of the Name of the LORD Almighty.[b]

A Prophecy About Egypt

19:1 [c]Isa 13:1; Jer 43:12 [d]Joel 3:19 [e]Ex 12:12 [f]Ps 18:10; 104:3; Rev 1:7 [g]Jos 2:11

19 An oracle[c] concerning Egypt:[de]

See, the LORD rides on a swift cloud[f]
and is coming to Egypt.
The idols of Egypt tremble before him,
and the hearts of the Egyptians melt[g] within them.

19:2 [h]Jdg 7:22; Mt 10:21,36 [i]2Ch 20:23

2 "I will stir up Egyptian against Egyptian—
brother will fight against brother,[h]
neighbor against neighbor,
city against city,
kingdom against kingdom.[i]
3 The Egyptians will lose heart,
and I will bring their plans to nothing;
they will consult the idols and the spirits of the dead,
the mediums and the spiritists.[j]

19:3 [j]Isa 8:19; 47:13; Da 2:2,10

4 I will hand the Egyptians over
to the power of a cruel master,
and a fierce king[k] will rule over them,"
declares the Lord, the LORD Almighty.

19:4 [k]Isa 20:4; Jer 46:26; Eze 29:19

19:5 [l]Jer 51:36

5 The waters of the river will dry up,[l]
and the riverbed will be parched and dry.

19:6 [m]Ex 7:18 [n]Isa 37:25; Eze 30:12 [o]Isa 15:6

6 The canals will stink;[m]
the streams of Egypt will dwindle and dry up.[n]
The reeds and rushes will wither,[o]
7 also the plants along the Nile,
at the mouth of the river.
Every sown field[p] along the Nile
will become parched, will blow away and be no more.

19:7 [p]Isa 23:3

19:8 [q]Eze 47:10 [r]Hab 1:15

8 The fishermen[q] will groan and lament,
all who cast hooks[r] into the Nile;
those who throw nets on the water
will pine away.
9 Those who work with combed flax will despair,
the weavers of fine linen[s] will lose hope.
10 The workers in cloth will be dejected,
and all the wage earners will be sick at heart.

19:9 [s]Pr 7:16; Eze 27:7

19:11 [t]Nu 13:22

11 The officials of Zoan[t] are nothing but fools;
the wise counselors of Pharaoh give senseless advice.

19:1 See the note on 13:1 for a discussion of "oracle."
19:2 The Libyans clashed with the "Ethiopians" (the Cushites; see the note on 18:1), as well as with the Saites of the Egyptian Twenty-fourth Dynasty.
19:3 For "mediums" and "spiritists," see "Akkadian Divination" on page 277.
19:4 The "cruel master" may be identified with Assyria's king (see 20:4). In 670 B.C. Esarhaddon subjugated Egypt.
19:5–10 The Nile was the lifeline of Egypt; its annual flooding provided essential water and produced the only fertile soil there.
19:6 Canals were used for irrigation.
19:7 Egypt's harvest was generally so abundant that some of the produce was available for export.
19:8 Fish, too, were typically in plentiful supply in the well-watered Egypt.
19:9 The processing of flax required large amounts of water—a resource readily available in lush Egypt, which was renowned as an exporter of fine linen.
19:11 Zoan (possibly synonymous with Tanis), a city in the north-eastern Nile delta region familiar to the Israelites from their centuries of residency in Egypt (see Nu 13:22; Ps 78:12,43), was the northern capital of the Egyptian Twenty-fifth Dynasty (see the note on 18:1).
Egypt was celebrated both for its "wise men" and for its profuse wisdom literature (see "Ancient Near Eastern Wisdom" on p. 960).

How can you say to Pharaoh,
"I am one of the wise men,[u]
a disciple of the ancient kings"?
12 Where are your wise men[v] now?
Let them show you and make known
what the LORD Almighty
has planned[w] against Egypt.
13 The officials of Zoan have become fools,
the leaders of Memphis[a][x] are deceived;
the cornerstones of her peoples
have led Egypt astray.
14 The LORD has poured into them
a spirit of dizziness;[y]
they make Egypt stagger in all that she does,
as a drunkard staggers around in his vomit.
15 There is nothing Egypt can do—
head or tail, palm branch or reed.[z]

16 In that day the Egyptians will be like women.[a] They will shudder with fear[b] at the uplifted hand[c]
that the LORD Almighty raises against them. 17 And the land of Judah will bring terror to the Egyptians;
everyone to whom Judah is mentioned will be terrified, because of what the LORD Almighty is planning[d]
against them.

18 In that day five cities in Egypt will speak the language of Canaan and swear allegiance[e] to the LORD
Almighty. One of them will be called the City of Destruction.[b]

19 In that day there will be an altar[f] to the LORD in the heart of Egypt, and a monument[g] to the LORD
at its border. 20 It will be a sign and witness to the LORD Almighty in the land of Egypt. When they cry out
to the LORD because of their oppressors, he will send them a savior and defender, and he will rescue[h]
them. 21 So the LORD will make himself known to the Egyptians, and in that day they will acknowledge[i]
the LORD. They will worship[j] with sacrifices and grain offerings; they will make vows to the LORD and
keep them. 22 The LORD will strike[k] Egypt with a plague; he will strike them and heal them. They will turn[l]
to the LORD, and he will respond to their pleas and heal[m] them.

23 In that day there will be a highway[n] from Egypt to Assyria. The Assyrians will go to Egypt and the
Egyptians to Assyria. The Egyptians and Assyrians will worship[o] together. 24 In that day Israel will be the
third, along with Egypt and Assyria, a blessing on the earth. 25 The LORD Almighty will bless them, say-
ing, "Blessed be Egypt my people,[p] Assyria my handiwork,[q] and Israel my inheritance.[r]"

A Prophecy Against Egypt and Cush

20 In the year that the supreme commander,[s] sent by Sargon king of Assyria, came to Ashdod and
attacked and captured it— 2 at that time the LORD spoke through Isaiah son of Amoz.[t] He said

19:11 [u]1Ki 4:30; Ac 7:22
19:12 [v]1Co 1:20 [w]Isa 14:24; Ro 9:17
19:13 [x]Jer 2:16; Eze 30:13,16
19:14 [y]Mt 17:17
19:15 [z]Isa 9:14
19:16 [a]Jer 51:30; Na 3:13 [b]Heb 10:31 [c]Isa 11:15
19:17 [d]Isa 14:24
19:18 [e]Zep 3:9
19:19 [f]Jos 22:10 [g]Ge 28:18
19:20 [h]Isa 49:24-26
19:21 [i]Isa 11:9 [j]Isa 56:7; Mal 1:11
19:22 [k]Heb 12:11 [l]Isa 45:14; Hos 14:1 [m]Dt 32:39
19:23 [n]Isa 11:16 [o]Isa 27:13
19:25 [p]Ps 100:3 [q]Isa 29:23; 45:11; 60:21; 64:8; Eph 2:10 [r]Hos 2:23
20:1 [s]2Ki 18:17
20:2 [t]Isa 13:1

[a] *13* Hebrew *Noph* [b] *18* Most manuscripts of the Masoretic Text; some manuscripts of the Masoretic Text, Dead Sea Scrolls and Vulgate *City of the Sun* (that is, Heliopolis)

19:13 See the note on verse 11 for commentary on "Zoan." Memphis, too, was an important Egyptian city. Located 15 miles (24 km) south of the Nile delta, it had enjoyed the distinction of being Egypt's capital during the Old Kingdom period (c. 2686–2160 B.C.).
19:15 See the note on 9:14 for a discussion of the paired phrases, such as "head or tail" and "palm branch or reed."
19:18 "Speak the language of Canaan" may either refer symbolically to Egypt's allegiance to Israel's God (see vv. 21–22,25) or be a literal reference to Jews residing in Egypt. After Jerusalem's fall in 586 B.C., many Judahites had in fact taken refuge there (see Jer 44:1).

"City of Destruction" most likely refers to Heliopolis, the city of the Egyptian sun god, which was destroyed by Nebuchadnezzar (see Jer 43:13). A wordplay missed by the English reader involves the fact that "destruction" and "sun" are nearly identical in Hebrew.
19:19 Some scholars relate "altar" to the temple built in Egypt by the Jewish high priest Onias IV, who fled to Egypt during the second century B.C. But more appears to have been at stake. Indeed, the reference appears to be to a conversion to the Lord of a significant number of Egyptians.
19:23 With regard to "highway," compare the references to the highway to Jerusalem in 11:16 and 35:8–10 (see also the notes on 11:16; 40:3). The Egyptians and Assyrians had been at loggerheads for years (see 20:4), but in the future they would be linked in a bond of fellowship sealed by their common allegiance to Israel's Lord (cf. 25:3).
20:1 "The year" was most likely 712 B.C., about halfway through the reign of Sargon II (721 to 705 B.C.; see "The Annals of Sargon II" on p. 1072).

Ashdod, one of five major Philistine cities (see "The Archaeology of Philistia" on p. 370), was situated near the Mediterranean Sea, approximately 18 miles (29 km) northeast of Gaza. It had rebelled against Assyria in 713 B.C. under the Philistine King Azuri. Three fragments of an Assyrian monument commemorating Sargon's victory were discovered in 1963 at Ashdod.
20:2 For a discussion of "sackcloth," see the notes on Job 16:15 and Isaiah 15:3; see also "Sackcloth and Ashes: Rituals of Lamentation" on page 820. The Hebrew word here translated "stripped" could connote either full or partial nudity, such as wearing only a loincloth.

20:2 [u]Zec 13:4; Mt 3:4 [v]Eze 24:17,23 [w]1Sa 19:24 [x]Mic 1:8
20:3 [y]Isa 8:18 [z]Isa 37:9; 43:3
20:4 [a]Isa 19:4 [b]Isa 47:3; Jer 13:22,26
20:5 [c]2Ki 18:21; Isa 30:5
20:6 [d]Isa 10:3 [e]Jer 30:15-17; Mt 23:33; 1Th 5:3; Heb 2:3

to him, "Take off the sackcloth[u] from your body and the sandals[v] from your feet." And he did so, going
around stripped[w] and barefoot.[x]
³Then the LORD said, "Just as my servant Isaiah has gone stripped and barefoot for three years, as a
sign[y] and portent against Egypt and Cush,[a][z] ⁴so the king[a] of Assyria will lead away stripped and bare-
foot the Egyptian captives and Cushite exiles, young and old, with buttocks bared—to Egypt's shame.[b]
⁵Those who trusted in Cush and boasted in Egypt[c] will be afraid and put to shame. ⁶In that day the peo-
ple who live on this coast will say, 'See what has happened to those we relied on, those we fled to for help[d]
and deliverance from the king of Assyria! How then can we escape?[e]' "

A Prophecy Against Babylon

21:1 [f]Isa 13:21; Jer 51:43 [g]Zec 9:14

21 An oracle concerning the Desert[f] by the Sea:

> Like whirlwinds sweeping through the southland,[g]
> an invader comes from the desert,
> from a land of terror.

21:2 [h]Ps 60:3 [i]Isa 33:1 [j]Isa 22:6; Jer 49:34

> ²A dire[h] vision has been shown to me:
> The traitor betrays,[i] the looter takes loot.
> Elam,[j] attack! Media, lay siege!
> I will bring to an end all the groaning she caused.

21:3 [k]Ps 48:6; Isa 26:17

> ³At this my body is racked with pain,
> pangs seize me, like those of a woman in labor;[k]
> I am staggered by what I hear,
> I am bewildered by what I see.
> ⁴My heart falters,
> fear makes me tremble;
> the twilight I longed for
> has become a horror to me.

21:5 [l]Jer 51:39, 57; Da 5:2

> ⁵They set the tables,
> they spread the rugs,
> they eat, they drink![l]
> Get up, you officers,
> oil the shields!

⁶This is what the Lord says to me:

21:7 [m]ver 9

> "Go, post a lookout
> and have him report what he sees.
> ⁷When he sees chariots[m]
> with teams of horses,
> riders on donkeys
> or riders on camels,
> let him be alert,
> fully alert."

21:8 [n]Hab 2:1

⁸And the lookout[b][n] shouted,

> "Day after day, my lord, I stand on the watchtower;
> every night I stay at my post.

[a] 3 That is, the upper Nile region; also in verse 5 [b] 8 Dead Sea Scrolls and Syriac; Masoretic Text *A lion*

20:3 For "Cush," see the note on 18:1.

21:1 For "oracle," see the note on 13:1.

Isaiah 21:9 makes clear that the subject of this message—"the Desert by the Sea" (v. 1)—was Babylon. The mention of Media (v. 2) suggests that the destruction in view was the conquest by the Medes and Persians in 539 B.C., because prior to that time the Medes had been allies of Babylon. Yet the general time frame of chapters 13–23 seems to relate to events closer to Isaiah's time (i.e., Babylon's fall to the Assyrians in 689 B.C.). Isaiah may have been telescoping together more than one destruction in order to argue against the folly of trusting in Babylon.

21:2 The country of Elam lay to the northeast of the lower Tigris Valley. The Elamites, avowed enemies of both Assyria and Babylon, were much later on allied with the Persian army that conquered Babylon under Cyrus in 539 B.C.

21:6 "Go, post a lookout" was likely a command to station a watchman on Jerusalem's wall (see the note on SS 3:3).

9 Look, here comes a man in a chariot
with a team of horses.
And he gives back the answer:
'Babylon[o] has fallen,[p] has fallen!
All the images of its gods[q]
lie shattered on the ground!' "
10 O my people, crushed on the threshing floor,[r]
I tell you what I have heard
from the LORD Almighty,
from the God of Israel.

A Prophecy Against Edom

11 An oracle concerning Dumah[a]:[s]

Someone calls to me from Seir,[t]
"Watchman, what is left of the night?
Watchman, what is left of the night?"
12 The watchman replies,
"Morning is coming, but also the night.
If you would ask, then ask;
and come back yet again."

A Prophecy Against Arabia

13 An oracle[u] concerning Arabia:

You caravans of Dedanites,
who camp in the thickets of Arabia,
14 bring water for the thirsty;
you who live in Tema,[v]
bring food for the fugitives.
15 They flee[w] from the sword,
from the drawn sword,
from the bent bow
and from the heat of battle.

16 This is what the Lord says to me: "Within one year, as a servant bound by contract[x] would count it,
all the pomp[y] of Kedar[z] will come to an end. 17 The survivors of the bowmen, the warriors of Kedar, will
be few.[a]" The LORD, the God of Israel, has spoken.

A Prophecy About Jerusalem

22 An oracle[b] concerning the Valley[c] of Vision:

What troubles you now,
that you have all gone up on the roofs,

21:9 [o]Rev 14:8 [p]Jer 51:8; Rev 18:2 [q]Isa 46:1; Jer 50:2; 51:44
21:10 [r]Jer 51:33
21:11 [s]Ge 25:14 [t]Ge 32:3
21:13 [u]Isa 13:1
21:14 [v]Ge 25:15
21:15 [w]Isa 13:14
21:16 [x]Isa 16:14 [y]Isa 17:3 [z]Ps 120:5; Isa 60:7
21:17 [a]Isa 10:19
22:1 [b]Isa 13:1 [c]Ps 125:2; Jer 21:13; Joel 3:2,12,14

[a] 11 *Dumah* means *silence* or *stillness,* a wordplay on *Edom.*

21:9 Babylon fell twice—in 689 B.C. and again in 539 B.C. The stirring cry "Babylon has fallen" was adapted by the apostle John in Revelation 14:8 and 18:2. The defeat of a kingdom implied the disgrace of its deities.
21:10 Threshing was a common Old Testament metaphor signifying judgment or destruction in battle. (See "The Threshing Floor" on p. 608.)
21:11 For "oracle," see the note on 13:1.
Dumah, meaning "silence" or "stillness," is a wordplay on "Edom" (see the NIV text note), also known as "Seir," the homeland of Esau's descendants located south of the Dead Sea. Perhaps the meaning of this short oracle may be found in this pun.
21:13–17 The message in these verses was addressed to Arabian tribes who lived in the desert between Babylon and Judah. Both Dedan and Tema (v. 14) were located in an area of northwestern Arabia known as Kedar. Dedanites were merchants who used the thickets to hide their caravans from invaders. They were attacked by both the Assyrians and the Babylonians.
21:13 For "oracle," see the note on 13:1.
21:15 The simple bows of the Arabs were woefully inadequate against Assyria's swords and sophisticated, composite bows.
21:16 Kedar was the home of nomadic tribes in the Arabian Desert, southeast of Damascus. It was known for its flocks (60:7; Eze 27:21), tents and tent curtains, which were woven by hand from black goat hair.
22:1 For "oracle," see the note on 13:1.
God had been known to reveal himself in visions in the "Valley of Vision," probably a valley near Jerusalem (see the note on 22:7).
For "roofs," see the note on 15:3.

[2] O town full of commotion,
22:2 [d]Isa 32:13
O city of tumult and revelry?[d]
Your slain were not killed by the sword,
nor did they die in battle.
[3] All your leaders have fled together;
they have been captured without using the bow.
All you who were caught were taken prisoner together,
having fled while the enemy was still far away.
[4] Therefore I said, "Turn away from me;
22:4 [e]Isa 15:3; Lk 19:41 [f]Jer 9:1
let me weep[e] bitterly.
Do not try to console me
over the destruction of my people."[f]

[5] The Lord, the LORD Almighty, has a day
22:5 [g]La 1:5
of tumult and trampling and terror[g]
in the Valley of Vision,
a day of battering down walls
and of crying out to the mountains.
22:6 [h]Isa 21:2 [i]Jer 49:35 [j]2Ki 16:9
[6] Elam[h] takes up the quiver,[i]
with her charioteers and horses;
Kir[j] uncovers the shield.
[7] Your choicest valleys are full of chariots,
22:7 [k]2Ch 32:1-2
and horsemen are posted at the city gates;[k]
[8] the defenses of Judah are stripped away.

And you looked in that day
22:8 [l]2Ch 32:5 [m]1Ki 7:2
to the weapons[l] in the Palace of the Forest;[m]
[9] you saw that the City of David
had many breaches in its defenses;
you stored up water
22:9 [n]2Ch 32:4
in the Lower Pool.[n]
[10] You counted the buildings in Jerusalem
and tore down houses to strengthen the wall.
22:11 [o]2Ki 25:4; Jer 39:4 [p]2Ch 32:4
[11] You built a reservoir between the two walls[o]
for the water of the Old Pool,[p]
but you did not look to the One who made it,
or have regard for the One who planned it long ago.

[12] The Lord, the LORD Almighty,
called you on that day
22:12 [q]Joel 2:17 [r]Mic 1:16 [s]Joel 1:13
to weep[q] and to wail,
to tear out your hair[r] and put on sackcloth.[s]
[13] But see, there is joy and revelry,
slaughtering of cattle and killing of sheep,
22:13 [t]Isa 5:22; 28:7-8; 56:12; Lk 17:26-29 [u]1Co 15:32*
eating of meat and drinking of wine![t]
"Let us eat and drink," you say,
"for tomorrow we die!"[u]

22:14 [v]Isa 5:9 [w]Isa 13:11; 26:21; 30:13-14; Eze 24:13
[14] The LORD Almighty has revealed this in my hearing:[v] "Till your dying day this sin will not be atoned[w]
for," says the Lord, the LORD Almighty.

22:3 King Zedekiah and his army, having fled Jerusalem, were captured near Jericho (see 2Ki 25:4–6).
22:6 Elam was the region northeast of the lower Tigris Valley (see the note on 21:2). Kir may have been Media.
22:7 The Kidron Valley lay east of Jerusalem, while the Hinnom Valley was located to the south and west.
22:9 It appears that the "Old" or "Upper" Pool had been built prior to Hezekiah's time to capture the waters of the Gihon spring. Hezekiah, in constructing the Siloam tunnel, incorporated the "Lower" Pool that had been commisioned by Ahaz into what became the Pool of Siloam, a larger water reservoir (see 2Ki 20:20; see also "Hezekiah's Tunnel" on p. 564 and "The Pool of Siloam" on p. 1739).
22:12 It is impossible to determine whether the hair was torn out or shaved off (cf. Jer 16:6; Eze 27:31).
For "sackcloth," see the note on Isaiah 15:3.

[15]This is what the Lord, the LORD Almighty, says:

"Go, say to this steward,
to Shebna,[x] who is in charge of the palace:
[16]What are you doing here and who gave you permission
to cut out a grave[y] for yourself here,
hewing your grave on the height
and chiseling your resting place in the rock?
[17]"Beware, the LORD is about to take firm hold of you
and hurl you away, O you mighty man.
[18]He will roll you up tightly like a ball
and throw[z] you into a large country.
There you will die
and there your splendid chariots will remain—
you disgrace to your master's house!
[19]I will depose you from your office,
and you will be ousted from your position.

[20]"In that day I will summon my servant, Eliakim[a] son of Hilkiah. [21]I will clothe him with your robe
and fasten your sash around him and hand your authority over to him. He will be a father to those who
live in Jerusalem and to the house of Judah. [22]I will place on his shoulder the key[b] to the house of David;[c]
what he opens no one can shut, and what he shuts no one can open.[d] [23]I will drive him like a peg[e] into a
firm place;[f] he will be a seat[a] of honor[g] for the house of his father. [24]All the glory of his family will hang
on him: its offspring and offshoots—all its lesser vessels, from the bowls to all the jars.

[25]"In that day," declares the LORD Almighty, "the peg[h] driven into the firm place will give way; it will
be sheared off and will fall, and the load hanging on it will be cut down." The LORD has spoken.[i]

22:15 [x]2Ki 18:18; Isa 36:3
22:16 [y]Mt 27:60
22:18 [z]Isa 17:13
22:20 [a]2Ki 18:18; Isa 36:3
22:22 [b]Rev 3:7 [c]Isa 7:2 [d]Job 12:14
22:23 [e]Zec 10:4 [f]Ezr 9:8 [g]1Sa 2:7-8; Job 36:7
22:25 [h]ver 23 [i]Isa 46:11; Mic 4:4

A Prophecy About Tyre

23 An oracle concerning Tyre:[j]

Wail, O ships[k] of Tarshish![l]
For Tyre is destroyed
and left without house or harbor.
From the land of Cyprus[b]
word has come to them.

[2]Be silent, you people of the island
and you merchants of Sidon,
whom the seafarers have enriched.
[3]On the great waters
came the grain of the Shihor;

23:1 [j]Jos 19:29; 1Ki 5:1; Jer 47:4; Eze 26,27,28; Joel 3:4-8; Am 1:9-10; Zec 9:2-4 [k]1Ki 10:22 [l]Ge 10:4; Isa 2:16 *fn*

[a] 23 Or *throne* [b] 1 Hebrew *Kittim*

22:15 Shebna, evidently a foreigner (possibly Egyptian) and a contemporary of King Hezekiah, was second only to the king in position (see the note on v. 21; cf. 1Ki 4:6; 2Ki 15:5; Isa 36:3).
22:16 In 1870 an inscription was discovered in a tomb hewn from rock in the village of Silwan, in southeastern Jerusalem. Finally deciphered in 1953, the restored text reads as follows: "This is the tomb of Shebaniah who is over the house. There is no silver or gold here, just his bones and the bones of his maidservant with him. Cursed is the man who opens this." The words "over the house" mean that Shebaniah was the royal steward. He is possibly the Shebna of Isaiah 22, whom Isaiah criticized for having hewn out a tomb for himself (v. 16), and the "maidservant" of the inscription may have been a favorite concubine. Elaborate tombs from preexilic Judah are rare, and Isaiah opposed this kind of ostentation (see "Tombs in Ancient Israel" on p. 376). The inscription is now housed in the British Museum.
The location of an individual's burial site was considered to be of critical importance; Shebna desired a tomb worthy of a king (cf. 2Ch 16:14).
22:18 The use of a chariot signified high office (see Ge 41:43).
22:20–21 Shebna was demoted to "secretary" after having been replaced by Eliakim sometime prior to 701 B.C. (see 36:3).
22:22 For commentary on house doors and keys, see the note on Song of Songs 5:5.
23:1 For "oracle," see the note on 13:1.
Tyre was the main seaport along the Phoenician coast, about 35 miles (56 km) north of Mount Carmel. Part of the city was built on two rocky islands about a half mile (.8 km) from shore, making it relatively secure from attack. (But see "The Downfall of Tyre" on p. 1345.)
The "ships of Tarshish" were trading ships (see the note on 2:16).
23:2 The "island" is Tyre.
Sidon, the other prominent Phoenician city, was located about 25 miles (40 km) north of Tyre. (See "Sidon" on p. 1536 and "Phoenicia" on p. 488.) The commercial ventures of Tyre and Sidon affected the entire Mediterranean world (see vv. 3,8).
23:3 "Shihor" may well refer to the easternmost branch of the Nile (see the NIV text note on Jer 2:18). The Nile's annual flooding produced fertile soil and abundant crops.

23:3 [m]Isa 19:7 [n]Eze 27:3

the harvest of the Nile[a][m] was the revenue of Tyre,[n]
and she became the marketplace of the nations.

23:4 [o]Ge 10:15, 19

4 Be ashamed, O Sidon,[o] and you, O fortress of the sea,
for the sea has spoken:
"I have neither been in labor nor given birth;
I have neither reared sons nor brought up daughters."
5 When word comes to Egypt,
they will be in anguish at the report from Tyre.
6 Cross over to Tarshish;
wail, you people of the island.

23:7 [p]Isa 22:2; 32:13

7 Is this your city of revelry,[p]
the old, old city,
whose feet have taken her
to settle in far-off lands?
8 Who planned this against Tyre,
the bestower of crowns,
whose merchants are princes,
whose traders are renowned in the earth?

23:9 [q]Job 40:11 [r]Isa 13:11 [s]Isa 5:13; 9:15

9 The LORD Almighty planned it,
to bring low[q] the pride of all glory
and to humble[r] all who are renowned[s] on
the earth.

10 Till[b] your land as along the Nile,
O Daughter of Tarshish,
for you no longer have a harbor.

23:11 [t]Ex 14:21 [u]Isa 25:2; Zec 9:3-4

11 The LORD has stretched out his hand[t] over the sea
and made its kingdoms tremble.
He has given an order concerning Phoenicia[c]
that her fortresses be destroyed.[u]

23:12 [v]Rev 18:22 [w]Isa 47:1

12 He said, "No more of your reveling,[v]
O Virgin Daughter[w] of Sidon, now crushed!

"Up, cross over to Cyprus[d];
even there you will find no rest."
13 Look at the land of the Babylonians,[e]
this people that is now of no account!

23:13 [x]Isa 10:5 [y]Isa 10:7

The Assyrians[x] have made it
a place for desert creatures;
they raised up their siege towers,
they stripped its fortresses bare
and turned it into a ruin.[y]

23:14 [z]Isa 2:16 *fn*

14 Wail, you ships of Tarshish;[z]
your fortress is destroyed!

[a] *2,3* Masoretic Text; one Dead Sea Scroll *Sidon, / who cross over the sea; / your envoys* [3]*are on the great waters. / The grain of the Shihor, / the harvest of the Nile,* [b] *10* Dead Sea Scrolls and some Septuagint manuscripts; Masoretic Text *Go through* [c] *11* Hebrew *Canaan* [d] *12* Hebrew *Kittim* [e] *13* Or *Chaldeans*

23:4 Tyre was the "fortress of the sea" (see the note on v. 1).
23:6 See "Where Was Tarshish?" on page 1475.
23:7 Tyre, founded before 2000 B.C., was an "old, old city" that had settled "far-off lands," such as Carthage in North Africa and perhaps Tarshish.
23:8 Tyre's colonies were governed by their own kings.
23:10 The city of Tarshish is here personified as "Daughter of Tarshish."
23:11 Modern-day Lebanon covers approximately the same territory as ancient Phoenicia (see "Phoenicia" on p. 488).
23:12 "Virgin Daughter of Sidon" personifies Sidon, which was captured first by Esarhaddon in the seventh century B.C. and again by Nebuchadnezzar around 587 B.C.
23:13 The Assyrian Sennacherib destroyed Babylon in 689 B.C., and Phoenicia would look like the Babylon of that time.
See "Siege Warfare" on page 465.

15 At that time Tyre[a] will be forgotten for seventy years, the span of a king's life. But at the end of these
seventy years, it will happen to Tyre as in the song of the prostitute:

23:15 [a]Jer 25:22

16 "Take up a harp, walk through the city,
  O prostitute forgotten;
play the harp well, sing many a song,
  so that you will be remembered."

17 At the end of seventy years, the LORD will deal with Tyre. She will return to her hire as a prostitute[b]
and will ply her trade with all the kingdoms on the face of the earth. 18 Yet her profit and her earnings will
be set apart for the LORD;[c] they will not be stored up or hoarded. Her profits will go to those who live be-
fore the LORD,[d] for abundant food and fine clothes.

23:17 [b]Eze 16:26; Na 3:4; Rev 17:1
23:18 [c]Ex 28:36; Ps 72:10 [d]Isa 60:5-9; Mic 4:13

The LORD's Devastation of the Earth

24 See, the LORD is going to lay waste the earth[e]
  and devastate it;
he will ruin its face
  and scatter its inhabitants—
2 it will be the same
  for priest as for people,[f]
  for master as for servant,
  for mistress as for maid,
  for seller as for buyer,[g]
  for borrower as for lender,
  for debtor as for creditor.[h]
3 The earth will be completely laid waste
  and totally plundered.[i]
      The LORD has spoken this word.

24:1 [e]ver 20; Isa 2:19-21; 33:9
24:2 [f]Hos 4:9 [g]Eze 7:12 [h]Lev 25:35-37; Dt 23:19-20
24:3 [i]Isa 6:11-12

4 The earth dries up and withers,
  the world languishes and withers,
  the exalted[j] of the earth languish.
5 The earth is defiled[k] by its people;
  they have disobeyed[l] the laws,
violated the statutes
  and broken the everlasting covenant.
6 Therefore a curse consumes the earth;
  its people must bear their guilt.
Therefore earth's inhabitants are burned up,[m]
  and very few are left.
7 The new wine dries up and the vine withers;[n]
  all the merrymakers groan.[o]
8 The gaiety of the tambourines[p] is stilled,
  the noise[q] of the revelers has stopped,
  the joyful harp[r] is silent.[s]
9 No longer do they drink wine[t] with a song;
  the beer is bitter[u] to its drinkers.
10 The ruined city lies desolate;
  the entrance to every house is barred.

24:4 [j]Isa 2:12
24:5 [k]Ge 3:17; Nu 35:33 [l]Isa 10:6; 59:12
24:6 [m]Isa 1:31
24:7 [n]Joel 1:10-12 [o]Isa 16:8-10
24:8 [p]Isa 5:12 [q]Jer 7:34; 16:9; 25:10; Hos 2:11 [r]Rev 18:22 [s]Eze 26:13
24:9 [t]Isa 5:11,22 [u]Isa 5:20

23:15 Seventy years was also the approximate duration of Judah's Babylonian captivity (see Jer 25:11–12), as well as the length of time the Babylonian god Marduk (according to an inscription of King Esarhaddon) decreed that Babylon would remain devastated.

23:18 Earnings from prostitution were considered unfit to offer to the Lord (Dt 23:18), but the silver and gold of a city devoted to destruction (see "*Herem*, Holy War" on p. 419) were transferred to the temple treasury as God's possession (see Jos 6:17,19).

24:1—35:10 Isaiah 24 looks far into the future. It is world-embracing and may be called an apocalypse. The world judgment would be followed by songs of thanksgiving for divine blessing (chs. 25–26). A prophecy against Egypt follows (ch. 27). Then there are again six woes (chs. 28–34), the last being a frightful curse on Edom. This group of chapters also closes with a beautiful prophetic picture of future blessedness (ch. 35).

11 In the streets they cry out for wine;
all joy turns to gloom,[v]
all gaiety is banished from the earth.
12 The city is left in ruins,
its gate is battered to pieces.
13 So will it be on the earth
and among the nations,
as when an olive tree is beaten,[w]
or as when gleanings are left after the grape
harvest.

14 They raise their voices, they shout for joy;[x]
from the west they acclaim the LORD's majesty.
15 Therefore in the east give glory[y] to the LORD;
exalt[z] the name of the LORD, the God
of Israel,
in the islands of the sea.
16 From the ends of the earth we hear singing:
"Glory[a] to the Righteous One."

But I said, "I waste away, I waste away!
Woe to me!
The treacherous betray!
With treachery the treacherous betray![b]"
17 Terror and pit and snare[c] await you,
O people of the earth.
18 Whoever flees at the sound of terror
will fall into a pit;
whoever climbs out of the pit
will be caught in a snare.

The floodgates of the heavens[d] are opened,
the foundations of the earth shake.[e]
19 The earth is broken up,
the earth is split asunder,[f]
the earth is thoroughly shaken.
20 The earth reels like a drunkard,[g]
it sways like a hut in the wind;
so heavy upon it is the guilt of its rebellion[h]
that it falls—never to rise again.

21 In that day the LORD will punish[i]
the powers in the heavens above
and the kings on the earth below.
22 They will be herded together
like prisoners[j] bound in a dungeon;[k]
they will be shut up in prison
and be punished[a] after many days.[l]
23 The moon will be abashed, the sun[m]
ashamed;
for the LORD Almighty will reign[n]
on Mount Zion[o] and in Jerusalem,
and before its elders, gloriously.[p]

24:11 [v]Isa 16:10; 32:13; Jer 14:3
24:13 [w]Isa 17:6
24:14 [x]Isa 12:6
24:15 [y]Isa 66:19 [z]Isa 25:3; Mal 1:11
24:16 [a]Isa 28:5 [b]Isa 21:2; Jer 5:11
24:17 [c]Jer 48:43
24:18 [d]Ge 7:11 [e]Ps 18:7
24:19 [f]Dt 11:6
24:20 [g]Isa 19:14 [h]Isa 1:2,28; 43:27
24:21 [i]Isa 10:12
24:22 [j]Isa 10:4 [k]Isa 42:7,22 [l]Eze 38:8
24:23 [m]Isa 13:10 [n]Rev 22:5 [o]Heb 12:22 [p]Isa 60:19

[a] 22 Or *released*

24:15 "Islands of the sea" is most likely a reference to the Mediterranean coastlands and islands.

Praise to the LORD

25

O LORD, you are my God;
I will exalt you and praise your name,
for in perfect faithfulness
you have done marvelous things,[q]
things planned[r] long ago.
2 You have made the city a heap of rubble,[s]
the fortified[t] town a ruin,
the foreigners' stronghold[u] a city no more;
it will never be rebuilt.
3 Therefore strong peoples will honor you;
cities of ruthless[v] nations will revere you.
4 You have been a refuge[w] for the poor,
a refuge for the needy in his distress,
a shelter from the storm
and a shade from the heat.
For the breath of the ruthless[x]
is like a storm driving against a wall
5 and like the heat of the desert.
You silence[y] the uproar of foreigners;
as heat is reduced by the shadow of a cloud,
so the song of the ruthless is stilled.

6 On this mountain[z] the LORD Almighty will prepare
a feast[a] of rich food for all peoples,
a banquet of aged wine—
the best of meats and the finest of wines.[b]
7 On this mountain he will destroy
the shroud[c] that enfolds all peoples,
the sheet that covers all nations;
8 he will swallow up death[d] forever.
The Sovereign LORD will wipe away the tears[e]
from all faces;
he will remove the disgrace[f] of his people
from all the earth.
The LORD has spoken.

9 In that day they will say,

"Surely this is our God;[g]
we trusted in him, and he saved[h] us.
This is the LORD, we trusted in him;
let us rejoice[i] and be glad in his salvation."

10 The hand of the LORD will rest on this mountain;
but Moab[j] will be trampled under him
as straw is trampled down in the manure.
11 They will spread out their hands in it,
as a swimmer spreads out his hands to swim.
God will bring down[k] their pride[l]
despite the cleverness[a] of their hands.

25:1 [q]Ps 98:1 [r]Nu 23:19
25:2 [s]Isa 17:1 [t]Isa 17:3 [u]Isa 13:22
25:3 [v]Isa 13:11
25:4 [w]Isa 4:6; 17:10; 27:5; 33:16 [x]Isa 29:5; 49:25
25:5 [y]Jer 51:55
25:6 [z]Isa 2:2 [a]Isa 1:19; Mt 8:11; 22:4 [b]Pr 9:2
25:7 [c]2Co 3:15-16; Eph 4:18
25:8 [d]Hos 13:14; 1Co 15:54-55* [e]Isa 30:19; 35:10; 51:11; 65:19; Rev 7:17; 21:4 [f]Mt 5:11; 1Pe 4:14
25:9 [g]Isa 40:9 [h]Ps 20:5; Isa 33:22; 35:4; 49:25-26; 60:16 [i]Isa 35:2,10
25:10 [j]Am 2:1-3
25:11 [k]Isa 5:25; 14:26; 16:14 [l]Job 40:12

[a] *11* The meaning of the Hebrew for this word is uncertain.

25:6 A coronation (1Ki 1:25) or wedding (see Jdg 14:10) was celebrated by a banquet (cf. the "wedding supper of the Lamb" in Rev 19:9).

25:7 The "shroud" and "sheet" were associated with death—coverings or veils with which mourners concealed their faces.

25:12 [m]Isa 15:1

[12] He will bring down your high fortified walls
and lay them low;[m]
he will bring them down to the ground,
to the very dust.

A Song of Praise

26 In that day this song will be sung in the land of Judah:

26:1 [n]Isa 14:32 [o]Isa 60:18

We have a strong city;[n]
God makes salvation
its walls[o] and ramparts.
[2] Open the gates
that the righteous[p] nation may enter,
the nation that keeps faith.
[3] You will keep in perfect peace
him whose mind is steadfast,
because he trusts in you.
[4] Trust[q] in the LORD forever,
for the LORD, the LORD, is the Rock eternal.
[5] He humbles those who dwell on high,
he lays the lofty city low;
he levels it to the ground[r]
and casts it down to the dust.
[6] Feet trample it down—
the feet of the oppressed,
the footsteps of the poor.[s]

26:2 [p]Isa 54:14; 58:8; 62:2
26:4 [q]Isa 12:2; 50:10
26:5 [r]Isa 25:12
26:6 [s]Isa 3:15

[7] The path of the righteous is level;
O upright One, you make the way of the righteous
smooth.[t]
[8] Yes, LORD, walking in the way of your laws,[a][u]
we wait for you;
your name[v] and renown
are the desire of our hearts.
[9] My soul yearns for you in the night;
in the morning my spirit longs[w] for you.
When your judgments come upon the earth,
the people of the world learn righteousness.[x]
[10] Though grace is shown to the wicked,
they do not learn righteousness;
even in a land of uprightness they go on doing evil[y]
and regard[z] not the majesty of the LORD.
[11] O LORD, your hand is lifted high,
but they do not see[a] it.
Let them see your zeal for your people and be put to shame;
let the fire[b] reserved for your enemies consume them.

26:7 [t]Isa 42:16
26:8 [u]Isa 56:1 [v]Isa 12:4
26:9 [w]Ps 63:1; 78:34; Isa 55:6 [x]Mt 6:33
26:10 [y]Isa 32:6 [z]Isa 22:12-13; Hos 11:7; Jn 5:37-38; Ro 2:4
26:11 [a]Isa 44:9, 18 [b]Heb 10:27

[12] LORD, you establish peace for us;
all that we have accomplished you have done for us.
[13] O LORD, our God, other lords[c] besides you have ruled
over us,
but your name alone do we honor.[d]

26:13 [c]Isa 2:8; 10:5,11 [d]Isa 63:7

[a] 8 Or *judgments*

26:1 Ramparts were sloping fortifications of earth or stone (cf. 2Sa 20:15) used as protective barriers against invaders.

26:11 A king lifted his hand high as a symbol of his power (see Ps 89:13).

[14]They are now dead,[e] they live no more;
those departed spirits do not rise.
You punished them and brought them to ruin;[f]
you wiped out all memory of them.
[15]You have enlarged the nation, O LORD;
you have enlarged the nation.
You have gained glory for yourself;
you have extended all the borders[g] of the land.

[16]LORD, they came to you in their distress;[h]
when you disciplined them,
they could barely whisper a prayer.[a]
[17]As a woman with child and about to give birth[i]
writhes and cries out in her pain,
so were we in your presence, O LORD.
[18]We were with child, we writhed in pain,
but we gave birth[j] to wind.
We have not brought salvation[k] to the earth;
we have not given birth to people of the world.

[19]But your dead[l] will live;
their bodies will rise.
You who dwell in the dust,
wake up and shout for joy.
Your dew is like the dew of the morning;
the earth will give birth to her dead.[m]

[20]Go, my people, enter your rooms
and shut the doors[n] behind you;
hide[o] yourselves for a little while
until his wrath has passed by.[p]
[21]See, the LORD is coming[q] out of his dwelling[r]
to punish[s] the people of the earth for their sins.
The earth will disclose the blood[t] shed upon her;
she will conceal her slain no longer.

Deliverance of Israel

27

In that day,

the LORD will punish with his sword,[u]
his fierce, great and powerful sword,
Leviathan[v] the gliding serpent,
Leviathan the coiling serpent;
he will slay the monster[w] of the sea.

[2]In that day—

"Sing about a fruitful vineyard:[x]
[3] I, the LORD, watch over it;
I water[y] it continually.
I guard it day and night
so that no one may harm it.

[a] *16* The meaning of the Hebrew for this clause is uncertain.

26:14 [e]Dt 4:28 [f]Isa 10:3
26:15 [g]Isa 33:17
26:16 [h]Hos 5:15
26:17 [i]Jn 16:21
26:18 [j]Isa 33:11; 59:4 [k]Ps 17:14
26:19 [l]Isa 25:8; Eph 5:14 [m]Eze 37:1-14; Da 12:2
26:20 [n]Ex 12:23 [o]Ps 91:1,4 [p]Ps 30:5; Isa 54:7-8
26:21 [q]Jude 1:14 [r]Mic 1:3 [s]Isa 13:9,11; 30:12-14 [t]Job 16:18; Lk 11:50-51
27:1 [u]Isa 34:6; 66:16 [v]Job 3:8 [w]Ps 74:13
27:2 [x]Jer 2:21
27:3 [y]Isa 58:11

26:14 See the note on Psalm 6:5 for a discussion of the ancient Near Eastern perspective on the afterlife; see also "Sheol, Hades, Gehenna, the Abyss and Tartarus: Images of Hell" on page 946.
26:19 See the note on verse 14.
27:1 For "Leviathan," see the note on Psalm 104:26. Here it is a symbol of wicked nations, such as Egypt (see Isa 30:7 and 51:9, where "Rahab" is used).

27:4 [z]Isa 10:17; Mt 3:12; Heb 6:8
27:5 [a]Isa 25:4 [b]Job 22:21; Ro 5:1; 2Co 5:20
27:6 [c]Hos 14:5-6 [d]Isa 37:31
27:7 [e]Isa 37:36-38
27:8 [f]Isa 50:1; 54:7
27:9 [g]Ro 11:27* [h]Ex 34:13
27:10 [i]Isa 32:14; Jer 26:6 [j]Isa 17:2
27:11 [k]Dt 32:28; Isa 1:3; Jer 8:7 [l]Dt 32:18; Isa 43:1,7,15; 44:1-2,21,24 [m]Isa 9:17
27:12 [n]Ge 15:18 [o]Dt 30:4; Isa 11:12; 17:6
27:13 [p]Lev 25:9; Mt 24:31 [q]Isa 19:21,25

4 I am not angry.
If only there were briers and thorns confronting me!
I would march against them in battle;
I would set them all on fire.[z]
5 Or else let them come to me for refuge;[a]
let them make peace[b] with me,
yes, let them make peace with me."

6 In days to come Jacob will take root,
Israel will bud and blossom[c]
and fill all the world with fruit.[d]

7 Has ⌞the LORD⌟ struck her
as he struck[e] down those who struck her?
Has she been killed
as those were killed who killed her?
8 By warfare[a] and exile[f] you contend with her—
with his fierce blast he drives her out,
as on a day the east wind blows.
9 By this, then, will Jacob's guilt be atoned for,
and this will be the full fruitage of the removal of his sin:[g]
When he makes all the altar stones
to be like chalk stones crushed to pieces,
no Asherah poles[b][h] or incense altars
will be left standing.
10 The fortified city stands desolate,[i]
an abandoned settlement, forsaken like the desert;
there the calves graze,
there they lie down;[j]
they strip its branches bare.
11 When its twigs are dry, they are broken off
and women come and make fires with them.
For this is a people without understanding;[k]
so their Maker has no compassion on them,
and their Creator[l] shows them no favor.[m]

12 In that day the LORD will thresh from the flowing Euphrates[c] to the Wadi of Egypt,[n] and you, O Is-
raelites, will be gathered[o] up one by one. 13 And in that day a great trumpet[p] will sound. Those who were
perishing in Assyria and those who were exiled in Egypt[q] will come and worship the LORD on the holy
mountain in Jerusalem.

Woe to Ephraim

28:1 [r]ver 3; Isa 9:9 [s]ver 4 [t]Hos 7:5

28

Woe to that wreath, the pride of Ephraim's[r] drunkards,
to the fading flower, his glorious beauty,
set on the head of a fertile valley[s]—
to that city, the pride of those laid low by wine![t]

[a] *8* See Septuagint; the meaning of the Hebrew for this word is uncertain. [b] *9* That is, symbols of the goddess Asherah
[c] *12* Hebrew *River*

27:8 The "east wind" was a scorching desert wind (see the notes on Jer 4:11 and Hos 13:15).

27:9 When entering Canaan the Hebrews, who had made bricks in Egypt (Ex 5:7), readily turned to the abundant supply of stones, both from quarries and from stream beds. Limestone (Isa 27:9), gravel (La 3:16) and stones rounded by water in streams (1Sa 17:40; Job 14:19) were abundant.

For "Asherah poles" and "incense altars," see the note on Isaiah 17:8.

27:12 Threshing here symbolized God's judgment upon the nations into which his people had been dispersed (see "The Threshing Floor" on p. 608). The threshing would separate the Israelites from the Gentiles.

Wadi el-Arish, the southern border of the promised land (of which the Euphrates was the northern boundary), was most likely the "Wadi of Egypt."

27:13 For "trumpet," see the note on 18:3; see also "Trumpets in the Ancient World" on page 2057.

28:1 Samaria, the "wreath," was the capital of the northern kingdom. In the eighth century B.C. it was a beautiful, luxurious and indulgent city, situated on an imposing hill (see the note on 1Ki 16:24; see also "Omri and Samaria" on p. 512).

2 See, the Lord has one who is powerful[u] and strong.
Like a hailstorm[v] and a destructive wind,[w]
like a driving rain and a flooding[x] downpour,
he will throw it forcefully to the ground.

28:2 [u]Isa 40:10 [v]Isa 30:30; Eze 13:11 [w]Isa 29:6 [x]Isa 8:7

3 That wreath, the pride of Ephraim's[y] drunkards,
will be trampled underfoot.

28:3 [y]ver 1

4 That fading flower, his glorious beauty,
set on the head of a fertile valley,[z]
will be like a fig[a] ripe before harvest—
as soon as someone sees it and takes it in his hand,
he swallows it.

28:4 [z]ver 1 [a]Hos 9:10; Na 3:12

5 In that day the LORD Almighty
will be a glorious crown,[b]
a beautiful wreath
for the remnant of his people.

28:5 [b]Isa 62:3

6 He will be a spirit of justice[c]
to him who sits in judgment,[d]
a source of strength
to those who turn back the battle[e] at the gate.

28:6 [c]Isa 11:2-4; 32:1,16 [d]Jn 5:30 [e]2Ch 32:8

7 And these also stagger from wine[f]
and reel[g] from beer:
Priests[h] and prophets[i] stagger from beer
and are befuddled with wine;
they reel from beer,
they stagger when seeing visions,[j]
they stumble when rendering decisions.

28:7 [f]Isa 22:13 [g]Isa 56:10-12 [h]Isa 24:2 [i]Isa 9:15 [j]Isa 29:11; Hos 4:11

8 All the tables are covered with vomit[k]
and there is not a spot without filth.

28:8 [k]Jer 48:26

9 "Who is it he is trying to teach?[l]
To whom is he explaining his message?
To children weaned[m] from their milk,[n]
to those just taken from the breast?

28:9 [l]ver 26; Isa 30:20; 48:17; 50:4; 54:13 [m]Ps 131:2 [n]Heb 5:12-13

10 For it is:
Do and do, do and do,
rule on rule, rule on rule[a];
a little here, a little there."

11 Very well then, with foreign lips and strange tongues[o]
God will speak to this people,[p]

28:11 [o]Isa 33:19 [p]1Co 14:21*

12 to whom he said,
"This is the resting place, let the weary rest";[q]
and, "This is the place of repose"—
but they would not listen.

28:12 [q]Isa 11:10; Mt 11:28-29

13 So then, the word of the LORD to them will become:
Do and do, do and do,
rule on rule, rule on rule;
a little here, a little there—

[a] *10* Hebrew / *sav lasav sav lasav / kav lakav kav lakav* (possibly meaningless sounds; perhaps a mimicking of the prophet's words); also in verse 13

28:4 Fruit grew in abundance in the Holy Land. Its variety included grapes, figs, olives, mulberries, pomegranates, oranges, lemons, melons, dates, almonds and walnuts. Grapes were both eaten as fresh food and dried as raisins. They were the chief source of the wines, which were used both sweet and fermented. Olives were eaten as food, as well as used to make olive oil. There were two kinds of figs, early (28:4) and late (Jer 8:13). The late figs were dried and pressed into cakes. Dates were eaten both raw and dried. (See "Food and Agriculture" on p. 390.)

28:7 In the ancient Near East drinking wine and beer was a necessity, as finding clean drinking water was often difficult.

so that they will go and fall backward,
be injured[r] and snared and captured.[s]

28:13 rMt 21:44 sIsa 8:15
28:14 tIsa 1:10

14 Therefore hear the word of the LORD,[t] you scoffers
who rule this people in Jerusalem.
15 You boast, "We have entered into a covenant with death,
with the grave[a] we have made an agreement.
When an overwhelming scourge sweeps by,[u]
it cannot touch us,
for we have made a lie[v] our refuge
and falsehood[b] our hiding place.[w]"

28:15 uver 2,18; Isa 8:7-8; 30:28; Da 11:22 vIsa 9:15 wIsa 29:15

16 So this is what the Sovereign LORD says:

"See, I lay a stone in Zion,
a tested stone,[x]
a precious cornerstone for a sure foundation;
the one who trusts will never be dismayed.[y]
17 I will make justice[z] the measuring line
and righteousness the plumb line;[a]
hail will sweep away your refuge, the lie,
and water will overflow your hiding place.

28:16 xPs 118:22; Isa 8:14-15; Mt 21:42; Ac 4:11; Eph 2:20 yRo 9:33*; 10:11*; 1Pe 2:6*
28:17 zIsa 5:16 a2Ki 21:13

[a] 15 Hebrew *Sheol*; also in verse 18 [b] 15 Or *false gods*

ANCIENT TEXTS AND ARTIFACTS

The Abecedaries

ISAIAH 28 An abecedary is a type of ancient inscription containing letters in a standard alphabetical order. Many such writings appear to be nothing more than the elementary exercises of school children. However, these documents still yield valuable information concerning the development and transmission of the alphabet. The earliest abecedaries were found at **Ugarit** ("Map 1") and date to the fourteenth century B.C.[1] The order of the letters preserved in these early documents follows the arrangement later adopted by the Hebrew, Greek, Latin and Arabic alphabets. Many have argued that the names of the letters, though not preserved in these inscriptions, must have developed simultaneously with the fixed alphabetic order by serving as a mnemonic device to aid in remembering the pattern. By analogy, modern American children use a rhyming song to learn their alphabet.

Parts of Isaiah 28:9–13 are difficult to interpret; verse 10 in particular looks like a series of nonsense rhymes. The NIV renders this as "Do and do, do and do, rule on rule, rule on rule; a little here, a little there," but this translation is something of a guess. The translational difficulty in the Hebrew can perhaps be explained by the development of mnemonic tools such as rhyming for teaching children. The nonsensical Hebrew words that appear in this passage are probably consonants plus rhyming vowel sounds, simulating an elementary school lesson. Further evidence that the Israelites made use of the alphabet for memorization purposes can be found elsewhere in the Hebrew Bible. For example, Psalms 111 and 112 are acrostic poems that follow the order of the Hebrew alphabet.[2]

An abecedary (text for learning the alphabet) from Greece, c. 800 B.C.

© The Schøyen Collection; photography courtesy of Mr. Martin Schøyen

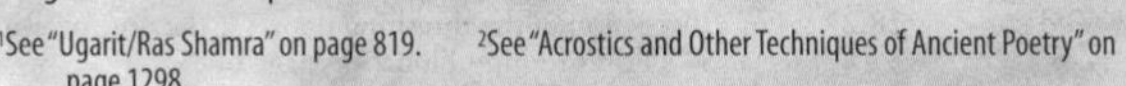

[1]See "Ugarit/Ras Shamra" on page 819. [2]See "Acrostics and Other Techniques of Ancient Poetry" on page 1298.

[18] Your covenant with death will be annulled;
your agreement with the grave will not stand.[b]
When the overwhelming scourge sweeps by,[c]
you will be beaten down[d] by it.
[19] As often as it comes it will carry you away;[e]
morning after morning, by day and by night,
it will sweep through."

The understanding of this message
will bring sheer terror.[f]
[20] The bed is too short to stretch out on,
the blanket too narrow to wrap around you.[g]
[21] The LORD will rise up as he did at Mount Perazim,[h]
he will rouse himself as in the Valley of Gibeon[i]—
to do his work,[j] his strange work,
and perform his task, his alien task.
[22] Now stop your mocking,
or your chains will become heavier;
the Lord, the LORD Almighty, has told me
of the destruction decreed[k] against the whole land.[l]
[23] Listen and hear my voice;
pay attention and hear what I say.
[24] When a farmer plows for planting, does he plow continually?
Does he keep on breaking up and harrowing the soil?
[25] When he has leveled the surface,
does he not sow caraway and scatter cummin?[m]
Does he not plant wheat in its place,[a]
barley in its plot,[a]
and spelt[n] in its field?
[26] His God instructs him
and teaches him the right way.

[27] Caraway is not threshed with a sledge,
nor is a cartwheel rolled over cummin;
caraway is beaten out with a rod,
and cummin with a stick.
[28] Grain must be ground to make bread;
so one does not go on threshing it forever.
Though he drives the wheels of his threshing cart over it,
his horses do not grind it.
[29] All this also comes from the LORD Almighty,
wonderful in counsel[o] and magnificent in wisdom.[p]

Woe to David's City

29

Woe[q] to you, Ariel, Ariel,[r]
the city where David settled!
Add year to year
and let your cycle of festivals[s] go on.

[a] 25 The meaning of the Hebrew for this word is uncertain.

28:18 [b]Isa 7:7 [c]ver 15 [d]Da 8:13
28:19 [e]2Ki 24:2 [f]Job 18:11
28:20 [g]Isa 59:6
28:21 [h]1Ch 14:11 [i]Jos 10:10,12; 1Ch 14:16 [j]Isa 10:12; Lk 19:41-44
28:22 [k]Isa 10:22 [l]Isa 10:23
28:25 [m]Mt 23:23 [n]Ex 9:32
28:29 [o]Isa 9:6 [p]Ro 11:33
29:1 [q]Isa 22:12-13 [r]2Sa 5:9 [s]Isa 1:14

28:21 God had earlier "broken out" against the Philistines on Mount Perazim (2Sa 5:20) and sent hail in the Valley of Gibeon to ravage the Amorites (see Jos 10:10–13). This time God would contest his own people, the Israelites.

28:25 Cummin is an herb used for seasoning, while spelt is a variety of wheat (see the note on Ex 9:32).

28:27 For a discussion of the threshing floor, see the note on Ruth 3:4–7; see also "The Threshing Floor" on page 608.

29:1 "Ariel" is Mount Zion, synonymous with Jerusalem (v. 8).

2 Yet I will besiege Ariel;
she will mourn and lament,[t]
she will be to me like an altar hearth.[a]
3 I will encamp against you all around;
I will encircle[u] you with towers
and set up my siege works against you.
4 Brought low, you will speak from the ground;
your speech will mumble[v] out of the dust.
Your voice will come ghostlike from the earth;
out of the dust your speech will whisper.

5 But your many enemies will become like fine dust,
the ruthless hordes like blown chaff.[w]
Suddenly,[x] in an instant,
6 the LORD Almighty will come
with thunder and earthquake[y] and great noise,
with windstorm and tempest and flames of a
devouring fire.
7 Then the hordes of all the nations[z] that fight against Ariel,
that attack her and her fortress and besiege her,
will be as it is with a dream,[a]
with a vision in the night—
8 as when a hungry man dreams that he is eating,
but he awakens,[b] and his hunger remains;
as when a thirsty man dreams that he is drinking,
but he awakens faint, with his thirst unquenched.
So will it be with the hordes of all the nations
that fight against Mount Zion.

9 Be stunned and amazed,
blind yourselves and be sightless;
be drunk,[c] but not from wine,[d]
stagger, but not from beer.
10 The LORD has brought over you a deep sleep:
He has sealed your eyes[e] (the prophets);[f]
he has covered your heads (the seers).[g]

11 For you this whole vision is nothing but words sealed[h] in a scroll. And if you give the scroll to some-
one who can read, and say to him, "Read this, please," he will answer, "I can't; it is sealed." 12 Or if you give
the scroll to someone who cannot read, and say, "Read this, please," he will answer, "I don't know how to
read."

13 The Lord says:

"These people come near to me with their mouth
and honor me with their lips,
but their hearts are far from me.[i]
Their worship of me
is made up only of rules taught by men.[b][j]
14 Therefore once more I will astound these people
with wonder upon wonder;[k]

29:2 [t]Isa 3:26; La 2:5
29:3 [u]Lk 19:43-44
29:4 [v]Isa 8:19
29:5 [w]Isa 17:13 [x]Isa 17:14; 1Th 5:3
29:6 [y]Mt 24:7; Mk 13:8; Lk 21:11; Rev 11:19
29:7 [z]Mic 4:11-12; Zec 12:9 [a]Job 20:8
29:8 [b]Ps 73:20
29:9 [c]Isa 51:17 [d]Isa 51:21-22
29:10 [e]Ps 69:23; Isa 6:9-10; Ro 11:8* [f]Mic 3:6 [g]1Sa 9:9
29:11 [h]Isa 8:16; Mt 13:11; Rev 5:1-2
29:13 [i]Eze 33:31 [j]Mt 15:8-9*; Mk 7:6-7*; Col 2:22
29:14 [k]Hab 1:5

[a] 2 The Hebrew for *altar hearth* sounds like the Hebrew for *Ariel.* [b] 13 Hebrew; Septuagint *They worship me in vain; / their teachings are but rules taught by men*

29:3 Attackers who wished to gain the advantage of combating a city's defenders on the same level would mount towers they had pushed up against the city wall (see "Siege Warfare" on p. 465).

29:4 In 8:19 Isaiah referred to mediums and spiritists as those who "whisper and mutter"; Judah was speaking as from the realm of the dead ("ground . . . dust . . . earth").

29:5 See the note on Psalm 1:4 for a commentary on "chaff."

the wisdom of the wise[l] will perish,
the intelligence of the intelligent will vanish.[m]"
15 Woe to those who go to great depths
to hide their plans from the LORD,
who do their work in darkness and think,
"Who sees us?[n] Who will know?"[o]
16 You turn things upside down,
as if the potter were thought to be like the clay!
Shall what is formed say to him who formed it,
"He did not make me"?
Can the pot say of the potter,[p]
"He knows nothing"?

17 In a very short time, will not Lebanon be turned into a fertile field[q]
and the fertile field seem like a forest?[r]
18 In that day the deaf[s] will hear the words of the scroll,
and out of gloom and darkness
the eyes of the blind will see.[t]
19 Once more the humble[u] will rejoice in the LORD;
the needy[v] will rejoice in the Holy One of Israel.
20 The ruthless will vanish,
the mockers[w] will disappear,
and all who have an eye for evil[x] will be cut down—
21 those who with a word make a man out to be guilty,
who ensnare the defender in court[y]
and with false testimony deprive the innocent of justice.[z]

22 Therefore this is what the LORD, who redeemed Abraham,[a] says to the house of Jacob:

"No longer will Jacob be ashamed;[b]
no longer will their faces grow pale.
23 When they see among them their children,[c]
the work of my hands,[d]
they will keep my name holy;
they will acknowledge the holiness of the Holy One of Jacob,
and will stand in awe of the God of Israel.
24 Those who are wayward[e] in spirit will gain understanding;[f]
those who complain will accept instruction."[g]

29:14 [l]Jer 8:9; 49:7 [m]Isa 6:9-10; 1Co 1:19*
29:15 [n]Ps 10:11-13; 94:7; Isa 57:12 [o]Job 22:13
29:16 [p]Isa 45:9; 64:8; Ro 9:20-21*
29:17 [q]Ps 84:6 [r]Isa 32:15
29:18 [s]Mk 7:37 [t]Isa 32:3; 35:5; Mt 11:5
29:19 [u]Isa 61:1; Mt 5:5; 11:29 [v]Isa 14:30; Mt 11:5; Jas 1:9; 2:5
29:20 [w]Isa 28:22 [x]Isa 59:4; Mic 2:1
29:21 [y]Am 5:10, 15 [z]Isa 5:23; 32:7
29:22 [a]Isa 41:8; 63:16 [b]Isa 49:23
29:23 [c]Isa 49:20-26 [d]Isa 19:25
29:24 [e]Isa 28:7; Heb 5:2 [f]Isa 41:20; 60:16 [g]Isa 30:21

Woe to the Obstinate Nation

30

"Woe[h] to the obstinate children,"[i]
declares the LORD,
"to those who carry out plans that are not mine,
forming an alliance,[j] but not by my Spirit,
heaping sin upon sin;
2 who go down to Egypt[k]
without consulting[l] me;
who look for help to Pharaoh's protection,[m]
to Egypt's shade for refuge.
3 But Pharaoh's protection will be to your shame,
Egypt's shade will bring you disgrace.[n]

30:1 [h]Isa 29:15 [i]Isa 1:2 [j]Isa 8:12
30:2 [k]Isa 31:1 [l]Nu 27:21 [m]Isa 36:9
30:3 [n]Isa 20:4-5; 36:6

29:17 "Lebanon" in this context may symbolize Assyria (see 10:34). Since the forests of Lebanon were unequaled (see 2:13 and its note), "fertile field" implied a lesser status.
30:1 After Shabako of Egypt became pharaoh in 715 B.C., the smaller nations in Aram (Syria) and Canaan sought his help in a coalition against Assyria. Judah apparently joined in this "alliance" (see 20:5).
30:2 The image of "shade" depicts a king in his role of providing protection (see Jdg 9:15; La 4:20). The Lord should have been Israel's shade (cf. Isa 49:2; 51:16; see also Ps 91:1; 121:5).

30:4 [o]Isa 19:11

[4] Though they have officials in Zoan[o]
and their envoys have arrived in Hanes,
[5] everyone will be put to shame
because of a people[p] useless to them,
who bring neither help nor advantage,
but only shame and disgrace."

30:5 [p]ver 7

[6] An oracle concerning the animals of the Negev:

30:6 [q]Ex 5:10,21; Isa 8:22; Jer 11:4 [r]Dt 8:15 [s]Isa 15:7

Through a land of hardship and distress,[q]
of lions and lionesses,
of adders and darting snakes,[r]
the envoys carry their riches on donkeys' backs,
their treasures[s] on the humps of camels,
to that unprofitable nation,
[7] to Egypt, whose help is utterly useless.
Therefore I call her
Rahab the Do-Nothing.

[8] Go now, write it on a tablet for them,
inscribe it on a scroll,[t]
that for the days to come
it may be an everlasting witness.
[9] These are rebellious people, deceitful[u] children,
children unwilling to listen to the LORD's
instruction.[v]
[10] They say to the seers,
"See no more visions[w]!"
and to the prophets,
"Give us no more visions of what is right!
Tell us pleasant things,[x]
prophesy illusions.[y]
[11] Leave this way,
get off this path,
and stop confronting[z] us
with the Holy One of Israel!"

30:8 [t]Isa 8:1; Hab 2:2

30:9 [u]Isa 28:15; 59:3-4 [v]Isa 1:10

30:10 [w]Jer 11:21; Am 7:13 [x]1Ki 22:8 [y]Eze 13:7; Ro 16:18

30:11 [z]Job 21:14

[12] Therefore, this is what the Holy One of Israel says:

"Because you have rejected this message,[a]
relied on oppression[b]
and depended on deceit,
[13] this sin will become for you
like a high wall,[c] cracked and bulging,
that collapses[d] suddenly,[e] in an instant.
[14] It will break in pieces like pottery,[f]
shattered so mercilessly
that among its pieces not a fragment will be found
for taking coals from a hearth
or scooping water out of a cistern."

30:12 [a]Isa 5:24 [b]Isa 5:7

30:13 [c]Ps 62:3 [d]1Ki 20:30 [e]Isa 29:5

30:14 [f]Ps 2:9; Jer 19:10-11

30:4 The Israelites had at one time served as slaves in Zoan (see 19:11 and its note).

"Hanes" may be a reference to Heracleopolis Magna, located approximately 50 miles (81 km) south of Cairo, or to Heracleopolis Parva in the Nile delta.

30:6 For "oracle," see the note on 13:1.

The Negev was the arid desert region in the southern portion of the Holy Land (see "The Negev: Its Climate and Features" on p. 34).

30:7 "Rahab" refers to a mythical sea monster (see the notes on Job 9:13; Ps 89:9–10)—here symbolic of Egypt. The name itself means "storm" or "arrogance." See also the note on Isaiah 27:1 (for "Leviathan").

30:8 See "Cuneiform and Clay Tablets in the Ancient Near East" on page 1108 and "Sumerian Scribal Education" on page 579.

30:10 Seers were essentially no different from prophets.

30:14 See the note on hearths and home heating at Psalm 102:3.

Cuneiform and Clay Tablets in the Ancient Near East

ISAIAH 30 In ancient **Mesopotamia** the most commonly used writing material was the clay tablet (cf. Isa 30:8). The earliest ones were produced at the **Sumerian** city of **Uruk** ("Map 1) during the fourth millennium B.C. Clay was available in such abundance and was so easy to mold into writing tablets that there was no obstacle to producing a great quantity of such tablets. Thus, over a half million tablet-documents have been discovered to date from the ancient Near East. Writing first involved carving into the clay with a sharp stick or nail—thus described as "nail-writing."

No one knows exactly how writing emerged, but it probably began with clay tokens that were used as record-keeping devices. Marks placed upon these tokens eventually evolved into writing. At first "nail-writing" was practiced by drawing pictures and pictographic symbols (e.g., a depiction of a man to represent a man). Today we use pictograms to communicate simple ideas. A stylized likeness of a man or woman can represent the men's or women's restroom; a cigarette with a circle around it and slash mark over it has come to be understood as "No smoking." But it is impossible to communicate complex speech with such symbols.

Cuneiform receipt for the purchase of three oxen; c. 2046 B.C.
Preserving Bible Times; © Dr. James C. Martin; permission of The British Museum

As the need for record keeping increased, pictograms became more abstract and began to be formed with quick, straight strokes instead of curving lines (the picture of the man became more stylized and abstract—a symbol rather than a recognizable picture). By the third millennium B.C. **cuneiform** had been invented. Cuneiform (Latin for "wedge-shaped") is so named for the shape of the mark made by a reed stylus, triangular at one end, that was pressed into wet clay to make wedge-shaped lines.

With the advent of cuneiform, writing became even more abstract. Signs could now represent not only words but also syllables, several of which could be combined to represent the syllables of a word. For example, the Sumerian word for "barley" is *she*. In cuneiform, the sign for barley might literally mean "barley," but it might also denote some other word with the syllable *she* in it. Using English for our analogy, in this system the symbol for "man" might represent a man, but it might also represent the syllable "man-" in "manner" or "manufacture." As the system became more sophisticated and uniform, the number of signs needed for writing was reduced. Whereas as many as 2,000 signs are known from the earliest tablets, there were only about 200 still in use by the second millennium B.C. This allowed writing to truly represent speech, with all of its complexities of vocabulary and grammar. Thus myths, legends, history and songs began to be recorded.

Another development was the linear arrangement of signs. Originally, tablets were divided into rectangular boxes into which related signs were drawn in no particular order. These boxes were arranged in vertical columns. As writing became more abstract and rapid (c. 2500 B.C.), the signs within the boxes came to be written from left to right. Later the boxes were no longer drawn, and the signs were written left to right across the face of the tablet. This also led to a standardization of sign height, much as one finds today in ruled paper.

Cuneiform was first developed for use with the Sumerian language[1] but was adapted for other Mesopotamian languages. The **Akkadians** adopted this form of writing, and as their realm of influence grew, cuneiform writing spread. By the second millennium B.C. the **Elamites**, **Hurrians** and **Hittites** were employing cuneiform to write their own languages.[2] Eventually Akkadian became the international language of diplomacy, and Akkadian cuneiform spread throughout the Near East. The **Amarna** Letters demonstrate that cuneiform was utilized in fourteenth-century B.C. **Canaan** and was readable in the Egyptian royal court.

Early pictographic script from Uruk III; Sumer, c. 3100 B.C.
© The Schøyen Collection; photography courtesy of Mr. Martin Schøyen

Around 1600 B.C. the **Phoenicians** invented the precursor to the modern alphabet. In a true alphabet signs represent not words or syllables but individual consonants and vowels. This allows for writing to use a very small number of signs. With an alphabet there are fewer signs to learn, allowing almost anyone to become literate. Also, spelling becomes more accurate and uniform, resulting in less ambiguity and confusion. The efficiency of the alphabet eventually led to the decline of cuneiform in Syria-Palestine. The **Aramaic** language, which was written alphabetically, replaced Akkadian as the *lingua franca* (language of common, commercial use) of the ancient Near Eastern world.

[1]See "Sumer" on page 10. [2]For more on these cultures, see "The Hurrians" on page 57 and "Anatolia and the Hittites" on page 144.

15 This is what the Sovereign LORD, the Holy One of Israel, says:

"In repentance and rest is your salvation,
  in quietness and trust[g] is your strength,
  but you would have none of it.
16 You said, 'No, we will flee on horses.'[h]
  Therefore you will flee!
You said, 'We will ride off on swift horses.'
  Therefore your pursuers will be swift!
17 A thousand will flee
  at the threat of one;
at the threat of five[i]
  you will all flee[j] away,
till you are left
  like a flagstaff on a mountaintop,
  like a banner on a hill."

18 Yet the LORD longs[k] to be gracious to you;
  he rises to show you compassion.
For the LORD is a God of justice.[l]
  Blessed are all who wait for him![m]

19 O people of Zion, who live in Jerusalem, you will weep no more.[n] How gracious he will be when
you cry for help! As soon as he hears, he will answer[o] you. 20 Although the Lord gives you the bread[p]
of adversity and the water of affliction, your teachers will be hidden[q] no more; with your own eyes
you will see them. 21 Whether you turn to the right or to the left, your ears will hear a voice[r] behind
you, saying, "This is the way; walk in it." 22 Then you will defile your idols[s] overlaid with silver and your
images covered with gold; you will throw them away like a menstrual cloth and say to them, "Away
with you!"

23 He will also send you rain[t] for the seed you sow in the ground, and the food that comes from the land
will be rich and plentiful. In that day your cattle will graze in broad meadows.[u] 24 The oxen and donkeys
that work the soil will eat fodder and mash, spread out with fork[v] and shovel. 25 In the day of great slaugh-
ter, when the towers[w] fall, streams of water will flow[x] on every high mountain and every lofty hill. 26 The
moon will shine like the sun,[y] and the sunlight will be seven times brighter, like the light of seven full
days, when the LORD binds up the bruises of his people and heals[z] the wounds he inflicted.

27 See, the Name[a] of the LORD comes from afar,
  with burning anger[b] and dense clouds of smoke;
his lips are full of wrath,[c]
  and his tongue is a consuming fire.
28 His breath[d] is like a rushing torrent,
  rising up to the neck.[e]
He shakes the nations in the sieve[f] of destruction;
  he places in the jaws of the peoples
  a bit[g] that leads them astray.
29 And you will sing
  as on the night you celebrate a holy festival;
your hearts will rejoice
  as when people go up with flutes
to the mountain[h] of the LORD,
  to the Rock of Israel.
30 The LORD will cause men to hear his majestic voice
  and will make them see his arm coming down

30:15 [g]Isa 32:17
30:16 [h]Isa 31:1,3
30:17 [i]Lev 26:8; Jos 23:10 [j]Lev 26:36; Dt 28:25
30:18 [k]Isa 42:14; 2Pe 3:9,15 [l]Isa 5:16 [m]Isa 25:9
30:19 [n]Isa 60:20; 61:3 [o]Ps 50:15; Isa 58:9; 65:24; Mt 7:7-11
30:20 [p]1Ki 22:27 [q]Ps 74:9; Am 8:11
30:21 [r]Isa 29:24
30:22 [s]Ex 32:4
30:23 [t]Isa 65:21-22 [u]Ps 65:13
30:24 [v]Mt 3:12; Lk 3:17
30:25 [w]Isa 2:15 [x]Isa 41:18
30:26 [y]Isa 24:23; 60:19-20; Rev 21:23; 22:5 [z]Dt 32:39; Isa 1:5
30:27 [a]Isa 59:19 [b]Isa 66:14 [c]Isa 10:5
30:28 [d]Isa 11:4 [e]Isa 8:8 [f]Am 9:9 [g]2Ki 19:28; Isa 37:29
30:29 [h]Ps 42:4

30:17 For "banner," see the note on 5:26.
30:20 Bread and water were the traditional fare of prisoners (see 1Ki 22:27).
30:24 "Mash" is a reference to a salted fodder.
30:28 "Rising up to the neck" is reminiscent of 8:8 ("reaching up to the neck"), where it is descriptive of the Assyria army.

with raging anger and consuming fire,
with cloudburst, thunderstorm and hail.
31 The voice of the LORD will shatter Assyria;[i]
with his scepter he will strike[j] them down.
32 Every stroke the LORD lays on them
with his punishing rod
will be to the music of tambourines and harps,
as he fights them in battle with the blows of his arm.[k]
33 Topheth[l] has long been prepared;
it has been made ready for the king.
Its fire pit has been made deep and wide,
with an abundance of fire and wood;
the breath of the LORD,
like a stream of burning sulfur,[m]
sets it ablaze.

30:31 [i]Isa 10:5, 12 [j]Isa 11:4
30:32 [k]Isa 11:15; Eze 32:10
30:33 [l]2Ki 23:10 [m]Ge 19:24

Woe to Those Who Rely on Egypt

31 Woe to those who go down to Egypt[n] for help,
who rely on horses,
who trust in the multitude of their chariots[o]
and in the great strength of their horsemen,
but do not look to the Holy One of Israel,
or seek help from the LORD.[p]
2 Yet he too is wise[q] and can bring disaster;[r]
he does not take back his words.[s]
He will rise up against the house of the wicked,[t]
against those who help evildoers.
3 But the Egyptians[u] are men and not God;[v]
their horses are flesh and not spirit.
When the LORD stretches out his hand,[w]
he who helps will stumble,
he who is helped[x] will fall;
both will perish together.

4 This is what the LORD says to me:

"As a lion[y] growls,
a great lion over his prey—
and though a whole band of shepherds
is called together against him,
he is not frightened by their shouts
or disturbed by their clamor—
so the LORD Almighty will come down[z]
to do battle on Mount Zion and on its heights.
5 Like birds hovering overhead,
the LORD Almighty will shield[a] Jerusalem;
he will shield it and deliver[b] it,
he will 'pass over' it and will rescue it."

6 Return to him you have so greatly revolted against, O Israelites. 7 For in that day every one of you will
reject the idols of silver and gold[c] your sinful hands have made.

31:1 [n]Dt 17:16; Isa 30:2,5 [o]Isa 2:7 [p]Ps 20:7; Da 9:13
31:2 [q]Ro 16:27 [r]Isa 45:7 [s]Nu 23:19 [t]Isa 32:6
31:3 [u]Isa 36:9 [v]Eze 28:9; 2Th 2:4 [w]Isa 9:17, 21 [x]Isa 30:5-7
31:4 [y]Nu 24:9; Hos 11:10; Am 3:8 [z]Isa 42:13
31:5 [a]Ps 91:4 [b]Isa 37:35; 38:6
31:7 [c]Isa 2:20; 30:22

30:32 In the aftermath of a decisive victory, women would typically rejoice with singing and dancing (see Ex 15:20–21; 1Sa 18:6; see also "Ancient Musical Instruments" on p. 797).
30:33 Topheth, a region outside Jerusalem where children were sacrificed to Molech, the god of the Ammonites (see 1Ki 11:7; see also "Human Sacrifice in the Ancient Near East" on p. 182), was thus a place of burning.
31:1 The Egyptian military force was well supplied with horses and chariots. (See "Horses and Chariots in Ancient Warfare" on p. 114.)

31:8 [d]Isa 10:12 [e]Isa 14:25; 37:7 [f]Ge 49:15

[8] "Assyria[d] will fall by a sword that is not of man;
a sword, not of mortals, will devour[e] them.
They will flee before the sword
and their young men will be put to forced labor.[f]

31:9 [g]Dt 32:31, 37 [h]Isa 10:17

[9] Their stronghold[g] will fall because of terror;
at sight of the battle standard their commanders will panic,"
declares the LORD,
whose fire[h] is in Zion,
whose furnace is in Jerusalem.

The Kingdom of Righteousness

32:1 [i]Eze 37:24 [j]Ps 72:1-4; Isa 9:7
32:2 [k]Isa 4:6

32 See, a king[i] will reign in righteousness
and rulers will rule with justice.[j]
[2] Each man will be like a shelter[k] from the wind
and a refuge from the storm,
like streams of water in the desert
and the shadow of a great rock in a thirsty land.

32:3 [l]Isa 29:18
32:4 [m]Isa 29:24
32:5 [n]1Sa 25:25
32:6 [o]Pr 19:3 [p]Isa 9:17 [q]Isa 9:16 [r]Isa 3:15

[3] Then the eyes of those who see will no longer be closed,[l]
and the ears of those who hear will listen.
[4] The mind of the rash will know and understand,[m]
and the stammering tongue will be fluent and clear.
[5] No longer will the fool[n] be called noble
nor the scoundrel be highly respected.
[6] For the fool speaks folly,[o]
his mind is busy with evil:
He practices ungodliness[p]
and spreads error[q] concerning the LORD;
the hungry he leaves empty[r]
and from the thirsty he withholds water.

32:7 [s]Jer 5:26-28 [t]Mic 7:3 [u]Isa 61:1
32:8 [v]Pr 11:25

[7] The scoundrel's methods are wicked,[s]
he makes up evil schemes[t]
to destroy the poor with lies,
even when the plea of the needy[u] is just.
[8] But the noble man makes noble plans,
and by noble deeds[v] he stands.

The Women of Jerusalem

32:9 [w]Isa 28:23 [x]Isa 47:8; Am 6:1; Zep 2:15
32:10 [y]Isa 5:5-6; 24:7
32:11 [z]Isa 47:2

[9] You women who are so complacent,
rise up and listen[w] to me;
you daughters who feel secure,[x]
hear what I have to say!
[10] In little more than a year
you who feel secure will tremble;
the grape harvest will fail,[y]
and the harvest of fruit will not come.
[11] Tremble, you complacent women;
shudder, you daughters who feel secure!
Strip off your clothes,[z]
put sackcloth around your waists.

31:8 The angel of the Lord single-handedly struck down 185,000 soldiers (see 37:36 and its note).
31:9 Nineveh, Assyria's "stronghold," was destroyed by the combined forces of the Medes and the Babylonians in 612 B.C. (see Na 3:7; see also "Nineveh" on p. 1497).
32:10 The "year" referenced here may be that of Sennacherib's impending invasion (701 B.C.). The summer harvest would be ruined by the extensive destruction of the Assyrian armies.
32:11 For a commentary on "sackcloth," see the note on 15:3; see also "Sackcloth and Ashes: Rituals of Lamentation" on page 820.

[12]Beat your breasts[a] for the pleasant fields,
for the fruitful vines
[13]and for the land of my people,
a land overgrown with thorns and briers[b]—
yes, mourn for all houses of merriment
and for this city of revelry.[c]
[14]The fortress[d] will be abandoned,
the noisy city deserted;[e]
citadel and watchtower[f] will become a wasteland forever,
the delight of donkeys,[g] a pasture for flocks,
[15]till the Spirit[h] is poured upon us from on high,
and the desert becomes a fertile field,[i]
and the fertile field seems like a forest.[j]
[16]Justice will dwell in the desert
and righteousness live in the fertile field.
[17]The fruit of righteousness will be peace;[k]
the effect of righteousness will be quietness and confidence[l] forever.
[18]My people will live in peaceful dwelling places,
in secure homes,
in undisturbed places of rest.[m]
[19]Though hail[n] flattens the forest[o]
and the city is leveled[p] completely,
[20]how blessed you will be,
sowing[q] your seed by every stream,
and letting your cattle and donkeys range free.[r]

32:12 [a]Na 2:7
32:13 [b]Isa 5:6 [c]Isa 22:2
32:14 [d]Isa 13:22 [e]Isa 6:11; 27:10 [f]Isa 34:13 [g]Ps 104:11
32:15 [h]Isa 11:2; Joel 2:28 [i]Ps 107:35; Isa 35:1-2 [j]Isa 29:17
32:17 [k]Ps 119:165; Ro 14:17; Jas 3:18 [l]Isa 30:15
32:18 [m]Hos 2:18-23
32:19 [n]Isa 28:17; 30:30 [o]Isa 10:19; Zec 11:2 [p]Isa 24:10; 27:10
32:20 [q]Ecc 11:1 [r]Isa 30:24

Distress and Help

33

Woe to you, O destroyer,
you who have not been destroyed!
Woe to you, O traitor,
you who have not been betrayed!
When you stop destroying,
you will be destroyed;[s]
when you stop betraying,
you will be betrayed.[t]

[2]O LORD, be gracious to us;
we long for you.
Be our strength[u] every morning,
our salvation[v] in time of distress.
[3]At the thunder of your voice, the peoples flee;
when you rise up,[w] the nations scatter.
[4]Your plunder, O nations, is harvested as by young locusts;
like a swarm of locusts men pounce on it.

[5]The LORD is exalted,[x] for he dwells on high;
he will fill Zion with justice[y] and righteousness.[z]
[6]He will be the sure foundation for your times,
a rich store of salvation[a] and wisdom and knowledge;
the fear[b] of the LORD is the key to this treasure.[a]

33:1 [s]Hab 2:8; Mt 7:2 [t]Isa 21:2
33:2 [u]Isa 40:10; 51:9; 59:16 [v]Isa 25:9
33:3 [w]Isa 59:16-18
33:5 [x]Ps 97:9 [y]Isa 28:6 [z]Isa 1:26
33:6 [a]Isa 51:6 [b]Isa 11:2-3; Mt 6:33

[a] 6 Or *is a treasure from him*

33:7 [c]2Ki 18:37
33:8 [d]Jdg 5:6; Isa 35:8
33:9 [e]Isa 3:26 [f]Isa 2:13; 35:2 [g]Isa 24:4
33:10 [h]Ps 12:5; Isa 2:21
33:11 [i]Ps 7:14; Isa 59:4; Jas 1:15 [j]Isa 26:18 [k]Isa 1:31
33:12 [l]Isa 10:17
33:13 [m]Ps 48:10; 49:1 [n]Isa 49:1
33:14 [o]Isa 32:11 [p]Isa 30:30; Heb 12:29
33:15 [q]Isa 58:8 [r]Ps 15:2; 24:4 [s]Ps 119:37
33:16 [t]Isa 25:4 [u]Isa 26:1 [v]Isa 49:10
33:17 [w]Isa 6:5 [x]Isa 26:15
33:18 [y]Isa 17:14

7 Look, their brave men cry aloud in the streets;
the envoys[c] of peace weep bitterly.
8 The highways are deserted,
no travelers are on the roads.[d]
The treaty is broken,
its witnesses[a] are despised,
no one is respected.
9 The land mourns[b][e] and wastes away,
Lebanon[f] is ashamed and withers;[g]
Sharon is like the Arabah,
and Bashan and Carmel drop their leaves.

10 "Now will I arise,[h]" says the LORD.
"Now will I be exalted;
now will I be lifted up.
11 You conceive[i] chaff,
you give birth[j] to straw;
your breath is a fire[k] that consumes you.
12 The peoples will be burned as if to lime;
like cut thornbushes they will be set ablaze.[l]"

13 You who are far away,[m] hear[n] what I have done;
you who are near, acknowledge my power!
14 The sinners in Zion are terrified;
trembling[o] grips the godless:
"Who of us can dwell with the consuming fire?[p]
Who of us can dwell with everlasting burning?"
15 He who walks righteously[q]
and speaks what is right,[r]
who rejects gain from extortion
and keeps his hand from accepting bribes,
who stops his ears against plots of murder
and shuts his eyes[s] against contemplating
evil—
16 this is the man who will dwell on the heights,
whose refuge[t] will be the mountain fortress.[u]
His bread will be supplied,
and water will not fail[v] him.

17 Your eyes will see the king[w] in his beauty
and view a land that stretches afar.[x]
18 In your thoughts you will ponder the former terror:[y]
"Where is that chief officer?
Where is the one who took the revenue?
Where is the officer in charge of the towers?"

[a] 8 Dead Sea Scrolls; Masoretic Text / *the cities* [b] 9 Or *dries up*

33:7 "Their brave men" were among those of Judah who would cry aloud in Jerusalem's streets in utter desolation during Sennacherib's coming invasion (see 10:28–34).

The "envoys of peace" may allude to the three officials who would confer with the Assyrian field commander (see 36:3,22).

33:8 Enemy garrisons and marauding bands made travel and trade virtually impossible, creating economic hardship.

The "treaty" perhaps refers to the agreement made when Hezekiah paid a large tribute to Sennacherib (see the note on 2Ki 18:13–14; see also "The Sennacherib Prism" on p. 659).

33:9 Fields and pastures throughout the region would be laid waste by the ruthless intruders.

Lebanon was renowned both for its towering cedars (see 2:13 and its note) and for its abundant wildlife (40:16). Sharon, a plain along the Mediterranean coast north of Joppa, boasted spectacular foliage and rich grazing lands (see 1Ch 27:29 and Isa 35:2; 65:10). Bashan, east of the Jordan and north of Gilead, was known for its oaks (Eze 27:6) and animals (Eze 39:18), and Carmel ("fertile field," as in Isa 29:17; 32:15, or "orchards," as in 16:10) was also an area of lush pastureland (see 35:2; Na 1:4).

33:18 "Revenue" was euphemistic for forced tribute (see the note on v. 8), and "towers" was a reference to Judah's fortifications—most likely under strict Assyrian control (see 2:15).

[19] You will see those arrogant people no more,
those people of an obscure speech,
with their strange, incomprehensible tongue.[z]
[20] Look upon Zion, the city of our festivals;
your eyes will see Jerusalem,
a peaceful abode,[a] a tent that will not be moved;[b]
its stakes will never be pulled up,
nor any of its ropes broken.
[21] There the LORD will be our Mighty One.
It will be like a place of broad rivers and streams.[c]
No galley with oars will ride them,
no mighty ship will sail them.
[22] For the LORD is our judge,[d]
the LORD is our lawgiver,[e]
the LORD is our king;[f]
it is he who will save[g] us.

[23] Your rigging hangs loose:
The mast is not held secure,
the sail is not spread.
Then an abundance of spoils will be divided
and even the lame[h] will carry off plunder.[i]
[24] No one living in Zion will say, "I am ill";[j]
and the sins of those who dwell there will be forgiven.[k]

33:19 [z]Isa 28:11; Jer 5:15
33:20 [a]Isa 32:18 [b]Ps 46:5; 125:1-2
33:21 [c]Isa 41:18; 48:18; 66:12
33:22 [d]Isa 11:4 [e]Isa 2:3; Jas 4:12 [f]Ps 89:18 [g]Isa 25:9
33:23 [h]2Ki 7:8 [i]2Ki 7:16
33:24 [j]Isa 30:26 [k]Jer 50:20; 1Jn 1:7-9

Judgment Against the Nations

34

Come near, you nations, and listen;
pay attention, you peoples![l]
Let the earth[m] hear, and all that is in it,
the world, and all that comes out of it![n]
[2] The LORD is angry with all nations;
his wrath is upon all their armies.
He will totally destroy[a][o] them,
he will give them over to slaughter.[p]
[3] Their slain will be thrown out,
their dead bodies will send up a stench;[q]
the mountains will be soaked with their blood.[r]
[4] All the stars of the heavens will be dissolved[s]
and the sky rolled up[t] like a scroll;
all the starry host will fall[u]
like withered leaves from the vine,
like shriveled figs from the fig tree.

[5] My sword[v] has drunk its fill in the heavens;
see, it descends in judgment on Edom,[w]
the people I have totally destroyed.[x]

34:1 [l]Isa 41:1; 43:9 [m]Ps 49:1 [n]Dt 32:1
34:2 [o]Isa 13:5 [p]Isa 30:25
34:3 [q]Joel 2:20; Am 4:10 [r]ver 7; Eze 14:19; 35:6; 38:22
34:4 [s]Isa 13:13; 2Pe 3:10 [t]Eze 32:7-8 [u]Joel 2:31; Mt 24:29*; Rev 6:13
34:5 [v]Dt 32:41-42; Jer 46:10; Eze 21:5 [w]Am 1:11-12 [x]Isa 24:6; Mal 1:4

[a] 2 The Hebrew term refers to the irrevocable giving over of things or persons to the LORD, often by totally destroying them; also in verse 5.

33:19 The "obscure speech" of the Assyrians, although related to Hebrew, was different enough to sound strange to Israelite ears.
34:1–17 Ironically, the language we may find offensive in this passage was probably comforting to Isaiah's early hearers. Blood and gore were an integral part of their daily lives—from the slaughter of animals for food and worship to brutal warfare. This "street language" confirmed to Judah that a day would come when God would bring justice.
34:2 For commentary on "totally destroy," see "*Herem*, Holy War" on page 419.
34:3 The lack of a proper burial was viewed as humiliating in the extreme (see 14:19 and its note).
34:5 Edom (see "Edom" on p. 1467) is here representative of all of the adversaries of God and of his people. The Edomites, descendants of Isaac's son Esau, would be driven from their homeland by the Nabatean Arabs, perhaps as early as 500 B.C.

[6] The sword of the LORD is bathed in blood,
it is covered with fat—
the blood of lambs and goats,
fat from the kidneys of rams.
For the LORD has a sacrifice in Bozrah
and a great slaughter in Edom.
[7] And the wild oxen will fall with them,
the bull calves and the great bulls.[y]
Their land will be drenched with blood,
and the dust will be soaked with fat.

[8] For the LORD has a day of vengeance,[z]
a year of retribution, to uphold Zion's cause.
[9] Edom's streams will be turned into pitch,
her dust into burning sulfur;
her land will become blazing pitch!
[10] It will not be quenched night and day;
its smoke will rise forever.[a]
From generation to generation it will lie desolate;[b]
no one will ever pass through it again.
[11] The desert owl[a c] and screech owl[a] will possess it;
the great owl[a] and the raven will nest there.

34:7 [y]Ps 68:30
34:8 [z]Isa 63:4
34:10 [a]Rev 14:10-11; 19:3 [b]Isa 13:20; 24:1; Eze 29:12; Mal 1:3
34:11 [c]Zep 2:14; Rev 18:2

[a] *11* The precise identification of these birds is uncertain.

34:6 The fat, considered the choicest portion of the meat, was regularly offered to the Lord as a sacrifice (see Lev 3:9–11). "Lambs and goats" here represent the people. Biblical authors frequently compared battles to sacrifices (see Jer 46:10; 50:27; Eze 39:17–19; cf. Rev 19:17–18).

Bozrah, a significant Edomite city located about 25 miles (40 km) southeast of the southern tip of the Dead Sea, was a sheepherding center. Its name means "grape-gathering" (cf. Isa 63:1–3).

34:7 "Wild oxen" and "great bulls" called to mind the armies and/or leaders of the nations.

34:8 The Edomites used every opportunity to oppose Israel (see 2Sa 8:13–14) and reveled in her destruction (see La 4:21; cf. Ps 137:7; Jer 49:8). But Edom's day of disaster was coming (see Isa 63:1–4).

34:9 Isaiah compared Edom's ultimate demise to the annihilation of Sodom and Gomorrah (see Ge 19:24; Jer 49:17–18; see also "The Destruction of Sodom and Gomorrah" on p. 32).

ANCIENT TEXTS AND ARTIFACTS

The Great Isaiah Scroll

ISAIAH 34 Among the greatest treasures of the **Dead Sea Scrolls** found at **Qumran** was the Great Isaiah Scroll or 1QIsa[a]. The technical name 1QIsa[a] means cave *1*, *Q*umran, *Isa*iah, and the first or "a" copy of Isaiah found in that cave. Scholars recognized this scroll as the earliest-known complete copy of Isaiah (c. 125–150 B.C.), replacing a copy dating back to the tenth century A.D.! Well preserved for nearly 2,000 years, this 24-foot-long (7.3 m) leather scroll has few holes and is essentially intact. In fact, it is the oldest complete copy discovered to date of any book of the Bible.

The traditional Hebrew text for the Old Testament is the **Masoretic Text** (or MT).[1] The MT is the Hebrew Bible in use today, and except for 1QIsa[a] and other fragments of Isaiah from Qumran or elsewhere, the oldest known extant copies of Isaiah are all in the MT tradition. Though separated by 1,100 years, the MT of Isaiah and 1QIsa[a] show amazing agreement, except in minute details of spelling and minor word variations. 1QIsa[a] demonstrates that the work of generations of Jewish scribes who produced the MT is trustworthy. We have every reason to believe that the MT is a reliable copy of the Hebrew Old Testament.

In addition, the discovery of this text suggests that as far back as the second century B.C. the text of Isaiah was viewed as having only one author. Many critical scholars maintain that chapters 1–39 were written by one author, while chapters 40–66 were composed by one or more different authors. However, chapters 39 and 40 appear in the same column in 1QIsa[a], suggesting that the ancient copyist viewed these two chapters as having originated from a single author.[2]

This ancient masterpiece now rests in a Jerusalem museum, the Great Shrine of the Book.

[1]See "Texts of the Old Testament" on page 1491. [2]See "The Authorship of Isaiah" on page 1055.

God will stretch out over Edom
the measuring line of chaos
and the plumb line[d] of desolation.
12 Her nobles will have nothing there to be called a kingdom,
all her princes[e] will vanish[f] away.
13 Thorns will overrun her citadels,
nettles and brambles her strongholds.[g]
She will become a haunt for jackals,[h]
a home for owls.
14 Desert creatures will meet with hyenas,[i]
and wild goats will bleat to each other;
there the night creatures will also repose
and find for themselves places of rest.
15 The owl will nest there and lay eggs,
she will hatch them, and care for her young under the shadow of her wings;
there also the falcons[j] will gather,
each with its mate.

16 Look in the scroll[k] of the LORD and read:

None of these will be missing,
not one will lack her mate.
For it is his mouth[l] that has given the order,
and his Spirit will gather them together.
17 He allots their portions;[m]
his hand distributes them by measure.
They will possess it forever
and dwell there from generation to generation.[n]

34:11 [d]2Ki 21:13; La 2:8
34:12 [e]Jer 27:20; 39:6 [f]Isa 41:11-12
34:13 [g]Isa 13:22; 32:13 [h]Ps 44:19; Jer 9:11; 10:22
34:14 [i]Isa 13:22
34:15 [j]Dt 14:13
34:16 [k]Isa 30:8 [l]Isa 1:20; 58:14
34:17 [m]Isa 17:14; Jer 13:25 [n]ver 10

Joy of the Redeemed

35

The desert[o] and the parched land will be glad;
the wilderness will rejoice and blossom.[p]
Like the crocus, 2 it will burst into bloom;
it will rejoice greatly and shout for joy.[q]
The glory of Lebanon[r] will be given to it,
the splendor of Carmel[s] and Sharon;
they will see the glory of the LORD,
the splendor of our God.[t]

3 Strengthen the feeble hands,
steady the knees[u] that give way;
4 say to those with fearful hearts,
"Be strong, do not fear;
your God will come,
he will come with vengeance;[v]
with divine retribution
he will come to save you."
5 Then will the eyes of the blind be opened[w]
and the ears of the deaf[x] unstopped.

35:1 [o]Isa 27:10; 41:18-19 [p]Isa 51:3
35:2 [q]Isa 25:9; 55:12 [r]Isa 32:15 [s]SS 7:5 [t]Isa 25:9
35:3 [u]Job 4:4; Heb 12:12
35:4 [v]Isa 1:24; 34:8
35:5 [w]Mt 11:5; Jn 9:6-7 [x]Isa 29:18; 50:4

34:14 Throughout the ancient Near East wild goats were traditionally associated with demons (see the note on 13:21, as well as "Goat-Demons and Desert Satyrs" on p. 177).
34:15 Both owls and falcons had been declared by God to be ceremonially unclean for the Israelites (Dt 14:13,15–17).
35:1 The "wilderness" here is the Arabah (see 33:9 and its note). For "crocus," see the NIV text note on Song of Songs 2:1 and "The Flowers of Ancient Israel" on page 1037.
35:2 Lebanon, Carmel and Sharon were all fertile areas renowned throughout the region for their luxuriant stands of trees and lush foliage (see the note on 33:9).

35:6 [y]Mt 15:30; Jn 5:8-9; Ac 3:8 [z]Isa 32:4; Mt 9:32-33; 12:22; Lk 11:14 [a]Isa 41:18; Jn 7:38
35:7 [b]Isa 49:10 [c]Isa 13:22

6 Then will the lame[y] leap like a deer,
and the mute tongue[z] shout for joy.
Water will gush forth in the wilderness
and streams[a] in the desert.
7 The burning sand will become a pool,
the thirsty ground bubbling springs.[b]
In the haunts where jackals[c] once lay,
grass and reeds and papyrus will grow.

35:8 [d]Isa 11:16; 33:8; Mt 7:13-14 [e]Isa 4:3; 1Pe 1:15 [f]Isa 52:1
35:9 [g]Isa 30:6 [h]Isa 34:14 [i]Isa 51:11; 62:12; 63:4
35:10 [j]Isa 25:9 [k]Isa 30:19; 51:11; Rev 7:17; 21:4

8 And a highway[d] will be there;
it will be called the Way of Holiness.[e]
The unclean[f] will not journey on it;
it will be for those who walk in that Way;
wicked fools will not go about on it.[a]
9 No lion[g] will be there,
nor will any ferocious beast[h] get up on it;
they will not be found there.
But only the redeemed[i] will walk there,
10 and the ransomed of the LORD will return.
They will enter Zion with singing;
everlasting joy[j] will crown their heads.
Gladness and joy will overtake them,
and sorrow and sighing will flee away.[k]

Sennacherib Threatens Jerusalem

36:1 [l]2Ch 32:1
36:2 [m]Isa 7:3
36:3 [n]Isa 22:20-21 [o]2Ki 18:18

36 In the fourteenth year of King Hezekiah's reign, Sennacherib[l] king of Assyria attacked all the for-
tified cities of Judah and captured them. 2 Then the king of Assyria sent his field commander
with a large army from Lachish to King Hezekiah at Jerusalem. When the commander stopped at the aq-
ueduct of the Upper Pool, on the road to the Washerman's Field,[m] 3 Eliakim[n] son of Hilkiah the palace ad-
ministrator, Shebna[o] the secretary, and Joah son of Asaph the recorder went out to him.
4 The field commander said to them, "Tell Hezekiah,

" 'This is what the great king, the king of Assyria, says: On what are you basing this confidence
of yours? 5 You say you have strategy and military strength—but you speak only empty words. On
whom are you depending, that you rebel[p] against me? 6 Look now, you are depending on Egypt,[q]
that splintered reed[r] of a staff, which pierces a man's hand and wounds him if he leans on it! Such
is Pharaoh king of Egypt to all who depend on him. 7 And if you say to me, "We are depending on
the LORD our God"—isn't he the one whose high places and altars Hezekiah removed,[s] saying to
Judah and Jerusalem, "You must worship before this altar"?[t]

36:5 [p]2Ki 18:7
36:6 [q]Isa 30:2,5 [r]Eze 29:6-7
36:7 [s]2Ki 18:4 [t]Dt 12:2-5

[a] 8 Or / *the simple will not stray from it*

35:9 Wild animals were known to render travel dangerous (see Dt 8:15; Jdg 14:5; see also "Lions and Other Wild Beasts in Ancient Israel" on p. 813).
36:1—39:8 This historical section of the book (cf. parallel passages in Kings and Chronicles) describes the blasphemous threats of Sennacherib against Jerusalem; Hezekiah's appeal to Isaiah, who ridiculed the invader; and the flight and death of the blasphemer (chs. 36–37)—one of the most thrilling episodes in the entire Bible. In all probability the events surrounding Hezekiah's illness and the envoy of Merodach-Baladan (chs. 38–39) took place prior to the destruction of Sennacherib's army. If so, the arrangement is topical and intended to prepare the reader for the prophecies of consolation to follow.
36:1 The year was 701 B.C., the fourteenth of Hezekiah's sole reign, which lasted from 715 to 686 (he had been coregent with his father prior to that time, beginning in approximately 729 B.C.). Sennacherib's reign over Assyria (705–681) was roughly parallel to that of Hezekiah of Judah (see "Hezekiah Against the Assyrians" on p. 1118). The Sennacherib Prism (see "The Sennacherib Prism" on p. 659) lists 46 of Hezekiah's fortified cities to which Sennacherib laid siege (see the note on 2Ki 18:13–14 and "Siege Warfare" on p. 465).
36:2 Lachish was an influential city about 30 miles (48 km) southwest of Jerusalem. It guarded the main approach to Judah's capital from that quarter (see "The Lachish Reliefs" on p. 559).
For "aqueduct," see the note on 22:9.
For "Washerman's Field," see 7:3 and its note.
36:3 For "Eliakim," see the note on 22:21. The palace administrator, second only to the king, was in charge of the palace (see 22:15 and its note). For "Shebna," see the same notes.
"Secretary" may have been an equivalent position to that of the modern secretary of state. The secretary's duties presumably included domestic and foreign correspondence, perhaps record keeping on important political events and various administrative functions (see 2Ki 12:10; Jer 36:12).
"Recorder" was a position in the court associated elsewhere with "secretary" (see 1Ki 4:3).
36:5 Hezekiah's rebellion consisted of his refusal to pay the expected tribute (see the note on 2Ki 18:7).
36:6 Hezekiah had been under pressure since 715 B.C. or earlier to join in an alliance with Egypt (see the note on 30:1).
36:7 As part of his reform initiative, Hezekiah had demolished the high places, the shrines often dedicated to Baal worship (see "The High Places" on p. 1318).
"This altar" was the one in Solomon's temple.

HEZEKIAH AGAINST THE ASSYRIANS

ISAIAH 36 After a lengthy coregency with his father, Ahaz, Hezekiah ascended to the throne of Judah in 715 B.C., six years after the northern kingdom had fallen to Sargon II[1] of **Assyria**. He promptly restored the long-neglected temple and invited the remnant of the northern tribes to celebrate the Passover in Jerusalem.[2] In the beginning of his reign Hezekiah remained a loyal subject of the Assyrian king, refusing to revolt when the Philistine states did so in 711 B.C. However, when Sargon died in battle in 705 B.C., the transfer of power to his successor, along with internal pressures from the Assyrian heartland, occasioned many of Assyria's vassals, including King Hezekiah, to attempt to regain their independence. Sennacherib ascended to the Assyrian throne facing rebellion on all sides.

Assyrian relief: Assyrian warriors with Judahite prisoner at Lachish

Preserving Bible Times; © Dr. James C. Martin; permission of The British Museum

In 701 B.C. Sennacherib laid siege to Lachish, which guarded access to Jerusalem and its rebellious king.[3] Hezekiah paid a heavy tribute at this time and released Padi, the pro-Assyrian king of Ekron, from prison in Jerusalem, while Sennacherib gave some cities of western Judah to loyal Philistine kings. Nevertheless Sennacherib sent forces to besiege Jerusalem, demoralize its people and try to persuade them to hand over their king (2Ki 18:19–35; 2Ch 32:10–19; Isa 36:4–20). The prophet Isaiah encouraged Hezekiah by prophesying the deliverance of Jerusalem and the return of Sennacherib to his own land. The angel of the Lord entered the Assyrian camp, slaying 185,000 soldiers. Sennacherib's own record boasts that he had shut up Hezekiah like a caged bird but does not explain how the siege ended. Sennacherib did in fact return to Nineveh, where he was later assassinated by two of his sons.[4]

Differences in the Biblical and Assyrian accounts of Sennacherib's dealings with Hezekiah have led many scholars to posit the theory that Sennacherib led two campaigns against Jerusalem: one in 701 B.C. and the other sometime between 688 and 681. According to this proposed reconstruction of events, the first siege of Jerusalem would have ended when Hezekiah sent tribute to Nineveh (2Ki 18:14–16).[5] Later, Hezekiah may have withheld tribute and relied upon Egypt as an ally powerful enough to resist Assyria. This may have roused Sennacherib to a second siege of Jerusalem, which ended when the Lord decimated the Assyrian army overnight.

Regardless of whether we accept the theory of one Assyrian campaign against Jerusalem or two, it is certain that Hezekiah went to great lengths to prepare and fortify his nation for the onslaught:

- He protected Jerusalem's water supply, channeling the Gihon spring through the city[6] and building a wall and additional towers to prevent access to the spring from without (2Ch 32:5; cf. the reference to the two walls in Isa 22:11).
- What is known as the Broad Wall was added to the western hill of Jerusalem, and an outer wall was added to the eastern side of the city, expanding Jerusalem's area fourfold to accommodate refugees from northern Israel and western Judah.
- Hezekiah stopped up water sources in outlying areas, fortified many Judahite cities and manufactured armaments.
- Hezekiah's efforts to safeguard Jerusalem against prolonged sieges may be evidenced by the countless jars discovered throughout ancient Judah. These large jars, bearing the Hebrew letters *lmlk* ("belonging to the king") and dating to the time of Hezekiah, suggest that he was preparing and equipping storehouses of food and supplies throughout the land.

Although Sennacherib inflicted dire casualties upon Judah, the Lord delivered the city from the hand of the Assyrian monarch. God's protection, along with Hezekiah's preparations for war, proved successful against a fearsome foe.

[1]See "The Annals of Sargon II" on page 1072. [2]See "The Passover" on page 656. [3]See "The Lachish Reliefs" on page 559. [4]See "The Death of Sennacherib" on page 562. [5]See "Nineveh" on page 1497. [6]See "Hezekiah's Tunnel" on page 564.

8“ ‘Come now, make a bargain with my master, the king of Assyria: I will give you two thousand
horses—if you can put riders on them! 9How then can you repulse one officer of the least of my
36:9 [u]Isa 31:3 master’s officials, even though you are depending on Egypt[u] for chariots and horsemen?[v] 10Fur-
[v]Isa 30:2-5 **36:10** [w]1Ki 13:18 thermore, have I come to attack and destroy this land without the LORD? The LORD himself told[w]
me to march against this country and destroy it.’ ”

11Then Eliakim, Shebna and Joah said to the field commander, “Please speak to your servants in Ar-
36:11 [x]Ezr 4:7 amaic,[x] since we understand it. Don’t speak to us in Hebrew in the hearing of the people on the wall.”
12But the commander replied, “Was it only to your master and you that my master sent me to say
these things, and not to the men sitting on the wall—who, like you, will have to eat their own filth and
drink their own urine?”
36:13 [y]2Ch 32:18 13Then the commander stood and called out in Hebrew,[y] “Hear the words of the great king, the king
of Assyria! 14This is what the king says: Do not let Hezekiah deceive you. He cannot deliver you! 15Do not
let Hezekiah persuade you to trust in the LORD when he says, ‘The LORD will surely deliver us; this city will
36:15 [z]Isa 37:10 not be given into the hand of the king of Assyria.’[z]
16“Do not listen to Hezekiah. This is what the king of Assyria says: Make peace with me and come out
36:16 [a]1Ki 4:25; Zec 3:10 [b]Pr 5:15 to me. Then every one of you will eat from his own vine and fig tree[a] and drink water from his own cis-
tern,[b] 17until I come and take you to a land like your own—a land of grain and new wine, a land of bread
and vineyards.
18“Do not let Hezekiah mislead you when he says, ‘The LORD will deliver us.’ Has the god of any na-
tion ever delivered his land from the hand of the king of Assyria? 19Where are the gods of Hamath and
Arpad? Where are the gods of Sepharvaim? Have they rescued Samaria from my hand? 20Who of all the
36:20 [c]1Ki 20:23 gods[c] of these countries has been able to save his land from me? How then can the LORD deliver Jerusa-
lem from my hand?”
21But the people remained silent and said nothing in reply, because the king had commanded, “Do not
36:21 [d]Pr 9:7-8; 26:4 answer him.”[d]
22Then Eliakim son of Hilkiah the palace administrator, Shebna the secretary, and Joah son of Asaph
the recorder went to Hezekiah, with their clothes torn, and told him what the field commander had said.

Jerusalem’s Deliverance Foretold

37 When King Hezekiah heard this, he tore his clothes and put on sackcloth and went into the tem-
ple of the LORD. 2He sent Eliakim the palace administrator, Shebna the secretary, and the lead-
37:2 [e]Isa 1:1 ing priests, all wearing sackcloth, to the prophet Isaiah son of Amoz.[e] 3They told him, “This is what Hez-
ekiah says: This day is a day of distress and rebuke and disgrace, as when children come to the point of
37:3 [f]Isa 26:18; 66:9; Hos 13:13 birth[f] and there is no strength to deliver them. 4It may be that the LORD your God will hear the words of
the field commander, whom his master, the king of Assyria, has sent to ridicule the living God, and that
37:4 [g]Isa 36:13, 18-20 [h]Isa 1:9 he will rebuke him for the words the LORD your God has heard.[g] Therefore pray for the remnant[h] that
still survives.”

36:8 Two thousand horses was a sizable number for any army. Horses and chariots were highly prized (see “Horses and Chariots in Ancient Warfare” on p. 114). “Riders” probably refers to charioteers, since cavalry was not employed by these nations at this early date (see v. 9). The army of Judah at the time consisted largely of foot soldiers. The city under siege would have contained few chariots, and it is not known whether the Israelites ever employed mounted men in combat.

36:11 For “Eliakim,” see the note on 22:20–21.

Aramaic had become the international language of the Near East, known and used by those experienced in diplomacy and commerce. It is surprising that the Assyrian officials were able to speak the Hebrew dialect of the common people of Judah. The Assyrians were masters of psychological warfare, and by speaking in Hebrew, which the people of Judah could understand, the commander hoped to undermine their morale.

36:12 The graphic imagery of eating one’s own filth and drinking one’s own urine was a repulsive, if unforgettable, depiction of the dreadfulness of the coming famine in the event Jerusalem were to be besieged (see “Siege Warfare” on p. 465).

36:17 The Assyrian strategy of deporting rebellious peoples was intended to reduce their will to revolt (see the notes on 2Ki 17:3–6,24–41; see also “Exile and Genocide in the Ancient Near East” on p. 1337).

Grain and new wine were two of the staples of Israel’s diet (see the note on Hag 1:11; see also “Food and Agriculture” on p. 390).

36:19 For commentary on “Hamath” and “Arpad,” see the note on 10:9.

Residents of Sepharvaim (probably located in northern Aram/Syria, not far from Hamath), though deported to Samaria, continued worshiping their own gods, Adrammelech and Anammelech (see 2Ki 17:24,31; see also the note on 2Ki 17:24–41). The Assyrians, assuming that each people group had its own deities, did not associate the God of Judah with the gods of Samaria.

37:1–5 Eliakim, the royal steward in charge of the king’s palace; Shebna the scribe; and Joah, son of Asaph, comprised the royal delegation that met with the Assyrian envoys when Sennacherib laid siege to Jerusalem in 701 B.C. (2Ki 18:13–36; Isa 36:1–21; see also “Hezekiah Against the Assyrians” on p. 1118). When its members reported the Assyrian threats to Hezekiah (2Ki 18:37; Isa 36:22), the king dispatched Eliakim and Shebna, along with the elders of the priests, to Isaiah to ask for his prayers (2Ki 19:1–5; Isa 37:1–5). A bulla of Eliakim acquired on the antiquities market reads, “Belonging to Eliakim (son of) Hilkiah,” corresponding to Eliakim’s full name in 22:20. Fingerprints on the bulla are likely those of Eliakim himself.

37:1 For a discussion of “sackcloth,” see the note on 15:3.

37:2 For annotations on “Eliakim” and “Shebna,” see the notes on 22:15, 20–21 and 36:3.

5When King Hezekiah's officials came to Isaiah, 6Isaiah said to them, "Tell your master, 'This is what
the LORD says: Do not be afraid[i] of what you have heard—those words with which the underlings of the 37:6 [i]Isa 7:4
king of Assyria have blasphemed me. 7Listen! I am going to put a spirit in him so that when he hears a
certain report,[j] he will return to his own country, and there I will have him cut down with the sword.' " 37:7 [j]ver 9
8When the field commander heard that the king of Assyria had left Lachish, he withdrew and found
the king fighting against Libnah.[k] 37:8 [k]Nu 33:20
9Now Sennacherib received a report[l] that Tirhakah, the Cushite[a] king ⌞of Egypt⌟, was marching out 37:9 [l]ver 7
to fight against him. When he heard it, he sent messengers to Hezekiah with this word: 10"Say to Heze-
kiah king of Judah: Do not let the god you depend on deceive you when he says, 'Jerusalem will not be
handed over to the king of Assyria.'[m] 11Surely you have heard what the kings of Assyria have done to all 37:10 [m]Isa 36:15
the countries, destroying them completely. And will you be delivered?[n] 12Did the gods of the nations that 37:11 [n]Isa 36:18-20
were destroyed by my forefathers[o] deliver them—the gods of Gozan, Haran,[p] Rezeph and the people of 37:12 [o]2Ki 18:11 [p]Ge 11:31; 12:1-4; Ac 7:2
Eden who were in Tel Assar? 13Where is the king of Hamath, the king of Arpad, the king of the city of
Sepharvaim, or of Hena or Ivvah?"

Hezekiah's Prayer

14Hezekiah received the letter from the messengers and read it. Then he went up to the temple of the
LORD and spread it out before the LORD. 15And Hezekiah prayed to the LORD: 16"O LORD Almighty, God of
Israel, enthroned between the cherubim, you alone are God[q] over all the kingdoms of the earth. You have 37:16 [q]Dt 10:17; Ps 86:10; 136:2-3
made heaven and earth. 17Give ear, O LORD, and hear;[r] open your eyes, O LORD, and see;[s] listen to all the 37:17 [r]2Ch 6:40 [s]Da 9:18
words Sennacherib has sent to insult the living God.
18"It is true, O LORD, that the Assyrian kings have laid waste all these peoples and their lands.[t] 19They 37:18 [t]2Ki 15:29; Na 2:11-12
have thrown their gods into the fire and destroyed them,[u] for they were not gods[v] but only wood and 37:19 [u]Isa 26:14 [v]Isa 41:24,29
stone, fashioned by human hands. 20Now, O LORD our God, deliver us from his hand, so that all kingdoms
on earth may know that you alone, O LORD, are God.[b][w] 37:20 [w]Ps 46:10

Sennacherib's Fall

21Then Isaiah son of Amoz[x] sent a message to Hezekiah: "This is what the LORD, the God of Israel, 37:21 [x]ver 2
says: Because you have prayed to me concerning Sennacherib king of Assyria, 22this is the word the LORD
has spoken against him:

"The Virgin Daughter of Zion
despises and mocks you.
The Daughter of Jerusalem
tosses her head[y] as you flee. 37:22 [y]Job 16:4
23Who is it you have insulted and blasphemed?[z] 37:23 [z]ver 4 [a]Isa 2:11
Against whom have you raised your voice
and lifted your eyes in pride?[a]
Against the Holy One of Israel!
24By your messengers
you have heaped insults on the Lord.
And you have said,
'With my many chariots
I have ascended the heights of the mountains,
the utmost heights of Lebanon.[b] 37:24 [b]Isa 14:8

[a] 9 That is, from the upper Nile region [b] 20 Dead Sea Scrolls (see also 2 Kings 19:19); Masoretic Text *alone are the LORD*

37:9 In 701 B.C. Tirhakah was still a prince. His brother Shebitku, Egypt's new pharaoh, sent him with an army to help Hezekiah withstand the Assyrian invasion. Tirhakah eventually ascended to the throne in 690. But since this portion of Isaiah was written after 681, it was natural for the prophet to refer to him as king.

37:12 Gozan was a city in northern Mesopotamia to which some of the Israelites had been deported by the Assyrians (see 2Ki 17:6 and its note).

Haran was a city west of Gozan where Abraham had lived for a number of years (see Ge 11:31; see also "Haran" on p. 47). Rezeph was a city between Haran and the Euphrates River. Eden, the Aramean city-state of Bit Adini, was located between the Euphrates and Balikh Rivers.

37:13 For "Hamath" and "Arpad," see the note on 10:9.

37:22 "Virgin Daughter of Zion" and "Daughter of Jerusalem" are both personifications of Jerusalem.

Tossing one's head was a gesture of mocking or scorn.

37:24 For "many chariots," see the note on 36:8.

Lebanon was famed for its fertile land, beautiful foliage and magnificent cedars (see the notes on 2:13; 9:10; 14:8; see also "Cedars of Lebanon" on p. 1043). For centuries the kings of Mesopotamia had used the cedars of Lebanon in their royal buildings (see 1Ki 5:8–10).

I have cut down its tallest cedars,
the choicest of its pines.
I have reached its remotest heights,
the finest of its forests.
25 I have dug wells in foreign lands[a]
and drunk the water there.
With the soles of my feet
I have dried up all the streams of Egypt.[c]
26 "Have you not heard?
Long ago I ordained[d] it.
In days of old I planned[e] it;
now I have brought it to pass,
that you have turned fortified cities
into piles of stone.[f]
27 Their people, drained of power,
are dismayed and put to shame.
They are like plants in the field,
like tender green shoots,
like grass sprouting on the roof,[g]
scorched[b] before it grows up.
28 "But I know where you stay
and when you come and go[h]
and how you rage[i] against me.
29 Because you rage against me
and because your insolence[j] has reached my ears,
I will put my hook in your nose[k]
and my bit in your mouth,
and I will make you return
by the way you came.[l]

30 "This will be the sign for you, O Hezekiah:

"This year you will eat what grows by itself,
and the second year what springs from that.
But in the third year sow and reap,
plant vineyards and eat their fruit.
31 Once more a remnant of the house of Judah
will take root below and bear fruit[m] above.
32 For out of Jerusalem will come a remnant,
and out of Mount Zion a band of survivors.
The zeal[n] of the LORD Almighty
will accomplish this.

33 "Therefore this is what the LORD says concerning the king of Assyria:

"He will not enter this city
or shoot an arrow here.
He will not come before it with shield
or build a siege ramp against it.

37:25 [c]Dt 11:10
37:26 [d]Ac 2:23; 4:27-28; 1Pe 2:8 [e]Isa 10:6; 25:1 [f]Isa 25:2
37:27 [g]Ps 129:6
37:28 [h]Ps 139:1-3 [i]Ps 2:1
37:29 [j]Isa 10:12 [k]Isa 30:28; Eze 38:4 [l]ver 34
37:31 [m]Isa 27:6
37:32 [n]Isa 9:7

[a] 25 Dead Sea Scrolls (see also 2 Kings 19:24); Masoretic Text does not have *in foreign lands.* [b] 27 Some manuscripts of the Masoretic Text, Dead Sea Scrolls and some Septuagint manuscripts (see also 2 Kings 19:26); most manuscripts of the Masoretic Text *roof / and terraced fields*

37:25 Neither the deprivation of desert lands nor the water of the Nile's branches hampered Sennacherib's relentless forward progress.
37:29 The Assyrians were notorious for leading away their captives by ropes tied to rings in their noses (see the note on 2Ki 19:28).
37:33 Siege ramps helped an invading army to bring up battering rams and scale a city's walls (see "Siege Warfare" on p. 465).

ANCIENT VOICES

There is no escaping from my fears
by myself,
I am seized by an evil sickness.
My sickness is an unlit darkness, not
visible to man.
The physician will not look upon it,
will not s[oothe?]* it with a bandage.
The exorcists will not recite a spell,
assuredly my sickness has not diagnosis.
My sickness: its (healing) herb has not
sprouted forth
on plain (or) mountain, no one gets it
for me.
Healing my sickness is with you (alone),
let me declare your exaltation:
"As my [mother] has abandoned me since
my childhood,
I am the one who has no [mother],
no one recites my lament to you,
you are my mother!
Except [for you], I do not have another
personal goddess,
no one pleads for mercy to you on
my behalf.
No one seeks [for mercy?] from you
for me,
you are my personal goddess!"

*Words or partial words in brackets or parentheses added by translator for clarity or where text has gaps

—THE LETTER-PRAYER OF KING SIN-IDDINAM TO NIN-ISINA

See "The Sumerian Prayer Letter of King Sin-Iddinam" article.

34 By the way that he came he will return;[o]
he will not enter this city,"
declares the LORD.

37:34 [o]ver 29

35 "I will defend[p] this city and save it,
for my sake[q] and for the sake of David[r]
my servant!"

37:35 [p]Isa 31:5; 38:6 [q]Isa 43:25; 48:9,11 [r]2Ki 20:6

36 Then the angel of the LORD went out and put to death a hun-
dred and eighty-five thousand men in the Assyrian[s] camp. When
the people got up the next morning—there were all the dead bod-
ies! 37 So Sennacherib king of Assyria broke camp and withdrew. He
returned to Nineveh[t] and stayed there.
38 One day, while he was worshiping in the temple of his god Nis-
roch, his sons Adrammelech and Sharezer cut him down with the
sword, and they escaped to the land of Ararat.[u] And Esarhaddon his
son succeeded him as king.

37:36 [s]Isa 10:12
37:37 [t]Ge 10:11
37:38 [u]Ge 8:4; Jer 51:27

Hezekiah's Illness

38 In those days Hezekiah became ill and was at the point of
death. The prophet Isaiah son of Amoz[v] went to him and
said, "This is what the LORD says: Put your house in order,[w] because
you are going to die; you will not recover."
2 Hezekiah turned his face to the wall and prayed to the LORD,
3 "Remember, O LORD, how I have walked[x] before you faithfully and
with wholehearted devotion[y] and have done what is good in your
eyes.[z]" And Hezekiah wept[a] bitterly.
4 Then the word of the LORD came to Isaiah: 5 "Go and tell Heze-
kiah, 'This is what the LORD, the God of your father David, says: I
have heard your prayer and seen your tears; I will add fifteen years[b]
to your life. 6 And I will deliver you and this city from the hand of the
king of Assyria. I will defend[c] this city.
7 " 'This is the LORD's sign[d] to you that the LORD will do what he
has promised: 8 I will make the shadow cast by the sun go back the
ten steps it has gone down on the stairway of Ahaz.' " So the sun-
light went back the ten steps it had gone down.[e]

38:1 [v]Isa 37:2 [w]2Sa 17:23
38:3 [x]Ne 13:14; Ps 26:3 [y]1Ch 29:19 [z]Dt 6:18 [a]Ps 6:8
38:5 [b]2Ki 18:2
38:6 [c]Isa 31:5; 37:35
38:7 [d]Isa 7:11,14
38:8 [e]Jos 10:13

9 A writing of Hezekiah king of Judah after his illness and recovery:

10 I said, "In the prime of my life[f]
must I go through the gates of death[a][g]
and be robbed of the rest of my years?[h]"
11 I said, "I will not again see the LORD,
the LORD, in the land of the living;[i]
no longer will I look on mankind,
or be with those who now dwell in this world.[b]
12 Like a shepherd's tent[j] my house
has been pulled down[k] and taken from me.

38:10 [f]Ps 102:24 [g]Ps 107:18; 2Co 1:9 [h]Job 17:11
38:11 [i]Ps 27:13; 116:9
38:12 [j]2Co 5:1,4; 2Pe 1:13-14 [k]Job 4:21

[a] 10 Hebrew *Sheol* [b] 11 A few Hebrew manuscripts; most Hebrew manuscripts *in the place of cessation*

37:36 Throughout the Old Testament we see instances of God dispatching angelic agents as carriers of plague (cf. Ex 12:12–13; 2Sa 24:15–16; 1Ch 21:22,27). The deaths of these soldiers fulfilled the prophecies of Isaiah 10:33–34, 30:31 and 31:8.
37:37 Nineveh was the capital of Assyria (see Jnh 1:2 and "Nineveh" on p. 1497).
37:38 Sennacherib was assassinated while in the temple of his god (see "The Death of Sennacherib" on p. 562). Sennacherib's designation of Esarhaddon, who was younger than several of his brothers, as heir apparent may well have sparked the abortive coup attempt by Adrammelech and Sharezer. Esarhaddon reigned from 681 to 669 B.C..

Ararat, or Urartu, lay north of Assyria in Armenia (see the note on Ge 8:4).
38:1 This account took place at some point prior to Sennacherib's invasion of 701 B.C. (see v. 6).

38:12 [l]Heb 1:12 [m]Job 7:6 [n]Ps 73:14
38:13 [o]Ps 51:8 [p]Job 10:16; Da 6:24
38:14 [q]Isa 59:11

Like a weaver I have rolled[l] up my life,
and he has cut me off from the loom;[m]
day and night[n] you made an end of me.
13 I waited patiently till dawn,
but like a lion he broke[o] all my bones;[p]
day and night you made an end of me.
14 I cried like a swift or thrush,
I moaned like a mourning dove.[q]

ANCIENT TEXTS AND ARTIFACTS

The Sumerian Prayer Letter of King Sin-Iddinam

A prayer letter from an Assyrian army commander to the god Shamash, asking for an oracle concerning a military campaign

Preserving Bible Times; © Dr. James C. Martin; permission of The British Museum

ISAIAH 38 The modern reader may be surprised that in Isaiah 38:9–20 Hezekiah's prayer is recorded as a "writing," or letter. The genre of the "prayer letter," however, is well attested in **Sumerian** and **Akkadian** literature. It is first known from the libraries of private individuals but later developed as a common means for royal figures to petition the gods. An example of this form of communication is the Sumerian prayer letter of King Sin-Iddinam of Larsa (c. mid-nineteenth century B.C.). Sin-Iddinam wrote to Nin-Isina, the patron goddess of the city of Isin (the rival city of Larsa), complaining that although he had been a faithful shepherd of the nation under his care, the city of Isin continued to raid his territory. Furthermore, he had been cursed with an incurable disease that defied diagnosis. Appealing to the goddess as though she were his own true mother, Sin-Iddinam begged Nin-Isina to petition her divine son Damu (the god of healing) on his behalf. The letter ends with the king on the brink of death, crying for Nin-Isina to have mercy and call upon Damu. A subsequent letter in the name of Nin-Isina to her divine son on behalf of King Sin-Iddinam appears to be the answer to the king's prayer.

Another prayer letter, this one an Akkadian missive written by a military officer, is addressed to the god Shamash. In it the officer asked for an oracle on the success of a planned campaign.

In Isaiah 38 King Hezekiah of Judah used the prayer letter genre to address **Yahweh**. Having been inflicted with a near-fatal illness, Hezekiah pleaded for healing while recounting his obedience and devotion to God. When the Lord heard his prayer and granted him 15 additional years of life, the king wrote another prayer letter, detailing the extent of his sickness and praising God for his healing restoration and loving faithfulness. In so doing Hezekiah demonstrated true loyalty: He did not call upon God only when experiencing life-threatening difficulty but remembered also to thank and praise him after his full recovery.

My eyes grew weak as I looked to the heavens.
I am troubled; O Lord, come to my aid!"[r]

15 But what can I say?
He has spoken to me, and he himself has done this.[s]
I will walk humbly[t] all my years
because of this anguish of my soul.[u]
16 Lord, by such things men live;
and my spirit finds life in them too.
You restored me to health
and let me live.[v]
17 Surely it was for my benefit
that I suffered such anguish.
In your love you kept me
from the pit[w] of destruction;
you have put all my sins[x]
behind your back.[y]
18 For the grave[a][z] cannot praise you,
death cannot sing your praise;[a]

38:14 [r]Job 17:3
38:15 [s]Ps 39:9 [t]1Ki 21:27 [u]Job 7:11
38:16 [v]Ps 119:25
38:17 [w]Ps 30:3 [x]Jer 31:34 [y]Isa 43:25; Mic 7:19
38:18 [z]Ecc 9:10 [a]Ps 6:5; 88:10-11; 115:17

[a] 18 Hebrew *Sheol*

38:17 The "pit of destruction" here refers to the grave.
38:18 For a discussion of Sheol, see the note on Job 17:13–16. See also "Sheol, Hades, Gehenna, the Abyss and Tartarus: Images of Hell" on page 946.

Sennacherib's Campaign Against Merodach-Baladan

ISAIAH 39 In Isaiah 39:1 Merodach-Baladan (a Hebrew form of his **Akkadian** name, Marduk-apla-iddina), the king of **Babylon**, sent envoys to Hezekiah. Merodach-Baladan, a ruler within the Chaldean tribe of Bit Yakin, spent his career trying to wrest Babylon from **Assyrian** control.

Although he paid tribute to the Assyrian Emperor Tiglath-Pileser III, Merodach-Baladan rebelled against Sargon II with help from the neighboring **Elamites**. By 710 B.C. Sargon II had defeated Merodach-Baladan and forced him to flee to Elam.[1] Upon Sargon's death his son Sennacherib became the Assyrian emperor, and once again Merodach-Baladan rebelled. Perhaps Hezekiah's aid was sought by Merodach-Baladan at this juncture, resulting in an alliance that may have led to the Assyrian siege of Jerusalem.[2] To address this sedition Sennacherib faced Merodach-Baladan at Kish and again forced him into exile. Although a seemingly loyal puppet named Bel-ibni was installed by Sennacherib over Babylon, Bel-ibni led another revolt, and Merodach-Baladan reasserted his power in the aftermath of the insurrection.

With the demise of Bel-ibni's mutiny in Babylon and Sennacherib's control secured yet again, the Assyrian emperor sought a final solution to the troublesome Merodach-Baladan. In 694 B.C. Sennacherib sent his army to flush his nemesis out of the marshes in southern Babylonia, But with the Assyrian army so far south, the Elamites exploited this weakness and again seized control of Babylon. Although Sennacherib was eventually able to oust the Elamite incursion, Merodach-Baladan escaped his grasp and apparently fled to Elam, where he lived out his days. His brief appearance within Isaiah (and in 2Ki 20:12) is appropriate, given the elusive nature of his career.

[1]See "The Annals of Sargon II" on page 1072. [2]See "Hezekiah Against the Assyrians" on page 1118.

38:18 [b]Ps 30:9 those who go down to the pit[b]
cannot hope for your faithfulness.
38:19 [c]Dt 6:7; Ps 118:17; 119:175 [d]Dt 11:19 19 The living, the living—they praise[c] you,
as I am doing today;
fathers tell their children[d]
about your faithfulness.

20 The LORD will save me,
38:20 [e]Ps 68:25 [f]Ps 33:2 [g]Ps 116:2 [h]Ps 116:17-19 and we will sing[e] with stringed instruments[f]
all the days of our lives[g]
in the temple[h] of the LORD.

21 Isaiah had said, "Prepare a poultice of figs and apply it to the boil, and he will recover."
22 Hezekiah had asked, "What will be the sign that I will go up to the temple of the LORD?"

Envoys From Babylon

39:1 [i]2Ch 32:31 39 At that time Merodach-Baladan son of Baladan king of Babylon[i] sent Hezekiah letters and a gift,
39:2 [j]2Ch 32:31 [k]2Ki 18:15 because he had heard of his illness and recovery. 2 Hezekiah received the envoys[j] gladly and
showed them what was in his storehouses—the silver, the gold,[k] the spices, the fine oil, his entire ar-
mory and everything found among his treasures. There was nothing in his palace or in all his kingdom
that Hezekiah did not show them.
3 Then Isaiah the prophet went to King Hezekiah and asked, "What did those men say, and where did
they come from?"
39:3 [l]Dt 28:49 "From a distant land,[l]" Hezekiah replied. "They came to me from Babylon."
4 The prophet asked, "What did they see in your palace?"
"They saw everything in my palace," Hezekiah said. "There is nothing among my treasures that I did
not show them."
5 Then Isaiah said to Hezekiah, "Hear the word of the LORD Almighty: 6 The time will surely come when
everything in your palace, and all that your fathers have stored up until this day, will be carried off to
39:6 [m]2Ki 24:13; Jer 20:5 Babylon.[m] Nothing will be left, says the LORD. 7 And some of your descendants, your own flesh and blood
who will be born to you, will be taken away, and they will become eunuchs in the palace of the king of
39:7 [n]2Ki 24:15; Da 1:1-7 Babylon.[n]"
8 "The word of the LORD you have spoken is good," Hezekiah replied. For he thought, "There will be
39:8 [o]2Ch 32:26 peace and security in my lifetime.[o]"

Comfort for God's People

40:1 [p]Isa 12:1; 49:13; 51:3,12; 52:9; 61:2; 66:13; Jer 31:13; Zep 3:14-17; 2Co 1:3 40 Comfort, comfort[p] my people,
says your God.
40:2 [q]Isa 35:4 [r]Isa 41:11-13; 49:25 [s]Isa 61:7; Jer 16:18; Zec 9:12; Rev 18:6 2 Speak tenderly[q] to Jerusalem,
and proclaim to her
that her hard service has been completed,[r]
that her sin has been paid for,
that she has received from the LORD's hand
double[s] for all her sins.

38:20 Instrumental music and hymns of praise were closely linked in worship (cf. Ps 33:1–3; 150; see also "Ancient Musical Instruments" on p. 797).
38:21 The plural verbs in this verse were likely addressed to the court physicians. Figs were used medicinally in ancient Ugarit (see "Ugarit/Ras Shamra" on p. 819).
39:7 For "eunuchs," compare Daniel 1:3–6 (where the Hebrew for "court officials" in v. 3 can also be rendered "eunuchs"); see also "The Eunuch" on page 1159.
The "king of Babylon" was Nebuchadnezzar (see "Nebuchadnezzar" on p. 571).
40:1—66:24 These chapters have been called the Book of Consolation. The words "Comfort, comfort my people" were clearly intended to engender within Israel a comfort and hope not to be gathered from Hezekiah's words, which they immediately follow. These chapters fall into three parts as suggested by the refrain-like words "'There is no peace,' says the LORD, 'for the wicked'" (48:22; cf. 57:21), which find their terrible echo in Isaiah's final words (66:24). See the separate notes on 40:1—48:22, 49:1—57:21 and 58:1—66:24.
40:1—48:22 Chapters 40–48 deal with the coming of Cyrus and the fall of Babylon as proof of the power of the God of Israel both to foretell and to fulfill, in amazing contrast to the idols of the heathen, which could do neither. The utter folly of idolatry is portrayed most vividly in 44:9–20 and 46:1–11. The last mention of Babylon (48:20) is clearly a description of flight from a doomed city, like that of Lot from Sodom. In the two remaining divisions of the book, 49:1—57:21 and 58:1—66:24, there is no mention of either Assyria or Babylon except by way of reminiscence (52:4).

[3] A voice of one calling:
"In the desert prepare
the way[t] for the LORD[a];
make straight in the wilderness
a highway for our God.[b][u]
[4] Every valley shall be raised up,
every mountain and hill made low;
the rough ground shall become level,[v]
the rugged places a plain.
[5] And the glory of the LORD will be revealed,
and all mankind together will see it.[w]
For the mouth of the LORD has spoken."[x]
[6] A voice says, "Cry out."
And I said, "What shall I cry?"

"All men are like grass,[y]
and all their glory is like the flowers of the field.
[7] The grass withers and the flowers fall,
because the breath[z] of the LORD blows on them.
Surely the people are grass.
[8] The grass withers and the flowers fall,
but the word[a] of our God stands forever.[b]"
[9] You who bring good tidings[c] to Zion,
go up on a high mountain.
You who bring good tidings to Jerusalem,[c]
lift up your voice with a shout,
lift it up, do not be afraid;
say to the towns of Judah,
"Here is your God!"[d]
[10] See, the Sovereign LORD comes[e] with power,
and his arm[f] rules[g] for him.
See, his reward[h] is with him,
and his recompense accompanies him.
[11] He tends his flock like a shepherd:[i]
He gathers the lambs in his arms
and carries them close to his heart;
he gently leads those that have young.

[12] Who has measured the waters[j] in the hollow of his hand,[k]
or with the breadth of his hand marked off the heavens?[l]
Who has held the dust of the earth in a basket,
or weighed the mountains on the scales
and the hills in a balance?
[13] Who has understood the mind[d] of the LORD,
or instructed him as his counselor?[m]
[14] Whom did the LORD consult to enlighten him,
and who taught him the right way?
Who was it that taught him knowledge[n]
or showed him the path of understanding?

40:3 [t]Mal 3:1 [u]Mt 3:3*; Mk 1:3*; Jn 1:23*
40:4 [v]Isa 45:2,13
40:5 [w]Isa 52:10; Lk 3:4-6* [x]Isa 1:20; 58:14
40:6 [y]Job 14:2
40:7 [z]Job 41:21
40:8 [a]Isa 55:11; 59:21 [b]Mt 5:18; 1Pe 1:24-25*
40:9 [c]Isa 52:7-10; 61:1; Ro 10:15 [d]Isa 25:9
40:10 [e]Rev 22:7 [f]Isa 59:16 [g]Isa 9:6-7 [h]Isa 62:11; Rev 22:12
40:11 [i]Eze 34:23; Mic 5:4; Jn 10:11
40:12 [j]Job 38:10 [k]Pr 30:4 [l]Heb 1:10-12
40:13 [m]Ro 11:34*; 1Co 2:16*
40:14 [n]Job 21:22; Col 2:3

[a] 3 Or *A voice of one calling in the desert: / "Prepare the way for the LORD* [b] 3 Hebrew; Septuagint *make straight the paths of our God* [c] 9 Or *O Zion, bringer of good tidings, / go up on a high mountain. / O Jerusalem, bringer of good tidings* [d] 13 Or *Spirit*; or *spirit*

40:3 "Prepar[ing] the way" was idiomatic for clearing away obstacles from the road (cf. 57:14; 62:10). It was customary in the ancient Near East to dispatch representatives ahead in preparation for a king's visit.

[15] Surely the nations are like a drop in a bucket;
they are regarded as dust on the scales;
he weighs the islands as though they were fine dust.
[16] Lebanon is not sufficient for altar fires,
nor its animals[o] enough for burnt offerings.
[17] Before him all the nations[p] are as nothing;[q]
they are regarded by him as worthless
and less than nothing.[r]

[18] To whom, then, will you compare God?[s]
What image[t] will you compare him to?
[19] As for an idol,[u] a craftsman casts it,
and a goldsmith[v] overlays it with gold[w]
and fashions silver chains for it.
[20] A man too poor to present such an offering
selects wood that will not rot.
He looks for a skilled craftsman
to set up an idol that will not topple.[x]

[21] Do you not know?
Have you not heard?
Has it not been told[y] you from the beginning?
Have you not understood[z] since the earth
was founded?[a]
[22] He sits enthroned above the circle of the earth,
and its people are like grasshoppers.[b]
He stretches out the heavens like a canopy,[c]
and spreads them out like a tent[d] to live in.
[23] He brings princes[e] to naught
and reduces the rulers of this world to nothing.[f]
[24] No sooner are they planted,
no sooner are they sown,
no sooner do they take root in the ground,
than he blows[g] on them and they wither,
and a whirlwind sweeps them away like chaff.

[25] "To whom will you compare me?[h]
Or who is my equal?" says the Holy One.
[26] Lift your eyes and look to the heavens:[i]
Who created[j] all these?
He who brings out the starry host[k] one by one,
and calls them each by name.
Because of his great power and mighty strength,
not one of them is missing.[l]

[27] Why do you say, O Jacob,
and complain, O Israel,
"My way is hidden from the LORD;
my cause is disregarded by my God"?[m]
[28] Do you not know?
Have you not heard?[n]
The LORD is the everlasting[o] God,
the Creator of the ends of the earth.

40:16 [o]Ps 50:9-11; Mic 6:7; Heb 10:5-9
40:17 [p]Isa 30:28 [q]Isa 29:7 [r]Da 4:35
40:18 [s]Ex 8:10; 1Sa 2:2; Isa 46:5 [t]Ac 17:29
40:19 [u]Ps 115:4 [v]Isa 41:7; Jer 10:3 [w]Isa 2:20
40:20 [x]1Sa 5:3
40:21 [y]Ps 19:1; 50:6; Ac 14:17 [z]Ro 1:19 [a]Isa 48:13; 51:13
40:22 [b]Nu 13:33; Ps 104:2; Isa 42:5 [c]Job 22:14 [d]Job 36:29
40:23 [e]Isa 34:12 [f]Job 12:21; Ps 107:40
40:24 [g]Isa 41:16
40:25 [h]ver 18
40:26 [i]Isa 51:6 [j]Ps 89:11-13; Isa 42:5 [k]Ps 147:4 [l]Isa 34:16
40:27 [m]Job 27:2; Lk 18:7-8
40:28 [n]ver 21 [o]Ps 90:2

40:16 Lebanon was a fertile region known throughout the ancient Near East for its stands of towering cedars (see "Cedars of Lebanon" on p. 1043), as well as for its birds and alpine animals.

He will not grow tired or weary,
and his understanding no one can fathom.[p]
29 He gives strength to the weary[q]
and increases the power of the weak.
30 Even youths grow tired and weary,
and young men[r] stumble and fall;
31 but those who hope[s] in the LORD
will renew their strength.[t]
They will soar on wings like eagles;[u]
they will run and not grow weary,
they will walk and not be faint.[v]

The Helper of Israel

41

"Be silent[w] before me, you islands![x]
Let the nations renew their strength!
Let them come forward[y] and speak;
let us meet together[z] at the place of judgment.

2 "Who has stirred[a] up one from the east,[b]
calling him in righteousness to his service[a]?
He hands nations over to him
and subdues kings before him.
He turns them to dust[c] with his sword,
to windblown chaff[d] with his bow.
3 He pursues them and moves on unscathed,
by a path his feet have not traveled before.
4 Who has done this and carried it through,
calling forth the generations from the beginning?[e]
I, the LORD—with the first of them
and with the last[f]—I am he."

5 The islands[g] have seen it and fear;
the ends of the earth tremble.
They approach and come forward;
6 each helps the other
and says to his brother, "Be strong!"
7 The craftsman encourages the goldsmith,[h]
and he who smooths with the hammer
spurs on him who strikes the anvil.
He says of the welding, "It is good."
He nails down the idol so it will not topple.

8 "But you, O Israel, my servant,
Jacob, whom I have chosen,
you descendants of Abraham[i] my friend,[j]
9 I took you from the ends of the earth,[k]
from its farthest corners I called you.
I said, 'You are my servant';
I have chosen[l] you and have not rejected you.

40:28 [p]Ps 147:5; Ro 11:33 **40:29** [q]Isa 50:4; Jer 31:25
40:30 [r]Isa 9:17; Jer 6:11; 9:21 **40:31** [s]Lk 18:1 [t]2Co 4:16 [u]Ex 19:4; Ps 103:5 [v]2Co 4:1; Heb 12:1-3
41:1 [w]Hab 2:20; Zec 2:13 [x]Isa 11:11 [y]Isa 48:16 [z]Isa 1:18; 34:1; 50:8
41:2 [a]Ezr 1:2 [b]ver 25; Isa 45:1, 13 [c]2Sa 22:43 [d]Isa 40:24
41:4 [e]ver 26; Isa 46:10 [f]Isa 44:6; 48:12; Rev 1:8,17; 22:13
41:5 [g]Eze 26:17-18
41:7 [h]Isa 40:19
41:8 [i]Isa 29:22; 51:2; 63:16 [j]2Ch 20:7; Jas 2:23 **41:9** [k]Isa 11:12 [l]Dt 7:6

[a] 2 Or / *whom victory meets at every step*

41:1 "Islands" refers to the Mediterranean coastlands and islands.
41:2 God would call "one from the east," Cyrus the Great, king of Persia (559–530 B.C.), to bring down the Babylonian Empire. This prophecy was fulfilled when Cyrus conquered Babylon in 539 B.C. (see the note on 13:17). He then issued a decree permitting the Jews to return to Jerusalem (see Ezr 1:1–4; 6:3–5; see also "Cyrus the Great" on p. 669). The Lord would give the nations into Cyrus's hand. Cyrus would scatter them like "windblown chaff" (see the note on Isa 17:13) with his "bow" (the Persians were renowned for their ability as archers).
41:5–7 By 546 B.C. Cyrus of Persia had fought his way victoriously to the western coast of Asia Minor, where his leading opponent was Croesus of Lydia.

41:10 [m]Jos 1:9; Isa 43:2,5; Ro 8:31 [n]ver 13-14; Isa 44:2; 49:8

10 So do not fear, for I am with you;[m]
do not be dismayed, for I am your God.
I will strengthen you and help[n] you;
I will uphold you with my righteous right hand.

41:11 [o]Isa 17:12 [p]Isa 45:24 [q]Ex 23:22 [r]Isa 29:8

11 "All who rage[o] against you
will surely be ashamed and disgraced;[p]
those who oppose[q] you
will be as nothing and perish.[r]

41:12 [s]Ps 37:35-36 [t]Isa 17:14

12 Though you search for your enemies,
you will not find them.[s]
Those who wage war against you
will be as nothing[t] at all.

41:13 [u]Isa 42:6; 45:1 [v]ver 10

13 For I am the LORD, your God,
who takes hold of your right hand[u]
and says to you, Do not fear;
I will help[v] you.
14 Do not be afraid, O worm Jacob,
O little Israel,
for I myself will help you," declares the LORD,
your Redeemer, the Holy One of Israel.

41:15 [w]Mic 4:13

15 "See, I will make you into a threshing sledge,[w]
new and sharp, with many teeth.
You will thresh the mountains and crush them,
and reduce the hills to chaff.

41:16 [x]Jer 51:2 [y]Isa 45:25

16 You will winnow[x] them, the wind will pick them up,
and a gale will blow them away.
But you will rejoice in the LORD
and glory[y] in the Holy One of Israel.

41:17 [z]Isa 43:20 [a]Isa 30:19

17 "The poor and needy search for water,[z]
but there is none;
their tongues are parched with thirst.
But I the LORD will answer[a] them;
I, the God of Israel, will not forsake them.

41:18 [b]Isa 30:25 [c]Isa 43:19 [d]Isa 35:7

18 I will make rivers flow[b] on barren heights,
and springs within the valleys.
I will turn the desert[c] into pools of water,
and the parched ground into springs.[d]

41:19 [e]Isa 60:13

19 I will put in the desert
the cedar and the acacia, the myrtle and the olive.
I will set pines in the wasteland,
the fir and the cypress together,[e]
20 so that people may see and know,
may consider and understand,
that the hand of the LORD has done this,

41:20 [f]Job 12:9

that the Holy One of Israel has created[f] it.

41:21 [g]Isa 43:15

21 "Present your case," says the LORD.
"Set forth your arguments," says Jacob's King.[g]

41:22 [h]Isa 43:9; 45:21

22 "Bring in ⌞your idols⌟ to tell us
what is going to happen.[h]

41:14 "Redeemer" in this context refers to the deliverer of Judah from Babylonian exile (in a new exodus). The Hebrew for this word is associated with an obligated family protector (see "The Kinsman-Redeemer" on p. 391), which here depicts the Lord as Israel's family defender.

41:15–16 "Threshing sledge," "thresh" and "winnow" are metaphors of judgment. For information on the threshing process, see the note on Ruth 1:22; see also "The Threshing Floor" on page 608.

Tell us what the former things were,
so that we may consider them
and know their final outcome.
Or declare to us the things to come,[i]
23 tell us what the future holds,
so we may know[j] that you are gods.
Do something, whether good or bad,[k]
so that we will be dismayed and filled with fear.
24 But you are less than nothing[l]
and your works are utterly worthless;
he who chooses you is detestable.[m]

25 "I have stirred up one from the north,[n] and he comes—
one from the rising sun who calls on my name.
He treads[o] on rulers as if they were mortar,
as if he were a potter treading the clay.
26 Who told of this from the beginning, so we could know,
or beforehand, so we could say, 'He was right'?
No one told of this,
no one foretold it,
no one heard any words[p] from you.
27 I was the first to tell[q] Zion, 'Look, here they are!'
I gave to Jerusalem a messenger of good tidings.[r]
28 I look but there is no one[s]—
no one among them to give counsel,[t]
no one to give answer when I ask them.
29 See, they are all false!
Their deeds amount to nothing;[u]
their images are but wind[v] and confusion.

41:22 [i]Isa 46:10
41:23 [j]Isa 42:9; 44:7-8; 45:3 [k]Jer 10:5
41:24 [l]Isa 37:19; 44:9; 1Co 8:4 [m]Ps 115:8
41:25 [n]ver 2 [o]2Sa 22:43
41:26 [p]Hab 2:18-19
41:27 [q]Isa 48:3, 16 [r]Isa 40:9
41:28 [s]Isa 50:2; 59:16; 63:5 [t]Isa 40:13-14
41:29 [u]ver 24 [v]Jer 5:13

The Servant of the Lord

42

"Here is my servant, whom I uphold,
my chosen one[w] in whom I delight;
I will put my Spirit[x] on him
and he will bring justice to the nations.
2 He will not shout or cry out,
or raise his voice in the streets.
3 A bruised reed he will not break,
and a smoldering wick he will not snuff out.
In faithfulness he will bring forth justice;[y]
4 he will not falter or be discouraged
till he establishes justice on earth.
In his law the islands will put their hope."[z]

5 This is what God the Lord says—
he who created the heavens and stretched them out,
who spread out the earth and all that comes out of it,[a]
who gives breath[b] to its people,
and life to those who walk on it:
6 "I, the Lord, have called[c] you in righteousness;[d]
I will take hold of your hand.

42:1 [w]Isa 43:10; Lk 9:35; 1Pe 2:4, 6 [x]Isa 11:2; Mt 3:16-17; Jn 3:34
42:3 [y]Ps 72:2
42:4 [z]Ge 49:10; Mt 12:18-21*
42:5 [a]Ps 24:2 [b]Ac 17:25
42:6 [c]Isa 43:1 [d]Jer 23:6

41:25 The residents of Jerusalem were accustomed to invasions originating primarily from the north (see the note on Ne 2:13). Cyrus, who came from the east (Isa 41:2), had conquered a number of kingdoms north of Babylon early in his reign. Although Cyrus used the Lord's name in his decree (Ezr 1:2), he did not personally acknowledge him as the one true God (see Isa 45:4–5).

42:1 "Servant" in ancient Near Eastern royal terminology meant something like "trusted envoy" or "confidential representative."
42:4 For "islands," see the note on 41:1.
42:6 For "Gentiles," see the note on Matthew 4:12–16.

42:6 [e]Isa 26:3 [f]Isa 49:8 [g]Lk 2:32; Ac 13:47

I will keep[e] you and will make you
to be a covenant[f] for the people
and a light for the Gentiles,[g]

42:7 [h]Isa 35:5 [i]Isa 49:9; 61:1 [j]Lk 4:19; 2Ti 2:26; Heb 2:14-15

7 to open eyes that are blind,[h]
to free[i] captives from prison[j]
and to release from the dungeon those who sit in darkness.

42:8 [k]Ex 3:15 [l]Isa 48:11

8 "I am the LORD; that is my name![k]
I will not give my glory to another[l]
or my praise to idols.
9 See, the former things have taken place,
and new things I declare;
before they spring into being
I announce them to you."

Song of Praise to the LORD

42:10 [m]Ps 33:3; 40:3; 98:1 [n]Isa 49:6 [o]1Ch 16:32; Ps 96:11

10 Sing to the LORD a new song,[m]
his praise from the ends of the earth,[n]
you who go down to the sea, and all that is in it,[o]
you islands, and all who live in them.

42:11 [p]Isa 32:16 [q]Isa 60:7 [r]Isa 52:7; Na 1:15

11 Let the desert[p] and its towns raise their voices;
let the settlements where Kedar[q] lives rejoice.
Let the people of Sela sing for joy;
let them shout from the mountaintops.[r]

42:12 [s]Isa 24:15

12 Let them give glory[s] to the LORD
and proclaim his praise in the islands.

42:13 [t]Isa 9:6 [u]Isa 26:11 [v]Hos 11:10 [w]Isa 66:14

13 The LORD will march out like a mighty[t] man,
like a warrior he will stir up his zeal;[u]
with a shout[v] he will raise the battle cry
and will triumph over his enemies.[w]

14 "For a long time I have kept silent,
I have been quiet and held myself back.
But now, like a woman in childbirth,
I cry out, I gasp and pant.

42:15 [x]Eze 38:20 [y]Isa 50:2; Na 1:4-6

15 I will lay waste[x] the mountains and hills
and dry up all their vegetation;
I will turn rivers into islands
and dry up[y] the pools.

42:16 [z]Lk 1:78-79 [a]Isa 32:3 [b]Lk 3:5 [c]Heb 13:5

16 I will lead[z] the blind[a] by ways they have not known,
along unfamiliar paths I will guide them;
I will turn the darkness into light before them
and make the rough places smooth.[b]
These are the things I will do;
I will not forsake[c] them.
17 But those who trust in idols,
who say to images, 'You are our gods,'
will be turned back in utter shame.[d]

42:17 [d]Ps 97:7; Isa 1:29; 44:11; 45:16

Israel Blind and Deaf

42:18 [e]Isa 35:5

18 "Hear, you deaf;[e]
look, you blind, and see!

42:11 "Desert" refers to the Arabah, the desert land from the Sea of Galilee to the southern end of the Dead Sea. For "Kedar," see the note on 21:16; and for "Sela" the note on 16:1.

19 Who is blind[f] but my servant,[g]
and deaf like the messenger[h] I send?
Who is blind like the one committed[i] to me,
blind like the servant of the LORD?
20 You have seen many things, but have paid no attention;
your ears are open, but you hear nothing."[j]
21 It pleased the LORD
for the sake of his righteousness
to make his law[k] great and glorious.
22 But this is a people plundered and looted,
all of them trapped in pits[l]
or hidden away in prisons.[m]
They have become plunder,
with no one to rescue them;
they have been made loot,
with no one to say, "Send them back."

23 Which of you will listen to this
or pay close attention[n] in time to come?
24 Who handed Jacob over to become loot,
and Israel to the plunderers?
Was it not the LORD,
against whom we have sinned?
For they would not follow[o] his ways;
they did not obey his law.
25 So he poured out on them his burning anger,
the violence of war.
It enveloped them in flames,[p] yet they did not understand;
it consumed them, but they did not take it to heart.[q]

42:19 [f]Isa 43:8; Eze 12:2 [g]Isa 41:8-9 [h]Isa 44:26 [i]Isa 26:3
42:20 [j]Jer 6:10
42:21 [k]ver 4
42:22 [l]Isa 24:18 [m]Isa 24:22
42:23 [n]Isa 48:18
42:24 [o]Isa 30:15
42:25 [p]2Ki 25:9 [q]Isa 29:13; 47:7; 57:1,11; Hos 7:9

Israel's Only Savior

43

But now, this is what the LORD says—
he who created you, O Jacob,
he who formed[r] you, O Israel:[s]
"Fear not, for I have redeemed[t] you;
I have summoned you by name;[u] you are mine.
2 When you pass through the waters,[v]
I will be with you;[w]
and when you pass through the rivers,
they will not sweep over you.
When you walk through the fire,[x]
you will not be burned;
the flames will not set you ablaze.[y]
3 For I am the LORD, your God,[z]
the Holy One of Israel, your Savior;
I give Egypt for your ransom,
Cush[a][a] and Seba in your stead.[b]
4 Since you are precious and honored in my sight,
and because I love[c] you,
I will give men in exchange for you,
and people in exchange for your life.

43:1 [r]ver 7 [s]Ge 32:28; Isa 44:21 [t]Isa 44:2,6 [u]Isa 42:6; 45:3-4
43:2 [v]Isa 8:7 [w]Dt 31:6,8 [x]Isa 29:6; 30:27 [y]Ps 66:12; Da 3:25-27
43:3 [z]Ex 20:2 [a]Isa 20:3 [b]Pr 21:18
43:4 [c]Isa 63:9

[a] 3 That is, the upper Nile region

43:3 The Persians' military success over Egypt, Cush and Seba may have been a God-given reward or "ransom" for Persia's kindness to Israel (see the note on 41:2; cf. Eze 29:19–20). For "Cush," see the note on 18:1. Seba was probably located either in southern Arabia or in eastern Africa.

43:5 [d]Isa 44:2 [e]Jer 30:10-11 [f]Isa 41:8
43:6 [g]Ps 107:3 [h]2Co 6:18
43:7 [i]Isa 56:5; 63:19; Jas 2:7 [j]ver 1,21; Ps 100:3; Eph 2:10
43:8 [k]Isa 6:9-10 [l]Isa 42:20; Eze 12:2
43:9 [m]Isa 41:1 [n]Isa 41:26
43:10 [o]Isa 41:8-9 [p]Isa 44:6,8
43:11 [q]Isa 45:21
43:12 [r]Dt 32:12; Ps 81:9 [s]Isa 44:8
43:13 [t]Ps 90:2 [u]Job 9:12; Isa 14:27
43:14 [v]Isa 13:14-15 [w]Isa 23:13
43:16 [x]Ps 77:19; Isa 11:15; 51:10
43:17 [y]Ps 118:12; Isa 1:31 [z]Ex 14:9

5 Do not be afraid,[d] for I am with you;[e]
I will bring your children[f] from the east
and gather you from the west.
6 I will say to the north, 'Give them up!'
and to the south,[g] 'Do not hold them back.'
Bring my sons from afar
and my daughters[h] from the ends of the earth—
7 everyone who is called by my name,[i]
whom I created for my glory,
whom I formed and made.[j]"

8 Lead out those who have eyes but are blind,[k]
who have ears but are deaf.[l]
9 All the nations gather together[m]
and the peoples assemble.
Which of them foretold[n] this
and proclaimed to us the former things?
Let them bring in their witnesses to prove they
were right,
so that others may hear and say, "It is true."
10 "You are my witnesses," declares the LORD,
"and my servant[o] whom I have chosen,
so that you may know and believe me
and understand that I am he.
Before me no god[p] was formed,
nor will there be one after me.
11 I, even I, am the LORD,
and apart from me there is no savior.[q]
12 I have revealed and saved and proclaimed—
I, and not some foreign god[r] among you.
You are my witnesses,[s]" declares the LORD, "that I am God.
13 Yes, and from ancient days[t] I am he.
No one can deliver out of my hand.
When I act, who can reverse it?"[u]

God's Mercy and Israel's Unfaithfulness

14 This is what the LORD says—
your Redeemer, the Holy One of Israel:
"For your sake I will send to Babylon
and bring down as fugitives[v] all the Babylonians,[a][w]
in the ships in which they took pride.
15 I am the LORD, your Holy One,
Israel's Creator, your King."

16 This is what the LORD says—
he who made a way through the sea,
a path through the mighty waters,[x]
17 who drew out[y] the chariots and horses,
the army and reinforcements together,[z]

[a] 14 Or *Chaldeans*

43:5 The "east" is a broad reference to the area encompassing Assyria and Babylonia. The "west" refers to places like the "islands" of 11:11 (see the note there).
43:6 The "north" included locations such as Hamath (see the note 11:11), while the "south" referred specifically to Egypt.
43:14 For commentary on "Redeemer," see the note on 41:14.

For "Babylon," see the note on 13:1; see also "Babylon" on page 1077. The Babylonians made use of the Persian Gulf and the Tigris and Euphrates Rivers for lucrative trade. Ironically, however, their impressive vessels (cf. 2:16) would one day become their means of flight (cf. Jer 51:13).

and they lay there, never to rise again,
extinguished, snuffed out like a wick:
18 "Forget the former things;
do not dwell on the past.
19 See, I am doing a new thing![a]
Now it springs up; do you not perceive it?
I am making a way in the desert[b]
and streams in the wasteland.
20 The wild animals honor me,
the jackals[c] and the owls,
because I provide water[d] in the desert
and streams in the wasteland,
to give drink to my people, my chosen,
21 the people I formed for myself
that they may proclaim my praise.[e]

22 "Yet you have not called upon me, O Jacob,
you have not wearied yourselves for me, O Israel.[f]
23 You have not brought me sheep for burnt offerings,
nor honored[g] me with your sacrifices.[h]
I have not burdened you with grain offerings
nor wearied you with demands[i] for incense.[j]
24 You have not bought any fragrant calamus[k] for me,
or lavished on me the fat of your sacrifices.
But you have burdened me with your sins
and wearied[l] me with your offenses.[m]

25 "I, even I, am he who blots out
your transgressions,[n] for my own sake,[o]
and remembers your sins no more.[p]
26 Review the past for me,
let us argue the matter together;[q]
state the case[r] for your innocence.
27 Your first father sinned;
your spokesmen[s] rebelled against me.
28 So I will disgrace the dignitaries of your temple,
and I will consign Jacob to destruction[a]
and Israel to scorn.[t]

Israel the Chosen

44 "But now listen, O Jacob, my servant,[u]
Israel, whom I have chosen.
2 This is what the LORD says—
he who made you, who formed you in the womb,
and who will help[v] you:
Do not be afraid, O Jacob, my servant,
Jeshurun,[w] whom I have chosen.
3 For I will pour water[x] on the thirsty land,
and streams on the dry ground;

43:19 [a]2Co 5:17; Rev 21:5 [b]Ex 17:6; Nu 20:11
43:20 [c]Isa 13:22 [d]Isa 48:21
43:21 [e]Ps 102:18; 1Pe 2:9
43:22 [f]Isa 30:11
43:23 [g]Zec 7:5-6; Mal 1:6-8 [h]Am 5:25 [i]Jer 7:22 [j]Ex 30:35; Lev 2:1
43:24 [k]Ex 30:23 [l]Isa 1:14; 7:13 [m]Mal 2:17
43:25 [n]Ac 3:19 [o]Isa 37:35; Eze 36:22 [p]Isa 38:17; Jer 31:34
43:26 [q]Isa 1:18 [r]Isa 41:1; 50:8
43:27 [s]Isa 9:15; 28:7; Jer 5:31
43:28 [t]Jer 24:9; Eze 5:15
44:1 [u]ver 21; Jer 30:10; 46:27-28
44:2 [v]Isa 41:10 [w]Dt 32:15
44:3 [x]Joel 3:18

[a] *28* The Hebrew term refers to the irrevocable giving over of things or persons to the LORD, often by totally destroying them.

43:20 Jackals and owls represent desert-dwelling creatures.
43:24 Calamus is associated with incense (see v. 23; see also SS 4:14 and its note; Jer 6:20; "Incense" on p. 1209).
For "fat," see the note on 34:6.

44:2 "Jeshurun" is a little-known designation for Israel, found elsewhere in the Old Testament only in Deuteronomy 32:15 (see the NIV text note there) and in Deuteronomy 33:5, 26.

44:3 [y]Joel 2:28; Ac 2:17 [z]Isa 61:9; 65:23

I will pour out my Spirit[y] on your offspring,
and my blessing on your descendants.[z]
4 They will spring up like grass in a meadow,
like poplar trees[a] by flowing streams.[b]

44:4 [a]Lev 23:40 [b]Job 40:22

5 One will say, 'I belong to the LORD';
another will call himself by the name of Jacob;
still another will write on his hand,[c] 'The LORD's,'[d]
and will take the name Israel.

44:5 [c]Ex 13:9 [d]Zec 8:20-22

The LORD, Not Idols

6 "This is what the LORD says—
Israel's King[e] and Redeemer,[f] the LORD Almighty:
I am the first and I am the last;[g]
apart from me there is no God.
7 Who then is like me? Let him proclaim it.
Let him declare and lay out before me
what has happened since I established my ancient people,
and what is yet to come—
yes, let him foretell[h] what will come.
8 Do not tremble, do not be afraid.
Did I not proclaim this and foretell it long ago?
You are my witnesses. Is there any God[i] besides me?
No, there is no other Rock;[j] I know not one."

44:6 [e]Isa 41:21 [f]Isa 43:1 [g]Isa 41:4; Rev 1:8,17; 22:13

44:7 [h]Isa 41:22, 26

44:8 [i]Isa 43:10 [j]Dt 4:35; 1Sa 2:2

9 All who make idols are nothing,
and the things they treasure are worthless.[k]
Those who would speak up for them are blind;
they are ignorant, to their own shame.
10 Who shapes a god and casts an idol,
which can profit him nothing?[l]
11 He and his kind will be put to shame;[m]
craftsmen are nothing but men.
Let them all come together and take their stand;
they will be brought down to terror and infamy.[n]

44:9 [k]Isa 41:24

44:10 [l]Isa 41:29; Jer 10:5; Ac 19:26

44:11 [m]Isa 1:29 [n]Isa 42:17

12 The blacksmith[o] takes a tool
and works with it in the coals;
he shapes an idol with hammers,
he forges it with the might of his arm.[p]
He gets hungry and loses his strength;
he drinks no water and grows faint.
13 The carpenter[q] measures with a line
and makes an outline with a marker;
he roughs it out with chisels
and marks it with compasses.
He shapes it in the form of man,[r]
of man in all his glory,
that it may dwell in a shrine.[s]
14 He cut down cedars,
or perhaps took a cypress or oak.
He let it grow among the trees of the forest,
or planted a pine, and the rain made it grow.

44:12 [o]Isa 40:19; 41:6-7 [p]Jer 10:3-5; Ac 17:29

44:13 [q]Isa 41:7 [r]Ps 115:4-7 [s]Jdg 17:4-5

44:4 Grass represents luxuriant growth also in 35:7 (cf. 37:27; 40:6–8).
44:12 See the note on coal/charcoal at Psalm 120:4.
44:14 Cedar, cypress and oak were the most valuable varieties of timber known at that time.

15 It is man's fuel[t] for burning;
some of it he takes and warms himself,
he kindles a fire and bakes bread.
But he also fashions a god and worships it;
he makes an idol and bows[u] down to it.
16 Half of the wood he burns in the fire;
over it he prepares his meal,
he roasts his meat and eats his fill.

44:15 [t]ver 19 [u]2Ch 25:14

Idols and Idol-Making

ISAIAH 44 The technical details of Isaiah's diatribe in 44:9–21 suggest that he was well acquainted with the idol-making practices of his day, including an important ritual known from **Mesopotamian** sources as the "mouth-washing" or "mouth-opening" ceremony (a similar rite is known from Egypt). Through a series of ritual acts and incantations, Mesopotamian craftsmen and priests believed that their deities were created and "brought to life" by means of the animation of the statues' sensory organs. An inert statue of wood or stone was thus in their view transformed into a living manifestation of the deity it represented.

However, some scholars argue that Isaiah's attack was based upon a superficial understanding of the mouth-washing/mouth-opening ritual. Isaiah claimed that the image remained a lifeless, artificial product, but at the close of the Mesopotamian rite was a disavowal of any human participation in the creation of the deity, suggesting that the pagans rejected the idea that human beings could manufacture a god. Furthermore, the mouth-washing texts include an acknowledgment that the transformation of the idol from man-made to divine was a work of the gods alone.

Was Isaiah aware of this important aspect of the mouth-washing ceremony? It is hard to imagine that he was not, considering how widely practiced it was in the ancient Near East. It seems, rather, that the prophet made a brilliant play on the idea by claiming that the transformation of the sensory organs occurred not in the wooden or stone image but *in the heart and mind of the worshiper*, who became dumb and blind (vv. 18–20) by being transformed into the inert image of the idol he or she worshiped. This same principle of "You are what you worship" is echoed in Psalms 115:1–8, 135:15–18 and in Jeremiah 10:14. However, for those who worshiped **Yahweh**, Isaiah promised a restoration of their sensory organs (Isa 32:3–4; 35:5–6), including eyes that would no longer be glazed over and minds that would experience understanding (44:18). Isaiah concluded his attack on idol-making with a fitting reminder to God's people that they had not created Yahweh. Rather, God reminded them, "*I* have made *you*" (v. 21, emphasis added).

Shrine image from Ur

Preserving Bible Times; © Dr. James C. Martin; permission of The British Museum

He also warms himself and says,
"Ah! I am warm; I see the fire."
17 From the rest he makes a god, his idol;
he bows down to it and worships.
He prays[v] to it and says,
"Save[w] me; you are my god."
18 They know nothing, they understand[x] nothing;
their eyes[y] are plastered over so they cannot see,
and their minds closed so they cannot understand.
19 No one stops to think,
no one has the knowledge or understanding[z]
to say,
"Half of it I used for fuel;
I even baked bread over its coals,
I roasted meat and I ate.
Shall I make a detestable[a] thing from what is left?
Shall I bow down to a block of wood?"
20 He feeds on ashes,[b] a deluded[c] heart misleads him;
he cannot save himself, or say,
"Is not this thing in my right hand a lie?[d]"

21 "Remember[e] these things, O Jacob,
for you are my servant, O Israel.
I have made you, you are my servant;[f]
O Israel, I will not forget you.[g]
22 I have swept away[h] your offenses like a cloud,
your sins like the morning mist.
Return[i] to me,
for I have redeemed[j] you."

23 Sing for joy,[k] O heavens, for the LORD has done this;
shout aloud, O earth[l] beneath.
Burst into song, you mountains,[m]
you forests and all your trees,
for the LORD has redeemed Jacob,
he displays his glory[n] in Israel.

Jerusalem to Be Inhabited

24 "This is what the LORD says—
your Redeemer,[o] who formed you in the womb:

I am the LORD,
who has made all things,
who alone stretched out the heavens,[p]
who spread out the earth by myself,

25 who foils[q] the signs of false prophets
and makes fools of diviners,[r]
who overthrows the learning of the wise[s]
and turns it into nonsense,[t]
26 who carries out the words[u] of his servants
and fulfills[v] the predictions of his messengers,

44:17 [v]1Ki 18:26 [w]Isa 45:20
44:18 [x]Isa 1:3 [y]Isa 6:9-10
44:19 [z]Isa 5:13; 27:11; 45:20 [a]Dt 27:15
44:20 [b]Ps 102:9 [c]Job 15:31; Ro 1:21-23,28; 2Th 2:11; 2Ti 3:13 [d]Isa 59:3,4,13; Ro 1:25
44:21 [e]Isa 46:8; Zec 10:9 [f]ver 1-2 [g]Isa 49:15
44:22 [h]Isa 43:25; Ac 3:19 [i]Isa 55:7 [j]1Co 6:20
44:23 [k]Isa 42:10 [l]Ps 148:7 [m]Ps 98:8 [n]Isa 61:3
44:24 [o]Isa 43:14 [p]Isa 42:5
44:25 [q]Ps 33:10 [r]Isa 47:13 [s]1Co 1:27 [t]2Sa 15:31; 1Co 1:19-20
44:26 [u]Zec 1:6 [v]Isa 55:11; Mt 5:18

44:19 Molech and Chemosh were "detestable" gods (1Ki 11:5,7; 2Ki 23:13; see the note on Lev 18:21; see also "Human Sacrifice in the Ancient Near East" on p. 182).
See the note on coal/charcoal at Psalm 120:4.

44:25 The Hebrew for "diviners" is used of Balaam (Jos 13:22), the medium at Endor (1Sa 28:8) and of false prophets (Jer 27:9). It is linked with soothsaying and sorcery (see 3:2–3 and its note, as well as Dt 18:9–11 and "Akkadian Divination" on p. 277).

who says of Jerusalem, 'It shall be inhabited,'
of the towns of Judah, 'They shall be built,'
and of their ruins, 'I will restore them,'[w]
27 who says to the watery deep, 'Be dry,
and I will dry up your streams,'
28 who says of Cyrus,[x] 'He is my shepherd
and will accomplish all that I please;
he will say of Jerusalem,[y] "Let it be rebuilt,"
and of the temple,[z] "Let its foundations be laid." '

44:26 [w]Isa 49:8-21
44:28 [x]2Ch 36:22 [y]Isa 14:32 [z]Ezr 1:2-4

45

"This is what the LORD says to his anointed,
to Cyrus, whose right hand I take hold[a] of
to subdue nations[b] before him
and to strip kings of their armor,
to open doors before him
so that gates will not be shut:
2 I will go before you
and will level[c] the mountains[a];
I will break down gates of bronze
and cut through bars of iron.[d]
3 I will give you the treasures[e] of darkness,
riches stored in secret places,[f]
so that you may know[g] that I am the LORD,
the God of Israel, who summons you by name.[h]
4 For the sake of Jacob my servant,[i]
of Israel my chosen,
I summon you by name
and bestow on you a title of honor,
though you do not acknowledge[j] me.
5 I am the LORD, and there is no other;[k]
apart from me there is no God.[l]
I will strengthen you,[m]
though you have not acknowledged me,
6 so that from the rising of the sun
to the place of its setting[n]
men may know there is none besides me.[o]
I am the LORD, and there is no other.
7 I form the light and create darkness,
I bring prosperity and create disaster;[p]
I, the LORD, do all these things.

8 "You heavens above, rain[q] down righteousness;[r]
let the clouds shower it down.
Let the earth open wide,
let salvation[s] spring up,
let righteousness grow with it;
I, the LORD, have created it.

9 "Woe to him who quarrels[t] with his Maker,
to him who is but a potsherd among the potsherds on the ground.

45:1 [a]Ps 73:23; Isa 41:13; 42:6 [b]Jer 50:35
45:2 [c]Isa 40:4 [d]Ps 107:16; Jer 51:30
45:3 [e]Jer 50:37 [f]Jer 41:8 [g]Isa 41:23 [h]Ex 33:12; Isa 43:1
45:4 [i]Isa 41:8-9 [j]Ac 17:23
45:5 [k]Isa 44:8 [l]Ps 18:31 [m]Ps 18:39
45:6 [n]Isa 43:5; Mal 1:11 [o]ver 5, 18
45:7 [p]Isa 31:2; Am 3:6
45:8 [q]Ps 72:6; Joel 3:18 [r]Ps 85:11; Isa 60:21; 61:10, 11; Hos 10:12 [s]Isa 12:3
45:9 [t]Job 15:25

[a] 2 Dead Sea Scrolls and Septuagint; the meaning of the word in the Masoretic Text is uncertain.

44:28 Throughout the ancient Near East the term "shepherd" was often applied to rulers (see 2Sa 5:2; Jer 23:2). Here it is used in reference to Cyrus the Great (see "Cyrus the Great" on p. 669). Cyrus's decree (Ezr 1:2–4; 6:3–5) authorizing the rebuilding of the temple eventually paved the way for a restored Jerusalem (see Isa 45:13).

45:2 Ordinarily the doors of city gates were wooden and their bars metal.

45:4 Cyrus did not personally "acknowledge" God (see the note on 41:25) but worshiped the chief Babylonian deity, Marduk, whom he praised in his inscriptions. (See "Cyrus the Great" on p. 669.)

45:9 [u]Isa 29:16; Ro 9:20-21*

Does the clay say to the potter,[u]
'What are you making?'
Does your work say,
'He has no hands'?
10 Woe to him who says to his father,
'What have you begotten?'
or to his mother,
'What have you brought to birth?'

11 "This is what the LORD says—
the Holy One of Israel, and its Maker:
Concerning things to come,
do you question me about my children,
or give me orders about the work of my hands?[v]
12 It is I who made the earth
and created mankind upon it.
My own hands stretched out the heavens;[w]
I marshaled their starry hosts.[x]
13 I will raise up Cyrus[a][y] in my righteousness:
I will make all his ways straight.

45:11 [v]Isa 19:25

45:12 [w]Ge 2:1; Isa 42:5 [x]Ne 9:6

45:13 [y]2Ch 36:22; Isa 41:2

[a] 13 Hebrew *him*

Cosmology in the Ancient Near East

ISAIAH 45 Cosmology deals with the order and nature of the universe. Observations of nature by ancient peoples were transformed into metaphors by which they understood their place in the world. Many myths attempted to explain the origin and purpose of the human race.

In the most prominent **Mesopotamian** myth of creation, which was annually enacted at New Year's religious festivals, the ordered universe emerged out of a cosmic struggle of the gods. The *Enuma Elish* vividly imagines the origins of the universe as a struggle between chaos and order.[1] In this myth Marduk, the storm-god, defeated Tiamat, the sea dragon, and from her body created the universe. He also killed her consort, the god Kingu, and from Kingu's blood created humanity for the purpose of serving the gods.

The actual process of humanity's creation is better described by another Mesopotamian myth, Atra-hasis,[2] in which Mami, the birth goddess and divine midwife, shaped clay moistened by the spittle of the gods and then pinched off pieces to deliver humans from the womb of the earth. The role of humanity, again, was to serve the gods by constructing their temples, working their lands and giving ritual service to the deities.

In the Memphite theology of Egypt, the god Ptah conceived the universe in his mind and brought it into being by his creative word. The fashioning of humanity, however, is ascribed to the potter god, Khnum, who molded people out of clay, crafting them on a potter's wheel, and then placed the fetus in the mother's womb. **Reliefs** in Hatshepsut's mortuary temple show Khnum sculpting her fetus and her *ka*, or "spirit," on the potter's wheel.

Yet another myth explains the origins of humanity as the joyful tears of the sun god, Ra (or Re; in Egyptian, *remut* means "tears" and *remet* means "humanity"). Although there is no clear Egyptian articulation of the purpose of humanity, there is an assertion that though human beings were created with equal opportunity to do good, they chose to devise evil in their hearts.

Biblical cosmology, treats natural phenomena from the standpoint of a monotheistic worldview. The primal waters are neither vilified nor deified. God commanded creation by the power of his word, shaping the cosmos in an orderly fashion and governing his world with wisdom (Ge 1; Pr 8:22–31). A person is not a servile being meant to fulfill the gods' need for food and worship; humanity is created in God's image and destined for communion with God and for the purpose of blessing (Ge 1:27–28).

[1]See "*The Enuma Elish* and the Biblical Concept of Creation" on page 888. [2]See "Humanity and the Divine: Comparing the Bible to the Myth of Atra-Hasis" on page 1176.

He will rebuild my city
and set my exiles free,
but not for a price or reward,[z]
says the LORD Almighty."

45:13 [z]Isa 52:3

14 This is what the LORD says:

"The products of Egypt and the merchandise of Cush,[a]
and those tall Sabeans—
they will come over to you
and will be yours;
they will trudge behind you,
coming over to you in chains.[a]
They will bow down before you
and plead[b] with you, saying,
'Surely God is with you,[c] and there is no other;
there is no other god.' "

45:14 [a]Isa 14:1-2 [b]Jer 16:19; Zec 8:20-23 [c]1Co 14:25

15 Truly you are a God who hides[d] himself,
O God and Savior of Israel.
16 All the makers of idols will be put to shame and disgraced;[e]
they will go off into disgrace together.
17 But Israel will be saved[f] by the LORD
with an everlasting salvation;[g]
you will never be put to shame or disgraced,
to ages everlasting.

45:15 [d]Ps 44:24
45:16 [e]Isa 44:9, 11
45:17 [f]Ro 11:26 [g]Isa 26:4

18 For this is what the LORD says—
he who created the heavens,
he is God;
he who fashioned and made the earth,
he founded it;
he did not create it to be empty,[h]
but formed it to be inhabited[i]—
he says:
"I am the LORD,
and there is no other.[j]
19 I have not spoken in secret,[k]
from somewhere in a land of darkness;
I have not said to Jacob's descendants,[l]
'Seek me in vain.'
I, the LORD, speak the truth;
I declare what is right.[m]

45:18 [h]Ge 1:2 [i]Ge 1:26; Isa 42:5 [j]ver 5
45:19 [k]Isa 48:16 [l]Isa 41:8 [m]Dt 30:11

20 "Gather together[n] and come;
assemble, you fugitives from the nations.
Ignorant[o] are those who carry[p] about idols of wood,
who pray to gods that cannot save.[q]
21 Declare what is to be, present it—
let them take counsel together.
Who foretold[r] this long ago,
who declared it from the distant past?

45:20 [n]Isa 43:9 [o]Isa 44:19 [p]Isa 46:1; Jer 10:5 [q]Isa 44:17; 46:6-7
45:21 [r]Isa 41:22

[a] 14 That is, the upper Nile region

45:14 For "Egypt," "Cush" and "Sabeans," see the notes on 18:1 and 43:3 ("Seba").

45:19 "Spoken in secret" and "land of darkness" most likely alluded to the furtive ways of mediums and spiritists (see 8:19; 29:4 and their notes).

Was it not I, the LORD?
  And there is no God apart from me,[s]
a righteous God and a Savior;
  there is none but me.

22 "Turn[t] to me and be saved,[u]
  all you ends of the earth;[v]
  for I am God, and there is no other.
23 By myself I have sworn,[w]
  my mouth has uttered in all integrity[x]
  a word that will not be revoked:[y]
Before me every knee will bow;
  by me every tongue will swear.[z]
24 They will say of me, 'In the LORD alone
  are righteousness[a] and strength.' "
All who have raged against him
  will come to him and be put to shame.[b]
25 But in the LORD all the descendants of Israel
  will be found righteous and will exult.[c]

45:21 [s]ver 5
45:22 [t]Zec 12:10 [u]Nu 21:8-9; 2Ch 20:12 [v]Isa 49:6,12
45:23 [w]Ge 22:16 [x]Heb 6:13 [y]Isa 55:11 [z]Ps 63:11; Isa 19:18; Ro 14:11*; Php 2:10-11
45:24 [a]Jer 33:16 [b]Isa 41:11
45:25 [c]Isa 41:16

Gods of Babylon

46

Bel[d] bows down, Nebo stoops low;
  their idols are borne by beasts of burden.[a]
The images that are carried[e] about are burdensome,
  a burden for the weary.
2 They stoop and bow down together;
  unable to rescue the burden,
  they themselves go off into captivity.[f]

3 "Listen[g] to me, O house of Jacob,
  all you who remain of the house of Israel,
you whom I have upheld since you were conceived,
  and have carried since your birth.
4 Even to your old age and gray hairs[h]
  I am he,[i] I am he who will sustain you.
I have made you and I will carry you;
  I will sustain you and I will rescue you.

5 "To whom will you compare me or count me equal?
  To whom will you liken me that we may be compared?[j]
6 Some pour out gold from their bags
  and weigh out silver on the scales;
they hire a goldsmith[k] to make it into a god,
  and they bow down and worship it.[l]
7 They lift it to their shoulders and carry[m] it;
  they set it up in its place, and there it stands.
  From that spot it cannot move.

46:1 [d]Isa 21:9; Jer 50:2; 51:44 [e]Isa 45:20
46:2 [f]Jdg 18:17-18; 2Sa 5:21
46:3 [g]ver 12
46:4 [h]Ps 71:18 [i]Isa 43:13
46:5 [j]Isa 40:18, 25
46:6 [k]Isa 40:19 [l]Isa 44:17
46:7 [m]ver 1

[a] *1* Or *are but beasts and cattle*

46:1–13 Isaiah 46 mocks the idols of the nations by declaring that the gods Bel and Nebo are stooped over and being carried off into captivity. We might be tempted to think that Isaiah was being too severe in depicting the gods of the nations as weak and prone to all of the troubles that befall humans, but when we read the myths of the pagans themselves, we realize that the prophet could have said a great deal more.

One western Semitic text describes the god El (also pronounced Ilu) attending a drinking party. He becomes drunk and on his way home spots a monster with horns and a tail (perhaps a kind of "pink elephant"). El soils himself and collapses. He is revived and, in order to sober him up, is given a drink made of olive oil, a kind of plant (the precise meaning of the word is unknown) and hair from a dog. (Ancient people thought that dog hair had a sobering effect; thus the modern expression "to take the hair of the dog.")

Some suggest that this text was originally intended to be humorous, but this is probably not the case. If anything, it appears to be the mythological justification for a specific curative for hangovers. Even if this account was intended as humor, it demonstrates that the pagans felt free to regard their own gods as capable of this kind of pathetic behavior.

Though one cries out to it, it does not answer;
it cannot save[n] him from his troubles.

8 "Remember[o] this, fix it in mind,
take it to heart, you rebels.
9 Remember the former things, those of long ago;[p]
I am God, and there is no other;
I am God, and there is none like me.[q]
10 I make known the end from the beginning,
from ancient times,[r] what is still to come.
I say: My purpose will stand,[s]
and I will do all that I please.
11 From the east I summon a bird of prey;
from a far-off land, a man to fulfill my purpose.
What I have said, that will I bring about;
what I have planned, that will I do.
12 Listen[t] to me, you stubborn-hearted,
you who are far from righteousness.[u]
13 I am bringing my righteousness near,
it is not far away;
and my salvation will not be delayed.
I will grant salvation to Zion,
my splendor[v] to Israel.

46:7 [n]Isa 44:17; Isa 45:20
46:8 [o]Isa 44:21
46:9 [p]Dt 32:7 [q]Isa 45:5,21
46:10 [r]Isa 45:21 [s]Pr 19:21; Ac 5:39
46:12 [t]ver 3 [u]Ps 119:150; Isa 48:1; Jer 2:5
46:13 [v]Isa 44:23

The Fall of Babylon

47 "Go down, sit in the dust,
Virgin Daughter[w] of Babylon;
sit on the ground without a throne,
Daughter of the Babylonians.[a][x]
No more will you be called
tender or delicate.[y]
2 Take millstones[z] and grind[a] flour;
take off your veil.[b]
Lift up your skirts,[c] bare your legs,
and wade through the streams.
3 Your nakedness[d] will be exposed
and your shame[e] uncovered.
I will take vengeance;[f]
I will spare no one."

4 Our Redeemer—the LORD Almighty is his name[g]—
is the Holy One of Israel.

5 "Sit in silence, go into darkness,[h]
Daughter of the Babylonians;
no more will you be called
queen of kingdoms.[i]
6 I was angry[j] with my people
and desecrated my inheritance;
I gave them into your hand,[k]
and you showed them no mercy.

47:1 [w]Isa 23:12 [x]Ps 137:8; Jer 50:42; 51:33; Zec 2:7 [y]Dt 28:56
47:2 [z]Ex 11:5; Mt 24:41 [a]Jdg 16:21 [b]Ge 24:65 [c]Isa 32:11
47:3 [d]Eze 16:37; Na 3:5 [e]Isa 20:4 [f]Isa 34:8
47:4 [g]Jer 50:34
47:5 [h]Isa 13:10 [i]Isa 13:19
47:6 [j]2Ch 28:9 [k]Isa 10:13

[a] *1* Or *Chaldeans*; also in verse 5

47:4 For "Redeemer," see the note on 41:14.
47:5 Babylon, an exceptionally beautiful city, was known as the "queen of kingdoms." (See "Babylon" on p. 1077.)
47:6–8 The Babylonians, who thought they could do whatever they wanted to captive nations (v. 6), made the fatal errors of believing themselves to be self-existent and self-perpetuating (v. 7).

Even on the aged
you laid a very heavy yoke.
7 You said, 'I will continue forever—
the eternal queen!'[l]
But you did not consider these things
or reflect[m] on what might happen.[n]

47:7 [l]ver 5; Rev 18:7 [m]Isa 42:23,25 [n]Dt 32:29

8 "Now then, listen, you wanton creature,
lounging in your security[o]
and saying to yourself,
'I am, and there is none besides me.[p]
I will never be a widow[q]
or suffer the loss of children.'
9 Both of these will overtake you
in a moment,[r] on a single day:
loss of children[s] and widowhood.
They will come upon you in full measure,
in spite of your many sorceries[t]
and all your potent spells.[u]

47:8 [o]Isa 32:9 [p]Isa 45:6; Zep 2:15 [q]Rev 18:7
47:9 [r]Ps 73:19; 1Th 5:3; Rev 18:8-10 [s]Isa 13:18 [t]Na 3:4 [u]Rev 18:23

10 You have trusted[v] in your wickedness
and have said, 'No one sees me.'[w]
Your wisdom[x] and knowledge mislead[y] you
when you say to yourself,
'I am, and there is none besides me.'
11 Disaster will come upon you,
and you will not know how to conjure it away.
A calamity will fall upon you
that you cannot ward off with a ransom;
a catastrophe you cannot foresee
will suddenly[z] come upon you.

47:10 [v]Ps 52:7; 62:10 [w]Isa 29:15 [x]Isa 5:21 [y]Isa 44:20
47:11 [z]1Th 5:3

12 "Keep on, then, with your magic spells
and with your many sorceries,[a]
which you have labored at since childhood.
Perhaps you will succeed,
perhaps you will cause terror.
13 All the counsel you have received has only worn you out![b]
Let your astrologers[c] come forward,
those stargazers who make predictions month by month,
let them save[d] you from what is coming upon you.
14 Surely they are like stubble;[e]
the fire will burn them up.
They cannot even save themselves
from the power of the flame.[f]
Here are no coals to warm anyone;
here is no fire to sit by.
15 That is all they can do for you—
these you have labored with
and trafficked[g] with since childhood.
Each of them goes on in his error;
there is not one that can save you.

47:12 [a]ver 9
47:13 [b]Isa 57:10; Jer 51:58 [c]Isa 44:25 [d]ver 15
47:14 [e]Isa 5:24; Na 1:10 [f]Isa 10:17; Jer 51:30,32,58
47:15 [g]Rev 18:11

47:9 The Babylonians attempted to control the spirit world through magic, astrology and divination. "Sorceries" and "spells" were magical practices employed to avoid danger and to inflict harm upon an enemy (see the note on 3:2–3; see also "Akkadian Divination" on p. 277).

47:13 See the note on astrology/astrologers at Daniel 2:2.
47:14 See the note on coal/charcoal at Psalm 120:4.

Stubborn Israel

48 "Listen to this, O house of Jacob,
you who are called by the name of Israel
and come from the line of Judah,
you who take oaths in the name of the LORD
and invoke[h] the God of Israel—
but not in truth[i] or righteousness—
2 you who call yourselves citizens of the holy city[j]
and rely[k] on the God of Israel—
the LORD Almighty is his name:
3 I foretold the former things[l] long ago,
my mouth announced[m] them and I made them known;
then suddenly I acted, and they came to pass.
4 For I knew how stubborn[n] you were;
the sinews of your neck[o] were iron,
your forehead[p] was bronze.
5 Therefore I told you these things long ago;
before they happened I announced them to you
so that you could not say,
'My idols did them;[q]
my wooden image and metal god ordained them.'
6 You have heard these things; look at them all.
Will you not admit them?

"From now on I will tell you of new things,
of hidden things unknown to you.
7 They are created now, and not long ago;
you have not heard of them before today.
So you cannot say,
'Yes, I knew of them.'
8 You have neither heard nor understood;
from of old your ear has not been open.
Well do I know how treacherous you are;
you were called a rebel[r] from birth.
9 For my own name's sake I delay my wrath;[s]
for the sake of my praise I hold it back from you,
so as not to cut you off.[t]
10 See, I have refined you, though not as silver;
I have tested you in the furnace[u] of affliction.
11 For my own sake,[v] for my own sake, I do this.
How can I let myself be defamed?[w]
I will not yield my glory to another.[x]

Israel Freed

12 "Listen[y] to me, O Jacob,
Israel, whom I have called:
I am he;
I am the first and I am the last.[z]
13 My own hand laid the foundations of the earth,[a]
and my right hand spread out the heavens;[b]
when I summon them,
they all stand up together.[c]

48:1 [h]Isa 58:2 [i]Jer 4:2
48:2 [j]Isa 52:1 [k]Isa 10:20; Mic 3:11; Ro 2:17
48:3 [l]Isa 41:22 [m]Isa 45:21
48:4 [n]Dt 31:27 [o]Ex 32:9; Ac 7:51 [p]Eze 3:9
48:5 [q]Jer 44:15-18
48:8 [r]Dt 9:7,24; Ps 58:3
48:9 [s]Ps 78:38; Isa 30:18 [t]Ne 9:31
48:10 [u]1Ki 8:51
48:11 [v]1Sa 12:22; Isa 37:35 [w]Dt 32:27; Jer 14:7,21; Eze 20:9,14,22,44 [x]Isa 42:8
48:12 [y]Isa 46:3 [z]Isa 41:4; Rev 1:17; 22:13
48:13 [a]Heb 1:10-12 [b]Ex 20:11 [c]Isa 40:26

48:12 The Hebrew word for "listen" (vv. 12,14,16) does not permit a separation between understanding and action. If people truly "heard" an admonition, they would without doubt obey it. If they did not, they had evidently failed to hear it.

48:14 [d]Isa 43:9 [e]Isa 46:10-11

14 “Come together,[d] all of you, and listen:
Which of ⌞the idols⌟ has foretold these things?
The LORD’s chosen ally
will carry out his purpose[e] against Babylon;
his arm will be against the Babylonians.[a]

48:15 [f]Isa 45:1

15 I, even I, have spoken;
yes, I have called[f] him.
I will bring him,
and he will succeed in his mission.

48:16 [g]Isa 41:1 [h]Isa 45:19 [i]Zec 2:9,11

16 “Come near[g] me and listen to this:

“From the first announcement I have not spoken in secret;[h]
at the time it happens, I am there.”

And now the Sovereign LORD has sent[i] me,
with his Spirit.

48:17 [j]Isa 49:7 [k]Isa 43:14 [l]Isa 49:10 [m]Ps 32:8

17 This is what the LORD says—
your Redeemer,[j] the Holy One[k] of Israel:
“I am the LORD your God,
who teaches you what is best for you,
who directs[l] you in the way[m] you should go.

48:18 [n]Dt 32:29 [o]Ps 119:165; Isa 66:12 [p]Isa 45:8

18 If only you had paid attention[n] to my commands,
your peace[o] would have been like a river,
your righteousness[p] like the waves of the sea.

48:19 [q]Ge 22:17 [r]Isa 56:5; 66:22

19 Your descendants would have been like the sand,
your children like its numberless grains;[q]
their name would never be cut off[r]
nor destroyed from before me.”

48:20 [s]Jer 50:8; 51:6,45; Zec 2:6-7; Rev 18:4 [t]Isa 49:13 [u]Isa 52:9; 63:9

20 Leave Babylon,
flee[s] from the Babylonians!
Announce this with shouts of joy[t]
and proclaim it.
Send it out to the ends of the earth;
say, “The LORD has redeemed[u] his servant Jacob.”

48:21 [v]Isa 41:17 [w]Isa 30:25 [x]Ex 17:6; Nu 20:11; Ps 105:41; Isa 35:6

21 They did not thirst[v] when he led them through the deserts;
he made water flow[w] for them from the rock;
he split the rock
and water gushed out.[x]

48:22 [y]Isa 57:21

22 “There is no peace,” says the LORD, “for the wicked.”[y]

The Servant of the LORD

49

49:1 [z]Isa 44:24; 46:3; Mt 1:20 [a]Isa 7:14; 9:6; 44:2; Jer 1:5; Gal 1:15

Listen to me, you islands;
hear this, you distant nations:
Before I was born[z] the LORD called[a] me;
from my birth he has made mention of my name.

[a] *14* Or *Chaldeans*; also in verse 20

48:17 For “Redeemer,” see the note on 41:14.

49:1—57:21 This section of the book forms a logical and climactic sequel to the preceding grouping of chapters (40–48). The figure of the “servant” is common to both. The word occurs ten times in chapters 40–53. Nine times the servant is called Israel, Jacob or Jacob-Israel, and six times the Lord calls him “my servant.” The title is used in three senses: of the servant as deaf and blind (42:18–19), sinful and needing redemption (44:22; cf. 43:25); of the servant as faithful and as having a mission to Israel and to the Gentiles (42:1–7; 49:1–6; 50:6–9); and finally of One who, himself innocent, suffers for the sins of others (52:13—53:12). The first three of these four passages, which are often called the “Servant Songs,” can refer to the pious in Israel as sharing with their Lord in his mission of salvation. In the last the reference to the Messiah is predominant and exclusive. This is one of the most precious chapters in the Bible, speaking both of the humiliation of the Savior and the glory that is to follow.

49:1 For “islands,” see the note on 41:1.

2 He made my mouth like a sharpened sword,[b] 49:2 [b]Isa 11:4; Rev 1:16
in the shadow of his hand he hid me;
he made me into a polished arrow
and concealed me in his quiver.
3 He said to me, "You are my servant,[c] 49:3 [c]Zec 3:8 [d]Isa 44:23
Israel, in whom I will display my splendor.[d]"
4 But I said, "I have labored to no purpose;
I have spent my strength in vain[e] and for nothing. 49:4 [e]Isa 65:23 [f]Isa 35:4
Yet what is due me is in the LORD's hand,
and my reward[f] is with my God."

5 And now the LORD says—
he who formed me in the womb to be his servant
to bring Jacob back to him
and gather Israel[g] to himself, 49:5 [g]Isa 11:12 [h]Isa 43:4
for I am honored[h] in the eyes of the LORD
and my God has been my strength—
6 he says:
"It is too small a thing for you to be my servant
to restore the tribes of Jacob
and bring back those of Israel I have kept.
I will also make you a light for the Gentiles,[i] 49:6 [i]Lk 2:32 [j]Ac 13:47*
that you may bring my salvation to the ends of the earth."[j]

7 This is what the LORD says—
the Redeemer and Holy One of Israel[k]— 49:7 [k]Isa 48:17 [l]Ps 22:6; 69:7-9 [m]Isa 52:15
to him who was despised[l] and abhorred by the nation,
to the servant of rulers:
"Kings[m] will see you and rise up,
princes will see and bow down,
because of the LORD, who is faithful,
the Holy One of Israel, who has chosen you."

Restoration of Israel

8 This is what the LORD says:

"In the time of my favor[n] I will answer you, 49:8 [n]Ps 69:13 [o]2Co 6:2* [p]Isa 26:3 [q]Isa 42:6 [r]Isa 44:26
and in the day of salvation I will help you;[o]
I will keep[p] you and will make you
to be a covenant for the people,[q]
to restore the land[r]
and to reassign its desolate inheritances,
9 to say to the captives,[s] 'Come out,' 49:9 [s]Isa 42:7; 61:1; Lk 4:19 [t]Isa 41:18
and to those in darkness, 'Be free!'

"They will feed beside the roads
and find pasture on every barren hill.[t]
10 They will neither hunger nor thirst,[u] 49:10 [u]Isa 33:16 [v]Ps 121:6; Rev 7:16 [w]Isa 14:1 [x]Isa 35:7
nor will the desert heat or the sun beat upon them.[v]
He who has compassion[w] on them will guide them
and lead them beside springs[x] of water.
11 I will turn all my mountains into roads,
and my highways[y] will be raised up.[z] 49:11 [y]Isa 11:16 [z]Isa 40:4
12 See, they will come from afar[a]— 49:12 [a]Isa 43:5-6
some from the north, some from the west,
some from the region of Aswan.[a]"

[a] 12 Dead Sea Scrolls; Masoretic Text *Sinim*

13 Shout for joy, O heavens;
rejoice, O earth;
burst into song, O mountains![b]
For the LORD comforts[c] his people
and will have compassion on his afflicted ones.

14 But Zion said, "The LORD has forsaken me,
the Lord has forgotten me."

15 "Can a mother forget the baby at her breast
and have no compassion on the child she has borne?
Though she may forget,
I will not forget you![d]
16 See, I have engraved[e] you on the palms of my hands;
your walls[f] are ever before me.
17 Your sons hasten back,
and those who laid you waste[g] depart from you.
18 Lift up your eyes and look around;
all your sons gather[h] and come to you.
As surely as I live,[i]" declares the LORD,
"you will wear[j] them all as ornaments;
you will put them on, like a bride.

19 "Though you were ruined and made desolate[k]
and your land laid waste,[l]
now you will be too small for your people,[m]
and those who devoured you will be far away.
20 The children born during your bereavement
will yet say in your hearing,
'This place is too small for us;
give us more space to live in.'[n]
21 Then you will say in your heart,
'Who bore me these?
I was bereaved and barren;
I was exiled and rejected.[o]
Who brought these up?
I was left[p] all alone,
but these—where have they come from?' "

22 This is what the Sovereign LORD says:

"See, I will beckon to the Gentiles,
I will lift up my banner[q] to the peoples;
they will bring your sons in their arms
and carry your daughters on their shoulders.[r]
23 Kings[s] will be your foster fathers,
and their queens your nursing mothers.[t]
They will bow down before you with their faces to
the ground;
they will lick the dust[u] at your feet.
Then you will know that I am the LORD;[v]
those who hope in me will not be disappointed."

49:13 [b]Isa 44:23 [c]Isa 40:1
49:15 [d]Isa 44:21
49:16 [e]SS 8:6 [f]Ps 48:12-13; Isa 62:6
49:17 [g]Isa 10:6
49:18 [h]Isa 43:5; 54:7; Isa 60:4 [i]Isa 45:23 [j]Isa 52:1
49:19 [k]Isa 54:1,3 [l]Isa 5:6 [m]Zec 10:10
49:20 [n]Isa 54:1-3
49:21 [o]Isa 5:13 [p]Isa 1:8
49:22 [q]Isa 11:10 [r]Isa 60:4
49:23 [s]Isa 60:3, 10-11 [t]Isa 60:16 [u]Ps 72:9 [v]Mic 7:17

49:17 "Sons" in this context may also be rendered "builders," based on the translation of this verse in the Dead Sea Scrolls and in some other ancient versions of Isaiah.
49:18 "Ornaments" here encompasses luxurious clothing and jewelry (see "Ancient Israelite Clothing and Jewelry on p. 1059), which represented both strength and joy. For information regarding the adornments of a bride, see "Weddings in Ancient Israel" on page 1039.
49:21 Here, as in 54:1, Israel is depicted as a barren woman—a disgrace and tragedy for a woman in ancient Near Eastern society.
49:22 For "banner," see the note on 5:26.

[24] Can plunder be taken from warriors,[w]
  or captives rescued from the fierce[a]?

[25] But this is what the LORD says:

"Yes, captives[x] will be taken from warriors,[y]
  and plunder retrieved from the fierce;
I will contend with those who contend with you,
  and your children I will save.[z]
[26] I will make your oppressors[a] eat[b] their own flesh;
  they will be drunk on their own blood,[c] as with wine.
Then all mankind will know[d]
  that I, the LORD, am your Savior,
  your Redeemer, the Mighty One of Jacob."

Israel's Sin and the Servant's Obedience

50 This is what the LORD says:

"Where is your mother's certificate of divorce[e]
  with which I sent her away?
Or to which of my creditors
  did I sell[f] you?
Because of your sins you were sold;[g]
  because of your transgressions your mother was sent away.
[2] When I came, why was there no one?
  When I called, why was there no one to answer?[h]
Was my arm too short[i] to ransom you?
  Do I lack the strength[j] to rescue you?
By a mere rebuke I dry up the sea,[k]
  I turn rivers into a desert;
their fish rot for lack of water
  and die of thirst.
[3] I clothe the sky with darkness
  and make sackcloth[l] its covering."

[4] The Sovereign LORD has given me an instructed tongue,[m]
  to know the word that sustains the weary.[n]
He wakens me morning by morning,[o]
  wakens my ear to listen like one being taught.
[5] The Sovereign LORD has opened my ears,[p]
  and I have not been rebellious;[q]
  I have not drawn back.
[6] I offered my back to those who beat[r] me,
  my cheeks to those who pulled out my beard;
I did not hide my face
  from mocking and spitting.[s]
[7] Because the Sovereign LORD helps[t] me,
  I will not be disgraced.
Therefore have I set my face like flint,[u]
  and I know I will not be put to shame.

49:24 [w]Mt 12:29; Lk 11:21
49:25 [x]Isa 14:2 [y]Jer 50:33-34 [z]Isa 25:9; 35:4
49:26 [a]Isa 9:4 [b]Isa 9:20 [c]Rev 16:6 [d]Eze 39:7
50:1 [e]Dt 24:1; Jer 3:8; Hos 2:2 [f]Ne 5:5; Mt 18:25 [g]Dt 32:30; Isa 52:3
50:2 [h]Isa 41:28 [i]Nu 11:23; Isa 59:1 [j]Ge 18:14 [k]Ex 14:22; Jos 3:16
50:3 [l]Rev 6:12
50:4 [m]Ex 4:12 [n]Mt 11:28 [o]Ps 5:3; 119:147; 143:8
50:5 [p]Isa 35:5 [q]Mt 26:39; Jn 8:29; 14:31; 15:10; Ac 26:19; Heb 5:8
50:6 [r]Isa 53:5; Mt 27:30; Mk 14:65; 15:19; Lk 22:63 [s]La 3:30; Mt 26:67
50:7 [t]Isa 42:1 [u]Eze 3:8-9

[a] 24 Dead Sea Scrolls, Vulgate and Syriac (see also Septuagint and verse 25); Masoretic Text *righteous*

49:26 During the siege of Jerusalem its ravenous inhabitants were reduced to cannibalism (La 4:10; cf. Zec 11:9 and its note; see also "Siege Warfare" on p. 465).
50:1 If a man's debts were not paid, his children could be sold into slavery (see 2Ki 4:1 and the note on Pr 6:1). But God has no creditors!
50:3 For "sackcloth," see the note on 15:3.
50:6 Beatings were standard punishment for criminals (see Pr 10:13; 19:29; 26:3; Mt 27:26; Jn 19:1), while pulling out someone's beard was a sign of disrespect and contempt (see 2Sa 10:4–5; Ne 13:25) and mocking and spitting demonstrated hatred (Job 30:10), insult or disgrace (Dt 25:9; Job 17:6; Mt 27:30).

[8]He who vindicates me is near.
Who then will bring charges against me?[v]
Let us face each other![w]
Who is my accuser?
Let him confront me!
[9]It is the Sovereign LORD who helps[x] me.
Who is he that will condemn me?
They will all wear out like a garment;
the moths[y] will eat them up.

[10]Who among you fears the LORD
and obeys the word of his servant?[z]
Let him who walks in the dark,
who has no light,
trust[a] in the name of the LORD
and rely on his God.
[11]But now, all you who light fires
and provide yourselves with flaming torches,[b]
go, walk in the light of your fires[c]
and of the torches you have set ablaze.
This is what you shall receive from my hand:
You will lie down in torment.[d]

50:8 [v]Isa 43:26; Ro 8:32-34 [w]Isa 41:1
50:9 [x]Isa 41:10 [y]Job 13:28; Isa 51:8
50:10 [z]Isa 49:3 [a]Isa 26:4
50:11 [b]Pr 26:18 [c]Jas 3:6 [d]Isa 65:13-15

Everlasting Salvation for Zion

51 "Listen[e] to me, you who pursue righteousness[f]
and who seek the LORD:
Look to the rock from which you were cut
and to the quarry from which you were hewn;
[2]look to Abraham,[g] your father,
and to Sarah, who gave you birth.
When I called him he was but one,
and I blessed him and made him many.[h]
[3]The LORD will surely comfort[i] Zion
and will look with compassion on all her ruins;[j]
he will make her deserts like Eden,[k]
her wastelands like the garden of the LORD.
Joy and gladness[l] will be found in her,
thanksgiving and the sound of singing.

[4]"Listen to me, my people;[m]
hear me, my nation:
The law will go out from me;
my justice[n] will become a light to the nations.[o]
[5]My righteousness draws near speedily,
my salvation is on the way,[p]
and my arm[q] will bring justice to the nations.
The islands will look to me
and wait in hope for my arm.
[6]Lift up your eyes to the heavens,
look at the earth beneath;
the heavens will vanish like smoke,[r]
the earth will wear out like a garment[s]
and its inhabitants die like flies.

51:1 [e]Isa 46:3 [f]ver 7; Ps 94:15; Ro 9:30-31
51:2 [g]Isa 29:22; Ro 4:16; Heb 11:11 [h]Ge 12:2
51:3 [i]Isa 40:1 [j]Isa 52:9 [k]Ge 2:8 [l]Isa 25:9; 66:10
51:4 [m]Ps 50:7 [n]Isa 2:4 [o]Isa 42:4,6
51:5 [p]Isa 46:13 [q]Isa 40:10; 63:1,5
51:6 [r]Mt 24:35; 2Pe 3:10 [s]Ps 102:25-26

51:5 For "arm," see the note on 52:10 and for "islands" the note on 41:1.

But my salvation will last forever,
my righteousness will never fail.

7 "Hear me, you who know what is right,[t]
you people who have my law in your hearts:[u]
Do not fear the reproach of men
or be terrified by their insults.[v]
8 For the moth will eat them up like a garment;[w]
the worm will devour them like wool.
But my righteousness will last forever,[x]
my salvation through all generations."

9 Awake, awake! Clothe yourself with strength,[y]
O arm of the LORD;
awake, as in days gone by,
as in generations of old.[z]
Was it not you who cut Rahab to pieces,
who pierced that monster[a] through?
10 Was it not you who dried up the sea,[b]
the waters of the great deep,
who made a road in the depths of the sea
so that the redeemed might cross over?
11 The ransomed[c] of the LORD will return.
They will enter Zion with singing;
everlasting joy will crown their heads.
Gladness and joy[d] will overtake them,
and sorrow and sighing will flee away.[e]

12 "I, even I, am he who comforts[f] you.
Who are you that you fear mortal men,[g]
the sons of men, who are but grass,[h]
13 that you forget[i] the LORD your Maker,[j]
who stretched out the heavens[k]
and laid the foundations of the earth,
that you live in constant terror[l] every day
because of the wrath of the oppressor,
who is bent on destruction?
For where is the wrath of the oppressor?
14 The cowering prisoners will soon be set free;
they will not die in their dungeon,
nor will they lack bread.[m]
15 For I am the LORD your God,
who churns up the sea[n] so that its waves roar—
the LORD Almighty is his name.
16 I have put my words in your mouth[o]
and covered you with the shadow of my hand[p]—
I who set the heavens in place,
who laid the foundations of the earth,
and who say to Zion, 'You are my people.' "

The Cup of the LORD's Wrath

17 Awake, awake![q]
Rise up, O Jerusalem,

51:7 [t]ver 1 [u]Ps 37:31 [v]Mt 5:11; Ac 5:41
51:8 [w]Isa 50:9 [x]ver 6
51:9 [y]Isa 52:1 [z]Dt 4:34 [a]Ps 74:13
51:10 [b]Ex 14:22
51:11 [c]Isa 35:9 [d]Jer 33:11 [e]Rev 7:17
51:12 [f]2Co 1:4 [g]Ps 118:6; Isa 2:22 [h]Isa 40:6-7; 1Pe 1:24
51:13 [i]Isa 17:10 [j]Isa 45:11 [k]Ps 104:2; Isa 48:13 [l]Isa 7:4
51:14 [m]Isa 49:10
51:15 [n]Jer 31:35
51:16 [o]Dt 18:18; Isa 59:21 [p]Ex 33:22
51:17 [q]Isa 52:1

51:9–11 See the note on 52:10 for the figurative implications of the Lord's arm.

51:9 For "Rahab," see the notes on 30:7 and on Job 9:13.
51:10 "Sea" in this context refers to the Red Sea.

TEXTUAL CRITICISM

ISAIAH 51 Any book copied by hand is likely to contain errors. Not surprisingly, there are copyists' errors (called textual or scribal errors) in ancient Biblical manuscripts. The original copies of the books were lost long ago. Thus our sources for the Biblical materials are limited to handwritten copies (of copies) of the originals. We do also have access to copies of ancient translations of the Bible into other languages, as well as citations of the Bible by early rabbis and church fathers.[1] Thus Hebrew and Greek manuscripts of the Bible, together with early translations and citations of Scripture, witness to the correct reading of a particular text.

How did scribal errors arise? Poor memory, impaired judgment, mishearing and errors of sight or misunderstanding often caused the best-intentioned scribes to omit, substitute or repeat letters or entire words. Sometimes scribes made matters worse when they deliberately altered the text in an attempt to rectify something they perceived as a problem (deliberate alterations are probably very rare, however). In time, the result was a series of accidental corruptions or intended improvements that departed from the original text.[2]

Textual criticism is the attempt to restore the Biblical authors' original words by comparing and contrasting the various copies and translations of the Bible. Here "criticism" does not mean "finding fault with" but "evaluating" the existing copies of the text. Significantly, while textual errors do exist among the Biblical witnesses, they do not destroy the Bible's credibility or message. Just as an alert reader can understand a book or newspaper article that has typographical errors in it, so too God's Word is able to speak for itself in spite of the minor corruptions that have arisen through scribal transmission. Most of the Biblical text is certain, and where variations do occur among existing copies, the original wording can usually be determined with a good degree of certainty by a thorough acquaintance with the available manuscripts. Most modern translations use footnotes to let readers know where the text is difficult or where scribal errors may exist.

Scroll container from Qumran, pre-A.D. 68

© The Schøyen Collection; photography courtesy of Mr. Martin Schøyen

An example of a textual problem is found in the last sentence of Isaiah 51:19. The New American Standard Bible translates the question "*How shall I* comfort you?", while the NIV words it "*Who* can console you?" (emphasis added for both translations). These different renderings reflect a differ ence of opinion over which manuscripts preserve the best reading. The NIV follows a reading that is found in a Hebrew manuscript from the **Dead Sea Scrolls**.[3] This translation is also supported by the Greek (**Septuagint**), Latin (**Vulgate**) and Syriac (**Peshitta**) translations of the Old Testament. On the other hand, the standard edition of the Hebrew Old Testament (the **Masoretic Text**) reads "How can I comfort you?" and was followed by the NASB translators.

The above example also makes the point that most scribal questions involve minor points in the text. We have good reason to be confident that the translations now available faithfully, albeit never perfectly, reflect what the prophets and other Biblical authors originally wrote. The presence of scribal errors is not a reason to consider the Bible untrustworthy.

[1]See "Texts of the Old Testament" on page 1491 and "The Old Testament of the Early Church" on page 1967. [2]See, for example, "Early Scribal Emendation" on page 448. [3]See "The Great Isaiah Scroll" on page 1115.

you who have drunk from the hand of the LORD
the cup of his wrath,[r]
you who have drained to its dregs
the goblet that makes men stagger.[s]
18 Of all the sons[t] she bore
there was none to guide her;[u]
of all the sons she reared
there was none to take her by the hand.
19 These double calamities[v] have come upon you—
who can comfort you?—
ruin and destruction, famine[w] and sword—
who can[a] console you?
20 Your sons have fainted;
they lie at the head of every street,[x]
like antelope caught in a net.
They are filled with the wrath of the LORD
and the rebuke of your God.
21 Therefore hear this, you afflicted one,
made drunk,[y] but not with wine.
22 This is what your Sovereign LORD says,
your God, who defends[z] his people:
"See, I have taken out of your hand
the cup[a] that made you stagger;
from that cup, the goblet of my wrath,
you will never drink again.
23 I will put it into the hands of your tormentors,[b]
who said to you,
'Fall prostrate[c] that we may walk[d] over you.'
And you made your back like the ground,
like a street to be walked over."

52 Awake, awake,[e] O Zion,
clothe yourself with strength.[f]
Put on your garments of splendor,[g]
O Jerusalem, the holy city.[h]
The uncircumcised and defiled
will not enter you again.[i]
2 Shake off your dust;[j]
rise up, sit enthroned, O Jerusalem.
Free yourself from the chains on your neck,
O captive Daughter of Zion.

3 For this is what the LORD says:

"You were sold for nothing,[k]
and without money[l] you will be redeemed."

4 For this is what the Sovereign LORD says:

"At first my people went down to Egypt[m] to live;
lately, Assyria has oppressed them.

51:17 [r]Job 21:20; Rev 14:10; 16:19 [s]Ps 60:3
51:18 [t]Ps 88:18 [u]Isa 49:21
51:19 [v]Isa 47:9 [w]Isa 14:30
51:20 [x]Isa 5:25; Jer 14:16
51:21 [y]ver 17; Isa 29:9
51:22 [z]Isa 49:25 [a]ver 17
51:23 [b]Isa 49:26; Jer 25:15-17,26, 28; 49:12 [c]Zec 12:2 [d]Jos 10:24
52:1 [e]Isa 51:17 [f]Isa 51:9 [g]Ex 28:2,40; Ps 110:3; Zec 3:4 [h]Ne 11:1; Mt 4:5; Rev 21:2 [i]Na 1:15; Rev 21:27
52:2 [j]Isa 29:4
52:3 [k]Ps 44:12 [l]Isa 45:13
52:4 [m]Ge 46:6

[a] *19* Dead Sea Scrolls, Septuagint, Vulgate and Syriac; Masoretic Text / *how can I*

51:18 Grown children in the ancient Near East were expected to undertake the care of their ailing or infirm parents (cf. 1Ti 5:8).
51:23 "Your tormentors" is a reference to the Babylonians.
52:1 "Garments of splendor" may have been a reference to the priestly robes that in a sense "belonged" to Jerusalem as a "holy city" (see the note on 49:18). The descriptive phrase "uncircumcised and defiled" depicted Judah's foreign invaders (see Jdg 14:33; Isa 5:8).
52:2 "Daughter of Zion" personified Jerusalem.

52:5 [n]Eze 36:20; Ro 2:24*
52:6 [o]Isa 49:23

[5]"And now what do I have here?" declares the LORD.
"For my people have been taken away for nothing,
and those who rule them mock,[a]"
declares the LORD.
"And all day long
my name is constantly blasphemed.[n]
[6]Therefore my people will know[o] my name;
therefore in that day they will know
that it is I who foretold it.
Yes, it is I."

52:7 [p]Isa 40:9; Ro 10:15* [q]Na 1:15; Eph 6:15 [r]Ps 93:1

[7]How beautiful on the mountains
are the feet of those who bring good news,[p]
who proclaim peace,[q]
who bring good tidings,
who proclaim salvation,
who say to Zion,
"Your God reigns!"[r]

52:8 [s]Isa 62:6

[8]Listen! Your watchmen[s] lift up their voices;
together they shout for joy.
When the LORD returns to Zion,
they will see it with their own eyes.

52:9 [t]Ps 98:4 [u]Isa 51:3 [v]Isa 48:20

[9]Burst into songs of joy[t] together,
you ruins[u] of Jerusalem,
for the LORD has comforted his people,
he has redeemed Jerusalem.[v]

52:10 [w]Isa 66:18 [x]Ps 98:2-3; Lk 3:6

[10]The LORD will lay bare his holy arm
in the sight of all the nations,[w]
and all the ends of the earth will see
the salvation[x] of our God.

52:11 [y]Isa 48:20 [z]Isa 1:16; 2Co 6:17* [a]2Ti 2:19

[11]Depart,[y] depart, go out from there!
Touch no unclean thing![z]
Come out from it and be pure,[a]
you who carry the vessels of the LORD.

52:12 [b]Ex 12:11 [c]Mic 2:13 [d]Ex 14:19

[12]But you will not leave in haste[b]
or go in flight;
for the LORD will go before you,[c]
the God of Israel will be your rear guard.[d]

The Suffering and Glory of the Servant

52:13 [e]Isa 42:1 [f]Isa 57:15; Php 2:9

[13]See, my servant[e] will act wisely[b];
he will be raised and lifted up and highly exalted.[f]
[14]Just as there were many who were appalled at him[c]—
his appearance was so disfigured beyond that of any man
and his form marred beyond human likeness—

[a] 5 Dead Sea Scrolls and Vulgate; Masoretic Text *wail* [b] 13 Or *will prosper* [c] 14 Hebrew *you*

52:7 This verse is a reference to messengers who ran from the scene of a battle to bring news of the outcome to a waiting king and people (see 2Sa 18:26; Na 1:15). Here the news is the return from exile (Isa 52:11–12; see 40:9; 41:27).
52:8 Watchmen were stationed on Jerusalem's walls (see the note on SS 3:3).
52:10 The reference here to the Lord's arm is a figure for personal, active power. Much as God lays "bare his holy arm," we might say of a man about to undertake some task that he has "rolled up his sleeves." The Lord's arm (53:1) is figurative as well of his personal intervention. In particular the figure of the arm looks back to what God had done at the time of the exodus (Ex 6:6; Dt 4:34; 5:15; Isa 51:9–10).
52:11 Cyrus allowed the people to take back the articles of the temple seized by Nebuchadnezzar (Ezr 1:7–11). From the beginning, the priests and Levites had been responsible for them (see Nu 3:6–8; 2Ch 5:4–7).
52:14 Those who would generations later witness Jesus' suffering

15 so will he sprinkle many nations,[a]
and kings will shut their mouths because of him.
For what they were not told, they will see,
and what they have not heard, they will understand.[g]

53 Who has believed our message[h]
and to whom has the arm of the LORD been revealed?[i]
2 He grew up before him like a tender shoot,
and like a root out of dry ground.
He had no beauty or majesty to attract us to him,
nothing in his appearance[j] that we should desire him.
3 He was despised and rejected by men,
a man of sorrows, and familiar with suffering.[k]
Like one from whom men hide their faces
he was despised,[l] and we esteemed him not.

4 Surely he took up our infirmities
and carried our sorrows,[m]
yet we considered him stricken by God,[n]
smitten by him, and afflicted.
5 But he was pierced for our transgressions,[o]
he was crushed for our iniquities;
the punishment that brought us peace was upon him,
and by his wounds we are healed.[p]
6 We all, like sheep, have gone astray,
each of us has turned to his own way;
and the LORD has laid on him
the iniquity of us all.

7 He was oppressed and afflicted,
yet he did not open his mouth;[q]
he was led like a lamb to the slaughter,
and as a sheep before her shearers is silent,
so he did not open his mouth.
8 By oppression[b] and judgment he was taken away.
And who can speak of his descendants?
For he was cut off from the land of the living;[r]
for the transgression[s] of my people he was stricken.[c]
9 He was assigned a grave with the wicked,
and with the rich[t] in his death,
though he had done no violence,[u]
nor was any deceit in his mouth.[v]

10 Yet it was the LORD's will[w] to crush[x] him and cause him to suffer,[y]
and though the LORD makes[d] his life a guilt offering,
he will see his offspring[z] and prolong his days,
and the will of the LORD will prosper in his hand.

52:15 [g]Ro 15:21*; Eph 3:4-5
53:1 [h]Ro 10:16* [i]Jn 12:38*
53:2 [j]Isa 52:14
53:3 [k]ver 4,10; Lk 18:31-33 [l]Ps 22:6; Jn 1:10-11
53:4 [m]Mt 8:17* [n]Jn 19:7
53:5 [o]Ro 4:25; 1Co 15:3; Heb 9:28 [p]1Pe 2:24-25
53:7 [q]Mk 14:61
53:8 [r]Da 9:26; Ac 8:32-33* [s]ver 12
53:9 [t]Mt 27:57-60 [u]Isa 42:1-3 [v]1Pe 2:22*
53:10 [w]Isa 46:10 [x]ver 5 [y]ver 3 [z]Ps 22:30

[a] 15 Hebrew; Septuagint *so will many nations marvel at him* [b] 8 Or *From arrest* [c] 8 Or *away. / Yet who of his generation considered / that he was cut off from the land of the living / for the transgression of my people, / to whom the blow was due?* [d] 10 Hebrew *though you make*

and death on the cross—not those who saw Jesus in some earlier context—would be "appalled" by his appearance, for he would at that point be "disfigured," a term used of a "blemished animal," one unfit for offering to the Lord (Mal 1:14). This prophecy makes clear that Christ's treatment at the time of his passion and crucifixion would be absolutely inhumane.

53:1 See the note on 52:10 for the figurative implications of the Lord's arm.

53:6 In the same way Israel's priests laid their hands on the head of a scapegoat, symbolically transferring the people's sins to it (see Lev 16:20–22), so our burden of sin was laid upon Christ (see 1Pe 2:24).

53:8 Jesus died without descendants, which was considered a tragedy for a man as well as for a woman (2Sa 18:18).

53:10 Restitution was typically required for a guilt offering; the offender was expected to sacrifice a ram (see Lev 5:15).

"Offspring" refers here to Christ's spiritual progeny and "prolong his days" to his eternal life.

53:11 [a]Jn 10:14-18 [b]Ro 5:18-19

11 After the suffering[a] of his soul,
he will see the light ⌞of life⌟[a] and be satisfied[b];
by his knowledge[c] my righteous servant will justify[b] many,
and he will bear their iniquities.

53:12 [c]Php 2:9 [d]Mt 26:28,38,39,42 [e]Mk 15:27*; Lk 22:37*; 23:32

12 Therefore I will give him a portion among the great,[d][c]
and he will divide the spoils with the strong,[e]
because he poured out his life unto death,[d]
and was numbered with the transgressors.[e]
For he bore the sin of many,
and made intercession for the transgressors.

The Future Glory of Zion

54:1 [f]Isa 49:20 [g]1Sa 2:5; Gal 4:27*

54 "Sing, O barren woman,
you who never bore a child;
burst into song, shout for joy,
you who were never in labor;
because more are the children[f] of the desolate woman
than of her who has a husband,[g]"
says the LORD.

54:2 [h]Isa 49:19-20 [i]Ex 35:18; 39:40

2 "Enlarge the place of your tent,[h]
stretch your tent curtains wide,
do not hold back;
lengthen your cords,
strengthen your stakes.[i]
3 For you will spread out to the right and to the left;
your descendants will dispossess nations
and settle in their desolate[j] cities.

54:3 [j]Isa 49:19

4 "Do not be afraid; you will not suffer shame.
Do not fear disgrace; you will not be humiliated.
You will forget the shame of your youth
and remember no more the reproach[k] of your widowhood.

54:4 [k]Isa 51:7

54:5 [l]Jer 3:14 [m]Isa 48:17 [n]Isa 6:3

5 For your Maker is your husband[l]—
the LORD Almighty is his name—
the Holy One of Israel is your Redeemer;[m]
he is called the God of all the earth.[n]

54:6 [o]Isa 49:14-21 [p]Isa 50:1-2; 62:4,12

6 The LORD will call you back[o]
as if you were a wife deserted[p] and distressed in spirit—
a wife who married young,
only to be rejected," says your God.

54:7 [q]Isa 26:20 [r]Isa 49:18

7 "For a brief moment[q] I abandoned you,
but with deep compassion I will bring you back.[r]

54:8 [s]Isa 60:10 [t]ver 10

8 In a surge of anger[s]
I hid my face from you for a moment,
but with everlasting kindness[t]
I will have compassion on you,"
says the LORD your Redeemer.

54:9 [u]Ge 8:21

9 "To me this is like the days of Noah,
when I swore that the waters of Noah would never again cover the earth.[u]

[a] 11 Dead Sea Scrolls (see also Septuagint); Masoretic Text does not have *the light ⌞of life⌟*. [b] 11 Or (with Masoretic Text) [11]*He will see the result of the suffering of his soul / and be satisfied* [c] 11 Or *by knowledge of him* [d] 12 Or *many* [e] 12 Or *numerous*

54:1 In the ancient Near East, infertility was a terrible fate for a woman. Widowhood also was a disgrace, for a woman could contribute to society only through her husband. There was still one worse humiliation: divorce—the assumption being that the woman was in some way deficient.

So now I have sworn not to be angry[v] with you,
never to rebuke you again.
10 Though the mountains be shaken[w]
and the hills be removed,
yet my unfailing love for you will not be shaken[x]
nor my covenant[y] of peace be removed,"
says the LORD, who has compassion[z] on you.

11 "O afflicted[a] city, lashed by storms[b] and not comforted,[c]
I will build you with stones of turquoise,[a] [d]
your foundations[e] with sapphires.[b]
12 I will make your battlements of rubies,
your gates of sparkling jewels,
and all your walls of precious stones.
13 All your sons will be taught by the LORD,[f]
and great will be your children's peace.[g]

54:9 [v]Isa 12:1
54:10 [w]Ps 46:2 [x]Isa 51:6 [y]Ps 89:34 [z]ver 8
54:11 [a]Isa 14:32 [b]Isa 28:2; 29:6 [c]Isa 51:19 [d]1Ch 29:2; Rev 21:18 [e]Isa 28:16; Rev 21:19-20
54:13 [f]Jn 6:45* [g]Isa 48:18

[a] *11* The meaning of the Hebrew for this word is uncertain. [b] *11* Or *lapis lazuli*

54:11 Turquoise was used in the construction of Solomon's temple (1Ch 29:2). For "sapphires," see Exodus 24:10, Ezekiel 1:26 and 10:1.

54:12 "Battlements" were parapets on the tops of walls for the partial concealment and the protection of soldiers.

Precious Stones of the Biblical World

ISAIAH 54 Precious stones have been known and sought after since earliest antiquity—gathered as loose rocks, chiseled out of sandstone or mined in shafts (Job 28:1–11). One of the first, and finest, examples of jewelry known in the ancient world comes from the royal tombs of Ur (c. 2500 B.C.). Among the funerary hoard is a queen's diadem (crown or royal headband), exquisitely fashioned of hammered gold beech leaves and floral motifs in lapis lazuli, as well as bead necklaces of gold, lapis, cornelian and agate. Valued for their rarity and beauty, gemstones served a wide variety of purposes in the ancient world:

✣ *Adornment:* Precious stones were used for ornamentation in both life and death (Isa 3:20–21).

✣ *Currency:* Gems were coveted as a mark of wealth (2Ch 32:27) and exchanged as a form of currency preceding coinage.[1] Their light weight, ease of transport and durability made precious stones in the form of jewelry the most common bridal gift and dowry (Ge 24:22; Isa 61:10; Eze 16:11–13). As a woman's personal possessions, they also became her inheritance.

✣ *Seals:* Hard stones such as jasper, agate and onyx were among the favorites for engraved seals. Inscribed with pictorial scenes or letters identifying their owner (Ge 38:18; 1Ki 21:8), signet rings were pressed, and cylinder seals rolled, on wax or clay to leave their impression. Jewels naturally served as insignia of royalty (Zec 9:16) and, by extension, of royal authority (Ge 41:42).[2]

✣ *Signs of National Power:* Gemstones were exchanged as gifts between rulers (2Ch 9:9) and seized as spoils of war (Jdg 8:26).

✣ *Ceremonial:* Ceremonial use of precious stones included their dedication to the Lord as an offering (Ex 35:22; Nu 31:50). The most abundant use of gems in ancient Israel was in the adornment of the temple (1Ch 29:2) and its chief ministrant, who wore a jewel-encrusted breastplate (Ex 28:17–21).

✣ *Theological Symbols:* The value, luminosity and enduring nature of gems rendered them a most apropos literary image for the glory of the Lord (Eze 1:26) and for the recreated, eschatological (end time) people of God (Isa 54:12; Rev 21:18–21).

[1]See "Banking and Money in the Ancient World" on page 696. [2]See "Signet Rings" on page 728.

54:14 [h]Isa 9:4

[14] In righteousness you will be established:
Tyranny[h] will be far from you;
you will have nothing to fear.
Terror will be far removed;
it will not come near you.
[15] If anyone does attack you, it will not be my doing;
whoever attacks you will surrender[i] to you.

54:15 [i]Isa 41:11-16

[16] "See, it is I who created the blacksmith
who fans the coals into flame
and forges a weapon fit for its work.
And it is I who have created the destroyer to work havoc;
[17] no weapon forged against you will prevail,[j]
and you will refute[k] every tongue that accuses you.
This is the heritage of the servants of the LORD,
and this is their vindication from me,"
declares the LORD.

54:17 [j]Isa 29:8 [k]Isa 45:24-25

Invitation to the Thirsty

55 "Come, all you who are thirsty,[l]
come to the waters;
and you who have no money,
come, buy[m] and eat!
Come, buy wine and milk[n]
without money and without cost.[o]
[2] Why spend money on what is not bread,
and your labor on what does not satisfy?[p]
Listen, listen to me, and eat what is good,[q]
and your soul will delight in the richest of fare.
[3] Give ear and come to me;
hear me, that your soul may live.[r]
I will make an everlasting covenant[s] with you,
my faithful love[t] promised to David.[u]
[4] See, I have made him a witness to the peoples,
a leader and commander[v] of the peoples.
[5] Surely you will summon nations[w] you know not,
and nations that do not know you will hasten to you,
because of the LORD your God,
the Holy One of Israel,
for he has endowed you with splendor."[x]

55:1 [l]Jn 4:14; 7:37 [m]La 5:4; Mt 13:44; Rev 3:18 [n]SS 5:1 [o]Hos 14:4; Mt 10:8; Rev 21:6
55:2 [p]Ps 22:26; Ecc 6:2; Hos 8:7 [q]Isa 1:19
55:3 [r]Lev 18:5; Ro 10:5 [s]Isa 61:8 [t]Isa 54:8 [u]Ac 13:34*
55:4 [v]Jer 30:9; Eze 34:23-24
55:5 [w]Isa 49:6 [x]Isa 60:9

[6] Seek the LORD while he may be found;[y]
call[z] on him while he is near.
[7] Let the wicked forsake his way
and the evil man his thoughts.[a]
Let him turn[b] to the LORD, and he will have mercy[c]
on him,
and to our God, for he will freely pardon.[d]

55:6 [y]Ps 32:6; Isa 49:8; 2Co 6:1-2 [z]Isa 65:24
55:7 [a]Isa 32:7; 59:7 [b]Isa 44:22 [c]Isa 54:10 [d]Isa 1:18; 40:2

[8] "For my thoughts are not your thoughts,
neither are your ways my ways,"[e]
declares the LORD.

55:8 [e]Isa 53:6

54:16 See the note on coal/charcoal at Psalm 120:4.
55:1 Spiritual thirst is primarily in view (see Ps 42:1–2; 63:1; Isa 41:17; 44:3). In hard times even water had to be purchased (see La 5:4), but here the water (a symbol of spiritual refreshment)—as well as the "wine" and "milk" (symbols of abundance, enjoyment and nourishment)—were free: The death of the servant (Isa 53:5–9) would pay for the free gift of life (see Ro 6:23).

[9]"As the heavens are higher than the earth,[f]
so are my ways higher than your ways
and my thoughts than your thoughts.
[10]As the rain[g] and the snow
come down from heaven,
and do not return to it
without watering the earth
and making it bud and flourish,
so that it yields seed for the sower and bread for the eater,[h]
[11]so is my word that goes out from my mouth:
It will not return to me empty,[i]
but will accomplish what I desire
and achieve the purpose[j] for which I sent it.
[12]You will go out in joy
and be led forth in peace;[k]
the mountains and hills
will burst into song before you,
and all the trees[l] of the field
will clap their hands.[m]
[13]Instead of the thornbush will grow the pine tree,
and instead of briers[n] the myrtle[o] will grow.
This will be for the LORD's renown,[p]
for an everlasting sign,
which will not be destroyed."

55:9 [f]Ps 103:11
55:10 [g]Isa 30:23 [h]2Co 9:10
55:11 [i]Isa 45:23 [j]Isa 44:26
55:12 [k]Isa 54:10, 13 [l]1Ch 16:33 [m]Ps 98:8
55:13 [n]Isa 5:6 [o]Isa 41:19 [p]Isa 63:12

Salvation for Others

56 This is what the LORD says:

"Maintain justice[q]
and do what is right,
for my salvation[r] is close at hand
and my righteousness will soon be revealed.
[2]Blessed[s] is the man who does this,
the man who holds it fast,
who keeps the Sabbath[t] without desecrating it,
and keeps his hand from doing any evil."

[3]Let no foreigner who has bound himself to the LORD say,
"The LORD will surely exclude me from his people."
And let not any eunuch[u] complain,
"I am only a dry tree."

[4]For this is what the LORD says:

"To the eunuchs who keep my Sabbaths,
who choose what pleases me
and hold fast to my covenant—
[5]to them I will give within my temple and its walls[v]
a memorial and a name
better than sons and daughters;

56:1 [q]Isa 1:17 [r]Ps 85:9
56:2 [s]Ps 119:2 [t]Ex 20:8,10; Isa 58:13
56:3 [u]Jer 38:7 *fn*; Ac 8:27
56:5 [v]Isa 26:1; 60:18

56:3 At least for several generations (see Ex 12:43; Dt 23:3,7–8), resident aliens from certain nations had been excluded from worship in Israel. But the work of the Lord's servant would eliminate this restriction (see 60:10). Eunuchs (see "The Eunuch" on p. 1159) had also been barred from the assembly of the Lord (see Dt 23:1), although they could still be a part of God's people (Ac 8:27,38–40).
56:5 The Hebrew phrase for "a memorial and a name" (*yad vashem*) was many centuries later chosen as the name of the principal Holocaust monument in Jerusalem in modern Israel.

56:5 [w]Isa 48:19; 55:13
56:6 [x]Isa 60:7, 10; 61:5 [y]ver 2,4

I will give them an everlasting name
that will not be cut off.[w]
6 And foreigners who bind themselves to the LORD
to serve[x] him,
to love the name of the LORD,
and to worship him,
all who keep the Sabbath[y] without desecrating it
and who hold fast to my covenant—

The Eunuch

ISAIAH 56 The compassion of God is poignantly illustrated in the reference to the eunuch in Isaiah 56:3–5, an allusion that must be understood in light of Deuteronomy 23:1, a text forbidding eunuchs from entering the assembly of the Lord. The word translated "eunuch" in Isaiah is *saris*, which is most likely a loanword from an **Akkadian** phrase meaning "one at the head of [the king]." As is probably true in Hebrew, the Akkadian meaning evolved from the more general sense of "officer, official" to "castrated official." Potiphar, in Genesis 39:1, was a *saris*, but this early use of the word meant only "official," not "eunuch." However, the time frame and context of Isaiah 56:3–4 require that the reader understand *saris* as "a castrated person."

Although some have attempted to relate this reference to some kind of historical reality, specifically to a return of **exiles** who had served as castrated officials in foreign courts (perhaps including Nehemiah), the primary focus should remain on the message: What defiles a person before God is not physical deformity but an unrepentant heart (cf. Mt 15:10–20).

The divine promise to give a "memorial" and a name to the faithful eunuch is quite profound. A eunuch could never have attained a memorial or passed along his name by means of having children. Also, the deliberate choice of the Hebrew noun "hand" (translated "memorial") and the verb "cut off" in verse 5 is remarkable. In the ancient Near East the word *hand* was often used euphemistically for the male genitals. God will provide a symbolic overturning in eternity of what has been taken away from the eunuch in the present. The prophetic foreshadowing, possibly of Nehemiah and certainly of the Ethiopian eunuch in Acts 8, is striking.

Lexical listing of titles and professions, with the world's oldest known signature on the reverse; Sumer, thirty-first century B.C.

© The Schøyen Collection; photography courtesy of Mr. Martin Schøyen

[7] these I will bring to my holy mountain[z]
and give them joy in my house of prayer.
Their burnt offerings and sacrifices[a]
will be accepted on my altar;
for my house will be called
a house of prayer for all nations.[b]"[c]
[8] The Sovereign LORD declares—
he who gathers the exiles of Israel:
"I will gather[d] still others to them
besides those already gathered."

56:7 [z]Isa 2:2 [a]Ro 12:1; Heb 13:15 [b]Mt 21:13*; Lk 19:46* [c]Mk 11:17*
56:8 [d]Isa 11:12; 60:3-11; Jn 10:16

God's Accusation Against the Wicked

[9] Come, all you beasts of the field,[e]
come and devour, all you beasts of the forest!
[10] Israel's watchmen[f] are blind,
they all lack knowledge;
they are all mute dogs,
they cannot bark;
they lie around and dream,
they love to sleep.[g]
[11] They are dogs with mighty appetites;
they never have enough.
They are shepherds[h] who lack understanding;[i]
they all turn to their own way,
each seeks his own gain.[j]
[12] "Come," each one cries, "let me get wine!
Let us drink our fill of beer!
And tomorrow will be like today,
or even far better."[k]

56:9 [e]Isa 18:6; Jer 12:9
56:10 [f]Eze 3:17 [g]Na 3:18
56:11 [h]Eze 34:2 [i]Isa 1:3 [j]Isa 57:17; Eze 13:19; Mic 3:11
56:12 [k]Ps 10:6; Lk 12:18-19

57 The righteous perish,[l]
and no one ponders it in his heart;[m]
devout men are taken away,
and no one understands
that the righteous are taken away
to be spared from evil.[n]
[2] Those who walk uprightly[o]
enter into peace;
they find rest as they lie in death.

[3] "But you—come here, you sons of a sorceress,
you offspring of adulterers[p] and prostitutes![q]
[4] Whom are you mocking?
At whom do you sneer
and stick out your tongue?
Are you not a brood of rebels,
the offspring of liars?
[5] You burn with lust among the oaks
and under every spreading tree;[r]

57:1 [l]Ps 12:1 [m]Isa 42:25 [n]2Ki 22:20
57:2 [o]Isa 26:7
57:3 [p]Mt 16:4 [q]Isa 1:21
57:5 [r]2Ki 16:4

56:7 For commentary on Old Testament expressions of joy, see the note on Psalm 96:11.
56:10 Israel's prophets are described as blind "watchmen" (see the note on Eze 3:17) and "mute dogs" (dogs guarded the sheep): They were useless.
57:3 A "sorceress" was a woman who practiced magic or consulted evil spirits (see 3:2–3 and its note; see also Dt 18:10; Isa 47:12; and "Akkadian Divination" on p. 277).
"Adulterers" and "prostitutes" here connote spiritual adultery—that is, idolatry (see vv. 5–8; cf. Ex 34:15).
57:5 Pagan rituals involving sexual immorality were often conducted under oak trees, which were considered sacred (see the note

57:5 [s]Lev 18:21; Ps 106:37-38; Eze 16:20
57:6 [t]Jer 3:9 [u]Jer 7:18 [v]Jer 5:9,29; 9:9
57:7 [w]Jer 3:6; Eze 16:16
57:8 [x]Eze 16:26; 23:7 [y]Eze 23:18
57:9 [z]Eze 23:16, 40
57:10 [a]Jer 2:25; 18:12
57:11 [b]Pr 29:25 [c]Jer 2:32; 3:21 [d]Ps 50:21
57:12 [e]Isa 29:15; Mic 3:2-4,8
57:13 [f]Jer 22:20; 30:15 [g]Ps 37:9 [h]Isa 65:9-11
57:14 [i]Isa 62:10; Jer 18:15

you sacrifice your children[s] in the ravines
and under the overhanging crags.
6 ⌞The idols⌟[t] among the smooth stones of the ravines are your portion;
they, they are your lot.
Yes, to them you have poured out drink offerings[u]
and offered grain offerings.
In the light of these things, should I relent?[v]
7 You have made your bed on a high and lofty hill;[w]
there you went up to offer your sacrifices.
8 Behind your doors and your doorposts
you have put your pagan symbols.
Forsaking me, you uncovered your bed,
you climbed into it and opened it wide;
you made a pact with those whose beds you love,[x]
and you looked on their nakedness.[y]
9 You went to Molech[a] with olive oil
and increased your perfumes.
You sent your ambassadors[b][z] far away;
you descended to the grave[c] itself!
10 You were wearied by all your ways,
but you would not say, 'It is hopeless.'[a]
You found renewal of your strength,
and so you did not faint.

11 "Whom have you so dreaded and feared[b]
that you have been false to me,
and have neither remembered[c] me
nor pondered this in your hearts?
Is it not because I have long been silent[d]
that you do not fear me?
12 I will expose your righteousness and your works,[e]
and they will not benefit you.
13 When you cry out[f] for help,
let your collection ⌞of idols⌟ save you!
The wind will carry all of them off,
a mere breath will blow them away.
But the man who makes me his refuge
will inherit the land[g]
and possess my holy mountain."[h]

Comfort for the Contrite

14 And it will be said:

"Build up, build up, prepare the road!
Remove the obstacles out of the way of my people."[i]

[a] 9 Or *to the king* [b] 9 Or *idols* [c] 9 Hebrew *Sheol*

---

on 1:29), and "spreading" trees were associated with the high places of pagan worship (1Ki 14:23; cf. Jer 2:20; 3:13; see also "The High Places" on p. 1318).

Child sacrifice was often linked to the worship of either Molech (cf. v. 9; see the note on 30:33) or Baal (Jer 19:5; see the notes on Jer 7:31,32). Psalm 106:37–38 speaks of children being sacrificed to idols and demons (see "Human Sacrifice in the Ancient Near East" on p. 182).

57:6 "Ravines" may be a reference to the Hinnom Valley (see Jer 7:31 and its note).

"Drink offerings" were popular pagan libations (liquid offerings poured out for a god).

57:7 "High and lofty hill" calls to mind a pagan "high place" or mountain shrine (see Jer 3:6; Eze 6:3; 16:16; 22:9; see also "The High Places" on p. 1318).

57:9 Molech was the principal god of the Ammonites (see the note on v. 5).

Olive oil was used as a base for perfume (see SS 4:10, where the Hebrew word for "oil" is translated "perfume"; see also the note on Pr 7:17 and "Perfumes and Anointing Oils" on p. 1746).

[15]For this is what the high and lofty[j] One says—
he who lives forever,[k] whose name is holy:
"I live in a high and holy place,
but also with him who is contrite[l] and lowly in spirit,[m]
to revive the spirit of the lowly
and to revive the heart of the contrite.[n]
[16]I will not accuse forever,
nor will I always be angry,[o]
for then the spirit of man would grow faint before me—
the breath of man that I have created.
[17]I was enraged by his sinful greed;[p]
I punished him, and hid my face in anger,
yet he kept on in his willful ways.[q]
[18]I have seen his ways, but I will heal[r] him;
I will guide him and restore comfort[s] to him,
[19] creating praise on the lips[t] of the mourners in Israel.
Peace, peace,[u] to those far and near,"[v]
says the LORD. "And I will heal them."
[20]But the wicked[w] are like the tossing sea,
which cannot rest,
whose waves cast up mire and mud.
[21]"There is no peace,"[x] says my God, "for the wicked."[y]

57:15 [j]Isa 52:13 [k]Dt 33:27 [l]Ps 147:3 [m]Ps 34:18; 51:17; Isa 66:2 [n]Isa 61:1
57:16 [o]Ps 85:5; 103:9; Mic 7:18
57:17 [p]Isa 56:11 [q]Isa 1:4
57:18 [r]Isa 30:26 [s]Isa 61:1-3
57:19 [t]Isa 6:7; Heb 13:15 [u]Eph 2:17 [v]Ac 2:39
57:20 [w]Job 18:5-21
57:21 [x]Isa 59:8 [y]Isa 48:22

True Fasting

58

"Shout it aloud,[z] do not hold back.
Raise your voice like a trumpet.
Declare to my people their rebellion[a]
and to the house of Jacob their sins.
[2]For day after day they seek[b] me out;
they seem eager to know my ways,
as if they were a nation that does what is right
and has not forsaken the commands of
its God.
They ask me for just decisions
and seem eager for God to come near[c] them.
[3]'Why have we fasted,'[d] they say,
'and you have not seen it?
Why have we humbled ourselves,
and you have not noticed?'[e]

"Yet on the day of your fasting, you do as you please[f]
and exploit all your workers.
[4]Your fasting ends in quarreling and strife,[g]
and in striking each other with wicked fists.
You cannot fast as you do today
and expect your voice to be heard[h] on high.
[5]Is this the kind of fast[i] I have chosen,
only a day for a man to humble[j] himself?
Is it only for bowing one's head like a reed
and for lying on sackcloth and ashes?[k]

58:1 [z]Isa 40:6 [a]Isa 48:8
58:2 [b]Isa 48:1; Tit 1:16; Jas 4:8 [c]Isa 29:13
58:3 [d]Lev 16:29 [e]Mal 3:14 [f]Isa 22:13; Zec 7:5-6
58:4 [g]1Ki 21:9-13; Isa 59:6 [h]Isa 59:2
58:5 [i]Zec 7:5 [j]1Ki 21:27 [k]Job 2:8

58:1—66:24 This final section of the prophecy continues the same general theme as that of the previous section (chs 49–57) and reaches its height in 66:1–3, a passage that foretells that day of which Jesus spoke to the woman of Samaria, when the true worshipers will worship not in temples made with hands but "in spirit and truth" (Jn 4:23). Yet here again, as constantly elsewhere in Isaiah, warning and denunciation alternate with offers and assurances of blessing. The book closes with a reference to the torments of the reprobate.
58:3 The Israelites were going through the motions of religion—specifically fasting—for the same reason the pagans participated in their rituals: in an attempt to manipulate God to act in their favor.

Is that what you call a fast,
  a day acceptable to the LORD?

6 "Is not this the kind of fasting I have chosen:
to loose the chains of injustice[l]
  and untie the cords of the yoke,
to set the oppressed[m] free
  and break every yoke?
7 Is it not to share your food with the hungry[n]
  and to provide the poor wanderer with shelter[o]—
when you see the naked, to clothe[p] him,
  and not to turn away from your own flesh and blood?[q]
8 Then your light will break forth like the dawn,[r]
  and your healing[s] will quickly appear;
then your righteousness[a] will go before you,
  and the glory of the LORD will be your rear guard.[t]
9 Then you will call,[u] and the LORD will answer;
  you will cry for help, and he will say: Here am I.

"If you do away with the yoke of oppression,
  with the pointing finger[v] and malicious talk,[w]
10 and if you spend yourselves in behalf of the hungry
  and satisfy the needs of the oppressed,[x]
then your light[y] will rise in the darkness,
  and your night will become like the noonday.[z]
11 The LORD will guide you always;
  he will satisfy your needs[a] in a sun-scorched land
  and will strengthen your frame.
You will be like a well-watered garden,[b]
  like a spring[c] whose waters never fail.
12 Your people will rebuild the ancient ruins[d]
  and will raise up the age-old foundations;[e]
you will be called Repairer of Broken Walls,
  Restorer of Streets with Dwellings.

13 "If you keep your feet from breaking the Sabbath[f]
  and from doing as you please on my holy day,
if you call the Sabbath a delight[g]
  and the LORD's holy day honorable,
and if you honor it by not going your own way
  and not doing as you please or speaking idle words,
14 then you will find your joy[h] in the LORD,
  and I will cause you to ride on the heights[i] of the land
  and to feast on the inheritance of your father Jacob."
    The mouth of the LORD has spoken.[j]

Sin, Confession and Redemption

59

Surely the arm of the LORD is not too short[k] to save,
  nor his ear too dull to hear.[l]
2 But your iniquities have separated
  you from your God;

58:6 [l]Ne 5:10-11 [m]Jer 34:9
58:7 [n]Eze 18:16; Lk 3:11 [o]Isa 16:4; Heb 13:2 [p]Job 31:19-20; Mt 25:36 [q]Ge 29:14; Lk 10:31-32
58:8 [r]Job 11:17 [s]Isa 30:26 [t]Ex 14:19
58:9 [u]Ps 50:15 [v]Pr 6:13 [w]Ps 12:2; Isa 59:13
58:10 [x]Dt 15:7-8 [y]Isa 42:16 [z]Job 11:17
58:11 [a]Ps 107:9 [b]SS 4:15 [c]Jn 4:14
58:12 [d]Isa 49:8 [e]Isa 44:28
58:13 [f]Isa 56:2 [g]Ps 84:2,10
58:14 [h]Job 22:26 [i]Dt 32:13 [j]Isa 1:20
59:1 [k]Nu 11:23; Isa 50:2 [l]Isa 58:9; 65:24

[a] 8 Or *your righteous One*

58:6 During the Jerusalem siege Hebrew slaves were released—only to be reclaimed by their masters after further consideration (see Jer 34:8–11).

your sins have hidden his face from you,
so that he will not hear.[m]
3 For your hands are stained with blood,[n]
your fingers with guilt.
Your lips have spoken lies,
and your tongue mutters wicked things.
4 No one calls for justice;
no one pleads his case with integrity.
They rely on empty arguments and speak lies;
they conceive trouble and give birth to evil.[o]
5 They hatch the eggs of vipers
and spin a spider's web.[p]
Whoever eats their eggs will die,
and when one is broken, an adder is hatched.
6 Their cobwebs are useless for clothing;
they cannot cover themselves with what
they make.[q]
Their deeds are evil deeds,
and acts of violence[r] are in their hands.
7 Their feet rush into sin;
they are swift to shed innocent blood.[s]
Their thoughts are evil thoughts;[t]
ruin and destruction mark their ways.[u]
8 The way of peace they do not know;
there is no justice in their paths.
They have turned them into crooked roads;
no one who walks in them will know peace.[v]

9 So justice is far from us,
and righteousness does not reach us.
We look for light, but all is darkness;[w]
for brightness, but we walk in deep shadows.
10 Like the blind[x] we grope along the wall,
feeling our way like men without eyes.
At midday we stumble[y] as if it were twilight;
among the strong, we are like the dead.[z]
11 We all growl like bears;
we moan mournfully like doves.[a]
We look for justice, but find none;
for deliverance, but it is far away.

12 For our offenses[b] are many in your sight,
and our sins testify[c] against us.
Our offenses are ever with us,
and we acknowledge our iniquities:
13 rebellion and treachery against the LORD,
turning our backs[d] on our God,
fomenting oppression[e] and revolt,
uttering lies[f] our hearts have conceived.
14 So justice is driven back,
and righteousness[g] stands at a distance;
truth[h] has stumbled in the streets,
honesty cannot enter.

59:2 [m]Isa 1:15; 58:4
59:3 [n]Isa 1:15
59:4 [o]Job 15:35; Ps 7:14
59:5 [p]Job 8:14
59:6 [q]Isa 28:20 [r]Isa 58:4
59:7 [s]Pr 6:17 [t]Mk 7:21-22 [u]Ro 3:15-17*
59:8 [v]Isa 57:21; Lk 1:79
59:9 [w]Isa 5:30; 8:20
59:10 [x]Dt 28:29 [y]Isa 8:15 [z]La 3:6
59:11 [a]Isa 38:14; Eze 7:16
59:12 [b]Ezr 9:6 [c]Isa 3:9
59:13 [d]Pr 30:9; Mt 10:33; Tit 1:16 [e]Isa 5:7 [f]Mk 7:21-22
59:14 [g]Isa 1:21 [h]Isa 48:1

59:3 On the subject of defilement in the Old and New Testaments, see the note on Song of Songs 5:3.

[15]Truth is nowhere to be found,
and whoever shuns evil becomes a prey.

The LORD looked and was displeased
that there was no justice.
[16]He saw that there was no one,[i]
he was appalled that there was no one to intervene;
so his own arm worked salvation[j] for him,
and his own righteousness sustained him.
[17]He put on righteousness as his breastplate,[k]
and the helmet[l] of salvation on his head;
he put on the garments[m] of vengeance
and wrapped himself in zeal[n] as in a cloak.
[18]According to what they have done,
so will he repay
wrath to his enemies
and retribution to his foes;
he will repay the islands their due.
[19]From the west,[o] men will fear the name of the LORD,
and from the rising of the sun,[p] they will revere his glory.
For he will come like a pent-up flood
that the breath of the LORD drives along.[a]

[20]"The Redeemer will come to Zion,
to those in Jacob who repent of their sins,"[q]
declares the LORD.

[21]"As for me, this is my covenant with them," says the LORD. "My Spirit,[r] who is on you, and my words
that I have put in your mouth will not depart from your mouth, or from the mouths of your children, or
from the mouths of their descendants from this time on and forever," says the LORD.

59:16 [i]Isa 41:28 [j]Ps 98:1; Isa 63:5
59:17 [k]Eph 6:14 [l]Eph 6:17; 1Th 5:8 [m]Isa 63:3 [n]Isa 9:7
59:19 [o]Isa 49:12 [p]Ps 113:3
59:20 [q]Ac 2:38-39; Ro 11:26-27*
59:21 [r]Isa 11:2; 44:3

The Glory of Zion

60 "Arise,[s] shine, for your light[t] has come,
and the glory of the LORD rises upon you.
[2]See, darkness covers the earth
and thick darkness[u] is over the peoples,
but the LORD rises upon you
and his glory appears over you.
[3]Nations[v] will come to your light,
and kings[w] to the brightness of your dawn.

[4]"Lift up your eyes and look about you:
All assemble[x] and come to you;
your sons come from afar,
and your daughters[y] are carried on the arm.[z]
[5]Then you will look and be radiant,
your heart will throb and swell with joy;
the wealth on the seas will be brought to you,
to you the riches of the nations will come.
[6]Herds of camels will cover your land,
young camels of Midian[a] and Ephah.[b]

60:1 [s]Isa 52:2 [t]Eph 5:14
60:2 [u]Jer 13:16; Col 1:13
60:3 [v]Isa 45:14; Rev 21:24 [w]Isa 49:23
60:4 [x]Isa 11:12 [y]Isa 43:6 [z]Isa 49:20-22
60:6 [a]Ge 25:2 [b]Ge 25:4

[a] 19 Or *When the enemy comes in like a flood, / the Spirit of the LORD will put him to flight*

59:18 For "islands," see the note on 41:1.
59:20 For "Redeemer," see the note on 41:14.
60:6 Camel caravans would convey wealth to Jerusalem (see "Caravan Trading and Routes in the Ancient Near East" on p. 63). Ironically, it had been on camels that the Midianites, who roamed the deserts of the Transjordan, had once devastated Israel (Jdg 6:1–6; Isa 9:4; for "Midian," see "Midian" on p. 92).
Ephah was a son of Midian (Ge 25:4) and Sheba a prosperous

And all from Sheba[c] will come,
bearing gold and incense[d]
and proclaiming the praise[e] of the LORD.
7 All Kedar's[f] flocks will be gathered to you,
the rams of Nebaioth will serve you;
they will be accepted as offerings on my altar,
and I will adorn my glorious temple.[g]

8 "Who are these[h] that fly along like clouds,
like doves to their nests?
9 Surely the islands[i] look to me;
in the lead are the ships of Tarshish,[a][j]
bringing[k] your sons from afar,
with their silver and gold,
to the honor of the LORD your God,
the Holy One of Israel,
for he has endowed you with splendor.[l]

10 "Foreigners[m] will rebuild your walls,
and their kings[n] will serve you.
Though in anger I struck you,
in favor I will show you compassion.[o]

60:6 [c]Ps 72:10 [d]Isa 43:23; Mt 2:11 [e]Isa 42:10
60:7 [f]Ge 25:13 [g]ver 13; Hag 2:3, 7,9
60:8 [h]Isa 49:21
60:9 [i]Isa 11:11 [j]Isa 2:16 *fn* [k]Isa 14:2; 43:6 [l]Isa 55:5
60:10 [m]Isa 14:1-2 [n]Isa 49:23; Rev 21:24 [o]Isa 54:8

[a] 9 Or *the trading ships*

land in southern Arabia, roughly the equivalent of modern Yemen (see Ge 25:3; 1Ki 10:1 and its note; see also "Sheba" on p. 498). The queen of Sheba had brought gold and spices to Solomon (1Ki 10:2), and the book of Jeremiah mentions the incense of Sheba (Jer 6:20; see also "Incense" on p. 1209).

60:9 For "islands," see the note on 41:1 and for "ships of Tarshish" the note on 2:16. Every three years vessels from Tarshish had delivered silver and gold to Solomon (1Ki 10:22).

60:10 In 444 B.C. Artaxerxes issued the decree allowing Nehemiah to rebuild Jerusalem's walls (Ne 2:8).

ANCIENT TEXTS AND ARTIFACTS

The Offering of King Ashyahu

ISAIAH 60 Isaiah 60:9 describes the expectation that one day the ships of Tarshish would come bringing silver and gold to honor the God of Israel. "Tarshish" may have been either in Spain or in Sardinia,[1] and the "hammered silver . . . brought from Tarshish" (Jer 10:9) was imported silver of high value. An **ostracon** dated through **paleography** to around the time of King Josiah (640–609 B.C.)[2] reads, "So King Ashyahu has commanded you to give by the agency of Zakaryahu silver of Tarshish for the house of the LORD: three shekels." But who was Ashyahu?

The names of Hebrew kings sometimes had elements inverted. For example, the name Ahaziah (2Ki 8:25) was inverted to Jehoahaz in 2 Chronicles 21:17. Both names mean "Yahweh holds," but in Ahaziah the word for "holds" is first and "Yahweh" is second (in the ending "-iah"), while in Jehoahaz "Yahweh" is first (as "Jeho-") and "holds" ("-ahaz") comes second. Ashyahu could be an inverted form of Joash, king of Judah (r. 835–796 B.C.), but it is more likely an inversion of Josiah, king of Judah (r. 640–609 B.C.). Zakaryahu was probably the Zechariah of 2 Chronicles 35:8, a temple administrator in Josiah's reign, and the ostracon seems to be a receipt for the offering. When Isaiah prophesied that one day Gentiles would bring the silver of Tarshish to **Yahweh**'s temple, he was alluding to a means of honoring God that was already being practiced in his own day by his own people.

[1]See "Where Was Tarshish?" on page 1475. [2]See "The Tragic Reign of King Josiah" on page 569.

60:11 [p]ver 18; Isa 62:10; Rev 21:25 [q]ver 5; Rev 21:26 [r]Ps 149:8

11 Your gates[p] will always stand open,
they will never be shut, day or night,
so that men may bring you the wealth of the nations[q]—
their kings[r] led in triumphal procession.

60:12 [s]Isa 14:2

12 For the nation or kingdom that will not serve[s] you will perish;
it will be utterly ruined.

60:13 [t]Isa 35:2 [u]Isa 41:19 [v]1Ch 28:2; Ps 132:7

13 "The glory of Lebanon[t] will come to you,
the pine, the fir and the cypress together,[u]
to adorn the place of my sanctuary;
and I will glorify the place of my feet.[v]

60:14 [w]Isa 14:2 [x]Isa 49:23; Rev 3:9 [y]Heb 12:22

14 The sons of your oppressors[w] will come bowing
before you;
all who despise you will bow down[x] at your feet
and will call you the City of the LORD,
Zion[y] of the Holy One of Israel.

60:15 [z]Isa 1:7-9; 6:12 [a]Isa 33:8 [b]Isa 4:2 [c]Isa 65:18

15 "Although you have been forsaken[z] and hated,
with no one traveling[a] through,
I will make you the everlasting pride[b]
and the joy[c] of all generations.

60:16 [d]Isa 49:23; 66:11,12 [e]Isa 59:20

16 You will drink the milk of nations
and be nursed[d] at royal breasts.
Then you will know that I, the LORD, am your Savior,
your Redeemer,[e] the Mighty One of Jacob.
17 Instead of bronze I will bring you gold,
and silver in place of iron.
Instead of wood I will bring you bronze,
and iron in place of stones.
I will make peace your governor
and righteousness your ruler.

60:18 [f]Isa 26:1

18 No longer will violence be heard in your land,
nor ruin or destruction within your borders,
but you will call your walls Salvation[f]
and your gates Praise.

60:19 [g]Rev 22:5 [h]Zec 2:5; Rev 21:23

19 The sun will no more be your light by day,
nor will the brightness of the moon shine on you,
for the LORD will be your everlasting light,[g]
and your God will be your glory.[h]

60:20 [i]Isa 30:26 [j]Isa 35:10

20 Your sun[i] will never set again,
and your moon will wane no more;
the LORD will be your everlasting light,
and your days of sorrow[j] will end.

60:21 [k]Rev 21:27 [l]Ps 37:11,22; Isa 57:13; 61:7 [m]Mt 15:13 [n]Isa 19:25; 29:23; Eph 2:10 [o]Isa 52:1

21 Then will all your people be righteous[k]
and they will possess[l] the land forever.
They are the shoot I have planted,[m]
the work of my hands,[n]
for the display of my splendor.[o]
22 The least of you will become a thousand,
the smallest a mighty nation.
I am the LORD;
in its time I will do this swiftly."

60:13 Lebanon's magnificent cedars and pine trees had been used in the construction of Solomon's temple (1Ki 5:10,18). Isaiah promised that the glory of the Solomonic era would return.

The Year of the LORD's Favor

61

The Spirit[p] of the Sovereign LORD is on me,
because the LORD has anointed[q] me
to preach good news to the poor.[r]
He has sent me to bind up[s] the brokenhearted,
to proclaim freedom for the captives[t]
and release from darkness for the prisoners,[a]
2 to proclaim the year of the LORD's favor[u]
and the day of vengeance[v] of our God,
to comfort[w] all who mourn,
3 and provide for those who grieve in Zion—
to bestow on them a crown of beauty
instead of ashes,
the oil of gladness
instead of mourning,
and a garment of praise
instead of a spirit of despair.
They will be called oaks of righteousness,
a planting of the LORD
for the display of his splendor.[x]

4 They will rebuild the ancient ruins[y]
and restore the places long devastated;
they will renew the ruined cities
that have been devastated for generations.
5 Aliens[z] will shepherd your flocks;
foreigners will work your fields and vineyards.
6 And you will be called priests[a] of the LORD,
you will be named ministers of our God.
You will feed on the wealth[b] of nations,
and in their riches you will boast.

7 Instead of their shame
my people will receive a double[c] portion,
and instead of disgrace
they will rejoice in their inheritance;
and so they will inherit a double portion in their land,
and everlasting joy will be theirs.

8 "For I, the LORD, love justice;[d]
I hate robbery and iniquity.
In my faithfulness I will reward them
and make an everlasting covenant[e] with them.
9 Their descendants will be known among the nations
and their offspring among the peoples.
All who see them will acknowledge
that they are a people the LORD has blessed."

10 I delight greatly in the LORD;
my soul rejoices[f] in my God.

61:1 [p]Isa 11:2 [q]Ps 45:7 [r]Mt 11:5; Lk 7:22 [s]Isa 57:15 [t]Isa 42:7; 49:9
61:2 [u]Isa 49:8; Lk 4:18-19* [v]Isa 34:8 [w]Isa 57:18; Mt 5:4
61:3 [x]Isa 60:20-21
61:4 [y]Isa 49:8; Eze 36:33; Am 9:14
61:5 [z]Isa 14:1-2
61:6 [a]Ex 19:6; 1Pe 2:5 [b]Isa 60:11
61:7 [c]Isa 40:2; Zec 9:12
61:8 [d]Ps 11:7; Isa 5:16 [e]Isa 55:3
61:10 [f]Isa 25:9; Hab 3:18

[a] *1* Hebrew; Septuagint *the blind*

61:3 "Crown of beauty" here refers to a headdress (translated "turban" in Eze 24:17). In 3:20 the prophet had predicted that the women of Jerusalem would lose their finery, including their magnificent head coverings. Anointing with olive oil was a common practice on joyous occasions (see Ps 23:5; 45:7; 104:15; 133:1–2; cf. 2Sa 14:2).
61:10 See "Weddings in Ancient Israel" on page 1039.

61:10 [g]Ps 132:9; Isa 52:1 [h]Isa 49:18; Rev 21:2

For he has clothed me with garments of salvation
and arrayed me in a robe of righteousness,[g]
as a bridegroom adorns his head like a priest,
and as a bride[h] adorns herself with her jewels.

61:11 [i]Ps 85:11

11 For as the soil makes the sprout come up
and a garden causes seeds to grow,
so the Sovereign LORD will make righteousness[i] and praise
spring up before all nations.

Zion's New Name

62:1 [j]Isa 1:26

62 For Zion's sake I will not keep silent,
for Jerusalem's sake I will not remain quiet,
till her righteousness[j] shines out like the dawn,
her salvation like a blazing torch.

62:2 [k]Isa 52:10; 60:3 [l]ver 4,12

2 The nations[k] will see your righteousness,
and all kings your glory;
you will be called by a new name[l]
that the mouth of the LORD will bestow.

62:3 [m]Isa 28:5; Zec 9:16; 1Th 2:19

3 You will be a crown[m] of splendor in the LORD's hand,
a royal diadem in the hand of your God.

62:4 [n]Isa 54:6 [o]Jer 32:41; Zep 3:17 [p]Jer 3:14; Hos 2:19

4 No longer will they call you Deserted,[n]
or name your land Desolate.
But you will be called Hephzibah,[a]
and your land Beulah[b];
for the LORD will take delight[o] in you,
and your land will be married.[p]
5 As a young man marries a maiden,
so will your sons[c] marry you;
as a bridegroom rejoices over his bride,

62:5 [q]Isa 65:19

so will your God rejoice[q] over you.

62:6 [r]Isa 52:8; Eze 3:17

6 I have posted watchmen[r] on your walls, O Jerusalem;
they will never be silent day or night.
You who call on the LORD,
give yourselves no rest,

62:7 [s]Mt 15:21-28; Lk 18:1-8

7 and give him no rest[s] till he establishes Jerusalem
and makes her the praise of the earth.

62:8 [t]Dt 28:30-33; Isa 1:7; Jer 5:17

8 The LORD has sworn by his right hand
and by his mighty arm:
"Never again will I give your grain[t]
as food for your enemies,
and never again will foreigners drink the new wine
for which you have toiled;
9 but those who harvest it will eat it
and praise the LORD,
and those who gather the grapes will drink it
in the courts of my sanctuary."

62:10 [u]Isa 60:11

10 Pass through, pass through the gates![u]
Prepare the way for the people.

[a] 4 *Hephzibah* means *my delight is in her.* [b] 4 *Beulah* means *married.* [c] 5 Or *Builder*

62:10 For commentary on "prepare the way" and "build up the highway," see the notes on 11:16, 19:23 and 40:3.
For "banner," see the note on 5:26.

Build up, build up the highway![v][w]
Remove the stones.
Raise a banner[x] for the nations.

11 The LORD has made proclamation
to the ends of the earth:
"Say to the Daughter of Zion,[y]
'See, your Savior comes![z]
See, his reward is with him,
and his recompense accompanies him.' "[a]
12 They will be called[b] the Holy People,[c]
the Redeemed[d] of the LORD;
and you will be called Sought After,
the City No Longer Deserted.[e]

God's Day of Vengeance and Redemption

63 Who is this coming from Edom,
from Bozrah,[f] with his garments stained crimson?
Who is this, robed in splendor,
striding forward in the greatness of his strength?

"It is I, speaking in righteousness,
mighty to save."[g]

2 Why are your garments red,
like those of one treading the winepress?

3 "I have trodden the winepress[h] alone;
from the nations no one was with me.
I trampled them in my anger
and trod them down in my wrath;[i]
their blood spattered my garments,[j]
and I stained all my clothing.
4 For the day of vengeance was in my heart,
and the year of my redemption has come.
5 I looked, but there was no one[k] to help,
I was appalled that no one gave support;
so my own arm[l] worked salvation for me,
and my own wrath sustained me.[m]
6 I trampled the nations in my anger;
in my wrath I made them drunk[n]
and poured their blood[o] on the ground."

Praise and Prayer

7 I will tell of the kindnesses[p] of the LORD,
the deeds for which he is to be praised,
according to all the LORD has done for us—
yes, the many good things he has done
for the house of Israel,
according to his compassion[q] and many kindnesses.
8 He said, "Surely they are my people,[r]
sons who will not be false to me";
and so he became their Savior.

62:10 [v]Isa 57:14 [w]Isa 11:16 [x]Isa 11:10
62:11 [y]Zec 9:9; Mt 21:5 [z]Rev 22:12 [a]Isa 40:10
62:12 [b]ver 4 [c]1Pe 2:9 [d]Isa 35:9 [e]Isa 42:16
63:1 [f]Am 1:12 [g]Zep 3:17
63:3 [h]Rev 14:20; 19:15 [i]Isa 22:5 [j]Rev 19:13
63:5 [k]Isa 41:28 [l]Ps 44:3; 98:1 [m]Isa 59:16
63:6 [n]Isa 29:9 [o]Isa 34:3
63:7 [p]Isa 54:8 [q]Ps 51:1; Eph 2:4
63:8 [r]Isa 51:4

62:11 "Daughter of Zion" personifies Jerusalem.
63:1 Edom (see "Edom" on p. 1467) and one of its leading cities, Bozrah (see the note on 34:6), symbolize a world that hates God's people.
63:2–3 See "The Winepress" on page 1171.

9 In all their distress he too was distressed,
and the angel of his presence[s] saved them.
In his love and mercy he redeemed[t] them;
he lifted them up and carried[u] them
all the days of old.
10 Yet they rebelled[v]
and grieved his Holy Spirit.[w]
So he turned and became their enemy[x]
and he himself fought against them.

63:9 [s]Ex 33:14 [t]Dt 7:7-8 [u]Dt 1:31
63:10 [v]Ps 78:40 [w]Ps 51:11; Ac 7:51; Eph 4:30 [x]Ps 106:40

The Winepress

Mosaic from Paphos (inscriptions says "The First Winedrinkers")
Preserving Bible Times; © Dr. James C. Martin

ISAIAH 63 The winepress was a key component of ancient wine production.[1] In its most basic form it consisted of three sections: an upper and a lower vat and a channel connecting the two. After the grapes had lain in the sun for a few days to increase their sugar content, they were placed in the upper vat and trodden with bare feet. The juice moved down the channel to the smaller, but deeper, lower vat. The husks that remained after having been trodden were pressed by a wooden plank, one end of which was secured to a side of the vat while the other was weighed with stones to facilitate the pressing process.

Some of the more elaborate winepresses that have been discovered have had three or four vats. The extra vats improved the settling process and reduced the amount of sediment in the wine. The juice would ferment in the lowest vat, a process requiring four to seven days. After this period the wine would be poured into jars or wineskins. Often there would be a spout in the lowest vat that would channel the wine into these containers. The jars or wineskins would hold the wine as the fermentation process was completed, a period of two to four months.

Isaiah used the imagery of treading the winepress to express divine judgment against the nations (Isa 63:1–6). The act of treading represents God's vengeance against his enemies, whether through war or other disasters. The juice produced from the grapes represents the blood of the defeated, while the intoxication produced by overindulgence of the wine represents the effect of God's wrath on those he judges (v. 6). At the same time, however, God's vengeance against his enemies is coupled with his redemption of his own people (v. 4).

[1]See "Wine and Alcoholic Beverages in the Ancient World" on page 2015.

[11]Then his people recalled[a] the days of old,
the days of Moses and his people—
where is he who brought them through the sea,[y]
with the shepherd of his flock?
Where is he who set
his Holy Spirit[z] among them,
[12]who sent his glorious arm of power
to be at Moses' right hand,
who divided the waters[a] before them,
to gain for himself everlasting renown,
[13]who led[b] them through the depths?
Like a horse in open country,
they did not stumble;[c]
[14]like cattle that go down to the plain,
they were given rest by the Spirit of the LORD.
This is how you guided your people
to make for yourself a glorious name.

[15]Look down from heaven[d] and see
from your lofty throne,[e] holy and glorious.
Where are your zeal[f] and your might?
Your tenderness and compassion[g] are withheld from us.
[16]But you are our Father,
though Abraham does not know us
or Israel acknowledge[h] us;
you, O LORD, are our Father,
our Redeemer[i] from of old is your name.
[17]Why, O LORD, do you make us wander from your ways
and harden our hearts so we do not revere[j] you?
Return[k] for the sake of your servants,
the tribes that are your inheritance.
[18]For a little while your people possessed your holy place,
but now our enemies have trampled down your sanctuary.[l]
[19]We are yours from of old;
but you have not ruled over them,
they have not been called by your name.[b]

64

Oh, that you would rend the heavens[m] and come down,[n]
that the mountains[o] would tremble before you!
[2]As when fire sets twigs ablaze
and causes water to boil,
come down to make your name known to your enemies
and cause the nations to quake[p] before you!
[3]For when you did awesome[q] things that we did not expect,
you came down, and the mountains trembled before you.
[4]Since ancient times no one has heard,
no ear has perceived,
no eye has seen any God besides you,
who acts on behalf of those who wait for him.[r]
[5]You come to the help of those who gladly do right,[s]
who remember your ways.

63:11 [y]Ex 14:22, 30 [z]Nu 11:17
63:12 [a]Ex 14:21-22; Isa 11:15
63:13 [b]Dt 32:12 [c]Jer 31:9
63:15 [d]Dt 26:15; Ps 80:14 [e]Ps 123:1 [f]Isa 9:7; 26:11 [g]Jer 31:20; Hos 11:8
63:16 [h]Job 14:21 [i]Isa 41:14; 44:6
63:17 [j]Isa 29:13 [k]Nu 10:36
63:18 [l]Ps 74:3-8
64:1 [m]Ps 18:9; 144:5 [n]Mic 1:3 [o]Ex 19:18
64:2 [p]Ps 99:1; Jer 5:22; 33:9
64:3 [q]Ps 65:5
64:4 [r]Isa 30:18; 1Co 2:9*
64:5 [s]Isa 26:8

[a] 11 Or *But may he recall* [b] 19 Or *We are like those you have never ruled, / like those never called by your name*

63:11 The "sea" is the Red Sea, and the "shepherd" refers to Moses. **63:12** For "arm of power," see the note on 52:10.

But when we continued to sin against them,
you were angry.
How then can we be saved?
6 All of us have become like one who is unclean,
and all our righteous[t] acts are like filthy rags;
we all shrivel up like a leaf,[u]
and like the wind our sins sweep us away.
7 No one[v] calls on your name
or strives to lay hold of you;
for you have hidden[w] your face from us
and made us waste away[x] because of our sins.

8 Yet, O LORD, you are our Father.[y]
We are the clay, you are the potter;[z]
we are all the work of your hand.
9 Do not be angry[a] beyond measure, O LORD;
do not remember our sins[b] forever.
Oh, look upon us, we pray,
for we are all your people.
10 Your sacred cities have become a desert;
even Zion is a desert, Jerusalem a desolation.
11 Our holy and glorious temple,[c] where our fathers praised you,
has been burned with fire,
and all that we treasured[d] lies in ruins.
12 After all this, O LORD, will you hold yourself back?[e]
Will you keep silent[f] and punish us beyond measure?

64:6 [t]Isa 46:12; 48:1 [u]Ps 90:5-6
64:7 [v]Isa 59:4 [w]Dt 31:18; Isa 1:15; 54:8 [x]Isa 9:18
64:8 [y]Isa 63:16 [z]Isa 29:16
64:9 [a]Isa 57:17; 60:10 [b]Isa 43:25
64:11 [c]Ps 74:3-7 [d]La 1:7,10
64:12 [e]Ps 74:10-11; Isa 42:14 [f]Ps 83:1

Judgment and Salvation

65 "I revealed myself to those who did not ask for me;
I was found by those who did not seek me.[g]
To a nation[h] that did not call on my name,
I said, 'Here am I, here am I.'
2 All day long I have held out my hands
to an obstinate people,[i]
who walk in ways not good,
pursuing their own imaginations[j]—
3 a people who continually provoke me
to my very face,[k]
offering sacrifices in gardens[l]
and burning incense on altars of brick;
4 who sit among the graves
and spend their nights keeping secret vigil;
who eat the flesh of pigs,[m]
and whose pots hold broth of unclean meat;
5 who say, 'Keep away; don't come near me,
for I am too sacred[n] for you!'

65:1 [g]Hos 1:10; Ro 9:24-26; 10:20* [h]Eph 2:12
65:2 [i]Isa 1:2,23; Ro 10:21* [j]Ps 81:11-12; Isa 66:18
65:3 [k]Job 1:11 [l]Isa 1:29
65:4 [m]Lev 11:7
65:5 [n]Mt 9:11; Lk 7:39; 18:9-12

64:6 "Unclean" has to do with ritual or ceremonial uncleanness (see 6:5; Lev 13:45–46). "Filthy rags" refers to the cloths a woman used during menstruation, a time when she was considered "unclean" in the ceremonial sense (see Lev 15:19–24,33–34; Eze 36:17).

65:3 For "gardens," see the note on 1:29.

"Burning incense" refers to the practice of worshipers of the Queen of Heaven (see "Incense" on p. 1209 and "The Queen of Heaven" on p. 1267).

65:4 People may have sat among graves in an attempt to consult the dead (see Dt 18:11; Isa 8:19; 57:9; see also "Ancient Necromancy" on p. 435).

The flesh of pigs was considered ceremonially unclean (see Lev 11:7–8; Isa 66:3,17).

Such people are smoke in my nostrils,
a fire that keeps burning all day.

6 "See, it stands written before me:
I will not keep silent[o] but will pay back[p] in full;
I will pay it back into their laps[q]—
7 both your sins[r] and the sins of your fathers,"[s]
says the LORD.
"Because they burned sacrifices on the mountains
and defied me on the hills,[t]
I will measure into their laps
the full payment for their former deeds."

8 This is what the LORD says:

"As when juice is still found in a cluster of grapes
and men say, 'Don't destroy it,
there is yet some good in it,'
so will I do in behalf of my servants;
I will not destroy them all.
9 I will bring forth descendants[u] from Jacob,
and from Judah those who will possess[v] my mountains;
my chosen people will inherit them,
and there will my servants live.[w]
10 Sharon[x] will become a pasture for flocks,
and the Valley of Achor[y] a resting place for herds,
for my people who seek[z] me.

11 "But as for you who forsake[a] the LORD
and forget my holy mountain,
who spread a table for Fortune
and fill bowls of mixed wine for Destiny,
12 I will destine you for the sword,[b]
and you will all bend down for the slaughter;
for I called but you did not answer,[c]
I spoke but you did not listen.[d]
You did evil in my sight
and chose what displeases me."

13 Therefore this is what the Sovereign LORD says:

"My servants will eat,[e]
but you will go hungry;
my servants will drink,
but you will go thirsty;[f]
my servants will rejoice,
but you will be put to shame.[g]
14 My servants will sing
out of the joy of their hearts,
but you will cry out[h]
from anguish of heart
and wail in brokenness of spirit.

65:6 [o]Ps 50:3 [p]Jer 16:18 [q]Ps 79:12
65:7 [r]Isa 22:14 [s]Ex 20:5 [t]Isa 57:7
65:9 [u]Isa 45:19 [v]Am 9:11-15 [w]Isa 32:18
65:10 [x]Isa 35:2 [y]Jos 7:26 [z]Isa 51:1
65:11 [a]Dt 29:24-25; Isa 1:28
65:12 [b]Isa 27:1 [c]Pr 1:24-25; Isa 41:28; 66:4 [d]2Ch 36:15-16; Jer 7:13
65:13 [e]Isa 1:19 [f]Isa 41:17 [g]Isa 44:9
65:14 [h]Mt 8:12; Lk 13:28

65:10 Sharon, a plain along the Mediterranean coast north of Joppa, was renowned for its lush foliage and excellent grazing land (see 1Ch 27:29; Isa 35:2; 65:10).

The Valley of Achor was near Jericho. Since Sharon and Achor were located on the western and eastern edges of the land, respectively, these references probably represent the whole country.

65:11 "Fortune" and "Destiny" were the pagan gods of good fortune and fate.

15 You will leave your name
to my chosen ones as a curse;[i]
the Sovereign LORD will put you to death,
but to his servants he will give another name.
16 Whoever invokes a blessing in the land
will do so by the God of truth;[j]
he who takes an oath in the land
will swear[k] by the God of truth.
For the past troubles will be forgotten
and hidden from my eyes.

New Heavens and a New Earth

17 "Behold, I will create
new heavens and a new earth.[l]
The former things will not be remembered,[m]
nor will they come to mind.
18 But be glad and rejoice[n] forever
in what I will create,
for I will create Jerusalem to be a delight
and its people a joy.
19 I will rejoice[o] over Jerusalem
and take delight in my people;
the sound of weeping and of crying[p]
will be heard in it no more.

20 "Never again will there be in it
an infant who lives but a few days,
or an old man who does not live out his years;[q]
he who dies at a hundred
will be thought a mere youth;
he who fails to reach[a] a hundred
will be considered accursed.
21 They will build houses[r] and dwell in them;
they will plant vineyards and eat their fruit.[s]
22 No longer will they build houses and others
live in them,
or plant and others eat.
For as the days of a tree,[t]
so will be the days[u] of my people;
my chosen ones will long enjoy
the works of their hands.
23 They will not toil in vain
or bear children doomed to misfortune;
for they will be a people blessed[v] by the LORD,
they and their descendants[w] with them.
24 Before they call[x] I will answer;
while they are still speaking[y] I will hear.
25 The wolf and the lamb[z] will feed together,
and the lion will eat straw like the ox,
but dust will be the serpent's[a] food.
They will neither harm nor destroy
on all my holy mountain,"
says the LORD.

65:15 [i]Zec 8:13
65:16 [j]Ps 31:5 [k]Isa 19:18
65:17 [l]Isa 66:22; 2Pe 3:13 [m]Isa 43:18; Jer 3:16
65:18 [n]Ps 98:1-9; Isa 25:9
65:19 [o]Isa 35:10; 62:5 [p]Isa 25:8; Rev 7:17
65:20 [q]Ecc 8:13
65:21 [r]Isa 32:18 [s]Isa 37:30; Am 9:14
65:22 [t]Ps 92:12-14 [u]Ps 21:4; 91:16
65:23 [v]Dt 28:3-12; Isa 61:9 [w]Ac 2:39
65:24 [x]Isa 55:6 [y]Da 9:20-23; 10:12
65:25 [z]Isa 11:6 [a]Ge 3:14; Mic 7:17

[a] 20 Or / *the sinner who reaches*

Judgment and Hope

66 This is what the LORD says:

"Heaven is my throne,[b]
and the earth is my footstool.[c]
Where is the house[d] you will build for me?
Where will my resting place be?
2 Has not my hand made all these things,[e]
and so they came into being?"
declares the LORD.

"This is the one I esteem:
he who is humble and contrite in spirit,[f]
and trembles at my word.[g]
3 But whoever sacrifices a bull[h]
is like one who kills a man,
and whoever offers a lamb,
like one who breaks a dog's neck;
whoever makes a grain offering
is like one who presents pig's blood,

66:1 [b]Mt 23:22 [c]1Ki 8:27; Mt 5:34-35 [d]2Sa 7:7; Jn 4:20-21; Ac 7:49*; 17:24
66:2 [e]Isa 40:26; Ac 7:50* [f]Isa 57:15; Mt 5:3-4; Lk 18:13-14 [g]Ezr 9:4
66:3 [h]Isa 1:11

66:1 See "Thrones in the Ancient World" on page 899.

ANCIENT TEXTS AND ARTIFACTS

Humanity and the Divine: Comparing the Bible to the Myth of Atra-Hasis

ISAIAH 66 The Bible, along with numerous other ancient Near Eastern texts, recounts the stories of creation and of a great flood.[1] The commonality of a flood story can be misleading, however, causing the reader to suppose that the Bible has essentially the same outlook as that found in other ancient cultures. In fact, the Biblical understanding of God and of his relationship to the world sets the Old Testament record apart from pagan notions of the divine.

One **Old Babylonian** text that recounts the events of creation and the flood is called Atra-hasis (named after the hero of the story, a Noah-like figure). The tale begins with a lower class of gods, the Igigi, who are discontented because they have been forced to do all of the drudge work for the higher gods (e.g., dig irrigation canals and clear marshlands). One night their frustration boils over and they march against the houses of the high gods. Cooler heads prevail, however, and the high gods offer a solution: They will create human beings to do the drudge work for the Igigi. A god is sacrificed, his blood is mixed with clay and humans are formed under the direction of the mother goddess, Mami.

The humans multiply, however, and this creates a new problem: The people make so much noise that the gods cannot sleep. They try to reduce the human population through disease and famine, but it swells again. Finally, they determine to strike humanity with a flood. One man, Atra-hasis, is warned of the coming deluge, however, so that not all humans are wiped out. A solution is finally found: Through infant mortality and the sterility of some women, the human race will be kept to a manageable number.

By contrast, Isaiah 66:1–2 reads, "This is what the LORD says: 'Heaven is my throne, and the earth is my footstool. Where is the house you will build for me? Where will my resting place be? Has not my hand made all these things, and so they came into being?' declares the LORD. 'This is the one I esteem: he who is humble and contrite in spirit, and trembles at my word.'" God needs no one to do his drudge work, nor is he disturbed by the most raucous or boisterous behavior of people. What he does seek is a humble heart. This is in keeping with what we see in Genesis, where God created only by his word, needing no assistance, and where he judged people for their sin—not because their decible level annoyed him. Superficial similarities between the Bible and the ancient Near Eastern myths should not blind us to their profound differences in outlook.

[1]See "Ancient Creation Narratives" on page 5, "Ancient Flood Narratives" on page 13 and "Cosmology in the Ancient Near East" on page 1139.

66:3 [i]Lev 2:2 [j]Isa 57:17

and whoever burns memorial incense,[i]
like one who worships an idol.
They have chosen their own ways,[j]
and their souls delight in their
abominations;
4 so I also will choose harsh treatment for
them
and will bring upon them what they
dread.[k]

66:4 [k]Pr 10:24 [l]Pr 1:24; Jer 7:13 [m]2Ki 21:2,4,6 [n]Isa 65:12

For when I called, no one answered,[l]
when I spoke, no one listened.
They did evil[m] in my sight
and chose what displeases me."[n]

5 Hear the word of the LORD,
you who tremble at his word:
"Your brothers who hate[o] you,
and exclude you because of my name, have said,
'Let the LORD be glorified,
that we may see your joy!'
Yet they will be put to shame.[p]

66:5 [o]Ps 38:20; Isa 60:15 [p]Lk 13:17

66:6 [q]Isa 65:6; Joel 3:7

6 Hear that uproar from the city,
hear that noise from the temple!
It is the sound of the LORD
repaying[q] his enemies all they deserve.

66:7 [r]Isa 54:1 [s]Rev 12:5

7 "Before she goes into labor,[r]
she gives birth;
before the pains come upon her,
she delivers a son.[s]
8 Who has ever heard of such a thing?
Who has ever seen[t] such things?

66:8 [t]Isa 64:4

Can a country be born in a day
or a nation be brought forth in a moment?
Yet no sooner is Zion in labor
than she gives birth to her children.

66:9 [u]Isa 37:3

9 Do I bring to the moment of birth[u]
and not give delivery?" says the LORD.
"Do I close up the womb
when I bring to delivery?" says your God.

66:10 [v]Dt 32:43; Ro 15:10 [w]Ps 26:8

10 "Rejoice[v] with Jerusalem and be glad for her,
all you who love[w] her;
rejoice greatly with her,
all you who mourn over her.

66:11 [x]Isa 60:16

11 For you will nurse[x] and be satisfied
at her comforting breasts;
you will drink deeply
and delight in her overflowing abundance."

12 For this is what the LORD says:

66:12 [y]Isa 48:18 [z]Ps 72:3; Isa 60:5; 61:6

"I will extend peace to her like a river,[y]
and the wealth[z] of nations like a flooding stream;

Ancient Voices

Mami made ready to speak,
And said to the great gods:
"You ordered me the task and I have
completed (it)*!
I have done away with your heavy
forced labor,
I have imposed your drudgery on man."

*Word in parentheses added by translator for clarity

—Atra-Hasis

See "Humanity and the Divine: Comparing the Bible to the Myth of Atra-Hasis" article.

66:12 Childhood in Old Testament times was brief, although boys and girls laughed, played and sang. Some of them had whistles, rattles and dolls, and the youngest ones sat on their mother's laps. In later Judaism a boy's coming of age was celebrated in a manner that reinforced his position within the home and also within the religious family of the synagogue. As soon as they were old enough, both boys and girls were expected to gather fuel (Jer 7:18), care for cattle and tend flocks.

you will nurse and be carried[a] on her arm
and dandled on her knees.
13 As a mother comforts her child,
so will I comfort[b] you;
and you will be comforted over Jerusalem."

14 When you see this, your heart will rejoice
and you will flourish like grass;
the hand of the LORD will be made known to his servants,
but his fury[c] will be shown to his foes.
15 See, the LORD is coming with fire,
and his chariots[d] are like a whirlwind;
he will bring down his anger with fury,
and his rebuke[e] with flames of fire.
16 For with fire[f] and with his sword[g]
the LORD will execute judgment upon all men,
and many will be those slain by the LORD.

17 "Those who consecrate and purify themselves to go into the gardens,[h] following the one in the midst
of[a] those who eat the flesh of pigs[i] and rats and other abominable things—they will meet their end[j] to-
gether," declares the LORD.
18 "And I, because of their actions and their imaginations, am about to come[b] and gather all nations
and tongues, and they will come and see my glory.
19 "I will set a sign[k] among them, and I will send some of those who survive to the nations—to Tar-
shish,[l] to the Libyans[c] and Lydians[m] (famous as archers), to Tubal[n] and Greece, and to the distant is-
lands[o] that have not heard of my fame or seen my glory.[p] They will proclaim my glory among the nations.
20 And they will bring all your brothers, from all the nations, to my holy mountain in Jerusalem as an of-
fering to the LORD—on horses, in chariots and wagons, and on mules and camels," says the LORD. "They
will bring them, as the Israelites bring their grain offerings, to the temple of the LORD in ceremonially
clean vessels.[q] 21 And I will select some of them also to be priests[r] and Levites," says the LORD.

22 "As the new heavens and the new earth[s] that I make will endure before me," declares the LORD, "so
will your name and descendants endure.[t] 23 From one New Moon to another and from one Sabbath[u] to
another, all mankind will come and bow down[v] before me," says the LORD. 24 "And they will go out and look
upon the dead bodies of those who rebelled against me; their worm[w] will not die, nor will their fire be
quenched,[x] and they will be loathsome to all mankind."

[a] 17 Or *gardens behind one of your temples, and* [b] 18 The meaning of the Hebrew for this clause is uncertain. [c] 19 Some Septuagint manuscripts *Put* (Libyans); Hebrew *Pul*

66:12 [a]Isa 60:4
66:13 [b]Isa 40:1; 2Co 1:4
66:14 [c]Isa 10:5
66:15 [d]Ps 68:17 [e]Ps 9:5
66:16 [f]Isa 30:30 [g]Isa 27:1
66:17 [h]Isa 1:29 [i]Lev 11:7 [j]Ps 37:20; Isa 1:28
66:19 [k]Isa 11:10; 49:22 [l]Isa 2:16 [m]Eze 27:10 [n]Ge 10:2 [o]Isa 11:11 [p]1Ch 16:24; Isa 24:15
66:20 [q]Isa 52:11
66:21 [r]Ex 19:6; Isa 61:6; 1Pe 2:5,9
66:22 [s]Isa 65:17; Heb 12:26-27; 2Pe 3:13; Rev 21:1 [t]Jn 10:27-29; 1Pe 1:4-5
66:23 [u]Eze 46:1-3 [v]Isa 19:21
66:24 [w]Isa 14:11 [x]Isa 1:31; Mk 9:48*

66:17 Pagan religions required worshipers to "consecrate and purify themselves" by performing special rituals.

For "gardens," see the note on 1:29 and for "flesh of pigs" the note on 65:4.

66:19 For "Tarshish," see "Where Was Tarshish?" on page 1475. "Libyans" were people who lived west of Egypt, and "Lydians" were probably peoples from western Asia Minor, who were renowned for their skill as archers (see Jer 46:9). "Tubal," usually mentioned in conjunction with Meshech (see Ge 10:2; Eze 27:13; 38:2–3; 39:1), was probably a region southeast of the Black Sea. For "islands," see the note on Isaiah 41:1.

66:23 For a discussion of "New Moon," see the note on 1:14.

66:24 This verse is quoted in part in Mark 9:48 (see also Mk 9:47, where the Greek *gehenna* is translated "hell"). The Valley of Hinnom (Hebrew *ge' hinnom,* the source of "Gehenna"), southwest of Jerusalem, became a picture of hell. See "Sheol, Hades, Gehenna, the Abyss and Tartarus: Images of Hell" on page 946.

INTRODUCTION TO *Jeremiah*

AUTHOR, PLACE AND DATE OF WRITING

Virtually no one disputes that the book of Jeremiah was written by Jeremiah, son of Hilkiah (1:1). The prophet Jeremiah dictated most of his prophecies from Jerusalem to his faithful secretary, Baruch, who wrote them down verbatim (36:4). Jeremiah wrote these words over the course of his prolonged ministry (c. 626–580 B.C.). Chapter 52, an addendum (see 51:64; cf. 2Ki 24:18—25:30, which is nearly identical), was added, possibly by Baruch, sometime after Jehoiachin's release from captivity (c. 560 B.C.).

Reclusive, analytical and self-critical by nature—he has aptly been called the "weeping prophet"—Jeremiah also preached an unpopular message. The people of Judah were in apostasy, God would not protect them and they were obliged to submit to Babylonian demands. Above all, and despite the promise that someday God would give Israel a new covenant (Jer 31), the prophet's overall message was one of doom and gloom: Jerusalem was soon to fall. Because of his negative stance, Jeremiah was widely despised and continuously in danger (11:18–23; 26:8; 38:6). On at least one occasion the text of his message was destroyed by the king (36:20–24). Even Jeremiah's scribe, Baruch, was dismayed about his own future (ch. 45). Jeremiah, an old man, lived to see his words fulfilled and Jerusalem destroyed.

The precise shape of Jeremiah's work is problematic, since two distinctly different versions of his book have survived. One, in the standard Hebrew version known as the Masoretic Text, is the basis for our English translations of the book. The other, found in the Septuagint, appears to represent a variant edition. The Septuagint version is shorter than its counterpart from the Masoretic Text, and its chapters are laid out in a somewhat different order. Many interpreters believe the Septuagint version of Jeremiah to have been based on an alternative Hebrew text. How do scholars account for the two distinct versions of this expanded prophecy, and how can we be certain that what we read is what the prophet intended? The turmoil surrounding Jeremiah's life and that of his book probably accounts for the two different versions. No doubt more than one collection of his messages was in circulation as Jerusalem fell and the Jews were scattered (Jeremiah himself was taken captive to Egypt; ch. 43). Thus, it is not surprising that different "editions" of his work were copied and handed down (see "The Problem of the Septuagint Version of Jeremiah" on p. 1240).

Jeremiah began his ministry during the thirteenth year of King Josiah (640–609 B.C.) and continued preaching through the reigns of Jehoahaz (609), Jehoiakim (609–598), Jehoiachin (598–597) and Zedekiah (597–586), living on into the first years after the fall of Jerusalem. His ministry covered a broad time period—in excess of 40 years—and his book is a compilation of his messages and of accounts of incidents throughout his life.

AUDIENCE

Jeremiah was written to the people of Judah and to Jerusalem, its capital city.

CULTURAL FACTS AND HIGHLIGHTS

Jeremiah wrote during a period of political and military unrest, during which the entire region, including the small and vulnerable state of Judah, found itself at the mercy of the day's superpowers—Assyria, Egypt and, increasingly, Babylonia—as they vied for domination.

Ironically, Jeremiah's ministry began during the time of Josiah's attempt to reform the nation of Judah and purge it of idolatry (2Ki 22–23). Yet the prophet's message, with its focus on judgment, was consistently rejected by the people. Despite Josiah's attempts to turn Judah back to God, the people were obstinate and complacent, fully meriting the sentence that would befall them.

TIMELINE

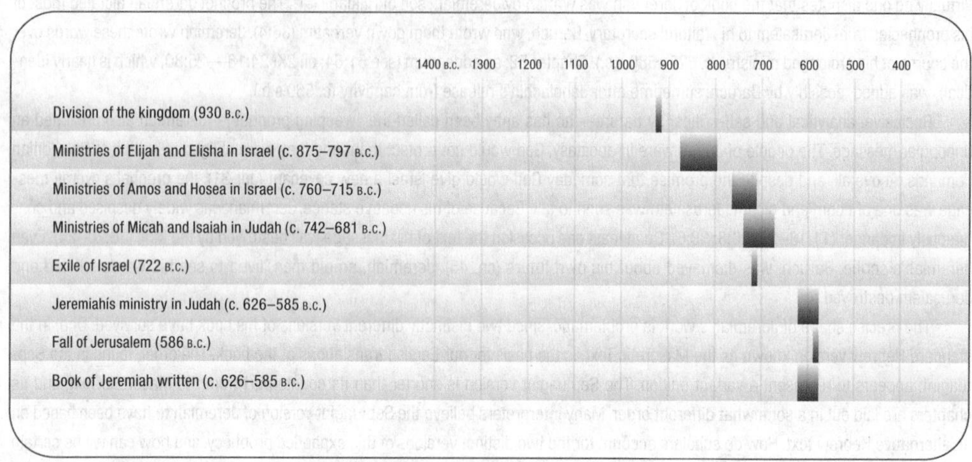

AS YOU READ

Be alert for Jeremiah's frequent self-revelations. What was this ostensibly dour individual all about underneath the rough exterior? Look for passages that reinforce his deep love, not only for the God he extolled but also for his countrymen and women. Marvel as he prayed for his people, despite God's instructions that he not bother to do so (Jer 7:16; 11:14; 14:11).

Pay attention to the role of symbolism and the use of visual aids in this rich book. What personal sacrifices did Jeremiah make in order to follow God's leading (e.g., 16:1–4)?

Look for the ever-present juxtaposition of judgment with the invitation to repentance, which, if sincere, might have been expected to postpone the otherwise inevitable.

Finally, watch for clues about Jeremiah's perception of God, who to him was ultimate and supreme, not only over his own people but over all the nations.

DID YOU KNOW?

- The ancient world considered child sacrifice a supremely religious act, since it gave the god what was most precious to the worshiper (7:31).
- "Jew" is a shortened form of "Judahite" (an inhabitant of the kingdom of Judah, where a remnant of the Israelites was still living).
- The Recabites were related to Moses' father-in-law, Jethro the Kenite. Though not ethnic Jews, this nomadic tribe lived among or near the Israelites and zealously attempted to be faithful to the Lord (35:2).
- The name Ben-Hadad designated a king as the adopted "son" (*ben* means "son") of the Aramean god Hadad. Comparable to the term *pharaoh* in Egypt, several kings from Damascus used this title/name (49:27).
- A little known fact of ancient shepherding is that a goat would often lead a flock of sheep (50:8).
- Marshes were sometimes set on fire to destory the reeds in order to prevent fugitives from hiding among them (51:32).

THEMES

Jeremiah's themes include:

1. *Repentance.* Jeremiah called God's people to repent and return to God in order to avoid divine judgment (e.g., 7:1–15). The people responded negatively (5:20–25; 8:4–7), and, as a consequence, some of the oracles asserted that the coming judgment was certain, with no possibility of repentance (6:16–21).

2. *Judgment.* Jeremiah announced that Judah's covenant rebellion would bring judgment (11:1—13:27). The prophet pointed out that the people had broken the covenant by their idolatry (2:11; 7:30; 9:13–14; 10:1–16; 16:10–13; 22:9; 29:10; 44:2–3,8,17–19,25), their attempts to save themselves through military alliances (2:36) and their injustice and ethical violations (7:5–11; 9:3–11; 17:19–27; 21:11—22:30). Their sin would not go unpunished (5:20–29).

3. *Restoration.* Jeremiah's prophetic vision extended beyond judgment to restoration. Jeremiah 30:1—33:26 (called the "book of consolation") describes a new covenant (31:31–33)—infinitely better than those that had preceded it. While these salvation oracles would come to preliminary fulfillment with the defeat of Babylon and the return of the people in 538 B.C., Jesus himself ultimately fulfilled the new covenant (1Co 11:25; 2Co 3:6; Heb 9:15; 12:24).

OUTLINE

I. Jeremiah's Call (1)
II. Warnings and Exhortations to Judah (2–29)
III. Promises of Restoration (30–33)
IV. Historical Insertion (34–35)
V. The Sufferings of Jeremiah (36–38)
VI. Fall of Jerusalem and Following Events (39–45)
VII. Judgment Against the Nations (46–51)
VIII. Historical Appendix (52)

1 The words of Jeremiah son of Hilkiah, one of the priests at Anathoth[a] in the territory of Benjamin. 1:1 [a]Jos 21:18; 1Ch 6:60; Jer 32:7-9
[2]The word of the LORD came to him in the thirteenth year of the reign of Josiah son of Amon king
of Judah, [3]and through the reign of Jehoiakim[b] son of Josiah king of Judah, down to the fifth month 1:3 [b]2Ki 23:34 [c]2Ki 24:17; Jer 39:2 [d]Jer 52:15
of the eleventh year of Zedekiah[c] son of Josiah king of Judah, when the people of Jerusalem went into
exile.[d]

The Call of Jeremiah

[4]The word of the LORD came to me, saying,

[5]"Before I formed you in the womb I knew[a][e] you, 1:5 [e]Ps 139:16 [f]Isa 49:1 [g]ver 10; Jer 25:15-26
before you were born[f] I set you apart;
I appointed you as a prophet to the nations.[g]"

[6]"Ah, Sovereign LORD," I said, "I do not know how to speak;[h] I am only a child."[i] 1:6 [h]Ex 4:10; 6:12 [i]1Ki 3:7

[a] 5 Or *chose*

1:1 Anathoth, located about three miles (four km) northeast of Jerusalem, was a Levitical town in the territory of Benjamin. The name comes from the Canaanite deity Anat(h), goddess of war. After the exile Benjamites again settled there (Ne 11:31–32).
1:2 Josiah (r. 640–609 B.C.) was the last godly king of Judah. Jeremiah supported his attempts at spiritual reformation and renewal (see 2Ki 22:3—23:25).
1:3 Zedekiah (r. 597–586 B.C.) was the last king of Judah. Judah's people were exiled when Jerusalem and Solomon's temple were destroyed by Nebuchadnezzar in 586 B.C.

FUNCTION OF THE PROPHETS

Period	Function	Audience	Message	Examples
PRE-MONARCHY	Mouthpiece-leader	People	National guidance Maintenance of justice Spiritual overseer	Moses Deborah
				TRANSITION: Samuel
PRE-CLASSICAL	Mouthpiece-leader	King and court	Military advice Pronouncement of rebuke or blessing	Nathan Elijah Elisha Micaiah
CLASSICAL	Mouthpiece-social/spiritual commentator	People	Rebuke concerning current condition of society; leads to warnings of captivity, destruction, exile and promise of eventual restoration Call for justice and repentance	TRANSITION: North—Jonah South—Isaiah
				Writing prophets Best example Jeremiah

Chronological and Background Charts of the Old Testament, p. 52

7But the LORD said to me, "Do not say, 'I am only a child.' You must go to everyone I send you to and
1:8 [j]Eze 2:6 [k]Jos 1:5; Jer 15:20 say whatever I command you. 8Do not be afraid[j] of them, for I am with you[k] and will rescue you," de-
clares the LORD.
1:9 [l]Isa 6:7 [m]Ex 4:12 9Then the LORD reached out his hand and touched[l] my mouth and said to me, "Now, I have put my
words in your mouth.[m] 10See, today I appoint you over nations and kingdoms to uproot and tear down,
1:10 [n]Jer 18:7-10; 24:6; 31:4,28 to destroy and overthrow, to build and to plant."[n]
1:11 [o]Jer 24:3; Am 7:8 11The word of the LORD came to me: "What do you see, Jeremiah?"[o]
"I see the branch of an almond tree," I replied.
12The LORD said to me, "You have seen correctly, for I am watching[a] to see that my word is fulfilled."
1:13 [p]Zec 4:2 13The word of the LORD came to me again: "What do you see?"[p]
"I see a boiling pot, tilting away from the north," I answered.
14The LORD said to me, "From the north disaster will be poured out on all who live in the land. 15I am
about to summon all the peoples of the northern kingdoms," declares the LORD.

"Their kings will come and set up their thrones
in the entrance of the gates of Jerusalem;
they will come against all her surrounding walls
1:15 [q]Jer 4:16; 9:11 and against all the towns of Judah.[q]
16I will pronounce my judgments on my people
1:16 [r]Dt 28:20 [s]Jer 17:13 [t]Jer 7:9; 19:4 because of their wickedness[r] in forsaking me,[s]
in burning incense to other gods[t]
and in worshiping what their hands have made.

1:17 [u]Eze 2:6 17"Get yourself ready! Stand up and say to them whatever I command you. Do not be terrified[u] by
1:18 [v]Isa 50:7 them, or I will terrify you before them. 18Today I have made you[v] a fortified city, an iron pillar and a
bronze wall to stand against the whole land—against the kings of Judah, its officials, its priests and the
1:19 [w]Jer 20:11 [x]ver 8 people of the land. 19They will fight against you but will not overcome you, for I am with you[w] and will
rescue[x] you," declares the LORD.

Israel Forsakes God

2 The word of the LORD came to me: 2"Go and proclaim in the hearing of Jerusalem:

2:2 [y]Eze 16:8-14, 60; Hos 2:15 [z]Dt 2:7 " 'I remember the devotion of your youth,[y]
how as a bride you loved me
and followed me through the desert,[z]
through a land not sown.
2:3 [a]Dt 7:6 [b]Ex 19:6 [c]Jas 1:18; Rev 14:4 [d]Isa 41:11; Jer 30:16 [e]Jer 50:7 3Israel was holy[a] to the LORD,[b]
the firstfruits[c] of his harvest;
all who devoured[d] her were held guilty,[e]
and disaster overtook them,' "
declares the LORD.

4Hear the word of the LORD, O house of Jacob,
all you clans of the house of Israel.

5This is what the LORD says:

"What fault did your fathers find in me,
that they strayed so far from me?

[a] 12 The Hebrew for *watching* sounds like the Hebrew for *almond tree.*

1:13 More than a dozen Hebrew and Greek words are translated "pot." Most of them referred to utensils for holding liquids and solid substances such as grain or ashes. The Hebrew *sîr* stood for the most common pot used in cooking (see also 2Ki 4:38).

1:15 The "northern kingdoms" is most likely a reference to Babylon and her allies.

The city gate was the place where the ruling council sat (see "The City Gate" on p. 392); the Babylonians replaced Judah's royal authority with their own.

1:16 Burning incense was a common feature of pagan worship (see the notes on Isa 15:3; Jer 19:13).

1:18 "Fortified city," "iron pillar" and "bronze wall" are all symbols of security and strength. God would give Jeremiah the ability to withstand the abuse and persecution that his divine commission would bring.

They followed worthless idols
and became worthless[f] themselves. 2:5 [f]2Ki 17:15
6 They did not ask, 'Where is the LORD,
who brought us up out of Egypt[g] 2:6 [g]Hos 13:4
and led us through the barren wilderness, [h]Dt 8:15 [i]Dt 32:10
through a land of deserts[h] and rifts,[i]
a land of drought and darkness,[a]
a land where no one travels and no one lives?'
7 I brought you into a fertile land
to eat its fruit and rich produce.[j] 2:7 [j]Nu 13:27; Dt 8:7-9; 11:10-12 [k]Ps 106:34-39; Jer 16:18
But you came and defiled my land
and made my inheritance detestable.[k]
8 The priests did not ask,
'Where is the LORD?'
Those who deal with the law did not know me;[l] 2:8 [l]Jer 4:22
the leaders rebelled against me. [m]Jer 23:13
The prophets prophesied by Baal,[m] [n]Jer 16:19
following worthless idols.[n]

9 "Therefore I bring charges[o] against you again," 2:9 [o]Eze 20:35-36; Mic 6:2

declares the LORD.

"And I will bring charges against your children's children.
10 Cross over to the coasts of Kittim[b] and look,
send to Kedar[c] and observe closely;
see if there has ever been anything like this:
11 Has a nation ever changed its gods?
(Yet they are not gods[p] at all.) 2:11 [p]Isa 37:19; Jer 16:20
But my people have exchanged their[d] Glory[q] [q]Ps 106:20; Ro 1:23
for worthless idols.
12 Be appalled at this, O heavens,
and shudder with great horror,"

declares the LORD.

13 "My people have committed two sins:
They have forsaken me,
the spring of living water,[r] 2:13 [r]Ps 36:9; Jn 4:14
and have dug their own cisterns,
broken cisterns that cannot hold water.
14 Is Israel a servant, a slave[s] by birth? 2:14 [s]Ex 4:22
Why then has he become plunder?
15 Lions[t] have roared; 2:15 [t]Jer 4:7; 50:17 [u]Isa 1:7
they have growled at him.
They have laid waste[u] his land;
his towns are burned and deserted.
16 Also, the men of Memphis[e][v] and Tahpanhes[w] 2:16 [v]Isa 19:13 [w]Jer 43:7-9
have shaved the crown of your head.[f]

[a] 6 Or *and the shadow of death* [b] 10 That is, Cyprus and western coastlands [c] 10 The home of Bedouin tribes in the Syro-Arabian desert [d] 11 Masoretic Text; an ancient Hebrew scribal tradition *my* [e] 16 Hebrew *Noph* [f] 16 Or *have cracked your skull*

2:10 Kittim (probably Cyprus) represents the western nations and regions, while Kedar (see the note on 49:28) signifies the eastern nations and regions.
2:13 A good cistern's entire interior was coated with plaster to prevent water loss (see "Wells, Cisterns and Aqueducts in the Ancient World" on p. 1259).
2:16 Memphis, an important Egyptian city located 15 miles (24 km) south of the Nile delta (see "Memphis" on p. 1270), was Egypt's capital during the Old Kingdom period (c. 2686–2160 B.C.).

Tahpanhes was probably the city later called Daphnai by the Greeks. Known today as Tell Defneh, it is located just south of Lake Menzaleh in the eastern Nile delta region of Egypt.

Having one's head shaved was a sign of disgrace and devastation (see the notes on Isa 3:24; 7:20; see also "Beards and Hairstyles in the Biblical World" on p. 1084).

2:17 [x]Jer 4:18
2:18 [y]Isa 30:2 [z]Jos 13:3
2:19 [a]Jer 3:11,22 [b]Isa 3:9; Hos 5:5 [c]Job 20:14; Am 8:10 [d]Ps 36:1
2:20 [e]Lev 26:13 [f]Isa 57:7; Jer 17:2 [g]Dt 12:2
2:21 [h]Ex 15:17 [i]Ps 80:8 [j]Isa 5:4
2:23 [k]Pr 30:12 [l]Jer 9:14 [m]Jer 7:31 [n]ver 33; Jer 31:22
2:24 [o]Jer 14:6
2:25 [p]Dt 32:16; Jer 3:13; 14:10
2:26 [q]Jer 48:27

17 Have you not brought this on yourselves[x]
by forsaking the LORD your God
when he led you in the way?
18 Now why go to Egypt[y]
to drink water from the Shihor[a]?[z]
And why go to Assyria
to drink water from the River[b]?
19 Your wickedness will punish you;
your backsliding[a] will rebuke[b] you.
Consider then and realize
how evil and bitter[c] it is for you
when you forsake the LORD your God
and have no awe[d] of me,"
declares the Lord, the LORD Almighty.

20 "Long ago you broke off your yoke[e]
and tore off your bonds;
you said, 'I will not serve you!'
Indeed, on every high hill[f]
and under every spreading tree[g]
you lay down as a prostitute.
21 I had planted[h] you like a choice vine[i]
of sound and reliable stock.
How then did you turn against me
into a corrupt,[j] wild vine?
22 Although you wash yourself with soda
and use an abundance of soap,
the stain of your guilt is still before me,"
declares the Sovereign LORD.
23 "How can you say, 'I am not defiled;[k]
I have not run after the Baals'?[l]
See how you behaved in the valley;[m]
consider what you have done.
You are a swift she-camel
running[n] here and there,
24 a wild donkey[o] accustomed to the desert,
sniffing the wind in her craving—
in her heat who can restrain her?
Any males that pursue her need not tire themselves;
at mating time they will find her.
25 Do not run until your feet are bare
and your throat is dry.
But you said, 'It's no use!
I love foreign gods,[p]
and I must go after them.'

26 "As a thief is disgraced[q] when he is caught,
so the house of Israel is disgraced—

[a] *18* That is, a branch of the Nile [b] *18* That is, the Euphrates

2:20 High hills and spreading trees were associated with rituals of pagan worship (see the note on Isa 57:5).
2:22 Soda (mineral alkali) and soap (vegetable alkali) were used for cleaning. Oil was one of the main ingredients used for making soap.
2:23 The "Baals" (plural) is a reference to the many local forms of this Canaanite deity (see the note on Jdg 2:13; see also "Baal and the Fertility Cults" on p. 1414).

The "valley" probably refers to the Hinnom Valley, known also as the Valley of Ben Hinnom (Jer 7:31–32; 19:2,6; 32:35). Located southwest of Jerusalem, it was used as a trash dump and also as a place for sacrificing children to pagan gods. Called "Gehenna" in the New Testament, it became a picture of hell. (See "Human Sacrifice in the Ancient Near East" on p. 182 and "Sheol, Hades, Gehenna, the Abyss and Tartarus: Images of Hell" on p. 946.)

they, their kings and their officials,
their priests and their prophets.
27 They say to wood, 'You are my father,'
and to stone,[r] 'You gave me birth.'
They have turned their backs to me
and not their faces;[s]
yet when they are in trouble,[t] they say,
'Come and save us!'
28 Where then are the gods[u] you made for yourselves?
Let them come if they can save you
when you are in trouble![v]
For you have as many gods
as you have towns,[w] O Judah.

29 "Why do you bring charges against me?
You have all[x] rebelled against me,"
declares the LORD.
30 "In vain I punished your people;
they did not respond to correction.
Your sword has devoured your prophets[y]
like a ravening lion.

31 "You of this generation, consider the word of the LORD:

"Have I been a desert to Israel
or a land of great darkness?[z]
Why do my people say, 'We are free to roam;
we will come to you no more'?
32 Does a maiden forget her jewelry,
a bride her wedding ornaments?
Yet my people have forgotten me,
days without number.
33 How skilled you are at pursuing love!
Even the worst of women can learn from your ways.
34 On your clothes men find
the lifeblood[a] of the innocent poor,
though you did not catch them breaking in.[b]
Yet in spite of all this
35 you say, 'I am innocent;
he is not angry with me.'
But I will pass judgment[c] on you
because you say, 'I have not sinned.'[d]
36 Why do you go about so much,
changing[e] your ways?
You will be disappointed by Egypt[f]
as you were by Assyria.
37 You will also leave that place
with your hands on your head,[g]
for the LORD has rejected those you trust;
you will not be helped[h] by them.

2:27 [r]Jer 3:9 [s]Jer 18:17; 32:33 [t]Jdg 10:10; Isa 26:16
2:28 [u]Isa 45:20 [v]Dt 32:37 [w]2Ki 17:29; Jer 11:13
2:29 [x]Jer 5:1; 6:13; Da 9:11
2:30 [y]Ne 9:26; Ac 7:52; 1Th 2:15
2:31 [z]Isa 45:19
2:34 [a]2Ki 21:16 [b]Ex 22:2
2:35 [c]Jer 25:31 [d]1Jn 1:8,10
2:36 [e]Jer 31:22 [f]Isa 30:2,3,7
2:37 [g]2Sa 13:19 [h]Jer 37:7

2:28 Every ancient Near Eastern town of any importance had its own patron deity, and many towns were named after their respective deities (see, e.g., the note on 1:1).

2:37 Ancient reliefs depict captives with wrists tied together above their heads.

3:1 [h]Dt 24:1-4 [i]Jer 2:20,25; Eze 16:26,29

3

“If a man divorces[h] his wife
and she leaves him and marries another man,
should he return to her again?
Would not the land be completely defiled?
But you have lived as a prostitute with many lovers[i]—
would you now return to me?”
declares the LORD.

3:2 [k]Ge 38:14; Eze 16:25 [l]Jer 2:7

2 “Look up to the barren heights and see.
Is there any place where you have not been ravished?
By the roadside[k] you sat waiting for lovers,
sat like a nomad[a] in the desert.
You have defiled the land[l]
with your prostitution and wickedness.

3:3 [m]Lev 26:19 [n]Jer 14:4 [o]Jer 6:15; 8:12; Zep 3:5

3 Therefore the showers have been withheld,[m]
and no spring rains[n] have fallen.
Yet you have the brazen look of a prostitute;
you refuse to blush with shame.[o]
4 Have you not just called to me:

3:4 [p]ver 19 [q]Jer 2:2
3:5 [r]Ps 103:9; Isa 57:16

‘My Father,[p] my friend from my youth,[q]
5 will you always be angry?[r]
Will your wrath continue forever?’
This is how you talk,
but you do all the evil you can.”

Unfaithful Israel

3:6 [s]Jer 17:2 [t]Jer 2:20
3:7 [u]Eze 16:46
3:8 [v]Eze 16:47; 23:11
3:9 [w]ver 2 [x]Isa 57:6 [y]Jer 2:27
3:10 [z]Jer 12:2

6 During the reign of King Josiah, the LORD said to me, “Have you seen what faithless Israel has done?
She has gone up on every high hill and under every spreading tree[s] and has committed adultery[t] there.
7 I thought that after she had done all this she would return to me but she did not, and her unfaithful sis-
ter[u] Judah saw it. 8 I gave faithless Israel her certificate of divorce and sent her away because of all her adul-
teries. Yet I saw that her unfaithful sister Judah had no fear;[v] she also went out and committed adultery.
9 Because Israel’s immorality mattered so little to her, she defiled the land[w] and committed adultery with
stone[x] and wood.[y] 10 In spite of all this, her unfaithful sister Judah did not return to me with all her heart,
but only in pretense,[z]” declares the LORD.

3:11 [a]Eze 16:52; 23:11 [b]ver 7
3:12 [c]2Ki 17:3-6 [d]ver 14; Jer 31:21,22; Eze 33:11 [e]Ps 86:15

11 The LORD said to me, “Faithless Israel is more righteous[a] than unfaithful[b] Judah. 12 Go, proclaim this
message toward the north:[c]

“ ‘Return,[d] faithless Israel,’ declares the LORD,
‘I will frown on you no longer,
for I am merciful,’ declares the LORD,
‘I will not be angry[e] forever.

3:13 [f]Dt 30:1-3; Jer 14:20; 1Jn 1:9 [g]Jer 2:25 [h]Dt 12:2 [i]ver 25

13 Only acknowledge[f] your guilt—
you have rebelled against the LORD your God,
you have scattered your favors to foreign gods[g]
under every spreading tree,[h]
and have not obeyed[i] me,’ ”
declares the LORD.

[a] 2 Or *an Arab*

3:1 On the subject of defilement in the Old and New Testaments, see the note on Song of Songs 5:3.
3:2 Pagan gods were consulted and worshiped on hilltops (see “The High Places” on p. 1318), and prostitutes often sat along the roadside (see Ge 38:14).
3:3 The rainy season in the region now known as Palestine begins in October and ends in April.
3:6 For information on King Josiah, see “The Tragic Reign of King Josiah” on page 569. For commentary on the phrases “on every high hill” and “under every spreading tree,” see the note on 2:20. “Israel” refers to the northern kingdom, which was destroyed in 722/721 B.C.
3:7 Israel’s “unfaithful sister” refers to the southern kingdom of Judah. See Ezekiel 23 for descriptions and comparisons of Samaria (Israel’s capital) and Jerusalem (Judah’s capital) as adulterous sisters (i.e., spiritually idolatrous).
3:12 The “north” refers to Assyria’s northern provinces, to which many Israelites had been exiled.
3:13 For “under every spreading tree,” see the note on 2:20.

14 “Return,[j] faithless people,” declares the LORD, “for I am your husband. I will choose you—one 3:14 [j]Hos 2:19
from a town and two from a clan—and bring you to Zion. 15 Then I will give you shepherds[k] after 3:15 [k]Ac 20:28
my own heart, who will lead you with knowledge and understanding. 16 In those days, when your
numbers have increased greatly in the land,” declares the LORD, “men will no longer say, ‘The ark of
the covenant of the LORD.’ It will never enter their minds or be remembered;[l] it will not be missed, 3:16 [l]Isa 65:17
nor will another one be made. 17 At that time they will call Jerusalem The Throne[m] of the LORD, and 3:17 [m]Jer 17:12;
all nations will gather in Jerusalem to honor[n] the name of the LORD. No longer will they follow the Eze 43:7 [n]Isa 60:9
stubbornness of their evil hearts.[o] 18 In those days the house of Judah will join the house of Isra- [o]Jer 11:8
el,[p] and together[q] they will come from a northern[r] land to the land[s] I gave your forefathers as an 3:18 [p]Hos 1:11
inheritance. [q]Isa 11:13; Jer 50:4 [r]Jer 16:15; 31:8 [s]Am 9:15

19 “I myself said,

“ ‘How gladly would I treat you like sons
and give you a desirable land,
the most beautiful inheritance of any nation.’
I thought you would call me ‘Father’[t] 3:19 [t]ver 4; Isa 63:16
and not turn away from following me.
20 But like a woman unfaithful to her husband,
so you have been unfaithful to me, O house of Israel,”

declares the LORD.

21 A cry is heard on the barren heights,[u] 3:21 [u]ver 2
the weeping and pleading of the people of Israel,
because they have perverted their ways
and have forgotten the LORD their God.

22 “Return,[v] faithless people; 3:22 [v]Hos 14:4
I will cure[w] you of backsliding.” [w]Jer 33:6; Hos 6:1

“Yes, we will come to you,
for you are the LORD our God.
23 Surely the ⌊idolatrous⌋ commotion on the hills
and mountains is a deception;
surely in the LORD our God
is the salvation[x] of Israel. 3:23 [x]Ps 3:8; Jer 17:14
24 From our youth shameful[y] gods have consumed 3:24 [y]Hos 9:10
the fruits of our fathers’ labor—
their flocks and herds,
their sons and daughters.
25 Let us lie down in our shame,[z] 3:25 [z]Ezr 9:6 [a]Jer 22:21
and let our disgrace cover us.
We have sinned against the LORD our God,
both we and our fathers;
from our youth[a] till this day
we have not obeyed the LORD our God.”

4

“If you will return[b], O Israel, 4:1 [b]Jer 3:1,22; Joel 2:12
return to me,” [c]Jer 35:15

declares the LORD.

“If you put your detestable idols[c] out of my sight
and no longer go astray,

3:15 Throughout the ancient Near East the term “shepherd” was a term often applied to rulers (see “Shepherding in the Ancient World” on p. 1363).
3:17 During Israel’s early history the Lord sat “enthroned between the cherubim” above the ark (1Sa 4:4; see Ex 25:18–20 and its note; see also “Thrones in the Ancient World” on p. 899), but Jerusalem itself would someday be his throne.
3:24 Children were sacrificed to pagan gods (see the note on 7:31; see also “Human Sacrifice in the Ancient Near East” on p. 182).

4:2 [d]Dt 10:20; Isa 65:16 [e]Jer 12:16 [f]Ge 22:18; Gal 3:8

2 and if in a truthful, just and righteous way
you swear,[d] 'As surely as the LORD lives,'[e]
then the nations will be blessed[f] by him
and in him they will glory."

3 This is what the LORD says to the men of Judah and to Jerusalem:

4:3 [g]Hos 10:12 [h]Mk 4:18

"Break up your unplowed ground[g]
and do not sow among thorns.[h]
4 Circumcise yourselves to the LORD,
circumcise your hearts,[i]
you men of Judah and people of Jerusalem,
or my wrath[j] will break out and burn like fire
because of the evil you have done—
burn with no one to quench[k] it.

4:4 [i]Dt 10:16; Jer 9:26; Ro 2:28-29 [j]Zep 2:2 [k]Am 5:6

Disaster From the North

5 "Announce in Judah and proclaim in Jerusalem
and say:
'Sound the trumpet throughout the land!'
Cry aloud and say:
'Gather together!
Let us flee to the fortified cities!'[l]
6 Raise the signal to go to Zion!
Flee for safety without delay!
For I am bringing disaster from the north,[m]
even terrible destruction."

4:5 [l]Jos 10:20; Jer 8:14
4:6 [m]Jer 1:13-15; 50:3

7 A lion[n] has come out of his lair;
a destroyer of nations has set out.
He has left his place
to lay waste[o] your land.
Your towns will lie in ruins[p]
without inhabitant.
8 So put on sackcloth,[q]
lament and wail,
for the fierce anger[r] of the LORD
has not turned away from us.

4:7 [n]2Ki 24:1; Jer 2:15 [o]Isa 1:7 [p]Jer 25:9
4:8 [q]Isa 22:12; Jer 6:26 [r]Jer 30:24

9 "In that day," declares the LORD,
"the king and the officials will lose heart,
the priests will be horrified,
and the prophets will be appalled."[s]

4:9 [s]Isa 29:9

10 Then I said, "Ah, Sovereign LORD, how completely you have deceived[t] this people and Jerusalem by
saying, 'You will have peace,'[u] when the sword is at our throats."
11 At that time this people and Jerusalem will be told, "A scorching wind[v] from the barren heights in

4:10 [t]2Th 2:11 [u]Jer 14:13
4:11 [v]Eze 17:10; Hos 13:15

4:5 The trumpet, usually made of a ram's or bull's horn, was sounded to warn of impending doom (see "The Shofar" on p. 898 and "Trumpets in the Ancient World" on p. 2057). People living in the countryside would take refuge in the nearest walled town in order to avoid being captured by the enemy.

4:6 For "raise the signal," see the note on Isaiah 5:26.

The "disaster from the north" was the Babylonian invasion. From the perspective of the writer, invasions came primarily from the north.

4:7 The lion was a symbol of Babylon, referred to here as the "destroyer" (also in 6:26; 15:8; 48:8,32). Note, however, that in 51:1 and 51:56 the "destroyer" refers to Persia and her allies (see also 51:48,53).

4:8 Sackcloth was the coarse garb of mourners (see the notes on 1Ki 20:31–32 and Job 16:15, as well as "Sackcloth and Ashes: Rituals of Lamentation" on p. 820).

4:10 The Hebrew for "throat" is usually translated "soul" or "life" (see "Heart, Breath, Throat and Intestines: Ancient Hebrew Anthropology" on p. 968).

4:11 The "scorching wind" refers to the sirocco or khamsin, a hot, dry wind that brings sand and dust.

God's coming judgment would not be a winnowing (separating grain from chaff) or a cleansing (blowing dust from the grain) but a destruction, for the judgment coming would sweep away good and bad alike (v. 12). (See the note on Ru 1:22 and "The Threshing Floor" on p. 608.)

the desert blows toward my people, but not to winnow or cleanse; 12 a wind too strong for that comes
from me.[a] Now I pronounce my judgments[w] against them."

13 Look! He advances like the clouds,[x]
his chariots[y] come like a whirlwind,[z]
his horses are swifter than eagles.[a]
Woe to us! We are ruined!
14 O Jerusalem, wash[b] the evil from your heart and
be saved.
How long will you harbor wicked thoughts?
15 A voice is announcing from Dan,[c]
proclaiming disaster from the hills of Ephraim.
16 "Tell this to the nations,
proclaim it to Jerusalem:
'A besieging army is coming from a distant land,
raising a war cry[d] against the cities of Judah.
17 They surround[e] her like men guarding a field,
because she has rebelled[f] against me,' "
declares the LORD.

18 "Your own conduct and actions[g]
have brought this upon you.[h]
This is your punishment.
How bitter[i] it is!
How it pierces to the heart!"

19 Oh, my anguish, my anguish![j]
I writhe in pain.
Oh, the agony of my heart!
My heart pounds within me,
I cannot keep silent.[k]
For I have heard the sound of the trumpet;
I have heard the battle cry.[l]
20 Disaster follows disaster;[m]
the whole land lies in ruins.
In an instant my tents[n] are destroyed,
my shelter in a moment.
21 How long must I see the battle standard
and hear the sound of the trumpet?

22 "My people are fools;[o]
they do not know me.[p]
They are senseless children;
they have no understanding.
They are skilled in doing evil;[q]
they know not how to do good."[r]

23 I looked at the earth,
and it was formless and empty;[s]
and at the heavens,
and their light was gone.

4:12 [w]Jer 1:16
4:13 [x]Isa 19:1 [y]Isa 66:15 [z]Isa 5:28 [a]Dt 28:49; Hab 1:8
4:14 [b]Jas 4:8
4:15 [c]Jer 8:16
4:16 [d]Eze 21:22
4:17 [e]2Ki 25:1,4 [f]Jer 5:23
4:18 [g]Ps 107:17; Isa 50:1 [h]Jer 2:17 [i]Jer 2:19
4:19 [j]Isa 16:11; 22:4; Jer 9:10 [k]Jer 20:9 [l]Nu 10:9
4:20 [m]Ps 42:7; Eze 7:26 [n]Jer 10:20
4:22 [o]Jer 10:8 [p]Jer 2:8 [q]Jer 13:23; 1Co 14:20 [r]Ro 16:19
4:23 [s]Ge 1:2

[a] 12 Or *comes at my command*

4:14 As the royal city of Judah and the most important metropolis of the nation, Jerusalem was addressed as representative of the nation.
4:15 Dan was close to the northern border of Israel, while Ephraim was a few miles north of Jerusalem. The prophet envisioned the enemy's fearfully rapid approach toward the holy city.
4:19 For "the sound of the trumpet," see the note on verse 5.
4:20 "Shelter" literally means "tent curtains" (as in Isa 54:2), which were usually made of goat hair (see Ex 26:7) and were therefore strong enough to protect from cold and rain (see Jer 10:20).
4:21 For "battle standard" and "sound of the trumpet," see the notes on verses 5 and 6; see also "The Shofar" on page 898 and "Trumpets in the Ancient World" on page 2057.

ARCHAEOLOGICAL SITES

JERUSALEM

JEREMIAH 4 Evidence for habitation of Jerusalem goes back to the **Chalcolithic Age**,[1,2] but it appears that the city was first fortified during the **Middle Bronze** period. First Chronicles 11:4 suggests that the pre-Israelite city was also called Jebus.[3] Even so, the name "Jerusalem," or something like it, appears to be very ancient. An eighteenth-century B.C. Egyptian **execration text** mentions a *Rosh-lamem*, and this appears to have been Jerusalem. The 12-acre Jebusite city captured by David's men was located south of what would become the temple mount and was bounded on the east by the Kidron Valley and on the west by the Tyropoeon Valley. It was surrounded during the **Late Bronze** and **Iron Ages** by walls that were hardly modified until Nehemiah's time. The city was watered by the Gihon spring, located below a protective tower just outside the northeastern walls. En-Rogel, a spring outside the city to the south, also provided water.

Solomon expanded the city to 32 acres. The threshing floor of Araunah, on a second hill just north of David's city, served as a platform for the temple-palace complex built by Solomon and was enclosed within a new wall. The depression between the two hills was filled in between newly constructed retaining walls on the eastern and western sides; this area was perhaps known as the Ophel ("swelling"). Few, if any, traces remain of Solomon's temple, which was destroyed by the **Babylonians**.[4] Zerubbabel's temple, built on the same foundation, was later greatly improved and expanded by Herod,[5] then destroyed by the Romans in A.D. 70.[6] The Dome of the Rock and the al-Aqsa mosque presently cover the temple mount.

Over the course of time the city expanded, with new towers, gates and conduits for water added. Uzziah strengthened the walls with towers along the western wall and the temple mount (2Ch 26:15). The Tower of Hananel, at the northwestern corner of the temple mount, also existed during this period. Jotham constructed the upper gate of the temple (2Ki 15:35).

The population increased from an influx of northern refugees after the fall of **Samaria** in 722 B.C., and the city grew to 125 acres. Hezekiah extended the walls to enclose a hill to the west, known as the Mishneh ("second quarter") and constructed a tunnel to ensure water flow from the Gihon spring to the Lower Pool (2Chr 32:30);[7] an earlier tunnel directed water to an "Old" or Upper Pool.[8] These improvements helped preserve the city from Sennacherib's siege of 701 B.C.[9]

Manasseh constructed a second wall near the Gihon spring (2Ch 33:14). Sixteen gates are named in descriptions of preexilic and fifth-century B.C. Jerusalem and three others in descriptions of Nehemiah's Jerusalem; others may have existed. Some are named for nearby roads or associated geographic features, while others reflect the activities of citizens (e.g., Fish Gate, Sheep Gate, Water Gate).

Nebuchadnezzar destroyed Jerusalem in 586 B.C., but the temple and walls were rebuilt during the **Persian** period following a half century without occupation. However, the newly inhabited area encompassed only the original Davidic and Solomonic quarters. An era of peace under the **Ptolemies** and then the Romans allowed Judea to prosper. **Hasmonean** Jerusalem expanded to 165 acres, then to 230 acres under Herod, who constructed a large, fortified palace along the western wall, protected by three towers in the northwestern corner. Another fortress protected the temple complex to the north, but this area and the lower city were the first to fall to the attack of the Romans under Titus in A.D. 70.

Kidron Valley with Jerusalem's Golden Gate in background
Photograph: © Todd Bolen/Bible Places.com

Jerusalem is sacred to Jews, Christians and Moslems and has been inhabited almost continuously since ancient times. These factors have ensured that much has been preserved—but much also has been lost. As later generations rebuilt over ancient sites, archaeological evidence vanished forever. Members of one religion at times deliberately destroyed what was sacred to another. Also, modern archaeologists have a limited ability to dig in the city for the simple reason that it is currently inhabited. Thus, although Jerusalem is by far the most important city of the Bible, many questions remain unanswered.

[1]See Glossary on page 2080 for definitions of bolded words. [2]See "Archaeological Periods" chart on page xx in the front of this Bible. [3]See "The Jebusites" on page 596. [4]See "Solomon's Temple and Other Ancient Temples" on page 620. [5]See "Herod's Temple" on page 1648. [6]See "Josephus and the Fall of Jerusalem" on page 1606. [7]See "Hezekiah's Tunnel" on page 564. [8]See "The Pool of Siloam" on page 1739. [9]See "Hezekiah Against the Assyrians" on page 1118.

[24] I looked at the mountains,
and they were quaking;[t]
all the hills were swaying.
[25] I looked, and there were no people;
every bird in the sky had flown away.[u]
[26] I looked, and the fruitful land was a desert;
all its towns lay in ruins
before the LORD, before his fierce anger.

[27] This is what the LORD says:

"The whole land will be ruined,
though I will not destroy[v] it completely.
[28] Therefore the earth will mourn[w]
and the heavens above grow dark,[x]
because I have spoken and will not relent,[y]
I have decided and will not turn back.[z]"
[29] At the sound of horsemen and archers[a]
every town takes to flight.[b]
Some go into the thickets;
some climb up among the rocks.
All the towns are deserted;[c]
no one lives in them.

[30] What are you doing,[d] O devastated one?
Why dress yourself in scarlet
and put on jewels[e] of gold?
Why shade your eyes with paint?[f]
You adorn yourself in vain.
Your lovers[g] despise you;
they seek your life.

[31] I hear a cry as of a woman in labor,[h]
a groan as of one bearing her first child—
the cry of the Daughter of Zion gasping for breath,[i]
stretching out her hands[j] and saying,
"Alas! I am fainting;
my life is given over to murderers."

Not One Is Upright

5 "Go up and down[k] the streets of Jerusalem,
look around and consider,
search through her squares.
If you can find but one person[l]
who deals honestly and seeks the truth,
I will forgive[m] this city.
[2] Although they say, 'As surely as the LORD lives,'[n]
still they are swearing falsely."
[3] O LORD, do not your eyes[o] look for truth?
You struck[p] them, but they felt no pain;
you crushed them, but they refused correction.[q]
They made their faces harder than stone[r]
and refused to repent.

4:24 [t]Isa 5:25; Eze 38:20
4:25 [u]Jer 9:10; 12:4; Zep 1:3
4:27 [v]Jer 5:10, 18; 12:12; 30:11; 46:28
4:28 [w]Jer 12:4, 11; 14:2; Hos 4:3 [x]Isa 5:30; 50:3 [y]Nu 23:19 [z]Jer 23:20; 30:24
4:29 [a]Jer 6:23 [b]2Ki 25:4 [c]ver 7
4:30 [d]Isa 10:3-4 [e]Eze 23:40 [f]2Ki 9:30 [g]La 1:2; Eze 23:9,22
4:31 [h]Jer 13:21 [i]Isa 42:14 [j]Isa 1:15; La 1:17
5:1 [k]2Ch 16:9; Eze 22:30 [l]Ge 18:32 [m]Ge 18:24
5:2 [n]Jer 4:2
5:3 [o]2Ch 16:9 [p]Isa 9:13 [q]Jer 2:30; Zep 3:2 [r]Jer 7:26; 19:15; Eze 3:8-9

4:30 The "paint" was antimony, a black powder used to enlarge the eyes and make them more attractive (see the note on 2Ki 9:30).

4:31 "Daughter of Zion" is a personification of Jerusalem.

[4]I thought, "These are only the poor;
they are foolish,
for they do not know[s] the way of the LORD,
the requirements of their God.
[5]So I will go to the leaders[t]
and speak to them;
surely they know the way of the LORD,
the requirements of their God."
But with one accord they too had broken off the yoke
and torn off the bonds.[u]
[6]Therefore a lion from the forest will attack them,
a wolf from the desert will ravage them,
a leopard[v] will lie in wait near their towns
to tear to pieces any who venture out,
for their rebellion is great
and their backslidings many.[w]

[7]"Why should I forgive you?
Your children have forsaken me
and sworn[x] by gods that are not gods.[y]
I supplied all their needs,
yet they committed adultery[z]
and thronged to the houses of prostitutes.
[8]They are well-fed, lusty stallions,
each neighing for another man's wife.[a]
[9]Should I not punish them for this?"[b]
declares the LORD.
"Should I not avenge myself
on such a nation as this?

[10]"Go through her vineyards and ravage them,
but do not destroy them completely.[c]
Strip off her branches,
for these people do not belong to the LORD.
[11]The house of Israel and the house of Judah
have been utterly unfaithful[d] to me,"
declares the LORD.

[12]They have lied about the LORD;
they said, "He will do nothing!
No harm will come to us;[e]
we will never see sword or famine.[f]
[13]The prophets[g] are but wind
and the word is not in them;
so let what they say be done to them."

[14]Therefore this is what the LORD God Almighty says:

"Because the people have spoken these words,
I will make my words in your mouth[h] a fire[i]
and these people the wood it consumes.
[15]O house of Israel," declares the LORD,
"I am bringing a distant nation[j] against you—

5:4 [s]Jer 8:7
5:5 [t]Mic 3:1,9 [u]Ps 2:3; Jer 2:20
5:6 [v]Hos 13:7 [w]Jer 30:14
5:7 [x]Jos 23:7; Zep 1:5 [y]Dt 32:21; Jer 2:11; Gal 4:8 [z]Nu 25:1
5:8 [a]Jer 29:23; Eze 22:11
5:9 [b]ver 29; Jer 9:9
5:10 [c]Jer 4:27
5:11 [d]Jer 3:20
5:12 [e]Jer 23:17 [f]2Ch 36:16; Jer 14:13
5:13 [g]Jer 14:15
5:14 [h]Jer 1:9; Hos 6:5 [i]Jer 23:29
5:15 [j]Dt 28:49; Isa 5:26; Jer 4:16

5:6 See "Lions and Other Wild Beasts in Ancient Israel" on page 813.
5:15 Babylon was an "ancient and enduring nation," with a history reaching back more than 2,000 years. Although related to Hebrew, the languages of Assyria and Babylonia were not understood by the average Israelite.

an ancient and enduring nation,
a people whose language[k] you do not know,
whose speech you do not understand.
16 Their quivers are like an open grave;
all of them are mighty warriors.
17 They will devour[l][m] your harvests and food,
devour[n][o] your sons and daughters;
they will devour[p] your flocks and herds,
devour your vines and fig trees.
With the sword they will destroy
the fortified cities in which you trust.[q]

18 "Yet even in those days," declares the LORD, "I will not destroy[r] you completely. 19 And when the peo-
ple ask,[s] 'Why has the LORD our God done all this to us?' you will tell them, 'As you have forsaken me and
served foreign gods[t] in your own land, so now you will serve foreigners[u] in a land not your own.'

20 "Announce this to the house of Jacob
and proclaim it in Judah:
21 Hear this, you foolish and senseless people,
who have eyes[v] but do not see,
who have ears but do not hear:[w]
22 Should you not fear[x] me?" declares the LORD.
"Should you not tremble in my presence?
I made the sand a boundary for the sea,
an everlasting barrier it cannot cross.
The waves may roll, but they cannot prevail;
they may roar, but they cannot cross it.
23 But these people have stubborn and rebellious[y] hearts;
they have turned aside and gone away.
24 They do not say to themselves,
'Let us fear the LORD our God,
who gives autumn and spring rains[z] in season,
who assures us of the regular weeks of harvest.'[a]
25 Your wrongdoings have kept these away;
your sins have deprived you of good.

26 "Among my people are wicked men
who lie in wait[b] like men who snare birds
and like those who set traps to catch men.
27 Like cages full of birds,
their houses are full of deceit;[c]
they have become rich[d] and powerful
28 and have grown fat[e] and sleek.
Their evil deeds have no limit;
they do not plead the case of the fatherless[f] to win it,
they do not defend the rights of the poor.[g]
29 Should I not punish them for this?"
declares the LORD.
"Should I not avenge myself
on such a nation as this?

30 "A horrible[h] and shocking thing
has happened in the land:

5:15 [k]Isa 28:11
5:17 [l]Jer 8:16 [m]Lev 26:16 [n]Jer 50:7,17 [o]Dt 28:32 [p]Dt 28:31 [q]Dt 28:33
5:18 [r]Jer 4:27
5:19 [s]Dt 29:24-26; 1Ki 9:9 [t]Jer 16:13 [u]Dt 28:48
5:21 [v]Isa 6:10; Eze 12:2 [w]Mt 13:15; Mk 8:18
5:22 [x]Dt 28:58
5:23 [y]Dt 21:18
5:24 [z]Ps 147:8; Joel 2:23 [a]Ge 8:22; Ac 14:17
5:26 [b]Ps 10:8; Pr 1:11
5:27 [c]Jer 9:6 [d]Jer 12:1
5:28 [e]Dt 32:15 [f]Zec 7:10 [g]Isa 1:23; Jer 7:6
5:30 [h]Jer 23:14; Hos 6:10

5:16 For the grave and its insatiability, destruction and death, see the note on Job 18:13–14, Psalm 6:5, 49:14.

5:27 Cages were traps or baskets woven of wicker.

5:31 [i]Eze 13:6; Mic 2:11

[31]The prophets prophesy lies,[i]
the priests rule by their own authority,
and my people love it this way.
But what will you do in the end?

Jerusalem Under Siege

6

6:1 [j]2Ch 11:6 [k]Ne 3:14 [l]Jer 4:6

"Flee for safety, people of Benjamin!
Flee from Jerusalem!
Sound the trumpet in Tekoa![j]
Raise the signal over Beth Hakkerem![k]
For disaster looms out of the north,[l]
even terrible destruction.
[2]I will destroy the Daughter of Zion,
so beautiful and delicate.

6:3 [m]Jer 12:10 [n]2Ki 25:4; Lk 19:43

[3]Shepherds[m] with their flocks will come against her;
they will pitch their tents around[n] her,
each tending his own portion."

6:4 [o]Jer 15:8

[4]"Prepare for battle against her!
Arise, let us attack at noon![o]
But, alas, the daylight is fading,
and the shadows of evening grow long.
[5]So arise, let us attack at night
and destroy her fortresses!"

[6]This is what the LORD Almighty says:

6:6 [p]Dt 20:19-20 [q]Jer 32:24

"Cut down the trees[p]
and build siege ramps[q] against Jerusalem.
This city must be punished;
it is filled with oppression.
[7]As a well pours out its water,
so she pours out her wickedness.

6:7 [r]Ps 55:9; Eze 7:11,23 [s]Jer 20:8

Violence[r] and destruction[s] resound in her;
her sickness and wounds are ever before me.
[8]Take warning, O Jerusalem,

6:8 [t]Eze 23:18; Hos 9:12

or I will turn away[t] from you
and make your land desolate
so no one can live in it."

[9]This is what the LORD Almighty says:

"Let them glean the remnant of Israel
as thoroughly as a vine;
pass your hand over the branches again,
like one gathering grapes."

6:1 Jeremiah himself was from Benjamin, a tribe bordering Judah north of Jerusalem.

Tekoa, 6 miles (9.7 km) south of Bethlehem and 11 miles (17.7 km) from Jerusalem, was the hometown of the prophet Amos (see Am 1:1).

Beth Hakkerem is mentioned elsewhere only in Nehemiah 3:14. It has been identified with Ramat Rahel, a fire-signal point 2 miles (3.2 km) south of Jerusalem (see "Ramat Rahel" on p. 1229).

For the phrase "out of the north," see the note on Jeremiah 4:6.

6:3 "Shepherds" refers to rulers. Although "flocks" sometimes represents a ruler's people (see 13:17,20; 25:34–36), here it points to his armies, which would destroy everything in their path.

6:4 Since ancient battles had religious connotations, soldiers had to prepare themselves ritually as well as militarily.

An attack at noon relied on the element of surprise, since the usual time of a military strike was early in the morning (see, e.g., Jos 8:10,14).

6:5 Attacking soldiers normally slept at night and resumed their siege the following morning; the phrase "at night" underscores their eagerness and determination.

6:6 Siege ramps helped the invading army to bring up battering rams and scale Jerusalem's walls (see 33:4; see also "Siege Warfare" on p. 465).

6:9 For "glean," see the notes on Ruth 1:22, 2:2.

[10]To whom can I speak and give warning?
Who will listen to me?
Their ears are closed[a][u]
so they cannot hear.
The word[v] of the LORD is offensive to them;
they find no pleasure in it.
[11]But I am full of the wrath[w] of the LORD,
and I cannot hold it in.[x]

"Pour it out on the children in the street
and on the young men[y] gathered together;
both husband and wife will be caught in it,
and the old, those weighed down with years.
[12]Their houses will be turned over to others,[z]
together with their fields and their wives,[a]
when I stretch out my hand[b]
against those who live in the land,"
declares the LORD.

[13]"From the least to the greatest,
all are greedy for gain;[c]
prophets and priests alike,
all practice deceit.[d]
[14]They dress the wound of my people
as though it were not serious.
'Peace, peace,' they say,
when there is no peace.[e]
[15]Are they ashamed of their loathsome conduct?
No, they have no shame at all;
they do not even know how to blush.[f]
So they will fall among the fallen;
they will be brought down when I punish them,"
says the LORD.

[16]This is what the LORD says:

"Stand at the crossroads and look;
ask for the ancient paths,[g]
ask where the good way[h] is, and walk in it,
and you will find rest[i] for your souls.
But you said, 'We will not walk in it.'
[17]I appointed watchmen[j] over you and said,
'Listen to the sound of the trumpet!'
But you said, 'We will not listen.'[k]
[18]Therefore hear, O nations;
observe, O witnesses,
what will happen to them.
[19]Hear, O earth:[l]
I am bringing disaster on this people,
the fruit of their schemes,[m]
because they have not listened to my words
and have rejected my law.[n]

6:10 [u]Ac 7:51 [v]Jer 20:8
6:11 [w]Jer 7:20 [x]Job 32:20; Jer 20:9 [y]Jer 9:21
6:12 [z]Dt 28:30 [a]Jer 8:10; 38:22 [b]Isa 5:25
6:13 [c]Isa 56:11 [d]Jer 8:10
6:14 [e]Jer 4:10; 8:11; Eze 13:10
6:15 [f]Jer 3:3; 8:10-12
6:16 [g]Jer 18:15 [h]Ps 119:3 [i]Mt 11:29
6:17 [j]Eze 3:17 [k]Jer 11:7-8; 25:4
6:19 [l]Isa 1:2; Jer 22:29 [m]Pr 1:31 [n]Jer 8:9

[a] 10 Hebrew *uncircumcised*

6:17 For "watchmen," see the note on Ezekiel 3:17. Here the term refers to true prophets.
For "sound of the trumpet," see the note on 4:5.

THE LAST DAYS OF JERUSALEM

The Golden Gate of Jerusalem
Photograph courtesy of © Dr. Gary Pratico

JEREMIAH 6 Jerusalem, after a 30-month siege, fell to the Babylonian king **Nebuchadnezzar** on July 18, 586 B.C.[1] Contemporary writings of Jeremiah, Ezekiel, the Babylonian Chronicle, the Lachish Letters and Egyptian records all provide details of this period.

The Judeans hoped for the restoration of King Jehoiachin, exiled in **Babylon** along with 10,000 Judean soldiers and artisans since 597 B.C. Babylonian ration tablets report distributions to Jehoiachin from 595 until 570 B.C.[2] A weakened Judah, ruled by Zedekiah, struggled against pressures from two sides: the ambitions of Pharaoh Apries (also known as Hophra) to gain control over the Levant (Syria-Palestine) and Babylonian interest in maintaining control of the same territory.

Zedekiah was summoned to Babylon, perhaps to proclaim his loyalty, but was soon involved in an anti-Babylonian coalition with Edom, **Moab**, Ammon, Tyre and Sidon. When he withheld annual tribute, Nebuchadnezzar responded, laying siege against Jerusalem on January 15, 588 B.C. A year later Zedekiah proclaimed the release of Hebrew slaves in the city, probably to add them to the meager ranks of the city's defenders. The Babylonians laid siege to Lachish[3] and Azekah, prompting an unsuccessful Egyptian intervention at Lachish. Nebuchadnezzar broke off the siege of Jerusalem for a month to deal with the Egyptians, prompting Zedekiah to rescind his order for the release of the Hebrew slaves. Some Judeans used the occasion to flee or to surrender to the Babylonians, following Jeremiah's advice.

The siege quickly resumed, and Jerusalem's wall was breached on July 18, 586 B.C. Owing to famine within the city, resistance was feeble. Zedekiah fled but was captured and blinded shortly after having been forced to witness his own sons being put to death. Jerusalem was ransacked, the temple burned and many exiled to Babylon. Others fled to Egypt after assassinating Gedaliah, the Babylonian governor.[4]

[1]See "Nebuchadnezzar" on page 571. [2]See "Jehoiachin in Captivity and Evil-Merodach" on page 1292. [3]See "The Lachish Ostraca" on page 1252. [4]See "The Seals of Jaazaniah, Ishmael and Elishama" on page 573 and "Gedaliah, Governor of Judah, and Baalis, King of Ammon" on page1261.

[20] What do I care about incense from Sheba
or sweet calamus[o] from a distant land?
Your burnt offerings are not acceptable;[p]
your sacrifices[q] do not please me."[r]

[21] Therefore this is what the LORD says:

"I will put obstacles before this people.
Fathers and sons alike will stumble[s] over them;
neighbors and friends will perish."

[22] This is what the LORD says:

"Look, an army is coming
from the land of the north;[t]
a great nation is being stirred up
from the ends of the earth.
[23] They are armed with bow and spear;
they are cruel and show no mercy.[u]
They sound like the roaring sea
as they ride on their horses;[v]
they come like men in battle formation
to attack you, O Daughter of Zion."

[24] We have heard reports about them,
and our hands hang limp.
Anguish[w] has gripped us,
pain like that of a woman in labor.[x]
[25] Do not go out to the fields
or walk on the roads,
for the enemy has a sword,
and there is terror on every side.[y]
[26] O my people, put on sackcloth[z]
and roll in ashes;[a]
mourn with bitter wailing
as for an only son,[b]
for suddenly the destroyer
will come upon us.

[27] "I have made you a tester[c] of metals
and my people the ore,
that you may observe
and test their ways.
[28] They are all hardened rebels,[d]
going about to slander.[e]
They are bronze and iron;[f]
they all act corruptly.
[29] The bellows blow fiercely
to burn away the lead with fire,

6:20 [o]Ex 30:23 [p]Am 5:22 [q]Ps 50:8-10; Jer 7:21; Mic 6:7-8 [r]Isa 1:11
6:21 [s]Isa 8:14
6:22 [t]Jer 1:15; 10:22
6:23 [u]Isa 13:18 [v]Jer 4:29
6:24 [w]Jer 4:19 [x]Jer 4:31; 50:41-43
6:25 [y]Jer 49:29
6:26 [z]Jer 4:8 [a]Jer 25:34; Mic 1:10 [b]Zec 12:10
6:27 [c]Jer 9:7
6:28 [d]Jer 5:23 [e]Jer 9:4 [f]Eze 22:18

6:20 Sheba, located in southwestern Arabia, was the center of the spice trade (see "Sheba" on p. 498).

Calamus, which probably came from India, is associated with incense (see Ex 30:25; SS 4:14 and its note; see also "Incense" on p. 1209). The Hebrew for this word is translated "cane" in Exodus 30:23.

6:22 For "the land of the north," see the note on 4:6.

6:23 The Hebrew for "spear" is translated "javelin" in 1 Samuel 17:6. Another possible rendering is "sword," as attested in The War of the Sons of Light Against the Sons of Darkness, one of the Dead Sea Scrolls.

6:26 Sackcloth was the coarse garb of mourners (see the notes on 1Ki 20:31–32 and Job 16:15, as well as "Sackcloth and Ashes: Rituals of Lamentation" on p. 820).

An only son was a father's most precious "possession" (see Ge 22:12,16; Am 8:10; Zec 12:10; Ro 8:32).

For "destroyer," see the note on 4:7.

6:29 In ancient times lead was added to silver ore as part of the refining process. When the crucible was heated the lead oxidized and acted as a flux to remove the alloys. Here the process failed because the ore was not sufficiently pure (cf. Eze 24:11–13).

but the refining goes on in vain;
the wicked are not purged out.
30 They are called rejected silver,
6:30 because the LORD has rejected them."[g]

g Ps 119:119; Jer 7:29; Hos 9:17

False Religion Worthless

7:2 h Jer 17:19 **7** This is the word that came to Jeremiah from the LORD: 2 "Stand[h] at the gate of the LORD's house and
there proclaim this message:
" 'Hear the word of the LORD, all you people of Judah who come through these gates to worship the
7:3 i Jer 18:11; LORD. 3 This is what the LORD Almighty, the God of Israel, says: Reform your ways[i] and your actions, and
26:13 7:4 j Mic 3:11 I will let you live in this place. 4 Do not trust in deceptive[j] words and say, "This is the temple of the LORD,
the temple of the LORD, the temple of the LORD!" 5 If you really change your ways and your actions and deal
7:5 k Jer 22:3 with each other justly,[k] 6 if you do not oppress the alien, the fatherless or the widow and do not shed in-
7:6 l Jer 2:34; nocent blood[l] in this place, and if you do not follow other gods[m] to your own harm, 7 then I will let you
19:4 m Dt 8:19 7:7 n Dt 4:40 live in this place, in the land[n] I gave your forefathers for ever and ever. 8 But look, you are trusting in de-
ceptive words that are worthless.
7:9 o Jer 11:13,17 9 " 'Will you steal and murder, commit adultery and perjury,[a] burn incense to Baal[o] and follow other
p Ex 20:3 7:10 q Jer 32:34; gods[p] you have not known, 10 and then come and stand before me in this house,[q] which bears my Name,
Eze 23:38-39 7:11 r Isa 56:7 and say, "We are safe"—safe to do all these detestable things? 11 Has this house,[r] which bears my Name,
s Mt 21:13*; Mk 11:17*; become a den of robbers[s] to you? But I have been watching![t] declares the LORD.
Lk 19:46* t Jer 29:23 12 " 'Go now to the place in Shiloh[u] where I first made a dwelling for my Name, and see what I did[v] to
7:12 u Jos 18:1 v 1Sa 4:10-11,22; it because of the wickedness of my people Israel. 13 While you were doing all these things, declares the
Ps 78:60-64 7:13 w 2Ch 36:15 LORD, I spoke to you again and again,[w] but you did not listen;[x] I called you, but you did not answer.[y]
x Isa 65:12 y Jer 35:17 14 Therefore, what I did to Shiloh I will now do to the house that bears my Name,[z] the temple you trust
7:14 z 1Ki 9:7 in, the place I gave to you and your fathers. 15 I will thrust you from my presence, just as I did all your
7:15 a Ps 78:67 brothers, the people of Ephraim.'[a]

7:16 b Ex 32:10; 16 "So do not pray for this people nor offer any plea[b] or petition for them; do not plead with me, for I
Dt 9:14; Jer 15:1 will not listen to you. 17 Do you not see what they are doing in the towns of Judah and in the streets of Je-
rusalem? 18 The children gather wood, the fathers light the fire, and the women knead the dough and
7:18 c Jer 44:17-19 make cakes of bread for the Queen of Heaven.[c] They pour out drink offerings[d] to other gods to provoke[e]
d Jer 19:13 e 1Ki 14:9 me to anger. 19 But am I the one they are provoking? declares the LORD. Are they not rather harming them-
7:19 f Jer 9:19 selves, to their own shame?[f]
7:20 g Jer 42:18; La 2:3-5 20 " 'Therefore this is what the Sovereign LORD says: My anger[g] and my wrath will be poured out on
this place, on man and beast, on the trees of the field and on the fruit of the ground, and it will burn and
not be quenched.
21 " 'This is what the LORD Almighty, the God of Israel, says: Go ahead, add your burnt offerings to your
7:21 h Isa 1:11; Am 5:21-22 other sacrifices[h] and eat[i] the meat yourselves! 22 For when I brought your forefathers out of Egypt and
i Hos 8:13 spoke to them, I did not just give them commands about burnt offerings and sacrifices,[j] 23 but I gave
7:22 j 1Sa 15:22; Ps 51:16; Hos 6:6 them this command: Obey[k] me, and I will be your God and you will be my people.[l] Walk in all the ways
7:23 k Ex 19:5 l Lev 26:12 I command you, that it may go well[m] with you. 24 But they did not listen or pay attention;[n] instead, they
m Ex 15:26 7:24 n Ps 81:11-12; Jer 11:8 followed the stubborn inclinations of their evil hearts. They went backward and not forward. 25 From the

a 9 Or *and swear by false gods*

7:2 "The gate" here may have been the "New Gate" (26:10; 36:10), which was located within the wall between the inner and outer courts of the temple.

7:9 For the phrase "burn incense to Baal," see the note on 1:16.

7:11 As thieves hid in caves and presumed they were safe, so the people of Judah falsely trusted in the temple to protect them in spite of their sins.

7:12 The tabernacle had been set up in Shiloh after the conquest of Canaan (Jos 18:1; see "The Tabernacle at Shiloh" on p. 401) and was still there at the end of the period of the judges (see 1Sa 1:9 and the NIV text note there). Modern Khirbet Seilun, about 18 miles (29 km) north of Jerusalem, preserves the name of the ancient site, and archaeological excavations there indicate that it was destroyed by the Philistines in about 1050 B.C. (see "The Destruction of Shiloh" on p. 1200). The tabernacle itself, however, was not included in that destruction, but it was still in existence at Gibeon during David's reign (see 1Ch 21:29). Several buildings were apparently erected at Shiloh near the tabernacle in connection with various aspects of public worship, along with a large complex of silos and storage buildings. Such structures would have been destroyed with the city itself.

7:15 Ephraim was another name for Israel. Ironically, Shiloh was located within this tribal territory.

7:18 For commentary on Hebrew childhood, see the note on Isaiah 66:12.

This verse describes entire families participating in idolatrous worship. "The Queen of Heaven" was a Babylonian title for Ishtar (also called Anat, Astarte or Ashtoreth). She was an important goddess in the Babylonian pantheon, whose worship involved extremely lascivious practices (1Ki 14:24; 2Ki 23:7). Cakes were made in her image (Jer 44:19), and drink offerings were offered to her (44:19,25), as well as to other gods. (See "The Queen of Heaven" on p. 1267.)

THE DESTRUCTION OF SHILOH

JEREMIAH 7 Located in the middle of Israel's hill country, Shiloh ("Maps 5–6") was the nation's first holy city.

At the conclusion of the conquest, around 1400 B.C.,[1] Joshua erected the tabernacle at Shiloh, thereby establishing this location as Israel's religious center (Jos 18:1). Thereafter, yearly pilgrimages were made to Shiloh for worship and sacrifice (Jdg 21:19; 1Sa 1:3,21; 2:19).[2] It remained the central shrine of Israel for over 300 years, until the city was destroyed, presumably by the Philistines, in the early eleventh century B.C. Israel remained without a primary religious locus for more than a century after that, until Solomon constructed the temple in Jerusalem around 966–959 B.C. (1Ki 6:37–38).[3]

The glacis at Shiloh
© Dr. James C. Martin

In the early eleventh century B.C. the Philistines defeated Israel at Ebenezer and the ark of the covenant was captured (1Sa 4:1–11).[4] Although this is not specifically stated in Scripture, it appears that the Philistines followed up their victory by destroying Shiloh (Ps 78:58–61; Jer 7:12–14; 26:6). One way or another, it is clear that Shiloh ceased to exist at about this time since, after Ebenezer, this city is no longer mentioned in the Bible. Therefore, when the Philistines returned the ark, it was taken to Beth Shemesh rather than to Shiloh.[5] Following the defeat at Ebenezer, Samuel took up residence at Ramah and ministered in Bethel, Gilgal and Mizpah (1Sa 7:16–17).[6]

Shiloh was first inhabited during the **Middle Bronze** II period.[7] This pre-Israelite site at that time covered an area of about four acres and was surrounded by a wall of field stones and an earthen **glacis**. This site was destroyed in the sixteenth century B.C.; large storage containers, bronze weapons and silver jewelry were unearthed there. Remains from the **Late Bronze** I period suggest that this location was a cultic or ritual center, but since no masonry has been found from the period, it was probably not a regular settlement at that time.

Excavations at Shiloh have revealed a significant building complex from the **Iron** I period, which takes us through the time of Eli. The Iron I period excavations produced fourteen silos and two Israelite storage buildings with rooms full of large, collared-rim jars (a type of pottery used by the Israelites). This period of habitation was terminated by a fierce conflagration, probably the work of the Philistines in around 1050 B.C.

No evidence of the tabernacle has been discovered, but the situation of the storage buildings suggests that they were part of a larger complex on the summit, constituting a public storage facility, exhibiting sophisticated construction techniques, including stone drum pillars, wooden columns and paved floors. The bedrock was cut to level the floor and hew out a cistern, which was then plastered. Inside, archaeologists uncovered the richest assemblage of pottery ever unearthed from the late twelfth through early eleventh centuries B.C., including over 20 large storage jars. The fire that destroyed this complex resulted in a thick layer of ash containing carbonized roof beams and bricks burned to a reddish-yellow hue. Shiloh ultimately became proverbial for divine judgment on an apostate shrine (Jer 7:12). The discovery of Iron II material verifies that the site was at least sporadically utilized after the destruction—probably by transient peoples, since no permanent settlement evidence from this period exists.

[1]See "The Conquest of Canaan" on page 310. [2]See "Israelite Shrines and Worship Before the Temple of Solomon" on page 398 and "The Tabernacle at Shiloh" on page 401. [3]See "Solomon's Temple and Other Ancient Temples" on page 620. [4]See "The Tabernacle and the Ark" on page 153. [5]See "Beth Shemesh" on page 405. [6]See "Bethel" on page 59, "The Camp at Gilgal" on page 308 and "Mizpah" on page 383. [7]See "Archaeological Periods" chart on page xx in the front of this Bible.

time your forefathers left Egypt until now, day after day, again and again I sent you my servants the proph-
7:25 oJer 25:4 ets.[o] 26 But they did not listen to me or pay attention. They were stiff-necked and did more evil than their
7:26 pJer 16:12 forefathers.'[p]
7:27 qEze 2:7 rEze 3:7 27 "When you tell[q] them all this, they will not listen[r] to you; when you call to them, they will not an-
swer. 28 Therefore say to them, 'This is the nation that has not obeyed the LORD its God or responded to
7:29 sJob 1:20; Isa 15:2; Mic 1:16 tJer 6:30 correction. Truth has perished; it has vanished from their lips. 29 Cut off[s] your hair and throw it away;
take up a lament on the barren heights, for the LORD has rejected and abandoned[t] this generation that is
under his wrath.

The Valley of Slaughter

30 " 'The people of Judah have done evil in my eyes, declares the LORD. They have set up their detest-
7:30 uEze 7:20-22 vJer 32:34 able idols[u] in the house that bears my Name and have defiled[v] it. 31 They have built the high places of To-
7:31 w2Ki 23:10 xPs 106:38 yJer 19:5 pheth[w] in the Valley of Ben Hinnom to burn their sons and daughters[x] in the fire—something I did not
command, nor did it enter my mind.[y] 32 So beware, the days are coming, declares the LORD, when people
7:32 zJer 19:6 aJer 19:11 will no longer call it Topheth or the Valley of Ben Hinnom, but the Valley of Slaughter,[z] for they will bury[a]
7:33 bDt 28:26 the dead in Topheth until there is no more room. 33 Then the carcasses of this people will become food[b]
for the birds of the air and the beasts of the earth, and there will be no one to frighten them away. 34 I will
7:34 cIsa 24:8; Eze 26:13 dRev 18:23 eLev 26:34 bring an end to the sounds[c] of joy and gladness and to the voices of bride and bridegroom[d] in the towns
of Judah and the streets of Jerusalem, for the land will become desolate.[e]

8 " 'At that time, declares the LORD, the bones of the kings and officials of Judah, the bones of the priests
and prophets, and the bones of the people of Jerusalem will be removed from their graves. 2 They will
8:2 f2Ki 23:5; Ac 7:42 be exposed to the sun and the moon and all the stars of the heavens, which they have loved and served[f]
and which they have followed and consulted and worshiped. They will not be gathered up or buried, but
will be like refuse lying on the ground. 3 Wherever I banish them, all the survivors of this evil nation will
8:3 gJob 3:22; Rev 9:6 prefer death to life,[g] declares the LORD Almighty.'

Sin and Punishment

4 "Say to them, 'This is what the LORD says:

8:4 hPr 24:16 " 'When men fall down, do they not get up?[h]
When a man turns away, does he not return?
5 Why then have these people turned away?
Why does Jerusalem always turn away?
8:5 iJer 5:27 jJer 7:24; 9:6 They cling to deceit;[i]
they refuse to return.[j]
6 I have listened attentively,
but they do not say what is right.
8:6 kRev 9:20 lPs 14:1-3 No one repents[k] of his wickedness,
saying, "What have I done?"
Each pursues his own course[l]
like a horse charging into battle.
7 Even the stork in the sky
knows her appointed seasons,

7:29 Cutting off one's hair was a sign of mourning.
7:30 Manasseh had placed a carved Asherah pole in the temple (2Ki 21:7; see the note on 1Ki 14:15; see also "Devotion to Asherah in the Khirbet El-Qom Inscription" on p. 638). King Josiah, Jeremiah's contemporary, removed the pole and other accessories to idol worship (2Ki 23:4–7). But less than 20 years after Josiah's death Ezekiel reported numerous idols again present in the temple courts (see Eze 8:3,5–6,10,12).
7:31 "High places" were cult centers, usually (but not here) located on natural heights.

Topheth was located in the Valley of Ben Hinnom (see the note on 2:23). The word *topheth* is of Aramaic origin and means "fireplace," although in cultures outside Israel it was used as a common noun meaning "place of child sacrifice." The Old Testament Topheth had a fire pit (see Isa 30:33) into which children were apparently thrown as human sacrifices (see the note on Isa 57:5; see also "Human Sacrifice in the Ancient Near East" on p. 182). The ancient world considered this a supremely religious act, since it gave the god what was most precious to the worshiper. Some Judahites must have believed that they were appeasing the Lord by these rituals, but God had prohibited such sacrifice (see Lev 18:21 and its note)—although it was practiced by Ahaz (see 2Ki 16:2–3) and Manasseh (2Ki 21:1,6).
7:32 Their place of sacrifice would become their cemetery when the people of Judah were slaughtered by the Babylonian invaders (see 19:6). See "Sheol, Hades, Gehenna, the Abyss and Tartarus: Images of Hell" on page 946.
7:33 A proper burial was of critical importance in ancient times, since to remain unburied was considered a dreadful fate (see "Tombs in Ancient Israel" on p. 376 and "Jewish Burial Practices" on p. 1688).
8:1 Removal of bones from their graves was viewed as a gross indignity and sacrilege (see 2Ki 23:16,18; Am 2:1).

and the dove, the swift and the thrush
observe the time of their migration.
But my people do not know[m]
the requirements of the LORD.

8 " 'How can you say, "We are wise,
for we have the law[n] of the LORD,"
when actually the lying pen of the scribes
has handled it falsely?

9 The wise[o] will be put to shame;
they will be dismayed and trapped.
Since they have rejected the word[p] of the LORD,
what kind of wisdom do they have?
10 Therefore I will give their wives to other men
and their fields to new owners.[q]
From the least to the greatest,
all are greedy for gain;[r]
prophets and priests alike,
all practice deceit.
11 They dress the wound of my people
as though it were not serious.
"Peace, peace," they say,
when there is no peace.[s]
12 Are they ashamed of their loathsome conduct?
No, they have no shame[t] at all;
they do not even know how to blush.
So they will fall among the fallen;
they will be brought down when they are punished,[u]
says the LORD.[v]

13 " 'I will take away their harvest,
declares the LORD.
There will be no grapes on the vine.[w]
There will be no figs[x] on the tree,
and their leaves will wither.[y]
What I have given them
will be taken[z] from them.[a]' "

14 "Why are we sitting here?
Gather together!
Let us flee to the fortified cities[a]
and perish there!
For the LORD our God has doomed us to perish
and given us poisoned water[b] to drink,
because we have sinned[c] against him.
15 We hoped for peace[d]
but no good has come,
for a time of healing
but there was only terror.[e]

8:7 [m]Isa 1:3; Jer 5:4-5
8:8 [n]Ro 2:17
8:9 [o]Jer 6:15 [p]Jer 6:19
8:10 [q]Jer 6:12 [r]Isa 56:11
8:11 [s]Jer 6:14
8:12 [t]Jer 3:3 [u]Ps 52:5-7; Isa 3:9 [v]Jer 6:15
8:13 [w]Joel 1:7 [x]Lk 13:6 [y]Mt 21:19 [z]Jer 5:17
8:14 [a]Jer 4:5; 35:11 [b]Dt 29:18; Jer 9:15; 23:15 [c]Jer 14:7,20
8:15 [d]ver 11 [e]Jer 14:19

[a] 13 The meaning of the Hebrew for this sentence is uncertain.

8:8 This is the earliest mention of scribes as a recognizable group. They were apparently organized on the basis of families (see 1Ch 2:55; 2Ch 34:13; see also "Sumerian Scribal Education" on p. 579 and "The Scribe" on p. 682).

8:13—9:24 This section is read aloud in synagogues every year on the ninth of Ab, the day the temple in Jerusalem was destroyed by the Babylonians in 586 B.C..

8:13 For commentary on fruit available in the Holy Land, see the note on Isaiah 28:4 and "Food and Agriculture" on page 390.

8:16 [f]Jer 4:15

[16] The snorting of the enemy's horses
is heard from Dan;[f]
at the neighing of their stallions
the whole land trembles.
They have come to devour
the land and everything in it,
the city and all who live there."

8:17 [g]Nu 21:6; Dt 32:24 [h]Ps 58:5

[17] "See, I will send venomous snakes[g] among you,
vipers that cannot be charmed,[h]
and they will bite you,"
declares the LORD.

8:18 [i]La 5:17

[18] O my Comforter[a] in sorrow,
my heart is faint[i] within me.

8:19 [j]Jer 9:16 [k]Dt 32:21

[19] Listen to the cry of my people
from a land far away:[j]
"Is the LORD not in Zion?
Is her King no longer there?"

"Why have they provoked me to anger with their images,
with their worthless foreign idols?"[k]

[20] "The harvest is past,
the summer has ended,
and we are not saved."

8:21 [l]Jer 14:17

8:22 [m]Ge 37:25 [n]Jer 30:12

[21] Since my people are crushed, I am crushed;
I mourn,[l] and horror grips me.
[22] Is there no balm in Gilead?[m]
Is there no physician there?
Why then is there no healing[n]
for the wound of my people?

9

9:1 [o]Jer 13:17; La 2:11,18 [p]Isa 22:4

9:2 [q]Jer 5:7-8; 23:10; Hos 4:2

[1] Oh, that my head were a spring of water
and my eyes a fountain of tears!
I would weep[o] day and night
for the slain of my people.[p]
[2] Oh, that I had in the desert
a lodging place for travelers,
so that I might leave my people
and go away from them;
for they are all adulterers,[q]
a crowd of unfaithful people.

9:3 [r]Ps 64:3

[3] "They make ready their tongue
like a bow, to shoot lies;[r]
it is not by truth
that they triumph[b] in the land.
They go from one sin to another;
they do not acknowledge me,"
declares the LORD.

[a] *18* The meaning of the Hebrew for this word is uncertain. [b] *3* Or *lies; / they are not valiant for truth*

8:16 Dan was close to the northern border of Israel. This tribal group would have been the first to feel the effects of the Babylonian invasion.

8:22 The territory of Gilead, east of the Jordan River and north of the Jabbok River, was an important source of spices and medicinal herbs. Spices had many uses—in food preparation and in the manufacture of incense and cosmetics—and the "balm" of Gilead was famous for its healing effects.

4 "Beware of your friends;
do not trust your brothers.[s]
For every brother is a deceiver,[a][t]
and every friend a slanderer.
5 Friend deceives friend,
and no one speaks the truth.
They have taught their tongues to lie;
they weary themselves with sinning.
6 You[b] live in the midst of deception;[u]
in their deceit they refuse to acknowledge me,"
declares the LORD.

9:4 [s]Mic 7:5-6 [t]Ge 27:35
9:6 [u]Jer 5:27

7 Therefore this is what the LORD Almighty says:

"See, I will refine[v] and test[w] them,
for what else can I do
because of the sin of my people?
8 Their tongue[x] is a deadly arrow;
it speaks with deceit.
With his mouth each speaks cordially to his neighbor,
but in his heart he sets a trap[y] for him.
9 Should I not punish them for this?"
declares the LORD.
"Should I not avenge[z] myself
on such a nation as this?"

9:7 [v]Isa 1:25 [w]Jer 6:27
9:8 [x]ver 3 [y]Jer 5:26
9:9 [z]Jer 5:9,29

10 I will weep and wail for the mountains
and take up a lament concerning the desert pastures.
They are desolate and untraveled,
and the lowing of cattle is not heard.
The birds of the air[a] have fled
and the animals are gone.

9:10 [a]Jer 4:25; 12:4; Hos 4:3

11 "I will make Jerusalem a heap of ruins,
a haunt of jackals;[b]
and I will lay waste the towns of Judah
so no one can live there."[c]

9:11 [b]Isa 34:13 [c]Isa 25:2; Jer 26:9

12 What man is wise[d] enough to understand this? Who has been instructed by the LORD and can ex-
plain it? Why has the land been ruined and laid waste like a desert that no one can cross?
13 The LORD said, "It is because they have forsaken my law, which I set before them; they have not
obeyed me or followed my law.[e] 14 Instead, they have followed[f] the stubbornness of their hearts;[g] they
have followed the Baals, as their fathers taught them." 15 Therefore, this is what the LORD Almighty, the
God of Israel, says: "See, I will make this people eat bitter food[h] and drink poisoned water.[i] 16 I will scat-
ter them among nations[j] that neither they nor their fathers have known,[k] and I will pursue them with
the sword[l] until I have destroyed them."[m]

9:12 [d]Ps 107:43; Hos 14:9
9:13 [e]2Ch 7:19; Ps 89:30-32
9:14 [f]Jer 2:8,23 [g]Jer 7:24
9:15 [h]La 3:15 [i]Jer 8:14
9:16 [j]Lev 26:33 [k]Dt 28:64 [l]Eze 5:2 [m]Jer 44:27; Eze 5:12

17 This is what the LORD Almighty says:

"Consider now! Call for the wailing women[n] to come;
send for the most skillful of them.

9:17 [n]2Ch 35:25; Ecc 12:5; Am 5:16

a 4 Or *a deceiving Jacob* *b* 6 That is, Jeremiah (the Hebrew is singular)

9:17–22 Jeremiah, the weeping prophet, made numerous references to mourning. He taught the mourning women their dirge (in these verses), heard the land lament because of the destruction by the Babylonians (v. 10; 12:4,11; 14:2; 23:10) and mentioned Rachel's mourning (31:15–16). He urged Israel to mourn for its sins (4:8; 6:26; 7:29) and secretly grieved for the nation himself (9:1; 13:17).

9:17 "Wailing women" were professional mourners who were paid to mourn at funerals and on the other sorrowful occasions (see 2Ch 35:25; Ecc 12:5; Am 5:16; and "Sackcloth and Ashes: Rituals of Lamentation" on p. 820). In the earliest times their purpose was probably to protect the living from the spirits of the departed, who were greatly feared. By Jeremiah's time, however, the mourning women served merely as another manifestation of grief for the departed.

The Israelite Town and Home

Archaeology of Beersheba, showing the three parallel chambers characteristic of Israelite buildings

Preserving Bible Times; © Dr. James C. Martin

JEREMIAH 9 The typical Israelite town followed the same basic design throughout the **Iron Age**[1] (1200–600 B.C.). Examining its layout, a Westerner might feel bewildered by an evidently unorganized array of walls and streets. But this was no labyrinth; the paths and walls first joined together families and only secondarily connected all the family units into a single community.

Each home probably housed a nuclear family but was also part of an extended family compound. This familial structure, a patriarchal social unit based upon patrilineal descent, was based on the concept of a "father's house" (Hebrew *bet av*). The larger family unit consisted of the paternal head, along with his wife, his sons and their wives, the grandchildren and finally the slaves.[2] When David was a youth his grown brothers were still part of the *bet av* of Jesse in Bethlehem (1Sa 16). Similarly, in Genesis 12:1 God commanded the already aging Abram to leave his *bet av*.

The four-room house was the most common type of Israelite residence. Most were two-story, rectangular structures, but the distinctive feature was the layout of the rooms. The main floor was entered through a door at the center of the (short) front wall, which led into a long hallway flanked on both sides by other corridor-like rooms. Across the back of the house was the fourth room. Actually, the four rooms could be subdivided into a number of different configurations. Even so, this basic design, along with a modified version called the three-room house, set the standard for Israelite architecture.

Such houses often had internal pillars of stone or wood. Walls were composed of sun-dried mud bricks (with plaster on the outer walls) and were built up on a few courses of foundation stones. Wooden beams served as the base for the second story, as well as the ceiling for the ground level. The roof consisted of compressed, mud-caked twigs placed over wooden beams and topped with plaster, a combination in constant need of maintenance. Windows were probably slits in the walls necessary for ventilation, since chimneys were not used, but still kept small for security purposes. The annexes or subdivisions located by archaeologists within some of these houses may have been "widow's quarters" for grandmothers. Servants shared the family compound.

The function of the four-room house within Israelite culture remains debated, but it was well suited to the agricultural nature of Israelite society.[3] The three parallel rooms may have been inspired by the need to accommodate stalls for domestic animals. In the coldest months livestock would have remained in these stalls, providing some warmth not only for the animals but also for the family upstairs. The cross-room at the back probably functioned as a storage compartment (a house excavated at Shechem included a storage pit in this area). The flat roof served as a kind of summer patio (cf. Ac 10:9), as well as a place to bathe (2Sa 11:2).[4]

Most towns were surrounded by a wall for security. Many had a double or **casemate wall**, often with homes integrated into it. Sometimes the backs of houses served as the outer defensive wall of the city, an arrangement especially common during the Iron II period. The main gate in the outer wall was not just the place through which people could exit and enter but also the primary meeting place. Inhabitants would continuously see one another going and coming and would meet there after a day in the fields. Traveling merchants encountered the townspeople at the gate, which became the site for the city market. Legal issues were discussed there as well. There are countless references in the Bible to "the gate" as the social, commercial and judicial hub of a city (e.g., Ru 4:1; 2Ki 7:1; Ps 127:5).[5]

The design of Israelite towns and houses in many ways mirrored Israel's social values and customs. These traditional structures endured through many historical changes. Tragically, the remains of these cities often attest to violent destruction and to chaotic upheavals that brought recurrent disruption and turmoil to a settled, agrarian society. Jeremiah 9 anticipates such a scenario.

See also "The Ancient City" on page 1790.

[1]See "Archaeological Periods" chart on page xx in the front of this Bible. [2]See "The Role of the Patriarch in Family Life" on page 30 and "The Israelite Family" on page 997. [3]See "Food and Agriculture" on page 390. [4]See "Bathing" on page 456. [5]See "The City Gate" on page 392.

[18]Let them come quickly
and wail over us
till our eyes overflow with tears
and water streams from our eyelids.[o]
[19]The sound of wailing is heard from Zion:
'How ruined[p] we are!
How great is our shame!
We must leave our land
because our houses are in ruins.' "

[20]Now, O women, hear the word of the LORD;
open your ears to the words of his mouth.
Teach your daughters how to wail;
teach one another a lament.[q]
[21]Death has climbed in through our windows
and has entered our fortresses;
it has cut off the children from the streets
and the young men[r] from the public squares.

[22]Say, "This is what the LORD declares:

" 'The dead bodies of men will lie
like refuse[s] on the open field,
like cut grain behind the reaper,
with no one to gather them.' "

[23]This is what the LORD says:

"Let not the wise man boast of his wisdom[t]
or the strong man boast of his strength[u]
or the rich man boast of his riches,[v]
[24]but let him who boasts boast[w] about this:
that he understands and knows me,
that I am the LORD,[x] who exercises kindness,[y]
justice and righteousness[z] on earth,
for in these I delight,"
declares the LORD.

[25]"The days are coming," declares the LORD, "when I will punish all who are circumcised only in the
flesh[a]— [26]Egypt, Judah, Edom, Ammon, Moab and all who live in the desert in distant places.[ab] For all
these nations are really uncircumcised, and even the whole house of Israel is uncircumcised in heart.[c]"

9:18 [o]Jer 14:17
9:19 [p]Jer 4:13
9:20 [q]Isa 32:9-13
9:21 [r]2Ch 36:17
9:22 [s]Jer 8:2
9:23 [t]Ecc 9:11 [u]1Ki 20:11 [v]Eze 28:4-5
9:24 [w]1Co 1:31*; Gal 6:14 [x]2Co 10:17* [y]Ps 51:1; Mic 7:18 [z]Ps 36:6
9:25 [a]Ro 2:8-9
9:26 [b]Jer 25:23 [c]Lev 26:41; Ac 7:51; Ro 2:28

God and Idols

10 Hear what the LORD says to you, O house of Israel. [2]This is what the LORD says:

"Do not learn the ways of the nations[d]
or be terrified by signs in the sky,
though the nations are terrified by them.
[3]For the customs of the peoples are worthless;
they cut a tree out of the forest,
and a craftsman[e] shapes it with his chisel.

10:2 [d]Lev 20:23
10:3 [e]Isa 40:19

[a] 26 Or *desert and who clip the hair by their foreheads*

9:21 Death is personified here. Canaanite mythology included a deity named Mot (a name related to the Hebrew word for "death"), the god of infertility and the netherworld, whose devouring throat supposedly reached from earth to sky (see the notes on Job 18:13–14; Ps 6:5; 49:14).
9:22 The concept of death as the "grim reaper" comes largely from this verse.
9:23 An almost exact parallel to these words occurs in the Aramaic Words of Ahiqar, written about a century after Jeremiah's time: "Let not the rich man say, 'In my riches I am glorious.'"
9:26 Those "who live . . . in distant places" refers to Arab tribes (see 25:23; 49:32) that were later attacked by the Babylonians under Nebuchadnezzar (see 49:28–33).
10:3 The word "craftsman" is often used of idol-makers who usually, but not always (see Isa 40:19), worked with wood (see Isa 41:7; see also "Idols and Idol-Making" on p. 1136).

4 They adorn it with silver and gold;
they fasten it with hammer and nails
10:4 [f]Isa 41:7
so it will not totter.[f]
5 Like a scarecrow in a melon patch,
10:5 [g]1Co 12:2 [h]Ps 115:5,7 [i]Isa 41:24; 46:7
their idols cannot speak;[g]
they must be carried
because they cannot walk.[h]
Do not fear them;
they can do no harm
nor can they do any good."[i]

6 No one is like you, O LORD;
10:6 [j]Ps 48:1
you are great,[j]
and your name is mighty in power.
7 Who should not revere you,
10:7 [k]Ps 22:28; Rev 15:4
O King of the nations?[k]
This is your due.
Among all the wise men of the nations
and in all their kingdoms,
there is no one like you.
8 They are all senseless and foolish;[l]
10:8 [l]Isa 40:19; Jer 4:22
they are taught by worthless wooden idols.
9 Hammered silver is brought from Tarshish
and gold from Uphaz.
10:9 [m]Ps 115:4; Isa 40:19
What the craftsman and goldsmith have made[m]
is then dressed in blue and purple—
all made by skilled workers.
10 But the LORD is the true God;
he is the living God, the eternal King.
When he is angry, the earth trembles;
10:10 [n]Ps 76:7
the nations cannot endure his wrath.[n]

10:11 [o]Ps 96:5; Isa 2:18
11 "Tell them this: 'These gods, who did not make the heavens and the earth, will perish[o] from the
earth and from under the heavens.' "[a]

12 But God made the earth by his power;
he founded the world by his wisdom
10:12 [p]Ge 1:1,8; Job 9:8; Isa 40:22
and stretched out the heavens[p] by his
understanding.
10:13 [q]Job 36:29 [r]Ps 135:7
13 When he thunders,[q] the waters in the heavens roar;
he makes clouds rise from the ends of the earth.
He sends lightning with the rain[r]
and brings out the wind from his storehouses.

14 Everyone is senseless and without knowledge;
every goldsmith is shamed by his idols.
His images are a fraud;
they have no breath in them.

[a] *11* The text of this verse is in Aramaic.

10:4 Wooden idols were plated with precious metals to make them more attractive (see Isa 30:22; 40:19).
10:5 Verse 70 in the Apocryphal Epistle of Jeremiah uses the same imagery found in this verse.
"Melon" might be more accurately translated as "cucumber."
10:9 See "Where Was Tarshish?" on page 1475.
10:11 The pronoun "them" is a reference to pagan idolaters, who would have been more likely to understand Aramaic (the language of diplomacy during this period) than Hebrew. Aramaic and Hebrew were similar, but still so different that the common people of Jerusalem did not understand the former. The whole of verse 11 is in Aramaic, an answer by the Jews to their Aramaic-speaking conquerors who would seduce them to worship idols.
10:13 See the note on Psalm 135:7.
10:14 The Hebrew here for "images" is translated "metal god" in Isaiah 48:5 and "metal images" in Daniel 11:8. (See "Idols and Idol-Making" on p. 1136.)

[15]They are worthless,[s] the objects of mockery;
when their judgment comes, they will perish.
[16]He who is the Portion[t] of Jacob is not like these,
for he is the Maker of all things,[u]
including Israel, the tribe of his inheritance[v]—
the LORD Almighty is his name.[w]

10:15 [s]Isa 41:24; Jer 14:22
10:16 [t]Dt 32:9; Ps 119:57 [u]ver 12 [v]Ps 74:2 [w]Jer 31:35; 32:18

Coming Destruction

[17]Gather up your belongings[x] to leave the land,
you who live under siege.
[18]For this is what the LORD says:
"At this time I will hurl[y] out
those who live in this land;
I will bring distress on them
so that they may be captured."

10:17 [x]Eze 12:3-12
10:18 [y]1Sa 25:29

[19]Woe to me because of my injury!
My wound[z] is incurable!
Yet I said to myself,
"This is my sickness, and I must endure[a] it."
[20]My tent[b] is destroyed;
all its ropes are snapped.
My sons are gone from me and are no more;[c]
no one is left now to pitch my tent
or to set up my shelter.
[21]The shepherds are senseless
and do not inquire of the LORD;
so they do not prosper
and all their flock is scattered.[d]
[22]Listen! The report is coming—
a great commotion from the land of the north!
It will make the towns of Judah desolate,
a haunt of jackals.[e]

10:19 [z]Jer 14:17 [a]Mic 7:9
10:20 [b]Jer 4:20 [c]Jer 31:15; La 1:5
10:21 [d]Jer 23:2
10:22 [e]Jer 9:11

Jeremiah's Prayer

[23]I know, O LORD, that a man's life is not his own;
it is not for man to direct his steps.[f]
[24]Correct me, LORD, but only with justice—
not in your anger,[g]
lest you reduce me to nothing.[h]
[25]Pour out your wrath on the nations[i]
that do not acknowledge you,
on the peoples who do not call on your name.[j]
For they have devoured[k] Jacob;
they have devoured him completely
and destroyed his homeland.[l]

10:23 [f]Pr 20:24
10:24 [g]Ps 6:1; 38:1 [h]Jer 30:11
10:25 [i]Zep 3:8 [j]Job 18:21; Ps 14:4 [k]Ps 79:7; Jer 8:16 [l]Ps 79:6-7

The Covenant Is Broken

11 This is the word that came to Jeremiah from the LORD: [2]"Listen to the terms of this covenant and
tell them to the people of Judah and to those who live in Jerusalem. [3]Tell them that this is what
the LORD, the God of Israel, says: 'Cursed[m] is the man who does not obey the terms of this covenant—

11:3 [m]Dt 27:26; Gal 3:10

10:20 For "shelter," see the note on 4:20.
10:21 For "shepherds," see the note on 3:15.
10:22 This verse describes the sound of the approaching Babylonian invaders.
11:2 "Terms" (lit., "words") is a technical reference to covenant stipulations (see the note on Ex 20:1–17). "This covenant" is a reference to the covenant established by God with Israel through Moses at Mount Sinai (see Ex 19–24). Periodic public reading of covenants was a common and necessary practice (see Dt 31:10–13; Jos 8:34–35).

4 the terms I commanded your forefathers when I brought them out of Egypt, out of the iron-smelting fur-
nace.[n] I said, 'Obey[o] me and do everything I command you, and you will be my people,[p] and I will be
your God. 5 Then I will fulfill the oath I swore[q] to your forefathers, to give them a land flowing with milk
and honey'—the land you possess today."

I answered, "Amen, LORD."

6 The LORD said to me, "Proclaim all these words in the towns of Judah and in the streets of Jerusalem:
'Listen to the terms of this covenant and follow[r] them. 7 From the time I brought your forefathers up from
Egypt until today, I warned them again and again,[s] saying, "Obey me." 8 But they did not listen or pay at-
tention;[t] instead, they followed the stubbornness of their evil hearts. So I brought on them all the curs-
es[u] of the covenant I had commanded them to follow but that they did not keep.' "

9 Then the LORD said to me, "There is a conspiracy[v] among the people of Judah and those who live in
Jerusalem. 10 They have returned to the sins of their forefathers,[w] who refused to listen to my words.
They have followed other gods[x] to serve them. Both the house of Israel and the house of Judah have
broken the covenant I made with their forefathers. 11 Therefore this is what the LORD says: 'I will bring
on them a disaster[y] they cannot escape. Although they cry[z] out to me, I will not listen[a] to them. 12 The
towns of Judah and the people of Jerusalem will go and cry out to the gods to whom they burn incense,[b]
but they will not help them at all when disaster[c] strikes. 13 You have as many gods as you have towns,
O Judah; and the altars you have set up to burn incense[d] to that shameful[e] god Baal are as many as the
streets of Jerusalem.'

11:4 [n]Dt 4:20; 1Ki 8:51 [o]Ex 24:8 [p]Jer 7:23; 31:33 **11:5** [q]Ex 13:5; Dt 7:12; Ps 105:8-11 **11:6** [r]Dt 15:5; Ro 2:13; Jas 1:22 **11:7** [s]2Ch 36:15 **11:8** [t]Jer 7:26 [u]Lev 26:14-43 **11:9** [v]Eze 22:25 **11:10** [w]Dt 9:7 [x]Jdg 2:12-13 **11:11** [y]2Ki 22:16 [z]Jer 14:12; Eze 8:18 [a]ver 14; Pr 1:28; Isa 1:15; Zec 7:13 **11:12** [b]Jer 44:17 [c]Dt 32:37 **11:13** [d]Jer 7:9 [e]Jer 3:24

11:12 For "burn incense," see the notes on 1:16 and 19:13. **11:13** See the notes on 1:16 and 2:28; see also 2 Chronicles 28:24.

Incense

JEREMIAH 11 Ritual incense in ancient Israel was a mixture of finely pulverized aromatic gum resins and frankincense, which was salted to produce a visible cloud of sweet-smelling smoke (Ex 30:34–35). Acquired from Syria and Arabia via ancient spice trade routes (Jer 6:20), its cost and fragrance rendered it a valuable commodity and an offering fitting for the Lord.

Incense was burned as a regular sacrifice at daybreak and again at twilight on a three-foot-long, gold-plated altar standing before the Most Holy Place (Ex 30:7–8). The aromatic cloud was the only physical entity to penetrate the veil that sealed off the divine Presence from the ministering priesthood. Thus it became a sign of earthly acts of devotion ascending to God's dwelling place, likened in Scripture to prayer rising to heaven as a cloud of smoke rises in the sky (Ps 141:2; Rev 5:8; 8:3–4). Incense could also be offered in portable censers, which were like cups attached to the ends of long handles or bowls set upon pedestals. The annual Day of Atonement was one occasion when the high priest would carry a fire pan of burning coals behind the veil. There he would sprinkle the spice mixture upon the coals, producing an effusive incense cloud to conceal the sight of the divine Presence (Lev 16:12–13).[1]

Consecrated for ritual use, incense was "holy to the LORD" (Ex 30:37). It was made according to a specific formula and offered at prescribed times by the appropriate temple personnel.[2] Those who burned it illicitly or unworthily were struck down by divine wrath (Lev 10:1–2; Nu 16:35; 2Ch 26:19). Idolatrous Israel exhibited her devotion to other gods by offering incense to them in homes, public city streets, sacred gardens and even in the temple itself (Isa 17:8; Jer 32:29; Eze 8:10–11). The kingdom of God, by contrast, will be characterized by a pilgrimage of the nations to adore the Lord in true worship and with offerings of incense (Isa 60:6; Mal 1:11; Mt 2:11).

[1]See "The Day of Atonement" on page 176. [2]See "The Levites and the Priests" on page 648.

14"Do not pray[f] for this people nor offer any plea or petition for them, because I will not listen[g] when
they call to me in the time of their distress.

15"What is my beloved doing in my temple
as she works out her evil schemes with many?
Can consecrated meat avert ⌞your punishment⌟?
When you engage in your wickedness,
then you rejoice.[a]"
16The LORD called you a thriving olive tree
with fruit beautiful in form.
But with the roar of a mighty storm
he will set it on fire,[h]
and its branches will be broken.[i]

17The LORD Almighty, who planted[j] you, has decreed disaster for you, because the house of Israel and the
house of Judah have done evil and provoked me to anger by burning incense to Baal.[k]

Plot Against Jeremiah

18Because the LORD revealed their plot to me, I knew it, for at that time he showed me what they were
doing. 19I had been like a gentle lamb led to the slaughter; I did not realize that they had plotted[l] against
me, saying,

"Let us destroy the tree and its fruit;
let us cut him off from the land of the living,[m]
that his name be remembered[n] no more."
20But, O LORD Almighty, you who judge righteously
and test the heart and mind,[o]
let me see your vengeance upon them,
for to you I have committed my cause.

21"Therefore this is what the LORD says about the men of Anathoth who are seeking your life[p] and
saying, 'Do not prophesy in the name of the LORD or you will die[q] by our hands'— 22therefore this is
what the LORD Almighty says: 'I will punish them. Their young men[r] will die by the sword, their sons and
daughters by famine. 23Not even a remnant[s] will be left to them, because I will bring disaster on the men
of Anathoth in the year of their punishment.[t]' "

Jeremiah's Complaint

12 You are always righteous,[u] O LORD,
when I bring a case before you.
Yet I would speak with you about your justice:
Why does the way of the wicked prosper?[v]
Why do all the faithless live at ease?
2You have planted[w] them, and they have taken root;
they grow and bear fruit.
You are always on their lips
but far from their hearts.[x]
3Yet you know me, O LORD;
you see me and test[y] my thoughts about you.
Drag them off like sheep to be butchered!
Set them apart for the day of slaughter![z]
4How long will the land lie parched[b][a]
and the grass in every field be withered?[b]

11:14 [f]Ex 32:10 [g]ver 11
11:16 [h]Jer 21:14 [i]Isa 27:11; Ro 11:17-24
11:17 [j]Isa 5:2; Jer 12:2 [k]Jer 7:9
11:19 [l]Jer 18:18; 20:10 [m]Job 28:13; Isa 53:8 [n]Ps 83:4
11:20 [o]Ps 7:9
11:21 [p]Jer 12:6 [q]Jer 26:8,11; 38:4
11:22 [r]Jer 18:21
11:23 [s]Jer 6:9 [t]Jer 23:12
12:1 [u]Ezr 9:15 [v]Jer 5:27-28
12:2 [w]Jer 11:17 [x]Isa 29:13; Jer 3:10; Mt 15:8; Tit 1:16
12:3 [y]Ps 7:9; 11:5; 139:1-4; Jer 11:20 [z]Jer 17:18
12:4 [a]Jer 4:28 [b]Joel 1:10-12

[a] 15 Or *Could consecrated meat avert your punishment? / Then you would rejoice* [b] 4 Or *land mourn*

11:16 Although an olive tree might not bear fruit for 40 years, it was a symbol of long life and productivity (see "Food and Agriculture" on p. 390).

11:17 This prophecy was fulfilled when Judah was destroyed in 586 B.C.

11:21 For "Anathoth," see the note on 1:1.

12:4 [c]Jer 4:25; 9:10

Because those who live in it are wicked,
the animals and birds have perished.[c]
Moreover, the people are saying,
"He will not see what happens to us."

God's Answer

5 "If you have raced with men on foot
and they have worn you out,
how can you compete with horses?
If you stumble in safe country,[a]
how will you manage in the thickets[d] by[b] the Jordan?

12:5 [d]Jer 49:19; 50:44

6 Your brothers, your own family—
even they have betrayed you;
they have raised a loud cry against you.[e]
Do not trust them,
though they speak well of you.[f]

12:6 [e]Pr 26:24-25; Jer 9:4 [f]Ps 12:2

7 "I will forsake my house,
abandon[g] my inheritance;
I will give the one I love
into the hands of her enemies.

12:7 [g]Jer 7:29

8 My inheritance has become to me
like a lion in the forest.
She roars at me;
therefore I hate her.[h]

12:8 [h]Hos 9:15; Am 6:8

9 Has not my inheritance become to me
like a speckled bird of prey
that other birds of prey surround and attack?
Go and gather all the wild beasts;
bring them to devour.[i]

12:9 [i]Isa 56:9; Jer 15:3; Eze 23:25

10 Many shepherds[j] will ruin my vineyard
and trample down my field;
they will turn my pleasant field
into a desolate wasteland.[k]

12:10 [j]Jer 23:1 [k]Isa 5:1-7

11 It will be made a wasteland,
parched and desolate before me;[l]
the whole land will be laid waste
because there is no one who cares.

12:11 [l]ver 4; Isa 42:25; Jer 23:10

12 Over all the barren heights in the desert
destroyers will swarm,
for the sword of the LORD[m] will devour
from one end of the land to the other;[n]
no one will be safe.

12:12 [m]Jer 47:6 [n]Jer 3:2

13 They will sow wheat but reap thorns;
they will wear themselves out but gain nothing.[o]
So bear the shame of your harvest
because of the LORD's fierce anger."[p]

12:13 [o]Lev 26:20; Dt 28:38; Mic 6:15; Hag 1:6 [p]Jer 4:26

14 This is what the LORD says: "As for all my wicked neighbors who seize the inheritance I gave my people Israel, I will uproot[q] them from their lands and I will uproot the house of Judah from among them.

12:14 [q]Zec 2:7-9

[a] 5 Or *If you put your trust in a land of safety* [b] 5 Or *the flooding of*

12:5 The Hebrew for the word here translated "thickets" is uncertain. Thickets provided shelter for lions (see 49:19; 50:44; Zec 11:3; see also "Lions and Other Wild Beasts in Ancient Israel" on p. 813).

12:9 The "birds of prey" and "wild beasts" represent Judah's enemies.

12:10 For "shepherds," see the note on 3:15. God's "vineyard" was Judah.

15But after I uproot them, I will again have compassion and will bring[r] each of them back to his own inheritance and his own country. 16And if they learn well the ways of my people and swear by my name, saying, 'As surely as the LORD lives'[s]—even as they once taught my people to swear by Baal[t]—then they will be established among my people.[u] 17But if any nation does not listen, I will completely uproot and destroy[v] it," declares the LORD.

12:15 [r]Am 9:14-15
12:16 [s]Jer 4:2 [t]Jos 23:7 [u]Isa 49:6; Jer 3:17
12:17 [v]Isa 60:12

A Linen Belt

13 This is what the LORD said to me: "Go and buy a linen belt and put it around your waist, but do not let it touch water." 2So I bought a belt, as the LORD directed, and put it around my waist.

3Then the word of the LORD came to me a second time: 4"Take the belt you bought and are wearing around your waist, and go now to Perath[a] and hide it there in a crevice in the rocks." 5So I went and hid it at Perath, as the LORD told me.[w]

13:5 [w]Ex 40:16

6Many days later the LORD said to me, "Go now to Perath and get the belt I told you to hide there." 7So I went to Perath and dug up the belt and took it from the place where I had hidden it, but now it was ruined and completely useless.

8Then the word of the LORD came to me: 9"This is what the LORD says: 'In the same way I will ruin the pride of Judah and the great pride[x] of Jerusalem. 10These wicked people, who refuse to listen to my words, who follow the stubbornness of their hearts[y] and go after other gods[z] to serve and worship them, will be like this belt—completely useless! 11For as a belt is bound around a man's waist, so I bound the whole house of Israel and the whole house of Judah to me,' declares the LORD, 'to be my people for my renown[a] and praise and honor.[b] But they have not listened.'[c]

13:9 [x]Lev 26:19
13:10 [y]Jer 11:8; 16:12 [z]Jer 9:14
13:11 [a]Jer 32:20; 33:9 [b]Ex 19:5-6 [c]Jer 7:26

Wineskins

12"Say to them: 'This is what the LORD, the God of Israel, says: Every wineskin should be filled with wine.' And if they say to you, 'Don't we know that every wineskin should be filled with wine?' 13then tell them, 'This is what the LORD says: I am going to fill with drunkenness[d] all who live in this land, including the kings who sit on David's throne, the priests, the prophets and all those living in Jerusalem. 14I will smash them one against the other, fathers and sons alike, declares the LORD. I will allow no pity or mercy or compassion[e] to keep me from destroying[f] them.' "

13:13 [d]Ps 60:3; 75:8; Isa 51:17; 63:6; Jer 51:57
13:14 [e]Jer 16:5 [f]Dt 29:20; Eze 5:10

Threat of Captivity

15Hear and pay attention,
    do not be arrogant,
    for the LORD has spoken.
16Give glory[g] to the LORD your God
    before he brings the darkness,
before your feet stumble[h]
    on the darkening hills.
You hope for light,
    but he will turn it to thick darkness
    and change it to deep gloom.[i]
17But if you do not listen,[j]
    I will weep in secret
    because of your pride;
my eyes will weep bitterly,
    overflowing with tears,[k]
    because the LORD's flock[l] will be taken captive.[m]

13:16 [g]Jos 7:19 [h]Jer 23:12 [i]Isa 59:9
13:17 [j]Mal 2:2 [k]Jer 9:1 [l]Ps 80:1; Jer 23:1 [m]Jer 14:18

[a] 4 Or possibly *the Euphrates*; also in verses 5-7

12:16 For "Baal," see the note on Judges 2:13; see also "Baal and the Fertility Cults" on page 1414.
13:1 The priests' garments were made of linen (see Eze 44:17–18), a symbol of Israel's holiness as a "kingdom of priests" (see Ex 19:6). For "linen belt," see "Ancient Israelite Clothing and Jewelry" on page 1059.
13:4 Perath may have been the same as Parah (Jos 18:23), near the modern Wadi Farah, 3 miles (4.8 km) northeast of Anathoth. Alternatively, it may refer to the Euphrates River (see the NIV text note).

18 Say to the king and to the queen mother,
"Come down from your thrones,
for your glorious crowns
will fall from your heads."
19 The cities in the Negev will be shut up,
and there will be no one to open them.
13:19 [n]Jer 20:4; 52:30
All Judah[n] will be carried into exile,
carried completely away.

20 Lift up your eyes and see
13:20 [o]Jer 6:22; Hab 1:6 [p]Jer 23:2
those who are coming from the north.[o]
Where is the flock[p] that was entrusted to you,
the sheep of which you boasted?
21 What will you say when ⌞the LORD⌟ sets over you
13:21 [q]Jer 38:22 [r]Jer 4:31
those you cultivated as your special allies?[q]
Will not pain grip you
like that of a woman in labor?[r]
22 And if you ask yourself,
"Why has this happened to me?"—
13:22 [s]Jer 9:2-6; 16:10-12 [t]Eze 16:37; Na 3:5-6
it is because of your many sins[s]
that your skirts have been torn off
and your body mistreated.[t]
23 Can the Ethiopian[a] change his skin
or the leopard its spots?
Neither can you do good
who are accustomed to doing evil.

13:24 [u]Ps 1:4 [v]Lev 26:33
24 "I will scatter you like chaff[u]
driven by the desert wind.[v]
25 This is your lot,
13:25 [w]Job 20:29; Mt 24:51
the portion[w] I have decreed for you,"
declares the LORD,

"because you have forgotten me
and trusted in false gods.
26 I will pull up your skirts over your face
13:26 [x]La 1:8; Eze 16:37; Hos 2:10
that your shame may be seen[x]—
27 your adulteries and lustful neighings,
13:27 [y]Jer 2:20 [z]Eze 6:13 [a]Hos 8:5
your shameless prostitution![y]
I have seen your detestable acts
on the hills and in the fields.[z]
Woe to you, O Jerusalem!
How long will you be unclean?"[a]

Drought, Famine, Sword

14 This is the word of the LORD to Jeremiah concerning the drought:

14:2 [b]Isa 3:26; Jer 8:21
2 "Judah mourns,[b]
her cities languish;

[a] 23 Hebrew *Cushite* (probably a person from the upper Nile region)

13:18 "King" and "queen mother" are probably references to Jehoiachin and Nehushta, respectively (2Ki 24:8). If so, the date was 597 B.C., about 12 years after Josiah's death.
13:19 See "The Negev: Its Climate and Features" on page 34.
13:20 "The north" refers to Babylonia (see 4:6 and its note; see also the note on Isa 41:25).
13:21 "Special allies" may refer to Egypt and Babylon, who alternated in dominating Judah.
13:22 To have one's skirt torn off was to be publicly disgraced, like a common prostitute.
13:24 See the notes on Psalm 1:4, Isaiah 17:13 and Jer 4:11.
14:1 Drought, water rights and water distribution were, then as now, major issues in the region now known as Palestine.
14:2 "Cities" is literally "gates." Taking possession of the gate of a city was tantamount to occupying the city itself.

they wail for the land,
and a cry goes up from Jerusalem.
3 The nobles send their servants for water;
they go to the cisterns
but find no water.[c]
They return with their jars unfilled;
dismayed and despairing,
they cover their heads.[d]
4 The ground is cracked
because there is no rain in the land;[e]
the farmers are dismayed
and cover their heads.
5 Even the doe in the field
deserts her newborn fawn
because there is no grass.[f]
6 Wild donkeys stand on the barren heights[g]
and pant like jackals;
their eyesight fails
for lack of pasture."

7 Although our sins testify[h] against us,
O LORD, do something for the sake of your name.
For our backsliding[i] is great;
we have sinned[j] against you.
8 O Hope[k] of Israel,
its Savior in times of distress,
why are you like a stranger in the land,
like a traveler who stays only a night?
9 Why are you like a man taken by surprise,
like a warrior powerless to save?[l]
You are among[m] us, O LORD,
and we bear your name;[n]
do not forsake us!

10 This is what the LORD says about this people:

"They greatly love to wander;
they do not restrain their feet.[o]
So the LORD does not accept[p] them;
he will now remember[q] their wickedness
and punish them for their sins."[r]

11 Then the LORD said to me, "Do not pray[s] for the well-being of this people. 12 Although they fast, I
will not listen to their cry;[t] though they offer burnt offerings[u] and grain offerings, I will not accept[v] them.
Instead, I will destroy them with the sword, famine and plague."
13 But I said, "Ah, Sovereign LORD, the prophets keep telling them, 'You will not see the sword or suffer
famine.[w] Indeed, I will give you lasting peace in this place.' "
14 Then the LORD said to me, "The prophets are prophesying lies[x] in my name. I have not sent[y] them
or appointed them or spoken to them. They are prophesying to you false visions,[z] divinations,[a] idolatries[a]
and the delusions of their own minds. 15 Therefore, this is what the LORD says about the prophets who are
prophesying in my name: I did not send them, yet they are saying, 'No sword or famine will touch this
land.' Those same prophets will perish[b] by sword and famine.[c] 16 And the people they are prophesying
to will be thrown out into the streets of Jerusalem because of the famine and sword. There will be no one

14:3 [c]2Ki 18:31; Job 6:19-20 [d]2Sa 15:30
14:4 [e]Jer 3:3
14:5 [f]Isa 15:6
14:6 [g]Job 39:5-6; Jer 2:24
14:7 [h]Hos 5:5 [i]Jer 5:6 [j]Jer 8:14
14:8 [k]Jer 17:13
14:9 [l]Isa 50:2 [m]Jer 8:19 [n]Isa 63:19; Jer 15:16
14:10 [o]Ps 119:101; Jer 2:25 [p]Jer 6:20; Am 5:22 [q]Hos 9:9 [r]Jer 44:21-23; Hos 8:13
14:11 [s]Ex 32:10
14:12 [t]Isa 1:15; Jer 11:11 [u]Jer 7:21 [v]Jer 6:20
14:13 [w]Jer 5:12
14:14 [x]Jer 27:14 [y]Jer 23:21,32 [z]Jer 23:16 [a]Eze 12:24
14:15 [b]Eze 14:9 [c]Jer 5:12-13

[a] 14 Or *visions, worthless divinations*

14:4 Unlike Egypt, where the Nile waters the ground, the area now known as Palestine depends upon adequate rainfall.

14:16 See the note on 7:33.

14:16 [d]Ps 79:3 [e]Jer 7:33 [f]Pr 1:31

to bury[d] them or their wives, their sons or their daughters.[e] I will pour out on them the calamity they deserve.[f]

17 "Speak this word to them:

14:17 [g]Jer 9:1 [h]Jer 8:21

" 'Let my eyes overflow with tears[g]
night and day without ceasing;
for my virgin daughter—my people—
has suffered a grievous wound,
a crushing blow.[h]

ANCIENT TEXTS AND ARTIFACTS

The Arad Ostraca

The Early Bronze city of Arad
Photograph courtesy of © Dr. Gary Pratico

JEREMIAH 14 Jeremiah 14 reflects the panic and dismay of the people as they sought to preserve life and home in the face of overwhelming military threats. We see evidence of the same conditions reflected in a series of notes written on pieces of clay from this time period.

The site of Arad ("Map 7"), an ancient Judean desert fortress, has yielded approximately 200 **ostraca** (ink-inscribed potsherds) of Hebrew and **Aramaic** inscriptions that constitute the largest collection of written texts recovered from Biblical times. These broken pottery pieces preserve the history of the citadel and grant a glimpse into the life of its occupants during the last decades of the kingdom of Judah. The majority of the **sherds**, written in **paleo-Hebrew**, are military communiqués dating back to approximately 600 B.C. They are addressed to the commander of the fortress, Eliashiv ben Eshiyahu, with instructions to ration flour, wine and oil to soldiers serving in the Negev, as well as to the "Kittim," an estimated 25 Aegean mercenary soldiers serving in the Judean military. A number of the ostraca contain listings of names, most likely used for recording the distribution of rations. Ostracon #24 speaks of an imminent Edomite invasion. In this letter the commander requested that reinforcement troops be sent from Arad and from the smaller fortress of Qinah to Ramat Negev, a town 6 miles (10 km) away, in order to repulse the Edomite threat.

In the vicinity of the Arad sanctuary, sherds with individual, personal names, possibly used as lots for priestly duties, were uncovered. Among those represented are Pashhur and Meremoth (Ezr 8:33; Jer 20:1), as well as "the sons of Korah" (2Ch 20:19; Ps 84:1), all priestly families mentioned in the Bible. Ostracon #18 contains the earliest extrabiblical mention of the temple as "the house of **Yahweh**." In addition to their historical value, these ostraca have contributed greatly to the study of Hebrew orthography (conventional or standardized spelling of words) and its development.

An ostracon from Arad
Preserving Bible Times; © Dr. James C. Martin; permission of The Israel Museum

18 If I go into the country,
I see those slain by the sword;
if I go into the city,
I see the ravages of famine.[i] 14:18 [i]Eze 7:15
Both prophet and priest
have gone to a land they know not.' "

19 Have you rejected Judah completely?[j] 14:19 [j]Jer 7:29 [k]Jer 30:12-13 [l]Jer 8:15
Do you despise Zion?
Why have you afflicted us
so that we cannot be healed?[k]
We hoped for peace
but no good has come,
for a time of healing
but there is only terror.[l]
20 O LORD, we acknowledge our wickedness
and the guilt of our fathers;
we have indeed sinned[m] against you. 14:20 [m]Da 9:7-8
21 For the sake of your name[n] do not despise us; 14:21 [n]ver 7 [o]Jer 3:17
do not dishonor your glorious throne.[o]
Remember your covenant with us
and do not break it.
22 Do any of the worthless idols of the nations bring rain?[p] 14:22 [p]Ps 135:7
Do the skies themselves send down showers?
No, it is you, O LORD our God.
Therefore our hope is in you,
for you are the one who does all this.

15 Then the LORD said to me: "Even if Moses[q] and Samuel[r] were to stand before me, my heart would 15:1 [q]Ex 32:11; Nu 14:13-20 [r]1Sa 7:9 [s]Jer 7:16; Eze 14:14,20 [t]2Ki 17:20
not go out to this people.[s] Send them away from my presence![t] Let them go! 2 And if they ask
you, 'Where shall we go?' tell them, 'This is what the LORD says:

" 'Those destined for death, to death;
those for the sword, to the sword;[u] 15:2 [u]Jer 43:11 [v]Jer 14:12 [w]Rev 13:10
those for starvation, to starvation;[v]
those for captivity, to captivity.'[w]

3 "I will send four kinds of destroyers[x] against them," declares the LORD, "the sword to kill and the dogs 15:3 [x]Lev 26:16 [y]Dt 28:26 [z]Lev 26:22; Eze 14:21
to drag away and the birds[y] of the air and the beasts of the earth to devour and destroy.[z] 4 I will make them
abhorrent[a] to all the kingdoms of the earth[b] because of what Manasseh[c] son of Hezekiah king of Judah 15:4 [a]Jer 24:9; 29:18 [b]Dt 28:25 [c]2Ki 21:2; 23:26-27
did in Jerusalem.

5 "Who will have pity[d] on you, O Jerusalem? 15:5 [d]Isa 51:19; Jer 13:14; 21:7; Na 3:7
Who will mourn for you?
Who will stop to ask how you are?
6 You have rejected[e] me," declares the LORD. 15:6 [e]Jer 6:19; 7:24 [f]Zep 1:4
"You keep on backsliding.
So I will lay hands[f] on you and destroy you;
I can no longer show compassion.
7 I will winnow them with a winnowing fork
at the city gates of the land.

14:22 Only the Lord (not Baal, the weather god) could send showers to end the drought (see v. 1).
15:1 Standing was a common posture for prayer (see Ge 18:22; Mk 11:25).
15:3 The seventh-century B.C. vassal treaties of Esarhaddon present similar curses: "May Ninurta, leader of the gods, fell you with his fierce arrow, fill the plain with your corpses, and give your flesh to the eagles and vultures to feed on . . . May dogs and pigs eat your flesh."
15:4 Manasseh was the most wicked king in Judah's history (see 2Ki 21:1–11,16), and his sins were a primary cause of the nation's eventual destruction (see 2Ki 21:12–15; 23:26–27; 24:3–4).
15:7 For "winnow," see the note on Ruth 1:22. Winnowing is often a figure of judgment.

15:7 [g]Jer 18:21

I will bring bereavement and destruction on my people,[g]
for they have not changed their ways.
8 I will make their widows more numerous
than the sand of the sea.

15:8 [h]Jer 6:4

At midday I will bring a destroyer[h]
against the mothers of their young men;
suddenly I will bring down on them
anguish and terror.

15:9 [i]1Sa 2:5 [j]Jer 21:7

9 The mother of seven will grow faint[i]
and breathe her last.
Her sun will set while it is still day;
she will be disgraced and humiliated.
I will put the survivors to the sword[j]
before their enemies,"
declares the LORD.

15:10 [k]Job 3:1 [l]Jer 1:19 [m]Lev 25:36

10 Alas, my mother, that you gave me birth,[k]
a man with whom the whole land strives and contends![l]
I have neither lent[m] nor borrowed,
yet everyone curses me.

11 The LORD said,

15:11 [n]Jer 40:4 [o]Jer 21:1-2; 37:3; 42:1-3

"Surely I will deliver you[n] for a good purpose;
surely I will make your enemies plead[o] with you
in times of disaster and times of distress.

15:12 [p]Jer 28:14

12 "Can a man break iron—
iron from the north[p]—or bronze?

15:13 [q]Ps 44:12 [r]Jer 17:3

13 Your wealth and your treasures
I will give as plunder, without charge,[q]
because of all your sins
throughout your country.[r]

15:14 [s]Dt 28:36; Jer 16:13 [t]Dt 32:22; Ps 21:9

14 I will enslave you to your enemies
in[a] a land you do not know,[s]
for my anger will kindle a fire[t]
that will burn against you."

15:15 [u]Jer 12:3 [v]Ps 69:7-9

15 You understand, O LORD;
remember me and care for me.
Avenge me on my persecutors.[u]
You are long-suffering—do not take me away;
think of how I suffer reproach for your sake.[v]

15:16 [w]Eze 3:3; Rev 10:10 [x]Ps 119:72,103 [y]Jer 14:9

16 When your words came, I ate[w] them;
they were my joy and my heart's delight,[x]
for I bear your name,[y]
O LORD God Almighty.

15:17 [z]Ps 1:1; 26:4-5; Jer 16:8

17 I never sat[z] in the company of revelers,
never made merry with them;
I sat alone because your hand was on me
and you had filled me with indignation.

[a] *14* Some Hebrew manuscripts, Septuagint and Syriac (see also Jer. 17:4); most Hebrew manuscripts *I will cause your enemies to bring you / into*

15:8 Military attacks at noon were unexpected (see the note on 6:4).

The "destroyer" was Babylon (see the note on 4:7).

15:12 Iron is a symbol of great strength.

"The north" refers to Babylonia (see 4:6 and its note; see also the note on Isa 41:25).

15:17 Jeremiah never married (see 16:2) and had few friends.

18 Why is my pain unending
and my wound grievous and incurable?[a]
Will you be to me like a deceptive brook,
like a spring that fails?[b]

19 Therefore this is what the LORD says:

"If you repent, I will restore you
that you may serve[c] me;
if you utter worthy, not worthless, words,
you will be my spokesman.
Let this people turn to you,
but you must not turn to them.
20 I will make you a wall to this people,
a fortified wall of bronze;
they will fight against you
but will not overcome you,
for I am with you
to rescue and save you,"[d]
declares the LORD.
21 "I will save you from the hands of the wicked
and redeem[e] you from the grasp of the cruel."[f]

Day of Disaster

16 Then the word of the LORD came to me: 2 "You must not marry[g] and have sons or daughters in
this place." 3 For this is what the LORD says about the sons and daughters born in this land and
about the women who are their mothers and the men who are their fathers:[h] 4 "They will die of deadly
diseases. They will not be mourned or buried[i] but will be like refuse lying on the ground.[j] They will per-
ish by sword and famine, and their dead bodies will become food for the birds of the air and the beasts
of the earth."[k]
5 For this is what the LORD says: "Do not enter a house where there is a funeral meal; do not go to
mourn or show sympathy, because I have withdrawn my blessing, my love and my pity from this peo-
ple," declares the LORD. 6 "Both high and low will die in this land.[l] They will not be buried or mourned,
and no one will cut[m] himself or shave[n] his head for them. 7 No one will offer food to comfort those who
mourn[o] for the dead—not even for a father or a mother—nor will anyone give them a drink to console
them.
8 "And do not enter a house where there is feasting and sit down to eat and drink.[p] 9 For this is what
the LORD Almighty, the God of Israel, says: Before your eyes and in your days I will bring an end to the
sounds[q] of joy and gladness and to the voices of bride and bridegroom in this place.[r]
10 "When you tell these people all this and they ask you, 'Why has the LORD decreed such a great di-
saster against us? What wrong have we done? What sin have we committed against the LORD our God?'[s]
11 then say to them, 'It is because your fathers forsook me,' declares the LORD, 'and followed other gods
and served and worshiped them. They forsook me and did not keep my law.[t] 12 But you have behaved
more wickedly than your fathers.[u] See how each of you is following the stubbornness of his evil heart[v]
instead of obeying me. 13 So I will throw you out of this land into a land neither you nor your fathers have
known,[w] and there you will serve other gods[x] day and night, for I will show you no favor.'[y]
14 "However, the days are coming," declares the LORD, "when men will no longer say, 'As surely as the
LORD lives, who brought the Israelites up out of Egypt,'[z] 15 but they will say, 'As surely as the LORD lives, who
brought the Israelites up out of the land of the north and out of all the countries where he had banished
them.'[a] For I will restore[b] them to the land I gave their forefathers.

15:18 [a]Jer 30:15; Mic 1:9 [b]Job 6:15
15:19 [c]Zec 3:7
15:20 [d]Jer 20:11; Eze 3:8
15:21 [e]Jer 50:34 [f]Ge 48:16
16:2 [g]1Co 7:26-27
16:3 [h]Jer 6:21
16:4 [i]Jer 25:33 [j]Ps 83:10; Jer 9:22 [k]Ps 79:1-3; Jer 15:3; 34:20
16:6 [l]Eze 9:5-6 [m]Lev 19:28 [n]Jer 41:5; 47:5
16:7 [o]Eze 24:17; Hos 9:4
16:8 [p]Ecc 7:2-4; Jer 15:17
16:9 [q]Isa 24:8; Eze 26:13; Hos 2:11 [r]Rev 18:23
16:10 [s]Dt 29:24; Jer 5:19
16:11 [t]Dt 29:25-26; 1Ki 9:9; Ps 106:35-43; Jer 22:9
16:12 [u]Jer 7:26 [v]Ecc 9:3; Jer 13:10
16:13 [w]Dt 28:36; Jer 5:19 [x]Dt 4:28 [y]Jer 15:5
16:14 [z]Dt 15:15; Jer 23:7-8
16:15 [a]Isa 11:11; Jer 23:8 [b]Jer 24:6

15:19 "Serve" is literally "stand before"—an appropriate posture for an obedient servant (see Nu 16:9; Dt 10:8).
16:6 Theses actions were prohibited in the law (see Lev 19:27–28; 21:5; Dt 14:1; see also "Tattoos and Self-Laceration in Ancient Religion" on p. 180), but the Israelites sometimes practiced them as a sign of mourning.
16:7 Food was customarily offered to mourners (see 2Sa 3:35; 12:16–17; Eze 24:17,22; Hos 9:4), and wine was given to cheer and console (Pr 31:6; Ecc 2:3). In later Judaism a special cup of wine (the "cup of consolation") was offered to the chief mourner.
16:15 The "land of the north" is Babylonia (see 4:6 and its note; see also the note on Isa 41:25).

16 “But now I will send for many fishermen,” declares the LORD, “and they will catch them.[c] After that
I will send for many hunters, and they will hunt[d] them down on every mountain and hill and from the
crevices of the rocks.[e] 17 My eyes are on all their ways; they are not hidden[f] from me, nor is their sin con-
cealed from my eyes.[g] 18 I will repay them double[h] for their wickedness and their sin, because they have
defiled my land[i] with the lifeless forms of their vile images and have filled my inheritance with their de-
testable idols.”

19 O LORD, my strength and my fortress,
my refuge in time of distress,
to you the nations will come[j]
from the ends of the earth and say,
“Our fathers possessed nothing but false gods,[k]
worthless idols that did them no good.
20 Do men make their own gods?
Yes, but they are not gods!”[l]

21 “Therefore I will teach them—
this time I will teach them
my power and might.
Then they will know
that my name is the LORD.

17

“Judah’s sin is engraved with an iron tool,[m]
inscribed with a flint point,
on the tablets of their hearts[n]
and on the horns of their altars.
2 Even their children remember
their altars and Asherah poles[a][o]
beside the spreading trees
and on the high hills.[p]
3 My mountain in the land
and your[b] wealth and all your treasures
I will give away as plunder,[q]
together with your high places,[r]
because of sin throughout your country.[s]
4 Through your own fault you will lose
the inheritance[t] I gave you.
I will enslave you to your enemies[u]
in a land[v] you do not know,
for you have kindled my anger,
and it will burn[w] forever.”

5 This is what the LORD says:

“Cursed is the one who trusts in man,[x]
who depends on flesh for his strength
and whose heart turns away from the LORD.

16:16 [c]Am 4:2; Hab 1:14-15 [d]Am 9:3; Mic 7:2 [e]1Sa 26:20 **16:17** [f]1Co 4:5; Heb 4:13 [g]Pr 15:3 **16:18** [h]Isa 40:2; Rev 18:6 [i]Nu 35:34; Jer 2:7
16:19 [j]Isa 2:2; Jer 3:17 [k]Ps 4:2
16:20 [l]Ps 115:4-7; Isa 37:19; Jer 2:11
17:1 [m]Job 19:24 [n]Pr 3:3; 2Co 3:3
17:2 [o]2Ch 24:18 [p]Jer 2:20
17:3 [q]2Ki 24:13 [r]Jer 26:18; Mic 3:12 [s]Jer 15:13
17:4 [t]La 5:2 [u]Dt 28:48; Jer 12:7 [v]Jer 16:13 [w]Jer 7:20; 15:14
17:5 [x]Isa 2:22; 30:1-3

[a] 2 That is, symbols of the goddess Asherah [b] 2,3 Or *hills* / [3] *and the mountains of the land. / Your*

16:21 “Name” often stands for “person” or “being” in the Old Testament. The name of the Lord is the manifestation of his character. It has no separate existence apart from God but is synonymous with the Lord himself in his gracious manifestation and accessibility to his people (see “YHWH: The Name of God in the Old Testament” on p. 89).

17:1 Engraving with an iron tool was the method used to inscribe the most permanent of records (see Job 19:24). Flint, an extremely hard stone, was used to make tools and weapons.

17:2 For “Asherah poles,” see the note on 1 Kings 14:15; see also “The Kuntillet Ajrûd Inscriptions: The Lord’s Asherah?” on page 1220.

For “spreading trees” and “high hills,” see the notes on 2:20 and Isaiah 57:5 and Jeremiah 2:20; see also “The High Places” on page 1318.

17:3 “My mountain” is Mount Zion, the location of the temple in Jerusalem (see “Zaphon, Olympus, Sinai and Zion: The Mountain of God” on p. 843).

High places were locales of idolatrous worship (see the note on 1Ki 3:2; see also “The High Places” on p. 1318).

[6]He will be like a bush in the wastelands;
he will not see prosperity when it comes.
He will dwell in the parched places of the desert,
in a salt[y] land where no one lives.

[7]"But blessed is the man who trusts[z] in the LORD,
whose confidence is in him.
[8]He will be like a tree planted by the water
that sends out its roots by the stream.
It does not fear when heat comes;
its leaves are always green.
It has no worries in a year of drought[a]
and never fails to bear fruit."[b]

[9]The heart[c] is deceitful above all things
and beyond cure.
Who can understand it?

[10]"I the LORD search the heart[d]
and examine the mind,[e]

17:6 [y]Dt 29:23; Job 39:6
17:7 [z]Ps 34:8; 40:4; Pr 16:20
17:8 [a]Jer 14:1-6 [b]Ps 1:3; 92:12-14
17:9 [c]Ecc 9:3; Mt 13:15; Mk 7:21-22
17:10 [d]1Sa 16:7; Rev 2:23 [e]Ps 17:3; 139:23; Jer 11:20; 20:12; Ro 8:27

17:9 The "heart" is the "wellspring of life" (Pr 4:23; see also Ps 4:7 and its note).
17:10 "Mind" is literally "kidneys" (see the notes on Ps 7:9; 139:13). The Hebrew for this word is translated "hearts" in 12:2. See "Heart, Breath, Throat and Intestines: Ancient Hebrew Anthropology" on page 968.

ANCIENT TEXTS AND ARTIFACTS

The Kuntillet Ajrûd Inscriptions: The Lord's Asherah?

JEREMIAH 17 The Hebrew word *Asherim* (NIV "Asherah poles") in Jeremiah 17:2 denotes either the **Canaanite** goddess named Asherah (the singular form of the word) or some object associated with pagan worship in Israel and Judah. Of the 40 occurrences of the term in the Old Testament, only four of them refer to the proper name given to the goddess; the remaining usages all signify something either constructed of wood or planted. We may assume that a wooden object—perhaps a tree or a pole—was used to symbolize the goddess in Canaanite religion. The passages that speak of Asherim being "made" may refer to wooden figurines of the goddess.

Early Bible translations (the **Septuagint** and the **Vulgate**),[1] as well as an ancient commentary (the Jewish **Mishnah**), understood Asherim to refer to a group of trees. The translation "grove" in the KJV preserves the Septuagint and Vulgate understanding. This tradition, while possible in some cases, is probably incorrect, since the KJV of Jeremiah 17:2 speaks of "groves by the green trees."[2]

The Canaanite goddess Asherah is well attested in the texts from the ancient city of **Ugarit**,[3] where she is portrayed as the consort, or partner, of El and the mother of other gods. Jeremiah's condemnation of idolatry in Judah, particularly of the type associated with the Asherim, is illuminated by a **cache** of inscriptions found at a site called Kuntillet Ajrûd, located 31 miles (50 km) south of Kadesh Barnea in the northern Sinai. Especially enlightening are three texts from this site that say, "I bless you by Yahweh of Samaria and by his Asherah," "I bless you by Yahweh of Teman and by his Asherah" and "to Yahweh of Teman and to his Asherah." The Asherah cited at Kuntillet Ajrûd may be the same wooden cultic object so frequently mentioned in the Bible. It is more likely, however, that the use of the term here provides firsthand evidence for an idolatrous merging of orthodox Yahwistic faith and is a reference not to an idol but to a goddess, a supposed consort of **Yahweh**. This is Canaanite paganism—precisely the type of idolatry and syncretism that Jeremiah was attempting to combat.[4]

[1]See "The Ancient Translations" on page 1492. [2]See "Trees of Ancient Israel" on page 1357. [3]See "Ugarit/Ras Shamra" on page 819. [4]See also "Devotion to Asherah in the Khirbet El-Qom Inscription" on page 1220.

17:10 [f]Ps 62:12; Jer 32:19 [g]Ro 2:6

to reward[f] a man according to his conduct,
according to what his deeds deserve."[g]

11 Like a partridge that hatches eggs it did not lay
is the man who gains riches by unjust means.
When his life is half gone, they will desert him,
and in the end he will prove to be a fool.[h]

17:11 [h]Lk 12:20

12 A glorious throne,[i] exalted from the beginning,
is the place of our sanctuary.

17:12 [i]Jer 3:17

13 O LORD, the hope[j] of Israel,
all who forsake[k] you will be put to shame.
Those who turn away from you will be written in the dust
because they have forsaken the LORD,
the spring of living water.

17:13 [j]Jer 14:8 [k]Isa 1:28; Jer 2:17

14 Heal me, O LORD, and I will be healed;
save me and I will be saved,
for you are the one I praise.[l]

17:14 [l]Ps 109:1

15 They keep saying to me,
"Where is the word of the LORD?
Let it now be fulfilled!"[m]

17:15 [m]Isa 5:19; 2Pe 3:4

16 I have not run away from being your shepherd;
you know I have not desired the day of despair.
What passes my lips is open before you.

17 Do not be a terror[n] to me;
you are my refuge[o] in the day of disaster.

17:17 [n]Ps 88:15-16 [o]Jer 16:19; Na 1:7

18 Let my persecutors be put to shame,
but keep me from shame;
let them be terrified,
but keep me from terror.
Bring on them the day of disaster;
destroy them with double destruction.[p]

17:18 [p]Ps 35:1-8

Keeping the Sabbath Holy

19 This is what the LORD said to me: "Go and stand at the gate of the people, through which the kings
of Judah go in and out; stand also at all the other gates of Jerusalem.[q] 20 Say to them, 'Hear the word of
the LORD, O kings of Judah and all people of Judah and everyone living in Jerusalem[r] who come through
these gates.[s] 21 This is what the LORD says: Be careful not to carry a load on the Sabbath[t] day or bring it
through the gates of Jerusalem. 22 Do not bring a load out of your houses or do any work on the Sabbath,
but keep the Sabbath day holy, as I commanded your forefathers.[u] 23 Yet they did not listen or pay atten-
tion;[v] they were stiff-necked[w] and would not listen or respond to discipline.[x] 24 But if you are careful to
obey me, declares the LORD, and bring no load through the gates of this city on the Sabbath, but keep the
Sabbath day holy by not doing any work on it, 25 then kings who sit on David's throne[y] will come through
the gates of this city with their officials. They and their officials will come riding in chariots and on hors-
es, accompanied by the men of Judah and those living in Jerusalem, and this city will be inhabited for-
ever. 26 People will come from the towns of Judah and the villages around Jerusalem, from the territory
of Benjamin and the western foothills, from the hill country and the Negev,[z] bringing burnt offerings

17:19 [q]Jer 7:2; 26:2 **17:20** [r]Jer 19:3 [s]Jer 22:2 **17:21** [t]Nu 15:32-36; Ne 13:15-21; Jn 5:10 **17:22** [u]Ex 20:8; 31:13; Isa 56:2-6; Eze 20:12 **17:23** [v]Jer 7:26 [w]Jer 19:15 [x]Jer 7:28 **17:25** [y]2Sa 7:13; Isa 9:7; Jer 22:2, 4; Lk 1:32 **17:26** [z]Jer 32:44; 33:13; Zec 7:7

17:12 See the note on 3:17.
17:13 The word "dust" is literally "earth," which sometimes refers to the netherworld, as is also the case in Canaanite and Mesopotamian literature. "Written in the dust" would then mean "destined for death." For the Old Testament view of the afterlife, see the note on Psalm 6:5 and "Sheol, Hades, Gehenna, the Abyss and Tartarus: Images of Hell" on page 946.
17:15 This accusation must have been voiced before the first invasion of Judah by the Babylonians in 605 B.C., after the battle of Carchemish (see 46:2).
17:19 The word "people" here is literally "sons of the people." The Hebrew for this word is elsewhere translated "common people" (26:23; 2Ki 23:6) and "lay people" (2Ch 35:5,7). The latter meaning seems intended here; therefore the "gate of the people" is likely the east gate of the temple, where the people assembled in large numbers and which the kings frequently used.
17:26 See "The Negev: Its Climate and Features" on page 34.

and sacrifices, grain offerings, incense and thank offerings to the house of the LORD. 27 But if you do not
obey[a] me to keep the Sabbath day holy by not carrying any load as you come through the gates of Jeru- 17:27 [a]Jer 22:5
salem on the Sabbath day, then I will kindle an unquenchable fire[b] in the gates of Jerusalem that will [b]Jer 7:20 [c]2Ki 25:9; Am 2:5
consume her fortresses.' "[c]

At the Potter's House

18 This is the word that came to Jeremiah from the LORD: 2 "Go down to the potter's house, and there
I will give you my message." 3 So I went down to the potter's house, and I saw him working at the
wheel. 4 But the pot he was shaping from the clay was marred in his hands; so the potter formed it into
another pot, shaping it as seemed best to him.

5 Then the word of the LORD came to me: 6 "O house of Israel, can I not do with you as this potter
does?" declares the LORD. "Like clay[d] in the hand of the potter, so are you in my hand, O house of Isra- 18:6 [d]Isa 45:9; Ro 9:20-21
el. 7 If at any time I announce that a nation or kingdom is to be uprooted,[e] torn down and destroyed, 8 and 18:7 [e]Jer 1:10
if that nation I warned repents of its evil, then I will relent[f] and not inflict on it the disaster[g] I had 18:8 [f]Jer 26:13; Jnh 3:8-10
planned. 9 And if at another time I announce that a nation or kingdom is to be built[h] up and planted, [g]Eze 18:21; Hos 11:8-9
10 and if it does evil[i] in my sight and does not obey me, then I will reconsider[j] the good I had intended 18:9 [h]Jer 1:10; 31:28
to do for it. 18:10 [i]Eze 33:18 [j]1Sa 2:29-30

11 "Now therefore say to the people of Judah and those living in Jerusalem, 'This is what the LORD says:
Look! I am preparing a disaster[k] for you and devising a plan against you. So turn[l] from your evil ways,[m] 18:11 [k]Jer 4:6 [l]2Ki 17:13;
each one of you, and reform your ways and your actions.' 12 But they will reply, 'It's no use.[n] We will con- Isa 1:16-19 [m]Jer 7:3
tinue with our own plans; each of us will follow the stubbornness of his evil heart.' " 18:12 [n]Isa 57:10; Jer 2:25

13 Therefore this is what the LORD says:

"Inquire among the nations:
Who has ever heard anything like this?[o] 18:13 [o]Isa 66:8; Jer 2:10 [p]Jer 5:30
A most horrible[p] thing has been done
by Virgin Israel.
14 Does the snow of Lebanon
ever vanish from its rocky slopes?
Do its cool waters from distant sources
ever cease to flow?[a]
15 Yet my people have forgotten me;
they burn incense to worthless
idols,[q] 18:15 [q]Jer 10:15
which made them stumble in their ways [r]Jer 6:16 [s]Isa 57:14; 62:10
and in the ancient paths.[r]
They made them walk in bypaths
and on roads not built up.[s]
16 Their land will be laid waste,[t] 18:16 [t]Jer 25:9
an object of lasting scorn;[u] [u]Jer 19:8 [v]Ps 22:7
all who pass by will be appalled
and will shake their heads.[v]

[a] 14 The meaning of the Hebrew for this sentence is uncertain.

17:27 Commercial business transactions, which took place at the city gates (see "The City Gate" on p. 392), were prohibited on the Sabbath (see Ex 20:8–10; Ne 10:31; 13:15–22). The gates of Jerusalem were therefore symbols of the people's flagrant violation of the Sabbath. As such these gates would be the first structures destroyed.

18:2 The potter's workshop was located on the slopes of the Valley of Ben Hinnom near the Potsherd Gate (see 2:23 and its note); hence Jeremiah "went down to the potter's house" (v. 3), descending from Jerusalem into the valley.

18:3 The word "wheel" is literally "two stones." Both wheels were attached to a single upright shaft, one end of which was sunk permanently into the ground. The potter would spin the lower wheel with his foot and work the clay on the upper wheel. This process is described in the Apocryphal book of Ecclesiasticus (38:29–30). See "The Potsherd: Pottery in the Bible" on page 738 and "Pottery-Making in Bible Times" on page 1223.

See the note on labor in the ancient Near Eastern world at Jeremiah 36:2.

18:4–6 The Hebrew word for "potter" is translated "Maker" in 10:16 with reference to God. Biblical imagery often pictures humankind as being fashioned of clay by a potter (see Job 4:19; Ro 9:20–21).

18:14 Mount Lebanon is one of the highest of the northern mountains, reaching an altitude of over 10,000 feet (3,048 m).

18:15 For "burn incense," see the notes on Isaiah 15:3 and Jeremiah 19:13.

Pottery-Making in Bible Times

JEREMIAH 18 Archaeologists have discovered a great deal of evidence related to pottery-making in ancient Israel, including the remains of workshops, potter's wheels, tools, unfired vessels, prepared clay and kilns. A large production area was excavated at **Late Bronze**[1] and **Iron Age** Megiddo,[2] for example. Production typically followed the method described below:

- After the clay had been extracted from the ground, it was brought to the workshop and prepared. Foreign objects were removed and water added as a softening agent.
- The clay was "wedged" (pressed to remove air) by a process of kneading or treading (cf. Isa 41:25).
- Sometimes potters employed levigation, a method of removing impurities by suspension in water.
- Tempering agents were added to harden the clay or to reduce its propensity to crack. Among the tempers used at various times were straw, sand, salt, animal dung and grog (ground-up pieces of broken pottery).
- A formed vessel was air-dried to a leather-hard condition. Wherever possible, pottery was dried in caves; the cooler temperature allowed for slow, even drying.
- A vessel might be decorated with a slip (a thin, colored coat of watery clay) or an incised pattern.
- Pots were stacked in a kiln and baked. The kiln had to be hot enough for the pottery to glow red—about 1,472ºF (800ºC)—a temperature that had to be maintained for two or three days).

Basic techniques were developed during the **Neolithic period.** The discovery of pottery-making technology was a major revolution of the ancient world; in fact, researchers differentiate between "pre-pottery" and "pottery" Neolithic phases. Fundamental principles worked out during this time included the selection of appropriate clays, the use of tempering agents and the development of proper firing techniques. There were some significant innovations later on, although many observable differences were simply matters of style.

Bethlehem tomb pottery grouping, characteristic of seventh century B.C. (see typical fertility figurine on the left)

Preserving Bible Times; © Dr. James C. Martin; permission of The British Museum

Early potters understood the importance of turning the clay in order to shape vessels, but an innovation of the **Middle Bronze** period, the "kick wheel," allowed potters to create delicate pottery. Since the wheel was turned rapidly by foot, it allowed the potter to use both hands for shaping. Potters could "throw" the clay, shaping a single lump on a wheel with the aid of centrifugal force. They also began to use fine clays that were slippery and plastic or pliable. The finer clays required more controlled drying and firing processes, since vessels made of such clay could more easily shrink and crack.

Toward the end of the Middle Bronze Age potters learned to decorate pots with slips and paint. While clay dries, salts suspended in the water form a layer on the surface. Since this "scum" prevents paints from absorbing properly and distorts their colors, a white firing slip was applied. This would adhere to the vessel so that the red or black painted decorations would not be affected by the scum.

The **Late Bronze Age** saw a decline in pottery-making skills. Late Bronze potters reverted to using less malleable, coarser clays that were easier to work with; they were less prone to cracking, and attaching handles was easier. Use of these coarser clays resulted in heavier, thicker pottery. The use of the high-speed wheel may have died out; slips, if applied at all, were thinner; and pottery was less likely to be painted.

During the **Iron Age** the quality of pottery-making improved markedly. The kick wheel came back into use, and techniques were developed for fast production and for making vessels with thin walls but sturdy bases. Potters used string to separate vessels from the remaining clay on the wheel ("string-cutting"); sometimes they partially dried vessels and then shaved them down prior to firing. This allowed for strong but lightweight pottery. Small vessels, like cups, were typically thrown, but larger items were built up using the coil technique.

When Jeremiah "went down to the potter's house" (Jer 18:3), he descended from Jerusalem to the Hinnom Valley, on the western and southern sides of the city, where the potters' quarter was located (19:2). He discovered the potter forming a vessel at a fast kick wheel. When the clay did not form properly, the potter started over, reshaping the lump into another vessel. This provided an object lesson for Jeremiah on the sovereignty of God, who molds and shapes people and events as he wills (18:5–6).

See also "The Potsherd: Pottery in the Bible" on page 738.

[1]See "Archaeological Periods" chart on page xx in the front of this Bible. [2]See "Megiddo" on page 1541.

17 Like a wind[w] from the east,
I will scatter them before their enemies;
I will show them my back and not my face[x]
in the day of their disaster."

18:17 [w]Jer 13:24 [x]Jer 2:27

18 They said, "Come, let's make plans[y] against Jeremiah; for the teaching of the law by the priest[z] will
not be lost, nor will counsel from the wise, nor the word from the prophets.[a] So come, let's attack him with
our tongues[b] and pay no attention to anything he says."

18:18 [y]Jer 11:19 [z]Mal 2:7 [a]Jer 5:13 [b]Ps 52:2

19 Listen to me, O LORD;
hear what my accusers are saying!
20 Should good be repaid with evil?
Yet they have dug a pit[c] for me.
Remember that I stood before you
and spoke in their behalf[d]
to turn your wrath away from them.

18:20 [c]Ps 35:7; 57:6 [d]Ps 106:23

21 So give their children over to famine;[e]
hand them over to the power of the sword.
Let their wives be made childless and widows;[f]
let their men be put to death,
their young men slain by the sword in battle.

18:21 [e]Jer 11:22 [f]Ps 109:9

22 Let a cry[g] be heard from their houses
when you suddenly bring invaders against them,
for they have dug a pit to capture me
and have hidden snares[h] for my feet.

18:22 [g]Jer 6:26 [h]Ps 140:5

23 But you know, O LORD,
all their plots to kill[i] me.
Do not forgive[j] their crimes
or blot out their sins from your sight.
Let them be overthrown before you;
deal with them in the time of your anger.

18:23 [i]Jer 11:21 [j]Ps 109:14

19 This is what the LORD says: "Go and buy a clay jar from a potter.[k] Take along some of the elders[l]
of the people and of the priests 2 and go out to the Valley of Ben Hinnom,[m] near the entrance of
the Potsherd Gate. There proclaim the words I tell you, 3 and say, 'Hear the word of the LORD, O kings[n] of
Judah and people of Jerusalem. This is what the LORD Almighty, the God of Israel, says: Listen! I am go-
ing to bring a disaster[o] on this place that will make the ears of everyone who hears of it tingle.[p] 4 For they
have forsaken[q] me and made this a place of foreign gods; they have burned sacrifices[r] in it to gods that
neither they nor their fathers nor the kings of Judah ever knew, and they have filled this place with the
blood of the innocent.[s] 5 They have built the high places of Baal to burn their sons[t] in the fire as offer-
ings to Baal—something I did not command or mention, nor did it enter my mind.[u] 6 So beware, the
days are coming, declares the LORD, when people will no longer call this place Topheth or the Valley of Ben
Hinnom,[v] but the Valley of Slaughter.[w]
7 " 'In this place I will ruin[a] the plans of Judah and Jerusalem. I will make them fall by the sword be-

19:1 [k]Jer 18:2 [l]Nu 11:17
19:2 [m]Jos 15:8
19:3 [n]Jer 17:20 [o]Jer 6:19 [p]1Sa 3:11
19:4 [q]Dt 28:20; Isa 65:11 [r]Lev 18:21 [s]2Ki 21:16; Jer 2:34
19:5 [t]Lev 18:21; Ps 106:37-38 [u]Jer 7:31; 32:35
19:6 [v]Jos 15:8 [w]Jer 7:32

[a] 7 The Hebrew for *ruin* sounds like the Hebrew for *jar* (see verses 1 and 10).

18:17 For "wind from the east," see the note on 4:11.
18:18 Reading the law to the Israelites (and teaching it to them) was one of the primary duties of the priests (Dt 33:10; Mal 2:4–9; see "The Levites and the Priests" on p. 648).
19:1 The Hebrew for "jar" implies a vessel with a narrow neck (perhaps the water decanter frequently found in excavations), ranging from 5 to 12 inches (12.7 to 30.5 cm) in height.

The Hebrew for "elders" means "bearded ones," possibly reflecting the age, wisdom, experience and influence necessary for a man expected to function as an elder. As heads of local families and tribes, elders had a recognized position also among the Babylonians, Hittites, Egyptians, Moabites and Midianites. Elders in Israel were of two kinds: The "elders of the people" performed primarily civil functions, such as counsel, arbitration, sentencing and military leadership. The "elders . . . of the priests" carried out primarily religious functions.

19:2 For the "Valley of Ben Hinnom," see the notes on 2:23 and 7:31.

The Jerusalem Targum (an ancient Aramaic paraphrase) identifies the Potsherd Gate (so called because it overlooked the main dump for broken pottery) with the Dung Gate of Nehemiah 2:13 (see the note there).
19:4 The pronoun "they" includes all those who attempted to combine the worship of idols with that of the one true God. The Hebrew for "burned sacrifices" is always translated "burned incense" elsewhere in Jeremiah (see the note on 1:16).

"The blood of the innocent" refers to the blood of godly people shed by wicked King Manasseh (see 15:4 and its note; see also 2Ki 21:16).
19:7 See the note on 7:33.

19:7 [x]Lev 26:17; Dt 28:25 [y]Jer 16:4; 34:20 [z]Ps 79:2
19:8 [a]Jer 18:16
19:9 [b]Lev 26:29; Dt 28:49-57; La 4:10 [c]Isa 9:20

fore their enemies,[x] at the hands of those who seek their lives, and I will give their carcasses[y] as food[z] to
the birds of the air and the beasts of the earth. 8 I will devastate this city and make it an object of scorn;[a]
all who pass by will be appalled and will scoff because of all its wounds. 9 I will make them eat[b] the flesh
of their sons and daughters, and they will eat one another's flesh during the stress of the siege imposed
on them by the enemies[c] who seek their lives.'

19:10 [d]ver 1
19:11 [e]Ps 2:9; Isa 30:14 [f]Jer 7:32
19:13 [g]Jer 32:29; 52:13 [h]Dt 4:19; Ac 7:42 [i]Jer 7:18; Eze 20:28

10 "Then break the jar[d] while those who go with you are watching, 11 and say to them, 'This is what the
LORD Almighty says: I will smash[e] this nation and this city just as this potter's jar is smashed and can-
not be repaired. They will bury[f] the dead in Topheth until there is no more room. 12 This is what I will do
to this place and to those who live here, declares the LORD. I will make this city like Topheth. 13 The hous-
es[g] in Jerusalem and those of the kings of Judah will be defiled like this place, Topheth—all the houses
where they burned incense on the roofs to all the starry hosts[h] and poured out drink offerings[i] to other
gods.' "

19:14 [j]2Ch 20:5; Jer 26:2
19:15 [k]Ne 9:16; Jer 7:26; 17:23

14 Jeremiah then returned from Topheth, where the LORD had sent him to prophesy, and stood in the
court[j] of the LORD's temple and said to all the people, 15 "This is what the LORD Almighty, the God of Is-
rael, says: 'Listen! I am going to bring on this city and the villages around it every disaster I pronounced
against them, because they were stiff-necked[k] and would not listen to my words.' "

Jeremiah and Pashhur

20:1 [l]1Ch 24:14 [m]2Ki 25:18
20:2 [n]Jer 1:19 [o]Job 13:27 [p]Jer 37:13; 38:7; Zec 14:10
20:3 [q]ver 10
20:4 [r]Jer 29:21 [s]Jer 21:10 [t]Jer 52:27
20:5 [u]Jer 17:3 [v]2Ki 20:17
20:6 [w]Jer 14:15; La 2:14

20 When the priest Pashhur son of Immer,[l] the chief officer[m] in the temple of the LORD, heard Jer-
emiah prophesying these things, 2 he had Jeremiah the prophet beaten[n] and put in the stocks[o] at
the Upper Gate of Benjamin[p] at the LORD's temple. 3 The next day, when Pashhur released him from the
stocks, Jeremiah said to him, "The LORD's name for you is not Pashhur, but Magor-Missabib.[a][q] 4 For this
is what the LORD says: 'I will make you a terror to yourself and to all your friends; with your own eyes[r]
you will see them fall by the sword of their enemies. I will hand[s] all Judah over to the king of Babylon,
who will carry[t] them away to Babylon or put them to the sword. 5 I will hand over to their enemies all the
wealth[u] of this city—all its products, all its valuables and all the treasures of the kings of Judah. They
will take it away[v] as plunder and carry it off to Babylon. 6 And you, Pashhur, and all who live in your house
will go into exile to Babylon. There you will die and be buried, you and all your friends to whom you have
prophesied[w] lies.' "

Jeremiah's Complaint

7 O LORD, you deceived[b] me, and I was deceived[b];
you overpowered me and prevailed.
I am ridiculed all day long;
everyone mocks me.

[a] 3 *Magor-Missabib* means *terror on every side.* [b] 7 Or *persuaded*

19:9 When Jerusalem's food supply ran out during the Babylonian siege in 586 B.C., cannibalism resulted (see La 2:20; 4:10; Eze 5:10). Such shocking activity was not unprecedented in Israel (see 2Ki 6:28–29) and would recur in A.D. 70 during the Roman siege of Jerusalem (see Zec 11:9 and its note): "A woman . . . who . . . had fled to Jerusalem . . . killed her son, roasted him, and ate one half, concealing and saving the rest" (Josephus, *Wars*, 6.3.4).

19:11 Egyptians of the Twelfth Dynasty (1963–1786 B.C.) inscribed the names of their enemies on pottery bowls and then smashed them, hoping in so doing to break their power (see "Curses and Imprecations" on p. 883).

19:13 Incense to pagan deities was often burned on rooftops (see 32:29; see also the notes on Isa 15:3; Jer 1:16). The kings of Judah had erected pagan altars on the roof of the palace in Jerusalem (see 2Ki 23:12), and the Ugaritic Epic of Kirta from the fourteenth century B.C. describes a similar practice: "Go to the top of a tower, bestride the top of the wall . . . Honor Baal with your sacrifice . . . Then descend . . . from the housetops" (see "The Kirta Epic" on p. 736).

Although it was prohibited, worship of the sun, moon and stars was common in Judah throughout much of the later history of the monarchy (see 2Ki 17:16; 21:3,5; 23:4–5; Zep 1:5).

For the phrase "drink offerings to other gods," see the note on Jeremiah 7:18.

20:1 Different men with the name "Pashhur" appear in the book of Jeremiah (see 21:1; 38:1 and their notes; see also "The Arad Ostraca" on p. 1215). Here Pashhur was a priest whose father, Immer, may have been a descendant of the head of the sixteenth division of priests in the Jerusalem temple (see 1Ch 24:14). Pashhur, as "chief officer" in the temple, was second only to the chief priest. Among other things, he headed the security detail for the large complex.

20:2 Jeremiah was probably beaten in accordance with the Mosaic Law (Dt 25:2–3) and then placed in "stocks" (lit., "restraint, confinement").

The Upper Gate of Benjamin was most likely the same as "the north gate of the inner court" (Eze 8:3; see also Eze 9:2). The phrase "at the LORD's temple" distinguishes the temple's Gate of Benjamin from "the Benjamin Gate" in the city wall (Jer 37:13; 38:7). Both gates were in the northern part of the city, facing the territory of Benjamin.

20:4 "The king of Babylon" refers to Nebuchadnezzar, who acceded to the Babylonian throne in 605 B.C. (see "Nebuchadnezzar" on p. 571).

20:5 This prophecy was fulfilled in 597 and 586 B.C.

20:6 The priest Pashhur had pretended to be a prophet. He probably went into exile in 597 B.C., because shortly after that year (see 29:2) two other men in succession replaced him as chief officer in the temple (see 29:25–26).

[8] Whenever I speak, I cry out
proclaiming violence and destruction.[x]
So the word of the LORD has brought me
insult and reproach[y] all day long.
[9] But if I say, "I will not mention him
or speak any more in his name,"
his word is in my heart like a fire,[z]
a fire shut up in my bones.
I am weary of holding it in;[a]
indeed, I cannot.
[10] I hear many whispering,
"Terror[b] on every side!
Report[c] him! Let's report him!"
All my friends[d]
are waiting for me to slip,[e] saying,
"Perhaps he will be deceived;
then we will prevail[f] over him
and take our revenge on him."

[11] But the LORD[g] is with me like a mighty warrior;
so my persecutors[h] will stumble and not prevail.[i]
They will fail and be thoroughly disgraced;[j]
their dishonor will never be forgotten.
[12] O LORD Almighty, you who examine the righteous
and probe the heart and mind,[k]
let me see your vengeance[l] upon them,
for to you I have committed[m] my cause.

20:8 [x]Jer 6:7 [y]2Ch 36:16; Jer 6:10
20:9 [z]Ps 39:3 [a]Job 32:18-20; Ac 4:20
20:10 [b]Ps 31:13; Jer 6:25 [c]Isa 29:21 [d]Ps 41:9 [e]Lk 11:53-54 [f]1Ki 19:2
20:11 [g]Jer 1:8; Ro 8:31 [h]Jer 17:18 [i]Jer 15:20 [j]Jer 23:40
20:12 [k]Jer 17:10 [l]Ps 54:7; 59:10 [m]Ps 62:8; Jer 11:20

ANCIENT TEXTS AND ARTIFACTS

The Desire for Justice in the Eloquent Peasant

JEREMIAH 21 Desire for justice was a major theme in many ancient writings. The Egyptian tale of the Eloquent Peasant (from the **Middle Kingdom**) is a prime example. An impoverished man, traveling to Egypt in search of food, was beaten and robbed of his provisions by a landholder named Nemty-nakht. When Nemty-nakht refused to return the poor man's possessions, the peasant appealed to the high steward of the district. The peasant's eloquent remarks concerning justice and equity were subsequently reported to the king, who, hoping to prompt more speeches from the peasant, ordered the high steward to make no reply to him but to secretly record all of his orations praising justice and admonishing against partiality. Taking the steward's silence as a sign of corruption, the peasant delivered nine beautifully crafted speeches regarding the duties of a righteous judge and the malignancy of corrupt officials. The king was so pleased with the peasant's articulate description of justice that he not only ordered the return of the man's stolen goods but apparently awarded him Nemty-nakht's possessions as well.

The cry for justice was also a common theme among the prophets of Israel. Jeremiah warned the king's house to deliver the poor from the oppressor who was robbing them (Jer 21:11–14). Refusal to execute justice would be met by the wrath of God. But God also promised a remedy for the corrupt rulers of his people: He would raise up a righteous branch from David's line to reign as king and to administer justice. This promised savior would be called "The LORD Our Righteousness" (23:6). Thus, Biblical Israel shared with other ancient cultures a desire for justice but received in response the promise of a unique answer to that desire.[1]

[1]See also "The Poor and the Afflicted in Ancient Wisdom Literature" on page 981.

13 Sing to the LORD!
Give praise to the LORD!
20:13 [n]Ps 35:10
He rescues[n] the life of the needy
from the hands of the wicked.

20:14 [o]Job 3:3; Jer 15:10
14 Cursed be the day I was born![o]
May the day my mother bore me not be blessed!
15 Cursed be the man who brought my father the news,
who made him very glad, saying,
"A child is born to you—a son!"
20:16 [p]Ge 19:25
16 May that man be like the towns[p]
the LORD overthrew without pity.
May he hear wailing in the morning,
a battle cry at noon.
20:17 [q]Job 10:18-19
17 For he did not kill me in the womb,[q]
with my mother as my grave,
her womb enlarged forever.
18 Why did I ever come out of the womb
to see trouble and sorrow
20:18 [r]Ps 90:9
and to end my days in shame?[r]

God Rejects Zedekiah's Request

21:1 [s]2Ki 24:18; Jer 52:1 [t]Jer 38:1 [u]2Ki 25:18; Jer 29:25; 37:3
21:2 [v]Jer 37:3,7 [w]2Ki 25:1 [x]Ps 44:1-4; Jer 32:17

21 The word came to Jeremiah from the LORD when King Zedekiah[s] sent to him Pashhur[t] son of
Malkijah and the priest Zephaniah[u] son of Maaseiah. They said: 2 "Inquire[v] now of the LORD for
us because Nebuchadnezzar[a][w] king of Babylon is attacking us. Perhaps the LORD will perform wonders[x]
for us as in times past so that he will withdraw from us."
3 But Jeremiah answered them, "Tell Zedekiah, 4 'This is what the LORD, the God of Israel, says: I am
21:4 [y]Jer 32:5 [z]Jer 37:8-10
about to turn[y] against you the weapons of war that are in your hands, which you are using to fight the
king of Babylon and the Babylonians[b] who are outside the wall besieging[z] you. And I will gather them
21:5 [a]Jer 6:12
inside this city. 5 I myself will fight against you with an outstretched hand[a] and a mighty arm in anger and
fury and great wrath. 6 I will strike down those who live in this city—both men and animals—and they
21:6 [b]Jer 14:12
21:7 [c]2Ki 25:7; Jer 52:9 [d]Jer 37:17; 39:5 [e]2Ch 36:17; Eze 7:9; Hab 1:6
will die of a terrible plague.[b] 7 After that, declares the LORD, I will hand over Zedekiah[c] king of Judah, his
officials and the people in this city who survive the plague, sword and famine, to Nebuchadnezzar king
of Babylon[d] and to their enemies who seek their lives. He will put them to the sword; he will show them
no mercy or pity or compassion.'[e]
8 "Furthermore, tell the people, 'This is what the LORD says: See, I am setting before you the way of life
21:9 [f]Jer 14:12 [g]Jer 38:2,17; 39:18; 45:5
and the way of death. 9 Whoever stays in this city will die by the sword, famine or plague.[f] But whoever
goes out and surrenders to the Babylonians who are besieging you will live; he will escape with his life.[g]
21:10 [h]Jer 44:11, 27; Am 9:4 [i]Jer 32:28; 38:2-3 [j]Jer 52:13
10 I have determined to do this city harm[h] and not good, declares the LORD. It will be given into the hands[i]
of the king of Babylon, and he will destroy it with fire.'[j]
21:11 [k]Jer 13:18
11 "Moreover, say to the royal house[k] of Judah, 'Hear the word of the LORD; 12 O house of David, this is
what the LORD says:

21:12 [l]Jer 22:3
" 'Administer justice[l] every morning;
rescue from the hand of his oppressor
the one who has been robbed,

[a] 2 Hebrew *Nebuchadrezzar,* of which *Nebuchadnezzar* is a variant; here and often in Jeremiah and Ezekiel [b] 4 Or *Chaldeans*; also in verse 9

20:16 "The towns the LORD overthrew" is a reference to Sodom and Gomorrah (see Ge 19:24–25,29; see also "The Destruction of Sodom and Gomorrah" on p. 32). By Jeremiah's time their wickedness had long been proverbial (see Dt 29:23; Jer 3:14; see also the note on Isa 1:9).

For "battle cry," see the note on Jeremiah 4:5. An attack at noon would have been a surprise (see the note on 6:4).

21:1 This "Pashhur" is not the same as the Pashhur of 20:1–6 (see 38:1), nor is this "Zephaniah" the prophet Zephaniah (see 29:25,29; 37:3; 52:24; see also Zep 1:1).

21:2 To "inquire ... of the LORD" was to make a request for knowledge or information (see Ge 25:22; 2Ki 22:13); it was not necessarily a plea for help.

In about 588 B.C. Nebuchadnezzar (see "Nebuchadnezzar" on p. 571) attacked Jerusalem because Zedekiah, the king of Judah, had rebelled against Babylon (see Jer 52:3).

21:4 The "Babylonians" were the Chaldeans (see the NIV text note), a Bedouin people until about 1000 B.C., at which time they had settled in southern Mesopotamia. They became the nucleus of Nebuchadnezzar's empire. (See "The Chaldeans" on p. 1402.)

or my wrath will break out and burn like fire
because of the evil you have done—
burn with no one to quench[m] it.
[13] I am against[n] you, ⌊Jerusalem,⌋
you who live above this valley[o]
on the rocky plateau,
declares the LORD—
you who say, "Who can come against us?
Who can enter our refuge?"[p]
[14] I will punish you as your deeds[q] deserve,
declares the LORD.
I will kindle a fire[r] in your forests[s]
that will consume everything around you.' "

21:12 [m]Isa 1:31
21:13 [n]Eze 13:8 [o]Ps 125:2 [p]Jer 49:4; Ob 1:3-4
21:14 [q]Isa 3:10-11 [r]2Ch 36:19; Jer 52:13 [s]Eze 20:47

Judgment Against Evil Kings

22 This is what the LORD says: "Go down to the palace of the king of Judah and proclaim this mes-
sage there: [2]'Hear the word of the LORD, O king of Judah, you who sit on David's throne[t]—you,
your officials and your people who come through these gates.[u] [3]This is what the LORD says: Do what is
just[v] and right. Rescue from the hand of his oppressor[w] the one who has been robbed. Do no wrong or
violence to the alien, the fatherless or the widow,[x] and do not shed innocent blood in this place. [4]For if
you are careful to carry out these commands, then kings[y] who sit on David's throne will come through
the gates of this palace, riding in chariots and on horses, accompanied by their officials and their peo-
ple. [5]But if you do not obey[z] these commands, declares the LORD, I swear[a] by myself that this palace will
become a ruin.' "

22:2 [t]Jer 17:25; Lk 1:32 [u]Jer 17:20
22:3 [v]Mic 6:8; Zec 7:9 [w]Ps 72:4; Jer 21:12 [x]Ex 22:22
22:4 [y]Jer 17:25
22:5 [z]Jer 17:27 [a]Heb 6:13

[6]For this is what the LORD says about the palace of the king of Judah:

"Though you are like Gilead to me,
like the summit of Lebanon,
I will surely make you like a desert,[b]
like towns not inhabited.
[7] I will send destroyers[c] against you,
each man with his weapons,
and they will cut[d] up your fine cedar beams
and throw them into the fire.

22:6 [b]Mic 3:12
22:7 [c]Jer 4:7 [d]Isa 10:34

[8]"People from many nations will pass by this city and will ask one another, 'Why has the LORD done
such a thing to this great city?'[e] [9]And the answer will be: 'Because they have forsaken the covenant of the
LORD their God and have worshiped and served other gods.[f]' "

[10] Do not weep for the dead[g] ⌊king⌋ or mourn[h] his loss;
rather, weep bitterly for him who is exiled,
because he will never return
nor see his native land again.

[11]For this is what the LORD says about Shallum[a][i] son of Josiah, who succeeded his father as king of Ju-
dah but has gone from this place: "He will never return. [12]He will die[j] in the place where they have led him
captive; he will not see this land again."

22:8 [e]Dt 29:25-26; 1Ki 9:8-9; Jer 16:10-11
22:9 [f]2Ki 22:17; 2Ch 34:25
22:10 [g]Ecc 4:2 [h]ver 18
22:11 [i]2Ki 23:31
22:12 [j]2Ki 23:34

[a] 11 Also called *Jehoahaz*

21:13 Jerusalem is surrounded on three sides by valleys (see the note on Isa 22:7).
21:14 The Hebrew for "forests" is singular and may refer figuratively to the "Palace of the Forest of Lebanon" (see the note on 1Ki 7:2).
22:1 The palace was at a lower elevation than the temple (see 26:10; 36:10–12); hence the words "Go down."
"The king of Judah" probably refers to Zedekiah.
22:6 Gilead and Lebanon were renowned for their forests, and Lebanon supplied cedar for the royal palace (see "Cedars of Lebanon" on p. 1043).
22:7 This is a vivid description of the Babylonians (the "destroyers"; see the note on 4:7) smashing the carved paneling of the Jerusalem temple with their axes and hatchets (see Ps 74:3–6).
22:10 The people were not to weep for Josiah ("the dead king"), who was killed at Megiddo and mourned by the people long after his death (see 2Ch 35:24–25). Rather, they were to mourn for Jehoahaz/Shallum, who was carried off to Egypt in 609 B.C. by the Egyptian pharaoh Neco (2Ki 23:34).
22:11 For "Shallum," see 1 Chronicles 3:15. "Shallum" was the king's personal name and "Jehoahaz" his throne name.

22:13 [k]Mic 3:10; Hab 2:9 [l]Lev 19:13; Jas 5:4
22:14 [m]Isa 5:8-9 [n]2Sa 7:2
22:15 [o]2Ki 23:25 [p]Ps 128:2; Isa 3:10
22:16 [q]Ps 72:1-4,12-13
22:17 [r]2Ki 24:4

13 "Woe to him who builds[k] his palace by
unrighteousness,
his upper rooms by injustice,
making his countrymen work for nothing,
not paying[l] them for their labor.
14 He says, 'I will build myself a great palace[m]
with spacious upper rooms.'
So he makes large windows in it,
panels it with cedar[n]
and decorates it in red.

15 "Does it make you a king
to have more and more cedar?
Did not your father have food and drink?
He did what was right and just,[o]
so all went well[p] with him.
16 He defended the cause of the poor and needy,[q]
and so all went well.
Is that not what it means to know me?"
declares the LORD.
17 "But your eyes and your heart
are set only on dishonest gain,
on shedding innocent blood[r]
and on oppression and extortion."

22:13–14 Rooms ("upper rooms") built on the flat rooftops of houses (2Ki 4:10–11) and palaces (Jer 22:13–14) featured latticed windows (2Ki 1:2) that afforded comfort in the heat of summer (see "The Israelite Town and Home" on p. 1205). The windows described here may well have been the same type as those uncovered in the ruins of Beth Hakkerem (see the note on Jer 6:1) by archaeologists in the early 1960s (see "Ramat Rahel," below). The extravagant paneling described here was similarly deplored by Haggai (see Hag 1:4).

ARCHAEOLOGICAL SITES

RAMAT RAHEL

JEREMIAH 22 Ramat Rahel, located between Jerusalem and Bethlehem,[1] was fortified during the eighth century B.C. and occupied, with some breaks, until the eighth century A.D. An Israelite citadel during the late seventh century B.C., it included a palace and administrative buildings. Archaeologists have discovered small, decorative capitals (the tops of columns that bear their weight) and columns with traces of red paint that formed the banister and railing of a window. Larger capitals were found with recesses at the top for ceiling beams, which were typically made of cedar wood.[2] These finds remarkably match the description of Jehoiakim's palace in Jeremiah 22:13–15; indeed, Ramat Rahel may have served as the king's summer palace (cf. Jer 36:22).

In addition, numerous jar handles were discovered there. Of those found, 145 were stamped with the Hebrew word *lmlk*, which means either "(belonging) to the king" (indicating that they were a royal stock) or "(certified) by the king" (specifying that they conformed to royal standards of weights and measures). Another handle was found stamped with the Hebrew words for "belonging to Eliakim, steward of Jehoiachin." This Eliakim may have been a subordinate of Jehoiachin, the son of Jehoiakim, who was exiled to Babylon in 597 B.C.[3] Later jar handles, stamped with "Jerusalem," "Judah," "Judah, the Governor," etc., indicate the site's use as an administrative center during the **Persian period**.

Evidence suggests that Ramat Rahel may be identified with Beth Hakkerem, which means "house of the vineyard" (Ne 3:14; Jer 6:1). Herodian remains include coins dated up to A.D. 69, the year before the destruction of Herod's temple.[4]

[1]See "Jerusalem" on page 1191 and "Bethlehem" on page 1487. [2]See "Cedars of Lebanon" on page 1043. [3]See "Jehoiachin in Captivity and Evil-Merodach" on page 1292. [4]See "Herod's Temple" on page 1648 and "Coins and Numismatics" on page 1699.

18 Therefore this is what the LORD says about Jehoiakim son of Josiah king of Judah:

"They will not mourn for him:
'Alas, my brother! Alas, my sister!'
They will not mourn for him:
'Alas, my master! Alas, his splendor!'
19 He will have the burial of a donkey—
dragged away and thrown[s] **22:19** [s]Jer 36:30
outside the gates of Jerusalem.

20 "Go up to Lebanon and cry out,
let your voice be heard in Bashan,
cry out from Abarim,[t] **22:20** [t]Nu 27:12
for all your allies are crushed.
21 I warned you when you felt secure,
but you said, 'I will not listen!'
This has been your way from your youth;[u] **22:21** [u]Jer 3:25; 32:30 [v]Jer 7:23-28
you have not obeyed[v] me.
22 The wind will drive all your shepherds away,
and your allies will go into exile.
Then you will be ashamed and disgraced
because of all your wickedness.
23 You who live in 'Lebanon,[a]'
who are nestled in cedar buildings,
how you will groan when pangs come upon you,
pain[w] like that of a woman in labor! **22:23** [w]Jer 4:31

24 "As surely as I live," declares the LORD, "even if you, Jehoiachin[b][x] son of Jehoiakim king of Judah, **22:24** [x]2Ki 24:6, 8; Jer 37:1
were a signet ring on my right hand, I would still pull you off. 25 I will hand you over[y] to those who seek **22:25** [y]2Ki 24:16; Jer 34:20
your life, those you fear—to Nebuchadnezzar king of Babylon and to the Babylonians.[c] 26 I will hurl[z] you **22:26** [z]2Ki 24:8; 2Ch 36:10
and the mother who gave you birth into another country, where neither of you was born, and there you
both will die. 27 You will never come back to the land you long to return to."

28 Is this man Jehoiachin a despised, broken pot,[a] **22:28** [a]Ps 31:12; Jer 48:38; Hos 8:8 [b]Jer 15:1 [c]Jer 17:4
an object no one wants?
Why will he and his children be hurled[b] out,
cast into a land[c] they do not know?
29 O land,[d] land, land, **22:29** [d]Jer 6:19; Mic 1:2
hear the word of the LORD!
30 This is what the LORD says:
"Record this man as if childless,[e] **22:30** [e]1Ch 3:18; Mt 1:12 [f]Jer 10:21
a man who will not prosper[f] in his lifetime,

[a] 23 That is, the palace in Jerusalem (see 1 Kings 7:2) [b] 24 Hebrew *Coniah,* a variant of *Jehoiachin;* also in verse 28
[c] 25 Or *Chaldeans*

22:19 A burial like that of a donkey was tantamount to no burial at all (see 36:30; see also the note on 7:33).
22:20 Lebanon, Bashan and Abarim were mountainous regions—the first two in the north and the third in the south—from which the whole land of Israel could be rhetorically addressed.

"Allies" (lit., "lovers") here refers to nations joined together by treaty. Judah's onetime allies included Egypt, Assyria (see 2:36), Edom, Moab, Ammon and Phoenicia (see 27:3), all of whom had been—or soon would be—conquered by Babylonia (see 27:6–7; 28:14; see also "Edom" on p. 1467, "Moab" on p. 292, "Ammon" on p. 364 and "Phoenicia" on p. 488.)
22:22 The initial fulfillment of this verse took place in 597 B.C.
22:23 See "Cedars of Lebanon" on page 1043.
22:24–30 These verses contain a prophecy against King Jehoiachin (fulfilled in 24:1; 29:2), who was also known as Coniah, a shortened form of Jeconiah. (See "Jehoiachin in Captivity and Evil-Merodach" on p. 1292.)
22:24 This curse on Jehoiachin was apparently reversed in Haggai 2:23.

For "signet ring," see the note on Haggai 2:23 and "Signet Rings" on page 728.
22:26 This was fulfilled in 597 B.C. when Jehoiachin and his mother, Nehushta, were exiled in Babylonia (see "Jehoiachin in Captivity and Evil-Merodach" on p. 1292).
22:30 The phrase "as if childless" is not meant in the sense of Jehoiachin's having no children at all (he had at least seven; see 1Ch 3:17–18); rather, he had none to sit on the throne of David in Judah. Jehoiachin's grandson Zerubbabel (1Ch 3:17–19; Mt 1:12) became governor of Judah (see Hag 1:1), but not king. Zedekiah was a son of Josiah (see Jer 37:1), not of Jehoiachin, and he and his sons died before Jehoiachin did (see 52:10–11). Jehoiachin therefore was Judah's last surviving Davidic king—until Jesus Christ.

for none of his offspring will prosper,
none will sit on the throne[g] of David
or rule anymore in Judah."

22:30 [g]Ps 94:20

The Righteous Branch

23 "Woe to the shepherds[h] who are destroying and scattering[i] the sheep of my pasture!"[j] declares
the LORD. 2 Therefore this is what the LORD, the God of Israel, says to the shepherds who tend my
people: "Because you have scattered my flock and driven them away and have not bestowed care on them,
I will bestow punishment on you for the evil[k] you have done," declares the LORD. 3 "I myself will gather
the remnant[l] of my flock out of all the countries where I have driven them and will bring them back to
their pasture, where they will be fruitful and increase in number. 4 I will place shepherds[m] over them who
will tend them, and they will no longer be afraid[n] or terrified, nor will any be missing,[o]" declares the
LORD.

23:1 [h]Jer 10:21; Eze 34:1-10; Zec 11:15-17 [i]Isa 56:11 [j]Eze 34:31
23:2 [k]Jer 21:12
23:3 [l]Isa 11:10-12; Jer 32:37; Eze 34:11-16
23:4 [m]Jer 3:15; 31:10; Eze 34:23 [n]Jer 30:10; 46:27-28 [o]Jn 6:39

5 "The days are coming," declares the LORD,
"when I will raise up to David[a] a righteous Branch,[p]
a King who will reign[q] wisely
and do what is just and right[r] in the land.
6 In his days Judah will be saved
and Israel will live in safety.
This is the name[s] by which he will be called:
The LORD Our Righteousness.[t]

23:5 [p]Isa 4:2 [q]Isa 9:7 [r]Isa 11:1; Zec 6:12
23:6 [s]Jer 33:16; Mt 1:21-23 [t]Ro 3:21-22; 1Co 1:30

7 "So then, the days are coming," declares the LORD, "when people will no longer say, 'As surely as the LORD
lives, who brought the Israelites up out of Egypt,'[u] 8 but they will say, 'As surely as the LORD lives, who
brought the descendants of Israel up out of the land of the north and out of all the countries where he
had banished them.' Then they will live in their own land."[v]

23:7 [u]Jer 16:14
23:8 [v]Isa 43:5-6; Am 9:14-15

Lying Prophets

9 Concerning the prophets:

My heart is broken within me;
all my bones tremble.
I am like a drunken man,
like a man overcome by wine,
because of the LORD
and his holy words.[w]
10 The land is full of adulterers;[x]
because of the curse[b] the land lies parched[c]
and the pastures[y] in the desert are withered.[z]
The ⌞prophets⌟ follow an evil course
and use their power unjustly.

23:9 [w]Jer 20:8-9
23:10 [x]Jer 9:2 [y]Ps 107:34; Jer 9:10 [z]Hos 4:2-3

11 "Both prophet and priest are godless;[a]
even in my temple[b] I find their wickedness,"
declares the LORD.

23:11 [a]Jer 6:13; 8:10; Zep 3:4 [b]Jer 7:10

12 "Therefore their path will become slippery;[c]
they will be banished to darkness
and there they will fall.
I will bring disaster on them
in the year they are punished,[d]"
declares the LORD.

23:12 [c]Ps 35:6; Jer 13:16 [d]Jer 11:23

[a] 5 Or *up from David's line* [b] 10 Or *because of these things* [c] 10 Or *land mourns*

23:5 "Branch" is a Messianic title. The Targum (ancient Aramaic paraphrase) reads "Messiah" here.

13 "Among the prophets of Samaria
I saw this repulsive thing:
They prophesied by Baal[e]
and led my people Israel astray.
14 And among the prophets of Jerusalem
I have seen something horrible:[f]
They commit adultery and live a lie.[g]
They strengthen the hands of evildoers,[h]
so that no one turns from his wickedness.
They are all like Sodom[i] to me;
the people of Jerusalem are like Gomorrah."[j]

15 Therefore, this is what the LORD Almighty says concerning the prophets:

"I will make them eat bitter food
and drink poisoned water,[k]
because from the prophets of Jerusalem
ungodliness has spread throughout the land."

16 This is what the LORD Almighty says:

"Do not listen[l] to what the prophets are prophesying to you;
they fill you with false hopes.
They speak visions[m] from their own minds,
not from the mouth[n] of the LORD.
17 They keep saying to those who despise me,
'The LORD says: You will have peace.'[o]
And to all who follow the stubbornness[p] of their hearts
they say, 'No harm[q] will come to you.'
18 But which of them has stood in the council of the LORD
to see or to hear his word?
Who has listened and heard his word?
19 See, the storm[r] of the LORD
will burst out in wrath,
a whirlwind swirling down
on the heads of the wicked.
20 The anger[s] of the LORD will not turn back[t]
until he fully accomplishes
the purposes of his heart.
In days to come
you will understand it clearly.
21 I did not send[u] these prophets,
yet they have run with their message;
I did not speak to them,
yet they have prophesied.
22 But if they had stood in my council,
they would have proclaimed my words to my people
and would have turned[v] them from their evil ways
and from their evil deeds.

23 "Am I only a God nearby,[w]"
declares the LORD,
"and not a God far away?
24 Can anyone hide[x] in secret places
so that I cannot see him?"
declares the LORD.
"Do not I fill heaven and earth?"[y]
declares the LORD.

23:13 [e]Jer 2:8
23:14 [f]Jer 5:30 [g]Jer 29:23 [h]Eze 13:22 [i]Ge 18:20 [j]Isa 1:9-10; Jer 20:16
23:15 [k]Jer 8:14; 9:15
23:16 [l]Jer 27:9-10,14; Mt 7:15 [m]Jer 14:14 [n]Jer 9:20
23:17 [o]Jer 8:11 [p]Jer 13:10 [q]Jer 5:12; Am 9:10; Mic 3:11
23:19 [r]Jer 25:32; 30:23
23:20 [s]2Ki 23:26 [t]Jer 30:24
23:21 [u]Jer 14:14; 27:15
23:22 [v]Jer 25:5; Zec 1:4
23:23 [w]Ps 139:1-10
23:24 [x]Job 22:12-14 [y]1Ki 8:27

23:25 [z]Jer 14:14 [a]ver 28,32; 25"I have heard what the prophets say who prophesy lies[z] in my name. They say, 'I had a dream![a] I
Jer 29:8 had a dream!' 26How long will this continue in the hearts of these lying prophets, who prophesy the de-
23:26 [b]1Ti 4:1-2 23:27 [c]Dt 13:1-3; lusions[b] of their own minds? 27They think the dreams they tell one another will make my people forget[c]
Jer 29:8 [d]Jdg 3:7; 8:33-34 my name, just as their fathers forgot[d] my name through Baal worship. 28Let the prophet who has a dream
tell his dream, but let the one who has my word speak it faithfully. For what has straw to do with grain?"
23:29 [e]Jer 5:14 declares the LORD. 29"Is not my word like fire,"[e] declares the LORD, "and like a hammer that breaks a rock
in pieces?

23:30 [f]Ps 34:16 [g]Dt 18:20; 30"Therefore," declares the LORD, "I am against[f] the prophets[g] who steal from one another words sup-
Jer 14:15 posedly from me. 31Yes," declares the LORD, "I am against the prophets who wag their own tongues and
23:31 [h]ver 17 yet declare, 'The LORD declares.'[h] 32Indeed, I am against those who prophesy false dreams,[i]" declares the
23:32 [i]ver 25 [j]Jer 7:8; La 2:14 LORD. "They tell them and lead my people astray with their reckless lies, yet I did not send or appoint
them. They do not benefit[j] these people in the least," declares the LORD.

False Oracles and False Prophets

23:33 [k]Mal 1:1 33"When these people, or a prophet or a priest, ask you, 'What is the oracle[a][k] of the LORD?' say to them,
[l]ver 39 'What oracle?[b] I will forsake[l] you, declares the LORD.' 34If a prophet or a priest or anyone else claims, 'This
23:34 [m]La 2:14 is the oracle[m] of the LORD,' I will punish[n] that man and his household. 35This is what each of you keeps
[n]Zec 13:3 23:35 [o]Jer 33:3; on saying to his friend or relative: 'What is the LORD's answer?'[o] or 'What has the LORD spoken?' 36But you
42:4 must not mention 'the oracle of the LORD' again, because every man's own word becomes his oracle and
23:36 [p]Gal 1:7-8; so you distort[p] the words of the living God, the LORD Almighty, our God. 37This is what you keep saying
2Pe 3:16 to a prophet: 'What is the LORD's answer to you?' or 'What has the LORD spoken?' 38Although you claim,
'This is the oracle of the LORD,' this is what the LORD says: You used the words, 'This is the oracle of the
LORD,' even though I told you that you must not claim, 'This is the oracle of the LORD.' 39Therefore, I will
23:39 [q]Jer 7:15 surely forget you and cast[q] you out of my presence along with the city I gave to you and your fathers. 40I
23:40 [r]Jer 20:11; Eze 5:14-15 will bring upon you everlasting disgrace[r]—everlasting shame that will not be forgotten."

Two Baskets of Figs

24:1 [s]2Ki 24:16; **24** After Jehoiachin[c][s] son of Jehoiakim king of Judah and the officials, the craftsmen and the arti-
2Ch 36:9; Jer 29:2 sans of Judah were carried into exile from Jerusalem to Babylon by Nebuchadnezzar king of Bab-
[t]Am 8:1-2 ylon, the LORD showed me two baskets of figs[t] placed in front of the temple of the LORD. 2One basket had
24:2 [u]Isa 5:4 very good figs, like those that ripen early; the other basket had very poor[u] figs, so bad they could not be
eaten.

24:3 [v]Jer 1:11; 3Then the LORD asked me, "What do you see,[v] Jeremiah?"
Am 8:2 "Figs," I answered. "The good ones are very good, but the poor ones are so bad they cannot be eaten."
4Then the word of the LORD came to me: 5"This is what the LORD, the God of Israel, says: 'Like these
good figs, I regard as good the exiles from Judah, whom I sent away from this place to the land of the
24:6 [w]Jer 29:10; Babylonians.[d] 6My eyes will watch over them for their good, and I will bring them back[w] to this land. I
Eze 11:17 [x]Jer 33:7; 42:10 will build[x] them up and not tear them down; I will plant them and not uproot them. 7I will give them a
24:7 [y]Isa 51:16; Jer 31:33; heart to know me, that I am the LORD. They will be my people,[y] and I will be their God, for they will re-
Heb 8:10 [z]Jer 32:40 turn[z] to me with all their heart.[a]
[a]Eze 11:19 8" 'But like the poor[b] figs, which are so bad they cannot be eaten,' says the LORD, 'so will I deal with Zed-
24:8 [b]Jer 29:17 [c]Jer 39:6 ekiah king of Judah, his officials[c] and the survivors[d] from Jerusalem, whether they remain in this land
[d]Jer 39:9 [e]Jer 44:1,26 or live in Egypt.[e] 9I will make them abhorrent[f] and an offense to all the kingdoms of the earth, a reproach
24:9 [f]Jer 15:4; 34:17 [g]Dt 28:25; and a byword,[g] an object of ridicule and cursing,[h] wherever I banish[i] them. 10I will send the sword,[j] fam-
1Ki 9:7 [h]Jer 29:18 [i]Dt 28:37 ine and plague[k] against them until they are destroyed from the land I gave to them and their fathers.' "
24:10 [j]Isa 51:19 [k]Jer 27:8

[a] 33 Or *burden* (see Septuagint and Vulgate) [b] 33 Hebrew; Septuagint and Vulgate *'You are the burden.* (The Hebrew for *oracle* and *burden* is the same.) [c] 1 Hebrew *Jeconiah,* a variant of *Jehoiachin* [d] 5 Or *Chaldeans*

23:26 "Hearts" and "minds" are alternative renderings of the same Hebrew word (see the note on Ps 7:9).
23:27 To forget the Lord's name was tantamount to forgetting him (see the note on 16:21). When Judah's ancestors forgot God, they began to serve Baal (see Jdg 3:7; 1Sa 12:9–10).
23:33 For "oracle," see the note on Isaiah 13:1.
24:1 Jehoiachin was carried into exile in 597 B.C. (see "Jehoiachin in Captivity and Evil-Merodach" on p. 1292). Officials, craftsmen and artisans were also deported, with only the poorest and weakest people being left behind in Judah. (For information on deportation, see the notes on 2Ki 17:24–41; 24:10–12; see also "Exile and Genocide in the Ancient Near East" on p. 1337.)
24:2 The first figs in June are especially juicy and delicious (see Isa 28:4; Hos 9:10; Mic 7:1; Na 3:12; see also "Food and Agriculture" on p. 390).
24:8 Those who "live in Egypt" may refer to those deported with Jehoahaz in 609 B.C. (see 2Ki 23:31–34; Jer 22:10–12) and/or to those who fled to Egypt after the Babylonians had defeated the Egyptians in the battle of Carchemish in 605 (see 46:2).

THE RELIABILITY OF THE BIBLE

THE 70 YEARS OF CAPTIVITY

JEREMIAH 25 The prophetic expression describing the time of Judah's captivity as "seventy years" (Jer 25:11,12; 29:10) has prompted speculation throughout the history of interpretation.

◆ The numeric systems of the ancient Near East were predominantly hexagesimal (based upon ascending groups of six), and the maximum number that could be easily calculated was 60. The number 70 may have been used to symbolically represent a numeric value of staggering proportions or perhaps the number of years representing a generation (Ps 90:10; Isa 23:15). The number 70 may have been used in the same way in Jeremiah 25, as in Isaiah's announcement that Tyre would be desolate for 70 years (Isa 23:15,17), and a similar usage may be reflected in the Black Stone of Esarhaddon, in which Marduk decreed displeasure against **Babylon** for 70 years.

◆ The original context of the prophetic word was the fourth year of Jehoiakim of Judah and the first of **Nebuchadnezzar** (605 B.C.).[1] "Until this very day" (Jer 25:3) Jeremiah anticipated a period of devastation and judgment during which Judah would serve Babylon.[2] Upon the completion of this interval, the prophet expected that divine judgment would be visited upon Babylon (vv. 12–13) and Judah and that Jerusalem would be restored (29:10–14).

King Jehoiakim began to serve the Babylonians by politically consigning Judah as a vassal state in 604 B.C. (2Ki 24:1). Almost 70 years later Babylon was captured by the **Persians**,[3] bringing about the end of Babylonian sovereignty over Judah and initiating the process of exilic return under Cyrus the Great (539/538 B.C.).[4]

The interpretation of Jeremiah's 70 years of captivity as the approximate period between 604–539/538 B.C. is more explicitly stated in later Biblical texts. According to 2 Chronicles 36:20–21, divine judgment was executed against the Judahites by the Babylonian king in that "they became servants to him and his sons until the kingdom of Persia came to power . . . until the seventy years were completed." Both the Chronicler (2Ch 36:22) and Ezra (Ezr 1:1) interpreted the edict of Cyrus, which authorized the return of the exiles and the rebuilding of the temple in Jerusalem (Ezr 1:2–4; 6:1–12), as the fulfillment of the prophetic word of Jeremiah.

A different calculation of the "seventy years of captivity" appears to underlie Zechariah 1:12 and 7:5. There it denotes the interval between the physical destruction of the temple (586 B.C.) and its rededication (515 B.C.).

[1]See "Nebuchadnezzar" on page 571. [2]See "Babylon" on page 1077. [3]See "Ancient Persian History Through Darius" on page 717. [4]See "Cyrus the Great" on page 669.

Seventy Years of Captivity

25 The word came to Jeremiah concerning all the people of Judah in the fourth year of Jehoiakim[l] — 25:1 [l]2Ki 24:2; Jer 36:1
son of Josiah king of Judah, which was the first year of Nebuchadnezzar[m] king of Babylon. 2 So — [m]2Ki 24:1
Jeremiah the prophet said to all the people of Judah[n] and to all those living in Jerusalem: 3 For twenty- — 25:2 [n]Jer 18:11
three years—from the thirteenth year of Josiah[o] son of Amon king of Judah until this very day—the — 25:3 [o]Jer 1:2
word of the LORD has come to me and I have spoken to you again and again,[p] but you have not listened.[q] — [p]Jer 11:7; 26:5 [q]Jer 7:26
4 And though the LORD has sent all his servants the prophets[r] to you again and again, you have not lis- — 25:4 [r]Jer 7:25
tened or paid any attention. 5 They said, "Turn now, each of you, from your evil ways and your evil prac-
tices, and you can stay in the land the LORD gave to you and your fathers for ever and ever. 6 Do not fol-
low other gods[s] to serve and worship them; do not provoke me to anger with what your hands have made. — 25:6 [s]Dt 8:19
Then I will not harm you."
7 "But you did not listen to me," declares the LORD, "and you have provoked me with what your hands
have made,[t] and you have brought harm[u] to yourselves." — 25:7 [t]Dt 32:21 [u]2Ki 21:15
8 Therefore the LORD Almighty says this: "Because you have not listened to my words, 9 I will summon[v] — 25:9 [v]Isa 13:3-5 [w]Jer 1:15
all the peoples of the north[w] and my servant[x] Nebuchadnezzar king of Babylon," declares the LORD, "and — [x]Jer 27:6

25:1 The date was 605 B.C. (see the note on Da 1:1; see also "The Problem of the Chronology of the Kings of Judah and Israel" on p. 508).

25:3 The "twenty-three years" includes nineteen years under Josiah and four under Jehoiakim (see v. 1). The "thirteenth year of Josiah" was 626 B.C. (or possibly as early as 627).

25:9 The "peoples of the north" is a reference to Babylonia and her allies.

The description of Nebuchadnezzar as God's "servant" is used not in the sense of "worshiper" but of "vassal" or agent in God's employ. In the book of Daniel this king would bear witness, through his own humiliation, that God is sovereign (Da 4:1–37; see "Neb-

I will bring them against this land and its inhabitants and against all the surrounding nations. I will com-
pletely destroy[a] them and make them an object of horror and scorn,[y] and an everlasting ruin. 10 I will
banish from them the sounds[z] of joy and gladness, the voices of bride and bridegroom,[a] the sound of
millstones[b] and the light of the lamp.[c] 11 This whole country will become a desolate wasteland,[d] and these
nations will serve the king of Babylon seventy years.[e]

12 "But when the seventy years[f] are fulfilled, I will punish the king of Babylon and his nation, the land
of the Babylonians,[b] for their guilt," declares the LORD, "and will make it desolate[g] forever. 13 I will bring
upon that land all the things I have spoken against it, all that are written in this book and prophesied by
Jeremiah against all the nations. 14 They themselves will be enslaved[h] by many nations[i] and great kings;
I will repay[j] them according to their deeds and the work of their hands."

25:9 [y]Jer 18:16
25:10 [z]Isa 24:8; Eze 26:13 [a]Jer 7:34 [b]Ecc 12:3-4 [c]Rev 18:22-23
25:11 [d]Jer 4:26-27; 12:11-12 [e]2Ch 36:21
25:12 [f]Jer 29:10 [g]Isa 13:19-22; 14:22-23
25:14 [h]Jer 27:7 [i]Jer 50:9; 51:27-28 [j]Jer 51:6

The Cup of God's Wrath

15 This is what the LORD, the God of Israel, said to me: "Take from my hand this cup[k] filled with the wine
of my wrath and make all the nations to whom I send you drink it. 16 When they drink it, they will stag-
ger[l] and go mad[m] because of the sword I will send among them."

17 So I took the cup from the LORD's hand and made all the nations to whom he sent[n] me drink it: 18 Je-
rusalem and the towns of Judah, its kings and officials, to make them a ruin and an object of horror and
scorn and cursing,[o] as they are today;[p] 19 Pharaoh king of Egypt, his attendants, his officials and all his
people, 20 and all the foreign people there; all the kings of Uz;[q] all the kings of the Philistines (those of Ash-
kelon,[r] Gaza, Ekron, and the people left at Ashdod); 21 Edom, Moab and Ammon;[s] 22 all the kings of Tyre
and Sidon;[t] the kings of the coastlands[u] across the sea; 23 Dedan, Tema, Buz and all who are in distant
places[c];[v] 24 all the kings of Arabia[w] and all the kings of the foreign people who live in the desert; 25 all the
kings of Zimri, Elam[x] and Media; 26 and all the kings of the north,[y] near and far, one after the other—
all the kingdoms on the face of the earth. And after all of them, the king of Sheshach[d][z] will drink it too.

27 "Then tell them, 'This is what the LORD Almighty, the God of Israel, says: Drink, get drunk[a] and vom-
it, and fall to rise no more because of the sword[b] I will send among you.' 28 But if they refuse to take the
cup from your hand and drink, tell them, 'This is what the LORD Almighty says: You must drink it! 29 See,
I am beginning to bring disaster[c] on the city that bears my Name,[d] and will you indeed go unpunished?[e]
You will not go unpunished, for I am calling down a sword upon all[f] who live on the earth, declares the
LORD Almighty.'

30 "Now prophesy all these words against them and say to them:

" 'The LORD will roar[g] from on high;
he will thunder[h] from his holy dwelling
and roar mightily against his land.

25:15 [k]Isa 51:17; Ps 75:8; Rev 14:10
25:16 [l]Na 3:11 [m]Jer 51:7
25:17 [n]Jer 1:10
25:18 [o]Jer 24:9 [p]Jer 44:22
25:20 [q]Job 1:1 [r]Jer 47:5
25:21 [s]Jer 49:1
25:22 [t]Jer 47:4 [u]Jer 31:10
25:23 [v]Jer 9:26; 49:32
25:24 [w]2Ch 9:14
25:25 [x]Ge 10:22
25:26 [y]Jer 50:3,9 [z]Jer 51:41
25:27 [a]ver 16,28; Hab 2:16 [b]Eze 21:4
25:29 [c]Jer 13:12-14 [d]1Pe 4:17 [e]Pr 11:31 [f]ver 30-31
25:30 [g]Isa 16:10; 42:13 [h]Joel 3:16; Am 1:2

[a] *9* The Hebrew term refers to the irrevocable giving over of things or persons to the LORD, often by totally destroying them.
[b] *12* Or *Chaldeans* [c] *23* Or *who clip the hair by their foreheads* [d] *26* *Sheshach* is a cryptogram for Babylon.

---

uchadnezzar's Madness" on p. 1391). Compare Isaiah 44:28, where the pagan ruler Cyrus is called the Lord's "shepherd," and Isaiah 45:1, where Cyrus is referred to as the Lord's "anointed."

25:11–12 The round number of "seventy years" (as in Ps 90:10; Isa 23:15) represents the period from 605 (see the notes on Jer 25:1; Da 1:1) to 538 B.C., which marked the beginning of Judah's return from exile (see 2Ch 36:20–23, as well as the note on Da 9:1). The 70 years of Zechariah 1:12 are not necessarily the same as those here and in 29:10 but probably represent the period from 586 (when Solomon's temple was destroyed) to 516 B.C. (when Zerubbabel's was completed). For a discussion of the calculation of the 70 years of captivity, see "The 70 Years of Captivity" on page 1234.

25:12 This was fulfilled when the city of Babylon was captured near the end of Jeremiah's 70 years by the Medes and Persians in 539 B.C. (see the note on vv. 11–12).

25:13 After the word "book," the Septuagint inserts the material found in chapters 46–51, although rearranged. (See "The Problem of the Septuagint Version of Jeremiah" on p. 1240 and "The Septuagint and the Masoretic Text" on p. 1254.)

25:14 "Many nations" is a reference to Media, Persia and their allies. The "great kings" refers to Cyrus and his associates.

25:20 For "Uz," see the note on Job 1:1.

For "Philistines," see "The Archaeology of Philistia" on page 370 and "Technological Supremacy of the Philistines' Iron Weapons" on page 414. The five main cities of the Philistines were Ashkelon, Gaza, Ekron, Ashdod and Gath (see the note on Jdg 1:18). According to the Greek historian Herodotus (2.157), the Egyptian pharaoh Psammetichus I (664–610 B.C.) destroyed Ashdod after a long siege, but it was inhabited again by Nehemiah's time. Gath was destroyed and apparently not rebuilt (in later centuries it is not mentioned with the other four cities; see Am 1:6–8; Zep 2:4; Zec 9:5–6).

25:21 See "Edom" on page 1467, "Moab" on page 292 and "Ammon" on page 364.

25:22 See "The Downfall of Tyre" on page 1345 and "Sidon" on page 1536.

The "coastlands across the sea" refer to the Mediterranean islands and maritime regions, some of which were Phoenician colonies (see Eze 27:15; Da 11:18 and their notes).

25:23 Dedan was located in an area of northwestern Arabia; the Dedanites were an Arab tribe associated with caravan trade. Tema was a desert oasis in northern Arabia about 400 miles (645 km) southwest of Babylon. Buz was a desert region in the east.

25:25 Elam lay east of Mesopotamia, northeast of the lower Tigris Valley (southwestern Iran).

Media lay east of Mesopotamia, northwest of Persia and south-southwest of the Caspian Sea (in northwestern Iran). The Medes were an Indo-European tribe related to the Persians. After the rise of Cyrus in 550 B.C. they became subordinate to the Persians. The name of the area was retained as late as the New Testament era.

25:26 "Sheshach" is a cryptogram for Babylon, formed by substituting the first consonant of the Hebrew alphabet for the last, the second for the next-to-last, etc. The purpose of this device is not fully understood.

25:30 See "The Winepress" on page 1171.

He will shout like those who tread the grapes,
shout against all who live on the earth.
31 The tumult will resound to the ends of the earth,
for the LORD will bring charges[i] against the nations;
he will bring judgment on all mankind
and put the wicked to the sword,' "
declares the LORD.

25:31 [i]Hos 4:1; Joel 3:2; Mic 6:2

32 This is what the LORD Almighty says:

"Look! Disaster is spreading
from nation to nation;[j]
a mighty storm[k] is rising
from the ends of the earth."

25:32 [j]Isa 34:2 [k]Jer 23:19

33 At that time those slain[l] by the LORD will be everywhere—from one end of the earth to the other. They
will not be mourned or gathered[m] up or buried,[n] but will be like refuse lying on the ground.

25:33 [l]Isa 66:16; Eze 39:17-20 [m]Jer 16:4 [n]Ps 79:3

34 Weep and wail, you shepherds;
roll[o] in the dust, you leaders of the flock.
For your time to be slaughtered[p] has come;
you will fall and be shattered like fine pottery.
35 The shepherds will have nowhere to flee,
the leaders of the flock no place to escape.[q]
36 Hear the cry of the shepherds,
the wailing of the leaders of the flock,
for the LORD is destroying their pasture.
37 The peaceful meadows will be laid waste
because of the fierce anger of the LORD.
38 Like a lion[r] he will leave his lair,
and their land will become desolate
because of the sword[a] of the oppressor
and because of the LORD's fierce anger.

25:34 [o]Jer 6:26 [p]Isa 34:6; Jer 50:27
25:35 [q]Job 11:20
25:38 [r]Jer 4:7

Jeremiah Threatened With Death

26 Early in the reign of Jehoiakim[s] son of Josiah king of Judah, this word came from the LORD: 2 "This
is what the LORD says: Stand in the courtyard[t] of the LORD's house and speak to all the people of
the towns of Judah who come to worship in the house of the LORD. Tell[u] them everything I command
you; do not omit[v] a word. 3 Perhaps they will listen and each will turn[w] from his evil way. Then I will re-
lent[x] and not bring on them the disaster I was planning because of the evil they have done. 4 Say to them,
'This is what the LORD says: If you do not listen[y] to me and follow my law,[z] which I have set before you,
5 and if you do not listen to the words of my servants the prophets, whom I have sent to you again and
again (though you have not listened[a]), 6 then I will make this house like Shiloh[b] and this city an object
of cursing[c] among all the nations of the earth.' "

26:1 [s]2Ki 23:36
26:2 [t]Jer 19:14 [u]Jer 1:17; Mt 28:20; Ac 20:27 [v]Dt 4:2
26:3 [w]Jer 36:7 [x]Jer 18:8
26:4 [y]Lev 26:14 [z]1Ki 9:6
26:5 [a]Jer 25:4
26:6 [b]Jos 18:1 [c]2Ki 22:19

7 The priests, the prophets and all the people heard Jeremiah speak these words in the house of the
LORD. 8 But as soon as Jeremiah finished telling all the people everything the LORD had commanded him
to say, the priests, the prophets and all the people seized him and said, "You must die! 9 Why do you proph-
esy in the LORD's name that this house will be like Shiloh and this city will be desolate and deserted?"[d]
And all the people crowded around Jeremiah in the house of the LORD.

26:9 [d]Jer 9:11

10 When the officials of Judah heard about these things, they went up from the royal palace to the
house of the LORD and took their places at the entrance of the New Gate of the LORD's house. 11 Then the

[a] 38 Some Hebrew manuscripts and Septuagint (see also Jer. 46:16 and 50:16); most Hebrew manuscripts *anger*

25:34–36 See the note on 3:15.
26:2 The "courtyard of the LORD's house" may have been near the New Gate (see v. 10; see also the note on 7:2).
26:6 See "The Destruction of Shiloh" on page 1200.
26:10 The "officials of Judah" were responsible for making legal decisions concerning disputes taking place in the temple precincts. The New Gate may have been the same as the "Upper Gate of Benjamin" (see 20:2 and its note).

priests and the prophets said to the officials and all the people, "This man should be sentenced to death[e] because he has prophesied against this city. You have heard it with your own ears!"

12 Then Jeremiah said to all the officials[f] and all the people: "The LORD sent me to prophesy[g] against this house and this city all the things you have heard.[h] 13 Now reform[i] your ways and your actions and obey the LORD your God. Then the LORD will relent and not bring the disaster he has pronounced against you. 14 As for me, I am in your hands;[j] do with me whatever you think is good and right. 15 Be assured, however, that if you put me to death, you will bring the guilt of innocent blood on yourselves and on this city and on those who live in it, for in truth the LORD has sent me to you to speak all these words in your hearing."

16 Then the officials[k] and all the people said to the priests and the prophets, "This man should not be sentenced to death![l] He has spoken to us in the name of the LORD our God."

17 Some of the elders of the land stepped forward and said to the entire assembly of people, 18 "Micah[m] of Moresheth prophesied in the days of Hezekiah king of Judah. He told all the people of Judah, 'This is what the LORD Almighty says:

" 'Zion[n] will be plowed like a field,
Jerusalem will become a heap of rubble,[o]
the temple hill[p] a mound overgrown with thickets.'[a][q]

19 "Did Hezekiah king of Judah or anyone else in Judah put him to death? Did not Hezekiah[r] fear the LORD and seek his favor? And did not the LORD relent,[s] so that he did not bring the disaster[t] he pronounced against them? We are about to bring a terrible disaster[u] on ourselves!"

20 (Now Uriah son of Shemaiah from Kiriath Jearim[v] was another man who prophesied in the name of the LORD; he prophesied the same things against this city and this land as Jeremiah did. 21 When King Jehoiakim[w] and all his officers and officials heard his words, the king sought to put him to death. But Uriah heard of it and fled[x] in fear to Egypt. 22 King Jehoiakim, however, sent Elnathan[y] son of Acbor to Egypt, along with some other men. 23 They brought Uriah out of Egypt and took him to King Jehoiakim, who had him struck down with a sword and his body thrown into the burial place of the common people.)

24 Furthermore, Ahikam[z] son of Shaphan supported Jeremiah, and so he was not handed over to the people to be put to death.

Judah to Serve Nebuchadnezzar

27 Early in the reign of Zedekiah[b][a] son of Josiah king of Judah, this word came to Jeremiah from the LORD: 2 This is what the LORD said to me: "Make a yoke[b] out of straps and crossbars and put it on your neck. 3 Then send word to the kings of Edom, Moab, Ammon,[c] Tyre and Sidon through the envoys who have come to Jerusalem to Zedekiah king of Judah. 4 Give them a message for their masters and say, 'This is what the LORD Almighty, the God of Israel, says: "Tell this to your masters: 5 With my great power and outstretched arm[d] I made the earth and its people and the animals that are on it, and I give[e] it to anyone I please. 6 Now I will hand all your countries over to my servant[f] Nebuchadnezzar[g] king of

26:11 [e]Dt 18:20; Jer 18:23; 38:4; Mt 26:66; Ac 6:11
26:12 [f]Jer 1:18 [g]Am 7:15; Ac 4:18-20; 5:29 [h]ver 2,15
26:13 [i]Jer 7:5; Joel 2:12-14
26:14 [j]Jer 38:5
26:16 [k]Ac 23:9 [l]Ac 5:34-39; 23:29
26:18 [m]Mic 1:1 [n]Isa 2:3 [o]Ne 4:2; Jer 9:11 [p]Mic 4:1; Zec 8:3 [q]Jer 17:3
26:19 [r]2Ch 32:24-26; Isa 37:14-20 [s]Ex 32:14; 2Sa 24:16 [t]Jer 44:7 [u]Hab 2:10
26:20 [v]Jos 9:17
26:21 [w]1Ki 19:2 [x]Mt 10:23
26:22 [y]Jer 36:12, 25
26:24 [z]2Ki 22:12
27:1 [a]2Ch 36:11
27:2 [b]Jer 28:10, 13
27:3 [c]Jer 25:21
27:5 [d]Dt 9:29 [e]Ps 115:16
27:6 [f]Jer 25:9 [g]Jer 21:7; Eze 29:18-20

[a] *18* Micah 3:12 [b] *1* A few Hebrew manuscripts and Syriac (see also Jer. 27:3, 12 and 28:1); most Hebrew manuscripts *Jehoiakim* (Most Septuagint manuscripts do not have this verse.)

26:20 This Uriah is not mentioned elsewhere in the Old Testament, although his name may appear in one of the Lachish letters (see "The Lachish Ostraca" on p. 1252).

See "Kiriath Jearim" on page 406.

26:21 "Officers" (lit., "strong men") may refer to the royal bodyguard. Uriah's flight to Egypt was a fatal mistake (see v. 23), for he could on that account have been accused of treason and sedition.

26:22 Elnathan, the son of Acbor, was one of King Jehoiakim's highest officials (see 36:12) and perhaps Jehoiakim's father-in-law (see 2Ki 24:6,8). A man named Acbor (perhaps the father of this Elnathan) was one of King Josiah's officials (see 2Ki 22:12,14).

26:23 Mutual rights of extradition were a part of the treaty imposed on Judah by Egypt when Jehoiakim became the vassal of the Egyptian pharaoh Neco II (see 2Ki 23:34–35).

Commoners were buried in the Kidron Valley east of Jerusalem (see 2Ki 23:6; see also "Tombs in Ancient Israel" on p. 376).

26:24 Ahikam son of Shaphan was one of King Josiah's officials (see 2Ki 22:12,14; see also "The Huldah Delegation and Nathan-Melech, the Official" on p. 567), along with a man named Acbor (see the note on Jer 26:22). Ahikam was also the father of Gedaliah, who later became governor of Judah after Jerusalem was destroyed in 586 B.C. (see 40:5).

27:2 This yoke, the kind worn by oxen, was a symbol of political submission.

27:3 Edom, Moab and Ammon were lands to the east and south of Judah (see the note on 25:21), while Tyre and Sidon were prominent cities in Phoenicia, north of Judah (see the note on 25:22).

Envoys came to Zedekiah, perhaps to discuss rebellion against Babylonia. They may have counted on support from Egypt, where Psammetichus II had become pharaoh a year earlier (594 B.C.). Zedekiah went to Babylon in 593 (see 51:59), perhaps to be interrogated by Nebuchadnezzar. In any case, Zedekiah rebelled against him (see 52:3).

27:6 For the phrase "my servant Nebuchadnezzar," see the note on 25:9.

Babylon; I will make even the wild animals subject to him.[h] 7 All nations will serve[i] him and his son and
his grandson until the time[j] for his land comes; then many nations and great kings will subjugate[k] him.
8 " ' "If, however, any nation or kingdom will not serve Nebuchadnezzar king of Babylon or bow its
neck under his yoke, I will punish that nation with the sword, famine and plague, declares the LORD, un-
til I destroy it by his hand. 9 So do not listen to your prophets, your diviners, your interpreters of dreams,
your mediums[l] or your sorcerers who tell you, 'You will not serve the king of Babylon.' 10 They prophesy
lies[m] to you that will only serve to remove you far from your lands; I will banish you and you will perish.
11 But if any nation will bow its neck under the yoke[n] of the king of Babylon and serve him, I will let that
nation remain in its own land to till it and to live there, declares the LORD." ' "

12 I gave the same message to Zedekiah king of Judah. I said, "Bow your neck under the yoke of the king
of Babylon; serve him and his people, and you will live. 13 Why will you and your people die[o] by the sword,
famine and plague with which the LORD has threatened any nation that will not serve the king of Bab-
ylon? 14 Do not listen to the words of the prophets who say to you, 'You will not serve the king of Babylon,'
for they are prophesying lies[p] to you. 15 'I have not sent[q] them,' declares the LORD. 'They are prophesying
lies in my name.[r] Therefore, I will banish you and you will perish,[s] both you and the prophets who proph-
esy to you.' "

16 Then I said to the priests and all these people, "This is what the LORD says: Do not listen to the proph-
ets who say, 'Very soon now the articles[t] from the LORD's house will be brought back from Babylon.' They
are prophesying lies to you. 17 Do not listen to them. Serve the king of Babylon, and you will live. Why
should this city become a ruin? 18 If they are prophets and have the word of the LORD, let them plead[u]
with the LORD Almighty that the furnishings remaining in the house of the LORD and in the palace of the
king of Judah and in Jerusalem not be taken to Babylon. 19 For this is what the LORD Almighty says about
the pillars, the Sea,[v] the movable stands and the other furnishings[w] that are left in this city, 20 which Neb-
uchadnezzar king of Babylon did not take away when he carried[x] Jehoiachin[a][y] son of Jehoiakim king of
Judah into exile from Jerusalem to Babylon, along with all the nobles of Judah and Jerusalem— 21 yes,
this is what the LORD Almighty, the God of Israel, says about the things that are left in the house of the
LORD and in the palace of the king of Judah and in Jerusalem: 22 'They will be taken[z] to Babylon and there
they will remain until the day[a] I come for them,' declares the LORD. 'Then I will bring[b] them back and re-
store them to this place.' "

The False Prophet Hananiah

28 In the fifth month of that same year, the fourth year, early in the reign of Zedekiah[c] king of Ju-
dah, the prophet Hananiah son of Azzur, who was from Gibeon,[d] said to me in the house of the
LORD in the presence of the priests and all the people: 2 "This is what the LORD Almighty, the God of Is-
rael, says: 'I will break the yoke[e] of the king of Babylon. 3 Within two years I will bring back to this place
all the articles[f] of the LORD's house that Nebuchadnezzar king of Babylon removed from here and took
to Babylon. 4 I will also bring back to this place Jehoiachin[a][g] son of Jehoiakim king of Judah and all the
other exiles from Judah who went to Babylon,' declares the LORD, 'for I will break the yoke of the king of
Babylon.' "

27:6 [h]Jer 28:14; Da 2:37-38 **27:7** [i]2Ch 36:20 [j]Jer 25:12 [k]Jer 25:14; Da 5:28 **27:9** [l]Dt 18:11 **27:10** [m]Jer 23:25 **27:11** [n]Jer 21:9 **27:13** [o]Eze 18:31 **27:14** [p]Jer 14:14 **27:15** [q]Jer 23:21 [r]Jer 29:9 [s]Jer 6:15 **27:16** [t]2Ki 24:13; 2Ch 36:7,10; Jer 28:3; Da 1:2 **27:18** [u]1Sa 7:8 **27:19** [v]2Ki 25:13 [w]Jer 52:17-23 **27:20** [x]2Ch 36:10; Jer 24:1 [y]Jer 22:24 **27:22** [z]2Ki 25:13 [a]2Ch 36:21 [b]Ezr 1:7; 7:19 **28:1** [c]Jer 27:1,3 [d]Jos 9:3 **28:2** [e]Jer 27:12 **28:3** [f]2Ki 24:13 **28:4** [g]Jer 22:24-27

[a] 20,4 Hebrew *Jeconiah,* a variant of *Jehoiachin*

27:9 In the ancient Near East great significance was given to dreams, and dream interpretations were sought from experts trained in the techniques and methods of the day. Both the Egyptians and the Babylonians compiled "dream books," which contained sample dreams with a key to their interpretation. These books preserved the data concerning past dreams and interpretations, providing the security of "scientific" documentation. (See "Dream Oracles in the Ancient World" on p. 741.)

Diviners, mediums and sorcerers were forbidden in Israel (see Lev 19:26; Dt 18:10–11; see also "Akkadian Divination" on p. 277).

27:16 Some of the articles from the temple were carried off to Babylon by Nebuchadnezzar in 605 B.C. (see Da 1:1–2), others in 597 (see 2Ki 24:13) and still others in 586 (see Jer 27:21–22; 52:17–23).

27:22 This prophetic prediction was fulfilled when the articles were carried away in 586 B.C. (see 52:17–23) and returned in 538/537 (see Ezr 1:7–11).

28:1–17 Following the Babylonian capture of Jerusalem in 597 B.C. (see "The Last Days of Jerusalem" on p. 1197), Nebuchadnezzar plundered the temple, took King Jehoiachin and many other Judahites captive and appointed Zedekiah king (2Ki 24:15–17). Four years later Hananiah, the son of Azzur, a prophet from Gibeon, made a prediction in the temple before the priests and people, stipulating that within two years the temple vessels, Jehoiachin (also called Jeconiah) and the exiles would be returned (Jer 28:1–4; see "Jehoiachin in Captivity and Evil-Merodach" on p. 1292). God's response through the prophet Jeremiah was that the captives would remain in captivity and that, because he had lied to the people, Hananiah would die that very year (vv. 12–16). Two months later this did indeed occur (vv. 1,17).

A seal of Hananiah has been discovered in Jerusalem. The inscription, surrounded by a pomegranate-garland border, reads, "Belonging to Hananiah son of Azzur."

28:1 The date was 593 B.C.

28:3 Hananiah's prediction directly contradicted the words of Jeremiah (see 27:16–22).

28:4 Hananiah's prediction again contradicted Jeremiah's prophecy (see 22:24–27), which was fulfilled (see 52:34). Jehoiachin went to Babylon in 597 B.C. (see "Jehoiachin in Captivity and Evil-Merodach" on p. 1292).

5 Then the prophet Jeremiah replied to the prophet Hananiah before the priests and all the people who
were standing in the house of the LORD. 6 He said, "Amen! May the LORD do so! May the LORD fulfill the
words you have prophesied by bringing the articles of the LORD's house and all the exiles back to this
place from Babylon. 7 Nevertheless, listen to what I have to say in your hearing and in the hearing of all
the people: 8 From early times the prophets who preceded you and me have prophesied war, disaster and
28:8 [h]Lev 26:14-17; Isa 5:5-7 plague[h] against many countries and great kingdoms. 9 But the prophet who prophesies peace will be rec-
28:9 [i]Dt 18:22 ognized as one truly sent by the LORD only if his prediction comes true.[i]"
28:10 [j]Jer 27:2 10 Then the prophet Hananiah took the yoke[j] off the neck of the prophet Jeremiah and broke it, 11 and
28:11 [k]Jer 14:14; 27:10 he said[k] before all the people, "This is what the LORD says: 'In the same way will I break the yoke of Neb-
uchadnezzar king of Babylon off the neck of all the nations within two years.' " At this, the prophet Jer-
emiah went on his way.

12 Shortly after the prophet Hananiah had broken the yoke off the neck of the prophet Jeremiah, the
word of the LORD came to Jeremiah: 13 "Go and tell Hananiah, 'This is what the LORD says: You have bro-
ken a wooden yoke, but in its place you will get a yoke of iron. 14 This is what the LORD Almighty, the God
28:14 [l]Dt 28:48 of Israel, says: I will put an iron yoke[l] on the necks of all these nations to make them serve[m] Nebuchad-
[m]Jer 25:11 [n]Jer 27:6 nezzar king of Babylon, and they will serve him. I will even give him control over the wild animals.[n]' "
28:15 [o]Jer 29:31 15 Then the prophet Jeremiah said to Hananiah the prophet, "Listen, Hananiah! The LORD has not sent[o]
[p]Jer 20:6; 29:21; La 2:14; Eze 13:6 you, yet you have persuaded this nation to trust in lies.[p] 16 Therefore, this is what the LORD says: 'I am
28:16 [q]Ge 7:4 about to remove you from the face of the earth.[q] This very year you are going to die, because you have
[r]Dt 13:5; Jer 29:32 preached rebellion[r] against the LORD.' "

17 In the seventh month of that same year, Hananiah the prophet died.

A Letter to the Exiles

29 This is the text of the letter that the prophet Jeremiah sent from Jerusalem to the surviving el-
ders among the exiles and to the priests, the prophets and all the other people Nebuchadnezzar
29:1 [s]2Ch 36:10 had carried into exile from Jerusalem to Babylon.[s] 2 (This was after King Jehoiachin[a][t] and the queen
29:2 [t]2Ki 24:12; Jer 22:24-28 mother, the court officials and the leaders of Judah and Jerusalem, the craftsmen and the artisans had
gone into exile from Jerusalem.) 3 He entrusted the letter to Elasah son of Shaphan and to Gemariah son
of Hilkiah, whom Zedekiah king of Judah sent to King Nebuchadnezzar in Babylon. It said:

29:4 [u]Jer 24:5 4 This is what the LORD Almighty, the God of Israel, says to all those I carried[u] into exile from
29:5 [v]ver 28 Jerusalem to Babylon: 5 "Build[v] houses and settle down; plant gardens and eat what they produce.
6 Marry and have sons and daughters; find wives for your sons and give your daughters in marriage,
so that they too may have sons and daughters. Increase in number there; do not decrease. 7 Also,
29:7 [w]Ezr 6:10; 1Ti 2:1-2 seek the peace and prosperity of the city to which I have carried you into exile. Pray[w] to the LORD
for it, because if it prospers, you too will prosper." 8 Yes, this is what the LORD Almighty, the God of
29:8 [x]Jer 37:9 Israel, says: "Do not let the prophets and diviners among you deceive[x] you. Do not listen to the
[y]Jer 23:27 29:9 [z]Jer 14:14; 27:15 dreams you encourage them to have.[y] 9 They are prophesying lies[z] to you in my name. I have not
sent them," declares the LORD.

29:10 10 This is what the LORD says: "When seventy years[a] are completed for Babylon, I will come to
[a]2Ch 36:21; Jer 25:12; Da 9:2 you and fulfill my gracious promise to bring you back[b] to this place. 11 For I know the plans[c] I have
[b]Jer 21:22 29:11 [c]Ps 40:5 for you," declares the LORD, "plans to prosper you and not to harm you, plans to give you hope and
29:12 [d]Ps 145:19 a future. 12 Then you will call upon me and come and pray to me, and I will listen[d] to you. 13 You will
29:13 [e]Mt 7:7 [f]Dt 4:29; Jer 24:7 seek[e] me and find me when you seek me with all your heart.[f] 14 I will be found by you," declares
29:14 [g]Dt 30:3; Jer 30:3 the LORD, "and will bring you back[g] from captivity.[b] I will gather you from all the nations and places

[a] 2 Hebrew *Jeconiah,* a variant of *Jehoiachin* [b] 14 Or *will restore your fortunes*

28:13 The wooden yoke of submission (see the note on 27:2) would be exchanged for the iron yoke of servitude (see 28:14; 38:17–23).
28:16 Preaching rebellion was punishable by death (see Dt 13:5).
28:17 Hananiah died within two months (see v. 1), in fulfillment of Jeremiah's prediction (v. 16).
29:2 The "queen mother" (Nehushta), as well as the officials, craftsmen and artisans, was deported (see the note on 24:1; see also "Exile and Genocide in the Ancient Near East" on p. 1337).
29:3 Jeremiah's letter was placed in the ancient equivalent of a diplomatic pouch to ensure its safe arrival.

Gemariah was a common name in Jeremiah's time (see, e.g., 36:10). It has been found on one of the Lachish ostraca (see "The Lachish Ostraca" on p. 1252), as well as in at least two of the Elephantine papyri (see the note on 32:10–11; see also "The Elephantine Community" on p. 1264). Gemariah's father, Hilkiah, may have been the same Hilkiah who was high priest under Josiah. (See "Gemariah, the Official, and Jerahmeel, the King's Son" on p. 1255.)
29:7 Seeking and praying for the prosperity of one's captors was an unprecedented and unique concept in the ancient world.
29:8 See the note on 27:9.

THE PROBLEM OF THE SEPTUAGINT VERSION OF JEREMIAH

JEREMIAH 29 The book of Jeremiah has come down to us in two different versions: the Greek version, known as the **Septuagint**, and the Hebrew version, known as the **Masoretic Text**. There are significant differences between the two in terms of wording, structure and length.

- *Wording*: The Septuagint version of Jeremiah lacks approximately 2,700 words when compared with the Masoretic Text. At the same time, the Greek text contains some 100 words not found in the Hebrew.
- *Structure*: Chapters in the Septuagint version of Jeremiah do not follow the same order as those in the Masoretic Text. The most striking example of divergent arrangement concerns the oracles against foreign nations. In the Hebrew text these appear as chapters 46–51. In the Septuagint these same oracles fall in the middle of Jeremiah, between 25:13 and 25:15, with verse 14 being omitted.

  Furthermore, the order of the oracles is different. The Hebrew sequence is Egypt, Philistia, **Moab**, Ammon, Edom, Damascus, Kedar, **Elam** and **Babylon**. The Septuagint, on the other hand, addresses Elam, Egypt, Babylon, Philistia, Edom, Ammon, Kedar, Damascus and Moab, in that order.
- *Length*: The overall lengths of the two versions is unequal. The Septuagint text of Jeremiah is nearly one eighth shorter than the Hebrew version—the equivalent of seven to eight chapters.

Several partial Jeremiah manuscripts in Hebrew found among the **Dead Sea Scrolls** in Cave 4 may shed light on this complex issue. Two significant manuscripts agree with the Masoretic Text, but another text, a fragment containing Jeremiah 9:22—10:18, may reflect the wording of the Septuagint. This evidence suggests that the book of Jeremiah may have circulated in two distinct Hebrew editions, one of which we see through the window of the Septuagint translation and the other as the traditional version of the Masoretic Text. Even if the Septuagint does reflect the fact that the book circulated in more than one "edition," this does not imply that the Hebrew text of Jeremiah is untrustworthy. It simply appears that two versions of the text of Jeremiah emerged fairly early and that for a long time both circulated among the Jews. The book of Jeremiah itself suggests a rather involved and difficult history (see ch. 36). Jerusalem was destroyed and the people scattered, with some going to Babylon but others, including Jeremiah himself, traveling to Egypt. In light of the turmoil of these times, it is not surprising that there were different collections of the prophet's messages. The two anthologies of his sermons and writings could have circulated from very early and yet both be authentic collections of Jeremiah's prophecies. It is important, then, to note that the Septuagint is based upon a different version of the same book, as opposed to being a different book.[1]

Interior of Cave 4
Photograph: © Todd Bolen/Bible Places.com

[1]See "The Septuagint and the Masoretic Text" on page 1254, "Texts of the Old Testament" on page 1491 and "The Ancient Translations" on page 1492.

where I have banished you," declares the LORD, "and will bring you back to the place from which I
29:14 [h]Jer 23:3-4 carried you into exile."[h]
[15]You may say, "The LORD has raised up prophets for us in Babylon," [16]but this is what the LORD
says about the king who sits on David's throne and all the people who remain in this city, your
countrymen who did not go with you into exile— [17]yes, this is what the LORD Almighty says: "I will
29:17 [i]Jer 27:8 send the sword, famine and plague[i] against them and I will make them like poor figs[j] that are so
[j]Jer 24:8-10 bad they cannot be eaten. [18]I will pursue them with the sword, famine and plague and will make
29:18 [k]Jer 15:4 them abhorrent[k] to all the kingdoms of the earth and an object of cursing and horror,[l] of scorn and
[l]Dt 28:25; Jer 42:18 reproach, among all the nations where I drive them. [19]For they have not listened to my words,"[m]
29:19 [m]Jer 6:19 [n]Jer 25:4 declares the LORD, "words that I sent to them again and again by my servants the prophets.[n] And
you exiles have not listened either," declares the LORD.
29:20 [o]Jer 24:5 [20]Therefore, hear the word of the LORD, all you exiles whom I have sent[o] away from Jerusalem
to Babylon. [21]This is what the LORD Almighty, the God of Israel, says about Ahab son of Kolaiah
29:21 [p]ver 9; Jer 14:14 and Zedekiah son of Maaseiah, who are prophesying lies[p] to you in my name: "I will hand them
over to Nebuchadnezzar king of Babylon, and he will put them to death before your very eyes. [22]Be-
cause of them, all the exiles from Judah who are in Babylon will use this curse: 'The LORD treat you
29:22 [q]Da 3:6 like Zedekiah and Ahab, whom the king of Babylon burned[q] in the fire.' [23]For they have done out-
29:23 [r]Jer 23:14 [s]Heb 4:13 rageous things in Israel; they have committed adultery[r] with their neighbors' wives and in my
name have spoken lies, which I did not tell them to do. I know[s] it and am a witness to it," declares
the LORD.

Message to Shemaiah

[24]Tell Shemaiah the Nehelamite, [25]"This is what the LORD Almighty, the God of Israel, says: You sent
29:25 [t]2Ki 25:18; Jer 21:1 letters in your own name to all the people in Jerusalem, to Zephaniah[t] son of Maaseiah the priest, and
to all the other priests. You said to Zephaniah, [26]'The LORD has appointed you priest in place of Jehoiada
29:26 [u]2Ki 9:11; Hos 9:7; Jn 10:20 to be in charge of the house of the LORD; you should put any madman[u] who acts like a prophet into the
[v]Jer 20:2 stocks[v] and neck-irons. [27]So why have you not reprimanded Jeremiah from Anathoth, who poses as a
29:28 [w]ver 1 prophet among you? [28]He has sent this message[w] to us in Babylon: It will be a long time.[x] Therefore build[y]
[x]ver 10 [y]ver 5 houses and settle down; plant gardens and eat what they produce.' "
[29]Zephaniah the priest, however, read the letter to Jeremiah the prophet. [30]Then the word of the LORD
29:31 [z]ver 24 came to Jeremiah: [31]"Send this message to all the exiles: 'This is what the LORD says about Shemaiah[z] the
[a]Jer 14:14; 28:15 Nehelamite: Because Shemaiah has prophesied to you, even though I did not send[a] him, and has led you
to believe a lie, [32]this is what the LORD says: I will surely punish Shemaiah the Nehelamite and his descen-
29:32 [b]1Sa 2:30-33 dants.[b] He will have no one left among this people, nor will he see the good[c] things I will do for my peo-
[c]ver 10 [d]Jer 28:16 ple, declares the LORD, because he has preached rebellion[d] against me.' "

Restoration of Israel

30 This is the word that came to Jeremiah from the LORD: [2]"This is what the LORD, the God of Isra-
30:2 [e]Isa 30:8 el, says: 'Write[e] in a book all the words I have spoken to you. [3]The days are coming,' declares the
30:3 [f]Jer 29:14 [g]Jer 16:15 LORD, 'when I will bring[f] my people Israel and Judah back from captivity[a] and restore[g] them to the land
I gave their forefathers to possess,' says the LORD."
[4]These are the words the LORD spoke concerning Israel and Judah: [5]"This is what the LORD says:

30:5 [h]Jer 6:25 " 'Cries of fear[h] are heard—
terror, not peace.

[a] 3 Or *will restore the fortunes of my people Israel and Judah*

29:22 The Babylonians used fire as a method of execution (see Da 3:6,24). This is attested in sections 25, 110 and 157 of the Code of Hammurabi (an ancient Babylonian law code; see "Hammurabi" on p. 271).
29:24 Shemaiah was a false prophet (see v. 31).
29:25 This Zephaniah was not the prophet of that name (see the note on 21:1).
29:26 This Jehoiada was not the priest during the days of King Joash (see 2Ki 12:7).
29:27 For "Anathoth," see the note on 1:1.
29:32 See the note on 28:16.

30:1—33:26 Chapters 30–33 are often called Jeremiah's "book of consolation." The entire section can be dated to 587 B.C., the year before Jerusalem was destroyed by Nebuchadnezzar and its people exiled to Babylon.
30:2 For information on writing materials and literacy in ancient Israel, see the note on Exodus 17:14; see also "Sumerian Scribal Education" on page 539, "The Scribe" on page 682 and "Writing Materials in the Ancient World" on page 2037.
30:3 The northern kingdom of Israel was exiled in 721 B.C., and the southern kingdom of Judah would meet the same fate in 586 B.C.

[6] Ask and see:
Can a man bear children?
Then why do I see every strong man
with his hands on his stomach like a woman in labor,[i]
every face turned deathly pale?
[7] How awful that day[j] will be!
None will be like it.
It will be a time of trouble[k] for Jacob,
but he will be saved[l] out of it.

[8] " 'In that day,' declares the LORD Almighty,
'I will break the yoke[m] off their necks
and will tear off their bonds;
no longer will foreigners enslave them.[n]
[9] Instead, they will serve the LORD their God
and David[o] their king,[p]
whom I will raise up for them.
[10] " 'So do not fear,[q] O Jacob my servant;[r]
do not be dismayed, O Israel,'
declares the LORD.

'I will surely save[s] you out of a distant place,
your descendants from the land of their exile.
Jacob will again have peace and security,[t]
and no one will make him afraid.
[11] I am with you and will save you,'
declares the LORD.
'Though I completely destroy all the nations
among which I scatter you,
I will not completely destroy[u] you.
I will discipline[v] you but only with justice;
I will not let you go entirely unpunished.'[w]

[12] "This is what the LORD says:
" 'Your wound is incurable,
your injury beyond healing.[x]
[13] There is no one to plead your cause,
no remedy for your sore,
no healing[y] for you.
[14] All your allies[z] have forgotten you;
they care nothing for you.
I have struck you as an enemy[a] would
and punished you as would the cruel,[b]
because your guilt is so great
and your sins[c] so many.
[15] Why do you cry out over your wound,
your pain that has no cure?
Because of your great guilt and many sins
I have done these things to you.

[16] " 'But all who devour[d] you will be devoured;
all your enemies will go into exile.[e]

30:6 [i]Jer 4:31
30:7 [j]Isa 2:12; Joel 2:11 [k]Zep 1:15 [l]ver 10
30:8 [m]Isa 9:4 [n]Eze 34:27
30:9 [o]Isa 55:3-4; Lk 1:69; Ac 2:30; 13:23 [p]Eze 34:23-24; 37:24; Hos 3:5
30:10 [q]Isa 43:5; Jer 46:27-28 [r]Isa 44:2 [s]Jer 29:14 [t]Isa 35:9
30:11 [u]Jer 4:27; 46:28 [v]Jer 10:24 [w]Am 9:8
30:12 [x]Jer 15:18
30:13 [y]Jer 8:22; 14:19; 46:11
30:14 [z]Jer 22:20; La 1:2 [a]Job 13:24 [b]Job 30:21 [c]Jer 5:6
30:16 [d]Isa 33:1; Jer 2:3; 10:25 [e]Isa 14:2; Joel 3:4-8

30:8 For "yoke," see the note on 27:2.
30:9 "David their king" refers to the Messiah (see the note on 23:5). The Targum (ancient Aramaic paraphrase) here reads "Messiah, the son of David, their king."
30:14 For "allies," see the note on 22:20.

30:16 [f]Jer 50:10

Those who plunder[f] you will be plundered;
all who make spoil of you I will despoil.
17 But I will restore you to health
and heal your wounds,'
declares the LORD,

30:17 [g]Jer 33:24

'because you are called an outcast,[g]
Zion for whom no one cares.'

18 "This is what the LORD says:

30:18 [h]ver 3; Jer 31:23 [i]Ps 102:13 [j]Jer 31:4,24,38

" 'I will restore the fortunes[h] of Jacob's tents
and have compassion[i] on his dwellings;
the city will be rebuilt[j] on her ruins,
and the palace will stand in its proper place.

30:19 [k]Isa 35:10; 51:11 [l]Isa 51:3 [m]Ps 126:1-2; Jer 31:4 [n]Jer 33:22 [o]Isa 60:9

19 From them will come songs[k] of thanksgiving[l]
and the sound of rejoicing.[m]
I will add to their numbers,[n]
and they will not be decreased;
I will bring them honor,[o]
and they will not be disdained.

30:20 [p]Isa 54:13; Jer 31:17 [q]Isa 54:14

20 Their children[p] will be as in days of old,
and their community will be established[q]
before me;
I will punish all who oppress them.

30:21 [r]ver 9 [s]Nu 16:5

21 Their leader[r] will be one of their own;
their ruler will arise from among them.
I will bring him near[s] and he will come close to me,
for who is he who will devote himself
to be close to me?'
declares the LORD.

22 " 'So you will be my people,
and I will be your God.' "

30:23 [t]Jer 23:19

23 See, the storm[t] of the LORD
will burst out in wrath,
a driving wind swirling down
on the heads of the wicked.

30:24 [u]Jer 4:8 [v]Jer 4:28 [w]Jer 23:19-20

24 The fierce anger[u] of the LORD will not turn back[v]
until he fully accomplishes
the purposes of his heart.
In days to come
you will understand[w] this.

31:1 [x]Jer 30:22

31 "At that time," declares the LORD, "I will be the God[x] of all the clans of Israel, and they will be my people."

2 This is what the LORD says:

31:2 [y]Nu 14:20 [z]Ex 33:14

"The people who survive the sword
will find favor[y] in the desert;
I will come to give rest[z] to Israel."

30:18 The Hebrew for "ruins" is *tel(l)*, referring to a mound resulting from the accumulation of years or centuries of debris caused by a successive series of towns having been built on the same site (see "Glossary" on page 2080).

30:20 The phrase "days of old" probably refers to the early days of the united kingdom, and especially to the reign of David.

30:21 Although the Targum renders "leader" and "ruler" as "Messiah" in this context, the terms probably refer in the first place to the rulers of Judah immediately following the exile. But Jesus Christ ultimately fulfilled the promise.

[3]The LORD appeared to us in the past,[a] saying:

"I have loved[a] you with an everlasting love;
I have drawn[b] you with loving-kindness.
[4]I will build you up again
and you will be rebuilt, O Virgin Israel.
Again you will take up your tambourines
and go out to dance with the joyful.[c]
[5]Again you will plant vineyards
on the hills of Samaria;[d]
the farmers will plant them
and enjoy their fruit.[e]
[6]There will be a day when watchmen cry out
on the hills of Ephraim,
'Come, let us go up to Zion,
to the LORD our God.' "[f]

[7]This is what the LORD says:

"Sing with joy for Jacob;
shout for the foremost[g] of the nations.
Make your praises heard, and say,
'O LORD, save[h] your people,
the remnant[i] of Israel.'
[8]See, I will bring them from the land of the north[j]
and gather[k] them from the ends of the earth.
Among them will be the blind[l] and the lame,[m]
expectant mothers and women in labor;
a great throng will return.
[9]They will come with weeping;[n]
they will pray as I bring them back.
I will lead[o] them beside streams of water
on a level[p] path where they will not stumble,
because I am Israel's father,[q]
and Ephraim is my firstborn son.

[10]"Hear the word of the LORD, O nations;
proclaim it in distant coastlands:[r]
'He who scattered Israel will gather[s] them
and will watch over his flock like a shepherd.'[t]
[11]For the LORD will ransom Jacob
and redeem[u] them from the hand of those stronger[v] than they.
[12]They will come and shout for joy on the heights[w] of Zion;
they will rejoice in the bounty[x] of the LORD—
the grain, the new wine and the oil,[y]
the young of the flocks and herds.
They will be like a well-watered garden,[z]
and they will sorrow[a] no more.

31:3 [a]Dt 4:37 [b]Hos 11:4
31:4 [c]Jer 30:19
31:5 [d]Jer 50:19 [e]Isa 65:21; Am 9:14
31:6 [f]Isa 2:3; Jer 50:4-5; Mic 4:2
31:7 [g]Dt 28:13; Isa 61:9 [h]Ps 14:7; 28:9 [i]Isa 37:31
31:8 [j]Jer 3:18; 23:8 [k]Dt 30:4; Eze 34:12-14 [l]Isa 42:16 [m]Eze 34:16; Mic 4:6
31:9 [n]Ps 126:5 [o]Isa 63:13 [p]Isa 49:11 [q]Ex 4:22; Jer 3:4
31:10 [r]Isa 66:19; Jer 25:22 [s]Jer 50:19 [t]Isa 40:11; Eze 34:12
31:11 [u]Isa 44:23; 48:20 [v]Ps 142:6
31:12 [w]Eze 17:23; Mic 4:1 [x]Joel 3:18 [y]Hos 2:21-22 [z]Isa 58:11 [a]Isa 65:19; Jn 16:22; Rev 7:17

[a] 3 Or *LORD has appeared to us from afar*

31:4 Tambourines were used on joyful occasions (see Ps 68:25; see also "Ancient Musical Instruments" on p. 797), especially following a military victory. Dancing in ancient times was often a religious activity (see 2Sa 6:14; Ps 149:3 and its note; 150:4).
31:5 Sargon II conquered Samaria in 722/721 B.C. (see 2Ki 17:24), but the northern kingdom's former capital would someday be resettled by God's people.
31:6 Watchmen were stationed at the city gates (see Ne 11:19) and on the walls (see 2Sa 18:24–27; 2Ki 9:17–20; Isa 62:6) and also patrolled the streets at night (see SS 5:7). They were accountable to warn of danger, as well as to observe and report upon the appearance of the various phases of the moon in order to fix the times of the important feasts.

In ancient Israel a person always went "up" to Jerusalem (see, e.g., Ezr 1:3; 7:7; Isa 2:3; Jn 2:13), not only because its elevation was above the surrounding countryside but also because it was the royal city and the center of the nation's religious life.

31:13 [b]Isa 61:3 [c]Ps 30:11; Isa 51:11
31:14 [d]ver 25
31:15 [e]Jos 18:25 [f]Ge 37:35 [g]Jer 10:20; Mt 2:17-18*
31:16 [h]Isa 25:8; 30:19 [i]Ru 2:12 [j]Jer 30:3; Eze 11:17
31:18 [k]Job 5:17 [l]Hos 4:16 [m]Ps 80:3
31:19 [n]Eze 36:31 [o]Eze 21:12; Lk 18:13
31:20 [p]Hos 4:4; 11:8 [q]Isa 55:7; 63:15; Mic 7:18
31:21 [r]Jer 50:5 [s]Isa 52:11 [t]ver 4

13 Then maidens will dance and be glad,
young men and old as well.
I will turn their mourning[b] into gladness;
I will give them comfort and joy[c] instead of sorrow.
14 I will satisfy[d] the priests with abundance,
and my people will be filled with my bounty,"
declares the LORD.

15 This is what the LORD says:

"A voice is heard in Ramah,[e]
mourning and great weeping,
Rachel weeping for her children
and refusing to be comforted,[f]
because her children are no more."[g]

16 This is what the LORD says:

"Restrain your voice from weeping
and your eyes from tears,[h]
for your work will be rewarded,[i]"
declares the LORD.

"They will return[j] from the land of the enemy.
17 So there is hope for your future,"
declares the LORD.

"Your children will return to their own land.

18 "I have surely heard Ephraim's moaning:
'You disciplined[k] me like an unruly calf,[l]
and I have been disciplined.
Restore[m] me, and I will return,
because you are the LORD my God.
19 After I strayed,[n]
I repented;
after I came to understand,
I beat[o] my breast.
I was ashamed and humiliated
because I bore the disgrace of my youth.'
20 Is not Ephraim my dear son,
the child in whom I delight?
Though I often speak against him,
I still remember[p] him.
Therefore my heart yearns for him;
I have great compassion[q] for him,"
declares the LORD.

21 "Set up road signs;
put up guideposts.
Take note of the highway,[r]
the road that you take.
Return,[s] O Virgin[t] Israel,
return to your towns.

31:15 Ramah was located about five miles (eight km) north of Jerusalem. The people of Jerusalem passed through Ramah on their way to exile in Babylonia.

Rachel, the grandmother of Ephraim and Manasseh (see Ge 30:22–24; 48:1–2), the two most powerful tribes in the northern kingdom, is here a personification of the northern kingdom (sometimes called "Ephraim"). See "Rachel's Tomb" on page 411.

31:19 Beating one's breast was an expression of grief and mourning. Similar expressions are found in other ancient literature, such as the Babylonian Descent of Ishtar (see "The Descent of Ishtar" on p. 356) and Homer's *Iliad* (15.397–398; 16.125) and *Odyssey* (13.198–199). See also "Sackcloth and Ashes: Rituals of Lamentation" on page 820.

31:21 "Road signs" were tombstone-shaped markers (see 2Ki 23:17; Eze 39:15).

22 How long will you wander,[u]
O unfaithful[v] daughter?
The LORD will create a new thing on earth—
a woman will surround[a] a man."

23 This is what the LORD Almighty, the God of Israel, says: "When I bring them back from captivity,[b w]
the people in the land of Judah and in its towns will once again use these words: 'The LORD bless you,
O righteous dwelling,[x] O sacred mountain.'[y] 24 People will live[z] together in Judah and all its towns—
farmers and those who move about with their flocks. 25 I will refresh the weary and satisfy the faint."[a]
26 At this I awoke[b] and looked around. My sleep had been pleasant to me.
27 "The days are coming," declares the LORD, "when I will plant[c] the house of Israel and the house of
Judah with the offspring of men and of animals. 28 Just as I watched over them to uproot and tear down,
and to overthrow, destroy and bring disaster,[d] so I will watch over them to build and to plant,"[e] declares
the LORD. 29 "In those days people will no longer say,

'The fathers[f] have eaten sour grapes,
and the children's teeth are set on edge.'[g]

30 Instead, everyone will die for his own sin;[h] whoever eats sour grapes—his own teeth will be set on
edge.

31 "The time is coming," declares the LORD,
"when I will make a new covenant[i]
with the house of Israel
and with the house of Judah.
32 It will not be like the covenant[j]
I made with their forefathers[k]
when I took them by the hand
to lead them out of Egypt,
because they broke my covenant,
though I was a husband to[c] them,[d]"
declares the LORD.
33 "This is the covenant I will make with the house of Israel
after that time," declares the LORD.
"I will put my law in their minds
and write it on their hearts.[l]
I will be their God,
and they will be my people.[m]
34 No longer will a man teach[n] his neighbor,
or a man his brother, saying, 'Know the LORD,'
because they will all know[o] me,
from the least of them to the greatest,"
declares the LORD.
"For I will forgive[p] their wickedness
and will remember their sins[q] no more."

35 This is what the LORD says,

he who appoints[r] the sun
to shine by day,

31:22 [u]Jer 2:23 [v]Jer 3:6
31:23 [w]Jer 30:18 [x]Isa 1:26 [y]Ps 48:1; Zec 8:3
31:24 [z]Zec 8:4-8
31:25 [a]Jn 4:14
31:26 [b]Zec 4:1
31:27 [c]Eze 36:9-11; Hos 2:23
31:28 [d]Jer 18:8; 44:27 [e]Jer 1:10
31:29 [f]La 5:7 [g]Eze 18:2
31:30 [h]Isa 3:11; Gal 6:7
31:31 [i]Jer 32:40; Eze 37:26; Lk 22:20; Heb 8:8-12*; 10:16-17
31:32 [j]Ex 24:8 [k]Dt 5:3
31:33 [l]2Co 3:3 [m]Jer 24:7; Heb 10:16
31:34 [n]1Jn 2:27 [o]Jn 6:45 [p]Isa 54:13; Jer 33:8; 50:20 [q]Mic 7:19; Ro 11:27; Heb 10:17*
31:35 [r]Ps 136:7-9

[a] 22 Or *will go about* ⌊*seeking*⌋; or *will protect* [b] 23 Or *I restore their fortunes* [c] 32 Hebrew; Septuagint and Syriac */ and I turned away from* [d] 32 Or *was their master*

31:23 For "sacred mountain," see "Zaphon, Olympus, Sinai and Zion: The Mountain of God" on page 843.
31:29 This saying was apparently a popular proverb that had originated in a misunderstanding of such passages as Exodus 20:5 and Numbers 14:18, which teach that sins can have a negative effect upon an individual's descendants. In Jeremiah's time many people assumed that God's judgment against them was due not to their own sins but to those of their ancestors.
31:31 This verse contains the only Old Testament use of the phrase "new covenant," which (together with its use in the NT) has come down to us (via Latin) as "new testament," the name that was later applied to the distinctively Christian part of the Biblical canon.
31:32 The "covenant [God] made with their forefathers" was the covenant at Sinai, which eventually became known as the "old covenant" (2Co 3:14) or "first covenant" (Heb 8:7; 9:15,18).

who decrees the moon and stars
31:35 [s]Ge 1:16 [t]Jer 10:16 — to shine by night,[s]
who stirs up the sea
so that its waves roar—
the LORD Almighty is his name:[t]
31:36 [u]Isa 54:9-10; Jer 33:20-26 [v]Ps 89:36-37 — 36 "Only if these decrees[u] vanish from my sight,"
declares the LORD,
"will the descendants[v] of Israel ever cease
to be a nation before me."

37 This is what the LORD says:

31:37 [w]Jer 33:22 [x]Jer 33:24-26; Ro 11:1-5 — "Only if the heavens above can be measured[w]
and the foundations of the earth below be searched out
will I reject[x] all the descendants of Israel
because of all they have done,"
declares the LORD.

31:38 [y]Jer 30:18 [z]Ne 3:1 [a]2Ki 14:13; Zec 14:10 — 38 "The days are coming," declares the LORD, "when this city will be rebuilt[y] for me from the Tower of
Hananel[z] to the Corner Gate.[a] 39 The measuring line will stretch from there straight to the hill of Gareb
31:40 [b]Jer 7:31-32 [c]Jer 8:2 [d]2Sa 15:23; Jn 18:1 [e]2Ki 11:16 [f]Joel 3:17; Zec 14:21 — and then turn to Goah. 40 The whole valley[b] where dead bodies[c] and ashes are thrown, and all the terraces out to the Kidron Valley[d] on the east as far as the corner of the Horse Gate,[e] will be holy[f] to the LORD.
The city will never again be uprooted or demolished."

Jeremiah Buys a Field

32:1 [g]2Ki 25:1 [h]Jer 25:1; 39:1 — 32 This is the word that came to Jeremiah from the LORD in the tenth[g] year of Zedekiah king of Judah, which was the eighteenth[h] year of Nebuchadnezzar. 2 The army of the king of Babylon was
32:2 [i]Ne 3:25; Jer 37:21 — then besieging Jerusalem, and Jeremiah the prophet was confined in the courtyard of the guard[i] in the
royal palace of Judah.
32:3 [j]Jer 26:8-9 [k]ver 28; Jer 34:2-3 — 3 Now Zedekiah king of Judah had imprisoned him there, saying, "Why do you prophesy[j] as you do?
You say, 'This is what the LORD says: I am about to hand this city over to the king of Babylon, and he will
32:4 [l]Jer 38:18, 23; 39:5-7; 52:9 — capture[k] it. 4 Zedekiah king of Judah will not escape[l] out of the hands of the Babylonians[a] but will certainly be handed over to the king of Babylon, and will speak with him face to face and see him with his
32:5 [m]Jer 39:7; Eze 12:13 [n]Jer 21:4 — own eyes. 5 He will take[m] Zedekiah to Babylon, where he will remain until I deal with him, declares the
LORD. If you fight against the Babylonians, you will not succeed.' "[n]
6 Jeremiah said, "The word of the LORD came to me: 7 Hanamel son of Shallum your uncle is going to
32:7 [o]Lev 25:24-25; Ru 4:3-4; Mt 27:10* — come to you and say, 'Buy my field at Anathoth, because as nearest relative it is your right and duty[o] to buy it.'
8 "Then, just as the LORD had said, my cousin Hanamel came to me in the courtyard of the guard and
said, 'Buy my field at Anathoth in the territory of Benjamin. Since it is your right to redeem it and possess it, buy it for yourself.'
"I knew that this was the word of the LORD; 9 so I bought the field at Anathoth from my cousin Hana-
32:9 [p]Ge 23:16 — mel and weighed out for him seventeen shekels[b] of silver.[p] 10 I signed and sealed the deed, had it wit-
32:10 [q]Ru 4:9 — nessed,[q] and weighed out the silver on the scales. 11 I took the deed of purchase—the sealed copy

[a] 4 Or *Chaldeans*; also in verses 5, 24, 25, 28, 29 and 43 [b] 9 That is, about 7 ounces (about 200 grams)

31:38 The Tower of Hananel and the Corner Gate were at the eastern and western ends of the northern wall, respectively.
31:39 Gareb and Goah were probably west of Jerusalem.
31:40 The "valley" most likely refers to the Hinnom Valley (see the note on 2:23).
The Horse Gate was probably at the easternmost point in the city wall—a gate through which one could reach the Kidron Valley.
32:1 The date was 587 B.C., the year before Jerusalem fell to the Babylonians. The siege began in 588.
32:2 King Zedekiah had imprisoned Jeremiah in the courtyard of the guard, where the prophet remained until Jerusalem fell.
32:5 Zedekiah was taken to Babylon, where he eventually died (see 52:11).
32:7 In the Old Testament the word "uncle" is used to denote any kinsman on the father's side (cf. Lev 10:4).
For "Anathoth," see the note on 1:1.
32:8 Hanamel's request for Jeremiah to buy the land was in accordance with the ancient law of redemption (see Lev 25:23–25; see also the note on Ru 4:1–3 and "The Kinsman-Redeemer" on p. 391).
32:9 The shekel was the most common unit of weight in ancient times. Coinage was not yet commonly used in Judah.
32:10–11 The deed was sealed to guarantee its content and to prevent tampering. An unsealed copy was also available for ready reference, the authenticity of which could be guaranteed by the sealed copy if the unsealed copy should be lost, damaged or changed (deliberately or otherwise). Examples of tied and sealed papyri have been found at Elephantine in southern Egypt (see "The Elephantine Community" on p. 1264 and "Scrolls, Seals and Codices" on p. 2053).

containing the terms and conditions, as well as the unsealed copy— 12and I gave this deed to Baruch[r] **32:12** [r]ver 16;
son of Neriah,[s] the son of Mahseiah, in the presence of my cousin Hanamel and of the witnesses who had Jer 36:4; 43:3,6;
signed the deed and of all the Jews sitting in the courtyard of the guard. 45:1 [s]Jer 51:59
13"In their presence I gave Baruch these instructions: 14'This is what the LORD Almighty, the God of
Israel, says: Take these documents, both the sealed and unsealed copies of the deed of purchase, and put
them in a clay jar so they will last a long time. 15For this is what the LORD Almighty, the God of Israel, says:
Houses, fields and vineyards will again be bought in this land.'[t] **32:15** [t]ver 43-44;
16"After I had given the deed of purchase to Baruch son of Neriah, I prayed to the LORD: Jer 30:18; Am 9:14-15

17"Ah, Sovereign LORD,[u] you have made the heavens and the earth by your great power and out- **32:17** [u]Jer 1:6
stretched arm.[v] Nothing is too hard[w] for you. 18You show love[x] to thousands but bring the punish- [v]2Ki 19:15;
ment for the fathers' sins into the laps of their children[y] after them. O great and powerful God, Ps 102:25 [w]Mt 19:26
whose name is the LORD Almighty,[z] 19great are your purposes and mighty are your deeds.[a] Your **32:18** [x]Dt 5:10 [y]Ex 20:5 [z]Jer 10:16
eyes are open to all the ways of men;[b] you reward everyone according to his conduct and as his **32:19** [a]Isa 28:29
deeds deserve.[c] 20You performed miraculous signs and wonders in Egypt[d] and have continued [b]Pr 5:21; Jer 16:17
them to this day, both in Israel and among all mankind, and have gained the renown that is still [c]Jer 17:10; Mt 16:27
yours. 21You brought your people Israel out of Egypt with signs and wonders, by a mighty hand[e] **32:20** [d]Ex 9:16 **32:21** [e]Ex 6:6;
and an outstretched arm and with great terror.[f] 22You gave them this land you had sworn to give 1Ch 17:21; Da 9:15 [f]Dt 26:8
their forefathers, a land flowing with milk and honey.[g] 23They came in and took possession[h] of it, **32:22** [g]Ex 3:8; Jer 11:5
but they did not obey you or follow your law;[i] they did not do what you commanded them to do. **32:23** [h]Ps 44:2; 78:54-55
So you brought all this disaster[j] upon them. [i]Ne 9:26; Jer 11:8 [j]Da 9:14
24"See how the siege ramps are built up to take the city. Because of the sword, famine and
plague,[k] the city will be handed over to the Babylonians who are attacking it. What you said[l] has **32:24** [k]Jer 14:12
happened, as you now see. 25And though the city will be handed over to the Babylonians, you, [l]Dt 4:25-26;
O Sovereign LORD, say to me, 'Buy the field with silver and have the transaction witnessed.' " Jos 23:15-16

32:12 See "Baruch, Scribe of Jeremiah," below.
32:14 Documents discovered in clay jars at Elephantine and Qumran (west of the Dead Sea) were preserved almost intact for more than 2,000 years (see "The Elephantine Community" on p. 1264, "Biblical Interpretation at Qumran and Among the Early Rabbis" on p. 1603 and "Qumran and the New Testament" on p. 1679) .
32:15 Jeremiah's deed of purchase would have enabled him (or his heirs) to reclaim the field when normal economic conditions resumed after the exile.

ANCIENT TEXTS AND ARTIFACTS

Baruch, Scribe of Jeremiah

JEREMIAH 32 Baruch, a well-known figure in the book of Jeremiah, was Jeremiah's secretary, representative and advisor, with an official title of "scribe" (Jer 36:26,32). Evidence suggests that he was a royal scribe from a prominent family involved in this profession.[1] Jeremiah 32 describes how Baruch drew up and filed a deed of purchase for the prophet (vv. 6–15). Jeremiah also dictated his prophecies to Baruch, who wrote them down on leather scrolls with pen and ink (36:4,18). Baruch was forced to hide with Jeremiah because of official opposition to Jeremiah's prophecies (36:26). Curiously, after the fall of Jerusalem,[2] when Jeremiah told the Jews left behind in Judah that God forbade them to flee to Egypt, the angry Jews blamed Baruch for that message (42:1—43:7, especially 43:3). Jeremiah 45 gives us a glimpse of the man Baruch. He was distraught over all that had happened and wondered what would become of him, but God responded with both an admonition and a promise.

Two seal impressions of Baruch, both made from the same seal, have been acquired on the antiquities market in Israel. One of them is on display in the Israel Museum. The three-line inscription on each of them reads, "Belonging to Berekyahu, son of Neriyahu, the scribe." Berekyahu is a longer form of Baruch's name; it includes the divine element "Yahu," or **Yahweh**. The other seal, including a fingerprint (no doubt that of Baruch himself) is held in a private collection.

[1]See "The Scribe" on page 682. [2]See "The Last Days of Jerusalem" on page 1197.

26 Then the word of the LORD came to Jeremiah: 27 "I am the LORD, the God of all mankind.[m] Is anything
too hard for me? 28 Therefore, this is what the LORD says: I am about to hand this city over to the Babylo-
nians and to Nebuchadnezzar[n] king of Babylon, who will capture it.[o] 29 The Babylonians who are attack-
ing this city will come in and set it on fire; they will burn it down,[p] along with the houses[q] where the
people provoked me to anger by burning incense on the roofs to Baal and by pouring out drink offerings[r]
to other gods.

30 "The people of Israel and Judah have done nothing but evil in my sight from their youth;[s] indeed,
the people of Israel have done nothing but provoke[t] me with what their hands have made,[u] declares the
LORD. 31 From the day it was built until now, this city has so aroused my anger and wrath that I must re-
move[v] it from my sight. 32 The people of Israel and Judah have provoked me by all the evil[w] they have
done—they, their kings and officials, their priests and prophets, the men of Judah and the people of Je-
rusalem. 33 They turned their backs[x] to me and not their faces; though I taught[y] them again and again,
they would not listen or respond to discipline. 34 They set up their abominable idols in the house that
bears my Name and defiled[z] it. 35 They built high places for Baal in the Valley of Ben Hinnom to sacrifice
their sons and daughters[a] to Molech,[a] though I never commanded, nor did it enter my mind,[b] that they
should do such a detestable thing and so make Judah sin.

36 "You are saying about this city, 'By the sword, famine and plague[c] it will be handed over to the king
of Babylon'; but this is what the LORD, the God of Israel, says: 37 I will surely gather[d] them from all the
lands where I banish them in my furious anger and great wrath; I will bring them back to this place and
let them live in safety.[e] 38 They will be my people,[f] and I will be their God. 39 I will give them singleness[g]
of heart and action, so that they will always fear me for their own good and the good of their children
after them. 40 I will make an everlasting covenant[h] with them: I will never stop doing good to them, and
I will inspire them to fear me, so that they will never turn away from me.[i] 41 I will rejoice in doing them
good[j] and will assuredly plant[k] them in this land with all my heart and soul.

42 "This is what the LORD says: As I have brought all this great calamity on this people, so I will give
them all the prosperity I have promised[l] them. 43 Once more fields will be bought[m] in this land of which
you say, 'It is a desolate waste, without men or animals, for it has been handed over to the Babylonians.'
44 Fields will be bought for silver, and deeds[n] will be signed, sealed and witnessed in the territory of Ben-
jamin, in the villages around Jerusalem, in the towns of Judah and in the towns of the hill country, of the
western foothills and of the Negev,[o] because I will restore[p] their fortunes,[b] declares the LORD."

Promise of Restoration

33 While Jeremiah was still confined in the courtyard[q] of the guard, the word of the LORD came to
him a second time: 2 "This is what the LORD says, he who made the earth,[r] the LORD who formed
it and established it—the LORD is his name:[s] 3 'Call[t] to me and I will answer you and tell you great and
unsearchable things you do not know.' 4 For this is what the LORD, the God of Israel, says about the hous-
es in this city and the royal palaces of Judah that have been torn down to be used against the siege[u]
ramps[v] and the sword 5 in the fight with the Babylonians[c]: 'They will be filled with the dead bodies of the
men I will slay in my anger and wrath.[w] I will hide my face[x] from this city because of all its wickedness.

6 " 'Nevertheless, I will bring health and healing to it; I will heal my people and will let them enjoy
abundant peace and security. 7 I will bring Judah[y] and Israel back from captivity[d][z] and will rebuild them
as they were before.[a] 8 I will cleanse[b] them from all the sin they have committed against me and will for-
give[c] all their sins of rebellion against me. 9 Then this city will bring me renown, joy, praise[d] and honor[e]
before all nations on earth that hear of all the good things I do for it; and they will be in awe and will
tremble at the abundant prosperity and peace I provide for it.'

10 "This is what the LORD says: 'You say about this place, "It is a desolate waste, without men or ani-
mals."[f] Yet in the towns of Judah and the streets of Jerusalem that are deserted, inhabited by neither men

32:27 [m]Nu 16:22
32:28 [n]2Ch 36:17 [o]ver 3
32:29 [p]2Ch 36:19; Jer 21:10; 37:8, 10; 52:13 [q]Jer 19:13 [r]Jer 44:18
32:30 [s]Jer 22:21 [t]Jer 8:19 [u]Jer 25:7
32:31 [v]2Ki 23:27; 24:3
32:32 [w]Isa 1:4-6; Da 9:8
32:33 [x]Jer 2:27; Eze 8:16 [y]Jer 7:13
32:34 [z]Jer 7:30
32:35 [a]Lev 18:21 [b]Jer 7:31; 19:5
32:36 [c]ver 24
32:37 [d]Jer 23:3,6 [e]Dt 30:3; Eze 34:28
32:38 [f]Jer 24:7; 2Co 6:16*
32:39 [g]Eze 11:19
32:40 [h]Isa 55:3 [i]Jer 24:7
32:41 [j]Dt 30:9 [k]Jer 24:6; 31:28; Am 9:15
32:42 [l]Jer 31:28
32:43 [m]ver 15
32:44 [n]ver 10 [o]Jer 17:26 [p]Jer 33:7,11,26
33:1 [q]Jer 32:2-3; 37:21; 38:28
33:2 [r]Jer 10:16 [s]Ex 3:15; 15:3
33:3 [t]Isa 55:6; Jer 29:12
33:4 [u]Eze 4:2 [v]Jer 32:24; Hab 1:10
33:5 [w]Jer 21:4-7 [x]Isa 8:17
33:7 [y]Jer 32:44 [z]Jer 30:3; Am 9:14 [a]Isa 1:26
33:8 [b]Heb 9:13-14 [c]Jer 31:34; Mic 7:18; Zec 13:1
33:9 [d]Jer 13:11 [e]Isa 62:7; Jer 3:17
33:10 [f]Jer 32:43

[a] 35 Or *to make their sons and daughters pass through* ⌊*the fire*⌋ [b] 44 Or *will bring them back from captivity* [c] 5 Or *Chaldeans*
[d] 7 Or *will restore the fortunes of Judah and Israel*

32:29 See the note on 19:13.
32:35 For "Molech," see "Human Sacrifice in the Ancient Near East" on page 182.
32:44 For "the Negev," see "The Negev: Its Climate and Features" on page 34.
33:1–26 This section is not found in the Septuagint. See "The Septuagint and the Masoretic Text" on page 1254 and "The Problem of the Septuagint Version of Jeremiah" on page 1240.
33:1 See the note on 32:2.
33:4 The houses were torn down so that their stones could be used to rebuild the city's walls. For "siege ramps," see "Siege Warfare" on page 465.

nor animals, there will be heard once more 11the sounds of joy and gladness,[g] the voices of bride and
bridegroom, and the voices of those who bring thank offerings[h] to the house of the LORD, saying,

> "Give thanks to the LORD Almighty,
> for the LORD is good;[i]
> his love endures forever."[j]

For I will restore the fortunes of the land as they were before,' says the LORD.
12"This is what the LORD Almighty says: 'In this place, desolate[k] and without men or animals—in all its
towns there will again be pastures for shepherds to rest their flocks.[l] 13In the towns of the hill country, of
the western foothills and of the Negev,[m] in the territory of Benjamin, in the villages around Jerusalem and
in the towns of Judah, flocks will again pass under the hand[n] of the one who counts them,' says the LORD.
14" 'The days are coming,' declares the LORD, 'when I will fulfill the gracious promise[o] I made to the
house of Israel and to the house of Judah.

> 15" 'In those days and at that time
> I will make a righteous[p] Branch[q] sprout from David's line;
> he will do what is just and right in the land.
> 16In those days Judah will be saved[r]
> and Jerusalem will live in safety.
> This is the name by which it[a] will be called:
> The LORD Our Righteousness.'[s]

17For this is what the LORD says: 'David will never fail[t] to have a man to sit on the throne of the house of
Israel, 18nor will the priests, who are Levites,[u] ever fail to have a man to stand before me continually to
offer burnt offerings, to burn grain offerings and to present sacrifices.[v]' "
19The word of the LORD came to Jeremiah: 20"This is what the LORD says: 'If you can break my cov-
enant with the day[w] and my covenant with the night, so that day and night no longer come at their ap-
pointed time, 21then my covenant[x] with David my servant—and my covenant with the Levites who are
priests ministering before me—can be broken and David will no longer have a descendant to reign on
his throne.[y] 22I will make the descendants of David my servant and the Levites who minister before me
as countless[z] as the stars of the sky and as measureless as the sand on the seashore.' "
23The word of the LORD came to Jeremiah: 24"Have you not noticed that these people are saying, 'The
LORD has rejected the two kingdoms[b][a] he chose'? So they despise[b] my people and no longer regard them
as a nation.[c] 25This is what the LORD says: 'If I have not established my covenant with day and night[d] and
the fixed laws of heaven and earth,[e] 26then I will reject[f] the descendants of Jacob[g] and David my servant
and will not choose one of his sons to rule over the descendants of Abraham, Isaac and Jacob. For I will
restore their fortunes[c][h] and have compassion on them.' "

Warning to Zedekiah

34 While Nebuchadnezzar king of Babylon and all his army and all the kingdoms and peoples[i] in
the empire he ruled were fighting against Jerusalem[j] and all its surrounding towns, this word
came to Jeremiah from the LORD: 2"This is what the LORD, the God of Israel, says: Go to Zedekiah[k] king
of Judah and tell him, 'This is what the LORD says: I am about to hand this city over to the king of Bab-
ylon, and he will burn it down.[l] 3You will not escape from his grasp but will surely be captured and hand-
ed over[m] to him. You will see the king of Babylon with your own eyes, and he will speak with you face to
face. And you will go to Babylon.
4" 'Yet hear the promise of the LORD, O Zedekiah king of Judah. This is what the LORD says concern-
ing you: You will not die by the sword; 5you will die peacefully. As people made a funeral fire[n] in honor
of your fathers, the former kings who preceded you, so they will make a fire in your honor and lament,
"Alas,[o] O master!" I myself make this promise, declares the LORD.' "

33:11 [g]Isa 51:3 [h]Lev 7:12 [i]1Ch 16:8; Ps 136:1 [j]1Ch 16:34; 2Ch 5:13; Ps 100:4-5
33:12 [k]Jer 32:43 [l]Isa 65:10; Eze 34:11-15
33:13 [m]Jer 17:26 [n]Lev 27:32
33:14 [o]Jer 29:10
33:15 [p]Ps 72:2 [q]Isa 4:2; 11:1; Jer 23:5
33:16 [r]Isa 45:17 [s]1Co 1:30
33:17 [t]2Sa 7:13; 1Ki 2:4; Ps 89:29-37; Lk 1:33
33:18 [u]Dt 18:1 [v]Heb 13:15
33:20 [w]Ps 89:36
33:21 [x]Ps 89:34 [y]2Ch 7:18
33:22 [z]Ge 15:5
33:24 [a]Eze 37:22 [b]Ne 4:4 [c]Jer 30:17
33:25 [d]Jer 31:35-36 [e]Ps 74:16-17
33:26 [f]Jer 31:37 [g]Isa 14:1 [h]ver 7
34:1 [i]Jer 27:7 [j]2Ki 25:1; Jer 39:1
34:2 [k]2Ch 36:11 [l]ver 22; Jer 32:29; 37:8
34:3 [m]2Ki 25:7; Jer 21:7; 32:4
34:5 [n]2Ch 16:14; 21:19 [o]Jer 22:18

[a] 16 Or *he* [b] 24 Or *families* [c] 26 Or *will bring them back from captivity*

34:1 Nebuchadnezzar's empire was vast (see "Nebuchadnezzar" on p. 571). As was common in ancient times, the nations subject to him were expected to supply troops to fight alongside him as their overlord. In a fourteenth-century B.C. treaty between the Hittite ruler Mursilis II and Duppi-Tessub, king of the Amorites, Mursilis stated, "If you do not send your son or brother with your foot soldiers and charioteers to help the Hittite king, you act in disregard of the gods of the oath."

34:5 The "funeral fire" was a memorial fire in honor of the deceased (see 2Ch 16:14; 21:19). This is not a reference to cremation, which, though practiced, was reserved primarily for serious offenders (Lev 20:14; 21:9; Jos 7:15,25).

6 Then Jeremiah the prophet told all this to Zedekiah king of Judah, in Jerusalem, 7 while the army of
the king of Babylon was fighting against Jerusalem and the other cities of Judah that were still holding
34:7 [p]Jos 10:3 [q]Jos 10:10; 2Ch 11:9 out—Lachish[p] and Azekah.[q] These were the only fortified cities left in Judah.

Freedom for Slaves

8 The word came to Jeremiah from the LORD after King Zedekiah had made a covenant with all the
34:8 [r]2Ki 11:17 [s]Ex 21:2; Lev 25:10,39-41; Ne 5:5-8 people[r] in Jerusalem to proclaim freedom[s] for the slaves. 9 Everyone was to free his Hebrew slaves, both
male and female; no one was to hold a fellow Jew in bondage.[t] 10 So all the officials and people who en-
34:9 [t]Lev 25:39-46 tered into this covenant agreed that they would free their male and female slaves and no longer hold
them in bondage. They agreed, and set them free. 11 But afterward they changed their minds and took
back the slaves they had freed and enslaved them again.
12 Then the word of the LORD came to Jeremiah: 13 "This is what the LORD, the God of Israel, says: I
34:13 [u]Ex 24:8 made a covenant with your forefathers[u] when I brought them out of Egypt, out of the land of slavery. I
said, 14 'Every seventh year each of you must free any fellow Hebrew who has sold himself to you. After
34:14 [v]Ex 21:2 [w]Dt 15:12; 2Ki 17:14 he has served you six years, you must let him go free.'[a][v] Your fathers, however, did not listen to me or pay
attention[w] to me. 15 Recently you repented and did what is right in my sight: Each of you proclaimed free-
34:15 [x]ver 8 [y]Jer 7:10-11; 32:34 dom to his countrymen.[x] You even made a covenant before me in the house that bears my Name.[y] 16 But
34:16 [z]Eze 3:20; 18:24 [a]Ex 20:7; Lev 19:12 now you have turned around[z] and profaned[a] my name; each of you has taken back the male and female
slaves you had set free to go where they wished. You have forced them to become your slaves again.
17 "Therefore, this is what the LORD says: You have not obeyed me; you have not proclaimed freedom
34:17 [b]Mt 7:2; Gal 6:7 [c]Dt 28:25, 64; Jer 29:18 for your fellow countrymen. So I now proclaim 'freedom' for you,[b] declares the LORD—'freedom' to fall
by the sword, plague and famine. I will make you abhorrent to all the kingdoms of the earth.[c] 18 The men
who have violated my covenant and have not fulfilled the terms of the covenant they made before me, I

[a] *14* Deut. 15:12

34:9 "Jew" is a shortened form of "Judahite" (an inhabitant of the kingdom of Judah, where a remnant of the Israelites was still living). Strictly speaking, the term "Jew" is properly applied only to the Old Testament people of God and their descendants from the time of the Babylonian exile forward.

34:11 When the Babylonian siege was temporaily lifted due to Egyptian intervention, the people of Judah reclaimed the slaves they had freed (in violation of Dt 15:12).

34:18 See "The Hittite Ritual of Passing Between the Pieces of a Sacrifice" on page 1251.

ANCIENT TEXTS AND ARTIFACTS

The Hittite Ritual of Passing Between the Pieces of a Sacrifice

JEREMIAH 34 Jeremiah 34:18–20 refers to Zedekiah's covenant with God, in which the people passed between the parts of a calf cut in two. A similar ceremony is described in Genesis 15. What was the significance of passing between the pieces of an animal that had been split in half? Ancient texts supply us with several parallels to the Biblical rite:

✣ A Middle **Hittite** text describes a purification ceremony. This ceremony required defeated troops to march between the severed halves of a human, a billy goat, a puppy and a piglet, with fires burning on each side. The troops were first to perform the ritual near a river, where they would sprinkle themselves with water as they marched; then they were to enact it in the plain in like manner.

✣ In an eighth-century B.C. **Aramaic** treaty between Ashurnirari V of Assyria and his **vassal** Matilu of Arpad, Matilu and his sons are likened to a spring lamb whose knuckle is placed in the mouth of its severed head, lest he should "sin" against the treaty with his lord.

✣ Esarhaddon (680–669 B.C.) of **Assyria** declared in a treaty that his vassal and the vassal's children, if he were to break the Assyrian king's covenant, were to be treated in the same manner as the animals that lay slaughtered and gutted before them.

The Hittite ritual is similar to its Biblical counterpart, but the Assyrian texts may help us to understand its true significance. Essentially, these rites served as self-imprecation oaths, by which people called down curses upon their own heads should they fail to keep their part of the covenant they were solemnly ratifying. The ritual was a way of saying, "May what happened to these animals happen to us if we break this covenant." Zedekiah's covenant symbolized what would befall covenant-breakers. In this case Zedekiah and his people did break the covenant, and the death and destruction the ritual enacted were indeed the outcome.

will treat like the calf they cut in two and then walked between its pieces.[d] 19The leaders of Judah and Je-
rusalem, the court officials,[e] the priests and all the people of the land who walked between the pieces of
the calf, 20I will hand over[f] to their enemies who seek their lives.[g] Their dead bodies will become food
for the birds of the air and the beasts of the earth.[h]
21"I will hand Zedekiah[i] king of Judah and his officials[j] over to their enemies who seek their lives, to
the army of the king of Babylon, which has withdrawn[k] from you. 22I am going to give the order, declares
the LORD, and I will bring them back to this city. They will fight against it, take[l] it and burn[m] it down.
And I will lay waste the towns of Judah so no one can live there."

34:18 [d]Ge 15:10
34:19 [e]Zep 3:3-4
34:20 [f]Jer 21:7 [g]Jer 11:21 [h]Dt 28:26; Jer 7:33; 19:7
34:21 [i]Jer 32:4 [j]Jer 39:6; 52:24-27 [k]Jer 37:5
34:22 [l]Jer 39:1-2 [m]Jer 39:8

ANCIENT TEXTS AND ARTIFACTS

The Lachish Ostraca

JEREMIAH 34 In 1935 18 **ostraca** (broken pieces of pottery used for writing) were discovered in a guard room below the gate tower inside the outer wall at Lachish ("Map 4"), a fortified town protecting the southern Judean hill country, and in 1938 three more were found. While a few of the ostraca are unreadable, and four are administrative lists, the remaining are letters dating to the period from 597 to 587 B.C. They are extremely important, not only for their value in studying the development of Hebrew grammar and syntax, but also for their illumination of the political situation and general turmoil as Judah prepared for the inevitable attack by Nebuchadnezzar.

The most significant of the letters are numbers 3, 4 and 6. Number 3 is from Hoshaiah, a subordinate officer writing to Yaosh, probably the governor or military commander of Lachish. He reported that Coniah, son of Elnathan, had traveled to Egypt to obtain military assistance. Jeremiah 37:6–8 indicates that king Zedekiah had believed that Egyptian forces would come to his aid but that the Lord had declared otherwise: The pharaoh's army would not stave off the Babylonian onslaught. Some suggest that Elnathan might have been the official of Zedekiah mentioned in 26:22 and 36:12,25. The letter concludes with a warning message from an unnamed prophet.

In letter number 4 the author appears to say that he was watching for the fire signals of Lachish; those of Azekah were not visible. This may indicate that Azekah had already capitulated at the time the ostracon was inscribed. Azekah was the only other fortified city besides Lachish still standing in Judah just prior to Jerusalem's fall.

Letter number 6 is concerned with the words of certain princes and officials of the sort intended to demoralize troops facing imminent war. A prophet is mentioned, but the name is illegible except for the ending "-yahu" (i.e., "**Yahweh**"). It may be that the prophet was either Uriah or Jeremiah (both their names end in "-yahu" in Hebrew), although of course we cannot know. Jeremiah had already prophesied that God would hand over Jerusalem to Babylon; many had thus regarded him as a traitor and a bad influence upon the people.

A Lachish ostracon
Preserving Bible Times; © Dr. James C. Martin; . permission of The Israel Museum

The Recabites

35:1 [n]2Ch 36:5 — **35** This is the word that came to Jeremiah from the LORD during the reign of Jehoiakim[n] son of Jo-
35:2 [o]2Ki 10:15; — siah king of Judah: 2“Go to the Recabite[o] family and invite them to come to one of the side rooms[p]
1Ch 2:55 [p]1Ki 6:5 — of the house of the LORD and give them wine to drink.”
3So I went to get Jaazaniah son of Jeremiah, the son of Habazziniah, and his brothers and all his
sons—the whole family of the Recabites. 4I brought them into the house of the LORD, into the room of
35:4 [q]Dt 33:1 — the sons of Hanan son of Igdaliah the man of God.[q] It was next to the room of the officials, which was
[r]1Ch 9:19 [s]2Ki 12:9 — over that of Maaseiah son of Shallum[r] the doorkeeper.[s] 5Then I set bowls full of wine and some cups be-
fore the men of the Recabite family and said to them, “Drink some wine.”
35:6 [t]2Ki 10:15 — 6But they replied, “We do not drink wine, because our forefather Jonadab[t] son of Recab gave us
[u]Lev 10:9; Nu 6:2-4; Lk 1:15 — this command: ‘Neither you nor your descendants must ever drink wine.[u] 7Also you must never
build houses, sow seed or plant vineyards; you must never have any of these things, but must al-
35:7 [v]Heb 11:9 — ways live in tents.[v] Then you will live a long time in the land[w] where you are nomads.’ 8We have
[w]Ex 20:12; Eph 6:2-3 — obeyed everything our forefather[x] Jonadab son of Recab commanded us. Neither we nor our wives
35:8 [x]Pr 1:8; Col 3:20 — nor our sons and daughters have ever drunk wine 9or built houses to live in or had vineyards, fields
35:9 [y]1Ti 6:6 — or crops.[y] 10We have lived in tents and have fully obeyed everything our forefather Jonadab com-
35:11 [z]2Ki 24:1 — manded us. 11But when Nebuchadnezzar king of Babylon invaded[z] this land, we said, ‘Come, we
[a]Jer 8:14 — must go to Jerusalem[a] to escape the Babylonian[a] and Aramean armies.’ So we have remained in Je-
rusalem.”
12Then the word of the LORD came to Jeremiah, saying: 13“This is what the LORD Almighty, the God of
35:13 [b]Jer 6:10; 32:33 — Israel, says: Go and tell the men of Judah and the people of Jerusalem, ‘Will you not learn a lesson[b] and
obey my words?’ declares the LORD. 14‘Jonadab son of Recab ordered his sons not to drink wine and this
command has been kept. To this day they do not drink wine, because they obey their forefather’s com-
35:14 [c]Jer 7:13; 25:3 [d]Isa 30:9 — mand. But I have spoken to you again and again,[c] yet you have not obeyed[d] me. 15Again and again I sent
35:15 [e]Jer 7:25 [f]Jer 26:3 — all my servants the prophets[e] to you. They said, “Each of you must turn[f] from your wicked ways and re-
[g]Isa 1:16-17; Jer 4:1; 18:11; — form[g] your actions; do not follow other gods to serve them. Then you will live in the land[h] I have given
Eze 18:30 [h]Jer 25:5 — to you and your fathers.” But you have not paid attention or listened[i] to me. 16The descendants of Jona-
[i]Jer 7:26 — dab son of Recab have carried out the command their forefather[j] gave them, but these people have not
35:16 [j]Mal 1:6 — obeyed me.’
17“Therefore, this is what the LORD God Almighty, the God of Israel, says: ‘Listen! I am going to bring
35:17 [k]Jos 23:15; — on Judah and on everyone living in Jerusalem every disaster[k] I pronounced against them. I spoke to
Jer 21:4-7 [l]Pr 1:24; Ro 10:21 — them, but they did not listen;[l] I called to them, but they did not answer.’ ”[m]
[m]Isa 65:12; 66:4; — 18Then Jeremiah said to the family of the Recabites, “This is what the LORD Almighty, the God of Is-
Jer 7:13 — rael, says: ‘You have obeyed the command of your forefather Jonadab and have followed all his instruc-
tions and have done everything he ordered.’ 19Therefore, this is what the LORD Almighty, the God of Is-
35:19 [n]Jer 33:17 [o]Jer 15:19 — rael, says: ‘Jonadab son of Recab will never fail[n] to have a man to serve[o] me.’ ”

[a] *11* Or *Chaldean*

35:1–19 Chapters 35–36 are a flashback to the reign of Jehoiakim. The mention of “Babylonian and Aramean armies” (v. 11) dates chapter 35 to no earlier than the eighth year of King Jehoiakim, who began his reign in 609 B.C. His capital city of Jerusalem was besieged in 605 by Nebuchadnezzar, against whom he rebelled three or four years later—an unwise act that led to raids on his territory by Babylonians, Arameans and others.

35:2 The Recabites were related to Moses’ father-in-law, Jethro the Kenite (Ex 3:1; Jdg 1:16; 1Ch 2:55; see also “The Kenites” on p. 434). Though not ethnic Jews, this nomadic tribe lived among or near the Israelites and zealously attempted to be faithful to the Lord. They got their name from their forefather Recab, whose son Jonadab (or Jehonadab) had helped to remove Baal worship temporarily from Israel 250 years earlier (2Ki 10:15–28). The Recabites from one generation to the next took a permanent vow not to drink wine and obeyed Jonadab’s other instructions, including living in tents rather than in houses and towns—until the Babylonian invasion forced them to take refuge in Jerusalem. Their faithfulness to their community’s values contrasted starkly with the lack of integrity in Judah as a whole, and particularly in Jerusalem, regarding the people’s covenant with God.

The question has been raised whether the Recabites were included within the Nazirite classification (Nazirites, such as Samson and John the Baptist, were Israelites who consecrated themselves, taking a vow of separation and self-imposed abstinence for the purpose of some special service). It appears, however, that the Recabites had more the status of a Hebrew nomadic group, since they were not merely forbidden to drink wine but were also required to refrain from owning real estate, opting instead to live in tents (see vv. 7,10).

The side rooms of the temple were used for storage and/or as living quarters.

35:3 Jaazaniah was a common name in Jeremiah’s time; it appears on a stamp seal discovered at Tell en-Nasbeh north of Jerusalem dating to about 600 B.C. (see “The Seals of Jaazaniah, Ishmael and Elishama” on p. 573), as well as on one of the Lachish ostraca (see “The Lachish Ostraca” on p. 1252).

The Jeremiah mentioned here was not the prophet by that name.

35:4 Three doorkeepers (see 52:24) guarded the entrances to the temple (see 2Ki 12:9).

35:5 These “bowls” were large vessels, from which smaller cups would be filled.

35:19 Various traditions in the Jewish Mishnah (rabbinic interpretations and applications of Pentateuchal laws) claim that the Recabites were later given special duties to perform in connection with the Jerusalem temple built after the return from Babylonian exile.

THE SEPTUAGINT AND THE MASORETIC TEXT

JEREMIAH 35 Most of the Old Testament was originally written in Hebrew, and thus we would expect the current Hebrew version to be the best witness we have to these books in their initial form. However, some scholars believe that the Greek version of the Old Testament, the **Septuagint**, is a superior witness to what the prophets originally wrote.

The Septuagint is the ancient Greek translation of the Hebrew Old Testament. However, we should not think of it as a uniform and consistent translation like the NIV. Much to the contrary, the Septuagint was translated by numerous scholars with varying skill levels and philosophies of translation, and it was also revised many times. The first portion to be translated was the **Pentateuch** in the third century B.C. The rest was completed over the next couple of centuries, and the entire corpus underwent continuous revisions for hundreds of years. A modern copy of the Septuagint is really an amalgam of manuscripts and fragments, and it inevitably includes many revisions slipped in by later scribes (even though modern editors do strive to get back to the earliest version, called the "Old Greek" text). One reality is clear, however: At some points the text of the Septuagint is different from what we see in the standard Hebrew Old Testament, the **Masoretic Text**:

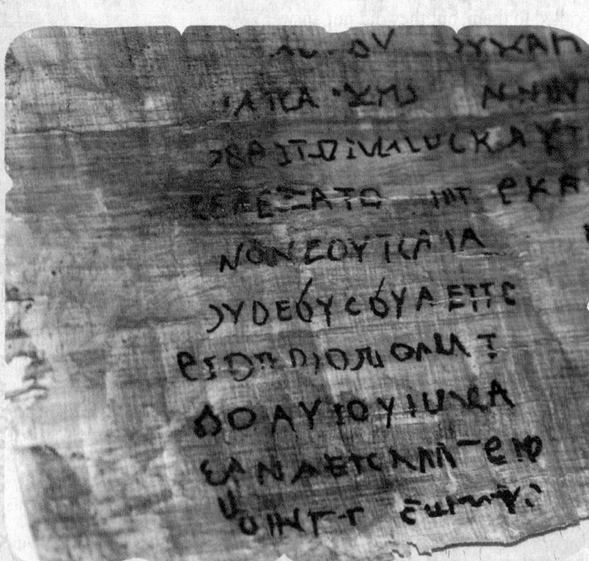

Replica of a portion of the second century B.C. Fouad 266 papyrus—the oldest Septuagint papyrus to date

© Dr. James C. Martin; Jerusalem Bible Society; Photographed by permission

- Sometimes the Greek variants were interpretive in nature, such as in the misunderstanding of a Hebrew term or phrase. For example, the Hebrew phrase translated as "For the director of music" in the headings of many psalms (e.g., Ps 4)[1] is somewhat oddly translated as "Into the ending" in the Septuagint.
- Sometimes, however, it appears that a particular translator was working with a Hebrew original of the Old Testament that was somewhat different from what we now see in the standard Hebrew Bible, the Masoretic Text. For example, Hosea 13:4 in the Masoretic Text (as translated by the NIV) says, "But I am the LORD your God, [who brought you] out of Egypt. You shall acknowledge no God but me, no Savior except me." The Septuagint rendition of this verse, however, is significantly longer: "I am the LORD your God who fixed heaven and created earth; and I did not show them to you to go after them. And I led you up from Egypt and you should acknowledge no God but me. Except for me there is no Savior." It is obvious that the Septuagint rendering here was based upon an original that included words not found in the standard version of the Hebrew, but it is an open question whether these extra words are original to the book of Hosea or reflect a later addition.

In no other portion of the Old Testament are the differences between the Septuagint and the Masoretic Text so pronounced as in the book of Jeremiah. This suggests that for a time two different Hebrew versions of Jeremiah were circulating, one reflected in the Masoretic Text and the other in the Septuagint.[2] Even so, we have no reason to doubt that the Masoretic Text is overall the best witness we have to the original text of the Old Testament. In the vast majority of cases where the Masoretic Text and the Septuagint differ, the Masoretic Text is intrinsically more probable than the Septuagint. Modern translations of the Old Testament are rightly based upon the Hebrew Masoretic Text and not upon the Greek Septuagint.[3]

[1]See "The Psalm Superscripts" on page 795. [2]See "The Problem of the Septuagint Version of Jeremiah" on page 1240. [3]See also "Textual Criticism" on page 1151, "Texts of the Old Testament" on page 1491 and "The Ancient Translations" on page 1492.

Jehoiakim Burns Jeremiah's Scroll

36:1 [p]2Ch 36:5
36:2 [q]Ex 17:14; Jer 30:2; Hab 2:2 [r]Jer 1:2; 25:3
36:3 [s]ver 7; Eze 12:3 [t]Mk 4:12 [u]Jer 26:3; Jnh 3:8; Ac 3:19 [v]Jer 18:8
36:4 [w]Jer 32:12 [x]ver 18 [y]Eze 2:9
36:6 [z]ver 9
36:7 [a]Jer 26:3 [b]Dt 31:17
36:9 [c]ver 22 [d]2Ch 20:3
36:10 [e]Jer 52:25 [f]Jer 26:10

36 In the fourth year of Jehoiakim[p] son of Josiah king of Judah, this word came to Jeremiah from
the LORD: 2“Take a scroll[q] and write on it all the words I have spoken to you concerning Israel,
Judah and all the other nations from the time I began speaking to you in the reign of Josiah[r] till now.
3Perhaps[s] when the people of Judah hear[t] about every disaster I plan to inflict on them, each of them
will turn[u] from his wicked way; then I will forgive[v] their wickedness and their sin.”
4So Jeremiah called Baruch[w] son of Neriah, and while Jeremiah dictated[x] all the words the LORD had
spoken to him, Baruch wrote them on the scroll.[y] 5Then Jeremiah told Baruch, “I am restricted; I cannot
go to the LORD's temple. 6So you go to the house of the LORD on a day of fasting[z] and read to the people from
the scroll the words of the LORD that you wrote as I dictated. Read them to all the people of Judah who
come in from their towns. 7Perhaps they will bring their petition before the LORD, and each will turn[a] from
his wicked ways, for the anger[b] and wrath pronounced against this people by the LORD are great.”
8Baruch son of Neriah did everything Jeremiah the prophet told him to do; at the LORD's temple he
read the words of the LORD from the scroll. 9In the ninth month[c] of the fifth year of Jehoiakim son of Jo-
siah king of Judah, a time of fasting[d] before the LORD was proclaimed for all the people in Jerusalem and
those who had come from the towns of Judah. 10From the room of Gemariah son of Shaphan the secre-
tary,[e] which was in the upper courtyard at the entrance of the New Gate[f] of the temple, Baruch read to
all the people at the LORD's temple the words of Jeremiah from the scroll.
11When Micaiah son of Gemariah, the son of Shaphan, heard all the words of the LORD from the scroll,

---

36:2 For “scroll,” see the note on Exodus 17:14.
Although most workers in the simple culture of Old Testament times were what we today would call “unskilled,” there were certain exceptions. The potter (ch. 18) has left behind unnumbered examples of his skill. Some technology in the working of metals was known, and the remains of smelting furnaces have been discovered. Stone masons, scribes (36:2,4; Eze 9:2), dyers, weavers and workers in precious stones and ivory carried on their work. But in general life was simple, work arduous, hours long and wages meager. By New Testament times the picture had changed, and the more complex civilization of the Roman world, with its skilled and more diversified occupations and better standards of living, had come to the Holy Land.

36:6 A day of fasting was often proclaimed during a national emergency. Perhaps in this case it was called due to the Babylonian attack.

36:8 If the book were arranged in chronological order, chapter 45 would appear after this verse.

36:9 The month and year were December 604 B.C.

36:10 Gemariah's name has been found in Jerusalem on a seal impression. (See “Gemariah, the Official, and Jerahmeel, the King's Son,” below.) For the “New Gate,” see the notes on 7:2 and 26:10.

ANCIENT TEXTS AND ARTIFACTS

Gemariah, the Official, and Jerahmeel, the King's Son

JEREMIAH 36 During the fourth year of king Jehoiakim (605 B.C.), God directed Jeremiah to record on a scroll prophecies against the nations and particularly against Jerusalem and Judah (Jer 36:1–3).[1] Baruch, Jeremiah's secretary,[2] documented the prophecies and later read the scroll in the chamber of Gemariah, the son of Shaphan the scribe (vv. 4–10). When Gemariah's son Micaiah notified the king's officials of the scroll, they requested Baruch to read its words to them (vv. 11–19), after which they confiscated the scroll and read it to the king (vv. 20–21). As the scroll was being read, each portion already read was cut away and burned, even though Gemariah and others pleaded with the king not to do so (vv. 22–25). The prophecies made the king so angry that he dispatched his son Jerahmeel and several others to arrest Baruch and Jeremiah, “but the LORD had hidden them” (v. 26; cf. v. 19). God then directed Jeremiah to replicate the first scroll, including in the new one additional indictments against Jehoiakim (vv. 27–32).

A clay seal impression of Gemariah was unearthed in excavations in Jerusalem of the 587 B.C. destruction level.[3] It reads, “Belonging to Gemariah (son of) Shaphan.” Researchers are in possession of a seal and a seal impression of Jerahmeel, both acquired on the antiquities market, which read, “Belonging to Jerahmeel the king's son.”

[1]See “Scrolls, Seals and Codices” on page 2053. [2]See “Baruch, Scribe of Jeremiah” on page 1248. [3]See “The Last Days of Jerusalem” on page 1197.

12 he went down to the secretary's room in the royal palace, where all the officials were sitting: Elishama
the secretary, Delaiah son of Shemaiah, Elnathan[g] son of Acbor, Gemariah son of Shaphan, Zedekiah son 36:12 [g]Jer 26:22
of Hananiah, and all the other officials. 13 After Micaiah told them everything he had heard Baruch read
to the people from the scroll, 14 all the officials sent Jehudi[h] son of Nethaniah, the son of Shelemiah, the 36:14 [h]ver 21
son of Cushi, to say to Baruch, "Bring the scroll from which you have read to the people and come." So
Baruch son of Neriah went to them with the scroll in his hand. 15 They said to him, "Sit down, please, and
read it to us."

So Baruch read it to them. 16 When they heard all these words, they looked at each other in fear and
said to Baruch, "We must report all these words to the king." 17 Then they asked Baruch, "Tell us, how did
you come to write all this? Did Jeremiah dictate it?"

18 "Yes," Baruch replied, "he dictated[i] all these words to me, and I wrote them in ink on the scroll." 36:18 [i]ver 4

19 Then the officials said to Baruch, "You and Jeremiah, go and hide.[j] Don't let anyone know where you 36:19 [j]1Ki 17:3
are."

20 After they put the scroll in the room of Elishama the secretary, they went to the king in the court-
yard and reported everything to him. 21 The king sent Jehudi[k] to get the scroll, and Jehudi brought it from 36:21 [k]ver 14
the room of Elishama the secretary and read it to the king[l] and all the officials standing beside him. 22 It [l]2Ki 22:10
was the ninth month and the king was sitting in the winter apartment,[m] with a fire burning in the fire- 36:22 [m]Am 3:15
pot in front of him. 23 Whenever Jehudi had read three or four columns of the scroll, the king cut them
off with a scribe's knife and threw them into the firepot, until the entire scroll was burned in the fire.[n] 36:23 [n]1Ki 22:8
24 The king and all his attendants who heard all these words showed no fear,[o] nor did they tear their 36:24 [o]Ps 36:1
clothes.[p] 25 Even though Elnathan, Delaiah and Gemariah urged the king not to burn the scroll, he would [p]Ge 37:29;
not listen to them. 26 Instead, the king commanded Jerahmeel, a son of the king, Seraiah son of Azriel 2Ki 22:11; Isa 37:1
and Shelemiah son of Abdeel to arrest[q] Baruch the scribe and Jeremiah the prophet. But the LORD had 36:26 [q]Mt 23:34
hidden[r] them. [r]Jer 15:21

27 After the king burned the scroll containing the words that Baruch had written at Jeremiah's dictation,[s] 36:27 [s]ver 4
the word of the LORD came to Jeremiah: 28 "Take another scroll and write on it all the words that were on
the first scroll, which Jehoiakim king of Judah burned up. 29 Also tell Jehoiakim king of Judah, 'This is what
the LORD says: You burned that scroll and said, "Why did you write on it that the king of Babylon would
certainly come and destroy this land and cut off both men and animals from it?"[t] 30 Therefore, this is what 36:29 [t]Isa 30:10
the LORD says about Jehoiakim king of Judah: He will have no one to sit on the throne of David; his body
will be thrown out[u] and exposed to the heat by day and the frost by night. 31 I will punish him and his chil- 36:30 [u]Jer 22:19
dren and his attendants for their wickedness; I will bring on them and those living in Jerusalem and the
people of Judah every disaster[v] I pronounced against them, because they have not listened.' " 36:31 [v]Pr 29:1

32 So Jeremiah took another scroll and gave it to the scribe Baruch son of Neriah, and as Jeremiah dic-
tated,[w] Baruch wrote[x] on it all the words of the scroll that Jehoiakim king of Judah had burned[y] in the 36:32 [w]ver 4
fire. And many similar words were added to them. [x]Ex 34:1 [y]ver 23

36:12 For "Elnathan," see the note on 26:22.

36:18 Ink is mentioned only here in the Old Testament (but see also 2Co 3:3; 2Jn 12; 3Jn 13). In ancient times ink was made from soot or lampblack mixed with gum arabic, oil or a metallic substance (see "Writing Materials in the Ancient World" on p. 2037).

36:22 The "winter apartment" (lit., "winter house") was probably a large room in a king's palace (see "Ramat Rahel" on p. 1229). In the highlands, as at Jerusalem, it became quite cold in winter (Ezr 10:9,13), especially since the houses were inadequately heated.

In the region now known as Palestine stoves were usually made of clay. Some were small, portable fireplaces that burned charcoal, while others were built outside the house and heated with dry sticks, grass and even dung. The hearth or firepot mentioned in Jeremiah 36:22 was a bronze heater—a brazier that only the well-to-do could afford. For cooking, the stove was molded so as to hold the pot or pan above the fire bowl through which air passed from vents at the bottom. The fire by which Peter warmed himself during the trial of Jesus was probably in a brazier (Mk 14:67). See the note on hearths and home heating at Psalm 102:3.

36:23 The scroll, or roll, was the usual form of a book in Bible times. It had been used in Egypt from very early times, the earliest ones having been made of papyrus, the paper-like tissue take from the reeds growing along the Nile. As the successive columns of Jeremiah's scroll were read, the king cut them off and burned them. Since the burning of skins in an open fire pot would have produced an intolerably bad odor, we may surmise that this roll was made of papyrus imported from Egypt. Several sheets, glued together to the desired length, were rolled on rods so that the beginning of the scroll was on the right and the end on the left (the Hebrews wrote from right to left).

A "scribe's knife" was used to sharpen reed pens. Knives in the ancient Near East were not used for eating. Meat was cut into small pieces before being served, and bread was broken at the table. The Philistines had metal knives long before they came into general use in Israel (see 1Sa 13:19,22).

36:26 Jerahmeel's name, along with his title, has been found on a seal impression discovered in a burnt archive near Jerusalem (see "Gemariah, the Official, and Jerahmeel, the King's Son" on p. 1255). He is called a "son of the king." However, since Jehoiakim was only about thirty years old (see 2Ki 23:36), the phrase is most likely not to be understood literally but may perhaps mean "member of the royal court" (cf. 1Ki 22:26; Jer 38:6; Zep 1:8).

36:30 Jehoiakim's son Jehoiachin (see 2Ki 24:6) ruled for only three months and then was captured and carried off to exile in Babylonia, where he eventually died (see "Jehoiachin in Captivity and Evil-Merodach" on p. 1292).

36:32 Obviously this scroll (see "The Scribe" on p. 682) was not our present book, which carries on the history for at least 20 more years. This account is of great interest in that it gives the only detailed Old Testament description of the writing of a prophetic book. That Jeremiah dictated to a secretary was normal for the times. Writing was a specialized skill, often restricted to a professional class. Learned

Jeremiah in Prison

37 Zedekiah[z] son of Josiah was made king[a] of Judah by Nebuchadnezzar king of Babylon; he reigned
in place of Jehoiachin[a][b] son of Jehoiakim. 2 Neither he nor his attendants nor the people of the
land paid any attention[c] to the words the LORD had spoken through Jeremiah the prophet.
3 King Zedekiah, however, sent Jehucal son of Shelemiah with the priest Zephaniah[d] son of Maaseiah
to Jeremiah the prophet with this message: "Please pray[e] to the LORD our God for us."
4 Now Jeremiah was free to come and go among the people, for he had not yet been put in prison.[f]
5 Pharaoh's army had marched out of Egypt,[g] and when the Babylonians[b] who were besieging Jerusalem
heard the report about them, they withdrew[h] from Jerusalem.[i]
6 Then the word of the LORD came to Jeremiah the prophet: 7 "This is what the LORD, the God of Isra-
el, says: Tell the king of Judah, who sent you to inquire[j] of me, 'Pharaoh's army, which has marched out
to support you, will go back to its own land, to Egypt.[k] 8 Then the Babylonians will return and attack this
city; they will capture it and burn[l] it down.'
9 "This is what the LORD says: Do not deceive[m] yourselves, thinking, 'The Babylonians will surely leave
us.' They will not! 10 Even if you were to defeat the entire Babylonian[c] army that is attacking you and only
wounded men were left in their tents, they would come out and burn this city down."
11 After the Babylonian army had withdrawn[n] from Jerusalem because of Pharaoh's army, 12 Jeremiah
started to leave the city to go to the territory of Benjamin to get his share of the property[o] among the
people there. 13 But when he reached the Benjamin Gate, the captain of the guard, whose name was Iri-
jah son of Shelemiah, the son of Hananiah, arrested him and said, "You are deserting to the Babylonians!"
14 "That's not true!" Jeremiah said. "I am not deserting to the Babylonians." But Irijah would not lis-
ten to him; instead, he arrested[p] Jeremiah and brought him to the officials. 15 They were angry with Jer-
emiah and had him beaten[q] and imprisoned in the house[r] of Jonathan the secretary, which they had
made into a prison.
16 Jeremiah was put into a vaulted cell in a dungeon, where he remained a long time. 17 Then King Zed-
ekiah sent for him and had him brought to the palace, where he asked[s] him privately,[t] "Is there any word
from the LORD?"
"Yes," Jeremiah replied, "you will be handed over[u] to the king of Babylon."
18 Then Jeremiah said to King Zedekiah, "What crime[v] have I committed against you or your officials
or this people, that you have put me in prison? 19 Where are your prophets who prophesied to you, 'The
king of Babylon will not attack you or this land'? 20 But now, my lord the king, please listen. Let me bring
my petition before you: Do not send me back to the house of Jonathan the secretary, or I will die there."
21 King Zedekiah then gave orders for Jeremiah to be placed in the courtyard of the guard and given
bread from the street of the bakers each day until all the bread[w] in the city was gone.[x] So Jeremiah re-
mained in the courtyard of the guard.[y]

Jeremiah Thrown Into a Cistern

38 Shephatiah son of Mattan, Gedaliah son of Pashhur, Jehucal[d][z] son of Shelemiah, and Pashhur
son of Malkijah heard what Jeremiah was telling all the people when he said, 2 "This is what the

37:1 [z]2Ki 24:17 [a]Eze 17:13 [b]2Ki 24:8,12; 2Ch 36:10; Jer 22:24
37:2 [c]2Ki 24:19; 2Ch 36:12,14
37:3 [d]Jer 29:25; 52:24 [e]1Ki 13:6; Jer 21:1-2; 42:2
37:4 [f]ver 15; Jer 32:2
37:5 [g]Eze 17:15 [h]Jer 34:21 [i]2Ki 24:7
37:7 [j]2Ki 22:18 [k]Jer 2:36; La 4:17
37:8 [l]Jer 34:22; 39:8
37:9 [m]Jer 29:8
37:11 [n]ver 5
37:12 [o]Jer 32:9
37:14 [p]Jer 40:4
37:15 [q]Jer 20:2 [r]Jer 38:26
37:17 [s]Jer 15:11 [t]Jer 38:16 [u]Jer 21:7
37:18 [v]1Sa 26:18; Jn 10:32; Ac 25:8
37:21 [w]Isa 33:16; Jer 38:9 [x]2Ki 25:3; Jer 52:6 [y]Jer 32:2; 38:6,13,28
38:1 [z]Jer 37:3

a *1* Hebrew *Coniah,* a variant of *Jehoiachin* *b* *5* Or *Chaldeans*; also in verses 8, 9, 13 and 14 *c* *10* Or *Chaldean*; also in verse 11
d *1* Hebrew *Jucal,* a variant of *Jehucal*

---

men might have been able to read but scorned to write. The document was probably written on a blank papyrus scroll imported from Egypt.

Two seal impressions with the words "the scribe Baruch son of Neriah" have been found in the same burnt archive as that mentioned in the note on verse 26. See "Baruch, Scribe of Jeremiah" on page 1248.

37:1 In 597 B.C. Nebuchadnezzar made Zedekiah king in place of Jehoiachin. This fulfilled the prophecy concerning Jehoiakim in 36:30 (see also the note there).

37:5 "Pharaoh's army" refers to the troops of Hophra (see 44:30; see also "Hophra, King of Egypt" on p. 1266) that were probably sent in response to Zedekiah's request for help as he attempted to defend Jerusalem from the Babylonian attack. Lachish Ostracon #3 (see "The Lachish Ostraca" on p. 1252) mentions a visit to Egypt made by the commander of Judah's army.

37:7 Hophra would soon be defeated by Nebuchadnezzar (see "Hophra, King of Egypt" on p. 1266).

37:12 While there was a brief lull in the Babylonian invasion, Jeremiah wanted to settle matters of estate with the other members of his family.

37:13 As Jeremiah approached the Benjamin Gate (see the note on 38:7), he was accused of desertion. Such an accusation was understandable, since the prophet had recommended surrendering to the Babylonians (see 21:9; 38:2) and since many other Judahites were in fact defecting (see 38:19; 39:9; 52:15).

37:16 The "dungeon" was actually a cistern (see the note on 38:6).

37:21 "The courtyard of the guard" was a less objectionable prison than the dungeon (see the note on 38:1).

"The street of the bakers" may have been near the Tower of the Ovens, which was located on the northern end of the western wall.

38:1 For "Pashhur," see the note on 20:1. For "Pashhur son of Malkijah," see the note on 21:1.

Even though Jeremiah was confined in the courtyard of the guard (see 37:21), he was allowed to have visitors and to speak freely to them (see 32:8,12).

LORD says: 'Whoever stays in this city will die by the sword, famine or plague,[a] but whoever goes over to
the Babylonians[a] will live. He will escape with his life; he will live.'[b] 3And this is what the LORD says: 'This
city will certainly be handed over to the army of the king of Babylon, who will capture it.' "[c]
4Then the officials[d] said to the king, "This man should be put to death.[e] He is discouraging the sol-
diers who are left in this city, as well as all the people, by the things he is saying to them. This man is not
seeking the good of these people but their ruin."
5"He is in your hands," King Zedekiah answered. "The king can do nothing to oppose you."
6So they took Jeremiah and put him into the cistern of Malkijah, the king's son, which was in the
courtyard of the guard.[f] They lowered Jeremiah by ropes into the cistern; it had no water in it, only mud,
and Jeremiah sank down into the mud.
7But Ebed-Melech,[g] a Cushite,[b] an official[c][h] in the royal palace, heard that they had put Jeremiah into
the cistern. While the king was sitting in the Benjamin Gate,[i] 8Ebed-Melech went out of the palace and
said to him, 9"My lord the king, these men have acted wickedly in all they have done to Jeremiah the
prophet. They have thrown him into a cistern, where he will starve to death when there is no longer any
bread[j] in the city."
10Then the king commanded Ebed-Melech the Cushite, "Take thirty men from here with you and lift
Jeremiah the prophet out of the cistern before he dies."
11So Ebed-Melech took the men with him and went to a room under the treasury in the palace. He
took some old rags and worn-out clothes from there and let them down with ropes to Jeremiah in the cis-
tern. 12Ebed-Melech the Cushite said to Jeremiah, "Put these old rags and worn-out clothes under your
arms to pad the ropes." Jeremiah did so, 13and they pulled him up with the ropes and lifted him out of
the cistern. And Jeremiah remained in the courtyard of the guard.[k]

Zedekiah Questions Jeremiah Again

14Then King Zedekiah sent for Jeremiah the prophet and had him brought to the third entrance to
the temple of the LORD. "I am going to ask you something," the king said to Jeremiah. "Do not hide[l] any-
thing from me."
15Jeremiah said to Zedekiah, "If I give you an answer, will you not kill me? Even if I did give you coun-
sel, you would not listen to me."
16But King Zedekiah swore this oath secretly[m] to Jeremiah: "As surely as the LORD lives, who has giv-
en us breath,[n] I will neither kill you nor hand you over to those who are seeking your life."[o]
17Then Jeremiah said to Zedekiah, "This is what the LORD God Almighty, the God of Israel, says: 'If
you surrender to the officers of the king of Babylon, your life will be spared and this city will not be
burned down; you and your family will live.[p] 18But if you will not surrender to the officers of the king of
Babylon, this city will be handed over[q] to the Babylonians and they will burn[r] it down; you yourself will
not escape[s] from their hands.' "
19King Zedekiah said to Jeremiah, "I am afraid[t] of the Jews who have gone over[u] to the Babylonians,
for the Babylonians may hand me over to them and they will mistreat me."
20"They will not hand you over," Jeremiah replied. "Obey[v] the LORD by doing what I tell you. Then it
will go well with you, and your life[w] will be spared. 21But if you refuse to surrender, this is what the LORD
has revealed to me: 22All the women[x] left in the palace of the king of Judah will be brought out to the of-
ficials of the king of Babylon. Those women will say to you:

" 'They misled you and overcame you—
those trusted friends of yours.
Your feet are sunk in the mud;
your friends have deserted you.'

38:2 [a]Jer 34:17 [b]Jer 21:9; 39:18; 45:5
38:3 [c]Jer 21:4, 10; 32:3
38:4 [d]Jer 36:12 [e]Jer 26:11
38:6 [f]Jer 37:21
38:7 [g]Jer 39:16 [h]Ac 8:27 [i]Job 29:7
38:9 [j]Jer 37:21
38:13 [k]Jer 37:21
38:14 [l]1Sa 3:17
38:16 [m]Jer 37:17 [n]Isa 42:5; 57:16 [o]ver 4
38:17 [p]2Ki 24:12; Jer 21:9
38:18 [q]ver 3; Jer 34:3 [r]Jer 37:8 [s]Jer 24:8; 32:4
38:19 [t]Isa 51:12; Jn 12:42 [u]Jer 39:9
38:20 [v]Jer 11:4 [w]Isa 55:3
38:22 [x]Jer 6:12

[a] 2 Or *Chaldeans*; also in verses 18, 19 and 23 [b] 7 Probably from the upper Nile region [c] 7 Or *a eunuch*

38:4 The word "discouraging" is literally "weakening the hands of," as in a similar expression found in Lachish Ostracon #6 (see "The Lachish Ostraca" on p. 1252): "The words of the officials are not good; they serve only to weaken our hands."
38:6 A cistern was a pit with a relatively small opening at the top (see "Wells, Cisterns and Aqueducts in the Ancient World" on p. 1259).
38:7 Since a city gateway was often used as a courtroom or town hall (see "The City Gate" on p. 392), Zedekiah may have been there settling legal matters and so would have been in a position to help Ebed-Melech.
38:11 The "room under the treasury" may have been a wardrobe storeroom (see 2Ki 10:22).
38:17–18 "The officers of the king of Babylon" were the men in charge of the siege of Jerusalem (see 39:3,13).
38:22 Women in a conquered king's harem became the property of the conquerors.

CULTURAL AND HISTORICAL NOTES

Wells, Cisterns and Aqueducts in the Ancient World

JEREMIAH 38 The semiarid climate of the Mediterranean basin made water acquisition and storage a critical issue.

Aqueduct at Greek Neapolis (modern Kavala)
Preserving Bible Times; © Dr. James C. Martin

Wells

A well is a deep reservoir fed by percolation from the soil, by a spring or by groundwater. The lower part is usually dug into impermeable rock or built with rock and then coated with a thick layer of lime plaster, which prevents seepage. It is possible either to tap into a natural spring or to dig down to the groundwater level. Archaeologists date the first such use of plaster to around 1200 B.C.

A very ancient well in Jerusalem, known as "Job's well," is nearly 44 yards (40.2 m) deep. Water was taken from it by lowering a drawing vessel attached to a rope. The high concentration of pottery **sherds** found in Near Eastern wells suggests that clay pots were used for this purpose, although wooden pails found in the Athenian agora (marketplace) seem to have served the same function.[1] Wells were often dug in rural areas in order to provide water for flocks and herds (Ge 26:18; 2Ch 26:9–10). A stone slab or wooden planks covered the mouth of the well when it was not in use to prevent people or animals from falling in and to lower the risk of pollution from surface debris (see Ge 29:10; Ex 21:33–34).

Cisterns

A cistern is a collection chamber that gathers runoff. Cisterns typically have a bottle or bell shape, with a narrow top to prevent evaporation. The entire interior is coated with plaster, so that every drop of water is preserved. Water was drawn from a cistern in the same fashion as from a well. Homes could have private cisterns (see 2Ki 18:31; Pr 5:15); in fact, excavations at Tell en-Nasbeh, a site north of Jerusalem that is usually identified as the Biblical Mizpah, revealed 50 cisterns from the ninth century B.C.[2] Cities had larger, public cisterns. In the temple area of Jerusalem, for example, excavators discovered 37 large cisterns, the largest of which is known as the "Great Sea." About 14 yards (13 m) deep, it can hold over two million gallons (9,917 cu yd) of water! Also in Jerusalem is the Pool of Siloam, constructed by Hezekiah (2Ch 32:30) and embellished by Herod—the Upper Pool of Isaiah 7:3. In order to ensure a steady and reliable supply of water to this reservoir, Hezekiah undertook the construction of a tunnel aqueduct that travels over 547 yards (500 m) through solid rock from the spring to the cistern. Dry cisterns also served as detention cells (Ge 37:22–24; Jer 38:6).[3]

Aqueducts

The first aqueducts (artificial water channels similar to pipelines) were simple channels dug into the ground. Eventually the channels were formed by plastering fieldstones together and covering the aqueduct with stone slabs to prevent contamination. Shallow settling basins were dug intermittently, allowing the heavier sediment to drop out of the water. Pools and reservoirs were often placed along the aqueduct to control water flow. The earliest known substantial aqueduct—from the early eighth century B.C.—is at Urartu in Turkey. The **Assyrian** king Sennacherib constructed a 34-mile (55-km) aqueduct to Nineveh.[4] Excavators have found numerous inscriptions along the course of the conduit praising Sennacherib for this impressive deed.

The masters of aqueduct construction, however, were the Romans. To this day the landscape of numerous Mediterranean countries is dotted with the remains of these engineering masterpieces. Ancient Rome was serviced by 11 aqueducts, the largest of which were the Marcia and the Anio Novus. Altogether the 11 aqueducts provided the capital with over 264,019,630,000 gallons (1,310,013,110 cu yd) of water every 24 hours—by far the largest volume of water carried to any ancient city.

The Romans are also famous for their ability to carry water across challenging terrain. Valleys were traversed in one of two ways. If the distance from the proposed water line to the valley floor was less than about 55 yards (50 m), an arched bridge was constructed, containing a channel running along the top. The aqueduct was built so that the water ran downhill on a gentle slope. The tallest aqueduct of this type is the Pont du Gard in southern France. It rises 54 yards (49 m) above the valley and supplied water to Nîmes beginning in 19 B.C. Pergamum was the first major city in **Asia Minor** (western Turkey) to establish an alliance with Rome and to construct Roman style aqueducts. Providing water to the upper city was a constant challenge, but engineers resolved the problem with a complex siphoning system.

[1]See "The Ancient Agora" on page 1799. [2]See "Mizpah" on page 383. [3]See "The Pool of Siloam" on page 1739. [4]See "Nineveh" on page 1497.

[23]"All your wives and children[y] will be brought out to the Babylonians. You yourself will not escape
from their hands but will be captured[z] by the king of Babylon; and this city will[a] be burned down."
[24]Then Zedekiah said to Jeremiah, "Do not let anyone know about this conversation, or you may die.
[25]If the officials hear that I talked with you, and they come to you and say, 'Tell us what you said to the
king and what the king said to you; do not hide it from us or we will kill you,' [26]then tell them, 'I was
pleading with the king not to send me back to Jonathan's house[a] to die there.' "
[27]All the officials did come to Jeremiah and question him, and he told them everything the king had
ordered him to say. So they said no more to him, for no one had heard his conversation with the king.
[28]And Jeremiah remained in the courtyard of the guard[b] until the day Jerusalem was captured.

38:23 [y]2Ki 25:6 [z]Jer 41:10
38:26 [a]Jer 37:15
38:28 [b]Jer 37:21; 39:14

The Fall of Jerusalem

39 This is how Jerusalem was taken: [1]In the ninth year of Zedekiah king of Judah, in the tenth
month, Nebuchadnezzar king of Babylon marched against Jerusalem with his whole army and
laid siege[c] to it. [2]And on the ninth day of the fourth month of Zedekiah's eleventh year, the city wall was
broken through. [3]Then all the officials[d] of the king of Babylon came and took seats in the Middle Gate:
Nergal-Sharezer of Samgar, Nebo-Sarsekim[b] a chief officer, Nergal-Sharezer a high official and all the
other officials of the king of Babylon. [4]When Zedekiah king of Judah and all the soldiers saw them, they
fled; they left the city at night by way of the king's garden, through the gate between the two walls, and
headed toward the Arabah.[c]
[5]But the Babylonian[d] army pursued them and overtook Zedekiah[e] in the plains of Jericho. They cap-
tured him and took him to Nebuchadnezzar king of Babylon at Riblah[f] in the land of Hamath, where he

39:1 [c]2Ki 25:1; Jer 52:4; Eze 24:2
39:3 [d]Jer 21:4
39:5 [e]Jer 32:4 [f]2Ki 23:33

[a] 23 Or *and you will cause this city to* [b] 3 Or *Nergal-Sharezer, Samgar-Nebo, Sarsekim* [c] 4 Or *the Jordan Valley*
[d] 5 Or *Chaldean*

39:1 The final Babylonian siege of Jerusalem began on January 15, 588 B.C.
39:2 The siege ended on July 18, 586 B.C. It had lasted for just over two and a half years (see "Siege Warfare" on p. 465 and "The Last Days of Jerusalem" on p. 1197).
39:3 The Middle Gate may have been located in the wall separating the citadel of Mount Zion from the lower city, therefore serving as a strategic vantage point for the invaders. Nergal-Sharezer was probably Neriglissar, who later became a successor of Nebuchadnezzar as ruler of Babylonia (560–556 B.C.).
39:4 The Arabah includes the valley of the Jordan (from the Sea of Galilee to the southern end of the Dead Sea) and the valley extending down to the Gulf of Aqaba.
39:5 Riblah, Nebuchadnezzar's headquarters, was a city north of Damascus on the Orontes River.

Nebuzaradan, Captain of the Guard

JEREMIAH 39 When Zedekiah, king of Judah, rebelled against Babylonian rule in 588 B.C., **Nebuchadnezzar** responded quickly, capturing Jerusalem the following year.[1] Nebuzaradan, a high-ranking officer in the Babylonian army, was responsible for supervising the burning of the city, tearing down the defenses, deporting 832 captives to **Babylon**, plundering the temple and rounding up Judean officials to appear before Nebuchadnezzar (2Ki 25:8–21; Jer 39:8–9; 52:15–27).[2]

Nebuchadnezzar left Nebuzaradan with specific instructions to deal kindly with Jeremiah, who had been imprisoned along with those going to Babylon (Jer 39:11–14; 40:1). Nebuzaradan released the prophet and gave him a choice of going to Babylon or remaining in Judah (40:2–4). Jeremiah opted to remain in Judah and joined the newly appointed Judean leader, Gedaliah, at Mizpah (39:14; 40:5–6).[3] Five years later Nebuzaradan returned to Jerusalem and deported another 745 persons to Babylon (52:30).

A clay prism listing court officials was found during excavations in Nebuchadnezzar's palace in Babylon. Among the names is that of Nebuzaradan, along with the title "Chancellor." The prism is thought to date to around 570 B.C. and thus to reflect a political appointment for Nebuzaradan following his military career.

[1]See "The Last Days of Jerusalem" on page 1197. [2]See "Nebuchadnezzar" on page 571. [3]See "Gedaliah, Governor of Judah, and Baalis, King of Ammon" on page 1261.

pronounced sentence on him. [6]There at Riblah the king of Babylon slaughtered the sons of Zedekiah be-
39:7 [g]Eze 12:13 fore his eyes and also killed all the nobles of Judah. [7]Then he put out Zedekiah's eyes[g] and bound him
[h]Jer 32:5 with bronze shackles to take him to Babylon.[h]
39:8 [i]Jer 38:18 [8]The Babylonians[a] set fire[i] to the royal palace and the houses of the people and broke down the walls[j]
[j]Ne 1:3 of Jerusalem. [9]Nebuzaradan commander of the imperial guard carried into exile to Babylon the people
39:9 [k]Jer 40:1 who remained in the city, along with those who had gone over to him, and the rest of the people.[k] [10]But
Nebuzaradan the commander of the guard left behind in the land of Judah some of the poor people, who
owned nothing; and at that time he gave them vineyards and fields.

[11]Now Nebuchadnezzar king of Babylon had given these orders about Jeremiah through Nebuzara-
39:12 [l]Pr 16:7; 1Pe 3:13 dan commander of the imperial guard: [12]"Take him and look after him; don't harm[l] him but do for him
whatever he asks." [13]So Nebuzaradan the commander of the guard, Nebushazban a chief officer, Nergal-
Sharezer a high official and all the other officers of the king of Babylon [14]sent and had Jeremiah taken
39:14 [m]Jer 38:28 out of the courtyard of the guard.[m] They turned him over to Gedaliah son of Ahikam,[n] the son of Sha-
[n]2Ki 22:12 [o]Jer 40:5 phan, to take him back to his home. So he remained among his own people.[o]

[15]While Jeremiah had been confined in the courtyard of the guard, the word of the LORD came to him:
39:16 [p]Jer 38:7 [16]"Go and tell Ebed-Melech[p] the Cushite, 'This is what the LORD Almighty, the God of Israel, says: I am
[q]Jer 21:10; Da 9:12 about to fulfill my words against this city through disaster,[q] not prosperity. At that time they will be ful-
39:17 [r]Ps 41:1-2 filled before your eyes. [17]But I will rescue[r] you on that day, declares the LORD; you will not be handed over
39:18 [s]Jer 45:5 to those you fear. [18]I will save you; you will not fall by the sword[s] but will escape with your life,[t] because
[t]Jer 21:9; 38:2 [u]Jer 17:7 you trust[u] in me, declares the LORD.' "

Jeremiah Freed

40 The word came to Jeremiah from the LORD after Nebuzaradan commander of the imperial guard
had released him at Ramah. He had found Jeremiah bound in chains among all the captives from

[a] 8 Or *Chaldeans*

39:14 Gedaliah became the governor of Judah (see "Gedaliah, Governor of Judah, and Baalis, King of Ammon," below) and resided in Mizpah (see "Mizpah" on p. 383). An early sixth-century B.C. seal impression found at Lachish reads: "Belonging to Gedaliah, who is over the house."
40:1 For "Ramah," see the note on 31:15.

ANCIENT TEXTS AND ARTIFACTS

Gedaliah, Governor of Judah, and Baalis, King of Ammon

JEREMIAH 40 Nebuchadnezzar appointed Gedaliah, who came from a family of royal administrators, as governor of Judah in 587 B.C. (2Ki 25:22). Gedaliah attempted to rebuild the country following the destruction of Jerusalem by the Babylonians (Jer 40:9–12).[1] Unfortunately, he became a victim of the political forces of the day when Baalis, king of Ammon, recruited Ishmael to assassinate him (vv. 13–14; 41:1–2). Ishmael, of the line of David (2Ki 25:25), may have had designs upon the leadership of the country, and Baalis may have wanted to set up a puppet king whom he could control.

Archaeologists have found a **bulla** of Gedaliah on the surface at Lachish, 27 miles (44 km) southwest of Jerusalem. The inscription reads "Belonging to Gedaliah Over(seer of) the (royal) house," a title designating the chief steward of the royal palace. Individuals bearing this title took on major state responsibilities and were active in political and diplomatic activities. Evidently Gedaliah held this post prior to the fall of Jerusalem.

A seal and a seal impression with the name of Baalis have been discovered as well.

✣ The seal, acquired on the antiquities market, is that of Baalis himself. It depicts a winged sphinx with the words "Belonging to Baalis" above it, the letters for "king" on either side and "Sons of Ammon" (i.e., Ammonites) below it.

✣ The seal impression was unearthed at Tell el-Umeiri, just south of Amman in Jordan. It reads "Belonging to Milkomor servant of Baalis."

[1]See "The Last Days of Jerusalem" on page 1197.

Jerusalem and Judah who were being carried into exile to Babylon. 2When the commander of the guard
found Jeremiah, he said to him, "The LORD your God decreed this disaster for this place.[v] 3And now the 40:2 [v]Jer 50:7
LORD has brought it about; he has done just as he said he would. All this happened because you people
sinned[w] against the LORD and did not obey[x] him. 4But today I am freeing you from the chains on your 40:3 [w]Da 9:11
wrists. Come with me to Babylon, if you like, and I will look after you; but if you do not want to, then [x]Dt 29:24-28; Ro 2:5-9
don't come. Look, the whole country lies before you; go wherever you please."[y] 5However, before Jeremi- 40:4 [y]Ge 13:9; Jer 39:11-12
ah turned to go,[a] Nebuzaradan added, "Go back to Gedaliah[z] son of Ahikam, the son of Shaphan, whom 40:5 [z]2Ki 25:22
the king of Babylon has appointed over the towns of Judah, and live with him among the people, or go [a]Jer 39:14
anywhere else you please."[a]

Then the commander gave him provisions and a present and let him go. 6So Jeremiah went to Geda-
liah son of Ahikam at Mizpah[b] and stayed with him among the people who were left behind in the land. 40:6 [b]Jdg 20:1; 1Sa 7:5-17

Gedaliah Assassinated

7When all the army officers and their men who were still in the open country heard that the king of
Babylon had appointed Gedaliah son of Ahikam as governor over the land and had put him in charge of
the men, women and children who were the poorest[c] in the land and who had not been carried into ex- 40:7 [c]Jer 39:10
ile to Babylon, 8they came to Gedaliah at Mizpah[d]—Ishmael[e] son of Nethaniah, Johanan and Jonathan 40:8 [d]ver 13
the sons of Kareah, Seraiah son of Tanhumeth, the sons of Ephai the Netophathite,[f] and Jaazaniah[b] the [e]ver 14; Jer 41:1, 2 [f]2Sa 23:28
son of the Maacathite,[g] and their men. 9Gedaliah son of Ahikam, the son of Shaphan, took an oath to re- [g]Dt 3:14
assure them and their men. "Do not be afraid to serve[h] the Babylonians,[c]" he said. "Settle down in the land 40:9 [h]Jer 27:11
and serve the king of Babylon, and it will go well with you.[i] 10I myself will stay at Mizpah[j] to represent [i]Jer 38:20 40:10 [j]ver 6
you before the Babylonians who come to us, but you are to harvest the wine, summer fruit and oil, and [k]Dt 1:39
put them in your storage jars, and live in the towns you have taken over."[k]

11When all the Jews in Moab,[l] Ammon, Edom and all the other countries heard that the king of Bab- 40:11 [l]Nu 25:1
ylon had left a remnant in Judah and had appointed Gedaliah son of Ahikam, the son of Shaphan, as gov-
ernor over them, 12they all came back to the land of Judah, to Gedaliah at Mizpah, from all the countries
where they had been scattered.[m] And they harvested an abundance of wine and summer fruit. 40:12 [m]Jer 43:5

13Johanan son of Kareah and all the army officers still in the open country came to Gedaliah at Miz-
pah[n] 14and said to him, "Don't you know that Baalis king of the Ammonites[o] has sent Ishmael son of 40:13 [n]ver 8
Nethaniah to take your life?" But Gedaliah son of Ahikam did not believe them. 40:14 [o]2Sa 10:1-19; Jer 25:21; 41:10

15Then Johanan son of Kareah said privately to Gedaliah in Mizpah, "Let me go and kill Ishmael son
of Nethaniah, and no one will know it. Why should he take your life and cause all the Jews who are gath-
ered around you to be scattered and the remnant of Judah to perish?"

16But Gedaliah son of Ahikam said to Johanan son of Kareah, "Don't do such a thing! What you are
saying about Ishmael is not true."

41 In the seventh month Ishmael[p] son of Nethaniah, the son of Elishama, who was of royal blood 41:1 [p]Jer 40:8
and had been one of the king's officers, came with ten men to Gedaliah son of Ahikam at Miz-
pah. While they were eating together there, 2Ishmael[q] son of Nethaniah and the ten men who were with 41:2 [q]Ps 41:9; 109:5 [r]Jer 40:5
him got up and struck down Gedaliah son of Ahikam, the son of Shaphan, with the sword, killing the [s]2Sa 3:27; 20:9-10
one whom the king of Babylon had appointed[r] as governor over the land.[s] 3Ishmael also killed all the 41:5 [t]Lev 19:27
Jews who were with Gedaliah at Mizpah, as well as the Babylonian[d] soldiers who were there. [u]Ge 33:18; Jdg 9:1-57; 1Ki 12:1

4The day after Gedaliah's assassination, before anyone knew about it, 5eighty men who had shaved [v]Jos 18:1
off their beards,[t] torn their clothes and cut themselves came from Shechem,[u] Shiloh[v] and Samaria,[w] [w]1Ki 16:24

[a] 5 Or *Jeremiah answered* [b] 8 Hebrew *Jezaniah,* a variant of *Jaazaniah* [c] 9 Or *Chaldeans*; also in verse 10 [d] 3 Or *Chaldean*

40:5 For "Gedaliah," see the note on 39:14.
40:6 For "Mizpah," see "Mizpah" on page 383.
40:8 For "Jaazaniah," see "The Seals of Jaazaniah, Ishmael and Elishama" on page 573.
40:10 Nebuzaradan, the commander of the imperial guard, had arrived in Jerusalem in August of 586 B.C. (see "Nebuzaradan, Captain of the Guard" on p. 1260), at a time when the grapes, figs and olives were harvested (see "Food and Agriculture" on p. 390).
40:14 Three royal inscriptions have been found that may relate to "Baalis king of the Ammonites": (1) "King Ba'lay," as his name is written on an early sixth-century B.C. bottle discovered in Jordan; (2) "Ba'alYasha," an Ammonite king whose name appears on a stamp seal found at Tell el 'Umeiri in Jordan in 1984; and (3) "Baalis king of [the Ammonites]," as his name reads on an Ammonite stamp seal that came to light in 1998.

For "Ammonites," see "Ammon" on page 364.
41:1 Ishmael's loyalty to Zedekiah might explain his assassination of Gedaliah, whom he considered to be a Babylonian puppet ruler (see "The Seals of Jaazaniah, Ishmael and Elishama" on p. 573).

Hospitality was one of the most highly regarded virtues of the ancient world. Ancient custom with respect to hospitality normally meant that a host tried to protect a guest from harm. Gedaliah likely assumed that his guests in turn would not harm him, much less kill him.
41:5 Shaving off one's beard, tearing one's clothing and cutting oneself were all signs of mourning (see 16:6 and its note; see also "Sack-

41:5 [x]2Ki 25:9 bringing grain offerings and incense with them to the house of the LORD.[x] 6 Ishmael son of Nethaniah
41:6 [y]2Sa 3:16 went out from Mizpah to meet them, weeping[y] as he went. When he met them, he said, "Come to Geda-
liah son of Ahikam." 7 When they went into the city, Ishmael son of Nethaniah and the men who were
with him slaughtered them and threw them into a cistern. 8 But ten of them said to Ishmael, "Don't kill
41:8 [z]Isa 45:3 us! We have wheat and barley, oil and honey, hidden in a field."[z] So he let them alone and did not kill
them with the others. 9 Now the cistern where he threw all the bodies of the men he had killed along with
41:9 [a]1Ki 15:22; 2Ch 16:6 [b]Jdg 6:2 Gedaliah was the one King Asa[a] had made as part of his defense[b] against Baasha[c] king of Israel. Ishma-
[c]2Ch 16:1 el son of Nethaniah filled it with the dead.
41:10 [d]Jer 40:7, 12 10 Ishmael made captives of all the rest of the people[d] who were in Mizpah—the king's daughters
[e]Jer 40:14 along with all the others who were left there, over whom Nebuzaradan commander of the imperial guard
had appointed Gedaliah son of Ahikam. Ishmael son of Nethaniah took them captive and set out to cross
over to the Ammonites.[e]
41:11 [f]Jer 40:8 11 When Johanan[f] son of Kareah and all the army officers who were with him heard about all the
crimes Ishmael son of Nethaniah had committed, 12 they took all their men and went to fight Ishmael
41:12 [g]2Sa 2:13 son of Nethaniah. They caught up with him near the great pool[g] in Gibeon. 13 When all the people[h] Ish-
41:13 [h]ver 10 mael had with him saw Johanan son of Kareah and the army officers who were with him, they were
glad. 14 All the people Ishmael had taken captive at Mizpah turned and went over to Johanan son of Ka-
41:15 [i]Job 21:30; reah. 15 But Ishmael son of Nethaniah and eight of his men escaped[i] from Johanan and fled to the Am-
Pr 28:17 monites.

Flight to Egypt

16 Then Johanan son of Kareah and all the army officers who were with him led away all the survi-
41:16 [j]Jer 43:4 vors[j] from Mizpah whom he had recovered from Ishmael son of Nethaniah after he had assassinated
Gedaliah son of Ahikam: the soldiers, women, children and court officials he had brought from Gibeon.
41:17 [k]2Sa 19:37 17 And they went on, stopping at Geruth Kimham[k] near Bethlehem on their way to Egypt[l] 18 to escape the
[l]Jer 42:14 **41:18** Babylonians.[a] They were afraid[m] of them because Ishmael son of Nethaniah had killed Gedaliah[n] son of
[m]Isa 51:12; Jer 42:16; Ahikam, whom the king of Babylon had appointed as governor over the land.
Lk 12:4-5 [n]Jer 40:5 **42** Then all the army officers, including Johanan[o] son of Kareah and Jezaniah[b] son of Hoshaiah,
42:1 [o]Jer 40:13; 41:11 [p]Jer 6:13; and all the people from the least to the greatest[p] approached 2 Jeremiah the prophet and said to
44:12 him, "Please hear our petition and pray[q] to the LORD your God for this entire remnant.[r] For as you now
42:2 [q]Jer 36:7; Ac 8:24; Jas 5:16 see, though we were once many, now only a few[s] are left. 3 Pray that the LORD your God will tell us where
[r]Isa 1:9 [s]Lev 26:22; we should go and what we should do."[t]
La 1:1 **42:3** [t]Ps 86:11; 4 "I have heard you," replied Jeremiah the prophet. "I will certainly pray[u] to the LORD your God as you
Pr 3:6 **42:4** [u]Ex 8:29; have requested; I will tell you everything the LORD says and will keep nothing back from you."[v]
1Sa 12:23 [v]1Ki 22:14; 5 Then they said to Jeremiah, "May the LORD be a true and faithful witness[w] against us if we do not act
1Sa 3:17 **42:5** [w]Ge 31:50 in accordance with everything the LORD your God sends you to tell us. 6 Whether it is favorable or unfa-
42:6 [x]Dt 5:29; 6:3; Jer 7:23 vorable, we will obey the LORD our God, to whom we are sending you, so that it will go well[x] with us, for
[y]Ex 24:7; we will obey[y] the LORD our God."
Jos 24:24 7 Ten days later the word of the LORD came to Jeremiah. 8 So he called together Johanan son of Kareah
42:8 [z]ver 1 and all the army officers[z] who were with him and all the people from the least to the greatest. 9 He said
42:9 [a]2Ki 22:15 to them, "This is what the LORD, the God of Israel, to whom you sent me to present your petition, says:[a]
42:10 [b]Jer 24:6 10 'If you stay in this land, I will build[b] you up and not tear you down; I will plant[c] you and not uproot you,[d]
[c]Jer 31:28 [d]Eze 36:36

[a] *18* Or *Chaldeans* [b] *1* Hebrew; Septuagint (see also 43:2) *Azariah*

---

cloth and Ashes: Rituals of Lamentation" on p. 820 and "Beards and Hairstyles in the Biblical World" on p. 1084). In this context the mourning was probably over the destruction of Jerusalem.

Shechem, Shiloh and Samaria had been worship centers in the north (see "Shechem" on p. 340, "The Tabernacle at Shiloh" on p. 401 and "The Destruction of Shiloh" on p. 1200). After the northern kingdom was destroyed in 722/721 B.C., many Israelites made periodic pilgrimages to Jerusalem.

They were bringing bloodless offerings, since the altar of the Jerusalem temple had been destroyed. Even though the temple itself was in ruins, the site was still considered holy.

41:6 Gedaliah had made his residence in Mizpah (see "Mizpah" on p. 383).

41:7 For "cistern," see "Wells, Cisterns and Aqueducts in the Ancient World" on page 1259.

41:9 Since cisterns were essential for storing water during times of siege, Asa had probably built these as part of the fortifications at Mizpah (see 1Ki 15:22). Archaeologists have discovered numerous cisterns in the ruins of ancient Mizpah (modern Tell en-Nasbeh), 7.5 miles (12 km) north of Jerusalem (see "Mizpah" on p. 383).

41:10 The phrase "king's daughters" refers here to women who had been members of King Zedekiah's court; they were not necessarily daughters of the king himself.

For "Ammonites," see "Ammon" on page 364.

41:12 See "Gibeon" on page 318 and "The Pool of Gibeon" on page 444.

42:1 "Jezaniah son of Hoshaiah" may be the same as "Jaazaniah the son of the Maacathite" (see "The Seals of Jaazaniah, Ishmael and Elishama" on p. 573). Apparently Jezaniah was also known as Azariah, as was King Uzziah.

for I am grieved over the disaster I have inflicted on you.[e] 11 Do not be afraid of the king of Babylon,[f]
whom you now fear.[g] Do not be afraid of him, declares the LORD, for I am with you and will save[h] you and
deliver you from his hands.[i] 12 I will show you compassion so that he will have compassion on you and
restore you to your land.'[j]
13 "However, if you say, 'We will not stay in this land,' and so disobey[k] the LORD your God, 14 and if you
say, 'No, we will go and live in Egypt,[l] where we will not see war or hear the trumpet or be hungry for
bread,' 15 then hear the word of the LORD, O remnant of Judah. This is what the LORD Almighty, the God of
Israel, says: 'If you are determined to go to Egypt and you do go to settle there, 16 then the sword[m] you fear
will overtake you there, and the famine you dread will follow you into Egypt, and there you will die. 17 In-
deed, all who are determined to go to Egypt to settle there will die by the sword, famine and plague;[n] not
one of them will survive or escape the disaster I will bring on them.' 18 This is what the LORD Almighty,
the God of Israel, says: 'As my anger and wrath[o] have been poured out on those who lived in Jerusalem,[p]
so will my wrath be poured out on you when you go to Egypt. You will be an object of cursing and hor-
ror,[q] of condemnation and reproach; you will never see this place again.'[r]
19 "O remnant of Judah, the LORD has told you, 'Do not go to Egypt.'[s] Be sure of this: I warn you today
20 that you made a fatal mistake[a] when you sent me to the LORD your God and said, 'Pray to the LORD our
God for us; tell us everything he says and we will do it.'[t] 21 I have told you today, but you still have not
obeyed the LORD your God in all he sent me to tell you.[u] 22 So now, be sure of this: You will die by the
sword, famine and plague[v] in the place where you want to go to settle."[w]

[a] 20 Or *you erred in your hearts*

42:10 [e]Jer 18:8
42:11 [f]Jer 27:11 [g]Nu 14:9 [h]Isa 43:5 [i]Jer 1:8; Ro 8:31
42:12 [j]Ps 106:44-46
42:13 [k]Jer 44:16
42:14 [l]Nu 11:4-5
42:16 [m]Eze 11:8
42:17 [n]ver 22; Jer 44:13
42:18 [o]Dt 29:18-20; Jer 7:20 [p]2Ch 36:19; Jer 39:1-9 [q]Jer 29:18 [r]Jer 22:10
42:19 [s]Dt 17:16; Isa 30:7
42:20 [t]ver 2
42:21 [u]Eze 2:7; Zec 7:11-12
42:22 [v]ver 17; Eze 6:11 [w]Hos 9:6

The Elephantine Community

JEREMIAH 43 The island of Elephantine is situated along the southern border of Egypt, near modern-day Aswan. This site functioned as an important military outpost throughout its long history. While its soldiers were usually Egyptian, other ethnic groups, including Jews, were periodically stationed at this garrison. By the time **Persian** rule commenced in 525 B.C., not only was there a Jewish community in Elephantine but also an established, thriving temple to **Yahweh**. We learn from Jeremiah 43 that a portion of the Jews of Judah fled to Egypt before the Babylonian invasion. Some scholars assume that a fragment of this group became the source of the Elephantine Jewish population. Others argue for a much earlier immigration of Jews to the area.

Evidence indicates that the Elephantine temple was a fully functioning sanctuary that performed animal sacrifices. Although this temple existed alongside temples to Egyptian gods for over a century, the priests of Khnum, the ram god, convinced the Egyptian authorities to have the temple destroyed in 410 B.C. (apparently because the Jewish practice of sacrificing sheep was offensive to the worshipers of Khnum). Soon thereafter the Jewish colony ceased to exist.

The knowledge we possess of this small, ancient community comes through a series of **papyri** found in the region. The majority of these texts are written in **Aramaic**, the international language of the Persian Empire.[1] While these documents reveal much concerning the daily life, customs and legal system of these people, most important to us are the archives of letters written between the Jews of Elephantine and the Jews of the region now known as Palestine. In these letters the Elephantine community requested and gained permission and aid to rebuild its temple. It remains unclear, however, whether that goal was ever accomplished.

[1] See "Languages of the Old Testament World" on page 672.

43 When Jeremiah finished telling the people all the words of the LORD their God—everything the
LORD had sent him to tell them[x]— 2Azariah son of Hoshaiah and Johanan[y] son of Kareah and
all the arrogant men said to Jeremiah, “You are lying! The LORD our God has not sent you to say, ‘You must
not go to Egypt to settle there.’ 3But Baruch son of Neriah is inciting you against us to hand us over to
the Babylonians,[a] so they may kill us or carry us into exile to Babylon.”[z]
4So Johanan son of Kareah and all the army officers and all the people disobeyed the LORD’s com-
mand[a] to stay in the land of Judah.[b] 5Instead, Johanan son of Kareah and all the army officers led away
all the remnant of Judah who had come back to live in the land of Judah from all the nations where they
had been scattered.[c] 6They also led away all the men, women and children and the king’s daughters whom
Nebuzaradan commander of the imperial guard had left with Gedaliah son of Ahikam, the son of Sha-
phan, and Jeremiah the prophet and Baruch son of Neriah. 7So they entered Egypt in disobedience to
the LORD and went as far as Tahpanhes.[d]
8In Tahpanhes[e] the word of the LORD came to Jeremiah: 9“While the Jews are watching, take some
large stones with you and bury them in clay in the brick pavement at the entrance to Pharaoh’s palace in
Tahpanhes. 10Then say to them, ‘This is what the LORD Almighty, the God of Israel, says: I will send for
my servant[f] Nebuchadnezzar king of Babylon, and I will set his throne over these stones I have buried
here; he will spread his royal canopy above them. 11He will come and attack Egypt,[g] bringing death to
those destined for death, captivity to those destined for captivity, and the sword to those destined for
the sword.[h] 12He[b] will set fire to the temples of the gods[i] of Egypt; he will burn their temples and take
their gods captive. As a shepherd wraps[j] his garment around him, so will he wrap Egypt around himself
and depart from there unscathed. 13There in the temple of the sun[c] in Egypt he will demolish the sacred
pillars and will burn down the temples of the gods of Egypt.’ ”

Disaster Because of Idolatry

44 This word came to Jeremiah concerning all the Jews living in Lower Egypt—in Migdol,[k] Tahpan-
hes[l] and Memphis[d][m]—and in Upper Egypt[e]:[n] 2“This is what the LORD Almighty, the God of Is-
rael, says: You saw the great disaster I brought on Jerusalem and on all the towns of Judah. Today they lie
deserted and in ruins[o] 3because of the evil they have done. They provoked me to anger by burning in-
cense and by worshiping other gods[p] that neither they nor you nor your fathers[q] ever knew. 4Again and
again[r] I sent my servants the prophets,[s] who said, ‘Do not do this detestable thing that I hate!’ 5But they
did not listen or pay attention; they did not turn from their wickedness or stop burning incense to oth-
er gods.[t] 6Therefore, my fierce anger was poured out; it raged against the towns of Judah and the streets
of Jerusalem and made them the desolate ruins they are today.
7“Now this is what the LORD God Almighty, the God of Israel, says: Why bring such great disaster[u] on
yourselves by cutting off from Judah the men and women,[v] the children and infants, and so leave your-
selves without a remnant? 8Why provoke me to anger with what your hands have made,[w] burning in-
cense to other gods in Egypt, where you have come to live?[x] You will destroy yourselves and make your-
selves an object of cursing and reproach[y] among all the nations on earth. 9Have you forgotten the
wickedness committed by your fathers and by the kings and queens of Judah and the wickedness com-
mitted by you and your wives in the land of Judah and the streets of Jerusalem?[z] 10To this day they have
not humbled themselves or shown reverence, nor have they followed my law[a] and the decrees I set be-
fore you and your fathers.[b]
11“Therefore, this is what the LORD Almighty, the God of Israel, says: I am determined to bring disaster[c]

43:1 [x]Jer 26:8; 42:9-22 **43:2** [y]Jer 42:1 **43:3** [z]Jer 38:4 **43:4** [a]Jer 42:5-6 [b]Jer 42:10 **43:5** [c]Jer 40:12 **43:7** [d]Jer 2:16; 44:1 **43:8** [e]Jer 2:16 **43:10** [f]Isa 44:28; Jer 25:9; 27:6 **43:11** [g]Jer 46:13-26; Eze 29:19-20 [h]Jer 15:2; 44:13; Zec 11:9 **43:12** [i]Jer 46:25; Eze 30:13 [j]Ps 104:2; 109:18-19 **44:1** [k]Ex 14:2 [l]Jer 43:7,8 [m]Isa 19:13 [n]Isa 11:11; Jer 46:14 **44:2** [o]Isa 6:11; Jer 9:11; 34:22 **44:3** [p]ver 8; Dt 13:6-11; 29:26 [q]Dt 32:17; Jer 19:4 **44:4** [r]Jer 7:13 [s]Jer 7:25; 25:4; 26:5 **44:5** [t]Jer 11:8-10 **44:7** [u]Jer 26:19 [v]Jer 51:22 **44:8** [w]Jer 25:6-7 [x]1Co 10:22 [y]Jer 42:18 **44:9** [z]ver 17,21 **44:10** [a]Jos 1:7 [b]1Ki 9:6-9 **44:11** [c]Jer 21:10; Am 9:4

[a] *3* Or *Chaldeans* [b] *12* Or *I* [c] *13* Or *in Heliopolis* [d] *1* Hebrew *Noph* [e] *1* Hebrew *in Pathros*

43:2 For “Azariah,” see the note on 42:1.
43:3 See “Baruch, Scribe of Jeremiah” on page 1248.
43:6 For “king’s daughters,” see the note on 41:10.
43:7 For “Tahpanhes,” see the note on 2:16.
43:9 “Pharaoh’s palace” is not necessarily a reference to his principal residence. One of the Elephantine papyri mentions the “king’s house,” apparently a more modest dwelling for the pharaoh’s use when he visited Elephantine in southern Egypt (see “The Elephantine Community” on p. 1264).
43:11 A fragmentary text now owned by the British Museum in London states that Nebuchadnezzar carried out a punitive expedition against Egypt in his thirty-seventh year (568–567 B.C.), during the reign of Pharaoh Amasis.
43:13 The “temple of the sun in Egypt” probably refers to the temple in the Egyptian city of Heliopolis (Greek for “city of the sun”), called *On* in Hebrew.
“Sacred pillars” refer to obelisks, for which ancient Heliopolis was famous.
44:1 Jews lived in Egypt as a result of previous deportations. For Lower and Upper Egypt, see the note on Isaiah 11:11. Migdol was probably in northern Egypt. For “Tahpanhes,” see the note on Jeremiah 2:16. For “Memphis,” see the note on Isaiah 19:13 and “Memphis” on page 1270.
44:3 For “burning incense,” see the note on 19:13.

on you and to destroy all Judah. 12 I will take away the remnant[d] of Judah who were determined to go to
Egypt to settle there. They will all perish in Egypt; they will fall by the sword or die from famine. From
the least to the greatest, they will die by sword or famine.[e] They will become an object of cursing and hor-
ror, of condemnation and reproach.[f] 13 I will punish those who live in Egypt with the sword, famine and
plague,[g] as I punished Jerusalem. 14 None of the remnant of Judah who have gone to live in Egypt will es-
cape or survive to return to the land of Judah, to which they long to return and live; none will return ex-
cept a few fugitives."[h]
15 Then all the men who knew that their wives were burning incense to other gods, along with all the
women who were present—a large assembly—and all the people living in Lower and Upper Egypt,[a]
said to Jeremiah, 16 "We will not listen[i] to the message you have spoken to us in the name of the LORD! 17 We
will certainly do everything we said we would:[j] We will burn incense to the Queen of Heaven[k] and will
pour out drink offerings to her just as we and our fathers, our kings and our officials did in the towns of
Judah and in the streets of Jerusalem. At that time we had plenty of food and were well off and suffered
no harm.[l] 18 But ever since we stopped burning incense to the Queen of Heaven and pouring out drink
offerings to her, we have had nothing and have been perishing by sword and famine.[m]"

44:12 [d]ver 7 [e]Isa 1:28 [f]Jer 29:18; 42:15-18
44:13 [g]Jer 42:17
44:14 [h]ver 28; Jer 22:24-27; Ro 9:27
44:16 [i]Jer 11:8-10
44:17 [j]Dt 23:23 [k]ver 25; Jer 7:18 [l]Hos 2:5-13
44:18 [m]Mal 3:13-15

[a] 15 Hebrew *in Egypt and Pathros*

44:17 For "Queen of Heaven," see the note on 7:18.
44:18 The people had stopped burning incense to the Queen of Heaven (as a result of King Josiah's reform movement, which had begun in 621 B.C.). But beginning with Josiah's death in 609 a series of disasters, including invasion and exile, had struck Judah. The people understandably (though mistakenly) attributed their misfortune to their failure to worship the Queen of Heaven.

Hophra, King of Egypt

JEREMIAH 44 Hophra (known to Egyptologists by the Greek form of his name, Apries), the fourth king of the Twenty-sixth (Saite) Dynasty, ruled Egypt from 589 to 570 B.C. His palace has been excavated at Memphis.[1] When **Nebuchadnezzar** invaded Judah in 588 B.C., Zedekiah requested help from Egypt (Eze 17:15), and Hophra responded by sending troops. This resulted in Nebuchadnezzar lifting the siege of Jerusalem to deal with the Egyptian threat (Jer 37:5,11). The relief was short-lived, however, because Nebuchadnezzar quickly drove off the Egyptians and returned to capture Jerusalem (2Ki 25:1–21; Jer 37:6–10; 39:1–10; 52:1–29).[2]

After Gedaliah, the new governor of Judah, was assassinated in 586 B.C.,[3] the remaining Judean leadership fled to Egypt, taking Jeremiah with them (41:16—43:7). While in Egypt the prophet declared that God would hand over Hophra to his enemies (44:30). Indeed, Jeremiah's words reflect a disdain for Hophra. In 46:17 he declared, "There they will exclaim, 'Pharaoh king of Egypt is only a loud noise; he has missed his opportunity.'" (This could also be translated, "There they will call Pharaoh, king of Egypt, 'Noisy has missed his opportunity.'") The Hebrew for "he has missed" in this verse sounds like the name Hophra.

Hophra's downfall does suggest a degree of ineptitude. In 570 B.C. he sent a force of Egyptians against a Greek colony in Cyrene in eastern Libya. The Egyptian army was badly defeated, leading to a soldiers' revolt against Hophra's leadership. Hophra sent his general, Amasis, to quell the rebellion, but Amasis joined it instead! Forced by Amasis into exile, Hophra made his way to the Babylonian court of Nebuchadnezzar II.[4] He returned three years later with the Babylonian army in an attempt to regain the throne but was defeated and lost his life in the process. Nevertheless, Amasis buried him with full honors in the royal cemetery at Sais in Egypt's western delta.

[1]See "Memphis" on page 1270. [2]See "The Last Days of Jerusalem" on page 1197. [3]See "Gedaliah, Governor of Judah, and Baalis, King of Ammon" on page 1261. [4]See "Nebuchadnezzar" on page 571.

44:19 [n]Jer 7:18 — 19 The women added, "When we burned incense to the Queen of Heaven[n] and poured out drink offer-
ings to her, did not our husbands know that we were making cakes like her image and pouring out drink
offerings to her?"
20 Then Jeremiah said to all the people, both men and women, who were answering him, 21 "Did not
44:21 [o]Isa 64:9; Jer 14:10 [p]Jer 11:13 [q]ver 9 [r]Ps 79:8 — the LORD remember[o] and think about the incense[p] burned in the towns of Judah and the streets of Jeru-
salem[q] by you and your fathers,[r] your kings and your officials and the people of the land? 22 When the
LORD could no longer endure your wicked actions and the detestable things you did, your land became
44:22 [s]Jer 25:18 [t]Ge 19:13; Ps 107:33-34 — an object of cursing[s] and a desolate waste without inhabitants, as it is today.[t] 23 Because you have burned
incense and have sinned against the LORD and have not obeyed him or followed his law or his decrees or
44:23 [u]Jer 40:2 [v]1Ki 9:9; Jer 7:13-15; Da 9:11-12 — his stipulations, this disaster[u] has come upon you, as you now see."[v]
24 Then Jeremiah said to all the people, including the women,[w] "Hear the word of the LORD, all you
44:24 [w]ver 15 [x]Jer 43:7 — people of Judah in Egypt.[x] 25 This is what the LORD Almighty, the God of Israel, says: You and your wives
have shown by your actions what you promised when you said, 'We will certainly carry out the vows we
44:25 [y]ver 17 [z]Eze 20:39 — made to burn incense and pour out drink offerings to the Queen of Heaven.'[y]
44:26 [a]Ge 22:16; Isa 48:1; Heb 6:13-17 [b]Dt 32:40; Ps 50:16 — "Go ahead then, do what you promised! Keep your vows![z] 26 But hear the word of the LORD, all Jews liv-
ing in Egypt: 'I swear[a] by my great name,' says the LORD, 'that no one from Judah living anywhere in Egypt
will ever again invoke my name or swear, "As surely as the Sovereign LORD lives."[b] 27 For I am watching over

44:19 Since Ishtar (the "Queen of Heaven"; see the note on 7:18) was a Babylonian goddess of fertility, women were particularly involved in her worship.

The Queen of Heaven

JEREMIAH 44 In the Bible the enigmatic title "Queen of Heaven" appears only in Jeremiah 7:18, 44:17–19, 25, but similar titles occur throughout the ancient Near East and apply to several goddesses. Anat is called the "Lady of Heaven," and the **Canaanite** Astarte (Ashtoreth in the Bible) and her **Mesopotamian** counterpart, Ishtar, also bear the title "Queen of Heaven."[1] These goddesses are connected to the worship of the planet Venus; astral worship was particularly popular during the seventh century B.C. (2Ki 21:3; 23:11).

The exiled Judahites conceived of this queen as a fertility goddess (Jer 44:17–18), in whose image the women made "cakes" (v. 19). This cultic practice may also be indicated by a discovery at **Mari** of a baking mold in the form of a naked female with hands supporting her breasts—a well-known fertility motif. Moreover, Jeremiah's word for these cakes derives from the **Akkadian** for a type of bread that was often presented to Ishtar. Jeremiah described how a family would gather wood, make a fire, prepare the bread, pour out libations and burn incense (7:18; 44:18). Religious texts dedicated to Ishtar recount very similar steps. The Judahites were apparently following ritual practices associated with the Mesopotamian Ishtar and the Canaanite Astarte/Ashtoreth (1Ki 11:5). The Queen of Heaven exemplified the religious syncretism that plagued Israel for centuries and ultimately led to God's judgment upon his people.

Still today, believers in the God of the Bible are wise to beware of a gradual assimilation of unbiblical and even pagan concepts. The notion of a "Queen of Heaven" was just such an assimilation.[2]

[1]For more on Ishtar, see "The Descent of Ishtar" on page 356 and "Sexuality and Religion in the Sumerian Hymns to Ishtar" on page 1340. [2]For other examples, see "The Golden Calf" on page 143, "Devotion to Asherah in the Khirbet El-Qom Inscription" on page 638 and "The Kuntillet Ajrûd Inscriptions: The Lord's Asherah?" on page 1220.

them for harm,[c] not for good; the Jews in Egypt will perish by sword and famine until they are all de-
stroyed. 28 Those who escape the sword and return to the land of Judah from Egypt will be very few.[d]
Then the whole remnant of Judah who came to live in Egypt will know whose word will stand—mine
or theirs.[e]

29 " 'This will be the sign to you that I will punish you in this place,' declares the LORD, 'so that you will
know that my threats of harm against you will surely stand.'[f] 30 This is what the LORD says: 'I am going to
hand Pharaoh[g] Hophra king of Egypt over to his enemies who seek his life, just as I handed Zedekiah[h]
king of Judah over to Nebuchadnezzar king of Babylon, the enemy who was seeking his life.' "[i]

44:27 [c]Jer 31:28
44:28 [d]ver 13-14; Isa 10:19 [e]ver 17,25-26
44:29 [f]Pr 19:21
44:30 [g]Jer 46:26; Eze 30:21 [h]2Ki 25:1-7 [i]Jer 39:5

A Message to Baruch

45 This is what Jeremiah the prophet told Baruch[j] son of Neriah in the fourth year of Jehoiakim[k] son
of Josiah king of Judah, after Baruch had written on a scroll the words Jeremiah was then dictat-
ing: 2 "This is what the LORD, the God of Israel, says to you, Baruch: 3 You said, 'Woe to me! The LORD has
added sorrow to my pain; I am worn out with groaning[l] and find no rest.' "

4 ⌞The LORD said,⌟ "Say this to him: 'This is what the LORD says: I will overthrow what I have built and
uproot what I have planted,[m] throughout the land.[n] 5 Should you then seek great things for yourself? Seek
them not.[o] For I will bring disaster on all people, declares the LORD, but wherever you go I will let you es-
cape with your life.' "[p]

45:1 [j]Jer 32:12; 36:4,18,32 [k]2Ch 36:5
45:3 [l]Ps 69:3
45:4 [m]Jer 11:17 [n]Isa 5:5-7; Jer 18:7-10
45:5 [o]Mt 6:25-27,33 [p]Jer 21:9; 38:2; 39:18

A Message About Egypt

46 This is the word of the LORD that came to Jeremiah the prophet concerning the nations:[q]

2 Concerning Egypt:

This is the message against the army of Pharaoh Neco[r] king of Egypt, which was defeated at Carche-
mish[s] on the Euphrates River by Nebuchadnezzar king of Babylon in the fourth year of Jehoiakim[t] son
of Josiah king of Judah:

46:1 [q]Jer 1:10; 25:15-38
46:2 [r]2Ki 23:29 [s]2Ch 35:20 [t]Jer 45:1

3 "Prepare your shields,[u] both large and small,
    and march out for battle!
4 Harness the horses,
    mount the steeds!
Take your positions
    with helmets on!
Polish[v] your spears,
    put on your armor![w]
5 What do I see?
    They are terrified,
they are retreating,
    their warriors are defeated.
They flee[x] in haste
    without looking back,
    and there is terror[y] on every side,"
        declares the LORD.

6 "The swift cannot flee[z]
    nor the strong escape.
In the north by the River Euphrates
    they stumble and fall.[a]

7 "Who is this that rises like the Nile,
    like rivers of surging waters?[b]

46:3 [u]Isa 21:5; Jer 51:11-12
46:4 [v]Eze 21:9-11 [w]1Sa 17:5,38; 2Ch 26:14; Ne 4:16
46:5 [x]ver 21 [y]Jer 49:29
46:6 [z]Isa 30:16 [a]ver 12,16; Da 11:19
46:7 [b]Jer 47:2

44:30 Hophra was pharaoh from 589 to 570 B.C. (see the note on 37:5; see also "Hophra, King of Egypt" on p. 1266).

45:1 The date was 605 B.C. Chapter 45 fits chronologically between 36:8 and 36:9 (see the note on 36:8).

See "Baruch, Scribe of Jeremiah" on page 1248. For "scroll," see the notes on Exodus 17:14 and Jeremiah 36:23.

46:2 Neco ruled Egypt from 610 until 595 B.C. In 605 he was defeated by Nebuchadnezzar at Carchemish (see "Josiah, Zechariah and Neco II" on p. 663). Egypt's defeat by Babylonia at Carchemish was decisive, ending Egypt's ancient claims and pretensions to power in Syro-Palestine.

46:4 Egypt was the primary source of fine horses during this time period (see 1Ki 10:28).

8 Egypt rises like the Nile,
like rivers of surging waters.
She says, 'I will rise and cover the earth;
I will destroy cities and their people.'
9 Charge, O horses!
46:9 [c]Jer 47:3 [d]Isa 66:19 Drive furiously, O charioteers![c]
March on, O warriors—
men of Cush[a] and Put who carry shields,
men of Lydia[d] who draw the bow.
46:10 [e]Joel 1:15 [f]Dt 32:42 [g]Zep 1:7 10 But that day[e] belongs to the Lord, the LORD Almighty—
a day of vengeance, for vengeance on his foes.
The sword will devour[f] till it is satisfied,
till it has quenched its thirst with blood.
For the Lord, the LORD Almighty, will offer sacrifice[g]
in the land of the north by the River Euphrates.

46:11 [h]Jer 8:22 [i]Isa 47:1 [j]Jer 30:13; Mic 1:9 11 "Go up to Gilead and get balm,[h]
O Virgin[i] Daughter of Egypt.
But you multiply remedies in vain;
there is no healing[j] for you.
12 The nations will hear of your shame;
your cries will fill the earth.
One warrior will stumble over another;
46:12 [k]Isa 19:4; Na 3:8-10 both will fall[k] down together."

13 This is the message the LORD spoke to Jeremiah the prophet about the coming of Nebuchadnezzar
46:13 [l]Isa 19:1 king of Babylon to attack Egypt:[l]

14 "Announce this in Egypt, and proclaim it in Migdol;
46:14 [m]Jer 43:8 proclaim it also in Memphis[b] and Tahpanhes:[m]
'Take your positions and get ready,
for the sword devours those around you.'
15 Why will your warriors be laid low?
46:15 [n]Isa 66:15-16 They cannot stand, for the LORD will push them down.[n]
46:16 [o]Lev 26:37 [p]ver 6 16 They will stumble[o] repeatedly;
they will fall[p] over each other.
They will say, 'Get up, let us go back
to our own people and our native lands,
away from the sword of the oppressor.'
17 There they will exclaim,
'Pharaoh king of Egypt is only a loud noise;
46:17 [q]Isa 19:11-16 he has missed his opportunity.[q]'

46:18 [r]Jer 48:15 [s]Jos 19:22 [t]1Ki 18:42 18 "As surely as I live," declares the King,[r]
whose name is the LORD Almighty,
"one will come who is like Tabor[s] among the mountains,
like Carmel[t] by the sea.
46:19 [u]Isa 20:4 19 Pack your belongings for exile,[u]
you who live in Egypt,

[a] 9 That is, the upper Nile region [b] 14 Hebrew *Noph*; also in verse 19

46:9 Cush (see "Cush" on p. 1519) is Nubia, or modern Sudan. Located south of Egypt, this territory was also known as Ethiopia (not to be confused with modern Ethiopia, which is located farther to the southeast). Put is either Libya or the land the ancient Egyptians called Punt (modern Somalia). Lydia is either a region in west-central Asia Minor or in Africa. Men from Cush, Put and Lydia served as mercenaries in the Egyptian army.
46:11 For "Gilead" and its healing "balm," see the note on 8:22. Egypt was renowned for its expertise in the healing arts, so this statement is ironic.
46:13 This occurred in 568/567 B.C., long after the battle of Carchemish (see the note on v. 2).
46:14 For Migdol, Tahpanhes and Memphis, see the note on 44:1.
46:15 The Hebrew for "be laid low" is translated "Apis has fled" in the Septuagint. Apis was a bull god worshiped in Egypt, especially at Memphis (see the note on 44:1).
46:17 After the battle of Carchemish (see v. 2), Nebuchadnezzar returned to Babylonia upon learning of his father's death. Egypt failed to press its advantage at that time.
46:18 Tabor and Carmel are two prominent mountains in Israel.

for Memphis will be laid waste
and lie in ruins without inhabitant.

20 "Egypt is a beautiful heifer,
but a gadfly is coming
against her from the north.[v]

46:20 [v]ver 24; Jer 47:2

46:20 The use of the word "heifer" may be an ironic reference to Egyptian bull worship (see the note on v. 15).

ARCHAEOLOGICAL SITES

MEMPHIS

JEREMIAH 46 In proclaiming God's condemnation of Egypt, Jeremiah called for heralds to announce a message of judgment in Memphis ("Maps 8a–8b"). This city (from Men-neferu, meaning "the goodness endures") was situated on the Nile at the border between Upper and Lower Egypt. It was founded by Menes, the first king of the united "Two Lands,"[1] and was sacred to the god Ptah. Its fortunes changed through the centuries, but it remained throughout an important city and religious center:

✣ Memphis, the capital of the **Old Kingdom**, was the location of the great temple of Ptah.

✣ It served as a **Hyksos** royal city during the time that Lower Egypt was under the control of these foreign rulers (eighteenth century B.C.).[2]

✣ It was a favorite residence of **New Kingdom** pharaohs (sixteenth–eleventh centuries B.C.), many of whom built temples, palaces or other buildings there. Memphis served as a military base for campaigns against Syria-Palestine for the great warrior-pharaoh of this time, Thutmose III (1479–1425 B.C.). Syrian and **Phoenician** merchants and mercenaries arriving during the New Kingdom period built temples there to Baal, Astarte and other Canaanite deities.

✣ The city was the center for the cult of the "Apis bulls," which were believed to be living representatives of the god Ptah.[3] Whenever one of these bulls died, it was embalmed and buried in a tomb called the Serapaeum. The shrine benefited from the attention of Pharaoh Shishak, who took an enormous amount of plunder from Israel.[4] He constructed a mortuary and embalming house (c. 910 B.C.) for the Apis bull at Memphis.

✣ As Egypt weakened, Memphis fell into the hands of a variety of foreign rulers. The city was captured by the Ethiopian Pi-Ankhy (c. 717 B.C.); by the **Assyrians** Esarhaddon (671 B.C.) and Ashurbanipal (666 B.C.); and by the **Persian** Cambyses (525 B.C.).[5] Memphis sometimes served as the headquarters for foreign rulers. For example, **Ptolemy** I, founder of the Greek dynasty that ruled Egypt after the conquests of Alexander the Great, made it his capital city.

✣ Jewish refugees entered the city after the Babylonian destruction of Jerusalem (587 B.C.; Jer 44:1).[6]

✣ The Christian emperor Theodosius ordered the temples of Memphis destroyed in A.D. 395, and the city was dismantled during the Arab period (after A.D. 642), after which al-Fustat and Cairo were constructed on the same or a nearby site. Archaeological remains include many temples, two colossal statues of **Rameses II**, a large necropolis (elaborate ancient cemetery), palaces and nearby clusters of pyramids.

Goddess Hathor: carving from Memphis, Egypt
Preserving Bible Times; © Dr. James C. Martin

[1]See "A Breakdown of Ancient Egyptian History" on page 104. [2]See "The Hyksos and the Old Testament" on page 121. [3]See "The Golden Calf" on page 143. [4]See "The Campaign of Shishak" on page 635. [5]See "Ancient Persian History Through Darius" on page 717. [6]See "The Last Days of Jerusalem" on page 1197.

46:21 [w]2Ki 7:6 [x]ver 5 [y]Ps 37:13

21 The mercenaries[w] in her ranks
are like fattened calves.
They too will turn and flee[x] together,
they will not stand their ground,
for the day[y] of disaster is coming upon them,
the time for them to be punished.
22 Egypt will hiss like a fleeing serpent
as the enemy advances in force;
they will come against her with axes,
like men who cut down trees.
23 They will chop down her forest,"
declares the LORD,
"dense though it be.

46:23 [z]Jdg 7:12

They are more numerous than locusts,[z]
they cannot be counted.
24 The Daughter of Egypt will be put to shame,
handed over to the people of the north.[a]"

46:24 [a]Jer 1:15

46:25 [b]Eze 30:14; Na 3:8 [c]Jer 43:12 [d]Isa 20:6
46:26 [e]Jer 44:30 [f]Eze 32:11 [g]Eze 29:11-16
46:27 [h]Isa 41:13; 43:5 [i]Isa 11:11; Jer 50:19

25 The LORD Almighty, the God of Israel, says: "I am about to bring punishment on Amon god of
Thebes,[a][b] on Pharaoh, on Egypt and her gods[c] and her kings, and on those who rely[d] on Pharaoh. 26 I will
hand them over[e] to those who seek their lives, to Nebuchadnezzar king[f] of Babylon and his officers. Later, however, Egypt will be inhabited[g] as in times past," declares the LORD.

27 "Do not fear,[h] O Jacob my servant;
do not be dismayed, O Israel.
I will surely save you out of a distant place,
your descendants from the land of their exile.[i]
Jacob will again have peace and security,
and no one will make him afraid.
28 Do not fear, O Jacob my servant,
for I am with you,"[j] declares the LORD.
"Though I completely destroy[k] all the nations
among which I scatter you,
I will not completely destroy you.
I will discipline you but only with justice;
I will not let you go entirely unpunished."

46:28 [j]Isa 8:9-10 [k]Jer 4:27

A Message About the Philistines

47:1 [l]Ge 10:19; Am 1:6; Zec 9:5-7

47 This is the word of the LORD that came to Jeremiah the prophet concerning the Philistines before Pharaoh attacked Gaza:[l]

2 This is what the LORD says:

47:2 [m]Isa 8:7; 14:31

"See how the waters are rising in the north;[m]
they will become an overflowing torrent.
They will overflow the land and everything in it,
the towns and those who live in them.
The people will cry out;
all who dwell in the land will wail

[a] 25 Hebrew *No*

46:22 Throughout much of Egypt's history the pharaoh wore a cobra cast in metal on the front of his headdress as a symbol of his sovereignty.
46:25 Amon was the chief god of Egypt during much of its history. Wicked King Manasseh may have named his son after this Egyptian deity (see 2Ki 21:18).

Thebes was the capital of Upper (southern) Egypt. (See "Thebes" on p. 1354.)
47:1 The Philistines, neighbors and often enemies of Judah since the days of Israel's judges, lived along the Mediterranean coast. Two Philistine cities are named in this chapter: Gaza (vv. 1,5) and Ashkelon (vv. 5,7). For more information on the Philistines, see "The Archaeology of Philistia" on page 370 and "Technological Supremacy of the Philistines' Iron Weapons" on page 414.
47:2 "The land" refers to Phoenicia (see "Phoenicia" on p. 488) and Philistia (see "The Archaeology of Philistia" on p. 370). "The towns" include Tyre and Sidon (see v. 4), as well as Gaza, Ashkelon and other Philistine cities.

3 at the sound of the hoofs of galloping steeds,
at the noise of enemy chariots
and the rumble of their wheels.
Fathers will not turn to help their children;
their hands will hang limp.
4 For the day has come
to destroy all the Philistines
and to cut off all survivors
who could help Tyre[n] and Sidon.[o]
The LORD is about to destroy the Philistines,[p]
the remnant from the coasts of Caphtor.[a][q]
5 Gaza will shave[r] her head in mourning;
Ashkelon[s] will be silenced.
O remnant on the plain,
how long will you cut yourselves?
6 " 'Ah, sword[t] of the LORD,' ⌞you cry,⌟
'how long till you rest?
Return to your scabbard;
cease and be still.'
7 But how can it rest
when the LORD has commanded it,
when he has ordered it
to attack Ashkelon and the coast?"

47:4 [n]Am 1:9-10; Zec 9:2-4 [o]Jer 25:22 [p]Ge 10:14; Joel 3:4 [q]Dt 2:23
47:5 [r]Jer 41:5; Mic 1:16 [s]Jer 25:20
47:6 [t]Jer 12:12

A Message About Moab

48 Concerning Moab:

This is what the LORD Almighty, the God of Israel, says:

"Woe to Nebo,[u] for it will be ruined.
Kiriathaim[v] will be disgraced and captured;
the stronghold[b] will be disgraced and shattered.
2 Moab will be praised[w] no more;
in Heshbon[c][x] men will plot her downfall:
'Come, let us put an end to that nation.'
You too, O Madmen,[d] will be silenced;
the sword will pursue you.
3 Listen to the cries from Horonaim,[y]
cries of great havoc and destruction.
4 Moab will be broken;
her little ones will cry out.[e]
5 They go up the way to Luhith,[z]
weeping bitterly as they go;

48:1 [u]Nu 32:38 [v]Nu 32:37
48:2 [w]Isa 16:14 [x]Nu 21:25
48:3 [y]Isa 15:5
48:5 [z]Isa 15:5

[a] 4 That is, Crete [b] 1 Or / *Misgab* [c] 2 The Hebrew for *Heshbon* sounds like the Hebrew for *plot.* [d] 2 The name of the Moabite town Madmen sounds like the Hebrew for *be silenced.* [e] 4 Hebrew; Septuagint / *proclaim it to Zoar*

47:4 See "The Downfall of Tyre" on page 1345. For "Sidon," see "Sidon" on page 1536. Caphtor is most likely Crete, one of many islands in the Mediterranean believed to have been the original homeland of the Philistines. See also the note on Zephaniah 2:5.
47:5 The "plain" is roughly equivalent to the modern Gaza Strip; it lay west of the foothills that separated Philistia from Judah.
Shaving one's head and cutting oneself were signs of mourning (see the note on 41:5).
47:7 The immediate fulfillment of this prophecy took place under Nebuchadnezzar in 604 B.C.
48:1 Josephus (*Antiquities*, 10.9.7) implied that Jeremiah's prophecy concerning the future destruction of Moab was fulfilled in the "twenty-third year of Nebuchadnezzar's reign" (582 B.C.). For information on Moab, see "Moab" on page 292.
Nebo was a town north of the Arnon River that had originally been allotted to the tribe of Reuben. Kiriathaim was an ancient town also allotted to Reuben. Nebo, Kiriathaim and several other towns referred to in this chapter are mentioned in an important Moabite inscription written by Mesha, king of Moab (see 2Ki 3:4), and discovered in 1868 in Dhiban, Jordan. See "The Mesha (Moabite) Stone" on page 530.
48:2 Heshbon, situated approximately 18 miles (29 km) east of the northern tip of the Dead Sea, was King Sihon's capital before Israel captured the city. Heshbon was originally allotted to Reuben but was later reassigned to Gad as a Levitical town (see "Levitical Towns" on p. 335).

on the road down to Horonaim
anguished cries over the destruction are heard.
6 Flee! Run for your lives;
become like a bush[a] in the desert.[a]
7 Since you trust in your deeds and riches,
you too will be taken captive,
and Chemosh[b] will go into exile,[c]
together with his priests and officials.
8 The destroyer will come against every town,
and not a town will escape.
The valley will be ruined
and the plateau destroyed,
because the LORD has spoken.
9 Put salt on Moab,
for she will be laid waste[b];
her towns will become desolate,
with no one to live in them.

10 "A curse on him who is lax in doing the LORD's work!
A curse on him who keeps his sword[d] from bloodshed![e]

11 "Moab has been at rest[f] from youth,
like wine left on its dregs,[g]
not poured from one jar to another—
she has not gone into exile.
So she tastes as she did,
and her aroma is unchanged.
12 But days are coming,"
declares the LORD,
"when I will send men who pour from jars,
and they will pour her out;
they will empty her jars
and smash her jugs.
13 Then Moab will be ashamed[h] of Chemosh,
as the house of Israel was ashamed
when they trusted in Bethel.

14 "How can you say, 'We are warriors,[i]
men valiant in battle'?
15 Moab will be destroyed and her towns invaded;
her finest young men will go down in the slaughter,[j]"
declares the King,[k] whose name is the LORD Almighty.[l]
16 "The fall of Moab is at hand;[m]
her calamity will come quickly.

48:6 [a]Jer 17:6
48:7 [b]Nu 21:29 [c]Isa 46:1-2; Jer 49:3
48:10 [d]Jer 47:6 [e]1Ki 20:42; 2Ki 13:15-19
48:11 [f]Zec 1:15 [g]Zep 1:12
48:13 [h]Hos 10:6
48:14 [i]Ps 33:16
48:15 [j]Jer 50:27 [k]Jer 46:18 [l]Jer 51:57
48:16 [m]Isa 13:22

[a] 6 Or *like Aroer* [b] 9 Or *Give wings to Moab, / for she will fly away*

48:7 Chemosh was the national god of Moab (see 1Ki 11:7,33; 2Ki 23:13). Images of pagan deities were often carried about from place to place (see Jer 43:12; Am 5:26).
48:8 The "destroyer" probably refers here to Nebuchadnezzar (see the note on 4:7).
48:9 Salt was scattered over the land to render the soil unproductive and barren.
48:11 A copy of the Hebrew text of this verse has been found inscribed on a large clay seal dating to the early Christian era and apparently used for stamping the bitumen with which the mouths of wine jars were sealed.

Wine was an apt figure for Moab, since this nation was noted for her vineyards. The best wine was aged while being "left on its dregs," a reference to thickening and congealing at the bottom of a container. The implication is that the people were complacent, indifferent and unmoved by prophetic warnings—like thick, syrupy wine.
48:13 "The house of Israel" refers to the northern kingdom, which was destroyed and exiled in 722/721 B.C.

Bethel may refer to the well-known town where one of Jeroboam's golden calves was placed (see 1Ki 12:25–33; see also "Bethel" on p. 59 and "The High Place at Dan" on p. 504). Alternatively, in parallelism with Chemosh, it may refer to the western Semitic deity known from contemporary Babylonian inscriptions as well as from the Elephantine papyri a century later.

17 Mourn for her, all who live around her,
all who know her fame;
say, 'How broken is the mighty scepter,
how broken the glorious staff!'

18 "Come down from your glory
and sit on the parched ground,[n]
O inhabitants of the Daughter of Dibon,[o]
for he who destroys Moab
will come up against you
and ruin your fortified cities.[p]
19 Stand by the road and watch,
you who live in Aroer.[q]
Ask the man fleeing and the woman escaping,
ask them, 'What has happened?'
20 Moab is disgraced, for she is shattered.
Wail[r] and cry out!
Announce by the Arnon[s]
that Moab is destroyed.
21 Judgment has come to the plateau—
to Holon, Jahzah[t] and Mephaath,[u]
22 to Dibon,[v] Nebo and Beth Diblathaim,
23 to Kiriathaim, Beth Gamul and Beth Meon,[w]
24 to Kerioth[x] and Bozrah—
to all the towns of Moab, far and near.
25 Moab's horn[a][y] is cut off;
her arm[z] is broken,"
declares the LORD.

26 "Make her drunk,[a]
for she has defied the LORD.
Let Moab wallow in her vomit;
let her be an object of ridicule.
27 Was not Israel the object of your ridicule?[b]
Was she caught among thieves,
that you shake your head[c] in scorn[d]
whenever you speak of her?
28 Abandon your towns and dwell among the rocks,
you who live in Moab.
Be like a dove[e] that makes its nest
at the mouth of a cave.[f]

29 "We have heard of Moab's pride[g]—
her overweening pride and conceit,

48:18 [n]Isa 47:1 [o]Nu 21:30; Jos 13:9 [p]ver 8
48:19 [q]Dt 2:36
48:20 [r]Isa 16:7 [s]Nu 21:13
48:21 [t]Nu 21:23; Isa 15:4 [u]Jos 13:18
48:22 [v]Jos 13:9, 17
48:23 [w]Jos 13:17
48:24 [x]Am 2:2
48:25 [y]Ps 75:10 [z]Ps 10:15; Eze 30:21
48:26 [a]Jer 25:16, 27
48:27 [b]Jer 2:26 [c]Job 16:4; Jer 18:16 [d]Mic 7:8-10
48:28 [e]Ps 55:6-7 [f]Jdg 6:2
48:29 [g]Job 40:12; Isa 16:6

[a] 25 *Horn* here symbolizes strength.

48:17 Scepters and staffs were symbols of authority and dominion.
48:18 Dibon was a city east of the Dead Sea and about 4 miles (6.5 km) north of the Arnon River. In was an important (apparently at one time royal) Moabite town. Dibon has been identified as modern Dhiban, Jordan, where the famous Moabite Stone of King Mesha was discovered in 1868. See "The Mesha (Moabite) Stone" on page 530.
48:20 The Arnon, Moab's most important river, served as the border between Moab and the region of the Amorites. It flows west into the midpoint of the Dead Sea.
48:22 For "Dibon," see the note on verse 18 and for "Nebo" the note on verse 1. "Beth Diblathaim" may be the same as, or may have been near, Almon Diblathaim (see Nu 33:46).
48:23 For "Kiriathaim," see the note on verse 1. Beth Gamul may be modern Khirbet Jumeil, five miles (eight km) east of Aroer. "Beth Meon" is the same as Baal Meon (see Nu 32:38) and Beth Baal Meon (see Jos 13:17).
48:24 Kerioth was probably a major (although otherwise unidentified) city with a shrine of Chemosh, the national god of Moab.

This Bozrah is not the same as the Bozrah in Edom (see 49:13,22) but is another name for Bezer in Moab, which was located about 20 miles (32 km) east of the northeast corner of the Dead Sea.
48:29 Moab's pride had long since become proverbial (see Isa 25:10–11; Zep 2:8–10).

her pride and arrogance
and the haughtiness of her heart.
30 I know her insolence but it is futile,"
declares the LORD,
"and her boasts accomplish nothing.

48:31 [h]Isa 15:5-8 [i]2Ki 3:25

31 Therefore I wail[h] over Moab,
for all Moab I cry out,
I moan for the men of Kir Hareseth.[i]
32 I weep for you, as Jazer weeps,

48:32 [j]Isa 16:8-9

O vines of Sibmah.[j]
Your branches spread as far as the sea;
they reached as far as the sea of Jazer.
The destroyer has fallen
on your ripened fruit and grapes.
33 Joy and gladness are gone
from the orchards and fields of Moab.

48:33 [k]Isa 16:10 [l]Joel 1:12

I have stopped the flow of wine[k] from the presses;
no one treads them with shouts of joy.[l]
Although there are shouts,
they are not shouts of joy.

34 "The sound of their cry rises

48:34 [m]Nu 32:3 [n]Isa 15:4 [o]Ge 13:10 [p]Isa 15:5 [q]Isa 15:6

from Heshbon to Elealeh[m] and Jahaz,[n]
from Zoar[o] as far as Horonaim[p] and Eglath Shelishiyah,
for even the waters of Nimrim are dried up.[q]
35 In Moab I will put an end

48:35 [r]Isa 15:2; 16:12 [s]Jer 11:13

to those who make offerings on the high places[r]
and burn incense[s] to their gods,"
declares the LORD.

48:36 [t]Isa 16:11 [u]Isa 15:7

36 "So my heart laments[t] for Moab like a flute;
it laments like a flute for the men of Kir Hareseth.
The wealth they acquired[u] is gone.

48:37 [v]Isa 15:2; Jer 41:5 [w]Ge 37:34

37 Every head is shaved[v]
and every beard cut off;
every hand is slashed
and every waist is covered with sackcloth.[w]
38 On all the roofs in Moab
and in the public squares
there is nothing but mourning,
for I have broken Moab

48:38 [x]Jer 22:28

like a jar[x] that no one wants,"
declares the LORD.

39 "How shattered she is! How they wail!
How Moab turns her back in shame!
Moab has become an object of ridicule,
an object of horror to all those around her."

40 This is what the LORD says:

48:40 [y]Dt 28:49; Hab 1:8 [z]Isa 8:8

"Look! An eagle is swooping[y] down,
spreading its wings[z] over Moab.

48:31 Kir Hareseth, the original capital of Moab, is usually identified with present-day Kerak, located about 11 miles (18 km) east of the Dead Sea and 15 miles (24 km) south of the Arnon River.
48:32 For information on Jazer and Sibmah, see the note on Isaiah 16:8. For "destroyer," see the note on verse 48:8.
48:36 Flutes were played by mourners at funerals (see "Ancient Musical Instruments" on p. 797).
48:37 These were signs of mourning (see "Sackcloth and Ashes: Rituals of Lamentation" on p. 820).
48:40 The eagle was Nebuchadnezzar.

[41] Kerioth[a] will be captured
and the strongholds taken.
In that day the hearts of Moab's warriors
will be like the heart of a woman in labor.[a]
[42] Moab will be destroyed[b] as a nation[c]
because she defied[d] the LORD.
[43] Terror and pit and snare[e] await you,
O people of Moab,"
declares the LORD.

[44] "Whoever flees[f] from the terror
will fall into a pit,
whoever climbs out of the pit
will be caught in a snare;
for I will bring upon Moab
the year[g] of her punishment,"
declares the LORD.

[45] "In the shadow of Heshbon
the fugitives stand helpless,
for a fire has gone out from Heshbon,
a blaze from the midst of Sihon;[h]
it burns the foreheads of Moab,
the skulls[i] of the noisy boasters.
[46] Woe to you, O Moab![j]
The people of Chemosh are destroyed;
your sons are taken into exile
and your daughters into captivity.

[47] "Yet I will restore[k] the fortunes of Moab
in days to come,"
declares the LORD.

Here ends the judgment on Moab.

A Message About Ammon

49 Concerning the Ammonites:[l]

This is what the LORD says:

"Has Israel no sons?
Has she no heirs?
Why then has Molech[b] taken possession of Gad?
Why do his people live in its towns?
[2] But the days are coming,"
declares the LORD,
"when I will sound the battle cry[m]
against Rabbah[n] of the Ammonites;

48:41 [a]Isa 21:3
48:42 [b]Ps 83:4; Isa 16:14 [c]ver 2 [d]ver 26
48:43 [e]Isa 24:17
48:44 [f]1Ki 19:17; Isa 24:18 [g]Jer 11:23
48:45 [h]Nu 21:21, 26-28 [i]Nu 24:17
48:46 [j]Nu 21:29
48:47 [k]Jer 12:15; 49:6,39
49:1 [l]Am 1:13; Zep 2:8-9
49:2 [m]Jer 4:19 [n]Dt 3:11

[a] *41* Or *The cities* [b] *1* Or *their king*; Hebrew *malcam*; also in verse 3

48:45 For "Heshbon," see the note on verse 2. The town was apparently controlled by the Ammonites at this time (see 49:3). Sihon was the king who ruled Heshbon at the time of the conquest (see Nu 21:27; see also "The Kingdoms of Sihon and Og" on p. 244). The idea seems to have been that a new Sihon ruled over Heshbon and that he, too, would see his city go down in flames.
48:46 For "Chemosh," see the note on verse 7.
49:1 Ammon (see "Ammon" on p. 364) was located north of Moab and east of the Jordan River. The chief god of the Ammonites was Molech, also known as Milcom, the god to whom child sacrifices were tragically offered in Judah (32:35; cf. Lev 20:2–5; 2Ki 23:10).

This verse probably refers to the time after Tiglath-Pileser III's conquest of Transjordan (734–732 B.C.), when the Ammonites evidently recovered from their defeat and overran some of the territory owned by the Israelite tribe of Gad.
49:2 Rabbah (Philadelphia in NT times) was the capital of Ammon (see "Rabbah" on p. 606 and "Ammon" on p. 364). Its remains form part of the impressive citadel at the heart of modern Amman, Jordan.

For "mound of ruins," see the note on 30:18.

it will become a mound of ruins,
and its surrounding villages will be set on fire.
Then Israel will drive out
49:2 [o]Isa 14:2; Eze 21:28-32; 25:2-11 — those who drove her out,[o]"
says the LORD.

49:3 [p]Jos 8:28 [q]Jer 48:7 — 3 "Wail, O Heshbon, for Ai[p] is destroyed!
Cry out, O inhabitants of Rabbah!
Put on sackcloth and mourn;
rush here and there inside the walls,
for Molech will go into exile,[q]
together with his priests and officials.
4 Why do you boast of your valleys,
boast of your valleys so fruitful?
O unfaithful daughter,
49:4 [r]Jer 9:23; 1Ti 6:17 [s]Jer 21:13 — you trust in your riches[r] and say,
'Who will attack me?'[s]
5 I will bring terror on you
from all those around you,"
declares the Lord, the LORD Almighty.
"Every one of you will be driven away,
and no one will gather the fugitives.

49:6 [t]ver 39; Jer 48:47 — 6 "Yet afterward, I will restore[t] the fortunes of the Ammonites,"
declares the LORD.

A Message About Edom

49:7 [u]Ge 25:30; Eze 25:12 [v]Ge 36:11,15,34 — 7 Concerning Edom:[u]

This is what the LORD Almighty says:

"Is there no longer wisdom in Teman?[v]
Has counsel perished from the prudent?
Has their wisdom decayed?
8 Turn and flee, hide in deep caves,
49:8 [w]Jer 25:23 — you who live in Dedan,[w]
for I will bring disaster on Esau
at the time I punish him.
9 If grape pickers came to you,
would they not leave a few grapes?
If thieves came during the night,
would they not steal only as much as they wanted?
10 But I will strip Esau bare;
I will uncover his hiding places,
so that he cannot conceal himself.
His children, relatives and neighbors will perish,
49:10 [x]Mal 1:2-5 — and he will be no more.[x]
49:11 [y]Hos 14:3 — 11 Leave your orphans;[y] I will protect their lives.
Your widows too can trust in me."

49:3 For "Heshbon," see the note on 48:2 and for "Molech" the note on verse 1.
49:4 "Unfaithful daughter" is a personification of the Ammonites. According to Josephus (*Antiquities*, 10.9.7) Nebuchadnezzar destroyed Ammon in 582 B.C.
49:7 Edom was located in a remote region south of Moab and the Dead Sea (see "Edom" on p. 1467). Edom and Teman, an important Edomite town, were both noted for their wisdom.
49:8 Dedan was both a tribe and a region located in southern Edom (see the note on Isa 21:13–17).

Esau (the brother of the patriarch Jacob) was another name for Edom, just as Israel was another name for Jacob. The fact that Esau (the forefather of the Edomites) was Jacob's brother made Edom's enmity toward Israel all the more reprehensible (see Am 1:11; Ob 10).

[12]This is what the LORD says: "If those who do not deserve to drink the cup[z] must drink it, why should
you go unpunished?[a] You will not go unpunished, but must drink it. [13]I swear[b] by myself," declares the
LORD, "that Bozrah[c] will become a ruin and an object of horror, of reproach and of cursing; and all its
towns will be in ruins forever."

[14]I have heard a message from the LORD:
An envoy was sent to the nations to say,
"Assemble yourselves to attack it!
Rise up for battle!"

[15]"Now I will make you small among the nations,
despised among men.
[16]The terror you inspire
and the pride of your heart have deceived you,
you who live in the clefts of the rocks,
who occupy the heights of the hill.
Though you build your nest[d] as high as the eagle's,
from there I will bring you down,"
declares the LORD.

[17]"Edom will become an object of horror;[e]
all who pass by will be appalled and will scoff
because of all its wounds.[f]
[18]As Sodom and Gomorrah[g] were overthrown,
along with their neighboring towns,"
says the LORD,
"so no one will live there;
no man will dwell[h] in it.

[19]"Like a lion coming up from Jordan's thickets[i]
to a rich pastureland,
I will chase Edom from its land in an instant.
Who is the chosen one I will appoint for this?
Who is like me and who can challenge me?[j]
And what shepherd can stand against me?"
[20]Therefore, hear what the LORD has planned against
Edom,
what he has purposed[k] against those who live
in Teman:
The young of the flock[l] will be dragged away;
he will completely destroy[m] their pasture because
of them.
[21]At the sound of their fall the earth will tremble;[n]
their cry[o] will resound to the Red Sea.[a]
[22]Look! An eagle will soar and swoop[p] down,
spreading its wings over Bozrah.
In that day the hearts of Edom's warriors
will be like the heart of a woman in labor.[q]

49:12 [z]Jer 25:15 [a]Jer 25:28-29
49:13 [b]Ge 22:16 [c]Ge 36:33; Isa 34:6
49:16 [d]Job 39:27; Am 9:2
49:17 [e]ver 13 [f]Jer 50:13; Eze 35:7
49:18 [g]Ge 19:24; Dt 29:23 [h]ver 33
49:19 [i]Jer 12:5 [j]Jer 50:44
49:20 [k]Isa 14:27 [l]Jer 50:45 [m]Mal 1:3-4
49:21 [n]Eze 26:15 [o]Jer 50:46; Eze 26:18
49:22 [p]Hos 8:1 [q]Isa 13:8; Jer 48:40-41

[a] *21* Hebrew *Yam Suph*; that is, Sea of Reeds

49:13 This Bozrah is not the Bozrah of 48:24 (see the note there). The Edomite Bozrah was probably the capital of Edom in the days of Jeremiah.
49:16 "Rocks" may be a reference to Petra ("rock" in Greek), the most spectacular of the mountain strongholds for which Edom was noted.
49:18 Calamities of various kinds were often compared with the one that had befallen Sodom and Gomorrah (see "The Destruction of Sodom and Gomorrah" on p. 32).
49:19 For "shepherd," see the note on 3:15.
49:20 For "Teman," see the note on verse 7.
"Flock" refers to the people of Edom.
49:22 The eagle probably represents Nebuchadnezzar, as in 48:40. A more complete subjugation of the Edomites, however, was accomplished by the Nabatean Arabs (perhaps the "desert jackals" of Mal 1:3) beginning about 550 B.C.
For "Bozrah," see the note on verse 13.

A Message About Damascus

49:23 [r]Ge 14:15; 2Ch 16:2; Ac 9:2 [s]Isa 10:9; Am 6:2; Zec 9:2 [t]2Ki 18:34 [u]Ge 49:4; Isa 57:20

23 Concerning Damascus:[r]

"Hamath[s] and Arpad[t] are dismayed,
for they have heard bad news.
They are disheartened,
troubled like[a] the restless sea.[u]
24 Damascus has become feeble,
she has turned to flee
and panic has gripped her;
anguish and pain have seized her,
pain like that of a woman in labor.
25 Why has the city of renown not been abandoned,
the town in which I delight?
26 Surely, her young men will fall in the streets;
all her soldiers will be silenced[v] in that day,"
declares the LORD Almighty.
27 "I will set fire[w] to the walls of Damascus;
it will consume the fortresses of Ben-Hadad.[x]"

49:26 [v]Jer 50:30

49:27 [w]Jer 43:12; Am 1:4 [x]1Ki 15:18

A Message About Kedar and Hazor

49:28 [y]Ge 25:13 [z]Jdg 6:3

28 Concerning Kedar[y] and the kingdoms of Hazor, which Nebuchadnezzar king of Babylon attacked:

This is what the LORD says:

"Arise, and attack Kedar
and destroy the people of the East.[z]
29 Their tents and their flocks will be taken;
their shelters will be carried off
with all their goods and camels.
Men will shout to them,
'Terror[a] on every side!'

49:29 [a]Jer 6:25; 46:5

30 "Flee quickly away!
Stay in deep caves, you who live in Hazor,"
declares the LORD.
"Nebuchadnezzar king of Babylon has plotted against you;
he has devised a plan against you.

31 "Arise and attack a nation at ease,
which lives in confidence,"
declares the LORD,
"a nation that has neither gates nor bars;[b]
its people live alone.
32 Their camels will become plunder,
and their large herds will be booty.

49:31 [b]Eze 38:11

[a] 23 Hebrew *on* or *by*

49:23 For "Damascus", see the note on Isaiah 17:1. Hamath was an important city on the Orontes River in the kingdom of Aram, and Arpad was a city near Hamath.
49:27 Hadad was a well-known Aramean deity, and the name Ben-Hadad designated a king as the adopted "son" (*ben* means "son") of this god. Comparable to the term *pharaoh* in Egypt, several kings from Damascus used this title/name (see, e.g., 2Ki 6:24).
49:28 Kedar, a region in northern Arabia, to the east of Judah, was known for its flocks (60:7; Eze 27:21), tents and tent curtains, which were woven by hand from black goat hair.

Hazor is something of a mystery, since no location by that name is known in northern Arabia. It is not the city north of the Sea of Galilee frequently mentioned in the Old Testament. The "kingdoms of Hazor" may have included Dedan, Tema, Buz and other Arab regions (see the note on 25:23).

Both Kedar and Hazor likely refer to groups of Arab tribesmen who were attacked by the Babylonians under Nebuchadnezzar in 599 B.C. For more than two millennia a mysterious "time warp" has kept nomadic Arab herders from the encroachment (good or bad) of modern civilization. While Kedar and Hazor may no longer exist, many places like them still dot the desert regions of the Middle East and northern Africa.
49:31 A nation that had "neither gates nor bars" refers to one whose people lived in unwalled villages.

I will scatter to the winds those who are in distant places[a] [c]
and will bring disaster on them from every side,"
declares the LORD.

33 "Hazor will become a haunt of jackals,
a desolate[d] place forever.
No one will live there;
no man will dwell[e] in it."

49:32 [c]Jer 9:26
49:33 [d]Jer 10:22 [e]ver 18; Jer 51:37

A Message About Elam

34 This is the word of the LORD that came to Jeremiah the prophet concerning Elam,[f] early in the reign
of Zedekiah[g] king of Judah:

35 This is what the LORD Almighty says:

"See, I will break the bow[h] of Elam,
the mainstay of their might.
36 I will bring against Elam the four winds[i]
from the four quarters of the heavens;
I will scatter them to the four winds,
and there will not be a nation
where Elam's exiles do not go.
37 I will shatter Elam before their foes,
before those who seek their lives;
I will bring disaster upon them,
even my fierce anger,"[j]
declares the LORD.

"I will pursue them with the sword[k]
until I have made an end of them.
38 I will set my throne in Elam
and destroy her king and officials,"
declares the LORD.

39 "Yet I will restore[l] the fortunes of Elam
in days to come,"
declares the LORD.

49:34 [f]Ge 10:22 [g]2Ki 24:18
49:35 [h]Isa 22:6
49:36 [i]ver 32
49:37 [j]Jer 30:24 [k]Jer 9:16
49:39 [l]Jer 48:47

A Message About Babylon

50 This is the word the LORD spoke through Jeremiah the prophet concerning Babylon[m] and the
land of the Babylonians[b]:

2 "Announce and proclaim[n] among the nations,
lift up a banner and proclaim it;
keep nothing back, but say,
'Babylon will be captured;[o]
Bel[p] will be put to shame,
Marduk[q] filled with terror.
Her images will be put to shame
and her idols filled with terror.'
3 A nation from the north will attack her
and lay waste her land.

50:1 [m]Ge 10:10; Isa 13:1
50:2 [n]Jer 4:16 [o]Jer 51:31 [p]Isa 46:1 [q]Jer 51:47

[a] 32 *Or who clip the hair by their foreheads* [b] 1 Or *Chaldeans*; also in verses 8, 25, 35 and 45

49:34 Elam was located in the southern part of modern Iran. The Elamites, perpetual enemies of both Assyria and Babylon, became part of the Persian army that conquered Babylon under Cyrus in 539 B.C.
49:35 The Elamites were skilled archers.
50:2 This prophecy regarding Babylon was fulfilled in 539 B.C. (See "Babylon" on p. 1077.) For "Bel," see the note on Isaiah 46:1. The chief god of Babylon, as well as his images and idols, was doomed.
50:3 In Jeremiah, the foe from the north is almost always Babylon. Here, however, the reference is probably to Persia.

50:3 [r]ver 13; Isa 14:22-23 [s]Zep 1:3

No one will live[r] in it;
both men and animals[s] will flee away.

50:4 [t]Jer 3:18; Hos 1:11 [u]Ezr 3:12; Jer 31:9 [v]Hos 3:5

4 "In those days, at that time,"
declares the LORD,
"the people of Israel and the people of Judah together[t]
will go in tears[u] to seek[v] the LORD their God.
5 They will ask the way to Zion
and turn their faces toward it.

50:5 [w]Jer 33:7 [x]Isa 55:3; Jer 32:40; Heb 8:6-10

They will come[w] and bind themselves to the LORD
in an everlasting covenant[x]
that will not be forgotten.

50:6 [y]Isa 53:6; Mt 9:36; 10:6 [z]Jer 3:6; Eze 34:6 [a]ver 19

6 "My people have been lost sheep;[y]
their shepherds have led them astray
and caused them to roam on the mountains.
They wandered over mountain and hill[z]
and forgot their own resting place.[a]
7 Whoever found them devoured them;

50:7 [b]Jer 2:3 [c]Jer 14:8

their enemies said, 'We are not guilty,[b]
for they sinned against the LORD, their true pasture,
the LORD, the hope[c] of their fathers.'

50:8 [d]Isa 48:20; Jer 51:6; Rev 18:4

8 "Flee[d] out of Babylon;
leave the land of the Babylonians,
and be like the goats that lead the flock.
9 For I will stir up and bring against Babylon
an alliance of great nations from the land of the north.
They will take up their positions against her,
and from the north she will be captured.
Their arrows will be like skilled warriors
who do not return empty-handed.
10 So Babylonia[a] will be plundered;
all who plunder her will have their fill,"
declares the LORD.

50:11 [e]Isa 47:6

11 "Because you rejoice and are glad,
you who pillage my inheritance,[e]
because you frolic like a heifer threshing grain
and neigh like stallions,
12 your mother will be greatly ashamed;
she who gave you birth will be disgraced.
She will be the least of the nations—
a wilderness, a dry land, a desert.
13 Because of the LORD's anger she will not be inhabited
but will be completely desolate.

50:13 [f]Jer 18:16 [g]Jer 49:17

All who pass Babylon will be horrified and scoff[f]
because of all her wounds.[g]

50:14 [h]ver 29,42

14 "Take up your positions around Babylon,
all you who draw the bow.[h]
Shoot at her! Spare no arrows,
for she has sinned against the LORD.

[a] 10 Or *Chaldea*

50:6 For "shepherds," see the note on 3:15.
The phrase "mountain and hill" refers to sites where pagan gods were worshiped (see "The High Places" on p. 1318).

[15]Shout[i] against her on every side!
She surrenders, her towers fall,
her walls[j] are torn down.
Since this is the vengeance[k] of the LORD,
take vengeance on her;
do to her[l] as she has done to others.
[16]Cut off from Babylon the sower,
and the reaper with his sickle at harvest.
Because of the sword[m] of the oppressor
let everyone return to his own people,[n]
let everyone flee to his own land.[o]

[17]"Israel is a scattered flock
that lions[p] have chased away.
The first to devour him
was the king[q] of Assyria;
the last to crush his bones
was Nebuchadnezzar[r] king[s] of Babylon."

[18]Therefore this is what the LORD Almighty, the God of Israel, says:

"I will punish the king of Babylon and his land
as I punished the king[t] of Assyria.[u]
[19]But I will bring[v] Israel back to his own pasture
and he will graze on Carmel and Bashan;
his appetite will be satisfied
on the hills[w] of Ephraim and Gilead.
[20]In those days, at that time,"
declares the LORD,
"search will be made for Israel's guilt,
but there will be none,
and for the sins[x] of Judah,
but none will be found,
for I will forgive[y] the remnant[z] I spare.

[21]"Attack the land of Merathaim
and those who live in Pekod.[a]
Pursue, kill and completely destroy[a] them,"
declares the LORD.

"Do everything I have commanded you.
[22]The noise[b] of battle is in the land,
the noise of great destruction!
[23]How broken and shattered
is the hammer of the whole earth!
How desolate[c] is Babylon
among the nations!

50:15 [i]Jer 51:14 [j]Jer 51:44,58 [k]Jer 51:6 [l]Ps 137:8; Rev 18:6
50:16 [m]Jer 25:38 [n]Isa 13:14 [o]Jer 51:9
50:17 [p]Jer 2:15 [q]2Ki 17:6 [r]2Ki 24:10,14 [s]2Ki 25:7
50:18 [t]Isa 10:12 [u]Eze 31:3
50:19 [v]Jer 31:10; Eze 34:13 [w]Jer 31:5; 33:12
50:20 [x]Mic 7:18, 19 [y]Jer 31:34 [z]Isa 1:9
50:21 [a]Eze 23:23
50:22 [b]Jer 4:19-21; 51:54
50:23 [c]Isa 14:16

[a] *21* The Hebrew term refers to the irrevocable giving over of things or persons to the LORD, often by totally destroying them; also in verse 26.

50:17 Lions symbolized both Assyria and Babylon (see the note on 4:7). The Assyrians destroyed Israel (the northern kingdom) "first" (722/721 B.C.), and the Babylonians sacked Judah (the southern kingdom) "last" (586 B.C.).
50:18 Nineveh, the proud Assyrian capital, fell in 612 B.C., and Assyria herself was conquered by a coalition of Medes and Babylonians in 609.
50:19 Carmel, Bashan, Ephraim and Gilead were all known for their lush pasturelands.
50:21 Merathaim is probably a pun on the Babylonian word *marratu*, which sometimes referred to a region in southern Babylonia that was characterized by briny waters. Pekod is a pun on *Puqudu*, the Babylonian name for an Aramean tribe living on the eastern bank of the lower Tigris River.

For "completely destroy," see the NIV text note. The Hebrew for this expression usually denotes the ruin of everyone and everything that could possibly be destroyed. Objects like gold, silver and bronze, not subject to such damage, were stored in a secure place as God's possession. The annihilation of people and things rendered them useless to the conquerors but put them in the hands of God, so the phrase is sometimes translated "destroyed" and sometimes "devoted" (see "*Herem*, Holy War" on p. 419).

HERODOTUS AND THE FALL OF BABYLON

JEREMIAH 50 The Greek historian Herodotus (c. 480–425 B.C.) produced one of the most famous books of ancient Greece, the *History*. Its focus is the series of wars between **Persia** and the Greeks that lasted from approximately 490 to 479 B.C. Herodotus devoted a great deal of attention to the background of the wars and in the process gave a fairly sweeping view of the eastern Mediterranean world during the sixth and fifth centuries B.C.

The Greek word *historiai* (literally "investigations") aptly describes how Herodotus went about collecting and recording information about the customs and histories of the peoples he encountered. He is regarded as the father of Western history writing because he tried to confine himself to human events and to avoid myths.

Brick inscription reads: "Cyrus, king of the world, king of Anshan, son of Cambyses, king of Anshan. The great gods delivered all the lands into my hands, and I made this land to dwell in peace."

© Dr. James C. Martin; The British Museum. Photographed by permission.

At times, however, claims from Herodotus are of questionable value. It is incorrect to assert, as some have, that Herodotus simply invented his stories. He did, however, include rumor, legend and gossip in his histories and sometimes may have misunderstood his sources.

Herodotus's account of the fall of Babylon (*History*, 1.189–191) in 539 B.C. relates to the prophetic account in Jeremiah 50–51, as well as to Daniel's indication that Babylon fell overnight during a festival (Da 5:30–31). Herodotus began with a fantastic tale of how Cyrus's horse drowned in the Gyndes River and how he, to punish the river by making it weak and shallow, compelled his army to spend a summer diverting it into 360 channels. Arriving at Babylon, Cyrus faced the prospect of a prolonged siege. Babylon was large enough to store food for many years, so any attempt to starve the city into submission would have been futile.

But, Herodotus noted, the city had one peculiar characteristic: The Euphrates River ran through the middle of Babylon and divided it into two parts. Cyrus decided that the river channels under the walls provided the only chance of gaining entry, but the volume of water and the strength of the current were too great. Yet the Persian king hatched an ingenious plan: He posted soldiers at the points at which the Euphrates entered and left the city and instructed his men to move through the river when it became fordable. Meanwhile, the noncombatants went upstream and diverted much of the river into an artificial marsh. When the water level had dropped sufficiently, the Persian soldiers made their way in and captured the Babylonian capital.[1]

What are we to make of this account? Most historians believe that Herodotus's version of events is at least to some degree confused and misleading. In his actual conquest of Babylonia, Cyrus's forces proceeded down from the north and rapidly overcame resistance. A second front was opened against Babylon by a certain Ugbaru, governor of Gutium. Ugbaru proceeded to capture Babylon for Cyrus with astonishing speed, and Cyrus himself entered the city shortly thereafter.

Several factors may have contributed to the Persian victory. First, Cyrus may have kept the bulk of the Babylonian forces occupied with his army while Ugbaru came in from the rear. Second, the Babylonian regime was unpopular, and the people seem to have welcomed Cyrus as a liberator. Third, Ugbaru appears to have entered Babylon by subterfuge (as is reflected in the version of the story about the diversion of the Euphrates).

It is certain, however, that Babylon fell suddenly. Herodotus is correct in stating that the Euphrates bisected the city, and the Nabonidus Chronicle confirms that it fell without a battle. Thus the account about diverting the Euphrates may be true. Both Daniel 5 and Herodotus indicate that Babylon fell during a rowdy festival. Herodotus stated: "Owing to the sheer size of the city, so say the inhabitants, those in the outlying areas were captured without those in the center knowing about it."

Daniel 5 recounts the story of Belshazzar's feast,[2] and can be regarded as an independent witness. Herodotus, in this account as elsewhere, was colorful and not always fully reliable, but he appears to have preserved something of (and perhaps a good deal of) the true story.[3]

[1]See "Cyrus the Great" on page 669. [2]See "Nabonidus and Belshazzar" on page 1394. [3]See also "Historians in the Ancient World" on page 939.

[24] I set a trap[d] for you, O Babylon,
and you were caught before you knew it;
you were found and captured[e]
because you opposed[f] the LORD.
[25] The LORD has opened his arsenal
and brought out the weapons[g] of his wrath,
for the Sovereign LORD Almighty has work to do
in the land of the Babylonians.[h]
[26] Come against her from afar.
Break open her granaries;
pile her up like heaps of grain.
Completely destroy[i] her
and leave her no remnant.
[27] Kill all her young bulls;
let them go down to the slaughter!
Woe to them! For their day has come,
the time for them to be punished.
[28] Listen to the fugitives and refugees from Babylon
declaring in Zion[j]
how the LORD our God has taken vengeance,[k]
vengeance for his temple.

[29] "Summon archers against Babylon,
all those who draw the bow.[l]
Encamp all around her;
let no one escape.
Repay[m] her for her deeds;[n]
do to her as she has done.
For she has defied[o] the LORD,
the Holy One of Israel.
[30] Therefore, her young men[p] will fall in the streets;
all her soldiers will be silenced in that day,"
declares the LORD.
[31] "See, I am against[q] you, O arrogant one,"
declares the Lord, the LORD Almighty,
"for your day has come,
the time for you to be punished.
[32] The arrogant one will stumble and fall
and no one will help her up;
I will kindle a fire[r] in her towns
that will consume all who are around her."

[33] This is what the LORD Almighty says:

"The people of Israel are oppressed,[s]
and the people of Judah as well.
All their captors hold them fast,
refusing to let them go.[t]
[34] Yet their Redeemer is strong;
the LORD Almighty[u] is his name.
He will vigorously defend their cause[v]
so that he may bring rest[w] to their land,
but unrest to those who live in Babylon.

50:24 [d]Da 5:30-31 [e]Jer 51:31 [f]Job 9:4
50:25 [g]Isa 13:5 [h]Jer 51:25,55
50:26 [i]Isa 14:22-23
50:28 [j]Isa 48:20; Jer 51:10 [k]ver 15
50:29 [l]ver 14 [m]Rev 18:6 [n]Jer 51:56 [o]Isa 47:10
50:30 [p]Isa 13:18; Jer 49:26
50:31 [q]Jer 21:13
50:32 [r]Jer 21:14; 49:27
50:33 [s]Isa 58:6 [t]Isa 14:17
50:34 [u]Jer 51:19 [v]Jer 15:21; 51:36 [w]Isa 14:7

50:24 The Persian attack in 539 B.C. would catch the city of Babylon completely by surprise (see "Herodotus and the Fall of Babylon" on p. 1283).

50:26 For "completely destroy," see the note on verse 21.

50:35 [x]Jer 47:6 [y]Da 5:7
50:36 [z]Jer 49:22
50:37 [a]Jer 51:21 [b]Jer 51:30; Na 3:13
50:38 [c]Jer 51:36 [d]ver 2
50:39 [e]Isa 13:19-22; 34:13-15; Jer 51:37; Rev 18:2
50:40 [f]Ge 19:24
50:41 [g]Jer 6:22 [h]Isa 13:4; Jer 51:22-28
50:42 [i]ver 14 [j]Isa 13:18 [k]Isa 5:30 [l]Jer 6:23
50:44 [m]Nu 16:5 [n]Job 41:10; Isa 46:9; Jer 49:19
50:45 [o]Ps 33:11; Isa 14:24; Jer 51:11
50:46 [p]Rev 18:9-10

35 "A sword[x] against the Babylonians!"
declares the LORD—
"against those who live in Babylon
and against her officials and wise[y] men!
36 A sword against her false prophets!
They will become fools.
A sword against her warriors![z]
They will be filled with terror.
37 A sword against her horses and chariots[a]
and all the foreigners in her ranks!
They will become women.[b]
A sword against her treasures!
They will be plundered.
38 A drought on[a] her waters!
They will dry[c] up.
For it is a land of idols,[d]
idols that will go mad with terror.

39 "So desert creatures and hyenas will live there,
and there the owl will dwell.
It will never again be inhabited
or lived in from generation to generation.[e]
40 As God overthrew Sodom and Gomorrah[f]
along with their neighboring towns,"
declares the LORD,
"so no one will live there;
no man will dwell in it.

41 "Look! An army is coming from the north;[g]
a great nation and many kings
are being stirred up from the ends of the earth.[h]
42 They are armed with bows[i] and spears;
they are cruel and without mercy.[j]
They sound like the roaring sea[k]
as they ride on their horses;
they come like men in battle formation
to attack you, O Daughter of Babylon.[l]
43 The king of Babylon has heard reports about them,
and his hands hang limp.
Anguish has gripped him,
pain like that of a woman in labor.
44 Like a lion coming up from Jordan's thickets
to a rich pastureland,
I will chase Babylon from its land in an instant.
Who is the chosen[m] one I will appoint for this?
Who is like me and who can challenge me?[n]
And what shepherd can stand against me?"
45 Therefore, hear what the LORD has planned against Babylon,
what he has purposed[o] against the land of the
Babylonians:
The young of the flock will be dragged away;
he will completely destroy their pasture because of them.
46 At the sound of Babylon's capture the earth will tremble;
its cry[p] will resound among the nations.

[a] 38 Or *A sword against*

51 This is what the LORD says:

"See, I will stir up the spirit of a destroyer
against Babylon and the people of Leb Kamai.[a]
2 I will send foreigners to Babylon
to winnow[q] her and to devastate her land;
they will oppose her on every side
in the day of her disaster.
3 Let not the archer string his bow,[r]
nor let him put on his armor.[s]
Do not spare her young men;
completely destroy[b] her army.
4 They will fall[t] down slain in Babylon,[c]
fatally wounded in her streets.[u]
5 For Israel and Judah have not been forsaken[v]
by their God, the LORD Almighty,
though their land[d] is full of guilt[w]
before the Holy One of Israel.

6 "Flee[x] from Babylon!
Run for your lives!
Do not be destroyed because of her sins.[y]
It is time for the LORD's vengeance;[z]
he will pay[a] her what she deserves.
7 Babylon was a gold cup[b] in the LORD's hand;
she made the whole earth drunk.
The nations drank her wine;
therefore they have now gone mad.
8 Babylon will suddenly fall[c] and be broken.
Wail over her!
Get balm[d] for her pain;
perhaps she can be healed.

9 " 'We would have healed Babylon,
but she cannot be healed;
let us leave[e] her and each go to his own land,
for her judgment[f] reaches to the skies,
it rises as high as the clouds.'

10 " 'The LORD has vindicated[g] us;
come, let us tell in Zion
what the LORD our God has done.'[h]

11 "Sharpen the arrows,[i]
take up the shields![j]
The LORD has stirred up the kings of the Medes,[k]
because his purpose[l] is to destroy Babylon.
The LORD will take vengeance,
vengeance for his temple.[m]

51:2 [q]Isa 41:16; Jer 15:7; Mt 3:12
51:3 [r]Jer 50:29 [s]Jer 46:4
51:4 [t]Isa 13:15 [u]Jer 49:26; 50:30
51:5 [v]Isa 54:6-8 [w]Hos 4:1
51:6 [x]Jer 50:8 [y]Nu 16:26; Rev 18:4 [z]Jer 50:15 [a]Jer 25:14
51:7 [b]Jer 25:15-16; Rev 14:8-10; 17:4
51:8 [c]Isa 21:9; Rev 14:8 [d]Jer 46:11
51:9 [e]Isa 13:14; Jer 50:16 [f]Rev 18:4-5
51:10 [g]Mic 7:9 [h]Jer 50:28
51:11 [i]Jer 50:9 [j]Jer 46:4 [k]ver 28 [l]Jer 50:45 [m]Jer 50:28

[a] *1 Leb Kamai* is a cryptogram for Chaldea, that is, Babylonia. [b] *3* The Hebrew term refers to the irrevocable giving over of things or persons to the LORD, often by totally destroying them. [c] *4* Or *Chaldea* [d] *5* Or / *and the land ⌞of the Babylonians⌟*

51:1 For "destroyer," see the note on 4:7; here it includes the "kings of the Medes" (51:11).

Leb Kamai is a cryptogram (see the note on 25:26) for Chaldea (Babylonia).

51:3 For "completely destroy," see the note on 50:21.

51:8 Balm was an odoriferous resin perhaps obtained in Gilead (Ge 37:25; Jer 8:22; 46:11) and exported from the region now known as Palestine. It was used as an ointment for healing wounds. Balm came from a small tree not found today in Gilead.

[12] Lift up a banner against the walls of Babylon!
Reinforce the guard,
station the watchmen,
prepare an ambush!
The LORD will carry out his purpose,
his decree against the people of Babylon.
[13] You who live by many waters[n]
and are rich in treasures,[o]
your end has come,
the time for you to be cut off.
[14] The LORD Almighty has sworn by himself:[p]
I will surely fill you with men, as with a swarm of locusts,[q]
and they will shout[r] in triumph over you.

[15] "He made the earth by his power;
he founded the world by his wisdom
and stretched[s] out the heavens by his understanding.
[16] When he thunders,[t] the waters in the heavens roar;
he makes clouds rise from the ends of the earth.
He sends lightning with the rain
and brings out the wind from his storehouses.[u]

[17] "Every man is senseless and without knowledge;
every goldsmith is shamed by his idols.
His images are a fraud;[v]
they have no breath in them.
[18] They are worthless,[w] the objects of mockery;
when their judgment comes, they will perish.
[19] He who is the Portion of Jacob is not like these,
for he is the Maker of all things,
including the tribe of his inheritance—
the LORD Almighty is his name.

[20] "You are my war club,[x]
my weapon for battle—
with you I shatter[y] nations,
with you I destroy kingdoms,
[21] with you I shatter horse and rider,[z]
with you I shatter chariot and driver,
[22] with you I shatter man and woman,
with you I shatter old man and youth,
with you I shatter young man and maiden,[a]
[23] with you I shatter shepherd and flock,
with you I shatter farmer and oxen,
with you I shatter governors and officials.[b]

[24] "Before your eyes I will repay[c] Babylon and all who live in Babylonia[a] for all the wrong they have
done in Zion," declares the LORD.

[25] "I am against you, O destroying mountain,
you who destroy the whole earth,"
declares the LORD.

51:13 [n]Rev 17:1, 15 [o]Isa 45:3; Hab 2:9
51:14 [p]Am 6:8 [q]ver 27; Na 3:15 [r]Jer 50:15
51:15 [s]Ge 1:1; Job 9:8; Ps 104:2
51:16 [t]Ps 18:11-13 [u]Ps 135:7; Jnh 1:4
51:17 [v]Isa 44:20; Hab 2:18-19
51:18 [w]Jer 18:15
51:20 [x]Isa 10:5 [y]Mic 4:13
51:21 [z]Ex 15:1
51:22 [a]2Ch 36:17; Isa 13:17-18
51:23 [b]ver 57
51:24 [c]Jer 50:15

[a] *24* Or *Chaldea*; also in verse 35

51:13 The "many waters" (the rivers) of Babylon, including the mighty Euphrates and a magnificent system of irrigation canals, were proverbial.

"I will stretch out my hand against you,
roll you off the cliffs,
and make you a burned-out mountain.[d] 51:25 [d]Zec 4:7
26 No rock will be taken from you for a cornerstone,
nor any stone for a foundation,
for you will be desolate[e] forever,"
declares the LORD. 51:26 [e]ver 29; Isa 13:19-22; Jer 50:12

27 "Lift up a banner[f] in the land! 51:27 [f]Isa 13:2; Jer 50:2 [g]Jer 25:14 [h]Ge 8:4 [i]Ge 10:3
Blow the trumpet among the nations!
Prepare the nations for battle against her;
summon against her these kingdoms:[g]
Ararat,[h] Minni and Ashkenaz.[i]
Appoint a commander against her;
send up horses like a swarm of locusts.
28 Prepare the nations for battle against her—
the kings of the Medes,[j] 51:28 [j]ver 11
their governors and all their officials,
and all the countries they rule.
29 The land trembles and writhes,
for the LORD's purposes against Babylon
stand—
to lay waste the land of Babylon
so that no one will live there.[k] 51:29 [k]ver 43; Isa 13:20
30 Babylon's warriors[l] have stopped fighting; 51:30 [l]Jer 50:36 [m]Isa 19:16 [n]Isa 45:2; La 2:9; Na 3:13
they remain in their strongholds.
Their strength is exhausted;
they have become like women.[m]
Her dwellings are set on fire;
the bars[n] of her gates are broken.
31 One courier[o] follows another 51:31 [o]2Sa 18:19-31
and messenger follows messenger
to announce to the king of Babylon
that his entire city is captured,
32 the river crossings seized,
the marshes set on fire,
and the soldiers terrified.[p]" 51:32 [p]Jer 50:36

33 This is what the LORD Almighty, the God of Israel, says:

"The Daughter of Babylon is like a threshing
floor[q] 51:33 [q]Isa 21:10 [r]Isa 17:5; Hos 6:11
at the time it is trampled;
the time to harvest[r] her will soon come."

34 "Nebuchadnezzar[s] king of Babylon has devoured us, 51:34 [s]Jer 50:17
he has thrown us into confusion,
he has made us an empty jar.
Like a serpent he has swallowed us
and filled his stomach with our delicacies,
and then has spewed us out.

51:27 The name Ararat is related to the Assyrian Urartu, which became an extensive and mountainous kingdom, including much of the territory north of Mesopotamia and east of modern Turkey. Minni, a region mentioned in Assyrian inscriptions, was located somewhere in Armenia. Ashkenaz refers to the homeland of the later Scythians, located in the upper Euphrates region.

51:32 "River crossings" probably refers to fords and ferries (and perhaps bridges).

The marshes were set on fire to destroy the reeds in order to prevent fugitives from hiding among them.

[35] May the violence done to our flesh[a] be upon Babylon,"
say the inhabitants of Zion.
"May our blood be on those who live in Babylonia,"
says Jerusalem.[t]

51:35 [t]ver 24; Ps 137:8

[36] Therefore, this is what the LORD says:

"See, I will defend your cause[u]
and avenge[v] you;
I will dry up[w] her sea
and make her springs dry.

51:36 [u]Ps 140:12; Jer 50:34; La 3:58 [v]ver 6; Ro 12:19 [w]Jer 50:38

[37] Babylon will be a heap of ruins,
a haunt[x] of jackals,
an object of horror and scorn,
a place where no one lives.[y]

51:37 [x]Isa 13:22; Rev 18:2 [y]Jer 50:13,39

[38] Her people all roar like young lions,
they growl like lion cubs.
[39] But while they are aroused,
I will set out a feast for them
and make them drunk,
so that they shout with laughter—
then sleep forever and not awake,"
declares the LORD.[z]

51:39 [z]ver 57

[40] "I will bring them down
like lambs to the slaughter,
like rams and goats.

[41] "How Sheshach[b][a] will be captured,[b]
the boast of the whole earth seized!
What a horror Babylon will be
among the nations!

51:41 [a]Jer 25:26 [b]Isa 13:19

[42] The sea will rise over Babylon;
its roaring waves[c] will cover her.

51:42 [c]Isa 8:7

[43] Her towns will be desolate,
a dry and desert land,
a land where no one lives,
through which no man travels.[d]

51:43 [d]ver 29,62; Isa 13:20; Jer 2:6

[44] I will punish Bel[e] in Babylon
and make him spew out[f] what he has swallowed.
The nations will no longer stream to him.
And the wall[g] of Babylon will fall.

51:44 [e]Isa 46:1 [f]ver 34 [g]ver 58; Jer 50:15

[45] "Come out[h] of her, my people!
Run[i] for your lives!
Run from the fierce anger of the LORD.

51:45 [h]Rev 18:4 [i]ver 6; Isa 48:20; Jer 50:8

[46] Do not lose heart or be afraid[j]
when rumors[k] are heard in the land;
one rumor comes this year, another the next,
rumors of violence in the land
and of ruler against ruler.

51:46 [j]Jer 46:27 [k]2Ki 19:7

[47] For the time will surely come
when I will punish the idols[l] of Babylon;

51:47 [l]ver 52; Isa 46:1-2; Jer 50:2

[a] 35 Or *done to us and to our children* [b] 41 *Sheshach* is a cryptogram for Babylon.

51:36 See the note on verse 13.

51:44 For "Bel," see the note on Isaiah 46:1–13. Babylon was renowned for its secure walls (see "Babylon" on p. 1077).

her whole land will be disgraced[m]
and her slain will all lie fallen within her.
48 Then heaven and earth and all that is in them
will shout[n] for joy over Babylon,
for out of the north[o]
destroyers will attack her,"
declares the LORD.

49 "Babylon must fall because of Israel's slain,
just as the slain in all the earth
have fallen because of Babylon.[p]
50 You who have escaped the sword,
leave[q] and do not linger!
Remember[r] the LORD in a distant land,
and think on Jerusalem."

51 "We are disgraced,[s]
for we have been insulted
and shame covers our faces,
because foreigners have entered
the holy places of the LORD's house."[t]

52 "But days are coming," declares the LORD,
"when I will punish her idols,[u]
and throughout her land
the wounded will groan.

51:47 [m]Jer 50:12
51:48 [n]Isa 44:23; Rev 18:20 [o]ver 11
51:49 [p]Ps 137:8; Jer 50:29
51:50 [q]ver 45 [r]Ps 137:6
51:51 [s]Ps 44:13-16; 79:4 [t]La 1:10
51:52 [u]ver 47

51:51 Nebuchadnezzar defiled the Jerusalem temple in 586 B.C. The same kind of sacrilege would occur under Antiochus Epiphanes in 168 B.C. and again under the Romans in A.D. 70.

ANCIENT TEXTS AND ARTIFACTS

Seraiah the Quartermaster

JEREMIAH 51 A seal acquired on the antiquities market reads "Belonging to Seraiah (son of) Neriah." This Seraiah is known from the Biblical text. His lineage is given as "son of Neriah, the son of Mahseiah" (Jer 51:59). This is the same lineage as that of Baruch, Jeremiah's secretary (32:12),[1] indicating that Seraiah was Baruch's brother.

Seraiah was the royal quartermaster during the reign of Zedekiah, king of Judah from 597 to 586 B.C. (51:59). In Zedekiah's fourth year (594 B.C.) Seraiah accompanied the king on a mission to **Babylon**, possibly to reaffirm Judah's loyalty to **Nebuchadnezzar**, the Babylonian king.[2] The trip would have taken four months each way (Ezr 7:9; 8:31). Just five years later Zedekiah revolted, resulting in the downfall of the kingdom.

God revealed to Jeremiah his coming judgment of Babylon (Jer 50–51), and the prophecy was recorded on a scroll (51:60). Jeremiah took advantage of Seraiah's journey by requesting that he take the scroll with him and read it aloud in Babylon, after which he was to cast it into the Euphrates River to illustrate Babylon's coming fate (vv. 61–64). Jeremiah's prophecies came to pass 55 years later when Cyrus the Great conquered Babylon in 539 B.C.[3]

[1]See "Baruch, Scribe of Jeremiah" on page 1248. [2]See "Nebuchadnezzar" on page 571. [3]See "Cyrus the Great" on page 669 and "Herodotus and the Fall of Babylon" on page 1283.

51:53 [v]Ge 11:4; Isa 14:13-14 [w]Jer 49:16

53 Even if Babylon reaches the sky[v]
and fortifies her lofty stronghold,
I will send destroyers[w] against her,"
declares the LORD.

51:54 [x]Jer 50:22

54 "The sound of a cry comes from Babylon,
the sound of great destruction[x]
from the land of the Babylonians.[a]
55 The LORD will destroy Babylon;
he will silence her noisy din.

51:55 [y]Ps 18:4

Waves[y] ⌞of enemies⌟ will rage like great waters;
the roar of their voices will resound.

51:56 [z]ver 48 [a]Ps 46:9 [b]ver 6; Ps 94:1-2; Hab 2:8

56 A destroyer[z] will come against Babylon;
her warriors will be captured,
and their bows will be broken.[a]
For the LORD is a God of retribution;
he will repay[b] in full.
57 I will make her officials and wise men drunk,
her governors, officers and warriors as well;

51:57 [c]Ps 76:5; Jer 25:27 [d]Jer 46:18; 48:15

they will sleep[c] forever and not awake,"
declares the King,[d] whose name is the LORD Almighty.

58 This is what the LORD Almighty says:

51:58 [e]ver 44 [f]ver 64 [g]Hab 2:13

"Babylon's thick wall[e] will be leveled
and her high gates set on fire;
the peoples[f] exhaust themselves for nothing,
the nations' labor is only fuel for the flames."[g]

51:59 [h]Jer 36:4 [i]Jer 52:1 [j]Jer 28:1

59 This is the message Jeremiah gave to the staff officer Seraiah son of Neriah,[h] the son of Mahseiah,
when he went to Babylon with Zedekiah[i] king of Judah in the fourth[j] year of his reign. 60 Jeremiah had
written on a scroll[k] about all the disasters that would come upon Babylon—all that had been recorded
concerning Babylon. 61 He said to Seraiah, "When you get to Babylon, see that you read all these words
aloud. 62 Then say, 'O LORD, you have said you will destroy this place, so that neither man nor animal will
live in it; it will be desolate[l] forever.' 63 When you finish reading this scroll, tie a stone to it and throw it
into the Euphrates. 64 Then say, 'So will Babylon sink to rise no more because of the disaster I will bring
upon her. And her people[m] will fall.' "

51:60 [k]Jer 30:2; 36:2

51:62 [l]Isa 13:20; Jer 50:13,39

51:64 [m]ver 58 [n]Job 31:40

The words of Jeremiah end[n] here.

The Fall of Jerusalem

52:1 [o]2Ki 24:17 [p]Jos 10:29; 2Ki 8:22

52:2 [q]Jer 36:30

52:3 [r]Isa 3:1 [s]Eze 17:12-16

52:4 [t]Zec 8:19

52 Zedekiah[o] was twenty-one years old when he became king, and he reigned in Jerusalem eleven
years. His mother's name was Hamutal daughter of Jeremiah; she was from Libnah.[p] 2 He did evil
in the eyes of the LORD, just as Jehoiakim[q] had done. 3 It was because of the LORD's anger that all this hap-
pened to Jerusalem and Judah,[r] and in the end he thrust them from his presence.
Now Zedekiah rebelled[s] against the king of Babylon.
4 So in the ninth year of Zedekiah's reign, on the tenth[t] day of the tenth month, Nebuchadnezzar king

[a] 54 Or *Chaldeans*

51:56 The "destroyer" here refers to Persia (see the note on 4:7).
51:58 Babylon was famous for its walls (see the note on v. 44), as well as for the Ishtar Gate, which was almost 40 feet (12 m) high.
51:59 As "the staff officer" (lit., "resting-place officer"), Seraiah was responsible for determining when and where his men on the march were to spend the night. An ancient seal bearing the inscription "Belonging to Seraiah son of Neriah" no doubt refers to the man mentioned here (see "Seraiah the Quartermaster" on p. 1290), who was also a brother of Jeremiah's secretary, Baruch (see "Baruch, Scribe of Jeremiah" on p. 1248). This event likely occurred in 593 B.C., when Nebuchadnezzar summoned Zedekiah to Babylon to be interrogated (see the note on 27:3).
51:60 For "scroll," see the notes on Exodus 17:14 and Jeremiah 36:23.
52:1 Jeremiah 52, an appendix to the book, was written by someone other than the prophet Jeremiah—perhaps Baruch (see "Baruch, Scribe of Jeremiah" on p. 1248). This chapter closely parallels the conclusion of 2 Kings. Rather than one copying the other, however, it is likely that the two relied upon the same sources.

Note that the Jeremiah mentioned in this verse is not the prophet Jeremiah.

of Babylon marched against Jerusalem[u] with his whole army. They camped outside the city and built 52:4 [u]2Ki 25:1-7;
siege works all around it.[v] 5 The city was kept under siege until the eleventh year of King Zedekiah. Jer 39:1 [v]Eze 24:1-2
6 By the ninth day of the fourth month the famine in the city had become so severe that there was no
food for the people to eat.[w] 7 Then the city wall was broken through, and the whole army fled. They left 52:6 [w]Isa 3:1
the city at night through the gate between the two walls near the king's garden, though the Babylonians[a]
were surrounding the city. They fled toward the Arabah,[b] 8 but the Babylonian[c] army pursued King Zed-
ekiah and overtook him in the plains of Jericho. All his soldiers were separated from him and scattered,
9 and he was captured.[x] 52:9 [x]Jer 32:4

He was taken to the king of Babylon at Riblah[y] in the land of Hamath,[z] where he pronounced sentence [y]Nu 34:11 [z]Nu 13:21
on him. 10 There at Riblah the king of Babylon slaughtered the sons[a] of Zedekiah before his eyes; he also 52:10 [a]Jer 22:30
killed all the officials of Judah. 11 Then he put out Zedekiah's eyes, bound him with bronze shackles and
took him to Babylon, where he put him in prison till the day of his death.[b] 52:11 [b]Eze 12:13
12 On the tenth day of the fifth[c] month, in the nineteenth year of Nebuchadnezzar king of Babylon, 52:12 [c]Zec 7:5; 8:19 [d]Jer 39:9
Nebuzaradan[d] commander of the imperial guard, who served the king of Babylon, came to Jerusalem.
13 He set fire[e] to the temple[f] of the LORD, the royal palace and all the houses of Jerusalem. Every impor- 52:13 [e]2Ch 36:19;
tant building he burned down. 14 The whole Babylonian army under the commander of the imperial Ps 74:8; La 2:6
guard broke down all the walls[g] around Jerusalem. 15 Nebuzaradan the commander of the guard carried [f]Ps 79:1; Mic 3:12 52:14 [g]Ne 1:3
into exile some of the poorest people and those who remained in the city, along with the rest of the crafts-
men[d] and those who had gone over to the king of Babylon. 16 But Nebuzaradan left behind[h] the rest of the 52:16 [h]Jer 40:6
poorest people of the land to work the vineyards and fields.
17 The Babylonians broke up the bronze pillars,[i] the movable stands[j] and the bronze Sea[k] that were at 52:17 [i]1Ki 7:15 [j]1Ki 7:27-37
the temple of the LORD and they carried all the bronze to Babylon.[l] 18 They also took away the pots, shov- [k]1Ki 7:23
els, wick trimmers, sprinkling bowls, dishes and all the bronze articles used in the temple service.[m] 19 The [l]Jer 27:19-22 52:18 [m]Ex 27:3; 1Ki 7:45

[a] 7 Or *Chaldeans*; also in verse 17 [b] 7 Or *the Jordan Valley* [c] 8 Or *Chaldean*; also in verse 14 [d] 15 Or *populace*

52:12 The "tenth day" reads "seventh day" in the parallel account in 2 Kings 25:8. One of the numbers is a copyist's error, but scholars cannot determine which (see "Textual Criticism" on p. 1151).

For Nebuzaradan, see "Nebuzaradan, Captain of the Guard" on page 1260.

Jehoiachin in Captivity and Evil-Merodach

JEREMIAH 52 Jehoiachin ruled Judah for only three months and then, at age eighteen, was taken captive to Babylon in 597 B.C. (2Ki 24:8–15). During excavations in Babylon approximately 300 clay tablets containing administrative records were uncovered in a building adjacent to **Nebuchadnezzar**'s palace.[1] Four of them were found to be highly significant for Old Testament studies, as they mention Jehoiachin. Dating from 595 to 570 B.C., all four are receipts for rations of oil issued to Jehoiachin and his entourage. Jehoiachin is referred to as "Jehoiachin king of the land of Judah." Three of the tablets list oil for Jehoiachin's five sons (cf. 1Ch 3:17–18), and oil was also given to five named and eight unnamed Judeans.

Evil-Merodach succeeded Nebuchadnezzar on the throne but ruled for only one year, from 561–560 B.C. He released Jehoiachin from confinement and allowed him to eat at the king's table (Jer 52:31–34). Inscriptions found in Babylon show that Evil-Merodach continued his father's building projects. He was deposed, and perhaps murdered, however, by his brother-in-law Nergal-Sharezer, a former military officer (39:3,13).

[1] See "Babylon" on page 1077 and "Nebuchadnezzar" on page 571.

52:19 [n]1Ki 7:50 commander of the imperial guard took away the basins, censers,[n] sprinkling bowls, pots, lampstands,
dishes and bowls used for drink offerings—all that were made of pure gold or silver.
20The bronze from the two pillars, the Sea and the twelve bronze bulls under it, and the movable
52:20 [o]1Ki 7:47 stands, which King Solomon had made for the temple of the LORD, was more than could be weighed.[o]
21Each of the pillars was eighteen cubits high and twelve cubits in circumference[a]; each was four fingers
52:21 [p]1Ki 7:15 thick, and hollow.[p] 22The bronze capital[q] on top of the one pillar was five cubits[b] high and was decorat-
52:22 [q]1Ki 7:16 ed with a network and pomegranates of bronze all around. The other pillar, with its pomegranates, was
52:23 [r]1Ki 7:20 similar. 23There were ninety-six pomegranates on the sides; the total number of pomegranates[r] above the
surrounding network was a hundred.
52:24 [s]2Ki 25:18 24The commander of the guard took as prisoners Seraiah[s] the chief priest, Zephaniah[t] the priest next
[t]Jer 21:1; 37:3 in rank and the three doorkeepers. 25Of those still in the city, he took the officer in charge of the fighting
men, and seven royal advisers. He also took the secretary who was chief officer in charge of conscript-
52:26 [u]ver 12 ing the people of the land and sixty of his men who were found in the city. 26Nebuzaradan[u] the com-
mander took them all and brought them to the king of Babylon at Riblah. 27There at Riblah, in the land
of Hamath, the king had them executed.
52:27 [v]Jer 20:4 So Judah went into captivity, away[v] from her land. 28This is the number of the people Nebuchadnez-
52:28 [w]2Ki 24:14-16; 2Ch 36:20 zar carried into exile:[w]

in the seventh year, 3,023 Jews;
29in Nebuchadnezzar's eighteenth year,
832 people from Jerusalem;
30in his twenty-third year,
745 Jews taken into exile by Nebuzaradan the commander of the imperial guard.
There were 4,600 people in all.

Jehoiachin Released

31In the thirty-seventh year of the exile of Jehoiachin king of Judah, in the year Evil-Merodach[c] be-
came king of Babylon, he released Jehoiachin king of Judah and freed him from prison on the twenty-
fifth day of the twelfth month. 32He spoke kindly to him and gave him a seat of honor higher than those
of the other kings who were with him in Babylon. 33So Jehoiachin put aside his prison clothes and for the
52:33 [x]2Sa 9:7 rest of his life ate regularly at the king's table.[x] 34Day by day the king of Babylon gave Jehoiachin a regu-
52:34 [y]2Sa 9:10 lar allowance[y] as long as he lived, till the day of his death.

[a] *21* That is, about 27 feet (about 8.1 meters) high and 18 feet (about 5.4 meters) in circumference [b] *22* That is, about 7 1/2 feet (about 2.3 meters) [c] *31* Also called *Amel-Marduk*

52:28–30 These verses record three deportations during Nebuchadnezzar's reign: (1) those taken in 597 B.C. (this number probably included only adult males, since the figures in 2Ki 24 are significantly higher); (2) those deported, rather than killed, when Jerusalem fell in 586 B.C.; and (3) those exiled in 581 B.C.—perhaps as punishment for Gedaliah's assassination (Jer 41:1–3). For information on deportation, see "Exile and Genocide in the Ancient Near East" on page 1337.

52:31–34 Evil-Merodach released Jehoiachin, king of Judah, from his 37-year Babylonian imprisonment and gave him a position of prominence among the captive kings, as well as a daily allowance of food for the rest of his life (2Ki 25:27–30; Jer 52:31–34)—but did not permit him to return to Judah (see "Jehoiachin in Captivity and Evil-Merodach" on p. 1292). Cuneiform tablets recovered from Babylon and assigned a date during Nebuchadnezzar's reign refer to provisions supplied to Jehoiachin and to other royal prisoners. The latest of these tablets is at least eight years older than the date of Jehoiachin's release, referred to in Scripture. Evil-Merodach may have increased the king's allowance from the small amount mentioned in these tablets.

52:31 The "twenty-fifth day" reads "twenty-seventh day" in the parallel account in 2 Kings 25:27 (see "Early Scribal Emendation" on p. 448).

INTRODUCTION TO 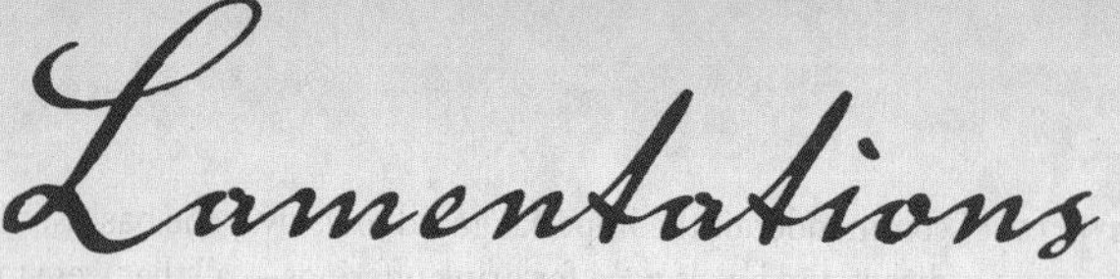

AUTHOR, PLACE AND DATE OF WRITING

Lamentations is anonymous, although Jewish tradition attributes it to Jeremiah, partly on the basis of 2 Chronicles 35:25: "Jeremiah composed laments for Josiah, and to this day all the men and women singers commemorate Josiah in the laments." Most scholars agree that the laments referred to in the above verse are not those of Lamentations, but the Septuagint version of Lamentations does begin, "Now it came about after the captivity of Israel and the desolation of Jerusalem, Jeremiah sat down weeping and he made this lament over Jerusalem." Despite this seemingly clear statement, it is impossible to determine whether or not this ancient tradition is correct.

Lamentations 1–4 comprises a series of cleverly executed acrostic poems (see "Acrostics and Other Techniques of Ancient Poetry" on p. 1298). This highly structured poetry seems out of character with what we know of Jeremiah, as seen in the book by his name. On the other hand, it is not impossible that the prophet would have composed a series of laments in this fashion for liturgical purposes, using a structure that would neither have been needed nor appropriate for his book of prophecy.

The book appears to have been written from Jerusalem by someone for whom the memory of the city's fall was fresh and poignant; there is no indication that Jerusalem had already been reinhabited by the Jews. Thus, a date after 586 B.C. but before 538 seems reasonable.

AUDIENCE

Lamentations was written as an expression for the exiled Jewish people of their pain, grief and horror at the destruction of Jerusalem and the temple.

Lamentations had a liturgical function: to give the exiles a formal ritual for grieving over the calamity that had befallen them and for reflecting upon the meaning of Jerusalem's destruction (see "Ancient Near Eastern Laments" on p. 1305).

CULTURAL FACTS AND HIGHLIGHTS

Whoever did write these stirring words, despite his poetic discipline, was clearly wrestling with the ways in which God, the Lord of history, was dealing with his wayward people. The author clearly understood that the Babylonians were merely human agents of the divine judgment—that God himself had destroyed his own city and temple (1:12–15; 2:1–8,17,22; 4:11).

The book stands in the tradition of other ancient Near Eastern works of the same genre, including Lamentation Over the Destruction of Ur, Lamentation Over the Destruction of Sumer and Ur and Lamentation Over the Destruction of Nippur.

Traditions related to this book continue into the present day:

- Orthodox Jews customarily read aloud the entire book on the ninth day of the month Ab, the traditional date of the destruction of Solomon's temple (in 586 B.C.).
- Many Jews read it each week at the Wailing Wall in Jerusalem's Old City.
- In the Roman Catholic tradition Lamentations is traditionally read during the final three days of Holy Week, just prior to Easter.

TIMELINE

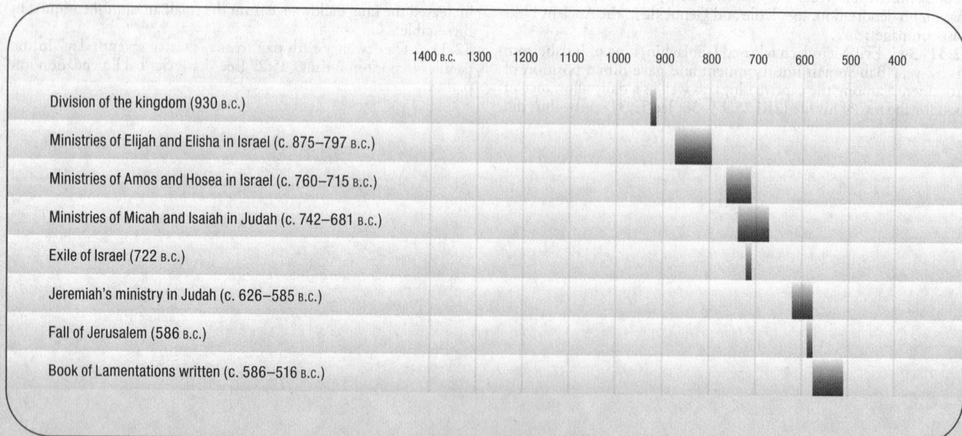

AS YOU READ

From chapter 3 on the author seems to vacillate randomly between despair and hope, but be alert to the developing threads of his theology as he presents his case before the Lord. Pay particular attention to passages such as 3:21–27, 31–33, as well as to the book's closing verses (5:19–22). What do you think of the author's reflection that "it is good for a man to bear the yoke while he is young" (3:27)? Does the final verse of the book leave you feeling as though the author were trailing off on an afterthought too horrible to imagine? How does your perspective as a New Testament Christian likely differ from that of the book's early readers with regard to these questions?

DID YOU KNOW?

- Ramparts were sloping, wall-like fortifications of earth or stone that were used as a protective barrier against invaders (2:8).
- The Hebrews divided the night into three watches: (1) sunset–10:00 P.M., (2) 10:00 P.M.–2:00 A.M. and (3) 2:00 A.M.–sunrise (2:19).
- The threat of starvation during the siege of Jerusalem had compelled some mothers to cook and eat their own children (2:20).

THEMES

The themes of the book of Lamentations include:

1. *Judgment.* Simply put, sin has consequences. Lamentations demonstrates that God often uses human agents to execute his judgment (1:14–15; 2:1–8,17,22; 4:11).

2. *Appropriate response to judgment.* The fitting response to judgment is repentance (3:40–42) and a cry for forgiveness and restoration (5:21–22). The Israelites had sinned (1:8,14,18; 2:14; 4:13) but appealed to God for help, expecting him to forgive and restore.

3. *God's character.* God is just, but he is also the God of hope (3:21,24–25), love (3:22), compassion (3:22), faithfulness (3:23) and salvation (3:26).

OUTLINE

I. Jerusalem's Sorrow (1)
II. The Lord's Anger Against His People (2)
III. The Hope of Consolation (3)
IV. Contrast Between the Past and Present (4)
V. Judah's Appeal for God's Forgiveness (5)

1[a]

How deserted lies the city,
once so full of people!
How like a widow[a] is she,
who once was great[b] among the nations!
She who was queen among the provinces
has now become a slave.[c]

2 Bitterly she weeps[d] at night,
tears are upon her cheeks.
Among all her lovers[e]
there is none to comfort her.
All her friends have betrayed[f] her;
they have become her enemies.[g]

3 After affliction and harsh labor,
Judah has gone into exile.[h]
She dwells among the nations;
she finds no resting place.[i]
All who pursue her have overtaken her
in the midst of her distress.

4 The roads to Zion mourn,
for no one comes to her appointed feasts.
All her gateways are desolate,[j]
her priests groan,
her maidens grieve,
and she is in bitter anguish.[k]

5 Her foes have become her masters;
her enemies are at ease.
The LORD has brought her grief[l]
because of her many sins.
Her children have gone into exile,[m]
captive before the foe.

6 All the splendor has departed
from the Daughter of Zion.[n]
Her princes are like deer
that find no pasture;
in weakness they have fled
before the pursuer.

1:1 [a]Isa 47:8 [b]1Ki 4:21 [c]Isa 3:26; Jer 40:9
1:2 [d]Ps 6:6 [e]Jer 3:1 [f]Jer 4:30; Mic 7:5 [g]ver 16
1:3 [h]Jer 13:19 [i]Dt 28:65
1:4 [j]Jer 9:11 [k]Joel 1:8-13
1:5 [l]Jer 30:15 [m]Jer 39:9; 52:28-30
1:6 [n]Jer 13:18

[a] This chapter is an acrostic poem, the verses of which begin with the successive letters of the Hebrew alphabet.

Title This book, titled in many English versions *The Lamentations of Jeremiah,* is placed between Jeremiah and Ezekiel in the Septuagint, the Vulgate and the English Bible (see Glossary on p. 2080 for definitions of the Septuagint and the Vulgate). In the Hebrew text, however, it appears in the Sacred Writings as the third of the Megilloth or "five scrolls." Its Hebrew title, *êkhâh* ("Oh, how[!]"), is derived from the word with which the book begins. The Talmud renamed the work *Qinoth* ("Lamentations" or "elegies") as a more accurate designation of its content. This approach was adopted in the Septuagint title *Thrçnoi* ("Elegies") and the *Threni* ("Lamentations") of the Latin versions.

1:1—5:22 Lamentations is comprised of five poems, each lamenting the desolation that had overtaken Jerusalem in 586 B.C. The first four compositions are highly artificial in structure, consisting of acrostics based on the Hebrew alphabet (see the introduction to this book; see also "Acrostics and Other Techniques of Ancient Poetry" on p. 1298). Each verse of chapters 1 and 2 begins with a word whose initial consonant is successively one of the 22 letters of the Hebrew alphabet. Slight variations of the regular order occur in 2:16–17, 3:47–48 and 4:16–17. In the third chapter a triple alphabetical arrangement is followed, so that all three lines in each stanza begin with the same letter. The fifth chapter is not an acrostic, although like the others it contains 22 stanzas, and it is a prayer rather than an elegy. Alphabetical forms of this kind probably served as a useful stimulus to memory at a time when manuscripts were rare and costly.

Some writers have regarded the mechanical structure of most of the book as incompatible with the grief and sincere penitence of the writer. These two ideas need not be inconsistent, however, particularly if the book was composed with a view to consistent liturgical usage. Judging from the manner in which this work has survived among the Jews, it seems well possible that this was the author's intention.

1:1 It was common in the Old Testament for cities to be portrayed as women.

1:2 "Lovers" and "friends" refer to the international allies to whom the people of Jerusalem and Judah looked for security (see the note on Jer 22:20). All of them, like Edom (see "Edom" on p. 1467) and Ammon (see "Ammon" on p. 364), had betrayed the Judahites.

1:3 The people of Judah had been deported to Babylonia (see the note on Jer 52:28–30; see also "Exile and Genocide in the Ancient Near East" on p. 1337).

1:4 For information regarding Israel's seven annual feasts, see "The Festivals of Israel" on page 186. See also "The Jewish Calendar" on page 241.

1:6 "Daughter of Zion" is a personification of Jerusalem. See the note on 1:1, above.

1:7 [o]Jer 37:7; La 4:17

[7] In the days of her affliction and wandering
Jerusalem remembers all the treasures
that were hers in days of old.
When her people fell into enemy hands,
there was no one to help her.[o]
Her enemies looked at her
and laughed at her destruction.

1:8 [p]ver 20; Isa 59:2-13 [q]Jer 13:22,26 [r]ver 21,22

[8] Jerusalem has sinned[p] greatly
and so has become unclean.
All who honored her despise her,
for they have seen her nakedness;[q]
she herself groans[r]
and turns away.

1:9 [s]Dt 32:28-29; Isa 47:7; Eze 24:13 [t]Jer 13:18 [u]Ecc 4:1; Jer 16:7 [v]Ps 25:18

[9] Her filthiness clung to her skirts;
she did not consider her future.[s]
Her fall[t] was astounding;
there was none to comfort[u] her.
"Look, O LORD, on my affliction,[v]
for the enemy has triumphed."

1:10 [w]Isa 64:11 [x]Ps 74:7-8; Jer 51:51 [y]Dt 23:3

[10] The enemy laid hands
on all her treasures;[w]
she saw pagan nations
enter her sanctuary[x]—
those you had forbidden[y]
to enter your assembly.

1:11 [z]Ps 38:8 [a]Jer 52:6

[11] All her people groan[z]
as they search for bread;[a]
they barter their treasures for food
to keep themselves alive.
"Look, O LORD, and consider,
for I am despised."

1:12 [b]Jer 18:16 [c]ver 18 [d]Isa 13:13; Jer 30:24

[12] "Is it nothing to you, all you who pass by?[b]
Look around and see.
Is any suffering like my suffering[c]
that was inflicted on me,
that the LORD brought on me
in the day of his fierce anger?[d]

1:13 [e]Job 30:30 [f]Jer 44:6 [g]Hab 3:16

[13] "From on high he sent fire,
sent it down into my bones.[e]
He spread a net for my feet
and turned me back.
He made me desolate,[f]
faint[g] all the day long.

1:14 [h]Dt 28:48; Isa 47:6

[14] "My sins have been bound into a yoke[a];[h]
by his hands they were woven together.

[a] 14 Most Hebrew manuscripts; Septuagint *He kept watch over my sins*

1:8 "Unclean" refers here to the ceremonial uncleanness of a woman during her menstrual period (see Lev 12:2,5; 15:19).

1:9 "Filthiness" refers not to a lack of physical cleanliness but to ceremonial uncleanness, here caused by willful sin.

1:10 While foreigners were not permitted to enter the temple (Dt 23:1–8; Jer 51:51; Eze 44:9), they were allowed to be a part of Israel (Eze 47:22). The later temple of the New Testament era featured a large outer court of the Gentiles that covered several acres, along with an inner court that was subdivided into the courts of the women, men (Israelites) and priests. A written warning at the entrance to the temple prohibited Gentiles from entering, upon pain of death (see "The Dividing Wall of the Court of the Gentiles in Herod's Temple" on p. 1917).

1:11 Food shortages were an ever-present problem for the Judahites during and after the siege of Jerusalem See "Siege Warfare" on page 465 and "The Last Days of Jerusalem" on page 1197.

They have come upon my neck
and the Lord has sapped my strength.
He has handed me over[i]
to those I cannot withstand.

15 "The Lord has rejected
all the warriors in my midst;[j]
he has summoned an army[k] against me
to[a] crush my young men.[l]
In his winepress the Lord has trampled
the Virgin Daughter of Judah.

16 "This is why I weep
and my eyes overflow with tears.[m]
No one is near to comfort[n] me,
no one to restore my spirit.
My children are destitute
because the enemy has prevailed."[o]

1:14 [i]Jer 32:5
1:15 [j]Jer 37:10 [k]Isa 41:2 [l]Isa 28:18; Jer 18:21
1:16 [m]La 2:11, 18; 3:48-49 [n]Ps 69:20; Ecc 4:1 [o]ver 2; Jer 13:17; 14:17

[a] 15 Or *has set a time for me / when he will*

1:15 The winepress was a common metaphor of divine judgment (see "The Winepress" on p. 1171). "Virgin Daughter of Judah" is a personification of Judah.

Acrostics and Other Techniques of Ancient Poetry

LAMENTATIONS 1 All poetry, except perhaps free verse, maintains some kind of repetition. Sometimes it is metrical, as in iambic pentameter; based on rhyme; or based on the number of syllables per line, as in Haiku. Biblical Hebrew poetry did not employ rhyme and, although there is some dispute about this issue, probably did not use meter or syllable counting. Long ago, however, scholars recognized that ancient Hebrew poetry often employed parallelism, which may be loosely described as "saying the same thing twice." Lamentations 2:7 illustrates the principle:

> The Lord has rejected his altar
> and abandoned his sanctuary.

Each line contains a subject, "Lord" (understood but not explicitly mentioned in line 2), a verb (has rejected/[has] abandoned) and a direct object (his altar/his sanctuary), and each direct object is composed of a pronoun and a noun. This is often called "synonymous parallelism." Yet Hebrew parallelism is often much more complex and subtle than the above example suggests (e.g., contrasting thoughts are often used as well, such as in Pr 22:12). Also, not all Hebrew poetry uses synonymous parallelism, nor is all synonymous parallelism poetry; it can occur as well in Hebrew prose.

Biblical Hebrew makes use of several other devices to establish the repetition poetry requires. Certain words may be repeated across several lines, or consecutive lines of poetry may begin with the same Hebrew letter. Another device is "inclusion," in which the first and last lines of a poem or strophe (also called "stanza," it refers to a major division in a poem) are identical, and the main topic is elaborated between them (e.g., Ps 8). Sometimes a Hebrew poem will repeat a full line at every other line, as in Psalm 136. It appears that Hebrew poetry follows certain constraints regarding, for example, the number of verbs allowed per line; this, too, can create poetic symmetry.

Sometimes a Hebrew poem may be an acrostic: The first letters of each consecutive line or strophe, taken in total, list the Hebrew alphabet in order. For example, the first verse of Lamentations 1 begins with *aleph* (the first letter of the Hebrew alphabet), the second verse with *beth* (the second letter of the alphabet), the third with *gimel* (the third letter), and so forth. Fundamentally, the acrostic is a type of repetition used in some Hebrew poetry.

Our understanding of Hebrew poetry is limited by the fact that no one living today has ever heard how it was originally sung. Sadly, much of the oral art of Hebrew poetry has been forever lost to us.

1:17 [p]Jer 4:31

[17] Zion stretches out her hands,[p]
but there is no one to comfort her.
The LORD has decreed for Jacob
that his neighbors become his foes;
Jerusalem has become
an unclean thing among them.

1:18 [q]1Sa 12:14 [r]ver 12 [s]Dt 28:32, 41

[18] "The LORD is righteous,
yet I rebelled[q] against his command.
Listen, all you peoples;
look upon my suffering.[r]
My young men and maidens
have gone into exile.[s]

1:19 [t]Jer 14:15; La 2:20

[19] "I called to my allies
but they betrayed me.
My priests and my elders
perished[t] in the city
while they searched for food
to keep themselves alive.

1:20 [u]Jer 4:19 [v]La 2:11 [w]Dt 32:25; Eze 7:15

[20] "See, O LORD, how distressed[u] I am!
I am in torment[v] within,
and in my heart I am disturbed,
for I have been most rebellious.
Outside, the sword bereaves;
inside, there is only death.[w]

1:21 [x]ver 8 [y]ver 4 [z]La 2:15 [a]Isa 47:11; Jer 30:16

[21] "People have heard my groaning,[x]
but there is no one to comfort me.[y]
All my enemies have heard of my distress;
they rejoice[z] at what you have done.
May you bring the day[a] you have announced
so they may become like me.

1:22 [b]Ne 4:5

[22] "Let all their wickedness come before you;
deal with them
as you have dealt with me
because of all my sins.[b]
My groans are many
and my heart is faint."

2:1 [c]La 3:44 [d]Ps 99:5; 132:7

2[a]

How the Lord has covered the Daughter
of Zion
with the cloud of his anger[b][c]
He has hurled down the splendor of Israel
from heaven to earth;
he has not remembered his footstool[d]
in the day of his anger.

2:2 [e]La 3:43 [f]Ps 21:9

[2] Without pity[e] the Lord has swallowed[f] up
all the dwellings of Jacob;

[a] This chapter is an acrostic poem, the verses of which begin with the successive letters of the Hebrew alphabet. [b] 1 Or *How the Lord in his anger / has treated the Daughter of Zion with contempt*

1:17 For "unclean thing," see the note on verse 8.
1:19 For "allies," see the note on verse 2.
1:20 The Sumerian Lamentation Over the Destruction of Ur contains a striking parallel: "Inside it we die of famine, outside we are killed by weapons" (lines 403–404).
2:1 "Daughter of Zion" is a personification of Jerusalem.

in his wrath he has torn down
the strongholds[g] of the Daughter of Judah.
He has brought her kingdom and its princes
down to the ground[h] in dishonor.

2:2 [g]Ps 89:39-40; Mic 5:11 [h]Isa 25:12

3 In fierce anger he has cut off
every horn[a] [i] of Israel.
He has withdrawn his right hand[j]
at the approach of the enemy.
He has burned in Jacob like a flaming fire
that consumes everything around it.[k]

2:3 [i]Ps 75:5,10 [j]Ps 74:11 [k]Isa 42:25; Jer 21:4-5,14

4 Like an enemy he has strung his bow;[l]
his right hand is ready.
Like a foe he has slain
all who were pleasing to the eye;[m]
he has poured out his wrath like fire[n]
on the tent of the Daughter of Zion.

2:4 [l]Job 16:13; La 3:12-13 [m]Eze 24:16,25 [n]Isa 42:25; Jer 7:20

5 The Lord is like an enemy;[o]
he has swallowed up Israel.
He has swallowed up all her palaces
and destroyed her strongholds.[p]
He has multiplied mourning and lamentation
for the Daughter of Judah.[q]

2:5 [o]Jer 30:14 [p]ver 2 [q]Jer 9:17-20

6 He has laid waste his dwelling like a garden;
he has destroyed his place of meeting.[r]
The LORD has made Zion forget
her appointed feasts and her Sabbaths;[s]
in his fierce anger he has spurned
both king and priest.[t]

2:6 [r]Jer 52:13 [s]La 1:4; Zep 3:18 [t]La 4:16

7 The Lord has rejected his altar
and abandoned his sanctuary.
He has handed over to the enemy
the walls of her palaces;[u]
they have raised a shout in the house of the LORD
as on the day of an appointed feast.

2:7 [u]Ps 74:7-8; Isa 64:11; Jer 33:4-5

8 The LORD determined to tear down
the wall around the Daughter of Zion.
He stretched out a measuring line[v]
and did not withhold his hand from destroying.
He made ramparts and walls lament;
together they wasted away.[w]

2:8 [v]2Ki 21:13; Isa 34:11 [w]Isa 3:26

9 Her gates[x] have sunk into the ground;
their bars he has broken and destroyed.
Her king and her princes are exiled[y] among
the nations,
the law[z] is no more,

2:9 [x]Ne 1:3 [y]Dt 28:36; 2Ki 24:15 [z]2Ch 15:3

[a] 3 Or / *all the strength*; or *every king*; *horn* here symbolizes strength.

2:3 "Horn" here symbolizes strength.
2:7 See "Temple Abandonment" on page 1323.
2:8 Ramparts were sloping, wall-like fortifications of earth or stone that were used as a protective barrier against invaders (see "Siege Warfare" on p. 465).
2:9 There were no longer any priests (see v. 20) to teach and interpret the covenant law, and the Lord was no longer communicating through prophets.

and her prophets no longer find
visions[a] from the LORD.

2:9 [a]Jer 14:14

10 The elders of the Daughter of Zion
sit on the ground in silence;
they have sprinkled dust on their heads[b]
and put on sackcloth.[c]
The young women of Jerusalem
have bowed their heads to the ground.[d]

2:10 [b]Job 2:12 [c]Isa 15:3 [d]Job 2:13; Isa 3:26

11 My eyes fail from weeping,[e]
I am in torment within,[f]
my heart is poured out[g] on the ground
because my people are destroyed,
because children and infants faint[h]
in the streets of the city.

2:11 [e]La 1:16; 3:48-51 [f]La 1:20 [g]ver 19; Ps 22:14 [h]La 4:4

12 They say to their mothers,
"Where is bread and wine?"
as they faint like wounded men
in the streets of the city,
as their lives ebb away
in their mothers' arms.[i]

2:12 [i]La 4:4

13 What can I say for you?
With what can I compare you,
O Daughter of Jerusalem?
To what can I liken you,
that I may comfort you,
O Virgin Daughter of Zion?[j]
Your wound is as deep as the sea.[k]
Who can heal you?

2:13 [j]Isa 37:22 [k]Jer 14:17; La 1:12

14 The visions of your prophets
were false and worthless;
they did not expose your sin
to ward off your captivity.[l]
The oracles they gave you
were false and misleading.[m]

2:14 [l]Isa 58:1 [m]Jer 2:8; 23:25-32,33-40; 29:9; Eze 13:3; 22:28

15 All who pass your way
clap their hands at you;[n]
they scoff[o] and shake their heads
at the Daughter of Jerusalem:
"Is this the city that was called
the perfection of beauty,[p]
the joy of the whole earth?"[q]

2:15 [n]Eze 25:6 [o]Jer 19:8 [p]Ps 50:2 [q]Ps 48:2

16 All your enemies open their mouths
wide against you;[r]
they scoff and gnash their teeth[s]
and say, "We have swallowed her up.[t]
This is the day we have waited for;
we have lived to see it."

2:16 [r]Ps 56:2; La 3:46 [s]Job 16:9 [t]Ps 35:25

2:10 For "elders" see the note on Jeremiah 19:1.

Sackcloth was the coarse garb of mourners (see the notes on 1Ki 20:31–32 and Job 16:15, as well as "Sackcloth and Ashes: Rituals of Lamentation" on p. 820).

2:13 "Daughter of Jerusalem" and "Virgin Daughter of Zion" in this verse both personify Jerusalem.

[17] The LORD has done what he planned;
he has fulfilled his word,
which he decreed long ago.[u]
He has overthrown you without pity,[v]
he has let the enemy gloat over you,
he has exalted the horn[a] of your foes.[w]

[18] The hearts of the people
cry out to the Lord.[x]
O wall of the Daughter of Zion,
let your tears[y] flow like a river
day and night;[z]
give yourself no relief,
your eyes no rest.[a]

[19] Arise, cry out in the night,
as the watches of the night begin;
pour out your heart[b] like water
in the presence of the Lord.[c]
Lift up your hands to him
for the lives of your children,
who faint[d] from hunger
at the head of every street.

[20] "Look, O LORD, and consider:
Whom have you ever treated like this?
Should women eat their offspring,[e]
the children they have cared for?[f]
Should priest and prophet be killed[g]
in the sanctuary of the Lord?

[21] "Young and old lie together
in the dust of the streets;
my young men and maidens
have fallen by the sword.[h]
You have slain them in the day of your anger;
you have slaughtered them without pity.[i]

[22] "As you summon to a feast day,
so you summoned against me terrors[j] on every side.
In the day of the LORD's anger
no one escaped or survived;
those I cared for and reared,[k]
my enemy has destroyed."

3[b]

I am the man who has seen affliction
by the rod of his wrath.[l]
[2] He has driven me away and made me walk
in darkness[m] rather than light;
[3] indeed, he has turned his hand against me[n]
again and again, all day long.

2:17 [u]Dt 28:15-45 [v]ver 2; Eze 5:11 [w]Ps 89:42
2:18 [x]Ps 119:145 [y]La 1:16 [z]Jer 9:1 [a]La 3:49
2:19 [b]1Sa 1:15; Ps 62:8 [c]Isa 26:9 [d]Isa 51:20
2:20 [e]Dt 28:53; Jer 19:9 [f]La 4:10 [g]Ps 78:64; Jer 14:15
2:21 [h]2Ch 36:17; Ps 78:62-63; Jer 6:11 [i]Jer 13:14; La 3:43; Zec 11:6
2:22 [j]Ps 31:13; Jer 6:25 [k]Hos 9:13
3:1 [l]Job 19:21; Ps 88:7
3:2 [m]Jer 4:23
3:3 [n]Isa 5:25

[a] *17 Horn* here symbolizes strength. [b] This chapter is an acrostic poem; the verses of each stanza begin with the successive letters of the Hebrew alphabet, and the verses within each stanza begin with the same letter.

2:17 "Exalted the horn" means "increased the strength."
2:19 The Hebrews divided the night into three watches: (1) sunset–10:00 P.M., (2) 10:00 P.M.–2:00 A.M. and (3) 2:00 A.M.–sunrise. Lifting one's hands was a common posture of prayer.
2:20 See the note on Jeremiah 19:9.

4 He has made my skin and my flesh grow old
and has broken my bones.[o]
5 He has besieged me and surrounded me
with bitterness[p] and hardship.[q]
6 He has made me dwell in darkness
like those long dead.[r]

7 He has walled me in so I cannot escape;[s]
he has weighed me down with chains.[t]
8 Even when I call out or cry for help,
he shuts out my prayer.[u]
9 He has barred my way with blocks of stone;
he has made my paths crooked.[v]

10 Like a bear lying in wait,
like a lion in hiding,
11 he dragged me from the path and mangled[w] me
and left me without help.
12 He drew his bow[x]
and made me the target[y] for his arrows.[z]

13 He pierced my heart
with arrows from his quiver.[a]
14 I became the laughingstock[b] of all my people;
they mock me in song[c] all day long.
15 He has filled me with bitter herbs
and sated me with gall.[d]

16 He has broken my teeth with gravel;[e]
he has trampled me in the dust.
17 I have been deprived of peace;
I have forgotten what prosperity is.
18 So I say, "My splendor is gone
and all that I had hoped from the LORD."[f]

19 I remember my affliction and my wandering,
the bitterness and the gall.
20 I well remember them,
and my soul is downcast[g] within me.[h]
21 Yet this I call to mind
and therefore I have hope:

22 Because of the LORD's great love we are not consumed,
for his compassions never fail.[i]
23 They are new every morning;
great is your faithfulness.[j]
24 I say to myself, "The LORD is my portion;[k]
therefore I will wait for him."

25 The LORD is good to those whose hope is in him,
to the one who seeks him;[l]
26 it is good to wait quietly
for the salvation of the LORD.[m]

3:4 [o]Ps 51:8; Isa 38:13; Jer 50:17
3:5 [p]ver 19 [q]Jer 23:15
3:6 [r]Ps 88:5-6
3:7 [s]Job 3:23 [t]Jer 40:4
3:8 [u]Job 30:20; Ps 22:2
3:9 [v]Isa 63:17; Hos 2:6
3:11 [w]Hos 6:1
3:12 [x]La 2:4 [y]Job 7:20 [z]Ps 7:12-13; 38:2
3:13 [a]Job 6:4
3:14 [b]Jer 20:7 [c]Job 30:9
3:15 [d]Jer 9:15
3:16 [e]Pr 20:17
3:18 [f]Job 17:15
3:20 [g]Ps 42:5 [h]Ps 42:11
3:22 [i]Ps 78:38; Mal 3:6
3:23 [j]Zep 3:5
3:24 [k]Ps 16:5
3:25 [l]Isa 25:9; 30:18
3:26 [m]Ps 37:7; 40:1

3:6 For commentary on the Old Testament view of the afterlife, see the note on Psalm 6:5; see also "Sheol, Hades, Gehenna, the Abyss and Tartarus: Images of Hell" on page 946.
3:10 See "Lions and Other Wild Beasts in Ancient Israel" on page 813.
3:13 For "heart" (lit., "kidneys"), see the notes on Psalms 4:7 and 7:9.
3:16 See the note on stones and gravel at Isaiah 27:9.

27 It is good for a man to bear the yoke
while he is young.

28 Let him sit alone in silence,[n]
for the LORD has laid it on him.
29 Let him bury his face in the dust—
there may yet be hope.[o]
30 Let him offer his cheek to one who would strike him,[p]
and let him be filled with disgrace.

31 For men are not cast off
by the Lord forever.[q]
32 Though he brings grief, he will show compassion,
so great is his unfailing love.[r]
33 For he does not willingly bring affliction
or grief to the children of men.[s]

34 To crush underfoot
all prisoners in the land,
35 to deny a man his rights
before the Most High,
36 to deprive a man of justice—
would not the Lord see such things?[t]

37 Who can speak and have it happen
if the Lord has not decreed it?[u]
38 Is it not from the mouth of the Most High
that both calamities and good things come?[v]
39 Why should any living man complain
when punished for his sins?[w]

40 Let us examine our ways and test them,[x]
and let us return to the LORD.[y]
41 Let us lift up our hearts and our hands
to God in heaven,[z] and say:
42 "We have sinned and rebelled[a]
and you have not forgiven.[b]

43 "You have covered yourself with anger and
pursued us;
you have slain without pity.[c]
44 You have covered yourself with a cloud[d]
so that no prayer[e] can get through.
45 You have made us scum[f] and refuse
among the nations.

46 "All our enemies have opened their mouths
wide against us.[g]
47 We have suffered terror and pitfalls,[h]
ruin and destruction.[i]"
48 Streams of tears flow from my eyes[j]
because my people are destroyed.[k]

49 My eyes will flow unceasingly,
without relief,[l]

3:28 [n]Jer 15:17
3:29 [o]Jer 31:17
3:30 [p]Job 16:10; Isa 50:6
3:31 [q]Ps 94:14; Isa 54:7
3:32 [r]Ps 78:38; Hos 11:8
3:33 [s]Eze 33:11
3:36 [t]Jer 22:3; Hab 1:13
3:37 [u]Ps 33:9-11
3:38 [v]Job 2:10; Isa 45:7; Jer 32:42
3:39 [w]Jer 30:15; Mic 7:9
3:40 [x]2Co 13:5 [y]Ps 119:59; 139:23-24
3:41 [z]Ps 25:1; 28:2
3:42 [a]Da 9:5 [b]Jer 5:7-9
3:43 [c]La 2:2,17, 21
3:44 [d]Ps 97:2 [e]ver 8
3:45 [f]1Co 4:13
3:46 [g]La 2:16
3:47 [h]Jer 48:43 [i]Isa 24:17-18; 51:19
3:48 [j]La 1:16 [k]La 2:11
3:49 [l]Jer 14:17

3:29 To "bury his face in the dust" was to demonstrate humble submission to God.

3:34 To "crush underfoot" recalls the treatment by the Babylonians in 586 B.C.

Ancient Near Eastern Laments

Tombs in Hierapolis in the Lycus Valley of Asia Minor (Turkey)
Photograph: © Todd Bolen/Bible Places.com

LAMENTATIONS 3 Mourning over calamities and deaths are common in human society, and both Israel and other ancient societies had ritualized means for expressing lamentation and grief.[1] A lament could be for a single person who had died or for an entire city that had met disaster. Both kinds of laments are well represented in the Bible.

✣ For individuals:

A number of texts indicate mourning for soldiers and kings killed in combat. David composed a lament for Saul and Jonathan (2Sa 1).[2] Second Chronicles 35:24 describes a national lamentation for Josiah after his death in battle, and David commanded respectful mourning for Abner (2Sa 3:31).

People naturally mourn the death of a loved one. Abraham grieved for Sarah (Ge 23:2), and David mourned excessively for Absalom (2Sa 18:33), considering the awkward circumstances with regard to his loyal troops. Luke 8:52–53 reflects the presence of professional mourners carrying out ritual lamentation for a deceased girl.

Job repeatedly bewailed the calamities that had befallen him (e.g., Job 3:1–26; 30:26–31). In his case personal disasters of several kinds (the deaths of loved ones, the loss of wealth and status, and personal sickness) were the occasions for his laments.

✣ For cities and states:

The entire book of Lamentations is a series of lament songs for Jerusalem, which had been destroyed in 586 B.C.[3]

Prophets often grieved for states and cities (Jer 6:26 [for Jerusalem]; Eze 27 [for Tyre]; Eze 32 [for Egypt]; and Mic 1:8–9 [for Jerusalem]).

The tradition of ritual mourning and the composition of lamentation texts is also found elsewhere in the ancient world. There are numerous examples of mourning over deceased individuals:

✣ Egyptian funerary texts tend to focus on the afterlife, but Egyptian funerals were carried out with elaborate bereavement ceremonies. The Egyptian Song of the Harper, for example, alludes to such mourning.[4] Egyptian artwork contains depictions of weeping mourners in funeral processions.

✣ In the Epic of Gilgamesh (from **Mesopotamia**)[5], the hero laments bitterly over the death of his friend, Enkidu.[6]

✣ A remarkable **Akkadian** poem bemoans a woman who had died in childbirth from the perspective of the deceased woman herself. She laments the fact that death has suddenly seized her and taken her away from her home, and she poignantly recalls how her husband grieved at her passing.

✣ In the Greek world, dirges were sung over the dead and elaborate funerals were carried out, as is reflected in various passages in the *Iliad* and *Odyssey*, as well as in Greek tragedy.

✣ Ritual mourning was a fixture in pagan religions that included a myth of a dying-and-rising god (such as Baal, Tammuz and Osiris). Worshipers would, in ritual fashion, lament the god's death.[7]

Examples of mourning over a city occur in Sumerian literature. There we find lamentations for Ur, **Sumer**, Nippur, Eridu and **Uruk**, all dating from the Isin-Larsa period (c. 1950–1700 B.C.). For example, after Ur was destroyed by **Elamites**, a mourner bemoaned the fall of the city in great detail and in a manner reminiscent of the Biblical book of Lamentations. Although he had pleaded with the gods for the safety of Ur, they had decreed that the city be destroyed. The song describes the warriors being struck down, citizens perishing by fire and hunger and even children expiring in their mothers' laps. Similarly, the Biblical book of Lamentations depicts Jerusalem's fall as being by the will of God and speaks at length of the suffering of the people. In spite of these similarities, however, direct linkage between Lamentations and the Sumerian texts is improbable. Both are part of a broad literary tradition, and both reflect the universal human response to calamity.

[1]See "Sackcloth and Ashes: Rituals of Lamentation" on page 820. [2]See "Songs of Warriors" on page 474. [3]See "The Last Days of Jerusalem" on page 1197. [4]See "The Harper Songs From the Tomb of Neferhotep" on page 1015 and "The Harper Song From the Tomb of King Intef" on page 1018. [5]See Glossary on page 2080 for definitions of bolded words. [6]For more on Gilgamesh, see "The Serpent Motif in Other Ancient Near Eastern Literature" on page 8 and "Ecclesiastes and the Epic of Gilgamesh" on page 1027. [7]See "Mourning for Tammuz" on page 1320.

50 until the LORD looks down
from heaven and sees.[m]
51 What I see brings grief to my soul
because of all the women of my city.

52 Those who were my enemies without cause
hunted me like a bird.[n]
53 They tried to end my life in a pit[o]
and threw stones at me;
54 the waters closed over my head,[p]
and I thought I was about to be cut off.

55 I called on your name, O LORD,
from the depths of the pit.[q]
56 You heard my plea:[r] "Do not close your ears
to my cry for relief."
57 You came near when I called you,
and you said, "Do not fear."[s]

58 O Lord, you took up my case;[t]
you redeemed my life.[u]
59 You have seen, O LORD, the wrong done to me.[v]
Uphold my cause!
60 You have seen the depth of their vengeance,
all their plots against me.[w]

61 O LORD, you have heard their insults,
all their plots against me—
62 what my enemies whisper and mutter
against me all day long.[x]
63 Look at them! Sitting or standing,
they mock me in their songs.

64 Pay them back what they deserve, O LORD,
for what their hands have done.[y]
65 Put a veil over their hearts,[z]
and may your curse be on them!
66 Pursue them in anger and destroy them
from under the heavens of the LORD.

3:50 [m]Isa 63:15
3:52 [n]Ps 35:7
3:53 [o]Jer 37:16
3:54 [p]Ps 69:2; Jnh 2:3-5
3:55 [q]Ps 130:1; Jnh 2:2
3:56 [r]Ps 55:1
3:57 [s]Isa 41:10
3:58 [t]Jer 51:36 [u]Ps 34:22; Jer 50:34
3:59 [v]Jer 18:19-20
3:60 [w]Jer 11:20; 18:18
3:62 [x]Eze 36:3
3:64 [y]Ps 28:4
3:65 [z]Isa 6:10

4[a]

How the gold has lost its luster,
the fine gold become dull!
The sacred gems are scattered
at the head of every street.[a]

2 How the precious sons of Zion,
once worth their weight in gold,
are now considered as pots of clay,
the work of a potter's hands!

3 Even jackals offer their breasts
to nurse their young,

4:1 [a]Eze 7:19

[a] This chapter is an acrostic poem, the verses of which begin with the successive letters of the Hebrew alphabet.

4:1–22 This lament over the conquest of Jerusalem by the Babylonians was apparently written by someone who had experienced the long siege of the city and the subsequent deportation of its people. See "Siege Warfare" on page 1536, "The Last Days of Jerusalem" on page 1197 and "Exile and Genocide in the Ancient Near East" on page 1337.

4:1 "Gold" and "gems" are metaphors for God's chosen people (see "Precious Stones of the Biblical World" on p. 1156). For similar imagery, see Song of Songs 5:11–12, 14–15, and Zechariah 9:16.

4:3 [b]Job 39:16

but my people have become heartless
like ostriches in the desert.[b]

4:4 [c]Ps 22:15 [d]La 2:11,12

4 Because of thirst the infant's tongue
sticks to the roof of its mouth;[c]
the children beg for bread,
but no one gives it to them.[d]

4:5 [e]Jer 6:2 [f]Am 6:3-7

5 Those who once ate delicacies
are destitute in the streets.
Those nurtured in purple[e]
now lie on ash heaps.[f]

4:6 [g]Ge 19:25

6 The punishment of my people
is greater than that of Sodom,[g]
which was overthrown in a moment
without a hand turned to help her.

7 Their princes were brighter than snow
and whiter than milk,
their bodies more ruddy than rubies,
their appearance like sapphires.[a]

4:8 [h]Job 30:28 [i]Ps 102:3-5

8 But now they are blacker[h] than soot;
they are not recognized in the streets.
Their skin has shriveled on their bones;[i]
it has become as dry as a stick.

4:9 [j]Jer 15:2; 16:4

9 Those killed by the sword are better off
than those who die of famine;
racked with hunger, they waste away
for lack of food from the field.[j]

4:10 [k]Lev 26:29; Dt 28:53-57; Jer 19:9; La 2:20; Eze 5:10

10 With their own hands compassionate women
have cooked their own children,[k]
who became their food
when my people were destroyed.

4:11 [l]Jer 17:27 [m]Dt 32:22; Jer 7:20; Eze 22:31

11 The LORD has given full vent to his wrath;
he has poured out his fierce anger.
He kindled a fire[l] in Zion
that consumed her foundations.[m]

4:12 [n]1Ki 9:9; Jer 21:13

12 The kings of the earth did not believe,
nor did any of the world's people,
that enemies and foes could enter
the gates of Jerusalem.[n]

4:13 [o]Jer 5:31; 6:13; Eze 22:28; Mic 3:11

13 But it happened because of the sins of her
prophets
and the iniquities of her priests,[o]
who shed within her
the blood of the righteous.

[a] 7 Or *lapis lazuli*

4:5 Purple was the color of royalty.
Ashes were symbolic of mourning (see "Sackcloth and Ashes: Rituals of Lamentation" on p. 820).

4:6 For "Sodom," see the note on Jeremiah 20:16. That ancient city was destroyed "in a moment," sparing it the suffering of a lengthy siege (like that of Jerusalem).

4:7 For "rubies" and "sapphires," see "Precious Stones of the Biblical World" on page 1156.

4:10 The threat of starvation during the siege of Jerusalem had driven some mothers to cook and eat their own children. The writer underscored the pain and despair of his generation by noting how drawn-out and painful it is to starve, as opposed to dying by the sword.

ANCIENT VOICES

Indeed, the Nile overflows none plough for it;
Everyone says: "We do not know what has happened throughout the land."
Indeed, women are barren, and none conceive,
Khnum does not create because of the condition of the land,
Indeed, many dead are buried in the river,
The stream is a grave and the tomb has become a stream.
Indeed the noblemen are in mourning and the poor man is full of joy,

—THE ADMONITIONS OF AN EGYPTIAN SAGE: THE ADMONITIONS OF IPUWER

See "Calamity and Distress at Ipuwer" article.

14 Now they grope through the streets
like men who are blind.[p]
They are so defiled with blood[q]
that no one dares to touch their garments.

15 "Go away! You are unclean!" men cry to them.
"Away! Away! Don't touch us!"
When they flee and wander about,
people among the nations say,
"They can stay here no longer."[r]

16 The LORD himself has scattered them;
he no longer watches over them.[s]
The priests are shown no honor,
the elders[t] no favor.

17 Moreover, our eyes failed,
looking in vain[u] for help;[v]
from our towers we watched
for a nation[w] that could not save us.

18 Men stalked us at every step,
so we could not walk in our streets.
Our end was near, our days were numbered,
for our end had come.[x]

19 Our pursuers were swifter
than eagles[y] in the sky;
they chased us[z] over the mountains
and lay in wait for us in the desert.

20 The LORD's anointed,[a] our very life breath,
was caught in their traps.[b]
We thought that under his shadow
we would live among the nations.

21 Rejoice and be glad, O Daughter of Edom,
you who live in the land of Uz.
But to you also the cup[c] will be passed;
you will be drunk and stripped naked.[d]

22 O Daughter of Zion, your punishment will end;[e]
he will not prolong your exile.
But, O Daughter of Edom, he will punish your sin
and expose your wickedness.[f]

5

Remember, O LORD, what has happened to us;
look, and see our disgrace.[g]
2 Our inheritance[h] has been turned over to aliens,
our homes[i] to foreigners.

4:14 [p]Isa 59:10 [q]Jer 2:34; 19:4
4:15 [r]Lev 13:46
4:16 [s]Isa 9:14-16 [t]La 5:12
4:17 [u]Isa 20:5; Eze 29:16 [v]La 1:7 [w]Jer 37:7
4:18 [x]Eze 7:2-12; Am 8:2
4:19 [y]Dt 28:49 [z]Isa 5:26-28
4:20 [a]2Sa 19:21 [b]Jer 39:5; Eze 12:12-13; 19:4,8
4:21 [c]Jer 25:15 [d]Isa 34:6-10; Am 1:11-12; Ob 1:16
4:22 [e]Isa 40:2; Jer 33:8 [f]Ps 137:7; Mal 1:4
5:1 [g]Ps 44:13-16; 89:50
5:2 [h]Ps 79:1 [i]Zep 1:13

4:15 "Unclean!" was the prescribed cry of the person with a much dreaded skin disease (see Lev 13:45; see also "Skin Diseaes in the Ancient World" on p. 171).
4:17 Egypt was one of the nations to whom Judah had looked for help (see Eze 29:16; see also the notes on Jer 22:20; 27:3; 37:5).
4:20 "The LORD's anointed" refers to King Zedekiah of the dynasty of David—under whom the people of Judah felt secure because of God's covenant with David.
"Our very life breath" (lit., "the breath of our nostrils") was a title used also of Pharaoh Rameses II in an inscription found at Abydos in Egypt.
4:21 "Daughter of Edom" is a personification of Edom (see "Edom" on p. 1467). Because of Edom's close relationship with Israel from earliest times and its persistent hostility, Edom often served as a representative of all Israel's enemies.
For "Uz," see the note on Job 1:1.
5:1–22 The circumstances described suggest the time immediately after the fall of Jerusalem, when all was chaotic in the land.
5:2 "Our inheritance" refers to the land of Judah.

3 We have become orphans and fatherless,
our mothers like widows.[j]
4 We must buy the water we drink;
our wood can be had only at a price.[k]
5 Those who pursue us are at our heels;
we are weary[l] and find no rest.
6 We submitted to Egypt and Assyria[m]
to get enough bread.
7 Our fathers sinned and are no more,
and we bear their punishment.[n]
8 Slaves[o] rule over us,
and there is none to free us from their hands.[p]
9 We get our bread at the risk of our lives
because of the sword in the desert.
10 Our skin is hot as an oven,
feverish from hunger.[q]

5:3 [j]Jer 15:8; 18:21
5:4 [k]Isa 3:1
5:5 [l]Ne 9:37
5:6 [m]Hos 9:3
5:7 [n]Jer 14:20; 16:12
5:8 [o]Ne 5:15 [p]Zec 11:6
5:10 [q]La 4:8-9

5:3 See "The Care of Widows and Orphans in the Bible and the Ancient Near East" on page 285.
5:6 By this time "Egypt and Assyria" (as a pair) was a conventional way of referring to the great world powers to which the Israelites had frequently turned for protective alliances (see the note on Jer 22:20).
5:8 "Slaves" is an ironic reference to the Babylonian officials who now ruled over Jerusalem.
5:9 The "sword in the desert" probably refers to marauding bandits.

ANCIENT TEXTS AND ARTIFACTS

Calamity and Distress in Ipuwer

LAMENTATIONS 5 Composed between 2000 and 1800 B.C., the text known as The Admonitions of Ipuwer laments the state of affairs in Egypt. Although it is found in a single Egyptian manuscript from the Nineteenth Dynasty, the work was in all probability written much earlier. The sage Ipuwer recounted the calamities that had befallen the nation, as well as the distress of the people, livestock and even the land. Much of the discussion is couched in terms that demonstrate reversals of the normal state of affairs: Slaves had become masters; the rich were reduced to poverty; servant girls ruled households; foreigners assumed leading positions of state; kings once buried in great pyramids now lay exposed on bare ground. Ipuwer blamed these disasters on the sun god Ra (Re), who, the sage pointed out, did not differentiate between good and evil people and had been unable to perceive the evil brooding in the hearts of the violent. Although there are differing interpretations of the text, it appears that Ipuwer also criticized the ineptitude of the reigning king and looked forward to the arrival of a redemptive ruler who would restore order and peace.

The book of Lamentations, written between 586 and 516 B.C., also deals with the themes of national calamity and distress. Here we also see reversals of fortunes: Jerusalem, once a queen, was now a slave (1:1), ruled by "slaves" (i.e., Babylonians; 5:8); gold and gems had lost their value (4:2); the rich sat in ash pits (4:5); and those who had been pure and polished in appearance were now so blackened with soot as to be unrecognizable (4:7–8). As in Ipuwer, foreigners had gained the upper hand (5:2), and princes and elders were being shown disrespect (v. 12). Unlike Ipuwer, however, the author of Lamentations did not blame the disaster on God's passivity. Rather, he understood that the Lord was justly judging the sins of the people (1:5,8,18; 3:38–42; 4:13). Although God was displaying his righteous anger (2:1–4; 4:11), his love and compassion were ever near (3:21–26,31–32). The judgment on the sins of Judah was his means of refining and restoring a remnant to himself.

Apart from that issue, Ipuwer does have some striking parallels to other parts of the Bible. The author bemoaned a situation of social upheaval in Egypt in which criminals, lowlifes and slaves had become wealthy and powerful and even maidservants felt free to be impudent toward their mistresses. This is similar to Ecclesiastes 10:6–7: "Fools are put in many high positions, while the rich occupy the low ones. I have seen slaves on horseback, while princes go on foot like slaves." Also, Ipuwer contains a striking reference to the Nile being turned to blood.[1]

[1]See "'The River Is Blood' in the Admonitions of Ipuwer" on page 908.

[11]Women have been ravished[r] in Zion,
 and virgins in the towns of Judah.
[12]Princes have been hung up by their hands;
 elders are shown no respect.[s]
[13]Young men toil at the millstones;
 boys stagger under loads of wood.
[14]The elders are gone from the city gate;
 the young men have stopped their music.[t]
[15]Joy is gone from our hearts;
 our dancing has turned to mourning.[u]
[16]The crown[v] has fallen from our head.
 Woe to us, for we have sinned![w]
[17]Because of this our hearts[x] are faint,
 because of these things our eyes[y] grow dim
[18]for Mount Zion, which lies desolate,[z]
 with jackals prowling over it.

[19]You, O LORD, reign forever;
 your throne endures[a] from generation to generation.
[20]Why do you always forget us?[b]
 Why do you forsake us so long?
[21]Restore[c] us to yourself, O LORD, that we may return;
 renew our days as of old
[22]unless you have utterly rejected us
 and are angry with us beyond measure.[d]

5:11 [r]Zec 14:2
5:12 [s]La 4:16
5:14 [t]Isa 24:8; Jer 7:34
5:15 [u]Jer 25:10
5:16 [v]Ps 89:39 [w]Isa 3:11
5:17 [x]Isa 1:5 [y]Ps 6:7
5:18 [z]Mic 3:12
5:19 [a]Ps 45:6; 102:12,24-27
5:20 [b]Ps 13:1; 44:24
5:21 [c]Ps 80:3
5:22 [d]Isa 64:9

5:12 To be "hung up" was an added indignity following execution.
5:14 The "city gate" was often used as the municipal court, as well as a place for conversation and entertainment (see "The City Gate" on p. 392).
5:18 The Hebrew for "jackals" can also mean "foxes."
5:22 A similarly somber ending characterizes not only other laments but also other Old Testament books (e.g., Isa and Mal).

INTRODUCTION TO 

AUTHOR, PLACE AND DATE OF WRITING

Ezekiel is named in Ezekiel 1:3 as the author of this book. Although some scholars have challenged this, arguing that Ezekiel was a late, postexilic work (perhaps as late as 200 B.C.), the vast majority consider this skepticism unfounded.

Ezekiel was carried into exile in Babylon, most likely along with Judah's king Jehoiachin, in 597 B.C. This prophet, who came from a priestly family, was married and lived in his own house in Babylon, enjoying relative freedom of movement. His intellect was keen and his knowledge wide-ranging.

Many of the visions and events recounted in Ezekiel can be dated with pinpoint accuracy. Ezekiel 1:2 is dated to the fifth year, fourth month and fifth day: July 31, 593 B.C. Ezekiel 8:1 specifies the sixth year, sixth month and fifth day: September 17, 592, and 20:1 designates the seventh year, fifth month and tenth day: August 14, 591. Other dates are stipulated at 24:1; 26:1; 29:1,17; 30:20; 31:1; 32:1, 17; 33:21; 40:1. The last dated vision (40:1) is reported to have come on April 28, 573 B.C. Thus, Ezekiel's visions spanned 25 years, from 593 to 573 B.C. The date in 1:1 (thirtieth year, fourth month, fifth day) is an apparent reference to Ezekiel's own life—that is, his age.

AUDIENCE

The book was written from Babylon during the exile and, although Ezekiel was carried to Jerusalem in a vision (ch. 8), was intended for the exiles. In particular, the prophet was given the distressing task of dashing the hopes of the early deportees that Jerusalem would be spared destruction and that they could soon return home. Beginning in 593, Ezekiel prepared his fellow captives for the heartrending events to come in 586: Jerusalem would be sacked and the temple burned to the ground.

CULTURAL FACTS AND HIGHLIGHTS

Ezekiel lived during a time of international upheaval. The once mighty Assyrian Empire, which had been the northern kingdom's nemesis and ultimate undoing, was beginning to crumble, but Babylon was flexing its muscles in alarming ways. Indeed, this resurgent power would dominate the international scene until being crushed itself by Persia in 539 B.C.

Ezekiel graphically portrayed the sinfulness of the Jerusalem of his day, as well as its consequent, certain judgment (see, e.g., ch. 16). In addition, he predicted the nature of that coming destruction (see, e.g., chs. 4–5) and provided its theological justification: The city was not inviolable, because God had abandoned his own temple (see "Temple Abandonment" on p. 1323). It is important to note, however, that the tragic tone is mitigated by hope: God allowed his spokesman to infuse his countrymen and women with anticipation not only of their own nation's restoration but also of his coming judgment upon their oppressors for generations of idolatry and violence perpetrated against his people.

TIMELINE

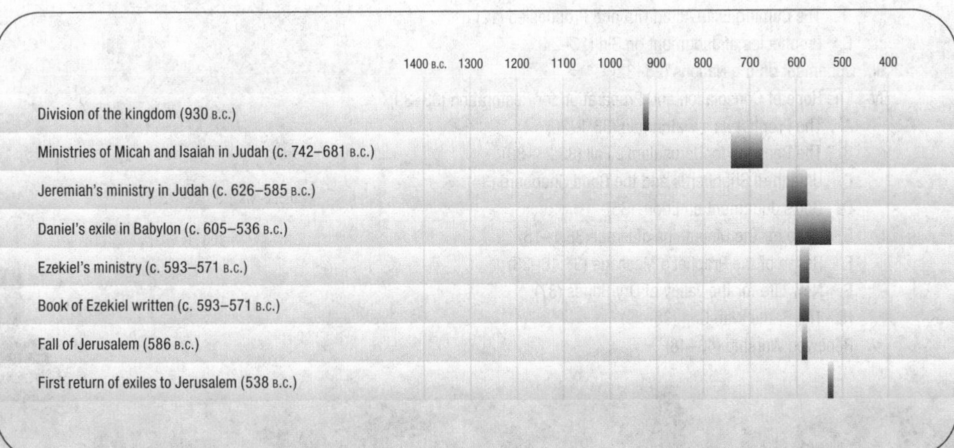

AS YOU READ

Ezekiel is a highly structured and symmetrical book (see outline). Be alert for contrasts, such as the following: the vision of the defiled temple, fit only for destruction (chs. 8–11), versus that of the restored and purified temple (chs. 40–48); the God of wrath (ch. 1) versus the God of comfort (48:35); Ezekiel's callings to be a watchman (1) announcing divine judgment (ch. 3) and (2) announcing the coming new age (ch. 33); the rebuke against the mountains of Israel (ch. 6) versus the prediction of their consolation (ch. 36). Notice Ezekiel's nontraditional prose, and listen for the hammering effect of his frequent repetitions. Pay special attention to the book's four major visions (chs. 1–3; 8–11; 37:1–14; 40–48), twelve symbolic acts (3:22–26; 4:1–3; 4:4–8; 4:9–11; 4:12–14; 5:1–3; 12:1–16; 12:17–20; 21:6–7; 21:18–24; 24:15–24; 37:15–28) and five parables (chs. 15; 16; 17; 19; 23).

DID YOU KNOW?

- The practice of rubbing newborns with salt has been observed among Arab peasants as recently as A.D. 1918 (16:4).
- The inner courtyard of Ezekiel's visionary temple was a perfect square—the "shape" of perfection, or holiness (40:47).
- The Dead Sea contains so much salt that nothing can live in it (47:8).

THEMES

The book of Ezekiel includes the following themes:

1. *Judgment.* The prophet Ezekiel used unusual means to prophesy God's coming judgment. He baked food using human excrement for fuel (4:9–17); shaved his head and beard, burning a third of the hair (5:1–4); dug a hole in the city wall and proceeded through it (12:1–6); and lay down without moving for extended periods of time (3:24–27; 4:4–8). These visible acts were matched by prophetic visions and images (1:1–28; 8:1—11:25; 40:1—48:35). God would judge both his people (1:1—24:27) and foreign nations (25:1—32:32) for their sinful behavior.

2. *God's sovereignty.* God is sovereign over the course of human history. His judgments are often a means of his self-revelation.

3. *Future hope.* There would be hope for God's people after judgment (33:1—39:29).

OUTLINE

- I. Ezekiel's Call and Commission (1–3)
- II. Judgment Against Judah and Jerusalem (4–24)
  - A. The Siege of Jerusalem Symbolized (4–5)
  - B. Prophecy of God's Judgment on His People (6–7)
  - C. Prophecy of the Temple Corrupted by Idolatry (8–11)
  - D. The Coming Exile Acted Out and Prophesied (12)
  - E. Prophecies of Judgment on Sin (13–24)
- III. Judgment on the Nations (25–32)
- IV. The Hope of Consolation and Preparation for Restoration (33–39)
  - A. The Prophet as a Watchman (33:1–20)
  - B. The Reasons for Jerusalem's Fall (33:21–33)
  - C. Unfaithful Shepherds and the Good Shepherd (34)
  - D. God's Judgment on Edom (35)
  - E. Hope for the Mountains of Israel (36:1–15)
  - F. Recap of the Prophet's Message (36:16–38)
  - G. New Life for the Valley of Dry Bones (37)
  - H. The Battle With Gog (38–39)
- V. Renewed Worship (40–48)

The Living Creatures and the Glory of the LORD

1:1 [a]Eze 11:24-25 [b]Mt 3:16; Ac 7:56 [c]Ex 24:10
1:2 [d]2Ki 24:15
1:3 [e]2Ki 3:15; Eze 3:14,22
1:4 [f]Jer 1:14 [g]Eze 8:2
1:5 [h]Rev 4:6 [i]ver 26
1:6 [j]Eze 10:14
1:7 [k]Da 10:6; Rev 1:15
1:8 [l]Eze 10:8
1:9 [m]Eze 10:22
1:10 [n]Eze 10:14; Rev 4:7
1:11 [o]Isa 6:2
1:13 [p]Rev 4:5
1:14 [q]Ps 29:7
1:16 [r]Eze 10:9-11; Da 10:6
1:17 [s]ver 9
1:18 [t]Eze 10:12; Rev 4:6
1:20 [u]ver 12
1:21 [v]Eze 10:17
1:22 [w]Eze 10:1

1 In the[a] thirtieth year, in the fourth month on the fifth day, while I was among the exiles[a] by the Ke-
bar River, the heavens were opened[b] and I saw visions[c] of God.
2On the fifth of the month—it was the fifth year of the exile of King Jehoiachin[d]— 3the word of the
LORD came to Ezekiel the priest, the son of Buzi,[b] by the Kebar River in the land of the Babylonians.[c]
There the hand of the LORD was upon him.[e]
4I looked, and I saw a windstorm coming out of the north[f]—an immense cloud with flashing light-
ning and surrounded by brilliant light. The center of the fire looked like glowing metal,[g] 5and in the fire
was what looked like four living creatures.[h] In appearance their form was that of a man,[i] 6but each of
them had four faces[j] and four wings. 7Their legs were straight; their feet were like those of a calf and
gleamed like burnished bronze.[k] 8Under their wings on their four sides they had the hands of a man.[l] All
four of them had faces and wings, 9and their wings touched one another. Each one went straight ahead;
they did not turn as they moved.[m]
10Their faces looked like this: Each of the four had the face of a man, and on the right side each
had the face of a lion, and on the left the face of an ox; each also had the face of an eagle.[n] 11Such
were their faces. Their wings[o] were spread out upward; each had two wings, one touching the wing
of another creature on either side, and two wings covering its body. 12Each one went straight ahead.
Wherever the spirit would go, they would go, without turning as they went. 13The appearance of the
living creatures was like burning coals of fire or like torches. Fire moved back and forth among the
creatures; it was bright, and lightning[p] flashed out of it. 14The creatures sped back and forth like
flashes of lightning.[q]
15As I looked at the living creatures, I saw a wheel on the ground beside each creature with its four fac-
es. 16This was the appearance and structure of the wheels: They sparkled like chrysolite,[r] and all four
looked alike. Each appeared to be made like a wheel intersecting a wheel. 17As they moved, they would
go in any one of the four directions the creatures faced; the wheels did not turn[s] about[d] as the creatures
went. 18Their rims were high and awesome, and all four rims were full of eyes[t] all around.
19When the living creatures moved, the wheels beside them moved; and when the living creatures
rose from the ground, the wheels also rose. 20Wherever the spirit would go, they would go,[u] and the wheels
would rise along with them, because the spirit of the living creatures was in the wheels. 21When the crea-
tures moved, they also moved; when the creatures stood still, they also stood still; and when the creatures
rose from the ground, the wheels rose along with them, because the spirit of the living creatures was in
the wheels.[v]
22Spread out above the heads of the living creatures was what looked like an expanse,[w] sparkling like
ice, and awesome. 23Under the expanse their wings were stretched out one toward the other, and each

[a] *1* Or ⌞*my*⌟ [b] *3* Or *Ezekiel son of Buzi the priest* [c] *3* Or *Chaldeans* [d] *17* Or *aside*

1:1 The "thirtieth year" probably refers to Ezekiel's age (see the NIV text note). According to Numbers 4:3, a person entered active priestly ministry in his thirtieth year. Denied the ministry of the priesthood, Ezekiel received another commission—that of prophet.

The Kebar River is usually identified as a canal of the Euphrates near the city of Nippur, south of Babylon, and possibly a place of prayer for the exiles (see Ps 137:1; cf. Ac 16:13). Ezekiel lived there with other Jewish exiles (Eze 1:3; 3:15), in contrast to Daniel, who carried out his quite different work in the Babylonian court.

The "captivity" of the Jews consisted in their deportation to a foreign land (see "Exile and Genocide in the Ancient Near East" on p. 1337). Once they had arrived in Babylon, however, the exiles seem to have been completely free to settle and live their lives as they pleased. Records have been found at Nippur of a Jewish business house, the Murashu Sons, indicating the possibilities open to the exiles. Many of the Jews became so settled in their adopted land that they declined to leave it at the end of the exile, and from that time to the present the majority of Hebrews have lived outside of Palestine.

1:2 Ezekiel was one of about 10,000 Jews who had been exiled to Babylon along with King Jehoiachin in 597 B.C. (2Ki 24:14–15). They joined those already exiled in 605 B.C. (cf. Da 1:1–2).

1:3 Ezekiel's name occurs elsewhere in the book only in 24:24.

Ezekiel was a powerful preacher. Possessing a deeply introspective and religious nature, he used allegory, vivid figures and symbolic actions to reinforce his message. His favorite expression to denote divine inspiration, "the hand of the LORD was upon me" (3:22; cf. 3:14), demonstrates how strongly he felt impelled to communicate the message given to him. His preaching was directed to his Jewish compatriots in exile and, like Jeremiah's, it was often resented, for it held out little hope for the immediate future. No doubt his message was ultimately received, however, for the exile became a time of religious purging. In Babylon the Jews were cured permanently of their idolatry, and Ezekiel, their major religious leader, must be given much credit for that.

1:4 In ancient times people identified their gods with observable, awe-inspiring natural phenomena, especially storms (see "Storm Gods, Storm Imagery and Theophany" on p. 808). Baal, the Canaanite fertility and weather god, is pictured as standing on a bull, a popular symbol of fertility and strength. The storm cloud was Baal's chariot, thunder his voice and lightning his spear and arrows (see the note on Ps 68:4; see also "Baal and the Fertility Cults" on p. 1414).

1:5 The "living creatures," called cherubim in 10:15, were throne attendants (see Ex 25:18–20 and its note). They were often depicted in the paintings and sculptures of the Middle Ages.

1:10 The lion was the strongest and most ferocious of the wild animals known in Israel and Mesopotamia (see "Lions and Other Wild Beasts in Ancient Israel" on p. 813); the ox was the most powerful of domesticated animals and the eagle the mightiest of the birds.

1:16 The precise identification of chrysolite is uncertain. It appears also with regard to the priestly breastplate in Exodus 28:20 (see "Precious Stones of the Biblical World" on p. 1156).

had two wings covering its body. 24 When the creatures moved, I heard the sound of their wings, like the
roar of rushing waters, like the voice[x] of the Almighty,[a] like the tumult of an army.[y] When they stood 1:24 [x]Eze 10:5; 43:2; Da 10:6; Rev 1:15; 19:6 [y]2Ki 7:6
still, they lowered their wings.
25 Then there came a voice from above the expanse over their heads as they stood with lowered wings.
26 Above the expanse over their heads was what looked like a throne of sapphire,[b][z] and high above on the 1:26 [z]Ex 24:10; Eze 10:1 [a]Rev 1:13
throne was a figure like that of a man.[a] 27 I saw that from what appeared to be his waist up he looked like
glowing metal, as if full of fire, and that from there down he looked like fire; and brilliant light surround-
ed him.[b] 28 Like the appearance of a rainbow[c] in the clouds on a rainy day, so was the radiance around 1:27 [b]Eze 8:2
him.[d] 1:28 [c]Ge 9:13; Rev 10:1 [d]Rev 4:2 [e]Eze 8:4 [f]Eze 3:23; Da 8:17; Rev 1:17
This was the appearance of the likeness of the glory[e] of the LORD. When I saw it, I fell facedown,[f] and
I heard the voice of one speaking.

Ezekiel's Call

2 He said to me, "Son of man, stand[g] up on your feet and I will speak to you." 2 As he spoke, the Spirit 2:1 [g]Da 10:11
came into me and raised me[h] to my feet, and I heard him speaking to me. 2:2 [h]Eze 3:24; Da 8:18
3 He said: "Son of man, I am sending you to the Israelites, to a rebellious nation that has rebelled
against me; they and their fathers have been in revolt against me to this very day.[i] 4 The people to whom 2:3 [i]Jer 3:25; Eze 20:8-24
I am sending you are obstinate and stubborn.[j] Say to them, 'This is what the Sovereign LORD says.' 2:4 [j]Eze 3:7
5 And whether they listen or fail to listen[k]—for they are a rebellious house[l]—they will know that a 2:5 [k]Eze 3:11 [l]Eze 3:27 [m]Eze 33:33
prophet has been among them.[m] 6 And you, son of man, do not be afraid[n] of them or their words. Do
not be afraid, though briers and thorns[o] are all around you and you live among scorpions. Do not be 2:6 [n]Jer 1:8,17 [o]Isa 9:18; Mic 7:4 [p]Eze 3:9
afraid of what they say or terrified by them, though they are a rebellious house.[p] 7 You must speak my
words to them, whether they listen or fail to listen, for they are rebellious.[q] 8 But you, son of man, lis- 2:7 [q]Jer 1:7; Eze 3:10-11
ten to what I say to you. Do not rebel like that rebellious house;[r] open your mouth and eat[s] what I give 2:8 [r]Isa 50:5 [s]Jer 15:16; Rev 10:9
you."
9 Then I looked, and I saw a hand[t] stretched out to me. In it was a scroll, 10 which he unrolled before 2:9 [t]Eze 8:3
me. On both sides of it were written words of lament and mourning and woe.[u] 2:10 [u]Rev 8:13

3 And he said to me, "Son of man, eat what is before you, eat this scroll; then go and speak to the house
of Israel." 2 So I opened my mouth, and he gave me the scroll to eat.
3 Then he said to me, "Son of man, eat this scroll I am giving you and fill your stomach with it." So I
ate[v] it, and it tasted as sweet as honey[w] in my mouth. 3:3 [v]Jer 15:16 [w]Ps 19:10; Ps 119:103; Rev 10:9-10
4 He then said to me: "Son of man, go now to the house of Israel and speak my words to them. 5 You
are not being sent to a people of obscure speech and difficult language,[x] but to the house of Israel— 3:5 [x]Isa 28:11; Jnh 1:2
6 not to many peoples of obscure speech and difficult language, whose words you cannot understand.
Surely if I had sent you to them, they would have listened to you.[y] 7 But the house of Israel is not willing 3:6 [y]Mt 11:21-23
to listen to you because they are not willing to listen to me, for the whole house of Israel is hardened and
obstinate.[z] 8 But I will make you as unyielding and hardened as they are.[a] 9 I will make your forehead like 3:7 [z]Eze 2:4; Jn 15:20-23
the hardest stone, harder than flint. Do not be afraid of them or terrified by them, though they are a re- 3:8 [a]Jer 1:18
bellious house.[b]" 3:9 [b]Isa 50:7; Eze 2:6; Mic 3:8
10 And he said to me, "Son of man, listen carefully and take to heart all the words I speak to you. 11 Go
now to your countrymen in exile and speak to them. Say to them, 'This is what the Sovereign LORD says,'
whether they listen or fail to listen.[c]" 3:11 [c]Eze 2:4-5,7
12 Then the Spirit lifted me up,[d] and I heard behind me a loud rumbling sound—May the glory of 3:12 [d]Eze 8:3; Ac 8:39
the LORD be praised in his dwelling place!— 13 the sound of the wings of the living creatures brushing
against each other and the sound of the wheels beside them, a loud rumbling sound.[e] 14 The Spirit then 3:13 [e]Eze 1:24; 10:5,16-17
lifted me up and took me away, and I went in bitterness and in the anger of my spirit, with the strong hand
of the LORD upon me. 15 I came to the exiles who lived at Tel Abib near the Kebar River.[f] And there, where 3:15 [f]Ps 137:1 [g]Job 2:13
they were living, I sat among them for seven days[g]—overwhelmed.

[a] 24 Hebrew *Shaddai* [b] 26 Or *lapis lazuli*

1:26 See "Thrones in the Ancient World" on page 899 and "Precious Stones of the Biblical World" on page 1156.

1:28 In the Old Testament God's glory is depicted as a substantial, even concrete Presence—the visible manifestation of his attendance among his people, often associated with the temple in Jerusalem (see 1Ki 8:11; Ps 26:8; 63:2; 96:6; 102:16).

2:9–10 Normally, ancient scrolls were written on one side only (see the note on Ex 17:14).

3:15 This is the only mention in the book of the specific place where the exiles were living (modern Tel Aviv).

Seven days was the traditional period of mourning (see Ge 50:10; 1Sa 31:13).

FILLED WITH THE SPIRIT

	Person	Reference
SKILL	Bezalel	Exodus 31:3; 35:30–31
LEADERSHIP	Moses	Numbers 11:17
	Joshua	Deuteronomy 34:9
	Othniel	Judges 3:10
	Gideon	Judges 6:34
	Jephthah	Judges 11:29
	Samson	Judges 14:6,19; 15:14
	David	1 Samuel 16:13
	Saul	1 Samuel 10:10; 11:6; 19:23
PROPHECY	Seventy Elders	Numbers 11:25
	Balaam	Numbers 24:2
	Messengers of Saul	1 Samuel 19:20
	Amasa	1 Chronicles 12:18
	Azarash	2 Chronicles 15:1
	Zechariah	2 Chronicles 24:20
	Isaiah	Isaiah 61:1
	Ezekiel	Ezekiel 3:24; 11:15

Chronological and Background Charts of the Old Testament, p. 111

Warning to Israel

[16]At the end of seven days the word of the LORD came to me:[h] [17]"Son of man, I have made you a watch-
man[i] for the house of Israel; so hear the word I speak and give them warning from me. [18]When I say to
a wicked man, 'You will surely die,' and you do not warn him or speak out to dissuade him from his evil
ways in order to save his life, that wicked man will die for[a] his sin, and I will hold you accountable for his
blood.[j] [19]But if you do warn the wicked man and he does not turn from his wickedness or from his evil
ways, he will die for his sin; but you will have saved yourself.[k]

3:16 [h]Jer 42:7
3:17 [i]Isa 52:8; Jer 6:17; Eze 33:7-9
3:18 [j]ver 20; Eze 33:6
3:19 [k]2Ki 17:13; Eze 14:14,20; Ac 18:6; 20:26; 1Ti 4:14-16

[a] *18* Or *in*; also in verses 19 and 20

3:17 In ancient Israel watchmen were stationed at the city gates (see Ne 11:19) and on the city walls to serve as the eyes of the city (see 2Sa 18:24–27; 2Ki 9:17–20; SS 3:3; 5:7; Isa 52:8; 62:6), with a primary goal to warn of approaching danger (see Ps 127:1; Isa 21:6; 56:10; Jer 6:17; Eze 33:2–3; Hos 9:8). They also patrolled the streets at night (see SS 5:7).

20“Again, when a righteous man turns from his righteousness and does evil, and I put a stumbling block before him, he will die. Since you did not warn him, he will die for his sin. The righteous things he did will not be remembered, and I will hold you accountable for his blood.[l] 21But if you do warn the righteous man not to sin and he does not sin, he will surely live because he took warning, and you will have saved yourself.[m]”

22The hand of the LORD[n] was upon me there, and he said to me, “Get up and go[o] out to the plain,[p] and there I will speak to you.” 23So I got up and went out to the plain. And the glory of the LORD was standing there, like the glory I had seen by the Kebar River,[q] and I fell facedown.[r]

24Then the Spirit came into me and raised me[s] to my feet. He spoke to me and said: “Go, shut yourself inside your house. 25And you, son of man, they will tie with ropes; you will be bound so that you cannot go out among the people.[t] 26I will make your tongue stick to the roof of your mouth so that you will be silent and unable to rebuke them, though they are a rebellious house.[u] 27But when I speak to you, I will open your mouth and you shall say to them, ‘This is what the Sovereign LORD says.’[v] Whoever will listen let him listen, and whoever will refuse let him refuse; for they are a rebellious house.[w]

Siege of Jerusalem Symbolized

4 “Now, son of man, take a clay tablet, put it in front of you and draw the city of Jerusalem on it. 2Then lay siege to it: Erect siege works against it, build a ramp[x] up to it, set up camps against it and put battering rams around it.[y] 3Then take an iron pan, place it as an iron wall between you and the city and turn your face toward it. It will be under siege, and you shall besiege it. This will be a sign[z] to the house of Israel.[a]

4“Then lie on your left side and put the sin of the house of Israel upon yourself.[a] You are to bear their sin for the number of days you lie on your side. 5I have assigned you the same number of days as the years of their sin. So for 390 days you will bear the sin of the house of Israel.

6“After you have finished this, lie down again, this time on your right side, and bear the sin of the house of Judah. I have assigned you 40 days, a day for each year.[b] 7Turn your face toward the siege of Jerusalem and with bared arm prophesy against her. 8I will tie you up with ropes so that you cannot turn from one side to the other until you have finished the days of your siege.[c]

9“Take wheat and barley, beans and lentils, millet and spelt;[d] put them in a storage jar and use them to make bread for yourself. You are to eat it during the 390 days you lie on your side. 10Weigh out twenty shekels[b] of food to eat each day and eat it at set times. 11Also measure out a sixth of a hin[c] of water and drink it at set times. 12Eat the food as you would a barley cake; bake it in the sight of the people, using human excrement[e] for fuel.” 13The LORD said, “In this way the people of Israel will eat defiled food among the nations where I will drive them.”[f]

14Then I said, “Not so, Sovereign LORD![g] I have never defiled myself. From my youth until now I have never eaten anything found dead[h] or torn by wild animals. No unclean meat has ever entered my mouth.[i]”

15“Very well,” he said, “I will let you bake your bread over cow manure instead of human excrement.”

16He then said to me: “Son of man, I will cut off[j] the supply of food in Jerusalem. The people will eat rationed food in anxiety and drink rationed water in despair,[k] 17for food and water will be scarce. They will be appalled at the sight of each other and will waste away because of[d] their sin.[l]

3:20 [l]Ps 125:5; Eze 18:24; 33:12, 18
3:21 [m]Ac 20:31
3:22 [n]Eze 1:3 [o]Ac 9:6 [p]Eze 8:4
3:23 [q]Eze 1:1 [r]Eze 1:28
3:24 [s]Eze 2:2
3:25 [t]Eze 4:8
3:26 [u]Eze 2:5; 24:27; 33:22
3:27 [v]ver 11 [w]Eze 12:3; 24:27; 33:22
4:2 [x]Jer 6:6 [y]Eze 21:22
4:3 [z]Isa 8:18; 20:3; Eze 12:3-6; 24:24,27 [a]Jer 39:1
4:6 [b]Nu 14:34; Da 9:24-26; 12:11-12
4:8 [c]Eze 3:25
4:9 [d]Isa 28:25
4:12 [e]Isa 36:12
4:13 [f]Hos 9:3
4:14 [g]Jer 1:6; Eze 9:8; 20:49 [h]Lev 11:39 [i]Ex 22:31; Dt 14:3; Ac 10:14
4:16 [j]Ps 105:16; Eze 5:16 [k]ver 10-11; Lev 26:26; Isa 3:1; Eze 12:19
4:17 [l]Lev 26:39; Eze 24:23; 33:10

[a] 4 Or *your side* [b] 10 That is, about 8 ounces (about 0.2 kilogram) [c] 11 That is, about 2/3 quart (about 0.6 liter) [d] 17 Or *away in*

4:1–3 This is the first of several symbolic acts performed by the prophet. After inscribing a likeness of the city of Jerusalem on a moist clay tablet, such as those commonly used in Babylonia (see the note on 4:1), Ezekiel was to place around it models of siege works to represent the city under attack (see “Siege Warfare” on p. 465). He was then to place an iron pan (perhaps a baking griddle used for baking flat loaves of bread) between himself and the symbolized city to indicate the unbreakable strength of the siege.

4:1 Ancient writing was done with a stylus on blocks of soft clay, which varied in size according to need (see “Cuneiform and Clay Tablets in the Ancient Near East” on p. 1108 and “Writing Materials in the Ancient World” on p. 2037). Ezekiel used such a tile in drawing a prophetic picture of the doom awaiting Jerusalem (NIV, “tablet”). When a permanent record was desired, the inscribed tile was baked in a furnace. So skilled were the scribes of the day that many of their tiles remain in perfect condition after 3,000 years.

4:9 These food items would have constituted a scant, vegetarian diet, representing the meager provisions of a besieged city. No Israelite meal was complete without bread. Sometimes honey and oil were mixed into the dough as it was being made in the kneading troughs or in wooden bowls. In times of poverty bread was made with beans, millet and spelt. Bread was usually eaten warm and seldom by itself; it was generally served with sour wine or meat gravy (Jn 13:26; 21:13).

4:12 See the note on Isaiah 9:5. When thoroughly dried, cow manure was commonly used in the Near East as a fuel for baking; it is still sometimes used in that way today. Ezekiel showed his sensitivity to things ceremonially unclean, and God graciously responded to the prophet’s objection by allowing this substitute for human excrement.

5 "Now, son of man, take a sharp sword and use it as a barber's razor[m] to shave[n] your head and your beard.[o] Then take a set of scales and divide up the hair. 2 When the days of your siege come to an end, burn a third of the hair with fire inside the city. Take a third and strike it with the sword all around the city. And scatter a third to the wind. For I will pursue them with drawn sword.[p] 3 But take a few strands of hair and tuck them away in the folds of your garment.[q] 4 Again, take a few of these and throw them into the fire and burn them up. A fire will spread from there to the whole house of Israel.

5 "This is what the Sovereign LORD says: This is Jerusalem, which I have set in the center of the nations, with countries all around her. 6 Yet in her wickedness she has rebelled against my laws and decrees more than the nations and countries around her. She has rejected my laws and has not followed my decrees.[r]

7 "Therefore this is what the Sovereign LORD says: You have been more unruly than the nations around you and have not followed my decrees or kept my laws. You have not even[a] conformed to the standards of the nations around you.[s]

8 "Therefore this is what the Sovereign LORD says: I myself am against you, Jerusalem, and I will inflict punishment on you in the sight of the nations.[t] 9 Because of all your detestable idols, I will do to you what I have never done before and will never do again.[u] 10 Therefore in your midst fathers will eat their children, and children will eat their fathers.[v] I will inflict punishment on you and will scatter all your survivors to the winds.[w] 11 Therefore as surely as I live, declares the Sovereign LORD, because you have defiled my sanctuary with all your vile images[x] and detestable practices,[y] I myself will withdraw my favor; I will not look on you with pity or spare you.[z] 12 A third of your people will die of the plague or perish by famine inside you; a third will fall by the sword outside your walls; and a third I will scatter to the winds and pursue with drawn sword.[a]

13 "Then my anger will cease and my wrath[b] against them will subside, and I will be avenged.[c] And when I have spent my wrath upon them, they will know that I the LORD have spoken in my zeal.

14 "I will make you a ruin and a reproach among the nations around you, in the sight of all who pass by.[d] 15 You will be a reproach and a taunt, a warning and an object of horror to the nations around you when I inflict punishment on you in anger and in wrath and with stinging rebuke.[e] I the LORD have spoken.[f] 16 When I shoot at you with my deadly and destructive arrows of famine, I will shoot to destroy you. I will bring more and more famine upon you and cut off your supply of food.[g] 17 I will send famine and wild beasts against you, and they will leave you childless. Plague and bloodshed[h] will sweep through you, and I will bring the sword against you. I the LORD have spoken.[i]"

A Prophecy Against the Mountains of Israel

6 The word of the LORD came to me: 2 "Son of man, set your face against the mountains[j] of Israel; prophesy against them 3 and say: 'O mountains of Israel, hear the word of the Sovereign LORD. This is what the Sovereign LORD says to the mountains and hills, to the ravines and valleys:[k] I am about to bring a sword against you, and I will destroy your high places.[l] 4 Your altars will be demolished and your incense altars[m] will be smashed; and I will slay your people in front of your idols. 5 I will lay the dead bodies of the Israelites in front of their idols, and I will scatter your bones[n] around your altars. 6 Wherever you live, the towns will be laid waste and the high places demolished, so that your altars will be laid waste and devastated, your idols[o] smashed and ruined, your incense altars[p] broken down, and what you have made wiped out.[q] 7 Your people will fall slain among you, and you will know that I am the LORD.

8 " 'But I will spare some, for some of you will escape[r] the sword when you are scattered among the lands and nations.[s] 9 Then in the nations where they have been carried captive, those who escape will remember me—how I have been grieved[t] by their adulterous hearts, which have turned away from me, and by their eyes, which have lusted after their idols.[u] They will loathe themselves for the evil they have

5:1 [m]Isa 7:20 [n]Eze 44:20 [o]Lev 21:5
5:2 [p]ver 12; Lev 26:33
5:3 [q]Jer 39:10
5:6 [r]Jer 11:10; Eze 16:47-51; Zec 7:11
5:7 [s]2Ch 33:9; Jer 2:10-11; Eze 16:47
5:8 [t]Eze 15:7
5:9 [u]Da 9:12; Mt 24:21
5:10 [v]Lev 26:29; La 2:20 [w]Lev 26:33; Ps 44:11; Eze 12:14; Zec 2:6
5:11 [x]Eze 7:20 [y]2Ch 36:14; Eze 8:6 [z]Eze 7:4,9
5:12 [a]ver 2,17; Jer 15:2; 21:9; Eze 6:11-12; 12:14
5:13 [b]Eze 21:17; 36:6 [c]Isa 1:24
5:14 [d]Lev 26:32; Ne 2:17; Ps 74:3-10; 79:1-4
5:15 [e]1Ki 9:7; Jer 22:8-9; 24:9 [f]Eze 25:17
5:16 [g]Dt 32:24
5:17 [h]Eze 38:22 [i]Eze 14:21
6:2 [j]Eze 36:1
6:3 [k]Eze 36:4 [l]Lev 26:30
6:4 [m]2Ch 14:5
6:5 [n]Jer 8:1-2
6:6 [o]Mic 1:7; Zec 13:2 [p]Lev 26:30 [q]Isa 6:11; Eze 5:14
6:8 [r]Jer 44:28 [s]Isa 6:13; Jer 44:14; Eze 12:16; 14:22
6:9 [t]Ps 78:40; Isa 7:13 [u]Eze 20:7,24

[a] 7 Most Hebrew manuscripts; some Hebrew manuscripts and Syriac *You have*

5:1 See "Beards and Hairstyles in the Biblical World" on page 1084.
5:10 Cannibalism, the most gruesome practice associated with life under siege (see 2Ki 6:28; see also "Siege Warfare" on p. 465), was threatened as a consequence of breaking the covenant (Dt 28:53; see Jer 19:9 and its note; La 2:20; Zec 11:9 and its note).
5:17 These judgments—famine, disease ("plague"), sword ("bloodshed"; i.e., violent death at human hands) and wild beasts (see "Lions and Other Wild Beasts in Ancient Israel" on p. 813)—were the four main causes of death among the peoples of the ancient Near East.
6:3 The "mountains of Israel" were the heavily cultivated central highlands, which also provided the principal sites for "high places" (see "The High Places" on p. 1318).
6:4 Incense altars, constructed of burnt clay and about 2 feet (61 cm) in height, were typically inscribed with animal figures and idols of Canaanite gods.

done and for all their detestable practices.[v] 10 And they will know that I am the LORD; I did not threaten 6:9 [v]Eze 20:43; 36:31
in vain to bring this calamity on them.
11 " 'This is what the Sovereign LORD says: Strike your hands together and stamp your feet and cry out
"Alas!" because of all the wicked and detestable practices of the house of Israel, for they will fall by the
sword, famine and plague.[w] 12 He that is far away will die of the plague, and he that is near will fall by the 6:11 [w]Eze 5:12; 21:14,17; 25:6
sword, and he that survives and is spared will die of famine. So will I spend my wrath upon them.[x] 13 And 6:12 [x]Eze 5:12
they will know that I am the LORD, when their people lie slain among their idols around their altars, on
every high hill and on all the mountaintops, under every spreading tree and every leafy oak[y]—places 6:13 [y]Isa 57:5

The High Places

EZEKIEL 6 English Bible readers are often bewildered by the regular references to the "high places" of Israel. The Hebrew word for "high place" is *bamah* (lit.,"height"). The term refers to local, open-air shrines that were frequently described as being located on a hill but could in reality have been found anywhere, including a city, gate or valley (Jer 7:31). Some surmise that a shrine was called a "high place" because of its location; others suggest that the name refers to its construction. Regardless, a *bamah* might have been either a shrine perched upon a hilltop, such as in Petra,[1] or an elevated platform like the mound of unhewn stones uncovered at **Megiddo**[2,3] (see "Map 6").

A typical high place consisted of a manmade platform or altar with associated buildings (1Ki 12:31; 2Ki 17:29). It is likely that many high places were located in spots that had originally been sacred to the **Canaanites**—and that the conquering Israelites were supposed to have destroyed (Nu 33:52). In Israel's early history in Canaan, high places became venues for the offering of animal sacrifices and incense to **Yahweh** (1Sa 9:12ff.). The rationale offered was that people "were still sacrificing at the high places, because a temple had not yet been built for the Name of the LORD" (1Ki 3:2).[4] It may be that Elijah chose Mount Carmel for his contest with the prophets of Baal (1Ki 18) because the site was sacred to both Israelites and pagans.

Gibeon ("Map 4") was known as "the most important high place" (1Ki 3:4);[5] although the ark was transferred by David from there to Jerusalem, the tabernacle and bronze altar remained at Gibeon (2Ch 1:3–5).[6] Also, Gibeon was the place at which the prophet Samuel celebrated festivals and where Solomon received a vision from the Lord.

Once worship of the Lord had been centralized in Jerusalem, however, high places came to pose a threat to the purity of Israel's faith. When Israelites worshiped the Lord away from the temple and its priestly oversight, they were at risk of being influenced by local, pagan cults and traditions. Prophets attacked high places for their syncretism: They were all too frequently locations at which the gods Molech, Chemosh and Asherah were worshiped, indiscriminately, alongside the God of Israel (1Ki 11:7–8; 2Ki 23:13). High places were regarded as centers of apostasy because they competed with Jerusalem for Israel's devotion (2Ki 17:9–11).

In the historical narratives kings are routinely evaluated by whether or not they demolished these sanctuaries. Josiah's reforms dealt a powerful blow to the high places (2Ki 23:15–20); even so, attachment to them survived. These locations of temptation are cited specifically as a cause for God's judgment upon Judah (Eze 6:3–7).[7]

Altar from Megiddo
Preserving Bible Times; © Dr. James C. Martin

[1]See "Aretas IV of Nabatea and Petra" on page 1898. [2]See Glossary on page 2080 for definitions of bolded words. [3]See "Megiddo" on page 1541. [4]See "Israelite Shrines and Worship Before the Temple of Solomon" on page 398. [5]See "Gibeon" on page 318. [6]See "The Tabernacle and the Ark" on page 153. [7]See also "The High Place at Dan" on page 504.

where they offered fragrant incense to all their idols.[z] 14And I will stretch out my hand[a] against them
and make the land a desolate waste from the desert to Diblah[a]—wherever they live. Then they will know
that I am the LORD.[b]' "

The End Has Come

7 The word of the LORD came to me: 2"Son of man, this is what the Sovereign LORD says to the land of
Israel: The end![c] The end has come upon the four corners[d] of the land. 3The end is now upon you
and I will unleash my anger against you. I will judge you according to your conduct and repay you for all
your detestable practices. 4I will not look on you with pity[e] or spare you; I will surely repay you for your
conduct and the detestable practices among you. Then you will know that I am the LORD.
5"This is what the Sovereign LORD says: Disaster![f] An unheard-of[b] disaster is coming. 6The end has
come! The end has come! It has roused itself against you. It has come! 7Doom has come upon you—you
who dwell in the land. The time has come, the day is near;[g] there is panic, not joy, upon the mountains.
8I am about to pour out my wrath[h] on you and spend my anger against you; I will judge you according
to your conduct and repay you for all your detestable practices.[i] 9I will not look on you with pity or spare
you; I will repay you in accordance with your conduct and the detestable practices among you. Then you
will know that it is I the LORD who strikes the blow.
10"The day is here! It has come! Doom has burst forth, the rod[j] has budded, arrogance has blossomed!
11Violence has grown into[c] a rod to punish wickedness; none of the people will be left, none of that
crowd—no wealth, nothing of value.[k] 12The time has come, the day has arrived. Let not the buyer rejoice
nor the seller grieve, for wrath is upon the whole crowd.[l] 13The seller will not recover the land he has sold
as long as both of them live, for the vision concerning the whole crowd will not be reversed. Because of
their sins, not one of them will preserve his life.[m] 14Though they blow the trumpet and get everything
ready, no one will go into battle, for my wrath is upon the whole crowd.
15"Outside is the sword, inside are plague and famine; those in the country will die by the sword, and
those in the city will be devoured by famine and plague.[n] 16All who survive and escape will be in the
mountains, moaning like doves[o] of the valleys, each because of his sins.[p] 17Every hand will go limp,[q] and
every knee will become as weak as water. 18They will put on sackcloth and be clothed with terror.[r] Their
faces will be covered with shame and their heads will be shaved.[s] 19They will throw their silver into the
streets, and their gold will be an unclean thing. Their silver and gold will not be able to save them in the
day of the LORD's wrath.[t] They will not satisfy their hunger or fill their stomachs with it, for it has made
them stumble[u] into sin.[v] 20They were proud of their beautiful jewelry and used it to make their detest-
able idols and vile images.[w] Therefore I will turn these into an unclean thing for them. 21I will hand it all
over as plunder to foreigners and as loot to the wicked of the earth, and they will defile it.[x] 22I will turn
my face[y] away from them, and they will desecrate my treasured place; robbers will enter it and dese-
crate it.
23"Prepare chains, because the land is full of bloodshed[z] and the city is full of violence. 24I will bring
the most wicked of the nations to take possession of their houses; I will put an end to the pride of the
mighty, and their sanctuaries[a] will be desecrated.[b] 25When terror comes, they will seek peace, but there
will be none.[c] 26Calamity upon calamity[d] will come, and rumor upon rumor. They will try to get a vision
from the prophet; the teaching of the law by the priest will be lost, as will the counsel of the elders.[e] 27The
king will mourn, the prince will be clothed with despair,[f] and the hands of the people of the land will
tremble. I will deal with them according to their conduct,[g] and by their own standards I will judge them.
Then they will know that I am the LORD.[h]"

6:13 [z]1Ki 14:23; Jer 2:20; Eze 20:28; Hos 4:13
6:14 [a]Isa 5:25 [b]Eze 14:13
7:2 [c]Am 8:2,10 [d]Rev 7:1; 20:8
7:4 [e]Eze 5:11
7:5 [f]2Ki 21:12
7:7 [g]Eze 12:23; Zep 1:14
7:8 [h]Isa 42:25; Eze 9:8; 14:19; Na 1:6 [i]Eze 20:8, 21; 36:19
7:10 [j]Ps 89:32; Isa 10:5
7:11 [k]Jer 16:6; Zep 1:18
7:12 [l]ver 7; Isa 5:13-14; Eze 30:3
7:13 [m]Lev 25:24-28
7:15 [n]Dt 32:25; Jer 14:18; La 1:20; Eze 5:12
7:16 [o]Isa 59:11 [p]Ezr 9:15; Eze 6:8
7:17 [q]Isa 13:7; Eze 21:7; 22:14
7:18 [r]Ps 55:5 [s]Isa 15:2-3; Eze 27:31; Am 8:10
7:19 [t]Eze 13:5; Zep 1:7,18 [u]Eze 14:3 [v]Pr 11:4
7:20 [w]Jer 7:30
7:21 [x]2Ki 24:13
7:22 [y]Eze 39:23-24
7:23 [z]2Ki 21:16
7:24 [a]Eze 24:21 [b]2Ch 7:20; Eze 28:7
7:25 [c]Eze 13:10, 16
7:26 [d]Jer 4:20 [e]Isa 47:11; Eze 20:1-3; Mic 3:6
7:27 [f]Ps 109:19; Eze 26:16 [g]Eze 18:20 [h]ver 4

[a] *14* Most Hebrew manuscripts; a few Hebrew manuscripts *Riblah* [b] *5* Most Hebrew manuscripts; some Hebrew manuscripts and Syriac *Disaster after* [c] *11* Or *The violent one has become*

6:14 Diblah may be Beth Diblathaim (Jer 48:22), a city in Moab, or Riblah, a city north of Damascus on the Orontes River. In Ezekiel this was the northern limit of God's judgments that were to fall on the Holy Land for the people's odious idolatry.
7:15 See the note on 5:17 with regard to this threefold threat.
7:18 Sackcloth was the coarse garb of mourners (see the notes at 1Ki 20:31–32 and Job 16:15, as well as "Sackcloth and Ashes: Rituals of Lamentation" on p. 820).
7:19 Wooden idols were often plated with precious metals to make them more attractive (see Isa 2:20; 30:22; 40:19).
7:20 Jewelry was sometimes melted down to make idols (see Ex 32:2–4).
7:26 There would be no guidance from God through the prophets, no reading or teaching of the law by the priests and no direction from the elders (see the note on Jer 19:1).
7:27 "The people of the land" were the full citizens of Judah (those holding inherited family property and those subject to military service).

Idolatry in the Temple

8 In the sixth year, in the sixth month on the fifth day, while I was sitting in my house and the elders[i]
of Judah were sitting before[j] me, the hand of the Sovereign LORD came upon me there.[k] 2 I looked, and
I saw a figure like that of a man.[a] From what appeared to be his waist down he was like fire, and from
there up his appearance was as bright as glowing metal.[l] 3 He stretched out what looked like a hand and
took me by the hair of my head. The Spirit lifted me up[m] between earth and heaven and in visions of
God he took me to Jerusalem, to the entrance to the north gate of the inner court, where the idol that
provokes to jealousy[n] stood. 4 And there before me was the glory[o] of the God of Israel, as in the vision I
had seen in the plain.[p]
5 Then he said to me, "Son of man, look toward the north." So I looked, and in the entrance north of
the gate of the altar I saw this idol[q] of jealousy.
6 And he said to me, "Son of man, do you see what they are doing—the utterly detestable[r] things the
house of Israel is doing here, things that will drive me far from my sanctuary? But you will see things that
are even more detestable."
7 Then he brought me to the entrance to the court. I looked, and I saw a hole in the wall. 8 He said to
me, "Son of man, now dig into the wall." So I dug into the wall and saw a doorway there.
9 And he said to me, "Go in and see the wicked and detestable things they are doing here." 10 So I went
in and looked, and I saw portrayed all over the walls all kinds of crawling things and detestable animals

8:1 [i]Eze 14:1 [j]Eze 33:31 [k]Eze 1:1-3
8:2 [l]Eze 1:4,26-27
8:3 [m]Eze 3:12; 11:1 [n]Ex 20:5; Dt 32:16
8:4 [o]Eze 1:28 [p]Eze 3:22
8:5 [q]Ps 78:58; Jer 32:34
8:6 [r]Eze 5:11

[a] 2 Or *saw a fiery figure*

8:1—11:25 Ezekiel 8–11 contains a unique vision of events that were transpiring in Jerusalem, made possible when "the Spirit lifted [Ezekiel] up . . . and took [him] to Jerusalem" (8:3). Elsewhere in the book an intimate knowledge of events in faraway Jerusalem is implied (e.g., 24:1–2). It appears impossible that Ezekiel in Babylon could have known in such detail events in Jerusalem except by divine inspiration. Therefore many scholars are now of the opinion that Ezekiel really prophesied in Jerusalem until the city fell. The clear statements of the book, however, indicate his presence with the Jews in Babylon when he "saw" (8:6,9–10) the events taking place at Jerusalem.

8:1 The date was September 17, 592 B.C. (see the note on 1:2), and Ezekiel was sitting in his house. The exiles were permitted to build houses and enjoyed freedom of movement, assembly and worship.

8:3 This idol may have been a statue of Asherah, the Canaanite goddess of fertility (see 2Ki 21:7; 23:6; see also the note on Jdg 3:7, as well as "Devotion to Asherah in the Khirbet El-Qom Inscription" on p. 638 and "The Kuntillet Ajrûd Inscriptions: The Lord's Asherah?" on p. 1220).

8:10 The nation's leaders were secretly practicing animal worship, probably reflecting Egyptian influence (cf. 2Ki 23:31–35).

ANCIENT TEXTS AND ARTIFACTS

Mourning for Tammuz

EZEKIEL 8 Among the pagan rituals the prophet Ezekiel was shown in Ezekiel 8 was a group of women "mourning for Tammuz" (v. 14). Numerous pagan religions feature a dying-and-rising god (such as Tammuz, Baal or Osiris), whose restoration comes about partly through the aid of his consort (partner) goddess (Ishtar, Anat or Isis, respectively, for the previous examples). The myths of the dying gods are not all the same; each is distinctive, and the various versions of these myths are sometimes contradictory and difficult to unravel.[1] Tammuz was sometimes regarded as a **Mesopotamian** version of the fertility god Baal but actually appears to have been a relatively minor shepherd god—who may or may not be thought to have returned from the dead.

It is clear that the cult of Tammuz was of very ancient origin, from **Sumer**. Even so, it persisted for millennia in the Near East and was especially popular, for unknown reasons, with women. One text from the **Seleucid** period (after 300 B.C.) contains a liturgy of the goddess Ishtar (also called Inanna),[2] who was weeping over him. This text contains echoes of Sumerian lamentation from 2,000 years earlier. Indeed, the Tammuz cult still existed among Sabean women in the tenth century A.D.! Although the women in Ezekiel 8 could have been professional mourners in the employ of the temple, it appears that they were ordinary people who had been swept up in a popular religious cult that had particularly strong appeal to women.

[1] See "Power Over Egypt in the Hymn to Osiris" on page 877 and "Baal and the Fertility Cults" on page 1414. [2] See "The Queen of Heaven" on page 1267.

8:10 [s]Ex 20:4 and all the idols of the house of Israel.[s] 11 In front of them stood sev-
enty elders of the house of Israel, and Jaazaniah son of Shaphan was
8:11 [t]Nu 16:17 standing among them. Each had a censer[t] in his hand, and a fra-
[u]Nu 16:35 grant cloud of incense[u] was rising.
12 He said to me, "Son of man, have you seen what the elders of
the house of Israel are doing in the darkness, each at the shrine of his
8:12 [v]Ps 10:11; own idol? They say, 'The LORD does not see[v] us; the LORD has forsak-
Isa 29:15; Eze 9:9 en the land.' " 13 Again, he said, "You will see them doing things that
are even more detestable."
14 Then he brought me to the entrance to the north gate of the
house of the LORD, and I saw women sitting there, mourning for
Tammuz. 15 He said to me, "Do you see this, son of man? You will see
things that are even more detestable than this."
16 He then brought me into the inner court of the house of the
LORD, and there at the entrance to the temple, between the portico
8:16 [w]Joel 2:17 and the altar,[w] were about twenty-five men. With their backs toward
[x]Dt 4:19; 17:3; the temple of the LORD and their faces toward the east, they were
Job 31:28; Jer 2:27; Eze 11:1,12 bowing down to the sun in the east.[x]
17 He said to me, "Have you seen this, son of man? Is it a trivial
matter for the house of Judah to do the detestable things they are
8:17 [y]Eze 9:9 doing here? Must they also fill the land with violence[y] and continually provoke me to anger?[z] Look at
[z]Eze 16:26 them putting the branch to their nose! 18 Therefore I will deal with them in anger; I will not look on them
8:18 [a]Eze 9:10; 24:14 [b]Isa 1:15; Jer 11:11; Mic 3:4; Zec 7:13 with pity[a] or spare them. Although they shout in my ears, I will not listen[b] to them."

Idolaters Killed

9 Then I heard him call out in a loud voice, "Bring the guards of the city here, each with a weapon in
his hand." 2 And I saw six men coming from the direction of the upper gate, which faces north, each
9:2 [c]Lev 16:4; Eze 10:2; with a deadly weapon in his hand. With them was a man clothed in linen[c] who had a writing kit at his
Rev 15:6 side. They came in and stood beside the bronze altar.
9:3 [d]Eze 10:4 3 Now the glory[d] of the God of Israel went up from above the cherubim,[e] where it had been, and moved
[e]Eze 11:22 to the threshold of the temple. Then the LORD called to the man clothed in linen who had the writing kit
9:4 [f]Ex 12:7; 2Co 1:22; at his side 4 and said to him, "Go throughout the city of Jerusalem and put a mark[f] on the foreheads of
Rev 7:3; 9:4 those who grieve and lament[g] over all the detestable things that are done in it.[h]"
[g]Ps 119:136; Jer 13:17; 5 As I listened, he said to the others, "Follow him through the city and kill, without showing pity[i] or
Eze 21:6 [h]Ps 119:53 compassion. 6 Slaughter old men, young men and maidens, women and children, but do not touch any-
9:5 [i]Eze 5:11 9:6 [j]Eze 8:11-13, one who has the mark. Begin at my sanctuary." So they began with the elders[j] who were in front of the
16 [k]2Ch 36:17; Jer 25:29; 1Pe 4:17 temple.[k]
7 Then he said to them, "Defile the temple and fill the courts with the slain. Go!" So they went out and
9:8 [l]Jos 7:6 began killing throughout the city. 8 While they were killing and I was left alone, I fell facedown,[l] crying
[m]Eze 11:13; Am 7:1-6 out, "Ah, Sovereign LORD! Are you going to destroy the entire remnant of Israel in this outpouring of your
wrath on Jerusalem?[m]"
9 He answered me, "The sin of the house of Israel and Judah is exceedingly great; the land is full of
9:9 [n]Eze 22:29 bloodshed and the city is full of injustice.[n] They say, 'The LORD has forsaken the land; the LORD does not
[o]Job 22:13; Eze 8:12 see.'[o] 10 So I will not look on them with pity[p] or spare them, but I will bring down on their own heads
9:10 [p]Eze 7:4; 8:18 [q]Isa 65:6; what they have done.[q]"
Eze 11:21 11 Then the man in linen with the writing kit at his side brought back word, saying, "I have done as you
commanded."

ANCIENT VOICES

The goddess of Kesh wept, waiting in the alleyway, she the lord of whose house a lynx had put an end to.
The goddess of Dunnu wept: "For whom the couch, for whom the coverlet?
For whom are guarded by me the coverlets, (now)* deathly still?"
The daughter of Nippur wept: "it is for the Gutians to finish the task!"
Her cheeks were sore (from weeping), she was deprived of her husband in whom she delighted.

*Words in parentheses added by translator for clarity or where text has gaps

—A NEO-BABYLONIAN LAMENT FOR TAMMMUZ

See "Mourning for Tammuz" article.

8:11 This Jaazaniah is not the same person as in 11:1.
8:14 This is the only Biblical reference to Tammuz, the Babylonian fertility god, who supposedly died each year at the height of the summer heat and then rose each spring (see "Mourning for Tammuz" on p. 1320). According to some interpreters, the god is alluded to in Daniel 11:37 as "the one desired by women."
8:16 Almost all ancient temples were oriented toward the east. These "twenty-five men" were worshiping the sun, which required them to turn their backs to the temple.
8:17 The phrase "putting the branch to their nose" may describe a ceremonial gesture in pagan worship that is not documented elsewhere in the Bible, but the translation is uncertain.
9:2 See the note regarding labor in the ancient Near Eastern world at Jeremiah 36:2.
9:4 The "mark" here refers to a *taw*, the last letter of the Hebrew alphabet, which originally looked like an *X* (see Rev 7:2–4).

The Glory Departs From the Temple

10 I looked, and I saw the likeness of a throne[r] of sapphire[a][s] above the expanse[t] that was over the
heads of the cherubim. 2The LORD said to the man clothed in linen,[u] "Go in among the wheels[v]
beneath the cherubim. Fill[w] your hands with burning coals from among the cherubim and scatter them
over the city." And as I watched, he went in.

3Now the cherubim were standing on the south side of the temple when the man went in, and a cloud
filled the inner court. 4Then the glory of the LORD[x] rose from above the cherubim and moved to the
threshold of the temple. The cloud filled the temple, and the court was full of the radiance of the glory
of the LORD. 5The sound of the wings of the cherubim could be heard as far away as the outer court, like
the voice[y] of God Almighty[b] when he speaks.

6When the LORD commanded the man in linen, "Take fire from among the wheels, from among the cher-
ubim," the man went in and stood beside a wheel. 7Then one of the cherubim reached out his hand to the
fire that was among them. He took up some of it and put it into the hands of the man in linen, who took it
and went out. 8(Under the wings of the cherubim could be seen what looked like the hands of a man.)[z]

9I looked, and I saw beside the cherubim four wheels, one beside each of the cherubim; the wheels
sparkled like chrysolite.[a] 10As for their appearance, the four of them looked alike; each was like a wheel
intersecting a wheel. 11As they moved, they would go in any one of the four directions the cherubim
faced; the wheels did not turn about[c] as the cherubim went. The cherubim went in whatever direction
the head faced, without turning as they went. 12Their entire bodies, including their backs, their hands and
their wings, were completely full of eyes,[b] as were their four wheels.[c] 13I heard the wheels being called
"the whirling wheels." 14Each of the cherubim[d] had four faces:[e] One face was that of a cherub, the sec-
ond the face of a man, the third the face of a lion, and the fourth the face of an eagle.[f]

15Then the cherubim rose upward. These were the living creatures[g] I had seen by the Kebar River.
16When the cherubim moved, the wheels beside them moved; and when the cherubim spread their wings
to rise from the ground, the wheels did not leave their side. 17When the cherubim stood still, they also
stood still; and when the cherubim rose, they rose with them, because the spirit of the living creatures
was in them.[h]

18Then the glory of the LORD departed from over the threshold of the temple and stopped above the
cherubim.[i] 19While I watched, the cherubim spread their wings and rose from the ground, and as they
went, the wheels went with them.[j] They stopped at the entrance to the east gate of the LORD's house, and
the glory of the God of Israel was above them.

20These were the living creatures I had seen beneath the God of Israel by the Kebar River,[k] and I re-
alized that they were cherubim. 21Each had four faces[l] and four wings,[m] and under their wings was what
looked like the hands of a man. 22Their faces had the same appearance as those I had seen by the Kebar
River. Each one went straight ahead.

10:1 [r]Rev 4:2 [s]Ex 24:10 [t]Eze 1:22
10:2 [u]Eze 9:2 [v]Eze 1:15 [w]Rev 8:5
10:4 [x]Eze 1:28; 9:3
10:5 [y]Job 40:9; Eze 1:24
10:8 [z]Eze 1:8
10:9 [a]Eze 1:15-16; Rev 21:20
10:12 [b]Rev 4:6-8 [c]Eze 1:15-21
10:14 [d]1Ki 7:36 [e]Eze 1:6 [f]Eze 1:10; Rev 4:7
10:15 [g]Eze 1:3,5
10:17 [h]Eze 1:20-21
10:18 [i]Ps 18:10
10:19 [j]Eze 11:1, 22
10:20 [k]Eze 1:1
10:21 [l]Eze 41:18 [m]Eze 1:6

Judgment on Israel's Leaders

11 Then the Spirit lifted me up and brought me to the gate of the house of the LORD that faces east.
There at the entrance to the gate were twenty-five men, and I saw among them Jaazaniah son of

[a] *1* Or *lapis lazuli* [b] *5* Hebrew *El-Shaddai* [c] *11* Or *aside*

10:1–22 That the cherubim were more than clouds or statues is plain from the description Ezekiel gave (9:3; 10:1–22), which shows that they are the "living creatures" of chapter 1. The four faces of each of the cherubim (1:10) stand for the four "excellencies" of the created order: the lion, the greatest of the wild beasts; the eagle, the greatest of the birds; the ox, the greatest of the domestic beasts; and man, the crown of creation. Ezekiel saw, over the heads of the cherubim, the throne of the God who is thus absolutely sovereign over his whole creation, in all its variety of life and being and in all its complexity of movement.

Ezekiel's vision explains the Old Testament allusion to the Lord as seated (or enthroned) on/between the cherubim (e.g., Ps. 99:1); it is a metaphor of his total sovereignty. Likewise, when the Lord rides on the cherubim (e.g., here and in Ps 18:10), the thought is that all creation is subject to his sovereign rule and "intervention" and that all its powers are at his disposal.

To sum up: The cherubim are the living chariot or carriers of God when appearing to human beings. They are heavenly creatures, servants of God in theophany and judgment, appearing in winged human-animal form with the faces of lion, eagle, ox and man. Their representations in the tabernacle and later in the temple as statues, as well as in embroidery and carving, did not constitute a breach of the second commandment (Ex 20:4). They are significant in prophecy (Ezekiel) and in the Apocalypse (Revelation). Their service is rendered immediately to God, and they never come closer to people than when one took fire in his hand and gave it "into the hands of the man in linen" (Eze 10:7). Yet because the mercy seat, on which the blood of atonement was sprinkled, lay "between the cherubim," nothing can more nearly touch our salvation. In the Old Testament sanctuary, where everything was done and taught by visible, tangible types and symbols, physical representations of the living, heavenly cherubim were essential. In Ezekiel's new temple, and in the heavenly sanctuary of Hebrews and Revelation, they are no longer needed, for the redeemed themselves stand in the presence of the living cherubim. The carvings of 41:18 are memorials only.

10:1 See the note on 1:26.

10:15 For "Kebar River," see the note on 1:1.

10:18 See "Temple Abandonment" on page 1323.

11:1 These were the "twenty-five men" of 8:16. They were the "leaders of the people," a small council of high officials who wielded

11:1 [n]Eze 8:16; 10:19; 43:4-5
11:3 [o]Jer 1:13; Eze 24:3 [p]ver 7, 11
11:4 [q]Eze 3:4,17
11:5 [r]Jer 17:10
11:6 [s]Eze 7:23; 22:6
11:7 [t]Eze 24:3-13; Mic 3:2-3
11:8 [u]Pr 10:24
11:9 [v]Ps 106:41 [w]Dt 28:36; Eze 5:8
11:10 [x]2Ki 14:25
11:11 [y]ver 3
11:12 [z]Lev 18:4; Eze 18:9 [a]Eze 8:10

Azzur and Pelatiah son of Benaiah, leaders of the people.[n] 2The LORD said to me, "Son of man, these are
the men who are plotting evil and giving wicked advice in this city. 3They say, 'Will it not soon be time
to build houses?[a] This city is a cooking pot,[o] and we are the meat.'[p] 4Therefore prophesy[q] against them;
prophesy, son of man."
5Then the Spirit of the LORD came upon me, and he told me to say: "This is what the LORD says: That
is what you are saying, O house of Israel, but I know what is going through your mind.[r] 6You have killed
many people in this city and filled its streets with the dead.[s]
7"Therefore this is what the Sovereign LORD says: The bodies you have thrown there are the meat and
this city is the pot, but I will drive you out of it.[t] 8You fear the sword, and the sword is what I will bring
against you, declares the Sovereign LORD.[u] 9I will drive you out of the city and hand you over[v] to foreign-
ers and inflict punishment on you.[w] 10You will fall by the sword, and I will execute judgment on you at
the borders of Israel.[x] Then you will know that I am the LORD. 11This city will not be a pot[y] for you, nor
will you be the meat in it; I will execute judgment on you at the borders of Israel. 12And you will know
that I am the LORD, for you have not followed my decrees[z] or kept my laws but have conformed to the
standards of the nations around you.[a]"

[a] 3 Or *This is not the time to build houses.*

significant power in Judah and had been able to remain in Jerusalem when many other Jews were exiled by the Babylonians in 597 B.C. They arrogantly boasted that they were the "meat" (v. 3), the best portion—implying that the exiles were the refuse.

This Jaazaniah is not the Jaazaniah of 8:11 (see the note there).

11:3 For information on a typical Israelite house, see "The Israelite Town and Home" on page 1205.

11:11 "The borders of Israel" is a reference to Riblah (see 2Ki 25:20–21).

Temple Abandonment

EZEKIEL 10 The desecration or destruction of temples in the ancient Near East represented grave national and religious calamities. Temples were considered the abodes of deities who served as guardians of lands, peoples and nations, and elaborate temple liturgies were aimed at securing the presence of the deity. Conquering armies plundered temples as a demonstrable sign that the gods of the victors had triumphed over those of the vanquished (Isa 36:18–20; 37:12). Sacred objects were regularly transported and then installed in the sanctuary of the conquering deity. For example, when the Philistines captured the ark of the covenant from Israel, they placed it in the temple of their god, **Dagon** (1Sa 5:1–5).[1]

From the perspective of the vanquished, it appeared that the temple had been abandoned by the deity. This gave rise to a genre of ritual laments for temples and cities that had been destroyed. A significant example of this motif is found in the **Sumerian** lamentation over the destruction of Ur.

The prophets used similar language to explain the destruction of the Jerusalem temple (La 2:7; cf. Eze 10). Biblical laments assert that the Lord had abandoned his sanctuary because Israel had first abandoned her God.

The idea of temple abandonment occurs as well with respect to the second temple. Second Maccabees, an **Apocryphal** book, reports that the **Seleucid** king Antiochus IV Epiphanes plundered the sanctuary of Jerusalem, an act that should have brought down divine judgment upon his head.[2] The text explains that such desecration was possible because God had temporarily abandoned the sanctuary on account of the sins of his people (2Mc 5:17). Other sources suggest that God abandoned the temple just prior to its destruction by the Romans in A.D. 70. The ancient Jewish historian Josephus described a sound like that of a great multitude from within the sanctuary, announcing the departure of God's presence (*Jewish Wars*, 6.5.3).[3] Second Baruch, a Jewish apocalyptic text written sometime after A.D. 70, narrates a visionary account of the angel of the Lord descending into the Most Holy Place, removing the sacred vessels and proclaiming: "Enter enemies and come adversaries because he who guarded the house has abandoned it" (2Bar 6:7–9; 8:2).

[1]See "Dagon" on page 404. [2]See "Ancient Near Eastern Laments" on page 1305. [3]See "Antiochus IV Epiphanes" on page 1406. [4]See "Josephus and the Fall of Jerusalem" on page 1606.

13 Now as I was prophesying, Pelatiah[b] son of Benaiah died. Then I fell facedown and cried out in a loud voice, "Ah, Sovereign LORD! Will you completely destroy the remnant of Israel?[c]"

14 The word of the LORD came to me: 15 "Son of man, your brothers—your brothers who are your blood relatives[a] and the whole house of Israel—are those of whom the people of Jerusalem have said, 'They are[b] far away from the LORD; this land was given to us as our possession.'[d]

Promised Return of Israel

16 "Therefore say: 'This is what the Sovereign LORD says: Although I sent them far away among the nations and scattered them among the countries, yet for a little while I have been a sanctuary[e] for them in the countries where they have gone.'

17 "Therefore say: 'This is what the Sovereign LORD says: I will gather you from the nations and bring you back from the countries where you have been scattered, and I will give you back the land of Israel again.'[f]

18 "They will return to it and remove all its vile images[g] and detestable idols.[h] 19 I will give them an undivided heart[i] and put a new spirit in them; I will remove from them their heart of stone[j] and give them a heart of flesh.[k] 20 Then they will follow my decrees and be careful to keep my laws.[l] They will be my people, and I will be their God.[m] 21 But as for those whose hearts are devoted to their vile images and detestable idols, I will bring down on their own heads what they have done, declares the Sovereign LORD.[n]"

22 Then the cherubim, with the wheels beside them, spread their wings, and the glory of the God of Israel was above them.[o] 23 The glory[p] of the LORD went up from within the city and stopped above the mountain[q] east of it. 24 The Spirit[r] lifted me up and brought me to the exiles in Babylonia[c] in the vision[s] given by the Spirit of God.

Then the vision I had seen went up from me, 25 and I told the exiles everything the LORD had shown me.[t]

11:13 [b]ver 1 [c]Eze 9:8
11:15 [d]Eze 33:24
11:16 [e]Ps 90:1; 91:9; Isa 8:14
11:17 [f]Jer 3:18; 24:5-6; Eze 28:25; 34:13
11:18 [g]Eze 5:11 [h]Eze 37:23
11:19 [i]Jer 32:39 [j]Zec 7:12 [k]Eze 18:31; 36:26; 2Co 3:3
11:20 [l]Ps 105:45 [m]Eze 14:11; 36:26-28
11:21 [n]Eze 9:10; 16:43
11:22 [o]Eze 10:19
11:23 [p]Eze 8:4; 10:4 [q]Zec 14:4
11:24 [r]Eze 8:3 [s]2Co 12:2-4
11:25 [t]Eze 3:4,11

The Exile Symbolized

12 The word of the LORD came to me: 2 "Son of man, you are living among a rebellious people. They have eyes to see but do not see and ears to hear but do not hear, for they are a rebellious people.[u]

3 "Therefore, son of man, pack your belongings for exile and in the daytime, as they watch, set out and go from where you are to another place. Perhaps[v] they will understand,[w] though they are a rebellious house.[x] 4 During the daytime, while they watch, bring out your belongings packed for exile. Then in the evening, while they are watching, go out like those who go into exile.[y] 5 While they watch, dig through the wall and take your belongings out through it. 6 Put them on your shoulder as they are watching and carry them out at dusk. Cover your face so that you cannot see the land, for I have made you a sign[z] to the house of Israel."

7 So I did as I was commanded.[a] During the day I brought out my things packed for exile. Then in the evening I dug through the wall with my hands. I took my belongings out at dusk, carrying them on my shoulders while they watched.

8 In the morning the word of the LORD came to me: 9 "Son of man, did not that rebellious house of Israel ask you, 'What are you doing?'[b]

10 "Say to them, 'This is what the Sovereign LORD says: This oracle concerns the prince in Jerusalem and the whole house of Israel who are there.' 11 Say to them, 'I am a sign to you.'

"As I have done, so it will be done to them. They will go into exile as captives.[c]

12 "The prince among them will put his things on his shoulder at dusk[d] and leave, and a hole will be

12:2 [u]Isa 6:10; Eze 2:6-8; Mt 13:15
12:3 [v]Jer 36:3 [w]Jer 26:3 [x]2Ti 2:25-26
12:4 [y]ver 12; Jer 39:4
12:6 [z]ver 12; Isa 8:18; 20:3; Eze 4:3; 24:24
12:7 [a]Eze 24:18; 37:10
12:9 [b]Eze 17:12; 20:49; 24:19
12:11 [c]2Ki 25:7; Jer 15:2; 52:15
12:12 [d]Jer 39:4

[a] 15 Or *are in exile with you* (see Septuagint and Syriac) [b] 15 Or *those to whom the people of Jerusalem have said, 'Stay* [c] 24 Or *Chaldea*

11:16 The Hebrew word for "sanctuary" refers almost exclusively to the tabernacle or temple. God's sanctuary was his established earthly abode, the place where he chose to dwell among his people. Psalm 114:2 states that "Judah became God's sanctuary, Israel his dominion." God himself is, in the final analysis, a sanctuary for his people (Isa 8:14).

11:23 The Mount of Olives is a flattened, rounded ridge with four identifiable summits. Its name is derived from the olive groves that covered it in ancient times. It is of cretaceous limestone formation, something over a mile (almost 2 km) in length, and forms the highest level of the range of hills to the east of Jerusalem (Eze 11:23; Zec 14:4), rising 250 feet (79 m) higher than the temple mount, and up to 2,600 feet (813 m) above sea level. See "The Mount of Olives" on page 1543.

12:5 This was a directive not to dig through the city wall, which was constructed of stone and was many feet thick, but through the sun-dried, brick wall of his own house (see "The Israelite Town and Home" on p. 1205).

12:10 See the note on verse 12.

12:12 The "prince" is Zedekiah.

dug in the wall for him to go through. He will cover his face so that he cannot see the land.[e] 13 I will spread my net[f] for him, and he will be caught in my snare;[g] I will bring him to Babylonia, the land of the Chaldeans, but he will not see[h] it, and there he will die.[i] 14 I will scatter to the winds all those around him—his staff and all his troops—and I will pursue them with drawn sword.[j]

15 "They will know that I am the LORD, when I disperse them among the nations and scatter them through the countries. 16 But I will spare a few of them from the sword, famine and plague, so that in the nations where they go they may acknowledge all their detestable practices. Then they will know that I am the LORD.[k]"

17 The word of the LORD came to me: 18 "Son of man, tremble as you eat your food,[l] and shudder in fear as you drink your water. 19 Say to the people of the land: 'This is what the Sovereign LORD says about those living in Jerusalem and in the land of Israel: They will eat their food in anxiety and drink their water in despair, for their land will be stripped of everything[m] in it because of the violence of all who live there.[n] 20 The inhabited towns will be laid waste and the land will be desolate. Then you will know that I am the LORD.[o]' "

21 The word of the LORD came to me: 22 "Son of man, what is this proverb you have in the land of Israel: 'The days go by and every vision comes to nothing'?[p] 23 Say to them, 'This is what the Sovereign LORD says: I am going to put an end to this proverb, and they will no longer quote it in Israel.' Say to them, 'The days are near when every vision will be fulfilled.[q] 24 For there will be no more false visions or flattering divinations[r] among the people of Israel. 25 But I the LORD will speak what I will, and it shall be fulfilled without delay. For in your days, you rebellious house, I will fulfill whatever I say, declares the Sovereign LORD.[s]' "

26 The word of the LORD came to me: 27 "Son of man, the house of Israel is saying, 'The vision he sees is for many years from now, and he prophesies about the distant future.'[t]

28 "Therefore say to them, 'This is what the Sovereign LORD says: None of my words will be delayed any longer; whatever I say will be fulfilled, declares the Sovereign LORD.' "

False Prophets Condemned

13 The word of the LORD came to me: 2 "Son of man, prophesy against the prophets of Israel who are now prophesying. Say to those who prophesy out of their own imagination: 'Hear the word of the LORD![u] 3 This is what the Sovereign LORD says: Woe to the foolish[a] prophets[v] who follow their own spirit and have seen nothing![w] 4 Your prophets, O Israel, are like jackals among ruins. 5 You have not gone up to the breaks in the wall to repair[x] it for the house of Israel so that it will stand firm in the battle on the day of the LORD.[y] 6 Their visions are false and their divinations a lie. They say, "The LORD declares," when the LORD has not sent them; yet they expect their words to be fulfilled.[z] 7 Have you not seen false visions and uttered lying divinations when you say, "The LORD declares," though I have not spoken?

8 " 'Therefore this is what the Sovereign LORD says: Because of your false words and lying visions, I am against you, declares the Sovereign LORD. 9 My hand will be against the prophets who see false visions and utter lying divinations. They will not belong to the council of my people or be listed in the records[a] of the house of Israel, nor will they enter the land of Israel. Then you will know that I am the Sovereign LORD.[b]

10 " 'Because they lead my people astray,[c] saying, "Peace," when there is no peace, and because, when a flimsy wall is built, they cover it with whitewash,[d] 11 therefore tell those who cover it with whitewash that it is going to fall. Rain will come in torrents, and I will send hailstones hurtling down, and violent winds will burst forth.[e] 12 When the wall collapses, will people not ask you, "Where is the whitewash you covered it with?"

13 " 'Therefore this is what the Sovereign LORD says: In my wrath I will unleash a violent wind, and in

[a] 3 Or *wicked*

12:12 [e]Jer 52:7
12:13 [f]Eze 17:20; 19:8; Hos 7:12 [g]Isa 24:17-18 [h]Jer 39:7 [i]Jer 52:11; Eze 17:16
12:14 [j]2Ki 25:5; Eze 5:10,12
12:16 [k]Jer 22:8-9; Eze 6:8-10; 14:22
12:18 [l]La 5:9; Eze 4:16
12:19 [m]Eze 6:6-14; Mic 7:13; Zec 7:14 [n]Eze 4:16; 23:33
12:20 [o]Isa 7:23-24; Jer 4:7
12:22 [p]Eze 11:3; Am 6:3; 2Pe 3:4
12:23 [q]Ps 37:13; Joel 2:1; Zep 1:14
12:24 [r]Jer 14:14; Eze 13:23; Zec 13:2-4
12:25 [s]Isa 14:24; Hab 1:5
12:27 [t]Da 10:14
13:2 [u]ver 17; Jer 23:16; 37:19
13:3 [v]La 2:14 [w]Jer 23:25-32
13:5 [x]Isa 58:12; Eze 22:30 [y]Eze 7:19
13:6 [z]Jer 28:15; Eze 22:28
13:9 [a]Jer 17:13 [b]Eze 20:38
13:10 [c]Jer 50:6 [d]Eze 7:25; 22:28
13:11 [e]Eze 38:22

12:13 For "Chaldeans," see "The Chaldeans" on page 1402. Zedekiah would not see the land because Nebuchadnezzar's men would put out his eyes (see 2Ki 25:7).

12:16 For commentary on this threefold threat, see the note on 5:17.

12:19 For "the people of the land," see the note on 7:27.

13:4 Jackals travel in packs and feed on dead flesh—a powerfully negative image.

13:10–16 Untempered mortar (a KJV term; Hebrew, *tâphçl*) was mortar made of clay instead of slaked lime. It was smeared on the walls of houses made of small stones or mud bricks so as to prolong the life of the building. Ezekiel used the term (NIV "whitewash") symbolically to refer to the flimsiness of the work of the false prophets. Recent scholarship holds to the belief that this passage does indeed refer to whitewash applied over a poorly constructed wall to disguise its weakness.

my anger hailstones[f] and torrents of rain will fall with destructive fury.[g] 14 I will tear down the wall you
have covered with whitewash and will level it to the ground so that its foundation[h] will be laid bare. When
it[a] falls,[i] you will be destroyed in it; and you will know that I am the LORD. 15 So I will spend my wrath
against the wall and against those who covered it with whitewash. I will say to you, "The wall is gone and
so are those who whitewashed it, 16 those prophets of Israel who prophesied to Jerusalem and saw vi-
sions of peace for her when there was no peace, declares the Sovereign LORD.[j]" '

17 "Now, son of man, set your face against the daughters[k] of your people who prophesy out of their
own imagination. Prophesy against them[l] 18 and say, 'This is what the Sovereign LORD says: Woe to the
women who sew magic charms on all their wrists and make veils of various lengths for their heads in
order to ensnare people. Will you ensnare the lives of my people but preserve your own? 19 You have pro-
faned[m] me among my people for a few handfuls of barley and scraps of bread. By lying to my people,
who listen to lies, you have killed those who should not have died and have spared those who should not
live.[n]

20 " 'Therefore this is what the Sovereign LORD says: I am against your magic charms with which you
ensnare people like birds and I will tear them from your arms; I will set free the people that you ensnare
like birds. 21 I will tear off your veils and save my people from your hands, and they will no longer fall
prey to your power. Then you will know that I am the LORD.[o] 22 Because you disheartened the righteous
with your lies, when I had brought them no grief, and because you encouraged the wicked not to turn
from their evil ways and so save their lives,[p] 23 therefore you will no longer see false visions or practice
divination.[q] I will save my people from your hands. And then you will know that I am the LORD.[r]' "

Idolaters Condemned

14 Some of the elders of Israel came to me and sat down in front of me.[s] 2 Then the word of the LORD
came to me: 3 "Son of man, these men have set up idols in their hearts and put wicked stumbling
blocks[t] before their faces. Should I let them inquire of me at all?[u] 4 Therefore speak to them and tell them,
'This is what the Sovereign LORD says: When any Israelite sets up idols in his heart and puts a wicked
stumbling block before his face and then goes to a prophet, I the LORD will answer him myself in keep-
ing with his great idolatry. 5 I will do this to recapture the hearts of the people of Israel, who have all de-
serted[v] me for their idols.'[w]

6 "Therefore say to the house of Israel, 'This is what the Sovereign LORD says: Repent! Turn from your
idols and renounce all your detestable practices![x]

7 " 'When any Israelite or any alien[y] living in Israel separates himself from me and sets up idols in his
heart and puts a wicked stumbling block before his face and then goes to a prophet to inquire of me, I
the LORD will answer him myself. 8 I will set my face against[z] that man and make him an example and a
byword.[a] I will cut him off from my people. Then you will know that I am the LORD.

9 " 'And if the prophet[b] is enticed[c] to utter a prophecy, I the LORD have enticed that prophet, and I will
stretch out my hand against him and destroy him from among my people Israel.[d] 10 They will bear their
guilt—the prophet will be as guilty as the one who consults him. 11 Then the people of Israel will no lon-
ger stray[e] from me, nor will they defile themselves anymore with all their sins. They will be my people,
and I will be their God, declares the Sovereign LORD.[f]' "

Judgment Inescapable

12 The word of the LORD came to me: 13 "Son of man, if a country sins against me by being unfaithful
and I stretch out my hand against it to cut off its food supply[g] and send famine upon it and kill its men
and their animals,[h] 14 even if these three men—Noah,[i] Daniel[b][j] and Job[k]—were in it, they could save only
themselves by their righteousness,[l] declares the Sovereign LORD.

13:13 [f]Rev 11:19; 16:21 [g]Ex 9:25; Isa 30:30
13:14 [h]Mic 1:6 [i]Jer 6:15
13:16 [j]Isa 57:21; Jer 6:14
13:17 [k]Rev 2:20 [l]ver 2
13:19 [m]Eze 20:39; 22:26 [n]Pr 28:21
13:21 [o]Ps 91:3
13:22 [p]Jer 23:14; Eze 33:14-16
13:23 [q]ver 6; Eze 12:24 [r]Mic 3:6
14:1 [s]Eze 8:1; 20:1
14:3 [t]ver 7; Eze 7:19 [u]Isa 1:15; Eze 20:31
14:5 [v]Zec 11:8 [w]Jer 2:11
14:6 [x]Isa 2:20; 30:22
14:7 [y]Ex 12:48; 20:10
14:8 [z]Eze 15:7 [a]Eze 5:15
14:9 [b]Jer 14:15 [c]Jer 4:10 [d]1Ki 22:23
14:11 [e]Eze 48:11 [f]Eze 11:19-20; 37:23
14:13 [g]Lev 26:26 [h]Eze 5:16; 6:14; 15:8
14:14 [i]Ge 6:8 [j]ver 20; Eze 28:3; Da 1:6; 6:13 [k]Job 1:1 [l]Job 42:9; Jer 15:1; Eze 18:20

[a] 14 Or *the city* [b] 14 Or *Danel*; the Hebrew spelling may suggest a person other than the prophet Daniel; also in verse 20.

13:18 Exactly what the women were doing with the magic charms is not known, but that it was some kind of black magic or voodoo is clear. The Biblical writers consistently avoided explicit description of occult practices.
14:1 For "elders," see the note on Jeremiah 19:1.
14:3 "Inquire" is a technical term for seeking an oracle from a prophet (see 2Ki 1:16; 3:11; 8:8) and does not necessarily imply a request for help.

14:14 These ancient men of renown were selected because of their proverbial righteousness. As the NIV text note indicates, another Daniel may be referred to (Ugaritic literature speaks of an honored "Danel"), since the Biblical Daniel's righteousness had probably not become proverbial by this time (Daniel and Ezekiel were contemporaries).

14:15 [m]Eze 5:17 15“Or if I send wild beasts[m] through that country and they leave it childless and it becomes desolate
[n]Lev 26:22 so that no one can pass through it because of the beasts,[n] 16as surely as I live, declares the Sovereign
LORD, even if these three men were in it, they could not save their own sons or daughters. They alone
14:16 [o]Eze 18:20 would be saved, but the land would be desolate.[o]
14:17 17“Or if I bring a sword[p] against that country and say, ‘Let the sword pass throughout the land,’ and I
[p]Lev 26:25; Eze 5:12; 21:3-4 kill its men and their animals,[q] 18as surely as I live, declares the Sovereign LORD, even if these three men
[q]Eze 25:13; Zep 1:3 were in it, they could not save their own sons or daughters. They alone would be saved.
14:19 [r]Eze 7:8 19“Or if I send a plague into that land and pour out my wrath[r] upon it through bloodshed, killing its
[s]Eze 38:22 men and their animals,[s] 20as surely as I live, declares the Sovereign LORD, even if Noah, Daniel and
Job were in it, they could save neither son nor daughter. They would save only themselves by their righ-
14:20 [t]ver 14 teousness.[t]
21“For this is what the Sovereign LORD says: How much worse will it be when I send against Jerusa-
lem my four dreadful judgments—sword and famine and wild beasts and plague—to kill its men and
14:21 [u]Jer 15:3; Eze 5:17; 33:27; Am 4:6-10; Rev 6:8 their animals![u] 22Yet there will be some survivors—sons and daughters who will be brought out of it.[v]
They will come to you, and when you see their conduct[w] and their actions, you will be consoled regard-
14:22 [v]Eze 12:16 ing the disaster I have brought upon Jerusalem—every disaster I have brought upon it. 23You will be
[w]Eze 20:43 consoled when you see their conduct and their actions, for you will know that I have done nothing in it
14:23 [x]Jer 22:8-9 without cause, declares the Sovereign LORD.[x]”

Jerusalem, A Useless Vine

15:2 [y]Isa 5:1-7; Jer 2:21; Hos 10:1 **15** The word of the LORD came to me: 2“Son of man, how is the wood of a vine[y] better than that of
a branch on any of the trees in the forest? 3Is wood ever taken from it to make anything useful?
Do they make pegs from it to hang things on? 4And after it is thrown on the fire as fuel and the fire burns
15:4 [z]Eze 19:14; Jn 15:6 both ends and chars the middle, is it then useful for anything?[z] 5If it was not useful for anything when
it was whole, how much less can it be made into something useful when the fire has burned it and it is
charred?
6“Therefore this is what the Sovereign LORD says: As I have given the wood of the vine among the trees
15:7 [a]Ps 34:16; Eze 14:8 of the forest as fuel for the fire, so will I treat the people living in Jerusalem. 7I will set my face against[a]
[b]Isa 24:18; Am 9:1-4 them. Although they have come out of the fire, the fire will yet consume them. And when I set my face
15:8 [c]Eze 14:13 against them, you will know that I am the LORD.[b] 8I will make the land desolate[c] because they have been
[d]Eze 17:20 unfaithful,[d] declares the Sovereign LORD.”

An Allegory of Unfaithful Jerusalem

16 The word of the LORD came to me: 2“Son of man, confront Jerusalem with her detestable prac-
16:2 [e]Eze 20:4; 22:2 tices[e] 3and say, ‘This is what the Sovereign LORD says to Jerusalem: Your ancestry[f] and birth were
16:3 [f]Eze 21:30 [g]ver 45 in the land of the Canaanites; your father was an Amorite and your mother a Hittite.[g] 4On the day you
16:4 [h]Hos 2:3 were born[h] your cord was not cut, nor were you washed with water to make you clean, nor were you
rubbed with salt or wrapped in cloths. 5No one looked on you with pity or had compassion enough to do
any of these things for you. Rather, you were thrown out into the open field, for on the day you were born
you were despised.
6“ ‘Then I passed by and saw you kicking about in your blood, and as you lay there in your blood I said
16:6 [i]Ex 19:4 to you, “Live!”[a][i] 7I made you grow[j] like a plant of the field. You grew up and developed and became the
16:7 [j]Dt 1:10 [k]Ex 1:7 most beautiful of jewels.[b] Your breasts were formed and your hair grew, you who were naked and bare.[k]
8“ ‘Later I passed by, and when I looked at you and saw that you were old enough for love, I spread the
16:8 [l]Ru 3:9 corner of my garment[l] over you and covered your nakedness. I gave you my solemn oath and entered
[m]Jer 2:2; Hos 2:7, 19-20 into a covenant with you, declares the Sovereign LORD, and you became mine.[m]

[a] 6 A few Hebrew manuscripts, Septuagint and Syriac; most Hebrew manuscripts *“Live!” And as you lay there in your blood I said to you, “Live!”* [b] 7 Or *became mature*

15:4 See the note on Isaiah 9:5 regarding fuel.
15:7 The “fire” they had “come out of” refers to the siege of Jerusalem in 597 B.C., which resulted in the exile of which Ezekiel was a part. The “fire” that would “yet consume them” refers to the more devastating siege that would come in 586 B.C.
16:3 For information on Jerusalem’s “ancestry and birth,” see “Jerusalem” on page 1191. For “Amorite” and “Hittite,” see “Lesser Known Peoples of the Old Testament” on page 265.
16:4 The practice of rubbing newborns with salt has been observed among Arab peasants as recently as A.D. 1918.
16:5 The abandonment of infants to die of exposure, common in ancient pagan societies, was abhorrent to Israel.
16:8 This action was symbolic of entering a marriage relationship (see Ru 3:9 and its note).

9“ ‘I bathed[a] you with water and washed[n] the blood from you and put ointments on you. 10I clothed
you with an embroidered[o] dress and put leather sandals on you. I dressed you in fine linen[p] and covered
you with costly garments.[q] 11I adorned you with jewelry:[r] I put bracelets[s] on your arms and a necklace[t]
around your neck, 12and I put a ring on your nose,[u] earrings on your ears and a beautiful crown[v] on your
head. 13So you were adorned with gold and silver; your clothes were of fine linen and costly fabric and
embroidered cloth. Your food was fine flour, honey and olive oil.[w] You became very beautiful and rose to
be a queen.[x] 14And your fame[y] spread among the nations on account of your beauty,[z] because the splen-
dor I had given you made your beauty perfect, declares the Sovereign LORD.

15“ ‘But you trusted in your beauty and used your fame to become a prostitute. You lavished your fa-
vors on anyone who passed by[a] and your beauty became his.[b][b] 16You took some of your garments to
make gaudy high places, where you carried on your prostitution.[c] Such things should not happen, nor
should they ever occur. 17You also took the fine jewelry I gave you, the jewelry made of my gold and sil-
ver, and you made for yourself male idols and engaged in prostitution with them.[d] 18And you took your
embroidered clothes to put on them, and you offered my oil and incense before them. 19Also the food I
provided for you—the fine flour, olive oil and honey I gave you to eat—you offered as fragrant incense
before them. That is what happened, declares the Sovereign LORD.[e]

20“ ‘And you took your sons and daughters[f] whom you bore to me[g] and sacrificed them as food to the
idols. Was your prostitution not enough?[h] 21You slaughtered my children and sacrificed them[c] to the
idols.[i] 22In all your detestable practices and your prostitution you did not remember the days of your
youth,[j] when you were naked and bare, kicking about in your blood.[k]

23“ ‘Woe! Woe to you, declares the Sovereign LORD. In addition to all your other wickedness, 24you built
a mound for yourself and made a lofty shrine[l] in every public square.[m] 25At the head of every street you
built your lofty shrines and degraded your beauty, offering your body with increasing promiscuity to
anyone who passed by.[n] 26You engaged in prostitution with the Egyptians, your lustful neighbors, and
provoked[o] me to anger with your increasing promiscuity.[p] 27So I stretched out my hand[q] against you and
reduced your territory; I gave you over to the greed of your enemies, the daughters of the Philistines,[r] who
were shocked by your lewd conduct. 28You engaged in prostitution with the Assyrians[s] too, because you
were insatiable; and even after that, you still were not satisfied. 29Then you increased your promiscuity
to include Babylonia,[d][t] a land of merchants, but even with this you were not satisfied.

30“ ‘How weak-willed you are, declares the Sovereign LORD, when you do all these things, acting like
a brazen prostitute![u] 31When you built your mounds at the head of every street and made your lofty
shrines[v] in every public square, you were unlike a prostitute, because you scorned payment.

32“ ‘You adulterous wife! You prefer strangers to your own husband! 33Every prostitute receives a fee,
but you give gifts[w] to all your lovers, bribing them to come to you from everywhere for your illicit fa-
vors.[x] 34So in your prostitution you are the opposite of others; no one runs after you for your favors. You
are the very opposite, for you give payment and none is given to you.

16:9 [n]Ru 3:3
16:10 [o]Ex 26:36 [p]Eze 27:16 [q]ver 18
16:11 [r]Eze 23:40 [s]Isa 3:19; Eze 23:42 [t]Ge 41:42
16:12 [u]Isa 3:21 [v]Isa 28:5; Jer 13:18
16:13 [w]1Sa 10:1 [x]Dt 32:13-14; 1Ki 4:21
16:14 [y]1Ki 10:24 [z]La 2:15
16:15 [a]ver 25 [b]Isa 57:8; Jer 2:20; Eze 23:3; 27:3
16:16 [c]2Ki 23:7
16:17 [d]Eze 7:20
16:19 [e]Hos 2:8
16:20 [f]Jer 7:31 [g]Ex 13:2 [h]Ps 106:37-38; Isa 57:5; Eze 23:37
16:21 [i]2Ki 17:17; Jer 19:5
16:22 [j]Jer 2:2; Hos 11:1 [k]ver 6
16:24 [l]ver 31; Isa 57:7 [m]Ps 78:58; Jer 2:20; 3:2; Eze 20:28
16:25 [n]ver 15; Pr 9:14
16:26 [o]Eze 8:17 [p]Eze 20:8; 23:19-21
16:27 [q]Eze 20:33 [r]2Ch 28:18
16:28 [s]2Ki 16:7
16:29 [t]Eze 23:14-17
16:30 [u]Jer 3:3
16:31 [v]ver 24
16:33 [w]Isa 30:6; 57:9 [x]Hos 8:9-10

[a] 9 Or *I had bathed* [b] 15 Most Hebrew manuscripts; one Hebrew manuscript (see some Septuagint manuscripts) *by. Such a thing should not happen* [c] 21 Or *and made them pass through ⌊the fire⌋* [d] 29 Or *Chaldea*

16:10–13 The items mentioned here are representative of the very best materials, garments and ornamentations (see “Ancient Israelite Clothing and Jewelry” on p. 1059 and “Precious Stones of the Biblical World” on p. 1156). Many of these clothing and jewelry items were used in wedding ceremonies (see “Weddings in Ancient Israel” on p. 1039).

16:10 Embroidery refers in the Old Testament to ornamental needlework on cloth. Several Hebrew words are used in connection with this and related skills. In Exodus 28:39 *shâvats* probably refers to a checkered weaving (ASV, RSV) or plaiting of a coat with colored threads. Hebrew *râqam* (Ex 35:35; 38:23) means “to variegate” or “to weave in colored threads.” “Embroidered” is used to translate Hebrew *riqmâh,* “variegated” (Eze 16:10,13,18). In Exodus 28:4 Hebrew *tashbçts,* “tessellated stuff,” is rendered by the ASV and RSV as “checkerwork” and by the NIV as “woven.” *Riqmâh* is also translated “various colors” and “varied colors” (Eze 17:3). Apart from the use of these Hebrew terms to describe the colors of gems and feathers, they seem to have referred to weaving into cloth or drawing in with a needle or appliqué colored threads to make checkered and other designs for hangings in the tabernacle; the coats, girdles and ephod of the priests; royal garments; and clothing in general. The details of such work provided in the Bible impress us with the rich and gorgeously colorful character of needlework that may be called embroidery, but they furnish no exact idea of its appearance or method of manufacture.

16:12 The ancient Hebrews had no specific word for earrings; these jewels were just rings or hoops made of gold (though sometimes the metal is not specified), worn by both men and women, either on the nose or in the ears: A nose ring is specified in some passages (here, as well as in Ge 24:47; Isa 3:21) and earrings in others (here, as well as in Ge 35:4; Ex 32:2–3). In the remaining passages where such rings or hoops are mentioned, they may be either nose rings or earrings (Ex 35:22; Nu 31:50; Jdg 8:24–26; Job 42:11; Pr 11:22; 25:12; Hos 2:13). It is probable that pendants were suspended from earrings. In Isaiah 3:20 the Hebrew term *lachash* is translated “amulets” (NASB), “charms” (NIV) or ”earrings” (KJV).

16:20 Child sacrifice, or the burning of a child while still alive, seems to have been associated with Molech, the god worshiped by the Ammonites and others (see “Human Sacrifice in the Ancient Near East” on p. 182). God had expressly prohibited such practices (see Lev 18:21; Dt 18:10; cf. Lev 20:2–5; Dt 12:31).

16:24 Centers of idol worship were set up not only in the countryside but also in Jerusalem itself.

16:27 After the 701 B.C. siege of Jerusalem the Assyrian king Sennacherib gave some of Jerusalem’s territory to the Philistines.

35 " 'Therefore, you prostitute, hear the word of the LORD! 36 This is what the Sovereign LORD says: Be-
cause you poured out your wealth[a] and exposed your nakedness in your promiscuity with your lov-
ers, and because of all your detestable idols, and because you gave them your children's blood,[y] 37 there-
fore I am going to gather all your lovers, with whom you found pleasure, those you loved as well as
those you hated. I will gather them against you from all around and will strip you in front of them,
and they will see all your nakedness.[z] 38 I will sentence you to the punishment of women who commit
adultery and who shed blood;[a] I will bring upon you the blood vengeance of my wrath and jealous
anger.[b] 39 Then I will hand you over to your lovers, and they will tear down your mounds and destroy
your lofty shrines. They will strip you of your clothes and take your fine jewelry and leave you naked
and bare.[c] 40 They will bring a mob against you, who will stone[d] you and hack you to pieces with their
swords. 41 They will burn down[e] your houses and inflict punishment on you in the sight of many wom-
en.[f] I will put a stop[g] to your prostitution, and you will no longer pay your lovers. 42 Then my wrath
against you will subside and my jealous anger will turn away from you; I will be calm and no longer
angry.[h]

43 " 'Because you did not remember[i] the days of your youth but enraged me with all these things, I
will surely bring down[j] on your head what you have done, declares the Sovereign LORD. Did you not add
lewdness to all your other detestable practices?[k]

44 " 'Everyone who quotes proverbs will quote this proverb about you: "Like mother, like daughter."
45 You are a true daughter of your mother, who despised her husband and her children; and you are a true
sister of your sisters, who despised their husbands and their children. Your mother was a Hittite and your
father an Amorite.[l] 46 Your older sister was Samaria, who lived to the north of you with her daughters; and
your younger sister, who lived to the south of you with her daughters, was Sodom.[m] 47 You not only walked
in their ways and copied their detestable practices, but in all your ways you soon became more depraved
than they.[n] 48 As surely as I live, declares the Sovereign LORD, your sister Sodom and her daughters nev-
er did what you and your daughters have done.[o]

49 " 'Now this was the sin of your sister Sodom:[p] She and her daughters were arrogant,[q] overfed and
unconcerned; they did not help the poor and needy.[r] 50 They were haughty and did detestable things be-
fore me. Therefore I did away with them as you have seen.[s] 51 Samaria did not commit half the sins you
did. You have done more detestable things than they, and have made your sisters seem righteous by all
these things you have done.[t] 52 Bear your disgrace, for you have furnished some justification for your sis-
ters. Because your sins were more vile than theirs, they appear more righteous than you. So then, be
ashamed and bear your disgrace, for you have made your sisters appear righteous.

53 " 'However, I will restore[u] the fortunes of Sodom and her daughters and of Samaria and her daugh-
ters, and your fortunes along with them, 54 so that you may bear your disgrace[v] and be ashamed of all you
have done in giving them comfort. 55 And your sisters, Sodom with her daughters and Samaria with her
daughters, will return to what they were before; and you and your daughters will return to what you were
before.[w] 56 You would not even mention your sister Sodom in the day of your pride, 57 before your wick-
edness was uncovered. Even so, you are now scorned by the daughters of Edom[b][x] and all her neighbors
and the daughters of the Philistines—all those around you who despise you. 58 You will bear the conse-
quences of your lewdness and your detestable practices, declares the LORD.[y]

59 " 'This is what the Sovereign LORD says: I will deal with you as you deserve, because you have de-
spised my oath by breaking the covenant.[z] 60 Yet I will remember the covenant I made with you in the
days of your youth, and I will establish an everlasting covenant[a] with you. 61 Then you will remember
your ways and be ashamed[b] when you receive your sisters, both those who are older than you and those
who are younger. I will give them to you as daughters, but not on the basis of my covenant with you. 62 So
I will establish my covenant with you, and you will know that I am the LORD.[c] 63 Then, when I make atone-
ment[d] for you for all you have done, you will remember and be ashamed and never again open your
mouth[e] because of your humiliation, declares the Sovereign LORD.[f] ' "

16:36 [y]Jer 19:5; Eze 23:10
16:37 [z]Jer 13:22
16:38 [a]Eze 23:45 [b]Lev 20:10; Eze 23:25
16:39 [c]Eze 23:26; Hos 2:3
16:40 [d]Jn 8:5,7
16:41 [e]Dt 13:16 [f]Eze 23:10 [g]Eze 23:27,48
16:42 [h]Isa 54:9; Eze 5:13; 39:29
16:43 [i]Ps 78:42 [j]Eze 22:31 [k]ver 22; Eze 11:21
16:45 [l]Eze 23:2
16:46 [m]Ge 13:10-13; Eze 23:4
16:47 [n]2Ki 21:9; Eze 5:7
16:48 [o]Mt 10:15; 11:23-24
16:49 [p]Ge 13:13 [q]Ps 138:6 [r]Eze 18:7,12,16; Lk 12:16-20
16:50 [s]Ge 18:20-21; 19:5
16:51 [t]Jer 3:8-11
16:53 [u]Isa 19:24-25
16:54 [v]Jer 2:26; Eze 14:22
16:55 [w]Mal 3:4
16:57 [x]2Ki 16:6
16:58 [y]Eze 23:49
16:59 [z]Eze 17:19
16:60 [a]Jer 32:40; Eze 37:26
16:61 [b]Eze 20:43
16:62 [c]Jer 24:7; Eze 20:37,43-44; Hos 2:19-20
16:63 [d]Ps 65:3; 79:9 [e]Ro 3:19 [f]Ps 39:9; Da 9:7-8

[a] 36 Or *lust* [b] 57 Many Hebrew manuscripts and Syriac; most Hebrew manuscripts, Septuagint and Vulgate *Aram*

16:38 The prescribed punishment for adultery was death (see Lev 20:10; Dt 22:22) by stoning (Dt 22:21–24; Eze 16:40) or burning (see Ge 38:24).
16:45 For "Hittite" and "Amorite," see "Lesser Known Peoples of the Old Testament" on page 265.
16:46 Historically, Samaria was not founded as a royal city until after 880 B.C., so "older" in this allegory apparently alludes to the fact that Samaria ruled over a significantly larger kingdom than Jerusalem did.
16:47 The wickedness of ancient Sodom was proverbial by this time.
16:57 See "Edom" on page 1467.

Two Eagles and a Vine

17 The word of the LORD came to me: 2"Son of man, set forth an allegory and tell the house of Isra-
el a parable.[g] 3Say to them, 'This is what the Sovereign LORD says: A great eagle[h] with powerful
wings, long feathers and full plumage of varied colors came to Lebanon.[i] Taking hold of the top of a ce-
dar, 4he broke off its topmost shoot and carried it away to a land of merchants, where he planted it in a
city of traders.
5" 'He took some of the seed of your land and put it in fertile soil. He planted it like a willow by abun-
dant water,[j] 6and it sprouted and became a low, spreading vine. Its branches turned toward him, but its
roots remained under it. So it became a vine and produced branches and put out leafy boughs.
7" 'But there was another great eagle with powerful wings and full plumage. The vine now sent out
its roots toward him from the plot where it was planted and stretched out its branches to him for water.[k]
8It had been planted in good soil by abundant water so that it would produce branches, bear fruit and
become a splendid vine.'
9"Say to them, 'This is what the Sovereign LORD says: Will it thrive? Will it not be uprooted and stripped
of its fruit so that it withers? All its new growth will wither. It will not take a strong arm or many people
to pull it up by the roots. 10Even if it[l] is transplanted, will it thrive? Will it not wither completely when the
east wind strikes it—wither away in the plot where it grew?' "
11Then the word of the LORD came to me: 12"Say to this rebellious house, 'Do you not know what these
things mean?[m]' Say to them: 'The king of Babylon went to Jerusalem and carried off her king and her
nobles,[n] bringing them back with him to Babylon.[o] 13Then he took a member of the royal family and
made a treaty with him, putting him under oath.[p] He also carried away the leading men of the land, 14so
that the kingdom would be brought low,[q] unable to rise again, surviving only by keeping his treaty. 15But
the king rebelled[r] against him by sending his envoys to Egypt to get horses and a large army.[s] Will he suc-
ceed? Will he who does such things escape? Will he break the treaty and yet escape?[t]
16" 'As surely as I live, declares the Sovereign LORD, he shall die[u] in Babylon, in the land of the king who
put him on the throne, whose oath he despised and whose treaty he broke.[v] 17Pharaoh[w] with his mighty
army and great horde will be of no help to him in war, when ramps[x] are built and siege works erected to
destroy many lives.[y] 18He despised the oath by breaking the covenant. Because he had given his hand in
pledge[z] and yet did all these things, he shall not escape.
19" 'Therefore this is what the Sovereign LORD says: As surely as I live, I will bring down on his head
my oath that he despised and my covenant that he broke.[a] 20I will spread my net[b] for him, and he will be
caught in my snare. I will bring him to Babylon and execute judgment[c] upon him there because he was
unfaithful to me. 21All his fleeing troops will fall by the sword,[d] and the survivors[e] will be scattered to
the winds.[f] Then you will know that I the LORD have spoken.
22" 'This is what the Sovereign LORD says: I myself will take a shoot from the very top of a cedar and
plant it; I will break off a tender sprig from its topmost shoots and plant it on a high and lofty mountain.[g]
23On the mountain heights of Israel I will plant it; it will produce branches and bear fruit and become a
splendid cedar. Birds of every kind will nest in it; they will find shelter in the shade of its branches.[h] 24All
the trees of the field[i] will know that I the LORD bring down the tall tree and make the low tree grow tall.
I dry up the green tree and make the dry tree flourish.
" 'I the LORD have spoken, and I will do it.[j]' "

17:2 [g]Eze 20:49
17:3 [h]Hos 8:1 [i]Jer 22:23
17:5 [j]Dt 8:7-9; Isa 44:4
17:7 [k]Eze 31:4
17:10 [l]Hos 13:15
17:12 [m]Eze 12:9 [n]2Ki 24:15 [o]Eze 24:19
17:13 [p]2Ch 36:13
17:14 [q]Eze 29:14
17:15 [r]Jer 52:3 [s]Dt 17:16 [t]Jer 34:3; 38:18
17:16 [u]Jer 52:11; Eze 12:13 [v]2Ki 24:17
17:17 [w]Jer 37:7 [x]Eze 4:2 [y]Isa 36:6; Jer 37:5; Eze 29:6-7
17:18 [z]1Ch 29:24
17:19 [a]Eze 16:59
17:20 [b]Eze 12:13; 32:3 [c]Jer 2:35; Eze 20:36
17:21 [d]Eze 12:14 [e]2Ki 25:11 [f]2Ki 25:5
17:22 [g]Jer 23:5; Eze 20:40; 36:1, 36; 37:22
17:23 [h]Ps 92:12; Isa 2:2; Eze 31:6; Da 4:12; Hos 14:5-7; Mt 13:32
17:24 [i]Ps 96:12 [j]Eze 19:12; 21:26; 22:14; Am 9:11

The Soul Who Sins Will Die

18 The word of the LORD came to me: 2"What do you people mean by quoting this proverb about the
land of Israel:

17:1–24 This parable symbolizes King Zedekiah's vacillating royal policy that led to his downfall. The parable is presented in verses 1–10, its explanation follows in verses 11–21, and verses 22–24 append a promise of better times to come.
17:2 The Hebrew for "riddles" can sometimes, as here, refer to allegories. On the popularity and function of riddles in the ancient world, see the note on Judges 14:12–14.
17:3 The "great eagle" is Nebuchadnezzar (see "Nebuchadnezzar" on p. 571).
For "varied colors," see the note on 16:10.
17:4 The "topmost shoot" is Jehoiachin; the "land of merchants" the country of Babylonia; and the "city of traders" the city of Babylon.
17:5 The "seed" is Zedekiah, the brother of Jehoahaz and Jehoiakim and the uncle of Jehoiachin. Nebuchadnezzar made Zedekiah king of Judah after taking King Jehoiachin captive to Babylon (2Ki 24:17; see "Jehoiachin in Captivity and Evil Merodach" on p. 1292).
17:7 The second "great eagle" is an Egyptian pharaoh, probably Psammetichus II (595–589 B.C.) but possibly Hophra (589–570). Hophra (Jer 44:30) was most likely the pharaoh who offered help to Jerusalem in 586 (see Jer 37:5; see also "Hophra, King of Egypt" on p. 1266), after Zedekiah appealed to Egypt for military aid (Eze 17:15), an act of rebellion against Nebuchadnezzar.
17:10 The "east wind" refers to the sirocco or khamsin, a hot, dry wind that brings with it storms of sand and dust. Here it stands for Nebuchadnezzar and his Babylonian forces.

“ ‘The fathers eat sour grapes,
and the children’s teeth are set on edge’?[k]

18:2 [k]Isa 3:15; Jer 31:29; La 5:7

3 “As surely as I live, declares the Sovereign LORD, you will no longer quote this proverb in Israel. 4 For
every living soul belongs to me, the father as well as the son—both alike belong to me. The soul who sins
is the one who will die.[l]

18:4 [l]ver 20; Isa 42:5; Ro 6:23

5 “Suppose there is a righteous man
who does what is just and right.
6 He does not eat at the mountain[m] shrines
or look to the idols[n] of the house of Israel.
He does not defile his neighbor’s wife
or lie with a woman during her period.
7 He does not oppress[o] anyone,
but returns what he took in pledge[p] for a loan.
He does not commit robbery
but gives his food to the hungry
and provides clothing for the naked.[q]
8 He does not lend at usury
or take excessive interest.[a][r]
He withholds his hand from doing wrong
and judges fairly[s] between man and man.
9 He follows my decrees
and faithfully keeps my laws.
That man is righteous;[t]
he will surely live,[u]
declares the Sovereign LORD.

18:6 [m]Eze 22:9 [n]Dt 4:19; Eze 6:13; 20:24
18:7 [o]Ex 22:21 [p]Ex 22:26; Dt 24:12 [q]Dt 15:11; Mt 25:36
18:8 [r]Ex 22:25; Lev 25:35-37; Dt 23:19-20 [s]Zec 8:16
18:9 [t]Hab 2:4 [u]Lev 18:5; Eze 20:11; Am 5:4

10 “Suppose he has a violent son, who sheds blood[v] or does any of these other things[b] 11 (though the
father has done none of them):

18:10 [v]Ex 21:12

“He eats at the mountain shrines.
He defiles his neighbor’s wife.
12 He oppresses the poor[w] and needy.
He commits robbery.
He does not return what he took in pledge.
He looks to the idols.
He does detestable things.[x]
13 He lends at usury and takes excessive interest.[y]

18:12 [w]Am 4:1 [x]2Ki 21:11; Isa 59:6-7; Jer 22:17; Eze 8:6,17
18:13 [y]Ex 22:25 [z]Eze 33:4-5

Will such a man live? He will not! Because he has done all these detestable things, he will surely be put to death and his blood will be on his own head.[z]

14 “But suppose this son has a son who sees all the sins his father commits, and though he sees them,
he does not do such things:[a]

18:14 [a]2Ch 34:21; Pr 23:24

15 “He does not eat at the mountain shrines
or look to the idols of the house of Israel.
He does not defile his neighbor’s wife.

[a] 8 Or *take interest*; similarly in verses 13 and 17 [b] 10 Or *things to a brother*

18:6 Pagan rites included eating meat sacrificed to idols on the high places (see “The High Places” on p. 1318).

18:8 In the Old Testament there is no trace of any system of commercial credit. Large commercial loans were not made in ancient Israel. Only the poor borrowed, and they did so to obtain the necessities of life. The Law of Moses forbade lending at interest to fellow Israelites (Ex 22:25) but permitted charging interest to foreigners (Dt 23:20). A needy Israelite might sell himself as a servant (Lev 25:39; 2Ki 4:1). The prophets condemned the taking of interest as a heinous sin (Jer 15:10; Eze 18:13,17). In the New Testament references to the receiving of interest occur in two parables—of the minas (Lk 19:23) and of the talents (Mt 25:27). In both cases the practice is distinctly encouraged.

During Israel’s time in Babylon many abuses arose regarding the lending of money (Eze 18:17). Because of this Nehemiah, after his return from exile, took measures to have the practice stopped (Ne 5:10–12).

[16] He does not oppress anyone
or require a pledge for a loan.
He does not commit robbery
but gives his food to the hungry
and provides clothing for the naked.[b]
[17] He withholds his hand from sin[a]
and takes no usury or excessive interest.
He keeps my laws and follows my decrees.

He will not die for his father's sin; he will surely live. [18] But his father will die for his own sin, because he
practiced extortion, robbed his brother and did what was wrong among his people.

[19] "Yet you ask, 'Why does the son not share the guilt of his father?' Since the son has done what is just
and right and has been careful to keep all my decrees, he will surely live.[c] [20] The soul who sins is the one
who will die. The son will not share the guilt of the father, nor will the father share the guilt of the son.
The righteousness of the righteous man will be credited to him, and the wickedness of the wicked will
be charged against him.[d]

[21] "But if a wicked man turns away from all the sins he has committed and keeps all my decrees and
does what is just and right, he will surely live; he will not die.[e] [22] None of the offenses he has committed
will be remembered against him. Because of the righteous things he has done, he will live.[f] [23] Do I take
any pleasure in the death of the wicked? declares the Sovereign LORD. Rather, am I not pleased[g] when
they turn from their ways and live?[h]

[24] "But if a righteous man turns from his righteousness and commits sin and does the same detestable
things the wicked man does, will he live? None of the righteous things he has done will be remembered.
Because of the unfaithfulness he is guilty of and because of the sins he has committed, he will die.[i]

[25] "Yet you say, 'The way of the Lord is not just.' Hear, O house of Israel: Is my way unjust?[j] Is it not
your ways that are unjust? [26] If a righteous man turns from his righteousness and commits sin, he will
die for it; because of the sin he has committed he will die. [27] But if a wicked man turns away from the
wickedness he has committed and does what is just and right, he will save his life.[k] [28] Because he consid-
ers all the offenses he has committed and turns away from them, he will surely live; he will not die. [29] Yet
the house of Israel says, 'The way of the Lord is not just.' Are my ways unjust, O house of Israel? Is it not
your ways that are unjust?

[30] "Therefore, O house of Israel, I will judge you, each one according to his ways, declares the Sover-
eign LORD. Repent![l] Turn away from all your offenses; then sin will not be your downfall.[m] [31] Rid your-
selves of all the offenses you have committed, and get a new heart[n] and a new spirit. Why will you die,
O house of Israel?[o] [32] For I take no pleasure in the death of anyone, declares the Sovereign LORD. Repent
and live![p]

18:16 [b]Ps 41:1; Isa 58:10
18:19 [c]Ex 20:5; Dt 5:9; Jer 15:4; Zec 1:3-6
18:20 [d]Dt 24:16; 1Ki 8:32; 2Ki 14:6; Isa 3:11; Mt 16:27; Ro 2:9
18:21 [e]Eze 33:12,19
18:22 [f]Ps 18:20-24; Isa 43:25; Mic 7:19
18:23 [g]Ps 147:11 [h]Eze 33:11; 1Ti 2:4
18:24 [i]1Sa 15:11; 2Ch 24:17-20; Eze 3:20; 20:27; 2Pe 2:20-22
18:25 [j]Ge 18:25; Jer 12:1; Eze 33:17; Zep 3:5; Mal 2:17; 3:13-15
18:27 [k]Isa 1:18
18:30 [l]Mt 3:2 [m]Eze 7:3; 33:20; Hos 12:6
18:31 [n]Ps 51:10 [o]Isa 1:16-17; Eze 11:19; 36:26
18:32 [p]Eze 33:11

A Lament for Israel's Princes

19 "Take up a lament[q] concerning the princes[r] of Israel [2] and say:

" 'What a lioness was your mother
among the lions!
She lay down among the young lions
and reared her cubs.
[3] She brought up one of her cubs,
and he became a strong lion.
He learned to tear the prey
and he devoured men.
[4] The nations heard about him,
and he was trapped in their pit.

19:1 [q]Eze 26:17; 27:2,32 [r]2Ki 24:6

[a] 17 Septuagint (see also verse 8); Hebrew *from the poor*

19:1 A "lament" was a chant, usually composed for the funeral of a fallen leader, but the word was often used sarcastically by Old Testament prophets to predict the destruction ("death") of a nation (see "Ancient Near Eastern Laments" on p. 1305).

19:2 The "lioness" is a personification of Israel, Judah or Jerusalem.
19:3 "One of her cubs" is Jehoahaz (also called Shallum), who ruled for only three months and whose reign was characterized by oppressive policies (Jer 22:13).

19:4 [s]2Ki 23:33-34; 2Ch 36:4
19:5 [t]2Ki 23:34
19:6 [u]2Ki 24:9; 2Ch 36:9
19:7 [v]Eze 30:12
19:8 [w]2Ki 24:2 [x]2Ki 24:11
19:9 [y]2Ch 36:6 [z]2Ki 24:15
19:10 [a]Ps 80:8-11
19:11 [b]Eze 31:3; Da 4:11
19:12 [c]Eze 17:10 [d]Isa 27:11; Eze 28:17; Hos 13:15
19:13 [e]Eze 20:35 [f]Hos 2:3
19:14 [g]Eze 20:47 [h]Eze 15:4

They led him with hooks
to the land of Egypt.[s]
5 " 'When she saw her hope unfulfilled,
her expectation gone,
she took another of her cubs
and made him a strong lion.[t]
6 He prowled among the lions,
for he was now a strong lion.
He learned to tear the prey
and he devoured men.[u]
7 He broke down[a] their strongholds
and devastated[v] their towns.
The land and all who were in it
were terrified by his roaring.
8 Then the nations[w] came against him,
those from regions round about.
They spread their net for him,
and he was trapped in their pit.[x]
9 With hooks they pulled him into a cage
and brought him to the king of Babylon.[y]
They put him in prison,
so his roar was heard no longer
on the mountains of Israel.[z]

10 " 'Your mother was like a vine in your vineyard[b]
planted by the water;
it was fruitful and full of branches
because of abundant water.[a]
11 Its branches were strong,
fit for a ruler's scepter.
It towered high
above the thick foliage,
conspicuous for its height
and for its many branches.[b]
12 But it was uprooted[c] in fury
and thrown to the ground.
The east wind made it shrivel,
it was stripped of its fruit;
its strong branches withered
and fire consumed them.[d]
13 Now it is planted in the desert,[e]
in a dry and thirsty land.[f]
14 Fire spread from one of its main[c] branches
and consumed[g] its fruit.
No strong branch is left on it
fit for a ruler's scepter.'[h]

This is a lament and is to be used as a lament."

[a] 7 Targum (see Septuagint); Hebrew *He knew* [b] 10 Two Hebrew manuscripts; most Hebrew manuscripts *your blood*
[c] 14 Or *from under its*

19:5 "Another of her cubs" may have been Jehoiachin but was more probably Zedekiah (the description in v. 7 appears to more appropriately describe Zedekiah). Both were taken to Babylon (v. 9). If the reference is to Jehoiachin (2Ki 24:15), this was a true lament; if to Zedekiah, it was a prediction (2Ki 25:7).
19:10 The one previously pictured as a lioness (see v. 2) is here depicted as a vine.
19:11 For "scepter," see the note on Zechariah 10:11.
19:12 For "east wind," see the note on 17:10.
19:13 The "desert" is Babylonia—which to Israel seemed like a wilderness (see 20:35).
19:14 "Fire" here represents rebellion (see 2Ki 24:20), and "one of its main branches" refers to Zedekiah.

Rebellious Israel

20 In the seventh year, in the fifth month on the tenth day, some of the elders of Israel came to in-
quire of the LORD, and they sat down in front of me.[i]
2 Then the word of the LORD came to me: 3 "Son of man, speak to the elders of Israel and say to them,
'This is what the Sovereign LORD says: Have you come to inquire[j] of me? As surely as I live, I will not let
you inquire of me, declares the Sovereign LORD.[k]'
4 "Will you judge them? Will you judge them, son of man? Then confront them with the detestable
practices of their fathers[l] 5 and say to them: 'This is what the Sovereign LORD says: On the day I chose[m]
Israel, I swore with uplifted hand to the descendants of the house of Jacob and revealed myself to them
in Egypt. With uplifted hand I said to them, "I am the LORD your God.[n]" 6 On that day I swore to them
that I would bring them out of Egypt into a land I had searched out for them, a land flowing with milk
and honey,[o] the most beautiful of all lands.[p] 7 And I said to them, "Each of you, get rid of the vile imag-
es[q] you have set your eyes on, and do not defile yourselves with the idols of Egypt. I am the LORD your
God.[r]"
8 " 'But they rebelled against me and would not listen to me; they did not get rid of the vile images
they had set their eyes on, nor did they forsake the idols of Egypt.[s] So I said I would pour out my wrath
on them and spend my anger against them in Egypt.[t] 9 But for the sake of my name I did what would
keep it from being profaned in the eyes of the nations they lived among and in whose sight I had revealed
myself to the Israelites by bringing them out of Egypt.[u] 10 Therefore I led them out of Egypt and brought
them into the desert.[v] 11 I gave them my decrees and made known to them my laws, for the man who
obeys them will live by them.[w] 12 Also I gave them my Sabbaths as a sign[x] between us, so they would
know that I the LORD made them holy.
13 " 'Yet the people of Israel rebelled[y] against me in the desert. They did not follow my decrees but re-
jected my laws—although the man who obeys them will live by them—and they utterly desecrated my
Sabbaths. So I said I would pour out my wrath[z] on them and destroy them in the desert.[a] 14 But for the
sake of my name I did what would keep it from being profaned in the eyes of the nations in whose sight
I had brought them out.[b] 15 Also with uplifted hand I swore to them in the desert that I would not bring
them into the land I had given them—a land flowing with milk and honey, most beautiful of all lands[c]—
16 because they rejected my laws and did not follow my decrees and desecrated my Sabbaths. For their
hearts[d] were devoted to their idols.[e] 17 Yet I looked on them with pity and did not destroy them or put an
end to them in the desert. 18 I said to their children in the desert, "Do not follow the statutes of your fa-
thers[f] or keep their laws or defile yourselves with their idols. 19 I am the LORD your God;[g] follow my de-
crees and be careful to keep my laws.[h] 20 Keep my Sabbaths holy, that they may be a sign between us.
Then you will know that I am the LORD your God.[i]"
21 " 'But the children rebelled against me: They did not follow my decrees, they were not careful to
keep my laws—although the man who obeys them will live by them—and they desecrated my Sab-
baths. So I said I would pour out my wrath on them and spend my anger against them in the desert.
22 But I withheld[j] my hand, and for the sake of my name I did what would keep it from being profaned
in the eyes of the nations in whose sight I had brought them out. 23 Also with uplifted hand I swore to
them in the desert that I would disperse them among the nations and scatter[k] them through the coun-
tries, 24 because they had not obeyed my laws but had rejected my decrees and desecrated my Sabbaths,[l]
and their eyes ⌞lusted⌟ after[m] their fathers' idols.[n] 25 I also gave them over[o] to statutes that were not good
and laws they could not live by;[p] 26 I let them become defiled through their gifts—the sacrifice of every
firstborn[a]—that I might fill them with horror so they would know that I am the LORD.[q]'
27 "Therefore, son of man, speak to the people of Israel and say to them, 'This is what the Sovereign
LORD says: In this also your fathers blasphemed[r] me by forsaking me:[s] 28 When I brought them into the

20:1 [i]Eze 8:1
20:3 [j]Eze 14:3 [k]Mic 3:7
20:4 [l]Eze 16:2; 22:2; Mt 23:32
20:5 [m]Dt 7:6 [n]Ex 6:7
20:6 [o]Ex 3:8; Jer 32:22 [p]Dt 8:7; Ps 48:2; Da 8:9
20:7 [q]Ex 20:4 [r]Ex 20:2; Lev 18:3; Dt 29:18
20:8 [s]Eze 7:8 [t]Isa 63:10
20:9 [u]Eze 36:22; 39:7
20:10 [v]Ex 13:18
20:11 [w]Lev 18:5; Dt 4:7-8; Ro 10:5
20:12 [x]Ex 31:13
20:13 [y]Ps 78:40 [z]Dt 9:8 [a]Nu 14:29; Ps 95:8-10; Isa 56:6
20:14 [b]Eze 36:23
20:15 [c]Ps 95:11; 106:26
20:16 [d]Nu 15:39 [e]Am 5:26
20:18 [f]Zec 1:4
20:19 [g]Ex 20:2 [h]Dt 5:32-33; 6:1-2; 8:1; 11:1; 12:1
20:20 [i]Jer 17:22
20:22 [j]Ps 78:38
20:23 [k]Lev 26:33; Dt 28:64
20:24 [l]ver 13 [m]Eze 6:9 [n]ver 16
20:25 [o]Ps 81:12 [p]2Th 2:11
20:26 [q]2Ki 17:17
20:27 [r]Ro 2:24 [s]Eze 18:24

[a] 26 Or *—making every firstborn pass through ⌞the fire⌟*

20:1 The date was August 14, 591 B.C. For "elders of Israel," see the note on Jeremiah 19:1. For "inquire," see the note on Ezekiel 14:3.
20:5 Raising one's hand was a standard oath-taking practice in ancient times.
20:9 For "name," see the note on Jeremiah 16:21. The phrase used here is equivalent to "for my own sake."
20:12 Israel's observance of the Sabbath was to serve as a sign that the nation constituted the Lord's holy people (see "Sabbath, Sabbath Year and the Jubilee" on p. 189). Jewish legalism later corrupted the Sabbath law (see Mt 12:1–14).
20:25–26 This most likely refers to God's requirement that Israel dedicate to him every firstborn male (Ex 13:2; 22:29)—which kings Ahaz and Manasseh, under the influence of the pagan religions of Israel's neighbors, radicalized into a law calling for actual sacrifice of the firstborn (see the note on 16:20; see also "Human Sacrifice in the Ancient Near East" on p. 182).

20:28 [t]Ps 78:55, 58 [u]Eze 6:13 land[t] I had sworn to give them and they saw any high hill or any leafy tree, there they offered their sac-
rifices, made offerings that provoked me to anger, presented their fragrant incense and poured out their
drink offerings.[u] 29Then I said to them: What is this high place you go to?' " (It is called Bamah[a] to this
day.)

Judgment and Restoration

30"Therefore say to the house of Israel: 'This is what the Sovereign LORD says: Will you defile your-
20:30 [v]ver 43 [w]Jer 16:12 selves[v] the way your fathers did and lust after their vile images?[w] 31When you offer your gifts—the sac-
20:31 [x]Eze 16:20 rifice of your sons[x] in[b] the fire—you continue to defile yourselves with all your idols to this day. Am I to
[y]Ps 106:37-39; Jer 7:31 let you inquire of me, O house of Israel? As surely as I live, declares the Sovereign LORD, I will not let you
inquire of me.[y]

32" 'You say, "We want to be like the nations, like the peoples of the world, who serve wood and stone."
But what you have in mind will never happen. 33As surely as I live, declares the Sovereign LORD, I will
20:33 [z]Jer 21:5 rule over you with a mighty hand and an outstretched arm and with outpoured wrath.[z] 34I will bring
20:34 [a]2Co 6:17* you from the nations[a] and gather you from the countries where you have been scattered—with a mighty
[b]Isa 27:12-13; Jer 44:6; La 2:4 hand and an outstretched arm and with outpoured wrath.[b] 35I will bring you into the desert of the na-
20:35 [c]Jer 2:35 tions and there, face to face, I will execute judgment[c] upon you. 36As I judged your fathers in the desert
20:36 [d]Nu 11:1-35; 1Co 10:5-10 of the land of Egypt, so I will judge you, declares the Sovereign LORD.[d] 37I will take note of you as you
20:37 [e]Lev 27:32; pass under my rod,[e] and I will bring you into the bond of the covenant.[f] 38I will purge[g] you of those who
Jer 33:13 [f]Eze 16:62 revolt and rebel against me. Although I will bring them out of the land where they are living, yet they will
20:38 [g]Eze 34:17-22; not enter the land of Israel. Then you will know that I am the LORD.[h]
Am 9:9-10 [h]Ps 95:11; 39" 'As for you, O house of Israel, this is what the Sovereign LORD says: Go and serve your idols,[i] every
Jer 44:14; one of you! But afterward you will surely listen to me and no longer profane my holy name with your
Eze 13:9; Mal 3:3; gifts and idols.[j] 40For on my holy mountain, the high mountain of Israel, declares the Sovereign LORD,
Heb 4:3 there in the land the entire house of Israel will serve me, and there I will accept them. There I will re-
20:39 [i]Jer 44:25 quire your offerings[k] and your choice gifts,[c] along with all your holy sacrifices.[l] 41I will accept you as fra-
[j]Isa 1:13; Eze 43:7; Am 4:4 grant incense when I bring you out from the nations and gather you from the countries where you have
20:40 [k]Isa 60:7 [l]Isa 56:7; Mal 3:4 been scattered, and I will show myself holy[m] among you in the sight of the nations.[n] 42Then you will
20:41 [m]Eze 28:25; know that I am the LORD,[o] when I bring you into the land of Israel,[p] the land I had sworn with uplifted
36:23 [n]Eze 11:17 hand to give to your fathers. 43There you will remember your conduct and all the actions by which you
20:42 [o]Eze 38:23 [p]Eze 34:13; 36:24 have defiled yourselves, and you will loathe yourselves for all the evil you have done.[q] 44You will know that
20:43 [q]Eze 6:9; 16:61; Hos 5:15 I am the LORD, when I deal with you for my name's sake[r] and not according to your evil ways and your
20:44 [r]Eze 36:22 [s]Eze 24:24 corrupt practices, O house of Israel, declares the Sovereign LORD.[s]' "

Prophecy Against the South

45The word of the LORD came to me: 46"Son of man, set your face toward the south; preach against the
20:46 [t]Eze 21:2; Am 7:16 south and prophesy against[t] the forest of the southland.[u] 47Say to the southern forest: 'Hear the word of
[u]Isa 30:6; Jer 13:19 the LORD. This is what the Sovereign LORD says: I am about to set fire to you, and it will consume all your
trees, both green and dry. The blazing flame will not be quenched, and every face from south to north
20:47 [v]Isa 9:18-19; 13:8; will be scorched by it.[v] 48Everyone will see that I the LORD have kindled it; it will not be quenched.[w]' "
Jer 21:14 20:48 [w]Jer 7:20 49Then I said, "Ah, Sovereign LORD! They are saying of me, 'Isn't he just telling parables?[x]' "
20:49 [x]Mt 13:13; Jn 16:25

Babylon, God's Sword of Judgment

21 The word of the LORD came to me: 2"Son of man, set your face against Jerusalem and preach
21:2 [y]Eze 20:46 against the sanctuary. Prophesy against[y] the land of Israel 3and say to her: 'This is what the LORD
21:3 [z]Jer 21:13 says: I am against you.[z] I will draw my sword from its scabbard and cut off from you both the righteous

[a] 29 *Bamah* means *high place.* [b] 31 Or *—making your sons pass through* [c] 40 Or *and the gifts of your firstfruits*

20:37 The rod was an instrument of authority that was also used by shepherds for counting, guiding, rescuing and protecting sheep. The staff was used for support. (See "Shepherding in the Ancient World" on p. 1363.)

20:40 "My holy mountain" refers to Jerusalem or Zion (see "Zaphon, Olympus, Sinai and Zion: The Mountain of God" on p. 843).

20:41 For "fragrant incense," see "Incense" on page 1209. Here the term is used in a metaphorical sense.

20:46 Ezekiel was to prophesy to Judah and Jerusalem. Any Babylonian invasion would traverse Israel from north to south (see the note on 26:7).

20:47 "From south to north" here expresses totality, not direction.

21:3 Here the "sword" refers to Babylon and Nebuchadnezzar (v. 19). The judgment to come on Israel would be complete—no one would escape its devastating effects, not even the righteous in the land.

and the wicked.[a] 4 Because I am going to cut off the righteous and the wicked, my sword will be un-
sheathed against everyone from south to north.[b] 5 Then all people will know that I the LORD have drawn
my sword from its scabbard; it will not return[c] again.'[d]

6 "Therefore groan, son of man! Groan before them with broken heart and bitter grief.[e] 7 And when
they ask you, 'Why are you groaning?' you shall say, 'Because of the news that is coming. Every heart will
melt and every hand go limp;[f] every spirit will become faint and every knee become as weak as water.'
It is coming! It will surely take place, declares the Sovereign LORD."

8 The word of the LORD came to me: 9 "Son of man, prophesy and say, 'This is what the Lord says:

" 'A sword, a sword,
sharpened and polished—
10 sharpened for the slaughter,[g]
polished to flash like lightning!

" 'Shall we rejoice in the scepter of my son ⌞Judah⌟? The sword despises every such stick.

11 " 'The sword is appointed to be polished,[h]
to be grasped with the hand;
it is sharpened and polished,
made ready for the hand of the slayer.
12 Cry out and wail, son of man,
for it is against my people;
it is against all the princes of Israel.
They are thrown to the sword
along with my people.
Therefore beat your breast.[i]

13 " 'Testing will surely come. And what if the scepter ⌞of Judah⌟, which the sword despises, does not
continue? declares the Sovereign LORD.'

14 "So then, son of man, prophesy
and strike your hands[j] together.
Let the sword strike twice,
even three times.
It is a sword for slaughter—
a sword for great slaughter,
closing in on them from every side.[k]
15 So that hearts may melt[l]
and the fallen be many,
I have stationed the sword for slaughter[a]
at all their gates.
Oh! It is made to flash like lightning,
it is grasped for slaughter.[m]
16 O sword, slash to the right,
then to the left,
wherever your blade is turned.
17 I too will strike my hands[n] together,
and my wrath[o] will subside.
I the LORD have spoken."

[a] *15* Septuagint; the meaning of the Hebrew for this word is uncertain.

21:3 [a]ver 9-11; Job 9:22
21:4 [b]Eze 20:47
21:5 [c]ver 30 [d]Na 1:9
21:6 [e]Isa 22:4
21:7 [f]Eze 22:14; 7:17
21:10 [g]Ps 110:5-6; Isa 34:5-6
21:11 [h]Jer 46:4
21:12 [i]Jer 31:19
21:14 [j]Nu 24:10 [k]Eze 6:11; 30:24
21:15 [l]2Sa 17:10 [m]Ps 22:14
21:17 [n]ver 14; Eze 22:13 [o]Eze 5:13

21:4 See the note on 20:47.
21:9 This is a sword song, possibly accompanied by dancing or symbolic actions. Such songs may have been sung by warriors about to go into battle.
21:10 A scepter represented rule, government or kingdom. See the note on Zechariah 10:11.
21:11 The "slayer" is Nebuchadnezzar (v. 19).
21:12 These were acts of mourning (see "Sackcloth and Ashes: Rituals of Lamentation" on p. 820).

[18]The word of the LORD came to me: [19]"Son of man, mark out two roads for the sword of the king of
Babylon to take, both starting from the same country. Make a signpost where the road branches off to the
city. [20]Mark out one road for the sword to come against Rabbah of the Ammonites[p] and another against
Judah and fortified Jerusalem. [21]For the king of Babylon will stop at the fork in the road, at the junction

21:20 [p]Dt 3:11; Jer 49:2; Am 1:14

21:19 The "king of Babylon" is Nebuchadnezzar (see "Nebuchadnezzar" on p. 571). The "same country" refers to Babylonia or possibly to Aram (Syria); Nebuchadnezzar headquartered his campaign at Riblah in northern Aram (see 2Ki 25:6).
21:20 Rabbah (see "Rabbah" on p. 606), was the capital of Ammon (see "Ammon" on p. 364). The city was called Philadelphia in the New Testament era and today is Amman, the capital of Jordan.
21:21 Divination with arrows (see "Akkadian Divination" on p. 277) was used to seek good omens for a coming military campaign. Apparently arrows were labeled (e.g., "Rabbah," "Jerusalem"), placed

Exile and Genocide in the Ancient Near East

EZEKIEL 21 Although nations in the ancient Near East were almost continuously at war—and many of these wars had no long-term effects—sometimes a nation or city did suffer a calamitous defeat. Such a conquest could lead to the near eradication of the defeated people. The scenario often began with the destruction of a conquered city, including the razing of its walls. This was followed by a looting of the palace or local seat of government affairs. The religious artifacts of the defeated city were typically carried off and its temple demolished.[1] The deportation of the survivors into exile then began. In some cases only royalty, government officials and well-educated members of society were initially deported. If the conquered territory remained rebellious, however, additional mass deportations of the general populace were undertaken. Sometimes the conquering power would resettle the area with outsiders in order to ensure that the cultural heritage of the conquered territory was effectively eliminated.

Inscription at Medinet Habu in Egypt, in which the hands of slain enemy soldiers are piled up
Photograph: © Todd Bolen/Bible Places.com

Historical annals demonstrate that **Assyrian** kings attempted to deal with unruly populations through massive deportations. When a rebellious city was defeated, its nobility, skilled workers and soldiers were resettled closer to the Assyrian heartland, where they could be more easily controlled. The remaining population was less likely to have the military and economic means to revolt again. The practice of deportation became increasingly popular among later kings. Sargon II (the king most likely responsible for the deportation of the Israelites in 721 B.C.)[2] counted over 239,000 deportees, while Sennacherib (who unsuccessfully besieged Jerusalem in 701 B.C.)[3] listed over 469,000 exiles during his reign.

Exiles were often treated with extreme cruelty. Assyrian **reliefs** depict long lines of captives being led away bound and naked. Sometimes, however, captives fared well and were able to rise to positions of authority (e.g., Daniel, Nehemiah, Esther). Personal names in Assyrian inscriptions indicate that some Israelites did rise to leadership positions within the Assyrian administration.

At times deliberate genocide—the attempt to completely destroy a nation or ethnic group—was carried out. Information concerning genocide in the ancient world is somewhat limited, but the Bible testifies to two basic forms: paranoid infanticide, or the mass murder of infants due to suspicious fear (e.g., Ex 1), and ethnic targeting, the singling out of a race of people for annihilation (e.g., Est 3).

[1]See "Temple Abandonment" on page 1323. [2]See "The Annals of Sargon II" on page 1072. [3]See "Hezekiah Against the Assyrians" on page 1118.

Ivory plaque from Megiddo showing stripped captives
Preserving Bible Times; © Dr. James C. Martin; permission of The Israel Museum

of the two roads, to seek an omen: He will cast lots[q] with arrows, he will consult his idols, he will exam-
ine the liver.[r] 22 Into his right hand will come the lot for Jerusalem, where he is to set up battering rams,
to give the command to slaughter, to sound the battle cry, to set battering rams against the gates, to build
a ramp and to erect siege works.[s] 23 It will seem like a false omen to those who have sworn allegiance to
him, but he will remind[t] them of their guilt and take them captive.
24 "Therefore this is what the Sovereign LORD says: 'Because you people have brought to mind your
guilt by your open rebellion, revealing your sins in all that you do—because you have done this, you will
be taken captive.
25 " 'O profane and wicked prince of Israel, whose day has come, whose time of punishment has
reached its climax,[u] 26 this is what the Sovereign LORD says: Take off the turban, remove the crown.[v] It
will not be as it was: The lowly will be exalted and the exalted will be brought low.[w] 27 A ruin! A ruin! I
will make it a ruin! It will not be restored until he comes to whom it rightfully belongs; to him I will
give it.'[x]
28 "And you, son of man, prophesy and say, 'This is what the Sovereign LORD says about the Ammon-
ites[y] and their insults:

" 'A sword,[z] a sword,
    drawn for the slaughter,
polished to consume
    and to flash like lightning!
29 Despite false visions concerning you
    and lying divinations about you,
it will be laid on the necks
    of the wicked who are to be slain,
whose day has come,
    whose time of punishment has reached its climax.[a]
30 Return the sword to its scabbard.[b]
    In the place where you were created,
in the land of your ancestry,[c]
    I will judge you.
31 I will pour out my wrath upon you
    and breathe out my fiery anger[d] against you;
I will hand you over to brutal men,
    men skilled in destruction.[e]
32 You will be fuel for the fire,[f]
    your blood will be shed in your land,
you will be remembered[g] no more;
    for I the LORD have spoken.' "

21:21 [q]Pr 16:33 [r]Nu 22:7; 23:23
21:22 [s]Eze 4:2; 26:9
21:23 [t]Nu 5:15
21:25 [u]Eze 35:5
21:26 [v]Jer 13:18 [w]Ps 75:7; Eze 17:24
21:27 [x]Ps 2:6; Jer 23:5-6; Eze 37:24; Hag 2:21-22
21:28 [y]Zep 2:8 [z]Jer 12:12
21:29 [a]ver 25; Eze 22:28; 35:5
21:30 [b]Jer 47:6 [c]Eze 16:3
21:31 [d]Eze 22:20-21 [e]Jer 51:20-23
21:32 [f]Mal 4:1 [g]Eze 25:10

Jerusalem's Sins

22 The word of the LORD came to me: 2 "Son of man, will you judge her? Will you judge this city of
bloodshed?[h] Then confront her with all her detestable practices[i] 3 and say: 'This is what the Sov-
ereign LORD says: O city that brings on herself doom by shedding blood[j] in her midst and defiles herself
by making idols, 4 you have become guilty because of the blood you have shed[k] and have become defiled
by the idols you have made. You have brought your days to a close, and the end of your years has come.[l]
Therefore I will make you an object of scorn to the nations and a laughingstock to all the countries.[m]
5 Those who are near and those who are far away will mock you, O infamous city, full of turmoil.

22:2 [h]Eze 24:6,9; Na 3:1 [i]Eze 16:2
22:3 [j]ver 6,13, 27; Eze 23:37,45
22:4 [k]2Ki 21:16 [l]Eze 21:25 [m]Eze 5:14

---

into a quiver and drawn out, one with each hand. Right-hand selection was seen as a good omen (see v. 22).

The Hebrew for "idols" is translated "household gods" in Genesis 31:19 (see the note there). Consulting them is referred to in Hosea 3:4 and Zechariah 10:2. Some household gods (Ge 31:19–35) were small enough to hide in a saddle, while others were life-sized (1Sa 19:13–16).

Inspecting the color and configurations of sheep livers to foretell the future was common practice in ancient Babylonia and Rome, but it is not mentioned elsewhere in the Bible.

21:22 See "Siege Warfare" on page 465.

21:25 The "prince of Israel" is Zedekiah.

21:26 Linen headdresses, twisted as turbans, were common for men, wealthy women, bridegrooms and priests (Ex 28:40; Isa 3:20; 61:10; see "Ancient Israelite Clothing and Jewelry" on p. 1059). Only here is such a headdress mentioned as royal headwear. It was also worn by priests as a setting for the crown (Ex 29:6; Lev 8:9).

21:28 See the note on verse 9.

21:31 "Brutal men" refers to the people of the East, as in 25:4.

21:32 See the note on Isaiah 9:5 regarding fuel.

22:2 "This city" is Jerusalem.

6“ ‘See how each of the princes of Israel who are in you uses his power to shed blood.[n] 7In you they have treated father and mother with contempt;[o] in you they have oppressed the alien and mistreated the fatherless and the widow.[p] 8You have despised my holy things and desecrated my Sabbaths.[q] 9In you are slanderous men[r] bent on shedding blood; in you are those who eat at the mountain shrines[s] and commit lewd acts.[t] 10In you are those who dishonor their fathers’ bed; in you are those who violate women during their period, when they are ceremonially unclean.[u] 11In you one man commits a detestable offense with his neighbor’s wife, another shamefully defiles his daughter-in-law,[v] and another violates his sister,[w] his own father’s daughter. 12In you men accept bribes[x] to shed blood; you take usury and excessive interest[a] and make unjust gain from your neighbors[y] by extortion. And you have forgotten me, declares the Sovereign LORD.

13“ ‘I will surely strike my hands[z] together at the unjust gain[a] you have made and at the blood[b] you have shed in your midst. 14Will your courage endure or your hands be strong in the day I deal with you? I the LORD have spoken,[c] and I will do it.[d] 15I will disperse you among the nations and scatter[e] you through the countries; and I will put an end to your uncleanness.[f] 16When you have been defiled[b] in the eyes of the nations, you will know that I am the LORD.’ ”

17Then the word of the LORD came to me: 18“Son of man, the house of Israel has become dross[g] to me; all of them are the copper, tin, iron and lead left inside a furnace. They are but the dross of silver.[h] 19Therefore this is what the Sovereign LORD says: ‘Because you have all become dross, I will gather you into Jerusalem. 20As men gather silver, copper, iron, lead and tin into a furnace to melt it with a fiery blast, so will I gather you in my anger and my wrath and put you inside the city and melt you.[i] 21I will gather you and I will blow on you with my fiery wrath, and you will be melted inside her. 22As silver is melted[j] in a furnace, so you will be melted inside her, and you will know that I the LORD have poured out my wrath upon you.’ ”[k]

23Again the word of the LORD came to me: 24“Son of man, say to the land, ‘You are a land that has had no rain or showers[c] in the day of wrath.’[l] 25There is a conspiracy[m] of her princes[d] within her like a roaring lion tearing its prey; they devour people,[n] take treasures and precious things and make many widows[o] within her. 26Her priests do violence to my law[p] and profane my holy things; they do not distinguish between the holy and the common;[q] they teach that there is no difference between the unclean and the clean;[r] and they shut their eyes to the keeping of my Sabbaths, so that I am profaned among them.[s] 27Her officials within her are like wolves tearing their prey; they shed blood and kill people to make unjust gain.[t] 28Her prophets whitewash[u] these deeds for them by false visions and lying divinations. They say, ‘This is what the Sovereign LORD says’—when the LORD has not spoken.[v] 29The people of the land practice extortion and commit robbery; they oppress the poor and needy and mistreat the alien,[w] denying them justice.[x]

30“I looked for a man among them who would build up the wall[y] and stand before me in the gap on behalf of the land so I would not have to destroy it, but I found none.[z] 31So I will pour out my wrath on them and consume them with my fiery anger, bringing down[a] on their own heads all they have done, declares the Sovereign LORD.[b]”

Two Adulterous Sisters

23 The word of the LORD came to me: 2“Son of man, there were two women, daughters of the same mother.[c] 3They became prostitutes in Egypt,[d] engaging in prostitution[e] from their youth. In that land their breasts were fondled and their virgin bosoms caressed. 4The older was named Oholah, and her sister was Oholibah. They were mine and gave birth to sons and daughters. Oholah is Samaria, and Oholibah is Jerusalem.

5“Oholah engaged in prostitution while she was still mine; and she lusted after her lovers, the Assyrians[f]—warriors[g] 6clothed in blue, governors and commanders, all of them handsome young men, and mounted horsemen. 7She gave herself as a prostitute to all the elite of the Assyrians and defiled herself

22:6 [n]Isa 1:23
22:7 [o]Dt 5:16; 27:16 [p]Ex 22:21-22
22:8 [q]Eze 23:38-39
22:9 [r]Lev 19:16 [s]Eze 18:11 [t]Hos 4:10,14
22:10 [u]Lev 18:8, 19
22:11 [v]Lev 18:15 [w]Lev 18:9; 2Sa 13:14
22:12 [x]Dt 27:25; Mic 7:3 [y]Lev 19:13
22:13 [z]Eze 21:17 [a]Isa 33:15 [b]ver 3
22:14 [c]Eze 24:14 [d]Eze 17:24; 21:7
22:15 [e]Dt 4:27; Zec 7:14 [f]Eze 23:27
22:18 [g]Ps 119:119; Isa 1:22 [h]Jer 6:28-30
22:20 [i]Mal 3:2
22:22 [j]Isa 1:25 [k]Eze 20:8,33
22:24 [l]Eze 24:13
22:25 [m]Jer 11:9 [n]Hos 6:9 [o]Jer 15:8
22:26 [p]Mal 2:7-8 [q]Eze 44:23 [r]Lev 10:10 [s]1Sa 2:12-17; Jer 2:8,26; Hag 2:11-14
22:27 [t]Isa 1:23
22:28 [u]Eze 13:10 [v]Eze 13:2,6-7
22:29 [w]Ex 22:21; 23:9 [x]Isa 5:7
22:30 [y]Eze 13:5 [z]Ps 106:23; Jer 5:1
22:31 [a]Eze 16:43 [b]Eze 7:8-9; 9:10; Ro 2:8
23:2 [c]Jer 3:7; Eze 16:45
23:3 [d]Jos 24:14 [e]Lev 17:7
23:5 [f]2Ki 16:7; Hos 5:13 [g]Hos 8:9

[a] 12 Or *usury and interest* [b] 16 Or *When I have allotted you your inheritance* [c] 24 Septuagint; Hebrew *has not been cleansed or rained on* [d] 25 Septuagint; Hebrew *prophets*

22:9 See the note on 18:6.
22:11 All of the sins mentioned in this verse were specifically forbidden in the Mosaic Law (Lev 18:7–20; 20:10–21; Dt 22:22–23,30; 27:22).
22:25 Ezekiel began to speak plainly concerning the “dross” of verses 18–22. All of Jerusalem’s leaders and people were included: princes (here), priests (v. 26), officials (v. 27), prophets (v. 28) and people (v. 29).
23:5 See “Sexuality and Religion in the Sumerian Hymns to Ishtar” on page 1340.

with all the idols of everyone she lusted after.[h] 8She did not give up the prostitution she began in Egypt,[i] 23:7 hHos 5:3; 6:10
when during her youth men slept with her, caressed her virgin bosom and poured out their lust upon her.[j] 23:8 iEx 32:4
9"Therefore I handed her over[k] to her lovers, the Assyrians, for whom she lusted.[l] 10They stripped[m] jEze 16:15 23:9 k2Ki 18:11
her naked, took away her sons and daughters and killed her with the sword. She became a byword among lHos 11:5 23:10 mHos 2:10
women,[n] and punishment was inflicted on her.[o] nEze 16:41 oEze 16:36
11"Her sister Oholibah saw this, yet in her lust and prostitution she was more depraved than her sis-
ter.[p] 12She too lusted after the Assyrians—governors and commanders, warriors in full dress, mounted 23:11 pJer 3:8-11; Eze 16:51
horsemen, all handsome young men.[q] 13I saw that she too defiled herself; both of them went the same 23:12 q2Ki 16:7-15; 2Ch 28:16
way.
14"But she carried her prostitution still further. She saw men portrayed on a wall,[r] figures of Chalde- 23:14 rEze 8:10 sJer 22:14
ans[a] portrayed in red,[s] 15with belts around their waists and flowing turbans on their heads; all of them
looked like Babylonian chariot officers, natives of Chaldea.[b] 16As soon as she saw them, she lusted after
them and sent messengers to them in Chaldea. 17Then the Babylonians came to her, to the bed of love,
and in their lust they defiled her. After she had been defiled by them, she turned away from them in dis-
gust. 18When she carried on her prostitution openly and exposed her nakedness, I turned away[t] from 23:18 tPs 78:59; 106:40; Jer 6:8
her in disgust, just as I had turned away from her sister.[u] 19Yet she became more and more promiscuous uJer 12:8; Am 5:21
as she recalled the days of her youth, when she was a prostitute in Egypt. 20There she lusted after her lov-

[a] 14 Or *Babylonians* [b] 15 Or *Babylonia*; also in verse 16

23:10 "Stripped her naked" is a reference to the fall of Samaria to the Assyrians in 722 B.C.

23:14 See "The Chaldeans" on page 1402.

ANCIENT TEXTS AND ARTIFACTS

Sexuality and Religion in the Sumerian Hymns to Ishtar

EZEKIEL 23 The sexual imagery employed by Ezekiel to demonstrate the apostasy of Israel and Judah is quite explicit. Equating the lovers of Oholah (**Samaria**) and Oholibah (Jerusalem) with the foreign nations of Egypt and **Assyria**, Ezekiel made use of Hosea's image of Israel and Judah as prostituting women. The link the prophets established between sexuality and paganism could hardly have surprised the Israelites; they saw the evidence all around them and knew that from ancient times many of the gods of the nations were known to have highly erotic characteristics.

The **Sumerian** goddess Inanna, who later merged with the **Akkadian** goddess Ishtar,[1] was the preeminent goddess among the **Mesopotamians**. In the mythology of Inanna/Ishtar, she is associated with prostitution.[2] The explicit nature of Ezekiel 23 is in many ways evocative of Mesopotamian texts that praise Ishtar. In one of these texts Ishtar meets her lover, Dumuzi (Tammuz). Referring to her sexual parts as "a well-watered field," she asks, "Who will plow it?" The answer is that "Dumuzi will plow it for you." Another text praises Inanna's breasts as "a fertile field."

Many of these texts may have been associated with a ritual involving sacred prostitution. Such rites were performed with regularity on the assumption that doing so would evoke the goddess's blessing. Although we cannot be certain of the extent to which Ezekiel may have been thinking of Inanna/Ishtar in his caustic portrayal of Jerusalem and Samaria, it is interesting to note the sexually explicit parallels between Ezekiel 23 and the numerous hymns to this Mesopotamian deity.

[1]See "The Descent of Ishtar" on page 356. [2]See "Prostitution in the Ancient World" on page 284.

Sumerian jewelry from Ur

Preserving Bible Times; © Dr. James C. Martin; permission of The British Museum

ers, whose genitals were like those of donkeys and whose emission was like that of horses. 21 So you longed
for the lewdness of your youth, when in Egypt your bosom was caressed and your young breasts fon-
23:21 [v]Eze 16:26 dled.[a][v]
22 "Therefore, Oholibah, this is what the Sovereign LORD says: I will stir up your lovers against you,
23:22 [w]Eze 16:37 those you turned away from in disgust, and I will bring them against you from every side[w]— 23 the Bab-
23:23 [x]2Ki 20:14-18 ylonians[x] and all the Chaldeans, the men of Pekod[y] and Shoa and Koa, and all the Assyrians with them,
[y]Jer 50:21 handsome young men, all of them governors and commanders, chariot officers and men of high rank,
[z]2Ki 24:2 **23:24** [a]Jer 47:3; all mounted on horses.[z] 24 They will come against you with weapons,[b] chariots and wagons[a] and with a
Eze 26:7,10; Na 2:4 throng of people; they will take up positions against you on every side with large and small shields and
[b]Jer 39:5-6 with helmets. I will turn you over to them for punishment,[b] and they will punish you according to their
standards. 25 I will direct my jealous anger against you, and they will deal with you in fury. They will cut
off your noses and your ears, and those of you who are left will fall by the sword. They will take away
23:25 [c]ver 47 your sons and daughters,[c] and those of you who are left will be consumed by fire.[d] 26 They will also strip[e]
[d]Eze 20:47-48 **23:26** [e]Jer 13:22 you of your clothes and take your fine jewelry.[f] 27 So I will put a stop[g] to the lewdness and prostitution
[f]Isa 3:18-23; Eze 16:39 you began in Egypt. You will not look on these things with longing or remember Egypt anymore.
23:27 [g]Eze 16:41 **23:28** [h]Jer 34:20 28 "For this is what the Sovereign LORD says: I am about to hand you over[h] to those you hate, to those
you turned away from in disgust. 29 They will deal with you in hatred and take away everything you have
worked for. They will leave you naked and bare, and the shame of your prostitution will be exposed. Your
23:29 [i]Dt 28:48 lewdness and promiscuity[i] 30 have brought this upon you, because you lusted after the nations and de-
23:30 [j]Eze 6:9 **23:31** [k]Jer 25:15 filed yourself with their idols.[j] 31 You have gone the way of your sister; so I will put her cup[k] into your
[l]2Ki 21:13 hand.[l]

32 "This is what the Sovereign LORD says:

"You will drink your sister's cup,
a cup large and deep;
it will bring scorn and derision,
23:32 [m]Ps 60:3; Isa 51:17; Jer 25:15 for it holds so much.[m]
33 You will be filled with drunkenness and sorrow,
the cup of ruin and desolation,
23:33 [n]Jer 25:15-16 the cup of your sister Samaria.[n]
23:34 [o]Ps 75:8; Isa 51:17 34 You will drink it[o] and drain it dry;
you will dash it to pieces
and tear your breasts.

I have spoken, declares the Sovereign LORD.

23:35 [p]Isa 17:10; Jer 3:21 [q]1Ki 14:9 35 "Therefore this is what the Sovereign LORD says: Since you have forgotten[p] me and thrust me behind
your back,[q] you must bear the consequences of your lewdness and prostitution."
23:36 [r]Eze 16:2 36 The LORD said to me: "Son of man, will you judge Oholah and Oholibah? Then confront[r] them with
[s]Isa 58:1; Eze 22:2; Mic 3:8 their detestable practices,[s] 37 for they have committed adultery and blood is on their hands. They com-
mitted adultery with their idols; they even sacrificed their children, whom they bore to me,[c] as food for
23:37 [t]Eze 16:36 them.[t] 38 They have also done this to me: At that same time they defiled my sanctuary and desecrated
my Sabbaths. 39 On the very day they sacrificed their children to their idols, they entered my sanctuary
23:39 [u]2Ki 21:4 [v]Jer 7:10 and desecrated[u] it. That is what they did in my house.[v]
23:40 [w]Isa 57:9 40 "They even sent messengers for men who came from far away,[w] and when they arrived you bathed
[x]2Ki 9:30 [y]Jer 4:30; Eze 16:13-19 yourself for them, painted your eyes[x] and put on your jewelry.[y] 41 You sat on an elegant couch,[z] with a ta-
23:41 [z]Est 1:6; Pr 7:17; Am 6:4 ble[a] spread before it on which you had placed the incense and oil that belonged to me.
[a]Isa 65:11; Eze 44:16

[a] *21* Syriac (see also verse 3); Hebrew *caressed because of your young breasts* [b] *24* The meaning of the Hebrew for this word is uncertain. [c] *37* Or *even made the children they bore to me pass through ⌊the fire⌋*

23:23 Babylonians and Chaldeans were often identified with one another; here they are distinguished probably because the Chaldeans were relative newcomers (see "The Chaldeans" on p. 1402). Pekod refers to Aramaic people located east of Babylon, while Shoa and Koa were Babylonian allies of uncertain origin and location.

23:34 Beating the breasts was a sign of mourning. Here it was intensified to the point of the tearing of flesh in a frantic attempt to find relief from intolerable suffering.

23:37 See the note on 16:20.

23:40 For information on bathing practices, see "Bathing" on page 456. From ancient times women painted their eyelids in order to enhance the beauty of their faces (see also 2Ki 9:30; Jer 4:30). Oriental women still paint their eyelids with antimony or *kohl* (a black powder made of the smoke black from the burning of frankincense) to make them look full and sparkling, the blackened margin contrasting with the white of the eye.

23:41 This verse describes the scene of a banquet.

42 "The noise of a carefree crowd was around her; Sabeans[a] were brought from the desert along with
men from the rabble, and they put bracelets[b] on the arms of the woman and her sister and beautiful
crowns on their heads.[c] 43 Then I said about the one worn out by adultery, 'Now let them use her as a pros-
titute,[d] for that is all she is.' 44 And they slept with her. As men sleep with a prostitute, so they slept with
those lewd women, Oholah and Oholibah. 45 But righteous men will sentence them to the punishment of
women who commit adultery and shed blood, because they are adulterous and blood is on their hands.[e]
46 "This is what the Sovereign LORD says: Bring a mob[f] against them and give them over to terror and
plunder. 47 The mob will stone them and cut them down with their swords; they will kill their sons and
daughters and burn[g] down their houses.[h]
48 "So I will put an end to lewdness in the land, that all women may take warning and not imitate you.[i]
49 You will suffer the penalty for your lewdness and bear the consequences of your sins of idolatry. Then
you will know that I am the Sovereign LORD.[j]"

The Cooking Pot

24 In the ninth year, in the tenth month on the tenth day, the word of the LORD came to me:[k] 2 "Son of
man, record this date, this very date, because the king of Babylon has laid siege to Jerusalem this
very day.[l] 3 Tell this rebellious house[m] a parable[n] and say to them: 'This is what the Sovereign LORD says:

" 'Put on the cooking pot;[o] put it on
and pour water into it.
4 Put into it the pieces of meat,
all the choice pieces—the leg and the shoulder.
Fill it with the best of these bones;
5 take the pick of the flock.[p]
Pile wood beneath it for the bones;
bring it to a boil
and cook the bones in it.[q]

6 " 'For this is what the Sovereign LORD says:

" 'Woe to the city of bloodshed,[r]
to the pot now encrusted,
whose deposit will not go away!
Empty it piece by piece
without casting lots[s] for them.

7 " 'For the blood she shed is in her midst:
She poured it on the bare rock;
she did not pour it on the ground,
where the dust would cover it.[t]
8 To stir up wrath and take revenge
I put her blood on the bare rock,
so that it would not be covered.

9 " 'Therefore this is what the Sovereign LORD says:

" 'Woe to the city of bloodshed!
I, too, will pile the wood high.

[a] 42 Or *drunkards*

23:42 [b]Ge 24:30 [c]Eze 16:11-12
23:43 [d]ver 3
23:45 [e]Lev 20:10; Eze 16:38; Hos 6:5
23:46 [f]Eze 16:40
23:47 [g]2Ch 36:19 [h]2Ch 36:17; Eze 16:40-41
23:48 [i]2Pe 2:6
23:49 [j]Eze 7:4; 9:10; 20:38
24:1 [k]Eze 8:1
24:2 [l]2Ki 25:1; Jer 39:1; 52:4
24:3 [m]Isa 1:2; Eze 2:3,6 [n]Eze 17:2; 20:49 [o]Jer 1:13; Eze 11:3
24:5 [p]Jer 52:10 [q]Jer 52:24-27
24:6 [r]Eze 22:2 [s]Ob 1:11; Na 3:10
24:7 [t]Lev 17:13

23:42 Saba, situated between the Nile and the Atbara, is a region about 400 miles (667 km) long and 200 miles (333 km) broad that was known to the Hebrews as Cush (see "Cush" on p. 1519). The ancient historian Strabo stated that a harbor named Saba was located on the western coast of the Red Sea. Josephus identified the Sabeans with the people of Saba in Upper (southern) Egypt, which he claimed that Moses had besieged and captured while in the service of the Egyptians. Another Sabean race, mentioned in Genesis 10:28 and 25:3, was located in Arabia. These Sabeans built a unique civilization and a great empire. The queen of Sheba, who made a visit of state to the court of Solomon, came from there (see "Sheba" on p. 498).

24:1–2 See the note on 8:1—11:25.

24:1 The date was January 15, 588 B.C., some two and a half years after the preceding dated oracle (see 20:1).

24:4 The "choice pieces" were the people of Jerusalem who thought they had been spared the exile in 597 B.C. because of their goodness.

24:5 "Wood" refers to Nebuchadnezzar's siege equipment (see "Siege Warfare" on p. 465).

24:6 After the siege of Jerusalem in 597 B.C., the Babylonians may have cast lots to see which of the local inhabitants they would take with them into exile. This time everyone would go.

10 So heap on the wood
and kindle the fire.
Cook the meat well,
mixing in the spices;
and let the bones be charred.
11 Then set the empty pot on the coals
till it becomes hot and its copper glows
so its impurities may be melted
24:11 [u]Jer 21:10; Eze 22:15 — and its deposit burned away.[u]
12 It has frustrated all efforts;
its heavy deposit has not been removed,
not even by fire.

13" 'Now your impurity is lewdness. Because I tried to cleanse you but you would not be cleansed
24:13 [v]Jer 6:28-30; Eze 16:42; 22:24 — from your impurity, you will not be clean again until my wrath against you has subsided.[v]

14" 'I the LORD have spoken. The time has come for me to act. I will not hold back; I will not have pity,
24:14 [w]Eze 36:19 [x]Eze 18:30 — nor will I relent. You will be judged according to your conduct and your actions,[w] declares the Sovereign
LORD.[x]' "

Ezekiel's Wife Dies

15 The word of the LORD came to me: 16 "Son of man, with one blow I am about to take away from you
24:16 [y]Jer 13:17; 16:5; 22:10 — the delight of your eyes. Yet do not lament or weep or shed any tears.[y] 17 Groan quietly; do not mourn for
the dead. Keep your turban fastened and your sandals on your feet; do not cover the lower part of your
24:17 [z]Jer 16:7 — face or eat the customary food ⌞of mourners⌟.[z]"

18 So I spoke to the people in the morning, and in the evening my wife died. The next morning I did
as I had been commanded.

24:19 [a]Eze 12:9; 37:18 — 19 Then the people asked me, "Won't you tell us what these things have to do with us?[a]"

20 So I said to them, "The word of the LORD came to me: 21 Say to the house of Israel, 'This is what the
Sovereign LORD says: I am about to desecrate my sanctuary—the stronghold in which you take pride,
24:21 [b]Ps 27:4 [c]Eze 23:25 [d]Jer 7:14,15; Eze 23:47 — the delight of your eyes,[b] the object of your affection. The sons and daughters[c] you left behind will fall
by the sword.[d] 22 And you will do as I have done. You will not cover the lower part of your face or eat the
24:22 [e]Jer 16:7 — customary food ⌞of mourners⌟.[e] 23 You will keep your turbans on your heads and your sandals on your
24:23 [f]Job 27:15 [g]Ps 78:64 — feet. You will not mourn[f] or weep but will waste away because of[a] your sins and groan among yourselves.[g]
24:24 [h]Isa 20:3; Eze 4:3; 12:11 — 24 Ezekiel will be a sign[h] to you; you will do just as he has done. When this happens, you will know that I
am the Sovereign LORD.'

25 "And you, son of man, on the day I take away their stronghold, their joy and glory, the delight of
24:25 [i]Jer 11:22 — their eyes, their heart's desire, and their sons and daughters[i] as well— 26 on that day a fugitive will come
24:26 [j]1Sa 4:12; Job 1:15-19 — to tell you[j] the news. 27 At that time your mouth will be opened; you will speak with him and will no lon-
24:27 [k]Eze 3:26; 33:22 — ger be silent. So you will be a sign to them, and they will know that I am the LORD.[k]"

A Prophecy Against Ammon

25:2 [l]Eze 21:28; Zep 2:8-9 [m]Jer 49:1-6 — 25 The word of the LORD came to me: 2 "Son of man, set your face against the Ammonites[l] and proph-
esy against them.[m] 3 Say to them, 'Hear the word of the Sovereign LORD. This is what the Sover-
25:3 [n]Eze 26:2; 36:2 [o]Pr 17:5 — eign LORD says: Because you said "Aha![n]" over my sanctuary when it was desecrated and over the land of
Israel when it was laid waste and over the people of Judah when they went into exile,[o] 4 therefore I am go-
25:4 [p]Jdg 6:3 [q]Dt 28:33,51; Jdg 6:33 — ing to give you to the people of the East[p] as a possession. They will set up their camps and pitch their tents
among you; they will eat your fruit and drink your milk.[q] 5 I will turn Rabbah[r] into a pasture for camels
25:5 [r]Dt 3:11; Eze 21:20

[a] 23 Or *away in*

24:11 Jerusalem, emptied of inhabitants, would be set ablaze.
24:17 Mourners normally removed their turbans and poured dust on their heads. Removing one's sandals was a sign of grief and covering one's face a gesture of shame. See "Sackcloth and Ashes: Rituals of Lamentation" on page 820.
24:18 Ezekiel's wife died on the same day the temple was burned—August 14, 586 B.C.
24:21 God would "desecrate" his own temple by allowing Nebuchadnezzar to burn it down.
25:2 See "Ammon" on page 364.
25:4 "People of the East" is probably a reference to nomadic tribes of the desert east of Ammon, although the term could refer to Nebuchadnezzar and his army (see 21:31).
25:5 For "Rabbah," see the note on 21:20.

and Ammon into a resting place for sheep.[s] Then you will know that I am the LORD. 6 For this is what the **25:5** [s]Isa 17:2
Sovereign LORD says: Because you have clapped your hands and stamped your feet, rejoicing with all the
malice of your heart against the land of Israel,[t] 7 therefore I will stretch out my hand[u] against you and give **25:6** [t]Ob 1:12; Zep 2:8
you as plunder to the nations. I will cut you off from the nations and exterminate you from the coun- **25:7** [u]Zep 1:4
tries. I will destroy[v] you, and you will know that I am the LORD.[w] ' " [v]Eze 21:31 [w]Am 1:14-15

A Prophecy Against Moab

8 "This is what the Sovereign LORD says: 'Because Moab[x] and Seir said, "Look, the house of Judah has **25:8** [x]Jer 48:1; Am 2:1
become like all the other nations," 9 therefore I will expose the flank of Moab, beginning at its frontier
towns—Beth Jeshimoth[y], Baal Meon[z] and Kiriathaim[a]—the glory of that land. 10 I will give Moab along **25:9** [y]Nu 33:49
with the Ammonites to the people of the East as a possession, so that the Ammonites will not be remem- [z]Nu 32:3; Jos 13:17
bered[b] among the nations; 11 and I will inflict punishment on Moab. Then they will know that I am the [a]Nu 32:37; Jos 13:19
LORD.' " **25:10** [b]Eze 21:32

A Prophecy Against Edom

12 "This is what the Sovereign LORD says: 'Because Edom[c] took revenge on the house of Judah and be- **25:12** [c]2Ch 28:17
came very guilty by doing so, 13 therefore this is what the Sovereign LORD says: I will stretch out my hand
against Edom and kill its men and their animals.[d] I will lay it waste, and from Teman to Dedan[e] they **25:13** [d]Eze 29:8
will fall by the sword. 14 I will take vengeance on Edom by the hand of my people Israel, and they will deal [e]Jer 25:23
with Edom in accordance with my anger[f] and my wrath; they will know my vengeance, declares the Sov- **25:14** [f]Eze 35:11
ereign LORD.' "

A Prophecy Against Philistia

15 "This is what the Sovereign LORD says: 'Because the Philistines[g] acted in vengeance and took re- **25:15** [g]2Ch 28:18
venge with malice in their hearts, and with ancient hostility sought to destroy Judah, 16 therefore this is
what the Sovereign LORD says: I am about to stretch out my hand against the Philistines,[h] and I will cut **25:16** [h]Jer 47:1-7
off the Kerethites[i] and destroy those remaining along the coast. 17 I will carry out great vengeance on [i]1Sa 30:14; Zep 2:4-5
them and punish them in my wrath. Then they will know that I am the LORD, when I take vengeance on
them.' "

A Prophecy Against Tyre

26 In the eleventh year, on the first day of the month, the word of the LORD came to me: 2 "Son of
man, because Tyre[j] has said of Jerusalem, 'Aha![k] The gate to the nations is broken, and its doors **26:2** [j]2Sa 5:11; Isa 23 [k]Eze 25:3
have swung open to me; now that she lies in ruins I will prosper,' 3 therefore this is what the Sovereign LORD
says: I am against you, O Tyre, and I will bring many nations against you, like the sea[l] casting up its waves. **26:3** [l]Isa 5:30; Jer 50:42; 51:42
4 They will destroy[m] the walls of Tyre[n] and pull down her towers; I will scrape away her rubble and make **26:4** [m]Isa 23:1, 11 [n]Am 1:10

25:8–11 The nations around Judah were addressed in clockwise order, starting with Ammon, east of the Jordan River, and moving south, then west and north.
25:8 See "Moab" on page 292. For "Seir," see "Edom" on page 1467.
25:9 Beth Jeshimoth was a town located in the plains of Moab. Baal Meon and Kiriathaim were Moabite towns mentioned in an inscribed monument of Mesha, king of Moab, discovered in 1868 in Dhiban, Jordan. See "The Mesha (Moabite) Stone" on page 530.
25:12–14 The Edomites (see "Edom" on p. 1467) had not just gloated over Judah's downfall in 586 B.C. but had participated in it. In Obadiah 10–14 Edom is accused of aiding Babylon, seizing Judah's wealth, cutting down the fugitives and handing over the survivors. Even though the Edomites, as descendants of Jacob's brother Esau, were related to the Israelites, their history demonstrated a lack of compassion for their brothers (cf. Nu 20:14–21). God would use his own people to execute judgment upon Edom.
25:13 Teman was a district near Petra in central Edom (see "Edom" on p. 1467), and Dedan was a tribe and territory in southern Edom.
25:15–17 Like the Edomites, the Philistines (see "The Archaeology of Philistia" on p. 370) were charged with trying to settle old scores. As longtime enemies of Israel, they sought to work out their "ancient hostility" (v. 15) by taking vengeance on God's chosen people. They, in turn, would experience God's retribution and would belatedly recognize his sovereign power. The Kerethites, related or perhaps identical to the Philistines, would be "cut off" (v. 16; *Kereth* sounds like the Hebrew word for "cut off").
25:16 In the Old Testament the Kerethites (1Sa 30:14), thought to be a Philistine tribe, are identified as Cretans; indeed, the Philistines are though to have originated in Crete. See also the note on Zephaniah 2:5.
26:1 The date is uncertain, as the number of the month is missing. The entire year dates from April 23, 587, to April 13, 586 B.C. The oracle must date from the end of that year, in the eleventh or the twelfth month (February 13 or March 15, 586). But there is a problem with these dates: This oracle describes Tyre's gloating over the destruction of Jerusalem (v. 2), yet Jerusalem did not fall until on or about July 18, 586 B.C. (see "The Last Days of Jerusalem" on p. 1197), and was not burned until August 14, 586—several months after the date given here for Tyre's celebration of the fact that Jerusalem "now . . . lies in ruins" (Eze 26:2). Many interpreters believe that the probable reading of the original Hebrew text was "In the eleventh month of the twelfth year, on the first day of the month," and that the words "month of the twelfth" must have been inadvertently omitted by a copyist (see "Textual Criticism" on p. 1151). The restored reading would yield the date February 3, 585, which would fit nicely the chronology in 33:21 (see also the note there).
26:2 For information on Tyre, see the note on Isaiah 23:1; see also "The Downfall of Tyre" on page 1345.

The Downfall of Tyre

EZEKIEL 26 The Phoenician city of Tyre ("Map 7"), in modern Lebanon, was an important commercial center located on the Mediterranean coast. It consisted of both a mainland city and an island city one half mile (.32 km) offshore, both well fortified.

Tyre was occupied by the middle of the third millennium B.C. It is first mentioned in the records of the Syrian city of **Ebla** ("Map 1") and again in the Egyptian execration texts of the eighteenth century B.C.;[1] it also appears in the **Amarna** Letters and in the Ugaritic texts. The city suffered from the invasions of the **Sea Peoples** around 1200 B.C. but became highly prosperous during the **Iron I**[2] Age. It sent its ships all over the world during the early first millennium and was instrumental in founding the city of Carthage in northern Africa ("Map 14") in the ninth century B.C. Hiram of Tyre provided workmen and cedar trees for the construction of David's palace in Jerusalem (2Sa 5:11) and also supplied cedars (1Ki 5:1–12) and craftsmen (1Ki 7:13–47) for Solomon's temple.

Ahab, king of the northern kingdom of Israel from approximately 874 to 853 B.C., married a princess from Tyre, the infamous Baal worshiper Jezebel (1Ki 16:31–32). Jezebel was the daughter of Ethbaal I, who seized the throne of Tyre in 887 B.C. and ruled there for 32 years. He had been a priest of Astarte, and Jezebel appears to have shared his devotion to the fertility gods of Canaan. This was a high point in Tyre's history; thus it is not surprising from a political point of view that the Israelite house of Omri desired to be on good terms with the Tyrians and so arranged the marriage between his son Ahab and Jezebel.

During the seventh century B.C. Tyre struggled to remain independent of Assyria. It was defeated at Ashkelon ("Map 7") when, with the support of Tirhakah of Egypt, it sought to resist Esarhaddon of Assyria.

Ezekiel wrote his prophecy against Tyre during the eleventh year of Jehoiakim's captivity (586 B.C.), predicting that Nebuchadnezzar would march against the city (Eze 26). Nebuchadnezzar did indeed turn his attention to the affluent city of Tyre following his destruction of Jerusalem and proceeded to besiege the city for 13 years, from 585 to 572 B.C. The Babylonians succeeded in capturing the mainland city but were unable, without a navy, to defeat the island fortress. Tyre was exhausted by the long struggle, however, and with the rise of the Persian Empire came under the domination of the Persians.

The next major event of Tyre's history occurred when Alexander the Great invaded the Persian Empire in 332 B.C. Probably because the city served as a center for the Persian fleet, Alexander attacked Tyre. Not wishing to undergo a long siege, as had Nebuchadnezzar before him, Alexander constructed a causeway (200–300 yards wide) from the mainland to the island fortress. Pulling down the buildings on the mainland, he repurposed the stones, timber and debris to build the causeway. Ezekiel had stated with respect to Tyre that God would "scrape away her rubble and make her a bare rock" (Eze 26:4) and "throw [her] stones, timber and rubble into the sea" (v. 12). Tyre was literally scraped bare like a rock. Today the famed causeway is an isthmus as a result of encroaching sand.

Alexander the Great routs the Persians in this carving from the Alexander sarcophagus, now in Istanbul, Turkey

Preserving Bible Times; © Dr. James C. Martin; permission of The Istanbul Archaeological Museum

With the death of Alexander, Tyre fell under the influence of the Greek kingdoms (first the **Ptolemies** of Egypt and then the **Seleucids** of Syria). She began to emerge again as an important trade city during the Seleucid period and once again exerted considerable influence over the Jewish state. By the time the Romans had assumed control of the eastern Mediterranean, Tyre was a major city of the region and a transportation center (see Ac 21:3–7). The region of Tyre and Sidon served as something of a retreat area for Jesus and his disciples (Mt 15:21), and people flocked from Tyre to hear his message (Mk 3:8).

[1]See "Curses and Imprecations" on page 883. [2]See "Archaeological Periods" chart on page xx in the front of this Bible.

her a bare rock. 5 Out in the sea[o] she will become a place to spread fishnets, for I have spoken, declares
the Sovereign LORD. She will become plunder[p] for the nations, 6 and her settlements on the mainland will
be ravaged by the sword. Then they will know that I am the LORD.
7 "For this is what the Sovereign LORD says: From the north I am going to bring against Tyre Nebu-
chadnezzar[a][q] king of Babylon, king of kings,[r] with horses and chariots,[s] with horsemen and a great army.
8 He will ravage your settlements on the mainland with the sword; he will set up siege works[t] against you,
build a ramp[u] up to your walls and raise his shields against you. 9 He will direct the blows of his batter-
ing rams against your walls and demolish your towers with his weapons. 10 His horses will be so many
that they will cover you with dust. Your walls will tremble at the noise of the war horses, wagons and
chariots[v] when he enters your gates as men enter a city whose walls have been broken through. 11 The
hoofs[w] of his horses will trample all your streets; he will kill your people with the sword, and your strong
pillars[x] will fall to the ground.[y] 12 They will plunder your wealth and loot your merchandise; they will
break down your walls and demolish your fine houses and throw your stones, timber and rubble into
the sea.[z] 13 I will put an end[a] to your noisy songs, and the music of your harps[b] will be heard no more.[c]
14 I will make you a bare rock, and you will become a place to spread fishnets. You will never be rebuilt,[d]
for I the LORD have spoken, declares the Sovereign LORD.
15 "This is what the Sovereign LORD says to Tyre: Will not the coastlands[e] tremble[f] at the sound of your
fall, when the wounded groan and the slaughter takes place in you? 16 Then all the princes of the coast will
step down from their thrones and lay aside their robes and take off their embroidered garments. Clothed[g]
with terror, they will sit on the ground, trembling[h] every moment, appalled[i] at you. 17 Then they will take
up a lament[j] concerning you and say to you:

" 'How you are destroyed, O city of renown,
peopled by men of the sea!
You were a power on the seas,
you and your citizens;
you put your terror
on all who lived there.[k]
18 Now the coastlands tremble
on the day of your fall;
the islands in the sea
are terrified at your collapse.'[l]

19 "This is what the Sovereign LORD says: When I make you a desolate city, like cities no longer inhab-
ited, and when I bring the ocean depths over you and its vast waters cover you,[m] 20 then I will bring you
down with those who go down to the pit,[n] to the people of long ago. I will make you dwell in the earth
below, as in ancient ruins, with those who go down to the pit, and you will not return or take your place[b]
in the land of the living.[o] 21 I will bring you to a horrible end and you will be no more. You will be sought,
but you will never again be found, declares the Sovereign LORD."[p]

A Lament for Tyre

27 The word of the LORD came to me: 2 "Son of man, take up a lament concerning Tyre. 3 Say to Tyre,
situated at the gateway to the sea,[q] merchant of peoples on many coasts, 'This is what the Sov-
ereign LORD says:

" 'You say, O Tyre,
"I am perfect in beauty.[r]"

26:5 [o]Eze 27:32 [p]Eze 29:19
26:7 [q]Jer 27:6 [r]Ezr 7:12; Da 2:37 [s]Eze 23:24; Na 2:3-4
26:8 [t]Jer 6:6 [u]Eze 21:22
26:10 [v]Jer 4:13
26:11 [w]Isa 5:28 [x]Jer 43:13 [y]Isa 26:5
26:12 [z]Isa 23:8; Eze 27:3-27; 28:8
26:13 [a]Jer 7:34 [b]Isa 14:11 [c]Jer 25:10; Rev 18:22
26:14 [d]Job 12:14; Mal 1:4
26:15 [e]Eze 27:35 [f]Jer 49:21
26:16 [g]Job 8:22 [h]Hos 11:10 [i]Eze 32:10
26:17 [j]Eze 19:1; 27:32 [k]Isa 14:12
26:18 [l]Isa 23:5; 41:5; Eze 27:35
26:19 [m]Isa 8:7-8
26:20 [n]Eze 32:18; Am 9:2; Jnh 2:2,6 [o]Eze 32:24,30
26:21 [p]Eze 27:36; 28:19; Rev 18:21
27:3 [q]ver 33 [r]Eze 28:2

[a] 7 Hebrew *Nebuchadrezzar,* of which *Nebuchadnezzar* is a variant; here and often in Ezekiel and Jeremiah [b] 20 Septuagint; Hebrew *return, and I will give glory*

26:7 Nebuchadnezzar (see "Nebuchadnezzar" on p. 571) would descend upon Tyre from the north, after first marching his army up the Euphrates River valley rather than across the Arabian Desert.
26:8 See "Siege Warfare" on page 465.
26:14 This prophecy was eventually fulfilled by Alexander's devastating siege in 332 B.C. (see "The Downfall of Tyre" on p. 1345).
26:16 The "princes of the coast" (called "kings" in 27:35) were probably trading partners with Tyre. Their actions in this verse demonstrate their grief and terror at Tyre's downfall.
For information on "robes" and "embroidered garments," see "Ancient Israelite Clothing and Jewelry" on p. 1059.
26:17 For "lament," see the note on 19:1.
26:19 "Ocean depths" refers to the primeval, chaotic mass—the "deep" of Genesis 1:2. Tyre's collapse into the sea is described in almost cosmic terms.
26:20 These are references to the shadowy underworld (see the note on Ps 6:5; see also "Sheol, Hades, Gehenna, the Abyss and Tartarus: Images of Hell" on p. 946).
27:2 For "lament," see the note on 19:1.

[4] Your domain was on the high seas;
your builders brought your beauty to perfection.
[5] They made all your timbers
27:5 sDt 3:9 — of pine trees from Senir[a];[s]
they took a cedar from Lebanon
to make a mast for you.
27:6 tNu 21:33; Jer 22:20; Zec 11:2 uGe 10:4; Isa 23:12 — [6] Of oaks[t] from Bashan
they made your oars;
of cypress wood[b] from the coasts of Cyprus[c][u]
they made your deck, inlaid with ivory.
[7] Fine embroidered linen from Egypt was your sail
and served as your banner;
27:7 vEx 25:4; Jer 10:9 — your awnings were of blue and purple[v]
from the coasts of Elishah.
27:8 wGe 10:18 x1Ki 9:27 — [8] Men of Sidon and Arvad[w] were your oarsmen;
your skilled men, O Tyre, were aboard as your
seamen.[x]
27:9 yJos 13:5; 1Ki 5:18 — [9] Veteran craftsmen of Gebal[d][y] were on board
as shipwrights to caulk your seams.
All the ships of the sea and their sailors
came alongside to trade for your wares.

27:10 zEze 38:5 aEze 30:5 — [10] " 'Men of Persia,[z] Lydia and Put[a]
served as soldiers in your army.
They hung their shields and helmets on your walls,
bringing you splendor.
[11] Men of Arvad and Helech
manned your walls on every side;
men of Gammad
were in your towers.
They hung their shields around your walls;
they brought your beauty to perfection.

27:12 bGe 10:4 cver 18,33 — [12] " 'Tarshish[b] did business with you because of your great wealth of goods;[c] they exchanged silver,
iron, tin and lead for your merchandise.
27:13 dGe 10:2; Isa 66:19; Eze 38:2 eRev 18:13 — [13] " 'Greece, Tubal and Meshech[d] traded with you; they exchanged slaves[e] and articles of bronze for
your wares.
27:14 fGe 10:3; Eze 38:6 — [14] " 'Men of Beth Togarmah[f] exchanged work horses, war horses and mules for your merchandise.

[a] 5 That is, Hermon [b] 6 Targum; the Masoretic Text has a different division of the consonants. [c] 6 Hebrew *Kittim*
[d] 9 That is, Byblos

27:4–11 The Phoenicians, confined to their coastal strip with the timber resources of the Lebanon range in their hinterland, were prompted by geography to exploit the sea and became, in the process, the great navigators of the ancient world—hence the symbolic vessel with ivory-inlaid decks and embroidered purple sails of Ezekiel's metaphor in his denunciation of Tyre. See "Phoenicia" on page 488 and "Seafaring in the Ancient World" on page 1473.

27:5 Mount Hermon ("Senir") marks the southern edge of the Anti-Lebanon range. A line drawn from Damascus to Tyre will pass through Mount Hermon at its middle point and will practially coincide with the northern boundary of Palestine. The ridge of Hermon is about 20 miles (33 km) long. It has three peaks, two of them rising over 9,000 feet (2,743 m). Hermon has had several names: the ancient Amorites called it "Shenir" or "Senir" (Dt 3:9; cf. Ps 29:6; Eze 27:5, where it is identified as a source of fir trees for Tyre); the Sidonians called it "Sirion" (Dt 3:9, although Ps 29:6 would separate the two); and the Arabs referred to it as "Jebel-esh-Sheikh" or "Mountain of the Old Man," perhaps because of its white head but more likely on account of its dignity. Here Ezekiel called it "Senir" and identified it as a source of fir trees for Tyre.

27:6 For "Bashan," see the note on 39:18.

Cyprus (Hebrew, *Kittim*) was originally the name of a town in today's southern Cyprus, then colonized by Phoenicia (see "Phoenicia" on p. 488).

27:7 Elishah was not only a city on the eastern side of Cyprus but also the oldest name for Cyprus.

27:8 Sidon was a harbor city 25 miles (40 km) north of Tyre (see "Sidon" on p. 1536).

Arvad was a Phoenician island-city off the Mediterranean coast north of Sidon.

27:9 Gebal refers to Byblos (see "Byblos" on p. 1349), an important ancient city on the coast between Sidon and Arvad.

27:10 For "Lydia" and "Put," see the note on Jeremiah 46:9.

27:11 For "Arvad," see the note on verse 8. "Helech" is Cilicia, the mountainous region in southeastern Asia Minor. "Gammad" is either northern Asia Minor or a coastal town near Arvad.

27:12 See "Where Was Tarshish?" on page 1475.

27:13 Tubal and Meshech were peoples and territories in Asia Minor (see the note on Isa 66:19).

27:14 Beth Togarmah was located in eastern Asia Minor, modern Armenia. Asia Minor was known for its horses.

15 “ ‘The men of Rhodes[a][g] traded with you, and many coastlands[h] were your customers; they paid
you with ivory[i] tusks and ebony.
16 “ ‘Aram[b][j] did business with you because of your many products; they exchanged turquoise,[k] pur-
ple fabric, embroidered work, fine linen, coral and rubies for your merchandise.
17 “ ‘Judah and Israel traded with you; they exchanged wheat from Minnith[l] and confections,[c] honey,
oil and balm for your wares.
18 “ ‘Damascus,[m] because of your many products and great wealth of goods, did business with you in
wine from Helbon and wool from Zahar.
19 “ ‘Danites and Greeks from Uzal bought your merchandise; they exchanged wrought iron, cassia
and calamus for your wares.
20 “ ‘Dedan traded in saddle blankets with you.
21 “ ‘Arabia and all the princes of Kedar[n] were your customers; they did business with you in lambs,
rams and goats.
22 “ ‘The merchants of Sheba[o] and Raamah traded with you; for your merchandise they exchanged
the finest of all kinds of spices[p] and precious stones, and gold.
23 “ ‘Haran,[q] Canneh and Eden[r] and merchants of Sheba, Asshur and Kilmad traded with you. 24 In
your marketplace they traded with you beautiful garments, blue fabric, embroidered work and multicol-
ored rugs with cords twisted and tightly knotted.

25 “ ‘The ships of Tarshish[s] serve
as carriers for your wares.
You are filled with heavy cargo
in the heart of the sea.
26 Your oarsmen take you
out to the high seas.
But the east wind[t] will break you to pieces
in the heart of the sea.
27 Your wealth,[u] merchandise and wares,
your mariners, seamen and shipwrights,
your merchants and all your soldiers,
and everyone else on board
will sink into the heart of the sea
on the day of your shipwreck.
28 The shorelands will quake[v]
when your seamen cry out.
29 All who handle the oars
will abandon their ships;
the mariners and all the seamen
will stand on the shore.

27:15 [g]Ge 10:7 [h]Jer 25:22 [i]1Ki 10:22; Rev 18:12
27:16 [j]Jdg 10:6; Isa 7:1-8 [k]Eze 28:13
27:17 [l]Jdg 11:33
27:18 [m]Ge 14:15; Eze 47:16-18
27:21 [n]Ge 25:13; Isa 60:7
27:22 [o]Ge 10:7, 28; 1Ki 10:1-2; Isa 60:6 [p]Ge 43:11
27:23 [q]2Ki 19:12 [r]Isa 37:12
27:25 [s]Isa 2:16 *fn*
27:26 [t]Ps 48:7; Jer 18:17
27:27 [u]Pr 11:4
27:28 [v]Eze 26:15

[a] *15* Septuagint; Hebrew *Dedan* [b] *16* Most Hebrew manuscripts; some Hebrew manuscripts and Syriac *Edom*
[c] *17* The meaning of the Hebrew for this word is uncertain.

27:15 Rhodes, a large island off the southwestern coast of Asia Minor, served as the gateway to the Aegean islands and was an early major trading center (see Ac 21:1).
27:16 See “Syria/Aram” on page 534.
27:17 Minnith was an Ammonite town, apparently famous for its wheat.

“Balm,” referring to gum or oil from one of several plants, was a product of Gilead (see the note on Jer 8:22).
27:18 See “Damascus” on page 1087. Helbon was a town north of Damascus, still in existence and still a wine-making center. Zahar is modern Sahra, an area northwest of Damascus where the grazing of livestock is still common today.
27:19 Uzal may be a reference to Yemen or to the area between Haran and the Tigris.

Cassia (similar to the cinnamon tree) and calamus (see the note on SS 4:14) are aromatic spices.
27:20 For “Dedan,” see the note on 25:13.
27:21 “Arabia” and “Kedar” (see the notes on Isa 21:16 and Jer 49:28) refer in general to the nomadic tribes from Aram to the Arabian Desert.
27:22 See “Sheba” on page 498. Raamah was a city in southern Arabia.
27:23 Haran was a city east of Carchemish, in modern eastern Turkey (see “Haran” on p. 47). In ancient times it was a center for trade, as well as for the worship of the moon god, Sin. The locations of Canneh (often identified with Calneh) and Kilmad are uncertain; both were presumably in Mesopotamia. Eden was a district south of Haran. For “Sheba,” see the article on page 498. “Asshur” can mean the city, the country (Assyria) or the people (Assyrians). The city, south of Nineveh, probably gave its name to the country.
27:25 See “Where Was Tarshish?” on page 1475.
27:26 For “east wind,” see the note on 17:10.

[30] They will raise their voice
and cry bitterly over you;
they will sprinkle dust[w] on their heads
and roll[x] in ashes.[y]
[31] They will shave their heads because of you
and will put on sackcloth.

27:30 [w]2Sa 1:2 [x]Jer 6:26 [y]Rev 18:18-19

27:30–31 These actions were all signs of mourning (see "Sackcloth and Ashes: Rituals of Lamentation" on p. 820).

ARCHAEOLOGICAL SITES

BYBLOS

EZEKIEL 27 As one of the few natural harbors on the coastline of the Levant (Syria-Palestine), Byblos (also called Gebal; see "Map 1" and "Map 5") was an important trade and religious center in antiquity. First settled during the sixth millennium B.C., this ancient port city was located at the foot of Mount Lebanon and had access to the abundant cedar groves of the western flank of the range.[1]

Lumber for building materials was especially in demand in Egypt. Oils and resins from the trees were used for mummification, as well as for cosmetic and medicinal purposes. The shipping of lumber followed sea lanes along the coast between Byblos and the Nile delta. In return, Byblos received commodities such as metals, **papyrus** reed and perfumes. With its import of Egyptian papyrus reed, the city became famous for the manufacturing of paper and rope during the **Iron Age**.[2] This economic partnership with Egypt began during the late fourth through the early third millenniums B.C. and reached its high point during the **Old Kingdom** (c. 2700–2100 B.C.) and **Middle Kingdom** (c. 1990–1786 B.C.) periods. The city's economic network was not limited to Egypt, however. Trade extended to the Mediterranean, the southern Levant, Syria, **Mesopotamia** and even into **Anatolia** and modern-day Iran.

During the **Iron Age** (1200–586 B.C.) Tyre and Sidon's economic domination eclipsed their counterpart to the north.[3] Byblos was reduced to functioning as a supplier of lumber and craftsmanship. When Solomon commissioned his building projects in partnership with Hiram of Tyre, stonecutters from Byblos were subcontracted for **ashlar** masonry (cf. 1Ki 5:18; 6:7).[4]

The great empires of the first millennium B.C. took notice of Byblos's value as a supplier of lumber. In their ruthless campaigns into the region later known as Palestine, the **Assyrians** and **Babylonians** exacted tribute from Byblos in the form of timber. The **Persian** and Roman Empires later secured the area as a source of supplies for maintaining their powerful navies.

Classical and postclassical building activities at the site virtually destroyed crucial occupational layers, including the **Late Bronze** and Iron Age levels. However, rich artifactual deposits and temple architecture provide a window into the character of Byblos as a religious center and a repository of **Phoenician** religious traditions. Enclosed within a fortification wall, the **acropolis** contained several religious buildings:

- The Balaat Gebal temple, dedicated to the goddess "Lady of Byblos," was first erected around 3100 B.C., and a royal inscription from Byblos provides evidence that a temple to Balaat was still present during the fifth century B.C.
- The Obelisk temple complex (early second millennium B.C.) contained over 26 votive pillars within its precinct. Similar religious pillars would later be prohibited for the worship of **Yahweh** (cf. Dt. 12:3–4).
- Excavators discovered an abundance of votive offerings in the form of golden axes, seals, amulets, figurines and inscribed offerings. These were placed into jars within temple foundations or in sacred rooms.
- A **Middle Bronze Age** royal **necropolis** also attests to the affluence of the city. We know from documentary sources that in **Roman times** the city retained its status as a pilgrim center for the cult of Adonis.

Gradual deforestation and the closing of pagan temples (late fourth century A.D.) probably contributed to Byblos's ultimate decline.

[1]See "Cedars of Lebanon" on page 1043. [2]See "Archaeological Periods" chart on page xx in the front of this Bible. [3]See "The Downfall of Tyre" on page 1345 and "Sidon" on page 1536. [4]See "Solomon's Temple and Other Ancient Temples" on page 620.

They will weep[z] over you with anguish of soul
and with bitter mourning.[a]
32 As they wail and mourn over you,
they will take up a lament[b] concerning you:
"Who was ever silenced like Tyre,
surrounded by the sea?"
33 When your merchandise went out on the seas,
you satisfied many nations;
with your great wealth[c] and your wares
you enriched the kings of the earth.
34 Now you are shattered by the sea
in the depths of the waters;
your wares and all your company
have gone down with you.[d]
35 All who live in the coastlands[e]
are appalled at you;
their kings shudder with horror
and their faces are distorted with fear.
36 The merchants among the nations hiss at you;[f]
you have come to a horrible end
and will be no more.[g]' "

27:31 [z]Isa 16:9 [a]Isa 22:12; Eze 7:18
27:32 [b]Eze 26:17
27:33 [c]ver 12; Eze 28:4-5
27:34 [d]Zec 9:4
27:35 [e]Eze 26:15
27:36 [f]Jer 18:16; 19:8; 49:17; 50:13; Zep 2:15 [g]Ps 37:10,36; Eze 26:21

A Prophecy Against the King of Tyre

28 The word of the LORD came to me: 2"Son of man, say to the ruler of Tyre, 'This is what the Sovereign LORD says:

" 'In the pride of your heart
you say, "I am a god;
I sit on the throne[h] of a god
in the heart of the seas."
But you are a man and not a god,
though you think you are as wise as a god.[i]
3 Are you wiser than Daniel[a]?[j]
Is no secret hidden from you?
4 By your wisdom and understanding
you have gained wealth for yourself
and amassed gold and silver
in your treasuries.[k]
5 By your great skill in trading
you have increased your wealth,
and because of your wealth
your heart has grown proud.[l]

6" 'Therefore this is what the Sovereign LORD says:

" 'Because you think you are wise,
as wise as a god,
7 I am going to bring foreigners against you,
the most ruthless of nations;[m]
they will draw their swords against your beauty and wisdom
and pierce your shining splendor.

28:2 [h]Isa 14:13 [i]Ps 9:20; 82:6-7; Isa 31:3; 2Th 2:4
28:3 [j]Da 1:20; 5:11-12
28:4 [k]Zec 9:3
28:5 [l]Job 31:25; Ps 52:7; 62:10; Hos 12:8; 13:6
28:7 [m]Eze 30:11; 31:12; 32:12; Hab 1:6

[a] 3 Or *Danel*; the Hebrew spelling may suggest a person other than the prophet Daniel.

28:2 The "ruler of Tyre" may refer to the city of Tyre as a ruler or to Ethbaal II, Tyre's king (see v. 12)—not to be confused with Ethbaal I (see 1Ki 16:31).

28:3 For "Daniel," see the note on 14:14.

28:7 "Foreigners" is a reference to the Babylonians.

28:8 [n]Eze 32:30 [o]Eze 27:27

[8] They will bring you down to the pit,[n]
and you will die a violent death
in the heart of the seas.[o]
[9] Will you then say, "I am a god,"
in the presence of those who kill you?
You will be but a man, not a god,
in the hands of those who slay you.
[10] You will die the death of the uncircumcised[p]
at the hands of foreigners.

28:10 [p]Eze 31:18; 32:19,24

I have spoken, declares the Sovereign LORD.' "

28:12 [q]Eze 19:1 [r]Eze 27:2-4

[11] The word of the LORD came to me: [12] "Son of man, take up a lament[q] concerning the king of Tyre
and say to him: 'This is what the Sovereign LORD says:

" 'You were the model of perfection,
full of wisdom and perfect in beauty.[r]
[13] You were in Eden,[s]
the garden of God;[t]
every precious stone adorned you:
ruby, topaz and emerald,
chrysolite, onyx and jasper,
sapphire,[a] turquoise[u] and beryl.[b]
Your settings and mountings[c] were made of gold;
on the day you were created they were prepared.
[14] You were anointed[v] as a guardian cherub,[w]
for so I ordained you.
You were on the holy mount of God;
you walked among the fiery stones.
[15] You were blameless in your ways
from the day you were created
till wickedness was found in you.
[16] Through your widespread trade
you were filled with violence,[x]
and you sinned.
So I drove you in disgrace from the mount of God,
and I expelled you, O guardian cherub,[y]
from among the fiery stones.
[17] Your heart became proud[z]
on account of your beauty,
and you corrupted your wisdom
because of your splendor.
So I threw you to the earth;
I made a spectacle of you before kings.
[18] By your many sins and dishonest trade
you have desecrated your sanctuaries.
So I made a fire come out from you,
and it consumed you,

28:13 [s]Ge 2:8 [t]Eze 31:8-9 [u]Eze 27:16

28:14 [v]Ex 30:26; 40:9 [w]Ex 25:17-20

28:16 [x]Hab 2:17 [y]Ge 3:24

28:17 [z]Eze 31:10

[a] 13 Or *lapis lazuli* [b] 13 The precise identification of some of these precious stones is uncertain. [c] 13 The meaning of the Hebrew for this phrase is uncertain.

28:8 The "pit" is a metaphor for the grave (see the note on Ps 6:5).
28:10 The term "uncircumcised" is used here in the sense of barbarian or uncouth. The Phoenicians (see "Phoenicia" on p. 488), like the Israelites, Arabs and Egyptians, practiced circumcision.
28:12 For "lament," see the note on 19:1.
28:13 Ezekiel used imagery of the creation and the fall as he pictured the king as a fully clothed priest, ordained (v. 14) to guard God's holy place. The nine stones were among the twelve worn by the priest (Ex 28:17–20; see "Precious Stones of the Biblical World" on p. 1156).
28:14 The account in Genesis 3 has cherubim (plural) stationed at the border of the garden after the expulsion of Adam and Eve.
For the phrase "holy mount of God," see "Zaphon, Olympus, Sinai and Zion: The Mountain of God" on page 843.

and I reduced you to ashes[a] on the ground
in the sight of all who were watching.
19 All the nations who knew you
are appalled at you;
you have come to a horrible end
and will be no more.[b] ' "

A Prophecy Against Sidon

20 The word of the LORD came to me: 21 "Son of man, set your face against[c] Sidon;[d] prophesy against
her 22 and say: 'This is what the Sovereign LORD says:

" 'I am against you, O Sidon,
and I will gain glory[e] within you.
They will know that I am the LORD,
when I inflict punishment[f] on her
and show myself holy within her.
23 I will send a plague upon her
and make blood flow in her streets.
The slain will fall within her,
with the sword against her on every side.
Then they will know that I am the LORD.[g]

24 " 'No longer will the people of Israel have malicious neighbors who are painful briers and sharp
thorns.[h] Then they will know that I am the Sovereign LORD.

25 " 'This is what the Sovereign LORD says: When I gather[i] the people of Israel from the nations where
they have been scattered,[j] I will show myself holy[k] among them in the sight of the nations. Then they
will live in their own land, which I gave to my servant Jacob.[l] 26 They will live there in safety[m] and will
build houses and plant vineyards; they will live in safety when I inflict punishment on all their neigh-
bors who maligned them. Then they will know that I am the LORD their God.[n] ' "

A Prophecy Against Egypt

29 In the tenth year, in the tenth month on the twelfth day, the word of the LORD came to me:[o] 2 "Son
of man, set your face against Pharaoh king of Egypt[p] and prophesy against him and against all
Egypt.[q] 3 Speak to him and say: 'This is what the Sovereign LORD says:

" 'I am against you, Pharaoh[r] king of Egypt,
you great monster[s] lying among your streams.
You say, "The Nile is mine;
I made it for myself."
4 But I will put hooks[t] in your jaws
and make the fish of your streams stick to your scales.
I will pull you out from among your streams,
with all the fish sticking to your scales.[u]
5 I will leave you in the desert,
you and all the fish of your streams.
You will fall on the open field
and not be gathered or picked up.

28:18 [a]Mal 4:3
28:19 [b]Jer 51:64; Eze 26:21; 27:36
28:21 [c]Eze 6:2 [d]Ge 10:15; Jer 25:22
28:22 [e]Eze 39:13 [f]Eze 30:19
28:23 [g]Eze 38:22
28:24 [h]Nu 33:55; Jos 23:13; Eze 2:6
28:25 [i]Ps 106:47; Jer 32:37 [j]Isa 11:12 [k]Eze 20:41 [l]Jer 23:8; Eze 11:17; 34:27; 37:25
28:26 [m]Jer 23:6 [n]Isa 65:21; Jer 32:15; Eze 38:8; Am 9:14-15
29:1 [o]ver 17; Eze 26:1
29:2 [p]Jer 25:19 [q]Isa 19:1-17; Jer 46:2; Eze 30:1-26; 31:1-18; 32:1-32
29:3 [r]Jer 44:30 [s]Ps 74:13; Isa 27:1; Eze 32:2
29:4 [t]2Ki 19:28 [u]Eze 38:4

28:21 See "Sidon" on page 1536.
28:26 Houses and vineyards were representative of the basic necessities of the good life (see "The Israelite Town and Home" on p. 1205).
29:1 The date was January 7, 587 B.C.
29:2 "Pharaoh" refers to Hophra (see "Hophra, King of Egypt" on p. 1266).
29:3 The "great monster" is probably the crocodile (see the note on Ps 74:13–15).

Egypt's "streams" include the Nile delta and Egypt's many irrigation canals.

29:5 Being left as "food to the beasts" would have been particularly frustrating to the pharaoh in terms of his glorified hopes for an afterlife, as symbolized by the pyramids and expressed in the Egyptian "Book of the Dead."
29:6 Hophra had been a "staff of reed" in that he had sent troops to aid Zedekiah when Nebuchadnezzar had invaded Judah in 588 B.C. This action had resulted in Nebuchadnezzar's temporarily lifting the siege of Jerusalem in order to deal with the Egyptian threat (Jer 37:5,11). But the relief for Judah was short-lived; Nebuchadnezzar quickly drove off the Egyptians and returned to capture Jerusalem.

I will give you as food
to the beasts of the earth and the birds of the air.[v]
6 Then all who live in Egypt will know that I am the LORD.

" 'You have been a staff of reed[w] for the house of Israel. 7 When they grasped you with their hands, you
splintered[x] and you tore open their shoulders; when they leaned on you, you broke and their backs were
wrenched.[a][y]
8 " 'Therefore this is what the Sovereign LORD says: I will bring a sword against you and kill your
men and their animals.[z] 9 Egypt will become a desolate wasteland. Then they will know that I am the
LORD.
" 'Because you said, "The Nile is mine; I made it,[a]" 10 therefore I am against you and against your
streams, and I will make the land of Egypt a ruin and a desolate waste from Migdol to Aswan,[b] as far as
the border of Cush.[b] 11 No foot of man or animal will pass through it; no one will live there for forty years.[c]
12 I will make the land of Egypt desolate among devastated lands, and her cities will lie desolate forty
years among ruined cities. And I will disperse the Egyptians among the nations and scatter them through
the countries.[d]
13 " 'Yet this is what the Sovereign LORD says: At the end of forty years I will gather the Egyptians from
the nations where they were scattered. 14 I will bring them back from captivity and return them to Up-
per Egypt,[c][e] the land of their ancestry. There they will be a lowly[f] kingdom. 15 It will be the lowliest of
kingdoms and will never again exalt itself above the other nations.[g] I will make it so weak that it will
never again rule over the nations. 16 Egypt will no longer be a source of confidence[h] for the people of Is-
rael but will be a reminder of their sin in turning to her for help. Then they will know that I am the Sov-
ereign LORD.[i] ' "

17 In the twenty-seventh year, in the first month on the first day, the word of the LORD came to me:[j]
18 "Son of man, Nebuchadnezzar[k] king of Babylon drove his army in a hard campaign against Tyre; ev-
ery head was rubbed bare[l] and every shoulder made raw. Yet he and his army got no reward from the
campaign he led against Tyre. 19 Therefore this is what the Sovereign LORD says: I am going to give Egypt
to Nebuchadnezzar king of Babylon, and he will carry off its wealth. He will loot and plunder the land as
pay for his army.[m] 20 I have given him Egypt as a reward for his efforts because he and his army did it for
me, declares the Sovereign LORD.[n]
21 "On that day I will make a horn[d][o] grow for the house of Israel, and I will open your mouth[p] among
them. Then they will know that I am the LORD.[q]"

A Lament for Egypt

30 The word of the LORD came to me: 2 "Son of man, prophesy and say: 'This is what the Sovereign
LORD says:

" 'Wail[r] and say,
"Alas for that day!"
3 For the day is near,[s]
the day of the LORD[t] is near—
a day of clouds,
a time of doom for the nations.

29:5 [v]Jer 7:33; 34:20; Eze 32:4-6; 39:4
29:6 [w]2Ki 18:21; Isa 36:6
29:7 [x]Isa 36:6 [y]Eze 17:15-17
29:8 [z]Eze 14:17; 32:11-13
29:9 [a]Eze 30:7-8, 13-19
29:10 [b]Eze 30:6
29:11 [c]Eze 32:13
29:12 [d]Jer 46:19; Eze 30:7,23,26
29:14 [e]Eze 30:14 [f]Eze 17:14
29:15 [g]Zec 10:11
29:16 [h]Isa 36:4,6 [i]Isa 30:2; Hos 8:13
29:17 [j]Eze 24:1
29:18 [k]Jer 27:6; Eze 26:7-8 [l]Jer 48:37
29:19 [m]Jer 43:10-13; Eze 30:4,10,24-25
29:20 [n]Isa 10:6-7; 45:1; Jer 25:9
29:21 [o]Ps 132:17 [p]Eze 33:22 [q]Eze 24:27
30:2 [r]Isa 13:6
30:3 [s]Eze 7:7; Joel 2:1,11; Ob 1:15 [t]ver 18; Eze 7:12,19

[a] *7* Syriac (see also Septuagint and Vulgate); Hebrew *and you caused their backs to stand* [b] *10* That is, the upper Nile region [c] *14* Hebrew *to Pathros* [d] *21* *Horn* here symbolizes strength.

29:8 The "sword" is Nebuchadnezzar (see the note on 21:3).
29:10 Migdol was probably a city in northern Egypt and Aswan a town in southern Egypt. "From Migdol to Aswan" (see 30:6) probably indicated all of Egypt, just as "from Dan to Beersheba" signified all of Israel (see, e.g., Jdg 20:1 and its note).
29:11 "Forty years" was sometimes used symbolically to signify a long and difficult period.
29:14 For "Upper Egypt," see the note on Isaiah 11:11.
29:17 The date was April 26, 571 B.C.
29:18 Nebuchadnezzar besieged Tyre for 13 years, from 585 to 572 B.C. (see "The Downfall of Tyre" on p. 1345 and "Siege Warfare" on p. 465).
The phrase "every head was rubbed bare" probably refers to the loss of hair that resulted from the wearing of leather helmets. It has also been posited that hair loss was believed to have been the result of hard work (see "Beards and Hairstyles in the Biblical World" on p. 1084).
30:1 No date is given, but this third oracle against Egypt was probably given between January and April of 587 B.C., while Jerusalem was under siege.

ARCHAEOLOGICAL SITES

THEBES

EZEKIEL 30 For much of Egyptian history, Thebes was the leading city of southern Egypt.[1] Located on the eastern bank of the Nile some 450 miles (726 km) south of Cairo, Thebes was the center of worship for the god Amon, "king of the gods." The city reached its zenith between 1500 and 1000 B.C., when it functioned as the center of a vast empire and ranked as one of the wealthiest and most famous cities in the ancient world. Ancient Thebes, located at modern Luxor and Karnak, comprises the largest collection of antiquities in the world, covering an area of 16 to 18 square miles (26 to 29 sq km). The magnificent temple of Amon, located on the eastern bank of the Nile at Karnak, is the largest temple ever constructed and, until modern times, held the distinction of being the largest columned building in the world. Its magnificent columns, 34 feet (10 m) in circumference, soar to a height of 69 feet (21 m).

Pharaohs recorded their achievements on the temple walls. One of these inscriptions, the Bubastite Portal, constitutes Pharaoh Sheshonk's (Biblical Shishak's) record of his campaign against Judah and Israel in 925 B.C. and can be compared with 1 Kings 14:25–26 and 2 Chronicles 12:2–9.[2] On the western side of the Nile is the royal **necropolis**, including numerous mortuary temples and tombs of the kings and queens of the **New Kingdom** (Eighteenth–Twentieth Dynasties, c. 1570–1070 B.C.). Here may be found, for example, the beautiful mortuary temple of Queen Hatshepsut (c. 1479–1457 B.C.) and the famous tomb of Tutankhamen (c. 1336–1327). Another important mortuary temple is that of Rameses III (c. 1184–1153 B.C.). This pharaoh recorded on its walls his 1176 B.C. victory over the **Sea Peoples**, among whom were the Philistines, who settled on the southwestern coast of the region now known as Palestine. Although the New Kingdom pharaohs were the major builders of Thebes and Karnak, other pharaohs also sought to contribute to their glory. The Twenty-sixth (Nubian) Dynasty sought to revive classical Egyptian culture and further enhanced the splendor of the temple of Amon at Karnak in the late eighth century B.C.

Nahum 3:8–10 vividly describes the **Assyrian** attack on Thebes that took place around 663 B.C., and the prophets Jeremiah and Ezekiel both wrote words of condemnation against the city, a center of paganism. Jeremiah, in about 600 B.C., declared that God would punish Amon of Thebes, the pharaoh and the gods of Egypt: They would be given into the hand of **Nebuchadnezzar**, king of **Babylon** (Jer 46:25–26; cf. Eze 30:10–19).[3] A fragmentary clay tablet attests to an attack upon Egypt by Nebuchadnezzar in approximately 569 B.C. The Persians also sacked the city under Cambyses (c. 525 B.C.) and Artaxerxes III (c. 342).[4] During the **Ptolemaic** period, Thebes was the focal point for Egyptian resistance to Ptolemaic (Greek) rule,[5] and three separate rebellions were suppressed. By the **Roman period** the glory of Thebes had come to an end.

[1]See "A Breakdown of Ancient Egyptian History" on page 104, and locate "Thebes" on the "Egypt" map on page 346. [2]See "The Campaign of Shishak" on page 635. [3]See "Nebuchadnezzar" on page 571. [4]See "Ancient Persian History Through Darius" on page 717. [5]See "The Ptolemies" on page 1399.

Temple at Egyptian Thebes
Preserving Bible Times; © Dr. James C. Martin

4 A sword will come against Egypt,
and anguish will come upon Cush.[a]
When the slain fall in Egypt,
her wealth will be carried away
and her foundations torn down.[u]

5 Cush and Put,[v] Lydia and all Arabia, Libya[b] and the people[w] of the covenant land will fall by the sword
along with Egypt.

6 " 'This is what the LORD says:

" 'The allies of Egypt will fall
and her proud strength will fail.
From Migdol to Aswan[x]
they will fall by the sword within her,
declares the Sovereign LORD.
7 " 'They will be desolate
among desolate lands,
and their cities will lie
among ruined cities.[y]
8 Then they will know that I am the LORD,
when I set fire to Egypt
and all her helpers are crushed.

9 " 'On that day messengers will go out from me in ships to frighten Cush[z] out of her complacency.
Anguish[a] will take hold of them on the day of Egypt's doom, for it is sure to come.[b]

10 " 'This is what the Sovereign LORD says:

" 'I will put an end to the hordes of Egypt
by the hand of Nebuchadnezzar king of Babylon.[c]
11 He and his army—the most ruthless of nations[d]—
will be brought in to destroy the land.
They will draw their swords against Egypt
and fill the land with the slain.
12 I will dry up[e] the streams of the Nile[f]
and sell the land to evil men;
by the hand of foreigners
I will lay waste the land and everything in it.

I the LORD have spoken.

13 " 'This is what the Sovereign LORD says:

" 'I will destroy the idols[g]
and put an end to the images in Memphis.[c][h]
No longer will there be a prince in Egypt,[i]
and I will spread fear throughout the land.
14 I will lay[j] waste Upper Egypt,[d]
set fire to Zoan[k]
and inflict punishment on Thebes.[e][l]
15 I will pour out my wrath on Pelusium,[f]
the stronghold of Egypt,
and cut off the hordes of Thebes.

30:4 [u]Eze 29:19
30:5 [v]Eze 27:10 [w]Jer 25:20
30:6 [x]Eze 29:10
30:7 [y]Eze 29:12
30:9 [z]Isa 18:1-2 [a]Isa 23:5 [b]Eze 32:9-10
30:10 [c]Eze 29:19
30:11 [d]Eze 28:7
30:12 [e]Isa 19:6 [f]Eze 29:9
30:13 [g]Jer 43:12 [h]Isa 19:13 [i]Zec 10:11
30:14 [j]Eze 29:14 [k]Ps 78:12,43 [l]Jer 46:25

[a] *4* That is, the upper Nile region; also in verses 5 and 9 [b] *5* Hebrew *Cub* [c] *13* Hebrew *Noph*; also in verse 16 [d] *14* Hebrew *waste Pathros* [e] *14* Hebrew *No*; also in verses 15 and 16 [f] *15* Hebrew *Sin*; also in verse 16

30:4 The "sword" is Nebuchadnezzar (see the note on 21:3).
30:5 For "Cush," "Put" and "Lydia," see the note on Jeremiah 46:9.
30:6 See the note on 29:10.
30:11 "The most ruthless of nations" was a common descriptor for the Babylonians, who were known for their cruelty.
30:13 See "Memphis" on page 1270.
30:14 For "Upper Egypt," see the note on Isaiah 11:11. For "Zoan," see the note on Isaiah 19:11. See also "Thebes" on page 1354.
30:15 Pelusium was a fortress in the eastern delta region of the Nile.

[16]I will set fire to Egypt;
Pelusium will writhe in agony.
Thebes will be taken by storm;
Memphis will be in constant distress.
[17]The young men of Heliopolis[a][m] and Bubastis[b]
will fall by the sword,
and the cities themselves will go into captivity.
[18]Dark will be the day at Tahpanhes
when I break the yoke of Egypt;[n]
there her proud strength will come to an end.
She will be covered with clouds,
and her villages will go into captivity.[o]
[19]So I will inflict punishment on Egypt,
and they will know that I am the LORD.' "

[20]In the eleventh year, in the first month on the seventh day, the word of the LORD came to me:[p] [21]"Son
of man, I have broken the arm[q] of Pharaoh king of Egypt. It has not been bound up for healing[r] or put
in a splint so as to become strong enough to hold a sword. [22]Therefore this is what the Sovereign LORD
says: I am against Pharaoh king of Egypt.[s] I will break both his arms, the good arm as well as the bro-
ken one, and make the sword fall from his hand.[t] [23]I will disperse the Egyptians among the nations and
scatter them through the countries.[u] [24]I will strengthen[v] the arms of the king of Babylon and put my
sword[w] in his hand, but I will break the arms of Pharaoh, and he will groan before him like a mortally
wounded man. [25]I will strengthen the arms of the king of Babylon, but the arms of Pharaoh will fall limp.
Then they will know that I am the LORD, when I put my sword into the hand of the king of Babylon and
he brandishes it against Egypt. [26]I will disperse the Egyptians among the nations and scatter them
through the countries. Then they will know that I am the LORD.[x]"

30:17 [m]Ge 41:45
30:18 [n]Lev 26:13 [o]ver 3
30:20 [p]Eze 26:1; 29:17; 31:1
30:21 [q]Jer 48:25 [r]Jer 30:13; 46:11
30:22 [s]Jer 46:25 [t]Ps 37:17
30:23 [u]Eze 29:12
30:24 [v]Zec 10:6, 12 [w]Eze 21:14; Zep 2:12
30:26 [x]Eze 29:12

A Cedar in Lebanon

31 In the eleventh year,[y] in the third month on the first day, the word of the LORD came to me:[z] [2]"Son
of man, say to Pharaoh king of Egypt and to his hordes:

" 'Who can be compared with you in majesty?
[3]Consider Assyria, once a cedar in Lebanon,
with beautiful branches overshadowing the forest;
it towered on high,
its top above the thick foliage.[a]
[4]The waters nourished it,
deep springs made it grow tall;
their streams flowed
all around its base
and sent their channels
to all the trees of the field.
[5]So it towered higher
than all the trees of the field;
its boughs increased
and its branches grew long,
spreading because of abundant waters.[b]

31:1 [y]Jer 52:5 [z]Eze 30:20
31:3 [a]Isa 10:34
31:5 [b]Eze 17:5

[a] 17 Hebrew *Awen* (or *On*) [b] 17 Hebrew *Pi Beseth*

30:17 Heliopolis (meaning "city of the sun") was the Greek name for On, located 6 miles (9.7 km) northeast of Cairo. Bubastis, at one time the capital of "Lower" (northern) Egypt, was located 40 miles (65 km) northeast of Cairo.
30:18 Tahpanhes was located in extreme northeastern Egypt.
30:20 The date was April 29, 587 B.C.
30:21 This refers to Pharaoh Hophra's defeat by Nebuchadnezzar during the previous year (see the note on 29:6).
31:1 The date was June 21, 587 B.C.
31:3 Although Assyria had once been a great empire, comparable to a cedar of Lebanon (see "Cedars of Lebanon" on p. 1043), it ultimately passed from history after it was destroyed by the Babylonians (see "Assyria From the Neo-Assyrian Period Forward" on p. 1502).
31:4 "Waters" refers here to the Tigris and Euphrates Rivers.

[6] All the birds of the air
nested in its boughs,
all the beasts of the field
gave birth under its branches;
all the great nations
31:6 [c]Eze 17:23; Mt 13:32 lived in its shade.[c]
[7] It was majestic in beauty,
with its spreading boughs,

CULTURAL AND HISTORICAL NOTES

Trees of Ancient Israel

Three-trunked olive tree
Preserving Bible Times; © Dr. James C. Martin

The majestic cedar grows upwards of 115 feet (35 m) and may live as long as 500 years, or 12 1/2 generations![1]

It is no wonder, therefore, that the oak and terebinth were often associated with the divine presence and marked important sites of worship, especially for the patriarchs (Ge 13:18; 18:1).[2] In fact, the trees themselves were often considered sacred objects of worship. They were sometimes planted beside altars in **Canaanite** temple courtyards and were associated with El's consort (partner), the goddess Asherah (cf. Dt 7:5; 2Ki 17:16).[3] The powerful cedar was also frequently planted in palace and temple gardens, symbolizing both king and deity in its grandeur and life-giving benefit to the land (see Ps 104:16; Isa 51:3; Eze 28:13; 31:8–9). Consequently, it became the ideal symbol for great rulers

EZEKIEL 31 Trees in ancient Israel, including its many native species of oak, pine and terebinth, as well as imported cedars from Lebanon, were precious natural resources highly valued for their use in construction and manufacturing, food production, environmental protection (such as erosion prevention) and the production of oils, perfumes, spices, rope and other by-products. Besides their great commercial value, some were prized for their symbolic significance, particularly because of their awe-inspiring size and strength and the sense of permanence they evoked. For example, some oak species in the region reach heights of over 80 feet (24 m) and live as long as 300 years.

and their empires, such as the **Assyrian** Empire, which once cast its shadow over Israel and the rest of the ancient Near East, reaching its apex in the early seventh century B.C. The imposing Assyrian Empire, however, was itself felled abruptly within a few years' time (Eze 31).[4]

[1]See "Cedars of Lebanon" on page 1043. [2]See "Hebron" on page 446. [3]See "Israelite Shrines and Worship Before the Temple of Solomon" on page 398 and "The Kuntillet Ajrûd Inscriptions: The Lord's Asherah?" on page 1220. [4]See "Assyria From the Neo-Assyrian Period Forward" on page 1502.

for its roots went down
to abundant waters.
[8]The cedars[d] in the garden of God 31:8 [d]Ps 80:10 [e]Ge 2:8-9
could not rival it,
nor could the pine trees
equal its boughs,
nor could the plane trees
compare with its branches—
no tree in the garden of God
could match its beauty.[e]
[9]I made it beautiful
with abundant branches,
the envy of all the trees of Eden[f] 31:9 [f]Ge 2:8 [g]Ge 13:10; Eze 28:13
in the garden of God.[g]

[10]" 'Therefore this is what the Sovereign LORD says: Because it towered on high, lifting its top above
the thick foliage, and because it was proud[h] of its height, [11]I handed it over to the ruler of the nations, 31:10 [h]Isa 14:13-14; Eze 28:17
for him to deal with according to its wickedness. I cast it aside,[i] [12]and the most ruthless of foreign na- 31:11 [i]Da 5:20
tions[j] cut it down and left it. Its boughs fell on the mountains and in all the valleys;[k] its branches lay bro- 31:12 [j]Eze 28:7 [k]Eze 32:5; 35:8
ken in all the ravines of the land. All the nations of the earth came out from under its shade and left it.[l] [l]Eze 32:11-12; Da 4:14
[13]All the birds of the air settled on the fallen tree, and all the beasts of the field were among its branch-
es.[m] [14]Therefore no other trees by the waters are ever to tower proudly on high, lifting their tops above 31:13 [m]Isa 18:6; Eze 29:5; 32:4
the thick foliage. No other trees so well-watered are ever to reach such a height; they are all destined for
death,[n] for the earth below, among mortal men, with those who go down to the pit.[o] 31:14 [n]Ps 82:7 [o]Ps 63:9; Eze 26:20; 32:24
[15]" 'This is what the Sovereign LORD says: On the day it was brought down to the grave[a] I covered the
deep springs with mourning for it; I held back its streams, and its abundant waters were restrained. Be-
cause of it I clothed Lebanon with gloom, and all the trees of the field withered away. [16]I made the na-
tions tremble[p] at the sound of its fall when I brought it down to the grave with those who go down to the 31:16 [p]Eze 26:15 [q]Isa 14:8
pit. Then all the trees[q] of Eden, the choicest and best of Lebanon, all the trees that were well-watered, [r]Eze 14:22; 32:31
were consoled[r] in the earth below.[s] [17]Those who lived in its shade, its allies among the nations, had also [s]Isa 14:15; Eze 32:18
gone down to the grave with it, joining those killed by the sword.[t] 31:17 [t]Ps 9:17
[18]" 'Which of the trees of Eden can be compared with you in splendor and majesty? Yet you, too, will
be brought down with the trees of Eden to the earth below; you will lie among the uncircumcised,[u] with 31:18 [u]Jer 9:26; Eze 32:19,21
those killed by the sword.
" 'This is Pharaoh and all his hordes, declares the Sovereign LORD.' "

A Lament for Pharaoh

32 In the twelfth year, in the twelfth month on the first day, the word of the LORD came to me:[v] [2]"Son 32:1 [v]Eze 31:1; 33:21
of man, take up a lament[w] concerning Pharaoh king of Egypt and say to him: 32:2 [w]Eze 19:1; 27:2 [x]Eze 19:3,6; Na 2:11-13 [y]Eze 29:3; 34:18

" 'You are like a lion[x] among the nations;
you are like a monster in the seas
thrashing about in your streams,
churning the water with your feet
and muddying the streams.[y]

[3]" 'This is what the Sovereign LORD says:

" 'With a great throng of people
I will cast my net over you,
and they will haul you up in my net.[z] 32:3 [z]Eze 12:13

[a] *15* Hebrew *Sheol*; also in verses 16 and 17

31:11 The "ruler of the nations" is probably Nabopolassar or possibly Nebuchadnezzar.
31:12 For "most ruthless," see the note on 30:11.
31:14 For "pit," see the note on 28:8.
32:1 The date was March 3, 585 B.C. If the Septuagint is followed ("eleventh year"), the chronological order of the Egypt oracles is preserved (making the date March 13, 586).
32:2 For "lament," see the note on 19:1. The lion was a figure for royalty and grandeur, and the seas and streams represent the Nile's many canals. For "monster," see the note on 29:3.

[4] I will throw you on the land
and hurl you on the open field.
I will let all the birds of the air settle on you
and all the beasts of the earth gorge themselves on you.[a]
[5] I will spread your flesh on the mountains
and fill the valleys[b] with your remains.
[6] I will drench the land with your flowing blood[c]
all the way to the mountains,
and the ravines will be filled with your flesh.
[7] When I snuff you out, I will cover the heavens
and darken their stars;
I will cover the sun with a cloud,
and the moon will not give its light.[d]
[8] All the shining lights in the heavens
I will darken over you;
I will bring darkness over your land,
declares the Sovereign LORD.
[9] I will trouble the hearts of many peoples
when I bring about your destruction among the nations,
among[a] lands you have not known.
[10] I will cause many peoples to be appalled at you,
and their kings will shudder with horror because of you
when I brandish my sword before them.
On the day[e] of your downfall
each of them will tremble
every moment for his life.[f]

[11] " 'For this is what the Sovereign LORD says:

" 'The sword of the king of Babylon[g]
will come against you.
[12] I will cause your hordes to fall
by the swords of mighty men—
the most ruthless of all nations.[h]
They will shatter the pride of Egypt,
and all her hordes will be overthrown.[i]
[13] I will destroy all her cattle
from beside abundant waters
no longer to be stirred by the foot of man
or muddied by the hoofs of cattle.[j]
[14] Then I will let her waters settle
and make her streams flow like oil,
declares the Sovereign LORD.
[15] When I make Egypt desolate
and strip the land of everything in it,
when I strike down all who live there,
then they will know that I am the LORD.[k]'

32:4 [a]Isa 18:6; Eze 31:12-13
32:5 [b]Eze 31:12
32:6 [c]Isa 34:3
32:7 [d]Isa 13:10; 34:4; Eze 30:3; Joel 2:2,31; 3:15; Mt 24:29; Rev 8:12
32:10 [e]Jer 46:10 [f]Eze 26:16; 27:35
32:11 [g]Jer 46:26
32:12 [h]Eze 28:7 [i]Eze 31:11-12
32:13 [j]Eze 29:8, 11
32:15 [k]Ex 7:5; 14:4,18; Ps 107:33-34; Eze 6:7

[a] 9 Hebrew; Septuagint *bring you into captivity among the nations, / to*

32:7–8 Cosmologically, the great divisions of the universe in the Old Testament were the earth and the heavens (Ge 1:1; 14:19)—or heaven, earth and the waters under the earth (Ex 20:4). In the visible heavens are the stars and planets (Ge 1:14–17; Eze 32:7–8). Later Jews divided the heavens into seven strata; there is no evidence for this in the Bible, although Paul spoke of being caught up into the third heaven (2Co 12:2).

32:10 For "my sword," see the note on 21:3.

32:11 The "king of Babylon" was Nebuchadnezzar (see "Nebuchadnezzar" on p. 571).

32:12 For "most ruthless of all nations," see the note on 30:11. The "pride of Egypt" was her army ("her hordes").

16 "This is the lament[l] they will chant for her. The daughters of the nations will chant it; for Egypt and
all her hordes they will chant it, declares the Sovereign LORD."

17 In the twelfth year, on the fifteenth day of the month, the word of the LORD came to me:[m] 18 "Son of
man, wail for the hordes of Egypt and consign[n] to the earth below both her and the daughters of mighty
nations, with those who go down to the pit.[o] 19 Say to them, 'Are you more favored than others? Go down
and be laid among the uncircumcised.'[p] 20 They will fall among those killed by the sword. The sword is
drawn; let her be dragged[q] off with all her hordes. 21 From within the grave[a][r] the mighty leaders will say
of Egypt and her allies, 'They have come down and they lie with the uncircumcised, with those killed by
the sword.'

22 "Assyria is there with her whole army; she is surrounded by the graves of all her slain, all who have
fallen by the sword. 23 Their graves are in the depths of the pit[s] and her army lies around her grave. All
who had spread terror in the land of the living are slain, fallen by the sword.

24 "Elam[t] is there, with all her hordes around her grave. All of them are slain, fallen by the sword.[u] All
who had spread terror in the land of the living[v] went down uncircumcised to the earth below. They bear
their shame with those who go down to the pit.[w] 25 A bed is made for her among the slain, with all her
hordes around her grave. All of them are uncircumcised, killed by the sword. Because their terror had
spread in the land of the living, they bear their shame with those who go down to the pit; they are laid
among the slain.

26 "Meshech and Tubal[x] are there, with all their hordes around their graves. All of them are uncircum-
cised, killed by the sword because they spread their terror in the land of the living. 27 Do they not lie with
the other uncircumcised warriors who have fallen, who went down to the grave with their weapons of
war, whose swords were placed under their heads? The punishment for their sins rested on their bones,
though the terror of these warriors had stalked through the land of the living.

28 "You too, O Pharaoh, will be broken and will lie among the uncircumcised, with those killed by the
sword.

29 "Edom[y] is there, her kings and all her princes; despite their power, they are laid with those killed by
the sword. They lie with the uncircumcised, with those who go down to the pit.[z]

30 "All the princes of the north[a] and all the Sidonians[b] are there; they went down with the slain in dis-
grace despite the terror caused by their power. They lie uncircumcised with those killed by the sword
and bear their shame with those who go down to the pit.

31 "Pharaoh—he and all his army—will see them and he will be consoled[c] for all his hordes that
were killed by the sword, declares the Sovereign LORD. 32 Although I had him spread terror in the land of
the living, Pharaoh and all his hordes will be laid among the uncircumcised, with those killed by the
sword, declares the Sovereign LORD."

Ezekiel a Watchman

33 The word of the LORD came to me: 2 "Son of man, speak to your countrymen and say to them:
'When I bring the sword[d] against a land, and the people of the land choose one of their men and
make him their watchman,[e] 3 and he sees the sword coming against the land and blows the trumpet[f] to
warn the people, 4 then if anyone hears the trumpet but does not take warning[g] and the sword comes
and takes his life, his blood will be on his own head.[h] 5 Since he heard the sound of the trumpet but did
not take warning, his blood will be on his own head. If he had taken warning, he would have saved him-
self. 6 But if the watchman sees the sword coming and does not blow the trumpet to warn the people and
the sword comes and takes the life of one of them, that man will be taken away because of his sin, but I
will hold the watchman accountable for his blood.'[i]

7 "Son of man, I have made you a watchman for the house of Israel; so hear the word I speak and give

32:16 [l]2Sa 1:17; 2Ch 35:25; Eze 26:17
32:17 [m]ver 1
32:18 [n]Jer 1:10 [o]Eze 31:14,16; Mic 1:8
32:19 [p]ver 29-30; Eze 28:10; 31:18
32:20 [q]Ps 28:3
32:21 [r]Isa 14:9
32:23 [s]Isa 14:15
32:24 [t]Ge 10:22 [u]Jer 49:37 [v]Job 28:13 [w]Eze 26:20
32:26 [x]Ge 10:2; Eze 27:13
32:29 [y]Isa 34:5-15; Jer 49:7; Eze 35:15; Ob 1:1 [z]Eze 25:12-14
32:30 [a]Jer 25:26; Eze 38:6; 39:2 [b]Jer 25:22; Eze 28:21
32:31 [c]Eze 14:22; 31:16
33:2 [d]Jer 12:12 [e]Eze 3:11
33:3 [f]Hos 8:1
33:4 [g]2Ch 25:16 [h]Jer 6:17; Eze 18:13; Zec 1:4; Ac 18:6
33:6 [i]Eze 3:18

[a] 21 Hebrew *Sheol*; also in verse 27

32:17 No month is given. The entire year dated from April 13, 586, to April 1, 585 B.C. The Septuagint suggests the first month, the fifteenth day of which would be April 27, 586.
32:18 The "earth below" refers to the grave (see "Sheol, Hades, Gehenna, the Abyss and Tartarus: Images of Hell" on p. 946).
32:19 For "uncircumcised," see the note on 28:10.
32:22 See "Assyria From the Neo-Assyrian Period Forward" on page 1502.
32:24 Elam (in present-day Iran) was a country east of Assyria.
32:26 Meshech and Tubal were peoples and territories in Asia Minor, to the north of Israel (see the note on Isa 66:19).
32:29 See "Edom" on page 1467.
32:30 For "Sidonians," see "Sidon" on page 1536.
33:3 The "trumpet," an instrument not of music but for signaling in both religious and military contexts, was made from a ram's horn (see "The Shofar" on p. 898).

33:7 [j]Jer 26:2; Eze 3:17 them warning from me.[j] 8When I say to the wicked, 'O wicked man, you will surely die,[k]' and you do not
33:8 [k]ver 14 [l]Eze 18:4 speak out to dissuade him from his ways, that wicked man will die for[a] his sin, and I will hold you ac-
countable for his blood.[l] 9But if you do warn the wicked man to turn from his ways and he does not do
33:9 [m]Eze 3:17-19 so, he will die for his sin, but you will have saved yourself.[m]
10"Son of man, say to the house of Israel, 'This is what you are saying: "Our offenses and sins weigh
33:10 [n]Eze 24:23 [o]Lev 26:39; Eze 4:17 us down, and we are wasting away[n] because of[b] them. How then can we live?[o]" ' 11Say to them, 'As sure-
ly as I live, declares the Sovereign LORD, I take no pleasure in the death of the wicked, but rather that they
33:11 [p]Eze 18:32; 2Pe 3:9 [q]Eze 18:23 turn from their ways and live.[p] Turn! Turn from your evil ways! Why will you die, O house of Israel?'[q]
12"Therefore, son of man, say to your countrymen, 'The righteousness of the righteous man will not
save him when he disobeys, and the wickedness of the wicked man will not cause him to fall when he
turns from it. The righteous man, if he sins, will not be allowed to live because of his former righteous-
33:12 [r]2Ch 7:14; Eze 3:20 ness.'[r] 13If I tell the righteous man that he will surely live, but then he trusts in his righteousness and
does evil, none of the righteous things he has done will be remembered; he will die for the evil he has
33:13 [s]Eze 18:24; Heb 10:38; 2Pe 2:20-21 done.[s] 14And if I say to the wicked man, 'You will surely die,' but he then turns away from his sin and
does what is just[t] and right— 15if he gives back what he took in pledge for a loan, returns what he has
33:14 [t]Eze 18:27 stolen,[u] follows the decrees that give life, and does no evil, he will surely live; he will not die.[v] 16None of
33:15 [u]Ex 22:1-4; Lev 6:2-5 [v]Eze 20:11; Lk 19:8 the sins he has committed will be remembered against him. He has done what is just and right; he will
surely live.[w]
33:16 [w]Isa 43:25; Eze 18:22 17"Yet your countrymen say, 'The way of the Lord is not just.' But it is their way that is not just. 18If a
33:18 [x]Eze 3:20; Eze 18:26 righteous man turns from his righteousness and does evil, he will die for it.[x] 19And if a wicked man turns
away from his wickedness and does what is just and right, he will live by doing so. 20Yet, O house of Is-
rael, you say, 'The way of the Lord is not just.' But I will judge each of you according to his own ways."

Jerusalem's Fall Explained

33:21 [y]Eze 24:26 [z]2Ki 25:4,10; Jer 39:1-2; Eze 32:1 21In the twelfth year of our exile, in the tenth month on the fifth day, a man who had escaped[y] from
Jerusalem came to me and said, "The city has fallen![z]" 22Now the evening before the man arrived, the
33:22 [a]Eze 1:3 [b]Lk 1:64 [c]Eze 3:26-27; 24:27 hand of the LORD was upon me,[a] and he opened my mouth[b] before the man came to me in the morning.
So my mouth was opened and I was no longer silent.[c]
23Then the word of the LORD came to me: 24"Son of man, the people living in those ruins[d] in the land
33:24 [d]Eze 36:4 [e]Isa 51:2; Jer 40:7; Eze 11:15; Ac 7:5 of Israel are saying, 'Abraham was only one man, yet he possessed the land. But we are many; surely the
land has been given to us as our possession.'[e] 25Therefore say to them, 'This is what the Sovereign LORD
33:25 [f]Ge 9:4; Dt 12:16 [g]Jer 7:9-10; Eze 22:6,27 says: Since you eat meat with the blood[f] still in it and look to your idols and shed blood, should you then
possess the land?[g] 26You rely on your sword, you do detestable things, and each of you defiles his neigh-
33:26 [h]Eze 22:11 bor's wife.[h] Should you then possess the land?'
27"Say this to them: 'This is what the Sovereign LORD says: As surely as I live, those who are left in the
ruins will fall by the sword, those out in the country I will give to the wild animals to be devoured, and
33:27 [i]1Sa 13:6; Isa 2:19; Jer 42:22; Eze 39:4 those in strongholds and caves will die of a plague.[i] 28I will make the land a desolate waste, and her proud
strength will come to an end, and the mountains of Israel will become desolate so that no one will cross
them. 29Then they will know that I am the LORD, when I have made the land a desolate waste because of
all the detestable things they have done.'
30"As for you, son of man, your countrymen are talking together about you by the walls and at the
doors of the houses, saying to each other, 'Come and hear the message that has come from the LORD.' 31My
33:31 [j]Eze 8:1 [k]Ps 78:36-37; Isa 29:13; Eze 22:27; Mt 13:22; 1Jn 3:18 people come to you, as they usually do, and sit before[j] you to listen to your words, but they do not put them
into practice. With their mouths they express devotion, but their hearts are greedy for unjust gain.[k] 32In-
deed, to them you are nothing more than one who sings love songs with a beautiful voice and plays an
33:32 [l]Mk 6:20 instrument well, for they hear your words but do not put them into practice.[l]
33"When all this comes true—and it surely will—then they will know that a prophet has been among
33:33 [m]1Sa 3:20; Jer 28:9; Eze 2:5 them.[m]"

[a] *8* Or *in*; also in verse 9 [b] *10* Or *away in*

33:21 The date was January 8, 585 B.C., five months after the Jerusalem temple had been burned (August 14, 586). The journey between Jerusalem and Babylon could have been made in four months (Ezr 7:9).
33:24 The "people living in those ruins" were the residents of Jerusalem not included in the exile of 586 B.C.
33:25 Eating meat with the blood in it had been forbidden by God (e.g., Ge 9:4).
33:27 For commentary on the threefold threat, see the note on 5:17.

Shepherds and Sheep

34 The word of the LORD came to me: 2 "Son of man, prophesy against the shepherds of Israel; proph-
esy and say to them: 'This is what the Sovereign LORD says: Woe to the shepherds of Israel who
only take care of themselves! Should not shepherds take care of the flock?[n] 3 You eat the curds, clothe
yourselves with the wool and slaughter the choice animals, but you do not take care of the flock.[o] 4 You
have not strengthened the weak or healed the sick or bound up the injured. You have not brought back
the strays or searched for the lost. You have ruled them harshly and brutally.[p] 5 So they were scattered be-
cause there was no shepherd,[q] and when they were scattered they became food for all the wild animals.[r]
6 My sheep wandered over all the mountains and on every high hill. They were scattered over the whole
earth, and no one searched or looked for them.[s]

7 " 'Therefore, you shepherds, hear the word of the LORD: 8 As surely as I live, declares the Sovereign
LORD, because my flock lacks a shepherd and so has been plundered and has become food for all the wild
animals, and because my shepherds did not search for my flock but cared for themselves rather than for
my flock, 9 therefore, O shepherds, hear the word of the LORD: 10 This is what the Sovereign LORD says: I am
against[t] the shepherds and will hold them accountable for my flock. I will remove them from tending
the flock so that the shepherds can no longer feed themselves. I will rescue[u] my flock from their mouths,
and it will no longer be food for them.[v]

11 " 'For this is what the Sovereign LORD says: I myself will search for my sheep and look after them.
12 As a shepherd[w] looks after his scattered flock when he is with them, so will I look after my sheep. I will
rescue them from all the places where they were scattered on a day of clouds and darkness.[x] 13 I will bring
them out from the nations and gather them from the countries, and I will bring them into their own
land. I will pasture them on the mountains of Israel, in the ravines and in all the settlements in the land.[y]
14 I will tend them in a good pasture, and the mountain heights of Israel[z] will be their grazing land. There
they will lie down in good grazing land, and there they will feed in a rich pasture[a] on the mountains of
Israel.[b] 15 I myself will tend my sheep and have them lie down, declares the Sovereign LORD.[c] 16 I will search
for the lost and bring back the strays. I will bind up the injured and strengthen the weak,[d] but the sleek
and the strong I will destroy. I will shepherd the flock with justice.[e]

17 " 'As for you, my flock, this is what the Sovereign LORD says: I will judge between one sheep and an-
other, and between rams and goats.[f] 18 Is it not enough for you to feed on the good pasture? Must you
also trample the rest of your pasture with your feet? Is it not enough for you to drink clear water? Must
you also muddy the rest with your feet? 19 Must my flock feed on what you have trampled and drink what
you have muddied with your feet?

20 " 'Therefore this is what the Sovereign LORD says to them: See, I myself will judge between the fat
sheep and the lean sheep. 21 Because you shove with flank and shoulder, butting all the weak sheep with
your horns[g] until you have driven them away, 22 I will save my flock, and they will no longer be plun-
dered. I will judge between one sheep and another.[h] 23 I will place over them one shepherd, my servant
David, and he will tend[i] them; he will tend them and be their shepherd. 24 I the LORD will be their God,[j]
and my servant David will be prince among them. I the LORD have spoken.[k]

25 " 'I will make a covenant of peace with them and rid the land of wild beasts[l] so that they may live
in the desert and sleep in the forests in safety.[m] 26 I will bless[n] them and the places surrounding my hill.[a]
I will send down showers in season;[o] there will be showers of blessing.[p] 27 The trees of the field will yield
their fruit and the ground will yield its crops; the people will be secure in their land. They will know that
I am the LORD, when I break the bars of their yoke[q] and rescue them from the hands of those who en-
slaved them.[r] 28 They will no longer be plundered by the nations, nor will wild animals devour them.
They will live in safety, and no one will make them afraid.[s] 29 I will provide for them a land renowned[t]
for its crops, and they will no longer be victims of famine[u] in the land or bear the scorn[v] of the nations.[w]

34:2 [n]Ps 78:70-72; Isa 40:11; Jer 3:15; 23:1; Mic 3:11; Jn 10:11; 21:15-17
34:3 [o]Isa 56:11; Eze 22:27; Zec 11:16
34:4 [p]Zec 11:15-17
34:5 [q]Nu 27:17 [r]ver 28; Isa 56:9
34:6 [s]Ps 142:4; 1Pe 2:25
34:10 [t]Jer 21:13 [u]Ps 72:14 [v]1Sa 2:29-30; Zec 10:3
34:12 [w]Isa 40:11; Jer 31:10; Lk 19:10 [x]Eze 30:3
34:13 [y]Jer 23:3
34:14 [z]Eze 20:40 [a]Ps 23:2 [b]Eze 36:29-30
34:15 [c]Ps 23:1-2
34:16 [d]Mic 4:6 [e]Isa 10:16; Lk 5:32
34:17 [f]Mt 25:32-33
34:21 [g]Dt 33:17
34:22 [h]Ps 72:12-14; Jer 23:2-3
34:23 [i]Isa 40:11
34:24 [j]Eze 36:28 [k]Jer 30:9
34:25 [l]Lev 26:6 [m]Isa 11:6-9; Hos 2:18
34:26 [n]Ge 12:2 [o]Ps 68:9 [p]Dt 11:13-15; Isa 44:3
34:27 [q]Lev 26:13 [r]Jer 30:8
34:28 [s]Jer 30:10; Eze 39:26
34:29 [t]Isa 4:2 [u]Eze 36:29 [v]Eze 36:6 [w]Eze 36:15

[a] 26 Or *I will make them and the places surrounding my hill a blessing*

34:2 The "shepherds of Israel" included her kings and officials, as well as the priests and prophets (see "Shepherding in the Ancient World" on p. 1363).
34:5 Ezekiel often used the term "scattered" to describe Israel's exile and dispersion.
34:17 "Rams and goats" was a reference to people of power and influence who were oppressing the poorer Israelites.
34:25 Wild beasts, deserts and sleeping in the forest all represented danger (see "Lions and Other Wild Beasts in Ancient Israel" on p. 813).
34:26 The rainy season in the region begins with the autumn rains and ends with the spring rains.
34:27 Yokes had holes through which wooden pegs ("bars") were inserted. Cords attached to the bars were then tied below an animal's neck, forming a collar.

CULTURAL AND HISTORICAL NOTES

Shepherding in the Ancient World

A shepherd with his flock

Photograph: © Todd Bolen/Bible Places.com

EZEKIEL 34 The keeping of sheep was widespread in the ancient world from earliest history; shepherding was practiced from **Mesopotamia** to the Roman world. Sheep provided meat, wool, milk and cheese. Shepherds sometimes practiced transhumance (seasonal movement of livestock between lowland pastures and mountains) and lived as nomads, but often they did not. Shepherds led their sheep to pasture and water, protected them from wild animals,[1] kept a careful count of them and gave special attention to those needing help, such as ewes about to lamb. At night, the shepherd often stayed with the sheep, sometimes settling them in simple enclosures or even in caves. In a shepherding family, both boys and girls could be required to work with the flock (e.g., Rachel in Ge 29:6 and David in 1Sa 16:11). A shepherd's life could be arduous, requiring long hours outdoors.

On the other hand, shepherding was often idealized, as in the pastoral poetry of Greece and Rome (e.g., Virgil's ten eclogues: poetry in which sheep converse with each other). Shepherds apparently spent a good deal of their idle time creating music and poetry while watching the sheep graze; the shield of Achilles featured an image of two piping shepherds (Homer's *Iliad*, 18.525), and David's career as the psalmist of Israel began among sheep and other shepherds.[2]

In the ancient world the shepherd was a standard metaphor for a ruler. The Mesopotamian lawgivers Lipit-Ishtar of Isin and **Hammurabi** of **Babylon** were both called "shepherds," and the crook held by the pharaoh may have represented the shepherd's staff. In Babylonian mythology Marduk was said to be a shepherd of the gods, while in the Old Testament God is referred to as the shepherd both of Israel (Ps 80:1) and of the faithful believer (Ps 23). At the same time, God expected the kings of Israel to function as shepherds of his people (2Sa 5:2) and harshly condemned those who abused that authority (Eze 34). Jesus, in fulfillment of verses 11–16, proclaimed himself to be the good shepherd (Jn 10:1–18).

[1]See "Lions and Other Wild Beasts in Ancient Israel" on page 813. [2]See "David" on page 443.

30 Then they will know that I, the LORD their God, am with them and that they, the house of Israel, are my
people, declares the Sovereign LORD.[x] 31 You my sheep, the sheep of my pasture,[y] are people, and I am
your God, declares the Sovereign LORD.' "

A Prophecy Against Edom

35 The word of the LORD came to me: 2 "Son of man, set your face against Mount Seir; prophesy
against it 3 and say: 'This is what the Sovereign LORD says: I am against you, Mount Seir, and I will
stretch out my hand[z] against you and make you a desolate waste.[a] 4 I will turn your towns into ruins and
you will be desolate. Then you will know that I am the LORD.[b]

5 " 'Because you harbored an ancient hostility and delivered the Israelites over to the sword at the time
of their calamity, the time their punishment reached its climax,[c] 6 therefore as surely as I live, declares the
Sovereign LORD, I will give you over to bloodshed and it will pursue you.[d] Since you did not hate blood-
shed, bloodshed will pursue you. 7 I will make Mount Seir a desolate waste and cut off from it all who
come and go. 8 I will fill your mountains with the slain; those killed by the sword will fall on your hills and
in your valleys and in all your ravines.[e] 9 I will make you desolate forever; your towns will not be inhab-
ited. Then you will know that I am the LORD.[f]

10 " 'Because you have said, "These two nations and countries will be ours and we will take possession[g]
of them," even though I the LORD was there, 11 therefore as surely as I live, declares the Sovereign LORD, I
will treat you in accordance with the anger[h] and jealousy you showed in your hatred of them and I will
make myself known among them when I judge you.[i] 12 Then you will know that I the LORD have heard all
the contemptible things you have said against the mountains of Israel. You said, "They have been laid
waste and have been given over to us to devour.[j]" 13 You boasted against me and spoke against me with-
out restraint, and I heard it.[k] 14 This is what the Sovereign LORD says: While the whole earth rejoices, I
will make you desolate.[l] 15 Because you rejoiced[m] when the inheritance of the house of Israel became
desolate, that is how I will treat you. You will be desolate, O Mount Seir,[n] you and all of Edom.[o] Then they
will know that I am the LORD.' "

A Prophecy to the Mountains of Israel

36 "Son of man, prophesy to the mountains of Israel and say, 'O mountains of Israel, hear the word
of the LORD. 2 This is what the Sovereign LORD says: The enemy said of you, "Aha![p] The ancient
heights[q] have become our possession.[r]" ' 3 Therefore prophesy and say, 'This is what the Sovereign LORD
says: Because they ravaged and hounded you from every side so that you became the possession of the
rest of the nations and the object of people's malicious talk and slander,[s] 4 therefore, O mountains of Is-
rael, hear the word of the Sovereign LORD: This is what the Sovereign LORD says to the mountains and
hills, to the ravines and valleys,[t] to the desolate ruins and the deserted towns that have been plundered
and ridiculed by the rest of the nations around you[u]— 5 this is what the Sovereign LORD says: In my burn-
ing zeal I have spoken against the rest of the nations, and against all Edom, for with glee and with mal-
ice in their hearts they made my land their own possession so that they might plunder its pastureland.'[v]
6 Therefore prophesy concerning the land of Israel and say to the mountains and hills, to the ravines and
valleys: 'This is what the Sovereign LORD says: I speak in my jealous wrath because you have suffered the
scorn of the nations.[w] 7 Therefore this is what the Sovereign LORD says: I swear with uplifted hand that
the nations around you will also suffer scorn.

8 " 'But you, O mountains of Israel, will produce branches and fruit[x] for my people Israel, for they will
soon come home. 9 I am concerned for you and will look on you with favor; you will be plowed and sown,
10 and I will multiply the number of people upon you, even the whole house of Israel. The towns will be
inhabited and the ruins rebuilt.[y] 11 I will increase the number of men and animals upon you, and they will
be fruitful and become numerous. I will settle people on you as in the past[z] and will make you prosper
more than before.[a] Then you will know that I am the LORD. 12 I will cause people, my people Israel, to walk
upon you. They will possess you, and you will be their inheritance;[b] you will never again deprive them
of their children.

13 " 'This is what the Sovereign LORD says: Because people say to you, "You devour men[c] and deprive
your nation of its children," 14 therefore you will no longer devour men or make your nation childless, de-

34:30 [x]Eze 14:11; 37:27
34:31 [y]Ps 100:3; Jer 23:1
35:3 [z]Jer 6:12 [a]Eze 25:12-14
35:4 [b]ver 9
35:5 [c]Ps 137:7; Eze 21:29
35:6 [d]Isa 63:2-6
35:8 [e]Eze 31:12
35:9 [f]Jer 49:13
35:10 [g]Ps 83:12; Eze 36:2,5
35:11 [h]Eze 25:14 [i]Ps 9:16; Mt 7:2
35:12 [j]Jer 50:7
35:13 [k]Da 11:36
35:14 [l]Jer 51:48
35:15 [m]Ob 1:12 [n]ver 3 [o]Isa 34:5-6,11; Jer 50:11-13; La 4:21
36:2 [p]Eze 25:3 [q]Dt 32:13 [r]Eze 35:10
36:3 [s]Ps 44:13-14
36:4 [t]Eze 6:3 [u]Dt 11:11; Ps 79:4; Eze 34:28
36:5 [v]Jer 50:11; Eze 25:12-14; 35:10,15
36:6 [w]Ps 123:3-4; Eze 34:29
36:8 [x]Isa 27:6
36:10 [y]ver 33; Isa 49:17-23
36:11 [z]Mic 7:14 [a]Jer 31:28; Eze 16:55
36:12 [b]Eze 47:14,22
36:13 [c]Nu 13:32

35:2 Mount Seir stands for Edom (see the note on 25:12–14; see also "Edom" on p. 1467).
35:5 Edom looted Jerusalem in 586 B.C.
36:2 "Ancient heights" refers to the promised land or, more specifically, to the heights of Zion.

clares the Sovereign LORD. 15No longer will I make you hear the taunts of the nations, and no longer will
you suffer the scorn of the peoples or cause your nation to fall, declares the Sovereign LORD.[d]' "
16Again the word of the LORD came to me: 17"Son of man, when the people of Israel were living in
their own land, they defiled it by their conduct and their actions. Their conduct was like a woman's
monthly uncleanness in my sight.[e] 18So I poured out[f] my wrath on them because they had shed blood
in the land and because they had defiled it with their idols. 19I dispersed them among the nations, and
they were scattered[g] through the countries; I judged them according to their conduct and their actions.[h]
20And wherever they went among the nations they profaned[i] my holy name, for it was said of them, 'These
are the LORD's people, and yet they had to leave his land.'[j] 21I had concern for my holy name, which the
house of Israel profaned among the nations where they had gone.[k]
22"Therefore say to the house of Israel, 'This is what the Sovereign LORD says: It is not for your sake,
O house of Israel, that I am going to do these things, but for the sake of my holy name, which you have
profaned[l] among the nations where you have gone.[m] 23I will show the holiness of my great name, which
has been profaned among the nations, the name you have profaned among them. Then the nations will
know that I am the LORD, declares the Sovereign LORD, when I show myself holy[n] through you before their
eyes.[o]
24" 'For I will take you out of the nations; I will gather you from all the countries and bring you back
into your own land.[p] 25I will sprinkle[q] clean water on you, and you will be clean; I will cleanse[r] you from
all your impurities and from all your idols.[s] 26I will give you a new heart[t] and put a new spirit in you; I
will remove from you your heart of stone and give you a heart of flesh.[u] 27And I will put my Spirit[v] in you
and move you to follow my decrees and be careful to keep my laws. 28You will live in the land I gave your
forefathers; you will be my people,[w] and I will be your God.[x] 29I will save you from all your uncleanness.
I will call for the grain and make it plentiful and will not bring famine[y] upon you. 30I will increase the
fruit of the trees and the crops of the field, so that you will no longer suffer disgrace among the nations
because of famine.[z] 31Then you will remember your evil ways and wicked deeds, and you will loathe
yourselves for your sins and detestable practices.[a] 32I want you to know that I am not doing this for your
sake, declares the Sovereign LORD. Be ashamed and disgraced for your conduct, O house of Israel![b]
33" 'This is what the Sovereign LORD says: On the day I cleanse you from all your sins, I will resettle
your towns, and the ruins will be rebuilt. 34The desolate land will be cultivated instead of lying desolate
in the sight of all who pass through it. 35They will say, "This land that was laid waste has become like the
garden of Eden;[c] the cities that were lying in ruins, desolate and destroyed, are now fortified and inhab-
ited."[d] 36Then the nations around you that remain will know that I the LORD have rebuilt what was de-
stroyed and have replanted what was desolate. I the LORD have spoken, and I will do it.'[e]
37"This is what the Sovereign LORD says: Once again I will yield to the plea of the house of Israel and
do this for them: I will make their people as numerous as sheep, 38as numerous as the flocks for offer-
ings[f] at Jerusalem during her appointed feasts. So will the ruined cities be filled with flocks of people.
Then they will know that I am the LORD."

The Valley of Dry Bones

37 The hand of the LORD was upon me,[g] and he brought me out by the Spirit[h] of the LORD and set
me in the middle of a valley;[i] it was full of bones.[j] 2He led me back and forth among them, and
I saw a great many bones on the floor of the valley, bones that were very dry. 3He asked me, "Son of man,
can these bones live?"

I said, "O Sovereign LORD, you alone know.[k]"
4Then he said to me, "Prophesy to these bones and say to them, 'Dry bones, hear the word of the LORD![l]
5This is what the Sovereign LORD says to these bones: I will make breath[a] enter you, and you will come
to life.[m] 6I will attach tendons to you and make flesh come upon you and cover you with skin; I will put
breath in you, and you will come to life. Then you will know that I am the LORD.[n]' "
7So I prophesied as I was commanded. And as I was prophesying, there was a noise, a rattling sound,
and the bones came together, bone to bone. 8I looked, and tendons and flesh appeared on them and skin
covered them, but there was no breath in them.

36:15 [d]Ps 89:50-51; Eze 34:29
36:17 [e]Jer 2:7
36:18 [f]2Ch 34:21
36:19 [g]Dt 28:64 [h]Eze 39:24
36:20 [i]Ro 2:24 [j]Isa 52:5; Jer 33:24; Eze 12:16
36:21 [k]Ps 74:18; Isa 48:9
36:22 [l]Ro 2:24* [m]Ps 106:8
36:23 [n]Eze 20:41 [o]Ps 126:2; Isa 5:16
36:24 [p]Eze 34:13; 37:21
36:25 [q]Heb 9:13; 10:22 [r]Ps 51:2,7 [s]Zec 13:2
36:26 [t]Jer 24:7 [u]Ps 51:10; Eze 11:19
36:27 [v]Eze 37:14
36:28 [w]Jer 30:22 [x]Eze 14:11; 37:14,27
36:29 [y]Eze 34:29
36:30 [z]Lev 26:4-5; Eze 34:27; Hos 2:21-22
36:31 [a]Eze 6:9; 20:43
36:32 [b]Dt 9:5
36:35 [c]Joel 2:3 [d]Isa 51:3
36:36 [e]Eze 17:22; 22:14; 37:14; 39:27-28
36:38 [f]1Ki 8:63; 2Ch 35:7-9
37:1 [g]Eze 1:3; 8:3 [h]Eze 11:24; Lk 4:1; Ac 8:39 [i]Jer 7:32 [j]Jer 8:2; Eze 40:1
37:3 [k]Dt 32:39; 1Sa 2:6; Isa 26:19
37:4 [l]Jer 22:29
37:5 [m]Ge 2:7; Ps 104:29-30
37:6 [n]Eze 38:23; Joel 2:27; 3:17

[a] 5 The Hebrew for this word can also mean *wind* or *spirit* (see verses 6-14).

37:2 "Very dry" bones referred to corpses long dead, far beyond any hope of resuscitation.

9 Then he said to me, "Prophesy to the breath;[o] prophesy, son of man, and say to it, 'This is what the
Sovereign LORD says: Come from the four winds, O breath, and breathe into these slain, that they may
live.' " 10 So I prophesied as he commanded me, and breath entered them; they came to life and stood up
on their feet—a vast army.[p]

11 Then he said to me: "Son of man, these bones are the whole house of Israel. They say, 'Our bones are
dried up and our hope is gone; we are cut off.'[q] 12 Therefore prophesy and say to them: 'This is what the Sov-
ereign LORD says: O my people, I am going to open your graves and bring you up from them; I will bring
you back to the land of Israel.[r] 13 Then you, my people, will know that I am the LORD, when I open your
graves and bring you up from them. 14 I will put my Spirit[s] in you and you will live, and I will settle you in
your own land. Then you will know that I the LORD have spoken, and I have done it, declares the LORD.[t] "

One Nation Under One King

15 The word of the LORD came to me: 16 "Son of man, take a stick of wood and write on it, 'Belonging
to Judah and the Israelites[u] associated with him.[v]' Then take another stick of wood, and write on it,
'Ephraim's stick, belonging to Joseph and all the house of Israel associated with him.' 17 Join them togeth-
er into one stick so that they will become one in your hand.[w]

18 "When your countrymen ask you, 'Won't you tell us what you mean by this?'[x] 19 say to them, 'This
is what the Sovereign LORD says: I am going to take the stick of Joseph—which is in Ephraim's hand—
and of the Israelite tribes associated with him, and join it to Judah's stick, making them a single stick
of wood, and they will become one in my hand.'[y] 20 Hold before their eyes the sticks you have written on
21 and say to them, 'This is what the Sovereign LORD says: I will take the Israelites out of the nations
where they have gone. I will gather them from all around and bring them back into their own land.[z] 22 I
will make them one nation in the land, on the mountains of Israel. There will be one king over all of
them and they will never again be two nations or be divided into two kingdoms.[a] 23 They will no lon-
ger defile[b] themselves with their idols and vile images or with any of their offenses, for I will save them
from all their sinful backsliding,[a] and I will cleanse them. They will be my people, and I will be their
God.[c]

24 " 'My servant David[d] will be king over them, and they will all have one shepherd.[e] They will follow
my laws and be careful to keep my decrees.[f] 25 They will live in the land I gave to my servant Jacob, the
land where your fathers lived.[g] They and their children and their children's children will live there for-
ever,[h] and David my servant will be their prince forever.[i] 26 I will make a covenant of peace[j] with them;
it will be an everlasting covenant. I will establish them and increase their numbers,[k] and I will put my
sanctuary among them forever.[l] 27 My dwelling place[m] will be with them; I will be their God, and they
will be my people.[n] 28 Then the nations will know that I the LORD make Israel holy,[o] when my sanctuary
is among them forever.' "

A Prophecy Against Gog

38 The word of the LORD came to me: 2 "Son of man, set your face against Gog, of the land of Magog,[p]
the chief prince of[b] Meshech and Tubal;[q] prophesy against him 3 and say: 'This is what the Sov-
ereign LORD says: I am against you, O Gog, chief prince of[c] Meshech and Tubal.[r] 4 I will turn you around,
put hooks[s] in your jaws and bring you out with your whole army—your horses, your horsemen fully
armed, and a great horde with large and small shields, all of them brandishing their swords.[t] 5 Persia,
Cush[d][u] and Put[v] will be with them, all with shields and helmets, 6 also Gomer[w] with all its troops, and
Beth Togarmah[x] from the far north with all its troops—the many nations with you.

37:9 [o]Ps 104:30
37:10 [p]Rev 11:11
37:11 [q]La 3:54
37:12 [r]Dt 32:39; 1Sa 2:6; Isa 26:19; Hos 13:14; Am 9:14-15
37:14 [s]Joel 2:28-29 [t]Eze 36:27-28, 36
37:16 [u]1Ki 12:20; 2Ch 10:17-19 [v]Nu 17:2-3; 2Ch 15:9
37:17 [w]ver 24; Isa 11:13; Jer 50:4; Hos 1:11
37:18 [x]Eze 24:19
37:19 [y]Zec 10:6
37:21 [z]Isa 43:5-6; Eze 36:24; 39:27
37:22 [a]Isa 11:13; Jer 3:18; Hos 1:11
37:23 [b]Eze 36:25; 43:7 [c]Eze 11:18; 36:28
37:24 [d]Hos 3:5 [e]Isa 40:11; Eze 34:23 [f]Ps 78:70-71
37:25 [g]Eze 28:25 [h]Am 9:15 [i]Isa 11:1
37:26 [j]Isa 55:3 [k]Jer 30:19 [l]Eze 16:62
37:27 [m]Lev 26:11; Jn 1:14 [n]2Co 6:16*
37:28 [o]Ex 31:13; Eze 20:12
38:2 [p]Ge 10:2 [q]Rev 20:8
38:3 [r]Eze 39:1
38:4 [s]2Ki 19:28 [t]Eze 29:4; Da 11:40
38:5 [u]Ge 10:6 [v]Eze 27:10
38:6 [w]Ge 10:2 [x]Eze 27:14

[a] 23 Many Hebrew manuscripts (see also Septuagint); most Hebrew manuscripts *all their dwelling places where they sinned*
[b] 2 Or *the prince of Rosh,* [c] 3 Or *Gog, prince of Rosh,* [d] 5 That is, the upper Nile region

37:9 Ezekiel saw a battlefield littered with the bones of those who had been killed in battle.
37:12 The scene shifts from a battlefield to a cemetery with sealed graves.
37:23 On the subject of defilement in the Old and New Testaments, see the note on Song of Songs 5:3.
37:24 The coming ruler is likened to a shepherd (see "Shepherding in the Ancient World" on p. 1363).
38:2 The identity of Gog is unknown; several identifications have been attempted, notably Gyges, king of Lydia (c. 660 B.C.). It may be that the name was purposely left vague, standing for a mysterious, undisclosed enemy of God's people. Magog was one of the sons of Japheth, and thus the name of a people. The word as used here may simply mean "land of Gog." Israel had long experienced the hostility of the Hamites and other Semitic peoples; the future coalition here envisioned includes—and in fact is led by—peoples descended from Japheth.
38:5 For "Cush" and "Put," see the note on Jeremiah 46:9. The invading forces from the north (see Eze 38:2 and its note) would be joined by armies from the south.
38:6 The people of Gomer (the later Cimmerians) lived near the Black Sea. For "Beth Togarmah," see the note on 27:14.

38:7 [y]Isa 8:9 7“ ‘Get ready; be prepared,[y] you and all the hordes gathered about you, and take command of them.
38:8 [z]Isa 24:22 8After many days[z] you will be called to arms. In future years you will invade a land that has recovered
[a]Isa 11:11 [b]Jer 23:6 from war, whose people were gathered from many nations[a] to the mountains of Israel, which had long
been desolate. They had been brought out from the nations, and now all of them live in safety.[b] 9You and
38:9 [c]Isa 28:2 [d]Jer 4:13; all your troops and the many nations with you will go up, advancing like a storm;[c] you will be like a
Joel 2:2 cloud[d] covering the land.
10“ ‘This is what the Sovereign LORD says: On that day thoughts will come into your mind and you
38:10 [e]Ps 36:4; will devise an evil scheme.[e] 11You will say, “I will invade a land of unwalled villages; I will attack a peace-
Mic 2:1 38:11 [f]Jer 49:31; ful and unsuspecting people—all of them living without walls and without gates and bars.[f] 12I will plun-
Zec 2:4 der and loot and turn my hand against the resettled ruins and the people gathered from the nations, rich
38:13 [g]Eze 27:22 in livestock and goods, living at the center of the land.” 13Sheba[g] and Dedan and the merchants of Tar-
[h]Isa 10:6; Jer 15:13 shish and all her villages[a] will say to you, “Have you come to plunder? Have you gathered your hordes to
loot, to carry off silver and gold, to take away livestock and goods and to seize much plunder?[h]” ’
14“Therefore, son of man, prophesy and say to Gog: ‘This is what the Sovereign LORD says: In that day,
38:14 [i]ver 8; Zec 2:5 when my people Israel are living in safety,[i] will you not take notice of it? 15You will come from your place
in the far north, you and many nations with you, all of them riding on horses, a great horde, a mighty
38:15 [j]Eze 39:2 army.[j] 16You will advance against my people Israel like a cloud[k] that covers the land. In days to come,
38:16 [k]ver 9 [l]Isa 29:23; Eze 39:21 O Gog, I will bring you against my land, so that the nations may know me when I show myself holy
through you before their eyes.[l]
17“ ‘This is what the Sovereign LORD says: Are you not the one I spoke of in former days by my servants
the prophets of Israel? At that time they prophesied for years that I would bring you against them. 18This
is what will happen in that day: When Gog attacks the land of Israel, my hot anger will be aroused, de-
clares the Sovereign LORD. 19In my zeal and fiery wrath I declare that at that time there shall be a great
38:19 [m]Ps 18:7; Eze 5:13; Hag 2:6, 21 earthquake in the land of Israel.[m] 20The fish of the sea, the birds of the air, the beasts of the field, every
creature that moves along the ground, and all the people on the face of the earth will tremble at my pres-
38:20 [n]Hos 4:3; Na 1:5 ence. The mountains will be overturned, the cliffs will crumble and every wall will fall to the ground.[n]
38:21 [o]Eze 14:17 [p]1Sa 14:20; 21I will summon a sword[o] against Gog on all my mountains, declares the Sovereign LORD. Every man’s
2Ch 20:23; Hag 2:22 sword will be against his brother.[p] 22I will execute judgment[q] upon him with plague and bloodshed; I will
38:22 [q]Isa 66:16; Jer 25:31 pour down torrents of rain, hailstones[r] and burning sulfur on him and on his troops and on the many
[r]Ps 18:12; Rev 16:21 nations with him. 23And so I will show my greatness and my holiness, and I will make myself known in
38:23 [s]Eze 36:23 the sight of many nations. Then they will know that I am the LORD.[s]’
39 “Son of man, prophesy against Gog and say: ‘This is what the Sovereign LORD says: I am against
39:1 [t]Eze 38:2,3 you, O Gog, chief prince of[b] Meshech and Tubal.[t] 2I will turn you around and drag you along. I
will bring you from the far north and send you against the mountains of Israel. 3Then I will strike your
39:3 [u]Hos 1:5 [v]Ps 76:3 bow[u] from your left hand and make your arrows[v] drop from your right hand. 4On the mountains of Is-
rael you will fall, you and all your troops and the nations with you. I will give you as food to all kinds of
39:4 [w]ver 17-20; Eze 29:5; 33:27 carrion birds and to the wild animals.[w] 5You will fall in the open field, for I have spoken, declares the
39:6 [x]Eze 30:8; Am 1:4 [y]Jer 25:22 Sovereign LORD. 6I will send fire[x] on Magog and on those who live in safety in the coastlands,[y] and they
will know that I am the LORD.
7“ ‘I will make known my holy name among my people Israel. I will no longer let my holy name be
39:7 [z]Ex 20:7 [a]Isa 12:6; profaned,[z] and the nations will know that I the LORD am the Holy One in Israel.[a] 8It is coming! It will
Eze 36:16,23 surely take place, declares the Sovereign LORD. This is the day I have spoken of.
9“ ‘Then those who live in the towns of Israel will go out and use the weapons for fuel and burn them
up—the small and large shields, the bows and arrows, the war clubs and spears. For seven years they will
39:9 [b]Ps 46:9 use them for fuel.[b] 10They will not need to gather wood from the fields or cut it from the forests, because
they will use the weapons for fuel. And they will plunder those who plundered them and loot those who
39:10 [c]Isa 14:2; 33:1; Hab 2:8 looted them, declares the Sovereign LORD.[c]
11“ ‘On that day I will give Gog a burial place in Israel, in the valley of those who travel east toward[c]

[a] 13 Or *her strong lions* [b] 1 Or *Gog, prince of Rosh,* [c] 11 Or *of*

38:11 A “land of unwalled villages” describes a place of peace, where walls (fortifications) were unnecessary.
38:12 The Hebrew for “center” also means “navel,” a graphic image reflecting the belief that Israel was the vital link between God and the world. Since the Hebrew for “land” can also mean “earth,” theologically Jerusalem is both the center of the land of Israel and the center of the world.
38:13 See “Sheba” on page 498. For “Dedan,” see the note on 25:13. See also “Where Was Tarshish?” on page 1475.
39:1 For “Gog,” see the note on 38:2.

the Sea.[a] It will block the way of travelers, because Gog and all his hordes will be buried there. So it will
be called the Valley of Hamon Gog.[b][d]
12 " 'For seven months the house of Israel will be burying them in order to cleanse the land.[e] 13 All the
people of the land will bury them, and the day I am glorified[f] will be a memorable day for them, declares
the Sovereign LORD.
14 " 'Men will be regularly employed to cleanse the land. Some will go throughout the land and, in ad-
dition to them, others will bury those that remain on the ground. At the end of the seven months they
will begin their search. 15 As they go through the land and one of them sees a human bone, he will set up
a marker beside it until the gravediggers have buried it in the Valley of Hamon Gog. 16 (Also a town called
Hamonah[c] will be there.) And so they will cleanse the land.'
17 "Son of man, this is what the Sovereign LORD says: Call out to every kind of bird[g] and all the wild
animals: 'Assemble and come together from all around to the sacrifice I am preparing for you, the great
sacrifice on the mountains of Israel. There you will eat flesh and drink blood. 18 You will eat the flesh of
mighty men and drink the blood of the princes of the earth as if they were rams and lambs, goats and
bulls—all of them fattened animals from Bashan.[h] 19 At the sacrifice I am preparing for you, you will eat
fat till you are glutted and drink blood till you are drunk. 20 At my table you will eat your fill of horses and
riders, mighty men and soldiers of every kind,' declares the Sovereign LORD.[i]
21 "I will display my glory among the nations, and all the nations will see the punishment I inflict and
the hand I lay upon them.[j] 22 From that day forward the house of Israel will know that I am the LORD their
God. 23 And the nations will know that the people of Israel went into exile for their sin, because they were
unfaithful to me. So I hid my face from them and handed them over to their enemies, and they all fell by
the sword.[k] 24 I dealt with them according to their uncleanness and their offenses, and I hid my face from
them.[l]
25 "Therefore this is what the Sovereign LORD says: I will now bring Jacob back from captivity[d][m] and
will have compassion[n] on all the people of Israel, and I will be zealous for my holy name.[o] 26 They will for-
get their shame and all the unfaithfulness they showed toward me when they lived in safety[p] in their
land with no one to make them afraid.[q] 27 When I have brought them back from the nations and have
gathered them from the countries of their enemies, I will show myself holy through them in the sight of
many nations.[r] 28 Then they will know that I am the LORD their God, for though I sent them into exile
among the nations, I will gather them to their own land, not leaving any behind. 29 I will no longer hide
my face from them, for I will pour out my Spirit[s] on the house of Israel, declares the Sovereign LORD."

The New Temple Area

40 In the twenty-fifth year of our exile, at the beginning of the year, on the tenth of the month, in
the fourteenth year after the fall of the city[t]—on that very day the hand of the LORD was upon
me[u] and he took me there. 2 In visions[v] of God he took me to the land of Israel and set me on a very high
mountain,[w] on whose south side were some buildings that looked like a city. 3 He took me there, and I saw
a man whose appearance was like bronze;[x] he was standing in the gateway with a linen cord and a mea-
suring rod[y] in his hand. 4 The man said to me, "Son of man, look with your eyes and hear with your ears
and pay attention to everything I am going to show you, for that is why you have been brought here. Tell[z]
the house of Israel everything you see.[a]"

The East Gate to the Outer Court

5 I saw a wall completely surrounding the temple area. The length of the measuring rod in the man's
hand was six long cubits, each of which was a cubit[e] and a handbreadth.[f] He measured[b] the wall; it was
one measuring rod thick and one rod high.

39:11 [d]Eze 38:2
39:12 [e]Dt 21:23
39:13 [f]Eze 28:22
39:17 [g]Rev 19:17
39:18 [h]Ps 22:12; Jer 51:40
39:20 [i]Rev 19:17-18
39:21 [j]Ex 9:16; Isa 37:20; Eze 38:16
39:23 [k]Isa 1:15; 59:2; Jer 22:8-9; 44:23
39:24 [l]Jer 2:17, 19; 4:18; Eze 36:19
39:25 [m]Jer 33:7; Eze 34:13 [n]Jer 30:18 [o]Isa 27:12-13
39:26 [p]1Ki 4:25 [q]Isa 17:2; Eze 34:28; Mic 4:4
39:27 [r]Eze 36:23-24; 37:21; 38:16
39:29 [s]Joel 2:28; Ac 2:17
40:1 [t]2Ki 25:7; Jer 39:1-10; 52:4-11; Eze 33:21 [u]Eze 1:3
40:2 [v]Da 7:1,7 [w]Eze 17:22; Rev 21:10
40:3 [x]Eze 1:7; Da 10:6; Rev 1:15 [y]Eze 47:3; Zec 2:1-2; Rev 11:1; 21:15
40:4 [z]Jer 26:2 [a]Eze 44:5
40:5 [b]Eze 42:20

[a] *11* That is, the Dead Sea [b] *11* *Hamon Gog* means *hordes of Gog.* [c] *16* *Hamonah* means *horde.* [d] *25* Or *now restore the fortunes of Jacob* [e] *5* The common cubit was about 1 1/2 feet (about 0.5 meter). [f] *5* That is, about 3 inches (about 8 centimeters)

39:12 Ritual purity is a major theme in Ezekiel. Corpses were considered particularly unclean (see Lev 5:2; 21:11).
39:13 For "people of the land," see the note on 7:27.
39:14 Absolute ritual purity was the aim (see the note on v. 12).
39:18 Bashan, east of the Sea of Galilee, was known for its rich pastureland, sleek cattle and magnificent oak trees.
40:1 The date was April 28, 573 B.C.
40:2 The "very high mountain" is a reference to Mount Zion. Height here signifies importance, as the earthly seat of God's reign (see "Zaphon, Olympus, Sinai and Zion: The Mountain of God" on p. 843).
40:3 The "man" was "like bronze," indicating that he was other than human. He was "standing in the gateway" (presumably of the outer court; see vv. 17–19), holding a "linen cord" (for longer measurements) and a "measuring rod" (for shorter measurements).
40:5 Ezekiel was using the long cubit (about 21 in. or 53.3 cm), an

40:6 [c]Eze 8:16 [6]Then he went to the gate facing east.[c] He climbed its steps and measured the threshold of the gate;
40:7 [d]ver 36 it was one rod deep.[a] [7]The alcoves[d] for the guards were one rod long and one rod wide, and the project-
ing walls between the alcoves were five cubits thick. And the threshold of the gate next to the portico fac-
ing the temple was one rod deep.
[8]Then he measured the portico of the gateway; [9]it[b] was eight cubits deep and its jambs were two
cubits thick. The portico of the gateway faced the temple.
[10]Inside the east gate were three alcoves on each side; the three had the same measurements,
and the faces of the projecting walls on each side had the same measurements. [11]Then he mea-
sured the width of the entrance to the gateway; it was ten cubits and its length was thirteen cu-
bits. [12]In front of each alcove was a wall one cubit high, and the alcoves were six cubits square.
[13]Then he measured the gateway from the top of the rear wall of one alcove to the top of the op-
posite one; the distance was twenty-five cubits from one parapet opening to the opposite one.
[14]He measured along the faces of the projecting walls all around the inside of the gateway—six-
40:14 [e]Ex 27:9 ty cubits. The measurement was up to the portico[c] facing the courtyard.[d][e] [15]The distance from the
entrance of the gateway to the far end of its portico was fifty cubits. [16]The alcoves and the project-
ing walls inside the gateway were surmounted by narrow parapet openings all around, as was the
portico; the openings all around faced inward. The faces of the projecting walls were decorated
40:16 [f]ver 21-22; 2Ch 3:5; Eze 41:26 with palm trees.[f]

The Outer Court

40:17 [g]Rev 11:2 [17]Then he brought me into the outer court.[g] There I saw some rooms and a pavement that had been
[h]Eze 41:6 [i]Eze 42:1 constructed all around the court; there were thirty rooms[h] along the pavement.[i] [18]It abutted the sides
of the gateways and was as wide as they were long; this was the lower pavement. [19]Then he measured
40:19 [j]Eze 46:1 the distance from the inside of the lower gateway to the outside of the inner court;[j] it was a hundred
[k]ver 23,27 cubits[k] on the east side as well as on the north.

The North Gate

[20]Then he measured the length and width of the gate facing north, leading into the outer court.
40:21 [l]ver 7 [21]Its alcoves[l]—three on each side—its projecting walls and its portico had the same measurements
as those of the first gateway. It was fifty cubits long and twenty-five cubits wide. [22]Its openings, its por-
40:22 [m]ver 49 tico[m] and its palm tree decorations had the same measurements as those of the gate facing east. Sev-
en steps led up to it, with its portico opposite them. [23]There was a gate to the inner court facing the
north gate, just as there was on the east. He measured from one gate to the opposite one; it was a hun-
40:23 [n]ver 19 dred cubits.[n]

The South Gate

[24]Then he led me to the south side and I saw a gate facing south. He measured its jambs and its por-
tico, and they had the same measurements as the others. [25]The gateway and its portico had narrow open-
40:25 [o]ver 33 ings all around, like the openings of the others. It was fifty cubits long and twenty-five cubits wide.[o]
[26]Seven steps led up to it, with its portico opposite them; it had palm tree decorations on the faces of the
40:26 [p]ver 22 projecting walls on each side.[p] [27]The inner court[q] also had a gate facing south, and he measured from
40:27 [q]ver 32 this gate to the outer gate on the south side; it was a hundred cubits.

[a] *6* Septuagint; Hebrew *deep, the first threshold, one rod deep* [b] *8,9* Many Hebrew manuscripts, Septuagint, Vulgate and Syriac; most Hebrew manuscripts *gateway facing the temple; it was one rod deep. 9Then he measured the portico of the gateway; it* [c] *14* Septuagint; Hebrew *projecting wall* [d] *14* The meaning of the Hebrew for this verse is uncertain.

---

older standard of measurement than the shorter cubit (about 18 in. or 45.7 cm), so the measuring rod of verse 3 was about 10 feet (3 m) long.

40:6 The "gate facing east" was that of the outer court. The three gates (east, north and south) of the outer court were similar to the three in the inner court (v. 32), each having six alcoves for the guards (three on each side) and a portico (vv. 8–9). Comparable gate plans have been discovered at Megiddo, Gezer and Hazor, all dating from the time of Solomon (see the note on 1Ki 9:15; see also "The Building Activity of Solomon" on p. 497). The guards restricted access by anyone who might profane the temple area (see Ezr 2:62).

There were three sets of stairs leading to the temple. The first set (mentioned here) had seven steps (Eze 40:22), the next (inner court) eight (v. 31) and the last (temple) ten (Eze 40:49)—the specific number of steps to the temple is not found in the Hebrew text but does appear in the Septuagint. The rising numbers may indicate increasing degrees of sacredness.

40:16 The walls were decorated with palm trees, as in Solomon's temple (see 1Ki 6:18,29,32,35; see also the note on 1Ki 6:18 and "Solomon's Temple and Other Ancient Temples" on p. 620).

40:19 Over 170 feet (52 m) separated the outer wall from the inner wall and constituted the width of the outer court.

40:20–27 The north and south gates were identical to the east gate (vv. 6–16), and all three outer-court gates were similar to the three in the inner court (vv. 28–37). See also the note on verse 6.

Gates to the Inner Court

28 Then he brought me into the inner court through the south gate, and he measured the south gate; it had the same measurements[r] as the others. 29 Its alcoves, its projecting walls and its portico had the same measurements as the others. The gateway and its portico had openings all around. It was fifty cubits long and twenty-five cubits wide. 30 (The porticoes[s] of the gateways around the inner court were twenty-five cubits wide and five cubits deep.) 31 Its portico[t] faced the outer court; palm trees decorated its jambs, and eight steps led up to it.

32 Then he brought me to the inner court on the east side, and he measured the gateway; it had the same measurements as the others. 33 Its alcoves, its projecting walls and its portico had the same measurements as the others. The gateway and its portico had openings all around. It was fifty cubits long and twenty-five cubits wide. 34 Its portico[u] faced the outer court; palm trees decorated the jambs on either side, and eight steps led up to it.

35 Then he brought me to the north gate[v] and measured it. It had the same measurements as the others, 36 as did its alcoves,[w] its projecting walls and its portico, and it had openings all around. It was fifty cubits long and twenty-five cubits wide. 37 Its portico[a] faced the outer court; palm trees decorated the jambs on either side, and eight steps led up to it.

The Rooms for Preparing Sacrifices

38 A room with a doorway was by the portico in each of the inner gateways, where the burnt offerings[x] were washed. 39 In the portico of the gateway were two tables on each side, on which the burnt offerings,[y] sin offerings[z] and guilt offerings[a] were slaughtered. 40 By the outside wall of the portico of the gateway, near the steps at the entrance to the north gateway were two tables, and on the other side of the steps were two tables. 41 So there were four tables on one side of the gateway and four on the other—eight tables in all—on which the sacrifices were slaughtered. 42 There were also four tables of dressed stone[b] for the burnt offerings, each a cubit and a half long, a cubit and a half wide and a cubit high. On them were placed the utensils for slaughtering the burnt offerings and the other sacrifices.[c] 43 And double-pronged hooks, each a handbreadth long, were attached to the wall all around. The tables were for the flesh of the offerings.

Rooms for the Priests

44 Outside the inner gate, within the inner court, were two rooms, one[b] at the side of the north gate and facing south, and another at the side of the south[c] gate and facing north. 45 He said to me, "The room facing south is for the priests who have charge of the temple,[d] 46 and the room facing north[e] is for the priests who have charge of the altar.[f] These are the sons of Zadok,[g] who are the only Levites who may draw near to the LORD to minister before him.[h]"

47 Then he measured the court: It was square—a hundred cubits long and a hundred cubits wide. And the altar was in front of the temple.

The Temple

48 He brought me to the portico of the temple[i] and measured the jambs of the portico; they were five cubits wide on either side. The width of the entrance was fourteen cubits and its projecting walls were[d] three cubits wide on either side. 49 The portico[j] was twenty cubits wide, and twelve[e] cubits from front to back. It was reached by a flight of stairs,[f] and there were pillars[k] on each side of the jambs.

41 Then the man brought me to the outer sanctuary[l] and measured the jambs; the width of the jambs was six cubits[g] on each side.[h] 2 The entrance was ten cubits wide, and the projecting walls on each side of it were five cubits wide. He also measured the outer sanctuary; it was forty cubits long and twenty cubits wide.[m]

40:28 [r]ver 35
40:30 [s]ver 21
40:31 [t]ver 22
40:34 [u]ver 22
40:35 [v]Eze 44:4; 47:2
40:36 [w]ver 7
40:38 [x]2Ch 4:6; Eze 42:13
40:39 [y]Eze 46:2 [z]Lev 4:3,28 [a]Lev 7:1
40:42 [b]Ex 20:25 [c]ver 39
40:45 [d]1Ch 9:23
40:46 [e]Eze 42:13 [f]Nu 18:5 [g]1Ki 2:35 [h]Nu 16:5; Eze 43:19; 44:15; 45:4; 48:11
40:48 [i]1Ki 6:2
40:49 [j]ver 22; 1Ki 6:3 [k]1Ki 7:15
41:1 [l]ver 23
41:2 [m]2Ch 3:3

[a] 37 Septuagint (see also verses 31 and 34); Hebrew *jambs* [b] 44 Septuagint; Hebrew *were rooms for singers, which were* [c] 44 Septuagint; Hebrew *east* [d] 48 Septuagint; Hebrew *entrance was* [e] 49 Septuagint; Hebrew *eleven* [f] 49 Hebrew; Septuagint *Ten steps led up to it* [g] 1 The common cubit was about 1 1/2 feet (about 0.5 meter). [h] 1 One Hebrew manuscript and Septuagint; most Hebrew manuscripts *side, the width of the tent*

40:38 There were rooms beside the portico of each gate in the inner courtyard for washing sacrifices; the porticoes themselves were for slaughtering animals. The temple's main function was sacrifice—the people needed regular atonement for their sins to enable them to stand in God's presence.

40:46 For "sons of Zadok," see the note on 44:15.

40:47 The inner courtyard formed a perfect square—the "shape" of perfection, or holiness. At its geometric center was the altar, the place of sacrifice.

41:1 The outer sanctuary was the largest of the temple's three rooms.

ANCIENT TEXTS AND ARTIFACTS

The Temple Scroll

EZEKIEL 41 Arriving at Ezekiel 41, many modern readers come to believe they are facing a portion of Scripture that is nearly pointless and certainly tedious. In addition, we may be confused by the fact that the description of the temple and its rituals given here is unlike anything we have heretofore seen in the law or elsewhere. A famous text from the **Dead Sea Scrolls**, however, illustrates just how significant the issues of temple and ritual were to ancient Jews. It also shows that the Jews were open to the possibility of a new vision of the ritual of the temple. This critical text is known as the Temple Scroll.

Fragment of the Temple Scroll from Qumran

Preserving Bible Times; © Dr. James C. Martin; permission of The Israel Museum/Shrine of the Book

With 66 columns preserved, the Temple Scroll (officially designated 11QTemple) is the longest of the Dead Sea Scrolls. Its authorship is unknown, and proposed dates of composition range from the fifth century B.C. to the first century A.D.; there are good reasons, however, for dating it at some point within the first century B.C.

This text is a reworking of various legal passages from Exodus 34 through Deuteronomy. The rewritten texts include instructions concerning the construction of a temple in Jerusalem, regulations for sacrifice and purity and Deuteronomic laws (laws relating to, or in the style of, the book of Deuteronomy). The scroll uses a distinctive type of rabbinical exegesis often called "midrashic" to reconcile difficulties in the **Pentateuch** and to create a new, unified law.

This rewritten **Torah** does not merely paraphrase or restate the **canonical** texts. On the contrary, the author made several notable omissions and additions, conforming these more ancient laws to the ideas of his own community. The scroll radically revised the festival calendar by including several festivals that were not part of the earlier Biblical cycle of holy days.[1] The instructions for the building of the temple, although containing similarities to Ezekiel's temple, differ from those found elsewhere in the Bible. Also intriguing is that the author changed Moses' words to the people from the third person to the first person. The result is that the revised instructions are placed on the lips of God himself!

This style of Biblical interpretation has caused some scholars to suggest that the **Qumran** community members believed that the Temple Scroll had the same authority as the Old Testament canon itself.[2] The Temple Scroll could in some sense be regarded as a new iteration or version of the law. It appears to envision a new temple and temple worship that would replace the current temple and serve as a kind of interim worship before the beginning of the Messianic Age. The Temple Scroll illustrates the fact that a great variety of failed religious viewpoints, some of which might rightly be called eccentric, had developed in Judaism during the **intertestamental period**.[3] The Temple Scroll probably represents the viewpoint of an extremist minority.

On the other hand, it is important to realize that the layout, rituals and holy days of the temple were of vital concern to ancient Jews. These issues may seem tedious to modern readers, but this only serves to illustrate the difference between our world and theirs. Ritual laws of the day were a kind of code that served to communicate religious ideals among the ancient Jews. In this sense the existence of texts such as the Temple Scroll is helpful when considering a passage such as Ezekiel 41–48. A new vision of the temple and its ritual signaled for Ezekiel's early readers a new era. The Qumran Temple Scroll communicated an eccentric and failed vision for the future of the people of God. Ezekiel, on the other hand, communicated the orthodox, canonical vision, but he did so within the same cultural world and using the same code as the Temple Scroll. Any credible interpretation of Ezekiel 41–48 must take into account the theological message ancient Israelites would have drawn from this (to us, mystifying) temple description.

[1]See "The Festivals of Israel" on page 186. [2]See "The Old Testament Canon" on page 1552. [3]See "The Intertestamental Period" on page 1551 and "Jewish Eschatology in the First Century A.D." on page 1846.

3 Then he went into the inner sanctuary and measured the jambs of the entrance; each was two cu-
bits wide. The entrance was six cubits wide, and the projecting walls on each side of it were seven cubits
wide. 4 And he measured the length of the inner sanctuary; it was twenty cubits, and its width was twen-
ty cubits across the end of the outer sanctuary.[n] He said to me, "This is the Most Holy Place.[o]"
5 Then he measured the wall of the temple; it was six cubits thick, and each side room around the tem-
ple was four cubits wide. 6 The side rooms were on three levels, one above another, thirty[p] on each level.
There were ledges all around the wall of the temple to serve as supports for the side rooms, so that the
supports were not inserted into the wall of the temple.[q] 7 The side rooms all around the temple were wid-
er at each successive level. The structure surrounding the temple was built in ascending stages, so that
the rooms widened as one went upward. A stairway[r] went up from the lowest floor to the top floor through
the middle floor.
8 I saw that the temple had a raised base all around it, forming the foundation of the side rooms. It
was the length of the rod, six long cubits. 9 The outer wall of the side rooms was five cubits thick. The
open area between the side rooms of the temple 10 and the ⌞priests'⌟ rooms was twenty cubits wide all
around the temple. 11 There were entrances to the side rooms from the open area, one on the north and
another on the south; and the base adjoining the open area was five cubits wide all around.
12 The building facing the temple courtyard on the west side was seventy cubits wide. The wall of the
building was five cubits thick all around, and its length was ninety cubits.
13 Then he measured the temple; it was a hundred cubits long, and the temple courtyard and the build-
ing with its walls were also a hundred cubits long. 14 The width of the temple courtyard on the east, in-
cluding the front of the temple, was a hundred cubits.[s]
15 Then he measured the length of the building facing the courtyard at the rear of the temple, includ-
ing its galleries[t] on each side; it was a hundred cubits.
The outer sanctuary, the inner sanctuary and the portico facing the court, 16 as well as the thresholds
and the narrow windows[u] and galleries around the three of them—everything beyond and including the
threshold was covered with wood. The floor, the wall up to the windows, and the windows were covered.[v]
17 In the space above the outside of the entrance to the inner sanctuary and on the walls at regular inter-
vals all around the inner and outer sanctuary 18 were carved[w] cherubim[x] and palm trees.[y] Palm trees al-
ternated with cherubim. Each cherub had two faces:[z] 19 the face of a man toward the palm tree on one side
and the face of a lion toward the palm tree on the other. They were carved all around the whole temple.[a]
20 From the floor to the area above the entrance, cherubim and palm trees were carved on the wall of the
outer sanctuary.
21 The outer sanctuary[b] had a rectangular doorframe, and the one at the front of the Most Holy Place
was similar. 22 There was a wooden altar[c] three cubits high and two cubits square[a]; its corners, its base[b]
and its sides were of wood. The man said to me, "This is the table[d] that is before the LORD." 23 Both the out-
er sanctuary[e] and the Most Holy Place had double doors.[f] 24 Each door had two leaves—two hinged
leaves[g] for each door. 25 And on the doors of the outer sanctuary were carved cherubim and palm trees
like those carved on the walls, and there was a wooden overhang on the front of the portico. 26 On the
sidewalls of the portico were narrow windows with palm trees carved on each side. The side rooms of the
temple also had overhangs.[h]

Rooms for the Priests

42 Then the man led me northward into the outer court and brought me to the rooms[i] opposite the
temple courtyard[j] and opposite the outer wall on the north side.[k] 2 The building whose door faced
north was a hundred cubits[c] long and fifty cubits wide. 3 Both in the section twenty cubits from the inner
court and in the section opposite the pavement of the outer court, gallery[l] faced gallery at the three

41:4 [n]1Ki 6:20 [o]Ex 26:33; Heb 9:3-8
41:6 [p]Eze 40:17 [q]1Ki 6:5
41:7 [r]1Ki 6:8
41:14 [s]Eze 40:47
41:15 [t]Eze 42:3
41:16 [u]1Ki 6:4 [v]ver 25-26; 1Ki 6:15; Eze 42:3
41:18 [w]1Ki 6:18 [x]Ex 37:7; 2Ch 3:7 [y]1Ki 6:29; 7:36 [z]Eze 10:21
41:19 [a]Eze 10:14
41:21 [b]ver 1
41:22 [c]Ex 30:1 [d]Ex 25:23; Eze 23:41; 44:16; Mal 1:7,12
41:23 [e]ver 1 [f]1Ki 6:32
41:24 [g]1Ki 6:34
41:26 [h]ver 15-16; Eze 40:16
42:1 [i]ver 13 [j]Eze 41:12-14 [k]Eze 40:17
42:3 [l]Eze 41:15

[a] 22 Septuagint; Hebrew *long* [b] 22 Septuagint; Hebrew *length* [c] 2 The common cubit was about 1 1/2 feet (about 0.5 meter).

41:4 The inner sanctuary, the only square space within the temple building itself, was accessed by passing through three openings of increasing narrowness (40:48—41:3), which may indicate increasing degrees of sacredness (see the note on 40:6).
41:6 These 90 side rooms were probably storerooms for the priests, possibly for the tithes (see Mal 3:10).
41:13 The temple itself was a perfect square (see the note on 40:47).
41:18 The "cherubim" were probably similar in appearance to the statues of winged figures that stood guard at the entrances to palaces and temples elsewhere in ancient Mesopotamia (see also the note on Ex 25:18–20).
41:22 A wooden altar (3 ft 5 in.—1.06 m—square by 5 ft—1.52 m—high) standing outside the Most Holy Place was used as a table. Ezekiel made no mention of an altar of incense or of lampstands like those in Solomon's temple and in the tabernacle before it. Also "missing" were the "Sea" and the ark of the covenant.

levels.[m] 4In front of the rooms was an inner passageway ten cubits wide and a hundred cubits[a] long.
Their doors were on the north.[n] 5Now the upper rooms were narrower, for the galleries took more space
from them than from the rooms on the lower and middle floors of the building. 6The rooms on the third
floor had no pillars, as the courts had; so they were smaller in floor space than those on the lower and
middle floors. 7There was an outer wall parallel to the rooms and the outer court; it extended in front of
the rooms for fifty cubits. 8While the row of rooms on the side next to the outer court was fifty cubits long,
the row on the side nearest the sanctuary was a hundred cubits long. 9The lower rooms had an entrance[o]
on the east side as one enters them from the outer court.

10On the south side[b] along the length of the wall of the outer court, adjoining the temple courtyard and
opposite the outer wall, were rooms[p] 11with a passageway in front of them. These were like the rooms on
the north; they had the same length and width, with similar exits and dimensions. Similar to the doorways
on the north 12were the doorways of the rooms on the south. There was a doorway at the beginning of the
passageway that was parallel to the corresponding wall extending eastward, by which one enters the rooms.

13Then he said to me, "The north[q] and south rooms facing the temple courtyard are the priests' rooms,
where the priests who approach the LORD will eat the most holy offerings. There they will put the most
holy offerings—the grain offerings, the sin offerings[r] and the guilt offerings[s]—for the place is holy.[t]
14Once the priests enter the holy precincts, they are not to go into the outer court until they leave behind
the garments[u] in which they minister, for these are holy. They are to put on other clothes before they go
near the places that are for the people.[v]"

15When he had finished measuring what was inside the temple area, he led me out by the east gate[w]
and measured the area all around: 16He measured the east side with the measuring rod; it was five hun-
dred cubits.[c] 17He measured the north side; it was five hundred cubits[d] by the measuring rod. 18He mea-
sured the south side; it was five hundred cubits by the measuring rod. 19Then he turned to the west side
and measured; it was five hundred cubits by the measuring rod. 20So he measured[x] the area on all four
sides. It had a wall around it,[y] five hundred cubits long and five hundred cubits wide,[z] to separate the holy
from the common.[a]

The Glory Returns to the Temple

43 Then the man brought me to the gate facing east,[b] 2and I saw the glory of the God of Israel com-
ing from the east. His voice was like the roar of rushing waters,[c] and the land was radiant with
his glory.[d] 3The vision I saw was like the vision I had seen when he[e] came to destroy the city and like the
visions I had seen by the Kebar River, and I fell facedown. 4The glory[e] of the LORD entered the temple
through the gate facing east.[f] 5Then the Spirit[g] lifted me up[h] and brought me into the inner court, and
the glory of the LORD filled the temple.

6While the man was standing beside me, I heard someone speaking to me from inside the temple.
7He said: "Son of man, this is the place of my throne and the place for the soles of my feet. This is where
I will live among the Israelites forever. The house of Israel will never again defile my holy name—nei-
ther they nor their kings—by their prostitution[f] and the lifeless idols[g] of their kings at their high plac-
es.[i] 8When they placed their threshold next to my threshold and their doorposts beside my doorposts,
with only a wall between me and them, they defiled my holy name by their detestable practices. So I de-
stroyed them in my anger. 9Now let them put away from me their prostitution and the lifeless idols of
their kings, and I will live among them forever.[j]

10"Son of man, describe the temple to the people of Israel, that they may be ashamed[k] of their sins. Let
them consider the plan, 11and if they are ashamed of all they have done, make known to them the design
of the temple—its arrangement, its exits and entrances—its whole design and all its regulations[h] and
laws. Write these down before them so that they may be faithful to its design and follow all its regulations.[l]

12"This is the law of the temple: All the surrounding area[m] on top of the mountain will be most holy.
Such is the law of the temple.

42:3 [m] Eze 41:16
42:4 [n] Eze 46:19
42:9 [o] Eze 44:5; 46:19
42:10 [p] ver 1
42:13 [q] Eze 40:46 [r] Lev 10:17; 6:25 [s] Lev 14:13 [t] Ex 29:31; Lev 6:29; 7:6; 10:12-13; Nu 18:9-10
42:14 [u] Eze 44:19 [v] Ex 29:9; Lev 8:7-9
42:15 [w] Eze 43:1
42:20 [x] Eze 40:5 [y] Zec 2:5 [z] Eze 45:2; Rev 21:16 [a] Eze 22:26
43:1 [b] Eze 10:19; 42:15; 44:1; 46:1
43:2 [c] Rev 1:15 [d] Isa 6:3; Eze 11:23; Rev 18:1
43:4 [e] Eze 1:28 [f] Eze 10:19
43:5 [g] Eze 11:24 [h] Eze 3:12; 8:3
43:7 [i] Lev 26:30
43:9 [j] Eze 37:26-28
43:10 [k] Eze 16:61
43:11 [l] Eze 44:5
43:12 [m] Eze 40:2

[a] 4 Septuagint and Syriac; Hebrew *and one cubit* [b] 10 Septuagint; Hebrew *Eastward* [c] 16 See Septuagint of verse 17; Hebrew *rods*; also in verses 18 and 19. [d] 17 Septuagint; Hebrew *rods* [e] 3 Some Hebrew manuscripts and Vulgate; most Hebrew manuscripts *I* [f] 7 Or *their spiritual adultery*; also in verse 9 [g] 7 Or *the corpses*; also in verse 9 [h] 11 Some Hebrew manuscripts and Septuagint; most Hebrew manuscripts *regulations and its whole design*

42:20 The total area was a perfect square (see the note on 40:47).
43:2 For "the glory of the God of Israel," see the note on 1:28.
43:3 For "Kebar River," see the note on 1:1.
43:5 Ezekiel was transported into the inner court but not into the temple proper.

The Altar

13"These are the measurements of the altar[n] in long cubits, that cubit being a cubit[a] and a handbreadth[b]: Its gutter is a cubit deep and a cubit wide, with a rim of one span[c] around the edge. And this is the height of the altar: 14From the gutter on the ground up to the lower ledge it is two cubits high and a cubit wide, and from the smaller ledge up to the larger ledge it is four cubits high and a cubit wide. 15The altar hearth is four cubits high, and four horns[o] project upward from the hearth. 16The altar hearth is square, twelve cubits long and twelve cubits wide. 17The upper ledge also is square, fourteen cubits long and fourteen cubits wide, with a rim of half a cubit and a gutter of a cubit all around. The steps[p] of the altar face east."

18Then he said to me, "Son of man, this is what the Sovereign LORD says: These will be the regulations for sacrificing burnt offerings[q] and sprinkling blood[r] upon the altar when it is built: 19You are to give a young bull[s] as a sin offering to the priests, who are Levites, of the family of Zadok,[t] who come near[u] to minister before me, declares the Sovereign LORD. 20You are to take some of its blood and put it on the four horns of the altar and on the four corners of the upper ledge[v] and all around the rim, and so purify the altar[w] and make atonement for it. 21You are to take the bull for the sin offering and burn it in the designated part of the temple area outside the sanctuary.[x]

22"On the second day you are to offer a male goat without defect for a sin offering, and the altar is to be purified as it was purified with the bull. 23When you have finished purifying it, you are to offer a young bull and a ram from the flock, both without defect.[y] 24You are to offer them before the LORD, and the priests are to sprinkle salt[z] on them and sacrifice them as a burnt offering to the LORD.

25"For seven days[a] you are to provide a male goat daily for a sin offering; you are also to provide a young bull and a ram from the flock, both without defect.[b] 26For seven days they are to make atonement for the altar and cleanse it; thus they will dedicate it. 27At the end of these days, from the eighth day[c] on, the priests are to present your burnt offerings and fellowship offerings[d][d] on the altar. Then I will accept you, declares the Sovereign LORD."

The Prince, the Levites, the Priests

44 Then the man brought me back to the outer gate of the sanctuary, the one facing east,[e] and it was shut. 2The LORD said to me, "This gate is to remain shut. It must not be opened; no one may enter through it.[f] It is to remain shut because the LORD, the God of Israel, has entered through it. 3The prince himself is the only one who may sit inside the gateway to eat in the presence[g] of the LORD. He is to enter by way of the portico of the gateway and go out the same way.[h]"

4Then the man brought me by way of the north gate to the front of the temple. I looked and saw the glory of the LORD filling the temple[i] of the LORD, and I fell facedown.[j]

5The LORD said to me, "Son of man, look carefully, listen closely and give attention to everything I tell you concerning all the regulations regarding the temple of the LORD. Give attention to the entrance of the temple and all the exits of the sanctuary.[k] 6Say to the rebellious house[l] of Israel, 'This is what the Sovereign LORD says: Enough of your detestable practices, O house of Israel! 7In addition to all your other detestable practices, you brought foreigners uncircumcised in heart[m] and flesh into my sanctuary, desecrating my temple while you offered me food, fat and blood, and you broke my covenant.[n] 8Instead of carrying out your duty in regard to my holy things, you put others in charge of my sanctuary.[o] 9This is what the Sovereign LORD says: No foreigner uncircumcised in heart and flesh is to enter my sanctuary, not even the foreigners who live among the Israelites.[p]

43:13 [n]2Ch 4:1
43:15 [o]Ex 27:2
43:17 [p]Ex 20:26
43:18 [q]Ex 40:29 [r]Lev 1:5,11; Heb 9:21-22
43:19 [s]Lev 4:3; Eze 45:18-19 [t]Eze 44:15 [u]Nu 16:40; Eze 40:46
43:20 [v]ver 17 [w]Lev 16:19
43:21 [x]Ex 29:14; Heb 13:11
43:23 [y]Ex 29:1
43:24 [z]Lev 2:13; Mk 9:49-50
43:25 [a]Lev 8:33 [b]Ex 29:37
43:27 [c]Lev 9:1 [d]Lev 17:5
44:1 [e]Eze 43:1
44:2 [f]Eze 43:4-5
44:3 [g]Ex 24:9-11 [h]Eze 46:2,8
44:4 [i]Isa 6:4; Rev 15:8 [j]Eze 1:28; 3:23
44:5 [k]Eze 40:4; 43:10-11
44:6 [l]Eze 3:9
44:7 [m]Lev 26:41 [n]Ge 17:14; Ex 12:48; Lev 22:25
44:8 [o]Lev 22:2; Nu 18:7
44:9 [p]Joel 3:17; Zec 14:21

[a] *13* The common cubit was about 1 1/2 feet (about 0.5 meter). [b] *13* That is, about 3 inches (about 8 centimeters) [c] *13* That is, about 9 inches (about 22 centimeters) [d] *27* Traditionally *peace offerings*

43:13–17 The importance of the altar is evident from its detailed description and its place at the geometric center of the temple complex. Ezekiel's altar was much larger than Solomon's. It was over 20 feet—6 meters—tall (including the horns, v. 15) and was made up of three slabs of decreasing size, like an Egyptian pyramid or Babylonian ziggurat. Exodus 20:26 prohibited the use of steps leading up to an altar, but here they were required because of its size. (See "Ancient Altars" on p. 125 and "The Horned Altar" on p. 924.)

44:2 The eastern gate was to remain shut because God had entered through it (43:1–2), thus rendering it holy. Related reasons may be that God would never again leave as before (10:19; 11:23) and that sun worship would be rendered impossible (see 8:16). Today the eastern gate (called the Golden Gate) of the sacred Muslim area (*Haram esh-Sharif*) in Jerusalem is sealed shut as a result of a later but possibly related tradition.

44:7–9 The *nokhrî* was a foreigner who did not have religious fellowship with Israel, since his allegiance was claimed by another people and another deity. Such a person was forbidden to enter the sanctuary.

44:9 Nehemiah enforced this restriction when he dismissed Tobiah (Ne 13:8), an Ammonite (Ne 2:10; see Dt 23:3). Foreigners could, however, be a part of the people of Israel (see Eze 47:22).

10“ ‘The Levites who went far from me when Israel went astray[q] and who wandered from me after
their idols must bear the consequences of their sin.[r] 11 They may serve in my sanctuary, having charge
of the gates of the temple and serving in it; they may slaughter the burnt offerings[s] and sacrifices for the
people and stand before the people and serve them.[t] 12 But because they served them in the presence of
their idols and made the house of Israel fall into sin, therefore I have sworn with uplifted hand[u] that they
must bear the consequences of their sin, declares the Sovereign LORD.[v] 13 They are not to come near to
serve me as priests or come near any of my holy things or my most holy offerings; they must bear the
shame[w] of their detestable practices.[x] 14 Yet I will put them in charge of the duties of the temple and all
the work that is to be done in it.[y]

15“ ‘But the priests, who are Levites and descendants of Zadok and who faithfully carried out the du-
ties of my sanctuary when the Israelites went astray from me, are to come near to minister before me;
they are to stand before me to offer sacrifices of fat and blood, declares the Sovereign LORD.[z] 16 They alone
are to enter my sanctuary; they alone are to come near my table[a] to minister before me and perform my
service.[b]

17“ ‘When they enter the gates of the inner court, they are to wear linen clothes;[c] they must not wear
any woolen garment while ministering at the gates of the inner court or inside the temple. 18 They are to
wear linen turbans[d] on their heads and linen undergarments[e] around their waists. They must not wear
anything that makes them perspire.[f] 19 When they go out into the outer court where the people are, they
are to take off the clothes they have been ministering in and are to leave them in the sacred rooms, and
put on other clothes, so that they do not consecrate[g] the people by means of their garments.[h]

20“ ‘They must not shave their heads or let their hair grow long, but they are to keep the hair of their
heads trimmed.[i] 21 No priest is to drink wine when he enters the inner court.[j] 22 They must not marry
widows or divorced women; they may marry only virgins of Israelite descent or widows of priests.[k]
23 They are to teach my people the difference between the holy and the common[l] and show them how to
distinguish between the unclean and the clean.[m]

24“ ‘In any dispute, the priests are to serve as judges[n] and decide it according to my ordinances. They
are to keep my laws and my decrees for all my appointed feasts, and they are to keep my Sabbaths holy.[o]

25“ ‘A priest must not defile himself by going near a dead person; however, if the dead person was his
father or mother, son or daughter, brother or unmarried sister, then he may defile himself.[p] 26 After he is
cleansed, he must wait seven days.[q] 27 On the day he goes into the inner court of the sanctuary to minis-
ter in the sanctuary, he is to offer a sin offering for himself, declares the Sovereign LORD.

28“ ‘I am to be the only inheritance[r] the priests have. You are to give them no possession in Israel; I
will be their possession. 29 They will eat the grain offerings, the sin offerings and the guilt offerings; and
everything in Israel devoted[*a*] to the LORD[s] will belong to them.[t] 30 The best of all the firstfruits[u] and of all
your special gifts will belong to the priests. You are to give them the first portion of your ground meal[v]
so that a blessing[w] may rest on your household.[x] 31 The priests must not eat anything, bird or animal,
found dead or torn by wild animals.[y]

Division of the Land

45 “ ‘When you allot the land as an inheritance,[z] you are to present to the LORD a portion of the land
as a sacred district, 25,000 cubits long and 20,000[*b*] cubits wide; the entire area will be holy.[a] 2 Of
this, a section 500 cubits square[b] is to be for the sanctuary, with 50 cubits around it for open land. 3 In
the sacred district, measure off a section 25,000 cubits[*c*] long and 10,000 cubits[*d*] wide. In it will be the

44:10 q2Ki 23:8 rNu 18:23
44:11 s2Ch 29:34 tNu 3:5-37; 16:9; 1Ch 26:12-19
44:12 uPs 106:26 v2Ki 16:10-16
44:13 wEze 16:61 xNu 18:3
44:14 yNu 18:4; 1Ch 23:28-32
44:15 zJer 33:18; Eze 40:46; Zec 3:7
44:16 aEze 41:22 bNu 18:5
44:17 cEx 39:27-28; Rev 19:8
44:18 dEx 28:39; Isa 3:20 eEx 28:42 fLev 16:4
44:19 gLev 6:27; Eze 46:20 hLev 6:10-11; Eze 42:14
44:20 iLev 21:5; Nu 6:5
44:21 jLev 10:9
44:22 kLev 21:7
44:23 lEze 22:26 mMal 2:7
44:24 nDt 17:8-9; 1Ch 23:4 o2Ch 19:8
44:25 pLev 21:1-4
44:26 qNu 19:14
44:28 rNu 18:20; Dt 10:9; 18:1-2; Jos 13:33
44:29 sLev 27:21 tNu 18:9,14
44:30 uNu 18:12-13 vNu 15:18-21 wMal 3:10 xNe 10:35-37
44:31 yEx 22:31; Lev 22:8
45:1 zEze 47:21-22 aEze 48:8-9, 29
45:2 bEze 42:20

a 29 The Hebrew term refers to the irrevocable giving over of things or persons to the LORD. *b* 1 Septuagint (see also verses 3 and 5 and 48:9); Hebrew *10,000* *c* 3 That is, about 7 miles (about 12 kilometers) *d* 3 That is, about 3 miles (about 5 kilometers)

44:15 In contrast to the Israelites in general and to other Levites in particular (whose access was restricted), the “descendants of Zadok” received the privileges of sole access (v. 16) to the inner court, as well as the responsibility of offering sacrifices inside the sanctuary proper. Zadok, a descendant of Aaron, had served as priest (along with Abiathar) in David’s time. God had chosen Zadok and his descendants to minister in the temple after Abiathar was removed for supporting Adonijah rather than Solomon as David’s successor (1Ki 2:35). The key issue here was loyalty.

For the Zadokites, access to God’s presence implied heavy lifestyle restrictions. If they were to minister in the presence of the all-holy God, there were things they could not touch, places they could not go, food they could not eat and clothes they could not wear.

44:18 After the fall, God told Adam that he would have to work hard enough to sweat in order to procure his food (Ge 3:19). In contrast, priests in the future temple were not to wear anything that might cause them to perspire.

44:25 Contact with the dead rendered a person ceremonially unclean (Lev 21:1–3; Hag 2:13).

45:2 The “open land” was to serve as a buffer between the more and the less holy, although the entire area was holy.

45:3 The middle strip of the holy square was specifically for the temple.

sanctuary, the Most Holy Place. 4 It will be the sacred portion of the land for the priests,[c] who minister
in the sanctuary and who draw near to minister before the LORD. It will be a place for their houses as well
as a holy place for the sanctuary.[d] 5 An area 25,000 cubits long and 10,000 cubits wide will belong to the
Levites, who serve in the temple, as their possession for towns to live in.[a][e]

6 " 'You are to give the city as its property an area 5,000 cubits wide and 25,000 cubits long, adjoining
the sacred portion; it will belong to the whole house of Israel.[f]

7 " 'The prince will have the land bordering each side of the area formed by the sacred district and
the property of the city. It will extend westward from the west side and eastward from the east side, run-
ning lengthwise from the western to the eastern border parallel to one of the tribal portions.[g] 8 This land
will be his possession in Israel. And my princes will no longer oppress my people but will allow the house
of Israel to possess the land according to their tribes.[h]

9 " 'This is what the Sovereign LORD says: You have gone far enough, O princes of Israel! Give up your
violence and oppression and do what is just and right.[i] Stop dispossessing my people, declares the Sov-
ereign LORD. 10 You are to use accurate scales,[j] an accurate ephah[b][k] and an accurate bath.[c] 11 The ephah[l]
and the bath are to be the same size, the bath containing a tenth of a homer[d] and the ephah a tenth of a
homer; the homer is to be the standard measure for both. 12 The shekel[e] is to consist of twenty gerahs.[m]
Twenty shekels plus twenty-five shekels plus fifteen shekels equal one mina.[f]

Offerings and Holy Days

13 " 'This is the special gift you are to offer: a sixth of an ephah from each homer of wheat and a
sixth of an ephah from each homer of barley. 14 The prescribed portion of oil, measured by the bath,
is a tenth of a bath from each cor (which consists of ten baths or one homer, for ten baths are equiv-
alent to a homer). 15 Also one sheep is to be taken from every flock of two hundred from the well-wa-
tered pastures of Israel. These will be used for the grain offerings, burnt offerings[n] and fellowship
offerings[g] to make atonement[o] for the people, declares the Sovereign LORD. 16 All the people of the
land will participate in this special gift for the use of the prince in Israel. 17 It will be the duty of the
prince to provide the burnt offerings, grain offerings and drink offerings at the festivals, the New
Moons and the Sabbaths[p]—at all the appointed feasts of the house of Israel. He will provide the sin
offerings, grain offerings, burnt offerings and fellowship offerings to make atonement for the house
of Israel.[q]

18 " 'This is what the Sovereign LORD says: In the first month[r] on the first day you are to take a young
bull without defect[s] and purify the sanctuary.[t] 19 The priest is to take some of the blood of the sin offer-
ing and put it on the doorposts of the temple, on the four corners of the upper ledge[u] of the altar[v] and
on the gateposts of the inner court. 20 You are to do the same on the seventh day of the month for anyone
who sins unintentionally[w] or through ignorance; so you are to make atonement for the temple.

21 " 'In the first month on the fourteenth day you are to observe the Passover,[x] a feast lasting seven
days, during which you shall eat bread made without yeast. 22 On that day the prince is to provide a bull
as a sin offering for himself and for all the people of the land.[y] 23 Every day during the seven days of the
Feast he is to provide seven bulls and seven rams[z] without defect as a burnt offering to the LORD, and a
male goat for a sin offering.[a] 24 He is to provide as a grain offering[b] an ephah for each bull and an ephah
for each ram, along with a hin[h] of oil for each ephah.[c]

25 " 'During the seven days of the Feast,[d] which begins in the seventh month on the fifteenth day, he
is to make the same provision for sin offerings, burnt offerings, grain offerings and oil.[e]

45:4 [c]Eze 40:46 [d]Eze 48:10-11
45:5 [e]Eze 48:13
45:6 [f]Eze 48:15-18
45:7 [g]Eze 48:21
45:8 [h]Nu 26:53; Eze 46:18
45:9 [i]Jer 22:3; Zec 7:9-10; 8:16
45:10 [j]Dt 25:15; Pr 11:1; Am 8:4-6; Mic 6:10-11 [k]Lev 19:36
45:11 [l]Isa 5:10
45:12 [m]Ex 30:13; Lev 27:25; Nu 3:47
45:15 [n]Lev 1:4 [o]Lev 6:30
45:17 [p]Lev 23:38; Isa 66:23 [q]1Ki 8:62; 2Ch 31:3; Eze 46:4-12
45:18 [r]Ex 12:2 [s]Lev 22:20; Heb 9:14 [t]Lev 16:16,33
45:19 [u]Eze 43:17 [v]Lev 16:18-19; Eze 43:20
45:20 [w]Lev 4:27
45:21 [x]Ex 12:11; Lev 23:5-6
45:22 [y]Lev 4:14
45:23 [z]Job 42:8 [a]Nu 28:16-25
45:24 [b]Nu 28:12-13 [c]Eze 46:5-7
45:25 [d]Dt 16:13 [e]Lev 23:34-43; Nu 29:12-38

[a] *5* Septuagint; Hebrew *temple; they will have as their possession 20 rooms* [b] *10* An ephah was a dry measure. [c] *10* A bath was a liquid measure. [d] *11* A homer was a dry measure. [e] *12* A shekel weighed about 2/5 ounce (about 11.5 grams). [f] *12* That is, 60 shekels; the common mina was 50 shekels. [g] *15* Traditionally *peace offerings*; also in verse 17 [h] *24* That is, probably about 4 quarts (about 4 liters)

45:4 The "land for the priests" was intended for their livelihood, not their ownership (see 44:28).

45:5 A section of land of equal size just to the north was designated for the Levites to dwell on, even though it was located within the holy area. The Levites, as opposed to the Zadokite priests, were permitted to hold land as a possession.

45:6 While the former Jerusalem had contained the temple area, the new holy city would be adjacent to the temple.

45:10 In a culture with no bureau of weights and measures, cheating in business transactions by falsification of standards was common practice (see Dt 25:13–16). The prophets consistently condemned such practices as sin (Am 8:5; Mic 6:10–11).

45:13—46:24 This section varies so much from the Pentateuch that Jewish rabbis have exerted great effort to reconcile the two. In fact, the difficulty of harmonizing them at one time put the book of Ezekiel in danger of exclusion from the canon of Jewish Scriptures.

45:16 For "people of the land," see the note on 7:27.

45:25 The feast mentioned here is the Feast of Ingathering (Ex 23:16; 34:22), also called the Feast of Tabernacles (see "The Festivals of Israel" on p. 186).

46 " 'This is what the Sovereign LORD says: The gate of the inner court[f] facing east[g] is to be shut on
the six working days, but on the Sabbath day and on the day of the New Moon[h] it is to be opened.
2 The prince is to enter from the outside through the portico[i] of the gateway and stand by the gatepost.
The priests are to sacrifice his burnt offering and his fellowship offerings.[a] He is to worship at the thresh-
old of the gateway and then go out, but the gate will not be shut until evening.[j] 3 On the Sabbaths and
New Moons the people of the land are to worship in the presence of the LORD at the entrance to that gate-
way.[k] 4 The burnt offering the prince brings to the LORD on the Sabbath day is to be six male lambs and
a ram, all without defect. 5 The grain offering given with the ram is to be an ephah,[b] and the grain offer-
ing with the lambs is to be as much as he pleases, along with a hin[c] of oil for each ephah.[l] 6 On the day of
the New Moon[m] he is to offer a young bull, six lambs and a ram, all without defect. 7 He is to provide as
a grain offering one ephah with the bull, one ephah with the ram, and with the lambs as much as he
wants to give, along with a hin of oil with each ephah.[n] 8 When the prince enters, he is to go in through
the portico[o] of the gateway, and he is to come out the same way.[p]

9 " 'When the people of the land come before the LORD at the appointed feasts,[q] whoever enters by the
north gate to worship is to go out the south gate; and whoever enters by the south gate is to go out the
north gate. No one is to return through the gate by which he entered, but each is to go out the opposite
gate. 10 The prince is to be among them, going in when they go in and going out when they go out.[r]

11 " 'At the festivals and the appointed feasts, the grain offering is to be an ephah with a bull, an ephah
with a ram, and with the lambs as much as one pleases, along with a hin of oil for each ephah.[s] 12 When
the prince provides[t] a freewill offering[u] to the LORD—whether a burnt offering or fellowship offerings—
the gate facing east is to be opened for him. He shall offer his burnt offering or his fellowship offerings
as he does on the Sabbath day. Then he shall go out, and after he has gone out, the gate will be shut.[v]

13 " 'Every day you are to provide a year-old lamb without defect for a burnt offering to the LORD; morn-
ing by morning you shall provide it.[w] 14 You are also to provide with it morning by morning a grain of-
fering, consisting of a sixth of an ephah with a third of a hin of oil to moisten the flour. The presenting
of this grain offering to the LORD is a lasting ordinance.[x] 15 So the lamb and the grain offering and the oil
shall be provided morning by morning for a regular[y] burnt offering.[z]

16 " 'This is what the Sovereign LORD says: If the prince makes a gift from his inheritance to one of his
sons, it will also belong to his descendants; it is to be their property by inheritance.[a] 17 If, however, he
makes a gift from his inheritance to one of his servants, the servant may keep it until the year of free-
dom;[b] then it will revert to the prince. His inheritance belongs to his sons only; it is theirs. 18 The prince
must not take any of the inheritance[c] of the people, driving them off their property. He is to give his sons
their inheritance out of his own property, so that none of my people will be separated from his prop-
erty.' "

19 Then the man brought me through the entrance[d] at the side of the gate to the sacred rooms facing
north, which belonged to the priests, and showed me a place at the western end. 20 He said to me, "This
is the place where the priests will cook the guilt offering and the sin offering and bake the grain offer-
ing, to avoid bringing them into the outer court and consecrating[e] the people."[f]

21 He then brought me to the outer court and led me around to its four corners, and I saw in each cor-
ner another court. 22 In the four corners of the outer court were enclosed[d] courts, forty cubits long and
thirty cubits wide; each of the courts in the four corners was the same size. 23 Around the inside of each
of the four courts was a ledge of stone, with places for fire built all around under the ledge. 24 He said to
me, "These are the kitchens where those who minister at the temple will cook the sacrifices of the people."

The River From the Temple

47 The man brought me back to the entrance of the temple, and I saw water[g] coming out from un-
der the threshold of the temple toward the east (for the temple faced east). The water was com-
ing down from under the south side of the temple, south of the altar.[h] 2 He then brought me out through

46:1 [f]Eze 40:19 [g]1Ch 9:18 [h]ver 6; Isa 66:23
46:2 [i]ver 8 [j]ver 12; Eze 44:3
46:3 [k]Lk 1:10
46:5 [l]ver 11; Eze 45:24
46:6 [m]ver 1; Nu 10:10
46:7 [n]Eze 45:24
46:8 [o]ver 2 [p]Eze 44:3
46:9 [q]Ex 23:14; 34:20
46:10 [r]2Sa 6:14-15; Ps 42:4
46:11 [s]ver 5
46:12 [t]Eze 45:17 [u]Lev 7:16 [v]ver 2
46:13 [w]Ex 29:38; Nu 28:3
46:14 [x]Da 8:11
46:15 [y]Ex 29:42 [z]Ex 29:38; Nu 28:5-6
46:16 [a]2Ch 21:3
46:17 [b]Lev 25:10
46:18 [c]Lev 25:23; Eze 45:8; Mic 2:1-2
46:19 [d]Eze 42:9
46:20 [e]Lev 6:27 [f]Zec 14:20
47:1 [g]Isa 55:1 [h]Ps 46:4; Joel 3:18; Rev 22:1

[a] 2 Traditionally *peace offerings*; also in verse 12 [b] 5 That is, probably about 3/5 bushel (about 22 liters) [c] 5 That is, probably about 4 quarts (about 4 liters) [d] 22 The meaning of the Hebrew for this word is uncertain.

46:3 For "people of the land," see the note on 7:27.
46:6 The "day of the New Moon" was the first day of the month.
46:17 "The year of freedom" was the Year of Jubilee, which was to be held every fiftieth year.
47:1 Ezekiel was standing in the inner court.
47:2 Ezekiel was brought out through the north gate because the east gate was closed (44:2).

the north gate and led me around the outside to the outer gate facing east, and the water was flowing
from the south side.
3 As the man went eastward with a measuring line[i] in his hand, he measured off a thousand cubits[a] **47:3** [i]Eze 40:3
and then led me through water that was ankle-deep. 4 He measured off another thousand cubits and led
me through water that was knee-deep. He measured off another thousand and led me through water that
was up to the waist. 5 He measured off another thousand, but now it was a river that I could not cross, be-
cause the water had risen and was deep enough to swim in—a river that no one could cross.[j] 6 He asked **47:5** [j]Isa 11:9; Hab 2:14
me, "Son of man, do you see this?"

[a] 3 That is, about 1,500 feet (about 450 meters)

The Geography of Ezekiel 47

En Gedi and the Dead Sea
Photograph: © Todd Bolen/Bible Places.com

EZEKIEL 47 The Great Rift Valley is an enormous depression roughly extending from north to south from Turkey to Lebanon and Syria, through the Galilee and Jordan Valleys, down to the Dead Sea and from there to the Gulf of Aqaba. The geologic depression continues in the form of the Gulf of Aqaba itself, creating a division between Arabia and the Sinai. From there it reappears on land in Africa and extends as far south as modern Mozambique.

In Palestine the depression created by the Great Rift Valley, known as the Arabah, runs from the Sea of Galilee to the Gulf of Aqaba (although at times the term Arabah is used to refer specifically to the desert valley extending from the Dead Sea to the Gulf of Aqaba). Waters from the Sea of Galilee flow south via the Jordan and are joined by the waters of the Yarmuk and Jabbok Rivers, both of which flow into the Jordan, which in turn empties into the Dead Sea. Water leaves the Dead Sea only by evaporation; there is no natural exit to the sea. For this reason the Dead Sea (or "Salt Sea") has a high concentration of minerals, prohibiting survival of aquatic life and rendering this body of water in effect "dead."

In Ezekiel's vision waters from the temple, located in the western central mountain region, flow eastward into the Arabah and the Jordan River Valley. The water from there flows into the Dead Sea and freshens its waters. In the vision this creates an environment favorable to the growth of trees, plants and fish. Fishermen in this visualization would spread their nets for fishing from En Gedi (located at the center of the western Dead Sea shoreline; see "Map 4")[1] to En Eglaim, an as yet unidentified ancient location.

Biblical scholars differ regarding whether this vision is to be read symbolically or literally. If it is to have a literal fulfillment, something must happen beyond what the text indicates. A simple infusion of fresh water would not in fact revive the Dead Sea, which already receives fresh water. The problem is that the water has no outlet. In favor of a more symbolic interpretation, Jesus may have been alluding to this passage in John 7:38.

[1]See "En Gedi" on page 643.

Then he led me back to the bank of the river. 7 When I arrived there, I saw a great number of trees on each side of the river.[k] 8 He said to me, "This water flows toward the eastern region and goes down into the Arabah,[a][l] where it enters the Sea.[b] When it empties into the Sea,[b] the water there becomes fresh.[m] 9 Swarms of living creatures will live wherever the river flows. There will be large numbers of fish, because this water flows there and makes the salt water fresh; so where the river flows everything will live.[n] 10 Fishermen[o] will stand along the shore; from En Gedi[p] to En Eglaim there will be places for spreading nets.[q] The fish will be of many kinds[r]—like the fish of the Great Sea.[c][s] 11 But the swamps and marshes will not become fresh; they will be left for salt.[t] 12 Fruit trees of all kinds will grow on both banks of the river.[u] Their leaves will not wither, nor will their fruit[v] fail. Every month they will bear, because the water from the sanctuary flows to them. Their fruit will serve for food and their leaves for healing.[w]"

The Boundaries of the Land

13 This is what the Sovereign LORD says: "These are the boundaries[x] by which you are to divide the land for an inheritance among the twelve tribes of Israel, with two portions for Joseph.[y] 14 You are to divide it equally among them. Because I swore with uplifted hand to give it to your forefathers, this land will become your inheritance.[z]

15 "This is to be the boundary of the land:

"On the north side it will run from the Great Sea by the Hethlon road[a] past Lebo[d] Hamath to Zedad, 16 Berothah[e][b] and Sibraim (which lies on the border between Damascus and Hamath),[c] as far as Hazer Hatticon, which is on the border of Hauran. 17 The boundary will extend from the sea to Hazar Enan,[f] along the northern border of Damascus, with the border of Hamath to the north. This will be the north boundary.[d]

18 "On the east side the boundary will run between Hauran and Damascus, along the Jordan between Gilead and the land of Israel, to the eastern sea and as far as Tamar.[g] This will be the east boundary.

19 "On the south side it will run from Tamar as far as the waters of Meribah Kadesh,[e] then along the Wadi ⌞of Egypt⌟[f] to the Great Sea.[g] This will be the south boundary.

20 "On the west side, the Great Sea will be the boundary to a point opposite Lebo[h] Hamath.[h] This will be the west boundary.[i]

21 "You are to distribute this land among yourselves according to the tribes of Israel. 22 You are to allot it as an inheritance for yourselves and for the aliens[j] who have settled among you and who have children. You are to consider them as native-born Israelites; along with you they are to be allotted an inheritance among the tribes of Israel.[k] 23 In whatever tribe the alien settles, there you are to give him his inheritance," declares the Sovereign LORD.

The Division of the Land

48 "These are the tribes, listed by name: At the northern frontier, Dan[l] will have one portion; it will follow the Hethlon road[m] to Lebo[i] Hamath;[n] Hazar Enan and the northern border of Damascus next to Hamath will be part of its border from the east side to the west side.

47:7 [k]ver 12; Rev 22:2
47:8 [l]Dt 3:17; Jos 3:16 [m]Isa 41:18
47:9 [n]Isa 12:3; 55:1; Jn 4:14; 7:37-38
47:10 [o]Mt 4:19 [p]Jos 15:62 [q]Eze 26:5 [r]Ps 104:25; Mt 13:47 [s]Nu 34:6
47:11 [t]Dt 29:23
47:12 [u]ver 7; Rev 22:2 [v]Ps 1:3 [w]Ge 2:9; Jer 17:8
47:13 [x]Nu 34:2-12 [y]Ge 48:5
47:14 [z]Ge 12:7; Dt 1:8; Eze 20:5-6
47:15 [a]Eze 48:1
47:16 [b]2Sa 8:8 [c]Nu 13:21; Eze 48:1
47:17 [d]Eze 48:1
47:19 [e]Dt 32:51 [f]Isa 27:12 [g]Eze 48:28
47:20 [h]Eze 48:1 [i]Nu 34:6
47:22 [j]Isa 14:1 [k]Nu 26:55-56; Isa 56:6-7; Ro 10:12; Eph 2:12-16; 3:6; Col 3:11
48:1 [l]Ge 30:6 [m]Eze 47:15-17 [n]Eze 47:20

[a] *8* Or *the Jordan Valley* [b] *8* That is, the Dead Sea [c] *10* That is, the Mediterranean; also in verses 15, 19 and 20 [d] *15* Or *past the entrance to* [e] *15,16* See Septuagint and Ezekiel 48:1; Hebrew *road to go into Zedad, 16Hamath, Berothah* [f] *17* Hebrew *Enon,* a variant of *Enan* [g] *18* Septuagint and Syriac; Hebrew *Israel. You will measure to the eastern sea* [h] *20* Or *opposite the entrance to* [i] *1* Or *to the entrance to*

47:8 The Arabah here refers to the Jordan Valley, the waterless region between Jerusalem and the Dead Sea (see "The Geography of Ezekiel 47" on p. 1378).

"The Sea" usually refers to the Mediterranean Sea, but here it is a reference to the Dead Sea, the lowest (1,300 ft—nearly 400 m—below sea level) and saltiest (25 percent) body of water in the world (see the note on Zec 14:8). It contains so much salt, in fact, that nothing can live in it. That it should sustain such an abundance of life indicates the wonderful, renewing power of this "river of the water of life" (Rev 22:1).

47:10 See "En Gedi" on page 643.

En Eglaim may be Ain Feshkha, at the northwestern corner of the Dead Sea, although some suggest a location on the eastern bank.

The "Great Sea" is the Mediterranean.

47:11 For the phrase "left for salt," see the note on Leviticus 2:13.

47:13–20 The boundaries were similar to the original area God had promised the Israelites through Moses in Numbers 34:1–12—stretching from Lebo Hamath in the north to the Wadi of Egypt and Meribah Kadesh in the south, from the Mediterranean in the west roughly to the Jordan River and the Dead Sea in the east. Strikingly absent is the area east of the Jordan River, which, though occupied by Israel for much of its history, was not part of God's original promise.

47:22–23 There would be a land inheritance not just for native Israelites but also for resident aliens. In earlier Old Testament legislation aliens were protected as a powerless class. Because they could not own land, they lacked full citizenship rights. But they could participate fully in Israel's religious life, and some had relocated for this reason. God recognized these proselytes/converts by giving them a hereditary portion of the renewed land.

48:1–29 The tribes were assigned equal portions of land, running in strips from east to west. This was a fair way to divide a country whose major topographic features ran from north to south. But,

[2]"Asher[o] will have one portion; it will border the territory of Dan from east to west.

[3]"Naphtali[p] will have one portion; it will border the territory of Asher from east to west.

[4]"Manasseh[q] will have one portion; it will border the territory of Naphtali from east to west.

[5]"Ephraim[r] will have one portion; it will border the territory of Manasseh[s] from east to west.[t]

[6]"Reuben[u] will have one portion; it will border the territory of Ephraim from east to west.

[7]"Judah[v] will have one portion; it will border the territory of Reuben from east to west.

[8]"Bordering the territory of Judah from east to west will be the portion you are to present as a special gift. It will be 25,000 cubits[a] wide, and its length from east to west will equal one of the tribal portions; the sanctuary will be in the center of it.[w]

[9]"The special portion you are to offer to the LORD will be 25,000 cubits long and 10,000 cubits[b] wide.[x] [10]This will be the sacred portion for the priests. It will be 25,000 cubits long on the north side, 10,000 cubits wide on the west side, 10,000 cubits wide on the east side and 25,000 cubits long on the south side. In the center of it will be the sanctuary of the LORD.[y] [11]This will be for the consecrated priests, the Zadokites,[z] who were faithful in serving me[a] and did not go astray as the Levites did when the Israelites went astray.[b] [12]It will be a special gift to them from the sacred portion of the land, a most holy portion, bordering the territory of the Levites.

[13]"Alongside the territory of the priests, the Levites will have an allotment 25,000 cubits long and 10,000 cubits wide. Its total length will be 25,000 cubits and its width 10,000 cubits.[c] [14]They must not sell or exchange any of it. This is the best of the land and must not pass into other hands, because it is holy to the LORD.[d]

[15]"The remaining area, 5,000 cubits wide and 25,000 cubits long, will be for the common use of the city, for houses and for pastureland. The city will be in the center of it [16]and will have these measurements: the north side 4,500 cubits, the south side 4,500 cubits, the east side 4,500 cubits, and the west side 4,500 cubits.[e] [17]The pastureland for the city will be 250 cubits on the north, 250 cubits on the south, 250 cubits on the east, and 250 cubits on the west. [18]What remains of the area, bordering on the sacred portion and running the length of it, will be 10,000 cubits on the east side and 10,000 cubits on the west side. Its produce will supply food for the workers of the city.[f] [19]The workers from the city who farm it will come from all the tribes of Israel. [20]The entire portion will be a square, 25,000 cubits on each side. As a special gift you will set aside the sacred portion, along with the property of the city.

[21]"What remains on both sides of the area formed by the sacred portion and the city property will belong to the prince. It will extend eastward from the 25,000 cubits of the sacred portion to the eastern border, and westward from the 25,000 cubits to the western border. Both these areas running the length of the tribal portions will belong to the prince, and the sacred portion with the temple sanctuary will be in the center of them.[g] [22]So the property of the Levites and the property of the city will lie in the center of the area that belongs to the prince. The area belonging to the prince will lie between the border of Judah and the border of Benjamin.

[23]"As for the rest of the tribes: Benjamin[h] will have one portion; it will extend from the east side to the west side.

[24]"Simeon[i] will have one portion; it will border the territory of Benjamin from east to west.

[25]"Issachar[j] will have one portion; it will border the territory of Simeon from east to west.

[26]"Zebulun[k] will have one portion; it will border the territory of Issachar from east to west.

[27]"Gad[l] will have one portion; it will border the territory of Zebulun from east to west.

[28]"The southern boundary of Gad will run south from Tamar[m] to the waters of Meribah Kadesh, then along the Wadi ⌊of Egypt⌋ to the Great Sea.[c][n]

[29]"This is the land you are to allot as an inheritance to the tribes of Israel, and these will be their portions," declares the Sovereign LORD.

The Gates of the City

[30]"These will be the exits of the city: Beginning on the north side, which is 4,500 cubits long, [31]the

48:2 [o]Jos 19:24-31
48:3 [p]Jos 19:32-39
48:4 [q]Jos 17:1-11
48:5 [r]Jos 16:5-9 [s]Jos 17:7-10 [t]Jos 17:17
48:6 [u]Jos 13:15-21
48:7 [v]Jos 15:1-63
48:8 [w]ver 21
48:9 [x]Eze 45:1
48:10 [y]ver 21; Eze 45:3-4
48:11 [z]2Sa 8:17 [a]Lev 8:35 [b]Eze 14:11; 44:15
48:13 [c]Eze 45:5
48:14 [d]Lev 25:34; 27:10,28
48:16 [e]Rev 21:16
48:18 [f]Eze 45:6
48:21 [g]ver 8,10; Eze 45:7
48:23 [h]Jos 18:11-28
48:24 [i]Ge 29:33; Jos 19:1-9
48:25 [j]Jos 19:17-23
48:26 [k]Jos 19:10-16
48:27 [l]Jos 13:24-28
48:28 [m]Ge 14:7 [n]Eze 47:19

[a] *8* That is, about 7 miles (about 12 kilometers) [b] *9* That is, about 3 miles (about 5 kilometers) [c] *28* That is, the Mediterranean

more significantly, it oriented the land along the sacred east-west axis of the temple. The tribal strips themselves were undefined, with the borders between tribes unmarked by geographic indicators. This contrasted with the historical division of the land in Joshua 14–21, in which tribal boundaries were clearly defined.

48:11 For "Zadokites," see the note on 44:15.

48:30–35 The new city, like the temple, is pictured as a perfect square. Its 12 gates were named after the 12 tribes of Israel. Since Levi was included in this list, Joseph (v. 32) represented Ephraim and Manasseh in order to keep the number at 12.

gates of the city will be named after the tribes of Israel. The three gates on the north side will be the gate
of Reuben, the gate of Judah and the gate of Levi.
[32]"On the east side, which is 4,500 cubits long, will be three gates: the gate of Joseph, the gate of Ben-
jamin and the gate of Dan.
[33]"On the south side, which measures 4,500 cubits, will be three gates: the gate of Simeon, the gate of
Issachar and the gate of Zebulun.
[34]"On the west side, which is 4,500 cubits long, will be three gates: the gate of Gad, the gate of Asher
and the gate of Naphtali.
[35]"The distance all around will be 18,000 cubits.
"And the name of the city from that time on will be:

THE LORD IS THERE.[o]"

48:35 [o]Isa 12:6; 24:23; Jer 3:17; 14:9; 33:16; Joel 3:21; Zec 2:10; Rev 21:3

INTRODUCTION TO 

AUTHOR, PLACE AND DATE OF WRITING

The book of Daniel gives the Bible interpreter two clear alternatives: Either it was recounted by Daniel himself or by a person close to him and is historically trustworthy, or it was written by a religious zealot during the Maccabean revolt and is pure fiction.

The question of authorship is essentially dependent upon the issue of when the book was written. The supposition that it was recorded by Daniel or an associate from Babylon and later Persia implies a date of approximately 530 B.C. The suggestion that it was instead composed during the Maccabean wars places the date of writing at approximately 165 B.C. The arguments for either side are complex, but there is good reason for considering Daniel to be historically trustworthy and written early in the Persian period (see "When Was Daniel Written?" on p. 1385).

AUDIENCE

Based upon the assumption of an early date of composition (530 B.C.), Daniel wrote to his fellow Jewish exiles in Babylon to remind them of God's sovereign control over world history and to encourage them with God's promises of restoration.

CULTURAL FACTS AND HIGHLIGHTS

Advocates of a late date of composition (c. 165 B.C.) argue that the book was intended essentially to encourage Jews locked at that time in conflict with the ruthless Seleucid king Antiochus IV (see "Antiochus IV Epiphanes" on p. 1406). From the perspective of scholars holding to this view, Daniel was meant to persuade the struggling Jews of that much later time that there were historical examples of godly Jews having overcome pagan kings and their persecutions of God's people (Da 3–6). In addition, these researchers argue, the prophecies of chapters 2, 7, 8 and 11 were intended to encourage the people that all of the troubles they were enduring under Antiochus had been foreseen and that the fullness of the kingdom of God would come immediately after Antiochus's downfall. Intrinsic to this interpretation is the presupposition that all of these historical examples and prophecies were in fact aspects of a pious fraud.

Against this, and apart from the fact that the inclusion of a "pious fraud" in the Bible would be, to say the least, theologically troublesome, it may be helpful to note that the pagan kings in Daniel are at times portrayed in positive terms (4:1–3,36–37; 6:19–28). If the historical context of Daniel were the much later Jewish war against Antiochus IV, a man who set up an image to Zeus and sacrificed pigs (ritually unclean animals) at the Jerusalem temple—a man who in fact tried to eradicate Judaism—this positive portrayal of pagan kings by a zealous Jewish combatant would be inexplicable.

But what is the purpose of Daniel if it is understood to be a historical document from 530 B.C.? Evidently the book was intended to encourage Jews of the exile and Diaspora to remain faithful in the face of a prolonged period during which Israel would remain at best an obscure, subservient nation under the rule of a series of Gentile world powers. Some Gentile rulers would be harsh and oppressive, while others would be tolerant and even supportive of the Jews. Yet through it all, generations of Daniel's readers could take heart in the fact that God had foreseen their trouble and would go on to see them through it.

TIMELINE

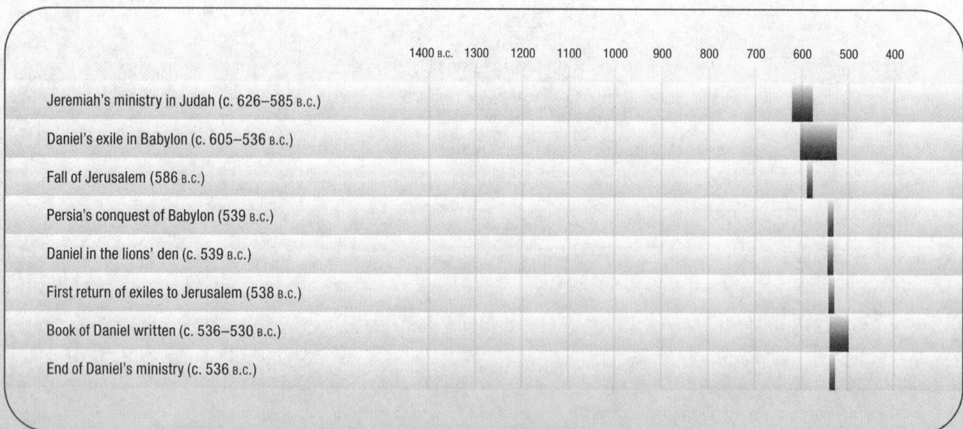

AS YOU READ

The riveting narratives in chapters 1–6 will easily hold the reader's attention. Look for examples of uncompromising faith in the face of the worst possible odds—that is, without God's sovereignty taken into account.

As you tackle the apocalyptic literature found in the rest of the book, you might find an in-depth Bible commentary a welcome companion. A well-researched commentary will no doubt point out and discuss similarities between this highly symbolic portion of Daniel and the book of Revelation at the end of the New Testament.

DID YOU KNOW?

- Daniel had been carried off to Babylon as part of a deportation in 605 B.C., but he was still there in 539 B.C. and still alive when the first exiles returned to Jerusalem (Da 1:1).
- Belshazzar, Nabonidus's son, was coregent with his father and ruled Babylon during Nabonidus's ten-year absence from the capital city (5:1).
- The identity of "King Darius" is puzzling. In this instance, "Darius" was evidently a throne name for someone ruling on orders from Cyrus or else Cyrus's throne name in Babylon (6:1).

THEMES

Daniel's themes include:

1. *God's sovereignty.* The narratives in Daniel emphasize God's faithfulness and absolute autonomy over world history (2:47; 3:17–18; 4:28–37; 5:18–31). Despite appearances, God is in control over global events, kingdoms and governments (5:21).

2. *Faithfulness to God.* God rewards those who are sincerely devoted to him and acknowledge him (cf. 1:8 with 1:15–20; 2:17–18 with 2:19; 2:27–28 with 2:48–49; 3:12,16–18 with 3:26–30; 5:16–18 with 5:29; 6:7–12 with 6:19–24). The book reveals that it is possible for God's oppressed people to survive and even thrive in a culture hostile to their faith.

3. *Prophecies of future events.* Daniel's four visions contain predictions of future periods of persecution, as well as of the return of the triumphant Christ (7:11,26–27; 8:25; 9:27; 11:45; 12:13). Daniel's visions encourage God's faithful people who are living under oppression and persecution by offering a divine perspective upon reality that differs from the purely visible: God will ultimately win the victory, so believers of any era can live their lives in the expectation of final triumph (2:44; 7:27; Rev 11:15).

OUTLINE

I. The Captivity, Faithfulness and Elevation of Daniel and His Three Friends (1)

II. The Destinies of the Nations (2–7)
   - A. Nebuchadnezzar's Dream of a Statue (2)
   - B. Nebuchadnezzar's Golden Image and Its Worship (3)
   - C. Nebuchadnezzar's Vision of a Large Tree (4)
   - D. Belshazzar's and Babylon's Downfall (5)
   - E. Daniel's Deliverance From the Lions' Den (6)
   - F. Daniel's Dream of Four Beasts (7)

III. Israel's Destiny (8–12)
   - A. Daniel's Vision of a Ram and a Goat (8)
   - B. Daniel's Prayer and His Vision of the 70 "Sevens" (9)
   - C. Daniel's Vision of Israel's Future (10–12)

Daniel's Training in Babylon

1 In the third year of the reign of Jehoiakim king of Judah, Nebuchadnezzar[a] king of Babylon came to 1:1 [a]2Ki 24:1
Jerusalem and besieged it.[b] 2 And the Lord delivered Jehoiakim king of Judah into his hand, along [b]2Ch 36:6
with some of the articles from the temple of God. These he carried off to the temple of his god in Bab-
ylonia[a] and put in the treasure house of his god.[c] 1:2 [c]2Ch 36:7;
3 Then the king ordered Ashpenaz, chief of his court officials, to bring in some of the Israelites from Jer 27:19-20; Zec 5:5-11
the royal family and the nobility[d]— 4 young men without any physical defect, handsome, showing apti- 1:3 [d]2Ki 20:18;
tude for every kind of learning, well informed, quick to understand, and qualified to serve in the king's 24:15; Isa 39:7
palace. He was to teach them the language and literature of the Babylonians.[b] 5 The king assigned them
a daily amount of food and wine[e] from the king's table. They were to be trained for three years, and af- 1:5 [e]ver 8,10
ter that they were to enter the king's service.[f] [f]ver 19
6 Among these were some from Judah: Daniel,[g] Hananiah, Mishael and Azariah. 7 The chief official 1:6 [g]Eze 14:14
gave them new names: to Daniel, the name Belteshazzar;[h] to Hananiah, Shadrach; to Mishael, Meshach; 1:7 [h]Da 4:8; 5:12
and to Azariah, Abednego.[i] [i]Da 2:49; 3:12
8 But Daniel resolved not to defile[j] himself with the royal food and wine, and he asked the chief offi- 1:8 [j]Eze 4:13-14
cial for permission not to defile himself this way. 9 Now God had caused the official to show favor[k] and 1:9 [k]Ge 39:21;
sympathy[l] to Daniel, 10 but the official told Daniel, "I am afraid of my lord the king, who has assigned Pr 16:7 [l]1Ki 8:50; Ps 106:46
your[c] food and drink. Why should he see you looking worse than the other young men your age? The
king would then have my head because of you."
11 Daniel then said to the guard whom the chief official had appointed over Daniel, Hananiah, Mish-
ael and Azariah, 12 "Please test your servants for ten days: Give us nothing but vegetables to eat and wa-
ter to drink. 13 Then compare our appearance with that of the young men who eat the royal food, and
treat your servants in accordance with what you see." 14 So he agreed to this and tested them for ten days.
15 At the end of the ten days they looked healthier and better nourished than any of the young men who
ate the royal food.[m] 16 So the guard took away their choice food and the wine they were to drink and gave 1:15 [m]Ex 23:25
them vegetables instead.[n] 1:16 [n]ver 12-13
17 To these four young men God gave knowledge and understanding[o] of all kinds of literature and 1:17 [o]1Ki 3:12
learning.[p] And Daniel could understand visions and dreams of all kinds.[q] [p]Da 2:23; Jas 1:5 [q]Da 2:19,30; 7:1; 8:1
18 At the end of the time[r] set by the king to bring them in, the chief official presented them to Nebu- 1:18 [r]ver 5
chadnezzar. 19 The king talked with them, and he found none equal to Daniel, Hananiah, Mishael and Az- 1:19 [s]Ge 41:46
ariah; so they entered the king's service.[s] 20 In every matter of wisdom and understanding about which 1:20 [t]1Ki 4:30;
the king questioned them, he found them ten times better than all the magicians and enchanters in his Da 2:13,28
whole kingdom.[t]
21 And Daniel remained there until the first year of King Cyrus.[u] 1:21 [u]Da 6:28; 10:1

[a] 2 Hebrew *Shinar* [b] 4 Or *Chaldeans* [c] 10 The Hebrew for *your* and *you* in this verse is plural.

1:1 According to the Babylonian system of computing the years of a king's reign, the third year of Jehoiakim would have been 605 B.C., since his first full year of kingship began on New Year's Day after his accession in 608. But according to the system in Judah, which counted the year of accession as the first year of reign, this was "the fourth year of Jehoiakim" (see Jer 25:1; 46:2 and its note; see also "The Problem of the Chronology of the Kings of Judah and Israel" on p. 508).

Since the first chapter of the book of Daniel begins and ends with chronological markers, we are able to date Daniel's career. Although Jerusalem was destroyed by the Babylonians in 586 B.C., Daniel had been carried off to Babylon as part of an earlier deportation in 605 B.C. Daniel 1:21 tells us that he was still there in 539 B.C. Since Daniel mentioned in 10:1 that he received a vision during the third year of Cyrus, we know that he was still alive when the first exiles returned to Jerusalem.

1:2 Articles from the temple were "carried off" when Judah was exiled to Babylonia. The first deportation (605 B.C.) included Daniel and the second (597) Ezekiel. A third deportation took place in 586, when the Babylonians destroyed the city of Jerusalem and Solomon's temple (see "Exile and Genocide in the Ancient Near East" on p. 1337).

Nebuchadnezzar's god was Marduk, the god of cosmic order and the chief god of the Babylonian pantheon.

1:4 The "language and literature of the Babylonians" included the classical literature in Sumerian and Akkadian cuneiform, a complicated syllabic writing system (see "Sumer" on p. 10 and "Cuneiform and Clay Tablets in the Ancient Near East" on p. 1108). The language of normal communication in multiracial Babylon was Aramaic, which was written in an easily learned alphabetic script and understood by all (see the note on 2:4).

1:7 The new names implied submission to Nebuchadnezzar's authority (see Ge 17:5; 2Ki 23:34 and their notes). The names of pagan gods were incorporated into the meanings of these Babylonian names: Belteshazzar probably means "Bel (i.e., Marduk), protect his life!"; Shadrach "command of Aku (the Sumerian moon god)"; Meshach "Who is what Aku is?"; and Abednego "servant of Nego/Nebo/Nabu."

1:8 Daniel considered the food and drink from Nebuchadnezzar's table to be ritually contaminated because the first portion of the food had been offered to idols and a portion of the wine had been poured out on a pagan altar (see "'Temple Restaurants' and Food Sacrificed to Idols" on p. 1871 for a NT equivalent). In addition, ceremonially unclean animals were eaten, and even those considered clean were neither slaughtered nor prepared according to the regulations of the Mosaic Law (see "Clean and Unclean Foods in the Bible and the Ancient Near East" on p. 168).

1:17 With God's help Daniel and his friends mastered the essential Babylonian literature (see the note on 1:4), as well as the subtleties of astrology and divination by dreams (see the note on Ge 40:8; see also "Dream Oracles of the Ancient World" on p. 741).

1:20 "Magicians and enchanters" refers to those trained in the magic "arts" of divination (see the note on Dt 18:10–18; see also "Akkadian Divination" on p. 277).

1:21 Daniel spent about 70 years in Babylonia and was still living in the year 537 B.C. (10:1), affording him the satisfaction of seeing the first exiles return to Judah from Babylonian captivity.

WHEN WAS DANIEL WRITTEN?

DANIEL 1 The dating of Daniel is controversial (see also the book introduction). Traditional scholarship holds that the book was composed in the sixth century B.C., concurrent with the historical information it provides. But common arguments for dating Daniel in the second century B.C. are as follows:

◆ Jesus ben Sirach (Sir 44–50),[1] writing in approximately 180 B.C., cited numerous Old Testament heroes—but not Daniel.

◆ Belshazzar is called "king" of **Babylon**[2] in Daniel 5; the actual king was Nabonidus.

◆ Darius the Mede (ch. 6) is otherwise unknown.

◆ The stories of Nebuchadnezzar's insanity[3] and of the fiery furnace read like pious legends—far-fetched miracle stories common in **intertestamental** Jewish texts.

◆ Half of Daniel was written in Aramaic,[4] a language Jews spoke during the **intertestamental period**. Daniel 3 also includes three Greek words—suggesting that the book was written after Greek culture had invaded the Near East.

◆ But this evidence is not as strong as it appears:

◆ Ben Sirach also omits mention of other famous Israelites, including Ezra. Also, Sirach may himself have been influenced by Daniel. In Sirach 36:10 he prayed, "Hasten the day, and remember the appointed time"—verbiage resembling Daniel 11:27, 35. It may be that ben Sirach offhandedly cited Daniel, which of course implies that the book already existed in his lifetime.

◆ The book demonstrates familiarity with the history and culture of the seventh and sixth centuries B.C. Daniel rightly portrays the position of Belshazzar, coregent with Nabonidus. He could have appropriately been called "king" (5:1), but in 5:16 Belshazzar offered to make the one who could interpret the writing on the wall "the third highest ruler in the kingdom." As Belshazzar was himself the second ruler,[5] this was the highest honor he could confer.

◆ Darius the Mede is not mentioned by that name outside the Bible.[6] This is the kind of historical puzzle scholars frequently encounter in ancient texts. In contrast, intertestamental Jewish works of religious fiction lack historical credibility in a way that has no parallel in historical works. The Apocryphal book of Judith, for example, written during the reign of Antiochus IV, contains absurd historical blunders and is altogether unlike Daniel.

◆ The miracles of Daniel are outside the ability of history or archaeology to prove. Still, the following observations are pertinent:

Miracles do not prove that a work is fictional.

Nebuchadnezzar's madness was a rare but authentic clinical condition called boanthropy. "Made-up" miracle stories contain outrageous elements with no clinical analogy (e.g., in Tb 2:9–10, another Apocryphal book, Tobit goes blind because of sparrow droppings in his eyes).

Basalt stela representing Nabonidus (555–539 B.C.), the last ruler of the Neo-Babylonian Empire

© Dr. James C. Martin; the British Museum; photographed by permission

◆ The fact that half of Daniel is written in Aramaic is a mystery with regard to any proposed reconstruction of its history.

But the Aramaic of Daniel is "official," or "imperial"—the standardized Aramaic used in official correspondence when Aramaic was the lingua franca of the Near East (see 2Ki 18:26; Ezr 4:7; Da 2:4), not the colloquial, regional Aramaic of second-century B.C. Palestine, at which time the common language of the region was Greek.

All three of the Greek words of 3:5 are musical terms. Greek poets and musicians were renowned, so their musical vocabulary came into use early. What would be surprising is how little Greek appears in Daniel, if the book had been written in the second century B.C., when the world was thoroughly **Hellenized**.

The Persian words in Daniel are of an older, pre-Hellenistic Persian.

◆ The Dead Sea Scrolls have thrown new light on Daniel. Cave 1 at **Qumran** contained several fragments of the book (1QDan[a-b]) in a script suggesting a second-century B.C. date. Other Daniel fragments from Cave 4 are in a style suggestive of a late **Hasmonean** or early Herodian date. It would be unlikely that such an unusual book, written as late as 165 B.C., would have been so quickly accepted and circulated as authoritative Scripture.

[1]Sirach is an Apocryphal book; see "The Apocrypha" on page 1973. [2]See Glossary on page 2080 for definitions of bolded words. [3]See "Nebuchadnezzar's Madness" on page 1391. [4]See "Languages of the Old Testament World" on page 672. [5]See "Nabonidus and Belshazzar" on page 1394. [6]See "Darius the Mede" on page 1396.

Nebuchadnezzar's Dream

2 In the second year of his reign, Nebuchadnezzar had dreams;[v] his mind was troubled[w] and he could
not sleep.[x] 2So the king summoned the magicians,[y] enchanters, sorcerers[z] and astrologers[a][a] to tell
him what he had dreamed.[b] When they came in and stood before the king, 3he said to them, "I have had
a dream that troubles[c] me and I want to know what it means.[b]"
4Then the astrologers answered the king in Aramaic,[c][d] "O king, live forever![e] Tell your servants the
dream, and we will interpret it."
5The king replied to the astrologers, "This is what I have firmly decided: If you do not tell me what my
dream was and interpret it, I will have you cut into pieces[f] and your houses turned into piles of rubble.[g]
6But if you tell me the dream and explain it, you will receive from me gifts and rewards and great hon-
or.[h] So tell me the dream and interpret it for me."
7Once more they replied, "Let the king tell his servants the dream, and we will interpret it."
8Then the king answered, "I am certain that you are trying to gain time, because you realize that this
is what I have firmly decided: 9If you do not tell me the dream, there is just one penalty[i] for you. You have
conspired to tell me misleading and wicked things, hoping the situation will change. So then, tell me the
dream, and I will know that you can interpret it for me."[j]
10The astrologers answered the king, "There is not a man on earth who can do what the king asks! No
king, however great and mighty, has ever asked such a thing of any magician or enchanter or astrolo-
ger.[k] 11What the king asks is too difficult. No one can reveal it to the king except the gods,[l] and they do
not live among men."
12This made the king so angry and furious[m] that he ordered the execution[n] of all the wise men of
Babylon. 13So the decree was issued to put the wise men to death, and men were sent to look for Daniel
and his friends to put them to death.[o]
14When Arioch, the commander of the king's guard, had gone out to put to death the wise men of
Babylon, Daniel spoke to him with wisdom and tact. 15He asked the king's officer, "Why did the king is-
sue such a harsh decree?" Arioch then explained the matter to Daniel. 16At this, Daniel went in to the king
and asked for time, so that he might interpret the dream for him.
17Then Daniel returned to his house and explained the matter to his friends Hananiah, Mishael and
Azariah.[p] 18He urged them to plead for mercy[q] from the God of heaven concerning this mystery,[r] so that
he and his friends might not be executed with the rest of the wise men of Babylon. 19During the night
the mystery[s] was revealed to Daniel in a vision.[t] Then Daniel praised the God of heaven 20and said:

"Praise be to the name of God for ever and ever;[u]
  wisdom and power[v] are his.
21 He changes times and seasons;[w]
  he sets up kings and deposes[x] them.
He gives wisdom[y] to the wise
  and knowledge to the discerning.
22 He reveals deep and hidden things;[z]
  he knows what lies in darkness,[a]
  and light[b] dwells with him.
23 I thank and praise you, O God of my fathers:[c]
  You have given me wisdom[d] and power,
you have made known to me what we asked of you,
  you have made known to us the dream of the king."

2:1 [v]Job 33:15, 18; Da 4:5 [w]Ge 41:8 [x]Est 6:1; Da 6:18
2:2 [y]Ge 41:8 [z]Ex 7:11 [a]ver 10; Da 5:7 [b]Da 4:6
2:3 [c]Da 4:5
2:4 [d]Ezr 4:7 [e]Da 3:9; 5:10
2:5 [f]ver 12 [g]Ezr 6:11; Da 3:29
2:6 [h]ver 48; Da 5:7,16
2:9 [i]Est 4:11 [j]Isa 41:22-24
2:10 [k]ver 27
2:11 [l]Da 5:11
2:12 [m]Da 3:13,19 [n]ver 5
2:13 [o]Da 1:20
2:17 [p]Da 1:6
2:18 [q]Isa 37:4 [r]Jer 33:3
2:19 [s]ver 28 [t]Job 33:15; Da 1:17
2:20 [u]Ps 113:2; 145:1-2 [v]Jer 32:19
2:21 [w]Da 7:25 [x]Job 12:19; Ps 75:6-7 [y]Jas 1:5
2:22 [z]Job 12:22; Ps 25:14; Da 5:11 [a]Ps 139:11-12; Jer 23:24; Heb 4:13 [b]Isa 45:7; Jas 1:17
2:23 [c]Ex 3:15 [d]Da 1:17

[a] *2* Or *Chaldeans*; also in verses 4, 5 and 10 [b] *3* Or *was* [c] *4* The text from here through chapter 7 is in Aramaic.

2:1 The date was 604 B.C. (see 1:1 and its note).

2:2 See "Akkadian Divination" on page 277.

Although the translation "astrologers" appears several times in the English Bible (e.g., Da 3:8; 4:7; 5:7,11), the only unequivocal reference to the practice and its practitioners is found in Isaiah 47:13 ("those stargazers who make predictions month by month") and in Jeremiah 10:2 (where people are urged not to be "terrified by signs in the sky"). It was characteristic of both Babylonian and Egyptian wisdom to ponder the movement of the stars, taking note of variations and conjunctions in order to predict events on Earth.

2:4 Since the astrologers were of varied racial backgrounds, they communicated in Aramaic, the commonly understood language of the time. From this point until the end of chapter 7 the entire narrative is in Aramaic.

2:14 Arioch was also the name of a Mesopotamian king who had lived centuries earlier (Ge 14:1).

2:18 "Mystery," a key word in Daniel (vv. 19,27–30,47; 4:9), also appears frequently in the writings of the Qumran sect (the Dead Sea Scrolls). In the New Testament the Greek equivalent refers to the secret purposes of God (see Ro 11:25; Rev 10:7).

Daniel Interprets the Dream

2:24 [e]ver 14 24 Then Daniel went to Arioch,[e] whom the king had appointed to execute the wise men of Babylon, and
said to him, "Do not execute the wise men of Babylon. Take me to the king, and I will interpret his dream
for him."

2:25 [f]Da 1:6; 5:13; 6:13 25 Arioch took Daniel to the king at once and said, "I have found a man among the exiles from Judah[f]
who can tell the king what his dream means."

2:26 [g]Da 1:7 26 The king asked Daniel (also called Belteshazzar),[g] "Are you able to tell me what I saw in my dream
and interpret it?"

27 Daniel replied, "No wise man, enchanter, magician or diviner can explain to the king the mystery
2:27 [h]ver 10 he has asked about,[h] 28 but there is a God in heaven who reveals mysteries.[i] He has shown King Nebuchad-
2:28 [i]Ge 40:8; Am 4:13 [j]Ge 49:1; Da 10:14 [k]Da 4:5 nezzar what will happen in days to come.[j] Your dream and the visions that passed through your mind[k]
as you lay on your bed are these:

29 "As you were lying there, O king, your mind turned to things to come, and the revealer of mysteries
2:30 [l]Isa 45:3; Da 1:17; Am 4:13 showed you what is going to happen. 30 As for me, this mystery has been revealed[l] to me, not because I
have greater wisdom than other living men, but so that you, O king, may know the interpretation and
that you may understand what went through your mind.

2:31 [m]Hab 1:7 31 "You looked, O king, and there before you stood a large statue—an enormous, dazzling statue,[m]
awesome in appearance. 32 The head of the statue was made of pure gold, its chest and arms of silver, its
belly and thighs of bronze, 33 its legs of iron, its feet partly of iron and partly of baked clay. 34 While you
2:34 [n]Zec 4:6 [o]ver 44-45; Ps 2:9; Isa 60:12; Da 8:25 were watching, a rock was cut out, but not by human hands.[n] It struck the statue on its feet of iron and
clay and smashed them.[o] 35 Then the iron, the clay, the bronze, the silver and the gold were broken to piec-
es at the same time and became like chaff on a threshing floor in the summer. The wind swept them
2:35 [p]Ps 1:4; 37:10; Isa 17:13 [q]Isa 2:3; Mic 4:1 away[p] without leaving a trace. But the rock that struck the statue became a huge mountain[q] and filled the
whole earth.

2:37 [r]Eze 26:7 [s]Jer 27:7 36 "This was the dream, and now we will interpret it to the king. 37 You, O king, are the king of kings.[r]
The God of heaven has given you dominion[s] and power and might and glory; 38 in your hands he has
placed mankind and the beasts of the field and the birds of the air. Wherever they live, he has made you
2:38 [t]Jer 27:6; Da 4:21-22 ruler over them all.[t] You are that head of gold.

39 "After you, another kingdom will rise, inferior to yours. Next, a third kingdom, one of bronze, will
rule over the whole earth. 40 Finally, there will be a fourth kingdom, strong as iron—for iron breaks and
2:40 [u]Da 7:7,23 smashes everything—and as iron breaks things to pieces, so it will crush and break all the others.[u] 41 Just
as you saw that the feet and toes were partly of baked clay and partly of iron, so this will be a divided king-
dom; yet it will have some of the strength of iron in it, even as you saw iron mixed with clay. 42 As the toes
were partly iron and partly clay, so this kingdom will be partly strong and partly brittle. 43 And just as
you saw the iron mixed with baked clay, so the people will be a mixture and will not remain united, any
more than iron mixes with clay.

44 "In the time of those kings, the God of heaven will set up a kingdom that will never be destroyed,
2:44 [v]Ps 2:9; 1Co 15:24 [w]Isa 60:12 [x]Ps 145:13; Isa 9:7; Da 4:34; 6:26; 7:14,27; Mic 4:7,13; Lk 1:33 nor will it be left to another people. It will crush[v] all those kingdoms[w] and bring them to an end, but
it will itself endure forever.[x] 45 This is the meaning of the vision of the rock[y] cut out of a mountain,
but not by human hands[z]—a rock that broke the iron, the bronze, the clay, the silver and the gold to
pieces.

2:45 [y]Isa 28:16 [z]Da 8:25 "The great God has shown the king what will take place in the future. The dream is true and the in-
terpretation is trustworthy."

2:46 [a]Da 8:17; Ac 10:25 [b]Ac 14:13 46 Then King Nebuchadnezzar fell prostrate[a] before Daniel and paid him honor and ordered that
an offering[b] and incense be presented to him. 47 The king said to Daniel, "Surely your God is the God
2:47 [c]Da 11:36 [d]Da 4:25 [e]ver 22, 28 of gods[c] and the Lord of kings[d] and a revealer of mysteries,[e] for you were able to reveal this mys-
tery."

48 Then the king placed Daniel in a high position and lavished many gifts on him. He made him rul-
2:48 [f]ver 6; Da 4:9; 5:11 er over the entire province of Babylon and placed him in charge of all its wise men.[f] 49 Moreover, at Dan-
iel's request the king appointed Shadrach, Meshach and Abednego administrators over the province of
2:49 [g]Da 1:7 Babylon,[g] while Daniel himself remained at the royal court.

2:32–43 See "The Kingdoms of Daniel's Prophecies" on page 1388. **2:35** See "The Threshing Floor" on page 608.

The Kingdoms of Daniel's Prophecies

DANIEL 2 Daniel 2 and 7 together present a prophetic look at four kingdoms that would dominate the world. They are represented both by an image of four metals (ch. 2) and by a vision of four beasts (ch. 7). One interpretation holds that these kingdoms are **Babylon**, Media, **Persia** and Greece, respectively. However, Media never attained the status of a world power. Its independent period was contemporary with that of Babylon, but it was ruled as part of Persia after Babylon's fall in 539 B.C. In approximately 550 B.C. Cyrus, the king of Persia, defeated the last king of Media, Astyages, and merged the two kingdoms.[1] In fact, the book of Daniel treats Media and Persia as a single power (cf. 5:28; 6:8,12,15; 8:20).

A more plausible interpretation holds that these kingdoms are Babylon, Media-Persia, Greece and Rome, according well with the symbolism and factual history of the kingdoms mentioned. The first kingdom is identified as Babylon (2:38),[2] the head of gold (v. 32) and winged lion (7:4). The lion was a recognized symbol of Babylonian royalty, as demonstrated by statues and **reliefs** of lions excavated from Babylon's ruins. The plucking of wings and subsequent transformation into a man perhaps represents Nebuchadnezzar's illness and restoration.[3]

The second, bear-like beast, "raised up on one of its sides" (7:5), corresponds to the Persian domination in the Medo-Persian Empire after the defeat of Astyages by Cyrus II (the fact that the bear is raised on one side symbolizes the ascendancy of the Persians over the Medes).[4] Similarly, the ram of Daniel 8 is described as having two horns, one longer than the other, identified as the kings of Media and Persia (8:20). Under Cyrus and his son Cambyses three kingdoms were "chewed up," as represented by the three ribs in the bear's mouth (7:5). These kingdoms were Lydia (546 B.C.), the Chaldean Empire (539 B.C.) and Egypt (525 B.C.).

The third beast, a four-winged, four-headed leopard (7:6), represents the Greek Empire.[5] The swiftness and agility of the leopard (cf. Hab 1:8 on Babylonia) symbolizes the speed of Alexander the Great, who conquered all the known world between 334 and 323 B.C. After his untimely death the kingdom was divided among four of his generals, as symbolized by the four heads of the leopard: (1) Cassander over Greece and Macedonia; (2) Lysimachus over Thrace and Asia Minor; (3) Seleucus over Syria and the Middle East;[6] and (4) **Ptolemy** over Egypt.[7] At the same time, the number four should probably not be pressed here; the Greek kingdoms after the death of Alexander were for some time quite unstable, and various dynasties rose and fell (Lysimachus, e.g., was slain in battle in 281 B.C., and no dynasty followed him). The number four is probably just representative of the several Greek kingdoms that at various times controlled parts of the Near East and, in particular, the Holy Land.

The final kingdom, "different from all the former beasts" (7:7), denotes Rome.[8] The two iron legs of the image (2:33) may reflect that the empire could generally be characterized as having two major parts, one in the east (where Greek was the principal language) and the other in the west (where Latin dominated). The ten horns may represent the various rulers and dynasties who governed the Roman Empire (again, "ten" here represents a plurality and should not be pressed for ten specific historical counterparts). Throughout its history the empire was ruled by the republic, by various generals who seized power during the late republic (examples include Marius, Sulla and Julius Caesar) and by various dynasties that ruled after Augustus had consolidated power under himself. Vying for power through intrigue, assassination and outright civil war was a regular feature of Roman history, and this seems to be reflected in the diversity of the image (iron mixed with clay).

An interesting motif of the four kingdoms is that they become increasingly large, diverse, violent and unstable. Babylon is portrayed as highly unified, while Persia is in two parts (one dominant over the other). Greece has four heads and Rome has a multiplicity of divisions.

A flask in the form of a comic Greek actor

Preserving Bible Times; © Dr. James C. Martin; permission of The British Museum

[1]See "Cyrus the Great" on page 669. [2]See "Babylon" on page 1077. [3]See "Nebuchadnezzar's Madness" on page 1391. [4]See "Ancient Persian History Through Darius" on page 717. [5]See "Greece: From Independent City-states Through Alexander the Great" on page 1814. [6]See "The Seleucids" on page 1408. [7]See "The Ptolemies" on page 1399. [8]See "Rome" on page 1838 and "The Roman Empire" on page 1845.

The Image of Gold and the Fiery Furnace

3 King Nebuchadnezzar made an image[h] of gold, ninety feet high and nine feet[a] wide, and set it up on
the plain of Dura in the province of Babylon. 2He then summoned the satraps, prefects, governors,
advisers, treasurers, judges, magistrates and all the other provincial officials[i] to come to the dedication
of the image he had set up. 3So the satraps, prefects, governors, advisers, treasurers, judges, magistrates
and all the other provincial officials assembled for the dedication of the image that King Nebuchadnez-
zar had set up, and they stood before it.

4Then the herald loudly proclaimed, "This is what you are commanded to do, O peoples, nations and
men of every language:[j] 5As soon as you hear the sound of the horn, flute, zither, lyre, harp, pipes and all
kinds of music, you must fall down and worship the image of gold that King Nebuchadnezzar has set
up.[k] 6Whoever does not fall down and worship will immediately be thrown into a blazing furnace."[l]

7Therefore, as soon as they heard the sound of the horn, flute, zither, lyre, harp and all kinds of mu-
sic, all the peoples, nations and men of every language fell down and worshiped the image of gold that
King Nebuchadnezzar had set up.[m]

8At this time some astrologers[b][n] came forward and denounced the Jews. 9They said to King Nebu-
chadnezzar, "O king, live forever![o] 10You have issued a decree,[p] O king, that everyone who hears the sound
of the horn, flute, zither, lyre, harp, pipes and all kinds of music must fall down and worship the image
of gold,[q] 11and that whoever does not fall down and worship will be thrown into a blazing furnace. 12But
there are some Jews whom you have set over the affairs of the province of Babylon—Shadrach, Meshach
and Abednego[r]—who pay no attention[s] to you, O king. They neither serve your gods nor worship the im-
age of gold you have set up."[t]

13Furious[u] with rage, Nebuchadnezzar summoned Shadrach, Meshach and Abednego. So these men
were brought before the king, 14and Nebuchadnezzar said to them, "Is it true, Shadrach, Meshach and
Abednego, that you do not serve my gods[v] or worship the image[w] of gold I have set up? 15Now when you
hear the sound of the horn, flute, zither, lyre, harp, pipes and all kinds of music, if you are ready to fall
down and worship the image I made, very good. But if you do not worship it, you will be thrown imme-
diately into a blazing furnace. Then what god[x] will be able to rescue[y] you from my hand?"

16Shadrach, Meshach and Abednego[z] replied to the king, "O Nebuchadnezzar, we do not need to de-
fend ourselves before you in this matter. 17If we are thrown into the blazing furnace, the God we serve is
able to save[a] us from it, and he will rescue[b] us from your hand, O king. 18But even if he does not, we want
you to know, O king, that we will not serve your gods or worship the image of gold you have set up.[c]"

19Then Nebuchadnezzar was furious with Shadrach, Meshach and Abednego, and his attitude toward
them changed. He ordered the furnace heated seven[d] times hotter than usual 20and commanded some

3:1 [h]Isa 46:6; Jer 16:20; Hab 2:19
3:2 [i]ver 27; Da 6:7
3:4 [j]Da 4:1; 6:25
3:5 [k]ver 10,15
3:6 [l]ver 11,15, 21; Jer 29:22; Da 6:7; Mt 13:42, 50; Rev 13:15
3:7 [m]ver 5
3:8 [n]Da 2:10
3:9 [o]Ne 2:3; Da 5:10; 6:6
3:10 [p]Da 6:12 [q]ver 4-6
3:12 [r]Da 2:49 [s]Da 6:13 [t]Est 3:3
3:13 [u]Da 2:12
3:14 [v]Isa 46:1; Jer 50:2 [w]ver 1
3:15 [x]Isa 36:18-20 [y]Ex 5:2; 2Ch 32:15
3:16 [z]Da 1:7
3:17 [a]Ps 27:1-2 [b]Job 5:19; Jer 1:8
3:18 [c]ver 28; Jos 24:15
3:19 [d]Lev 26:18-28

[a] 1 Aramaic *sixty cubits high and six cubits wide* (about 27 meters high and 2.7 meters wide) [b] 8 Or *Chaldeans*

3:1–30 Advanced techniques for smelting and refining metals in furnaces were developed early in human civilizations. The current system of demarcating broad archaeological periods is itself based on the successive emergence of stone, bronze and eventually ironworks. The most common alloys refined were copper, silver, lead and gold. Brick kilns were usually constructed either as circular domes or as taller, chimney-like structures. One kiln discovered at Nippur (from approximately 2000 B.C.) is fashioned like a railway tunnel, with one end blocked and the other serving as an entrance. Kilns were heated with charcoal to extreme temperatures of 900–1000°C (1652–1832°F).

As depicted in Daniel 3, punishment by burning is well attested in the ancient Near East:

- The Bible prescribes death by burning for prostitution by a priest's daughter (Lev 21:9) and for certain forms of incest (Lev 20:14).
- Burning was proposed in the case of Tamar (Ge 38:24) and actually carried out against Achan and his family after they had already been stoned to death (Jos 7:15,25).
- The Code of Hammurabi (an ancient Babylonian law code) stipulates burning for various crimes. The Assyrian king Ashurnasirpal II is reported to have burned prisoners alive.
- Jeremiah records that Nebuchadnezzar, king of Babylon, roasted two false prophets, Ahab and Zedekiah, in the fire (Jer 29:21–22; see also "Nebuchadnezzar" on p. 571).
- In Syria, Antiochus IV Epiphanes later executed the illegitimate high priest Menelaus by casting him onto a funnel that fed directly into a high tower filled with ashes (2Mc 13:4–8; second Maccabees is an Apocryphal book, not found in the traditional Protestant canon).
- Later Jewish tradition contains an account of Abraham being delivered from a fiery furnace after having refused to worship idols.

3:1 Large statues of this kind, though made of wood, were plated with gold. This particular statute was 90 feet (27 m) high and probably represented the god Nabu, whose name formed the first element in Nebuchadnezzar's name.

"Dura" was either the name of a place now marked by a series of mounds (located a few miles south of Babylon) or a common noun meaning "walled enclosure."

3:2 The seven classifications of government officials were to pledge full allegiance to the newly established empire as they stood before the image.

3:4 Babylon had become a cosmopolitan city whose population included people of many different national and ethnic origins.

3:5 "Zither," "harp" and "pipes" (or perhaps "small drum") are Greek loanwords in Daniel. Greek musicians and instruments are mentioned in Assyrian inscriptions written before the time of Nebuchadnezzar. See "Ancient Musical Instruments" on page 797.

3:8 The term "Jew" is a shortened form of "Judahite" (see the note on Jer 34:9).

3:15 Boastful taunts were characteristic of proud Mesopotamian rulers (see Isa 36:18–20).

of the strongest soldiers in his army to tie up Shadrach, Meshach and Abednego and throw them into
the blazing furnace. 21So these men, wearing their robes, trousers, turbans and other clothes, were bound
and thrown into the blazing furnace. 22The king's command was so urgent and the furnace so hot that
the flames of the fire killed the soldiers who took up Shadrach, Meshach and Abednego,[e] 23and these — 3:22 [e]Da 1:7
three men, firmly tied, fell into the blazing furnace.
24Then King Nebuchadnezzar leaped to his feet in amazement and asked his advisers, "Weren't there
three men that we tied up and threw into the fire?"
They replied, "Certainly, O king."
25He said, "Look! I see four men walking around in the fire, unbound and unharmed, and the fourth
looks like a son of the gods."
26Nebuchadnezzar then approached the opening of the blazing furnace and shouted, "Shadrach, Me-
shach and Abednego, servants of the Most High God,[f] come out! Come here!" — 3:26 [f]Da 4:2,34
So Shadrach, Meshach and Abednego came out of the fire, 27and the satraps, prefects, governors
and royal advisers[g] crowded around them.[h] They saw that the fire[i] had not harmed their bodies, nor — 3:27 [g]ver 2
was a hair of their heads singed; their robes were not scorched, and there was no smell of fire on — [h]Isa 43:2; Heb 11:32-34
them. — [i]Da 6:23
28Then Nebuchadnezzar said, "Praise be to the God of Shadrach, Meshach and Abednego, who has
sent his angel[j] and rescued his servants! They trusted[k] in him and defied the king's command and were — 3:28 [j]Ps 34:7; Da 6:22; Ac 5:19
willing to give up their lives rather than serve or worship any god except their own God.[l] 29Therefore I — [k]Job 13:15; Ps 26:1; 84:12; Jer 17:7 [l]ver 18
decree[m] that the people of any nation or language who say anything against the God of Shadrach, Me-
shach and Abednego be cut into pieces and their houses be turned into piles of rubble,[n] for no other god — 3:29 [m]Da 6:26 [n]Ezr 6:11
can save[o] in this way." — [o]Da 6:27
30Then the king promoted Shadrach, Meshach and Abednego in the province of Babylon.[p] — 3:30 [p]Da 2:49

Nebuchadnezzar's Dream of a Tree

4 King Nebuchadnezzar,

To the peoples, nations and men of every language,[q] who live in all the world: — 4:1 [q]Da 3:4 [r]Da 6:25

May you prosper greatly![r]

2It is my pleasure to tell you about the miraculous signs[s] and wonders that the Most High God[t] — 4:2 [s]Ps 74:9 [t]Da 3:26
has performed for me.

3How great are his signs,
how mighty his wonders![u] — 4:3 [u]Ps 105:27; Da 6:27 [v]Da 2:44
His kingdom is an eternal kingdom;
his dominion endures[v] from generation to generation.

4I, Nebuchadnezzar, was at home in my palace, contented[w] and prosperous. 5I had a dream[x] — 4:4 [w]Ps 30:6 4:5 [x]Da 2:1
that made me afraid. As I was lying in my bed, the images and visions that passed through my — [y]Da 2:28
mind[y] terrified me. 6So I commanded that all the wise men of Babylon be brought before me to

---

3:23 Interspersed among the canonical books of the Old Testament in the old Latin Vulgate Bible are certain additional books and chapters. It is to these that Protestant usage generally assigns the term "Apocrypha" (see "The Apocrypha" on p. 1973). Additions to the book of Daniel are included in this body of literature (see "The Books of the Apocrypha" on p. 1974):

Between 3:23 and 3:24 of canonical Daniel both Greek and Latin versions insert: (1) a prayer of national confession with supplication for deliverance, offered by Daniel's friend Azariah (cf. 1:7) while he and his two companions were in the fiery furnace; (2) a psalm of praise (dependent upon Ps 148 and 136) uttered by the three; and (3) a narrative framework containing details not warranted by the genuine Daniel. This section may be of composite authorship and was probably written in Hebrew.

In addition, in the Vulgate (fourth century A.D. Latin translation) Susanna follows canonical Daniel as chapter 13; in Greek manuscripts this is prefixed to chapter 1. Two crucial wordplays at the climax of the tale suggest that it was composed in Greek, but there is no consensus on this issue. Susanna's origin and date are unknown; one theory is that the work was composed in Alexandria in about 100 B.C. The story relates how two Israelite elders in Babylon, their lustful advances having been resisted by Susanna, falsely accused her of adultery. But young Daniel effected Susanna's deliverance, as well as the elders' doom, by ensnaring them in contradictory testimony.

Bel and the Dragon, fables ridiculing heathenism, appear as chapter 13 of Daniel in the Greek (the Septuagint) and as chapter 14 in the Latin (the Vulgate). They date from the first or second century B.C., and their original language is uncertain. Daniel then played detective to expose to Cyrus the fraud of the priests who clandestinely consumed the food-offerings of Bel (Baal—i.e., Marduk). After destroying Bel, Daniel concocted a recipe that exploded a sacred dragon. Consigned to a den of lions, Daniel was miraculously fed and delivered.

3:25 Nebuchadnezzar, speaking as a pagan polytheist, was content to conceive of the fourth figure as a lesser heavenly being ("angel," v. 28) sent by the all-powerful God of the Jews (see also 6:22).

4:6 See "Dream Oracles in the Ancient World" on page 741.

4:6 [z]Da 2:2
4:7 [a]Ge 41:8
[b]Isa 44:25; Da 2:2
[c]Da 2:10
4:8 [d]Da 1:7
[e]Da 5:11,14

interpret[z] the dream for me. 7 When the magicians,[a] enchanters, astrologers[a] and diviners[b] came,
I told them the dream, but they could not interpret it for me.[c] 8 Finally, Daniel came into my pres-
ence and I told him the dream. (He is called Belteshazzar,[d] after the name of my god, and the spir-
it of the holy gods[e] is in him.)

[a] 7 Or *Chaldeans*

4:8 Daniel's Babylonian name, Belteshazzar, was formed from Bel ("lord"), a title for the Babylonian god Marduk (see the note on 1:7).

Nebuchadnezzar's Madness

DANIEL 4 Nebuchadnezzar reigned from 605–562 B.C. over **Babylon** at the peak of its power.[1] Inscriptions reveal his great pride over his achievements in building temples and greatly fortifying the city of Babylon. The book of Daniel records that God struck Nebuchadnezzar with a strange affliction in order to humble him. Extrabiblical records deal with his infirmity only obliquely. The ancient Jewish historian Josephus cited a report by the Babylonian priest Berossus that Nebuchadnezzar died following a period of weakness.[2] The Christian writer Eusebius preserved a tradition from the Greek historian Megasthenes (c. 300 B.C.) that Nebuchadnezzar, having ascended to the roof of his palace, became inspired by some god. (In antiquity insanity was looked upon as possession by a deity.)

Babylonian brick with inscription of Nebuchadnezzar

Preserving Bible Times; © Dr. James C. Martin; permission of The British Museum

The illness described in Daniel 4:22–34 appears to have been a delusional disorder. The typical onset for this kind of malady occurs in later life; it frequently lasts from months to years and remits spontaneously, often without subsequent relapse. Lycanthropy, in which patients imagine themselves to be wolves, is one such disorder. Nebuchadnezzar's condition has been described as boanthropy, or cow-like behavior. However, the imagery implied by his behavior may be related to a figure of the Gilgamesh Epic. This myth, known from the library of Ashurbanipal (668–626 B.C.), tells of Enkidu, a savage, animal-like creature who was hairy, unclothed and ate grass until becoming civilized—the antithesis of what would be expected of a cultured, self-sufficient builder of cities like Nebuchadnezzar.[3]

Little is known of Nebuchadnezzar's final years in power. The seven "times," or periods (4:16,23,32), of the illness could represent years, months or various other units of time. If his illness lasted seven years, then its onset must have been toward the end of Nebuchadnezzar's reign, after the completion of his numerous building projects.

[1]See "Nebuchadnezzar" on page 571 and "Babylon" on page 1077. [2]See "Historians in the Ancient World" on page 939. [3]For more on Gilgamesh, see "Ecclesiastes and the Epic of Gilgamesh" on page 1027.

[9]I said, "Belteshazzar, chief[f] of the magicians, I know that the spirit of the holy gods[g] is in you,
and no mystery is too difficult for you. Here is my dream; interpret it for me. [10]These are the vi-
sions I saw while lying in my bed:[h] I looked, and there before me stood a tree in the middle of the
land. Its height was enormous.[i] [11]The tree grew large and strong and its top touched the sky; it
was visible to the ends of the earth. [12]Its leaves were beautiful, its fruit abundant, and on it was
food for all. Under it the beasts of the field found shelter, and the birds of the air lived in its branch-
es;[j] from it every creature was fed.

[13]"In the visions I saw while lying in my bed,[k] I looked, and there before me was a messenger,[a]
a holy one,[l] coming down from heaven. [14]He called in a loud voice: 'Cut down the tree and trim off
its branches; strip off its leaves and scatter its fruit. Let the animals flee from under it and the birds
from its branches.[m] [15]But let the stump and its roots, bound with iron and bronze, remain in the
ground, in the grass of the field.

" 'Let him be drenched with the dew of heaven, and let him live with the animals among the
plants of the earth. [16]Let his mind be changed from that of a man and let him be given the mind
of an animal, till seven times[b] pass by for him.[n]

[17]" 'The decision is announced by messengers, the holy ones declare the verdict, so that the liv-
ing may know that the Most High[o] is sovereign[p] over the kingdoms of men and gives them to any-
one he wishes and sets over them the lowliest[q] of men.'

[18]"This is the dream that I, King Nebuchadnezzar, had. Now, Belteshazzar, tell me what it means,
for none of the wise men in my kingdom can interpret it for me.[r] But you can,[s] because the spir-
it of the holy gods is in you."[t]

Daniel Interprets the Dream

[19]Then Daniel (also called Belteshazzar) was greatly perplexed for a time, and his thoughts ter-
rified[u] him. So the king said, "Belteshazzar, do not let the dream or its meaning alarm you."

Belteshazzar answered, "My lord, if only the dream applied to your enemies and its meaning to
your adversaries! [20]The tree you saw, which grew large and strong, with its top touching the sky,
visible to the whole earth, [21]with beautiful leaves and abundant fruit, providing food for all, giv-
ing shelter to the beasts of the field, and having nesting places in its branches for the birds of the
air— [22]you, O king, are that tree![v] You have become great and strong; your greatness has grown
until it reaches the sky, and your dominion extends to distant parts of the earth.[w]

[23]"You, O king, saw a messenger, a holy one,[x] coming down from heaven and saying, 'Cut down
the tree and destroy it, but leave the stump, bound with iron and bronze, in the grass of the field,
while its roots remain in the ground. Let him be drenched with the dew of heaven; let him live like
the wild animals, until seven times pass by for him.'[y]

[24]"This is the interpretation, O king, and this is the decree[z] the Most High has issued against
my lord the king: [25]You will be driven away from people and will live with the wild animals; you
will eat grass like cattle and be drenched with the dew of heaven. Seven times will pass by for you
until you acknowledge that the Most High[a] is sovereign over the kingdoms of men and gives them
to anyone he wishes.[b] [26]The command to leave the stump of the tree with its roots[c] means that your
kingdom will be restored to you when you acknowledge that Heaven rules.[d] [27]Therefore, O king,
be pleased to accept my advice: Renounce your sins by doing what is right, and your wickedness
by being kind to the oppressed.[e] It may be that then your prosperity will continue.[f]"

The Dream Is Fulfilled

[28]All this happened[g] to King Nebuchadnezzar. [29]Twelve months later, as the king was walking
on the roof of the royal palace of Babylon, [30]he said, "Is not this the great Babylon I have built as
the royal residence, by my mighty power and for the glory of my majesty?"[h]

4:9 [f]Da 2:48 [g]Da 5:11-12
4:10 [h]ver 5 [i]Eze 31:3-4
4:12 [j]Eze 17:23; Mt 13:32
4:13 [k]Da 7:1 [l]ver 23; Dt 33:2; Da 8:13
4:14 [m]Eze 31:12; Mt 3:10
4:16 [n]ver 23,32
4:17 [o]ver 2,25; Ps 83:18 [p]Jer 27:5-7; Da 2:21; 5:18-21 [q]Da 11:21
4:18 [r]Ge 41:8; Da 5:8,15 [s]Ge 41:15 [t]ver 7-9
4:19 [u]Da 7:15, 28; 8:27; 10:16-17
4:22 [v]2Sa 12:7 [w]Jer 27:7; Da 2:37-38; 5:18-19
4:23 [x]ver 13 [y]Da 5:21
4:24 [z]Job 40:12; Ps 107:40
4:25 [a]ver 17; Ps 83:18 [b]Jer 27:5; Da 5:21
4:26 [c]ver 15 [d]Da 2:37
4:27 [e]Isa 55:6-7 [f]1Ki 21:29; Ps 41:3; Eze 18:22
4:28 [g]Nu 23:19
4:30 [h]Isa 37:24-25; Da 5:20; Hab 2:4

[a] 13 Or *watchman*; also in verses 17 and 23 [b] 16 Or *years*; also in verses 23, 25 and 32

4:9 See the note on 1:20.
4:11 In one of Nebuchadnezzar's building inscriptions Babylon is compared to a spreading tree (cf. v. 22). The phrase "its top touched the sky" was often used of Mesopotamian temple-towers (see the note on Ge 11:4).
4:16 "Seven" signifies completeness, and "times" can refer to indefinite periods.
4:22 Nebuchadnezzar's empire was the largest and most powerful in that part of the world up to that time (see "Nebuchadnezzar" on p. 571).
4:25 See "Nebuchadnezzar's Madness" on page 1391.
4:26 The term "Heaven" was a Jewish way of referring to God.
4:30 Babylon was grand indeed, and Nebuchadnezzar had much to do with creating its splendor (see "Babylon" on p. 1077).

31 The words were still on his lips when a voice came from heaven, "This is what is decreed for
you, King Nebuchadnezzar: Your royal authority has been taken from you. 32 You will be driven
away from people and will live with the wild animals; you will eat grass like cattle. Seven times
will pass by for you until you acknowledge that the Most High is sovereign over the kingdoms of
men and gives them to anyone he wishes."

33 Immediately what had been said about Nebuchadnezzar was fulfilled. He was driven away
from people and ate grass like cattle. His body was drenched with the dew of heaven until his hair
grew like the feathers of an eagle and his nails like the claws of a bird.[i]

4:33 [i]Da 5:20-21

34 At the end of that time, I, Nebuchadnezzar, raised my eyes toward heaven, and my sanity was
restored. Then I praised the Most High; I honored and glorified him who lives forever.[j]

4:34 [j]Da 12:7; Rev 4:10 [k]Ps 145:13; Da 2:44; 5:21; 6:26; Lk 1:33

His dominion is an eternal dominion;
his kingdom endures from generation to generation.[k]
35 All the peoples of the earth
are regarded as nothing.[l]
He does as he pleases[m]
with the powers of heaven
and the peoples of the earth.
No one can hold back his hand
or say to him: "What have you done?"[n]

4:35 [l]Isa 40:17 [m]Ps 115:3; 135:6 [n]Isa 45:9; Ro 9:20

36 At the same time that my sanity was restored, my honor and splendor were returned to me
for the glory of my kingdom.[o] My advisers and nobles sought me out, and I was restored to my
throne and became even greater than before. 37 Now I, Nebuchadnezzar, praise and exalt and glo-
rify the King of heaven, because everything he does is right and all his ways are just.[p] And those
who walk in pride he is able to humble.[q]

4:36 [o]Pr 22:4

4:37 [p]Dt 32:4; Ps 33:4-5 [q]Ex 18:11; Job 40:11-12; Da 5:20,23

The Writing on the Wall

5 King Belshazzar gave a great banquet[r] for a thousand of his nobles and drank wine with them.
2 While Belshazzar was drinking his wine, he gave orders to bring in the gold and silver goblets[s] that
Nebuchadnezzar his father[a] had taken from the temple in Jerusalem, so that the king and his nobles, his
wives and his concubines might drink from them.[t] 3 So they brought in the gold goblets that had been tak-
en from the temple of God in Jerusalem, and the king and his nobles, his wives and his concubines drank
from them. 4 As they drank the wine, they praised the gods of gold and silver, of bronze, iron, wood and
stone.[u]

5 Suddenly the fingers of a human hand appeared and wrote on the plaster of the wall, near the
lampstand in the royal palace. The king watched the hand as it wrote. 6 His face turned pale and he was
so frightened[v] that his knees knocked together and his legs gave way.[w]

5:1 [r]Est 1:3
5:2 [s]2Ki 24:13; Jer 52:19 [t]Est 1:7; Da 1:2
5:4 [u]Ps 135:15-18; Hab 2:19; Rev 9:20
5:6 [v]Da 4:5 [w]Eze 7:17

[a] 2 Or *ancestor*; or *predecessor*; also in verses 11, 13 and 18

4:34 The history of Daniel the prophet is confirmed both by the words of Jesus (Mt 24:15) and by references to Daniel's righteousness and wisdom by his prophetic contemporary, Ezekiel (Eze 14:14,20; 28:3, although some scholars relate the latter passages to the Danel of the Ugaritic epic material). The book of Daniel presents a timeless demonstration of separation from impurity, of courage against compromise, of efficaciousness in prayer and of dedication to him whose "kingdom endures from generation to generation."

5:1–4 The ancient Greek historians Herodotus and Xenophon both attested to the orgy of revelry, as well as to the blasphemy, that occurred on such occasions (see "Herodotus and the Fall of Babylon" on p. 1283).

5:1–2 The name Belshazzar was for many years regarded as a fictitious literary creation of a post-captivity author assuming the pen name of Daniel (c. 165 B.C.). Now, however, it is well authenticated through archaeological studies that Belshazzar was a historic personage. In Daniel 5 he is referred to as the son of Nebuchadnezzar (vv. 2,11,13, 18,22). This conforms with general Semitic usage, in which one's descendant is often referred to as his "son." Nebuchadnezzar died in 562 B.C. after a 42-year reign and was followed by Amel-Marduk (562–560), the Evil-Merodach of Jeremiah 52:31 and 2 Kings 25:27. Evil-Merodach was replaced by Mergal Shar-usar (Nergal-Sharezer), who reigned from 560 to 556 and was succeeded in turn by Labasi-Marduk, his weak son, who reigned for only a few months and was then overthrown by revolution.

One of the conspirators, Nabonidus (Nabonaid), then ascended the throne. Though a revolutionary, he was still a man of culture and religious zeal for the gods of Babylon. He is sometimes styled "the world's first archaeologist." Nabonidus was the last true king of Babylon and the father of Belshazzar (see "Nabonidus and Belshazzar" on p. 1394 and "Babylon" on p. 1077). Nabonidus made Belshazzar coregent when he retired to Arabia, presumably to consolidate the weakening empire. This explains Belshazzar's offered reward to Daniel of becoming "the third highest ruler in the kingdom" (vv. 7,16).

The Nabonidus Chronicle was written after the capture of Babylon in 539 B.C. Cyrus of Persia claimed that he had been able to take the city without a struggle, going on to describe his leniency toward the population and regarding himself as an "Enlightened Despot" and executioner of the will of the gods. His estimation of the character of Belshazzar was exceedingly low, not at all out of harmony with what is presented in the Biblical account.

5:5–31 There has been much discussion about the original form of the inscription, as well as about its interpretation. The words seem to refer to three weights in common use: the mina, the shekel and the

[7]The king called out for the enchanters, astrologers[a] and diviners[x] to be brought and said to these
wise[y] men of Babylon, "Whoever reads this writing and tells me what it means will be clothed in purple
and have a gold chain placed around his neck,[z] and he will be made the third highest ruler in the king-
dom."[a]
[8]Then all the king's wise men came in, but they could not read the writing or tell the king what it
meant.[b] [9]So King Belshazzar became even more terrified[c] and his face grew more pale. His nobles were
baffled.
[10]The queen,[b] hearing the voices of the king and his nobles, came into the banquet hall. "O king, live
forever!"[d] she said. "Don't be alarmed! Don't look so pale! [11]There is a man in your kingdom who has the
spirit of the holy gods[e] in him. In the time of your father he was found to have insight and intelligence
and wisdom[f] like that of the gods. King Nebuchadnezzar your father—your father the king, I say—ap-
pointed him chief of the magicians, enchanters, astrologers and diviners.[g] [12]This man Daniel, whom the
king called Belteshazzar,[h] was found to have a keen mind and knowledge and understanding, and also

5:7 [x]Isa 44:25 [y]Da 4:6-7 [z]Ge 41:42 [a]Da 2:5-6,48; 6:2-3
5:8 [b]Da 2:10,27
5:9 [c]Isa 21:4
5:10 [d]Da 3:9
5:11 [e]Da 4:8-9, 19 [f]ver 14; Da 1:17 [g]Da 2:47-48
5:12 [h]Da 1:7

[a] 7 Or *Chaldeans*; also in verse 11 [b] 10 Or *queen mother*

half mina. Or they may have been terms used in Mesopotamian counting houses: "numbered, numbered, weighed and divisions."

The mysterious message was the fact that "God ha[d] numbered" the days of the kingdom (v. 26) and that the king had "been weighed on the scales and found wanting" (v. 27). His kingdom was to be "divided and given to the Medes and Persians" (v. 28). There was not much time between interpretation and fulfillment: "That very night Belshazzar, king of the Babylonians, was slain" (v. 30).

5:10 The "queen" could have been (1) the wife of Nebuchadnezzar, (2) the daughter of Nebuchadnezzar and the wife of Nabonidus or (3) the wife of Nabonidus but not the daughter of Nebuchadnezzar.

5:11 Nebuchadnezzar had died in 562 B.C.; the year was now 539.

ANCIENT PEOPLES, LANDS AND RULERS

Nabonidus and Belshazzar

DANIEL 5 Belshazzar (meaning "Bel protect the king") was the son of the **Babylonian** king Nabonidus (r. 556–539 B.C.) and the principal monarch from approximately 550 to 540 B.C. Although Nabonidus claimed to be a rightful heir to **Nebuchadnezzar**'s kingdom, it is clear that he was not originally in line to become king. An inscription found in Harran indicates that Nabonidus's mother, Adad-guppi, was responsible for his rise to power. Some suggest that she was a daughter of Nebuchadnezzar; hence Nebuchadnezzar would have been Belshazzar's "(grand)father" or "(fore)father" (Da 5:2). Others propose that Belshazzar may have played an active role in advancing his father to the throne—by murdering a man named Labasi-Marduk who had a better claim to succession.

A Babylonian text, the Verse Account of Nabonidus, relates that Nabonidus placed the military troops under Belshazzar's command and entrusted the kingship to him before departing to the west. During the approximate ten-year reign of Belshazzar, Nabonidus remained on campaign in Tema (Arabia). Nabonidus also was apparently devoted to the god Sin; he had no interest in the worship of Marduk (the chief Babylonian god) and even ceased to observe the traditional New Year festival. He was thus despised as a heretical and negligent monarch. Curiously, Nabonidus seems to have been one of history's first archaeologists, having carried out excavations at Agade, **Uruk** and Ur.

Though always referred to as "son of the king" in **Assyrian** sources, Belshazzar exercised all the functions of kingship, including receiving tribute, granting leases and attending to the upkeep of the temples, as attested in several business letters and contracts contemporary to his reign. He was apparently as impious as his father (seen in his lack of regard for the God of Israel), and ruthless as well. As "second" ruler, he promised Daniel the position of "third" ruler (v. 16). Little is known of Belshazzar's final years in power. Babylon was well fortified when the **Persians** attacked in 539 B.C., but Cyrus is said to have diverted the waters of the Euphrates and opened an access into the city. Herodotus and Xenophon relate that Cyrus found the city in celebration and took it with relative ease.[1] Nabonidus returned to Babylon in 539 B.C. but was captured at Borsippa and exiled to Carmania in the east.[2]

[1]See "Herodotus and the Fall of Babylon" on page 1283. [2]See also "The Sippar Cylinder of Nabonidus" on page 664 and "The Prayer of Nabonidus" on page 1400.

5:12 [i]ver 14-16; Da 6:3 the ability to interpret dreams, explain riddles and solve difficult problems.[i] Call for Daniel, and he will
tell you what the writing means."
13 So Daniel was brought before the king, and the king said to him, "Are you Daniel, one of the exiles
5:13 [j]Da 6:13 my father the king brought from Judah?[j] 14 I have heard that the spirit of the gods is in you and that you
have insight, intelligence and outstanding wisdom. 15 The wise men and enchanters were brought before
me to read this writing and tell me what it means, but they could not explain it. 16 Now I have heard that
you are able to give interpretations and to solve difficult problems. If you can read this writing and tell
me what it means, you will be clothed in purple and have a gold chain placed around your neck, and you
will be made the third highest ruler in the kingdom."
17 Then Daniel answered the king, "You may keep your gifts for yourself and give your rewards to some-
5:17 [k]2Ki 5:16 one else.[k] Nevertheless, I will read the writing for the king and tell him what it means.
18 "O king, the Most High God gave your father Nebuchadnezzar sovereignty and greatness and glory
5:18 [l]Jer 27:7; Da 2:37-38 and splendor.[l] 19 Because of the high position he gave him, all the peoples and nations and men of every
5:19 [m]Da 2:12-13; 3:6 language dreaded and feared him. Those the king wanted to put to death, he put to death;[m] those he
wanted to spare, he spared; those he wanted to promote, he promoted; and those he wanted to humble,
5:20 [n]Da 4:30 [o]Jer 13:18 [p]Job 40:12; Isa 14:13-15 he humbled. 20 But when his heart became arrogant and hardened with pride,[n] he was deposed from his
royal throne and stripped[o] of his glory.[p] 21 He was driven away from people and given the mind of an an-
imal; he lived with the wild donkeys and ate grass like cattle; and his body was drenched with the dew
5:21 [q]Eze 17:24 [r]Da 4:16-17,35 of heaven, until he acknowledged that the Most High God is sovereign[q] over the kingdoms of men and
sets over them anyone he wishes.[r]
5:22 [s]Ex 10:3; 2Ch 33:23 22 "But you his son,[a] O Belshazzar, have not humbled[s] yourself, though you knew all this. 23 Instead, you
5:23 [t]Jer 50:29 [u]Ps 115:4-8; Hab 2:19 [v]Job 12:10 [w]Job 31:4; Jer 10:23 have set yourself up against[t] the Lord of heaven. You had the goblets from his temple brought to you, and
you and your nobles, your wives and your concubines drank wine from them. You praised the gods of sil-
ver and gold, of bronze, iron, wood and stone, which cannot see or hear or understand.[u] But you did not
honor the God who holds in his hand your life[v] and all your ways.[w] 24 Therefore he sent the hand that
wrote the inscription.
25 "This is the inscription that was written:

MENE, MENE, TEKEL, PARSIN[b]

26 "This is what these words mean:

5:26 [x]Jer 27:7 [y]Isa 13:6 *Mene*[c]: God has numbered the days[x] of your reign and brought it to an end.[y]
5:27 [z]Ps 62:9 27 *Tekel*[d]: You have been weighed on the scales and found wanting.[z]
5:28 [a]Isa 13:17 [b]Da 6:28 28 *Peres*[e]: Your kingdom is divided and given to the Medes[a] and Persians."[b]

29 Then at Belshazzar's command, Daniel was clothed in purple, a gold chain was placed around his
neck, and he was proclaimed the third highest ruler in the kingdom.
5:30 [c]ver 1 [d]Isa 21:9; Jer 51:31 30 That very night Belshazzar,[c] king of the Babylonians,[f] was slain,[d] 31 and Darius[e] the Mede took over
5:31 [e]Da 6:1; 9:1 the kingdom, at the age of sixty-two.

Daniel in the Den of Lions

6:1 [f]Da 5:31 [g]Est 1:1 6 It pleased Darius[f] to appoint 120 satraps[g] to rule throughout the kingdom, 2 with three admin-
6:2 [h]Da 2:48-49 [i]Ezr 4:22 istrators over them, one of whom was Daniel.[h] The satraps were made accountable[i] to them so
that the king might not suffer loss. 3 Now Daniel so distinguished himself among the administrators
and the satraps by his exceptional qualities that the king planned to set him over the whole king-
6:3 [j]Ge 41:41; Est 10:3; Da 5:12-14 dom.[j] 4 At this, the administrators and the satraps tried to find grounds for charges against Daniel in
his conduct of government affairs, but they were unable to do so. They could find no corruption in

[a] 22 Or *descendant*; or *successor* [b] 25 Aramaic *UPARSIN* (that is, *AND PARSIN*) [c] 26 *Mene* can mean *numbered* or *mina* (a unit of money). [d] 27 *Tekel* can mean *weighed* or *shekel.* [e] 28 *Peres* (the singular of *Parsin*) can mean *divided* or *Persia* or *a half mina* or *a half shekel.* [f] 30 Or *Chaldeans*

5:16 For "third highest ruler," see the note on verses 1–2.
5:21 See "Nebuchadnezzar's Madness" on page 1391.
5:26–28 See the NIV text notes. Three weights (mina, shekel and half mina/shekel) may be intended, symbolizing three rulers, respectively: Nebuchadnezzar, either Evil-Merodach or Nabonidus, and Belshazzar. For an alternative interpretation, see the note on verses 5–31.
5:29 The three symbols of a ruler's authority were his signet ring (see "Signet Rings" on p. 728), his royal robes and the gold chain he wore around the neck (see Ge 41:42).
5:30 See "Herodotus and the Fall of Babylon" on page 1283.
5:31 See "Darius the Mede" on page 1396.

him, because he was trustworthy and neither corrupt nor negligent. 5Finally these men said, "We will
never find any basis for charges against this man Daniel unless it has something to do with the law
of his God."[k] 6:5 [k]Ac 24:13-16
6So the administrators and the satraps went as a group to the king and said: "O King Darius, live for-
ever![l] 7The royal administrators, prefects, satraps, advisers and governors[m] have all agreed that the king 6:6 [l]Ne 2:3; Da 2:4
should issue an edict and enforce the decree that anyone who prays to any god or man during the next 6:7 [m]Da 3:2
thirty days, except to you, O king, shall be thrown into the lions' den.[n] 8Now, O king, issue the decree and [n]Ps 59:3; 64:2-6; Da 3:6
put it in writing so that it cannot be altered—in accordance with the laws of the Medes and Persians,
which cannot be repealed."[o] 9So King Darius put the decree in writing. 6:8 [o]Est 1:19
10Now when Daniel learned that the decree had been published, he went home to his upstairs room
where the windows opened toward[p] Jerusalem. Three times a day he got down on his knees[q] and prayed, 6:10 [p]1Ki 8:48-49 [q]Ps 95:6
giving thanks to his God, just as he had done before.[r] 11Then these men went as a group and found Dan- [r]Ac 5:29
iel praying and asking God for help. 12So they went to the king and spoke to him about his royal decree:
"Did you not publish a decree that during the next thirty days anyone who prays to any god or man ex-
cept to you, O king, would be thrown into the lions' den?"
The king answered, "The decree stands—in accordance with the laws of the Medes and Persians, 6:12 [s]Est 1:19; Da 3:8-12
which cannot be repealed."[s] 6:13 [t]Da 2:25; 5:13 [u]Est 3:8; Da 3:12
13Then they said to the king, "Daniel, who is one of the exiles from Judah,[t] pays no attention[u] to you,

6:7 The lions' den was a pit with a relatively small opening at the top (see v. 17), making it impossible for a prisoner to escape.

Darius the Mede

DANIEL 6 Daniel 6 informs us that after the **Persian** conquest of **Babylon**,[1] the city was ruled by a king called "Darius the Mede." This statement poses a problem: There is no record of such an individual outside of the Bible—a fact that has brought the historicity and authorship of Daniel into question. Many believe that an unknown author wrote Daniel hundreds of years after the fall of Babylon and that the figure Darius the Mede, like most of Daniel, is pure fiction.[2] But is it appropriate to patently dismiss Darius the Mede on the assumption that he never existed?

✣ Darius the Mede cannot be the Persian king known as Darius I, since this later Darius was the *successor* of Cyrus, not his *predecessor.*[3] Furthermore, Darius the Mede, who was purported to be sixty-two years old at the time of the fall of Babylon (5:31), was born in 601/600 B.C., whereas history indicates that Darius I was born in 521 B.C. Those who believe that Daniel is not a historical book sometimes suggest that the author was simply confused about Persian history and thought that Darius I preceded Cyrus the Great. If this were the case, however, the author's ignorance would truly be astounding; Cyrus the Great, the creator of the Persian Empire, is a prominent figure in the Old Testament. Also, Darius I is always presented as a Persian, but Darius the Mede is obviously asserted to be a Mede.

✣ Darius the Mede could have been Cyrus the Great.[4] Daniel 6:28 might, according to this theory, be translated, "Daniel prospered during the reign of Darius, that is, in the reign of Cyrus the Persian." Normally, however, this would be translated simply, "*and* in the reign of Cyrus the Persian" (emphasis added), as most versions render it. Though a possibility, this interpretation is not persuasive.

✣ Darius the Mede could also have been a subordinate king appointed by Cyrus to rule over Babylon. The Hebrew of 9:1 supports this position, stating that Darius *was made* king, using a passive verb. Also, the **Aramaic** of Daniel 5:31 states that Darius "received the kingdom (NIV "took over the kingdom")." Normally an author would not speak of a conqueror "receiving" a kingdom. Thus, it may be conjectured that Darius the Mede was not a "king" of the same standing as Cyrus but rather a subordinate. It is important to note that the book of Daniel never refers to this Darius as the king either of Persia or of the Medes but simply as the ruler of Babylon. Darius the Mede's personal name might have been Gubaru, that of a governor appointed by Cyrus. Gubaru is mentioned in **cuneiform** documents, including the Nabonidus Chronicles.

[1]See "Babylon" on page 1077. [2]See "When Was Daniel Written?" on page 1385. [3]See "Darius I" on page 676. [4]See "Cyrus the Great" on page 669.

O king, or to the decree you put in writing. He still prays three times a day." 14 When the king heard this,
6:14 [v]Mk 6:26 he was greatly distressed;[v] he was determined to rescue Daniel and made every effort until sundown to
save him.

15 Then the men went as a group to the king and said to him, "Remember, O king, that according to
6:15 [w]Est 8:8 the law of the Medes and Persians no decree or edict that the king issues can be changed."[w]

6:16 [x]ver 7 16 So the king gave the order, and they brought Daniel and threw him into the lions' den.[x] The king
[y]Job 5:19; Ps 37:39-40 said to Daniel, "May your God, whom you serve continually, rescue[y] you!"

6:17 [z]Mt 27:66 17 A stone was brought and placed over the mouth of the den, and the king sealed[z] it with his own sig-
net ring and with the rings of his nobles, so that Daniel's situation might not be changed. 18 Then the king
6:18 [a]2Sa 12:17 returned to his palace and spent the night without eating[a] and without any entertainment being brought
[b]Est 6:1; Da 2:1 to him. And he could not sleep.[b]

19 At the first light of dawn, the king got up and hurried to the lions' den. 20 When he came near the den,
he called to Daniel in an anguished voice, "Daniel, servant of the living God, has your God, whom you
6:20 [c]Da 3:17 serve continually, been able to rescue you from the lions?"[c]

6:21 [d]Da 2:4 21 Daniel answered, "O king, live forever![d] 22 My God sent his angel,[e] and he shut the mouths of the li-
6:22 [e]Da 3:28 [f]Ps 91:11-13; ons.[f] They have not hurt me, because I was found innocent in his sight.[g] Nor have I ever done any wrong
Heb 11:33 [g]Ac 12:11; before you, O king."
2Ti 4:17

23 The king was overjoyed and gave orders to lift Daniel out of the den. And when Daniel was lifted
6:23 [h]Da 3:27 [i]1Ch 5:20 from the den, no wound[h] was found on him, because he had trusted[i] in his God.

24 At the king's command, the men who had falsely accused Daniel were brought in and thrown into
6:24 [j]Dt 19:18-19; Est 7:9-10; the lions' den,[j] along with their wives and children.[k] And before they reached the floor of the den, the li-
Ps 54:5 ons overpowered them and crushed all their bones.[l]
[k]Dt 24:16; 2Ki 14:6 [l]Isa 38:13

25 Then King Darius wrote to all the peoples, nations and men of every language throughout the land:
6:25 [m]Da 4:1 "May you prosper greatly![m]

26 "I issue a decree that in every part of my kingdom people must fear and reverence the God
6:26 [n]Ps 99:1-3; Da 3:29 [o]Da 2:44; 4:34 of Daniel.[n]

"For he is the living God
and he endures forever;
his kingdom will not be destroyed,
his dominion will never end.[o]
27 He rescues and he saves;
6:27 [p]Da 4:3 [q]ver 22 he performs signs and wonders[p]
in the heavens and on the earth.
He has rescued Daniel
from the power of the lions."[q]

6:28 [r]2Ch 36:22; Da 1:21 28 So Daniel prospered during the reign of Darius and the reign of Cyrus[a][r] the Persian.

Daniel's Dream of Four Beasts

7:1 [s]Da 5:1 [t]Da 1:17 [u]Jer 36:4 7 In the first year of Belshazzar[s] king of Babylon, Daniel had a dream, and visions passed through his
mind[t] as he was lying on his bed. He wrote[u] down the substance of his dream.

7:2 [v]Rev 7:1 2 Daniel said: "In my vision at night I looked, and there before me were the four winds of heaven[v]
7:3 [w]Rev 13:1 churning up the great sea. 3 Four great beasts,[w] each different from the others, came up out of the sea.

7:4 [x]Jer 4:7 [y]Eze 17:3 4 "The first was like a lion,[x] and it had the wings of an eagle.[y] I watched until its wings were torn off
and it was lifted from the ground so that it stood on two feet like a man, and the heart of a man was giv-
en to it.

5 "And there before me was a second beast, which looked like a bear. It was raised up on one of its
7:5 [z]Da 2:39 sides, and it had three ribs in its mouth between its teeth. It was told, 'Get up and eat your fill of flesh!'[z]

[a] 28 *Or Darius, that is, the reign of Cyrus*

6:17 See "Signet Rings" on page 728.
6:24 It was the Persian custom for a man's family to share in his guilt (cf. Est 9:24–25).
7:1 The date here is uncertain—perhaps 553 B.C. The events of chapter 7 actually preceded those of chapter 5.
7:4–7 See "The Kingdoms of Daniel's Prophecies" on page 1388 and "The Ptolemies" on page 1399.
7:4 The lion with an eagle's wings is a cherub symbolizing the Neo-Babylonian Empire (see Ge 3:24 and its note).

6“After that, I looked, and there before me was another beast, one that looked like a leopard.[a] And 7:6 [a]Rev 13:2
on its back it had four wings like those of a bird. This beast had four heads, and it was given authority
to rule.
7“After that, in my vision at night I looked, and there before me was a fourth beast—terrifying and
frightening and very powerful. It had large iron[b] teeth; it crushed and devoured its victims and trampled 7:7 [b]Da 2:40
underfoot whatever was left. It was different from all the former beasts, and it had ten horns.[c] [c]Rev 12:3
8“While I was thinking about the horns, there before me was another horn, a little[d] one, which came 7:8 [d]Da 8:9
up among them; and three of the first horns were uprooted before it. This horn had eyes like the eyes of [e]Rev 9:7 [f]Ps 12:3;
a man[e] and a mouth that spoke boastfully.[f] Rev 13:5-6
9“As I looked,

“thrones were set in place,
  and the Ancient of Days took his seat.
His clothing was as white as snow;
  the hair of his head was white like wool.[g] 7:9 [g]Rev 1:14
His throne was flaming with fire, [h]Eze 1:15; 10:6
  and its wheels[h] were all ablaze.
10 A river of fire[i] was flowing,
  coming out from before him.[j] 7:10 [i]Ps 50:3; 97:3; Isa 30:27
Thousands upon thousands attended him; [j]Dt 33:2; Ps 68:17;
  ten thousand times ten thousand stood before him. Rev 5:11 [k]Rev 20:11-15
The court was seated,
  and the books[k] were opened.

11“Then I continued to watch because of the boastful words the horn was speaking. I kept looking
until the beast was slain and its body destroyed and thrown into the blazing fire.[l] 12(The other beasts 7:11 [l]Rev 19:20
had been stripped of their authority, but were allowed to live for a period of time.)
13“In my vision at night I looked, and there before me was one like a son of man,[m] coming with the 7:13 [m]Mt 8:20*;
clouds of heaven.[n] He approached the Ancient of Days and was led into his presence. 14He was given au- Rev 1:13* [n]Mt 24:30;
thority,[o] glory and sovereign power; all peoples, nations and men of every language worshiped him.[p] Rev 1:7 7:14 [o]Mt 28:18
His dominion is an everlasting dominion that will not pass away, and his kingdom is one that will nev- [p]Ps 72:11; 102:22;
er be destroyed.[q] 1Co 15:27; Eph 1:22 [q]Da 2:44; Heb 12:28; Rev 11:15

The Interpretation of the Dream

15“I, Daniel, was troubled in spirit, and the visions that passed through my mind disturbed me.[r] 16I 7:15 [r]Da 4:19
approached one of those standing there and asked him the true meaning of all this.
“So he told me and gave me the interpretation[s] of these things: 17‘The four great beasts are four king- 7:16 [s]Da 8:16;
doms that will rise from the earth. 18But the saints of the Most High will receive the kingdom and will 9:22; Zec 1:9
possess it forever—yes, for ever and ever.’[t] 7:18 [t]Isa 60:12-14; Rev 2:26;
19“Then I wanted to know the true meaning of the fourth beast, which was different from all the 20:4
others and most terrifying, with its iron teeth and bronze claws—the beast that crushed and devoured
its victims and trampled underfoot whatever was left. 20I also wanted to know about the ten horns on
its head and about the other horn that came up, before which three of them fell—the horn that looked
more imposing than the others and that had eyes and a mouth that spoke boastfully. 21As I watched, this
horn was waging war against the saints and defeating them,[u] 22until the Ancient of Days came and pro- 7:21 [u]Rev 13:7
nounced judgment in favor of the saints of the Most High, and the time came when they possessed the
kingdom.
23“He gave me this explanation: ‘The fourth beast is a fourth kingdom that will appear on earth. It
will be different from all the other kingdoms and will devour the whole earth, trampling it down and
crushing it.[v] 24The ten horns[w] are ten kings who will come from this kingdom. After them another king 7:23 [v]Da 2:40
will arise, different from the earlier ones; he will subdue three kings. 25He will speak against the Most 7:24 [w]Rev 17:12

7:9 “Ancient of Days” is a reference to God. See “Thrones in the Ancient World” on page 899.

For a discussion of literal and figurative references to hair in the Bible, see the note on Psalm 40:12. See also “Beards and Hairstyles in the Biblical World” on page 1084.

7:24 For commentary on the “ten kings,” see “The Kingdoms of Daniel’s Prophecies” on page 1388.

7:25 [x]Isa 37:23; Da 11:36 [y]Da 2:21 [z]Da 8:24; 12:7; Rev 12:14
7:27 [a]Da 2:44; 4:34; Lk 1:33; Rev 11:15; 22:5 [b]Ps 22:27; 72:11; 86:9
7:28 [c]Da 4:19

High[x] and oppress his saints and try to change the set times[y] and the laws. The saints will be handed
over to him for a time, times and half a time.[a][z]
26"'But the court will sit, and his power will be taken away and completely destroyed forever. 27Then
the sovereignty, power and greatness of the kingdoms under the whole heaven will be handed over to
the saints, the people of the Most High. His kingdom will be an everlasting[a] kingdom, and all rulers will
worship[b] and obey him.'
28"This is the end of the matter. I, Daniel, was deeply troubled[c] by my thoughts, and my face turned
pale, but I kept the matter to myself."

[a] 25 Or *for a year, two years and half a year*

The Ptolemies

DANIEL 7 Daniel 7:6 describes a vision in which a kingdom is represented by a leopard with four wings and four heads. The wings represent great speed, but the heads signify that the kingdom was split into several domains. The leopard symbolizes the Greek kingdom of Alexander the Great, a kingdom that was established with lightning speed but that broke into several parts, ruled by various Greek dynasties, after his death.[1]

The **Ptolemies** were a dynasty of Greek kings who ruled Egypt from just after the death of Alexander the Great to the time of the annexation of Egypt by Rome. Their history is closely connected to that of the region later known as Palestine in the third century B.C. (the Ptolemies ruled Palestine and thus also Jerusalem from 323–200 B.C.).[2] Important Ptolemaic rulers were as follows:

✣ *Ptolemy I Soter* (323/305–282 B.C.): Immediately after the death of Alexander in 323, his general Ptolemy headed to Egypt and seized control of the administration, assuming the title "king" in 305. Ptolemy was highly intelligent and, after having taken control of a wealthy and relatively isolated domain (Egypt), was able to begin a dynasty that would last for over two centuries. His capital, Alexandria, was a Greek city in Egypt.[3] Ptolemy was the "king of the South" in 11:5.

✣ *Ptolemy II Philadelphus* (282–246 B.C.): The reign of this king was prosperous and marked by impressive building projects, such as the completion of the lighthouse of Pharos and the library of Alexandria. He was also engaged in wars with the **Seleucids** over control of Palestine and **Anatolia**. Ptolemy II did much to establish Greek culture and education in Egypt and elsewhere but offended his Greek subjects by marrying his full sister, Arsinoë.

✣ *Ptolemy II Euergetes* (246–222 B.C.): The reign of this king was marked by further wars with the Seleucids, brought about by the fact that the Seleucid king, Seleucus II, murdered Ptolemy's sister Berenice and her son.[4] Berenice was the "daughter of the king of the South" in 11:6.

✣ *Ptolemy IV Philopator* (222–205 B.C.): This king is often described as a weak ruler, although he did defeat Antiochus III of Syria at Raphia in 217 B.C. He deployed Egyptian troops in his army (instead of using exclusively Greek soldiers), and some believe that this sowed the seed for future native revolts by the Egyptians. He is the "king of the South" of 11:11.

✣ *Ptolemy V Theos Epiphanes* (204–180 B.C.): During the administration of this regent Palestine was lost to the Seleucid kingdom (200 B.C.). The Rosetta Stone commemorates his coronation.[5]

✣ *Ptolemy VI Philometor* (180–145 B.C.): During his reign Ptolemaic control of Egypt nearly collapsed. Antiochus IV fought his way to Memphis in Egypt in around 168 B.C. and no doubt would have taken control of the country had he not been forced out by a delegation from Rome.

✣ Thereafter, Ptolemaic power declined as members of the royal family struggled for control and as Rome began to take an increasingly important role in the affairs of Egypt. The last Ptolemy to rule Egypt was the famous *Cleopatra VII* (51–30 B.C.). Intelligent and resourceful (she was the only Ptolemy who gained the loyalty of Egyptians by learning to speak Egyptian, but she also murdered her brother, Ptolemy XIV, in order to secure the throne for herself), she used sexual relations with Julius Caesar and later with Mark Antony to better her political position in dealing with Rome. Her alliance with Antony proved her undoing, however. He was defeated by Octavian (Augustus) at Actium in 31 B.C.,[6] and she committed suicide when she realized that Octavian was implacable toward her.

[1]See "Greece: From the Independent City-states Through Alexander the Great" on page 1814. [2]See "The History of the Holy Land" on page xxi. [3]See "Alexandria" on page 1085. [4]See "The Seleucids" on page 1408. [5]See "The Rosetta Stone and the Deciphering of Hieroglyphs" on page 101. [6]See "Caesar Augustus, Emperor of Rome; the Census; and Quirinius, Governor of Syria" on page 1667.

Daniel's Vision of a Ram and a Goat

8 In the third year of King Belshazzar's reign, I, Daniel, had a vision, after the one that had already ap-
peared to me. 2 In my vision I saw myself in the citadel of Susa[d] in the province of Elam;[e] in the vi- 8:2 dEst 1:2 eGe 10:22
sion I was beside the Ulai Canal. 3 I looked up,[f] and there before me was a ram with two horns, standing 8:3 fDa 10:5
beside the canal, and the horns were long. One of the horns was longer than the other but grew up later.
4 I watched the ram as he charged toward the west and the north and the south. No animal could stand
against him, and none could rescue from his power. He did as he pleased[g] and became great. 8:4 gDa 11:3,16
5 As I was thinking about this, suddenly a goat with a prominent horn between his eyes came from the
west, crossing the whole earth without touching the ground. 6 He came toward the two-horned ram I had
seen standing beside the canal and charged at him in great rage. 7 I saw him attack the ram furiously,
striking the ram and shattering his two horns. The ram was powerless to stand against him; the goat
knocked him to the ground and trampled on him,[h] and none could rescue the ram from his power. 8 The 8:7 hDa 7:7
goat became very great, but at the height of his power his large horn was broken off,[i] and in its place four 8:8 i2Ch 26:16-21; Da 5:20
prominent horns grew up toward the four winds of heaven.[j] jDa 7:2; Rev 7:1
9 Out of one of them came another horn, which started small but grew in power to the south and to
the east and toward the Beautiful Land.[k] 10 It grew until it reached[l] the host of the heavens, and it threw 8:9 kDa 11:16 8:10 lIsa 14:13
some of the starry host down to the earth[m] and trampled[n] on them. 11 It set itself up to be as great as the mRev 12:4 nDa 7:7
Prince of the host;[o] it took away the daily sacrifice[p] from him, and the place of his sanctuary was brought 8:11 oDa 11:36-37 pEze 46:13-14

8:1—12:13 These chapters were written in Hebrew (see the note on 2:4).
8:1 The date was about 551 B.C. The events of chapter 8 actually preceded those of chapter 5.
8:2 The "citadel of Susa" was the acropolis (upper fortified area) and palace complex, which was distinguished from the surrounding city. Several archaeological investigations have been conducted at the site since the mid-nineteenth century. Xerxes had made extensive renovations in the palace structures (see "Susa" on p. 729). For "Elam," see the note on Jeremiah 25:25.
8:3 The ram represents the Medo-Persian Empire (v. 20), and the longer of his two horns reflects the predominant position of Persia (see 7:5 and "The Kingdoms of Daniel's Prophecies" on p. 1388).
8:5 The charging goat is Greece and the "prominent horn" is Alexander the Great, "the first king" (v. 21).
8:7 Greece crushed the Medo-Persian Empire.
8:8 With the death of Alexander the Great (the "large horn") at the height of his power (323 B.C.), his kingdom was divided among his four generals.
8:9–12 The horn that "started small" (v. 9) is Antiochus IV Epiphanes (see "Antiochus IV Epiphanes" on p. 1406).

ANCIENT TEXTS AND ARTIFACTS

The Prayer of Nabonidus

DANIEL 8 Nabonidus was the father of King Belshazzar of Babylon, with whom he ruled as coregent for at least several years.[1] A Qumran scroll dating between 75 and 50 B.C., commonly called The Prayer of Nabonidus, or 4QprNab, is an **Apocryphal** account of a healing of Nabonidus that is probably based on Daniel 4. This text tells us that King Nabonidus was inflicted with a physical ailment for seven years, until a Jewish exorcist pardoned his sins. This Jewish man then encouraged Nabonidus to document the event and to give praise to God, who pardoned him. In the final section of the scroll Nabonidus declared that his prior supplications to the gods of the world concerning his ailment had gone unanswered.

The scroll suggests that Nabonidus journeyed to Tema, Arabia, and remained there for a number of years. This detail is accurate. In fact, it was during his stay in Tema that Belshazzar reigned in Babylon. Therefore, 8:1 refers to Belshazzar as king, for the Babylonians saw him as their ruling authority. Apart from that, however, there is little reason to regard The Prayer of Nabonidus as historical. It appears that the story is based on the Biblical account of the healing of Nebuchadnezzar.[2] Other Apocryphal books, such as Bel and the Dragon, are also popular legends that grew out of the canonical book of Daniel.[3] As such, The Prayer of Nabonidus can neither confirm nor refute the historical reliability of the story of Daniel 4.

[1]See "Nabonidus and Belshazzar" on page 1394. [2]See "Nebuchadnezzar's Madness" on page 1391. [3]See "The Apocrypha" on page 1973.

8:11 qDa 11:31; 12:11 low.[q] 12 Because of rebellion, the host ⌞of the saints⌟[a] and the daily
sacrifice were given over to it. It prospered in everything it did, and
truth was thrown to the ground.

8:13 rDa 4:23 sDa 12:6 tLk 21:24; Rev 11:2 13 Then I heard a holy one[r] speaking, and another holy one said
to him, "How long will it take for the vision to be fulfilled[s]—the vi-
sion concerning the daily sacrifice, the rebellion that causes desola-
tion, and the surrender of the sanctuary and of the host that will be
trampled[t] underfoot?"

14 He said to me, "It will take 2,300 evenings and mornings; then
8:14 uDa 12:11-12 the sanctuary will be reconsecrated."[u]

The Interpretation of the Vision

8:15 vver 1 wDa 10:16-18 15 While I, Daniel, was watching the vision[v] and trying to under-
stand it, there before me stood one who looked like a man.[w] 16 And
8:16 xDa 9:21; Lk 1:19 I heard a man's voice from the Ulai calling, "Gabriel,[x] tell this man
the meaning of the vision."

17 As he came near the place where I was standing, I was terrified
8:17 yEze 1:28; Da 2:46; Rev 1:17 zHab 2:3 and fell prostrate.[y] "Son of man," he said to me, "understand that the
vision concerns the time of the end."[z]

18 While he was speaking to me, I was in a deep sleep, with my
8:18 aDa 10:9 bEze 2:2; Da 10:16-18 face to the ground.[a] Then he touched me and raised me to my feet.[b]

19 He said: "I am going to tell you what will happen later in the
time of wrath, because the vision concerns the appointed time of
8:19 cHab 2:3 the end.[bc] 20 The two-horned ram that you saw represents the kings
8:21 dDa 10:20 eDa 11:3 of Media and Persia. 21 The shaggy goat is the king of Greece,[d] and
the large horn between his eyes is the first king.[e] 22 The four horns
that replaced the one that was broken off represent four kingdoms that will emerge from his nation but
will not have the same power.

23 "In the latter part of their reign, when rebels have become completely wicked, a stern-faced king, a
master of intrigue, will arise. 24 He will become very strong, but not by his own power. He will cause as-
tounding devastation and will succeed in whatever he does. He will destroy the mighty men and the holy
8:24 fDa 7:25; 11:36 people.[f] 25 He will cause deceit to prosper, and he will consider himself superior. When they feel secure,
8:25 gDa 11:36 hDa 2:34; 11:21 he will destroy many and take his stand against the Prince of princes.[g] Yet he will be destroyed, but not
by human power.[h]

8:26 iDa 10:1 jRev 22:10 kDa 10:14 26 "The vision of the evenings and mornings that has been given you is true,[i] but seal[j] up the vision,
for it concerns the distant future."[k]

27 I, Daniel, was exhausted and lay ill for several days. Then I got up and went about the king's busi-
8:27 lDa 2:48 mDa 7:28 ness.[l] I was appalled[m] by the vision; it was beyond understanding.

Daniel's Prayer

9:1 nDa 5:31 **9** In the first year of Darius[n] son of Xerxes[c] (a Mede by descent), who was made ruler over the Bab-
ylonian[d] kingdom— 2 in the first year of his reign, I, Daniel, understood from the Scriptures, ac-
cording to the word of the LORD given to Jeremiah the prophet, that the desolation of Jerusalem would last
9:2 o2Ch 36:21; Jer 29:10; Zec 7:5 seventy[o] years. 3 So I turned to the Lord God and pleaded with him in prayer and petition, in fasting, and
9:3 pNe 1:4; Jer 29:12 in sackcloth and ashes.[p]

[a] 12 Or *rebellion, the armies* [b] 19 Or *because the end will be at the appointed time* [c] 1 Hebrew *Ahasuerus* [d] 1 Or *Chaldean*

ANCIENT VOICES

The words of the prayer that Nabonidus, king of Babylon, the Great King, prayed when by divine decree he was afflicted with a foul ulcer while in Teiman: "I, Nabonidus, was afflicted with a foul ulcer for seven years, and because God laid it upon me, I sought him and he healed me, and a soothsayer forgave my sin. This soothsayer was a Jew, from the Jewish exile, and he said to me, 'Proclaim this and write it down, in order to give honor and majesty to the name of the Most High God!' And so I wrote this: 'I was afflicted while in Teiman with a foul ulcer by a decree of the Most High God. For seven years I prayed before the gods of silver, gold, bronze, iron, wood, stone and clay, because I supposed that they were gods . . .'" (the text is fragmentary and illegible at this point).

—THE PRAYER OF NABONIDUS
From the Dead Sea Scrolls, 4Q242,
trans. by Duane Garrett

See "The Prayer of Nabonidus" article.

8:14 This could refer to 2,300 full days. But as morning and evening sacrifices were offered daily at the temple (9:21; Ex 29:38–39), "2,300 evenings and mornings" quite possibly refers to the number of sacrifices consecutively offered on 1,150 days—the interval between the desecration of the altar by Antiochus and its reconsecration by Judas Maccabeus in December of 165 B.C.

8:17 The term "son of man" here is not to be confused with the "one like a son of man" in 7:13.

8:21 See verse 5 and its note.

8:22 See verse 8 and its note.

8:23–25 These verses describe Antiochus IV and his rise to power by political intrigue and deceit. Antiochus called himself Epiphanes ("God manifest"). He died in 164 B.C. at Tabae in Persia as the result of either illness or accident. In reality, God (the "Prince of princes," v. 5) destroyed him.

9:1 The date was 538 B.C. For Darius, see "Darius the Mede" on page 1396. The Xerxes mentioned here is not the later Xerxes of the book of Esther.

9:2 See "The 70 Years of Captivity" on page 1234.

9:3 Sackcloth was the coarse garb of mourners (see the notes on 1Ki 20:31–32 and Job 16:15, as well as "Sackcloth and Ashes: Rituals of Lamentation" on p. 820).

4 I prayed to the LORD my God and confessed:

"O Lord, the great and awesome God,[q] who keeps his covenant of love[r] with all who love him 9:4 [q]Dt 7:21
and obey his commands, 5 we have sinned and done wrong.[s] We have been wicked and have re- [r]Dt 7:9 9:5 [s]Ps 106:6
belled; we have turned away[t] from your commands and laws.[u] 6 We have not listened to your ser- [t]Isa 53:6 [u]ver 11; La 1:20
vants the prophets,[v] who spoke in your name to our kings, our princes and our fathers, and to all 9:6 [v]2Ch 36:16; Jer 44:5
the people of the land.
7 "Lord, you are righteous, but this day we are covered with shame[w]—the men of Judah and 9:7 [w]Ps 44:15
people of Jerusalem and all Israel, both near and far, in all the countries where you have scattered[x] [x]Dt 4:27; Am 9:9
us because of our unfaithfulness to you.[y] 8 O LORD, we and our kings, our princes and our fathers [y]Jer 3:25
are covered with shame because we have sinned against you. 9 The Lord our God is merciful and
forgiving,[z] even though we have rebelled against him;[a] 10 we have not obeyed the LORD our God or 9:9 [z]Ps 130:4
kept the laws he gave us through his servants the prophets.[b] 11 All Israel has transgressed your law [a]Ne 9:17; Jer 14:7
and turned away, refusing to obey you. 9:10 [b]2Ki 17:13-15; 18:12
"Therefore the curses and sworn judgments written in the Law of Moses, the servant of God,
have been poured out on us, because we have sinned[c] against you. 12 You have fulfilled[d] the words 9:11 [c]Isa 1:4-6; Jer 8:5-10
spoken against us and against our rulers by bringing upon us great disaster. Under the whole heav- 9:12 [d]Isa 44:26; Zec 1:6 [e]Jer 44:2-6; Eze 5:9
en nothing has ever been done like what has been done to Jerusalem.[e] 13 Just as it is written in the
Law of Moses, all this disaster has come upon us, yet we have not sought the favor of the LORD our
God by turning from our sins and giving attention to your truth.[f] 14 The LORD did not hesitate to 9:13 [f]Isa 9:13; Jer 2:30
bring the disaster[g] upon us, for the LORD our God is righteous in everything he does; yet we have 9:14 [g]Jer 44:27 [h]Ne 9:33
not obeyed him.[h]

The Chaldeans

DANIEL 9 The Chaldeans were a seminomadic ethnic group first mentioned in ancient sources from the ninth century B.C. as a people from the land of Kaldu. Living in the southern frontier of **Babylon**, they were organized into tribal "houses," each of which was headed by a tribal leader. As these tribes assimilated into the predominant culture and subsequently inherited the empire of Babylonia, the terms "Chaldean" and "Babylonian" became synonymous (Isa 47:1; Da 9:1).

The first notable Chaldean recorded in Scripture was Merodach-Baladan, king of Babylon, who sent envoys to Hezekiah of Judah for the purpose of forming an anti-Assyrian coalition (2Ki 20:12–19; Isa 39:1). Merodach-Baladan united the Chaldean tribes and, with **Elamite** assistance, managed to overthrow **Assyrian** dominance in the region and to rule for a decade before being driven out (c. 722–710 B.C.).[1] By 626 B.C., as Assyrian power declined, Chaldean power in Babylon experienced a resurgence during the reigns of Nabopolassar and his son **Nebuchadnezzar**. This last dynasty of Babylon is thus known as the Chaldean, or **Neo-Babylonian** Empire.

The reign of the Chaldeans brought the greatest flowering and fame of the Babylonian Empire. Nebuchadnezzar, under whose rule the kingdom of Judah was conquered and exiled (Jer 52),[2] in addition to his military achievements is credited with the grandest rebuilding of Babylon's cultural and religious life.[3] The city came to be regarded as one of the wonders of the ancient world and was, in the prophet's words, "Babylon, the jewel of kingdoms, the glory of the Babylonians' pride" (Isa 13:19).

Because Babylon was famed as a city of learning, the term "Chaldean" came to stand for priests, astrologers and the educated class (Da 2:10; 4:7; 5:7). This Chaldean/Neo-Babylonian period marked the beginning of accurate historical, economic and astronomical record keeping, as well as the rise of **Aramaic** as the lingua franca (common, commercial language) of the Near East (2:4).[4] Ultimately the Neo-Babylonian Empire fell to Cyrus of **Persia**,[5] and the glory of **Mesopotamia** faded into history.

[1]See "Sennacherib's Campaign Against Merodach-Baladan" on page 1124. [2]See "The Last Days of Jerusalem" on page 1197. [3]See "Nebuchadnezzar" on page 571.
[4]See "Languages of the Old Testament World" on page 672. [5]See "Cyrus the Great" on page 669.

15“Now, O Lord our God, who brought your people out of Egypt with a mighty hand[i] and who
made for yourself a name[j] that endures to this day, we have sinned, we have done wrong. 16O Lord,
in keeping with all your righteous acts,[k] turn away your anger and your wrath from Jerusalem,[l]
your city, your holy hill.[m] Our sins and the iniquities of our fathers have made Jerusalem and your
people an object of scorn[n] to all those around us.

17“Now, our God, hear the prayers and petitions of your servant. For your sake, O Lord, look
with favor[o] on your desolate sanctuary. 18Give ear, O God, and hear; open your eyes and see[p]
the desolation of the city that bears your Name.[q] We do not make requests of you because we
are righteous, but because of your great mercy. 19O Lord, listen! O Lord, forgive![r] O Lord, hear
and act! For your sake, O my God, do not delay, because your city and your people bear your
Name.”

9:15 [i]Jer 32:21 [j]Ne 9:10
9:16 [k]Ps 31:1 [l]Jer 32:32 [m]Zec 8:3 [n]Eze 5:14
9:17 [o]Nu 6:24-26; Ps 80:19
9:18 [p]Ps 80:14 [q]Isa 37:17; Jer 7:10-12; 25:29
9:19 [r]Ps 44:23

The Seventy “Sevens”

20While I was speaking and praying, confessing my sin and the sin of my people Israel and making
my request to the LORD my God for his holy hill[s]— 21while I was still in prayer, Gabriel,[t] the man I had
seen in the earlier vision, came to me in swift flight about the time of the evening sacrifice.[u] 22He in-
structed me and said to me, “Daniel, I have now come to give you insight and understanding. 23As soon
as you began to pray, an answer was given, which I have come to tell you, for you are highly esteemed.[v]
Therefore, consider the message and understand the vision:[w]

24“Seventy ‘sevens’[a] are decreed for your people and your holy city to finish[b] transgression, to put an
end to sin, to atone[x] for wickedness, to bring in everlasting righteousness,[y] to seal up vision and proph-
ecy and to anoint the most holy.[c]

25“Know and understand this: From the issuing of the decree[d] to restore and rebuild[z] Jerusalem un-
til the Anointed One,[e][a] the ruler, comes, there will be seven ‘sevens,’ and sixty-two ‘sevens.’ It will be re-
built with streets and a trench, but in times of trouble. 26After the sixty-two ‘sevens,’ the Anointed One
will be cut off[b] and will have nothing.[f] The people of the ruler who will come will destroy the city and
the sanctuary. The end will come like a flood:[c] War will continue until the end, and desolations have been
decreed. 27He will confirm a covenant with many for one ‘seven.’[g] In the middle of the ‘seven’[g] he will put
an end to sacrifice and offering. And on a wing ⌊of the temple⌋ he will set up an abomination that caus-
es desolation, until the end that is decreed[d] is poured out on him.[h]”[i]

9:20 [s]ver 3; Ps 145:18; Isa 58:9
9:21 [t]Da 8:16; Lk 1:19 [u]Ex 29:39
9:23 [v]Da 10:19; Lk 1:28 [w]Da 10:11-12; Mt 24:15
9:24 [x]Isa 53:10 [y]Isa 56:1
9:25 [z]Ezr 4:24 [a]Jn 4:25
9:26 [b]Isa 53:8 [c]Na 1:8
9:27 [d]Isa 10:22

Daniel’s Vision of a Man

10 In the third year of Cyrus[e] king of Persia, a revelation was given to Daniel (who was called Bel-
teshazzar).[f] Its message was true[g] and it concerned a great war.[j] The understanding of the mes-
sage came to him in a vision.

2At that time I, Daniel, mourned[h] for three weeks. 3I ate no choice food; no meat or wine touched my
lips; and I used no lotions at all until the three weeks were over.

4On the twenty-fourth day of the first month, as I was standing on the bank of the great river, the Ti-
gris,[i] 5I looked up and there before me was a man dressed in linen,[j] with a belt of the finest gold[k] around
his waist. 6His body was like chrysolite, his face like lightning,[l] his eyes like flaming torches,[m] his arms
and legs like the gleam of burnished bronze,[n] and his voice like the sound of a multitude.

10:1 [e]Da 1:21 [f]Da 1:7 [g]Da 8:26
10:2 [h]Ezr 9:4
10:4 [i]Ge 2:14
10:5 [j]Eze 9:2; Rev 15:6 [k]Jer 10:9
10:6 [l]Mt 17:2 [m]Rev 19:12 [n]Rev 1:15

[a] 24 Or *‘weeks’*; also in verses 25 and 26 [b] 24 Or *restrain* [c] 24 Or *Most Holy Place*; or *most holy One* [d] 25 Or *word*
[e] 25 Or *an anointed one*; also in verse 26 [f] 26 Or *off and will have no one*; or *off, but not for himself* [g] 27 Or *‘week’*
[h] 27 Or *it* [i] 27 Or *And one who causes desolation will come upon the pinnacle of the abominable ⌊temple⌋, until the end that is decreed is poured out on the desolated ⌊city⌋* [j] 1 Or *true and burdensome*

9:18 The “city that bears your Name” is Jerusalem.

9:20 The “holy hill” is Zion (see “Zaphon, Olympus, Sinai and Zion: The Mountain of God” on p. 843).

9:24–27 “The Seventy Weeks” is a name often applied to Daniel 9:24–27, a prophecy that presumably, in contrast to the general prophecies in Daniel 2 and 7, pinpointed the exact time within the fourth kingdom when the Messiah would appear. Almost all scholars agree that the “weeks” designate 490 years. The prophecy is (1) divided—the successive periods are described as 7, 62, 1; (2) dated—“from” and “until” in 9:25; (3) determinative—Its purposes regard Israel (v. 24), redemption (v. 24), the Messiah (vv. 24,26–27), the sacrifices (v. 27) and Jerusalem (vv. 25–27); and (4) debated (see below).

Three primary views are held. (1) The *critical view* posits that the “prophecy” was written by a pseudo-Daniel in 165 B.C. and synchronizes (inaccurately) with the history between 586 B.C. (Jerusalem’s fall) and 164 B.C. (Antiochus). (2) The *dispensational view* has the sixty-ninth week terminating before Jesus’ crucifixion, leaving the seventieth (the present age being a “great parenthesis”) to be fulfilled in the great tribulation. (3) The *conservative* or *traditional view* asserts that the seventieth week was introduced by Jesus’ baptism and bisected (three and a half years) by his death, thus causing the sacrifices to cease (v. 27).

10:1 The date was 537 B.C., the third year after Cyrus’s conquest of Babylonia in 539 (see the note on 1:1 regarding the computation of the years of a king’s reign).

10:3 See the note on 1:8.

7 I, Daniel, was the only one who saw the vision; the men with me did not see it,[o] but such terror over-
whelmed them that they fled and hid themselves. 8 So I was left alone,[p] gazing at this great vision; I had
no strength left,[q] my face turned deathly pale and I was helpless.[r] 9 Then I heard him speaking, and as I
listened to him, I fell into a deep sleep, my face to the ground.[s]
10 A hand touched me[t] and set me trembling on my hands and knees.[u] 11 He said, "Daniel, you who
are highly esteemed,[v] consider carefully the words I am about to speak to you, and stand up,[w] for I have
now been sent to you." And when he said this to me, I stood up trembling.
12 Then he continued, "Do not be afraid, Daniel. Since the first day that you set your mind to gain un-
derstanding and to humble[x] yourself before your God, your words were heard, and I have come in re-
sponse to them.[y] 13 But the prince of the Persian kingdom resisted me twenty-one days. Then Michael,[z]
one of the chief princes, came to help me, because I was detained there with the king of Persia. 14 Now I
have come to explain[a] to you what will happen to your people in the future, for the vision concerns a
time yet to come.[b]"
15 While he was saying this to me, I bowed with my face toward the ground and was speechless.[c]
16 Then one who looked like a man[a] touched my lips, and I opened my mouth and began to speak.[d] I said
to the one standing before me, "I am overcome with anguish[e] because of the vision, my lord, and I am
helpless. 17 How can I, your servant, talk with you, my lord? My strength is gone and I can hardly breathe."[f]
18 Again the one who looked like a man touched[g] me and gave me strength. 19 "Do not be afraid, O man
highly esteemed," he said. "Peace![h] Be strong now; be strong."[i]
When he spoke to me, I was strengthened and said, "Speak, my lord, since you have given me
strength."[j]
20 So he said, "Do you know why I have come to you? Soon I will return to fight against the prince of
Persia, and when I go, the prince of Greece[k] will come; 21 but first I will tell you what is written in the
Book of Truth.[l] (No one supports me against them except Michael,[m] your prince. 11 1 And in the
first year of Darius[n] the Mede, I took my stand to support and protect him.)

10:7 [o]2Ki 6:17-20; Ac 9:7 **10:8** [p]Ge 32:24 [q]Da 8:27 [r]Hab 3:16 **10:9** [s]Da 8:18 **10:10** [t]Jer 1:9 [u]Rev 1:17 **10:11** [v]Da 9:23 [w]Eze 2:1 **10:12** [x]Da 9:3 [y]Da 9:20 **10:13** [z]ver 21; Da 12:1; Jude 1:9 **10:14** [a]Da 9:22 [b]Da 2:28; 8:26; Hab 2:3 **10:15** [c]Eze 24:27; Lk 1:20 **10:16** [d]Isa 6:7; Jer 1:9; Da 8:15-18 [e]Isa 21:3 **10:17** [f]Da 4:19 **10:18** [g]ver 16 **10:19** [h]Jdg 6:23; Isa 35:4 [i]Jos 1:9 [j]Isa 6:1-8 **10:20** [k]Da 8:21; 11:2 **10:21** [l]Da 11:2 [m]ver 13; Jude 1:9 **11:1** [n]Da 5:31

[a] *16* Most manuscripts of the Masoretic Text; one manuscript of the Masoretic Text, Dead Sea Scrolls and Septuagint *Then something that looked like a man's hand*

11:1 See "Daruis the Mede" on page 1396.

ARCHAEOLOGICAL SITES

PERSEPOLIS

DANIEL 10 Persepolis (meaning "Persian city") was a capital city of the **Achaemenid** kings. Its remains, known as Takht-i Jamshid, are located northeast of Shiraz, Iran, 140 miles (226 km) inland from the Persian Gulf. Trilingual inscriptions on the site report the building activities of several generations of Persian monarchs.[1] Darius I (521–486 B.C.)[2] began construction of the city after having created a platform of 33 acres, 40 feet (12.2 m) above the plain. He erected fortifications, a monumental stairway to the platform, a palace, an audience hall and other buildings. The audience hall, or *Apadana*, employed 72 stone columns, each 65 feet (20 m) in height, of which 13 still stand. Its eastern stairway was decorated with images of delegations of Persians, Medes, Egyptians, **Assyrians**, Greeks and others bearing tribute and in their customary dress.

Xerxes I (r. 486–465 B.C.) added a larger palace, harem and treasury. He began the "throne-hall of 100 columns" and built the "Gate of All Nations," ornamented with colossal winged and human-headed bulls. Thousands of **Elamite** tablets from the reigns of Darius, Xerxes and Artaxerxes I[3] were recovered from the treasury, among which are featured a number of Jewish names, including Baruch, Zechariah, Abijah and Hezeki(ah). Artaxerxes I (465–425 B.C.) completed the throne-hall, and Artaxerxes III (359–338 B.C.) added a staircase to Darius's palace. Alexander the Great destroyed the city in 330 B.C. as retribution for Xerxes' destruction of Athens in 480 B.C.[4] Tombs of the Achaemenid kings, cut into cliffs at Naqsh-i Rustam, are located 3.5 miles (5.7 km) north of the city.

[1]See "Ancient Persian History Through Darius" on page 717 and "Ancient Persian History From Xerxes Forward" on page 718. [2]See "Darius I" on page 676. [3]See "Artaxerxes I, King of Persia" on page 681. [4]See "Athens" on page 1804.

The Kings of the South and the North

11:2 [o]Da 10:21 2“Now then, I tell you the truth:[o] Three more kings will appear in Persia, and then a fourth, who will
[p]Da 10:20 be far richer than all the others. When he has gained power by his wealth, he will stir up everyone against
the kingdom of Greece.[p] 3Then a mighty king will appear, who will rule with great power and do as he
11:3 [q]Da 8:4,21 pleases.[q] 4After he has appeared, his empire will be broken up and parceled out toward the four winds
11:4 [r]Da 7:2; 8:22 of heaven.[r] It will not go to his descendants, nor will it have the power he exercised, because his empire
will be uprooted and given to others.

5“The king of the South will become strong, but one of his commanders will become even stronger
than he and will rule his own kingdom with great power. 6After some years, they will become allies. The
daughter of the king of the South will go to the king of the North to make an alliance, but she will not re-
tain her power, and he and his power[a] will not last. In those days she will be handed over, together with
her royal escort and her father[b] and the one who supported her.

7“One from her family line will arise to take her place. He will attack the forces of the king of the
11:7 [s]ver 6 North[s] and enter his fortress; he will fight against them and be victorious. 8He will also seize their gods,[t]
11:8 [t]Isa 37:19; 46:1-2 [u]Jer 43:12 their metal images and their valuable articles of silver and gold and carry them off to Egypt.[u] For some
years he will leave the king of the North alone. 9Then the king of the North will invade the realm of the
king of the South but will retreat to his own country. 10His sons will prepare for war and assemble a great
11:10 [v]Isa 8:8; Jer 46:8; Da 9:26 army, which will sweep on like an irresistible flood[v] and carry the battle as far as his fortress.

11“Then the king of the South will march out in a rage and fight against the king of the North, who
11:11 [w]Da 8:7-8 will raise a large army, but it will be defeated.[w] 12When the army is carried off, the king of the South will
be filled with pride and will slaughter many thousands, yet he will not remain triumphant. 13For the king
of the North will muster another army, larger than the first; and after several years, he will advance with
a huge army fully equipped.

14“In those times many will rise against the king of the South. The violent men among your own peo-
ple will rebel in fulfillment of the vision, but without success. 15Then the king of the North will come and
11:15 [x]Eze 4:2 build up siege ramps[x] and will capture a fortified city. The forces of the South will be powerless to resist;
11:16 [y]Da 8:4 even their best troops will not have the strength to stand. 16The invader will do as he pleases;[y] no one will
[z]Jos 1:5; Da 8:7 [a]Da 8:9 be able to stand against him.[z] He will establish himself in the Beautiful Land and will have the power to
destroy it.[a] 17He will determine to come with the might of his entire kingdom and will make an alliance
with the king of the South. And he will give him a daughter in marriage in order to overthrow the king-
11:17 [b]Ps 20:4 dom, but his plans[c] will not succeed[b] or help him. 18Then he will turn his attention to the coastlands[c] and
11:18 [c]Isa 66:19; Jer 25:22 will take many of them, but a commander will put an end to his insolence and will turn his insolence back
[d]Hos 12:14 upon him.[d] 19After this, he will turn back toward the fortresses of his own country but will stumble and
11:19 [e]Ps 27:2 [f]Ps 37:36; Eze 26:21 fall,[e] to be seen no more.[f]
20“His successor will send out a tax collector to maintain the royal splendor.[g] In a few years, howev-
11:20 [g]Isa 60:17 er, he will be destroyed, yet not in anger or in battle.

11:21 [h]Da 4:17 21“He will be succeeded by a contemptible[h] person who has not been given the honor of royalty.[i] He
[i]Da 8:25 will invade the kingdom when its people feel secure, and he will seize it through intrigue. 22Then an over-
11:22 [j]Da 8:10-11 whelming army will be swept away before him; both it and a prince of the covenant will be destroyed.[j]
11:23 [k]Da 8:25 23After coming to an agreement with him, he will act deceitfully,[k] and with only a few people he will rise
to power. 24When the richest provinces feel secure, he will invade them and will achieve what neither his
11:24 [l]Ne 9:25 fathers nor his forefathers did. He will distribute plunder, loot and wealth among his followers.[l] He will
plot the overthrow of fortresses—but only for a time.

25“With a large army he will stir up his strength and courage against the king of the South. The king
of the South will wage war with a large and very powerful army, but he will not be able to stand because

[a] 6 Or *offspring* [b] 6 Or *child* (see Vulgate and Syriac) [c] 17 Or *but she*

11:2 “Three more kings” is a reference to Cambyses (530–522 B.C.), Pseudo Smerdis or Gaumata (522) and Darius I (522–486). The “fourth” king was Xerxes I (486–465; see the note on Est 1:1), who attempted to conquer Greece in 480.
11:3 The “mighty king” was Alexander the Great (336–323).
11:5–45 See “The Ptolemies” on page 1399, “The Seleucids” on page 1408 and “Antiochus IV Epiphanes” on page 1406.
11:8 “Their gods” refers to the images of Syrian deities, as well as to those of the Egyptian gods the Persian Cambyses had carried off after conquering Egypt in 525 B.C.
11:12 The Greek historian Polybius recorded that Antiochus lost nearly 10,000 infantrymen at Raphia (Ptolemy’s fortress southwest of Gaza) in 217 B.C.
11:15 The “fortified city” refers to the Mediterranean port of Sidon (see “Sidon” on p. 1536).
11:18 “Coastlands” is a reference to Asia Minor and perhaps also to mainland Greece.

of the plots devised against him. 26Those who eat from the king's provisions will try to destroy him; his
army will be swept away, and many will fall in battle. 27The two kings, with their hearts bent on evil,[m] will
sit at the same table and lie[n] to each other, but to no avail, because an end will still come at the appoint-
ed time.[o] 28The king of the North will return to his own country with great wealth, but his heart will be
set against the holy covenant. He will take action against it and then return to his own country.

11:27 [m]Ps 64:6 [n]Ps 12:2; Jer 9:5 [o]Hab 2:3

11:28 In 169 B.C. Antiochus plundered the temple in Jerusalem, set up a garrison there and massacred many Jews in the city (see "Antiochus IV Epiphanes" on p. 1406).

Antiochus IV Epiphanes

DANIEL 11 Antiochus IV Epiphanes ruled the **Seleucid** (Syrian) kingdom from 175 to 164 B.C.[1] Epiphanes means "manifest," and the name indicates that he claimed to be the earthly manifestation of Zeus.[2] Antiochus attempted to unify his empire by imposing **Hellenistic** culture upon all its inhabitants. This policy brought him into sharp conflict with the Jews of the region later known as Palestine.

Most Biblical scholars believe Antiochus IV to have been the "small" horn in Daniel 8:9 and the "contemptible person" of 11:21. His relations with the Jews are recorded in 1 and 2 Maccabees (**Apocryphal** books) and are prophetically depicted in Daniel 8:9–12,23–25 and 11:21–34. He was infamous for establishing pagan worship in the Jerusalem temple.

In about 174 B.C. Jason, the leader of a pro-Greek faction in the Jerusalem priesthood, bribed Antiochus to install him as high priest, after which Jason set about turning Jerusalem into a Greek city (2Mc 4:7–22). In 171 B.C., however, another man, Menelaus, in turn bought the priesthood from Antiochus. Jason, believing that Antiochus had died, seized Jerusalem by force. But Antiochus returned in 169 and carried out a massacre of the city. He then moved upon Egypt but was humiliated by the Roman legate C. Popilius Laenas and forced to make an undignified withdrawal to the north. Thereafter, this tyrant vigorously sought to **Hellenize** Jerusalem.

In 167 B.C. Antiochus dispatched his tax collector Apollonius against Jerusalem with 22,000 men. They attacked on the Sabbath, killing most of the male population and enslaving the women and children. Jerusalem's walls were demolished and a Seleucid military garrison stationed immediately south of the temple. All Jewish rites were outlawed, resulting in the cessation of the daily sacrifice. An altar to Zeus was erected over the Jewish altar of burnt offerings, and worship of Zeus was instituted in the temple. On December 25, 167 B.C., a pig was sacrificed on the Zeus altar; this was the "abomination that causes desolation" in Daniel 9:27, 11:31 and 12:11.

Enraged, the Jews rebelled against their Greek overlords and, under Judas Maccabeus, defeated the armies that Antiochus had sent against them. After a three-year struggle Jewish forces gained major concessions from the Greeks, and the Maccabees became the de facto rulers of Judea. Most notably, they purified the temple and reinstated the daily sacrifice, an event commemorated in the feast of Hanukkah. Antiochus himself, who had moved off to the east to campaign in **Elam**, died in **Persia** in 164 B.C.[3]

[1]See "The Seleucids" on page 1408. [2]See "The Gods of the Greeks and Romans" on page 1908. [3]See also "The Intertestamental Period" on page 1551.

Roman bronze of a man leading a boar to be sacrificed (Jews did not sacrifice swine of any kind)

Preserving Bible Times; © Dr. James C. Martin; permission of The British Museum

[29]"At the appointed time he will invade the South again, but this time the outcome will be different
from what it was before. [30]Ships of the western coastlands[a][p] will oppose him, and he will lose heart. Then
he will turn back and vent his fury against the holy covenant. He will return and show favor to those who
forsake the holy covenant.

[31]"His armed forces will rise up to desecrate the temple fortress and will abolish the daily sacrifice.
Then they will set up the abomination that causes desolation.[q] [32]With flattery he will corrupt those who
have violated the covenant, but the people who know their God will firmly resist[r] him.

[33]"Those who are wise will instruct[s] many, though for a time they will fall by the sword or be burned
or captured or plundered.[t] [34]When they fall, they will receive a little help, and many who are not sincere[u]
will join them. [35]Some of the wise will stumble, so that they may be refined,[v] purified and made spot-
less until the time of the end, for it will still come at the appointed time.

The King Who Exalts Himself

[36]"The king will do as he pleases. He will exalt and magnify himself above every god and will say un-
heard-of things[w] against the God of gods.[x] He will be successful until the time of wrath[y] is completed,
for what has been determined must take place. [37]He will show no regard for the gods of his fathers or for
the one desired by women, nor will he regard any god, but will exalt himself above them all. [38]Instead of
them, he will honor a god of fortresses; a god unknown to his fathers he will honor with gold and silver,
with precious stones and costly gifts. [39]He will attack the mightiest fortresses with the help of a foreign
god and will greatly honor those who acknowledge him. He will make them rulers over many people and
will distribute the land at a price.[b]

[40]"At the time of the end the king of the South[z] will engage him in battle, and the king of the North
will storm[a] out against him with chariots and cavalry and a great fleet of ships. He will invade many
countries and sweep through them like a flood.[b] [41]He will also invade the Beautiful Land. Many coun-
tries will fall, but Edom,[c] Moab[d] and the leaders of Ammon will be delivered from his hand. [42]He will ex-
tend his power over many countries; Egypt will not escape. [43]He will gain control of the treasures of gold
and silver and all the riches of Egypt,[e] with the Libyans[f] and Nubians in submission. [44]But reports from
the east and the north will alarm him, and he will set out in a great rage to destroy and annihilate many.
[45]He will pitch his royal tents between the seas at[c] the beautiful holy mountain. Yet he will come to his
end, and no one will help him.

The End Times

12 "At that time Michael,[g] the great prince who protects your people, will arise. There will be a
time of distress[h] such as has not happened from the beginning of nations until then. But at
that time your people—everyone whose name is found written in the book[i]—will be delivered.[j]
[2]Multitudes who sleep in the dust of the earth will awake: some to everlasting life, others to shame
and everlasting contempt.[k] [3]Those who are wise[d][l] will shine[m] like the brightness of the heavens, and
those who lead many to righteousness, like the stars for ever and ever.[n] [4]But you, Daniel, close up
and seal[o] the words of the scroll until the time of the end.[p] Many will go here and there to increase
knowledge."

[5]Then I, Daniel, looked, and there before me stood two others, one on this bank of the river and one
on the opposite bank.[q] [6]One of them said to the man clothed in linen,[r] who was above the waters of the
river, "How long will it be before these astonishing things are fulfilled?"[s]

11:30 [p]Ge 10:4
11:31 [q]Da 8:11-13; 9:27; Mt 24:15*; Mk 13:14*
11:32 [r]Mic 5:7-9
11:33 [s]Mal 2:7 [t]Mt 24:9; Jn 16:2; Heb 11:32-38
11:34 [u]Mt 7:15; Ro 16:18
11:35 [v]Ps 78:38; Da 12:10; Zec 13:9; Jn 15:2
11:36 [w]Rev 13:5-6 [x]Dt 10:17; Isa 14:13-14; Da 7:25; 8:11-12, 25; 2Th 2:4 [y]Isa 10:25; 26:20
11:40 [z]Isa 21:1 [a]Isa 5:28 [b]Eze 38:4
11:41 [c]Isa 11:14 [d]Jer 48:47
11:43 [e]Eze 30:4 [f]2Ch 12:3; Na 3:9
12:1 [g]Da 10:13 [h]Da 9:12; Mt 24:21; Mk 13:19; Rev 16:18 [i]Ex 32:32; Ps 56:8 [j]Jer 30:7
12:2 [k]Isa 26:19; Mt 25:46; Jn 5:28-29
12:3 [l]Da 11:33 [m]Mt 13:43; Jn 5:35 [n]1Co 15:42
12:4 [o]Isa 8:16 [p]ver 9,13; Rev 22:10
12:5 [q]Da 10:4
12:6 [r]Eze 9:2 [s]Da 8:13

[a] 30 Hebrew *of Kittim* [b] 39 Or *land for a reward* [c] 45 Or *the sea and* [d] 3 Or *who impart wisdom*

11:31 The "abomination that causes desolation" refers to the altar to the pagan god Zeus that was set up in 167 B.C. by Antiochus IV Epiphanes; it prefigures a similar abomination that Jesus predicted would be erected (see Mt 24:15; Lk 21:20).

11:34 This verse refers to the Jewish rebellion led by Judas Maccabeus. After a three-year struggle the Maccabees were successful and the altar of the temple was rededicated.

11:36–45 Daniel concluded his predictions about Antiochus IV Epiphanes in verse 35 and now began to prophesy concerning the more distant future. Daniel's language in these verses seems larger than life and does not fit what is known from history about Antiochus. Further, this prophecy refers to the "time of the end" (v. 40; cf. v. 35). At the conclusion of the conflict between the antichrist and his political enemies, he will meet his end at the "beautiful holy mountain" (v. 45; see "Zaphon, Olympus, Sinai and Zion: The Mountain of God" on p. 843), the temple mount of Jerusalem—perhaps in connection with the battle of Armageddon (Rev 16:13–16).

12:2 This is the first clear reference to a resurrection of both the righteous and the wicked (see the note on Ps 6:5; see also "Sheol, Hades, Gehenna, the Abyss and Tartarus: Images of Hell" on p. 946).

12:5 Two was the minimum number of required witnesses to an oath (see Dt 17:6; 19:15; Da 12:7).

[7]The man clothed in linen, who was above the waters of the river, lifted his right hand and his left
hand toward heaven, and I heard him swear by him who lives forever,[t] saying, "It will be for a time, times
and half a time.[a][u] When the power of the holy people[v] has been finally broken, all these things will be
completed.[w]"
[8]I heard, but I did not understand. So I asked, "My lord, what will the outcome of all this be?"
[9]He replied, "Go your way, Daniel, because the words are closed up and sealed until the time of the

12:7 [t]Rev 10:5-6 [u]Da 7:25 [v]Da 8:24 [w]Lk 21:24; Rev 10:7

[a] 7 Or *a year, two years and half a year*

The Seleucids

DANIEL 12 After the death of Alexander the Great, his massive empire was divided among his generals, who vied for power. One of the major victors was Seleucus I (born c. 358 B.C.), who seized control of a domain centered in Syria. His dynasty, the **Seleucids**, governed there from 321 to 64 B.C.:

✣ *Seleucus I Nicator* (r. 312–281 B.C.): A childhood friend of Alexander, he took control of **Babylon**. A rival Greek general, Antigonus Monophthalmus, forced him to take refuge in Egypt with another Greek general, Ptolemy.[1] Seleucus I returned to power in Syria and Babylon in 312 B.C. In 301 B.C. he moved his capital west to Syrian Antioch, a city he had founded. By the terms of a peace treaty he should have gained control of Palestine—which Ptolemy refused to relinquish. Thereafter, the Seleucids regarded Palestine as rightfully theirs.

✣ *Antiochus I Soter* (r. 281–261 B.C.): The son of Seleucus I, he fought with Ptolemy II of Egypt in a struggle for control of Palestine and **Anatolia** (Turkey).

✣ *Antiochus II Theos* (r. 261–246 B.C.): This ruler was successful against Ptolemy II in the ongoing struggle for control of Anatolia. Ptolemy persuaded him to marry his daughter Berenice, a union that caused dynastic troubles among the Seleucids. Seleucus's first wife, Laodice, established a rival court at Ephesus[2] and, after Antiochus's death, had Berenice and her son murdered. This resulted in renewed war between the Seleucids and the Ptolemies (the latter now under Ptolemy III, Berenice's brother). Antiochus II is the "king of the North" in Daniel 11:6.

✣ *Seleucus II Callinicus* (246–225 B.C.): Son of Antiochus II and Laodice, his reign began with a war against Ptolemy III. During his lifetime the Seleucid Empire nearly collapsed.

✣ *Seleucus III Soter* (225–223 B.C.): His brief reign focused upon a failed campaign to regain control of Anatolia.

✣ *Antiochus III the Great* (223–187 B.C.): The younger son of Seleucus II, he was the Seleucids' most successful warrior-king. He first campaigned south into Palestine against the Ptolemies but was stopped at Raphia by Ptolemy IV in 217 B.C. Turning east, he won victories against Bactria and Parthia. In a new war against the Ptolemies, now under Ptolemy V, he wrested control of Palestine in 200 B.C., after which he focused on regaining Anatolia. War broke out between Rome and the Seleucids, and Antiochus III was defeated in several battles. Antiochus III is the "king of the North" in 11:11–13.

✣ *Seleucus IV Philopator* (187–175 B.C.): The son of Antiochus III, his reign was hampered by the financial strain of heavy tribute payments to Rome.

✣ *Antiochus IV Epiphanes*[3] (175–164 B.C.): A younger son of Antiochus III and a usurper of the throne after the assassination of Seleucus IV, Antiochus was the most infamous Seleucid. He attempted to extirpate Judaism and replace it with a Hellenistic culture; his enormities are recorded in 2 Maccabees 5, an **Apocryphal** book. His oppression prompted Jewish rebellion in the **Maccabean revolt**. Antiochus Epiphanes almost conquered Egypt in 168 B.C. but turned back when the Roman C. Popilius Laenas warned him to proceed no further.

✣ *Antiochus V Eupator* (164–162 B.C.): Two men, Philip and Lysias, contended for control of this boy during his brief reign; the confusion left an opening for the Jewish Maccabees against the Greeks. Though not entirely successful, they did win religious concessions.

✣ *Demetrius I Soter* (162–150 B.C.): A son of Seleucus IV, he had Philip and Lysias put to death and assumed the throne himself. Wars with the Jews continued. Judas Maccabeus was killed in battle and replaced by his brother Jonathan, who defeated the Seleucids.

✣ Thereafter Seleucid power weakened steadily. A usurper named Alexander Balas contended ineffectively for the Seleucid throne. *Demetrius II*, son of Demetrius I, seized power and ruled from around 145 to 140 and again from approximately 129 to 125 B.C. (between which times he was a prisoner of the Parthians). Meanwhile, Antiochus VI Epiphanes Dionysus (a son of Alexander Balas), Antiochus VII Sidetes (a brother of Demetrius II) and Tryphon (another usurper) vied for power. This situation made the Jews power brokers, further illustrating how far the Seleucids had declined. The last Seleucid ruler was *Antiochus XIII Asiaticus* (69–64 B.C.); in the final year of his reign Pompey the Great made Syria a Roman province.[4]

[1]See "The Ptolemies" on page 1399. [2]See "Early History of Ephesus" on page 1965. [3]See "Antiochus IV Epiphanes" on page 1406. [4]See also "The Intertestamental Period" on page 1551.

12:9 [x]ver 4
12:10 [y]Da 11:35 [z]Isa 32:7; Rev 22:11 [a]Hos 14:9
12:11 [b]Da 8:11; 9:27; Mt 24:15*; Mk 13:14*
12:12 [c]Isa 30:18 [d]Da 8:14
12:13 [e]Isa 57:2 [f]Ps 16:5; Rev 14:13

end.[x] 10Many will be purified, made spotless and refined,[y] but the wicked will continue to be wicked.[z]
None of the wicked will understand, but those who are wise will understand.[a]
11“From the time that the daily sacrifice is abolished and the abomination that causes desolation[b] is
set up, there will be 1,290 days. 12Blessed is the one who waits[c] for and reaches the end of the 1,335 days.[d]
13“As for you, go your way till the end. You will rest,[e] and then at the end of the days you will rise to
receive your allotted inheritance.[f]”

INTRODUCTION TO  Hosea

AUTHOR, PLACE AND DATE OF WRITING

Hosea the prophet in all likelihood wrote the book that bears his name. Some scholars have argued that parts of the book are secondary (written by someone else), but their arguments have produced no consensus and have persuaded few. Some hold, for example, that references to Judah and to the house of David were added at a later time (e.g., Hos 3:5; Hosea was primarily a prophet to the northern kingdom of Israel). Others contend that the "optimistic" messages are add-ons (e.g., 14:4–7; Hosea primarily preached a message of condemnation). These arguments presuppose that Hosea was a one-dimensional prophet, incapable of speaking to both Israel and Judah or of preaching both condemnation and hope.

Another major issue regarding Hosea is the nature of his relationship to Gomer, his wife. It seems astonishing that Hosea would have been commanded by God to marry an immoral woman (1:2). The account in the first three chapters of this prophetic work has been subjected to every conceivable interpretation (e.g., that it is only the record of a vision or parable, that Gomer was actually faithful but played the part of a faithless woman for the sake of Hosea's message, or that Gomer was actually guilty of idolatry but not of promiscuity). None of these suggestions is persuasive. The text seems clear that God commanded Hosea to marry a dissolute woman and that the prophet took Gomer in direct obedience to that command. This is the ultimate kind of prophetic sign—a scenario in which a prophet engages in shocking and otherwise inexplicable behavior in order to make his point for his audience (see Isa 20:2–4; Eze 24:15–24).

Hosea dated his message to the reign of Jeroboam II of Israel and to those of Uzziah, Jotham, Ahaz and Hezekiah of Judah (Hos 1:1). This places the years of his prophetic ministry from around 755 to 715 B.C. and indicates that the prophet lived to see the destruction of Samaria, the capital of Israel, in 722 B.C.

AUDIENCE

Hosea initially delivered his message of doom orally to the northern kingdom of Israel. After the fall of Samaria his words were transcribed to scrolls as a record of prophecy fulfilled and as a warning of judgment, a call to repentance and a promise of restoration.

CULTURAL FACTS AND HIGHLIGHTS

Hosea was written primarily as a message of judgment to the northern kingdom during the years of its precipitous decline prior to its fall to Assyria. For the most part the prophet's words are filled with condemnation and promises of destruction for the nation, but readers who find this tedious do well to recognize that his predictions, in all their horror, were fulfilled within about 30 years of the beginning of his ministry.

TIMELINE

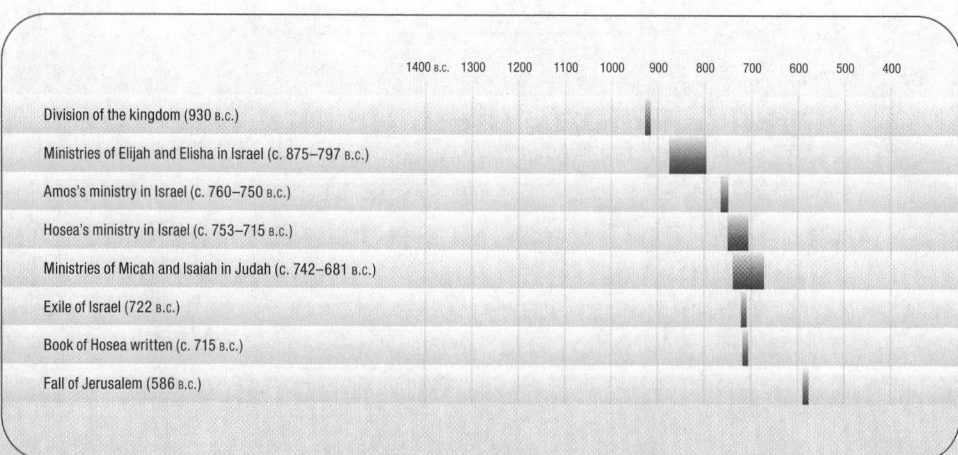

AS YOU READ

The first three chapters of this book are a moving story that makes for fascinating reading. Make the attempt to enter vicariously into the drama from the perspective of the prophet himself or from that of one of the other players, such as the forgiven Gomer. What relevance does this story have to the history of your own life and salvation?

DID YOU KNOW?

- Clay tablets from Ugarit tell of fertility rites carried out by the Canaanites at the high places, and pagan rituals involving sexual immorality were often conducted under oak trees, which were considered sacred (4:13).
- "Harlots" were common prostitutes, while "shrine prostitutes" were women of the sanctuaries who served as partners for men in the sexual activity that was part of their religious ritual (4:14).
- The "festival of our king" probably refers to a coronation or birthday celebration that developed into a drunken orgy (7:5). King Elah died in drunkenness (1Ki 16:9).
- Four Israelite kings were assassinated within 20 years, Zechariah and Shallum during a mere seven-month period (Hos 7:7).

THEMES

The prophecy of Hosea includes the following themes:

1. *God's faithfulness, mercy and unfailing love.* Hosea's unconditional love for his adulterous wife represents God's relentless love for the faithless Israelites (1:2; 2:19; 6:6; 10:12; 12:6). In fact, God's covenantal relationship with his people is likened to the intimacy experienced in marriage (2:2–5; 3:3; 4:10–19; 5:3–7; 6:10; 8:9; 9:1), reinforcing the theme of God's passionate devotion to his people.

2. *Judgment for sin.* At the root of Israel's idolatry was her failure to acknowledge God (2:8,13,20; 4:1,6; 5:4; 6:3,6; 13:4), an unfaithfulness that would result in the punishment of exile (7:16; 8:14; 9:3,6,17; 11:5).

3. *Repentance and restoration.* God would not leave his people under judgment and in exile forever but pledged to heal Israel of the wounds caused by her disobedience and to reestablish his people in the land (14:1–9). Hosea demonstrates the recurring theme that repentance brings restoration (1:10–11; 2:14–23; 3:5; 11:10–11; 14:4–7).

OUTLINE

- I. Hosea's Marriage (1–3)
- II. Hosea's Message (4–14)
  - A. Israel's Unfaithfulness (4:1—6:3)
  - B. Israel's Punishment (6:4—10:15)
  - C. God Is Faithful (11–14)

1 The word of the LORD that came to Hosea son of Beeri during the reigns of Uzziah, Jotham, Ahaz and
Hezekiah, kings of Judah,[a] and during the reign of Jeroboam[b] son of Jehoash[a] king of Israel:[c]

Hosea's Wife and Children

2 When the LORD began to speak through Hosea, the LORD said to him, "Go, take to yourself an adul-
terous[d] wife and children of unfaithfulness, because the land is guilty of the vilest adultery[e] in depart-
ing from the LORD." 3 So he married Gomer daughter of Diblaim, and she conceived and bore him a son.
4 Then the LORD said to Hosea, "Call him Jezreel,[f] because I will soon punish the house of Jehu for the
massacre at Jezreel, and I will put an end to the kingdom of Israel. 5 In that day I will break Israel's bow
in the Valley of Jezreel.[g]"
6 Gomer[h] conceived again and gave birth to a daughter. Then the LORD said to Hosea, "Call her Lo-Ru-
hamah,[b] for I will no longer show love to the house of Israel,[i] that I should at all forgive them. 7 Yet I will
show love to the house of Judah; and I will save them—not by bow,[j] sword or battle, or by horses and
horsemen, but by the LORD their God.[k]"

1:1 [a]Isa 1:1; Mic 1:1 [b]2Ki 13:13 [c]Am 1:1
1:2 [d]Jer 3:1; Hos 2:2,5; 3:1 [e]Dt 31:16; Jer 3:14; Eze 23:3-21; Hos 5:3
1:4 [f]2Ki 10:1-14; Hos 2:22
1:5 [g]2Ki 15:29
1:6 [h]ver 3 [i]Hos 2:4
1:7 [j]Ps 44:6 [k]Zec 4:6

[a] *1* Hebrew *Joash*, a variant of *Jehoash* [b] *6 Lo-Ruhamah* means *not loved.*

1:1 Although the introduction to the book lists only one king from the northern kingdom of Israel (Jeroboam II, r. 793–753 B.C.), the list of kings from the southern kingdom of Judah demonstrates that Hosea preached during the reigns of several other northern kings, until just before Israel's exile to Assyria in 722 B.C. Hosea's ministry in Israel came shortly after that of Amos and partially overlapped those of Micah and Isaiah in Judah.

1:4–5 Located east of Megiddo, the Valley of Jezreel provides the only major pass through the mountain range that crosses Israel from north to south; it was therefore a major battleground in ancient times (see "The Valley of Jezreel" on p. 1412). Jeroboam II was of the dynasty of Jehu (841–814 B.C.), which was established at Jezreel by the overthrow of Ahab's son Joram (see 2Ki 9:14–29). Jehu's dynasty ended with the murder of Zechariah in 753 (2Ki 15:8–10).

1:7 God delivered Judah from Assyria in 722 B.C. and again in 701 (see 2Ki 19:32–36).

The Valley of Jezreel

HOSEA 1 The Valley of Jezreel, located between the Jordan River and the Mediterranean Sea, divides Galilee in the north from **Samaria**[1] in the south. It is part of a larger valley that constitutes the only east-west passage across the Holy Land. It is also a fertile stretch of land that formed an important junction in the trade route between Egypt in the south and Damascus in the north.[2] All of these factors, plus its relatively flat geography, have made it tremendously important and have contributed to its violent history.

During the conquest, when this area was occupied by **Canaanites**,[3] the Joseph tribes were unable to wrest Jezreel from its occupants (for Jezreel, see "Map 7"). The problem was that the flat land allowed for the effective use of chariots, which the Israelites did not have in their arsenal (Jos 17:16). During the Judges period Sisera, the general of the Canaanite king Jabin, had dominated this region with his 900 chariots (Jdg 4:3). Jezreel is of great importance in Hosea, a book of prophecy directed against the northern kingdom of Israel.

✣ In Hosea 1:4 the prophet, adhering to God's direct instruction, named his first son Jezreel in an ironic allusion to the slaughter at Jezreel carried out by Jehu against the house of Ahab, and particularly against Jezebel, for their support of the prophets of Baal (2Ki 9:1—10:11). The irony is that Jehu's own dynasty would be wiped out because of its continued adherence to the cult of Baal.

✣ Hosea 1:5 proclaimed that God would break the bow of Israel in the Valley of Jezreel. This obviously pointed to a military defeat for the northern kingdom. This prophecy came to pass in 733 B.C. when Tiglath-Pileser III conquered the area.[4]

✣ Even so, Hosea promised that God would one day redeem Israel. Making use of the fact that Jezreel means "God sows," 2:17–22 promised that one day God would make Israel flourish again like a lush garden.

[1]See Glossary on page 2080 for definitions of bolded words. [2]See "Damascus" on page 1087. [3]See "The Conquest of Canaan" on page 310. [4]See "Menahem and Pekah of Israel, Jotham of Judah and Tiglath-Pileser III of Assyria" on page 553.

8 After she had weaned Lo-Ruhamah, Gomer had another son. 9 Then the LORD said, "Call him Lo-
Ammi,[a] for you are not my people, and I am not your God.

1:10 [l]Ge 22:17; Jer 33:22 [m]ver 9; Ro 9:26*

10 "Yet the Israelites will be like the sand on the seashore, which cannot be measured or counted.[l] In
the place where it was said to them, 'You are not my people,' they will be called 'sons of the living God.'[m]

1:11 [n]Isa 11:12, 13 [o]Jer 23:5-8 [p]Eze 37:15-28

11 The people of Judah and the people of Israel will be reunited,[n] and they will appoint one leader[o] and
will come up out of the land,[p] for great will be the day of Jezreel.

2:1 [q]ver 23

2 "Say of your brothers, 'My people,' and of your sisters, 'My loved one.'[q]

Israel Punished and Restored

2:2 [r]ver 5; Isa 50:1; Hos 1:2 [s]Eze 23:45

2 "Rebuke your mother,[r] rebuke her,
for she is not my wife,
and I am not her husband.
Let her remove the adulterous[s] look from her face
and the unfaithfulness from between her breasts.
3 Otherwise I will strip her naked

2:3 [t]Eze 16:4,22 [u]Isa 32:13-14

and make her as bare as on the day she was born;[t]
I will make her like a desert,[u]
turn her into a parched land,
and slay her with thirst.

2:4 [v]Eze 8:18

4 I will not show my love to her children,[v]
because they are the children of adultery.
5 Their mother has been unfaithful
and has conceived them in disgrace.

2:5 [w]Jer 3:6 [x]Jer 44:17-18

She said, 'I will go after my lovers,[w]
who give me my food and my water,
my wool and my linen, my oil and my drink.'[x]
6 Therefore I will block her path with thornbushes;

2:6 [y]Job 3:23; 19:8; La 3:9

I will wall her in so that she cannot find her way.[y]
7 She will chase after her lovers but not catch them;

2:7 [z]Hos 5:13 [a]Jer 2:2; 3:1 [b]Eze 16:8

she will look for them but not find them.[z]
Then she will say,
'I will go back to my husband as at first,[a]
for then I was better off[b] than now.'

2:8 [c]Isa 1:3 [d]Eze 16:15-19; Hos 8:4

8 She has not acknowledged[c] that I was the one
who gave her the grain, the new wine and oil,
who lavished on her the silver and gold—
which they used for Baal.[d]

[a] 9 *Lo-Ammi* means *not my people.*

2:2 See "Marriage and Divorce in Ancient Israel" on page 1548. Although the Old Testament seems to have permitted divorce for rather general reasons (Dt 24:1), it was usually either for adultery or childlessness. The bill of divorce could be a simple repudiation, such as, "She is not my wife, and I am not her husband."

Among the ancient Sumerians it was easy for a man to divorce his wife, especially if she had failed to produce children. Among the Babylonians, the Code of Hammurabi (eighteenth century B.C.; see "Hammurabi" on p. 271) provided for divorce under certain circumstances but included the return of the dowry to the wife, a situation that would have given many men cause for contemplation. Where there was no dowry, the husband was required to make a payment of silver according to a schedule based on the social status of the wife's family. But if the wife had been negligent in her household duties, she could be sent away without payment or simply replaced and demoted to the position of a servant or a slave (Code of Hammurabi, 141,143). Simpler and more severe was the Middle Assyrian law code, which stated that, with no fault specified, the wife could be divorced and sent away empty-handed (Middle Assyrian Laws, 37). Generally speaking, it was an unusual and, therefore, more complex situation if a wife instituted divorce proceedings. Divorce was discouraged in the fourth century B.C. in Egypt, and later by the Hebrews, through the imposition of a substantial fine on the husband, known as "divorce money."

2:3 It was the husband's responsibility to supply his wife's clothing (see Ex 21:10; Eze 16:10).

2:7 The catalyst of Hosea's prophetic message was his marriage to Gomer. There are two major views of this relationship. One holds that Gomer was pure when she married Hosea but later proved unfaithful. Another posits that she was a harlot/prostitute when the prophet married her. Either way, the shock effect of Hosea's marital difficulties would have had a telling impact on the people of his community. The children born of this marriage were given symbolic names indicating divine displeasure with Israel (see "Naming of Children" on p. 28). After Gomer had pursued her illicit lovers, she was to be brought back and with patient love readmitted to Hosea's home, there to await in penitence and grief the time of restoration to full favor. This was a clear picture of wayward Israel in her relationship with God, highlighting the unending faithfulness of the Almighty.

2:8 The Canaanite god Baal was believed to control both the weather and the fertility of crops, animals and people (see the note on Jdg 2:13; see also "The Ugaritic Text of the Myth of Baal" on p. 905 and "Baal and the Fertility Cults" on p. 1414).

Silver and gold were used for casting idols (see Hos 8:4; 13:2).

9 "Therefore I will take away my grain[e] when it ripens,
and my new wine[f] when it is ready.
I will take back my wool and my linen,
intended to cover her nakedness.
10 So now I will expose her lewdness
before the eyes of her lovers;
no one will take her out of my hands.[g]

2:9 [e]Hos 8:7 [f]Hos 9:2
2:10 [g]Eze 16:37

Baal and the Fertility Cults

HOSEA 2 The worship of the **Canaanite** storm god Baal was an object of singular condemnation by Hosea and other prophets. The vehemence of the prophetic condemnation of the cult reflects just how extensive and pernicious the problem was. We learn about Baal first through Biblical texts. Examples include:

- Numbers 25 (the narrative of Baal of Peor, showing the prominence of sacred prostitution within the cult)[1]
- First Kings 18 (the contest involving Elijah and the prophets of Baal on Mount Carmel, illustrating the popularity of the Baal cult and its use of self-laceration for demonstrating devotion to Baal)[2]
- Hosea 2 (v. 8 indicates that the people associated Baal with prosperity, and vv. 16–17 suggest that many people identified Baal and **Yahweh** almost as one and the same.)

We also learn a great deal about Baal from ancient texts in the form of **cuneiform** tablets, especially those from **Ugarit** and from **Phoenician** inscriptions. The hymns and epic poems of Ugarit provide us with something of the "theology" of the Baal cult.[3]

The basic meaning of the word *baal* is "lord," and this appropriately suggests Baal's importance in Canaanite religion. He was called "prince Baal (Lord) of the earth." Although the god El was nominally the supreme deity in Ugaritic mythology, Baal purportedly exercised a direct role in ruling the pantheon and effectively supplanted El. Baal's consort (partner) is usually identified as the goddess Anat, although sometimes another goddess, Asherah, assumes that role. Baal was declared king after having supposedly defeated the god Yam ("sea") in battle. In another myth he was slain by the god Mot ("Death"), but with the aid of Anat he revived and defeated Mot.

Not only was Baal exalted as a chief deity, but he also functioned specifically as the Canaanite storm god, the "rider of the clouds."[4] The birth of healthy offspring and the staving off of famine were major concerns in the ancient Near East, and consequently fertility took on religious significance. In Egypt the god Osiris was identified with the Nile and its perennial flooding—the basis of Egypt's agricultural life. In **Mesopotamia** the cult of Tammuz and his consort, Inanna, represented the power of fertility and included the practice of sacred prostitution.[5]

For Israel—an agrarian society situated in a dry climate—the veneration of a god who could send rain proved to be an irresistible enticement. One Canaanite myth attributed agricultural fertility to the "rain of Baal." Hosea 2:5 indicates the acceptance of Baal's role at every level of life: "food" and "water" for sustenance, "wool" and "linen" for material goods and "oil" and "drink" for cultic rituals or personal luxury. Although sacred prostitution was not a part of every fertility cult, Israel incorporated this aspect as well (4:10–14), and the sexual temptation of the cult proved too much for many Israelites to withstand. The situation was exacerbated by an enormous number of local shrines where "the Baals" were worshiped under various titles (such as Baal Peor, Baal Hammon, Baal Zaphon, Baal of Lebanon or Baal of Sidon; see 2:13,17).[6] This phenomenon is attested by the wide variety of representations of Baal in Phoenician inscriptions.

The fact that the Israelites identified Baal with Yahweh is telling. Although Baal worship, viewed from a distance, was obviously horrendous, those who were involved in it were so influenced by the dominant culture that they remained convinced that they were devout and orthodox followers of the Lord—when they were all the while worshiping Baal.

[1]See "Prostitution in the Ancient World" on page 284. [2]See "Tattoos and Self-Laceration in Ancient Religion" on page 180. [3]See "Tablets From Ugarit and Canaanite Religion" on page 304, "Ugarit/Ras Shamra" on page 819 and "The Ugarit Text of the Myth of Baal" on page 905. [4]See "Storm Gods, Storm Imagery and Theophany" on page 808. [5]See "Mourning for Tammuz" on page 1320. [6]For an example of such a shrine or temple, see "Abimelech at Shechem" on page 363.

2:11 [h]Jer 7:34 [i]Isa 1:14; Jer 16:9; Hos 3:4; Am 8:10
2:12 [j]Isa 7:23; Jer 8:13 [k]Isa 5:6 [l]Hos 13:8
2:13 [m]Hos 11:2 [n]Eze 16:17 [o]Hos 4:13 [p]Hos 4:6; 8:14; 13:6
2:15 [q]Jos 7:24, 26 [r]Ex 15:1-18 [s]Jer 2:2 [t]Hos 12:9
2:17 [u]Ex 23:13; Ps 16:4 [v]Jos 23:7
2:18 [w]Job 5:22 [x]Isa 2:4 [y]Jer 23:6; Eze 34:25
2:19 [z]Isa 62:4 [a]Isa 1:27
2:20 [b]Jer 31:34; Hos 6:6; 13:4
2:21 [c]Isa 55:10; Zec 8:12
2:22 [d]Jer 31:12; Joel 2:19

11 I will stop[h] all her celebrations:
her yearly festivals, her New Moons,
her Sabbath days—all her appointed feasts.[i]
12 I will ruin her vines[j] and her fig trees,
which she said were her pay from her lovers;
I will make them a thicket,[k]
and wild animals will devour them.[l]
13 I will punish her for the days
she burned incense to the Baals;[m]
she decked herself with rings and jewelry,[n]
and went after her lovers,[o]
but me she forgot,[p]"
declares the LORD.

14 "Therefore I am now going to allure her;
I will lead her into the desert
and speak tenderly to her.
15 There I will give her back her vineyards,
and will make the Valley of Achor[a][q] a door of hope.
There she will sing[b][r] as in the days of her youth,[s]
as in the day she came up out of Egypt.[t]

16 "In that day," declares the LORD,
"you will call me 'my husband';
you will no longer call me 'my master.[c]'
17 I will remove the names of the Baals from her lips;[u]
no longer will their names be invoked.[v]
18 In that day I will make a covenant for them
with the beasts of the field and the birds of the air
and the creatures that move along the ground.[w]
Bow and sword and battle
I will abolish[x] from the land,
so that all may lie down in safety.[y]
19 I will betroth[z] you to me forever;
I will betroth you in[d] righteousness and justice,[a]
in[e] love and compassion.
20 I will betroth you in faithfulness,
and you will acknowledge[b] the LORD.

21 "In that day I will respond,"
declares the LORD—
"I will respond[c] to the skies,
and they will respond to the earth;
22 and the earth will respond to the grain,
the new wine and oil,[d]
and they will respond to Jezreel.[f]

[a] 15 *Achor* means *trouble.* [b] 15 Or *respond* [c] 16 Hebrew *baal* [d] 19 Or *with*; also in verse 20 [e] 19 Or *with* [f] 22 *Jezreel* means *God plants.*

2:11 See "The Festivals of Israel" on page 186 and "Sabbath, Sabbath Year and the Jubilee" on page 189.
2:12 Israel attributed her agricultural produce to the false gods she worshiped rather than to the Lord (see v. 8 and its note; cf. Dt 11:13–14).
2:13 "Baals" is plural, suggesting that various gods are intended. Incense to pagan deities was often burned on rooftops (see Jer 19:13 and its note; see also "Incense" on p. 1209).
For earrings or nose rings, see the note on Ezekiel 16:12.
2:15 The Valley of Achor (meaning "trouble") was near Jericho.
2:16 The word *baal* appears in the Old Testament with a variety of meanings. Originally it was not a proper noun, but later it came to be used as such. Sometimes it is used in the primary sense of "master" or "owner" (as in Ex 21:28,34; Jdg 19:22; Isa 16:8). Since the Hebrew husband was regarded as the literal owner of his wife, *baal* was the common term for husband used here—see the NIV text note—as well as in Exodus 21:3 and 2 Samuel 11:26. Most often, however, the word refers to the Semitic deity or deities called Baal.
2:19–20 See "Marriage and Divorce in Ancient Israel" on page 1548.

[23] I will plant[e] her for myself in the land;
I will show my love to the one I called 'Not my loved one.[a][f]'
I will say to those called 'Not my people,[b]' 'You are my people';[g]
and they will say, 'You are my God.[h]' "

2:23 [e]Jer 31:27 [f]Hos 1:6 [g]Hos 1:10 [h]Ro 9:25*; 1Pe 2:10

Hosea's Reconciliation With His Wife

3 The LORD said to me, "Go, show your love to your wife again, though she is loved by another and is
an adulteress.[i] Love her as the LORD loves the Israelites, though they turn to other gods and love the
sacred raisin cakes.[j]"
[2] So I bought her for fifteen shekels[c] of silver and about a homer and a lethek[d] of barley. [3] Then I told
her, "You are to live with[e] me many days; you must not be a prostitute or be intimate with any man, and
I will live with[e] you."
[4] For the Israelites will live many days without king or prince,[k] without sacrifice[l] or sacred stones,
without ephod or idol.[m] [5] Afterward the Israelites will return and seek the LORD their God and David their
king.[n] They will come trembling to the LORD and to his blessings in the last days.[o]

3:1 [i]Hos 1:2 [j]2Sa 6:19
3:4 [k]Hos 13:11 [l]Da 11:31; Hos 2:11 [m]Jdg 17:5-6; Zec 10:2
3:5 [n]Eze 34:23-24 [o]Jer 50:4-5

The Charge Against Israel

4 Hear the word of the LORD, you Israelites,
because the LORD has a charge to bring
against you who live in the land:
"There is no faithfulness, no love,
no acknowledgment[p] of God in the land.
[2] There is only cursing,[f] lying[q] and murder,[r]
stealing[s] and adultery;
they break all bounds,
and bloodshed follows bloodshed.
[3] Because of this the land mourns,[g][t]
and all who live in it waste away;[u]
the beasts of the field and the birds of the air
and the fish of the sea are dying.[v]

[4] "But let no man bring a charge,
let no man accuse another,
for your people are like those
who bring charges against a priest.[w]
[5] You stumble[x] day and night,
and the prophets stumble with you.
So I will destroy your mother[y]—
[6] my people are destroyed from lack of knowledge.[z]

"Because you have rejected knowledge,
I also reject you as my priests;
because you have ignored the law[a] of your God,
I also will ignore your children.

4:1 [p]Jer 7:28
4:2 [q]Hos 7:3; 10:4 [r]Hos 6:9 [s]Hos 7:1
4:3 [t]Jer 4:28 [u]Isa 33:9 [v]Jer 4:25; Zep 1:3
4:4 [w]Dt 17:12; Eze 3:26
4:5 [x]Eze 14:7 [y]Hos 2:2
4:6 [z]Hos 2:13; Mal 2:7-8 [a]Hos 8:1,12

[a] 23 Hebrew *Lo-Ruhamah* [b] 23 Hebrew *Lo-Ammi* [c] 2 That is, about 6 ounces (about 170 grams) [d] 2 That is, probably about 10 bushels (about 330 liters) [e] 3 Or *wait for* [f] 2 That is, to pronounce a curse upon [g] 3 Or *dries up*

3:1 Raisin cakes were offered to Baal in thanksgiving for a good harvest (see "Baal and the Fertility Cults" on p. 1414).
3:2 The fact that Hosea "bought" Gomer means at the least that she had become indebted to someone, if not even that she had become a slave. Fifteen shekels was half the usual price of a slave (see Ex 21:32). It appears that half her price was paid in money (silver) and half in produce (barley)—for a total value of 30 shekels. See "Banking and Money in the Ancient World" on page 696.
3:4 For "sacred stones," see the note on 1 Kings 14:23–24.
The ephod is here a symbol of idols (see Jdg 8:27; see also the note on Jdg 17:4–5 and "The Ephod" on p. 399).

4:1—14:9 The remainder of Hosea's prophecy is an indictment of Israel, delivered at various times from the later days of Jeroboam II up to approximately 730 B.C. The style of this section is vigorous, although the Hebrew text has suffered in transmission, making for difficulties in translation. Although the book is generally held to be unified, critical writers have maintained that interpolations and editorial material appear throughout the work.
4:4–9 This was an indictment against the priests, whose duty it was to act as guardians of God's law and to furnish religious instruction (see "The Levites and the Priests" on p. 648).

4:7 [b]Hab 2:16 [c]Hos 10:1,6; 13:6
4:8 [d]Isa 56:11; Mic 3:11
4:9 [e]Isa 24:2 [f]Jer 5:31; Hos 8:13; 9:9,15
4:10 [g]Lev 26:26; Mic 6:14 [h]Hos 7:14; 9:17
4:11 [i]Hos 5:4 [j]Pr 20:1
4:12 [k]Jer 2:27 [l]Hab 2:19

7 The more the priests increased,
the more they sinned against me;
they exchanged[a] their[b] Glory[b] for something disgraceful.[c]
8 They feed on the sins of my people
and relish their wickedness.[d]
9 And it will be: Like people, like priests.[e]
I will punish both of them for their ways
and repay them for their deeds.[f]

10 "They will eat but not have enough;[g]
they will engage in prostitution but not increase,
because they have deserted[h] the LORD
to give themselves 11 to prostitution,[i]
to old wine and new,
which take away the understanding[j] 12 of my people.
They consult a wooden idol[k]
and are answered by a stick of wood.[l]

[a] 7 Syriac and an ancient Hebrew scribal tradition; Masoretic Text *I will exchange* [b] 7 Masoretic Text; an ancient Hebrew scribal tradition *my*

4:12 Idols were often carved from wood (see Jer 2:27; 10:8; Hab 2:19) but were sometimes also plated with gold or silver (see Jer 10:4 and its note). See "Idols and Idol-Making" on page 1136.

ARCHAEOLOGICAL SITES

BETH AVEN: A LESSON IN THE DIFFICULTY OF BIBLICAL GEOGRAPHY

HOSEA 4 Beth Aven is mentioned seven times in the Old Testament (Jos 7:2; 18:12–13; 1Sa 13:5; 14:23; Hos 4:15; 5:8; 10:5). In Joshua and Samuel it is an actual place-name, but in the book of Hosea Beth Aven ("house of wickedness") is a derogatory reference to Bethel ("house of God"). Thus, there appear to have been at least two sites referred to as Beth Aven. But the location of the actual Beth Aven has been a source of confusion.

Joshua 7:2 suggests that Beth Aven was east of Bethel, usually identified as the modern Beitin. Joshua 18:12–13 stipulates that the northern border of the tribe of Benjamin ran from the Jordan past the region of Jericho to the "desert of Beth Aven" and from there on in a southerly direction to Bethel. Based on these descriptions Beth Aven must have been northeast of Bethel. But 1 Samuel 13:5 indicates that Beth Aven was west of Micmash, usually identified with modern Mukhmas.[1] The problem is that Micmash was south of Bethel, and it is of course impossible to see how Beth Aven could have been both northeast of Bethel and west of Micmash, which is south of Bethel.

It may be that there were two sites actually named Beth Aven, the one being the site referred to in Joshua, northeast of Bethel, and the other the one of 1 Samuel, west of Micmash. The situation is further complicated by the fact that, as mentioned above, Beth Aven was also used as a secondary name for Bethel itself!

Another proposal argues that there was just one village named Beth Aven; however, this proposal depends upon relocating several sites. If Bethel was actually located at a site called el Bireh (near modern Ramallah in the West Bank) rather than at Beitin, then Beitin may have been Beth Aven, as it can be said to be both northeast of el Bireh and west of Mukhmas. The locating of Bethel at el Bireh is not yet widely accepted, however.[2]

All of these sites are in the general area of the hill country north of Jerusalem, and so a general notion of the locations of Beth Aven and the other sites is not in question. Even so, this illustrates the difficulty scholars frequently encounter in precisely identifying Biblical sites. Modern readers of the Bible do well to bear in mind that the exact locations of many sites mentioned in the text are uncertain.

[1]See "The Pass at Micmash" on page 417. [2]See "Bethel" on page 59.

A spirit of prostitution leads them astray;[m]
they are unfaithful to their God.
13 They sacrifice on the mountaintops
and burn offerings on the hills,
under oak,[n] poplar and terebinth,
where the shade is pleasant.[o]
Therefore your daughters turn to prostitution[p]
and your daughters-in-law to adultery.[q]

14 "I will not punish your daughters
when they turn to prostitution,
nor your daughters-in-law
when they commit adultery,
because the men themselves consort with harlots[r]
and sacrifice with shrine prostitutes—
a people without understanding will come to ruin!

15 "Though you commit adultery, O Israel,
let not Judah become guilty.

"Do not go to Gilgal;[s]
do not go up to Beth Aven.[a]
And do not swear, 'As surely as the LORD lives!'
16 The Israelites are stubborn,
like a stubborn heifer.
How then can the LORD pasture them
like lambs[t] in a meadow?
17 Ephraim is joined to idols;
leave him alone!
18 Even when their drinks are gone,
they continue their prostitution;
their rulers dearly love shameful ways.
19 A whirlwind[u] will sweep them away,
and their sacrifices will bring them shame.[v]

4:12 [m]Isa 44:20
4:13 [n]Isa 1:29 [o]Jer 3:6; Hos 11:2 [p]Jer 2:20; Am 7:17 [q]Hos 2:13
4:14 [r]ver 11
4:15 [s]Hos 9:15; 12:11; Am 4:4
4:16 [t]Isa 5:17; 7:25
4:19 [u]Hos 12:1; 13:15 [v]Isa 1:29

Judgment Against Israel

5 "Hear this, you priests!
Pay attention, you Israelites!
Listen, O royal house!
This judgment is against you:
You have been a snare[w] at Mizpah,
a net spread out on Tabor.
2 The rebels are deep in slaughter.[x]
I will discipline all of them.[y]

5:1 [w]Hos 6:9; 9:8
5:2 [x]Hos 4:2 [y]Hos 9:15

[a] *15 Beth Aven* means *house of wickedness* (a name for Bethel, which means *house of God*).

4:13 Pagan altars were commonly constructed on mountaintops (see "The High Places" on p. 1318). Clay tablets from Ugarit tell of fertility rites carried out by the Canaanites at the high places (see "Baal and the Fertility Cults" on p. 1414), and pagan rituals involving sexual immorality were often conducted under oak trees, which were considered sacred (see the note on Isa 1:29).
4:14 "Harlots" were common prostitutes (see Ge 34:31; Lev 21:14; Eze 16:31), while "shrine prostitutes" were women of the sanctuaries who served as partners for men in the sexual activity that was a part of their religious ritual (cf. Ge 38:21; Dt 23:18). See "Prostitution in the Ancient World" on page 284.
4:15 Gilgal was near Jericho (see "The Camp at Gilgal" on p. 308). The Israelites had established a religious shrine there.

See "Beth Aven: A Lesson in the Difficulty of Biblical Geography" on page 1417.
4:17 For "Ephraim," see the note on 5:3.

"Idols" refers to the Baals (see the notes on 2:8,13) and to the golden calves set up by Jeroboam I (see the note on 8:5).
5:1 The "snare" and "net," devices for catching animals and birds, function here as metaphors for Israel's corruption.

Mizpah refers either to Mizpah in Gilead, east of the Jordan (Ge 31:43–49), or to Mizpah in Benjamin.

Tabor is a mountain at the southeastern edge of the Jezreel Valley.

[3]I know all about Ephraim;
Israel is not hidden from me.
Ephraim, you have now turned to prostitution;
Israel is corrupt.[z]

[4]"Their deeds do not permit them
to return to their God.
A spirit of prostitution[a] is in their heart;
they do not acknowledge[b] the LORD.
[5]Israel's arrogance testifies[c] against them;
the Israelites, even Ephraim, stumble in
their sin;
Judah also stumbles with them.
[6]When they go with their flocks and herds
to seek the LORD,[d]
they will not find him;
he has withdrawn[e] himself from them.
[7]They are unfaithful[f] to the LORD;
they give birth to illegitimate[g] children.
Now their New Moon festivals
will devour[h] them and their fields.

[8]"Sound the trumpet in Gibeah,[i]
the horn in Ramah.[j]
Raise the battle cry in Beth Aven[a];[k]
lead on, O Benjamin.
[9]Ephraim will be laid waste
on the day of reckoning.[l]
Among the tribes of Israel
I proclaim what is certain.[m]
[10]Judah's leaders are like those
who move boundary stones.[n]
I will pour out my wrath[o] on them
like a flood of water.
[11]Ephraim is oppressed,
trampled in judgment,
intent on pursuing idols.[b][p]
[12]I am like a moth[q] to Ephraim,
like rot to the people of Judah.

[13]"When Ephraim saw his sickness,
and Judah his sores,
then Ephraim turned to Assyria,[r]
and sent to the great king for help.[s]
But he is not able to cure[t] you,
not able to heal your sores.[u]

5:3 [z]Hos 6:10
5:4 [a]Hos 4:11 [b]Hos 4:6
5:5 [c]Hos 7:10
5:6 [d]Mic 6:6-7 [e]Pr 1:28; Isa 1:15; Eze 8:6
5:7 [f]Hos 6:7 [g]Hos 2:4 [h]Hos 2:11-12
5:8 [i]Hos 9:9; 10:9 [j]Isa 10:29 [k]Hos 4:15
5:9 [l]Isa 37:3; Hos 9:11-17 [m]Isa 46:10; Zec 1:6
5:10 [n]Dt 19:14 [o]Eze 7:8
5:11 [p]Hos 9:16; Mic 6:16
5:12 [q]Isa 51:8
5:13 [r]Hos 7:11; 8:9 [s]Hos 10:6 [t]Hos 14:3 [u]Jer 30:12

[a] *8 Beth Aven* means *house of wickedness* (a name for Bethel, which means *house of God*). [b] *11* The meaning of the Hebrew for this word is uncertain.

5:3 Hosea frequently used "Ephraim" as a synonym for Israel. As the northern kingdom's largest tribe, Ephraim had come to be associated with the nation as a whole.

5:8 Some interpreters suggest that the Syro-Ephraimite War (see "The Syro-Ephraimite War" on p. 1066) forms the background for the oracle in chapters 4–5.

The "trumpet," made from a ram's horn, sounded the alarm to warn of an approaching army (see "The Shofar" on p. 898).

See "Gibeah" on page 380 and "Beth Aven: A Lesson in the Difficulty of Biblical Geography" on page 1417. Ramah was 2 miles (3.2 km) north of Jerusalem.

5:10 For a discussion of the removal of boundary stones, see the note on Deuteronomy 19:14.

5:13 Assyrian records confirm the tribute paid to Tiglath-Pileser III by the Israelite kings Menahem and Hoshea (see "Menahem and Pekah of Israel, Jotham of Judah and Tiglath-Pileser III of Assyria" on p. 553 and "Hoshea, King of Israel, and Shalmaneser V, King of Assyria" on p. 556).

[14]For I will be like a lion[v] to Ephraim,
like a great lion to Judah.
I will tear them to pieces and go away;
I will carry them off, with no one to rescue
them.[w]
[15]Then I will go back to my place
until they admit their guilt.
And they will seek my face;[x]
in their misery[y] they will earnestly seek me.[z]"

Israel Unrepentant

6 "Come, let us return to the LORD.
He has torn us to pieces[a]
but he will heal us;
he has injured us
but he will bind up our wounds.[b]
[2]After two days he will revive us;[c]
on the third day he will restore us,
that we may live in his presence.
[3]Let us acknowledge the LORD;
let us press on to acknowledge him.
As surely as the sun rises,
he will appear;
he will come to us like the winter rains,[d]
like the spring rains that water the earth.[e]"

[4]"What can I do with you, Ephraim?[f]
What can I do with you, Judah?
Your love is like the morning mist,
like the early dew that disappears.[g]
[5]Therefore I cut you in pieces with my prophets,
I killed you with the words of my mouth;[h]
my judgments flashed like lightning
upon you.[i]
[6]For I desire mercy, not sacrifice,[j]
and acknowledgment[k] of God rather than
burnt offerings.
[7]Like Adam,[a] they have broken the covenant[l]—
they were unfaithful[m] to me there.
[8]Gilead is a city of wicked men,
stained with footprints of blood.
[9]As marauders lie in ambush for a man,
so do bands of priests;
they murder on the road to Shechem,
committing shameful crimes.[n]
[10]I have seen a horrible[o] thing
in the house of Israel.
There Ephraim is given to prostitution
and Israel is defiled.[p]

[11]"Also for you, Judah,
a harvest[q] is appointed.

5:14 [v]Am 3:4 [w]Mic 5:8
5:15 [x]Hos 3:5 [y]Jer 2:27 [z]Isa 64:9
6:1 [a]Hos 5:14 [b]Dt 32:39; Jer 30:17; Hos 14:4
6:2 [c]Ps 30:5
6:3 [d]Joel 2:23 [e]Ps 72:6
6:4 [f]Hos 11:8 [g]Hos 7:1; 13:3
6:5 [h]Jer 1:9-10; 23:29 [i]Heb 4:12
6:6 [j]Isa 1:11; Mt 9:13*; 12:7* [k]Hos 2:20
6:7 [l]Hos 8:1 [m]Hos 5:7
6:9 [n]Jer 7:9-10; Eze 22:9; Hos 7:1
6:10 [o]Jer 5:30 [p]Hos 5:3
6:11 [q]Jer 51:33; Joel 3:13

[a] 7 Or *As at Adam*; or *Like men*

6:4 For "Ephraim," see the note on 5:3. **6:9** See "Shechem" on page 340.

7

"Whenever I would restore the fortunes of my people,
1 whenever I would heal Israel,
the sins of Ephraim are exposed
and the crimes of Samaria revealed.[r]
They practice deceit,[s]
thieves break into houses,[t]
bandits rob in the streets;
2 but they do not realize
that I remember[u] all their evil deeds.
Their sins engulf them;[v]
they are always before me.

3 "They delight the king with their wickedness,
the princes with their lies.[w]
4 They are all adulterers,[x]
burning like an oven
whose fire the baker need not stir
from the kneading of the dough till it rises.
5 On the day of the festival of our king
the princes become inflamed with wine,[y]
and he joins hands with the mockers.
6 Their hearts are like an oven;[z]
they approach him with intrigue.
Their passion smolders all night;
in the morning it blazes like a flaming fire.
7 All of them are hot as an oven;
they devour their rulers.
All their kings fall,
and none of them calls[a] on me.

8 "Ephraim mixes[b] with the nations;
Ephraim is a flat cake not turned over.
9 Foreigners sap his strength,[c]
but he does not realize it.
His hair is sprinkled with gray,
but he does not notice.
10 Israel's arrogance testifies against him,[d]
but despite all this
he does not return to the LORD his God
or search[e] for him.

11 "Ephraim is like a dove,[f]
easily deceived and senseless—
now calling to Egypt,
now turning to Assyria.[g]

7:1 [r]Hos 6:4 [s]ver 13 [t]Hos 4:2
7:2 [u]Jer 14:10; Hos 8:13 [v]Jer 2:19
7:3 [w]Hos 4:2; Mic 7:3
7:4 [x]Jer 9:2
7:5 [y]Isa 28:1,7
7:6 [z]Ps 21:9
7:7 [a]ver 16
7:8 [b]ver 11; Ps 106:35; Hos 5:13
7:9 [c]Isa 1:7; Hos 8:7
7:10 [d]Hos 5:5 [e]Isa 9:13
7:11 [f]Hos 11:11 [g]Hos 5:13; 12:1

7:1 "Ephraim" and "Samaria" (the capital city of the northern kingdom) are both alternate names for the northern kingdom of Israel.
7:4–7 There were three principal types of ovens in the ancient Near East. In Egypt there was in nearly every house a structure of clay built on the floor. In this, or on it, baking was done. In the region now known as Palestine and in Syria a barrel-shaped hole in the ground was coated with clay and heated by a quick, hot fire of brambles or dry dung mixed with straw. The dough, beaten very thin, was spread on the inside and almost immediately taken out, fully baked. In some places, a curved plate of iron was placed over the sunken oven, but in cities the oven was a chamber of stone, from which the fire was raked when the oven was very hot and into which the unbaked loaves were then placed.
7:4 See the note on verse 8.
7:5 The "festival of our king" probably refers to a coronation or birthday celebration that developed into a drunken orgy. King Elah died in drunkenness (see 1Ki 16:9).
7:7 Four kings were assassinated within 20 years, Zechariah and Shallum during a mere seven-month period (2Ki 15:10–14).
7:8 Bread (in the form of a "flat cake") was baked on hot stones. If it was not turned, it would burn on the bottom and be undone on the top.
7:9 The drain of tribute both to Assyria (see the note on 5:13) and to Egypt (v. 11) had weakened the country economically.
7:11 Menahem turned to Assyria (2Ki 15:19–20), while Hoshea alternated in his allegiance between Assyria and Egypt (2Ki 17:3–4). See the note on Hosea 5:13.

12 When they go, I will throw my net[h] over them; 7:12 [h]Eze 12:13
I will pull them down like birds of the air.
When I hear them flocking together,
I will catch them.
13 Woe[i] to them, 7:13 [i]Hos 9:12 [j]Jer 14:10; Eze 34:4-6; Hos 9:17 [k]ver 1; Mt 23:37
because they have strayed[j] from me!
Destruction to them,
because they have rebelled against me!
I long to redeem them
but they speak lies against me.[k]
14 They do not cry out to me from their hearts[l] 7:14 [l]Jer 3:10 [m]Am 2:8 [n]Hos 13:16
but wail upon their beds.
They gather together[a] for grain and new wine[m]
but turn away from me.[n]
15 I trained them and strengthened them,
but they plot evil[o] against me. 7:15 [o]Na 1:9,11
16 They do not turn to the Most High;
they are like a faulty bow.[p] 7:16 [p]Ps 78:9,57 [q]Eze 23:32 [r]Hos 9:3
Their leaders will fall by the sword
because of their insolent words.
For this they will be ridiculed[q]
in the land of Egypt.[r]

Israel to Reap the Whirlwind

8

"Put the trumpet to your lips!
An eagle[s] is over the house of the LORD 8:1 [s]Dt 28:49; Jer 4:13 [t]Hos 4:6; 6:7
because the people have broken my covenant
and rebelled against my law.[t]
2 Israel cries out to me,
'O our God, we acknowledge you!'
3 But Israel has rejected what is good;
an enemy will pursue him.
4 They set up kings without my consent;
they choose princes without my approval.[u] 8:4 [u]Hos 13:10 [v]Hos 2:8
With their silver and gold
they make idols[v] for themselves
to their own destruction.
5 Throw out your calf-idol, O Samaria![w] 8:5 [w]Hos 10:5 [x]Jer 13:27
My anger burns against them.
How long will they be incapable of purity?[x]
6 They are from Israel!
This calf—a craftsman has made it;
it is not God.
It will be broken in pieces,
that calf of Samaria.

7 "They sow the wind
and reap the whirlwind.[y] 8:7 [y]Pr 22:8; Isa 66:15; Hos 10:12-13; Na 1:3
The stalk has no head;
it will produce no flour.

[a] 14 Most Hebrew manuscripts; some Hebrew manuscripts and Septuagint *They slash themselves*

8:1 For "trumpet," see "The Shofar" on page 898.
8:3 "An enemy" refers to the Assyrians.
8:4 After Jeroboam II five other kings ruled over Israel within 13 years (2Ki 15:8–30), three of whom seized the throne by violence (see Hos 7:7 and its note).
8:5 Jeroboam I (930–909 B.C.), Israel's first king, had set up golden calves in Bethel and Dan, saying, "Here are your gods" (see 1Ki 12:28–33; see also "The High Place at Dan" on p. 504).

8:7 [z]Hos 2:9
8:8 [a]Jer 51:34 [b]Jer 22:28
8:10 [c]Eze 16:37; 22:20 [d]Jer 42:2
8:11 [e]Hos 10:1; 12:11
8:13 [f]Jer 7:21 [g]Hos 7:2 [h]Hos 4:9 [i]Hos 9:3,6
8:14 [j]Dt 32:18; Hos 2:13 [k]Jer 17:27

Were it to yield grain,
foreigners would swallow it up.[z]
8 Israel is swallowed up;[a]
now she is among the nations
like a worthless[b] thing.
9 For they have gone up to Assyria
like a wild donkey wandering alone.
Ephraim has sold herself to lovers.
10 Although they have sold themselves among the nations,
I will now gather them together.[c]
They will begin to waste away[d]
under the oppression of the mighty king.

11 "Though Ephraim built many altars for sin offerings,
these have become altars for sinning.[e]
12 I wrote for them the many things of my law,
but they regarded them as something alien.
13 They offer sacrifices given to me
and they eat[f] the meat,
but the LORD is not pleased with them.
Now he will remember[g] their wickedness
and punish their sins:[h]
They will return to Egypt.[i]
14 Israel has forgotten[j] his Maker
and built palaces;
Judah has fortified many towns.
But I will send fire upon their cities
that will consume their fortresses."[k]

Punishment for Israel

9:1 [l]Isa 22:12-13 [m]Hos 10:5
9:2 [n]Hos 2:9
9:3 [o]Lev 25:23 [p]Hos 8:13 [q]Eze 4:13; Hos 7:11
9:4 [r]Jer 6:20; Hos 8:13 [s]Hag 2:13-14

9 Do not rejoice, O Israel;
do not be jubilant[l] like the other nations.
For you have been unfaithful[m] to your God;
you love the wages of a prostitute
at every threshing floor.
2 Threshing floors and winepresses will not feed the people;
the new wine[n] will fail them.
3 They will not remain[o] in the LORD's land;
Ephraim will return to Egypt[p]
and eat unclean[a] food in Assyria.[q]
4 They will not pour out wine offerings to the LORD,
nor will their sacrifices please[r] him.
Such sacrifices will be to them like the bread of mourners;
all who eat them will be unclean.[s]
This food will be for themselves;
it will not come into the temple of the LORD.

[a] 3 That is, ceremonially unclean

8:9 The northern kingdom of Israel ("Ephraim") sought Assyrian protection. Menahem (2Ki 15:19) and Hoshea (2Ki 17:3), kings of Israel, paid tribute to Assyria (see the note on Hos 5:13).
8:13 Both the offerer and the priests ate parts of the sacrifices (see Lev 7:11–18,28–36; Dt 12:7; Jer 7:21).
9:1 At threshing time, the threshing floor (see "The Threshing Floor" on p. 608) was a man's world. At the end of a hard day the threshers feasted there and then stayed all night to protect the grain (see Ru 3:2–3). Prostitutes were not uncommon visitors.
9:3 For "Ephraim," see the note on 5:3. Israel was threatened with exile to the very lands upon which it had depended. Any foreign country, along with whatever grew there, was considered unclean; the produce was the product of fertility credited to pagan gods (see the notes on 2:8,12; see also "Baal and the Fertility Cults" on p. 1414).
9:4 The "bread of mourners" was unclean, coming as it did from a house where there had been a death (see Nu 19:14; Dt 26:14; Jer 16:7). All who touched it also became ceremonially unclean.

5 What will you do[t] on the day of your appointed
feasts,[u]
on the festival days of the LORD?
6 Even if they escape from destruction,
Egypt will gather them,
and Memphis[v] will bury them.
Their treasures of silver will be taken over by briers,
and thorns[w] will overrun their tents.
7 The days of punishment[x] are coming,
the days of reckoning are at hand.
Let Israel know this.
Because your sins[y] are so many
and your hostility so great,
the prophet is considered a fool,[z]
the inspired man a maniac.
8 The prophet, along with my God,
is the watchman over Ephraim,[a]
yet snares[a] await him on all his paths,
and hostility in the house of his God.
9 They have sunk deep into corruption,
as in the days of Gibeah.[b]
God will remember[c] their wickedness
and punish them for their sins.

10 "When I found Israel,
it was like finding grapes in the desert;
when I saw your fathers,
it was like seeing the early fruit on the fig tree.
But when they came to Baal Peor,[d]
they consecrated themselves to that shameful idol[e]
and became as vile as the thing they loved.
11 Ephraim's glory will fly away like a bird[f]—
no birth, no pregnancy, no conception.[g]
12 Even if they rear children,
I will bereave them of every one.
Woe[h] to them
when I turn away from them![i]
13 I have seen Ephraim, like Tyre,
planted in a pleasant place.[j]
But Ephraim will bring out
their children to the slayer."

14 Give them, O LORD—
what will you give them?
Give them wombs that miscarry
and breasts that are dry.[k]

9:5 [t]Isa 10:3; Jer 5:31 [u]Hos 2:11
9:6 [v]Isa 19:13 [w]Isa 5:6; Hos 10:8
9:7 [x]Isa 34:8; Jer 10:15; Mic 7:4 [y]Jer 16:18 [z]Isa 44:25; La 2:14; Eze 14:9-10
9:8 [a]Hos 5:1
9:9 [b]Jdg 19:16-30; Hos 5:8; 10:9 [c]Hos 8:13
9:10 [d]Nu 25:1-5; Ps 106:28-29 [e]Jer 11:13; Hos 4:14
9:11 [f]Hos 4:7; 10:5 [g]ver 14
9:12 [h]Hos 7:13 [i]Dt 31:17
9:13 [j]Eze 27:3
9:14 [k]ver 11; Lk 23:29

[a] 8 Or *The prophet is the watchman over Ephraim, / the people of my God*

9:6 Memphis was the capital of Lower (northern) Egypt. See "Memphis" on page 1270.
9:7 A prophet was often considered a "fool" or "maniac" because his behavior was sometimes bizarre (see 2Ki 9:11; Jer 29:26; cf. 1Sa 21:15).
9:8 For "watchman," see the note on Ezekiel 3:17. Israel demonstrated hostility only toward those watchmen (the true prophets) whom God had sent to warn his people of coming judgment (see Jer 1:19; 11:19; 15:10; Am 7:10–13).
9:9 The word "corrupt" is used of the Israelites who worshiped the golden calf (Ex 32:7; Dt 9:12), while "the days of Gibeah" refers to the debased behavior of the Benjamites described in Judges 19 (see also "Gibeah" on p. 380).
9:10 Peor was a mountain (Nu 23:28), and "Baal Peor" refers to the god of Peor (see Nu 25).
9:13 Tyre was renowned for its wealth and security (see "The Downfall of Tyre" on p. 1345).

9:15 [l]Hos 4:15 [m]Hos 7:2 [n]Isa 1:23; Hos 4:9; 5:2

15 "Because of all their wickedness in Gilgal,[l]
I hated them there.
Because of their sinful deeds,[m]
I will drive them out of my house.
I will no longer love them;
all their leaders are rebellious.[n]

9:16 [o]Hos 5:11 [p]Hos 8:7 [q]ver 12

16 Ephraim[o] is blighted,
their root is withered,
they yield no fruit.[p]
Even if they bear children,
I will slay[q] their cherished offspring."

9:17 [r]Hos 4:10 [s]Dt 28:65; Hos 7:13

17 My God will reject them
because they have not obeyed[r] him;
they will be wanderers among the nations.[s]

10:1 [t]Eze 15:2 [u]1Ki 14:23 [v]Hos 8:11; 12:11

10

Israel was a spreading vine;[t]
he brought forth fruit for himself.
As his fruit increased,
he built more altars;[u]
as his land prospered,
he adorned his sacred stones.[v]

10:2 [w]1Ki 18:21 [x]Hos 13:16 [y]ver 8 [z]Mic 5:13

2 Their heart is deceitful,[w]
and now they must bear their guilt.[x]
The LORD will demolish their altars[y]
and destroy their sacred stones.[z]

3 Then they will say, "We have no king
because we did not revere the LORD.
But even if we had a king,
what could he do for us?"

10:4 [a]Hos 4:2 [b]Eze 17:19; Am 5:7

4 They make many promises,
take false oaths[a]
and make agreements;[b]
therefore lawsuits spring up
like poisonous weeds in a plowed field.

10:5 [c]Hos 5:8 [d]2Ki 23:5 [e]Hos 8:5; 9:1,3, 11

5 The people who live in Samaria fear
for the calf-idol of Beth Aven.[a][c]
Its people will mourn over it,
and so will its idolatrous priests,[d]
those who had rejoiced over its splendor,
because it is taken from them into exile.[e]

10:6 [f]Hos 11:5 [g]Hos 5:13 [h]Isa 30:3; Hos 4:7

6 It will be carried to Assyria[f]
as tribute for the great king.[g]
Ephraim will be disgraced;[h]
Israel will be ashamed of its wooden idols.[b]

10:7 [i]Hos 13:11

7 Samaria and its king will float away[i]
like a twig on the surface of the waters.

[a] 5 *Beth Aven* means *house of wickedness* (a name for Bethel, which means *house of God*). [b] 6 Or *its counsel*

9:15 For "Gilgal," see the note on 4:15.
10:1 For "sacred stones," see the note on 1 Kings 14:23–24.
10:3–4 The last kings of Israel were notoriously corrupt and deceitful.
10:5 The "calf-idol of Beth Aven" was the idol that Jeroboam I had set up at Bethel (see the note on 8:5; see also "The High Place at Dan" on p. 504 and "Beth Aven: A Lesson in the Difficulty of Biblical Geography" on p. 1417).
10:6 For "tribute for the great king," see the note on 5:13. For "Ephraim," see the note on 5:3.

8 The high places of wickedness[a][j] will be destroyed—
it is the sin of Israel.
Thorns[k] and thistles will grow up
and cover their altars.[l]
Then they will say to the mountains, "Cover us!"
and to the hills, "Fall on us!"[m]

9 "Since the days of Gibeah,[n] you have sinned, O Israel,
and there you have remained.[b]
Did not war overtake
the evildoers in Gibeah?
10 When I please, I will punish[o] them;
nations will be gathered against them
to put them in bonds for their double sin.
11 Ephraim is a trained heifer
that loves to thresh;
so I will put a yoke
on her fair neck.
I will drive Ephraim,
Judah must plow,
and Jacob must break up the ground.
12 Sow for yourselves righteousness,[p]
reap the fruit of unfailing love,
and break up your unplowed ground;[q]
for it is time to seek[r] the LORD,
until he comes
and showers righteousness[s] on you.
13 But you have planted wickedness,
you have reaped evil,[t]
you have eaten the fruit of deception.
Because you have depended on your own strength
and on your many warriors,[u]
14 the roar of battle will rise against your people,
so that all your fortresses will be devastated[v]—
as Shalman devastated Beth Arbel on the day of battle,
when mothers were dashed to the ground with
their children.[w]
15 Thus will it happen to you, O Bethel,
because your wickedness is great.
When that day dawns,
the king of Israel will be completely destroyed.[x]

10:8 [j]1Ki 12:28-30; Hos 4:13 [k]Hos 9:6 [l]ver 2; Isa 32:13 [m]Lk 23:30*; Rev 6:16
10:9 [n]Hos 5:8
10:10 [o]Eze 5:13; Hos 4:9
10:12 [p]Pr 11:18 [q]Jer 4:3 [r]Hos 12:6 [s]Isa 45:8
10:13 [t]Job 4:8; Hos 7:3; 11:12; Gal 6:7-8 [u]Ps 33:16
10:14 [v]Isa 17:3 [w]Hos 13:16
10:15 [x]ver 7

God's Love for Israel

11 "When Israel was a child, I loved him,
and out of Egypt I called my son.[y]
2 But the more I[c] called Israel,
the further they went from me.[d]

11:1 [y]Ex 4:22; Hos 12:9,13; 13:4; Mt 2:15*

[a] 8 Hebrew *aven,* a reference to Beth Aven (a derogatory name for Bethel) [b] 9 Or *there a stand was taken* [c] 2 Some Septuagint manuscripts; Hebrew *they* [d] 2 Septuagint; Hebrew *them*

10:8 See "The High Places" on page 1318.
10:9 For "the days of Gibeah," see the note on 9:9.
10:11 The English word *fair* translates more than a dozen Hebrew and Greek words, none of which has the modern sense of blond or fair-skinned. Here it carries the meaning of beautiful or attractive (cf. Ac 7:20).
10:14 This event is otherwise unknown, as is true of the names mentioned. In any event, atrocities against civilians were common in ancient warfare (see the note on Ps 137:9; see also "Warfare in the Ancient World" on p. 950 and "Siege Warfare" on p. 465).
10:15 For "Bethel," see the note on 8:5; see also "Bethel" on page 59.
11:2 For "Baals," see the note on 2:13.

11:2 [z]Hos 2:13 [a]2Ki 17:15; Isa 65:7; Jer 18:15

They sacrificed to the Baals[z]
and they burned incense to images.[a]
3 It was I who taught Ephraim to walk,

11:3 [b]Dt 1:31; Hos 7:15 [c]Jer 30:17

taking them by the arms;[b]
but they did not realize
it was I who healed[c] them.
4 I led them with cords of human kindness,

11:4 [d]Jer 31:2-3 [e]Lev 26:13 [f]Ex 16:32; Ps 78:25

with ties of love;[d]
I lifted the yoke[e] from their neck
and bent down to feed[f] them.

11:5 [g]Hos 7:16 [h]Hos 10:6

5 "Will they not return to Egypt[g]
and will not Assyria[h] rule over them
because they refuse to repent?

11:6 [i]Hos 13:16

6 Swords[i] will flash in their cities,
will destroy the bars of their gates
and put an end to their plans.

11:7 [j]Jer 3:6-7; 8:5

7 My people are determined to turn from me.[j]
Even if they call to the Most High,
he will by no means exalt them.

11:8 [k]Hos 6:4 [l]Ge 14:8

8 "How can I give you up, Ephraim?[k]
How can I hand you over, Israel?
How can I treat you like Admah?
How can I make you like Zeboiim?[l]
My heart is changed within me;
all my compassion is aroused.

11:9 [m]Dt 13:17; Jer 30:11 [n]Mal 3:6 [o]Nu 23:19

9 I will not carry out my fierce anger,[m]
nor will I turn and devastate[n] Ephraim.
For I am God, and not man[o]—
the Holy One among you.
I will not come in wrath.[a]
10 They will follow the LORD;
he will roar like a lion.
When he roars,

11:10 [p]Hos 6:1-3

his children will come trembling from the west.[p]
11 They will come trembling
like birds from Egypt,

11:11 [q]Isa 11:11 [r]Eze 28:26

like doves from Assyria.[q]
I will settle them in their homes,"[r]
declares the LORD.

Israel's Sin

11:12 [s]Hos 4:2

12 Ephraim has surrounded me with lies,[s]
the house of Israel with deceit.
And Judah is unruly against God,
even against the faithful Holy One.

12

12:1 [t]Eze 17:10

1 Ephraim feeds on the wind;[t]
he pursues the east wind all day
and multiplies lies and violence.

[a] 9 Or *come against any city*

11:3 For "Ephraim," see the note on 5:3.
11:8 Admah and Zeboiim were cities of the plain located east and/or southeast of the Dead Sea. They were overthrown when Sodom was destroyed (Ge 19:24–25), symbolizing total destruction.
11:10 "The west" refers to the islands and coastlands of the Mediterranean Sea.
12:1 For "Ephraim," see the note on 5:3.

THE RELIABILITY OF THE BIBLE

HOSEA'S USE OF THE OLD TESTAMENT

HOSEA 12 Hosea was one of Israel's first prophets whose message was put into writing. Nevertheless Hosea's message, like those of Israel's other "writing prophets," cannot be understood in isolation from the law and the books of Joshua and Judges, books to which Hosea often alluded. For example, he used other Old Testament accounts as follows:

◆ The promises to Abraham await their final fulfillment (Hos 1:10; cf. Ge 22:17).

◆ God's dealings with Jacob are applicable and relevant for his descendants (Ge 25:25–26; 28:11–16; 29:16–30; 32:24–27; Hos 12:2–4,12).

◆ Israel's bondage in Egypt was a type or representation of her coming bondage to the **Assyrians** (8:13; 9:3,6).

◆ The **exodus** was a sign of God's great mercy and compassion (11:1; 13:4–6), but also an event that soon would be reversed in Israel's **exile** and captivity (10:5–8; 11:1–5). This event would be repeated in the nation's restoration under the Davidic king (1:11; 2:15; 3:5; 11:11; 12:9).

◆ The Ten Commandments were the fundamental rules by which the nation was to live and by which she would be judged (Ex 20:1–17; Hos 4:1–2; 13:4).

◆ God's covenant with Israel (8:1–3,12) was a source of great blessings (2:8,18–23; 13:4; 14:4–8) but would also bring curses on those who broke it (4:6; 8:1–10; cf. Dt 28).

◆ Israel's tendency toward apostasy was reflected in the people's idolatry during their period of desert wandering and continuing into Hosea's day (Hos 9:10; 13:4–6).

◆ The city of Gibeah (see "Map 5") was a notable example of wickedness in the past (Jdg 19:12–30) and in Hosea's day as well (Hos 10:9).

◆ Sodom, Gomorrah, Admah and Zeboiim (locations uncertain) were notorious examples of God's judgment (Dt 29:23; Hos 11:8).

Hosea's allusions to Genesis through Judges are highly significant. First, they help to establish the fact that these books had already been written by the time of Hosea, in the eighth century B.C. (Many scholars consider these books to be from the sixth century B.C. and even later.) Second, Hosea's construal of these books helps us to understand early Biblical interpretation, which in turn gives us a better understanding of how the New Testament interprets the Old.

He makes a treaty with Assyria
and sends olive oil to Egypt.[u]
2 The LORD has a charge[v] to bring against Judah;
he will punish Jacob[a] according to his ways
and repay him according to his deeds.[w]
3 In the womb he grasped his brother's heel;[x]
as a man he struggled[y] with God.
4 He struggled with the angel and overcame him;
he wept and begged for his favor.
He found him at Bethel[z]
and talked with him there—
5 the LORD God Almighty,
the LORD is his name[a] of renown!
6 But you must return to your God;
maintain love and justice,[b]
and wait for your God always.[c]

12:1 [u]2Ki 17:4
12:2 [v]Mic 6:2 [w]Hos 4:9
12:3 [x]Ge 25:26 [y]Ge 32:24-29
12:4 [z]Ge 28:12-15; 35:15
12:5 [a]Ex 3:15
12:6 [b]Mic 6:8 [c]Hos 6:1-3; 10:12; Mic 7:7

[a] 2 *Jacob* means *he grasps the heel* (figuratively, *he deceives*).

12:4 In Hosea's time Bethel was the most important royal sanctuary in the northern kingdom (see the note on 8:5; see also "Bethel" on p. 59).

12:7 [d]Am 8:5
12:8 [e]Ps 62:10; Rev 3:17
12:9 [f]Lev 23:43; Hos 11:1 [g]Ne 8:17
12:10 [h]Eze 20:49 [i]2Ki 17:13; Jer 7:25
12:11 [j]Hos 6:8 [k]Hos 4:15 [l]Hos 8:11
12:12 [m]Ge 28:5 [n]Ge 29:18
12:13 [o]Ex 13:3; Isa 63:11-14
12:14 [p]Eze 18:13 [q]Da 11:18
13:1 [r]Jdg 12:1 [s]Jdg 8:1 [t]Hos 11:2
13:2 [u]Isa 46:6; Jer 10:4 [v]Isa 44:17-20
13:3 [w]Hos 6:4 [x]Isa 17:13 [y]Da 2:35 [z]Ps 68:2

7 The merchant uses dishonest scales;[d]
he loves to defraud.
8 Ephraim boasts,
"I am very rich; I have become wealthy.[e]
With all my wealth they will not find in me
any iniquity or sin."

9 "I am the LORD your God,
⌞who brought you⌟ out of[a] Egypt;[f]
I will make you live in tents[g] again,
as in the days of your appointed feasts.
10 I spoke to the prophets,
gave them many visions
and told parables[h] through them."[i]

11 Is Gilead wicked?[j]
Its people are worthless!
Do they sacrifice bulls in Gilgal?[k]
Their altars will be like piles of stones
on a plowed field.[l]
12 Jacob fled to the country of Aram[b];[m]
Israel served to get a wife,
and to pay for her he tended sheep.[n]
13 The LORD used a prophet to bring Israel up from Egypt,
by a prophet he cared for him.[o]
14 But Ephraim has bitterly provoked him to anger;
his Lord will leave upon him the guilt of his bloodshed[p]
and will repay him for his contempt.[q]

The LORD's Anger Against Israel

13 When Ephraim spoke, men trembled;[r]
he was exalted[s] in Israel.
But he became guilty of Baal worship[t] and died.
2 Now they sin more and more;
they make idols for themselves from their silver,[u]
cleverly fashioned images,
all of them the work of craftsmen.
It is said of these people,
"They offer human sacrifice
and kiss[c] the calf-idols.[v]"
3 Therefore they will be like the morning mist,
like the early dew that disappears,[w]
like chaff[x] swirling from a threshing floor,[y]
like smoke[z] escaping through a window.

[a] 9 Or *God / ever since you were in* [b] 12 That is, Northwest Mesopotamia [c] 2 Or *"Men who sacrifice / kiss*

12:7 For "dishonest scales," see the notes on Proverbs 11:1 and 16:11.
12:9 For the "appointed feasts," see "The Festivals of Israel" on page 186.
12:11 Gilead was overrun by Assyria in 734–732 B.C. (2Ki 15:29). For "Gilgal," see the note on Hosea 4:15.
12:14 For "Ephraim," see the note on 5:3.
"Bloodshed" refers to violence committed against others, including human sacrifice (see "Human Sacrifice in the Ancient Near East" on p. 182).
13:1 For "Ephraim," see the note on 5:3. From Ephraim came such prominent leaders as Joshua (Nu 13:8,16; Jos 24:29–30) and Jeroboam I (1Ki 11:26; 12:20). "Israel" here refers to the 12 tribes.
13:2 For "human sacrifice," see "Human Sacrifice in the Ancient Near East" on page 182.
In the ancient Near East kissing was an act of worship toward heathen gods (1Ki 19:18,20; Job 31:27; Hos 13:2). For "calf-idols," see the note on 8:5.
13:3 "Mist," "dew," "chaff" and "smoke" are all figurative descriptors for Ephraim, which was soon to vanish as a nation. For commentary on chaff, see the notes on Psalm 1:4 and Isaiah 5:24. For "smoke," see the note on hearths and home heating at Psalm 102:3.

4 "But I am the LORD your God,
⌞who brought you⌟ out of[a] Egypt.[a]
You shall acknowledge no God but me,[b]
no Savior[c] except me.
5 I cared for you in the desert,
in the land of burning heat.
6 When I fed them, they were satisfied;
when they were satisfied, they became proud;
then they forgot me.[d]
7 So I will come upon them like a lion,
like a leopard I will lurk by the path.
8 Like a bear robbed of her cubs,[e]
I will attack them and rip them open.
Like a lion I will devour them;
a wild animal will tear them apart.[f]

9 "You are destroyed, O Israel,
because you are against me,[g] against your helper.[h]
10 Where is your king,[i] that he may save you?
Where are your rulers in all your towns,
of whom you said,
'Give me a king and princes'?[j]
11 So in my anger I gave you a king,
and in my wrath I took him away.[k]
12 The guilt of Ephraim is stored up,
his sins are kept on record.[l]
13 Pains as of a woman in childbirth[m] come to him,
but he is a child without wisdom;
when the time arrives,
he does not come to the opening of the womb.[n]

14 "I will ransom them from the power of the grave[b];[o]
I will redeem them from death.
Where, O death, are your plagues?
Where, O grave,[b] is your destruction?[p]

"I will have no compassion,
15 even though he thrives[q] among his brothers.
An east wind[r] from the LORD will come,
blowing in from the desert;
his spring will fail
and his well dry up.[s]
His storehouse will be plundered[t]
of all its treasures.
16 The people of Samaria must bear their guilt,[u]
because they have rebelled[v] against their God.

13:4 [a]Hos 12:9 [b]Ex 20:3 [c]Isa 43:11; 45:21-22
13:6 [d]Dt 32:12-15; Hos 2:13
13:8 [e]2Sa 17:8 [f]Ps 50:22
13:9 [g]Jer 2:17-19 [h]Dt 33:29
13:10 [i]2Ki 17:4 [j]1Sa 8:6; Hos 8:4
13:11 [k]1Ki 14:10; Hos 10:7
13:12 [l]Dt 32:34
13:13 [m]Isa 13:8; Mic 4:9-10 [n]Isa 66:9
13:14 [o]Ps 49:15; Eze 37:12-13 [p]1Co 15:55*
13:15 [q]Hos 10:1 [r]Eze 19:12 [s]Jer 51:36 [t]Jer 20:5
13:16 [u]Hos 10:2 [v]Hos 7:14

[a] 4 Or *God / ever since you were in* [b] 14 Hebrew *Sheol*

13:7–8 The Lord, previously pictured as a shepherd (4:16), would attack like the wild beasts that often ravaged the flocks. See "Shepherding in the Ancient World" on page 1363 and "Lions and Other Wild Beasts in Ancient Israel" on page 813.
13:14 For "grave," see the NIV text note; see also the note on Psalm 6:5 and "Sheol, Hades, Gehenna, the Abyss and Tartarus: Images of Hell" on page 946.
13:15 In a literal sense, wind from the east came to Palestine over the desert, making it a hot, dry wind (see Jer 4:11and its note). An east wind brought the plague of locusts on Egypt (Ex 10:13) and dried up the sea so the Israelites could cross over on dry land (Ex 14:21). Many references mention the destructive results of the east wind: thin and withered heads of grain (Ge 41:6), broken ships (Ps 48:7; Eze 27:26), withered plants (Eze 17:10), dried fountains (Hos 13:15) and Jonah's fainting spell (Jnh 4:8). In addition, the east wind was used as a means of judgment by God (Isa 27:8; Jer 18:17). Here the "east wind" is a figure for Assyria, an instrument of destruction. Assyria invaded the northern kingdom in 734 B.C., then crushed it and exiled its people in 722.
13:16 For commentary on wartime atrocities against women and children, see the note on 10:14.

13:16 [w]Hos 11:6 [x]2Ki 8:12; Hos 10:14 [y]2Ki 15:16; Isa 13:16

They will fall by the sword;[w]
their little ones will be dashed[x] to the ground,
their pregnant women[y] ripped open."

Repentance to Bring Blessing

14

14:1 [z]Hos 5:5

Return, O Israel, to the LORD your God.
Your sins have been your downfall![z]
2 Take words with you
and return to the LORD.
Say to him:
"Forgive all our sins
and receive us graciously,[a]
that we may offer the fruit of our lips.[a][b]
3 Assyria cannot save us;
we will not mount war-horses.[c]
We will never again say 'Our gods'[d]
to what our own hands have made,
for in you the fatherless[e] find compassion."

14:2 [a]Mic 7:18-19 [b]Heb 13:15

14:3 [c]Ps 33:17; Isa 31:1 [d]Hos 8:6 [e]Ps 10:14; 68:5

4 "I will heal[f] their waywardness
and love them freely,[g]
for my anger has turned away from them.
5 I will be like the dew to Israel;
he will blossom like a lily.[h]
Like a cedar of Lebanon[i]
he will send down his roots;[j]
6 his young shoots will grow.
His splendor will be like an olive tree,[k]
his fragrance like a cedar of Lebanon.[l]
7 Men will dwell again in his shade.[m]
He will flourish like the grain.
He will blossom like a vine,
and his fame will be like the wine[n] from Lebanon.[o]
8 O Ephraim, what more have I[b] to do with idols?[p]
I will answer him and care for him.
I am like a green pine tree;
your fruitfulness comes from me."

14:4 [f]Hos 6:1 [g]Zep 3:17

14:5 [h]SS 2:1 [i]Isa 35:2 [j]Job 29:19

14:6 [k]Ps 52:8; Jer 11:16 [l]SS 4:11

14:7 [m]Ps 91:1-4 [n]Hos 2:22 [o]Eze 17:23

14:8 [p]ver 3

9 Who is wise?[q] He will realize these things.
Who is discerning? He will understand them.[r]
The ways of the LORD are right;[s]
the righteous walk[t] in them,
but the rebellious stumble in them.

14:9 [q]Ps 107:43 [r]Pr 10:29; Isa 1:28 [s]Ps 111:7-8; Zep 3:5; Ac 13:10 [t]Isa 26:7

[a] 2 Or *offer our lips as sacrifices of bulls* [b] 8 Or *What more has Ephraim*

14:5 "Dew" is here a symbol of God's blessing (see Dt 33:13; Mic 5:7).
See "Cedars of Lebanon" on page 1043.

14:8 For "Ephraim," see the note on 5:3.

INTRODUCTION TO *Joel*

AUTHOR, PLACE AND DATE OF WRITING

Little is known of the author of this short book besides his name, and even that is somewhat in doubt. His given name, Joel, was common, but his father's name may either have been Pethuel, as the Hebrew of Joel 1:1 has it, or Bethuel, as in the Greek Septuagint. This confusion serves to point out how little we really know of the man.

Joel did not date his book, so scholars are forced to look for textual hints as to the time of writing. Suggestions range from the ninth century B.C. to the late postexilic period. Although certainty is impossible, there are reasons for suggesting a seventh century B.C. date for this prophecy (see "The Date of the Book of Joel" on p. 1435). The book was written from Judah.

AUDIENCE

Joel warned the people of the southern kingdom of coming judgment and urged them to repent and turn to God.

CULTURAL FACTS AND HIGHLIGHTS

Locust plagues, common in Old Testament days, still devastate parts of the world today and are remembered with horror by many Midwesterners in the United States from their experiences in the early to mid twentieth century.

This book was written in response to such a devastating blight (Joel 1). Its text, however, is more than a historical record or lamentation. Joel used the locust plague as a basis for developing a theology, employed by other minor prophets, of the "day of the LORD," an event that would bring both judgment and salvation. The phrase as it appears in the book is versatile, applying alike to a locust plague (ch. 1), an invading army (2:1–10), the final battle at the last judgment (ch. 3) and a salvation event—the outpouring of God's Spirit (2:28).

TIMELINE

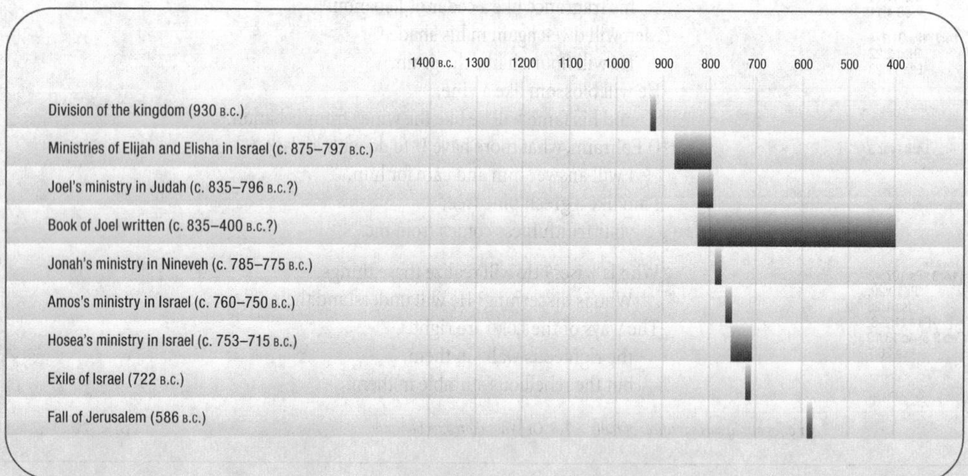

AS YOU READ

Be aware as you engage with this prophet of the contrasts in his depictions of judgment and hope. Pay particular attention to the section titled "The Day of the LORD" (2:28–32).

DID YOU KNOW?

- Drunkenness is the only specific sin mentioned in the book of Joel (1:5).
- A call for national prayer and fasting signaled an extraordinary event (1:13–14).
- The "trumpet," made from a ram's horn, was used to signal of approaching danger (2:1).
- Latticed windows with no glass would not have prevented the locusts from entering the houses (2:9).

THEMES

Joel's themes include:

1. *Judgment.* Joel's description of the coming day of judgment upon Judah foreshadowed a greater future day of reckoning. The soon-to-come accounting would be against God's own people, while the later, greater judgment would target their enemies. Joel described the judgment against God's own people as "the great and dreadful day of the LORD" (2:31), "a day of darkness and gloom, a day of clouds and blackness" (2:2). The greater future judgment referred to a day when the nations would be held accountable for their mistreatment of God's people (3:2–16,19), who themselves would be protected and blessed (3:16–18,20–21).

2. *Repentance and salvation.* Joel called upon everyone to repent: old and young (1:2–3; 2:16), drunkards (1:5), farmers (1:11) and priests (1:13; 2:17). External evidence of change is insufficient (2:12); God requires sincere repentance. In response to heartfelt remorse and trust in his grace, love and compassion (2:13), God forgives and restores (2:18–32). Most notable in this book is his promise of the outpouring of the Holy Spirit upon all people—young and old, men and women (2:28–29)—and the promise of salvation for "everyone who calls on the name of the LORD" (2:32).

OUTLINE

- I. The Locust Invasion and Call to Repentance (1:1—2:17)
  - A. A Call to Mourning and Prayer (1:1–14)
  - B. The Announcement of the Day of the Lord (1:15—2:11)
  - C. A Call to Repentance and Prayer (2:12–17)
- II. Salvation in the Day of the Lord (2:18—3:21)
  - A. The Lord's Restoration of Judah (2:18–27)
  - B. The Lord's Renewal of His People (2:28–32)
  - C. The Coming of the Day of the Lord (3)

1 The word of the LORD that came[a] to Joel[b] son of Pethuel.

1:1 [a]Jer 1:2 [b]Ac 2:16

An Invasion of Locusts

2 Hear this,[c] you elders;
listen, all who live in the land.[d]
Has anything like this ever happened in your days
or in the days of your forefathers?[e]
3 Tell it to your children,[f]
and let your children tell it to their children,
and their children to the next generation.
4 What the locust swarm has left
the great locusts have eaten;
what the great locusts have left
the young locusts have eaten;
what the young locusts have left
other locusts[a] have eaten.[g]

5 Wake up, you drunkards, and weep!
Wail, all you drinkers of wine;[h]
wail because of the new wine,
for it has been snatched from your lips.
6 A nation has invaded my land,
powerful and without number;[i]
it has the teeth[j] of a lion,
the fangs of a lioness.
7 It has laid waste[k] my vines
and ruined my fig trees.[l]
It has stripped off their bark
and thrown it away,
leaving their branches white.

8 Mourn like a virgin[b] in sackcloth[m]
grieving for the husband[c] of her youth.
9 Grain offerings and drink offerings[n]
are cut off from the house of the LORD.
The priests are in mourning,
those who minister before the LORD.
10 The fields are ruined,
the ground is dried up[d];[o]
the grain is destroyed,
the new wine[p] is dried up,
the oil fails.

1:2 [c]Hos 5:1 [d]Hos 4:1 [e]Joel 2:2
1:3 [f]Ex 10:2; Ps 78:4
1:4 [g]Dt 28:39; Na 3:15
1:5 [h]Joel 3:3
1:6 [i]Joel 2:2,11, 25 [j]Rev 9:8
1:7 [k]Isa 5:6 [l]Am 4:9
1:8 [m]ver 13; Isa 22:12; Am 8:10
1:9 [n]Hos 9:4; Joel 2:14,17
1:10 [o]Isa 24:4 [p]Hos 9:2

[a] 4 The precise meaning of the four Hebrew words used here for locusts is uncertain. [b] 8 Or *young woman* [c] 8 Or *betrothed*
[d] 10 Or *ground mourns*

1:2 "Elders" refers either to the older men of the community or to the recognized officials (see the note on Jer 19:1).
1:4 See "Locusts in the Ancient Near East" on page 1438.
1:5 Drunkenness is the only specific sin mentioned in this book. In this context drunkenness represents a self-indulgent lifestyle pursued by those who value the material more than the spiritual.
1:6 The locusts are compared here to a nation, and elsewhere in the book they are called the Lord's "army" (2:11,25). The reverse comparison—that of armies to locusts with regard to numbers—is as old as Ugaritic literature (fifteenth century B.C.) and is common in the Old Testament (see Jdg 6:5; Jer 46:23; 51:14,27; Na 3:15).
1:8 Sackcloth was the coarse garb of mourners (see the notes on 1Ki 20:31–32 and Job 16:15, as well as "Sackcloth and Ashes: Rituals of Lamentation" on p. 820).

In Israel, when a woman was pledged to be married to a man, he was already called her husband and she his wife, even though she was still a virgin (see Dt 22:23–24; see also "Marriage and Divorce in Ancient Israel" on p. 1548). This verse refers to a "husband" who died before the marriage had been consummated.
1:9 The grain offering (Lev 2:1–2) and the drink offering, which was a libation of wine (Lev 23:13), were part of the daily offering (Ex 29:40; Nu 28:5–8). The locusts had left nothing that could be given as a sacrifice.
1:10 Grain, wine and oil were the three staples of the agricultural society of that day (see "Food and Agriculture" on p. 390).

THE DATE OF THE BOOK OF JOEL

JOEL 1 The book of Joel itself gives no indication of its date of authorship. This is unusual in the Old Testament prophetic literature; most prophets indicated that they preached during the reigns of certain kings (e.g., Hos 1:1; Hag 1:1) or provided other chronological indicators (Am 1:1). The dates suggested for Joel range from the ninth century B.C. (making him the earliest of the writing prophets) to the late **postexilic**[1] period (making him one of the latest). The following arguments are often raised in the discussion:

◆ Joel is the second of the minor prophets, and thus the book is early, since they are roughly presented in chronological order. But there are exceptions to this rule: Obadiah, for example, almost certainly was written later than Micah, and Hosea later than Amos.

◆ No kings are mentioned, and therefore the book is postexilic. On the other hand, postexilic prophets sometimes dated their books by **Persian** kings (Hag 1:1; Zec 1:1). Thus, the non-mention of any king does not imply anything in particular about the book's date.

◆ Joel does mention priests and elders, and therefore the book was written when the nation was governed by these groups rather than by a king, making the book postexilic. However, the elders are mentioned only in a context of calling for ritual lamentation (2:15–17).[2] They are not said to have been in a governing position, and the reference may in fact have been literally to a group of elderly men (1:2). Again, nothing here helps us to date the book.

◆ Joel never alludes in any way to the northern kingdom (usually called Israel or **Samaria**), suggesting that the northern kingdom may no longer have existed and that the book was thus written after the fall of Samaria (722 B.C.)[3]

◆ Jerusalem had walls (2:7–9). Thus, the book was written either before its fall (586 B.C.)[4] or late in the postexilic period, after the walls had been restored.

◆ Worship was carried out at the temple (2:15–17), indicating that the book was written either before its destruction or after its restoration.

◆ All who lived in the land could gather in Jerusalem (1:14). This suggests that the population of the community was relatively small, as in the late preexilic or the postexilic period.

A few other fine points regarding the language and circumstances of Joel are debated but have produced no consensus.

All in all, the above considerations speak against a date that was very early, very late or during the **exile**. Apparently the northern kingdom no longer existed, but the temple was functioning and Jerusalem's walls were intact. A seventh-century B.C. date seems reasonable, but the fact remains that the book itself does not tell us when it was written.

[1]See Glossary on page 2080 for definitions of bolded words. [2]See "Ancient Near Eastern Laments" on page 1305. [3]See "Hoshea, King of Israel, and Shalmaneser V, King of Assyria" on page 556. [4]See "The Last Days of Jerusalem" on page 1197.

Jerusalem's "broad wall" after its restoration

© Dr. James C. Martin

[11] Despair, you farmers,[q]
wail, you vine growers;
grieve for the wheat and the barley,
because the harvest of the field is destroyed.[r]
[12] The vine is dried up
and the fig tree is withered;
the pomegranate, the palm and the apple tree—
all the trees of the field—are dried up.[s]
Surely the joy of mankind
is withered away.

1:11 [q]Jer 14:3-4; Am 5:16 [r]Isa 17:11
1:12 [s]Hag 2:19

A Call to Repentance

[13] Put on sackcloth,[t] O priests, and mourn;
wail, you who minister[u] before the altar.
Come, spend the night in sackcloth,
you who minister before my God;
for the grain offerings and drink offerings[v]
are withheld from the house of your God.
[14] Declare a holy fast;[w]
call a sacred assembly.
Summon the elders
and all who live in the land
to the house of the LORD your God,
and cry out[x] to the LORD.

[15] Alas for that[y] day!
For the day of the LORD[z] is near;
it will come like destruction from the Almighty.[a]

[16] Has not the food been cut off[a]
before our very eyes—
joy and gladness
from the house of our God?[b]
[17] The seeds are shriveled
beneath the clods.[b][c]
The storehouses are in ruins,
the granaries have been broken down,
for the grain has dried up.
[18] How the cattle moan!
The herds mill about
because they have no pasture;
even the flocks of sheep are suffering.

[19] To you, O LORD, I call,[d]
for fire[e] has devoured the open pastures[f]
and flames have burned up all the trees of the field.
[20] Even the wild animals pant for you;[g]
the streams of water have dried up[h]
and fire has devoured the open pastures.

1:13 [t]Jer 4:8 [u]Joel 2:17 [v]ver 9
1:14 [w]2Ch 20:3 [x]Jnh 3:8
1:15 [y]Jer 30:7 [z]Isa 13:6,9; Joel 2:1,11,31
1:16 [a]Isa 3:7 [b]Dt 12:7
1:17 [c]Isa 17:10-11
1:19 [d]Ps 50:15 [e]Am 7:4 [f]Jer 9:10
1:20 [g]Ps 104:21 [h]1Ki 17:7

[a] 15 Hebrew *Shaddai* [b] 17 The meaning of the Hebrew for this word is uncertain.

1:13–14 Joel challenged Judah's spiritual leaders, the priests, to call for a "sacred assembly" (v. 14). The call for national prayer and fasting signaled an extraordinary event (cf. Ne 9:1–3; Jer 36:9) or calamity—here an unprecedented locust invasion, apparently accompanied by a terrible drought.

For "elders" (v. 14), see the note on verse 2.

1:15 Sometimes abbreviated as "that day," the term "the day of the LORD" often refers to the decisive intervention of God in history, such as through the invasion of locusts in Joel. It can also herald Christ's coming to consummate history.

1:20 Because of its scarcity in Palestine, water is much appreciated there, and its absence is extremely serious (see also 1Ki 17:1ff., Jer 14:3). In fact, rain was viewed in Old Testament days as a direct sign of God's favor. The rivers of Palestine tend to be small and carry little,

An Army of Locusts

2:1 [i]Jer 4:5 [j]ver 15 [k]Joel 1:15; Zep 1:14-16 [l]Ob 1:15
2:2 [m]Am 5:18 [n]Da 9:12 [o]Joel 1:6 [p]Joel 1:2
2:3 [q]Ge 2:8 [r]Ps 105:34-35
2:4 [s]Rev 9:7
2:5 [t]Rev 9:9 [u]Isa 5:24; 30:30
2:6 [v]Isa 13:8 [w]Na 2:10
2:7 [x]Isa 5:27
2:9 [y]Jer 9:21
2:10 [z]Ps 18:7 [a]Mt 24:29 [b]Isa 13:10; Eze 32:8
2:11 [c]Joel 1:15

2 Blow the trumpet[i] in Zion;[j]
sound the alarm on my holy hill.
Let all who live in the land tremble,
for the day of the LORD[k] is coming.
It is close at hand[l]—
2 a day of darkness[m] and gloom,[n]
a day of clouds and blackness.
Like dawn spreading across the mountains
a large and mighty army[o] comes,
such as never was of old[p]
nor ever will be in ages to come.

3 Before them fire devours,
behind them a flame blazes.
Before them the land is like the garden of Eden,[q]
behind them, a desert waste[r]—
nothing escapes them.
4 They have the appearance of horses;[s]
they gallop along like cavalry.
5 With a noise like that of chariots[t]
they leap over the mountaintops,
like a crackling fire[u] consuming stubble,
like a mighty army drawn up for battle.

6 At the sight of them, nations are in anguish;[v]
every face turns pale.[w]
7 They charge like warriors;
they scale walls like soldiers.
They all march in line,
not swerving[x] from their course.
8 They do not jostle each other;
each marches straight ahead.
They plunge through defenses
without breaking ranks.
9 They rush upon the city;
they run along the wall.
They climb into the houses;
like thieves they enter through the windows.[y]

10 Before them the earth shakes,[z]
the sky trembles,
the sun and moon are darkened,[a]
and the stars no longer shine.[b]
11 The LORD[c] thunders
at the head of his army;

---

if any, water in summer. Consequently, in Bible times Israel depended on rain as its source of water, supplying springs and fountains. Cisterns were a necessity for the storage of water (see "Wells, Cisterns and Aqueducts in the Ancient World" on p. 1259), but if water was stored too long it became brackish and filthy and a menace to health. In the summer there was no rain, so vegetation was dependent upon the heavy dews. Irrigation was carried on wherever there was sufficient water. When this vital resource was scarce, as during a time of siege, it had to be rationed. Drinking water, carried in goatskins, was often sold in the streets. Wells and pools, although comparatively scarce, are often mentioned in the Bible (Ge 21:19; 24:11; Jn 4:6; 9:7).

2:1 The trumpet, made of a ram's horn, was used to signal approaching danger (see "The Shofar" on p. 898).

Zion here refers to Jerusalem as the capital of the nation.

For "the day of the LORD," see the note on 1:15.

2:9 Latticed windows with no glass would not have prevented the locusts from entering the houses (see "The Israelite Town and Home" on p. 1205).

2:11 Just as Isaiah viewed the Assyrians (see Isa 10:5) and Jeremiah the Babylonians (Jer 25:9; 43:10) as the Lord's weapons, so Joel saw the locusts as the Lord's army—the army with which he would come against his enemies in the day of the Lord.

his forces are beyond number,
and mighty are those who obey his command.
The day of the LORD is great;[d]
it is dreadful.
Who can endure it?[e]

2:11 [d]Zep 1:14; Rev 18:8 [e]Eze 22:14

Rend Your Heart

12 "Even now," declares the LORD,
"return[f] to me with all your heart,
with fasting and weeping and mourning."

2:12 [f]Jer 4:1; Hos 12:6

13 Rend your heart[g]
and not your garments.[h]
Return to the LORD your God,
for he is gracious and compassionate,
slow to anger and abounding in love,[i]
and he relents from sending calamity.[j]

2:13 [g]Ps 34:18; Isa 57:15 [h]Job 1:20 [i]Ex 34:6 [j]Jer 18:8

14 Who knows? He may turn[k] and have pity
and leave behind a blessing[l]—
grain offerings and drink offerings[m]
for the LORD your God.

2:14 [k]Jer 26:3 [l]Hag 2:19 [m]Joel 1:13

2:14 See the note on 1:9.

Locusts in the Ancient Near East

JOEL 2 The book of Joel describes a calamity that befell ancient Judah when it was struck by a locust plague. Locusts in fact can do an astonishing amount of damage to agriculture. Over the past few hundred years, a number of observers have left accounts of the sudden and complete devastation of crops produced by a swarm of locusts in Africa, the Near East and the American Midwest. The situation in the ancient world was exacerbated by the fact that almost all farming was subsistence farming.[1] Catastrophic crop failure within a single year meant starvation or near-starvation, as importation of food in sufficient quantities to make a difference was not feasible.

Joel 1:4 uses four different Hebrew words to describe the locusts. Translators struggle to distinguish among them. For example, the New American Standard Bible says: "What the *gnawing locust* has left, the *swarming locust* has eaten; And what the *swarming locust* has left, the *creeping locust* has eaten; And what the *creeping locust* has left, the *stripping locust* has eaten" (emphases added). The NIV puts it this way: "What the *locust swarm* has left the *great locusts* have eaten; what the *great locusts* have left the *young locusts* have eaten; what the *young locusts* have left *other locusts* have eaten" (emphases added). One translation is not necessarily better than another; both are trying to bring out the fact that four different Hebrew words for "locust"—the original meanings of which have been lost—appear in the original.

What do these four words represent? Are four different species of locust implied? This is possible, but it may be that the reference is to the four different instars (stages of insect growth) of a single species. Under this scenario, it would appear that the first term (NASB *gnawing locust*; NIV *locust swarm*) is the third stage of growth. The second term (NASB *swarming locust*; NIV *great locusts*) is the fourth and final instar—an adult locust. The third term (NASB *creeping locust*; NIV *young locusts*) is the larval stage, representing the offspring of the previous generation of locusts as the first instar of the insect. The fourth term (NASB *stripping locust*; NIV *other locusts*) is the nymph, the second instar of the locust. This suggests that a swarm of locusts moved in, devastated the land and laid their eggs. The eggs then hatched, and the voracious larvae and nymphs devoured every green thing that remained. The repetition seen in 1:4 clearly makes the point that nothing was left by the time the last stage of locusts had eaten its fill.

[1]See "Food and Agriculture" on page 390.

2:15 [n]Nu 10:2 [o]Jer 36:9 [p]Joel 1:14

15 Blow the trumpet[n] in Zion,
declare a holy fast,[o]
call a sacred assembly.[p]

2:16 [q]Ex 19:10, 22 [r]Ps 19:5

16 Gather the people,
consecrate[q] the assembly;
bring together the elders,
gather the children,
those nursing at the breast.
Let the bridegroom[r] leave his room
and the bride her chamber.

2:17 [s]Eze 8:16; Mt 23:35 [t]Dt 9:26-29; Ps 44:13 [u]Ps 42:3

17 Let the priests, who minister before the LORD,
weep between the temple porch and the altar.[s]
Let them say, "Spare your people, O LORD.
Do not make your inheritance an object of scorn,[t]
a byword among the nations.
Why should they say among the peoples,
'Where is their God?[u]' "

The LORD's Answer

2:18 [v]Zec 1:14

18 Then the LORD will be jealous[v] for his land
and take pity on his people.

19 The LORD will reply[a] to them:

2:19 [w]Jer 31:12 [x]Eze 34:29

"I am sending you grain, new wine and oil,[w]
enough to satisfy you fully;
never again will I make you
an object of scorn[x] to the nations.

2:20 [y]Jer 1:14-15 [z]Zec 14:8 [a]Isa 34:3

20 "I will drive the northern army[y] far from you,
pushing it into a parched and barren land,
with its front columns going into the eastern[z] sea[b]
and those in the rear into the western sea.[c]
And its stench[a] will go up;
its smell will rise."

Surely he has done great things.[d]

2:21 [b]Isa 54:4; Zep 3:16-17 [c]Ps 126:3

21 Be not afraid,[b] O land;
be glad and rejoice.
Surely the LORD has done great things.[c]

2:22 [d]Ps 65:12 [e]Joel 1:18-20

22 Be not afraid, O wild animals,
for the open pastures are becoming green.[d]
The trees are bearing their fruit;
the fig tree and the vine yield their riches.[e]

2:23 [f]Ps 149:2; Isa 12:6; 41:16; Hab 3:18; Zec 10:7

23 Be glad, O people of Zion,
rejoice[f] in the LORD your God,

[a] 18,19 Or *LORD was jealous . . . / and took pity . . . / [19]The LORD replied* [b] 20 That is, the Dead Sea [c] 20 That is, the Mediterranean [d] 20 Or *rise. / Surely it has done great things."*

2:15 Here the trumpet is sounded not as an alarm (cf. v. 1) but as a call to religious assembly (see "The Shofar" on p. 898).

For "fast" and "assembly," see the note on 1:13–14.

2:16 The Hebrew for "assembly" refers to the religious community.

For "elders," see the note on 1:2.

The "chamber" refers to the place where the marriage was consummated (see the note on SS 1:16–17; see also "Weddings in Ancient Israel" on p. 1039).

2:17 For "byword," see "Bywords and Insults in the Ancient World" on page 431.

2:19 See the note on 1:10.

2:20 Since enemies in ancient times did not invade from the sea or across the desert, Canaan's geographical location made her vulnerable only from the south (Egypt) and from the north (Assyria and Babylon). The hordes of locusts are pictured here as a vast army of Israel's most feared enemies.

For "the eastern sea" (the Dead Sea), see the note on Zechariah 14:8.

2:23 The phrase "the autumn rains in righteousness" can also be translated "the teacher of righteousness." The religious sect at

for he has given you
the autumn rains in righteousness.[a]
He sends you abundant showers,
both autumn and spring rains,[g] as before. 2:23 [g]Lev 26:4
[24] The threshing floors will be filled with grain;
the vats will overflow[h] with new wine[i] and oil. 2:24 [h]Lev 26:10; Mal 3:10 [i]Am 9:13

[25] "I will repay you for the years the locusts have eaten—
the great locust and the young locust,
the other locusts and the locust swarm[b]—
my great army that I sent among you.
[26] You will have plenty to eat, until you are full,[j] 2:26 [j]Lev 26:5 [k]Isa 62:9 [l]Ps 126:3; Isa 25:1
and you will praise[k] the name of the LORD
your God,
who has worked wonders[l] for you;
never again will my people be shamed.
[27] Then you will know that I am in Israel,
that I am the LORD[m] your God, 2:27 [m]Joel 3:17
and that there is no other;
never again will my people be shamed.

The Day of the LORD

[28] "And afterward,
I will pour out my Spirit[n] on all people. 2:28 [n]Eze 39:29
Your sons and daughters will prophesy,
your old men will dream dreams,
your young men will see visions.
[29] Even on my servants,[o] both men and women, 2:29 [o]1Co 12:13; Gal 3:28
I will pour out my Spirit in those days.
[30] I will show wonders in the heavens[p] 2:30 [p]Lk 21:11 [q]Mk 13:24-25
and on the earth,[q]
blood and fire and billows of smoke.
[31] The sun will be turned to darkness[r] 2:31 [r]Mt 24:29 [s]Isa 13:9-10; Mal 4:1,5
and the moon to blood
before the coming of the great and dreadful day
of the LORD.[s]
[32] And everyone who calls
on the name of the LORD will be saved;[t] 2:32 [t]Ac 2:17-21*; Ro 10:13* [u]Isa 46:13 [v]Ob 1:17 [w]Isa 11:11; Mic 4:7; Ro 9:27
for on Mount Zion[u] and in Jerusalem
there will be deliverance,[v]
as the LORD has said,
among the survivors[w]
whom the LORD calls.

[a] 23 Or / *the teacher for righteousness:* [b] 25 The precise meaning of the four Hebrew words used here for locusts is uncertain.

Qumran, which produced most of the Dead Sea Scrolls, claimed that its most revered teacher of the law, whom its members called the "Teacher of Righteousness," was the fulfillment of this prophecy (see "Biblical Interpretation at Qumran and Among the Early Rabbis" on p. 1603). The immediate context, however, seems to support the translation in the NIV text.

2:24 See "The Threshing Floor" on page 608; for "vats," see "The Winepress" on page 1171.

2:25 See "Locusts in the Ancient Near East" on page 1438.

2:28 See the note on prophetesses at Exodus 15:20–21.

2:31 There are a number of allusions in the Bible to eclipses of the sun and of the moon. In Isaiah 13:10 it is stated, "The rising sun will be darkened," while we find here the statement, "The sun will be turned to darkness and the moon to blood." These two descriptions accord quite well with observations of eclipses of the sun and of the moon. As the shadow of the moon sweeps across the face of the sun, it appears that the sun is turned to darkness, and when the earth comes directly between the sun and the moon there is an eclipse of the moon. When the eclipse is complete, it is still possible to see the surface of the moon, due to the fact that the atmosphere of the earth bends the light rays from their straight path. The sunlight is bent somewhat as it passes the earth and is then reflected by the moon and returned to the earth. Just as the sun appears to be red when it is setting, due to the passage of the light through more atmosphere, so the eclipsed light appears strange in color. The Bible uses the apt expression "turned . . . to blood" to describe this astronomical phenomenon.

The Nations Judged

3 "In those days and at that time,
3:1 xJer 16:15 when I restore the fortunes[x] of Judah and Jerusalem,
2 I will gather all nations
and bring them down to the Valley of Jehoshaphat.[a]
3:2 yEze 36:5 There I will enter into judgment[y] against them
concerning my inheritance, my people Israel,
for they scattered my people among the nations
and divided up my land.
3 They cast lots for my people
and traded boys for prostitutes;
3:3 zAm 2:6 they sold girls for wine[z]
that they might drink.

[a] *2 Jehoshaphat* means *the LORD judges*; also in verse 12.

3:2 Called the "valley of decision" in verse 14, the "Valley of Jehoshaphat" seems to have been a symbolic name for a valley near Jerusalem that is here depicted as the place of God's ultimate judgment on the nations gathered against Jerusalem (see the NIV text note). There King Jehoshaphat had witnessed one of the Lord's historic victories over the nations (see 2Ch 20:1–30).

3:3 The events described here happened to Judah at the time of the captivity (586 B.C.) and are mentioned in Obadiah 11. The Israelites were treated by their enemies as mere chattel, to be traded off for the pleasures of prostitution and wine. (See "Casting Lots" on p. 744.)

The Greeks and the Old Testament

JOEL 3 Alexander the Great conquered the ancient Near East during the late fourth century B.C. and began a process of "Hellenizing" the region (spreading Greek language and culture). Unfortunately, this has wrongly given some modern interpreters the notion that any sign of a Greek presence in an Old Testament text is evidence that the text was not written until after the time of Alexander. Thus, for example, the book of Daniel is often dated to the second century B.C., partially on the ground that Daniel 3 includes a few Greek words (e.g., *sumponia*, analogous to the Greek *sumphonia*, perhaps referring to some wind instrument). However, Greek musicians were famous in the ancient world far earlier than the time of Alexander the Great, and no doubt some of the Greek musical terminology was adopted by other cultures.[1]

An interesting case is Joel 3:6, where the prophet castigated the Philistines and **Phoenicians** for having taken Israelites as slaves and sold them to Greeks, thus removing Jews far from their homeland. Some have taken this to be an indication that the book of Joel is **postexilic**, but this is not necessarily the case. The Greeks were well known as a seafaring people, and undoubtedly preexilic Israelites had some contact with Greeks. It is significant in the Joel text, however, that Greece is perceived to be far away from the land of Israel. In preexilic times very few Israelites had ever ventured there, and most had never encountered a Greek. Thus they would have perceived Greece to be a remote and far-flung place. However, during the postexilic period, and certainly after Alexander's time, contact with Greeks was frequent and the Greek language widely spoken. Travel to Greece was also more common during this era.

The perception of Greeks as a faraway people in verse 6, therefore, actually suggests a preexilic date for the book. In addition, in the seventh century B.C. Greece was in the midst of a great economic expansion and needed many slaves.[2] This, too, fits well with what we see in Joel 3 if the book is dated to the seventh century B.C.[3]

[1]See "When Was Daniel Written?" on page 1385. [2]See "Greece: From Independent City-states Through Alexander the Great" on page 1814. [3]See "The Date of the Book of Joel" on page 1435.

4 "Now what have you against me, O Tyre and Sidon[a] and all you regions of Philistia? Are you repay-
ing me for something I have done? If you are paying me back, I will swiftly and speedily return on your
own heads what you have done.[b] 5 For you took my silver and my gold and carried off my finest treasures
to your temples.[c] 6 You sold the people of Judah and Jerusalem to the Greeks, that you might send them
far from their homeland.

7 "See, I am going to rouse them out of the places to which you sold them,[d] and I will return on your
own heads what you have done. 8 I will sell your sons[e] and daughters to the people of Judah,[f] and they
will sell them to the Sabeans, a nation far away." The LORD has spoken.

9 Proclaim this among the nations:
Prepare for war![g]
Rouse the warriors![h]
Let all the fighting men draw near and attack.
10 Beat your plowshares into swords
and your pruning hooks[i] into spears.
Let the weakling[j] say,
"I am strong!"
11 Come quickly, all you nations from every side,
and assemble[k] there.
Bring down your warriors,[l] O LORD!

12 "Let the nations be roused;
let them advance into the Valley of Jehoshaphat,
for there I will sit
to judge[m] all the nations on every side.
13 Swing the sickle,
for the harvest[n] is ripe.
Come, trample the grapes,
for the winepress[o] is full
and the vats overflow—
so great is their wickedness!"

14 Multitudes, multitudes
in the valley of decision!
For the day of the LORD[p] is near
in the valley of decision.
15 The sun and moon will be darkened,
and the stars no longer shine.
16 The LORD will roar from Zion
and thunder from Jerusalem;[q]
the earth and the sky will tremble.[r]
But the LORD will be a refuge for his people,
a stronghold[s] for the people of Israel.

3:4 [a]Mt 11:21 [b]Isa 34:8
3:5 [c]2Ch 21:16-17
3:7 [d]Isa 43:5-6; Jer 23:8
3:8 [e]Isa 60:14 [f]Isa 14:2
3:9 [g]Isa 8:9 [h]Jer 46:4
3:10 [i]Isa 2:4; Mic 4:3 [j]Zec 12:8
3:11 [k]Eze 38:15-16; Zep 3:8 [l]Isa 13:3
3:12 [m]Isa 2:4
3:13 [n]Hos 6:11; Mt 13:39; Rev 14:15-19 [o]Rev 14:20
3:14 [p]Isa 34:2-8; Joel 1:15
3:16 [q]Am 1:2 [r]Eze 38:19 [s]Jer 16:19

3:4–6 Tyre and Philistia (for Philistia, see "The Archaeology of Philistia" on p. 370 and the note on Eze 25:15–17) were longtime enemies of Israel. But God would punish them by allowing Sidon (see "Sidon" on p. 1536) to be destroyed and many of its people to be enslaved by Artaxerxes III in about 345 B.C., as well as by allowing Tyre to be captured by the Greeks under Alexander the Great in 332. Artaxerxes III sold the Sidonians as slaves in 345 B.C. (see "The Downfall of Tyre" on p. 1345).

3:6 *Javan* (Greek *Iōnia*) had come to be the name by which the Hebrews referred to Greece. From 700 to 830 B.C. the Ionians carried on extensive trade in the Near East; hence all people of Greece were called *Javan*. The Greeks were trading with the Phoenicians as early as 800 B.C. (see "Phoenicia" on p. 480 and "The Greeks and the Old Testament" on p. 1441), and the Phoenicians often sold captives from Judah to the Greeks. These later became the agents of God's vengeance against Greece (see Zec 9:13, noting the contrast of "your sons, O Zion" with "your sons, O Greece"). Critics have suggested that the Hebrews of preexilic days were not familiar with the Ionians, but discoveries have demonstrated that by Solomon's day (tenth century B.C.) the Hebrews were engaged in regular trade with them.

3:8 Sabeans were probably southern Arabians from Sheba (see "Sheba" on p. 498).

3:10 The pruning hook, an agricultural tool used in the cultivation of the vine, had a sharp, knifelike end for pruning (see also Isa 2:4; Mic 4:3).

3:11 "There" refers to the Valley of Jehoshaphat (see vv. 2,12; see also the note on v. 2).

3:14 The "valley of decision" is the Valley of Jehoshaphat (judgment) of verses 2 and 12 (see the note on v. 2).

3:16 For "Zion," see "Zaphon, Olympus, Sinai and Zion: The Mountain of God" on page 843.

Blessings for God's People

3:17 [t]Joel 2:27 [u]Isa 4:3

17 "Then you will know that I, the LORD your God,[t]
dwell in Zion,[u] my holy hill.
Jerusalem will be holy;
never again will foreigners invade her.

3:18 [v]Ex 3:8 [w]Isa 30:25; 35:6 [x]Rev 22:1-2 [y]Eze 47:1; Am 9:13

18 "In that day the mountains will drip new wine,
and the hills will flow with milk;[v]
all the ravines of Judah will run with water.[w]
A fountain will flow out of the LORD's house[x]
and will water the valley of acacias.[a][y]
19 But Egypt will be desolate,
Edom a desert waste,

3:19 [z]Ob 1:10

because of violence[z] done to the people of Judah,
in whose land they shed innocent blood.

3:20 [a]Am 9:15

20 Judah will be inhabited forever[a]
and Jerusalem through all generations.

3:21 [b]Eze 36:25

21 Their bloodguilt, which I have not pardoned,
I will pardon.[b]"

The LORD dwells in Zion!

[a] 18 Or *Valley of Shittim*

3:18 Since the acacia is one of the few trees that flourishes in dry soil, the picture here is that of a well-watered desert.

3:19 As ancient enemies of Israel, Egypt and Edom probably represented all the nations hostile to God's people (see "Edom" on p. 1467).

INTRODUCTION TO *Amos*

AUTHOR, PLACE AND DATE OF WRITING

The prophet Amos, the book's author (1:1), described himself as a shepherd and farmer—specifically, a tender of sycamore-fig trees (7:14)—although his strong verbal skills and wide-ranging knowledge negate the suggestion that he was simply an ignorant peasant. His denial that he was a prophet did not signify that he lacked a prophetic calling but indicated that he was not a professional prophet who earned his living by providing kings with the oracles they wanted to hear (7:14–15). Amos's hometown, Tekoa, was located in the highlands of Judah approximately 11 miles (7 km) south of Jerusalem, although his message was directed primarily to the northern kingdom of Israel. Some scholars believe that parts of Amos are secondary (not written by Amos), but that conclusion is unnecessary (see "The Unity of Amos" on page 1460).

Amos provided pointers that have assisted scholars with dating his message: He mentioned the names of the kings during whose reigns he preached (Jeroboam II of Israel and Uzziah of Judah), suggesting a date of approximately 760 B.C., as well as the fact that he preached two years prior to an earthquake (1:1); there is also the possible suggestion that an eclipse occurred during his ministry (8:9). Archaeological evidence from Hazor points to a severe earthquake in the mid-eighth century B.C., and an eclipse did take place in 763 (as well as earlier, in 784).

Amos most likely centered his ministry efforts around Bethel in the north (7:10–13), Israel's primary religious sanctuary, where the upper echelons of the northern kingdom worshiped.

AUDIENCE

Although Amos was from Judah, his message was directed primarily to the northern kingdom, suggesting that the Israelites were conscious of their common identity as God's people despite the political division that had split the nation. It is conceivable that he was specifically called to Jeroboam's court because his status as a peasant would have been in such contrast to the wealth and professionalism of Samaria (see especially ch. 7).

CULTURAL FACTS AND HIGHLIGHTS

Amos ministered during a period in which the dominant empires of the day (Egypt, Babylon and particularly Assyria) were relatively weak and both Israel and Judah were enjoying a period of prosperity and imperial expansion. Amos decried the wealth and arrogance of his time, symbolized by what he called "houses adorned with ivory" (3:15; see "The Samaria Ivories" on p. 1449). This prosperity was misleading, however: In a little over a quarter of a century Samaria, Israel's capital, would lie in ruins.

TIMELINE

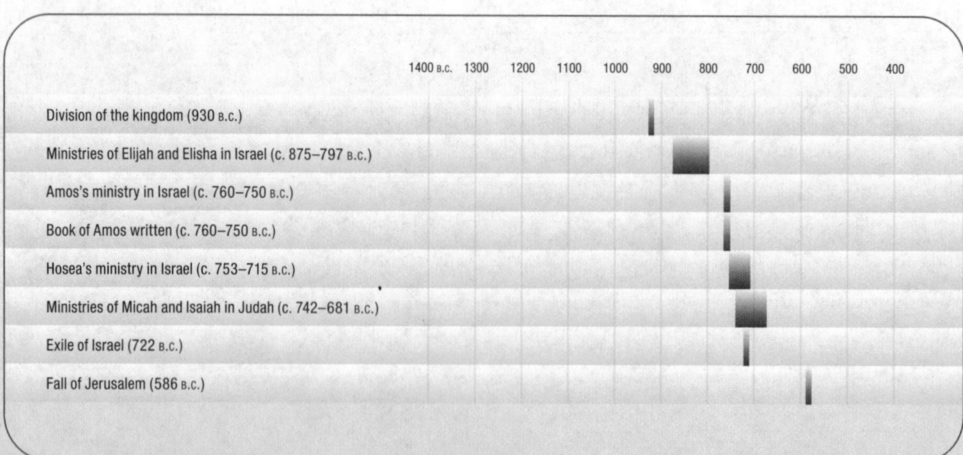

AS YOU READ

Pay particular attention to the strong social emphasis of this book. In what specific ways are these social themes relevant to any society during a period of prosperity and comfort?

DID YOU KNOW?

- "Fortresses" may refer not only to citadels but also to the fortress-like, palatial dwellings of the rich and powerful (1:4).
- In ancient times many people believed that burning the bones of the dead deprived the person's spirit of the rest that was widely believed to result from decent burial (2:1).
- Since Israel had extended its influence over Damascus by this time, the rich merchants of Samaria may have maintained luxurious houses in Damascus, along with market privileges in that city (3:12).
- The well-fed cattle raised in Bashan were considered the best breed in ancient Canaan (4:1).
- The reference to burning the dead bodies may actually refer to lighting a memorial fire in honor of the dead, as cremation was not generally practiced (6:10).

THEMES

Amos's themes include:

1. *Social justice.* Amos demonstrated that periods of unusual prosperity can lead to spiritual complacency and ethical laxity (6:1–6). Oppression of the poor (2:6–7a; 5:12; 8:4,6), injustice in the courts (2:7a; 5:7,12; 6:12), sexual immorality (2:7b), religious abuses (2:8), violence (3:10), idolatry (5:26), corrupt business practices (8:5)—all told the story: "The times [were] evil" (5:13). Amos taught that true faith is expressed through actions, particularly those that concern social justice.

2. *Judgment.* Injustice and exploitation of the poor would be punished (2:13–16; 6:8,14; 8:9—9:10), and those who lived opulently at the expense of others would lose everything they had (3:15—4:3; 5:16–17; 6:4–7). God would expose the hypocrisy and false piety of his people (4:4–5; 5:21–23), but he first called them to turn to him (5:4–6) and "live" (5:6). After judgment God would restore his people (9:11–15).

OUTLINE

I. Introduction (1:1–2)
II. Judgments on the Nations (1:3—2:16)
III. Judgments on God's People (3:1—5:17)
IV. Announcements of Exile (5:18—6:14)
V. Visions of Amos (7:1—9:10)
VI. Restored Israel's Hope for the Future (9:11–15)

1 The words of Amos, one of the shepherds of Tekoa[a]—what he saw concerning Israel two years be-
fore the earthquake,[b] when Uzziah[c] was king of Judah and Jeroboam[d] son of Jehoash[a] was king of
Israel.[e]
2 He said:

"The LORD roars[f] from Zion
and thunders from Jerusalem;[g]
the pastures of the shepherds dry up,[b]
and the top of Carmel[h] withers."[i]

1:1 [a]2Sa 14:2 [b]Zec 14:5 [c]2Ch 26:23 [d]2Ki 14:23 [e]Hos 1:1
1:2 [f]Isa 42:13 [g]Joel 3:16 [h]Am 9:3 [i]Jer 12:4

Judgment on Israel's Neighbors

3 This is what the LORD says:

"For three sins of Damascus,[j]
even for four, I will not turn back ⌞my wrath⌟.[k]
Because she threshed Gilead
with sledges having iron teeth,
4 I will send fire[l] upon the house of Hazael
that will consume the fortresses[m] of Ben-Hadad.[n]
5 I will break down the gate[o] of Damascus;
I will destroy the king who is in[c] the Valley of Aven[d]
and the one who holds the scepter in Beth Eden.
The people of Aram will go into exile to Kir,[p]"
says the LORD.

6 This is what the LORD says:

"For three sins of Gaza,[q]
even for four, I will not turn back ⌞my wrath⌟.
Because she took captive whole communities
and sold them to Edom,[r]
7 I will send fire upon the walls of Gaza
that will consume her fortresses.
8 I will destroy the king[e] of Ashdod[s]
and the one who holds the scepter in Ashkelon.

1:3 [j]Isa 8:4; 17:1-3 [k]Am 2:6
1:4 [l]Jer 49:27 [m]Jer 17:27 [n]1Ki 20:1; 2Ki 6:24
1:5 [o]Jer 51:30 [p]2Ki 16:9
1:6 [q]1Sa 6:17; Zep 2:4 [r]Ob 1:11
1:8 [s]2Ch 26:6

[a] *1* Hebrew *Joash,* a variant of *Jehoash* [b] *2* Or *shepherds mourn* [c] *5* Or *the inhabitants of* [d] *5* *Aven* means *wickedness.*
[e] *8* Or *inhabitants*

1:1 Tekoa lay 12 miles (20 km) south of Jerusalem and the same distance northeast of Hebron. It had been fortified by Rehoboam (2Ch 11:6). Previous to this, Joab, David's cousin and general, had sent to Tekoa for a "wise woman" and plotted with her to persuade David to bring back Absalom. The prophet Amos described himself both as one of the shepherds of Tekoa (Am 1:1) and later as one who cared for sycamore-fig trees (7:14), offering insight into the civilization of the city and surrounding countryside. Ruins of Tekoa survive as Takua.

Evidently a major earthquake had occurred, probably the one mentioned in Zechariah 14:5 (see the note there). Recent geological studies have detected a mammoth seismic event in this area dating to about the mid-eighth century B.C.

1:2 "Zion" refers to Jerusalem (see "Zaphon, Olympus, Sinai and Zion: The Mountain of God" on p. 843).

Amos, a shepherd, used shepherding imagery to warn the people of coming danger (see "Shepherding in the Ancient World" on p. 1363). The Lord's judgment would be felt by the whole land, from the "pastures" (the lowest and driest regions) to the "top of Carmel" (the highest and greenest area).

1:3—2:5 Amos pronounced God's judgment on: (1) Aram (and its capital, Damascus), for war atrocities; (2) Philistia (and its major cities of Gaza, Ashdod, Ashkelon and Ekron), for slave raids on defenseless villages; (3) Tyre, also for slave trafficking; (4) Edom (and its major cities, Teman and Bozrah)—Israel's "brother" through Esau (see Ge 25:21–30; 27:38–40)—for years of hostility toward Israel; (5) Ammon (and its capital, Rabbah), for brutal genocide bred by territorial greed; (6) Moab, for showing absolute disrespect for the dead; and (7) Judah (and its capital, Jerusalem), for rejecting God's law in general and for worshiping false gods in particular.

1:3 Damascus, the capital of Aram, was a perpetual enemy of Israel in that day (see "Damascus" on p. 1087 and "Syria/Aram" on p. 534).

For information on the harvesting process, which included threshing the heads of grain by driving a wooden sledge over the cut grain, see the note on Ruth 1:22.

1:4 Hazael was the king of Damascus (see "Hazael, the Nemesis of Israel" on p. 539), and Ben-Hadad (r. 796–775 B.C.) was Hazael's son and one of several kings with this name (see "Ben-Hadad III of Aram and Jehoash of Israel" on p. 548).

"Fortresses" may refer not only to citadels but also to the fortress-like palatial dwellings of the rich and powerful.

1:5 The "Valley of Aven" may be the Beqaa Valley, located between the Lebanon and Anti-Lebanon mountains, but it may also refer to the river valley in which Damascus is located. "Beth Eden" is probably Damascus, a lush, garden-like spot of that region. Kir is an unidentified site, possibly in the vicinity of Elam (see the notes on Isa 21:2; 22:6), from which the Arameans are said to have come (9:7).

For "scepter," see the note on Zechariah 10:11.

1:6–8 Gaza, Ashdod, Ashkelon and Ekron were four of the five major Philistine cities (see "The Archaeology of Philistia" on p. 370).

1:8 [t]Ps 81:14 [u]Eze 25:16 [v]Isa 14:28-32; Zep 2:4-7

I will turn my hand[t] against Ekron,
till the last of the Philistines[u] is dead,"
says the Sovereign LORD.[v]

9 This is what the LORD says:

1:9 [w]1Ki 5:1; 9:11-14; Isa 23:1-18; Jer 25:22; Joel 3:4; Mt 11:21

"For three sins of Tyre,[w]
even for four, I will not turn back ⌊my wrath⌋.
Because she sold whole communities of captives to Edom,
disregarding a treaty of brotherhood,
10 I will send fire upon the walls of Tyre
that will consume her fortresses.[x]"

1:10 [x]Zec 9:1-4

11 This is what the LORD says:

1:11 [y]Nu 20:14-21; 2Ch 28:17; Jer 49:7-22 [z]Eze 25:12-14

"For three sins of Edom,[y]
even for four, I will not turn back ⌊my wrath⌋.
Because he pursued his brother with a sword,
stifling all compassion,[a]
because his anger raged continually
and his fury flamed unchecked,[z]
12 I will send fire upon Teman[a]
that will consume the fortresses of Bozrah."

1:12 [a]Ob 1:9-10

13 This is what the LORD says:

1:13 [b]Jer 49:1-6; Eze 21:28; 25:2-7 [c]Hos 13:16

"For three sins of Ammon,[b]
even for four, I will not turn back ⌊my wrath⌋.
Because he ripped open the pregnant women[c] of Gilead
in order to extend his borders,
14 I will set fire to the walls of Rabbah[d]
that will consume her fortresses
amid war cries[e] on the day of battle,
amid violent winds on a stormy day.
15 Her king[b] will go into exile,
he and his officials together,"
says the LORD.

1:14 [d]Dt 3:11 [e]Am 2:2

2 This is what the LORD says:

"For three sins of Moab,
even for four, I will not turn back ⌊my wrath⌋.
Because he burned, as if to lime,
the bones of Edom's king,
2 I will send fire upon Moab
that will consume the fortresses of Kerioth.[c]
Moab will go down in great tumult
amid war cries and the blast of the trumpet.

[a] 11 Or *sword / and destroyed his allies* [b] 15 Or / *Molech*; Hebrew *malcam* [c] 2 Or *of her cities*

Gath, the fifth significant city (cf. 6:2), may already have been subdued by Uzziah (see 2Ch 26:6). Philistia was eventually destroyed by Nebuchadnezzar (see "Nebuchadnezzar" on p. 571).

See "Edom" on page 1467.

1:9–10 Tyre, the dominant Phoenician merchant city of the time, boasted of its secure position on its nearly impregnable island (see "The Downfall of Tyre" on p. 1345).

1:12 Teman and Bozrah were major cities of Edom. Teman is thought to have been near Petra (see the note on Ob 9), while Bozrah is identified with Buseirah or "el Buseirah" ("the little Bozrah"), 37 miles (60 km) to the north. The word *bozrah* means "sheepfold" and appears in Micah 2:12 (NIV "sheep in a pen").

1:13–14 This prophecy against Ammon (see "Ammon" on p. 364) and its capital, Rabbah (see "Rabbah" on p. 606), was fulfilled through the Assyrian king Tiglath-Pileser III around 732 B.C.

2:1 See "Moab" on page 292.

In ancient times burning the bones of the dead was thought to have deprived the person's spirit of the rest that was widely believed to result from a decent burial.

2:2 *Kerioth* may be a plural noun meaning "cities" (see the NIV text note) or the name of a major town and a shrine of Chemosh, the national god of Moab.

For "trumpet," see "The Shofar" on page 898.

3 I will destroy her ruler[f]
and kill all her officials with him,"[g]
says the LORD.

4 This is what the LORD says:

"For three sins of Judah,[h]
even for four, I will not turn back ⌊my wrath⌋.
Because they have rejected the law[i] of the LORD
and have not kept his decrees,[j]
because they have been led astray[k] by false gods,[a][l]
the gods[b] their ancestors followed,[m]
5 I will send fire upon Judah
that will consume the fortresses of Jerusalem.[n]"

Judgment on Israel

6 This is what the LORD says:

"For three sins of Israel,
even for four, I will not turn back ⌊my wrath⌋.
They sell the righteous for silver,
and the needy for a pair of sandals.[o]
7 They trample on the heads of the poor
as upon the dust of the ground
and deny justice to the oppressed.
Father and son use the same girl
and so profane my holy name.[p]
8 They lie down beside every altar
on garments taken in pledge.[q]
In the house of their god
they drink wine[r] taken as fines.

9 "I destroyed the Amorite[s] before them,
though he was tall as the cedars
and strong as the oaks.
I destroyed his fruit above
and his roots[t] below.

10 "I brought you up out of Egypt,[u]
and I led you forty years in the desert[v]
to give you the land of the Amorites.[w]
11 I also raised up prophets[x] from among your sons
and Nazirites[y] from among your young men.
Is this not true, people of Israel?"
declares the LORD.

12 "But you made the Nazirites drink wine
and commanded the prophets not to prophesy.[z]

[a] 4 Or *by lies* [b] 4 Or *lies*

2:3 [f]Ps 2:10 [g]Isa 40:23
2:4 [h]2Ki 17:19; Hos 12:2 [i]Jer 6:19 [j]Eze 20:24 [k]Isa 9:16 [l]Isa 28:15 [m]2Ki 22:13; Jer 16:12
2:5 [n]Jer 17:27; Hos 8:14
2:6 [o]Joel 3:3; Am 8:6
2:7 [p]Am 5:11-12; 8:4
2:8 [q]Ex 22:26 [r]Am 4:1; 6:6
2:9 [s]Nu 21:23-26; Jos 10:12 [t]Eze 17:9; Mal 4:1
2:10 [u]Ex 20:2; Am 3:1 [v]Dt 2:7 [w]Ex 3:8; Am 9:7
2:11 [x]Dt 18:18; Jer 7:25 [y]Nu 6:2-3; Jdg 13:5
2:12 [z]Isa 30:10; Jer 11:21; Am 7:12-13; Mic 2:6

2:7 Israel's law, as well as numerous other laws of the ancient Near East, commanded kings and rulers to care for the poor and the oppressed and to protect them from injustice (see "The Care of Widows and Orphans in the Bible and the Ancient Near East" on p. 285).

Whether the girl being "used" was a household servant (in which case father and son alike were abusing her as a family prostitute) is unclear. In any case, Israelite law required that in the case of illicit sexual relations with a girl, marriage was obligatory (Ex 22:16; Dt 22:28–29). For a father and son to engage in sexual relations with the same girl or woman was strictly forbidden (Lev 18:7–8,15; 20:11–12).

2:8 The law prohibited retaining a man's cloak overnight as security for a debt (see Ex 22:26–27) or taking a widow's cloak at all (Dt 24:17).

2:9 "Amorite" is here used to include all of the inhabitants of Canaan.

2:11 Prophets were God's faithful spokespersons (see "Prophets in the Bible and Pagan Nations" on p. 1457), and Nazirites were others who were uniquely dedicated to him (see the note on Nu 6:1–21). These persons, though outside the priesthood, were used by God through word and example to call his people to faithfulness.

2:14 [a]Jer 9:23 [b]Ps 33:16; Isa 30:16-17
2:15 [c]Eze 39:3
2:16 [d]Jer 48:41

[13] "Now then, I will crush you
as a cart crushes when loaded with grain.
[14] The swift will not escape,
the strong[a] will not muster their strength,
and the warrior will not save his life.[b]
[15] The archer[c] will not stand his ground,
the fleet-footed soldier will not get away,
and the horseman will not save his life.
[16] Even the bravest warriors[d]
will flee naked on that day,"

declares the LORD.

Witnesses Summoned Against Israel

3:1 [e]Am 2:10
3:2 [f]Dt 7:6; Lk 12:47 [g]Jer 14:10
3:4 [h]Ps 104:21; Hos 5:14

3 Hear this word the LORD has spoken against you, O people of Israel—against the whole family I
brought up out of Egypt:[e]

[2] "You only have I chosen[f]
of all the families of the earth;
therefore I will punish you
for all your sins.[g]"

[3] Do two walk together
unless they have agreed to do so?
[4] Does a lion roar in the thicket
when he has no prey?[h]
Does he growl in his den
when he has caught nothing?

2:13 For a discussion of sheaves and threshing, see the note on Ruth 2:7. See also "The Threshing Floor" on page 608 and "Food and Agriculture" on page 390.

2:16 For "that day," see the note on Joel 1:15.

ANCIENT TEXTS AND ARTIFACTS

The Samaria Ivories

AMOS 3 The reference to "houses adorned with ivory" in Amos 3:15 finds confirmation in the discovery of the Samaria Ivories, a collection of hundreds of pieces of artwork, including over 200 fragments uncovered in the rubbish heap of a building on the city's **acropolis.**[1] This "ivory building" is associated with the Israelite king Ahab (c. 874–853 B.C.), who is said to have constructed a palace "inlaid with ivory" in **Samaria** (1Ki 22:39).[2] An alabaster jar found with the largest of the ivories and incised with the name of the Egyptian pharaoh Osorkon II (874–850 B.C.) is contemporary with Ahab. There are also other ivories discovered throughout Syria-Palestine and **Mesopotamia** that date to the same general period and resemble the Samarian artifacts in craftsmanship and style.[3]

The artistic features of these ivories appear to have originated in **Phoenicia**,[4] an area strongly influenced by Egyptian motifs and artwork. Characters from Egyptian mythology often appear in the collection, which also includes ivory plaques incised with Hebrew script—most likely inlays for palace furniture. These plaques could be related to the "beds inlaid with ivory" of which Amos spoke in 6:4.

[1]See Glossary on page 2080 for definitions of bolded words. [2]See "Omri and Samaria" on page 512 and "Ahab and the Battle of Qarqar" on page 524. [3]See "The Nimrud Ivories" on page 1455. [4]See "Phoenicia" on page 488.

5 Does a bird fall into a trap on the ground
where no snare has been set?
Does a trap spring up from the earth
when there is nothing to catch?
6 When a trumpet sounds in a city,
do not the people tremble?
When disaster comes to a city,
has not the LORD caused it?[i]
7 Surely the Sovereign LORD does nothing
without revealing his plan[j]
to his servants the prophets.[k]
8 The lion has roared—
who will not fear?
The Sovereign LORD has spoken—
who can but prophesy?[l]
9 Proclaim to the fortresses of Ashdod
and to the fortresses of Egypt:
"Assemble yourselves on the mountains of Samaria;[m]
see the great unrest within her
and the oppression among her people."

10 "They do not know how to do right,[n]" declares the LORD,
"who hoard plunder[o] and loot in their fortresses."[p]

11 Therefore this is what the Sovereign LORD says:

"An enemy will overrun the land;
he will pull down your strongholds
and plunder your fortresses.[q]"

12 This is what the LORD says:

"As a shepherd saves from the lion's[r] mouth
only two leg bones or a piece of an ear,
so will the Israelites be saved,
those who sit in Samaria
on the edge of their beds
and in Damascus on their couches.[a][s]"

13 "Hear this and testify[t] against the house of Jacob," declares the Lord, the LORD God Almighty.

14 "On the day I punish Israel for her sins,
I will destroy the altars of Bethel;[u]
the horns of the altar will be cut off
and fall to the ground.
15 I will tear down the winter house[v]
along with the summer house;[w]
the houses adorned with ivory[x] will be destroyed
and the mansions will be demolished,"

declares the LORD.

3:6 [i] Isa 14:24-27; 45:7
3:7 [j] Ge 18:17; Da 9:22; Jn 15:15; Rev 10:7 [k] Jer 23:22
3:8 [l] Jer 20:9; Jnh 1:1-3; 3:1-3; Ac 4:20
3:9 [m] Am 4:1; 6:1
3:10 [n] Jer 4:22; Am 5:7; 6:12 [o] Hab 2:8 [p] Zep 1:9
3:11 [q] Am 2:5; 6:14
3:12 [r] 1Sa 17:34 [s] Am 6:4
3:13 [t] Eze 2:7
3:14 [u] Am 5:5-6
3:15 [v] Jer 36:22 [w] Jdg 3:20 [x] 1Ki 22:39

[a] 12 The meaning of the Hebrew for this line is uncertain.

3:9 For "fortresses," see the note on 1:4.
3:11 The "enemy" here refers to Assyria.
3:12 A piece of the sheep was saved to prove to the owner that it had been eaten by a wild animal, not stolen by the shepherd.

Since Israel had extended its influence over Damascus by this time, the rich merchants of Samaria may have maintained luxurious houses in Damascus, along with market privileges in that city (see 1Ki 20:34).

3:14 Israel's sins were rooted in the false shrines erected by Jeroboam I at Bethel and Dan (1Ki 12:26–33; see also "The High Place at Dan" on p. 504).

The horns of the altar were the last refuge for a condemned individual (cf. 1Ki 1:50–53). To cut off its horns rendered an altar useless for religious purposes.

3:15 Extensive excavations of Samaria were carried out by G. Reisner, C.S. Fisher and D.H. Lyon in 1908 and 1910–1911, as well as

Israel Has Not Returned to God

4:1 [y]Ps 22:12; Eze 39:18 [z]Am 3:9 [a]Am 2:8; 5:11; 8:6

4 Hear this word, you cows of Bashan[y] on Mount Samaria,[z]
you women who oppress the poor and crush the needy
and say to your husbands, "Bring us some drinks![a]"
2 The Sovereign LORD has sworn by his holiness:
"The time will surely come
when you will be taken away[b] with hooks,
the last of you with fishhooks.
3 You will each go straight out
through breaks in the wall,[c]
and you will be cast out toward Harmon,[a]"
declares the LORD.

4:2 [b]Am 6:8
4:3 [c]Eze 12:5

4 "Go to Bethel and sin;
go to Gilgal[d] and sin yet more.
Bring your sacrifices every morning,[e]
your tithes[f] every three years.[b][g]
5 Burn leavened bread[h] as a thank offering
and brag about your freewill offerings[i]—
boast about them, you Israelites,
for this is what you love to do,"
declares the Sovereign LORD.

4:4 [d]Hos 4:15 [e]Nu 28:3 [f]Dt 14:28 [g]Eze 20:39; Am 5:21-22
4:5 [h]Lev 7:13 [i]Lev 22:18-21

6 "I gave you empty stomachs[c] in every city
and lack of bread in every town,
yet you have not returned to me,"
declares the LORD.[j]

4:6 [j]Isa 3:1; Jer 5:3; Hag 2:17

7 "I also withheld rain from you
when the harvest was still three months away.
I sent rain on one town,
but withheld it from another.[k]
One field had rain;
another had none and dried up.
8 People staggered from town to town for water[l]
but did not get enough to drink,
yet you have not returned[m] to me,"
declares the LORD.[n]

4:7 [k]Ex 9:4,26; Dt 11:17; 2Ch 7:13
4:8 [l]Eze 4:16-17 [m]Jer 3:7 [n]Jer 14:4

9 "Many times I struck your gardens and vineyards,
I struck them with blight and mildew.[o]

4:9 [o]Dt 28:22

[a] 3 Masoretic Text; with a different word division of the Hebrew (see Septuagint) *out, O mountain of oppression* [b] 4 Or *tithes on the third day* [c] 6 Hebrew *you cleanness of teeth*

---

by J.W. Crowfoot, K. Kenyon and others in 1931–1935. Impressive remains of a palace from the time of Omri and Ahab have been located on the city's acropolis (fortified height). Ostraca written in ancient Hebrew were found dating to the reign of Jeroboam II, as well as numerous ivory plaques reminiscent of the "palace [Ahab had] built and inlaid with ivory" (1Ki 22:39; see also Am 6:4 and "The Samaria Ivories" on page 1449.

4:1 The well-fed cattle raised in Bashan were considered the best breed in ancient Canaan. The phrase "cows of Bashan" was therefore a harsh but fitting symbol for Israel's wealthy, pampered, self-indulgent women, who maintained their lifestyles by exploiting the poor and speaking demandingly—even to their husbands.

For "Mount Samaria," see the note on 6:1.

The Scriptures demonstrate that drunkenness was one of the major vices of antiquity (e.g., Ge 9:21; 19:33,35; 1Sa 25:36; 2Sa 11:13; 13:28; 1Ki 16:9; 20:16), and the prophets often denounced it as a great social evil of the wealthy in Israel. Women, who spent much of their lives in the home and were perhaps more subject to boredom than men, are often criticized in ancient texts for excessive drinking.

4:2 According to Assyrian reliefs, prisoners of war were led away with ropes fastened to hooks that pierced their noses or lower lips (see 2Ki 19:28; Isa 37:29 and their notes). The Hebrew word here translated "hooks" may, in fact, refer to ropes.

The fishhook in ancient times served as the means not only of catching fish but also of keeping them, at least for a time (cf. Am 4:2 with Job 41:1–2).

4:4 Bethel and Gilgal were popular places of worship in Amos's day (see "Bethel" on p. 59 and "The Camp at Gilgal" on p. 308).

4:5 The burning of leavened bread in the sacrifices was strictly forbidden (see Lev 2:11; 6:17).

4:7–8 Lack of rain three months before harvest would have prevented the full development of the grain.

4:9 Mildew is a pale fungus that discolors and spoils grains and fruits in warm, damp weather. In Scripture it is always associated with "blight," a disease or injury of plants marked by the formation of lesions, withering and the death of parts, such as leaves and tubers (Dt 28:22; 1Ki 8:37; Hag 2:17). For "locusts," see "Locusts in the Ancient Near East" on page 1438.

Locusts devoured your fig and olive trees,[p]
yet you have not returned[q] to me,"
declares the LORD.

4:9 [p]Joel 1:7 [q]Jer 3:10; Hag 2:17

10 "I sent plagues[r] among you
as I did to Egypt.
I killed your young men with the sword,
along with your captured horses.
I filled your nostrils with the stench of your camps,
yet you have not returned to me,"
declares the LORD.[s]

4:10 [r]Ex 9:3; Dt 28:27 [s]Isa 9:13

11 "I overthrew some of you
as I[a] overthrew Sodom and Gomorrah.[t]
You were like a burning stick snatched from the fire,
yet you have not returned to me,"
declares the LORD.

4:11 [t]Ge 19:24; Jer 23:14

12 "Therefore this is what I will do to you, Israel,
and because I will do this to you,
prepare to meet your God, O Israel."

13 He who forms the mountains,[u]
creates the wind,
and reveals his thoughts[v] to man,
he who turns dawn to darkness,
and treads the high places of the earth[w]—
the LORD God Almighty is his name.[x]

4:13 [u]Ps 65:6 [v]Da 2:28 [w]Mic 1:3 [x]Isa 47:4; Am 5:8, 27; 9:6

A Lament and Call to Repentance

5 Hear this word, O house of Israel, this lament[y] I take up concerning you:

5:1 [y]Eze 19:1

2 "Fallen is Virgin[z] Israel,
never to rise again,
deserted in her own land,
with no one to lift her up.[a]"

5:2 [z]Jer 14:17 [a]Jer 50:32; Am 8:14

3 This is what the Sovereign LORD says:

"The city that marches out a thousand strong for Israel
will have only a hundred left;
the town that marches out a hundred strong
will have only ten left.[b]"

5:3 [b]Isa 6:13; Am 6:9

4 This is what the LORD says to the house of Israel:

"Seek me and live;[c]
5 do not seek Bethel,
do not go to Gilgal,[d]
do not journey to Beersheba.[e]
For Gilgal will surely go into exile,
and Bethel will be reduced to nothing.[b][f]"

5:4 [c]Isa 55:3; Jer 29:13

5:5 [d]1Sa 11:14; Am 4:4 [e]Am 8:14 [f]1Sa 7:16

[a] *11* Hebrew *God* [b] *5* Or *grief;* or *wickedness;* Hebrew *aven,* a reference to Beth Aven (a derogatory name for Bethel)

4:11 Sodom and Gomorrah had long since become proverbial for their wickedness and for the divine judgment upon sin (see "The Destruction of Sodom and Gomorrah" on p. 32).
5:1 See "Ancient Near Eastern Laments" on page 1305.
5:2 "Deserted" refers here to a dead body that had been left in an open field—a disgrace and an indignity.
5:5 For "Bethel" and "Gilgal," see the note on 4:4. Beersheba, located in the south of Judah, had evidently become a place of pilgrimage and idolatry (see 8:14; see also "Beersheba" on p. 518).

5:6 [g]Isa 55:6 [h]ver 14 [i]Dt 4:24 [j]Am 3:14

[6] Seek[g] the LORD and live,[h]
or he will sweep through the house of Joseph
like a fire;[i]
it will devour,
and Bethel[j] will have no one to quench it.

5:7 [k]Am 6:12

[7] You who turn justice into bitterness[k]
and cast righteousness to the ground

5:8 [l]Job 9:9 [m]Isa 42:16 [n]Ps 104:20; Am 8:9 [o]Ps 104:6-9; Am 4:13

[8] (he who made the Pleiades and Orion,[l]
who turns blackness into dawn[m]
and darkens day into night,[n]
who calls for the waters of the sea
and pours them out over the face of the land—
the LORD is his name[o]—
[9] he flashes destruction on the stronghold
and brings the fortified city to ruin),[p]
[10] you hate the one who reproves in court[q]
and despise him who tells the truth.[r]

5:9 [p]Mic 5:11
5:10 [q]Isa 29:21 [r]1Ki 22:8

5:11 [s]Am 8:6 [t]Am 3:15 [u]Mic 6:15

[11] You trample on the poor[s]
and force him to give you grain.
Therefore, though you have built stone mansions,[t]
you will not live in them;
though you have planted lush vineyards,
you will not drink their wine.[u]
[12] For I know how many are your offenses
and how great your sins.

You oppress the righteous and take bribes
and you deprive the poor of justice in
the courts.[v]
[13] Therefore the prudent man keeps quiet in
such times,
for the times are evil.

5:12 [v]Isa 5:23; Am 2:6-7

[14] Seek good, not evil,
that you may live.
Then the LORD God Almighty will be with you,
just as you say he is.
[15] Hate evil,[w] love good;
maintain justice in the courts.
Perhaps the LORD God Almighty will have mercy[x]
on the remnant[y] of Joseph.

5:15 [w]Ps 97:10; Ro 12:9 [x]Joel 2:14 [y]Mic 5:7,8

[16] Therefore this is what the Lord, the LORD God Almighty, says:

5:16 [z]Jer 9:17 [a]Joel 1:11

"There will be wailing[z] in all the streets
and cries of anguish in every public square.
The farmers[a] will be summoned to weep
and the mourners to wail.
[17] There will be wailing in all the vineyards,
for I will pass through[b] your midst,"

says the LORD.[c]

5:17 [b]Ex 12:12 [c]Isa 16:10; Jer 48:33

5:6 The "house of Joseph" refers to the northern kingdom of Israel, which was dominated by the tribe of Ephraim, whose members were descended from Joseph's son.

Bethel was the primary religious center of the northern kingdom (see "Bethel" on p. 59 and "The High Place at Dan" on p. 504).

5:10 Legal proceedings were conducted at the city gate (see "The City Gate" on p. 392).

5:16 In ancient funeral processions wailing relatives, often accompanied by hired mourners and musicians (usually fremale), preceded the body to the grave (see also Jer 9:17–18; Mt 9:23).

The Day of the Lord

[18] Woe to you who long
for the day of the LORD![d]
Why do you long for the day of the LORD?
That day will be darkness,[e] not light.[f]
[19] It will be as though a man fled from a lion
only to meet a bear,
as though he entered his house
and rested his hand on the wall
only to have a snake bite him.[g]
[20] Will not the day of the LORD be darkness, not light—
pitch-dark, without a ray of brightness?[h]

[21] "I hate, I despise your religious feasts;[i]
I cannot stand your assemblies.[j]
[22] Even though you bring me burnt offerings and grain offerings,
I will not accept them.
Though you bring choice fellowship offerings,[a]
I will have no regard for them.[k][l]
[23] Away with the noise of your songs!
I will not listen to the music of your harps.[m]
[24] But let justice[n] roll on like a river,
righteousness like a never-failing stream![o]

[25] "Did you bring me sacrifices[p] and offerings
forty years[q] in the desert, O house of Israel?
[26] You have lifted up the shrine of your king,
the pedestal of your idols,
the star of your god[b]—
which you made for yourselves.
[27] Therefore I will send you into exile beyond Damascus,"
says the LORD, whose name is God Almighty.[r]

5:18 [d]Joel 1:15 [e]Joel 2:2 [f]Isa 5:19,30; Jer 30:7
5:19 [g]Job 20:24; Isa 24:17-18; Jer 15:2-3; 48:44
5:20 [h]Isa 13:10; Zep 1:15
5:21 [i]Lev 26:31 [j]Isa 1:11-16
5:22 [k]Am 4:4; Mic 6:6-7 [l]Isa 66:3
5:23 [m]Am 6:5
5:24 [n]Jer 22:3 [o]Mic 6:8
5:25 [p]Isa 43:23 [q]Dt 32:17
5:27 [r]Am 4:13; Ac 7:42-43*

Woe to the Complacent

6

Woe to you[s] who are complacent in Zion,
and to you who feel secure on Mount Samaria,
you notable men of the foremost nation,
to whom the people of Israel come![t]
[2] Go to Calneh[u] and look at it;
go from there to great Hamath,[v]
and then go down to Gath[w] in Philistia.
Are they better off than[x] your two kingdoms?
Is their land larger than yours?
[3] You put off the evil day
and bring near a reign of terror.[y]
[4] You lie on beds inlaid with ivory
and lounge on your couches.

6:1 [s]Lk 6:24 [t]Isa 32:9-11
6:2 [u]Ge 10:10 [v]2Ki 18:34 [w]2Ch 26:6 [x]Na 3:8
6:3 [y]Isa 56:12; Am 9:10

[a] 22 Traditionally *peace offerings* [b] 26 Or *lifted up Sakkuth your king / and Kaiwan your idols, / your star-gods*; Septuagint *lifted up the shrine of Molech / and the star of your god Rephan, / their idols*

5:18 For "the day of the LORD," see the note on Joel 1:15.
5:23 See "Ancient Musical Instruments" on page 797.
6:1 Samaria, Israel's capital city founded by King Omri, was situated at a crossroads near the main north-south road through the highlands of Israel, 34 miles (nearly 55 km) north of Jerusalem. Situated on a high hill, the city dominated the surrounding countryside.
6:2 Calneh and Hamath, cities located in northern Aram (Syria), had fallen in Jeroboam's campaign (see 2Ki 14:25,28), and the wall of Gath had been broken down by Uzziah (2Ch 26:6).
6:4 See "The Nimrud Ivories" on page 1455, as well as the note on 3:15.

The meat of lambs was considered a delicacy among the ancient Hebrews (Dt 32:14; 2Sa 12:3–6). Meat was scarce, and the killing of a lamb would have marked an important occasion. Lambs had been used for sacrifices from the earliest times (Ge 4:4; 22:7).

6:4 [z]Eze 34:2-3; Am 3:12
6:5 [a]Isa 5:12; Am 5:23 [b]1Ch 15:16
6:6 [c]Am 2:8 [d]Eze 9:4

You dine on choice lambs
and fattened calves.[z]
5 You strum away on your harps[a] like David
and improvise on musical instruments.[b]
6 You drink wine[c] by the bowlful
and use the finest lotions,
but you do not grieve[d] over the ruin of Joseph.
7 Therefore you will be among the first to go into exile;
your feasting and lounging will end.

The LORD Abhors the Pride of Israel

6:8 [e]Ge 22:16; Heb 6:13 [f]Lev 26:30 [g]Ps 47:4 [h]Am 4:2 [i]Dt 32:19

8 The Sovereign LORD has sworn by himself[e]—the LORD God Almighty declares:

"I abhor[f] the pride of Jacob[g]
and detest his fortresses;
I will deliver up[h] the city
and everything in it.[i]"

6:5 See "Ancient Musical Instruments" on page 797.
6:6 The use of perfume in the form of ointment or impregnated oil was a Middle Eastern practice long before it spread to the Mediterranean world. In all probability perfume was originally used for ceremonial purposes, first religious and then secular, and became a personal habit with the growing sophistication of society and the need for deodorants in hot lands. So universal was the practice that its suspension was viewed as an accepted sign of mourning (Dt 28:40; Ru 3:3; 2Sa 14:2; Da 10:3; Mic 6:15).
6:8 "Fortresses" may refer to the palace-fortresses that were the status symbols of Israel's rich and famous—as well as to the citadels that were a tribute to Israel's past military victories (v. 13).

ANCIENT TEXTS AND ARTIFACTS

The Nimrud Ivories

AMOS 6 Amos 6:4 spoke of "beds inlaid with ivory" and attested to the availability of ivory in Israel, as well as to the high esteem in which it was held. Indeed, throughout the Near East elephant ivory was treasured as a medium for artwork. A large collection of carved ivories was discovered in the palace area of Nimrud, an **Assyrian**[1] city on the eastern bank of the Tigris. These ivory carvings were artistic masterpieces in the form of human figures, animals (both real and mythological), plants and abstractions. Many of these carved pieces were originally covered in gold. On the other hand, many of the objects were used for practical purposes. For example, one ivory piece was the handle of a fly-whisk or a fan, and another carving was used as a blinder for a horse.

In 1961 fragments of an ivory plaque were unearthed at Nimrud. Surprisingly, in light of how far removed this site is from Israel, this plaque had a Hebrew inscription. Because of the broken condition of the find, a complete and certain translation is impossible. Even so, the plaque appears to contain the phrases, "the great king" (evidently referring to the king of Assyria; 2Ki 18:19) and "may **Yahweh** shatter." The plaque dates to around 750 B.C. and was either part of the tribute given to the Assyrians or taken as booty by the Assyrian army after the Assyrians had destroyed **Samaria** in 722 B.C.[1]

Examples from the Nimrud Ivories
Preserving Bible Times; © Dr. James C. Martin; permission of The British Museum

[1]See "Hoshea, King of Israel, and Shalmaneser V, King of Assyria" on page 556 and "The Samaria Ivories" on page 1449.

[9]If ten[j] men are left in one house, they too will die. [10]And if a relative who is to burn the bodies[k] comes
to carry them out of the house and asks anyone still hiding there, "Is anyone with you?" and he says, "No,"
then he will say, "Hush![l] We must not mention the name of the LORD."

> [11]For the LORD has given the command,
> and he will smash the great house[m] into pieces
> and the small house into bits.[n]
>
> [12]Do horses run on the rocky crags?
> Does one plow there with oxen?
> But you have turned justice into poison[o]
> and the fruit of righteousness into bitterness[p]—
> [13]you who rejoice in the conquest of Lo Debar[a]
> and say, "Did we not take Karnaim[b] by our own strength?[q]"
>
> [14]For the LORD God Almighty declares,
> "I will stir up a nation[r] against you, O house of Israel,
> that will oppress you all the way
> from Lebo[c] Hamath[s] to the valley of the Arabah.[t]"

6:9 [j]Am 5:3
6:10 [k]1Sa 31:12 [l]Am 8:3
6:11 [m]Am 3:15 [n]Isa 55:11
6:12 [o]Hos 10:4 [p]Am 5:7
6:13 [q]Job 8:15; Isa 28:14-15
6:14 [r]Jer 5:15 [s]1Ki 8:65 [t]Am 3:11

Locusts, Fire and a Plumb Line

7 This is what the Sovereign LORD showed me:[u] He was preparing swarms of locusts[v] after the king's
share had been harvested and just as the second crop was coming up. [2]When they had stripped the
land clean,[w] I cried out, "Sovereign LORD, forgive! How can Jacob survive?[x] He is so small![y]"

[3]So the LORD relented.[z]

"This will not happen," the LORD said.[a]

[4]This is what the Sovereign LORD showed me: The Sovereign LORD was calling for judgment by fire;[b]
it dried up the great deep and devoured[c] the land. [5]Then I cried out, "Sovereign LORD, I beg you, stop! How
can Jacob survive? He is so small![d]"

[6]So the LORD relented.[e]

"This will not happen either," the Sovereign LORD said.

[7]This is what he showed me: The Lord was standing by a wall that had been built true to plumb, with
a plumb line in his hand. [8]And the LORD asked me, "What do you see,[f] Amos?[g]"

"A plumb line,[h]" I replied.

Then the Lord said, "Look, I am setting a plumb line among my people Israel; I will spare them no
longer.[i]

> [9]"The high places of Isaac will be destroyed
> and the sanctuaries[j] of Israel will be ruined;
> with my sword I will rise against the house of Jeroboam.[k]"

Amos and Amaziah

[10]Then Amaziah the priest of Bethel[l] sent a message to Jeroboam[m] king of Israel: "Amos is raising a

7:1 [u]Am 8:1 [v]Joel 1:4
7:2 [w]Ex 10:15 [x]Isa 37:4 [y]Eze 11:13
7:3 [z]Dt 32:36; Jer 26:19; Jnh 3:10 [a]Hos 11:8
7:4 [b]Isa 66:16 [c]Dt 32:22
7:5 [d]ver 1-2; Joel 2:17
7:6 [e]Jnh 3:10
7:8 [f]Jer 1:11,13 [g]Isa 28:17; La 2:8; Am 8:2 [h]2Ki 21:13 [i]Jer 15:6; Eze 7:2-9
7:9 [j]Lev 26:31 [k]2Ki 15:9; Isa 63:18; Hos 10:8
7:10 [l]1Ki 12:32 [m]2Ki 14:23

[a] 13 Lo Debar means *nothing.* [b] 13 Karnaim means *horns; horn* here symbolizes strength. [c] 14 Or *from the entrance to*

6:10 The reference to burning the dead bodies may actually be to lighting a memorial fire in honor of the dead, as cremation was not generally practiced (see the note on Jer 34:5).

6:12 The ancient plow, which scratched the surface but did not turn over the soil, was thus a "scratch plow." It consisted of a branched stick with the larger branch, usually the trunk of a small tree, hitched to the animals that pulled it, the other branch braced and terminating in the share, which was at first simply the sharpened end of the branch but was later a metal point. The plow was ordinarily drawn by a yoke of oxen (Job 1:14).

6:13 Lo Debar and Karnaim, cities in Transjordan, may have been regained from Hazael by Jehoash (2Ki 10:32–33; 13:25) or by Jeroboam II (see 2Ki 14:25), then taken by the Assyrians soon after Amos's day (2Ki 15:29)—beginning the sequence of events that would lead to the loss of all the territory conquered by Jeroboam II.

6:14 "From Lebo Hamath to the valley of the Arabah" encompassed an area from the Orontes River in northern Lebanon to the Dead Sea—thus the whole land (see 2Ki 14:25). For information on the Arabah, see "The Geography of Ezekiel 47" on page 1378.

7:1 See "Locusts in the Ancient Near East" on page 1438.

The "king's share" was apparently taken from the earlier crop as payment for the royal taxes. The "second crop" referred to further growth in the fields after the grains and the early hay had been harvested. The flocks and herds pastured on these crops until the summer dry season halted all growth.

7:2 See "Famine in the Ancient Near East" on page 70.

7:4 The "great deep" probably refers to the Mediterranean Sea.

7:9 See "The High Places" on page 1318.

7:10 [n]Jer 38:4 [o]Jer 26:8-11

conspiracy[n] against you in the very heart of Israel. The land cannot bear all his words.[o] 11 For this is what Amos is saying:

"'Jeroboam will die by the sword,
and Israel will surely go into exile,
away from their native land.'"

7:11 "Jeroboam" refers to Jeroboam's "house" (v. 9)—his dynasty. Jeroboam died naturally (2Ki 14:29), but his son and successor, Zechariah (2Ki 15:8), was assassinated (2Ki 15:10).

Prophets in the Bible and Pagan Nations

AMOS 7 Prophecy was a common feature in the world of the Old Testament. Men and women who were called by God to speak on his behalf were known by a variety of Hebrew terms that may be variously translated as "prophet [prophetess]," "seer," "visionary" and "man of God." Since there was no substantial difference among these terms, the **Septuagint** often translates "prophet," "seer" and "visionary" with the single Greek word for "prophet." Early prophets in Israel seem to have been connected to a prophetic group (e.g., "the company of the prophets" who followed Elisha; 2Ki 2:3) while later prophets appear to have been more independent. Archaeological confirmation of prophetic activity in Israel is seen in the Lachish **ostracon** that speaks of a certain person called the "prophet."[1]

Hebrew text of Amos; Iraq, c. A.D. 1000

© The Schøyen Collection; photography courtesy of Mr. Martin Schøyen

Yet prophecy was not a phenomenon unique to Israel, as the Bible itself attests (cf. "prophets of Baal" and "prophets of Asherah" in 1Ki 18:19). Ancient texts have yielded numerous examples of pagan prophets:

✣ The archive from the city of **Mari** on the Middle Euphrates,[2] dated to the mid-eighteenth century B.C., speaks of a number of men and women who addressed the king on behalf of the gods. Like the Biblical terms for prophets, multiple titles were given to these individuals at Mari, including on one occasion the term *nabu*, the **Akkadian** equivalent of the Hebrew *navi* ("prophet"). While some of the Mari prophets were connected to religious sites as priests or servants of a temple, many appear to have been ordinary people from various walks of life. Ecstatic behavior, seen among Biblical prophets in Samuel's day (1Sa 19:24) and later in Ezekiel's (Eze 4:4), was also evident at Mari.

✣ An ecstatic seer called a "man of god" is attested in the fourteenth century B.C. **Hittite** Prayer of Mursilis.[3]

✣ The eleventh-century B.C. Egyptian story of Wen Amon tells of a page in the court of the king of Byblos[4] who was seemingly possessed by a god during an offertory ritual, as evidenced by his ecstatic behavior.

✣ An inscription from the eighth-century B.C. Syrian state of Hamath recounts the story of a man named Zakir praying to Baal for his besieged city and subsequently receiving assurance of divine assistance through seers and other inspired people.

✣ Late eighth-century B.C. plaster texts from Deir Allah speak of a certain Balaam, who is said to be "a seer of the gods" and who, later in the story, sees a vision from the god El.[5]

As God's spokesman in 7:14, Amos eschewed any prophetic title, perhaps because of unwanted associations with the term in his day. As seen in so many other parts of Scripture, the words of Amos enforce the reality that God uses everyday people to carry out his will.

[1]See "The Lachish Ostraca" on page 1252. [2]See "Mari" on page 54. [3]See "Plague Prayers of Mursilis II" on page 477. [4]See "Byblos" on page 1349. [5]See "Balaam, the Son of Beor" on page 229.

12 Then Amaziah said to Amos, "Get out, you seer! Go back to the land of Judah. Earn your bread there
and do your prophesying there.[p] 13 Don't prophesy anymore at Bethel, because this is the king's sanctu-
ary and the temple of the kingdom.[q]"
14 Amos answered Amaziah, "I was neither a prophet[r] nor a prophet's son, but I was a shepherd, and
I also took care of sycamore-fig trees. 15 But the LORD took me from tending the flock[s] and said to me, 'Go,
prophesy to my people Israel.'[t] 16 Now then, hear the word of the LORD. You say,

" 'Do not prophesy against[u] Israel,
and stop preaching against the house of Isaac.'

17 "Therefore this is what the LORD says:

" 'Your wife will become a prostitute[v] in the city,
and your sons and daughters will fall by the sword.
Your land will be measured and divided up,
and you yourself will die in a pagan[a] country.
And Israel will certainly go into exile,
away from their native land.[w]' "

A Basket of Ripe Fruit

8 This is what the Sovereign LORD showed me: a basket of ripe fruit. 2 "What do you see,[x] Amos?[y]" he
asked.

"A basket of ripe fruit," I answered.

Then the LORD said to me, "The time is ripe for my people Israel; I will spare them no longer.[z]
3 "In that day," declares the Sovereign LORD, "the songs in the temple will turn to wailing.[b][a] Many, many
bodies—flung everywhere! Silence![b]"

4 Hear this, you who trample the needy
and do away with the poor[c] of the land,[d]

5 saying,

"When will the New Moon be over
that we may sell grain,
and the Sabbath be ended
that we may market wheat?"—
skimping the measure,
boosting the price
and cheating with dishonest scales,[e]
6 buying the poor with silver
and the needy for a pair of sandals,
selling even the sweepings with the wheat.[f]

7 The LORD has sworn by the Pride of Jacob:[g] "I will never forget[h] anything they have done.

8 "Will not the land tremble[i] for this,
and all who live in it mourn?
The whole land will rise like the Nile;
it will be stirred up and then sink
like the river of Egypt.[j]

7:12 [p]Mt 8:34
7:13 [q]Am 2:12; Ac 4:18
7:14 [r]2Ki 2:5; 4:38
7:15 [s]2Sa 7:8 [t]Jer 7:1-2; Eze 2:3-4
7:16 [u]Eze 20:46; Mic 2:6
7:17 [v]Hos 4:13 [w]2Ki 17:6; Eze 4:13; Hos 9:3
8:2 [x]Jer 24:3 [y]Am 7:8 [z]Eze 7:2-9
8:3 [a]Am 5:16 [b]Am 5:23; 6:10
8:4 [c]Pr 30:14 [d]Ps 14:4; Am 2:7
8:5 [e]2Ki 4:23; Ne 13:15-16; Hos 12:7; Mic 6:10-11
8:6 [f]Am 2:6
8:7 [g]Am 6:8 [h]Hos 8:13
8:8 [i]Hos 4:3 [j]Ps 18:7; Jer 46:8; Am 9:5

[a] 17 Hebrew *an unclean* [b] 3 Or *"the temple singers will wail*

7:12 For "seer," see "Prophets in the Bible and Pagan Nations" on page 1457.

7:14 The Hebrew word here translated "shepherd"—a term not found elsewhere in the Old Testament—is related to a word for "cattle," suggesting that Amos may also have tended cattle.

Sycamore-fig trees are large trees that yield fig-like fruit. To ensure good fruit, the gardener had to slit the top of each fig—which may be the procedure referred to by the obscure Hebrew word here rendered "took care of."

7:17 With the exile of Amaziah, the death of their children and the loss of the family estate, Amaziah's wife would be reduced to prostitution in order to survive (see "Prostitution in the Ancient World" on p. 284).

8:5 Commerce ceased on the Sabbath and during religious festivals (see Nu 28:9–15; 2Ki 4:23).

For "dishonest scales," see the notes on Proverbs 11:1 and 16:11; see also "Weights and Measures" on page 1459.

8:8 Because of the heavy seasonal rains in Ethiopia, the Nile in Egypt annually rose by as much as 25 feet (8 m), flooding the whole area except for the towns and villages situated above the valley. Its waters carried a large amount of rich soil, which was thus deposited on the land—perhaps referred to by the words "stirred up."

[9]"In that day," declares the Sovereign LORD,

"I will make the sun go down at noon
and darken the earth in broad daylight.[k]
[10]I will turn your religious feasts into mourning
and all your singing into weeping.

8:9 [k]Job 5:14; Isa 59:9-10; Jer 15:9; Am 5:8; Mic 3:6

8:9 For "that day," see the note on Joel 1:15.
8:10 An only son represented the future of his entire family, so his death would have caused intense mourning (see "Sackcloth and Ashes: Rituals of Lamentation" on p. 820).

Weights and Measures

AMOS 8 Weights in the ancient world were crafted of either metal or semiprecious stones, often carved in the shapes of ducks, lions or turtles. They had a flat base and were inscribed with their weight standard. The law called for standardized weights and measures (Lev 19:35–36), and yet, of the weights that have been found, very few of the same denomination are identical. It is important to note that ancient weights were never able to achieve the precision of modern standards, due in part to the method of production, as well as to standards that varied at different times and in different regions. Thus, they must be thought of as commonly accepted estimates. Those who knowingly used dishonest weights and balances came under prophetic critique for defrauding God and their fellow human beings (Am 8:5–6; Mic 6:11; Mal 3:8–10).

The talent, the largest standard weight used for gold, silver, iron and bronze (1Ki 10:14; 2Ki 23:33), weighed approximately 75 pounds (34 kg).[1] The mina, .017 of a talent, most likely was incorporated as a **postexilic**[2] measure and was made infamous in the judgment of Belshazzar, who was "weighed" by God and found to be deficient (Da 5:27).[2] The shekel, derived from the verb "to weigh," was the primary weight unit of ancient Israel, yet its valuation displays a certain degree of variability. The common shekel was approximately .41 ounces or 11.6 grams, the royal shekel about .46 ounces or 13 grams (2Sa 14:26) and the sanctuary shekel about .35 ounces or 9.9 grams (Lev 5:15). Subdivisions of the shekel include the beka, valued at half a sanctuary shekel (Ex 38:26), and the gerah, valued at .05 of a sanctuary shekel (Ex 30:13).

Since height and length were measured in ancient cultures by laying the forearm or hand upon an object, linear measures were named after the parts of the arm by which they were counted. The cubit, or "forearm," was the distance from the elbow to the tip of the middle finger and was used to measure height, depth and distance (Jos 3:4; 1Sa 17:4; Zec 5:2). While the Bible records varying cubit standards in the Hebrew system of measurement, the "ordinary cubit" was approximately 17.5 inches (44.5 cm). Other measures in decreasing size were: the span (Ex 39:9), counted as the breadth of an outstretched hand from thumb to little finger and equaling half a cubit; the palm (1Ki 7:26), the width of the base of the hand; and the width of the finger (Jer 52:21).

Capacity measures throughout the ancient Near East bore common names and were essentially similar. The homer, a "donkey load," was equivalent to a cor, both equaling an average of 158.5 quarts (150 l) and used for cereals such as wheat and barley.[3] The ephah, measuring .10 of a homer, was a vessel large enough to hold a person (Zec 5:6–8). An omer, meaning "small bowl," was equivalent to .10 of an ephah and identified as the daily bread ration (Ex 16:32, 36). The bath[3] and hin[3] were the two major liquid measures used for water, wine and oil. The bath was the liquid equivalent of the ephah (2Ch 2:10; Isa 5:10), while the hin, named after a measuring vessel, was equal to .1666 of a bath (6.34 qts or 6 l).

[1]See "Weights and Measures" on page 1459 in the back of this Bible. [2]See "Nabonidus and Belshazzar" on page 1394. [3]A different assessment of the cor is reflected in the table of Weights and Measures on page 2079 in the back of this Bible. It is difficult at this time to determine which of the two figures—220 liters or 150 liters—is correct, and the standard may have varied from time to time. Differing assessments also apply to the bath and the hin.

THE UNITY OF AMOS

AMOS 9 Some scholars have argued that the latter part of Amos 9 is stylistically inferior to the rest of the book and that the book of Amos is actually a haphazard collection of writings from various authors that was compiled many years after the time of the prophet (Amos himself lived during the eighth century B.C.). In particular, many scholars believe that Amos did not write 9:11–15. However, this perspective denies the inherent unity that permeates the book. The linguistic and structural elements of Amos create a solid, cohesive work of literature. Indications of the book's integration are as follows:

◆ Precise structure allows the work to be divided into logical sections, as outlined below (see also the briefer outline in the introduction):

Amos 1–2 describes judgment on eight nations with the pattern, "For three sins . . . , even for four . . ."

3:1–15 has an introduction and three parts; each begins with a lion metaphor (vv. 4,8,12).

4:1–13 describes deficits in Israel: The women lacked compassion, the shrines lacked holiness and the land lacked rain and crops.

8:7—9:15 is held together by parallels that not only show this as coherent text but imply that 9:11–15 belongs with the preceding text.

8:7–8: Yahweh swears an oath not to forget Israel's sins (v. 7); the land will rise [heave] like the Nile (v. 8).

8:9–14: "In that day" (v. 9) there will be darkness and famine for Israel (vv. 10–14).

9:1–10: Yahweh stands on the altar and makes a solemn declaration to pursue Israelites wherever they flee (vv. 1–4; this parallels God's oath in 8:7) and says that Samaria will rise like the Nile (vv. 5–10; this parallels v. 8:8).

9:11–15: "In that day" (v. 11; this parallels 8:9) there will be deliverance for Israel and abundant harvest (9:13; this parallels the famine in 8:11).

◆ The book employs *inclusion*, a literary device whereby the first and last sections (in this case, chs. 1 and 9) share several literary connections. For example,

Amos 1:2 refers to Carmel, which is not mentioned again until 9:3.

Judah, "David's fallen tent" (v. 11), would be restored and rebuilt. This parallels the mention of "Zion" (Jerusalem) in 1:2.

Other parallels in vocabulary, literary technique and theme between chapter 9 and the rest of the book demonstrate that the text of Amos is indeed unified linguistically and artistically from beginning to end.

[1]See "Famine in the Ancient Near East" on page 70].

AN ALTERNATIVE OUTLINE FOR THE BOOK OF AMOS (see also introduction)

1:3—2:16	Judgment on eight nations ("For three sins . . . , even for four . . .")
1:3–5	Damascus
1:6–8	Gaza
1:9–10	Tyre
1:11–12	Edom
1:13–15	Ammon
2:1–3	Moab
2:4–5	Judah
2:6–16	Israel
3:1–15	The lion roars.
3:1–2	Introduction
3:3–7	Rhetorical question: Will the lion roar when it has no prey?
3:8–11	Answer: The lion has roared, and Israel is the prey of the nations.
3:12–15	Aftermath: Israel will be consumed like a lamb in a lion's mouth.
4:1–13	All is wrong in Israel.
4:1–3	The women are not compassionate.
4:4–5	The shrines are not holy.
4:6–13	The land is not fruitful.
5:1—6:14	Decadence and destruction
5:1–3	*A.** Lamentation over the house of Israel
5:4–7	*B.* False religious hopes
5:8–9	*C.* Yahweh is God over heaven and the stars.
5:10–15	*D.* The rich oppress the poor and take vineyards for wine.
5:16–17	*A.* Lamentation in the city and the vineyards
5:18–24	*B.* False religious hopes
5:25–27	*C.* Yahweh against the idols, the "star of your god"
6:1–7	*D.* They recline at feasts and drink wine.
6:8–14	Yahweh swears that Israel will be desolate.
7:1—8:6	Visions of judgment and false religion
7:1–9	*A.* Visions of destruction and a plumb line
7:10–17	*B.* A false priest
8:1–3	*A.* A vision of ripe fruit
8:4–6	*B.* False Sabbath observance
8:7—9:15	The day of Yahweh
8:7–8	*A.* Yahweh swears an oath not to forget (7). *B.* The land will rise like the Nile (8).
8:9–14	*B.* "In that day" there will be darkness and famine for Israel.
9:1–10	*B.* Yahweh stands on the altar and makes a solemn declaration to pursue the Israelites wherever they flee (1–4). Also, Samaria will rise like the Nile (5–10).
9:11–15	*B.* "In that day" there will be deliverance for Israel and an abundant harvest.

*Italicized letters demonstrate parallel structure.

Prepared by Duane A. Garrett

8:10 [l]Jer 48:37 [m]Jer 6:26; Zec 12:10 [n]Eze 7:18

I will make all of you wear sackcloth[l]
and shave your heads.
I will make that time like mourning for an only son[m]
and the end of it like a bitter day.[n]

[11] "The days are coming," declares the Sovereign LORD,
"when I will send a famine through the land—
not a famine of food or a thirst for water,
but a famine of hearing the words of the LORD.[o]
[12] Men will stagger from sea to sea
and wander from north to east,
searching for the word of the LORD,
but they will not find it.[p]

8:11 [o]1Sa 3:1; 2Ch 15:3; Eze 7:26
8:12 [p]Eze 20:3, 31

[13] "In that day

"the lovely young women and strong young men
will faint because of thirst.[q]
[14] They who swear by the shame[a] of Samaria,
or say, 'As surely as your god lives, O Dan,'[r]
or, 'As surely as the god[b] of Beersheba[s] lives'—
they will fall,
never to rise again.[t]"

8:13 [q]Isa 41:17; Hos 2:3
8:14 [r]1Ki 12:29 [s]Am 5:5 [t]Am 5:2

Israel to Be Destroyed

9 I saw the Lord standing by the altar, and he said:

"Strike the tops of the pillars
so that the thresholds shake.
Bring them down on the heads[u] of all the people;
those who are left I will kill with the sword.
Not one will get away,
none will escape.
[2] Though they dig down to the depths of the grave,[c][v]
from there my hand will take them.
Though they climb up to the heavens,[w]
from there I will bring them down.[x]
[3] Though they hide themselves on the top of Carmel,[y]
there I will hunt them down and seize them.[z]
Though they hide from me at the bottom of the sea,
there I will command the serpent to bite them.[a]
[4] Though they are driven into exile by their enemies,
there I will command the sword[b] to slay them.
I will fix my eyes upon them
for evil[c] and not for good.[d]"[e]

9:1 [u]Ps 68:21
9:2 [v]Ps 139:8 [w]Jer 51:53 [x]Ob 1:4
9:3 [y]Am 1:2 [z]Ps 139:8-10 [a]Jer 16:16-17
9:4 [b]Lev 26:33; Eze 5:12 [c]Jer 21:10 [d]Jer 39:16 [e]Jer 44:11

[5] The Lord, the LORD Almighty,
he who touches the earth and it melts,[f]
and all who live in it mourn—
the whole land rises like the Nile,
then sinks like the river of Egypt[g]—

9:5 [f]Ps 46:2; Mic 1:4 [g]Am 8:8

[a] 14 Or *by Ashima*; or *by the idol*   [b] 14 Or *power*   [c] 2 Hebrew *to Sheol*

8:12 The phrases "sea to sea" and "north to east" encompass the entire land of Israel, from the Mediterranean to the Dead Sea and even across the Jordan River through the Transjordan.

8:14 Dan and Beersheba were cities that not only marked the northern and southern limits of Israel (see the note on Jdg 20:1) but were also noted as sites where pagan shrines had been erected (see 1Ki 12:29, Am 5:5; see also "The High Place at Dan" on p. 504 and "Beersheba" on p. 518).

9:3 For "the top of Carmel," see the note on 1:2.

The "serpent" refers to a fierce monster of the sea from pagan mythology (see the note on Ps 74:13–15).

[6]he who builds his lofty palace[a] in the heavens
and sets its foundation[b] on the earth,
who calls for the waters of the sea
and pours them out over the face of the land—
the LORD is his name.[h]

[7]"Are not you Israelites
the same to me as the Cushites[c]?"[i]
declares the LORD.
"Did I not bring Israel up from Egypt,
the Philistines from Caphtor[d][j]
and the Arameans from Kir?[k]

[8]"Surely the eyes of the Sovereign LORD
are on the sinful kingdom.
I will destroy it
from the face of the earth—
yet I will not totally destroy
the house of Jacob,"
declares the LORD.[l]

[9]"For I will give the command,
and I will shake the house of Israel
among all the nations
as grain[m] is shaken in a sieve,[n]
and not a pebble will reach the ground.

[10]All the sinners among my people
will die by the sword,
all those who say,
'Disaster will not overtake or meet us.'[o]

Israel's Restoration

[11]"In that day I will restore
David's fallen tent.
I will repair its broken places,
restore its ruins,
and build it as it used to be,[p]

[12]so that they may possess the remnant of Edom[q]
and all the nations that bear my name,[e][r]"
declares the LORD, who will do these things.[s]

[13]"The days are coming," declares the LORD,

"when the reaper will be overtaken by the plowman[t]
and the planter by the one treading grapes.
New wine will drip from the mountains
and flow from all the hills.[u]

[14]I will bring back my exiled[f] people Israel;
they will rebuild the ruined cities[v] and live in them.

9:6 [h]Ps 104:1-3, 5-6,13; Am 5:8
9:7 [i]Isa 20:4; 43:3 [j]Dt 2:23; Jer 47:4 [k]2Ki 16:9; Isa 22:6; Am 1:5; 2:10
9:8 [l]Jer 44:27
9:9 [m]Lk 22:31 [n]Isa 30:28
9:10 [o]Am 6:3
9:11 [p]Ps 80:12
9:12 [q]Nu 24:18 [r]Isa 43:7 [s]Ac 15:16-17*
9:13 [t]Lev 26:5 [u]Joel 3:18
9:14 [v]Isa 61:4

[a] 6 The meaning of the Hebrew for this phrase is uncertain. [b] 6 The meaning of the Hebrew for this word is uncertain.
[c] 7 That is, people from the upper Nile region [d] 7 That is, Crete [e] 12 Hebrew; Septuagint *so that the remnant of men / and all the nations that bear my name may seek ⌞the Lord⌟* [f] 14 Or *will restore the fortunes of my*

9:7 The Cushites were a dark-skinned people who lived south of Egypt (see "Cush" on p. 1519).

Caphtor is Crete, one of many islands in the Mediterranean believed to have been the original homeland of the Philistines (see "The Ekron Inscriptions of Akhayus" on p. 428; see also the note on Zep 2:5).

For "Kir," see the note on Amos 1:5.

9:9 Grain was sifted with a sieve to remove any foreign matter, such as small stones or refuse gathered with it when it was scooped up from the ground. Only the grain dropped through, while the refuse was screened out and discarded. (For information on the harvesting process, see the note on Ru 1:22.)

9:11 This verse is regarded in the Jewish Talmud as Messianic.

9:12 See "Edom" on page 1467.

9:14 [w]Jer 30:18; 31:28; Eze 28:25-26
9:15 [x]Isa 60:21 [y]Jer 24:6; Eze 34:25-28; 37:12,25

They will plant vineyards and drink their wine;
they will make gardens and eat their fruit.[w]
15 I will plant[x] Israel in their own land,
never again to be uprooted
from the land I have given them,"

says the LORD your God.[y]

INTRODUCTION TO

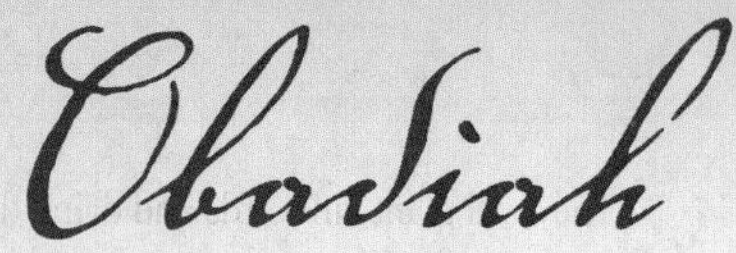

AUTHOR, PLACE AND DATE OF WRITING

We know nothing about Obadiah beyond his name, nor is the place of the book's composition certain. The name itself (meaning "servant of Yahweh") was fairly common, and the prophet Obadiah was clearly not the Obadiah of 1 Kings 18:3–16.

Obadiah did not specify that his message came at the time of any specific king or event. On the other hand, Obadiah 11–14 indicates that a major calamity had recently struck Judah and that the Edomites had capitalized on Judah's troubles to their own advantage. Some scholars have proposed that this event was some preexilic setback that Judah had endured (e.g., 2Ch 21:16–17), but common sense and a broad consensus suggest that the calamity was in fact the fall of Jerusalem in 586 B.C. From the Nabonidus Chronicle, an important Akkadian source for the history of the Neo-Babylonian Empire (now housed in the British Museum), we learn that Edom itself fell in 553 B.C. to Nabonidus of Babylon. This combination of factors suggests that Obadiah was written between 586 and 553 B.C.

AUDIENCE

Obadiah was written to the people of Judah about the Edomites (descendants of Esau), condemning them for their treachery and violence toward the people of Judah, as well as for their arrogance and indifference toward God.

CULTURAL FACTS AND HIGHLIGHTS

Obadiah represents the culmination of prolonged tensions between Israel and Edom. Conflict between these nations dated back to the patriarchal period, when their respective ancestors, the twin brothers Esau and Jacob, had been at odds, and throughout their history the two nations had fought frequently (Nu 20:14–21; 1Sa 14:47; 1Ki 11:14; Isa 34:5). For all that, the people of Judah felt that the hostility shown them by Edom at what was possibly the lowest moment in their history was cruel and unjustified. The fact that God had rejected Esau (Ge 25:23; Mal 1:2–3; Ro 9:13) in no way excused Edom's disdain for Israel. Obadiah assured his readers that Edom's callousness and opportunism would not escape judgment, as indeed it did not.

The Old Testament contains other prophecies against Edom (Jer 49:7–22; La 4:21–22; Eze 25:12–14; 35:1–15), but Obadiah is the only book dedicated entirely to this purpose.

TIMELINE

AS YOU READ

Consider Obadiah's prophetic statements about the coming deliverance and restoration of God's people in light of the book of Revelation, which informs believers that, while sometimes it appears that evil has the upper hand, Christ's certain return will result in the ultimate victory of righteousness.

DID YOU KNOW?

- Edom's arrogance was grounded in its virtually impregnable mountain strongholds (v. 3).
- The Edomites safeguarded their wealth—accumulated from trade—in vaults in the rocks (v. 6).
- Edom, particularly Teman, was known for its wise men. Eliphaz, one of Job's three friends, was a Temanite (v. 8).

THEMES

The book of Obadiah includes the following themes:

1. *Judgment for Edom.* This briefest of Old Testament books assured God's people that God would punish those who abused them.

2. *Deliverance and restoration for Israel.* Obadiah teaches that God is sovereign over all nations. Although the enemies of God's people may have experienced momentary glimpses of glory, they would ultimately be defeated by God and their lands given to his people (vv. 19–21).

OUTLINE

I. Title and Introduction (1)
II. The Doom of Edom (2–14)
III. Edom in the Day of the Lord (15–21)

[1]The vision of Obadiah.

This is what the Sovereign LORD says about Edom[a]—

We have heard a message from the LORD:
An envoy[b] was sent to the nations to say,
"Rise, and let us go against her for battle"[c]—

[2]"See, I will make you small among the nations;
you will be utterly despised.
[3]The pride[d] of your heart has deceived you,
you who live in the clefts of the rocks[a]
and make your home on the heights,
you who say to yourself,
'Who can bring me down to the ground?'[e]
[4]Though you soar like the eagle
and make your nest[f] among the stars,
from there I will bring you down,"[g]
declares the LORD.[h]

[5]"If thieves came to you,
if robbers in the night—
Oh, what a disaster awaits you—
would they not steal only as much as they wanted?
If grape pickers came to you,
would they not leave a few grapes?[i]
[6]But how Esau will be ransacked,
his hidden treasures pillaged!
[7]All your allies[j] will force you to the border;
your friends will deceive and overpower you;
those who eat your bread[k] will set a trap for you,[b]
but you will not detect it.

[8]"In that day," declares the LORD,
"will I not destroy[l] the wise men of Edom,
men of understanding in the mountains of Esau?
[9]Your warriors, O Teman,[m] will be terrified,
and everyone in Esau's mountains
will be cut down in the slaughter.
[10]Because of the violence[n] against your brother Jacob,[o]
you will be covered with shame;
you will be destroyed forever.[p]
[11]On the day you stood aloof
while strangers carried off his wealth
and foreigners entered his gates
and cast lots[q] for Jerusalem,
you were like one of them.

1:1 [a]Isa 63:1-6; Jer 49:7-22; Eze 25:12-14; Am 1:11-12 [b]Isa 18:2 [c]Jer 6:4-5
1:3 [d]Isa 16:6 [e]Isa 14:13-15; Rev 18:7
1:4 [f]Hab 2:9 [g]Isa 14:13 [h]Job 20:6
1:5 [i]Dt 24:21
1:7 [j]Jer 30:14 [k]Ps 41:9
1:8 [l]Job 5:12; Isa 29:14
1:9 [m]Ge 36:11,34
1:10 [n]Joel 3:19 [o]Ps 137:7; Am 1:11-12 [p]Eze 35:9
1:11 [q]Na 3:10

[a] 3 Or *of Sela* [b] 7 The meaning of the Hebrew for this clause is uncertain.

1–7 For the Nabateans (alluded to but not named in these verses), see the note on Malachi 1:1–7. See also "Aretas IV of Nabatea and Petra" on page 1898.
1 See "Edom" on page 1467.
3 Edom's arrogance was grounded in its location "on the heights." Sela (perhaps the later Petra), the capital of Edom, was located some 50 miles (80 km) south of the southern end of the Dead Sea. Situated on a rocky plateau towering 1,000 feet (305 m) above the surrounding landscape, it was a natural fortress.
6 The ancient Greek historian Diodorus Siculus indicated that the Edomites safeguarded their wealth—accumulated from trade—in vaults in the rocks.
8 For "that day," see the note on Joel 1:15.
Edom, particularly Teman, was known for its wise men (see "The Sage" on p. 1025). Eliphaz, one of Job's three friends, was a Temanite (see the note on Job 2:11).
"Esau" is another name for Edom.
9 Teman means "south," and the name probably refers to Edom as the southland. Some, however, identify Teman with Tawilan, a site about 3 miles (4.8 km) east of Petra.
"Esau mountains" is a reference to Mount Seir.
11 The book's principal clue to its date of writing is in verses 11 and 14. If "the day you stood aloof" (v. 11) alludes to the events of 2 Kings 8:20–22 and 2 Chronicles 21:16–18, when the Edomites

[12]You should not look down on your brother
in the day of his misfortune,
nor rejoice[r] over the people of Judah
in the day of their destruction,[s]
nor boast so much
in the day of their trouble.[t]
[13]You should not march through the gates of my people
in the day of their disaster,
nor look down on them in their calamity[u]
in the day of their disaster,
nor seize their wealth
in the day of their disaster.

1:12 [r]Eze 35:15 [s]Pr 17:5 [t]Mic 4:11
1:13 [u]Eze 35:5

and others rebelled against King Jehoram early in the ninth century B.C., it probably would be dated quite early. But if the reference is to Psalm 137:7, 2 Chronicles 36:20 and Ezekiel 25:13–14, the prophecy would point to the period after the destruction of Jerusalem in 586 B.C. Still another view is that the Edomite raid mentioned in 2 Chronicles 28:16–18 was the impetus for Obadiah's prophecy (in the eighth century B.C., during the reign of Ahaz of Judah). The majority of scholars, however, believe that Obadiah was referring to the 586 B.C. destruction of Jerusalem and that Psalm 137:7 is the closest parallel to this prophecy.

For "cast lots for Jerusalem," see the note on Ezekiel 24:6; see also "Casting Lots" on page 744.

12 The word "day" in the Bible is often misinterpreted because of its various uses. It often denotes time from sunrise to sunset (Ge 1:5; Ps 74:16), and at an early date it was divided into three parts—morning, noon and evening (Ps 55:17; Da 6:10). Probably due to Medo-Persian influence after the exile, it was divided into 12 hours (Jn 11:9). Time could not be determined by clocks, so the length of an hour depended on the time of the year. The word also refers to time in general (here, as well as in Jdg 18:30; Job 18:20; Ob 12), length of life (Ge 5:4) or a time of opportunity (Jn 9:4).

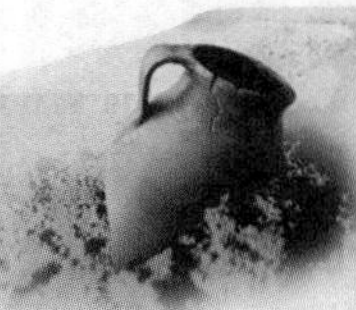

ARCHAEOLOGICAL SITES

EDOM

OBADIAH Edom was located south of the Dead Sea and north of the Gulf of Aqaba (see "Map 4"). The region boasts numerous mountains over 5,000 feet (1,524 m) in height, some pasturage and a few oases. Many Edomite dwellings were cut into the faces of these high, craggy mountains and gave rise to Obadiah's description of the Edomites as people "who live in the clefts of the rocks" and "soar like the eagle" (Ob 3–4). Some such ancient abodes are still visible today.

Edom prospered through its control of the major north-south caravan route, the "King's Highway,"[1] as well as through the mining of iron and copper. A pre-Edomite **Early Bronze**[2] agricultural civilization flourished in this region, organized under seminomadic clan chiefs. Pharaohs were involved in Edom's copper mines from the fourteenth to the twelfth centuries B.C., and thus the area is mentioned often in Egyptian documents.

As descendants of Esau, the twin brother of the patriarch Jacob, the Edomites were considered "brothers" by Israel (cf. vv. 10–12). Moses unsuccessfully attempted to negotiate passage for the Israelites through the territory of the king of Edom. Saul fought against the Edomites, but David conquered Edom. His general, Joab, killed many adult males during a six-month occupation, although Hadad, a royal heir, escaped to Egypt (1Ki 11:14–22). Edom revolted from under Joram (c. 851 B.C.), but later Amaziah (c. 800 B.C.) captured its capital, Sela, and renamed it Joktheel. Edomites sometimes raided Judah (e.g., 2Ch 20; 28:16–17).

From 734 B.C. until the fall of Jerusalem, Edom was under **Assyrian** domination.[3] Assyrian records mention three Edomite kings as tributaries: Qaus-malaku (732 B.C.), Aiarammu (701 B.C.) and Qaus-gabri (629 B.C.). Edom prospered under Assyrian control, and its population increased considerably. Evidence of Edomite settlement during this period appears at several sites in southern Judah. Obadiah indicates that the Edomites participated in the 586 B.C. destruction of Jerusalem.[4]

During the **postexilic period** Edom proper was overrun by Arabs until the Nabateans became established there.[5] Edomites (who were during the postexilic period called Idumeans) established Hebron as their capital.[6] John Hyrcanus forcibly converted the Idumeans to Judaism in approximately 120 B.C. Antipater, an Idumean, became governor of Judea, and his son Herod ruled the region as king.[7] After the Roman destruction of Jerusalem (A.D. 70) Idumea and the Idumeans disappeared from history.

[1]See "Caravan Trading and Routes in the Ancient Near East" on page 63. [2]See Glossary on page 2080 for definitions of bolded words. [3]See "Assyria From the Neo-Assyrian Period Forward" on page 1502. [4]See "The Last Days of Jerusalem" on page 1197. [5]See "Aretas IV of Nabatea and Petra" on page 1898. [6]See "Hebron" on page 446. [7]See "Herod the Great" on page 1627.

[14] You should not wait at the crossroads
to cut down their fugitives,
nor hand over their survivors
in the day of their trouble.

[15] "The day of the LORD is near[v]
for all nations.
As you have done, it will be done to you;
your deeds[w] will return upon your own head.
[16] Just as you drank on my holy hill,
so all the nations will drink[x] continually;
they will drink and drink
and be as if they had never been.
[17] But on Mount Zion will be deliverance;[y]
it will be holy,[z]
and the house of Jacob
will possess its inheritance.
[18] The house of Jacob will be a fire
and the house of Joseph a flame;
the house of Esau will be stubble,
and they will set it on fire and consume[a] it.
There will be no survivors
from the house of Esau."

The LORD has spoken.

[19] People from the Negev will occupy
the mountains of Esau,
and people from the foothills will possess
the land of the Philistines.[b]
They will occupy the fields of Ephraim and Samaria,[c]
and Benjamin will possess Gilead.
[20] This company of Israelite exiles who are in Canaan
will possess ⌞the land⌟ as far as Zarephath;[d]
the exiles from Jerusalem who are in Sepharad
will possess the towns of the Negev.[e]
[21] Deliverers will go up on[c] Mount Zion
to govern the mountains of Esau.
And the kingdom will be the LORD's.[f]

1:15 [v]Eze 30:3 [w]Jer 50:29; Hab 2:8
1:16 [x]Jer 25:15; 49:12
1:17 [y]Am 9:11-15 [z]Isa 4:3
1:18 [a]Zec 12:6
1:19 [b]Isa 11:14 [c]Jer 31:5
1:20 [d]1Ki 17:9-10 [e]Jer 33:13
1:21 [f]Ps 22:28; Zec 14:9,16; Rev 11:15

[c] *21* Or *from*

---

15 For "the day of the LORD," see the note on Joel 1:15.
17 "Mount Zion" is Jerusalem (see "Zaphon, Olympus, Sinai and Zion: The Mountain of God" on p. 843).
19 See "The Negev: Its Climate and Features" on page 34.
The Philistines were one of the Sea Peoples, who had arrived on the Canaanite shores at the end of the Bronze Age (see "The Archaeology of Philistia" on p. 370).
Gilead, located southeast of the Sea of Galilee, was a fertile region known for its good pasturage.
20 Zarephath (present-day Sarafand, Lebanon) was a coastal town located between Tyre and Sidon. (See "Zarephath" on p. 514.)
Sepharad is usually taken to refer to Sardis in Asia Minor (present-day Turkey), though some think that Sparta (the city in Greece) might be intended. Another possibility is that it may be identified with Shaparda, which Sargon II, who exiled Israelites to the cities of the Medes and claimed to have conquered Judah, mentioned as a district in southwestern Media. Among the Jews of the postbiblical period the term was used with reference to Spain.

INTRODUCTION TO 

AUTHOR, PLACE AND DATE OF WRITING

The book of Jonah is among the most controversial in the Old Testament, interpreted by various scholars as either history or fiction. If the story is factual, then Jonah either wrote it himself or was the author's primary source. Almost everything in the book stems from the direct experiences of the prophet, and even details outside of his personal knowledge (e.g., the sailors making a sacrifice to the Lord at 1:16 and the ritual lamentation of the king of Nineveh at 3:6) could have been surmised or learned by him at a later time. If the story is a fictionalized account, its authorship is unknown.

The matter of the date of the book of Jonah is closely related to the question of whether the work is historical or fictional. The events of the book of Jonah, if historical, probably took place around 770–750 B.C. If this is the case, the work was almost certainly written during the eighth century B.C. If it is merely a story, it could have been written at any time after the eighth century, although scholars who believe this story is fiction concur that the work is probably postexilic, written at a time when Nineveh was only a distant memory.

See "The Historicity of the Book of Jonah" on page 1474.

AUDIENCE

Assuming that Jonah's story is a factual account, the book was addressed to the northern kingdom (Israel) during the reign of Jeroboam II (793–753 B.C.), a time of great territorial and commercial expansion.

CULTURAL FACTS AND HIGHLIGHTS

Nineveh's historical situation during this period may explain the readiness of the king and his people to accept Jonah's message. Assyrian power was at a particularly low point during the reign of Assur-dan III (773–756 B.C.). Assyria had suffered military reverses, diplomatic setbacks, famine and domestic uprisings. In addition, an eclipse had taken place on June 15, 763 B.C., and this could have been regarded as a terrible omen (there had also been an eclipse in 784 B.C.). With all of this going on, it is not surprising that the Ninevites would have been especially jittery and ready to pay attention to a foreign prophet who suddenly appeared in their city.

TIMELINE

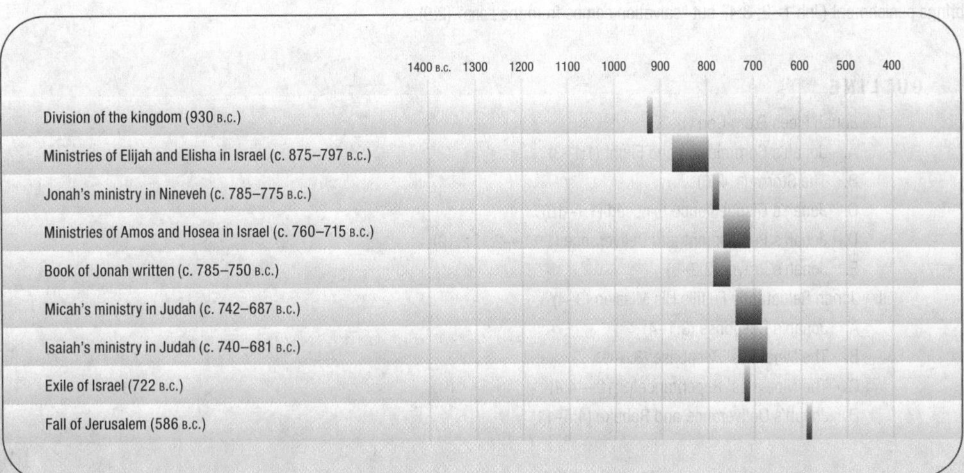

AS YOU READ

Be attuned to the prophet's negative attitude as he nevertheless followed through—after a major act of rebellion and a dramatic turnabout—with his God-given mandate. Notice, for instance, his pronouncement to God that he was "angry enough to die" when the vine withered and his shade was gone (4:9). What do these details say about God's willingness and ability to use human beings, whatever their limitations or petty complaints?

How does the book's abrupt ending (an unanswered, rhetorical question of God) leave you feeling? Do you sense a need for closure of the human story, or is the divine "last word" sufficient from your perspective?

DID YOU KNOW?

- The sailors understood Jonah's description of God as being characteristic of the highest deity, for in the religions of the ancient Near East the supreme god was usually the master of the seas (1:9)
- The Hebrew for "great fish" and the Greek for "huge fish" in Matthew 12:40 are both general terms for a large sea creature, not necessarily (but possibly) a whale (1:17).
- The Assyrians, instead of numbering their years, named them after certain rulers and powerful men (3:4).

THEMES

Jonah's themes include:

1. *God's sovereignty.* God is in control of life, nature and all circumstances (1:4,9,15,17; 2:10; 4:6–8). The God of all peoples, he is concerned about everyone and everything (including the animals) he has created (4:11). Finally, he will bring his all-encompassing plan to completion.

2. *God's compassion and mercy.* God loves even the adversaries of his people and will show them mercy when they repent (3:10; 4:2,11). He demands obedience (1:1–17) but is also the God of second chances.

3. *Mission.* Jonah foreshadows the New Testament mission to proclaim God's message to the whole world (1:1–2; 3:1–2), even to those who oppose it (4:11; Mt 5:44). As God's ambassadors they are to announce this call: "Be reconciled to God" (2Co 5:20), for wickedness brings punishment (Jnh 1–2; 3:4), but "salvation comes from the LORD" (2:9).

OUTLINE

- I. Jonah Flees From God (1–2)
  - A. Jonah's Commission and Flight (1:1–3)
  - B. The Storm (1:4–6)
  - C. Jonah's Disobedience Exposed (1:7–10)
  - D. Jonah's Punishment and Deliverance (1:11—2:1; 2:10)
  - E. Jonah's Prayer (2:2–9)
- II. Jonah Reluctantly Fulfills His Mission (3–4)
  - A. Jonah's Response (3:1–4)
  - B. The Ninevites' Response (3:5–9)
  - C. The Ninevites' Repentance (3:10—4:4)
  - D. Jonah's Deliverance and Rebuke (4:5–11)

Jonah Flees From the Lord

1:1 [a]Mt 12:39-41 [b]2Ki 14:25 **1** The word of the LORD came to Jonah[a] son of Amittai:[b] 2“Go to the great city of Nineveh[c] and preach
1:2 [c]Ge 10:11 against it, because its wickedness has come up before me.”
1:3 [d]Ps 139:7 [e]Jos 19:46; 3But Jonah ran[d] away from the LORD and headed for Tarshish. He went down to Joppa,[e] where he found
Ac 9:36,43 a ship bound for that port. After paying the fare, he went aboard and sailed for Tarshish to flee from the
LORD.
4Then the LORD sent a great wind on the sea, and such a violent storm arose that the ship threatened
1:4 [f]Ps 107:23-26 to break up.[f] 5All the sailors were afraid and each cried out to his own god. And they threw the cargo into
1:5 [g]Ac 27:18-19 the sea to lighten the ship.[g]
But Jonah had gone below deck, where he lay down and fell into a deep sleep. 6The captain went to him
1:6 [h]Jnh 3:8 [i]Ps 107:28 and said, “How can you sleep? Get up and call[h] on your god! Maybe he will take notice of us, and we will
not perish.”[i]
7Then the sailors said to each other, “Come, let us cast lots to find out who is responsible for this ca-
1:7 [j]Jos 7:10-18; 1Sa 14:42 lamity.”[j] They cast lots and the lot fell on Jonah.
8So they asked him, “Tell us, who is responsible for making all this trouble for us? What do you do?
Where do you come from? What is your country? From what people are you?”
1:9 [k]Ac 17:24 [l]Ps 146:6 9He answered, “I am a Hebrew and I worship the LORD, the God of heaven,[k] who made the sea and the
land.[l]”
10This terrified them and they asked, “What have you done?” (They knew he was running away from
the LORD, because he had already told them so.)
11The sea was getting rougher and rougher. So they asked him, “What should we do to you to make
the sea calm down for us?”
12“Pick me up and throw me into the sea,” he replied, “and it will become calm. I know that it is my
1:12 [m]2Sa 24:17; 1Ch 21:17 fault that this great storm has come upon you.”[m]
13Instead, the men did their best to row back to land. But they could not, for the sea grew even wild-
1:13 [n]Pr 21:30 er than before.[n] 14Then they cried to the LORD, “O LORD, please do not let us die for taking this man’s life.
1:14 [o]Dt 21:8 [p]Ps 115:3 Do not hold us accountable for killing an innocent man,[o] for you, O LORD, have done as you pleased.”[p]
1:15 [q]Ps 107:29; Lk 8:24 15Then they took Jonah and threw him overboard, and the raging sea grew calm.[q] 16At this the men great-
1:16 [r]Mk 4:41 ly feared[r] the LORD, and they offered a sacrifice to the LORD and made vows to him.
1:17 [s]Mt 12:40; 16:4; Lk 11:30 17But the LORD provided a great fish to swallow Jonah,[s] and Jonah was inside the fish three days and
three nights.

Jonah’s Prayer

2 From inside the fish Jonah prayed to the LORD his God. 2He said:

2:2 [t]Ps 18:6; 120:1 “In my distress I called to the LORD,[t]
and he answered me.

1:2 In about 700 B.C. Sennacherib made Nineveh the capital of Assyria, a status it retained until its fall in 612 B.C. (see “Nineveh” on p. 1497). Nineveh was over 500 miles (800 km) from Gath Hepher, Jonah’s hometown. According to the prophet Nahum, Nineveh’s flagrant sins included plotting evil against the Lord, cruelty and plundering in war, prostitution, witchcraft and commercial exploitation (Na 1:11; 2:12–13; 3:1,4,16,19).

1:3 Tarshish was in the west, meaning that Jonah was heading in the opposite direction of Nineveh (see “Where Was Tarshish?” on p. 1475). See also “Joppa” on page 1472.

Regular passenger service by land or sea were unknown, and there is no evidence that the pattern of procedure changed from Old Testament times to New. Nine centuries after the approximate date of Jonah’s flight a record similar to Jonah’s reads: “When we had sailed across the open sea off the coast of Cilicia and Pamphylia, we landed at Myra in Lycia. There the centurion found an Alexandrian ship sailing for Italy and put us on board” (Ac 27:5–6). Travelers evidently made their own arrangements, attached themselves to official parties, accompanied caravans and coordinated their movements with those of trade and commerce.

1:5 Apparently the sailors, who may have come from various ports, worshiped a variety of pagan gods.

1:7 The casting of lots was common practice in the ancient Near East (see “Casting Lots” on p. 744).

1:9 Commonly used as an ethnic designation in the Bible, the word “Hebrew” was typically intended by non-Israelites as a disparaging term. Outside the Bible, people known as the *Habiru/Apiru* (a word probably related to “Hebrew”) are described to as a landless, dependent, immigrant (foreign) social class rather than as a specific ethnic group. Negative descriptions of them are given in the Amarna Letters (see “The Amarna Tablets and the Habiru” on p. 347).

The sailors understood Jonah’s description of God as being characteristic of the highest deity, for in the religions of the ancient Near East the supreme god was generally considered the master of the seas (see the note on Jos 3:10–11).

1:13 The Hebrew translated “to row” literally means “to dig” (with oars), indicating strenuous effort. The ship could have been driven by sails, oars or both (see “Seafaring in the Ancient World” on p. 1473).

1:16 There is no evidence that the sailors renounced all other gods. Ancient pagans were ready to recognize the existence and power of many gods. At the least, however, the sailors acknowledged that the God of Israel was in control of the present events.

1:17 The Hebrew for “great fish” and the Greek for “huge fish” in Matthew 12:40 are both general terms for a large fish, not necessarily a whale. This great fish is not to be confused with the sinister “serpent” of the sea (Am 9:3)—otherwise called “Leviathan” (Isa 27:1), the “monster of the deep” (Job 7:12; see also the note on Ps 32:6).

The phrase “three days and three nights” as used here may, as in Matthew 12:40, refer to a period of time including one full day and parts of two others (see the notes on Mt 12:40; 1Co 15:4).

From the depths of the grave[a] I called for help,
and you listened to my cry.
3 You hurled me into the deep,[u]
into the very heart of the seas,
and the currents swirled about me;
all your waves and breakers
swept over me.[v]

2:3 [u]Ps 88:6 [v]Ps 42:7

[a] 2 Hebrew *Sheol*

ARCHAEOLOGICAL SITES

JOPPA

JONAH 1 Joppa ("Map 7"), which means "beautiful," was located on the Mediterranean coast at Jaffa, just south of modern Tel Aviv. It was the only natural harbor between Acco ("Map 6") and Egypt. Timber from Lebanon passed through this seaport on its way to Jerusalem for use in the construction of the temples built by Solomon (2Ch 2:16)[1] and Zerubbabel (Ezr 3:7). The prophet Jonah departed from Joppa in an attempt to flee God's call to go to Nineveh.[2] The Danites had earlier received this city as part of their tribal allotment (Jos 19:46) but had moved north to Laish because of their inability to gain control of their allotted territory.[3]

One of the few port cities on the coast of the Holy Land, Joppa was a city that attracted kings from the entire region. It is mentioned frequently in ancient sources, which attest to the wide variety of powers that controlled the city:

✣ The Egyptian Harris Papyrus describes how the city was taken by Thutmose III (fifteenth century B.C.), who, in a Trojan-horse maneuver, sent the city's ruler a gift of baskets in which were hidden his soldiers.

✣ The city is also mentioned in two of the **Amarna**[4] Letters (fourteenth century B.C.), which indicate that Joppa was an Egyptian stronghold during the Eighteenth Dynasty.[5]

✣ Egyptian dominance evidently continued into the Nineteenth Dynasty; stone doorjambs excavated in Joppa were inscribed with the name and titles of **Rameses II** (thirteenth century B.C.).

✣ In light of its location on the northern edge of Philistine territory, a Philistine presence is to be expected after the twelfth century B.C., and indeed Philistine pottery from the eleventh century B.C. has been unearthed there.

✣ The city was evidently under Israelite jurisdiction during the Solomonic period (2Ch 2:16) and perhaps again under the dynasty of Omri, although available sources do not explicitly claim Israelite control during either of these periods.

✣ The city was also conquered by the **Assyrians**. Sennacherib (in his "prism stele") lists Joppa among the cities he captured during his 701 B.C. campaign.[6]

✣ Joppa remained a prized city during the **Persian period.** A **sarcophagus** inscription of Eshmunezer, king of the **Phoenician** city of Sidon ("Map 7"), reveals that Joppa, through a donation of the Persian king, was subject to Phoenician authority. Eshmunezer claims that the "Lord of Kings" (the Persian ruler) conferred upon him control of Dor and Joppa, "which are in the plain of Sharon," as a reward for his faithful service.

✣ The Phoenicians were not always loyal to Persia, however, and in the fourth century B.C. they engaged in a rebellion against Persian rule. Artaxerxes III destroyed Sidon in 358 B.C.,[7] and Joppa became liberated from Phoenician rule.

✣ Soon afterward, however, Joppa came under the control of a series of Greek rulers. Two coins of Alexander the Great, who entered this region around 332 B.C., have been uncovered there. The city did enjoy a degree of independence under the **Ptolemaic** Greek rulers of Egypt.

✣ Joppa was conquered by the Jewish **Hasmonean** ruler Simon Maccabeus around 144 B.C. This was a matter of great importance to the Jewish state, as it offered an outlet to the sea. The Hasmonean Alexander Jannaeus struck a large quantity of coins stamped with an anchor on one side to celebrate Jewish control over the city.

✣ Roman rule began with the conquests of Pompey the Great (64 B.C.). Judea thus lost control of Joppa, but Augustus placed it under the authority of Herod in approximately 30 B.C.[8]

As the port city of Judea, Joppa was important to the New Testament church. It was in Joppa that the apostle Peter raised Tabitha from the dead (Ac 9:36–43), experienced his vision indicating that God would accept the faith of Gentiles and subsequently preached the gospel to Cornelius (Ac 10).

[1]See "Solomon's Temple and Other Ancient Temples" on page 620. [2]See "Nineveh" on page 1497. [3]See "The Migration of the Danites" on page 378. [4]See Glossary on page 2080 for definitions of bolded words. [5]See "The Amarna Tablets and the Habiru" on page 347. [6]See "The Sennacherib Prism" on page 659. [7]See "Sidon" on page 1536. [8]See "Herod the Great" on page 1627.

2:4 [w]Ps 31:22
2:5 [x]Ps 69:1-2
2:7 [y]Ps 77:11-12 [z]2Ch 30:27 [a]Ps 11:4; 18:6

4 I said, 'I have been banished
from your sight;[w]
yet I will look again
toward your holy temple.'
5 The engulfing waters threatened me,[b]
the deep surrounded me;
seaweed was wrapped around my head.[x]
6 To the roots of the mountains I sank down;
the earth beneath barred me in forever.
But you brought my life up from the pit,
O LORD my God.

7 "When my life was ebbing away,
I remembered[y] you, LORD,
and my prayer[z] rose to you,
to your holy temple.[a]

[b] 5 Or *waters were at my throat*

2:6 "The pit" refers to the grave (see the note on Ps 6:5; see also "Sheol, Hades, Gehenna, the Abyss and Tartarus: Images of Hell" on p. 946).

Seafaring in the Ancient World

JONAH 2 Seafaring in the ancient Near East extends back well into the third millennium B.C., a period during which Egyptian sources refer to the "Byblos ship" (a term that signified any large, seafaring vessel). Such ships carried the valuable cedars of Lebanon and other prized timber from the northern Levant (Syria-Palestine) to Egypt.[1] During the second millennium B.C. **Ugaritic** letters also report seafaring trade along coastal Canaan.[2] A shipwrecked vessel from around 1300 B.C. near Uluburun, Turkey, managed to preserve its cargo of olives, pomegranates, figs, various spices and nuts. Twelfth-century B.C. pictures from Mendinet Habu carved into the temple of the Egyptian pharaoh Rameses III depict the naval battle between the Egyptians and the **Sea Peoples**, a mysterious new emigrant group who brought with them naval technology that revolutionized seafaring in the Near East.

The **Phoenicians** were especially great naval innovators, building a maritime trading empire that extended west to Carthage and beyond.[3] Two eighth-century Phoenician shipwrecked crafts laden with wine amphorae have been located in the Mediterranean, approximately 31 miles (50 km) from Ashkelon ("Map 6"). The Bible also speaks of Phoenician maritime skill in 1 Kings 9:26–28, where Solomon is said to have established a fleet at Ezion Geber, on the shore of the Red Sea, staffed by Phoenician sailors to make the run to Ophir for the gold trade. It is clear that seafaring already boasted a long history by the time of Jonah.

Joppa, on the Mediterranean coast, was one of the major seaports in the region during Jonah's day. Ships of Tarshish were heavy, seagoing vessels perhaps named for a geographical location or for their metallurgical cargo. Scholars once speculated that ships of this time hugged the coast and did not venture into deeper waters, but this is no longer believed to have been the case; the ship Jonah took was probably capable of going far out to sea. The most likely geographical candidates for Tarshish are Tartessus in southwestern Spain or Tarsus in southeastern **Asia Minor**[4] ("Map 12"). Despite this ambiguity, it is clear that Jonah knew he could flee west from Joppa aboard a ship. Yet he would soon discover that not even these mighty vessels and their advanced Phoenician technology could separate the Lord's prophet from the God of Israel.

[1]See "Cedars of Lebanon" on page 1043. [2]See "Ugarit/Ras Shamra" on page 819. [3]See "Phoenicia" on page 488. [4]See "Where Was Tarshish?" on page 1475.

THE HISTORICITY OF THE BOOK OF JONAH

JONAH 3 There is no question that Jonah was a historical person; he is mentioned in 2 Kings 14:25, where he is said to have predicted the expansion of Israel during the reign of Jeroboam II. The fact that Jonah was cited for having made a prediction of military success suggests that he was one of the more nationalistic and militaristic prophets, perhaps not too different from Zedekiah, whom the prophet Micaiah opposed in 1 Kings 22. This, in itself, however, sheds no light on whether the book of Jonah is a factual, historical account. If it is pure fiction, its author could have used this prophet as a character because he wanted to make a point about divine compassion: God, in showing mercy to the Ninevites, humbled this angry, super-patriotic prophet.

Arguments against reading Jonah as history are as follows:

- Jonah 3:9 is similar to Joel 2:14, suggesting that Jonah was a late work, written long after the lifetime of the historical prophet.
- The story of Jonah's being swallowed alive by a "great fish" seems too far-fetched to be believable.
- Jonah's psalm (ch. 2) makes no sense in context. The prophet is depicted as praising God for his salvation while still inside the fish.
- The account lacks evidence of a real understanding of Nineveh and its history. For example, the author greatly exaggerated the city's size in claiming that it would require three days to cross it on foot (3:3).
- There is no historical record that Nineveh experienced a mass revival or conversion (ch. 3).

It is possible, however, to convincingly address these arguments:

- It is notoriously difficult to prove which Old Testament text is original when two books contain similar wording. There would be no way in this case to determine whether Jonah or Joel was original or whether the authors of both were merely employing common language.
- The story of the great fish is miraculous only in the sense that God supernaturally provided a whale to swallow Jonah. There are three critical issues here:

The great fish may indeed have been a large whale, which would not normally have been found in the eastern Mediterranean, but the provision of the whale so far from its usual habitat is the miraculous part of the account.

The word for "belly" (a term used in some translations, though not in the NIV) in Hebrew is imprecise and does not necessarily mean "stomach." Jonah may have been in the oral cavity of a large-mouthed whale.

A whale, being a mammal, is a warm-blooded air breather that periodically resurfaces for air. It therefore would have provided Jonah with oxygen, while its body heat would have prevented the prophet from being overcome with hypothermia.

- The psalm of Jonah 2 is intelligible if we reconstruct events as follows: (1) Jonah, cast overboard during a storm and unable to swim, sank immediately (2:6). (2) A whale scooped him up and carried him to the surface, allowing him to breathe. (3) When the whale kept Jonah near the surface, the prophet recognized God's provision and was able to praise him.
- Jonah 3:3 says literally that Nineveh was a "three-day walk," a possible reference to walking straight across the middle of the city or around its perimeter. But Jonah was required to walk to every neighborhood and proclaim his message of warning.
- The Ninevites' repentance by no means indicates that they became worshipers of **Yahweh** or converted to the Israelites' religion but suggests that they ritually asked God to spare them. Historically, this was a short-lived event—unlikely to have shown up in the city's annals.

Those who regard Jonah as postexilic fiction typically view the work as a counter to the nationalistic zeal of Ezra and Nehemiah. The book presents pagans as ready to repent (chs. 1 and 3) and portrays the Israelite prophet as disobedient, angry and vengeful. There is no doubt that the book of Jonah makes the point that God is compassionate to all people and cares about the Gentiles just as he does about Israel. It is unnecessary, however, to take it to be a postexilic work or a critique of Ezra and Nehemiah. If, as suggested above, Jonah was a nationalistic prophet along the lines of Zedekiah in 1 Kings 22, the events he experienced and the book itself were a corrective to this misguided zeal. God is, as Jonah himself confessed, the maker both of the sea and of the dry land (Jnh 1:9), and he does not play favorites in the manner Jonah would have liked.

2:8 [b]2Ki 17:15; Jer 10:8

8 "Those who cling to worthless idols[b]
forfeit the grace that could be theirs.
9 But I, with a song of thanksgiving,
will sacrifice[c] to you.

2:9 [c]Ps 50:14,23; Hos 14:2 [d]Ecc 5:4-5 [e]Ps 3:8

What I have vowed[d] I will make good.
Salvation[e] comes from the LORD."

10 And the LORD commanded the fish, and it vomited Jonah onto dry land.

Jonah Goes to Nineveh

3:1 [f]Jnh 1:1

3 Then the word of the LORD came to Jonah[f] a second time: 2 "Go to the great city of Nineveh and pro-
claim to it the message I give you."
3 Jonah obeyed the word of the LORD and went to Nineveh. Now Nineveh was a very important city—
a visit required three days. 4 On the first day, Jonah started into the city. He proclaimed: "Forty more days

3:2 For "great city," see the note on 1:2.
A prophet was the bearer of a message from God, not primarily a foreteller of coming events (see "Prophets in the Bible and Pagan Nations" on p. 1457).
3:3 The later imperial city of Nineveh had a perimeter of about 8 miles (13 km), enclosing an area of approximately 1,700 acres (see "Nineveh" on p. 1497).
3:4 The Assyrians, instead of numbering their years, named them after certain rulers and powerful men. "Eponym" lists of this sort are critical for establishing ancient Near Eastern chronology.
An eclipse of the sun is recorded for the reign of Ashur-Dan III (763 B.C.), an event that would have been regarded as an ill omen. It was at about this time that Jonah was sent by the Lord to warn the people of Nineveh. But God gave the city a respite for nearly 200 years.
Forty was often used symbolically in Old Testament times as a round number (see also Ex 24:18; 1Ki 19:8).

Where Was Tarshish?

JONAH 4 It is impossible to say with certainty where Tarshish was located. What is known is that Nineveh was to the east[1] and that Jonah was trying to get as far as possible from Nineveh by boarding a ship and sailing westward. If Tarshish were a specific port, it certainly would have been located somewhere along the coast of the Mediterranean Sea, as may be suggested by several Old Testament texts (Ps 48:7; Isa 23:6; Eze 27:25) and by an inscription of Esarhaddon of **Assyria**. Many suggest that it was a city associated with mining and metallurgy, since the name Tarshish may be derived from a word referring to smelting or refining (see also Eze 27:12). Places that could satisfy these requirements include:

- Tartessus in southwestern Spain. This would be appropriate to the story, for it would have been difficult to sail any farther from Nineveh.
- The island of Sardinia. A ninth-century B.C. Phoenician inscription suggests the possible presence of Tarshish there.
- Carthage in North Africa ("Map 14"). This is supported by the **Septuagint** version of Ezekiel 27:12, which identifies Carthage with Tarshish (but there was also a Carthage in Spain).
- Tarsus in **Anatolia** (modern Turkey). This city would later become the hometown of Paul.

Some scholars, however, believe that the term "Tarshish" refers not to a specific location but simply to the "open sea." If this is the case, the author's intent may have been simply to describe Jonah as going off to sea.[2] The church father Jerome, in his commentary on Jonah, accepted this interpretation.

Regardless of the intended destination of the ship Jonah boarded, it is obvious that the reluctant prophet sought to sail in the opposite direction from the destination to which God was calling him.

[1]See "Nineveh" on page 1497, and locate this city on "'Map 8a' and 'Map 8b.'" [2]See "Seafaring in the Ancient World" on page 1473.

and Nineveh will be overturned." 5The Ninevites believed God. They declared a fast, and all of them, from
the greatest to the least, put on sackcloth.[g] — 3:5 [g]Da 9:3; Lk 11:32
6When the news reached the king of Nineveh, he rose from his throne, took off his royal robes, cov-
ered himself with sackcloth and sat down in the dust.[h] 7Then he issued a proclamation in Nineveh: — 3:6 [h]Job 2:8,13; Eze 27:30-31

"By the decree of the king and his nobles:

Do not let any man or beast, herd or flock, taste anything; do not let them eat or drink.[i] 8But — 3:7 [i]2Ch 20:3
let man and beast be covered with sackcloth. Let everyone call[j] urgently on God. Let them give up — 3:8 [j]Ps 130:1; Jnh 1:6
their evil ways and their violence. 9Who knows?[k] God may yet relent and with compassion turn[l] — 3:9 [k]2Sa 12:22 [l]Joel 2:14
from his fierce anger so that we will not perish."

10When God saw what they did and how they turned from their evil ways, he had compassion[m] and — 3:10 [m]Am 7:6 [n]Jer 18:8 [o]Ex 32:14
did not bring upon them the destruction[n] he had threatened.[o]

Jonah's Anger at the LORD's Compassion

4 But Jonah was greatly displeased and became angry.[p] 2He prayed to the LORD, "O LORD, is this not — 4:1 [p]ver 4; Lk 15:28
what I said when I was still at home? That is why I was so quick to flee to Tarshish. I knew[q] that you — 4:2 [q]Jer 20:7-8
are a gracious and compassionate God, slow to anger and abounding in love,[r] a God who relents from — [r]Ex 34:6; Ps 86:5, 15 [s]Joel 2:13
sending calamity.[s] 3Now, O LORD, take away my life,[t] for it is better for me to die[u] than to live." — 4:3 [t]1Ki 19:4 [u]Job 7:15
4But the LORD replied, "Have you any right to be angry?"[v] — 4:4 [v]Mt 20:11-15
5Jonah went out and sat down at a place east of the city. There he made himself a shelter, sat in its
shade and waited to see what would happen to the city. 6Then the LORD God provided a vine and made
it grow up over Jonah to give shade for his head to ease his discomfort, and Jonah was very happy about
the vine. 7But at dawn the next day God provided a worm, which chewed the vine so that it withered.[w] — 4:7 [w]Joel 1:12
8When the sun rose, God provided a scorching east wind, and the sun blazed on Jonah's head so that he
grew faint. He wanted to die, and said, "It would be better for me to die than to live."
9But God said to Jonah, "Do you have a right to be angry about the vine?"
"I do," he said. "I am angry enough to die."
10But the LORD said, "You have been concerned about this vine, though you did not tend it or make it
grow. It sprang up overnight and died overnight. 11But Nineveh[x] has more than a hundred and twenty — 4:11 [x]Jnh 1:2; 3:2 [y]Jnh 3:10
thousand people who cannot tell their right hand from their left, and many cattle as well. Should I not
be concerned[y] about that great city?"

3:5–6 These were customary signs of repentance and/or mourning (see "Sackcloth and Ashes: Rituals of Lamentation" on p. 820).
4:2 For "Tarshish," see the note on 1:3.
4:5 A prophet was the bearer of a message from God, not primarily a foreteller of coming events (see "Prophets in the Bible and Pagan Nations" on p. 1457).
4:11 For "great city," see the note on 1:2.

INTRODUCTION TO 

AUTHOR, PLACE AND DATE OF WRITING

The author of this book, Micah, tells us that he was from Moresheth (1:1), a village in the Shephelah of Judah also known as Moresheth Gath (1:14). We know virtually nothing else about him, although he is one of the few Old Testament prophets to be cited by name in another's writings (Jer 26:18, citing Mic 3:12). This signifies that Micah's book was recognized as canonical by the time of Jeremiah's ministry (the nature of the citation suggests that there was consensus by that time that Micah had been a true prophet). In addition, Habakkuk 2:12 is a modification of Micah 3:10, and 4:2–3 is almost identical to Isaiah 2:2–4, although in this case we cannot be sure whether the oracle originated with Micah or with Isaiah.

Today some scholars believe that only part of the book of Micah came from the prophet himself and that the rest is secondary (written by someone else). The prophecies of judgment in particular are thought to be authentic, with the more optimistic predictions—those that promise salvation for Judah—coming from some other prophet. This approach to the text, which is founded on the premise that a given prophet had only a single, uncomplicated message, is misguided and simplistic.

Micah 1:1 informs the reader that Micah preached during the reigns of Jotham, Ahaz and Hezekiah. This would place his ministry during the second half of the eighth century B.C., making him a contemporary of Isaiah, Amos and Hosea.

AUDIENCE

Micah ministered primarily to the southern kingdom of Judah, but he also addressed the northern kingdom of Israel and predicted the fall of Samaria (1:6), which took place in 722 B.C. His message was aimed in particular at greedy and oppressive landowners (2:1–5) who supported Israel's corrupt political and religious leaders who had led the nation into moral decay.

CULTURAL FACTS AND HIGHLIGHTS

The background of this book is the same as that found in the earlier portions of Isaiah. Biblical passages covering this period are 2 Kings 15:32—20:21, 2 Chronicles 27–32 and Isaiah 7, 20, 36–39. Several significant historical events occurred during this period:

- In 734–732 B.C. Tiglath-Pileser III of Assyria led a military campaign against Aram (Syria), Philistia and parts of Israel and Judah. The northern kingdom lost most of its territory, including all of Gilead and much of Galilee.
- In 722–721 Samaria fell, and the northern kingdom was conquered by Assyria.
- In 701 Judah joined a revolt against Assyria but was overrun by King Sennacherib and his army. Jerusalem, however, was spared.

Micah condemned the sin of Judah and anticipated divine judgment against the nation (3:1–4; 4:10a), yet he also forecast her ultimate triumph over all the other nations on Earth (4:10b–13). Even in this Micah was not simply a patriotic Jew looking forward to victory over the Gentiles; to the contrary, he expected Israel in the long term to be a blessing to all the nations (4:2–3). In short, Micah was advancing a theology to deal with the current dilemma of the chosen people of God and the house of David falling under judgment. Far from implying the failure of the covenant promises, this very judgment would be the means by which God would fulfill those covenants.

TIMELINE

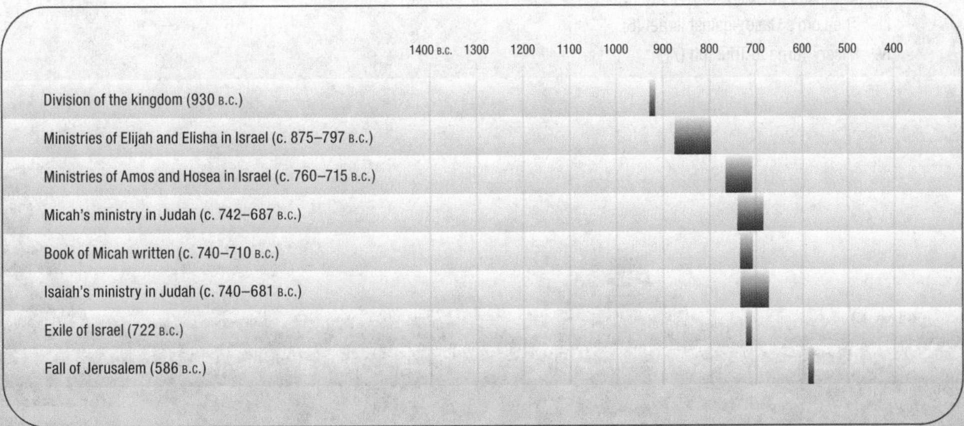

AS YOU READ

Be aware of the alternating oracles of doom and hope in this prophetic book. Do you view such changes in perspective in this and other prophetic works as "mood swings" on the part of the author or as faithful representation of the messages given to the prophet by the God who is characterized by both "kindness and sternness" (cf. Ro 11:22)?

DID YOU KNOW?

- Going barefoot was a sign of mourning, as was wearing sackcloth. It is possible that Micah actually walked barefoot through Jerusalem, wearing only a loincloth of sackcloth (1:8).
- The Hebrew for "parting gifts" is translated "wedding gift" in 1 Kings 9:16. Jerusalem would give up Moresheth Gath to Assyria, as a father gives a "wedding gift" to his daughter when she marries (1:14).
- "Seers" is an older term for "prophets" (3:7).
- A plowshare (4:3) was an iron point mounted on a wooden beam (ancient plows did not include what we know as a plowshare).
- To sit under one's own vine and fig tree was a proverbial picture of peace, security and contentment (4:4).
- "Seven . . . even eight" is figurative for "an indefinite number" (5:5).
- A hopeful element was actually quite common in laments (7:7).

THEMES

The prophecy of Micah includes the following themes:

1. *Judgment against oppressors.* Micah predicted that God would justly judge "the sins of the house of Israel" (1:5). The landowners and religious and political leaders had abused their power and conspired to do evil (2:1; 7:3), coveted and defrauded others of their property (2:2; 6:10), stolen and plundered (2:8), hated good and loved evil (3:2), oppressed the poor (3:3), despised justice and distorted truth (3:9), accepted bribes (3:11; 7:3), used their religious positions for profit (3:11), engaged in dishonest business practices (6:11), acted with violence and deceit (6:12) and murdered their own people (7:2). God would bring disaster upon Samaria (1:6–7), Jerusalem (1:12; 3:12; 4:10), the greedy landowners (2:3–5), the corrupted leaders (3:4) and the false prophets (3:5–7).

2. *Restoration.* Micah declared that after judgment God would mercifully forgive and restore his people (7:9), bringing them back from exile in Babylon (4:10) and restoring Jerusalem's dominion (4:8,13).

3. *Justice.* Micah asked a deceptively simple question: "What does the LORD require of you?" The answer: "To act justly and to love mercy and to walk humbly with your God" (6:8). Israel had failed to live up to this divine expectation, and the nation would suffer the horrible consequences.

OUTLINE

I. Judgment Against Israel and Judah (1–3)
II. Israel and Judah Have Hope (4–5)
III. The Lord's Case Against Israel (6)
IV. Misery Turns to Triumph (7)

1:1 [a]Jer 26:18 [b]1Ch 3:12 [c]1Ch 3:13 [d]Hos 1:1 [e]Isa 1:1
1:2 [f]Ps 50:7 [g]Jer 6:19 [h]Ge 31:50; Dt 4:26; Isa 1:2 [i]Ps 11:4

1 The word of the LORD that came to Micah of Moresheth[a] during the reigns of Jotham,[b] Ahaz[c] and Hezekiah, kings of Judah[d]—the vision[e] he saw concerning Samaria and Jerusalem.

2 Hear, O peoples, all of you,[f]
listen, O earth[g] and all who are in it,
that the Sovereign LORD may witness[h] against you,
the Lord from his holy temple.[i]

1:1 Micah, a shortened form of the name Micaiah (or Michael), means "Who is like God?"

ARCHAEOLOGICAL SITES

ADULLAM

The Cave of Adullam
Photograph: © Todd Bolen/Bible Places.com

MICAH 1 Located 16 miles (26 km) southwest of Jerusalem, Adullam was one of several strategic cities in the Shephelah ("Map 2") to be the object of grim prophecies from Micah. As Adullam had been a place of refuge during the time of David's distress, so now the city would host the strong and the wealthy who were fleeing before the **Assyrian**[1] army.

Adullam is mentioned early in Scripture in connection with Judah and Tamar (Ge 38), as well as with Joshua's conquest (Jos 12:15),[2] but it is most prominent as the place where David sought safety—a "no man's land" between Israelite and Philistine territory (1Sa 22). While he was there, David was joined by family members and other refugees, until he had become the leader of a 400-man force. The **superscripts** of Psalms 34, 57 and 142 may indicate that David wrote these psalms while residing at the cave of Adullam.[3]

Numerous caves mark the prominent hill of Adullam today, but the site has not yet been excavated. David's grandson Rehoboam fortified Adullam as part of his strategy of protecting Judah's western flank (2Ch 11:7), but the site may have been destroyed in the invasion of Sennacherib that was anticipated by Micah.[4] Following the **Babylonian** exile, however, Adullam was reinhabited (Ne 11:30).

[1]See Glossary on page 2080 for definitions of bolded words. [2]See "The Conquest of Canaan" on page 310. [3]See "The Psalm Superscripts" on page 795. [4]See "The Sennacherib Prism" on page 659.

Judgment Against Samaria and Jerusalem

[3] Look! The LORD is coming from his dwelling[j] place;
he comes down and treads the high places of the earth.[k]
[4] The mountains melt[l] beneath him
and the valleys split apart,[m]
like wax before the fire,
like water rushing down a slope.
[5] All this is because of Jacob's transgression,
because of the sins of the house of Israel.
What is Jacob's transgression?
Is it not Samaria?[n]
What is Judah's high place?
Is it not Jerusalem?

[6] "Therefore I will make Samaria a heap of rubble,
a place for planting vineyards.
I will pour her stones[o] into the valley
and lay bare her foundations.[p]
[7] All her idols[q] will be broken to pieces;
all her temple gifts will be burned with fire;
I will destroy all her images.[r]
Since she gathered her gifts from the wages of prostitutes,[s]
as the wages of prostitutes they will again be used."

1:3 [j]Isa 18:4 [k]Am 4:13
1:4 [l]Ps 46:2,6 [m]Nu 16:31; Na 1:5
1:5 [n]Am 8:14
1:6 [o]Am 5:11 [p]Eze 13:14
1:7 [q]Eze 6:6 [r]Dt 9:21 [s]Dt 23:17-18

Weeping and Mourning

[8] Because of this I will weep[t] and wail;
I will go about barefoot and naked.
I will howl like a jackal
and moan like an owl.
[9] For her wound[u] is incurable;
it has come to Judah.[v]
It[a] has reached the very gate[w] of my people,
even to Jerusalem itself.
[10] Tell it not in Gath[b];
weep not at all.[c]
In Beth Ophrah[d]
roll in the dust.
[11] Pass on in nakedness[x] and shame,
you who live in Shaphir.[e]
Those who live in Zaanan[f]
will not come out.
Beth Ezel is in mourning;
its protection is taken from you.

1:8 [t]Isa 15:3
1:9 [u]Jer 46:11 [v]2Ki 18:13 [w]Isa 3:26
1:11 [x]Eze 23:29

[a] 9 Or *He* [b] 10 *Gath* sounds like the Hebrew for *tell.* [c] 10 Hebrew; Septuagint may suggest *not in Acco.* The Hebrew for *in Acco* sounds like the Hebrew for *weep.* [d] 10 *Beth Ophrah* means *house of dust.* [e] 11 *Shaphir* means *pleasant.* [f] 11 *Zaanan* sounds like the Hebrew for *come out.*

1:3–4 See "Storm Gods, Storm Imagery and Theophany" on page 808.
1:6–7 This prophecy was fulfilled during Micah's lifetime when Assyria destroyed Samaria in 722–721 B.C.
1:7 Prostitution is often an Old Testament symbol for idolatry or spiritual unfaithfulness. The wealth that Samaria had gained from her idolatry would be taken by the Assyrians and placed in their own temples to be used again in the worship of idols.
1:8 Going barefoot was a sign of mourning (see "Sackcloth and Ashes: Rituals of Lamentation" on p. 820). It is possible that Micah actually walked barefoot through Jerusalem, wearing only a loincloth of sackcloth ("naked").
1:9 The city gate was the place where the leaders of the city met to hold court, where the marketplace was located and where official business was transacted (see "The City Gate" on p. 392).
1:10–15 The towns mentioned in these verses lay in the Shephelah, the foothills between the Mediterranean coastal plain and the mountains of Judah.
1:10 Sitting in the dust was a sign of mourning.
1:11 Zaanan, located, like Moresheth, in the Shephelah region of Judah, has never been identified with certainty, but it may be Zenan.
Beth Ezel, a town in southern Judea in the Philistine plain, was for a time thought to be the same as Azel (Zec 14:5) but has now been identified with Deir el-Asal.

1:12 [y]Jer 14:19
1:13 [z]Jos 10:3
1:14 [a]2Ki 16:8 [b]Jos 15:44 [c]Jer 15:18
1:15 [d]Jos 15:44 [e]Jos 12:15
1:16 [f]Job 1:20

12 Those who live in Maroth[a] writhe in pain,
waiting for relief,[y]
because disaster has come from the LORD,
even to the gate of Jerusalem.
13 You who live in Lachish,[b][z]
harness the team to the chariot.
You were the beginning of sin
to the Daughter of Zion,
for the transgressions of Israel
were found in you.
14 Therefore you will give parting gifts[a]
to Moresheth Gath.
The town of Aczib[c][b] will prove deceptive[c]
to the kings of Israel.
15 I will bring a conqueror against you
who live in Mareshah.[d][d]
He who is the glory of Israel
will come to Adullam.[e]
16 Shave[f] your heads in mourning
for the children in whom you delight;
make yourselves as bald as the vulture,
for they will go from you into exile.

Man's Plans and God's

2:1 [g]Ps 36:4
2:2 [h]Isa 5:8 [i]Jer 22:17
2:3 [j]Jer 18:11; Am 3:1-2 [k]Isa 2:12
2:4 [l]Jer 4:13

2 Woe to those who plan iniquity,
to those who plot evil on their beds![g]
At morning's light they carry it out
because it is in their power to do it.
2 They covet fields[h] and seize them,
and houses, and take them.
They defraud[i] a man of his home,
a fellowman of his inheritance.

3 Therefore, the LORD says:

"I am planning disaster[j] against this people,
from which you cannot save yourselves.
You will no longer walk proudly,[k]
for it will be a time of calamity.
4 In that day men will ridicule you;
they will taunt you with this mournful song:
'We are utterly ruined;[l]
my people's possession is divided up.
He takes it from me!
He assigns our fields to traitors.' "

[a] 12 *Maroth* sounds like the Hebrew for *bitter.* [b] 13 *Lachish* sounds like the Hebrew for *team.* [c] 14 *Aczib* means *deception.* [d] 15 *Mareshah* sounds like the Hebrew for *conqueror.*

1:13 Lachish was one of the largest towns in Judah. Later, Sennacherib would decorate his palace at Nineveh with a relief picturing his exploits there (see "The Lachish Reliefs" on p. 559).

Micah condemned Lachish's chariots as "the beginning of sin to the Daughter of Zion," perhaps because the city was used as a staging point for the extravagant importation of Egyptian horses (cf. Dt 17:16; 1Ki 10:28–29).

1:14 The Hebrew for "parting gifts" is translated "wedding gift" in 1 Kings 9:16. Jerusalem would give up Moresheth Gath to Assyria, as a father gives a "wedding gift" to his daughter when she marries.

The only Biblical reference to Moresheth Gath, a town in the Judah-Philistine border area, appears in this verse, although verse 1 identifies the prophet as coming from Moresheth. "Gath" may have been added to the name to indicate that this was the Moresheth that was near Gath. It may be identified with Tell ej-Judeideh, located about five miles (eight km) west of Gath in the Shephelah region.

Aczib, a city of Judah (Jos 15:44) may be Tell el-beida, southwest of Adullam. The same location is variously called Kezib (Ge 38:5) and Cozeba (2Ch 4:22).

2:2 Land was intended to be the permanent possession of a particular family (see the notes on Nu 27:1–11; 1Ki 21:1–7; see also "Inheritance in the Ancient Near East" on p. 250).

[5]Therefore you will have no one in the assembly of the LORD
to divide the land[m] by lot.

2:5 [m]Jos 18:4

False Prophets

[6]"Do not prophesy," their prophets say.
"Do not prophesy about these things;
disgrace[n] will not overtake us.[o]"
[7]Should it be said, O house of Jacob:
"Is the Spirit of the LORD angry?
Does he do such things?"

2:6 [n]Mic 6:16 [o]Am 2:12

"Do not my words do good[p]
to him whose ways are upright?[q]
[8]Lately my people have risen up
like an enemy.
You strip off the rich robe
from those who pass by without a care,
like men returning from battle.
[9]You drive the women of my people
from their pleasant homes.[r]
You take away my blessing
from their children forever.
[10]Get up, go away!
For this is not your resting place,[s]
because it is defiled,[t]
it is ruined, beyond all remedy.
[11]If a liar and deceiver[u] comes and says,
'I will prophesy for you plenty of wine and beer,'
he would be just the prophet for this people![v]

2:7 [p]Ps 119:65 [q]Ps 15:2; 84:11
2:9 [r]Jer 10:20
2:10 [s]Dt 12:9 [t]Lev 18:25-29; Ps 106:38-39
2:11 [u]Jer 5:31 [v]Isa 30:10

Deliverance Promised

[12]"I will surely gather all of you, O Jacob;
I will surely bring together the remnant[w] of Israel.
I will bring them together like sheep in a pen,
like a flock in its pasture;
the place will throng with people.
[13]One who breaks open the way will go up before[x] them;
they will break through the gate and go out.
Their king will pass through before them,
the LORD at their head."

2:12 [w]Mic 4:7; 5:7; 7:18
2:13 [x]Isa 52:12

Leaders and Prophets Rebuked

3 Then I said,

"Listen, you leaders[y] of Jacob,
you rulers of the house of Israel.
Should you not know justice,
[2] you who hate good and love evil;
who tear the skin from my people
and the flesh from their bones;[z]
[3]who eat my people's flesh,[a]
strip off their skin
and break their bones in pieces;[b]
who chop them up like meat for the pan,
like flesh for the pot?[c]"

3:1 [y]Jer 5:5
3:2 [z]Ps 53:4; Eze 22:27
3:3 [a]Ps 14:4 [b]Zep 3:3 [c]Eze 11:7

2:6 See "Prophets in the Bible and Pagan Nations" on page 1457.

CHRONOLOGY OF THE PROPHETS

	To Israel	To Judah	To Foreign Nation
Assyrian Age	Amos: c. 763–750 B.C. Hosea: c. 755–715 B.C.	Isaiah: c. 740–700 B.C. Micah: c. 737–690 B.C.	Jonah: c. 770–750 B.C.
Babylonian Age		Habakkuk: c. 630–605 B.C. Zephaniah: c. 640–609 B.C. Jeremiah: c. 627–580 B.C. Daniel: c. 605–530 B.C. Ezekiel: c. 593–570 B.C.	Nahum: c. 663–615 B.C.
Persian Age		Haggai: 520 B.C. Zechariah: c. 520–518 B.C. Joel: c. 800–500 B.C. Malachi: c. 433 B.C.	Obadiah: c. 586–553 B.C.

Chronological and Background Charts of the Old Testament, p. 52

4 Then they will cry out to the LORD,
but he will not answer them.[d]
At that time he will hide his face[e] from them
because of the evil they have done.

5 This is what the LORD says:

"As for the prophets
who lead my people astray,[f]
if one feeds them,
they proclaim 'peace';
if he does not,
they prepare to wage war against him.
6 Therefore night will come over you, without visions,
and darkness, without divination.[g]
The sun will set for the prophets,[h]
and the day will go dark for them.
7 The seers will be ashamed[i]
and the diviners disgraced.[j]
They will all cover their faces
because there is no answer from God."

3:4 [d]Ps 18:41; Isa 1:15 [e]Dt 31:17
3:5 [f]Isa 3:12; 9:16
3:6 [g]Isa 8:19-22 [h]Isa 29:10
3:7 [i]Mic 7:16 [j]Isa 44:25

3:5 The false prophets predicted peace for Judah, while Micah forecast destruction and captivity (see v. 12; 4:10).

3:7 "Seers" is an older term for "prophets" (see "Prophets in the Bible and Pagan Nations" on p. 1457).

[8] But as for me, I am filled with power,
with the Spirit of the LORD,
and with justice and might,
to declare to Jacob his transgression,
to Israel his sin.[k]
[9] Hear this, you leaders of the house of Jacob,
you rulers of the house of Israel,
who despise justice
and distort all that is right;[l]
[10] who build[m] Zion with bloodshed,[n]
and Jerusalem with wickedness.[o]
[11] Her leaders judge for a bribe,
her priests teach for a price,
and her prophets tell fortunes for money.[p]
Yet they lean upon the LORD and say,
"Is not the LORD among us?
No disaster will come upon us."[q]
[12] Therefore because of you,
Zion will be plowed like a field,
Jerusalem will become a heap of rubble,[r]
the temple hill a mound overgrown with thickets.

3:8 [k]Isa 58:1
3:9 [l]Ps 58:1-2; Isa 1:23
3:10 [m]Jer 22:13 [n]Hab 2:12 [o]Eze 22:27
3:11 [p]Isa 1:23; Jer 6:13; Hos 4:8, 18 [q]Jer 7:4
3:12 [r]Jer 26:18

The Mountain of the LORD

4 In the last days

the mountain[s] of the LORD's temple will be established
as chief among the mountains;
it will be raised above the hills,[t]
and peoples will stream to it.[u]

[2] Many nations will come and say,

"Come, let us go up to the mountain of the LORD,[v]
to the house of the God of Jacob.[w]
He will teach us his ways,[x]
so that we may walk in his paths."
The law will go out from Zion,
the word of the LORD from Jerusalem.
[3] He will judge between many peoples
and will settle disputes for strong nations far and wide.[y]
They will beat their swords into plowshares
and their spears into pruning hooks.[z]
Nation will not take up sword against nation,
nor will they train for war anymore.[a]
[4] Every man will sit under his own vine
and under his own fig tree,[b]
and no one will make them afraid,[c]
for the LORD Almighty has spoken.[d]
[5] All the nations may walk
in the name of their gods;[e]

4:1 [s]Zec 8:3 [t]Eze 17:22 [u]Ps 22:27; 86:9; Jer 3:17
4:2 [v]Jer 31:6 [w]Zec 2:11; 14:16 [x]Ps 25:8-9; Isa 54:13
4:3 [y]Isa 11:4 [z]Joel 3:10 [a]Isa 2:4
4:4 [b]1Ki 4:25 [c]Lev 26:6 [d]Isa 1:20; Zec 3:10
4:5 [e]2Ki 17:29

3:12 Micah's preaching may have been instrumental in the reformation under King Hezekiah (see 2Ki 18:1–6; 2Ch 29–31; Jer 26:18–19). The destruction of Jerusalem eventually occurred in 586 B.C.

4:1–3 This passage is practically identical to Isaiah 2:2–4. Many have questioned whether Micah quoted Isaiah or vice versa, or whether both quoted a common oracle.

4:3 A plowshare was an iron point mounted on a wooden beam (ancient plows did not include what we know as a plowshare).

The pruning hook, an agricultural tool used in the cultivation of the vine, had a sharp, knifelike end for pruning (see also Isa 2:4; Joel 3:10).

4:4 To sit under one's own vine and fig tree was a proverbial picture of peace, security and contentment.

we will walk in the name of the LORD
our God for ever and ever.[f]

4:5 [f]Jos 24:14-15; Isa 26:8; Zec 10:12

The LORD's Plan

6 "In that day," declares the LORD,

"I will gather the lame;
I will assemble the exiles[g]
and those I have brought to grief.[h]
7 I will make the lame a remnant,[i]
those driven away a strong nation.
The LORD will rule over them in Mount Zion
from that day and forever.[j]
8 As for you, O watchtower of the flock,
O stronghold[a] of the Daughter of Zion,
the former dominion will be restored[k] to you;
kingship will come to the Daughter of
Jerusalem."

4:6 [g]Ps 147:2 [h]Eze 34:13,16; 37:21; Zep 3:19
4:7 [i]Mic 2:12 [j]Da 7:14; Lk 1:33; Rev 11:15
4:8 [k]Isa 1:26

9 Why do you now cry aloud—
have you no king?[l]
Has your counselor perished,
that pain seizes you like that of a woman in
labor?[m]
10 Writhe in agony, O Daughter of Zion,
like a woman in labor,
for now you must leave the city
to camp in the open field.
You will go to Babylon;[n]
there you will be rescued.
There the LORD will redeem[o] you
out of the hand of your enemies.

4:9 [l]Jer 8:19 [m]Jer 30:6
4:10 [n]2Ki 20:18; Isa 43:14 [o]Isa 48:20

11 But now many nations
are gathered against you.
They say, "Let her be defiled,
let our eyes gloat[p] over Zion!"
12 But they do not know
the thoughts of the LORD;
they do not understand his plan,[q]
he who gathers them like sheaves to the
threshing floor.
13 "Rise and thresh, O Daughter of Zion,
for I will give you horns of iron;
I will give you hoofs of bronze
and you will break to pieces many nations."[r]

You will devote their ill-gotten gains to the LORD,
their wealth to the Lord of all the earth.

4:11 [p]La 2:16; Ob 1:12
4:12 [q]Isa 55:8; Ro 11:33-34
4:13 [r]Da 2:44

[a] 8 Or *hill*

4:6 For "that day," see the note on Joel 1:15.
4:9—5:15 This section has as its background the wars of Hezekiah's day (see "Hezekiah Against the Assyrians" on p. 1118). The Assyrians under Sennacherib captured 40 cities of Judah and received tribute from Hezekiah (cf. 2Ki 18:13–16).
4:12–13 Threshing was done in one of two ways: (1) by beating the sheaves with a rod or flail or (2) by trampling them under the feet of oxen that pulled a wooden sled around the threshing floor (Isa 28:27). Threshing was done out-of-doors on a hard surface of the ground. The word "threshing" also was used figuratively to describe God's judgment (see Isa 21:10; 41:15; 1Co 9:10; "The Threshing Floor" on p. 608; and the note on Ruth 2:7).

A Promised Ruler From Bethlehem

5

Marshal your troops, O city of troops,[a]
for a siege is laid against us.
They will strike Israel's ruler
on the cheek[s] with a rod.

2 "But you, Bethlehem[t] Ephrathah,[u]
though you are small among the clans[b] of Judah,
out of you will come for me
one who will be ruler over Israel,
whose origins[c] are from of old,[v]
from ancient times."[d][w]

3 Therefore Israel will be abandoned
until the time when she who is in labor gives birth
and the rest of his brothers return
to join the Israelites.

4 He will stand and shepherd his flock[x]
in the strength of the LORD,
in the majesty of the name of the LORD his God.
And they will live securely, for then his greatness[y]
will reach to the ends of the earth.
5 And he will be their peace.[z]

Deliverance and Destruction

When the Assyrian invades[a] our land
and marches through our fortresses,
we will raise against him seven shepherds,
even eight leaders of men.[b]

6 They will rule[e] the land of Assyria with the sword,
the land of Nimrod[c] with drawn sword.[f][d]
He will deliver us from the Assyrian
when he invades our land
and marches into our borders.[e]

7 The remnant[f] of Jacob will be
in the midst of many peoples
like dew from the LORD,
like showers on the grass,[g]
which do not wait for man
or linger for mankind.

8 The remnant of Jacob will be among the nations,
in the midst of many peoples,
like a lion among the beasts of the forest,[h]
like a young lion among flocks of sheep,
which mauls and mangles[i] as it goes,
and no one can rescue.[j]

5:1 [s]La 3:30
5:2 [t]Jn 7:42 [u]Ge 48:7 [v]Ps 102:25 [w]Mt 2:6*
5:4 [x]Isa 40:11; 49:9; Eze 34:11-15,23; Mic 7:14 [y]Isa 52:13; Lk 1:32
5:5 [z]Isa 9:6; Lk 2:14; Col 1:19-20 [a]Isa 8:7 [b]Isa 10:24-27
5:6 [c]Ge 10:8 [d]Zep 2:13 [e]Na 2:11-13
5:7 [f]Mic 2:12 [g]Isa 44:4
5:8 [h]Ge 49:9 [i]Mic 4:13; Zec 10:5 [j]Ps 50:22; Hos 5:14

[a] 1 Or *Strengthen your walls, O walled city* [b] 2 Or *rulers* [c] 2 Hebrew *goings out* [d] 2 Or *from days of eternity* [e] 6 Or *crush* [f] 6 Or *Nimrod in its gates*

5:1 This prophecy was fulfilled when Jerusalem was besieged and her kings seized and taken to Babylon (Judah's last king, Zedekiah, was blinded). See "The Last Days of Jerusalem" on page 1197.
5:2 Against the Babylonian danger to Judah, God held out Messianic hope. The mention of Bethlehem Ephrathah (see "Bethlehem" on p. 1487) identifies the Messiah as belonging to David's line (cf. Isa 11:1; Jer 23:5; Eze 37:24). The "clans of Judah" is read as the "rulers of Judah" in Matthew 2:6 by using different (and probably correct) vowels with the Hebrew consonants. "You, Bethlehem," is masculine and is therefore most likely a direct reference to the Messiah from Bethlehem (the gender would be feminine if the city alone were being addressed).
5:5 Assyria here represents all of the enemies of God's people in every age.
"Seven ... even eight" is figurative for "an indefinite number."

5:9 [k]Ps 10:12
[9] Your hand will be lifted up[k] in triumph over your enemies,
and all your foes will be destroyed.

[10] "In that day," declares the LORD,

5:10 [l]Hos 14:3; Zec 9:10
"I will destroy your horses from among you
and demolish your chariots.[l]

5:6 Nimrod refers to Assyria (see Ge 10:8–12).

5:10 For "that day," see the note on Joel 1:15.

ARCHAEOLOGICAL SITES

BETHLEHEM

MICAH 5 Situated five miles (eight km) south of Jerusalem along the main ridge route ("Map 6"), Bethlehem ("house of bread") was an insignificant town during Old Testament times, except for being the birthplace of David, who was also anointed there by Samuel (1Sa 16).[1] The book of Ruth, which deals with David's paternal ancestors, is for the most part set in this village. The Old Testament does record a few other minor historical details about Bethlehem, however.[2] For a time a Philistine garrison controlled the town (2Sa 23:14–16). Also, Bethlehem was one of the villages that Rehoboam fortified in his effort to hold on to Judah after the defection of the northern tribes (2Ch 11:5–12). Micah prophesied that the Messiah would come from this otherwise insignificant community (5:2–5), but it was not unfitting that the Messianic "son of David" should be born in the birthplace of David.

Archaeologically, little is known of ancient Bethlehem. The site was occupied from prehistoric times (some prehistoric flints and split animal bones have been unearthed there). Bethlehem may be mentioned in one of the **Amarna** Letters, but this reference is disputed. Most archaeological research at Bethlehem, in fact, focuses on the Church of the Nativity and on the history of the site through the **Byzantine**, Islamic and Crusader periods.

Modern Bethlehem
Photograph: © Todd Bolen/Bible Places.com

Jesus' birth in Bethlehem is noted in the two Gospel infancy narratives (Mt 2:1; Lk 2:4),[3] and the testimony is clear that the Jewish leaders knew of Micah's prophecy that the Messiah would be born there (Mt 2:4–6; Jn 7:42). Although the slaughter of the infant and toddler boys of the town by Herod the Great is not attested in other ancient sources, the account fits the character of this paranoid "king."[4] The small size of the village at the time, clustered as it was on the hillside where the Church of the Nativity was later built, indicates that probably only a few dozen little boys were killed as the result of Herod's irrational fury. Heinous as this infanticide was, the incident would probably not have attracted the attention of ancient historians.

Very early church tradition locates Jesus' birth in a cave in Bethlehem, over which the emperor Hadrian constructed a shrine to a Roman deity. Later, the Christian emperor Constantine erected a church building over the cave.[5] After its partial destruction by the Samaritans in the sixth century A.D., the Church of the Nativity was rebuilt by the emperor Justinian and still stands today as one of the most ancient church buildings in existence.

[1]See "David" on page 443. [2]See "Rachel's Tomb" on page 411. [3]See "The Birthplace of Jesus" on page 1668. [4]See "Herod the Great" on page 1627. [5]See "Constantine and Queen Helena's Role in Preserving Holy Sites" on page 1758.

[11] I will destroy the cities[m] of your land
and tear down all your strongholds.[n]
[12] I will destroy your witchcraft
and you will no longer cast spells.[o]
[13] I will destroy your carved images
and your sacred stones from among you;
you will no longer bow down
to the work of your hands.[p]
[14] I will uproot from among you your Asherah
poles[a][q]
and demolish your cities.
[15] I will take vengeance[r] in anger and wrath
upon the nations that have not obeyed me."

5:11 [m]Isa 6:11 [n]Hos 10:14; Am 5:9
5:12 [o]Dt 18:10-12; Isa 2:6; 8:19
5:13 [p]Eze 6:9; Zec 13:2
5:14 [q]Ex 34:13
5:15 [r]Isa 65:12

The LORD's Case Against Israel

6 Listen to what the LORD says:

"Stand up, plead your case before the mountains;[s]
let the hills hear what you have to say.
[2] Hear,[t] O mountains, the LORD's accusation;[u]
listen, you everlasting foundations of the earth.
For the LORD has a case against his people;
he is lodging a charge[v] against Israel.

[3] "My people, what have I done to you?
How have I burdened[w] you? Answer me.
[4] I brought you up out of Egypt
and redeemed you from the land of slavery.[x]
I sent Moses[y] to lead you,
also Aaron[z] and Miriam.[a]
[5] My people, remember
what Balak[b] king of Moab counseled
and what Balaam son of Beor answered.
Remember ⌊your journey⌋ from Shittim[c] to Gilgal,[d]
that you may know the righteous acts[e] of
the LORD."

[6] With what shall I come before the LORD
and bow down before the exalted God?
Shall I come before him with burnt offerings,
with calves a year old?[f]
[7] Will the LORD be pleased with thousands of rams,[g]
with ten thousand rivers of oil?[h]
Shall I offer my firstborn[i] for my transgression,
the fruit of my body for the sin of my soul?[j]
[8] He has showed you, O man, what is good.
And what does the LORD require of you?
To act justly[k] and to love mercy
and to walk humbly[l] with your God.[m]

6:1 [s]Ps 50:1; Eze 6:2
6:2 [t]Dt 32:1 [u]Hos 12:2 [v]Ps 50:7
6:3 [w]Jer 2:5
6:4 [x]Dt 7:8 [y]Ex 4:16 [z]Ps 77:20 [a]Ex 15:20
6:5 [b]Nu 22:5-6 [c]Nu 25:1 [d]Jos 5:9-10 [e]Jdg 5:11; 1Sa 12:7
6:6 [f]Ps 40:6-8; 51:16-17
6:7 [g]Isa 40:16 [h]Ps 50:8-10 [i]Lev 18:21 [j]2Ki 16:3
6:8 [k]Isa 1:17; Jer 22:3 [l]Isa 57:15 [m]Dt 10:12-13; 1Sa 15:22; Hos 6:6

[a] *14* That is, symbols of the goddess Asherah

5:14 For "Asherah poles," see the note on 1 Kings 14:15.
6:1—7:6 The condemnations of this section include several references to the Pentateuch and to other historical books (6:5–16; cf. also 5:6 with Ge 10:8–9). The response of Micah 6:8 is famous. Some have argued that it teaches salvation apart from sacrifice, but it actually alludes to Deuteronomy 10:12 and involves Israel's duty to obey *all* of the Mosaic injunctions. Jesus probably referred to this verse in his condemnation of the formalistic Pharisees (Mt 23:23; see "The Pharisees" on p. 1566).
6:5 See "Shittim" on page 233 and "The Camp at Gilgal" on page 308.

Israel's Guilt and Punishment

9 Listen! The LORD is calling to the city—
and to fear your name is wisdom—
"Heed the rod and the One who appointed it.[a]
10 Am I still to forget, O wicked house,
your ill-gotten treasures
and the short ephah,[b] which is accursed?[n]
11 Shall I acquit a man with dishonest scales,[o]
with a bag of false weights?
12 Her rich men are violent;[p]
her people are liars[q]
and their tongues speak deceitfully.[r]
13 Therefore, I have begun to destroy[s] you,
to ruin you because of your sins.
14 You will eat but not be satisfied;[t]
your stomach will still be empty.[c]
You will store up but save nothing,[u]
because what you save I will give to the sword.
15 You will plant but not harvest;[v]
you will press olives but not use the oil on
yourselves,
you will crush grapes but not drink the wine.[w]
16 You have observed the statutes of Omri[x]
and all the practices of Ahab's[y] house,
and you have followed their traditions.[z]
Therefore I will give you over to ruin[a]
and your people to derision;
you will bear the scorn[b] of the nations.[d]"

6:10 [n]Eze 45:9-10; Am 3:10; 8:4-6
6:11 [o]Lev 19:36; Hos 12:7
6:12 [p]Isa 1:23 [q]Isa 3:8 [r]Jer 9:3
6:13 [s]Isa 1:7; 6:11
6:14 [t]Isa 9:20 [u]Isa 30:6
6:15 [v]Dt 28:38; Jer 12:13 [w]Am 5:11; Zep 1:13
6:16 [x]1Ki 16:25 [y]1Ki 16:29-33 [z]Jer 7:24 [a]Jer 25:9 [b]Jer 51:51

Israel's Misery

7

What misery is mine!
I am like one who gathers summer fruit
at the gleaning of the vineyard;
there is no cluster of grapes to eat,
none of the early figs that I crave.
2 The godly have been swept from the land;[c]
not one upright man remains.
All men lie in wait to shed blood;[d]
each hunts his brother with a net.[e]

7:2 [c]Ps 12:1 [d]Mic 3:10 [e]Jer 5:26

[a] *9* The meaning of the Hebrew for this line is uncertain. [b] *10* An ephah was a dry measure. [c] *14* The meaning of the Hebrew for this word is uncertain. [d] *16* Septuagint; Hebrew *scorn due my people*

6:9–16 These verses follow the outline of a divine covenant lawsuit: (1) an opening statement (v. 9); (2) a listing of commercial and social sins (vv. 10–12); (3) an announcement of divine punishment (vv. 13–15); and (4) a summary statement (v. 16).
6:10 An ephah was about half a bushel.
6:11 For "dishonest scales" and "false weights," see the notes on Proverbs 11:1 and 16:11; see also "Weights and Measures" on page 1459. A Hebrew balance consisted of a horizontal bar, either suspended from a cord that was held in the hand or pivoted on a perpendicular rod. Scales were suspended from the ends of the bar, one for the object to be weighed and the other for the weight. At first the weights were of stone. Weighing with such balances could be accurately done, but the system was liable to fraud.
6:14–15 This was a curse for disobedience (see Dt 28:38–39).
6:15 In the Bible oil is almost always olive oil, perhaps the only exception being Esther 2:12, where it is oil of myrrh. The olives were sometimes beaten (Lev 24:2), sometimes trodden (Mic 6:15), but generally crushed in a mill designed for that purpose.
6:16 Omri reigned from about 886 to 874 B.C. After he had prevailed over Tibni, he transferred the capital of the northern kingdom to Samaria, a location that was easily defended. This was perhaps his most significant accomplishment (v. 24). Although Omri is dismissed by one Hebrew historian as an evil influence (1Ki 16:25–26), he is the first Hebrew monarch to be mentioned in nonbiblical records, implying that he was a highly regarded king in his day. Mesha included Omri's name in the Mesha Stele (c. 847 B.C.), reflecting the fact that Omri subdued Moab. Sargon II (c. 721 B.C.; see "The Annals of Sargon II" on p. 1072) referred to Israel as "Omri-Land," and Tiglath-Pileser III spoke in his annals of the "house of Omri" (see "Omri and Samaria" on p. 512).

Omri and Ahab together committed more evil than all the other kings who had preceded them, cumulatively (see 1Ki 16:25,30; see also "Ahab and the Battle of Qarqar" on p. 524).

[3] Both hands are skilled in doing evil;[f]
the ruler demands gifts,
the judge accepts bribes,
the powerful dictate what they desire—
they all conspire together.
[4] The best of them is like a brier,[g]
the most upright worse than a thorn hedge.
The day of your watchmen has come,
the day God visits you.
Now is the time of their confusion.[h]
[5] Do not trust a neighbor;
put no confidence in a friend.[i]
Even with her who lies in your embrace
be careful of your words.
[6] For a son dishonors his father,
a daughter rises up against her mother,[j]
a daughter-in-law against her mother-in-law—
a man's enemies are the members of his own
household.[k]

[7] But as for me, I watch in hope[l] for the LORD,
I wait for God my Savior;
my God will hear[m] me.

Israel Will Rise

[8] Do not gloat over me,[n] my enemy!
Though I have fallen, I will rise.[o]
Though I sit in darkness,
the LORD will be my light.[p]
[9] Because I have sinned against him,
I will bear the LORD's wrath,[q]
until he pleads my case
and establishes my right.
He will bring me out into the light;
I will see his righteousness.[r]
[10] Then my enemy will see it
and will be covered with shame,[s]
she who said to me,
"Where is the LORD your God?"
My eyes will see her downfall;[t]
even now she will be trampled[u] underfoot
like mire in the streets.

[11] The day for building your walls[v] will come,
the day for extending your boundaries.
[12] In that day people will come to you
from Assyria and the cities of Egypt,
even from Egypt to the Euphrates
and from sea to sea
and from mountain to mountain.[w]
[13] The earth will become desolate because of its inhabitants,
as the result of their deeds.[x]

7:3 [f]Pr 4:16
7:4 [g]Eze 2:6 [h]Isa 22:5; Hos 9:7
7:5 [i]Jer 9:4
7:6 [j]Eze 22:7 [k]Mt 10:35-36*
7:7 [l]Ps 130:5; Isa 25:9 [m]Ps 4:3
7:8 [n]Pr 24:17 [o]Ps 37:24; Am 9:11 [p]Isa 9:2
7:9 [q]La 3:39-40 [r]Isa 46:13
7:10 [s]Ps 35:26 [t]Isa 51:23 [u]Zec 10:5
7:11 [v]Isa 54:11
7:12 [w]Isa 19:23-25
7:13 [x]Isa 3:10-11

7:4 The prophets were likened to watchmen assigned to warn of approaching danger—in this case, impending judgment (see Eze 3:17; Hos 9:8 and their notes).

7:7 A hopeful element is actually quite common in laments (see "Ancient Near Eastern Laments" on p. 1305).

7:12 For "that day," see the note on Joel 1:15.

TEXTS OF THE OLD TESTAMENT

MICAH 7 For anyone who regards the Old Testament as the Word of God, a critically important question is, How do I know that the text we now have accurately reflects what the ancient authors wrote and that scribal errors have not seriously distorted it? As a matter of fact, the ancient texts and versions of the Old Testament are themselves the tools scholars use to confirm that the Old Testament as it has been handed down to us does indeed reflect the original.

The Old Testament was originally written in Hebrew (with a few chapters in **Aramaic**). As Jews spread out in the **Diaspora** they began to speak other languages, and, as Christianity spread among Gentiles, people who knew no Hebrew whatsoever wanted to read Scripture. Thus, translations of the Old Testament were produced in Greek, Aramaic, Egyptian, Latin and other languages. At the same time Jewish scribes continued to copy and preserve the Hebrew Old Testament. Today there are thousands of Old Testament texts available on leather and papyrus scrolls and in fragments—some more than 2,000 years old.

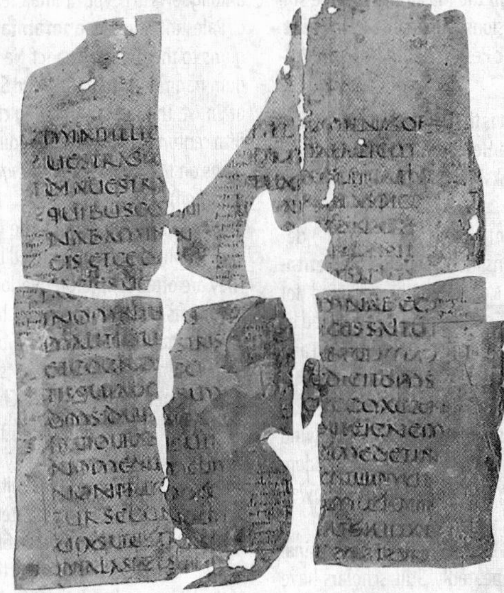

Fragment of Ezekiel in the Old Latin Version; Northern Italy, fifth century A.D.

© The Schøyen Collection; photography courtesy of Mr. Martin Schøyen

The Hebrew Manuscripts

Not one original Biblical manuscript still exists, but the most significant witnesses to the original Hebrew text are the **Masoretic Text** and the **Dead Sea Scrolls**:

◆ *The Masoretic Text*: This is the Hebrew Bible as it exists today.

Its origin: Until the sixth century A.D. only the consonants of the Hebrew Old Testament were written down; the language contained no vowels. The tradition of correct pronunciation of ancient Hebrew words was passed down orally. But between A.D. 500 and 1000 a group of Jewish scholars known as the Masoretes (from *maser*—"to hand down; transmit") developed a system of adding vowels, accents and notes that guaranteed more accurate reading and copying of the ancient texts.

Its quality: No other text from the ancient world was as carefully safeguarded as the Masoretic Text. Its tradition came to be regarded as authoritative and can still be considered highly trustworthy.

Early manuscripts: The earliest complete Masoretic manuscript, the Leningrad Codex (A.D. 1009), is used for the standard edition of the Hebrew Bible. Another ancient copy, although partially lost, is the Aleppo Codex (A.D. 925).

◆ *The Dead Sea Scrolls*: With the discovery in 1947 of 800 scrolls in the Judean Desert, dating from approximately 250 B.C. to A.D. 135 and including every Old Testament book except Esther,[1] the age of the most ancient extant Old Testament manuscripts increased by a thousand years! The Dead Sea Scrolls contain Hebrew, Greek and Aramaic manuscripts and fragments, many of which are Biblical in nature. Significantly, a great number of the Hebrew Bible manuscripts found reflect essentially the same text as that inherited by the Masoretes, confirming the antiquity and authority of the Masoretic Text.

[1]See "The Canonicity of Esther" on page 730.

THE ANCIENT TRANSLATIONS

MICAH 7 Since the discovery of the Dead Sea Scrolls, the ancient versions or translations of the Bible have become less important for establishing the original Old Testament text.[1] Nevertheless, readings that differ from the Masoretic Text are still evaluated in at least four early versions: the Greek **Septuagint**, the Aramaic **Targums**, the **Syriac** Peshitta and the Latin **Vulgate**.

◆ *Septuagint*: The most important is the Septuagint, which contains the Greek translation of the Hebrew Bible, along with a number of noncanonical Greek works known by Protestant Christians as the **Apocrypha**.[2]

Its origin: The title "Septuagint" (Latin for "seventy") derives from the tradition that 72 translators rendered the **Pentateuch** into Greek around 285 B.C. Originally designed for Greek-speaking Jews in Egypt, the Septuagint was completed by various translators in or around Alexandria between the third and first centuries B.C. The Bible of the early church, it is frequently quoted in the New Testament and by early church fathers.

Its structure: The Septuagint is organized in the following order: the Pentateuch, followed by the historical, poetic, wisdom and prophetic books. The Septuagint order is loosely followed by our English translations.

Its original text: We do not have a perfect copy of the original Septuagint, which was revised repeatedly. Still, scholars have largely been able to reconstruct the text, and the work is ongoing.

Its quality: The Septuagint is varied in character—the work of numerous translators from different times and with varying capabilities and styles (ranging from rigidly literal to loosely paraphrastic).

Comparison to the Masoretic Text: The Septuagint is similar to the Hebrew Masoretic Text; when translated into English, many parts are almost identical. Yet the two are sometimes quite different.[3]

Its value: The Septuagint is the most useful version for helping us establish the original Old Testament text because it: (1) is the earliest translation of the entire Old Testament, (2) is well attested in numerous manuscripts and (3) differs in a number of important places from the Masoretic Text, providing an alternative rendering to what appears there.[4]

◆ *Aramaic Targums*: This is not a single work but a series of interpretations of Old Testament books.

Their origin: Just as Greek became the common language among Jews in Egypt, Aramaic replaced Hebrew among the Jews of Palestine and **Mesopotamia**. Jewish tradition dates the Targums to the time of Ezra (cf. Ne 8:8), but the oldest known Targum fragments from the Dead Sea Scrolls date to near the time of Christ. The Targum tradition climaxed between the third and fifth centuries A.D. with the production of the official rabbinic Targums on the Torah (*Targum Onqelos*) and the Prophets (*Targum Jonathan*).

Their quality and value: The Targums provide a paraphrastic translation, often accompanied by commentary or explanation. They are often so interpretive, loosely translated and filled with comments that it is hard to use them to confirm the original text.

◆ *Peshitta*: The authorized Bible of the Syrian Church is the Peshitta (meaning "simple" or "straightforward"). Whether the Old Testament Peshitta had a Christian or Jewish origin is difficult to discern. In its earliest form, dating no later than the fourth century A.D., the Old Testament Peshitta was a relatively literal translation of a Hebrew text similar to the Masoretic Text. In time, however, the Syriac was updated and the text smoothed over, though we still have remnants of the original.

◆ *The Vulgate*: By the mid-fourth century A.D. the Christian Bible of the Western church was the Latin translation of the Septuagint. But between A.D. 390 and 405 the Christian scholar Jerome set out to reclaim "the truth of the Hebrew text." Assisted by later Septuagint versions, Jerome translated the Hebrew Old Testament into Latin. His work now makes up the Old Testament portion of the Latin Bible called the Vulgate ("common" or "popular"). Because Jerome was largely dependent on the Septuagint and his own translation varies in literalness, the Old Testament Vulgate must be used cautiously as a witness to the Hebrew original.

When the Hebrew of the Masoretic Text is compared to that of the Dead Sea Scrolls and then to the various other versions, the Masoretic Text is in the vast majority of instances vindicated and regarded as accurately reflecting the original words of the Biblical authors.

[1]See "Textual Criticism" on page 1151. [2]See "The Apocrypha" on page 1973. [3]For an example, see "The Problem of the Septuagint Version of Jeremiah" on page 1240. [4]See "The Septuagint and the Masoretic Text" on page 1254.

Prayer and Praise

7:14 [y]Mic 5:4 [z]Ps 23:4 [a]Jer 50:19

[14] Shepherd[y] your people with your staff,[z]
the flock of your inheritance,
which lives by itself in a forest,
in fertile pasturelands.[a]
Let them feed in Bashan and Gilead[a]
as in days long ago.

7:15 [b]Ex 3:20; Ps 78:12

[15] "As in the days when you came out of Egypt,
I will show them my wonders.[b]"

7:16 [c]Isa 26:11

[16] Nations will see and be ashamed,[c]
deprived of all their power.
They will lay their hands on their mouths
and their ears will become deaf.
[17] They will lick dust like a snake,
like creatures that crawl on the ground.
They will come trembling out of their dens;

7:17 [d]Isa 25:3; 49:23; 59:19

they will turn in fear[d] to the LORD our God
and will be afraid of you.
[18] Who is a God like you,

7:18 [e]Isa 43:25; Jer 50:20 [f]Ps 103:8-13 [g]Mic 2:12 [h]Ex 34:9 [i]Ps 103:9 [j]Jer 32:41

who pardons sin[e] and forgives[f] the transgression
of the remnant[g] of his inheritance?[h]
You do not stay angry[i] forever
but delight to show mercy.[j]
[19] You will again have compassion on us;
you will tread our sins underfoot

7:19 [k]Isa 43:25 [l]Jer 31:34

and hurl all our iniquities[k] into the depths of the sea.[l]
[20] You will be true to Jacob,
and show mercy to Abraham,

7:20 [m]Dt 7:8; Lk 1:72

as you pledged on oath to our fathers[m]
in days long ago.

[a] 14 Or *in the middle of Carmel*

7:14 Throughout the ancient Near East the term "shepherd" was often applied to rulers (see 2Sa 5:2; Jer 23:2; see also "Shepherding in the Ancient World" on p. 1363). Bashan and Gilead were fertile areas with rich pasturelands (for Bashan, see the note on Eze 39:18).

INTRODUCTION TO 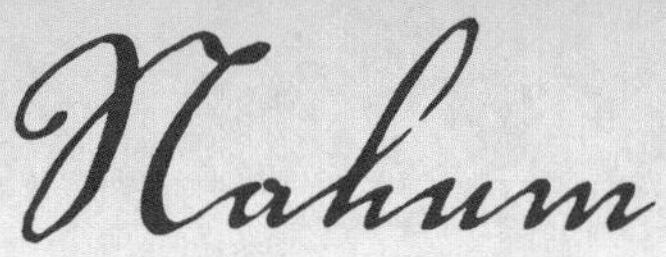

Nahum

AUTHOR, PLACE AND DATE OF WRITING

We know nothing of the author of this book, the prophet Nahum, other than that he came from Elkosh, a village of unknown location. Based on his harsh condemnation of Nineveh, some interpreters suggest that he was a kind of “super-patriot” prophet similar to Hananiah, a false prophet condemned by Jeremiah (Jer 28). This is an unnecessary conclusion; even Jeremiah spoke words of judgment against other nations (Jer 46–51). Nahum did not simply cheer for the fall of Nineveh; he set this event within the context of the Biblical theology of the justice of God.

Nahum 3:8–10 mentions the destruction of Thebes in Egypt, which took place in 663 B.C., and the book of Nahum anticipates the fall of Nineveh, which occurred in 612 B.C. We can therefore assume that the book was written during the latter half of seventh century B.C., or about 630.

AUDIENCE

Nahum addressed his prophecy to the people of Nineveh, the capital city of the ruthless Assyrians, as well as to the nation of Judah. His message of doom for Nineveh (approximately 100 years after the Ninevites’ evidently short-lived repentance under Jonah’s ministry) was a comfort to the people of Judah, who had seen the northern kingdom of Israel defeated and carried into exile by the Assyrians and who were themselves suffering under that nation’s cruelty. Nahum reminded his readers that God is just and that the evil nations of the world cannot and will not escape his judgment.

CULTURAL FACTS AND HIGHLIGHTS

Nahum prophesied the fall of Nineveh, the capital of the Neo-Assyrian Empire at the height of its power (see “Nineveh” on p. 1497). The brutality of the Assyrians was legendary, and their treatment of Israel and Judah had been particularly harsh.

TIMELINE

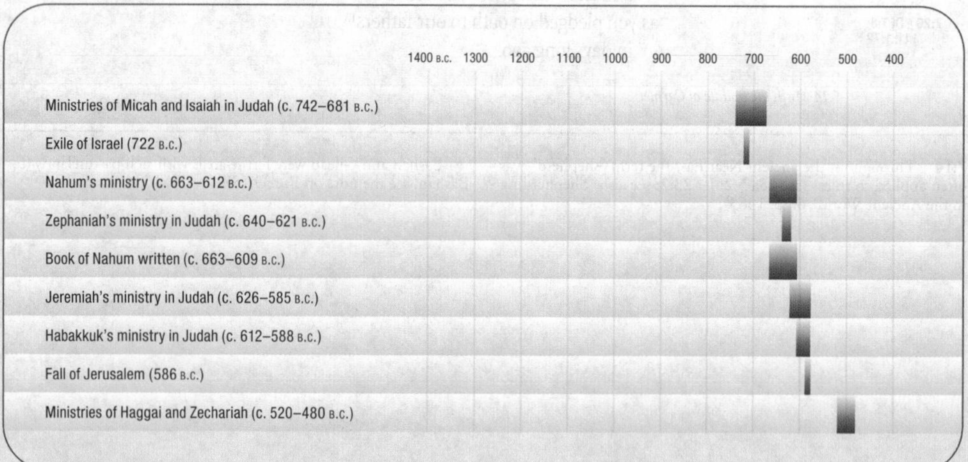

AS YOU READ

Pay attention to the literary devices Nahum employed in this poetic book, noting and appreciating his rich vocabulary and the intense moods he attempted to evoke; his masterful use of simile and metaphor; his vivid word pictures; his effective use of repetition; his penchant for short, staccato phrases (see, e.g., 3:1–3); and his frequent rhetorical questions.

DID YOU KNOW?

- It was common practice for peoples in the ancient world to identify their deities with observable, awe-inspiring natural phenomena (1:3–6).
- Nineveh's wall, which was almost 8 miles (13 km) long with 15 gates, was surrounded by a moat 150 feet (nearly 46 m) wide. The moat had to be filled in before attackers could reach the city wall. The "protective shield" refers to a large defensive shelter covered with hides to deflect stones and arrows (2:5).
- The lion is an appropriate image for Assyria, which was known for its viciousness. Nineveh itself contained numerous lion sculptures (2:11).
- The Assyrian king Shalmaneser III boasted of having erected a pyramid of chopped-off heads in front of an enemy's city. Other Assyrian kings stacked corpses like cordwood by the gates of defeated cities (3:3).
- Atrocities against civilians were common in ancient warfare: Infants were routinely killed, leaders often put in chains and lots cast to determine which prisoners of war would be taken into exile and resettled in other lands (3:10).
- Nineveh's destruction was so complete that the decimated city was never rebuilt. Within a few centuries it was covered with wind-blown sand, leaving no trace except a mound that is known today as Tell Kuyunjik, "the mound of many sheep" (3:19).

THEMES

Nahum's themes include:

1. *Judgment.* According to the prophet the instrument of Nineveh's destruction would be God himself (1:2–3,8,14–15). The Ninevites had failed to live in the light of their earlier and evidently transitory repentance. Nahum made ample use of the divine warrior theme, the picture of God as a military figure who wages war against those who resist him. Nahum taught that God punishes violence (2:12; 3:1,4), idolatry (2:14), ruthless business practices (3:16), materialism (2:9; 3:4) and cruelty (3:19).

2. *Deliverance.* Nahum's prophecy of judgment was intended to bring hope to the people of Judah, who had suffered Assyrian abuse for many years. God cares for his people and will punish those who abuse them. He will protect them (1:7), free them from oppression (1:13,15) and restore them (2:2).

OUTLINE

- I. The Lord As Nineveh's Judge (1)
  - A. God's Anger Against Nineveh (1:2–8)
  - B. God's Judgment on Nineveh and Victory for Judah (1:9–15)
- II. Nineveh's Fall (2)
  - A. The Siege (2:1–10)
  - B. The Desolation (2:11–13)
- III. Woe to Nineveh (3)
  - A. Nineveh's Sins (3:1–4)
  - B. Nineveh's Coming Doom (3:5–19)

1 An oracle[a] concerning Nineveh.[b] The book of the vision of Nahum the Elkoshite.

The LORD's Anger Against Nineveh

[2] The LORD is a jealous[c] and avenging God;
the LORD takes vengeance[d] and is filled with wrath.
The LORD takes vengeance on his foes
and maintains his wrath against his enemies.
[3] The LORD is slow to anger[e] and great in power;
the LORD will not leave the guilty unpunished.[f]
His way is in the whirlwind and the storm,
and clouds[g] are the dust of his feet.
[4] He rebukes the sea and dries it up;
he makes all the rivers run dry.
Bashan and Carmel[h] wither
and the blossoms of Lebanon fade.
[5] The mountains quake[i] before him
and the hills melt away.[j]
The earth trembles at his presence,
the world and all who live in it.
[6] Who can withstand his indignation?
Who can endure[k] his fierce anger?
His wrath is poured out like fire;[l]
the rocks are shattered[m] before him.

[7] The LORD is good,[n]
a refuge in times of trouble.
He cares for[o] those who trust in him,
[8] but with an overwhelming flood
he will make an end of ⌊Nineveh⌋;
he will pursue his foes into darkness.

[9] Whatever they plot against the LORD
he[a] will bring to an end;
trouble will not come a second time.
[10] They will be entangled among thorns[p]
and drunk from their wine;
they will be consumed like dry stubble.[b][q]
[11] From you, ⌊O Nineveh,⌋ has one come forth
who plots evil against the LORD
and counsels wickedness.

[12] This is what the LORD says:

"Although they have allies and are numerous,
they will be cut off[r] and pass away.
Although I have afflicted you, ⌊O Judah,⌋
I will afflict you no more.[s]

1:1 [a]Isa 13:1; 19:1; Jer 23:33-34 [b]Jnh 1:2; Na 2:8; Zep 2:13
1:2 [c]Ex 20:5 [d]Dt 32:41; Ps 94:1
1:3 [e]Ne 9:17 [f]Ex 34:7 [g]Ps 104:3
1:4 [h]Isa 33:9
1:5 [i]Ex 19:18 [j]Mic 1:4
1:6 [k]Mal 3:2 [l]Jer 10:10 [m]1Ki 19:11
1:7 [n]Jer 33:11 [o]Ps 1:6
1:10 [p]2Sa 23:6 [q]Isa 5:24; Mal 4:1
1:12 [r]Isa 10:34 [s]Isa 54:6-8; La 3:31-32

[a] 9 Or *What do you foes plot against the LORD? / He* [b] 10 The meaning of the Hebrew for this verse is uncertain.

1:1 See "Oracles of the Ancient World" on page 1507, as well as "Nineveh" on page 1497. Here the capital city stands for the entire Assyrian Empire.

Nahum is called the Elkoshite. The third- and fourth-century A.D. theologian Jerome stated that a town in Galilee named Elkosh had been shown to him. The Nestorians locate the town and the tomb of the prophet near the Tigris, north of Mosul, Iraq. Another tradition places Elkosh "beyond Jordan," but emendations of that text and other considerations lead some to believe that Elkosh was actually located in southern Judah.

1:3–6 It was common practice for peoples in the ancient world to identify their deities with observable, awe-inspiring natural phenomena (see "Storm Gods, Storm Imagery and Theophany" on p. 808).

1:4 Bashan, Carmel and Lebanon were known for their fertility, including their vineyards, trees and animals (see the notes on SS 7:5; Isa 2:13; 33:9; Eze 39:18).

1:11 The "one" may refer to the Assyrian king Ashurbanipal (669–627 B.C.), the last great Assyrian emperor, whose western expeditions succeeded in subduing Egypt and to whom King Manasseh had to submit as a vassal (see 2Ch 33:11–13; Ezr 4:9–10; see also "The Seal of Manasseh" on p. 565).

ARCHAEOLOGICAL SITES

NINEVEH

NAHUM 1 Located at Mosul, Iraq, Nineveh ("Maps 8a–8b") was an ancient city first inhabited as early as the seventh millennium B.C. The prominence of this city in the Bible, however, is due to its distinction as one of the capital cities of the **Assyrian** Empire,[1] which dominated the ancient Near East for most of the period from 900 to 612 B.C. Nineveh was at the height of its power under the Assyrian kings Sennacherib, Esarhaddon and Ashurbanipal. Numerous important archaeological finds at Nineveh come from the period during which these kings reigned:

Assyrian slingers attack a city in an Assyrian panel dated c. 700 B.C.

Preserving Bible Times; © Dr. James C. Martin

- The walls of the city, nearly 8 miles (13 km) long, enclosed an area covering approximately 1,700 acres.
- Portions of the palace, covering three large city blocks, have been excavated. Painted, sculptured **reliefs** depicting Sennacherib's exploits, including his defeat of Lachish in 701 B.C. (2Ki 18:14,17),[2] lined the walls.
- The city boasted an enormous number of parks and water gardens, which may account for the focus on waters in Nahum 2:8.
- Sennacherib's account of his conquest of Judah in 701 B.C. (2Ki 18:13—19:36) was found here. Hezekiah is mentioned by name in Sennacherib's version.[3]
- Other records mention Manasseh, king of Judah, who supplied building materials for Esarhaddon's palace at Nineveh and troops for Ashurbanipal's invasion of Egypt.[4]
- One of the most significant finds was Ashurbanipal's library. It contained about 1,500 different texts, some with multiple copies, including archival, literary, magical, medical, divinatory and ritual tablets.[5]

The book of Nahum, as well as Zephaniah 2:13–15, predicts the defeat and destruction of Nineveh. These prophecies were fulfilled when a coalition of **Babylonians**, Medes and Scythians overthrew the city in 612 B.C., as described in the Babylonian Chronicle.

[1]See Glossary on page 2080 for definitions of bolded words. [2]See "The Lachish Reliefs" on page 559. [3]See "The Sennacherib Prism" on page 659. [4]See "The Seal of Manasseh" on page 565. [5]See "The Coronation of Ashurbanipal" on page 868.

Assyrian archers at Lachish in Judah

Preserving Bible Times; © Dr. James C. Martin

[13] Now I will break their yoke[t] from your neck
and tear your shackles away."

[14] The LORD has given a command concerning you, ⌞Nineveh⌟:
"You will have no descendants to bear your name.[u]
I will destroy the carved images[v] and cast idols
that are in the temple of your gods.
I will prepare your grave,[w]
for you are vile."

[15] Look, there on the mountains,
the feet of one who brings good news,[x]
who proclaims peace![y]
Celebrate your festivals,[z] O Judah,
and fulfill your vows.
No more will the wicked invade you;[a]
they will be completely destroyed.

1:13 [t]Isa 9:4
1:14 [u]Isa 14:22 [v]Mic 5:13 [w]Eze 32:22-23
1:15 [x]Isa 40:9; Ro 10:15 [y]Isa 52:7 [z]Lev 23:2-4 [a]Isa 52:1

Nineveh to Fall

2 An attacker[b] advances against you, ⌞Nineveh⌟.
Guard the fortress,
watch the road,
brace yourselves,
marshal all your strength!

[2] The LORD will restore[c] the splendor[d] of Jacob
like the splendor of Israel,
though destroyers have laid them waste
and have ruined their vines.

[3] The shields of his soldiers are red;
the warriors are clad in scarlet.[e]
The metal on the chariots flashes
on the day they are made ready;
the spears of pine are brandished.[a]
[4] The chariots[f] storm through the streets,
rushing back and forth through the squares.
They look like flaming torches;
they dart about like lightning.

[5] He summons his picked troops,
yet they stumble[g] on their way.
They dash to the city wall;
the protective shield is put in place.
[6] The river gates[h] are thrown open
and the palace collapses.

2:1 [b]Jer 51:20
2:2 [c]Eze 37:23 [d]Isa 60:15
2:3 [e]Eze 23:14-15
2:4 [f]Jer 4:13
2:5 [g]Jer 46:12
2:6 [h]Na 3:13

[a] 3 Hebrew; Septuagint and Syriac / *the horsemen rush to and fro*

1:13 The yoke was a common ancient Near Eastern symbol of political submission. Here it symbolizes Judah's submission as Assyria's vassal.

1:14–15 God used the Babylonians and Medes to destroy Nineveh in 612 B.C. For the fulfillment of this prophecy, see Ezekiel 32:22–23.

2:1—3:9 Nabopolassar was the first ruler of the Neo-Babylonian Empire (626–605 B.C.). Allied with Medes and Scythians, he overthrew the Assyrian Empire, destroying Nineveh in 612, as prophesied in this passage and in Zephaniah 2:13–15.

2:1 The "attacker" refers to the alliance of the Medes under Cyaxares and the Babylonians under Nabopolassar.

2:5 The pronoun "he" refers either to the king of Assyria or to Nabopolassar.

Nineveh's wall, which was almost 8 miles (13 km) long with 15 gates, was surrounded by a moat 150 feet (nearly 46 m) wide. The moat had to be filled in before attackers could reach the city's wall, after which battering rams could be moved up (see "Siege Warfare" on p. 465). The "protective shield" refers to a large, defensive framework covered with hides to deflect stones and arrows.

2:6 "River gates" may be a reference to the dams on the Khoser River, which ran through the city to the Tigris River (see "The Tigris and Euphrates Rivers" on p. 604). The dams were either already in place or quickly built to back up the river water; they were then sud-

[7] It is decreed[a] that ⌞the city⌟
be exiled and carried away.
Its slave girls moan[i] like doves
and beat upon their breasts.[j]
[8] Nineveh is like a pool,
and its water is draining away.
"Stop! Stop!" they cry,
but no one turns back.
[9] Plunder the silver!
Plunder the gold!
The supply is endless,
the wealth from all its treasures!
[10] She is pillaged, plundered, stripped!
Hearts melt, knees give way,
bodies tremble, every face grows pale.[k]

[11] Where now is the lions' den,[l]
the place where they fed their young,
where the lion and lioness went,
and the cubs, with nothing to fear?
[12] The lion killed[m] enough for his cubs
and strangled the prey for his mate,
filling his lairs with the kill
and his dens with the prey.

[13] "I am against[n] you,"
declares the LORD Almighty.
"I will burn up your chariots in smoke,[o]
and the sword will devour your young lions.
I will leave you no prey on the earth.
The voices of your messengers
will no longer be heard."

2:7 [i]Isa 59:11 [j]Isa 32:12
2:10 [k]Isa 29:22
2:11 [l]Isa 5:29
2:12 [m]Jer 51:34
2:13 [n]Jer 21:13; Na 3:5 [o]Ps 46:9

Woe to Nineveh

3 Woe to the city of blood,[p]
full of lies,
full of plunder,
never without victims!
[2] The crack of whips,
the clatter of wheels,
galloping horses
and jolting chariots!
[3] Charging cavalry,
flashing swords
and glittering spears!

3:1 [p]Eze 22:2; Mic 3:10

[a] 7 The meaning of the Hebrew for this word is uncertain.

denly released to ensure that the flooding would damage the city's walls. One ancient historian (the author of the Babylonian Chronicles) spoke of a flood that washed away some of the wall, making it easier for invaders to enter the city.
2:7 Slave girls occupied the lowest rung of the social order (see "Slavery and Labor Law in the Ancient Near East" on p. 127).
2:8 Some think that this verse refers to the Tigris and the smaller rivers that may have encircled and run through parts of the city, as well as to a system of dams that may have been used to make the city more secure (see the note on v. 6).
2:10 That a great quantity of plunder was carried off is confirmed in the Babylonian Chronicles.
2:11 The lion is an appropriate image for Assyria, known for its viciousness (see the notes on 3:1,3). Nineveh itself contained numerous lion sculptures.
2:12 Nineveh was filled with the spoils of war from numerous conquered nations.
3:1 The Assyrians were noted for their ruthlessness, brutality and terrible atrocities. Many of their victims were beheaded, impaled or burned.
3:3 The Assyrian king Shalmaneser III boasted of erecting a pyramid of chopped-off heads in front of an enemy's city. Other Assyrian kings stacked corpses like cordwood by the gates of defeated cities.

Many casualties,
piles of dead,
bodies without number,
people stumbling over the corpses[q]—
4 all because of the wanton lust of a harlot,
alluring, the mistress of sorceries,[r]
who enslaved nations by her prostitution[s]
and peoples by her witchcraft.

5 "I am against[t] you," declares the LORD
Almighty.
"I will lift your skirts[u] over your face.
I will show the nations your nakedness[v]
and the kingdoms your shame.
6 I will pelt you with filth,[w]
I will treat you with contempt[x]
and make you a spectacle.[y]
7 All who see you will flee from you and say,
'Nineveh[z] is in ruins—who will mourn
for her?'[a]
Where can I find anyone to comfort[b] you?"
8 Are you better than[c] Thebes,[a][d]
situated on the Nile,[e]
with water around her?
The river was her defense,
the waters her wall.
9 Cush[b][f] and Egypt were her boundless
strength;
Put[g] and Libya[h] were among her allies.
10 Yet she was taken captive[i]
and went into exile.
Her infants were dashed[j] to pieces
at the head of every street.
Lots were cast for her nobles,
and all her great men were put in chains.
11 You too will become drunk;[k]
you will go into hiding[l]
and seek refuge from the enemy.

12 All your fortresses are like fig trees
with their first ripe fruit;
when they are shaken,
the figs[m] fall into the mouth of the eater.

3:3 [q]2Ki 19:35; Isa 34:3
3:4 [r]Isa 47:9 [s]Isa 23:17; Eze 16:25-29
3:5 [t]Na 2:13 [u]Jer 13:22 [v]Isa 47:3
3:6 [w]Job 9:31 [x]1Sa 2:30; Jer 51:37 [y]Isa 14:16
3:7 [z]Na 1:1 [a]Jer 15:5 [b]Isa 51:19
3:8 [c]Am 6:2 [d]Jer 46:25 [e]Isa 19:6-9
3:9 [f]2Ch 12:3 [g]Eze 27:10 [h]Eze 30:5
3:10 [i]Isa 20:4 [j]Isa 13:16; Hos 13:16
3:11 [k]Isa 49:26 [l]Isa 2:10
3:12 [m]Isa 28:4

[a] 8 Hebrew *No Amon* [b] 9 That is, the upper Nile region

3:4 Nineveh was a city of luxury, wealth and witchcraft (see "Akkadian Divination" on p. 277).
3:5 Public disgrace and humiliation constituted a common punishment for prostitutes and adulteresses.
3:8 "No Amon" (see the NIV text note), better known by its Greek name, Thebes, was the great capital of Upper (southern) Egypt. The city was destroyed by the Assyrians in 663 B.C. (see "Thebes" on p. 1354). Located 450 miles (726 km) south of Cairo, it is now known by the names Karnak and Luxor and is famed for its huge necropolis (large, elaborate cemetery) on the western side of the Nile. Amon, an Egyptian deity, appears in the Old Testament linked with this city. During the period of the Theban Dynasties (from 1991 B.C.), Amon became the state god of the Egyptian empire. His city and priesthood came to such glory that Nahum was able to recall its downfall as evidence to great Nineveh that its time of desolation would surely come as well.
3:9 For "Cush" and "Put," see the note on Jeremiah 46:9.
3:10 Atrocities against civilians were common in ancient warfare (see the note on Ps 137:9; see also "Warfare in the Ancient World" on p. 950 and "Siege Warfare" on p. 465): Infants were routinely killed (see the note on Isa 13:16), leaders were often put in chains and lots were cast to determine which prisoners of war would be taken into exile and distributed to other lands (see "Casting Lots" on p. 744). The Assyrian king Ashurbanipal gave this description of his treatment of a captured leader: "I . . . put a dog chain on him and made him occupy a kennel at the eastern gate of Nineveh."

Assyria Through the Middle Assyrian Period

NAHUM 3 The heartland of **Assyria** lay in a small area in northern **Mesopotamia**, centered on the Tigris River. Villages were established in this area by 7000 B.C., although traces of human activity appear from thousands of years earlier. The great cities of Assyria included **Asshur** (founded c. 2700 B.C.), Nineveh[1] (founded c. 3000 B.C.) and Kalhu (Biblical Calah, modern Nimrud; founded c. 878 B.C.; "Map 8b"). Although Assyria was dominated early on by **Babylonia**, it eventually became the most powerful empire in the ancient Near East. Its history was one of continual expansion and retraction.

Old Assyrian Period (c. 2334–1275 B.C.)

Early in its history Assyria was a group of independent cities. The empire of Sargon of Akkad (c. 2334–2279 B.C.) exercised authority in Assyria, and a king in Sargon's line, Manishtushu (c. 2269–2255 B.C.), is said to have built a temple in Nineveh. With the collapse of the power of Akkad, Assyria came under another Mesopotamian power, the Third Dynasty of Ur (c. 2112–2004 B.C.). Sometime later Asshur won its independence and began to establish trading colonies in **Anatolia**. Thousands of **cuneiform** documents from the Anatolian town of Kanish (modern Kultepe) provide detailed information about prosperous Assyrian merchant colonies from approximately 1900 to 1750 B.C.

At the same time **Amorite** tribes from the west began to invade Mesopotamia. An Amorite ruler, Shamshi-Adad I (c. 1814–1782 B.C.), dominated most of the Assyrian heartland, including Asshur. He installed his sons as governors of **Mari**[2] on the Euphrates River and Ekallatum, south of Asshur on the Tigris.[3] Shamshi-Adad himself ventured west, establishing a vast empire stretching over northern Mesopotamia into Syria. After his death in 1781 B.C., Shamshi-Adad's son Ishme-Dagan I was unable to maintain his father's empire. **Hammurabi** of Babylon conquered Mari and Asshur, while the **Hurrians**[4] invaded from the northeast. For he next 400 years there is virtually no documentation from the Assyrian cities, except for the Assyrian King List.[5]

The reign of Ashur-uballit I (1364–1329 B.C.), who unified and consolidated the city-states of Assyria into a stable political entity, marks the beginning of Assyria as a political state. Letters uncovered at **Amarna**[6] demonstrate that he corresponded as an equal with Egypt's **Amenhotep IV**. Although the Babylonian king considered Ashur-uballit I his **vassal**, Ashur-uballit I was able to exert considerable influence in Babylon when his daughter was given in marriage to the Babylonian king; the son of this union became the next ruler of Babylon.

Much Babylonian literature and learning was imported to Assyria, a practice later Assyrian monarchs would continue. Following the reign of Ashur-uballit, his successors lost influence in Babylonia; however, they (particularly Adad-narari I) were able to push westward into **Mitanni**[7] and as far as Carchemish ("Map 8b"), continuing to lay the groundwork for empire building.

Inscription listing peoples conquered by Tiglath-Pileser I of Assyria
Preserving Bible Times; © Dr. James C. Martin; permission of The British Museum

Middle Assyrian Period (c. 1274–935 B.C.)

The Assyrian Empire emerged under the next two kings, Shalmaneser I (c. 1274–1245 B.C.) and Tukulti-Ninurta I (c. 1244–1208 B.C.). As the son of Ashur-uballit, Shalmaneser I campaigned especially in the west against the Hittites and also against the Hurrians of Mitanni. Tukulti-Ninurta continued the military expeditions of his father, even gaining temporary control of Babylonia. The first recorded deportation occurred under Tukulti-Ninurta, who relocated **Hittites** from Syria to the Assyrian heartland as laborers. Tukulti-Ninurta also established a new capital on the eastern bank of the Tigris—and was murdered in his own new palace.

With the collapse of the Hittite Empire,[8] other peoples began to move. The Mushki (probably the Phrygians) migrated into Anatolia, and the Arameans (Syrians) pushed against Assyria from the west, causing a decline in Assyrian control. In the ensuing instability Babylonia was able to regain its independence, and Assyrian control over other areas weakened.

Ashur-resha-ishi I (c. 1133–1116 B.C.) restored and reunified the core area of Assyria, and Tiglath-Pileser I (c. 1115–1077 B.C.) built upon this foundation, expanding the empire in all directions. He campaigned successfully against the Mushki and the Arameans to the west, bringing all of Syria and southern Anatolia under Assyrian domination. He also marched south into Babylonia, capturing many of its leading cities. Assyrian culture surged under the prosperity brought about by these military conquests. Upon the death of Tiglath-Pileser, however, the fortunes of Assyria once again declined until the reign of Ashur-dan II (c. 934–912 B.C.).

[1]See "Nineveh" on page 1497. [2]See "Mari" on page 54. [3]See "The Tigris and Euphrates Rivers" on page 604. [4]See "The Hurrians" on page 57. [5]See "The Assyrian King Lists" on page 652. [6]See "The Amarna Tablets and the Habiru" on page 347. [7]See "Mitanni" on page 257. [8]See "Anatolia and the Hittites" on page 144.

Assyria From the Neo-Assyrian Period Forward

NAHUM 3

Neo-Assyrian Period (c. 934–612 B.C.)

Ashur-dan II returned stability to Assyria and reclaimed western territory lost to the Arameans. The next two kings reconsolidated and expanded the state. Military outposts were established throughout the empire to replenish troops on campaign.

Ashurnasirpal II (884–859 B.C.) built a new capital at Calah ("Map 8a")—later Nimrud. He marched north to the Zagros Mountains and west to Syria-Palestine, exacting tribute and subjecting defeated peoples to forced labor in Calah. His son **Shalmaneser III** (859–824 B.C.) continued to expand the empire north and west. His annals record a conflict involving a coalition of ten kings, including Ahab of Israel, who provided 2,000 chariots and several thousand soldiers for the battle of Qarqar in 853 B.C.[1] Shalmaneser, unable to defeat the coalition, returned to engage these nations again during subsequent years. Eventually Jehu of Israel paid tribute to the Assyrian king, as depicted on the Black Obelisk of Shalmaneser III.[2] On the southern front Shalmaneser assisted the Babylonian king in dispelling Aramean invaders.

Toward the end of Shalmaneser's reign Assyria began to decline due to internal revolutions. For 80 years after his death, Assyrian kings attempted to retain control over outlying territories. The famous queen Semiramis ruled Assyria during the minority of her son, Adad-narari III (810–782 B.C.), who in turn subjugated Damascus; received tribute from nearby kings, including Israel's Joash; and was recognized as sovereign by the Chaldean tribes.[3]

Tiglath-Pileser III (744–727 B.C.) strengthened royal authority and regained lost Syrian territories. He continued his march through Syria and Palestine down to Egypt, receiving tribute from Damascus, Byblos, Tyre and Samaria (cf. 2Ch 28:19–21). When Damascus and Samaria rebelled, Tiglath-Pileser quelled the uprising, making them vassal states (cf. 2Ki 15:30). He installed an appointee as king of Babylonia, later taking that throne himself.

During the short reign of Shalmaneser V (726–722 B.C.), Samaria was besieged. Assyrian records attribute Samaria's capitulation to Shalmaneser V or to Sargon II (722–705 B.C.).

Royal inscription of Sargon II of Assyria; Nimrud, c. 710 B.C.

© The Schøyen Collection; photography courtesy of Mr. Martin Schøyen

Most likely the fall of Samaria was a foregone conclusion when Shalmaneser was assassinated and Sargon II usurped the throne in 722 B.C.[4] Massive deportation of Israelites to Assyria followed. Sargon II gained control of Syria-Palestine, defeating a coalition of Syrians and Egyptians at Qarqar in 720 B.C. From 720 to 710 he also fought against and eventually prevailed over the Babylonian king Marduk-apal-iddina (Merodach-Baladan of Isa 39:1).

Sargon's son Sennacherib (701–681 B.C.) is famous for his siege of Jerusalem. Hezekiah of Judah was encouraged to rebel against Assyria on the basis of resurgent Egyptian strength. Egypt, however, was soundly defeated by Sennacherib, who then pressed against Hezekiah. Jerusalem, though besieged, miraculously escaped defeat (2Ki 18–19). Sennacherib destroyed Babylon in 689 B.C. but was assassinated by two of his sons and succeeded by another son, Esarhaddon.[5]

Under Esarhaddon (680–669 B.C.) the Egyptian army was defeated, after which Egypt was ruled by Assyrian-appointed governors. With most of Syria-Palestine submissive, Esarhaddon rebuilt Babylon and oversaw extensive work in Nineveh, Asshur and Calah. Before his death in 669 B.C. he required his officials to swear allegiance to his son Ashurbanipal.[6] Esarhaddon conferred the Babylonian throne, however, upon another son, Shamash-shuma-ukin.

Ashurbanipal focused on Egypt, which was attempting to regain independence. Although Memphis and Thebes[7] were captured in 663 B.C., Egypt was freed from Assyrian domination when troubles in other parts of the empire required Ashurbanipal's attention. Civil war broke out between Ashurbanipal and his brother Shamash-shuma-ukin in 652 B.C. Ashurbanipal emerged victorious four years later after a long siege of Babylon.

Although Assyria emerged as victor, it never recovered from the drain on its military and resources. Ashurbanipal's successors were unable to restore the empire's greatness. Nabopolassar of Babylonia retrieved much territory from Assyria during the latter portion of the seventh century B.C. and the Babylonians and Medes invaded the heartland, capturing Asshur in 614 B.C. In 612 the Assyrian capital of Nineveh fell following a short siege. Although Ashur-uballit II attempted to rule an independent Assyrian state from Harran, he was no match for Babylonia and her allies. The once formidable Assyrian Empire had come to a decisive end.

[1]See "Ahab and the Battle of Qarqar" on page 524. [2]See "Jehu/The Black Obelisk of Shalmaneser III" on page 544. [3]See "The Chaldeans" on page 1402. [4]See "The Annals of Sargon II" on page 1072. [5]See "The Death of Sennacherib" on page 562. [6]See "The Coronation of Ashurbanipal" on page 868. [7]See "Memphis" on page 1270 and "Thebes" on page 1354.

3:13 [n]Isa 19:16; Jer 50:37 [o]Na 2:6 [p]Isa 45:2

[13] Look at your troops—
they are all women![n]
The gates[o] of your land
are wide open to your enemies;
fire has consumed their bars.[p]

3:14 [q]2Ch 32:4 [r]Na 2:1

[14] Draw water for the siege,[q]
strengthen your defenses![r]
Work the clay,
tread the mortar,
repair the brickwork!
[15] There the fire will devour you;
the sword will cut you down
and, like grasshoppers, consume you.
Multiply like grasshoppers,
multiply like locusts![s]

3:15 [s]Joel 1:4

[16] You have increased the number of your merchants
till they are more than the stars of the sky,
but like locusts they strip the land
and then fly away.

3:17 [t]Jer 51:27

[17] Your guards are like locusts,[t]
your officials like swarms of locusts
that settle in the walls on a cold day—
but when the sun appears they fly away,
and no one knows where.

3:18 [u]Ps 76:5-6 [v]Isa 56:10 [w]1Ki 22:17

[18] O king of Assyria, your shepherds[a] slumber;[u]
your nobles lie down to rest.[v]
Your people are scattered[w] on the mountains
with no one to gather them.

3:19 [x]Jer 30:13; Mic 1:9 [y]Job 27:23; La 2:15; Zep 2:15

[19] Nothing can heal your wound;[x]
your injury is fatal.
Everyone who hears the news about you
claps his hands[y] at your fall,
for who has not felt
your endless cruelty?

[a] 18 Or *rulers*

3:13 Comparing troops to women was an insult, implying that the soldiers were weak and unable to stand against the invading armies.

"Bars" refers to the bars of the city gates.

3:14 Drawing water was a normal practice in preparation for a siege (see "Siege Warfare" on p. 465).

3:15 History and archaeology confirm that Nineveh was burned. Assyria's king (see v. 18) died in the flames of his own palace.

3:16 Assyria at the time boasted vast trading and commercial enterprises.

3:17 Farmers of the ancient Near East feared locusts, because they came in huge swarms and devoured everything in their path (see "Locusts in the Ancient Near East" on p. 1438).

For centuries no one knew where ancient Nineveh lay buried. Its remains were finally uncovered by archaeologists in 1845.

3:18 Sin-Shar-Ishkun was the king of Assyria at the time of Nineveh's fall.

3:19 Nineveh's destruction was so complete that the city was never rebuilt. Within a few centuries it was covered with windblown sand, leaving no trace but a mound that is known today as Tell Kuyunjik, "the mound of many sheep."

INTRODUCTION TO

AUTHOR, PLACE AND DATE OF WRITING

The book of Habakkuk divides naturally into two clearly defined sections: A segment in which the prophet seeks and receives answers from God in response to some hard questions (Hab 1–2) is followed by a psalm of praise (ch. 3). The author, Habakkuk, is unknown to modern readers beyond the little we can glean from the book itself. The prophet's name appears both in the title of the book at 1:1 and at 3:1, where it serves as the superscript to the psalm (see "The Psalm Superscripts" on p. 795). In spite of this many scholars have questioned whether Habakkuk wrote the entire book, and in particular whether the psalm of chapter 3 was composed by the same man who wrote chapters 1 and 2. Interestingly, the Habakkuk Pesher (a *pesher* is an ancient Jewish commentary on a Biblical book) from Qumran (found among the Dead Sea Scrolls) contains only the text of Habakkuk 1–2. This commentary dates to the first century B.C.

Other ancient manuscripts do, however, support the unity of Habakkuk. The Scroll of the Minor Prophets from Wadi Murabbaat (in the Judean desert), dating to the second century A.D., does contain all three chapters of Habakkuk, as does an ancient Greek text of the prophecy contained in the Greek Scroll of the Minor Prophets from Nahal Hever from the first century A.D. In light of this evidence, together with the fact that the book explicitly claims that Habakkuk wrote all three chapters, there is no reason to question the text's single authorship.

The prophet was clearly aware that Jerusalem and Judah were under threat from the Babylonians (1:6); therefore, most scholars date the manuscript to the late seventh century B.C., perhaps soon after the reign of Josiah.

AUDIENCE

The book of Habakkuk, presented as a dialogue between God and the prophet, was composed for the benefit of the people of Judah. Habakkuk was troubled by Judah's idolatry, indifference to God and social injustice and wondered how long God would ignore the blatant wickedness of his people. God responded by revealing that his judgment would come through the Babylonians.

CULTURAL FACTS AND HIGHLIGHTS

Habakkuk, like Job, raised the question of the justice of God, but he did so in the historical context of the coming destruction of Jerusalem and in the literary context of the prophets—not through the more philosophical genre of Wisdom Literature. Habakkuk 1:3 asks how God could tolerate injustice, referring to the disregard for the law in Judah (1:4), and 1:6 delineates God's answer: He would punish his people through the Babylonians. This answer perplexed Habakkuk even more: How could a just God use the Babylonians, a people even more wicked than Judah, to chastise his own people? Habakkuk reminded God that the Babylonians were a pagan and ruthless nation who, for whatever reason, seemed never to suffer on this account (1:16–17). God assured his prophet by asserting that those who plunder many nations will themselves be plundered (2:8); he then went on to catalog a series of woes against all who practice evil (2:9–20). Habakkuk's prayer psalm was his response to this revelation. In short, the book of Habakkuk is a defense of the justice of God, a call for believers to maintain their faith even in the face of difficult times (2:4).

TIMELINE

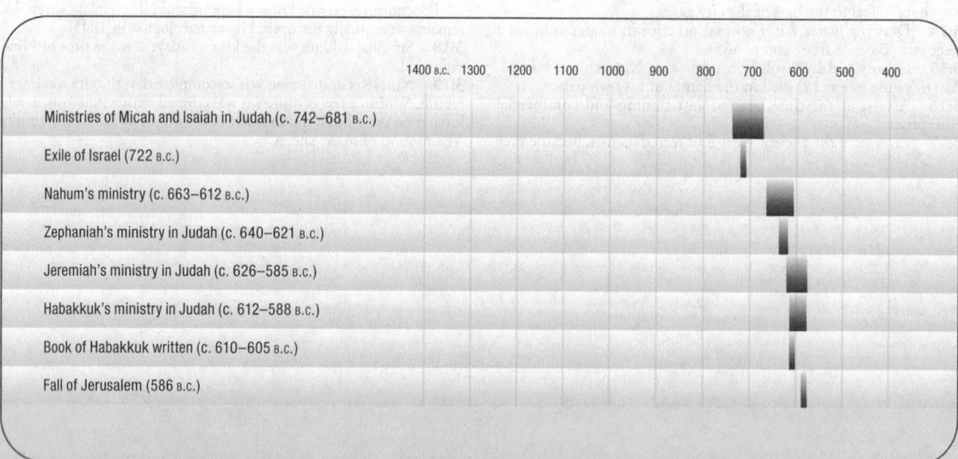

AS YOU READ

Attempt to enter vicariously into Habakkuk's frame of mind as he wrestled with God over what appeared to him to be evident injustice. You might want to take the time to compare and contrast Habakkuk's approach to God with Job's (skim through the book of Job and look for the passages in which Job addressed his Maker). Follow up by comparing Habakkuk's public expression of faith in chapter 3 with Job's eventual affirmations of God's love and goodness.

DID YOU KNOW?

- Habakkuk is probably a Babylonian name, referring to a kind of garden plant (1:1).
- The timbers of the highly prized cedars of Lebanon had been ravaged for centuries by the kings of Assyria and Babylon to adorn their temples and palaces. Assyrian inscriptions record hunting expeditions in the Lebanon range, and the invading Babylonians may have engaged in such sport as well (2:17).
- Old Testament writers frequently combined recollections of the mighty acts of God with conventional images of a fearsome manifestation of his power: He is depicted as riding on the mighty thunderstorm as his chariot, his arrows flying in all directions, a cloudburst of rain descending upon the earth and the mountains quaking before him (3:3).
- "Plague" was one of the elements of the characteristic triad of divine punishment: sword, famine and plague (3:5).

THEMES

Habakkuk's themes include:

1. *Justice.* Habakkuk affirmed that God is holy and just (1:12–13; 3:3), never indifferent to sin and injustice. He will eventually punish the wicked (1:5–11; 2:2–20) and has in fact fixed an "appointed time" (2:3) in history for revealing his justice and judgment on evil. Habakkuk apprises the faithful of every generation that the current situation is never to be construed as the true and ultimate state of affairs. The righteous may have to wait for vindication, but it will certainly come.

2. *Faith.* Faith is needed to endure injustice (2:4). Even when life seems confusing, God's people are to wait patiently for his deliverance, trusting that he will eventually make all things right (2:3). "The righteous will live by his faith" (2:4), not by what appears on the face of things to be true (1:4; see Heb 11:1). As Abraham waited patiently for God to fulfill his promise (Heb 6:13–15)—and as Habakkuk and the faithful remnant were to wait for him to respond in justice (2:3; 3:16)—so believers of every age are to wait in faith for God to carry out his purposes (Ro 1:17; 5:1–2).

OUTLINE

I. Habakkuk's First Question (1:1–4)
II. God's Answer (1:5–11)
III. Habakkuk's Second Question (1:12—2:1)
IV. God's Answer (2:2–20)
V. Habakkuk's Prayer (3)

1 The oracle[a] that Habakkuk the prophet received.

1:1 [a]Na 1:1

Habakkuk's Complaint

2 How long, O LORD, must I call for help,
but you do not listen?[b]
Or cry out to you, "Violence!"
but you do not save?[c]
3 Why do you make me look at injustice?
Why do you tolerate[d] wrong?
Destruction and violence[e] are before me;
there is strife,[f] and conflict abounds.
4 Therefore the law[g] is paralyzed,
and justice never prevails.
The wicked hem in the righteous,
so that justice is perverted.[h]

1:2 [b]Ps 13:1-2; 22:1-2 [c]Jer 14:9
1:3 [d]ver 13 [e]Jer 20:8 [f]Ps 55:9
1:4 [g]Ps 119:126 [h]Job 19:7; Isa 1:23; 5:20; Eze 9:9

The LORD's Answer

5 "Look at the nations and watch—
and be utterly amazed.[i]
For I am going to do something in your days
that you would not believe,
even if you were told.[j]
6 I am raising up the Babylonians,[a][k]
that ruthless and impetuous people,
who sweep across the whole earth
to seize dwelling places not their own.[l]
7 They are a feared and dreaded people;[m]
they are a law to themselves
and promote their own honor.
8 Their horses are swifter[n] than leopards,
fiercer than wolves at dusk.
Their cavalry gallops headlong;
their horsemen come from afar.
They fly like a vulture swooping to devour;
9 they all come bent on violence.
Their hordes[b] advance like a desert wind
and gather prisoners[o] like sand.
10 They deride kings
and scoff at rulers.[p]

1:5 [i]Isa 29:9 [j]Ac 13:41*
1:6 [k]2Ki 24:2 [l]Jer 13:20
1:7 [m]Isa 18:7; Jer 39:5-9
1:8 [n]Jer 4:13
1:9 [o]Hab 2:5
1:10 [p]2Ch 36:6

[a] 6 Or *Chaldeans* [b] 9 The meaning of the Hebrew for this word is uncertain.

1:1—2:20 One of the more interesting finds at Qumran (origin of the Dead Sea Scrolls) was a commentary on chapters 1 and 2 of Habakkuk. Unfortunately, it casts little light on the meaning of these chapters, although it does provide a glimpse of how the Essene community living there in the first century B.C. understood the book. See "The Zealots and the Essenes" on page 1576, "Biblical Interpretation at Qumran and Among the Early Rabbis" on page 1603 and "Qumran and the New Testament" on page 1679.

1:1 For "oracle," see the note on Isaiah 13:1 and "Oracles of the Ancient World" on page 1507.

Habakkuk is probably a Babylonian name, referring to a kind of garden plant. As indicated in the introduction, of the man Habakkuk nothing is known outside of the book that bears his name. Legendary references to Habakkuk (in the Apocryphal Bel and the Dragon and elsewhere) appear to have no historical value. The musical references in chapter 3 have led some to believe that the prophet was a member of a Levitical musical guild, but even this is uncertain.

1:2–4 Habakkuk's complaint began like a lament (see "Ancient Near Eastern Laments" on p. 1305), with injustice as its theme. The likely historical context was the corruption of Judah's government under the cruel and oppressive King Jehoiakim (cf. 2Ki 23:34–37; Jer 22:18–19). Justice was perverted because the rich controlled the courts through bribery (cf. Mic 3:11; 7:3).

1:6 God would punish the apostate nation of Judah by an invasion of the Babylonians, a powerful people who would regain their independence from Assyria in 626 B.C., destroy Assyrian power completely in 612–605 and flourish until 539. In this context the Chaldeans (see the NIV text note and "The Chaldeans" on p. 1402) are synonymous with the Babylonians.

1:8 The speed with which Babylonia conquered her enemies had by this time become proverbial.

1:9 The cruelty of the Babylonians was well known. Like their Assyrian predecessors, they deported conquered peoples as a matter of deliberate national policy (see the notes on 2Ki 17:24–41; 24:10–12; see also "Exile and Genocide in the Ancient Near East" on p. 1337).

1:10 For "earthen ramps," see "Siege Warfare" on page 465.

They laugh at all fortified cities;
they build earthen ramps and capture them.
1:11 [q]Jer 4:11-12 [r]Da 4:30
[11] Then they sweep past like the wind[q] and go on—
guilty men, whose own strength is their god."[r]

Habakkuk's Second Complaint

[12] O LORD, are you not from everlasting?
1:12 [s]Isa 31:1 [t]Isa 10:6
My God, my Holy One,[s] we will not die.
O LORD, you have appointed[t] them to execute judgment;
O Rock, you have ordained them to punish.
[13] Your eyes are too pure to look on evil;
1:13 [u]La 3:34-36
you cannot tolerate wrong.[u]
Why then do you tolerate the treacherous?
Why are you silent while the wicked
swallow up those more righteous than themselves?
[14] You have made men like fish in the sea,
like sea creatures that have no ruler.

1:11 The Babylonians were so proud and confident of their military might that it had virtually become their god (see v. 16).

Oracles of the Ancient World

HABAKKUK 1 An oracle is any divine pronouncement through a prophet that directs human action in the present or foretells future events. In the Old Testament an oracle always refers to a communication from God through a prophet (2Ki 9:25; Isa 13:1; Hab 1:1; Mal 1:1). The three New Testament instances of oracles all have Israel's God as their source and refer to the revelation begun in the Old Testament and finalized in Christ (Ac 7:38; Ro 3:2; Heb 5:12 with 1:1–2). Significantly, Scripture (Nu 22–24; 1Ki 18:20–40), along with numerous extrabiblical texts from Syria-Palestine, **Anatolia**,[1] **Mesopotamia** and (to a lesser extent) Egypt, attest to the fact that peoples of other nations believed that they, too, received oracles from their gods.[2]

✣ The Bible presents the classical prophets as ambassadors of the heavenly court (2Ki 17:13) who authoritatively presented the revelation of God to his people (2Ch 36:15–16; Isa 44:26).

✣ Prophets sometimes mentioned the Holy Spirit's role in inspiration (Joel 2:28–29; Mic 3:8; Zec 7:12).

✣ At times the source of the message is said to have been a dream or vision (Isa 6:1–13; Jer 31:26; Zec 2:1), but ordinarily the mode of inspiration is unspecified.

✣ Sometimes oracles provided a divine answer to human questions (2Sa 2:1; Hab 1–2), but often they were initiated by God.

✣ The divine revelations were at times framed as parables or allegories (2Sa 12:1–7), and sometimes oracles were acted out (2Ki 13:14–20; Eze 4).

✣ The prophets pronounced oracles of warning against both individuals (1Sa 13:13–14) and nations (Isa 17; Eze 15; Am 4:1–3) but also oracles of salvation that predicted a day when God would restore his people (Jer 31:31–34; Eze 36:16–32; Am 9:13–15; Zec 8:1–8).

Prophets of the pagan deities sometimes delivered messages similar to those of Israel's prophets. Like Israel's God, these gods purportedly demanded homage and declared judgments. But Biblical prophecy was distinct in at least three ways:

✣ Only **Yahweh** among the gods of the ancient world spoke in order to establish, maintain and enforce a covenant relationship with his people (Dt 4:5–9).

✣ Whereas many pagan oracles were ambiguous as to their intent and fulfillment, Biblical oracles were generally clear and specific (Dt 18:14–22).

✣ Only from Israel's prophets did a staunch monotheism confront polytheistic idolatry (Dt 5:7–10; 6:4–5; Ps 115; Isa 40:18–31).

[1]See Glossary on page 2080 for definitions of bolded words. [2]See "Prophets in the Bible and Pagan Nations" on page 1457.

[15]The wicked foe pulls all of them up with hooks,[v]
he catches them in his net,[w]
he gathers them up in his dragnet;
and so he rejoices and is glad.
[16]Therefore he sacrifices to his net
and burns incense[x] to his dragnet,
for by his net he lives in luxury
and enjoys the choicest food.
[17]Is he to keep on emptying his net,
destroying nations without mercy?[y]

1:15 [v]Isa 19:8 [w]Jer 16:16
1:16 [x]Jer 44:8
1:17 [y]Isa 14:6; 19:8

2

I will stand at my watch[z]
and station myself on the ramparts;[a]
I will look to see what he will say[b] to me,
and what answer I am to give to this complaint.[a][c]

2:1 [z]Isa 21:8 [a]Ps 48:13 [b]Ps 85:8 [c]Ps 5:3

The LORD's Answer

[2]Then the LORD replied:

"Write[d] down the revelation
and make it plain on tablets
so that a herald[b] may run with it.
[3]For the revelation awaits an appointed time;
it speaks of the end[e]
and will not prove false.
Though it linger, wait[f] for it;
it[c] will certainly come and will not delay.[g]

2:2 [d]Rev 1:19
2:3 [e]Da 8:17; 10:14 [f]Ps 27:14 [g]Eze 12:25; Heb 10:37-38

[4]"See, he is puffed up;
his desires are not upright—
but the righteous will live by his faith[d][h]—
[5]indeed, wine[i] betrays him;
he is arrogant and never at rest.
Because he is as greedy as the grave[e]
and like death is never satisfied,[j]
he gathers to himself all the nations
and takes captive all the peoples.

2:4 [h]Ro 1:17*; Gal 3:11*; Heb 10:37-38*
2:5 [i]Pr 20:1 [j]Pr 27:20; 30:15-16

[6]"Will not all of them taunt[k] him with ridicule and scorn, saying,

" 'Woe to him who piles up stolen goods
and makes himself wealthy by extortion!
How long must this go on?'
[7]Will not your debtors[f] suddenly arise?
Will they not wake up and make you tremble?
Then you will become their victim.[m]

2:6 [k]Isa 14:4 [l]Am 2:8
2:7 [m]Pr 29:1

[a] *1* Or *and what to answer when I am rebuked* [b] *2* Or *so that whoever reads it* [c] *3* Or *Though he linger, wait for him; / he*
[d] *4* Or *faithfulness* [e] *5* Hebrew *Sheol* [f] *7* Or *creditors*

1:15 For "hooks," see the note on Amos 4:2. Babylonia's victims were as powerless as fish swimming into a net. Mesopotamian reliefs symbolically portray conquerors capturing their enemies in fishnets.
2:1 For "watch," see the note on Micah 7:4. "Ramparts" refer to the walls of Jerusalem.
2:2–20 Habakkuk 2 recounts the Lord's revelation of the fall of Babylon. The foolishness of puffed-up desire (v. 4) led to five "woes" from the mouths of Babylon's captives or threatened victims—Judah in particular. These woes condemned the Babylonians' (1) greed for conquest (vv. 6–8); (2) pride in their building projects accomplished at others' expense (vv. 9–11); (3) self-centered injustice (vv. 12–13); (4) violence in stripping others of their possessions and dignity (vv. 15–17); and (5) idol worship (vv. 18–19).
2:2–3 The Hebrew for "revelation" refers specifically to a prophet's vision (see "Oracles of the Ancient World" on p. 1507).
2:3 The message that follows deals with the fall of Babylon to take place in 539 B.C., about 66 years after Habakkuk's prophecy.
2:4 The pronoun "he" in this context is used collectively of the Babylonians.
2:5 The "grave" as used here is a reference to the shadowy world of the dead. For commentary on its insatiable appetite, see the notes on Job 18:13–14 and Psalm 6:5; 49:14; see also "Sheol, Hades, Gehenna, the Abyss and Tartarus: Images of Hell" on page 946.

2:8 [n]Isa 33:1; Zec 2:8-9 [o]ver 17
2:9 [p]Jer 22:13
2:10 [q]Jer 26:19 [r]ver 16
2:11 [s]Jos 24:27; Lk 19:40
2:12 [t]Mic 3:10
2:13 [u]Isa 50:11 [v]Isa 47:13
2:14 [w]Nu 14:21 [x]Isa 11:9
2:16 [y]ver 10 [z]La 4:21 [a]Isa 51:22
2:17 [b]Jer 51:35 [c]Jer 50:15 [d]ver 8
2:18 [e]Jer 5:21 [f]Ps 115:4-5; Jer 10:14
2:19 [g]1Ki 18:27 [h]Jer 10:4
2:20 [i]Ps 11:4 [j]Isa 41:1
3:2 [k]Ps 44:1 [l]Ps 119:120

8 Because you have plundered many nations,
the peoples who are left will plunder you.[n]
For you have shed man's blood;[o]
you have destroyed lands and cities and everyone in them.

9 "Woe to him who builds[p] his realm by unjust gain
to set his nest on high,
to escape the clutches of ruin!
10 You have plotted the ruin[q] of many peoples,
shaming[r] your own house and forfeiting your life.
11 The stones[s] of the wall will cry out,
and the beams of the woodwork will echo it.

12 "Woe to him who builds a city with bloodshed[t]
and establishes a town by crime!
13 Has not the LORD Almighty determined
that the people's labor is only fuel for the fire,[u]
that the nations exhaust themselves for nothing?[v]
14 For the earth will be filled with the knowledge of the glory[w] of the LORD,
as the waters cover the sea.[x]

15 "Woe to him who gives drink to his neighbors,
pouring it from the wineskin till they are drunk,
so that he can gaze on their naked bodies.
16 You will be filled with shame[y] instead of glory.
Now it is your turn! Drink and be exposed[a]![z]
The cup[a] from the LORD's right hand is coming around to you,
and disgrace will cover your glory.
17 The violence[b] you have done to Lebanon will overwhelm you,
and your destruction of animals will terrify you.[c]
For you have shed man's blood;[d]
you have destroyed lands and cities and everyone in them.

18 "Of what value is an idol,[e] since a man has carved it?
Or an image that teaches lies?
For he who makes it trusts in his own creation;
he makes idols that cannot speak.[f]
19 Woe to him who says to wood, 'Come to life!'
Or to lifeless stone, 'Wake up!'[g]
Can it give guidance?
It is covered with gold and silver;[h]
there is no breath in it.
20 But the LORD is in his holy temple;[i]
let all the earth be silent[j] before him."

Habakkuk's Prayer

3 A prayer of Habakkuk the prophet. On *shigionoth.*[b]

2 LORD, I have heard[k] of your fame;
I stand in awe[l] of your deeds, O LORD.

[a] *16* Masoretic Text; Dead Sea Scrolls, Aquila, Vulgate and Syriac (see also Septuagint) *and stagger* [b] *1* Probably a literary or musical term

2:17 The timbers of the highly prized cedars of Lebanon (see "Cedars of Lebanon" on p. 1043) had been ravaged for centuries by the kings of Assyria and Babylon to adorn their temples and palaces. Assyrian inscriptions record hunting expeditions in the Lebanon range, and the invading Babylonians may have engaged in such sport as well.

3:1 *Shigionoth* is probably a literary or musical term. This chapter may have been a hymn that existed independently and was added at a later time.

Renew[m] them in our day,
 in our time make them known;
 in wrath remember mercy.[n]

3 God came from Teman,
 the Holy One from Mount Paran. *Selah*[a]
His glory covered the heavens
 and his praise filled the earth.[o]
4 His splendor was like the sunrise;
 rays flashed from his hand,
 where his power was hidden.
5 Plague went before him;
 pestilence followed his steps.
6 He stood, and shook the earth;
 he looked, and made the nations tremble.
The ancient mountains crumbled
 and the age-old hills collapsed.[p]
 His ways are eternal.
7 I saw the tents of Cushan in distress,
 the dwellings of Midian[q] in anguish.[r]

8 Were you angry with the rivers,[s] O LORD?
 Was your wrath against the streams?
Did you rage against the sea
 when you rode with your horses
 and your victorious chariots?[t]
9 You uncovered your bow,
 you called for many arrows.[u] *Selah*
You split the earth with rivers;
10 the mountains saw you and writhed.
Torrents of water swept by;
 the deep roared[v]
 and lifted its waves[w] on high.

11 Sun and moon stood still[x] in the heavens
 at the glint of your flying arrows,[y]
 at the lightning of your flashing spear.
12 In wrath you strode through the earth
 and in anger you threshed[z] the nations.
13 You came out to deliver[a] your people,
 to save your anointed one.
You crushed[b] the leader of the land of wickedness,
 you stripped him from head to foot. *Selah*

3:2 [m]Ps 85:6 [n]Isa 54:8
3:3 [o]Ps 48:10
3:6 [p]Ps 114:1-6
3:7 [q]Jdg 7:24-25 [r]Ex 15:14
3:8 [s]Ex 7:20 [t]Ps 68:17
3:9 [u]Ps 7:12-13
3:10 [v]Ps 98:7 [w]Ps 93:3
3:11 [x]Jos 10:13 [y]Ps 18:14
3:12 [z]Isa 41:15
3:13 [a]Ps 20:6; 28:8 [b]Ps 68:21; 110:6

[a] 3 A word of uncertain meaning; possibly a musical term; also in verses 9 and 13

3:3 Teman, meaning "southland," was a village in Edom, south of the Dead Sea.

Mount Paran, often associated with Mount Sinai and Mount Seir and the giving of the Law (see Dt 33:2), was probably northwest of the Gulf of Aqaba and south of Kadesh Barnea, between Edom and Sinai.

It was common practice for peoples in the ancient world to identify their deities with observable, awe-inspiring natural phenomena (see vv. 3–15; see also "Storm Gods, Storm Imagery and Theophany" on p. 808). Old Testament writers frequently combined recollections of the mighty acts of God with conventional images of a fearsome manifestation of his power: He is depicted as riding on the mighty thunderstorm as his chariot, his arrows flying in all directions, a cloudburst of rain descending upon the earth and the mountains quaking before him (see Jdg 5:4–5; Ps 18:7–15; 68:7–10; 77:16–19; Mic 1:3).

Selah is thought to be a literary or musical term (see the note on v. 1).

3:5 "Plague" was one of the elements of the characteristic triad of divine punishment: "sword, famine and plague" (Jer 14:12; cf. Lev 26:25–26).

3:6 See the note on verse 3.

3:7 Cushan and Midian were Arab tribes living near Edom.

3:8–11 See the note on verse 3, as well as those on Psalms 32:6, 68:4 and 135:7.

3:12 "Threshing" is often used in the prophetic books as a term for judgment. For information on the harvesting process, see the note on Ruth 1:22; see also "The Threshing Floor" on page 608.

3:14 [c]Jdg 7:22 [d]Ps 64:2-5

[14] With his own spear you pierced his head
when his warriors stormed out to scatter us,[c]
gloating as though about to devour
the wretched[d] who were in hiding.

3:15 [e]Ex 15:8; Ps 77:19

[15] You trampled the sea with your horses,
churning the great waters.[e]

[16] I heard and my heart pounded,
my lips quivered at the sound;
decay crept into my bones,
and my legs trembled.
Yet I will wait patiently for the day of calamity
to come on the nation invading us.

3:17 [f]Joel 1:10-12,18 [g]Jer 5:17

[17] Though the fig tree does not bud
and there are no grapes on the vines,
though the olive crop fails
and the fields produce no food,[f]
though there are no sheep in the pen
and no cattle in the stalls,[g]

3:18 [h]Isa 61:10; Php 4:4

[18] yet I will rejoice in the LORD,[h]
I will be joyful in God my Savior.

3:19 [i]Dt 33:29; Ps 46:1-5 [j]Dt 32:13; 2Sa 22:34; Ps 18:33

[19] The Sovereign LORD is my strength;[i]
he makes my feet like the feet of a deer,
he enables me to go on the heights.[j]

For the director of music. On my stringed instruments.

3:19 "Director" probably refers to the conductor of the temple musicians. This chapter may have formed part of the temple prayers that were chanted with the accompaniment of instruments, including the harp and lyre (see the note on v. 1; see also "Ancient Musical Instruments" on p. 797).

INTRODUCTION TO

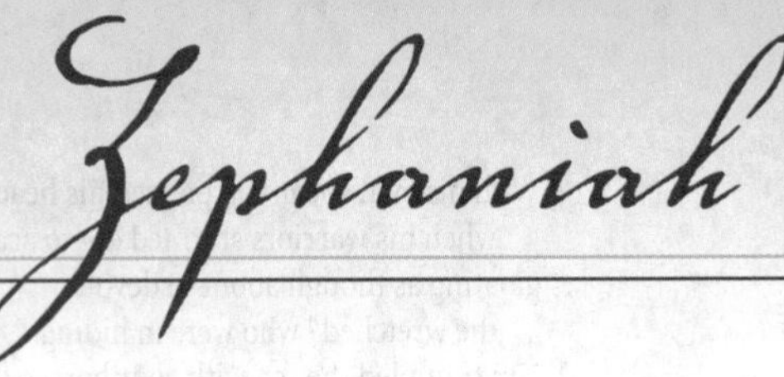

AUTHOR, PLACE AND DATE OF WRITING

We know nothing about Zephaniah beyond what we read in 1:1 and what we can infer from the rest of the book. It is unusual that the prophet traced his ancestry back four generations; some suggest that he did this because the Hezekiah who was his great-great-grandfather was in fact King Hezekiah of Judah. Unlike Micah, who focused on Judah's common people, Zephaniah was evidently at home in the political arena and in distinguished court circles.

The book is dated to the reign of Josiah, placing it within the span of 640–609 B.C. The reference to the "remnant of Baal" in 1:4 has been taken by many to suggest that the reform initiatives of Josiah were already well underway and that most of the conspicuous shrines to Baal had already been removed. Others assert that Zephaniah appears to allude to Deuteronomy in several places (e.g., Zep 1:13 echoes Dt 28:30 and Zep 1:17 resonates with Dt 28:29), implying that the Book of the Law (2Ki 22) had been found and read aloud by the time of Zephaniah's writing. This suggests that the prophecy may well have been written toward the end of the seventh century B.C.

AUDIENCE

Zephaniah wrote to the people of Judah to warn them of God's impending judgment, to urge them to repent and to offer them the hope of restoration.

CULTURAL FACTS AND HIGHLIGHTS

The focus of Zephaniah's message is "the day of the LORD," which the prophet conceived to be a day of judgment first for Judah (Zep 1) and only afterward for the other nations (ch. 2), although he also anticipated a final day of salvation (ch. 3). It is possible that Zephaniah recognized that Josiah's rigorous reform efforts had not fully penetrated to the hearts of the people. Sadly, any resurgence of covenant faithfulness that Josiah had inspired was doomed to be short-lived. Judgment was both deserved and unavoidable.

TIMELINE

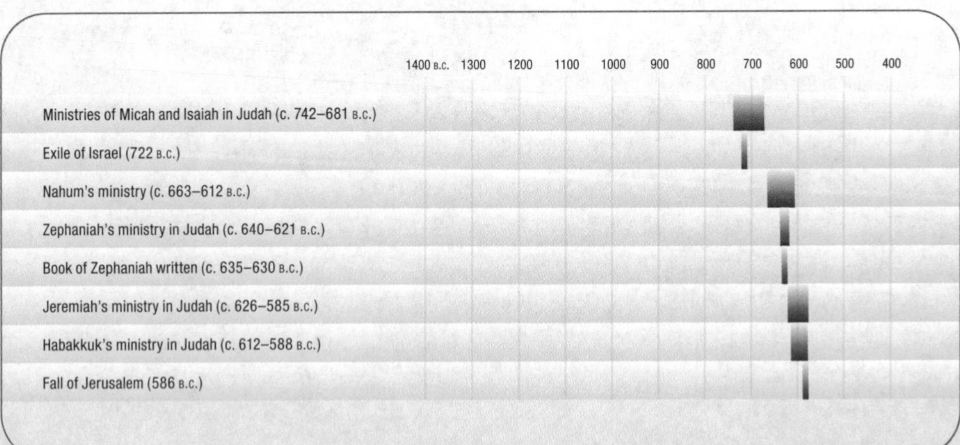

AS YOU READ

As with Habakkuk and several other Old Testament writing prophets, be aware of the stark contrast between the author's graphic images of horror and doom and his comforting words of hope for restoration.

DID YOU KNOW?

- Incense to pagan deities was often burned on rooftops (see Isa 15:3; Jer 1:16), and the kings of Judah had gone so far as to erect pagan altars on the roof of the palace in Jerusalem (Zep 1:5).
- There was evidently a general and widespread pagan idea that the threshold of a home, temple or other building was the dwelling place of spirits (1:9).
- Nineveh was destroyed in 612 B.C. and its location was later forgotten—until it was discovered by archaeologists in 1845 (2:13).

THEMES

Zephaniah's themes include:

1. *Judgment.* Zephaniah's main theme was the imminent coming of "the day of the LORD" (1:7,14). That day would be one of universal judgment (1:2–3) as well as of specific judgment against Judah (1:4–6) and other nations (2:4–15). The book emphasizes that religious syncretism—a mixing of the worship of God with idolatry (1:4–6)—brings destruction (1:9–13) but that seeking God, and God alone, in humility results in salvation (2:1–3).

2. *Restoration.* Zephaniah assured his audience that judgment would be followed by restoration. God would purify his own (3:9), bring rejoicing to Jerusalem (3:14–17) and restore both his people and Jerusalem's glory (3:18–20).

OUTLINE

I. Introduction: Announcement of Total Judgment (1:1–3)
II. The Day of the Lord Coming on Judah and the Nations (1:4–18)
III. God's Judgment on the Nations (2:1—3:8)
IV. The Promise of Redemption (3:9–20)

1 The word of the LORD that came to Zephaniah son of Cushi, the son of Gedaliah, the son of Amariah, the son of Hezekiah, during the reign of Josiah[a] son of Amon king of Judah:

1:1 [a]2Ki 22:1; 2Ch 34:1-35:25

Warning of Coming Destruction

2 "I will sweep away everything
from the face of the earth,"[b]
declares the LORD.
3 "I will sweep away both men and animals;
I will sweep away the birds of the air[c]
and the fish of the sea.
The wicked will have only heaps of rubble[a]
when I cut off man from the face of the earth,"[d]
declares the LORD.

1:2 [b]Ge 6:7
1:3 [c]Jer 4:25 [d]Hos 4:3

Against Judah

4 "I will stretch out my hand[e] against Judah
and against all who live in Jerusalem.
I will cut off from this place every remnant of Baal,[f]
the names of the pagan and the idolatrous priests[g]—
5 those who bow down on the roofs
to worship the starry host,
those who bow down and swear by the LORD
and who also swear by Molech,[b][h]
6 those who turn back from following[i] the LORD
and neither seek[j] the LORD nor inquire[k] of him.
7 Be silent[l] before the Sovereign LORD,
for the day of the LORD[m] is near.
The LORD has prepared a sacrifice;[n]
he has consecrated those he has invited.
8 On the day of the LORD's sacrifice
I will punish[o] the princes
and the king's sons[p]
and all those clad
in foreign clothes.
9 On that day I will punish
all who avoid stepping on the threshold,[c]
who fill the temple of their gods
with violence and deceit.[q]

1:4 [e]Jer 6:12 [f]Mic 5:13 [g]Hos 10:5
1:5 [h]Jer 5:7
1:6 [i]Isa 1:4; Jer 2:13 [j]Isa 9:13 [k]Hos 7:7
1:7 [l]Hab 2:20; Zec 2:13 [m]ver 14; Isa 13:6 [n]Isa 34:6; Jer 46:10
1:8 [o]Isa 24:21 [p]Jer 39:6
1:9 [q]Am 3:10

[a] 3 The meaning of the Hebrew for this line is uncertain. [b] 5 Hebrew *Malcam,* that is, Milcom [c] 9 See 1 Samuel 5:5.

1:1 Zephaniah prophesied during the reign of King Josiah (640–609 B.C.), making him a contemporary of Jeremiah, Nahum and perhaps Habakkuk. His prophecy is probably to be dated relatively early in Josiah's reign, before that king's attempt at reform.

This prophet was very probably related to the kings of Judah as follows: Amariah and King Manasseh were brothers; Gedaliah and King Amon were cousins; Cushi and King Josiah were second cousins; and Zephaniah was third cousin of the three kings Jehoahaz, Jehoiakim and Zechariah, thus putting the prophet into familiar relationship with the court, to which his message seems to have been specifically directed (e.g., v. 8). His principal work seems to have been early in Josiah's reign, like that of his contemporaries Nahum and (perhaps) Habakkuk, and before the greater prophecies of his other contemporary, Jeremiah.

1:5 Incense to pagan deities was often burned on rooftops (see Isa 15:3; Jer 1:16), and the kings of Judah had erected pagan altars on the roof of the palace in Jerusalem (see 2Ki 23:12). The Ugaritic Epic of Kirta from the fourteenth century B.C. (see "The Kirta Epic" on p. 736) describes a similar practice: "Go to the top of a tower, bestride the top of the wall ... Honor Baal with your sacrifice ... Then descend ... from the housetops."

Even though it was prohibited, worship of the sun, moon and stars was common in Judah throughout much of the later history of the monarchy (see 2Ki 17:16; 21:3,5; 23:4–5).

The god Molech, whose rituals sometimes involved child sacrifice (see "Human Sacrifice in the Ancient Near East" on p. 182), was worshiped by the Ammonites. Although Molech worship was forbidden to the Israelites (see Lev 18:21; 20:1–5), Solomon set up an altar to Molech on the Mount of Olives (1Ki 11:7) and Manasseh established Molech rituals in the Valley of Ben Hinnom (see 2Ch 33:6; Jer 7:31; 32:35).

1:8 "Foreign clothes" refers to dress that indicated conformity to Babylonian, Egyptian or Assyrian ways (see "Ancient Israelite Clothing and Jewelry" on p. 1059).

1:9 Apparently there was a general and relatively widespread pagan idea that the threshold was the dwelling place of spirits. This notion had developed during the time of Samuel, when the Philistine god Dagon had been found broken and lying on the threshold of its temple after the Philistines had placed the ark of the covenant next to their idol in Dagon's temple (see 1Sa 5:1–5).

1:10 [r]2Ch 33:14
1:11 [s]Jas 5:1 [t]Hos 9:6
1:12 [u]Am 6:1 [v]Jer 48:11 [w]Eze 8:12
1:13 [x]Jer 15:13 [y]Dt 28:30,39; Am 5:11; Mic 6:15

10 "On that day," declares the LORD,
"a cry will go up from the Fish Gate,[r]
wailing from the New Quarter,
and a loud crash from the hills.
11 Wail,[s] you who live in the market district[a];
all your merchants will be wiped out,
all who trade with[b] silver will be ruined.[t]
12 At that time I will search Jerusalem with lamps
and punish those who are complacent,[u]
who are like wine left on its dregs,[v]
who think, 'The LORD will do nothing,[w]
either good or bad.'
13 Their wealth will be plundered,[x]
their houses demolished.
They will build houses
but not live in them;
they will plant vineyards
but not drink the wine.[y]

The Great Day of the LORD

1:14 [z]ver 7; Joel 1:15 [a]Eze 7:7
1:15 [b]Isa 22:5; Joel 2:2
1:16 [c]Jer 4:19 [d]Isa 2:15
1:17 [e]Isa 59:10 [f]Ps 79:3 [g]Jer 9:22
1:18 [h]Eze 7:19 [i]ver 2-3; Zep 3:8 [j]Ge 6:7

14 "The great day of the LORD[z] is near[a]—
near and coming quickly.
Listen! The cry on the day of the LORD will be bitter,
the shouting of the warrior there.
15 That day will be a day of wrath,
a day of distress and anguish,
a day of trouble and ruin,
a day of darkness and gloom,
a day of clouds and blackness,[b]
16 a day of trumpet and battle cry[c]
against the fortified cities
and against the corner towers.[d]
17 I will bring distress on the people
and they will walk like blind[e] men,
because they have sinned against the LORD.
Their blood will be poured out[f] like dust
and their entrails like filth.[g]
18 Neither their silver nor their gold
will be able to save them
on the day of the LORD's wrath.[h]
In the fire of his jealousy
the whole world will be consumed,[i]
for he will make a sudden end
of all who live in the earth.[j]"

2:1 [k]2Ch 20:4; Joel 1:14 [l]Jer 3:3; 6:15

2

Gather together,[k] gather together,
O shameful[l] nation,

[a] 11 Or *the Mortar* [b] 11 Or *in*

1:10 The Fish Gate was located in the northern wall of Jerusalem, in the northwestern corner. Jerusalem was particularly vulnerable to attacks from the north (see the note on Ne 2:13).

The "New Quarter," also called the "Second District" (see Ne 11:9), was probably a suburb west of the temple area.

1:11 The "market district" may have been an area in the Tyropoeon Valley, just south of Mount Moriah.

1:12 People would later try to escape the Babylonians by hiding in houses, streets, sewers and tombs.

The phrase "left on its dregs" refers to the winemaking process (see "The Winepress" on p. 1171). The best wine was aged while being left on its dregs, a reference to its being allowed to thicken and congeal at the bottom of a container. The implication is that the people were complacent, indifferent and unmoved by prophetic warnings—that they were like thick, syrupy wine.

[2] before the appointed time arrives
and that day sweeps on like chaff,[m]
before the fierce anger[n] of the LORD comes upon you,
before the day of the LORD's wrath comes upon you.
[3] Seek[o] the LORD, all you humble of the land,
you who do what he commands.
Seek righteousness, seek humility;[p]
perhaps you will be sheltered[q]
on the day of the LORD's anger.

Against Philistia

[4] Gaza[r] will be abandoned
and Ashkelon left in ruins.
At midday Ashdod will be emptied
and Ekron uprooted.
[5] Woe to you who live by the sea,
O Kerethite[s] people;
the word of the LORD is against you,[t]
O Canaan, land of the Philistines.

"I will destroy you,
and none will be left."[u]

[6] The land by the sea, where the Kerethites[a] dwell,
will be a place for shepherds and sheep pens.[v]
[7] It will belong to the remnant of the house of Judah;
there they will find pasture.
In the evening they will lie down
in the houses of Ashkelon.
The LORD their God will care for them;
he will restore their fortunes.[b][w]

Against Moab and Ammon

[8] "I have heard the insults[x] of Moab
and the taunts of the Ammonites,
who insulted[y] my people
and made threats against their land.
[9] Therefore, as surely as I live,"
declares the LORD Almighty, the God of Israel,
"surely Moab[z] will become like Sodom,[a]
the Ammonites[b] like Gomorrah—
a place of weeds and salt pits,
a wasteland forever.

2:2 [m]Isa 17:13; Hos 13:3 [n]La 4:11
2:3 [o]Am 5:6 [p]Ps 45:4; Am 5:14-15 [q]Ps 57:1
2:4 [r]Am 1:6,7-8; Zec 9:5-7
2:5 [s]Eze 25:16 [t]Am 3:1 [u]Isa 14:30
2:6 [v]Isa 5:17
2:7 [w]Ps 126:4; Jer 32:44
2:8 [x]Jer 48:27 [y]Eze 25:3
2:9 [z]Isa 15:1-16:14; Jer 48:1-47 [a]Dt 29:23 [b]Jer 49:1-6; Eze 25:1-7

[a] *6* The meaning of the Hebrew for this word is uncertain. [b] *7* Or *will bring back their captives*

2:2 For "like chaff," see the note on Psalm 1:4.
2:4 Gaza, Ashdod, Ashkelon and Ekron were four of the five major Philistine cities (see "The Archaeology of Philistia" on p. 370), all located west of Judah "by the sea" (v. 6). Gath, the fifth major city, may already have been subdued by Uzziah (see 2Ch 26:6). Philistia was eventually destroyed by Nebuchadnezzar (see "Nebuchadnezzar" on p. 571).
2:5 Caphtor is the place from which the Philistines originally came (Am 9:7). Jeremiah (Jer 47:4) called it an island. There are a number of theories regarding the matter, but the one most widely accepted is that the Philistines originated on the isle of Crete in the Mediterranean. There is evidence of ancient connection between Crete and Philistia (here and in Eze 25:16; the Septuagint renders Kerethites "Cretans," indicating the belief that the Kerethites came from Crete), and the Philistines are called Kerethites. It is possible that Caphtor includes along with Crete the other islands in the vicinity, among them Caria and Lycia.

Canaan means "land of purple" (as does Phoenicia, the Greek name for the same general region)—so called because Canaan was a major producer and exporter of purple dye, highly prized by ancient royalty. The territory was much later called Palestine after the Philistines. (See "Canaan" on p. 324, "Phoenicia" on p. 488 and "The Archaeology of Philistia" on p. 370.)
2:8 The Moabites and Ammonites were peoples living east of Judah (see "Moab" on p. 292 and "Ammon" on p. 364). Although Israel's "cousins" through Abraham's nephew Lot (Ge 19:30–38), they were longtime enemies of Israel (Nu 22:1–6; Jdg 3:12–14; 11:12–33; Eze 25:2–7).
2:9 Sodom and Gomorrah had long since become proverbial for their wickedness and for divine judgment upon sin (see "The Destruction of Sodom and Gomorrah" on p. 32).

2:9 [c]Isa 11:14 [d]Am 2:1-3

The remnant of my people will plunder[c] them;
the survivors of my nation will inherit their land.[d]"

2:10 [e]Isa 16:6 [f]Jer 48:27

10 This is what they will get in return for their pride,[e]
for insulting[f] and mocking the people of the LORD Almighty.

2:11 [g]Joel 2:11 [h]Zep 1:4 [i]Zep 3:9

11 The LORD will be awesome[g] to them
when he destroys all the gods[h] of the land.
The nations on every shore will worship him,[i]
every one in its own land.

Against Cush

2:12 [j]Isa 18:1; 20:4 [k]Jer 46:10

12 "You too, O Cushites,[a][j]
will be slain by my sword.[k]"

Against Assyria

13 He will stretch out his hand against the north
and destroy Assyria,

2:13 [l]Na 1:1 [m]Mic 5:6

leaving Nineveh[l] utterly desolate
and dry as the desert.[m]
14 Flocks and herds will lie down there,
creatures of every kind.

2:14 [n]Isa 14:23

The desert owl[n] and the screech owl
will roost on her columns.
Their calls will echo through the windows,
rubble will be in the doorways,
the beams of cedar will be exposed.

2:15 [o]Isa 32:9 [p]Isa 47:8 [q]Eze 28:2 [r]Na 3:19

15 This is the carefree[o] city
that lived in safety.[p]
She said to herself,
"I am, and there is none besides me."[q]
What a ruin she has become,
a lair for wild beasts!
All who pass by her scoff[r]
and shake their fists.

The Future of Jerusalem

3:1 [s]Jer 6:6 [t]Eze 23:30

3 Woe to the city of oppressors,[s]
rebellious and defiled![t]

3:2 [u]Jer 22:21 [v]Jer 7:28 [w]Ps 73:28; Jer 5:3

2 She obeys[u] no one,
she accepts no correction.[v]
She does not trust in the LORD,
she does not draw near[w] to her God.
3 Her officials are roaring lions,

3:3 [x]Eze 22:27

her rulers are evening wolves,[x]
who leave nothing for the morning.
4 Her prophets are arrogant;

3:4 [y]Jer 9:4 [z]Eze 22:26

they are treacherous[y] men.
Her priests profane the sanctuary
and do violence to the law.[z]

[a] *12* That is, people from the upper Nile region

2:13–15 Nabopolassar was the first ruler of the Neo-Babylonian Empire, (626–605 B.C.). Allied with Medes and Scythians, he overthrew the Assyrian Empire, destroying Nineveh in 612, as prophesied in Nahum 2:1—3:9 and Zephaniah 2:13–15.
2:13 Although Nineveh (see "Nineveh" on p. 1497) lay east of Judah, Assyrian armies ordinarily invaded Canaan from the north (see the note on Ne 2:13), having first marched west along the Euphrates instead of through the Arabian desert. Nineveh was destroyed in 612 B.C. and its location was later forgotten—until it was discovered by archaeologists in 1845 (see the note on Na 3:19).
2:15 This verse anticipates Nineveh's impending destruction.

[5] The LORD within her is righteous;
he does no wrong.[a]
Morning by morning he dispenses his justice,
and every new day he does not fail,
yet the unrighteous know no shame.

[6] "I have cut off nations;
their strongholds are demolished.
I have left their streets deserted,
with no one passing through.
Their cities are destroyed;[b]
no one will be left—no one at all.
[7] I said to the city,
'Surely you will fear me
and accept correction!'
Then her dwelling would not be cut off,
nor all my punishments come upon her.
But they were still eager
to act corruptly[c] in all they did.
[8] Therefore wait[d] for me," declares the LORD,
"for the day I will stand up to testify.[a]
I have decided to assemble the nations,[e]
to gather the kingdoms
and to pour out my wrath on them—
all my fierce anger.
The whole world will be consumed[f]
by the fire of my jealous anger.

[9] "Then will I purify the lips of the peoples,
that all of them may call[g] on the name of the LORD
and serve[h] him shoulder to shoulder.
[10] From beyond the rivers of Cush[b][i]
my worshipers, my scattered people,
will bring me offerings.[j]
[11] On that day you will not be put to shame[k]
for all the wrongs you have done to me,
because I will remove from this city
those who rejoice in their pride.
Never again will you be haughty
on my holy hill.
[12] But I will leave within you
the meek[l] and humble,
who trust[m] in the name of the LORD.
[13] The remnant[n] of Israel will do no wrong;[o]
they will speak no lies,[p]
nor will deceit be found in their mouths.
They will eat and lie down[q]
and no one will make them afraid.[r]"

[14] Sing, O Daughter of Zion;[s]
shout aloud,[t] O Israel!

3:5 [a]Dt 32:4
3:6 [b]Lev 26:31
3:7 [c]Hos 9:9
3:8 [d]Ps 27:14 [e]Joel 3:2 [f]Zep 1:18
3:9 [g]Zep 2:11 [h]Isa 19:18
3:10 [i]Ps 68:31 [j]Isa 60:7
3:11 [k]Joel 2:26-27
3:12 [l]Isa 14:32 [m]Na 1:7
3:13 [n]Isa 10:21; Mic 4:7 [o]Ps 119:3 [p]Rev 14:5 [q]Eze 34:15; Zep 2:7 [r]Eze 34:25-28
3:14 [s]Zec 2:10 [t]Isa 12:6

[a] 8 Septuagint and Syriac; Hebrew *will rise up to plunder* [b] 10 That is, the upper Nile region

3:10 For "Cush," see the note on Isaiah 18:1 and "Cush" on page 1519. In this context it represents the most distant area imaginable, the implication being that even the most widely dispersed would be restored.

3:11 "My holy hill" is Mount Zion, the site of the Jerusalem temple (see "Zaphon, Olympus, Sinai and Zion: The Mountain of God" on p. 843).

ANCIENT PEOPLES, LANDS AND RULERS

Cush

ZEPHANIAH 3 Biblical Cush lay south of Egypt. Most references to the term "Cush" probably refer to Lower and Upper Nubia, the region directly south of Egypt, with its northern limit at the First Cataract of the Nile and its southern boundary at the Sixth Cataract. Sometimes the term may have been used more broadly for parts of Africa south of Egypt, but Cush is not to be equated with modern Ethiopia.

Ancient sources confirm that Cush was a land of great wealth; in fact, the Egyptian name Nubia may come from the word *nub*, or "gold." Egyptian trade lists record the precious minerals and other luxury items that traveled north from Cush along the Nile commerce routes. Among these commodities were gold, silver, cosmetics, balsam, frankincense and myrrh. Exotic animal products, such as ostrich eggs, rhinoceros horns and panther skins, were also available from or through Cush. Job 28:19 speaks of Cush as the source of the precious stone topaz.

Throughout Egyptian history Nubia and Egypt struggled against each other. For the most part Egypt was dominant—especially when Egyptian power was at its height under the **New Kingdom**[1] pharaohs.[2] Sometimes, however, Nubians extended their reach into Egypt—as during the **Second Intermediate period.** While the **Hyksos** ruled Lower (northern) Egypt, the Nubians penetrated from the south.[3] The Nubians themselves, however, were thoroughly Egyptianized.

Cushites appear several times in the Old Testament. Numbers 12:1 recounts that Moses had a Cushite wife; 2 Samuel 18:21–31 mentions that David's army had a Cushite messenger; and 2 Chronicles 14:9 refers to a "Zerah the Cushite," who fought against Asa of Judah.

View of the Nile from Kitchener's Island in the Aswan region of Upper Egypt

Photograph: © Todd Bolen/Bible Places.com

From the Biblical perspective, however, the most significant Cushite or Nubian power was represented by the Twenty-fifth Dynasty of Egypt (c. 780–656 B.C.). Under the Nubian pharaohs Piye (Piankhi), Shabaka, Shebitku and Tarhaqa (Biblical Tirhakah; 2Ki 19:9), the unified Egypt and Nubia became powerful and prosperous.

Shabaka, for example, carried out an extensive rebuilding campaign in Egypt, seeking to revive ancient pharaonic traditions such as building in the temple precinct at Karnak, near Thebes.[4] Also, the Nubian military pushed northward out of Egypt and confronted the **Assyrians**. Shebitku checked the expansion of Sennacherib at Eltekeh (in the coastal plain of Israel) in 701 B.C.

Although the Nubian-Egyptian forces were a power to be reckoned with, Isaiah warned Judah against placing any hope in them for protection from Assyria (Isa 20:3–6). Indeed, Nubian fortunes soon fell before the Assyrians. Tarhaqa, although an energetic and capable ruler, was defeated and driven back by Esarhaddon of Assyria, who actually captured Memphis in 671 B.C.[5] After that point Nubian power in Egypt collapsed.

[1]See Glossary on page 2080 for definitions of bolded words. [2]See "A Breakdown of Ancient Egyptian History" on page 104. [3]See "The Hyksos and the Old Testament" on page 121. [4]See "Thebes" on page 1354. [5]See "Memphis" on page 1270.

Be glad and rejoice with all your heart,
O Daughter of Jerusalem!
15 The LORD has taken away your punishment,
he has turned back your enemy.
The LORD, the King of Israel, is with you;[u]
never again will you fear[v] any harm.
16 On that day they will say to Jerusalem,
"Do not fear, O Zion;
do not let your hands hang limp.[w]
17 The LORD your God is with you,
he is mighty to save.[x]
He will take great delight[y] in you,
he will quiet you with his love,
he will rejoice over you with singing."

18 "The sorrows for the appointed feasts
I will remove from you;
they are a burden and a reproach to you.[a]
19 At that time I will deal
with all who oppressed you;
I will rescue the lame
and gather those who have been scattered.[z]
I will give them praise[a] and honor
in every land where they were put to shame.
20 At that time I will gather you;
at that time I will bring[b] you home.
I will give you honor[c] and praise
among all the peoples of the earth
when I restore your fortunes[b d]
before your very eyes,"
says the LORD.

3:15 [u]Eze 37:26-28 [v]Isa 54:14

3:16 [w]Job 4:3; Isa 35:3-4; Heb 12:12

3:17 [x]Isa 63:1 [y]Isa 62:4

3:19 [z]Eze 34:16; Mic 4:6 [a]Isa 60:18

3:20 [b]Jer 29:14; Eze 37:12 [c]Isa 56:5; 66:22 [d]Joel 3:1

[a] 18 Or *"I will gather you who mourn for the appointed feasts; / your reproach is a burden to you* [b] 20 Or *I bring back your captives*

INTRODUCTION TO Haggai

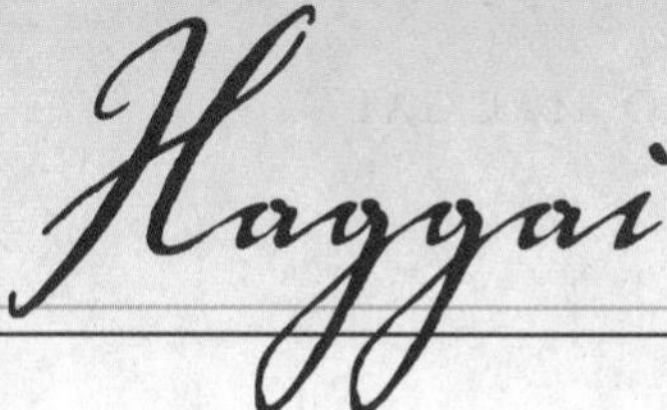

AUTHOR, PLACE AND DATE OF WRITING

There is little question that Haggai the prophet wrote the book that bears his name. We know nothing about him beyond what we find in his book.

Haggai precisely dated his messages, all of which were delivered between August and December of 520 B.C.

AUDIENCE

Zerubbabel had returned to Jerusalem in 538 B.C. along with about 50,000 Jews to rebuild the temple. Over the years the returnees had become discouraged by opposition and had abandoned the project. Haggai's messages were delivered to encourage the Jews to complete the temple rebuilding project.

CULTURAL FACTS AND HIGHLIGHTS

Haggai's words were directed to the postexilic community 18 years after the initial return from exile. The temple had still not been repaired, and the leadership was deeply discouraged, not only by local opposition but also by the lethargy of its own people. Darius of Persia was interested in the religions of his empire, and, in light of the impetus offered by his support, the Jews themselves were more to blame for their inactivity than were their opponents.

The prophet's message was essentially an exhortation to persevere in the effort to reestablish the community and the temple. From the perspective of some interpreters, however, Haggai's message was more than that; it was in their view a call to open rebellion against Persian authority. Those who espouse this viewpoint see Haggai as a Messianic zealot who believed that the eschatological kingdom would dawn if only Zerubbabel would be bold enough to cast off foreign domination. This interpretation, however, seems to read far more into the text than is justified (see "Did Haggai Lead a Messianic Rebellion?" on p. 1524.

TIMELINE

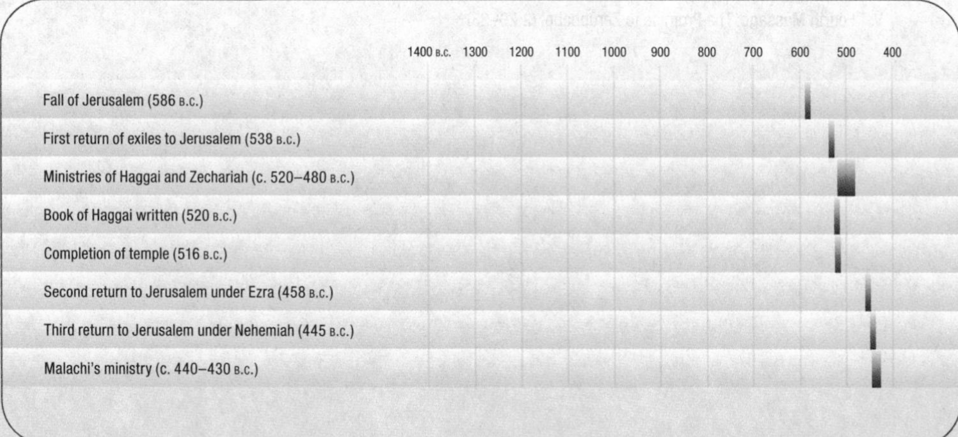

AS YOU READ

You might want to approach this short book equipped with a ledger, either mental or physical, on which you "list" the consequences of obedience and disobedience. Considering the pros and cons, does a clear "winner" come through?

DID YOU KNOW?

- In the arid climate of this region, dew is typically abundant during the growing season and is often as valuable as rain (1:10).
- A garment coming into contact with "consecrated meat" (meat from an animal set apart for a sacrifice) became "holy" (see Lev 6:27) but could not pass on that holiness to a third object. Ceremonial uncleanness was transmitted much more easily than holiness, since anything touched by an unclean person became unclean (Hag 2:12–13).
- A signet was a kind of seal, the impression of which in clay or wax functioned as a signature. A signet, worn on one's finger or on a cord around one's neck, could be used as a pledge or guarantee of full payment of a debt (2:23).

THEMES

Haggai's themes include:

1. *Priorities.* The people had neglected the rebuilding of God's temple while focusing their efforts on constructing beautiful homes for themselves (1:2–4,9). Haggai instructed them that God's temple and work were to be their top priority. They were to "give careful thought" (1:5,7; 2:15,18) to their ways, for God's pleasure and honor were to be their overriding goals (1:8).

2. *Obedience.* There are consequences for disobeying God (1:6,11; 2:16–17). But when God's people follow him (1:12) he graciously provides the enthusiasm (1:14), strength (2:4–5) and resources (2:8) to do his will. God promised the postexilic community that, in return for their obedience, he would bless them with his presence (2:9), peace (2:9) and prosperity (2:19).

OUTLINE

I. First Message: The Call to Rebuild the Temple (1:1–11)
II. The Response of Zerubbabel and the People (1:12–15)
III. Second Message: The Promised Glory (2:1–9)
IV. Third Message: A Defiled People Blessed (2:10–19)
V. Fourth Message: The Promise to Zerubbabel (2:20–23)

A Call to Build the House of the LORD

1 In the second year of King Darius,[a] on the first day of the sixth month, the word of the LORD came
through the prophet Haggai[b] to Zerubbabel[c] son of Shealtiel, governor[d] of Judah, and to Joshua[a][e] son
of Jehozadak,[f] the high priest:
2 This is what the LORD Almighty says: "These people say, 'The time has not yet come for the LORD's
house to be built.' "
3 Then the word of the LORD came through the prophet Haggai:[g] 4 "Is it a time for you yourselves to be
living in your paneled houses,[h] while this house remains a ruin?[i]"
5 Now this is what the LORD Almighty says: "Give careful thought[j] to your ways. 6 You have planted
much, but have harvested little.[k] You eat, but never have enough. You drink, but never have your fill. You
put on clothes, but are not warm. You earn wages,[l] only to put them in a purse with holes in it."
7 This is what the LORD Almighty says: "Give careful thought to your ways. 8 Go up into the mountains
and bring down timber and build the house, so that I may take pleasure[m] in it and be honored," says the
LORD. 9 "You expected much, but see, it turned out to be little. What you brought home, I blew away. Why?"
declares the LORD Almighty. "Because of my house, which remains a ruin,[n] while each of you is busy with
his own house. 10 Therefore, because of you the heavens have withheld their dew and the earth its crops.[o]
11 I called for a drought[p] on the fields and the mountains, on the grain, the new wine, the oil and what-
ever the ground produces, on men and cattle, and on the labor of your hands.[q]"

12 Then Zerubbabel[r] son of Shealtiel, Joshua son of Jehozadak, the high priest, and the whole rem-
nant[s] of the people obeyed[t] the voice of the LORD their God and the message of the prophet Haggai, be-
cause the LORD their God had sent him. And the people feared[u] the LORD.
13 Then Haggai, the LORD's messenger, gave this message of the LORD to the people: "I am with[v] you,"
declares the LORD. 14 So the LORD stirred up the spirit of Zerubbabel[w] son of Shealtiel, governor of Judah,
and the spirit of Joshua son of Jehozadak, the high priest, and the spirit of the whole remnant[x] of the
people. They came and began to work on the house of the LORD Almighty, their God, 15 on the twenty-
fourth day of the sixth month[y] in the second year of King Darius.

The Promised Glory of the New House

2 On the twenty-first day of the seventh month, the word of the LORD came through the prophet Hag-
gai: 2 "Speak to Zerubbabel son of Shealtiel, governor of Judah, to Joshua son of Jehozadak, the high
priest, and to the remnant of the people. Ask them, 3 'Who of you is left who saw this house[z] in its former
glory? How does it look to you now? Does it not seem to you like nothing?[a] 4 But now be strong, O Zerub-
babel,' declares the LORD. 'Be strong,[b] O Joshua son of Jehozadak, the high priest. Be strong, all you people

1:1 [a]Ezr 4:24 [b]Ezr 5:1 [c]Mt 1:12-13 [d]Ezr 5:3 [e]Ezr 2:2 [f]1Ch 6:15; Ezr 3:2
1:3 [g]Ezr 5:1
1:4 [h]2Sa 7:2 [i]ver 9; Jer 33:12
1:5 [j]La 3:40
1:6 [k]Dt 28:38 [l]Hag 2:16; Zec 8:10
1:8 [m]Ps 132:13-14
1:9 [n]ver 4
1:10 [o]Lev 26:19; Dt 28:23
1:11 [p]Dt 28:22; 1Ki 17:1 [q]Hag 2:17
1:12 [r]ver 1 [s]ver 14; Isa 1:9; Hag 2:2 [t]Isa 50:10 [u]Dt 31:12
1:13 [v]Mt 28:20; Ro 8:31
1:14 [w]Ezr 5:2 [x]ver 12
1:15 [y]ver 1
2:3 [z]Ezr 3:12 [a]Zec 4:10
2:4 [b]1Ch 28:20; Zec 8:9; Eph 6:10

[a] *1* A variant of *Jeshua;* here and elsewhere in Haggai

1:1 The date was August 29, 520 B.C. "King Darius" refers to Darius Hystaspes, also called Darius I or Darius the Great (see "Darius I" on p. 676), who ruled Persia from 521 to 486 B.C. Archaeologically, Darius is most famous for his Behistun Inscription, a trilingual inscription emblazoned high on a cliff face in western Iran, through which cuneiform inscriptions were deciphered and the culture and history of ancient Mesopotamia were brought to light.

The "first day" was the New Moon, the day on which prophets were sometimes consulted. New Moon festivals included special sacrifices and feasts, as well as a cessation from work.

For "Zerubbabel," see the note on Ezra 1:8 and for "Joshua" the note on Ezra 2:2. Jehozadak had been taken captive by Nebuchadnezzar (1Ch 6:15).

1:2 After the foundation of the temple had been laid in 536 B.C. (see Ezr 3:8–10), the people became discouraged and halted the work until 520 (see Ezr 4:1–5,24).

1:3 During a four-month period in 520 B.C., Haggai received a series of prophetic messages (see "Prophets in the Bible and Pagan Nations" on p. 1457 and "Oracles of the Ancient World" on p. 1507). Haggai's call to rebuild the temple did not represent the first initiative to restore this structure. According to Ezra 5:13–16 the project had begun immediately following the decree of Cyrus in 538 B.C. (cf. Ezr 1). Although the returned exiles had rebuilt the foundation shortly thereafter (Ezr 3:8–11), they had allowed opposition to prevent them from making further progress on the temple itself (Ezr 4:23–24).

1:4 "Paneled houses" is usually a reference to royal dwellings, which boasted cedar paneling (see 1Ki 7:3,7; Jer 22:14–15).

1:10 In the arid climate of this region, dew is typically abundant during the growing season and is often as valuable as rain.

1:11 Drought, which was often a precursor to famine (see "Famine in the Ancient Near East" on p. 70), affected the "mountains" because the hills were cultivated, especially through terracing. Grain, wine and oil were the three basic crops of the land (see "Food and Agriculture" on p. 390), and olive oil was used as food, ointment and medicine.

1:13 "Messenger" is often synonymous with "prophet" (see "Prophets in the Bible and Pagan Nations" on p. 1457).

1:15 The date was September 21, 520 B.C.

2:1 The date was October 17, 520 B.C., the last day of the Feast of Tabernacles. Even though the crops in this instance were meager, this was a time set aside for celebrating the summer harvest (see "The Festivals of Israel" on p. 186).

2:3 Some of the older exiles had seen Solomon's temple (see "Solomon's Temple and Other Ancient Temples" on p. 620) before its destruction by the Babylonians in 586 B.C. This verse makes reference to the "former glory" of "this house" because Zerubbabel's temple was considered a continuation of Solomon's. Ezra 3:12 describes the reaction of the older returnees when the foundation of the temple was completed.

of the land,' declares the LORD, 'and work. For I am with[c] you,' declares the LORD Almighty. 5 'This is what
I covenanted with you when you came out of Egypt.[d] And my Spirit[e] remains among you. Do not fear.'
6 "This is what the LORD Almighty says: 'In a little while[f] I will once more shake the heavens and the
earth,[g] the sea and the dry land. 7 I will shake all nations, and the desired of all nations will come, and I

2:4 [c]2Sa 5:10; Ac 7:9
2:5 [d]Ex 29:46 [e]Ne 9:20; Isa 63:11
2:6 [f]Isa 10:25 [g]Heb 12:26*

2:7 The phrase "desired of all nations" occurs only here in the entire Bible. Again, when the temple was erected in Ezra's time, the prophet was directed to encourage the older men who had seen the more magnificent temple of Solomon and were disappointed with what they saw now, by assuring them that God was with them; that in a little while he would shake the heavens, the earth, the sea, the

Did Haggai Lead a Messianic Rebellion?

HAGGAI 2 The book of Haggai is one of the shortest documents in the Bible, consisting of four messages totaling only about 600 words. It is also one of the most precisely dated books in all of Scripture. Its four oracles are reported to have been received by the prophet within the space of 15 weeks during the fall of the second year of the **Persian**[1] king Darius I, who reigned from 521–486 B.C.[2]

During this period Judah existed as part of a large administrative district or satrapy of the Persian Empire called *abar naharah* ("Beyond the River"; cf. Ezr 4:10; Ne 2:7). Each satrapy contributed annual tribute and was ruled by a Persian governor. Nevertheless, Persian imperial policy beginning with Cyrus the Great and continuing under Darius encouraged a significant degree of local autonomy.[3] An extension of this policy led to Persian support for the construction of local temples and sanctuaries (2Ch 36:23; Isa 44:26–28). Haggai's central concern within this historical context was to encourage the full reconstruction of the temple in Jerusalem. His messages were directed at the principal leaders of the Jerusalem community—Zerubbabel, the governor, and Joshua, the high priest.

Certain aspects of Haggai's imagery have led some to conclude that this prophet hoped not only for the rebuilding of the temple but also for the restoration of the Davidic monarchy. In his final oracle Haggai applied lofty titles to Zerubbabel, the son of Shealtiel and grandson of the last Davidic king, Jehoiachin:

- Zerubbabel is called "my servant" (Hag 2:23), a title frequently applied to David (1Ki 11:34; Ps 78:70; Eze 34:23) and to Isaiah's Messianic "servant" (Isa 42:1; 49:6; 52:13; 53:11).
- God declared that he would shake the heavens and the earth, overthrowing thrones of kingdoms and the power of the nations (Hag 2:21–22). The Messianic kingdom was about to begin, with Zerubbabel at the top.
- Zerubbabel is said to have been chosen and honored like a royal signet ring (v. 23).[4]

Two questions have been raised: Did Haggai believe Zerubbabel to be the Messiah? Did the prophet call for a rebellion against Persian rule?

In reality, Haggai neither exhorted Zerubbabel to claim a Messianic office nor urged the Jews to revolt against Persia.[5] Nothing in the book suggests an expectation on Haggai's part that the promises of Zion's final exaltation would be imminently fulfilled or that Zerubbabel would be the agent of their fulfillment. To the contrary, Zerubbabel was simply exhorted to perform his task in rebuilding the Jerusalem temple in anticipation of a greater future yet to come. Zerubbabel was called upon to live up to the heritage handed down from his ancestor David, but beyond the rebuilding of the temple no specific actions were called for.

It is true that the book of Haggai reflects the hope, common to all the prophets, for a glorious future for Zion:

- God will shake the universe (vv. 6,21).
- He will remove the dominion of the nations (v. 22) and bring their tribute to Israel (vv. 7–8; cf. Ex 12:35–36).
- He will accomplish a second **exodus** (Hag 2:5,22) and install his chosen king (v. 23).
- He will once again dwell in the midst of his people (1:13; 2:4,9).

[1]See Glossary on page 2080 for definitions of bolded words. [2]See "Darius I" on page 676. [3]See "Cyrus the Great" on page 669. [4]See "Signet Rings" on page 728. [5]See "Ancient Persian History Through Darius" on page 717 and "Ancient Persian History From Xerxes Forward" on page 718.

2:7 [h]Isa 60:7 will fill this house[h] with glory,' says the LORD Almighty. 8'The silver is mine and the gold is mine,' declares
2:9 [i]Ps 85:9 the LORD Almighty. 9'The glory[i] of this present house will be greater than the glory of the former house,'
says the LORD Almighty. 'And in this place I will grant peace,' declares the LORD Almighty."

Blessings for a Defiled People

2:10 [j]ver 1 10On the twenty-fourth day of the ninth month,[j] in the second year of Darius, the word of the LORD
2:11 [k]Lev 10:10-11; Dt 17:8-11; Mal 2:7 came to the prophet Haggai: 11"This is what the LORD Almighty says: 'Ask the priests[k] what the law says:
12If a person carries consecrated meat in the fold of his garment, and that fold touches some bread or
2:12 [l]Lev 6:27; Mt 23:19 stew, some wine, oil or other food, does it become consecrated?[l]' "
The priests answered, "No."
13Then Haggai said, "If a person defiled by contact with a dead body touches one of these things, does
it become defiled?"
2:13 [m]Lev 22:4-6 "Yes," the priests replied, "it becomes defiled.[m]"
14Then Haggai said, " 'So it is with this people and this nation in my sight,' declares the LORD. 'What-
2:14 [n]Isa 1:13 ever they do and whatever they offer[n] there is defiled.
2:15 [o]Hag 1:5 [p]Ezr 3:10 [q]Ezr 4:24 15" 'Now give careful thought[o] to this from this day on[a]—consider how things were before one stone
was laid[p] on another in the LORD's temple.[q] 16When anyone came to a heap of twenty measures, there
2:16 [r]Hag 1:6 were only ten. When anyone went to a wine vat to draw fifty measures, there were only twenty.[r] 17I struck
2:17 [s]Hag 1:11 [t]Dt 28:22; 1Ki 8:37; Am 4:9 [u]Am 4:6 all the work of your hands[s] with blight,[t] mildew and hail, yet you did not turn to me,' declares the LORD.[u]
18'From this day on, from this twenty-fourth day of the ninth month, give careful thought to the day when
2:18 [v]Zec 8:9 the foundation[v] of the LORD's temple was laid. Give careful thought: 19Is there yet any seed left in the
barn? Until now, the vine and the fig tree, the pomegranate and the olive tree have not borne fruit.
" 'From this day on I will bless you.' "

Zerubbabel the LORD's Signet Ring

20The word of the LORD came to Haggai a second time on the twenty-fourth day of the month: 21"Tell
2:21 [w]Ezr 5:2 Zerubbabel[w] governor of Judah that I will shake the heavens and the earth. 22I will overturn royal thrones
2:22 [x]Da 2:44 [y]Mic 5:10 [z]Jdg 7:22 and shatter the power of the foreign kingdoms.[x] I will overthrow chariots[y] and their drivers; horses and
their riders will fall, each by the sword of his brother.[z]
2:23 [a]Isa 43:10 23" 'On that day,' declares the LORD Almighty, 'I will take you, my servant[a] Zerubbabel son of Shealtiel,'
declares the LORD, 'and I will make you like my signet ring, for I have chosen you,' declares the LORD Al-
mighty."

[a] 15 Or *to the days past*

---

dry land and the nations; and that "the desired of all nations" would come to fill the house with his glory. Many expositors refer the prophecy to Christ's first advent, and others to his coming second advent, while others deny a Messianic application altogether, translating "the desired of all nations" as "the desirable things of all nations"—their precious gifts (cf. Isa 60:5,11; 61:6).

2:8 Silver and gold had earlier been provided for Solomon's temple (1Ch 29:2,7), as they were provided now for Zerubbabel's (Ezr 6:5).

2:10 The date was December 18, 520 B.C.

2:11 One of the responsibilities of the priests was to teach and interpret the Law of Moses (see the note on Jer 18:18; see also "The Levites and the Priests" on p. 648).

2:12–13 A garment coming into contact with "consecrated meat" (meat from an animal set apart for a sacrifice) became "holy" (see Lev 6:27) but could not pass along that holiness to a third object. Ceremonial uncleanness was transmitted much more easily than holiness, since anything touched by an unclean person became unclean (see Nu 19:11–13,22; see also "Sacrifices and Offerings in the Bible and the Ancient Near East" on p. 158 and "Ritual Purity in Israel and the Ancient Near East" on p. 166.)

2:16 For "wine vat," see "The Winepress" on page 1171.

2:17 The blight was probably caused by a scorching east wind (the sirocco), which blows in from the desert in late spring and early fall, often withering vegetation.

2:19 Grapes, figs and pomegranates ripened in August and September; olives, from September to November (see "Food and Agriculture" on p. 390). These harvests, like the earlier grain crops, in this instance had produced little (see 1:11 and its note).

2:23 For "that day," see the note on Joel 1:15.

A signet was a kind of seal, the impression of which in clay or wax functioned as a signature (see Est 8:8). A signet, worn on one's finger (as here and in Est 3:10) or on a cord around one's neck (see "Signet Rings" on p. 728), could be used as a pledge or guarantee of full payment. Its mention here apparently reversed the curse placed upon King Jehoiachin in Jeremiah 22:24. Zerubbabel was himself a guarantee that the future glory of the temple would be realized.

INTRODUCTION TO *Zechariah*

AUTHOR, PLACE AND DATE OF WRITING

The author of this book was a priest named Zechariah, the son of Berekiah, the son of Iddo (1:1). Zechariah is mentioned alongside Haggai in Ezra 5:1 and 6:14, and he played a role in the restoration of the postexilic community. Today, however, many scholars believe that Zechariah wrote only chapters 1–8 of the book by his name, not chapters 9–14; these researchers refer to the two sections of the book, respectively, as "Proto-Zechariah" and "Deutero-Zechariah." The arguments for dividing the text can be satisfactorily answered, however, allowing interpreters to affirm that Zechariah did indeed write the entire book (see "Zechariah's Authorship" at on 1531).

The prophecies of chapters 1–8, dated in the text (1:1,7; 7:1), were delivered from 520 to 518 B.C. Those of chapters 9–14, on the other hand, are undated, and there are reasons to believe that Zechariah wrote these later chapters long after the initial eight. It is perhaps significant that Zechariah and Haggai did not undertake any leadership role in the community until 520 B.C., about 18 years after the return from exile (c. 538). The suggestion that they were children at the time of the return is probably confirmed in 2:4, where the prophet in 520 B.C. is called a "young man."

AUDIENCE

Zechariah encouraged the Jews who had returned from exile in Babylon to complete the rebuilding of the temple and prophesied concerning Jerusalem's future place in God's kingdom.

CULTURAL FACTS AND HIGHLIGHTS

The book of Zechariah was essentially a message of hope and encouragement for the postexilic Jews. The prophet's earlier messages in the first eight chapters, like those of Haggai, aimed at prompting the Jews to put an end to their procrastination and defeatism and to give themselves wholeheartedly to the task of rebuilding the community and the temple (e.g., 1:16–17; 2:10–13; 4:7–10). In the latter part of the book, despite a critique of the nation's leadership (10:3), the positive tone continues (e.g., ch. 9). In short, the book of Zechariah served as an encouragement to the postexilic community—a people who thought that all of Israel's glory was in the past—that far greater realities lay ahead. They must, however, perform their duty in the present.

TIMELINE

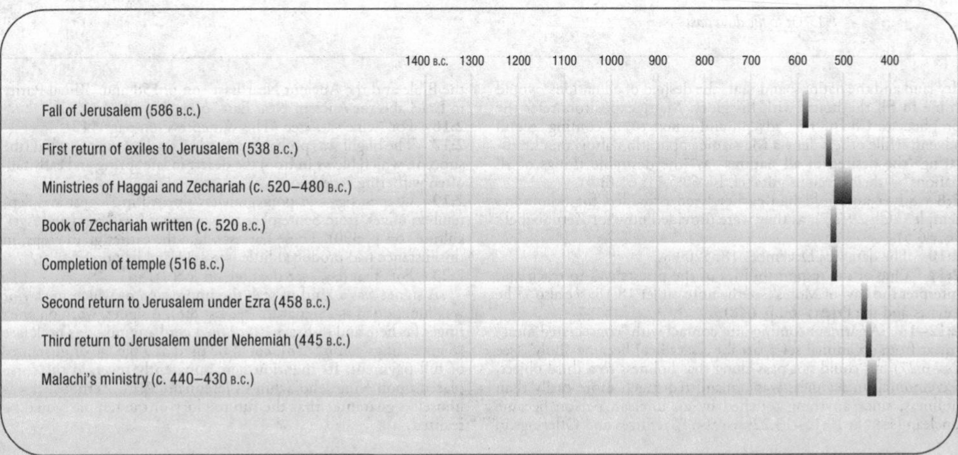

AS YOU READ

Zechariah's name, fittingly, means "The LORD (Yahweh) remembers." As you engage with this prophet, who was a contemporary of Haggai and shared his overall viewpoint, look for evidences that confirm the assertion that God does indeed remember.

DID YOU KNOW?

- Zechariah experienced all eight visions during the course of one night. They were not dreams, for the prophet was fully awake (1:8).
- The "land of the north" was Babylonia, which in fact lay to the east. But since a desert separated Assyria and Babylonia from Israel/Judah, invading armies regularly attacked from the north (2:6).
- Taking off his filthy clothing deprived Joshua of his priestly office but was also symbolic of the removal of sin. Putting a clean turban on his head reinstated him to his high-priestly function so that Israel once again had a divinely authorized priestly mediator (3:4–5).
- A "waterless pit" or empty cistern was sometimes used as a detention cell (9:11).
- Wounds on a person's body were at times suspected to have been self-inflicted as a component of idolatrous worship practices (13:6).

THEMES

Zechariah's themes include:

1. *Israel's near future.* The first eight chapters of Zechariah fit its historical setting and focus on the near future of the restored Jewish community. Zechariah encouraged the returnees as they struggled to rebuild the temple, all the while calling them to repent of their sins (1:2–6) and exhorting them to exhibit compassion and mercy toward the vulnerable (7:4–14). Zechariah's night visions expressed God's continuing concern for the protection and restoration of his people (1:16–17,20; 2:11–12; 8:3–23), as well as the importance of Zerubbabel and Joshua in God's plan (3:1–14; 6:9–15).

2. *Israel's distant future.* The last six chapters of Zechariah focus on the distant future of the restored Jewish community. These prophecies reveal God's plan to bring further and greater blessings to Jerusalem: God would avenge his people by destroying their enemies (9:1–8); Israel's ultimate King would arrive in Jerusalem, ushering in a time of peace (9:9–17); and God would gather his scattered people (10:1—11:3). The final chapters culminate in a vision of God's ultimate victory over those who continue to resist his will (12:1–9) and of his cleansing of the land and people (13:1–9). The Divine Warrior will return, and all humans will submit to his rule (14:1–21). Zechariah's vision of a coming king and an ultimate, divine victory over evil points not only to Christ's earthly ministry but also to his ultimate return as described in the book of Revelation.

OUTLINE

I. A Call to Repentance (1:1–6)
II. Eight Night Visions and Prophecies (1:7—6:8)
III. The Crowning of Joshua the High Priest (6:9–15)
IV. Fasting and the Future (7–8)
V. The Advent and Rejection of Messiah (9–11)
VI. The Advent and Reception of Messiah (12–14)

A Call to Return to the LORD

1 In the eighth month of the second year of Darius,[a] the word of the LORD came to the prophet Zech-
ariah[b] son of Berekiah,[c] the son of Iddo:[d]
2 “The LORD was very angry[e] with your forefathers. 3 Therefore tell the people: This is what the LORD Al-
mighty says: ‘Return to me,’ declares the LORD Almighty, ‘and I will return to you,’[f] says the LORD Almighty.
4 Do not be like your forefathers,[g] to whom the earlier prophets proclaimed: This is what the LORD Almighty
says: ‘Turn from your evil ways[h] and your evil practices.’ But they would not listen or pay attention to me,[i]
declares the LORD. 5 Where are your forefathers now? And the prophets, do they live forever? 6 But did not
my words and my decrees, which I commanded my servants the prophets, overtake your forefathers?
“Then they repented and said, ‘The LORD Almighty has done to us what our ways and practices de-
serve,[j] just as he determined to do.’ ”

The Man Among the Myrtle Trees

7 On the twenty-fourth day of the eleventh month, the month of Shebat, in the second year of Darius,
the word of the LORD came to the prophet Zechariah son of Berekiah, the son of Iddo.
8 During the night I had a vision—and there before me was a man riding a red[k] horse! He was stand-
ing among the myrtle trees in a ravine. Behind him were red, brown and white horses.[l]
9 I asked, “What are these, my lord?”
The angel[m] who was talking with me answered, “I will show you what they are.”
10 Then the man standing among the myrtle trees explained, “They are the ones the LORD has sent to
go throughout the earth.”[n]
11 And they reported to the angel of the LORD, who was standing among the myrtle trees, “We have
gone throughout the earth and found the whole world at rest and in peace.”[o]
12 Then the angel of the LORD said, “LORD Almighty, how long will you withhold mercy from Jerusalem
and from the towns of Judah, which you have been angry with these seventy[p] years?” 13 So the LORD spoke
kind and comforting words to the angel who talked with me.[q]
14 Then the angel who was speaking to me said, “Proclaim this word: This is what the LORD Almighty
says: ‘I am very jealous[r] for Jerusalem and Zion, 15 but I am very angry with the nations that feel secure.[s]
I was only a little angry, but they added to the calamity.’[t]
16 “Therefore, this is what the LORD says: ‘I will return[u] to Jerusalem with mercy, and there my house
will be rebuilt. And the measuring line[v] will be stretched out over Jerusalem,’ declares the LORD Almighty.
17 “Proclaim further: This is what the LORD Almighty says: ‘My towns will again overflow with pros-
perity, and the LORD will again comfort[w] Zion and choose[x] Jerusalem.’ ”[y]

Four Horns and Four Craftsmen

18 Then I looked up—and there before me were four horns! 19 I asked the angel who was speaking to
me, “What are these?”

1:1 [a]Ezr 4:24; 6:15 [b]Ezr 5:1 [c]Mt 23:35; Lk 11:51 [d]ver 7; Ne 12:4
1:2 [e]2Ch 36:16
1:3 [f]Mal 3:7; Jas 4:8
1:4 [g]2Ch 36:15 [h]Ps 106:6 [i]2Ch 24:19; Ps 78:8; Jer 6:17
1:6 [j]Jer 12:14-17; La 2:17
1:8 [k]Rev 6:4 [l]Zec 6:2-7
1:9 [m]Zec 4:1,4-5
1:10 [n]Zec 6:5-8
1:11 [o]Isa 14:7
1:12 [p]Da 9:2
1:13 [q]Zec 4:1
1:14 [r]Joel 2:18; Zec 8:2
1:15 [s]Jer 48:11 [t]Ps 123:3-4; Am 1:11
1:16 [u]Zec 8:3 [v]Zec 2:1-2
1:17 [w]Isa 51:3 [x]Isa 14:1 [y]Zec 2:12

1:1 The date was October–November 520 B.C. Zechariah was not only a prophet but also a member of a priestly family. Born in Babylonia, he was among those who returned to Judah in 538/537 B.C. under the leadership of Zerubbabel and Joshua. Zechariah was a contemporary of Haggai but continued his ministry long after him.

See “Prophets in the Bible and Pagan Nations” on page 1457.

1:4 The “earlier prophets” included Isaiah, Jeremiah and Ezekiel.

1:7—6:15 Zechariah was the grandson of Iddo, the head of one of the priestly families that returned from the exile (Ne 12:4,16; see also the introduction to Zechariah and the note on 1:1). Twenty years after the return the temple still lay a blackened ruin, and the discouraged populace could not imagine how it could be restored. At this critical moment God raised up the prophets Haggai and Zechariah to encourage the Jews to rebuild the temple. The prophecies of the two men were delivered at almost the same time. Haggai appeared first, in August of 520 B.C., and within a month of his appeal the foundation of the temple was laid. Soon afterward Zechariah uttered his first prophecy (1:1–6). Haggai finished his recorded prophecies in the same year. The following year Zechariah delivered a message consisting of eight symbolic visions, along with an appendix (1:7—6:15). Two years later he gave a third message in answer to an inquiry by the men of Bethel regarding the observance of a fast. The two prophecies in chapters 9–14 are not dated but were probably given at a much later period (see the introduction).

1:7 The date was February 15, 519 B.C., about three months after that of verse 1.

1:8–17 The purpose of this first of eight symbolic night visions was to assure the Israelites of God’s special care for and interest in them. See also the notes on 1:18–21, 2:1–13, 3:1–10, 4:1–14, 5:1–4, 5:5–11 and 6:1–8.

1:8 Zechariah experienced all eight visions (1:7—6:8) during the course of one night. They were not dreams (see 4:1), for the prophet was fully awake.

1:11 For “angel of the LORD,” see “Angels and Guardian Spirits in the Bible and the Ancient Near East” on page 1529.

1:12 See “The 70 Years of Captivity” on page 1234.

1:15 While the Persian Empire as a whole was secure at this time, the Israelites in Judah were oppressed and still under foreign domination.

1:18–21 The four horns and the four craftsmen taught the Israelites that, with their enemies destroyed, there was no longer any opposition to the building of God’s house.

1:18 Zechariah’s second vision was a vivid picture of the destruction of the nations that had devastated Israel (v. 19). If the number four is to be taken literally, the reference is probably to Assyria, Egypt, Babylonia and Persia.

1:19 [z]Am 6:13 He answered me, "These are the horns[z] that scattered Judah, Israel and Jerusalem."
20Then the LORD showed me four craftsmen. 21I asked, "What are these coming to do?"
He answered, "These are the horns that scattered Judah so that no one could raise his head, but the
1:21 [a]Ps 75:4 [b]Ps 75:10 craftsmen have come to terrify them and throw down these horns of the nations who lifted up their
horns[a] against the land of Judah to scatter its people."[b]

1:20 If the number four is to be understood literally, the reference here, unlike that in verse 18, may be to Egypt, Babylonia, Persia and Greece.

CULTURAL AND HISTORICAL NOTES

Angels and Guardian Spirits in the Bible and the Ancient Near East

Protective spirit; relief from Assyria

Preserving Bible Times; © Dr. James C. Martin; permission of The British Museum

ZECHARIAH 1 Both the Hebrew and the Greek words that are translated into English as "angel" also mean "messenger." This reflects the fact that an angel is a messenger from God. It was sometimes difficult to determine whether a messenger from God during Bible times was human or angelic (Jdg 13:2–22), since angels were often perceived as humanlike in appearance and evidently seemed to be either male or female (Zec 5:9). The situation is also confusing in the case of "the angel of the LORD," since this being sometimes appears to have been a mere angel but at other times God himself.

Human messengers in the ancient Near East acted as heralds, envoys and ambassadors, bearing the authority of the sender. In like manner angels functioned in the Bible as God's representatives. The "message" an angel carried may have been verbal, but it may also have been an action indicative of a judgment (2Sa 24:15–17), a ministry to believers (1Ki 19:5–8) or a service as a guardian of God's people (Ps 91:11).

Beings analogous to angels also appear in the mythology of Israel's neighbors:

- Lists of gods from **Mesopotamia**[1] often name the servants of the great gods. These lesser divinities purportedly functioned as messengers and agents for the high gods. Sometimes the myths present these lower gods as a kind of heavenly peasant class who did menial work for the high gods but who, if pushed too hard, were inclined to rebel against their heavenly overlords.[2]
- Lesser deities or "personal gods" in the ancient world also functioned as protective spirits with regard to individuals (analogous to the idea of guardian angels or patron saints). They were thought to watch over the lives of devotees in return for their allegiance.[3]
- Another group of lower deities encompassed the gatekeepers, typically depicted as fearsome, hybrid creatures, such as winged bulls or lions with human heads. Colossal statues of such creatures flanked the entrances of temples and palaces and were thought to ward off evil spirits, serving as guardians and attendants of both gods and kings. The British Museum now houses several of these statues, averaging over 9.8 feet (3 m) in height. Their Egyptian counterparts were the sphinx and the uraeus serpent.

Biblical cherubim and seraphim are analogous to the supernatural gatekeepers of the ancient Near East. Cherubim secured the way into Eden after the expulsion of the man and woman (Ge 3:24), and figures of winged cherubim also symbolically guarded the ark of the covenant and the Tent of Meeting (Ex 25:18–22; 26:1).[4] Seraphim served as attendants in the heavenly throne room in Isaiah's vision (Isa 6). Cherubim are sometimes described in terms reminiscent of the hybrid creatures of ancient Near Eastern art (Ex 37:9; Eze 10:1–11), and some interpreters believe that the seraphim were serpentine. Both cherubim and seraphim are closely associated with God's holiness, sovereignty and purity.

[1]See Glossary on page 2080 for definitions of bolded words. [2]See "Humanity and the Divine: Comparing the Bible to the Myth of Atra-Hasis" on page 1176.
[3]See "A Man and His God" on page 771. [4]See "The Tabernacle and the Ark" on page 153.

A Man With a Measuring Line

2 Then I looked up—and there before me was a man with a measuring line in his hand! 2I asked,
"Where are you going?"
He answered me, "To measure Jerusalem, to find out how wide and how long it is."[c]
3Then the angel who was speaking to me left, and another angel came to meet him 4and said to him:
"Run, tell that young man, 'Jerusalem will be a city without walls[d] because of the great number[e] of men
and livestock in it. 5And I myself will be a wall[f] of fire around it,' declares the LORD, 'and I will be its glory[g]
within.'
6"Come! Come! Flee from the land of the north," declares the LORD, "for I have scattered you to the
four winds of heaven,"[h] declares the LORD.
7"Come, O Zion! Escape, you who live in the Daughter of Babylon!"[i] 8For this is what the LORD Al-
mighty says: "After he has honored me and has sent me against the nations that have plundered
you—for whoever touches you touches the apple of his eye[j]— 9I will surely raise my hand against
them so that their slaves will plunder them.[a][k] Then you will know that the LORD Almighty has
sent me.[l]
10"Shout and be glad, O Daughter of Zion.[m] For I am coming,[n] and I will live among you,"[o] declares
the LORD. 11"Many nations will be joined with the LORD in that day and will become my people. I will live
among you and you will know that the LORD Almighty has sent me to you. 12The LORD will inherit[p] Judah
as his portion in the holy land and will again choose[q] Jerusalem. 13Be still[r] before the LORD, all mankind,
because he has roused himself from his holy dwelling."

2:2 [c]Eze 40:3; Rev 21:15
2:4 [d]Eze 38:11 [e]Isa 49:20; Jer 30:19; 33:22
2:5 [f]Isa 26:1 [g]Rev 21:23
2:6 [h]Eze 17:21
2:7 [i]Isa 48:20
2:8 [j]Dt 32:10
2:9 [k]Isa 14:2 [l]Zec 4:9
2:10 [m]Zep 3:14 [n]Zec 9:9 [o]Lev 26:12; Zec 8:3
2:12 [p]Dt 32:9; Ps 33:12; Jer 10:16 [q]Zec 1:17
2:13 [r]Hab 2:20

Clean Garments for the High Priest

3 Then he showed me Joshua[b][s] the high priest standing before the angel of the LORD, and Satan[c][t]
standing at his right side to accuse him. 2The LORD said to Satan, "The LORD rebuke you,[u] Satan!
The LORD, who has chosen[v] Jerusalem, rebuke you! Is not this man a burning stick snatched from the
fire?"[w]
3Now Joshua was dressed in filthy clothes as he stood before the angel. 4The angel said to those who
were standing before him, "Take off his filthy clothes."
Then he said to Joshua, "See, I have taken away your sin,[x] and I will put rich garments[y] on you."
5Then I said, "Put a clean turban[z] on his head." So they put a clean turban on his head and clothed him,
while the angel of the LORD stood by.
6The angel of the LORD gave this charge to Joshua: 7"This is what the LORD Almighty says: 'If you will
walk in my ways and keep my requirements, then you will govern my house[a] and have charge of my
courts, and I will give you a place among these standing here.
8" 'Listen, O high priest Joshua and your associates seated before you, who are men symbolic[b] of
things to come: I am going to bring my servant, the Branch.[c] 9See, the stone I have set in front of Josh-
ua! There are seven eyes[d] on that one stone,[d] and I will engrave an inscription on it,' says the LORD Al-
mighty, 'and I will remove the sin[e] of this land in a single day.
10" 'In that day each of you will invite his neighbor to sit under his vine and fig tree,[f]' declares the
LORD Almighty."

3:1 [s]Hag 1:1; Zec 6:11 [t]Ps 109:6
3:2 [u]Jude 1:9 [v]Isa 14:1 [w]Am 4:11; Jude 1:23
3:4 [x]Eze 36:25; Mic 7:18 [y]Isa 52:1; Rev 19:8
3:5 [z]Ex 29:6
3:7 [a]Dt 17:8-11; Eze 44:15-16
3:8 [b]Eze 12:11 [c]Isa 4:2
3:9 [d]Isa 28:16 [e]Jer 50:20
3:10 [f]1Ki 4:25; Mic 4:4

[a] 8,9 Or *says after . . . eye: 9"I . . . plunder them."* [b] 1 A variant of *Jeshua*; here and elsewhere in Zechariah [c] 1 *Satan* means *accuser.* [d] 9 Or *facets*

2:1–13 The man with the measuring line taught the Israelites that Jerusalem would expand until it outgrew its walls and that God would be its only sure defense.
2:6 The "land of the north" was Babylonia, which in fact lay to the east. But since a desert separated Assyria and Babylonia from Israel/Judah, invading armies regularly attacked from the north.
2:8 For "the apple of his eye," see "Early Scribal Emendation" on page 448.
2:11 For "that day," see the note on Joel 1:15.
2:12 The land was rendered holy chiefly because it was the site of the earthly throne and sanctuary of the holy King (see "Zaphon, Olympus, Sinai and Zion: The Mountain of God" on p. 843).
3:1–10 In this fourth vision Joshua, the high priest, clad in filthy garments that represented his own sins and those of the people, was cleansed and given charge of the temple. He is depicted here as a type or representation of the future Messiah-Branch who would take away all iniquity.
3:1 The names Joshua and Jeshua were common in ancient times. The Greek equivalent is spelled "Jesus" in English.
3:4–5 Taking off his filthy clothing deprived Joshua of his priestly office but was also symbolic of the removal of sin. Putting a clean turban on his head reinstated him to his high-priestly function, so that Israel once again had a divinely authorized priestly mediator.
3:8 The word "branch" represents eighteen different Hebrew and four different Greek words in the Bible and is most notably used as a title applied to the Messiah as the offspring of David (here; see also Jer 23:5; 33:15).
3:10 For "that day," see the note on Joel 1:15 and for "sit under his vine and fig tree" the note on Micah 4:4.

ZECHARIAH'S AUTHORSHIP

ZECHARIAH 4 Before the sixteenth century A.D. the authorship of Zechariah was uncontested. The book was believed to have been written in its entirety by the prophet Zechariah, the son of Berekiah, the son of Iddo (1:1). Zechariah began his ministry in 520 B.C., a mere two months after Haggai commenced his own.

During the seventeenth century A.D., on the basis of Matthew 27:9 (which quotes Zec 11:12–13 but ascribes it to the prophet Jeremiah), the suggestion was made that the latter half of Zechariah (chs. 9–14) was actually written by Jeremiah. Since then the unity of Zechariah has been questioned by many critical scholars. Some hold that the entire work was written before the time of Zechariah, while others are convinced that it was written long after his day. The various arguments include:

Kidron Valley: the traditional (not actual) tomb of Zechariah

Photograph: © Todd Bolen/Bible Places.com

◆ The first eight chapters allude to the historical situation during the restoration of the temple and include the dates when the visions occurred, while the last six chapters contain no such allusions or dates.

◆ There are marked differences in style and vocabulary between chapters 1–8 and 9–14.

◆ The reference to Greece in 9:13 suggests to some scholars a composition date in the late fourth century B.C., after Greece under Alexander the Great had conquered the Near East. Since **Persia**, not Greece, was the prevailing power in Zechariah's day, many believe this particular verse to have been written after the fall of the Persian Empire.[1]

There is little disagreement that chapters 9–14 are different from 1–8 or that the two sections were written at different times. This does not necessarily preclude, however, the assumption that Zechariah did in fact write the entire book.

◆ The fact that Zechariah 1–8 dates its prophecies, while chapters 9–14 do not, can be accounted for without postulating a second author:

The first section relates to the crucial events of 520 to 518 B.C., focusing on specific individuals and time frames. This specificity in purpose requires a more concrete historical setting.

The second section is for the most part eschatological (focused on the end times) and oriented toward the distant future.

The first section was most likely written well before the second. Zechariah was a young man in 520 B.C. (2:4) but may have written chapters 9–14 decades later.

◆ The prophet need not have maintained one writing style throughout his ministry. The apocalyptic-type visions of chapters 1–8 are reminiscent of what we see in Ezekiel (completed c. 575 B.C.) and Daniel (completed c. 530 B.C.). Zechariah 9–14, on the other hand, returns to a more classical style of prophecy.

◆ With regard to 9:13, the Hebrew Scriptures already refer to Greece ("Javan") before Zechariah's time (Isa 66:19; Eze 27:13); Greece was a significant power already in the sixth century B.C.[2] By 520 B.C. the Greeks were a considerable irritation to the Persian Empire, and within a few decades the Persians would assemble one of the greatest armies of ancient history to deal with them—and suffer a catastrophic defeat. Indeed, the Persians may already have experienced a major setback in Greece by the time of the writing of Zechariah 9–14, and yet those chapters could still be the work of Zechariah himself (the battle of Marathon was fought in 492 B.C.).

Several solutions have been offered for Matthew's reference to Jeremiah. Some have argued that since the **Talmud** places Jeremiah at the head of the collection of prophetic books, any prophetic quote might be considered as belonging to the literary collection of Jeremiah. Others suggest that Matthew originally ascribed the passage to Zechariah but that the name Jeremiah crept in through scribal error. Matthew may have been *quoting* Zechariah but *referring* the reader to the prophecy found in Jeremiah 19:1–13 and 32:6–8, which had been repeated and expanded in Zechariah's work.

In addition to the arguments presented above, the work shows internal signs of unity. The first and second sections are both concerned with the divine protection of Jerusalem, judgment against Israel's enemies, the Messiah (Zec. 3:8; 9:9) and the outpouring of the Spirit (4:6; 12:10).

[1]See "Ancient Persian History Through Darius" on page 717 and "Ancient Persian History From Xerxes Forward" on page 718. [2]See "The Greeks and the Old Testament" on page 1441 and "Greece: From Independent City-states Through Alexander the Great" on page 1814.

The Gold Lampstand and the Two Olive Trees

4 Then the angel who talked with me returned and wakened[g] me, as a man is wakened from his sleep.[h]
2He asked me, "What do you see?"[i]
I answered, "I see a solid gold lampstand[j] with a bowl at the top and seven lights[k] on it, with seven
channels to the lights. 3Also there are two olive trees[l] by it, one on the right of the bowl and the other on
its left."
4I asked the angel who talked with me, "What are these, my lord?"
5He answered, "Do you not know what these are?"
"No, my lord," I replied.[m]
6So he said to me, "This is the word of the LORD to Zerubbabel:[n] 'Not by might nor by power, but by
my Spirit,'[o] says the LORD Almighty.
7"What[a] are you, O mighty mountain? Before Zerubbabel you will become level ground.[p] Then he will
bring out the capstone[q] to shouts of 'God bless it! God bless it!' "
8Then the word of the LORD came to me: 9"The hands of Zerubbabel have laid the foundation[r] of this
temple; his hands will also complete it.[s] Then you will know that the LORD Almighty has sent me[t] to you.
10"Who despises the day of small things?[u] Men will rejoice when they see the plumb line in the hand
of Zerubbabel.
"(These seven are the eyes[v] of the LORD, which range throughout the earth.)"
11Then I asked the angel, "What are these two olive trees[w] on the right and the left of the lampstand?"
12Again I asked him, "What are these two olive branches beside the two gold pipes that pour out gold-
en oil?"
13He replied, "Do you not know what these are?"
"No, my lord," I said.
14So he said, "These are the two who are anointed[x] to[b] serve the Lord of all the earth."

The Flying Scroll

5 I looked again—and there before me was a flying scroll![y]
2He asked me, "What do you see?"
I answered, "I see a flying scroll, thirty feet long and fifteen feet wide.[c]"
3And he said to me, "This is the curse[z] that is going out over the whole land; for according to what it
says on one side, every thief[a] will be banished, and according to what it says on the other, everyone who
swears falsely[b] will be banished. 4The LORD Almighty declares, 'I will send it out, and it will enter the
house of the thief and the house of him who swears falsely by my name. It will remain in his house and
destroy it, both its timbers and its stones.[c]' "

The Woman in a Basket

5Then the angel who was speaking to me came forward and said to me, "Look up and see what this
is that is appearing."
6I asked, "What is it?"
He replied, "It is a measuring basket.[d]" And he added, "This is the iniquity[e] of the people throughout
the land."

4:1 [g]Da 8:18 [h]Jer 31:26
4:2 [i]Jer 1:13 [j]Ex 25:31; Rev 1:12 [k]Rev 4:5
4:3 [l]ver 11; Rev 11:4
4:5 [m]Zec 1:9
4:6 [n]Ezr 5:2 [o]Isa 11:2-4; Hos 1:7
4:7 [p]Jer 51:25 [q]Ps 118:22
4:9 [r]Ezr 3:11 [s]Ezr 3:8; 6:15; Zec 6:12 [t]Zec 2:9
4:10 [u]Hag 2:3 [v]Zec 3:9; Rev 5:6
4:11 [w]ver 3; Rev 11:4
4:14 [x]Ex 29:7; 40:15; Da 9:24-26; Zec 3:1-7
5:1 [y]Eze 2:9; Rev 5:1
5:3 [z]Isa 24:6; 43:28; Mal 3:9; 4:6 [a]Ex 20:15; Mal 3:8 [b]Isa 48:1
5:4 [c]Lev 14:34-45; Hab 2:9-11; Mal 3:5

[a] 7 Or *Who* [b] 14 Or *two who bring oil and* [c] 2 Hebrew *twenty cubits long and ten cubits wide* (about 9 meters long and 4.5 meters wide) [d] 6 Hebrew *an ephah*; also in verses 7-11 [e] 6 Or *appearance*

4:1–14 The fifth of Zechariah's night visions—of a seven-branched lampstand fed by two olive trees—assured the returnees that the people of God would receive his grace through their spiritual and temporal leaders, through whose efforts the prosperity of the nation would be accomplished.

4:1–3 The bowl providing fuel for the lampstand signified an abundant supply of oil, thus symbolizing the fullness of God's power through his Spirit. On either side of the bowl stood an olive tree, together representing two men chosen by God to serve him—Joshua the priest (3:1–10) and Zerubbabel, the governor of Judah (Hag 1:1). Zerubbabel, the heir to David's throne (Hag 2:20–23; Mt 1:13), is not referred to as a king. The roles of priest and prince (king) melded together here, and the New Testament depicts Jesus as the fulfillment of this priest-king ideal.

4:8 This verse introduces a prophetic oracle (see "Oracles of the Ancient World" on p. 1507).

5:1–4 The vision of the flying scroll taught the people that the land would be purified from wickedness when the temple was build and God's law taught.

5:3 Although theft and perjury may have been the most common forms of lawbreaking at the time, they are probably intended here as representative sins. The people of Judah were guilty of infractions against the whole law.

5:5–11 A woman (typifying the flagrant sins of Israel) was carried off in this vision in a basket to the land of Babylon—a lesson to the returnees that God not only forgives the sins of his people but carries those sins away from their land.

[7]Then the cover of lead was raised, and there in the basket sat a woman! [8]He said, "This is wickedness,"
5:8 [d]Mic 6:11 and he pushed her back into the basket and pushed the lead cover down over its mouth.[d]
[9]Then I looked up—and there before me were two women, with the wind in their wings! They had
5:9 [e]Lev 11:19 wings like those of a stork,[e] and they lifted up the basket between heaven and earth.
[10]"Where are they taking the basket?" I asked the angel who was speaking to me.
5:11 [f]Ge 10:10 [11]He replied, "To the country of Babylonia[a][f] to build a house[g] for it. When it is ready, the basket will
[g]Jer 29:5,28 [h]Da 1:2 be set there in its place."[h]

Four Chariots

6:1 [i]ver 5 **6** I looked up again—and there before me were four chariots[i] coming out from between two moun-
6:2 [j]Rev 6:5 6:3 [k]Rev 6:2 tains—mountains of bronze! [2]The first chariot had red horses, the second black,[j] [3]the third white,[k]
and the fourth dappled—all of them powerful. [4]I asked the angel who was speaking to me, "What are
these, my lord?"
6:5 [l]Eze 37:9; Mt 24:31; Rev 7:1 [5]The angel answered me, "These are the four spirits[b][l] of heaven, going out from standing in the pres-
ence of the Lord of the whole world. [6]The one with the black horses is going toward the north country,
the one with the white horses toward the west,[c] and the one with the dappled horses toward the south."
6:7 [m]Zec 1:10 [7]When the powerful horses went out, they were straining to go throughout the earth.[m] And he said,
"Go throughout the earth!" So they went throughout the earth.
6:8 [n]Eze 5:13; 24:13 [8]Then he called to me, "Look, those going toward the north country have given my Spirit[d] rest[n] in the
land of the north."

A Crown for Joshua

[9]The word of the LORD came to me: [10]"Take ⌞silver and gold⌟ from the exiles Heldai, Tobijah and
6:10 [o]Ezr 7:14-16; Jer 28:6 Jedaiah, who have arrived from Babylon.[o] Go the same day to the house of Josiah son of Zephaniah.
6:11 [p]Ps 21:3 [q]Zec 3:1 [r]Ezr 3:2 [11]Take the silver and gold and make a crown,[p] and set it on the head of the high priest, Joshua[q] son
of Jehozadak.[r] [12]Tell him this is what the LORD Almighty says: 'Here is the man whose name is the
6:12 [s]Isa 4:2; Zec 3:8 [t]Ezr 3:8-10; Zec 4:6-9 Branch,[s] and he will branch out from his place and build the temple of the LORD.[t] [13]It is he who will
build the temple of the LORD, and he will be clothed with majesty and will sit and rule on his throne.
6:13 [u]Ps 110:4 And he will be a priest[u] on his throne. And there will be harmony between the two.' [14]The crown will
be given to Heldai,[e] Tobijah, Jedaiah and Hen[f] son of Zephaniah as a memorial in the temple of the
6:15 [v]Isa 60:10 [w]Zec 2:9-11 [x]Isa 58:12; Jer 7:23; Zec 3:7 LORD. [15]Those who are far away will come and help to build the temple of the LORD,[v] and you will
know that the LORD Almighty has sent me to you.[w] This will happen if you diligently obey[x] the LORD
your God."

Justice and Mercy, Not Fasting

7 In the fourth year of King Darius, the word of the LORD came to Zechariah on the fourth day of the
7:1 [y]Ne 1:1 ninth month, the month of Kislev.[y] [2]The people of Bethel had sent Sharezer and Regem-Melech, to-
7:2 [z]Jer 26:19; Zec 8:21 gether with their men, to entreat[z] the LORD [3]by asking the priests of the house of the LORD Almighty and
7:3 [a]Zec 12:12-14 [b]Jer 52:12-14; Zec 8:19 the prophets, "Should I mourn[a] and fast in the fifth[b] month, as I have done for so many years?"

[a] 11 Hebrew *Shinar* [b] 5 Or *winds* [c] 6 Or *horses after them* [d] 8 Or *spirit* [e] 14 Syriac; Hebrew *Helem* [f] 14 Or *and the gracious one, the*

5:8 "Wickedness" is a general word denoting moral, religious and civil evil—frequently used as an antonym of "righteousness" (e.g., Pr 13:6; Eze 33:12).
5:9 The two women were agents of God (see "Angels and Guardian Spirits in the Bible and the Ancient Near East" on p. 1529).
6:1–8 In this final of Zechariah's night visions, four war chariots went forth to protect God's people, confirming God's protective providence.
6:1 The "two mountains" may have been Mount Zion and the Mount of Olives, with the Kidron Valley between them. (See "Zaphon, Olympus, Sinai and Zion: The Mountain of God" on p. 843 and "The Mount of Olives" on p. 1543.)
6:11 The Hebrew word here translated "crown" is not the same as that used for the high priest's turban but refers instead to an ornate crown (cf. Rev 19:12).
6:12–13 Zerubbabel and Joshua represent, respectively, the two separate offices of king and priest (see the note on 4:1–3). The "Branch" (6:12) would hold both offices (v. 13). According to the Aramaic Targum (a paraphrase), the Jerusalem Talmud (a collection of religious instructions) and the Midrash (practical exposition), Jews early on regarded this verse as Messianic.
7:1–7 After the return from captivity, four annual fasts were held in memory of the national calamities through which the nation had passed. They are mentioned only in this passage and in 8:19. These fasts, established during the captivity, were held during the fourth, fifth, seventh and tenth months. The Mishnah (*Taarith*, iv, 6) and Jerome (*Zachariam*, viii) provide information on the historical events that these fasts were intended to commemorate (see the notes on 7:5; 8:19). By the time of Christ these fasts had fallen into disuse and were not revived until after the destruction of Jerusalem by the Romans in A.D. 70.
7:1 The date was December 7, 518 B.C., not quite two years after Zechariah's eight visions (see the note on 1:7).

4 Then the word of the LORD Almighty came to me: 5 "Ask all the people of the land and the priests, 'When you fasted[c] and mourned in the fifth and seventh months for the past seventy years, was it really for me that you fasted? 6 And when you were eating and drinking, were you not just feasting for yourselves? 7 Are these not the words the LORD proclaimed through the earlier prophets[d] when Jerusalem and its surrounding towns were at rest[e] and prosperous, and the Negev and the western foothills[f] were settled?' "

8 And the word of the LORD came again to Zechariah: 9 "This is what the LORD Almighty says: 'Administer true justice;[g] show mercy and compassion to one another. 10 Do not oppress the widow or the fatherless, the alien[h] or the poor. In your hearts do not think evil of each other.'[i]

11 "But they refused to pay attention; stubbornly they turned their backs and stopped up their ears.[j] 12 They made their hearts as hard as flint[k] and would not listen to the law or to the words that the LORD Almighty had sent by his Spirit through the earlier prophets.[l] So the LORD Almighty was very angry.[m]

13 " 'When I called, they did not listen;[n] so when they called, I would not listen,'[o] says the LORD Almighty.[p] 14 'I scattered[q] them with a whirlwind[r] among all the nations, where they were strangers. The land was left so desolate behind them that no one could come or go. This is how they made the pleasant land desolate.[s]' "

The LORD Promises to Bless Jerusalem

8 Again the word of the LORD Almighty came to me. 2 This is what the LORD Almighty says: "I am very jealous for Zion; I am burning with jealousy for her."

3 This is what the LORD says: "I will return[t] to Zion and dwell in Jerusalem.[u] Then Jerusalem will be called the City of Truth, and the mountain of the LORD Almighty will be called the Holy Mountain."

4 This is what the LORD Almighty says: "Once again men and women of ripe old age will sit in the streets of Jerusalem,[v] each with cane in hand because of his age. 5 The city streets will be filled with boys and girls playing there.[w]"

6 This is what the LORD Almighty says: "It may seem marvelous to the remnant of this people at that time,[x] but will it seem marvelous to me?[y]" declares the LORD Almighty.

7 This is what the LORD Almighty says: "I will save my people from the countries of the east and the west.[z] 8 I will bring them back[a] to live in Jerusalem; they will be my people,[b] and I will be faithful and righteous to them as their God."

9 This is what the LORD Almighty says: "You who now hear these words spoken by the prophets[c] who were there when the foundation was laid for the house of the LORD Almighty, let your hands be strong[d] so that the temple may be built. 10 Before that time there were no wages[e] for man or beast. No one could go about his business safely because of his enemy, for I had turned every man against his neighbor. 11 But now I will not deal with the remnant of this people as I did in the past,"[f] declares the LORD Almighty.

12 "The seed will grow well, the vine will yield its fruit,[g] the ground will produce its crops,[h] and the heavens will drop their dew.[i] I will give all these things as an inheritance[j] to the remnant of this people. 13 As you have been an object of cursing[k] among the nations, O Judah and Israel, so will I save you, and you will be a blessing.[l] Do not be afraid, but let your hands be strong."

14 This is what the LORD Almighty says: "Just as I had determined to bring disaster[m] upon you and showed no pity when your fathers angered me," says the LORD Almighty, 15 "so now I have determined to do good[n] again to Jerusalem and Judah. Do not be afraid. 16 These are the things you are to do: Speak the

7:5 [c]Isa 58:5
7:7 [d]Zec 1:4 [e]Jer 22:21 [f]Jer 17:26
7:9 [g]Zec 8:16
7:10 [h]Ex 22:21 [i]Ex 22:22; Isa 1:17
7:11 [j]Jer 8:5; 11:10; 17:23
7:12 [k]Jer 17:1; Eze 11:19 [l]Ne 9:29 [m]Da 9:12
7:13 [n]Pr 1:24 [o]Isa 1:15; Jer 11:11; 14:12; Mic 3:4 [p]Pr 1:28
7:14 [q]Dt 4:27; 28:64-67 [r]Jer 23:19 [s]Jer 44:6
8:3 [t]Zec 1:16 [u]Zec 2:10
8:4 [v]Isa 65:20
8:5 [w]Jer 30:20; 31:13
8:6 [x]Ps 118:23; 126:1-3 [y]Jer 32:17,27
8:7 [z]Ps 107:3; Isa 11:11; 43:5
8:8 [a]Zec 10:10 [b]Eze 11:19-20; 36:28; Zec 2:11
8:9 [c]Ezr 5:1 [d]Hag 2:4
8:10 [e]Hag 1:6
8:11 [f]Isa 12:1
8:12 [g]Joel 2:22 [h]Ps 67:6 [i]Ge 27:28 [j]Ob 1:17
8:13 [k]Jer 42:18 [l]Ge 12:2
8:14 [m]Jer 31:28; Eze 24:14
8:15 [n]ver 13; Jer 29:11; Mic 7:18-20

7:5 The fast of the fifth month commemorated the burning of the temple and the other important buildings (2Ki 25:8–10), while that of the seventh month marked the anniversary of Gedaliah's assassination (2Ki 25:22–25; Jer 39:14; 40:5–16; 41:1–18; 43:6; see detail in the paragraph to follow). Since these fasts commemorated events related to the destruction of Jerusalem and the temple, the 70 years here are to be reckoned from 586 B.C. (see "The 70 Years of Captivity" on p. 1234). Strictly speaking, 68 years had transpired; 70 is a round number.

Gedaliah—a son of Shaphan, King Josiah's secretary and the governor of Mizpah—had shared Jeremiah's views and protected him from the anti-Chaldeans. Nebuchadnezzar had made Gedaliah governor, but he had ruled for only two months before his treacherous murder. See "Gedaliah, Governor of Judah, and Baalis, King of Ammon" on page 1261.

7:7 For "earlier prophets," see the note on 1:4.

For "the Negev," see "The Negev: Its Climate and Features" on page 34.

7:10 In the ancient Near East the ideal king was expected to protect the oppressed and needy members of society. For commentary on the Biblical concern for such people, see "The Care of Widows and Orphans in the Bible and the Ancient Near East" on page 285.

8:1 See the note on 4:8.

8:3 For "the Holy Mountain," see "Zaphon, Olympus, Sinai and Zion: The Mountain of God" on page 843.

8:9 The "prophets" include Haggai (1:1) and Zechariah (1:1; see also Ezr 5:1–2).

8:16 "Courts" is literally "gates" (see the note on Pr 24:7; see also "The City Gate" on p. 392).

8:16 [o]Ps 15:2; Eph 4:25 [p]Zec 7:9 **8:17** [q]Pr 3:29 [r]Pr 6:16-19 **8:19** [s]Jer 39:2 [t]Jer 52:12 [u]2Ki 25:25 [v]Jer 52:4 [w]Ps 30:11 [x]ver 16 **8:21** [y]Zec 7:2 **8:22** [z]Ps 117:1; Isa 60:3; Zec 2:11 **8:23** [a]Isa 45:14; 1Co 14:25

truth[o] to each other, and render true and sound judgment in your courts;[p] 17 do not plot evil[q] against
your neighbor, and do not love to swear falsely.[r] I hate all this," declares the LORD.
18 Again the word of the LORD Almighty came to me. 19 This is what the LORD Almighty says: "The fasts
of the fourth,[s] fifth,[t] seventh[u] and tenth[v] months will become joyful[w] and glad occasions and happy fes-
tivals for Judah. Therefore love truth[x] and peace."
20 This is what the LORD Almighty says: "Many peoples and the inhabitants of many cities will yet
come, 21 and the inhabitants of one city will go to another and say, 'Let us go at once to entreat[y] the LORD
and seek the LORD Almighty. I myself am going.' 22 And many peoples and powerful nations will come to
Jerusalem to seek the LORD Almighty and to entreat him."[z]
23 This is what the LORD Almighty says: "In those days ten men from all languages and nations will
take firm hold of one Jew by the hem of his robe and say, 'Let us go with you, because we have heard that
God is with you.' "[a]

Judgment on Israel's Enemies

An Oracle

9:1 [b]Isa 17:1 **9:2** [c]Jer 49:23 [d]Eze 28:1-19 **9:3** [e]Job 27:16; Eze 28:4 **9:4** [f]Isa 23:1; Eze 26:3-5; 28:18

9 The word of the LORD is against the land of Hadrach
and will rest upon Damascus[b]—
for the eyes of men and all the tribes of Israel
are on the LORD— [a]
2 and upon Hamath[c] too, which borders on it,
and upon Tyre[d] and Sidon, though they are very skillful.
3 Tyre has built herself a stronghold;
she has heaped up silver like dust,
and gold like the dirt of the streets.[e]
4 But the Lord will take away her possessions
and destroy her power on the sea,
and she will be consumed by fire.[f]
5 Ashkelon will see it and fear;
Gaza will writhe in agony,
and Ekron too, for her hope will wither.
Gaza will lose her king
and Ashkelon will be deserted.

[a] 1 Or *Damascus. / For the eye of the LORD is on all mankind, / as well as on the tribes of Israel,*

8:17 To "swear falsely" was to commit perjury (see the note on 5:3).

8:18 See the note on 4:8.

8:19 The fast of the fourth month lamented the breaching of the walls of Jerusalem by Nebuchadnezzar (2Ki 25:3–4; Jer 39:2), while that of the tenth month mourned the beginning of Nebuchadnezzar's siege of Jerusalem (2Ki 25:1; Jer 39:1; Eze 24:1–2). For the fasts of the fifth and seventh months, see the note on Zechariah 7:5.

8:23 In Hebrew, the number ten is used to indicate a large or complete number.

For "Jew," see the note on Jeremiah 34:9.

9:1–8 As history shows, the agent of God's judgment was Alexander the Great (333–332 B.C.).

9:1–2 Hadrach is Hatarikka, north of Hamath (see the note on Isa 10:9) on the Orontes River. Damascus was the capital city of Aram (see "Damascus" on p. 1087), and Tyre and Sidon were Phoenician (modern Lebanese) coastal cities (see "The Downfall of Tyre" on p. 1345 and "Sidon" on p. 1536).

9:3–4 Tyre was a center of trade and commerce, and her wealth—much of which was gained through exploitation of commercial sea lanes in the Mediterranean—was proverbial. Tyre consisted of both a mainland city and an island city one half mile (.8 km) offshore, both well fortified. Tyre fell to Alexander the Great in July of 332 B.C., following a seven-month siege (see "The Downfall of Tyre" on p. 1345).

9:5 Ashkelon, Gaza and Ekron were three of the five major Philistine cities (see "The Archaeology of Philistia" on p. 370). As the northernmost city of Philistia, Ekron would be the first to suffer. Her hope that Tyre would stem the tide would meet with disappointment. Detail regarding the subsequent history of each of these cities follows:

Zechariah prophesied that Ashkelon would see the destruction of Tyre and that the city itself would be destroyed. Apparently, however, it was rebuilt, for Herod the Great (see "Herod the Great" on p. 1627) was born there, and Roman ruins have been excavated. During the Crusades it came to life again, and Richard Coeur de Lion held court there. Later still, the town reverted to the Saracens. Archaeological remains are sparse: a ruined and overgrown Byzantine church; a quadrangle with some preserved columns and foundation walls of an odium (tiered council chamber), attributed by the excavators to Herod the Great; some statues belonging to the facade of the odium; and a third-century A.D. painted tomb. The oldest evidence of occupation there, from the area near the beach, dates to approximately 2000 B.C.

The predictions that Gaza would be forsaken (Zep 2:5) and that its king would perish (Zec 9:4; i.e., its Persian satrap, or petty king subordinate to the great king of Persia) were fulfilled by Alexander the Great, who took the city in 332 B.C., after it had resisted his siege for two months. He bound Betis the satrap to a chariot and dragged him around the city, and he killed 10,000 of its inhabitants and sold the rest as slaves. The town was desolated again by fire and sword by the Maccabees in 96 B.C. In turn, Gaza passed under the control of Syria and Rome.

Philip would centuries later meet the Ethiopian eunuch on "the road—the desert road—that goes down from Jerusalem to Gaza" (Ac 8:26). Once Gaza was the seat of a Christian church and bishop in the midst of Greek culture and temples, but most of its inhabitants turned to Islam in A.D. 634. Today of its 20,000 residents only a few

6 Foreigners will occupy Ashdod,
and I will cut off the pride of the Philistines.
7 I will take the blood from their mouths,
the forbidden food from between their teeth.
Those who are left will belong to our God
and become leaders in Judah,
and Ekron will be like the Jebusites.

---

hundred are Christians. Modern Ghuzzeh, the metropolis of the Gaza Strip, is crowded with Arab refugees today. North of Ghuzzeh lies an extensive olive grove whose fruit is used to make soap. The city's trade in grain is considerable, the grain still being ground by millstones such as Samson was forced to work at in his prison house at Gaza (Jdg 16:21). The tel el Muntar, or "hill of the watchman" ("watchtower" is mentioned in 2Ki 18:8), southeast of Gaza, is the hill up which Samson carried the gates of the city (Jdg 16:3).

In Assyrian inscriptions Ekron appears as *Amquarruna.* Sennacherib assaulted the city and killed its officials because of their disloyalty to Assyria. Esarhaddon called on 22 cities that paid tribute to him (Ekron being one) to help transport building supplies for his palace. Ashurbanipal included Ekron in his listing of cities that paid him tribute. The Greek form of Ekron, *Accaron,* appears in 1 Maccabees 10:89 (an Apocryphal book) and in accounts of the Crusades. Its modern site is 'Agir or Catrah, both on the Wadi Surar.

9:6 "Foreigners" is a reference to people of mixed nationality; they characterized Israel during the postexilic period (Ne 13:23–24).

Ashdod was the fourth remaining city in the Philistine group (see the note on Zep 9:5). At one time the Philistines' control of Canaan (see "Canaan" on p. 324 and "The Archaeology of Philistia" on p. 370) was so extensive that the land was eventually named after them ("Palestine").

In the Septuagint and in the New Testament Ashdod is Azotus. Philip the evangelist found himself there after the Holy Spirit had taken him away from the Ethiopian eunuch (Ac 8:40).

9:7 The Philistines offered idolatrous sacrifices and ate food that was forbidden because it was ceremonially unclean (see Lev 11; see also "Clean and Unclean Foods in the Bible and the Ancient Near East" on p. 168).

The Jebusites were ancient inhabitants of Jerusalem (see "Lesser Known Peoples of the Old Testament" on p. 265 and "The Jebusites" on p. 596).

ARCHAEOLOGICAL SITES

SIDON

ZECHARIAH 9 Sidon is located at a natural harbor on the coast of Lebanon, in ancient **Phoenicia,**[1] between Tyre and Beirut ("Map 7"). It was, in fact, one of the oldest and most important cities in the region. Sidon's prominence is reflected in the fact that it is mentioned in **Hittite**, **Ugaritic**, Egyptian and **Assyrian** records. The Sidonians were engaged throughout their long history in fishing, seafaring, commerce and the manufacture of purple dye. An enormous mound of murex shells, from which this striking dye was extracted, still exists in modern Sidon. Its inhabitants were also known for their fine craftsmanship; they produced beautiful works in materials such as ivory and silver.[2] References to "Greater Sidon" in Joshua 11:8 and 19:28 reflect a precise knowledge of the name of the town. The **Assyrian** record of Sennacherib's campaign in 701 B.C. states that he captured both "Greater Sidon" and "Little Sidon."

When Joshua divided the promised land, Sidon was allotted to the tribe of Asher, but this tribe was unable to drive out the Sidonians (Jdg 1:31; 3:1–3). Later, during the **divided monarchy** period, Ahab married Jezebel, daughter of Ethbaal, king of Sidon, in a union that resulted in the introduction of pagan worship into the northern kingdom (1Ki 16:31–33). The prophets Jeremiah (Jer 25:22; 27:3–6; 47:4), Ezekiel (Eze 28:20–24), Joel (Joel 3:4–8) and Zechariah (Zec 9:1–2) all pronounced judgment against Sidon. She was among the cities God had given to **Nebuchadnezzar**[3] of **Babylon** (Jer 27:6), and a text excavated at Babylon lists the king of Sidon among Nebuchadnezzar's captives. Sidon was also a center for the **Persian** fleet during the reign of Xerxes.

Excavations at ancient Sidon have been limited by recent military hostilities, as well as by urban development. Recently there have been indications of the possibility of excavating remains of ancient Sidon under the sea (Greek historians indicate that in 146 B.C. the city was struck by an earthquake, which caused a large portion of it to sink beneath the ocean).

[1]See "Phoenicia" on page 488. [2]See "Ancient Craftsmanship" on page 141. [3]See "Nebuchadnezzar" on page 571.

[8]But I will defend my house
against marauding forces.
Never again will an oppressor overrun my people,
for now I am keeping watch.[g]

9:8 [g]Isa 52:1; 54:14

The Coming of Zion's King

[9]Rejoice greatly, O Daughter of Zion!
Shout, Daughter of Jerusalem!
See, your king[a] comes to you,
righteous and having salvation,[h]
gentle and riding on a donkey,
on a colt, the foal of a donkey.[i]
[10]I will take away the chariots from Ephraim
and the war-horses from Jerusalem,
and the battle bow will be broken.[j]
He will proclaim peace to the nations.
His rule will extend from sea to sea
and from the River[b] to the ends of the earth.[c][k]
[11]As for you, because of the blood of my covenant[l] with you,
I will free your prisoners[m] from the waterless pit.
[12]Return to your fortress,[n] O prisoners of hope;
even now I announce that I will restore twice as much to you.
[13]I will bend Judah as I bend my bow
and fill it with Ephraim.[o]
I will rouse your sons, O Zion,
against your sons, O Greece,[p]
and make you like a warrior's sword.[q]

9:9 [h]Isa 9:6-7; 43:3-11; Jer 23:5-6; Zep 3:14-15; Zec 2:10 [i]Mt 21:5*; Jn 12:15*
9:10 [j]Hos 1:7; 2:18; Mic 4:3; 5:10; Zec 10:4 [k]Ps 72:8
9:11 [l]Ex 24:8 [m]Isa 42:7
9:12 [n]Joel 3:16
9:13 [o]Isa 49:2 [p]Joel 3:6 [q]Jer 51:20

The LORD Will Appear

[14]Then the LORD will appear over them;[r]
his arrow will flash like lightning.[s]
The Sovereign LORD will sound the trumpet;
he will march in the storms[t] of the south,
15 and the LORD Almighty will shield[u] them.
They will destroy
and overcome with slingstones.
They will drink and roar as with wine;
they will be full like a bowl
used for sprinkling[d] the corners[v] of the altar.
[16]The LORD their God will save them on that day
as the flock of his people.
They will sparkle in his land
like jewels in a crown.[w]

9:14 [r]Isa 31:5 [s]Ps 18:14; Hab 3:11 [t]Isa 21:1; 66:15
9:15 [u]Isa 37:35; Zec 12:8 [v]Ex 27:2
9:16 [w]Isa 62:3; Jer 31:11

[a] 9 Or *King* [b] 10 That is, the Euphrates [c] 10 Or *the end of the land* [d] 15 Or *bowl, / like*

9:8 After his conquest of the region Alexander the Great spared the temple and the city of Jerusalem.
9:9 A donkey was a lowly animal of peace (contrast the war-horse of v. 10), as well as a princely mount. The royal mount used by David and his sons was the mule (see 2Sa 13:29). This verse, quoted in the New Testament as Messianic, refers ultimately to the triumphal entry of Jesus into Jerusalem as King (Mt 21:5; Jn 12:15).
9:10 For "chariots" and "war-horses," see "Horses and Chariots in Ancient Warfare" on page 114.
9:11 "Waterless pit" refers to an empty cistern, sometimes used as a detention cell (see "Wells, Cisterns and Aqueducts in the Ancient World" on p. 1259).
9:13 The initial fulfillment of this verse is evidently found in the conflict in the second century B.C. between the Maccabees ("Zion") and the Seleucids of Syria ("Greece" after the breakup of Alexander's empire). But the complete fulfillment looks beyond that to the future, when God's people will gain the victory over their enemies. (See "The Seleucids" on p. 1408 and "The Intertestamental Period" on p. 1551.)
9:15–16 Although the book of 1 Maccabees (an Apocryphal work never accepted into the standard Protestant canon) likely records an initial fulfillment of verse 15, the phrase "on that day" (v. 16; see the note on Joel 1:15) gives the passage an eschatological, or end times, tone.

[17] How attractive and beautiful they will be!
Grain will make the young men thrive,
and new wine the young women.

The LORD Will Care for Judah

10 Ask the LORD for rain in the springtime;
it is the LORD who makes the storm clouds.
He gives showers of rain to men,
and plants of the field to everyone.
[2] The idols[x] speak deceit,
diviners see visions that lie;
they tell dreams that are false,
they give comfort in vain.
Therefore the people wander like sheep
oppressed for lack of a shepherd.[y]

[3] "My anger burns against the shepherds,
and I will punish the leaders;[z]
for the LORD Almighty will care
for his flock, the house of Judah,
and make them like a proud horse in battle.
[4] From Judah will come the cornerstone,
from him the tent peg,[a]
from him the battle bow,[b]
from him every ruler.
[5] Together they[a] will be like mighty men
trampling the muddy streets in battle.[c]
Because the LORD is with them,
they will fight and overthrow the horsemen.[d]

[6] "I will strengthen the house of Judah
and save the house of Joseph.
I will restore them
because I have compassion on them.[e]
They will be as though
I had not rejected them,
for I am the LORD their God
and I will answer[f] them.
[7] The Ephraimites will become like mighty men,
and their hearts will be glad as with wine.[g]
Their children will see it and be joyful;
their hearts will rejoice in the LORD.
[8] I will signal[h] for them
and gather them in.
Surely I will redeem them;
they will be as numerous[i] as before.

10:2 [x] Eze 21:21 [y] Eze 34:5; Hos 3:4; Mt 9:36
10:3 [z] Jer 25:34
10:4 [a] Isa 22:23 [b] Zec 9:10
10:5 [c] 2Sa 22:43 [d] Am 2:15; Hag 2:22
10:6 [e] Zec 8:7-8 [f] Zec 13:9
10:7 [g] Zec 9:15
10:8 [h] Isa 5:26 [i] Jer 33:22; Eze 36:11

[a] 4,5 Or *ruler, all of them together.* / [5] *They*

10:1 The Lord, not the Canaanite god Baal, controls the weather, conferring life and fertility upon the land (see the note on Jdg 2:13; see also "Baal and the Fertility Cults" on p. 1414).
10:2 "Idols" refers to household gods that were used for divination during the period of the judges (see Jdg 17:5; see also "Akkadian Divination" on p. 277). Resorting to such sources for information and guidance was expressly forbidden to God's people (Dt 18:9–14).

It was common practice in the ancient Near East to refer to leaders as "shepherds" and to the people as their "sheep" or "flock" (see "Shepherding in the Ancient World" on p. 1363).
10:4 The Targum (ancient Aramaic paraphrase) indicates that this verse is Messianic.
10:5 This verse was partly fulfilled in the Maccabean victories (see "The Intertestamental Period" on p. 1551).
10:8 The use of the word "signal" (lit., "whistle") is a continuation of the shepherd metaphor (see the note on v. 2).

The Hebrew for "redeem" is often used of ransoming from slavery or captivity (see the note on Hos 3:2; see also "Slavery and Labor Law in the Ancient Near East" on p. 127 and "The Kinsman-Redeemer" on p. 391).

9 Though I scatter them among the peoples,
10:9 [j]Eze 6:9 yet in distant lands they will remember me.[j]
They and their children will survive,
and they will return.
10 I will bring them back from Egypt
10:10 [k]Isa 11:11 [l]Jer 50:19 [m]Isa 49:19 and gather them from Assyria.[k]
I will bring them to Gilead[l] and Lebanon,
and there will not be room[m] enough for them.
11 They will pass through the sea of trouble;
the surging sea will be subdued
10:11 [n]Isa 19:5-7; 51:10 [o]Zep 2:13 [p]Eze 30:13 and all the depths of the Nile will dry up.[n]
Assyria's pride[o] will be brought down
and Egypt's scepter[p] will pass away.
12 I will strengthen them in the LORD
10:12 [q]Mic 4:5 and in his name they will walk,[q]"

declares the LORD.

11:1 [r]Eze 31:3 **11** Open your doors, O Lebanon,[r]
so that fire may devour your cedars!
2 Wail, O pine tree, for the cedar has fallen;
the stately trees are ruined!
Wail, oaks of Bashan;
11:2 [s]Isa 32:19 the dense forest[s] has been cut down!
3 Listen to the wail of the shepherds;
their rich pastures are destroyed!
Listen to the roar of the lions;
11:3 [t]Jer 2:15; 50:44 the lush thicket of the Jordan is ruined![t]

Two Shepherds

4 This is what the LORD my God says: "Pasture the flock marked for slaughter. 5 Their buyers slaughter
them and go unpunished. Those who sell them say, 'Praise the LORD, I am rich!' Their own shepherds do
11:5 [u]Jer 50:7; Eze 34:2-3 not spare them.[u] 6 For I will no longer have pity on the people of the land," declares the LORD. "I will hand
11:6 [v]Zec 14:13 [w]Isa 9:19-21; Jer 13:14; Mic 5:8; 7:2-6 everyone over to his neighbor[v] and his king. They will oppress the land, and I will not rescue them from
their hands."[w]
7 So I pastured the flock marked for slaughter, particularly the oppressed of the flock. Then I took two
staffs and called one Favor and the other Union, and I pastured the flock. 8 In one month I got rid of the
three shepherds.
The flock detested me, and I grew weary of them 9 and said, "I will not be your shepherd. Let the dy-
11:9 [x]Jer 15:2; 43:11 ing die, and the perishing perish.[x] Let those who are left eat one another's flesh."
11:10 [y]ver 7 [z]Ps 89:39; Jer 14:21 10 Then I took my staff called Favor[y] and broke it, revoking[z] the covenant I had made with all the na-
tions. 11 It was revoked on that day, and so the afflicted of the flock who were watching me knew it was
the word of the LORD.
12 I told them, "If you think it best, give me my pay; but if not, keep it." So they paid me thirty pieces
11:12 [a]Ex 21:32; Mt 26:15 of silver.[a]

10:10 Egypt and Assyria probably represent all the countries to which the Israelites had been dispersed.

Gilead, a region southeast of the Sea of Galilee, was known for its fertile pasturelands.

Lebanon was famed for its great trees, particularly its cedars (see "Cedars of Lebanon" on p. 1043), as well as for its hordes of birds and alpine animals. It was a beautiful and majestic region.

10:11 A scepter was a rod held in the hand of a king as a token of authority. It indicated sovereignty in general, and perhaps even conquest (see also Nu 24:17; Isa 14:5; Am 1:5,8). God's kingship is also represented in this way (Ps 45:6). The use of the scepter by an oriental monarch is illustrated by the account of King Xerxes, who held out his scepter to Esther as a mark of favor (Est 5:1–2). The scepter of Xerxes was fashioned of gold, but Ezekiel referred to scepters made from vine branches (Eze 19:11,14). When Jesus was mocked as a king, a reed or staff was placed in his hand as a scepter (Mt 27:29).

11:2 For "Bashan," see the note on Ezekiel 39:18. The Israelites had taken this region from the Amorite king Og at the time of the conquest of Canaan (Nu 21:33–35), and it had later been allotted to the half-tribe of Manasseh (Jos 13:29–30; 17:5).

11:3 Lions used the thickets for their lairs (see "Lions and Other Wild Beasts in Ancient Israel" on p. 813).

11:4–5 The "flock" refers to Israel (see the note on 10:2)—the sheep (the Jews) had been bought as slaves by outsiders. This prophecy was partly fulfilled in A.D. 70, when Jerusalem and the temple were destroyed, and the following years. "Those who sell them" refers, on the other hand, to their own shepherds (i.e., their rulers or leaders).

11:8 The three shepherds cannot be specifically identified.

11:9 According to the ancient Jewish historian Josephus (see "Historians in the Ancient World" on p. 939), cannibalism occurred during the Roman siege of Jerusalem in A.D. 70 (see the note on Jer 19:9; see also "Josephus and the Fall of Jerusalem" on p. 1606).

13 And the LORD said to me, "Throw it to the potter"—the handsome price at which they priced me! So I took the thirty pieces of silver and threw them into the house of the LORD to the potter.[b]

14 Then I broke my second staff called Union, breaking the brotherhood between Judah and Israel.

15 Then the LORD said to me, "Take again the equipment of a foolish shepherd. 16 For I am going to raise up a shepherd over the land who will not care for the lost, or seek the young, or heal the injured, or feed the healthy, but will eat the meat of the choice sheep, tearing off their hoofs.

> 17 "Woe to the worthless shepherd,[c]
> who deserts the flock!
> May the sword strike his arm[d] and his
> right eye!
> May his arm be completely withered,
> his right eye totally blinded!"[e]

Jerusalem's Enemies to Be Destroyed

An Oracle

12 This is the word of the LORD concerning Israel. The LORD, who stretches out the heavens,[f] who lays the foundation of the earth,[g] and who forms the spirit of man[h] within him, declares: 2 "I am going to make Jerusalem a cup[i] that sends all the surrounding peoples reeling.[j] Judah[k] will be besieged as well as Jerusalem. 3 On that day, when all the nations[l] of the earth are gathered against her, I will make Jerusalem an immovable rock[m] for all the nations. All who try to move it will injure[n] themselves. 4 On that day I will strike every horse with panic and its rider with madness," declares the LORD. "I will keep a watchful eye over the house of Judah, but I will blind all the horses of the nations.[o] 5 Then the leaders of Judah will say in their hearts, 'The people of Jerusalem are strong, because the LORD Almighty is their God.'

6 "On that day I will make the leaders of Judah like a firepot[p] in a woodpile, like a flaming torch among sheaves. They will consume[q] right and left all the surrounding peoples, but Jerusalem will remain intact in her place.

7 "The LORD will save the dwellings of Judah first, so that the honor of the house of David and of Jerusalem's inhabitants may not be greater than that of Judah.[r] 8 On that day the LORD will shield[s] those who live in Jerusalem, so that the feeblest among them will be like David, and the house of David will be like God,[t] like the Angel of the LORD going before[u] them. 9 On that day I will set out to destroy all the nations that attack Jerusalem.[v]

Mourning for the One They Pierced

10 "And I will pour out on the house of David and the inhabitants of Jerusalem a spirit[a] of grace and supplication.[w] They will look on[b] me, the one they have pierced,[x] and they will mourn for him as one mourns for an only child, and grieve bitterly for him as one grieves for a firstborn son. 11 On that day the weeping in Jerusalem will be great, like the weeping of Hadad Rimmon in the plain of Megiddo.[y] 12 The land will mourn,[z] each clan by itself, with their wives by themselves: the clan of the house of David and their wives, the clan of the house of Nathan and their wives, 13 the clan of the house of Levi and their wives, the clan of Shimei and their wives, 14 and all the rest of the clans and their wives.

[a] 10 Or *the Spirit* [b] 10 Or *to*

11:13 [b]Mt 27:9-10*; Ac 1:18-19
11:17 [c]Jer 23:1 [d]Eze 30:21-22 [e]Jer 23:1
12:1 [f]Isa 42:5; Jer 51:15 [g]Ps 102:25; Heb 1:10 [h]Isa 57:16
12:2 [i]Ps 75:8 [j]Isa 51:23 [k]Zec 14:14
12:3 [l]Zec 14:2 [m]Da 2:34-35 [n]Mt 21:44
12:4 [o]Ps 76:6
12:6 [p]Isa 10:17-18; Zec 11:1 [q]Ob 1:18
12:7 [r]Jer 30:18; Am 9:11
12:8 [s]Joel 3:16; Zec 9:15 [t]Ps 82:6 [u]Mic 7:8
12:9 [v]Zec 14:2-3
12:10 [w]Isa 44:3; Eze 39:29; Joel 2:28-29 [x]Jn 19:34,37*; Rev 1:7
12:11 [y]2Ki 23:29
12:12 [z]Mt 24:30; Rev 1:7

11:14 The breaking up of the nation into parties hostile to each other was characteristic of later Jewish history. This trend greatly hindered the popular cause in the war against Rome (cf. Jn 11:48).

11:16 A selfish, greedy, corrupt leader would arise and afflict the flock (the people of Israel).

11:17 The prophecy of "the worthless shepherd" may have found partial historical fulfillment in such leaders as Simeon Bar Kokhba, who led the Jewish revolt against the Romans in A.D. 132–135 and who was hailed as the Messiah by Rabbi Akiba (see "The Intertestamental Period" on p. 1551). But it would seem that the final stage of the progressive fulfillment of this prophecy awaits the rise of the ultimate antichrist (cf. Eze 34:2–4; Da 11:36–39; Jn 5:43; 2Th 2:3–10; Rev 13:1–8).

12:3 For "that day," see the note on Joel 1:15.

12:6 See the note on hearths and home heating at Psalm 102:3.

12:11 Hadad Rimmon (today called Rummaneh, "place of pomegranates") probably refers in this context to a site in the valley of Megiddo (see "Megiddo" on p. 1541) where the people mourned the death of Judah's last good king, Josiah (2Ch 35:20–27). Alternatively, it may refer to a Semitic storm god (see 2Ki 5:18), whose name means "Hadad the thunderer" in Babylonian (as in the Epic of Gilgamesh). (See "Ecclesiastes and the Epic of Gilgamesh" on p. 1027 and "Syria/Aram" on p. 729.) See also Ezekiel 8:14 for an example of the practice of weeping for a Babylonian deity (see "Mourning for Tammuz" on p. 1320).

ARCHAEOLOGICAL SITES

MEGIDDO

Early Bronze Age temple and altar at Megiddo
Photograph: © Todd Bolen/Bible Places.com

ZECHARIAH 12 The city of **Megiddo** ("Map 6") controlled the pass between the Valley of Jezreel and the Sharon plain. Routes that traveled northwest to the **Phoenician** coast and east to Damascus were also controlled by this city[1] Many critical battles took place at Megiddo, one of the most strategic cities in the region now called Palestine.

An archaeological excavation of Tell el-Mutesellim during the first decade of the twentieth century located the city, including numerous layers of occupation. Megiddo was first inhabited during the **Neolithic Age**.[2] The Megiddo of the **Early Bronze** I period boasted the largest known temple in the Levant (Syria-Palestine) for that time period. Excavation revealed numerous levels of occupation through the **Middle Bronze** and **Late Bronze** Ages; some levels indicate periods when the city was prosperous and others when it was impoverished. During the earlier part of the Late Bronze Age Megiddo was under Egyptian domination, having been captured by Pharaoh Thutmose III in approximately 1479 B.C. Several of the **Amarna** Letters[3] from the ruler of Megiddo profess loyalty to Egypt.

During the conquest of the promised land Megiddo was allotted to the tribe of Manasseh (Jos 17:11).[4] The king of Megiddo is listed among those defeated by Joshua (Jos 12:21), but Manasseh could not take the city (Jdg 1:27). It appears that Megiddo was subsequently a Canaanite city with a Philistine presence. Apparently David conquered it for Israel.

An occupation level from the tenth century B.C., the age of Solomon, indicates that the city was used as a government administrative center for Israel. This level evidences the same kind of multichambered gates and double walls (called **casemate walls**) found in **Hazor** and Gezer during the same time period.[5] On the basis of 1 Kings 9:15 we can conclude that the style of construction used in these cities was of a sort favored by Solomon's engineers.[6] Pharaoh Shishak (r. c. 945–924 B.C.) appears to have destroyed Megiddo during a campaign that included an attack on Judah and Jerusalem.[7]

Megiddo was rebuilt and used again as a military or administrative center during the ninth and eighth centuries B.C. However, the city once again fell to a foreign power when Tiglath-Pileser III, king of **Assyria**, conquered it around 733 B.C., after which it was used as an Assyrian administrative center. With the fall of the Assyrian Empire, Megiddo came under the control of Judah. It was the location of the confrontation between King Josiah and Pharaoh Neco that resulted in Josiah's death.[8] In Zechariah 12:11 "the weeping of Hadad Rimmon in the plain of Megiddo" probably refers to mourning over this calamity. During the **Persian** Age the city was abandoned.

A number of remarkable archaeological finds have emerged from Megiddo:

- A large, round sacrificial area from an Early Bronze temple complex
- A plaque depicting a **Hittite** king standing beneath a winged sun disk
- A fragment of an **Akkadian** tablet containing a part of the Gilgamesh epic
- Ivory carvings of the Egyptian god Bes and of lotus patterns
- A painted pitcher, called the "Orpheus Jug," portraying a lyre player leading a procession of animals
- Palace structures dating from the Israelite period (tenth–eighth centuries B.C.) reflecting that the city was for a time a significant Israelite administrative center
- A **stele** from Pharaoh Shishak, confirming that this Egyptian monarch did take the city during the time of Rehoboam
- A remarkable jasper seal with a roaring lion and the inscription "of Shema, servant of Jeroboam" (i.e., Jeroboam II)
- A large building excavated there with three aisles running its length, separated by rows of pillars. (Its function has been debated, with some suggesting a storehouse or barracks, but it was probably a stable for horses from the time of Ahab.)

These finds, from different ages and from across the ancient Near East, attest to the abiding significance of Megiddo.

[1]See "Phoenicia" on page 488 and "Damascus" on page 1087. [2]See "Archaeological Periods" chart on page xx in the front of this Bible. [3]See "The Amarna Tablets and the Habiru" on page 347. [4]See "The Conquest of Canaan" on page 310. [5]See "Hazor" on page 322 and "Gezer" on page 588. [6]See "The Building Activity of Solomon" on page 497. [7]See "The Campaign of Shishak" on page 635. [8]See "Josiah, Zechariah and Neco II" on page 663.

Cleansing From Sin

13 "On that day a fountain[a] will be opened to the house of David and the inhabitants of Jerusalem,
to cleanse[b] them from sin and impurity.
[2]"On that day, I will banish the names of the idols[c] from the land, and they will be remembered no
more," declares the LORD Almighty. "I will remove both the prophets[d] and the spirit of impurity from the
land. [3]And if anyone still prophesies, his father and mother, to whom he was born, will say to him, 'You
must die, because you have told lies in the LORD's name.' When he prophesies, his own parents will stab
him.[e]
[4]"On that day every prophet will be ashamed[f] of his prophetic vision. He will not put on a prophet's
garment[g] of hair[h] in order to deceive. [5]He will say, 'I am not a prophet. I am a farmer; the land has been
my livelihood since my youth.[a]'[i] [6]If someone asks him, 'What are these wounds on your body[b]?' he will
answer, 'The wounds I was given at the house of my friends.'

The Shepherd Struck, the Sheep Scattered

[7]"Awake, O sword,[j] against my shepherd,[k]
against the man who is close to me!"
declares the LORD Almighty.
"Strike the shepherd,
and the sheep will be scattered,[l]
and I will turn my hand against the little ones.
[8]In the whole land," declares the LORD,
"two-thirds will be struck down and perish;
yet one-third will be left in it.[m]
[9]This third I will bring into the fire;[n]
I will refine them like silver[o]
and test them like gold.
They will call[p] on my name
and I will answer[q] them;
I will say, 'They are my people,'[r]
and they will say, 'The LORD is our God.[s]' "

The LORD Comes and Reigns

14 A day of the LORD[t] is coming when your plunder will be divided among you.
[2]I will gather all the nations to Jerusalem to fight against it; the city will be captured, the hous-
es ransacked, and the women raped. Half of the city will go into exile, but the rest of the people will not
be taken from the city.[u]
[3]Then the LORD will go out and fight[v] against those nations, as he fights in the day of battle. [4]On that
day his feet will stand on the Mount of Olives,[w] east of Jerusalem, and the Mount of Olives will be split
in two from east to west, forming a great valley, with half of the mountain moving north and half mov-
ing south. [5]You will flee by my mountain valley, for it will extend to Azel. You will flee as you fled from

[a] 5 Or *farmer; a man sold me in my youth* [b] 6 Or *wounds between your hands*

13:1 [a]Jer 17:13 [b]Ps 51:2; Heb 9:14
13:2 [c]Ex 23:13; Eze 36:25; Hos 2:17 [d]1Ki 22:22; Jer 23:14-15
13:3 [e]Dt 13:6-11; 18:20; Jer 23:34; Eze 14:9
13:4 [f]Jer 6:15; Mic 3:6-7 [g]Mt 3:4 [h]2Ki 1:8; Isa 20:2
13:5 [i]Am 7:14
13:7 [j]Jer 47:6 [k]Isa 40:11; 53:4; Eze 37:24 [l]Mt 26:31*; Mk 14:27*
13:8 [m]Eze 5:2-4, 12
13:9 [n]Mal 3:2 [o]Isa 48:10; 1Pe 1:6-7 [p]Ps 50:15 [q]Zec 10:6 [r]Jer 30:22 [s]Jer 29:12
14:1 [t]Isa 13:9; Mal 4:1
14:2 [u]Isa 13:6; Zec 13:8
14:3 [v]Zec 9:14-15
14:4 [w]Eze 11:23

13:2 "Prophets" refers here to false prophets. False prophecy was still a problem during the postexilic period (see Ne 6:12–14) and would again be so in the future (see Mt 24:4–5,11,23–24; 2Th 2:2–4).
13:4 Matthew 3:4 and Mark 1:6 state that John the Baptist wore a garment of camel's hair. It is probable, however, that this article of clothing was not actually made of the relatively expensive woven camel's hair but of dressed camel's skin. Such garments are still used in the Near East. Some scholars suspect that Elijah's mantle was made of camel's hair (2Ki 1:8).
13:6 Apparently the accuser suspected that the false prophet's wounds were self-inflicted to arouse his prophetic ecstasy in idolatrous rites (as in 1Ki 18:28; see also "Tattoos and Self-Laceration in Ancient Religion" on p. 180).
13:7 "My shepherd" is a reference to the royal (Messianic) Good Shepherd. Jesus quoted phrases from this verse (regarding the striking of the shepherd and the scattering of the sheep) not long before his arrest (Mt 26:31; Mk 14:27). He applied the scattering of the sheep to the dispersal of the apostles (Mt 26:56; Mk 14:49–50), who in turn are probably typological of the dispersion of the Jews in A.D. 70 and subsequent years.
14:4 For commentary on the Mount of Olives, see the note on Ezekiel 11:23 and "The Mount of Olives" on page 1543.
14:5 Four earthquakes are recorded in Scripture: the one that occurred at Mount Horeb for Elijah's benefit (1Ki 19:11); the one referred to by Amos (Am 1:1) and Zechariah (here) as occurring in the reign of Uzziah, king of Judah; the one that happened at the resurrection of Jesus (Mt 28:2); and the one that freed Paul and Silas from prison (Ac 16:26). An earthquake is mentioned in Isaiah 29:6 as a form of judgment from the Lord on the enemies of his people. This is in line with the steady Biblical testimony that all natural phenomena—earthquake, wind, storm, rain, hail and the rest—are under divine, sovereign control and are part of God's armory for ruling the world in righteousness.

14:5 [x]Am 1:1 [y]Isa 29:6; 66:15-16 [z]Mt 16:27; 25:31
14:6 [a]Isa 13:10; Jer 4:23
14:7 [b]Jer 30:7 [c]Rev 21:23-25; 22:5 [d]Isa 30:26

the earthquake[a][x] in the days of Uzziah king of Judah. Then the LORD my God will come,[y] and all the holy ones with him.[z]

6On that day there will be no light,[a] no cold or frost. 7It will be a unique[b] day, without daytime or nighttime[c]—a day known to the LORD. When evening comes, there will be light.[d]

[a] 5 Or [5]*My mountain valley will be blocked and will extend to Azel. It will be blocked as it was blocked because of the earthquake*

ARCHAEOLOGICAL SITES

THE MOUNT OF OLIVES

ZECHARIAH 14 The Mount of Olives forms a ridge running north and south for about two miles (three km) just across the Kidron Valley ("Map 10") east of Jerusalem.[1] Zechariah 14:4 speaks of a split in this mountain that will run from east to west in the eschatological (end times) future. This gulch will provide an avenue of escape, so the text tells us, when Jerusalem comes under a terrible siege (v. 2).

The Mount of Olives is explicitly mentioned in the Old Testament only here and in 2 Samuel 15:30; however, the "hill east of Jerusalem" where Solomon constructed shrines to pagan gods (1Ki 11:7–8; cf. 2Ki 23:13) was probably the same location. In these Old Testament references there seems to be some association of the Mount of Olives with crisis and judgment. This trend continues in the New Testament, where the Mount of Olives is prominent in the ministry of Jesus:

- When Jesus in his triumphal entry approached Jerusalem, moving downward from the Mount of Olives, he wept over the city's coming destruction (Lk 19:30–44).
- The cursing of the fig tree (Mt 21:17–19), a symbol of judgment on Israel, appears to have occurred there.
- From this vantage point Jesus delivered his "Olivet Discourse" (Mt 24; Mk 13), a prophecy of judgment.
- Jesus' agony in the garden of Gethsemane (Mt 26:30–42), as well as Judas's betrayal of him (Jn 18:1–3), both occurred there.

[1]See "Jerusalem" on page 1191.

The Kidron Valley and the Mount of Olives as seen from the City of David

Photograph: © Todd Bolen/Bible Places.com

8 On that day living water[e] will flow out from Jerusalem, half to the eastern[f] sea[a] and half to the western sea,[b] in summer and in winter.

9 The LORD will be king over the whole earth.[g] On that day there will be one LORD, and his name the only name.[h]

10 The whole land, from Geba[i] to Rimmon, south of Jerusalem, will become like the Arabah. But Jerusalem will be raised up[j] and remain in its place,[k] from the Benjamin Gate to the site of the First Gate, to the Corner Gate, and from the Tower of Hananel to the royal winepresses. 11 It will be inhabited; never again will it be destroyed. Jerusalem will be secure.[l]

12 This is the plague with which the LORD will strike all the nations that fought against Jerusalem: Their flesh will rot while they are still standing on their feet, their eyes will rot in their sockets, and their tongues will rot in their mouths.[m] 13 On that day men will be stricken by the LORD with great panic. Each man will seize the hand of another, and they will attack each other.[n] 14 Judah[o] too will fight at Jerusalem. The wealth of all the surrounding nations will be collected[p]—great quantities of gold and silver and clothing. 15 A similar plague[q] will strike the horses and mules, the camels and donkeys, and all the animals in those camps.

16 Then the survivors from all the nations that have attacked Jerusalem will go up year after year to worship the King, the LORD Almighty, and to celebrate the Feast of Tabernacles.[r] 17 If any of the peoples of the earth do not go up to Jerusalem to worship the King, the LORD Almighty, they will have no rain.[s] 18 If the Egyptian people do not go up and take part, they will have no rain. The LORD[c] will bring on them the plague he inflicts on the nations that do not go up to celebrate the Feast of Tabernacles.[t] 19 This will be the punishment of Egypt and the punishment of all the nations that do not go up to celebrate the Feast of Tabernacles.

20 On that day HOLY TO THE LORD will be inscribed on the bells of the horses, and the cooking pots[u] in the LORD's house will be like the sacred bowls[v] in front of the altar. 21 Every pot in Jerusalem and Judah will be holy[w] to the LORD Almighty, and all who come to sacrifice will take some of the pots and cook in them. And on that day[x] there will no longer be a Canaanite[d][y] in the house of the LORD Almighty.[z]

14:8 [e]Eze 47:1-12; Jn 7:38; Rev 22:1-2 [f]Joel 2:20
14:9 [g]Dt 6:4; Isa 45:24; Rev 11:15 [h]Eph 4:5-6
14:10 [i]1Ki 15:22 [j]Jer 30:18; Am 9:11 [k]Zec 12:6
14:11 [l]Eze 34:25-28
14:12 [m]Lev 26:16; Dt 28:22
14:13 [n]Zec 11:6
14:14 [o]Zec 12:2 [p]Isa 23:18
14:15 [q]ver 12
14:16 [r]Isa 60:6-9
14:17 [s]Jer 14:4; Am 4:7
14:18 [t]ver 12
14:20 [u]Eze 46:20 [v]Zec 9:15
14:21 [w]Ro 14:6-7; 1Co 10:31 [x]Ne 8:10 [y]Zec 9:8 [z]Eze 44:9

[a] *8* That is, the Dead Sea [b] *8* That is, the Mediterranean [c] *18* Or *part, then the LORD* [d] *21* Or *merchant*

14:8 The Dead Sea is alternately called in Scripture the Salt Sea (Ge 14:3), the Sea of the Arabah (Dt 3:17) or the eastern sea (here and in Joel 2:20). It has the earth's lowest surface, 1,300 feet (400 m) below sea level. Occupying a geologic fault that extends from Syria through the Red Sea into Africa, it measures 47 by 10 miles (76 x 16 km), or approximately 300 square miles (777 sq km). Its cliffs rise 1,500–2,500 feet (457–762 m) on either shore. North of Lisan, "the tongue," the water's depth attains 1,300 feet (400 m), although southward it averages less than 10 feet (3 m). The Dead Sea is slowly expanding, as the muddy Jordan extends its northern delta. Salt concentration reaches 25 percent, four times that of ocean water. Magnesium bromide prevents organic life, and the climate is arid and the heat extreme.

14:10 This verse describes the entire city of, as well as the area around, Jerusalem: Geba was located about 6 miles (10 km) north-northeast of Jerusalem at the northern boundary of Judah. Rimmon was about 35 miles (56 km) south-southwest of Jerusalem, where the hill country of Judah slopes away into the Negev. The Arabah runs from the Sea of Galilee to the Gulf of Aqaba, although at times the term *Arabah* is used to refer specifically to the desert valley extending from the Dead Sea to the Gulf of Aqaba (see "The Geography of Ezekiel 47" on p. 1378). The Benjamin Gate, the First Gate and the Tower of Hananel were all probably located at the northeastern part of the city wall, while the Corner Gate was at its northwestern corner. The "royal winepresses" were just south of the city.

14:16 See "The Festivals of Israel" on page 186.

14:18 The Nile was the lifeline of Egypt; its annual flooding provided essential water and produced the only fertile soil there. Drought in the upper reaches of the Nile would have caused the annual flooding of the Nile to fail.

14:20 The phrase "HOLY TO THE LORD" was engraved upon the golden plate worn on the high priest's turban (Ex 28:36–38) as a reminder of his consecration to the Lord's service.

14:21 For "Canaanite," see "Lesser Known Peoples of the Old Testament" on page 265. Here the term represents anyone who was spiritually or morally unclean—anyone not included among the chosen people of God.

INTRODUCTION TO 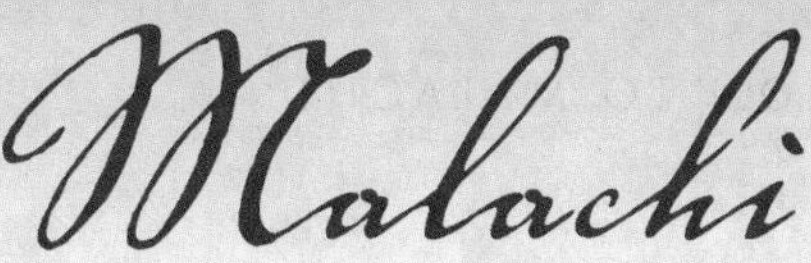

AUTHOR, PLACE AND DATE OF WRITING

The author of this book is identified as Malachi, but the meaning of the name, "my messenger," has raised questions. Some suggest that this is not a proper name at all but a common noun and that Malachi 1:1 should simply be translated as "An oracle: The word of the LORD to Israel through my messenger." This would imply that the book is anonymous and that this opening verse (written in the form of a pronouncement of God) simply asserts that the unnamed prophet was God's messenger. This is in fact the understanding of the Septuagint, which translates the term in 1:1 as "his messenger." "My messenger" would indeed be a peculiar name for a man, but it may be a shortened form of Malachiyahu, meaning "Yahweh's messenger." If so, it can be considered to be the prophet's proper name.

The date of this prophet's ministry is not given, but there are a number of clues: Sacrifices were being made at the temple (1:7–10); the Jews were under a governor (1:8), which suggests the Persian period; and Jewish men were marrying foreign wives (2:11), a problem that existed during the time of Ezra and Nehemiah. This information suggests that the book was written at some point during the fifth century B.C.

AUDIENCE

Malachi was written to the Jews who had returned from Babylon. The temple in Jerusalem had by this time been rebuilt (516 B.C.), but the people had fallen into a state of spiritual apathy. They were both disillusioned about their future and skeptical of God's promises.

CULTURAL FACTS AND HIGHLIGHTS

The book of Malachi exhorted the postexilic Jews to worship God rightly and to live faithfully as they awaited the fulfillment of his promises. Problems addressed by Malachi include the offering of substandard animals as sacrifices (1:8), negligence of duty among the priests (2:7–8), intermarriage with pagans (2:11), general immorality (3:5), a failure to tithe (3:10) and a widespread cynicism about the individual's duty to God (3:14). At the same time the book encouraged the people to maintain hope in the coming kingdom of God (3:1–4; 4:2–4). It is noteworthy that this prophecy has little to say about the old patterns of paganism of the preexilic Israelites, who had been enticed over and over again into the fertility cult of Baal. This generation was not guilty of the gross idolatry of its forefathers. Rather, these Israelites had embraced a kind of dead orthodoxy, in which they tried to get by with the minimum that their faith required.

TIMELINE

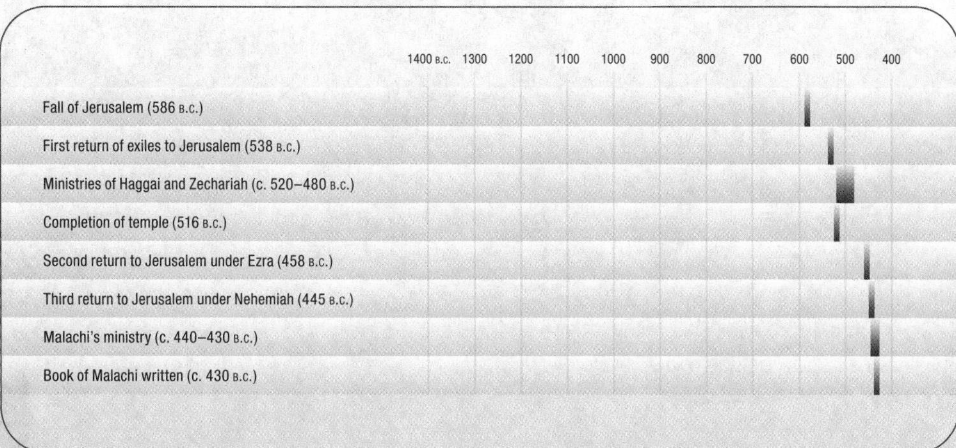

AS YOU READ

Watch for the prophet's effective use of repetition and for his vivid and memorable figures of speech. Pay attention to the series of questions asked by both God and the people. Notice how frequently the Lord's statements are followed by sarcastic questions introduced by "[But] you ask" (e.g., 1:2,6–7; 2:14,17; 3:7–8,13; cf. 1:13).

DID YOU KNOW?

- Marriages to foreign (pagan) women were stricly forbidden in the covenant law, not for ethnic or cultural reasons but because of the danger of their leading to apostasy (2:11).
- "Launderer's soap," called "fuller's soap" in some versions, was an alkali prepared from the ashes of certain plants and used for cleansing and "fulling" (shrinking or thickening) new woolen cloth (3:2).

THEMES

Malachi's themes include:

1. *Israel's unfaithfulness.* Malachi rebuked the people of Israel for their lapse into unfaithfulness. The priests had shown contempt for God's name by offering diseased or imperfect animals (1:6–14) and by violating the covenant (2:1–9). The men of Israel had married idolatrous Gentile women and had broken the marriage covenants by divorcing their Israelite wives (2:10–16), and the people were failing to honor God with the tithe (3:8–12). Malachi demonstrated that God demands his people's best (1:7–8)—both in their service and in their lifestyles.

2. *Judgment.* God will judge those who practice evil (2:17—3:5; 4:1) but save and reward those who honor him (3:16–18; 4:2–3). Faithful service to God will be remembered and rewarded (3:13–18).

OUTLINE

I. God's Covenant Love for Israel (1:1–5)
II. Israel's Unfaithfulness Rebuked (1:6—2:16)
   A. The Unfaithfulness of the Priests (1:6—2:9)
   B. The Unfaithfulness of the People (2:10–16)
III. The Lord's Coming (2:17—4:6)
   A. His Coming Will Bring Purification and Judgment (2:17—3:5)
   B. Repentance Is Appropriate Preparation for the Lord's Coming (3:6–18)
   C. The Day of the Lord Is Certain to Come (4)

1:1 [a]Na 1:1 [b]1Pe 4:11 **1** An oracle:[a] The word[b] of the LORD to Israel through Malachi.[a]

Jacob Loved, Esau Hated

1:2 [c]Dt 4:37 [d]Ro 9:13* 2"I have loved[c] you," says the LORD.
"But you ask, 'How have you loved us?'
"Was not Esau Jacob's brother?" the LORD says. "Yet I have loved Jacob,[d] 3but Esau I have hated, and I
1:3 [e]Isa 34:10 [f]Eze 35:3-9 have turned his mountains into a wasteland[e] and left his inheritance to the desert jackals.[f]"
1:4 [g]Isa 9:10 [h]Eze 25:12-14 4Edom may say, "Though we have been crushed, we will rebuild[g] the ruins."
But this is what the LORD Almighty says: "They may build, but I will demolish. They will be called the
Wicked Land, a people always under the wrath of the LORD.[h] 5You will see it with your own eyes and say,
1:5 [i]Ps 35:27; Mic 5:4 [j]Am 1:11-12 'Great[i] is the LORD—even beyond the borders of Israel!'[j]

Blemished Sacrifices

6"A son honors his father, and a servant his master. If I am a father, where is the honor due me? If I
1:6 [k]Isa 1:2 [l]Job 5:17 am a master, where is the respect[k] due me?" says the LORD Almighty.[l] "It is you, O priests, who show con-
tempt for my name.
"But you ask, 'How have we shown contempt for your name?'
1:7 [m]ver 12; Lev 21:6 7"You place defiled food[m] on my altar.
"But you ask, 'How have we defiled you?'
"By saying that the LORD's table is contemptible. 8When you bring blind animals for sacrifice, is
1:8 [n]Lev 22:22; Dt 15:21 [o]Isa 43:23 that not wrong? When you sacrifice crippled or diseased animals,[n] is that not wrong? Try offering
them to your governor! Would he be pleased with you? Would he accept you?" says the LORD Al-
mighty.[o]
1:9 [p]Lev 23:33-44 9"Now implore God to be gracious to us. With such offerings[p] from your hands, will he accept you?"—
says the LORD Almighty.
10"Oh, that one of you would shut the temple doors, so that you would not light useless fires on my al-
1:10 [q]Hos 5:6 [r]Isa 1:11-14; Jer 14:12 tar! I am not pleased[q] with you," says the LORD Almighty, "and I will accept no offering[r] from your hands.
11My name will be great among the nations, from the rising to the setting of the sun. In every place in-
1:11 [s]Isa 60:6-7; Rev 8:3 cense[s] and pure offerings will be brought to my name, because my name will be great among the na-
tions," says the LORD Almighty.
1:12 [t]ver 7 12"But you profane it by saying of the Lord's table, 'It is defiled,' and of its food,[t] 'It is contemptible.'
1:13 [u]Isa 43:22-24 13And you say, 'What a burden!'[u] and you sniff at it contemptuously," says the LORD Almighty.
"When you bring injured, crippled or diseased animals and offer them as sacrifices, should I accept
them from your hands?" says the LORD. 14"Cursed is the cheat who has an acceptable male in his flock and
1:14 [v]Lev 22:18-21 [w]1Ti 6:15 vows to give it, but then sacrifices a blemished animal[v] to the Lord. For I am a great king,[w]" says the LORD
Almighty, "and my name is to be feared among the nations.

[a] 1 *Malachi* means *my messenger.*

1:1–7 The Nabateans, an Arabian tribe named in the Apocrypha but not in the Bible, were nonetheless important to Bible history. Between the sixth and fourth centuries B.C. they moved to Edom and Moab (as alluded to here and in Ob 1–7). During Hellenistic times they were a formidable foe to the Greek successors of Alexander the Great, their capital, Petra, being inaccessible and virtually impregnable. While their king, Aretas I, befriended the early Maccabees, they were in conflict with the later Maccabees. By New Testament times their territory stretched from the Mediterranean Sea south of Gaza and the Red Sea, to the Euphrates, including Damascus. The Nabateans lost Damascus when the Romans came to the aid of the Jews against them, but they later recovered it, so that their king Aretas IV controlled it when Paul was there (2Co 11:32). Aretas IV struggled for power against the Herodian rulers and was victorious over Herod Antipas, who had divorced Aretas's daughter to marry Herodias. Nabatea was absorbed into the Roman province of Arabia in A.D. 106. (See "Aretas IV or Nabatea and Petra" on p. 1898.)

The Nabateans, a nomadic people influenced by the Aramean, Hellenistic and Roman cultures, developed skill in pottery, fine specimens of which have been recovered. The architecture of Petra, "the rose-red city," is remarkable; its religious high places, pillars and figures carved out of sandstone cliffs of a canyon are accessible only on foot or muleback. By 100 B.C. the Nabateans developed water storage and irrigations systems in the highlands of Transjordan, the remains of which are still impressive. Yet the Nabateans in the Sinai peninsula and other outlying districts remained nomadic. They were traders between Egypt and Mesopotamia, dealing also in wares from India and China, both overland by caravan and by sea from a port on the Aqaba.

1:1 For "oracle," see the note on Isaiah 13:1; see also "Oracles of the Ancient World" on page 1507.

1:2–4 Between about 550 and 400 B.C. the Nabatean Arabs gradually forced the Edomites (descendants of Esau) from their homeland (see the note on vv. 1–7 and "Edom" on p. 1467).

1:7 Since the priests ate from the sacrifices, the altar was also the table from which they received their food (see the note on Lev 3:11; see also "The Levites and the Priests" on p. 648).

1:8 The "governor" probably refers to the Persian governor.

1:11 See "Sacrifices and Offerings in the Bible and the Ancient Near East" on page 158 and "Incense" on page 1209.

1:14 An animal sacrificed in fulfillment of a vow had to be a male without defect or blemish (see Lev 22:18–23).

Admonition for the Priests

2 "And now this admonition is for you, O priests.[x] 2If you do not listen, and if you do not set your heart 2:1 [x]ver 7
to honor my name," says the LORD Almighty, "I will send a curse[y] upon you, and I will curse your 2:2 [y]Dt 28:20
blessings. Yes, I have already cursed them, because you have not set your heart to honor me.
3"Because of you I will rebuke[a] your descendants[b]; I will spread on your faces the offal[z] from your 2:3 [z]Ex 29:14

[a] 3 Or *cut off* (see Septuagint) [b] 3 Or *will blight your grain*

2:3 The "offal" was the content of the intestines of a sacrificial animal.

Marriage and Divorce in Ancient Israel

MALACHI 2 At the heart of the Hebrew concept of marriage is the notion of covenant—a legally binding agreement with spiritual and emotional ramifications (Pr 2:17). God serves as witness to the marriage covenant, blessing its faithfulness but hating its betrayal (Mal 2:14–16). The Lord's intimate involvement renders this legal commitment a spiritual union, "so they are no longer two, but one" (Mt 19:6). The purpose of marriage as articulated in the Bible is to find true companionship (Ge 2:18; Pr 18:22), produce godly offspring (Mal 2:15; 1Co 7:14) and fulfill God's calling upon an individual's life (Ge 1:28).

It was customary in ancient Israel for parents to arrange a marriage (Ge 24:47–53; 38:6; 1Sa 18:17), although marrying for love was not uncommon (Jdg 14:2). Arranged marriages highlight the nature of the marriage covenant as a commitment intended to outlast youthful infatuation. The declaration at the first marriage, "This is now bone of my bones and flesh of my flesh" (Ge 2:23), is a kinship formula (Ge 29:14; 2Sa 5:1; 19:12–13). Marriage binds husband and wife together into an entity greater than either partner as an individual, and it does so in order to assure continuity of the family lineage. Marriage within the kinship group was encouraged so as not to alienate family land holdings (Ge 24:4; Nu 36:6–9),[1] and in the event that a woman's husband died and left her childless, the law provided for the husband's brother to act as a levirate in order to raise up offspring for the deceased (Ge 38:8; Dt 25:5–6).[2]

An engagement period preceded the wedding celebration and the consummation of the marriage union. The pledge of engagement was regarded as being as binding as the marriage itself, and a betrothed woman was considered legally married (Dt 22:23–29). The engagement was concluded by the payment of a bride-price to the woman's father (Ge 29:18; Jdg 1:12). This may be understood as a compensation given to the family for the loss of their daughter. The father enjoyed its usage temporarily, but the money reverted to the daughter at the father's death or in the event she were widowed. In addition, gifts were given to the bride and her family at the acceptance of a marriage proposal (Ge 24:53). Thus, marriage and its attendant economic investment brought the bride and groom's families into legal relationship with one another (Ge 31:50).

Israelite law included a provision for divorce—initiated by the husband only. Marriages were dissolved contractually with a certificate of divorce (Dt 24:1). This divorce document most likely recorded a formula of repudiation declared orally before witnesses: "She is not my wife, and I am not her husband" (Hos 2:2). The declaration might have been accompanied by a sign, the act of removing the woman's outer garment as an annulment of the promise made at the time of the wedding to protect and provide for her (Ru 3:9; Eze 16:8, 37; Hos 2:3,9).[3] A man was not permitted to divorce his wife if he had forcefully violated her while she was yet unbetrothed (Dt 22:28–29) or if he had falsely accused her of nonvirginal status at the time they had wed (Dt 22:13–19).[4]

[1]See "Inheritance in the Ancient Near East" on page 250. [2]See "Levirate Marriage" on page 64. [3]See "Weddings in Ancient Israel" on page 1039. [4]See also "Husbands and Wives: Family Life in the Greco-Roman World" on page 1922.

2:3 [a]1Ki 14:10 festival sacrifices, and you will be carried off with it.[a] 4And you will know that I have sent you this ad-
2:4 [b]Nu 3:12 monition so that my covenant with Levi[b] may continue," says the LORD Almighty. 5"My covenant was with
2:5 [c]Dt 33:9 [d]Nu 25:12 him, a covenant[c] of life and peace,[d] and I gave them to him; this called for reverence and he revered me
2:6 [e]Dt 33:10 and stood in awe of my name. 6True instruction[e] was in his mouth and nothing false was found on his
[f]Jer 23:22; Jas 5:19-20 lips. He walked with me in peace and uprightness, and turned many from sin.[f]
2:7 [g]Jer 18:18 [h]Lev 10:11 7"For the lips of a priest[g] ought to preserve knowledge, and from his mouth men should seek instruc-
[i]Nu 27:21 tion[h]—because he is the messenger[i] of the LORD Almighty. 8But you have turned from the way and by
2:8 [j]Jer 18:15 your teaching have caused many to stumble;[j] you have violated the covenant with Levi," says the LORD Al-
2:9 [k]1Sa 2:30 mighty. 9"So I have caused you to be despised[k] and humiliated before all the people, because you have
not followed my ways but have shown partiality in matters of the law."

Judah Unfaithful

2:10 [l]1Co 8:6 [m]Ex 19:5 10Have we not all one Father[a]?[l] Did not one God create us? Why do we profane the covenant[m] of our
fathers by breaking faith with one another?
11Judah has broken faith. A detestable thing has been committed in Israel and in Jerusalem: Judah
2:11 [n]Ne 13:23 has desecrated the sanctuary the LORD loves by marrying[n] the daughter of a foreign god.[o] 12As for the
[o]Ezr 9:1; Jer 3:7-9 man who does this, whoever he may be, may the LORD cut him off[p] from the tents of Jacob[b]—even though
2:12 [p]Eze 24:21 [q]Mal 1:10 he brings offerings[q] to the LORD Almighty.
13Another thing you do: You flood the LORD's altar with tears. You weep and wail because he no lon-
2:13 [r]Jer 14:12 ger pays attention[r] to your offerings or accepts them with pleasure from your hands. 14You ask, "Why?"
2:14 [s]Pr 5:18 It is because the LORD is acting as the witness between you and the wife of your youth,[s] because you have
broken faith with her, though she is your partner, the wife of your marriage covenant.
2:15 [t]Ge 2:24; Mt 19:4-6 15Has not ⌞the LORD⌟ made them one?[t] In flesh and spirit they are his. And why one? Because he was
[u]1Co 7:14 seeking godly offspring.[c][u] So guard yourself in your spirit, and do not break faith with the wife of your
youth.
2:16 [v]Dt 24:1; Mt 5:31-32; 16"I hate divorce,[v]" says the LORD God of Israel, "and I hate a man's covering himself[d] with violence
19:4-9 as well as with his garment," says the LORD Almighty.
So guard yourself in your spirit, and do not break faith.

The Day of Judgment

2:17 [w]Isa 43:24 17You have wearied[w] the LORD with your words.
"How have we wearied him?" you ask.
By saying, "All who do evil are good in the eyes of the LORD, and he is pleased with them" or "Where
is the God of justice?"

3:1 [x]Isa 40:3; Mt 11:10*; 3 "See, I will send my messenger, who will prepare the way before me.[x] Then suddenly the Lord you
Mk 1:2*; Lk 7:27* are seeking will come to his temple; the messenger of the covenant, whom you desire, will come," says
the LORD Almighty.
3:2 [y]Eze 22:14; Rev 6:17 2But who can endure[y] the day of his coming? Who can stand when he appears? For he will be like a
[z]Zec 13:9; Mt 3:10-12 refiner's fire[z] or a launderer's soap. 3He will sit as a refiner and purifier of silver;[a] he will purify[b] the Le-
3:3 [a]Da 12:10 [b]Isa 1:25 vites and refine them like gold and silver. Then the LORD will have men who will bring offerings in righ-
3:4 [c]2Ch 7:12; Ps 51:19; teousness, 4and the offerings[c] of Judah and Jerusalem will be acceptable to the LORD, as in days gone by,
Mal 1:11 [d]2Ch 7:3 as in former years.[d]

[a] 10 Or *father* [b] 12 Or *12May the LORD cut off from the tents of Jacob anyone who gives testimony in behalf of the man who does this* [c] 15 Or *15But the one ⌞who is our father⌟ did not do this, not as long as life remained in him. And what was he seeking? An offspring from God* [d] 16 Or *his wife*

2:4 God's "covenant with Levi" refers to God's choice of the tribe of Levi for the priesthood (see Dt 21:5; see also "The Levites and the Priests" on p. 648).

2:6–7 Priests were responsible for teaching the Law of Moses to the people (see Lev 10:11) and for serving as God's messengers (see the note on Hag 1:13).

2:11 Marriages to foreign (pagan) women were strictly forbidden in the covenant law, not for ethnic or cultural reasons but because of the danger that they would lead to apostasy (see Ex 34:15–16; Dt 7:2–5; Jos 23:12–13).

2:14 From the earliest times (Ge 39:9), even outside the people of God (Ge 26:10), adultery was regarded as a serious sin. Along with other sexual offenses (e.g., Ge 34:7; Dt 22:21; Jdg 19:23; 2Sa 13:12), adultery was called an "outrageous thing" (Jer 29:23)—the Hebrew word being *nĕvālāh* ("wicked thing"); that is, behavior lacking moral principle or any recognition of proper obligation. Marriage is a covenant relationship; for this reason it imposes obligations not only on the partners but also on the community within which they have entered into their solemn, mutual vows. See "Marriage and Divorce in Ancient Israel" on page 1548.

3:2 The "day of his coming" refers to the day of the Lord (see the note on Joel 1:15).

"Launderer's soap," called "fuller's soap" in some versions, was an alkali prepared from the ashes of certain plants and used for cleansing and "fulling" (shrinking or thickening) new woolen cloth. The term is used figuratively here.

KEY VERSES IN THE PROPHETIC BOOKS

Book	Reference	Subject or Message
Isaiah	55:6–7	Seek the Lord
Jeremiah	31:31–33	New covenant
Lamentations	3:22–23	God's faithfulness
Ezekiel	36:22–23	Holiness of God
Daniel	4:34–35	Sovereignty of God
Hosea	10:1–2	Israel's faithlessness
Joel	2:28–32	Day of the Lord
Amos	5:14–15	Call to return
Obadiah	v. 15	God's judgment on nations
Jonah	3:10	God's mercy
Micah	3:8–12	Role of the prophet
Nahum	1:15	Future deliverance
Habakkuk	3:16–18	Submission to God's plan and timing
Zephaniah	3:11–13	Restoration of remnant
Haggai	1:8	Rebuild the temple
Zechariah	1:14–17	God's continued concern for Jerusalem
Malachi	3:1–3	Purification to come

Old Testament Today, p. 229

5 “So I will come near to you for judgment. I will be quick to testify against sorcerers, adulterers and
perjurers,[e] against those who defraud laborers of their wages,[f] who oppress the widows[g] and the father-
less, and deprive aliens of justice, but do not fear me,” says the LORD Almighty.

3:5 [e]Jer 7:9 [f]Lev 19:13; Jas 5:4 [g]Ex 22:22

Robbing God

6 “I the LORD do not change.[h] So you, O descendants of Jacob, are not destroyed. 7 Ever since the time
of your forefathers you have turned away[i] from my decrees and have not kept them. Return to me, and I
will return to you,”[j] says the LORD Almighty.
“But you ask, ‘How are we to return?’
8 “Will a man rob God? Yet you rob me.
“But you ask, ‘How do we rob you?’
“In tithes[k] and offerings. 9 You are under a curse—the whole nation of you—because you are rob-
bing me. 10 Bring the whole tithe into the storehouse,[l] that there may be food in my house. Test me in
this,” says the LORD Almighty, “and see if I will not throw open the floodgates[m] of heaven and pour out

3:6 [h]Nu 23:19; Jas 1:17 **3:7** [i]Jer 7:26; Ac 7:51 [j]Zec 1:3
3:8 [k]Ne 13:10-12
3:10 [l]Ne 13:12 [m]2Ki 7:2

3:5 Sorcerers were common in the ancient Near East (see “Akkadian Divination” on p. 277).

“Perjury” (or “perjurers”) is a word rarely found in our English Bible (but see also Jer 7:9; 1Ti 1:10). It is closely related to several other Biblical words, such as “oath” or “punishment.” For “oaths,” see Leviticus 19:12 and Ezekiel 16:59; see also “Oaths in Jewish and Christian Practice” on page 1988.

3:10 “Storehouse” refers to the treasury rooms of the temple, which were used to store provisions and valuable objects.

The Intertestamental Period

MALACHI 3 The **intertestamental period**[1] designates the time between Malachi (c. 400 B.C.), and the birth of Jesus. This was also part of the **Second Temple** period—the time between construction of the **postexilic** temple in 515 B.C. and destruction of the Herodian temple by the Romans in A.D. 70.[2]

Israel's historical experience changed rapidly during successive periods of Persian, Greek and Roman sovereignty. After defeating the **Babylonians**, the Persian king Cyrus II issued an edict in 538 B.C. allowing some Jews to return to Israel and authorizing temple reconstruction (Ezr 1:2–4).[3] Israel, a satrapy, or province, of the Persian Empire, was ruled by governors and priests. In 332 B.C. Alexander the Great overtook Judah. After his death in 323 B.C. his generals competed for control of the vast Greek Empire. Israel existed under Egyptian **Ptolemaic** sovereignty from 302 to 200 B.C. and under Syrian Seleucid control from 200 to 152 B.C.[4]

Antiochus III, the first **Seleucid** king, allowed Israel to live under the high priests' jurisdiction. Antiochus IV Epiphanes, however, sought to reorganize Jerusalem as a Greek city in 174 B.C. In 168 B.C., Antiochus IV issued an edict prohibiting Jewish observance of the Sabbath, circumcision, dietary laws and temple sacrifices (1Mc 1:41–64),[5] and he desecrated the temple by erecting an altar to Zeus (see Da 11:31).[6]

This edict incited the **Maccabean revolt**, which began in 167 B.C. when an aged priest, Mattathias, defied it by killing a Syrian official and a Jew who was preparing to sacrifice to Zeus. After Mattathias's death his five sons, and especially Judas Maccabeus, assumed leadership. The temple was cleansed and rededicated, an event still commemorated as Hanukkah. Maccabean success led Israel to independent statehood in 142 B.C. The Maccabean priest-kings (the **Hasmoneans**) ruled Israel from 163 to 142 B.C., until the Roman general Pompey incorporated Judea into the Roman Empire.[7]

The Romans conferred the status of client king (a king who rules in submission to a foreign ruler and with his support) to Herod the Great, who ruled from 37 to 4 B.C.[8] Herod's vast building programs and lavish expansion of the Jerusalem temple endeared him to some, although his willingness to slaughter all opposition sealed his memory as a cruel tyrant (Mt 2:1–20). His son Archelaus slaughtered 3,000 Jews during Passover. After his banishment in A.D. 6 Judea was reduced to a Roman province, governed by prefects and procurators from A.D. 6 to 66 (the most famous being Pontius Pilate).[9] The insensitivity of Roman leadership and the memory of Maccabean success led Judea to revolt. The four-year rebellion, though bitterly fought, ended with the destruction of the temple in A.D. 70.[10] A second revolt flared from 132 to 135 under Bar Kokhba and Rabbi Akiba. After massive losses on both sides, Jerusalem was converted into a pagan city, Aelia Capitolina, to which Jews were denied access.

Macherus: a site occupied by Jews during the Hasmonean period, rebuilt as an outpost by Herod the Great against Nabatea and occupied by Jews in their war against the Romans until A.D. 72

Photograph: © Todd Bolen/Bible Places.com

The intertestamental period brought significant religious developments, attesting to the developing diversity within Judaism and providing the context for the New Testament:

- The closure of the Hebrew Scripture gave the Jews an authoritative canon.[11]
- The translation of the Old Testament into Greek (the **Septuagint**) produced a Bible that would supply the linguistic background for many New Testament concepts.[12]
- The progression of foreign nations ruling the Jewish homeland recalled Daniel's prophecies and heightened Messianic expectation.
- Israel's tumultuous leadership changes contributed to the formation of diverse sects, including the Pharisees, Sadducees, Essenes, Samaritans, Zealots and Messianic pretenders.[13]
- The literary efforts of Palestinian and Babylonian Jews, together with those of Hellenistic Jewish communities, created a large corpus of writings, including the **Dead Sea Scrolls**,[14] the works of Philo and Josephus,[15] the **Apocrypha**,[16] the **pseudepigrapha** and the earliest rabbinic sayings.

[1]See Glossary on page 2080 for definitions of bolded words. [2]See "Herod's Temple" on page 1648. [3]See "Cyrus the Great" on page 669. [4]See "The Ptolemies" on page 1399 and "The Seleucids" on page 1408. [5]First Maccabees is an Apocryphal book (see Glossary on p. 2080). [6]See "Antiochus IV Epiphanes" on page 1406. [7]See "The Roman Empire" on page 1845. [8]See "Herod the Great" on page 1627. [9]See "Pontius Pilate" on page 1714. [10]See "Josephus and the Fall of Jerusalem" on page 1606. [11]See "The Old Testament Canon" on page 1552. [12]See "The Ancient Translations" on page 1492. [13]See "The Pharisees" on page 1566, "The Sadducees" on page 1600, "The Zealots and the Essenes" on page 1576 and "The Samaritans" on page 1737. [14]See, for example, "The Great Isaiah Scroll" on page 1115 and "The Temple Scroll" on page 1371. [15]See "Historians in the Ancient World" on page 939. [16]See "The Apocrypha" on page 1973.

THE OLD TESTAMENT CANON

MALACHI 4 Canon (from Greek *kanon*: "rule; standard of measure") refers to writings that are authoritative for faith and religious practice by virtue of their divine inspiration. Secondarily, it designates a listing of such authoritative books.

Canonical writings were known in the ancient Near East in extrabiblical contexts. The Pyramid Texts profess to incorporate direct quotations from Egyptian gods. **Mesopotamian** seers recorded revelations they claimed to have received from the gods in dreams and visions. These compositions were deposited in temples to be preserved by priests. Important religious and secular documents were copied with meticulous care and often contained curses against anyone who would alter their contents. In particular, treaties were preserved in duplicate, with a copy deposited in the temple of each king, to be carefully guarded and periodically reread.

These practices find parallels in the treatment of Biblical writings. As a covenant or treaty document,[1] early Mosaic legislation was preserved in the ark of the covenant (Dt 31:9),[2] first within the tabernacle and later in the temple; faithfully copied without alteration (Dt 4:2; 12:32); and publicly read every seven years (Dt 31:10–13).

The author of a canonical writing was to be an Israelite prophet who spoke in the Lord's name. Fulfillment of short-range prophecies authenticated the prophet in the eyes of his countrymen (e.g., Jer 28:15–17), after which his prophetic messages were to be held in reverence and obeyed.

The intrinsic authority of canonical books was recognized from the date of their composition, with later prophets at times citing the works of their predecessors as authoritative Scripture (e.g., Jer 26:18 cites Mic 3:12, and Da 9:2 refers to Jer 25:11–12). Rabbinical writings and the ancient Jewish historian Josephus[3] bear witness that prophetic authorship was essential for a book to be included in the canon. The closing of the Old Testament canon coincided with the cessation of this prophetic activity.

Early witnesses number the books of the Old Testament canon at 24. This total actually corresponds to our 39 books, with the 12 minor prophets counted as one book and the books of Samuel, Kings, Chronicles and Ezra–Nehemiah as one apiece. Some lists join Lamentations to Jeremiah and Ruth to Judges in order to force the total to correspond to the 22 letters of the Hebrew alphabet. All told, these books were often referred to under three different categories: the Law, the Prophets and the Writings. The 39 books of our Old Testament already appear as such in the **Septuagint**,[4] and fragments of all of them except for Esther[5] have been found among the **Dead Sea Scrolls** (dated 150 B.C.–A.D. 150). Jesus and the apostles acknowledged the same canon by their Old Testament quotations and use of such phrases as "the Law and the Prophets."

The status of some books was debated by Jewish scholars at Jamnia in A.D. 90—under the assumption that they were already accepted as canonical. The deliberations resolved difficulties of interpretation in light of other canonical books, such as apparent contradictions (e.g., the differences between Eze 40–48 and Lev), apparent skepticism (in Ecc), eroticism (in SS), and the lack of any direct reference to God (in Est).

Qumran jars containing ancient manuscripts
Preserving Bible Times; © Dr. James C. Martin

Some scholars argue that the Jewish canon of Alexandria, Egypt, included **Apocryphal** books.[6] However, Philo of Alexandria (c. 20 B.C.–A.D. 50) never alluded to any of them as Scripture, and many early church fathers (e.g., Origen, Athanasius, Chrysostom and Jerome) were either openly uncomfortable treating them as canonical or only rarely quoted them. The earliest manuscripts of the Septuagint (fourth–fifth centuries A.D.) include some of the Apocryphal books, probably as supplementary religious literature, but the list does not correspond to the 14 Apocryphal books designated as such at the Council of Trent in 1546. Many additional noncanonical works were cited by Jews in pre-Christian times, as is evident from the large amount of religious literature discovered at **Qumran**. But the 39 Old Testament canonical books correspond to those Israel has regarded as Scripture from ancient times.[7]

[1]See "Deuteronomy and the Covenant Treaty Form" on page 255. [2]See "The Tabernacle and the Ark" on page 153. [3]See "Historians in the Ancient World" on page 939. [4]See "The Ancient Translations" at on page 1492. [5]See "The Canonicity of Esther" on page 730. [6]See "The Apocrypha" on page 1973. [7]See also "The Old Testament of the Early Church" on page 1967 and "The New Testament Canon" on page 2022.

so much blessing that you will not have room enough for it. [11]I will prevent pests from devouring your
crops, and the vines in your fields will not cast their fruit," says the LORD Almighty. [12]"Then all the na-
3:12 [n]Isa 61:9 tions will call you blessed,[n] for yours will be a delightful land,"[o] says the LORD Almighty.
[o]Isa 62:4 3:13 [p]Mal 2:17 [13]"You have said harsh things[p] against me," says the LORD.
"Yet you ask, 'What have we said against you?'
3:14 [q]Ps 73:13 [14]"You have said, 'It is futile[q] to serve God. What did we gain by carrying out his requirements and go-
[r]Isa 58:3 ing about like mourners[r] before the LORD Almighty? [15]But now we call the arrogant blessed. Certainly
3:15 [s]Jer 7:10 the evildoers[s] prosper, and even those who challenge God escape.' "
3:16 [t]Ps 34:15 [16]Then those who feared the LORD talked with each other, and the LORD listened and heard.[t] A scroll[u]
[u]Ps 56:8 of remembrance was written in his presence concerning those who feared the LORD and honored his
name.
3:17 [v]Dt 7:6 [17]"They will be mine," says the LORD Almighty, "in the day when I make up my treasured possession.[a][v]
[w]Ps 103:13; Isa 26:20 I will spare[w] them, just as in compassion a man spares his son who serves him. [18]And you will again see
3:18 [x]Ge 18:25 the distinction between the righteous[x] and the wicked, between those who serve God and those who do
not.

The Day of the LORD

4:1 [y]Joel 2:31 **4** "Surely the day is coming;[y] it will burn like a furnace. All the arrogant and every evildoer will be
[z]Isa 5:24; Ob 1:18 stubble,[z] and that day that is coming will set them on fire," says the LORD Almighty. "Not a root or a
4:2 [a]Lk 1:78; Eph 5:14 branch will be left to them. [2]But for you who revere my name, the sun of righteousness[a] will rise with
[b]Isa 30:26 healing[b] in its wings. And you will go out and leap[c] like calves released from the stall. [3]Then you will
[c]Isa 35:6 4:3 [d]Job 40:12 trample[d] down the wicked; they will be ashes[e] under the soles of your feet on the day when I do these
[e]Eze 28:18 things," says the LORD Almighty.
4:4 [f]Ps 147:19 [4]"Remember the law[f] of my servant Moses, the decrees and laws I gave him at Horeb for all Israel.
4:5 [g]Mt 11:14; Lk 1:17 [5]"See, I will send you the prophet Elijah[g] before that great and dreadful day of the LORD comes.[h] [6]He
[h]Joel 2:31 4:6 [i]Lk 1:17 will turn the hearts of the fathers to their children,[i] and the hearts of the children to their fathers; or else
[j]Isa 11:4; Rev 19:15 I will come and strike[j] the land with a curse."[k]
[k]Zec 5:3

[a] 17 Or *Almighty, "my treasured possession, in the day when I act*

4:1 For "the day," see the note on Joel 1:15.
4:3 See "The Winepress" on page 1171.
4:4 "Horeb" is Mount Sinai (see "The Location of Mount Sinai" on p. 123).

THE New Testament

INTRODUCTION TO 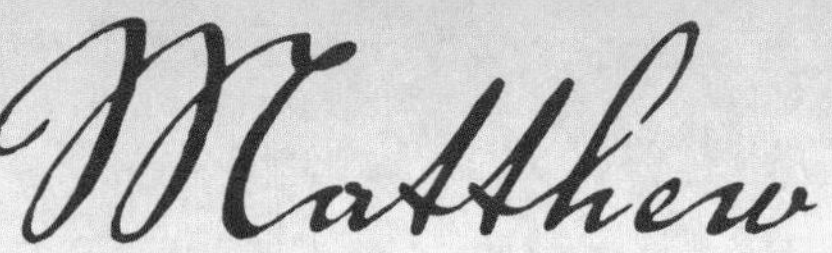

AUTHOR, PLACE AND DATE OF WRITING

Tradition associates this Gospel with the apostle Matthew, although intense debate has swirled around a statement from the early church father Papias (c. 130) that survives only in Eusebius (*Ecclesiastical History*, 3.39.16). It is usually translated (in part), "Matthew collected the oracles (*logia*) in the Hebrew language (*Hebraidi dialekto*)." For generations most scholars interpreted Papias as claiming that Matthew had composed in Hebrew a Gospel that was for the most part a record of Jesus' sayings or "oracles." The present Gospel of Matthew (written in Greek) was supposedly an expanded translation of this Hebrew text. Some have even associated Matthew with the hypothetical document Q (see "The Synoptic Problem and 'Q'" on p. 1685).

More recent investigation, however, has shown that this view is probably mistaken. *Logia* probably means a "Gospel," while *Hebraidi dialekto* likely signifies "in a Jewish style," not "in the Hebrew language."

There has also been much debate regarding the dating of Matthew's Gospel. Many think it was written between A.D. 70 and 80, although some suggest a much earlier date (in the 50s or 60s). The Jewish nature of Matthew's Gospel may suggest that it was written in the Holy Land, though many suggest an origination in Syrian Antioch.

AUDIENCE

Matthew's original readers were predominately Jews who already believed in Jesus and confessed him as the Son of God (14:33; 16:16; 27:54).

CULTURAL FACTS AND HIGHLIGHTS

Matthew's purpose was to prove to a Jewish audience that Jesus is the Messiah: (1) He emphasized Jesus' fulfillment of Old Testament prophecy (e.g., 1:22–23; 2:15); (2) used typical Jewish terminology, such as "kingdom of heaven"; (3) told the story of Jesus as a retelling of the story of Israel (e.g., Jesus came out of Egypt—analogous to the exodus; passed through the Jordan—analogous to the Red Sea; suffered in the wilderness—analogous to the wilderness wandering; gave his law on a mountain—analogous to Sinai; and so forth); and (4) traced Jesus' ancestry to Abraham and frequently referred to the Messianic title "Son of David" instead of to "Son of God" (as in the Gospel of John).

TIMELINE

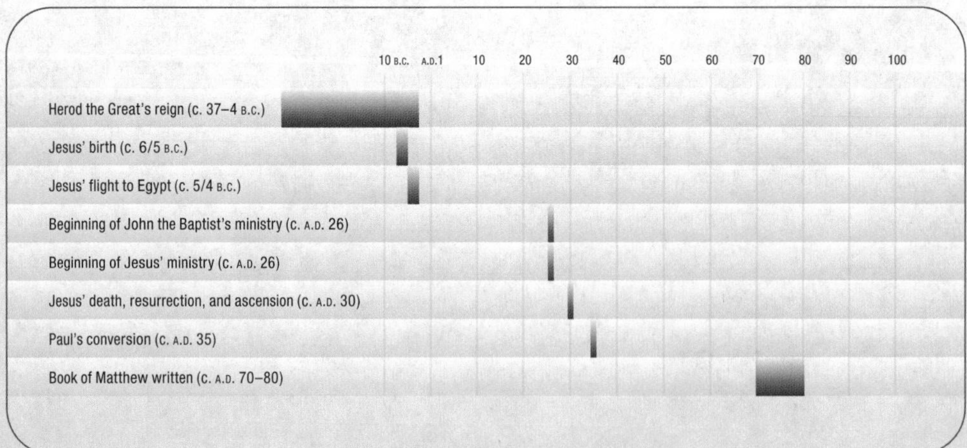

AS YOU READ

Notice Matthew's systematic, yet artistic, style. He did not tell Jesus' story in strict chronological sequence but grouped facts topically. Watch for the many references to the "kingdom of heaven," and note Jesus' teachings about what it means to be a citizen of that kingdom.

DID YOU KNOW?

- There were no sexual relations during a Jewish betrothal period, yet it was a much more binding relationship than a modern engagement—breakable only by divorce (1:18).
- No one living in the desert hesitated to eat insects, and locusts were among the ceremonially clean foods of which the Jews were free to partake (3:4).
- Most of the salt used in Israel came from the Dead Sea and was full of impurities, causing it to lose some of its flavor (5:13).
- People in ancient times commonly hid valuables in fields (e.g., when a marauding army approached), since there were no banks (13:44).
- A person who stepped on a grave became ceremonially unclean, so graves were whitewashed to make them easily visible, especially at night (23:27).

THEMES

Matthew's themes include:

1. *Jesus, the Messiah.* Matthew clearly taught that Jesus was the fulfillment of Old Testament promises, especially that of the coming Messiah (King).

2. *Righteousness.* Citizens of the kingdom of heaven are called to be righteous, and ethical issues are a major focus in Matthew. Jesus' first recorded words in Matthew had to do with fulfilling righteousness (3:15), and he demanded that his disciples invest their treasures in God's kingdom, not in earthly possessions. Love for others is also emphasized.

3. *The believer's commission.* In its closing verses (28:16–20) Matthew reveals the plan for the expansion of the kingdom of heaven. Believers are to be "salt" and "light" (5:13–16), spreading the Good News of the kingdom to all the world.

OUTLINE

- I. Jesus' Childhood (1–2)
- II. The Beginnings of Jesus' Ministry (3:1—4:11)
  - A. John the Baptist (3)
  - B. The Temptation (4:1–11)
- III. Jesus' Ministry in Galilee (4:12—14:12)
  - A. His Early Ministry (4:12–25)
  - B. The Sermon on the Mount (5–7)
  - C. Miracles (8–9)
  - D. Ministry (10:1—14:12)
- IV. Ministry in Other Areas (14:13—17:21)
- V. Jesus Returns to Galilee (17:22—18:35)
- VI. Jesus' Ministry in Judea and Perea (19–20)
- VII. Passion Week (21–27)
  - A. The Triumphal Entry (21:1–11)
  - B. The Cleansing of the Temple (21:12–17)
  - C. Questions From the Jewish Leaders (21:18—23:39)
  - D. The Olivet Discourse (24–25)
  - E. The Anointing of Jesus' Feet (26:1–13)
  - F. The Arrest, Trials and Death of Jesus (26:14—27:66)
- VIII. The Resurrection (28)

The Genealogy of Jesus

1 A record of the genealogy of Jesus Christ the son of David,[a] the son of Abraham:[b]

[2] Abraham was the father of Isaac,[c]
Isaac the father of Jacob,[d]
Jacob the father of Judah and his brothers,[e]
[3] Judah the father of Perez and Zerah, whose mother was Tamar,[f]
Perez the father of Hezron,
Hezron the father of Ram,
[4] Ram the father of Amminadab,
Amminadab the father of Nahshon,
Nahshon the father of Salmon,
[5] Salmon the father of Boaz, whose mother was Rahab,
Boaz the father of Obed, whose mother was Ruth,
Obed the father of Jesse,
[6] and Jesse the father of King David.[g]

David was the father of Solomon, whose mother had been Uriah's wife,[h]
[7] Solomon the father of Rehoboam,
Rehoboam the father of Abijah,
Abijah the father of Asa,
[8] Asa the father of Jehoshaphat,
Jehoshaphat the father of Jehoram,
Jehoram the father of Uzziah,
[9] Uzziah the father of Jotham,
Jotham the father of Ahaz,
Ahaz the father of Hezekiah,
[10] Hezekiah the father of Manasseh,[i]
Manasseh the father of Amon,
Amon the father of Josiah,
[11] and Josiah the father of Jeconiah[a] and his brothers at the time of the exile to Babylon.[j]

[12] After the exile to Babylon:
Jeconiah was the father of Shealtiel,[k]
Shealtiel the father of Zerubbabel,[l]
[13] Zerubbabel the father of Abiud,
Abiud the father of Eliakim,
Eliakim the father of Azor,
[14] Azor the father of Zadok,
Zadok the father of Akim,
Akim the father of Eliud,
[15] Eliud the father of Eleazar,
Eleazar the father of Matthan,
Matthan the father of Jacob,
[16] and Jacob the father of Joseph, the husband of Mary,[m] of whom was born Jesus, who is called Christ.[n]

[17] Thus there were fourteen generations in all from Abraham to David, fourteen from David to the exile to Babylon, and fourteen from the exile to the Christ.[b]

1:1 [a]2Sa 7:12-16; Isa 9:6,7; 11:1; Jer 23:5,6; Mt 9:27; Lk 1:32, 69; Ro 1:3; Rev 22:16 [b]Ge 22:18; Gal 3:16
1:2 [c]Ge 21:3,12 [d]Ge 25:26 [e]Ge 29:35
1:3 [f]Ge 38:27-30
1:6 [g]1Sa 16:1; 17:12 [h]2Sa 12:24
1:10 [i]2Ki 20:21
1:11 [j]2Ki 24:14-16; Jer 27:20; Da 1:1,2
1:12 [k]1Ch 3:17 [l]1Ch 3:19; Ezr 3:2
1:16 [m]Lk 1:27 [n]Mt 27:17

[a] *11* That is, Jehoiachin; also in verse 12 [b] *17* Or *Messiah.* "The Christ" (Greek) and "the Messiah" (Hebrew) both mean "the Anointed One."

1:1 The Hebrews kept extensive records of a family's ancestry (cf. 1Ch 1–9). These were used for practical and legal purposes: to establish a person's heritage, inheritance, legitimacy and rights (see "Genealogies in Ancient Israel" on p. 1559). Luke followed the traditional approach of tracing lineage through males (Lk 3:23–38), but Matthew included five women (Bathsheba is not named but is described), three of whom were outsiders to Israel.
1:17 In the New Testament the word "generation" translates four Greek words, all having reference to descent: (1) *genea,* most frequently found in the Synoptic (or parallel) Gospels (Matthew, Mark

Genealogies in Ancient Israel

MATTHEW 1 In societies organized around kinship, genealogies (lists of names tracing the ancestry of a given individual or group) serve as public records that document history, establish identity and/or legitimate office. The key to legitimacy and identity is a direct, irrefutable familial tie with the past. Such lists may *ascend* from the individual, using the formula "*x* the son of *y*, the son of *z* . . ." (1Ch 6:33–43; Ezr 7:1–5; Lk 3:23–38) or *descend* from a common ancestor, using the pattern "*x* was the father of *y*, *y* the father of *z* . . ." (Ge 5:1–32; Ru 4:18–23; Mt 1:1–17). These two basic types of genealogies can be combined (cf. v. 1 and vv. 2–17). In addition, genealogical rolls may either contain a simple succession of names or may be supplemented with expansive content pertaining to the deeds of certain prominent individuals on the list.[1]

Genealogies feature prominently in both the early and later history of Israel. There are ten principal genealogical lists in Genesis alone, (e.g., "the written account of Adam's line" in Ge 5). These records served to establish and protect identity in that they regulated a variety of social interactions, including marriage and land inheritance (Dt 25:5–10; Ezr 10:18–43).[2] Thus the registration of families who had returned from exile was a profound concern during the **postexilic period**[3] (1Ch 1–9; Ezr 8:2–14; Ne 7:7–63).[4] Genealogies were especially important in ancient Israel because the right to hold important offices was a hereditary privilege. For example, the priesthood was assured to the sons of Levi (Ex 6:16–26; Nu 3:10; 1Ch 6:1–53),[5] while kingship was reserved for the descendants of Judah (Ge 49:10) and more specifically for the son of David (2Sa 7:12–16; Ps 89:29; Isa 9:7; 11:1–3).

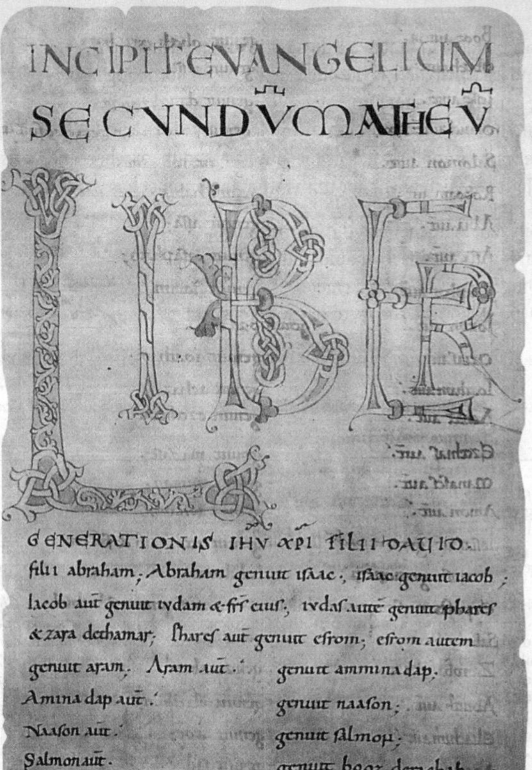
INCIPIT EVANGELIUM
SECUNDUM MATHEV
LIBER
GENERATIONIS IHU XPI FILII DAUID.
filii abraham; Abraham genuit isaac; isaac genuit iacob;
Iacob aut genuit iudam & frs eius; iudas autem genuit phares
& zara de thamar; Phares aut genuit esrom; esrom autem
genuit aram; Aram aut. genuit amminadap.
Amina dap aut. genuit naason;
Naason aut. genuit salmon;
Salmon aut. genuit booz de rachab.

The opening of the Gospel of Matthew in the Liesborn Gospels; Germany, tenth century A.D.

© The Schøyen Collection; photography courtesy of Mr. Martin Schøyen

In the New Testament era certain genealogical records were stored in a public archive in the temple mount, while others were maintained by private families. Early Christian preaching radically redefined genealogical descent by considering all who identified with Jesus as true, legal descendants of Abraham, "heirs according to the promise" (Gal 3:29; cf. Mt 3:9; Jn 8:33,39; Ro 4:16).[6]

The New Testament preserves two pertinent genealogical lists, both of which present the human ancestry of Jesus as the son of David (Mt 1:1–17; Lk 3:23–38). The two listings are different, and the reasons for this variation have been extensively debated. It may be that the register in Luke preserves the *biological* family tree of Joseph, while that in Matthew records the *legal* line of descent that authenticated Joseph's (and Jesus') claim to David's throne. Others suggest that the genealogy in Matthew is Joseph's, while the one in Luke is Mary's.

[1]See also "The Sumerian King List" on page 12. [2]See also "The Rights of the Firstborn" on page 43 and "Levirate Marriage" on page 64. [3]See Glossary on page 2080 for definitions of bolded words. [4]See "The Postexilic Period of the Old Testament: The Persian Period" on page 699. [5]See "The Levites and the Priests" on page 648. [6]See "Adoption in the Roman World" on page 1849.

The Birth of Jesus Christ

18 This is how the birth of Jesus Christ came about: His mother Mary was pledged to be married to Jo-
seph, but before they came together, she was found to be with child through the Holy Spirit.[o] 19 Because **1:18** [o]Lk 1:35
Joseph her husband was a righteous man and did not want to expose her to public disgrace, he had in
mind to divorce[p] her quietly. **1:19** [p]Dt 24:1
20 But after he had considered this, an angel of the Lord appeared to him in a dream and said, "Joseph
son of David, do not be afraid to take Mary home as your wife, because what is conceived in her is from
the Holy Spirit. 21 She will give birth to a son, and you are to give him the name Jesus,[a][q] because he will **1:21** [q]Lk 1:31
save his people from their sins."[r] [r]Lk 2:11; Ac 5:31; 13:23,28
22 All this took place to fulfill what the Lord had said through the prophet: 23 "The virgin will be with
child and will give birth to a son, and they will call him Immanuel"[b][s]—which means, "God with us." **1:23** [s]Isa 7:14; 8:8,10
24 When Joseph woke up, he did what the angel of the Lord had commanded him and took Mary home
as his wife. 25 But he had no union with her until she gave birth to a son. And he gave him the name Jesus.[t] **1:25** [t]ver 21

The Visit of the Magi

2 After Jesus was born in Bethlehem in Judea,[u] during the time of King Herod,[v] Magi[c] from the east **2:1** [u]Lk 2:4-7 [v]Lk 1:5
came to Jerusalem 2 and asked, "Where is the one who has been born king of the Jews?[w] We saw his **2:2** [w]Jer 23:5; Mt 27:11; Mk 15:2; Jn 1:49; 18:33-37
star[x] in the east[d] and have come to worship him." [x]Nu 24:17
3 When King Herod heard this he was disturbed, and all Jerusalem with him. 4 When he had called to-
gether all the people's chief priests and teachers of the law, he asked them where the Christ[e] was to be
born. 5 "In Bethlehem[y] in Judea," they replied, "for this is what the prophet has written: **2:5** [y]Jn 7:42

6 " 'But you, Bethlehem, in the land of Judah,
are by no means least among the rulers of Judah;
for out of you will come a ruler
who will be the shepherd of my people Israel.'[f]"[z] **2:6** [z]2Sa 5:2; Mic 5:2

7 Then Herod called the Magi secretly and found out from them the exact time the star had appeared.

[a] *21 Jesus* is the Greek form of *Joshua,* which means *the LORD saves.* [b] *23* Isaiah 7:14 [c] *1* Traditionally *Wise Men*
[d] *2* Or *star when it rose* [e] *4* Or *Messiah* [f] *6* Micah 5:2

---

and Luke), signifying the lines of descent from an ancestor (e.g., this v.); all the people living in a given period (e.g., 11:16); a class of people characterized by a certain quality (e.g., 12:39); or a period of time (Ac 13:36; Col 1:26); (2) *genesis,* in Matthew 1:1, in a heading to verses 2:17, used to mean "genealogy;" (3) *gennçma,* in the phrase "brood of vipers" (3:7; 12:34; 23:33; Lk 3:7); and (4) *genos,* meaning "race" (1Pe 2:9; KJV "generation").

1:18 There were no sexual relations during a Jewish betrothal period, but this was a much more binding relationship than a modern engagement—breakable only by divorce. Verse 20 makes it clear that Mary and Joseph were legally bound to each other, though not yet living together as husband and wife. See "Marriage and Divorce in Ancient Israel" on page 1548.

1:19 In Deuteronomy 22:24 a betrothed woman is called a "wife," although the preceding verse speaks of her as being "a virgin pledged to be married." During the betrothal period, sexual unfaithfulness was considered adultery, the penalty for which was death by stoning (Lev 20:10; Dt 22:23–24). Joseph planned to have a private divorce—the only choice that would have allowed him to maintain his personal righteousness according to the Law of Moses and yet save Mary from public disgrace and possible death.

1:20 See "Dream Oracles in the Ancient World" on page 741.

1:21 For Jesus as Savior, see the note on Luke 2:11.

2:1–12 The word *epiphany,* which is not found in the Bible itself, comes from a Greek term meaning "manifestation." The word originally marked a feast to celebrate the baptism of Jesus (3:16–17)—and still does so in the churches of Eastern Orthodoxy. The Lord had similarly "revealed his glory" at his first miracle in Cana of Galilee (Jn 2:11). From the fourth century, however, Epiphany has been linked with Christ's manifestation of himself to the Magi, the first Gentiles who believed in him (Mt 2:1–12). In England it has become customary for the monarch to offer gold, myrrh and frankincense in the Chapel Royal every year on January 6, the day the feast is observed.

2:1 Bethlehem, a village about 5 miles (8 km) south of Jerusalem (see "Bethlehem" on p. 1487 and "The Birthplace of Jesus" on p. 1668), is called "Bethlehem in Judea" to distinguish it from the town of Bethlehem about 7 miles (11.3 km) northwest of Nazareth.

Originally a religious caste among the Persians, Magi were devoted to astrology, divination and the interpretation of dreams. This led to an extension in the meaning of the word, and by the first century B.C. the terms *magi* and *Chaldean* were applied generally to fortune tellers and to the exponents of esoteric religious cults throughout the Mediterranean world. "Magus" or "sorcerer" is the name given to Simon in Acts 8:9, to Bar-Jesus in Acts 13:6 and to Elymas in Acts 13:8. The legend of "the Three Kings" is late and medieval.

The Magi were likely from Persia or southern Arabia, both of which lay east of the Holy Land. Herod (see "Herod the Great" on p. 1627) was "disturbed" (v. 3) by the Magi's announcement because he knew he was not the rightful heir to Israel's throne, having usurped power by aligning himself with Rome. The Magi's visit likely caused him to fear that invading forces from the east might join others within Israel to replace him with a king from the true line of the anticipated Messiah. The religious leaders had aligned themselves politically with Herod. If his power base were threatened, so was theirs.

2:2 The "star" was probably not an ordinary star, planet or comet, though some interpreters have identified it with the conjunction of Jupiter and Saturn or with some other astronomical phenomenon.

2:4 The chief priests were in charge of worship in the temple in Jerusalem. They included the ruling high priest, Caiaphas; the former high priest, Annas; and the high priestly families, all of whom were included in the Sanhedrin—the ruling Jewish council (see "The Sanhedrin" on p. 1821).

The teachers of the law were Jewish scholars of the day, professionally trained in the development, teaching and application of Old Testament law. Their authority was strictly human and traditional. They too were members of the Sanhedrin.

8 He sent them to Bethlehem and said, "Go and make a careful search for the child. As soon as you find
him, report to me, so that I too may go and worship him."
9 After they had heard the king, they went on their way, and the star they had seen in the east[a] went
ahead of them until it stopped over the place where the child was. 10 When they saw the star, they were
overjoyed. 11 On coming to the house, they saw the child with his mother Mary, and they bowed down
2:11 [a]Isa 60:3 and worshiped him.[a] Then they opened their treasures and presented him with gifts[b] of gold and of in-
[b]Ps 72:10 2:12 [c]Heb 11:7 cense and of myrrh. 12 And having been warned[c] in a dream[d] not to go back to Herod, they returned to
[d]ver 13,19,22; Mt 27:19 their country by another route.

The Escape to Egypt

2:13 [e]Ac 5:19 [f]ver 12,19,22 13 When they had gone, an angel[e] of the Lord appeared to Joseph in a dream.[f] "Get up," he said, "take
the child and his mother and escape to Egypt. Stay there until I tell you, for Herod is going to search for
the child to kill him."
14 So he got up, took the child and his mother during the night and left for Egypt, 15 where he stayed
until the death of Herod. And so was fulfilled what the Lord had said through the prophet: "Out of Egypt
2:15 [g]Ex 4:22,23; Hos 11:1 I called my son."[b][g]
16 When Herod realized that he had been outwitted by the Magi, he was furious, and he gave orders to
kill all the boys in Bethlehem and its vicinity who were two years old and under, in accordance with the
time he had learned from the Magi. 17 Then what was said through the prophet Jeremiah was fulfilled:

18 "A voice is heard in Ramah,
weeping and great mourning,
Rachel weeping for her children
and refusing to be comforted,
2:18 [h]Jer 31:15 because they are no more."[c][h]

The Return to Nazareth

2:19 [i]ver 12,13, 22 19 After Herod died, an angel of the Lord appeared in a dream[i] to Joseph in Egypt 20 and said, "Get up,
take the child and his mother and go to the land of Israel, for those who were trying to take the child's
life are dead."
21 So he got up, took the child and his mother and went to the land of Israel. 22 But when he heard that
Archelaus was reigning in Judea in place of his father Herod, he was afraid to go there. Having been
2:22 [j]ver 12,13, 19; Mt 27:19 warned in a dream,[j] he withdrew to the district of Galilee,[k] 23 and he went and lived in a town called Naz-
[k]Lk 2:39 2:23 [l]Lk 1:26; Jn 1:45,46 areth.[l] So was fulfilled[m] what was said through the prophets: "He will be called a Nazarene."[n]
[m]Mt 1:22 [n]Mk 1:24

John the Baptist Prepares the Way

3:1 [o]Lk 1:13,57-66; 3:2-19 3 In those days John the Baptist[o] came, preaching in the Desert of Judea 2 and saying, "Repent, for the
3:2 [p]Da 2:44; Mt 4:17; 6:10; Lk 11:20; 21:31; Jn 3:3,5; Ac 1:3,6 kingdom of heaven[p] is near." 3 This is he who was spoken of through the prophet Isaiah:

"A voice of one calling in the desert,
'Prepare the way for the Lord,
3:3 [q]Isa 40:3; Mal 3:1; Lk 1:76; Jn 1:23 make straight paths for him.' "[d][q]

[a] 9 Or *seen when it rose* [b] 15 Hosea 11:1 [c] 18 Jer. 31:15 [d] 3 Isaiah 40:3

2:11 The Magi's gifts (gold, incense and myrrh) were the most valuable, transportable and marketable items of the day, ideal for sustaining Mary and Joseph in another country (v. 14). Myrrh is probably to be identified with labdanum, an aromatic gum exuded from the leaves of the cistus rose. Its oil was used in beauty treatments and was sometimes mixed with wine and drunk to relieve pain. (See "Incense" on p. 1209.)
2:12 See "Dream Oracles in the Ancient World" on page 741.
2:16 The number killed has often been exaggerated as being in the thousands. In so small a village as Bethlehem, the actual number was probably not large—although the act was no less brutal.
2:22 Archelaus, one of the sons of Herod the Great, ruled over Judea and Samaria for only 10 years (4 B.C.–A.D. 6). Unusually cruel and tyrannical, he was deposed, after which Judea became a Roman province, administered by governors appointed by the emperor. See "The Postexilic Period of the Old Testament: the Roman and Herodian Periods" on page 701, "Herod's Successors and Uneasy Relations Between Rome and the Jews" on page 1631 and "The Roman Governor" on page 1824.
2:23 The word "Nazarene" was derived from Nazareth, the hometown of Jesus, who was often called a Nazarene. Used by his disciples and associates, the term had a friendly meaning (Ac 2:22; 3:6; 10:38). Jesus, in fact, applied it to himself (Ac 22:8). On the lips of his enemies, however, it was a title of scorn (Mt 26:71; Mk 14:67). It is not altogether certain what Matthew intended here. It is generally thought that he was referring to Isaiah 11:1, where the Messiah is called a *netser*, or shoot, out of the root of Jesse. The name Nazareth may be derived from the same word. Matthew saw a fulfillment of Isaiah's prophecy in Jesus' parents' taking up their residence in Nazareth. See "Nazareth" on page 1623.
3:1 The desert of Judea was an area that stretched some 20 miles (32 km) from the Jerusalem-Bethlehem plateau down to the Jordan River and the Dead Sea—perhaps the same region where John the Baptist lived (cf. Lk 1:80). The community of Qumran lived in this area too (see "Qumran and the New Testament" on p. 1679 and "Biblical Interpretation at Qumran and Among the Early Rabbis" on p. 1603).

Baptism in the Ancient World

MATTHEW 3 Ritual immersion in water, or baptism, represented a powerful and frequently used religious symbol in ancient Judaism.[1] This sacramental ceremony was enacted to symbolize purification and the removal of sin or was sometimes used as an initiation rite to consecrate a change of status or a conversion.

✣ In the Old Testament, rites of immersion were associated with maintaining ritual purity, especially for priests (Lev 15; 16:4,24).[2]

✣ During the New Testament period, water itself and immersion in water functioned as the primary means by which ritual impurity was removed within Pharisaic Judaism (Mt 15:2; Jn 2:6).[3]

✣ Baptism was practiced by the Essene community at **Qumran** as a symbolic act by which one was "made holy by the waters of repentance" (1QS 3:9).[4]

✣ During the first century A.D. certain groups within Judaism began to practice proselyte baptism, a rite that required converts, in addition to male circumcision, to undergo immersion in a ritual bath prior to their full reception into the community.[5]

✣ Purification through immersion in ritual baths was required for all Jews in order to preserve that state of purity without which they could neither enter the temple nor participate in its services during major festivals (Nu 9:10; Jn 11:55; Ac 21:24–27; Josephus, *Wars*, 1.11.6).[6]

✣ A number of Jewish ritual baths, or *miqvaot* (singular *miqveh*), have been excavated in Jerusalem, Jericho and elsewhere. By rabbinical law these had to hold at least 60 gallons (227 l) of water and be deep enough to completely immerse the body.

Within emerging Christianity the rite of baptism acquired fundamental importance. Baptism in water defined the central symbolic act required by John in the course of his preparatory preaching in the wilderness (Mt 3; Mk 1:4). It is precisely this act for which he was divinely commissioned and later received the epithet "the Baptist" (Mt 3:1; Josephus, *Antiquities*, 18.5.2). John summoned his hearers to be baptized in light of the imminent advent of God's judgment upon the earth (Mt 3:5–6; Lk 3:17). His baptism thus evoked prophetic images of cleansing with water for forgiveness, purification and the repentance that would characterize the Messianic age (Jer 31; Eze 36:25; Zec 13:1).

The Gospels present the baptism of John as a necessary precursor to the public ministry of Jesus, who would baptize "with the Holy Spirit and with fire" (Mt 3:11; see Mk 1:8; Jn 1:31). The risen Jesus sanctioned this sacramental act as an important aspect of conversion, requiring baptism "in the name of the Father and of the Son and of the Holy Spirit" (Mt 28:19). Other New Testament texts record slight variations in the wording of the baptismal formula, such as "in the name of Jesus Christ" (Ac 2:38; 10:48), "into the name of the Lord Jesus" (Ac 8:16; 19:5) or simply "into Christ" (Gal 3:27). The place of baptism within early Christianity occasioned sustained reflection by various New Testament authors upon the meaning of this symbolic act. Within the New Testament canon baptism is viewed as the symbolic identification of the believer with the death and resurrection of Jesus (Ro 6; Col 2:12), through which the believer becomes "clothed . . . with Christ" (Gal 3:27), as well as a clear expression of repentance before God (1Pe 3:21).[7]

A Jewish ritual bath or "mikveh"

Preserving Bible Times; © Dr. James C. Martin

[1]See "Bathing" on page 456. [2]See "Ritual Purity in Israel and the Ancient Near East" on page 166. [3]See "The Pharisees" on page 1566. [4]See also "The Zealots and the Essenes" on page 1576, "Biblical Interpretation at Qumran and Among the Early Rabbis" on page 1603 and "Qumran and the New Testament" on page 1679. [5]See "Proselytes in Second Temple Judaism" on page 1776. [6]See also "The Jewish Priesthood and Religious Life in the First Century A.D." on page 1704. [7]See also "Baptism for the Dead" on page 1881.

3:4 [r]2Ki 1:8 4 John's clothes were made of camel's hair, and he had a leather belt around his waist.[r] His food was
[s]Lev 11:22 locusts[s] and wild honey. 5 People went out to him from Jerusalem and all Judea and the whole region of
the Jordan. 6 Confessing their sins, they were baptized by him in the Jordan River.
7 But when he saw many of the Pharisees and Sadducees coming to where he was baptizing, he said
3:7 [t]Mt 12:34; 23:33 [u]Ro 1:18; 1Th 1:10 to them: "You brood of vipers![t] Who warned you to flee from the coming wrath?[u] 8 Produce fruit in
keeping with repentance.[v] 9 And do not think you can say to yourselves, 'We have Abraham as our fa-
3:8 [v]Ac 26:20 ther.' I tell you that out of these stones God can raise up children for Abraham. 10 The ax is already at
the root of the trees, and every tree that does not produce good fruit will be cut down and thrown into
3:10 [w]Mt 7:19; Lk 13:6-9; Jn 15:2,6 the fire.[w]
11 "I baptize you with[a] water for repentance. But after me will come one who is more powerful than I,
3:11 [x]Mk 1:8 [y]Isa 4:4; Ac 2:3,4 whose sandals I am not fit to carry. He will baptize you with the Holy Spirit[x] and with fire.[y] 12 His win-
nowing fork is in his hand, and he will clear his threshing floor, gathering his wheat into the barn and
3:12 [z]Mt 13:30 burning up the chaff with unquenchable fire."[z]

The Baptism of Jesus

3:13 [a]Mk 1:4 13 Then Jesus came from Galilee to the Jordan to be baptized by John.[a] 14 But John tried to deter him,
saying, "I need to be baptized by you, and do you come to me?"
15 Jesus replied, "Let it be so now; it is proper for us to do this to fulfill all righteousness." Then John
consented.
16 As soon as Jesus was baptized, he went up out of the water. At that moment heaven was opened, and
3:16 [b]Isa 11:2; 42:1 he saw the Spirit of God[b] descending like a dove and lighting on him. 17 And a voice from heaven[c] said,
3:17 [c]Mt 17:5; Jn 12:28 [d]Ps 2:7; 2Pe 1:17,18 [e]Isa 42:1; Mt 12:18; 17:5; Mk 1:11; 9:7; Lk 9:35 "This is my Son,[d] whom I love; with him I am well pleased."[e]

The Temptation of Jesus

4 Then Jesus was led by the Spirit into the desert to be tempted by the devil. 2 After fasting forty days
4:2 [f]Ex 34:28; 1Ki 19:8 and forty nights,[f] he was hungry. 3 The tempter[g] came to him and said, "If you are the Son of God,[h]
4:3 [g]1Th 3:5 [h]Mt 3:17; Jn 5:25; Ac 9:20 tell these stones to become bread."
4 Jesus answered, "It is written: 'Man does not live on bread alone, but on every word that comes from
4:4 [i]Dt 8:3 the mouth of God.'[b]"[i]
4:5 [j]Ne 11:1; Da 9:24; Mt 27:53 5 Then the devil took him to the holy city[j] and had him stand on the highest point of the temple. 6 "If
you are the Son of God," he said, "throw yourself down. For it is written:

" 'He will command his angels concerning you,
and they will lift you up in their hands,
4:6 [k]Ps 91:11,12 so that you will not strike your foot against a stone.'[c]"[k]

4:7 [l]Dt 6:16 7 Jesus answered him, "It is also written: 'Do not put the Lord your God to the test.'[d]"[l]

[a] *11* Or *in* [b] *4* Deut. 8:3 [c] *6* Psalm 91:11,12 [d] *7* Deut. 6:16

3:4 Leather belts were used to bind up loose outer garments. Camel's hair and a leather belt may also have been worn by Elijah and other Old Testament prophets (see 2Ki 1:8; Zec 13:4). It is probable, however, that such articles of clothing were not actually made of the relatively expensive woven camel's hair but of dressed camel's skin. Such garments are still used in the Near East.

No one living in the desert hesitated to eat insects, and locusts were among the ceremonially clean foods of which the Jews were free to partake (Lev 11:21–22; see "Clean and Unclean Foods in the Bible and the Ancient Near East" on page 168 and "Locusts in the Ancient Near East" on p. 1438).

3:6 See "Baptism in the Ancient World" on page 1562.

3:7 The Pharisees, the party of the synagogue, were a legalistic and separatist group who strictly kept the Law of Moses and the unwritten "tradition of the elders" (see the note on 15:2). Although they were comparatively few in number, the Pharisees enjoyed the support of the people and influenced popular opinion, if not national policy. They were the only party to survive the destruction of the temple in A.D. 70 and were the spiritual progenitors of modern Judaism. See "The Pharisees" on page 1566.

The Sadducees were a Jewish party that represented the wealthy and sophisticated classes. They were more politically minded than the Pharisees and denied the resurrection, angels and spirits. They were located largely in Jerusalem and made the temple and its administration their primary interest. Though they too were a relatively small group, in Jesus' day they exerted powerful political and religious influence. See "The Sadducees" on page 1600.

3:11 See the note on John 1:27.

3:16–17 For commentary on Epiphany, which originally celebrated the event of Jesus' baptism, see the note on 2:1–12.

4:1 The temptations took place (1) in the desert region of the lower Jordan Valley, (2) on a high mountain (possibly one of the abrupt cliffs near Jericho that present an unsurpassed panorama) and (3) on the highest point of the temple, from which the priests sounded the trumpet to call the city's attention to important events.

4:5 The temple, including the entire temple area, had been rebuilt by Herod the Great (see "Herod's Temple" on p. 1648), and during the renovation the courtyard had been greatly enlarged. To accomplish this, a huge platform had been erected to compensate for the sharp falling off of the land to the southeast. An enormous retaining wall constructed of massive stones had been built to support the platform. On the platform stood the temple building, porches and courtyards, flanked by beautiful colonnades.

[8]Again, the devil took him to a very high mountain and showed him all the kingdoms of the world
and their splendor. [9]"All this I will give you," he said, "if you will bow down and worship me."

[10]Jesus said to him, "Away from me, Satan![m] For it is written: 'Worship the Lord your God, and serve
him only.'[a]"[n]

[11]Then the devil left him, and angels came and attended him.[o]

Jesus Begins to Preach

[12]When Jesus heard that John had been put in prison,[p] he returned to Galilee.[q] [13]Leaving Nazareth,
he went and lived in Capernaum,[r] which was by the lake in the area of Zebulun and Naphtali— [14]to ful-
fill what was said through the prophet Isaiah:

[15]"Land of Zebulun and land of Naphtali,
the way to the sea, along the Jordan,
Galilee of the Gentiles—
[16]the people living in darkness
have seen a great light;
on those living in the land of the shadow of death
a light has dawned."[b][s]

[17]From that time on Jesus began to preach, "Repent, for the kingdom of heaven[t] is near."

The Calling of the First Disciples

[18]As Jesus was walking beside the Sea of Galilee,[u] he saw two brothers, Simon called Peter[v] and his
brother Andrew. They were casting a net into the lake, for they were fishermen. [19]"Come, follow me,"[w]
Jesus said, "and I will make you fishers of men." [20]At once they left their nets and followed him.

[21]Going on from there, he saw two other brothers, James son of Zebedee and his brother John.[x] They
were in a boat with their father Zebedee, preparing their nets. Jesus called them, [22]and immediately they
left the boat and their father and followed him.

Jesus Heals the Sick

[23]Jesus went throughout Galilee,[y] teaching in their synagogues,[z] preaching the good news[a] of the
kingdom,[b] and healing every disease and sickness among the people.[c] [24]News about him spread all over
Syria,[d] and people brought to him all who were ill with various diseases, those suffering severe pain, the
demon-possessed,[e] those having seizures,[f] and the paralyzed,[g] and he healed them. [25]Large crowds from
Galilee, the Decapolis,[c] Jerusalem, Judea and the region across the Jordan followed him.[h]

4:10 [m]1Ch 21:1 [n]Dt 6:13
4:11 [o]Mt 26:53; Lk 22:43; Heb 1:14
4:12 [p]Mt 14:3 [q]Mk 1:14
4:13 [r]Mk 1:21; Lk 4:23,31; Jn 2:12; 4:46,47
4:16 [s]Isa 9:1,2; Lk 2:32
4:17 [t]Mt 3:2
4:18 [u]Mt 15:29; Mk 7:31; Jn 6:1 [v]Mt 16:17,18
4:19 [w]Mk 10:21, 28,52
4:21 [x]Mt 20:20
4:23 [y]Mk 1:39; Lk 4:15,44 [z]Mt 9:35; 13:54; Mk 1:21; Lk 4:15; Jn 6:59 [a]Mk 1:14 [b]Mt 3:2; Ac 20:25 [c]Mt 8:16; 15:30; Ac 10:38
4:24 [d]Lk 2:2 [e]Mt 8:16,28; 9:32; 15:22; Mk 1:32; 5:15,16, 18 [f]Mt 17:15 [g]Mt 8:6; 9:2; Mk 2:3
4:25 [h]Mk 3:7,8; Lk 6:17

[a] *10* Deut. 6:13   [b] *16* Isaiah 9:1,2   [c] *25* That is, the Ten Cities

---

4:12–16 The northern part of Naphtali was inhabited by a mixed race of Jews and pagans (Jdg 1:33). Its Israelite population had been carried away captive to Assyria and had been replaced by a colony of pagan immigrants (2Ki 15:29; 17:24). Hence the region was called "Galilee of the nations" and its people "Gentiles" (Isa 9:1; Mt 4:13,15–16). During and after the captivity the predominant mixture of Gentile races impoverished the worship of Judaism, and for the same reason the Galilean accent and dialect were noticeably peculiar (26:73). This caused the southern Jews of "purer" blood and orthodox tradition to despise the Galileans (Jn 1:46; 7:52).

Yet Galilee's very darkness was the Lord's reason for granting more of the light of his presence and ministry to this region than to self-satisfied and privileged Judea. Christ was sent for "a light for the Gentiles" (Isa 42:6), as well as to the "lost sheep of Israel" (Mt 15:24). Galilee's very debasement made some of its people feel more acutely their need of the Savior. This and its comparative freedom from priestly and pharisaical prejudice may have been additional reasons for its receiving the larger share of the Lord's ministry. See "Galilee in Jesus' Time" on page 1587.

4:13 Capernaum was evidently a sizable town in Jesus' day (see "Capernaum" on p. 1643). Peter's house there became Jesus' base of operations during his extended ministry in Galilee. A fifth-century basilica now stands over the supposed site of Peter's house, and a fourth-century synagogue is located a short distance from it (see "Houses in the Holy Land of the First Century A.D.: Peter's House in Capernaum; Insulae" on p. 1584).

4:15 The "way to the sea" was the trade route through the tribal territories of Zebulun (including Nazareth) and Naphtali (including Capernaum) to the Mediterranean. Ever since the region had been reduced to an Assyrian province in 732 B.C. (see 2Ki 15:29), it had experienced turmoil and a strong Gentile influence.

4:21 James and John were probably washing, mending and hanging up their nets to dry in preparation for the next day's work. In 1986 the remains of a 2,000-year-old typical fisherman's boat were located off the northwestern shore of the Sea of Galilee. Its discoverers named it the Jesus Boat. See "Fishing in New Testament Times" on page 1676.

4:23 The synagogues (see "Ancient Synagogues" on p. 1783) provided a place for Jesus to teach on the Sabbath. During the week he preached to larger crowds in the open air.

4:24 Syria is the area north of Galilee and between Damascus and the Mediterranean Sea (see "Syria/Aram" on p. 534).

The Greek word translated "those having seizures" originally meant "moonstruck" and reflects the ancient superstition that seizures were caused by changes of the moon.

4:25 The Decapolis was a league of free cities characterized by Greek culture. All but one, Scythopolis (Beth Shan), were situated east of the Sea of Galilee and the Jordan River. The league stretched from a point northeast of the Sea of Galilee southward to Philadelphia (modern Amman, Jordan).

The Beatitudes

5 Now when he saw the crowds, he went up on a mountainside and sat down. His disciples came to
him, 2 and he began to teach them, saying:

3 "Blessed are the poor in spirit,
for theirs is the kingdom of heaven.[i]
4 Blessed are those who mourn,
for they will be comforted.[j]
5 Blessed are the meek,
for they will inherit the earth.[k]
6 Blessed are those who hunger and thirst for righteousness,
for they will be filled.[l]
7 Blessed are the merciful,
for they will be shown mercy.
8 Blessed are the pure in heart,[m]
for they will see God.[n]
9 Blessed are the peacemakers,
for they will be called sons of God.[o]
10 Blessed are those who are persecuted because of righteousness,[p]
for theirs is the kingdom of heaven.

11 "Blessed are you when people insult you,[q] persecute you and falsely say all kinds of evil against you
because of me. 12 Rejoice and be glad,[r] because great is your reward in heaven, for in the same way they
persecuted the prophets who were before you.[s]

Salt and Light

13 "You are the salt of the earth. But if the salt loses its saltiness, how can it be made salty again? It is
no longer good for anything, except to be thrown out and trampled by men.[t]
14 "You are the light of the world.[u] A city on a hill cannot be hidden. 15 Neither do people light a lamp
and put it under a bowl. Instead they put it on its stand, and it gives light to everyone in the house.[v] 16 In
the same way, let your light shine before men, that they may see your good deeds and praise[w] your Fa-
ther in heaven.

The Fulfillment of the Law

17 "Do not think that I have come to abolish the Law or the Prophets; I have not come to abolish them
but to fulfill them.[x] 18 I tell you the truth, until heaven and earth disappear, not the smallest letter, not the

5:3 [i]ver 10,19; Mt 25:34
5:4 [j]Isa 61:2,3; Rev 7:17
5:5 [k]Ps 37:11; Ro 4:13
5:6 [l]Isa 55:1,2
5:8 [m]Ps 24:3,4 [n]Heb 12:14; Rev 22:4
5:9 [o]ver 44,45; Ro 8:14
5:10 [p]1Pe 3:14
5:11 [q]1Pe 4:14
5:12 [r]Ac 5:41; 1Pe 4:13,16 [s]Mt 23:31,37; Ac 7:52; 1Th 2:15
5:13 [t]Mk 9:50; Lk 14:34,35
5:14 [u]Jn 8:12
5:15 [v]Mk 4:21; Lk 8:16
5:16 [w]Mt 9:8
5:17 [x]Ro 3:31

5:1—7:29 The site of the Sermon on the Mount (see also Lk 6:20–49) is not identified in the Gospels. Tradition has associated it with Karn Hattin, near Capernaum, but with very little factual basis.

The word *sermon* in this context is misleading to the modern mind. Matthew did not say that Jesus arose, entered the pulpit and delivered a sermon that he had formally prepared in a quiet library. The crowds were following him (Mt 5:1; Lk 6:17) to see his miracles. He went up the mountain a little way so that his immediate followers would be nearer than the rest and then came down with them to a level place (Lk 6:17), still in "the mountain." Presently he sat down and began to teach, with special attention to the disciples who were nearby.

The Biblical writers, of course, used no quotation marks, and it is important for us to understand that they did not claim to record Jesus' quotations word for word. Neither did they claim to include all that was spoken on any given occasion. They did assert, however, that their words were a true presentation of the substance of what they quoted. The "sermon," then, is a student's (Matthew's) report of a class lecture and discussion. The fact that there are digressions from a formal outline (Mt 5:25–26,29–30), in fact, evidences the genuineness of the record.

5:3–11 The word *beatitude* is not found in the English Bible. It means either (1) the joys of heaven or (2) a declaration of blessedness, especially as made by Christ. Beatitudes occur frequently in the Old Testament (e.g., Ps 32:1–2; 41:1; 65:4), and the Gospels contain isolated beatitudes by Jesus (Mt 11:6; 13:16; 16:17; 24:46 with the Lukan parallels; Jn 13:17; 20:29). But the word is most commonly used of the declarations of blessedness made by Jesus in the discourse recorded here by Matthew, as well as the one recounted by Luke (Lk 6:20–22)—called, respectively, the "Sermon on the Mount" and the "Sermon on the Plain." Scholars do not agree whether we have here two different records of the same discourse or records of two different but similar speeches/dialogues.

5:8 The heart was considered the center of one's being, including mind, will and emotions (see the note on Ps 4:7). See also "Heart, Breath, Throat and Intestines: Ancient Hebrew Anthropology" on page 968.

5:13 Salt was used for flavoring and for preserving (see also the note on Lev 2:13). Most of the salt used in Israel came from the Dead Sea and was full of impurities, causing it to lose some of its flavor.

5:15 In Jesus' day people used small clay lamps that burned olive oil drawn up by a wick. The common New Testament mention of lamps is in connection with their household usage (5:15; Mk 4:21; Lk 8:16; 11:33; 15:8). Because they gave off only modest light, they were strategically positioned for maximum benefit. Such lamps were generally placed on a "lampstand," often a niche built into the wall. It appears that the Hebrews were accustomed to burning lamps overnight in their chambers, perhaps because of a dread of darkness but more likely to keep away prowlers. The use of oil-fed lamps in a marriage procession is mentioned in Matthew 25:1. Since such lamps contained only a few spoonfuls of oil, a reserve supply would have been a necessity.

5:18 The Greek word *iota* (translated here "smallest letter") is the nearest Greek equivalent to the Hebrew *yodh*, the smallest letter of

least stroke of a pen, will by any means disappear from the Law until everything is accomplished.[y] 19 Any- **5:18** [y]Lk 16:17
one who breaks one of the least of these commandments[z] and teaches others to do the same will be **5:19** [z]Jas 2:10
called least in the kingdom of heaven, but whoever practices and teaches these commands will be called
great in the kingdom of heaven. 20 For I tell you that unless your righteousness surpasses that of the Phar-
isees and the teachers of the law, you will certainly not enter the kingdom of heaven.

Murder

21 "You have heard that it was said to the people long ago, 'Do not murder,[a][a] and anyone who murders **5:21** [a]Ex 20:13;
will be subject to judgment.' 22 But I tell you that anyone who is angry with his brother[b] will be subject to Dt 5:17
judgment.[b] Again, anyone who says to his brother, 'Raca,[c]' is answerable to the Sanhedrin.[c] But anyone **5:22** [b]1Jn 3:15
who says, 'You fool!' will be in danger of the fire of hell.[d] [c]Mt 26:59 [d]Jas 3:6
23 "Therefore, if you are offering your gift at the altar and there remember that your brother has some-
thing against you, 24 leave your gift there in front of the altar. First go and be reconciled to your brother;
then come and offer your gift.

[a] *21* Exodus 20:13 [b] *22* Some manuscripts *brother without cause* [c] *22* An Aramaic term of contempt

---

the Hebrew alphabet. The Greek word translated here as "least stroke of a pen" means "horn" and was used to designate the slight embellishment or extension of certain letters of the Hebrew alphabet (somewhat like the bottom [descender] of the letter *j*).

5:20 For "teachers of the law" in the New Testament, see the note on Acts 5:35.

5:22 *Raca*, possibly related to the Aramaic word for "empty," may thus mean "Empty-headed!"

The Greek word for hell is *ge(h)enna*, which derives its name from a deep ravine south of Jerusalem, the "Valley of (the Sons of) Hinnom." During the reigns of the wicked kings Ahaz and Manasseh, human sacrifices to the Ammonite god Molech were offered there. It became a sort of perpetually burning city dump and later a figure for the place of final punishment. See "Human Sacrifice in the Ancient Near East" on page 182 and "Sheol, Hades, Gehenna, the Abyss and Tartarus: Images of Hell" on page 946.

The Pharisees

MATTHEW 5 The Pharisees were an influential political and religious sect during the **Second Temple** period.[1] During this time of increasing foreign influence, they promoted the faithful observance of Jewish law at both a national and an individual level. The exact meaning of the term *Pharisee* remains uncertain. The noun derives from the Hebrew verb meaning "to separate" or "to distinguish." The title appears to have been applied originally in a negative sense when the Pharisees were expelled from membership in the Sanhedrin under John Hyrcanus (135–104 B.C.), though it was later understood in a positive sense either as "those who separated themselves" from all sources of ritual uncleanness (see Mk 7:1–23; Gal 2:12–13) or "those who interpreted the law precisely" (see Ac 22:3; 26:5; Josephus's *Antiquities*, 17.2.4).

The Pharisees believed that God was the sovereign Creator, who expressed his will to humanity through Scripture. Moreover, he granted humanity the gifts of responsible moral choice and reason in order to apply the Scriptures to this life in preparation for the resurrection, judgment and the life to come (cf. Ac 23:6–8). Members of this sect carefully observed the Mosaic Law, systematically interpreting and adapting it to the conditions of their own time in order to maintain a sense of purity among the populace (Mt 23:2–3). This system of interpretation and way of life were transmitted by generations of teachers and became known variously as the oral law, the tradition of the elders (Mk 7:3–5; Gal 1:14), the works of the law (Ro 3:20–28; Gal 2:16—3:10) or simply the *Halakhah* (from a Hebrew word meaning "walk"; *Halakhah* is traditional Jewish teaching that governs behavior and religious practice).

The Pharisees saw themselves as the heirs of a vast body of interpretative tradition that enabled them to function as reliable guides for the Jewish people during a tumultuous era (Ro 2:17–20). Although some Pharisees came to believe in Jesus as the Christ (Ac 15:5; Php 3:4–11), the majority justified their opposition to him on the grounds that Jesus ostensibly taught on his own authority (Mt 7:29; Jn 3:1–3; 8:13), as well as on the basis of his interpretations of various issues that were of vital concern to them.

Jesus criticized the Pharisees on the grounds that, for all of their commendable observance of rules and traditions, they were fundamentally unrepentant, neither knowing God nor loving people (Mt 23).

[1]See "The Intertestamental Period" on page 1551 and "The Jewish Priesthood and Religious Life in the First Century A.D." on page 1704.

25“Settle matters quickly with your adversary who is taking you
to court. Do it while you are still with him on the way, or he may
hand you over to the judge, and the judge may hand you over to the
officer, and you may be thrown into prison. 26I tell you the truth, you
will not get out until you have paid the last penny.[a]

Adultery

5:27 [e]Ex 20:14; Dt 5:18 27“You have heard that it was said, ‘Do not commit adultery.’[b][e]
28But I tell you that anyone who looks at a woman lustfully has al-
5:28 [f]Pr 6:25 ready committed adultery with her in his heart.[f] 29If your right eye
5:29 [g]Mt 18:6,8, 9; Mk 9:42-47 causes you to sin,[g] gouge it out and throw it away. It is better for you
to lose one part of your body than for your whole body to be thrown
into hell. 30And if your right hand causes you to sin, cut it off and
throw it away. It is better for you to lose one part of your body than
for your whole body to go into hell.

Divorce

31“It has been said, ‘Anyone who divorces his wife must give her
5:31 [h]Dt 24:1-4 a certificate of divorce.’[c][h] 32But I tell you that anyone who divorces
his wife, except for marital unfaithfulness, causes her to become an
adulteress, and anyone who marries the divorced woman commits
5:32 [i]Lk 16:18 adultery.[i]

Ancient Voices

Now there was a certain Jewish sect whose members made themselves out both to be prudent in the great matters of the laws of their fathers and to be favored by heaven. They brought the women of the harem under their influence. They are called the Pharisees, and they were especially shrewd in dealing with a powerful king and were quickly stirred up to fighting and making trouble. And so, when all the Jews had confirmed with oaths their good-will to Caesar and to the king's government, these men, more than six thousand, did not swear. And when the king imposed a fine upon them, the wife of Pheroras paid the fine for them.

—Josephus on The Pharisees
From Flavius Josephus, *Antiquities*, 17.2, trans. by Duane Garrett

See "The Pharisees" article.

Oaths

5:33 [j]Lev 19:12 [k]Nu 30:2; Dt 23:21; Mt 23:16-22 33“Again, you have heard that it was said to the people long ago, ‘Do not break your oath,[j] but keep the
5:34 [l]Jas 5:12 oaths you have made to the Lord.’[k] 34But I tell you, Do not swear at all:[l] either by heaven, for it is God's
[m]Isa 66:1; Mt 23:22 throne;[m] 35or by the earth, for it is his footstool; or by Jerusalem, for it is the city of the Great King.[n] 36And
5:35 [n]Ps 48:2 do not swear by your head, for you cannot make even one hair white or black. 37Simply let your ‘Yes’ be
5:37 [o]Jas 5:12 [p]Mt 6:13; 13:19, 38; Jn 17:15; 2Th 3:3; 1Jn 2:13,14; 3:12; 5:18,19 ‘Yes,’ and your ‘No,’ ‘No’;[o] anything beyond this comes from the evil one.[p]

An Eye for an Eye

5:38 [q]Ex 21:24; Lev 24:20; Dt 19:21 38“You have heard that it was said, ‘Eye for eye, and tooth for tooth.’[d][q] 39But I tell you, Do not resist an
evil person. If someone strikes you on the right cheek, turn to him the other also.[r] 40And if someone
5:39 [r]Lk 6:29; Ro 12:17,19; 1Co 6:7; 1Pe 3:9 wants to sue you and take your tunic, let him have your cloak as well. 41If someone forces you to go one
mile, go with him two miles. 42Give to the one who asks you, and do not turn away from the one who
5:42 [s]Dt 15:8; Lk 6:30 wants to borrow from you.[s]

Love for Enemies

5:43 [t]Lev 19:18 [u]Dt 23:6 43“You have heard that it was said, ‘Love your neighbor[e][t] and hate your enemy.’[u] 44But I tell you: Love
5:44 [v]Lk 6:27,28; 23:34; Ac 7:60; Ro 12:14; 1Co 4:12; 1Pe 2:23 your enemies[f] and pray for those who persecute you,[v] 45that you may be sons[w] of your Father in heaven.
5:45 [w]ver 9 [x]Job 25:3 He causes his sun to rise on the evil and the good, and sends rain on the righteous and the unrighteous.[x]
5:46 [y]Lk 6:32 46If you love those who love you, what reward will you get?[y] Are not even the tax collectors doing that?
47And if you greet only your brothers, what are you doing more than others? Do not even pagans do that?
5:48 [z]Lev 19:2; 1Pe 1:16 48Be perfect, therefore, as your heavenly Father is perfect.[z]

[a] *26* Greek *kodrantes* [b] *27* Exodus 20:14 [c] *31* Deut. 24:1 [d] *38* Exodus 21:24; Lev. 24:20; Deut. 19:21 [e] *43* Lev. 19:18
[f] *44* Some late manuscripts *enemies, bless those who curse you, do good to those who hate you*

5:26 The penny was the smallest Roman copper coin.
5:32 The Greek word translated here as “marital unfaithfulness” refers to illicit sexual activity—in this case, adultery.
5:33–37 See “Oaths in Jewish and Christian Practice” on page 1988 and “Speech Ethics” on page 2005.
5:39 Striking someone on the cheek was more an insult than considered was an act of violence (see “Bywords and Insults in the Ancient World” on p. 431).
5:40 The tunic was an undergarment and the cloak a loose outer one. Since the outer garment was wrapped around the individual for sleeping, Old Testament law prohibited anyone from taking it as a pledge overnight (see Ex 22:26–27; Dt 24:12–13; see also “Ancient Israelite Clothing and Jewelry” on p. 1059 and “Dress and Fashion in the Greco-Roman World” on p. 2004).
5:43 Hatred of one's enemies was an accepted part of the Jewish ethic at that time in some circles.
5:46 Traditionally known as “publicans;” tax collectors were men employed by Roman tax contractors to collect taxes (see “Roman Taxation” on p. 1855). Because they worked for Rome and often demanded unreasonable payments, the tax collectors gained a bad reputation and were generally hated and considered traitors.

Giving to the Needy

6 “Be careful not to do your ‘acts of righteousness’ before men, to be seen by them.[a] If you do, you will 6:1 [a]Mt 23:5
have no reward from your Father in heaven.
2“So when you give to the needy, do not announce it with trumpets, as the hypocrites do in the syn-
agogues and on the streets, to be honored by men. I tell you the truth, they have received their reward in
full. 3But when you give to the needy, do not let your left hand know what your right hand is doing, 4so
that your giving may be in secret. Then your Father, who sees what is done in secret, will reward you.[b] 6:4 [b]ver 6,18; Col 3:23,24

Prayer

5“And when you pray, do not be like the hypocrites, for they love to pray standing[c] in the synagogues 6:5 [c]Mk 11:25; Lk 18:10-14
and on the street corners to be seen by men. I tell you the truth, they have received their reward in full.
6But when you pray, go into your room, close the door and pray to your Father,[d] who is unseen. Then 6:6 [d]2Ki 4:33
your Father, who sees what is done in secret, will reward you. 7And when you pray, do not keep on bab-
bling[e] like pagans, for they think they will be heard because of their many words.[f] 8Do not be like them, 6:7 [e]Ecc 5:2 [f]1Ki 18:26-29
for your Father knows what you need[g] before you ask him. 6:8 [g]ver 32
9“This, then, is how you should pray:

“ ‘Our Father in heaven,
hallowed be your name,
10your kingdom[h] come, 6:10 [h]Mt 3:2 [i]Mt 26:39
your will be done[i]
on earth as it is in heaven.
11Give us today our daily bread.[j] 6:11 [j]Pr 30:8
12Forgive us our debts,
as we also have forgiven our debtors.[k] 6:12 [k]Mt 18:21-35
13And lead us not into temptation,[l] 6:13 [l]Jas 1:13 [m]Mt 5:37
but deliver us from the evil one.[a]’[m]

14For if you forgive men when they sin against you, your heavenly Father will also forgive you.[n] 15But if 6:14 [n]Mt 18:21-35; Mk 11:25,26; Eph 4:32; Col 3:13
you do not forgive men their sins, your Father will not forgive your sins.[o] 6:15 [o]Mt 18:35

Fasting

16“When you fast, do not look somber[p] as the hypocrites do, for they disfigure their faces to show 6:16 [p]Isa 58:5
men they are fasting. I tell you the truth, they have received their reward in full. 17But when you fast, put
oil on your head and wash your face, 18so that it will not be obvious to men that you are fasting, but only
to your Father, who is unseen; and your Father, who sees what is done in secret, will reward you.[q] 6:18 [q]ver 4,6

Treasures in Heaven

19“Do not store up for yourselves treasures on earth,[r] where moth and rust destroy,[s] and where thieves 6:19 [r]Pr 23:4; Heb 13:5 [s]Jas 5:2,3
break in and steal. 20But store up for yourselves treasures in heaven,[t] where moth and rust do not de- 6:20 [t]Mt 19:21; Lk 12:33; 18:22; 1Ti 6:19;
stroy, and where thieves do not break in and steal.[u] 21For where your treasure is, there your heart will be [u]Lk 12:33
also.[v] 6:21 [v]Lk 12:34

[a] 13 Or *from evil*; some late manuscripts *one, / for yours is the kingdom and the power and the glory forever. Amen.*

6:1–2 In later Judaism the righteousness of almsgiving became somewhat legalistic and professional. The lame man at the gate called Beautiful exemplified professional begging in that he daily “asked . . . for money” (Ac 3:2–3). Perversion in receiving alms is seen in the beggar’s cry, couching the tacit “bless yourself by giving to me.” Perversion in giving alms, on the other hand, is seen in benefactors who “announce it with trumpets,” probably to be taken figuratively (cf. today’s expression “toot your own horn”). Their desire “to be seen” by people involves the same term from which we derive our word “theater.”

Almsgiving was of two kinds: “alms of the dish” (food and money received daily for distribution) and “alms of the chest” (coins received on the Sabbath for widows, orphans, strangers and the poor).

6:5 Pious Jews prayed publicly at set times—usually morning, afternoon and evening (cf. Ps 55:17; Da 6:10; Ac 3:1).

6:6 The Greek word here translated “room” probably means “storeroom,” because unlike most of the rooms in the house, this one had a door that could be shut.

6:16 “Disfigure” here refers to disguising one’s face to publicize physical hardships endured while fasting (see “Fasting in the Bible and the Ancient Near East” on p. 1569). During the fasting period religious individuals in Jesus’ day might have somehow marked their faces, remained ungroomed and/or sprinkled ashes on their heads and faces. This was a pretentious way of letting others see and appreciate their extensive efforts to increase their godliness.

6:19 Houses in the Holy Land had walls made of mud bricks and could easily be broken into (see “Houses in the Holy Land of the First Century A.D.: Peter’s House in Capernaum; Insulae” on p. 1584).

[22]"The eye is the lamp of the body. If your eyes are good, your whole body will be full of light. [23]But if
your eyes are bad, your whole body will be full of darkness. If then the light within you is darkness, how
great is that darkness!
[24]"No one can serve two masters. Either he will hate the one and love the other, or he will be devoted
to the one and despise the other. You cannot serve both God and Money.[w]

6:24 [w]Lk 16:13

Do Not Worry

[25]"Therefore I tell you, do not worry[x] about your life, what you will eat or drink; or about your body,
what you will wear. Is not life more important than food, and the body more important than clothes?
[26]Look at the birds of the air; they do not sow or reap or store away in barns, and yet your heavenly Fa-
ther feeds them.[y] Are you not much more valuable than they?[z] [27]Who of you by worrying can add a sin-
gle hour to his life[a]?[a]
[28]"And why do you worry about clothes? See how the lilies of the field grow. They do not labor or spin.
[29]Yet I tell you that not even Solomon in all his splendor[b] was dressed like one of these. [30]If that is how
God clothes the grass of the field, which is here today and tomorrow is thrown into the fire, will he not
much more clothe you, O you of little faith?[c] [31]So do not worry, saying, 'What shall we eat?' or 'What shall

6:25 [x]ver 27,28, 31,34; Lk 10:41; 12:11,22; Php 4:6; 1Pe 5:7
6:26 [y]Job 38:41; Ps 147:9 [z]Mt 10:29-31
6:27 [a]Ps 39:5
6:29 [b]1Ki 10:4-7
6:30 [c]Mt 8:26; 14:31; 16:8

[a] 27 Or *single cubit to his height*

6:30 Grass was commonly used to heat clay ovens in the Holy Land.

7:6 See "Dogs in the Ancient World" on page 1002.

Fasting in the Bible and the Ancient Near East

MATTHEW 6

Fasting in the Old Testament

While the Day of Atonement was the only required day of fasting in the Old Testament,[1] there were occasions throughout the year for voluntary fasting. Rather than avoiding specific foods, fasting usually involved abstinence from all food for a predetermined period of time. It was always accompanied by prayer and was used to express grief, penitence or humble devotion to God. Fasting was encouraged at times of national crisis as an indication that Israel or Judah was wholeheartedly dedicated to the Lord (Jdg 20:26; Joel 1:14). Individuals in particular distress also fasted (1Sa 1:7; 2Sa 12:22). The duration of a given fast ranged from several hours to as long as 40 days. After the exile there were at least four commonly practiced periods of fasting (Zec 8:19). For example, a tradition began of fasting on the ninth of Ab (the fifth month, spanning our July and August). This fast was intended to commemorate the destruction of the Jerusalem temple, and it became customary to read Lamentations on that day.[2]

Fasting in Pagan Religion

Fasting was also practiced in some forms of Greek pagan religion. One of the initiatory rites of the Eleusinian mystery religion involved a fast, and the cults of Isis and Cybele also entailed some fasting. Abstinence from food, as well as sexual abstinence, was often thought to be a necessary preparation before undergoing a ritual. The Greeks rarely practiced lengthy fasts, but many cults had a number of taboos involving food (the Pythagoreans, e.g., were vegetarian).[3]

Fasting in the New Testament and the Church

Fasting remained common throughout the New Testament era. The Pharisees fasted twice a week, on Mondays and Thursdays (Lk 18:12).[4] Jesus, the disciples of John the Baptist and Paul practiced substantial fasts as well. Matthew 6:16–18 indicates that fasting remains a legitimate form of worship for Christians. During the first few centuries of the Christian church a theology of asceticism with heroic acts of prolonged fasting arose. But Jesus' words also provide a reminder that true fasting is directed toward God, not toward impressing others. Like the prophets before him (Isa 58:1–12; Jer 14:10–12; Zec 7), Jesus proclaimed that true fasting is an indication of the heart's inclination toward God.

[1]See "The Day of Atonement" on page 176. [2]See also "Israelite Shrines and Worship Before the Temple of Solomon" on page 398 and "Sackcloth and Ashes: Rituals of Lamentation" on page 820. [3]For more information on pagan religion, see "The Gods of the Greeks and Romans" on page 1908 and "The Mystery Religions" on page 1939. [4]See "The Pharisees" on page 1566.

we drink?' or 'What shall we wear?' 32For the pagans run after all these things, and your heavenly Father
knows that you need them.[d] 33But seek first his kingdom and his righteousness, and all these things will
be given to you as well.[e] 34Therefore do not worry about tomorrow, for tomorrow will worry about itself.
Each day has enough trouble of its own.

Judging Others

7 "Do not judge, or you too will be judged.[f] 2For in the same way you judge others, you will be judged,
and with the measure you use, it will be measured to you.[g]
3"Why do you look at the speck of sawdust in your brother's eye and pay no attention to the plank in
your own eye? 4How can you say to your brother, 'Let me take the speck out of your eye,' when all the time
there is a plank in your own eye? 5You hypocrite, first take the plank out of your own eye, and then you
will see clearly to remove the speck from your brother's eye.
6"Do not give dogs what is sacred; do not throw your pearls to pigs. If you do, they may trample them
under their feet, and then turn and tear you to pieces.

Ask, Seek, Knock

7"Ask and it will be given to you;[h] seek and you will find; knock and the door will be opened to you.
8For everyone who asks receives; he who seeks finds;[i] and to him who knocks, the door will be opened.
9"Which of you, if his son asks for bread, will give him a stone? 10Or if he asks for a fish, will give him
a snake? 11If you, then, though you are evil, know how to give good gifts to your children, how much more
will your Father in heaven give good gifts to those who ask him! 12So in everything, do to others what you
would have them do to you,[j] for this sums up the Law and the Prophets.[k]

The Narrow and Wide Gates

13"Enter through the narrow gate.[l] For wide is the gate and broad is the road that leads to destruction,
and many enter through it. 14But small is the gate and narrow the road that leads to life, and only a few
find it.

A Tree and Its Fruit

15"Watch out for false prophets.[m] They come to you in sheep's clothing, but inwardly they are fero-
cious wolves.[n] 16By their fruit you will recognize them.[o] Do people pick grapes from thornbushes, or figs
from thistles?[p] 17Likewise every good tree bears good fruit, but a bad tree bears bad fruit. 18A good tree
cannot bear bad fruit, and a bad tree cannot bear good fruit. 19Every tree that does not bear good fruit
is cut down and thrown into the fire.[q] 20Thus, by their fruit you will recognize them.
21"Not everyone who says to me, 'Lord, Lord,'[r] will enter the kingdom of heaven, but only he who does
the will of my Father who is in heaven.[s] 22Many will say to me on that day,[t] 'Lord, Lord, did we not proph-
esy in your name, and in your name drive out demons and perform many miracles?'[u] 23Then I will tell
them plainly, 'I never knew you. Away from me, you evildoers!'[v]

The Wise and Foolish Builders

24"Therefore everyone who hears these words of mine and puts them into practice[w] is like a wise man
who built his house on the rock. 25The rain came down, the streams rose, and the winds blew and beat
against that house; yet it did not fall, because it had its foundation on the rock. 26But everyone who hears
these words of mine and does not put them into practice is like a foolish man who built his house on
sand. 27The rain came down, the streams rose, and the winds blew and beat against that house, and it fell
with a great crash."

28When Jesus had finished saying these things,[x] the crowds were amazed at his teaching,[y] 29because
he taught as one who had authority, and not as their teachers of the law.

6:32 [d]ver 8
6:33 [e]Mt 19:29; Mk 10:29-30
7:1 [f]Lk 6:37; Ro 14:4,10,13; 1Co 4:5; Jas 4:11,12
7:2 [g]Mk 4:24; Lk 6:38
7:7 [h]Mt 21:22; Mk 11:24; Jn 14:13,14; 15:7,16; 16:23,24; Jas 1:5-8; 4:2,3; 1Jn 3:22; 5:14,15
7:8 [i]Pr 8:17; Jer 29:12,13
7:12 [j]Lk 6:31 [k]Ro 13:8-10; Gal 5:14
7:13 [l]Lk 13:24
7:15 [m]Jer 23:16; Mt 24:24; Mk 13:22; Lk 6:26; 2Pe 2:1; 1Jn 4:1; Rev 16:13 [n]Ac 20:29
7:16 [o]Mt 12:33; Lk 6:44 [p]Jas 3:12
7:19 [q]Mt 3:10
7:21 [r]Hos 8:2; Mt 25:11 [s]Ro 2:13; Jas 1:22
7:22 [t]Mt 10:15 [u]1Co 13:1-3
7:23 [v]Ps 6:8; Mt 25:12,41; Lk 13:25-27
7:24 [w]Jas 1:22-25
7:28 [x]Mt 11:1; 13:53; 19:1; 26:1 [y]Mt 13:54; Mk 1:22; 6:2; Lk 4:32; Jn 7:46

7:12 The so-called Golden Rule is found in negative form in Rabbinic Judaism and also in Hinduism, Buddhism and Confucianism. It also occurred in various forms in Greek and Roman ethical teaching. Jesus, in contrast, stated it in positive form.

7:13–14 The image of two paths was common in Judaism. Sometimes the analogy was of separate roads leading in opposite directions—to paradise or to hell. At other times a narrow path of life's hardships was pictured as ultimately leading to a broad path of eternal blessing.

7:24–27 The Sea of Galilee served as a natural setting for this parable. The sand ringing the lake was rock hard during the hot summer. But a wise builder would dig down, as far as ten feet (three m) below the surface sand to the bedrock, knowing that this was the only way to erect a foundation able to withstand the winter rains, which were notoriously torrential and capable of causing disastrous flooding.

The Man With Leprosy

8:2 [z]Lk 5:12 [a]Mt 9:18; 15:25; 18:26; 20:20
8 When he came down from the mountainside, large crowds followed him. 2 A man with leprosy[a][z]
came and knelt before him[a] and said, "Lord, if you are willing, you can make me clean."
3 Jesus reached out his hand and touched the man. "I am willing," he said. "Be clean!" Immediately he
8:4 [b]Mt 9:30; Mk 5:43; 7:36; 8:30 [c]Lev 14:2-32
was cured[b] of his leprosy. 4 Then Jesus said to him, "See that you don't tell anyone.[b] But go, show yourself
to the priest and offer the gift Moses commanded,[c] as a testimony to them."

The Faith of the Centurion

5 When Jesus had entered Capernaum, a centurion came to him, asking for help. 6 "Lord," he said, "my
servant lies at home paralyzed and in terrible suffering."
7 Jesus said to him, "I will go and heal him."
8 The centurion replied, "Lord, I do not deserve to have you come under my roof. But just say the word,
8:8 [d]Ps 107:20
and my servant will be healed.[d] 9 For I myself am a man under authority, with soldiers under me. I tell
this one, 'Go,' and he goes; and that one, 'Come,' and he comes. I say to my servant, 'Do this,' and he does it."
10 When Jesus heard this, he was astonished and said to those following him, "I tell you the truth, I
8:10 [e]Mt 15:28
have not found anyone in Israel with such great faith.[e] 11 I say to you that many will come from the east
8:11 [f]Ps 107:3; Isa 49:12; 59:19; Mal 1:11 [g]Lk 13:29
and the west,[f] and will take their places at the feast with Abraham, Isaac and Jacob in the kingdom of
heaven.[g] 12 But the subjects of the kingdom[h] will be thrown outside, into the darkness, where there will
8:12 [h]Mt 13:38 [i]Mt 13:42,50; 22:13; 24:51; 25:30; Lk 13:28
be weeping and gnashing of teeth."[i]
13 Then Jesus said to the centurion, "Go! It will be done just as you believed it would."[j] And his servant
8:13 [j]Mt 9:22
was healed at that very hour.

Jesus Heals Many

14 When Jesus came into Peter's house, he saw Peter's mother-in-law lying in bed with a fever. 15 He
touched her hand and the fever left her, and she got up and began to wait on him.
16 When evening came, many who were demon-possessed were brought to him, and he drove out the
8:16 [k]Mt 4:23,24 **8:17** [l]Mt 1:22 [m]Isa 53:4
spirits with a word and healed all the sick.[k] 17 This was to fulfill[l] what was spoken through the prophet
Isaiah:

> "He took up our infirmities
> and carried our diseases."[c][m]

The Cost of Following Jesus

8:18 [n]Mk 4:35
18 When Jesus saw the crowd around him, he gave orders to cross to the other side of the lake.[n] 19 Then
a teacher of the law came to him and said, "Teacher, I will follow you wherever you go."
8:20 [o]Da 7:13; Mt 12:8,32,40; 16:13,27,28; 17:9; 19:28; Mk 2:10; 8:31
20 Jesus replied, "Foxes have holes and birds of the air have nests, but the Son of Man[o] has no place to
lay his head."
21 Another disciple said to him, "Lord, first let me go and bury my father."
8:22 [p]Mt 4:19
22 But Jesus told him, "Follow me,[p] and let the dead bury their own dead."

Jesus Calms the Storm

23 Then he got into the boat and his disciples followed him. 24 Without warning, a furious storm came
up on the lake, so that the waves swept over the boat. But Jesus was sleeping. 25 The disciples went and
woke him, saying, "Lord, save us! We're going to drown!"

a *2* The Greek word was used for various diseases affecting the skin—not necessarily leprosy. *b* *3* Greek *made clean*
c *17* Isaiah 53:4

8:1 See the note on 5:1.
8:2 Our picture of leprosy brings to mind the dreaded and debilitating Hansen's disease, but other skin conditions may have been regarded as leprosy (see the NIV text note; see also "Skin Diseases in the Ancient World" on p. 171).
8:3 See the note on Mark 1:41.
8:5 For "Capernaum," see the note on 4:13. A centurion was a Roman military officer who was placed in charge of a *centuria*, a command that could be as small as 60 men or as large as 160 men, but that was typically comprised of 80 men.
8:12 For the meaning of gnashing with one's teeth, see the note on Psalm 35:16.
8:14 For "Peter's house," see "Houses in the Holy Land of the First Century A.D.: Peter's House in Capernaum; Insulae" on page 1584. For "fever," see "Disease and Medicine in the Ancient World" on page 1674.
8:24 Crossing the Sea of Galilee after dark was common for fishermen, who used trammel nets through the night (see "Fishing in New Testament Times" on p. 1676). The lake's setting results in sudden violent storms that produce waves seven feet (two m) or higher (see the note on Mk 4:37). This must have been a powerful storm for these seasoned fishermen to be so afraid.

Demons and the Bible

MATTHEW 8 Many readers assume that the belief in demons attested in the New Testament is simply a function of its authors' sharing in the superstitious beliefs and practices of all ancient peoples. The question of the reality of demons, of course, cannot be settled by archaeology. Researchers can demonstrate, however, that the notion that the New Testament writers simply shared the prescientific views of their contemporaries is simplistic and misleading.

Demons in the Ancient Near East

Ancient Near Eastern society was awash in texts containing magical incantations and amulets intended to protect people from evil spirits (spells for defense against demons are called "apotropaic spells"). For example, one of the feared demons of Neo-Assyrian times was the lion-headed female figure Lamashtu, who was thought especially to attack pregnant women and babies. For protection women wore a necklace with a pendant of the god Pazuzu. An enormous number of apotropaic spells have survived from Babylonia, employing magical words and rituals involving plants, animal parts and other sacred objects.[1] Even today in the eastern Mediterranean it is not uncommon to see amulets intended to ward off the "evil eye."

Demons in Nonbiblical Jewish Literature

Ancient Jewish literature was also fascinated with magic as a means of dealing with demons. The Apocryphal book of Tobit tells the story of one "Sarah, daughter of Raguel," who had been married—and widowed on her wedding night through the intervention of the demon Asmodeus—seven times. Meanwhile Tobias, the son of the blind Tobit, journeyed to Media, where Sarah lived, traveling in the company of a man who turned out to be the angel Raphael. While Tobias was sitting by the Tigris River a fish tried to eat his foot. Raphael instructed Tobias to seize the fish and extract its gall, heart and liver. If he would burn the heart and liver in the presence of an individual afflicted by a demon, that person would be delivered. Arriving in Media, Raphael informed Tobias that he was to marry Sarah but that he could thwart the demon, Asmodeus, by burning the fish's liver and heart when he went in to her. Tobias safely took Sarah as his wife, after which he used the fish gall to cure his father's blindness.

The Testimony of Solomon further illustrates the widespread belief in apotropaic magic. This is a **pseudepigraphical** work (one that falsely claims to have been written by a famous person of the Old Testament) attributed to Solomon. In this work Solomon received a powerful ring from the angel Michael. With it he could imprison or control demons and deliver people from affliction. For example, Solomon forced the demon Lix Tetrax to help build the temple by hurling stones up to the workers.

Demons in the Old Testament

The Old Testament is remarkably reticent about evil spirits, so much so that it seems to have no developed demonology. Even so, three facts stand out:

✣ There are no incantations, rituals or amulets prescribed for giving an individual protection from spirits. Considering how much of the Torah is devoted to ritual and to sacred objects, this is a remarkable omission.

✣ God is said to have complete authority over the spirits, which cannot operate in the world without his approval. If a "lying spirit" goes out, it is only with divine consent (1Ki 22:23; cf. Job 1–2).

✣ The main concern of the Old Testament writers was that people avoid seeking to avail themselves of magical powers through contact with spirits (e.g., Dt 18:10–12).

Demons in the New Testament

The New Testament demonstrates two realities about evil spirits:

✣ Jesus alone (Lk 4:41) has absolute power over them, but this was a matter of divine authority, not magic or sorcery.

✣ The New Testament mocks the claims of magicians by describing their inability to deal with real spirits. The failed efforts of Simon the sorcerer (Ac 8:9–24) and the sons of Sceva (Ac 19:14–16) to obtain apostolic authority illustrates the point that the miracles of the New Testament had nothing in common with ancient magic.[2]

Jesus had no use for demonic spirits and did not seek to employ them to do his bidding.

Hand inscription as an amulet to ward off evil

Preserving Bible Times; © Dr. James C. Martin; permission of The Israel Museum

[1]For Ancient Near Eastern examples, see "A Hittite Ritual Against Plague" on page 758 and "A Pagan's Prayer of Thanks" on page 922. [2]See "Miracle Workers and Magicians in the First Century A.D." on page 1706 and "Magic in the Greco-Roman World" on page 1911.

8:26 [q]Mt 6:30 [r]Ps 65:7; 89:9; 107:29

26 He replied, "You of little faith,[q] why are you so afraid?" Then he
got up and rebuked the winds and the waves, and it was completely
calm.[r]
27 The men were amazed and asked, "What kind of man is this?
Even the winds and the waves obey him!"

The Healing of Two Demon-possessed Men

28 When he arrived at the other side in the region of the Gada-
8:28 [s]Mt 4:24
renes,[a] two demon-possessed[s] men coming from the tombs met
him. They were so violent that no one could pass that way. 29 "What
8:29 [t]Jdg 11:12; 2Sa 16:10; 1Ki 17:18; Mk 1:24; Lk 4:34; Jn 2:4 [u]2Pe 2:4
do you want with us,[t] Son of God?" they shouted. "Have you come
here to torture us before the appointed time?"[u]
30 Some distance from them a large herd of pigs was feeding.
31 The demons begged Jesus, "If you drive us out, send us into the
herd of pigs."
32 He said to them, "Go!" So they came out and went into the pigs,
and the whole herd rushed down the steep bank into the lake and
died in the water. 33 Those tending the pigs ran off, went into the
town and reported all this, including what had happened to the de-
mon-possessed men. 34 Then the whole town went out to meet
Jesus. And when they saw him, they pleaded with him to leave their
8:34 [v]Lk 5:8; Ac 16:39
region.[v]

Jesus Heals a Paralytic

9 Jesus stepped into a boat, crossed over and came to his own
9:1 [w]Mt 4:13 9:2 [x]Mt 4:24 [y]ver 22 [z]Jn 16:33 [a]Lk 7:48
town.[w] 2 Some men brought to him a paralytic,[x] lying on a mat.
When Jesus saw their faith,[y] he said to the paralytic, "Take heart,[z]
son; your sins are forgiven."[a]
3 At this, some of the teachers of the law said to themselves, "This
9:3 [b]Mt 26:65; Jn 10:33 9:4 [c]Ps 94:11; Mt 12:25; Lk 6:8; 9:47; 11:17
fellow is blaspheming!"[b]
4 Knowing their thoughts,[c] Jesus said, "Why do you entertain evil
thoughts in your hearts? 5 Which is easier: to say, 'Your sins are for-
given,' or to say, 'Get up and walk'? 6 But so that you may know that
9:6 [d]Mt 8:20
the Son of Man[d] has authority on earth to forgive sins . . ." Then he
said to the paralytic, "Get up, take your mat and go home." 7 And the
man got up and went home. 8 When the crowd saw this, they were
9:8 [e]Mt 5:16; 15:31; Lk 7:16; 13:13; 17:15; 23:47; Jn 15:8; Ac 4:21; 11:18; 21:20
filled with awe; and they praised God,[e] who had given such author-
ity to men.

The Calling of Matthew

9 As Jesus went on from there, he saw a man named Matthew sit-
ting at the tax collector's booth. "Follow me," he told him, and Mat-
thew got up and followed him.

[a] *28* Some manuscripts *Gergesenes*; others *Gerasenes*

ANCIENT VOICES

And he explained the matter (of Tobias' desire to marry Sarah)* to Raguel, and Raguel said to Tobias, "Eat and drink, and be merry tonight. For it is fitting that you should marry my child. I must, however, explain to you the true situation. I have given her to seven men, and they died during the night when they went in to her. But for now, be merry." But Tobias said, "I will not taste anything here until you settle matters with me." And Raguel said, "Receive her from this moment in accordance with your decision. You are her relative, and she is yours. May God, the Merciful, guide and prosper you most wonderfully." Then Raguel called for his daughter Sarah, and he took her hand and presented her to Tobias as his wife. And he said, "Now in accordance with the Law of Moses receive her, and go to your father. And he blessed them." Then he called for Edna his wife; he then took a scroll and wrote out a marriage certificate and sealed it. Then they began their dinner. Raguel then addressed his wife Edna and said to her, "Dear, prepare the other room, and take her there." And she did as he said and took her there; and she wept. Then she wiped away the tears of her daughter and said to her, "Take courage, child! May the Lord of heaven and earth give you joy instead of this grief. Take courage, child!" When they had finished dining they took Tobias to her. As he went in, Tobias remembered the words of Raphael, and he took some incense embers and placed the fish's heart and liver on them so that it produced smoke. When the demon smelled the fragrance he fled to remotest Upper Egypt, and the angel Raphael tied him up.

*Words in parentheses added by translator where text has gaps

—TOBIAS TAKES SARAH AS HIS WIFE AND THWARTS A DEMON, ACCORDING TO THE BOOK OF TOBIT

From Tobit 7:10—8:3 (Rahlfs' Septuagint), trans. by Duane Garrett

See "Demons and the Bible" article.

8:28 The "region of the Gadarenes" was most likely the area around the city of Gadara, 6 miles (9.7 km) southeast of the Sea of Galilee. Mark and Luke identified the region by the capital city Gerasa, located about 35 miles (56 km) southeast of the Sea. See "Gergesenes, Gerasenes or Gadarenes?" on page 1635.

8:30 Large numbers of Gentiles lived in Galilee (see "Galilee in Jesus' Time" on p. 1587). Jews did not raise pigs, since they were considered the most ceremonially unclean of all animals.

8:31 The demons' plea to move into the swine would have been welcome to Jews, who considered "unclean" pigs on a par with demons (see "Clean and Unclean Foods in the Bible and the Ancient Near East" on p. 168). But this incident took place in Gentile territory; the pigs were most likely being raised commercially.

9:3 For "teachers of the law" in the New Testament, see the note on Acts 2:4.

9:9 Matthew, the son of Alphaeus (Mk 2:14) and a tax collector, was also called Levi (Mk 2:14; Lk 5:27). Since double names were common among the Jews, there can be little doubt that Levi and Matthew were one and the same person. Levi probably changed his name to Matthew ("gift of Yahweh") when he became a disciple of Jesus.

Matthew may have collected tolls from commercial traffic or taxes for the fish caught on the Sea of Galilee—a heavy toll to extract

10 While Jesus was having dinner at Matthew's house, many tax collectors and "sinners" came and ate
with him and his disciples. 11 When the Pharisees saw this, they asked his disciples, "Why does your teach-
er eat with tax collectors and 'sinners'?"[f]
12 On hearing this, Jesus said, "It is not the healthy who need a doctor, but the sick. 13 But go and learn
what this means: 'I desire mercy, not sacrifice.'[a] [g] For I have not come to call the righteous, but sinners."[h]

Jesus Questioned About Fasting

14 Then John's disciples came and asked him, "How is it that we and the Pharisees fast,[i] but your dis-
ciples do not fast?"
15 Jesus answered, "How can the guests of the bridegroom mourn while he is with them?[j] The time
will come when the bridegroom will be taken from them; then they will fast.[k]
16 "No one sews a patch of unshrunk cloth on an old garment, for the patch will pull away from the gar-
ment, making the tear worse. 17 Neither do men pour new wine into old wineskins. If they do, the skins
will burst, the wine will run out and the wineskins will be ruined. No, they pour new wine into new wine-
skins, and both are preserved."

A Dead Girl and a Sick Woman

18 While he was saying this, a ruler came and knelt before him[l] and said, "My daughter has just died.
But come and put your hand on her,[m] and she will live." 19 Jesus got up and went with him, and so did his
disciples.
20 Just then a woman who had been subject to bleeding for twelve years came up behind him and
touched the edge of his cloak.[n] 21 She said to herself, "If I only touch his cloak, I will be healed."
22 Jesus turned and saw her. "Take heart, daughter," he said, "your faith has healed you."[o] And the wom-
an was healed from that moment.[p]
23 When Jesus entered the ruler's house and saw the flute players and the noisy crowd,[q] 24 he said, "Go
away. The girl is not dead[r] but asleep."[s] But they laughed at him. 25 After the crowd had been put outside,
he went in and took the girl by the hand, and she got up. 26 News of this spread through all that region.[t]

Jesus Heals the Blind and Mute

27 As Jesus went on from there, two blind men followed him, calling out, "Have mercy on us, Son of Da-
vid!"[u]
28 When he had gone indoors, the blind men came to him, and he asked them, "Do you believe that I
am able to do this?"
"Yes, Lord," they replied.
29 Then he touched their eyes and said, "According to your faith will it be done to you";[v] 30 and their
sight was restored. Jesus warned them sternly, "See that no one knows about this."[w] 31 But they went out
and spread the news about him all over that region.[x]
32 While they were going out, a man who was demon-possessed[y] and could not talk[z] was brought to
Jesus. 33 And when the demon was driven out, the man who had been mute spoke. The crowd was amazed
and said, "Nothing like this has ever been seen in Israel."[a]
34 But the Pharisees said, "It is by the prince of demons that he drives out demons."[b]

9:11 [f]Mt 11:19; Lk 5:30; 15:2; Gal 2:15
9:13 [g]Hos 6:6; Mic 6:6-8; Mt 12:7 [h]1Ti 1:15
9:14 [i]Lk 18:12
9:15 [j]Jn 3:29 [k]Ac 13:2,3; 14:23
9:18 [l]Mt 8:2 [m]Mk 5:23
9:20 [n]Mt 14:36; Mk 3:10
9:22 [o]Mk 10:52; Lk 7:50; 17:19; 18:42 [p]Mt 15:28
9:23 [q]2Ch 35:25; Jer 9:17,18
9:24 [r]Ac 20:10 [s]Jn 11:11-14
9:26 [t]Mt 4:24
9:27 [u]Mt 15:22; Mk 10:47; Lk 18:38-39
9:29 [v]ver 22
9:30 [w]Mt 8:4
9:31 [x]ver 26; Mk 7:36
9:32 [y]Mt 4:24 [z]Mt 12:22-24
9:33 [a]Mk 2:12
9:34 [b]Mt 12:24; Lk 11:15

[a] *13* Hosea 6:6

---

from struggling Galileans. The Romans imposed tribute or tax (typically a road toll) on all their subjects for the maintenance of their provincial government (see the note on Mt 5:46; see also "Roman Taxation" on p. 1855).

The readiness with which Matthew responded to Jesus' call seems to indicate that he had previously come into contact with Jesus and his teachings and had already decided to dedicate his life to Jesus' cause. That Jesus should have chosen as his disciple a Jewish tax collector who was in the employ of the Roman government is indeed remarkable. Tax collectors were bitterly hated by their own countrymen and regarded as little more than traitors. However, Matthew's background and talents must have been of great value to Jesus. As a tax collector Matthew was skilled at writing and keeping records. Apart from the mention of Matthew in the lists of the apostles (10:3; Mk 3:18; Ac 1:13), no further notices of him are found in the New Testament.

9:10 See "Jewish Meals and Meal Customs" on page 1575.

9:11 For information on the Pharisees, see the note on 3:7.

9:17 See "Wine and Alcoholic Beverages in the Ancient World" on page 2015. In ancient times goatskins were used to hold wine. As the fresh grape juice fermented, the wine would expand, and the new wineskin would stretch. But a used skin, already stretched, would break.

9:20 The hemorrhaging woman was considered ritually unclean and was excluded from social and religious relations. Jesus' healing of her removed the public stigma of her condition and smoothed the way for her reentry into social and religious life.

9:23 Musicians were hired to play in mourning ceremonies (see "Sackcloth and Ashes: Rituals of Lamentation" on p. 820).

9:25 Touching a corpse rendered a person "unclean" (see Nu 19:14–16), but Jesus restored the girl to life, transforming uncleanness to purity.

The Workers Are Few

9:35 cMt 4:23 9:36 dMt 14:14 eNu 27:17; Eze 34:5,6; Zec 10:2; Mk 6:34 9:37 fJn 4:35 gLk 10:2

35 Jesus went through all the towns and villages, teaching in their synagogues, preaching the good
news of the kingdom and healing every disease and sickness.[c] 36 When he saw the crowds, he had com-
passion on them,[d] because they were harassed and helpless, like sheep without a shepherd.[e] 37 Then he
said to his disciples, "The harvest[f] is plentiful but the workers are few.[g] 38 Ask the Lord of the harvest,
therefore, to send out workers into his harvest field."

Jewish Meals and Meal Customs

MATTHEW 9

The Origin of New Testament Dietary Practices

The references to dining and meals in the New Testament, and especially in the Gospels, combine features of Greco-Roman practice with Jewish religious tradition. From Greco-Roman customs we see the following:

- Communal meals, or banquets, provided an important social and religious venue for defining and experiencing fellowship (Mt 9:10; 11:19).
- The meal was followed by a period of music or extended conversation.
- The normal posture for eating was reclining on one's side (Lk 7:36; 22:14).

The majority of the dietary practices we see in the Gospels, however, were derived from Judaism. From Jewish religious teachings we see the following:

- The holiness of meals within Judaism was extended through interpretation to the complex system of the kosher laws.

Acceptable animals were those that both chewed the cud and had cloven hoofs.

Fish possessing scales and fins, as well as certain types of birds, were also permitted.

The Bible prohibited certain types of food deemed to be pagan or acquired by cruel means. This included the consumption of meat taken from a still living animal or from one found dead, the drinking of blood or the boiling of a kid in its mother's milk.

- The Biblical injunction against fellowship with sinners (Ps 1:1; Pr 13:20; 14:7) was developed in Jewish tradition as a warning against improper or excessively intimate association with the wicked, especially at mealtimes (1Co 15:33; Sir 6:7–12; 12:13–18).[1]
- The demands of the Levitical system of dietary purity greatly restricted the possibility of shared meals between Jews and Gentiles (Ac 10:28; Gal 2:12).
- The Pharisees, known for their exacting interpretation of Scripture, applied the even higher purity restrictions of the temple to their own table fellowship.[2] In this way they attempted to eat their meals in a state of ritual purity appropriate for priests as a way of sanctifying all of life to God.[3]

The Significance of the New Testament Dietary Practices

Interpreters have given a variety of explanations for Jewish dietary laws.[4] Some contend that they were primarily intended for hygiene and good health, while others argue that the avoidance of idolatrous practices was the main reason for kosher laws. Still others simply suggest that these laws functioned as an artificial boundary to remind Jews that they were different from Gentiles. Most Jews seem to have believed these elaborate restrictions to have been a concrete, daily expression of holiness (Lev 11:44–45), which was also expressed in Jewish meals through the act of tithing all means of sustenance, the recitation of blessings before and after each meal (Dt 8:10; Jn 6:11; 1Co 11:24) and the marking of each festival on the liturgical calendar through the eating of distinctive foods prepared in a distinctive manner.[5]

The observance of the dietary laws acquired new significance during the Maccabean era when "many in Israel stood firm and were resolved in their hearts not to eat unclean food. They chose to die rather than to be defiled by food or to profane the holy covenant" (1Mc 1:62–63).[6] This historical reality, together with inherited prophetic imagery, led to the notion of a great Messianic banquet in which the righteous would enjoy the hospitality of God in the age to come (Isa 25:6–8; Mt 22:1–10; Rev 19:9–17).

[1] Sirach is an Apocryphal book. [2] See "The Pharisees" on page 1566. [3] See "Ritual Purity in Israel and the Ancient Near East" on page 166 and "The Jewish Priesthood and Religious Life in the First Century A.D." on page 1704. [4] See "Clean and Unclean Foods in the Bible and the Ancient Near East" on page 168. [5] See "The Festivals of Israel" on page 186. [6] First Maccabees is an Apocryphal book.

Jesus Sends Out the Twelve

10 He called his twelve disciples to him and gave them authority to drive out evil[a] spirits[h] and to heal
every disease and sickness.
2 These are the names of the twelve apostles: first, Simon (who is called Peter) and his brother An-
drew; James son of Zebedee, and his brother John; 3 Philip and Bartholomew; Thomas and Matthew the
tax collector; James son of Alphaeus, and Thaddaeus; 4 Simon the Zealot and Judas Iscariot, who betrayed
him.[i]
5 These twelve Jesus sent out with the following instructions: "Do not go among the Gentiles or enter
any town of the Samaritans.[j] 6 Go rather to the lost sheep of Israel.[k] 7 As you go, preach this message: 'The
kingdom of heaven[l] is near.' 8 Heal the sick, raise the dead, cleanse those who have leprosy,[b] drive out de-
mons. Freely you have received, freely give. 9 Do not take along any gold or silver or copper in your belts;[m]
10 take no bag for the journey, or extra tunic, or sandals or a staff; for the worker is worth his keep.[n]
11 "Whatever town or village you enter, search for some worthy person there and stay at his house un-
til you leave. 12 As you enter the home, give it your greeting.[o] 13 If the home is deserving, let your peace rest

10:1 [h]Mk 3:13-15; Lk 9:1
10:4 [i]Mt 26:14-16,25,47; Jn 13:2,26,27
10:5 [j]2Ki 17:24; Lk 9:52; Jn 4:4-26,39,40; Ac 8:5,25
10:6 [k]Jer 50:6; Mt 15:24
10:7 [l]Mt 3:2
10:9 [m]Lk 22:35
10:10 [n]1Ti 5:18
10:12 [o]1Sa 25:6

[a] *1* Greek *unclean* [b] *8* The Greek word was used for various diseases affecting the skin—not necessarily leprosy.

10:3 For "Bartholomew," see the note on Luke 6:14.

Thaddaeus is mentioned only twice in Scripture—in two of the four lists of the apostles (here and in Mk 3:18). In Matthew 10:3, the KJV renders this as "Lebbaeus, whose surname was Thaddaeus." The other two lists (Lk 6:16 and Ac 1:13) insert Judas, the son of James instead of this name. Nothing else is known with certainty about this individual, but he may be mentioned in John 14:22. An unauthentic "Gospel of Thaddaeus" used to exist.

10:4 The label "the Zealot" either describes Simon's religious zeal or is a reference to his membership in the party of the Zealots, a Jewish revolutionary group violently opposed to Roman rule over the Holy Land (see "The Zealots and the Essenes" below).

The Zealots were members of a Jewish patriotic party started during the time of Quirinius to resist Roman aggression. According to Josephus (*Jewish Wars*, 4.3.9; 5.1; 7.8.1), the Zealots resorted to violence and assassination in their hatred of the Romans, their fanatical violence eventually provoking the Roman war. Simon the Zealot was distinguished from Simon Peter by this epithet (Lk 6:15; Ac 1:13).

10:5 Samaritans were a mixed-blood race resulting from the intermarriage of Israelites left behind when the people of the northern kingdom were exiled and Gentiles brought into the land by the Assyrians (see the notes on 2Ki 17:24–41; 24:10–12). Bitter hostility existed between Jews and Samaritans in Jesus' day. See "The Samaritans" on page 1737.

10:8 See the NIV text note; see also "Skin Diseases in the Ancient World" on page 171.

10:9 For "belts," see the note on Luke 10:4.

10:10 See "Ancient Israelite Clothing and Jewelry" on page 1059 and "Dress and Fashion in the Greco-Roman World" on page 2004.

10:12 The Jewish greeting was *shalom*, meaning "peace."

CULTURAL AND HISTORICAL NOTES

The Zealots and the Essenes

MATTHEW 10 The Zealots were radical Jews who sought the violent overthrow of the Roman regime in Judea under the rallying cry "No king but God!" They came to prominence during the Jewish revolt against Rome in A.D. 66–73, but the roots of violent rebellion stretch back much further. While scholars debate whether there was a continuous, organized movement of insurrection throughout the first century A.D., it is at least interesting to note that some of the leaders of the uprising in A.D. 66 were direct descendants of men who had fought against Rome during the first century B.C.[1] When Jesus advocated nonviolent resistance to enemies, he may have been directly opposing this kind of armed revolution.[2]

The Essenes were another protest group in early Judaism. This faction most likely grew out of mid-second-century B.C. reform movements that arose during the Maccabean revolt. By the first century A.D. the Essenes were a significant force for renewal in Judaism. Like the Pharisees, they were concerned with purity and called for a strict adherence to the Law, although the two groups disagreed with the Pharisees on particular points of interpretation and practice.[3] The Essenes were noted for their ascetic tendencies, their nonparticipation in temple worship and their desire to isolate themselves in tight-knit communities. Some of the more radical Essenes who followed the so-called Teacher of Righteousness eventually gave up hope of renewal through normal channels and withdrew to the Judean wilderness to live together near the Dead Sea.

[1] See "The Intertestamental Period" on page 1551. [2] See "Messianic Conflicts and the Fall of Jerusalem" on page 1632. [3] See "The Pharisees" on page 1566 and "Ritual Purity in Israel and the Ancient Near East" on page 166.

on it; if it is not, let your peace return to you. [14]If anyone will not welcome you or listen to your words,
shake the dust off your feet[p] when you leave that home or town. [15]I tell you the truth, it will be more bear-
able for Sodom and Gomorrah[q] on the day of judgment[r] than for that town.[s] [16]I am sending you out like
sheep among wolves.[t] Therefore be as shrewd as snakes and as innocent as doves.[u]

[17]"Be on your guard against men; they will hand you over to the local councils[v] and flog you in their
synagogues.[w] [18]On my account you will be brought before governors and kings[x] as witnesses to them
and to the Gentiles. [19]But when they arrest you, do not worry about what to say or how to say it.[y] At that
time you will be given what to say, [20]for it will not be you speaking, but the Spirit of your Father[z] speak-
ing through you.

[21]"Brother will betray brother to death, and a father his child; children will rebel against their parents[a]
and have them put to death. [22]All men will hate you because of me, but he who stands firm to the end
will be saved.[b] [23]When you are persecuted in one place, flee to another. I tell you the truth, you will not
finish going through the cities of Israel before the Son of Man comes.

[24]"A student is not above his teacher, nor a servant above his master.[c] [25]It is enough for the student
to be like his teacher, and the servant like his master. If the head of the house has been called Beelze-
bub,[a][d] how much more the members of his household!

[26]"So do not be afraid of them. There is nothing concealed that will not be disclosed, or hidden that will
not be made known.[e] [27]What I tell you in the dark, speak in the daylight; what is whispered in your ear,
proclaim from the roofs. [28]Do not be afraid of those who kill the body but cannot kill the soul. Rather, be
afraid of the One[f] who can destroy both soul and body in hell. [29]Are not two sparrows sold for a penny[b]?
Yet not one of them will fall to the ground apart from the will of your Father. [30]And even the very hairs of
your head are all numbered.[g] [31]So don't be afraid; you are worth more than many sparrows.[h]

[32]"Whoever acknowledges me before men,[i] I will also acknowledge him before my Father in heaven.
[33]But whoever disowns me before men, I will disown him before my Father in heaven.[j]

[34]"Do not suppose that I have come to bring peace to the earth. I did not come to bring peace, but a
sword. [35]For I have come to turn

> " 'a man against his father,
> a daughter against her mother,
> a daughter-in-law against her mother-in-law[k]—
> [36] a man's enemies will be the members of his own household.'[c][l]

[37]"Anyone who loves his father or mother more than me is not worthy of me; anyone who loves his
son or daughter more than me is not worthy of me;[m] [38]and anyone who does not take his cross and fol-
low me is not worthy of me.[n] [39]Whoever finds his life will lose it, and whoever loses his life for my sake
will find it.[o]

[40]"He who receives you receives me,[p] and he who receives me receives the one who sent me.[q] [41]Any-
one who receives a prophet because he is a prophet will receive a prophet's reward, and anyone who re-
ceives a righteous man because he is a righteous man will receive a righteous man's reward. [42]And if any-
one gives even a cup of cold water to one of these little ones because he is my disciple, I tell you the truth,
he will certainly not lose his reward."[r]

Jesus and John the Baptist

11 After Jesus had finished instructing his twelve disciples,[s] he went on from there to teach and
preach in the towns of Galilee.[d]

[2]When John heard in prison[t] what Christ was doing, he sent his disciples [3]to ask him, "Are you the one
who was to come,[u] or should we expect someone else?"

10:14 [p]Ne 5:13; Lk 10:11; Ac 13:51
10:15 [q]2Pe 2:6 [r]Mt 12:36; 2Pe 2:9; 1Jn 4:17 [s]Mt 11:22,24
10:16 [t]Lk 10:3 [u]Ro 16:19
10:17 [v]Mt 5:22 [w]Mt 23:34; Mk 13:9; Ac 5:40; 26:11
10:18 [x]Ac 25:24-26
10:19 [y]Ex 4:12
10:20 [z]Ac 4:8
10:21 [a]ver 35,36; Mic 7:6
10:22 [b]Mt 24:13; Mk 13:13
10:24 [c]Lk 6:40; Jn 13:16; 15:20
10:25 [d]Mk 3:22
10:26 [e]Mk 4:22; Lk 8:17
10:28 [f]Isa 8:12, 13; Heb 10:31
10:30 [g]1Sa 14:45; 2Sa 14:11; Lk 21:18; Ac 27:34
10:31 [h]Mt 12:12
10:32 [i]Ro 10:9
10:33 [j]Mk 8:38; 2Ti 2:12
10:35 [k]ver 21
10:36 [l]Mic 7:6
10:37 [m]Lk 14:26
10:38 [n]Mt 16:24; Lk 14:27
10:39 [o]Lk 17:33; Jn 12:25
10:40 [p]Mt 18:5; Gal 4:14 [q]Lk 9:48; Jn 12:44; 13:20
10:42 [r]Mt 25:40; Mk 9:41; Heb 6:10
11:1 [s]Mt 7:28
11:2 [t]Mt 14:3
11:3 [u]Ps 118:26; Jn 11:27; Heb 10:37

[a] 25 Greek *Beezeboul* or *Beelzeboul* [b] 29 Greek *an assarion* [c] 36 Micah 7:6 [d] 1 Greek *in their towns*

10:14 Shaking the dust off one's feet was a symbolic act practiced by the Pharisees when they left a ceremonially unclean Gentile area. Here it represented an act of solemn warning to those who rejected God's message.
10:15 See "The Destruction of Sodom and Gomorrah" on page 32.
10:17 "Local councils" refers to the lower courts, connected with local synagogues (see "Ancient Synagogues" on p. 1783). They tried less serious cases and flogged those found guilty.

10:25 *Beelzebub* is the Greek form of the Hebrew name Baal-Zebub. It is widely thought to mean "lord of the flies" and to be a parody on and mockery of Baal-Zebul, an ancient name of the god Baal that meant "Prince Baal." The precise meaning of Beelzebub/Baal-Zebul is unknown, however, nor do we know how it came to be regarded as a name for Satan.
10:40–42 During times of persecution, hospitality was especially important and could entail danger for the host(s).

4 **Jesus replied,** "Go back and report to John what you hear and see: 5 The blind receive sight, the lame
walk, those who have leprosy[a] are cured, the deaf hear, the dead are raised, and the good news is preached
to the poor.[v] 6 Blessed is the man who does not fall away on account of me."[w]
7 As John's[x] disciples were leaving, Jesus began to speak to the crowd about John: "What did you go out
into the desert to see? A reed swayed by the wind? 8 If not, what did you go out to see? A man dressed in
fine clothes? No, those who wear fine clothes are in kings' palaces. 9 Then what did you go out to see? A
prophet?[y] Yes, I tell you, and more than a prophet. 10 This is the one about whom it is written:

> " 'I will send my messenger ahead of you,
> who will prepare your way before you.'[b][z]

11 I tell you the truth: Among those born of women there has not risen anyone greater than John the Bap-
tist; yet he who is least in the kingdom of heaven is greater than he. 12 From the days of John the Baptist
until now, the kingdom of heaven has been forcefully advancing, and forceful men lay hold of it. 13 For all
the Prophets and the Law prophesied until John. 14 And if you are willing to accept it, he is the Elijah who
was to come.[a] 15 He who has ears, let him hear.[b]
16 "To what can I compare this generation? They are like children sitting in the marketplaces and call-
ing out to others:

> 17 " 'We played the flute for you,
> and you did not dance;
> we sang a dirge,
> and you did not mourn.'

11:5 [v]Isa 35:4-6; 61:1; Lk 4:18,19
11:6 [w]Mt 13:21
11:7 [x]Mt 3:1
11:9 [y]Mt 21:26; Lk 1:76
11:10 [z]Mal 3:1; Mk 1:2
11:14 [a]Mal 4:5; Mt 17:10-13; Mk 9:11-13; Lk 1:17; Jn 1:21
11:15 [b]Mt 13:9, 43; Mk 4:23; Lk 14:35; Rev 2:7

[a] *5* The Greek word was used for various diseases affecting the skin—not necessarily leprosy. [b] *10* Mal. 3:1

11:5 For "leprosy," see the NIV text note; see also "Skin Diseases in the Ancient World" on page 171.
11:16–17 The New Testament word for "market" is *agora*, the civic center where people gathered for recreation (vv. 16–17), where the unemployed loafed (20:3,6) and where the proud paraded (Mk 12:38; Lk 11:43). The agora was both a courtroom (Ac 16:19) and a forum (Ac 17:17). From a corner shop the market developed into a great urban multipurpose center. See "The Ancient Agora" on page 1799.

ARCHAEOLOGICAL SITES

KORAZIN

MATTHEW 11 Early in his ministry Jesus left his hometown of Nazareth and settled in Capernaum, located on the northern shore of the Sea of Galilee.[1] He ministered in Capernaum and in the nearby towns of Korazin (often spelled Chorazin) and Bethsaida (see "Map 11" to locate all three towns). Korazin is mentioned in the Bible only in Matthew 11:21 and the parallel passage in Luke 10:13, where all three towns came under Jesus' condemnation for their failure to repent. They were, after all, "the cities in which most of his miracles had been performed" (Mt 11:20).

Korazin is located about an hour's walk (2.5 mi or 4 km) north of Capernaum on a basalt plateau known as the Korazin Plateau, about 800 feet (244 m) above the Sea of Galilee. It is described in Jewish sources as a medium-sized town noted for its wheat production. The main road to Damascus passed by a little to the north, so commerce, as well as agriculture, played an important role in the economy of the community.

The ruins of Korazin cover an area of more than 80 acres. Excavations and literary sources indicate that the city was founded in the first century A.D. and thrived until the Arab conquest in the eighth century. A civic center and a number of domestic complexes, all made of local black basalt stone and dating from the third to eighth centuries A.D., have been uncovered. The civic center, arranged in an east-west direction on the gently sloping plateau, is comprised of a synagogue, ritual bath complex, cisterns and public buildings. After the Arab conquest Korazin declined and was eventually abandoned.

[1]See "Capernaum" on page 1643.

11:18 [c]Mt 3:4 18For John came neither eating[c] nor drinking,[d] and they say, 'He has a demon.' 19The Son of Man came
[d]Lk 1:15 eating and drinking, and they say, 'Here is a glutton and a drunkard, a friend of tax collectors and "sin-
11:19 [e]Mt 9:11 ners." '[e] But wisdom is proved right by her actions."

Woe on Unrepentant Cities

20Then Jesus began to denounce the cities in which most of his miracles had been performed, be-
11:21 [f]Mk 6:45; Lk 9:10; Jn 12:21 cause they did not repent. 21"Woe to you, Korazin! Woe to you, Bethsaida![f] If the miracles that were
[g]Mt 15:21; Lk 6:17; Ac 12:20 performed in you had been performed in Tyre and Sidon,[g] they would have repented long ago in sack-
[h]Jnh 3:5-9 cloth and ashes.[h] 22But I tell you, it will be more bearable for Tyre and Sidon on the day of judgment
11:22 [i]ver 24; Mt 10:15 than for you.[i] 23And you, Capernaum,[j] will you be lifted up to the skies? No, you will go down to the
11:23 [j]Mt 4:13 [k]Isa 14:13-15 depths.[a][k] If the miracles that were performed in you had been performed in Sodom, it would have re-
11:24 [l]Mt 10:15 mained to this day. 24But I tell you that it will be more bearable for Sodom on the day of judgment
than for you."[l]

Rest for the Weary

11:25 [m]Lk 22:42; Jn 11:41 25At that time Jesus said, "I praise you, Father,[m] Lord of heaven and earth, because you have hidden
[n]1Co 1:26-29 these things from the wise and learned, and revealed them to little children.[n] 26Yes, Father, for this was
your good pleasure.
11:27 [o]Mt 28:18 [p]Jn 3:35; 13:3; 27"All things have been committed to me[o] by my Father.[p] No one knows the Son except the Father,
17:2 [q]Jn 10:15 and no one knows the Father except the Son and those to whom the Son chooses to reveal him.[q]
11:28 [r]Jn 7:37 28"Come to me,[r] all you who are weary and burdened, and I will give you rest. 29Take my yoke upon
11:29 [s]Jn 13:15; Php 2:5; you and learn from me,[s] for I am gentle and humble in heart, and you will find rest for your souls.[t] 30For
1Pe 2:21; 1Jn 2:6 [t]Jer 6:16 11:30 [u]1Jn 5:3 my yoke is easy and my burden is light."[u]

Lord of the Sabbath

12 At that time Jesus went through the grainfields on the Sabbath. His disciples were hungry and
12:1 [v]Dt 23:25 began to pick some heads of grain[v] and eat them. 2When the Pharisees saw this, they said to
12:2 [w]ver 10; Lk 13:14; 14:3; him, "Look! Your disciples are doing what is unlawful on the Sabbath."[w]
Jn 5:10; 7:23; 9:16 3He answered, "Haven't you read what David did when he and his companions were hungry?[x] 4He en-
12:3 [x]1Sa 21:6 tered the house of God, and he and his companions ate the consecrated bread—which was not lawful
12:4 [y]Lev 24:5,9 for them to do, but only for the priests.[y] 5Or haven't you read in the Law that on the Sabbath the priests
12:5 [z]Nu 28:9,10; Jn 7:22,23 in the temple desecrate the day[z] and yet are innocent? 6I tell you that one[b] greater than the temple is
12:6 [a]ver 41,42 12:7 [b]Hos 6:6; here.[a] 7If you had known what these words mean, 'I desire mercy, not sacrifice,'[c][b] you would not have
Mic 6:6-8; Mt 9:13 condemned the innocent. 8For the Son of Man[c] is Lord of the Sabbath."
12:8 [c]Mt 8:20 9Going on from that place, he went into their synagogue, 10and a man with a shriveled hand was there.
12:10 [d]ver 2; Lk 13:14; 14:3; Looking for a reason to accuse Jesus, they asked him, "Is it lawful to heal on the Sabbath?"[d]
Jn 9:16 11He said to them, "If any of you has a sheep and it falls into a pit on the Sabbath, will you not take
12:11 [e]Lk 14:5 12:12 [f]Mt 10:31 hold of it and lift it out?[e] 12How much more valuable is a man than a sheep![f] Therefore it is lawful to do
good on the Sabbath."
13Then he said to the man, "Stretch out your hand." So he stretched it out and it was completely re-
12:14 [g]Mt 26:4; 27:1; Mk 3:6; Lk 6:11; Jn 5:18; 11:53 stored, just as sound as the other. 14But the Pharisees went out and plotted how they might kill Jesus.[g]

[a] 23 Greek *Hades* [b] 6 Or *something*; also in verses 41 and 42 [c] 7 Hosea 6:6

11:21 See "Korazin" on page 1578.

Tyre and Sidon were cities on the Phoenician coast north of the Holy Land (see "The Downfall of Tyre" on p. 1345 and "Sidon" on p. 1536).

For "sackcloth," see "Sackcloth and Ashes: Rituals of Lamentation" on page 820.

11:23 For "Capernaum," see the note on 4:13.

11:28 "The Pharisees placed burdens on the people by insisting on a strict adherence to the law (see 23:4; see also "Biblical Interpretation at Qumran and Among the Early Rabbis" on p. 1603).

11:29–30 The chief work of a carpenter was making roofs, doors, window shutters, lattice squares and divan frames for houses, plows, and yokes. So Jesus knew about yokes, as well as about various other aspects of farm life.

The image of a yoke was commonly used in the Old Testament to describe Israel's subjection to foreign oppression (Lev 26:13; Isa 10:24–27). By Jesus' time, it also had become a metaphor in Judaism for the law. Jesus' invitation was a stark contrast to the military burden of foreign oppressors or to the religious burden imposed by the Pharisees (see "The Pharisees" on p. 1566).

12:1 "Grainfields" included those for wheat and barley, the latter eaten by poorer people.

12:2 To a Pharisee, "what is unlawful" could have referred either to a Scriptural command or to a rabbi's interpretation of that command (see the note on 3:7; see also "The Pharisees" on p. 1566 and "Bible Interpretation at Qumran and Among the Early Rabbis" on p. 1603). The disciples could have been cited for any of several rabbinic taboos.

12:4 Each Sabbath, 12 fresh loaves of bread were to be set out on a table in the Holy Place (Ex 25:30; Lev 24:5–9). The old loaves were to be eaten by the priests.

12:9 For "synagogue," see the note on Mark 1:21.

God's Chosen Servant

15 Aware of this, Jesus withdrew from that place. Many followed him, and he healed all their sick,[h] **12:15** [h]Mt 4:23
16 warning them not to tell who he was.[i] 17 This was to fulfill what was spoken through the prophet Isaiah: **12:16** [i]Mt 8:4

18 "Here is my servant whom I have chosen,
the one I love, in whom I delight;[j] **12:18** [j]Mt 3:17
I will put my Spirit on him,
and he will proclaim justice to the nations.
19 He will not quarrel or cry out;
no one will hear his voice in the streets.
20 A bruised reed he will not break,
and a smoldering wick he will not snuff out,
till he leads justice to victory.
21 In his name the nations will put their hope."[a][k] **12:21** [k]Isa 42:1-4

Jesus and Beelzebub

22 Then they brought him a demon-possessed man who was blind and mute, and Jesus healed him,
so that he could both talk and see.[l] 23 All the people were astonished and said, "Could this be the Son of **12:22** [l]Mt 4:24; 9:32-33
David?"[m] **12:23** [m]Mt 9:27
24 But when the Pharisees heard this, they said, "It is only by Beelzebub,[b][n] the prince of demons, that **12:24** [n]Mk 3:22
this fellow drives out demons."[o] [o]Mt 9:34
25 Jesus knew their thoughts[p] and said to them, "Every kingdom divided against itself will be ruined, **12:25** [p]Mt 9:4
and every city or household divided against itself will not stand. 26 If Satan[q] drives out Satan, he is divid- **12:26** [q]Mt 4:10
ed against himself. How then can his kingdom stand? 27 And if I drive out demons by Beelzebub, by whom
do your people[r] drive them out? So then, they will be your judges. 28 But if I drive out demons by the Spir- **12:27** [r]Ac 19:13
it of God, then the kingdom of God has come upon you.
29 "Or again, how can anyone enter a strong man's house and carry off his possessions unless he first
ties up the strong man? Then he can rob his house.
30 "He who is not with me is against me, and he who does not gather with me scatters.[s] 31 And so I tell **12:30** [s]Mk 9:40; Lk 11:23
you, every sin and blasphemy will be forgiven men, but the blasphemy against the Spirit will not be for-
given.[t] 32 Anyone who speaks a word against the Son of Man will be forgiven, but anyone who speaks **12:31** [t]Mk 3:28, 29; Lk 12:10
against the Holy Spirit will not be forgiven, either in this age[u] or in the age to come.[v] **12:32** [u]Tit 2:12
33 "Make a tree good and its fruit will be good, or make a tree bad and its fruit will be bad, for a tree [v]Mk 10:30; Lk 20:34,35;
is recognized by its fruit.[w] 34 You brood of vipers,[x] how can you who are evil say anything good? For out Eph 1:21; Heb 6:5
of the overflow of the heart the mouth speaks.[y] 35 The good man brings good things out of the good stored **12:33** [w]Mt 7:16, 17; Lk 6:43,44
up in him, and the evil man brings evil things out of the evil stored up in him. 36 But I tell you that men **12:34** [x]Mt 3:7; 23:33 [y]Mt 15:18;
will have to give account on the day of judgment for every careless word they have spoken. 37 For by your Lk 6:45
words you will be acquitted, and by your words you will be condemned."

The Sign of Jonah

38 Then some of the Pharisees and teachers of the law said to him, "Teacher, we want to see a mirac-
ulous sign from you."[z] **12:38** [z]Mt 16:1; Mk 8:11,12;
39 He answered, "A wicked and adulterous generation asks for a miraculous sign! But none will be giv- Lk 11:16; Jn 2:18;
en it except the sign of the prophet Jonah.[a] 40 For as Jonah was three days and three nights in the belly of 6:30; 1Co 1:22
a huge fish,[b] so the Son of Man[c] will be three days and three nights in the heart of the earth.[d] 41 The men **12:39** [a]Mt 16:4; Lk 11:29
of Nineveh[e] will stand up at the judgment with this generation and condemn it; for they repented at the **12:40** [b]Jnh 1:17 [c]Mt 8:20 [d]Mt 16:21
preaching of Jonah,[f] and now one[c] greater than Jonah is here. 42 The Queen of the South will rise at the **12:41** [e]Jnh 1:2 [f]Jnh 3:5

[a] *21* Isaiah 42:1-4 [b] *24* Greek *Beezeboul* or *Beelzeboul*; also in verse 27 [c] *41* Or *something*; also in verse 42

12:22–24 Ancient exorcists used a variety of incantations and spells; potions and herbs; and material articles, like rings, to try to manipulate the spirit world. Jesus commanded demons from his own authority, and they immediately submitted. The Pharisees attributed Jesus' power to Satan. This charge of practicing magic under the influence of Satan was punishable by stoning.

12:38 For "teachers of the law" in the New Testament, see the note on 2:4.

12:40 To count a part of a day as a whole day was a common Jewish reckoning of time.

The Greek word translated here "huge fish" does not necessarily mean "whale" but rather denotes a large "sea creature."

12:41 See "Nineveh" on page 1497.

12:42 In 1 Kings 10:1 the "Queen of the South" is called the queen of Sheba, a country in southwestern Arabia (modern Yemen). See "Sheba" on page 498.

12:42 g1Ki 10:1; 2Ch 9:1
judgment with this generation and condemn it; for she came[g] from the ends of the earth to listen to Sol-
omon's wisdom, and now one greater than Solomon is here.
43"When an evil[a] spirit comes out of a man, it goes through arid places seeking rest and does not find
it. 44Then it says, 'I will return to the house I left.' When it arrives, it finds the house unoccupied, swept
clean and put in order. 45Then it goes and takes with it seven other spirits more wicked than itself, and
12:45 h2Pe 2:20
they go in and live there. And the final condition of that man is worse than the first.[h] That is how it will
be with this wicked generation."

[a] 43 Greek *unclean*

CULTURAL AND HISTORICAL NOTES

The Family of Joseph, Mary and Jesus

MATTHEW 12 The Gospel accounts provide limited details about Jesus' immediate family. We know, of course, that he was born to Mary and that his stepfather was Joseph. A carpenter by trade, Joseph is mentioned only in the narratives of Jesus' birth and early childhood, leaving many to believe that he died prior to the time of Jesus' public ministry. The Gospels record the names of four of Jesus' brothers—James, Joseph, Simon and Judas (Mt 13:55)—and mention sisters without providing names.

Those who believe that Mary remained a virgin throughout her entire life suggest that these siblings were Joseph's children from a previous marriage. Scripture itself, however, makes no claim that Mary maintained her virginity following Jesus' birth, and it is more likely that the brothers and sisters of Jesus were simply the natural children born to Mary and Joseph after Jesus' birth. In ancient Jewish culture it would have been unthinkable for a man and woman to live together in a permanently unconsummated marriage. Matthew 1:25 in fact implies that Mary and Joseph did have normal sexual relations after Jesus' birth.

Although the relationship between Jesus and his family was characterized by tension and misunderstanding (e.g., Mk 3:31–34), at least two of his brothers later became his followers. James, a leader of the Jerusalem church (Ac 12:17), was martyred in the early sixties. Tradition ascribes the New Testament epistle of James to him. Similarly, the epistle of Jude is attributed to Jesus' brother Judas.

A carpenter's shop

Preserving Bible Times; © Dr. James C. Martin; permission of Eretz Israel Museum

Jesus' Mother and Brothers

46While Jesus was still talking to the crowd, his mother[i] and brothers[j] stood outside, wanting to speak
to him. 47Someone told him, "Your mother and brothers are standing outside, wanting to speak to you."[a]
48He replied to him, "Who is my mother, and who are my brothers?" 49Pointing to his disciples, he
said, "Here are my mother and my brothers. 50For whoever does the will of my Father in heaven[k] is my
brother and sister and mother."

The Parable of the Sower

13 That same day Jesus went out of the house[l] and sat by the lake. 2Such large crowds gathered
around him that he got into a boat[m] and sat in it, while all the people stood on the shore. 3Then
he told them many things in parables, saying: "A farmer went out to sow his seed. 4As he was scattering
the seed, some fell along the path, and the birds came and ate it up. 5Some fell on rocky places, where it
did not have much soil. It sprang up quickly, because the soil was shallow. 6But when the sun came up,
the plants were scorched, and they withered because they had no root. 7Other seed fell among thorns,
which grew up and choked the plants. 8Still other seed fell on good soil, where it produced a crop—a
hundred,[n] sixty or thirty times what was sown. 9He who has ears, let him hear."[o]
10The disciples came to him and asked, "Why do you speak to the people in parables?"
11He replied, "The knowledge of the secrets of the kingdom of heaven has been given to you,[p] but not
to them. 12Whoever has will be given more, and he will have an abundance. Whoever does not have, even
what he has will be taken from him.[q] 13This is why I speak to them in parables:

> "Though seeing, they do not see;
> though hearing, they do not hear or understand.[r]

14In them is fulfilled the prophecy of Isaiah:

> " 'You will be ever hearing but never understanding;
> you will be ever seeing but never perceiving.
> 15For this people's heart has become calloused;
> they hardly hear with their ears,
> and they have closed their eyes.
> Otherwise they might see with their eyes,
> hear with their ears,
> understand with their hearts
> and turn, and I would heal them.'[b][s]

16But blessed are your eyes because they see, and your ears because they hear.[t] 17For I tell you the truth,
many prophets and righteous men longed to see what you see[u] but did not see it, and to hear what you
hear but did not hear it.
18"Listen then to what the parable of the sower means: 19When anyone hears the message about the
kingdom[v] and does not understand it, the evil one[w] comes and snatches away what was sown in his
heart. This is the seed sown along the path. 20The one who received the seed that fell on rocky places is
the man who hears the word and at once receives it with joy. 21But since he has no root, he lasts only a
short time. When trouble or persecution comes because of the word, he quickly falls away.[x] 22The one who
received the seed that fell among the thorns is the man who hears the word, but the worries of this life
and the deceitfulness of wealth[y] choke it, making it unfruitful. 23But the one who received the seed that
fell on good soil is the man who hears the word and understands it. He produces a crop, yielding a hun-
dred, sixty or thirty times what was sown."[z]

The Parable of the Weeds

24Jesus told them another parable: "The kingdom of heaven is like[a] a man who sowed good seed in

[a] *47* Some manuscripts do not have verse 47. [b] *15* Isaiah 6:9,10

12:46 [i]Mt 1:18; 2:11,13,14,20; Lk 1:43; 2:33,34, 48,51; Jn 2:1,5; 19:25,26 [j]Mt 13:55; Jn 2:12; 7:3,5; Ac 1:14; 1Co 9:5; Gal 1:19
12:50 [k]Jn 15:14
13:1 [l]ver 36; Mt 9:28
13:2 [m]Lk 5:3
13:8 [n]Ge 26:12
13:9 [o]Mt 11:15
13:11 [p]Mt 11:25; 16:17; 19:11; Jn 6:65; 1Co 2:10,14; Col 1:27; 1Jn 2:20,27
13:12 [q]Mt 25:29; Lk 19:26
13:13 [r]Dt 29:4; Jer 5:21; Eze 12:2
13:15 [s]Isa 6:9, 10; Jn 12:40; Ac 28:26,27; Ro 11:8
13:16 [t]Mt 16:17
13:17 [u]Jn 8:56; Heb 11:13; 1Pe 1:10-12
13:19 [v]Mt 4:23 [w]Mt 5:37
13:21 [x]Mt 11:6
13:22 [y]Mt 19:23; 1Ti 6:9,10,17
13:23 [z]ver 8
13:24 [a]ver 31,33, 45,47; Mt 18:23; 20:1; 22:2; 25:1; Mk 4:26,30

13:2 Rabbis usually taught from a sitting position.
13:3 For information on sowing seed, see the note on Luke 8:5.

13:5 "Rocky places" refers not to ground covered with small stones but to shallow soil on top of solid rock. Any moisture that fell there soon evaporated, and the germinating seed withered and died.

his field. 25 But while everyone was sleeping, his enemy came and sowed weeds among the wheat, and
went away. 26 When the wheat sprouted and formed heads, then the weeds also appeared.
27 "The owner's servants came to him and said, 'Sir, didn't you sow good seed in your field? Where
then did the weeds come from?'
28 " 'An enemy did this,' he replied.
"The servants asked him, 'Do you want us to go and pull them up?'
29 " 'No,' he answered, 'because while you are pulling the weeds, you may root up the wheat with them.
30 Let both grow together until the harvest. At that time I will tell the harvesters: First collect the weeds
13:30 [b]Mt 3:12 and tie them in bundles to be burned; then gather the wheat and bring it into my barn.' "[b]

The Parables of the Mustard Seed and the Yeast

13:31 [c]ver 24 [d]Mt 17:20; 31 He told them another parable: "The kingdom of heaven is like[c] a mustard seed,[d] which a man took
Lk 17:6 and planted in his field. 32 Though it is the smallest of all your seeds, yet when it grows, it is the largest of
13:32 [e]Ps 104:12; garden plants and becomes a tree, so that the birds of the air come and perch in its branches."[e]
Eze 17:23; 31:6; Da 4:12 33 He told them still another parable: "The kingdom of heaven is like[f] yeast that a woman took and
13:33 [f]ver 24 [g]Ge 18:6 [h]Gal 5:9 mixed into a large amount[a] of flour[g] until it worked all through the dough."[h]
34 Jesus spoke all these things to the crowd in parables; he did not say anything to them without us-
13:34 [i]Mk 4:33; Jn 16:25 ing a parable.[i] 35 So was fulfilled what was spoken through the prophet:

"I will open my mouth in parables,
13:35 [j]Ps 78:2; Ro 16:25,26; 1Co 2:7; Eph 3:9; Col 1:26 I will utter things hidden since the creation of the world."[b][j]

The Parable of the Weeds Explained

36 Then he left the crowd and went into the house. His disciples came to him and said, "Explain to us
13:36 [k]Mt 15:15 the parable[k] of the weeds in the field."
13:37 [l]Mt 8:20 37 He answered, "The one who sowed the good seed is the Son of Man.[l] 38 The field is the world, and
13:38 [m]Jn 8:44, 45; 1Jn 3:10 the good seed stands for the sons of the kingdom. The weeds are the sons of the evil one,[m] 39 and the en-
13:39 [n]Joel 3:13 [o]Mt 24:3; 28:20 emy who sows them is the devil. The harvest[n] is the end of the age,[o] and the harvesters are angels.[p]
[p]Rev 14:15 40 "As the weeds are pulled up and burned in the fire, so it will be at the end of the age. 41 The Son of Man[q]
13:41 [q]Mt 8:20 [r]Mt 24:31 will send out his angels,[r] and they will weed out of his kingdom everything that causes sin and all who
13:42 [s]ver 50; Mt 8:12 do evil. 42 They will throw them into the fiery furnace, where there will be weeping and gnashing of teeth.[s]
13:43 [t]Da 12:3 [u]Mt 11:15 43 Then the righteous will shine like the sun[t] in the kingdom of their Father. He who has ears, let him hear.[u]

The Parables of the Hidden Treasure and the Pearl

13:44 [v]ver 24 [w]Isa 55:1; 44 "The kingdom of heaven is like[v] treasure hidden in a field. When a man found it, he hid it again, and
Php 3:7,8 then in his joy went and sold all he had and bought that field.[w]
13:45 [x]ver 24 45 "Again, the kingdom of heaven is like[x] a merchant looking for fine pearls. 46 When he found one of
great value, he went away and sold everything he had and bought it.

The Parable of the Net

13:47 [y]ver 24 [z]Mt 22:10 47 "Once again, the kingdom of heaven is like[y] a net that was let down into the lake and caught all
kinds[z] of fish. 48 When it was full, the fishermen pulled it up on the shore. Then they sat down and col-
lected the good fish in baskets, but threw the bad away. 49 This is how it will be at the end of the age. The
13:49 [a]Mt 25:32 angels will come and separate the wicked from the righteous[a] 50 and throw them into the fiery furnace,
13:50 [b]Mt 8:12 where there will be weeping and gnashing of teeth.[b]

[a] 33 Greek *three satas* (probably about 1/2 bushel or 22 liters) [b] 35 Psalm 78:2

13:26 Zizanion, a kind of weed referred to as "darnel" or "tares," has poisonous seeds but looks like wheat in its early stages of growth. Yet it is easily distinguishable at harvest.

13:31–32 The mustard seed is not the smallest seed known today, but it was the smallest used by farmers and gardeners in the Holy Land at that time. Under favorable conditions the mature plant could reach about ten feet (three m) in height. Using the mustard seed as a metaphor for the kingdom no doubt shocked Jesus' audience, who expected God's kingdom to be great and expansive.

13:33 Scripture almost always uses yeast as a negative image (see the note on Mk 8:15). But Jesus cited it to symbolize the positive, hidden permeation and growth of the kingdom of heaven within an unsuspecting world.

13:42 For the meaning of gnashing with one's teeth, see the note on Psalm 35:16.

13:44 People in ancient times commonly hid valuables in fields (e.g., when a marauding army approached), since there were no banks—although there were "bankers" (see 25:27 and its note; see also "Banking and Money in the Ancient World" on p. 696). These treasures might go hidden and unclaimed for generations.

13:48 See "Fishing in New Testament Times" on page 1676.

ARCHAEOLOGICAL SITES

HOUSES IN THE HOLY LAND OF THE FIRST CENTURY A.D.: PETER'S HOUSE IN CAPERNAUM; INSULAE

MATTHEW 14 Housing conditions in the first-century Holy Land varied dramatically according to people's financial situations. The best preserved homes are those that were built for the upper classes and constructed with obvious craftsmanship from lasting materials. Of these, the most splendid examples are the remains of Herod the Great's lavish palaces in Jerusalem, Masada and Jericho.[1]

These structures, along with other luxurious houses discovered in Jerusalem's upper city, reflect the stylistic conventions of contemporary Roman villas. The villa was structured around an open, colonnaded courtyard and contained a large reception room and dining area to accommodate large gatherings. Floors were covered with detailed stone mosaics, and walls were painted with frescoes. These upper-class houses and palaces in Judea also contained distinctively Jewish features, such as ritual baths alongside ordinary bathrooms,[2] the absence of human or animal representation in mosaics and frescoes and the presence of Jewish symbols (e.g., the menorah).

Since relatively few people lived in palatial homes, many more examples of middle-class dwellings have been revealed through archaeology. An important example, discovered in Jerusalem in 1970, is known as the "burnt house." This home was completely buried with soot and ash from the destruction of the city in A.D. 70 and, therefore, has been well preserved. The floor plan reflects a common pattern of three medium-sized rooms, a small storage room, a small kitchen and a stepped, ritual bath built around a paved courtyard. The walls were covered with a thin layer of limestone plaster, and the floors consisted of pressed earth. Furnishings within the house included rectangular stone tables, bowls, plates, cups and cylindrical weights, one of which identifies the owner as Bar Karos.

A key found at Qumran

Preserving Bible Times; © Dr. James C. Martin; permission of The Israel Museum/Shrine of the Book

Other significant examples of first-century houses have been unearthed in Capernaum ("Map 9").[3] Excavations near the ruins of the ancient synagogue there revealed a group of approximately 12 homes constructed of black basalt rocks and small pebbles and arranged around a central courtyard containing ovens and grinding stones. These single-story dwellings had floors of beaten black earth and stairways leading to flat roofs. The less-substantial roofs were probably built with tree branches covered with mud and straw (cf. Mk 2:4).

The largest of these homes attracted particular attention in that it featured a crushed limestone floor and had plastered walls filled with decorations (including flowers, pomegranates and numerous crosses) and inscriptions, which were fragmentary and in many languages: 124 in Greek, 18 in Syriac, 15 in Hebrew and 1 in Latin. Most of the inscriptions were short prayers, such as "Christ have mercy" or "Lord Jesus Christ help." Others contained the name of Peter, suggesting that this home was venerated in antiquity as a place of Christian pilgrimage and associated with the memory of Peter. Thus, this dwelling has become known as the house of Peter in Capernaum (Mt 8:14; Mk 1:29; Lk 4:38).

The lowest urban classes inhabited crowded tenement buildings called *insulae*—multistoried buildings divided into numerous apartments called *cenaculi*. The lowest floor generally contained a shop in which the proprietor also lived. The upper floors were accessed through outside staircases. The *insulae* usually lacked any system of heating, running water or sewage. Eutychus most likely fell from the third floor window of an *insula* while listening to Paul preach Christ in Troas (Ac 20:7–12).

[1]See "Herod the Great" on page 1627, "Masada" on page 1775 and "New Testament Jericho" on page 1646. [2]See "Baptism in the Ancient World" on page 1562. [3]See "Capernaum" on page 1643 and "The Capernaum Synagogue" on page 1591.

51“Have you understood all these things?” Jesus asked.
“Yes,” they replied.
52He said to them, “Therefore every teacher of the law who has been instructed about the kingdom
of heaven is like the owner of a house who brings out of his storeroom new treasures as well as old.”

A Prophet Without Honor

13:53 [c]Mt 7:28
53When Jesus had finished these parables,[c] he moved on from there. 54Coming to his hometown, he
13:54 [d]Mt 4:23 [e]Mt 7:28
began teaching the people in their synagogue,[d] and they were amazed.[e] “Where did this man get this
13:55 [f]Lk 3:23; Jn 6:42 [g]Mt 12:46
wisdom and these miraculous powers?” they asked. 55“Isn’t this the carpenter’s son?[f] Isn’t his mother’s[g]
name Mary, and aren’t his brothers James, Joseph, Simon and Judas? 56Aren’t all his sisters with us? Where
13:57 [h]Jn 6:61 [i]Lk 4:24; Jn 4:44
then did this man get all these things?” 57And they took offense[h] at him.
But Jesus said to them, “Only in his hometown and in his own house is a prophet without honor.”[i]
58And he did not do many miracles there because of their lack of faith.

John the Baptist Beheaded

14:1 [j]Mk 8:15; Lk 3:1,19; 13:31; 23:7,8; Ac 4:27; 12:1 [k]Lk 9:7-9
14 At that time Herod[j] the tetrarch heard the reports about Jesus,[k] 2and he said to his attendants,
14:2 [l]Mt 3:1
“This is John the Baptist;[l] he has risen from the dead! That is why miraculous powers are at work
in him.”
14:3 [m]Mt 4:12; 11:2 [n]Lk 3:19,20
3Now Herod had arrested John and bound him and put him in prison[m] because of Herodias, his broth-
14:4 [o]Lev 18:16; 20:21
er Philip’s wife,[n] 4for John had been saying to him: “It is not lawful for you to have her.”[o] 5Herod wanted
14:5 [p]Mt 11:9
to kill John, but he was afraid of the people, because they considered him a prophet.[p]
6On Herod’s birthday the daughter of Herodias danced for them and pleased Herod so much 7that he
promised with an oath to give her whatever she asked. 8Prompted by her mother, she said, “Give me here
on a platter the head of John the Baptist.” 9The king was distressed, but because of his oaths and his din-
14:10 [q]Mt 17:12
ner guests, he ordered that her request be granted 10and had John beheaded[q] in the prison. 11His head
was brought in on a platter and given to the girl, who carried it to her mother. 12John’s disciples came
14:12 [r]Ac 8:2
and took his body and buried it.[r] Then they went and told Jesus.

Jesus Feeds the Five Thousand

13When Jesus heard what had happened, he withdrew by boat privately to a solitary place. Hearing of
this, the crowds followed him on foot from the towns. 14When Jesus landed and saw a large crowd, he
14:14 [s]Mt 9:36 [t]Mt 4:23
had compassion on them[s] and healed their sick.[t]
15As evening approached, the disciples came to him and said, “This is a remote place, and it’s already
getting late. Send the crowds away, so they can go to the villages and buy themselves some food.”
16Jesus replied, “They do not need to go away. You give them something to eat.”
14:17 [u]Mt 16:9
17“We have here only five loaves[u] of bread and two fish,” they answered.
18“Bring them here to me,” he said. 19And he directed the people to sit down on the grass. Taking the
14:19 [v]1Sa 9:13; Mt 26:26; Mk 8:6; Lk 24:30; Ac 2:42; 27:35; 1Ti 4:4
five loaves and the two fish and looking up to heaven, he gave thanks and broke the loaves.[v] Then he gave
them to the disciples, and the disciples gave them to the people. 20They all ate and were satisfied, and
the disciples picked up twelve basketfuls of broken pieces that were left over. 21The number of those who
ate was about five thousand men, besides women and children.

13:54 Jesus’ hometown was “Nazareth” (see the note on 2:23). For information on teaching in the synagogue, see the note on Mark 1:21.
13:55 For “carpenter’s son,” see the note on Mark 6:3. Apparently Joseph was not living at the time of this incident. See “The Family of Joseph, Mary and Jesus” on page 1581.
14:1 A tetrarch was the ruler of a fourth part of a region. “Herod the tetrarch” (Herod Antipas) was one of several sons of Herod the Great (see “Herod the Great” on p. 1627). When Herod the Great died, his kingdom was divided among three of his sons (see “Herod’s Successors and Uneasy Relations Between Rome and the Jews” on p. 1631). Herod Antipas ruled over Galilee and Perea (4 B.C.–A.D. 39).
14:3 Herodias was a granddaughter of Herod the Great. First she married her uncle, Herod Philip I (Herod the Great also had another son named Philip, called Philip II, born of a different wife). Philip I lived in Rome and did not rule after the death of his father, Herod the Great. While a guest in the home of Herodias and Philip I, Herod Antipas persuaded Herodias to leave her husband (his half brother) for him. When Herod Antipas married Herodias, John the Baptist publicly condemned him for marrying his half brother’s wife. Such a marriage would have been considered an incestuous affront to God’s law (Lev 18:16; 20:21). John was a threat to Herod politically, so Herod had him arrested to counter his influence with the people. Josephus stated that John was imprisoned at Machaerus, a fortress in Perea on the eastern side of the Dead Sea.
14:6 For Hebrew/Jewish feasting, see the note on 22:2–14.
According to Josephus, the “daughter of Herodias” (and Philip I) was Salome. She later married her granduncle, the other Philip (Philip II).
14:20 The New Testament makes reference to two kinds of baskets. The *kophinos* (here and in Mk 6:43; Jn 6:13) was a relatively small basket that could be carried on the back to hold provisions. Twelve of these baskets were used to gather the food that remained after the feeding of the five thousand. The *spuris* was considerably larger, as we know from its use in letting Paul down from the wall at Damascus (Ac 9:25). Seven of these were used to gather the food that was left after the feeding of the four thousand (Mt 16:9–10).
14:21 All four Gospels record this miracle, but only Matthew noted that the number 5,000 resulted from a tally of men only. Jews

Jesus Walks on the Water

22 Immediately Jesus made the disciples get into the boat and go on ahead of him to the other side,
while he dismissed the crowd. 23 After he had dismissed them, he went up on a mountainside by himself
to pray.[w] When evening came, he was there alone, 24 but the boat was already a considerable distance[a] **14:23** [w]Lk 3:21
from land, buffeted by the waves because the wind was against it.
25 During the fourth watch of the night Jesus went out to them, walking on the lake. 26 When the dis-
ciples saw him walking on the lake, they were terrified. "It's a ghost,"[x] they said, and cried out in fear. **14:26** [x]Lk 24:37
27 But Jesus immediately said to them: "Take courage![y] It is I. Don't be afraid."[z] **14:27** [y]Mt 9:2; Ac 23:11
28 "Lord, if it's you," Peter replied, "tell me to come to you on the water." [z]Da 10:12; Mt 17:7; 28:10;
29 "Come," he said. Lk 1:13,30; 2:10;
Then Peter got down out of the boat, walked on the water and came toward Jesus. 30 But when he saw Ac 18:9; 23:11;
the wind, he was afraid and, beginning to sink, cried out, "Lord, save me!" Rev 1:17
31 Immediately Jesus reached out his hand and caught him. "You of little faith,"[a] he said, "why did you **14:31** [a]Mt 6:30
doubt?"
32 And when they climbed into the boat, the wind died down. 33 Then those who were in the boat wor-
shiped him, saying, "Truly you are the Son of God."[b] **14:33** [b]Ps 2:7; Mt 4:3
34 When they had crossed over, they landed at Gennesaret. 35 And when the men of that place recog-
nized Jesus, they sent word to all the surrounding country. People brought all their sick to him 36 and
begged him to let the sick just touch the edge of his cloak,[c] and all who touched him were healed. **14:36** [c]Mt 9:20

Clean and Unclean

15 Then some Pharisees and teachers of the law came to Jesus from Jerusalem and asked, 2 "Why
do your disciples break the tradition of the elders? They don't wash their hands before they eat!"[d] **15:2** [d]Lk 11:38
3 Jesus replied, "And why do you break the command of God for the sake of your tradition? 4 For God
said, 'Honor your father and mother'[b][e] and 'Anyone who curses his father or mother must be put to **15:4** [e]Ex 20:12; Dt 5:16; Eph 6:2
death.'[c][f] 5 But you say that if a man says to his father or mother, 'Whatever help you might otherwise [f]Ex 21:17;
have received from me is a gift devoted to God,' 6 he is not to 'honor his father[d]' with it. Thus you nulli- Lev 20:9
fy the word of God for the sake of your tradition. 7 You hypocrites! Isaiah was right when he prophesied
about you:

> 8 " 'These people honor me with their lips,
> but their hearts are far from me.
> 9 They worship me in vain;
> their teachings are but rules taught by men.[g]'[e][h]" **15:9** [g]Col 2:20-22 [h]Isa 29:13; Mal 2:2

10 Jesus called the crowd to him and said, "Listen and understand. 11 What goes into a man's mouth
does not make him 'unclean,'[i] but what comes out of his mouth, that is what makes him 'unclean.' "[j] **15:11** [i]Ac 10:14,15 [j]ver 18
12 Then the disciples came to him and asked, "Do you know that the Pharisees were offended when
they heard this?"
13 He replied, "Every plant that my heavenly Father has not planted[k] will be pulled up by the roots. **15:13** [k]Isa 60:21; 61:3; Jn 15:2
14 Leave them; they are blind guides.[f][l] If a blind man leads a blind man, both will fall into a pit."[m] **15:14** [l]Mt 23:16, 24; Ro 2:19 [m]Lk 6:39

[a] 24 Greek *many stadia* [b] 4 Exodus 20:12; Deut. 5:16 [c] 4 Exodus 21:17; Lev. 20:9 [d] 6 Some manuscripts *father or his mother* [e] 9 Isaiah 29:13 [f] 14 Some manuscripts *guides of the blind*

---

did not permit women and children to eat with men in public, so they were no doubt fed in a separate area. The total number of people may have stretched to 10,000 or more. The remote region offered no food for the people, but neither would such abundant staples likely have been on hand in the nearby villages.

14:25 The fourth watch was roughly 3:00–6:00 A.M. According to Roman reckoning, the night was divided into four watches: (1) 6:00–9:00 P.M., (2) 9:00 P.M.–midnight, (3) midnight–3:00 A.M. and (4) 3:00–6:00 A.M. The Jews had only three watches during the night: (1) sunset–10:00 P.M., (2) 10:00 P.M.–2:00 A.M. and (3) 2:00 A.M.–sunrise. It is helpful to bear in mind that these times are approximate. The ancient people did not have precise or standardized timekeeping devices (some used a kind of water-clock). Also, nighttime hours were longer in winter, when the nights were longer, and shorter in summer.

14:34 Mentioned only here and in Mark 6:53, Gennesaret is a plain stretching about three miles (five km) along the northwestern shore of the Sea of Galilee, extending about a mile (almost two km) inland (modern Ghuweir). With a rich, loamy, well-watered soil, it was and still is extraordinarily fertile, the only easily tillable land bordering the Sea of Galilee. Fig, olive, palm and walnut trees, all of which ordinarily require diverse conditions, grow well there.

15:1 For "teachers of the law," see the note on 2:4.

15:2 After the Babylonian exile, the Jewish rabbis began to make meticulous rules and regulations governing the daily life of the people. These were interpretations and applications of the Law of Moses, handed down from generation to generation. In Jesus' day this "tradition of the elders" was in oral form. It was not until about A.D. 200 that it was put into writing in the Mishnah. (See "Biblical Interpretation at Qumran and Among the Early Rabbis" on p. 1603.)

15:15 [n]Mt 13:36
15:16 [o]Mt 16:9
15:18 [p]Mt 12:34; Lk 6:45; Jas 3:6
15:19 [q]Gal 5:19-21
15:20 [r]Ro 14:14

15Peter said, "Explain the parable to us."[n]
16"Are you still so dull?"[o] Jesus asked them. 17"Don't you see that whatever enters the mouth goes into
the stomach and then out of the body? 18But the things that come out of the mouth come from the heart,[p]
and these make a man 'unclean.' 19For out of the heart come evil thoughts, murder, adultery, sexual im-
morality, theft, false testimony, slander.[q] 20These are what make a man 'unclean';[r] but eating with un-
washed hands does not make him 'unclean.'"

The Faith of the Canaanite Woman

15:21 [s]Mt 11:21
15:22 [t]Mt 9:27 [u]Mt 4:24

21Leaving that place, Jesus withdrew to the region of Tyre and Sidon.[s] 22A Canaanite woman from
that vicinity came to him, crying out, "Lord, Son of David,[t] have mercy on me! My daughter is suffering
terribly from demon-possession."[u]
23Jesus did not answer a word. So his disciples came to him and urged him, "Send her away, for she
keeps crying out after us."

15:24 [v]Mt 10:6, 23; Ro 15:8
15:25 [w]Mt 8:2

24He answered, "I was sent only to the lost sheep of Israel."[v]
25The woman came and knelt before him.[w] "Lord, help me!" she said.
26He replied, "It is not right to take the children's bread and toss it to their dogs."

15:21 Tyre was a Gentile city located in Phoenicia (modern Lebanon), which bordered Galilee to the northwest. Sidon was about 25 miles (40 km) north of Tyre. (See "The Downfall of Tyre" on p. 1345 and "Sidon" on p. 1536.)
15:22 The term "Canaanite" is found many times in the Old Testament, but only here in the New. In New Testament times there was no country known as Canaan. Some think that this was the Semitic manner of referring to the people of Phoenicia at this time.
15:24 For "the lost sheep of Israel," see the note on 4:12–16.

Galilee in Jesus' Time

MATTHEW 15 Jesus grew up in Nazareth ("Map 9"), about 15 miles (24 km) from the Sea of Galilee.[1] This region had been settled by Jews since ancient times and had remained a bastion of Judaism down through the centuries. Certain aspects of this area help to define the cultural environment in which Jesus lived, spoke and acted:

✣ Economically, the region benefited from the fish of the Sea of Galilee, trade with the **Phoenician**[2] coastal cities and reasonably productive agricultural yields, including wheat, grapes, figs and olives.[3]

✣ In terms of religion, although cut off from Judea by **Samaria**, Galilean Jews appear to have been as orthodox as their Judean counterparts. Galilee did experience upheaval in the Jewish revolt of A.D. 66–70, but the region was not necessarily marked by revolutionary sentiment before that time.

✣ Politically, Galilee lay within the territory of Herod Antipas. While the Gospels say little about Antipas, the incidents surrounding the death of John the Baptist profoundly distressed the common people. Certainly Jesus realized that preaching would be unsettling to worldly monarchs like Antipas.

✣ Galilee is thought to have had a strong Gentile presence. The city of Sepphoris, just a few miles from Nazareth, is believed by many to have been largely Hellenized.[4] However, it is doubtful that Gentile customs had any major influence on Jesus' preaching; the cultural separation between a city like Sepphoris and a Galilean village was much greater than the physical distance. Furthermore, we have no suggestion in the Gospels or other records that Jesus frequented urban centers like Sepphoris or Tiberias.[5]

[1]See "Nazareth" on page 1623. [2]See Glossary on page 2080 for definitions of bolded words. [3]See "Phoenicia" on page 488. [4]See "Sepphoris" on page 1638. [5]See "Tiberias" on page 1732.

27“Yes, Lord,” she said, “but even the dogs eat the crumbs that fall from their masters’ table.”
28Then Jesus answered, “Woman, you have great faith![x] Your request is granted.” And her daughter 15:28 [x]Mt 9:22
was healed from that very hour.

Jesus Feeds the Four Thousand

29Jesus left there and went along the Sea of Galilee. Then he went up on a mountainside and sat down.
30Great crowds came to him, bringing the lame, the blind, the crippled, the mute and many others, and
laid them at his feet; and he healed them.[y] 31The people were amazed when they saw the mute speaking, 15:30 [y]Mt 4:23
the crippled made well, the lame walking and the blind seeing. And they praised the God of Israel.[z] 15:31 [z]Mt 9:8
32Jesus called his disciples to him and said, “I have compassion for these people;[a] they have already 15:32 [a]Mt 9:36
been with me three days and have nothing to eat. I do not want to send them away hungry, or they may
collapse on the way.”
33His disciples answered, “Where could we get enough bread in this remote place to feed such a
crowd?”
34“How many loaves do you have?” Jesus asked.
“Seven,” they replied, “and a few small fish.”
35He told the crowd to sit down on the ground. 36Then he took the seven loaves and the fish, and when
he had given thanks, he broke them[b] and gave them to the disciples, and they in turn to the people. 37They 15:36 [b]Mt 14:19
all ate and were satisfied. Afterward the disciples picked up seven basketfuls of broken pieces that were
left over.[c] 38The number of those who ate was four thousand, besides women and children. 39After Jesus 15:37 [c]Mt 16:10
had sent the crowd away, he got into the boat and went to the vicinity of Magadan.

The Demand for a Sign

16 The Pharisees and Sadducees[d] came to Jesus and tested him by asking him to show them a sign 16:1 [d]Ac 4:1
from heaven.[e] [e]Mt 12:38
2He replied,[a] “When evening comes, you say, ‘It will be fair weather, for the sky is red,’ 3and in the
morning, ‘Today it will be stormy, for the sky is red and overcast.’ You know how to interpret the appear-
ance of the sky, but you cannot interpret the signs of the times.[f] 4A wicked and adulterous generation 16:3 [f]Lk 12:54-56
looks for a miraculous sign, but none will be given it except the sign of Jonah.”[g] Jesus then left them and 16:4 [g]Mt 12:39
went away.

The Yeast of the Pharisees and Sadducees

5When they went across the lake, the disciples forgot to take bread. 6“Be careful,” Jesus said to them.
“Be on your guard against the yeast of the Pharisees and Sadducees.”[h] 16:6 [h]Lk 12:1
7They discussed this among themselves and said, “It is because we didn’t bring any bread.”
8Aware of their discussion, Jesus asked, “You of little faith,[i] why are you talking among yourselves 16:8 [i]Mt 6:30
about having no bread? 9Do you still not understand? Don’t you remember the five loaves for the five
thousand, and how many basketfuls you gathered?[j] 10Or the seven loaves for the four thousand, and how 16:9 [j]Mt 14:17-21
many basketfuls you gathered?[k] 11How is it you don’t understand that I was not talking to you about 16:10 [k]Mt 15:34-38
bread? But be on your guard against the yeast of the Pharisees and Sadducees.” 12Then they understood
that he was not telling them to guard against the yeast used in bread, but against the teaching of the
Pharisees and Sadducees.[l] 16:12 [l]Ac 4:1

Peter’s Confession of Christ

13When Jesus came to the region of Caesarea Philippi, he asked his disciples, “Who do people say the
Son of Man is?”
14They replied, “Some say John the Baptist;[m] others say Elijah; and still others, Jeremiah or one of the 16:14 [m]Mt 3:1; 14:2 [n]Mk 6:15; Jn 1:21
prophets.”[n]

[a] 2 Some early manuscripts do not have the rest of verse 2 and all of verse 3.

15:35 For Hebrew/Jewish feasting, see the note on 22:2–14.

15:39 Magadan was also called Magdala, the home of Mary Magdalene. Mark 8:10 renders this “Dalmanutha.”

16:1 For information on the Pharisees and Sadducees, see the note on 3:7. Normally these two groups were opponents, but they had a common enemy in Jesus.

16:6 For “yeast,” see the notes on 13:33 and Mark 8:15.

16:9–10 For “basket,” see the note on 14:20.

16:13 Caesarea Philippi is to be distinguished from the magnificent city of Caesarea Maritima, which Herod the Great had built on the Mediterranean coast. See “Caesarea Philippi” on page 1589 and “Caesarea Maritima” on page 1786.

ARCHAEOLOGICAL SITES

CAESAREA PHILIPPI

MATTHEW 16 The area of Caesarea Philippi ("Map 9") was first known (c. 200 B.C.) by the name Panion, meaning "sanctuary of Pan," a pagan god associated with fields and herds. In 23 B.C. Augustus assigned the area to Herod I to rule for the Romans,[1] and Herod's son, Philip, took control of the region after his father's death. Philip constructed an administrative capitol building at Panion and changed the name to Caesarea Philippi, honoring both Caesar and himself. (Caesarea Philippi is not to be confused with Caesarea Maritima, a city on the Mediterranean coast.)

There is no record of any civilian habitation at the time, so Caesarea Philippi was an administrative center and not yet a city during Jesus' lifetime. The Gospel accounts carefully observe this fact, recording that Jesus and the disciples frequented the villages (Mk 8:27) or the region (Mt 6:13) of Caesarea Philippi.

In the year A.D. 53 or 54 Agrippa II became king of the principality and transformed Caesarea Philippi into a Greco-Roman city. The magnificent administrative palace was converted into a public bath house, and a long colonnaded street was constructed through the middle of the city. Fresh water was supplied through underground pipes and a new aqueduct. In A.D. 70 the city was the scene of notorious savagery.[2] The Roman general Titus, after destroying Jerusalem, brought a large number of Jewish prisoners to Caesarea Philippi, where they were massacred in games as a public spectacle. The city reached its peak in the second and third centuries A.D. but appears to have undergone a sharp decline from the fourth century on.

Although the site has been a popular tourist destination since the nineteenth century, systematic excavations did not begin until 1988. Work has focused on the sanctuary of Pan and the central area of the city. Much of the Roman-period architecture was destroyed during the Middle Ages, when the location was used as a military outpost by both Muslims and crusaders. Stone blocks were mined from the ancient buildings to be reused in later structures, making the work of reconstructing the ancient city more difficult. Archaeologists have uncovered numerous medieval pieces of pottery, metal and glass and are confident that further exploration will reveal remains from the Biblical era. The city's athletic facilities and a temple built for Augustus by Herod I are among the important edifices yet to be excavated.

Roman period glass drinking horn
Preserving Bible Times; © Dr. James C. Martin; permission of Eretz Israel Museum

[1]See "Herod the Great" on page 1627. [2]See also "Josephus and the Fall of Jerusalem" on page 1606 and "The Early Persecution of the Church" on page 2067.

Cave sacred to the god Pan at Caesarea Philippi
Preserving Bible Times; © Dr. James C. Martin

15“But what about you?” he asked. “Who do you say I am?”
16Simon Peter answered, “You are the Christ,[a] the Son of the living God.”[o]
17Jesus replied, “Blessed are you, Simon son of Jonah, for this was not revealed to you by man,[p] but by
my Father in heaven. 18And I tell you that you are Peter,[b][q] and on this rock I will build my church,[r] and
the gates of Hades[c] will not overcome it.[d] 19I will give you the keys[s] of the kingdom of heaven; whatever
you bind on earth will be[e] bound in heaven, and whatever you loose on earth will be[e] loosed in heaven.”[t]
20Then he warned his disciples not to tell anyone[u] that he was the Christ.

Jesus Predicts His Death

21From that time on Jesus began to explain to his disciples that he must go to Jerusalem and suffer
many things[v] at the hands of the elders, chief priests and teachers of the law, and that he must be killed
and on the third day[w] be raised to life.[x]
22Peter took him aside and began to rebuke him. “Never, Lord!” he said. “This shall never happen to
you!”
23Jesus turned and said to Peter, “Get behind me, Satan![y] You are a stumbling block to me; you do not
have in mind the things of God, but the things of men.”
24Then Jesus said to his disciples, “If anyone would come after me, he must deny himself and take up
his cross and follow me.[z] 25For whoever wants to save his life[f] will lose it, but whoever loses his life for
me will find it.[a] 26What good will it be for a man if he gains the whole world, yet forfeits his soul? Or what
can a man give in exchange for his soul? 27For the Son of Man[b] is going to come[c] in his Father's glory with
his angels, and then he will reward each person according to what he has done.[d] 28I tell you the truth,
some who are standing here will not taste death before they see the Son of Man coming in his kingdom.”

The Transfiguration

17 After six days Jesus took with him Peter, James and John the brother of James, and led them up
a high mountain by themselves. 2There he was transfigured before them. His face shone like the
sun, and his clothes became as white as the light. 3Just then there appeared before them Moses and Eli-
jah, talking with Jesus.
4Peter said to Jesus, “Lord, it is good for us to be here. If you wish, I will put up three shelters—one
for you, one for Moses and one for Elijah.”
5While he was still speaking, a bright cloud enveloped them, and a voice from the cloud said, “This is
my Son, whom I love; with him I am well pleased.[e] Listen to him!”[f]
6When the disciples heard this, they fell facedown to the ground, terrified. 7But Jesus came and
touched them. “Get up,” he said. “Don't be afraid.”[g] 8When they looked up, they saw no one except Jesus.
9As they were coming down the mountain, Jesus instructed them, “Don't tell anyone[h] what you have
seen, until the Son of Man[i] has been raised from the dead.”[j]
10The disciples asked him, “Why then do the teachers of the law say that Elijah must come first?”
11Jesus replied, “To be sure, Elijah comes and will restore all things.[k] 12But I tell you, Elijah has al-
ready come,[l] and they did not recognize him, but have done to him everything they wished.[m] In the same
way the Son of Man is going to suffer[n] at their hands.” 13Then the disciples understood that he was talk-
ing to them about John the Baptist.

The Healing of a Boy With a Demon

14When they came to the crowd, a man approached Jesus and knelt before him. 15“Lord, have mercy
on my son,” he said. “He has seizures[o] and is suffering greatly. He often falls into the fire or into the wa-
ter. 16I brought him to your disciples, but they could not heal him.”

16:16 [o]Mt 4:3; Ps 42:2; Jn 11:27; Ac 14:15; 2Co 6:16; 1Th 1:9; 1Ti 3:15; Heb 10:31; 12:22
16:17 [p]1Co 15:50; Gal 1:16; Eph 6:12; Heb 2:14
16:18 [q]Jn 1:42 [r]Eph 2:20
16:19 [s]Isa 22:22; Rev 3:7 [t]Mt 18:18; Jn 20:23
16:20 [u]Mk 8:30
16:21 [v]Mk 10:34; Lk 17:25 [w]Jn 2:19 [x]Mt 17:22,23; 27:63; Mk 9:31; Lk 9:22; 18:31-33; 24:6,7
16:23 [y]Mt 4:10
16:24 [z]Mt 10:38; Lk 14:27
16:25 [a]Jn 12:25
16:27 [b]Mt 8:20 [c]Ac 1:11 [d]Job 34:11; Ps 62:12; Jer 17:10; Ro 2:6; 2Co 5:10; Rev 22:12
17:5 [e]Mt 3:17; 2Pe 1:17 [f]Ac 3:22,23
17:7 [g]Mt 14:27
17:9 [h]Mk 8:30 [i]Mt 8:20 [j]Mt 16:21
17:11 [k]Mal 4:6; Lk 1:16,17
17:12 [l]Mt 11:14 [m]Mt 14:3,10 [n]Mt 16:21
17:15 [o]Mt 4:24

[a] *16* Or *Messiah*; also in verse 20 [b] *18* Peter means *rock.* [c] *18* Or *hell* [d] *18* Or *not prove stronger than it* [e] *19* Or *have been* [f] *25* The Greek word means either *life* or *soul*; also in verse 26.

16:18 In the Gospels the word “church” is used only by Matthew (see also 18:17) although in the Septuagint the word is used for the congregation of Israel. In Greek circles of Jesus' day it indicated the assembly of free, voting citizens in a city.

For “Hades,” see the note on Psalm 6:5; see also “Sheol, Hades, Gehenna, the Abyss and Tartarus: Images of Hell” on page 946.

17:4 For “three shelters,” see the note on Mark 9:5.

17:5 For God's *shekînâh* glory (his visible presence), see the note on Exodus14:19.

17:10 Traditional Jewish eschatology held that Elijah had to appear before the coming of the Messiah (see “Jewish Eschatology in the First Century A.D.” on p. 1846).

17:15 For “seizures,” see the note on 4:24.

ARCHAEOLOGICAL SITES

THE CAPERNAUM SYNAGOGUE

The Capernaum Synagogue
Photograph courtesy of © Dr. Gary Pratico

MATTHEW 17 The city of Capernaum ("Map 9") features prominently in the Gospel narratives as a location from which Jesus conducted much of his public ministry (Mt 4:13; Mk 2:1).[1] He performed many miracles there and is reported to have frequently entered the Capernaum synagogue in order to teach (Mk 1:21; 3:1–5; Lk 4:31; Jn 6:59). According to Luke 7:5 the synagogue of Capernaum was constructed under the auspices of a Roman centurion who felt great love for the people of Israel.

The ruins of a synagogue were recognized by Edward Robinson in 1852 at the site of Tell Hum. Charles Wilson conducted the first excavation there in 1865–1866. In 1894 the Franciscan Custody of the Holy Land acquired the site from the Turks, built a monastery, covered the ruins and planted crops over them in order to keep them safe until the political situation would permit careful excavation. During the years 1905–1926 the ancient synagogue was excavated and partially restored by German and Franciscan teams.

The wait had been worthwhile. The teams discovered a large, ornate, limestone synagogue planned as a rectangular basilica approximately 60 feet (18 m) wide by 80 feet (24.5 m) long. The floor plan consisted of a central nave flanked by aisles. Stone benches lined the eastern and western walls. The focal point of the structure faced south, toward Jerusalem. For a number of years scholars believed that these visible ruins represented the actual structure in which Jesus had taught. However, continuing excavations begun in 1968 have revealed the remains of an earlier structure, built of black basalt stone, with a similar floor plan. The 4-foot-thick (1.2 m) basalt walls are slightly out of line with the limestone walls and, therefore, could not have served as their foundation. In 1981 a basalt cobblestone floor was discovered, together with pottery from the first century A.D. Thus, it is no doubt this earlier structure from which Jesus declared, "I am the living bread that came down from heaven. If anyone eats of this bread, he will live forever" (Jn 6:51).[2]

Architectural motifs from the synagogue
Photographs courtesy of © Dr. Gary Pratico

[1]See "Capernaum" on page 1643. [2]See also "Ancient Synagogues" on page 1783.

17“O unbelieving and perverse generation,” Jesus replied, “how long shall I stay with you? How long
shall I put up with you? Bring the boy here to me.” 18Jesus rebuked the demon, and it came out of the boy,
and he was healed from that moment.
19Then the disciples came to Jesus in private and asked, “Why couldn't we drive it out?”
20He replied, “Because you have so little faith. I tell you the truth, if you have faith[p] as small as a mus- **17:20** [p]Mt 21:21
tard seed,[q] you can say to this mountain, ‘Move from here to there’ and it will move.[r] Nothing will be im- [q]Mt 13:31; Mk 11:23; Lk 17:6
possible for you.[a]” [r]1Co 13:2
22When they came together in Galilee, he said to them, “The Son of Man[s] is going to be betrayed into **17:22** [s]Mt 8:20
the hands of men. 23They will kill him,[t] and on the third day[u] he will be raised to life.”[v] And the disci- **17:23** [t]Ac 2:23; 3:13 [u]Mt 16:21
ples were filled with grief. [v]Mt 16:21

The Temple Tax

24After Jesus and his disciples arrived in Capernaum, the collectors of the two-drachma tax[w] came to **17:24** [w]Ex 30:13
Peter and asked, “Doesn't your teacher pay the temple tax[b]?”
25“Yes, he does,” he replied.
When Peter came into the house, Jesus was the first to speak. “What do you think, Simon?” he asked.
“From whom do the kings of the earth collect duty and taxes[x]—from their own sons or from others?” **17:25** [x]Mt 22:17-21; Ro 13:7
26“From others,” Peter answered.
“Then the sons are exempt,” Jesus said to him. 27“But so that we may not offend[y] them, go to the lake **17:27** [y]Jn 6:61
and throw out your line. Take the first fish you catch; open its mouth and you will find a four-drachma
coin. Take it and give it to them for my tax and yours.”

The Greatest in the Kingdom of Heaven

18 At that time the disciples came to Jesus and asked, “Who is the greatest in the kingdom of heaven?”
2He called a little child and had him stand among them. 3And he said: “I tell you the truth, un-
less you change and become like little children,[z] you will never enter the kingdom of heaven.[a] 4There- **18:3** [z]Mt 19:14; 1Pe 2:2 [a]Mt 3:2
fore, whoever humbles himself like this child is the greatest in the kingdom of heaven.[b] **18:4** [b]Mk 9:35
5“And whoever welcomes a little child like this in my name welcomes me.[c] 6But if anyone causes one **18:5** [c]Mt 10:40
of these little ones who believe in me to sin,[d] it would be better for him to have a large millstone hung **18:6** [d]Mt 5:29
around his neck and to be drowned in the depths of the sea.[e] [e]Mk 9:42; Lk 17:2
7“Woe to the world because of the things that cause people to sin! Such things must come, but woe to
the man through whom they come![f] 8If your hand or your foot causes you to sin,[g] cut it off and throw it **18:7** [f]Lk 17:1
away. It is better for you to enter life maimed or crippled than to have two hands or two feet and be thrown **18:8** [g]Mt 5:29; Mk 9:43,45
into eternal fire. 9And if your eye causes you to sin,[h] gouge it out and throw it away. It is better for you to **18:9** [h]Mt 5:29
enter life with one eye than to have two eyes and be thrown into the fire of hell.[i] [i]Mt 5:22

The Parable of the Lost Sheep

10“See that you do not look down on one of these little ones. For I tell you that their angels[j] in heaven **18:10** [j]Ge 48:16; Ps 34:7; Ac 12:11, 15; Heb 1:14
always see the face of my Father in heaven.[c]
12“What do you think? If a man owns a hundred sheep, and one of them wanders away, will he not
leave the ninety-nine on the hills and go to look for the one that wandered off? 13And if he finds it, I tell
you the truth, he is happier about that one sheep than about the ninety-nine that did not wander off. 14In
the same way your Father in heaven is not willing that any of these little ones should be lost.

A Brother Who Sins Against You

15“If your brother sins against you,[d] go and show him his fault,[k] just between the two of you. If he lis- **18:15**
tens to you, you have won your brother over. 16But if he will not listen, take one or two others along, so [k]Lev 19:17; Lk 17:3; Gal 6:1; Jas 5:19,20

[a] *20* Some manuscripts *you.* [21]*But this kind does not go out except by prayer and fasting.* [b] *24* Greek *the two drachmas*
[c] *10* Some manuscripts *heaven.* [11]*The Son of Man came to save what was lost.* [d] *15* Some manuscripts do not have *against you.*

17:20 For “mustard seed,” see the note on 13:31–32.
17:24 Unlike Matthew, who had collected taxes for the occupying Roman forces (9:9), these tax collectors represented the Jewish religious establishment in Jerusalem, overseeing the temple and its tax. The two-drachma tax was the annual temple tax required of every male twenty years of age and older (Ex 30:13; 2Ch 24:9; Ne 10:32). It was worth half a shekel (approximately two days' wages) and was used for the upkeep of the temple.
18:6 The “large millstone” (lit., “millstone of a donkey”) was a millstone (either of two circular stones used for grinding grain) turned by a donkey. As such, it was far larger and heavier than the small millstones used by women each morning for grinding grain.

18:16 [l]Nu 35:30; Dt 17:6; 19:15; Jn 8:17; 2Co 13:1; 1Ti 5:19; Heb 10:28
18:17 [m]1Co 6:1-6 [n]Ro 16:17; 2Th 3:6,14
18:18 [o]Mt 16:19; Jn 20:23
18:19 [p]Mt 7:7

that 'every matter may be established by the testimony of two or three witnesses.'[a] [l] 17If he refuses to lis-
ten to them, tell it to the church;[m] and if he refuses to listen even to the church, treat him as you would
a pagan or a tax collector.[n]
18"I tell you the truth, whatever you bind on earth will be[b] bound in heaven, and whatever you loose
on earth will be[b] loosed in heaven.[o]
19"Again, I tell you that if two of you on earth agree about anything you ask for, it will be done for you[p]
by my Father in heaven. 20For where two or three come together in my name, there am I with them."

The Parable of the Unmerciful Servant

18:21 [q]Mt 6:14 [r]Lk 17:4
18:22 [s]Ge 4:24
18:23 [t]Mt 13:24 [u]Mt 25:19
18:25 [v]Lk 7:42 [w]Lev 25:39; 2Ki 4:1; Ne 5:5,8
18:26 [x]Mt 8:2
18:35 [y]Mt 6:14; Jas 2:13

21Then Peter came to Jesus and asked, "Lord, how many times shall I forgive my brother when he sins
against me?[q] Up to seven times?"[r]
22Jesus answered, "I tell you, not seven times, but seventy-seven times.[c] [s]
23"Therefore, the kingdom of heaven is like[t] a king who wanted to settle accounts[u] with his servants.
24As he began the settlement, a man who owed him ten thousand talents[d] was brought to him. 25Since
he was not able to pay,[v] the master ordered that he and his wife and his children and all that he had be
sold[w] to repay the debt.
26"The servant fell on his knees before him.[x] 'Be patient with me,' he begged, 'and I will pay back ev-
erything.' 27The servant's master took pity on him, canceled the debt and let him go.
28"But when that servant went out, he found one of his fellow servants who owed him a hundred de-
narii.[e] He grabbed him and began to choke him. 'Pay back what you owe me!' he demanded.
29"His fellow servant fell to his knees and begged him, 'Be patient with me, and I will pay you back.'
30"But he refused. Instead, he went off and had the man thrown into prison until he could pay the
debt. 31When the other servants saw what had happened, they were greatly distressed and went and told
their master everything that had happened.
32"Then the master called the servant in. 'You wicked servant,' he said, 'I canceled all that debt of yours
because you begged me to. 33Shouldn't you have had mercy on your fellow servant just as I had on you?'
34In anger his master turned him over to the jailers to be tortured, until he should pay back all he owed.
35"This is how my heavenly Father will treat each of you unless you forgive your brother from your
heart."[y]

Divorce

19:1 [z]Mt 7:28
19:2 [a]Mt 4:23
19:3 [b]Mt 5:31
19:4 [c]Ge 1:27; 5:2
19:5 [d]Ge 2:24; 1Co 6:16; Eph 5:31
19:7 [e]Dt 24:1-4; Mt 5:31

19 When Jesus had finished saying these things,[z] he left Galilee and went into the region of Judea
to the other side of the Jordan. 2Large crowds followed him, and he healed them[a] there.
3Some Pharisees came to him to test him. They asked, "Is it lawful for a man to divorce his wife[b] for
any and every reason?"
4"Haven't you read," he replied, "that at the beginning the Creator 'made them male and female,'[f] [c]
5and said, 'For this reason a man will leave his father and mother and be united to his wife, and the two
will become one flesh'?[g] [d] 6So they are no longer two, but one. Therefore what God has joined together,
let man not separate."
7"Why then," they asked, "did Moses command that a man give his wife a certificate of divorce and
send her away?"[e]
8Jesus replied, "Moses permitted you to divorce your wives because your hearts were hard. But it was

[a] *16* Deut. 19:15 [b] *18* Or *have been* [c] *22* Or *seventy times seven* [d] *24* That is, millions of dollars [e] *28* That is, a few dollars [f] *4* Gen. 1:27 [g] *5* Gen. 2:24

18:17 "Church" here refers to the local congregation (see the note on 16:18).

For "tax collector," see the note on 5:46.

18:21 The standard teaching within Judaism (based on Job 33:29–30; Am 1:3; 2:6) was that three instances of forgiveness reflected a forgiving spirit. Peter's offer to more than double that number was generous, probably reflecting his desire for the completeness the number seven usually represented. Jesus' response—in essence that Peter was to forgive countless times—was astonishing.

18:28 For "a hundred denarii," see the note on 20:2.

18:30 See "Imprisonment in the Roman World: In Prison Versus House Arrest" on page 1826.

19:1 For "Judea," see the note on Mark 10:1. The "other side of the Jordan" refers to the eastern side, known later as Transjordan or Perea and today simply as Jordan.

19:3 For "Pharisees," see the note on 3:7.

There was a dispute between the schools of Shammai and Hillel over the interpretation of Deuteronomy 24:1–4. Shammai held that "something indecent" (Dt 24:1) meant "marital unfaithfulness" (Mt 19:9)—the only allowable cause for divorce. Hillel emphasized the preceding clause, "who becomes displeasing to him" (Dt 24:1). He advocated a man to divorce his wife if she did anything he disliked—even if she burned his food while cooking it. Jesus clearly took the side of Shammai, but only after pointing back to God's original ideal for marriage.

not this way from the beginning. 9 I tell you that anyone who divorces his wife, except for marital unfaith-
fulness, and marries another woman commits adultery."[f] 19:9 [f]Mt 5:32; Lk 16:18
10 The disciples said to him, "If this is the situation between a husband and wife, it is better not to
marry."
11 Jesus replied, "Not everyone can accept this word, but only those to whom it has been given.[g] 12 For 19:11 [g]Mt 13:11; 1Co 7:7-9,17
some are eunuchs because they were born that way; others were made that way by men; and others have
renounced marriage[a] because of the kingdom of heaven. The one who can accept this should accept it."

[a] 12 Or *have made themselves eunuchs*

The Legend of the Needle's Eye Gate

MATTHEW 19 Since the Middle Ages commentators have considered the possibility that Jesus' statement concerning the "eye of a needle" (Mt 19:24) may have been a reference to certain doors or gates that actually existed in his day. Some homes did in fact have large doors that would allow a fully loaded camel to enter into the courtyard. Since such doors were cumbersome and required great effort to open, there were often smaller doors cut within them, permitting easy passage of people and smaller animals into the house. Some interpreters have argued that this smaller door was the "needle's eye gate," while others have suggested that the needle's eye referred to smaller doors within larger city gates, such as those at Jaffa and Hebron.[1] Passage through the smaller gate, it was said, would have forced a camel to its knees. Thus, the point of Jesus' teaching in verse 24 is supposedly that a rich man can enter the kingdom of heaven only if he falls down to his knees.

As illustrative as these theories are, they in fact diminish the force of Jesus' words. The point is not that salvation is difficult without God but that it is *impossible* without him. Jesus' contrast of the largest animal known in Palestine with the smallest of holes created a vivid and memorable illustration. The fact that modern-day gates have been so named can most likely be attributed to the influence of this and similar statements within the **Talmud** and the Koran. In other words, the term "needle's eye gate" most likely did not precede the teaching; rather, the popularity of the term evidently came about because of the teaching. But in Jesus' original setting, it is very likely that a needle's eye was simply a needle's eye and not a gate at all.

Bible readers do well to beware of legendary, pseudo-archaeological interpretations, which can be quite misleading and even distort or undermine the true meaning of a Biblical text.

The Greek text of the Gospel of Matthew; Egypt, fourth century A.D.

© The Schøyen Collection; photography courtesy of Mr. Martin Schøyen

[1]See "The City Gate" on page 392.

The Little Children and Jesus

19:13 [h]Mk 5:23 — 13 Then little children were brought to Jesus for him to place his hands on them[h] and pray for them.
But the disciples rebuked those who brought them.
14 Jesus said, "Let the little children come to me, and do not hinder them, for the kingdom of heaven
19:14 [i]Mt 25:34 [j]Mt 18:3; 1Pe 2:2 — belongs[i] to such as these."[j] 15 When he had placed his hands on them, he went on from there.

The Rich Young Man

19:16 [k]Mt 25:46 [l]Lk 10:25 — 16 Now a man came up to Jesus and asked, "Teacher, what good thing must I do to get eternal life[k]?"[l]
17 "Why do you ask me about what is good?" Jesus replied. "There is only One who is good. If you want
19:17 [m]Lev 18:5 — to enter life, obey the commandments."[m]
18 "Which ones?" the man inquired.
19:18 [n]Jas 2:11 — Jesus replied, " 'Do not murder, do not commit adultery,[n] do not steal, do not give false testimony,
19:19 [o]Ex 20:12-16; Dt 5:16-20 [p]Lev 19:18; Mt 5:43 — 19 honor your father and mother,'[a][o] and 'love your neighbor as yourself.'[b]"[p]
20 "All these I have kept," the young man said. "What do I still lack?"
19:21 [q]Mt 5:48 [r]Lk 12:33; Ac 2:45; 4:34-35 [s]Mt 6:20 — 21 Jesus answered, "If you want to be perfect,[q] go, sell your possessions and give to the poor,[r] and you
will have treasure in heaven.[s] Then come, follow me."
22 When the young man heard this, he went away sad, because he had great wealth.
19:23 [t]Mt 13:22; 1Ti 6:9,10 — 23 Then Jesus said to his disciples, "I tell you the truth, it is hard for a rich man[t] to enter the kingdom
of heaven. 24 Again I tell you, it is easier for a camel to go through the eye of a needle than for a rich man
to enter the kingdom of God."
25 When the disciples heard this, they were greatly astonished and asked, "Who then can be saved?"
19:26 [u]Ge 18:14; Job 42:2; Jer 32:17; Zec 8:6; Lk 1:37; 18:27; Ro 4:21 — 26 Jesus looked at them and said, "With man this is impossible, but with God all things are possible."[u]
19:27 [v]Mt 4:19 — 27 Peter answered him, "We have left everything to follow you![v] What then will there be for us?"
19:28 [w]Mt 20:21; 25:31 [x]Lk 22:28-30; Rev 3:21; 4:4; 20:4 — 28 Jesus said to them, "I tell you the truth, at the renewal of all things, when the Son of Man sits on his
glorious throne,[w] you who have followed me will also sit on twelve thrones, judging the twelve tribes of
Israel.[x] 29 And everyone who has left houses or brothers or sisters or father or mother[c] or children or
19:29 [y]Mt 6:33; 25:46 — fields for my sake will receive a hundred times as much and will inherit eternal life.[y] 30 But many who are
19:30 [z]Mt 20:16; Mk 10:31; Lk 13:30 — first will be last, and many who are last will be first.[z]

The Parable of the Workers in the Vineyard

20:1 [a]Mt 13:24 [b]Mt 21:28,33 — **20** "For the kingdom of heaven is like[a] a landowner who went out early in the morning to hire men
to work in his vineyard.[b] 2 He agreed to pay them a denarius for the day and sent them into his
vineyard.
3 "About the third hour he went out and saw others standing in the marketplace doing nothing. 4 He
told them, 'You also go and work in my vineyard, and I will pay you whatever is right.' 5 So they went.
"He went out again about the sixth hour and the ninth hour and did the same thing. 6 About the elev-
enth hour he went out and found still others standing around. He asked them, 'Why have you been stand-
ing here all day long doing nothing?'
7 " 'Because no one has hired us,' they answered.
"He said to them, 'You also go and work in my vineyard.'
20:8 [c]Lev 19:13; Dt 24:15 — 8 "When evening came,[c] the owner of the vineyard said to his foreman, 'Call the workers and pay them
their wages, beginning with the last ones hired and going on to the first.'
9 "The workers who were hired about the eleventh hour came and each received a denarius. 10 So when
those came who were hired first, they expected to receive more. But each one of them also received a de-
20:11 [d]Jnh 4:1 — narius. 11 When they received it, they began to grumble[d] against the landowner. 12 'These men who were
hired last worked only one hour,' they said, 'and you have made them equal to us who have borne the
20:12 [e]Jnh 4:8; Lk 12:55; Jas 1:11 — burden of the work and the heat[e] of the day.'

[a] *19* Exodus 20:12-16; Deut. 5:16-20 [b] *19* Lev. 19:18 [c] *29* Some manuscripts *mother or wife*

19:21–22 For a discussion of asceticism in the believer's life, see the note on Leviticus 10:9.
19:24 See the note on Mark 10:25; see also "The Legend of the Needle's Eye Gate" on page 1594.
20:2 The denarius was the usual daily wage. A Roman soldier also received one denarius a day.
20:3 The third hour was 9:00 A.M.
For the multiple functions of the *agora*, or marketplace, see the note on 11:16–17, as well as "The Ancient Agora" on page 1799.
20:5 The sixth hour was noon and the ninth hour 3:00 P.M.
20:6 The eleventh hour, then, was 5:00 P.M.
20:8 Because farm workers were poor, the Law of Moses required that they be paid at the end of each day.

13“But he answered one of them, ‘Friend,[f] I am not being unfair to you. Didn’t you agree to work for 20:13 [f]Mt 22:12; 26:50
a denarius? 14Take your pay and go. I want to give the man who was hired last the same as I gave you.
15Don’t I have the right to do what I want with my own money? Or are you envious because I am gener-
ous?’[g] 20:15 [g]Dt 15:9; Mk 7:22
16“So the last will be first, and the first will be last.”[h] 20:16 [h]Mt 19:30

Jesus Again Predicts His Death

17Now as Jesus was going up to Jerusalem, he took the twelve disciples aside and said to them, 18“We
are going up to Jerusalem,[i] and the Son of Man[j] will be betrayed to the chief priests and the teachers of 20:18 [i]Lk 9:51 [j]Mt 8:20 [k]Mt 16:21; 27:1,2
the law.[k] They will condemn him to death 19and will turn him over to the Gentiles to be mocked and
flogged[l] and crucified.[m] On the third day[n] he will be raised to life!”[o] 20:19 [l]Mt 16:21 [m]Ac 2:23 [n]Mt 16:21 [o]Mt 16:21

A Mother’s Request

20Then the mother of Zebedee’s sons[p] came to Jesus with her sons and, kneeling down,[q] asked a fa- 20:20 [p]Mt 4:21 [q]Mt 8:2
vor of him.
21“What is it you want?” he asked.
She said, “Grant that one of these two sons of mine may sit at your right and the other at your left in
your kingdom.”[r] 20:21 [r]Mt 19:28

20:15 “Are you envious?” literally means, “Is your eye evil?” The “evil eye” in the ancient world coveted what belonged to another.

20:21 For information on these positions of honor, see “The ‘Right Hand’ in Ancient Thinking” on page 1983.

A King Riding on a Donkey: Cultural / Political Significance in the Ancient Near East

MATTHEW 21 Jesus’ entrance into Jerusalem on Palm Sunday represents one of the most significant public events of his ministry. Each of the four Gospels records this incident, though with distinctive details (Mt 21:1–11; Mk 11:1–10; Lk 19:29–38; Jn 12:12–15). Central to each report is Jesus’ deliberate choice to enter the city riding upon a donkey. Scholars have noted three significant points regarding this chosen mount. These aspects are not mutually exclusive, and each contributes to a more complete appreciation of the meaning of Jesus’ symbolic action and its decisive consequences:

✣ The donkey was a traditional mount for kings and rulers in the ancient Near East (Jdg 10:4; 12:14; 2Sa 16:2); Jesus was therefore making an implicit claim to be the king of his people.[1]

✣ The act of riding into Jerusalem on a donkey near the time of the Passover celebration invoked a central image of Messianic expectation, linked to key Biblical texts such as Genesis 49:10, Isaiah 62:11 and Zechariah 9:9. Two of the four Evangelists explained the significance of Jesus’ entrance explicitly as the fulfillment of Scripture (Mt 21:5; Jn 12:15). In Jewish literature and teaching, moreover, the image of a king on a donkey approaching Jerusalem was consistently understood to signify the arrival of the Messianic King. Thus, Jesus was claiming to be the Messiah and proclaiming that the age of restoration was dawning through his own person.[2]

✣ In light of the frequent Old Testament association of horses with war and human pride, the donkey may have presented an image of peaceful humility. Jesus, in this interpretation, was making a statement regarding the nature of his kingship (cf. Dt 17:16; 2Sa 15:1; Ps 20:6–9; 33:16–18; 147:10–11; Pr 21:31; Zec 9:9–10).

[1]See “The Ancient Near Eastern King” on page 839. [2]See “Jewish Eschatology in the First Century A.D.” on page 1846.

[22]"You don't know what you are asking," Jesus said to them. "Can you drink the cup[s] I am going to
drink?"
"We can," they answered.
[23]Jesus said to them, "You will indeed drink from my cup,[t] but to sit at my right or left is not for me
to grant. These places belong to those for whom they have been prepared by my Father."
[24]When the ten heard about this, they were indignant[u] with the two brothers. [25]Jesus called them to-
gether and said, "You know that the rulers of the Gentiles lord it over them, and their high officials exer-
cise authority over them. [26]Not so with you. Instead, whoever wants to become great among you must be
your servant,[v] [27]and whoever wants to be first must be your slave— [28]just as the Son of Man[w] did not
come to be served, but to serve,[x] and to give his life as a ransom[y] for many."

Two Blind Men Receive Sight

[29]As Jesus and his disciples were leaving Jericho, a large crowd followed him. [30]Two blind men were
sitting by the roadside, and when they heard that Jesus was going by, they shouted, "Lord, Son of David,[z]
have mercy on us!"
[31]The crowd rebuked them and told them to be quiet, but they shouted all the louder, "Lord, Son of
David, have mercy on us!"
[32]Jesus stopped and called them. "What do you want me to do for you?" he asked.
[33]"Lord," they answered, "we want our sight."
[34]Jesus had compassion on them and touched their eyes. Immediately they received their sight and
followed him.

The Triumphal Entry

21 As they approached Jerusalem and came to Bethphage on the Mount of Olives,[a] Jesus sent two
disciples, [2]saying to them, "Go to the village ahead of you, and at once you will find a donkey tied
there, with her colt by her. Untie them and bring them to me. [3]If anyone says anything to you, tell him that
the Lord needs them, and he will send them right away."
[4]This took place to fulfill what was spoken through the prophet:

[5]"Say to the Daughter of Zion,
'See, your king comes to you,
gentle and riding on a donkey,
on a colt, the foal of a donkey.' "[a][b]

[6]The disciples went and did as Jesus had instructed them. [7]They brought the donkey and the colt,
placed their cloaks on them, and Jesus sat on them. [8]A very large crowd spread their cloaks[c] on the road,
while others cut branches from the trees and spread them on the road. [9]The crowds that went ahead of
him and those that followed shouted,

"Hosanna[b] to the Son of David!"[d]

"Blessed is he who comes in the name of the Lord!"[c][e]

"Hosanna[b] in the highest!"[f]

20:22 [s]Isa 51:17, 22; Jer 49:12; Mt 26:39,42; Mk 14:36; Lk 22:42; Jn 18:11
20:23 [t]Ac 12:2; Rev 1:9
20:24 [u]Lk 22:24, 25
20:26 [v]Mt 23:11; Mk 9:35
20:28 [w]Mt 8:20 [x]Lk 22:27; Jn 13:13-16; 2Co 8:9; Php 2:7 [y]Isa 53:10; Mt 26:28; 1Ti 2:6; Tit 2:14; Heb 9:28; 1Pe 1:18,19
20:30 [z]Mt 9:27
21:1 [a]Mt 24:3; 26:30; Mk 14:26; Lk 19:37; 21:37; 22:39; Jn 8:1; Ac 1:12
21:5 [b]Isa 62:11; Zec 9:9
21:8 [c]2Ki 9:13
21:9 [d]ver 15; Mt 9:27 [e]Ps 118:26; Mt 23:39 [f]Lk 2:14

a 5 Zech. 9:9 *b* 9 A Hebrew expression meaning "Save!" which became an exclamation of praise; also in verse 15
c 9 Psalm 118:26

20:22 To "drink the cup" was a figure of speech meaning to "undergo" or to "experience."
20:26–27 A "servant" (*diakonos*, v. 26) was a person who worked in another's service; he or she could either be free or a slave. A "slave" (*doulos*, v. 27) was the property of another (although the NIV often translates *doulos* as "servant"). Paul used both titles to describe himself and others who gave their lives for the welfare of humanity and the church. John later called himself a *doulos* of Jesus (Rev 1:1), as did Peter (2Pe 1:1) and Jesus' own brothers (Jas 1:1; Jude 1).
20:28 The Greek word translated "ransom" was used most commonly for the price paid to redeem a slave.
20:29 See "New Testament Jericho" on page 1646.
21:1–11 Through what we call the "Triumphal Entry," Jesus intentionally declared his Messianic identity to Israel. His descent from the Mount of Olives into Jerusalem evoked images of Zechariah's prophecy of God fighting, with his feet on the Mount of Olives, on Israel's behalf (Zec 14:3–21). Further excitement would have been stirred by Jesus riding on a colt, fulfilling Zechariah's prophecy of the Messianic King coming to liberate his people (see Zec 9:9; see also "A King Riding on a Donkey: Cultural/Political Significance in the Ancient Near East" on p. 1596).
21:1 See "The Mount of Olives" on page 1543.
21:8 Spreading their cloaks on the roads was an act of royal homage. The word "branches" means "leaves" or "leafy branches," which were readily available in nearby fields. Only John mentioned palm branches (see Jn 12:13), which may have come from Jericho, since they are not native to Jerusalem (see "Palm Branches in Israel" on p. 2056.
21:9 "Hosanna" (Hebrew *hôšā'-nā*; Greek *hôsanna*, "save now") originated as a prayer ("Save now, pray"; Ps 118:25) but by New Testament times had lost its primary meaning and had become an

10 When Jesus entered Jerusalem, the whole city was stirred and asked, "Who is this?"
11 The crowds answered, "This is Jesus, the prophet[g] from Nazareth in Galilee."

21:11 [g]Lk 7:16, 39; 24:19; Jn 1:21,25; 6:14; 7:40

Jesus at the Temple

12 Jesus entered the temple area and drove out all who were buying[h] and selling there. He overturned
the tables of the money changers[i] and the benches of those selling doves.[j] 13 "It is written," he said to
them, " 'My house will be called a house of prayer,'[a][k] but you are making it a 'den of robbers.'[b]"[l]
14 The blind and the lame came to him at the temple, and he healed them.[m] 15 But when the chief priests
and the teachers of the law saw the wonderful things he did and the children shouting in the temple area,
"Hosanna to the Son of David,"[n] they were indignant.[o]
16 "Do you hear what these children are saying?" they asked him.

"Yes," replied Jesus, "have you never read,

> " 'From the lips of children and infants
> you have ordained praise'[c]?"[p]

17 And he left them and went out of the city to Bethany,[q] where he spent the night.

21:12 [h]Dt 14:26 [i]Ex 30:13 [j]Lev 1:14
21:13 [k]Isa 56:7 [l]Jer 7:11
21:14 [m]Mt 4:23
21:15 [n]ver 9; Mt 9:27 [o]Lk 19:39
21:16 [p]Ps 8:2
21:17 [q]Mt 26:6; Mk 11:1; Lk 24:50; Jn 11:1, 18; 12:1

The Fig Tree Withers

18 Early in the morning, as he was on his way back to the city, he was hungry. 19 Seeing a fig tree by the
road, he went up to it but found nothing on it except leaves. Then he said to it, "May you never bear fruit
again!" Immediately the tree withered.[r]
20 When the disciples saw this, they were amazed. "How did the fig tree wither so quickly?" they asked.
21 Jesus replied, "I tell you the truth, if you have faith and do not doubt,[s] not only can you do what was
done to the fig tree, but also you can say to this mountain, 'Go, throw yourself into the sea,' and it will be
done. 22 If you believe, you will receive whatever you ask for[t] in prayer."

21:19 [r]Isa 34:4; Jer 8:13
21:21 [s]Mt 17:20; Lk 17:6; 1Co 13:2; Jas 1:6
21:22 [t]Mt 7:7

The Authority of Jesus Questioned

23 Jesus entered the temple courts, and, while he was teaching, the chief priests and the elders of the
people came to him. "By what authority[u] are you doing these things?" they asked. "And who gave you this
authority?"
24 Jesus replied, "I will also ask you one question. If you answer me, I will tell you by what authority I
am doing these things. 25 John's baptism—where did it come from? Was it from heaven, or from men?"

They discussed it among themselves and said, "If we say, 'From heaven,' he will ask, 'Then why didn't
you believe him?' 26 But if we say, 'From men'—we are afraid of the people, for they all hold that John was
a prophet."[v]
27 So they answered Jesus, "We don't know."

Then he said, "Neither will I tell you by what authority I am doing these things.

21:23 [u]Ac 4:7; 7:27
21:26 [v]Mt 11:9; Mk 6:20

The Parable of the Two Sons

28 "What do you think? There was a man who had two sons. He went to the first and said, 'Son, go and
work today in the vineyard.'[w]
29 " 'I will not,' he answered, but later he changed his mind and went.
30 "Then the father went to the other son and said the same thing. He answered, 'I will, sir,' but he did
not go.

21:28 [w]ver 33; Mt 20:1

[a] *13* Isaiah 56:7 [b] *13* Jer. 7:11 [c] *16* Psalm 8:2

---

exclamation of praise (see also Mk 11:9–10; Jn 12:13). That it is transliterated instead of translated in three of the Gospels (Luke omited it) is evidence of the change of meaning. Not that the Hebrew word no longer had any connection with salvation: The context, which is reminiscent of Psalm 118:25–26, if not a direct quotation from or allusion to it, shows that in its application to God the Father and to Jesus, "Hosanna" was concerned with Messianic salvation.

21:11 See "Nazareth" on page 1623.

21:12 The "buying" and "selling" of animals (at exhorbitant prices) took place in the large outer court of the Gentiles, which covered several acres (see the note on Mk 11:15).

21:14 The Jewish authorities typically restricted the lame, blind, deaf or mute from full temple access to symbolize the purity expected in those approaching God.

21:17 Bethany was a village on the eastern slope of the Mount of Olives, about 2 miles (3.2 km) from Jerusalem. It was the home of Mary, Martha and Lazarus (see "Bethany and the Tomb of Lazarus" on p. 1743).

21:23 Several courts surrounded the main temple buildings, including the court of the women, the court of the men (Israelite), and the court of the Gentiles.

For "chief priests," see the note on 2:4. The "elders" were the lay members of the Sanhedrin (see "The Sanhedrin" on p. 1821), the high court of the Jews.

31 "Which of the two did what his father wanted?"
"The first," they answered.
21:31 [x]Lk 7:29 Jesus said to them, "I tell you the truth, the tax collectors[x] and the prostitutes[y] are entering the king-
[y]Lk 7:50 **21:32** [z]Mt 3:1-12 dom of God ahead of you. 32 For John came to you to show you the way of righteousness,[z] and you did not
[a]Lk 3:12,13; 7:29 [b]Lk 7:36-50 believe him, but the tax collectors[a] and the prostitutes[b] did. And even after you saw this, you did not re-
[c]Lk 7:30 pent[c] and believe him.

The Parable of the Tenants

21:33 [d]Ps 80:8 33 "Listen to another parable: There was a landowner who planted[d] a vineyard. He put a wall around it,
[e]Isa 5:1-7 [f]Mt 25:14,15 dug a winepress in it and built a watchtower.[e] Then he rented the vineyard to some farmers and went away
21:34 [g]Mt 22:3 on a journey.[f] 34 When the harvest time approached, he sent his servants[g] to the tenants to collect his fruit.
21:35 35 "The tenants seized his servants; they beat one, killed another, and stoned a third.[h] 36 Then he sent
[h]2Ch 24:21; Mt 23:34,37; other servants[i] to them, more than the first time, and the tenants treated them the same way. 37 Last of
Heb 11:36,37 **21:36** [i]Mt 22:4 all, he sent his son to them. 'They will respect my son,' he said.
21:38 [j]Heb 1:2 38 "But when the tenants saw the son, they said to each other, 'This is the heir.[j] Come, let's kill him[k] and
[k]Mt 12:14 [l]Ps 2:8 take his inheritance.'[l] 39 So they took him and threw him out of the vineyard and killed him.
40 "Therefore, when the owner of the vineyard comes, what will he do to those tenants?"
21:41 [m]Mt 8:11,12 41 "He will bring those wretches to a wretched end,"[m] they replied, "and he will rent the vineyard to oth-
[n]Ac 13:46; 18:6; 28:28 er tenants,[n] who will give him his share of the crop at harvest time."
42 Jesus said to them, "Have you never read in the Scriptures:

> " 'The stone the builders rejected
> has become the capstone[a];
> the Lord has done this,
> and it is marvelous in our eyes'[b]?[o]

21:42 [o]Ps 118:22,23; Ac 4:11; 1Pe 2:7
21:43 [p]Mt 8:12 43 "Therefore I tell you that the kingdom of God will be taken away from you[p] and given to a people
who will produce its fruit. 44 He who falls on this stone will be broken to pieces, but he on whom it falls
21:44 [q]Lk 2:34 will be crushed."[c][q]
45 When the chief priests and the Pharisees heard Jesus' parables, they knew he was talking about
them. 46 They looked for a way to arrest him, but they were afraid of the crowd because the people held
21:46 [r]ver 11,26 that he was a prophet.[r]

The Parable of the Wedding Banquet

22:2 [s]Mt 13:24 22 Jesus spoke to them again in parables, saying: 2 "The kingdom of heaven is like[s] a king who pre-
22:3 [t]Mt 21:34 pared a wedding banquet for his son. 3 He sent his servants[t] to those who had been invited to the
banquet to tell them to come, but they refused to come.
22:4 [u]Mt 21:36 4 "Then he sent some more servants[u] and said, 'Tell those who have been invited that I have prepared
my dinner: My oxen and fattened cattle have been butchered, and everything is ready. Come to the wed-
ding banquet.'

[a] 42 Or *cornerstone* [b] 42 Psalm 118:22,23 [c] 44 Some manuscripts do not have verse 44.

21:31 For "tax collectors," see the note on 5:46.
21:33 For "winepress," see "The Winepress" on page 1171.
A watchtower was for guarding the vineyard, especially when the grapes ripened, as well as for shelter.
21:41 "Other tenants" is a reference to Gentiles. By the second century A.D. the church was composed almost entirely of Gentiles.
21:45 For "chief priests," see the note on 2:4. For "Pharisees," see the note on 3:7.
22:2–14 The Hebrews, like other peoples of the ancient Near East, were enormously fond of social feasting. At the three great religious feasts, which all males were expected to attend, each family held its own feast. Sacrifices also were accompanied by an extensive meal (Ex 34:15; Jdg 16:23–25), and there were feasts on birthdays (Ge 40:20; Job 1:4; Mt 14:6), at marriages (Ge 29:22; Mt 22:2), at funerals (2Sa 3:35; Jer 16:7), at the laying of foundations (Pr 9:1–5), for vintage (Jdg 9:27), for sheep-shearing (1Sa 25:2,36) and on other occasions.
A banquet always included wine drinking. At a large banquet a second invitation was often sent on the day of the feast, or a servant escorted the invitees to the banquet (see also Lk 14:17). The host provided robes for the guests, which were worn in his honor and as a token of his regard. Guests were welcomed by the host with a kiss (Lk 7:45), and their feet were washed because of the dusty roads (Ge 18:4; Jdg 19:21; Lk 7:44). The guest's head was anointed (Ps 23:5; Lk 7:46), as well as sometimes his beard, his feet and his clothing. His head was decorated with garlands (Isa 28:1). The guests were seated according to their respective rank (1Sa 9:22; Lk 14:8), their hands were washed (2Ki 3:11) and prayers were offered for blessing on the food (1Sa 9:13; Mt 15:35; Lk 22:17).
The banquet was put under the superintendence of a "governor of the feast," usually one of the guests, whose task it was to taste the food and drinks and to supervise the toasts and amusements. The most honored guests received either larger or more choice portions than the others (Ge 43:34; 1Sa 9:23–24), and portions were sometimes sent to friends not attending the feast (2Sa 11:8; Ne 8:10). Often the meal was enlivened with music, singing and dancing (2Sa 19:35; Lk 15:25) or with riddles (Jdg 14:12). A great banquet sometimes lasted seven days, but excess in eating and drinking was condemned by the sacred writers (Ecc 10:16–17; Isa 5:11–12).

5"But they paid no attention and went off—one to his field, another to his business. 6The rest seized
his servants, mistreated them and killed them. 7The king was enraged. He sent his army and destroyed
those murderers[v] and burned their city. 22:7 [v]Lk 19:27
8"Then he said to his servants, 'The wedding banquet is ready, but those I invited did not deserve to
come. 9Go to the street corners[w] and invite to the banquet anyone you find.' 10So the servants went out 22:9 [w]Eze 21:21
into the streets and gathered all the people they could find, both good and bad,[x] and the wedding hall 22:10 [x]Mt 13:47, 48
was filled with guests.
11"But when the king came in to see the guests, he noticed a man there who was not wearing wed-
ding clothes. 12'Friend,'[y] he asked, 'how did you get in here without wedding clothes?' The man was 22:12 [y]Mt 20:13; 26:50
speechless.
13"Then the king told the attendants, 'Tie him hand and foot, and throw him outside, into the dark-
ness, where there will be weeping and gnashing of teeth.'[z] 22:13 [z]Mt 8:12
14"For many are invited, but few are chosen."[a] 22:14 [a]Rev 17:14

22:7 Burning a city was a common military practice. Here the reference may be an allusion to the coming destruction of Jerusalem in A.D. 70.
22:11 It appears to have been the custom for a host at a wedding feast to provide the guests with wedding garments. This would have been necessary for the guests at this banquet in particular, for they were brought in directly from the streets. The failure of the man in question to avail himself of the wedding garment was therefore a direct insult to the host. (See "Weddings in Ancient Israel" on p. 1039.)
22:13 For the meaning of gnashing with one's teeth, see the note on Psalm 35:16.

The Sadducees

MATTHEW 22 The Sadducees were a religious and political sect during the **Second Temple** period,[1] drawn primarily from the ruling priestly and aristocratic elements in Jewish society.[2] This party controlled the temple worship, and many of its adherents were also members of the supreme Jewish legal council, called the Sanhedrin (Ac 23:6). Two separate accounts of the Sadducees' origin link the name of the sect to two different historical figures, both named Zadok.

✣ The name Sadducee may be derived from Zadok, the high priest in the days of David and Solomon (2Sa 8:17; 1Ki 1:34). In Ezekiel's vision of restoration, the descendants of this Zadok are entrusted with oversight of the temple worship (Eze 40:46; 43:19; 44:15). Zadok's descendants did in fact constitute the temple hierarchy down to the second century B.C.

✣ According to rabbinic tradition, however, the sect of the Sadducees was founded by a disciple of Antigonus of Sokho (c. 200 B.C.), also named Zadok.

The Sadducees' major opponents were the Pharisees.[3] Contrary to this rival faction, the Sadducees denied the resurrection of the dead (Mt 22:23–33; Ac 4:1–2; 23:6–8), the immortality of the soul, the doctrine of reward and punishment and the validity of the oral law (regulations passed down by rabbinic tradition). They accepted as binding only those laws based directly upon the written text of the **Pentateuch**. It is for this reason that Jesus defended the doctrine of the resurrection to them from the standpoint of Exodus 3:6 rather than from the prophets (Mt 22:32). The influence of the Sadducees virtually ceased with the destruction of the temple in A.D. 70,[4] leaving postbiblical Judaism to develop along Pharisaic lines. Later rabbinic teaching contains numerous examples and anti-Sadducee propaganda.

[1]See Glossary on page 2080 for definitions of bolded words. [2]See "The Jewish Priesthood and Religious Life in the First Century A.D." on page 1704. [3]See "The Pharisees" on page 1566. [4]See "Josephus and the Fall of Jerusalem" on page 1606.

Paying Taxes to Caesar

15 Then the Pharisees went out and laid plans to trap him in his words. 16 They sent their disciples to
22:16 [b]Mk 3:6 him along with the Herodians.[b] "Teacher," they said, "we know you are a man of integrity and that you
teach the way of God in accordance with the truth. You aren't swayed by men, because you pay no atten-
22:17 [c]Mt 17:25 tion to who they are. 17 Tell us then, what is your opinion? Is it right to pay taxes[c] to Caesar or not?"
18 But Jesus, knowing their evil intent, said, "You hypocrites, why are you trying to trap me? 19 Show me
the coin used for paying the tax." They brought him a denarius, 20 and he asked them, "Whose portrait is
this? And whose inscription?"
21 "Caesar's," they replied.
22:21 [d]Ro 13:7 Then he said to them, "Give to Caesar what is Caesar's,[d] and to God what is God's."
22:22 [e]Mk 12:12 22 When they heard this, they were amazed. So they left him and went away.[e]

Marriage at the Resurrection

22:23 [f]Ac 4:1 [g]Ac 23:8; 1Co 15:12 23 That same day the Sadducees,[f] who say there is no resurrection,[g] came to him with a question.
24 "Teacher," they said, "Moses told us that if a man dies without having children, his brother must
22:24 [h]Dt 25:5,6 marry the widow and have children for him.[h] 25 Now there were seven brothers among us. The first
one married and died, and since he had no children, he left his wife to his brother. 26 The same thing
happened to the second and third brother, right on down to the seventh. 27 Finally, the woman died.
28 Now then, at the resurrection, whose wife will she be of the seven, since all of them were married
to her?"
22:29 [i]Jn 20:9 29 Jesus replied, "You are in error because you do not know the Scriptures[i] or the power of God. 30 At
22:30 [j]Mt 24:38 the resurrection people will neither marry nor be given in marriage;[j] they will be like the angels in heav-
en. 31 But about the resurrection of the dead—have you not read what God said to you, 32 'I am the God
22:32 [k]Ex 3:6; Ac 7:32 of Abraham, the God of Isaac, and the God of Jacob'[a]?[k] He is not the God of the dead but of the living."
22:33 [l]Mt 7:28 33 When the crowds heard this, they were astonished at his teaching.[l]

The Greatest Commandment

22:34 [m]Ac 4:1 34 Hearing that Jesus had silenced the Sadducees,[m] the Pharisees got together. 35 One of them, an ex-
22:35 [n]Lk 7:30; 10:25; 11:45; 14:3 pert in the law,[n] tested him with this question: 36 "Teacher, which is the greatest commandment in the
Law?"
37 Jesus replied: " 'Love the Lord your God with all your heart and with all your soul and with all your
22:37 [o]Dt 6:5 mind.'[b][o] 38 This is the first and greatest commandment. 39 And the second is like it: 'Love your neighbor
22:39 [p]Lev 19:18; Mt 5:43; 19:19; Gal 5:14 as yourself.'[c][p] 40 All the Law and the Prophets hang on these two commandments."[q]

22:40 [q]Mt 7:12

Whose Son Is the Christ?

41 While the Pharisees were gathered together, Jesus asked them, 42 "What do you think about the
Christ[d]? Whose son is he?"
22:42 [r]Mt 9:27 "The son of David,"[r] they replied.
43 He said to them, "How is it then that David, speaking by the Spirit, calls him 'Lord'? For he says,

[a] 32 Exodus 3:6 [b] 37 Deut. 6:5 [c] 39 Lev. 19:18 [d] 42 Or *Messiah*

22:15–17 The Pharisees were ardent nationalists, opposed to Roman rule, while the hated Herodians, as their name indicates, supported the rule of the Herods. The Herodians are mentioned in the New Testament only three times (see also Mk 3:6; 12:13), in each case in the context of joining with the Pharisees to oppose Jesus. Nothing more is known about them than what the Gospels state. It appears that they were neither a religious sect nor a political party, but simply Jews who supported the dynasty of Herod and therefore the rule of Rome.

22:17 For information on paying taxes to Caesar, see the note on Mark 12:14; see also "Tiberius Caesar, the Caesar of Jesus' Ministry" on page 1708 and "Roman Taxation" on page 1855.

22:19 The denarius was the common Roman coin of that day (see the note on 20:2; see also "Coins and Numismatics" on p. 1699). On one side of this coin was the portrait of the Roman emperor Tiberius; on the other an inscription in Latin: "Tiberius Caesar Augustus, son of the divine Augustus." The coin was issued by Tiberius and was used for paying taxes to him.

22:23 The Sadducees did not believe in the resurrection of the dead because they accepted only the books of Moses (the first five OT books). Jesus' reference to angels had a double edge, since the Sadducees also denied their existence (cf. Ac 23:8). For information on the Sadducees, see the note on 3:7 and "The Sadducees" on page 1600.

22:24 The reference here is to the levirate law, which had been given to protect the widow and to guarantee continuance of the family line. See "Levirate Marriage" on page 64.

22:41–42 The Jews did not generally believe that the coming Messiah would be divine, and Jesus was far more than what the Pharisees had understood that the "son of David" would be infinitely more than a human descendant of David. Since the Pharisees did not adequately understand the Old Testament prophecies regarding the Messiah, they could not possibly comprehend his true identity.

44 " 'The Lord said to my Lord:
"Sit at my right hand
until I put your enemies
under your feet." '[a] [s]

45 If then David calls him 'Lord,' how can he be his son?" 46 No one could say a word in reply, and from that day on no one dared to ask him any more questions.[t]

[a] 44 Psalm 110:1

22:44 [s]Ps 110:1; Ac 2:34,35; 1Co 15:25; Heb 1:13; 10:13
22:46 [t]Mk 12:34; Lk 20:40

22:44 For the "right hand" as a position of honor, see "The 'Right Hand' in Ancient Thinking" on page 1983.

RABBINIC WRITINGS

Writings	Divisions	Dates	Contributors	Contents	Comments
Midrash[1]	Halakhah[2]	100 B.C.–A.D. 300	Tannaim[4]	Legal sections commenting only on Torah	Halakhah is the legal part of the Gemara, usually derived from the Old Testament.
	Haggadah[3]			Narratives and sermons on entire Old Testament	Haggadah embraces nonlegal interests (i.e., history, folklore, parables and scientific knowledge, such as medicine and astronomy) infrequently encountered in the Mishnah.
Tosefta[5]		A.D. 100–300	Tannaim	Teachings not found in the Mishnah	
Palestinian Talmud	Gemara[6]	A.D. 200	Amoraim[7]	Commentary on the Mishnah	
Babylonian Talmud	Mishnah[8]	A.D. 200	Tannaim	Legal portions commenting on Torah	The Mishnah was divided into six sections: *Seeds*, concerning ritual laws dealing with cultivation of the soil; *Festivals*, concerning rules and regulations on the Sabbath and holy days; *Women*, on marriage, divorce and other family issues; *Damages*, mainly regarding compensation on damages; *Holy Things*, rules and laws on sacrifices and other issues pertaining to the ancient temple and its ritual; *Purifications*, pertaining to the subject of cleanness and purity.
	Gemara	A.D. 500	Amoraim	Commentary on the Mishnah	

[1] Midrash refers to the exposition of the Law in running commentary.
[2] Halakah literally means "going" or "walking" and was extended to the statements by which one is guided.
[3] Haggadah is a type of Jewish interpretation intended for edification.
[4] The Tannaim are "repeaters" or teachers of the Oral Law before the completion of the Mishnah. They date from Ezra—through Hillel, Akiba, and Meir—to Judah Hanasi.
[5] Tosefta means "supplement."
[6] Gemara literally means the "completion" of the Talmud.
[7] The Amoraim were sages who labored in Judaism after the completion of the Mishnah.
[8] Mishnah means "repetition"; the Oral Law had to be repeated verbally with great accuracy from generation to generation.

Chronological and Background Charts of the New Testament, p. 85

CULTURAL AND HISTORICAL NOTES

Biblical Interpretation at Qumran and Among the Early Rabbis

MATTHEW 23 **Qumran**[1] is the location at which the Dead Sea Scrolls were discovered. The ancient community that was once located there produced a library of well over 800 manuscripts, most of them related to Biblical interpretation.[2] This collection includes a wide variety of documents:

- Paraphrases: Some texts "re-wrote" portions of the Biblical narratives with interpretive and expansive paraphrases (e.g., the Genesis Apocryphon and the Temple Scroll).
- Commentaries: *Pesharim*, annotations on the prophetic books and the Psalms, sought to interpret or explain Biblical texts.
- Anthologies: These texts stitch together various Biblical passages on a particular theme—something like a modern "topical Bible."
- Original writings composed in a Biblical style: These documents use Biblical expressions, style and vocabulary to evoke the authority of Scripture. The Teacher of Righteousness, the dominant leader of the Qumran community, believed that God had revealed all the mysteries of the prophetic writings to him. Biblical interpretation in Qumran reflected his understanding that the Scriptures were full of hidden references to his community and to its conflicts with other Jewish leaders and with the outside world. Some of the documents from Qumran suggest that the community perceived itself as authorized not only to provide inspired interpretations of the Scriptures but also to generate new inspired works on an equal footing with Scripture.

Mikveh (ritual immersion tank) at Qumran
Photograph courtesy of © Dr. Gary Pratico

Interpretation at Qumran focused on the rules that governed the community and upon the prophetic interpretations that supported its ideals and hopes.

Early rabbinic Biblical interpretation was primarily concerned with *Halakhah*—the rules that governed daily life and religious practice. The demand for precise application of Biblical law among the Jews meant that *Halakhah* had to give guidance about what a person could eat or wear or what action was permissible under specific circumstances. As times and situations changed, new questions arose about what was allowable or required; thus interpretation was an ongoing task, resulting in a continuing process of refinements to previous legal judgments.

Those refinements took place in a dialogic fashion, as rabbis debated the proper application of Biblical texts and legal principles. In their deliberations they tended to cite or string together a series of verses on the basis of some similarity, such as the fact that each verse had a specific word in common. For example, rabbis might cite or associate several verses from different parts of the Bible that have in common the word *grapes*—even if the verses they cited had nothing to do with one another and used the word in radically different contexts. This strategy treated the Bible as a "hypertext" (a complex web of associations in which one could jump from one passage to another); such interpretation was like solving a puzzle whose pieces needed to be constantly turned, rotated and rearranged. The desired, ideal outcome: When the right combination of Biblical passages was placed side by side, they revealed the otherwise elusive meaning of the particular text under consideration.

The process was not altogether arbitrary. A series of rules was developed to control the interpretive process. The first seven of these were attributed to Hillel, a famous rabbi of the first century A.D. The two most important principles were the argument *a fortiori* (meaning that a principle that works in a lesser case should also apply to a more important one) and the principle of verbal analogy (meaning that two different passages sharing words in common can be used to interpret each other).

In Matthew 23 Jesus upbraided the scribes and Pharisees[3] for establishing elaborate and meticulous rules that attended to fine points on less significant matters but that ignored weightier issues. He particularly rejected their tendency to focus on the lesser issue of external, ritual purity while ignoring the greater issue of the internal contamination of their hearts.

[1]See Glossary on page 2080 for definitions of bolded words. [2]See "The Temple Scroll" on page 1371 and "Qumran and the New Testament" on page 1679. [3]See "The Pharisees" on page 1566.

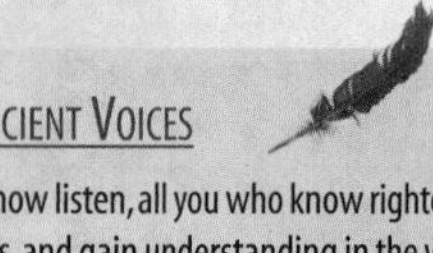

Ancient Voices

So now listen, all you who know righteousness, and gain understanding in the works of God! For he has a dispute with all flesh and will execute judgment against all who despise him. For when they were unfaithful, so that they abandoned him, he hid his face from Israel and from his sanctuary and gave them over to the sword. But when he remembered his covenant with their ancestors, he left behind a remnant for Israel and did not give them over to complete destruction. And during the time of wrath (390 years after he had given them into the hand of Nebuchadnezzar, king of Babylon), he visited them. He caused a root from Israel and from Aaron to sprout up, so that they might inherit his land and prosper from the richness of the land. And they recognized their evil and knew that they were guilty men. But for twenty years they were like blind men groping for their way. And God took note of their deeds, that they sought him with their whole heart, and he raised up a Teacher of Righteousness for them, to guide them in the way of God's heart.

—How God Raised Up the Teacher of Righteousness for the Jewish Community, According to the Dead Sea Scrolls

From the Dead Sea Scrolls, The Damascus Document 1.1–11, trans. by Duane Garrett

See "Biblical Interpretation at Qumran and Among the Early Rabbis" article on the previous page.

Seven Woes

23 Then Jesus said to the crowds and to his disciples: 2"The
teachers of the law[u] and the Pharisees sit in Moses' seat. 3So — **23:2** [u]Ezr 7:6,25;
you must obey them and do everything they tell you. But do not do — Ne 8:4
what they do, for they do not practice what they preach. 4They tie
up heavy loads and put them on men's shoulders, but they them-
selves are not willing to lift a finger to move them.[v] — **23:4** [v]Lk 11:46;
5"Everything they do is done for men to see:[w] They make their — Ac 15:10; Gal 6:13
phylacteries[a][x] wide and the tassels on their garments[y] long; 6they — **23:5** [w]Mt 6:1,2,5, 16 [x]Ex 13:9;
love the place of honor at banquets and the most important seats in — Dt 6:8 [y]Nu 15:38; Dt 22:12
the synagogues;[z] 7they love to be greeted in the marketplaces and — **23:6** [z]Lk 11:43; 14:7; 20:46
to have men call them 'Rabbi.'[a] — **23:7** [a]ver 8; Mk 9:5; 10:51;
8"But you are not to be called 'Rabbi,' for you have only one Mas- — Jn 1:38,49
ter and you are all brothers. 9And do not call anyone on earth 'fa-
ther,' for you have one Father,[b] and he is in heaven. 10Nor are you to — **23:9** [b]Mal 1:6;
be called 'teacher,' for you have one Teacher, the Christ.[b] 11The great- — Mt 7:11
est among you will be your servant.[c] 12For whoever exalts himself — **23:11** [c]Mt 20:26;
will be humbled, and whoever humbles himself will be exalted.[d] — Mk 9:35 **23:12** [d]Lk 14:11
13"Woe to you, teachers of the law and Pharisees, you hypocrites![e] — **23:13** [e]ver 15,23, 25,27,29
You shut the kingdom of heaven in men's faces. You yourselves do — [f]Lk 11:52
not enter, nor will you let those enter who are trying to.[c][f]
15"Woe to you, teachers of the law and Pharisees, you hypocrites!
You travel over land and sea to win a single convert,[g] and when he — **23:15** [g]Ac 2:11; 6:5; 13:43
becomes one, you make him twice as much a son of hell[h] as you are. — [h]Mt 5:22
16"Woe to you, blind guides![i] You say, 'If anyone swears by the — **23:16** [i]ver 24;
temple, it means nothing; but if anyone swears by the gold of the — Mt 15:14 [j]Mt 5:33-35
temple, he is bound by his oath.'[j] 17You blind fools! Which is greater:
the gold, or the temple that makes the gold sacred?[k] 18You also say, — **23:17** [k]Ex 30:29
'If anyone swears by the altar, it means nothing; but if anyone swears
by the gift on it, he is bound by his oath.' 19You blind men! Which is
greater: the gift, or the altar that makes the gift sacred?[l] 20Therefore, — **23:19** [l]Ex 29:37
he who swears by the altar swears by it and by everything on it.
21And he who swears by the temple swears by it and by the one who
dwells[m] in it. 22And he who swears by heaven swears by God's throne — **23:21** [m]1Ki 8:13; Ps 26:8
and by the one who sits on it.[n] — **23:22** [n]Ps 11:4; Mt 5:34
23"Woe to you, teachers of the law and Pharisees, you hypocrites! You give a tenth[o] of your spices— — **23:23** [o]Lev 27:30
mint, dill and cummin. But you have neglected the more important matters of the law—justice, mercy — [p]Mic 6:8; Lk 11:42
and faithfulness.[p] You should have practiced the latter, without neglecting the former. 24You blind guides![q] — **23:24** [q]ver 16
You strain out a gnat but swallow a camel.
25"Woe to you, teachers of the law and Pharisees, you hypocrites! You clean the outside of the cup and

[a] 5 That is, boxes containing Scripture verses, worn on forehead and arm [b] *10* Or *Messiah* [c] *13* Some manuscripts *to.* *14Woe to you, teachers of the law and Pharisees, you hypocrites! You devour widows' houses and for a show make lengthy prayers. Therefore you will be punished more severely.*

23:2 For "teachers of the law," see the note on 2:4.
"Moses' seat" was a position of authority. The Pharisees considered themselves to be the authorized successors of Moses as teachers of the law.

23:4 "Heavy loads" refer to the oral tradition (see the note on 15:2), a distinctive feature of the Pharisees' brand of Judaism. It was intended to make the Old Testament relevant to life situations, but its massive obligations were far more burdensome than Scripture itself. (See "Biblical Interpretation at Qumran and Among the Early Rabbis" on p. 1603.)

23:5 For "phylacteries," see the note on Exodus 13:1. For "tassels," see "Fringe (Tassels) on Garments" on page 217.

23:6 For "most important seats in the synagogues," see the note on Mark 12:39.

23:15 The Greek word for "convert" is found in the New Testament only here and in Acts 2:11, 6:5 and 13:43. See "Proselytes in Second Temple Judaism" on page 1776.

23:16–22 When the teachers of the law (see the note on 2:4) and the Pharisees (see the note on 3:7) took oaths, they differentiated between which were binding and which were not. This allowed for evasive oath-taking. Jesus rejected all such subtleties and insisted that people simply tell the truth. (See "Oaths in Jewish and Christian Practice" on p. 1988.)

23:23 Cummin is a spice indigenous to western Asia and resembling caraway in taste and appearance.

23:24 The strict Pharisee would carefully strain his drinking water through a cloth to make certain he did not swallow a gnat, the smallest of ceremonially unclean animals. But, figuratively, he was willing to swallow a camel—one of the largest.

23:25 [r]Mk 7:4 dish,[r] but inside they are full of greed and self-indulgence.[s] 26Blind Pharisee! First clean the inside of
[s]Lk 11:39 the cup and dish, and then the outside also will be clean.
23:27 [t]Lk 11:44; 27"Woe to you, teachers of the law and Pharisees, you hypocrites! You are like whitewashed tombs,[t]
Ac 23:3 which look beautiful on the outside but on the inside are full of dead men's bones and everything unclean.
28In the same way, on the outside you appear to people as righteous but on the inside you are full of hy-
pocrisy and wickedness.
23:29 [u]Lk 11:47, 29"Woe to you, teachers of the law and Pharisees, you hypocrites! You build tombs for the prophets[u]
48 and decorate the graves of the righteous. 30And you say, 'If we had lived in the days of our forefathers, we
would not have taken part with them in shedding the blood of the prophets.' 31So you testify against
23:31 [v]Ac 7:51- yourselves that you are the descendants of those who murdered the prophets.[v] 32Fill up, then, the mea-
52; 23:32 [w]1Th 2:16 sure[w] of the sin of your forefathers!
23:33 [x]Mt 3:7; 33"You snakes! You brood of vipers![x] How will you escape being condemned to hell?[y] 34Therefore I
12:34 [y]Mt 5:22; 23:34 am sending you prophets and wise men and teachers. Some of them you will kill and crucify;[z] others
[z]2Ch 36:15,16; Lk 11:49 you will flog in your synagogues[a] and pursue from town to town.[b] 35And so upon you will come all the
[a]Mt 10:17 [b]Mt 10:23 righteous blood that has been shed on earth, from the blood of righteous Abel[c] to the blood of Zechari-
23:35 [c]Ge 4:8; Heb 11:4 [d]Zec 1:1 ah son of Berekiah,[d] whom you murdered between the temple and the altar.[e] 36I tell you the truth, all
[e]2Ch 24:21; 23:36 [f]Mt 10:23; this will come upon this generation.[f]
24:34 37"O Jerusalem, Jerusalem, you who kill the prophets and stone those sent to you,[g] how often I have
23:37 [g]2Ch 24:21; longed to gather your children together, as a hen gathers her chicks under her wings, but you were not
Mt 5:12; 23:38 [h]1Ki 9:7,8; willing. 38Look, your house is left to you desolate.[h] 39For I tell you, you will not see me again until you say,
Jer 22:5; 23:39 [i]Ps 118:26; 'Blessed is he who comes in the name of the Lord.'[a]"[i]
Mt 21:9

Signs of the End of the Age

24 Jesus left the temple and was walking away when his disciples came up to him to call his atten-
tion to its buildings. 2"Do you see all these things?" he asked. "I tell you the truth, not one stone
24:2 [j]Lk 19:44 here will be left on another;[j] every one will be thrown down."
24:3 [k]Mt 21:1 3As Jesus was sitting on the Mount of Olives,[k] the disciples came to him privately. "Tell us," they said,
"when will this happen, and what will be the sign of your coming and of the end of the age?"
4Jesus answered: "Watch out that no one deceives you. 5For many will come in my name, claiming, 'I
24:5 [l]ver 11,23, 24; 1Jn 2:18 am the Christ,[b]' and will deceive many.[l] 6You will hear of wars and rumors of wars, but see to it that you
are not alarmed. Such things must happen, but the end is still to come. 7Nation will rise against nation,
24:7 [m]Isa 19:2 and kingdom against kingdom.[m] There will be famines[n] and earthquakes in various places. 8All these
[n]Ac 11:28 are the beginning of birth pains.
24:9 [o]Mt 10:17 9"Then you will be handed over to be persecuted[o] and put to death,[p] and you will be hated by all na-
[p]Jn 16:2 tions because of me. 10At that time many will turn away from the faith and will betray and hate each oth-
24:11 [q]Mt 7:15 er, 11and many false prophets[q] will appear and deceive many people. 12Because of the increase of wick-
24:13 [r]Mt 10:22; 24:14 [s]Mt 4:23 edness, the love of most will grow cold, 13but he who stands firm to the end will be saved.[r] 14And this
[t]Lk 2:1; 4:5; Ac 11:28; 17:6; gospel of the kingdom[s] will be preached in the whole world[t] as a testimony to all nations, and then the
Ro 10:18; Col 1:6, 23; Rev 3:10; end will come.
16:14; 24:15 [u]Ac 6:13 15"So when you see standing in the holy place[u] 'the abomination that causes desolation,'[c][v] spoken of
[v]Da 9:27; 11:31; 12:11

[a] 39 Psalm 118:26 [b] 5 Or *Messiah*; also in verse 23 [c] 15 Daniel 9:27; 11:31; 12:11

23:27 A person who stepped on a grave became thereby ceremonially unclean (see Nu 19:16), so graves were whitewashed to make them easily visible, especially at night. They appeared clean and beautiful on the outside but were dirty and rotten on the inside.
24:2 This prophecy was fulfilled literally in A.D. 70, when the Romans under Titus completely destroyed Jerusalem and the temple buildings. Stones were even pried apart to collect the gold leaf that melted from the roof when the temple was set on fire (see the note on Mk 13:1). Excavations in 1968 uncovered large numbers of these stones, toppled from the walls by the invaders. (See "Herod's Temple" on p. 1648 and "Josephus and the Fall of Jerusalem" on p. 1606.)
24:3 See "The Mount of Olives" on page 1543.
24:7 See the note on famine at Ruth 1:1, as well as "Famine in the Ancient Near East" on page 70.
24:15 The "abomination that causes desolation" is the detestable thing causing the desolation of the holy place. The primary reference in Daniel (Da 9:27; 11:31; 12:11) was to 168 B.C., when Antiochus Epiphanes (see "Antiochus IV Epiphanes" on p. 1406) erected a pagan altar to Zeus on the sacred altar in the temple of Jerusalem. According to some, there were still two more stages in the progressive fulfillment of the predictions in Daniel and Matthew: (1) the Roman destruction of the temple in A.D. 70 and (2) the setting up of an image of the antichrist in Jerusalem (see 2Th 2:4; Rev 13:14–15).

Although the book of Daniel stands as the last of the Major Prophets in the English Bible, it appears in the Hebrew Old Testament (which consists of "the Law, the Prophets and the Writings") as one of the "Writings." For although Jesus Christ spoke of Daniel's *function* as prophetic, his position was that of a governmental official and inspired writer rather than of a ministering prophet (see Ac 2:29–30).

Josephus and the Fall of Jerusalem

The Arch of Titus

Preserving Bible Times; © Dr. James C. Martin; on licence Ministero per i Beni le Attivita Culturali-Soprintendza Archeologica di Roma

MATTHEW 24 The Jewish historian Josephus is our primary source of information about the fall of Jerusalem. During the Jewish revolt of A.D. 66–70 Josephus began as a rebel leader, but midway he switched his allegiance to the Roman side of the conflict. He accompanied the Roman general Titus to the siege of Jerusalem and was thus an eyewitness of the harrowing events of the city's fall.[1]

As the Romans slowly crushed the revolt in outlying areas, refugees flooded into Jerusalem for the climactic battle of the war. The Jews inside the city were torn by internal dissent, with various rebel groups vying for control. There was horrendous loss of life, and conditions worsened as the Romans laid siege to Jerusalem in the spring of A.D. 70. Titus's troops took the outer wall around May and captured the strategic Fortress of Antonia. The destruction of the temple was imminent, but many of the Jewish defenders likely believed that God would defend them and his temple at the last.[2] Nonetheless, at the end of August the Romans successfully attacked the temple, setting fire to its gates and overwhelming its defenders. With the sanctuary fallen, the Jews lost hope, and carnage ensued.

Josephus described it thus: "No pity was shown on account of age or out of respect for anyone's dignity—children and elderly, lay people and priests alike were slain. The battle surged ahead and surrounded everybody, including both those who begged for mercy and those who resisted. The flames spread out to a great distance and its noise mixed with the groans of the perishing; and such was the height of the ridge and the magnitude of the burning that one would have imagined the whole city was aflame" (*Wars*, 6.5.1). Thus was Jesus' prophecy regarding the destruction of the temple fulfilled (Mt 24:2).

[1]See "The Roman Army and the Occupation of the Holy Land" on page 1829. [2]See "Herod's Temple" on page 1648.

Interior of arch, depicting troops carrying away plunder from the temple in Jerusalem

Preserving Bible Times; © Dr. James C. Martin; on licence Ministero per i Beni le Attivita Culturali-Soprintendza Archeologica di Roma

through the prophet Daniel—let the reader understand— 16 then
let those who are in Judea flee to the mountains. 17 Let no one on the
24:17 w1Sa 9:25; Mt 10:27; Lk 12:3; Ac 10:9 roof of his house[w] go down to take anything out of the house. 18 Let
no one in the field go back to get his cloak. 19 How dreadful it will be
24:19 xLk 23:29 in those days for pregnant women and nursing mothers![x] 20 Pray that
your flight will not take place in winter or on the Sabbath. 21 For then
there will be great distress, unequaled from the beginning of the
24:21 yDa 12:1; Joel 2:2 world until now—and never to be equaled again.[y] 22 If those days
had not been cut short, no one would survive, but for the sake of the
24:22 zver 24,31 elect[z] those days will be shortened. 23 At that time if anyone says to
24:23 aLk 17:23; 21:8 you, 'Look, here is the Christ!' or, 'There he is!' do not believe it.[a] 24 For
false Christs and false prophets will appear and perform great signs
24:24 b2Th 2:9-11; Rev 13:13 and miracles[b] to deceive even the elect—if that were possible. 25 See,
I have told you ahead of time.

26 "So if anyone tells you, 'There he is, out in the desert,' do not go
out; or, 'Here he is, in the inner rooms,' do not believe it. 27 For as
24:27 cLk 17:24 dMt 8:20 lightning[c] that comes from the east is visible even in the west, so will
be the coming of the Son of Man.[d] 28 Wherever there is a carcass,
24:28 eLk 17:37 there the vultures will gather.[e]

29 "Immediately after the distress of those days

" 'the sun will be darkened,
and the moon will not give its light;
the stars will fall from the sky,
and the heavenly bodies will be
24:29 fIsa 13:10; 34:4; Eze 32:7; Joel 2:10,31; Zep 1:15; Rev 6:12,13; 8:12 shaken.'[a][f]

30 "At that time the sign of the Son of Man will appear in the sky,
and all the nations of the earth will mourn. They will see the Son of
24:30 gDa 7:13; Rev 1:7 Man coming on the clouds of the sky,[g] with power and great glory.
24:31 hMt 13:41 iIsa 27:13; Zec 9:14; 1Co 15:52; 1Th 4:16; Rev 8:2; 10:7; 11:15 31 And he will send his angels[h] with a loud trumpet call,[i] and they
will gather his elect from the four winds, from one end of the heav-
ens to the other.

32 "Now learn this lesson from the fig tree: As soon as its twigs get
tender and its leaves come out, you know that summer is near.
33 Even so, when you see all these things, you know that it[b] is near,
24:33 jJas 5:9 right at the door.[j] 34 I tell you the truth, this generation[c] will certainly not pass away until all these things
24:34 kMt 16:28; 23:36 24:35 lMt 5:18 have happened.[k] 35 Heaven and earth will pass away, but my words will never pass away.[l]

The Day and Hour Unknown

36 "No one knows about that day or hour, not even the angels in heaven, nor the Son,[d] but only the Fa-
24:36 mAc 1:7 24:37 nGe 6:5; 7:6-23 ther.[m] 37 As it was in the days of Noah,[n] so it will be at the coming of the Son of Man. 38 For in the days
24:38 oMt 22:30 before the flood, people were eating and drinking, marrying and giving in marriage,[o] up to the day Noah
entered the ark; 39 and they knew nothing about what would happen until the flood came and took them
all away. That is how it will be at the coming of the Son of Man. 40 Two men will be in the field; one will
24:40 pLk 17:34 be taken and the other left.[p] 41 Two women will be grinding with a hand mill; one will be taken and the
24:41 qLk 17:35 other left.[q]

Ancient Voices

The number of those that fell by famine in the city was boundless, and unspeakable was the suffering that accompanied their deaths. If in any household there was a passing shadow of food, a fight ensued, and even those who had been closest in love gave way to struggling with each other, trying to grab the most pathetic sustenance. People refused to believe that even the dying had nothing; instead, robbers searched people as they expired, thinking that someone with food under his cloak would fake his own death. They stumbled about like mad dogs, mouths gaping open for hunger, pounding against doors like drunken men. Being at wit's end, they burst into the same houses two or three times in a single hour. The need for something to chew on was so great that they gathered up and tried to eat things that the vilest of animals would treat as inedible. At the end, they would not refuse belts and shoes, and they stripped off and chewed the leather of their shields. Shreds of old hay became food for some, and some gathered stalks and sold the smallest quantity for four Attic drachmas.

—Starvation in Jerusalem at the End of the Roman Siege

From Flavius Josephus, *The Jewish Wars*, 6.3, trans. by Duane Garrett

See "Josephus and the Fall of Jerusalem" article.

[a] *29* Isaiah 13:10; 34:4 [b] *33* Or *he* [c] *34* Or *race* [d] *36* Some manuscripts do not have *nor the Son.*

24:16 "Mountains" refers to the Transjordan mountains, where Pella was located. Christians in Jerusalem fled there during the Roman siege shortly before A.D. 70.
24:17 For "roof," see the notes on Mark 2:4 and Luke 17:31.
24:20 Matthew alone included the phrase "on the Sabbath" because he was writing to Jews, who were forbidden to travel more than about .75 miles (.81 km) on the Sabbath.
24:21 Josephus, the Jewish historian who was present at the time, described the destruction of Jerusalem in almost identical language (see "Josephus and the Fall of Jerusalem" on p. 1606).
24:26 "Inner rooms" probably refers to storerooms, which were surrounded by other rooms, so that no one could dig in from the outside.
24:41 The grinding of grain into flour between two heavy stones was a domestic art usually performed by women; hence the import of Jesus' parable (see also Lk 17:35).

42 “Therefore keep watch, because you do not know on what day your Lord will come.[r] 43 But under-
stand this: If the owner of the house had known at what time of night the thief was coming,[s] he would
have kept watch and would not have let his house be broken into. 44 So you also must be ready,[t] because
the Son of Man will come at an hour when you do not expect him.
45 “Who then is the faithful and wise servant,[u] whom the master has put in charge of the servants in his
household to give them their food at the proper time? 46 It will be good for that servant whose master finds
him doing so when he returns.[v] 47 I tell you the truth, he will put him in charge of all his possessions.[w] 48 But
suppose that servant is wicked and says to himself, ‘My master is staying away a long time,’ 49 and he then
begins to beat his fellow servants and to eat and drink with drunkards.[x] 50 The master of that servant will
come on a day when he does not expect him and at an hour he is not aware of. 51 He will cut him to pieces
and assign him a place with the hypocrites, where there will be weeping and gnashing of teeth.[y]

The Parable of the Ten Virgins

25 “At that time the kingdom of heaven will be like[z] ten virgins who took their lamps[a] and went out
to meet the bridegroom.[b] 2 Five of them were foolish and five were wise.[c] 3 The foolish ones took
their lamps but did not take any oil with them. 4 The wise, however, took oil in jars along with their lamps.
5 The bridegroom was a long time in coming, and they all became drowsy and fell asleep.[d]
6 “At midnight the cry rang out: ‘Here’s the bridegroom! Come out to meet him!’
7 “Then all the virgins woke up and trimmed their lamps. 8 The foolish ones said to the wise, ‘Give us
some of your oil; our lamps are going out.’[e]
9 “ ‘No,’ they replied, ‘there may not be enough for both us and you. Instead, go to those who sell oil and
buy some for yourselves.’
10 “But while they were on their way to buy the oil, the bridegroom arrived. The virgins who were ready
went in with him to the wedding banquet.[f] And the door was shut.
11 “Later the others also came. ‘Sir! Sir!’ they said. ‘Open the door for us!’
12 “But he replied, ‘I tell you the truth, I don’t know you.’
13 “Therefore keep watch, because you do not know the day or the hour.[g]

The Parable of the Talents

14 “Again, it will be like a man going on a journey,[h] who called his servants and entrusted his proper-
ty to them. 15 To one he gave five talents[a] of money, to another two talents, and to another one talent, each
according to his ability.[i] Then he went on his journey. 16 The man who had received the five talents went
at once and put his money to work and gained five more. 17 So also, the one with the two talents gained
two more. 18 But the man who had received the one talent went off, dug a hole in the ground and hid his
master’s money.
19 “After a long time the master of those servants returned and settled accounts with them.[j] 20 The
man who had received the five talents brought the other five. ‘Master,’ he said, ‘you entrusted me with five
talents. See, I have gained five more.’
21 “His master replied, ‘Well done, good and faithful servant! You have been faithful with a few things;
I will put you in charge of many things.[k] Come and share your master’s happiness!’
22 “The man with the two talents also came. ‘Master,’ he said, ‘you entrusted me with two talents; see,
I have gained two more.’
23 “His master replied, ‘Well done, good and faithful servant! You have been faithful with a few things;
I will put you in charge of many things.[l] Come and share your master’s happiness!’
24 “Then the man who had received the one talent came. ‘Master,’ he said, ‘I knew that you are a hard
man, harvesting where you have not sown and gathering where you have not scattered seed. 25 So I was
afraid and went out and hid your talent in the ground. See, here is what belongs to you.’
26 “His master replied, ‘You wicked, lazy servant! So you knew that I harvest where I have not sown

[a] *15* A talent was worth more than a thousand dollars.

24:42 [r]Mt 25:13; Lk 12:40
24:43 [s]Lk 12:39
24:44 [t]1Th 5:6
24:45 [u]Mt 25:21, 23
24:46 [v]Rev 16:15
24:47 [w]Mt 25:21, 23
24:49 [x]Lk 21:34
24:51 [y]Mt 8:12
25:1 [z]Mt 13:24 [a]Lk 12:35-38; Ac 20:8; Rev 4:5 [b]Rev 19:7; 21:2
25:2 [c]Mt 24:45
25:5 [d]1Th 5:6
25:8 [e]Lk 12:35
25:10 [f]Rev 19:9
25:13 [g]Mt 24:42, 44; Mk 13:35; Lk 12:40
25:14 [h]Mt 21:33; Lk 19:12
25:15 [i]Mt 18:24, 25
25:19 [j]Mt 18:23
25:21 [k]ver 23; Mt 24:45,47; Lk 16:10
25:23 [l]ver 21

24:51 For the meaning of gnashing with one’s teeth, see the note on Psalm 35:16.
25:1 “Virgins” may be a reference to the bridesmaids, who were responsible for preparing the bride to meet the bridegroom (see “Weddings in Ancient Israel” on p. 1039).
25:7 The charred ends of the rags were cut off and olive oil was added.
25:9 Torches required large amounts of oil to keep burning, and the oil had to be replenished almost every 15 minutes.
25:15 The term “talent” was first used for a unit of weight (about 75 pounds [34 kg]), then later for a unit of coinage. The present-day use of “talent” to indicate an ability or gift is derived from this parable.

and gather where I have not scattered seed? 27Well then, you should have put my money on deposit with the bankers, so that when I returned I would have received it back with interest.

28" 'Take the talent from him and give it to the one who has the ten talents. 29For everyone who has will be given more, and he will have an abundance. Whoever does not have, even what he has will be taken from him.[m] 30And throw that worthless servant outside, into the darkness, where there will be weeping and gnashing of teeth.'[n]

25:29 [m]Mt 13:12; Mk 4:25; Lk 8:18; 19:26
25:30 [n]Mt 8:12

The Sheep and the Goats

31"When the Son of Man comes[o] in his glory, and all the angels with him, he will sit on his throne[p] in heavenly glory. 32All the nations will be gathered before him, and he will separate[q] the people one from another as a shepherd separates the sheep from the goats.[r] 33He will put the sheep on his right and the goats on his left.

34"Then the King will say to those on his right, 'Come, you who are blessed by my Father; take your inheritance, the kingdom[s] prepared for you since the creation of the world.[t] 35For I was hungry and you gave me something to eat, I was thirsty and you gave me something to drink, I was a stranger and you invited me in,[u] 36I needed clothes and you clothed me,[v] I was sick and you looked after me,[w] I was in prison and you came to visit me.'[x]

37"Then the righteous will answer him, 'Lord, when did we see you hungry and feed you, or thirsty and give you something to drink? 38When did we see you a stranger and invite you in, or needing clothes and clothe you? 39When did we see you sick or in prison and go to visit you?'

40"The King will reply, 'I tell you the truth, whatever you did for one of the least of these brothers of mine, you did for me.'[y]

41"Then he will say to those on his left, 'Depart from me,[z] you who are cursed, into the eternal fire[a] prepared for the devil and his angels.[b] 42For I was hungry and you gave me nothing to eat, I was thirsty and you gave me nothing to drink, 43I was a stranger and you did not invite me in, I needed clothes and you did not clothe me, I was sick and in prison and you did not look after me.'

44"They also will answer, 'Lord, when did we see you hungry or thirsty or a stranger or needing clothes or sick or in prison, and did not help you?'

45"He will reply, 'I tell you the truth, whatever you did not do for one of the least of these, you did not do for me.'[c]

46"Then they will go away to eternal punishment, but the righteous to eternal life."[d][e]

25:31 [o]Mt 16:27; Lk 17:30 [p]Mt 19:28
25:32 [q]Mal 3:18 [r]Eze 34:17,20
25:34 [s]Mt 3:2; 5:3,10,19; 19:14; Ac 20:32; 1Co 15:50; Gal 5:21; Jas 2:5 [t]Heb 4:3; 9:26; Rev 13:8; 17:8
25:35 [u]Job 31:32; Isa 58:7; Eze 18:7; Heb 13:2
25:36 [v]Isa 58:7; Eze 18:7; Jas 2:15,16 [w]Jas 1:27 [x]2Ti 1:16
25:40 [y]Pr 19:17; Mt 10:40,42; Heb 6:10; 13:2
25:41 [z]Mt 7:23 [a]Isa 66:24; Mt 3:12; 5:22; Mk 9:43,48; Lk 3:17; Jude 7 [b]2Pe 2:4
25:45 [c]Pr 14:31; 17:5
25:46 [d]Mt 19:29; Jn 3:15,16,36; 17:2,3; Ro 2:7; Gal 6:8; 5:11,13, 20 [e]Da 12:2; Jn 5:29; Ac 24:15; Ro 2:7,8; Gal 6:8

The Plot Against Jesus

26 When Jesus had finished saying all these things,[f] he said to his disciples, 2"As you know, the Passover[g] is two days away—and the Son of Man will be handed over to be crucified."

3Then the chief priests and the elders of the people assembled[h] in the palace of the high priest, whose name was Caiaphas,[i] 4and they plotted to arrest Jesus in some sly way and kill him.[j] 5"But not during the Feast," they said, "or there may be a riot[k] among the people."

26:1 [f]Mt 7:28
26:2 [g]Jn 11:55; 13:1
26:3 [h]Ps 2:2 [i]ver 57; Jn 11:47-53; 18:13,14,24, 28
26:4 [j]Mt 12:14
26:5 [k]Mt 27:24

Jesus Anointed at Bethany

6While Jesus was in Bethany[l] in the home of a man known as Simon the Leper, 7a woman came to him with an alabaster jar of very expensive perfume, which she poured on his head as he was reclining at the table.

8When the disciples saw this, they were indignant. "Why this waste?" they asked. 9"This perfume could have been sold at a high price and the money given to the poor."

26:6 [l]Mt 21:17

25:27 Bankers sat at small tables and exchanged money (see "Banking and Money in the Ancient World" on p. 696). For a discussion of interest, see note on Ezekiel 18:8.

25:30 For the meaning of gnashing with one's teeth, see the note on Psalm 35:16.

26:3 For "chief priests," see the note on 2:4 and for "elders" the note on 21:23.

Caiaphas was the high priest from A.D. 18–36. He was the son-in-law of Annas, a former high priest, who served from A.D. 6–15 and still wielded much influence following his tenure in office. Caiaphas knew well how to maneuver the political scene. The reputation of the office had been ruined, since the Roman governor appointed and deposed the office-holder. The Jewish Qumran community (which produced the Dead Sea Scrolls) was especially critical of this Roman puppet, whom they called the "Wicked Priest." (See "Qumran and the New Testament" on p. 1679 and "Biblical Interpretation at Qumran and Among the Early Rabbis" on p. 1603.) In 1991 an ossuary (a limestone chest containing the bones of the dead) was discovered in Jerusalem, inscribed with the name Caiaphas. See "The High Priests Annas and Caiaphas" on page 1772.

26:6 For "Bethany," see the note on 21:17.

26:7 Most "alabaster" of ancient times was actually marble.

26:9 See the note on Mark 14:5; see also "Perfumes and Anointing Oils" on page 1746.

10Aware of this, Jesus said to them, "Why are you bothering this woman? She has done a beautiful
thing to me. 11The poor you will always have with you,[m] but you will not always have me. 12When she 26:11 [m]Dt 15:11
poured this perfume on my body, she did it to prepare me for burial.[n] 13I tell you the truth, wherever this 26:12 [n]Jn 19:40
gospel is preached throughout the world, what she has done will also be told, in memory of her."

Judas Agrees to Betray Jesus

14Then one of the Twelve—the one called Judas Iscariot[o]—went to the chief priests 15and asked, 26:14 [o]ver 25,47; Mt 10:4
"What are you willing to give me if I hand him over to you?" So they counted out for him thirty silver
coins.[p] 16From then on Judas watched for an opportunity to hand him over. 26:15 [p]Ex 21:32; Zec 11:12

The Lord's Supper

17On the first day of the Feast of Unleavened Bread,[q] the disciples came to Jesus and asked, "Where 26:17 [q]Ex 12:18-20
do you want us to make preparations for you to eat the Passover?"

18He replied, "Go into the city to a certain man and tell him, 'The Teacher says: My appointed time[r] is 26:18 [r]Jn 7:6,8, 30; 12:23; 13:1; 17:1
near. I am going to celebrate the Passover with my disciples at your house.' " 19So the disciples did as
Jesus had directed them and prepared the Passover.

20When evening came, Jesus was reclining at the table with the Twelve. 21And while they were eating,
he said, "I tell you the truth, one of you will betray me."[s] 26:21 [s]Lk 22:21-23; Jn 13:21

22They were very sad and began to say to him one after the other, "Surely not I, Lord?"

23Jesus replied, "The one who has dipped his hand into the bowl with me will betray me.[t] 24The Son 26:23 [t]Ps 41:9; Jn 13:18
of Man will go just as it is written about him.[u] But woe to that man who betrays the Son of Man! It would 26:24 [u]Isa 53; Da 9:26; Mk 9:12; Lk 24:25-27,46; Ac 17:2,3; 26:22, 23
be better for him if he had not been born."

25Then Judas, the one who would betray him, said, "Surely not I, Rabbi?"[v]

Jesus answered, "Yes, it is you."[a] 26:25 [v]Mt 23:7

26While they were eating, Jesus took bread, gave thanks and broke it,[w] and gave it to his disciples, say- 26:26 [w]Mt 14:19; 1Co 10:16
ing, "Take and eat; this is my body."

27Then he took the cup, gave thanks and offered it to them, saying, "Drink from it, all of you. 28This is
my blood of the[b] covenant,[x] which is poured out for many for the forgiveness of sins.[y] 29I tell you, I will 26:28 [x]Ex 24:6-8; Heb 9:20
not drink of this fruit of the vine from now on until that day when I drink it anew with you[z] in my Fa- [y]Mt 20:28; Mk 1:4
ther's kingdom." 26:29 [z]Ac 10:41

30When they had sung a hymn, they went out to the Mount of Olives.[a] 26:30 [a]Mt 21:1; Mk 14:26

Jesus Predicts Peter's Denial

31Then Jesus told them, "This very night you will all fall away on account of me,[b] for it is written: 26:31 [b]Mt 11:6 [c]Zec 13:7; Jn 16:32

> " 'I will strike the shepherd,
> and the sheep of the flock will be scattered.'[c]

[a] 25 Or *"You yourself have said it"* [b] 28 Some manuscripts *the new* [c] 31 Zech. 13:7

26:12 Embalming had to do with preparation of a dead body with oil and spices to preserve it from decay. Embalming was of Egyptian origin, and the only clear Biblical instances of the practice are in the cases of Jacob and Joseph (Ge 50:2–3,6).

Jesus commented on the use of spices for burial (see also Mk 14:8; Jn 12:7), and his body was buried with 75 pounds (34 kg) of myrrh and spices, wrapped in a linen cloth (Jn 19:39–40). Evidently the women who watched the burial considered this inadequate, for they prepared and brought to the sepulcher more spices (Mk 16:1; Lk 23:35–36; 24:1).

Earlier, Martha had assumed that the body of Lazarus was decaying, making it clear that her brother had not been embalmed (Jn 11:39), but his body had been so bound that it had to be loosened (Jn 11:44). The widow's son at Nain had simply been carried out for burial (Lk 7:11–17), while Ananias (and presumably Sapphira) were later merely wrapped up (Ac 5:6,10). The Biblical concept of the future life by that point made embalming unnecessary.

See also "Jewish Burial Practices" on page 1688 and "Perfumes and Anointing Oils" on page 1746.

26:14 For "Iscariot," see the note on Mark 3:19 and for "chief priests" the note on Matthew2:4.

26:15 Thirty silver coins is equivalent to 120 denarii. Laborers customarily received one denarius for a day's work.

26:17 The "first day of the Feast of Unleavened Bread" was the fourteenth of Nisan (March–April). It was also called the preparation of the Passover. The Passover meal was eaten on the evening of the fourteenth after sunset and therefore technically on the fifteenth, since the Jewish day ended at sunset. The Feast of Unleavened Bread lasted for seven days, from the fifteenth to the twenty-first of Nisan. See "The Festivals of Israel" on page 186 and "The Passover" on page 656. Jesus reconstituted the feast, inaugurating the new covenant (see "The Last Supper and the Passover" on p. 1611).

26:20 For "reclining at the table," see the note on Mark 14:18; see also "Jewish Meals and Meal Customs" on page 1575 and "Triclinia" on page 1748.

26:23 It was the custom—still practiced by some in the Middle East—to take a piece of bread, or a piece of meat wrapped in bread, and dip it into a bowl of sauce (made of stewed fruit) on the table. A special courtesy consisted in picking out a choice piece of meat from the central dish and handing it to a guest.

In that culture, as among Arabs today, to eat with a person was tantamount to saying, "I am your friend and will not hurt you."

26:27 The "cup" refers to either the first or the third of the four cups shared during regular observance of the Passover meal.

26:28 For "blood of the covenant," see "The Last Supper and the Passover" on page 1611.

26:30 The Passover fellowship was concluded with the singing of the second half of the Egyptian Hallel Psalms (Ps 115–118). Psalms 113–114 were sung before the meal. (See also "Early Christian Hymnody" on p. 2007.)

26:32 [d]Mt 28:7, 10,16
[32]But after I have risen, I will go ahead of you into Galilee."[d]
[33]Peter replied, "Even if all fall away on account of you, I never will."
[34]"I tell you the truth," Jesus answered, "this very night, before the rooster crows, you will disown me
26:34 [e]ver 75; Jn 13:38 three times."[e]
26:35 [f]Jn 13:37 [35]But Peter declared, "Even if I have to die with you,[f] I will never disown you." And all the other dis-
ciples said the same.

26:34 "Before the rooster crows" may have been a reference to the third of the Roman watches (see the note on 14:25).

The Last Supper and the Passover

MATTHEW 26 Exodus 12 records the deaths of all firstborn males in Egypt, except for those born to Israelites whom God spared or "passed over" when the avenging angel saw the blood of the lamb on their doorposts. Passover is the annual festival commemorating God's miraculous deliverance of the Israelites from Egyptian bondage.[1] Every year thousands of first-century Jews would make a pilgrimage to Jerusalem to celebrate this holy day (the fourteenth day of the first month).[2] The Passover celebration involved a sacrifice on behalf of each family present, followed by a sacrificial meal consisting of unleavened bread, bitter herbs and wine. The following day (the fifteenth) was the first day of the seven-day Festival of Unleavened Bread. During the eight days of these two festivals no one was permitted to eat bread with leaven; this was commemorative of the need to prepare to leave Egypt in haste at the time of the exodus (there being no time to wait for the dough to rise).

There has been a good deal of debate over whether the Last Supper of Jesus was a Passover meal. It certainly appears that Jesus understood it to be such (Mk 14:12–16; Lk 22:15). Arguments against it being a Passover meal include the following:

✣ John 19:14 indicates that Jesus was crucified on the day of the *preparation* for the Passover; thus the previous evening could not have been that of the Passover.

✣ The Passover is traditionally eaten with one's family, whereas the Last Supper was shared among a group of men, some of whom (such as Simon Peter) were married but who for the most part were unrelated to one another.

✣ The Gospel accounts of the Last Supper do not mention the lamb or the bitter herbs of the Passover, nor do they use the normal Greek word for "unleavened bread," speaking instead of ordinary bread.

✣ Passover wine was consumed using individual cups, but the wine of the Last Supper was drunk from a common cup.

On the other hand, many elements associated with the Passover were present at the Last Supper:

✣ The meal was consumed at night, which was the time for the celebration of Passover.

✣ The drinking of wine was obligatory at Passover, and wine was central to the Last Supper.

✣ During New Testament times Jews ordinarily sat when taking meals, but Jesus and the disciples habitually reclined while taking the Passover. At the Last Supper they reclined.[3]

✣ At Passover, a dish of hors d'oeuvres preceded the breaking of bread; such a dish is mentioned in Matthew 26:23.

✣ A hymn was sung at Passover, as in verse 30.

Some of the arguments against the Last Supper having been a Passover meal probably indicate that Jesus was transforming the Passover and creating a new institution for the new covenant:

✣ Jesus' taking the meal with his disciples implies that the church is the family of God (see Mk 3:31–34).

✣ Jesus may well have used unleavened bread at the Last Supper, but the Evangelists may have used the ordinary word for bread to avoid the implication that it is essential that the Lord's Supper be taken with unleavened bread.

✣ The lack of mention of a lamb is probably significant. Jesus was presenting himself as the sacrificial Lamb of the new covenant, and the mention of a literal lamb would have been a misleading distraction in the narrative.

[1]See "The Festivals of Israel" on page 186 and "The Passover" on page 656. [2]See "The Jewish Calendar" on page 241. [3]See "Jewish Meals and Meal Customs" on page 1575.

Gethsemane

36 Then Jesus went with his disciples to a place called Gethsemane, and he said to them, "Sit here while I go over there and pray." 37 He took Peter and the two sons of Zebedee[g] along with him, and he began to be sorrowful and troubled. 38 Then he said to them, "My soul is overwhelmed with sorrow[h] to the point of death. Stay here and keep watch with me."[i]

39 Going a little farther, he fell with his face to the ground and prayed, "My Father, if it is possible, may this cup[j] be taken from me. Yet not as I will, but as you will."[k]

40 Then he returned to his disciples and found them sleeping. "Could you men not keep watch with me[l] for one hour?" he asked Peter. 41 "Watch and pray so that you will not fall into temptation.[m] The spirit is willing, but the body is weak."

42 He went away a second time and prayed, "My Father, if it is not possible for this cup to be taken away unless I drink it, may your will be done."

43 When he came back, he again found them sleeping, because their eyes were heavy. 44 So he left them and went away once more and prayed the third time, saying the same thing.

45 Then he returned to the disciples and said to them, "Are you still sleeping and resting? Look, the hour[n] is near, and the Son of Man is betrayed into the hands of sinners. 46 Rise, let us go! Here comes my betrayer!"

Jesus Arrested

47 While he was still speaking, Judas, one of the Twelve, arrived. With him was a large crowd armed with swords and clubs, sent from the chief priests and the elders of the people. 48 Now the betrayer had arranged a signal with them: "The one I kiss is the man; arrest him." 49 Going at once to Jesus, Judas said, "Greetings, Rabbi!"[o] and kissed him.

50 Jesus replied, "Friend,[p] do what you came for."[a]

Then the men stepped forward, seized Jesus and arrested him. 51 With that, one of Jesus' companions reached for his sword,[q] drew it out and struck the servant of the high priest, cutting off his ear.[r]

52 "Put your sword back in its place," Jesus said to him, "for all who draw the sword will die by the sword.[s] 53 Do you think I cannot call on my Father, and he will at once put at my disposal more than twelve legions of angels?[t] 54 But how then would the Scriptures be fulfilled[u] that say it must happen in this way?"

55 At that time Jesus said to the crowd, "Am I leading a rebellion, that you have come out with swords and clubs to capture me? Every day I sat in the temple courts teaching,[v] and you did not arrest me. 56 But this has all taken place that the writings of the prophets might be fulfilled."[w] Then all the disciples deserted him and fled.

Before the Sanhedrin

57 Those who had arrested Jesus took him to Caiaphas,[x] the high priest, where the teachers of the law and the elders had assembled. 58 But Peter followed him at a distance, right up to the courtyard of the high priest.[y] He entered and sat down with the guards[z] to see the outcome.

59 The chief priests and the whole Sanhedrin[a] were looking for false evidence against Jesus so that they could put him to death. 60 But they did not find any, though many false witnesses[b] came forward.

26:37 [g]Mt 4:21
26:38 [h]Jn 12:27 [i]ver 40,41
26:39 [j]Mt 20:22 [k]ver 42; Ps 40:6-8; Isa 50:5; Jn 5:30; 6:38
26:40 [l]ver 38
26:41 [m]Mt 6:13
26:45 [n]ver 18
26:49 [o]ver 25
26:50 [p]Mt 20:13; 22:12
26:51 [q]Lk 22:36, 38 [r]Jn 18:10
26:52 [s]Ge 9:6; Rev 13:10
26:53 [t]2Ki 6:17; Da 7:10; Mt 4:11
26:54 [u]ver 24
26:55 [v]Mk 12:35; Lk 21:37; Jn 7:14, 28; 18:20
26:56 [w]ver 24
26:57 [x]ver 3
26:58 [y]Jn 18:15 [z]Jn 7:32,45,46
26:59 [a]Mt 5:22
26:60 [b]Ps 27:12; 35:11; Ac 6:13

[a] 50 Or *"Friend, why have you come?"*

26:36–56 Gethsemane ("olive press") was the place of Jesus' agony and arrest (see also Mk 14:32–52; Lk 22:39–54; Jn 18:1–12). Luke indicated that this place was one to which Jesus customarily went and that it was located on the Mount of Olives (see "Mount of Olives" on p. 1543). John 18:1, without naming the site, explains that this was a garden across the Kidron Valley from Jerusalem. The traditional site, cared for by the Franciscans, is not far from the road, near the bridge over the Kidron, and is laid out in neat gardens. Within are eight large olive trees. If Emperor Titus destroyed all of the trees around Jerusalem during the siege of A.D. 70, as the historian Josephus asserted, these trees cannot be as old as the time of Jesus, but they are certainly ancient, and they add to the atmosphere of a place of Christian devotion. Armenian, Greek and Russian churches claim other olive groves nearby as the correct site.

26:48 See "The Jewish Custom of Kissing" on page 1682.

26:49 For a discussion of salutations in the Bible, see the note on Ruth 2:4.

26:53 A Roman legion at full strength included 6,000 soldiers.

26:57 For "Caiaphas," see the note on verse 3; see also "The Jewish Priesthood and Religious Life in the First Century A.D." on page 1704. For "teachers of the law," see the note on 2:4 and for "elders" the note on 21:23.

26:59 The "whole Sanhedrin" (the ecclesiastical court)—70 members plus the high priest—was convened (see "The Sanhedrin" on p. 1821). When a capital case was considered, the sages required that 23 members be present for a quorum. Scholars have long noted the irregularities of the Jewish legal proceedings against Jesus, among them: (1) a trial held at night; (2) at the high priest's home; (3) on the eve of a festival day; (4) beginning with reasons for conviction instead of acquittal; (5) based on false and contradictory witnesses; and (6) the verdict rendered on the day of trial.

26:60 [c]Dt 19:15
26:61 [d]Jn 2:19
26:63 [e]Mt 27:12,14 [f]Lev 5:1 [g]Mt 16:16

Finally two[c] came forward 61and declared, "This fellow said, 'I am able to destroy the temple of God and rebuild it in three days.' "[d]

62Then the high priest stood up and said to Jesus, "Are you not going to answer? What is this testimony that these men are bringing against you?" 63But Jesus remained silent.[e]

The high priest said to him, "I charge you under oath[f] by the living God:[g] Tell us if you are the Christ,[a] the Son of God."

26:64 [h]Ps 110:1 [i]Da 7:13; Rev 1:7
26:65 [j]Mk 14:63

64"Yes, it is as you say," Jesus replied. "But I say to all of you: In the future you will see the Son of Man sitting at the right hand of the Mighty One[h] and coming on the clouds of heaven."[i]

65Then the high priest tore his clothes[j] and said, "He has spoken blasphemy! Why do we need any more witnesses? Look, now you have heard the blasphemy. 66What do you think?"

26:66 [k]Lev 24:16; Jn 19:7
26:67 [l]Mt 16:21; 27:30
26:68 [m]Lk 22:63-65

"He is worthy of death,"[k] they answered.

67Then they spit in his face and struck him with their fists.[l] Others slapped him 68and said, "Prophesy to us, Christ. Who hit you?"[m]

Peter Disowns Jesus

69Now Peter was sitting out in the courtyard, and a servant girl came to him. "You also were with Jesus of Galilee," she said.

70But he denied it before them all. "I don't know what you're talking about," he said.

71Then he went out to the gateway, where another girl saw him and said to the people there, "This fellow was with Jesus of Nazareth."

72He denied it again, with an oath: "I don't know the man!"

73After a little while, those standing there went up to Peter and said, "Surely you are one of them, for your accent gives you away."

74Then he began to call down curses on himself and he swore to them, "I don't know the man!"

26:75 [n]ver 34; Jn 13:38

Immediately a rooster crowed. 75Then Peter remembered the word Jesus had spoken: "Before the rooster crows, you will disown me three times."[n] And he went outside and wept bitterly.

Judas Hangs Himself

27:1 [o]Mt 12:14; Mk 15:1; Lk 22:66
27:2 [p]Mt 20:19 [q]Mk 15:1; Lk 13:1; Ac 3:13; 1Ti 6:13
27:3 [r]Mt 10:4 [s]Mt 26:14,15
27:4 [t]ver 24
27:5 [u]Lk 1:9,21 [v]Ac 1:18

27 Early in the morning, all the chief priests and the elders of the people came to the decision to put Jesus to death.[o] 2They bound him, led him away and handed him over[p] to Pilate, the governor.[q]

3When Judas, who had betrayed him,[r] saw that Jesus was condemned, he was seized with remorse and returned the thirty silver coins[s] to the chief priests and the elders. 4"I have sinned," he said, "for I have betrayed innocent blood."

"What is that to us?" they replied. "That's your responsibility."[t]

5So Judas threw the money into the temple[u] and left. Then he went away and hanged himself.[v]

27:8 [w]Ac 1:19
27:9 [x]Mt 1:22
27:10 [y]Zec 11:12,13; Jer 32:6-9

6The chief priests picked up the coins and said, "It is against the law to put this into the treasury, since it is blood money." 7So they decided to use the money to buy the potter's field as a burial place for foreigners. 8That is why it has been called the Field of Blood[w] to this day. 9Then what was spoken by Jeremiah the prophet was fulfilled:[x] "They took the thirty silver coins, the price set on him by the people of Israel, 10and they used them to buy the potter's field, as the Lord commanded me."[b][y]

Jesus Before Pilate

27:11 [z]Mt 2:2

11Meanwhile Jesus stood before the governor, and the governor asked him, "Are you the king of the Jews?"[z]

[a] 63 Or *Messiah*; also in verse 68 [b] 10 See Zech. 11:12,13; Jer. 19:1-13; 32:6-9.

26:63 Jesus was legally obliged to reply after having been "charged" under oath.
26:64 For the "right hand" as a position of honor, see "The 'Right Hand' in Ancient Thinking" on page 1983.
26:65 Ordinarily the high priest was forbidden by law to tear his clothing (Lev 10:6; 21:10), but this was considered a highly unusual circumstance. The high priest interpreted Jesus' answer (Mt 26:64) as blasphemy (see the note on Mk 14:64).
26:73 Peter had a Galilean accent that was conspicuous in Jerusalem. See the note on 4:12–16.
27:1 The Sanhedrin (see "The Sanhedrin" on p. 1821) could not have convened a legal session at night, so at daybreak they held a special meeting to make the death sentence official.
27:2 The Sanhedrin had been deprived by the Roman government of the right to carry out capital punishment, except in the case of a foreigner who entered the sacred precincts of the temple. So Jesus had to be handed over to Pilate for execution.
27:3 The word "remorse" (*metamelomai*) is different from the normal word for repentance (*metanoeo*). Repentance is a change of heart. Remorse, a weaker emotion, means feeling regret. Judas was remorseful but stopped short of repentance.
27:8 For "the Field of Blood," see the note on Acts 1:18–19.
27:11 The "governor" was Pontius Pilate (see "Pontius Pilate" on p. 1714 and "The Roman Governor" on p. 1824).

"Yes, it is as you say," Jesus replied.
12 When he was accused by the chief priests and the elders, he gave no answer.[a] 13 Then Pilate asked
him, "Don't you hear the testimony they are bringing against you?"[b] 14 But Jesus made no reply,[c] not even
to a single charge—to the great amazement of the governor.
15 Now it was the governor's custom at the Feast to release a prisoner[d] chosen by the crowd. 16 At that
time they had a notorious prisoner, called Barabbas. 17 So when the crowd had gathered, Pilate asked
them, "Which one do you want me to release to you: Barabbas, or Jesus who is called Christ?"[e] 18 For he
knew it was out of envy that they had handed Jesus over to him.
19 While Pilate was sitting on the judge's seat,[f] his wife sent him this message: "Don't have anything to
do with that innocent[g] man, for I have suffered a great deal today in a dream[h] because of him."
20 But the chief priests and the elders persuaded the crowd to ask for Barabbas and to have Jesus executed.[i]
21 "Which of the two do you want me to release to you?" asked the governor.
"Barabbas," they answered.
22 "What shall I do, then, with Jesus who is called Christ?"[j] Pilate asked.
They all answered, "Crucify him!"
23 "Why? What crime has he committed?" asked Pilate.
But they shouted all the louder, "Crucify him!"
24 When Pilate saw that he was getting nowhere, but that instead an uproar[k] was starting, he took wa-
ter and washed his hands[l] in front of the crowd. "I am innocent of this man's blood,"[m] he said. "It is your
responsibility!"[n]
25 All the people answered, "Let his blood be on us and on our children!"[o]
26 Then he released Barabbas to them. But he had Jesus flogged,[p] and handed him over to be crucified.

The Soldiers Mock Jesus

27 Then the governor's soldiers took Jesus into the Praetorium[q] and gathered the whole company of sol-
diers around him. 28 They stripped him and put a scarlet robe on him,[r] 29 and then twisted together a
crown of thorns and set it on his head. They put a staff in his right hand and knelt in front of him and
mocked him. "Hail, king of the Jews!" they said.[s] 30 They spit on him, and took the staff and struck him
on the head again and again.[t] 31 After they had mocked him, they took off the robe and put his own clothes
on him. Then they led him away to crucify him.[u]

The Crucifixion

32 As they were going out,[v] they met a man from Cyrene,[w] named Simon, and they forced him to car-
ry the cross.[x] 33 They came to a place called Golgotha (which means The Place of the Skull).[y] 34 There they
offered Jesus wine to drink, mixed with gall;[z] but after tasting it, he refused to drink it. 35 When they had
crucified him, they divided up his clothes by casting lots.[a][a] 36 And sitting down, they kept watch[b] over him
there. 37 Above his head they placed the written charge against him: THIS IS JESUS, THE KING OF THE JEWS.

[a] 35 A few late manuscripts *lots that the word spoken by the prophet might be fulfilled: "They divided my garments among themselves and cast lots for my clothing"* (Psalm 22:18)

27:12 [a]Mt 26:63; Mk 14:61; Jn 19:9 **27:13** [b]Mt 26:62 **27:14** [c]Mk 14:61 **27:15** [d]Jn 18:39 **27:17** [e]ver 22; Mt 1:16 **27:19** [f]Jn 19:13 [g]ver 24 [h]Ge 20:6; Nu 12:6; 1Ki 3:5; Job 33:14-16; Mt 1:20; 2:12,13, 19,22 **27:20** [i]Ac 3:14 **27:22** [j]Mt 1:16 **27:24** [k]Mt 26:5 [l]Ps 26:6 [m]Dt 21:6-8 [n]ver 4 **27:25** [o]Jos 2:19; Ac 5:28 **27:26** [p]Isa 53:5; Jn 19:1 **27:27** [q]Jn 18:28, 33; 19:9 **27:28** [r]Jn 19:2 **27:29** [s]Isa 53:3; Jn 19:2,3 **27:30** [t]Mt 16:21; 26:67 **27:31** [u]Isa 53:7 **27:32** [v]Heb 13:12 [w]Ac 2:10; 6:9; 11:20; 13:1 [x]Mk 15:21; Lk 23:26 **27:33** [y]Jn 19:17 **27:34** [z]ver 48; Ps 69:21 **27:35** [a]Ps 22:18 **27:36** [b]ver 54

27:16 Barabbas had taken part in a rebellion, presumably against the Romans, so he may have been a folk hero among some of the Jews. Matthew referred to him as a notorious prisoner, and the other evangelists stated that he had been arrested with others for robbery, sedition and murder (see also Mk 15:15; Lk 23:18; Jn 18:40). The custom here mentioned of releasing a prisoner on the Passover is otherwise unknown. The reading "Jesus Barabbas" for his full name in Matthew 27:16–17 was found by Origen in many manuscripts and is still found in some early versions, probably due to a scribe's error in transcription.
27:18 See "Dream Oracles in the Ancient World" on page 741.
27:19 For "judge's seat," see "The Judgment Seat" on page 1819, and for the importance of dreams, see "Dream Oracles in the Ancient World" on page 741.
27:26 The Romans used a whip made of several strips of leather, into which were embedded (near the ends) pieces of bone and lead. The Jews limited the number of stripes to a maximum of 40 (in practice to 39 in case of a miscount; see Dt 25:3), but no such limitation was recognized by the Romans. Roman floggings were so brutal that sometimes the victim died before crucifixion. For additional information on Roman flogging, see "The Shroud of Turin Controversy" on page 1658.
27:27 The Praetorium was the governor's official residence in Jerusalem (see "The Roman Governor" on p. 1824).
27:28–31 Roman soldiers in Jerusalem at the time were known to play a cruel game with condemned prisoners, especially revolutionary brigands. The prisoner was dressed up like a burlesque king and used as a game pawn. (His "scarlet robe" was the outer cloak of a Roman soldier, thorns were twisted into a crown and the "staff" was his mock scepter.) With each roll of the "dice," the prisoner "king" moved around a game board etched in the floor. For the entertainment of the troops, they hurled verbal and physical abuse at the mock king.
27:29 For "staff," see the note on "sceptor" at Zechariah 10:11.
27:34 Tradition says that the women of Jerusalem customarily furnished this pain-killing narcotic to prisoners who were crucified (see "Wine and Alcoholic Beverages in the Ancient World" on p. 2015).
27:35 For "crucified," see the note on Mark 15:24; see also "Crucifixion" on page 1757. For "casting lots," see "Casting Lots" on page 744.

The Location of Jesus' Tomb

MATTHEW 27 According to the New Testament, Jesus was buried in a new tomb hewn out of rock (Mt 27:60; Mk 15:46; Lk 23:53) in a garden near the crucifixion site (Jn 19:41), just outside the city (Jn 19:20; Heb 13:12). In addition, the entrance was low and sealed with a stone (Mt 27:60; Mk 15:46; Jn 20:11), and on the right side it was possible to sit where the body of Jesus had lain (Mk 16:5; Jn 20:12). Based upon the Biblical description and upon other known first-century tombs, the tomb of Jesus can be reconstructed as having had a small forecourt, a low entry passage and a burial chamber with benches, or "couches," on three sides for the placement of the deceased.

There are two main contenders for the location of Jesus' tomb in the Old City of Jerusalem: the Garden Tomb, 275 yards (251 m) north of the Damascus Gate, and the Church of the Holy Sepulchre in the Christian Quarter. The Garden Tomb, however, has no authentic ancient tradition associated with it. It was suggested as the site of Jesus' burial after the renowned British military hero Charles Gordon, while visiting Jerusalem in 1883, suggested that Calvary would have been located on a nearby hill. His identification was based on a fanciful interpretation of ancient Jerusalem as being in the shape of a skeleton, with the skull (i.e., Golgotha) positioned at a hill north of the Damascus Gate. This led to the identification of a tomb on the western side of the hill as Jesus' burial place, once referred to as Gordon's Tomb. Modern investigations of the Garden Tomb and others in the vicinity, however, indicate that they were part of a cemetery dating to the divided monarchy period rather than to the first century A.D.

The Church of the Holy Sepulchre location, on the other hand, has a tradition going back to early Christian times. When the Roman emperor Hadrian rebuilt Jerusalem in A.D. 130/131, he constructed a temple to Jupiter and Venus over the site of the present Church of the Holy Sepulchre. In A.D. 325 Constantine ordered the removal of Hadrian's temple. Local Christian tradition had claimed this to be the site of Jesus' tomb, and, remarkably, when Hadrian's temple was cleared away, a tomb area was indeed discovered beneath it. Constantine had a church constructed on the site and built a small structure, *or edicule,* within the building to enclose the tomb itself. The present Church of the Holy Sepulchre is the continuation of Constantine's church.[1]

Jerusalem: "The Garden Tomb"
Photograph courtesy of © Dr. Gary Pratico

In favor of the authenticity of this location is the fact that there was a continuous Christian presence in Jerusalem from Jesus' death until Constantine uncovered the tomb. This Christian community doubtless would have venerated the site of Jesus' burial, preserving the memory of the location of his tomb. Also, the site of the church was an old quarry during the time of Jesus, although at least part of it had been made into a garden (Jn 19:41). The fact that the site of the Church of the Holy Sepulchre had been a quarry implies that it was outside the walls of the city (it is today inside the Old City). This agrees with the fact that Jesus was crucified outside the walls. Within this area at least four tombs cut into the western rock face have been discovered, only one of which corresponds to the type in which Jesus was buried.

The church was destroyed in 614 and rebuilt in 626. The edicule was destroyed in 1009 by the Egyptian caliph al-Hakim Bi-Amr Allah. Contemporary accounts suggest that the southern wall, the burial couch and part of the northern wall survived this destruction. The rebuilt edicule has suffered damage and neglect over the centuries since that time, so that today it is a hodgepodge of reconstructions and repairs. Although absolute certainty is impossible, the evidence points to the Church of the Holy Sepulchre as being the actual site of Jesus' tomb.

[1]See "Constantine and Queen Helena's Role in Preserving Holy Sites" on page1758.

38Two robbers were crucified with him,[c] one on his right and one on his left. 39Those who passed by 27:38 [c]Isa 53:12
hurled insults at him, shaking their heads[d] 40and saying, "You who are going to destroy the temple and 27:39 [d]Ps 22:7; 109:25; La 2:15
build it in three days,[e] save yourself![f] Come down from the cross, if you are the Son of God!"[g] 27:40 [e]Mt 26:61; Jn 2:19 [f]ver 42 [g]Mt 4:3,6
41In the same way the chief priests, the teachers of the law and the elders mocked him. 42"He saved oth-
ers," they said, "but he can't save himself! He's the King of Israel![h] Let him come down now from the cross, 27:42 [h]Jn 1:49; 12:13 [i]Jn 3:15
and we will believe[i] in him. 43He trusts in God. Let God rescue him[j] now if he wants him, for he said, 'I am 27:43 [j]Ps 22:8
the Son of God.' " 44In the same way the robbers who were crucified with him also heaped insults on him.

The Death of Jesus

45From the sixth hour until the ninth hour darkness[k] came over all the land. 46About the ninth hour
Jesus cried out in a loud voice, *"Eloi, Eloi,[a] lama sabachthani?"*—which means, "My God, my God, why 27:45 [k]Am 8:9
have you forsaken me?"[b][l] 27:46 [l]Ps 22:1
47When some of those standing there heard this, they said, "He's calling Elijah."
48Immediately one of them ran and got a sponge. He filled it with wine vinegar,[m] put it on a stick, and 27:48 [m]ver 34; Ps 69:21
offered it to Jesus to drink. 49The rest said, "Now leave him alone. Let's see if Elijah comes to save him."
50And when Jesus had cried out again in a loud voice, he gave up his spirit.[n] 27:50 [n]Jn 19:30
51At that moment the curtain of the temple[o] was torn in two from top to bottom. The earth shook 27:51 [o]Ex 26:31-33; Heb 9:3,8
and the rocks split.[p] 52The tombs broke open and the bodies of many holy people who had died were [p]ver 54
raised to life. 53They came out of the tombs, and after Jesus' resurrection they went into the holy city[q] 27:53 [q]Mt 4:5
and appeared to many people.
54When the centurion and those with him who were guarding[r] Jesus saw the earthquake and all that 27:54 [r]ver 36 [s]Mt 4:3; 17:5
had happened, they were terrified, and exclaimed, "Surely he was the Son[c] of God!"[s]
55Many women were there, watching from a distance. They had followed Jesus from Galilee to care
for his needs.[t] 56Among them were Mary Magdalene, Mary the mother of James and Joses, and the moth- 27:55 [t]Lk 8:2,3
er of Zebedee's sons.[u] 27:56 [u]Mk 15:47; Lk 24:10; Jn 19:25

The Burial of Jesus

57As evening approached, there came a rich man from Arimathea, named Joseph, who had himself be-
come a disciple of Jesus. 58Going to Pilate, he asked for Jesus' body, and Pilate ordered that it be given to
him. 59Joseph took the body, wrapped it in a clean linen cloth, 60and placed it in his own new tomb[v] that 27:60 [v]Mt 27:66; 28:2; Mk 16:4
he had cut out of the rock. He rolled a big stone in front of the entrance to the tomb and went away. 61Mary
Magdalene and the other Mary were sitting there opposite the tomb.

The Guard at the Tomb

62The next day, the one after Preparation Day, the chief priests and the Pharisees went to Pilate. 63"Sir,"
they said, "we remember that while he was still alive that deceiver said, 'After three days I will rise again.'[w] 27:63 [w]Mt 16:21
64So give the order for the tomb to be made secure until the third day. Otherwise, his disciples may come
and steal the body and tell the people that he has been raised from the dead. This last deception will be
worse than the first."
65"Take a guard,"[x] Pilate answered. "Go, make the tomb as secure as you know how." 66So they went 27:65 [x]ver 66; Mt 28:11
and made the tomb secure by putting a seal[y] on the stone[z] and posting the guard.[a] 27:66 [y]Da 6:17 [z]ver 60; Mt 28:2 [a]Mt 28:11

[a] 46 Some manuscripts *Eli, Eli* [b] 46 Psalm 22:1 [c] 54 Or *a son*

27:38 These "robbers" were probably insurrectionists (see the note on Mk 15:27, as well as "Messianic Conflicts and the Fall of Jerusalem" on p. 1632).
27:41 For "chief priests" and "teachers of the law," see the note on 2:4. For "elders," see the note on 21:23.
27:45 It was dark from noon until 3:00 P.M.
27:46 There are several Aramaic words and phrases in the New Testament, among them *Talitha koum* (Mk 5:41), *Ephphatha* (Mk 7:34), *Eloi, Eloi, lama sabachthani* (Mt 27:46; Mk 15:34), *Maranatha* (1Co 16:22 footnote) and *Abba* (Mk 14:36; Ro 8:15; Gal 4:6). It has been generally assumed that Aramaic was the colloquial language of the Holy Land from the time of the return of the exiles from Babylon, but some scholars believe that Hebrew was spoken in Galilee during New Testament times. It is probably safe to assume that our Lord habitually spoke Aramaic and occasionally Greek and that he could both read and speak Hebrew.
27:48 Wine vinegar was a sour wine, the drink of laborers and common soldiers (see "Wine and Alcoholic Beverages in the Ancient World" on p. 2015).
27:54 For "centurion," see the note on 8:5.
27:57 Arimathea was a village in the hill country of Ephraim, about 20 miles (32 km) northwest of Jerusalem. It may perhaps be identified with Ramathaim, the birthplace of the prophet Samuel (see 1Sa 1:1).
27:59 For "linen cloth," see "The Shroud of Turin Controversy" on page 1658.
27:60 For "new tomb," see the note on Mark 15:46; see also "Jewish Burial Practices" on page 1688 and "The Location of Jesus' Tomb" on page 1615.
27:62 The "next day" was Saturday, the Sabbath. Friday was the preparation day for the Sabbath (sunset Friday to sunset Saturday).
27:65 "Take a guard" refers either to a guard of Roman soldiers or to one of the Jews' own temple police. See "The Soldiers Guarding the Tomb" on page 1618.
27:66 The seal was a security device, likely a cord attached both to the stone (cf. v. 60) and to the tomb, with wax imprinted with the Roman seal anchoring both ends so that tampering could be detected (cf. Da 6:17). The soldiers standing guard added additional security.

THE RESURRECTION OF JESUS

MATTHEW 28 All four Gospels are clear in their teaching that Jesus arose bodily from the dead. They differ, however, in their accounts of the appearances of the risen Christ:

- Matthew 28:9–10 notes an appearance of Jesus to Mary Magdalene and "the other Mary" (v. 1) near the empty tomb, followed by a manifestation to the remaining 11 disciples in Galilee (vv. 16–17).
- The most ancient manuscripts of Mark, meanwhile, do not feature an account of the appearance of the risen Christ, although an angel assured the women at the tomb that the disciples would see him in Galilee.
- Luke's narrative focuses on the vicinity of Jerusalem, with Jesus revealing himself to two disciples on the road to Emmaus and later to larger groups of his followers in Jerusalem and Bethany.
- John features an appearance to Mary Magdalene outside the empty tomb, two appearances (perhaps in Jerusalem) to the disciples—once with Thomas absent and once with this disciple present—and an appearance by the Sea of Galilee to a number of disciples who were fishing.[1]

Are these accounts in conflict, as some scholars have suggested? Most of them are left without specific time references, so there is no need to posit any chronological problems with the texts. Luke, however, has been understood to indicate that all of the resurrection appearances and the ascension to heaven happened on the same day, namely Easter Sunday, leaving no room for the manifestations recorded in Matthew and John. But is this really an insurmountable problem?[2]

Luke was clearly interested in the Jerusalem appearances as a transition from his Gospel to the book of Acts. But while the appearances to the Emmaus travelers and to the rest of the disciples must have taken place on Easter Sunday (cf. Lk 24:13 with vv. 33,36), there is room for a chronological break either after Luke 24:43 (i.e., Jesus ate with the disciples, some undetermined time period ensued and then he spoke the words beginning in v. 44) or after verse 49 (i.e., Jesus met with the disciples and sometime later met them again in Jerusalem, led them to Bethany and ascended to heaven).

Like many ancient writers,[3] Luke was not concerned about giving an exhaustive, chronological account in his Gospel. It is difficult to imagine that he was unaware of traditions concerning Jesus' appearances in Galilee, and we have no reason to suspect that he would have rejected them. It would appear that he simply wished to move his readers as smoothly as possible from his Gospel to the accounts in Acts and that he carefully selected from among the postresurrection appearances of Jesus those centered in the Jerusalem area.

Tomb remains from the Shephelah in Israel

Preserving Bible Times; © Dr. James C. Martin

[1]See "Fishing in New Testament Times" on page 1676. [2]See "The Historical Value of Luke–Acts" on page 1697. [3]See "Historians in the Ancient World" on page 939.

The Resurrection

28 After the Sabbath, at dawn on the first day of the week, Mary Magdalene and the other Mary[b]
went to look at the tomb.
2 There was a violent earthquake,[c] for an angel[d] of the Lord came down from heaven and, going to the
tomb, rolled back the stone and sat on it. 3 His appearance was like lightning, and his clothes were white
as snow.[e] 4 The guards were so afraid of him that they shook and became like dead men.
5 The angel said to the women, "Do not be afraid,[f] for I know that you are looking for Jesus, who was
crucified. 6 He is not here; he has risen, just as he said.[g] Come and see the place where he lay. 7 Then go
quickly and tell his disciples: 'He has risen from the dead and is going ahead of you into Galilee.[h] There
you will see him.' Now I have told you."
8 So the women hurried away from the tomb, afraid yet filled with joy, and ran to tell his disciples.
9 Suddenly Jesus met them.[i] "Greetings," he said. They came to him, clasped his feet and worshiped him.
10 Then Jesus said to them, "Do not be afraid. Go and tell my brothers[j] to go to Galilee; there they will
see me."

28:1 [b]Mt 27:56
28:2 [c]Mt 27:51 [d]Jn 20:12
28:3 [e]Da 10:6; Mk 9:3; Jn 20:12
28:5 [f]ver 10; Mt 14:27
28:6 [g]Mt 16:21
28:7 [h]ver 10,16; Mt 26:32
28:9 [i]Jn 20:14-18
28:10 [j]Jn 20:17; Ro 8:29; Heb 2:11-13,17

The Guards' Report

11 While the women were on their way, some of the guards[k] went into the city and reported to the chief
priests everything that had happened. 12 When the chief priests had met with the elders and devised a
plan, they gave the soldiers a large sum of money, 13 telling them, "You are to say, 'His disciples came dur-

28:11 [k]Mt 27:65, 66

28:2 For earthquakes, see the note on Zechariah 14:5.

The Soldiers Guarding the Tomb

MATTHEW 28 Only Matthew mentions that soldiers guarded the tomb of Jesus.[1] Matthew 27:62–66 records that the chief priests and Pharisees[2] recalled Jesus' own prediction that he would rise again, and they cited their fear that the disciples might steal his body to support their request for an authorized guard. Pilate's reply in 27:65 literally means "You have a guard," and on this basis some have surmised that the guard in question was the temple guard under the high priest's own jurisdiction. However, the language of 28:14 precludes this possibility and requires a Roman guard under Pilate's direct control. Moreover, it is unclear why the chief priests and Pharisees would have requested permission for a guard that they themselves could have directed. Thus, the phrase of 27:65 should probably be rendered as "Take a guard" (as in the NIV).[3]

The tomb of Jesus was already sealed by a large stone (27:60), which was then probably affixed with an official seal that, if broken, would have attested to the opening of the tomb (cf. Da 6:17).[4] Matthew 28:11–15 records that some of the guards reported the things they had seen and were bribed into circulating a false report about their own negligence and the theft of Jesus' body. The ensuing rumor is assumed in John 20:2, 15 and appears later in Justin Martyr's second-century *Dialogue With Trypho* (108:2).

The Roman concern for safeguarding tombs is reflected in an imperial inscription bearing the title *Diatagma Kaisaros*, acquired at Nazareth during the nineteenth century.[5] The marble slab, containing 21 lines of Greek text, dates from between 50 B.C. and A.D. 50. The text attests to the sanctity of tombs and threatens with capital punishment any who would defile a tomb by removing the body. Scholars have considered the possibility that, in light of the disturbances between Jews and early Christians over what happened to the body of Jesus, the *Diatagma Kaisaros* may reflect an early Roman response. Although the present state of research does not allow for absolute certainty, the presence of this authentic decree lends historical credibility to Matthew's account.

[1]See "The Location of Jesus' Tomb" on page 1615. [2]See "The Pharisees" on page 1566. [3]See "The Roman Army and the Occupation of the Holy Land" on page 1829. [4]See "Jewish Burial Practices" on page 1688. [5]See "Nazareth" on page 1623.

28:14 [l]Mt 27:2
28:16 [m]ver 7,10; Mt 26:32
28:18 [n]Da 7:13, 14; Lk 10:22; Jn 3:35; 17:2; 1Co 15:27; Eph 1:20-22; Php 2:9,10
28:19 [o]Mk 16:15, 16; Lk 24:47; Ac 1:8; 14:21 [p]Ac 2:38; 8:16; Ro 6:3,4
28:20 [q]Ac 2:42 [r]Mt 18:20; Ac 18:10 [s]Mt 13:39

ing the night and stole him away while we were asleep.' 14 If this report gets to the governor,[l] we will sat-
isfy him and keep you out of trouble." 15 So the soldiers took the money and did as they were instructed.
And this story has been widely circulated among the Jews to this very day.

The Great Commission

16 Then the eleven disciples went to Galilee, to the mountain where Jesus had told them to go.[m] 17 When
they saw him, they worshiped him; but some doubted. 18 Then Jesus came to them and said, "All author-
ity in heaven and on earth has been given to me.[n] 19 Therefore go and make disciples of all nations,[o] bap-
tizing them in[a] the name of the Father and of the Son and of the Holy Spirit,[p] 20 and teaching[q] them to
obey everything I have commanded you. And surely I am with you[r] always, to the very end of the age."[s]

[a] *19* Or *into*; see Acts 8:16; 19:5; Romans 6:3; 1 Cor. 1:13; 10:2 and Gal. 3:27.

28:19 See "Baptism in the Ancient World" on page 1562.

INTRODUCTION TO 

AUTHOR, PLACE AND DATE OF WRITING

Although the book does not name its author, tradition going back to the church father Papias (c. 130) claims that John Mark wrote this Gospel on the basis of the reminiscences of the apostle Peter (Papias claims to have received this tradition from someone called "the elder"). See also the introduction to Matthew for reference to this church father. John Mark appears repeatedly in the New Testament and is associated with Paul (Col 4:10), Barnabas (Ac 15:39) and Peter (1Pe 5:13).

Some church fathers (e.g., Irenaeus) asserted that Mark wrote after the death of Peter, which would place his Gospel at about A.D. 67. Clement of Alexandria, however, claimed that it was written while Peter was in Rome, which could place it any time after about A.D. 45. We know that Mark was associated with Peter late in Peter's life (1Pe 5:13), but that does not exclude the possibility of an earlier association between the two. A date between 50 and 70 is probable, and some point in the 60s seems preferable.

AUDIENCE

Mark addressed his Gospel to Gentile Christians, perhaps to those facing increasingly trying conditions in Rome. Because Mark's Gospel was written to a Gentile audience, he often explained Jewish customs or translated Aramaic for his readers (Mk 3:17; 7:2–4; 15:22), and only once did he quote directly from the Old Testament law.

CULTURAL FACTS AND HIGHLIGHTS

The notorious fire of Rome in A.D. 64—probably set by Nero himself but blamed on Christians—resulted in widespread persecution and martyrdom. Some interpreters, assuming a Roman audience for Mark's Gospel and a historical setting during the time of Nero's persecutions, believe that Mark was especially written to encourage Christians to persevere in the face of persecution (see, e.g., 3:22; 8:34–38; 13:8–13). However, Mark's general purpose appears to have been precisely what Papias claimed it was: to preserve Peter's account of the life and teachings of Jesus.

TIMELINE

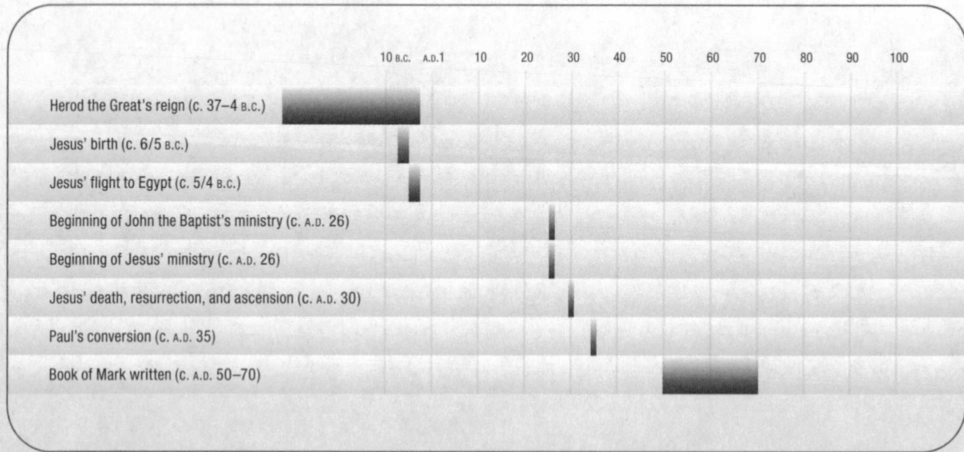

AS YOU READ

Attempt to enter vicariously into Mark's vivid account of Jesus' ministry. Note not only what Jesus said but also what he did and the emotional impact his words and actions had on others. Watch for revelations of Jesus' humanity, as Mark revealed him to be at the same time the Son of God and the Son of Man.

DID YOU KNOW?

- A synagogue could be established in any town where there were at least ten married Jewish men (1:21).
- In addition to being labeled traitors, tax collectors were notorious for their dishonesty. They were banned from serving as witnesses or judges and were expelled from the synagogue (2:14).
- Jesus spoke Aramaic but undoubtedly also understood Greek and read from the Scriptures in classical Hebrew (5:41).
- Jewish rabbis counted 613 individual statutes in the law and attempted to differentiate between "heavy" and "light" commands (12:28).
- During the Passover and the week-long Feast of Unleavened Bread, the population of Jerusalem increased from about 50,000 to several hundred thousand (14:2).
- Death during crucifixion was due to heart failure (15:24).

THEMES

The Gospel of Mark includes the following themes:

1. *Jesus, the Son of God.* Mark's account reveals Jesus' authority (a) as a teacher (1:21–22); (b) to forgive sins (2:5–12); and (c) over the Sabbath (2:27–28), unclean spirits (3:20–27), nature (4:35–41; 6:45–52), the law (7:1–20), the temple (11:12–19,27–33; 12:1–12) and the mystery of the kingdom of God (4:10–11).

2. *Jesus, the Son of Man.* Jesus did not shrink from ritual defilement, physical contamination or moral pollution. His loving touch displayed his compassion and accessibility.

3. *Jesus, the Messiah.* Jesus' suffering, rejection and death were central to God's way of salvation. Mark revealed the disciples' initial inability to recognize Jesus' Messianic identity and role.

4. *Jesus, a model of suffering.* Jesus spoke openly of his suffering and death and warned his disciples that they also would face tribulation.

5. *Jesus, the Savior of all who believe.* Jesus is the Savior of all who receive him by faith. Mark's Gospel focuses on Jesus' ministry in Gentile regions, explains Jewish terms and customs, records the confession of faith of a Gentile (15:39) and the sending of the first Gentile missionary (5:18–19) and calls the temple "a house of prayer for *all* nations" (11:17, emphasis added).

OUTLINE

- I. The Beginnings of Jesus' Ministry (1:1–13)
- II. Jesus' Ministry in Galilee (1:14—6:29)
  - A. His Early Ministry (1:14—3:12)
  - B. His Later Ministry (3:13—6:29)
- III. Ministry in Other Areas (6:30—9:32)
- IV. Final Ministry in Galilee (9:33–50)
- V. Jesus' Ministry in Judea and Perea (10)
- VI. The Passion of Jesus (11:1—14:11)
  - A. The Triumphal Entry (11:1–11)
  - B. The Cleansing of the Temple (11:12–19)
  - C. Last Questions From the Jewish Leaders (11:20—12:44)
  - D. The Olivet Discourse (13)
  - E. The Anointing of Jesus' Head (14:1–11)
- VII. The Arrest, Trial and Death of Jesus (14:12—15:47)
- VIII. The Resurrection of Jesus (16)

John the Baptist Prepares the Way

1 The beginning of the gospel about Jesus Christ, the Son of God.[a][a] 1:1 [a]Mt 4:3

2 It is written in Isaiah the prophet:

"I will send my messenger ahead of you,
who will prepare your way"[b][b]— 1:2 [b]Mal 3:1; Mt 11:10; Lk 7:27
3 "a voice of one calling in the desert,
'Prepare the way for the Lord,
make straight paths for him.' "[c][c] 1:3 [c]Isa 40:3; Jn 1:23

4 And so John[d] came, baptizing in the desert region and preaching a baptism of repentance[e] for the for- 1:4 [d]Mt 3:1 [e]Ac 13:24
giveness of sins.[f] 5 The whole Judean countryside and all the people of Jerusalem went out to him. Con- [f]Lk 1:77
fessing their sins, they were baptized by him in the Jordan River. 6 John wore clothing made of camel's hair,
with a leather belt around his waist, and he ate locusts[g] and wild honey. 7 And this was his message: "Af- 1:6 [g]Lev 11:22
ter me will come one more powerful than I, the thongs of whose sandals I am not worthy to stoop down
and untie.[h] 8 I baptize you with[d] water, but he will baptize you with the Holy Spirit."[i] 1:7 [h]Ac 13:25 1:8 [i]Isa 44:3; Joel 2:28; Ac 1:5; 2:4; 11:16; 19:4-6

The Baptism and Temptation of Jesus

9 At that time Jesus came from Nazareth[j] in Galilee and was baptized by John in the Jordan. 10 As Jesus 1:9 [j]Mt 2:23
was coming up out of the water, he saw heaven being torn open and the Spirit descending on him like a
dove.[k] 11 And a voice came from heaven: "You are my Son,[l] whom I love; with you I am well pleased." 1:10 [k]Jn 1:32 1:11 [l]Mt 3:17
12 At once the Spirit sent him out into the desert, 13 and he was in the desert forty days, being tempt-
ed by Satan.[m] He was with the wild animals, and angels attended him. 1:13 [m]Mt 4:10

The Calling of the First Disciples

14 After John was put in prison, Jesus went into Galilee,[n] proclaiming the good news of God.[o] 15 "The 1:14 [n]Mt 4:12 [o]Mt 4:23
time has come,"[p] he said. "The kingdom of God is near. Repent and believe the good news!"[q] 1:15 [p]Gal 4:4; Eph 1:10 [q]Ac 20:21
16 As Jesus walked beside the Sea of Galilee, he saw Simon and his brother Andrew casting a net into
the lake, for they were fishermen. 17 "Come, follow me," Jesus said, "and I will make you fishers of men."
18 At once they left their nets and followed him.
19 When he had gone a little farther, he saw James son of Zebedee and his brother John in a boat, pre-
paring their nets. 20 Without delay he called them, and they left their father Zebedee in the boat with the
hired men and followed him.

Jesus Drives Out an Evil Spirit

21 They went to Capernaum, and when the Sabbath came, Jesus went into the synagogue and began
to teach.[r] 22 The people were amazed at his teaching, because he taught them as one who had authority, 1:21 [r]Mt 4:23; Mk 10:1
not as the teachers of the law.[s] 23 Just then a man in their synagogue who was possessed by an evil[e] spir- 1:22 [s]Mt 7:28,29

[a] *1* Some manuscripts do not have *the Son of God.* [b] *2* Mal. 3:1 [c] *3* Isaiah 40:3 [d] *8* Or *in* [e] *23* Greek *unclean*; also in verses 26 and 27

1:4 The "desert region" was the arid region west of the Dead Sea. See "Baptism in the Ancient World" on page 1562.

1:5 The Jordan River was the principal river in the Holy Land, beginning in the snows of Mount Hermon and ending in the Dead Sea. At its closest point to Jerusalem, it is about 20 miles (32 km) away. The Jordan is important in that in the New Testament it was there that John that Baptist carried on his ministry (see also Mt 3:6; Jn 1:28; 3:26), and thus in this river Jesus himself was baptized (Mt 3:13; Mk 1:9; Lk 4:1). No other event occurs in the New Testament directly related to the Jordan River. The theme of the Jordan River is frequently found in the ritual of the church and in its hymnology and poetry. A frequent motif is describing death as a crossing of the Jordan, a metaphor based on the story of Elijah (2Ki 2:4–9).

1:6 For "camel's hair," see the notes on Zechariah 13:4 and Matthew 3:4.

1:9 See "Nazareth" on page 1623.

1:13 In Jesus' day there were many more wild animals in Israel than there are today. See "Lions and Other Wild Beasts in Ancient Israel" on page 813.

1:14 See the note on Matthew 14:3; see also "Imprisonment in the Roman World: In Prison Versus House Arrest" on page 1826.

1:16 The Sea of Galilee is a beautiful lake, almost 700 feet (213 m) below sea level, 14 miles (22.5 km) long and 6 miles (10 km) wide, fed by the waters of the upper Jordan River. It was also called the Lake of Gennesaret (Lk 5:1) and the Sea of Tiberias (Jn 6:1; 21:1), and in Old Testament times it was known as the Sea of Kinnereth (e.g., Nu 34:11) because it is shaped like a harp.

1:21 For "Capernaum," see the note on Matthew 4:13.

The synagogue was a vitally important religious institution among the Jews of that day. Originating during the exile, it provided a place where Jews could study the Scriptures and worship God. A synagogue could be established in any town where there were at least ten married Jewish men. Jesus, like Paul (see Ac 13:14–15), took advantage of the custom that allowed visiting teachers to participate in the worship service by invitation of the synagogue leaders. (See "The Capernaum Synagogue" on p. 1591 and "Ancient Synagogues" on p. 1783.)

1:23 See "Demons and the Bible" on page 1572.

1:24 [t]Mt 8:29 [u]Mt 2:23; Lk 24:19; Ac 24:5 [v]Lk 1:35; Jn 6:69; Ac 3:14 1:25 [w]ver 34 1:26 [x]Mk 9:20 1:27 [y]Mk 10:24, 32

it cried out, 24 "What do you want with us,[t] Jesus of Nazareth?[u] Have you come to destroy us? I know who
you are—the Holy One of God!"[v]
25 "Be quiet!" said Jesus sternly. "Come out of him!"[w] 26 The evil spirit shook the man violently and
came out of him with a shriek.[x]
27 The people were all so amazed[y] that they asked each other, "What is this? A new teaching—and

1:24 The name "Holy One of God" points to Christ's divine origin rather than to his Messiahship. The name may have been used by the demons in accordance with the occult belief that the precise use of a person's name conferred upon the speaker a certain degree of control over him or her.

ARCHAEOLOGICAL SITES

NAZARETH

MARK 1 The town of Nazareth ("Map 9") is located north of the Jezreel Valley in the hills of lower Galilee, approximately 3 miles (4.8 km) south of Sepphoris.[1] While Sepphoris was an opulent Greco-Roman city during Jesus' youth and functioned as the capital of Galilee until A.D. 20, Nazareth remained in relative obscurity.[2] Nazareth occupied about 60 acres, with a population of only about 500. In his writings Josephus named some 45 Galilean towns but never once mentioned Nazareth, and neither does the Talmud, which names 63 other Galilean sites. The insignificance of Nazareth provoked disparaging comments already in Jesus' day, such as Nathanael's retort: "Can any good thing come from [Nazareth]?" (Jn 1:46).

Nevertheless, the New Testament explicitly identifies Jesus as "the prophet from Nazareth in Galilee" (Mt 21:11). This humble town was the residence of Mary and Joseph (Lk 2:39) and the place where Jesus grew up (Mt 2:23; Lk 4:16). It was also the jumping-off point for his public ministry (Mk 1:9) and the site of his first rejection (Lk 4:16–30).[3] He is frequently referred to in the Gospel narratives simply as "Jesus of Nazareth" (Mk 1:24; Lk 18:37), and the *titulus* (official placard) that Pilate affixed to the cross dubbed him "JESUS OF NAZARETH, THE KING OF THE JEWS" (Jn 19:19).[4] Even his earliest followers were labeled "the Nazarene sect" (Ac 24:5).

Both Matthew and John, however, connected the origin of Jesus from Nazareth with an important precedent in the Bible. Matthew 2:23 states that Jesus fulfilled the prophecy, "He will be called a Nazarene." What was Matthew referring to? No Old Testament text contains those specific words, and Matthew did not indicate the source of his reference. Some have conjectured that he was alluding to Isaiah 11:1, in which the Messiah is called a "Branch" (the Hebrew word for branch, *netzer*, sounds similar to Nazareth). Others have proposed that Matthew was referring to the concept of the Nazirite, a person consecrated to God's service (Nu 6:1–21; Jdg 13). But John also linked his first mention of Jesus' origins in Nazareth to his assertion that Jesus was the fulfillment of what Moses and the prophets had written (Jn 1:45). John did not claim that Jesus' coming from Nazareth in and of itself fulfilled Scripture, but he did report Nathanael's astonishment at the idea that the Messiah could have hailed from such a little-known hometown (Jn 1:46).

Archaeological excavations conducted beneath the Church of the Annunciation have revealed that ancient Nazareth was an agricultural village. Pottery was found there dating from the **Iron Age** II[5] (900–600 B.C.) to the **Byzantine** period (A.D. 330–640). Excavations have also uncovered a number of Jewish tombs, including four that were sealed with rolling stones, typical of tombs used up to A.D. 70 and similar to the one in which Jesus was laid.[6] In addition, a third-century A.D. Jewish-Christian synagogue was discovered there. Oriented toward Jerusalem, it contained Jewish-Christian iconography within its mosaic floor. The synagogue that Jesus attended as a young man and in which he first proclaimed his Messianic identity (Lk 4) probably stood beneath this later structure.[7] The present-day Basilica of the Annunciation at Nazareth was dedicated in 1969 and represents the largest Christian church structure in the Middle East.

[1]See "Sepphoris" on page 1638. [2]See "Galilee in Jesus' Time" on page 1587. [3]See "The Life of Jesus" on page 1636. [4]See "Pontius Pilate" on page 1714.
[5]See Glossary on page 2080 for definitions of bolded words. See also "Archaeological Periods" chart on page xx in the front of this Bible. [6]See "The Location of Jesus' Tomb" on page 1615 and "Jewish Burial Practices" on page 1688. [7]See "Ancient Synagogues" on page 1783.

with authority! He even gives orders to evil spirits and they obey him." 28 News about him spread quick-
ly over the whole region[z] of Galilee. 1:28 [z]Mt 9:26

Jesus Heals Many

29 As soon as they left the synagogue,[a] they went with James and John to the home of Simon and An- 1:29 [a]ver 21,23
drew. 30 Simon's mother-in-law was in bed with a fever, and they told Jesus about her. 31 So he went to her,
took her hand and helped her up.[b] The fever left her and she began 1:31 [b]Lk 7:14
to wait on them.

32 That evening after sunset the people brought to Jesus all the
sick and demon-possessed.[c] 33 The whole town gathered at the door, 1:32 [c]Mt 4:24
34 and Jesus healed many who had various diseases.[d] He also drove 1:34 [d]Mt 4:23
out many demons, but he would not let the demons speak because [e]Mk 3:12;
they knew who he was.[e] Ac 16:17,18

Jesus Prays in a Solitary Place

35 Very early in the morning, while it was still dark, Jesus got up,
left the house and went off to a solitary place, where he prayed.[f] 36 Si- 1:35 [f]Lk 3:21
mon and his companions went to look for him, 37 and when they
found him, they exclaimed: "Everyone is looking for you!"

38 Jesus replied, "Let us go somewhere else—to the nearby vil-
lages—so I can preach there also. That is why I have come."[g] 39 So he 1:38 [g]Isa 61:1
traveled throughout Galilee, preaching in their synagogues[h] and 1:39 [h]Mt 4:23
driving out demons.[i] [i]Mt 4:24

Ancient Voices

Besides, nothing is sacred or safe from his lust: not the household matron, nor the virgin daughter, nor the smooth-cheeked boy engaged to one's daughter, and not even the innocent son! If none of these are available, he will take sexual advantage of his friend's grandmother!

—Juvenal the Satirist on the Lusts of Wealthy Hellenistic Men

From Juvenal, *Satire 3*, lines 109ff, trans. by Duane Garrett. Certain Latin vulgarities are not translated literally.

See "Cynics and Satirists in the Greco-Roman World" article.

A Man With Leprosy

40 A man with leprosy[a] came to him and begged him on his knees,[j] "If you are willing, you can make 1:40 [j]Mk 10:17
me clean."

41 Filled with compassion, Jesus reached out his hand and touched the man. "I am willing," he said. "Be
clean!" 42 Immediately the leprosy left him and he was cured.

43 Jesus sent him away at once with a strong warning: 44 "See that you don't tell this to anyone.[k] But go, 1:44 [k]Mt 8:4
show yourself to the priest[l] and offer the sacrifices that Moses commanded for your cleansing,[m] as a tes- [l]Lev 13:49
timony to them." 45 Instead he went out and began to talk freely, spreading the news. As a result, Jesus [m]Lev 14:1-32
could no longer enter a town openly but stayed outside in lonely places.[n] Yet the people still came to him 1:45 [n]Lk 5:15,16
from everywhere.[o] [o]Mk 2:13; Lk 5:17; Jn 6:2

Jesus Heals a Paralytic

2 A few days later, when Jesus again entered Capernaum, the people heard that he had come home. 2 So
many[p] gathered that there was no room left, not even outside the door, and he preached the word to 2:2 [p]ver 13; Mk 1:45
them. 3 Some men came, bringing to him a paralytic,[q] carried by four of them. 4 Since they could not get 2:3 [q]Mt 4:24
him to Jesus because of the crowd, they made an opening in the roof above Jesus and, after digging
through it, lowered the mat the paralyzed man was lying on. 5 When Jesus saw their faith, he said to the
paralytic, "Son, your sins are forgiven."[r] 2:5 [r]Lk 7:48

6 Now some teachers of the law were sitting there, thinking to themselves, 7 "Why does this fellow talk
like that? He's blasphemy! Who can forgive sins but God alone?"[s] 2:7 [s]Isa 43:25

[a] *40* The Greek word was used for various diseases affecting the skin—not necessarily leprosy.

1:29 Jesus and the disciples probably went to Simon and Andrew's house for a meal, since the main Sabbath meal was traditionally served immediately following the synagogue service. See "Houses in the Holy Land of the First Century A.D.: Peter's House in Capernaum; Insulae" on page 1584.

1:32 The people waited until the Sabbath was over ("after sunset") before carrying anything (see the note on Lk 4:40).

1:40 See the NIV text note, as well as "Skin Diseases in the Ancient World" on page 171.

1:41 According to the Mosaic Law, touching a leprous person resulted in defilement (see Lev 5:2; 13:45–46).

1:44 Only a priest could declare a leprous person healed—that is, "clean" (Lev 13:6,13,17,23). By receiving a ritual certification of cleansing, the man could be reinstated into society.

2:1 When in Capernaum, Jesus probably made his home at Peter's house (see the note on Mt 4:13).

2:4 A typical house in the Middle East had a flat roof accessible by means of an outside staircase. The roof was often made of a thick layer of clay (packed with a stone roller), supported by mats of branches across wooden beams.

2:6 For "teachers of the law," see the notes on Matthew 2:4 and Luke 5:17.

2:7 According to Jewish theology even the Messiah could not forgive sins. Jesus' forgiveness of sin was a claim to deity—which his detractors considered to be blasphemous (see the note on 14:64).

8Immediately Jesus knew in his spirit that this was what they were thinking in their hearts, and he said
to them, "Why are you thinking these things? 9Which is easier: to say to the paralytic, 'Your sins are for-
2:10 [t]Mt 8:20 given,' or to say, 'Get up, take your mat and walk'? 10But that you may know that the Son of Man[t] has au-
thority on earth to forgive sins . . ." He said to the paralytic, 11"I tell you, get up, take your mat and go
home." 12He got up, took his mat and walked out in full view of them all. This amazed everyone and they
2:12 [u]Mt 9:8 [v]Mt 9:33 praised God,[u] saying, "We have never seen anything like this!"[v]

The Calling of Levi

2:13 [w]Mk 1:45; Lk 5:15; Jn 6:2 13Once again Jesus went out beside the lake. A large crowd came to him,[w] and he began to teach them.
2:14 [x]Mt 4:19 14As he walked along, he saw Levi son of Alphaeus sitting at the tax collector's booth. "Follow me,"[x] Jesus
told him, and Levi got up and followed him.
15While Jesus was having dinner at Levi's house, many tax collectors and "sinners" were eating with
him and his disciples, for there were many who followed him. 16When the teachers of the law who were
2:16 [y]Ac 23:9 [z]Mt 9:11 Pharisees[y] saw him eating with the "sinners" and tax collectors, they asked his disciples: "Why does he
eat with tax collectors and 'sinners'?"[z]
17On hearing this, Jesus said to them, "It is not the healthy who need a doctor, but the sick. I have not
2:17 [a]Lk 19:10; 1Ti 1:15 come to call the righteous, but sinners."[a]

2:14 Levi, also called Matthew, was probably collecting tolls and customs for Rome at a toll booth on the major international road that went west from Damascus through Capernaum to the Mediterranean coast and then south to Egypt. In addition to being labeled traitors, tax collectors were notorious for their dishonesty. They could not serve as witnesses or as judges and were expelled from the synagogue. In the eyes of the Jewish community their disgrace extended even to their families. (See "Roman Taxation" on p. 1855.)
2:16 Not all "teachers of the law" (see the note on Mt 2:4) were Pharisees (see also the note on Mt 3:7).

Cynics and Satirists in the Greco-Roman World

MARK 2 The Cynics were members of a loosely organized school of philosophy founded in late fifth-century B.C. Greece. They rejected a conventional value system that emphasized such social constructs as wealth and status, seeking instead to live a virtuous life as defined by living according to nature. Cynics believed that society placed value on worthless things. They espoused primitivism as a way of life; some have compared them to the "hippies" of America in the 1960s. Their value system was based upon the equation that living a life void of any artificial value will inevitably lead to happiness. Anecdotes about Cynics abound. Alexander the Great reportedly visited Diogenes the Cynic and asked him to request anything at all. Diogenes, who was sunbathing at the time of the visit, responded simply by asking Alexander to move in order to stop blocking the sun. On the other hand, Socrates was reported to have told the Cynic philosopher Anthisthenes (who made a point of always wearing ragged clothing), "I can see your pride through the holes in your cloak."

Satire flourished in Roman culture. Satirists, like their predecessors the Cynics, were fundamentally social critics. One significant difference is that satire was more an art form than a philosophy (although Cynics did also engage in literary satire). Satirists wrote plays, novels and poems that ridiculed the vice and moral decay found in contemporary Roman society. Horace (died 8 B.C.) and Juvenal (d. early second century A.D.) can probably be regarded as the greatest Roman satirists. Both the Cynics and the Satirists sought to ridicule what they saw as the foolish trappings of society. For example, in *Satire 3* Juvenal attacked the debauchery of the **Hellenistic** upper classes, and in *Satire 6* he listed in great detail the supposed vices of Roman wives. However, the extant writings of both Cynics and Satirists are often characterized by perverse kinds of self-indulgence, as well as by ferocious anger, crassness and obscenity (especially on the part of the Satirists).

Recently it has become fashionable in some scholarly circles to argue that Jesus himself was a Jewish follower of a cynical philosophy. In reality, other than the simplicity of his life, Jesus had nothing in common with the Greek Cynics. Roman authorities clashed with Cynics because the latter tended to be anarchic. Jesus, who taught, for instance, that people should pay their taxes (Mk 12:17),[1] could hardly be classified as anarchic.[2]

[1]See "Roman Taxation" on page 1855. [2]See also "Greek Philosophical Schools" on page 1937.

Ancient Voices

He then returned to Jericho and came to be in such a foul state that, while only barely able to hold back death itself, he proceeded to attempt an atrocious deed. He gathered the most renowned men from every village of the whole Jewish nation to a place called the Hippodrome and shut them in. He then summoned his sister Salome and her husband Alexas and said to them, "I know that the Jews will be feasting over my death. But I can have mourning for other reasons and have a splendid funeral if you will just obey my commands. Station soldiers around these men who are now under guard, and kill them as soon as I expire. Then all Judea and every household, however unwillingly, will weep over me."

—Herod the Great Makes His Funeral Arrangements

From Flavius Josephus, *The Jewish Wars*, 1.33, trans. by Duane Garrett

See "Herod the Great" article.

Jesus Questioned About Fasting

18 Now John's disciples and the Pharisees were fasting.[b] Some 2:18 [b]Mt 6:16-18; Ac 13:2
people came and asked Jesus, "How is it that John's disciples and the
disciples of the Pharisees are fasting, but yours are not?"
19 Jesus answered, "How can the guests of the bridegroom fast
while he is with them? They cannot, so long as they have him with
them. 20 But the time will come when the bridegroom will be taken
from them,[c] and on that day they will fast. 2:20 [c]Lk 17:22
21 "No one sews a patch of unshrunk cloth on an old garment. If
he does, the new piece will pull away from the old, making the tear
worse. 22 And no one pours new wine into old wineskins. If he does,
the wine will burst the skins, and both the wine and the wineskins
will be ruined. No, he pours new wine into new wineskins."

Lord of the Sabbath

23 One Sabbath Jesus was going through the grainfields, and as
his disciples walked along, they began to pick some heads of grain.[d] 2:23 [d]Dt 23:25
24 The Pharisees said to him, "Look, why are they doing what is un-
lawful on the Sabbath?"[e] 2:24 [e]Mt 12:2
25 He answered, "Have you never read what David did when he
and his companions were hungry and in need? 26 In the days of Abi-
athar the high priest,[f] he entered the house of God and ate the con- 2:26 [f]1Ch 24:6; 2Sa 8:17
secrated bread, which is lawful only for priests to eat.[g] And he also [g]Lev 24:5-9
gave some to his companions."[h] [h]1Sa 21:1-6
27 Then he said to them, "The Sabbath was made for man,[i] not man 2:27 [i]Ex 23:12; Dt 5:14 [j]Col 2:16
for the Sabbath.[j] 28 So the Son of Man[k] is Lord even of the Sabbath." 2:28 [k]Mt 8:20

3 Another time he went into the synagogue,[l] and a man with a shriveled hand was there. 2 Some of 3:1 [l]Mt 4:23; Mk 1:21
them were looking for a reason to accuse Jesus, so they watched him closely[m] to see if he would heal 3:2 [m]Mt 12:10
him on the Sabbath.[n] 3 Jesus said to the man with the shriveled hand, "Stand up in front of everyone." [n]Lk 14:1
4 Then Jesus asked them, "Which is lawful on the Sabbath: to do good or to do evil, to save life or to
kill?" But they remained silent.
5 He looked around at them in anger and, deeply distressed at their stubborn hearts, said to the man,
"Stretch out your hand." He stretched it out, and his hand was completely restored. 6 Then the Pharisees
went out and began to plot with the Herodians[o] how they might kill Jesus.[p] 3:6 [o]Mt 22:16; Mk 12:13 [p]Mt 12:14

Crowds Follow Jesus

7 Jesus withdrew with his disciples to the lake, and a large crowd from Galilee followed.[q] 8 When they 3:7 [q]Mt 4:25
heard all he was doing, many people came to him from Judea, Jerusalem, Idumea, and the regions across
the Jordan and around Tyre and Sidon.[r] 9 Because of the crowd he told his disciples to have a small boat 3:8 [r]Mt 11:21

2:18 Some Pharisees were also "scribes" (i.e., teachers of the law; see the note on Mt 2:4), who often had disciples. Or perhaps the phrase "disciples of the Pharisees" is used in a nontechnical way to refer to people influenced by the Pharisees.

In the Mosaic Law only the fast of the Day of Atonement was required (see Lev 16:29,31; 23:27–32; Nu 29:7). After the Babylonian exile four other yearly fasts were observed by the Jews (see the notes on Zec 7:5; 8:19). In Jesus' time the Pharisees fasted twice a week—on Mondays and Thursdays.

2:19 A Jewish wedding was a particularly joyous occasion, and the celebration associated with it often lasted a week (see "Weddings in Ancient Israel" on p. 1039). It was unthinkable to fast during such festivities, because fasting was associated with sorrow (see "Fasting in the Bible and the Ancient Near East" on p. 1569).

2:22 See the note on Matthew 9:17.

2:24 According to Jewish tradition (in the Mishnah; see the note on Mt 15:2), harvesting—which is what Jesus' disciples technically were doing—was forbidden on the Sabbath (see Ex 34:21).

2:26 For "consecrated bread," see the note on Matthew 12:4.

2:27 Jewish tradition had so multiplied the requirements and restrictions for keeping the Sabbath that the burden had become all but intolerable (see the note on Mt 15:2; see also "Biblical Interpretation at Qumran and Among the Early Rabbis" on p. 1603).

3:2 Jewish tradition prescribed that aid could be given to the sick on the Sabbath only when the person's life was threatened—obviously not the case here.

3:6 Herodians were evidently influential Jews who favored the Herodian dynasty, meaning that they were supporters of Rome, from which the Herods received their authority. They joined the Pharisees in opposing Jesus because they feared he might have an unsettling political influence on the people. (See 12:13; see also the note on Matthew 22:16.)

3:8 This geographical list indicates that members of the crowd hailed not only from the areas in the vicinity of Capernaum (see "Capernaum" on p. 1643) but also from a considerable distance away. The regions mentioned included virtually all of Israel and its surrounding neighbors.

Idumea is the Greek form of the Hebrew *Edom*, but here it refers to an area south of Judea, not to earlier Edomite territory.

ANCIENT PEOPLES, LANDS AND RULERS

Herod the Great

MARK 3 Herod the Great began his career as military governor of Galilee in 47 B.C.[1] The Roman Senate then appointed him king of Judea in 40 B.C. After violently suppressing a significant opposition from the aristocracy in Jerusalem, he formally began his reign in 37 B.C. and ruled until his death in 4 B.C. Herod's father, Antipater, was an Idumean convert to Judaism,[2] and his mother, Cypros, was a Nabatean. Herod curried favor with the Jews but was staunchly allied to Rome and embraced Greco-Roman culture and religion. He is known for his extensive building programs; evidence of some of this activity can still be seen today. In this arena, Herod's accomplishments were impressive and included the following:

Herodium

Photograph courtesy of © Dr. Gary Pratico

- Temples to Roma, Augustus and Baal Shamim; the Pythian temple at Rhodes; and, of course, the Jerusalem temple.[3]
- Palaces at Masada, Jericho, Ascalon and elsewhere.[4]
- Gymnasia, baths, fountains, colonnades, markets and other public buildings throughout the eastern Roman Empire.
- Entire cities, such as Caesarea Maritima and Sebaste.[5]

Herod's rise to power came about during a tumultuous period in Roman history—the civil wars of the First and Second Triumvirates. Herod often backed the losing side; for example, he was on the side of Antony and Cleopatra when they were at war with and finally defeated by Octavian (later known as Caesar Augustus).[6] Nevertheless, Herod had remarkable political instincts and was able to save his life and power by quickly submitting and swearing allegiance to Octavian. Indeed, every move he made was designed in some way to ensure that he eliminated his enemies and held on to the support of the people who mattered. For example, Herod divorced his first wife, Doris, and became engaged to Mariamne, granddaughter of the high priest Hyrcanus II (Herod ultimately executed both of them).

His tenuous hold on power—a single misstep and he could have lost everything—may have contributed to the paranoia that led him to execute so many, including his own children. Jesus was born during the reign of Herod (Mt 2:1), who, near the end of his life, gained eternal infamy by having the baby boys of Bethlehem put to death (Mt 2:16). Caesar Augustus is reported to have once made the pun that he would rather be Herod's pig (in Greek, *hus*) than his son (*huios*), a reference to the fact that as a nominal Jew Herod at least had scruples about killing pigs—if none about executing his own family members.

The holy family fled to Egypt to escape Herod's wrath (Mt 2:13–14). While they were there Herod died of disease in his palace at Jericho, which has been excavated. His body was carried in an elaborate procession to Herodium (see "Map 9"), near Bethlehem, where he was interred with splendor. In spite of extensive excavations at Herodium, Herod's tomb has never been located.

Herod's kingdom was divided among three of his four surviving sons: Archelaus, ruler of Judea and **Samaria**[7] (Mt 2:22); Herod Antipas, **tetrarch** of Galilee and Perea (Mt 14:1–10); and Philip II, tetrarch of Iturea and Trachonitis (Lk 3:1). Other members of Herod's extensive family (he had ten wives) are mentioned in the New Testament: a fourth son, Philip I (Mt 14:3–11; Mk 6:17–28; Lk 3:19); a granddaughter Herodias, who married two of his sons (her uncles), Philip I and Herod Antipas (Mt 14:3–11; Mk 6:17–28; Lk 3:19); a grandson Herod Agrippa I (Ac 12:1–23; 23:35); a great-grandson Agrippa II (Ac 25:13—26:32); great-granddaughters Bernice (Ac 25:13–27; 26:30), Drusilla (Ac 24:24) and Salome (Mt 14:6–11; Mk 6:22–28).[7]

[1]See "Galilee in Jesus' Time" on page 1587. [2]See "Proselytes in Second Temple Judaism" on page 1776. [3]See "Herod's Temple" on page 1648 and "The Dividing Wall of the 'Court of the Gentiles' in Herod's Temple" on page 1917. [4]See "Masada" on page 1775 and "New Testament Jericho" on page 1646. [5]See "Caesarea Maritima" on page 1786. [6]See "Caesar Augustus, Emperor of Rome; the Census; and Quirinius, Governor of Syria" on page 1667. [7]See also "Politics in the Holy Land Leading Up to the Time of Jesus" on page 1630.

FIRST-CENTURY EMPERORS, ROMAN PROCURATORS OVER JUDEA, AND RULERS IN PALESTINE

Emperors	Procurators	Kings, Tetrarchs, Ethnarch
AUGUSTUS, 27 B.C.–A.D. 14 (Lk 2:1)	Coponius, A.D. 6–10	HEROD the Great, King over all Palestine, 37–4 B.C. (Mt 2:1–19; Lk 1:5)
	M. Ambivius, 10–13	ARCHELAUS, Ethnarch of Judea, Samaria and Idumea, 4 B.C.–A.D. 6 (Mt 2:22)
	Annius Rufus, 13–15	
TIBERIUS, A.D. 14–37 (Lk 3:1)	Valerius Gratus, 15–26	HEROD PHILIP, Tetrarch of Iturea, Trachonitus, Gaulanitis, Auranitis and Batanea, 4 B.C.–A.D. 34 (Lk 3:1)
	PONTIUS PILATE, 26–36 (Lk 3:1; 23:1)	
Caligula, 37–41	Marcellus, 36–38	HEROD ANTIPAS, Tetrarch of Galilee and Perea, 4 B.C.–A.D. 39 (Mk 6:14–29; Lk 3:1; 13:31–35; 23:7–12)
	Marullus, 38–41	
CLAUDIUS, 41–54 (Ac 11:28; 18:2; 23:26)	Cuspius Fadus, 44–46	HEROD AGRIPPA I, 37–44; by A.D. 41 King over all Palestine (Ac 12:1–24)
	Tiberius Alexander, 46–48	
Nero, 54–68 (Emperor at deaths of Paul and Peter)	Ventidius Cumanus, 48–52	
	M. Antonius FELIX, 52–59 (Ac 23:26—24:27)	HEROD AGRIPPA II, 48–70, Tetrarch of Chalcis and northern territory (Ac 25:13—26:32)
	Porcius FESTUS, 59–61 (Ac 25)	
Galba, 68	Albinus, 61–65	
Otho, 69	Gessius Florus, 65–70	
Vitellius, 69		
Vespasian, 69–79	Vettulenus Cerialis, 70–72	
Titus, 79–81	Lucilius Bassus, 72–75	
Domitian, 81–96	M. Salvienus, 75–86	
	Flavius Silva, 86	
	Pompeius Longinus, 86	
Nerva, 96–98		
Trajan, 98–117		

Names in caps are mentioned by name in the New Testament

Chronological and Background Charts of the New Testament, p. 63

ready for him, to keep the people from crowding him. [10]For he had healed many,[s] so that those with dis- 3:10 [s]Mt 4:23 [t]Mt 9:20
eases were pushing forward to touch him.[t] [11]Whenever the evil[a] spirits saw him, they fell down before
him and cried out, "You are the Son of God."[u] [12]But he gave them strict orders not to tell who he was.[v] 3:11 [u]Mt 4:3; Mk 1:23,24 3:12 [v]Mt 8:4; Mk 1:24,25,34; Ac 16:17,18

The Appointing of the Twelve Apostles

[13]Jesus went up on a mountainside and called to him those he wanted, and they came to him.[w] [14]He 3:13 [w]Mt 5:1
appointed twelve—designating them apostles[b][x]—that they might be with him and that he might send 3:14 [x]Mk 6:30

[a] 11 Greek *unclean*; also in verse 30 [b] 14 Some manuscripts do not have *designating them apostles.*

3:13 The "mountainside" probably refers to the hill country of Galilee around the lake.

3:15 [y]Mt 10:1 them out to preach 15 and to have authority to drive out demons.[y] 16 These are the twelve he appointed:
3:16 [z]Jn 1:42 Simon (to whom he gave the name Peter);[z] 17 James son of Zebedee and his brother John (to them he
gave the name Boanerges, which means Sons of Thunder); 18 Andrew, Philip, Bartholomew, Matthew,
Thomas, James son of Alphaeus, Thaddaeus, Simon the Zealot 19 and Judas Iscariot, who betrayed him.

Jesus and Beelzebub

3:20 [a]ver 7 [b]Mk 6:31 20 Then Jesus entered a house, and again a crowd gathered,[a] so that he and his disciples were not even
able to eat.[b] 21 When his family heard about this, they went to take charge of him, for they said, "He is out
3:21 [c]Jn 10:20; Ac 26:24 of his mind."[c]
3:22 [d]Mt 15:1 [e]Mt 10:25; 11:18; 12:24; Jn 7:20; 8:48,52; 10:20 [f]Mt 9:34 22 And the teachers of the law who came down from Jerusalem[d] said, "He is possessed by Beelzebub[a]![e]
By the prince of demons he is driving out demons."[f]
23 So Jesus called them and spoke to them in parables:[g] "How can Satan[h] drive out Satan? 24 If a king-
3:23 [g]Mk 4:2 [h]Mt 4:10 dom is divided against itself, that kingdom cannot stand. 25 If a house is divided against itself, that house
cannot stand. 26 And if Satan opposes himself and is divided, he cannot stand; his end has come. 27 In
fact, no one can enter a strong man's house and carry off his possessions unless he first ties up the strong
3:27 [i]Isa 49:24, 25 man. Then he can rob his house.[i] 28 I tell you the truth, all the sins and blasphemies of men will be for-
given them. 29 But whoever blasphemes against the Holy Spirit will never be forgiven; he is guilty of an
3:29 [j]Mt 12:31, 32; Lk 12:10 eternal sin."[j]
30 He said this because they were saying, "He has an evil spirit."

Jesus' Mother and Brothers

3:31 [k]ver 21 31 Then Jesus' mother and brothers arrived.[k] Standing outside, they sent someone in to call him. 32 A
crowd was sitting around him, and they told him, "Your mother and brothers are outside looking for
you."
33 "Who are my mother and my brothers?" he asked.
34 Then he looked at those seated in a circle around him and said, "Here are my mother and my broth-
ers! 35 Whoever does God's will is my brother and sister and mother."

The Parable of the Sower

4:1 [l]Mk 2:13; 3:7 4 Again Jesus began to teach by the lake.[l] The crowd that gathered around him was so large that he got
into a boat and sat in it out on the lake, while all the people were along the shore at the water's edge.
4:2 [m]ver 11; Mk 3:23 2 He taught them many things by parables,[m] and in his teaching said: 3 "Listen! A farmer went out to sow
4:3 [n]ver 26 his seed.[n] 4 As he was scattering the seed, some fell along the path, and the birds came and ate it up. 5 Some
fell on rocky places, where it did not have much soil. It sprang up quickly, because the soil was shallow.
6 But when the sun came up, the plants were scorched, and they withered because they had no root. 7 Oth-
er seed fell among thorns, which grew up and choked the plants, so that they did not bear grain. 8 Still oth-
er seed fell on good soil. It came up, grew and produced a crop, multiplying thirty, sixty, or even a hun-
4:8 [o]Jn 15:5; Col 1:6 dred times."[o]
4:9 [p]ver 23; Mt 11:15 9 Then Jesus said, "He who has ears to hear, let him hear."[p]
10 When he was alone, the Twelve and the others around him asked him about the parables. 11 He told
4:11 [q]Mt 3:2 [r]1Co 5:12,13; Col 4:5; 1Th 4:12; 1Ti 3:7 them, "The secret of the kingdom of God[q] has been given to you. But to those on the outside[r] everything
is said in parables 12 so that,

> " 'they may be ever seeing but never perceiving,
> and ever hearing but never understanding;
> 4:12 [s]Isa 6:9,10; Mt 13:13-15 otherwise they might turn and be forgiven!'[b]"[s]

[a] 22 Greek *Beezeboul* or *Beelzeboul* [b] 12 Isaiah 6:9,10

3:18 For "Bartholomew," see the note on Luke 6:14 and for "Thaddaeus" the note on Matthew 10:3. For "Zealot," see the note on Matthew 10:4.
3:19 "Iscariot" probably means "the man from Kerioth," perhaps the town of Kerioth Hezron, 12 miles (19 km) south of Hebron.
3:21 Jesus' family may have come to Capernaum from Nazareth, about 30 miles (48 km) away.
3:22 For "Beelzebub," see the note on Matthew 10:25.
3:32 See "The Family of Joseph, Mary and Jesus" on page 1581.
3:35 In the first-century world, family was the basis of a person's social and economic life, the source of his or her identity.
4:1 Sitting was the usual position for Jewish teachers.
4:3–8 In that day seed was scattered by hand—which, by its nature, left some on unproductive ground. In Eastern practice the seed was sometimes sown first and the field plowed afterward. Roads and pathways intersected many fields, and the traffic made much of the surface too hard for seed to take root.

13 Then Jesus said to them, "Don't you understand this parable? How then will you understand any
parable? 14 The farmer sows the word.[t] 15 Some people are like seed along the path, where the word is — **4:14** [t]Mk 16:20; Lk 1:2; Ac 4:31;
sown. As soon as they hear it, Satan[u] comes and takes away the word that was sown in them. 16 Others, — 8:4; 16:6; 17:11; Php 1:14
like seed sown on rocky places, hear the word and at once receive it with joy. 17 But since they have no — **4:15** [u]Mt 4:10
root, they last only a short time. When trouble or persecution comes because of the word, they quickly
fall away. 18 Still others, like seed sown among thorns, hear the word; 19 but the worries of this life, the de-
ceitfulness of wealth[v] and the desires for other things come in and choke the word, making it unfruitful. — **4:19** [v]Mt 19:23;
20 Others, like seed sown on good soil, hear the word, accept it, and produce a crop — thirty, sixty or even — 1Ti 6:9,10,17; 1Jn 2:15-17
a hundred times what was sown."

Politics in the Holy Land Leading Up to the Time of Jesus

MARK 4 The Holy Land just prior to and during the time of Jesus was formally under the supervision of the Roman governor of Syria. The Roman period began in 63 B.C. and culminated with the destruction of the temple in A.D. 70 and the establishment of Jerusalem as a pagan city in A.D. 135. As a critical epoch in the history of Israel, ancient contemporaries and modern interpreters view these years as a period of tremendous change, expectation and consequence.

Arrival of Rome and the End of the Hasmoneans

Roman control debuted in Israel in the wake of a conflict for succession between two sons of the Hasmonean queen Salome Alexandra: Hyrcanus II, who had served as high priest, and Aristobulus II, who had been the chief military commander. Although Hyrcanus initially yielded to his brother, he was pressed by the Idumean leader Antipater to fight for the throne. Both sides sent delegations before the Roman general Pompey in Damascus, who eventually sided with Hyrcanus. In the meantime, the supporters of Aristobulus had barricaded themselves in the temple of Jerusalem. Pompey's forces besieged the temple mount for three months, eventually taking the area. Josephus recorded that Pompey desecrated the temple by entering into the Most Holy Place (*Wars*, 1.7.1–6). Hyrcanus was confirmed in power, although denied the title of king and stripped of all coastal and **Transjordanian** Greek cities. After another rebellion in 57 B.C. by Aristobulus's son Alexander, Hyrcanus retained only the high priesthood and the temple, while the province of Judea was divided into five administrative districts.

During the course of a Roman civil war between Pompey and Julius Caesar, the Idumean Antipater encouraged Hyrcanus to support Caesar and to send auxiliary troops to his aid in Egypt (47 B.C.). As a gesture of thanks, Julius Caesar conferred upon Hyrcanus the title Ethnarch of the Jews (an Ethnarch was a man appointed by Rome to be ruler of a people) and named Antipater as the first procurator of Judea.[1] Antipater named his two sons, Phasael and Herod, as prefects over Judea and Galilee, respectively. Herod quickly distinguished himself and was named prefect of Syria by the Roman governor.[2]

Herod the Great

Caesar's assassination in 44 B.C. was a blow to Jewish communities throughout the empire and produced a period of instability in Rome. During this interval the eastern empire was attacked by Parthians from Mesopotamia. They named Antigonus, the son of Aristobulus, as high priest and king in Jerusalem. Phasael was captured and slain, while Herod fled to Rome. After the defeat of the Parthians, Mark Antony and Octavian (Julius Caesar's heir)[3] conferred the title King of the Jews upon Herod in 37 B.C.

Herod ruled from Jerusalem with the support of Rome from 37 to 34 B.C. He functioned as a client-king (a king who rules under the authority of an outside power) and was considered a "friend and ally of the Roman people" (a title conferred by the senate upon non-Romans whose support they valued). He was dependent upon Rome for his kingship and was compelled to swear an oath of allegiance to Caesar (Josephus, *Antiquities*, 17.2.4). In return he promised stability, order and tax revenue. Herod earned an international reputation as a great benefactor and builder of cities and temples, but his legacy within Judaism is almost entirely negative. Josephus recorded the contemporary evaluation that Jews suffered more during the reign of Herod than during the entire period prior to Herod since the Babylonian exile (Josephus, *Wars*, 2.6.2).

[1]See "The Roman Governor" on page 1824. [2]See "Herod the Great" on page 1627. [3]See "Caesar Augustus, Emperor of Rome; the Census; and Quirinius, Governor of Syria" on page 1667.

A Lamp on a Stand

4:21 wMt 5:15 4:22 xJer 16:17; Mt 10:26; Lk 8:17; 12:2 4:23 yver 9; Mt 11:15 4:24 zMt 7:2; Lk 6:38 4:25 aMt 13:12; 25:29

[21]He said to them, "Do you bring in a lamp to put it under a bowl or a bed? Instead, don't you put it
on its stand?[w] [22]For whatever is hidden is meant to be disclosed, and whatever is concealed is meant to
be brought out into the open.[x] [23]If anyone has ears to hear, let him hear."[y]
[24]"Consider carefully what you hear," **he continued.** "With the measure you use, it will be measured to
you—and even more.[z] [25]Whoever has will be given more; whoever does not have, even what he has will
be taken from him."[a]

4:21 For "lamps," see the note on Matthew 5:15.

Herod's Successors and Uneasy Relations Between Rome and the Jews

MARK 4

Herod's Successors

When Herod died in 4 B.C., the predominantly Gentile area northeast of the Sea of Galilee, known as Iturea and Trachonitis, was given as a tetrarchy to Philip, the half brother of Antipas (Mt 14:3; Lk 3:1). Philip ruled his territory well from his newly constructed capital, Caesarea Philippi.[1] When he died in A.D. 34 his tetrarchy was incorporated into the Roman province of Syria. Galilee and Perea were assigned to Philip's half brother Antipas (also known as Herod the **tetrarch**; cf. Mt 14:1; Lk 3:1). Herod Antipas ruled from Sepphoris, near Nazareth, and later from Tiberias until his banishment by the Roman emperor Caligula in A.D. 39.[2] He is often remembered for his illegal marriage to his brother's wife, Herodias, and for his imprisonment and execution of John the Baptist (Mt 14:3; Josephus, *Antiquities*, 18.5.1–2).

Judea and **Samaria** were placed under the control of Herod's son Archelaus (the full brother of Antipas and half brother of Philip), who was given the title of ethnarch (cf. Mt 2:22). Archelaus began his reign by slaughtering 3,000 people during the Jewish Passover, and he was eventually banished for incompetence by Augustus to Gaul in 6 A.D. (Josephus, *Antiquities*, 17.13.2). At this point Judea became a Roman province, ruled directly by a series of Roman prefects (A.D. 6–41) and then procurators (A.D. 44–66), who maintained their residence in Caesarea and at the Fortress of Antonia near the temple in Jerusalem. The most important prefecture for early Christianity was that of Pontius Pilate (A.D. 26–36).[3]

The Uneasy Relations Between Rome and the Jews

The first act of direct Roman rule was the taking of a census by Quirinius, legate of Syria, in order to determine the amount of tribute owed by Judea (cf. Lk 2:1–3; Ac 5:37).[4] The census itself and the paying of tribute provoked great animosity within Judean society. Under the prefects, internal Jewish affairs were governed by the high priestly aristocracy and judicial cases were determined by the Sanhedrin, or court of seventy-one.[5] The prefects reserved the power of the sword, or the right of capital punishment. However, Jewish leadership seems to have retained this power in cases that dealt exclusively with religious crimes, especially those having to do with the sanctity of the temple. It is for this reason that Jesus, Paul and Stephen were tried on the accusation of "speaking against" or "defiling" the temple (Mt 26:61; Ac 6:13–14; 21:28). The prefects further maintained their authority over the high priests through the power of appointment and by means of Roman custody of the high priestly garments (Josephus, *Antiquities*, 20.1.1).

After a brief return to Herodian rule under Agrippa from A.D. 41–44 (cf. Ac 12:20–23), Judea, Samaria and Galilee were ruled by a series of procurators until the outbreak of war in A.D. 66. Agrippa's son reigned over a small kingdom in the north from A.D. 48–66 (Ac 25:13), and several later procurators are known from the New Testament, including Marcus Antonius Felix (A.D. 52–59; Ac 23:24) and Porcius Festus (A.D. 59–62; Ac 24:27), under both of whom Paul was imprisoned.

The reality of Roman control during the time of Jesus produced various reactions within Israelite society. Archaeology has revealed the large extent to which the upper classes adopted Greco-Roman customs and welcomed this new relationship. Evidence for such **Hellenization** can be observed in both public and private architecture, civic institutions and the widespread use of the Greek language. At the same time, Roman control generated widespread animosity and concern for the vitality of traditional Jewish values and expectations.

[1]See "Caesarea Philippi" on page 1589. [2]See "Sepphoris" on page 1638 and "Tiberias" on page 1732. [3]See "Pontius Pilate" on page 1714. [4]See "Caesar Augustus, Emperor of Rome; the Census; and Quirinius, Governor of Syria" on page 1667. [5]See "The Sanhedrin" on page 1821.

The Parable of the Growing Seed

[26]He also said, "This is what the kingdom of God is like.[b] A man scatters seed on the ground. [27]Night 4:26 [b]Mt 13:24
and day, whether he sleeps or gets up, the seed sprouts and grows, though he does not know how. [28]All
by itself the soil produces grain—first the stalk, then the head, then the full kernel in the head. [29]As soon
as the grain is ripe, he puts the sickle to it, because the harvest has come."[c] 4:29 [c]Rev 14:15

4:29 The sickle was a tool used for cutting grain. Earlier sickles varied in size, shape and the material from which they were made. The earliest type seems to have been constructed of wood. It resembled our modern scythes, except that it was smaller, and its cutting edge was made of flint. Later sickles were constructed of metal. These were used primarily for cutting grain, but upon occasion they were also employed for pruning. Mark here used the sickle in a figurative sense as the instrument of God's judgment (see also Rev 14:14–20).

Messianic Conflicts and the Fall of Jerusalem

MARK 4

Messianic Movements and Other Conflicts

One of the most explicit Messianic images of the Old Testament, the vision of four successive empires in Daniel 2 and 7, was understood to signal the advent of the Messianic kingdom after the downfall of Rome.[1] For this reason a number of Messianic movements arose within this period. According to Josephus, the actions of Messianic teachers and the failure of Judean and Roman leaders to deal effectively with them propelled the nation toward open revolt. A review of select Messianic incidents reveals the tension, potential violence and general atmosphere in which Jesus proclaimed the "good news of the kingdom" (Mt 4:23):

✣ Near the time of Herod's death in 4 B.C., two leading Jewish teachers incited their students to remove the large, golden eagle (the symbol of Rome) that Herod had erected over the great gate of the temple. Herod arrested the teachers and their students and proceeded to burn them alive, also deposing the reigning high priest for his assumed complicity (Josephus, *Antiquities*, 17.6.2).

✣ The census of Quirinius in A.D. 6 prompted an open revolt, led by Judas of Galilee, which was violently suppressed (*Antiquities*, 18.1.1; Ac 5:37).

✣ When Pilate became prefect in A.D. 26 he commanded his troops to bring standards bearing the image of Caesar into Jerusalem. A large crowd followed him to Caesarea and sat outside his palace for five days and nights in protest. When he surrounded them with troops, they fell prostrate, exposed their necks and confessed themselves willing to die rather than to have the (Mosaic) Law transgressed (*Antiquities*, 18.3.1).

✣ Pilate later used funds from the temple treasury to build an aqueduct and crushed all public opposition to this action (*Antiquities*, 18.3.2).

✣ He also slaughtered a group of Galileans while they were offering sacrifices in Jerusalem (Lk 13:1).

✣ John the Baptist appeared in Judea around A.D. 29, preaching repentance, the imminent advent of God and public criticism of Herod Antipas. He was arrested and subsequently executed (Mk 6:16–29).

✣ A few years later Pilate crucified Jesus of Nazareth on the charge that he claimed to be "THE KING OF THE JEWS" (Mt 27:37; *Antiquities*, 18.3.3).

✣ In A.D. 36 Pilate brutally suppressed a Messianic movement in Samaria, which precipitated his removal from office (*Antiquities*, 18.4.1–2).

✣ In A.D. 41 the emperor Caligula sought to have a statue of himself erected in the temple of Jerusalem. Tens of thousands of Jews protested, demanding that they be slain first (*Antiquities*, 18.8.2–3).

✣ Around A.D. 45 a would-be prophet, Theudas, led a large crowd to the Jordan, promising to part the river at his own command as the sign of a new exodus. Roman troops slaughtered most of his followers and carried the head of Theudas to Jerusalem (*Antiquities*, 20.5.1; Ac 5:36).

Many other such incidents are described in ancient sources, providing an important window into the complex and challenging world of the Holy Land during the time of Jesus.

The End of Jerusalem

All of these tensions ultimately led to the Jewish revolt and the destruction of Jerusalem.[2] Josephus blamed the incompetence and insensitivity of the later procurators for the disastrous revolt. Despite initial Jewish success, the rebellion was crushed and the temple destroyed by the Roman general Titus in A.D. 70. After the war Judea was governed by a legate of senatorial rank who was under the direct supervision of the emperor. A second Jewish revolt in A.D. 132–135, led by the Messianic pretender Bar Kokhba ("son of the star"; cf. Nu 24:17), resulted in a great slaughter of Jews and the forcible removal of surviving Jews from the land. The Romans renamed the province Palestine and converted the temple into a pagan shrine. Jerusalem itself became a Roman city, named Aelia Capitolina.

[1]See "The Kingdoms of Daniel's Prophecies" on page 1388. [2]See "Josephus and the Fall of Jerusalem" on page 1606.

The Parable of the Mustard Seed

4:30 [d]Mt 13:24 30 Again he said, "What shall we say the kingdom of God is like,[d] or what parable shall we use to de-
scribe it? 31 It is like a mustard seed, which is the smallest seed you plant in the ground. 32 Yet when plant-
ed, it grows and becomes the largest of all garden plants, with such big branches that the birds of the air
can perch in its shade."
4:33 [e]Jn 16:12 33 With many similar parables Jesus spoke the word to them, as much as they could understand.[e] 34 He
4:34 [f]Jn 16:25 did not say anything to them without using a parable.[f] But when he was alone with his own disciples, he
explained everything.

Jesus Calms the Storm

35 That day when evening came, he said to his disciples, "Let us go over to the other side." 36 Leaving
4:36 [g]ver 1; Mk 3:9; 5:2,21; 6:32,45 the crowd behind, they took him along, just as he was, in the boat.[g] There were also other boats with
him. 37 A furious squall came up, and the waves broke over the boat, so that it was nearly swamped. 38 Je-
sus was in the stern, sleeping on a cushion. The disciples woke him and said to him, "Teacher, don't you
care if we drown?"
39 He got up, rebuked the wind and said to the waves, "Quiet! Be still!" Then the wind died down and
it was completely calm.
4:40 [h]Mt 14:31; Mk 16:14 40 He said to his disciples, "Why are you so afraid? Do you still have no faith?"[h]
41 They were terrified and asked each other, "Who is this? Even the wind and the waves obey him!"

The Healing of a Demon-possessed Man

5:2 [i]Mk 4:1 5 They went across the lake to the region of the Gerasenes.[a] 2 When Jesus got out of the boat,[i] a man
[j]Mk 1:23 with an evil[b] spirit[j] came from the tombs to meet him. 3 This man lived in the tombs, and no one
could bind him any more, not even with a chain. 4 For he had often been chained hand and foot, but he
tore the chains apart and broke the irons on his feet. No one was strong enough to subdue him. 5 Night
and day among the tombs and in the hills he would cry out and cut himself with stones.
6 When he saw Jesus from a distance, he ran and fell on his knees in front of him. 7 He shouted at the
5:7 [k]Mt 8:29 [l]Mt 4:3; Lk 1:32; 6:35; Ac 16:17; Heb 7:1 top of his voice, "What do you want with me,[k] Jesus, Son of the Most High God?[l] Swear to God that you
won't torture me!" 8 For Jesus had said to him, "Come out of this man, you evil spirit!"
9 Then Jesus asked him, "What is your name?"
5:9 [m]ver 15 "My name is Legion,"[m] he replied, "for we are many." 10 And he begged Jesus again and again not to
send them out of the area.
11 A large herd of pigs was feeding on the nearby hillside. 12 The demons begged Jesus, "Send us among
the pigs; allow us to go into them." 13 He gave them permission, and the evil spirits came out and went
into the pigs. The herd, about two thousand in number, rushed down the steep bank into the lake and
were drowned.
14 Those tending the pigs ran off and reported this in the town and countryside, and the people went
out to see what had happened. 15 When they came to Jesus, they saw the man who had been possessed
5:15 [n]ver 9 [o]ver 16,18; Mt 4:24 by the legion[n] of demons,[o] sitting there, dressed and in his right mind; and they were afraid. 16 Those
who had seen it told the people what had happened to the demon-possessed man—and told about the
pigs as well. 17 Then the people began to plead with Jesus to leave their region.
18 As Jesus was getting into the boat, the man who had been demon-possessed begged to go with him.
5:19 [p]Mt 8:4 19 Jesus did not let him, but said, "Go home to your family and tell them[p] how much the Lord has done
5:20 [q]Mt 4:25; Mk 7:31 for you, and how he has had mercy on you." 20 So the man went away and began to tell in the Decapolis[c][q]
how much Jesus had done for him. And all the people were amazed.

[a] *1* Some manuscripts *Gadarenes*; other manuscripts *Gergesenes* [b] *2* Greek *unclean*; also in verses 8 and 13 [c] *20* That is, the Ten Cities

---

4:35 Jesus left the territory of Galilee to go to the "region of the Gerasenes" (5:1; see the note there).
4:37 Situated in a basin surrounded by mountains, the Sea of Galilee is particularly susceptible to sudden, violent storms. Cool air from the Mediterranean is drawn down through the narrow mountain passes and clashes with the hot, humid air lying over the lake.
5:1 "Across the lake" refers to the eastern side of the lake, the territory largely inhabited by Gentiles, as indicated by the presence of the large herd of swine—animals Jews considered ceremonially unclean and therefore unfit to eat.
5:3 It was not unusual for the same cave to provide burial for the dead and shelter for the living. Very poor people often lived in such caves.
5:9 A legion, the largest single unit in the Roman army, included both light and heavy infantry, cavalry and auxiliaries. A legion at full strength consisted of about 6,000 soldiers. The term in the New Testament represents a vast number (see also Mt 26:53; Lk 8:30). For the application here, see "Demons and the Bible" on page 1572.
5:11 For "pigs," see the note on Luke 8:32.
5:20 For "Decapolis," see the note on Matthew 4:25.

A Dead Girl and a Sick Woman

21 When Jesus had again crossed over by boat to the other side of the lake,[r] a large crowd gathered **5:21** [r]Mt 9:1
around him while he was by the lake.[s] 22 Then one of the synagogue rulers,[t] named Jairus, came there. [s]Mk 4:1 **5:22** [t]ver 35,36,
Seeing Jesus, he fell at his feet 23 and pleaded earnestly with him, "My little daughter is dying. Please come 38; Lk 13:14; Ac 13:15; 18:8,17
and put your hands on[u] her so that she will be healed and live." 24 So Jesus went with him. **5:23** [u]Mt 19:13;
A large crowd followed and pressed around him. 25 And a woman was there who had been subject to Mk 6:5; 7:32; 8:23; 16:18;
bleeding[v] for twelve years. 26 She had suffered a great deal under the care of many doctors and had spent all Lk 4:40; 13:13; Ac 6:6
she had, yet instead of getting better she grew worse. 27 When she heard about Jesus, she came up behind **5:25** [v]Lev 15:25-30
him in the crowd and touched his cloak, 28 because she thought, "If I just touch his clothes,[w] I will be healed." **5:28** [w]Mt 9:20
29 Immediately her bleeding stopped and she felt in her body that she was freed from her suffering.[x] **5:29** [x]ver 34
30 At once Jesus realized that power[y] had gone out from him. He turned around in the crowd and asked, **5:30** [y]Lk 5:17; 6:19
"Who touched my clothes?"
31 "You see the people crowding against you," his disciples answered, "and yet you can ask, 'Who
touched me?' "
32 But Jesus kept looking around to see who had done it. 33 Then the woman, knowing what had hap-
pened to her, came and fell at his feet and, trembling with fear, told him the whole truth. 34 He said to her,
"Daughter, your faith has healed you.[z] Go in peace[a] and be freed from your suffering." **5:34** [z]Mt 9:22 [a]Ac 15:33
35 While Jesus was still speaking, some men came from the house of Jairus, the synagogue ruler.[b] "Your **5:35** [b]ver 22
daughter is dead," they said. "Why bother the teacher any more?"
36 Ignoring what they said, Jesus told the synagogue ruler, "Don't be afraid; just believe."
37 He did not let anyone follow him except Peter, James and John the brother of James.[c] 38 When they **5:37** [c]Mt 4:21
came to the home of the synagogue ruler,[d] Jesus saw a commotion, with people crying and wailing loud- **5:38** [d]ver 22
ly. 39 He went in and said to them, "Why all this commotion and wailing? The child is not dead but asleep."[e] **5:39** [e]Mt 9:24
40 But they laughed at him.
After he put them all out, he took the child's father and mother and the disciples who were with him,
and went in where the child was. 41 He took her by the hand[f] and said to her, *"Talitha koum!"* (which **5:41** [f]Mk 1:31 [g]Lk 7:14; Ac 9:40
means, "Little girl, I say to you, get up!").[g] 42 Immediately the girl stood up and walked around (she was
twelve years old). At this they were completely astonished. 43 He gave strict orders not to let anyone know
about this,[h] and told them to give her something to eat. **5:43** [h]Mt 8:4

A Prophet Without Honor

6 Jesus left there and went to his hometown,[i] accompanied by his disciples. 2 When the Sabbath came,[j] **6:1** [i]Mt 2:23 **6:2** [j]Mk 1:21
he began to teach in the synagogue,[k] and many who heard him were amazed.[l] [k]Mt 4:23 [l]Mt 7:28
"Where did this man get these things?" they asked. "What's this wisdom that has been given him, that
he even does miracles! 3 Isn't this the carpenter? Isn't this Mary's son and the brother of James, Joseph,[a]
Judas and Simon?[m] Aren't his sisters here with us?" And they took offense at him.[n] **6:3** [m]Mt 12:46 [n]Mt 11:6; Jn 6:61
4 Jesus said to them, "Only in his hometown, among his relatives and in his own house is a prophet
without honor."[o] 5 He could not do any miracles there, except lay his hands on[p] a few sick people and heal **6:4** [o]Lk 4:24; Jn 4:44
them. 6 And he was amazed at their lack of faith. **6:5** [p]Mk 5:23

[a] 3 Greek *Joses,* a variant of *Joseph*

5:21 Jesus returned to the western side of the lake, perhaps to Capernaum.
5:22 A ruler of the synagogue was a layman whose responsibilities were administrative and included such duties as looking after the building and supervising the worship. With some exceptions (see Ac 13:14–15), most synagogues had only one ruler. Sometimes the title was honorary, with no administrative responsibilities assigned.
5:26 The Jewish Talmud preserves a record of medicines and treatments prescribed for illnesses of this sort (see "Disease and Medicine in the Ancient World" on p. 1674).
5:34 For a discussion of salutations in the Bible, see the note on Ruth 2:4.
5:38 It was customary for professional mourners to be brought in at the time of death (see "Sackcloth and Ashes: Rituals of Lamentation" on p. 820).
5:41 There are several Aramaic words and phrases in the New Testament, among them *Talitha kowm* (here), *Ephphatha* (7:34), *Eloi, Eloi, lama sabachthani* (Mt 27:46; Mk 15:34), *Maranatha* (see the text note on 1Co 16:22) and *Abba* (Mk 14:36; Ro 8:15; Gal 4:6). It has been generally assumed that Aramaic was the colloquial language of the Holy Land from the time of the return of the exiles from Babylon, but some scholars believe that Hebrew was spoken in Galilee during New Testament times.

The other colloquial dialect of the New Testament period was Greek—the common dialect of Greek in its simplified and basic form that had become an alternative language throughout most of the eastern Mediterranean basin, and especially in the kingdoms of Alexander's successors. Jesus spoke Aramaic but undoubtedly also understood Greek and read from the Scriptures in classical Hebrew. Paul was fluent in all three languages and used them with equal facility, along with the addition of Latin.
6:1 For Jesus' hometown, see the note on Matthew 2:23.
6:2 For "teach in the synagogue," see the note on 1:21.
6:3 Only in Mark is Jesus himself referred to as a carpenter. The Greek word can also apply to a mason, smith or builder in general.

ARCHAEOLOGICAL SITES

GERGESENES, GERASENES OR GADARENES?

MARK 5 Three of the four Gospels record the miracle of the healing of the demoniac (and, as a consequence, of the pigs rushing into the sea), but a vexing issue remains: Did this take place in the region of the Gerasenes, the Gadarenes or the Gergesenes? All three can be found among the Greek manuscripts of the Gospels. On textual evidence alone, manuscripts of Matthew 8:28 probably favor "Gadarenes," but those of Mark 5:1 and Luke 8:26 both suggest "Gerasenes."

Gadara, modern Umm Qeis, was about 5 miles (8 km) from the Sea of Galilee and thus cannot have been the place where the miracle took place. Gerasa (Jerash) contains magnificent Roman ruins and a number of pagan temples, but it is 37 miles (60 km) southeast of Galilee and thereby also out of the question as the site of the miracle.

Gergesa (see "Map 9"), modern Kursi, is situated on the eastern shore of the Sea of Galilee and is also the only spot on this shore with a steep bank overlooking the sea (Mk 5:13). The church historian Eusebius identified this as the site of the miracle. The remains of a **Byzantine** monastery, built in the sixth century to commemorate this healing, have been found here. Based upon this evidence, it would appear that the earliest texts rendered the site "Gergesenes" but that, because the name was unfamiliar to many scribes and because of the similarity in pronunciation and spelling, it was erroneously copied as both "Gerasenes" and "Gadarenes."

(photos from top to bottom)
Jerash: the Arch of Hadrian
Umm Qeis: the site of Gadara
Jerash: the street of columns looking toward the modern city
Photographs courtesy of © Dr. Gary Pratico

THE LIFE OF JESUS

MARK 5 In what year was Jesus born, and when was he crucified? These are longstanding historical questions. The seemingly obvious answer to the first—that he was born in A.D. 1 (there is no year 0)—is incorrect, however, since the calculations on which our modern calendar is based were faulty.

The basic data of Jesus' life are well known. After his birth in Bethlehem,[1] he spent most of his youth and early years of ministry in Galilee.[2] Like many Jews, Jesus would have made trips to Jerusalem and Judea (noted especially in John's Gospel), but he is also reported to have journeyed at various times into the regions surrounding Galilee, such as **Phoenicia** (Mt 15:21)[3] and Caesarea Philippi (Mt 16:13).[4] But most of his life was spent in his hometown of Nazareth and in the fishing villages around the sea of Galilee.[5] Jesus' final period of ministry centered on Judea, with the crucifixion and resurrection events occurring in and about Jerusalem.

The chronology of Jesus' life, though clear in outline, cannot be fixed with absolute precision. Matthew and Luke both inform us that Jesus was born before the death of Herod (4 B.C.), though it would appear that his birth occurred toward the final years of Herod's reign,[6] suggesting an approximate date of 6–4 B.C. The next chronological marker comes from Luke 3:1, where we learn that John the Baptist's ministry began during the fifteenth year of the reign of the emperor Tiberius.[7] Since A.D. 14 is the generally accepted date for Tiberius's accession to the throne, John's ministry would have commenced between August of A.D. 28 and December of 29. Jesus began his own ministry shortly after John had embarked on his, at some point in A.D. 28 or 29, making Jesus about 32 or 33 years old at the time. This fits well with Luke's statement that Jesus was "about thirty years old" (Lk 3:23).

The duration of Jesus' public ministry was approximately three years. While the exact chronology of this period is difficult to ascertain, the final phase of his ministry allows for closer scrutiny. It is clear that Jesus was crucified under Pontius Pilate, who governed Judea from A.D. 26–36.[8] Moreover, it is likely that he was put to death on a Friday on the fourteenth day of the Jewish month Nisan, as the Passover lambs were being slaughtered in preparation for the Passover that Friday night; this is the clear implication of John's narrative (Jn 18:28; 19:31). While it is true that in the Synoptic Gospels Jesus referred to the Last Supper, which took place on a Thursday, as a "Passover" meal (e.g., Mk 14:12–16), this may be accounted for in a few different ways. It has been suggested, with some historical support, that some Jews (in this case Jesus and his Galilean companions) may have reckoned the feast days from sunrise to sunrise rather than from sunset to sunset. This explanation would accommodate the material both in John and in the Synoptics. It is also possible that Jesus deliberately held his meal on a different day from the Passover because of his intention to radically transform the meaning of the Passover.[9]

Taking Friday, Nisan 14, as the day of the crucifixion, astronomical data informs us that the only years from A.D. 29–36 that could have seen Nisan 14 on a Friday are A.D. 30, 33 and 36. A.D. 36 is easily dismissed as too late, while A.D. 30 seems too early (although some who begin Jesus' ministry in A.D. 28 and shorten his public ministry find it acceptable). This leaves A.D. 33 as the most likely date for the year of Jesus' death and resurrection.[10]

[1]See "Bethlehem" on page 1487 and "The Birthplace of Jesus" on page 1668. [2]See "Galilee in Jesus' Time" on page 1587. [3]See "Phoenicia" on page 488. [4]See "Caesarea Philippi" on page 1589. [5]See "Nazareth" on page 1623. [6]See "Herod the Great" on page 1627. [7]See "Tiberius Caesar, the Caesar of Jesus' Ministry" on page 1708. [8]See "Pontius Pilate" on page 1714. [9]See "The Last Supper and the Passover" on page 1611. [10]See "The Resurrection of Jesus" on page 1617.

Mosaic at a Christian church at Tabgha, on the northwestern shore of the Sea of Galilee, where tradition says Jesus gave the Sermon on the Mount

Preserving Bible Times; © Dr. James C. Martin

Jesus Sends Out the Twelve

6:6 [q]Mt 9:35; Mk 1:39; Lk 13:22 Then Jesus went around teaching from village to village.[q] 7 Calling the Twelve to him,[r] he sent them
6:7 [r]Mk 3:13 [s]Dt 17:6; Lk 10:1 out two by two[s] and gave them authority over evil[a] spirits.[t]
[t]Mt 10:1 8 These were his instructions: "Take nothing for the journey except a staff—no bread, no bag, no mon-
ey in your belts. 9 Wear sandals but not an extra tunic. 10 Whenever you enter a house, stay there until you
6:11 [u]Mt 10:14 leave that town. 11 And if any place will not welcome you or listen to you, shake the dust off your feet[u]
when you leave, as a testimony against them."
6:12 [v]Lk 9:6 12 They went out and preached that people should repent.[v] 13 They drove out many demons and anoint-
6:13 [w]Jas 5:14 ed many sick people with oil[w] and healed them.

John the Baptist Beheaded

14 King Herod heard about this, for Jesus' name had become well known. Some were saying,[b] "John
6:14 [x]Mt 3:1 the Baptist[x] has been raised from the dead, and that is why miraculous powers are at work in him."
6:15 [y]Mal 4:5 15 Others said, "He is Elijah."[y]
[z]Mt 21:11 [a]Mt 16:14; Mk 8:28 And still others claimed, "He is a prophet,[z] like one of the prophets of long ago."[a]
16 But when Herod heard this, he said, "John, the man I beheaded, has been raised from the dead!"
17 For Herod himself had given orders to have John arrested, and he had him bound and put in pris-
6:17 [b]Mt 4:12; 11:2; Lk 3:19,20 on.[b] He did this because of Herodias, his brother Philip's wife, whom he had married. 18 For John had
6:18 [c]Lev 18:16; 20:21 been saying to Herod, "It is not lawful for you to have your brother's wife."[c] 19 So Herodias nursed a grudge
against John and wanted to kill him. But she was not able to, 20 because Herod feared John and protected
6:20 [d]Mt 11:9; 21:26 him, knowing him to be a righteous and holy man.[d] When Herod heard John, he was greatly puzzled[c];
yet he liked to listen to him.
6:21 [e]Est 1:3; 2:18 [f]Lk 3:1 21 Finally the opportune time came. On his birthday Herod gave a banquet[e] for his high officials and
military commanders and the leading men of Galilee.[f] 22 When the daughter of Herodias came in and
danced, she pleased Herod and his dinner guests.
The king said to the girl, "Ask me for anything you want, and I'll give it to you." 23 And he promised her
6:23 [g]Est 5:3,6; 7:2 with an oath, "Whatever you ask I will give you, up to half my kingdom."[g]
24 She went out and said to her mother, "What shall I ask for?"
"The head of John the Baptist," she answered.
25 At once the girl hurried in to the king with the request: "I want you to give me right now the head
of John the Baptist on a platter."
26 The king was greatly distressed, but because of his oaths and his dinner guests, he did not want to
refuse her. 27 So he immediately sent an executioner with orders to bring John's head. The man went,
beheaded John in the prison, 28 and brought back his head on a platter. He presented it to the girl, and
she gave it to her mother. 29 On hearing of this, John's disciples came and took his body and laid it in a
tomb.

Jesus Feeds the Five Thousand

6:30 [h]Mt 10:2; Lk 9:10; 17:5; 30 The apostles[h] gathered around Jesus and reported to him all they had done and taught.[i] 31 Then, be-
22:14; 24:10; Ac 1:2,26 cause so many people were coming and going that they did not even have a chance to eat,[j] he said to
[i]Lk 9:10 them, "Come with me by yourselves to a quiet place and get some rest."
6:31 [j]Mk 3:20 6:32 [k]ver 45; 32 So they went away by themselves in a boat[k] to a solitary place. 33 But many who saw them leaving
Mk 4:36 recognized them and ran on foot from all the towns and got there ahead of them. 34 When Jesus landed
6:34 [l]Mt 9:36 and saw a large crowd, he had compassion on them, because they were like sheep without a shepherd.[l]
So he began teaching them many things.
35 By this time it was late in the day, so his disciples came to him. "This is a remote place," they said,
"and it's already very late. 36 Send the people away so they can go to the surrounding countryside and vil-
lages and buy themselves something to eat."

[a] 7 Greek *unclean* [b] 14 Some early manuscripts *He was saying* [c] 20 Some early manuscripts *he did many things*

6:9 At night an extra tunic was helpful as a covering to protect from the cold night air (see "Dress and Fashion in the Greco-Roman World" on p. 2004).
6:11 See the note on Matthew 10:14.
6:13 In the ancient world olive oil was widely used as a medicine (see "Disease and Medicine in the Ancient World" on p. 1674).
6:17 See the note on Matthew 14:3.
6:22 See the note on Matthew 14:6.

37 But he answered, "You give them something to eat."[m] 6:37 [m]2Ki 4:42-44
They said to him, "That would take eight months of a man's wages[a]! Are we to go and spend that much
on bread and give it to them to eat?"
38 "How many loaves do you have?" he asked. "Go and see."
When they found out, they said, "Five—and two fish."[n] 6:38 [n]Mt 15:34; Mk 8:5
39 Then Jesus directed them to have all the people sit down in groups on the green grass. 40 So they sat
down in groups of hundreds and fifties. 41 Taking the five loaves and the two fish and looking up to heav-
en, he gave thanks and broke the loaves.[o] Then he gave them to his disciples to set before the people. He also 6:41 [o]Mt 14:19
divided the two fish among them all. 42 They all ate and were satisfied, 43 and the disciples picked up twelve
basketfuls of broken pieces of bread and fish. 44 The number of the men who had eaten was five thousand.

Jesus Walks on the Water

45 Immediately Jesus made his disciples get into the boat[p] and go on ahead of him to Bethsaida,[q] while 6:45 [p]ver 32 [q]Mt 11:21
he dismissed the crowd. 46 After leaving them, he went up on a mountainside to pray.[r] 6:46 [r]Lk 3:21
47 When evening came, the boat was in the middle of the lake, and he was alone on land. 48 He saw the
disciples straining at the oars, because the wind was against them. About the fourth watch of the night he
went out to them, walking on the lake. He was about to pass by them, 49 but when they saw him walking
on the lake, they thought he was a ghost.[s] They cried out, 50 because they all saw him and were terrified. 6:49 [s]Lk 24:37

[a] 37 Greek *take two hundred denarii*

6:37 See the NIV text note. The usual pay for a day's work was one denarius (see the note on Mt 20:2).
6:38 These were barley loaves, a cheap bread that was a staple for the poor. Unlike our modern loaves, these were small and flat. One could easily eat several at a single meal.
6:39 Grass is green around the Sea of Galilee after the late winter or early spring rains.
6:43 Bread was regarded by Jews as a particularly significant and representative gift of God, and it was required that scraps that fell on the ground during a meal be picked up. Here the fragments were collected in small wicker baskets that were carried as a part of daily attire. Each of the disciples returned with his basket full. For "basketfuls," see the note on Matthew 14:20.
6:44 See the note on Matthew 14:21. The number could be easily calculated because of the division of the crowd into "groups of hundreds and fifties" (v. 40). The size of the crowd is amazing in light of the fact that the neighboring towns of Capernaum and Bethsaida probably had a population of only 2,000–3,000 each.
6:48 For "fourth watch," see the note on Matthew 14:25.

ARCHAEOLOGICAL SITES

SEPPHORIS

MARK 6 The city of Sepphoris (modern Zippori) is mentioned nowhere in the Bible, even though it was a town that Jesus must have known well. Located just four miles (six km) northwest of Nazareth,[1] Sepphoris had become quite prominent by the first century B.C. In the winter of 39/38 B.C., Herod the Great captured it and used it as his northern base.[2] At his death the city rebelled but was harshly defeated by the Roman governor, Varus. Herod Antipas inherited this territory from Herod the Great and set about rebuilding the town, transforming it into the most opulent city of Galilee.[3] A theater seating three thousand, possibly built by Herod Antipas, was located there. A beautiful mosaic of a woman's face has been unearthed there, dating much later, to the third or fourth century A.D. The first-century inhabitants of the city appear to have been staunchly pro-Roman, since they refused to join the Jewish revolt of A.D. 70. During the second century A.D., however, the city did become a center of Jewish learning.

The elaborate rebuilding of this city, carried out by Herod Antipas, occurred during the lifetimes of both Joseph and Jesus. Since the two were craftsmen (perhaps carpenters; see Mk 6:3), some suggest that they may in fact have worked at construction projects there. Sepphoris is the traditional birthplace of Jesus' mother, Mary.

[1]See "Nazareth" on page 1623. [2]See "Herod the Great" on page 1627. [3]See "Galilee in Jesus' Time" on page 1587.

6:50 [t]Mt 14:27 — Immediately he spoke to them and said, "Take courage! It is I. Don't be afraid."[t] [51]Then he climbed into
6:51 [u]ver 32 [v]Mk 4:39 — the boat[u] with them, and the wind died down.[v] They were completely amazed, [52]for they had not under-
6:52 [w]Mk 8:17-21 — stood about the loaves; their hearts were hardened.[w]
6:53 [x]Jn 6:24,25 — [53]When they had crossed over, they landed at Gennesaret and anchored there.[x] [54]As soon as they got
out of the boat, people recognized Jesus. [55]They ran throughout that whole region and carried the sick
on mats to wherever they heard he was. [56]And wherever he went—into villages, towns or countryside—
6:56 [y]Mt 9:20 — they placed the sick in the marketplaces. They begged him to let them touch even the edge of his cloak,[y]
and all who touched him were healed.

Clean and Unclean

7 The Pharisees and some of the teachers of the law who had come from Jerusalem gathered around
7:2 [z]Ac 10:14,28; 11:8; Ro 14:14 — Jesus and [2]saw some of his disciples eating food with hands that were "unclean,"[z] that is, unwashed.
[3](The Pharisees and all the Jews do not eat unless they give their hands a ceremonial washing, holding
7:3 [a]ver 5,8,9,13; Lk 11:38 — to the tradition of the elders.[a] [4]When they come from the marketplace they do not eat unless they wash.
7:4 [b]Mt 23:25; Lk 11:39 — And they observe many other traditions, such as the washing of cups, pitchers and kettles.[a])[b]
[5]So the Pharisees and teachers of the law asked Jesus, "Why don't your disciples live according to the
7:5 [c]ver 3; Gal 1:14; Col 2:8 — tradition of the elders[c] instead of eating their food with 'unclean' hands?"
[6]He replied, "Isaiah was right when he prophesied about you hypocrites; as it is written:

> " 'These people honor me with their lips,
> but their hearts are far from me.
> [7]They worship me in vain;
> 7:7 [d]Isa 29:13 — their teachings are but rules taught by men.'[b][d]

7:8 [e]ver 3 — [8]You have let go of the commands of God and are holding on to the traditions of men."[e]
[9]And he said to them: "You have a fine way of setting aside the commands of God in order to observe[c]
7:9 [f]ver 3 — your own traditions![f] [10]For Moses said, 'Honor your father and your mother,'[d][g] and, 'Anyone who curses
7:10 [g]Ex 20:12; Dt 5:16 [h]Ex 21:17; Lev 20:9 — his father or mother must be put to death.'[e][h] [11]But you say[i] that if a man says to his father or mother:
'Whatever help you might otherwise have received from me is Corban' (that is, a gift devoted to God),
7:11 [i]Mt 23:16,18 — [12]then you no longer let him do anything for his father or mother. [13]Thus you nullify the word of God[j] by
7:13 [j]Heb 4:12 [k]ver 3 — your tradition[k] that you have handed down. And you do many things like that."
[14]Again Jesus called the crowd to him and said, "Listen to me, everyone, and understand this. [15]Noth-
ing outside a man can make him 'unclean' by going into him. Rather, it is what comes out of a man that
makes him 'unclean.'[f]"
7:17 [l]Mk 9:28 — [17]After he had left the crowd and entered the house, his disciples asked him[l] about this parable. [18]"Are

[a] *4* Some early manuscripts *pitchers, kettles and dining couches* [b] *6,7* Isaiah 29:13 [c] *9* Some manuscripts *set up*
[d] *10* Exodus 20:12; Deut. 5:16 [e] *10* Exodus 21:17; Lev. 20:9 [f] *15* Some early manuscripts *'unclean.'* [16]*If anyone has ears to hear, let him hear.*

6:53 For "Gennesaret," see the note on Matthew 14:34.
7:3–13 On Judaism, see note on Exodus 20:1–21.
7:3–4 The fact that the conception of purity was deeply embedded within the religio-social structure of the children of Israel since very early times is well known to students of the Bible. The attitude of the Jews as a whole, and of the Pharisees as a class, is expressed in these verses. Religious purity was both ceremonial and ethical. Under the Mosaic Law, ceremonial purification was required in four specific instances: (1) the birth of a child, after which "uncleanness" was removed through circumcision (if male) and through the isolation of the mother for a varying period of time (Lev 12:2ff.); (2) contact with a corpse, the offering of a red heifer being prescribed as a sacrifice of purification (Nu 19:1–10); (3) certain conditions, such as skin diseases (Lev 13:8); and (4) uncleanness due to a running sore (Lev 15). Family purity was guarded through strict regulations concerning sex (Lev 20:1–21; Dt 22:20–21). In the New Testament, although there is a transference from the outward to the inner, there is no relaxing of the basic requirements for purity itself (Mt 5:27–28; 19:3–9; Mk 10:2–11; 1Co 5:9–13; 6:18–20; 7:8ff.).

For "ceremonial washing," see the note on John 2:6. In the time of Christ the Jews engaged in the ceremonial washing of hands before eating and used public baths as the Greeks and Romans did. For other traditions, see the note on "tradition of the elders" on Matthew 15:2.
7:4 The marketplace was the area where religious Jews would come into contact with Gentiles or with other Jews who did not observe the ceremonial law, thus becoming ceremonially unclean. (See "The Ancient Agora" on p. 1799.)
7:5 This disagreement about hand washing did not concern hygiene but purity—an issue high on the Pharisees' agenda. There is actually no Biblical requirement of washing hands prior to eating.
7:11 The word *Corban* (Hebrew *qorbân*, "an offering") occurs in the Hebrew text of the Old Testament with reference to an offering or sacrifice, whether bloody of otherwise, made to God (Lev 1:2–3; 2:1; 3:1; Nu 7:12–17). It is found in our English versions of the New Testament here in Mark 7:11, where it refers to money dedicated to God. The Talmud states that the Jews were much given to making rash vows to God, with no intention of carrying them out. By Jesus' time there arose the reprehensible practice of grown children avoiding the responsibility of looking after their parents' material needs by informing them that their money had been dedicated to God and that it would be wrong to divert it from that sacred purpose. This could be done by simply pronouncing the word "Corban." Ideally, the money thereafter belonged to God, but actually the one who had made the vow might keep it in his possession. By referring to this custom Jesus demonstrated the subtly deceptive reasoning of tradition that enabled the Jews to disregard plain commandments of God, like the one requiring children to honor their parents.
7:16 This verse (see the NIV text note) appears to be a scribal addition derived from either 4:9 or 4:23. (See "Early Scribal Emendation" on p. 448.)

you so dull?" he asked. "Don't you see that nothing that enters a man from the outside can make him 'un-
clean'? 19 For it doesn't go into his heart but into his stomach, and then out of his body." (In saying this,
Jesus declared all foods[m] "clean.")[n] — 7:19 [m]Ro 14:1-12; Col 2:16; 1Ti 4:3-5 [n]Ac 10:15
20 He went on: "What comes out of a man is what makes him 'unclean.' 21 For from within, out of men's
hearts, come evil thoughts, sexual immorality, theft, murder, adultery, 22 greed,[o] malice, deceit, lewdness, — 7:22 [o]Mt 20:15
envy, slander, arrogance and folly. 23 All these evils come from inside and make a man 'unclean.' "

The Faith of a Syrophoenician Woman

24 Jesus left that place and went to the vicinity of Tyre.[a][p] He entered a house and did not want anyone — 7:24 [p]Mt 11:21
to know it; yet he could not keep his presence secret. 25 In fact, as soon as she heard about him, a wom-
an whose little daughter was possessed by an evil[b] spirit[q] came and fell at his feet. 26 The woman was a — 7:25 [q]Mt 4:24
Greek, born in Syrian Phoenicia. She begged Jesus to drive the demon out of her daughter.
27 "First let the children eat all they want," he told her, "for it is not right to take the children's bread and
toss it to their dogs."
28 "Yes, Lord," she replied, "but even the dogs under the table eat the children's crumbs."
29 Then he told her, "For such a reply, you may go; the demon has left your daughter."
30 She went home and found her child lying on the bed, and the demon gone.

The Healing of a Deaf and Mute Man

31 Then Jesus left the vicinity of Tyre[r] and went through Sidon, down to the Sea of Galilee[s] and into — 7:31 [r]ver 24; Mt 11:21 [s]Mt 4:18
the region of the Decapolis.[c][t] 32 There some people brought to him a man who was deaf and could hardly — [t]Mt 4:25; Mk 5:20
talk,[u] and they begged him to place his hand on[v] the man. — 7:32 [u]Mt 9:32; Lk 11:14
33 After he took him aside, away from the crowd, Jesus put his fingers into the man's ears. Then he — [v]Mk 5:23
spit[w] and touched the man's tongue. 34 He looked up to heaven[x] and with a deep sigh[y] said to him, *"Eph-* — 7:33 [w]Mk 8:23 7:34 [x]Mk 6:41;
phatha!" (which means, "Be opened!"). 35 At this, the man's ears were opened, his tongue was loosened — Jn 11:41 [y]Mk 8:12
and he began to speak plainly.[z] — 7:35 [z]Isa 35:5,6
36 Jesus commanded them not to tell anyone.[a] But the more he did so, the more they kept talking about — 7:36 [a]Mt 8:4
it. 37 People were overwhelmed with amazement. "He has done everything well," they said. "He even makes
the deaf hear and the mute speak."

Jesus Feeds the Four Thousand

8 During those days another large crowd gathered. Since they had nothing to eat, Jesus called his dis-
ciples to him and said, 2 "I have compassion for these people;[b] they have already been with me three — 8:2 [b]Mt 9:36
days and have nothing to eat. 3 If I send them home hungry, they will collapse on the way, because some
of them have come a long distance."
4 His disciples answered, "But where in this remote place can anyone get enough bread to feed them?"
5 "How many loaves do you have?" Jesus asked.
"Seven," they replied.
6 He told the crowd to sit down on the ground. When he had taken the seven loaves and given thanks,
he broke them and gave them to his disciples to set before the people, and they did so. 7 They had a few
small fish as well; he gave thanks for them also and told the disciples to distribute them.[c] 8 The people — 8:7 [c]Mt 14:19
ate and were satisfied. Afterward the disciples picked up seven basketfuls of broken pieces that were left
over.[d] 9 About four thousand men were present. And having sent them away, 10 he got into the boat with — 8:8 [d]ver 20
his disciples and went to the region of Dalmanutha.

[a] *24* Many early manuscripts *Tyre and Sidon* [b] *25* Greek *unclean* [c] *31* That is, the Ten Cities

---

7:19 On defilement in the Old and New Testaments, see the note on Song of Songs 5:3.
7:24 For "Tyre," see the note on Matthew 15:21. A journey of about 30 miles (48 km) from Capernaum would have brought Jesus to "the vicinity of Tyre."
7:26 "Greek" here is probably equivalent to "Gentile." At that time Phoenicia belonged administratively to Syria. Mark may have used the term to distinguish this woman from the Libyan Phoenicians of North Africa.
7:27 Jews commonly referred to Gentiles as "dogs."
7:31 The commercially magnificent cities of Tyre and Sidon had been heavily influenced by Hellenism; the sophistication of Greek culture was apparent in their coinage and architecture. Each was also a proud, historic center of Canaanite paganism, with tombs of ancient kings and temples to various deities.

Apparently Jesus traveled north from Tyre to Sidon (a distance of about 25 mi or 40 km) and then southeast through the territory of Herod Philip to the eastern side of the Sea of Galilee. The route was circuitous—possibly in order to avoid entering Galilee, where Herod Antipas was in power and where many people wanted to take Jesus by force and make him king. Herod had intimated a hostile interest in Jesus.

For "Decapolis," see the note on Matthew 4:25.
7:34 For the use of the Aramaic language in New Testament times, see the note on 5:41.
8:10 South of the Plain of Gennesaret (see the note on Mt 14:34)

11 The Pharisees came and began to question Jesus. To test him, they asked him for a sign from heav-
8:11 [e]Mt 12:38 en.[e] 12 He sighed deeply[f] and said, "Why does this generation ask for a miraculous sign? I tell you the
8:12 [f]Mk 7:34 truth, no sign will be given to it." 13 Then he left them, got back into the boat and crossed to the other
side.

The Yeast of the Pharisees and Herod

14 The disciples had forgotten to bring bread, except for one loaf they had with them in the boat. 15 "Be
8:15 [g]1Co 5:6-8 [h]Lk 12:1 [i]Mt 14:1; Mk 12:13 careful," Jesus warned them. "Watch out for the yeast[g] of the Pharisees[h] and that of Herod."[i]
16 They discussed this with one another and said, "It is because we have no bread."
17 Aware of their discussion, Jesus asked them: "Why are you talking about having no bread? Do you
8:17 [j]Isa 6:9,10; Mk 6:52 still not see or understand? Are your hearts hardened?[j] 18 Do you have eyes but fail to see, and ears but
fail to hear? And don't you remember? 19 When I broke the five loaves for the five thousand, how many
basketfuls of pieces did you pick up?"
8:19 [k]Mt 14:20; Mk 6:41-44; Lk 9:17; Jn 6:13 "Twelve,"[k] they replied.
20 "And when I broke the seven loaves for the four thousand, how many basketfuls of pieces did you
pick up?"
8:20 [l]ver 6-9; Mt 15:37 They answered, "Seven."[l]
8:21 [m]Mk 6:52 21 He said to them, "Do you still not understand?"[m]

The Healing of a Blind Man at Bethsaida

8:22 [n]Mt 11:21 [o]Mk 10:46; Jn 9:1 22 They came to Bethsaida,[n] and some people brought a blind man[o] and begged Jesus to touch him.
8:23 [p]Mk 7:33 [q]Mk 5:23 23 He took the blind man by the hand and led him outside the village. When he had spit[p] on the man's eyes
and put his hands on[q] him, Jesus asked, "Do you see anything?"
24 He looked up and said, "I see people; they look like trees walking around."
25 Once more Jesus put his hands on the man's eyes. Then his eyes were opened, his sight was restored,
and he saw everything clearly. 26 Jesus sent him home, saying, "Don't go into the village.[a]"

Peter's Confession of Christ

27 Jesus and his disciples went on to the villages around Caesarea Philippi. On the way he asked them,
"Who do people say I am?"
8:28 [r]Mt 3:1 [s]Mal 4:5 28 They replied, "Some say John the Baptist;[r] others say Elijah;[s] and still others, one of the prophets."
29 "But what about you?" he asked. "Who do you say I am?"
8:29 [t]Jn 6:69; 11:27 Peter answered, "You are the Christ.[b]"[t]
8:30 [u]Mt 8:4; 16:20; 17:9; Mk 9:9; Lk 9:21 30 Jesus warned them not to tell anyone about him.[u]

Jesus Predicts His Death

8:31 [v]Mt 8:20 [w]Mt 16:21 31 He then began to teach them that the Son of Man[v] must suffer many things[w] and be rejected by the
[x]Mt 27:1,2 [y]Ac 2:23; 3:13 elders, chief priests and teachers of the law,[x] and that he must be killed[y] and after three days[z] rise again.[a]
[z]Mt 16:21 [a]Mt 16:21 32 He spoke plainly[b] about this, and Peter took him aside and began to rebuke him.
8:32 [b]Jn 18:20 8:33 [c]Mt 4:10 33 But when Jesus turned and looked at his disciples, he rebuked Peter. "Get behind me, Satan!"[c] he
said. "You do not have in mind the things of God, but the things of men."
34 Then he called the crowd to him along with his disciples and said: "If anyone would come after me,
8:34 [d]Mt 10:38; Lk 14:27 he must deny himself and take up his cross and follow me.[d] 35 For whoever wants to save his life[c] will
8:35 [e]Jn 12:25 lose it, but whoever loses his life for me and for the gospel will save it.[e] 36 What good is it for a man to gain

[a] 26 Some manuscripts *Don't go and tell anyone in the village* [b] 29 Or *Messiah.* "The Christ" (Greek) and "the Messiah" (Hebrew) both mean "the Anointed One." [c] 35 The Greek word means either *life* or *soul*; also in verse 36.

a cave has been found bearing the name "Talmanutha," perhaps the spot where Jesus landed. Matthew stated that Jesus "went to the vicinity of Magadan" (Mt 15:39). Dalmanutha and Magadan (or Magdala), located on the western shore of the Sea of Galilee, may be names either for the same place or for two sites located close to each other.

8:11 For "Pharisees," see the note on Matthew 3:7.

8:15 Yeast is generally a symbol of evil or corruption in the New Testament. The metaphor includes the idea of a tiny amount of yeast being able to ferment a large amount of dough. In this context the reference is to the evil disposition of both the Pharisees and Herod Antipas.

8:22 Bethsaida was on the northeastern shore of the Sea of Galilee. Philip the tetrarch later rebuilt the ruined city and named it "Julias," after Julia, the daughter of Caesar Augustus.

8:23 For commentary on Jesus' chosen method of healing (spitting on the man's eyes), see "Miracle Workers and Magicians in the First Century A.D." on page 1706.

8:27 For "Caesarea Philippi," see the note on Matthew 16:13.

8:29 Because popular Jewish ideas associated with the term "Christ" were largely political and national, Jesus seldom used the term.

8:31 For "elders," see the note on Matthew 21:23. For "chief priests" and "teachers of the law," see the note on Matthew 2:4.

the whole world, yet forfeit his soul? 37Or what can a man give in exchange for his soul? 38If anyone is
ashamed of me and my words in this adulterous and sinful generation, the Son of Man[f] will be ashamed
of him[g] when he comes[h] in his Father's glory with the holy angels."

9 And he said to them, "I tell you the truth, some who are standing here will not taste death before
they see the kingdom of God come[i] with power."[j]

The Transfiguration

2After six days Jesus took Peter, James and John[k] with him and led them up a high mountain, where
they were all alone. There he was transfigured before them. 3His clothes became dazzling white,[l] whiter
than anyone in the world could bleach them. 4And there appeared before them Elijah and Moses, who
were talking with Jesus.
5Peter said to Jesus, "Rabbi,[m] it is good for us to be here. Let us put up three shelters—one for you,
one for Moses and one for Elijah." 6(He did not know what to say, they were so frightened.)
7Then a cloud appeared and enveloped them, and a voice came from the cloud:[n] "This is my Son,
whom I love. Listen to him!"[o]
8Suddenly, when they looked around, they no longer saw anyone with them except Jesus.
9As they were coming down the mountain, Jesus gave them orders not to tell anyone[p] what they had
seen until the Son of Man[q] had risen from the dead. 10They kept the matter to themselves, discussing
what "rising from the dead" meant.
11And they asked him, "Why do the teachers of the law say that Elijah must come first?"
12Jesus replied, "To be sure, Elijah does come first, and restores all things. Why then is it written that
the Son of Man[r] must suffer much[s] and be rejected?[t] 13But I tell you, Elijah has come,[u] and they have
done to him everything they wished, just as it is written about him."

The Healing of a Boy With an Evil Spirit

14When they came to the other disciples, they saw a large crowd around them and the teachers of the
law arguing with them. 15As soon as all the people saw Jesus, they were overwhelmed with wonder and
ran to greet him.
16"What are you arguing with them about?" he asked.
17A man in the crowd answered, "Teacher, I brought you my son, who is possessed by a spirit that has
robbed him of speech. 18Whenever it seizes him, it throws him to the ground. He foams at the mouth,
gnashes his teeth and becomes rigid. I asked your disciples to drive out the spirit, but they could not."
19"O unbelieving generation," Jesus replied, "how long shall I stay with you? How long shall I put up
with you? Bring the boy to me."
20So they brought him. When the spirit saw Jesus, it immediately threw the boy into a convulsion. He
fell to the ground and rolled around, foaming at the mouth.[v]
21Jesus asked the boy's father, "How long has he been like this?"
"From childhood," he answered. 22"It has often thrown him into fire or water to kill him. But if you can
do anything, take pity on us and help us."
23" 'If you can'?" said Jesus. "Everything is possible for him who believes."[w]
24Immediately the boy's father exclaimed, "I do believe; help me overcome my unbelief!"
25When Jesus saw that a crowd was running to the scene,[x] he rebuked the evil[a] spirit. "You deaf and
mute spirit," he said, "I command you, come out of him and never enter him again."
26The spirit shrieked, convulsed him violently and came out. The boy looked so much like a corpse
that many said, "He's dead." 27But Jesus took him by the hand and lifted him to his feet, and he stood up.
28After Jesus had gone indoors, his disciples asked him privately,[y] "Why couldn't we drive it out?"
29He replied, "This kind can come out only by prayer.[b]"
30They left that place and passed through Galilee. Jesus did not want anyone to know where they were,
31because he was teaching his disciples. He said to them, "The Son of Man[z] is going to be betrayed into

8:38 [f]Mt 8:20 [g]Mt 10:33; Lk 12:9 [h]1Th 2:19
9:1 [i]Mk 13:30; Lk 22:18 [j]Mt 24:30; 25:31
9:2 [k]Mt 4:21
9:3 [l]Mt 28:3
9:5 [m]Mt 23:7
9:7 [n]Ex 24:16 [o]Mt 3:17
9:9 [p]Mk 8:30 [q]Mt 8:20
9:12 [r]Mt 8:20 [s]Mt 16:21 [t]Lk 23:11
9:13 [u]Mt 11:14
9:20 [v]Mk 1:26
9:23 [w]Mt 21:21; Mk 11:23; Jn 11:40
9:25 [x]ver 15
9:28 [y]Mk 7:17
9:31 [z]Mt 8:20

[a] 25 Greek *unclean* [b] 29 Some manuscripts *prayer and fasting*

9:5 Peter may have desired to erect new tents of meeting where God could again communicate with his people (see Ex 29:42). Or he may have been thinking of the booths used at the Feast of Tabernacles (see Lev 23:42; see also "The Festivals of Israel" on p. 186).
9:10 As Jews they were familiar with the doctrine of the resurrection; it was the resurrection of the Son of Man that baffled them; their theology had no place for a suffering and dying Messiah.
9:14 For "teachers of the law," see the note on Matthew 2:4.
9:18 For "seizes him," see the note on Matthew 4:24.

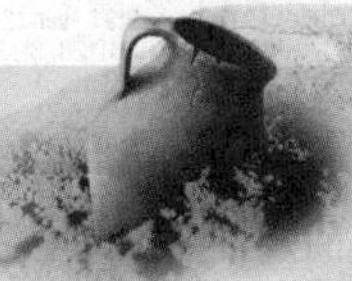

ARCHAEOLOGICAL SITES

CAPERNAUM

The Capernaum synagogue
Preserving Bible Times; © Dr. James C. Martin

MARK 9 Jesus chose as the headquarters for his Galilean ministry the city of Capernaum ("Map 9"), on the northwestern shore of the Sea of Galilee.[1] In Matthew 9:1 Capernaum is referred to, in fact, as Jesus' "own town." Jesus stayed in Peter's house there and frequented the Capernaum synagogue. Residents of the town were simple folk who made their living from fishing, agriculture, industry and trade. The road leading to Damascus passed nearby, providing a commercial link with regions to the north and south.

It was in the vicinity of Capernaum that Jesus chose several of his disciples: the resident fishermen Peter and his brother Andrew (Mk 1:16–18); John and James, the sons of Zebedee, also local fishermen (1:19–20); and Matthew, a tax collector (2:13–14). In addition, Jesus performed several miracles there. He cured Peter's mother-in-law of a fever (1:29–31), healed many townspeople of diseases and demon-possession (1:32–34) and restored a paralytic on a pallet let down with ropes by his friends through a roof (2:1–5). Elsewhere in the town Jesus healed the servant of the Roman centurion under whose auspices the local synagogue had been constructed (Lk 7:1–10).

The remains of what was probably a first-century synagogue were discovered beneath those of a later, **Byzantine**-period synagogue. The first-century structure archaeologists uncovered featured a basalt floor 60 feet (18 m) wide by 79 feet (24 m) long. Too large to have been a private dwelling, this was very possibly the synagogue at which Jesus taught (Mk 1:21). Impressive remains of the Byzantine-era synagogue can still be seen by visitors today.[2]

A site that may have been the location of Peter's house has also been excavated. The remains are located 84 feet (26 m) south of the synagogue, at the bottom of three layers of construction. The topmost layer has been identified as the ruins of a fifth-century octagonal church; the second layer, a fourth-century house-church; and the lowest layer, a simple, first-century home. The house had narrow walls, which would have been too weak to support a second story or a roof of masonry; it probably had a roof of branches covered with earth. Thus, this house or one like it could have been the scene of Jesus' healing of the paralytic man who was lowered through the roof (2:4).[3]

[1]See "Galilee in Jesus' Time" on page 1587. [2]See "The Capernaum Synagogue" on page 1591. [3]See "Houses in the Holy Land of the First Century A.D.: Peter's House in Capernaum; Insulae" on page 1584.

the hands of men. They will kill him,[a] and after three days[b] he will rise."[c] 32 But they did not understand
what he meant[d] and were afraid to ask him about it.

Who Is the Greatest?

33 They came to Capernaum.[e] When he was in the house,[f] he asked them, "What were you arguing about
on the road?" 34 But they kept quiet because on the way they had argued about who was the greatest.[g]
35 Sitting down, Jesus called the Twelve and said, "If anyone wants to be first, he must be the very last,
and the servant of all."[h]
36 He took a little child and had him stand among them. Taking him in his arms,[i] he said to them,
37 "Whoever welcomes one of these little children in my name welcomes me; and whoever welcomes me
does not welcome me but the one who sent me."[j]

Whoever Is Not Against Us Is for Us

38 "Teacher," said John, "we saw a man driving out demons in your name and we told him to stop, be-
cause he was not one of us."[k]
39 "Do not stop him," Jesus said. "No one who does a miracle in my name can in the next moment say
anything bad about me, 40 for whoever is not against us is for us.[l] 41 I tell you the truth, anyone who gives
you a cup of water in my name because you belong to Christ will certainly not lose his reward.[m]

Causing to Sin

42 "And if anyone causes one of these little ones who believe in me to sin,[n] it would be better for him
to be thrown into the sea with a large millstone tied around his neck.[o] 43 If your hand causes you to sin,[p]
cut it off. It is better for you to enter life maimed than with two hands to go into hell,[q] where the fire nev-
er goes out.[a][r] 45 And if your foot causes you to sin,[s] cut it off. It is better for you to enter life crippled than
to have two feet and be thrown into hell.[b][t] 47 And if your eye causes you to sin,[u] pluck it out. It is better
for you to enter the kingdom of God with one eye than to have two eyes and be thrown into hell,[v] 48 where

" 'their worm does not die,
and the fire is not quenched.'[c][w]

49 Everyone will be salted[x] with fire.
50 "Salt is good, but if it loses its saltiness, how can you make it salty again?[y] Have salt in yourselves,[z]
and be at peace with each other."[a]

Divorce

10 Jesus then left that place and went into the region of Judea and across the Jordan.[b] Again crowds
of people came to him, and as was his custom, he taught them.[c]
2 Some Pharisees[d] came and tested him by asking, "Is it lawful for a man to divorce his wife?"
3 "What did Moses command you?" he replied.
4 They said, "Moses permitted a man to write a certificate of divorce and send her away."[e]
5 "It was because your hearts were hard[f] that Moses wrote you this law," Jesus replied. 6 "But at the be-
ginning of creation God 'made them male and female.'[d][g] 7 'For this reason a man will leave his father and
mother and be united to his wife,[e] 8 and the two will become one flesh.'[f][h] So they are no longer two, but
one. 9 Therefore what God has joined together, let man not separate."

9:31 [a]ver 12; Ac 2:23; 3:13 [b]Mt 16:21 [c]Mt 16:21
9:32 [d]Lk 2:50; 9:45; 18:34; Jn 12:16
9:33 [e]Mt 4:13 [f]Mk 1:29
9:34 [g]Lk 22:24
9:35 [h]Mt 18:4; 20:26; Mk 10:43; Lk 22:26
9:36 [i]Mk 10:16
9:37 [j]Mt 10:40
9:38 [k]Nu 11:27-29
9:40 [l]Mt 12:30; Lk 11:23
9:41 [m]Mt 10:42
9:42 [n]Mt 5:29 [o]Mt 18:6; Lk 17:2
9:43 [p]Mt 5:29 [q]Mt 5:30; 18:8 [r]Mt 25:41
9:45 [s]Mt 5:29 [t]Mt 18:8
9:47 [u]Mt 5:29 [v]Mt 5:29; 18:9
9:48 [w]Isa 66:24; Mt 25:41
9:49 [x]Lev 2:13
9:50 [y]Mt 5:13; Lk 14:34,35 [z]Col 4:6 [a]Ro 12:18; 2Co 13:11; 1Th 5:13
10:1 [b]Mk 1:5; Jn 10:40; 11:7 [c]Mt 4:23; Mk 2:13; 4:2; 6:6, 34
10:2 [d]Mk 2:16
10:4 [e]Dt 24:1-4; Mt 5:31
10:5 [f]Ps 95:8; Heb 3:15
10:6 [g]Ge 1:27; 5:2
10:8 [h]Ge 2:24; 1Co 6:16

[a] 43 Some manuscripts *out,* 44*where / " 'their worm does not die, / and the fire is not quenched.'* [b] 45 Some manuscripts *hell,* 46*where / " 'their worm does not die, / and the fire is not quenched.'* [c] 48 Isaiah 66:24 [d] 6 Gen. 1:27 [e] 7 Some early manuscripts do not have *and be united to his wife.* [f] 8 Gen. 2:24

9:33 The "house" probably refers to the one belonging to Peter and Andrew (see the note on Mt 4:13). See also "Houses in the Holy Land of the First Century A.D.: Peter's House in Capernaum; Insulae" on page 1584.
9:34 Rank and status were important in the life of Jewish groups at this time.
9:35 For "sitting down," see the note on 4:1.
9:42 For "large millstone," see the note on Matthew 18:6.
9:48 Worms were always present in the rubbish dump (see the note on hell at Mt 5:22).
9:50 For "salt," see the note on Matthew 5:13.
10:1 The "region of Judea" is the Greek and Roman equivalent to the Old Testament land of Judah, essentially the southern part of the Holy Land (now exclusive of Idumea), which formerly had been the southern kingdom.
For "Jordan," see the note on 1:5.
10:2 For "Pharisees," see the note on Matthew 3:7.
Jews of that day generally agreed that divorce was lawful, the only debated issue being the acceptable grounds for it (see the note on Mt 19:3).

10When they were in the house again, the disciples asked Jesus about this. 11He answered, "Anyone
10:11 [i]Mt 5:32; Lk 16:18 who divorces his wife and marries another woman commits adultery against her.[i] 12And if she divorces
10:12 [j]Ro 7:3; 1Co 7:10,11 her husband and marries another man, she commits adultery."[j]

The Little Children and Jesus

13People were bringing little children to Jesus to have him touch them, but the disciples rebuked them.
14When Jesus saw this, he was indignant. He said to them, "Let the little children come to me, and do not
10:14 [k]Mt 25:34 hinder them, for the kingdom of God belongs to such as these.[k] 15I tell you the truth, anyone who will not
10:15 [l]Mt 18:3 receive the kingdom of God like a little child will never enter it."[l] 16And he took the children in his arms,[m]
10:16 [m]Mk 9:36 put his hands on them and blessed them.

The Rich Young Man

10:17 [n]Mk 1:40 [o]Lk 10:25; Ac 20:32 17As Jesus started on his way, a man ran up to him and fell on his knees[n] before him. "Good teacher,"
he asked, "what must I do to inherit eternal life?"[o]

18"Why do you call me good?" Jesus answered. "No one is good—except God alone. 19You know the
commandments: 'Do not murder, do not commit adultery, do not steal, do not give false testimony, do not
10:19 [p]Ex 20:12-16; Dt 5:16-20 defraud, honor your father and mother.'[a]"[p]

20"Teacher," he declared, "all these I have kept since I was a boy."

21Jesus looked at him and loved him. "One thing you lack," he said. "Go, sell everything you have and
10:21 [q]Ac 2:45 [r]Mt 6:20; Lk 12:33 [s]Mt 4:19 give to the poor,[q] and you will have treasure in heaven.[r] Then come, follow me."[s]

22At this the man's face fell. He went away sad, because he had great wealth.

10:23 [t]Ps 52:7; 62:10; 1Ti 6:9,10, 17 23Jesus looked around and said to his disciples, "How hard it is for the rich[t] to enter the kingdom of
God!"

24The disciples were amazed at his words. But Jesus said again, "Children, how hard it is[b] to enter the
10:24 [u]Mt 7:13, 14 kingdom of God![u] 25It is easier for a camel to go through the eye of a needle than for a rich man to enter
10:25 [v]Lk 12:16-20 the kingdom of God."[v]

26The disciples were even more amazed, and said to each other, "Who then can be saved?"

27Jesus looked at them and said, "With man this is impossible, but not with God; all things are possi-
10:27 [w]Mt 19:26 ble with God."[w]

10:28 [x]Mt 4:19 28Peter said to him, "We have left everything to follow you!"[x]

29"I tell you the truth," Jesus replied, "no one who has left home or brothers or sisters or mother or fa-
10:30 [y]Mt 6:33 [z]Mt 12:32 [a]Mt 25:46 ther or children or fields for me and the gospel 30will fail to receive a hundred times as much[y] in this
present age (homes, brothers, sisters, mothers, children and fields—and with them, persecutions) and
10:31 [b]Mt 19:30 in the age to come,[z] eternal life.[a] 31But many who are first will be last, and the last first."[b]

Jesus Again Predicts His Death

32They were on their way up to Jerusalem, with Jesus leading the way, and the disciples were aston-
10:32 [c]Mk 3:16-19 ished, while those who followed were afraid. Again he took the Twelve[c] aside and told them what was go-
10:33 [d]Lk 9:51 [e]Mt 8:20 [f]Mt 27:1,2 ing to happen to him. 33"We are going up to Jerusalem,"[d] he said, "and the Son of Man[e] will be betrayed
to the chief priests and teachers of the law.[f] They will condemn him to death and will hand him over to
10:34 [g]Mt 16:21 [h]Ac 2:23; 3:13 [i]Mt 16:21 [j]Mt 16:21 the Gentiles, 34who will mock him and spit on him, flog him[g] and kill him.[h] Three days later[i] he will rise."[j]

The Request of James and John

35Then James and John, the sons of Zebedee, came to him. "Teacher," they said, "we want you to do for
us whatever we ask."

36"What do you want me to do for you?" he asked.

10:37 [k]Mt 19:28 37They replied, "Let one of us sit at your right and the other at your left in your glory."[k]

[a] *19* Exodus 20:12-16; Deut. 5:16-20 [b] *24* Some manuscripts *is for those who trust in riches*

10:11 In Jewish practice, divorce was effected by the husband himself, not by a judicial authority or court.

10:20 A Jewish boy assumed personal responsibility for obeying the commandments and thus became a "son of the commandment(s)" (Aramaic, *bar mitzvah*) when he was thirteen years old.

10:25 The camel was the largest animal in the Holy Land. The vivid contrast between the largest animal and the smallest opening represents that which, humanly speaking, is impossible. (See "The Legend of the Needle's Eye Gate" on p. 1594.) There is a rabbinical parallel phrase: "an elephant through a needle's eye."

10:29–30 For a discussion of asceticism in the believer's life, see the note on Leviticus 10:9.

10:37 Being seated at the right-hand of a king was the place of honor implying prestige, power and authority. The left-hand side was reserved for the second highest in terms of importance. (See "The 'Right Hand' in Ancient Thinking" on p. 1983.)

[38]"You don't know what you are asking,"[l] Jesus said. "Can you drink the cup[m] I drink or be baptized
with the baptism I am baptized with?"[n]
[39]"We can," they answered.
Jesus said to them, "You will drink the cup I drink and be baptized with the baptism I am baptized
with,[o] [40]but to sit at my right or left is not for me to grant. These places belong to those for whom they
have been prepared."

10:38 [l]Job 38:2 [m]Mt 20:22 [n]Lk 12:50

10:39 [o]Ac 12:2; Rev 1:9

10:38 For "drink the cup," see the note on Matthew 20:22.

ARCHAEOLOGICAL SITES

NEW TESTAMENT JERICHO

MARK 10 Mark 10:46–52 tells of Jesus' healing of blind Bartimaeus as he was going out from Jericho. The same account in Luke 18:35–43, however, records that this happened as Jesus was approaching Jericho. This appears to be a contradiction in the texts, but the explanation may be very simple—that in Jesus' day there were two cities called Jericho—an Old Testament Jericho and its New Testament counterpart. The Old Testament city was located at a site now called Tell es-Sultan[1] and the New Testament city at nearby Tulul Abu el-Alayiq.

The new town, which thrived from the late second century B.C. to the destruction of Jerusalem in A.D. 70,[2] extended south and west of the mound that covered the ruins of Old Testament Jericho. The heart of the newer city was the winter palace complex built by Herod the Great, situated about 2 miles (3.2 km) southwest of Old Testament Jericho.[3] Incorporating the foundations of earlier **Hasmonean** palaces, this complex covered an area of some 35 acres and was made up of luxurious palaces, villas, gardens, pools, theaters and athletic facilities. The Jewish historian Josephus mentioned many of these palatial facilities, as well as the murder of Aristobulus III in one of the pools (Josephus, *Antiquities* 15.3.3 and *Wars* 1.22.2).

Mark related the healing of Bartimaeus to Old Testament Jericho; thus the event occurred as Jesus was leaving that city and entering its New Testament counterpart. Luke, on the other hand, associated the incident with New Testament Jericho; following this, he recounted Jesus' encounter with Zacchaeus within the town (Luke 19:1–10). Thus, Luke wrote that Bartimaeus was healed as Jesus was approaching Jericho (18:35) and then that Jesus encountered Zacchaeus as he entered and was passing through the city (19:1).

[1]See "The Walls of Jericho" on page 312. [2]See "Josephus and the Fall of Jerusalem" on page 1606., [3]See "Herod the Great" on page 1627.

The region of Jericho
Photograph courtesy of © Dr. Gary Pratico

41 When the ten heard about this, they became indignant with James and John. 42 Jesus called them
together and said, "You know that those who are regarded as rulers of the Gentiles lord it over them, and
their high officials exercise authority over them. 43 Not so with you. Instead, whoever wants to become
10:43 [p]Mk 9:35 great among you must be your servant,[p] 44 and whoever wants to be first must be slave of all. 45 For even
10:45 [q]Mt 20:28 [r]Mt 20:28 the Son of Man did not come to be served, but to serve,[q] and to give his life as a ransom for many."[r]

Blind Bartimaeus Receives His Sight

46 Then they came to Jericho. As Jesus and his disciples, together with a large crowd, were leaving the
city, a blind man, Bartimaeus (that is, the Son of Timaeus), was sitting by the roadside begging. 47 When
10:47 [s]Mk 1:24 [t]Mt 9:27 he heard that it was Jesus of Nazareth,[s] he began to shout, "Jesus, Son of David,[t] have mercy on me!"
48 Many rebuked him and told him to be quiet, but he shouted all the more, "Son of David, have mer-
cy on me!"
49 Jesus stopped and said, "Call him."
So they called to the blind man, "Cheer up! On your feet! He's calling you." 50 Throwing his cloak aside,
he jumped to his feet and came to Jesus.
51 "What do you want me to do for you?" Jesus asked him.
10:51 [u]Mt 23:7 The blind man said, "Rabbi,[u] I want to see."
10:52 [v]Mt 9:22 [w]Mt 4:19 52 "Go," said Jesus, "your faith has healed you."[v] Immediately he received his sight and followed[w] Jesus
along the road.

The Triumphal Entry

11:1 [x]Mt 21:17 [y]Mt 21:1 **11** As they approached Jerusalem and came to Bethphage and Bethany[x] at the Mount of Olives,[y]
Jesus sent two of his disciples, 2 saying to them, "Go to the village ahead of you, and just as you
11:2 [z]Nu 19:2; Dt 21:3; 1Sa 6:7 enter it, you will find a colt tied there, which no one has ever ridden.[z] Untie it and bring it here. 3 If any-
one asks you, 'Why are you doing this?' tell him, 'The Lord needs it and will send it back here shortly.' "
11:4 [a]Mk 14:16 4 They went and found a colt outside in the street, tied at a doorway.[a] As they untied it, 5 some people
standing there asked, "What are you doing, untying that colt?" 6 They answered as Jesus had told them to,
and the people let them go. 7 When they brought the colt to Jesus and threw their cloaks over it, he sat on
it. 8 Many people spread their cloaks on the road, while others spread branches they had cut in the fields.
9 Those who went ahead and those who followed shouted,

"Hosanna![a]"

11:9 [b]Ps 118:25, 26; Mt 23:39 "Blessed is he who comes in the name of the Lord!"[b][b]

10 "Blessed is the coming kingdom of our father David!"

11:10 [c]Lk 2:14 "Hosanna in the highest!"[c]

11 Jesus entered Jerusalem and went to the temple. He looked around at everything, but since it was
11:11 [d]Mt 21:12, 17 already late, he went out to Bethany with the Twelve.[d]

Jesus Clears the Temple

12 The next day as they were leaving Bethany, Jesus was hungry. 13 Seeing in the distance a fig tree in
leaf, he went to find out if it had any fruit. When he reached it, he found nothing but leaves, because it

[a] 9 A Hebrew expression meaning "Save!" which became an exclamation of praise; also in verse 10 [b] 9 Psalm 118:25,26

10:46 Jericho was a very ancient city located 5 miles (8 km) west of the Jordan and about 15 miles (24 km) northeast of Jerusalem. In Jesus' time Old Testament Jericho was largely abandoned, but a new city, south of the old one, had been commissioned by Herod the Great. Mark specified that Jesus was "leaving the city," while Luke depicted him as approaching it. Luke may have been referring to the new Jericho, while Matthew (20:29) and Mark may have intended the old city. (See "New Testament Jericho" on p. 1646.)

The presence of a blind beggar just outside the city gates, on a road pilgrims followed on the way to Jerusalem, was a common sight in that day.

10:47 For "Nazareth," see the note on Matthew 2:23.

11:1 For "Bethany," see the note on Matthew 21:17; see also "Bethany and the Tomb of Lazarus" on page 1743. The Mount of Olives was directly east of Jerusalem, rising to a height of about 2,700 feet (823 m), some 200 feet (61 m) higher than Mount Zion. Its summit commands a magnificent view of the city and especially of the temple. See "The Mount of Olives" on page 1543.

11:8 For "branches," see the note on Matthew 21:8.

11:9–10 For "Hosanna," see the note on Matthew 21:9.

11:11 For "temple," see the note on Matthew 4:5. Apparently Jesus spent each night through Thursday of Passion Week in Bethany (see the note on Mt 21:17), at the home of his friends Mary, Martha and Lazarus.

11:13 Fig trees around Jerusalem normally begin to leaf in March or April but do not produce figs until their leaves are all out in June. This tree was an exception in that it was already, at Passover time, full of leaves.

ARCHAEOLOGICAL SITES

HEROD'S TEMPLE

MARK 11 For hundreds of years the Jerusalem temple was the center of Jewish life. However, in the centuries leading up to the New Testament era, the postexilic edifice rebuilt by Zerubbabel[1] suffered serious damage. The renovation and expansion of this dilapidated structure gave Herod the Great the opportunity to construct the greatest of his numerous building projects and perhaps the most impressive structure Jerusalem has ever seen.[2]

Work on Herod's temple began in 20–19 B.C., and though most of it was finished within ten years, adornment continued until A.D. 63. Herod faced a significant challenge: The size of the temple was limited by the Biblical precedent of Solomon's temple, a fairly modest structure.[3] But pagan temples of the New Testament era were becoming increasingly mammoth, and the Jerusalem temple if confined to Biblical standards would have seemed puny in comparison. Therefore, although the temple proper was left fairly small, the temple precincts in Herod's scheme were enormous. Zerubbabel's temple had to be torn down and the three surrounding valleys filled in. Massive retaining walls helped to support the platform of the temple precinct (the western retaining wall is the familiar "Wailing Wall"). The temple and its surrounding courtyards created a rhomboid shape, measuring 1,590 feet (485 m) on its western side, 1,536 feet (468 m) on the eastern side, 1,035 feet (315.5 m) on the northern side and 912 feet (278 m) on the southern side.

The temple area was essentially a series of concentric courts, each of increasing holiness as one proceeded closer to the temple proper.

✣ The first courtyard, the court of the Gentiles, was open to Jews and God-fearing Gentiles. This area contained the merchant and money-changing areas, and here the blind and lame begged and children were present (Mt 21:14–15).[4]

✣ Only Jewish men and women could enter the court of women, which contained chests for tithes that contributed to temple expenses and was the location of the poor widow's contribution (Mk 12:44).

✣ Only ritually clean Jewish men were permitted to proceed beyond into the court of Israel. When Jesus came to the temple and "looked around at everything" (11:11), he was surveying this area.

✣ Only priests could move farther into the temple area. The approach included an altar of uncut stones, the porch and finally the temple itself. Constructed of marble and gold, the temple was built to the same specifications as Solomon's earlier counterpart. Golden spikes lined the roof to prevent birds from alighting there and defiling the structure.

✣ Entering the temple proper, one first came to the Holy Place, which contained the lampstand, the table for the bread of the Presence and the incense altar, all cast in pure gold.

✣ Separated by a heavy, embroidered curtain, the Most Holy Place contained only a single rock, upon which the high priest offered incense and sprinkled blood once annually on the Day of Atonement (the ark of the covenant had long since been lost). Some surmise that the Most Holy Place was located where the Islamic holy place, the Dome of the Rock, now stands.

Mikveh (ritual bath) south of the temple mount

Photograph: © Todd Bolen/Bible Places.com

Other important structures were within the vicinity of the temple. The Fortress of Antonia, north of the temple vicinity, was the barracks for Roman troops in Jerusalem. Soldiers from the fortress could enter the temple area quickly if needed, as when a riot broke out during Paul's visit there (Ac 21:31–32). On the south side of the temple was the house for the Sanhedrin and a bathhouse for ritual immersion (a requirement for entering the temple area).[5] As a social center, the temple was the most important locale for education and debate in Judea (Lk 2:46), as well as the backdrop for many events recorded in the Gospels, most notably Jesus' ejection of the merchants. Jesus' actions and words upon that occasion created an "enacted parable." He was angry not only at the extortion but also at the moneychangers' occupation of the court of the Gentiles, which effectively limited access to this area.

For all its glory, this temple had a short life. Completed in A.D. 63, it was destroyed in A.D. 70 by the Romans. Jesus' words to his disciples in this regard were fulfilled: Not one stone was left upon another (Mt 24:2).[6]

[1]See "The Postexilic Period of the Old Testament: The Persian Period" on page 699. [2]See "Herod the Great" on page 1627. [3]See "Solomon's Temple and Other Ancient Temples" on page 620. [4]See "The Dividing Wall of the 'Court of the Gentiles' in Herod's Temple" on page 1917. [5]See "Baptism in the Ancient World" on page 1562. [6]See "Josephus and the Fall of Jerusalem" on page 1606.

11:13 [e]Lk 13:6-9 was not the season for figs.[e] 14 Then he said to the tree, "May no one ever eat fruit from you again." And
his disciples heard him say it.
15 On reaching Jerusalem, Jesus entered the temple area and began driving out those who were buy-
ing and selling there. He overturned the tables of the money changers and the benches of those selling
doves, 16 and would not allow anyone to carry merchandise through the temple courts. 17 And as he taught
them, he said, "Is it not written:

" 'My house will be called
11:17 [f]Isa 56:7 [g]Jer 7:11 a house of prayer for all nations'[a]?[f]

But you have made it 'a den of robbers.'[b]"[g]
18 The chief priests and the teachers of the law heard this and began looking for a way to kill him, for
11:18 [h]Mt 21:46; Mk 12:12; Lk 20:19 [i]Mt 7:28 they feared him,[h] because the whole crowd was amazed at his teaching.[i]
11:19 [j]Lk 21:37 19 When evening came, they[c] went out of the city.[j]

The Withered Fig Tree

20 In the morning, as they went along, they saw the fig tree withered from the roots. 21 Peter remem-
11:21 [k]Mt 23:7 bered and said to Jesus, "Rabbi,[k] look! The fig tree you cursed has withered!"
22 "Have[d] faith in God," Jesus answered. 23 "I tell you the truth, if anyone says to this mountain, 'Go,
throw yourself into the sea,' and does not doubt in his heart but believes that what he says will happen,
11:23 [l]Mt 21:21 it will be done for him.[l] 24 Therefore I tell you, whatever you ask for in prayer, believe that you have received
11:24 [m]Mt 7:7 it, and it will be yours.[m] 25 And when you stand praying, if you hold anything against anyone, forgive him,
11:25 [n]Mt 6:14 so that your Father in heaven may forgive you your sins.[e]"[n]

The Authority of Jesus Questioned

27 They arrived again in Jerusalem, and while Jesus was walking in the temple courts, the chief priests,
the teachers of the law and the elders came to him. 28 "By what authority are you doing these things?"
they asked. "And who gave you authority to do this?"
29 Jesus replied, "I will ask you one question. Answer me, and I will tell you by what authority I am do-
ing these things. 30 John's baptism—was it from heaven, or from men? Tell me!"
31 They discussed it among themselves and said, "If we say, 'From heaven,' he will ask, 'Then why didn't
you believe him?' 32 But if we say, 'From men' . . ." (They feared the people, for everyone held that John
11:32 [o]Mt 11:9 really was a prophet.)[o]
33 So they answered Jesus, "We don't know."
Jesus said, "Neither will I tell you by what authority I am doing these things."

The Parable of the Tenants

12:1 [p]Isa 5:1-7 12 He then began to speak to them in parables: "A man planted a vineyard.[p] He put a wall around
it, dug a pit for the winepress and built a watchtower. Then he rented the vineyard to some farm-
ers and went away on a journey. 2 At harvest time he sent a servant to the tenants to collect from them
some of the fruit of the vineyard. 3 But they seized him, beat him and sent him away empty-handed.
4 Then he sent another servant to them; they struck this man on the head and treated him shamefully.

[a] 17 Isaiah 56:7 [b] 17 Jer. 7:11 [c] 19 Some early manuscripts *he* [d] 22 Some early manuscripts *If you have* [e] 25 Some manuscripts *sins.* *26But if you do not forgive, neither will your Father who is in heaven forgive your sins.*

11:14 A fully leafed tree normally would have fruit, but Jesus cursed this one because it had none.

11:15 The "temple area" was the court of the Gentiles, the only part of the temple in which Gentiles were permitted to worship God and gather for prayer. Pilgrims attending the Passover Feast needed animals that met the ritual requirements for sacrifice, and the vendors set up their animal pens and money tables in the court of the Gentiles. Pilgrims also needed their money changed into the local currency because the annual temple tax (see the note on Mt 17:24) had to be paid in that currency.

11:16 Apparently the temple area was being used as a shortcut between the city and the Mount of Olives.

11:17 By allowing the court of the Gentiles to become a noisy, smelly marketplace, the Jewish religious leaders were interfering with God's provision of a "house of prayer for all nations."

11:18 For "chief priests" and "teachers of the law," see the note on Matthew 2:4.

11:23 The Dead Sea is visible from the Mount of Olives.

11:27 For "temple courts," see the note on Matthew 21:23. For "chief priests" and "teachers of the law," see the note on Matthew 2:4; for "elders," see the note on Matthew 21:23.

11:30 "Heaven" was a common Jewish substitute for the divine name, substituted in order to avoid a possible misuse of God's name.

12:1–12 In first-century Galilee large estates, owned by absentee landlords, were put in the hands of local peasants who cultivated the land as tenant farmers.

12:1 For "watchtower," see the note on Matthew 21:33.

12:2 In accordance with a kind of sharecropping agreement (see the note on vv. 1–12), a fixed amount was due the landowner. At the proper time he would have expected to receive his share.

5 He sent still another, and that one they killed. He sent many others; some of them they beat, others they killed.

6 "He had one left to send, a son, whom he loved. He sent him last of all,[q] saying, 'They will respect my son.'

12:6 [q]Heb 1:1-3

7 "But the tenants said to one another, 'This is the heir. Come, let's kill him, and the inheritance will be ours.' 8 So they took him and killed him, and threw him out of the vineyard.

9 "What then will the owner of the vineyard do? He will come and kill those tenants and give the vineyard to others. 10 Haven't you read this scripture:

> " 'The stone the builders rejected
> has become the capstone[a];[r]
> 11 the Lord has done this,
> and it is marvelous in our eyes'[b]?"[s]

12:10 [r]Ac 4:11
12:11 [s]Ps 118:22,23

12 Then they looked for a way to arrest him because they knew he had spoken the parable against them. But they were afraid of the crowd;[t] so they left him and went away.[u]

12:12 [t]Mk 11:18 [u]Mt 22:22

Paying Taxes to Caesar

13 Later they sent some of the Pharisees and Herodians[v] to Jesus to catch him[w] in his words. 14 They came to him and said, "Teacher, we know you are a man of integrity. You aren't swayed by men, because you pay no attention to who they are; but you teach the way of God in accordance with the truth. Is it right to pay taxes to Caesar or not? 15 Should we pay or shouldn't we?"

12:13 [v]Mt 22:16; Mk 3:6 [w]Mt 12:10

But Jesus knew their hypocrisy. "Why are you trying to trap me?" he asked. "Bring me a denarius and let me look at it." 16 They brought the coin, and he asked them, "Whose portrait is this? And whose inscription?"

"Caesar's," they replied.

17 Then Jesus said to them, "Give to Caesar what is Caesar's and to God what is God's."[x]

12:17 [x]Ro 13:7

And they were amazed at him.

Marriage at the Resurrection

18 Then the Sadducees,[y] who say there is no resurrection,[z] came to him with a question. 19 "Teacher," they said, "Moses wrote for us that if a man's brother dies and leaves a wife but no children, the man must marry the widow and have children for his brother.[a] 20 Now there were seven brothers. The first one married and died without leaving any children. 21 The second one married the widow, but he also died, leaving no child. It was the same with the third. 22 In fact, none of the seven left any children. Last of all, the woman died too. 23 At the resurrection[c] whose wife will she be, since the seven were married to her?"

12:18 [y]Ac 4:1 [z]Ac 23:8; 1Co 15:12
12:19 [a]Dt 25:5

24 Jesus replied, "Are you not in error because you do not know the Scriptures[b] or the power of God? 25 When the dead rise, they will neither marry nor be given in marriage; they will be like the angels in heaven.[c] 26 Now about the dead rising—have you not read in the book of Moses, in the account of the bush, how God said to him, 'I am the God of Abraham, the God of Isaac, and the God of Jacob'[d]?[d] 27 He is not the God of the dead, but of the living. You are badly mistaken!"

12:24 [b]2Ti 3:15-17
12:25 [c]1Co 15:42,49,52
12:26 [d]Ex 3:6

The Greatest Commandment

28 One of the teachers of the law[e] came and heard them debating. Noticing that Jesus had given them a good answer, he asked him, "Of all the commandments, which is the most important?"

12:28 [e]Lk 10:25-28; 20:39

29 "The most important one," answered Jesus, "is this: 'Hear, O Israel, the Lord our God, the Lord is

[a] 10 Or *cornerstone* [b] 11 Psalm 118:22,23 [c] 23 Some manuscripts *resurrection, when men rise from the dead,*
[d] 26 Exodus 3:6

12:13 For "Herodians," see the note on 3:6.
12:14 Subject peoples were required to pay a poll tax to the Roman emperor (see "Roman Taxation" on p. 1855). The tax was highly unpopular, and some Jews flatly refused to pay it, believing that doing so constituted an admission of the Roman right to rule.
12:15 For "denarius," see the notes on Matthew 20:2 and 22:19.
12:16 See "Tiberius Caesar, the Caesar of Jesus' Ministry" on page 1708 and "The Imperial Cult" on page 1651.
12:18 For "Sadducees," see the note on Matthew 3:7. The Sadducees denied the resurrection (see the note on Mt 22:23).
12:19 See the note on Matthew 22:24.
12:28 Jewish rabbis counted 613 individual statutes in the law and attempted to differentiate between "heavy" (or "great") and "light" (or "little") commands.
12:29 This Old Testament citation came to be known as the *Shema,* named after the first word of Deuteronomy 6:4 in Hebrew, which means "hear." The Shema became the Jewish confession of faith, recited by pious Jews every morning and evening. To this day its recitation begins every synagogue service.

one.[a] 30 Love the Lord your God with all your heart and with all your soul and with all your mind and with
all your strength.'[b][f] 31 The second is this: 'Love your neighbor as yourself.'[c][g] There is no commandment
greater than these."
32 "Well said, teacher," the man replied. "You are right in saying that God is one and there is no other
but him.[h] 33 To love him with all your heart, with all your understanding and with all your strength, and
to love your neighbor as yourself is more important than all burnt offerings and sacrifices."[i]
34 When Jesus saw that he had answered wisely, he said to him, "You are not far from the kingdom of
God."[j] And from then on no one dared ask him any more questions.[k]

[a] *29* Or *the Lord our God is one Lord* [b] *30* Deut. 6:4,5 [c] *31* Lev. 19:18

12:30 [f]Dt 6:4,5 **12:31** [g]Lev 19:18; Mt 5:43 **12:32** [h]Dt 4:35, 39; Isa 45:6,14; 46:9 **12:33** [i]1Sa 15:22; Hos 6:6; Mic 6:6-8; Heb 10:8 **12:34** [j]Mt 3:2 [k]Mt 22:46; Lk 20:40

The Imperial Cult

MARK 12 The Roman imperial cult was essentially a "religion" based upon the deification of Roman emperors. It had its origins in eastern and Greek practices, in which kings were often said to be gods. Roman emperors were regularly deified after their deaths by an act of the Senate. The attribution of deity was seen as the highest possible manifestation of gratitude and honor, and participation in the imperial cult was a religious way of expressing gratitude for the benefits experienced during that emperor's rule. There was no expectation that the deified emperor would continue to intervene in human affairs, and sacrifices were also made to the "genius," or spirit, embodied in his current, living successor.

The imperial cult had both a religious and a political function, serving as a unifying factor in the empire and as a test of loyalty.[1] Refusal to participate in the cult by offering sacrifices in honor of the emperor could result in execution. The New Testament's central confession that "Jesus is Lord," as well as references to Christ as "Savior" and the "Son of God," while based upon Jewish and Christian theology, also served to undermine the lofty assertions of the imperial cult. The silver denarius[2] mentioned in Mark 12:15 bore the image of the emperor Tiberius and the inscription "Augustus Tiberius Caesar, Son of the Divine Augustus," reflecting both the deification of Augustus and Tiberius's desire to highlight his filial relationship to his deified predecessor.[3]

Temple to Caesar near the Cave of Pan at Caesarea Philippi

Preserving Bible Times; © Dr. James C. Martin

The imperial cult placed early Christians in the empire in a dilemma. On the one hand the cult was fundamentally a manifestation of the antichrist, while on the other, Christians were called upon to respect the institution and power of government (Ro 13). This quandary was anticipated in the Jews' question about paying taxes, and Jesus' answer pointed to a paradox of the Christian life: Believers, though *in* the world, are not to be *of* it.

[1]See "The Roman Empire" on page 1845. [2]See "Coins and Numismatics" on page 1699. [3]See "Caesar Augustus, Emperor of Rome; the Census; and Quirinius, Governor of Syria" on page 1667 and "Tiberius Caesar, the Caesar of Jesus' Ministry" on page 1708.

Whose Son Is the Christ?

35 While Jesus was teaching in the temple courts,[l] he asked, "How is it that the teachers of the law say 12:35 [l]Mt 26:55
that the Christ[a] is the son of David?[m] 36 David himself, speaking by the Holy Spirit,[n] declared: [m]Mt 9:27 12:36 [n]2Sa 23:2

" 'The Lord said to my Lord: [o]Ps 110:1; Mt 22:44
"Sit at my right hand
until I put your enemies
under your feet." '[b][o]

37 David himself calls him 'Lord.' How then can he be his son?"

The large crowd[p] listened to him with delight. 12:37 [p]Jn 12:9

38 As he taught, Jesus said, "Watch out for the teachers of the law. They like to walk around in flowing
robes and be greeted in the marketplaces, 39 and have the most important seats in the synagogues and
the places of honor at banquets.[q] 40 They devour widows' houses and for a show make lengthy prayers. 12:39 [q]Lk 11:43
Such men will be punished most severely."

The Widow's Offering

41 Jesus sat down opposite the place where the offerings were put[r] and watched the crowd putting their 12:41 [r]2Ki 12:9; Jn 8:20
money into the temple treasury. Many rich people threw in large amounts. 42 But a poor widow came and
put in two very small copper coins,[c] worth only a fraction of a penny.[d]

43 Calling his disciples to him, Jesus said, "I tell you the truth, this poor widow has put more into the
treasury than all the others. 44 They all gave out of their wealth; but she, out of her poverty, put in every-
thing—all she had to live on."[s] 12:44 [s]2Co 8:12

Signs of the End of the Age

13 As he was leaving the temple, one of his disciples said to him, "Look, Teacher! What massive
stones! What magnificent buildings!"

2 "Do you see all these great buildings?" replied Jesus. "Not one stone here will be left on another; ev-
ery one will be thrown down."[t] 13:2 [t]Lk 19:44

3 As Jesus was sitting on the Mount of Olives[u] opposite the temple, Peter, James, John[v] and Andrew 13:3 [u]Mt 21:1 [v]Mt 4:21
asked him privately, 4 "Tell us, when will these things happen? And what will be the sign that they are all
about to be fulfilled?"

5 Jesus said to them: "Watch out that no one deceives you.[w] 6 Many will come in my name, claiming, 'I 13:5 [w]ver 22; Jer 29:8; Eph 5:6;
am he,' and will deceive many. 7 When you hear of wars and rumors of wars, do not be alarmed. Such things 2Th 2:3,10-12;
must happen, but the end is still to come. 8 Nation will rise against nation, and kingdom against kingdom. 1Ti 4:1; 2Ti 3:13; 1Jn 4:6
There will be earthquakes in various places, and famines. These are the beginning of birth pains.

9 "You must be on your guard. You will be handed over to the local councils and flogged in the syna-
gogues.[x] On account of me you will stand before governors and kings as witnesses to them. 10 And the 13:9 [x]Mt 10:17

[a] 35 Or *Messiah* [b] 36 Psalm 110:1 [c] 42 Greek *two lepta* [d] 42 Greek *kodrantes*

12:38–40 Jesus denounced the teachers of the law: (1) They wore special clothing—long robes that were fringed and almost reached to the ground; see "Fringe (Tassels) on Garments" on page 217—to set themselves apart from others and to boost their authority. (2) They basked in the esteem of those of lesser status. (3) They used their position to prey on the weak and vulnerable. (4) Instead of being humbly directed to God, their prayers were spoken to impress those listening. See also the note on Matthew 2:4.

12:38 For the multiple functions of the *agora*, or marketplace, see the note on Matthew 11:16–17, as well as "The Ancient Agora" on page 1799.

12:39 The synagogue had a bench positioned in front of the "ark" containing the sacred scrolls. Those who sat there were held in high honor and could be seen by all the worshipers in the synagogue. The great synagogue in Alexandria had 71 such seats, which were occupied by members of the great council of that city.

12:40 Since the teachers of the law (see the note on Mt 2:4) were not paid a regular wage, they were dependent upon the generosity of patrons for their livelihood. Such a system was open to abuses, and widows were especially vulnerable to exploitation.

12:41 The temple treasury was located in the court of the women, east of Herod's temple. Both men and women were allowed in this court, but women could go no farther into the temple buildings. In the court of women were 13 trumpet-shaped receptacles, shaped like inverted megaphones and positioned to receive the donations of the worshipers.

12:42 The smallest coins then in circulation in the Holy Land were small copper coins (see "Coins and Numismatics" on p. 1699).

13:1–37 Mark's is the Gospel of action. Only one long message of Jesus is recorded, the Olivet Discourse summarized in this chapter. Mark included 18 miracles of Jesus, about the same number as did Matthew or Luke. In contrast, though, he recounted only 4 of the parables, compared with 18 in Matthew and 19 in Luke.

13:1 According to Josephus (*Antiquities,* 15.11.3), these "massive stones" were white and some of them were 37 feet (11.3 m) high and 18 feet (5.5 m) wide. See also the note on Luke 21:5.

13:3 For "Mount of Olives," see the note on 11:1.

13:8 See the note on famine at Ruth 1:1. Also see "Famine in the Ancient Near East" on page 70.

13:9 For "local councils," see the note on Matthew 10:17.

Infraction of Jewish regulations was punishable by flogging, the maximum penalty being 39 strokes with a whip. (For a comparison to Roman flogging, see the note on Mt 27:26.)

For "synagogues," see the note on Mark 1:21.

gospel must first be preached to all nations. 11 Whenever you are arrested and brought to trial, do not
worry beforehand about what to say. Just say whatever is given you at the time, for it is not you speak-
13:11 [y]Mt 10:19, 20; Lk 12:11,12 ing, but the Holy Spirit.[y]
12 "Brother will betray brother to death, and a father his child. Children will rebel against their parents
13:12 [z]Mic 7:6; Mt 10:21; Lk 12:51-53 and have them put to death.[z] 13 All men will hate you because of me,[a] but he who stands firm to the end
will be saved.[b]
13:13 [a]Jn 15:21 [b]Mt 10:22 14 "When you see 'the abomination that causes desolation'[a][c] standing where it[b] does not belong—let
13:14 [c]Da 9:27; 11:31; 12:11 the reader understand—then let those who are in Judea flee to the mountains. 15 Let no one on the roof
of his house go down or enter the house to take anything out. 16 Let no one in the field go back to get his
13:17 [d]Lk 23:29 cloak. 17 How dreadful it will be in those days for pregnant women and nursing mothers![d] 18 Pray that this
will not take place in winter, 19 because those will be days of distress unequaled from the beginning, when
13:19 [e]Mk 10:6 [f]Da 9:26; 12:1; Joel 2:2 God created the world,[e] until now—and never to be equaled again.[f] 20 If the Lord had not cut short those
days, no one would survive. But for the sake of the elect, whom he has chosen, he has shortened them.
13:21 [g]Lk 17:23; 21:8 21 At that time if anyone says to you, 'Look, here is the Christ[c]!' or, 'Look, there he is!' do not believe it.[g]
13:22 [h]Mt 7:15 [i]Jn 4:48; 2Th 2:9, 10 22 For false Christs and false prophets[h] will appear and perform signs and miracles[i] to deceive the elect—
if that were possible. 23 So be on your guard;[j] I have told you everything ahead of time.
13:23 [j]2Pe 3:17 24 "But in those days, following that distress,

" 'the sun will be darkened,
and the moon will not give its light;
25 the stars will fall from the sky,
13:25 [k]Isa 13:10; 34:4; Mt 24:29 and the heavenly bodies will be shaken.'[d][k]

13:26 [l]Da 7:13; Mt 16:27; Rev 1:7 26 "At that time men will see the Son of Man coming in clouds[l] with great power and glory. 27 And he
will send his angels and gather his elect from the four winds, from the ends of the earth to the ends of
13:27 [m]Zec 2:6 the heavens.[m]
28 "Now learn this lesson from the fig tree: As soon as its twigs get tender and its leaves come out, you
know that summer is near. 29 Even so, when you see these things happening, you know that it is near,
13:30 [n]Lk 17:25 [o]Mk 9:1 right at the door. 30 I tell you the truth, this generation[e][n] will certainly not pass away until all these things
13:31 [p]Mt 5:18 have happened.[o] 31 Heaven and earth will pass away, but my words will never pass away.[p]

The Day and Hour Unknown

32 "No one knows about that day or hour, not even the angels in heaven, nor the Son, but only the Fa-
13:32 [q]Ac 1:7; 1Th 5:1,2 ther.[q] 33 Be on guard! Be alert[f]![r] You do not know when that time will come. 34 It's like a man going away:
13:33 [r]1Th 5:6 13:34 [s]Mt 25:14 He leaves his house and puts his servants[s] in charge, each with his assigned task, and tells the one at the
door to keep watch.
35 "Therefore keep watch because you do not know when the owner of the house will come back—
whether in the evening, or at midnight, or when the rooster crows, or at dawn. 36 If he comes suddenly,
13:37 [t]Lk 12:35-40 do not let him find you sleeping. 37 What I say to you, I say to everyone: 'Watch!' "[t]

Jesus Anointed at Bethany

14:1 [u]Jn 11:55; 13:1 [v]Mt 12:14 **14** Now the Passover[u] and the Feast of Unleavened Bread were only two days away, and the chief
priests and the teachers of the law were looking for some sly way to arrest Jesus and kill him.[v]
2 "But not during the Feast," they said, "or the people may riot."

[a] *14* Daniel 9:27; 11:31; 12:11 [b] *14* Or *he*; also in verse 29 [c] *21* Or *Messiah* [d] *25* Isaiah 13:10; 34:4 [e] *30* Or *race*
[f] *33* Some manuscripts *alert and pray*

13:14 For "abomination that causes desolation," see the note on Matthew 24:15.
13:15 For "roof," see the notes on 2:4 and Luke 17:31.
13:16 For "cloak," see the note on Matthew 5:40; see also "Ancient Israelite Clothing and Jewelry" on page 1059 and "Dress and Fashion in the Greco-Roman World" on page 2004.
13:18 The winter was the time when heavy rains caused streams to become swollen and impossible to cross, preventing many unfortunate people and animals from reaching a place of refuge.
13:28 See the note on 11:13.
13:32 For "that day," see the note on Joel 1:15.
13:35 This verse includes all four watches of the night used by the Romans (see the note on Mt 14:25).
14:1 The lambs used in the Passover (see "The Passover" on p. 656) were killed on the fourteenth day of Nisan (March-April), and the meal was eaten the same evening between sundown and midnight. Since the Jewish day began at sundown, the Passover feast took place on the fifteenth of Nisan.
The Feast of Unleavened Bread followed the Passover and lasted seven days (see "The Festivals of Israel" on p. 186).
For "chief priests" and "teachers of the law," see the note on Matthew 2:4.
14:2 During the Passover and the week-long Feast of Unleavened Bread, the population of Jerusalem increased from about 50,000 to several hundred thousand. It would have been too risky to apprehend Jesus with so large and excitable a crowd present.

CULTURAL AND HISTORICAL NOTES

The Upper Room

The Madaba Map
Preserving Bible Times; © Dr. James C. Martin

MARK 14 Christian tradition, supported by Cyril of Jerusalem (c. 310–386), identifies the site of Holy Zion Church in Jerusalem as the place where the upper room was located. This may well be correct, but the story is complicated and details are disputed by scholars.

First, it is unclear whether there were one or two "upper rooms." Mark 14:15 and Luke 22:12 each speaks of an upper room where the Last Supper was held,[1] but Acts 1:13 uses a different Greek word to refer to the upper room where the disciples met after the resurrection of Jesus. Even so, the two rooms may well have been one and the same.

The traditional location of the upper room at Holy Zion Church is called the Cenacle or, in Latin, the *Coenaculum.* It is located outside the Old City near the Zion Gate and may be seen on the sixth-century Madaba Map, an ancient mosaic map of the Holy Land. The Cenacle is also (erroneously) referred to as David's Tomb.

Holy Zion Church was damaged in the 1948 war, and this allowed Israeli archaeologist Jacob Pinkerfeld to investigate the site. He concluded that a Roman-period synagogue had stood on the spot, arguing that the building had a niche that could have been a repository for Torah scrolls and that it was oriented toward the temple mount. Christian scholars responded that this was probably a Jewish-Christian church built after the fall of Jerusalem in A.D. 70[2] to commemorate the site of the Last Supper (the present-day Holy Zion Church being a later structure built at the same site). They note that the building appears to have been constructed from reused stone from the fallen temple of Herod[3] and that it is actually oriented toward the Holy Sepulchre (obviously implying that the builders were Christian). Since then numerous scholars have weighed in on both sides of the issue, some favoring the interpretation of the structure as a synagogue and others as a church. The debate is also complicated by questions involving comments by ancient writers.

No one is suggesting that the actual building where the Last Supper took place has been located, but only that remains of a church that commemorated its location have been unearthed. We should note that the debate here centers not upon the historicity of the Last Supper account but simply upon whether or not the traditional identification of its location is accurate. The traditional Cenacle still remains the strongest candidate for being that location.

[1]See "The Last Supper and the Passover" on page 1611. [2]See "Josephus and the Fall of Jerusalem" on page 1606. [3]See "Herod's Temple" on page 1648.

14:3 [w]Mt 21:17 3 While he was in Bethany,[w] reclining at the table in the home of a man known as Simon the Leper, a
[x]Lk 7:37-39 woman came with an alabaster jar of very expensive perfume, made of pure nard. She broke the jar and
poured the perfume on his head.[x]
4 Some of those present were saying indignantly to one another, "Why this waste of perfume? 5 It could
have been sold for more than a year's wages[a] and the money given to the poor." And they rebuked her
harshly.
6 "Leave her alone," said Jesus. "Why are you bothering her? She has done a beautiful thing to me. 7 The
14:7 [y]Dt 15:11 poor you will always have with you, and you can help them any time you want.[y] But you will not always
have me. 8 She did what she could. She poured perfume on my body beforehand to prepare for my buri-
14:8 [z]Jn 19:40 14:9 [a]Mt 24:14; al.[z] 9 I tell you the truth, wherever the gospel is preached throughout the world,[a] what she has done will
Mk 16:15 also be told, in memory of her."
14:10 [b]Mk 3:16-19 10 Then Judas Iscariot, one of the Twelve,[b] went to the chief priests to betray Jesus to them.[c] 11 They
[c]Mt 10:4 were delighted to hear this and promised to give him money. So he watched for an opportunity to hand
him over.

The Lord's Supper

12 On the first day of the Feast of Unleavened Bread, when it was customary to sacrifice the Passover
14:12 [d]Ex 12:1-11; Dt 16:1-4; 1Co 5:7 lamb,[d] Jesus' disciples asked him, "Where do you want us to go and make preparations for you to eat the
Passover?"
13 So he sent two of his disciples, telling them, "Go into the city, and a man carrying a jar of water will
meet you. Follow him. 14 Say to the owner of the house he enters, 'The Teacher asks: Where is my guest
14:15 [e]Ac 1:13 room, where I may eat the Passover with my disciples?' 15 He will show you a large upper room,[e] fur-
nished and ready. Make preparations for us there."
16 The disciples left, went into the city and found things just as Jesus had told them. So they prepared
the Passover.
17 When evening came, Jesus arrived with the Twelve. 18 While they were reclining at the table eating,
he said, "I tell you the truth, one of you will betray me—one who is eating with me."
19 They were saddened, and one by one they said to him, "Surely not I?"
14:20 [f]Jn 13:18-27 20 "It is one of the Twelve," he replied, "one who dips bread into the bowl with me.[f] 21 The Son of Man[g]
14:21 [g]Mt 8:20 will go just as it is written about him. But woe to that man who betrays the Son of Man! It would be bet-
ter for him if he had not been born."
14:22 [h]Mt 14:19 22 While they were eating, Jesus took bread, gave thanks and broke it,[h] and gave it to his disciples, say-
ing, "Take it; this is my body."
14:23 [i]1Co 10:16 23 Then he took the cup, gave thanks and offered it to them, and they all drank from it.[i]
14:24 [j]Mt 26:28 24 "This is my blood of the[b] covenant,[j] which is poured out for many," he said to them. 25 "I tell you the

[a] 5 Greek *than three hundred denarii* [b] 24 Some manuscripts *the new*

14:3 For "Bethany," see the note on Matthew 21:17; see also "Bethany and the Tomb of Lazarus" on page 1743.

Reclining at the table was the usual posture for eating at a banquet (see "Jewish Meals and Meal Customs" on p. 1575 and "Triclinia" on p. 1748).

An alabaster jar was a sealed flask with a long neck that was broken off when the contents were used and that contained enough ointment for one application.

"Nard" refers to an aromatic oil extracted from the roots of a perennial herb that grows in India. It was inordinately expensive (see "Perfumes and Anointing Oils" on p. 1746). Anointing was a common custom at feasts.

14:5 It was a Jewish custom to give gifts to the poor on the evening of Passover.

14:8 Another Jewish custom was to anoint a dead body with aromatic oils in preparation for burial (see the notes on 16:1 and Mt 26:12, "Jewish Burial Practices" on p. 1688 and "Perfumes and Anointing Oils" on p. 1746).

14:10 For "Iscariot," see the note on 3:19. For "chief priests," see the note on Matthew 2:4.

14:11 For "money," see the note on Matthew 26:15.

14:12 "Preparations" would have included obtaining food and drink for the meal, such as unleavened bread, wine, bitter herbs and a lamb.

14:15 The Greek word *katalyma,* used of the upper room where the Last Supper was held, as well as of the place in Bethlehem that had turned away Mary and Joseph (Lk 2:7), was probably a spare room in a private house rather than in a public inn. The vast numbers who went to Jerusalem to attend the annual feasts were allowed to use such guest chambers at no cost. Apparently Jesus had made previous arrangements with the owner of the house. For information on the "upper room," see the note on Jeremiah 22:13–14 and "The Upper Room" on page 1654.

14:18 Originally the Passover meal was eaten standing (see Ex 12:11), but in Jesus' time it was customary to partake of it while reclining (see "Jewish Meals and Meal Customs" on p. 1575 and "Triclinia" on p. 1748).

14:20 See the note on Matthew 26:23.

14:22 At Jewish meals the head of the family would take the bread to be eaten, lift it up and praise God for his provision. After an "Amen" response, the bread would be broken, mediating the blessing to everyone who would partake. The same was true of the wine. By stating, "This is my body," Jesus was saying in effect, "This is myself." To the people around the table, a person's body represented or encompassed the whole person. Mark made it clear that all who were present drank from one cup. Drinking the cup of someone else meant entering into a communion relationship with that person, to the point of sharing his or her destiny, for good or ill.

14:23 The word "Eucharist," often used to refer to the Lord's Supper, is derived from the Greek term here translated "gave thanks."

14:24 For "blood of the covenant," see "The Last Supper and the Passover" on page 1611.

truth, I will not drink again of the fruit of the vine until that day when I drink it anew in the kingdom of
God."[k] 14:25 [k]Mt 3:2

26 When they had sung a hymn, they went out to the Mount of Olives.[l] 14:26 [l]Mt 21:1

Jesus Predicts Peter's Denial

27 "You will all fall away," Jesus told them, "for it is written:

> " 'I will strike the shepherd,
> and the sheep will be scattered.'[a][m] 14:27 [m]Zec 13:7

28 But after I have risen, I will go ahead of you into Galilee."[n] 14:28 [n]Mk 16:7

29 Peter declared, "Even if all fall away, I will not."

30 "I tell you the truth," Jesus answered, "today—yes, tonight—before the rooster crows twice[b] you
yourself will disown me three times."[o] 14:30 [o]ver 66-72; Lk 22:34; Jn 13:38

31 But Peter insisted emphatically, "Even if I have to die with you,[p] I will never disown you." And all the
others said the same. 14:31 [p]Lk 22:33; Jn 13:37

Gethsemane

32 They went to a place called Gethsemane, and Jesus said to his disciples, "Sit here while I pray."
33 He took Peter, James and John[q] along with him, and he began to be deeply distressed and troubled. 14:33 [q]Mt 4:21
34 "My soul is overwhelmed with sorrow to the point of death,"[r] he said to them. "Stay here and keep 14:34 [r]Jn 12:27
watch."

35 Going a little farther, he fell to the ground and prayed that if possible the hour[s] might pass from 14:35 [s]ver 41; Mt 26:18
him. 36 "*Abba*,[c] Father,"[t] he said, "everything is possible for you. Take this cup[u] from me. Yet not what I 14:36 [t]Ro 8:15; Gal 4:6 [u]Mt 20:22
will, but what you will."[v] [v]Mt 26:39

37 Then he returned to his disciples and found them sleeping. "Simon," he said to Peter, "are you asleep?
Could you not keep watch for one hour? 38 Watch and pray so that you will not fall into temptation.[w] The 14:38 [w]Mt 6:13
spirit is willing, but the body is weak."[x] [x]Ro 7:22,23

39 Once more he went away and prayed the same thing. 40 When he came back, he again found them
sleeping, because their eyes were heavy. They did not know what to say to him.

41 Returning the third time, he said to them, "Are you still sleeping and resting? Enough! The hour[y] 14:41 [y]ver 35; Mt 26:18
has come. Look, the Son of Man is betrayed into the hands of sinners. 42 Rise! Let us go! Here comes my
betrayer!"

Jesus Arrested

43 Just as he was speaking, Judas,[z] one of the Twelve, appeared. With him was a crowd armed with 14:43 [z]Mt 10:4
swords and clubs, sent from the chief priests, the teachers of the law, and the elders.

44 Now the betrayer had arranged a signal with them: "The one I kiss is the man; arrest him and lead
him away under guard." 45 Going at once to Jesus, Judas said, "Rabbi!"[a] and kissed him. 46 The men seized 14:45 [a]Mt 23:7
Jesus and arrested him. 47 Then one of those standing near drew his sword and struck the servant of the
high priest, cutting off his ear.

48 "Am I leading a rebellion," said Jesus, "that you have come out with swords and clubs to capture me?
49 Every day I was with you, teaching in the temple courts,[b] and you did not arrest me. But the Scriptures 14:49 [b]Mt 26:55 [c]Isa 53:7-12; Mt 1:22
must be fulfilled."[c] 50 Then everyone deserted him and fled.[d] 14:50 [d]ver 27

[a] 27 Zech. 13:7 [b] 30 Some early manuscripts do not have *twice.* [c] 36 Aramaic for *Father*

14:26 For "hymn," see the note on Matthew 26:30. For "Mount of Olives," see the note on Mark 11:1.
14:32 For "Gethsemane," see the note on Matthew 26:36–56.
14:36 For the use of the Aramaic language in New Testament times, see the note on Matthew 27:46.
14:43 The "crowd armed with swords and clubs" refers to the auxiliary police or servants of the court assigned to the task of maintaining public order beyond the precincts of the temple. John 18:3 indicates that at least some of the Roman cohort of soldiers were in the arresting group, along with officers of the temple guard. The fact that some carried clubs suggests that they were conscripted at the last moment.

For "chief priests" and "teachers of the law," see the note on Matthew 2:4. The warrant for Jesus' arrest had been issued by the Sanhedrin (see the note on Mark 14:55), the ruling Jewish council.
14:45 A kiss reflecting mutual trust and affection is still common in the Near East, corresponding to the handshake of the Western world. Rabbis were customarily greeted by their disciples with a kiss. See "The Jewish Custom of Kissing" on page 1682.
14:49 For "temple courts," see the note on Matthew 21:23.

51 A young man, wearing nothing but a linen garment, was following Jesus. When they seized him,
52 he fled naked, leaving his garment behind.

Before the Sanhedrin

53 They took Jesus to the high priest, and all the chief priests, elders and teachers of the law came to-
14:54 [e]Mt 26:3 [f]Jn 18:18 gether. 54 Peter followed him at a distance, right into the courtyard of the high priest.[e] There he sat with
the guards and warmed himself at the fire.[f]
14:55 [g]Mt 5:22 55 The chief priests and the whole Sanhedrin[g] were looking for evidence against Jesus so that they
could put him to death, but they did not find any. 56 Many testified falsely against him, but their state-
ments did not agree.
57 Then some stood up and gave this false testimony against him: 58 "We heard him say, 'I will destroy
14:58 [h]Mk 15:29; Jn 2:19 this man-made temple and in three days will build another,[h] not made by man.' " 59 Yet even then their
testimony did not agree.
60 Then the high priest stood up before them and asked Jesus, "Are you not going to answer? What is this
14:61 [i]Isa 53:7; Mt 27:12,14; Mk 15:5; Lk 23:9; Jn 19:9 [j]Mt 16:16; Jn 4:25,26 testimony that these men are bringing against you?" 61 But Jesus remained silent and gave no answer.[i]
Again the high priest asked him, "Are you the Christ,[a] the Son of the Blessed One?"[j]
62 "I am," said Jesus. "And you will see the Son of Man sitting at the right hand of the Mighty One and
14:62 [k]Rev 1:7 coming on the clouds of heaven."[k]
14:63 [l]Lev 10:6; 21:10; Nu 14:6; Ac 14:14 63 The high priest tore his clothes.[l] "Why do we need any more witnesses?" he asked. 64 "You have heard
the blasphemy. What do you think?"
14:64 [m]Lev 24:16 They all condemned him as worthy of death.[m] 65 Then some began to spit at him; they blindfolded
14:65 [n]Mt 16:21 him, struck him with their fists, and said, "Prophesy!" And the guards took him and beat him.[n]

Peter Disowns Jesus

14:66 [o]ver 54 66 While Peter was below in the courtyard,[o] one of the servant girls of the high priest came by. 67 When
14:67 [p]ver 54 [q]Mk 1:24 she saw Peter warming himself,[p] she looked closely at him.
"You also were with that Nazarene, Jesus,"[q] she said.
14:68 [r]ver 30,72 68 But he denied it. "I don't know or understand what you're talking about,"[r] he said, and went out into
the entryway.[b]
69 When the servant girl saw him there, she said again to those standing around, "This fellow is one
14:70 [s]ver 30,68, 72 [t]Ac 2:7 of them." 70 Again he denied it.[s]
After a little while, those standing near said to Peter, "Surely you are one of them, for you are a Galilean."[t]
71 He began to call down curses on himself, and he swore to them, "I don't know this man you're talk-
14:71 [u]ver 30,72 ing about."[u]
72 Immediately the rooster crowed the second time.[c] Then Peter remembered the word Jesus had spo-
14:72 [v]ver 30,68 ken to him: "Before the rooster crows twice[d] you will disown me three times."[v] And he broke down and
wept.

[a] *61* Or *Messiah* [b] *68* Some early manuscripts *entryway and the rooster crowed* [c] *72* Some early manuscripts do not have *the second time.* [d] *72* Some early manuscripts do not have *twice.*

14:51 The outer garment was ordinarily made of wool. The fine linen garment left behind in the hand of a guard indicates that the youth was from a wealthy family. (See "Ancient Israelite Clothing and Jewelry" on p. 1059 and "Dress and Fashion in the Greco-Roman World" on p. 2004.)

14:52 The absence of an undergarment suggests that he had dressed hastily to follow Jesus.

14:53 The high priest was Caiaphas (see the note on Mt 26:3).

For "chief priests" and "teachers of the law," see the note on Matthew 2:4. For "elders," see the note on Matthew 21:23.

14:54 The Sanhedrin (see "The Sanhedrin" on p. 1821) may have met at Caiaphas's house to ensure secrecy.

14:55 The Sanhedrin was the high court of the Jew. In New Testament times it was made up of three kinds of members: chief priests, elders and teachers of the law. Its total membership numbered 71, including the high priest, who was the presiding officer. Under Roman jurisdiction the Sanhedrin was given a great deal of authority, but it could not impose capital punishment. (For information on the chief priests and teachers of the law, see the note on Mt 2:4; for information on the elders, see the note on Mt 21:23.)

14:56 In Jewish judicial procedure, witnesses functioned as the prosecution. According to the law (Dt 17:6), a person could not be put to death except on the testimony of two or more witnesses.

14:63 See the note on Matthew 26:65.

14:64 Blasphemy not only involved reviling the name of God (see Lev 24:10–16) but also included any affront to his majesty or authority (see Mk 2:7; 3:28–29). Jesus' claim to be the Messiah and, in fact, to have majesty and authority belonging to God was therefore regarded by Caiaphas as blasphemy, for which the Mosaic Law prescribed death by stoning (Lev 24:16).

14:65 A Rabbinic interpretation of Isaiah 11:2–4 held that the Messiah could judge by smell without the aid of sight.

14:67 For "Nazarene," see the note on Matthew 2:23.

The fire by which Peter warmed himself during the trial of Jesus was probably a brazier (see the note on Jer 36:22).

14:68 Peter's response was an expression used in Jewish law courts for a formal, legal denial.

14:70 Peter's dialect showed him to be from Galilee, and his presence among the Judeans in the courtyard suggested that he was a follower of Jesus.

Jesus Before Pilate

15 Very early in the morning, the chief priests, with the elders, the teachers of the law[w] and the whole Sanhedrin,[x] reached a decision. They bound Jesus, led him away and handed him over to Pilate.[y]

15:1 [w]Mt 27:1; Lk 22:66 [x]Mt 5:22 [y]Mt 27:2

15:1 The Sanhedrin (see the note on 14:55) apparently accused Jesus before the civil authority for treason rather than blasphemy (see Lk 23:1–14). For information on Pilate, see the note on Luke 3:1 and "Pontius Pilate" on page 1714.

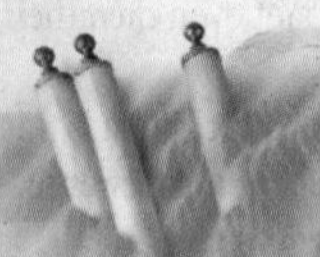

ANCIENT TEXTS AND ARTIFACTS

The Shroud of Turin Controversy

MARK 15 No other artifact in the history of scholarship has been the subject of as much debate and study as the Shroud of Turin. This piece of linen cloth is said to bear the front and rear images of a man apparently crucified in Roman fashion.[1] His injuries correspond to those suffered by Jesus. Proponents argue that this is the actual burial cloth of Christ, while opponents see to it as a clever hoax.

The History of the Shroud

The basic historical details, as we know them, are as follows:

- The shroud's first known appearance was in France in the 1350s. The original owner died in 1356 without having revealed where or how he had acquired the cloth.
- A fire in 1532 damaged the cloth, and repair patches were added.
- It has been housed in Turin since 1578.
- Some theorize that the shroud is the same as the Mandylion, a sacred relic of Constantinople that was said to have borne the divine and miraculous imprint of Jesus' face.

The Mandylion is said to have been discovered in 525 in Edessa in eastern Turkey. It found its way to the **Byzantine** capital in A.D. 944.

The shroud disappeared from Constantinople in 1204, when a crusader army looted the city. The leaders of the expedition were French, which could explain the shroud's westward journey.

Basic Facts About the Shroud

The shroud is a swath of linen cloth measuring 14 feet 3 inches (4.3 m) by 3 feet 7 inches (1.1 m). The figure on the cloth is naked, with hands folded across the pelvic area. He is bearded and between 5 feet 10 inches (1.8 m) and 6 feet 1 inch (1.9 m) in height. The cloth bears a number of extraordinary features:

- It's purple stains may be from blood.
- Potsherds or coins may have covered the eyes. Some argue that the outline of a coin from the time of Pontius Pilate is present,[2] but the fabric is so coarse and the image so unclear that substantiation is difficult.
- The image is barely visible up close, and only a rough outline can be discerned by standing farther away. However, when photographed and viewed in negative, the shroud reveals a clear image, formed in such a way that a three-dimensional reconstruction of the man's appearance is possible.
- The image, on the very surface of the cloth only, is said to be no more than two fibrils (filaments or fibers) deep.
- It was not painted on. Rather, some of the threads were themselves changed to produce the image. Adherents suggest that at the moment of the resurrection Jesus' body radiated energy and fixed his image upon the shroud.
- The traces of flogging on the body are said to accurately depict Roman scourging. The 100-plus lash marks evident on the image have a dumbbell shape, conceivably reflecting the use of a Roman flagrum.
- The shoulders are said to exhibit abrasions that could have been the result of the victim's having carried the crossbar of a cross.
- Studies on the soil and pollen preserved in the fibers suggest that the cloth originated in or near Jerusalem.

Recent Developments

Supporters of the shroud's authenticity argue that no individual in the Middle Ages could have had the expertise to deliberately create such a piece. In 1988, however, British scientists released the results of carbon 14 testing that dated the cloth to between 1260 and 1390. The shroud was judged to have been proven a fraud, yet subsequent researchers have argued that the sample for the carbon 14 test was taken from a part of the shroud that had been repaired and not from the original fabric.

In 2002 the shroud underwent substantial restoration, including the removal of the repair patches from 1532. Some researchers fear that this process will limit or invalidate any further testing. The enigma of the shroud continues. It remains either the most significant archaeological artifact ever found or one of the most ingenious forgeries in history.

[1]See "Crucifixion" on page 1757. [2]See "Pontius Pilate" on page 1714.

15:2 [z]ver 9,12, 2“Are you the king of the Jews?”[z] asked Pilate.
18,26; Mt 2:2 “Yes, it is as you say,” Jesus replied.
3The chief priests accused him of many things. 4So again Pilate asked him, “Aren’t you going to an-
swer? See how many things they are accusing you of.”
15:5 [a]Mk 14:61 5But Jesus still made no reply,[a] and Pilate was amazed.
6Now it was the custom at the Feast to release a prisoner whom the people requested. 7A man called
Barabbas was in prison with the insurrectionists who had committed murder in the uprising. 8The crowd
came up and asked Pilate to do for them what he usually did.
15:9 [b]ver 2 9“Do you want me to release to you the king of the Jews?”[b] asked Pilate, 10knowing it was out of envy
that the chief priests had handed Jesus over to him. 11But the chief priests stirred up the crowd to have
15:11 [c]Ac 3:14 Pilate release Barabbas[c] instead.
12“What shall I do, then, with the one you call the king of the Jews?” Pilate asked them.
13“Crucify him!” they shouted.
14“Why? What crime has he committed?” asked Pilate.
But they shouted all the louder, “Crucify him!”
15:15 [d]Isa 53:6 15Wanting to satisfy the crowd, Pilate released Barabbas to them. He had Jesus flogged,[d] and handed
him over to be crucified.

The Soldiers Mock Jesus

15:16 [e]Jn 18:28, 16The soldiers led Jesus away into the palace[e] (that is, the Praetorium) and called together the whole
33; 19:9 company of soldiers. 17They put a purple robe on him, then twisted together a crown of thorns and set
15:18 [f]ver 2 it on him. 18And they began to call out to him, “Hail, king of the Jews!”[f] 19Again and again they struck
him on the head with a staff and spit on him. Falling on their knees, they paid homage to him. 20And
when they had mocked him, they took off the purple robe and put his own clothes on him. Then they led
15:20 [g]Heb 13:12 him out[g] to crucify him.

The Crucifixion

15:21 [h]Mt 27:32 21A certain man from Cyrene,[h] Simon, the father of Alexander and Rufus,[i] was passing by on his
[i]Ro 16:13 [j]Mt 27:32; way in from the country, and they forced him to carry the cross.[j] 22They brought Jesus to the place called
Lk 23:26 **15:23** [k]ver 36; Golgotha (which means The Place of the Skull). 23Then they offered him wine mixed with myrrh,[k] but
Ps 69:21; Pr 31:6 **15:24** [l]Ps 22:18 he did not take it. 24And they crucified him. Dividing up his clothes, they cast lots[l] to see what each
would get.

15:2 Judgment in a Roman court was the sole responsibility of the imperial magistrate. A Roman governor would not have put a Jew on trial for his life simply on a charge of religious blasphemy (see 14:61–64). Thus, the chief priests presented the accusations against Jesus in a way Pilate would have taken seriously. If Jesus claimed to be a king, he would be guilty of a crime against Rome.
15:4 If Jesus made no defense, according to Roman law Pilate would have to pronounce against him.
15:6 For “custom,” see the note on John 18:39.
15:7 Barabbas was probably a member of the Zealots, a Jewish revolutionary group (see “The Zealots and the Essenes” on p. 1576).
The “uprising” mentioned here is unknown from other sources, although Mark spoke of it as though it were well known. Under the Roman governors such revolts were common (see “The Intertestamental Period” on p. 1551, “The Zealots and the Essenes” on p. 1576 and “Herod’s Successors and Uneasy Relations Between Rome and the Jews” on p. 1631).
15:15 For “Barabbas,” see the notes on verse 7 and Matthew 27:16. For “flogged,” see the note on Matthew 27:26.
15:16 For “Praetorium,” see the note on Matthew 27:27. The soldiers quartered in the Praetorium were recruited from non-Jewish inhabitants of the Holy Land and assigned to the military governor.
15:17 See the note on Matthew 27:28–31.
15:21 For “Cyrene,” see the note on Acts 6:9. Simon was probably a Jew who was in Jerusalem to celebrate the Passover.
The Bible contains several references to countries/areas that are a part of the modern continent of Africa. Egypt figures prominently in Old Testament history, and Ethiopia is mentioned a few times (e.g., Isa 45:14; Jer 13:23). In the New Testament Egypt, its Greek city of Alexandria (Ac 18:24), Ethiopia (Ac 8:27) and the port city of Cyrene (modern Libya) are mentioned primarily because of the Jewish settlements there. Jesus himself went into Egypt (Mt 2:13–14), and Jews from Africa were present on the day of Pentecost (Ac 2:10).
Men condemned to death were usually forced to carry a beam of their own cross, often weighing 30–40 pounds (13.6–18.2 kg), to the place of crucifixion (see “Crucifixion” on p. 1757).
15:22 The Place of the Skull may have been a small hill that looked like a skull, or it may have been so named because of the many executions that took place there. The Gospels and tradition do not agree as to its location. Both Matthew (Mt 27:33) and Mark locate it outside the city but close to it (Jn 19:20) on the public highway—the type of location usually chosen by the Romans for executions. Tradition locates it within the present city of Jerusalem.
15:23 The vinegar with which moderns are familiar is generally a sour fluid obtained by fermentation of cider, but in Bible times it came from wine. The Nazirite was to abstain from drinking it (Nu 6:3), and it was used as a condiment on bread (Ru 2:14). Its action on the teeth (Pr 10:26) and its fizzing with soda (Pr 25:20) were mentioned by Solomon. On the cross Jesus was offered vinegar (NIV “wine”) mixed with gall or with myrrh, a spice derived from plants native to the Arabian deserts and to parts of Africa (see also Mt 27:34), in fulfillment of Psalm 69:21, but he refused it. Later he was offered a mixture of water and vinegar on a sponge (Mt 27:48; see the note on Mk 15:36), a drink popular among the poor and used by Roman soldiers when in camp. (See “Wine and Alcoholic Beverages in the Ancient World” on p. 2015.)
15:24 Crucifixion was a Roman means of execution in which the prisoner was nailed (or tied) to a cross (see the note on Jn 19:17). If the method of securing the victim was nailing, heavy, wrought-iron nails were driven through the wrists and heel bones. Archaeologists have discovered near Jerusalem the bones of a crucified man, dating between A.D. 7 and 66, which shed light on the position of a person when nailed to a cross. Only slaves, the basest of criminals, and

[25]It was the third hour when they crucified him. [26]The written notice of the charge against him read:
THE KING OF THE JEWS.[m] [27]They crucified two robbers with him, one on his right and one on his left.[a]
[29]Those who passed by hurled insults at him, shaking their heads[n] and saying, "So! You who are going
to destroy the temple and build it in three days,[o] [30]come down from the cross and save yourself!"
[31]In the same way the chief priests and the teachers of the law mocked him[p] among themselves. "He
saved others," they said, "but he can't save himself! [32]Let this Christ,[b][q] this King of Israel,[r] come down now
from the cross, that we may see and believe." Those crucified with him also heaped insults on him.

The Death of Jesus

[33]At the sixth hour darkness came over the whole land until the ninth hour.[s] [34]And at the ninth hour
Jesus cried out in a loud voice, *"Eloi, Eloi, lama sabachthani?"*—which means, "My God, my God, why
have you forsaken me?"[c][t]
[35]When some of those standing near heard this, they said, "Listen, he's calling Elijah."
[36]One man ran, filled a sponge with wine vinegar,[u] put it on a stick, and offered it to Jesus to drink.
"Now leave him alone. Let's see if Elijah comes to take him down," he said.
[37]With a loud cry, Jesus breathed his last.[v]
[38]The curtain of the temple was torn in two from top to bottom.[w] [39]And when the centurion,[x] who
stood there in front of Jesus, heard his cry and[d] saw how he died, he said, "Surely this man was the Son[e]
of God!"[y]
[40]Some women were watching from a distance.[z] Among them were Mary Magdalene, Mary the moth-
er of James the younger and of Joses, and Salome.[a] [41]In Galilee these women had followed him and cared
for his needs. Many other women who had come up with him to Jerusalem were also there.[b]

The Burial of Jesus

[42]It was Preparation Day (that is, the day before the Sabbath).[c] So as evening approached, [43]Joseph of
Arimathea, a prominent member of the Council,[d] who was himself waiting for the kingdom of God,[e]
went boldly to Pilate and asked for Jesus' body. [44]Pilate was surprised to hear that he was already dead.
Summoning the centurion, he asked him if Jesus had already died. [45]When he learned from the centurion[f]

15:26 [m]ver 2
15:29 [n]Ps 22:7; 109:25 [o]Mk 14:58; Jn 2:19
15:31 [p]Ps 22:7
15:32 [q]Mk 14:61 [r]ver 2
15:33 [s]Am 8:9
15:34 [t]Ps 22:1
15:36 [u]ver 23; Ps 69:21
15:37 [v]Jn 19:30
15:38 [w]Heb 10:19,20
15:39 [x]ver 45 [y]Mk 1:1,11; 9:7; Mt 4:3
15:40 [z]Ps 38:11 [a]Mk 16:1; Lk 24:10; Jn 19:25
15:41 [b]Mt 27:55, 56; Lk 8:2,3
15:42 [c]Mt 27:62; Jn 19:31
15:43 [d]Mt 5:22 [e]Mt 3:2; Lk 2:25, 38
15:45 [f]ver 39

[a] 27 Some manuscripts *left,* [28]*and the scripture was fulfilled which says, "He was counted with the lawless ones"* (Isaiah 53:12)
[b] 32 Or *Messiah* [c] 34 Psalm 22:1 [d] 39 Some manuscripts do not have *heard his cry and* [e] 39 Or *a son*

---

offenders who were not Roman citizens were executed in this manner. First-century authors vividly described the agony and disgrace of being crucified. Crucifixion had earlier been practiced, especially in times of war, by the Phoenicians, Carthaginians and Egyptians. (See "Crucifixion" on p. 1757.)

The agony of the crucified victim was brought about by a number of factors, first of which was the painful but nonfatal character of the wounds inflicted. The second factor causing great suffering was the abnormal position of the body. The slightest movement brought on additional, excruciating torture. The third factor was the traumatic fever induced by hanging for such a long period of time.

What was the physical reason for Jesus' death? Recent medical studies have sought an answer to this question. When a person is suspended by the hands, the blood sinks rapidly into the lower extremities of the body. Within six to twelve minutes the blood pressure drops by half, while the pulse rate doubles. The heart is deprived of blood, and fainting follows. Death during crucifixion was due to heart failure. Victims did not generally succumb for two or three days, so death was sometimes hastened by the *crucifragium* or the breaking of the legs (cf. Jn 19:33). Sometimes a fire was kindled beneath the cross so that its fumes might suffocate the individual hanging there.

It was the accepted right of the executioner's squad to claim the minor possessions of the victim. Jesus' clothing probably consisted of an under and an outer garment, a belt, sandals and possibly a head covering.

See "Casting Lots" on page 744.

15:25 The "third hour" was 9:00 A.M. (see the note on Lk 23:44).

15:26 It was customary to write the charge on a wooden board that was carried before the victim as he walked to the place of execution, after which the board was affixed to the cross above his head.

15:27 According to Roman law, robbery was not a capital offense. Mark's term must signify men guilty of insurrection, who were crucified for high treason.

15:33 The sixth hour was 12:00 noon and the ninth hour 3:00 P.M. (See the note on Lk 23:44).

15:34 Jesus' words here were spoken in a dialect of Aramaic, one of the languages commonly spoken in the Holy Land in his day. For a discussion of the use of Aramaic in New Testament times, see the note on Matthew 5:41.

15:36 Known scientifically as *Porifera,* the sponge is a class of the sessile (attached to a base; not free to move about) aquatic animal family. A sponge filled with wine vinegar was offered to Jesus on the cross (see also Mt 27:48). John noted that the stalk of a hyssop plant was used to lift the sponge to the Lord's lips (Jn 19:29). Such use of a sponge to provide liquid refreshment was common in Biblical times. The sponge absorbed the wine or water contained in a vessel and then was squeezed into the upturned mouth of the user. For "wine vinegar," see the note on Matthew 27:48.

15:38 The "curtain of the temple" refers to the curtain that separated the Holy Place from the Most Holy Place.

15:39 For "centurion," see the note on Matthew 8:5.

15:42 It was a Friday and, since it was now late in the afternoon, there was an urgency to get Jesus' body down from the cross before sundown, when the Sabbath would begin.

15:43 For "Arimathea," see the note on Matthew 27:57. The "Council" refers to the Sanhedrin (see the note on Mk 14:55). For information on Pilate, see the note on Luke 3:1 and "Pontius Pilate" on page 1714. For information on Joseph's request for Jesus' body, see the note on Mark 15:45.

15:45 The remains of an executed criminal were often left unburied or at best deposited in a dishonored place in a pauper's field. The release of the body of one condemned for high treason, especially to a person who was not an immediate relative, was quite unusual.

THE ENDING OF MARK

MARK 16 There are several different endings to the Gospel of Mark found in the various Greek manuscripts. Most Greek texts and several ancient translations conclude with the ending familiar to us as Mark 16:9–20. The earliest Greek manuscript with that ending is from the fifth century, but evidence from the church fathers suggests that it was already in existence during the second century. Many scholars feel, however, that the vocabulary and themes of the traditional ending are inconsistent with the rest of the Gospel.

In the two oldest Greek manuscripts and in a number of ancient **versions**, Mark's Gospel ends at 16:8. Clement of Alexandria and Origen show no knowledge of any ending of this Gospel account beyond verse 8, and Eusebius and Jerome affirm that nearly all Greek manuscripts known to them were concluded with this verse. Most scholars believe that this is indeed the point at which the original Gospel probably ended and suggest that the other endings very likely developed during the second century, after the Gospel of Mark was read alongside the other Gospels and appeared, by comparison, to lack a satisfactory conclusion. Despite its abruptness, Mark 16:8 is arguably an appropriate ending for the Gospel, since one of its motifs is the fear caused by God's powerful work in and through Jesus (see, e.g., 5:15,33; 9:6). The women's fear suggests that God had performed one more climactic, powerful work, confirming the testimony of the empty tomb and the angelic announcement that Jesus had indeed arisen from the dead, just as he had promised (8:31; 9:9,31; 10:34).[1]

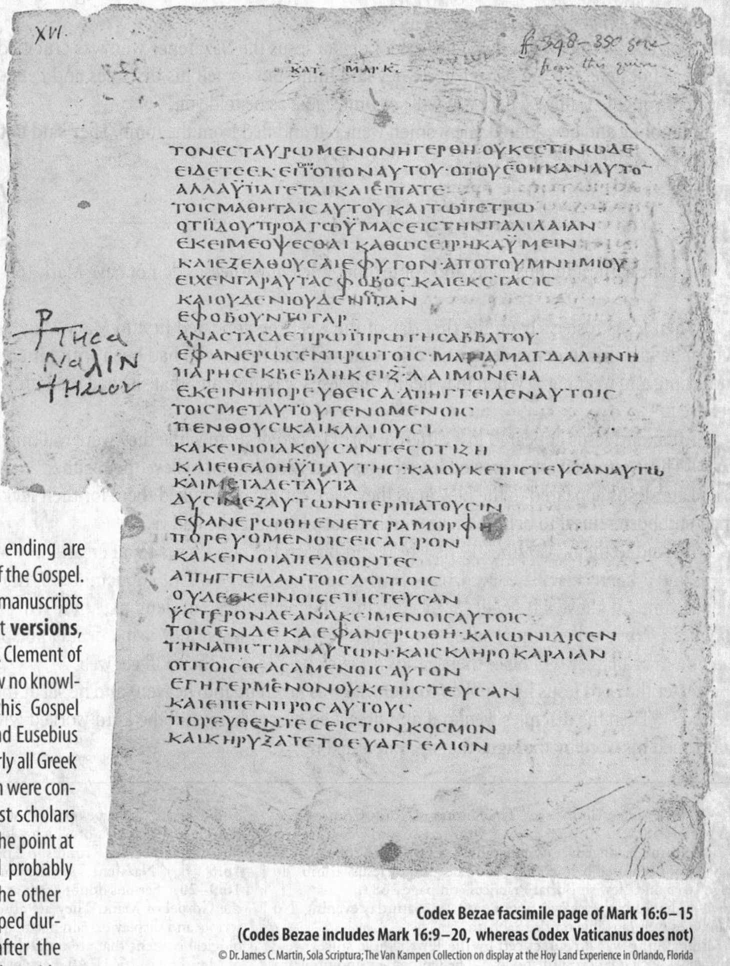

Codex Bezae facsimile page of Mark 16:6–15
(Codes Bezae includes Mark 16:9–20, whereas Codex Vaticanus does not)

© Dr. James C. Martin, Sola Scriptura; The Van Kampen Collection on display at the Hoy Land Experience in Orlando, Florida

[1] See also "The New Testament Texts" on page 1859.

that it was so, he gave the body to Joseph. 46 So Joseph bought some linen cloth, took down the body,
wrapped it in the linen, and placed it in a tomb cut out of rock. Then he rolled a stone against the entrance
of the tomb.[g] 47 Mary Magdalene and Mary the mother of Joses[h] saw where he was laid.

15:46 [g]Mk 16:3
15:47 [h]ver 40

The Resurrection

16 When the Sabbath was over, Mary Magdalene, Mary the mother of James, and Salome bought
spices[i] so that they might go to anoint Jesus' body. 2 Very early on the first day of the week, just
after sunrise, they were on their way to the tomb 3 and they asked each other, "Who will roll the stone
away from the entrance of the tomb?"[j]

4 But when they looked up, they saw that the stone, which was very large, had been rolled away. 5 As they
entered the tomb, they saw a young man dressed in a white robe[k] sitting on the right side, and they were
alarmed.

6 "Don't be alarmed," he said. "You are looking for Jesus the Nazarene,[l] who was crucified. He has ris-
en! He is not here. See the place where they laid him. 7 But go, tell his disciples and Peter, 'He is going
ahead of you into Galilee. There you will see him,[m] just as he told you.' "[n]

8 Trembling and bewildered, the women went out and fled from the tomb. They said nothing to any-
one, because they were afraid.

16:1 [i]Lk 23:56; Jn 19:39,40
16:3 [j]Mk 15:46
16:5 [k]Jn 20:12
16:6 [l]Mk 1:24
16:7 [m]Jn 21:1-23 [n]Mk 14:28

[The earliest manuscripts and some other ancient witnesses do not have Mark 16:9-20.]

9 When Jesus rose early on the first day of the week, he appeared first to Mary Magdalene,[o] out of
whom he had driven seven demons. 10 She went and told those who had been with him and who were
mourning and weeping. 11 When they heard that Jesus was alive and that she had seen him, they did not
believe it.[p]

12 Afterward Jesus appeared in a different form to two of them while they were walking in the coun-
try.[q] 13 These returned and reported it to the rest; but they did not believe them either.

14 Later Jesus appeared to the Eleven as they were eating; he rebuked them for their lack of faith and
their stubborn refusal to believe those who had seen him after he had risen.[r]

15 He said to them, "Go into all the world and preach the good news to all creation.[s] 16 Whoever be-
lieves and is baptized will be saved, but whoever does not believe will be condemned.[t] 17 And these signs
will accompany those who believe: In my name they will drive out demons;[u] they will speak in new
tongues;[v] 18 they will pick up snakes[w] with their hands; and when they drink deadly poison, it will not
hurt them at all; they will place their hands on[x] sick people, and they will get well."

19 After the Lord Jesus had spoken to them, he was taken up into heaven[y] and he sat at the right hand
of God.[z] 20 Then the disciples went out and preached everywhere, and the Lord worked with them and
confirmed his word by the signs that accompanied it.

16:9 [o]Jn 20:11-18
16:11 [p]ver 13,14; Lk 24:11
16:12 [q]Lk 24:13-32
16:14 [r]Lk 24:36-43
16:15 [s]Mt 28:18-20; Lk 24:47,48
16:16 [t]Jn 3:16, 18,36; Ac 16:31
16:17 [u]Mk 9:38; Lk 10:17; Ac 5:16; 8:7; 16:18; 19:13-16 [v]Ac 2:4; 10:46; 19:6; 1Co 12:10, 28,30
16:18 [w]Lk 10:19; Ac 28:3-5 [x]Ac 6:6
16:19 [y]Lk 24:50, 51; Jn 6:62; Ac 1:9-11; 1Ti 3:16 [z]Ps 110:1; Ro 8:34; Col 3:1; Heb 1:3; 12:2

15:46 For "linen cloth," see "The Shroud of Turin Controversy" on page 1658.

The tomb belonged to Joseph and was new (Mt 27:60); that is, it had not been used before. See "The Location of Jesus' Tomb" on page 1615 and "Jewish Burial Practices" on page 1688.

16:1 The Sabbath was over about 6:00 P.M. Saturday evening. No purchases were possible on the Sabbath.

Embalming was not practiced by the Jews. These spices were brought as an act of devotion and love. The women, by anointing his body, demonstrated that they had no expectation of Jesus' resurrection. (See the note on Mt 26:12, "Jewish Burial Practices" on p. 1688 and "Perfumes and Anointing Oils" on p. 1746.)

16:3 Setting the large stone in place was a relatively easy task, but once it had slipped into the groove cut in bedrock in front of the entrance it was very difficult to remove.

16:5 Inside the large opening of the facade of the tomb was a forechamber, at the back of which a low rectangular opening led to the burial chamber (see "Tombs in Ancient Israel" on p. 376).

16:6 For "Nazarene," see the note on Matthew 2:23.

16:9–20 Serious doubt exists as to whether these verses belong to the Gospel of Mark. They are absent from important early manuscripts and display certain peculiarities of vocabulary, style and theological content that are unlike the rest of Mark (see "The Ending of Mark" on p. 1661). After extensive study of all manuscripts, many scholars believe that one or more scribes took a hand at "writing a more appropriate ending," using the information from the other Gospels to avoid their own discomfort and to "fill in the blanks" for future generations (see "Early Scribal Emendation" on p. 448). Still, the book through verse 20 is included in the New Testament canon—the authorized Scripture of the church.

INTRODUCTION TO *Luke*

AUTHOR, PLACE AND DATE OF WRITING

The openings of Luke (1:1–4) and Acts (1:1–2) make clear that the two books are to be regarded as a single work in two volumes. Neither names its author, but the "we" sections of Acts (e.g., Ac 16:9–17; 27:1—28:16), in comparison with what can be known from Paul's letters about who was with him at various points in his career, point to Luke as the author of this work. Justin Martyr (c. 160), the Muratorian Canon (c. 170–180) and Irenaeus (c. 175–195) all supported the ascription of Luke–Acts to Luke.

Luke was one of Paul's most loyal followers (Col 4:14; 2Ti 4:11; Phm 24). Well educated in Greek culture and a physician by profession (Col 4:14), Luke may have been a Gentile convert; if so, his knowledge of the Old Testament was extraordinary. Syrian Antioch and Philippi are among the sites posited as his hometown.

It has been suggested that Luke wrote his Gospel from Caesarea or (more probably) Rome. A logical conclusion is that Luke began writing Luke at some point during Paul's Roman imprisonment and continued writing until his story caught up to his present situation, at the end of two years awaiting the conclusion of Paul's case in Rome. In this scenario, we may confidently date the Gospel to A.D. 61–62.

AUDIENCE

Luke directly addressed someone named Theophilus (1:3), possibly a non-Christian Roman official but definitely a person of high position and wealth. Yet underlying Luke's overt greeting, his Gospel, the most comprehensive of the four, was written to strengthen the faith of all believers and to answer the attacks of cultured non-Christians.

CULTURAL FACTS AND HIGHLIGHTS

In his prologue to his Gospel, Luke articulated his desire to give his readers a clear and coherent presentation of the words and deeds of Christ (1:1–4). By A.D. 62 there were undoubtedly many oral and some written accounts of Jesus' miracles and teachings, so there is no reason to question Luke's stated purpose.

TIMELINE

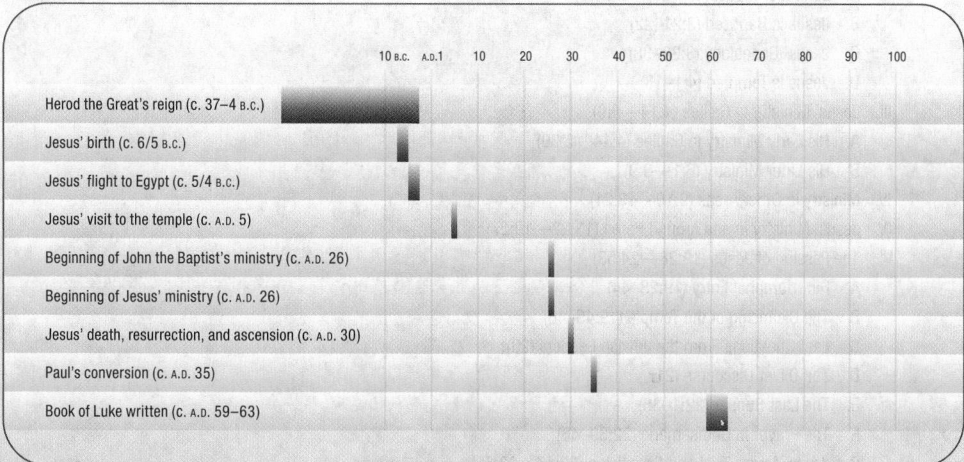

AS YOU READ

Notice that Luke's account gives prominence to Jesus' concern for the poor and oppressed. Pay particular attention to Jesus' interest in diverse ethnic, religious, economic and social groups.

DID YOU KNOW?

- Each priest was responsible for a week's service at the temple once every six months (1:23).
- Thirty was the age at which a Levite undertook his service (Nu 4:47) and at which a man was considered mature (3:23).
- In ancient times it was often assumed that a calamity would befall only those who were extremely sinful (13:2).
- Synagogues were used not only for worship and school but also for community administration and for confinement of accused persons while awaiting trial (21:12).

THEMES

Luke includes the following themes:

1. *The universality of the gospel.* Luke's account of Jesus' birth, ministry, death and resurrection emphasizes that the Good News of the gospel is intended for all peoples (2:14,32).

2. *Concern for social outcasts.* Luke's Gospel underscores Jesus' particular concern for social outcasts, women and the poor. Jesus' first public sermon recorded in Luke (4:16–21) cited Isaiah 61:1–2 in proclaiming good news, freedom, healing and release (4:18–19).

3. *Repentance.* The vocabulary of repentance is prominent in Luke, as manifested in the parable of the lost son (15:11–32), the parable of the tax collector and the Pharisee (18:9–14) and the story of Zacchaeus (19:1–10). Repentance requires a fundamental reorientation toward God, which then leads to reconciliation of human relationships.

4. *Wealth.* Luke stressed the ethical aspects of the Christian life, making it clear that repentance involves a change in attitude that reveals itself in the manner in which a person handles money (3:10–14).

OUTLINE

- I. The Births of John and Jesus (1–2)
- II. The Beginnings of Jesus' Ministry (3:1—4:13)
  - A. John the Baptist (3:1–20)
  - B. Jesus Is Baptized (3:21–22)
  - C. Jesus' Genealogy (3:23–38)
  - D. Jesus Is Tempted (4:1–13)
- III. Jesus' Ministry in Galilee (4:14—9:9)
  - A. His Early Ministry in Galilee (4:14—5:39)
  - B. His Later Ministry (6:1—9:9)
- IV. Ministry in Other Areas (9:10—13:21)
- V. Jesus' Ministry in and Around Perea (13:22—19:27)
- VI. The Passion of Jesus (19:28—24:53)
  - A. His Triumphal Entry (19:28–44)
  - B. The Cleansing of the Temple (19:45–48)
  - C. Last Questions From the Jewish Leaders (20)
  - D. The Olivet Discourse (21)
  - E. The Last Supper (22:1–38)
  - F. The Prayer in Gethsemane (22:39–46)
  - G. Jesus' Arrest, Trial and Crucifixion (22:47—23:56)
  - H. Jesus' Resurrection (24:1–49)
  - I. The Ascension (24:50–53)

Introduction

1 Many have undertaken to draw up an account of the things that have been fulfilled[a] among us, 2just
as they were handed down to us by those who from the first[a] were eyewitnesses[b] and servants of the
word.[c] 3Therefore, since I myself have carefully investigated everything from the beginning, it seemed
good also to me to write an orderly account[d] for you, most excellent[e] Theophilus,[f] 4so that you may know
the certainty of the things you have been taught.[g]

The Birth of John the Baptist Foretold

5In the time of Herod king of Judea[h] there was a priest named Zechariah, who belonged to the priest-
ly division of Abijah;[i] his wife Elizabeth was also a descendant of Aaron. 6Both of them were upright in
the sight of God, observing all the Lord's commandments and regulations blamelessly.[j] 7But they had
no children, because Elizabeth was barren; and they were both well along in years.
8Once when Zechariah's division was on duty and he was serving as priest before God,[k] 9he was chosen
by lot, according to the custom of the priesthood, to go into the temple of the Lord and burn incense.[l] 10And
when the time for the burning of incense came, all the assembled worshipers were praying outside.[m]
11Then an angel[n] of the Lord appeared to him, standing at the right side of the altar of incense.[o]
12When Zechariah saw him, he was startled and was gripped with fear.[p] 13But the angel said to him: "Do
not be afraid,[q] Zechariah; your prayer has been heard. Your wife Elizabeth will bear you a son, and you
are to give him the name John.[r] 14He will be a joy and delight to you, and many will rejoice because of
his birth,[s] 15for he will be great in the sight of the Lord. He is never to take wine or other fermented
drink,[t] and he will be filled with the Holy Spirit even from birth.[b][u] 16Many of the people of Israel will he
bring back to the Lord their God. 17And he will go on before the Lord,[v] in the spirit and power of Eli-
jah,[w] to turn the hearts of the fathers to their children[x] and the disobedient to the wisdom of the righ-
teous—to make ready a people prepared for the Lord."
18Zechariah asked the angel, "How can I be sure of this? I am an old man and my wife is well along in
years."[y]
19The angel answered, "I am Gabriel.[z] I stand in the presence of God, and I have been sent to speak
to you and to tell you this good news. 20And now you will be silent and not able to speak[a] until the day
this happens, because you did not believe my words, which will come true at their proper time."
21Meanwhile, the people were waiting for Zechariah and wondering why he stayed so long in the tem-
ple. 22When he came out, he could not speak to them. They realized he had seen a vision in the temple,
for he kept making signs[b] to them but remained unable to speak.
23When his time of service was completed, he returned home. 24After this his wife Elizabeth became
pregnant and for five months remained in seclusion. 25"The Lord has done this for me," she said. "In
these days he has shown his favor and taken away my disgrace[c] among the people."

1:2 [a]Mk 1:1; Jn 15:27; Ac 1:21, 22 [b]Heb 2:3; 1Pe 5:1; 2Pe 1:16; 1Jn 1:1 [c]Mk 4:14
1:3 [d]Ac 11:4 [e]Ac 24:3; 26:25 [f]Ac 1:1
1:4 [g]Jn 20:31
1:5 [h]Mt 2:1 [i]1Ch 24:10
1:6 [j]Ge 7:1; 1Ki 9:4
1:8 [k]1Ch 24:19; 2Ch 8:14
1:9 [l]Ex 30:7,8; 1Ch 23:13; 2Ch 29:11
1:10 [m]Lev 16:17
1:11 [n]Ac 5:19 [o]Ex 30:1-10
1:12 [p]Jdg 6:22, 23; 13:22
1:13 [q]ver 30; Mt 14:27 [r]ver 60, 63
1:14 [s]ver 58
1:15 [t]Nu 6:3; Jdg 13:4; Lk 7:33 [u]Jer 1:5; Gal 1:15
1:17 [v]ver 76 [w]Mt 11:14 [x]Mal 4:5,6
1:18 [y]ver 34; Ge 17:17
1:19 [z]ver 26; Da 8:16; 9:21; Mt 18:10
1:20 [a]Eze 3:26
1:22 [b]ver 62
1:25 [c]Ge 30:23; Isa 4:1

[a] *1* Or *been surely believed* [b] *15* Or *from his mother's womb*

1:3 It is reasonable to suppose that Theophilus, to whom Luke dedicated both his Gospel and the book of Acts (Ac 1:1), was a real person. The title "most excellent" demands this, while the name and title together suggest a person of some rank who became a Christian convert (Theophilus is very possibly a baptismal name). Nothing is known of the man himself. He was certainly not Seneca, as one conjecture would have it. It is impossible to decide whether he was pure Roman, Greek or Jew, or whether the omission in Acts of the honorable title used in the Gospel indicates a deepening friendship when the second book was dedicated, the abandonment of office or dismissal from office for professing the Christian faith.

1:5 "Herod king of Judea" refers to Herod the Great (r. 37–4 B.C.), whose kingdom also included Samaria, Galilee, Perea and Traconitis (see "Herod the Great" on p. 1627). The time referred to here is probably approximately 7–6 B.C.

From the time of David the priests were organized into 24 divisions, and Abijah was one of the "heads of the priestly families" (Ne 12:12,17; see 1Ch 24:10).

1:7 See the note on verse 25.

1:9 It was one of the priest's duties to keep the incense burning on the altar in front of the Most Holy Place. He supplied it with fresh incense before the morning sacrifice and again after the evening sacrifice (Ex 30:6–8). Ordinarily a priest would have this privilege very infrequently, and sometimes never, since duty assignments were determined by casting lots (see the notes on Pr 16:33; Ac 1:26; see also "Casting Lots" on p. 744 and "The Jewish Priesthood and Religious Life in the First Century A.D." on p. 1704).

1:11 See "Angels and Guardian Spirits in the Bible and the Ancient Near East" on page 1529.

1:15 It appears likely that John the Baptist, a Nazirite from birth, was to be subject to the Nazirite vow of abstinence from alcoholic drinks (see Nu 6:1–12 and its note; see also "Wine and Alcoholic Beverages in the Ancient World" on p. 2015).

It is thought by some that John was a member of the Essenes or Quruan community, but there is no clear evidence tht this was so, nor can it be proved that the men of Qumran were all Nazirites (see "The Zealots and Essenes" on p. 1576, "Biblical Interpretation at Qumran and Among Early Rabbis" on p. 1603 and "Qumrun and the New Testament" on p. 1679). The possibility that the apostle Paul was a Nazirite has frequently elicited discussion. Although it cannot be established that the apostle took such a vow, it is certain that he did assume the expenses of those who did (Ac 21:23ff.) According to Josephus, the court of Herod supported a large number of Nazirites.

1:21 The people were waiting for Zechariah to come out of the Holy Place and pronounce the Aaronic blessing (see Nu 6:24–26).

1:23 Each priest was responsible for a week's service at the temple once every six months.

1:25 Not only did the absence of children deprive the would-be parents of personal happiness, but being childless was generally thought to indicate divine disfavor and often brought social reproach.

The Birth of Jesus Foretold

26 In the sixth month, God sent the angel Gabriel[d] to Nazareth,[e] a town in Galilee, 27 to a virgin pledged
to be married to a man named Joseph,[f] a descendant of David. The virgin's name was Mary. 28 The angel
went to her and said, "Greetings, you who are highly favored! The Lord is with you."
29 Mary was greatly troubled at his words and wondered what kind of greeting this might be. 30 But
the angel said to her, "Do not be afraid,[g] Mary, you have found favor with God. 31 You will be with child
and give birth to a son, and you are to give him the name Jesus.[h] 32 He will be great and will be called the
Son of the Most High.[i] The Lord God will give him the throne of his father David, 33 and he will reign
over the house of Jacob forever; his kingdom[j] will never end."[k]
34 "How will this be," Mary asked the angel, "since I am a virgin?"
35 The angel answered, "The Holy Spirit will come upon you,[l] and the power of the Most High[m] will
overshadow you. So the holy one[n] to be born will be called[a] the Son of God.[o] 36 Even Elizabeth your rel-
ative is going to have a child in her old age, and she who was said to be barren is in her sixth month. 37 For
nothing is impossible with God."[p]
38 "I am the Lord's servant," Mary answered. "May it be to me as you have said." Then the angel left her.

Mary Visits Elizabeth

39 At that time Mary got ready and hurried to a town in the hill country of Judea,[q] 40 where she entered
Zechariah's home and greeted Elizabeth. 41 When Elizabeth heard Mary's greeting, the baby leaped in her
womb, and Elizabeth was filled with the Holy Spirit. 42 In a loud voice she exclaimed: "Blessed are you
among women,[r] and blessed is the child you will bear! 43 But why am I so favored, that the mother of my
Lord should come to me? 44 As soon as the sound of your greeting reached my ears, the baby in my womb
leaped for joy. 45 Blessed is she who has believed that what the Lord has said to her will be accomplished!"

Mary's Song

46 And Mary said:

"My soul glorifies the Lord[s]
47 and my spirit rejoices in God my Savior,[t]
48 for he has been mindful
of the humble state of his servant.[u]
From now on all generations will call me blessed,[v]
49 for the Mighty One has done great things[w] for me—
holy is his name.[x]
50 His mercy extends to those who fear him,
from generation to generation.[y]
51 He has performed mighty deeds with his arm;[z]
he has scattered those who are proud in their inmost thoughts.
52 He has brought down rulers from their thrones
but has lifted up the humble.
53 He has filled the hungry with good things[a]
but has sent the rich away empty.
54 He has helped his servant Israel,
remembering to be merciful[b]
55 to Abraham and his descendants[c] forever,
even as he said to our fathers."

56 Mary stayed with Elizabeth for about three months and then returned home.

1:26 [d]ver 19 [e]Mt 2:23 **1:27** [f]Mt 1:16,18,20; Lk 2:4 **1:30** [g]ver 13; Mt 14:27 **1:31** [h]Isa 7:14; Mt 1:21,25; Lk 2:21 **1:32** [i]ver 35,76; Mk 5:7 **1:33** [j]Mt 28:18 [k]Da 2:44; 7:14,27; Mic 4:7; Heb 1:8 **1:35** [l]Mt 1:18 [m]ver 32,76 [n]Mk 1:24 [o]Mt 4:3 **1:37** [p]Mt 19:26 **1:39** [q]ver 65 **1:42** [r]Jdg 5:24 **1:46** [s]Ps 34:2,3 **1:47** [t]1Ti 1:1; 2:3 **1:48** [u]Ps 138:6 [v]Lk 11:27 **1:49** [w]Ps 71:19 [x]Ps 111:9 **1:50** [y]Ex 20:6; Ps 103:17 **1:51** [z]Ps 98:1; Isa 40:10 **1:53** [a]Ps 107:9 **1:54** [b]Ps 98:3 **1:55** [c]Ge 17:19; Ps 132:11; Gal 3:16

[a] 35 Or *So the child to be born will be called holy,*

1:26 For "Nazareth," see the note on Matthew 2:23.
1:27 For "pledged to be married," see the notes on Matthew 1:18–19.
1:46–55 The familiar title of the song of praise by Mary comes from the Vulgate version of the Bible: *Magnificat mea anima* ("My soul doth magnify"). Mary spoke these words in response to the assurance from Elizabeth that God would surely fulfill the pronouncement of the angel Gabriel that Mary was the woman chosen to bring the Son of God into the world. The song resembles closely the poetry of the Old Testament; its similarity to Hannah's prayer in 1 Samuel 2:1–10 is striking. All of the Greek manuscripts of Luke ascribe the song to Mary, although three Latin manuscripts read Elizabeth instead of Mary in verse 46.

Caesar Augustus, Emperor of Rome; the Census; and Quirinius, Governor of Syria

LUKE 1

The Reign of Augustus

Caesar Augustus was ruler of the Roman Empire when Jesus was born (Lk 2:1). [1]He ruled for 45 years, from 31 B.C. to A.D. 14. Born Gaius Octavius, he was adopted by his maternal uncle, Julius Caesar (100–44 B.C.), and, as was common, assumed the name of his adoptive father. Thus, he was known as Gaius Julius Caesar Octavian. The name Augustus, "revered one," was bestowed upon him by the Roman Senate in 27 B.C.

Augustus put an end to the civil wars that had raged since the dictatorship of Julius Caesar and established the *Pax Romana* ("Roman peace") throughout the empire. For this, he received lavish honors in Rome and around the Roman world. Herod the Great built the city of Caesarea Maritima[2] and rebuilt **Samaria**[3] (the former capital of the northern kingdom)[4] in Augustus's honor. The Greek name of Samaria, *Sebastos*, means "Augustus."

The peace that characterized Augustus's reign was marred only by the disaster of the loss of three Roman legions in a battle with German tribes at the Teutoburg Forest in A.D. 9. Otherwise, Augustus used the stability of the times to carry out extensive building projects in Rome. Some of his structures have been excavated and can be seen today, such as the Forum of Augustus, the beautiful Altar of Peace and the Mausoleum of Augustus, where his ashes were placed.

Quirinius and the Census

At the time of Jesus' birth, Joseph and Mary were in Bethlehem to be counted for a census. Luke recorded that the census taken when Jesus was born "was the first census that took place while Quirinius was governor of Syria" (v. 2). Publius Sulpicius Quirinius was a well-known Roman military and political figure who was appointed to serve as governor of Syria in A.D. 6. At this time he carried out a census in Syria and Judea. This census is documented in the writings of the first-century Jewish historian Josephus (*Antiquities*, 18) and is mentioned in Acts 5:37. An obvious problem is that this census is too late to be related to the birth of Jesus, since Jesus was born prior to the death of Herod the Great in 4 B.C. How might one resolve this difficulty?

✣ It may be that Luke was aware of Quirinius's A.D. 6 census and that Luke 2:2 means that there had been an earlier census during the reign of Herod, which was also supervised by Quirinius. Some scholars believe that a fragmentary inscription called the *Lapis Tiburtinus* implies that Quirinius was twice governor of Syria, so that the A.D. 6 census was in fact his second census. This interpretation of the *Lapis Tiburtinus* is open to question, however; we do not know with certainty that this inscription actually dealt with Quirinius at all.

✣ It may be that this verse should be translated as, "This census was before the one made when Quirinius was governor." This would be a somewhat peculiar translation of the Greek, but a number of New Testament scholars nonetheless support it.

✣ The church father Tertullian believed that the census of Luke 2:2 took place during the governorship of Sentius Saturninus (8–6 B.C.) rather than that of Quirinius. It may be that the text of 2:2 has suffered some kind of corruption, although, except for Tertullian, there is no evidence for this.

[1]See "The Roman Empire" on page 1845. [2]See "Caesarea Maritima" on page 1786. [3]See Glossary on page 2080 for definitions of bolded words. [4]See "Omri and Samaria" on page 512.

Head of Caesar Augustus

Preserving Bible Times; © Dr. James C. Martin; permission of The Istanbul Archaeological Museum

The Birth of John the Baptist

57 When it was time for Elizabeth to have her baby, she gave birth to a son. 58 Her neighbors and rela-
tives heard that the Lord had shown her great mercy, and they shared her joy.
59 On the eighth day they came to circumcise[d] the child, and they were going to name him after his fa-
ther Zechariah, 60 but his mother spoke up and said, "No! He is to be called John."[e]
61 They said to her, "There is no one among your relatives who has that name."
62 Then they made signs[f] to his father, to find out what he would like to name the child. 63 He asked for
a writing tablet, and to everyone's astonishment he wrote, "His name is John."[g] 64 Immediately his mouth
was opened and his tongue was loosed, and he began to speak,[h] praising God. 65 The neighbors were all
filled with awe, and throughout the hill country of Judea[i] people were talking about all these things. 66 Ev-
eryone who heard this wondered about it, asking, "What then is this child going to be?" For the Lord's
hand was with him.[j]

Zechariah's Song

67 His father Zechariah was filled with the Holy Spirit and prophesied:[k]

68 "Praise be to the Lord, the God of Israel,[l]
because he has come and has redeemed his people.[m]
69 He has raised up a horn[a][n] of salvation for us
in the house of his servant David[o]
70 (as he said through his holy prophets of long ago),[p]
71 salvation from our enemies
and from the hand of all who hate us—
72 to show mercy to our fathers[q]
and to remember his holy covenant,[r]
73 the oath he swore to our father Abraham:[s]

1:59 [d]Ge 17:12; Lev 12:3; Lk 2:21; Php 3:5
1:60 [e]ver 13,63
1:62 [f]ver 22
1:63 [g]ver 13,60
1:64 [h]ver 20
1:65 [i]ver 39
1:66 [j]Ge 39:2; Ac 11:21
1:67 [k]Joel 2:28
1:68 [l]Ps 72:18 [m]Ps 111:9; Lk 7:16
1:69 [n]1Sa 2:1,10; Ps 18:2; 89:17; 132:17; Eze 29:21 [o]Mt 1:1
1:70 [p]Jer 23:5
1:72 [q]Mic 7:20 [r]Ps 105:8,9; 106:45; Eze 16:60
1:73 [s]Ge 22:16-18

[a] *69 Horn* here symbolizes strength.

1:59 It was an accepted practice in that day to name a child after his father (see "Naming of Children" on p. 28).
1:63 The "writing tablet" was probably a small wooden board covered with wax (see "Writing Materials in the Ancient World" on p. 2037).
1:69 "Horn" indicates strength, as in the horn of an animal.

The Birthplace of Jesus

LUKE 2 Bethlehem[1] of Judah ("Map 9"), located at modern Bethlehem, was already an ancient habitation during Old Testament times. Genesis 35:19 and 48:7 mention that the site was also called Ephrathah (or Ephrath), a name preserved in the prophecy of Micah 5:2. This town is the principal setting for the book of Ruth, the great-grandmother of King David, as well as the home of David (1Sa 16). During David's lifetime the city was sometimes under Philistine control (2Sa 23:14), although Rehoboam fortified it after the secession of the northern tribes (2Ch 11:5–6).

The archaeology of Bethlehem has focused almost entirely upon historical tradition surrounding the Church of the Nativity. Justin Martyr in the second century identified a cave near the village as the place of Jesus' birth, and the church was built over this grotto. Emperor Constantine constructed the first basilica there in approximately A.D. 326.[2] While this building was badly damaged in a Samaritan revolt (529), the church was rebuilt by Justinian (r. 527–565). The Christian population of Bethlehem severely declined after the Muslim conquest, although the church building was restored to some of its former glory during the Crusader period. It fell into near ruin again during the period of Turkish rule, but repairs were made beginning in 1670. To this day the church continues to be at the center of religious and political tensions.

[1]See "Bethlehem" on page 1487. [2]See "Constantine and Queen Helena's Role in Preserving Holy Sites" on page 1758.

1:74 [t]Heb 9:14
1:75 [u]Eph 4:24
1:76 [v]Mt 11:9 [w]ver 32,35 [x]ver 17; Mal 3:1
1:77 [y]Jer 31:34; Mk 1:4
1:78 [z]Mal 4:2
1:79 [a]Isa 9:2; 59:9; Mt 4:16; Ac 26:18
1:80 [b]Lk 2:40,52

74 to rescue us from the hand of our enemies,
and to enable us to serve him[t] without fear
75 in holiness and righteousness[u] before him all our days.

76 And you, my child, will be called a prophet[v] of the Most High;[w]
for you will go on before the Lord to prepare the way for him,[x]
77 to give his people the knowledge of salvation
through the forgiveness of their sins,[y]
78 because of the tender mercy of our God,
by which the rising sun[z] will come to us from heaven
79 to shine on those living in darkness
and in the shadow of death,[a]
to guide our feet into the path of peace."

80 And the child grew and became strong in spirit;[b] and he lived in the desert until he appeared pub-
licly to Israel.

The Birth of Jesus

2:1 [c]Mt 22:17; Lk 3:1 [d]Mt 24:14
2:2 [e]Mt 4:24
2:4 [f]Jn 7:42

2 In those days Caesar Augustus[c] issued a decree that a census should be taken of the entire Roman
world.[d] 2 (This was the first census that took place while Quirinius was governor of Syria.)[e] 3 And
everyone went to his own town to register.
4 So Joseph also went up from the town of Nazareth in Galilee to Judea, to Bethlehem[f] the town of Da-
vid, because he belonged to the house and line of David. 5 He went there to register with Mary, who was
pledged to be married to him and was expecting a child. 6 While they were there, the time came for the
baby to be born, 7 and she gave birth to her firstborn, a son. She wrapped him in cloths and placed him
in a manger, because there was no room for them in the inn.

The Shepherds and the Angels

2:9 [g]Lk 1:11; Ac 5:19
2:10 [h]Mt 14:27
2:11 [i]Mt 1:21; Jn 4:42; Ac 5:31 [j]Mt 1:16; 16:16, 20; Jn 11:27; Ac 2:36
2:12 [k]1Sa 2:34; 2Ki 19:29; Isa 7:14

8 And there were shepherds living out in the fields nearby, keeping watch over their flocks at night.
9 An angel[g] of the Lord appeared to them, and the glory of the Lord shone around them, and they were
terrified. 10 But the angel said to them, "Do not be afraid.[h] I bring you good news of great joy that will be
for all the people. 11 Today in the town of David a Savior[i] has been born to you; he is Christ[a][j] the Lord.
12 This will be a sign[k] to you: You will find a baby wrapped in cloths and lying in a manger."

[a] *11* Or *Messiah.* "The Christ" (Greek) and "the Messiah" (Hebrew) both mean "the Anointed One"; also in verse 26.

1:80 John's parents, already elderly at the time of his birth, probably died while he was young, and he apparently grew up in the desert of Judea, which lies between Jerusalem and the Dead Sea (see the note on Mt 3:1).

2:1 Luke was the only Gospel writer who related his narrative to dates of world history (see "The Historical Value of Luke–Acts" on p. 1697). Caesar Augustus (31 B.C.–A.D. 14) was the first and (according to many) the greatest Roman emperor. See "Caesar Augustus, Emperor of Rome; the Census; and Quirinius, Governor of Syria" on page 1667.

The census was used for military service and taxation (see "The Roman Army and the Occupation of the Holy Land" on p. 1829 and "Roman Taxation" on p. 1855). Jews, however, were exempt from Roman military service.

2:2 Quirinius may have been in office for two terms, with a census associated with each of them. This was the first, and Acts 5:37 refers to the second. See again "Caesar Augustus, Emperor of Rome; the Census; and Quirinius, Governor of Syria" on page 1667.

2:3 "Own town" probably refers to the village of their ancestral origin.

2:4 "Judea" was the Roman designation for the southern part of the Holy Land, earlier included in the kingdom of Judah.

Bethlehem, located 6 miles (10 km) south of Jerusalem, was at least a three-day trek from Nazareth. In Jesus' day Bethlehem was a village of fewer than 1,000 people; today it is a bustling town of 22,000. (See "Bethlehem" on p. 1487, "The Birthplace of Jesus" on p. 1668 and "Nazareth" on p. 1623.)

2:5 Mary, also of the house of David, was probably required to enroll. In Syria, the Roman province in which the Holy Land was located, women twelve years of age and older were required to pay a poll tax and therefore to register. (See "Roman Taxation" on p. 1855.)

For "pledged to be married," see the note on Matthew 1:18–19.

2:7 Newborn babies had their navels cut, and were washed with water, salted and wrapped in swaddling clothes (Eze 16:4; Lk 2:7,12).

The "manger" was the feeding trough of the animals. This is the only indication that Jesus was born in a stable. Very early tradition suggests that his birthplace was a cave, perhaps being used as a stable. Justin Martyr in the second century A.D. stated that Jesus' birth took place in a cave close to the village. Over this traditional manger site the emperor Constantine (A.D. 330) and his mother, Helena, constructed the Church of the Nativity (see "Constantine and Queen Helena's Role in Preserving Holy Sites" on p. 1758). In a part of this cave Jerome, the Latin scholar, spent 30 years translating the Bible into Latin. (See also "The Birthplace of Jesus" on p. 1668.)

In Jeremiah's time (Jer 41:17) the caravan inn of Kimham (see 2Sa 19:37–40) near Bethlehem was the usual starting point for a journey to Egypt. The inn mentioned in Luke 2:7 may have been similar or even the same. On the other hand, the reference may have been to a guest chambers within a private home (see the note on Mk 14:14).

2:8 The fact that the shepherds were "living out in the fields" does not necessarily imply that it was summer, the dry season. The flocks reserved for temple sacrifice were kept in the fields near Bethlehem throughout the year. The shepherds were keeping watch against thieves and predatory animals.

2:9 See "Angels and Guardian Spirits in the Bible and the Ancient Near East" on page 1529.

2:11 The Greeks applied the title *sôtçr* ("savior") to their gods; the term was also used by philosophers (e.g., Epicurus) of rulers (e.g.,

13 Suddenly a great company of the heavenly host appeared with the angel, praising God and
saying,

> 14 "Glory to God in the highest,
> and on earth peace[l] to men on whom his favor rests."

15 When the angels had left them and gone into heaven, the shepherds said to one another, "Let's go to
Bethlehem and see this thing that has happened, which the Lord has told us about."
16 So they hurried off and found Mary and Joseph, and the baby, who was lying in the manger. 17 When
they had seen him, they spread the word concerning what had been told them about this child, 18 and all
who heard it were amazed at what the shepherds said to them. 19 But Mary treasured up all these things
and pondered them in her heart.[m] 20 The shepherds returned, glorifying and praising God[n] for all the
things they had heard and seen, which were just as they had been told.

Jesus Presented in the Temple

21 On the eighth day, when it was time to circumcise him,[o] he was named Jesus, the name the angel
had given him before he had been conceived.[p]
22 When the time of their purification according to the Law of Moses[q] had been completed, Joseph
and Mary took him to Jerusalem to present him to the Lord 23 (as it is written in the Law of the Lord,
"Every firstborn male is to be consecrated to the Lord"[a]),[r] 24 and to offer a sacrifice in keeping with what
is said in the Law of the Lord: "a pair of doves or two young pigeons."[b][s]
25 Now there was a man in Jerusalem called Simeon, who was righteous and devout.[t] He was waiting
for the consolation of Israel,[u] and the Holy Spirit was upon him. 26 It had been revealed to him by the
Holy Spirit that he would not die before he had seen the Lord's Christ. 27 Moved by the Spirit, he went into
the temple courts. When the parents brought in the child Jesus to do for him what the custom of the Law
required,[v] 28 Simeon took him in his arms and praised God, saying:

> 29 "Sovereign Lord, as you have promised,[w]
> you now dismiss[c] your servant in peace.[x]
> 30 For my eyes have seen your salvation,[y]
> 31 which you have prepared in the sight of all people,
> 32 a light for revelation to the Gentiles
> and for glory to your people Israel."[z]

33 The child's father and mother marveled at what was said about him. 34 Then Simeon blessed them
and said to Mary, his mother:[a] "This child is destined to cause the falling[b] and rising of many in Israel,
and to be a sign that will be spoken against, 35 so that the thoughts of many hearts will be revealed. And
a sword will pierce your own soul too."
36 There was also a prophetess,[c] Anna, the daughter of Phanuel, of the tribe of Asher. She was very old;
she had lived with her husband seven years after her marriage, 37 and then was a widow until she was
eighty-four.[d][d] She never left the temple but worshiped night and day, fasting and praying.[e] 38 Coming up
to them at that very moment, she gave thanks to God and spoke about the child to all who were looking
forward to the redemption of Jerusalem.[f]
39 When Joseph and Mary had done everything required by the Law of the Lord, they returned to Gal-
ilee to their own town of Nazareth.[g] 40 And the child grew and became strong; he was filled with wisdom,
and the grace of God was upon him.[h]

2:14 [l]Lk 1:79; Ro 5:1; Eph 2:14, 17
2:19 [m]ver 51
2:20 [n]Mt 9:8
2:21 [o]Lk 1:59 [p]Lk 1:31
2:22 [q]Lev 12:2-8
2:23 [r]Ex 13:2,12, 15; Nu 3:13
2:24 [s]Lev 12:8
2:25 [t]Lk 1:6 [u]ver 38; Isa 52:9; Lk 23:51
2:27 [v]ver 22
2:29 [w]ver 26 [x]Ac 2:24
2:30 [y]Isa 52:10; Lk 3:6
2:32 [z]Isa 42:6; 49:6; Ac 13:47; 26:23
2:34 [a]Mt 12:46 [b]Isa 8:14; Mt 21:44; 1Co 1:23; 2Co 2:16; 1Pe 2:7,8
2:36 [c]Ac 21:9
2:37 [d]1Ti 5:9 [e]Ac 13:3; 14:23; 1Ti 5:5
2:38 [f]ver 25; Isa 40:2; Lk 1:68; 24:21
2:39 [g]ver 51; Mt 2:23
2:40 [h]ver 52; Lk 1:80

[a] 23 Exodus 13:2,12 [b] 24 Lev. 12:8 [c] 29 Or *promised, / now dismiss* [d] 37 Or *widow for eighty-four years*

Ptolemy I, Nero) or men who had conferred notable benefits upon their country. But in the New Testament it is a strictly religious term that is never applied to a mere man.

2:21 See "Circumcision in the Ancient World" on page 1840.

2:22 Following the birth of a son, the mother had to wait 40 days before going to the temple to offer sacrifice for her purification. If she could not afford both a lamb and a pigeon (or a dove), then two pigeons (or doves) were acceptable (see Lev 12:2–8 and the note on v. 2).

2:36–38 The Gospel of Luke is full of evidence of Jesus' understanding of and appreciation for women, thus setting a pattern for normal Christian living. Godly women stand out in Jesus' life and ministry, as reported by Luke, as well as elsewhere in the Gospels.

2:36 Other prophetesses were Miriam (Ex 15:20), Deborah (Jdg 4:4), Huldah (2Ki 22:14) and the daughters of Philip (Ac 21:9). See the note on prophetesses at Exodus 15:20–21.

2:37 Herod's temple was quite large and included rooms for various uses (see "Herod's Temple" on p. 1648), and Anna may have been allowed to live in one of them. This statement, however, probably means that she spent her waking hours attending to and worshiping in the temple.

The Boy Jesus at the Temple

2:41 [i]Ex 23:15; Dt 16:1-8 — 41 Every year his parents went to Jerusalem for the Feast of the Passover.[i] 42 When he was twelve years
old, they went up to the Feast, according to the custom. 43 After the Feast was over, while his parents were
returning home, the boy Jesus stayed behind in Jerusalem, but they were unaware of it. 44 Thinking he was
in their company, they traveled on for a day. Then they began looking for him among their relatives and
friends. 45 When they did not find him, they went back to Jerusalem to look for him. 46 After three days
they found him in the temple courts, sitting among the teachers, listening to them and asking them ques-
2:47 [j]Mt 7:28 — tions. 47 Everyone who heard him was amazed[j] at his understanding and his answers. 48 When his parents
2:48 [k]Mt 12:46 [l]Lk 3:23; 4:22 — saw him, they were astonished. His mother[k] said to him, "Son, why have you treated us like this? Your fa-
ther[l] and I have been anxiously searching for you."
2:49 [m]Jn 2:16 — 49 "Why were you searching for me?" he asked. "Didn't you know I had to be in my Father's house?"[m]
2:50 [n]Mk 9:32 — 50 But they did not understand what he was saying to them.[n]
2:51 [o]ver 39; Mt 2:23 [p]ver 19 — 51 Then he went down to Nazareth with them[o] and was obedient to them. But his mother treasured all
2:52 [q]ver 40; 1Sa 2:26; Lk 1:80 — these things in her heart.[p] 52 And Jesus grew in wisdom and stature, and in favor with God and men.[q]

John the Baptist Prepares the Way

3:1 [r]Mt 27:2 [s]Mt 14:1 — 3 In the fifteenth year of the reign of Tiberius Caesar—when Pontius Pilate[r] was governor of Judea,
Herod[s] tetrarch of Galilee, his brother Philip tetrarch of Iturea and Traconitis, and Lysanias te-
3:2 [t]Mt 26:3; Jn 18:13; Ac 4:6 [u]Mt 3:1 [v]Lk 1:13 — trarch of Abilene— 2 during the high priesthood of Annas and Caiaphas,[t] the word of God came to
John[u] son of Zechariah[v] in the desert. 3 He went into all the country around the Jordan, preaching a bap-
3:3 [w]ver 16; Mk 1:4 — tism of repentance for the forgiveness of sins.[w] 4 As is written in the book of the words of Isaiah the
prophet:

> "A voice of one calling in the desert,
> 'Prepare the way for the Lord,
> make straight paths for him.
> 5 Every valley shall be filled in,
> every mountain and hill made low.
> The crooked roads shall become straight,
> the rough ways smooth.
> 3:6 [x]Ps 98:2; Isa 40:3-5; 42:16; 52:10; Lk 2:30 — 6 And all mankind will see God's salvation.' "[a][x]

3:7 [y]Mt 12:34; 23:33 [z]Ro 1:18 — 7 John said to the crowds coming out to be baptized by him, "You brood of vipers![y] Who warned you
3:8 [a]Isa 51:2; Lk 19:9; Jn 8:33, 39; Ac 13:26; Ro 4:1,11,12,16, 17; Gal 3:7 — to flee from the coming wrath?[z] 8 Produce fruit in keeping with repentance. And do not begin to say to
yourselves, 'We have Abraham as our father.'[a] For I tell you that out of these stones God can raise up chil-
dren for Abraham. 9 The ax is already at the root of the trees, and every tree that does not produce good
3:9 [b]Mt 3:10 — fruit will be cut down and thrown into the fire."[b]
3:10 [c]ver 12,14; Ac 2:37; 16:30 — 10 "What should we do then?"[c] the crowd asked.

[a] *6* Isaiah 40:3-5

2:41 Annual attendance at three feasts by all adult males (normally accompanied by their families) was commanded in the law: Passover, Pentecost and Tabernacles (see Ex 23:14–17; Dt 16:16; see also "The Festivals of Israel" on p. 186). Distance prevented many from attending all three, but most Jews tried to be in Jerusalem for Passover.
2:42 At age twelve boys began preparing to take their places in the religious community during the following year.
2:46 The "teachers" were rabbis, experts in Judaism. In Jesus' day it was not unusual for students to gather at the feet of their rabbis to discuss theology, often in a question-and-answer, discussion format.
3:1–2 Ancient historians (see "Historians in the Ancient World" on p. 939) frequently dated an event by noting the year of the reign of the ruler then in power.
3:1 Several possible dates could be indicated by "the fifteenth year," but the date A.D. 25–26 best fits the chronology of the life of Christ.

Pontius Pilate was the Roman governor of Judea from A.D. 26 to 36 (see "Pontius Pilate" on p. 1714 and "The Roman Governor" on p. 1824). His official residence was in Caesarea on the Mediterranean coast. In 1961 archaeologists unearthed a stone step in the Roman amphitheater in Caesarea contemporary with Pilate and bearing a Latin inscription that included his name. When he came to Jerusalem, he stayed in the magnificent palace built by Herod the Great, located southwest of the temple area. Mark called this palace "the Praetorium" (Mk 15:16; see the notes there and on Mt 27:27), and it was there that the Roman trial of Jesus took place.

At the death of Herod the Great (4 B.C.), three of his sons—Archelaus, Herod Antipas and Herod Philip—were given jurisdiction over his divided kingdom. Herod Antipas became the tetrarch of Galilee and Perea (see the note on Mt 14:1; see also "Herod the Great" on p. 1627 and "Herod's Successors and Uneasy Relations Between Rome and the Jews" on p. 1631).
3:2 Annas was the high priest from A.D. 6 until he was deposed in 15. He was followed by his son Eleazar, his son-in-law Caiaphas and then four more sons. Even though Rome had replaced Annas, the Jews continued to recognize his authority (see Jn 18:13; Ac 4:6), so Luke included his name as well as that of the Roman appointee, Caiaphas (see the note on Mt 26:3; see also "The High Priests Annas and Caiaphas" on p. 1772 and "The Jewish Priesthood and Religious Life in the First Century A.D." on p. 1704).
3:4 Before a king made a journey to a distant country, the roads he would travel were improved. Similarly, moral and spiritual preparation for the Messiah was made by the ministry of John the Baptist.

11 John answered, "The man with two tunics should share with him who has none, and the one who
has food should do the same."[d]
12 Tax collectors also came to be baptized.[e] "Teacher," they asked, "what should we do?"
13 "Don't collect any more than you are required to,"[f] he told them.
14 Then some soldiers asked him, "And what should we do?"
He replied, "Don't extort money and don't accuse people falsely[g]—be content with your pay."
15 The people were waiting expectantly and were all wondering in their hearts if John[h] might possi-
bly be the Christ.[a][i] 16 John answered them all, "I baptize you with[b] water.[j] But one more powerful than I
will come, the thongs of whose sandals I am not worthy to untie. He will baptize you with the Holy Spir-
it and with fire.[k] 17 His winnowing fork[l] is in his hand to clear his threshing floor and to gather the wheat
into his barn, but he will burn up the chaff with unquenchable fire."[m] 18 And with many other words John
exhorted the people and preached the good news to them.
19 But when John rebuked Herod[n] the tetrarch because of Herodias, his brother's wife, and all the oth-
er evil things he had done, 20 Herod added this to them all: He locked John up in prison.[o]

The Baptism and Genealogy of Jesus

21 When all the people were being baptized, Jesus was baptized too. And as he was praying,[p] heaven
was opened 22 and the Holy Spirit descended on him[q] in bodily form like a dove. And a voice came from
heaven: "You are my Son,[r] whom I love; with you I am well pleased."[s]
23 Now Jesus himself was about thirty years old when he began his ministry.[t] He was the son, so it was
thought, of Joseph,[u]

the son of Heli, 24 the son of Matthat,
the son of Levi, the son of Melki,
the son of Jannai, the son of Joseph,
25 the son of Mattathias, the son of Amos,
the son of Nahum, the son of Esli,
the son of Naggai, 26 the son of Maath,
the son of Mattathias, the son of Semein,
the son of Josech, the son of Joda,
27 the son of Joanan, the son of Rhesa,
the son of Zerubbabel,[v] the son of Shealtiel,
the son of Neri, 28 the son of Melki,
the son of Addi, the son of Cosam,
the son of Elmadam, the son of Er,
29 the son of Joshua, the son of Eliezer,
the son of Jorim, the son of Matthat,
the son of Levi, 30 the son of Simeon,
the son of Judah, the son of Joseph,
the son of Jonam, the son of Eliakim,
31 the son of Melea, the son of Menna,
the son of Mattatha, the son of Nathan,[w]
the son of David, 32 the son of Jesse,

3:11 [d] Isa 58:7
3:12 [e] Lk 7:29
3:13 [f] Lk 19:8
3:14 [g] Ex 23:1; Lev 19:11
3:15 [h] Mt 3:1 [i] Jn 1:19,20; Ac 13:25
3:16 [j] ver 3; Mk 1:4 [k] Jn 1:26, 33; Ac 1:5; 11:16; 19:4
3:17 [l] Isa 30:24 [m] Mt 13:30; 25:41
3:19 [n] ver 1
3:20 [o] Mt 14:3,4; Mk 6:17-18
3:21 [p] Mt 14:23; Mk 1:35; 6:46; Lk 5:16; 6:12; 9:18,28; 11:1
3:22 [q] Isa 42:1; Jn 1:32,33; Ac 10:38 [r] Mt 3:17 [s] Mt 3:17
3:23 [t] Mt 4:17; Ac 1:1 [u] Lk 1:27
3:27 [v] Mt 1:12
3:31 [w] 2Sa 5:14; 1Ch 3:5

[a] 15 Or *Messiah* [b] 16 Or *in*

3:11 A tunic was something like a long undershirt (see "Ancient Israelite Clothing and Jewelry" on p. 1059 and "Dress and Fashion in the Greco-Roman World" on p. 2004).
3:12 For "tax collectors," see the notes on Matthew 5:46 and Mark 2:14.
3:14 Limited military forces were allowed for for the proection of certain Jewish leaders and institutions (such as those of Herod Antipas, the police guard of the temple, and escorts for tax collectors). The professions of tax collector and soldier as such were not condemned, but the common unethical practices associated with them were.
3:16 See "Baptism in the Ancient World" on page 1562.
3:17 See "The Threshing Floor" on page 608. For "chaff," see the note on Isaiah 5:24.
3:19–20 Herodias, the granddaughter of Herod the Great, had married her uncle Philip. But his brother Antipas had seen her at Rome, desired her and married her. John the Baptist reproved Herod Antipas for his immoral action and was put in prison for his impudence (Mt 14:3–12; Mk 6:14–29). This did not satisfy Herodias, who by a sordid scheme arranged his death. Later, when Antipas was banished to Spain, Herodias accompanied him and died there. See the note on Matthew 14:3; see also "Herod the Great" on page 1627 and "Herod's Successors and Uneasy Relations Between Rome and the Jews" on page 1631.
3:19 See the note on Matthew 14:3.
3:23 Thirty was the age at which a Levite undertook his service (Nu 4:47) and at which a man was considered mature. (See "The Life of Jesus" on p. 1636.)

the son of Obed, the son of Boaz,
the son of Salmon,[a] the son of Nahshon,
33 the son of Amminadab, the son of Ram,[b]
3:33 [x]Ru 4:18-22; 1Ch 2:10-12 the son of Hezron, the son of Perez,[x]
the son of Judah, 34 the son of Jacob,
the son of Isaac, the son of Abraham,
3:34 [y]Ge 11:24, 26 the son of Terah, the son of Nahor,[y]
35 the son of Serug, the son of Reu,
the son of Peleg, the son of Eber,
the son of Shelah, 36 the son of Cainan,
3:36 [z]Ge 11:12 [a]Ge 5:28-32 the son of Arphaxad,[z] the son of Shem,
the son of Noah, the son of Lamech,[a]
37 the son of Methuselah, the son of Enoch,
the son of Jared, the son of Mahalalel,
the son of Kenan, 38 the son of Enosh,
the son of Seth, the son of Adam,
3:38 [b]Ge 5:1,2, 6-9 the son of God.[b]

The Temptation of Jesus

4:1 [c]ver 14,18 [d]Lk 3:3,21 [e]Lk 2:27 4:2 [f]Ex 34:28; 1Ki 19:8

4 Jesus, full of the Holy Spirit,[c] returned from the Jordan[d] and was led by the Spirit[e] in the desert,
2 where for forty days[f] he was tempted by the devil. He ate nothing during those days, and at the end
of them he was hungry.
3 The devil said to him, "If you are the Son of God, tell this stone to become bread."
4:4 [g]Dt 8:3 4 Jesus answered, "It is written: 'Man does not live on bread alone.'[c]"[g]
4:5 [h]Mt 24:14 5 The devil led him up to a high place and showed him in an instant all the kingdoms of the world.[h]
4:6 [i]Jn 12:31; 14:30; 1Jn 5:19 6 And he said to him, "I will give you all their authority and splendor, for it has been given to me,[i] and I
can give it to anyone I want to. 7 So if you worship me, it will all be yours."
4:8 [j]Dt 6:13 8 Jesus answered, "It is written: 'Worship the Lord your God and serve him only.'[d]"[j]
9 The devil led him to Jerusalem and had him stand on the highest point of the temple. "If you are the
Son of God," he said, "throw yourself down from here. 10 For it is written:

" 'He will command his angels concerning you
to guard you carefully;
11 they will lift you up in their hands,
so that you will not strike your foot against
4:11 [k]Ps 91:11, 12 a stone.'[e]"[k]

4:12 [l]Dt 6:16 12 Jesus answered, "It says: 'Do not put the Lord your God to the test.'[f]"[l]
4:13 [m]Heb 4:15 [n]Jn 14:30 13 When the devil had finished all this tempting,[m] he left him[n] until an opportune time.

Jesus Rejected at Nazareth

4:14 [o]Mt 4:12 [p]Mt 9:26 14 Jesus returned to Galilee[o] in the power of the Spirit, and news about him spread through the whole
4:15 [q]Mt 4:23 countryside.[p] 15 He taught in their synagogues,[q] and everyone praised him.
4:16 [r]Mt 2:23 [s]Mt 13:54 16 He went to Nazareth,[r] where he had been brought up, and on the Sabbath day he went into the syn-
agogue,[s] as was his custom. And he stood up to read. 17 The scroll of the prophet Isaiah was handed to
him. Unrolling it, he found the place where it is written:

[a] 32 Some early manuscripts *Sala* [b] 33 Some manuscripts *Amminadab, the son of Admin, the son of Arni*; other manuscripts vary widely. [c] 4 Deut. 8:3 [d] 8 Deut. 6:13 [e] 11 Psalm 91:11,12 [f] 12 Deut. 6:16

4:1 The "desert" refers to the desert of Judea (see the notes on Mt 3:1; Luke 1:80).
4:9 The "highest point of the temple" refers either to the southeastern corner of the temple colonnade, from which there was a drop of some 100 feet (30.5 m) to the Kidron Valley below or to the pinnacle of the temple proper.
For "temple," see the note on Matthew 4:5.
4:15 For "taught in their synagogues," see the note on Mark 1:21.
4:16 See "Nazareth" on page 1623.
Jesus probably read from Isaiah in Hebrew, and then he or someone else paraphrased the passage in Aramaic, one of the other common languages of the day.
4:17 The books of the Old Testament were written on scrolls (see the note on Ex 17:14) that were kept in a special place in the synagogue and handed to the reader by a special attendant. The passage Jesus read about the Messiah (Isa 61:1–2) may have been one he had chosen or the assigned passage for the day.

18 "The Spirit of the Lord is on me,[t]
because he has anointed me
to preach good news to the poor.
He has sent me to proclaim freedom for the prisoners
and recovery of sight for the blind,
to release the oppressed,
19 to proclaim the year of the Lord's favor."[a][u]

4:18 [t]Jn 3:34

4:19 [u]Lev 25:10; Isa 61:1,2

[a] 19 Isaiah 61:1,2

Disease and Medicine in the Ancient World

LUKE 4 Ancient doctors were few in number, expensive, lacking in knowledge of effective treatments and, although learned for their time, still quite ignorant and superstitious. Temples to Asclepius, the Greco-Roman god of healing, were found all over the Mediterranean world. These temples were somewhat like the spas of today; therapy consisted more of rest, massage and a modified diet than of what we would call medicine. Religion also played a major role. A common healing method was "incubation," whereby the sick person would sleep in the confines of the temple of Asclepius in the hope of receiving a dream-revelation from the god. Those who had been healed made special contributions to the temples, which often included plaster reproductions of whatever parts of their bodies had been healed. These were set on display as testimonies to the healing power of the god.[1]

Diagnoses of medical conditions with prognoses of outcome; Babylonia, c. 1900–1700 B.C.

© The Schøyen Collection; photography courtesy of Mr. Martin Schøyen

The second-century orator and chronic invalid Aelius Aristides, in his *Sacred Tales*, gives us an insight into the need people had for healing and the methods employed to that end.[2] After falling ill on a journey to Rome and enduring brutal surgery at the hands of Roman doctors, Aristides became a devotee of Asclepius. The cures prescribed for him in the dreams included bathing in a churning river during winter, pouring mud on himself before sitting in the courtyard of the temple, walking about without shoes all winter and blood-letting from various parts of his body.

It was in such a world that Jesus performed his ministry of healing. Unlike many doctors connected to temples, Jesus healed without charge or fanfare. Also, he did not follow any specific ritual that might have been regarded as the key to tapping into magical, healing power.[3] Sometimes he would touch a person; in other instances he might place a daub of mud on a blind man's eyes (Jn 9:6) or simply speak a word (Mt 8:13). In short, Jesus' healings pointed to the power of God that dwelled within him; they did not encourage people to seek out rituals for magical healing but were part of his proclamation of the kingdom. Physical healing pointed always to the restoration of creation.

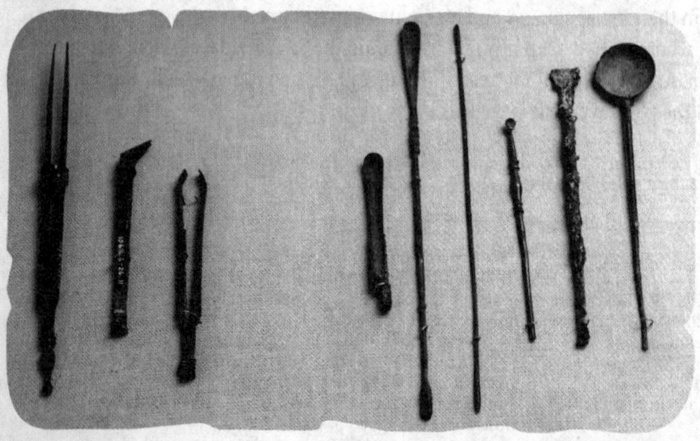

Ancient surgical instruments

Preserving Bible Times; © Dr. James C. Martin; permission of The British Museum

[1]See also "The Gods of the Greeks and Romans" on page 1908. [2]See "Miracle Workers and Magicians in the First Century A.D." on page 1706. [3]See "Magic in the Greco-Roman World" on page 1911.

[20]Then he rolled up the scroll, gave it back to the attendant and sat down.[v] The eyes of everyone in the synagogue were fastened on him, [21]and he began by saying to them, "Today this scripture is fulfilled in your hearing."

[22]All spoke well of him and were amazed at the gracious words that came from his lips. "Isn't this Joseph's son?" they asked.[w]

[23]Jesus said to them, "Surely you will quote this proverb to me: 'Physician, heal yourself! Do here in your hometown[x] what we have heard that you did in Capernaum.' "[y]

[24]"I tell you the truth," he continued, "no prophet is accepted in his hometown.[z] [25]I assure you that there were many widows in Israel in Elijah's time, when the sky was shut for three and a half years and there was a severe famine throughout the land.[a] [26]Yet Elijah was not sent to any of them, but to a widow in Zarephath in the region of Sidon.[b] [27]And there were many in Israel with leprosy[a] in the time of Elisha the prophet, yet not one of them was cleansed—only Naaman the Syrian."[c]

[28]All the people in the synagogue were furious when they heard this. [29]They got up, drove him out of the town,[d] and took him to the brow of the hill on which the town was built, in order to throw him down the cliff. [30]But he walked right through the crowd and went on his way.[e]

Jesus Drives Out an Evil Spirit

[31]Then he went down to Capernaum,[f] a town in Galilee, and on the Sabbath began to teach the people. [32]They were amazed at his teaching,[g] because his message had authority.[h]

[33]In the synagogue there was a man possessed by a demon, an evil[b] spirit. He cried out at the top of his voice, [34]"Ha! What do you want with us,[i] Jesus of Nazareth?[j] Have you come to destroy us? I know who you are[k]—the Holy One of God!"[l]

[35]"Be quiet!" Jesus said sternly.[m] "Come out of him!" Then the demon threw the man down before them all and came out without injuring him.

[36]All the people were amazed[n] and said to each other, "What is this teaching? With authority[o] and power he gives orders to evil spirits and they come out!" [37]And the news about him spread throughout the surrounding area.[p]

Jesus Heals Many

[38]Jesus left the synagogue and went to the home of Simon. Now Simon's mother-in-law was suffering from a high fever, and they asked Jesus to help her. [39]So he bent over her and rebuked[q] the fever, and it left her. She got up at once and began to wait on them.

[40]When the sun was setting, the people brought to Jesus all who had various kinds of sickness, and laying his hands on each one,[r] he healed them.[s] [41]Moreover, demons came out of many people, shouting, "You are the Son of God!"[t] But he rebuked[u] them and would not allow them to speak,[v] because they knew he was the Christ.[c]

[42]At daybreak Jesus went out to a solitary place. The people were looking for him and when they came to where he was, they tried to keep him from leaving them. [43]But he said, "I must preach the good news of the kingdom of God[w] to the other towns also, because that is why I was sent." [44]And he kept on preaching in the synagogues of Judea.[d][x]

4:20 [v]ver 17; Mt 26:55
4:22 [w]Mt 13:54, 55; Jn 6:42; 7:15
4:23 [x]ver 16 [y]Mk 1:21-28; 2:1-12
4:24 [z]Mt 13:57; Jn 4:44
4:25 [a]1Ki 17:1; 18:1; Jas 5:17,18
4:26 [b]1Ki 17:8-16; Mt 11:21
4:27 [c]2Ki 5:1-14
4:29 [d]Nu 15:35; Ac 7:58; Heb 13:12
4:30 [e]Jn 8:59; 10:39
4:31 [f]ver 23; Mt 4:13
4:32 [g]Mt 7:28 [h]ver 36; Mt 7:29
4:34 [i]Mt 8:29 [j]Mk 1:24 [k]Jas 2:19 [l]ver 41; Mk 1:24
4:35 [m]ver 39,41; Mt 8:26; Lk 8:24
4:36 [n]Mt 7:28 [o]ver 32; Mt 7:29; Mt 10:1
4:37 [p]ver 14; Mt 9:26
4:39 [q]ver 35,41
4:40 [r]Mk 5:23 [s]Mt 4:23
4:41 [t]Mt 4:3 [u]ver 35 [v]Mt 8:4
4:43 [w]Mt 3:2
4:44 [x]Mt 4:23

[a] *27* The Greek word was used for various diseases affecting the skin—not necessarily leprosy. [b] *33* Greek *unclean*; also in verse 36 [c] *41* Or *Messiah* [d] *44* Or *the land of the Jews*; some manuscripts *Galilee*

4:20 It was customary to stand while reading Scripture but to sit while teaching.

4:23 Jesus' hometown was Nazareth (see the note on Mt 2:23, as well as "Nazareth" on p. 1623), where he was raised, although he had been born in Bethlehem.

For "Capernaum," see the note on Matthew 4:13.

4:25 See the note on famine at Ruth 1:1. Also see "Famine in the Ancient Near East" on page 70.

4:26 Sidon, one of the oldest Phoenician cities, lay 20 miles (32 km) north of Tyre. See "Sidon" on page 1536.

4:31 Jesus often taught in the synagogues (see the note on Mk 1:21, as well as "The Capernaum Synagogue" on p. 1591).

4:33 To pagans, "demon" meant a supernatural being, whether good or bad, but Luke made it clear that this was an evil spirit. See "Demons and the Bible" on page 1572.

4:34 For "Holy One of God," see the note on Mark 1:24.

4:38 For "synagogue," see the note on Mark 1:21. Jesus probably went to Simon's house for a meal, since the main Sabbath meal was served immediately following the synagogue service. See "Houses in the Holy Land of the First Century A.D.: Peter's House in Capernaum; Insulae" on page 1584.

4:40 The Sabbath (v. 31) was over at sundown (about 6:00 P.M.). According to the tradition of the elders (see the note on Mt 15:2), Jews could not carry a burden or travel more than about .66 miles (1 km) on the Sabbath. Only after sundown could they carry the sick to Jesus, and their eagerness is seen in the fact that they set out while the sun was still setting.

4:41 See "Demons and the Bible" on page 1572.

The Calling of the First Disciples

5 One day as Jesus was standing by the Lake of Gennesaret,[a] with the people crowding around him and
listening to the word of God,[y] 2he saw at the water's edge two boats, left there by the fishermen, who 5:1 [y]Mk 4:14; Heb 4:12
were washing their nets. 3He got into one of the boats, the one belonging to Simon, and asked him to put
out a little from shore. Then he sat down and taught the people from the boat.[z] 5:3 [z]Mt 13:2
4When he had finished speaking, he said to Simon, "Put out into deep water, and let down[b] the nets
for a catch."[a] 5:4 [a]Jn 21:6
5Simon answered, "Master,[b] we've worked hard all night and haven't caught anything.[c] But because 5:5 [b]Lk 8:24,45; 9:33,49; 17:13 [c]Jn 21:3
you say so, I will let down the nets."
6When they had done so, they caught such a large number of fish that their nets began to break.[d] 7So 5:6 [d]Jn 21:11
they signaled their partners in the other boat to come and help them, and they came and filled both
boats so full that they began to sink.
8When Simon Peter saw this, he fell at Jesus' knees and said, "Go away from me, Lord; I am a sinful
man!"[e] 9For he and all his companions were astonished at the catch of fish they had taken, 10and so were 5:8 [e]Ge 18:27; Job 42:6; Isa 6:5
James and John, the sons of Zebedee, Simon's partners.
Then Jesus said to Simon, "Don't be afraid;[f] from now on you will catch men." 11So they pulled their 5:10 [f]Mt 14:27
boats up on shore, left everything and followed him.[g] 5:11 [g]ver 28; Mt 4:19

The Man With Leprosy

12While Jesus was in one of the towns, a man came along who was covered with leprosy.[c][h] When he saw 5:12 [h]Mt 8:2
Jesus, he fell with his face to the ground and begged him, "Lord, if you are willing, you can make me clean."

a *1* That is, Sea of Galilee *b* *4* The Greek verb is plural. *c* *12* The Greek word was used for various diseases affecting the skin—not necessarily leprosy.

5:1 Luke was the only Gospel writer to call this body of water the Lake of Gennesaret. The others referred to it as the Sea of Galilee (see Mk 1:16 and its note), and John twice called it the Sea of Tiberias (see Jn 6:1 and its note; see also 21:1).

5:2 After each period of fishing, the nets were washed, stretched and prepared for reuse (see "Fishing in New Testament Times" on p. 1676).

5:3 Sitting down was the usual position for teaching.

5:12 For "leprosy," see the NIV text note and "Skin Diseases in the Ancient World" on page 171.

Fishing in New Testament Times

LUKE 5 Fishing was an important part of the Galilean economy, as reflected in place-names like Bethsaida ("House of Fish") and Taricheae ("Preserved Fish Town"). The major types of fish in the Sea of Galilee would have been tilapia, carp and sardines. Much of the catch would have been dried for sale or manufactured into fish sauce and imported throughout the Mediterranean world. Fishing was thus embedded in the larger economy of the Roman Empire.[1]

In 1986 a fishing boat from the time of Jesus was discovered on the northwestern shore of the Sea of Galilee.[2] Largely made of cedar and oak, the boat measured 26.5 feet (8 m) long, 7.5 feet (2.3 m) wide and 4.5 feet (1.4 m) deep. It could hold approximately one ton—either five crew members and the catch or the crew and ten passengers. The fishermen could have used a large dragnet, which might have been hundreds of feet long, or a circular casting net approximately 6.3–8.8 yards (5.7–8 m) in diameter. A hook and line might also have been employed. Galilean fishermen were most often employees or partners in small, family-run business cooperatives. Storms were a real danger in that they could come in quickly off the Mediterranean through the wind tunnel formed by the Arbel Pass.

[1]See "The Roman Empire" on page 1845 and "Trade and Mercantilism in the Roman Empire" on page 2070. [2]See "Galilee in Jesus' Time" on page 1587.

13 Jesus reached out his hand and touched the man. "I am willing," he said. "Be clean!" And immedi-
ately the leprosy left him.
5:14 [i]Mt 8:4 14 Then Jesus ordered him, "Don't tell anyone,[i] but go, show yourself to the priest and offer the sacri-
[j]Lev 14:2-32 fices that Moses commanded[j] for your cleansing, as a testimony to them."
5:15 [k]Mt 9:26 15 Yet the news about him spread all the more,[k] so that crowds of people came to hear him and to be
5:16 [l]Mt 14:23; Lk 3:21 healed of their sicknesses. 16 But Jesus often withdrew to lonely places and prayed.[l]

Jesus Heals a Paralytic

5:17 [m]Mt 15:1; 17 One day as he was teaching, Pharisees and teachers of the law,[m] who had come from every village
Lk 2:46 [n]Mk 5:30; Lk 6:19 of Galilee and from Judea and Jerusalem, were sitting there. And the power of the Lord was present for
him to heal the sick.[n] 18 Some men came carrying a paralytic on a mat and tried to take him into the
house to lay him before Jesus. 19 When they could not find a way to do this because of the crowd, they
went up on the roof and lowered him on his mat through the tiles into the middle of the crowd, right in
front of Jesus.
5:20 [o]Lk 7:48,49 20 When Jesus saw their faith, he said, "Friend, your sins are forgiven."[o]
21 The Pharisees and the teachers of the law began thinking to themselves, "Who is this fellow who
5:21 [p]Isa 43:25 speaks blasphemy? Who can forgive sins but God alone?"[p]
22 Jesus knew what they were thinking and asked, "Why are you thinking these things in your hearts?
23 Which is easier: to say, 'Your sins are forgiven,' or to say, 'Get up and walk'? 24 But that you may know that
5:24 [q]Mt 8:20 the Son of Man[q] has authority on earth to forgive sins . . ." He said to the paralyzed man, "I tell you, get
up, take your mat and go home." 25 Immediately he stood up in front of them, took what he had been ly-
5:26 [r]Mt 9:8 ing on and went home praising God. 26 Everyone was amazed and gave praise to God.[r] They were filled
with awe and said, "We have seen remarkable things today."

The Calling of Levi

27 After this, Jesus went out and saw a tax collector by the name of Levi sitting at his tax booth. "Fol-
5:27 [s]Mt 4:19 low me,"[s] Jesus said to him, 28 and Levi got up, left everything and followed him.[t]
5:28 [t]ver 11; Mt 4:19 29 Then Levi held a great banquet for Jesus at his house, and a large crowd of tax collectors[u] and oth-
5:29 [u]Lk 15:1
5:30 [v]Ac 23:9 ers were eating with them. 30 But the Pharisees and the teachers of the law who belonged to their sect[v]
[w]Mt 9:11 complained to his disciples, "Why do you eat and drink with tax collectors and 'sinners'?"[w]
31 Jesus answered them, "It is not the healthy who need a doctor, but the sick. 32 I have not come to call
5:32 [x]Jn 3:17 the righteous, but sinners to repentance."[x]

Jesus Questioned About Fasting

5:33 [y]Lk 7:18; 33 They said to him, "John's disciples[y] often fast and pray, and so do the disciples of the Pharisees, but
Jn 1:35; 3:25,26 yours go on eating and drinking."
5:34 [z]Jn 3:29 34 Jesus answered, "Can you make the guests of the bridegroom[z] fast while he is with them? 35 But the
5:35 [a]Lk 9:22; 17:22; Jn 16:5-7 time will come when the bridegroom will be taken from them;[a] in those days they will fast."
36 He told them this parable: "No one tears a patch from a new garment and sews it on an old one. If
he does, he will have torn the new garment, and the patch from the new will not match the old. 37 And no
one pours new wine into old wineskins. If he does, the new wine will burst the skins, the wine will run
out and the wineskins will be ruined. 38 No, new wine must be poured into new wineskins. 39 And no one
after drinking old wine wants the new, for he says, 'The old is better.' "

5:14 See the note on Mark 1:44.

5:17 For "Pharisees" ("separated ones"), see the note on Matthew 3:7. Numbering about 6,000 and spread over the whole of the Holy Land, they were teachers in the synagogues, religious examples in the eyes of the people and self-appointed guardians of the law and its proper observance. They considered the interpretations and regulations handed down by tradition (see the note on Mt 15:2) to be virtually as authoritative as Scripture.

For "teachers of the law," see the note on Matthew 2:4. Also called "scribes" (see "The Scribe" on p. 682), they studied, interpreted and taught the law (both written and oral). The majority of these teachers belonged to the party of the Pharisees.

5:19 The reference to roofing tiles is apparently to clay roofing—tiles with which the roof was covered. Clay tiles were not commonly used as roofing material for houses in Palestine, roofs usually being covered with a mixture of clay and straw (see the note on Mk 2:4). It may be that Luke was using the expression "through the tiles" to mean "through the roof," without reference to the material used. For "roof," see also the note on Mark 2:4.

5:27 Tax collectors were regarded as corrupt conspirators with the occupying Roman government (see the notes on Mt 5:46; Mk 2:14).

5:29–32 See the note on Matthew 9:9. See also "Jewish Meals and Meal Customs" on page 1575 and "Triclinia" on page 1748.

5:38 For "new wineskins," see the note on Matthew 9:17.

ANCIENT VOICES

The book of the rule of the community: To seek God with the whole heart and the entire being, to do what is good and right before him, just as he commanded by the hand of Moses and by the hand of all his servants the prophets; to love all that he has chosen and hate all that he has rejected; to be far from all evil and to cling to all good deeds; to behave with integrity, righteousness, and justice in the land; and to walk no longer in the stubbornness of a guilty heart and lustful eyes, whereby one does all kinds of evil . . .

Now this is the rule for the men of the community, that is, for those who of their own volition turn away from all evil and cling to all that he commanded us according to his will. They should separate from the congregation of wicked men and become a community in doctrine and in common possession of property, and conduct their affairs under the direction of the sons of Zadok, who are the priests who keep the covenant, and under the direction of the full body of the men of the community, which is a community of men who hold fast to the covenant. Under their direction every decision will be made in every matter of doctrine, community property and enforcement of rules, so that they may together behave with integrity and humility, with righteousness and justice and love of kindness, and so that they may be careful to walk in all the ways of the community, and that no one may walk in the stubbornness of his heart and go astray, following his own heart and eyes and inclinations.

—EXCERPTS FROM THE COMMUNITY RULE OF QUMRAN

From the Dead Sea Scrolls, 1QS, beginnings of chapters 1 and 5, trans. by Duane Garrett

See "Qumran and the New Testament" article.

Lord of the Sabbath

6 One Sabbath Jesus was going through the grainfields, and
his disciples began to pick some heads of grain, rub them
in their hands and eat the kernels.[b] 2 Some of the Pharisees 6:1 [b]Dt 23:25
asked, "Why are you doing what is unlawful on the Sabbath?"[c] 6:2 [c]Mt 12:2
3 Jesus answered them, "Have you never read what David did
when he and his companions were hungry?[d] 4 He entered the 6:3 [d]1Sa 21:6
house of God, and taking the consecrated bread, he ate what is
lawful only for priests to eat.[e] And he also gave some to his com- 6:4 [e]Lev 24:5,9
panions." 5 Then Jesus said to them, "The Son of Man[f] is Lord of 6:5 [f]Mt 8:20
the Sabbath."

6 On another Sabbath[g] he went into the synagogue and was 6:6 [g]ver 1
teaching, and a man was there whose right hand was shriveled.
7 The Pharisees and the teachers of the law were looking for a
reason to accuse Jesus, so they watched him closely[h] to see if he 6:7 [h]Mt 12:10 [i]Mt 12:2
would heal on the Sabbath.[i] 8 But Jesus knew what they were
thinking[j] and said to the man with the shriveled hand, "Get up 6:8 [j]Mt 9:4
and stand in front of everyone." So he got up and stood there.

9 Then Jesus said to them, "I ask you, which is lawful on the
Sabbath: to do good or to do evil, to save life or to destroy it?"

10 He looked around at them all, and then said to the man,
"Stretch out your hand." He did so, and his hand was complete-
ly restored. 11 But they were furious[k] and began to discuss with 6:11 [k]Jn 5:18
one another what they might do to Jesus.

The Twelve Apostles

12 One of those days Jesus went out to a mountainside to pray,
and spent the night praying to God.[l] 13 When morning came, he 6:12 [l]Lk 3:21
called his disciples to him and chose twelve of them, whom he
also designated apostles:[m] 14 Simon (whom he named Peter), 6:13 [m]Mk 6:30
his brother Andrew, James, John, Philip, Bartholomew, 15 Mat-
thew,[n] Thomas, James son of Alphaeus, Simon who was called 6:15 [n]Mt 9:9
the Zealot, 16 Judas son of James, and Judas Iscariot, who be-
came a traitor.

Blessings and Woes

17 He went down with them and stood on a level place. A large
crowd of his disciples was there and a great number of people
from all over Judea, from Jerusalem, and from the coast of Tyre
and Sidon,[o] 18 who had come to hear him and to be healed of 6:17 [o]Mt 4:25; 11:21; Mk 3:7,8

6:1 See the notes on Matthew 12:1 and Mark 2:24.
6:4 For "consecrated bread," see the note on Matthew 12:4.
6:5 *Logia* is the Greek word for "sententious sayings" or "epigrams" purported to be nonbiblical sayings of Christ, the latest collection of which is the so-called Gospel of Thomas, discovered in 1945. The church has from the outset been aware of recorded sayings of Jesus not included in the Gospels. For instance, the apostle Paul spoke of "the words the Lord Jesus himself said: 'It is more blessed to give than to receive'" (Ac 20:35). The Muslims claim to have maintained some such sayings, one displayed on a mosque near Agra: "Jesus, on whom be peace, said, The world is merely a bridge; ye are to pass over it, and not build your dwellings upon it."

An ancient manuscript titled the Codex Bezae inserts a *logion* after Luke 6:5: "On the same day, seeing someone working on the Sabbath, he said to him, Man if you know what you are doing, blessed you are. If you do not know, you are accursed, and a transgressor of the law."
6:7 See the note on Mark 3:2.

6:14 Bartholomew is mentioned in all four of the lists of the apostles in the New Testament (Mt 10:3; Mk 3:18; Lk 6:14; Ac 1:13). There is no further reference to him in the New Testament, and the traditions concerning him are not trustworthy. Some scholars think that Bartholomew was the surname of Nathanael, who was led to Christ by Philip (Jn 1:45–46). The reason for this is that in the listing of the apostles in the Gospels the name Bartholomew immediately follows that of Philip, and the Synoptic Gospels never mention Nathanael, while John never mentions Bartholomew. This view has, however, not been conclusively established.
6:15 For "Zealot," see the note on Matthew 10:4.
6:16 "Judas son of James" is called "Thaddaeus" in Matthew 10:3 and Mark 3:18 (see the note of Mt 10:3).
6:17 The Sermon on the Plain (vv. 20–49) is Luke's counterpart to Matthew's Sermon on the Mount.

For information on Tyre and Sidon, see the notes on Matthew 15:21 and Mark 7:31.

Qumran and the New Testament

Scroll fragments from Qumran
Preserving Bible Times; © Dr. James C. Martin; permission of The Amman Museum

LUKE 6 The **Dead Sea Scrolls** (found at **Qumran**) are the texts of a Jewish religious community now called the Qumran community. Numerous scholars have pointed out that there are similarities between the beliefs and practices of the Qumran community and those of New Testament Christians. Some have gone so far as to view Christianity as an offshoot of the Qumran community. There is no doubt that the Dead Sea Scrolls provide a unique window into the world of early Judaism and that their value for understanding the New Testament is great, but it is possible to exaggerate the similarities and overlook the differences between the Qumran community and the early Christians.

To be sure, we can find significant examples of how the Qumran community parallels the New Testament church:

✣ The Qumran community saw itself as the remnant of Israel that had entered into a new covenant with God in the end times.

✣ The community relied on revelations given to the "Teacher of Righteousness," who had been persecuted by the Jerusalem authorities for his unorthodox beliefs.[1]

✣ Community members made a sustained effort to read the Old Testament Scriptures in light of the realities of the "last days" that had now come upon Israel.

But these similarities should not be allowed to mask some crucial differences:

✣ Unlike the Qumran community, the early Christians did not withdraw into the desert. Instead, they remained within the Jewish communities in the Holy Land and in the **Diaspora**.[2]

✣ Even more radical was the willingness of the early Christians to bring the Good News to the Gentiles, an idea completely absent from Qumran.

✣ The Qumran community abandoned the Jewish mainstream largely because of perceived defects in their calendar and in their interpretation of purity laws.[3] The early Christians, meanwhile, made it clear that such matters should not be allowed to become sources of division (cf. Mt 7:19; Col 2:20–23).

✣ Finally, while the instruction of the Teacher of Righteousness remained foundational for the Qumran community, this concept pales beside the Christian belief that Jesus has risen from the dead and sits exalted to reign at the right hand of God.

In sum, the Dead Sea Scrolls give us information on the kinds of issues of concern to Jews during the New Testament era: the identity of God's true people, questions of ritual and purity and the search for a fresh word of revelation in troubled times. But the community that emerged from Jesus' teaching was radically different from that of Qumran. In many ways Qumran depicts for us "the road not taken" by the early Christians.

[1]See "Biblical Interpretation at Qumran and Among the Early Rabbis" on page 1603. [2]See "The Church From the Resurrection to the Conversion of Paul" on page 1766 and "The Jewish Diaspora in the First Century A.D." on page 1769. [3]See "The Jewish Priesthood and Religious Life in the First Century A.D." on page 1704.

Caves 4a and 4b at Qumran
Photograph courtesy of © Dr. Gary Pratico

their diseases. Those troubled by evil[a] spirits were cured, 19and the people all tried to touch him,[p] because
power was coming from him and healing them all.[q]
20Looking at his disciples, he said:

"Blessed are you who are poor,
for yours is the kingdom of God.[r]
21 Blessed are you who hunger now,
for you will be satisfied.[s]
Blessed are you who weep now,
for you will laugh.[t]
22 Blessed are you when men hate you,
when they exclude you[u] and insult you[v]
and reject your name as evil,
because of the Son of Man.[w]

23"Rejoice in that day and leap for joy,[x] because great is your reward in heaven. For that is how their
fathers treated the prophets.[y]

24"But woe to you who are rich,[z]
for you have already received your comfort.[a]
25 Woe to you who are well fed now,
for you will go hungry.[b]
Woe to you who laugh now,
for you will mourn and weep.[c]
26 Woe to you when all men speak well of you,
for that is how their fathers treated the false prophets.[d]

Love for Enemies

27"But I tell you who hear me: Love your enemies, do good to those who hate you,[e] 28bless those who
curse you, pray for those who mistreat you.[f] 29If someone strikes you on one cheek, turn to him the oth-
er also. If someone takes your cloak, do not stop him from taking your tunic. 30Give to everyone who asks
you, and if anyone takes what belongs to you, do not demand it back.[g] 31Do to others as you would have
them do to you.[h]
32"If you love those who love you, what credit is that to you?[i] Even 'sinners' love those who love them.
33And if you do good to those who are good to you, what credit is that to you? Even 'sinners' do that. 34And
if you lend to those from whom you expect repayment, what credit is that to you?[j] Even 'sinners' lend to
'sinners,' expecting to be repaid in full. 35But love your enemies, do good to them,[k] and lend to them
without expecting to get anything back. Then your reward will be great, and you will be sons[l] of the Most
High,[m] because he is kind to the ungrateful and wicked. 36Be merciful,[n] just as your Father[o] is merciful.

Judging Others

37"Do not judge, and you will not be judged.[p] Do not condemn, and you will not be condemned. For-
give, and you will be forgiven.[q] 38Give, and it will be given to you. A good measure, pressed down, shak-
en together and running over, will be poured into your lap.[r] For with the measure you use, it will be mea-
sured to you."[s]
39He also told them this parable: "Can a blind man lead a blind man? Will they not both fall into a
pit?[t] 40A student is not above his teacher, but everyone who is fully trained will be like his teacher.[u]
41"Why do you look at the speck of sawdust in your brother's eye and pay no attention to the plank in
your own eye? 42How can you say to your brother, 'Brother, let me take the speck out of your eye,' when
you yourself fail to see the plank in your own eye? You hypocrite, first take the plank out of your eye, and
then you will see clearly to remove the speck from your brother's eye.

[a] 18 Greek *unclean*

6:19 [p]Mt 9:20 [q]Mt 14:36; Mk 5:30; Lk 5:17
6:20 [r]Mt 25:34
6:21 [s]Isa 55:1,2; Mt 5:6 [t]Isa 61:2, 3; Mt 5:4; Rev 7:17
6:22 [u]Jn 9:22; 16:2 [v]Isa 51:7 [w]Jn 15:21
6:23 [x]Mt 5:12 [y]Mt 5:12
6:24 [z]Jas 5:1 [a]Lk 16:25
6:25 [b]Isa 65:13 [c]Pr 14:13
6:26 [d]Mt 7:15
6:27 [e]ver 35; Mt 5:44; Ro 12:20
6:28 [f]Mt 5:44
6:30 [g]Dt 15:7,8, 10; Pr 21:26
6:31 [h]Mt 7:12
6:32 [i]Mt 5:46
6:34 [j]Mt 5:42
6:35 [k]ver 27 [l]Ro 8:14 [m]Mk 5:7
6:36 [n]Jas 2:13 [o]Mt 5:48; 6:1; Lk 11:2; 12:32; Ro 8:15; Eph 4:6; 1Pe 1:17; 1Jn 1:3; 3:1
6:37 [p]Mt 7:1 [q]Mt 6:14
6:38 [r]Ps 79:12; Isa 65:6,7 [s]Mt 7:2; Mk 4:24
6:39 [t]Mt 15:14
6:40 [u]Mt 10:24; Jn 13:16

6:20–49 For commentary on the Sermon on the Mount, see the note on Matthew 5:1—7:29.
6:29 For "cloak" and "tunic," see the note on Matthew 5:40.
6:31 See the note on Matthew 7:12.
6:38 "Poured into your lap" probably refers to the way an outer garment was worn, leaving a fold over the belt that could be used as a large pocket to hold a measure of wheat.

A Tree and Its Fruit

43“No good tree bears bad fruit, nor does a bad tree bear good fruit. 44Each tree is recognized by its
6:44 [v]Mt 12:33 own fruit.[v] People do not pick figs from thornbushes, or grapes from briers. 45The good man brings good
things out of the good stored up in his heart, and the evil man brings evil things out of the evil stored
6:45 [w]Pr 4:23; Mt 12:34,35; Mk 7:20 up in his heart. For out of the overflow of his heart his mouth speaks.[w]

The Wise and Foolish Builders

6:46 [x]Jn 13:13 [y]Mal 1:6; Mt 7:21 46“Why do you call me, ‘Lord, Lord,’[x] and do not do what I say?[y] 47I will show you what he is like who
6:47 [z]Lk 8:21; 11:28; Jas 1:22-25 comes to me and hears my words and puts them into practice.[z] 48He is like a man building a house, who
dug down deep and laid the foundation on rock. When a flood came, the torrent struck that house but
could not shake it, because it was well built. 49But the one who hears my words and does not put them
into practice is like a man who built a house on the ground without a foundation. The moment the tor-
rent struck that house, it collapsed and its destruction was complete.”

The Faith of the Centurion

7:1 [a]Mt 7:28 **7** When Jesus had finished saying all this[a] in the hearing of the people, he entered Capernaum. 2There
a centurion’s servant, whom his master valued highly, was sick and about to die. 3The centurion
heard of Jesus and sent some elders of the Jews to him, asking him to come and heal his servant. 4When
they came to Jesus, they pleaded earnestly with him, “This man deserves to have you do this, 5because
he loves our nation and has built our synagogue.” 6So Jesus went with them.

He was not far from the house when the centurion sent friends to say to him: “Lord, don’t trouble
yourself, for I do not deserve to have you come under my roof. 7That is why I did not even consider my-
7:7 [b]Ps 107:20 self worthy to come to you. But say the word, and my servant will be healed.[b] 8For I myself am a man un-
der authority, with soldiers under me. I tell this one, ‘Go,’ and he goes; and that one, ‘Come,’ and he comes.
I say to my servant, ‘Do this,’ and he does it.”

9When Jesus heard this, he was amazed at him, and turning to the crowd following him, he said, “I tell
you, I have not found such great faith even in Israel.” 10Then the men who had been sent returned to the
house and found the servant well.

Jesus Raises a Widow’s Son

11Soon afterward, Jesus went to a town called Nain, and his disciples and a large crowd went along with
him. 12As he approached the town gate, a dead person was being carried out—the only son of his moth-
7:13 [c]ver 19; Lk 10:1; 13:15; 17:5; 22:61; 24:34; Jn 11:2 er, and she was a widow. And a large crowd from the town was with her. 13When the Lord[c] saw her, his
heart went out to her and he said, “Don’t cry.”

14Then he went up and touched the coffin, and those carrying it stood still. He said, “Young man, I
7:14 [d]Mt 9:25; Mk 1:31; Lk 8:54; Jn 11:43; Ac 9:40 say to you, get up!”[d] 15The dead man sat up and began to talk, and Jesus gave him back to his mother.

7:16 [e]Lk 1:65 [f]Mt 9:8 [g]ver 39; Mt 21:11 [h]Lk 1:68 16They were all filled with awe[e] and praised God.[f] “A great prophet[g] has appeared among us,” they
said. “God has come to help his people.”[h] 17This news about Jesus spread throughout Judea[a] and the sur-
7:17 [i]Mt 9:26 rounding country.[i]

Jesus and John the Baptist

7:18 [j]Mt 3:1 [k]Lk 5:33 18John’s[j] disciples[k] told him about all these things. Calling two of them, 19he sent them to the Lord to
ask, “Are you the one who was to come, or should we expect someone else?”

20When the men came to Jesus, they said, “John the Baptist sent us to you to ask, ‘Are you the one who
was to come, or should we expect someone else?’ ”

[a] 17 Or *the land of the Jews*

7:1 For “Capernaum,” see the note on Matthew 4:13.
7:2 This centurion was probably a member of Herod Antipas’s forces, which were organized in Roman fashion, often in companies of 100 men.
7:3 The “elders of the Jews” (see the note on Mt 21:23) were highly respected Jews of the community, though not necessarily rulers of the synagogue.
7:11–17 For New Testament burial practices, see the note on Matthew 26:12. See also “Jewish Burial Practices” on page 1688 and “Perfumes and Anointing Oils” on page 1746.
7:11 Nain was a small village located about 6 miles (nearly 10 km) southeast of Nazareth. A village by that name is still located there today.
7:14 The man was probably being carried in an open coffin, suggested by Jewish custom (see “Jewish Burial Practices” on p. 1688) and by the fact that he sat up in response to Jesus’ command. By touching the coffin, Jesus risked ritual uncleanness (cf. Nu 19:16).

21 At that very time Jesus cured many who had diseases, sicknesses[l] and evil spirits, and gave sight to 7:21 [l]Mt 4:23
many who were blind. 22 So he replied to the messengers, "Go back and report to John what you have seen
and heard: The blind receive sight, the lame walk, those who have leprosy[a] are cured, the deaf hear, the
dead are raised, and the good news is preached to the poor.[m] 23 Blessed is the man who does not fall away 7:22 [m]Isa 29:18, 19; 35:5,6; 61:1, 2; Lk 4:18
on account of me."
24 After John's messengers left, Jesus began to speak to the crowd about John: "What did you go out into
the desert to see? A reed swayed by the wind? 25 If not, what did you go out to see? A man dressed in fine

[a] 22 The Greek word was used for various diseases affecting the skin—not necessarily leprosy.

The Jewish Custom of Kissing

LUKE 7 In the Biblical world, kissing could be either erotic or nonerotic in nature, but the nonerotic variety is most commonly mentioned in the Bible. In Old Testament narratives, relatives often kissed one another as a greeting, especially following a long absence (Ge 27:26–27; 29:11,13; 33:4; 45:15; Ex 18:7). Kissing was also a sign of farewell prior to a prolonged departure (Ge 31:28; Ru 1:9; 1Ki 19:20). Close, nonfamilial friends also greeted one another with a kiss, such as in the case of David and Jonathan (1Sa 20:41), and it was not uncommon to kiss a guest as a sign of hospitality. This ritual could also demonstrate homage or submission. In 1 Samuel 10:1, for example, Samuel anointed David king and kissed him as part of the ritual. Likewise, in Psalm 2:12 the kings of the earth are commanded to "kiss the Son" as a way of expressing homage to the Messiah.

By contrast, kissing for sexual pleasure is mentioned in Proverbs 7:13 and Song of Songs 1:2. In Biblical times public kissing was always of the nonerotic nature and was either between friends or relatives of the same sex or relatives of the opposite sex. Kissing one's lover—or even one's spouse—in public was taboo, because such an action might easily cross the boundary between nonerotic and erotic (SS 8:1).

Extrabiblical literature of the time also refers to both erotic and nonerotic kissing. Egyptian love poetry written from the thirteenth century B.C. speaks of the pleasures young men and women take in each other's kisses. Greco-Roman narratives contain many examples of the use of the kiss as a greeting but also suggest that the Greeks and Romans were uncomfortable with public kissing.

The custom of kissing remained common among the Jews throughout the New Testament period. Early Jewish sources suggest that there were three kinds of acceptable public kisses: those for greeting, for farewell or for expressing devotion. In Jesus' parable, a father greets a long lost son with a kiss (Lk 15:20). Judas's act of kissing Jesus (Mt 26:49; Lk 22:47) connoted affection, as well as, most likely, devotion to him as a teacher (thus Judas called out, "Greetings, Rabbi!"); it was therefore darkly ironic that this was the sign of his betrayal of Jesus. A distinctive case is that of the sinful woman in 7:36–50, who repeatedly kissed Jesus' feet, though she was neither a close friend nor a relative. Nevertheless, her kisses were not erotic but were a sign of devotion and repentance. Even so, her actions made some of the guests uncomfortable. When Simon criticized the woman's actions, Jesus pointed out that his host had failed to offer even the traditional kiss of greeting, whereas the woman had not ceased offering kisses of devotion.

Paul regularly called upon Christians to greet one another with a "holy kiss," a term that appears to have been a Christian innovation (Ro 16:16; 1Co 16:20; 2Co 13:12; 1Th 5:26). It is possible that the qualifier "holy" was added to make clear that such kisses were to be given in such a way that they had no erotic connotations. It is conceivable that such a kiss was given in concert with the celebration of the Lord's Supper and thus was holy by virtue of its association with that sacrament. At any rate, the gesture was clearly intended to reinforce the bond of love between believers.

clothes? No, those who wear expensive clothes and indulge in luxury are in palaces. [26]But what did you go
7:26 [n]Mt 11:9 out to see? A prophet?[n] Yes, I tell you, and more than a prophet. [27]This is the one about whom it is written:

> " 'I will send my messenger ahead of you,
> **7:27** [o]Mal 3:1; Mt 11:10; Mk 1:2 who will prepare your way before you.'[a] [o]

[28]I tell you, among those born of women there is no one greater than John; yet the one who is least in the
7:28 [p]Mt 3:2 kingdom of God[p] is greater than he."
[29](All the people, even the tax collectors, when they heard Jesus' words, acknowledged that God's way
7:29 [q]Mt 21:32; Mk 1:5; Lk 3:12 was right, because they had been baptized by John.[q] [30]But the Pharisees and experts in the law[r] reject-
7:30 [r]Mt 22:35 ed God's purpose for themselves, because they had not been baptized by John.)
[31]"To what, then, can I compare the people of this generation? What are they like? [32]They are like chil-
dren sitting in the marketplace and calling out to each other:

> " 'We played the flute for you,
> and you did not dance;
> we sang a dirge,
> and you did not cry.'

7:33 [s]Lk 1:15 [33]For John the Baptist came neither eating bread nor drinking wine,[s] and you say, 'He has a demon.' [34]The
Son of Man came eating and drinking, and you say, 'Here is a glutton and a drunkard, a friend of tax col-
7:34 [t]Lk 5:29,30; 15:1,2 lectors and "sinners." '[t] [35]But wisdom is proved right by all her children."

Jesus Anointed by a Sinful Woman

[36]Now one of the Pharisees invited Jesus to have dinner with him, so he went to the Pharisee's house
and reclined at the table. [37]When a woman who had lived a sinful life in that town learned that Jesus was
eating at the Pharisee's house, she brought an alabaster jar of perfume, [38]and as she stood behind him
at his feet weeping, she began to wet his feet with her tears. Then she wiped them with her hair, kissed
them and poured perfume on them.
7:39 [u]ver 16; Mt 21:11 [39]When the Pharisee who had invited him saw this, he said to himself, "If this man were a prophet,[u]
he would know who is touching him and what kind of woman she is—that she is a sinner."
[40]Jesus answered him, "Simon, I have something to tell you."
"Tell me, teacher," he said.
[41]"Two men owed money to a certain moneylender. One owed him five hundred denarii,[b] and the
other fifty. [42]Neither of them had the money to pay him back, so he canceled the debts of both. Now which
of them will love him more?"
[43]Simon replied, "I suppose the one who had the bigger debt canceled."
"You have judged correctly," Jesus said.
[44]Then he turned toward the woman and said to Simon, "Do you see this woman? I came into your
7:44 [v]Ge 18:4; 19:2; 43:24; Jdg 19:21; Jn 13:4-14; 1Ti 5:10 house. You did not give me any water for my feet,[v] but she wet my feet with her tears and wiped them with
her hair. [45]You did not give me a kiss,[w] but this woman, from the time I entered, has not stopped kissing
my feet. [46]You did not put oil on my head,[x] but she has poured perfume on my feet. [47]Therefore, I tell
7:45 [w]Lk 22:47, 48; Ro 16:16 you, her many sins have been forgiven—for she loved much. But he who has been forgiven little loves
7:46 [x]Ps 23:5; Ecc 9:8 little."
7:48 [y]Mt 9:2 [48]Then Jesus said to her, "Your sins are forgiven."[y]
[49]The other guests began to say among themselves, "Who is this who even forgives sins?"
7:50 [z]Mt 9:22; Mk 5:34; Lk 8:48 [a]Ac 15:33 [50]Jesus said to the woman, "Your faith has saved you;[z] go in peace."[a]

[a] *27* Mal. 3:1 [b] *41* A denarius was a coin worth about a day's wages.

7:29 For "tax collectors," see the notes on Matthew 5:46 and Mark 2:14.
7:30 The "experts in the law" were "scribes" (NIV "teachers of the law"), most of whom were Pharisees. (For "Pharisees" and "teachers of the law," see the notes on Mt 2:4; 3:7; Lk 5:17).
7:32 For "marketplace," see "The Ancient Agora" on page 1799.
7:37 For "alabaster jar," see the note on Mark 14:3; for "perfume," see "Perfumes and Anointing Oils" on page 1746.
7:38 Jesus reclined on a couch with his feet extended away from the table, which made it possible for the woman to wipe his feet with her hair and without disturbing him. (See "Jewish Meals and Meal Customs" on p. 1575 and "Triclinia" on p. 1758.)
7:41 For "denarii," see the NIV text note and the notes on Matthew 20:2 and 22:19.
7:44–46 For Hebrew/Jewish feasting, see the note on Matthew 22:2–14.
7:44 Providing water for a guest's feet was a minimal gesture of hospitality.
7:45 A kiss was a common greeting (see "The Jewish Custom of Kissing" on p. 1682).

The Parable of the Sower

8 After this, Jesus traveled about from one town and village to another, proclaiming the good news of
the kingdom of God.[b] The Twelve were with him, 2and also some women who had been cured of 8:1 [b]Mt 4:23
evil spirits and diseases: Mary (called Magdalene)[c] from whom seven demons had come out; 3Joanna 8:2 [c]Mt 27:55,56
the wife of Cuza, the manager of Herod's[d] household; Susanna; and many others. These women were 8:3 [d]Mt 14:1
helping to support them out of their own means.

4While a large crowd was gathering and people were coming to Jesus from town after town, he told
this parable: 5"A farmer went out to sow his seed. As he was scattering the seed, some fell along the path;
it was trampled on, and the birds of the air ate it up. 6Some fell on rock, and when it came up, the plants
withered because they had no moisture. 7Other seed fell among thorns, which grew up with it and choked
the plants. 8Still other seed fell on good soil. It came up and yielded a crop, a hundred times more than
was sown."

When he said this, he called out, "He who has ears to hear, let him hear."[e] 8:8 [e]Mt 11:15

9His disciples asked him what this parable meant. 10He said, "The knowledge of the secrets of the
kingdom of God has been given to you,[f] but to others I speak in parables, so that, 8:10 [f]Mt 13:11 [g]Isa 6:9; Mt 13:13,14

" 'though seeing, they may not see;
though hearing, they may not understand.'[a][g]

11"This is the meaning of the parable: The seed is the word of God.[h] 12Those along the path are the 8:11 [h]Heb 4:12
ones who hear, and then the devil comes and takes away the word from their hearts, so that they may not
believe and be saved. 13Those on the rock are the ones who receive the word with joy when they hear it,
but they have no root. They believe for a while, but in the time of testing they fall away.[i] 14The seed that 8:13 [i]Mt 11:6
fell among thorns stands for those who hear, but as they go on their way they are choked by life's wor-
ries, riches[j] and pleasures, and they do not mature. 15But the seed on good soil stands for those with a 8:14 [j]Mt 19:23; 1Ti 6:9,10,17
noble and good heart, who hear the word, retain it, and by persevering produce a crop.

A Lamp on a Stand

16"No one lights a lamp and hides it in a jar or puts it under a bed. Instead, he puts it on a stand, so
that those who come in can see the light.[k] 17For there is nothing hidden that will not be disclosed, and 8:16 [k]Mt 5:15; Mk 4:21; Lk 11:33
nothing concealed that will not be known or brought out into the open.[l] 18Therefore consider carefully 8:17 [l]Mt 10:26; Mk 4:22; Lk 12:2
how you listen. Whoever has will be given more; whoever does not have, even what he thinks he has will
be taken from him."[m] 8:18 [m]Mt 13:12; 25:29; Lk 19:26

Jesus' Mother and Brothers

19Now Jesus' mother and brothers came to see him, but they were not able to get near him because of
the crowd. 20Someone told him, "Your mother and brothers[n] are standing outside, wanting to see you." 8:20 [n]Jn 7:5
21He replied, "My mother and brothers are those who hear God's word and put it into practice."[o] 8:21 [o]Lk 6:47; 11:28; Jn 14:21

Jesus Calms the Storm

22One day Jesus said to his disciples, "Let's go over to the other side of the lake." So they got into a boat
and set out. 23As they sailed, he fell asleep. A squall came down on the lake, so that the boat was being
swamped, and they were in great danger.

[a] *10* Isaiah 6:9

8:2 Mary Magdalene's hometown was Magdala. She is not to be confused with the sinful woman of chapter 7 or with Mary of Bethany (Jn 11:1).
8:5 In that day seed was scattered by hand—a method which, by its nature, left some to fall on unproductive ground. In Eastern practice the seed was sometimes sown first and the field plowed afterward. Roads and pathways crisscrossed many fields, and the traffic made much of the surface too hard for the seed to take root.
8:6 See the note on Matthew 13:5.
8:16 In Jesus' day people used small clay lamps that burned olive oil drawn up by a wick. Because they gave off only modest light, they were placed on a stand for maximum benefit. The "jar" mentioned here was a large container holding about 8 quarts (8.8 l) of ground meal or flour.
8:19 Jesus' brothers did not believe in him at this time (Jn 7:5). Various interpretations concerning their relationship to Jesus arose in the early church: They were sons of Joseph by a previous marriage (according to Epiphanius) or Jesus' cousins (per Jerome). The most natural conclusion (suggested by Helvidius) is that they were the sons of Joseph and Mary and, as such, younger half brothers of Jesus. Four of these brothers are named in Mark 6:3, where sisters are also mentioned. Since Joseph is not referred to here, it is likely that he had died. (See "The Family of Joseph, Mary and Jesus" on p. 1581.)
8:22 For "lake," see the note on 5:1.
8:23 For "squall," see the note on Mark 4:37.

THE SYNOPTIC PROBLEM AND "Q"

LUKE 8 The bulk of the material recorded in Luke 8 also appears in Matthew and Mark. At times the authors used language that was nearly identical (cf. Mt 8:27 with Mk 4:41; Lk 8:25). They displayed further similarities in the order in which they arranged their material (cf. Mk 4:1–25 with Lk 8:4–18). Observations of this sort have prompted reflection on the precise relationship that exists among the **Synoptic Gospels** (the Gospels of Matthew, Mark and Luke). How are the similarities in wording and arrangement to be explained? The "Synoptic Problem" is the name that has been given to the question of these relationships.

Some explain the parallels in the synoptic accounts with appeals to historical accuracy or inspiration by the Holy Spirit. However, two accounts of the same incident may both be historically accurate without employing identical or nearly identical wording. Furthermore, as the Synoptic Gospels were inspired by the Holy Spirit, so was the Gospel of John, yet John's word choice and ordering of material are quite different from that of the synoptic authors.[1] Inspiration need not require or even imply precise agreement in wording or similar arrangement of material.

The stories of Jesus' life and ministry circulated widely in the first century, forming a body of oral tradition. Undoubtedly the evangelists all drew upon this common body of tradition in writing their Gospels. Although the role of common oral tradition should not be underestimated, it seems likely that the Synoptic Gospels share some sort of literary relationship and that the later Gospel writers used one or more of the earlier writings as a source for their works. Several hypotheses attempt to explain the precise literary relationship of the Synoptic Gospels, although no single proposal solves all of the difficulties.

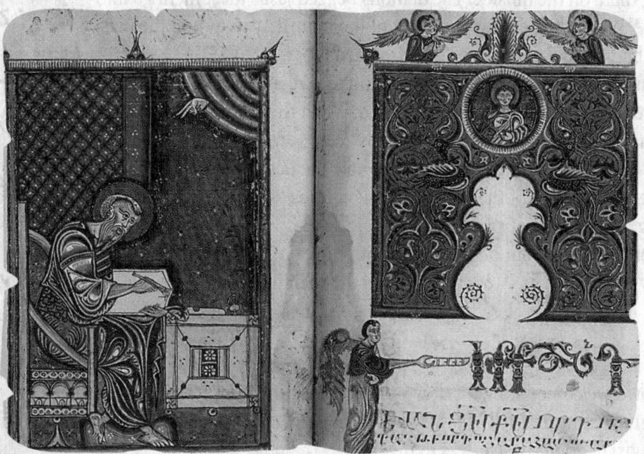

Armenian copy of the Gospels dated to 1435 A.D.
© The Schøyen Collection; photography courtesy of Mr. Martin Schøyen

One widely held solution to the Synoptic Problem is the Two-Source Hypothesis. These two sources are identified as Mark and "Q" (an unknown source).

◆ This theory claims that Mark was the first Gospel written (an idea referred to as "Markan priority") and that Matthew and Luke both independently used Mark as a source, often polishing its literary style and making editorial changes. Matthew and Luke also added material that is absent from Mark's Gospel.[2]

◆ Sometimes Matthew and Luke referred to the same or similar events, suggesting that they were drawing upon a second common source. This hypothetical source for Matthew and Luke has been given the name "**Q source**" (from the German *Quelle*, meaning "source"). No copies of "Q" exist, but by definition it is a source containing material common to Matthew and Luke but not found in Mark. Therefore "Q" is said to include such passages as the temptations of Jesus by the devil (Mt 4:2–11; Lk 4:2–13), the Beatitudes (Mt 5:3–12; Lk 6:20–23) and the Lord's Prayer (Mt 6:9–13; Lk 11:2–4).

Still, the very existence of "Q" is purely hypothetical and much debated, and alternative explanations for the history of the writing of the Synoptic Gospels have been proposed. Not all New Testament scholars believe in Markan priority, and some insist that more attention needs to be given to the fact that Matthew was an eyewitness to many of the events he recorded.

[1]See "Can John's Gospel Be Trusted?" on page 1761. [2]See "The Ending of Mark" on page 1661.

24 The disciples went and woke him, saying, "Master, Master,[p] we're going to drown!" **8:24** [p]Lk 5:5
He got up and rebuked[q] the wind and the raging waters; the storm subsided, and all was calm.[r] [q]Lk 4:35,39,41 [r]Ps 107:29;
25 "Where is your faith?" he asked his disciples. Jnh 1:15
In fear and amazement they asked one another, "Who is this? He commands even the winds and the
water, and they obey him."

The Healing of a Demon-possessed Man

26 They sailed to the region of the Gerasenes,[a] which is across the lake from Galilee. 27 When Jesus
stepped ashore, he was met by a demon-possessed man from the town. For a long time this man had not
worn clothes or lived in a house, but had lived in the tombs. 28 When he saw Jesus, he cried out and fell
at his feet, shouting at the top of his voice, "What do you want with me,[s] Jesus, Son of the Most High **8:28** [s]Mt 8:29
God?[t] I beg you, don't torture me!" 29 For Jesus had commanded the evil[b] spirit to come out of the man. [t]Mk 5:7
Many times it had seized him, and though he was chained hand and foot and kept under guard, he had
broken his chains and had been driven by the demon into solitary places.
30 Jesus asked him, "What is your name?"
"Legion," he replied, because many demons had gone into him. 31 And they begged him repeatedly
not to order them to go into the Abyss.[u] **8:31** [u]Rev 9:1,2, 11; 11:7; 17:8;
32 A large herd of pigs was feeding there on the hillside. The demons begged Jesus to let them go into 20:1,3
them, and he gave them permission. 33 When the demons came out of the man, they went into the pigs,
and the herd rushed down the steep bank into the lake[v] and was drowned. **8:33** [v]ver 22,23
34 When those tending the pigs saw what had happened, they ran off and reported this in the town
and countryside, 35 and the people went out to see what had happened. When they came to Jesus, they
found the man from whom the demons had gone out, sitting at Jesus' feet,[w] dressed and in his right **8:35** [w]Lk 10:39
mind; and they were afraid. 36 Those who had seen it told the people how the demon-possessed[x] man **8:36** [x]Mt 4:24
had been cured. 37 Then all the people of the region of the Gerasenes asked Jesus to leave them,[y] because **8:37** [y]Ac 16:39
they were overcome with fear. So he got into the boat and left.
38 The man from whom the demons had gone out begged to go with him, but Jesus sent him away,
saying, 39 "Return home and tell how much God has done for you." So the man went away and told all
over town how much Jesus had done for him.

A Dead Girl and a Sick Woman

40 Now when Jesus returned, a crowd welcomed him, for they were all expecting him. 41 Then a man
named Jairus, a ruler of the synagogue,[z] came and fell at Jesus' feet, pleading with him to come to his **8:41** [z]ver 49;
house 42 because his only daughter, a girl of about twelve, was dying. Mk 5:22
As Jesus was on his way, the crowds almost crushed him. 43 And a woman was there who had been
subject to bleeding[a] for twelve years,[c] but no one could heal her. 44 She came up behind him and touched **8:43** [a]Lev 15:25-30
the edge of his cloak,[b] and immediately her bleeding stopped. **8:44** [b]Mt 9:20
45 "Who touched me?" Jesus asked.
When they all denied it, Peter said, "Master,[c] the people are crowding and pressing against you." **8:45** [c]Lk 5:5
46 But Jesus said, "Someone touched me;[d] I know that power has gone out from me."[e] **8:46** [d]Mt 14:36;
47 Then the woman, seeing that she could not go unnoticed, came trembling and fell at his feet. In the Mk 3:10 [e]Lk 5:17; 6:19
presence of all the people, she told why she had touched him and how she had been instantly healed.
48 Then he said to her, "Daughter, your faith has healed you.[f] Go in peace."[g] **8:48** [f]Mt 9:22
49 While Jesus was still speaking, someone came from the house of Jairus, the synagogue ruler.[h] "Your [g]Ac 15:33 **8:49** [h]ver 41
daughter is dead," he said. "Don't bother the teacher any more."

[a] *26* Some manuscripts *Gadarenes*; other manuscripts *Gergesenes*; also in verse 37 [b] *29* Greek *unclean* [c] *43* Many manuscripts *years, and she had spent all she had on doctors*

8:24 See "Storm Gods, Storm Imagery and Theophany" on page 808.
8:26 The Gospels describe the location of this event in two ways: (1) the region of the Gerasenes (see the note on Mk 5:1); (2) the region of the Gadarenes (see the note on Mt 8:28). Some manuscripts of Matthew, Mark and Luke read "Gergesenes." For commentary on this discrepancy, see "Gergesenes, Gerasenes or Gadarenes?" on page 1635.
8:27 See "Demons and the Bible" on page 1572.
8:30 For "Legion," see the note on Mark 5:9.
8:31 The Abyss was the place of confinement for evil spirits and for Satan (see the note on Rev 9:1; see also "Sheol, Hades, Gehenna, the Abyss and Tartarus: Images of Hell" on p. 946).
8:32 Pigs were unclean to Jews, and eating them was strictly forbidden (Lev 11:7–8), but this was the Decapolis (see the note on Mt 4:25), a predominately Gentile territory.
8:41 The ruler of the synagogue was responsible for conducting services, selecting participants and maintaining order. See also the note on Mark 5:22.
8:43 See the note on Matthew 9:20.

50 Hearing this, Jesus said to Jairus, "Don't be afraid; just believe, and she will be healed."
51 When he arrived at the house of Jairus, he did not let anyone go in with him except Peter, John and
8:51 [i]Mt 4:21 8:52 [j]Lk 23:27 James,[i] and the child's father and mother. 52 Meanwhile, all the people were wailing and mourning[j] for her.
[k]Mt 9:24; Jn 11:11,13 "Stop wailing," Jesus said. "She is not dead but asleep."[k]
53 They laughed at him, knowing that she was dead. 54 But he took her by the hand and said, "My child,
8:54 [l]Lk 7:14 get up!"[l] 55 Her spirit returned, and at once she stood up. Then Jesus told them to give her something to
8:56 [m]Mt 8:4 eat. 56 Her parents were astonished, but he ordered them not to tell anyone what had happened.[m]

Jesus Sends Out the Twelve

9 When Jesus had called the Twelve together, he gave them power and authority to drive out all de-
9:1 [n]Mt 10:1 [o]Mt 4:23; Lk 5:17 mons[n] and to cure diseases,[o] 2 and he sent them out to preach the kingdom of God[p] and to heal the
9:2 [p]Mt 3:2 sick. 3 He told them: "Take nothing for the journey—no staff, no bag, no bread, no money, no extra tu-
9:3 [q]Lk 10:4; 22:35 nic.[q] 4 Whatever house you enter, stay there until you leave that town. 5 If people do not welcome you,
9:5 [r]Mt 10:14 shake the dust off your feet when you leave their town, as a testimony against them."[r] 6 So they set out and
went from village to village, preaching the gospel and healing people everywhere.
9:7 [s]Mt 14:1 [t]Mt 3:1 [u]ver 19 7 Now Herod[s] the tetrarch heard about all that was going on. And he was perplexed, because some
9:8 [v]Mt 11:14 [w]ver 19; Jn 1:21 were saying that John[t] had been raised from the dead,[u] 8 others that Elijah had appeared,[v] and still oth-
ers that one of the prophets of long ago had come back to life.[w] 9 But Herod said, "I beheaded John. Who,
9:9 [x]Lk 23:8 then, is this I hear such things about?" And he tried to see him.[x]

Jesus Feeds the Five Thousand

9:10 [y]Mk 6:30 [z]Mt 11:21 10 When the apostles[y] returned, they reported to Jesus what they had done. Then he took them with
him and they withdrew by themselves to a town called Bethsaida,[z] 11 but the crowds learned about it and
9:11 [a]ver 2; Mt 3:2 followed him. He welcomed them and spoke to them about the kingdom of God,[a] and healed those who
needed healing.
12 Late in the afternoon the Twelve came to him and said, "Send the crowd away so they can go to the
surrounding villages and countryside and find food and lodging, because we are in a remote place here."
13 He replied, "You give them something to eat."
They answered, "We have only five loaves of bread and two fish—unless we go and buy food for all
this crowd." 14 (About five thousand men were there.)
But he said to his disciples, "Have them sit down in groups of about fifty each." 15 The disciples did so,
and everybody sat down. 16 Taking the five loaves and the two fish and looking up to heaven, he gave
9:16 [b]Mt 14:19 thanks and broke them.[b] Then he gave them to the disciples to set before the people. 17 They all ate and
were satisfied, and the disciples picked up twelve basketfuls of broken pieces that were left over.

Peter's Confession of Christ

9:18 [c]Lk 3:21 18 Once when Jesus was praying[c] in private and his disciples were with him, he asked them, "Who do
the crowds say I am?"
9:19 [d]Mt 3:1 [e]ver 7,8 19 They replied, "Some say John the Baptist;[d] others say Elijah; and still others, that one of the proph-
ets of long ago has come back to life."[e]
20 "But what about you?" he asked. "Who do you say I am?"
9:20 [f]Jn 1:49; 6:66-69; 11:27 Peter answered, "The Christ[a] of God."[f]
9:21 [g]Mt 16:20; Mk 8:30 21 Jesus strictly warned them not to tell this to anyone.[g] 22 And he said, "The Son of Man[h] must suffer
9:22 [h]Mt 8:20 [i]Mt 16:21 many things[i] and be rejected by the elders, chief priests and teachers of the law,[j] and he must be killed[k]
[j]Mt 27:1,2 and on the third day[l] be raised to life."[m]
[k]Ac 2:23; 3:13 [l]Mt 16:21 23 Then he said to them all: "If anyone would come after me, he must deny himself and take up his
[m]Mt 16:21 cross daily and follow me.[n] 24 For whoever wants to save his life will lose it, but whoever loses his life for
9:23 [n]Mt 10:38; Lk 14:27 9:24 [o]Jn 12:25 me will save it.[o] 25 What good is it for a man to gain the whole world, and yet lose or forfeit his very self?

[a] *20* Or *Messiah*

8:52 For "wailing and mourning," see the note on Mark 5:38.
9:1 See "Demons and the Bible" on page 1572.
9:5 Shaking the dust off their feet was a sign of repudiation of the people there for their rejection of God's message, as well as a gesture indicating separation from everything associated with the place (see also the note on Mt 10:14).
9:7 For "Herod the tetrarch," see the note on Matthew 14:1.
9:10 For "Bethsaida," see the note on Mark 8:22.
9:14 See the note on Mark 6:44.
9:17 See the note on Mark 6:43.
9:22 The Jews were looking for a deliverer, not a suffering servant.

Jewish Burial Practices

LUKE 9 In the New Testament era, the death of a relative required immediate attention, along with a period of mourning after burial.[1] Because Jewish law prohibited dead bodies from remaining within the city walls of Jerusalem overnight, it was necessary to bury a corpse on the day of death. This tradition was practiced throughout Judea. Corpses were immediately washed, anointed with perfumes or oils and wrapped in linen. The linen was typically in strips, though there is evidence that some bodies were wrapped in single garments.

A tomb in Jerusalem from the Second Temple period
Photograph: © Todd Bolen/Bible Places.com

The dead were carried to the place of burial on a bier (Lk 7:14), typically accompanied by a large procession. A eulogizer might have preceded the body, while dirge singers and pipers typically joined the mourners. Depending upon the degree of wealth of the deceased, the body was either laid in an earthen grave to be covered with dirt and stones or placed within a tomb hewn from rock. Such tombs were often, but not always, sealed with rocks or millstones. Interment often involved **ossuaries**, chests in which the bones of decayed corpses were collected and later reburied.

After burial, mourning continued for seven days (though it could last up to 30 days), as the family and community participated with dirge singing, weeping, the application of dust or ashes upon the head and/or fasting. Within the context of such burial customs, Jesus' words were radical; he insisted that pursuing and joining the advancing kingdom of God takes precedence even over family loyalty and social convention.[2]

[1]See "Sackcloth and Ashes: Rituals of Lamentation" on page 820 and "Ancient Near Eastern Laments" on page 1305. [2]For information on Jesus' burial, see "The Location of Jesus' Tomb" on page 1615 and "The Soldiers Guarding the Tomb" on page 1618. For information on burials during the Old Testament period, see "Tombs in Ancient Israel" on page 376.

Ossuaries left in a cave
Preserving Bible Times; © Dr. James C. Martin

9:26 [p]Mt 10:33; 26 If anyone is ashamed of me and my words, the Son of Man will be ashamed of him[p] when he comes in
Lk 12:9; 2Ti 2:12 his glory and in the glory of the Father and of the holy angels.[q] 27 I tell you the truth, some who are stand-
[q]Mt 16:27 ing here will not taste death before they see the kingdom of God."

The Transfiguration

9:28 [r]Mt 4:21 28 About eight days after Jesus said this, he took Peter, John and James[r] with him and went up onto a
[s]Lk 3:21 mountain to pray.[s] 29 As he was praying, the appearance of his face changed, and his clothes became as
bright as a flash of lightning. 30 Two men, Moses and Elijah, 31 appeared in glorious splendor, talking with
9:31 [t]2Pe 1:15 Jesus. They spoke about his departure,[t] which he was about to bring to fulfillment at Jerusalem. 32 Peter
9:32 [u]Mt 26:43 and his companions were very sleepy,[u] but when they became fully awake, they saw his glory and the
9:33 [v]Lk 5:5 two men standing with him. 33 As the men were leaving Jesus, Peter said to him, "Master,[v] it is good for
us to be here. Let us put up three shelters—one for you, one for Moses and one for Elijah." (He did not
know what he was saying.)
34 While he was speaking, a cloud appeared and enveloped them, and they were afraid as they entered
9:35 [w]Isa 42:1 the cloud. 35 A voice came from the cloud, saying, "This is my Son, whom I have chosen;[w] listen to him."[x]
[x]Mt 3:17 36 When the voice had spoken, they found that Jesus was alone. The disciples kept this to themselves, and
9:36 [y]Mt 17:9 told no one at that time what they had seen.[y]

The Healing of a Boy With an Evil Spirit

37 The next day, when they came down from the mountain, a large crowd met him. 38 A man in the
crowd called out, "Teacher, I beg you to look at my son, for he is my only child. 39 A spirit seizes him and
he suddenly screams; it throws him into convulsions so that he foams at the mouth. It scarcely ever leaves
him and is destroying him. 40 I begged your disciples to drive it out, but they could not."
9:41 [z]Dt 32:5 41 "O unbelieving and perverse generation,"[z] Jesus replied, "how long shall I stay with you and put up
with you? Bring your son here."
42 Even while the boy was coming, the demon threw him to the ground in a convulsion. But Jesus re-
buked the evil[a] spirit, healed the boy and gave him back to his father. 43 And they were all amazed at the
greatness of God.
While everyone was marveling at all that Jesus did, he said to his disciples, 44 "Listen carefully to what
9:44 [a]ver 22 I am about to tell you: The Son of Man is going to be betrayed into the hands of men."[a] 45 But they did
9:45 [b]Mk 9:32 not understand what this meant. It was hidden from them, so that they did not grasp it,[b] and they were
afraid to ask him about it.

Who Will Be the Greatest?

9:46 [c]Lk 22:24 46 An argument started among the disciples as to which of them would be the greatest.[c] 47 Jesus, know-
9:47 [d]Mt 9:4 ing their thoughts,[d] took a little child and had him stand beside him. 48 Then he said to them, "Whoever
welcomes this little child in my name welcomes me; and whoever welcomes me welcomes the one who
9:48 [e]Mt 10:40 sent me.[e] For he who is least among you all—he is the greatest."[f]
[f]Mk 9:35
9:49 [g]Lk 5:5 49 "Master,"[g] said John, "we saw a man driving out demons in your name and we tried to stop him, be-
cause he is not one of us."
9:50 [h]Mt 12:30; 50 "Do not stop him," Jesus said, "for whoever is not against you is for you."[h]
Lk 11:23

Samaritan Opposition

9:51 [i]Mk 16:19 51 As the time approached for him to be taken up to heaven,[i] Jesus resolutely set out for Jerusalem.[j]
[j]Lk 13:22; 17:11; 52 And he sent messengers on ahead, who went into a Samaritan[k] village to get things ready for him; 53 but
18:31; 19:28
9:52 [k]Mt 10:5 the people there did not welcome him, because he was heading for Jerusalem. 54 When the disciples James

[a] 42 Greek *unclean*

9:28 Although Mount Tabor is the traditional site of the Mount of Transfiguration, its distance from Caesarea Philippi (the vicinity of the last scene), its height (about 1,800 ft or 549 m) and its occupation by a fortress make this identity unlikely. Mount Hermon fits the context much better by being both closer and much higher (over 9,000 ft or 2,743 m).
9:33 For "three shelters," see the note on Mark 9:5.
9:39 For "seizes him," see the note on Matthew 4:24.

9:52 Samaritans were particularly hostile to Jews who were on their way to observe religious festivals in Jerusalem. It was at least a three-day journey from Galilee to Jerusalem, through Samaria, and Samaritans regularly refused overnight shelter for the pilgrims. Because of this antipathy, Jews traveling between Galilee and Jerusalem frequently chose to remain on the east side of the Jordan River. (See "The Samaritans" on p. 1737.)

and John[l] saw this, they asked, "Lord, do you want us to call fire down from heaven to destroy them[a]?"[m] 55 But Jesus turned and rebuked them, 56 and[b] they went to another village.

The Cost of Following Jesus

57 As they were walking along the road,[n] a man said to him, "I will follow you wherever you go."

58 Jesus replied, "Foxes have holes and birds of the air have nests, but the Son of Man[o] has no place to lay his head."

59 He said to another man, "Follow me."[p]

But the man replied, "Lord, first let me go and bury my father."

60 Jesus said to him, "Let the dead bury their own dead, but you go and proclaim the kingdom of God."[q]

61 Still another said, "I will follow you, Lord; but first let me go back and say good-by to my family."[r]

62 Jesus replied, "No one who puts his hand to the plow and looks back is fit for service in the kingdom of God."

Jesus Sends Out the Seventy-two

10 After this the Lord[s] appointed seventy-two[c] others[t] and sent them two by two[u] ahead of him to every town and place where he was about to go.[v] 2 He told them, "The harvest is plentiful, but the workers are few. Ask the Lord of the harvest, therefore, to send out workers into his harvest field.[w] 3 Go! I am sending you out like lambs among wolves.[x] 4 Do not take a purse or bag or sandals; and do not greet anyone on the road.

5 "When you enter a house, first say, 'Peace to this house.' 6 If a man of peace is there, your peace will rest on him; if not, it will return to you. 7 Stay in that house, eating and drinking whatever they give you, for the worker deserves his wages.[y] Do not move around from house to house.

8 "When you enter a town and are welcomed, eat what is set before you.[z] 9 Heal the sick who are there and tell them, 'The kingdom of God[a] is near you.' 10 But when you enter a town and are not welcomed, go into its streets and say, 11 'Even the dust of your town that sticks to our feet we wipe off against you.[b] Yet be sure of this: The kingdom of God is near.'[c] 12 I tell you, it will be more bearable on that day for Sodom[d] than for that town.[e]

13 "Woe to you,[f] Korazin! Woe to you, Bethsaida! For if the miracles that were performed in you had been performed in Tyre and Sidon, they would have repented long ago, sitting in sackcloth[g] and ashes. 14 But it will be more bearable for Tyre and Sidon at the judgment than for you. 15 And you, Capernaum,[h] will you be lifted up to the skies? No, you will go down to the depths.[d]

16 "He who listens to you listens to me; he who rejects you rejects me; but he who rejects me rejects him who sent me."[i]

17 The seventy-two[j] returned with joy and said, "Lord, even the demons submit to us in your name."[k]

18 He replied, "I saw Satan[l] fall like lightning from heaven.[m] 19 I have given you authority to trample on snakes[n] and scorpions and to overcome all the power of the enemy; nothing will harm you. 20 However, do not rejoice that the spirits submit to you, but rejoice that your names are written in heaven."[o]

21 At that time Jesus, full of joy through the Holy Spirit, said, "I praise you, Father, Lord of heaven and earth, because you have hidden these things from the wise and learned, and revealed them to little children.[p] Yes, Father, for this was your good pleasure.

22 "All things have been committed to me by my Father.[q] No one knows who the Son is except the Father, and no one knows who the Father is except the Son and those to whom the Son chooses to reveal him."[r]

9:54 [l]Mt 4:21 [m]2Ki 1:10,12
9:57 [n]ver 51
9:58 [o]Mt 8:20
9:59 [p]Mt 4:19
9:60 [q]Mt 3:2
9:61 [r]1Ki 19:20
10:1 [s]Lk 7:13 [t]Lk 9:1,2,51,52 [u]Mk 6:7 [v]Mt 10:1
10:2 [w]Mt 9:37, 38; Jn 4:35
10:3 [x]Mt 10:16
10:7 [y]Mt 10:10; 1Co 9:14; 1Ti 5:18
10:8 [z]1Co 10:27
10:9 [a]Mt 3:2; 10:7
10:11 [b]Mt 10:14; Mk 6:11 [c]ver 9
10:12 [d]Mt 10:15 [e]Mt 11:24
10:13 [f]Lk 6:24-26 [g]Rev 11:3
10:15 [h]Mt 4:13
10:16 [i]Mt 10:40; Jn 13:20
10:17 [j]ver 1 [k]Mk 16:17
10:18 [l]Mt 4:10 [m]Isa 14:12; Rev 9:1; 12:8,9
10:19 [n]Mk 16:18; Ac 28:3-5
10:20 [o]Ex 32:32; Ps 69:28; Da 12:1; Php 4:3; Heb 12:23; Rev 13:8; 20:12; 21:27
10:21 [p]1Co 1:26-29
10:22 [q]Mt 28:18 [r]Jn 1:18

[a] *54* Some manuscripts *them, even as Elijah did* [b] *55,56* Some manuscripts *them. And he said, "You do not know what kind of spirit you are of, for the Son of Man did not come to destroy men's lives, but to save them."* *56* *And* [c] *1* Some manuscripts *seventy;* also in verse 17 [d] *15* Greek *Hades*

10:4 A "purse" (Greek *ballantion*) was a rather finely finished leather pouch or bag. Money was also carried in "belts" (Greek *zōnē*; Mt 10:9), which were really Middle Eastern girdles made of crude leather or woven camel's hair worn around the waist. Sometimes these "girdles" were finely tooled and contained "slots" in which gold and silver coins could be kept. If the "girdle" was made of cloth, the money was placed within the folds themselves.

For a discussion of salutations in the Bible, see the note at Ruth 2:4.

10:12 See "The Destruction of Sodom and Gomorrah" on page 32.

10:13–15 See "Korazin" on page 1578. For "Bethsaida," see the note on Mark 8:22, for "Tyre and Sidon," the notes on Matthew 15:21 and Mark 7:31, for "sackcloth and ashes," the article on page 820, and for "Capernaum," the note on Matthew 4:13.

[23]Then he turned to his disciples and said privately, "Blessed are the eyes that see what you see. [24]For
I tell you that many prophets and kings wanted to see what you see but did not see it, and to hear what
10:24 [s]1Pe 1:10-12 you hear but did not hear it."[s]

The Parable of the Good Samaritan

[25]On one occasion an expert in the law stood up to test Jesus. "Teacher," he asked, "what must I do to
10:25 [t]Mt 19:16; Lk 18:18 inherit eternal life?"[t]
[26]"What is written in the Law?" he replied. "How do you read it?"
[27]He answered: " 'Love the Lord your God with all your heart and with all your soul and with all your
10:27 [u]Dt 6:5 [v]Lev 19:18; Mt 5:43 strength and with all your mind'[a];[u] and, 'Love your neighbor as yourself.'[b]"[v]
10:28 [w]Lev 18:5; Ro 7:10 [28]"You have answered correctly," Jesus replied. "Do this and you will live."[w]
10:29 [x]Lk 16:15 [29]But he wanted to justify himself,[x] so he asked Jesus, "And who is my neighbor?"
[30]In reply Jesus said: "A man was going down from Jerusalem to Jericho, when he fell into the hands of
robbers. They stripped him of his clothes, beat him and went away, leaving him half dead. [31]A priest hap-
10:31 [y]Lev 21:1-3 pened to be going down the same road, and when he saw the man, he passed by on the other side.[y] [32]So
10:33 [z]Mt 10:5 too, a Levite, when he came to the place and saw him, passed by on the other side. [33]But a Samaritan,[z] as
he traveled, came where the man was; and when he saw him, he took pity on him. [34]He went to him and
bandaged his wounds, pouring on oil and wine. Then he put the man on his own donkey, took him to an
inn and took care of him. [35]The next day he took out two silver coins[c] and gave them to the innkeeper.
'Look after him,' he said, 'and when I return, I will reimburse you for any extra expense you may have.'
[36]"Which of these three do you think was a neighbor to the man who fell into the hands of robbers?"
[37]The expert in the law replied, "The one who had mercy on him."
Jesus told him, "Go and do likewise."

At the Home of Martha and Mary

10:38 [a]Jn 11:1; 12:2 [38]As Jesus and his disciples were on their way, he came to a village where a woman named Martha[a]
10:39 [b]Jn 11:1; 12:3 [c]Lk 8:35 opened her home to him. [39]She had a sister called Mary,[b] who sat at the Lord's feet[c] listening to what he
said. [40]But Martha was distracted by all the preparations that had to be made. She came to him and asked,
10:40 [d]Mk 4:38 "Lord, don't you care[d] that my sister has left me to do the work by myself? Tell her to help me!"
10:41 [e]Mt 6:25-34; Lk 12:11,22 [41]"Martha, Martha," the Lord answered, "you are worried[e] and upset about many things, [42]but only one
10:42 [f]Ps 27:4 thing is needed.[d][f] Mary has chosen what is better, and it will not be taken away from her."

Jesus' Teaching on Prayer

11:1 [g]Lk 3:21 [h]Jn 13:13 **11** One day Jesus was praying[g] in a certain place. When he finished, one of his disciples said to him,
"Lord,[h] teach us to pray, just as John taught his disciples."
[2]He said to them, "When you pray, say:

" 'Father,[e]
hallowed be your name,
11:2 [i]Mt 3:2 your kingdom[i] come.[f]
[3]Give us each day our daily bread.
[4]Forgive us our sins,
11:4 [j]Mt 18:35; Mk 11:25 [k]Mt 26:41; Jas 1:13 for we also forgive everyone who sins against us.[g][j]
And lead us not into temptation.[h]' "[k]

[a] *27* Deut. 6:5 [b] *27* Lev. 19:18 [c] *35* Greek *two denarii* [d] *42* Some manuscripts *but few things are needed—or only one*
[e] *2* Some manuscripts *Our Father in heaven* [f] *2* Some manuscripts *come. May your will be done on earth as it is in heaven.*
[g] *4* Greek *everyone who is indebted to us* [h] *4* Some manuscripts *temptation but deliver us from the evil one*

10:25 For "expert in the law," see the note on 7:30.
10:30 Jerusalem to Jericho was a distance of 17 miles (27 km) and a descent from about 25,000 feet (7,620 m) above sea level to some 800 feet (244 m) below sea level. The road ran through rocky, desert terrain, which provided natural hiding places for lurking robbers to waylay defenseless travelers.
10:33 Jews viewed Samaritans as half-breeds, both physically (see the note on Mt 10:5) and spiritually (see the notes on Jn 4:20,22, as well as "The Samaritan Temple on Mount Gerizim" on p. 1727). Samaritans and Jews practiced open hostility toward one another (see the note on Lk 9:52).
10:34 Oil and wine were used for their healing effects (see "Disease and Medicine in the Ancient World" on p. 1674 and "Wine and Alcoholic Beverages in the Ancient World" on p. 2015).
10:35 The "two silver coins" were denarii, worth two days' wages (see the note on Mt 20:2).
10:38 This "village" was Bethany (see the note on Mt 21:17).

[5]Then he said to them, "Suppose one of you has a friend, and he goes to him at midnight and says, 'Friend, lend me three loaves of bread, [6]because a friend of mine on a journey has come to me, and I have nothing to set before him.'

[7]"Then the one inside answers, 'Don't bother me. The door is already locked, and my children are with me in bed. I can't get up and give you anything.' [8]I tell you, though he will not get up and give him the bread because he is his friend, yet because of the man's boldness[a] he will get up and give him as much as he needs.[l]

[9]"So I say to you: Ask and it will be given to you;[m] seek and you will find; knock and the door will be opened to you. [10]For everyone who asks receives; he who seeks finds; and to him who knocks, the door will be opened.

[11]"Which of you fathers, if your son asks for[b] a fish, will give him a snake instead? [12]Or if he asks for an egg, will give him a scorpion? [13]If you then, though you are evil, know how to give good gifts to your children, how much more will your Father in heaven give the Holy Spirit to those who ask him!"

Jesus and Beelzebub

[14]Jesus was driving out a demon that was mute. When the demon left, the man who had been mute spoke, and the crowd was amazed.[n] [15]But some of them said, "By Beelzebub,[c] [o] the prince of demons, he is driving out demons."[p] [16]Others tested him by asking for a sign from heaven.[q]

[17]Jesus knew their thoughts[r] and said to them: "Any kingdom divided against itself will be ruined, and a house divided against itself will fall. [18]If Satan[s] is divided against himself, how can his kingdom stand? I say this because you claim that I drive out demons by Beelzebub. [19]Now if I drive out demons by Beelzebub, by whom do your followers drive them out? So then, they will be your judges. [20]But if I drive out demons by the finger of God,[t] then the kingdom of God[u] has come to you.

[21]"When a strong man, fully armed, guards his own house, his possessions are safe. [22]But when someone stronger attacks and overpowers him, he takes away the armor in which the man trusted and divides up the spoils.

[23]"He who is not with me is against me, and he who does not gather with me, scatters.[v]

[24]"When an evil[d] spirit comes out of a man, it goes through arid places seeking rest and does not find it. Then it says, 'I will return to the house I left.' [25]When it arrives, it finds the house swept clean and put in order. [26]Then it goes and takes seven other spirits more wicked than itself, and they go in and live there. And the final condition of that man is worse than the first."[w]

[27]As Jesus was saying these things, a woman in the crowd called out, "Blessed is the mother who gave you birth and nursed you."[x]

[28]He replied, "Blessed rather are those who hear the word of God[y] and obey it."[z]

The Sign of Jonah

[29]As the crowds increased, Jesus said, "This is a wicked generation. It asks for a miraculous sign,[a] but none will be given it except the sign of Jonah.[b] [30]For as Jonah was a sign to the Ninevites, so also will the Son of Man be to this generation. [31]The Queen of the South will rise at the judgment with the men of this generation and condemn them; for she came from the ends of the earth to listen to Solomon's wisdom,[c] and now one[e] greater than Solomon is here. [32]The men of Nineveh will stand up at the judgment with this generation and condemn it; for they repented at the preaching of Jonah,[d] and now one greater than Jonah is here.

The Lamp of the Body

[33]"No one lights a lamp and puts it in a place where it will be hidden, or under a bowl. Instead he puts it on its stand, so that those who come in may see the light.[e] [34]Your eye is the lamp of your body. When your eyes are good, your whole body also is full of light. But when they are bad, your body also is full of darkness. [35]See to it, then, that the light within you is not darkness. [36]Therefore, if your whole body is full of light, and no part of it dark, it will be completely lighted, as when the light of a lamp shines on you."

11:8 [l]Lk 18:1-6
11:9 [m]Mt 7:7
11:14 [n]Mt 9:32, 33
11:15 [o]Mk 3:22 [p]Mt 9:34
11:16 [q]Mt 12:38
11:17 [r]Mt 9:4
11:18 [s]Mt 4:10
11:20 [t]Ex 8:19 [u]Mt 3:2
11:23 [v]Mt 12:30; Mk 9:40; Lk 9:50
11:26 [w]2Pe 2:20
11:27 [x]Lk 23:29
11:28 [y]Heb 4:12 [z]Pr 8:32; Lk 6:47; 8:21; Jn 14:21
11:29 [a]ver 16; Mt 12:38 [b]Jnh 1:17; Mt 16:4
11:31 [c]1Ki 10:1; 2Ch 9:1
11:32 [d]Jnh 3:5
11:33 [e]Mt 5:15; Mk 4:21; Lk 8:16

[a] 8 Or *persistence* [b] 11 Some manuscripts *for bread, will give him a stone; or if he asks for* [c] 15 Greek *Beezeboul* or *Beelzeboul*; also in verses 18 and 19 [d] 24 Greek *unclean* [e] 31 Or *something*; also in verse 32

11:15 For "Beelzebub," see the note on Matthew 10:25.
11:31 For "Queen of the South," see the note on Matthew 12:42.
11:33 For "lamps," see the note on Matthew 5:15.

Six Woes

37 When Jesus had finished speaking, a Pharisee invited him to eat with him; so he went in and re-
clined at the table.[f] 38 But the Pharisee, noticing that Jesus did not first wash before the meal,[g] was sur-
prised.
39 Then the Lord[h] said to him, "Now then, you Pharisees clean the outside of the cup and dish, but in-
side you are full of greed and wickedness.[i] 40 You foolish people![j] Did not the one who made the outside
make the inside also? 41 But give what is inside ⌊the dish⌋[a] to the poor,[k] and everything will be clean for you.[l]
42 "Woe to you Pharisees, because you give God a tenth[m] of your mint, rue and all other kinds of gar-
den herbs, but you neglect justice and the love of God.[n] You should have practiced the latter without leav-
ing the former undone.[o]
43 "Woe to you Pharisees, because you love the most important seats in the synagogues and greetings
in the marketplaces.[p]
44 "Woe to you, because you are like unmarked graves,[q] which men walk over without knowing it."
45 One of the experts in the law[r] answered him, "Teacher, when you say these things, you insult us also."
46 Jesus replied, "And you experts in the law, woe to you, because you load people down with burdens
they can hardly carry, and you yourselves will not lift one finger to help them.[s]
47 "Woe to you, because you build tombs for the prophets, and it was your forefathers who killed them.
48 So you testify that you approve of what your forefathers did; they killed the prophets, and you build
their tombs.[t] 49 Because of this, God in his wisdom[u] said, 'I will send them prophets and apostles, some
of whom they will kill and others they will persecute.'[v] 50 Therefore this generation will be held respon-
sible for the blood of all the prophets that has been shed since the beginning of the world, 51 from the
blood of Abel[w] to the blood of Zechariah,[x] who was killed between the altar and the sanctuary. Yes, I tell
you, this generation will be held responsible for it all.[y]
52 "Woe to you experts in the law, because you have taken away the key to knowledge. You yourselves
have not entered, and you have hindered those who were entering."[z]
53 When Jesus left there, the Pharisees and the teachers of the law began to oppose him fiercely and
to besiege him with questions, 54 waiting to catch him in something he might say.[a]

Warnings and Encouragements

12 Meanwhile, when a crowd of many thousands had gathered, so that they were trampling on one
another, Jesus began to speak first to his disciples, saying: "Be on your guard against the yeast of
the Pharisees, which is hypocrisy.[b] 2 There is nothing concealed that will not be disclosed, or hidden that
will not be made known.[c] 3 What you have said in the dark will be heard in the daylight, and what you
have whispered in the ear in the inner rooms will be proclaimed from the roofs.
4 "I tell you, my friends,[d] do not be afraid of those who kill the body and after that can do no more.
5 But I will show you whom you should fear: Fear him who, after the killing of the body, has power to
throw you into hell. Yes, I tell you, fear him.[e] 6 Are not five sparrows sold for two pennies[b]? Yet not one of
them is forgotten by God. 7 Indeed, the very hairs of your head are all numbered.[f] Don't be afraid; you
are worth more than many sparrows.[g]
8 "I tell you, whoever acknowledges me before men, the Son of Man will also acknowledge him before
the angels of God.[h] 9 But he who disowns me before men will be disowned[i] before the angels of God.
10 And everyone who speaks a word against the Son of Man[j] will be forgiven, but anyone who blasphemes
against the Holy Spirit will not be forgiven.[k]
11 "When you are brought before synagogues, rulers and authorities, do not worry about how you will de-
fend yourselves or what you will say,[l] 12 for the Holy Spirit will teach you at that time what you should say."[m]

11:37 [f]Lk 7:36; 14:1
11:38 [g]Mk 7:3,4
11:39 [h]Lk 7:13 [i]Mt 23:25,26; Mk 7:20-23
11:40 [j]Lk 12:20; 1Co 15:36
11:41 [k]Lk 12:33 [l]Ac 10:15
11:42 [m]Lk 18:12 [n]Dt 6:5; Mic 6:8 [o]Mt 23:23
11:43 [p]Mt 23:6, 7; Mk 12:38-39; Lk 14:7; 20:46
11:44 [q]Mt 23:27
11:45 [r]Mt 22:35
11:46 [s]Mt 23:4
11:48 [t]Mt 23:29-32; Ac 7:51-53
11:49 [u]1Co 1:24, 30; Col 2:3 [v]Mt 23:34
11:51 [w]Ge 4:8 [x]2Ch 24:20,21 [y]Mt 23:35,36
11:52 [z]Mt 23:13
11:54 [a]Mt 12:10; Mk 12:13
12:1 [b]Mt 16:6,11, 12; Mk 8:15
12:2 [c]Mk 4:22; Lk 8:17
12:4 [d]Jn 15:14, 15
12:5 [e]Heb 10:31
12:7 [f]Mt 10:30 [g]Mt 12:12
12:8 [h]Lk 15:10
12:9 [i]Mk 8:38; 2Ti 2:12
12:10 [j]Mt 8:20 [k]Mt 12:31,32; Mk 3:28-29; 1Jn 5:16
12:11 [l]Mt 10:17, 19; Mk 13:11; Lk 21:12,14
12:12 [m]Ex 4:12; Mt 10:20; Mk 13:11; Lk 21:15

[a] *41* Or *what you have* [b] *6* Greek *two assaria*

11:37–52 For a note on expressions of vengeful attitudes toward enemies, see Psalm 69:22–28. See also "Curses and Imprecations" on page 883.
11:38 "Wash" refers to ceremonial washing (see the note on Jn 2:6).
11:42 For "Pharisees," see the notes on Matthew 3:7 and Luke 5:17.
A "tenth" was the tithe of all agricultural produce required by law (see Dt 14:22–29).
"Rue" refers to strongly scented herbs with bitter leaves.
11:43 For "important seats in the synagogues," see the note on Mark 12:39. For the multiple functions of the *agora*, or marketplace, see the note on Matthew 11:16–17, as well as "The Ancient Agora" on page 1799.
11:44 For "unmarked graves," see the note on Matthew 23:27.
11:45 For "experts in the law," see the note on 7:30.
11:46 For "load people down," see the note on Matthew 11:28.
12:3 For "inner rooms," see the note on Matthew 24:26.
12:5 For "hell," see the note on Matthew 5:22.

The Parable of the Rich Fool

13Someone in the crowd said to him, "Teacher, tell my brother to divide the inheritance with me."

14Jesus replied, "Man, who appointed me a judge or an arbiter between you?" 15Then he said to them, "Watch out! Be on your guard against all kinds of greed; a man's life does not consist in the abundance of his possessions."[n]

16And he told them this parable: "The ground of a certain rich man produced a good crop. 17He thought to himself, 'What shall I do? I have no place to store my crops.'

18"Then he said, 'This is what I'll do. I will tear down my barns and build bigger ones, and there I will store all my grain and my goods. 19And I'll say to myself, "You have plenty of good things laid up for many years. Take life easy; eat, drink and be merry." '

20"But God said to him, 'You fool![o] This very night your life will be demanded from you.[p] Then who will get what you have prepared for yourself?'[q]

21"This is how it will be with anyone who stores up things for himself but is not rich toward God."[r]

12:15 [n]Job 20:20; 31:24; Ps 62:10
12:20 [o]Jer 17:11; Lk 11:40 [p]Job 27:8 [q]Ps 39:6; 49:10
12:21 [r]ver 33

Do Not Worry

22Then Jesus said to his disciples: "Therefore I tell you, do not worry about your life, what you will eat; or about your body, what you will wear. 23Life is more than food, and the body more than clothes. 24Consider the ravens: They do not sow or reap, they have no storeroom or barn; yet God feeds them.[s] And how much more valuable you are than birds! 25Who of you by worrying can add a single hour to his life[a]? 26Since you cannot do this very little thing, why do you worry about the rest?

27"Consider how the lilies grow. They do not labor or spin. Yet I tell you, not even Solomon in all his splendor[t] was dressed like one of these. 28If that is how God clothes the grass of the field, which is here today, and tomorrow is thrown into the fire, how much more will he clothe you, O you of little faith![u] 29And do not set your heart on what you will eat or drink; do not worry about it. 30For the pagan world runs after all such things, and your Father[v] knows that you need them.[w] 31But seek his kingdom,[x] and these things will be given to you as well.[y]

32"Do not be afraid,[z] little flock, for your Father has been pleased to give you the kingdom.[a] 33Sell your possessions and give to the poor.[b] Provide purses for yourselves that will not wear out, a treasure in heaven[c] that will not be exhausted, where no thief comes near and no moth destroys.[d] 34For where your treasure is, there your heart will be also.[e]

12:24 [s]Job 38:41; Ps 147:9
12:27 [t]1Ki 10:4-7
12:28 [u]Mt 6:30
12:30 [v]Lk 6:36 [w]Mt 6:8
12:31 [x]Mt 3:2 [y]Mt 19:29
12:32 [z]Mt 14:27 [a]Mt 25:34
12:33 [b]Mt 19:21; Ac 2:45 [c]Mt 6:20 [d]Jas 5:2
12:34 [e]Mt 6:21

Watchfulness

35"Be dressed ready for service and keep your lamps burning, 36like men waiting for their master to return from a wedding banquet, so that when he comes and knocks they can immediately open the door for him. 37It will be good for those servants whose master finds them watching when he comes.[f] I tell you the truth, he will dress himself to serve, will have them recline at the table and will come and wait on them.[g] 38It will be good for those servants whose master finds them ready, even if he comes in the second or third watch of the night. 39But understand this: If the owner of the house had known at what hour the thief[h] was coming, he would not have let his house be broken into. 40You also must be ready,[i] because the Son of Man will come at an hour when you do not expect him."

41Peter asked, "Lord, are you telling this parable to us, or to everyone?"

42The Lord[j] answered, "Who then is the faithful and wise manager, whom the master puts in charge of his servants to give them their food allowance at the proper time? 43It will be good for that servant whom the master finds doing so when he returns. 44I tell you the truth, he will put him in charge of all his possessions. 45But suppose the servant says to himself, 'My master is taking a long time in coming,' and he then begins to beat the menservants and maidservants and to eat and drink and get drunk. 46The

12:37 [f]Mt 24:42, 46; 25:13 [g]Mt 20:28
12:39 [h]Mt 6:19; 1Th 5:2; 2Pe 3:10; Rev 3:3; 16:15
12:40 [i]Mk 13:33; Lk 21:36
12:42 [j]Lk 7:13

[a] 25 Or *single cubit to his height*

12:13 The elder son generally received a double portion of the inheritance (see "Inheritance in the Ancient Near East" on p. 250). Disputes over such matters were normally settled by rabbis.
12:27 "Lilies" probably represents flowers in general (see "The Flowers of Ancient Israel" on p. 1037).
12:28 For "grass," see the note on Matthew 6:30.
12:38 The night was divided into four watches by the Romans and three by the Jews (see the note on Mt 14:25). The "second or third watch" probably refers to the last two Jewish watches.
12:42 The "wise manager" was an outstanding slave (v. 43) who had been put in charge of the estate (see "Labor and Welfare in the Ancient World" on p. 1952 and "Slavery in the Greco-Roman World" on p. 1979).

master of that servant will come on a day when he does not expect him and at an hour he is not aware
12:46 [k]ver 40 of.[k] He will cut him to pieces and assign him a place with the unbelievers.
47 "That servant who knows his master's will and does not get ready or does not do what his master
12:47 [l]Dt 25:2 wants will be beaten with many blows.[l] 48 But the one who does not know and does things deserving
12:48 [m]Lev 5:17; Nu 15:27-30 punishment will be beaten with few blows.[m] From everyone who has been given much, much will be de-
manded; and from the one who has been entrusted with much, much more will be asked.

Not Peace but Division

49 "I have come to bring fire on the earth, and how I wish it were already kindled! 50 But I have a bap-
12:50 [n]Mk 10:38 [o]Jn 19:30 tism[n] to undergo, and how distressed I am until it is completed![o] 51 Do you think I came to bring peace
on earth? No, I tell you, but division. 52 From now on there will be five in one family divided against each
other, three against two and two against three. 53 They will be divided, father against son and son against
father, mother against daughter and daughter against mother, mother-in-law against daughter-in-law
12:53 [p]Mic 7:6; Mt 10:21 and daughter-in-law against mother-in-law."[p]

Interpreting the Times

54 He said to the crowd: "When you see a cloud rising in the west, immediately you say, 'It's going to
12:54 [q]Mt 16:2 rain,' and it does.[q] 55 And when the south wind blows, you say, 'It's going to be hot,' and it is. 56 Hypocrites!
You know how to interpret the appearance of the earth and the sky. How is it that you don't know how to
12:56 [r]Mt 16:3 interpret this present time?[r]
57 "Why don't you judge for yourselves what is right? 58 As you are going with your adversary to the
magistrate, try hard to be reconciled to him on the way, or he may drag you off to the judge, and the judge
12:58 [s]Mt 5:25 turn you over to the officer, and the officer throw you into prison.[s] 59 I tell you, you will not get out until
12:59 [t]Mt 5:26; Mk 12:42 you have paid the last penny.[a]"[t]

Repent or Perish

13:1 [u]Mt 27:2 **13** Now there were some present at that time who told Jesus about the Galileans whose blood Pilate[u]
had mixed with their sacrifices. 2 Jesus answered, "Do you think that these Galileans were worse
13:2 [v]Jn 9:2,3 sinners than all the other Galileans because they suffered this way?[v] 3 I tell you, no! But unless you re-
13:4 [w]Jn 9:7,11 pent, you too will all perish. 4 Or those eighteen who died when the tower in Siloam[w] fell on them—do
you think they were more guilty than all the others living in Jerusalem? 5 I tell you, no! But unless you re-
13:5 [x]Mt 3:2; Ac 2:38 pent,[x] you too will all perish."
6 Then he told this parable: "A man had a fig tree, planted in his vineyard, and he went to look for fruit
13:6 [y]Isa 5:2; Jer 8:13; Mt 21:19 on it, but did not find any.[y] 7 So he said to the man who took care of the vineyard, 'For three years now
I've been coming to look for fruit on this fig tree and haven't found any. Cut it down![z] Why should it use
13:7 [z]Mt 3:10 up the soil?'
8 " 'Sir,' the man replied, 'leave it alone for one more year, and I'll dig around it and fertilize it. 9 If it
bears fruit next year, fine! If not, then cut it down.' "

A Crippled Woman Healed on the Sabbath

13:10 [a]Mt 4:23 10 On a Sabbath Jesus was teaching in one of the synagogues,[a] 11 and a woman was there who had been
13:11 [b]ver 16 crippled by a spirit for eighteen years.[b] She was bent over and could not straighten up at all. 12 When Jesus
saw her, he called her forward and said to her, "Woman, you are set free from your infirmity." 13 Then he
13:13 [c]Mk 5:23 put his hands on her,[c] and immediately she straightened up and praised God.

[a] 59 Greek *lepton*

12:54–55 Wind from the west blew from the direction of the Mediterranean Sea, while wind from the south came from the desert. People used such indicators to forecast the weather.
12:58 For "prison," see "Imprisonment in the Roman World: In Prison Versus House Arrest" on page 1826.
13:1 Having people killed while they were offering sacrifices in the temple fits Pilate's reputation (see "Pontius Pilate" on page 1714, as well as "Messianic Conflicts and the Fall of Jerusalem" on p. 1632).
13:2 In ancient times it was often assumed that a calamity would befall only those who were extremely sinful.
13:4 The tower in Siloam was probably part of the ancient system of fortifications on the walls of the city of Jerusalem near the Pool of Siloam (see "The Pool of Siloam" on p. 1739). The collapse of this tower and the resulting death of 18 persons (possibly workmen employed on the aqueduct that Pilate was building; cf. Josephus, *Wars*, 2.9.4) is here cited by Jesus. Apparently the accident was well known to his hearers, although it is not mentioned elsewhere in the Bible.
13:11 Various disorders were caused by evil spirits: mental disturbances (Jn 10:20); a tendency toward unprovoked, violent actions (Lk 8:26–29), and bodily disease (13:11,16). See "Demons and the Bible" on page 1572.

14 Indignant because Jesus had healed on the Sabbath,[d] the synagogue ruler[e] said to the people, "There 13:14 [d]Mt 12:2;
are six days for work.[f] So come and be healed on those days, not on the Sabbath." Lk 14:3 [e]Mk 5:22 [f]Ex 20:9
15 The Lord answered him, "You hypocrites! Doesn't each of you on the Sabbath untie his ox or donkey
from the stall and lead it out to give it water?[g] 16 Then should not this woman, a daughter of Abraham,[h] 13:15 [g]Lk 14:5
whom Satan[i] has kept bound for eighteen long years, be set free on the Sabbath day from what bound her?" 13:16 [h]Lk 3:8; 19:9 [i]Mt 4:10
17 When he said this, all his opponents were humiliated,[j] but the people were delighted with all the 13:17 [j]Isa 66:5
wonderful things he was doing.

The Parables of the Mustard Seed and the Yeast

18 Then Jesus asked, "What is the kingdom of God[k] like?[l] What shall I compare it to? 19 It is like a mus- 13:18 [k]Mt 3:2
tard seed, which a man took and planted in his garden. It grew and became a tree,[m] and the birds of the [l]Mt 13:24 13:19 [m]Lk 17:6
air perched in its branches."[n] [n]Mt 13:32
20 Again he asked, "What shall I compare the kingdom of God to? 21 It is like yeast that a woman took
and mixed into a large amount[a] of flour until it worked all through the dough."[o] 13:21 [o]1Co 5:6

The Narrow Door

22 Then Jesus went through the towns and villages, teaching as he made his way to Jerusalem.[p] 23 Some- 13:22 [p]Lk 9:51
one asked him, "Lord, are only a few people going to be saved?"
He said to them, 24 "Make every effort to enter through the narrow door,[q] because many, I tell you, 13:24 [q]Mt 7:13
will try to enter and will not be able to. 25 Once the owner of the house gets up and closes the door, you
will stand outside knocking and pleading, 'Sir, open the door for us.'
"But he will answer, 'I don't know you or where you come from.'[r] 13:25 [r]Mt 7:23; 25:10-12
26 "Then you will say, 'We ate and drank with you, and you taught in our streets.'
27 "But he will reply, 'I don't know you or where you come from. Away from me, all you evildoers!'[s] 13:27 [s]Mt 7:23; 25:41
28 "There will be weeping there, and gnashing of teeth,[t] when you see Abraham, Isaac and Jacob and 13:28 [t]Mt 8:12
all the prophets in the kingdom of God, but you yourselves thrown out. 29 People will come from east and
west[u] and north and south, and will take their places at the feast in the kingdom of God. 30 Indeed there 13:29 [u]Mt 8:11
are those who are last who will be first, and first who will be last."[v] 13:30 [v]Mt 19:30

Jesus' Sorrow for Jerusalem

31 At that time some Pharisees came to Jesus and said to him, "Leave this place and go somewhere
else. Herod[w] wants to kill you." 13:31 [w]Mt 14:1
32 He replied, "Go tell that fox, 'I will drive out demons and heal people today and tomorrow, and on
the third day I will reach my goal.'[x] 33 In any case, I must keep going today and tomorrow and the next 13:32 [x]Heb 2:10
day—for surely no prophet[y] can die outside Jerusalem! 13:33 [y]Mt 21:11
34 "O Jerusalem, Jerusalem, you who kill the prophets and stone those sent to you, how often I have
longed to gather your children together, as a hen gathers her chicks under her wings,[z] but you were not 13:34 [z]Mt 23:37
willing! 35 Look, your house is left to you desolate.[a] I tell you, you will not see me again until you say, 13:35 [a]Jer 12:17; 22:5 [b]Ps 118:26;
'Blessed is he who comes in the name of the Lord.'[b]"[b] Mt 21:9; Lk 19:38

Jesus at a Pharisee's House

14 One Sabbath, when Jesus went to eat in the house of a prominent Pharisee,[c] he was being care- 14:1 [c]Lk 7:36;
fully watched.[d] 2 There in front of him was a man suffering from dropsy. 3 Jesus asked the Phar- 11:37 [d]Mt 12:10
isees and experts in the law,[e] "Is it lawful to heal on the Sabbath or not?"[f] 4 But they remained silent. So 14:3 [e]Mt 22:35 [f]Mt 12:2
taking hold of the man, he healed him and sent him away.
5 Then he asked them, "If one of you has a son[c] or an ox that falls into a well on the Sabbath day, will
you not immediately pull him out?"[g] 6 And they had nothing to say. 14:5 [g]Lk 13:15

[a] 21 Greek *three satas* (probably about 1/2 bushel or 22 liters) [b] 35 Psalm 118:26 [c] 5 Some manuscripts *donkey*

13:14 For "healed on the Sabbath," see the note on Mark 3:2; for "synagogue ruler," see the note on Luke 8:41 and "Ancient Synagogues" on page 1783.
13:19 For "mustard seed," see the note on Matthew 13:31–32.
13:21 For "yeast," see the note on Matthew 13:33.
13:28 For the meaning of gnashing with one's teeth, see the note on Psalm 35:16.
13:31 Jesus was probably in Perea, which was under Herod's jurisdiction (see the note on 3:1).
14:2 Dropsy, or edema, manifests itself in a excessive accumulation of fluid in the tissues and cavities of the body.
14:3 For "Pharisees," see the notes on Matthew 3:7 and Luke 5:17; for "experts in the law," see the note on Luke 7:30.

THE HISTORICAL VALUE OF LUKE-ACTS

LUKE 14 The historical accuracy of the Luke-Acts two-volume work is frequently challenged. Scholars dispute such issues as the dating of the reign of Quirinius (Lk 1:5; 2:2)[1] and references to Palestinian geography (4:44; 17:11) and raise additional historical questions regarding the numerous speeches in Acts (e.g., Ac 2:14–36) and the harmonious portrayal of the early church (Ac 4:32–35).[2] The most critical historical objection to Acts concerns the details of Paul's ministry. Although certain passages suggest that Luke was a traveling companion of Paul (Ac 16:10–17; 27:1—28:16), some scholars deem this tradition untenable on the basis of perceived difficulties in harmonizing the life and perspective of Paul as presented in Acts with details about his life found in his letters.[3]

Many of these perceived difficulties are lessened when we recall the purpose of Luke's accounts. In composing his volumes Luke did not intend to record a comprehensive history but to offer a selective historical account to meet a pastoral need for assurance of faith (Lk 1:4). Luke acknowledged his use of sources (1:2), which he investigated thoroughly in order to compose an orderly account (1:3). Where it is possible to verify Luke's use of sources, we find that the Gospel writer followed them meticulously.[4] Furthermore, Luke was precise concerning the titles of officials and municipalities in various towns (Ac 13:12; 17:6; 18:12; 19:31,35), details that reveal the author's commitment to accuracy.

Traditional site of Luke's tomb (the bull is an ancient Christian symbol for Luke)
Photograph: © Todd Bolen/Bible Places.com

[1]See "Caesar Augustus, Emperor of Rome; the Census; and Quirinius, Governor of Syria" on page 1667. [2]See "The Church From the Resurrection to the Conversion of Paul" on page 1766. [3]For an example of possible harmonization, see "Paul's Visits and Letters to Corinth" on page 1888. [4]See "The Synoptic Problem and 'Q'" on page 1685.

14:7 [h]Lk 11:43 [7]When he noticed how the guests picked the places of honor at the table,[h] he told them this parable:
[8]"When someone invites you to a wedding feast, do not take the place of honor, for a person more dis-
tinguished than you may have been invited. [9]If so, the host who invited both of you will come and say to
you, 'Give this man your seat.' Then, humiliated, you will have to take the least important place. [10]But
when you are invited, take the lowest place, so that when your host comes, he will say to you, 'Friend,
move up to a better place.' Then you will be honored in the presence of all your fellow guests. [11]For ev-
14:11 [i]Mt 23:12; Lk 18:14 eryone who exalts himself will be humbled, and he who humbles himself will be exalted."[i]
[12]Then Jesus said to his host, "When you give a luncheon or dinner, do not invite your friends, your
brothers or relatives, or your rich neighbors; if you do, they may invite you back and so you will be re-
14:13 [j]ver 21 paid. [13]But when you give a banquet, invite the poor, the crippled, the lame, the blind,[j] [14]and you will be
14:14 [k]Ac 24:15 blessed. Although they cannot repay you, you will be repaid at the resurrection of the righteous."[k]

The Parable of the Great Banquet

[15]When one of those at the table with him heard this, he said to Jesus, "Blessed is the man who will
14:15 [l]Isa 25:6; Mt 26:29; Lk 13:29; Rev 19:9 [m]Mt 3:2 eat at the feast[l] in the kingdom of God."[m]
[16]Jesus replied: "A certain man was preparing a great banquet and invited many guests. [17]At the time
of the banquet he sent his servant to tell those who had been invited, 'Come, for everything is now ready.'

14:7 For "places of honor at the table," see "Triclinia" on page 1748.
14:8 For Hebrew/Jewish feasting, see the note on Matthew 22:2–14.
14:16–17 It was the Jewish custom to send two invitations to a banquet: an advance invitation and a follow-up announcement when the feast was ready.

18 “But they all alike began to make excuses. The first said, ‘I have just bought a field, and I must go and see it. Please excuse me.’

19 “Another said, ‘I have just bought five yoke of oxen, and I’m on my way to try them out. Please excuse me.’

20 “Still another said, ‘I just got married, so I can’t come.’

21 “The servant came back and reported this to his master. Then the owner of the house became angry and ordered his servant, ‘Go out quickly into the streets and alleys of the town and bring in the poor, the crippled, the blind and the lame.’[n]

22 “ ‘Sir,’ the servant said, ‘what you ordered has been done, but there is still room.’

23 “Then the master told his servant, ‘Go out to the roads and country lanes and make them come in, so that my house will be full. 24 I tell you, not one of those men who were invited will get a taste of my banquet.’ ”[o]

14:21 [n]ver 13
14:24 [o]Mt 21:43; Ac 13:46

The Cost of Being a Disciple

25 Large crowds were traveling with Jesus, and turning to them he said: 26 “If anyone comes to me and does not hate his father and mother, his wife and children, his brothers and sisters—yes, even his own life—he cannot be my disciple.[p] 27 And anyone who does not carry his cross and follow me cannot be my disciple.[q]

28 “Suppose one of you wants to build a tower. Will he not first sit down and estimate the cost to see if he has enough money to complete it? 29 For if he lays the foundation and is not able to finish it, everyone who sees it will ridicule him, 30 saying, ‘This fellow began to build and was not able to finish.’

31 “Or suppose a king is about to go to war against another king. Will he not first sit down and consider whether he is able with ten thousand men to oppose the one coming against him with twenty thousand? 32 If he is not able, he will send a delegation while the other is still a long way off and will ask for terms of peace. 33 In the same way, any of you who does not give up everything he has cannot be my disciple.[r]

34 “Salt is good, but if it loses its saltiness, how can it be made salty again?[s] 35 It is fit neither for the soil nor for the manure pile; it is thrown out.[t]

“He who has ears to hear, let him hear.”[u]

14:26 [p]Mt 10:37; Jn 12:25
14:27 [q]Mt 10:38; Lk 9:23
14:33 [r]Php 3:7,8
14:34 [s]Mk 9:50
14:35 [t]Mt 5:13 [u]Mt 11:15

The Parable of the Lost Sheep

15 Now the tax collectors[v] and “sinners” were all gathering around to hear him. 2 But the Pharisees and the teachers of the law muttered, “This man welcomes sinners and eats with them.”[w]

3 Then Jesus told them this parable:[x] 4 “Suppose one of you has a hundred sheep and loses one of them. Does he not leave the ninety-nine in the open country and go after the lost sheep until he finds it?[y] 5 And when he finds it, he joyfully puts it on his shoulders 6 and goes home. Then he calls his friends and neighbors together and says, ‘Rejoice with me; I have found my lost sheep.’[z] 7 I tell you that in the same way there will be more rejoicing in heaven over one sinner who repents than over ninety-nine righteous persons who do not need to repent.[a]

15:1 [v]Lk 5:29
15:2 [w]Mt 9:11
15:3 [x]Mt 13:3
15:4 [y]Ps 23; 119:176; Jer 31:10; Eze 34:11-16; Lk 5:32; 19:10
15:6 [z]ver 9
15:7 [a]ver 10

The Parable of the Lost Coin

8 “Or suppose a woman has ten silver coins[a] and loses one. Does she not light a lamp, sweep the house and search carefully until she finds it? 9 And when she finds it, she calls her friends and neighbors together and says, ‘Rejoice with me; I have found my lost coin.’[b] 10 In the same way, I tell you, there is rejoicing in the presence of the angels of God over one sinner who repents.”[c]

15:9 [b]ver 6
15:10 [c]ver 7

The Parable of the Lost Son

11 Jesus continued: “There was a man who had two sons.[d] 12 The younger one said to his father, ‘Father, give me my share of the estate.’[e] So he divided his property[f] between them.

15:11 [d]Mt 21:28
15:12 [e]Dt 21:17 [f]ver 30

[a] 8 Greek *ten drachmas,* each worth about a day’s wages

14:34 For “salt,” see the note on Matthew 5:13.
15:1 For “tax collectors,” see the notes on Matthew 5:46 and Mark 2:14.
15:8 The “silver coins” were drachmas (see the NIV text note). A drachma was a Greek coin approximately equivalent to the Roman denarius (see the notes on Mt 20:2; 22:19), worth about a day’s wage.
For “lamp,” see the note on Matthew 5:15. Near Eastern houses frequently had no windows and only earthen floors, making the search for a single coin difficult (see “Houses in the Holy Land of the First Century A.D.: Peter’s House in Capernaum; Insulae” on p. 1584).
15:12 The father may have divided the inheritance (with a double portion to the older son; see the note on 12:13) but retained the income from it until his death. To give a younger son his portion of the inheritance upon request was highly unusual.

Coins and Numismatics

LUKE 15 Although silver and gold were highly valued in commercial exchange from very ancient times, throughout much of the Old Testament period precious metals were measured by weight and were not struck into coins.[1] The first coinage probably came from western Anatolia (Turkey) around the seventh century B.C. The practice may have been initiated by commercial traders rather than by governmental authorities, but most experts suggest that the Lydian kingdom was the first to coin silver and gold.

Money changer and servant on a Roman era funerary stele from Hungary

Preserving Bible Times; © Dr. James C. Martin; permission of Eretz Israel Museum

The use of coins gained widespread acceptance when the Persian Empire issued standardized coinage.[2] Kings and emperors soon realized that coins were an effective propaganda tool; the image of the king's face was stamped onto them, after which they were disseminated throughout his territories and beyond. Coinage was especially useful for the **Phoenicians**, since their economy was based on trade.[3]

Coins were introduced in Jerusalem by the fifth century B.C. Early Jewish coins of the **Persian** and **Hellenistic period**s often bear the inscription *Yehud* ("Judah") and are called "Yehud coins." It is surprising to observe that some of them also bear an image of the head of Pallas Athena, the Greek goddess, on the obverse and that of an owl, the sacred bird of Athena, on the reverse side.

Coin with the image of the goddess Athena

Preserving Bible Times; © Dr. James C. Martin

After the **Maccabean revolt**, the success of which allowed the Jews to throw off Greek rule in Jerusalem, the Jews developed a more native coinage that reflected their religious sensitivities. There is debate as to whether Alexander Jannaeus (103–76 B.C.) or John Hyrcanus I (135–104 B.C.) was the first **Hasmonean** ruler to strike coins. For the most part Jewish rulers from this period avoided stamping an image of the ruler's face on coins since such coins were not well received by pious Jews.

Hasmonean rule ultimately gave way to Herodian governance.[4] The coins of Herod the Great and his sons made use of a number of symbols (the pomegranate, grape cluster, ship's prow, helmet or tripod) but usually respected Jewish custom in not exhibiting the images of their faces.

A number of different coins were in use in the Holy Land during the New Testament period. The shekel was indigenous to the area. The mite, a copper coin of little value ("mite" is an Old English translation of the Greek *lepton*), may have been the copper prutah, a cheap coin minted during the Hasmonean period but still in use during Jesus' lifetime.

The silver denarius from Rome was circulated throughout the empire, due in large part to the universal presence of the Roman army.[5] The coin given in tribute to Rome in Jesus' day had the image of the emperor Tiberius Caesar on the obverse and of his mother Livia on the reverse side.[6] Therefore, when Jesus asked whose likeness was on the coin, the obvious answer was "Caesar's" (Mt 22:20–21).

A single denarius was equal to a day's wage; thus the loss of a single coin was significant (Lk 15:8). Other coins, such as the copper shekel, dated from an earlier period but still may have been in circulation in Jesus' time. Coins from the Hasmonean and earlier Herodian rulers also remained in circulation. The variety of coins and the inconsistency of their weights made the money changer a practical necessity of economic life.

Numismatics, the scientific study of coins, is one of the archaeologist's most useful tools, due to the particular advantages offered by coins as artifacts:

- Coins often bear the name and sometimes the likeness of the ruler of an area at the time of production. Therefore, they can be dated with a high degree of precision and can aid in the dating of surrounding structures.
- Coins tell much about the official propaganda of a particular period. By studying their portraiture and imagery, scholars gain insight into the persona a ruler attempted to create.
- Coins generally exist in large numbers, a fact that allows scholars to undertake highly accurate comparison and analysis of the numismatic evidence.

Still, scholars need to exercise caution, since some coins supposedly from the ancient world are actually modern forgeries.

[1]See "Banking and Money in the Ancient World" on page 696 and "Weights and Measures" on page 1459. [2]See "Ancient Persian History Through Darius" on page 717. [3]See "Phoenicia" on page 488. [4]See "Herod the Great" on page 1627. [5]See "The Roman Army and the Occupation of the Holy Land" on page 1829. [6]See "Tiberius Caesar, the Caesar of Jesus' Ministry" on page 1708.

13“Not long after that, the younger son got together all he had, set off for a distant country and there
squandered his wealth[g] in wild living. 14After he had spent everything, there was a severe famine in that **15:13** [g]ver 30; Lk 16:1
whole country, and he began to be in need. 15So he went and hired himself out to a citizen of that coun-
try, who sent him to his fields to feed pigs.[h] 16He longed to fill his stomach with the pods that the pigs **15:15** [h]Lev 11:7
were eating, but no one gave him anything.
17“When he came to his senses, he said, ‘How many of my father’s hired men have food to spare, and
here I am starving to death! 18I will set out and go back to my father and say to him: Father, I have sinned[i] **15:18** [i]Lev 26:40; Mt 3:2
against heaven and against you. 19I am no longer worthy to be called your son; make me like one of your
hired men.’ 20So he got up and went to his father.
“But while he was still a long way off, his father saw him and was filled with compassion for him; he
ran to his son, threw his arms around him and kissed him.[j] **15:20** [j]Ge 45:14, 15; 46:29; Ac 20:37
21“The son said to him, ‘Father, I have sinned against heaven and against you.[k] I am no longer wor- **15:21** [k]Ps 51:4
thy to be called your son.[a]’
22“But the father said to his servants, ‘Quick! Bring the best robe[l] and put it on him. Put a ring on his **15:22** [l]Zec 3:4; Rev 6:11
finger[m] and sandals on his feet. 23Bring the fattened calf and kill it. Let’s have a feast and celebrate. 24For [m]Ge 41:42
this son of mine was dead and is alive again;[n] he was lost and is found.’ So they began to celebrate.[o] **15:24** [n]Eph 2:1,5; 5:14; 1Ti 5:6 [o]ver 32
25“Meanwhile, the older son was in the field. When he came near the house, he heard music and danc-
ing. 26So he called one of the servants and asked him what was going on. 27‘Your brother has come,’ he
replied, ‘and your father has killed the fattened calf because he has him back safe and sound.’
28“The older brother became angry[p] and refused to go in. So his father went out and pleaded with **15:28** [p]Jnh 4:1
him. 29But he answered his father, ‘Look! All these years I’ve been slaving for you and never disobeyed
your orders. Yet you never gave me even a young goat so I could celebrate with my friends. 30But when
this son of yours who has squandered your property[q] with prostitutes[r] comes home, you kill the fattened **15:30** [q]ver 12,13 [r]Pr 29:3
calf for him!’
31“ ‘My son,’ the father said, ‘you are always with me, and everything I have is yours. 32But we had to
celebrate and be glad, because this brother of yours was dead and is alive again; he was lost and is
found.’ ”[s] **15:32** [s]ver 24; Mal 3:17

The Parable of the Shrewd Manager

16 Jesus told his disciples: “There was a rich man whose manager was accused of wasting his pos-
sessions.[t] 2So he called him in and asked him, ‘What is this I hear about you? Give an account of **16:1** [t]Lk 15:13, 30
your management, because you cannot be manager any longer.’
3“The manager said to himself, ‘What shall I do now? My master is taking away my job. I’m not strong
enough to dig, and I’m ashamed to beg— 4I know what I’ll do so that, when I lose my job here, people
will welcome me into their houses.’
5“So he called in each one of his master’s debtors. He asked the first, ‘How much do you owe my
master?’
6“ ‘Eight hundred gallons[b] of olive oil,’ he replied.
“The manager told him, ‘Take your bill, sit down quickly, and make it four hundred.’
7“Then he asked the second, ‘And how much do you owe?’
“ ‘A thousand bushels[c] of wheat,’ he replied.
“He told him, ‘Take your bill and make it eight hundred.’

[a] *21* Some early manuscripts *son. Make me like one of your hired men.* [b] *6* Greek *one hundred batous* (probably about 3 kiloliters) [c] *7* Greek *one hundred korous* (probably about 35 kiloliters)

15:15 To feed pigs was considered the ultimate indignity for Jews, who viewed them as “unclean” animals (Lev 11:7).
15:22–23 A long robe of distinction, a signet ring of authority, sandals like a son (slaves went barefoot) and the fattened calf for a special occasion—all these were signs of position and acceptance.
15:25 For Hebrew/Jewish feasting, see the note on Matthew 22:2–14.
15:29 A young goat was less expensive food than a fattened calf.
16:1 The “manager” was a steward or trusted slave who handled all of the business affairs of the owner (see the note on 12:42).
16:3–7 Knowing that he would lose his job, the manager planned for his future by discounting the debts owed to his master in order to obligate the debtors to himself. Interpreters disagree as to whether his procedure of discounting was in itself dishonest. Was he giving away what really belonged to his master, or was he forgoing interest payments his master did not have a right to charge? Originally the manager may have overcharged the debtors, a common way of circumventing the Mosaic Law, which prohibited taking interest from fellow Jews (see Ex 22:25–27; Lev 25:36). So, to reduce the debts, he may have returned the figures to their initial amounts, which would have both satisfied his master and gained the good favor of the debtors. In any event, the point remains the same: He was shrewd enough to use the means at his disposal to plan for his future well-being.

8“The master commended the dishonest manager because he had acted shrewdly. For the people of
this world[u] are more shrewd[v] in dealing with their own kind than are the people of the light.[w] 9I tell you,
use worldly wealth[x] to gain friends for yourselves, so that when it is gone, you will be welcomed into eter-
nal dwellings.[y]

10“Whoever can be trusted with very little can also be trusted with much,[z] and whoever is dishonest
with very little will also be dishonest with much. 11So if you have not been trustworthy in handling world-
ly wealth,[a] who will trust you with true riches? 12And if you have not been trustworthy with someone
else’s property, who will give you property of your own?

13“No servant can serve two masters. Either he will hate the one and love the other, or he will be de-
voted to the one and despise the other. You cannot serve both God and Money.”[b]

14The Pharisees, who loved money,[c] heard all this and were sneering at Jesus.[d] 15He said to them, “You
are the ones who justify yourselves[e] in the eyes of men, but God knows your hearts.[f] What is highly val-
ued among men is detestable in God’s sight.

Additional Teachings

16“The Law and the Prophets were proclaimed until John.[g] Since that time, the good news of the king-
dom of God is being preached,[h] and everyone is forcing his way into it. 17It is easier for heaven and earth
to disappear than for the least stroke of a pen to drop out of the Law.[i]

18“Anyone who divorces his wife and marries another woman commits adultery, and the man who
marries a divorced woman commits adultery.[j]

The Rich Man and Lazarus

19“There was a rich man who was dressed in purple and fine linen and lived in luxury every day.[k]
20At his gate was laid a beggar[l] named Lazarus, covered with sores 21and longing to eat what fell from the
rich man’s table.[m] Even the dogs came and licked his sores.

22“The time came when the beggar died and the angels carried him to Abraham’s side. The rich man
also died and was buried. 23In hell,[a] where he was in torment, he looked up and saw Abraham far away,
with Lazarus by his side. 24So he called to him, ‘Father Abraham,[n] have pity on me and send Lazarus to
dip the tip of his finger in water and cool my tongue, because I am in agony in this fire.’[o]

25“But Abraham replied, ‘Son, remember that in your lifetime you received your good things, while
Lazarus received bad things,[p] but now he is comforted here and you are in agony.[q] 26And besides all this,
between us and you a great chasm has been fixed, so that those who want to go from here to you cannot,
nor can anyone cross over from there to us.’

27“He answered, ‘Then I beg you, father, send Lazarus to my father’s house, 28for I have five brothers.
Let him warn them,[r] so that they will not also come to this place of torment.’

29“Abraham replied, ‘They have Moses[s] and the Prophets;[t] let them listen to them.’

30“ ‘No, father Abraham,’[u] he said, ‘but if someone from the dead goes to them, they will repent.’

31“He said to him, ‘If they do not listen to Moses and the Prophets, they will not be convinced even if
someone rises from the dead.’ ”

Sin, Faith, Duty

17 Jesus said to his disciples: “Things that cause people to sin[v] are bound to come, but woe to that
person through whom they come.[w] 2It would be better for him to be thrown into the sea with a
millstone tied around his neck than for him to cause one of these little ones[x] to sin.[y] 3So watch yourselves.

“If your brother sins, rebuke him,[z] and if he repents, forgive him.[a] 4If he sins against you seven times
in a day, and seven times comes back to you and says, ‘I repent,’ forgive him.”[b]

16:8 [u]Ps 17:14 [v]Ps 18:26 [w]Jn 12:36; Eph 5:8; 1Th 5:5 **16:9** [x]ver 11,13 [y]Mt 19:21; Lk 12:33 **16:10** [z]Mt 25:21, 23; Lk 19:17 **16:11** [a]ver 9,13 **16:13** [b]ver 9,11; Mt 6:24 **16:14** [c]1Ti 3:3 [d]Lk 23:35 **16:15** [e]Lk 10:29 [f]1Sa 16:7; Rev 2:23 **16:16** [g]Mt 11:12, 13 [h]Mt 4:23 **16:17** [i]Mt 5:18 **16:18** [j]Mt 5:31, 32; 19:9; Mk 10:11; Ro 7:2, 3; 1Co 7:10,11 **16:19** [k]Eze 16:49 **16:20** [l]Ac 3:2 **16:21** [m]Mt 15:27 **16:24** [n]ver 30; Lk 3:8 [o]Mt 5:22 **16:25** [p]Ps 17:14 [q]Lk 6:21,24,25 **16:28** [r]Ac 2:40; 20:23; 1Th 4:6 **16:29** [s]Lk 24:27, 44; Jn 5:45-47; Ac 15:21 [t]Lk 4:17; Jn 1:45 **16:30** [u]ver 24; Lk 3:8 **17:1** [v]Mt 5:29 [w]Mt 18:7 **17:2** [x]Mk 10:24; Lk 10:21 [y]Mt 5:29 **17:3** [z]Mt 18:15 [a]Eph 4:32; Col 3:13 **17:4** [b]Mt 18:21, 22

[a] 23 Greek *Hades*

16:19 Garments of “purple and fine linen” symbolize wealth.
16:22 “Abraham’s side” refers to the place of blessedness to which the righteous dead go. The figure derives either from the Roman custom of reclining on the left side at meals; Lazarus being in the place of honor at Abraham’s right, leaning on his breast; or its appropriateness for expressing the closest of fellowship (Jn 1:18; 13:23). Since Abraham was the founder of the Hebrew nation, such intimacy equated to the highest honor and bliss.
16:23 For “hell,” see the note on Matthew 5:22.
16:29 “Moses and the Prophets” was a way of designating the entire Old Testament.
17:2 For “millstone,” see the note on Matthew 18:6.
17:4 See the note on Matthew 18:21.

5 The apostles[c] said to the Lord,[d] "Increase our faith!"
6 He replied, "If you have faith as small as a mustard seed,[e] you can say to this mulberry tree, 'Be up-
rooted and planted in the sea,' and it will obey you.[f]
7 "Suppose one of you had a servant plowing or looking after the sheep. Would he say to the servant
when he comes in from the field, 'Come along now and sit down to eat'? 8 Would he not rather say, 'Prepare
my supper, get yourself ready and wait on me[g] while I eat and drink; after that you may eat and drink'?
9 Would he thank the servant because he did what he was told to do? 10 So you also, when you have done
everything you were told to do, should say, 'We are unworthy servants; we have only done our duty.' "[h]

Ten Healed of Leprosy

11 Now on his way to Jerusalem,[i] Jesus traveled along the border between Samaria and Galilee.[j] 12 As
he was going into a village, ten men who had leprosy[a][k] met him. They stood at a distance[l] 13 and called
out in a loud voice, "Jesus, Master,[m] have pity on us!"
14 When he saw them, he said, "Go, show yourselves to the priests."[n] And as they went, they were
cleansed.
15 One of them, when he saw he was healed, came back, praising God[o] in a loud voice. 16 He threw him-
self at Jesus' feet and thanked him—and he was a Samaritan.[p]
17 Jesus asked, "Were not all ten cleansed? Where are the other nine? 18 Was no one found to return and
give praise to God except this foreigner?" 19 Then he said to him, "Rise and go; your faith has made you
well."[q]

The Coming of the Kingdom of God

20 Once, having been asked by the Pharisees when the kingdom of God would come,[r] Jesus replied,
"The kingdom of God does not come with your careful observation, 21 nor will people say, 'Here it is,' or
'There it is,'[s] because the kingdom of God is within[b] you."
22 Then he said to his disciples, "The time is coming when you will long to see one of the days of the
Son of Man,[t] but you will not see it.[u] 23 Men will tell you, 'There he is!' or 'Here he is!' Do not go running
off after them.[v] 24 For the Son of Man in his day[c] will be like the lightning,[w] which flashes and lights up
the sky from one end to the other. 25 But first he must suffer many things[x] and be rejected[y] by this gen-
eration.[z]
26 "Just as it was in the days of Noah,[a] so also will it be in the days of the Son of Man. 27 People were
eating, drinking, marrying and being given in marriage up to the day Noah entered the ark. Then the
flood came and destroyed them all.
28 "It was the same in the days of Lot.[b] People were eating and drinking, buying and selling, plant-
ing and building. 29 But the day Lot left Sodom, fire and sulfur rained down from heaven and destroyed
them all.
30 "It will be just like this on the day the Son of Man is revealed.[c] 31 On that day no one who is on the
roof of his house, with his goods inside, should go down to get them. Likewise, no one in the field should
go back for anything.[d] 32 Remember Lot's wife![e] 33 Whoever tries to keep his life will lose it, and whoev-
er loses his life will preserve it.[f] 34 I tell you, on that night two people will be in one bed; one will be tak-
en and the other left. 35 Two women will be grinding grain together; one will be taken and the other left.[d]"[g]
37 "Where, Lord?" they asked.
He replied, "Where there is a dead body, there the vultures will gather."[h]

The Parable of the Persistent Widow

18 Then Jesus told his disciples a parable to show them that they should always pray and not give
up.[i] 2 He said: "In a certain town there was a judge who neither feared God nor cared about men.

17:5 [c]Mk 6:30 [d]Lk 7:13
17:6 [e]Mt 13:31; 17:20; Lk 13:19 [f]Mt 21:21; Mk 9:23
17:8 [g]Lk 12:37
17:10 [h]1Co 9:16
17:11 [i]Lk 9:51 [j]Lk 9:51,52; Jn 4:3,4
17:12 [k]Mt 8:2 [l]Lev 13:45,46
17:13 [m]Lk 5:5
17:14 [n]Lev 14:2; Mt 8:4
17:15 [o]Mt 9:8
17:16 [p]Mt 10:5
17:19 [q]Mt 9:22
17:20 [r]Mt 3:2
17:21 [s]ver 23
17:22 [t]Mt 8:20 [u]Mt 9:15; Lk 5:35
17:23 [v]Mt 24:23; Mk 13:21; Lk 21:8
17:24 [w]Mt 24:27
17:25 [x]Mt 16:21 [y]Lk 9:22; 18:32 [z]Mk 13:30; Lk 21:32
17:26 [a]Ge 7:6-24
17:28 [b]Ge 19:1-28
17:30 [c]Mt 10:23; 16:27; 24:3,27, 37,39; 25:31; 1Co 1:7; 1Th 2:19; 2Th 1:7; 2:8; 2Pe 3:4; Rev 1:7
17:31 [d]Mt 24:17, 18; Mk 13:15-16
17:32 [e]Ge 19:26
17:33 [f]Jn 12:25
17:35 [g]Mt 24:41
17:37 [h]Mt 24:28
18:1 [i]Isa 40:31; Lk 11:5-8; Ac 1:14; Ro 12:12; Eph 6:18; Col 4:2; 1Th 5:17

[a] 12 The Greek word was used for various diseases affecting the skin—not necessarily leprosy. [b] 21 Or *among* [c] 24 Some manuscripts do not have *in his day.* [d] 35 Some manuscripts *left.* [36]*Two men will be in the field; one will be taken and the other left.*

17:6 For "mustard seed," see the note on Matthew 13:31–32.
17:14 See the note on Mark 1:44.
17:16 For "Samaritan," see the note on 10:33.
17:31 It was customary to relax on flat rooftops, where people could catch the cool evening breezes (see the note on Mk 2:4).
17:35 The grinding of grain into flour between two heavy stones was a domestic art usually performed by women; hence the import of Jesus' parable (see also Mt 24:41).
17:36 A copyist probably inserted verse 36 here (see the NIV text note on v. 36) from Matthew 24:40. (See "Early Scribal Emendation" on p. 448.)

18:3 [j]Isa 1:17 3 And there was a widow in that town who kept coming to him with the plea, 'Grant me justice[j] against
my adversary.'
4 "For some time he refused. But finally he said to himself, 'Even though I don't fear God or care about
men, 5 yet because this widow keeps bothering me, I will see that she gets justice, so that she won't even-
18:5 [k]Lk 11:8 tually wear me out with her coming!' "[k]
18:6 [l]Lk 7:13 6 And the Lord[l] said, "Listen to what the unjust judge says. 7 And will not God bring about justice for
18:7 [m]Ex 22:23; his chosen ones, who cry out[m] to him day and night? Will he keep putting them off? 8 I tell you, he will
Ps 88:1; Rev 6:10 18:8 [n]Mt 8:20 see that they get justice, and quickly. However, when the Son of Man[n] comes,[o] will he find faith on the
[o]Mt 16:27 earth?"

The Parable of the Pharisee and the Tax Collector

18:9 [p]Lk 16:15 9 To some who were confident of their own righteousness[p] and looked down on everybody else,[q] Jesus
[q]Isa 65:5 18:10 [r]Ac 3:1 told this parable: 10 "Two men went up to the temple to pray,[r] one a Pharisee and the other a tax collec-
18:11 [s]Mt 6:5; Mk 11:25 tor. 11 The Pharisee stood up[s] and prayed about[a] himself: 'God, I thank you that I am not like other men—
18:12 [t]Isa 58:3; Mt 9:14 [u]Mal 3:8; robbers, evildoers, adulterers—or even like this tax collector. 12 I fast[t] twice a week and give a tenth[u] of
Lk 11:42 all I get.'
18:13 [v]Isa 66:2; 13 "But the tax collector stood at a distance. He would not even look up to heaven, but beat his breast[v]
Jer 31:19; Lk 23:48 and said, 'God, have mercy on me, a sinner.'[w]
[w]Lk 5:32; 1Ti 1:15 14 "I tell you that this man, rather than the other, went home justified before God. For everyone who
18:14 [x]Mt 23:12; Lk 14:11 exalts himself will be humbled, and he who humbles himself will be exalted."[x]

The Little Children and Jesus

15 People were also bringing babies to Jesus to have him touch them. When the disciples saw this, they
rebuked them. 16 But Jesus called the children to him and said, "Let the little children come to me, and do
not hinder them, for the kingdom of God belongs to such as these. 17 I tell you the truth, anyone who will
18:17 [y]Mt 11:25; 18:3 not receive the kingdom of God like a little child[y] will never enter it."

The Rich Ruler

18:18 [z]Lk 10:25 18 A certain ruler asked him, "Good teacher, what must I do to inherit eternal life?"[z]
19 "Why do you call me good?" Jesus answered. "No one is good—except God alone. 20 You know the
commandments: 'Do not commit adultery, do not murder, do not steal, do not give false testimony, hon-
18:20 [a]Ex 20:12-16; Dt 5:16-20; or your father and mother.'[b]"[a]
Ro 13:9 21 "All these I have kept since I was a boy," he said.
22 When Jesus heard this, he said to him, "You still lack one thing. Sell everything you have and give to
18:22 [b]Ac 2:45 [c]Mt 6:20 the poor,[b] and you will have treasure in heaven.[c] Then come, follow me."
23 When he heard this, he became very sad, because he was a man of great wealth. 24 Jesus looked at
18:24 [d]Pr 11:28 him and said, "How hard it is for the rich to enter the kingdom of God![d] 25 Indeed, it is easier for a cam-
el to go through the eye of a needle than for a rich man to enter the kingdom of God."
26 Those who heard this asked, "Who then can be saved?"
18:27 [e]Mt 19:26 27 Jesus replied, "What is impossible with men is possible with God."[e]
18:28 [f]Mt 4:19 28 Peter said to him, "We have left all we had to follow you!"[f]
29 "I tell you the truth," Jesus said to them, "no one who has left home or wife or brothers or parents
or children for the sake of the kingdom of God 30 will fail to receive many times as much in this age and,
18:30 [g]Mt 12:32 [h]Mt 25:46 in the age to come,[g] eternal life."[h]

Jesus Again Predicts His Death

18:31 [i]Lk 9:51 31 Jesus took the Twelve aside and told them, "We are going up to Jerusalem,[i] and everything that is
[j]Ps 22; Isa 53 [k]Mt 8:20 written by the prophets[j] about the Son of Man[k] will be fulfilled. 32 He will be handed over to the Gentiles.[l]
18:32 [l]Lk 23:1

[a] 11 Or *to*   [b] 20 Exodus 20:12-16; Deut. 5:16-20

18:3 Widows were particularly helpless and vulnerable because they had no family to uphold their cause (see "The Care of Widows and Orphans in the Bible and the Ancient Near East" on p. 285).
18:10 Periods for prayer were scheduled daily in connection with the morning and evening sacrifices. People could also go to the temple at any time for private prayer.

For "tax collector," see the notes on Matthew 5:46 and Mark 2:14.
18:12 For "fast twice a week," see the note on Mark 2:18; see also "Fasting in the Bible and the Ancient Near East" on page 1569.
18:13 For "beat his breast," see the note on 23:48.

The Jewish Priesthood and Religious Life in the First Century A.D.

LUKE 18 According to Biblical tradition the priesthood was entrusted to the hereditary, Levitical descendants of Aaron.[1] During the Solomonic age the high priesthood belonged to the family of Zadok (2Sa 15:24), which, together with the other anointed offices of prophet and king, exercised leadership over the nation. In the **Persian period** Judea was reconstituted as a temple-state under the exclusive political and religious hegemony of the high priests, who were themselves subordinate only to the king of Persia. The house of Zadok, from which the name Sadducees probably derived,[2] controlled the office until 174 B.C., when Jason effectively purchased the high priesthood from the **Seleucid** king Antiochus IV, who at that time controlled Judea. This accomplished a fundamental shift away from hereditary succession to the unprecedented situation of having a pagan ruler appoint the high priest in Israel, usually in return for pledges of loyalty and outright payment of money.

As a result of the **Maccabean** success against the Seleucid dynasty, the **Hasmonean** family established itself as a clan of priest-kings, even though they were descendants of neither the Zadokite family nor the royal line of David. Their questionable status produced tremendous strife among certain factions within Judaism, especially the Pharisees, who appealed for them to relinquish the high priesthood and to be content with governing the people. The Romans eventually prohibited the Hasmonean leaders from using the title of king and restricted their influence to political control of Judea and religious authority over all Jews everywhere.[3]

In 37 B.C. Herod the Great received Judea as a client kingdom from Caesar Augustus.[4] He promptly murdered Aristobulus, the last Hasmonean high priest, and transferred the office to the family of Boethus. From the inauguration of Herod's reign to the destruction of the temple in A.D. 70,[5] 28 different high priests were appointed. The only one to serve for any length of time was Joseph Caiaphas (A.D. 18–36), who is known from the Gospel accounts (Mt 26:57; Lk 3:2; Jn 11:49; 18:13).[6]

Despite considerable fluctuations in the priesthood during the **Second Temple** period, the office continued to enjoy tremendous prestige and influence. The high priest served as the supreme religious functionary in the temple liturgy, and he alone was granted access to the Most Holy Place on the annual Day of Atonement.[7] He also presided as the president of the supreme judiciary council, the Sanhedrin, comprised of members of the leading aristocratic members of society (cf. Ex 24:1; Mt 5:22; Mk 14:55; Lk 22:66; Jn 11:47; Ac 4:15; 5:21; 6:12; 22:30).[8]

Under the direct authority of the high priest were the chief priests, temple treasurer and the remainder of the common priests and Levites. During the first century A.D. there were approximately 7,200 common priests, divided into 24 courses or divisions. Members of each course were called from their homes to serve in the Jerusalem temple for one week at a time (Lk 1:8; Josephus, *Antiquities*, 7.14.7). The remainder of the temple duties were fulfilled by approximately 9,600 Levites, who were also divided into weekly courses (*Antiquities*, 7.14.7).

The religious life of first-century Jews was oriented around the temple, which was admired by pagans and a source of pride for Jews (Lk 21:5). While the great pilgrimage festivals demarcated the liturgical year,[9] individual piety was both cultivated and demonstrated through daily observances, such as morning and evening prayers, tithing, participation in public and private fasts, study and the keeping of the Sabbath. Jews maintained their unique identity through circumcision, dietary laws and an abiding determination to avoid mixed marriages. Synagogues also served as centers for communal prayer, study and the rehearsal of Jewish lifestyle obligations. Although their importance expanded after the destruction of the temple in A.D. 70, their origin dates from a much earlier period. Jesus spoke frequently in synagogues (Mt 4:23; 9:35; Jn 18:20), as did Paul (Ac 9:20; 17:10; 19:8). According to the **Talmud** there were some 480 synagogues in Jerusalem prior to the temple's destruction.[10]

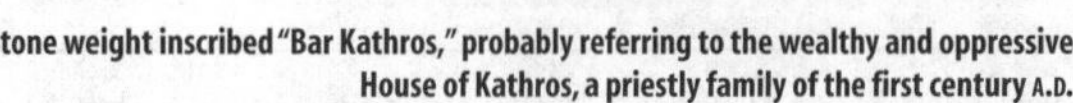

Stone weight inscribed "Bar Kathros," probably referring to the wealthy and oppressive House of Kathros, a priestly family of the first century A.D.

Preserving Bible Times; © Dr. James C. Martin; permission of The Wohl Archaeological Museum and Burnt House

[1]See "The Levites and the Priests" on page 648. [2]See "The Sadducees" on page 1600. [3]See "The Intertestamental Period" on page 1551. [4]See "Herod the Great" on page 1627 and "Caesar Augustus, Emperor of Rome; the Census; and Quirinius, Governor of Syria" on page 1667. [5]See "Josephus and the Fall of Jerusalem" on page 1606. [6]See "The High Priests Annas and Caiaphas" on page 1772. [7]See "The Day of Atonement" on page 176. [8]See "The Sanhedrin" on page 1821. [9]See "The Festivals of Israel" on page 186. [10]See "Ancient Synagogues" on page 1783.

18:32 [m]Mt 16:21; [n]Ac 2:23 They will mock him, insult him, spit on him, flog him[m] and kill him.[n] 33On the third day[o] he will rise
18:33 [o]Mt 16:21; [p]Mt 16:21 again."[p]

34The disciples did not understand any of this. Its meaning was hidden from them, and they did not
18:34 [q]Mk 9:32; Lk 9:45 know what he was talking about.[q]

A Blind Beggar Receives His Sight

18:35 [r]Lk 19:1 35As Jesus approached Jericho,[r] a blind man was sitting by the roadside begging. 36When he heard
18:37 [s]Lk 19:4 the crowd going by, he asked what was happening. 37They told him, "Jesus of Nazareth is passing by."[s]

18:38 [t]ver 39; Mt 9:27 38He called out, "Jesus, Son of David,[t] have mercy[u] on me!"

[u]Mt 17:15; Lk 18:13 39Those who led the way rebuked him and told him to be quiet, but he shouted all the more, "Son of
18:39 [v]ver 38 David, have mercy on me!"[v]

40Jesus stopped and ordered the man to be brought to him. When he came near, Jesus asked him,
41"What do you want me to do for you?"

"Lord, I want to see," he replied.

18:42 [w]Mt 9:22 42Jesus said to him, "Receive your sight; your faith has healed you."[w] 43Immediately he received his
18:43 [x]Mt 9:8; Lk 13:17 sight and followed Jesus, praising God. When all the people saw it, they also praised God.[x]

Zacchaeus the Tax Collector

19:1 [y]Lk 18:35 **19** Jesus entered Jericho[y] and was passing through. 2A man was there by the name of Zacchaeus; he
was a chief tax collector and was wealthy. 3He wanted to see who Jesus was, but being a short
19:4 [z]1Ki 10:27; 1Ch 27:28; man he could not, because of the crowd. 4So he ran ahead and climbed a sycamore-fig[z] tree to see him,
Isa 9:10; [a]Lk 18:37 since Jesus was coming that way.[a]

5When Jesus reached the spot, he looked up and said to him, "Zacchaeus, come down immediately. I
must stay at your house today." 6So he came down at once and welcomed him gladly.

19:7 [b]Mt 9:11 7All the people saw this and began to mutter, "He has gone to be the guest of a 'sinner.' "[b]

19:8 [c]Lk 7:13; [d]Lk 3:12,13 8But Zacchaeus stood up and said to the Lord,[c] "Look, Lord! Here and now I give half of my posses-
[e]Ex 22:1; Lev 6:4, 5; Nu 5:7; sions to the poor, and if I have cheated anybody out of anything,[d] I will pay back four times the amount."[e]
2Sa 12:6 9Jesus said to him, "Today salvation has come to this house, because this man, too, is a son of Abra-
19:9 [f]Lk 3:8; 13:16; Ro 4:16; Gal 3:7 ham.[f] 10For the Son of Man came to seek and to save what was lost."[g]

19:10 [g]Eze 34:12,16; Jn 3:17

The Parable of the Ten Minas

11While they were listening to this, he went on to tell them a parable, because he was near Jerusalem
19:11 [h]Mt 3:2; [i]Lk 17:20; Ac 1:6 and the people thought that the kingdom of God[h] was going to appear at once.[i] 12He said: "A man of no-
ble birth went to a distant country to have himself appointed king and then to return. 13So he called ten
19:13 [j]Mk 13:34 of his servants[j] and gave them ten minas.[a] 'Put this money to work,' he said, 'until I come back.'

14"But his subjects hated him and sent a delegation after him to say, 'We don't want this man to be
our king.'

15"He was made king, however, and returned home. Then he sent for the servants to whom he had
given the money, in order to find out what they had gained with it.

16"The first one came and said, 'Sir, your mina has earned ten more.'

19:17 [k]Pr 27:18; [l]Lk 16:10 17" 'Well done, my good servant!'[k] his master replied. 'Because you have been trustworthy in a very
small matter, take charge of ten cities.'[l]

18"The second came and said, 'Sir, your mina has earned five more.'

19"His master answered, 'You take charge of five cities.'

20"Then another servant came and said, 'Sir, here is your mina; I have kept it laid away in a piece of

[a] *13* A mina was about three months' wages.

18:35 For "approached Jericho," see the note on Mark 10:46.
19:1 For "entered Jericho," see again the note on Mark 10:46.
19:2 The position of "chief tax collector," referred to only here in the Bible, probably designated an individual in charge of a district, with other tax collectors under him. The region was prosperous at this time, so it was no wonder that Zacchaeus had grown rich. (For information on tax collectors, see the notes on Mt 5:46; Mk 2:14.)
19:4 A sycamore-fig tree is a sturdy tree 30–40 feet (9–12 m) high, with a short trunk and spreading branches, capable of withstanding the weight of a grown man (see the note on Am 7:14).
19:10 For Jesus as Savior, see the note on 2:11.
19:12 This parable has a historical background. Both Herod in 40 B.C. and Archelaus in 4 B.C. went to Rome to receive ruling authority from the emperor. There was a public outcry against Archelaus, who was unpopular and received a less comprehensive ruling mandate.
19:13 A mina was equivalent to about three months' wages.
19:14 Such an incident had occurred over 30 years earlier in the case of Archelaus (Josephus, *Wars*, 2.6.1; *Antiquities*, 17.9.3), as well as in a number of other instances (see the note on v. 12).

cloth. 21 I was afraid of you, because you are a hard man. You take out what you did not put in and reap
what you did not sow.'[m] 19:21 [m]Mt 25:24
22 "His master replied, 'I will judge you by your own words,[n] you wicked servant! You knew, did you, 19:22 [n]2Sa 1:16;
that I am a hard man, taking out what I did not put in, and reaping what I did not sow?[o] 23 Why then Job 15:6 [o]Mt 25:26
didn't you put my money on deposit, so that when I came back, I could have collected it with interest?'
24 "Then he said to those standing by, 'Take his mina away from him and give it to the one who has ten
minas.'
25 " 'Sir,' they said, 'he already has ten!'
26 "He replied, 'I tell you that to everyone who has, more will be given, but as for the one who has noth-
ing, even what he has will be taken away.[p] 27 But those enemies of mine who did not want me to be king 19:26 [p]Mt 13:12;
over them—bring them here and kill them in front of me.' " 25:29; Lk 8:18

The Triumphal Entry

28 After Jesus had said this, he went on ahead, going up to Jerusalem.[q] 29 As he approached Bethpha- 19:28 [q]Mk 10:32;
ge and Bethany[r] at the hill called the Mount of Olives,[s] he sent two of his disciples, saying to them, 30 "Go Lk 9:51 19:29 [r]Mt 21:17
to the village ahead of you, and as you enter it, you will find a colt tied there, which no one has ever rid- [s]Mt 21:1
den. Untie it and bring it here. 31 If anyone asks you, 'Why are you untying it?' tell him, 'The Lord
needs it.' "
32 Those who were sent ahead went and found it just as he had told them.[t] 33 As they were untying the 19:32 [t]Lk 22:13
colt, its owners asked them, "Why are you untying the colt?"
34 They replied, "The Lord needs it."
35 They brought it to Jesus, threw their cloaks on the colt and put Jesus on it. 36 As he went along, peo-
ple spread their cloaks[u] on the road. 19:36 [u]2Ki 9:13
37 When he came near the place where the road goes down the Mount of Olives,[v] the whole crowd of 19:37 [v]Mt 21:1
disciples began joyfully to praise God in loud voices for all the miracles they had seen:

19:23 For a discussion of interest, see the note on Ezekiel 18:8.
19:29 Bethphage was a village near the road running from Jericho to Jerusalem. For "Bethany," see the note on Matthew 21:17. See also "The Mount of Olives" on page 1543.

CULTURAL AND HISTORICAL NOTES

Miracle Workers and Magicians in the First Century A.D.

LUKE 19 Some historians have argued that Jesus was just one among many miracle workers operating during the first century A.D. While Jesus himself admitted that there were effective Jewish exorcists, and we have a few scattered reports of rabbis performing miracles, the evidence for miracle workers on a par with Jesus is minimal. For example, Apollonius of Tyana, a first-century sage, is sometimes claimed to have been Jesus' equal in this regard. In the fullest account of his life (published long after his death), Apollonius is credited with only a few amazing feats, generally involving his ability to foresee the future or to perceive demonic activity. His most striking "miracle," raising a girl from her funeral bier, was doubted even by his most loyal followers, who suspected that the young woman was not actually dead but that Apollonius had revived her from near death.

There were certainly "magicians" both within and outside of Judaism during the first century.[1] Archaeologists have discovered numerous papyri and **amulets** with magical formulas for gaining the love of a man or woman, exacting vengeance on an enemy or even winning at the horse races. Frequently these magicians would use natural objects in the course of performing their magical acts. Some critics have suggested that Jesus' use of saliva and mud in a few of his healings (Mk 8:33; Jn 9) points to magical rituals. But this conjecture misinterprets what Jesus was doing. For example, the use of mud in John 9 was intended to recall God's creation of humankind from the dirt: Jesus was symbolically recreating this man's eyes. In terms of the number and magnitude of his miracles, Jesus undeniably stands alone in the ancient world.

[1] See "Magic in the Greco-Roman World" on page 1911.

[38] "Blessed is the king who comes in the name of the Lord!"[a][w]

"Peace in heaven and glory in the highest!"[x]

[39] Some of the Pharisees in the crowd said to Jesus, "Teacher, rebuke your disciples!"[y]

[40] "I tell you," he replied, "if they keep quiet, the stones will cry out."[z]

[41] As he approached Jerusalem and saw the city, he wept over it[a] [42] and said, "If you, even you, had only known on this day what would bring you peace—but now it is hidden from your eyes. [43] The days will come upon you when your enemies will build an embankment against you and encircle you and hem you in on every side.[b] [44] They will dash you to the ground, you and the children within your walls.[c] They will not leave one stone on another,[d] because you did not recognize the time of God's coming[e] to you."

Jesus at the Temple

[45] Then he entered the temple area and began driving out those who were selling. [46] "It is written," he said to them, " 'My house will be a house of prayer'[b];[f] but you have made it 'a den of robbers.'[c]"[g]

[47] Every day he was teaching at the temple.[h] But the chief priests, the teachers of the law and the leaders among the people were trying to kill him.[i] [48] Yet they could not find any way to do it, because all the people hung on his words.

The Authority of Jesus Questioned

20 One day as he was teaching the people in the temple courts[j] and preaching the gospel,[k] the chief priests and the teachers of the law, together with the elders, came up to him. [2] "Tell us by what authority you are doing these things," they said. "Who gave you this authority?"[l]

[3] He replied, "I will also ask you a question. Tell me, [4] John's baptism[m]—was it from heaven, or from men?"

[5] They discussed it among themselves and said, "If we say, 'From heaven,' he will ask, 'Why didn't you believe him?' [6] But if we say, 'From men,' all the people[n] will stone us, because they are persuaded that John was a prophet."[o]

[7] So they answered, "We don't know where it was from."

[8] Jesus said, "Neither will I tell you by what authority I am doing these things."

The Parable of the Tenants

[9] He went on to tell the people this parable: "A man planted a vineyard,[p] rented it to some farmers and went away for a long time.[q] [10] At harvest time he sent a servant to the tenants so they would give him some of the fruit of the vineyard. But the tenants beat him and sent him away empty-handed. [11] He sent another servant, but that one also they beat and treated shamefully and sent away empty-handed. [12] He sent still a third, and they wounded him and threw him out.

[13] "Then the owner of the vineyard said, 'What shall I do? I will send my son, whom I love;[r] perhaps they will respect him.'

[14] "But when the tenants saw him, they talked the matter over. 'This is the heir,' they said. 'Let's kill him, and the inheritance will be ours.' [15] So they threw him out of the vineyard and killed him.

"What then will the owner of the vineyard do to them? [16] He will come and kill those tenants[s] and give the vineyard to others."

When the people heard this, they said, "May this never be!"

[17] Jesus looked directly at them and asked, "Then what is the meaning of that which is written:

" 'The stone the builders rejected
has become the capstone[d]'[e]?[t]

19:38 [w]Ps 118:26; Lk 13:35 [x]Lk 2:14
19:39 [y]Mt 21:15,16
19:40 [z]Hab 2:11
19:41 [a]Isa 22:4; Lk 13:34,35
19:43 [b]Isa 29:3; Jer 6:6; Eze 4:2; 26:8; Lk 21:20
19:44 [c]Ps 137:9 [d]Mt 24:2; Mk 13:2; Lk 21:6 [e]1Pe 2:12
19:46 [f]Isa 56:7 [g]Jer 7:11
19:47 [h]Mt 26:55 [i]Mt 12:14; Mk 11:18
20:1 [j]Mt 26:55 [k]Lk 8:1
20:2 [l]Jn 2:18; Ac 4:7; 7:27
20:4 [m]Mk 1:4
20:6 [n]Lk 7:29 [o]Mt 11:9
20:9 [p]Isa 5:1-7 [q]Mt 25:14
20:13 [r]Mt 3:17
20:16 [s]Lk 19:27
20:17 [t]Ps 118:22; Ac 4:11

[a] *38* Psalm 118:26 [b] *46* Isaiah 56:7 [c] *46* Jer. 7:11 [d] *17* Or *cornerstone* [e] *17* Psalm 118:22

19:43 This prophecy was fulfilled when the Romans took Jerusalem in A.D. 70, using an embankment to besiege the city (see "Siege Warfare" on p. 465).

19:45 The temple area (the outer court of the Gentiles) was the place where various items necessary for sacrifices were sold: animals, wine, oil, salt and doves. In addition, money was changed from Roman currency to the required Tyrean shekels in accordance with the law (Ex 30:11–14). This exchange had a built-in surcharge, some of which probably went to the high priest's family.

20:1 For "chief priests," see the note on Matthew 2:4, for "teachers of the law," the notes on Matthew 2:4 and Luke 5:17 and for "elders," the notes on Matthew 21:23 and Luke 7:3.

20:10 See the note on Mark 12:2.

20:14 Jewish law provided that a piece of property unclaimed by an heir would be declared ownerless and could then be claimed by others. The tenants assumed that the son came as the heir to claim his property and that if he were slain they could themselves claim the land.

18 Everyone who falls on that stone will be broken to pieces, but he on whom it falls will be crushed."[u] 20:18 [u]Isa 8:14, 15
19 The teachers of the law and the chief priests looked for a way to arrest him[v] immediately, because 20:19 [v]Lk 19:47
they knew he had spoken this parable against them. But they were afraid of the people.[w] [w]Mk 11:18

Paying Taxes to Caesar

20 Keeping a close watch on him, they sent spies, who pretended to be honest. They hoped to catch
Jesus in something he said[x] so that they might hand him over to the power and authority of the gover- 20:20 [x]Mt 12:10
nor.[y] 21 So the spies questioned him: "Teacher, we know that you speak and teach what is right, and that [y]Mt 27:2
you do not show partiality but teach the way of God in accordance with the truth.[z] 22 Is it right for us to 20:21 [z]Jn 3:2
pay taxes to Caesar or not?"
23 He saw through their duplicity and said to them, 24 "Show me a denarius. Whose portrait and in-
scription are on it?"
25 "Caesar's," they replied.
He said to them, "Then give to Caesar what is Caesar's,[a] and to God what is God's." 20:25 [a]Lk 23:2; Ro 13:7
26 They were unable to trap him in what he had said there in public. And astonished by his answer, they
became silent.

20:19 For "teachers of the law," see the notes on Matthew 2:4 and Luke 5:17 and for "chief priests" the note on Matthew 2:4.
20:22–25 Jesus was not a political revolutionary who challenged Rome, nor was he an ardent nationalist. No one could have charged him with political subversion. (See the note on Mk 12:14.)
20:24 For "denarius," see the notes on Matthew 20:2 and 22:19.
20:25 For "Caesar," see "Tiberius Caesar, the Caesar of Jesus' Ministry" on page 1708.

Tiberius Caesar, the Caesar of Jesus' Ministry

LUKE 20 Tiberius Caesar is generally referred to simply as "Caesar" in the Gospels. Ruling from A.D. 14 until 37, he was emperor during Jesus' adolescence and adulthood. In A.D. 18 Herod Antipas, son of Herod the Great and governor of Galilee, founded the city of Tiberias ("Map 9") in honor of the emperor. It was located at the site of hot springs at the southern end of the Sea of Galilee and remains there today.[1] In A.D. 26 Tiberius appointed Pontius Pilate governor of Judea, a position he held until Tiberius removed him from office in 36.[2] The beginning of John the Baptist's preaching, and thus the beginning of Jesus' ministry, is given by Luke as "the fifteenth year of the reign of Tiberius Caesar" (Lk 3:1). There is disagreement over the exact interpretation of this chronological notice, resulting in dates ranging from A.D. 25 to 29.

The most famous Biblical reference to Tiberius is in regard to payment of the Roman tax (Mt 22:15–21; Mk 12:13–17; Lk 20:20–26).[3] When the religious leaders tried to trick Jesus over the matter of paying taxes, Jesus, referring to a silver denarius coin, gave his familiar answer: "Give to Caesar what is Caesar's, and to God what is God's" (v. 25). The coin bore the image of Tiberius and was inscribed as "Tiberius, Son of the Divine Augustus" (Augustus being the former emperor).[4] Jesus' point was that people, who bear the image of God, ought to give themselves to God alone.

[1]See "Tiberias" on page 1732. [2]See "Pontius Pilate" on page 1714. [3]See "Roman Taxation" on page 1855. [4]See also "The Imperial Cult" on page 1651.

Tiberius Caesar
Preserving Bible Times; © Dr. James C. Martin; permission of The British Museum

The Resurrection and Marriage

20:27 [b]Ac 4:1 27 Some of the Sadducees,[b] who say there is no resurrection,[c] came to Jesus with a question. 28 "Teach-
[c]Ac 23:8; 1Co 15:12 er," they said, "Moses wrote for us that if a man's brother dies and leaves a wife but no children, the man
20:28 [d]Dt 25:5 must marry the widow and have children for his brother.[d] 29 Now there were seven brothers. The first one
married a woman and died childless. 30 The second 31 and then the third married her, and in the same
way the seven died, leaving no children. 32 Finally, the woman died too. 33 Now then, at the resurrection
whose wife will she be, since the seven were married to her?"
34 Jesus replied, "The people of this age marry and are given in marriage. 35 But those who are consid-
20:35 [e]Mt 12:32 ered worthy of taking part in that age[e] and in the resurrection from the dead will neither marry nor be
20:36 [f]Jn 1:12; 1Jn 3:1-2 given in marriage, 36 and they can no longer die; for they are like the angels. They are God's children,[f]
since they are children of the resurrection. 37 But in the account of the bush, even Moses showed that the
20:37 [g]Ex 3:6 dead rise, for he calls the Lord 'the God of Abraham, and the God of Isaac, and the God of Jacob.'[a][g] 38 He
is not the God of the dead, but of the living, for to him all are alive."
39 Some of the teachers of the law responded, "Well said, teacher!" 40 And no one dared to ask him any
20:40 [h]Mt 22:46; Mk 12:34 more questions.[h]

Whose Son Is the Christ?

20:41 [i]Mt 1:1 41 Then Jesus said to them, "How is it that they say the Christ[b] is the Son of David?[i] 42 David himself
declares in the Book of Psalms:

> " 'The Lord said to my Lord:
> "Sit at my right hand
> 43 until I make your enemies
> a footstool for your feet." '[c][j]

20:43 [j]Ps 110:1; Mt 22:44

44 David calls him 'Lord.' How then can he be his son?"
45 While all the people were listening, Jesus said to his disciples, 46 "Beware of the teachers of the law.
They like to walk around in flowing robes and love to be greeted in the marketplaces and have the most
20:46 [k]Lk 11:43 important seats in the synagogues and the places of honor at banquets.[k] 47 They devour widows' houses
and for a show make lengthy prayers. Such men will be punished most severely."

The Widow's Offering

21:1 [l]Mt 27:6; Jn 8:20 **21** As he looked up, Jesus saw the rich putting their gifts into the temple treasury.[l] 2 He also saw a
poor widow put in two very small copper coins.[d] 3 "I tell you the truth," he said, "this poor wid-
ow has put in more than all the others. 4 All these people gave their gifts out of their wealth; but she out
21:4 [m]2Co 8:12 of her poverty put in all she had to live on."[m]

Signs of the End of the Age

5 Some of his disciples were remarking about how the temple was adorned with beautiful stones and
with gifts dedicated to God. But Jesus said, 6 "As for what you see here, the time will come when not one
21:6 [n]Lk 19:44 stone will be left on another;[n] every one of them will be thrown down."
7 "Teacher," they asked, "when will these things happen? And what will be the sign that they are about
to take place?"
8 He replied: "Watch out that you are not deceived. For many will come in my name, claiming, 'I am he,'
21:8 [o]Lk 17:23 and, 'The time is near.' Do not follow them.[o] 9 When you hear of wars and revolutions, do not be fright-
ened. These things must happen first, but the end will not come right away."

[a] *37* Exodus 3:6 [b] *41* Or *Messiah* [c] *43* Psalm 110:1 [d] *2* Greek *two lepta*

20:27 For "Sadducees," see the note on Matthew 3:7.
20:28 The Sadducees were referring to the levirate law (see "Levirate Marriage" on p. 64).
20:46–47 See the notes on Mark 12:38–40.
21:1 For "temple treasury," see the note on Mark 12:41.
21:2 For "very small copper coins," see the note on Mark 12:42.
21:5 In describing the beauty of the temple, Josephus noted that "whatever was not overlaid with gold was purest white" (*Wars*, 5.5.6). Herod donated a golden vine for one of its decorations, and its grape clusters were as tall as a man. The full magnificence of the temple as elaborated and adorned by Herod has only recently come to light through archaeological investigations on the temple site (see "Herod's Temple" on p. 1648).
21:6 This was fulfilled in A.D. 70 when the Romans took Jerusalem and burned the temple (see "Josephus and the Fall of Jerusalem" on p. 1606).

10Then he said to them: "Nation will rise against nation, and kingdom against kingdom.[p] 11There will
be great earthquakes, famines and pestilences in various places, and fearful events and great signs from
heaven.[q]
12"But before all this, they will lay hands on you and persecute you. They will deliver you to syna-
gogues and prisons, and you will be brought before kings and governors, and all on account of my name.
13This will result in your being witnesses to them.[r] 14But make up your mind not to worry beforehand
how you will defend yourselves.[s] 15For I will give you[t] words and wisdom that none of your adversaries
will be able to resist or contradict. 16You will be betrayed even by parents, brothers, relatives and friends,[u]
and they will put some of you to death. 17All men will hate you because of me.[v] 18But not a hair of your
head will perish.[w] 19By standing firm you will gain life.[x]
20"When you see Jerusalem being surrounded by armies,[y] you will know that its desolation is near.
21Then let those who are in Judea flee to the mountains, let those in the city get out, and let those in the
country not enter the city.[z] 22For this is the time of punishment[a] in fulfillment[b] of all that has been writ-
ten. 23How dreadful it will be in those days for pregnant women and nursing mothers! There will be great
distress in the land and wrath against this people. 24They will fall by the sword and will be taken as pris-
oners to all the nations. Jerusalem will be trampled[c] on by the Gentiles until the times of the Gentiles are
fulfilled.
25"There will be signs in the sun, moon and stars. On the earth, nations will be in anguish and per-
plexity at the roaring and tossing of the sea.[d] 26Men will faint from terror, apprehensive of what is com-
ing on the world, for the heavenly bodies will be shaken.[e] 27At that time they will see the Son of Man[f] com-
ing in a cloud[g] with power and great glory. 28When these things begin to take place, stand up and lift up
your heads, because your redemption is drawing near."[h]
29He told them this parable: "Look at the fig tree and all the trees. 30When they sprout leaves, you can
see for yourselves and know that summer is near. 31Even so, when you see these things happening, you
know that the kingdom of God[i] is near.
32"I tell you the truth, this generation[a][j] will certainly not pass away until all these things have hap-
pened. 33Heaven and earth will pass away, but my words will never pass away.[k]
34"Be careful, or your hearts will be weighed down with dissipation, drunkenness and the anxieties
of life,[l] and that day will close on you unexpectedly[m] like a trap. 35For it will come upon all those who live
on the face of the whole earth. 36Be always on the watch, and pray[n] that you may be able to escape all that
is about to happen, and that you may be able to stand before the Son of Man."
37Each day Jesus was teaching at the temple,[o] and each evening he went out[p] to spend the night on the
hill called the Mount of Olives,[q] 38and all the people came early in the morning to hear him at the temple.[r]

Judas Agrees to Betray Jesus

22 Now the Feast of Unleavened Bread, called the Passover, was approaching,[s] 2and the chief priests
and the teachers of the law were looking for some way to get rid of Jesus,[t] for they were afraid of
the people. 3Then Satan[u] entered Judas, called Iscariot,[v] one of the Twelve. 4And Judas went to the chief
priests and the officers of the temple guard[w] and discussed with them how he might betray Jesus. 5They
were delighted and agreed to give him money.[x] 6He consented, and watched for an opportunity to hand
Jesus over to them when no crowd was present.

The Last Supper

7Then came the day of Unleavened Bread on which the Passover lamb had to be sacrificed.[y] 8Jesus sent
Peter and John,[z] saying, "Go and make preparations for us to eat the Passover."

[a] 32 Or *race*

21:10 [p]2Ch 15:6; Isa 19:2
21:11 [q]Isa 29:6; Joel 2:30
21:13 [r]Php 1:12
21:14 [s]Lk 12:11
21:15 [t]Lk 12:12
21:16 [u]Lk 12:52, 53
21:17 [v]Jn 15:21
21:18 [w]Mt 10:30
21:19 [x]Mt 10:22
21:20 [y]Lk 19:43
21:21 [z]Lk 17:31
21:22 [a]Isa 63:4; Da 9:24-27; Hos 9:7 [b]Mt 1:22
21:24 [c]Isa 5:5; 63:18; Da 8:13; Rev 11:2
21:25 [d]2Pe 3:10, 12
21:26 [e]Mt 24:29
21:27 [f]Mt 8:20 [g]Rev 1:7
21:28 [h]Lk 18:7
21:31 [i]Mt 3:2
21:32 [j]Lk 11:50; 17:25
21:33 [k]Mt 5:18
21:34 [l]Mk 4:19 [m]Lk 12:40,46; 1Th 5:2-7
21:36 [n]Mt 26:41
21:37 [o]Mt 26:55 [p]Mk 11:19 [q]Mt 21:1
21:38 [r]Jn 8:2
22:1 [s]Jn 11:55
22:2 [t]Mt 12:14
22:3 [u]Mt 4:10; Jn 13:2 [v]Mt 10:4
22:4 [w]ver 52; Ac 4:1; 5:24
22:5 [x]Zec 11:12
22:7 [y]Ex 12:18-20; Dt 16:5-8; Mk 14:12
22:8 [z]Ac 3:1,11; 4:13,19; 8:14

21:11 See the note on famine at Ruth 1:1, as well as "Famine in the Ancient Near East" on page 70.
21:12 Synagogues were used not only for worship and school but also for community administration and for confinement of accused persons while they were awaiting trial. See also the note on Mark 1:21 and "Ancient Synagogues" on page 1783.
21:21 When an army surrounded a city, it was natural to seek protection inside the walls, but Jesus directed his followers to seek the safety of the mountains because the city was doomed to destruction.
21:34 For "that day," see the note on Joel 1:15.
22:1 See the note on Matthew 26:17.
22:2 For "chief priests," see the note on Matthew 2:4 and for "teachers of the law" the notes on Matthew 2:4 and Luke 5:17.
22:4 The "officers of the temple guard" would have been Jews selected mostly from the Levites.
22:7 The Passover lamb was sacrificed on the fourteenth day of the month Nisan between 2:30 and 5:30 P.M. in the court of the priests. This was Thursday of Passion Week.
22:8 See "The Last Supper and the Passover" on page 1611.

9 "Where do you want us to prepare for it?" they asked.
10 He replied, "As you enter the city, a man carrying a jar of water will meet you. Follow him to the
house that he enters, 11 and say to the owner of the house, 'The Teacher asks: Where is the guest room,
where I may eat the Passover with my disciples?' 12 He will show you a large upper room, all furnished.
Make preparations there."
13 They left and found things just as Jesus had told them.[a] So they prepared the Passover.
14 When the hour came, Jesus and his apostles[b] reclined at the table.[c] 15 And he said to them, "I have
eagerly desired to eat this Passover with you before I suffer.[d] 16 For I tell you, I will not eat it again until
it finds fulfillment in the kingdom of God."[e]
17 After taking the cup, he gave thanks and said, "Take this and divide it among you. 18 For I tell you I
will not drink again of the fruit of the vine until the kingdom of God comes."
19 And he took bread, gave thanks and broke it,[f] and gave it to them, saying, "This is my body given
for you; do this in remembrance of me."
20 In the same way, after the supper he took the cup, saying, "This cup is the new covenant[g] in my
blood, which is poured out for you. 21 But the hand of him who is going to betray me is with mine on the
table.[h] 22 The Son of Man[i] will go as it has been decreed,[j] but woe to that man who betrays him." 23 They
began to question among themselves which of them it might be who would do this.
24 Also a dispute arose among them as to which of them was considered to be greatest.[k] 25 Jesus said
to them, "The kings of the Gentiles lord it over them; and those who exercise authority over them call
themselves Benefactors. 26 But you are not to be like that. Instead, the greatest among you should be like
the youngest,[l] and the one who rules like the one who serves.[m] 27 For who is greater, the one who is at the
table or the one who serves? Is it not the one who is at the table? But I am among you as one who serves.[n]
28 You are those who have stood by me in my trials. 29 And I confer on you a kingdom,[o] just as my Father
conferred one on me, 30 so that you may eat and drink at my table in my kingdom[p] and sit on thrones,
judging the twelve tribes of Israel.[q]

22:13 [a]Lk 19:32
22:14 [b]Mk 6:30 [c]Mt 26:20; Mk 14:17,18
22:15 [d]Mt 16:21
22:16 [e]Lk 14:15; Rev 19:9
22:19 [f]Mt 14:19
22:20 [g]Ex 24:8; Isa 42:6; Jer 31:31-34; Zec 9:11; 2Co 3:6; Heb 8:6; 9:15
22:21 [h]Ps 41:9
22:22 [i]Mt 8:20 [j]Ac 2:23; 4:28
22:24 [k]Mk 9:34; Lk 9:46
22:26 [l]1Pe 5:5 [m]Mk 9:35; Lk 9:48
22:27 [n]Mt 20:28; Lk 12:37
22:29 [o]Mt 25:34; 2Ti 2:12
22:30 [p]Lk 14:15 [q]Mt 19:28

22:10 It was extraordinary to see a man carrying a jar of water, since this was normally considered women's work.
22:14 For "reclined at the table," see the note on Mark 14:18.
22:17 The "cup" refers either to the first of the four cups shared during regular observance of the Passover meal or to the third cup. For Hebrew/Jewish feasting, see the note on Matthew 22:2–14.
22:25 See "The Benefactor," below.

The "Benefactor"

LUKE 22 In Luke 22:25 Jesus spoke of how Gentile rulers loved to call themselves "benefactors." The Greek word for "benefactor" is *euergetes*, and classical scholars speak of "euergetism," a social phenomenon of the Greco-Roman world in which rulers and wealthy people would gain a reputation for themselves as philanthropists on behalf of the people through acts of public generosity. This became extremely important during the Roman Republic, when senators struggled for success in the *cursus honorum* ("the path of honors"), the career track that took a citizen through various public offices to the height of Roman power, the rank of consul. In order to win popularity and votes, a senator would sponsor public games and spectacles, build parks and temples and perform other works of public service. Julius Caesar, for example, was lavish in his public beneficence during his rise to power. Roman rulers would also gain the support of the provinces by sponsoring public improvements around the Roman world. The Mediterranean region contains thousands of inscriptions commemorating the public generosity of such individuals.

Jesus' use of the word "benefactor" was obviously intended as irony—and for good reason. Although there are examples of real generosity from such donors, the practice was often inspired by political self-interest or financed by ruthless taxation of the provinces or other corrupt practices.[1] In addition, such benefactors often demanded the submission of those whom they had allegedly helped.

[1]See "Roman Taxation" on page 1855.

31“Simon, Simon, Satan has asked[r] to sift you[a] as wheat.[s] 32But I have prayed for you,[t] Simon, that 22:31 [r]Job 1:6-12 [s]Am 9:9
your faith may not fail. And when you have turned back, strengthen your brothers.”[u] 22:32 [t]Jn 17:9, 15; Ro 8:34 [u]Jn 21:15-17
33But he replied, “Lord, I am ready to go with you to prison and to death.”[v]
34Jesus answered, “I tell you, Peter, before the rooster crows today, you will deny three times that you 22:33 [v]Jn 11:16
know me.”

35Then Jesus asked them, “When I sent you without purse, bag or sandals,[w] did you lack anything?” 22:35 [w]Mt 10:9, 10; Lk 9:3; 10:4
“Nothing,” they answered.

36He said to them, “But now if you have a purse, take it, and also a bag; and if you don't have a sword,
sell your cloak and buy one. 37It is written: 'And he was numbered with the transgressors'[b];[x] and I tell 22:37 [x]Isa 53:12
you that this must be fulfilled in me. Yes, what is written about me is reaching its fulfillment.”

38The disciples said, “See, Lord, here are two swords.”
“That is enough,” he replied.

Jesus Prays on the Mount of Olives

39Jesus went out as usual[y] to the Mount of Olives,[z] and his disciples followed him. 40On reaching the 22:39 [y]Lk 21:37 [z]Mt 21:1
place, he said to them, “Pray that you will not fall into temptation.”[a] 41He withdrew about a stone's throw 22:40 [a]Mt 6:13
beyond them, knelt down[b] and prayed, 42“Father, if you are willing, take this cup[c] from me; yet not my 22:41 [b]Lk 18:11
will, but yours be done.”[d] 43An angel from heaven appeared to him and strengthened him.[e] 44And being 22:42 [c]Mt 20:22 [d]Mt 26:39
in anguish, he prayed more earnestly, and his sweat was like drops of blood falling to the ground.[c] 22:43 [e]Mt 4:11; Mk 1:13

45When he rose from prayer and went back to the disciples, he found them asleep, exhausted from
sorrow. 46“Why are you sleeping?” he asked them. “Get up and pray so that you will not fall into temp-
tation.”[f] 22:46 [f]ver 40

Jesus Arrested

47While he was still speaking a crowd came up, and the man who was called Judas, one of the Twelve,
was leading them. He approached Jesus to kiss him, 48but Jesus asked him, “Judas, are you betraying the
Son of Man with a kiss?”

49When Jesus' followers saw what was going to happen, they said, “Lord, should we strike with our
swords?”[g] 50And one of them struck the servant of the high priest, cutting off his right ear. 22:49 [g]ver 38

51But Jesus answered, “No more of this!” And he touched the man's ear and healed him.

52Then Jesus said to the chief priests, the officers of the temple guard,[h] and the elders, who had come 22:52 [h]ver 4
for him, “Am I leading a rebellion, that you have come with swords and clubs? 53Every day I was with
you in the temple courts,[i] and you did not lay a hand on me. But this is your hour[j]—when darkness 22:53 [i]Mt 26:55 [j]Jn 12:27
reigns.”[k] [k]Mt 8:12; Jn 1:5; 3:20

Peter Disowns Jesus

54Then seizing him, they led him away and took him into the house of the high priest.[l] Peter followed 22:54 [l]Mt 26:57; Mk 14:53
at a distance.[m] 55But when they had kindled a fire in the middle of the courtyard and had sat down to- [m]Mt 26:58; Mk 14:54;
gether, Peter sat down with them. 56A servant girl saw him seated there in the firelight. She looked close- Jn 18:15
ly at him and said, “This man was with him.”

57But he denied it. “Woman, I don't know him,” he said.

58A little later someone else saw him and said, “You also are one of them.”
“Man, I am not!” Peter replied.

59About an hour later another asserted, “Certainly this fellow was with him, for he is a Galilean.”[n] 22:59 [n]Lk 23:6

60Peter replied, “Man, I don't know what you're talking about!” Just as he was speaking, the rooster
crowed. 61The Lord[o] turned and looked straight at Peter. Then Peter remembered the word the Lord had 22:61 [o]Lk 7:13
spoken to him: “Before the rooster crows today, you will disown me three times.”[p] 62And he went outside [p]ver 34
and wept bitterly.

[a] *31* The Greek is plural. [b] *37* Isaiah 53:12 [c] *44* Some early manuscripts do not have verses 43 and 44.

22:34 See the note on Matthew 26:34.

22:47 The “crowd,” sent by the chief priests, elders and teachers of the law, carried swords and clubs. Included was a detachment of soldiers with officials of the Jews.

For “kiss,” see “The Jewish Custom of Kissing” on page 1682.

22:54 The high priest was Caiaphas (see the note on Mt 26:3). The gathering may have taken place at his house to ensure secrecy.

22:59 Peter was suspected on the basis of his Galilean accent (see the notes on Mt 26:73; Mk 14:70).

The Guards Mock Jesus

63The men who were guarding Jesus began mocking and beating him. 64They blindfolded him and de-
22:65 [q]Mt 16:21 manded, "Prophesy! Who hit you?" 65And they said many other insulting things to him.[q]

Jesus Before Pilate and Herod

22:66 [r]Mt 5:22 66At daybreak the council[r] of the elders of the people, both the chief priests and teachers of the law,
[s]Mt 27:1; Mk 15:1 met together,[s] and Jesus was led before them. 67"If you are the Christ,[a]" they said, "tell us."
22:68 [t]Lk 20:3-8 Jesus answered, "If I tell you, you will not believe me, 68and if I asked you, you would not answer.[t]
22:69 [u]Mk 16:19 69But from now on, the Son of Man will be seated at the right hand of the mighty God."[u]
22:70 [v]Mt 4:3 70They all asked, "Are you then the Son of God?"[v]
[w]Mt 27:11; Lk 23:3 He replied, "You are right in saying I am."[w]
71Then they said, "Why do we need any more testimony? We have heard it from his own lips."
23:1 [x]Mt 27:2; Mk 15:1; Jn 18:28 **23** Then the whole assembly rose and led him off to Pilate.[x] 2And they began to accuse him, saying,
23:2 [y]ver 14 [z]Lk 20:22 "We have found this man subverting our nation.[y] He opposes payment of taxes to Caesar[z] and
[a]Jn 19:12 claims to be Christ,[b] a king."[a]
3So Pilate asked Jesus, "Are you the king of the Jews?"
"Yes, it is as you say," Jesus replied.
4Then Pilate announced to the chief priests and the crowd, "I find no basis for a charge against this
23:4 [b]ver 14,22, 41; Mt 27:23; man."[b]
Jn 18:38; 1Ti 6:13; 5But they insisted, "He stirs up the people all over Judea[c] by his teaching. He started in Galilee[c] and
2Co 5:21 has come all the way here."
23:5 [c]Mk 1:14 **23:6** [d]Lk 22:59 6On hearing this, Pilate asked if the man was a Galilean.[d] 7When he learned that Jesus was under Her-
23:7 [e]Mt 14:1; Lk 3:1 od's jurisdiction, he sent him to Herod,[e] who was also in Jerusalem at that time.
8When Herod saw Jesus, he was greatly pleased, because for a long time he had been wanting to see
23:8 [f]Lk 9:9 him.[f] From what he had heard about him, he hoped to see him perform some miracle. 9He plied him
23:9 [g]Mk 14:61 with many questions, but Jesus gave him no answer.[g] 10The chief priests and the teachers of the law were
standing there, vehemently accusing him. 11Then Herod and his soldiers ridiculed and mocked him.
23:11 [h]Mk 15:17-19; Dressing him in an elegant robe,[h] they sent him back to Pilate. 12That day Herod and Pilate became
Jn 19:2,3 **23:12** [i]Ac 4:27 friends[i]—before this they had been enemies.
13Pilate called together the chief priests, the rulers and the people, 14and said to them, "You brought
me this man as one who was inciting the people to rebellion. I have examined him in your presence and
23:14 [j]ver 4 have found no basis for your charges against him.[j] 15Neither has Herod, for he sent him back to us; as you
23:16 [k]ver 22; Mt 27:26; can see, he has done nothing to deserve death. 16Therefore, I will punish him[k] and then release him.[d]"
Jn 19:1; Ac 16:37; 18With one voice they cried out, "Away with this man! Release Barabbas to us!"[l] 19(Barabbas had been
2Co 11:23,24 **23:18** [l]Ac 3:13, 14 thrown into prison for an insurrection in the city, and for murder.)
20Wanting to release Jesus, Pilate appealed to them again. 21But they kept shouting, "Crucify him!
Crucify him!"
22For the third time he spoke to them: "Why? What crime has this man committed? I have found in
23:22 [m]ver 16 him no grounds for the death penalty. Therefore I will have him punished and then release him."[m]

[a] 67 Or *Messiah* [b] 2 Or *Messiah*; also in verses 35 and 39 [c] 5 Or *over the land of the Jews* [d] 16 Some manuscripts *him." 17Now he was obliged to release one man to them at the Feast.*

22:64 Jesus' guards—probably the temple police who had arrested him—were mocking this unusual and vulnerable prisoner. The game appears to have been an early version of blindman's bluff, in which the guards blindfolded him and taunted him to "prophesy." One interpretation of Isaiah 11:2–4 was that the Messiah could judge by smell, without the need for sight.

22:66—23:25 Luke recounted four trials preceding Jesus' crucifixion. The first was conducted before the Sanhedrin, composed of leading Jews. Jesus then appeared twice before Pilate and once before a curious Herod.

22:66 Only after daylight could a legal trial take place for the whole council (the Sanhedrin) to pass the death sentence. (For information on the Sanhedrin, see the note on Mk 14:55.)

23:1 The "whole assembly" refers to the body of the Sanhedrin (see the note on Mk 14:55), who had met at the earliest hint of dawn.

For information on Pilate, see the note on Luke 3:1. Pilate's headquarters was in Caesarea, but he was in Jerusalem during Passover to prevent trouble from the large number of Jews assembled for the occasion (see the note on Mark 14:2).

23:5 "Judea" may here refer to the whole of the land of the Jews (including Galilee) or to the southern section only, where the region of Judea proper was governed by Pilate.

23:7 Herod Antipas was the tetrarch of Galilee and Perea (see the note on Mt 14:1). His headquarters was in Tiberias on the Sea of Galilee (see "Tiberias" on p. 1732); but, like Pilate, he had come to Jerusalem on account of the crowds at Passover (see the note on Lk 23:1).

23:16 Although Pilate found Jesus innocent as charged, he was willing to have him illegally beaten in order to satisfy the chief priests and the people and to warn against any possible trouble in the future. Scourging, though not intended to kill, was in reality sometimes fatal (see the note on Mt 27:26).

23:18 For "Barabbas," see the note on Matthew 27:16.

23:19 For "insurrection," see the note on Mark 15:7; see also "The Intertestamental Period" on page 1555. For "prison," see "Imprisonment in the Roman World: In Prison Versus House Arrest" on page 1826.

23 But with loud shouts they insistently demanded that he be crucified, and their shouts prevailed.
24 So Pilate decided to grant their demand. 25 He released the man who had been thrown into prison for
insurrection and murder, the one they asked for, and surrendered Jesus to their will.

The Crucifixion

26 As they led him away, they seized Simon from Cyrene,[n] who was on his way in from the country, and 23:26 [n]Mt 27:32
put the cross on him and made him carry it behind Jesus.[o] 27 A large number of people followed him, in- [o]Mk 15:21; Jn 19:17
cluding women who mourned and wailed[p] for him. 28 Jesus turned and said to them, "Daughters of Je- 23:27 [p]Lk 8:52
rusalem, do not weep for me; weep for yourselves and for your children.[q] 29 For the time will come when 23:28 [q]Lk 19:41-44; 21:23,24
you will say, 'Blessed are the barren women, the wombs that never bore and the breasts that never
nursed!'[r] 30 Then 23:29 [r]Mt 24:19

" 'they will say to the mountains, "Fall on us!"
and to the hills, "Cover us!" '[a][s] 23:30 [s]Isa 2:19; Hos 10:8; Rev 6:16

31 For if men do these things when the tree is green, what will happen when it is dry?"[t] 23:31 [t]Eze 20:47

[a] 30 Hosea 10:8

23:26 Cyrene was a leading city of Libya, west of Egypt (see the note on Ac 6:9). Simon was probably a Jew who was in Jerusalem to celebrate the Passover. Men condemned to death were usually forced to carry a beam of their own cross, often weighing 30–40 pounds (14–18 kg), to the place of crucifixion.

ANCIENT TEXTS AND ARTIFACTS

Pontius Pilate

LUKE 23 Pilate was the Roman governor of Judea from A.D. 26 to 36.[1] Ruling from Caesarea on the Mediterranean coast, he was primarily responsible for maintaining the peace and collecting taxes.[2] A number of artifacts remain from Pilate's governance of Judea:

✣ In 1961 an inscription bearing Pilate's name was found during excavation of the theater at Caesarea.[3] The surviving portion reads, "Tiberium [of the Caesareans?], Pontius Pilate, Prefect of Judea, [. . . has given . . .]." The inscription was most likely part of a building called a Tiberium, possibly a temple, dedicated to the emperor Tiberius. While the Tiberium fell into disuse, the stone bearing the inscription was used, ironically, to repair a stairway during a fourth-century remodeling of a theater built by Herod the Great.[4] It was in the stairwell that the Italian excavators discovered the inscription.

The name "Pilatus" (Pilate) in a replica of the Pilate inscription found at Caesarea

Photograph courtesy of © Dr. Gary Pratico

✣ Pilate built an aqueduct to bring water into Jerusalem from south of the city. Remnants of this structure can still be seen in Bethlehem.[5]

✣ A number of coins struck during Pilate's tenure have survived. As with coins of other Roman governors, they do not bear Pilate's name but instead carry the names Tiberius Caesar and Empress Julia. Pilate's coins incorporated symbols that would have offended the Jews. One was the *littus*, or augur's wand (augury or divination was forbidden by Mosaic Law; e.g., Dt 18:9–14). The other was the *simpulum*, a small ladle with a high handle used to make libations during sacrifices, a common symbol of the Roman priesthood.[6]

The trial of Jesus was probably carried out at Herod's palace, the Praetorium (Mt 27:27; Mk 15:16; Jn 18:28,33; 19:9), portions of which have been excavated. The only mention of Pilate in the New Testament apart from the trial of Jesus is in Luke 13:1. There Jesus was told about "the Galileans whose blood Pilate had mixed with their sacrifices," evidently a reference to an incident in which a number of Galileans were killed while offering sacrifices at the temple. This accords well with what we read about Pilate in the works of the ancient Jewish writers Josephus and Philo, who portrayed him as cruel and corrupt. Pilate was recalled to Rome after having massacred a group of Samaritans.

[1]See "The Roman Governor" on page 1824. [2]See "Roman Taxation" on page 1855. [3]See "Caesarea Maritima" on page 1786. [4]See "Herod the Great" on page 1627. [5]See "The Birthplace of Jesus" on page 1668. [6]See "Coins and Numismatics" on page 1699.

32 Two other men, both criminals, were also led out with him to be executed.[u] 33 When they came to
the place called the Skull, there they crucified him, along with the criminals—one on his right, the oth-
er on his left. 34 Jesus said, "Father,[v] forgive them, for they do not know what they are doing."[a][w] And they
divided up his clothes by casting lots.[x]

35 The people stood watching, and the rulers even sneered at him.[y] They said, "He saved others; let
him save himself if he is the Christ of God, the Chosen One."[z]

36 The soldiers also came up and mocked him.[a] They offered him wine vinegar[b] 37 and said, "If you
are the king of the Jews,[c] save yourself."

38 There was a written notice above him, which read: THIS IS THE KING OF THE JEWS.[d]

39 One of the criminals who hung there hurled insults at him: "Aren't you the Christ? Save yourself
and us!"[e]

40 But the other criminal rebuked him. "Don't you fear God," he said, "since you are under the same
sentence? 41 We are punished justly, for we are getting what our deeds deserve. But this man has done
nothing wrong."[f]

42 Then he said, "Jesus, remember me when you come into your kingdom.[b]"[g]

43 Jesus answered him, "I tell you the truth, today you will be with me in paradise."[h]

Jesus' Death

44 It was now about the sixth hour, and darkness came over the whole land until the ninth hour,[i]
45 for the sun stopped shining. And the curtain of the temple[j] was torn in two.[k] 46 Jesus called out with
a loud voice,[l] "Father, into your hands I commit my spirit."[m] When he had said this, he breathed his
last.[n]

47 The centurion, seeing what had happened, praised God[o] and said, "Surely this was a righteous man."
48 When all the people who had gathered to witness this sight saw what took place, they beat their breasts[p]
and went away. 49 But all those who knew him, including the women who had followed him from Galilee,[q]
stood at a distance,[r] watching these things.

Jesus' Burial

50 Now there was a man named Joseph, a member of the Council, a good and upright man, 51 who had
not consented to their decision and action. He came from the Judean town of Arimathea and he was
waiting for the kingdom of God.[s] 52 Going to Pilate, he asked for Jesus' body. 53 Then he took it down,
wrapped it in linen cloth and placed it in a tomb cut in the rock, one in which no one had yet been laid.
54 It was Preparation Day,[t] and the Sabbath was about to begin.

55 The women who had come with Jesus from Galilee[u] followed Joseph and saw the tomb and how his
body was laid in it. 56 Then they went home and prepared spices and perfumes.[v] But they rested on the
Sabbath in obedience to the commandment.[w]

23:32 [u]Isa 53:12; Mt 27:38; Mk 15:27; Jn 19:18
23:34 [v]Mt 11:25 [w]Mt 5:44 [x]Ps 22:18
23:35 [y]Ps 22:17 [z]Isa 42:1
23:36 [a]Ps 22:7 [b]Ps 69:21; Mt 27:48
23:37 [c]Lk 4:3,9
23:38 [d]Mt 2:2
23:39 [e]ver 35,37
23:41 [f]ver 4
23:42 [g]Mt 16:27
23:43 [h]2Co 12:3, 4; Rev 2:7
23:44 [i]Am 8:9
23:45 [j]Ex 26:31-33; Heb 9:3,8 [k]Heb 10:19,20
23:46 [l]Mt 27:50 [m]Ps 31:5; 1Pe 2:23 [n]Jn 19:30
23:47 [o]Mt 9:8
23:48 [p]Lk 18:13
23:49 [q]Lk 8:2 [r]Ps 38:11
23:51 [s]Lk 2:25, 38
23:54 [t]Mt 27:62
23:55 [u]ver 49
23:56 [v]Mk 16:1; Lk 24:1 [w]Ex 12:16; 20:10

[a] *34* Some early manuscripts do not have this sentence. [b] *42* Some manuscripts *come with your kingly power*

23:33 See "The Crucifixion" on page 1757.
23:34 It was the accepted right of the executioner's squad to claim the minor possessions of the victim. Jesus' clothing probably consisted of an under and an outer garment, a belt, sandals and possibly a head covering.
23:36 For "wine vinegar," see the note on Matthew 27:48.
23:38 For "written notice," see the note on Mark 15:26.
23:39 For "criminals," see the note on Matthew 27:38 ("robbers").
23:41 The criminals crucified with Jesus must have been robbers or brigands, judging by the severity of the punishment and the fact that one of them acknowledged that the death penalty imposed on them was just.
23:44 The "sixth hour" was 12:00 noon and the "ninth hour" 3:00 P.M., by the Jewish method of designating time. Jesus had been put on the cross at the third hour (9:00 A.M., see Mk 15:25). The "sixth hour" of John (Jn 19:14) may be Roman time (6:00 A.M.), when Pilate gave his decision (but see the note on Jn 19:14).
23:45 For "curtain," see the note on Mark 15:38.
23:48 Beating one's breast was a sign of anguish, grief or contrition (see "Sackcloth and Ashes: Rituals of Lamentation" on p. 820).
23:51 For "Arimathea," see the note on Matthew 27:57.
23:52 See the note on Mark 15:45.
23:53 For "linen cloth," see "The Shroud of Turin Controversy" on page 1658. In New Testament times linen was extensively used by Jews for burial shrouds, as at the burial of Jesus (see also Mt 27:59; Mk 15:46; Jn 19:40; 20:5ff). Egyptian mummies throughout Biblical times were also wrapped in linen sheets of vast proportions.

Rock-hewn tombs were usually made to accommodate several bodies (see "Tombs in Ancient Israel" on p. 376). This one, though finished, had not yet been used (see "The Location of Jesus' Tomb" on p. 1615 and "Jewish Burial Practices" on p. 1688).
23:54 "Preparation Day" refers to Friday, the day before the Sabbath, when preparation was made for keeping the Sabbath. It could be used for Passover preparation, but since in this instance it is followed by the Sabbath, it indicates Friday.
23:56 Yards of cloth and large quantities of spices were used in preparing a body for burial (see "Jewish Burial Practices" on p. 1688). Seventy-five pounds (34 kg) of myrrh and aloes were already used on that first evening (see Jn 19:39–40 and its note; see also "Perfumes and Anointing Oils" on p. 1746). More was purchased for the return of the women after the Sabbath.

The Resurrection

24 On the first day of the week, very early in the morning, the women took the spices they had pre-
pared[x] and went to the tomb. 2They found the stone rolled away from the tomb, 3but when they 24:1 [x]Lk 23:56
entered, they did not find the body of the Lord Jesus.[y] 4While they were wondering about this, sudden- 24:3 [y]ver 23,24
ly two men in clothes that gleamed like lightning[z] stood beside them. 5In their fright the women bowed 24:4 [z]Jn 20:12
down with their faces to the ground, but the men said to them, "Why do you look for the living among
the dead? 6He is not here; he has risen! Remember how he told you, while he was still with you in Gali-
lee:[a] 7'The Son of Man[b] must be delivered into the hands of sinful men, be crucified and on the third 24:6 [a]Mt 17:22,
day be raised again.' "[c] 8Then they remembered his words.[d] 23; Mk 9:30-31; Lk 9:22; 24:44
9When they came back from the tomb, they told all these things to the Eleven and to all the others. 24:7 [b]Mt 8:20 [c]Mt 16:21
10It was Mary Magdalene, Joanna, Mary the mother of James, and the others with them[e] who told this 24:8 [d]Jn 2:22 24:10 [e]Lk 8:1-3
to the apostles.[f] 11But they did not believe[g] the women, because their words seemed to them like non- [f]Mk 6:30
sense. 12Peter, however, got up and ran to the tomb. Bending over, he saw the strips of linen lying by them- 24:11 [g]Mk 16:11
selves,[h] and he went away,[i] wondering to himself what had happened. 24:12 [h]Jn 20:3-7 [i]Jn 20:10

On the Road to Emmaus

13Now that same day two of them were going to a village called Emmaus, about seven miles[a] from Je-
rusalem.[j] 14They were talking with each other about everything that had happened. 15As they talked and 24:13 [j]Mk 16:12
discussed these things with each other, Jesus himself came up and walked along with them;[k] 16but they 24:15 [k]ver 36
were kept from recognizing him.[l] 24:16 [l]Jn 20:14; 21:4

[a] *13* Greek *sixty stadia* (about 11 kilometers)

24:1 By Jewish time, Sunday began at sundown on Saturday. The women bought spices after sunset on Saturday and were ready to set out early the next morning. When they started out, it was dark (see Jn 20:1), and by the time they arrived at the tomb it was still early dawn (see Mt 28:1).

For New Testament burial practices, see the note on Matthew 26:12. See also "Jewish Burial Practices" on page 1688 and "Perfumes and Anointing Oils" on page 1746.

24:2 A tomb's entrance was ordinarily kept closed to prevent vandals and animals from disturbing the bodies. This stone, however, had been sealed by Roman authority for a different reason (see the note on Mt 27:66). Such stone doors weighed from one to three tons (.9 to 2.7 metric tons); hence the miracle of the stone being rolled away from Jesus' tomb (cf. Jn 20:1).

24:13 Emmaus is thought to have been about 6–7 miles (10–11 km) west of Jerusalem (see "Emmaus" on p. 1716). For commentary on Jesus' resurrection appearances, see "The Resurrection of Jesus" on page 1617.

ARCHAEOLOGICAL SITES

EMMAUS

LUKE 24 The problem of uncertainty over the location of Emmaus is compounded by a textual difficulty in Luke 24:13 that reads "60 stadia" in some Greek manuscripts but "160 stadia" in others (a stadium was 625 Roman ft, or about 190 m). Thus, 60 stadia was about 7 miles (12 km), while 160 stadia was roughly 18.4 miles (29.7 km). The reading of "60 stadia" in verse 13 is almost certainly correct and is the rendering adopted by all modern versions. Patristic readers (church fathers), however, preferred "160 stadia" and located Emmaus at Emmaus-Nicopolis (modern Khirbet Imwas), about 20 miles (32 km) west of Jerusalem. But Luke 24 indicates that the disciples walked with Jesus from Jerusalem to Emmaus, had a midday meal and then returned to Jerusalem that same afternoon. If Emmaus were Emmaus-Nicopolis, this would have been a 40-mile (64.5 km) trek within a single day!

Adopting the figure of 60 stadia, a good candidate for the location of Emmaus is el-Qubeibeh, located about 7 miles (11.3 km) northwest of Jerusalem. The crusaders favored this site, and the remains of a first-century village have been excavated there. There is no scholarly consensus, however, and the actual location of Emmaus remains open to question. A proposed site is indicated on "Map 9."

17He asked them, “What are you discussing together as you walk along?”
24:18 [m]Jn 19:25 They stood still, their faces downcast. 18One of them, named Cleopas,[m] asked him, “Are you only a
visitor to Jerusalem and do not know the things that have happened there in these days?”
19“What things?” he asked.
24:19 [n]Mk 1:24 “About Jesus of Nazareth,”[n] they replied. “He was a prophet,[o] powerful in word and deed before God
[o]Mt 21:11 **24:20** [p]Lk 23:13 and all the people. 20The chief priests and our rulers[p] handed him over to be sentenced to death, and
24:21 [q]Lk 1:68; they crucified him; 21but we had hoped that he was the one who was going to redeem Israel.[q] And what
2:38; 21:28 [r]Mt 16:21 is more, it is the third day[r] since all this took place. 22In addition, some of our women amazed us.[s] They
24:22 [s]ver 1-10 went to the tomb early this morning 23but didn’t find his body. They came and told us that they had seen
a vision of angels, who said he was alive. 24Then some of our companions went to the tomb and found it
24:24 [t]ver 12 just as the women had said, but him they did not see.”[t]
25He said to them, “How foolish you are, and how slow of heart to believe all that the prophets have
24:26 [u]Heb 2:10; spoken! 26Did not the Christ[a] have to suffer these things and then enter his glory?”[u] 27And beginning
1Pe 1:11 **24:27** [v]Ge 3:15; with Moses[v] and all the Prophets,[w] he explained to them what was said in all the Scriptures concerning
Nu 21:9; Dt 18:15 himself.[x]
[w]Isa 7:14; 9:6; 40:10,11; 53; 28As they approached the village to which they were going, Jesus acted as if he were going farther.
Eze 34:23; Da 9:24; 29But they urged him strongly, “Stay with us, for it is nearly evening; the day is almost over.” So he went
Mic 7:20; Mal 3:1 [x]Jn 1:45 in to stay with them.
24:30 [y]Mt 14:19 30When he was at the table with them, he took bread, gave thanks, broke it[y] and began to give it to
24:31 [z]ver 16 them. 31Then their eyes were opened and they recognized him,[z] and he disappeared from their sight.
24:32 [a]Ps 39:3 32They asked each other, “Were not our hearts burning within us[a] while he talked with us on the road and
[b]ver 27,45 opened the Scriptures[b] to us?”
33They got up and returned at once to Jerusalem. There they found the Eleven and those with them,
24:34 [c]1Co 15:5 assembled together 34and saying, “It is true! The Lord has risen and has appeared to Simon.”[c] 35Then the
24:35 [d]ver 30,31 two told what had happened on the way, and how Jesus was recognized by them when he broke the bread.[d]

Jesus Appears to the Disciples

36While they were still talking about this, Jesus himself stood among them and said to them, “Peace
24:36 [e]Jn 20:19, be with you.”[e]
21,26; 14:27 **24:37** [f]Mk 6:49 37They were startled and frightened, thinking they saw a ghost.[f] 38He said to them, “Why are you trou-
bled, and why do doubts rise in your minds? 39Look at my hands and my feet. It is I myself! Touch me
24:39 [g]Jn 20:27; 1Jn 1:1 and see;[g] a ghost does not have flesh and bones, as you see I have.”
40When he had said this, he showed them his hands and feet. 41And while they still did not believe it
because of joy and amazement, he asked them, “Do you have anything here to eat?” 42They gave him a
24:43 [h]Ac 10:41 piece of broiled fish, 43and he took it and ate it in their presence.[h]
24:44 [i]Lk 9:45; 44He said to them, “This is what I told you while I was still with you:[i] Everything must be fulfilled[j]
18:34 [j]Mt 16:21; Lk 9:22,44; that is written about me in the Law of Moses,[k] the Prophets and the Psalms.”[l]
18:31-33; 22:37 [k]ver 27 [l]Ps 2; 16; 45Then he opened their minds so they could understand the Scriptures. 46He told them, “This is what
22; 69; 72; 110; 118 is written: The Christ will suffer and rise from the dead on the third day, 47and repentance and forgive-
24:47 [m]Ac 5:31; ness of sins will be preached in his name[m] to all nations,[n] beginning at Jerusalem. 48You are witnesses[o]
10:43; 13:38 [n]Mt 28:19 of these things. 49I am going to send you what my Father has promised;[p] but stay in the city until you have
24:48 [o]Ac 1:8; 2:32; 5:32; 13:31; been clothed with power from on high.”
1Pe 5:1 **24:49** [p]Jn 14:16; Ac 1:4

The Ascension

24:50 [q]Mt 21:17 50When he had led them out to the vicinity of Bethany,[q] he lifted up his hands and blessed them.
24:51 [r]2Ki 2:11 51While he was blessing them, he left them and was taken up into heaven.[r] 52Then they worshiped him
24:53 [s]Ac 2:46 and returned to Jerusalem with great joy. 53And they stayed continually at the temple,[s] praising God.

[a] *26* Or *Messiah*; also in verse 46

24:21 The “third day” may be a reference to (1) the Jewish belief that after the third day the soul left the body or (2) Jesus’ prophecy that he would be resurrected on the third day (9:22).
24:27 “Moses and all the Prophets” was a way of designating the entire Old Testament.
24:36 For a discussion of salutations in the Bible, see the note on Ruth 2:4.
24:44 The “Law of Moses, the Prophets and the Psalms” are the three parts of the Hebrew Old Testament (see “The Old Testament of the Early Church” on p. 1967).
24:50 For “Bethany,” see the note on Matthew 21:17.
24:53 During the period of time immediately following Jesus’ ascension the believers met continually at the temple (Ac 2:46; 3:1; 5:21,42), where many rooms were available for meetings (see the note on Lk 2:37).

INTRODUCTION TO *John*

AUTHOR, PLACE AND DATE OF WRITING

The author of this book claimed to have been a disciple of Jesus and a trustworthy witness of the things he described (21:24). Most readers take for granted his identification with the "disciple whom Jesus loved" (21:20), an epithet applied to John, son of Zebedee, since the earliest traditions of the church.

John's Gospel is usually dated very late—toward the end of the first century—but there are reasons for believing that it was actually written much earlier. The John Rylands Papyrus (p^{52}) suggests that John was already in wide circulation during the second century A.D. (see "John Rylands papyrus [p^{52}]" on p. 1755). Some have even proposed a date prior to the destruction of the temple in A.D. 70 (see further discussion in "Cultural Facts and Highlights," below). It has been suggested that John may have written from Ephesus.

AUDIENCE

The Gospel of John was written to non-Jewish believers and to questioning unbelievers struggling with popular Greek philosophies claiming that Jesus was divine but not truly human (see "The Gnostics and Their Scriptures" on p. 2029). John expressed his primary purpose for writing in 20:31: "that you may believe that Jesus is the Christ, the Son of God."

CULTURAL FACTS AND HIGHLIGHTS

Those who advocate an early date for John's Gospel see no implication anywhere in the book that Jerusalem and the temple had already been destroyed. In fact, John's presentation of Jesus' cleansing of the temple, and his claim that Jesus' body *is* the true temple (ch. 2), would have been surprising had that edifice already been destroyed. On the contrary, nothing would have served as better vindication of Jesus' condemnation of the corruption at the temple and of his claim to have supplanted it in his own person. More than that, at 2:21, immediately after having reported that Jesus spoke of the destruction of "this temple," John, had he been writing after A.D. 70, would have ignored a perfect opportunity to point to the desolation of the Jerusalem temple when he instead clarified that Jesus was speaking of his own body.

TIMELINE

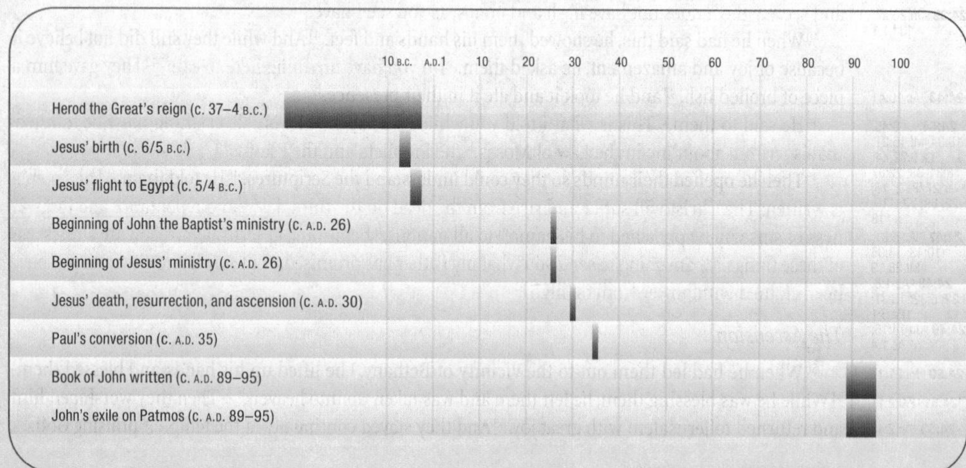

AS YOU READ

Look for "signs" in John's Gospel that point to Jesus as the Messiah, the Son of God. Note the various audiences Jesus addressed in this Gospel. To whom was he speaking at any given point? How did he interact with them? Did his style change based upon his audience?

DID YOU KNOW?

- Jewish religious teachers rarely spoke with women in public (4:27).
- Many Jews believed that the soul remained near the body for three days after death in the hope of returning to it (11:17).
- Jewish custom provided for three days of very heavy mourning, then four of heavy mourning, followed by lighter mourning for the remainder of thirty days (11:19).
- "God-fearers" were attracted to Judaism by its monotheism and morality but repelled by its nationalism and requirements such as circumcision. They worshiped in the synagogues but did not become proselytes/converts (12:20).

THEMES

John's Gospel includes the following themes:

1. *Jesus is God.* John identified Jesus as the Word who was with God in the beginning (1:1–2), the One who "came from the Father" (1:14) to make him known (1:18). Jesus is "equal with God" (5:18) and identified himself as God (8:58; 9:35–37; 10:36; 14:9).
2. *Jesus is the Messiah.* The miracles recorded in John function primarily as "signs" pointing to Jesus' Messianic identity—signs of God's presence in Jesus' works and words, each calling for a commitment: Who indeed is this Jesus?
3. *Choose belief or unbelief.* Jesus' miracles fostered belief in some (2:11; 9:1–39; 11:1–44) but only hardened the opposition of others (11:46–57). We commonly assert that "seeing is believing," but in John believing is seeing.

OUTLINE

I. Prologue (1:1–18)
II. Beginnings of Jesus' Ministry (1:19–51)
III. Jesus' Ministry (2–11)
IV. The Passion Week (12–19)
   A. The Anointing of Jesus' Feet by Mary (12:1–11)
   B. The Triumphal Entry (12:12–19)
   C. The Greeks Seek Jesus (12:20–36)
   D. Rejection by the Jews (12:37–50)
   E. Farewell Discourses (13–17)
   F. Jesus' Betrayal, Arrest and Trial (18:1—19:15)
   G. The Crucifixion and Burial (19:16–42)
V. The Resurrection (20:1–29)
VI. Statement of Purpose (20:30–31)
VII. Epilogue (21)

Ancient Voices

The *Logos* (speech, reason) is designed to distinguish the beneficial from the harmful, and thus also the right and the wrong. For this, in distinction from the other animals, is the distinctive property of man: that he alone has the ability to perceive good and bad and right and wrong and the other qualities. And it is communication of these things that makes a household and a city-state.

—Aristotle on the *Logos*

From Aristotle, *Politics*, 1253a, trans. by Duane Garrett

See "The *Logos* in Greek and Jewish Literature" article.

The Word Became Flesh

1 In the beginning was the Word,[a] and the Word was with God,[b]
and the Word was God.[c] 2He was with God in the beginning.[d]
3Through him all things were made; without him nothing was
made that has been made.[e] 4In him was life,[f] and that life was the
light[g] of men. 5The light shines in the darkness, but the darkness
has not understood[a] it.[h]
6There came a man who was sent from God; his name was John.[i]
7He came as a witness to testify[j] concerning that light, so that
through him all men might believe.[k] 8He himself was not the light;
he came only as a witness to the light. 9The true light[l] that gives light
to every man[m] was coming into the world.[b]
10He was in the world, and though the world was made through
him,[n] the world did not recognize him. 11He came to that which was
his own, but his own did not receive him. 12Yet to all who received
him, to those who believed[o] in his name,[p] he gave the right to be-
come children of God[q]— 13children born not of natural descent,[c] nor of human decision or a husband's
will, but born of God.[r]
14The Word became flesh[s] and made his dwelling among us. We have seen his glory, the glory of the
One and Only,[d] who came from the Father, full of grace and truth.[t]
15John testifies[u] concerning him. He cries out, saying, "This was he of whom I said, 'He who comes af-
ter me has surpassed me because he was before me.' "[v] 16From the fullness[w] of his grace we have all re-
ceived one blessing after another. 17For the law was given through Moses;[x] grace and truth came through
Jesus Christ.[y] 18No one has ever seen God,[z] but God the One and Only,[d, e][a] who is at the Father's side, has
made him known.

John the Baptist Denies Being the Christ

19Now this was John's testimony when the Jews[b] of Jerusalem sent priests and Levites to ask him who
he was. 20He did not fail to confess, but confessed freely, "I am not the Christ.[f]"[c]
21They asked him, "Then who are you? Are you Elijah?"[d]
He said, "I am not."

1:1 [a]Rev 19:13 [b]Jn 17:5; 1Jn 1:2 [c]Php 2:6
1:2 [d]Ge 1:1
1:3 [e]1Co 8:6; Col 1:16; Heb 1:2
1:4 [f]Jn 5:26; 11:25; 14:6 [g]Jn 8:12
1:5 [h]Jn 3:19
1:6 [i]Mt 3:1
1:7 [j]ver 15,19,32 [k]ver 12
1:9 [l]1Jn 2:8 [m]Isa 49:6
1:10 [n]Heb 1:2
1:12 [o]ver 7 [p]1Jn 3:23 [q]Gal 3:26
1:13 [r]Jn 3:6; Jas 1:18; 1Pe 1:23; 1Jn 3:9
1:14 [s]Gal 4:4; Php 2:7,8; 1Ti 3:16; Heb 2:14 [t]Jn 14:6
1:15 [u]ver 7 [v]ver 30; Mt 3:11
1:16 [w]Eph 1:23; Col 1:19
1:17 [x]Jn 7:19 [y]ver 14
1:18 [z]Ex 33:20; Jn 6:46; Col 1:15; 1Ti 6:16 [a]Jn 3:16, 18; 1Jn 4:9
1:19 [b]Jn 2:18; 5:10,16; 6:41,52
1:20 [c]Jn 3:28; Lk 3:15,16
1:21 [d]Mt 11:14

[a] 5 Or *darkness, and the darkness has not overcome* [b] 9 Or *This was the true light that gives light to every man who comes into the world* [c] 13 Greek *of bloods* [d] 14, 18 Or *the Only Begotten* [e] 18 Some manuscripts *but the only* (or *only begotten*) *Son* [f] 20 Or *Messiah.* "The Christ" (Greek) and "the Messiah" (Hebrew) both mean "the Anointed One"; also in verse 25.

1:1 Tradition holds the apostle John to have been the author of this Gospel, as well as that the date and place of authorship were sometime toward the close of the first century A.D. in Asia Minor (see the introduction). This tradition can be traced back from the ancient church historian Eusebius at the beginning of the fourth century to Theophilus (see Ac 1:1). The major witnesses, besides Eusebius, are Origen, Clement of Alexandria, Tertullian, Irenaeus, the writer of the Muratorian Canon and Theophilus himself. Irenaeus, one of the earliest of these witnesses, was a disciple of Polycarp, who, in turn, had been a disciple of the apostle John. The inference seems to be legitimate that this tradition can be traced back to the disciple whom Jesus loved. Moreover, because of his wide travels, the witness of Irenaeus may be called a representative testimony, the first conviction of the early church that this Greek church father knew so well. In fact, the early writers (mentioned above) show that in the last quarter of the second century the fourth Gospel was known and read throughout Christendom—in Africa, Asia Minor, Italy, Gaul, Syria—and that it was ascribed to the well-known apostle John.

Among even earlier witnesses, Justin Martyr (*Apology*, 1.61) quoted from John 3:3–5. He used a number of expressions from this Gospel (cf. his *Dialogue With Trypho*, ch. 105). His doctrine of the Logos (see "The *Logos* in Greek and Jewish Literature" on p. 1721 and "Greek Philosophical Schools" on p. 1937) presupposes acquaintance with the fourth Gospel, which his pupil Tatian included in his *Diatessaron* or *Harmony*. Ignatius, who went to his martyrdom about the year A.D. 110, alluded to John's Gospel again and again (*Epistles of Ignatius, Short Recension*). Very significant also is the testimonial of the elders of Ephesus (21:24). The traditional belief regarding the authorship and date of the fourth Gospel has received strong confirmation in the discovery of a very early Gospel of John fragment of a papyrus codex, which seems to have originated in the Christian community of Middle Egypt—see "John Rylands Papyrus (p^{52})" on page 1755. On the basis of solid evidence it has been established that this papyrus scrap belonged to a codex that circulated in that general region in the first part of the second century.

1:15 In ancient times the older person was given respect and regarded as greater than the younger. People would ordinarily have ranked Jesus lower in terms of respect than John, who was older. John the Baptist explained that this age relationship was only apparent, since Jesus, as the Word, had existed before he was born on Earth.

1:19 Here "Jews" refers to the delegation commissioned by the Sanhedrin (see the note on Mk 14:55) to investigate the activities of an unauthorized teacher.

"Levites" refers to the descendants of the tribe of Levi, who were assigned to specific duties in connection with the tabernacle (Nu 3:17–37) and later the temple. They also had teaching responsibilities (2Ch 35:3; Ne 8:7–9), and it was probably in this role that they were sent with the priests to John the Baptist.

1:21 The Jews remembered that Elijah had not died (2Ki 2:11) and believed that he would come back to Earth to announce the end time.

1:21 [e]Dt 18:15 "Are you the Prophet?"[e]
He answered, "No."
22Finally they said, "Who are you? Give us an answer to take back to those who sent us. What do you
say about yourself?"
1:23 [f]Mt 3:1 [g]Isa 40:3 23John replied in the words of Isaiah the prophet, "I am the voice of one calling in the desert,[f] 'Make
straight the way for the Lord.' "[a g]
24Now some Pharisees who had been sent 25questioned him, "Why then do you baptize if you are not
the Christ, nor Elijah, nor the Prophet?"
26"I baptize with[b] water," John replied, "but among you stands one you do not know. 27He is the one
1:27 [h]ver 15,30 who comes after me,[h] the thongs of whose sandals I am not worthy to untie."

[a] 23 Isaiah 40:3 [b] 26 Or *in*; also in verses 31 and 33

1:23 The Baptist applied the prophecy of Isaiah 40:3 to his own ministry of calling people to repent in preparation for the coming of the Messiah. The men of Qumran (see "Qumran and the New Testament" on p. 1679) applied the same words to themselves, but they prepared for the Lord's coming by isolating themselves from the world in an attempt to secure their own salvation. John concentrated on helping people come to the Messiah.
1:24 The Pharisees (see the notes on Mt 3:7; Lk 5:17) were the conservative religious party.
1:25 "The Christ" means "the Anointed One." In Old Testament times anointing signified being set apart for service, particularly as king (cf. 1Sa 16:1,13) or priest (Ex 28:41; 29:7; 30:30; 40:13,15). But people were looking not just for an anointed one but for *the* Anointed One, the Messiah.
1:26 See "Baptism in the Ancient World" on page 1562.
1:27 Disciples would perform all sorts of service for their rabbis (teachers), but loosing sandal thongs was expressly excluded, as this was considered a menial task, fit only for a slave.

The Logos in Greek and Jewish Literature

JOHN 1 John's theology of the Word (Greek *logos*) is rooted in the Old Testament but also addresses pressing philosophical concerns in the Greek world. The phrase "In the beginning was the Word" (Jn 1:1) obviously echoes Genesis 1, which records that God created simply by speaking (e.g., "Let there be light" in v. 3). That is, God created by means of his *word*. There can be little doubt that this is the primary background to the use of *logos* in John 1: God's word brought the universe into orderly existence. The Jewish **Targums**[1] echo this understanding of the divine Word. They frequently employ the term *memra* (derived from the Aramaic word for "speak") to describe God's creative activity, and this may have contributed to the language we find in John 1.

The word *logos*, however, also had a rich tradition in Greek thought. While *logos* can be a very general term, meaning simply "word, account, explanation or thing," the philosopher Heraclitus (c. 535–475 B.C.) used it in the sense of an *ordering principle for the universe*. Thus, the *logos* is the divine logic that gives order to the universe. Heraclitus appears to have associated it with fire and to have linked it with reason within human beings. This sense of *logos* was most fully developed by the Stoics, who taught that the universe was permeated with the *logos* that gave order and rationality to all things. In late Stoicism this *logos* could be equated with *pneuma*, "spirit," a kind of compound of fire and air, permeated by reason. There was a *logos* within each individual person (i.e., human reason) and a *logos* that pervaded the universe (i.e., the rationality that governs the world). By extension, the *logos* within human beings enabled them to move in harmony with the *logos* of the universe. Those who were governed by passions and emotions, however, were thought to have turned away from the universal *logos* and to have become bestial in their behavior. This concept provided the basis for the Stoic ethical system.[2]

What did John mean by describing Jesus as the *logos*? As noted above, the link to Genesis 1 is central; the *logos* is the one by whom "all things were made" (v. 3)—that is, Christ. But there may be a secondary application of the term that would speak to the educated Greek reader. Christ in his person is the *Logos*. The truth, the guiding principle of the universe and of the soul of every person, is not a mere abstraction of theoretical "rationality," but a person. By this person, the *Logos*, the individual may attain harmony with God and his creation.

[1]See Glossary on page 2080 for definitions of bolded words. [2]See "Greek Philosophical Schools" on page 1937.

28 This all happened at Bethany on the other side of the Jordan,[i] where John was baptizing.

1:28 [i]Jn 3:26; 10:40

Jesus the Lamb of God

29 The next day John saw Jesus coming toward him and said, "Look, the Lamb of God,[j] who takes away
the sin of the world! 30 This is the one I meant when I said, 'A man who comes after me has surpassed me
because he was before me.'[k] 31 I myself did not know him, but the reason I came baptizing with water
was that he might be revealed to Israel."

32 Then John gave this testimony: "I saw the Spirit come down from heaven as a dove and remain on
him.[l] 33 I would not have known him, except that the one who sent me to baptize with water[m] told me,
'The man on whom you see the Spirit come down and remain is he who will baptize with the Holy Spir-
it.'[n] 34 I have seen and I testify that this is the Son of God."[o]

1:29 [j]ver 36; Isa 53:7; 1Pe 1:19; Rev 5:6
1:30 [k]ver 15,27
1:32 [l]Mt 3:16; Mk 1:10
1:33 [m]Mk 1:4 [n]Mt 3:11; Mk 1:8
1:34 [o]ver 49; Mt 4:3

Jesus' First Disciples

35 The next day John[p] was there again with two of his disciples. 36 When he saw Jesus passing by, he
said, "Look, the Lamb of God!"[q]

37 When the two disciples heard him say this, they followed Jesus. 38 Turning around, Jesus saw them
following and asked, "What do you want?"

They said, "Rabbi"[r] (which means Teacher), "where are you staying?"

39 "Come," he replied, "and you will see."

So they went and saw where he was staying, and spent that day with him. It was about the tenth hour.

40 Andrew, Simon Peter's brother, was one of the two who heard what John had said and who had fol-
lowed Jesus. 41 The first thing Andrew did was to find his brother Simon and tell him, "We have found the
Messiah" (that is, the Christ).[s] 42 And he brought him to Jesus.

Jesus looked at him and said, "You are Simon son of John. You will be called[t] Cephas" (which, when
translated, is Peter[a]).[u]

1:35 [p]Mt 3:1
1:36 [q]ver 29
1:38 [r]ver 49; Mt 23:7
1:41 [s]Jn 4:25
1:42 [t]Ge 17:5,15 [u]Mt 16:18

Jesus Calls Philip and Nathanael

43 The next day Jesus decided to leave for Galilee. Finding Philip,[v] he said to him, "Follow me."[w]

44 Philip, like Andrew and Peter, was from the town of Bethsaida.[x] 45 Philip found Nathanael[y] and told
him, "We have found the one Moses wrote about in the Law,[z] and about whom the prophets also wrote[a]—
Jesus of Nazareth,[b] the son of Joseph."[c]

46 "Nazareth! Can anything good come from there?"[d] Nathanael asked.

"Come and see," said Philip.

47 When Jesus saw Nathanael approaching, he said of him, "Here is a true Israelite,[e] in whom there is
nothing false."[f]

48 "How do you know me?" Nathanael asked.

Jesus answered, "I saw you while you were still under the fig tree before Philip called you."

49 Then Nathanael declared, "Rabbi,[g] you are the Son of God;[h] you are the King of Israel."[i]

50 Jesus said, "You believe[b] because I told you I saw you under the fig tree. You shall see greater things
than that." 51 He then added, "I tell you[c] the truth, you[c] shall see heaven open,[j] and the angels of God as-
cending and descending[k] on the Son of Man."[l]

1:43 [v]Mt 10:3; Jn 6:5-7; 12:21, 22; 14:8,9 [w]Mt 4:19
1:44 [x]Mt 11:21; Jn 12:21
1:45 [y]Jn 21:2 [z]Lk 24:27 [a]Lk 24:27 [b]Mt 2:23; Mk 1:24 [c]Lk 3:23
1:46 [d]Jn 7:41,42, 52
1:47 [e]Ro 9:4,6 [f]Ps 32:2
1:49 [g]ver 38; Mt 23:7 [h]ver 34; Mt 4:3 [i]Mt 2:2; 27:42; Jn 12:13
1:51 [j]Mt 3:16 [k]Ge 28:12 [l]Mt 8:20

[a] 42 Both *Cephas* (Aramaic) and *Peter* (Greek) mean *rock.* [b] 50 Or *Do you believe . . . ?* [c] 51 The Greek is plural.

1:28 The Bethany mentioned elsewhere in the Gospels was only about 2 miles (3.2 km) from Jerusalem (see the note on Mt 21:17). The site of this other Bethany is uncertain, except that it was located on the eastern side of the Jordan (see "Bethany on the Other Side of the Jordan" on p. 1740).

1:35–37 John the Baptist encouraged two of his own disciples to follow Jesus. One was Andrew (v. 40), and the other is not named. In Matthew, Mark and Luke, the earliest converts to Jesus are identified as Andrew, Peter, James and John (see Mk 1:16–20). The unnamed disciple may be a concealed reference to the apostle John, the author of this Gospel and likely the mystery person behind the title "the disciple whom Jesus loved" (Jn 13:23; 21:7,20; see also 19:26; 20:2).

1:39 The tenth hour was about 4:00 P.M.

1:40 Andrew, one of the 12 apostles (Mt 10:2), was from Bethsaida but later lived with Peter at Capernaum (see Mk 1:29 and its note; see also the note on Mt 4:13), where they fished for a living (see Mt 4:18).

1:44 For "Bethsaida," see the note on Mark 8:22.

1:45 Joseph was Jesus' legal, though not his natural, father.

1:46 For "Nazareth," see the notes on Matthew 2:23 and 4:12–16.

1:48 The shade of a fig tree was a favorite place for study and prayer in hot weather.

Jesus Changes Water to Wine

2:1 ᵐJn 4:46; 21:2 ⁿMt 12:46

2 On the third day a wedding took place at Cana in Galilee.ᵐ Jesus' motherⁿ was there, 2and Jesus and
his disciples had also been invited to the wedding. 3When the wine was gone, Jesus' mother said to
him, "They have no more wine."

2:1 Cana is mentioned only in John's Gospel. It lay west of the Sea of Galilee, but the exact location is unknown. Most scholars believe that Khirbet Qana, situated about 9 miles (14.5 km) north of Nazareth and just north of the Beit Netofa Valley, is a likely candidate (see "Cana of Galilee" on p. 1723).

See "Weddings in Ancient Israel" on page 1039.

2:3 Running out of wine was more than a minor social embarrassment, since the family had an obligation to provide a feast of the socially required standard. There was no great variety in beverages, and people normally drank water or wine (see "Wine and Alcoholic Beverages in the Ancient World" on p. 2015).

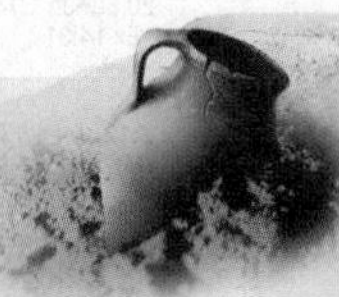

ARCHAEOLOGICAL SITES

CANA OF GALILEE

JOHN 2 John is the only New Testament writer who mentioned Cana of Galilee, and he only hinted at its location. The fact that Jesus' family had friends or relatives and were able to attend a wedding there suggests that Cana was not too far from Nazareth.[1] In addition, John 4:46–54 implies that the trip from Cana to Capernaum required somewhat more than a half-day's journey.[2]

Christian pilgrims have long associated Cana with the village of Kefr Kenna, located about 4 miles (6.5 km) northeast of Nazareth (see "Map 9"). This is probably incorrect, notwithstanding the presence there of churches claiming to preserve the tradition of the miracle at the wedding. Today most scholars agree that Khirbet Qana, located about 9 miles (14.5 km) north of Nazareth and just north of the Beit Netofa Valley, is the more likely candidate (although both Kefr Kenna and Khirbet Qana meet the requirements of John's Gospel).

Excavation at Khirbet Qana began in 1998. Remains have been found from the **Neolithic period** through to the modern period, but most physical evidence (pottery, coins and housing remains) dates from the **Roman** through the **Byzantine** periods. Remains of what could have been a first-century synagogue (although this has not yet been firmly established) have also been found, along with a ***miqveh*** (a pool for Jewish ritual cleansing). Cisterns held water for the village since there appears to have been no aqueduct.[3] John 2:6 mentions that water was stored in large stone jars. Archaeology is not likely to provide decisive proof that Khirbet Qana was Cana of Galilee, but even the prospect of uncovering artifacts there that existed when Jesus worked his first miracle is profoundly exciting.

[1]See "Nazareth" on page 1623. [2]See "Capernaum" on page 1643. [3]See "Wells, Cisterns and Aqueducts in the Ancient World" on page 1259.

Stone water vessels

Preserving Bible Times; © Dr. James C. Martin; permission of The Israel Museum

4“Dear woman,[o] why do you involve me?”[p] Jesus replied. “My time[q] has not yet come.”

5His mother said to the servants, “Do whatever he tells you.”[r]

6Nearby stood six stone water jars, the kind used by the Jews for ceremonial washing,[s] each holding from twenty to thirty gallons.[a]

7Jesus said to the servants, “Fill the jars with water”; so they filled them to the brim.

8Then he told them, “Now draw some out and take it to the master of the banquet.”

They did so, 9and the master of the banquet tasted the water that had been turned into wine.[t] He did not realize where it had come from, though the servants who had drawn the water knew. Then he called the bridegroom aside 10and said, “Everyone brings out the choice wine first and then the cheaper wine after the guests have had too much to drink; but you have saved the best till now.”

11This, the first of his miraculous signs,[u] Jesus performed at Cana in Galilee. He thus revealed his glory,[v] and his disciples put their faith in him.[w]

Jesus Clears the Temple

12After this he went down to Capernaum[x] with his mother and brothers[y] and his disciples. There they stayed for a few days.

13When it was almost time for the Jewish Passover,[z] Jesus went up to Jerusalem.[a] 14In the temple courts he found men selling cattle, sheep and doves, and others sitting at tables exchanging money. 15So he made a whip out of cords, and drove all from the temple area, both sheep and cattle; he scattered the coins of the money changers and overturned their tables. 16To those who sold doves he said, “Get these out of here! How dare you turn my Father’s house[b] into a market!”

17His disciples remembered that it is written: “Zeal for your house will consume me.”[b][c]

18Then the Jews demanded of him, “What miraculous sign can you show us to prove your authority to do all this?”[d]

19Jesus answered them, “Destroy this temple, and I will raise it again in three days.”[e]

20The Jews replied, “It has taken forty-six years to build this temple, and you are going to raise it in three days?” 21But the temple he had spoken of was his body.[f] 22After he was raised from the dead, his disciples recalled what he had said.[g] Then they believed the Scripture and the words that Jesus had spoken.

23Now while he was in Jerusalem at the Passover Feast,[h] many people saw the miraculous signs he was doing and believed in his name.[c] 24But Jesus would not entrust himself to them, for he knew all men. 25He did not need man’s testimony about man, for he knew what was in a man.[i]

Jesus Teaches Nicodemus

3 Now there was a man of the Pharisees named Nicodemus,[j] a member of the Jewish ruling council.[k] 2He came to Jesus at night and said, “Rabbi, we know you are a teacher who has come from God. For no one could perform the miraculous signs[l] you are doing if God were not with him.”[m]

3In reply Jesus declared, “I tell you the truth, no one can see the kingdom of God unless he is born again.[d]”[n]

4“How can a man be born when he is old?” Nicodemus asked. “Surely he cannot enter a second time into his mother’s womb to be born!”

5Jesus answered, “I tell you the truth, no one can enter the kingdom of God unless he is born of water and the Spirit.[o] 6Flesh gives birth to flesh, but the Spirit[e] gives birth to spirit.[p] 7You should not be sur-

2:4 [o]Jn 19:26 [p]Mt 8:29 [q]Mt 26:18; Jn 7:6
2:5 [r]Ge 41:55
2:6 [s]Mk 7:3,4; Jn 3:25
2:9 [t]Jn 4:46
2:11 [u]ver 23; Jn 3:2; 4:48; 6:2, 14,26,30; 12:37; 20:30 [v]Jn 1:14 [w]Ex 14:31
2:12 [x]Mt 4:13 [y]Mt 12:46
2:13 [z]Jn 11:55 [a]Dt 16:1-6; Lk 2:41
2:16 [b]Lk 2:49
2:17 [c]Ps 69:9
2:18 [d]Mt 12:38
2:19 [e]Mt 26:61; 27:40; Mk 14:58; 15:29
2:21 [f]1Co 6:19
2:22 [g]Lk 24:5-8; Jn 12:16; 14:26
2:23 [h]ver 13
2:25 [i]Mt 9:4; Jn 6:61,64; 13:11
3:1 [j]Jn 7:50; 19:39 [k]Lk 23:13
3:2 [l]Jn 9:16,33 [m]Ac 2:22; 10:38
3:3 [n]Jn 1:13; 1Pe 1:23
3:5 [o]Tit 3:5
3:6 [p]Jn 1:13; 1Co 15:50

[a] 6 Greek *two to three metretes* (probably about 75 to 115 liters) [b] 17 Psalm 69:9 [c] 23 Or *and believed in him* [d] 3 Or *born from above*; also in verse 7 [e] 6 Or *but spirit*

2:6 Jews became ceremonially defiled during the normal circumstances of daily life, and they were cleansed by pouring water over their hands. For a lengthy feast with many guests, a large amount of water was required for this purpose.
2:8–9 The “master of the banquet” was apparently one of the guests charged with serving as master of ceremonies (see “Weddings in Ancient Israel” on p. 1039).
2:10 Ordinarily, after the guests’ taste buds were dulled, the “cheaper wine” was served.
2:12 Situated on the shore of the lake, Capernaum was at a lower level than Cana; thus, one “went down” to Capernaum. For information on Capernaum, see the note on Matthew 4:13.
For “brothers,” see the note on Luke 8:19.
2:13 See the note on Luke 2:41.
2:14 See the note on Luke 19:45.
2:20 Herod’s new temple was not finally completed until A.D. 63/64. The meaning here is that work on the edifice had been going on for 46 years. Since construction had begun in about 19 or 20 B.C. (see “Herod’s Temple” on p. 1648), the year of the event recorded here is about A.D. 27.
3:1 For “Pharisees,” see the notes on Matthew 3:7 and Luke 5:17.

prised at my saying, 'You[a] must be born again.' 8 The wind blows wherever it pleases. You hear its sound,
but you cannot tell where it comes from or where it is going. So it is with everyone born of the Spirit."
9 "How can this be?"[q] Nicodemus asked.
10 "You are Israel's teacher,"[r] said Jesus, "and do you not understand these things? 11 I tell you the truth,
we speak of what we know,[s] and we testify to what we have seen, but still you people do not accept our
testimony.[t] 12 I have spoken to you of earthly things and you do not believe; how then will you believe if
I speak of heavenly things? 13 No one has ever gone into heaven[u] except the one who came from heav-
en[v]—the Son of Man.[b] 14 Just as Moses lifted up the snake in the desert,[w] so the Son of Man must be
lifted up,[x] 15 that everyone who believes[y] in him may have eternal life.[c]
16 "For God so loved[z] the world that he gave his one and only Son,[d] that whoever believes in him shall
not perish but have eternal life.[a] 17 For God did not send his Son into the world[b] to condemn the world,
but to save the world through him.[c] 18 Whoever believes in him is not condemned,[d] but whoever does not
believe stands condemned already because he has not believed in the name of God's one and only Son.[e][e]
19 This is the verdict: Light[f] has come into the world, but men loved darkness instead of light because
their deeds were evil. 20 Everyone who does evil hates the light, and will not come into the light for fear
that his deeds will be exposed.[g] 21 But whoever lives by the truth comes into the light, so that it may be
seen plainly that what he has done has been done through God."[f]

John the Baptist's Testimony About Jesus

22 After this, Jesus and his disciples went out into the Judean countryside, where he spent some time
with them, and baptized.[h] 23 Now John also was baptizing at Aenon near Salim, because there was plen-
ty of water, and people were constantly coming to be baptized. 24 (This was before John was put in pris-
on.)[i] 25 An argument developed between some of John's disciples and a certain Jew[g] over the matter of cer-
emonial washing.[j] 26 They came to John and said to him, "Rabbi,[k] that man who was with you on the
other side of the Jordan—the one you testified[l] about—well, he is baptizing, and everyone is going to
him."
27 To this John replied, "A man can receive only what is given him from heaven. 28 You yourselves can
testify that I said, 'I am not the Christ[h] but am sent ahead of him.'[m] 29 The bride belongs to the bride-
groom.[n] The friend who attends the bridegroom waits and listens for him, and is full of joy when he
hears the bridegroom's voice. That joy is mine, and it is now complete.[o] 30 He must become greater; I must
become less.
31 "The one who comes from above[p] is above all; the one who is from the earth belongs to the earth, and
speaks as one from the earth.[q] The one who comes from heaven is above all. 32 He testifies to what he has
seen and heard,[r] but no one accepts his testimony.[s] 33 The man who has accepted it has certified that God
is truthful. 34 For the one whom God has sent[t] speaks the words of God, for God[i] gives the Spirit[u] without
limit. 35 The Father loves the Son and has placed everything in his hands.[v] 36 Whoever believes in the Son
has eternal life,[w] but whoever rejects the Son will not see life, for God's wrath remains on him."[j]

Jesus Talks With a Samaritan Woman

4 The Pharisees heard that Jesus was gaining and baptizing more disciples than John,[x] 2 although in
fact it was not Jesus who baptized, but his disciples. 3 When the Lord learned of this, he left Judea[y]
and went back once more to Galilee.
4 Now he had to go through Samaria. 5 So he came to a town in Samaria called Sychar, near the plot of

3:9 [q]Jn 6:52,60
3:10 [r]Lk 2:46
3:11 [s]Jn 1:18; 7:16,17 [t]ver 32
3:13 [u]Pr 30:4; Ac 2:34; Eph 4:8-10 [v]Jn 6:38,42
3:14 [w]Nu 21:8,9 [x]Jn 8:28; 12:32
3:15 [y]ver 16,36
3:16 [z]Ro 5:8; Eph 2:4; 1Jn 4:9, 10 [a]ver 36; Jn 6:29,40; 11:25,26
3:17 [b]Jn 6:29,57; 10:36; 11:42; 17:8,21; 20:21 [c]Jn 12:47; 1Jn 4:14
3:18 [d]Jn 5:24 [e]1Jn 4:9
3:19 [f]Jn 1:4; 8:12
3:20 [g]Eph 5:11, 13
3:22 [h]Jn 4:2
3:24 [i]Mt 4:12; 14:3
3:25 [j]Jn 2:6
3:26 [k]Mt 23:7 [l]Jn 1:7
3:28 [m]Jn 1:20,23
3:29 [n]Mt 9:15 [o]Jn 16:24; 17:13; Php 2:2; 1Jn 1:4; 2Jn 12
3:31 [p]ver 13 [q]Jn 8:23; 1Jn 4:5
3:32 [r]Jn 8:26; 15:15 [s]ver 11
3:34 [t]ver 17 [u]Mt 12:18; Lk 4:18; Ac 10:38
3:35 [v]Mt 28:18; Jn 5:20,22; 17:2
3:36 [w]ver 15; Jn 5:24; 6:47
4:1 [x]Jn 3:22,26
4:3 [y]Jn 3:22

[a] *7* The Greek is plural. [b] *13* Some manuscripts *Man, who is in heaven* [c] *15* Or *believes may have eternal life in him*
[d] *16* Or *his only begotten Son* [e] *18* Or *God's only begotten Son* [f] *21* Some interpreters end the quotation after verse 15.
[g] *25* Some manuscripts *and certain Jews* [h] *28* Or *Messiah* [i] *34* Greek *he* [j] *36* Some interpreters end the quotation after verse 30.

3:22 This is the only record that Jesus had a baptizing ministry, although 4:2 makes clear that his disciples, not Jesus himself, baptized people (see "Baptism in the Ancient World" on p. 1562).
3:23 The location of Aenon is uncertain; it may have been about 8 miles (nearly 13 km) south of Scythopolis (Beth Shan), west of the Jordan.
3:25 The Dead Sea (Qumran) Scrolls show that some Jews were deeply interested in the right way to achieve ceremonial purification. (See "Biblical Interpretation at Qumran and Among the Early Rabbis" on p. 1603 and "Qumran and the New Testament" on p. 1679.)
3:29 See "Weddings in Ancient Israel" on page 1039.
4:1 For "Pharisees," see the notes on Matthew 3:7 and Luke 5:17.
4:4 "Samaria" here refers to the whole region, not simply the city. Jews often avoided Samaria by crossing the Jordan and traveling on its eastern side (see the notes on Mt 10:5; Lk 9:52). Perhaps the necessity of going through Samaria had to do with Jesus' mission rather than with geography.
4:5 Sychar was a small village near Shechem (see "Shechem" on p. 340).

ground Jacob had given to his son Joseph.[z] 6 Jacob's well was there, and Jesus, tired as he was from the
journey, sat down by the well. It was about the sixth hour.
7 When a Samaritan woman came to draw water, Jesus said to her, "Will you give me a drink?" 8 (His
disciples had gone into the town[a] to buy food.)
9 The Samaritan woman said to him, "You are a Jew and I am a Samaritan[b] woman. How can you ask
me for a drink?" (For Jews do not associate with Samaritans.[a])
10 Jesus answered her, "If you knew the gift of God and who it is that asks you for a drink, you would
have asked him and he would have given you living water."[c]
11 "Sir," the woman said, "you have nothing to draw with and the well is deep. Where can you get this
living water? 12 Are you greater than our father Jacob, who gave us the well[d] and drank from it himself,
as did also his sons and his flocks and herds?"
13 Jesus answered, "Everyone who drinks this water will be thirsty again, 14 but whoever drinks the wa-
ter I give him will never thirst.[e] Indeed, the water I give him will become in him a spring of water[f] well-
ing up to eternal life."[g]
15 The woman said to him, "Sir, give me this water so that I won't get thirsty[h] and have to keep com-
ing here to draw water."
16 He told her, "Go, call your husband and come back."
17 "I have no husband," she replied.
Jesus said to her, "You are right when you say you have no husband. 18 The fact is, you have had five hus-
bands, and the man you now have is not your husband. What you have just said is quite true."
19 "Sir," the woman said, "I can see that you are a prophet.[i] 20 Our fathers worshiped on this mountain,[j]
but you Jews claim that the place where we must worship is in Jerusalem."[k]
21 Jesus declared, "Believe me, woman, a time is coming[l] when you will worship the Father neither on
this mountain nor in Jerusalem.[m] 22 You Samaritans worship what you do not know;[n] we worship what
we do know, for salvation is from the Jews.[o] 23 Yet a time is coming and has now come[p] when the true
worshipers will worship the Father in spirit[q] and truth, for they are the kind of worshipers the Father
seeks. 24 God is spirit,[r] and his worshipers must worship in spirit and in truth."
25 The woman said, "I know that Messiah" (called Christ)[s] "is coming. When he comes, he will explain
everything to us."
26 Then Jesus declared, "I who speak to you am he."[t]

4:5 [z]Ge 33:19; 48:22; Jos 24:32
4:8 [a]ver 5,39
4:9 [b]Mt 10:5; Lk 9:52,53
4:10 [c]Isa 44:3; Jer 2:13; Zec 14:8; Jn 7:37,38; Rev 21:6; 22:1,17
4:12 [d]ver 6
4:14 [e]Jn 6:35 [f]Jn 7:38 [g]Mt 25:46
4:15 [h]Jn 6:34
4:19 [i]Mt 21:11
4:20 [j]Dt 11:29; Jos 8:33 [k]Lk 9:53
4:21 [l]Jn 5:28; 16:2 [m]Mal 1:11; 1Ti 2:8
4:22 [n]2Ki 17:28-41 [o]Isa 2:3; Ro 3:1,2; 9:4,5
4:23 [p]Jn 5:25; 16:32 [q]Php 3:3
4:24 [r]Php 3:3
4:25 [s]Mt 1:16
4:26 [t]Jn 8:24; 9:35-37

The Disciples Rejoin Jesus

27 Just then his disciples returned[u] and were surprised to find him talking with a woman. But no one
asked, "What do you want?" or "Why are you talking with her?"

4:27 [u]ver 8

[a] 9 Or *do not use dishes Samaritans have used*

4:6 At its most basic, a well is a pit or hole dug in the earth down to the water table (the level at which the ground is permanently saturated with water). For both safety and permanence, wells in Bible times were generally surrounded by walls of stone. In the case of some famous wells, like that of Jacob of Sychar (ch. 4), the walls were beautifully constructed with dressed stone. A well is to be distinguished from a cistern (which is merely for storing water; Jer 2:13), a spring (which is found at the surface of the ground) or a fountain (from which water actively flows; Jos 15:9). For additional commentary on wells, see the note on Joel 1:20. See also "Wells, Cisterns and Aqueducts in the Ancient World" on page 1259.

Modern Bir Ya'kub is doubtless the well referred to in this verse as "Jacob's well." For more than 23 centuries Samaritans and Jews have believed this to be true. The ground mentioned by John had been purchased by Jacob (Ge 33:19), and the area was later wrested by force from the Amorites (Ge 48:22). The well is near the base of Mount Gerizim, whose bluffs may have been intended in Jesus' phrase "this mountain" (Jn 4:21). A narrow opening 4 feet (1.3 m) long was dug through limestone. The depth of the well has not been determined. One explorer in A.D. 670 claimed that it was 240 feet (75 m), while another reported in 1697 that it was 105 feet (33 m). In 1861 a Major Anderson declared it to be only 75 feet (23 m) deep. When the well was cleaned out in 1935, it was found to be 138 feet (42 m) deep. For centuries tourists cast pebbles into the well until Greek Catholics purchased the site and put it under guard.

The sixth hour was 12:00 noon.

4:7 People normally drew water at the end of the day rather than in the heat of midday (see Ge 24:11). But the practice is attested by Josephus, who stated that the young women whom Moses helped (Ex 2:15–17) came to draw water at noon.

4:9 Jews would become ceremonially unclean if they used a drinking vessel handled by a Samaritan, since they held that all Samaritans were "unclean" (see "The Samaritans" on p. 1737).

4:11 See the note on verse 6.

4:18 The Jews held that a woman might be divorced twice or at the most three times. If the Samaritans had the same standard, this woman's life had been exceedingly immoral. Apparently she had not married her present partner.

4:20 The proper place of worship had long been a source of debate between Jews and Samaritans. Samaritans held that Mount Gerizim was especially sacred. They had built a temple there in about 400 B.C., which the Jews destroyed in 128. (See "The Samaritan Temple on Mount Gerizim" on p. 1727 and "The Samaritans" on p. 1737.)

4:22 The Samaritan Bible contained only the Pentateuch. Samaritans worshiped the true God, but their failure to accept much of his revelation meant that they knew little about him.

4:25 The Samaritans expected a Messiah, but their rejection of all the inspired writings after the Pentateuch meant that they knew little about him. They thought of him mainly as a teacher.

4:26 This is the only occasion before his trial in which Jesus specifically said that he was the Messiah (but see Mk 9:41). The term "Messiah" did not have the political overtones in Samaria that it had in Judea, which may be part of the reason Jesus used the designation here.

4:27 Jewish religious teachers rarely spoke with women in public.

4:29 ᵛver 17,18 ʷMt 12:23; Jn 7:26,31
4:31 ˣMt 23:7
4:32 ʸJob 23:12; Mt 4:4; Jn 6:27
4:34 ᶻMt 26:39; Jn 6:38; 17:4; 19:30 ᵃJn 19:30

28 Then, leaving her water jar, the woman went back to the town and said to the people, 29 "Come, see
a man who told me everything I ever did.[v] Could this be the Christ[a]?"[w] 30 They came out of the town and
made their way toward him.
31 Meanwhile his disciples urged him, "Rabbi,[x] eat something."
32 But he said to them, "I have food to eat[y] that you know nothing about."
33 Then his disciples said to each other, "Could someone have brought him food?"
34 "My food," said Jesus, "is to do the will[z] of him who sent me and to finish his work.[a] 35 Do you not
say, 'Four months more and then the harvest'? I tell you, open your eyes and look at the fields! They are

[a] 29 Or *Messiah*

ARCHAEOLOGICAL SITES

THE SAMARITAN TEMPLE ON MOUNT GERIZIM

JOHN 4 The rift between the Samaritans and the Judeans dates from an early period.[1] According to 2 Kings 17 the Samaritans were the descendants of Mesopotamian peoples who were forcibly settled in the lands of northern Israel by the king of **Assyria** in the wake of the exile of 722 B.C.[2] They combined the worship of **Yahweh** with idolatrous practices. The construction of a Samaritan temple to Yahweh on Mount Gerizim and the establishment of a rival, hereditary priesthood dates from the fourth century B.C. Josephus reported that the high priest Manasseh was threatened with expulsion from Jerusalem on account of his foreign wife, Nikaso, the daughter of the Samaritan Sanballat. Sanballat in turn promised to preserve the priesthood for Manasseh, to appoint him as governor over his lands and to build a temple similar to that in Jerusalem on Mount Gerizim, provided Manasseh would remain with his daughter (Josephus, *Antiquities*, 11.8.2).

The Samaritans, however, viewed themselves as the faithful descendants of Israel and saw the Judeans as apostate. They accepted only the **Pentateuch** as Scripture; in their version Mount Gerizim is described as the chosen place for the sanctuary (Dt 11:29–30; cf. Jn 4:20).

The history of the temple site at Mount Gerizim is full of turmoil:

- From the time of the building of the Samaritan temple (often dated to 388 B.C.), **Samaria** functioned as a temple-state under the leadership of its own priestly aristocracy.
- During a period of Greek domination, the Samaritan temple was renamed as the temple of Zeus, the Friend of Strangers (2Mc 6:2).[3]
- After the **Maccabean** success the Samaritan temple was attacked and destroyed by the **Hasmonean** priest-king John Hyrcanus in 128 B.C. (*Antiquities*, 13). This act sealed a permanent rift between the two communities and to a large extent underlies the hostility between Jews and Samaritans reflected in the New Testament (v. 9).
- Emperor Hadrian built another temple to Zeus there (fifth century A.D.).
- The Christian emperor Justinian constructed a church on this spot (sixth century), which was later destroyed by Arabs (seventh century).

Archaeologists have uncovered remains from Justinian's church, Hadrian's temple and the temple John Hyrcanus destroyed. The words of the woman at the well reflect Samaritan devotion to this site.

The Samaritans, like the Jews, expected a Messiah to come. They revered Moses as the true prophet and, based upon Deuteronomy 18, cherished hopes that a prophet like Moses would one day restore both themselves and their sanctuary. They described this Messianic figure as the Restorer. A Samaritan document called the *Memar Marqah*, though written in the fourth century A.D., contains earlier Samaritan traditions. It states, "Let the Restorer come safely and sacrifice a true offering. The Restorer will come in peace and reveal the truth and will purify the world and establish the heads of the people as they once were" (*Memar Marqah*, 2:33,70,180). The Samaritan woman reflected this expectation when she declared, "I know that Messiah . . . is coming. When he comes, he will explain everything to us" (v. 25). Jesus' reply was, as was frequently the case, understated: "I who speak to you am he" (v. 26).

[1] See "The Samaritans" on page 1737. [2] See "Hoshea, King of Israel, and Shalmaneser V, King of Assyria" on page 556. [3] Second Maccabees is an Apocryphal book.

ARCHAEOLOGICAL SITES

THE POOL OF BETHESDA IN JERUSALEM

Coupled with the elegant porticoes, the pools must have been an impressive sight. While the lavish complex of John's day likely dated to the reign of Herod the Great,[2] the pools were probably in use before that and may have been the site of an intermittent spring. The connection between the pool and the healing process is attested not only by the fourth Gospel but also by archaeological remains indicating that the Romans also sought healing there after taking over Jerusalem in approximately A.D. 135.

There is some controversy about the translation "Sheep Gate" in John 5:2. Early Christian tradition understands this to refer to the "Sheep Pool" rather than to the "Sheep Gate"; both translations are possible, but the historical evidence for the latter is not as strong. Eusebius noted that the waters of the pool were reddish in color and that some supposed this was because the entrails of the sacrificial animals were washed there. It is more likely that the red coloring was a simple factor of geology and that the pools had been built to provide an opportunity for ritual cleansing for visitors to the temple.[3]

[1]See "Qumran and the New Testament" on page 1679. [2]See "Herod the Great" on page 1627. [3]See "Baptism in the Ancient World" on page 1562.

Bethesda ***(above)*****, with the pools of Bethesda excavations** ***(right)***

Photographs: © Todd Bolen/Bible Places.com

JOHN 5 The pool at Bethesda was a familiar locale among the Jews of Jerusalem. It was mentioned, for example, in **Qumran**'s Copper Scroll as the "place of poured out water."[1] It was located near what are now the ruins of the basilica of Saint Anne to the north of the temple mount. The "pool" was actually two pools surrounded by four porticoes, with a fifth portico situated between them. The surface area of the enclosed water was over 3.10 square miles (5 sq km).

4:35 [b]Mt 9:37; Lk 10:2 ripe for harvest.[b] 36Even now the reaper draws his wages, even now he harvests[c] the crop for eternal life,[d]
4:36 [c]Ro 1:13 [d]Mt 25:46 so that the sower and the reaper may be glad together. 37Thus the saying 'One sows and another reaps'[e]
4:37 [e]Job 31:8; Mic 6:15 is true. 38I sent you to reap what you have not worked for. Others have done the hard work, and you have
reaped the benefits of their labor."

Many Samaritans Believe

4:39 [f]ver 5 [g]ver 29 39Many of the Samaritans from that town[f] believed in him because of the woman's testimony, "He
told me everything I ever did."[g] 40So when the Samaritans came to him, they urged him to stay with
them, and he stayed two days. 41And because of his words many more became believers.
42They said to the woman, "We no longer believe just because of what you said; now we have heard
4:42 [h]Lk 2:11; 1Jn 4:14 for ourselves, and we know that this man really is the Savior of the world."[h]

Jesus Heals the Official's Son

4:43 [i]ver 40 43After the two days[i] he left for Galilee. 44(Now Jesus himself had pointed out that a prophet has no
4:44 [j]Mt 13:57; Lk 4:24 honor in his own country.)[j] 45When he arrived in Galilee, the Galileans welcomed him. They had seen all
4:45 [k]Jn 2:23 that he had done in Jerusalem at the Passover Feast,[k] for they also had been there.
4:46 [l]Jn 2:1-11 46Once more he visited Cana in Galilee, where he had turned the water into wine.[l] And there was a
certain royal official whose son lay sick at Capernaum. 47When this man heard that Jesus had arrived
4:47 [m]ver 3,54 in Galilee from Judea,[m] he went to him and begged him to come and heal his son, who was close to
death.
4:48 [n]Da 4:2,3; Jn 2:11; Ac 2:43; 14:3; Ro 15:19; 2Co 12:12; Heb 2:4 48"Unless you people see miraculous signs and wonders,"[n] Jesus told him, "you will never believe."
49The royal official said, "Sir, come down before my child dies."
50Jesus replied, "You may go. Your son will live."
The man took Jesus at his word and departed. 51While he was still on the way, his servants met him
with the news that his boy was living. 52When he inquired as to the time when his son got better, they said
to him, "The fever left him yesterday at the seventh hour."
53Then the father realized that this was the exact time at which Jesus had said to him, "Your son will
4:53 [o]Ac 11:14 live." So he and all his household[o] believed.
4:54 [p]ver 48; Jn 2:11 54This was the second miraculous sign[p] that Jesus performed, having come from Judea to Galilee.

The Healing at the Pool

5 Some time later, Jesus went up to Jerusalem for a feast of the Jews. 2Now there is in Jerusalem near
5:2 [q]Ne 3:1; 12:39 [r]Jn 19:13, 17,20; 20:16; Ac 21:40; 22:2; 26:14 the Sheep Gate[q] a pool, which in Aramaic[r] is called Bethesda[a] and which is surrounded by five cov-
ered colonnades. 3Here a great number of disabled people used to lie—the blind, the lame, the para-
lyzed.[b] 5One who was there had been an invalid for thirty-eight years. 6When Jesus saw him lying there
and learned that he had been in this condition for a long time, he asked him, "Do you want to get well?"
7"Sir," the invalid replied, "I have no one to help me into the pool when the water is stirred. While I am
trying to get in, someone else goes down ahead of me."
5:8 [s]Mt 9:5,6; Mk 2:11; Lk 5:24 8Then Jesus said to him, "Get up! Pick up your mat and walk."[s] 9At once the man was cured; he picked
up his mat and walked.
5:9 [t]Jn 9:14 The day on which this took place was a Sabbath,[t] 10and so the Jews[u] said to the man who had been
5:10 [u]ver 16 [v]Ne 13:15-22; Jer 17:21; Mt 12:2 healed, "It is the Sabbath; the law forbids you to carry your mat."[v]
11But he replied, "The man who made me well said to me, 'Pick up your mat and walk.' "
12So they asked him, "Who is this fellow who told you to pick it up and walk?"

[a] 2 Some manuscripts *Bethzatha*; other manuscripts *Bethsaida* [b] 3 Some less important manuscripts *paralyzed—and they waited for the moving of the waters. 4From time to time an angel of the Lord would come down and stir up the waters. The first one into the pool after each such disturbance would be cured of whatever disease he had.*

4:39 "That town" is Sychar (v. 5).
4:42 For Jesus as Savior, see the note on Luke 2:11.
4:46 Evidently the "royal official" was an officer in Herod's service.
4:52 The seventh hour was about 1:00 P.M.
5:1 The "feast of the Jews" probably refers to Passover, Pentecost or Tabernacles (see "The Festivals of Israel" on p. 186).
5:2 Use of the present tense ("there is") may mean that the pool was still in existence when John wrote his Gospel, which has led some to suggest that John wrote before the destruction of Jerusalem. However, others observe that John sometimes used the present tense when speaking of the past.

Bethesda is generally identified with the twin pools near the present-day Saint Anne's Church. There would have been a colonnade on each of the four sides and another between the two pools (see "The Pool of Bethesda in Jerusalem" on p. 1728).
5:10 It was not the Law of Moses itself but its traditional interpretation that prohibited carrying loads of any kind on the Sabbath (see the note on Mt 15:2).

13 The man who was healed had no idea who it was, for Jesus had slipped away into the crowd that
was there.
14 Later Jesus found him at the temple and said to him, "See, you are well again. Stop sinning[w] or some-
thing worse may happen to you." 15 The man went away and told the Jews[x] that it was Jesus who had made
him well.

Life Through the Son

16 So, because Jesus was doing these things on the Sabbath, the Jews persecuted him. 17 Jesus said to
them, "My Father is always at his work[y] to this very day, and I, too, am working." 18 For this reason the Jews
tried all the harder to kill him;[z] not only was he breaking the Sabbath, but he was even calling God his
own Father, making himself equal with God.[a]
19 Jesus gave them this answer: "I tell you the truth, the Son can do nothing by himself;[b] he can do
only what he sees his Father doing, because whatever the Father does the Son also does. 20 For the Father
loves the Son[c] and shows him all he does. Yes, to your amazement he will show him even greater things
than these.[d] 21 For just as the Father raises the dead and gives them life,[e] even so the Son gives life[f] to
whom he is pleased to give it. 22 Moreover, the Father judges no one, but has entrusted all judgment to the
Son,[g] 23 that all may honor the Son just as they honor the Father. He who does not honor the Son does not
honor the Father, who sent him.[h]
24 "I tell you the truth, whoever hears my word and believes him who sent me has eternal life and will
not be condemned;[i] he has crossed over from death to life.[j] 25 I tell you the truth, a time is coming and
has now come[k] when the dead will hear[l] the voice of the Son of God and those who hear will live. 26 For
as the Father has life in himself, so he has granted the Son to have life in himself. 27 And he has given him
authority to judge[m] because he is the Son of Man.
28 "Do not be amazed at this, for a time is coming[n] when all who are in their graves will hear his voice
29 and come out—those who have done good will rise to live, and those who have done evil will rise to
be condemned.[o] 30 By myself I can do nothing;[p] I judge only as I hear, and my judgment is just,[q] for I
seek not to please myself but him who sent me.[r]

Testimonies About Jesus

31 "If I testify about myself, my testimony is not valid.[s] 32 There is another who testifies in my favor,[t]
and I know that his testimony about me is valid.
33 "You have sent to John and he has testified[u] to the truth. 34 Not that I accept human testimony;[v] but
I mention it that you may be saved. 35 John was a lamp that burned and gave light,[w] and you chose for a
time to enjoy his light.
36 "I have testimony weightier than that of John.[x] For the very work that the Father has given me to fin-
ish, and which I am doing,[y] testifies that the Father has sent me.[z] 37 And the Father who sent me has him-
self testified concerning me.[a] You have never heard his voice nor seen his form,[b] 38 nor does his word
dwell in you,[c] for you do not believe the one he sent.[d] 39 You diligently study[a] the Scriptures[e] because you
think that by them you possess eternal life. These are the Scriptures that testify about me,[f] 40 yet you re-
fuse to come to me to have life.
41 "I do not accept praise from men,[g] 42 but I know you. I know that you do not have the love of God in
your hearts. 43 I have come in my Father's name, and you do not accept me; but if someone else comes in
his own name, you will accept him. 44 How can you believe if you accept praise from one another, yet
make no effort to obtain the praise that comes from the only God[b]?[h]
45 "But do not think I will accuse you before the Father. Your accuser is Moses,[i] on whom your hopes
are set.[j] 46 If you believed Moses, you would believe me, for he wrote about me.[k] 47 But since you do not
believe what he wrote, how are you going to believe what I say?"[l]

[a] 39 Or *Study diligently* (the imperative)   [b] 44 Some early manuscripts *the Only One*

5:14 [w]Mk 2:5; Jn 8:11
5:15 [x]Jn 1:19
5:17 [y]Jn 9:4; 14:10
5:18 [z]Jn 7:1 [a]Jn 10:30,33; 19:7
5:19 [b]ver 30; Jn 8:28
5:20 [c]Jn 3:35 [d]Jn 14:12
5:21 [e]Ro 4:17; 8:11 [f]Jn 11:25
5:22 [g]ver 27; Jn 9:39; Ac 10:42; 17:31
5:23 [h]Lk 10:16; 1Jn 2:23
5:24 [i]Jn 3:18 [j]1Jn 3:14
5:25 [k]Jn 4:23 [l]Jn 8:43,47
5:27 [m]ver 22; Ac 10:42; 17:31
5:28 [n]Jn 4:21
5:29 [o]Da 12:2; Mt 25:46
5:30 [p]ver 19 [q]Jn 8:16 [r]Mt 26:39; Jn 4:34; 6:38
5:31 [s]Jn 8:14
5:32 [t]ver 37; Jn 8:18
5:33 [u]Jn 1:7
5:34 [v]1Jn 5:9
5:35 [w]2Pe 1:19
5:36 [x]1Jn 5:9 [y]Jn 14:11; 15:24 [z]Jn 3:17; 10:25
5:37 [a]Jn 8:18 [b]Dt 4:12; 1Ti 1:17; Jn 1:18
5:38 [c]1Jn 2:14 [d]Jn 3:17
5:39 [e]Ro 2:17,18 [f]Lk 24:27,44; Ac 13:27
5:41 [g]ver 44
5:44 [h]Ro 2:29
5:45 [i]Jn 9:28 [j]Ro 2:17
5:46 [k]Ge 3:15; Lk 24:27,44; Ac 26:22
5:47 [l]Lk 16:29,31

5:17 The Jews did not refer to God as "my Father," regarding the term as too intimate—although they might have used "our Father" or, in prayer, "my Father in heaven."
5:18 The Jews did not object to the idea that God is the Father of all, but they strongly protested Jesus' claim that he stood in a special relationship to the Father—a relationship so close as to make himself equal with God.
5:21 The Jews (with the exception of the Sadducees) firmly believed that God raises the dead. They also held that God did not give this privilege to anyone else. Jesus claimed a prerogative that, according to his opponents, belonged only to God.
5:22 The Jews believed that the Father is Judge of the world, so this teaching seemed heretical to them.
5:46 The authors of the New Testament books at times stressed and everywhere assumed that the Old Testament, rightly read, pervasively points to Christ (see Lk 24:25–27,44).

Jesus Feeds the Five Thousand

6 Some time after this, Jesus crossed to the far shore of the Sea of Galilee (that is, the Sea of Tiberias),
6:2 [m]Jn 2:11 2 and a great crowd of people followed him because they saw the miraculous signs[m] he had per-
6:3 [n]ver 15 formed on the sick. 3 Then Jesus went up on a mountainside[n] and sat down with his disciples. 4 The Jew-
6:4 [o]Jn 2:13; 11:55 ish Passover Feast[o] was near.
6:5 [p]Jn 1:43 5 When Jesus looked up and saw a great crowd coming toward him, he said to Philip,[p] "Where shall we
buy bread for these people to eat?" 6 He asked this only to test him, for he already had in mind what he
was going to do.
7 Philip answered him, "Eight months' wages[a] would not buy enough bread for each one to have a
bite!"
6:8 [q]Jn 1:40 8 Another of his disciples, Andrew, Simon Peter's brother,[q] spoke up, 9 "Here is a boy with five small bar-
6:9 [r]2Ki 4:43 ley loaves and two small fish, but how far will they go among so many?"[r]
10 Jesus said, "Have the people sit down." There was plenty of grass in that place, and the men sat down,
6:11 [s]ver 23; Mt 14:19 about five thousand of them. 11 Jesus then took the loaves, gave thanks,[s] and distributed to those who
were seated as much as they wanted. He did the same with the fish.
12 When they had all had enough to eat, he said to his disciples, "Gather the pieces that are left over.
Let nothing be wasted." 13 So they gathered them and filled twelve baskets with the pieces of the five bar-
ley loaves left over by those who had eaten.
6:14 [t]Jn 2:11 [u]Dt 18:15,18; Mt 11:3; 21:11 14 After the people saw the miraculous sign[t] that Jesus did, they began to say, "Surely this is the Proph-
6:15 [v]Jn 18:36 et who is to come into the world."[u] 15 Jesus, knowing that they intended to come and make him king[v] by
[w]Mt 14:23; Mk 6:46 force, withdrew again to a mountain by himself.[w]

Jesus Walks on the Water

16 When evening came, his disciples went down to the lake, 17 where they got into a boat and set off
across the lake for Capernaum. By now it was dark, and Jesus had not yet joined them. 18 A strong wind
was blowing and the waters grew rough. 19 When they had rowed three or three and a half miles,[b] they
6:19 [x]Job 9:8 saw Jesus approaching the boat, walking on the water;[x] and they were terrified. 20 But he said to them, "It
6:20 [y]Mt 14:27 is I; don't be afraid."[y] 21 Then they were willing to take him into the boat, and immediately the boat
reached the shore where they were heading.
6:22 [z]ver 2 [a]ver 15-21 22 The next day the crowd that had stayed on the opposite shore of the lake[z] realized that only one boat
had been there, and that Jesus had not entered it with his disciples, but that they had gone away alone.[a]
6:23 [b]ver 1 [c]ver 11 23 Then some boats from Tiberias[b] landed near the place where the people had eaten the bread after the
Lord had given thanks.[c] 24 Once the crowd realized that neither Jesus nor his disciples were there, they
got into the boats and went to Capernaum in search of Jesus.

Jesus the Bread of Life

6:25 [d]Mt 23:7 25 When they found him on the other side of the lake, they asked him, "Rabbi,[d] when did you get here?"
6:26 [e]ver 24 [f]ver 30; Jn 2:11 26 Jesus answered, "I tell you the truth, you are looking for me,[e] not because you saw miraculous signs[f]
but because you ate the loaves and had your fill. 27 Do not work for food that spoils, but for food that en-
6:27 [g]Isa 55:2 [h]ver 54; Mt 25:46; Jn 4:14 [i]Mt 8:20 [j]Ro 4:11; 1Co 9:2; 2Co 1:22; Eph 1:13; 4:30; 2Ti 2:19; Rev 7:3 dures[g] to eternal life,[h] which the Son of Man[i] will give you. On him God the Father has placed his seal[j]
of approval."
28 Then they asked him, "What must we do to do the works God requires?"
6:29 [k]1Jn 3:23 [l]Jn 3:17 29 Jesus answered, "The work of God is this: to believe[k] in the one he has sent."[l]
6:30 [m]Jn 2:11 [n]Mt 12:38 30 So they asked him, "What miraculous sign[m] then will you give that we may see it and believe you?[n]
6:31 [o]Nu 11:7-9 [p]Ex 16:4,15; Ne 9:15; Ps 78:24; 105:40 What will you do? 31 Our forefathers ate the manna[o] in the desert; as it is written: 'He gave them bread
from heaven to eat.'[c]"[p]

[a] 7 Greek *two hundred denarii* [b] 19 Greek *rowed twenty-five or thirty stadia* (about 5 or 6 kilometers) [c] 31 Exodus 16:4; Neh. 9:15; Psalm 78:24,25

6:1 The "far shore" refers to the northeastern shore, probably near Bethsaida (see Lk 9:10; see also the note on Mk 8:22).
The Sea of Tiberias was probably the official Roman name for the Sea of Galilee (see the note on Mk 1:16). The name came from the town of Tiberias (named after the emperor Tiberius Caesar), founded about A.D. 20 (see "Tiberias" on p. 1732).
6:5 Since Philip came from nearby Bethsaida (see the note on Mk 8:22), it was appropriate to ask him where they could purchase bread.
6:9 For "barley loaves," see the note on Mark 6:38.
6:10 See the note on Matthew 14:21.
6:12 For "gather the pieces," see the note on Mark 6:43.
6:13 For "basket," see the note on Matthew 14:20.
6:15 The people wanted to force Jesus to define his mission and work politically—to become a king who would rival the Herodians or the Romans. Jesus wanted no part of such a kingship.

32 Jesus said to them, "I tell you the truth, it is not Moses who has given you the bread from heaven,
but it is my Father who gives you the true bread from heaven. 33 For the bread of God is he who comes
down from heaven[q] and gives life to the world."
34 "Sir," they said, "from now on give us this bread."[r]
35 Then Jesus declared, "I am the bread of life.[s] He who comes to me will never go hungry, and he who
believes in me will never be thirsty.[t] 36 But as I told you, you have seen me and still you do not believe.
37 All that the Father gives me[u] will come to me, and whoever comes to me I will never drive away. 38 For
I have come down from heaven not to do my will but to do the will of him who sent me.[v] 39 And this is
the will of him who sent me, that I shall lose none of all that he has given me,[w] but raise them up at the
last day.[x] 40 For my Father's will is that everyone who looks to the Son and believes in him shall have eter-
nal life,[y] and I will raise him up at the last day."
41 At this the Jews began to grumble about him because he said, "I am the bread that came down from
heaven." 42 They said, "Is this not Jesus, the son of Joseph,[z] whose father and mother we know?[a] How can
he now say, 'I came down from heaven'?"[b]
43 "Stop grumbling among yourselves," Jesus answered. 44 "No one can come to me unless the Father
who sent me draws him,[c] and I will raise him up at the last day. 45 It is written in the Prophets: 'They will
all be taught by God.'[a][d] Everyone who listens to the Father and learns from him comes to me. 46 No one
has seen the Father except the one who is from God;[e] only he has seen the Father. 47 I tell you the truth,
he who believes has everlasting life. 48 I am the bread of life.[f] 49 Your forefathers ate the manna in the des-
ert, yet they died.[g] 50 But here is the bread that comes down from heaven,[h] which a man may eat and not
die. 51 I am the living bread that came down from heaven. If anyone eats of this bread, he will live forev-
er. This bread is my flesh, which I will give for the life of the world."[i]
52 Then the Jews began to argue sharply among themselves,[j] "How can this man give us his flesh to
eat?"

6:33 [q]ver 50
6:34 [r]Jn 4:15
6:35 [s]ver 48,51 [t]Jn 4:14
6:37 [u]ver 39; Jn 17:2,6,9,24
6:38 [v]Jn 4:34; 5:30
6:39 [w]Jn 10:28; 17:12; 18:9 [x]ver 40,44,54
6:40 [y]Jn 3:15,16
6:42 [z]Lk 4:22 [a]Jn 7:27,28 [b]ver 38,62
6:44 [c]ver 65; Jer 31:3; Jn 12:32
6:45 [d]Isa 54:13; Jer 31:33,34; Heb 8:10,11; 10:16
6:46 [e]Jn 1:18; 5:37; 7:29
6:48 [f]ver 35,51
6:49 [g]ver 31,58
6:50 [h]ver 33
6:51 [i]Heb 10:10
6:52 [j]Jn 7:43; 9:16; 10:19

[a] *45* Isaiah 54:13

6:45 "The Prophets" refers to the section of the Old Testament from which this quotation was taken. This section includes not only the "Latter Prophets"—Isaiah, Jeremiah and Ezekiel, which we call the Major Prophets, and the 12 Minor Prophets (lumped together by the Jews as "the Book of the Twelve")—but also the "Former Prophets" (Joshua, Judges, Samuel and Kings).

ARCHAEOLOGICAL SITES

TIBERIAS

JOHN 6 Herod Antipas, the son of Herod the Great and the tetrarch of Galilee (Mt 14:1; Lk 3:19),[1] founded the city of Tiberias (see "Map 9") around A.D. 20. The city was named in honor of the Roman emperor Tiberius, who ruled from A.D. 14–37.[2] Ancient Tiberias was located on the western shore of the Sea of Galilee 2 miles (3.2 km) south of Magdala and one mile north of the hot springs at Hammath. The site is commonly identified with a place called Khirbet Qunaytirah, which is actually north of modern Tiberias.

A large number of tombs discovered there during the initial stages of its construction[3] were cleared away and new buildings erected over them, but this act rendered the city unclean for pious Jews (cf. Nu 19:16). As a result Herod was forced to populate the town with a mixture of Galileans, foreigners and freed slaves. According to Josephus, a continual settlement of the city was ensured through land and housing grants, as well as through the emancipation of great numbers of slaves who were freed with the obligation to live there (Josephus, *Antiquities*, 18.2.3).[4]

Antipas built the city according to the Hellenistic-Roman conventions of his time, including within it a stadium, forum, public baths and a lavish royal palace adorned with animal statuary, which was offensive to Jews. Tiberias was thus a city that was thoroughly Gentile in atmosphere. But Antipas also constructed a large synagogue to accommodate its Jewish inhabitants.[5] As Tiberias grew in importance as both an urban and an administrative center, the Sea of Galilee became known as the Sea of Tiberias (Jn 6:1; 21:1).[6]

[1] See also "Herod the Great" on page 1627. [2] See "Tiberius Caesar, the Caesar of Jesus' Ministry" on page 1708. [3] See "Tombs in Ancient Israel" on page 376. [4] See "Slavery in the Greco-Roman World" on page 1979. [5] See "Ancient Synagogues" on page 1783. [6] See "Sepphoris" on page 1638 for a discussion of other building activities attributed to Herod Antipas.

53Jesus said to them, "I tell you the truth, unless you eat the flesh of the Son of Man[k] and drink his blood, you have no life in you. 54Whoever eats my flesh and drinks my blood has eternal life, and I will raise him up at the last day.[l] 55For my flesh is real food and my blood is real drink. 56Whoever eats my flesh and drinks my blood remains in me, and I in him.[m] 57Just as the living Father sent me[n] and I live because of the Father, so the one who feeds on me will live because of me. 58This is the bread that came down from heaven. Your forefathers ate manna and died, but he who feeds on this bread will live forever."[o] 59He said this while teaching in the synagogue in Capernaum.

Many Disciples Desert Jesus

60On hearing it, many of his disciples[p] said, "This is a hard teaching. Who can accept it?"

61Aware that his disciples were grumbling about this, Jesus said to them, "Does this offend you?[q] 62What if you see the Son of Man ascend to where he was before![r] 63The Spirit gives life;[s] the flesh counts for nothing. The words I have spoken to you are spirit[a] and they are life. 64Yet there are some of you who do not believe." For Jesus had known[t] from the beginning which of them did not believe and who would betray him. 65He went on to say, "This is why I told you that no one can come to me unless the Father has enabled him."[u]

66From this time many of his disciples[v] turned back and no longer followed him.

67"You do not want to leave too, do you?" Jesus asked the Twelve.[w]

68Simon Peter answered him,[x] "Lord, to whom shall we go? You have the words of eternal life. 69We believe and know that you are the Holy One of God."[y]

70Then Jesus replied, "Have I not chosen you,[z] the Twelve? Yet one of you is a devil!"[a] 71(He meant Judas, the son of Simon Iscariot, who, though one of the Twelve, was later to betray him.)

Jesus Goes to the Feast of Tabernacles

7 After this, Jesus went around in Galilee, purposely staying away from Judea because the Jews[b] there were waiting to take his life.[c] 2But when the Jewish Feast of Tabernacles[d] was near, 3Jesus' brothers[e] said to him, "You ought to leave here and go to Judea, so that your disciples may see the miracles you do. 4No one who wants to become a public figure acts in secret. Since you are doing these things, show yourself to the world." 5For even his own brothers did not believe in him.[f]

6Therefore Jesus told them, "The right time[g] for me has not yet come; for you any time is right. 7The world cannot hate you, but it hates me[h] because I testify that what it does is evil.[i] 8You go to the Feast. I am not yet[b] going up to this Feast, because for me the right time[j] has not yet come." 9Having said this, he stayed in Galilee.

10However, after his brothers had left for the Feast, he went also, not publicly, but in secret. 11Now at the Feast the Jews were watching for him[k] and asking, "Where is that man?"

12Among the crowds there was widespread whispering about him. Some said, "He is a good man."

Others replied, "No, he deceives the people."[l] 13But no one would say anything publicly about him for fear of the Jews.[m]

Jesus Teaches at the Feast

14Not until halfway through the Feast did Jesus go up to the temple courts and begin to teach.[n] 15The Jews[o] were amazed and asked, "How did this man get such learning[p] without having studied?"[q]

16Jesus answered, "My teaching is not my own. It comes from him who sent me.[r] 17If anyone chooses to do God's will, he will find out[s] whether my teaching comes from God or whether I speak on my own.

6:53 [k]Mt 8:20
6:54 [l]ver 39
6:56 [m]Jn 15:4-7; 1Jn 3:24; 4:15
6:57 [n]Jn 3:17
6:58 [o]ver 49-51; Jn 3:36
6:60 [p]ver 66
6:61 [q]Mt 11:6
6:62 [r]Mk 16:19; Jn 3:13; 17:5
6:63 [s]2Co 3:6
6:64 [t]Jn 2:25
6:65 [u]ver 37,44
6:66 [v]ver 60
6:67 [w]Mt 10:2
6:68 [x]Mt 16:16
6:69 [y]Mk 8:29; Lk 9:20
6:70 [z]Jn 15:16, 19 [a]Jn 13:27
7:1 [b]Jn 1:19 [c]Jn 5:18
7:2 [d]Lev 23:34; Dt 16:16
7:3 [e]Mt 12:46
7:5 [f]Mk 3:21
7:6 [g]Mt 26:18
7:7 [h]Jn 15:18,19 [i]Jn 3:19,20
7:8 [j]ver 6
7:11 [k]Jn 11:56
7:12 [l]ver 40,43
7:13 [m]Jn 9:22; 12:42; 19:38
7:14 [n]ver 28; Mt 26:55
7:15 [o]Jn 1:19 [p]Ac 26:24 [q]Mt 13:54
7:16 [r]Jn 3:11; 14:24
7:17 [s]Ps 25:14; Jn 8:43

[a] 63 Or *Spirit* [b] 8 Some early manuscripts do not have *yet.*

6:59 See "The Capernaum Synagogue" on page 1591.
6:60 The thought of eating the flesh of the Son of Man and drinking his blood was doubtless shocking to most of Jesus' Jewish hearers.
6:69 For "Holy One of God," see the note on Mark 1:24.
6:71 For "Iscariot," see the note on Mark 3:19.
7:1 Since 6:4 refers to the Passover Feast and 7:2 to the Feast of Tabernacles, the interval was about six months.
7:2 The Feast of Tabernacles celebrated the completion of harvest and commemorated God's goodness to the people during the desert wanderings (see "The Festivals of Israel" on p. 186).
7:3 For "brothers," see the note on Luke 8:19.
7:14 The crowds would have reached their peak halfway through the Feast. Teaching in the temple courts at such a time would have reached many (see "The Rabbis' Teaching Steps at the Southern Wall Excavations" on p. 1741).
7:15 The Jews wanted to know where Jesus had gone to school. Educational standards for rabbis were well established by Jesus' day. Advanced study under a rabbinic scholar was common (cf. Paul with Gamaliel in Ac 22:3). Jesus possessed no such credentials.

18 He who speaks on his own does so to gain honor for himself,[t] but he who works for the honor of the one who sent him is a man of truth; there is nothing false about him. 19 Has not Moses given you the law?[u] Yet not one of you keeps the law. Why are you trying to kill me?"[v]

20 "You are demon-possessed,"[w] the crowd answered. "Who is trying to kill you?"

21 Jesus said to them, "I did one miracle, and you are all astonished. 22 Yet, because Moses gave you circumcision[x] (though actually it did not come from Moses, but from the patriarchs),[y] you circumcise a child on the Sabbath. 23 Now if a child can be circumcised on the Sabbath so that the law of Moses may not be broken, why are you angry with me for healing the whole man on the Sabbath? 24 Stop judging by mere appearances, and make a right judgment."[z]

Is Jesus the Christ?

25 At that point some of the people of Jerusalem began to ask, "Isn't this the man they are trying to kill? 26 Here he is, speaking publicly, and they are not saying a word to him. Have the authorities[a] really concluded that he is the Christ[*a*]? 27 But we know where this man is from;[b] when the Christ comes, no one will know where he is from."

28 Then Jesus, still teaching in the temple courts,[c] cried out, "Yes, you know me, and you know where I am from.[d] I am not here on my own, but he who sent me is true.[e] You do not know him, 29 but I know him[f] because I am from him and he sent me."

30 At this they tried to seize him, but no one laid a hand on him,[g] because his time had not yet come. 31 Still, many in the crowd put their faith in him.[h] They said, "When the Christ comes, will he do more miraculous signs[i] than this man?"

32 The Pharisees heard the crowd whispering such things about him. Then the chief priests and the Pharisees sent temple guards to arrest him.

33 Jesus said, "I am with you for only a short time,[j] and then I go to the one who sent me.[k] 34 You will look for me, but you will not find me; and where I am, you cannot come."[l]

35 The Jews said to one another, "Where does this man intend to go that we cannot find him? Will he go where our people live scattered[m] among the Greeks,[n] and teach the Greeks? 36 What did he mean when he said, 'You will look for me, but you will not find me,' and 'Where I am, you cannot come'?"

37 On the last and greatest day of the Feast,[o] Jesus stood and said in a loud voice, "If anyone is thirsty, let him come to me and drink.[p] 38 Whoever believes in me, as[*b*] the Scripture has said,[q] streams of living water[r] will flow from within him."[s] 39 By this he meant the Spirit,[t] whom those who believed in him were later to receive.[u] Up to that time the Spirit had not been given, since Jesus had not yet been glorified.[v]

40 On hearing his words, some of the people said, "Surely this man is the Prophet."[w]

41 Others said, "He is the Christ."

Still others asked, "How can the Christ come from Galilee?[x] 42 Does not the Scripture say that the Christ will come from David's family[*c*][y] and from Bethlehem,[z] the town where David lived?" 43 Thus the people were divided[a] because of Jesus. 44 Some wanted to seize him, but no one laid a hand on him.[b]

Unbelief of the Jewish Leaders

45 Finally the temple guards went back to the chief priests and Pharisees, who asked them, "Why didn't you bring him in?"

46 "No one ever spoke the way this man does,"[c] the guards declared.

7:18 [t]Jn 5:41; 8:50,54 **7:19** [u]Jn 1:17 [v]ver 1; Mt 12:14 **7:20** [w]Jn 8:48; 10:20 **7:22** [x]Lev 12:3 [y]Ge 17:10-14 **7:24** [z]Isa 11:3,4; Jn 8:15 **7:26** [a]ver 48 **7:27** [b]Mt 13:55; Lk 4:22 **7:28** [c]ver 14 [d]Jn 8:14 [e]Jn 8:26,42 **7:29** [f]Mt 11:27 **7:30** [g]ver 32,44; Jn 10:39 **7:31** [h]Jn 8:30 [i]Jn 2:11 **7:33** [j]Jn 13:33; 16:16 [k]Jn 16:5, 10,17,28 **7:34** [l]Jn 8:21; 13:33 **7:35** [m]Jas 1:1 [n]Jn 12:20; 1Pe 1:1 **7:37** [o]Lev 23:36 [p]Isa 55:1; Rev 22:17 **7:38** [q]Isa 58:11 [r]Jn 4:10 [s]Jn 4:14 **7:39** [t]Joel 2:28; Ac 2:17,33 [u]Jn 20:22 [v]Jn 12:23; 13:31, 32 **7:40** [w]Mt 21:11; Jn 1:21 **7:41** [x]ver 52; Jn 1:46 **7:42** [y]Mt 1:1 [z]Mic 5:2; Mt 2:5, 6; Lk 2:4 **7:43** [a]Jn 9:16; 10:19 **7:44** [b]ver 30 **7:46** [c]Mt 7:28

a 26 Or *Messiah*; also in verses 27, 31, 41 and 42 *b* 37,38 Or / *If anyone is thirsty, let him come to me. / And let him drink,* [38]*who believes in me. / As* *c* 42 Greek *seed*

7:22 See "Circumcision in the Ancient World" on page 1840.

7:32 For "Pharisees," see the notes on Matthew 3:7 and Luke 5:17. For "chief priests," see the note on Matthew 2:4.

7:35 From the time of the exile, many Jews lived outside the Holy Land and were found in most cities throughout the Roman Empire (see "The Jewish Diaspora in the First Century A.D." on p. 1769).

7:37–38 The Feast of Tabernacles lasted seven days (Lev 23:34; Dt 16:13,15) but included a "closing assembly" on the eighth day (Lev 23:36). The celebration included a daily procession from the temple to the Pool of Siloam (see "The Pool of Siloam" on p. 1739). There a priest drew water that was then returned and poured out as an offering at the altar, accompanied by a recitation of Isaiah 12:3. On the final day of celebration (either the seventh or eighth day), Jesus announced that he himself was the source of "living water."

Teachers usually sat, so Jesus drew special attention to his message by standing.

7:42 There were different ideas about the Messiah's place of origin (see v. 27).

7:46 The guards knew they would be in trouble for failing to make the arrest but did not mention the hostility of the crowd, which would have given them something of an excuse before the Pharisees. They were favorably impressed by the teaching of Jesus and were not inclined to cause him trouble.

7:47 dver 12 47“You mean he has deceived you also?”[d] the Pharisees retorted. 48“Has any of the rulers or of the
7:48 eJn 12:42 Pharisees believed in him?[e] 49No! But this mob that knows nothing of the law—there is a curse on them.”
7:50 fJn 3:1; 19:39 50Nicodemus,[f] who had gone to Jesus earlier and who was one of their own number, asked, 51“Does
our law condemn anyone without first hearing him to find out what he is doing?”
52They replied, “Are you from Galilee, too? Look into it, and you will find that a prophet[a] does not
7:52 gver 41 come out of Galilee.”[g]

[The earliest manuscripts and many other ancient witnesses do not have John 7:53-8:11.]

53Then each went to his own home.
8:1 hMt 21:1 8 But Jesus went to the Mount of Olives.[h] 2At dawn he appeared again in the temple courts, where all
8:2 iver 20; Mt 26:55 the people gathered around him, and he sat down to teach them.[i] 3The teachers of the law and the
Pharisees brought in a woman caught in adultery. They made her stand before the group 4and said to
Jesus, “Teacher, this woman was caught in the act of adultery. 5In the Law Moses commanded us to stone
8:5 jLev 20:10; Dt 22:22 such women.[j] Now what do you say?” 6They were using this question as a trap,[k] in order to have a basis
8:6 kMt 22:15,18 lMt 12:10 for accusing him.[l]
But Jesus bent down and started to write on the ground with his finger. 7When they kept on ques-
tioning him, he straightened up and said to them, “If any one of you is without sin, let him be the first to
8:7 mDt 17:7 nRo 2:1,22 throw a stone[m] at her.”[n] 8Again he stooped down and wrote on the ground.
9At this, those who heard began to go away one at a time, the older ones first, until only Jesus was left,
with the woman still standing there. 10Jesus straightened up and asked her, “Woman, where are they?
Has no one condemned you?”
11“No one, sir,” she said.
8:11 oJn 3:17 pJn 5:14 “Then neither do I condemn you,”[o] Jesus declared. “Go now and leave your life of sin.”[p]

The Validity of Jesus' Testimony

8:12 qJn 6:35 rJn 1:4; 12:35 sPr 4:18; Mt 5:14 12When Jesus spoke again to the people, he said, “I am[q] the light of the world.[r] Whoever follows me
will never walk in darkness, but will have the light of life.”[s]
13The Pharisees challenged him, “Here you are, appearing as your own witness; your testimony is not
8:13 tJn 5:31 valid.”[t]

[a] 52 Two early manuscripts *the Prophet*

7:47 The Pharisees must have been greatly irritated. Ordinarily the chief priests would have rebuked the temple guards.
7:49 The Pharisees exaggerated the people's ignorance of Scripture (cf. v. 42), although the average Jew paid little attention to the minutiae that mattered so much to the Pharisees. The law (traditions of the elders; see the note on Mt 15:2) was too great a burden for people who earned their living by hard physical work, and consequently these regulations were widely disregarded.
7:52 For “Galilee,” see the note on Matthew 4:12–16. The chief priests and the Pharisees were angry—and wrong. Jonah had come from Galilee, and perhaps other prophets had as well.
7:53—8:11 Evidence indicates that this story was not originally contained in John's Gospel. No early New Testament text from either the east or west, and no early church father, includes these verses. Some suggest that they existed as an independent account that circulated freely for some time and was only later placed here in John's Gospel.
8:1 See “The Mount of Olives” on page 1543.
8:3 For “teachers of the law,” see the notes on Matthew 2:4 and Luke 5:17.

This sin cannot be committed by one individual alone, so the question arises as to why only one offender was brought in. The incident was staged to trap Jesus (see Jn 8:6 and its note), and provision had been made for the man to escape. The woman's accusers must have been especially eager to humiliate her, since they could have kept her in private custody while they spoke to Jesus.
8:4 Compromising circumstances were insufficient evidence of adultery; Jewish law required witnesses who had seen the act.
8:5 The accusers altered the law slightly. Stoning was not in fact prescribed unless the woman was a betrothed virgin (Dt 22:23–24). And the law required the execution of both parties (Lev 20:10; Dt 22:22), not just the woman.
8:6 The Romans did not allow the Jews to carry out death sentences (see 18:31 and its note), so if Jesus had indicated that she should be stoned he could have been seen as in conflict with the Romans. If he had stated the opposite, however, he could have been accused of lack of support for the law.
8:7 Since Jesus spoke of throwing a stone, he could not be accused of failure to uphold the law. But the qualifications for doing so prevented anyone from acting. (The phrase “without sin” is quite general, meaning “without any sin,” not “without this sin.”)
8:12 The Feast of Tabernacles included spectacular ceremonies that symbolized multiple themes: harvest, drought, the coming winter darkness and the desert wandering after the exodus. Four stands, each holding four golden bowls, were placed in the heavily used court of women. These large bowls were filled with oil and lit during the feast. On this final day of Tabernacles, Jesus was teaching in the treasury located within the court of women. It was in this setting, standing beneath 16 lit bowls of oil, that Jesus identified himself as the true light of the world.
8:13 For “Pharisees,” see the notes on Matthew 3:7 and Luke 5:17.

14 Jesus answered, "Even if I testify on my own behalf, my testimony is valid, for I know where I came from and where I am going.[u] But you have no idea where I come from[v] or where I am going. 15 You judge by human standards;[w] I pass judgment on no one.[x] 16 But if I do judge, my decisions are right, because I am not alone. I stand with the Father, who sent me.[y] 17 In your own Law it is written that the testimony of two men is valid.[z] 18 I am one who testifies for myself; my other witness is the Father, who sent me."[a]

19 Then they asked him, "Where is your father?"

"You do not know me or my Father,"[b] Jesus replied. "If you knew me, you would know my Father also."[c] 20 He spoke these words while teaching[d] in the temple area near the place where the offerings were put.[e] Yet no one seized him, because his time had not yet come.[f]

21 Once more Jesus said to them, "I am going away, and you will look for me, and you will die[g] in your sin. Where I go, you cannot come."[h]

22 This made the Jews ask, "Will he kill himself? Is that why he says, 'Where I go, you cannot come'?"

23 But he continued, "You are from below; I am from above. You are of this world; I am not of this world.[i] 24 I told you that you would die in your sins; if you do not believe that I am ⌊the one I claim to be⌋,[a][j] you will indeed die in your sins."

25 "Who are you?" they asked.

"Just what I have been claiming all along," Jesus replied. 26 "I have much to say in judgment of you. But he who sent me is reliable,[k] and what I have heard from him I tell the world."[l]

27 They did not understand that he was telling them about his Father. 28 So Jesus said, "When you have lifted up the Son of Man,[m] then you will know that I am ⌊the one I claim to be⌋ and that I do nothing on my own but speak just what the Father has taught me. 29 The one who sent me is with me; he has not left me alone,[n] for I always do what pleases him."[o] 30 Even as he spoke, many put their faith in him.[p]

The Children of Abraham

31 To the Jews who had believed him, Jesus said, "If you hold to my teaching,[q] you are really my disciples. 32 Then you will know the truth, and the truth will set you free."[r]

33 They answered him, "We are Abraham's descendants[b][s] and have never been slaves of anyone. How can you say that we shall be set free?"

34 Jesus replied, "I tell you the truth, everyone who sins is a slave to sin.[t] 35 Now a slave has no permanent place in the family, but a son belongs to it forever.[u] 36 So if the Son sets you free, you will be free indeed. 37 I know you are Abraham's descendants. Yet you are ready to kill me,[v] because you have no room for my word. 38 I am telling you what I have seen in the Father's presence,[w] and you do what you have heard from your father.[c]"

39 "Abraham is our father," they answered.

"If you were Abraham's children,"[x] said Jesus, "then you would[d] do the things Abraham did. 40 As it is, you are determined to kill me, a man who has told you the truth that I heard from God.[y] Abraham did not do such things. 41 You are doing the things your own father does."[z]

"We are not illegitimate children," they protested. "The only Father we have is God himself."[a]

The Children of the Devil

42 Jesus said to them, "If God were your Father, you would love me,[b] for I came from God[c] and now am here. I have not come on my own;[d] but he sent me.[e] 43 Why is my language not clear to you? Because you are unable to hear what I say. 44 You belong to your father, the devil,[f] and you want to carry out your father's desire.[g] He was a murderer from the beginning, not holding to the truth, for there is no truth in him. When he lies, he speaks his native language, for he is a liar and the father of lies.[h] 45 Yet because I tell the truth,[i] you do not believe me! 46 Can any of you prove me guilty of sin? If I am telling the truth, why don't you believe me? 47 He who belongs to God hears what God says.[j] The reason you do not hear is that you do not belong to God."

8:14 [u]Jn 13:3; 16:28 [v]Jn 7:28; 9:29
8:15 [w]Jn 7:24 [x]Jn 3:17
8:16 [y]Jn 5:30
8:17 [z]Dt 17:6; Mt 18:16
8:18 [a]Jn 5:37
8:19 [b]Jn 16:3 [c]Jn 14:7; 1Jn 2:23
8:20 [d]Mt 26:55 [e]Mk 12:41 [f]Mt 26:18; Jn 7:30
8:21 [g]Eze 3:18 [h]Jn 7:34; 13:33
8:23 [i]Jn 3:31; 17:14
8:24 [j]Jn 4:26; 13:19
8:26 [k]Jn 7:28 [l]Jn 3:32; 15:15
8:28 [m]Jn 3:14; 5:19; 12:32
8:29 [n]ver 16; Jn 16:32 [o]Jn 4:34; 5:30; 6:38
8:30 [p]Jn 7:31
8:31 [q]Jn 15:7; 2Jn 9
8:32 [r]Ro 8:2; Jas 2:12
8:33 [s]ver 37,39; Mt 3:9
8:34 [t]Ro 6:16; 2Pe 2:19
8:35 [u]Gal 4:30
8:37 [v]ver 39,40
8:38 [w]Jn 5:19, 30; 14:10,24
8:39 [x]ver 37; Ro 9:7; Gal 3:7
8:40 [y]ver 26
8:41 [z]ver 38,44 [a]Isa 63:16; 64:8
8:42 [b]1Jn 5:1 [c]Jn 16:27; 17:8 [d]Jn 7:28 [e]Jn 3:17
8:44 [f]1Jn 3:8 [g]ver 38,41 [h]Ge 3:4
8:45 [i]Jn 18:37
8:47 [j]Jn 18:37; 1Jn 4:6

[a] 24 Or *I am he*; also in verse 28 [b] 33 Greek *seed*; also in verse 37 [c] 38 Or *presence. Therefore do what you have heard from the Father.* [d] 39 Some early manuscripts *"If you are Abraham's children," said Jesus, "then*

8:33 The Jews' statement that they had "never been slaves of anyone" was an amazing disregard of their Roman overlords—as well as of their Egyptian, Assyrian, Babylonian, Persian and Syrian oppressors. Perhaps they meant that they had never accepted servitude to others as their proper status, since they were descendants of Abraham.

8:44 Jesus' words here did not apply to the Jewish people as a whole but to his Jewish opponents.

The Claims of Jesus About Himself

8:48 [k]Mt 10:5 — 48 The Jews answered him, "Aren't we right in saying that you are a Samaritan[k] and demon-pos-
[l]ver 52; Jn 7:20 — sessed?"[l]
49 "I am not possessed by a demon," said Jesus, "but I honor my Father and you dishonor me. 50 I am
8:50 [m]ver 54; Jn 5:41 — not seeking glory for myself;[m] but there is one who seeks it, and he is the judge. 51 I tell you the truth, if
8:51 [n]Jn 11:26 — anyone keeps my word, he will never see death."[n]
52 At this the Jews exclaimed, "Now we know that you are demon-possessed! Abraham died and so did
the prophets, yet you say that if anyone keeps your word, he will never taste death. 53 Are you greater than
8:53 [o]Jn 4:12 — our father Abraham?[o] He died, and so did the prophets. Who do you think you are?"
8:54 [p]ver 50 [q]Jn 16:14; 17:1,5 — 54 Jesus replied, "If I glorify myself,[p] my glory means nothing. My Father, whom you claim as your
8:55 [r]ver 19 [s]Jn 7:28,29 — God, is the one who glorifies me.[q] 55 Though you do not know him,[r] I know him.[s] If I said I did not, I
[t]Jn 15:10 8:56 [u]ver 37,39 — would be a liar like you, but I do know him and keep his word.[t] 56 Your father Abraham[u] rejoiced at the
[v]Mt 13:17; Heb 11:13 — thought of seeing my day; he saw it[v] and was glad."
8:58 [w]Jn 1:2; — 57 "You are not yet fifty years old," the Jews said to him, "and you have seen Abraham!"
17:5,24 [x]Ex 3:14 8:59 [y]Lev 24:16; — 58 "I tell you the truth," Jesus answered, "before Abraham was born,[w] I am!"[x] 59 At this, they picked up
Jn 10:31; 11:8 [z]Jn 12:36 — stones to stone him,[y] but Jesus hid himself,[z] slipping away from the temple grounds.

8:48 The Jews may have called Jesus a "Samaritan" to suggest that he was lax in Jewish observances or that he was a Samaritan by birth. (For information on Samaritans, see the note on Lk 10:33; see also "The Samaritans" on p. 1737.)

8:57 Jesus was about thirty years old when he began his ministry (see Lk 3:23 and its note).

8:59 Those who heard Jesus could not interpret his claim as other than blasphemy, for which stoning was the prescribed penalty (Lev 24:16).

The Samaritans

JOHN 8 The Samaritans believed themselves to be the descendants of the northern tribes, who had been exiled in 722 B.C. by **Assyria.**[1] In 2 Kings 17, however, the Samaritans are described as a mixed group, composed at least partly of pagans whom the king of Assyria had brought into the land from other nations. In Ezra 4 the Samaritans appear as troublemakers for the Jews who were seeking to reestablish themselves and their temple in the land following their return from exile.

This group did not identify itself with **Samaria** so much as with Mount Gerizim, near Shechem, which its members claimed was the place God had chosen for his sanctuary (see Dt 12:5,11,21,26; 14:24–25; 16:6; 17:8; 18:6; 26:2).[2] They believed that Israel had become apostate as soon as the sanctuary had been moved away from Shechem ("Map 4"), during the time of Eli, the priest.[3] The Samaritans rejected Jerusalem's special place in God's plans, and the ongoing tension regarding the proper place for the sanctuary of God is evident in John 4:20. Samaritans believed in the God of Israel, acknowledged Moses as his prophet and the **Pentateuch** as his revelation, and looked forward to the day when he would send the "prophet like [Moses]," as he had promised (Dt 18:18). They did not accept or acknowledge any Old Testament writings beyond the Pentateuch as **canonical.**

The Jewish high priest and ruler John Hyrcanus destroyed the Samaritan sanctuary on Mount Gerizim in 128 B.C., and tensions between Jews and Samaritans remained high throughout the first century A.D. Samaritans scattered bones in the Jerusalem temple during Passover in A.D. 6–7 and in A.D. 52 massacred a group of Galilean pilgrims on their way to Jerusalem (Josephus, *Antiquities*, 20.6.1 and *Wars*, 2.12.3). Typically Jews would avoid passing through Samaria when traveling between Judea and Galilee. The Jewish accusation against Jesus that he was a Samaritan and therefore demon-possessed is consistent with the strong anti-Samaritan sentiment that motivated the destruction of their sanctuary; Jewish writings from this time (such as Sir 50:25–26, Jubilees 30:5–6 and the Testament of Levi 7:2)[4] attest to this hostility (see also Jn 4:7–9). Samaritans were considered apostates and idolaters (based in part on Ge 35:4) and were viewed as more likely than Jews to be demonized. Jesus, however, apparently regarded the Samaritans as a genuine, albeit misguided, subgroup of the covenant people.

[1]See "Hoshea, King of Israel, and Shalmaneser V, King of Assyria" on page 556. [2]See "The Samaritan Temple on Mount Gerizim" on page 1727. [3]See "Shechem" on page 340. [4]Sirach is an Apocryphal book, while Jubilees and the Testament of Levi are pseudepigraphal.

Jesus Heals a Man Born Blind

9 As he went along, he saw a man blind from birth. 2His disciples asked him, "Rabbi,[a] who sinned,[b]
this man[c] or his parents,[d] that he was born blind?"
3"Neither this man nor his parents sinned," said Jesus, "but this happened so that the work of God
might be displayed in his life.[e] 4As long as it is day,[f] we must do the work of him who sent me. Night is
coming, when no one can work. 5While I am in the world, I am the light of the world."[g]
6Having said this, he spit[h] on the ground, made some mud with the saliva, and put it on the man's
eyes. 7"Go," he told him, "wash in the Pool of Siloam"[i] (this word means Sent). So the man went and
washed, and came home seeing.[j]
8His neighbors and those who had formerly seen him begging asked, "Isn't this the same man who
used to sit and beg?"[k] 9Some claimed that he was.
Others said, "No, he only looks like him."
But he himself insisted, "I am the man."
10"How then were your eyes opened?" they demanded.
11He replied, "The man they call Jesus made some mud and put it on my eyes. He told me to go to Si-
loam and wash. So I went and washed, and then I could see."[l]
12"Where is this man?" they asked him.
"I don't know," he said.

9:2 [a]Mt 23:7 [b]ver 34; Lk 13:2; Ac 28:4 [c]Eze 18:20 [d]Ex 20:5; Job 21:19
9:3 [e]Jn 11:4
9:4 [f]Jn 11:9; 12:35
9:5 [g]Jn 1:4; 8:12; 12:46
9:6 [h]Mk 7:33; 8:23
9:7 [i]ver 11; 2Ki 5:10; Lk 13:4 [j]Isa 35:5; Jn 11:37
9:8 [k]Ac 3:2,10
9:11 [l]ver 7

The Pharisees Investigate the Healing

13They brought to the Pharisees the man who had been blind. 14Now the day on which Jesus had made
the mud and opened the man's eyes was a Sabbath.[m] 15Therefore the Pharisees also asked him how he
had received his sight.[n] "He put mud on my eyes," the man replied, "and I washed, and now I see."
16Some of the Pharisees said, "This man is not from God, for he does not keep the Sabbath."[o]
But others asked, "How can a sinner do such miraculous signs?" So they were divided.[p]
17Finally they turned again to the blind man, "What have you to say about him? It was your eyes he
opened."
The man replied, "He is a prophet."[q]
18The Jews[r] still did not believe that he had been blind and had received his sight until they sent for
the man's parents. 19"Is this your son?" they asked. "Is this the one you say was born blind? How is it that
now he can see?"
20"We know he is our son," the parents answered, "and we know he was born blind. 21But how he can
see now, or who opened his eyes, we don't know. Ask him. He is of age; he will speak for himself." 22His
parents said this because they were afraid of the Jews,[s] for already the Jews had decided that anyone who
acknowledged that Jesus was the Christ[a] would be put out[t] of the synagogue.[u] 23That was why his par-
ents said, "He is of age; ask him."[v]
24A second time they summoned the man who had been blind. "Give glory to God,[b]"[w] they said. "We
know this man is a sinner."[x]
25He replied, "Whether he is a sinner or not, I don't know. One thing I do know. I was blind but now I
see!"
26Then they asked him, "What did he do to you? How did he open your eyes?"
27He answered, "I have told you already[y] and you did not listen. Why do you want to hear it again? Do
you want to become his disciples, too?"

9:14 [m]Jn 5:9
9:15 [n]ver 10
9:16 [o]Mt 12:2 [p]Jn 6:52; 7:43; 10:19
9:17 [q]Mt 21:11
9:18 [r]Jn 1:19
9:22 [s]Jn 7:13 [t]ver 34; Lk 6:22 [u]Jn 12:42; 16:2
9:23 [v]ver 21
9:24 [w]Jos 7:19 [x]ver 16
9:27 [y]ver 15

[a] 22 Or *Messiah* [b] 24 A solemn charge to tell the truth (see Joshua 7:19)

9:2 The rabbis taught, based on Exodus 34:7, that if a person suffered from a physical ailment from birth this must have been (1) because the individual's parents or grandparents had committed some sin or (2) because the sick person had sinned before birth.
9:6 See "Disease and Medicine in the Ancient World" on page 1674 and "Miracle Workers and Magicians in the First Century A.D." on page 1706.
9:7 The Pool of Siloam, a rock-cut pool on the southern end of the main ridge on which Jerusalem was built, served as part of the major water system developed by King Hezekiah (see the note on Joel 1:20, "The Pool of Siloam" on p. 1739 and "Hezekiah's Tunnel" on p. 564). This pool is still in existence today.
9:13 For "Pharisees," see the notes on Matthew 3:7 and Luke 5:17.
9:14 See the note on Mark 3:2, as well as "Sabbath, Sabbath Year and the Jubilee" on page 189.
9:22 Excommunication was reported as early as the time of Ezra (10:8), but there is practically no information about the way it was practiced in New Testament times. The synagogue was the center of Jewish community life (see the notes on Mk 1:21 and Lk 21:12; see also "Ancient Synagogues" on p. 1783), so excommunication cut a person off from many social relationships (though, in some forms, at least in later times, not from worship).

9:28 [z]Jn 5:45
9:29 [a]Jn 8:14
9:31 [b]Ge 18:23-32; Ps 34:15,16; 66:18; 145:19,20; Pr 15:29; Isa 1:15; 59:1,2; Jn 15:7; Jas 5:16-18; 1Jn 5:14,15
9:33 [c]ver 16; Jn 3:2
9:34 [d]ver 2 [e]ver 22,35; Isa 66:5
9:36 [f]Ro 10:14
9:37 [g]Jn 4:26
9:38 [h]Mt 28:9
9:39 [i]Jn 5:22 [j]Jn 3:19 [k]Lk 4:18 [l]Mt 13:13
9:40 [m]Ro 2:19
9:41 [n]Jn 15:22, 24
10:2 [o]ver 11,14

28 Then they hurled insults at him and said, "You are this fellow's disciple! We are disciples of Moses![z]
29 We know that God spoke to Moses, but as for this fellow, we don't even know where he comes from."[a]
30 The man answered, "Now that is remarkable! You don't know where he comes from, yet he opened
my eyes. 31 We know that God does not listen to sinners. He listens to the godly man who does his will.[b]
32 Nobody has ever heard of opening the eyes of a man born blind. 33 If this man were not from God,[c] he
could do nothing."
34 To this they replied, "You were steeped in sin at birth;[d] how dare you lecture us!" And they threw him
out.[e]

Spiritual Blindness

35 Jesus heard that they had thrown him out, and when he found him, he said, "Do you believe in the
Son of Man?"
36 "Who is he, sir?" the man asked. "Tell me so that I may believe in him."[f]
37 Jesus said, "You have now seen him; in fact, he is the one speaking with you."[g]
38 Then the man said, "Lord, I believe," and he worshiped him.[h]
39 Jesus said, "For judgment[i] I have come into this world,[j] so that the blind will see[k] and those who
see will become blind."[l]
40 Some Pharisees who were with him heard him say this and asked, "What? Are we blind too?"[m]
41 Jesus said, "If you were blind, you would not be guilty of sin; but now that you claim you can see, your
guilt remains.[n]

The Shepherd and His Flock

10 "I tell you the truth, the man who does not enter the sheep pen by the gate, but climbs in by some
other way, is a thief and a robber. 2 The man who enters by the gate is the shepherd of his sheep.[o]

9:34 "Threw him out" may mean "excommunicated him" (see the note on v. 22).
9:40 The Pharisees found it incredible that anyone would consider them spiritually blind (see the notes on Mt 3:7; Lk 5:17).
10:1–30 These verses should be understood in light of the Old Testament concept of a "shepherd" as a royal caretaker of God's people. The concept of a ruler being the "shepherd" of his nation and its people was common in the ancient Near East (see the note on Isa 44:28; see also "Shepherding in the Ancient World" on p. 1363).
10:1 The sheep pen was an enclosure with only one entrance. Its walls kept the sheep from wandering away.

ARCHAEOLOGICAL SITES

THE POOL OF SILOAM

JOHN 9 The water of the Pool of Siloam in Jerusalem was regarded as sacred. According to rabbinic tradition, during the celebration of the Feast of Booths water was drawn from the pool into a golden vessel and carried in procession to the temple (cf. Jn 7).[1] Jesus instructed the man born blind to wash in this same pool (9:1–7), although it was Jesus—the source of "living water" (7:38)—who did the healing.

The question of where the Pool of Siloam was located has been examined on the basis of reports from the Bible, Josephus, ancient pilgrims and archaeological findings. There were actually two pools. The first, the "Lower" or older "Pool of Shiloah" (cf. Isa 8:6; 22:9–11) collected water from the Gihon Spring, east of the city, via a short channel. The second, or "Upper" Pool, also received water from the Gihon Spring, but it came through an underground tunnel that had been cut through rock by King Hezekiah around 701 B.C.[2] Hezekiah strategically situated the Upper Pool within the city walls to serve as a secure water supply. The Lower Pool would have been located outside the city of his day. There is some dispute about which pool, the Upper or the Lower, was the "Siloam Pool" of Jesus' day, although it was probably the Upper Pool. Today the Upper Pool is known as the Siloam Pool, while the Lower Pool is dry.

[1]See "The Festivals of Israel" on page 186. [2]See "Hezekiah's Tunnel" on page 564.

[3]The watchman opens the gate for him, and the sheep listen to his voice.[p] He calls his own sheep by name
and leads them out. [4]When he has brought out all his own, he goes on ahead of them, and his sheep fol-
low him because they know his voice. [5]But they will never follow a stranger; in fact, they will run away
from him because they do not recognize a stranger's voice." [6]Jesus used this figure of speech,[q] but they
did not understand what he was telling them.

[7]Therefore Jesus said again, "I tell you the truth, I am the gate for the sheep. [8]All who ever came be-
fore me[r] were thieves and robbers, but the sheep did not listen to them. [9]I am the gate; whoever enters
through me will be saved.[a] He will come in and go out, and find pasture. [10]The thief comes only to steal
and kill and destroy; I have come that they may have life, and have it to the full.

[11]"I am the good shepherd.[s] The good shepherd lays down his life for the sheep.[t] [12]The hired hand is
not the shepherd who owns the sheep. So when he sees the wolf coming, he abandons the sheep and runs
away.[u] Then the wolf attacks the flock and scatters it. [13]The man runs away because he is a hired hand
and cares nothing for the sheep.

[14]"I am the good shepherd;[v] I know my sheep[w] and my sheep know me— [15]just as the Father knows
me and I know the Father[x]—and I lay down my life for the sheep. [16]I have other sheep[y] that are not of
this sheep pen. I must bring them also. They too will listen to my voice, and there shall be one flock[z] and

[a] 9 Or *kept safe*

10:3 [p]ver 4,5,14,16,27
10:6 [q]Jn 16:25
10:8 [r]Jer 23:1,2
10:11 [s]ver 14; Isa 40:11; Eze 34:11-16,23; Heb 13:20; 1Pe 5:4; Rev 7:17 [t]Jn 15:13; 1Jn 3:16
10:12 [u]Zec 11:16,17
10:14 [v]ver 11 [w]ver 27
10:15 [x]Mt 11:27
10:16 [y]Isa 56:8 [z]Jn 11:52; Eph 2:11-19

10:3–4 The watchman was apparently in charge of a large sheep pen, where several flocks were kept.

Shepherds in the Holy Land led their sheep (as opposed to driving them) and did not call sheep randomly, calling instead only those that belonged to them. The sheep responded to the voice of their own shepherd and followed only him.

ARCHAEOLOGICAL SITES

BETHANY ON THE OTHER SIDE OF THE JORDAN

JOHN 10 After a particularly difficult exchange with the Jews, Jesus escaped to the area on the eastern side of the Jordan River, "to the place where John had been baptizing"[1] (Jn 10:40). The name of this location is given in 1:28 in the NIV as "Bethany on the other side of the Jordan." Early pilgrims claimed that a place called Sapsaphas, north of the Dead Sea and east of the Jordan River, was the site at which Jesus was baptized and that a church there was dedicated to John the Baptist. Interestingly, the pilgrims also identified a hill in this vicinity as the point from which Elijah had been taken up to heaven in a chariot of fire (2Ki 2:1–14), perhaps mistakenly associating the first Elijah with John the Baptist, who was commonly called the second Elijah (Mt 11:14; 17:11–13; Lk 1:17). A place called Beth-abara (a possible variant name for Bethany) is shown on the sixth-century mosaic **Madaba map**, where it is labeled "Ainon (spring) where now is Sapsaphas."

Ancient Sapsaphas has been identified as Wadi el-Kharrar, a small riverbed slightly over 1 mile (1.6 km) long, 5 miles (8 km) north of the Dead Sea. Investigations there have located "Elijah's hill" at Tell el-Kharrar at the beginning of the wadi, about 1 mile from the Jordan River. Excavations at the hill have revealed three churches, three caves and three baptismal pools from the **Roman** and **Byzantine periods**. Approximately 330 yards (302 m) from the Jordan River there is indeed a church, identified by the excavators as the Church of Saint John the Baptist that was mentioned by the early pilgrims—the traditional site of Jesus' baptism (Jn 1:29–34).

Other scholars have suggested that the term "Bethany" is rather to be identified with the region of Batanea in the northern **Transjordan**. This suggests that Bethany ("Bethany beyond Jordan" on "Map 9") "on the other side of the Jordan" was a region, not a town. Some Jewish writings attest to possible linguistic links between the names Bethany and Batanea. In the generations immediately preceding Jesus' birth, pious Jewish sects moved into this area, many of whom were anticipating the coming of God's Anointed One from the north.[2] That John the Baptist could have begun his ministry among or have been associated with one or more of these groups is not unreasonable.

[1]See "Baptism in the Ancient World" on page 1562; see also Glossary on page 2080 for definitions of bolded words. [2]See "Jewish Eschatology in the First Century A.D." on page 1846.

10:16 [a]Eze 37:24; 1Pe 2:25 **10:17** [b]ver 11,15, 18 **10:18** [c]Mt 26:53 [d]Jn 15:10; Php 2:8; Heb 5:8 **10:19** [e]Jn 7:43; 9:16 **10:20** [f]Jn 7:20 [g]Mk 3:21 **10:21** [h]Mt 4:24 [i]Ex 4:11; Jn 9:32, 33

one shepherd.[a] 17 The reason my Father loves me is that I lay down my life[b]—only to take it up again. 18 No
one takes it from me, but I lay it down of my own accord.[c] I have authority to lay it down and authority
to take it up again. This command I received from my Father."[d]
19 At these words the Jews were again divided.[e] 20 Many of them said, "He is demon-possessed[f] and
raving mad.[g] Why listen to him?"
21 But others said, "These are not the sayings of a man possessed by a demon.[h] Can a demon open the
eyes of the blind?"[i]

ARCHAEOLOGICAL SITES

THE RABBIS' TEACHING STEPS AT THE SOUTHERN WALL EXCAVATIONS

JOHN 10 Those who came to worship at the temple of Herod approached from the southern precinct of Jerusalem.[1] Various routes converged into a large, stone-paved plaza under the shadow of an imposing southern **retaining wall** that was crowned with the rising spires of the royal **portico** (Lk 4:9; Josephus, *Antiquities*, 15.11.5). The plaza contained a number of ritual baths and served both as a significant center of public life and as a gathering place for the swelling crowds who made their way up to Jerusalem during the pilgrimage festivals.[2] Massive stairways rose from the plaza toward two arched gates built into the southern wall.

The largest of these monumental staircases was uncovered in 1968 and has been restored to much of its original splendor. It measures 215 feet (157 m) wide and rises some 22 feet (6.7 m) via 30 steps of trimmed and smoothed stone paving blocks. The width and spacing of the steps has led some to conjecture that the stairways were built to correspond to the rhythmic patterns that characterize the Psalms of Ascent (i.e., Ps 120–134). From these steps teachers could address those who had assembled in the plaza; it is probable that Jesus taught from this vantage point, even though the Gospels explicitly refer only to his teaching from the porticoes standing on the temple mount itself (Jn 10:23).

Excavations at the southern temple mount and the southern temple mount steps

Photographs: © Todd Bolen/Bible Places.com

[1]See "Herod's Temple" on page 1648. [2]See "The Festivals of Israel" on page 186.

The Unbelief of the Jews

22 Then came the Feast of Dedication[a] at Jerusalem. It was winter, 23 and Jesus was in the temple area
walking in Solomon's Colonnade.[j] 24 The Jews[k] gathered around him, saying, "How long will you keep us
in suspense? If you are the Christ,[b] tell us plainly."[l]
25 Jesus answered, "I did tell you,[m] but you do not believe. The miracles I do in my Father's name speak
for me,[n] 26 but you do not believe because you are not my sheep.[o] 27 My sheep listen to my voice; I know
them,[p] and they follow me.[q] 28 I give them eternal life, and they shall never perish; no one can snatch
them out of my hand.[r] 29 My Father, who has given them to me,[s] is greater than all[c];[t] no one can snatch
them out of my Father's hand. 30 I and the Father are one."[u]
31 Again the Jews picked up stones to stone him,[v] 32 but Jesus said to them, "I have shown you many
great miracles from the Father. For which of these do you stone me?"
33 "We are not stoning you for any of these," replied the Jews, "but for blasphemy, because you, a mere
man, claim to be God."[w]
34 Jesus answered them, "Is it not written in your Law,[x] 'I have said you are gods'[d]?[y] 35 If he called
them 'gods,' to whom the word of God came—and the Scripture cannot be broken— 36 what about the
one whom the Father set apart[z] as his very own[a] and sent into the world?[b] Why then do you accuse me
of blasphemy because I said, 'I am God's Son'?[c] 37 Do not believe me unless I do what my Father does.[d]
38 But if I do it, even though you do not believe me, believe the miracles, that you may know and under-
stand that the Father is in me, and I in the Father."[e] 39 Again they tried to seize him,[f] but he escaped
their grasp.[g]
40 Then Jesus went back across the Jordan[h] to the place where John had been baptizing in the early
days. Here he stayed 41 and many people came to him. They said, "Though John never performed a mi-
raculous sign,[i] all that John said about this man was true."[j] 42 And in that place many believed in Jesus.[k]

The Death of Lazarus

11 Now a man named Lazarus was sick. He was from Bethany,[l] the village of Mary and her sister
Martha.[m] 2 This Mary, whose brother Lazarus now lay sick, was the same one who poured per-
fume on the Lord and wiped his feet with her hair.[n] 3 So the sisters sent word to Jesus, "Lord, the one you
love[o] is sick."
4 When he heard this, Jesus said, "This sickness will not end in death. No, it is for God's glory[p] so that
God's Son may be glorified through it." 5 Jesus loved Martha and her sister and Lazarus. 6 Yet when he
heard that Lazarus was sick, he stayed where he was two more days.
7 Then he said to his disciples, "Let us go back to Judea."[q]
8 "But Rabbi,"[r] they said, "a short while ago the Jews tried to stone you,[s] and yet you are going back
there?"
9 Jesus answered, "Are there not twelve hours of daylight? A man who walks by day will not stumble,
for he sees by this world's light.[t] 10 It is when he walks by night that he stumbles, for he has no light."
11 After he had said this, he went on to tell them, "Our friend[u] Lazarus has fallen asleep;[v] but I am go-
ing there to wake him up."
12 His disciples replied, "Lord, if he sleeps, he will get better." 13 Jesus had been speaking of his death,
but his disciples thought he meant natural sleep.[w]
14 So then he told them plainly, "Lazarus is dead, 15 and for your sake I am glad I was not there, so that
you may believe. But let us go to him."
16 Then Thomas[x] (called Didymus) said to the rest of the disciples, "Let us also go, that we may die with
him."

10:23 [j]Ac 3:11; 5:12
10:24 [k]Jn 1:19 [l]Jn 16:25,29
10:25 [m]Jn 8:58 [n]Jn 5:36
10:26 [o]Jn 8:47
10:27 [p]ver 14 [q]ver 4
10:28 [r]Jn 6:39
10:29 [s]Jn 17:2,6, 24 [t]Jn 14:28
10:30 [u]Jn 17:21-23
10:31 [v]Jn 8:59
10:33 [w]Lev 24:16; Jn 5:18
10:34 [x]Jn 8:17; Ro 3:19 [y]Ps 82:6
10:36 [z]Jer 1:5 [a]Jn 6:69 [b]Jn 3:17 [c]Jn 5:17,18
10:37 [d]ver 25; Jn 15:24
10:38 [e]Jn 14:10, 11,20; 17:21
10:39 [f]Jn 7:30 [g]Lk 4:30; Jn 8:59
10:40 [h]Jn 1:28
10:41 [i]Jn 2:11; 3:30 [j]Jn 1:26,27, 30,34
10:42 [k]Jn 7:31
11:1 [l]Mt 21:17 [m]Lk 10:38
11:2 [n]Mk 14:3; Lk 7:38; Jn 12:3
11:3 [o]ver 5,36
11:4 [p]ver 40; Jn 9:3
11:7 [q]Jn 10:40
11:8 [r]Mt 23:7 [s]Jn 8:59; 10:31
11:9 [t]Jn 9:4; 12:35
11:11 [u]ver 3 [v]Ac 7:60
11:13 [w]Mt 9:24
11:16 [x]Mt 10:3; Jn 14:5; 20:24-28; 21:2; Ac 1:13

[a] 22 That is, Hanukkah [b] 24 Or *Messiah* [c] 29 Many early manuscripts *What my Father has given me is greater than all*
[d] 34 Psalm 82:6

10:22 The Feast of Dedication was the commemoration of the dedication of the temple by Judas Maccabeus in December, 165 B.C., after it had been profaned by Antiochus Epiphanes (see "Antiochus IV Epiphanes" on p. 1406 and "The Intertestamental Period" on p. 1551). This was the last great deliverance the Jews had experienced.
10:23 Solomon's Colonnade was a porch along the inner side of the wall enclosing the outer court. It had rows of columns 27 feet (over 8 m) high and a roof of cedar. Somewhat similar to a Greek *stoa* (see "The Ancient City" on p. 1790), it is commonly but erroneously thought to date back to Solomon's time.
10:30–31 Jesus' claim to be "one" with the Father could not have been clearer. In the people's minds, this "blasphemy" demanded death by stoning.
10:34 The "Law" in its strictest sense meant the Pentateuch, but the term was often used, as here, of the whole Old Testament (see "The Old Testament of the Early Church" on p. 1967).
11:2 For "poured perfume," see the note on 12:3.

Jesus Comforts the Sisters

11:17 [y]ver 6,39 — 17On his arrival, Jesus found that Lazarus had already been in the tomb for four days.[y] 18Bethany[z]
11:18 [z]ver 1 — was less than two miles[a] from Jerusalem, 19and many Jews had come to Martha and Mary to comfort
11:19 [a]ver 31; Job 2:11 — them in the loss of their brother.[a] 20When Martha heard that Jesus was coming, she went out to meet
11:20 [b]Lk 10:38-42 — him, but Mary stayed at home.[b]
11:21 [c]ver 32,37 — 21"Lord," Martha said to Jesus, "if you had been here, my brother would not have died.[c] 22But I know
11:22 [d]ver 41,42; Jn 9:31 — that even now God will give you whatever you ask."[d]
23Jesus said to her, "Your brother will rise again."
11:24 [e]Da 12:2; Jn 5:28,29; Ac 24:15 — 24Martha answered, "I know he will rise again in the resurrection[e] at the last day."
11:25 [f]Jn 1:4 — 25Jesus said to her, "I am the resurrection and the life.[f] He who believes in me will live, even though
he dies; 26and whoever lives and believes in me will never die. Do you believe this?"
11:27 [g]Lk 2:11 [h]Mt 16:16 [i]Jn 6:14 — 27"Yes, Lord," she told him, "I believe that you are the Christ,[b][g] the Son of God,[h] who was to come into
the world."[i]
11:28 [j]Mt 26:18; Jn 13:13 — 28And after she had said this, she went back and called her sister Mary aside. "The Teacher[j] is here,"
she said, "and is asking for you." 29When Mary heard this, she got up quickly and went to him. 30Now
11:30 [k]ver 20 — Jesus had not yet entered the village, but was still at the place where Martha had met him.[k] 31When the
11:31 [l]ver 19 — Jews who had been with Mary in the house, comforting her,[l] noticed how quickly she got up and went
out, they followed her, supposing she was going to the tomb to mourn there.
32When Mary reached the place where Jesus was and saw him, she fell at his feet and said, "Lord, if you
11:32 [m]ver 21 — had been here, my brother would not have died."[m]

[a] 18 Greek *fifteen stadia* (about 3 kilometers) [b] 27 Or *Messiah*

11:17 Many Jews believed that the soul remained near the body for three days after death in the hope of returning to it. If this idea was in the minds of these people, they obviously thought that all hope was gone—Lazarus was irrevocably dead.
11:18 For "Bethany," see the note on Matthew 21:17.
11:19 Jewish custom provided for three days of very heavy mourning, then four of heavy mourning, followed by lighter mourning for the remainder of 30 days. It was usual then, as now, for friends to visit the family to comfort them.
11:28 That Martha called Jesus "Teacher" is significant: Rabbis would ordinarily not teach women, although Jesus did so frequently.
11:31 Wailing at a tomb was common, and the Jews immediately assumed that this was in Mary's mind. (See "Sackcloth and Ashes: Rituals of Lamentation" on p. 820 and "Jewish Burial Practices" on p. 1688.)

ARCHAEOLOGICAL SITES

BETHANY AND THE TOMB OF LAZARUS

JOHN 11 The home of Lazarus and his sisters, Mary and Martha, was in Bethany (see "Map 9"), about 2 miles (3.2 km) from Jerusalem on the eastern slope of the Mount of Olives (Jn 11:1,18; according to 1:19–28, there was another Bethany "on the other side of the Jordan," where John the Baptist ministered).[1] The Bethany of Lazarus is today called el-Azariyeh, a name that preserves its association with Lazarus. Because of the close relationship between Jesus and the family of Lazarus, Jesus made Bethany the base of his Jerusalem ministry during Passion Week (Mk 11:11).

Excavations carried out by the Franciscans at Bethany have uncovered the remains of Christian churches dating back to the fourth century A.D. Of particular interest is the tomb of Lazarus. Eusebius remarked that Lazarus's tomb was a pilgrimage site during his day, and the presumed site remains so today. The tomb has been modified: Its original entrance was on the east, but now it is entered from the north side. Although it is impossible to verify that this is in fact the tomb of Lazarus, the tradition for this site is very old and should not be regarded as particularly suspect.

[1]See "Bethany on the Other Side of the Jordan" on page 1740.

33 When Jesus saw her weeping, and the Jews who had come along with her also weeping, he was deep-
ly moved[n] in spirit and troubled.[o] 34 "Where have you laid him?" he asked. 11:33 [n]ver 38
"Come and see, Lord," they replied. [o]Jn 12:27
35 Jesus wept.[p] 11:35 [p]Lk 19:41
36 Then the Jews said, "See how he loved him!"[q] 11:36 [q]ver 3
37 But some of them said, "Could not he who opened the eyes of the blind man[r] have kept this man 11:37 [r]Jn 9:6,7
from dying?"[s] [s]ver 21,32

Jesus Raises Lazarus From the Dead

38 Jesus, once more deeply moved,[t] came to the tomb. It was a cave with a stone laid across the en- 11:38 [t]ver 33
trance.[u] 39 "Take away the stone," he said. [u]Mt 27:60;
"But, Lord," said Martha, the sister of the dead man, "by this time there is a bad odor, for he has been Lk 24:2; Jn 20:1
there four days."[v] 11:39 [v]ver 17
40 Then Jesus said, "Did I not tell you that if you believed,[w] you would see the glory of God?"[x] 11:40 [w]ver 23-25
41 So they took away the stone. Then Jesus looked up[y] and said, "Father,[z] I thank you that you have [x]ver 4 11:41 [y]Jn 17:1
heard me. 42 I knew that you always hear me, but I said this for the benefit of the people standing here,[a] [z]Mt 11:25 11:42 [a]Jn 12:30
that they may believe that you sent me."[b] [b]Jn 3:17
43 When he had said this, Jesus called in a loud voice, "Lazarus, come out!"[c] 44 The dead man came 11:43 [c]Lk 7:14
out, his hands and feet wrapped with strips of linen,[d] and a cloth around his face.[e] 11:44 [d]Jn 19:40
Jesus said to them, "Take off the grave clothes and let him go." [e]Jn 20:7

The Plot to Kill Jesus

45 Therefore many of the Jews who had come to visit Mary,[f] and had seen what Jesus did,[g] put their 11:45 [f]ver 19
faith in him.[h] 46 But some of them went to the Pharisees and told them what Jesus had done. 47 Then the [g]Jn 2:23 [h]Ex 14:31;
chief priests and the Pharisees[i] called a meeting[j] of the Sanhedrin.[k] Jn 7:31 11:47 [i]ver 57
"What are we accomplishing?" they asked. "Here is this man performing many miraculous signs.[l] 48 If [j]Mt 26:3 [k]Mt 5:22
we let him go on like this, everyone will believe in him, and then the Romans will come and take away [l]Jn 2:11
both our place[a] and our nation."
49 Then one of them, named Caiaphas,[m] who was high priest that year,[n] spoke up, "You know nothing 11:49 [m]Mt 26:3
at all! 50 You do not realize that it is better for you that one man die for the people than that the whole na- [n]ver 51; Jn 18:13, 14
tion perish."[o] 11:50 [o]Jn 18:14
51 He did not say this on his own, but as high priest that year he prophesied that Jesus would die for
the Jewish nation, 52 and not only for that nation but also for the scattered children of God, to bring them
together and make them one.[p] 53 So from that day on they plotted to take his life.[q] 11:52 [p]Isa 49:6;
54 Therefore Jesus no longer moved about publicly among the Jews.[r] Instead he withdrew to a region Jn 10:16 11:53 [q]Mt 12:14
near the desert, to a village called Ephraim, where he stayed with his disciples. 11:54 [r]Jn 7:1
55 When it was almost time for the Jewish Passover,[s] many went up from the country to Jerusalem for 11:55 [s]Ex 12:13,
their ceremonial cleansing[t] before the Passover. 56 They kept looking for Jesus,[u] and as they stood in the 23,27; Mt 26:1,2; Mk 14:1; Jn 13:1
temple area they asked one another, "What do you think? Isn't he coming to the Feast at all?" 57 But the [t]2Ch 30:17,18 11:56 [u]Jn 7:11
chief priests and Pharisees had given orders that if anyone found out where Jesus was, he should report
it so that they might arrest him.

[a] 48 Or *temple*

11:33 The Greek word for "weeping," used twice in this verse, denotes a loud expression of grief, that is, "wailing."
11:35 The Greek word for "wept" in this verse is not the one for loud grief (as in v. 33) but refers instead to quiet mourning ("shed tears").
11:38 A "cave with a stone laid across the entrance" was a common type of burial place in the Holy Land at this time, especially for the wealthy (see "Bethany and the Tomb of Lazarus" on p. 1743).
11:39 For "four days," see the note on verse 17. See also the note on Matthew 26:12, "Jewish Burial Practices" on page 1688 and "Perfumes and Anointing Oils" on page 1746.
11:44 The "strips of linen" were narrow, like bandages. Sometimes a shroud, like a large sheet, was used. The "cloth around his face" was a separate item.
11:47 In all four Gospels, the Pharisees appear as Jesus' principal opponents throughout his public ministry (see the notes on Mt 3:7; Lk 5:17). But they lacked political power, and it was the chief priests (see the note on Mt 2:4) who were prominent in the events that led to Jesus' crucifixion.
11:49 For information on Caiaphas, see the note on Matthew 26:3; see also "The High Priests Annas and Caiaphas" on page 1772 and "The Jewish Priesthood and Religious Life in the First Century A.D." on page 1704.

Caiaphas was a Sadducee (see the note on Mt 3:7). Josephus noted that Sadducees "in their intercourse with their peers [were] as rude as to aliens" (*Wars*, 2.8.14).
11:54 After Lazarus's raising, Jesus withdrew to Ephraim, most likely a small town about 12 miles (19 km) north of Jerusalem. But as the Passover approached he returned to Bethany (12:1).
11:55 Being ceremonially clean was especially important at a time like Passover (see "Ritual Purity in Israel and the Ancient Near East" on p. 166 and "The Passover" on p. 656). Otherwise, it would not have been possible to keep the Feast (see the notes on 2:6; 18:28).

Jesus Anointed at Bethany

12:1 [v]Jn 11:55 [w]Mt 21:17 12 Six days before the Passover,[v] Jesus arrived at Bethany,[w] where Lazarus lived, whom Jesus had
12:2 [x]Lk 10:38-42 raised from the dead. 2 Here a dinner was given in Jesus' honor. Martha served,[x] while Lazarus
was among those reclining at the table with him. 3 Then Mary took about a pint[a] of pure nard, an expen-
12:3 [y]Mk 14:3 [z]Jn 11:2 sive perfume;[y] she poured it on Jesus' feet and wiped his feet with her hair.[z] And the house was filled
with the fragrance of the perfume.
12:4 [a]Mt 10:4 4 But one of his disciples, Judas Iscariot, who was later to betray him,[a] objected, 5 "Why wasn't this
perfume sold and the money given to the poor? It was worth a year's wages.[b]" 6 He did not say this be-
12:6 [b]Jn 13:29 cause he cared about the poor but because he was a thief; as keeper of the money bag,[b] he used to help
himself to what was put into it.
7 "Leave her alone," Jesus replied. "⌊It was intended⌋ that she should save this perfume for the day of
12:7 [c]Jn 19:40 12:8 [d]Dt 15:11 my burial.[c] 8 You will always have the poor among you,[d] but you will not always have me."
9 Meanwhile a large crowd of Jews found out that Jesus was there and came, not only because of him
12:9 [e]Jn 11:43, 44 but also to see Lazarus, whom he had raised from the dead.[e] 10 So the chief priests made plans to kill
12:11 [f]ver 17,18; Jn 11:45 [g]Jn 7:31 Lazarus as well, 11 for on account of him[f] many of the Jews were going over to Jesus and putting their
faith in him.[g]

The Triumphal Entry

12 The next day the great crowd that had come for the Feast heard that Jesus was on his way to Jeru-
salem. 13 They took palm branches and went out to meet him, shouting,

"Hosanna![c]"

12:13 [h]Ps 118:25,26 [i]Jn 1:49 "Blessed is he who comes in the name of the Lord!"[d][h]

"Blessed is the King of Israel!"[i]

14 Jesus found a young donkey and sat upon it, as it is written,

15 "Do not be afraid, O Daughter of Zion;
see, your king is coming,
12:15 [j]Zec 9:9 seated on a donkey's colt."[e][j]

12:16 [k]Mk 9:32 [l]Jn 2:22; 7:39; 14:26 16 At first his disciples did not understand all this.[k] Only after Jesus was glorified[l] did they realize that
these things had been written about him and that they had done these things to him.
12:17 [m]Jn 11:42 17 Now the crowd that was with him[m] when he called Lazarus from the tomb and raised him from the
dead continued to spread the word. 18 Many people, because they had heard that he had given this mirac-
12:18 [n]ver 11 ulous sign,[n] went out to meet him. 19 So the Pharisees said to one another, "See, this is getting us nowhere.
12:19 [o]Jn 11:47, 48 Look how the whole world has gone after him!"[o]

Jesus Predicts His Death

12:20 [p]Jn 7:35; Ac 11:20 20 Now there were some Greeks[p] among those who went up to worship at the Feast. 21 They came to
12:21 [q]Mt 11:21; Jn 1:44 Philip, who was from Bethsaida[q] in Galilee, with a request. "Sir," they said, "we would like to see Jesus."
22 Philip went to tell Andrew; Andrew and Philip in turn told Jesus.

[a] 3 Greek *a litra* (probably about 0.5 liter) [b] 5 Greek *three hundred denarii* [c] 13 A Hebrew expression meaning "Save!" which became an exclamation of praise [d] 13 Psalm 118:25,26 [e] 15 Zech. 9:9

12:1 For "Bethany," see the note on Matthew 21:17.
12:3 "Nard" is the name of both a plant and the fragrant oil it yielded. Since it was exorbitantly expensive, Mary's act of devotion was costly—the pint (473 ml) of nard would have cost about a year's wage for a day-laborer. Her action was also unusual, both because she poured the oil on Jesus' feet (normally it was poured on the head) and because she used her hair to wipe them (a respectable woman did not unbind her hair in public).
12:4 For "Iscariot," see the note on Mark 3:19.
12:5 It was a Jewish custom to give gifts to the poor on the evening of Passover.
12:7 Perfume was normally associated with festivity, but it was also used in burials. For New Testament burial practices, see the note on Matthew 26:12. See also "Jewish Burial Practices" on page 1688 and "Perfumes and Anointing Oils" on page 1746.
12:12 During the Passover and the week-long Feast of Unleavened Bread, the population of Jerusalem increased from about fifty thousand to several hundred thousand.
12:13 Palm branches were used in celebrations of victory (see "Palm Branches in Israel" on p. 2056). For "Hosanna!" see the note on Matthew 21:9.
12:14 See "A King Riding on a Donkey: Cultural/Political Significance in the Ancient Near East" on page 1596.
12:19 For "Pharisees," see the notes on Matthew 3:7 and Luke 5:17.
12:20 "Greeks" probably refers to "God-fearers," people attracted to Judaism by its monotheism and morality but repelled by its nationalism and requirements such as circumcision. They worshiped in the synagogues but did not become proselytes (cf. the note on Ac 16:14).
12:21 For "Bethsaida," see the note on Mark 8:22.

23 Jesus replied, "The hour has come for the Son of Man to be glorified.[r] 24 I tell you the truth, unless a
kernel of wheat falls to the ground and dies,[s] it remains only a single seed. But if it dies, it produces many
seeds. 25 The man who loves his life will lose it, while the man who hates his life in this world will keep
it[t] for eternal life. 26 Whoever serves me must follow me; and where I am, my servant also will be.[u] My
Father will honor the one who serves me.
27 "Now my heart is troubled,[v] and what shall I say? 'Father,[w] save me from this hour'?[x] No, it was for
this very reason I came to this hour. 28 Father, glorify your name!"

12:23 [r] Jn 13:32; 17:1
12:24 [s] 1Co 15:36
12:25 [t] Mt 10:39; Mk 8:35; Lk 14:26
12:26 [u] Jn 14:3; 17:24; 2Co 5:8; 1Th 4:17
12:27 [v] Mt 26:38, 39; Jn 11:33,38; 13:21 [w] Mt 11:25 [x] ver 23

Perfumes and Anointing Oils

Rotary olive crusher

Preserving Bible Times; © Dr. James C. Martin; permission of Eretz Israel Museum

JOHN 12 For several reasons people in the ancient world devoted great attention to the use of fragrances, perfumes and anointing oils:

✣ They were keenly aware of the presence and suggestive powers of odors. Perfumes had a cosmetic function and served as an aphrodisiac (e.g., SS 1:12–13), but there was also a kind of sacred perfume formula that was to be used only on Israel's priests and sanctuary objects (Ex 30:22–33).

✣ Oils served a hygienic purpose prior to the invention of soap and shampoo (e.g., anointing the scalp with oils killed head lice).

✣ Oils were used medicinally. Greek physicians regularly massaged patients and athletes with oil, and James 5:14 recommends anointing the sick with oil.[1]

✣ Perfumes and spices were used for special purposes, such as for embalming the dead (Jn 19:39–40).[2]

Most perfumes originated from plant sources. Examples include frankincense, myrrh, nard, saffron, aloes and calamus. Since none of these spices and fragrances were indigenous to the region of the Holy Land, they had to be imported from Arabia, Iran, India and elsewhere. These perfumes were therefore extravagantly expensive, as John 12:3–5 suggests.

The primary source of oil was the olive tree, which was widely cultivated throughout the Mediterranean world. In Greco-Roman times oils were scented with the fragrances of narcissus, cinnamon, saffron and other plants, and people regularly anointed themselves after a bath.[3] Fragrances were obtained in a variety of ways, depending upon the nature of the plant source (be it a root, flower, bark secretion, etc.), but often the raw material was either distilled or in some way pressed or crushed. The attention the New Testament gives to these ointments reflects something of the values of the culture of that time.

[1] See "Disease and Medicine in the Ancient World" on page 1674. [2] See "Jewish Burial Practices" on page 1688. [3] See "Bathing" on page 456.

Olive basket

Preserving Bible Times; © Dr. James C. Martin; permission of Eretz Israel Museum

12:28 [y]Mt 3:17 — Then a voice came from heaven,[y] "I have glorified it, and will glorify it again." 29 The crowd that was
there and heard it said it had thundered; others said an angel had spoken to him.
12:30 [z]Jn 11:42 12:31 [a]Jn 16:11 — 30 Jesus said, "This voice was for your benefit,[z] not mine. 31 Now is the time for judgment on this world;[a]
[b]Jn 14:30; 16:11; — now the prince of this world[b] will be driven out. 32 But I, when I am lifted up from the earth,[c] will draw
2Co 4:4; Eph 2:2; 1Jn 4:4 — all men to myself."[d] 33 He said this to show the kind of death he was going to die.[e]
12:32 [c]ver 34; Jn 3:14; 8:28 — 34 The crowd spoke up, "We have heard from the Law that the Christ[a] will remain forever,[f] so how can
[d]Jn 6:44 12:33 [e]Jn 18:32 — you say, 'The Son of Man[g] must be lifted up'?[h] Who is this 'Son of Man'?"
12:34 [f]Ps 110:4; Isa 9:7; — 35 Then Jesus told them, "You are going to have the light[i] just a little while longer. Walk while you have
Eze 37:25; Da 7:14 [g]Mt 8:20 — the light,[j] before darkness overtakes you.[k] The man who walks in the dark does not know where he is go-
[h]Jn 3:14 12:35 [i]ver 46 — ing. 36 Put your trust in the light while you have it, so that you may become sons of light."[l] When he had
[j]Eph 5:8 [k]1Jn 2:11 — finished speaking, Jesus left and hid himself from them.[m]

12:36 [l]Lk 16:8 [m]Jn 8:59

The Jews Continue in Their Unbelief

12:37 [n]Jn 2:11 — 37 Even after Jesus had done all these miraculous signs[n] in their presence, they still would not believe
in him. 38 This was to fulfill the word of Isaiah the prophet:

> "Lord, who has believed our message
> and to whom has the arm of the Lord been revealed?"[b] [o]

12:38 [o]Isa 53:1; Ro 10:16

39 For this reason they could not believe, because, as Isaiah says elsewhere:

> 40 "He has blinded their eyes
> and deadened their hearts,
> so they can neither see with their eyes,
> nor understand with their hearts,
> nor turn—and I would heal them."[c] [p]

12:40 [p]Isa 6:10; Mt 13:13,15

12:41 [q]Isa 6:1-4 [r]Lk 24:27 — 41 Isaiah said this because he saw Jesus' glory[q] and spoke about him.[r]
12:42 [s]ver 11; Jn 7:48 [t]Jn 7:13 — 42 Yet at the same time many even among the leaders believed in him.[s] But because of the Pharisees[t]
[u]Jn 9:22 — they would not confess their faith for fear they would be put out of the synagogue;[u] 43 for they loved praise
12:43 [v]Jn 5:44 — from men more than praise from God.[v]
44 Then Jesus cried out, "When a man believes in me, he does not believe in me only, but in the one who
12:44 [w]Mt 10:40; Jn 5:24 — sent me.[w] 45 When he looks at me, he sees the one who sent me.[x] 46 I have come into the world as a light,[y]
12:45 [x]Jn 14:9 — so that no one who believes in me should stay in darkness.
12:46 [y]Jn 1:4; 3:19; 8:12; 9:5 — 47 "As for the person who hears my words but does not keep them, I do not judge him. For I did not
12:47 [z]Jn 3:17 — come to judge the world, but to save it.[z] 48 There is a judge for the one who rejects me and does not ac-
12:48 [a]Jn 5:45 — cept my words; that very word which I spoke will condemn him[a] at the last day. 49 For I did not speak of
12:49 [b]Jn 14:31 — my own accord, but the Father who sent me commanded me[b] what to say and how to say it. 50 I know
that his command leads to eternal life. So whatever I say is just what the Father has told me to say."

Jesus Washes His Disciples' Feet

13:1 [c]Jn 11:55 — **13** It was just before the Passover Feast.[c] Jesus knew that the time had come[d] for him to leave this
[d]Jn 12:23 [e]Jn 16:28 — world and go to the Father.[e] Having loved his own who were in the world, he now showed them
the full extent of his love.[d]
2 The evening meal was being served, and the devil had already prompted Judas Iscariot, son of Simon,
13:3 [f]Mt 28:18 — to betray Jesus. 3 Jesus knew that the Father had put all things under his power,[f] and that he had come
[g]Jn 8:42; 16:27, 28,30 — from God[g] and was returning to God; 4 so he got up from the meal, took off his outer clothing, and
wrapped a towel around his waist. 5 After that, he poured water into a basin and began to wash his dis-
13:5 [h]Lk 7:44 — ciples' feet,[h] drying them with the towel that was wrapped around him.

[a] 34 Or *Messiah* [b] 38 Isaiah 53:1 [c] 40 Isaiah 6:10 [d] 1 Or *he loved them to the last*

12:34 The "Law" here seems to mean the Old Testament Scripture in general (see "The Old Testament of the Early Church" on p. 1967).

12:42 Many Jewish leaders believed in Jesus, though they remained secret devotees for fear of excommunication (see the note on 9:22). Two such cases in this Gospel are Nicodemus and Joseph of Arimathea (see 3:12; 19:38–39).

13:1 See "The Passover" on page 656.

13:5 The people of Jesus' time walked the dusty roads shod only in sandals, and their feet became dirt-encrusted. Etiquette demanded that, when a traveler entered a home as a guest, the host provide for the washing of his or her feet. This distasteful chore was generally delegated to the lowliest servant in the household (see the note on 1:27).

[6]He came to Simon Peter, who said to him, "Lord, are you going to wash my feet?"
[7]Jesus replied, "You do not realize now what I am doing, but later you will understand."[i] 13:7 [i]ver 12
[8]"No," said Peter, "you shall never wash my feet."
Jesus answered, "Unless I wash you, you have no part with me."
[9]"Then, Lord," Simon Peter replied, "not just my feet but my hands and my head as well!"
[10]Jesus answered, "A person who has had a bath needs only to wash his feet; his whole body is clean.
And you are clean,[j] though not every one of you." [11]For he knew who was going to betray him, and that 13:10 [j]Jn 15:3
was why he said not every one was clean.
[12]When he had finished washing their feet, he put on his clothes and returned to his place. "Do you
understand what I have done for you?" he asked them. [13]"You call me 'Teacher'[k] and 'Lord,'[l] and rightly 13:13 [k]Jn 11:28 [l]Lk 6:46; 1Co 12:3; Php 2:11
so, for that is what I am. [14]Now that I, your Lord and Teacher, have washed your feet, you also should
wash one another's feet.[m] [15]I have set you an example that you should do as I have done for you.[n] [16]I tell 13:14 [m]1Pe 5:5 13:15 [n]Mt 11:29
you the truth, no servant is greater than his master,[o] nor is a messenger greater than the one who sent 13:16 [o]Mt 10:24; Lk 6:40; Jn 15:20
him. [17]Now that you know these things, you will be blessed if you do them.[p] 13:17 [p]Mt 7:24, 25; Lk 11:28; Jas 1:25

Jesus Predicts His Betrayal

[18]"I am not referring to all of you;[q] I know those I have chosen.[r] But this is to fulfill the scripture: 'He
who shares my bread[s] has lifted up his heel[t] against me.'[a][u] 13:18 [q]ver 10 [r]Jn 15:16,19 [s]Mt 26:23 [t]Jn 6:70 [u]Ps 41:9

[a] *18* Psalm 41:9

13:10 A man would bathe himself before going to a feast (see "Bathing" on p. 456). When he arrived, he needed only to wash his feet to be considered entirely clean again.

13:18 To eat bread together was a mark of close fellowship.

ARCHAEOLOGICAL SITES

TRICLINIA

JOHN 13 The *triclinium* (plural *triclinia*) was the dining room in a Roman house. Some of the finest examples of *triclinia* have been excavated at Pompeii in the houses identified with Menander, Pansa, Castor and Pollux and the Golden Cupids.[1] In wealthier homes the walls of triclinia were often adorned with ornate frescoes of mythological or pastoral scenes. The room was typically placed such that it afforded a view of the garden, creating a scenic backdrop for the dining experience. It had an oblong shape and featured long couches placed along three of its walls; hence its name. The couch frames were usually made of wood with bronze adornments. Leather straps crisscrossed the open bottoms of the frames and supported stuffed cushions. The diners reclined on their left sides, freeing their right hands to take food from the low table in the center of the room.

The traditional Roman dinner party (*convivium*) involved nine guests, with three persons apiece on each of three couches. These would be arranged in three sides of a square, with entertainment taking place in the open space. Since multiple diners occupied each couch, each person would place his or her head close to the table and then angle the rest of the body away. The bodies of the diners, then, overlapped, with the head of one diner situated next to the chest of the adjacent guest (their feet were angled back and away from the table). For this reason, according to the historian Pliny, one diner was said to lie "in the bosom" of the other. The historian Livy recorded that a type of hierarchy developed in this reclining system. The inferior person's head lay near the torso of the superior.

By New Testament times many Jews had adopted the Roman style of dining.[2] The account of the Last Supper in John 13 suggests that Jesus and the disciples were following this custom in a modified form. The Last Supper was not a *convivium* meal but a Passover, and there had to be room for all of Jesus' inner circle of 12.[3] There was, of course, no entertainment, and so it may have been the case that four couches were arranged around a central table. The 13 diners were reclining as they ate, and John is said to have been leaning against the breast of Jesus, who was naturally in the position of a superior. John's position next to Jesus suggests that he was Jesus' closest friend, which is indeed implied in the narrative (v. 23).

[1]See "Pompeii" on page 1857. [2]See "Jewish Meals and Meal Customs" on page 1575. [3]See "The Last Supper and the Passover" on page 1611.

19 “I am telling you now before it happens, so that when it does happen you will believe[v] that I am
He.[w] 20 I tell you the truth, whoever accepts anyone I send accepts me; and whoever accepts me accepts
the one who sent me.”[x]
21 After he had said this, Jesus was troubled in spirit[y] and testified, “I tell you the truth, one of you is
going to betray me.”[z]
22 His disciples stared at one another, at a loss to know which of them he meant. 23 One of them, the dis-
ciple whom Jesus loved,[a] was reclining next to him. 24 Simon Peter motioned to this disciple and said,
“Ask him which one he means.”
25 Leaning back against Jesus, he asked him, “Lord, who is it?”[b]
26 Jesus answered, “It is the one to whom I will give this piece of bread when I have dipped it in the
dish.” Then, dipping the piece of bread, he gave it to Judas Iscariot, son of Simon. 27 As soon as Judas took
the bread, Satan entered into him.[c]
“What you are about to do, do quickly,” Jesus told him, 28 but no one at the meal understood why Jesus
said this to him. 29 Since Judas had charge of the money,[d] some thought Jesus was telling him to buy what
was needed for the Feast, or to give something to the poor. 30 As soon as Judas had taken the bread, he went
out. And it was night.[e]

Jesus Predicts Peter’s Denial

31 When he was gone, Jesus said, “Now is the Son of Man glorified[f] and God is glorified in him.[g] 32 If
God is glorified in him,[a] God will glorify the Son in himself,[h] and will glorify him at once.
33 “My children, I will be with you only a little longer. You will look for me, and just as I told the Jews,
so I tell you now: Where I am going, you cannot come.[i]
34 “A new command[j] I give you: Love one another.[k] As I have loved you, so you must love one anoth-
er.[l] 35 By this all men will know that you are my disciples, if you love one another.”[m]
36 Simon Peter asked him, “Lord, where are you going?”
Jesus replied, “Where I am going, you cannot follow now,[n] but you will follow later.”[o]
37 Peter asked, “Lord, why can’t I follow you now? I will lay down my life for you.”
38 Then Jesus answered, “Will you really lay down your life for me? I tell you the truth, before the roost-
er crows, you will disown me three times![p]

Jesus Comforts His Disciples

14 “Do not let your hearts be troubled.[q] Trust in God[b]; trust also in me. 2 In my Father’s house are
many rooms; if it were not so, I would have told you. I am going there[r] to prepare a place for you.
3 And if I go and prepare a place for you, I will come back and take you to be with me that you also may
be where I am.[s] 4 You know the way to the place where I am going.”

Jesus the Way to the Father

5 Thomas[t] said to him, “Lord, we don’t know where you are going, so how can we know the way?”
6 Jesus answered, “I am the way[u] and the truth and the life.[v] No one comes to the Father except through
me. 7 If you really knew me, you would know[c] my Father as well.[w] From now on, you do know him and
have seen him.”
8 Philip said, “Lord, show us the Father and that will be enough for us.”
9 Jesus answered: “Don’t you know me, Philip, even after I have been among you such a long time?
Anyone who has seen me has seen the Father.[x] How can you say, ‘Show us the Father’? 10 Don’t you believe
that I am in the Father, and that the Father is in me?[y] The words I say to you are not just my own.[z] Rath-
er, it is the Father, living in me, who is doing his work. 11 Believe me when I say that I am in the Father and
the Father is in me; or at least believe on the evidence of the miracles themselves.[a] 12 I tell you the truth,
anyone who has faith[b] in me will do what I have been doing.[c] He will do even greater things than these,
because I am going to the Father. 13 And I will do whatever you ask[d] in my name, so that the Son may
bring glory to the Father. 14 You may ask me for anything in my name, and I will do it.

13:19 [v]Jn 14:29; 16:4 [w]Jn 8:24
13:20 [x]Mt 10:40; Lk 10:16
13:21 [y]Jn 12:27 [z]Mt 26:21
13:23 [a]Jn 19:26; 20:2; 21:7,20
13:25 [b]Jn 21:20
13:27 [c]Lk 22:3
13:29 [d]Jn 12:6
13:30 [e]Lk 22:53
13:31 [f]Jn 7:39 [g]Jn 14:13; 17:4; 1Pe 4:11
13:32 [h]Jn 17:1
13:33 [i]Jn 7:33, 34
13:34 [j]1Jn 2:7-11; 3:11 [k]Lev 19:18; 1Th 4:9; 1Pe 1:22 [l]Jn 15:12; Eph 5:2; 1Jn 4:10, 11
13:35 [m]1Jn 3:14; 4:20
13:36 [n]ver 33; Jn 14:2 [o]Jn 21:18,19; 2Pe 1:14
13:38 [p]Jn 18:27
14:1 [q]ver 27
14:2 [r]Jn 13:33, 36
14:3 [s]Jn 12:26
14:5 [t]Jn 11:16
14:6 [u]Jn 10:9 [v]Jn 11:25
14:7 [w]Jn 8:19
14:9 [x]Jn 12:45; Col 1:15; Heb 1:3
14:10 [y]Jn 10:38 [z]Jn 5:19
14:11 [a]Jn 5:36; 10:38
14:12 [b]Mt 21:21 [c]Lk 10:17
14:13 [d]Mt 7:7

[a] 32 Many early manuscripts do not have *If God is glorified in him.* [b] 1 Or *You trust in God* [c] 7 Some early manuscripts *If you really have known me, you will know*

13:23 At a dinner, guests reclined on couches, leaning on the left elbow with the head toward the table (see “Jewish Meals and Meal Customs” on p. 1575 and “Triclinia” on p. 1748).

13:26 See the note on Matthew 26:23.

Jesus Promises the Holy Spirit

15“If you love me, you will obey what I command.[e] 16And I will ask the Father, and he will give you
another Counselor[f] to be with you forever— 17the Spirit of truth.[g] The world cannot accept him,[h] be-
cause it neither sees him nor knows him. But you know him, for he lives with you and will be[a] in you. 18I
will not leave you as orphans; I will come to you.[i] 19Before long, the world will not see me anymore, but
you will see me.[j] Because I live, you also will live.[k] 20On that day you will realize that I am in my Father,[l]
and you are in me, and I am in you. 21Whoever has my commands and obeys them, he is the one who
loves me.[m] He who loves me will be loved by my Father,[n] and I too will love him and show myself to him.”
22Then Judas[o] (not Judas Iscariot) said, “But, Lord, why do you intend to show yourself to us and not
to the world?”[p]
23Jesus replied, “If anyone loves me, he will obey my teaching.[q] My Father will love him, and we will
come to him and make our home with him.[r] 24He who does not love me will not obey my teaching. These
words you hear are not my own; they belong to the Father who sent me.[s]
25“All this I have spoken while still with you. 26But the Counselor,[t] the Holy Spirit, whom the Father
will send in my name,[u] will teach you all things[v] and will remind you of everything I have said to you.[w]
27Peace I leave with you; my peace I give you.[x] I do not give to you as the world gives. Do not let your
hearts be troubled and do not be afraid.
28“You heard me say, ‘I am going away and I am coming back to you.’[y] If you loved me, you would be
glad that I am going to the Father,[z] for the Father is greater than I.[a] 29I have told you now before it hap-
pens, so that when it does happen you will believe.[b] 30I will not speak with you much longer, for the
prince of this world[c] is coming. He has no hold on me, 31but the world must learn that I love the Father
and that I do exactly what my Father has commanded me.[d]
“Come now; let us leave.

14:15 [e]ver 21,23; Jn 15:10; 1Jn 5:3 **14:16** [f]Jn 15:26; 16:7 **14:17** [g]Jn 15:26; 16:13; 1Jn 4:6 [h]1Co 2:14 **14:18** [i]ver 3,28 **14:19** [j]Jn 7:33, 34; 16:16 [k]Jn 6:57 **14:20** [l]Jn 10:38 **14:21** [m]1Jn 5:3 [n]1Jn 2:5 **14:22** [o]Lk 6:16; Ac 1:13 [p]Ac 10:41 **14:23** [q]ver 15 [r]1Jn 2:24; Rev 3:20 **14:24** [s]Jn 7:16 **14:26** [t]Jn 15:26; 16:7 [u]Ac 2:33 [v]Jn 16:13; 1Jn 2:20,27 [w]Jn 2:22 **14:27** [x]Jn 16:33; Php 4:7; Col 3:15 **14:28** [y]ver 2-4, 18 [z]Jn 5:18 [a]Jn 10:29; Php 2:6 **14:29** [b]Jn 13:19; 16:4 **14:30** [c]Jn 12:31 **14:31** [d]Jn 10:18; 12:49

The Vine and the Branches

15 “I am the true vine,[e] and my Father is the gardener. 2He cuts off every branch in me that bears
no fruit, while every branch that does bear fruit he prunes[b] so that it will be even more fruitful.
3You are already clean because of the word I have spoken to you.[f] 4Remain in me, and I will remain in
you.[g] No branch can bear fruit by itself; it must remain in the vine. Neither can you bear fruit unless you
remain in me.
5“I am the vine; you are the branches. If a man remains in me and I in him, he will bear much fruit;[h]
apart from me you can do nothing. 6If anyone does not remain in me, he is like a branch that is thrown
away and withers; such branches are picked up, thrown into the fire and burned.[i] 7If you remain in me
and my words remain in you, ask whatever you wish, and it will be given you.[j] 8This is to my Father's
glory,[k] that you bear much fruit, showing yourselves to be my disciples.[l]
9“As the Father has loved me,[m] so have I loved you. Now remain in my love. 10If you obey my com-
mands,[n] you will remain in my love, just as I have obeyed my Father's commands and remain in his love.
11I have told you this so that my joy may be in you and that your joy may be complete.[o] 12My command
is this: Love each other as I have loved you.[p] 13Greater love has no one than this, that he lay down his life
for his friends.[q] 14You are my friends[r] if you do what I command.[s] 15I no longer call you servants, because
a servant does not know his master's business. Instead, I have called you friends, for everything that I
learned from my Father I have made known to you.[t] 16You did not choose me, but I chose you and ap-
pointed you[u] to go and bear fruit—fruit that will last. Then the Father will give you whatever you ask in
my name. 17This is my command: Love each other.[v]

15:1 [e]Isa 5:1-7 **15:3** [f]Jn 13:10; 17:17; Eph 5:26 **15:4** [g]Jn 6:56; 1Jn 2:6 **15:5** [h]ver 16 **15:6** [i]ver 2 **15:7** [j]Mt 7:7 **15:8** [k]Mt 5:16 [l]Jn 8:31 **15:9** [m]Jn 17:23, 24,26 **15:10** [n]Jn 14:15 **15:11** [o]Jn 17:13 **15:12** [p]Jn 13:34 **15:13** [q]Jn 10:11; Ro 5:7,8 **15:14** [r]Lk 12:4 [s]Mt 12:50 **15:15** [t]Jn 8:26 **15:16** [u]Jn 6:70; 13:18 **15:17** [v]ver 12

The World Hates the Disciples

18“If the world hates you,[w] keep in mind that it hated me first. 19If you belonged to the world, it would
love you as its own. As it is, you do not belong to the world, but I have chosen you[x] out of the world. That

15:18 [w]1Jn 3:13 **15:19** [x]ver 16

[a] *17* Some early manuscripts *and is* [b] *2* The Greek for *prunes* also means *cleans.*

14:16 “Counselor” means “Helper” or “Advocate.” It is a legal term but carries a broader meaning than “counsel for the defense,” referring instead to any person who helped someone in trouble with the law.

14:26 For “Counselor,” see the note on verse 16.

15:15 A servant was simply an agent, doing whatever his master commanded, often not understanding the purpose. But Jesus took his friends into his confidence.

15:16 Disciples normally chose the particular rabbi to whom they wanted to be attached, but this was not the case with Jesus' disciples: He chose them.

NON-BIBLICAL SOURCES FOR THE HISTORICAL JESUS

JOHN 15 Christian readers often wonder whether there are references to Jesus outside the New Testament. Although some opponents of Christianity, dismissing the New Testament, contend that there is little or no real evidence that Jesus ever lived, some verification does in fact exist from both Jewish and Roman sources. A few rabbinical texts have survived, as well as an important passage from the ancient Jewish historian Josephus.

One rabbinical text from the **Babylonian Talmud** is especially significant. This passage, called b. Sanhedrin 43[a], asserts that Jesus was "hanged" on Passover eve for being a sorcerer and enticer to apostasy, but that prior to his execution the Jewish officials had waited 40 days for someone to bring forward evidence in his defense. This contradicts the New Testament account but does affirm Jesus' existence, his condemnation by Jewish officials and his execution at the time of the Passover.

A Josephus text known as the "Testimonium Flavianum" is found in *Antiquities*, 18.63–64. (*Antiquities* was completed in A.D. 93, less than 60 years after Jesus' crucifixion.) Describing the days of Pontius Pilate, it states:

> At this time Jesus, a wise man (if it is appropriate to call him a man), appeared. For he was a worker of incredible deeds, a teacher of men who happily receive the truth, and he drew to himself many Jews—and many Greeks, too. This man was the Christ. And when Pilate had executed him at the instigation of the leading men among us, those who had first loved him did not give up. For he appeared to them on the third day alive again (the divine prophets had spoken concerning him of these and countless other wonders). And to this day the tribe of "Christians" (named after him) has not vanished.

Controversy surrounds the *Testimonium* because of its confessional tone, with some scholars arguing that it was an interpolation by a later Christian scribe. However, in *Antiquities*, 20.200 Josephus described the martyrdom of James, whom he identified simply as "the brother of Jesus, called Christ." Such a passing reference to Jesus suggests either that he felt Jesus needed no introduction or that Josephus himself had already introduced him to the reader.

There are several references to Christians and indirectly to Jesus in Roman literature. Two are particularly important:

◆ Suetonius, in Claudius 25.4 of *The Lives of the Caesars* (C. A.D. 120), described riots among the Jews at Rome during the reign of Claudius in A.D. 49. He stated that these riots were instigated by

A vine with its branch

© Dr. James C. Martin

"Chrestus," which numerous scholars suggest to be a garbled version of "Christ." The Roman authorities in 49 could easily have misunderstood the cause of Jewish upheavals in their city. If Jews had rioted because of the presence of Christians among them, Romans seeking to make sense of the troubles could have jumped to the conclusion that someone named "Chrestus" was at the center of it. Local authorities in Rome at this very early stage of Christian history would have possessed little knowledge of this new religion or of the degree of discord it had already created among the Jews. It is worth noting that this expulsion of Jews from Rome is also mentioned in Acts 18:2.

◆ The Roman historian Tacitus, writing in approximately A.D. 115, mentioned Christians in *Annals*, 15.44. Although he regarded Christianity as a superstition, he nevertheless made clear that Nero had wrongly implicated Christians as scapegoats for the fires at Rome in A.D. 64.[1] Of the term "Christian," he stated, "The author of this name, Christ, suffered the ultimate penalty at the hands of the procurator Pontius Pilate during the imperium of Tiberius." That Jesus was crucified during the reign of Tiberius (A.D. 14–37) is also indicated in the New Testament.[2]

To put the issue in perspective, it is important to realize in general how scanty evidence of any kind from the ancient world actually is. Many persons and episodes from ancient history would be unknown to us except for mention in a single historical document or inscription, and there are significant gaps in our knowledge. All things considered, the evidence for the historical Jesus in ancient sources, to say nothing of the New Testament and the Christian church, is ample.

[1]See "Nero, Persecutor of Christians" on page 1931. [2]See "Tiberius Caesar, the Caesar of Jesus' Ministry" on page 1708.

is why the world hates you.[y] 20 Remember the words I spoke to you: 'No servant is greater than his mas-
ter.'[a][z] If they persecuted me, they will persecute you also.[a] If they obeyed my teaching, they will obey
yours also. 21 They will treat you this way because of my name,[b] for they do not know the One who sent
me.[c] 22 If I had not come and spoken to them, they would not be guilty of sin. Now, however, they have
no excuse for their sin.[d] 23 He who hates me hates my Father as well. 24 If I had not done among them
what no one else did,[e] they would not be guilty of sin. But now they have seen these miracles, and yet they
have hated both me and my Father. 25 But this is to fulfill what is written in their Law: 'They hated me
without reason.'[b][f]

26 "When the Counselor[g] comes, whom I will send to you from the Father,[h] the Spirit of truth[i] who
goes out from the Father, he will testify about me.[j] 27 And you also must testify,[k] for you have been with
me from the beginning.[l]

16 "All this[m] I have told you so that you will not go astray.[n] 2 They will put you out of the synagogue;[o]
in fact, a time is coming when anyone who kills you will think he is offering a service to God.[p]
3 They will do such things because they have not known the Father or me.[q] 4 I have told you this, so that
when the time comes you will remember[r] that I warned you. I did not tell you this at first because I was
with you.

The Work of the Holy Spirit

5 "Now I am going to him who sent me,[s] yet none of you asks me, 'Where are you going?'[t] 6 Because I
have said these things, you are filled with grief. 7 But I tell you the truth: It is for your good that I am go-
ing away. Unless I go away, the Counselor[u] will not come to you; but if I go, I will send him to you.[v] 8 When
he comes, he will convict the world of guilt[c] in regard to sin and righteousness and judgment: 9 in regard
to sin,[w] because men do not believe in me; 10 in regard to righteousness,[x] because I am going to the Fa-
ther, where you can see me no longer; 11 and in regard to judgment, because the prince of this world[y] now
stands condemned.

12 "I have much more to say to you, more than you can now bear.[z] 13 But when he, the Spirit of truth,[a]
comes, he will guide you into all truth.[b] He will not speak on his own; he will speak only what he hears,
and he will tell you what is yet to come. 14 He will bring glory to me by taking from what is mine and
making it known to you. 15 All that belongs to the Father is mine.[c] That is why I said the Spirit will take
from what is mine and make it known to you.

16 "In a little while[d] you will see me no more, and then after a little while you will see me."[e]

The Disciples' Grief Will Turn to Joy

17 Some of his disciples said to one another, "What does he mean by saying, 'In a little while you
will see me no more, and then after a little while you will see me,'[f] and 'Because I am going to the Fa-
ther'?"[g] 18 They kept asking, "What does he mean by 'a little while'? We don't understand what he is
saying."

19 Jesus saw that they wanted to ask him about this, so he said to them, "Are you asking one another
what I meant when I said, 'In a little while you will see me no more, and then after a little while you will
see me'? 20 I tell you the truth, you will weep and mourn[h] while the world rejoices. You will grieve, but
your grief will turn to joy.[i] 21 A woman giving birth to a child has pain[j] because her time has come; but
when her baby is born she forgets the anguish because of her joy that a child is born into the world. 22 So
with you: Now is your time of grief,[k] but I will see you again[l] and you will rejoice, and no one will take
away your joy. 23 In that day you will no longer ask me anything. I tell you the truth, my Father will give
you whatever you ask in my name.[m] 24 Until now you have not asked for anything in my name. Ask and
you will receive, and your joy will be complete.[n]

25 "Though I have been speaking figuratively,[o] a time is coming[p] when I will no longer use this kind
of language but will tell you plainly about my Father. 26 In that day you will ask in my name.[q] I am not
saying that I will ask the Father on your behalf. 27 No, the Father himself loves you because you have loved

15:19 [y]Jn 17:14
15:20 [z]Jn 13:16 [a]2Ti 3:12
15:21 [b]Mt 10:22 [c]Jn 16:3
15:22 [d]Jn 9:41; Ro 1:20
15:24 [e]Jn 5:36
15:25 [f]Ps 35:19; 69:4
15:26 [g]Jn 14:16 [h]Jn 14:26 [i]Jn 14:17 [j]1Jn 5:7
15:27 [k]Lk 24:48; 1Jn 1:2; 4:14 [l]Lk 1:2
16:1 [m]Jn 15:18-27 [n]Mt 11:6
16:2 [o]Jn 9:22 [p]Isa 66:5; Ac 26:9,10; Rev 6:9
16:3 [q]Jn 15:21; 17:25; 1Jn 3:1
16:4 [r]Jn 13:19
16:5 [s]Jn 7:33 [t]Jn 13:36; 14:5
16:7 [u]Jn 14:16, 26; 15:26 [v]Jn 7:39
16:9 [w]Jn 15:22
16:10 [x]Ac 3:14; 7:52; 1Pe 3:18
16:11 [y]Jn 12:31
16:12 [z]Mk 4:33
16:13 [a]Jn 14:17 [b]Jn 14:26
16:15 [c]Jn 17:10
16:16 [d]Jn 7:33 [e]Jn 14:18-24
16:17 [f]ver 16 [g]ver 5
16:20 [h]Lk 23:27 [i]Jn 20:20
16:21 [j]Isa 26:17; 1Th 5:3
16:22 [k]ver 6 [l]ver 16
16:23 [m]Mt 7:7; Jn 15:16
16:24 [n]Jn 3:29; 15:11
16:25 [o]Mt 13:34; Jn 10:6 [p]ver 2
16:26 [q]ver 23,24

[a] *20* John 13:16 [b] *25* Psalms 35:19; 69:4 [c] *8* Or *will expose the guilt of the world*

15:21 For "name," see the note on Jeremiah 16:21.
15:25 For "Law," see the note on 12:34.
15:26 For "Counselor," see the note on 14:16.
16:2 For "put you out of the synagogue," see the note on 9:22.
16:20 "Weep" is here the verb for loud wailing, as in 11:33 (see the note there), which carries the idea of deep sorrow and its outward expression.
16:23,26 For "name," see the note on Jeremiah 16:21.

16:27 [r]Jn 14:21, 23
16:28 [s]Jn 13:3
16:29 [t]ver 25

me[r] and have believed that I came from God. 28 I came from the Father and entered the world; now I am
leaving the world and going back to the Father."[s]
29 Then Jesus' disciples said, "Now you are speaking clearly and without figures of speech.[t] 30 Now we
can see that you know all things and that you do not even need to have anyone ask you questions. This
makes us believe that you came from God."

16:32 [u]ver 2,25 [v]Mt 26:31 [w]Jn 8:16,29
16:33 [x]Jn 14:27 [y]Jn 15:18-21 [z]Ro 8:37; 1Jn 4:4

31 "You believe at last!"[a] Jesus answered. 32 "But a time is coming,[u] and has come, when you will be
scattered,[v] each to his own home. You will leave me all alone. Yet I am not alone, for my Father is with me.[w]
33 "I have told you these things, so that in me you may have peace.[x] In this world you will have trou-
ble.[y] But take heart! I have overcome[z] the world."

Jesus Prays for Himself

17:1 [a]Jn 11:41 [b]Jn 12:23; 13:31, 32
17:2 [c]ver 6,9,24; Da 7:14; Jn 6:37, 39
17:3 [d]ver 8,18, 21,23,25; Jn 3:17
17:4 [e]Jn 13:31 [f]Jn 4:34
17:5 [g]Php 2:6 [h]Jn 1:2

17 After Jesus said this, he looked toward heaven[a] and prayed:
"Father, the time has come. Glorify your Son, that your Son may glorify you.[b] 2 For you grant-
ed him authority over all people that he might give eternal life to all those you have given him.[c]
3 Now this is eternal life: that they may know you, the only true God, and Jesus Christ, whom you
have sent.[d] 4 I have brought you glory[e] on earth by completing the work you gave me to do.[f] 5 And
now, Father, glorify me in your presence with the glory I had with you[g] before the world began.[h]

Jesus Prays for His Disciples

17:6 [i]ver 26 [j]ver 2; Jn 6:37,39
17:8 [k]ver 14,26 [l]Jn 16:27 [m]ver 3, 18,21,23,25; Jn 3:17
17:9 [n]Lk 22:32
17:10 [o]Jn 16:15
17:11 [p]Jn 13:1 [q]Jn 7:33 [r]ver 21-23 [s]Jn 10:30
17:12 [t]Jn 6:39 [u]Jn 6:70
17:13 [v]Jn 3:29
17:14 [w]Jn 15:19 [x]Jn 8:23
17:15 [y]Mt 5:37
17:16 [z]ver 14
17:17 [a]Jn 15:3
17:18 [b]ver 3,8, 21,23,25 [c]Jn 20:21

6 "I have revealed you[b][i] to those whom you gave me[j] out of the world. They were yours; you gave
them to me and they have obeyed your word. 7 Now they know that everything you have given me
comes from you. 8 For I gave them the words you gave me[k] and they accepted them. They knew
with certainty that I came from you,[l] and they believed that you sent me.[m] 9 I pray for them.[n] I am
not praying for the world, but for those you have given me, for they are yours. 10 All I have is yours,
and all you have is mine.[o] And glory has come to me through them. 11 I will remain in the world
no longer, but they are still in the world,[p] and I am coming to you.[q] Holy Father, protect them by
the power of your name—the name you gave me—so that they may be one[r] as we are one.[s]
12 While I was with them, I protected them and kept them safe by that name you gave me. None has
been lost[t] except the one doomed to destruction[u] so that Scripture would be fulfilled.
13 "I am coming to you now, but I say these things while I am still in the world, so that they may
have the full measure of my joy[v] within them. 14 I have given them your word and the world has hat-
ed them,[w] for they are not of the world any more than I am of the world.[x] 15 My prayer is not that
you take them out of the world but that you protect them from the evil one.[y] 16 They are not of the
world, even as I am not of it.[z] 17 Sanctify[c] them by the truth; your word is truth.[a] 18 As you sent me
into the world,[b] I have sent them into the world.[c] 19 For them I sanctify myself, that they too may
be truly sanctified.

Jesus Prays for All Believers

17:21 [d]Jn 10:38 [e]ver 3,8,18,23, 25; Jn 3:17
17:22 [f]Jn 14:20
17:23 [g]Jn 3:17 [h]Jn 16:27
17:24 [i]Jn 12:26 [j]Jn 1:14 [k]ver 5; Mt 25:34
17:25 [l]Jn 15:21; 16:3 [m]ver 3,8,18, 21,23; Jn 3:17; 7:29; 16:27
17:26 [n]ver 6 [o]Jn 15:9

20 "My prayer is not for them alone. I pray also for those who will believe in me through their
message, 21 that all of them may be one, Father, just as you are in me and I am in you.[d] May they
also be in us so that the world may believe that you have sent me.[e] 22 I have given them the glory
that you gave me, that they may be one as we are one:[f] 23 I in them and you in me. May they be
brought to complete unity to let the world know that you sent me[g] and have loved them[h] even as
you have loved me.
24 "Father, I want those you have given me to be with me where I am,[i] and to see my glory,[j] the
glory you have given me because you loved me before the creation of the world.[k]
25 "Righteous Father, though the world does not know you,[l] I know you, and they know that you
have sent me.[m] 26 I have made you known to them,[n] and will continue to make you known in or-
der that the love you have for me may be in them[o] and that I myself may be in them."

[a] 31 Or *"Do you now believe?"* [b] 6 Greek *your name*; also in verse 26 [c] 17 Greek *hagiazo (set apart for sacred use* or *make holy)*; also in verse 19

17:1 The customary posture in prayer was looking upward toward heaven, though sometimes Jesus prostrated himself (see Mt 26:39).

Jesus Arrested

18 When he had finished praying, Jesus left with his disciples and crossed the Kidron Valley.[p] On 18:1 [p]2Sa 15:23
the other side there was an olive grove,[q] and he and his disciples went into it.[r] [q]ver 26 [r]Mt 26:36
2Now Judas, who betrayed him, knew the place, because Jesus had often met there with his disciples.[s] 18:2 [s]Lk 21:37; 22:39
3So Judas came to the grove, guiding[t] a detachment of soldiers and some officials from the chief priests 18:3 [t]Ac 1:16
and Pharisees.[u] They were carrying torches, lanterns and weapons. [u]ver 12
4Jesus, knowing all that was going to happen to him,[v] went out and asked them, "Who is it you want?"[w] 18:4 [v]Jn 6:64; 13:1,11 [w]ver 7
5"Jesus of Nazareth," they replied.
"I am he," Jesus said. (And Judas the traitor was standing there with them.) 6When Jesus said, "I am
he," they drew back and fell to the ground.
7Again he asked them, "Who is it you want?"[x] 18:7 [x]ver 4
And they said, "Jesus of Nazareth."
8"I told you that I am he," Jesus answered. "If you are looking for me, then let these men go." 9This
happened so that the words he had spoken would be fulfilled: "I have not lost one of those you gave
me."[a][y] 18:9 [y]Jn 17:12
10Then Simon Peter, who had a sword, drew it and struck the high priest's servant, cutting off his right
ear. (The servant's name was Malchus.)
11Jesus commanded Peter, "Put your sword away! Shall I not drink the cup[z] the Father has given me?" 18:11 [z]Mt 20:22

Jesus Taken to Annas

12Then the detachment of soldiers with its commander and the Jewish officials[a] arrested Jesus. They 18:12 [a]ver 3
bound him 13and brought him first to Annas, who was the father-in-law of Caiaphas,[b] the high priest 18:13 [b]ver 24; Mt 26:3
that year. 14Caiaphas was the one who had advised the Jews that it would be good if one man died for the
people.[c] 18:14 [c]Jn 11:49-51

Peter's First Denial

15Simon Peter and another disciple were following Jesus. Because this disciple was known to the high
priest,[d] he went with Jesus into the high priest's courtyard,[e] 16but Peter had to wait outside at the door. 18:15 [d]Mt 26:3 [e]Mt 26:58; Mk 14:54; Lk 22:54
The other disciple, who was known to the high priest, came back, spoke to the girl on duty there and
brought Peter in.
17"You are not one of his disciples, are you?" the girl at the door asked Peter.
He replied, "I am not."[f] 18:17 [f]ver 25
18It was cold, and the servants and officials stood around a fire[g] they had made to keep warm. Peter 18:18 [g]Jn 21:9
also was standing with them, warming himself.[h] [h]Mk 14:54,67

The High Priest Questions Jesus

19Meanwhile, the high priest questioned Jesus about his disciples and his teaching.
20"I have spoken openly to the world," Jesus replied. "I always taught in synagogues[i] or at the temple,[j] 18:20 [i]Mt 4:23 [j]Mt 26:55
where all the Jews come together. I said nothing in secret.[k] 21Why question me? Ask those who heard me. [k]Jn 7:26
Surely they know what I said."

[a] 9 John 6:39

18:1 The Kidron Valley lies east of Jerusalem and is dry except during the rainy season.

For "olive grove," see the note on Matthew 26:36–56.

18:3 The "officials" were equivalent to the temple guard sent by the chief priests and Pharisees (see the notes on Mt 2:4; 3:7; Mk 14:55).

Torches were long poles with oil-drenched rags at the top, whereas lanterns were terra-cotta holders into which household lamps could be inserted.

18:12 The reason for the bonds is not clear. Perhaps their use was standard procedure, much like the modern use of handcuffs.

18:13 Annas had been deposed from the high priesthood by the Romans in A.D.15 but was still regarded by many as the true high priest (see the note on Lk 3:2; see also "The High Priests Annas and Caiaphas" on p. 1772 and "The Jewish Priesthood and Religious Life in the First Century A.D." on p. 1704).

In Jewish law no one could be sentenced on the same day their trial was held. The two examinations—this one and that before Caiaphas—may have been conducted to give some form of legitimacy to the proceedings.

18:14 See 11:49–50.

18:15 "Known" refers to more than casual acquaintance; this disciple (perhaps John) had entrée into the high priest's house.

18:17 Slave girls were the least important persons imaginable at that time (see "Slavery in the Greco-Roman World" on p. 1979).

18:18 See the note on coal/charcoal at Psalm 120:4.

18:19–21 In a formal Jewish trial, the judge did not ask direct questions of the accused. Instead he called witnesses, whose words determined the outcome. If two or more agreed on the charge, the verdict was sealed. The accused was not required to prove his innocence. But the scene here was more like a police interrogation than a trial. Perhaps Annas regarded this as a preliminary inquiry, not a trial. By pointing out that Annas should be talking to witnesses, Jesus unmasked Annas's attempt to make Jesus incriminate himself. In essence, Jesus was demanding a trial.

18:22 [l]ver 3 [m]Mt 16:21; Jn 19:3
18:23 [n]Mt 5:39; Ac 23:2-5
18:24 [o]ver 13; Mt 26:3
18:25 [p]ver 18 [q]ver 17
18:26 [r]ver 10 [s]ver 1
18:27 [t]Jn 13:38
18:28 [u]Mt 27:2; Mk 15:1; Lk 23:1 [v]ver 33; Jn 19:9 [w]Jn 11:55

22 When Jesus said this, one of the officials[l] nearby struck him in the face.[m] "Is this the way you an-
swer the high priest?" he demanded.
23 "If I said something wrong," Jesus replied, "testify as to what is wrong. But if I spoke the truth, why
did you strike me?"[n] 24 Then Annas sent him, still bound, to Caiaphas[o] the high priest.[a]

Peter's Second and Third Denials

25 As Simon Peter stood warming himself,[p] he was asked, "You are not one of his disciples, are you?"
He denied it, saying, "I am not."[q]
26 One of the high priest's servants, a relative of the man whose ear Peter had cut off,[r] challenged him,
"Didn't I see you with him in the olive grove?"[s] 27 Again Peter denied it, and at that moment a rooster be-
gan to crow.[t]

Jesus Before Pilate

28 Then the Jews led Jesus from Caiaphas to the palace of the Roman governor.[u] By now it was early
morning, and to avoid ceremonial uncleanness the Jews did not enter the palace;[v] they wanted to be able
to eat the Passover.[w] 29 So Pilate came out to them and asked, "What charges are you bringing against
this man?"
30 "If he were not a criminal," they replied, "we would not have handed him over to you."

[a] 24 Or *(Now Annas had sent him, still bound, to Caiaphas the high priest.)*

18:22 The word "struck" means a blow or slap with the open hand—another illegality.
18:26 The light in the garden would have been dim, as it was in the courtyard (a charcoal fire glows but does not flame).
18:27 See the note on Matthew 26:34.
18:28 The Roman governor at that time was Pontius Pilate (see the note on Lk 3:1).

The chief priests evidently held a second session of the Sanhedrin (see "The Sanhedrin" on p. 1821) after daybreak to give some appearance of legality to what they were doing. This occasion would have been immediately after that, perhaps between 6:00 and 7:00 A.M.

Jews became ceremonially unclean as a result of entering a Gentile residence; hence their caution.

"Passover" here may refer to the combined festivals of Passover and Unleavened Bread, which together lasted seven days and included a number of meals.

ANCIENT TEXTS AND ARTIFACTS

John Rylands Papyrus (p[52])

JOHN 18 The John Rylands papyrus (p[52]) is the oldest copy yet discovered of any portion of the New Testament, dating back to the first half of the second century A.D. A tiny fragment of a **codex** (a leaf-form text, like a modern book, in contrast to a scroll) of the Gospel of John, it contains parts of John 18:31–33 on one side and verses 37–38 on the other.[1] It was acquired in Egypt in 1920 and now resides in the John Rylands Library in Manchester, England.

Despite its tiny size (less than 3.5 in. [9 cm] from top to bottom), this papyrus fragment is highly significant. It testifies that by the first half of the second century the Gospel of John was already being read in Egypt, far from Ephesus in Asia Minor, the most likely place of its composition.[2] It seems unlikely that John's Gospel could have been composed much later than the end of the first century, since it would have taken time for it to have been accepted and disseminated so far from its place of origin. The manuscript of which p[52] is a fragment may have been copied within 25 to 30 years of the composition of the Gospel itself. If we take into account that in some pieces of Greek or Latin literature the oldest manuscript available is dated to over a thousand years after the composition of the original text, that is in reality an extremely short period of time. An enormous number of Greek New Testament texts exist, and they give us good reason to be confident that the New Testament we read today accurately reflects what was in the original manuscripts.[3]

[1]See "Writing Materials in the Ancient World" on page 2037. [2]See "Early History of Ephesus" on page 1965 and "Ephesus During the Time of Paul" on page 1968.
[3]See "The New Testament Texts" on page 1859.

31 Pilate said, "Take him yourselves and judge him by your own law."
"But we have no right to execute anyone," the Jews objected. 32 This happened so that the words Jesus
had spoken indicating the kind of death he was going to die[x] would be fulfilled.
33 Pilate then went back inside the palace,[y] summoned Jesus and asked him, "Are you the king of the
Jews?"[z]
34 "Is that your own idea," Jesus asked, "or did others talk to you about me?"
35 "Am I a Jew?" Pilate replied. "It was your people and your chief priests who handed you over to me.
What is it you have done?"
36 Jesus said, "My kingdom[a] is not of this world. If it were, my servants would fight to prevent my ar-
rest by the Jews.[b] But now my kingdom is from another place."[c]
37 "You are a king, then!" said Pilate.
Jesus answered, "You are right in saying I am a king. In fact, for this reason I was born, and for this I
came into the world, to testify to the truth.[d] Everyone on the side of truth listens to me."[e]
38 "What is truth?" Pilate asked. With this he went out again to the Jews and said, "I find no basis for
a charge against him.[f] 39 But it is your custom for me to release to you one prisoner at the time of the
Passover. Do you want me to release 'the king of the Jews'?"
40 They shouted back, "No, not him! Give us Barabbas!" Now Barabbas had taken part in a rebellion.[g]

Jesus Sentenced to Be Crucified

19 Then Pilate took Jesus and had him flogged.[h] 2 The soldiers twisted together a crown of thorns
and put it on his head. They clothed him in a purple robe 3 and went up to him again and again,
saying, "Hail, king of the Jews!"[i] And they struck him in the face.[j]
4 Once more Pilate came out and said to the Jews, "Look, I am bringing him out[k] to you to let you know
that I find no basis for a charge against him."[l] 5 When Jesus came out wearing the crown of thorns and
the purple robe,[m] Pilate said to them, "Here is the man!"
6 As soon as the chief priests and their officials saw him, they shouted, "Crucify! Crucify!"
But Pilate answered, "You take him and crucify him.[n] As for me, I find no basis for a charge against
him."[o]
7 The Jews insisted, "We have a law, and according to that law he must die,[p] because he claimed to be
the Son of God."[q]
8 When Pilate heard this, he was even more afraid, 9 and he went back inside the palace.[r] "Where do
you come from?" he asked Jesus, but Jesus gave him no answer.[s] 10 "Do you refuse to speak to me?" Pilate
said. "Don't you realize I have power either to free you or to crucify you?"
11 Jesus answered, "You would have no power over me if it were not given to you from above.[t] There-
fore the one who handed me over to you[u] is guilty of a greater sin."
12 From then on, Pilate tried to set Jesus free, but the Jews kept shouting, "If you let this man go, you
are no friend of Caesar. Anyone who claims to be a king[v] opposes Caesar."
13 When Pilate heard this, he brought Jesus out and sat down on the judge's seat[w] at a place known as
the Stone Pavement (which in Aramaic[x] is Gabbatha). 14 It was the day of Preparation[y] of Passover Week,
about the sixth hour.[z]
"Here is your king,"[a] Pilate said to the Jews.

18:32 [x]Mt 20:19; 26:2; Jn 3:14; 8:28; 12:32,33
18:33 [y]ver 28,29; Jn 19:9 [z]Lk 23:3; Mt 2:2
18:36 [a]Mt 3:2 [b]Mt 26:53 [c]Lk 17:21; Jn 6:15
18:37 [d]Jn 3:32 [e]Jn 8:47; 1Jn 4:6
18:38 [f]Lk 23:4; Jn 19:4,6
18:40 [g]Ac 3:14
19:1 [h]Dt 25:3; Isa 50:6; 53:5; Mt 27:26
19:3 [i]Mt 27:29 [j]Jn 18:22
19:4 [k]Jn 18:38 [l]ver 6; Lk 23:4
19:5 [m]ver 2
19:6 [n]Ac 3:13 [o]ver 4; Lk 23:4
19:7 [p]Lev 24:16 [q]Mt 26:63-66; Jn 5:18; 10:33
19:9 [r]Jn 18:33 [s]Mk 14:61
19:11 [t]Ro 13:1 [u]Jn 18:28-30; Ac 3:13
19:12 [v]Lk 23:2
19:13 [w]Mt 27:19 [x]Jn 5:2
19:14 [y]Mt 27:62 [z]Mk 15:25 [a]ver 19,21

18:31–33 See "John Rylands Papyrus (p^{52})" on page 1755.
18:31 The Jews were looking for an execution, not a fair trial. The Sanhedrin (see "The Sanhedrin" on p. 1821) had been deprived by the Roman government of the right to carry out capital punishment, except in the case of a foreigner who entered the sacred precincts of the temple. So Jesus had to be handed over to Pilate for execution. This restriction was important, for otherwise Rome's supporters could have been quietly removed by local legal executions. Sometimes the Romans seem to have tolerated local executions (e.g., of Stephen, Ac 7), but normally they retained the sole right to inflict the death penalty.
18:32 Jewish execution was by stoning, but Jesus' death was to be by crucifixion, whereby he would bear the curse associated with that particular form of capital punishment (see Dt 21:22–23). The Romans, not the Jews, had to put Jesus to death.
18:39 Prisoners are known to have been released on special occasions in other places during this time period.
18:40 Barabbas was a rebel and a murderer (see the notes on Mt 27:16; Mk 15:7).
19:1 For information on Roman flogging, see the note on Matthew 27:26.
19:2 See the note on Matthew 27:28–31.
19:3 "Hail" is an interjection found only in the Gospels (see also Mt 27:29; Mk 15:18) as a translation of *chaire,* used as a greeting or salutation. A similar greeting is still to be heard in modern Greece.
19:12 Some people had official status as "Friends of Caesar," but the term seems to be used here in a general sense.
19:13 For "judge's seat," see "The Judgment Seat" on page 1891.
19:14 For "day of Preparation," see the note on verse 31.
The sixth hour was 12:00 noon. It is possible that Mark's Gospel contains a copyist's error (see "Textual Criticism" on p. 1151 and "Early Scribal Emendation" on p. 448), in that the Greek numerals for three and six could be confused. Or it may be that John was using Roman time, in which case the appearance before Pilate would have been at 6:00 A.M. and the crucifixion at 9:00 A.M. (the third hour according to Jewish reckoning).

[15]But they shouted, "Take him away! Take him away! Crucify him!"
"Shall I crucify your king?" Pilate asked.
19:16 [b]Mt 27:26; Mk 15:15; Lk 23:25 "We have no king but Caesar," the chief priests answered.
[16]Finally Pilate handed him over to them to be crucified.[b]

19:15 The chief priests' emphatic statement that they had no king but Caesar was a direct contradiction of the Old Testament declaration that God alone was Israel's king (1Sa 8:7; 10:19).

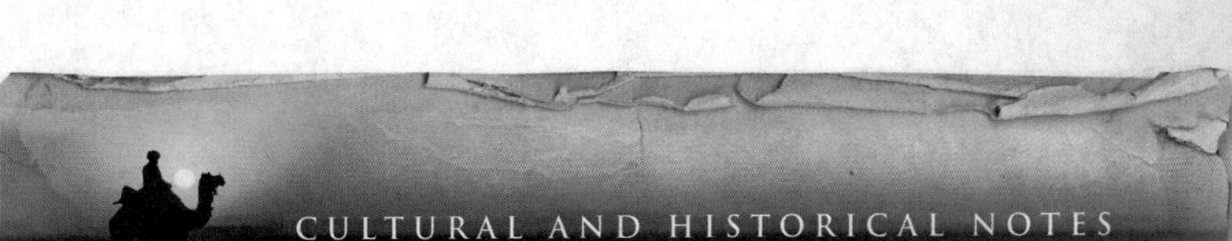

Crucifixion

JOHN 19 In the ancient world crucifixion was seen as a particularly disgraceful and grievous form of execution. **Assyrian** battle **reliefs** depict a precursor to crucifixion—impaling victims on poles outside the walls of conquered cities. The Persians made widespread use of crucifixion, although sometimes the crucifixion took place only after the victim had been executed by other means (Herodotus, *Histories*, 3.125.2–3). There are also reports that crucifixion was used by peoples as varied as the Assyrians, Scythians, Celts, Germans, Britons and inhabitants of India, although the reliability of some of these accounts is questionable. Common to most of these cultures was the perspective that crucifixion was a form of execution reserved for the worst offenders, as well as for slaves.

The practice of crucifixion became widespread under Alexander the Great (356–323 B.C.).[1] It became the common form of execution for traitors, defeated armies and rebellious slaves. Later, under the Roman Empire, only non-citizens, lower class Romans and violent offenders could be crucified.[2] The only possible exceptions were in cases of high treason or desertion during wartime. Slaves were particularly vulnerable to the imposition of crucifixion. Latin literature reflects the dread slaves felt at the prospect of this fate.[3] It was officially accepted as the most painful and disgraceful form of capital punishment, more so than decapitation, being thrown to wild animals or even being burned alive. For these reasons this heinous penalty was often imposed upon foreigners who were seen as threats to Roman rule.

There are also accounts of crucifixion being practiced among Jews. Josephus wrote that the Sadducean high priest Alexander Janneus (in office from 103 to 76 B.C.) committed the following atrocity against his enemies, the Pharisees: "While dining in a conspicuous place with his concubines, he commanded that about 800 of them be crucified, and while they were still alive before their eyes he had the throats of their children and wives cut" (Josephus, *Antiquities*, 13.14.2).[4]

Victims were often scourged or otherwise tortured prior to crucifixion. Crucifixions were carried out on either a single vertical stake or on a vertical stake with a crossbeam near or on its top. Sometimes blocks were attached to the stake as a seat, footrest or both. Depending upon the presence of these blocks, the victim might linger, alive, for up to three days. The blocks allowed a victim to rest some of his weight, increasing the chance of breathing and proper circulation. Without the blocks a victim's weight would rest totally upon his arms, which were attached to the crosspiece by ropes, nails or both. This would prohibit breathing and circulation and lead to both brain and heart failure. To end the torture, a victim's legs could be broken, after which death would quickly follow. Oftentimes the charge against the guilty party would be written out and nailed to the cross above his head. As a deterrent to would-be rebels and criminals, crucifixions were usually carried out in highly visible locations.

During Jesus' lifetime crucifixion was used by the Romans to exercise and gruesomely display their authority over others. This tortuous execution was viewed by the Jews as a cursed form of death. Deuteronomy 21:23 states that "anyone who is hung on a tree is under God's curse." Documents discovered at **Qumran** reveal that many Jews of Jesus' time applied this text to Roman crucifixion. This perspective of crucifixion demonstrates why the apostle Paul wrote that the cross of Christ was "a stumbling block to Jews and foolishness to Gentiles" (1Co 1:23). Who would have imagined that the Holy One of God would voluntarily take upon himself the curse that should have been ours? This emblem of shame has thus become the symbol of our salvation.

[1]See "Greece: From Independent City-states Through Alexander the Great" on page 1814. [2]See "The Roman Empire" on page 1845. [3]See "Slavery in the Greco-Roman World" on page 1979. [4]See also "The Sadducees" on page 1600 and "The Pharisees" on page 1566.

The Crucifixion

So the soldiers took charge of Jesus. 17 Carrying his own cross,[c] he went out to the place of the Skull[d]
(which in Aramaic[e] is called Golgotha). 18 Here they crucified him, and with him two others[f]—one on
each side and Jesus in the middle.

19:17 [c]Ge 22:6; Lk 14:27; 23:26 [d]Lk 23:33 [e]Jn 5:2
19:18 [f]Lk 23:32

19:17 A cross might have been shaped like a *T*, an *X*, a *Y* or an *I*, as well as in the traditional form. A condemned man would normally carry a beam of his own cross to the place of execution (see the note on Mk 15:21).

19:18 For "crucified," see "Crucifixion" on page 1757.

Constantine and Queen Helena's Role in Preserving Holy Sites

JOHN 19 The path of Christian pilgrimage and its appointed sites took distinctive shape during the fourth century A.D. (the early **Byzantine period**)[1] through the influence and direct involvement of Queen Helena and her son Constantine the Great. Flavia Iulia Helena was born in A.D. 248 in Bithynia. She married Constantius Chlorus and gave birth to the future emperor, Constantine the Great, in A.D. 273.

After Constantine's conversion to Christianity, he embarked upon an ambitious building program to adorn sacred sites. His most significant accomplishment was the discovery and excavation of the (probable) site of Jesus' burial.[2] According to Eusebius, the entire area had been covered with debris and converted into a pagan shrine. Constantine ordered the area to be cleared and purified. He then sponsored the construction of the Church of the Holy Sepulchre in A.D. 326 to mark the place of Jesus' suffering. Eusebius reported Constantine's aim as having been the construction of the most beautiful structure in the entire empire (*Life of Constantine*, 3.31).

The Arch of Constantine
Preserving Bible Times; © Dr. James C. Martin; on licence Ministero per i Beni le Attivita Culturali-Soprintendza Archeologica di Roma

During this same year Helena traveled to the eastern provinces and spent an appreciable amount of time touring the Holy Land. Under imperial sponsorship she dedicated two important churches: the Church of Nativity in Bethlehem, to mark the cave where Christ was thought to have been born,[3] and the Church of Ascension on the Mount of Olives to indicate the place of his ascension (*Life of Constantine*, 3.42).[4] Whether these sites are indeed the places where Jesus was born and buried are open to debate. Later legendary accounts also attribute to Helena the discovery of the actual cross upon which Jesus was crucified and of the *titulus*, the plaque announcing the charge against him: "JESUS OF NAZARETH, THE KING OF THE JEWS" (Jn 19:19).

[1]See Glossary on page 2080 for definitions of bolded words. [2]See "The Location of Jesus' Tomb" on page 1615. [3]See "The Birthplace of Jesus" on page 1668. [4]See "The Mount of Olives" on page 1543.

19:19 [g]Mk 1:24 [h]ver 14,21 — 19 Pilate had a notice prepared and fastened to the cross. It read: JESUS OF NAZARETH,[g] THE KING OF THE
19:20 [i]Heb 13:12 — JEWS.[h] 20 Many of the Jews read this sign, for the place where Jesus was crucified was near the city,[i] and
the sign was written in Aramaic, Latin and Greek. 21 The chief priests of the Jews protested to Pilate, "Do
19:21 [j]ver 14 — not write 'The King of the Jews,' but that this man claimed to be king of the Jews."[j]
22 Pilate answered, "What I have written, I have written."
23 When the soldiers crucified Jesus, they took his clothes, dividing them into four shares, one for each
of them, with the undergarment remaining. This garment was seamless, woven in one piece from top to
bottom.
24 "Let's not tear it," they said to one another. "Let's decide by lot who will get it."
19:24 [k]ver 28,36, 37; Mt 1:22 [l]Ps 22:18 — This happened that the scripture might be fulfilled[k] which said,

> "They divided my garments among them
> and cast lots for my clothing."[a][l]

So this is what the soldiers did.
19:25 [m]Mt 27:55, 56; Mk 15:40,41; Lk 23:49 — 25 Near the cross[m] of Jesus stood his mother,[n] his mother's sister, Mary the wife of Clopas, and Mary
[n]Mt 12:46 [o]Lk 24:18 — Magdalene.[o] 26 When Jesus saw his mother[p] there, and the disciple whom he loved[q] standing nearby, he
19:26 [p]Mt 12:46 — said to his mother, "Dear woman, here is your son," 27 and to the disciple, "Here is your mother." From that
[q]Jn 13:23 — time on, this disciple took her into his home.

The Death of Jesus

19:28 [r]ver 30; Jn 13:1 [s]ver 24, 36,37 — 28 Later, knowing that all was now completed,[r] and so that the Scripture would be fulfilled,[s] Jesus said,
"I am thirsty." 29 A jar of wine vinegar[t] was there, so they soaked a sponge in it, put the sponge on a stalk
19:29 [t]Ps 69:21 — of the hyssop plant, and lifted it to Jesus' lips. 30 When he had received the drink, Jesus said, "It is fin-
19:30 [u]Lk 12:50; Jn 17:4 — ished."[u] With that, he bowed his head and gave up his spirit.
19:31 [v]ver 14,42 — 31 Now it was the day of Preparation,[v] and the next day was to be a special Sabbath. Because the Jews
[w]Dt 21:23; Jos 8:29; 10:26, 27 — did not want the bodies left on the crosses[w] during the Sabbath, they asked Pilate to have the legs bro-
ken and the bodies taken down. 32 The soldiers therefore came and broke the legs of the first man who
19:32 [x]ver 18 — had been crucified with Jesus, and then those of the other.[x] 33 But when they came to Jesus and found
19:34 [y]Zec 12:10 — that he was already dead, they did not break his legs. 34 Instead, one of the soldiers pierced[y] Jesus' side with
[z]1Jn 5:6,8 19:35 [a]Lk 24:48 — a spear, bringing a sudden flow of blood and water.[z] 35 The man who saw it[a] has given testimony, and his
[b]Jn 15:27; 21:24 — testimony is true.[b] He knows that he tells the truth, and he testifies so that you also may believe. 36 These
19:36 [c]ver 24,28, 37; Mt 1:22 — things happened so that the scripture would be fulfilled:[c] "Not one of his bones will be broken,"[b][d] 37 and,
[d]Ex 12:46; Nu 9:12; Ps 34:20 — as another scripture says, "They will look on the one they have pierced."[c][e]

19:37 [e]Zec 12:10; Rev 1:7

The Burial of Jesus

38 Later, Joseph of Arimathea asked Pilate for the body of Jesus. Now Joseph was a disciple of Jesus,
but secretly because he feared the Jews. With Pilate's permission, he came and took the body away.

[a] *24* Psalm 22:18 [b] *36* Exodus 12:46; Num. 9:12; Psalm 34:20 [c] *37* Zech. 12:10

19:19 For "notice," see the note on Mark 15:26 and "Constantine and Queen Helena's Role in Preserving Holy Sites" on page 1758.

19:20 Aramaic was one of the languages of the Jewish people at that time (along with Hebrew); Latin was the official language of Rome and Greek the common language of communication throughout the empire. The threefold inscription may account for the slight differences in wording in the four Gospels.

19:23 Jesus' clothing probably consisted of an under and an outer garment, a belt, sandals and possibly a head covering. Since the undergarment was seamless, it was too valuable to be cut up.

19:27 By taking Mary to his home, the disciple took responsibility for her. It may be that Jesus' brothers still did not believe in him (see the note on Lk 8:19).

19:29 For "wine vinegar," see the note on Matthew 27:48.

Hyssop is the name given to a number of plants (see "Hyssop and the Rituals of Cleansing" on p. 847). See the note on Mark 15:36 for the procedure used in offering Jesus this liquid on a sponge lifted to his lips on a stalk of the hyssop plant.

19:31 The "day of Preparation" was normally Friday, the day people prepared for the Sabbath. Here the meaning is Friday of Passover week. "Special Sabbath" refers to the Sabbath that fell at Passover time. The Passover meal had been eaten on Thursday evening, the day of Preparation was Friday and the Sabbath came on Saturday. (See "The Last Supper and the Passover" on p. 1611.)

The victims' legs were broken to hasten death by prohibiting them from putting weight on their legs to facilitate breathing.

19:34 Jesus' side was most likely pierced to make doubly sure that he was dead, though perhaps this was simply an act of brutality. The "sudden flow of blood and water" was the result of the spear piercing his pericardium (the sac that surrounds the heart) and his heart itself.

19:35 See "Can John's Gospel Be Trusted?" on page 1761.

19:36–37 It was extraordinary that Jesus was the only one of the three whose legs were not broken (see the note on v. 31) and that he suffered an unusual spear thrust (see the note on v. 34) that did not break a bone.

19:38 Joseph, a wealthy (Mt 27:57) member of the Sanhedrin (Mk 15:43), had disagreed with Jesus' prosecution (Lk 23:50–51). Nicodemus was also a member of the Sanhedrin (3:1; 7:50–51).

The location of Arimathea is in doubt, but it is conjectured to be Ramathaim-Zophim, the Ramah of Samuel's residence, in the hill country of Ephraim, about 20 miles (33 km) northwest of Jerusalem and 6 miles (10 km) southeast of Antipatris.

Permission was required to take away the body of a victim of

39He was accompanied by Nicodemus,[f] the man who earlier had visited Jesus at night. Nicodemus
brought a mixture of myrrh and aloes, about seventy-five pounds.[a] 40Taking Jesus' body, the two of
them wrapped it, with the spices, in strips of linen.[g] This was in accordance with Jewish burial cus-
toms.[h] 41At the place where Jesus was crucified, there was a garden, and in the garden a new tomb, in
which no one had ever been laid. 42Because it was the Jewish day of Preparation[i] and since the tomb
was nearby,[j] they laid Jesus there.

The Empty Tomb

20 Early on the first day of the week, while it was still dark, Mary Magdalene[k] went to the tomb and
saw that the stone had been removed from the entrance.[l] 2So she came running to Simon Peter
and the other disciple, the one Jesus loved,[m] and said, "They have taken the Lord out of the tomb, and we
don't know where they have put him!"[n]
3So Peter and the other disciple started for the tomb.[o] 4Both were running, but the other disciple out-
ran Peter and reached the tomb first. 5He bent over and looked in[p] at the strips of linen[q] lying there but
did not go in. 6Then Simon Peter, who was behind him, arrived and went into the tomb. He saw the strips
of linen lying there, 7as well as the burial cloth that had been around Jesus' head.[r] The cloth was folded
up by itself, separate from the linen. 8Finally the other disciple, who had reached the tomb first,[s] also
went inside. He saw and believed. 9(They still did not understand from Scripture[t] that Jesus had to rise
from the dead.)[u]

Jesus Appears to Mary Magdalene

10Then the disciples went back to their homes, 11but Mary stood outside the tomb crying. As she wept,
she bent over to look into the tomb[v] 12and saw two angels in white,[w] seated where Jesus' body had been,
one at the head and the other at the foot.
13They asked her, "Woman, why are you crying?"[x]
"They have taken my Lord away," she said, "and I don't know where they have put him."[y] 14At this, she
turned around and saw Jesus standing there,[z] but she did not realize that it was Jesus.[a]
15"Woman," he said, "why are you crying?[b] Who is it you are looking for?"
Thinking he was the gardener, she said, "Sir, if you have carried him away, tell me where you have put
him, and I will get him."
16Jesus said to her, "Mary."
She turned toward him and cried out in Aramaic,[c] "Rabboni!"[d] (which means Teacher).
17Jesus said, "Do not hold on to me, for I have not yet returned to the Father. Go instead to my broth-
ers[e] and tell them, 'I am returning to my Father[f] and your Father, to my God and your God.' "
18Mary Magdalene[g] went to the disciples[h] with the news: "I have seen the Lord!" And she told them
that he had said these things to her.

Jesus Appears to His Disciples

19On the evening of that first day of the week, when the disciples were together, with the doors locked

19:39 [f]Jn 3:1; 7:50
19:40 [g]Lk 24:12; Jn 11:44; 20:5,7 [h]Mt 26:12
19:42 [i]ver 14,31 [j]ver 20,41
20:1 [k]ver 18; Jn 19:25 [l]Mt 27:60,66
20:2 [m]Jn 13:23 [n]ver 13
20:3 [o]Lk 24:12
20:5 [p]ver 11 [q]Jn 19:40
20:7 [r]Jn 11:44
20:8 [s]ver 4
20:9 [t]Mt 22:29; Jn 2:22 [u]Lk 24:26,46
20:11 [v]ver 5
20:12 [w]Mt 28:2, 3; Mk 16:5; Lk 24:4; Ac 5:19
20:13 [x]ver 15 [y]ver 2
20:14 [z]Mt 28:9; Mk 16:9 [a]Lk 24:16; Jn 21:4
20:15 [b]ver 13
20:16 [c]Jn 5:2 [d]Mt 23:7
20:17 [e]Mt 28:10 [f]Jn 7:33
20:18 [g]ver 1 [h]Lk 24:10,22,23

[a] 39 Greek *a hundred litrai* (about 34 kilograms)

---

crucifixion because otherwise people could have taken away the victim before he died and revived him. Joseph's request, however, was unusual (see the note on Mk 15:45). Joseph and Nicodemus could have been excommunicated from the synagogue (see the note on Jn 9:22) and ousted from the Sanhedrin for their actions.

19:39–40 Seventy-five pounds (34 kg) was a very large amount of myrrh and aloes, similar to what as used in royal burials (see the note on Mt 26:12; see also "Perfumes and Anointing Oils" on p. 1746).

The "strips of linen" (v. 40) were thin strips like bandages. There was also a shroud, a large sheet (Mt 27:59; Mk 15:46; Lk 23:53; see "The Shroud of Turin Controversy" on p. 1658 and "Jewish Burial Practices" on p. 1688). See also the note on Matthew 26:12.

19:41 See "The Location of Jesus' Tomb" on page 1615.

20:1 For "while it was still dark," see the note on Luke 24:1.

Tombs of New Testament times were either caves or holes dug into stone cliffs. Since only grave clothes are mentioned in connection with tombs, it seems certain that the Jews used neither caskets nor sarcophagi. Tombs carried no inscriptions or paintings. Embalming, learned long ago in Egypt (Ge 50:2), had soon become a lost art (Jn 11:39). A general opening gave access to vaults that opened on ledges to provide support for the stone doors. The door to such a grave weighed from 1 to 3 tons (.9 to 2.7 metric tons); hence the miracle of the stone being rolled away from Jesus' tomb (see also Lk 24:2).

20:6–7 If someone had stolen Jesus' body, the strips of linen and the burial cloth would most likely have been missing or at least strewn about the floor. However, the burial cloth was neatly folded up, separate from the linen.

20:9 See "The Resurrection of Jesus" on page 1617.

20:11 As in 11:33 (see the note there), "crying" means "wailing," a loud expression of grief.

20:12 See "Angels and Guardian Spirits in the Bible and the Ancient Near East" on page 1529.

20:17 "My brothers" probably refers to the disciples, as the members of Jesus' family most likely did not believe in him at this point (see the note on Lk 8:19), although they evidently became disciples not long afterward (see Ac 1:14 and its note; see also the note on Jude 1).

20:19 "Peace be with you!" was a common Hebrew greeting.

CAN JOHN'S GOSPEL BE TRUSTED?

First-century kochim tomb (Jesus' resurrection is the ultimate miracle recorded)

© Dr. James C. Martin

◆ In any attempt to assess the reliability of John, pride of place should be given to John's own testimony about the nature of his literary endeavor. John alone among the Gospels provides an explicit statement of purpose (see vv. 30–31). This purpose statement reflects the writer's intention to present selective accounts of Jesus' ministry, aimed at persuading the reader that Jesus of Nazareth really is the promised Messiah. The apostle was well aware that Jesus did many other things, commenting at the close of his Gospel account, "If every one of them were written down, I suppose that even the whole world would not have room for the books that would be written" (21:25). Many of the apparent Johannine omissions are thus essentially acknowledged by John and, therefore, are not to be considered as evidence against historicity.

◆ No other Gospel addresses the theme of truth as frequently as John's. He used a series of signs and a parade of witnesses to reinforce the main thesis of his work. The trustworthiness of these witnesses, including John's own explicit claim to have been an eyewitness (19:35), is integral to his purpose and should remind the reader that accuracy was deeply important to this apostle and author.

◆ This concern for accurate reporting is reflected in the exact recording of numbers (2:20; 21:11); the translation of foreign terms (1:38,41; 20:16); and the precise depictions of persons, places and customs (2:6; 4:20; 5:2; 19:40).

◆ A close reading of John reveals numerous agreements with the Synoptic Gospels, in terms both of broad themes and of specific details.

Modern readers of John are wise to refrain both from overstating the apparent contradictions and from excessive efforts at harmonizing John with the other Gospels. John successfully accomplished his stated aim: to present an eloquent, accurate and persuasive testimony that Jesus is indeed the Messiah, the Son of God (20:31).

JOHN 20 There are obvious and striking differences between the Gospel of John and the Synoptic Gospels (Mt, Mk and Lk). These include:

◆ John contains no narrative parables, no account of the transfiguration, no record of the Lord's Supper, no mention of Jesus' temptation and no report of Jesus casting out demons.

◆ John includes a vast amount of material not found in the synoptic tradition, such as the records of extended conversations with Nicodemus, the Samaritan woman and the disciples, as well as of significant miracles (e.g., the turning of water into wine and the resurrection of Lazarus).

◆ John recounts an extensive Judean ministry for Jesus, including several visits to Jerusalem, whereas the Synoptic Gospels focus on his Galilean ministry.

◆ Certain features of John's presentation also raise chronological difficulties for understanding Jesus' action in the temple (Jn 2) and the precise sequence of events during Passion Week.

◆ Perhaps most significant, notable stylistic differences emerge between John's Jesus, who discourses poetically on themes of light, life, witness and truth, and the synoptic Jesus, who argues forcefully and consistently on the theme of the kingdom of God.

The accumulation of these differences has generated speculation regarding the historical reliability of this document as a testimony concerning Jesus (20:31). There are, however, significant reasons for believing John to be historically accurate:

for fear of the Jews,[i] Jesus came and stood among them and said, "Peace[j] be with you!"[k] 20After he said
this, he showed them his hands and side.[l] The disciples were overjoyed[m] when they saw the Lord.
21Again Jesus said, "Peace be with you![n] As the Father has sent me,[o] I am sending you."[p] 22And with
that he breathed on them and said, "Receive the Holy Spirit.[q] 23If you forgive anyone his sins, they are for-
given; if you do not forgive them, they are not forgiven."[r]

Jesus Appears to Thomas

24Now Thomas[s] (called Didymus), one of the Twelve, was not with the disciples when Jesus came.
25So the other disciples told him, "We have seen the Lord!"
But he said to them, "Unless I see the nail marks in his hands and put my finger where the nails were,
and put my hand into his side,[t] I will not believe it."[u]
26A week later his disciples were in the house again, and Thomas was with them. Though the doors
were locked, Jesus came and stood among them and said, "Peace[v] be with you!"[w] 27Then he said to Thom-
as, "Put your finger here; see my hands. Reach out your hand and put it into my side. Stop doubting and
believe."[x]
28Thomas said to him, "My Lord and my God!"
29Then Jesus told him, "Because you have seen me, you have believed;[y] blessed are those who have
not seen and yet have believed."[z]
30Jesus did many other miraculous signs[a] in the presence of his disciples, which are not recorded in
this book.[b] 31But these are written that you may[a] believe[c] that Jesus is the Christ, the Son of God,[d] and
that by believing you may have life in his name.[e]

Jesus and the Miraculous Catch of Fish

21 Afterward Jesus appeared again to his disciples,[f] by the Sea of Tiberias.[b][g] It happened this way:
2Simon Peter, Thomas[h] (called Didymus), Nathanael[i] from Cana in Galilee,[j] the sons of Zebe-
dee,[k] and two other disciples were together. 3"I'm going out to fish," Simon Peter told them, and they said,
"We'll go with you." So they went out and got into the boat, but that night they caught nothing.[l]
4Early in the morning, Jesus stood on the shore, but the disciples did not realize that it was Jesus.[m]
5He called out to them, "Friends, haven't you any fish?"
"No," they answered.
6He said, "Throw your net on the right side of the boat and you will find some." When they did, they
were unable to haul the net in because of the large number of fish.[n]
7Then the disciple whom Jesus loved[o] said to Peter, "It is the Lord!" As soon as Simon Peter heard him
say, "It is the Lord," he wrapped his outer garment around him (for he had taken it off) and jumped into
the water. 8The other disciples followed in the boat, towing the net full of fish, for they were not far from
shore, about a hundred yards.[c] 9When they landed, they saw a fire[p] of burning coals there with fish on
it,[q] and some bread.
10Jesus said to them, "Bring some of the fish you have just caught."
11Simon Peter climbed aboard and dragged the net ashore. It was full of large fish, 153, but even with
so many the net was not torn. 12Jesus said to them, "Come and have breakfast." None of the disciples
dared ask him, "Who are you?" They knew it was the Lord. 13Jesus came, took the bread and gave it to
them, and did the same with the fish.[r] 14This was now the third time Jesus appeared to his disciples[s] af-
ter he was raised from the dead.

Jesus Reinstates Peter

15When they had finished eating, Jesus said to Simon Peter, "Simon son of John, do you truly love me
more than these?"

20:19 [i]Jn 7:13 [j]Jn 14:27 [k]ver 21, 26; Lk 24:36-39
20:20 [l]Lk 24:39, 40; Jn 19:34 [m]Jn 16:20,22
20:21 [n]ver 19 [o]Jn 3:17 [p]Mt 28:19; Jn 17:18
20:22 [q]Jn 7:39; Ac 2:38; 8:15-17; 19:2; Gal 3:2
20:23 [r]Mt 16:19; 18:18
20:24 [s]Jn 11:16
20:25 [t]ver 20 [u]Mk 16:11
20:26 [v]Jn 14:27 [w]ver 21
20:27 [x]ver 25; Lk 24:40
20:29 [y]Jn 3:15 [z]1Pe 1:8
20:30 [a]Jn 2:11 [b]Jn 21:25
20:31 [c]Jn 3:15; 19:35 [d]Mt 4:3 [e]Mt 25:46
21:1 [f]Jn 20:19, 26 [g]Jn 6:1
21:2 [h]Jn 11:16 [i]Jn 1:45 [j]Jn 2:1 [k]Mt 4:21
21:3 [l]Lk 5:5
21:4 [m]Lk 24:16; Jn 20:14
21:6 [n]Lk 5:4-7
21:7 [o]Jn 13:23
21:9 [p]Jn 18:18 [q]ver 10,13
21:13 [r]ver 9
21:14 [s]Jn 20:19, 26

[a] *31* Some manuscripts *may continue to* [b] *1* That is, Sea of Galilee [c] *8* Greek *about two hundred cubits* (about 90 meters)

20:30–31 See "Can John's Gospel Be Trusted?" on page 1761.
20:31 Jesus' name represents all that he is and stands for (see the note on Jer 16:21).
21:1 For the "Sea of Tiberias," see the note on 6:1.
21:3 Nighttime was favored by fishermen in ancient times (see "Fishing in New Testament Times" on p. 1676).
21:7 It is curious that Peter put on his outer garment (the word appears only here in the NT) before jumping into the water. But Jews regarded a greeting as a religious act that could be performed only when one was clothed. Peter may have been preparing himself to greet the Lord.
21:9 "Burning coals" is literally "charcoal" (see the note on 18:26). See also the note on coal/charcoal at Psalm 120:4.

21:15 [t]Mt 26:33, 35; Jn 13:37 [u]Lk 12:32
"Yes, Lord," he said, "you know that I love you."[t]
Jesus said, "Feed my lambs."[u]
16 Again Jesus said, "Simon son of John, do you truly love me?"
He answered, "Yes, Lord, you know that I love you."
21:16 [v]Mt 2:6; Ac 20:28; 1Pe 5:2,3
Jesus said, "Take care of my sheep."[v]
17 The third time he said to him, "Simon son of John, do you love me?"
21:17 [w]Jn 13:38 [x]Jn 16:30 [y]ver 16
Peter was hurt because Jesus asked him the third time, "Do you love me?"[w] He said, "Lord, you know
all things;[x] you know that I love you."
Jesus said, "Feed my sheep.[y] 18 I tell you the truth, when you were younger you dressed yourself and
went where you wanted; but when you are old you will stretch out your hands, and someone else will
21:19 [z]Jn 12:33; 18:32 [a]2Pe 1:14
dress you and lead you where you do not want to go." 19 Jesus said this to indicate the kind of death[z] by
which Peter would glorify God.[a] Then he said to him, "Follow me!"
21:20 [b]ver 7; Jn 13:23 [c]Jn 13:25
20 Peter turned and saw that the disciple whom Jesus loved[b] was following them. (This was the one who
had leaned back against Jesus at the supper and had said, "Lord, who is going to betray you?")[c] 21 When
Peter saw him, he asked, "Lord, what about him?"
21:22 [d]Mt 16:27; 1Co 4:5; Rev 2:25 [e]ver 19
21:23 [f]Ac 1:16
22 Jesus answered, "If I want him to remain alive until I return,[d] what is that to you? You must follow
me."[e] 23 Because of this, the rumor spread among the brothers[f] that this disciple would not die. But Jesus
did not say that he would not die; he only said, "If I want him to remain alive until I return, what is that
to you?"
21:24 [g]Jn 15:27 [h]Jn 19:35
24 This is the disciple who testifies to these things[g] and who wrote them down. We know that his tes-
timony is true.[h]
21:25 [i]Jn 20:30
25 Jesus did many other things as well.[i] If every one of them were written down, I suppose that even
the whole world would not have room for the books that would be written.

21:18–19 The early church understood the phrase "stretch out your hands" (v. 18) as a prophecy of crucifixion. Peter would be a martyr. Tradition indicates that he was in fact crucified upside down.

INTRODUCTION TO *Acts*

AUTHOR, PLACE AND DATE OF WRITING

Extrabiblical evidence and clues from the book itself suggest that Acts was written by the physician Luke, the traveling companion of Paul and the author of the Gospel of Luke. The date of writing has been debated, but A.D. 63–70 is the probable range, with an early date being the more likely. Although the place of writing is unknown, some have suggested Rome.

AUDIENCE

Like the Gospel of Luke, the book of Acts was originally addressed to an individual named Theophilus (1:1), but it was clearly intended for all believers.

CULTURAL FACTS AND HIGHLIGHTS

As a historical account of Christianity's origins, Acts records the relations between the church and the Roman Empire. It describes the founding of the church and the spread of the gospel throughout the known world. Luke's account covers a period of about 30 years and reaches from Jerusalem to Rome—and archaeological findings reveal that in each instance Luke used the proper terms for the time and place being described.

At a time when the church was facing growing suspicion from both the Roman authorities and the Jewish establishment, Luke demonstrated that the riots and disorders that followed Paul were not Paul's doing; in fact, on several occasions Paul was either exonerated by Roman officials or determined not to be a person of interest.

Although the first 12 chapters concentrate mainly on the apostle Peter, it would appear that Luke wrote Acts primarily as a vindication of the life and theology of Paul. The book describes his conversion; follows him in his missionary journeys; testifies to miracles he performed; gives accounts of conversions brought about by his preaching; describes how Gentiles were moved to turn from idols; shows that believers in churches around the world received him as a messenger from God; and, above all, provides accounts of the beatings, imprisonments, dangers and abuses he endured for the sake of Christ.

TIMELINE

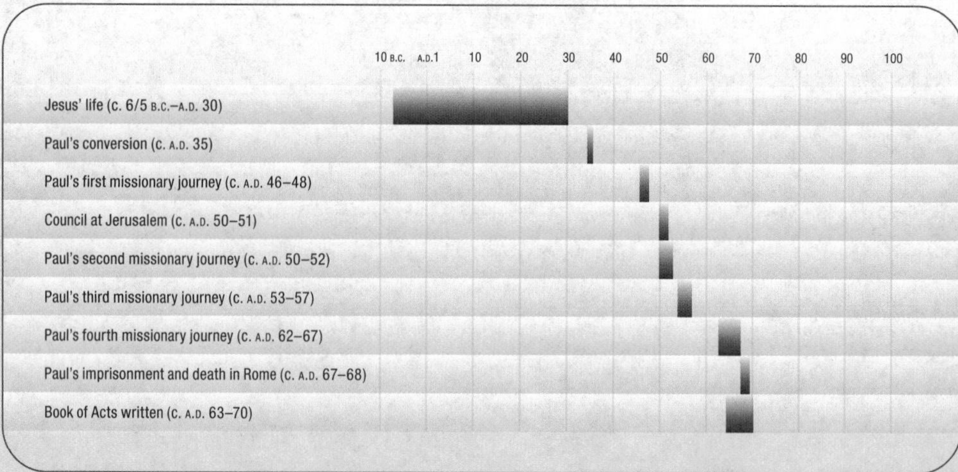

AS YOU READ

Note the adversities and struggles of the early church. Be encouraged and inspired by the enthusiasm that carried the gospel across ethnic and national boundaries, remembering that the same Spirit operating in Acts is at work in the church today.

DID YOU KNOW?

- "The Way" as an early name for Christianity occurs several times in Acts (e.g., 9:2).
- If a prisoner escaped, the life of the guard was demanded in his place (16:27).
- Blasphemy was the gravest accusation for a Jew, but treason—support of a rival king above Caesar—was the worst possible accusation against a Roman (17:7).
- Inscriptions in Greek and Latin on stone slabs (two of which have been discovered by archaeologists) were placed on the barrier between the inner and outer temple courts, warning Gentiles of the death penalty for proceeding further (21:28).
- The Romans considered sailing after September 15 doubtful and after November 11 suicidal (27:9).

THEMES

Acts includes the following themes:

1. *The Holy Spirit's empowerment for witness.* The central theme in Acts is the Spirit's power and witness. Peter and John asserted, "We cannot help speaking about what we have seen and heard" (4:20).

2. *Community.* Acts reveals a united, caring community of believers who enjoyed not only a common belief and worship but also a common experience as they shared their possessions and themselves with one another (2:42–47; 4:32–37).

3. *Reconciliation.* Despite the oneness of the faith community, conflicts did arise. But the church is intended to be inclusive: Jews and Gentiles (10:23–48)—even Samaritans (8:4–24)—were members of Christ's body. The inner working of Christ's Spirit alone engenders harmony and reconciliation.

4. *Persecution.* The Holy Spirit not only empowers believers to withstand opposition and suffering (6:10) but also enables the spread of the gospel, despite persecution (8:1–4; 11:19–21). Mistreatment for the sake of the faith actually spreads the gospel and builds up the faith of those who suffer, validating them as Christ's disciples (Jn 15:18—16:4).

OUTLINE

- I. The Beginnings of the Church (1–12)
  - A. The Church in Jerusalem (1–7)
  - B. The Church Is Scattered (8:1—9:31)
  - C. The Church Spreads to the Gentiles (9:32—12:25)
- II. Paul's Missionary Journeys (13:1—21:16)
  - A. Paul's First Missionary Journey (13–14)
  - B. The Jerusalem Conference (15:1–35)
  - C. Paul's Second Missionary Journey (15:36—18:22)
  - D. Paul's Third Missionary Journey (18:23—21:16)
- III. Paul's Arrest and Imprisonment (21:17—28:31)

Jesus Taken Up Into Heaven

1 In my former book,[a] Theophilus, I wrote about all that Jesus began to do and to teach[b] 2until the day
he was taken up to heaven,[c] after giving instructions[d] through the Holy Spirit to the apostles[e] he
had chosen.[f] 3After his suffering, he showed himself to these men and gave many convincing proofs that
he was alive. He appeared to them[g] over a period of forty days and spoke about the kingdom of God. 4On
one occasion, while he was eating with them, he gave them this command: "Do not leave Jerusalem, but
wait for the gift my Father promised, which you have heard me speak about.[h] 5For John baptized with[a]
water, but in a few days you will be baptized with the Holy Spirit."

1:1 aLk 1:1-4 bLk 3:23 **1:2** cver 9,11; Mk 16:19 dMt 28:19,20 eMk 6:30 fJn 13:18 **1:3** gMt 28:17; Lk 24:34,36; Jn 20:19,26; 21:1,14; 1Co 15:5-7 **1:4** hLk 24:49; Jn 14:16; Ac 2:33

[a] 5 Or *in*

1:1 For "book," see "Scrolls, Seals and Codices" on page 2053. For "Theophilus," see the note on Luke 1:1.
1:4–5 *Agrapha* ("unwritten things") are units of tradition concerning Christ, mostly sayings ascribed to Jesus transmitted to us outside of the canonical Gospels. The entire collection of agrapha, gathered from all sources, is not large, and when what is obviously Apocryphal or unauthentic is eliminated, the small remainder is of very little value. The best authenticated agrapha are those found in the New Testament itself, outside the Gospels: four in Acts (vv. 4–5; vv. 7–8; 11:16; 20:35), two in Paul's letters (1Co 11:24–25; 1Th 4:15–17) and one in James (1:12). Other sources of agrapha are: (1) ancient manuscripts of the New Testament (most often, sayings preserved in such manuscripts are textual variations); (2) patristic literature (the writings of the church fathers, such as Papias, bishop of Hierapolis from approximately A.D. 80–155; Justin Martyr; Clement of Alexandria; and Origen; (3) papyri discovered in Egypt during the twentieth century, especially those found by Grenfell and Hunt at Oxyrhynchus; (4) the Apocryphal gospels, such as the *Gospel According to the Hebrews,* the *Gospel According to the Egyptians* and the *Gospel of Thomas,* found near Nag Hammadi in Upper Egypt and dated to around A.D. 150—few of which may be regarded as genuine; and (5) Islamic sources (sayings ascribed to Jesus that are for the most part of no value).
1:5 See "Baptism in the Ancient World" on page 1562.

The Church From the Resurrection to the Conversion of Paul

ACTS 1 The book of Acts provides the only historical record of the activities of the earliest Christians from the time of Jesus' resurrection until the conversion of Paul. Acts 1–8 precedes the first mention of Paul, and these chapters provide a selective report, primarily detailing the activity of the apostles in Jerusalem following Jesus' resurrection.

The earliest believers began to establish a communal life. They were frequently in conflict with the Jewish authorities, and followers of Jesus soon were expelled from the temple. Seeds of dissension between **Hellenistic**[1] and Jewish Christianity began to sprout even during these early years (6:1). Meanwhile, although Acts does not tell much about early missionary work outside of Jerusalem, it is certain that the church saw extraordinary growth. The brothers of Jesus, who are mentioned among the earliest believers (1:14), are known to have been active in spreading the gospel throughout the region later known as Palestine. We are not given many details, but Acts intimates that communities of Christians were established in Antioch (11:19),[2] Damascus (9:2),[3] North Africa (8:27) and **Samaria** (8:5) prior to Paul's conversion. The Good News even reached Rome, the leading city of the Roman world, prior to the advent of Paul's missionary enterprise.[4]

It is highly likely that some pilgrims who had been present in Jerusalem during the crucifixion and resurrection of Jesus became believers (2:5). When these masses returned to their hometowns, they took the gospel with them. Persecution also played a role in the spread of the Good News and the growth of the early church. As believers migrated in order to avoid persecution, they established new Christian communities in the towns and cities where they settled.[5]

[1]See Glossary on page 2080 for definitions of bolded words. [2]See "Antioch of Syria, Center Of Christianity" on page 1904. [3]See "Damascus" on page 1087. [4]See "Rome" on page 1838. [5]See "The Geographic Expansion of the Church Under Persecution" on page 1781.

6So when they met together, they asked him, "Lord, are you at this time going to restore[i] the kingdom to Israel?"

7He said to them: "It is not for you to know the times or dates the Father has set by his own authority.[j] 8But you will receive power when the Holy Spirit comes on you;[k] and you will be my witnesses[l] in Jerusalem, and in all Judea and Samaria,[m] and to the ends of the earth."[n]

9After he said this, he was taken up[o] before their very eyes, and a cloud hid him from their sight.

10They were looking intently up into the sky as he was going, when suddenly two men dressed in white[p] stood beside them. 11"Men of Galilee,"[q] they said, "why do you stand here looking into the sky? This same Jesus, who has been taken from you into heaven, will come back[r] in the same way you have seen him go into heaven."

Matthias Chosen to Replace Judas

12Then they returned to Jerusalem[s] from the hill called the Mount of Olives,[t] a Sabbath day's walk[a] from the city. 13When they arrived, they went upstairs to the room[u] where they were staying. Those present were Peter, John, James and Andrew; Philip and Thomas, Bartholomew and Matthew; James son of Alphaeus and Simon the Zealot, and Judas son of James.[v] 14They all joined together constantly in prayer,[w] along with the women[x] and Mary the mother of Jesus, and with his brothers.[y]

15In those days Peter stood up among the believers[b] (a group numbering about a hundred and twenty) 16and said, "Brothers, the Scripture had to be fulfilled[z] which the Holy Spirit spoke long ago through the mouth of David concerning Judas,[a] who served as guide for those who arrested Jesus— 17he was one of our number[b] and shared in this ministry."[c]

18(With the reward[d] he got for his wickedness, Judas bought a field;[e] there he fell headlong, his body burst open and all his intestines spilled out. 19Everyone in Jerusalem heard about this, so they called that field in their language Akeldama, that is, Field of Blood.)

20"For," said Peter, "it is written in the book of Psalms,

> " 'May his place be deserted;
> let there be no one to dwell in it,'[c][f]

and,

> " 'May another take his place of leadership.'[d][g]

21Therefore it is necessary to choose one of the men who have been with us the whole time the Lord Jesus went in and out among us, 22beginning from John's baptism[h] to the time when Jesus was taken up from us. For one of these must become a witness[i] with us of his resurrection."

23So they proposed two men: Joseph called Barsabbas (also known as Justus) and Matthias. 24Then they prayed,[j] "Lord, you know everyone's heart.[k] Show us which of these two you have chosen 25to take over this apostolic ministry, which Judas left to go where he belongs." 26Then they cast lots, and the lot fell to Matthias; so he was added to the eleven apostles.[l]

1:6 [i]Mt 17:11
1:7 [j]Mt 24:36
1:8 [k]Ac 2:1-4 [l]Lk 24:48 [m]Ac 8:1-25 [n]Mt 28:19
1:9 [o]ver 2
1:10 [p]Lk 24:4; Jn 20:12
1:11 [q]Ac 2:7 [r]Mt 16:27
1:12 [s]Lk 24:52 [t]Mt 21:1
1:13 [u]Ac 9:37; 20:8 [v]Mt 10:2-4; Mk 3:16-19; Lk 6:14-16
1:14 [w]Ac 2:42; 6:4 [x]Lk 23:49,55 [y]Mt 12:46
1:16 [z]ver 20 [a]Jn 13:18
1:17 [b]Jn 6:70,71 [c]ver 25
1:18 [d]Mt 26:14,15 [e]Mt 27:3-10
1:20 [f]Ps 69:25 [g]Ps 109:8
1:22 [h]Mk 1:4 [i]ver 8
1:24 [j]Ac 6:6; 14:23 [k]1Sa 16:7; Jer 17:10; Ac 15:8; Rev 2:23
1:26 [l]Ac 2:14

[a] *12* That is, about 3/4 mile (about 1,100 meters) [b] *15* Greek *brothers* [c] *20* Psalm 69:25 [d] *20* Psalm 109:8

1:6 Like their fellow countrymen, the disciples were looking for the deliverance of the people of Israel from foreign domination and for the establishment of an earthly kingdom.
1:8 Judea was the region in which Jerusalem was located. Samaria was the adjoining region to the north. (See "The Geographic Expansion of the Church Under Persecution" on p. 1781.)
1:9 On God's *shekînâh* glory (his visible presence), see the note on Exodus 14:19.
1:11 The Twelve were called "men of Galilee" because the disciples, with the exception of Judas, who was no longer present, were all from Galilee.
1:12 The ascension occurred on the eastern slope of the mount between Jerusalem and Bethany (see "The Mount of Olives" on p. 1543).

A "Sabbath day's walk" was the distance drawn from rabbinical reasoning based on several Old Testament passages (Ex 16:29; Nu 35:5; Jos 3:4). A faithful Jew was to travel no farther than .75 miles (1.2 km) on the Sabbath (see the note on Mt 15:2).
1:13 The "room" was probably an upper room of a large house, such as the one where the Last Supper was held (see "The Upper Room" on p. 1654)—perhaps in the home of Mary, the mother of Mark (see the note on 12:12).

For "Bartholomew," see the note on Luke 6:14 and for "Zealot" the note on Matthew 10:4. See also the note on "Thaddaeus" (listed in Mt 10:3 and Mk 3:18 in place of "Judas son of James") at Matthew 10:3.
1:14 These "brothers" would have included James (see the note on Lk 8:19), who later became a leader in the Jerusalem church (12:17; 15:13; 21:18; Gal 1:19; 2:9).
1:18–19 These verses are a parenthesis, an explanation by Luke and not part of Peter's speech. *Akeldama* was the field purchased with the money Judas had received for betraying Jesus. Matthew 27:3–10, which includes a fuller account of the purchase, states that the priests bought it "as a burial place for foreigners." The field was called "the place of blood" ("the Field of Blood" here and in Mt 27:8) in Aramaic (the best translation, although some scholars prefer the rendering "field of sleep" or "cemetery").
1:26 By casting lots they submitted the decision to the ascended Lord. The use of rocks or sticks to designate the choice was common (see 1Ch 26:13–16; see also "Casting Lots" on p. 744).

The Holy Spirit Comes at Pentecost

2 When the day of Pentecost[m] came, they were all together[n] in one place. 2 Suddenly a sound like
the blowing of a violent wind came from heaven and filled the whole house where they were sit-
ting.[o] 3 They saw what seemed to be tongues of fire that separated and came to rest on each of them.
4 All of them were filled with the Holy Spirit and began to speak in other tongues[a][p] as the Spirit enabled
them.

5 Now there were staying in Jerusalem God-fearing[q] Jews from every nation under heaven. 6 When
they heard this sound, a crowd came together in bewilderment, because each one heard them speaking
in his own language. 7 Utterly amazed,[r] they asked: "Are not all these men who are speaking Galileans?[s]
8 Then how is it that each of us hears them in his own native language? 9 Parthians, Medes and Elamites;
residents of Mesopotamia, Judea and Cappadocia,[t] Pontus[u] and Asia,[v] 10 Phrygia[w] and Pamphylia,[x] Egypt
and the parts of Libya near Cyrene;[y] visitors from Rome 11 (both Jews and converts to Judaism); Cretans
and Arabs—we hear them declaring the wonders of God in our own tongues!" 12 Amazed and perplexed,
they asked one another, "What does this mean?"

13 Some, however, made fun of them and said, "They have had too much wine.[b]"[z]

Peter Addresses the Crowd

14 Then Peter stood up with the Eleven, raised his voice and addressed the crowd: "Fellow Jews and all
of you who live in Jerusalem, let me explain this to you; listen carefully to what I say. 15 These men are not
drunk, as you suppose. It's only nine in the morning![a] 16 No, this is what was spoken by the prophet Joel:

> 17 " 'In the last days, God says,
> I will pour out my Spirit on all people.[b]

2:1 [m]Lev 23:15, 16; Ac 20:16 [n]Ac 1:14
2:2 [o]Ac 4:31
2:4 [p]Mk 16:17; 1Co 12:10
2:5 [q]Ac 8:2
2:7 [r]ver 12 [s]Ac 1:11
2:9 [t]1Pe 1:1 [u]Ac 18:2 [v]Ac 16:6; Ro 16:5; 1Co 16:19; 2Co 1:8
2:10 [w]Ac 16:6; 18:23 [x]Ac 13:13; 15:38 [y]Mt 27:32
2:13 [z]1Co 14:23
2:15 [a]1Th 5:7
2:17 [b]Isa 44:3; Jn 7:37-39; Ac 10:45

[a] 4 Or *languages*; also in verse 11 [b] 13 Or *sweet wine*

2:1 The day of Pentecost was the fiftieth day after the Sabbath of Passover week (Lev 23:15–16), thus the first day of the week. Pentecost is also called the Feast of Weeks (Dt 16:10), the Feast of Harvest (Ex 23:16) and the day of firstfruits (Nu 28:26). See "The Festivals of Israel" on page 186 and "Pentecost" on page 275.

2:5 "God-fearing Jews" refers to devout Jews from different parts of the world who were then assembled in Jerusalem either as pilgrims attending the Feast of Pentecost or as current residents (cf. Lk 2:25).

2:9–11 Several countries and peoples are mentioned as being present at Pentecost (numbers indicate the sequence in which they are listed): (1) Parthians were inhabitants of the territory from the Tigris River to India. (2) Medes were inhabitants of Media, which lay east of Mesopotamia, northwest of Persia and south-southwest of the Caspian Sea. (3) Elamites inhabited Elam, north of the Persian Gulf and bounded on the west by the Tigris. (4) Mesopotamia lay between the Euphrates and the Tigris Rivers. (5) Judea was the homeland of the Jews, perhaps used here in the Old Testament sense "from the river of Egypt to . . . the Euphrates" (Ge 15:18), including Galilee. (6–8) Cappadocia, Pontus and Asia were districts in Asia Minor. Asia was a Roman province in western Asia Minor, now Turkish territory. (9–10) Phrygia and Pamphylia were districts in Asia Minor. (11) Egypt had become a refuge for Jews since the eighth century B.C. (Two of the five districts of Alexandria were Jewish.) (12) Libya was a region west of Egypt. (13) Cyrene was the capital of a district of Libya called Cyrenaica. (14) Rome was home to thousands of Jews. (15) Cretans lived on Crete, the fourth largest island in the Mediterranean Sea. The island is 156 miles (250 km) long and lies directly south of the Aegean Sea (see "Crete" on p. 1972). (16) Arabs were from a region to the southeast.

2:9 Cappadocia was a large inland region of Asia Minor that apparently had been given this name by the Persians, although its people were called "Syrians" by the Greeks. In the latter period of the Persian Empire the region had been divided into two territories, of which the more northerly was later called Pontus and the more southerly Cappadocia, the name it retained in New Testament times. It was bounded on the north by Pontus, on the east by Syria and Armenia, on the south by Cilicia and on the west by Lycaonia. The Romans built roads through the "Cilician gates" in the Taurus range so that Cappadocia could easily be accessed from the south. The Cappadocians were Aryans. Jews from this region were among the hearers of the first Christian sermon, along with men from other Anatolian provinces.

2:10 In Bible times Phrygia was an inland province of southwestern Asia Minor. Its tablelands, which rose to 4,000 feet (1,250 m), contained numerous cities and towns considerable in size and wealth. Historians agree that the province included greater or lesser territory at different times, its boundaries shifting with almost every generation. It seems that at one point in time it included a greater part of western Asia Minor, after which it was divided into Phrygia Major and Phrygia Minor; later the Romans divided it into three parts. Some Bible students believe that the term "Phrygia" is used loosely in Acts to include small provinces like Pisidia. Although a great deal of Christian activity took place in ancient Phrygia, with this reference the region passes from the Biblical record.

Pamphylia was a small Roman province of southern Asia Minor, extending 75 miles (125 km) inland to the Taurus Mountains. It was surrounded by Pisidia on the north, Cilicia to the east and Lycia to the southwest. It never became an important province, and its boundaries were often changed by sudden and arbitrary political decisions. The emperor Claudius brought the region into the Roman provincial system during the first century A.D. It is said that most of Pampylia's inhabitants were illiterate, and Christianity never flourished there as it did in other provinces in Asia Minor.

2:11 "Converts to Judaism" refers to Gentiles who undertook the full observance of the Mosaic Law and were therefore received into full fellowship with the Jews (see "Proselytes in Second Temple Judaism" on p. 1776; cf. "God-fearers" in the note on 10:2).

Crete is an island in the Mediterranean Sea with Cythera on the northwest and Rhodes on the northeast, forming a natural stepping stone between Europe and Asia Minor. The island is about 156 miles (250 km) long and about 35 miles (56 km) wide. Despite its enviable geographical position, Crete has for the most part not held a prominent place in history, partly because of internal dissensions. Crete was for a long time the center of a great power—the Minoan civilization—but that power collapsed around 1200 B.C. (see "Greece: From the Prehistoric Period Through the Mycenaean Empire" on p. 1810). In more modern times, Crete accepted Turkish rule and the Islamic faith until 1913, when it was formally incorporated into Greece, in which the Orthodox church predominates. See "Crete" on page 1972.

2:13 In the New Testament, the primary Greek word for "wine" is *oinos*. The word *gleukos* ("new, sweet wine") occurs only here. See "Wine and Alcoholic Beverages in the Ancient World" on page 2015.

2:15 On a festival day such as Pentecost, a Jew would not break his fast until at least 10:00 A.M. So it was extremely unlikely that a group of men would have been drunk at such an early hour.

2:17 [c]Ac 21:9 Your sons and daughters will prophesy,[c]
your young men will see visions,
your old men will dream dreams.
18 Even on my servants, both men and women,
I will pour out my Spirit in those days,
2:18 [d]Ac 21:9-12 and they will prophesy.[d]
19 I will show wonders in the heaven above
and signs on the earth below,
blood and fire and billows of smoke.
20 The sun will be turned to darkness
2:20 [e]Mt 24:29 and the moon to blood[e]
before the coming of the great and glorious day of the Lord.
21 And everyone who calls
2:21 [f]Ro 10:13 on the name of the Lord will be saved.'[a][f]

22 "Men of Israel, listen to this: Jesus of Nazareth was a man accredited by God to you by miracles,
2:22 [g]Jn 4:48; Ac 10:38 [h]Jn 3:2 wonders and signs,[g] which God did among you through him,[h] as you yourselves know. 23 This man

[a] *21* Joel 2:28-32

2:18 See the note on prophetesses at Exodus 15:20–21.

The Jewish Diaspora in the First Century A.D.

ACTS 2 Jews had been living outside the land of Israel at least since residents from the northern kingdom of Israel were taken as exiles by **Assyria** and those from the southern kingdom of Judah were exiled by **Babylon**.[1] During the **Hellenistic** era these Jews of the **Diaspora** were scattered throughout the Roman Empire and beyond.[2] The long list of place-names mentioned in Acts 2:9–11 is consistent with the literary and inscriptional evidence on the widespread geographic distribution of Jews at this time. Special mention may be made of the longstanding presence of a vibrant Jewish community in Babylonia (which contributed much to the intellectual vigor of the faith), of the large community at Rome (which lobbied passionately for the political interests of Judaism)[3] and of the community in Alexandria (which produced a wealth of scholarship, including the writings of Philo).[4]

Jews of the Diaspora struggled to preserve their unique ethnic and religious identity, while remaining good citizens of the cities in which they lived. In general, they appear to have succeeded on both counts. Their zeal in contributing to the half-shekel tax for the Jerusalem temple and their frequent pilgrimages to the Holy City are evidence that the vast majority maintained allegiance to their faith.

While serious outbreaks of violence against Jews did occur from time to time (notably in the years surrounding the Jewish revolt in A.D. 66–70 and later, under the reign of Hadrian), the Jewish people were generally permitted to maintain their unique customs—while continuing to make a contribution to the civic life of the empire.

[1]See "The Postexilic Period of the Old Testament: The Persian Period" on page 699, "The Postexilic Period of the Old Testament: The Hasmonean Period" on page 700, and "The Postexilic Period of the Old Testament: The Roman and Herodian Periods" on page 701. [2]See "The Roman Empire" on page 1845. [3]See "Rome" on page 1838. [4]See "Alexandria" on page 1805.

was handed over to you by God's set purpose and foreknowledge;[i] and you, with the help of wicked men,[a] put him to death by nailing him to the cross.[j] 24But God raised him from the dead,[k] freeing him from the agony of death, because it was impossible for death to keep its hold on him.[l] 25David said about him:

> " 'I saw the Lord always before me.
> Because he is at my right hand,
> I will not be shaken.
> 26Therefore my heart is glad and my tongue rejoices;
> my body also will live in hope,
> 27because you will not abandon me to the grave,
> nor will you let your Holy One see decay.[m]
> 28You have made known to me the paths of life;
> you will fill me with joy in your presence.'[b]

29"Brothers, I can tell you confidently that the patriarch[n] David died and was buried,[o] and his tomb is here[p] to this day. 30But he was a prophet and knew that God had promised him on oath that he would place one of his descendants on his throne.[q] 31Seeing what was ahead, he spoke of the resurrection of the Christ,[c] that he was not abandoned to the grave, nor did his body see decay.[r] 32God has raised this Jesus to life,[s] and we are all witnesses[t] of the fact. 33Exalted[u] to the right hand of God,[v] he has received from the Father[w] the promised Holy Spirit[x] and has poured out[y] what you now see and hear. 34For David did not ascend to heaven, and yet he said,

> " 'The Lord said to my Lord:
> "Sit at my right hand
> 35until I make your enemies
> a footstool for your feet." '[d][z]

36"Therefore let all Israel be assured of this: God has made this Jesus, whom you crucified, both Lord and Christ."[a]

37When the people heard this, they were cut to the heart and said to Peter and the other apostles, "Brothers, what shall we do?"[b]

38Peter replied, "Repent and be baptized,[c] every one of you, in the name of Jesus Christ for the forgiveness of your sins.[d] And you will receive the gift of the Holy Spirit. 39The promise is for you and your children[e] and for all who are far off[f]—for all whom the Lord our God will call."

40With many other words he warned them; and he pleaded with them, "Save yourselves from this corrupt generation."[g] 41Those who accepted his message were baptized, and about three thousand were added to their number that day.

The Fellowship of the Believers

42They devoted themselves to the apostles' teaching and to the fellowship, to the breaking of bread and to prayer.[h] 43Everyone was filled with awe, and many wonders and miraculous signs were done by the apostles.[i] 44All the believers were together and had everything in common.[j] 45Selling their possessions and goods, they gave to anyone as he had need.[k] 46Every day they continued to meet together in the temple courts.[l] They broke bread[m] in their homes and ate together with glad and sincere hearts, 47praising God and enjoying the favor of all the people.[n] And the Lord added to their number[o] daily those who were being saved.

2:23 [i]Lk 22:22; Ac 3:18; 4:28 [j]Lk 24:20; Ac 3:13
2:24 [k]ver 32; 1Co 6:14; 2Co 4:14; Eph 1:20; Col 2:12; Heb 13:20; 1Pe 1:21 [l]Jn 20:9
2:27 [m]ver 31; Ac 13:35
2:29 [n]Ac 7:8,9 [o]1Ki 2:10; Ac 13:36 [p]Ne 3:16
2:30 [q]2Sa 7:12; Ps 132:11
2:31 [r]Ps 16:10
2:32 [s]ver 24 [t]Ac 1:8
2:33 [u]Php 2:9 [v]Mk 16:19 [w]Ac 1:4 [x]Jn 7:39; 14:26 [y]Ac 10:45
2:35 [z]Ps 110:1; Mt 22:44
2:36 [a]Lk 2:11
2:37 [b]Lk 3:10,12, 14
2:38 [c]Ac 8:12,16, 36,38; 22:16 [d]Lk 24:47; Ac 3:19
2:39 [e]Isa 44:3 [f]Ac 10:45; Eph 2:13
2:40 [g]Dt 32:5
2:42 [h]Ac 1:14
2:43 [i]Ac 5:12
2:44 [j]Ac 4:32
2:45 [k]Mt 19:21
2:46 [l]Lk 24:53; Ac 5:21,42 [m]Ac 20:7
2:47 [n]Ro 14:18 [o]ver 41; Ac 5:14

[a] 23 Or *of those not having the law* (that is, Gentiles) [b] 28 Psalm 16:8-11 [c] 31 Or *Messiah.* "The Christ" (Greek) and "the Messiah" (Hebrew) both mean "the Anointed One"; also in verse 36. [d] 35 Psalm 110:1

2:27 For "grave," see "Sheol, Hades, Gehenna, the Abyss and Tartarus: Images of Hell" on page 946.

2:29 The tomb of David could be seen in Jerusalem and still contained the remains of David's body, so the words of Psalm 16:8–11 did not fully apply to him.

2:33 For "the right hand of God," see "The 'Right Hand' in Ancient Thinking" on page 1983.

2:38 For "baptized," see "Baptism in the Ancient World" on page 1562.

2:41 See "Before the Gentile Expansion: The Jewish Churches in the Holy Land" on page 1997.

2:42 For "the breaking of bread," see "The Love Feast" on page 1874.

2:46 "Temple courts" probably refers to Solomon's Colonnade (see the note on Jn 10:23).

Peter Heals the Crippled Beggar

3 One day Peter and John[p] were going up to the temple[q] at the time of prayer—at three in the afternoon.[r] 2Now a man crippled from birth[s] was being carried to the temple gate[t] called Beautiful, where he was put every day to beg[u] from those going into the temple courts. 3When he saw Peter and John about to enter, he asked them for money. 4Peter looked straight at him, as did John. Then Peter said, "Look at us!" 5So the man gave them his attention, expecting to get something from them.

6Then Peter said, "Silver or gold I do not have, but what I have I give you. In the name of Jesus Christ of Nazareth,[v] walk." 7Taking him by the right hand, he helped him up, and instantly the man's feet and ankles became strong. 8He jumped to his feet and began to walk. Then he went with them into the temple courts, walking and jumping,[w] and praising God. 9When all the people[x] saw him walking and praising God, 10they recognized him as the same man who used to sit begging at the temple gate called Beautiful,[y] and they were filled with wonder and amazement at what had happened to him.

Peter Speaks to the Onlookers

11While the beggar held on to Peter and John,[z] all the people were astonished and came running to them in the place called Solomon's Colonnade.[a] 12When Peter saw this, he said to them: "Men of Israel, why does this surprise you? Why do you stare at us as if by our own power or godliness we had made this man walk? 13The God of Abraham, Isaac and Jacob, the God of our fathers,[b] has glorified his servant Jesus. You handed him over to be killed, and you disowned him before Pilate,[c] though he had decided to let him go.[d] 14You disowned the Holy[e] and Righteous One[f] and asked that a murderer be released to you.[g] 15You killed the author of life, but God raised him from the dead.[h] We are witnesses of this. 16By faith in the name of Jesus, this man whom you see and know was made strong. It is Jesus' name and the faith that comes through him that has given this complete healing to him, as you can all see.

17"Now, brothers, I know that you acted in ignorance,[i] as did your leaders.[j] 18But this is how God fulfilled what he had foretold[k] through all the prophets,[l] saying that his Christ[*a*] would suffer.[m] 19Repent, then, and turn to God, so that your sins may be wiped out,[n] that times of refreshing may come from the Lord, 20and that he may send the Christ, who has been appointed for you—even Jesus. 21He must remain in heaven[o] until the time comes for God to restore everything,[p] as he promised long ago through his holy prophets.[q] 22For Moses said, 'The Lord your God will raise up for you a prophet like me from among your own people; you must listen to everything he tells you.[r] 23Anyone who does not listen to him will be completely cut off from among his people.'[*b*][s]

24"Indeed, all the prophets[t] from Samuel on, as many as have spoken, have foretold these days. 25And you are heirs[u] of the prophets and of the covenant[v] God made with your fathers. He said to Abraham, 'Through your offspring all peoples on earth will be blessed.'[*c*][w] 26When God raised up[x] his servant, he sent him first[y] to you to bless you by turning each of you from your wicked ways."

Peter and John Before the Sanhedrin

4 The priests and the captain of the temple guard[z] and the Sadducees[a] came up to Peter and John while they were speaking to the people. 2They were greatly disturbed because the apostles were teaching the people and proclaiming in Jesus the resurrection of the dead.[b] 3They seized Peter and John, and because it was evening, they put them in jail[c] until the next day. 4But many who heard the message believed, and the number of men grew[d] to about five thousand.

3:1 [p]Lk 22:8 [q]Ac 2:46 [r]Ps 55:17
3:2 [s]Ac 14:8 [t]Lk 16:20 [u]Jn 9:8
3:6 [v]ver 16; Ac 4:10
3:8 [w]Ac 14:10
3:9 [x]Ac 4:16,21
3:10 [y]ver 2
3:11 [z]Lk 22:8 [a]Jn 10:23; Ac 5:12
3:13 [b]Ac 5:30 [c]Mt 27:2 [d]Lk 23:4
3:14 [e]Mk 1:24; Ac 4:27 [f]Ac 7:52 [g]Mk 15:11; Lk 23:18-25
3:15 [h]Ac 2:24
3:17 [i]Lk 23:34 [j]Ac 13:27
3:18 [k]Ac 2:23 [l]Lk 24:27 [m]Ac 17:2,3; 26:22,23
3:19 [n]Ac 2:38
3:21 [o]Ac 1:11 [p]Mt 17:11 [q]Lk 1:70
3:22 [r]Dt 18:15,18; Ac 7:37
3:23 [s]Dt 18:19
3:24 [t]Lk 24:27
3:25 [u]Ac 2:39 [v]Ro 9:4,5 [w]Ge 12:3; 22:18; 26:4; 28:14
3:26 [x]ver 22; Ac 2:24 [y]Ac 13:46; Ro 1:16
4:1 [z]Lk 22:4 [a]Mt 3:7
4:2 [b]Ac 17:18
4:3 [c]Ac 5:18
4:4 [d]Ac 2:41

[*a*] *18* Or *Messiah*; also in verse 20 [*b*] *23* Deut. 18:15,18,19 [*c*] *25* Gen. 22:18; 26:4

3:1 The three stated times of prayer for later Judaism were mid-morning (the third hour, 9:00 A.M.), the time of the evening sacrifice (the ninth hour, 3:00 P.M.) and sunset.

3:2–3 The "gate called Beautiful" was the favorite entrance to the temple court. It was probably the bronze-sheathed gate that is elsewhere called the Nicanor Gate. Apparently it led from the court of the Gentiles to the court of women, east of the temple.

For a discussion of "begging" and almsgiving, see the note on Matthew 6:1–2.

3:8 The man proceeded from the outer court (the court of the Gentiles) into the court of women, containing the treasury, and from there into the court of Israel. From the outer court, nine gates led into the inner courts.

3:11 For "Solomon's Colonnade," see the note on John 10:23.

3:13 See "Pontius Pilate" on page 1714.

4:1 The "captain of the temple guard" was a member of one of the leading priestly families and was next in rank to the high priest.

The Sadducees were a Jewish sect whose members came from the priestly line and controlled the temple (see the note on Mt 3:7; see also "The Sadducees" on p. 1600). They did not believe in the resurrection or in a personal Messiah but held that the Messianic age—an ideal time—was then present and must be preserved. The high priest, one of their number, presided over the Sanhedrin (see the note on Mk 14:55; see also "The Sanhedrin" on p. 1821).

4:3 The evening sacrifices ended about 4:00 P.M., and the temple gates were closed for the day at that time. Any judgments involving life and death had to be begun and concluded within daylight hours.

4:4 See "Before the Gentile Expansion: The Jewish Churches in the Holy Land" on page 1997.

5The next day the rulers,[e] elders and teachers of the law met in Jerusalem. 6Annas the high priest was 4:5 [e]Lk 23:13
there, and so were Caiaphas,[f] John, Alexander and the other men of the high priest's family. 7They had 4:6 [f]Mt 26:3;
Peter and John brought before them and began to question them: "By what power or what name did you Lk 3:2
do this?"
8Then Peter, filled with the Holy Spirit, said to them: "Rulers and elders of the people![g] 9If we are be- 4:8 [g]ver 5;
ing called to account today for an act of kindness shown to a cripple[h] and are asked how he was healed, Lk 23:13 4:9 [h]Ac 3:6
10then know this, you and all the people of Israel: It is by the name of Jesus Christ of Nazareth, whom you
crucified but whom God raised from the dead,[i] that this man stands before you healed. 11He is 4:10 [i]Ac 2:24

" 'the stone you builders rejected,
which has become the capstone.[a][b][j] 4:11 [j]Ps 118:22; Isa 28:16; Mt 21:42

12Salvation is found in no one else, for there is no other name under heaven given to men by which we
must be saved."[k] 4:12 [k]Mt 1:21; Ac 10:43; 1Ti 2:5
13When they saw the courage of Peter and John[l] and realized that they were unschooled, ordinary 4:13 [l]Lk 22:8
men,[m] they were astonished and they took note that these men had been with Jesus. 14But since they [m]Mt 11:25
could see the man who had been healed standing there with them, there was nothing they could say. 15So
they ordered them to withdraw from the Sanhedrin[n] and then conferred together. 16"What are we going 4:15 [n]Mt 5:22
to do with these men?"[o] they asked. "Everybody living in Jerusalem knows they have done an outstand- 4:16 [o]Jn 11:47
ing miracle,[p] and we cannot deny it. 17But to stop this thing from spreading any further among the peo- [p]Ac 3:6-10
ple, we must warn these men to speak no longer to anyone in this name."
18Then they called them in again and commanded them not to speak or teach at all in the name of
Jesus.[q] 19But Peter and John replied, "Judge for yourselves whether it is right in God's sight to obey you 4:18 [q]Ac 5:40
rather than God.[r] 20For we cannot help speaking about what we have seen and heard." 4:19 [r]Ac 5:29

[a] *11* Or *cornerstone* [b] *11* Psalm 118:22

4:5 "Rulers, elders and teachers of the law" made up the Sanhedrin (see the note on Mk 14:55).
4:6 For information on Annas, see the note on Luke 3:2.
4:13 Peter and John had not been trained in the Rabbinic schools, nor did they hold official positions in recognized religious circles.
4:15 For "Sanhedrin," see the note on Mark 14:55 and "The Sanhedren" on page 1821.

The High Priests Annas and Caiaphas

ACTS 4 From the reign of Herod onward,[1] several high-caste priestly families ("houses") in Israel competed for the high priesthood.[2] Since high priests were regularly deposed by the political authorities (whether Herod or the Romans), numerous individuals undoubtedly served in the capacity of high priest during the first half of the first century A.D. To make matters even more complicated, it appears that even if an individual did not actually serve as high priest, he might still adopt the title if he belonged to one of the high-priestly families.

Annas (high priest from A.D. 6 to 15; five of his sons held the position after him) and his son-in-law Joseph Caiaphas (high priest from A.D. 18 to 36) were of the house of Hanan. The Gospels indicate that while Caiaphas was the official high priest during the time of Jesus, Annas still wielded considerable power. It is noteworthy that Ananus, one of the sons of Annas, was the high priest who engineered the execution of James, Jesus' brother, in A.D. 62 (Josephus, *Antiquities*, 20.9.1). According to Josephus, those who were "strict in the observance of the law" (likely the Pharisees)[3] were so disturbed at this action that they protested to King Agrippa and to the procurator Albinus. As a direct result, Ananus was deposed as high priest after only three months in office.

[1]See "Herod the Great" on page 1627. [2]See "The Jewish Priesthood and Religious Life in the First Century A.D." on page 1704; for historical background, see "The Levites and the Priests" on page 648. [3]See "The Pharisees" on page 1566.

21 After further threats they let them go. They could not decide how to punish them, because all the
4:21 [s]Ac 5:26 [t]Mt 9:8 people[s] were praising God[t] for what had happened. 22 For the man who was miraculously healed was
over forty years old.

The Believers' Prayer

23 On their release, Peter and John went back to their own people and reported all that the chief priests
and elders had said to them. 24 When they heard this, they raised their voices together in prayer to God.
"Sovereign Lord," they said, "you made the heaven and the earth and the sea, and everything in them.
4:25 [u]Ac 1:16 25 You spoke by the Holy Spirit through the mouth of your servant, our father David:[u]

> " 'Why do the nations rage
> and the peoples plot in vain?
> 26 The kings of the earth take their stand
> and the rulers gather together
> against the Lord
> and against his Anointed One.'[a][b][v]

4:26 [v]Ps 2:1,2; Da 9:25; Lk 4:18; Ac 10:38; Heb 1:9
4:27 [w]Mt 14:1 [x]Mt 27:2; Lk 23:12 [y]ver 30 27 Indeed Herod[w] and Pontius Pilate[x] met together with the Gentiles and the people[c] of Israel in this city
to conspire against your holy servant Jesus,[y] whom you anointed. 28 They did what your power and will
4:28 [z]Ac 2:23 had decided beforehand should happen.[z] 29 Now, Lord, consider their threats and enable your servants
4:29 [a]ver 13,31; Ac 9:27; 14:3; Php 1:14 to speak your word with great boldness.[a] 30 Stretch out your hand to heal and perform miraculous signs
4:30 [b]Jn 4:48 [c]ver 27 and wonders[b] through the name of your holy servant Jesus."[c]
31 After they prayed, the place where they were meeting was shaken.[d] And they were all filled with the
4:31 [d]Ac 2:2 [e]ver 29 Holy Spirit and spoke the word of God boldly.[e]

The Believers Share Their Possessions

32 All the believers were one in heart and mind. No one claimed that any of his possessions was his
4:32 [f]Ac 2:44 own, but they shared everything they had.[f] 33 With great power the apostles continued to testify[g] to the
4:33 [g]Lk 24:48 [h]Ac 1:22 resurrection[h] of the Lord Jesus, and much grace was upon them all. 34 There were no needy persons
4:34 [i]Mt 19:21; Ac 2:45 among them. For from time to time those who owned lands or houses sold them,[i] brought the money
4:35 [j]ver 37; Ac 5:2 [k]Ac 2:45; 6:1 from the sales 35 and put it at the apostles' feet,[j] and it was distributed to anyone as he had need.[k]
4:36 [l]Ac 9:27; 1Co 9:6 36 Joseph, a Levite from Cyprus, whom the apostles called Barnabas[l] (which means Son of Encour-
4:37 [m]ver 35; Ac 5:2 agement), 37 sold a field he owned and brought the money and put it at the apostles' feet.[m]

Ananias and Sapphira

5 Now a man named Ananias, together with his wife Sapphira, also sold a piece of property. 2 With his
wife's full knowledge he kept back part of the money for himself, but brought the rest and put it at
5:2 [n]Ac 4:35,37 the apostles' feet.[n]
5:3 [o]Mt 4:10 [p]Jn 13:2,27 [q]ver 9 3 Then Peter said, "Ananias, how is it that Satan[o] has so filled your heart[p] that you have lied to the Holy
Spirit[q] and have kept for yourself some of the money you received for the land? 4 Didn't it belong to you
before it was sold? And after it was sold, wasn't the money at your disposal? What made you think of do-
ing such a thing? You have not lied to men but to God."
5:5 [r]ver 10 [s]ver 11 5 When Ananias heard this, he fell down and died.[r] And great fear[s] seized all who heard what had hap-
5:6 [t]Jn 19:40 pened. 6 Then the young men came forward, wrapped up his body,[t] and carried him out and buried him.
7 About three hours later his wife came in, not knowing what had happened. 8 Peter asked her, "Tell
me, is this the price you and Ananias got for the land?"
5:8 [u]ver 2 "Yes," she said, "that is the price."[u]

[a] *26* That is, Christ or Messiah [b] *26* Psalm 2:1,2 [c] *27* The Greek is plural.

4:22 The man's age pointed to the fact that he had been lame for so long that any hope that his condition might someday naturally improve had vanished.
4:27 "Herod" refers to Herod Antipas, tetrarch of Galilee and Perea (see the note on Mt 14:1). Pontius Pilate was the Roman governor of Judea (see the note on Lk 3:1 and "Pontius Pilot" on p. 1714).
4:36 Although Levites owned no inherited land within the Holy Land, these regulations may not have applied to the Levites in other countries, such as Cyprus.

Cyprus is an island in the eastern part of the Mediterranean Sea. Jews had settled there from Maccabean times. It was the home of Barnabas (see the note on 13:1–2).
5:2 The couple had the right to keep back whatever they chose, but to make it appear that they had given all when they had not was sinful.
5:6 For New Testament burial practices, see the note on Matthew 26:12. See also "Jewish Burial Practices" on page 1688 and "Perfumes and Anointing Oils" on page 1746.

9Peter said to her, "How could you agree to test the Spirit of the Lord?[v] Look! The feet of the men who 5:9 [v]ver 3
buried your husband are at the door, and they will carry you out also."
10At that moment she fell down at his feet and died.[w] Then the young men came in and, finding her 5:10 [w]ver 5
dead, carried her out and buried her beside her husband. 11Great fear[x] seized the whole church and all 5:11 [x]ver 5; Ac 19:17
who heard about these events.

The Apostles Heal Many

12The apostles performed many miraculous signs and wonders[y] among the people. And all the believ- 5:12 [y]Ac 2:43
ers used to meet together[z] in Solomon's Colonnade.[a] 13No one else dared join them, even though they [z]Ac 4:32 [a]Ac 3:11
were highly regarded by the people.[b] 14Nevertheless, more and more men and women believed in the 5:13 [b]Ac 2:47; 4:21
Lord and were added to their number. 15As a result, people brought the sick into the streets and laid them
on beds and mats so that at least Peter's shadow might fall on some of them as he passed by.[c] 16Crowds 5:15 [c]Ac 19:12
gathered also from the towns around Jerusalem, bringing their sick and those tormented by evil[a] spir-
its, and all of them were healed.[d] 5:16 [d]Mk 16:17

The Apostles Persecuted

17Then the high priest and all his associates, who were members of the party[e] of the Sadducees,[f] were 5:17 [e]Ac 15:5 [f]Ac 4:1
filled with jealousy. 18They arrested the apostles and put them in the public jail.[g] 19But during the night 5:18 [g]Ac 4:3
an angel[h] of the Lord opened the doors of the jail[i] and brought them out. 20"Go, stand in the temple 5:19 [h]Mt 1:20; Lk 1:11; Ac 8:26; 27:23 [i]Ac 16:26
courts," he said, "and tell the people the full message of this new life."[j]
21At daybreak they entered the temple courts, as they had been told, and began to teach the people. 5:20 [j]Jn 6:63,68
When the high priest and his associates[k] arrived, they called together the Sanhedrin[l]—the full as- 5:21 [k]Ac 4:5,6 [l]ver 27,34,41; Mt 5:22
sembly of the elders of Israel—and sent to the jail for the apostles. 22But on arriving at the jail, the offi-
cers did not find them there. So they went back and reported, 23"We found the jail securely locked, with
the guards standing at the doors; but when we opened them, we found no one inside." 24On hearing this
report, the captain of the temple guard and the chief priests[m] were puzzled, wondering what would come 5:24 [m]Ac 4:1
of this.
25Then someone came and said, "Look! The men you put in jail are standing in the temple courts
teaching the people." 26At that, the captain went with his officers and brought the apostles. They did not
use force, because they feared that the people[n] would stone them. 5:26 [n]Ac 4:21
27Having brought the apostles, they made them appear before the Sanhedrin[o] to be questioned by the 5:27 [o]Mt 5:22
high priest. 28"We gave you strict orders not to teach in this name,"[p] he said. "Yet you have filled Jerusa- 5:28 [p]Ac 4:18 [q]Mt 23:35; 27:25; Ac 2:23,36; 3:14, 15; 7:52
lem with your teaching and are determined to make us guilty of this man's blood."[q]
29Peter and the other apostles replied: "We must obey God rather than men![r] 30The God of our fa- 5:29 [r]Ac 4:19
thers[s] raised Jesus from the dead[t]—whom you had killed by hanging him on a tree.[u] 31God exalted him 5:30 [s]Ac 3:13 [t]Ac 2:24 [u]Ac 10:39; 13:29; Gal 3:13; 1Pe 2:24
to his own right hand[v] as Prince and Savior[w] that he might give repentance and forgiveness of sins to Is-
rael.[x] 32We are witnesses of these things,[y] and so is the Holy Spirit,[z] whom God has given to those who
obey him." 5:31 [v]Ac 2:33 [w]Lk 2:11 [x]Mt 1:21; Lk 24:47; Ac 2:38
33When they heard this, they were furious[a] and wanted to put them to death. 34But a Pharisee named
Gamaliel,[b] a teacher of the law,[c] who was honored by all the people, stood up in the Sanhedrin and or- 5:32 [y]Lk 24:48 [z]Jn 15:26
dered that the men be put outside for a little while. 35Then he addressed them: "Men of Israel, consider 5:33 [a]Ac 2:37; 7:54 5:34 [b]Ac 22:3 [c]Lk 2:46

[a] 16 Greek *unclean*

5:11 This is the first use of the term "church" in Acts. It can denote either the local congregation (see 8:1; 11:22; 13:1) or the universal church (see 20:28). The Greek word for "church" (*ekklesia*) was already being used for political and other assemblies (see 19:32,41), and it appears in the Septuagint for Israel when gathered in religious assembly.

5:12 For "Solomon's Colonnade," see the note on John 10:23.

5:17 The official high priest recognized by Rome was Caiaphas, but the Jews considered Annas, Caiaphas's father-in-law, to be the actual high priest since the high priesthood was to be held for life (see the note on Lk 3:2).

For background on the Sadducees, see the note on Acts 4:1. After the Day of Pentecost the Sadducees were active against the infant church. Along with the priests and the captain of the temple, they arrested Peter and John and put them in prison. A little later they arrested all of the other apostles and made plans to kill them (see also 5:33). Their hostile attitude persisted throughout the apostolic times, and there is no record of any Sadducee being admitted into the Christian church. According to Josephus (*Antiquities*, 20.9.1), members of this sect were responsible for the death of James, the brother of the Lord. With the destruction of Jerusalem in A.D. 70 the Sadducean party disappeared. See also "The Sadducees" on page 1600.

5:18 For "public jail," see "Imprisonment in the Roman World: In Prison Versus House Arrest" on page 1826.

5:19 For "angel of the Lord," see "Angels and Guardian Spirits in the Bible and the Ancient Near East" on page 1529.

5:21 For "Sanhedrin," see the note on Mark 14:55 and "The Sanhedrin" on page 1821.

5:24 For "captain of the temple guard," see the note on 4:1.

5:34 Gamaliel was the most famous Jewish teacher of his time and traditionally was listed among the "heads of the schools" (see

ARCHAEOLOGICAL SITES

MASADA

ACTS 5 The remains of the plateau fortress called Masada (see "Map 9") still stand in the Judean desert, south of En Gedi.[1] The tableland, which overlooks the Dead Sea, rises more than 437 yards (400 m) above the surrounding land and measures a half mile (.8 km) in length. Masada was the location of several palaces in use during the New Testament era and became an important stronghold for Jewish zealots fighting against Roman occupation during the first century A.D.[2]

Masada was established during the second century B.C. and completed by Herod (r. 37–4 B.C.),[3] who erected on the site an elaborate palace, a rain collection system and fortified walls that permitted long periods of isolation. Control passed to the Romans in A.D. 6 and then to Jewish Zealots in 66. The Zealots transformed the palaces into military outposts, converted other buildings into ceremonial baths and a study house and constructed a synagogue.

A room at Masada where 11 lots were found with names of men (possibly these were chosen to kill the others and then commit suicide)

Photograph: © Todd Bolen/Bible Places.com

The Romans attacked Masada in A.D. 73. The army's slaves built a ramp nearly 219 yards (200 m) in height along the side of the cliffs in order to wage a full-scale attack. Recognizing that defeat was inevitable, Eleazer, Masada's leader, convinced the 960 inhabitants that death would be more satisfactory than Roman slavery. Ten men were assigned to kill all of the others, including women and children, and one of them was selected to kill the final ten, including himself. When the Romans reached the top of the plateau, there was no one left there to conquer.

Gamaliel's advice in Acts 5:38–39 proved true with Masada: Although the Zealots stationed there led remarkable uprisings, their well-constructed plans were eventually thwarted because they were of human origin and not from God.[4]

[1]See "En Gedi" on page 643. [2]See "The Zealots and the Essenes" on page 1576 and "The Roman Army and the Occupation of the Holy Land" on page 1829. [3]See "Herod the Great" on page 1627. [4]See "Gamaliel, Paul's Teacher" on page 1819.

Herod's swimming pool at Masada

Photograph: © Todd Bolen/Bible Places.com

carefully what you intend to do to these men. 36 Some time ago Theudas appeared, claiming to be
somebody, and about four hundred men rallied to him. He was killed, all his followers were dispersed,
and it all came to nothing. 37 After him, Judas the Galilean appeared in the days of the census[d] and led a 5:37 [d]Lk 2:1,2
band of people in revolt. He too was killed, and all his followers were scattered. 38 Therefore, in the pres-
ent case I advise you: Leave these men alone! Let them go! For if their purpose or activity is of human
origin, it will fail.[e] 39 But if it is from God, you will not be able to stop these men; you will only find your- 5:38 [e]Mt 15:13
selves fighting against God."[f] 5:39 [f]Pr 21:30; Ac 7:51; 11:17

40 His speech persuaded them. They called the apostles in and had them flogged.[g] Then they ordered 5:40 [g]Mt 10:17
them not to speak in the name of Jesus, and let them go.

41 The apostles left the Sanhedrin, rejoicing[h] because they had been counted worthy of suffering dis- 5:41 [h]Mt 5:12 [i]Jn 15:21
grace for the Name.[i] 42 Day after day, in the temple courts[j] and from house to house, they never stopped 5:42 [j]Ac 2:46
teaching and proclaiming the good news that Jesus is the Christ.[a]

[a] *42* Or *Messiah*

"Gamaliel, Paul's Teacher" on p. 1819). He was probably the grandson of Hillel. Like Hillel (see the note on Mt 19:3), he was moderate in his views, a characteristic that is apparent in his cautious recommendation on this occasion. Saul (Paul) was one of his students (Ac 22:3).

In New Testament times the scribes were a class of learned men who made the systematic study of the law and in its exposition their professional occupation (see "The Scribe" on p. 682). In the New Testament they are generally called "teachers of the law" (see the notes on Mt 2:4; Lk 5:17). These men were prominent in the Gospels, often associated with the Pharisees (Mt 5:20; 12:38; 15:1; 23:2,13; Mk 7:5; Lk 5:21,30; 6:7; 11:53; 15:2; Jn 8:3) but also mentioned alone, as they were not necessarily Pharisees (Mt 9:3; Mk 2:6; 3:22; 9:14; Lk 20:39). The Pharisees were a religious party (see the note on Mt 3:7 and "The Pharisees" on p. 1566), while the scribes held an office. The double designation distinguished these teachers of the law from the Pharisees, but many scribes belonged to the Pharisee party, which recognized the legal interpretations of the scribes. Certain expressions (e.g., "the Pharisees and the teachers of the law who belonged to their sect") imply that the Sadducees also had their scribes (Mk 2:16; Lk 5:30; Ac 23:9).

5:36–37 Josephus (*Antiquities,* 20.5.1) mentioned a Theudas who led a considerable revolt in A.D. 44 or 45. This cannot have been the Theudas of Gamaliel's speech, which was made some ten years earlier. To suggest that Luke used Josephus and confused Theudas and Judas (see the note to follow), reversing their chronological order, is to disregard Luke's customary accuracy. There is little correspondence between Luke's "four hundred" and Josephus's account of a more extensive rebellion. It is quite possible that the reference in Josephus was in fact an interpolation (altering or corruption) of Acts. There could have been more than one Theudas, and our knowledge of the history of the province is far too sketchy to dispute this clear possibility.

5:37 The Jewish historian Josephus referred to Judas the Galilean as a man from Gamala in Gaulanitis who refused to give tribute to Caesar (see the previous note). His revolt was crushed, but a movement started in his time may have lived on in the party of the Zealots, a Jewish revolutionary group violently opposed to Roman rule over the Holy Land (see "The Zealots and the Essenes" on p. 1576 and "Messianic Conflicts and the Fall of Jerusalem" on p. 1632).

5:40 The apostles were "flogged," that is, beaten with the Jewish penalty of "forty lashes minus one" (2Co 11:24). (To compare Jewish flogging with Roman flogging, see the note on Mt 27:26.)

Proselytes in Second Temple Judaism

ACTS 6 Although Jews were a distinct minority within the Roman Empire, they nonetheless managed to attract a significant number of sympathizers and converts to their community. Gentiles could have varying levels of adherence to Judaism:

✣ Benefactors, like the centurion in Luke 7:1–10, supported the Jewish community and presumably were sympathetic to Jewish beliefs.

✣ "God-fearers" were affiliated with the synagogue and showed keen interest in Judaism (see, e.g., Ac 10:2; 13:16; 17:4; there is also an important mention of God-fearers in an inscription from approximately A.D. 210 in Aphrodisias in modern Turkey).

✣ Full proselytes converted to Judaism and embraced all of its requirements. Josephus mentioned a certain Izates of the royal family of Adiabene, who embraced Judaism and arranged to have himself circumcised in order to accept fully the Jewish way of life (*Antiquities,* 20.2.3–4).

The number of Gentile converts to Judaism was not insignificant, but it is doubtful that there was a concentrated Jewish missionary movement among the Gentiles comparable to that in early Christianity. The majority of those who joined the Jewish community likely did so as an outcome of personal or business relationships with Jews (most notably marriage), or from a personal quest for truth.[2]

[1]See "Circumcision in the Ancient World" on page 1840. [2]See "Greek Philosophical Schools" on page 1937.

The Choosing of the Seven

6 In those days when the number of disciples was increasing,[k] the Grecian Jews[l] among them com-
plained against the Hebraic Jews because their widows[m] were being overlooked in the daily distri-
bution of food.[n] 2 So the Twelve gathered all the disciples together and said, "It would not be right for us
to neglect the ministry of the word of God in order to wait on tables. 3 Brothers,[o] choose seven men from
among you who are known to be full of the Spirit and wisdom. We will turn this responsibility over to
them 4 and will give our attention to prayer[p] and the ministry of the word."
5 This proposal pleased the whole group. They chose Stephen,[q] a man full of faith and of the Holy Spir-
it;[r] also Philip,[s] Procorus, Nicanor, Timon, Parmenas, and Nicolas from Antioch, a convert to Judaism.
6 They presented these men to the apostles, who prayed[t] and laid their hands on them.[u]
7 So the word of God spread.[v] The number of disciples in Jerusalem increased rapidly, and a large
number of priests became obedient to the faith.

Stephen Seized

8 Now Stephen, a man full of God's grace and power, did great wonders and miraculous signs[w] among
the people. 9 Opposition arose, however, from members of the Synagogue of the Freedmen (as it was
called)—Jews of Cyrene[x] and Alexandria as well as the provinces of Cilicia[y] and Asia.[z] These men be-
gan to argue with Stephen, 10 but they could not stand up against his wisdom or the Spirit by whom he
spoke.[a]
11 Then they secretly[b] persuaded some men to say, "We have heard Stephen speak words of blasphe-
my against Moses and against God."[c]
12 So they stirred up the people and the elders and the teachers of the law. They seized Stephen
and brought him before the Sanhedrin.[d] 13 They produced false witnesses, who testified, "This fel-
low never stops speaking against this holy place[e] and against the law. 14 For we have heard him say
that this Jesus of Nazareth will destroy this place and change the customs Moses handed down
to us."[f]
15 All who were sitting in the Sanhedrin[g] looked intently at Stephen, and they saw that his face was like
the face of an angel.

6:1 [k]Ac 2:41 [l]Ac 9:29 [m]Ac 9:39,41 [n]Ac 4:35
6:3 [o]Ac 1:16
6:4 [p]Ac 1:14
6:5 [q]ver 8; Ac 11:19 [r]Ac 11:24 [s]Ac 8:5-40; 21:8
6:6 [t]Ac 1:24; 8:17; 13:3; 2Ti 1:6 [u]Nu 8:10; Ac 9:17; 1Ti 4:14
6:7 [v]Ac 12:24; 19:20
6:8 [w]Jn 4:48
6:9 [x]Mt 27:32 [y]Ac 15:23,41; 22:3; 23:34 [z]Ac 2:9
6:10 [a]Lk 21:15
6:11 [b]1Ki 21:10 [c]Mt 26:59-61
6:12 [d]Mt 5:22
6:13 [e]Ac 21:28
6:14 [f]Ac 15:1; 21:21; 26:3; 28:17
6:15 [g]Mt 5:22

6:1 At this stage of the church's development, it was entirely Jewish in its composition (see "The Church From the Resurrection to the Conversion of Paul" on p. 1766). However, there were two groups of Jews within the fellowship: (1) Grecian Jews were Hellenists—Jews born in lands other than the Holy Land who spoke the Greek language and were more Grecian than Hebraic in their attitudes and outlooks (for "Greeks" and "Grecians," see the note on 16:1). (2) Hebraic Jews were Jews born in the Holy Land who spoke Palestinian Aramaic and/or Hebrew and preserved Jewish culture and customs.

Help was needed by widows who had no one else to care for them, so the church took on this responsibility (see "The Care of Widows and Orphans in the Bible and the Ancient Near East" on p. 285).

6:2 At this early stage, the apostles were responsible for church life in general, including the ministry of the Word of God and the care of the needy.

6:5 It is significant that a proselyte (see "Proselytes in Second Temple Judaism" on p. 1776) was included in the number and that Luke pointed out his place of origin as Syrian Antioch (see the note on 11:19), the city to which the gospel was soon to be taken and which was to become the "headquarters" for the forthcoming Gentile missionary effort (see "Antioch of Syria, Center of Christianity" on p. 1904).

6:6 Laying on of hands was a method used in the Old Testament period to confer blessing (Ge 48:13–20), to transfer guilt from sinner to sacrifice (Lev 1:4) and to commission a person for a new responsibility (Nu 27:23). In the New Testament period laying on of hands was observed in healing (Mk 1:41; Ac 28:8), blessing (Mk 10:16), ordaining or commissioning (Ac 6:6; 13:3; 1Ti 5:22) and the imparting of spiritual gifts (Ac 8:17; 19:6; 1Ti 4:14; 2Ti 1:6).

These seven men were appointed to responsibilities turned over to them by the Twelve. The Greek word used to describe their responsibility ("wait on") is the verb from which the noun "deacon" comes. The Greek noun for "deacon(s)" can also be translated "minister" or "servant." The men appointed on this occasion were simply called the Seven (Ac 21:8), just as the apostles were called the Twelve. It is disputed whether the Seven were the first deacons or were later replaced by deacons (see the note on 1Ti 3:8-13).

6:7 This "large number of priests," though involved by lineage and life service in the priestly observances of the old covenant, accepted the preaching of the apostles, which proclaimed a sacrifice that made the old sacrifices unnecessary (see Heb 8:13).

6:9 Freedmen (also called Libertines) were most likely originally captive Jews who had been brought to Rome by Pompey in 63 B.C., liberated subsequently and repatriated to Palestine, where, presumably, they had constructed a synagogue still occupied by their descendants a century after Pompey's Palestinian campaign.

Cyrene was the chief city in Libya and northern Africa, halfway between Alexandria and Carthage. One of its population groups was Jewish.

Alexandria was the capital of Egypt and second only to Rome in the empire (see "Alexandria" on p. 1805). Two of the five districts in Alexandria were Jewish.

Cilicia was a Roman province in the southeastern corner of Asia Minor adjoining Syria. Tarsus, the birthplace of Paul, was one of its principal towns (see the note on 22:3 and the more extensive note on 15:23).

Asia was a Roman province in the western part of Asia Minor. Ephesus, where Paul later ministered for a few years, was its capital (see "Ephesus During the Time of Paul" on p. 1968).

6:11 Stephen declared that the worship of God was no longer to be restricted to the temple (7:48–49), but his opponents twisted his words to trump up an accusation that Stephen was attacking the temple, the law, Moses and, ultimately, God.

6:12 For "elders," see the notes on Matthew 21:23 and Luke 7:3. For "teachers of the law," see the notes on Matthew 2:4 and Luke 5:17. For "Sanhedrin," see the note on Mark 14:55.

6:13 The "holy place" is a reference to the temple in Jerusalem.

Stephen's Speech to the Sanhedrin

7 Then the high priest asked him, "Are these charges true?"
2 To this he replied: "Brothers and fathers,[h] listen to me! The God of glory[i] appeared to our father
Abraham while he was still in Mesopotamia, before he lived in Haran.[j] 3 'Leave your country and your
people,' God said, 'and go to the land I will show you.'[a][k]
4 "So he left the land of the Chaldeans and settled in Haran. After the death of his father, God sent him
to this land where you are now living.[l] 5 He gave him no inheritance here, not even a foot of ground. But
God promised him that he and his descendants after him would possess the land,[m] even though at that
time Abraham had no child. 6 God spoke to him in this way: 'Your descendants will be strangers in a coun-
try not their own, and they will be enslaved and mistreated four hundred years.[n] 7 But I will punish the
nation they serve as slaves,' God said, 'and afterward they will come out of that country and worship me
in this place.'[b][o] 8 Then he gave Abraham the covenant of circumcision.[p] And Abraham became the father
of Isaac and circumcised him eight days after his birth.[q] Later Isaac became the father of Jacob,[r] and Ja-
cob became the father of the twelve patriarchs.[s]
9 "Because the patriarchs were jealous of Joseph,[t] they sold him as a slave into Egypt.[u] But God was
with him[v] 10 and rescued him from all his troubles. He gave Joseph wisdom and enabled him to gain the
goodwill of Pharaoh king of Egypt; so he made him ruler over Egypt and all his palace.[w]
11 "Then a famine struck all Egypt and Canaan, bringing great suffering, and our fathers could not
find food.[x] 12 When Jacob heard that there was grain in Egypt, he sent our fathers on their first visit.[y]
13 On their second visit, Joseph told his brothers who he was,[z] and Pharaoh learned about Joseph's fam-
ily. 14 After this, Joseph sent for his father Jacob and his whole family,[a] seventy-five in all.[b] 15 Then Jacob
went down to Egypt, where he and our fathers died.[c] 16 Their bodies were brought back to Shechem and
placed in the tomb that Abraham had bought from the sons of Hamor at Shechem for a certain sum of
money.[d]
17 "As the time drew near for God to fulfill his promise to Abraham, the number of our people in Egypt
greatly increased.[e] 18 Then another king, who knew nothing about Joseph, became ruler of Egypt.[f] 19 He
dealt treacherously with our people and oppressed our forefathers by forcing them to throw out their
newborn babies so that they would die.[g]
20 "At that time Moses was born, and he was no ordinary child.[c] For three months he was cared for in
his father's house.[h] 21 When he was placed outside, Pharaoh's daughter took him and brought him up as
her own son.[i] 22 Moses was educated in all the wisdom of the Egyptians[j] and was powerful in speech and
action.
23 "When Moses was forty years old, he decided to visit his fellow Israelites. 24 He saw one of them be-
ing mistreated by an Egyptian, so he went to his defense and avenged him by killing the Egyptian. 25 Mo-
ses thought that his own people would realize that God was using him to rescue them, but they did not.
26 The next day Moses came upon two Israelites who were fighting. He tried to reconcile them by saying,
'Men, you are brothers; why do you want to hurt each other?'
27 "But the man who was mistreating the other pushed Moses aside and said, 'Who made you ruler and
judge over us? 28 Do you want to kill me as you killed the Egyptian yesterday?'[d] 29 When Moses heard this,
he fled to Midian, where he settled as a foreigner and had two sons.[k]
30 "After forty years had passed, an angel appeared to Moses in the flames of a burning bush in the des-
ert near Mount Sinai. 31 When he saw this, he was amazed at the sight. As he went over to look more close-
ly, he heard the Lord's voice:[l] 32 'I am the God of your fathers, the God of Abraham, Isaac and Jacob.'[e] Mo-
ses trembled with fear and did not dare to look.[m]

7:2 h Ac 22:1 i Ps 29:3 j Ge 11:31; 15:7
7:3 k Ge 12:1
7:4 l Ge 12:5
7:5 m Ge 12:7; 17:8; 26:3
7:6 n Ex 12:40
7:7 o Ex 3:12
7:8 p Ge 17:9-14 q Ge 21:2-4 r Ge 25:26 s Ge 29:31-35; 30:5-13,17-24; 35:16-18,22-26
7:9 t Ge 37:4,11 u Ge 37:28; Ps 105:17 v Ge 39:2,21,23
7:10 w Ge 41:37-43
7:11 x Ge 41:54
7:12 y Ge 42:1,2
7:13 z Ge 45:1-4
7:14 a Ge 45:9,10 b Ge 46:26,27; Ex 1:5; Dt 10:22
7:15 c Ge 46:5-7; 49:33; Ex 1:6
7:16 d Ge 23:16-20; 33:18,19; 50:13; Jos 24:32
7:17 e Ex 1:7; Ps 105:24
7:18 f Ex 1:8
7:19 g Ex 1:10-22
7:20 h Ex 2:2; Heb 11:23
7:21 i Ex 2:3-10
7:22 j 1Ki 4:30; Isa 19:11
7:29 k Ex 2:11-15
7:31 l Ex 3:1-4
7:32 m Ex 3:6

a 3 Gen. 12:1 b 7 Gen. 15:13,14 c 20 Or *was fair in the sight of God* d 28 Exodus 2:14 e 32 Exodus 3:6

7:1 The high priest was probably Caiaphas (see the note on Mt 26:3; see also "The High Priests Annas and Caiaphas" on p. 1772).
7:2–53 Stephen's speech marks a decisive break between Judaism and Christianity and points forward to the vigorous explanations of the differences between the old faith and the new faith expounded in the writings of Paul and the author of Hebrews.
7:4 The "land of the Chaldeans" refers here to a district in southern Babylonia; the name was later applied to a region that included all of Babylonia.
7:8 For "covenant of circumcision," see Genesis 17:10 and its note.
7:16 Josephus preserves a tradition that Joseph's brothers were buried at Hebron. Stephen's rhetorical device (by which he recalled that Jacob and the 12 patriarchs were buried not in Egypt but in Canaan) is strange to modern ears but would have been well understood by his hearers.
7:23 Moses was eighty years old when he was sent to speak before the pharaoh (Ex 7:7) and one hundred twenty years old when he died (Dt 34:7). Stephen's words agree with a tradition that at Moses' first departure from Egypt he was forty years of age.
7:29 See "Midian" on page 92.
7:30 Mount Sinai is called Horeb in Exodus 3:1 (see "The Location of Mount Sinai" on p. 123).

33“Then the Lord said to him, ‘Take off your sandals; the place where you are standing is holy ground.[n]
34I have indeed seen the oppression of my people in Egypt. I have heard their groaning and have come
down to set them free. Now come, I will send you back to Egypt.’[a][o]
35“This is the same Moses whom they had rejected with the words, ‘Who made you ruler and judge?’[p]
He was sent to be their ruler and deliverer by God himself, through the angel who appeared to him in the
bush. 36He led them out of Egypt[q] and did wonders and miraculous signs in Egypt, at the Red Sea[b][r] and
for forty years in the desert.
37“This is that Moses who told the Israelites, ‘God will send you a prophet like me from your own peo-
ple.’[c][s] 38He was in the assembly in the desert, with the angel[t] who spoke to him on Mount Sinai, and with
our fathers;[u] and he received living words[v] to pass on to us.[w]
39“But our fathers refused to obey him. Instead, they rejected him and in their hearts turned back to
Egypt.[x] 40They told Aaron, ‘Make us gods who will go before us. As for this fellow Moses who led us out
of Egypt—we don’t know what has happened to him!’[d][y] 41That was the time they made an idol in the
form of a calf. They brought sacrifices to it and held a celebration in honor of what their hands had made.[z]
42But God turned away[a] and gave them over to the worship of the heavenly bodies.[b] This agrees with
what is written in the book of the prophets:

> “ ‘Did you bring me sacrifices and offerings
> forty years in the desert, O house of Israel?
> 43You have lifted up the shrine of Molech
> and the star of your god Rephan,
> the idols you made to worship.
> Therefore I will send you into exile’[e][c] beyond Babylon.

44“Our forefathers had the tabernacle of the Testimony[d] with them in the desert. It had been made as
God directed Moses, according to the pattern he had seen.[e] 45Having received the tabernacle, our fathers
under Joshua brought it with them when they took the land from the nations God drove out before them.[f]
It remained in the land until the time of David, 46who enjoyed God’s favor and asked that he might pro-
vide a dwelling place for the God of Jacob.[f][g] 47But it was Solomon who built the house for him.
48“However, the Most High does not live in houses made by men.[h] As the prophet says:

> 49“ ‘Heaven is my throne,
> and the earth is my footstool.[i]
> What kind of house will you build for me?
> says the Lord.
> Or where will my resting place be?
> 50Has not my hand made all these things?’[g][j]

51“You stiff-necked people,[k] with uncircumcised hearts[l] and ears! You are just like your fathers: You
always resist the Holy Spirit! 52Was there ever a prophet your fathers did not persecute?[m] They even killed
those who predicted the coming of the Righteous One. And now you have betrayed and murdered
him[n]— 53you who have received the law that was put into effect through angels[o] but have not obeyed it.”

The Stoning of Stephen

54When they heard this, they were furious[p] and gnashed their teeth at him. 55But Stephen, full of the
Holy Spirit, looked up to heaven and saw the glory of God, and Jesus standing at the right hand of God.[q]
56“Look,” he said, “I see heaven open[r] and the Son of Man[s] standing at the right hand of God.”
57At this they covered their ears and, yelling at the top of their voices, they all rushed at him, 58dragged
him out of the city[t] and began to stone him.[u] Meanwhile, the witnesses laid their clothes[v] at the feet of
a young man named Saul.[w]

7:33 [n]Ex 3:5; Jos 5:15
7:34 [o]Ex 3:7-10
7:35 [p]ver 27
7:36 [q]Ex 12:41; 33:1 [r]Ex 14:21
7:37 [s]Dt 18:15, 18; Ac 3:22
7:38 [t]ver 53 [u]Ex 19:17 [v]Dt 32:45-47; Heb 4:12 [w]Ro 3:2
7:39 [x]Nu 14:3,4
7:40 [y]Ex 32:1,23
7:41 [z]Ex 32:4-6; Ps 106:19,20; Rev 9:20
7:42 [a]Jos 24:20; Isa 63:10 [b]Jer 19:13
7:43 [c]Am 5:25-27
7:44 [d]Ex 38:21 [e]Ex 25:8,9,40
7:45 [f]Jos 3:14-17; 18:1; 23:9; 24:18; Ps 44:2
7:46 [g]2Sa 7:8-16; Ps 132:1-5
7:48 [h]1Ki 8:27; 2Ch 2:6
7:49 [i]Mt 5:34,35
7:50 [j]Isa 66:1,2
7:51 [k]Ex 32:9; 33:3,5 [l]Lev 26:41; Dt 10:16; Jer 4:4; 9:26
7:52 [m]2Ch 36:16; Mt 5:12 [n]Ac 3:14; 1Th 2:15
7:53 [o]ver 38; Gal 3:19; Heb 2:2
7:54 [p]Ac 5:33
7:55 [q]Mk 16:19
7:56 [r]Mt 3:16 [s]Mt 8:20
7:58 [t]Lk 4:29 [u]Lev 24:14,16; Dt 13:9 [v]Ac 22:20 [w]Ac 8:1

[a] *34* Exodus 3:5,7,8,10 [b] *36* That is, Sea of Reeds [c] *37* Deut. 18:15 [d] *40* Exodus 32:1 [e] *43* Amos 5:25-27 [f] *46* Some early manuscripts *the house of Jacob* [g] *50* Isaiah 66:1,2

7:38 According to Jewish interpretation at that time, the Law was given to Moses by angel mediation—after the manner of the original call of Moses (see Ex 3:2; see also Ac 7:53; Gal 3:19; Heb 2:2).
7:43 For “Molech,” see the note on Leviticus 18:21.
7:53 See the note on verse 38.
7:56 See “The ‘Right Hand’ in Ancient Thinking” on page 1983.
7:58 Because the witnesses laid their clothes at the feet of Saul, some have thought that this gesture marked Saul as being in charge of the execution.

59 While they were stoning him, Stephen prayed, "Lord Jesus, receive my spirit."[x] 60 Then he fell on his
knees[y] and cried out, "Lord, do not hold this sin against them."[z] When he had said this, he fell asleep.
8 And Saul[a] was there, giving approval to his death.

The Church Persecuted and Scattered

On that day a great persecution broke out against the church at Jerusalem, and all except the apostles
were scattered[b] throughout Judea and Samaria.[c] 2 Godly men buried Stephen and mourned deeply for
him. 3 But Saul[d] began to destroy the church.[e] Going from house to house, he dragged off men and wom-
en and put them in prison.

Philip in Samaria

4 Those who had been scattered[f] preached the word wherever they went.[g] 5 Philip[h] went down to a city
in Samaria and proclaimed the Christ[a] there. 6 When the crowds heard Philip and saw the miraculous
signs he did, they all paid close attention to what he said. 7 With shrieks, evil[b] spirits came out of many,[i]
and many paralytics and cripples were healed.[j] 8 So there was great joy in that city.

Simon the Sorcerer

9 Now for some time a man named Simon had practiced sorcery[k] in the city and amazed all the peo-
ple of Samaria. He boasted that he was someone great,[l] 10 and all the people, both high and low, gave him
their attention and exclaimed, "This man is the divine power known as the Great Power."[m] 11 They fol-
lowed him because he had amazed them for a long time with his magic. 12 But when they believed Phil-
ip as he preached the good news of the kingdom of God[n] and the name of Jesus Christ, they were bap-
tized,[o] both men and women. 13 Simon himself believed and was baptized. And he followed Philip
everywhere, astonished by the great signs and miracles[p] he saw.
14 When the apostles in Jerusalem heard that Samaria[q] had accepted the word of God, they sent Peter and
John[r] to them. 15 When they arrived, they prayed for them that they might receive the Holy Spirit,[s] 16 be-
cause the Holy Spirit had not yet come upon any of them;[t] they had simply been baptized into[c] the name
of the Lord Jesus.[u] 17 Then Peter and John placed their hands on them,[v] and they received the Holy Spirit.
18 When Simon saw that the Spirit was given at the laying on of the apostles' hands, he offered them
money 19 and said, "Give me also this ability so that everyone on whom I lay my hands may receive the
Holy Spirit."
20 Peter answered: "May your money perish with you, because you thought you could buy the gift of
God with money![w] 21 You have no part or share in this ministry, because your heart is not right[x] before
God. 22 Repent of this wickedness and pray to the Lord. Perhaps he will forgive you for having such a
thought in your heart. 23 For I see that you are full of bitterness and captive to sin."
24 Then Simon answered, "Pray to the Lord for me[y] so that nothing you have said may happen to me."
25 When they had testified and proclaimed the word of the Lord, Peter and John returned to Jerusa-
lem, preaching the gospel in many Samaritan villages.[z]

Philip and the Ethiopian

26 Now an angel[a] of the Lord said to Philip, "Go south to the road—the desert road—that goes down
from Jerusalem to Gaza." 27 So he started out, and on his way he met an Ethiopian[d][b] eunuch,[c] an impor-

[a] 5 Or *Messiah* [b] 7 Greek *unclean* [c] 16 Or *in* [d] 27 That is, from the upper Nile region

7:59 [x]Ps 31:5; Lk 23:46
7:60 [y]Ac 9:40 [z]Mt 5:44
8:1 [a]Ac 7:58 [b]Ac 11:19 [c]Ac 9:31
8:3 [d]Ac 7:58 [e]Ac 22:4,19; 26:10,11; 1Co 15:9; Gal 1:13,23; Php 3:6; 1Ti 1:13
8:4 [f]ver 1 [g]Ac 15:35
8:5 [h]Ac 6:5
8:7 [i]Mk 16:17 [j]Mt 4:24
8:9 [k]Ac 13:6 [l]Ac 5:36
8:10 [m]Ac 14:11; 28:6
8:12 [n]Ac 1:3 [o]Ac 2:38
8:13 [p]ver 6; Ac 19:11
8:14 [q]ver 1 [r]Lk 22:8
8:15 [s]Ac 2:38
8:16 [t]Ac 19:2 [u]Mt 28:19; Ac 2:38
8:17 [v]Ac 6:6
8:20 [w]2Ki 5:16; Da 5:17; Mt 10:8; Ac 2:38
8:21 [x]Ps 78:37
8:24 [y]Ex 8:8; Nu 21:7; 1Ki 13:6
8:25 [z]ver 40
8:26 [a]Ac 5:19
8:27 [b]Ps 68:31; 87:4; Zep 3:10 [c]Isa 56:3-5

8:1 See "The Geographic Expansion of the Church Under Persecution" on page 1781 and "The Early Persecution of the Church" on page 2067.

8:5 Philip, a Grecian Jew and one of the Seven in the Jerusalem church (see the note on 6:6), became an evangelist and brought the gospel to the Samaritans, a mixed race—a blend of Jews left behind after Israel's exile and Gentiles forcibly settled in the region by Assyria (2Ki 17:24; see the note on Lk 10:33 and "The Samaritans" on p. 1737).

Rather than "a city in Samaria," some manuscripts have "the city of Samaria," a reference to the old capital of Samaria, renamed Sebaste or Neapolis (modern Nablus).

8:9 In early Christian literature this "sorcerer" (Simon Magus) is described as the arch-heretic of the church and the "father" of Gnostic teaching (see "The Gnostics and Their Scriptures" on p. 2029).

For "sorcerer," see the note on "Magi" at Matthew 2:1.

8:14 The Jerusalem church assumed the responsibility of inspecting new evangelistic efforts and the communities of believers they produced (see 11:22).

8:16 See "Baptism in the Ancient World" on page 1562.

8:17 For "placed their hands on," see the note on 6:6.

8:25 For "Samaritan villages," see the note on Luke 10:33 and "The Samaritans" on page 1737.

8:26 For "angel of the Lord," see "Angels and Guardian Spirits in the Bible and the Ancient Near East" on page 1529.

From Jerusalem to Gaza was a distance of about 50 miles (80 km).

8:27 Ethiopia corresponded in this period to Nubia, from the upper Nile region at the first cataract (Aswan) to Khartoum.

For "eunuch," see "The Eunuch" on page 1159.

"Candace" was the traditional title of the queen mother of Ethiopia (much as "Pharaoh" was the designated name for Egyptian

8:27 [d]1Ki 8:41-43; Jn 12:20
8:29 [e]Ac 10:19; 11:12; 13:2; 20:23; 21:11

tant official in charge of all the treasury of Candace, queen of the Ethiopians. This man had gone to Je-
rusalem to worship,[d] 28 and on his way home was sitting in his chariot reading the book of Isaiah the
prophet. 29 The Spirit told[e] Philip, "Go to that chariot and stay near it."
30 Then Philip ran up to the chariot and heard the man reading Isaiah the prophet. "Do you understand
what you are reading?" Philip asked.
31 "How can I," he said, "unless someone explains it to me?" So he invited Philip to come up and sit
with him.
32 The eunuch was reading this passage of Scripture:

"He was led like a sheep to the slaughter,
and as a lamb before the shearer is silent,
so he did not open his mouth.
33 In his humiliation he was deprived of justice.
Who can speak of his descendants?
For his life was taken from the earth."[a][f]

8:33 [f]Isa 53:7,8

[a] 33 Isaiah 53:7,8

kings and "Caesar" for Roman emperors), responsible for performing the secular duties of the reigning king—who was thought to be too sacred for such activities.

If not a full-fledged proselyte, the Ethiopian was a Gentile God-fearer (see the notes on Jn 12:20; Ac10:2 cf. "converts" in the note on Ac 2:11; see also "Proselytes in Second Temple Judaism" on p. 1776).

8:30 It was customary practice to read aloud.

The Geographic Expansion of the Church Under Persecution

ACTS 8 The expansion of Christianity was a direct—if unanticipated—result of persecution. On the very day that Stephen became the first Christian martyr, a severe persecution broke out in Jerusalem. Christians who fled the city became scattered throughout Judea and **Samaria**[1], proclaiming the gospel wherever they went (8:1–4).

Philip headed north to an unidentified city in the region of Samaria, which many scholars conjecture to have been ancient Samaria (1Ki 20:1), then called Sebaste. Others point to Gitta, or to Sychar, which Jesus was reported in John 4 to have visited.

At any rate, so many converts were won through Philip's evangelistic endeavors that Peter and John came to join him. As they later returned to Jerusalem, they followed Philip's lead, preaching in Samaritan villages along the way (Ac 8:25).[2] Philip was then dispatched south of Jerusalem toward the ancient Philistine city of Gaza, where he experienced his encounter with the Ethiopian eunuch (vv. 26–39). In the Greco-Roman world, Ethiopia was considered to be the southernmost extent of civilization, so this incident may have previewed for early Christians the promise of the message going out "to the ends of the earth" (1:8).

Chapter 8 concludes with Philip, farther north on the Mediterranean coast, preaching from Azotus to Caesarea, where he eventually settled (21:8).[3] His travels would have taken him through Lydda and Joppa, probably the "cities" (8:40) in which he preached. It seems that Peter again followed Philip's path by stopping to preach in Lydda and Joppa, as well as to Cornelius in Caesarea (9:32—10:48).

Christianity also spread eastward to Damascus; Saul had been en route there when he had experienced his dramatic conversion (9:1–6).[4] In 11:19–26 Luke added additional detail about the scattering of the Jerusalem believers: Some disciples ventured north of Galilee into the region of **Phoenicia** and even farther to the city of Antioch,[5] while others journeyed westward to the island of Cyprus. By the end of Acts, Paul had reached Rome, the capital of the then-known world. It was from this city that the Good News eventually spread throughout the Roman Empire to provinces as far away as Africa and Europe.

[1]See "Omri and Samaria" on page 512. [2]See "The Samaritans" on page 1737. [3]See "Caesarea Maritima" on page 1786. [5]See "Damascus" on page 1087. [5]See "Antioch of Syria, Center of Christianity" on page 1904.

34 The eunuch asked Philip, "Tell me, please, who is the prophet talking about, himself or someone else?" 35 Then Philip began[g] with that very passage of Scripture[h] and told him the good news about Jesus.

36 As they traveled along the road, they came to some water and the eunuch said, "Look, here is water. Why shouldn't I be baptized?"[a][i] 38 And he gave orders to stop the chariot. Then both Philip and the eunuch went down into the water and Philip baptized him. 39 When they came up out of the water, the Spirit of the Lord suddenly took Philip away,[j] and the eunuch did not see him again, but went on his way rejoicing. 40 Philip, however, appeared at Azotus and traveled about, preaching the gospel in all the towns[k] until he reached Caesarea.[l]

Saul's Conversion

9 Meanwhile, Saul was still breathing out murderous threats against the Lord's disciples.[m] He went to the high priest 2 and asked him for letters to the synagogues in Damascus, so that if he found any there who belonged to the Way,[n] whether men or women, he might take them as prisoners to Jerusalem. 3 As he neared Damascus on his journey, suddenly a light from heaven flashed around him.[o] 4 He fell to the ground and heard a voice say to him, "Saul, Saul, why do you persecute me?"

5 "Who are you, Lord?" Saul asked.

"I am Jesus, whom you are persecuting," he replied. 6 "Now get up and go into the city, and you will be told what you must do."[p]

7 The men traveling with Saul stood there speechless; they heard the sound[q] but did not see anyone.[r] 8 Saul got up from the ground, but when he opened his eyes he could see nothing. So they led him by the hand into Damascus. 9 For three days he was blind, and did not eat or drink anything.

10 In Damascus there was a disciple named Ananias. The Lord called to him in a vision,[s] "Ananias!"

"Yes, Lord," he answered.

11 The Lord told him, "Go to the house of Judas on Straight Street and ask for a man from Tarsus[t] named Saul, for he is praying. 12 In a vision he has seen a man named Ananias come and place his hands on[u] him to restore his sight."

13 "Lord," Ananias answered, "I have heard many reports about this man and all the harm he has done to your saints[v] in Jerusalem.[w] 14 And he has come here with authority from the chief priests[x] to arrest all who call on your name."

15 But the Lord said to Ananias, "Go! This man is my chosen instrument[y] to carry my name before the Gentiles[z] and their kings[a] and before the people of Israel. 16 I will show him how much he must suffer for my name."[b]

17 Then Ananias went to the house and entered it. Placing his hands on[c] Saul, he said, "Brother Saul, the Lord—Jesus, who appeared to you on the road as you were coming here—has sent me so that you may see again and be filled with the Holy Spirit." 18 Immediately, something like scales fell from Saul's eyes, and he could see again. He got up and was baptized, 19 and after taking some food, he regained his strength.

8:35 [g]Mt 5:2 [h]Lk 24:27; Ac 17:2; 18:28; 28:23
8:36 [i]Ac 10:47
8:39 [j]1Ki 18:12; 2Ki 2:16; Eze 3:12,14; 8:3; 11:1,24; 43:5; 2Co 12:2
8:40 [k]ver 25 [l]Ac 10:1,24; 12:19; 21:8,16; 23:23,33; 25:1,4, 6,13
9:1 [m]Ac 8:3
9:2 [n]Ac 19:9,23; 22:4; 24:14,22
9:3 [o]1Co 15:8
9:6 [p]ver 16
9:7 [q]Jn 12:29 [r]Da 10:7; Ac 22:9
9:10 [s]Ac 10:3,17, 19
9:11 [t]ver 30; Ac 21:39; 22:3
9:12 [u]Mk 5:23
9:13 [v]ver 32; Ro 1:7; 16:2,15 [w]Ac 8:3
9:14 [x]ver 2,21
9:15 [y]Ac 13:2; Ro 1:1; Gal 1:15 [z]Ro 11:13; 15:15, 16; Gal 2:7,8; Eph 3:7,8 [a]Ac 25:22,23; 26:1
9:16 [b]Ac 20:23; 21:11; 2Co 11:23-27
9:17 [c]Ac 6:6

[a] 36 Some late manuscripts *baptized?" 37 Philip said, "If you believe with all your heart, you may." The eunuch answered, "I believe that Jesus Christ is the Son of God."*

8:36 There are several possible places where the eunuch could have been baptized: a brook in the Valley of Elah (which David had crossed to meet Goliath, 1Sa 17:40); the Wadi el-Hasi just north of Gaza; water from a spring or one of the many pools in the area.
8:40 Azotus, Old Testament Ashdod (see 1Sa 5:1), was one of the five major Philistine cities. It was about 19 miles (31 km) from Gaza and 60 miles (97 km) from Caesarea.

Caesarea, about 30 miles (48 km) north of Joppa, was rebuilt by Herod, and with its excellent harbor it served as the headquarters of the Roman governors (see "Caesarea Maritima" on p. 1786).
9:1 Saul was born in Tarsus (see the note on 22:3) and trained under Gamaliel (see "Gamaliel, Paul's Teacher" on p. 1819). We do not know that Saul was directly involved in the death of anyone other than Stephen (8:1), but there appear to have been similar cases (see "The Early Persecution of the Church" on p. 2067).

The high priest was probably Caiaphas (see the note on Mt 26:3).
9:2 Damascus, located in the Roman province of Syria, was the hub of a vast commercial network with far-flung lines of caravan trade reaching into northern Syria, Mesopotamia, Anatolia, Persia and Arabia. The city was situated in a plain watered by two rivers. Roman architecture overlaid the Hellenistic town plan with a great temple to Jupiter and a mile-long colonnaded street called Straight Street (see v. 11 and its note). The city gates and a section of the town wall may still be seen today, as well as the lengthy bazaar that ran along the line of the ancient street. Damascus, which also had a large Jewish population, was the nearest important city outside the Holy Land. The distance from Jerusalem to Damascus was about 150 miles (241 km), which equated to four to six days' travel. Damascus is one of the oldest continuously occupied towns in the world. Today this still-thriving city, the capital of Syria, is home to 1.7 million people.

"The Way" was a name for Christianity that appears a number of times in Acts.

The prisoners were taken to Jerusalem, where the full authority of the Sanhedrin could be exercised in trial for either acquittal or death.
9:5 In Rabbinic tradition such a voice from heaven would have been understood as the voice of God himself.
9:11 Straight Street probably followed the same route of the long, straight street that today runs through the city from east to west (see the note on v. 2), in decided contrast to the numerous crooked streets of the city. In fact, this name was given to any route in antiquity extending in a straight course across a city.

For information on Tarsus, see the note on 22:3.
9:15 "Their kings" refers to King Agrippa (26:1) and to Caesar in Rome (25:11–12; 28:19).
9:18 The Greek word *lepis,* meaning "rind, husk or flake," is used here to describe Saul's recovery from temporary blindness.

Ancient Synagogues

ACTS 9 The earliest archaeological evidence of ancient synagogues derives from Greek inscriptions found in Egypt dating from the third century B.C., although the synagogue as an institution dates from a much earlier time. Literary and **epigraphic** sources employ various terms for these structures, which indicate the range of functions for which they were used. The Greek term sometimes used, *proseuche*, literally "(a place of) prayer," attests to the synagogue as a location for worship and communal prayer; this usage is found in the New Testament (Ac 16:13,16). The later term *synagoge*, which eventually became dominant, means "a place of assembly" and suggests a range of corporate functions, most particularly the public reading, exposition and study of Scripture.

The Theodotus inscription unearthed in the Jerusalem excavations of 1913–1914 describes the essential functions of a first-century A.D. synagogue. This Greek dedicatory inscription mentions a certain Theodotus, the son and grandson of a priest and ruler of the synagogue (cf. Mk 5:35; Lk 13:14; Ac 18:8,17), who constructed the synagogue "for the reading of the Torah and the teaching of the commandments." The text also refers to guest rooms and accommodations for those traveling from abroad.

Ancient synagogues served as a central meeting place for local Jewish communities. The synagogue played a complementary role to the temple by providing a venue for local services of word and prayer, as well as a forum for communal assemblies, study, hospitality and even religious courts. Synagogues are mentioned in a wide variety of Jewish literary works.

✣ According to **Talmudic** sources there were some 480 synagogues in Jerusalem prior to the destruction of the temple. Josephus (*Against Apion*, 2.17) considered the public reading and learning of the **Torah** to be the essential element of the weekly synagogue service, a practice he perceived to have been ordained by Moses.

✣ Philo likewise referred to synagogues as schools at which the ancestral philosophy was taught (*Life of Moses*, 2.39).

✣ The New Testament corroborates this general picture (Ac 15:21) and also presents numerous examples of reading and teaching Scripture in synagogues by Jesus (Mt 4:23; 9:35; Mk 1:21; Lk 4:16–21; Jn 6:59; 18:20), Paul (Ac 9:20; 17:10; 19:8) and other early leaders (13:5; 14:1).

✣ According to rabbinic sources the synagogue service included the recitation of the *Shema* and its blessings (i.e., Nu 15:37–41; Dt 6:4–9; 11:13–21), the *Amidah* or Prayer of Eighteen Benedictions, the reading of the weekly Torah portion, a reading from the Prophets, an exposition or translation of the Scripture and the priestly benediction. Those in attendance were seated according to age and status (cf. Mt 23:6; Lk 20:46), and the entire congregation was orientated toward the Most Holy Place in Jerusalem (cf. 1Ki 8:48).

Synagogues were typically built in close proximity to rivers or other bodies of water that could provide for the ritual washings required of those participating in the service (cf. Ac 16:13).[1] Architectural styles of ancient synagogues varied considerably. In fact, the earliest synagogue meetings may have been held within large private dwellings, with synagogue buildings appearing as separate edifices approximately one century after the destruction of the Jerusalem temple in A.D. 70.[2]

The building was usually oriented toward Jerusalem, perhaps reflecting the practice of praying toward this sacred city (cf. 1Ki 8:44–48; Da 6:10). The Torah ark (the box containing the Torah) represented the visual focal point of the synagogue, communicating a holiness flowing from the temple in Jerusalem. Synagogues are distinguished archaeologically by the presence of Jewish religious symbols such as the menorah (candelabrum), shofar (ram's horn)[3] and a niche for the Torah. At a further stage of development, during the late **Roman** and **Byzantine** periods, Biblical scenes and even characters were depicted in elaborate stone mosaics. Surprisingly, even astrological symbols appear in some mosaics. Spectacular examples of such mosaics have been uncovered in excavations at the synagogues of Beth Alpa, Gerasa, Hammath and Dura Europos.[4]

[1]See "Baptism in the Ancient World" on page 1562. [2]See "Josephus and the Fall of Jerusalem" on page 1606. [3]See "The Shofar" on page 898. [4]See also "The Capernaum Synagogue" on page 1591.

The "Seat of Moses" from the Chorazin Synagogue

Preserving Bible Times; © Dr. James C. Martin; permission of The Israel Museum

Saul in Damascus and Jerusalem

Saul spent several days with the disciples[d] in Damascus.[e] 20 At once he began to preach in the syna- 9:19 [d]Ac 11:26 [e]Ac 26:20
gogues[f] that Jesus is the Son of God.[g] 21 All those who heard him were astonished and asked, "Isn't he the 9:20 [f]Ac 13:5,14
man who raised havoc in Jerusalem among those who call on this name?[h] And hasn't he come here to [g]Mt 4:3 9:21 [h]Ac 8:3
take them as prisoners to the chief priests?"[i] 22 Yet Saul grew more and more powerful and baffled the Jews [i]Gal 1:13,23
living in Damascus by proving that Jesus is the Christ.[a][j] 9:22 [j]Ac 18:5,28
23 After many days had gone by, the Jews conspired to kill him, 24 but Saul learned of their plan.[k] Day 9:24 [k]Ac 20:3,19
and night they kept close watch on the city gates in order to kill him. 25 But his followers took him by
night and lowered him in a basket through an opening in the wall.[l] 9:25 [l]1Sa 19:12; 2Co 11:32,33
26 When he came to Jerusalem,[m] he tried to join the disciples, but they were all afraid of him, not be- 9:26 [m]Ac 22:17; 26:20; Gal 1:17,
lieving that he really was a disciple. 27 But Barnabas[n] took him and brought him to the apostles. He told 18
them how Saul on his journey had seen the Lord and that the Lord had spoken to him,[o] and how in Da- 9:27 [n]Ac 4:36 [o]ver 3-6 [p]ver 20, 22
mascus he had preached fearlessly in the name of Jesus.[p] 28 So Saul stayed with them and moved about
freely in Jerusalem, speaking boldly in the name of the Lord. 29 He talked and debated with the Grecian 9:29 [q]Ac 6:1 [r]2Co 11:26
Jews,[q] but they tried to kill him.[r] 30 When the brothers[s] learned of this, they took him down to Caesarea[t] 9:30 [s]Ac 1:16 [t]Ac 8:40 [u]ver 11
and sent him off to Tarsus.[u]
31 Then the church throughout Judea, Galilee and Samaria[v] enjoyed a time of peace. It was strength- 9:31 [v]Ac 8:1
ened; and encouraged by the Holy Spirit, it grew in numbers, living in the fear of the Lord.

Aeneas and Dorcas

32 As Peter traveled about the country, he went to visit the saints[w] in Lydda. 33 There he found a man 9:32 [w]ver 13
named Aeneas, a paralytic who had been bedridden for eight years. 34 "Aeneas," Peter said to him, "Jesus
Christ heals you.[x] Get up and take care of your mat." Immediately Aeneas got up. 35 All those who lived 9:34 [x]Ac 3:6,16; 4:10
in Lydda and Sharon[y] saw him and turned to the Lord.[z] 9:35 [y]1Ch 5:16; 27:29; Isa 33:9; 35:2; 65:10 [z]Ac 11:21
36 In Joppa[a] there was a disciple named Tabitha (which, when translated, is Dorcas[b]), who was always
doing good[b] and helping the poor. 37 About that time she became sick and died, and her body was washed 9:36 [a]Jos 19:46; 2Ch 2:16; Ezr 3:7;
and placed in an upstairs room.[c] 38 Lydda was near Joppa; so when the disciples[d] heard that Peter was in Jnh 1:3; Ac 10:5 [b]1Ti 2:10; Tit 3:8
Lydda, they sent two men to him and urged him, "Please come at once!" 9:37 [c]Ac 1:13
39 Peter went with them, and when he arrived he was taken upstairs to the room. All the widows[e] stood 9:38 [d]Ac 11:26 9:39 [e]Ac 6:1
around him, crying and showing him the robes and other clothing that Dorcas had made while she was
still with them.
40 Peter sent them all out of the room;[f] then he got down on his knees[g] and prayed. Turning toward 9:40 [f]Mt 9:25 [g]Lk 22:41;
the dead woman, he said, "Tabitha, get up." She opened her eyes, and seeing Peter she sat up. 41 He took Ac 7:60
her by the hand and helped her to her feet. Then he called the believers and the widows and presented
her to them alive. 42 This became known all over Joppa, and many people believed in the Lord. 43 Peter
stayed in Joppa for some time with a tanner named Simon.[h] 9:43 [h]Ac 10:6

[a] 22 Or *Messiah* [b] 36 Both *Tabitha* (Aramaic) and *Dorcas* (Greek) mean *gazelle.*

9:20 It became Paul's regular practice to preach at every opportunity in the synagogues (see the notes on Mk 1:21 and Lk 21:12; see also "Ancient Synagogues" on p. 1783 and "The Jewish Priesthood and Religious Life in the First Century A.D." on p. 1704).

9:23 It is probable that the major part of this "many days" (in actuality a period of three years; Gal 1:17–18) was spent in Arabia, away from Damascus, although the borders of Arabia extended to the environs of Damascus. Upon Paul's return to Damascus, the governor under Aretas (see "Aretas IV of Nabatea and Petra" on p. 1898) gave orders for his arrest. The absence of Roman coins struck in Damascus between A.D. 34 and 62 may indicate that Aretas was in control during that period.

9:25 For information on the city walls, see "The Ancient City" on page 1790 and for "basket," see the note on Matthew 14:20.

9:30 For "Caesarea," see the note on 8:40 and for "Tarsus" the note on 22:3.

9:31 "Church" here refers not to various individual congregations but to the whole Christian body, including Christians in the districts of Judea, Galilee and Samaria.

9:32 Lydda, a town 2–3 miles (3–5 km) north of the road connecting Joppa and Jerusalem, lay about 12 miles (19 km) from Joppa (see the note on v. 36).

9:35 The fertile plain of Sharon runs about 50 miles (80 km) along the Mediterranean coast, roughly from Joppa to Caesarea. The reference here, however, may be to a village in the neighborhood of Lydda instead of to a district (an Egyptian papyrus refers to a town by that name in the Holy Land).

9:36 Joppa, about 38 miles (61 km) from Jerusalem, was the main seaport of Judea (see "Joppa" on p. 1472). Today it is known as Jaffa and is a suburb of Tel Aviv.

9:37 The body was washed in preparation for burial, a custom common to both Jews and Greeks. If burial was delayed, it was customary to lay the body in an upper room. In Jerusalem the body had to be buried the day the person died, but outside Jerusalem up to three days might be allowed for burial (see "Jewish Burial Practices" on p. 1688).

9:38 For "Lydda," see the note on verse 32 and for "Joppa" the note on verse 36.

9:43 Occupations were frequently used with personal names to further identify individuals, but in this case the occupation was especially significant. A tanner was involved in treating the skins of dead animals, thus contacting the unclean according to Jewish law; an individual involved in such a trade was despised by many.

Cornelius Calls for Peter

10:1 [i]Ac 8:40 10 At Caesarea[i] there was a man named Cornelius, a centurion in what was known as the Italian
10:2 [j]ver 22,35; Ac 13:16,26 Regiment. 2He and all his family were devout and God-fearing;[j] he gave generously to those in
10:3 [k]Ac 3:1 need and prayed to God regularly. 3One day at about three in the afternoon[k] he had a vision.[l] He dis-
[l]Ac 9:10 [m]Ac 5:19 tinctly saw an angel[m] of God, who came to him and said, "Cornelius!"
4Cornelius stared at him in fear. "What is it, Lord?" he asked.
10:4 [n]Mt 26:13 [o]Rev 8:4 The angel answered, "Your prayers and gifts to the poor have come up as a memorial offering[n] before
10:5 [p]Ac 9:36 God.[o] 5Now send men to Joppa[p] to bring back a man named Simon who is called Peter. 6He is staying with
10:6 [q]Ac 9:43 Simon the tanner,[q] whose house is by the sea."
7When the angel who spoke to him had gone, Cornelius called two of his servants and a devout sol-
10:8 [r]Ac 9:36 dier who was one of his attendants. 8He told them everything that had happened and sent them to Joppa.[r]

Peter's Vision

9About noon the following day as they were on their journey and approaching the city, Peter went up
10:9 [s]Mt 24:17 on the roof[s] to pray. 10He became hungry and wanted something to eat, and while the meal was being
10:10 [t]Ac 22:17 prepared, he fell into a trance.[t] 11He saw heaven opened and something like a large sheet being let down
to earth by its four corners. 12It contained all kinds of four-footed animals, as well as reptiles of the earth
and birds of the air. 13Then a voice told him, "Get up, Peter. Kill and eat."
10:14 [u]Ac 9:5 [v]Lev 11:4-8,13-20; 20:25; Dt 14:3-20; Eze 4:14 14"Surely not, Lord!"[u] Peter replied. "I have never eaten anything impure or unclean."[v]
15The voice spoke to him a second time, "Do not call anything impure that God has made clean."[w]
16This happened three times, and immediately the sheet was taken back to heaven.
10:15 [w]Mt 15:11; Ro 14:14,17,20; 1Co 10:25; 1Ti 4:3,4; Tit 1:15 17While Peter was wondering about the meaning of the vision, the men sent by Cornelius[x] found out
where Simon's house was and stopped at the gate. 18They called out, asking if Simon who was known as
10:17 [x]ver 7,8 Peter was staying there.
10:19 [y]Ac 8:29 19While Peter was still thinking about the vision, the Spirit said[y] to him, "Simon, three[a] men are look-
10:20 [z]Ac 15:7-9 ing for you. 20So get up and go downstairs. Do not hesitate to go with them, for I have sent them."[z]
21Peter went down and said to the men, "I'm the one you're looking for. Why have you come?"
22The men replied, "We have come from Cornelius the centurion. He is a righteous and God-fearing
10:22 [a]ver 2 [b]Ac 11:14 man,[a] who is respected by all the Jewish people. A holy angel told him to have you come to his house so
that he could hear what you have to say."[b] 23Then Peter invited the men into the house to be his guests.

Peter at Cornelius's House

10:23 [c]Ac 1:16 [d]ver 45; Ac 11:12 The next day Peter started out with them, and some of the brothers[c] from Joppa went along.[d] 24The
10:24 [e]Ac 8:40 following day he arrived in Caesarea.[e] Cornelius was expecting them and had called together his rela-
tives and close friends. 25As Peter entered the house, Cornelius met him and fell at his feet in reverence.
10:26 [f]Ac 14:15; Rev 19:10 26But Peter made him get up. "Stand up," he said, "I am only a man myself."[f]
27Talking with him, Peter went inside and found a large gathering of people. 28He said to them: "You
10:28 [g]Jn 4:9; 18:28; Ac 11:3 are well aware that it is against our law for a Jew to associate with a Gentile or visit him.[g] But God has
[h]Ac 15:8,9 shown me that I should not call any man impure or unclean.[h] 29So when I was sent for, I came without
raising any objection. May I ask why you sent for me?"

[a] 19 One early manuscript *two*; other manuscripts do not have the number.

10:1 For "Caesarea," see the note on 8:40.

A centurion commanded a century, a military unit that by New Testament times typically numbered 80 men (see the note on Mt 8:5). The Roman legion (about 6,000 men) generally included about 60 centuries, as well as cavalry and auxiliaries. A legion was typically comprised of ten cohorts or regiments, with six centuries per cohort. Centurions were carefully selected; all of them mentioned in the New Testament appear to have had noble qualities. The Roman centurions provided necessary stability to the entire Roman military system.

"Italy" (here referred to in the designation "the Italian Regiment") is the geographical term for the country of which Rome was the capital. Originally it applied only to the extreme south of what is now Italy, the region now called Calabria, but gradually the application of the name was extended, until in the first century A.D. it began to be used in the current sense. It is referred to three other times in the New Testament: 18:2, 27:1 and Hebrews 13:24.

10:2 God-fearers were non-Jews who believed in one God, attended the synagogue and respected the moral and ethical teachings of the Jews but who did not fully embrace all of the Jewish customs, such as the rite of circumcision (see the note on Jn 12:20; cf. "converts" in the note on Ac 2:11; see also "Proselytes in Second Temple Judaism" on p. 1776 and "Circumcision in the Ancient World" on p. 1840.)

10:3 Cornelius experienced his vision "at about three in the afternoon"—a traditional Jewish time of prayer—the hour of the evening incense (see the note on 3:1).

10:5 For "Joppa," see the note on 9:36.

10:6 For "tanner," see the note on 9:43.

10:9 For "roof," see the notes on Mark 2:4 and Luke 17:31.

10:15 On the subject of defilement in the Old and New Testaments, see the note on Song of Songs 5:3.

10:23 By providing lodging for them, Peter was already taking the first step toward accepting Gentiles. Such intimate relationship with Gentiles was contrary to prescribed Jewish practice.

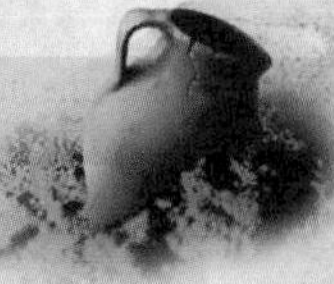

ARCHAEOLOGICAL SITES

CAESAREA MARITIMA

ACTS 10 Caesarea Maritima (also called Caesarea Augusta), located near the site of modern Tel Aviv, is to be distinguished from Caesarea Philippi, located north of the Sea of Galilee.[1] Caesarea Maritima was constructed by Herod the Great from 22 to 10 B.C.[2] Built to be one of the great cities of the Roman Empire, Caesarea was renowned for its beauty. The city boasted a temple dedicated to Augustus Caesar, a large hippodrome, a theater (including an inscription that mentions Pontius Pilate),[3] large waterfront warehouses and a sewer system. Five major roads led into Caesarea. Its harbor, Sebastos, was an engineering wonder that included artificial breakwaters and features that mitigated silt accumulation and wave damage. Ships entering the harbor passed through an entryway flanked by colossal statues of the imperial family. Underwater archaeology was carried out in the harbor area by the Caesarea Ancient Harbor Excavation Project (CAHEP) during the 1980s.

A section of the Roman aqueduct at Caesarea Maritima
Photograph courtesy of © Dr. Gary Pratico

Paul often traveled by way of the port at Caesarea (Ac 9:30; 18:22; 21:8; 27:2) and was guarded in Herod's Praetorium there during the last two years of procurator Antonius Felix's governorship (c. A.D. 58–59).[4] Caesarea, the Roman headquarters for the province, maintained a large Roman garrison. Vespasian and Titus used the city as a base of operations for the Roman army during the war of A.D. 66–72 against the Jews.[5]

Both Christians and Jews established schools of higher education in Caesarea Maritima. Christian scholars who worked there include Origen, Pamphilus and the church historian Eusebius. Numerous remains from the later **Byzantine**, Crusader and Muslim periods have also been excavated there.

[1]See "Caesarea Philippi" on page 1589. [2]See "Herod the Great" on page 1627. [3]See "Pontius Pilate" on page 1714. [4]See "Imprisonment in the Roman World: In Prison Versus House Arrest" on page 1826. [5]See "The Roman Army and the Occupation of the Holy Land" on page 1829.

The Roman theater at Caesarea
Photograph courtesy of © Dr. Gary Pratico

30 Cornelius answered: “Four days ago I was in my house praying at this hour, at three in the after-
noon. Suddenly a man in shining clothes stood before me 31 and said, ‘Cornelius, God has heard your
prayer and remembered your gifts to the poor. 32 Send to Joppa for Simon who is called Peter. He is a guest
in the home of Simon the tanner, who lives by the sea.’ 33 So I sent for you immediately, and it was good
of you to come. Now we are all here in the presence of God to listen to everything the Lord has com-
manded you to tell us.”
10:34 [i]Dt 10:17; 2Ch 19:7; 34 Then Peter began to speak: “I now realize how true it is that God does not show favoritism[i] 35 but ac-
Job 34:19; Ro 2:11; Gal 2:6; cepts men from every nation who fear him and do what is right.[j] 36 You know the message God sent to
Eph 6:9; Col 3:25; 1Pe 1:17 the people of Israel, telling the good news[k] of peace[l] through Jesus Christ, who is Lord of all.[m] 37 You know
10:35 [j]Ac 15:9 what has happened throughout Judea, beginning in Galilee after the baptism that John preached— 38 how
10:36 [k]Ac 13:32 [l]Lk 2:14 God anointed[n] Jesus of Nazareth with the Holy Spirit and power, and how he went around doing good and
[m]Mt 28:18; Ro 10:12 healing[o] all who were under the power of the devil, because God was with him.[p]
10:38 [n]Ac 4:26 [o]Mt 4:23 [p]Jn 3:2 39 “We are witnesses[q] of everything he did in the country of the Jews and in Jerusalem. They killed
10:39 [q]Lk 24:48 [r]Ac 5:30 him by hanging him on a tree,[r] 40 but God raised him from the dead[s] on the third day and caused him
10:40 [s]Ac 2:24 10:41 [t]Jn 14:17, to be seen. 41 He was not seen by all the people,[t] but by witnesses whom God had already chosen—by
22 [u]Lk 24:43; Jn 21:13 us who ate[u] and drank with him after he rose from the dead. 42 He commanded us to preach to the peo-
10:42 [v]Mt 28:19, 20 [w]Jn 5:22; ple[v] and to testify that he is the one whom God appointed as judge of the living and the dead.[w] 43 All the
Ac 17:31; prophets testify about him[x] that everyone[y] who believes in him receives forgiveness of sins through his
Ro 14:9; 2Co 5:10; 2Ti 4:1; name.”
1Pe 4:5 10:43 [x]Isa 53:11 44 While Peter was still speaking these words, the Holy Spirit came on[z] all who heard the message.
[y]Ac 15:9 45 The circumcised believers who had come with Peter[a] were astonished that the gift of the Holy Spirit had
10:44 [z]Ac 8:15, 16; 11:15; 15:8 been poured out[b] even on the Gentiles.[c] 46 For they heard them speaking in tongues[a] [d] and praising God.
10:45 [a]ver 23 [b]Ac 2:33,38 Then Peter said, 47 “Can anyone keep these people from being baptized with water?[e] They have re-
[c]Ac 11:18 10:46 [d]Mk 16:17 ceived the Holy Spirit just as we have.”[f] 48 So he ordered that they be baptized in the name of Jesus Christ.[g]
10:47 [e]Ac 8:36 [f]Ac 11:17 Then they asked Peter to stay with them for a few days.

10:48 [g]Ac 2:38; 8:16

Peter Explains His Actions

11:1 [h]Ac 1:16 **11** The apostles and the brothers[h] throughout Judea heard that the Gentiles also had received the
11:2 [i]Ac 10:45 word of God. 2 So when Peter went up to Jerusalem, the circumcised believers[i] criticized him
11:3 [j]Ac 10:25, 28; Gal 2:12 3 and said, “You went into the house of uncircumcised men and ate with them.”[j]
4 Peter began and explained everything to them precisely as it had happened: 5 “I was in the city of
11:5 [k]Ac 9:10; 10:9-32 Joppa praying, and in a trance I saw a vision.[k] I saw something like a large sheet being let down from
heaven by its four corners, and it came down to where I was. 6 I looked into it and saw four-footed ani-
mals of the earth, wild beasts, reptiles, and birds of the air. 7 Then I heard a voice telling me, ‘Get up, Pe-
ter. Kill and eat.’
8 “I replied, ‘Surely not, Lord! Nothing impure or unclean has ever entered my mouth.’
11:9 [l]Ac 10:15 9 “The voice spoke from heaven a second time, ‘Do not call anything impure that God has made clean.’[l]
10 This happened three times, and then it was all pulled up to heaven again.
11 “Right then three men who had been sent to me from Caesarea stopped at the house where I was
11:12 [m]Ac 8:29 [n]Ac 15:9; Ro 3:22 staying. 12 The Spirit told[m] me to have no hesitation about going with them.[n] These six brothers also went
with me, and we entered the man’s house. 13 He told us how he had seen an angel appear in his house and
say, ‘Send to Joppa for Simon who is called Peter. 14 He will bring you a message through which you and
11:14 [o]Jn 4:53; Ac 16:15,31-34; all your household[o] will be saved.’
1Co 1:11,16 11:15 [p]Ac 10:44 15 “As I began to speak, the Holy Spirit came on[p] them as he had come on us at the beginning.[q] 16 Then
[q]Ac 2:4 I remembered what the Lord had said: ‘John baptized with[b] water, but you will be baptized with the Holy

[a] 46 Or *other languages* [b] 16 Or *in*

10:30 The Jews counted a part of a day as a whole day.
“A man in shining clothes” was common language to describe an angel when appearing in the form of a man (see Mt 28:3; Mk 16:5; Jn 20:12; see also “Angels and Guardian Spirits in the Bible and the Ancient Near East” on p. 1529).
10:46 See “Tongue-Speaking in Christian and Pagan Worship” on page 1876.
11:1 At times “brothers” is used to refer to those of common Jewish lineage (2:29; 7:2), but in Christian contexts the term denotes those united in Christ (6:3; 10:23).
11:2 “Circumcised believers” refers to Jewish Christians.
11:3 “Uncircumcised men” refers to the Gentiles who would not observe the laws of clean and unclean food and who would violate Jewish regulations concerning food preparation.
11:5 For “Joppa,” see the note on 9:36.
11:14 “Household” refers not only to the family but also to slaves and employed individuals under Cornelius’s authority.

Spirit.'[r] 17 So if God gave them the same gift as he gave us,[s] who believed in the Lord Jesus Christ, who
was I to think that I could oppose God?"
18 When they heard this, they had no further objections and praised God, saying, "So then, God has
granted even the Gentiles repentance unto life."[t]

The Church in Antioch

19 Now those who had been scattered by the persecution in connection with Stephen[u] traveled as far
as Phoenicia, Cyprus and Antioch,[v] telling the message only to Jews. 20 Some of them, however, men from
Cyprus[w] and Cyrene,[x] went to Antioch and began to speak to Greeks also, telling them the good news
about the Lord Jesus. 21 The Lord's hand was with them,[y] and a great number of people believed and
turned to the Lord.[z]
22 News of this reached the ears of the church at Jerusalem, and they sent Barnabas[a] to Antioch.
23 When he arrived and saw the evidence of the grace of God,[b] he was glad and encouraged them all to
remain true to the Lord with all their hearts.[c] 24 He was a good man, full of the Holy Spirit and faith, and
a great number of people were brought to the Lord.[d]
25 Then Barnabas went to Tarsus[e] to look for Saul, 26 and when he found him, he brought him to An-
tioch. So for a whole year Barnabas and Saul met with the church and taught great numbers of people.
The disciples[f] were called Christians first[g] at Antioch.

11:16 [r]Mk 1:8; Ac 1:5
11:17 [s]Ac 10:45, 47
11:18 [t]Ro 10:12, 13; 2Co 7:10
11:19 [u]Ac 8:1,4 [v]ver 26,27; Ac 13:1; 18:22; Gal 2:11
11:20 [w]Ac 4:36 [x]Mt 27:32
11:21 [y]Lk 1:66 [z]Ac 2:47
11:22 [a]Ac 4:36
11:23 [b]Ac 13:43; 14:26; 20:24 [c]Ac 14:22
11:24 [d]ver 21; Ac 5:14
11:25 [e]Ac 9:11
11:26 [f]Ac 6:1,2; 13:52 [g]Ac 26:28

11:19 Phoenicia was a country about 15 miles (24 km) wide and 120 miles (193 km) long, stretching along the northeastern Mediterranean coast (modern Lebanon). Its important cities were Tyre and Sidon (see the notes on Mt 15:21; Mk 7:31; see also "Phoenicia" on p. 488).

Cyprus is an island in the eastern part of the Mediterranean Sea. Jews had settled there from Maccabean times. It was also the home of Barnabas (see the note on Ac 13:1–2).

Antioch—not to be confused with Pisidian Antioch (see the note on 13:14)—was the third city of the Roman Empire (after Rome and Alexandria). It lay 15 miles (24 km) inland from the northeastern corner of the Mediterranean. The first largely Gentile church was located there, and it was from this church that Paul's three missionary journeys were launched (see "Antioch of Syria, Center of Christianity" on p. 1904).

11:20 For "Cyprus," see the note on verse 19. Cyrene was the capital of a district of Libya (a region west of Egypt) called Cyrenaica. Archaeology has shown that the Greek plan was to make Cyrene the "Athens of Africa." The most interesting remains there are a great system of tombs cut out of solid rock into the cliff. Architecture and paintings adorn these tombs.

11:22 "Antioch" is Syrian Antioch (see the note on v. 19).

The sending of Barnabas (see the note on 13:1–2) was apparently in keeping with the Jerusalem church's policy of sending leaders to check on new ministries that came to their attention (see 8:14 and its note).

11:25 For "Tarsus," see the note on 22:3.

11:26 The term "Christian" was probably applied to these disciples in Syrian Antioch (see the note on v. 19) by the city's non-Christian population, possibly as a derogatory label meaning "little messiahs" or "belonging to Christ." *Christ* is the Greek word for Messiah—a redeemer most Jews thought they still awaited.

Claudius, Emperor of Rome

ACTS 11 Claudius, the Roman emperor from A.D. 41 to 54, was an effective ruler, with the style of administration becoming less despotic and more bureaucratic during his tenure. He expanded the empire and improved roads and aqueducts in Italy and the provinces. Classical writers have reported, however, that the reign of Claudius was a period of distress and scarcity due to scanty harvests and other causes.[1]

Early in his rule Claudius issued edicts favoring the Jews, reversing the policy of Caligula (Ac 37–41) and permitting Jews in all parts of the empire to freely observe their own laws and customs. Claudius made poor choices, however, in appointing procurators over Judea, and the situation there continued to deteriorate.[2] Jews in Rome were not allowed to assemble because of their large number. Later, around the year 50, he expelled the Jews from Rome (18:2). The historian Suetonius (c. 70–130) recorded this event (*Claudius*, 25.4), which is historically significant for its connection to the rise of Christianity.[3] For the infant Christian church, the reign of Claudius was a relatively quiet environment in which to grow, in contrast to the tumultuous reign of his successor, the infamous Nero (r. 54–68).[4]

[1]See "Famine in the Ancient Near East" on page 70. [2]See "The History of the Holy Land" on page xxi in the front of this Bible. [3]See "Nonbiblical Sources for the Historical Jesus" on page 1751 and "The Geographic Expansion of the Church Under Persecution" on page 1781. [4]See "Nero, Persecutor of Christians" on page 1931 and "The Early Persecution of the Church" on page 2067.

27During this time some prophets[h] came down from Jerusalem to Antioch. 28One of them, named Agabus,[i] stood up and through the Spirit predicted that a severe famine would spread over the entire Roman world.[j] (This happened during the reign of Claudius.)[k] 29The disciples,[l] each according to his ability, decided to provide help[m] for the brothers[n] living in Judea. 30This they did, sending their gift to the elders[o] by Barnabas and Saul.[p]

Peter's Miraculous Escape From Prison

12 It was about this time that King Herod arrested some who belonged to the church, intending to persecute them. 2He had James, the brother of John,[q] put to death with the sword. 3When he saw that this pleased the Jews,[r] he proceeded to seize Peter also. This happened during the Feast of Unleavened Bread.[s] 4After arresting him, he put him in prison, handing him over to be guarded by four squads of four soldiers each. Herod intended to bring him out for public trial after the Passover.

5So Peter was kept in prison, but the church was earnestly praying to God for him.[t]

6The night before Herod was to bring him to trial, Peter was sleeping between two soldiers, bound with two chains,[u] and sentries stood guard at the entrance. 7Suddenly an angel[v] of the Lord appeared and a light shone in the cell. He struck Peter on the side and woke him up. "Quick, get up!" he said, and the chains fell off Peter's wrists.[w]

8Then the angel said to him, "Put on your clothes and sandals." And Peter did so. "Wrap your cloak around you and follow me," the angel told him. 9Peter followed him out of the prison, but he had no idea that what the angel was doing was really happening; he thought he was seeing a vision.[x] 10They passed the first and second guards and came to the iron gate leading to the city. It opened for them by itself,[y] and they went through it. When they had walked the length of one street, suddenly the angel left him.

11Then Peter came to himself[z] and said, "Now I know without a doubt that the Lord sent his angel and rescued me[a] from Herod's clutches and from everything the Jewish people were anticipating."

12When this had dawned on him, he went to the house of Mary the mother of John, also called Mark,[b] where many people had gathered and were praying.[c] 13Peter knocked at the outer entrance, and a servant girl named Rhoda came to answer the door.[d] 14When she recognized Peter's voice, she was so overjoyed[e] she ran back without opening it and exclaimed, "Peter is at the door!"

15"You're out of your mind," they told her. When she kept insisting that it was so, they said, "It must be his angel."[f]

16But Peter kept on knocking, and when they opened the door and saw him, they were astonished. 17Peter motioned with his hand[g] for them to be quiet and described how the Lord had brought him out of prison. "Tell James[h] and the brothers[i] about this," he said, and then he left for another place.

18In the morning, there was no small commotion among the soldiers as to what had become of Peter. 19After Herod had a thorough search made for him and did not find him, he cross-examined the guards and ordered that they be executed.[j]

11:27 [h]Ac 13:1; 15:32; 1Co 12:28, 29; Eph 4:11
11:28 [i]Ac 21:10 [j]Mt 24:14 [k]Ac 18:2
11:29 [l]ver 26 [m]Ro 15:26; 2Co 9:2 [n]Ac 1:16
11:30 [o]Ac 14:23 [p]Ac 12:25
12:2 [q]Mt 4:21
12:3 [r]Ac 24:27 [s]Ex 12:15; 23:15
12:5 [t]Eph 6:18
12:6 [u]Ac 21:33
12:7 [v]Ac 5:19 [w]Ac 16:26
12:9 [x]Ac 9:10
12:10 [y]Ac 5:19; 16:26
12:11 [z]Lk 15:17 [a]Ps 34:7; Da 3:28; 6:22; 2Co 1:10; 2Pe 2:9
12:12 [b]ver 25; Ac 15:37,39; Col 4:10; Phm 24; 1Pe 5:13 [c]ver 5
12:13 [d]Jn 18:16, 17
12:14 [e]Lk 24:41
12:15 [f]Mt 18:10
12:17 [g]Ac 13:16; 19:33; 21:40 [h]Ac 15:13 [i]Ac 1:16
12:19 [j]Ac 16:27

11:28 See "Famine in the Ancient Near East" on page 70, as well as the note at Ruth 1:1. According to Josephus, a severe famine occurred in Judah (affecting Jerusalem) in A.D. 46.

Claudius was the emperor of Rome (see "Claudius, Emperor of Rome" on p. 1788) from A.D. 41 to 54.

11:30 This is the first reference to "elders" in Acts (see also the notes on 1Ti 3:1-7; 5:17). Since the apostles are not mentioned, they may have been absent from Jerusalem at this time.

12:1 "King Herod" is a reference here to Agrippa I, grandson of Herod the Great and son of Aristobulus. He was a nephew of Herod Antipas, who had beheaded John the Baptist (Mt 14:3–12) and tried Jesus (Lk 23:8–12). When Antipas was exiled, Agrippa received his tetrarchy, as well as those of Philip and Lysanias (see Lk 3:1 and its note). In A.D. 41 Judea and Samaria were added to his realm. (See "Herod's Successors and Uneasy Relations Between Rome and the Jews" on p. 1631.)

For "persecute them," see "The Early Persecution of the Church" on page 2067.

12:2 James was the brother of John the apostle and the son of Zebedee (Mt 4:21). This event took place about ten years after Jesus' death and resurrection.

"Put to death with the sword" implies beheaded, like John the Baptist.

12:3 For "Feast of Unleavened Bread," see the notes on Matthew 26:17 and Mark 14:1.

12:4 "Four squads" means one company of four soldiers for each of the four watches of the night (see the note on Mt 14:25).

"Passover" here refers to the whole week of the festival (see the note on Mt 26:17).

12:7 For "angel of the Lord," see "Angels and Guardian Spirits in the Bible and the Ancient Near East" on page 1529.

12:8 For "clothes and sandals," see "Dress and Fashion in the Greco-Roman World" on page 2004.

12:9 "Prison" probably refers to the Fortress of Antonia, located at the northwestern corner of the temple—the "barracks" where Paul was later held (see 21:34; see also "Herod's Temple" on p. 1648, "The Ancient City" on p. 1790 and "Imprisonment in the Roman World: In Prison Versus House Arrest" on p. 1826).

12:12 Mary was the aunt of Barnabas (see Col 4:10; see also the note on Ac 13:1–2). Apparently her home was a gathering place for Christians, and it may have been the location of the upper room where the Last Supper was held (see Mk 14:13–15; Ac 1:13; see also "The Upper Room" on p. 1826) and the place of prayer in Acts 4:31.

12:17 James was Jesus' brother (see the note on Lk 8:19 and "The Family of Joseph, Mary and Jesus" on p. 1581).

The Ancient City

ACTS 12 Ancient cities varied widely in size, structure and appearance. Models for the "ideal" city—such as those of the Greek engineer Hippodamus—existed, but reality was determined by topography; the availability of natural resources, especially water; and the need for provisions for protection, commerce and religious observance.

A city's outside walls were designed to protect residents from attack. Stone was the material of choice, yet mud brick and wood (which was vulnerable to burning) were also used. Major New Testament cities employed large, cut blocks (**ashlars**) for their walls. These fortifications were impressive for their depth and height, but during the Greco-Roman period walls were seldom comprised of solid rock. The outside and inside faces were stone, but a gap between them was filled with rubble, especially dirt. This added girth rendered a wall more resistant to bombardment, since the middle layer absorbed shock. It is common to find city walls between 5.5 yards and 7.7 yards (5 x 7 m) thick, as well as quite high. Fortified towers were often placed regularly along the course of the walls, giving guards the ability to monitor them and fire defensive weapons.

A second wall was typically constructed around the citadel (Greek *acropolis*), the highest point in the city and the last line of defense against an attack. Flavius Josephus reported that Herod the Great (37–4 B.C.)[1] expanded and strengthened Jerusalem's walls. Part of this project was the construction of the Tower of David on the city's citadel. Standing nearly 21 yards (19 m) above ground level and measuring 24 yards (22 m) by nearly 17 yards (15.5 m), it was a monument to the strength of Jerusalem's defenses. In 35 B.C. Herod also constructed the impressive Fortress of Antonia, the headquarters for the Roman military forces and perhaps also a prison (the likely location of Peter's incarceration),[2] beside the temple mount.

A city's market, located along the main road to maximize the flow of visitors and goods, was its social and commercial center. Known to the Greeks as the *agora* and to the Romans as the forum, this locale bustled with the sounds of haggling merchants, tethered animals and playing children.[3] During the **Hellenistic** period the Greeks surrounded the markets with *stoas* (open, roofed colonnades). The Lower Agora at Pergamum, built during the reign of Eumenes II (197–49 B.C.), is an excellent example. Surrounded by two-storied stoas, it featured two aisles opening to the interior of the agora. These were left clear for foot traffic, with small shops inhabiting the rear aisles, allowing customers to escape the relentless sun. A cistern in a nearby house fed a fountain in the central courtyard of the agora through a system of underground clay pipes.

A Roman era caryatid, a female figure that functions as an architectural column

Preserving Bible Times; © Dr. James C. Martin; permission of The Istanbul Archaeological Museum

The market was also the site of monuments to local heroes and deities and an informal meeting place for residents and visitors. Especially in port cities, it was the location for debate on religious and philosophical ideas. This was the scenario in Acts 17, when Paul engaged the Athenians in discussion in their agora, reasoning with Epicureans, Stoics and any others who happened to be there.[4] The subsequent debate with the council of the Areopagus would have occurred on Mars Hill, between the agora and the Acropolis.[5]

In the ancient world it was believed that each city had a primary protector deity responsible for its well-being, and it was customary to honor that deity with a temple on the citadel. For example, the temple to Athena Parthenos (the Parthenon) was constructed between 447 and 432 B.C. in honor of the patron goddess of Athens. In the polytheistic religions of antiquity, however, where dedication to a single deity was considered undesirable, temples to multiple gods were the rule. Athena, therefore, shared the Acropolis with sanctuaries to Poseidon, to the mythical king Erechtheus and to Nike (Victory). Rome displayed a similar variety of temples: to Roma, Venus, Diana, Apollo, Jupiter, Mars and other lesser deities and deified emperors,[6] as well as a temple dedicated to *all* the gods, the Pantheon.[7] This highlights the uniqueness of the Jerusalem landscape, with its lone temple to the one true God.

[1]See "Herod the Great" on page 1627. [2]See "Imprisonment in the Roman World: In Prison Versus House Arrest" on page 1826. [3]See "The Ancient Agora" on page 1799. [4]See "Greek Philosophical Schools" on page 1937. [5]See "Debate and Rhetoric in the Ancient World" on page 1797 and "The Areopagus" on page 1802. [6]See "The Imperial Cult" on page 1651. [7]See "The Gods of the Greeks and Romans" on page 1908.

Herod's Death

12:19 [k]Ac 8:40 Then Herod went from Judea to Caesarea[k] and stayed there a while. 20 He had been quarreling with the
12:20 [l]Mt 11:21 people of Tyre and Sidon;[l] they now joined together and sought an audience with him. Having secured
[m]1Ki 5:9,11; Eze 27:17 the support of Blastus, a trusted personal servant of the king, they asked for peace, because they depend-
ed on the king's country for their food supply.[m]
21 On the appointed day Herod, wearing his royal robes, sat on his throne and delivered a public ad-
dress to the people. 22 They shouted, "This is the voice of a god, not of a man." 23 Immediately, because
12:23 [n]1Sa 25:38; Herod did not give praise to God, an angel of the Lord struck him down,[n] and he was eaten by worms
2Sa 24:16,17 and died.
12:24 [o]Ac 6:7; 19:20 24 But the word of God continued to increase and spread.[o]
12:25 [p]Ac 4:36 25 When Barnabas[p] and Saul had finished their mission,[q] they returned from[a] Jerusalem, taking with
[q]Ac 11:30 [r]ver 12 them John, also called Mark.[r]

Barnabas and Saul Sent Off

13:1 [s]Ac 11:19 [t]Ac 11:27 **13** In the church at Antioch[s] there were prophets[t] and teachers: Barnabas,[u] Simeon called Niger,
[u]Ac 4:36; 11:22- Lucius of Cyrene, Manaen (who had been brought up with Herod[v] the tetrarch) and Saul. 2 While
26 [v]Mt 14:1 13:2 [w]Ac 8:29 they were worshiping the Lord and fasting, the Holy Spirit said,[w] "Set apart for me Barnabas and Saul for
[x]Ac 14:26 [y]Ac 22:21 the work[x] to which I have called them."[y] 3 So after they had fasted and prayed, they placed their hands on
13:3 [z]Ac 6:6 [a]Ac 14:26 them[z] and sent them off.[a]

On Cyprus

13:4 [b]ver 2,3 4 The two of them, sent on their way by the Holy Spirit,[b] went down to Seleucia and sailed from there
[c]Ac 4:36 13:5 [d]Ac 9:20 to Cyprus.[c] 5 When they arrived at Salamis, they proclaimed the word of God in the Jewish synagogues.[d]
[e]Ac 12:12 John[e] was with them as their helper.
6 They traveled through the whole island until they came to Paphos. There they met a Jewish sorcer-
13:6 [f]Ac 8:9 er[f] and false prophet[g] named Bar-Jesus, 7 who was an attendant of the proconsul,[h] Sergius Paulus. The
[g]Mt 7:15 13:7 [h]ver 8,12; proconsul, an intelligent man, sent for Barnabas and Saul because he wanted to hear the word of God.
Ac 19:38 13:8 [i]Ac 8:9 8 But Elymas the sorcerer[i] (for that is what his name means) opposed them and tried to turn the procon-
[j]ver 7 [k]Ac 6:7 13:9 [l]Ac 4:8 sul[j] from the faith.[k] 9 Then Saul, who was also called Paul, filled with the Holy Spirit,[l] looked straight at
13:10 [m]Mt 13:38; Elymas and said, 10 "You are a child of the devil[m] and an enemy of everything that is right! You are full of
Jn 8:44 [n]Hos 14:9 all kinds of deceit and trickery. Will you never stop perverting the right ways of the Lord?[n] 11 Now the

[a] 25 Some manuscripts *to*

12:20–23 Agrippa's sudden death was fully recorded by Josephus (*Antiquities*, 19.8). On the second day of a festival held in Caesarea in honor of Claudius, Agrippa donned a silver garment of "wonderful" texture and entered the amphitheater early in the morning. When the sun's rays shone on his garment, the brilliant glare caused his flatterers to cry out that he was a god. Josephus added that "the king did neither rebuke them nor reject their impious flattery." Almost immediately a severe pain arose in his abdomen, and five days later he died in great agony.

12:21 For "throne," see "The Judgment Seat" on page 1891.

13:1–2 Barnabas (called Joseph in 4:36) was a Levite from Cyprus who was known for his generosity and goodness (4:36; 11:24) and who had spoken on Paul's behalf to the apostles (9:27). The Jerusalem church had sent Barnabas to Syrian Antioch (11:22; see the note on 11:19) to lead the new church there, and he later brought Paul to Antioch to work as his associate (11:26). Paul and Barnabas spent about a year together in Antioch before receiving this call from God to set out on a missionary journey together. Paul and Barnabas would later have a disagreement over Barnabas's cousin John Mark, and the two would separate to go on separate missionary journeys—Barnabas and John Mark to Cyprus, Paul and Silas to Asia Minor (15:36–40).

13:3 For "placed their hands on," see the note on 6:6.

13:4 It was common to travel by sea (see "Travel in the Greco-Roman World" on p. 1946); accordingly they headed to Seleucia, the seaport of Syrian Antioch, 16 miles (26 km) to the west and 5 miles (8 km) upstream from the mouth of the Orontes River.

13:5 Salamis was a town on the eastern coast of the central plain of Cyprus (see the note on 4:36), near modern Famagusta. It was founded, according to tradition, by Teucer, who was from the island by the same name off the coast of Greece. The city possessed a good harbor and was populous and flourishing during the Hellenic and Roman periods. Nothing is said of the duration or success of the visit by Paul and Barnabas. Paul did not return to Salamis, but Barnabas doubtless did on his second missionary journey (15:39). According to tradition he was martyred there during the reign of Nero.

"John" was John Mark, a cousin of Barnabas.

13:6 Paphos, the headquarters of Roman rule, was located at the western end of Cyprus, nearly 100 miles (160 km) from Salamis. The Paphos of the Bible is really New Paphos, a Roman city rebuilt by Augustus; the old Greek city of Paphos, dedicated to the worship of Aphrodite, lay 10 miles (16 km) to the south. New Paphos is now known as Baffa.

For "sorcerer," see the note on "Magi" at Matthew 2:1.

13:7 Since Cyprus (see the note on 4:36) was a Roman senatorial province, a proconsul was assigned to it. A proconsul was a Roman official, generally of praetorian or consular rank, who served as deputy consul in the Roman provinces. The term of office was one year, although it could be longer in special instances. The powers of the proconsul were unlimited in both the military and civil areas, but when his term had expired he was held accountable for what he had done. Sergius Paulus, Paul's famous convert (see "Sergius Paulus, Proconsul of Cyprus" on p. 1792), and Gallio (18:12) were such officials mentioned in the Bible.

13:8 "Elymas" is a Semitic name meaning "sorcerer," "magician" or "wise man" (probably a self-assumed designation). See also the note on "Magi" at Matthew 2:1.

13:9 It was customary to have a given name, in this case Saul (designating a Hebrew with a Jewish background), and a later name, in this case Paul (denoting a Roman with a Hellenistic background).

hand of the Lord is against you.[o] You are going to be blind, and for a time you will be unable to see the
light of the sun."
Immediately mist and darkness came over him, and he groped about, seeking someone to lead him
by the hand. 12 When the proconsul[p] saw what had happened, he believed, for he was amazed at the teach-
ing about the Lord.

In Pisidian Antioch

13 From Paphos,[q] Paul and his companions sailed to Perga in Pamphylia, where John[r] left them to re-
turn to Jerusalem. 14 From Perga they went on to Pisidian Antioch.[s] On the Sabbath[t] they entered the syn-
agogue[u] and sat down. 15 After the reading from the Law[v] and the Prophets, the synagogue rulers sent
word to them, saying, "Brothers, if you have a message of encouragement for the people, please speak."
16 Standing up, Paul motioned with his hand[w] and said: "Men of Israel and you Gentiles who worship
God, listen to me! 17 The God of the people of Israel chose our fathers; he made the people prosper dur-
ing their stay in Egypt, with mighty power he led them out of that country,[x] 18 he endured their conduct[a][y]
for about forty years in the desert,[z] 19 he overthrew seven nations in Canaan[a] and gave their land to his
people[b] as their inheritance. 20 All this took about 450 years.
"After this, God gave them judges[c] until the time of Samuel the prophet.[d] 21 Then the people asked for
a king,[e] and he gave them Saul[f] son of Kish, of the tribe of Benjamin,[g] who ruled forty years. 22 After re-
moving Saul,[h] he made David their king.[i] He testified concerning him: 'I have found David son of Jesse
a man after my own heart;[j] he will do everything I want him to do.'
23 "From this man's descendants[k] God has brought to Israel the Savior[l] Jesus,[m] as he promised.[n] 24 Be-
fore the coming of Jesus, John preached repentance and baptism to all the people of Israel.[o] 25 As John was
completing his work,[p] he said: 'Who do you think I am? I am not that one.[q] No, but he is coming after me,
whose sandals I am not worthy to untie.'[r]
26 "Brothers, children of Abraham, and you God-fearing Gentiles, it is to us that this message of sal-
vation[s] has been sent. 27 The people of Jerusalem and their rulers did not recognize Jesus,[t] yet in con-
demning him they fulfilled the words of the prophets[u] that are read every Sabbath. 28 Though they found
no proper ground for a death sentence, they asked Pilate to have him executed.[v] 29 When they had car-
ried out all that was written about him,[w] they took him down from the tree[x] and laid him in a tomb.[y]
30 But God raised him from the dead,[z] 31 and for many days he was seen by those who had traveled with
him from Galilee to Jerusalem.[a] They are now his witnesses[b] to our people.
32 "We tell you the good news:[c] What God promised our fathers[d] 33 he has fulfilled for us, their children,
by raising up Jesus. As it is written in the second Psalm:

> " 'You are my Son;
> today I have become your Father.[b][c][e]

34 The fact that God raised him from the dead, never to decay, is stated in these words:

> " 'I will give you the holy and sure blessings promised to David.'[d][f]

13:11 [o]Ex 9:3; 1Sa 5:6,7; Ps 32:4
13:12 [p]ver 7
13:13 [q]ver 6 [r]Ac 12:12
13:14 [s]Ac 14:19, 21 [t]Ac 16:13 [u]Ac 9:20
13:15 [v]Ac 15:21
13:16 [w]Ac 12:17
13:17 [x]Ex 6:6,7; Dt 7:6-8
13:18 [y]Dt 1:31 [z]Ac 7:36
13:19 [a]Dt 7:1 [b]Jos 19:51
13:20 [c]Jdg 2:16 [d]1Sa 3:19,20
13:21 [e]1Sa 8:5, 19 [f]1Sa 10:1 [g]1Sa 9:1,2
13:22 [h]1Sa 15:23,26 [i]1Sa 16:13; Ps 89:20 [j]1Sa 13:14
13:23 [k]Mt 1:1 [l]Lk 2:11 [m]Mt 1:21 [n]ver 32
13:24 [o]Mk 1:4
13:25 [p]Ac 20:24 [q]Jn 1:20 [r]Mt 3:11; Jn 1:27
13:26 [s]Ac 4:12
13:27 [t]Ac 3:17 [u]Lk 24:27
13:28 [v]Mt 27:20-25; Ac 3:14
13:29 [w]Lk 18:31 [x]Ac 5:30 [y]Lk 23:53
13:30 [z]Mt 28:6; Ac 2:24
13:31 [a]Mt 28:16 [b]Lk 24:48
13:32 [c]Ac 5:42 [d]Ac 26:6; Ro 4:13
13:33 [e]Ps 2:7
13:34 [f]Isa 55:3

[a] 18 Some manuscripts *and cared for them* [b] 33 Or *have begotten you* [c] 33 Psalm 2:7 [d] 34 Isaiah 55:3

13:13 Perga, the capital of Pamphylia, a coastal province of Asia Minor between the provinces of Lycia and Cilicia, lay 5 miles (8 km) inland and 12 miles (19 km) east of the important seaport Attalia (see the note on 14:25). During Greek times a celebrated temple of Artemis (Diana) was located in the vicinity, which may have been the reason that Christianity never flourished there as it did in other cities in Asia Minor. Today it is known as Murtana, and the well-preserved ruins still reveal an immense theater that accommodated about 13,000 people.

13:14 For "Pisidian," see the note on 14:24.

Pisidian Antioch—not to be confused with Syrian Antioch (see the note on 11:19)—was named after Antiochus, the king of Syria after the death of Alexander the Great. It was located 110 miles (177 km) from Perga and 3,600 feet (1,100 m) above sea level. The city was the hub of good roads and trade and had a large Jewish population. It was a Roman colony, which meant that a contingent of retired military men was settled there. They had been given free land and made citizens of the city of Rome, with all of the accompanying privileges (see "Roman Citizenship" on p. 1930).

Paul's regular practice was to begin his preaching in the synagogue, as long as the Jews would allow it. His reason for doing so was grounded in his understanding of God's redemptive plan. He was not neglecting his Gentile mission, for "God-fearers" (see the notes on Jn 12:20; Ac 10:2; cf. "converts" in the note on 2:11) were a part of the audience. The synagogue provided a ready-made preaching situation with a building, regularly scheduled meetings and a people who knew the Old Testament Scriptures. It was customary to invite visitors, and especially visiting rabbis (such as Paul), to address the gathering. (See the notes on Mk 1:21; Lk 21:12.)

13:15 Sections from the Old Testament were read (see "The Old Testament of the Early Church" on p. 1967), followed by exposition and exhortation.

For "synagogue rulers," see the notes on Mark 5:22 and Luke 8:41.

13:28 See "Pontius Pilate" on page 1714.

[35]So it is stated elsewhere:

13:35 [g]Ps 16:10; Ac 2:27

" 'You will not let your Holy One see decay.'[a][g]

[36]"For when David had served God's purpose in his own generation, he fell asleep; he was buried
13:36 [h]1Ki 2:10; Ac 2:29 with his fathers[h] and his body decayed. [37]But the one whom God raised from the dead did not see
decay.

[38]"Therefore, my brothers, I want you to know that through Jesus the forgiveness of sins is pro-
13:38 [i]Lk 24:47; Ac 2:38 claimed to you.[i] [39]Through him everyone who believes is justified from everything you could not be
13:39 [j]Ro 3:28 justified from by the law of Moses.[j] [40]Take care that what the prophets have said does not happen
to you:

[41]" 'Look, you scoffers,
wonder and perish,
for I am going to do something in your days
that you would never believe,
13:41 [k]Hab 1:5 even if someone told you.'[b]"[k]

13:42 [l]ver 14 [42]As Paul and Barnabas were leaving the synagogue,[l] the people invited them to speak further about
these things on the next Sabbath. [43]When the congregation was dismissed, many of the Jews and devout
converts to Judaism followed Paul and Barnabas, who talked with them and urged them to continue in
13:43 [m]Ac 11:23; 14:22 the grace of God.[m]

[a] 35 Psalm 16:10 [b] 41 Hab. 1:5

Sergius Paulus, Proconsul of Cyprus

ACTS 13 Sergius Paulus was Paul's first recorded convert on his first missionary journey that took place around A.D. 46 (Ac 13:6–12).[1] This conversion took place in the city of Paphos on the island of Cyprus, off the coast of Syria. Paul and Barnabas landed at Seleucia, on the eastern coast of the island, and traveled overland to Paphos, on the western coast—a journey of about 105 miles (169 km) that would have taken at least a week. Cyprus was a Roman province ruled by a proconsul, or governor, from Paphos.[2] Cicero, in a letter to one Sextilius Rufus (c. 50 B.C.), indicated that Paphos was the administrative center for the island.

Romans typically had three names: a *praenomen*, a *nomen* and a *cognomen*. The *praenomen* was a personal name, the *nomen* a clan name and the *cognomen* the name of a particular branch within the clan. Thus, in the name Gaius Julius Caesar, Gaius was the personal name (*praenomen*), Julius the name of the clan (*nomen*) and Caesar the name of the extended family or subclan (*cognomen*) within the Julian clan.

The name Sergius Paulus provides only the *nomen* and the *cognomen*. Either of two inscriptions found in Cyprus may relate to the Sergius Paulus named in Acts 13:7. One records that a man named Paulus was proconsul around the year A.D. 50 (probably too late to relate to Paul's visit), while the other designates a Quintus Sergius Paulus as proconsul during the reign of Caligula, from A.D. 37–41. In addition, a Latin inscription from Rome refers to a Lucius Sergius Paulus, who held an administrative position during the reign of Claudius, from A.D. 41–54.[3]

These inscriptions demonstrate that the Roman family Sergius Paulus was prominent during the period of Acts, and it is entirely feasible that a member of that family could have been serving as proconsul of Cyprus at the time of Paul's first missionary journey.

[1]See "The Missionary Journeys of Paul" on page 1795. [2]See "The Roman Governor" on page 1824. [3]See "Claudius, Emperor of Rome" on page 1788.

44 On the next Sabbath almost the whole city gathered to hear the word of the Lord. 45 When the Jews
saw the crowds, they were filled with jealousy and talked abusively[n] against what Paul was saying.[o] **13:45** [n]Ac 18:6; 1Pe 4:4; Jude 10 [o]1Th 2:16
46 Then Paul and Barnabas answered them boldly: "We had to speak the word of God to you first.[p]
Since you reject it and do not consider yourselves worthy of eternal life, we now turn to the Gentiles.[q] **13:46** [p]ver 26; Ac 3:26 [q]Ac 18:6; 22:21; 28:28
47 For this is what the Lord has commanded us:

> " 'I have made you[a] a light for the Gentiles,[r] **13:47** [r]Lk 2:32 [s]Isa 49:6
> that you[a] may bring salvation to the ends of the earth.'[b]"[s]

48 When the Gentiles heard this, they were glad and honored the word of the Lord; and all who were
appointed for eternal life believed.
49 The word of the Lord spread through the whole region. 50 But the Jews incited the God-fearing wom-
en of high standing and the leading men of the city. They stirred up persecution against Paul and Bar-
nabas, and expelled them from their region.[t] 51 So they shook the dust from their feet[u] in protest against **13:50** [t]1Th 2:16
them and went to Iconium.[v] 52 And the disciples were filled with joy and with the Holy Spirit. **13:51** [u]Mt 10:14; Ac 18:6 [v]Ac 14:1, 19,21; 2Ti 3:11

In Iconium

14 At Iconium[w] Paul and Barnabas went as usual into the Jewish synagogue. There they spoke so ef- **14:1** [w]Ac 13:51
fectively that a great number of Jews and Gentiles believed. 2 But the Jews who refused to believe
stirred up the Gentiles and poisoned their minds against the brothers. 3 So Paul and Barnabas spent con-
siderable time there, speaking boldly[x] for the Lord, who confirmed the message of his grace by enabling **14:3** [x]Ac 4:29 [y]Jn 4:48; Heb 2:4
them to do miraculous signs and wonders.[y] 4 The people of the city were divided; some sided with the
Jews, others with the apostles.[z] 5 There was a plot afoot among the Gentiles and Jews, together with their **14:4** [z]Ac 17:4,5
leaders, to mistreat them and stone them.[a] 6 But they found out about it and fled[b] to the Lycaonian cities **14:5** [a]ver 19 **14:6** [b]Mt 10:23
of Lystra and Derbe and to the surrounding country, 7 where they continued to preach[c] the good news.[d] **14:7** [c]Ac 16:10 [d]ver 15,21

In Lystra and Derbe

8 In Lystra there sat a man crippled in his feet, who was lame from birth[e] and had never walked. 9 He **14:8** [e]Ac 3:2
listened to Paul as he was speaking. Paul looked directly at him, saw that he had faith to be healed[f] 10 and **14:9** [f]Mt 9:28,29
called out, "Stand up on your feet!" At that, the man jumped up and began to walk.[g] **14:10** [g]Ac 3:8
11 When the crowd saw what Paul had done, they shouted in the Lycaonian language, "The gods have
come down to us in human form!"[h] 12 Barnabas they called Zeus, and Paul they called Hermes because **14:11** [h]Ac 8:10; 28:6
he was the chief speaker. 13 The priest of Zeus, whose temple was just outside the city, brought bulls and
wreaths to the city gates because he and the crowd wanted to offer sacrifices to them.
14 But when the apostles Barnabas and Paul heard of this, they tore their clothes[i] and rushed out into **14:14** [i]Mk 14:63
the crowd, shouting: 15 "Men, why are you doing this? We too are only men,[j] human like you. We are **14:15** [j]Ac 10:26; Jas 5:17

[a] 47 The Greek is singular. [b] 47 Isaiah 49:6

13:45 See "Paul's Jewish Opponents" on page 1907.
13:51 For "shook the dust from their feet," see the notes on Matthew 10:14 and Luke 9:5.

In the first century Iconium was one of the chief cities in the southern part of the Roman province of Galatia. It was a city of immemorial antiquity, situated near the western end of a vast, level plain, with mountains a few miles toward the west, from which streams flowed that made it a veritable oasis. Two important trade routes passed through the city, and it lay on the road leading to Ephesus and Rome. Its geographical position made it the natural capital of Lycaonia (see the note on Ac 14:6). Archaeological inscriptions found there in 1910 show that the Phrygian language was spoken there for two centuries after the time of Paul, although at neighboring Lystra the natives spoke "the Lycaonian language (14:11). Hadrian made the city a Roman colony. It has had a continuous history and is now known as Konia—still the main trading center on the Lycaonian plain.

14:1 Paul made it his practice to preach in the synagogues of cities through which he passed (see the notes on 9:20; 13:14).

14:5 Stoning was a Jewish mode of execution for blasphemy (Lev 24:16).

14:6 Lycaonia was a district east of Pisidia (see the note on 14:24), north of the Taurus Mountains. In early Roman days it had been a part of the Roman province of Cilicia, but Trajan transferred it to Galatia (the situation during Paul's time), after which it reverted largely back to Cilicia under the boundary adjustments of Antonius Pius. Iconium, an ancient city rich in history, was its administrative capital (see the note on 13:51). The province generally was backward, its inhabitants still speaking a vernacular language during the first century A.D. In this verse it is implied that one crossed a frontier in passing from Iconium to Lystra.

Lystra, a Roman colony, was the probable home of Timothy (see 16:1)—although he was known in Iconium as well (see 16:2). Lystra lay about 20 miles (32 km) from Iconium and 130 miles (209 km) from Antioch.

Derbe, about 60 miles (97 km) from Lystra, was the home of Gaius (see 20:4). It was a border town in the southeastern part of the Lycaonian region of Galatia. An inscription naming the city has been discovered about 30 miles (48 km) east of what was previously thought to be its site.

14:12 Zeus, the most popular god in Galatia, was regularly linked with Hermes. The response of the Lystrans may be traced to the following legend: Zeus and Hermes once visited the Phrygian hill country, disguised as ordinary men. They were turned away from a thousand homes but finally were welcomed into the humble abode of an elderly couple. The gods turned that house into a temple and destroyed the houses of all who had rejected them.

14:13 The Greek for "city gates" can refer to the temple gates, the city gates or house gates.

14:14 Tearing one's clothes was a Jewish way of expressing great anguish (see "Sackcloth and Ashes: Rituals of Lamentation" on p. 820).

The Missionary Journeys of Paul

ACTS 14 Although the apostle Paul embarked upon numerous missionary travels, traditionally these have been divided into three major journeys. It is estimated that the first lasted from A.D. 46 to 48; the itinerary moved from Syrian Antioch to Cyprus and then on to southern Asia Minor (Turkey), where Paul visited several cities before returning to Syrian Antioch.[1] The second journey (A.D. 49–52) involved an overland trip from Syrian Antioch across Asia Minor to Troas in the northwest, followed by a sea voyage across the Aegean to Greece, with visits to Philippi, Thessalonica, Athens and Corinth.[2] Paul then crossed the Aegean to Ephesus (in Asia Minor) and from there made a lengthy sea voyage to Judea.[3] The third journey, from A.D. 53 to 58, once again took him across Asia Minor and into Greece.

Certain elements of Paul's strategy and style are evident in his missionary work:

✣ Paul was seldom without a fellow worker; his partners at various times included Barnabas, Silas, Luke and others. He also endeavored to train young Christians, such as John Mark, Timothy and Apollos, in the work of missions.

✣ Paul always endeavored to speak in terms that would be meaningful to a particular audience (1Co 9:22). This is perhaps best demonstrated during his second journey in the city of Athens, where Paul delivered his famous sermon on Mars Hill.[4] Facing an educated tribunal, he addressed his audience using logic and Greek poetry. Although his stay in Athens was not particularly successful overall, this strategy demonstrated a great strength of the apostle's style of communication.

✣ From time to time Paul participated in the trade of tent-making in order to support his travels (Ac 18:3). Even though he believed that a minister of the gospel is worthy of pay, he did not want to alienate or antagonize anyone on the issue of financial support (1Co 9:6).

✣ Paul tended to speak first at a local synagogue when preaching in a new city. This encounter generally met with forceful Jewish opposition, compelling him to move on to the Gentiles. This practice began in Pisidian Antioch (Ac 13:14), where Paul and Barnabas, after meeting with Jewish opposition, first proclaimed that they would then take the gospel to the Gentiles. This familiar pattern was once again repeated in Rome near the end of Paul's ministry (28:26–28).

✣ Paul had to deal with persecution from both Jews and Gentiles.

The apostle was opposed by some Jews simply for preaching Jesus and by others (who believed in Jesus) for not requiring Gentiles to become proselytes to Judaism. Jewish leaders sometimes tried to prejudice local authorities against Paul, causing his expulsion from Antioch on charges of disturbing the peace (13:50).

Paul was opposed by Gentiles because he led his converts to abandon their traditional gods (see 19:23–41).

Even though Paul was at times jailed and beaten by Roman authorities, he invoked his Roman citizenship at strategic points to further his ministry.[5]

✣ Paul demonstrated deep commitment to the churches he planted, and his emotional ties to the new converts were deep (2Co 6:4–13): He worked on behalf of these fledgling churches night and day (1Th 2:9) and prayed for them continuously. Throughout his journeys Paul revisited churches, analyzing their growth and ministering to them. Paul also wrote letters to the various churches throughout his missionary journeys.

[1]See "Antioch of Syria, Center of Christianity" on page 1904. [2]See "Philippi" on page 1927, "Thessalonica" on page 1944, "Athens" on page 1804 and "Corinth" on page 1887. [3]See "Ephesus During the Time of Paul" on page 1968. [4]See "The Areopagus" on page 1802. [5]See "Imprisonment in the Roman World: In Prison Versus House Arrest" on page 1826.

The Ingnatian Way, near Philippi
Preserving Bible Times; © Dr. James C. Martin

bringing you good news,[k] telling you to turn from these worthless things[l] to the living God,[m] who made
heaven and earth[n] and sea and everything in them.[o] 16In the past, he let[p] all nations go their own way.[q]
17Yet he has not left himself without testimony:[r] He has shown kindness by giving you rain from heav-
en and crops in their seasons;[s] he provides you with plenty of food and fills your hearts with joy." 18Even
with these words, they had difficulty keeping the crowd from sacrificing to them.
19Then some Jews[t] came from Antioch and Iconium[u] and won the crowd over. They stoned Paul[v] and
dragged him outside the city, thinking he was dead. 20But after the disciples[w] had gathered around him,
he got up and went back into the city. The next day he and Barnabas left for Derbe.

The Return to Antioch in Syria

21They preached the good news in that city and won a large number of disciples. Then they returned
to Lystra, Iconium[x] and Antioch, 22strengthening the disciples and encouraging them to remain true to
the faith.[y] "We must go through many hardships[z] to enter the kingdom of God," they said. 23Paul and
Barnabas appointed elders[a][a] for them in each church and, with prayer and fasting,[b] committed them to
the Lord,[c] in whom they had put their trust. 24After going through Pisidia, they came into Pamphylia,
25and when they had preached the word in Perga, they went down to Attalia.
26From Attalia they sailed back to Antioch,[d] where they had been committed to the grace of God[e] for
the work they had now completed.[f] 27On arriving there, they gathered the church together and reported
all that God had done through them[g] and how he had opened the door[h] of faith to the Gentiles. 28And
they stayed there a long time with the disciples.

The Council at Jerusalem

15 Some men[i] came down from Judea to Antioch and were teaching the brothers: "Unless you are
circumcised,[j] according to the custom taught by Moses,[k] you cannot be saved." 2This brought
Paul and Barnabas into sharp dispute and debate with them. So Paul and Barnabas were appointed, along
with some other believers, to go up to Jerusalem[l] to see the apostles and elders[m] about this question.
3The church sent them on their way, and as they traveled through Phoenicia and Samaria, they told how
the Gentiles had been converted.[n] This news made all the brothers very glad. 4When they came to Jeru-
salem, they were welcomed by the church and the apostles and elders, to whom they reported everything
God had done through them.[o]
5Then some of the believers who belonged to the party of the Pharisees stood up and said, "The Gen-
tiles must be circumcised and required to obey the law of Moses."
6The apostles and elders met to consider this question. 7After much discussion, Peter got up and ad-
dressed them: "Brothers, you know that some time ago God made a choice among you that the Gentiles
might hear from my lips the message of the gospel and believe. 8God, who knows the heart,[p] showed that
he accepted them by giving the Holy Spirit to them,[q] just as he did to us. 9He made no distinction between
us and them,[r] for he purified their hearts by faith.[s] 10Now then, why do you try to test God by putting on
the necks of the disciples a yoke[t] that neither we nor our fathers have been able to bear? 11No! We believe
it is through the grace[u] of our Lord Jesus that we are saved, just as they are."
12The whole assembly became silent as they listened to Barnabas and Paul telling about the miracu-
lous signs and wonders[v] God had done among the Gentiles through them.[w] 13When they finished, James[x]
spoke up: "Brothers, listen to me. 14Simon[b] has described to us how God at first showed his concern by

14:15 [k]ver 7,21; Ac 13:32 [l]1Sa 12:21; 1Co 8:4; 1Th 1:9 [m]Mt 16:16 [n]Ge 1:1; Jer 14:22 [o]Ps 146:6; Rev 14:7
14:16 [p]Ac 17:30 [q]Ps 81:12; Mic 4:5
14:17 [r]Ac 17:27; Ro 1:20 [s]Dt 11:14; Job 5:10; Ps 65:10
14:19 [t]Ac 13:45 [u]Ac 13:51 [v]2Co 11:25; 2Ti 3:11
14:20 [w]ver 22, 28; Ac 11:26
14:21 [x]Ac 13:51
14:22 [y]Ac 11:23; 13:43 [z]Jn 16:33; 1Th 3:3; 2Ti 3:12
14:23 [a]Ac 11:30; Tit 1:5 [b]Ac 13:3 [c]Ac 20:32
14:26 [d]Ac 11:19 [e]Ac 15:40 [f]Ac 13:1,3
14:27 [g]Ac 15:4, 12; 21:19 [h]1Co 16:9; 2Co 2:12; Col 4:3; Rev 3:8
15:1 [i]ver 24; Gal 2:12 [j]ver 5; Gal 5:2,3 [k]Ac 6:14
15:2 [l]Gal 2:2 [m]Ac 11:30
15:3 [n]Ac 14:27
15:4 [o]ver 12; Ac 14:27
15:8 [p]Ac 1:24 [q]Ac 10:44,47
15:9 [r]Ac 10:28, 34; 11:12 [s]Ac 10:43
15:10 [t]Mt 23:4; Gal 5:1
15:11 [u]Ro 3:24; Eph 2:5-8
15:12 [v]Jn 4:48 [w]Ac 14:27
15:13 [x]Ac 12:17

[a] *23* Or *Barnabas ordained elders*; or *Barnabas had elders elected* [b] *14* Greek *Simeon*, a variant of *Simon*; that is, Peter

---

14:19 The Jews stoned Paul inside the city rather than at the usual place of execution outside its walls (see "Paul's Jewish Opponents" on p. 1907).
14:20 For "Derbe," see the note on verse 6.
14:21 "Antioch" is Pisidian Antioch (see the note on 13:14).
14:24 Pisidia was a district about 120 miles (193 km) long and 50 miles (80 km) wide, located north of Pamphylia. Bandits frequented the region.

Pamphylia was a district 80 miles (129 km) long and 20 miles (32 km) wide at its widest part, located on the southern coast of Asia Minor. After A.D. 74 Pisidia was included in the Roman province of Pamphylia.
14:25 For "Perga," see the note on 13:13.

Attalia was the best harbor on the coast of Pamphylia.
14:26 For "sailed," see "Travel in the Greco-Roman World" on page 1946.

"Antioch" is Syrian Antioch (see the note on 11:19).
15:1 These "men" were probably from the party of the Pharisees (see the notes on Mt 3:7; Lk 5:17). They were believers (see Ac 15:5) who insisted that before anyone could become a true Christian that individual must keep the Law of Moses; for a man, the test of such compliance was circumcision. These Judaizers (or legalists) were given a hearing, not implying that they correctly represented the apostles and elders of Jerusalem.
15:2 For "sharp dispute and debate," see "Debate and Rhetoric in the Ancient World" on page 1797.
15:5 Some Pharisees (see the notes on Mt 3:7; Lk 5:17) became Christians but brought their Judaic beliefs with them. They believed that Gentiles must first become converts to Judaism and be circumcised (see v. 1) before being eligible to be saved by faith.
15:10 For "yoke," see the note on Matthew 11:28–30.

taking from the Gentiles a people for himself. 15 The words of the prophets are in agreement with this, as
it is written:

16 " 'After this I will return
and rebuild David's fallen tent.
Its ruins I will rebuild,
and I will restore it,
17 that the remnant of men may seek the Lord,
and all the Gentiles who bear my name,
says the Lord, who does these things'[a y]
18 that have been known for ages.[b]

19 "It is my judgment, therefore, that we should not make it difficult for the Gentiles who are turning
to God. 20 Instead we should write to them, telling them to abstain from food polluted by idols,[z] from sex-
ual immorality,[a] from the meat of strangled animals and from blood.[b] 21 For Moses has been preached
in every city from the earliest times and is read in the synagogues on every Sabbath."[c]

15:17 [y]Am 9:11,12
15:20 [z]1Co 8:7-13; 10:14-28; Rev 2:14,20 [a]1Co 10:7,8 [b]ver 29; Ge 9:4; Lev 3:17; Dt 12:16,23
15:21 [c]Ac 13:15; 2Co 3:14,15

[a] 17 Amos 9:11,12 [b] 17,18 Some manuscripts *things'— / 18 known to the Lord for ages is his work*

15:19–20 Circumcision was not required, but four stipulations were laid down. These involved areas of Gentile weakness that particularly repulsed Jewish believers. It would have helped both the individual and the relationship between Gentile and Jew if these requirements had been observed. They involved divine directives that the Jews believed were given before the Mosaic Law. Gentiles were to abstain from (1) food polluted by idols (see the note on 1Co 8:7); (2) sexual immorality, a sin taken too lightly by the Greeks and also associated with certain pagan religious festivals; (3) the meat of strangled animals, those retaining the blood that was forbidden to be eaten (see Ge 9:4); and (4) eating blood, a practice expressly forbidden under Jewish law (see Lev 17:10–12).

Debate and Rhetoric in the Ancient World

ACTS 15 Although the ability to speak persuasively has always been important, the formal study of rhetoric may be traced back to the fifth century B.C. Around 467 B.C. the tyrant Hieron died on the island of Syracuse, initiating a debate about land ownership among the inhabitants of the island. A man named Corax used this debate as an opportunity to offer training in the art of courtroom disputation and persuasion. A number of the city's inhabitants hired Corax as a private tutor, and the practice of systematic rhetoric was born. Corax's approach traveled to the cosmopolitan world of Athens,[1] and rhetoric quickly became one of the most significant intellectual disciplines.

The most renowned group to embrace rhetoric was the Sophists, a society of philosophers who believed that useful opinion was far more significant than knowledge or truth. They established an educational system that taught young men the "art" of language and persuasion. The Athenian political landscape, characterized at the time by change and unrest, offered the Sophists the opportunity to become quite wealthy in their pursuit. They prided themselves in their ability to debate from either side of an argument. This fact, which demonstrated their relative view of truth and justice, coupled with the exorbitant fees the Sophists charged, led many Athenians to distrust them.

The Greek philosopher Plato held only disdain for Sophists, believing that rhetoric's strength lay in its ability to attain and convey truth in the pursuit of justice—not in its power per se. The most renowned advocate, however, of systematic rhetoric in the ancient world was Aristotle, who insisted that value and truth had to be a part of the rhetorical process. A good rhetorician, he emphasized, needed to understand the argument as well as the human emotion surrounding it, maintain a worthy character, understand the relevant type of oratorical expression and be gifted with a natural persuasive ability. The persuasive process, he insisted, was accomplished by employing one or more of the three categories of appeal: *logos* (reason), *pathos* (emotional appeal) and *ethos* (virtue and goodwill).

Whether he was spreading the gospel via spoken word or pen, it is obvious that the apostle Paul to some degree employed the rhetorical training he had most certainly received (2Co 5:11). On the other hand, Paul was careful to avoid verbal trickery and insisted upon reliance on the power of God in winning people over (1Co 2:1–2). Even though systematic rhetoric has often been criticized as immoral or unethical, it is important to appreciate its value when it is properly employed.

[1] See "Athens" on page 1804.

The Council's Letter to Gentile Believers

22 Then the apostles and elders, with the whole church, decided to choose some of their own men and
send them to Antioch with Paul and Barnabas. They chose Judas (called Barsabbas) and Silas,[d] two men
who were leaders among the brothers. 23 With them they sent the following letter:

The apostles and elders, your brothers,

To the Gentile believers in Antioch,[e] Syria and Cilicia:[f]

Greetings.[g]

24 We have heard that some went out from us without our authorization and disturbed you, trou-
bling your minds by what they said.[h] 25 So we all agreed to choose some men and send them to you
with our dear friends Barnabas and Paul— 26 men who have risked their lives[i] for the name of our
Lord Jesus Christ. 27 Therefore we are sending Judas and Silas to confirm by word of mouth what we
are writing. 28 It seemed good to the Holy Spirit[j] and to us not to burden you with anything beyond
the following requirements: 29 You are to abstain from food sacrificed to idols, from blood, from the
meat of strangled animals and from sexual immorality.[k] You will do well to avoid these things.

Farewell.

30 The men were sent off and went down to Antioch, where they gathered the church together and de-
livered the letter. 31 The people read it and were glad for its encouraging message. 32 Judas and Silas, who
themselves were prophets, said much to encourage and strengthen the brothers. 33 After spending some
time there, they were sent off by the brothers with the blessing of peace[l] to return to those who had sent
them.[a] 35 But Paul and Barnabas remained in Antioch, where they and many others taught and preached[m]
the word of the Lord.

Disagreement Between Paul and Barnabas

36 Some time later Paul said to Barnabas, "Let us go back and visit the brothers in all the towns[n] where
we preached the word of the Lord and see how they are doing." 37 Barnabas wanted to take John, also
called Mark,[o] with them, 38 but Paul did not think it wise to take him, because he had deserted them[p] in
Pamphylia and had not continued with them in the work. 39 They had such a sharp disagreement that
they parted company. Barnabas took Mark and sailed for Cyprus, 40 but Paul chose Silas[q] and left, com-
mended by the brothers to the grace of the Lord.[r] 41 He went through Syria[s] and Cilicia,[t] strengthening
the churches.[u]

Timothy Joins Paul and Silas

16 He came to Derbe and then to Lystra,[v] where a disciple named Timothy[w] lived, whose mother
was a Jewess and a believer, but whose father was a Greek. 2 The brothers[x] at Lystra and Iconium[y]
spoke well of him. 3 Paul wanted to take him along on the journey, so he circumcised him because of the

[a] 33 Some manuscripts *them,* 34 *but Silas decided to remain there*

15:22 [d]ver 27,32, 40
15:23 [e]ver 1 [f]ver 41 [g]Ac 23:25, 26; Jas 1:1
15:24 [h]ver 1; Gal 1:7; 5:10
15:26 [i]Ac 9:23-25; 14:19
15:28 [j]Ac 5:32
15:29 [k]ver 20; Ac 21:25
15:33 [l]Mk 5:34; Ac 16:36; 1Co 16:11
15:35 [m]Ac 8:4
15:36 [n]Ac 13:4, 13,14,51; 14:1,6, 24,25
15:37 [o]Ac 12:12
15:38 [p]Ac 13:13
15:40 [q]ver 22 [r]Ac 11:23
15:41 [s]ver 23 [t]Ac 6:9 [u]Ac 16:5
16:1 [v]Ac 14:6 [w]Ac 17:14; 18:5; 19:22; Ro 16:21; 1Co 4:17; 2Co 1:1,19; 1Th 3:2,6; 1Ti 1:2,18; 2Ti 1:2,5,6
16:2 [x]ver 40 [y]Ac 13:51

15:22 Silas was a leader in the Jerusalem church, a prophet (v. 32), a Roman citizen (16:37–38) and Paul's companion on his second missionary journey (15:40).

15:23 "Antioch" is Syrian Antioch (see the note on 11:19).

Cilicia was a country in southeastern Asia Minor, bounded on the north and west by the Taurus range and on the south by the Mediterranean. It had two parts, the western region, called the Rugged, and the eastern side, called the Plain Cilicia, the chief city of which was Tarsus, the birthplace of Paul (21:39; 22:3; 23:34). The early inhabitants must have been Hittites, although later on the Syrians and Phoenicans settled there. The region came under Persian sway but, after Alexander, Seleucid rulers governed it from Antioch. Cilicia became a Roman province in 100 B.C. One of its governors was Cicero, the renowned orator (51–50 B.C.). The country was accessible by land only by way of its two famous mountain passes, the Cilician Gates and the Syrian Gates. Jews from Cilicia disputed with Stephen (6:9), and the gospel reached the area early, probably through Paul (9:30; Gal 1:21). On Paul's second missionary journey he confirmed the churches that had been established there (Ac 15:41), and on his way to Rome as a prisoner he sailed over the sea of Cilicia (27:5).

15:29 See the note on verses 19–20.

16:1 For "Derbe" and "Lystra," see the note on 14:6.

Timothy must have been in his teens at this time. His father was a Greek, while his mother was a Jewish Christian. (Statements concerning his mother's faith, combined with silence concerning the faith of his father, suggest that his father was neither a convert to Judaism nor a believer in Christ.) Although Timothy lived in Lystra (in modern Turkey), he was well known in Iconium as well (16:2; see the note on 13:51).

Greeks and Grecians are to be distinguished. *Greeks* were generally those of the Hellenic race (here and in 18:4; this designation probably applies as well to Jn 12:20), but the word may be used as well to indicate non-Jews, foreigners and aliens. *Grecians* were Greek-speaking Jews, people of the dispersion, from areas that were predominantly Greek (Ac 6:1).

16:3 Timothy was circumcised as a matter of expediency, so that his work among the Jews might be more effective. This was different from Titus's case (see Gal 2:3), where circumcision was refused because some were demanding it as being necessary for salvation.

16:3 zGal 2:3 Jews who lived in that area, for they all knew that his father was a Greek.[z] 4As they traveled from town
16:4 aAc 11:30 bAc 15:2 to town, they delivered the decisions reached by the apostles and elders[a] in Jerusalem[b] for the people to
cAc 15:28,29 16:5 dAc 9:31; 15:41 obey.[c] 5So the churches were strengthened[d] in the faith and grew daily in numbers.

Paul's Vision of the Man of Macedonia

16:6 eAc 18:23 fAc 18:23; Gal 1:2; 3:1 6Paul and his companions traveled throughout the region of Phrygia[e] and Galatia,[f] having been kept
gAc 2:9 by the Holy Spirit from preaching the word in the province of Asia.[g] 7When they came to the border of
16:7 hRo 8:9; Gal 4:6 Mysia, they tried to enter Bithynia, but the Spirit of Jesus[h] would not allow them to. 8So they passed by
16:8 iver 11; 2Co 2:12; Mysia and went down to Troas.[i] 9During the night Paul had a vision[j] of a man of Macedonia[k] standing
2Ti 4:13 and begging him, "Come over to Macedonia and help us." 10After Paul had seen the vision, we[l] got ready
16:9 jAc 9:10 kAc 20:1,3 at once to leave for Macedonia, concluding that God had called us to preach the gospel[m] to them.

16:6 The district of Phrygia was formerly the Hellenistic territory of Phrygia, but it had more recently been divided between the Roman provinces of Asia and Galatia. Iconium (see the note on 13:51) and Pisidian Antioch (see the note on 13:14) were located in Galatian Phrygia.

The name "Galatia" had been used to denote the Hellenistic kingdom, but in 25 B.C. the territory had been expanded considerably to become the Roman province of that name.

Asia had been a smaller area but was now a Roman province that included the Hellenistic districts of Mysia, Lydia, Carla and parts of Phrygia.

16:7 Mysia was located in the northwestern part of the province of Asia. Luke used old, Hellenistic names, but Paul preferred the provincial (Roman) names.

Bithynia was a region along the northern edge of Asia Minor fronting on the Black Sea, the Bosphorus and the Sea of Marmara. The area had been settled very early, and its known history goes back past the sixth century B.C., when Croesus made it a part of his kingdom. A king of Bithynia in the third century B.C. invited the Gauls into Asia, so originating the designation "Galatia." From the thirteenth century A.D. on the region has been Turkish, or at least ruled by the Turks.

16:8 Troas was located 10 miles (16 km) from ancient Troy. Alexandria Troas (its full name) was a Roman colony and an important seaport for connections between Macedonia and Greece on the one hand and Asia Minor on the other. A church was eventually started there, for Paul ministered to believers in Troas when he returned from his third journey on his way to Jerusalem (20:5–12).

16:9 Macedonia had become a Roman province in 148 B.C.

16:10 The pronoun "we" suggests that Paul and Luke may have met or joined forces at Troas. Some scholars believe that Luke joined the team as a doctor due to Paul's health concerns (cf. Gal 4:13).

The Ancient Agora

ACTS 16 In antiquity the *agora* (marketplace) was the social, political and administrative center of the city. Two such marketplaces are mentioned in Acts. In the Roman colony of Lydia, after Paul cast out a demon from a slave girl, her owners dragged Paul and Silas before the authorities in the agora (16:19). Later, while in Athens, Paul reasoned daily with philosophers in that city's agora (17:17–18). These Hellenic marketplaces would have been gathering places for the dissemination of ideas and for commerce, worship and the official business of the city authorities.

The ancient Athenian agora, lying at the foot of, and to the northwest of, the **Acropolis**, was impressive. Before the sixth century B.C. the space was used as a cemetery and domestic area during different periods. At the beginning of the sixth century, assemblies were held and dances performed on this site. Pisistratus erected a nine-spouted fountain and palace there, as well as a stadium for the Panathenaic games. The Panathenaic Way passed through the agora; its remains are still visible. When Athens became a democracy in the late sixth century B.C., a court was built in the agora, followed by several other public buildings on the western side of the area. Throughout the history of the marketplace, temples to various gods were erected, the most well preserved being the Temple of Hephaestus, built in the late fifth century B.C. The military headquarters was located there, as well as a prison. During the second century B.C. King Attalus of Pergamon constructed a *stoa* (an open, roofed colonnade) on the site with shops on one end. Today this ancient *stoa* is home to a museum dedicated to archaeological finds from the agora.

The Romans added more buildings and repaired those that had been damaged by war. A new marketplace, known as the Forum of Caesar and Augustus (popularly called the Roman Agora), was built to the east of the ancient one, and the two were connected by a street behind the Stoa of Attalus. The Roman Agora had a more commercial function. Interestingly, the water clock known as the Tower of the Winds (built during the first century A.D.) still stands. Other buildings from the first century A.D. include public lavatories and what was possibly the headquarters for law enforcement. Both the ancient and the Roman agoras would have been places of bustling activity during Paul's day.[1]

[1]See also "The Ancient City" on page 1790.

Lydia's Conversion in Philippi

11 From Troas[n] we put out to sea and sailed straight for Samothrace, and the next day on to Neapolis. 16:11 [n]ver 8
12 From there we traveled to Philippi,[o] a Roman colony and the leading city of that district of Macedonia.[p] 16:12 [o]Ac 20:6;
And we stayed there several days. Php 1:1; 1Th 2:2 [p]ver 9
13 On the Sabbath[q] we went outside the city gate to the river, where we expected to find a place of 16:13 [q]Ac 13:14
prayer. We sat down and began to speak to the women who had gathered there. 14 One of those listening
was a woman named Lydia, a dealer in purple cloth from the city of Thyatira,[r] who was a worshiper of 16:14 [r]Rev 1:11
God. The Lord opened her heart[s] to respond to Paul's message. 15 When she and the members of her [s]Lk 24:45
household[t] were baptized, she invited us to her home. "If you consider me a believer in the Lord," she 16:15 [t]Ac 11:14
said, "come and stay at my house." And she persuaded us.

Paul and Silas in Prison

16 Once when we were going to the place of prayer,[u] we were met by a slave girl who had a spirit[v] by 16:16 [u]ver 13 [v]Dt 18:11;
which she predicted the future. She earned a great deal of money for her owners by fortune-telling. 17 This 1Sa 28:3,7
girl followed Paul and the rest of us, shouting, "These men are servants of the Most High God,[w] who are 16:17 [w]Mk 5:7
telling you the way to be saved." 18 She kept this up for many days. Finally Paul became so troubled that
he turned around and said to the spirit, "In the name of Jesus Christ I command you to come out of her!"
At that moment the spirit left her.[x] 16:18 [x]Mk 16:17
19 When the owners of the slave girl realized that their hope of making money[y] was gone, they seized 16:19 [y]ver 16; Ac 19:25,26
Paul and Silas[z] and dragged[a] them into the marketplace to face the authorities. 20 They brought them be- [z]Ac 15:22
fore the magistrates and said, "These men are Jews, and are throwing our city into an uproar[b] 21 by ad- [a]Ac 8:3; 17:6; 21:30; Jas 2:6
vocating customs unlawful for us Romans[c] to accept or practice."[d] 16:20 [b]Ac 17:6 16:21 [c]ver 12
22 The crowd joined in the attack against Paul and Silas, and the magistrates ordered them to be [d]Est 3:8
stripped and beaten.[e] 23 After they had been severely flogged, they were thrown into prison, and the jail- 16:22
er[f] was commanded to guard them carefully. 24 Upon receiving such orders, he put them in the inner cell [e]2Co 11:25; 1Th 2:2
and fastened their feet in the stocks.[g] 16:23 [f]ver 27,36 16:24
25 About midnight Paul and Silas were praying and singing hymns[h] to God, and the other prisoners [g]Job 13:27; 33:11; Jer 20:2,3;
were listening to them. 26 Suddenly there was such a violent earthquake that the foundations of the pris- 29:26
on were shaken.[i] At once all the prison doors flew open,[j] and everybody's chains came loose.[k] 27 The jail- 16:25 [h]Eph 5:19 16:26 [i]Ac 4:31
er woke up, and when he saw the prison doors open, he drew his sword and was about to kill himself be- [j]Ac 12:10 [k]Ac 12:7
cause he thought the prisoners had escaped.[l] 28 But Paul shouted, "Don't harm yourself! We are all here!" 16:27 [l]Ac 12:19
29 The jailer called for lights, rushed in and fell trembling before Paul and Silas. 30 He then brought
them out and asked, "Sirs, what must I do to be saved?"[m] 16:30 [m]Ac 2:37

16:11 Samothrace is an island in the northeastern Aegean Sea. It was a convenient place for ships to anchor rather than sailing at night. Traveling by sea was common in New Testament times (see "Travel in the Greco-Roman World" on p. 1946).

Neapolis (modern Kavalla) was the seaport for Philippi, 10 miles (16 km) away.

16:12 Philippi was a city in eastern Macedonia named after Philip II, the father of Alexander the Great. Since it was a Roman colony, it was independent of provincial administration and had a governmental organization modeled after that of Rome. Many retired legionnaires from the Roman army settled there, but few Jews. (See "Philippi" on p. 1927.)

16:13 There were in fact so few Jews in Philippi that there was no synagogue (ten married men were required to establish one), so the Jews who were there met for prayer along the banks of the Gangites River. It was customary for such places of prayer to be located outdoors near running water.

16:14 Lydia was a businesswoman whose name may be associated with her place of origin, the Hellenistic district of Lydia. In fact, as "Lydia" was a common term to denote a woman from Lydia, some scholars have suggested that her personal name was unknown or that she may have been either the Euodia or the Syntyche mentioned in Philippians 4:2. At any rate, Lydia was a Gentile who, like Cornelius (see Ac 10:2), believed in the true God and followed the moral teachings of Scripture. She had not, however, become a full convert to Judaism (see the notes on Jn 12:20; Ac 10:2; cf. "converts" in the note on 2:11).

Thyatira was located in the Roman province of Asia, 20 miles (32 km) southeast of Pergamum (in the Hellenistic kingdom of Lydia). The city was famous for dyeing works, especially royal purple (crimson).

16:15 Private homes were central to the life of the early church. Beyond being centers for hospitality, they were places for teaching, worship, fellowship and witness (see "House Churches and Early Church Buildings" on p. 2033). Life was lived in community, so when Lydia believed, her whole household did as well.

16:16 The spirit by which the slave girl predicted the future was a demonic "python" spirit. The python was a mythical snake worshiped at Delphi and associated with the Delphic oracle. The term *python* had come to be used of the persons through whom the python spirit supposedly spoke. Since such persons spoke involuntarily, the term *ventriloquist* was used to describe them. To what extent this young woman actually predicted the future is unknown.

16:19 For the multiple functions of the *agora,* or marketplace, see the note on Matthew 11:16–17, as well as "The Ancient Agora" on page 1799.

16:22–24 The treatment described here was not permitted against Roman citizens. After being stripped, flogged (see the note on Mt 27:26) and sentenced without a trial, these men were sent to a maximum security area ("inner cell"). Prisoners in stocks were obliged to sleep sitting or lying on the floor, and changing positions was nearly impossible. (See "Imprisonment in the Roman World: In Prison Versus House Arrest" on p. 1826.)

16:25 For "hymns," see "Early Christian Hymnody" on page 2007.

16:26 For earthquakes, see the note on Zechariah 14:5.

16:27 If a prisoner escaped, the life of the guard was demanded in his place. To take his own life would have shortened the guard's shame and distress.

16:31 nAc 11:14 31They replied, "Believe in the Lord Jesus, and you will be saved—you and your household."[n] 32Then
16:33 over 25 they spoke the word of the Lord to him and to all the others in his house. 33At that hour of the night[o] the
jailer took them and washed their wounds; then immediately he and all his family were baptized. 34The
16:34 pAc 11:14 jailer brought them into his house and set a meal before them; he[p] was filled with joy because he had
come to believe in God—he and his whole family.
35When it was daylight, the magistrates sent their officers to the jailer with the order: "Release those
16:36 qver 23,27 men." 36The jailer[q] told Paul, "The magistrates have ordered that you and Silas be released. Now you can
rAc 15:33 leave. Go in peace."[r]
37But Paul said to the officers: "They beat us publicly without a trial, even though we are Roman cit-
16:37 sAc 22:25-29 izens,[s] and threw us into prison. And now do they want to get rid of us quietly? No! Let them come them-
selves and escort us out."
38The officers reported this to the magistrates, and when they heard that Paul and Silas were Roman
16:38 tAc 22:29 citizens, they were alarmed.[t] 39They came to appease them and escorted them from the prison, request-
16:39 uMt 8:34 16:40 vver 14 ing them to leave the city.[u] 40After Paul and Silas came out of the prison, they went to Lydia's house,[v]
wver 2; Ac 1:16 where they met with the brothers[w] and encouraged them. Then they left.

In Thessalonica

17:1 xver 11,13; Php 4:16; 17 When they had passed through Amphipolis and Apollonia, they came to Thessalonica,[x] where
1Th 1:1; 2Th 1:1; there was a Jewish synagogue. 2As his custom was, Paul went into the synagogue,[y] and on three
2Ti 4:10 17:2 yAc 9:20 Sabbath[z] days he reasoned with them from the Scriptures,[a] 3explaining and proving that the Christ[a] had
zAc 13:14 aAc 8:35 to suffer[b] and rise from the dead.[c] "This Jesus I am proclaiming to you is the Christ,[a]"[d] he said. 4Some
17:3 bLk 24:26; Ac 3:18 cLk 24:46 of the Jews were persuaded and joined Paul and Silas,[e] as did a large number of God-fearing Greeks and
dAc 9:22; 18:28 17:4 eAc 15:22 not a few prominent women.
5But the Jews were jealous; so they rounded up some bad characters from the marketplace, formed a
17:5 fver 13; 1Th 2:16 mob and started a riot in the city.[f] They rushed to Jason's[g] house in search of Paul and Silas in order to
gRo 16:21 17:6 hAc 16:19 bring them out to the crowd.[b] 6But when they did not find them, they dragged[h] Jason and some other
iMt 24:14 brothers before the city officials, shouting: "These men who have caused trouble all over the world[i] have
jAc 16:20 now come here,[j] 7and Jason has welcomed them into his house. They are all defying Caesar's decrees,
17:7 kLk 23:2; Jn 19:12 saying that there is another king, one called Jesus."[k] 8When they heard this, the crowd and the city offi-
17:9 lver 5 cials were thrown into turmoil. 9Then they made Jason[l] and the others post bond and let them go.

In Berea

17:10 mver 13; Ac 20:4 10As soon as it was night, the brothers sent Paul and Silas away to Berea.[m] On arriving there, they
17:11 nver 1 went to the Jewish synagogue. 11Now the Bereans were of more noble character than the Thessalonians,[n]
oLk 16:29; Jn 5:39 for they received the message with great eagerness and examined the Scriptures[o] every day to see if what
Paul said was true. 12Many of the Jews believed, as did also a number of prominent Greek women and
many Greek men.
13When the Jews in Thessalonica learned that Paul was preaching the word of God at Berea, they went

[a] 3 Or *Messiah* [b] 5 Or *the assembly of the people*

16:37 The public beating of a Roman citizen was illegal, let alone a beating without a trial.

17:1–9 The events described here occurred in the spring of A.D. 50, shortly after Claudius had expelled Jews from Rome (in 49) following riots associated with Jews and Christians. The authorities would have wanted to avoid such problems, and the Jewish opponents would have exploited those fears.

17:1 The Egnatian Way crossed the whole of present-day northern Greece in an east-west direction and included Philippi, Amphipolis, Apollonia and Thessalonica on its route. At several locations, such as Kavalla (Neapolis), Philippi and Apollonia, the road is still visible today. If a person traveled about 30 miles (48 km) a day, each city could be reached after one day's journey.

Thessalonica, situated about 100 miles (160 km) from Philippi, was the capital of the province of Macedonia and had a population of more than 200,000, including a colony of Jews (and a synagogue). See "Thessalonica" on page 1944.

17:2 For "synagogue," see the notes on 9:20 and 13:14.

17:4 For "God-fearing Greeks," see the notes on John 12:20 and Ac 10:2 (cf. "converts" in the note on 2:11).

These "prominent women" may have been the wives of the leading men of that city; alternatively, they may have been women who deserved notice and position in their own right.

17:5 For "marketplace," see "The Ancient Agora" on page 1799.

17:6 The Greek term *politarch* (lit., "city ruler"), translated here and in verse 8 as "city officials," is found nowhere else in Greek literature, but it was discovered in 1835 in a Greek inscription on an arch that had spanned the Egnatian Way on the western side of Thessalonica. (The arch was destroyed in 1867, but the block with the inscription was rescued and is now in the British Museum in London.) The term has since been found in 16 other inscriptions in surrounding towns of Macedonia, as well as elsewhere.

17:7 Blasphemy was the gravest accusation for a Jew, but treason—to support a rival king above Caesar—was the worst accusation for a Roman.

17:9 Jason was forced to guarantee a peaceful, quiet community; otherwise, he would have faced the confiscation of his properties and perhaps even death.

17:10 Berea (modern Verria) was located 50 miles (80 km) from Thessalonica in another district of Macedonia.

For "synagogue," see the notes on 9:20 and 13:14.

there too, agitating the crowds and stirring them up. 14The brothers immediately sent Paul to the coast,
but Silas[p] and Timothy[q] stayed at Berea. 15The men who escorted Paul brought him to Athens[r] and then
left with instructions for Silas and Timothy to join him as soon as possible.[s]

17:14 [p]Ac 15:22 [q]Ac 16:1 17:15 [r]ver 16,21, 22; Ac 18:1; 1Th 3:1 [s]Ac 18:5

In Athens

16While Paul was waiting for them in Athens, he was greatly distressed to see that the city was full of
idols. 17So he reasoned in the synagogue[t] with the Jews and the God-fearing Greeks, as well as in the
marketplace day by day with those who happened to be there. 18A group of Epicurean and Stoic philos-
ophers began to dispute with him. Some of them asked, "What is this babbler trying to say?" Others re-
marked, "He seems to be advocating foreign gods." They said this because Paul was preaching the good
news about Jesus and the resurrection.[u] 19Then they took him and brought him to a meeting of the Ar-
eopagus,[v] where they said to him, "May we know what this new teaching[w] is that you are presenting?

17:17 [t]Ac 9:20 17:18 [u]ver 31,32; Ac 4:2 17:19 [v]ver 22 [w]Mk 1:27

17:14–15 Although we might conclude that Paul traveled by ship to Athens, the route there follows a coastal road, and he may have walked the distance after having been escorted to the coast—some 20 miles (32 km).

Five centuries before Paul, Athens had been at the height of its glory in terms of art, philosophy and literature. The city had retained its reputation in philosophy through the years and still maintained a leading university in Paul's day (see "Athens" on p. 1804).

17:16–33 The Epicureans were followers of Epicurus, a Greek philosopher who had lived from 341–270 B.C. Epicurus taught that nature rather than reason is the true reality and that nothing exists but atoms and voice (matter and space). The chief purpose of humankind in his view was to achieve happiness. People have free will, he asserted, in order to plan and live lives of pleasure. Epicurus interpreted pleasure as avoidance of pain, so that the mere enjoyment of good health would have been considered "pleasure." He also considered it impossible to live a good life without having honor and justice. Such moderation was lost on later interpreters, however, who took "pleasure" to be synonymous with unrestrained sensual satisfaction. Epicureanism was widely espoused at the time of Christ, and Paul met it in Athens when he encountered the philosophers of that city. Epicureans were not impressed by his teaching of creation, judgment and resurrection, since all of these doctrines were denied by the Epicurean philosophy (see "Greek Philosopical Schools" on p. 1937).

17:17–19 In Athens Paul ministered in the synagogue (see the notes on 9:20; 13:14) to Jews and to "God-fearing Greeks" (see the notes on Jn 12:20; Ac 10:2; cf. "converts" in the note on 2:11), as well as in the marketplace (see "The Ancient Agora" on p. 1799). He also engaged in discussions with the philosophers (see "Greek Philosophical Schools" on p. 1937) and leaders of the city.

The Areopagus (see "The Areopagus" on p. 1802) was the main administrative body and chief court in Athens, representing that society's intellectual elite. The Council of the Areopagus had ruled Athens before it had become a democracy in 620 B.C. By New Testament times the Areopagus retained authority only in the areas of religion and morals and met in the Royal Portico at the northwestern corner of the agora. Its members considered themselves the custodians of teachings that introduced new religions and foreign gods.

17:17 For the multiple functions of the *agora,* or marketplace, see the note on Matthew 11:16–17, as well as "The Ancient Agora" on page 1799.

ARCHAEOLOGICAL SITES

THE AREOPAGUS

ACTS 17 In Acts 17:19 Paul was taken to a meeting of the Areopagus ("rock of Ares" or "rock of Areia," another name for Athena), where he used the Greek altar to an unknown god as a point of contact to preach the gospel to the Athenian citizens (vv. 22–31). Also known in antiquity as Mars Hill (Mars and Ares are both names for the Greek god of war), the site was used as an early meeting place by a council of nobility. The Council of the Areopagus had ruled Athens before it became a democracy in 620 B.C.[1] Thereafter, the power and prestige of the council declined, although it did retain some juridical prerogatives, especially the right to try those accused of murder. During the trial the accused would stand on the Rock of Insolence, while his accuser stood on the Rock of No-Mercy. (This procedure was still practiced a century after Paul's visit.) During the first century A.D. the council directed the internal affairs of Athens, especially in religious matters.

Although the location of Paul's speech is unknown, tradition places the Areopagus itself on a rocky hill just below the **Acropolis** and just above the agora. This hill rises approximately 380 feet (116 m). An ancient stairway carved into the rock is still used today, although centuries of wear have left the steps extremely slippery. On the crest may be seen the possible foundations of a building. Several finds suggest that the hill may have been an early religious site. On the other hand, since the council tried cases in the "Royal Stoa" (a building located at the northeastern corner of the Athenian agora), Paul's speech may have taken place there, before the Council of the Areopagus, instead of atop Mars Hill.

[1]See "Athens" on page 1804.

20 You are bringing some strange ideas to our ears, and we want to
know what they mean." 21 (All the Athenians and the foreigners who
lived there spent their time doing nothing but talking about and lis-
tening to the latest ideas.)
22 Paul then stood up in the meeting of the Areopagus and said:
"Men of Athens! I see that in every way you are very religious. 23 For as
I walked around and looked carefully at your objects of worship, I even
found an altar with this inscription: TO AN UNKNOWN GOD. Now what
you worship as something unknown[x] I am going to proclaim to you.
24 "The God who made the world and everything in it[y] is the Lord
of heaven and earth[z] and does not live in temples built by hands.[a]
25 And he is not served by human hands, as if he needed anything,
because he himself gives all men life and breath and everything
else.[b] 26 From one man he made every nation of men, that they
should inhabit the whole earth; and he determined the times set for
them and the exact places where they should live.[c] 27 God did this so
that men would seek him and perhaps reach out for him and find
him, though he is not far from each one of us.[d] 28 'For in him we live
and move and have our being.'[e] As some of your own poets have
said, 'We are his offspring.'
29 "Therefore since we are God's offspring, we should not think
that the divine being is like gold or silver or stone—an image made
by man's design and skill.[f] 30 In the past God overlooked[g] such igno-
rance,[h] but now he commands all people everywhere to repent.[i]
31 For he has set a day when he will judge[j] the world with justice[k] by
the man he has appointed.[l] He has given proof of this to all men by
raising him from the dead."[m]
32 When they heard about the resurrection of the dead,[n] some of
them sneered, but others said, "We want to hear you again on this
subject." 33 At that, Paul left the Council. 34 A few men became followers of Paul and believed. Among them
was Dionysius, a member of the Areopagus,[o] also a woman named Damaris, and a number of others.

In Corinth

18 After this, Paul left Athens[p] and went to Corinth.[q] 2 There he met a Jew named Aquila, a native of
Pontus, who had recently come from Italy with his wife Priscilla,[r] because Claudius[s] had ordered
all the Jews to leave Rome. Paul went to see them, 3 and because he was a tentmaker as they were, he

17:23 [x]Jn 4:22
17:24 [y]Isa 42:5; Ac 14:15 [z]Dt 10:14; Mt 11:25 [a]Ac 7:48
17:25 [b]Ps 50:10-12; Isa 42:5
17:26 [c]Dt 32:8; Job 12:23
17:27 [d]Dt 4:7; Jer 23:23,24; Ac 14:17
17:28 [e]Job 12:10; Da 5:23
17:29 [f]Isa 40:18-20; Ro 1:23
17:30 [g]Ac 14:16; Ro 3:25 [h]ver 23; 1Pe 1:14 [i]Lk 24:47; Tit 2:11,12
17:31 [j]Mt 10:15 [k]Ps 9:8; 96:13; 98:9 [l]Ac 10:42 [m]Ac 2:24
17:32 [n]ver 18,31
17:34 [o]ver 19,22
18:1 [p]Ac 17:15 [q]Ac 19:1; 1Co 1:2; 2Co 1:1,23; 2Ti 4:20
18:2 [r]Ro 16:3; 1Co 16:19; 2Ti 4:19 [s]Ac 11:28

Ancient Voices

We love beauty with simplicity, and we love the pursuit of knowledge without effeminacy. We employ wealth properly, for use rather than for noisy display, and we do not consider poverty to be a disgrace but do regard it as shameful for someone not to seek to escape poverty through labor. We citizens of Athens care for both our own domestic concerns and for the affairs of state; those of us engaged in business are not lacking in understanding of public matters. For we alone consider those who avoid engagement in public affairs not as "uninvolved" but as useless. And we, as we judge and reflect carefully on matters, do not consider words to be a hindrance to actions. Rather, the real hindrance to action is to enter into whatever must be done without taking forewarning through discussion.

—PERICLES EXTOLS THE VIRTUES OF ATHENIAN CULTURE

From the funeral oration of Pericles, as reported in Thucydides, *The Peloponnesian War*, 2.40, trans. by Duane Garrett

See "Athens" article on the next page.

17:21 See "Debate and Rhetoric in the Ancient World" on page 1797.
17:23 The Greeks were fearful of offending any god by failing to give him or her attention; they felt that they could cover any omissions by the label "unknown god" (see "The Gods of the Greeks and Romans" on p. 1908). Other Greek writers confirm that such altars could be seen in Athens.
17:28 There are two quotations here: The first is from the Cretan poet Epimenides (c. 600 B.C.) in his *Cretica*. The second is from the Cilician poet Aratus (c. 315–240) in his *Phaenomena*, as well as from Cleanthes (331–233). Paul quoted Greek poets elsewhere as well (see 1Co 15:33; Tit 1:12).

Cleanthes, the head of the Stoic school from 263 to 232 B.C., had infused religious fervor into Zeno's Stoicism, teaching that the universe is a living being with God its soul, advocating disinterest in ethics (maintaining that doing good to gain advantage is like feeding cattle for meat!) and asserting that evil thoughts are worse than evil deeds. Paul quoted here from his "Hymn to Zeus," a surviving poem.
17:32 Immortality of the soul was accepted by the Greeks, but not resurrection of a dead body.
17:33 "The Council" refers to the meeting of the Areopagus (see "The Areopagus" on p. 1802).
17:34 Later tradition states, though it cannot be proved, that Dionysius became the bishop of Athens.

Some have suggested that Damaris must have been a foreign, educated woman to have been present at a public meeting such as that of the Areopagus (see "The Areopagus" on p. 1802). It is also possible that she was a God-fearing Gentile (see the notes on Jn 12:20; Ac 10:2; cf. "converts" in the note on 2:11) who had heard Paul at the synagogue.
18:1 Paul traveled either by land along the isthmus (a distance of about 50 mi or 80 km) or by sea from Piraeus, the port of Athens, to Cenchrea, on the eastern shore of the isthmus of Corinth (see "Travel in the Greco-Roman World" on p. 1946).
18:2 Pontus, located in the northeastern region of Asia Minor, was a province lying along the Black Sea between Bithynia and Armenia.

For "Italy," see the note on 10:1.

Suetonius wrote that Claudius (see "Claudius, Emperor of Rome" on p. 1788) had given the expulsion order because of "[the Jews'] continual tumults instigated by Chrestus" (a common misspelling of "Christ"). If "Chrestus" does in fact refer to Christ, the riots obviously were "about" him rather than led "by" him.
18:3 Paul had evidently been taught the tent-making trade as a youth. It was the Jewish custom to provide manual training for sons, whether rich or poor. (See "Labor and Welfare in the Ancient World" on p. 1952.)

ARCHAEOLOGICAL SITES

ATHENS

ACTS 18 Athens ("Map 13") is situated five miles (eight km) from the Aegean Sea on the peninsula of Attica. Life there began at and has continued to revolve around the **Acropolis**, a rocky hill that rises 171 yards (156 m) above the city. It was there that Athenian culture began during the **Neolithic Age**[1] (4000–3000 B.C.). Agricultural settlement on the Acropolis continued through the **Bronze Age** (3000–1100 B.C.), giving rise to the Mycenaean culture (1550–1050 B.C.), which saw the advent of commerce and the arts in the city. This culture declined during the twelfth century B.C., when Athens entered the Dark Ages, which were to last until the eighth century B.C.

The recorded history of Athens dates to the end of the seventh century B.C. Solon, an aristocrat who gained authority around 594 B.C., introduced the concept of democracy into Athenian culture. The same Solon, who was also a poet, used his art to instill a sense of patriotism and care for the common good into the Athenian culture. The process of democratizing Athens was completed around the end of the sixth century B.C. under Cleisthenes.

Athens became a fortified city in the fifth century B.C. during the threat of **Persian** invasion. In 490 B.C. Darius sent an expeditionary force to attack Athens,[2] but the Athenians defeated him on the plain of Marathon. In 480 B.C. Xerxes, Darius's son, made another attempt but was again forced to retreat. Although Athens withstood the invasion, the city was ravaged.

The 30 years following saw the rebuilding of Athens and the continued development of democracy. This period reached its zenith during the radical democratization under Pericles. During the years of his influence (450–429 B.C.), Athens experienced the height of her glor; during this time the city saw the construction of the great temples of the Acropolis. Of the four great buildings, the first to be constructed was the Propylaea, a gateway offering access to temples dedicated to Athena Nike, as well as to the Erechtheum and the Parthenon, the masterpiece of ancient Greek architecture constructed from 447 to 432 B.C.

At the height of its power Athens dedicated itself to learning and art, with philosophy, rhetoric, drama and science becoming the foci of the educated populace.[3] Still, the city suffered from a short-sighted foreign policy (characterized by a harsh domination of other Greek states) that led to the Peloponnesian War (431–404 B.C.). This 27-year conflict between Sparta and Athens eventually saw the defeat of Athens. During the war the city fell victim to the military power of Sparta and to a plague that decimated a third of her population. In 404 B.C. Athens surrendered under the duress of a blockade. Sparta, beginning a tradition of treating Athens with respect, levied lenient terms against the defeated city.

The Acropolis of Athens
Photograph: © Todd Bolen/Bible Places.com

At the onset of the fourth century B.C. Athens attempted to reclaim some of her previous glory. This quest was buoyed by the rise within the city of great intellectual power. Socrates (d. 399 B.C.) had begun an unprecedented period of intellectual pursuit. Although he did not write, his philosophical method and intellectual prowess created an impressive model. He was followed by his illustrious student Plato (427–348 B.C.). The Academy, established by Plato in 385 B.C., gained wide fame and attracted the great minds of the period.[4]

In the middle of that century, however, Athens again faced invasion. In 338 B.C. Philip of Macedonia defeated the Athenian forces on the plain of Chaeronea. Due largely to the cultural stature it had achieved, Athens was once again spared harsh terms of peace. Macedonian rule continued until 228 B.C.

Athens later came under Roman influence. Many wealthy Romans sent their sons to study there, and the cultural prestige of Athens continued into the Christian era. The apostle Paul brought Christianity to Athens in A.D. 54, as he defended the gospel at a meeting of the Areopagus (Mars Hill). He began by mentioning the altar to the "unknown god" and proceeded to call for the Athenians' repentance. Although there is a monument dedicated to Paul's sermon on a hill traditionally known as the Areopagus, the location of the actual hill from which Paul spoke his sermon is uncertain.[5] In 529 B.C. Emperor Justinian, in an attempt to eradicate paganism from the empire, closed Athens' schools, effectively ending the age of Athenian intellectual glory.[6]

[1]See "Archaeological Periods" chart on page xx in the front of this Bible. [2]See "Darius I" on page 676. [3]See "Debate and Rhetoric in the Ancient World" on page 1797. [4]See "Greek Philosophical Schools" on page 1937. [5]See "The Areopagus" on page 1802. [6]See "Greece: From Independent City-states Through Alexander the Great" on page 1814 and "Greece: Roman Domination and the Growth of Christianity" on page 1816.

ARCHAEOLOGICAL SITES

ALEXANDRIA

Roman theater in Alexandria
Photograph: © Todd Bolen/Bible Places.com

ACTS 18 The city of Alexandria ("Map 14"), founded by Alexander the Great in 331 B.C. in the northwestern Egyptian delta between the Mediterranean Sea and Lake Mareotis, quickly became one of the great cities of the **Hellenistic** culture. A center for education, it boasted the most renowned library of ancient times. At its harbor stood the lighthouse of Pharos, one of the wonders of the ancient world. Recently, the harbor waters of Alexandria have been the site of submarine archaeology; researchers have discovered under the sea magnificent examples of Egyptian and Greek art and also what may be remnants of the great lighthouse.

Alexandria, home to a large Jewish community that flourished even though the Jews there sometimes clashed with other groups, was also a center of **Diaspora** Jewish learning.[1] By legend and no doubt in fact, much of the work of translating the Old Testament into Greek (the **Septuagint** version) was accomplished there.[2] The great Jewish philosopher and Biblical scholar Philo (died c. A.D. 50) also lived and worked in Alexandria. Acts 18:24 describes Apollos of Alexandria as a Jewish intellectual, and what we know of the city and its Jewish population accords well with this description.

With the rise of Christianity, Alexandria became a center of Christian learning. A number of Christian scholars, including Clement and Origen, made the city their home. Following the lead of Philo, who read the Old Testament as an allegory of philosophical truth, the city became the center of "Alexandrian" interpretation, a method of reading much of the Hebrew Bible as an allegory for Christian teaching.

Pompey's Pillar in Alexandria, Egypt
Photograph: © Todd Bolen/Bible Places.com

[1]See "The Jewish Diaspora in the First Century A.D." on page 1769. [2]See "Texts of the Old Testament" on page 1491, "The Ancient Translations" on page 1492 and "The Septuagint and Its Use in the New Testament" on page 1995.

Ancient Voices

So, the text (of Genesis 6:12) must be explained as follows: All flesh corrupts the perfect way of the Eternal and Incorruptible One, the way leading to God. One must understand that this way refers to Wisdom. Because the mind that is led along a straight and direct route attains its destination. That destination is the knowledge and comprehension of God. Every friend of the flesh hates and rejects and seeks to corrupt this path. No two things are so antagonistic to each other as the comprehension of God and the pleasure of the flesh.

—Philo of Alexandria on Genesis 6:12

From Philo, chapter 30 of "On the Unchangeableness of God," trans. by Duane Garrett

See "Alexandria" article on the previous page.

stayed and worked with them.[t] [4]Every Sabbath[u] he reasoned in the
synagogue, trying to persuade Jews and Greeks.
[5]When Silas[v] and Timothy[w] came from Macedonia,[x] Paul devot-
ed himself exclusively to preaching, testifying to the Jews that Jesus
was the Christ.[a][y] [6]But when the Jews opposed Paul and became abu-
sive,[z] he shook out his clothes in protest and said to them, "Your
blood be on your own heads![a] I am clear of my responsibility.[b] From
now on I will go to the Gentiles."[c]
[7]Then Paul left the synagogue and went next door to the house of
Titius Justus, a worshiper of God.[d] [8]Crispus,[e] the synagogue ruler,[f]
and his entire household[g] believed in the Lord; and many of the Co-
rinthians who heard him believed and were baptized.
[9]One night the Lord spoke to Paul in a vision: "Do not be afraid;
keep on speaking, do not be silent. [10]For I am with you,[h] and no one
is going to attack and harm you, because I have many people in this
city." [11]So Paul stayed for a year and a half, teaching them the word
of God.
[12]While Gallio was proconsul of Achaia,[i] the Jews made a united
attack on Paul and brought him into court. [13]"This man," they
charged, "is persuading the people to worship God in ways contrary
to the law."

[a] 5 Or *Messiah;* also in verse 28

18:3 [t]Ac 20:34; 1Co 4:12; 1Th 2:9; 2Th 3:8
18:4 [u]Ac 13:14
18:5 [v]Ac 15:22 [w]Ac 16:1 [x]Ac 16:9; 17:14, 15 [y]ver 28; Ac 17:3
18:6 [z]Ac 13:45 [a]2Sa 1:16; Eze 18:13; 33:4 [b]Ac 20:26 [c]Ac 13:46
18:7 [d]Ac 16:14
18:8 [e]1Co 1:14 [f]Mk 5:22 [g]Ac 11:14
18:10 [h]Mt 28:20
18:12 [i]ver 27

18:4 For "synagogue," see the notes on 9:20 and 13:14 and for "Greeks" the note on 16:1.
18:8 For "synagogue ruler," see the notes on Mark 5:22 and Luke 8:41.
18:10 Corinth was a large, strategic political, commercial and religious center (see "Corinth" on p. 1887). It was important that a strong church be established there.
18:12 Gallio's positive response to Paul was a key building block in the church's case for a strong legal standing in the empire.
For "court," see "The Judgment Seat" on page 1891.
18:13 The Jews were claiming that Paul was advocating a religion not recognized by Roman law as Judaism was. If he had been given the opportunity to speak, he could have argued that the gospel he was preaching was the faith of his fathers and thus authorized by Roman law.

Gallio, Proconsul of Achaia

ACTS 18 During his second missionary journey Paul spent 18 months at Corinth (v. 11), the capital of the Roman province of Achaia ("Map 13").[1] While there he was brought before Gallio, the Roman proconsul, (vv. 12–17).[2]

Gallio was born in Corduba, Spain, as Marcus Annaeus Novatus. His name was changed to Gallio when the orator and senator Lucius Junius Gallio adopted him. Gallio's biological father was Lucius Annaeus Seneca (Seneca the Elder), a well-known writer and rhetorician, and his younger brother was Lucius Annaeus Seneca, Jr. (Seneca the Younger), a renowned writer and politician. In A.D. 41 Gallio and his brother Seneca were banished to Corsica because of Seneca's alleged adultery with Julia Livilla, the sister of Emperor Caligula. Agrippina, Nero's mother, recalled the two in A.D. 49 so that Seneca could become Nero's tutor.[3]

Gallio was proconsul of Achaia in 51–52. The date is accurately known thanks to an inscription discovered in Delphi, Greece, a copy of a letter from Emperor Claudius referring to "Lucius Junius Gallio, my friend, and the proconsul of Achaia."[4] Seneca wrote of Gallio's charm and humility and dedicated two of his books to him. The Gallio inscription is of enormous importance in dating Paul's 18-month stay in Corinth. It suggests that he was there from the fall of 50 until the late spring of 52.[5]

[1]See "The Missionary Journeys of Paul" on page 1795 and "Corinth" on page 1887. [2]See "The Roman Governor" on page 1824. [3]See "Nero, Persecutor of Christians" on page 1931. [4]See "Claudius, Emperor of Rome" on page 1788. [5]See "Paul's Visits and Letters to Corinth" on page 1888.

[14]Just as Paul was about to speak, Gallio said to the Jews, "If you Jews were making a complaint about
some misdemeanor or serious crime, it would be reasonable for me to listen to you. [15]But since it in-
18:15 [j]Ac 23:29; 25:11,19 volves questions about words and names and your own law[j]—settle the matter yourselves. I will not be
18:17 [k]1Co 1:1 a judge of such things." [16]So he had them ejected from the court. [17]Then they all turned on Sosthenes[k]
the synagogue ruler and beat him in front of the court. But Gallio showed no concern whatever.

Priscilla, Aquila and Apollos

18:18 [l]Ac 1:16 [m]Ro 16:1 [n]Nu 6:2, 5,18; Ac 21:24 [18]Paul stayed on in Corinth for some time. Then he left the brothers[l] and sailed for Syria, accompa-
nied by Priscilla and Aquila. Before he sailed, he had his hair cut off at Cenchrea[m] because of a vow he
18:19 [o]ver 21,24; 1Co 15:32 had taken.[n] [19]They arrived at Ephesus,[o] where Paul left Priscilla and Aquila. He himself went into the
synagogue and reasoned with the Jews. [20]When they asked him to spend more time with them, he de-
18:21 [p]Ro 1:10; 1Co 4:19; Jas 4:15 clined. [21]But as he left, he promised, "I will come back if it is God's will."[p] Then he set sail from Ephesus.
[22]When he landed at Caesarea,[q] he went up and greeted the church and then went down to Antioch.[r]
18:22 [q]Ac 8:40 [r]Ac 11:19 [23]After spending some time in Antioch, Paul set out from there and traveled from place to place
18:23 [s]Ac 16:6 [t]Ac 14:22; 15:32, 41 throughout the region of Galatia[s] and Phrygia, strengthening all the disciples.[t]
[24]Meanwhile a Jew named Apollos,[u] a native of Alexandria, came to Ephesus. He was a learned man,
18:24 [u]Ac 19:1; 1Co 1:12; 3:5,6, 22; 4:6; 16:12; Tit 3:13 with a thorough knowledge of the Scriptures. [25]He had been instructed in the way of the Lord, and he
spoke with great fervor[a][v] and taught about Jesus accurately, though he knew only the baptism of John.[w]
18:25 [v]Ro 12:11 [w]Ac 19:3 [26]He began to speak boldly in the synagogue. When Priscilla and Aquila heard him, they invited him to
their home and explained to him the way of God more adequately.
18:27 [x]ver 12 [y]ver 18 [27]When Apollos wanted to go to Achaia,[x] the brothers[y] encouraged him and wrote to the disciples
there to welcome him. On arriving, he was a great help to those who by grace had believed. [28]For he vig-
18:28 [z]Ac 17:2 [a]ver 5; Ac 9:22 orously refuted the Jews in public debate, proving from the Scriptures[z] that Jesus was the Christ.[a]

Paul in Ephesus

19:1 [b]Ac 18:1 [c]Ac 18:19 **19** While Apollos was at Corinth,[b] Paul took the road through the interior and arrived at Ephesus.[c]
There he found some disciples [2]and asked them, "Did you receive the Holy Spirit when[b] you
believed?"
They answered, "No, we have not even heard that there is a Holy Spirit."
[3]So Paul asked, "Then what baptism did you receive?"
"John's baptism," they replied.
[4]Paul said, "John's baptism was a baptism of repentance. He told the people to believe in the one com-
19:4 [d]Jn 1:7; Ac 13:24,25 ing after him, that is, in Jesus."[d] [5]On hearing this, they were baptized into[c] the name of the Lord Jesus.
19:6 [e]Ac 6:6; 8:17 [f]Ac 2:4 [g]Mk 16:17; Ac 10:46 [6]When Paul placed his hands on them,[e] the Holy Spirit came on them,[f] and they spoke in tongues[d][g] and
prophesied. [7]There were about twelve men in all.
[8]Paul entered the synagogue[h] and spoke boldly there for three months, arguing persuasively about
19:8 [h]Ac 9:20 [i]Ac 1:3; 28:23 the kingdom of God.[i] [9]But some of them[j] became obstinate; they refused to believe and publicly ma-
19:9 [j]Ac 14:4 [k]ver 23; Ac 9:2 [l]ver 30; Ac 11:26 ligned the Way.[k] So Paul left them. He took the disciples[l] with him and had discussions daily in the lecture

[a] 25 Or *with fervor in the Spirit* [b] 2 Or *after* [c] 5 Or *in* [d] 6 Or *other languages*

18:17 It is not clear whether the Greeks beat Sosthenes, seeing the occasion as an opportunity to vent their feelings against the Jews, or the Jews beat their own synagogue ruler because he was unsuccessful in presenting their case—probably the former.

18:18 That Priscilla's name is mentioned first may indicate her prominent role or her higher social position.

People in Paul's day typically cut or shaved their hair after following through on a vow. Paul may have taken this vow (probably a temporary Nazarite vow) in connection with the vision he had received (vv. 9–10). If so, cutting his hair may have been an act of thanksgiving for his protection and for the positive response of the Corinthians to the gospel.

Paul's vow was probably a temporary Nazirite vow.

18:19 Ephesus was the leading commercial city of Asia Minor, the capital of provincial Asia and the warden of the temple of Artemis (Diana). (See "Artemis of the Ephesians" on p. 1808 and "Ephesus During the Time of Paul" on p. 1968.)

18:22 For "Caesarea," see the note on 8:40.

18:23 The phrase "region of Galatia and Phrygia" may indicate the southern part of Galatia in the Phrygian area.

18:24 Alexandria, located in Egypt, was the second most important city in the Roman Empire. It had a large Jewish population (see "Alexandria" on p. 1805).

18:27 Achaia was a Roman province, and Corinth was its capital.

19:1 Paul did not take the lower, direct route down the Lycus and Meander Valleys but instead took the upper, Phrygian route, approaching Ephesus from a more northerly direction.

For "Ephesus," see "Ephesus During the Time of Paul" on p. 1968.

19:4 See "Baptism in the Ancient World" on page 1562.

19:6 For "placed his hands on," see the note on 6:6.

For "spoke in tongues," see "Tongue-Speaking in Christian and Pagan Worship" on page 1876.

19:9 "The Way" was a name for Christianity occurring a number of times in Acts.

The "lecture hall of Tyrannus" was probably a school used regularly by Tyrannus, a philosopher or rhetorician. Instruction was probably given during the cooler, morning hours. One Greek manuscript adds that Paul did his instructing from 11:00 A.M. to 4:00 P.M. This would have been the hottest time of the day, but the hall was available and the people were not at their regular work.

Artemis of the Ephesians

ACTS 19 Artemis of Ephesus ("Map 13") was a tremendously popular deity; in fact, the Greek traveler Pausanias stated that she was the god(dess) most worshiped in private devotions in the Mediterranean world. Her cult idol was unusual—a stiff, elongated body with legs bound together in mummy-like fashion. The upper half of the front torso was covered with protuberances resembling human breasts, so that she was sometimes called the "many-breasted Artemis." She wore a necklace of acorns, for the oak tree was sacred to her, and on her breastplate appeared the signs of the zodiac. On her head rose a high crown, often topped with the turrets of the city of Ephesus.[1] This crown may have concealed a meteorite "which fell from heaven" (Ac 19:35). Frequently her skirt was decorated with rows of animals, an indicator of fertility, and along the sides were bees, depicted as both actual insects and as priestesses ("honey bees"), adorned with crowns and wings. Artemis herself was known as the queen bee, and her castrated priests were called "drones."

Her image, said to possess particular sanctity, appears on coins, papyri, wall paintings, **reliefs**, statuettes (cf. v. 24) and in larger statuary. Some 50 stone statues of Artemis have been excavated at ancient sites in widely separated parts of the ancient world. It was said that six magical words were inscribed upon the image of the Ephesian Artemis, although these have never been found. Incantations in the name of Artemis were said to have had a powerful force (v. 19), a claim attested by magical papyri.[2]

The first idol to Artemis was said to have been carved of wood and set in an oak tree at Ephesus by the Amazons. The sanctuary was soon surrounded by a village as it became a site of pilgrimage. On the site one temple succeeded another in size and splendor, until the final shrine was considered one of the wonders of the ancient world. Thousands of personnel served within the immense confines of the sanctuary, and huge sums of money were entrusted to the keeping of Artemis. As a result the temple complex became the major banking center of Asia.[3] Not only was Artemis the guardian deity of Ephesus, but she also figured as savior goddess in inscriptions. The dead were entrusted to her care, and she was thought to have lent her assistance to women in childbirth. Secret rituals known as "mysteries," portraying both birth and death, initiated her devotees.[4]

The book of Acts (19:23–41) records the first of many confrontations between the followers of Christ and those of Artemis. At last the cause of Christ prevailed: The great temple was demolished and the cult statues were hidden.

[1]See "Ephesus During the Time of Paul" on page 1968. [2]See also "Magic in the Greco-Roman World" on page 1911. [3]See "Banking and Money in the Ancient World" on page 696. [4]See also "The Mystery Religions" on page 1939.

Remains of Hadrian's temple in Ephesus, dedicated to Artemis
Preserving Bible Times; © Dr. James C. Martin

19:10 [m]Ac 20:31 hall of Tyrannus. 10This went on for two years,[m] so that all the Jews and Greeks who lived in the prov-
[n]ver 22,26,27 ince of Asia[n] heard the word of the Lord.
19:11 [o]Ac 8:13 11God did extraordinary miracles[o] through Paul, 12so that even handkerchiefs and aprons that had
19:12 [p]Ac 5:15 touched him were taken to the sick, and their illnesses were cured[p] and the evil spirits left them.
19:13 [q]Mt 12:27 [r]Mk 9:38 13Some Jews who went around driving out evil spirits[q] tried to invoke the name of the Lord Jesus over
those who were demon-possessed. They would say, "In the name of Jesus,[r] whom Paul preaches, I com-
mand you to come out." 14Seven sons of Sceva, a Jewish chief priest, were doing this. 15⌞One day⌟ the evil
spirit answered them, "Jesus I know, and I know about Paul, but who are you?" 16Then the man who had
the evil spirit jumped on them and overpowered them all. He gave them such a beating that they ran out
of the house naked and bleeding.
19:17 [s]Ac 18:19 [t]Ac 5:5,11 17When this became known to the Jews and Greeks living in Ephesus,[s] they were all seized with fear,[t]
and the name of the Lord Jesus was held in high honor. 18Many of those who believed now came and
openly confessed their evil deeds. 19A number who had practiced sorcery brought their scrolls together
and burned them publicly. When they calculated the value of the scrolls, the total came to fifty thousand
19:20 [u]Ac 6:7; 12:24 drachmas.[a] 20In this way the word of the Lord spread widely and grew in power.[u]
19:21 [v]Ac 20:16, 22; Ro 15:25 21After all this had happened, Paul decided to go to Jerusalem,[v] passing through Macedonia[w] and
[w]Ac 16:9 [x]Ac 18:12 Achaia.[x] "After I have been there," he said, "I must visit Rome also."[y] 22He sent two of his helpers,[z] Tim-
[y]Ro 15:24,28 19:22 [z]Ac 13:5 othy[a] and Erastus,[b] to Macedonia, while he stayed in the province of Asia[c] a little longer.

[a]Ac 16:1 [b]Ro 16:23; 2Ti 4:20 [c]ver 10, 26,27

The Riot in Ephesus

19:23 [d]Ac 9:2 23About that time there arose a great disturbance about the Way.[d] 24A silversmith named Deme-
trius, who made silver shrines of Artemis, brought in no little business for the craftsmen. 25He called
them together, along with the workmen in related trades, and said: "Men, you know we receive a good
19:25 [e]Ac 16:16, 19,20 income from this business.[e] 26And you see and hear how this fellow Paul has convinced and led astray
19:26 [f]Ac 18:19 large numbers of people here in Ephesus[f] and in practically the whole province of Asia. He says that
[g]Dt 4:28; Ps 115:4; man-made gods are no gods at all.[g] 27There is danger not only that our trade will lose its good name,
Isa 44:10-20; Jer 10:3-5; but also that the temple of the great goddess Artemis will be discredited, and the goddess herself,
Ac 17:29; 1Co 8:4; Rev 9:20 who is worshiped throughout the province of Asia and the world, will be robbed of her divine
majesty."
19:28 [h]Ac 18:19 28When they heard this, they were furious and began shouting: "Great is Artemis of the Ephesians!"[h]
19:29 [i]Ac 20:4; Ro 16:23; 1Co 1:14 [j]Ac 20:4; 27:2; Col 4:10; Phm 24 29Soon the whole city was in an uproar. The people seized Gaius[i] and Aristarchus,[j] Paul's traveling

[a] *19* A drachma was a silver coin worth about a day's wages.

19:12 Handkerchiefs were probably used by Paul in his trade of leatherworking, for tying around his head and waist.

19:13 For "demon-possessed," see "Demons and the Bible" on page 1572.

19:14 Sceva, "a Jewish chief priest," may have been related to the high priestly family of Jerusalem. But more likely he took this title himself to make a further impression with his magical wiles. Drawn by Paul's ability to drive out evil spirits, Jewish exorcists wanted to copy his work.

19:19 Scrolls bearing alleged magical formulas and secret information have been unearthed. Ephesus was a center for magical incantations. The high price of 50,000 drachmas (a drachma was worth about a day's wage) was due not to the quality of the books but to the supposed power gained by their secret knowledge of words and names.

19:21 Macedonia and Achaia were the two Roman provinces into which Greece was then divided.

19:22 Erastus, at one time "the city's director of public works" (see Ro 16:23 and its note), was an important figure at Corinth (see "The Erastus Inscription" on p. 1861).

19:23 "The Way" was a name for Christianity occurring a number of times in Acts.

19:24 Each trade had its guild, and Demetrius was probably a responsible leader of the guild for the manufacture of silver shrines and images.

Reproductions from the time of the emperor Domitian (A.D. 81–96) of the original Artemis image have been found in Ephesus. (See "Artemis of the Ephesians" on p. 1808.)

19:25 Since the temple of Artemis was one of the seven wonders of the ancient world (see the note on v. 27), people came from far and wide to view it. Their purchase of silver shrines and images produced a lucrative business for the craftsmen.

19:27 The temple of Artemis was the glory of Ephesus. It was 425 feet (130 m) long and 220 feet (67 m) wide, having 127 white marble columns 62 feet (19 m) high and less than 4 feet (1.2 m) apart. In the inner sanctuary stood the many-breasted image supposedly dropped from heaven.

19:29 In spite of the rudimentary dramatic structure discernible in the book of Job and the Song of Songs, Israel produced no drama and thus had no theaters. The word *theater* is from the Greek and is a noun derived from the verb *theaomai,* meaning "to view" or "to look upon." The Greek theater, and the Roman theater that followed it, were structures designed to seat the viewers at a dramatic representation. The theater was usually an open-air structure, a semicircle of stone seats built into the side of a hill and seating 5,000 people or more. The seats were cut concentrically (facing a common center), and at the foot of the auditorium a semicircular piece of level pavement provided the "orchestra" (the space where the chorus, an indispensable part of all Greek dramas, and the actions performed).

There were only three actors in a Greek tragedy to fill all of the roles involved in a play. On the tent was painted a rough representation of trees or a temple or a house. The Greek for "tent" is *skçnç;* hence "scenery" in the dramatic sense. Surviving Greek theaters are acoustically remarkable. They were commonly used for public gatherings, since they were likely to provide the largest places of assembly in the city. The ruins of the theater in Ephesus, a most imposing structure seating 25,000 people, have been excavated. Roman theaters tended to be more elaborate than those of the Greeks, contained a more finished stage and, perhaps in conformity with the needs of a more severe climate, were at least in part roofed over.

companions from Macedonia,[k] and rushed as one man into the theater. 30 Paul wanted to appear before 19:29 [k]Ac 16:9
the crowd, but the disciples would not let him. 31 Even some of the officials of the province, friends of
Paul, sent him a message begging him not to venture into the theater.
32 The assembly was in confusion: Some were shouting one thing, some another.[l] Most of the people 19:32 [l]Ac 21:34
did not even know why they were there. 33 The Jews pushed Alexander to the front, and some of the crowd
shouted instructions to him. He motioned[m] for silence in order to make a defense before the people. 19:33 [m]Ac 12:17

Greece: From the Prehistoric Period Through the Mycenaean Empire

ACTS 20 The habitation of Greece dates back to the prehistoric period, with the earliest identifiable farming communities in the fertile plains of Thessaly and Macedonia, two regions in northern Greece. Between 2200 and 2000 B.C. several waves of invaders overran the region and established settlements. It is believed that these tribes were the ethnic ancestors of the modern Greeks, although they left no evidence of an organized society.

The first great civilization in the area developed on Crete.[1] Modern scholars refer to this culture as that of the Minoans, a name that comes from Minos, a legendary king of Crete. We do not know what these people called themselves, since researchers have been unable as yet to decipher the script in which their language was written, known simply as Linear A.

The Minoans were highly accomplished artists, engineers, sailors and merchants (Minoan motifs appear in some Egyptian artwork). Eventually, Minoan civilization declined until it disappeared entirely by 1000 B.C. The collapse of the Minoan civilization is often attributed to a catastrophic volcanic eruption on the nearby island of Thera (modern Santorini) during the mid-second millennium B.C. (perhaps c. 1640 B.C.). Although that must have been a major trauma, the Minoans continued as a people long after that event. It was probably the pillaging of their territory by the **Sea Peoples**, beginning around 1200 B.C., that finally brought the Minoan age to an end. Today a traveler may visit the ruins of four grand Minoan palaces at Knossos, Phaestos, Malia and Zakros, replete with numerous famous frescoes, jewelry and other artwork.

Around 1400 B.C. the Mycenaean Empire rose to prominence. Its capital, Mycenae, was a heavily fortified city located in the northeastern part of the Peloponnesian peninsula. Its influence spread over the mainland and many of the islands, and the Mycenaeans developed their own written language, known to archaeologists as Linear B. In 1952 Michael Ventris, a British architect, managed to decipher this language, discovering it to be a pre-alphabetic form of Greek—making the Mycenaeans the first identifiable Greek speakers. Their most famous king, Agamemnon, was said by Homer to have led a Greek military campaign in approximately 1250 B.C. against the city of Troy, located on the western coast of modern Turkey. According to Homer, rulers of the various districts of Greece were obliged to provide men and supplies for this operation. For many years scholars doubted the historicity of the Trojan War, but archaeological discoveries of the nineteenth and twentieth centuries, including that of the city of Troy itself, have led most researchers to conclude that Homer's epic was based upon actual events, even if his account was mythologized.

By 1150 B.C. the great centers of Mycenaean civilization had been destroyed. The collapse of the Mycenaean civilization is often attributed to invaders from the north, but there is little clear evidence to support this hypothesis. It is possible that the end of Mycenaean civilization came as a result of changes in military strategy and weaponry that made the older military aristocracy of Mycenae obsolete and led to the emergence of roving troops of infantry (the Sea Peoples), bent upon conquest and plunder. Regardless of the cause, for several hundred years Greece was immersed in a dark age. Settlements became isolated on account of poverty and the rugged, mountainous terrain that separated Greece from her neighbors.

[1]See "Crete" on page 1972.

[34] But when they realized he was a Jew, they all shouted in unison for about two hours: "Great is Artemis of the Ephesians!"

[35] The city clerk quieted the crowd and said: "Men of Ephesus,[n] doesn't all the world know that the city of Ephesus is the guardian of the temple of the great Artemis and of her image, which fell from heaven? [36] Therefore, since these facts are undeniable, you ought to be quiet and not do anything rash. [37] You have brought these men here, though they have neither robbed temples[o] nor blasphemed our goddess. [38] If, then, Demetrius and his fellow craftsmen have a grievance against anybody, the courts are open and there are proconsuls.[p] They can press charges. [39] If there is anything further you want to bring up, it must be settled in a legal assembly. [40] As it is, we are in danger of being charged with rioting because of today's events. In that case we would not be able to account for this commotion, since there is no reason for it." [41] After he had said this, he dismissed the assembly.

Through Macedonia and Greece

20 When the uproar had ended, Paul sent for the disciples[q] and, after encouraging them, said good-by and set out for Macedonia.[r] [2] He traveled through that area, speaking many words of encouragement to the people, and finally arrived in Greece, [3] where he stayed three months. Because the Jews made a plot against him[s] just as he was about to sail for Syria, he decided to go back through Macedonia.[t] [4] He was accompanied by Sopater son of Pyrrhus from Berea, Aristarchus[u] and Secundus from Thessalonica,[v] Gaius[w] from Derbe, Timothy[x] also, and Tychicus[y] and Trophimus[z] from the province of Asia. [5] These men went on ahead and waited for us[a] at Troas.[b] [6] But we sailed from Philippi[c] after the Feast of Unleavened Bread, and five days later joined the others at Troas,[d] where we stayed seven days.

Eutychus Raised From the Dead at Troas

[7] On the first day of the week[e] we came together to break bread. Paul spoke to the people and, because he intended to leave the next day, kept on talking until midnight. [8] There were many lamps in the upstairs room[f] where we were meeting. [9] Seated in a window was a young man named Eutychus, who was sinking into a deep sleep as Paul talked on and on. When he was sound asleep, he fell to the ground from the third story and was picked up dead. [10] Paul went down, threw himself on the young man[g] and put his arms around him. "Don't be alarmed," he said. "He's alive!"[h] [11] Then he went upstairs again and broke bread[i] and ate. After talking until daylight, he left. [12] The people took the young man home alive and were greatly comforted.

19:35 [n] Ac 18:19
19:37 [o] Ro 2:22
19:38 [p] Ac 13:7,8,12
20:1 [q] Ac 11:26 [r] Ac 16:9
20:3 [s] ver 19; Ac 9:23,24; 23:12,15,30; 25:3; 2Co 11:26 [t] Ac 16:9
20:4 [u] Ac 19:29 [v] Ac 17:1 [w] Ac 19:29 [x] Ac 16:1 [y] Eph 6:21; Col 4:7; 2Ti 4:12; Tit 3:12 [z] Ac 21:29; 2Ti 4:20
20:5 [a] Ac 16:10 [b] Ac 16:8
20:6 [c] Ac 16:12 [d] Ac 16:8
20:7 [e] 1Co 16:2; Rev 1:10
20:8 [f] Ac 1:13
20:10 [g] 1Ki 17:21; 2Ki 4:34 [h] Mt 9:23,24
20:11 [i] ver 7

Ancient Voices

For most, the disease began for no apparent reason. Instead, people of sound health were suddenly stricken by severe head fever and by redness and inflammation in the eyes. Internally, the throat and tongue became blood red, and the breath became strange and came out foul. After this, sneezing and hoarseness set in, and in a little while pain descended to the chest, and it was accompanied by a hard cough. When it settled into the stomach, it upset it, and added to this, they vomited fluids of every kind named by physicians, which came with very great pain. In the majority of cases dry heaves followed, which produced violent spasms. Some had relief soon after this, but for others relief came much later. Externally, the body was neither excessively hot to the touch, nor was it pale, but it was reddish, livid and broken out into blisters and sores. But internally it burned so badly that one could not bear to have on even the lightest clothing or linen or endure anything other than to be naked; and people most wanted to throw themselves into cold water. And many suffering like this while not under someone's care did so; constrained by unceasing thirst they went into water tanks (although it actually made little difference whether one drank little or much).

—Thucydides Describes the Plague in Athens During the Peloponnesian War

From Thucydides, *The Peloponnesian War*, 2.49.1, trans. by Duane Garrett

See "Greece: From the Prehistoric Period Through the Mycenaean Empire" article.

19:38 The words "courts" and "proconsuls" are probably general terms, not intended to refer to more than one court or one proconsul. As the capital city of the province of Asia, Ephesus was the headquarters for the proconsul.

19:39 The "legal assembly" was the regular civil meeting ordinarily held three times a month.

20:4 These men seem to have been the delegates appointed to accompany Paul and the money given for the needy in Judea.

For information on Timothy, see the note on 16:1.

20:5 For "Troas," see the note on 16:8. This city was to be the rendezvous for Paul and those who went on ahead by sea from Neapolis, the seaport of Philippi.

20:6 For "Feast of Unleavened Bread," see the note on Matthew 26:17.

The voyage from Neapolis (the seaport of Philippi) to Troas took five days.

20:7 The "first day of the week" was Sunday. This is the first clear reference to believers meeting for worship on the first day of the week, but Sunday worship may have already become a regular practice. Although some scholars maintain that the meetings were held on Saturday evenings, since the Jewish day began at 6:00 the previous evening, Luke's method of counting days and reporting happenings in this Hellenistic city was probably not Jewish but Roman, which counted from midnight to midnight.

"Break bread" is a reference to the Lord's Supper.

20:9 See "Houses in the Holy Land of the First Century A.D.: Peter's House in Capernaum; Insulae" on page 1584.

A CHRONOLOGICAL HISTORY OF GREECE FROM 600 B.C. THROUGH 142 B.C.

	Events	Persons
600 B.C.	Peloponnesian league founded (c. 550)	Solon, the Archon (594)
		Anaximander
		Anaximenes
	Tyranny of Athens (c. 546)	Pythagoras
		Xenophanes
	Democracy at Athens (507)	Heraclitus
500	Ionian revolt against Darius I of Persia (499–493)	
	Attack on Athens by Darius I (490)	
	Persian attack on Greece under Xerxes (480–479)	Pindar
	Athenian alliance founded (478)	
		Lysias (459–380)
		Aeschylus (458)
	Citizenship Law of Pericles (451–450)	
	Athens' peace with Persia (449)	
		Sophocles (441)
		Herodotus
		Anaxagoras
		Hippocrates
	Peloponnesian War (431–404)	Socrates
		Aristophanes (431)
		Plato (429–380)
		Xenophon (428–354)
		Demosthenes
		Aristotle (d. 322)
		Euripides (d. 405)
400	Expedition of the 10,000 (401–400)	
	Spartan expedition in Asia Minor (400–394)	
	Sparta's peace with Persia (387)	
	Thebes' defeat of Sparta (371)	
		Menander (342–291)
		Epicurus (341–271)

	Events	Persons
400 B.C. con't	Philip II of Macedon conquers Greece (338) Alexander's attack on Persia (334) Death of Alexander (323) Beginning of Seleucid Era (311)	Zeno (336–264) Aratus of Soli (315–240)
300	First Syrian War (276–273) Second Syrian War (260–255) Third Syrian War (246–241) Antiochus III (the Great), Seleucid ruler of Syria (223–187) Antiochus III driven from Egypt; defeated at Raphia by Ptolemy IV (217)	Polybius (208–126)
200	Antiochus III's defeat of Egypt at battle of Panium and control of Palestine (198) Seleucids driven from Asia Minor by Romans (188) Syro-Palestine ruled by Antiochus IV (Epiphanes) (175–163) Antiochus's attack on Jerusalem and persecution of the Jews (168) Maccabean revolt against the Syrians (167) Syria's loss of political control over Judea (142)	

Chronological and Background Charts of the New Testament, pp, 50–51

Greece: From Independent City-states Through Alexander the Great

ACTS 20 During this period the autonomous city-state, or *polis*, developed. Fear of attack was constant, and most of the hundreds of city-states grew up around a high, easily defensible stronghold called a citadel or **acropolis**. During the Archaic period (seventh–sixth centuries B.C.) Greece began to rebound, and particular city-states asserted themselves. In the Peloponnesian peninsula (southwestern Greece), Sparta rose to prominence, as did Corinth and Argos in the north and east, respectively. In northern Greece Thebes exercised hegemony over the Boeotian League, a federation of cities in that area, while Athens and Megara vied for authority in the region of Attica.[1] Meanwhile, Greek colonies thrived across the eastern Mediterranean. The two major centers for Greek colonies were the western coastline of **Anatolia** (Turkey) and the lower half of Italy, including Sicily.

Soon after 500 B.C. the Greeks found themselves facing a formidable external threat. The **Persian** king Darius I had extended his influence as far east as modern Pakistan and as far west as Thrace and Macedonia.[2] The Greek cities of western Anatolia, with the help of several Greek city-states, rebelled against Persia in 499–493 B.C. After Darius crushed the revolt, he decided that all of Greece must be subdued, and he dispatched envoys throughout the region to demand allegiance. Manycity-states —but not Athens or Sparta—acquiesced. Darius, arriving in 490 with a sizable army, destroyed the city of Eretria and began pushing south toward Athens. His force of perhaps 20,000 soldiers met an inferior Athenian contingent of 9,000 at Marathon. The brilliant Athenian general Miltiades nonetheless led his men to a decisive victory (492 B.C.).

Following the death of Darius, his son Xerxes returned to Greece in 480 B.C. with a massive army. The Persian war machine moved south, overwhelming everything in its path. Sparta prepared for land defense, while Athens enlarged her navy. The Persians sacked Athens (which the Athenians had abandoned), but the Athenian navy managed to lure Xerxes into a battle in a narrow channel near the island of Salamis, where the trapped Persians were thoroughly defeated. Because his army was extremely vulnerable without support from the sea, Xerxes retreated, leaving a contingent of 60,000 troops that attempted to subdue the Greeks in the following year. They were destroyed by a Spartan-led army at Plataea, effectively ending the Persian threat.

Just prior to 500 B.C. Athens became the first democracy in history. The people had expelled a series of tyrants and established a popular assembly. The other city-states mistrusted the Athenians and their aberrant form of government, and Athens gave the others additional cause for concern: Following the expulsion of the Persians from Greece and, soon afterward, from some Greek cities of **Asia Minor**, Athens founded the Athenian League, a confederation of Greek cities around the Aegean Sea. Athens, as leader, became tremendously wealthy from the tribute it gathered. The glorious monuments on the Athenian Acropolis were funded by money extracted from the league's members, and by the mid-fifth century B.C. Athens had become Greece's wealthiest, as well as culturally dominant, city. The comic playwright Aristophanes; the tragic playwrights Aeschylus, Sophocles and Euripides; and the philosopher Socrates all inhabited the city at this time.

In 431 B.C. Sparta, Corinth, Megara and other allies responded with military force. The historian Thucydides recounted the events of the conflict in *The Peloponnesian War.* A plague ravaged the Athenian population in 430, yet Athens continued to hold up under the heavy threat. The turning point came when the Athenians launched a failed campaign to conquer Syracuse on the island of Sicily. The Spartans seized their advantage and forced an Athenian surrender in 404, pulling down its walls but sparing the city.

For much of the fourth century B.C. Greece was entangled in conflicts among a resurgent Athens, Sparta, Corinth and Thebes. Alliances among the four prominent cities were repeatedly formed and broken. The future of Greece, however, by this point lay to the north, with Philip II of Macedon, whose army swept south and crushed the confederated Greek army in 338 B.C. at Chaeronea, near Thebes. Several attempts at revolt proved pointless, and Macedonian control of Greece was strengthened under Philip's son, Alexander the Great, who launched an invasion of the Persian Empire and, in the course of a few years of lightning campaigns through Anatolia, the Levant, Egypt, Mesopotamia and Persia, brought that empire to its end.

[1]See "Athens" on page1804. [2]See "Darius I" on page 676.

Paul's Farewell to the Ephesian Elders

13 We went on ahead to the ship and sailed for Assos, where we were going to take Paul aboard. He had
made this arrangement because he was going there on foot. 14 When he met us at Assos, we took him
aboard and went on to Mitylene. 15 The next day we set sail from there and arrived off Kios. The day af-
ter that we crossed over to Samos, and on the following day arrived at Miletus.[j] 16 Paul had decided to
sail past Ephesus[k] to avoid spending time in the province of Asia, for he was in a hurry to reach Jerusa-
lem,[l] if possible, by the day of Pentecost.[m]

17 From Miletus, Paul sent to Ephesus for the elders[n] of the church. 18 When they arrived, he said to
them: "You know how I lived the whole time I was with you,[o] from the first day I came into the province
of Asia. 19 I served the Lord with great humility and with tears, although I was severely tested by the plots
of the Jews.[p] 20 You know that I have not hesitated to preach anything[q] that would be helpful to you but
have taught you publicly and from house to house. 21 I have declared to both Jews[r] and Greeks that they
must turn to God in repentance[s] and have faith in our Lord Jesus.[t]

22 "And now, compelled by the Spirit, I am going to Jerusalem,[u] not knowing what will happen to me
there. 23 I only know that in every city the Holy Spirit warns me[v] that prison and hardships are facing
me.[w] 24 However, I consider my life worth nothing to me,[x] if only I may finish the race and complete the
task[y] the Lord Jesus has given me[z]—the task of testifying to the gospel of God's grace.

25 "Now I know that none of you among whom I have gone about preaching the kingdom will ever see
me again.[a] 26 Therefore, I declare to you today that I am innocent of the blood of all men.[b] 27 For I have
not hesitated to proclaim to you the whole will of God.[c] 28 Keep watch over yourselves and all the flock
of which the Holy Spirit has made you overseers.[a] [d] Be shepherds of the church of God,[b] which he bought
with his own blood. 29 I know that after I leave, savage wolves[e] will come in among you and will not spare
the flock.[f] 30 Even from your own number men will arise and distort the truth in order to draw away dis-
ciples[g] after them. 31 So be on your guard! Remember that for three years[h] I never stopped warning each
of you night and day with tears.[i]

32 "Now I commit you to God[j] and to the word of his grace, which can build you up and give you an
inheritance[k] among all those who are sanctified.[l] 33 I have not coveted anyone's silver or gold or clothing.[m]
34 You yourselves know that these hands of mine have supplied my own needs and the needs of my com-
panions.[n] 35 In everything I did, I showed you that by this kind of hard work we must help the weak, re-
membering the words the Lord Jesus himself said: 'It is more blessed to give than to receive.' "

36 When he had said this, he knelt down with all of them and prayed.[o] 37 They all wept as they em-
braced him and kissed him.[p] 38 What grieved them most was his statement that they would never see his
face again.[q] Then they accompanied him to the ship.

On to Jerusalem

21 After we[r] had torn ourselves away from them, we put out to sea and sailed straight to Cos. The
next day we went to Rhodes and from there to Patara. 2 We found a ship crossing over to Phoe-
nicia,[s] went on board and set sail. 3 After sighting Cyprus and passing to the south of it, we sailed on to
Syria. We landed at Tyre, where our ship was to unload its cargo. 4 Finding the disciples[t] there, we stayed
with them seven days. Through the Spirit[u] they urged Paul not to go on to Jerusalem. 5 But when our time
was up, we left and continued on our way. All the disciples and their wives and children accompanied us
out of the city, and there on the beach we knelt to pray.[v] 6 After saying good-by to each other, we went
aboard the ship, and they returned home.

[a] 28 Traditionally *bishops* [b] 28 Many manuscripts *of the Lord*

20:15 [j]ver 17; 2Ti 4:20 **20:16** [k]Ac 18:19 [l]Ac 19:21 [m]Ac 2:1; 1Co 16:8 **20:17** [n]Ac 11:30 **20:18** [o]Ac 18:19-21; 19:1-41 **20:19** [p]ver 3 **20:20** [q]ver 27 **20:21** [r]Ac 18:5 [s]Ac 2:38 [t]Ac 24:24; 26:18; Eph 1:15; Col 2:5; Phm 5 **20:22** [u]ver 16 **20:23** [v]Ac 21:4 [w]Ac 9:16 **20:24** [x]Ac 21:13 [y]2Co 4:1 [z]Gal 1:1; Tit 1:3 **20:25** [a]ver 38 **20:26** [b]Ac 18:6 **20:27** [c]ver 20 **20:28** [d]1Pe 5:2 **20:29** [e]Mt 7:15 [f]ver 28 **20:30** [g]Ac 11:26 **20:31** [h]Ac 19:10 [i]ver 19 **20:32** [j]Ac 14:23 [k]Eph 1:14; Col 1:12; 3:24; Heb 9:15; 1Pe 1:4 [l]Ac 26:18 **20:33** [m]1Sa 12:3; 1Co 9:12; 2Co 7:2; 11:9; 12:14-17 **20:34** [n]Ac 18:3 **20:36** [o]Lk 22:41; Ac 21:5 **20:37** [p]Lk 15:20 **20:38** [q]ver 25 **21:1** [r]Ac 16:10 **21:2** [s]Ac 11:19 **21:4** [t]Ac 11:26 [u]ver 11; Ac 20:23 **21:5** [v]Ac 20:36

20:13 Assos was on the opposite side of the peninsula from Troas—about 20 miles (32 km) away by land. The journey along the coastline, however, was about 40 miles (64 km). Travel by sea was common in New Testament times (see "Travel in the Greco-Roman World" on p. 1946).

20:14 Mitylene was a harbor on the southeastern shore of the island of Lesbos.

20:15 Kios was a large island that lay along the western coast of Asia Minor. Samos was one of the most important islands in the Aegean, while Miletus was located about 35 miles (56 km) south of Ephesus, the destination of the ship on which Paul was traveling. He would have had to change ships to put into Ephesus, which would have resulted in lost time.

20:16 For "the day of Pentecost," see the note on 2:1.

20:28 "Overseers" refers to the "elders of the church" (v. 17).

21:1 Cos, one of the Sporades islands off the coast of Asia Minor, was the birthplace of Hippocrates, the father of medicine. A large Jewish settlement was located there.

"Rhodes" here refers to the leading city on the island of Rhodes, once noted for its "harbor colossus," one of the seven wonders of the ancient world (but demolished over two centuries before Paul's arrival there).

Patara was located on the southern coast of Lycia. Paul changed ships there from a vessel that hugged the shore of Asia Minor to one going directly to Tyre and Phoenicia (see "Travel in the Greco-Roman World" on p. 1946).

Greece: Roman Domination and the Growth of Christianity

The Parthenon in Athens
Preserving Bible Times; © Dr. James C. Martin

ACTS 20 Following Alexander's death in 323 B.C., a power struggle ensued among his leading generals. Greece eventually fell under the control of Antigonus and his descendants, referred to as the Antigonids. The malcontent Greeks countered by forming two federal states, the Aetolian League in the north and the Achaean League, led by Corinth, in the south. Beginning in 214 B.C. the Antigonid king Philip V attempted to punish these states and to tighten his grip on Greece. In response, the Greek states sought help from an emerging power in the west: Rome. The Romans, who had previously attempted to invade Philip's territories, answered by dispatching a sizable military force. In 197 B.C. the Roman general Titus Quinctius Flaminius soundly defeated Philip V's army in Thessaly. By 196 the "liberation" of Greece was complete, and the Roman province of Achaea was born.

The Romans held Greek civilization in the highest regard and adopted many of its customs and traditions. Rome protected the great cities and monuments of Greece, as long as Roman dominance was not challenged by the Greeks—who did test this on two occasions, both with disastrous results. In 172 B.C. Perseus, son of Philip V, invaded Greece in an attempt to win back the lands of his father. Many Greeks were sympathetic to Perseus, and, after his total defeat in 167, the Romans punished the Greeks by carrying a thousand noble Greek youths to Rome as hostages. In 146 B.C. the Achaean League, led by Corinth, rose in revolt. The Romans responded by sending the general Mummius, who defeated an insignificant Achaean force and entered Corinth unopposed. He burned the city, killed its inhabitants and took much of its valuable artwork back to Rome. This incident put an end to any realistic dreams of resurgent Greek independence.

Corinth was reestablished by Julius Caesar in 44 B.C. as a Roman colony, and the Greeks lived in relative peace within the Roman Empire from that point on. Corinth, which had major harbors opening to the eastern and western Mediterranean, grew to be Greece's commercial capital and most cosmopolitan city.[1] Athens retained its position as the cultural center of Greece, while Sparta and Thebes became insignificant. The impressive system of Roman roads brought commercial prowess to other locations in Greece, such as Thessalonica and Philippi.[2] Under Roman rule Greece enjoyed something it had never experienced while free: peace. In this ideal situation, the New Testament church took root and was able to thrive.[3]

[1]See "Corinth" on page 1887. [2]See "Thessalonica" on page 1944 and "Philippi" on page 1927. [3]See also "The Roman Empire" on page 1845.

21:7 wAc 12:20 7We continued our voyage from Tyre[w] and landed at Ptolemais, where we greeted the brothers[x] and
xAc 1:16 21:8 yAc 8:40 stayed with them for a day. 8Leaving the next day, we reached Caesarea[y] and stayed at the house of Phil-
zAc 6:5; 8:5-40 aEph 4:11; 2Ti 4:5 ip[z] the evangelist,[a] one of the Seven. 9He had four unmarried daughters who prophesied.[b]
21:9 bLk 2:36; Ac 2:17 10After we had been there a number of days, a prophet named Agabus[c] came down from Judea. 11Com-
21:10 cAc 11:28 ing over to us, he took Paul's belt, tied his own hands and feet with it and said, "The Holy Spirit says, 'In
21:11 dver 33 e1Ki 22:11 this way the Jews of Jerusalem will bind[d] the owner of this belt and will hand him over to the Gentiles.' "[e]
12When we heard this, we and the people there pleaded with Paul not to go up to Jerusalem. 13Then
Paul answered, "Why are you weeping and breaking my heart? I am ready not only to be bound, but also
21:13 fAc 20:24 gAc 9:16 to die[f] in Jerusalem for the name of the Lord Jesus."[g] 14When he would not be dissuaded, we gave up and
said, "The Lord's will be done."
21:16 hAc 8:40 iver 3,4 15After this, we got ready and went up to Jerusalem. 16Some of the disciples from Caesarea[h] accom-
panied us and brought us to the home of Mnason, where we were to stay. He was a man from Cyprus[i] and
one of the early disciples.

Paul's Arrival at Jerusalem

21:17 jAc 15:4 17When we arrived at Jerusalem, the brothers received us warmly.[j] 18The next day Paul and the rest
21:18 kAc 15:13 lAc 11:30 of us went to see James,[k] and all the elders[l] were present. 19Paul greeted them and reported in detail what
21:19 mAc 14:27 nAc 1:17 God had done among the Gentiles[m] through his ministry.[n]
20When they heard this, they praised God. Then they said to Paul: "You see, brother, how many thou-
21:20 oAc 22:3; Ro 10:2; Gal 1:14 sands of Jews have believed, and all of them are zealous[o] for the law.[p] 21They have been informed that you
pAc 15:1,5 teach all the Jews who live among the Gentiles to turn away from Moses,[q] telling them not to circumcise
21:21 qver 28 rAc 15:19-21; 1Co 7:18,19 their children[r] or live according to our customs.[s] 22What shall we do? They will certainly hear that you
sAc 6:14 have come, 23so do what we tell you. There are four men with us who have made a vow.[t] 24Take these
21:23 tAc 18:18 men, join in their purification rites[u] and pay their expenses, so that they can have their heads shaved.[v]
21:24 uver 26; Ac 24:18 vAc 18:18 Then everybody will know there is no truth in these reports about you, but that you yourself are living
in obedience to the law. 25As for the Gentile believers, we have written to them our decision that they
should abstain from food sacrificed to idols, from blood, from the meat of strangled animals and from
21:25 wAc 15:20, 29 sexual immorality."[w]
26The next day Paul took the men and purified himself along with them. Then he went to the temple
to give notice of the date when the days of purification would end and the offering would be made for
21:26 xNu 6:13-20; Ac 24:18 each of them.[x]

Paul Arrested

27When the seven days were nearly over, some Jews from the province of Asia saw Paul at the temple.
21:27 yAc 24:18; 26:21 They stirred up the whole crowd and seized him,[y] 28shouting, "Men of Israel, help us! This is the man who
21:28 zMt 24:15; Ac 24:5,6 teaches all men everywhere against our people and our law and this place. And besides, he has brought
21:29 aAc 20:4 Greeks into the temple area and defiled this holy place."[z] 29(They had previously seen Trophimus[a] the
bAc 18:19 Ephesian[b] in the city with Paul and assumed that Paul had brought him into the temple area.)

21:3 For "Cyprus," see the note on 4:36.
21:7 Ptolemais (modern Acco) was a city lying north of and across the bay from Mount Carmel. It was situated one day's journey from Tyre on the north and another 35 miles (56 km) to Caesarea on the south.
21:8 For "Caesarea," see the note on 8:40. Philip's evangelistic work may have focused on Caesarea for almost 25 years.
21:9 See the note on prophetesses at Exodus 15:20–21.
21:10 Evidently Agabus held the office of prophet, as Philip held the office of evangelist (v. 8). This is the same prophet who had been in Syrian Antioch (see the note on 11:19) prophesying the coming famine in Jerusalem, some 15 years earlier (11:27–29).
21:18 This James was the brother of Jesus (see the note on Lk 8:19). He wrote the letter of James and was the leader of the church in Jerusalem (see Gal 1:19; 2:9). Although called an apostle, he was not one of the Twelve.
21:20 See "Before the Gentile Expansion: The Jewish Churches in the Holy Land" on page 1997.
21:23 These men, evidently under the temporary Nazirite vow (see the note on Nu 6:1–21), became unclean before the completion time of the vow (perhaps due to contact with a dead body). For a discussion of the support of Nazirites by the apostle Paul, as well as by the court of Herod Agrippa, see the note on Luke 1:15.
21:24 In some instances purification rites included the offering of sacrifices. Such rites were observed by choice by some Jewish Christians but were not required of Christians, either Jew or Gentile.

Paul's part in sponsoring these men would have included (1) paying part or all of the cost of the sacrifices (in this case eight pigeons and four lambs; Nu 6:9–12) and (2) going to the temple to notify the priest when their days of purification would be fulfilled so that the priests would be prepared to sacrifice their offerings (Ac 21:26).
21:27 Seven days were required for purification, shaving their heads at the altar, the sacrifice of a sin offering and burnt offering for each and announcing the completion of the vow to the priests.
21:28 Inscriptions in Greek and Latin on stone slabs (two of which have been discovered by archaeologists) were placed on the barrier between the inner and outer temple courts, warning Gentiles of the death penalty for proceeding any further (see "The Dividing Wall of the Court of the Gentiles in Herod's Temple" on p. 1917). The Roman authorities were so anxious to appease the Jews in this regard that they authorized execution even if the offender was a Roman citizen.
21:29 Trophimus was a Gentile Ephesian. Paul probably did not take him into the forbidden area. If he had, these Jews should have attacked Trophimus rather than Paul.

30The whole city was aroused, and the people came running from all directions. Seizing Paul,[c] they — 21:30 [c]Ac 26:21
dragged him[d] from the temple, and immediately the gates were shut. 31While they were trying to kill — [d]Ac 16:19
him, news reached the commander of the Roman troops that the whole city of Jerusalem was in an up-
roar. 32He at once took some officers and soldiers and ran down to the crowd. When the rioters saw the
commander and his soldiers, they stopped beating Paul.[e] — 21:32 [e]Ac 23:27
33The commander came up and arrested him and ordered him to be bound[f] with two[g] chains.[h] Then — 21:33 [f]ver 11
he asked who he was and what he had done. 34Some in the crowd shouted one thing and some another,[i] — [g]Ac 12:6; [h]Ac 20:23;
and since the commander could not get at the truth because of the uproar, he ordered that Paul be tak- — Eph 6:20; 2Ti 2:9; 21:34 [i]Ac 19:32
en into the barracks.[j] 35When Paul reached the steps,[k] the violence of the mob was so great he had to be — [j]ver 37; Ac 23:10, 16,32
carried by the soldiers. 36The crowd that followed kept shouting, "Away with him!"[l] — 21:35 [k]ver 40; 21:36 [l]Lk 23:18; Jn 19:15; Ac 22:22

Paul Speaks to the Crowd

37As the soldiers were about to take Paul into the barracks,[m] he asked the commander, "May I say — 21:37 [m]ver 34
something to you?"
"Do you speak Greek?" he replied. 38"Aren't you the Egyptian who started a revolt and led four thou-
sand terrorists out into the desert[n] some time ago?"[o] — 21:38 [n]Mt 24:26 [o]Ac 5:36
39Paul answered, "I am a Jew, from Tarsus[p] in Cilicia,[q] a citizen of no ordinary city. Please let me speak — 21:39 [p]Ac 9:11 [q]Ac 22:3
to the people."
40Having received the commander's permission, Paul stood on the steps and motioned[r] to the crowd. — 21:40 [r]Ac 12:17 [s]Jn 5:2
22 When they were all silent, he said to them in Aramaic[a]:[s] 1"Brothers and fathers,[t] listen now to — 22:1 [t]Ac 7:2
my defense."
2When they heard him speak to them in Aramaic,[u] they became very quiet. — 22:2 [u]Ac 21:40
Then Paul said: 3"I am a Jew,[v] born in Tarsus[w] of Cilicia, but brought up in this city. Under[x] Gamali- — 22:3 [v]Ac 21:39 [w]Ac 9:11
el[y] I was thoroughly trained in the law of our fathers[z] and was just as zealous[a] for God as any of you are — [x]Lk 10:39
today. 4I persecuted[b] the followers of this Way to their death, arresting both men and women and throw- — [y]Ac 5:34 [z]Ac 26:5 [a]Ac 21:20
ing them into prison,[c] 5as also the high priest and all the Council[d] can testify. I even obtained letters — 22:4 [b]Ac 8:3 [c]ver 19,20
from them to their brothers[e] in Damascus,[f] and went there to bring these people as prisoners to Jerusa- — 22:5 [d]Lk 22:66 [e]Ac 13:26 [f]Ac 9:2
lem to be punished.
6"About noon as I came near Damascus, suddenly a bright light from heaven flashed around me.[g] 7I — 22:6 [g]Ac 9:3
fell to the ground and heard a voice say to me, 'Saul! Saul! Why do you persecute me?'
8" 'Who are you, Lord?' I asked.
" 'I am Jesus of Nazareth, whom you are persecuting,' he replied. 9My companions saw the light,[h] but — 22:9 [h]Ac 26:13 [i]Ac 9:7
they did not understand the voice[i] of him who was speaking to me.
10" 'What shall I do, Lord?' I asked.

[a] 40 Or possibly *Hebrew*; also in 22:2

21:30 The gates were shut by order of the temple officer in order to prevent further trouble inside the sacred precincts.
21:31 The "commander" (Greek, *chiliarch*) was responsible for 1,000 soldiers (a regiment). His name was Claudius Lysias (23:26), and he was stationed at the Fortress of Antonia.
21:32 "Officers" refers to centurions (see the note on 10:1). Since the plural is used, it is likely that at least two centurions and over 150 soldiers were involved.
21:33 Paul's hands were probably chained to that of a soldier on either side.
21:34 For "barracks," see the note on 12:9.
21:35 The Fortress of Antonia was connected to the northern end of the temple area by two flights of steps. The tower overlooked the temple area (see the note on v. 40; see also "Herod's Temple" on p. 1648).
21:38 Josephus told of an Egyptian false prophet who some years earlier had led 4,000 people (Josephus, through a misreading of a Greek capital letter, reported the number as 30,000) out to the Mount of Olives. Roman soldiers killed hundreds, but the leader escaped.
"Terrorists" (the Greek here is a loanword from Latin *sicarii*, meaning "dagger-men") were violent assassins.
21:39 For "Tarsus," see the note on 22:3.
21:40 The Tower of Antonia was a castle connected to the temple at Jerusalem, rebuilt by Herod the Great at the same time as the temple and named by him in honor of Mark Antony, his patron. A Roman legion was stationed in the castle to guard against excesses on the part of the people. When Paul was seized in the temple by the Jews, he was carried to this castle, from the stairs of which he addressed the people.
Aramaic was the most commonly used language among Palestinian Jews.
22:2 For "Aramaic," see the note on 21:40.
22:3 Paul was a citizen of Tarsus (21:39) as well as of Rome (see "Roman Citizenship" on p. 1930).
Tarsus was located 10 miles (16 km) inland on the Cydnus River and 30 miles (48 km) from the mountains, which were cut by a deep, narrow gorge called the Cilician Gates. The city was an important commercial center, university city and crossroads of travel. Jews had been living in Tarsus since Antiochus Epiphanes' refoundation in 171 B.C., and Paul belonged to a minority that had held Roman citizenship, most likely since Pompey's organization of the East in 66–62 B.C.
Paul must have come to Jerusalem at an early age. Another translation ("brought up in this city at the feet of Gamaliel, being thoroughly trained according to the law of our fathers") would suggest that Paul had come to Jerusalem when he was old enough to begin training under Gamaliel.
Gamaliel, the most honored rabbi of the first century, was probably the grandson of Hillel (see "Gamaliel, Paul's Teacher" on p. 1819).
22:5 Caiaphas, the high priest over 20 years earlier, was now dead, and Ananias was high priest (see 23:2 and its note).
The "Council" refers to the Sanhedrin (see the note on Mk 14:55; see also "The Sanhedrin" on p. 1821).

" 'Get up,' the Lord said, 'and go into Damascus. There you will be told all that you have been assigned
to do.'[j] 11 My companions led me by the hand into Damascus, because the brilliance of the light had blind-
ed me.[k]

12 "A man named Ananias came to see me.[l] He was a devout observer of the law and highly respect-
ed by all the Jews living there.[m] 13 He stood beside me and said, 'Brother Saul, receive your sight!' And at
that very moment I was able to see him.

14 "Then he said: 'The God of our fathers[n] has chosen you to know his will and to see[o] the Righteous
One[p] and to hear words from his mouth. 15 You will be his witness[q] to all men of what you have seen and
heard. 16 And now what are you waiting for? Get up, be baptized[r] and wash your sins away,[s] calling on his
name.'[t]

17 "When I returned to Jerusalem[u] and was praying at the temple, I fell into a trance[v] 18 and saw the
Lord speaking. 'Quick!' he said to me. 'Leave Jerusalem immediately, because they will not accept your tes-
timony about me.'

19 " 'Lord,' I replied, 'these men know that I went from one synagogue to another to imprison[w] and
beat[x] those who believe in you. 20 And when the blood of your martyr[a] Stephen was shed, I stood there
giving my approval and guarding the clothes of those who were killing him.'[y]

21 "Then the Lord said to me, 'Go; I will send you far away to the Gentiles.' "[z]

Paul the Roman Citizen

22 The crowd listened to Paul until he said this. Then they raised their voices and shouted, "Rid the
earth of him![a] He's not fit to live!"[b]

23 As they were shouting and throwing off their cloaks[c] and flinging dust into the air,[d] 24 the com-
mander ordered Paul to be taken into the barracks.[e] He directed[f] that he be flogged and questioned in

22:10 [j]Ac 16:30
22:11 [k]Ac 9:8
22:12 [l]Ac 9:17 [m]Ac 10:22
22:14 [n]Ac 3:13 [o]1Co 9:1; 15:8 [p]Ac 7:52
22:15 [q]Ac 23:11; 26:16
22:16 [r]Ac 2:38 [s]Heb 10:22 [t]Ro 10:13
22:17 [u]Ac 9:26 [v]Ac 10:10
22:19 [w]ver 4; Ac 8:3 [x]Mt 10:17
22:20 [y]Ac 7:57-60; 8:1
22:21 [z]Ac 9:15; 13:46
22:22 [a]Ac 21:36 [b]Ac 25:24
22:23 [c]Ac 7:58 [d]2Sa 16:13
22:24 [e]Ac 21:34 [f]ver 29

[a] 20 Or *witness*

22:24 For "commander," see the note on 21:31 and for "barracks" the notes on 12:9 and 21:35.

"Flogged" here means beaten with the scourge, a merciless instrument of torture. It was legal to use the scourge to force a confession from a slave or alien but never from a Roman citizen. This weapon consisted of a whip of leather thongs with pieces of bone or metal attached to the ends (see the note on Mt 27:26).

Gamaliel, Paul's Teacher

ACTS 22 Gamaliel was one of the greatest teachers of Judaism. His grandfather, Hillel, founded the more liberal of the two main schools of the Pharisees,[1] and Gamaliel was the first of seven leaders of the school of Hillel to be honored with the title *Rabban*, "Our Rabbi." Paul, while making his defense on the steps of the Fortress of Antonia after his arrest in the temple, stated that he had been brought up in Jerusalem and, under Gamaliel, "thoroughly trained in the law of our fathers" (Ac 22:3). Paul, in other words, had received the best possible Jewish education of his day.

Gamaliel is also mentioned in chapter 5 in connection with the appearance of Peter and the apostles before the Sanhedrin on the charge of teaching about Jesus.[2] The members of the Sanhedrin became incensed when Peter and the apostles declared "We must obey God rather than men!" (5:29) and were about to put them to death. But Gamaliel, "a Pharisee . . . a teacher of the law, who was honored by all the people" (5:34), as a member of the Sanhedrin persuaded them to let the apostles go, wisely observing, "If their purpose or activity is of human origin, it will fail. But if it is from God, you will not be able to stop these men" (5:38–39).

Gamaliel was a man of great intellect who studied not only Biblical law but also Greek literature (his love of Greek set him apart from many of his more zealous rabbinical colleagues). Gamaliel tended to be pragmatic in his interpretation of the law and was known for his tolerant attitude. He recommended that Sabbath observance be less rigorous and burdensome, regulated laws of divorce in order to protect women[3] and urged kindness toward Gentiles.

[1]See "The Pharisees" on page 1566. [2]See "The Sanhedrin" on page 1821. [3]See "Marriage and Divorce in Ancient Israel" on page 1548.

order to find out why the people were shouting at him like this. 25 As they stretched him out to flog him,
Paul said to the centurion standing there, "Is it legal for you to flog a Roman citizen who hasn't even been
found guilty?"[g]
26 When the centurion heard this, he went to the commander and reported it. "What are you going to
do?" he asked. "This man is a Roman citizen."
27 The commander went to Paul and asked, "Tell me, are you a Roman citizen?"
"Yes, I am," he answered.
28 Then the commander said, "I had to pay a big price for my citizenship."
"But I was born a citizen," Paul replied.
29 Those who were about to question him withdrew immediately. The commander himself was
alarmed when he realized that he had put Paul, a Roman citizen,[h] in chains.

Before the Sanhedrin

30 The next day, since the commander wanted to find out exactly why Paul was being accused by the
Jews,[i] he released him[j] and ordered the chief priests and all the Sanhedrin[k] to assemble. Then he brought
Paul and had him stand before them.
23 Paul looked straight at the Sanhedrin[l] and said, "My brothers,[m] I have fulfilled my duty to God in
all good conscience[n] to this day." 2 At this the high priest Ananias[o] ordered those standing near Paul
to strike him on the mouth.[p] 3 Then Paul said to him, "God will strike you, you whitewashed wall![q] You sit
there to judge me according to the law, yet you yourself violate the law by commanding that I be struck!"[r]
4 Those who were standing near Paul said, "You dare to insult God's high priest?"
5 Paul replied, "Brothers, I did not realize that he was the high priest; for it is written: 'Do not speak evil
about the ruler of your people.'[a]"[s]
6 Then Paul, knowing that some of them were Sadducees and the others Pharisees, called out in the
Sanhedrin, "My brothers,[t] I am a Pharisee,[u] the son of a Pharisee. I stand on trial because of my hope in
the resurrection of the dead."[v] 7 When he said this, a dispute broke out between the Pharisees and the
Sadducees, and the assembly was divided. 8 (The Sadducees say that there is no resurrection,[w] and that
there are neither angels nor spirits, but the Pharisees acknowledge them all.)
9 There was a great uproar, and some of the teachers of the law who were Pharisees[x] stood up and ar-
gued vigorously. "We find nothing wrong with this man,"[y] they said. "What if a spirit or an angel has spo-
ken to him?"[z] 10 The dispute became so violent that the commander was afraid Paul would be torn to
pieces by them. He ordered the troops to go down and take him away from them by force and bring him
into the barracks.[a]
11 The following night the Lord stood near Paul and said, "Take courage![b] As you have testified about
me in Jerusalem, so you must also testify in Rome."[c]

The Plot to Kill Paul

12 The next morning the Jews formed a conspiracy and bound themselves with an oath not to eat or

22:25 [g]Ac 16:37
22:29 [h]ver 24,25; Ac 16:38
22:30 [i]Ac 23:28 [j]Ac 21:33 [k]Mt 5:22
23:1 [l]Ac 22:30 [m]Ac 22:5 [n]Ac 24:16; 1Co 4:4; 2Co 1:12; 2Ti 1:3; Heb 13:18
23:2 [o]Ac 24:1 [p]Jn 18:22
23:3 [q]Mt 23:27 [r]Lev 19:15; Dt 25:1,2; Jn 7:51
23:5 [s]Ex 22:28
23:6 [t]Ac 22:5 [u]Ac 26:5; Php 3:5 [v]Ac 24:15,21; 26:8
23:8 [w]Mt 22:23
23:9 [x]Mk 2:16 [y]ver 29; Ac 25:25; 26:31 [z]Ac 22:7,17,18
23:10 [a]Ac 21:34
23:11 [b]Ac 18:9 [c]Ac 19:21; 28:23

[a] 5 Exodus 22:28

22:25 The Greek word translated "stretched him out" was used for tying a person to a post for whipping.

For "centurion," see the note on 10:1.

According to Roman law, Roman citizens were assured exclusion from all degrading forms of punishment: beating with rods, scourging or crucifixion (see "Roman Citizenship" on p. 1930).

22:28 There were three ways to obtain Roman citizenship: (1) receive it as a reward for some outstanding service to Rome; (2) buy it at a considerable price; (3) be born into a family of Roman citizens. How Paul's father or an earlier ancestor had gained citizenship no one knows. By 171 B.C. a large number of Jews were citizens of Tarsus (see the note on v. 3), and in the time of Pompey (106–48 B.C.) some of these could have received Roman citizenship as well (see "Roman Citizenship" on p. 1930).

22:30 The "chief priests" were those of the high priestly line of descent (mainly Sadducees; see the notes on Mt 2:4; 3:7), but the Sanhedrin (see the note on Mk 14:55) now included a considerable number of Pharisees (see the notes on Mt 3:7; Lk 5:17). These men constituted the ruling body of the Jews. The Jewish court was respected by the Roman governor (see "The Roman Governor" on p. 1824), whose approval had to be obtained before sentencing to capital punishment.

23:1 For "Sanhedrin," see the note on Mark 14:55, and "The Sanhedrin" on p. 1821.

23:2 Ananias, the son of Nebedaeus, was the high priest from A.D. 47 to 59. He is not to be confused with the high priest Annas (A.D. 6–15; see the note on Lk 3:2). Ananias was noted for cruelty and violence. When the revolt against Rome broke out, he was assassinated by his own people.

23:3 Paul called Ananias a "whitewashed wall"—a metaphor for a hypocrite (see the note on Mt 23:27)—because Ananias had acted improperly in ordering that Paul be struck (Ac 23:2). Striking someone prior to a conviction was illegal. In this case, Paul had not even been properly charged.

23:6 For "Sadducees," see the note on 4:1 and for "Pharisees" the notes on Matthew 3:7 and Luke 5:17.

23:10 For "commander," see the note on 21:31. For "barracks," see the notes on 12:9 and 21:35.

23:12 These Jews were probably from the Zealots (see "The Zealots and the Essenes" on p. 1576) or the "terrorists" (see the note on 21:38) later responsible for revolt against Rome.

For "bound themselves with an oath," see "Oaths in Jewish and Christian Practice" on page 1988.

23:12 [d]ver 14,21, 30; Ac 25:3 drink until they had killed Paul.[d] 13More than forty men were involved in this plot. 14They went to the
chief priests and elders and said, "We have taken a solemn oath not to eat anything until we have killed
23:14 [e]ver 12 23:15 [f]ver 1; Ac 22:30 Paul.[e] 15Now then, you and the Sanhedrin[f] petition the commander to bring him before you on the pre-
text of wanting more accurate information about his case. We are ready to kill him before he gets here."
23:16 [g]ver 10; Ac 21:34 16But when the son of Paul's sister heard of this plot, he went into the barracks[g] and told Paul.
17Then Paul called one of the centurions and said, "Take this young man to the commander; he has
something to tell him." 18So he took him to the commander.
23:18 [h]Eph 3:1 The centurion said, "Paul, the prisoner,[h] sent for me and asked me to bring this young man to you
because he has something to tell you."
19The commander took the young man by the hand, drew him aside and asked, "What is it you want
to tell me?"
23:20 [i]ver 1 [j]ver 14,15 20He said: "The Jews have agreed to ask you to bring Paul before the Sanhedrin[i] tomorrow on the pre-
text of wanting more accurate information about him.[j] 21Don't give in to them, because more than for-
23:21 [k]ver 13 [l]ver 12,14 ty[k] of them are waiting in ambush for him. They have taken an oath not to eat or drink until they have
killed him.[l] They are ready now, waiting for your consent to their request."
22The commander dismissed the young man and cautioned him, "Don't tell anyone that you have re-
ported this to me."

23:17 For "centurions," see the note on 10:1.

The Sanhedrin

ACTS 23 The Greek noun *synedrion* can be used generically to indicate a civic council or a local court. Within the New Testament, however, the Sanhedrin refers to the highest Jewish judicial council in Jerusalem, under the leadership of the high priest (Ac 5:21; 22:5; 23:1–2). According to rabbinic sources, the Jerusalem Sanhedrin was comprised of 71 members, reflecting the Biblical practice instituted by Moses (70 elders plus Moses; see Ex 24:1,9; Nu 11:16).

The idea of a ruling council composed of leading aristocratic citizens reflects the structure of Greek civic constitutions. The high priestly aristocracy played a leading role from the outset, but the Sanhedrin was gradually forced to make way for lay representatives drawn largely from the Pharisees. During the New Testament period, the Jerusalem Sanhedrin consisted of a sometimes mutually-hostile mixture of aristocratic, priestly Sadducees and learned, lay Pharisees (Ac 23:6–9).[1] Membership in the Sanhedrin was conferred by appointment and accompanied by a ceremony of ordination through the laying on of hands (cf. Nu 27:18–23; Dt 34:9).

The Sanhedrin functioned as the supreme Jewish court, trying appellate cases sent up from lower courts and maintaining an exclusive competence over certain cases. For example, a high priest or a false prophet could be tried only by the Jerusalem Sanhedrin. Even during the era of direct Roman rule, the Sanhedrin retained a significant degree of juridical authority. This was particularly true on matters deemed to be of importance specifically within Jewish law (Jn 18:31; Ac 18:15; 24:6).

The authority of the Sanhedrin to adjudicate capital crimes during the first century A.D. has been the focus of much research and debate. Prior to this time the Sanhedrin, like other supreme courts in the ancient world, clearly possessed such authority. But afterward the power of the sword appears to have lain exclusively in Roman hands. The real situation of the first century reflects a period of legal ambiguity, in which both Roman and Jewish leaders competed for ultimate control. On the one hand, key sources attest to a gradual increase in Roman claims to try and execute capital crimes (Josephus, *Antiquities*, 18.1.1; *Wars*, 2.8.1). Some Jewish and Christian sources suggest that capital authority was removed from Israel during this period (Jn 18:31). On the other hand, literary and archaeological sources suggest that the Sanhedrin did in fact possess authority in capital cases, especially in those pertaining to the desecration of the sanctuary or other specifically religious charges, such as blasphemy (Mt 26:59–66; Ac 6:11—7:60; 21:27–33; *Antiquities*, 20.9.1; *Wars*, 6.2.4).

[1]See "The Pharisees" on page 1566 and "The Sadducees" on page 1600.

Paul Transferred to Caesarea

23Then he called two of his centurions and ordered them, "Get ready a detachment of two hundred
soldiers, seventy horsemen and two hundred spearmen[a] to go to Caesarea[m] at nine tonight.[n] 24Provide 23:23 [m]Ac 8:40
mounts for Paul so that he may be taken safely to Governor Felix."[o] [n]ver 33 23:24 [o]ver 26,33;
25He wrote a letter as follows: Ac 24:1-3,10; 25:14

26Claudius Lysias,

To His Excellency,[p] Governor Felix: 23:26 [p]Lk 1:3; Ac 24:3; 26:25
Greetings.[q] [q]Ac 15:23

27This man was seized by the Jews and they were about to kill him,[r] but I came with my troops 23:27 [r]Ac 21:32
and rescued him,[s] for I had learned that he is a Roman citizen.[t] 28I wanted to know why they were [s]Ac 21:33 [t]Ac 22:25-29
accusing him, so I brought him to their Sanhedrin.[u] 29I found that the accusation had to do with 23:28 [u]Ac 22:30
questions about their law,[v] but there was no charge against him[w] that deserved death or impris- 23:29 [v]Ac 18:15;
onment. 30When I was informed[x] of a plot[y] to be carried out against the man, I sent him to you at 25:19 [w]ver 9; Ac 26:31
once. I also ordered his accusers[z] to present to you their case against him. 23:30 [x]ver 20,21 [y]Ac 20:3 [z]ver 35; Ac 24:19; 25:16

31So the soldiers, carrying out their orders, took Paul with them during the night and brought him as
far as Antipatris. 32The next day they let the cavalry[a] go on with him, while they returned to the bar- 23:32 [a]ver 23
racks.[b] 33When the cavalry[c] arrived in Caesarea,[d] they delivered the letter to the governor[e] and handed [b]Ac 21:34 23:33 [c]ver 23,24
Paul over to him. 34The governor read the letter and asked what province he was from. Learning that he [d]Ac 8:40 [e]ver 26
was from Cilicia,[f] 35he said, "I will hear your case when your accusers[g] get here." Then he ordered that 23:34 [f]Ac 6:9; 21:39
Paul be kept under guard[h] in Herod's palace. 23:35 [g]ver 30; Ac 24:19; 25:16 [h]Ac 24:27

The Trial Before Felix

24 Five days later the high priest Ananias[i] went down to Caesarea with some of the elders and a 24:1 [i]Ac 23:2
lawyer named Tertullus, and they brought their charges[j] against Paul before the governor.[k] 2When [j]Ac 23:30,35 [k]Ac 23:24
Paul was called in, Tertullus presented his case before Felix: "We have enjoyed a long period of peace un-
der you, and your foresight has brought about reforms in this nation. 3Everywhere and in every way, most
excellent[l] Felix, we acknowledge this with profound gratitude. 4But in order not to weary you further, I 24:3 [l]Lk 1:3; Ac 23:26; 26:25
would request that you be kind enough to hear us briefly.
5"We have found this man to be a troublemaker, stirring up riots[m] among the Jews[n] all over the world. 24:5 [m]Ac 16:20; 17:6 [n]Ac 21:28

[a] 23 The meaning of the Greek for this word is uncertain.

23:23 Moving a prisoner for his or her own safety or to avoid possible violence or the threat of a riot is a tactic still used today. The commander made every possible provision for Paul's security, sending him off in the company of 470 armed soldiers under cover of darkness.

23:24 For "Governor Felix," see the note on verse 34.

23:31 Antipatris, rebuilt by Herod the Great and named for his father (Antipater), was a military post between Samaria and Judea located 30 miles (48 km) from Jerusalem.

23:33 Caesarea was the headquarters of Roman rule for Samaria and Judea—28 miles (45 km) from Antipatris (see the note on 8:40).

23:34 The governor (see "The Roman Governor" on p. 1824) was Antonius Felix. The emperor Claudius had appointed him governor of Judea in about A.D. 52, a time when Felix's brother was the emperor's favorite minister. The brothers had formerly been slaves, then Freedmen, then high government officials. The historian Tacitus stated of Felix: "He held the power of a tyrant with the disposition of a slave." Felix married three queens in succession, one of whom was Drusilla (see the note on 24:24).

23:35 Herod's palace had been erected as a royal residence by Herod the Great but was now used as a Roman praetorium—the headquarters of the local Roman governor. Praetoria were located in Rome (Php 1:13), Ephesus, Jerusalem (Jn 18:28), Caesarea and other parts of the empire. (See "The Roman Governor" on p. 1824.)

24:1 For "Ananias," see the note on 23:2. The high priest himself made the 60-mile (96-km) journey to supervise the case personally.

The term "elders" was used of both the religious and the political councils. The Sanhedrin was made up of 71 elders (see "The Sanhedrin" on p. 1821).

A lawyer (lit., "orator") was one trained in forensic rhetoric who served as an attorney at law in a court trial.

Tertullus was a common variant of the name Tertius. Only a few words of his elaborate oration are included, but they are enough to reveal the nature of his rhetoric and the character of his accusation. He may have been a Roman, for there is a Latin ring to some of his phrases as they appear in Luke's Greek, and his name is Latin. Tertullus was obviously trained in the art of contemporary rhetoric, (see Debate and Rhetoric inthe Ancient World" on p. 1797) and Luke was impressed with his elaborate introduction, drawing positive attention toward Felix. This was a traditional courtesy, and the device, without the self-seeking flattery, is to be distinguished also in the opening phrases of Paul's reply in verse 10.

24:2 In his six years in office Felix had eliminated bands of robbers, thwarted organized assassins and crushed a movement led by an Egyptian (see the note on 21:38). But in general his record was not good. He was recalled by Rome two years later because of misrule (see the note on 24:27). His reforms and improvements are hard to identify historically.

24:5 To excite dissension in the empire was treason against Caesar, and to be a leader of a religious sect—the "Nazarene sect" refers to Christianity—without Roman approval was contrary to law.

He is a ringleader of the Nazarene[o] sect[p] 6 and even tried to desecrate the temple;[q] so we seized him. 8 By[a]
examining him yourself you will be able to learn the truth about all these charges we are bringing against
him."

9 The Jews joined in the accusation,[r] asserting that these things were true.

10 When the governor[s] motioned for him to speak, Paul replied: "I know that for a number of years
you have been a judge over this nation; so I gladly make my defense. 11 You can easily verify that no more
than twelve days[t] ago I went up to Jerusalem to worship. 12 My accusers did not find me arguing with
anyone at the temple,[u] or stirring up a crowd[v] in the synagogues or anywhere else in the city. 13 And they
cannot prove to you the charges they are now making against me.[w] 14 However, I admit that I worship the
God of our fathers[x] as a follower of the Way,[y] which they call a sect.[z] I believe everything that agrees with
the Law and that is written in the Prophets,[a] 15 and I have the same hope in God as these men, that there
will be a resurrection[b] of both the righteous and the wicked.[c] 16 So I strive always to keep my conscience
clear[d] before God and man.

17 "After an absence of several years, I came to Jerusalem to bring my people gifts for the poor[e] and
to present offerings. 18 I was ceremonially clean[f] when they found me in the temple courts doing this.
There was no crowd with me, nor was I involved in any disturbance.[g] 19 But there are some Jews from the
province of Asia, who ought to be here before you and bring charges if they have anything against me.[h]
20 Or these who are here should state what crime they found in me when I stood before the Sanhedrin—
21 unless it was this one thing I shouted as I stood in their presence: 'It is concerning the resurrection of
the dead that I am on trial before you today.' "[i]

22 Then Felix, who was well acquainted with the Way, adjourned the proceedings. "When Lysias the
commander comes," he said, "I will decide your case." 23 He ordered the centurion to keep Paul under
guard[j] but to give him some freedom[k] and permit his friends to take care of his needs.[l]

24 Several days later Felix came with his wife Drusilla, who was a Jewess. He sent for Paul and listened
to him as he spoke about faith in Christ Jesus.[m] 25 As Paul discoursed on righteousness, self-control[n] and
the judgment[o] to come, Felix was afraid and said, "That's enough for now! You may leave. When I find it
convenient, I will send for you." 26 At the same time he was hoping that Paul would offer him a bribe, so
he sent for him frequently and talked with him.

27 When two years had passed, Felix was succeeded by Porcius Festus,[p] but because Felix wanted to
grant a favor to the Jews,[q] he left Paul in prison.[r]

The Trial Before Festus

25 Three days after arriving in the province, Festus went up from Caesarea[s] to Jerusalem, 2 where
the chief priests and Jewish leaders appeared before him and presented the charges against Paul.[t]
3 They urgently requested Festus, as a favor to them, to have Paul transferred to Jerusalem, for they were
preparing an ambush to kill him along the way. 4 Festus answered, "Paul is being held[u] at Caesarea, and
I myself am going there soon. 5 Let some of your leaders come with me and press charges against the
man there, if he has done anything wrong."

6 After spending eight or ten days with them, he went down to Caesarea, and the next day he convened
the court[v] and ordered that Paul be brought before him. 7 When Paul appeared, the Jews who had come

24:5 [o]Mk 1:24 [p]ver 14; Ac 26:5; 28:22
24:6 [q]Ac 21:28
24:9 [r]1Th 2:16
24:10 [s]Ac 23:24
24:11 [t]Ac 21:27; ver 1
24:12 [u]Ac 25:8; 28:17 [v]ver 18
24:13 [w]Ac 25:7
24:14 [x]Ac 3:13 [y]Ac 9:2 [z]ver 5 [a]Ac 26:6,22; 28:23
24:15 [b]Ac 23:6; 28:20 [c]Da 12:2; Jn 5:28,29
24:16 [d]Ac 23:1
24:17 [e]Ac 11:29, 30; Ro 15:25-28, 31; 1Co 16:1-4, 15; 2Co 8:1-4; Gal 2:10
24:18 [f]Ac 21:26 [g]ver 12
24:19 [h]Ac 23:30
24:21 [i]Ac 23:6
24:23 [j]Ac 23:35 [k]Ac 28:16 [l]Ac 23:16; 27:3
24:24 [m]Ac 20:21
24:25 [n]Gal 5:23; 2Pe 1:6 [o]Ac 10:42
24:27 [p]Ac 25:1,4, 9,14 [q]Ac 12:3; 25:9 [r]Ac 23:35; 25:14
25:1 [s]Ac 8:40
25:2 [t]ver 15; Ac 24:1
25:4 [u]Ac 24:23
25:6 [v]ver 17

[a] 6-8 Some manuscripts *him and wanted to judge him according to our law. 7But the commander, Lysias, came and with the use of much force snatched him from our hands 8and ordered his accusers to come before you. By*

24:14 Paul admitted to his part in the Way (see the note on 19:23) but still believed the Law and the Prophets (i.e., the Old Testament Scriptures; see "The Old Testament of the Early Church" on p. 1967).

24:23 Perhaps Paul was under house arrest similar to that which he experienced while awaiting trial in Rome (28:30–31; see "Imprisonment in the Roman World: In Prison Versus House Arrest" on p. 1826)—in recognition of the fact that he was a Roman citizen who had not been found guilty of any crime.

24:24 Drusilla was the youngest of the three daughters of Herod Agrippa I, her sisters being Bernice and Mariamhe (see the note on "Bernice" at 25:13). At the age of fourteen she married Azizus, King of Emesa, but left him for Felix, procurator of Judea, who was captivated by her beauty and employed a Cyprian sorcerer to gain her for his wife. The couple had one son, Agrippa, who died in the eruption of Mount Vesuvius in A.D. 79.

24:27 Felix was recalled to Rome in A.D. 59/60 to answer for disturbances and irregularities in his rule, such as his mishandling of riots between Jewish and Syrian inhabitants. Festus is not mentioned in existing historical records before his arrival in Judea. He died in office after two years, but his record for that time reflects wisdom and honesty superior to those of either his predecessor, Felix, or his successor, Albinus.

See "Imprisonment in the Roman World: In Prison Versus House Arrest" on page 1826.

25:1 The trip from Caesarea to Jerusalem was 60 miles (97 km), requiring two days. Festus was anxious to go immediately to the center of Jewish rule and worship.

25:2 The "chief priests and Jewish leaders" is a reference to the Sanhedrin (see the note on Mk 14:55; see also "The Sanhedrin" on p. 1821).

25:6 For "court," see "The Judgment Seat" on page 1891.

down from Jerusalem stood around him, bringing many serious charges against him,[w] which they could
not prove.[x]
[8]Then Paul made his defense: "I have done nothing wrong against the law of the Jews or against the
temple[y] or against Caesar."
[9]Festus, wishing to do the Jews a favor,[z] said to Paul, "Are you willing to go up to Jerusalem and stand
trial before me there on these charges?"[a]
[10]Paul answered: "I am now standing before Caesar's court, where I ought to be tried. I have not done
any wrong to the Jews, as you yourself know very well. [11]If, however, I am guilty of doing anything de-
serving death, I do not refuse to die. But if the charges brought against me by these Jews are not true, no
one has the right to hand me over to them. I appeal to Caesar!"[b]
[12]After Festus had conferred with his council, he declared: "You have appealed to Caesar. To Caesar you
will go!"

25:7 [w]Mk 15:3; Lk 23:2,10; Ac 24:5,6 [x]Ac 24:13
25:8 [y]Ac 6:13; 24:12; 28:17
25:9 [z]Ac 24:27 [a]ver 20
25:11 [b]ver 21,25; Ac 26:32; 28:19

25:9 Paul wanted his trial to be conducted in Caesarea rather than to suffer at the hands of a Jewish religious court. As a Roman citizen, he could refuse to go to a local provincial court; instead, he looked to a higher Roman court.
25:11 Nero had become emperor by this time (see "Nero, Persecutor of Christians" on p. 1931). It was the right of every Roman citizen to have his case heard before Caesar himself (or his representative) in Rome (see "Rome" on p. 1838). This was the highest court of appeal, and winning such a case could have led to more than just Paul's acquittal: It could have resulted in official recognition of Christianity as distinct from Judaism.
25:12 Festus's "council" refers to the officials and legal experts who made up the advisory council for the Roman governor.

The Roman Governor

ACTS 25 Six Roman governors are mentioned in the New Testament: Quirinius (Syria; Lk 2:2), Pilate (Judea; Mt 27:2–65, etc.),[1] Sergius Paulus (Cyprus; Ac 13:6–12),[2] Gallio (Achaia; 18:12–17), Felix (Judea; 23:23—24:27; 25:14)[3] and Festus (Judea; 24:27—26:32). They administered their provinces from a capital city and lived in a palace-fortress called a praetorium. In Judea the Roman administrative center was at Caesarea Maritima on the Mediterranean coast; there Paul was held prisoner (23:33–35).[4] There was also a praetorium in Jerusalem where the governor would stay when he was in residence there; there Jesus was tried and mocked (Mt 27:27; Mk 15:16; Jn 18:28; 19:9).

When Archelaus, the son of Herod the Great, was stripped of his power in A.D. 6, the governance of the territory of Judea was transferred to the ruler of Syria, Quirinius.[5] Coponius was chosen as the new governor of Judea and was given the title of praefectus (prefect). The prefect alone controlled the appointment of high priests and retained the prerogative of capital punishment. In cases in which the sanctity of the temple had allegedly been violated, the Sanhedrin may also have been able to exercise the right to impose the death sentence, but even then the governor had to give his consent.[6] After A.D. 44 the governor's title was changed to procurator, an equestrian rank. Although the procurator continued to exercise full judicial powers, he lost the right to appoint and depose high priests.

Felix, a freed slave of the family of Emperor Claudius,[7] was governor of Judea from A.D. 52 to 60. During his tenure Felix married Drusilla, the great-granddaughter of Herod the Great (24:24).[8] His rule was marked by unrest, and he was ultimately recalled to Rome and tried for his misgovernment, resulting in banishment. Paul was confined at Caesarea for two years, until Festus replaced Felix in A.D. 60 (24:27).[9] Festus speedily acted upon Paul's case and granted his request to be tried in Rome (25:12). Festus's term was cut short when he died unexpectedly two years after his appointment. According to Josephus (*Antiquities*, 20.9.1), before Festus's successor arrived in Judea, the high priest Ananias usurped the procurator's sole right to impose capital punishment and had James the brother of Jesus executed, along with several others whom he claimed had broken Jewish law.[10]

[1]See "Pontius Pilate" on page 1714. [2]See "Sergius Paulus, Proconsul of Cyprus" on page 1793. [3]See "Gallio, Proconsul of Achaia" on page 1806. [4]See "Caesarea Maritima" on page 1786. [5]See "Caesar Augustus, Emperor of Rome; the Census; and Quirinius, Governor of Syria" on page 1667. [6]See "The Sanhedrin" on page 1821. [7]See "Claudius, Emperor of Rome" on page 1788. [8]See "Herod the Great" on page 1627. [9]See "Imprisonment in the Roman World: In Prison Versus House Arrest" on page 1826. [10]See "The High Priests Annas and Caiaphas" on page 1772.

Festus Consults King Agrippa

25:13 [c]Ac 8:40 13A few days later King Agrippa and Bernice arrived at Caesarea[c] to pay their respects to Festus.
14Since they were spending many days there, Festus discussed Paul's case with the king. He said: "There
25:14 [d]Ac 24:27 is a man here whom Felix left as a prisoner.[d] 15When I went to Jerusalem, the chief priests and elders of
25:15 [e]ver 2; the Jews brought charges against him[e] and asked that he be condemned.
Ac 24:1 16"I told them that it is not the Roman custom to hand over any man before he has faced his accus-
25:16 [f]ver 4,5; ers and has had an opportunity to defend himself against their charges.[f] 17When they came here with me,
Ac 23:30 25:17 [g]ver 6,10 I did not delay the case, but convened the court the next day and ordered the man to be brought in.[g]
18When his accusers got up to speak, they did not charge him with any of the crimes I had expected.
25:19 [h]Ac 18:15; 19Instead, they had some points of dispute[h] with him about their own religion[i] and about a dead man
23:29 [i]Ac 17:22 named Jesus who Paul claimed was alive. 20I was at a loss how to investigate such matters; so I asked if
25:20 [j]ver 9 he would be willing to go to Jerusalem and stand trial there on these charges.[j] 21When Paul made his ap-
25:21 [k]ver 11,12 peal to be held over for the Emperor's decision, I ordered him held until I could send him to Caesar."[k]
22Then Agrippa said to Festus, "I would like to hear this man myself."
25:22 [l]Ac 9:15 He replied, "Tomorrow you will hear him."[l]

Paul Before Agrippa

25:23 [m]ver 13; 23The next day Agrippa and Bernice[m] came with great pomp and entered the audience room with the
Ac 26:30 high ranking officers and the leading men of the city. At the command of Festus, Paul was brought in.
24Festus said: "King Agrippa, and all who are present with us, you see this man! The whole Jewish com-
25:24 [n]ver 2,3,7 munity[n] has petitioned me about him in Jerusalem and here in Caesarea, shouting that he ought not to
[o]Ac 22:22 25:25 [p]Ac 23:9 live any longer.[o] 25I found he had done nothing deserving of death,[p] but because he made his appeal to
[q]ver 11 the Emperor[q] I decided to send him to Rome. 26But I have nothing definite to write to His Majesty about
him. Therefore I have brought him before all of you, and especially before you, King Agrippa, so that as
a result of this investigation I may have something to write. 27For I think it is unreasonable to send on a
prisoner without specifying the charges against him."

26:1 [r]Ac 9:15; 26 Then Agrippa said to Paul, "You have permission to speak for yourself."[r]
25:22 So Paul motioned with his hand and began his defense: 2"King Agrippa, I consider myself for-
tunate to stand before you today as I make my defense against all the accusations of the Jews, 3and es-
26:3 [s]ver 7; pecially so because you are well acquainted with all the Jewish customs[s] and controversies.[t] Therefore,
Ac 6:14 [t]Ac 25:19 I beg you to listen to me patiently.
26:4 [u]Gal 1:13, 4"The Jews all know the way I have lived ever since I was a child,[u] from the beginning of my life in my
14; Php 3:5 26:5 [v]Ac 22:3 own country, and also in Jerusalem. 5They have known me for a long time[v] and can testify, if they are will-
[w]Ac 23:6; Php 3:5 26:6 [x]Ac 23:6; ing, that according to the strictest sect of our religion, I lived as a Pharisee.[w] 6And now it is because of
24:15; 28:20 [y]Ac 13:32; my hope[x] in what God has promised our fathers[y] that I am on trial today. 7This is the promise our twelve
Ro 15:8 26:7 [z]Jas 1:1 tribes[z] are hoping to see fulfilled as they earnestly serve God day and night.[a] O king, it is because of this
[a]1Th 3:10; 1Ti 5:5 [b]ver 2 hope that the Jews are accusing me.[b] 8Why should any of you consider it incredible that God raises the
26:8 [c]Ac 23:6 dead?[c]

25:13 "King Agrippa" was Herod Agrippa II. He was seventeen years old at the death of his father, Herod Agrippa I, in A.D. 44. Being too young to succeed his father, he was replaced by Roman governors. Eight years later, however, a gradual extension of his territorial authority began. Ultimately he ruled over territory north and northeast of the Sea of Galilee, over several Galilean cities and over some cities in Perea. At the Jewish revolt, when Jerusalem fell, he was on the side of the Romans. He died in about A.D. 100—the last of the Herods.

Bernice, the oldest daughter of Agrippa I, is mentioned three times in Acts (here; v. 23; 26:30). According to Josephus, she was first married to Marcus, after whose death she became the wife of Herod of Chalcis, her uncle (*Antiquities*, 19.5.1; 20.7.1–3). After Herod's death Bernice lived with Agrippa II, her brother, and was rumored to be involved in an incestuous relationship with him. Later she was married to Polemo of Cilicia. This marriage was of short duration, as she returned to Agrippa. She was later the mistress of Vespasian and Titus, who finally cast her aside.

It was customary for rulers to pay a complimentary visit to a new ruler at the time of his assignment. It was advantageous to each that they get along well together.

25:23 The "audience room" was not the judgment hall, for this was not a court trial. It was an auditorium appropriate for the pomp of the occasion, with a king, his sister, the Roman governor and the outstanding teachers of both the Jews and the Roman government present.

Five regiments were stationed at Caesarea, so their five commanders (the "high ranking officers") would have been in attendance.

25:26 Festus was required to send Caesar an explicit report on the case when an appeal was made. He hoped for some help from Agrippa in this matter. This was not an official trial but a special hearing to satisfy the curiosity of Agrippa and provide an assessment for Festus.

King Agrippa would have been sensitive to differences between Pharisees (see the notes on Mt 3:7 and Lk 5:17) and Sadducees (see the note on Mt 3:7), varying expectations of the Messiah, differences between Jews and Christians and Jewish customs pertinent to these issues.

26:3 As king, Agrippa controlled the temple treasury and the investments of the high priest and could appoint the high priest. He was consulted by the Romans on religious matters. This is one of the reasons Festus wanted him to assess Paul.

26:5 For "Pharisee," see the notes on Matthew 3:7 and Luke 5:17.

Imprisonment in the Roman World: In Prison Versus House Arrest

ACTS 26 Persons were imprisoned in Roman times while awaiting trial or execution, for political reasons or for ensuring compliance with a judicial order. Paul was detained for trial in Caesarea (Ac 23:33—24:27) and in Rome (Ac 28:16), John the Baptist was imprisoned for accusing Herod of adultery and thus threatening his political authority (Lk 3:19–20) and debtors were sometimes imprisoned to pressure them to pay their debts (Mt 18:30; Lk 12:58). Imprisonment as a method of formal punishment was rare.

Times of detention were neither limited nor strongly enforced, and ordinarily the prisoner was poorly treated. Many were beaten, tortured and given inadequate food and water, although a prisoner of higher status would often fare better. Herod Agrippa I, before he became ethnarch of Judea and **Samaria** (Ac 12), experienced various degrees of imprisonment. At first Emperor Tiberius[1] placed him in chains in a military camp under the prefect of the praetorians in Rome. Tiberius's sister-in-law, Antonia, lessened the severity of conditions during this incarceration, asking the guard to be more humane, to allow Agrippa to bathe every day and to permit his friends to bring him food and clothing. After Tiberius died Agrippa was allowed to live in his own private residence. He was still guarded and chained at the wrist to a guard each day but was permitted to handle his own affairs (Josephus, *Antiquities*, 18.6.6–11).

Paul was probably detained in the Praetorium, a fortress or governor's residence, while in Caesarea.[2] While in Rome he was allowed to dwell outside the military camp, as well as to find and rent his own quarters. He received this relatively mild treatment for three reasons:

- Paul was a Roman citizen.[3]
- He had received favorable verdicts from governors Festus and Agrippa.
- The praetorian prefect overseeing prisoners from the provinces in the years A.D. 51–62 was the honest Afranius Burrus.

Paul's trial took two years to conclude. According to Eusebius (*History*, 2.22,25), Paul was released but later detained again in Rome when Nero began to execute Christians.[4] Paul was at that point probably placed in the *tullianum*, the underground execution cell of the prison at Rome.

[1]See "Tiberius Caesar, the Caesar of Jesus' Ministry" on page 1708. [2]See "Caesarea Maritima" on page 1786. [3]See "Roman Citizenship" on page 1930. [4]See "Nero, Persecutor of Christians" on page 1931 and "The Early Persecution of the Church" on page 2067.

Agrippa's palace in Caesarea; probably the place of Paul's imprisonment

Preserving Bible Times; © Dr. James C. Martin

9“I too was convinced[d] that I ought to do all that was possible to oppose[e] the name of Jesus of Naza-
reth.[f] 10And that is just what I did in Jerusalem. On the authority of the chief priests I put many of the
saints[g] in prison,[h] and when they were put to death, I cast my vote against them.[i] 11Many a time I went
from one synagogue to another to have them punished,[j] and I tried to force them to blaspheme. In my
obsession against them, I even went to foreign cities to persecute them.

12“On one of these journeys I was going to Damascus with the authority and commission of the chief
priests. 13About noon, O king, as I was on the road, I saw a light from heaven, brighter than the sun, blaz-
ing around me and my companions. 14We all fell to the ground, and I heard a voice[k] saying to me in Ar-
amaic,[a] ‘Saul, Saul, why do you persecute me? It is hard for you to kick against the goads.’

15“Then I asked, ‘Who are you, Lord?’

“ ‘I am Jesus, whom you are persecuting,’ the Lord replied. 16‘Now get up and stand on your feet.[l] I
have appeared to you to appoint you as a servant and as a witness of what you have seen of me and
what I will show you.[m] 17I will rescue you[n] from your own people and from the Gentiles.[o] I am sending
you to them 18to open their eyes[p] and turn them from darkness to light,[q] and from the power of Satan
to God, so that they may receive forgiveness of sins[r] and a place among those who are sanctified by faith
in me.’[s]

19“So then, King Agrippa, I was not disobedient to the vision from heaven. 20First to those in Damas-
cus,[t] then to those in Jerusalem[u] and in all Judea, and to the Gentiles[v] also, I preached that they should
repent[w] and turn to God and prove their repentance by their deeds.[x] 21That is why the Jews seized me[y]
in the temple courts and tried to kill me.[z] 22But I have had God’s help to this very day, and so I stand here
and testify to small and great alike. I am saying nothing beyond what the prophets and Moses said would
happen[a]— 23that the Christ[b] would suffer and, as the first to rise from the dead,[b] would proclaim light
to his own people and to the Gentiles.”[c]

24At this point Festus interrupted Paul’s defense. “You are out of your mind,[d] Paul!” he shouted. “Your
great learning[e] is driving you insane.”

25“I am not insane, most excellent[f] Festus,” Paul replied. “What I am saying is true and reasonable.
26The king is familiar with these things,[g] and I can speak freely to him. I am convinced that none of this
has escaped his notice, because it was not done in a corner. 27King Agrippa, do you believe the prophets?
I know you do.”

28Then Agrippa said to Paul, “Do you think that in such a short time you can persuade me to be a
Christian?”[h]

29Paul replied, “Short time or long—I pray God that not only you but all who are listening to me to-
day may become what I am, except for these chains.”[i]

30The king rose, and with him the governor and Bernice[j] and those sitting with them. 31They left the
room, and while talking with one another, they said, “This man is not doing anything that deserves death
or imprisonment.”[k]

32Agrippa said to Festus, “This man could have been set free[l] if he had not appealed to Caesar.”[m]

Paul Sails for Rome

27 When it was decided that we[n] would sail for Italy,[o] Paul and some other prisoners were handed
over to a centurion named Julius, who belonged to the Imperial Regiment.[p] 2We boarded a ship
from Adramyttium about to sail for ports along the coast of the province of Asia,[q] and we put out to sea.
Aristarchus,[r] a Macedonian[s] from Thessalonica,[t] was with us.

3The next day we landed at Sidon;[u] and Julius, in kindness to Paul,[v] allowed him to go to his friends

26:9 [d]1Ti 1:13 [e]Jn 16:2 [f]Jn 15:21
26:10 [g]Ac 9:13 [h]Ac 8:3; 9:2,14, 21 [i]Ac 22:20
26:11 [j]Mt 10:17
26:14 [k]Ac 9:7
26:16 [l]Eze 2:1; Da 10:11 [m]Ac 22:14,15
26:17 [n]Jer 1:8,19 [o]Ac 9:15
26:18 [p]Isa 35:5 [q]Isa 42:7,16; Eph 5:8; Col 1:13; 1Pe 2:9 [r]Lk 24:47; Ac 2:38 [s]Ac 20:21,32
26:20 [t]Ac 9:19-25 [u]Ac 9:26-29; 22:17-20 [v]Ac 9:15; 13:46 [w]Ac 3:19 [x]Mt 3:8; Lk 3:8
26:21 [y]Ac 21:27, 30 [z]Ac 21:31
26:22 [a]Lk 24:27, 44; Ac 10:43; 24:14
26:23 [b]1Co 15:20,23; Col 1:18; Rev 1:5 [c]Lk 2:32
26:24 [d]Jn 10:20; 1Co 4:10 [e]Jn 7:15
26:25 [f]Ac 23:26
26:26 [g]ver 3
26:28 [h]Ac 11:26
26:29 [i]Ac 21:33
26:30 [j]Ac 25:23
26:31 [k]Ac 23:9
26:32 [l]Ac 28:18 [m]Ac 25:11
27:1 [n]Ac 16:10 [o]Ac 18:2; 25:12, 25 [p]Ac 10:1
27:2 [q]Ac 2:9 [r]Ac 19:29 [s]Ac 16:9 [t]Ac 17:1
27:3 [u]Mt 11:21 [v]ver 43

[a] *14* Or *Hebrew* [b] *23* Or *Messiah*

26:22 "The prophets and Moses" refers to the Old Testament Scriptures (see "The Old Testament of the Early Church" on p. 1967).

26:24 The governor felt that Paul's education and reading of the sacred Scriptures had led him to a mania about prophecy and resurrection.

26:27 As an expert on Jewish Scripture, this king knew what Paul was talking about.

26:30 For "Bernice," she the note on 25:13.

27:1 For "Italy," see the note on 10:1.

Luke had probably spent the two years of Paul's Caesarean imprisonment nearby, and now he joined those ready to sail.

The "centurion named Julius" is otherwise unknown. Perhaps he was given the specific duties of an imperial courier, which included delivering prisoners for trial.

The Roman legions were designated by number, and each of the regiments also had a designation. The identification "Augustan," or "Imperial" (belonging to the empire), was common.

27:2 Adramyttium was a harbor on the western coast of the province of Asia, southeast of Troas and east of Assos. At one of these stops Julius would have planned to transfer to a ship going to Rome (see "Rome" on p. 1838).

27:3 Sidon was about 70 miles (113 km) north of Caesarea.

so they might provide for his needs.[w] [4]From there we put out to sea again and passed to the lee of Cyprus because the winds were against us.[x] [5]When we had sailed across the open sea off the coast of Cilicia[y] and Pamphylia, we landed at Myra in Lycia. [6]There the centurion found an Alexandrian ship[z] sailing for Italy[a] and put us on board. [7]We made slow headway for many days and had difficulty arriving off Cnidus. When the wind did not allow us to hold our course,[b] we sailed to the lee of Crete,[c] opposite Salmone. [8]We moved along the coast with difficulty and came to a place called Fair Havens, near the town of Lasea.

[9]Much time had been lost, and sailing had already become dangerous because by now it was after the Fast.[a][d] So Paul warned them, [10]"Men, I can see that our voyage is going to be disastrous and bring great loss to ship and cargo, and to our own lives also."[e] [11]But the centurion, instead of listening to what Paul said, followed the advice of the pilot and of the owner of the ship. [12]Since the harbor was unsuitable to winter in, the majority decided that we should sail on, hoping to reach Phoenix and winter there. This was a harbor in Crete, facing both southwest and northwest.

The Storm

[13]When a gentle south wind began to blow, they thought they had obtained what they wanted; so they weighed anchor and sailed along the shore of Crete. [14]Before very long, a wind of hurricane force,[f] called the "northeaster," swept down from the island. [15]The ship was caught by the storm and could not head into the wind; so we gave way to it and were driven along. [16]As we passed to the lee of a small island called Cauda, we were hardly able to make the lifeboat secure. [17]When the men had hoisted it aboard, they passed ropes under the ship itself to hold it together. Fearing that they would run aground[g] on the sandbars of Syrtis, they lowered the sea anchor and let the ship be driven along. [18]We took such a violent battering from the storm that the next day they began to throw the cargo overboard.[h] [19]On the third day, they threw the ship's tackle overboard with their own hands. [20]When neither sun nor stars appeared for many days and the storm continued raging, we finally gave up all hope of being saved.

[21]After the men had gone a long time without food, Paul stood up before them and said: "Men, you should have taken my advice[i] not to sail from Crete;[j] then you would have spared yourselves this damage and loss. [22]But now I urge you to keep up your courage,[k] because not one of you will be lost; only the ship will be destroyed. [23]Last night an angel[l] of the God whose I am and whom I serve[m] stood beside me[n] [24]and said, 'Do not be afraid, Paul. You must stand trial before Caesar;[o] and God has graciously given

27:3 [w]Ac 24:23; 28:16
27:4 [x]ver 7
27:5 [y]Ac 6:9
27:6 [z]Ac 28:11 [a]ver 1
27:7 [b]ver 4 [c]ver 12,13,21
27:9 [d]Lev 16:29-31; 23:27-29; Nu 29:7
27:10 [e]ver 21
27:14 [f]Mk 4:37
27:17 [g]ver 26,39
27:18 [h]ver 19,38; Jnh 1:5
27:21 [i]ver 10 [j]ver 7
27:22 [k]ver 25,36
27:23 [l]Ac 5:19 [m]Ro 1:9 [n]Ac 18:9; 23:11; 2Ti 4:17
27:24 [o]Ac 23:11

[a] *9* That is, the Day of Atonement (Yom Kippur)

27:4 They sought the protecting shelter of the island by sailing north on the eastern side of the island, then west along the northern side. Prevailing winds in the summertime were westerly.

27:5–6 For a discussion of travel by land or sea in Bible times, see the note on Jonah 1:3 and "Travel in the Greco-Roman World" on page 1946.

Cilicia and Pamphylia were adjoining provinces on the southern shore of Asia Minor. From Sidon to Myra along this coast would ordinarily have entailed a voyage of from 10 to 15 days.

The growing importance of the city of Myra was associated with the development of navigation. Instead of hugging the coast from point to point, more ships were daring to run directly from Alexandria in Egypt to harbors like Myra on the southern coast of Asia Minor. Myra was considerably out of the way on the trip to Rome from Egypt, but the prevailing westerly wind would not allow a direct voyage toward the west. Myra became an important grain-storage city as well.

27:6 The "Alexandrian ship" had originated in Egypt (with grain cargo, v. 38) and was bound for Rome (see "Alexandria" on p. 1805 and "Rome" on p. 1838.

27:7 From Myra to Cnidus at the southwest point of Asia Minor was a trip of about 170 miles (273.5 km). The journey probably took another 10 to 15 days.

Crete is an island 156 miles (250 km) long. Rather than crossing the open sea to Greece, the ship was forced to bear south, seeking to sail west with the protection of the island of Crete on the north. (See "Crete" on p. 1972.)

27:8 Fair Havens was a port about midway on the southern coast of Crete. Lasea was a city about five miles (eight km) away.

27:9 "The Fast" was the Jewish Day of Atonement. It fell in the latter part of September or in October. The usual sailing season by Jewish calculation lasted from Pentecost (May-June) to Tabernacles, which fell five days after the Fast. The Romans considered the prospect of sailing after September 15 doubtful and after November 11 suicidal.

27:12 Phoenix was a small port city that served as a wintering place, having a harbor with protection against the storms. Its precise location is debated, although it was clearly located on the western end of Crete.

27:13 In ancient times every ship carried several anchors. In successive periods these were made of stone, iron, lead and perhaps other metals. Each had two flukes (the part of the anchor that fastens to the ground) and was held by a cable or a chain. The word "anchor" is used here and in verses 17, 29, 30 and 40, as well as in Hebrews 6:19 (in a figurative sense in this last reference).

27:14 A "northeaster" was a typhoon-like, east-northeast wind (the *Euroquilo*), which drove the ship away from its destination.

27:16 Cauda (now called Gavdo) was a small island about 23 miles (37 km) from Crete. It provided enough shelter to make preparation against the storm.

A "lifeboat" being towed behind the ship was interfering with its progress and with the steering. It may also have been in danger of being crushed against the ship in the wind and the waves and had to be taken aboard.

27:17 The ropes were probably passed crosswise underneath the ship in order to prevent it from being broken apart by the storm.

Syrtis, a long stretch of desolate banks of quicksand along northern Africa off the coast of Tunis and Tripoli, was still far away, but in such a storm the ship could have been driven a great distance.

The sea anchor was apparently lowered to keep the ship from running onto the sandbars of Syrtis. Alternatively, the Greek translated "sea anchor" may be rendered "mainsail."

27:18 Cargo was thrown overboard to lighten the ship. The crew retained some bags of grain, however.

27:19 A "ship's tackle"—spars, planks and perhaps the yardarm with the mainsail attached—were at times dragged behind, serving as a brake.

The Roman Army and the Occupation of the Holy Land

Roman soldier's helmet

Preserving Bible Times; © Dr. James C. Martin; permission of The Israel Museum

ACTS 27 The Roman army was arguably the greatest single military organization in world history, as it was consistently victorious and maintained its identity and traditions for nearly a thousand years. The early Roman armies were composed entirely of property-owning citizens because service in the army was regarded as a privilege. Wealthier citizens formed the cavalry and poorer citizens the infantry (a necessary arrangement, since troops provided their own gear). Allies provided the manpower for specialized forces, such as archers. As Rome grew to be a world power, however, this arrangement proved inadequate.

In 107 B.C. C. Marius reformed the army and accepted landless recruits, equipping them at state expense. This was the beginning of professional Roman armies that owed their allegiance to their generals and also expected from them rich rewards for years of loyal service. In 88 B.C. Sulla used his legions to seize power in Rome itself, and this precedent began a series of civil wars. Julius Caesar employed his armies to end the republic and establish himself as dictator, but the turmoil did not end until Augustus established the empire and placed all legions under his direct command.[1]

Although Rome produced a number of great generals, the secret of Roman success lay in the legendary discipline of its troops. Ancient battles, because they were fought face-to-face and were bloody affairs, tended to be extremely short, typically ending as soon as one side panicked, broke ranks and fled. Romans, when confronted, for example, with a furious onslaught of Gauls, simply refused to break ranks, and after a few minutes of fighting the Gauls turned and ran. The Carthaginian Hannibal, the greatest general Rome ever faced, inflicted a terrible defeat on the Roman army at Cannae in 216 B.C. Even so, Roman perseverance won out, and Hannibal ultimately lost the Second Punic War.

The presence of Roman armies in Judea created an explosive situation. The Jews despised the Romans as pagans and were offended at the presence of Roman war standards, with the idol-like eagle at the top, in close proximity to their temple. Fanatics and messianic pretenders, such as Bar-Kokhba, assured the Jews that God would intervene if they were to rise up against Rome. For their part, Romans sometimes infuriated Jews with needless insults. Two Jewish revolts (A.D. 66–70 and 132–135) both ended in catastrophic defeat for the Jewish people.

[1]See "Rome" on page 1838 and "The Roman Empire" on page 1845.

Roman roof tile found in Britain with the emblem of the twentieth legion, the boar

Preserving Bible Times; © Dr. James C. Martin

you the lives of all who sail with you.'[p] 25 So keep up your courage,[q] men, for I have faith in God that it will
happen just as he told me.[r] 26 Nevertheless, we must run aground[s] on some island."[t]

The Shipwreck

27 On the fourteenth night we were still being driven across the Adriatic[a] Sea, when about midnight
the sailors sensed they were approaching land. 28 They took soundings and found that the water was a
hundred and twenty feet[b] deep. A short time later they took soundings again and found it was ninety
feet[c] deep. 29 Fearing that we would be dashed against the rocks, they dropped four anchors from the
stern and prayed for daylight. 30 In an attempt to escape from the ship, the sailors let the lifeboat[u] down
into the sea, pretending they were going to lower some anchors from the bow. 31 Then Paul said to the
centurion and the soldiers, "Unless these men stay with the ship, you cannot be saved."[v] 32 So the soldiers
cut the ropes that held the lifeboat and let it fall away.

33 Just before dawn Paul urged them all to eat. "For the last fourteen days," he said, "you have been in
constant suspense and have gone without food—you haven't eaten anything. 34 Now I urge you to take
some food. You need it to survive. Not one of you will lose a single hair from his head."[w] 35 After he said
this, he took some bread and gave thanks to God in front of them all. Then he broke it[x] and began to
eat. 36 They were all encouraged[y] and ate some food themselves. 37 Altogether there were 276 of us on
board. 38 When they had eaten as much as they wanted, they lightened the ship by throwing the grain
into the sea.[z]

39 When daylight came, they did not recognize the land, but they saw a bay with a sandy beach,[a] where
they decided to run the ship aground if they could. 40 Cutting loose the anchors,[b] they left them in the sea
and at the same time untied the ropes that held the rudders. Then they hoisted the foresail to the wind
and made for the beach. 41 But the ship struck a sandbar and ran aground. The bow stuck fast and would
not move, and the stern was broken to pieces by the pounding of the surf.[c]

42 The soldiers planned to kill the prisoners to prevent any of them from swimming away and escap-
ing. 43 But the centurion wanted to spare Paul's life[d] and kept them from carrying out their plan. He or-
dered those who could swim to jump overboard first and get to land. 44 The rest were to get there on
planks or on pieces of the ship. In this way everyone reached land in safety.[e]

Ashore on Malta

28 Once safely on shore, we[f] found out that the island[g] was called Malta. 2 The islanders showed us
unusual kindness. They built a fire and welcomed us all because it was raining and cold. 3 Paul
gathered a pile of brushwood and, as he put it on the fire, a viper, driven out by the heat, fastened itself
on his hand. 4 When the islanders saw the snake hanging from his hand,[h] they said to each other, "This
man must be a murderer; for though he escaped from the sea, Justice has not allowed him to live."[i] 5 But
Paul shook the snake off into the fire and suffered no ill effects.[j] 6 The people expected him to swell up
or suddenly fall dead, but after waiting a long time and seeing nothing unusual happen to him, they
changed their minds and said he was a god.[k]

7 There was an estate nearby that belonged to Publius, the chief official of the island. He welcomed us

27:24 [p] ver 44
27:25 [q] ver 22,36 [r] Ro 4:20,21
27:26 [s] ver 17,39 [t] Ac 28:1
27:30 [u] ver 16
27:31 [v] ver 24
27:34 [w] Mt 10:30
27:35 [x] Mt 14:19
27:36 [y] ver 22,25
27:38 [z] ver 18; Jnh 1:5
27:39 [a] Ac 28:1
27:40 [b] ver 29
27:41 [c] 2Co 11:25
27:43 [d] ver 3
27:44 [e] ver 22,31
28:1 [f] Ac 16:10 [g] Ac 27:26,39
28:4 [h] Mk 16:18 [i] Lk 13:2,4
28:5 [j] Lk 10:19
28:6 [k] Ac 14:11

[a] *27* In ancient times the name referred to an area extending well south of Italy. [b] *28* Greek *twenty orguias* (about 37 meters)
[c] *28* Greek *fifteen orguias* (about 27 meters)

27:27 The Adriatic Sea is the sea between Italy, Malta, Crete and Greece. In ancient times it extended as far south as Sicily and Crete. (Some think that this sea included all of the area between Greece, Italy and Africa and that it was known as the Adrian, not the Adriatic, Sea.) The modern usage of "Adriatic" describes a smaller area.
27:28 The sailors measured the depth of the sea by letting down a weighted line.
27:30 Without a port for the ship, the sailors felt that their chance for survival was better in the single lifeboat, unencumbered by the many passengers.
27:31 The sailors were needed to successfully beach the ship the next day.
27:37 To note the number on board may have been necessary in preparation for the distribution of food or perhaps for the coming attempt to get ashore. The number (276) was not extraordinary for the time. Josephus referred to a ship that had 600 aboard (*Life,* 13).
27:38 The crew threw overboard the remaining bags of wheat (see v. 18), which had probably been kept for food supply. The lighter the ship, the farther it could sail in to shore.
27:40 The sailors lowered the stern rudders into place so that the ship could be steered toward the sandy shore. Ancient ships had a steering oar on either side of the stern.
27:42 If a prisoner escaped, the life of his guard was to be taken in his place. The soldiers did not want to risk having this happen.
28:1 Malta, which was included in the province of Sicily, was known as Melita by the Greeks and Romans. It is located 58 miles (93 km) south of that large island.
28:2 "Islanders" is literally "barbarians." All non-Greek-speaking people were called this by Greeks. Far from being uncivilized tribesmen, these men were Phoenician in ancestry and used a Phoenician dialect, although they were otherwise thoroughly Romanized.
It was raining and cold at the end of October or the beginning of November.
28:3 The islanders must have known that the "viper" was poisonous. There are no snakes on Malta today.

to his home and for three days entertained us hospitably. 8His father was sick in bed, suffering from fe-
28:8 [l]Jas 5:14,15 [m]Ac 9:40 ver and dysentery. Paul went in to see him and, after prayer,[l] placed his hands on him and healed him.[m]
9When this had happened, the rest of the sick on the island came and were cured. 10They honored us in
many ways and when we were ready to sail, they furnished us with the supplies we needed.

Arrival at Rome

11After three months we put out to sea in a ship that had wintered in the island. It was an Alexandri-
28:11 [n]Ac 27:6 an ship[n] with the figurehead of the twin gods Castor and Pollux. 12We put in at Syracuse and stayed there
three days. 13From there we set sail and arrived at Rhegium. The next day the south wind came up, and
28:14 [o]Ac 1:16 on the following day we reached Puteoli. 14There we found some brothers[o] who invited us to spend a
28:15 [p]Ac 1:16 week with them. And so we came to Rome. 15The brothers[p] there had heard that we were coming, and they
traveled as far as the Forum of Appius and the Three Taverns to meet us. At the sight of these men Paul
thanked God and was encouraged. 16When we got to Rome, Paul was allowed to live by himself, with a
28:16 [q]Ac 24:23; 27:3 soldier to guard him.[q]

Paul Preaches at Rome Under Guard

28:17 [r]Ac 25:2 17Three days later he called together the leaders of the Jews.[r] When they had assembled, Paul said to
[s]Ac 22:5 [t]Ac 25:8 [u]Ac 6:14 them: "My brothers,[s] although I have done nothing against our people[t] or against the customs of our an-
28:18 [v]Ac 22:24 [w]Ac 26:31,32 cestors,[u] I was arrested in Jerusalem and handed over to the Romans. 18They examined me[v] and want-
[x]Ac 23:9 ed to release me,[w] because I was not guilty of any crime deserving death.[x] 19But when the Jews object-
28:19 [y]Ac 25:11 ed, I was compelled to appeal to Caesar[y]—not that I had any charge to bring against my own people.
28:20 [z]Ac 26:6,7 [a]Ac 21:33 20For this reason I have asked to see you and talk with you. It is because of the hope of Israel[z] that I am
bound with this chain."[a]

21They replied, "We have not received any letters from Judea concerning you, and none of the broth-
28:21 [b]Ac 22:5 ers[b] who have come from there has reported or said anything bad about you. 22But we want to hear what
28:22 [c]Ac 24:5, 14 your views are, for we know that people everywhere are talking against this sect."[c]

23They arranged to meet Paul on a certain day, and came in even larger numbers to the place where
28:23 [d]Ac 19:8 [e]Ac 17:3 [f]Ac 8:35 he was staying. From morning till evening he explained and declared to them the kingdom of God[d] and
tried to convince them about Jesus[e] from the Law of Moses and from the Prophets.[f] 24Some were con-
28:24 [g]Ac 14:4 vinced by what he said, but others would not believe.[g] 25They disagreed among themselves and began
to leave after Paul had made this final statement: "The Holy Spirit spoke the truth to your forefathers
when he said through Isaiah the prophet:

> 26" 'Go to this people and say,
> "You will be ever hearing but never understanding;
> you will be ever seeing but never perceiving."
> 28:27 [h]Ps 119:70 27For this people's heart has become calloused;[h]
> they hardly hear with their ears,
> and they have closed their eyes.

28:11 The travelers had to remain there until the sailing season opened in late February or early March.

A "figurehead" is a carving mounted at the prow of the ship. This one was of Castor and Pollux, the two "sons of Zeus," the guardian deities of sailors.

28:12 Syracuse, the leading city on the island of Sicily, was located on its eastern coast.

28:13 Rhegium (modern Reggio) was a Greek colony on the coast of Italy, near the southwestern tip and close to the narrowest point (six mi, or ten km in width) of the strait separating that country from Sicily, opposite Messina. As a strategic point, it was the object of Rome's special care, and in consequence a loyal ally. The port was also a haven in extremely difficult water. The captain of the ship Paul was on, having tacked widely to make Rhegium, waited in the protection of the port for a favorable southerly wind to drive his ship through the currents of the strait on the course to Puteoli.

Puteoli (modern Pozzuoli) was almost 200 miles (322 km) from Rhegium. It was situated in the northern part of the Bay of Naples and was the chief port of Rome, though 75 miles (120 km) away. Its population included Jews as well as Christians.

28:14–15 The city of Rome appears several times in Scripture in a historical context, the most notable being Paul's enforced stay there. Paul landed at Puteoli, and, alerted by the little church there, members of Rome's Christian community met him at two stopping-places. On the evidence of a document called the Nazareth Decree, it appears that a group of believers had been established in Rome since the principate of Claudius in the late 40s A.D. Paul probably entered Rome by the Capena Gate. His "rented house" (v. 30) was no doubt located in some block of flats—an "insula" (see "Houses in the Holy Land of the First Century A.D.: Peter's House in Capernaum; Insulae" on p. 1584).

28:15 The Forum of Appius was a small town 43 miles (69 km) from Rome (see "Rome" on p. 1838).

Three Taverns was a town 33 miles (53 km) from Rome.

28:16 Paul had committed no flagrant crime and was not politically dangerous. He was accordingly allowed to have his own living quarters, but a guard was with him at all times, perhaps chained to him (see "Imprisonment in the Roman World: In Prison Versus House Arrest" on p. 1826).

28:17 The decree of the emperor Claudius (see 18:2 and its note) had been allowed to lapse, and Jews had returned to Rome with their leaders.

28:23 "The Law of Moses and . . . the Prophets" refers to the entire Old Testament Scriptures (see "The Old Testament of the Early Church" on p. 1967).

Otherwise they might see with their eyes,
hear with their ears,
understand with their hearts
and turn, and I would heal them.'[a][i]

28:27 [i]Isa 6:9,10

[28]"Therefore I want you to know that God's salvation[j] has been sent to the Gentiles,[k] and they will lis-
ten!"[b]

28:28 [j]Lk 2:30 [k]Ac 13:46

[30]For two whole years Paul stayed there in his own rented house and welcomed all who came to see
him. [31]Boldly and without hindrance he preached the kingdom of God[l] and taught about the Lord Jesus
Christ.

28:31 [l]ver 23; Mt 4:23

[a] 27 Isaiah 6:9,10 [b] 28 Some manuscripts *listen!"* [29]*After he said this, the Jews left, arguing vigorously among themselves.*

28:30 See the note on verses 14–15 for commentary on Paul's "rented house."

INTRODUCTION TO 

AUTHOR, PLACE AND DATE OF WRITING

That Paul is the author of Romans (1:1) is virtually undisputed. The book is generally dated to A.D. 57, probably during Paul's third missionary journey (Ac 20). He desired to carry the gospel to the west, having nearly completed his work in the eastern Mediterranean (Ro 15:19,24). Most scholars believe that Paul wrote this letter from Corinth.

AUDIENCE

Paul's original readers were the believers—predominately Gentiles (Ro 1:13)—in Rome. Paul introduced himself to the Roman church (one he had not personally founded) and explained why he intended to visit.

CULTURAL FACTS AND HIGHLIGHTS

For many years Paul had desired to visit Rome to minister there (1:13–15). Some surmise that he was hoping to use Rome as a base for his missionary venture to Spain and so wrote this letter to explain the nature of his work. Others suggest that the epistle had a pastoral purpose of healing divisions within the Roman church (14:1—15:6), while still others posit that it was apologetic in purpose, that Paul's gospel was under attack and that he needed to defend his core teaching that "the righteous will live by faith" (1:17) against the slanderous accusation that he was preaching an antinomian and libertine gospel (3:8). Whatever Paul's overriding purpose, it is clear that a major concern of the book is the relationship between Jew and Gentile in God's overall plan of redemption.

TIMELINE

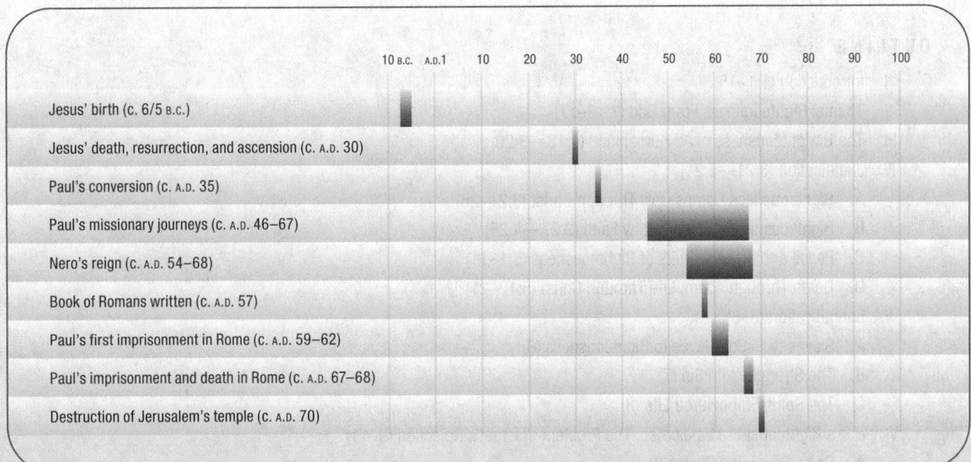

AS YOU READ

Be alert for the recurring topics of faith and works, law and grace, sin and righteousness, judgment and justification. Notice the systematic and comprehensive explanation of the gospel as presented by Paul: Gentiles came from a background of idolatry and unbelief, as over against Jews, whose heritage included knowing the law and promises of God; yet all have sinned (chs. 1–3). Justification is by faith and not by works, yet this does not provide license to live in sin (chs. 4–6). Jews, who had previously sought righteousness by works, did not find it, whereas Gentiles, who did not seek God through the law, found him and had been grafted into the true Israel of faith. This is by divine election and the plan of God—who has nevertheless remembered his people Israel (chs. 9–11). From this foundation of faith, Paul moved into concerns that relate to the everyday Christian life (chs. 12–15).

DID YOU KNOW?

- Jews of that day regarded themselves as superior to Gentiles because they (the Jews) possessed the Mosaic Law (2:1).
- Large amounts of wealth were often stored in pagan temples (2:22).
- In New Testament times baptism so closely followed conversion that the two were considered aspects of a single event (6:3–4).
- Adoption was common among the Greeks and Romans, both of whom granted an adopted son all of the privileges of a natural son, including inheritance rights (8:15).

THEMES

The book of Romans includes the following themes:

1. *God's faithfulness.* A central theme of Romans is God's covenant faithfulness. His fidelity to his promise to Abraham is revealed in salvation on the basis of faith. Both Jews and Gentiles find righteousness before God through faith in Jesus (3:21–26).

2. *Righteousness.* Neither Jew nor Gentile is on personal merit righteous before God; each, apart from Christ, is under his wrath (2:1—3:20). But there is Good News: Through Jesus' death, God credits *his own* righteousness to all who believe and rely on his promise of salvation in Christ (3:21—5:21). Through their union with Jesus, the power of the Holy Spirit enables Christians to live righteous lives here and now (6:1—8:39).

3. *Reconciliation.* Romans is marked by Paul's concern for racial reconciliation and cross-cultural sensitivity. His advice on resolving internal conflicts in the church (14:1—15:6) lifts up Christ's attitude as the example for our own (15:1–6). Paul reiterated Jesus' teaching that love of neighbor fulfills the law's intent (13:8–10).

OUTLINE

- I. Introduction (1:1–15)
- II. Theme: Righteousness From God (1:16–17)
- III. The Unrighteousness of All Humankind (1:18—3:20)
- IV. Justification (3:21—5:21)
  - A. Righteousness Comes Only Through Christ (3:21–26)
  - B. Righteousness Is Received by Faith (3:27—4:25)
  - C. Peace and Joy Are Fruits of Righteousness (5:1–11)
  - D. Death Through Adam, Life Through Christ (5:12–21)
- V. Sanctification (6–8)
  - A. Slaves to Sin or Slaves to Righteousness (6)
  - B. The Struggle With Sin (7)
  - C. The Spirit-Empowered Life (8)
- VI. God's Righteousness Vindicated: The Problem of Israel's Rejection (9–11)
  - A. God's Sovereign Choice (9:1–29)
  - B. Israel's Unbelief (9:30—10:21)
  - C. The Remnant and the Ingrafted Branches (11)
- VII. Righteousness Practiced (12:1—15:13)
- VIII. Conclusion (15:14—16:27)

1 Paul, a servant of Christ Jesus, called to be an apostle[a] and set apart[b] for the gospel of God[c]— 2the
gospel he promised beforehand through his prophets in the Holy Scriptures[d] 3regarding his Son,
who as to his human nature[e] was a descendant of David, 4and who through the Spirit[a] of holiness was
declared with power to be the Son of God[b] by his resurrection from the dead: Jesus Christ our Lord.
5Through him and for his name's sake, we received grace and apostleship to call people from among all
the Gentiles[f] to the obedience that comes from faith.[g] 6And you also are among those who are called to
belong to Jesus Christ.[h]

7To all in Rome who are loved by God[i] and called to be saints:

Grace and peace to you from God our Father and from the Lord Jesus Christ.[j]

Paul's Longing to Visit Rome

8First, I thank my God through Jesus Christ for all of you,[k] because your faith is being reported all
over the world.[l] 9God, whom I serve[m] with my whole heart in preaching the gospel of his Son, is my wit-
ness[n] how constantly I remember you 10in my prayers at all times; and I pray that now at last by God's
will the way may be opened for me to come to you.[o]

11I long to see you[p] so that I may impart to you some spiritual gift to make you strong— 12that is, that
you and I may be mutually encouraged by each other's faith. 13I do not want you to be unaware, broth-
ers, that I planned many times to come to you (but have been prevented from doing so until now)[q] in or-
der that I might have a harvest among you, just as I have had among the other Gentiles.

14I am obligated[r] both to Greeks and non-Greeks, both to the wise and the foolish. 15That is why I am
so eager to preach the gospel also to you who are at Rome.[s]

16I am not ashamed of the gospel,[t] because it is the power of God[u] for the salvation of everyone who
believes: first for the Jew,[v] then for the Gentile.[w] 17For in the gospel a righteousness from God is revealed,[x]
a righteousness that is by faith from first to last,[c] just as it is written: "The righteous will live by faith."[d][y]

God's Wrath Against Mankind

18The wrath of God[z] is being revealed from heaven against all the godlessness and wickedness of men
who suppress the truth by their wickedness, 19since what may be known about God is plain to them, be-
cause God has made it plain to them.[a] 20For since the creation of the world God's invisible qualities—
his eternal power and divine nature—have been clearly seen, being understood from what has been
made,[b] so that men are without excuse.

21For although they knew God, they neither glorified him as God nor gave thanks to him, but their
thinking became futile and their foolish hearts were darkened.[c] 22Although they claimed to be wise, they
became fools[d] 23and exchanged the glory of the immortal God for images[e] made to look like mortal man
and birds and animals and reptiles.

24Therefore God gave them over[f] in the sinful desires of their hearts to sexual impurity for the de-
grading of their bodies with one another.[g] 25They exchanged the truth of God for a lie,[h] and worshiped
and served created things[i] rather than the Creator—who is forever praised.[j] Amen.

26Because of this, God gave them over[k] to shameful lusts.[l] Even their women exchanged natural re-
lations for unnatural ones.[m] 27In the same way the men also abandoned natural relations with women

1:1 [a]1Co 1:1 [b]Ac 9:15 [c]2Co 11:7
1:2 [d]Gal 3:8
1:3 [e]Jn 1:14
1:5 [f]Ac 9:15 [g]Ac 6:7
1:6 [h]Rev 17:14
1:7 [i]Ro 8:39 [j]1Co 1:3
1:8 [k]1Co 1:4 [l]Ro 16:19
1:9 [m]2Ti 1:3 [n]Php 1:8
1:10 [o]Ro 15:32
1:11 [p]Ro 15:23
1:13 [q]Ro 15:22, 23
1:14 [r]1Co 9:16
1:15 [s]Ro 15:20
1:16 [t]2Ti 1:8 [u]1Co 1:18 [v]Ac 3:26 [w]Ro 2:9, 10
1:17 [x]Ro 3:21 [y]Hab 2:4; Gal 3:11; Heb 10:38
1:18 [z]Eph 5:6; Col 3:6
1:19 [a]Ac 14:17
1:20 [b]Ps 19:1-6
1:21 [c]Jer 2:5; Eph 4:17,18
1:22 [d]1Co 1:20, 27
1:23 [e]Ps 106:20; Jer 2:11; Ac 17:29
1:24 [f]Eph 4:19 [g]1Pe 4:3
1:25 [h]Isa 44:20 [i]Jer 10:14 [j]Ro 9:5
1:26 [k]ver 24,28 [l]1Th 4:5 [m]Lev 18:22,23

[a] 4 Or *who as to his spirit* [b] 4 Or *was appointed to be the Son of God with power* [c] 17 Or *is from faith to faith* [d] 17 Hab. 2:4

1:1–7 Ancient letters typically began with a simple identification of the sender and the recipients, followed by a greeting (see "Letter Writing in the Greco-Roman World" on p. 1889). New Testament letters follow this pattern, but in no other letter does the author elaborate as much as Paul did in Romans—perhaps because he was writing to a church he had never visited. Paul spent six verses identifying himself before mentioning his audience and extending them a greeting.

1:1 The Greek word translated "servant" here literally means a "slave," one who belonged completely to his owner and was not at liberty to leave (see "Labor and Welfare in the Ancient World" on p. 1952 and "Slavery in the Greco-Roman World" on p. 1979).

1:2 For "Holy Scriptures," see "The Old Testament of the Early Church" on page 1967.

1:7 See "Rome" on page 1838.

1:13 The Greek word translated "brothers" was commonly used in Paul's day to address a crowd or community that included both men and women (see Ac 1:14–16).

1:14 "Greeks" refers to those Gentiles who either spoke Greek or followed the Greek way of life, even though they may have been Latin-speaking citizens of the Roman Empire.

"Non-Greeks" (lit., "barbarians") is a word that probably imitated the unintelligible sound of their languages to Greek ears.

1:18 God's anger is not like the egoistic and unpredictable anger attributed to the mythic gods with whom Paul's Roman audience was familiar (see "The Gods of the Greeks and Romans" on p. 1908).

1:27 "Indecent acts" refer to sodomy, for which Sodom had become noted (Ge 19:5). God strictly forbade this practice (Dt 23:17). Typically this act took place in connection with heathen worship, and its presence was a sign of departure from the Lord (1Ki 14:24). Both Asa (1Ki 15:12) and Jehoshaphat took measures against this sin (1Ki 22:46), but its practice continued, until in the days of Josiah it was being practiced even in the Lord's house (2Ki 23:7).

and were inflamed with lust for one another. Men committed indecent acts with other men, and received
in themselves the due penalty for their perversion.[n] 1:27 [n]Lev 18:22; 20:13
28 Furthermore, since they did not think it worthwhile to retain the knowledge of God, he gave them
over[o] to a depraved mind, to do what ought not to be done. 29 They have become filled with every kind 1:28 [o]ver 24,26
of wickedness, evil, greed and depravity. They are full of envy, murder, strife, deceit and malice. They are
gossips,[p] 30 slanderers, God-haters, insolent, arrogant and boastful; they invent ways of doing evil; they 1:29 [p]2Co 12:20
disobey their parents;[q] 31 they are senseless, faithless, heartless,[r] ruthless. 32 Although they know God's 1:30 [q]2Ti 3:2
righteous decree that those who do such things deserve death,[s] they not only continue to do these very 1:31 [r]2Ti 3:3 1:32 [s]Ro 6:23
things but also approve[t] of those who practice them. [t]Ps 50:18; Lk 11:48; Ac 8:1; 22:20

Homosexuality in the Ancient World

ROMANS 1 In Romans 1:24–32 Paul described the depravity of the Gentiles. He cited homosexuality as the prime example and proof of their reprobation. In this behavior they demonstrated the reality that rejecting God leads to a perversion of everything that is good and right. Indeed, widespread homosexuality remains irrefutable proof that a culture stands under divine judgment.

Today, however, many interpreters assert that reading Romans 1 in light of the cultural backdrop of the Greco-Roman world reveals that Paul was not really condemning homosexuality itself but was reproving a particularly lustful, promiscuous version of this sexual inclination. In other words, according to these scholars homosexuality in the context of a caring, loving relationship is not only acceptable but outside the realm of Paul's concern.

Emperor Hadrian

Preserving Bible Times; © Dr. James C. Martin; permission of The Israel Museum

This interpretation is based upon a distortion of what we know of ancient practices and beliefs. Homosexuality was extremely common in the Greek world and by New Testament times had become widespread in the Roman world as well. Then, as now, there were homosexual orgies, but many other varieties of homosexual behavior were practiced as well, and we cannot say with certainty that pagan homosexual behavior was strictly of the orgiastic type. Greek men often engaged in homosexual relationships with adolescent boys; many, in fact, regarded this as a coming-of-age experience. Some homosexual attraction was described in highly romantic terms; both male and female poets celebrated their love for members of their own sex (Sappho, c. 630 B.C., was the most famous poet of this genre, although the precise nature of her relationship with the women of her poems is debated). The Roman emperor Hadrian was so overcome with passionate love for a young man named Antinous that when the object of his affection drowned, the grief-stricken emperor decreed that he be worshiped as a god.

The Jews, by contrast, regarded homosexuals as by nature depraved—an attitude founded upon Biblical texts such as Leviticus 18:22. Jewish writings of this period treated homosexual activity as meriting death and damnation. Paul, far from dissenting from this viewpoint, rigorously endorsed it (1Co 6:9). It is important to note, however, that neither Paul nor his Jewish contemporaries distinguished between lawful and illicit homosexuality. For them, such a sexual preference was by nature wrong in any context.

Evidence exists that even the Greeks may have been aware that this behavior was deviant. Aristophanes, the Greek comic poet, mocked homosexual behavior (even as he employed it as a comic device). For example, in *Women at the Thesmophoria* he ruthlessly ridiculed the notorious homosexuality of the poet Agathon. It would be an overstatement to claim that Aristophanes opposed homosexual practice, but his comedy betrayed an uneasy conscience about such behavior within the culture he inhabited. Plato, on the other hand, in his earlier dialogues spoke approvingly of homosexual behavior. Yet near the end of his career he observed in his *Laws* that homosexual intercourse was widely recognized to be unnatural.

God's Righteous Judgment

2:1 uRo 1:20 v2Sa 12:5-7; Mt 7:1,2 — 2 You, therefore, have no excuse,[u] you who pass judgment on
someone else, for at whatever point you judge the other, you
are condemning yourself, because you who pass judgment do
the same things.[v] 2 Now we know that God's judgment against
those who do such things is based on truth. 3 So when you, a
mere man, pass judgment on them and yet do the same things,
do you think you will escape God's judgment? 4 Or do you show
2:4 wRo 9:23; Eph 1:7,18; 2:7 xRo 11:22 yRo 3:25 zEx 34:6 a2Pe 3:9 — contempt for the riches[w] of his kindness,[x] tolerance[y] and pa-
tience,[z] not realizing that God's kindness leads you toward re-
pentance?[a]
5 But because of your stubbornness and your unrepentant heart,
you are storing up wrath against yourself for the day of God's wrath,
2:5 bJude 6 — when his righteous judgment[b] will be revealed. 6 God "will give to
2:6 cPs 62:12; Mt 16:27 — each person according to what he has done."[a][c] 7 To those who by per-
2:7 dver 10 e1Co 15:53,54 — sistence in doing good seek glory, honor[d] and immortality,[e] he will
give eternal life. 8 But for those who are self-seeking and who reject
2:8 f2Th 2:12 — the truth and follow evil,[f] there will be wrath and anger. 9 There will
2:9 g1Pe 4:17 — be trouble and distress for every human being who does evil: first for the Jew, then for the Gentile;[g] 10 but
2:10 hver 9 — glory, honor and peace for everyone who does good: first for the Jew, then for the Gentile.[h] 11 For God
2:11 iAc 10:34 — does not show favoritism.[i]
2:12 jRo 3:19; 1Co 9:20,21 — 12 All who sin apart from the law will also perish apart from the law, and all who sin under the law[j]
will be judged by the law. 13 For it is not those who hear the law who are righteous in God's sight, but
2:13 kJas 1:22, 23,25 — it is those who obey[k] the law who will be declared righteous. 14 (Indeed, when Gentiles, who do not
2:14 lAc 10:35 — have the law, do by nature things required by the law,[l] they are a law for themselves, even though they
do not have the law, 15 since they show that the requirements of the law are written on their hearts,
their consciences also bearing witness, and their thoughts now accusing, now even defending them.)
2:16 mEcc 12:14 nAc 10:42 oRo 16:25 — 16 This will take place on the day when God will judge men's secrets[m] through Jesus Christ,[n] as my gos-
pel[o] declares.

The Jews and the Law

17 Now you, if you call yourself a Jew; if you rely on the law and brag about your relationship to
2:17 pver 23; Mic 3:11; Ro 9:4 — God;[p] 18 if you know his will and approve of what is superior because you are instructed by the law;
19 if you are convinced that you are a guide for the blind, a light for those who are in the dark, 20 an in-
structor of the foolish, a teacher of infants, because you have in the law the embodiment of knowl-
edge and truth— 21 you, then, who teach others, do you not teach yourself? You who preach against
2:21 qMt 23:3,4 — stealing, do you steal?[q] 22 You who say that people should not commit adultery, do you commit adul-
2:22 rAc 19:37 2:23 sver 17 — tery? You who abhor idols, do you rob temples?[r] 23 You who brag about the law,[s] do you dishonor God
by breaking the law? 24 As it is written: "God's name is blasphemed among the Gentiles because of
2:24 tIsa 52:5; Eze 36:22 — you."[b][t]
2:25 uGal 5:3 vJer 4:4 — 25 Circumcision has value if you observe the law,[u] but if you break the law, you have become as though
2:26 wRo 8:4 x1Co 7:19 — you had not been circumcised.[v] 26 If those who are not circumcised keep the law's requirements,[w] will
they not be regarded as though they were circumcised?[x] 27 The one who is not circumcised physically
2:27 yMt 12:41, 42 — and yet obeys the law will condemn you[y] who, even though you have the[c] written code and circumci-
sion, are a lawbreaker.
2:28 zMt 3:9; Jn 8:39; Ro 9:6,7 aGal 6:15 — 28 A man is not a Jew if he is only one outwardly,[z] nor is circumcision merely outward and physical.[a]
2:29 bPhp 3:3; Col 2:11 cRo 7:6 dJn 5:44; 1Co 4:5; 2Co 10:18; 1Th 2:4; 1Pe 3:4 — 29 No, a man is a Jew if he is one inwardly; and circumcision is circumcision of the heart, by the Spirit,[b]
not by the written code.[c] Such a man's praise is not from men, but from God.[d]

[a] *6* Psalm 62:12; Prov. 24:12 [b] *24* Isaiah 52:5; Ezek. 36:22 [c] *27* Or *who, by means of a*

Ancient Voices

Whether one makes the observation lightheartedly or in all seriousness, one must observe that, when the male body unites for procreation with the female, the pleasure that goes along with this is understood to be in accordance with nature, but that when male joins with male, or female with female, it is outside the bounds of nature. This outrage was first done by people whose desire for pleasure was without self-control.

—Plato on Homosexuality

From Plato, *Laws*, 636c, trans. by Duane Garrett

See "Homosexuality in the Ancient World" article.

2:1 Jews of that day regarded themselves as superior to Gentiles because they (the Jews) possessed the Mosaic Law. According to Jews of that day, Gentiles were ignorant of God's revelation and immoral in their lifestyles.

2:22 Large amounts of wealth were often stored in pagan temples.
2:25 Circumcision was a sign of the covenant that God had made with Israel and a pledge of the covenant blessing (see Ge 17:10 and its note; see also "Circumcision in the Ancient World" on p. 1840).

ARCHAEOLOGICAL SITES

ROME

ROMANS 2 During the first century A.D. Rome boasted a population of approximately one million people. The city was home to numerous temples, such as the temple of Concord, the temple of Castor and the temple of Vesta, the last a modest but ancient structure dedicated to the hearth goddess and served by the vestal virgins. The ancient center of religious, cultural, commercial and political life was the Roman Forum, although in the first century several other large fora (such as the Forum of Augustus and the Forum of Julius Caesar) stood nearby.

Augustus Caesar and his lieutenant M. Vispanius Agrippa had overseen a great deal of construction in Rome a century earlier, during the late first century B.C.[1] Their works included the Pantheon (a temple dedicated to all of Rome's gods),[2] the Altar of Peace, the imperial residence on the Palatine hill, the temple of Julius Caesar, a triumphal arch, new aqueducts and sewer systems and numerous other structures. Augustus boasted that he had found Rome a city of stone and left it a city of marble.

Even so, many of Rome's residents lived in squalor. Massive apartment buildings called insulae (lit., "islands") were interspersed throughout the city.[3] Besides being crime-ridden, these areas were firetraps, and in A.D. 64 a massive conflagration gutted three of the fourteen regions of the city, leaving only four unscathed. Nero, who was emperor at the time, used the denuded land to build an extravagant residence for himself that he called the *domus aurea* ("gold house").[4] The famous Colosseum, an amphitheater seating 50,000, was dedicated in A.D. 80. The Arch of Titus, constructed in A.D. 81, commemorates the Roman sacking of Jerusalem.[5]

Rome was home to an ethnically mixed population, including a significant number of Jews.[6] Ethnic groups tended to cluster in distinct neighborhoods, and the city suffered from severe disparity of class. One-third to one-half of Rome's residents were slaves or recently freed slaves, although slaves were not necessarily at the bottom of the social ladder.[7] It is likely that the free poor experienced the most difficult lot and lived in the direst of conditions. The needy depended upon government largess and could quickly become a mob (thus the common saying that the people demanded "bread and circuses").

Rome, the center of trade within the empire, was easily accessible via a vast network of roads and seaways. Similar to the ethnic neighborhoods, the marketplace was organized into quarters that were clustered according to categories of trade. This made it easy for the foreign visitor to find others who shared in his craft and for consumers to locate items for purchase. Those who shared a particular profession frequently formed clubs and associations, enabling a shared social life as well as a shared business community.[8]

The Church of Saint Peter is located at the traditional (but unsubstantiated) burial site of the apostle Peter, while the Church of Saint Paul, outside the city walls, marks the traditional burial place of Paul; a slab found there dating to the time of Constantine is inscribed with the words *PAULO APOSTOLO MART[YRI]* ("to the Apostle Paul, martyr").[9]

[1]See "Caesar Augustus, Emperor of Rome; the Census; and Quirinius, Governor of Syria" on page 1667. [2]See "The Gods of the Greeks and Romans" on page 1908. [3]See "Houses in the Holy Land of the First Century A.D.: Peter's House in Capernaum; Insulae" on page 1584. [4]See "Nero, Persecutor of Christians" on page 1931. [5]See "Josephus and the Fall of Jerusalem" on page 1606. [6]See "The Jewish Diaspora in the First Century A.D." on page 1769. [7]See "Slavery in the Greco-Roman World" on page 1979. [8]See "Travel in the Greco-Roman World" on page 1946 and "Trade and Mercantilism in the Roman Empire" on page 2070. [9]See "Constantine and Queen Helena's Role in Preserving Holy Sites" on page1758.

The Palatine Hill in Rome

Preserving Bible Times; © Dr. James C. Martin; on licence Ministero per i Beni le Attivita Culturali-Soprintendza Archeologica di Roma

God's Faithfulness

3 What advantage, then, is there in being a Jew, or what value is there in circumcision? 2 Much in ev-
3:2 [e]Dt 4:8; Ps 147:19 ery way! First of all, they have been entrusted with the very words of God.[e]
3:3 [f]Heb 4:2 [g]2Ti 2:13 3 What if some did not have faith?[f] Will their lack of faith nullify God's faithfulness?[g] 4 Not at all! Let
3:4 [h]Jn 3:33 [i]Ps 116:11 [j]Ps 51:4 God be true,[h] and every man a liar.[i] As it is written:

"So that you may be proved right when you speak
and prevail when you judge."[a][j]

5 But if our unrighteousness brings out God's righteousness more clearly, what shall we say? That God
3:5 [k]Ro 6:19; Gal 3:15 is unjust in bringing his wrath on us? (I am using a human argument.)[k] 6 Certainly not! If that were so,
3:6 [l]Ge 18:25 how could God judge the world?[l] 7 Someone might argue, "If my falsehood enhances God's truthfulness
3:7 [m]ver 4 and so increases his glory,[m] why am I still condemned as a sinner?" 8 Why not say—as we are being slan-
3:8 [n]Ro 6:1 derously reported as saying and as some claim that we say—"Let us do evil that good may result"?[n]
Their condemnation is deserved.

No One Is Righteous

9 What shall we conclude then? Are we any better[b]? Not at all! We have already made the charge that
3:9 [o]ver 19,23; Gal 3:22 Jews and Gentiles alike are all under sin.[o] 10 As it is written:

"There is no one righteous, not even one;
11 there is no one who understands,
no one who seeks God.
12 All have turned away,
they have together become worthless;
there is no one who does good,
3:12 [p]Ps 14:1-3 not even one."[c][p]
13 "Their throats are open graves;
3:13 [q]Ps 5:9 [r]Ps 140:3 their tongues practice deceit."[d][q]
"The poison of vipers is on their lips."[e][r]
3:14 [s]Ps 10:7 14 "Their mouths are full of cursing and bitterness."[f][s]
15 "Their feet are swift to shed blood;
16 ruin and misery mark their ways,
17 and the way of peace they do not know."[g]
3:18 [t]Ps 36:1 18 "There is no fear of God before their eyes."[h][t]

3:19 [u]Jn 10:34 [v]Ro 2:12 19 Now we know that whatever the law says,[u] it says to those who are under the law,[v] so that every
mouth may be silenced and the whole world held accountable to God. 20 Therefore no one will be de-
3:20 [w]Ac 13:39; Gal 2:16 [x]Ro 7:7 clared righteous in his sight by observing the law;[w] rather, through the law we become conscious of sin.[x]

Righteousness Through Faith

3:21 [y]Ro 1:17; 9:30 [z]Ac 10:43 21 But now a righteousness from God,[y] apart from law, has been made known, to which the Law and
3:22 [a]Ro 9:30 the Prophets testify.[z] 22 This righteousness from God comes through faith[a] in Jesus Christ to all who

[a] *4* Psalm 51:4 [b] *9* Or *worse* [c] *12* Psalms 14:1-3; 53:1-3; Eccles. 7:20 [d] *13* Psalm 5:9 [e] *13* Psalm 140:3
[f] *14* Psalm 10:7 [g] *17* Isaiah 59:7,8 [h] *18* Psalm 36:1

3:8 Antinomianism is the view that the oral law does not apply to Christians, who are instead under the law of grace. Because salvation does not come through works but through grace, it is held, moral effort can be discounted. Paul found that this kind of heresy had crept into the church (1Co 5–6). Others had chosen to misrepresent Paul's teaching on grace (as in this verse), and Paul pointed out the absurdity of the charge (Ro 6:1,15). From the first century to our own day, some individuals or groups have sought to combine the spiritual life with moral license, but Scripture leaves no doubt that the new life in Christ means death to the old, evil desires (Gal 5:24).

3:10–18 Several factors explain why Old Testament quotations are not always cited verbatim in the New Testament: (1) New Testament quotations sometimes gave the general sense of the original and were not intended to be word-for-word citations. (2) Quotation marks were not used in Greek. (3) The quotations were often taken from the pre-Christian Greek translation (the Septuagint) of the Hebrew Old Testament, because Greek readers were for the most part unfamiliar with the Hebrew Bible. (4) Sometimes the New Testament writer, in order to drive home his point, would purposely enlarge, abbreviate or adapt an Old Testament passage or combine two or more passages. (See "The Septuagint and Its Use in the New Testament" on p. 1995.)

3:21 "The Law and the Prophets" refers to the entire Old Testament Scriptures (see "The Old Testament of the Early Church" on p. 1967).

3:22–25 Paul drew on several dimensions of human experience from his day. "Justification" is the language of the courtroom—what a judge does when he declares a defendant not guilty. "Redemption" comes from the world of commerce and slavery—one could redeem slaves by purchasing their freedom. "Sacrifice of atonement" obviously is the language of religion—the giving of an offering to take the place of the guilty.

believe. There is no difference,[b] 23 for all have sinned and fall short of the glory of God, 24 and are justi-
fied freely by his grace[c] through the redemption[d] that came by Christ Jesus. 25 God presented him as a sac-
rifice of atonement,[a][e] through faith in his blood.[f] He did this to demonstrate his justice, because in his
forbearance he had left the sins committed beforehand unpunished[g]— 26 he did it to demonstrate his
justice at the present time, so as to be just and the one who justifies those who have faith in Jesus.
27 Where, then, is boasting?[h] It is excluded. On what principle? On that of observing the law? No, but on
that of faith. 28 For we maintain that a man is justified by faith apart from observing the law.[i] 29 Is God the

[a] 25 Or *as the one who would turn aside his wrath, taking away sin*

3:22 [b]Ro 10:12; Gal 3:28; Col 3:11
3:24 [c]Ro 4:16; Eph 2:8 [d]Eph 1:7, 14; Col 1:14; Heb 9:12
3:25 [e]1Jn 4:10 [f]Heb 9:12,14 [g]Ac 17:30
3:27 [h]Ro 2:17,23; 4:2; 1Co 1:29-31; Eph 2:9
3:28 [i]ver 20,21; Ac 13:39; Eph 2:9

Circumcision in the Ancient World

ROMANS 3 The significance of circumcision among non-Israelites of the ancient world is debated among scholars (whether circumcision was a rite of marriage or of puberty or was practiced for hygienic purposes). But for Israel the rite served as a "sign" of the people's covenant pledge to "walk before [**Yahweh**][1] and be blameless" (Ge 17:1,11). The procedure was performed on the male reproductive organ in order to remind the recipient that the oath of allegiance was binding on both himself and his offspring. It is also probable that the cutting ritual within the covenant context (cf. Ge 15:7–18; Jer 34:17–20) pointed to the curse of being "cut off" that was to be brought upon all covenant violators (cf. Ge 17:14; Ex 4:25).

Greek text of Romans 3; Egypt, third century A.D.

© The Schøyen Collection; photography courtesy of Mr. Martin Schøyen

Israel's full removal of the foreskin made its brand of circumcision a mark of ethnic distinction, setting apart Israelite males from the Egyptians and from many of Israel's western Semitic neighbors (cf. Jer 9:24–25), who performed the rite only by slitting the foreskin; from the "uncircumcised" Philistines and the eastern Semites of Mesopotamia, who did not practice the ritual at all; and, finally, from the Greeks and Romans of the **intertestamental** and New Testament periods, who were repulsed by all forms of circumcision.

It is not surprising that for Israel the term "foreskin" bore a negative connotation, representing all that was opposed to God and his people. In contrast, the term "circumcision" was used metaphorically to point to one who had renounced pagan practices and was now fully devoted to Yahweh (Dt 10:16; Jer 4:4). Following the establishment of the Christian faith, all national markers such as physical circumcision lost their value, and God's people became distinguished solely by faith working itself out in love—the true sign of their identification with the Messiah through the transforming work of the Spirit (Ro 2:28–29; Gal 5:6; 6:14–16; cf. Dt 30:6; Jer 31:33; 32:39; Eze 36:26–27).

[1]See Glossary on page 2080 for definitions of bolded words.

God of Jews only? Is he not the God of Gentiles too? Yes, of Gentiles
3:29 [j]Ro 9:24 too,[j] 30 since there is only one God, who will justify the circumcised by
3:30 [k]Gal 3:8 faith and the uncircumcised through that same faith.[k] 31 Do we, then,
nullify the law by this faith? Not at all! Rather, we uphold the law.

Abraham Justified by Faith

4 What then shall we say that Abraham, our forefather, discov-
ered in this matter? 2 If, in fact, Abraham was justified by works,
4:2 [l]1Co 1:31 he had something to boast about—but not before God.[l] 3 What does
the Scripture say? "Abraham believed God, and it was credited to him
4:3 [m]ver 5,9,22; Ge 15:6; Gal 3:6; Jas 2:23 as righteousness."[a][m]
4 Now when a man works, his wages are not credited to him as a
4:4 [n]Ro 11:6 gift,[n] but as an obligation. 5 However, to the man who does not work
but trusts God who justifies the wicked, his faith is credited as righ-
teousness. 6 David says the same thing when he speaks of the bless-
edness of the man to whom God credits righteousness apart from
works:

> 7 "Blessed are they
> whose transgressions are forgiven,
> whose sins are covered.
> 8 Blessed is the man
> whose sin the Lord will never count
> against him."[b][o]

4:8 [o]Ps 32:1,2; 2Co 5:19

9 Is this blessedness only for the circumcised, or also for the un-
4:9 [p]Ro 3:30 [q]ver 3 circumcised?[p] We have been saying that Abraham's faith was cred-
ited to him as righteousness.[q] 10 Under what circumstances was it
credited? Was it after he was circumcised, or before? It was not after,
but before! 11 And he received the sign of circumcision, a seal of the
4:11 [r]Ge 17:10, 11 [s]ver 16,17; Lk 19:9 [t]Ro 3:22 righteousness that he had by faith while he was still uncircumcised.[r]
So then, he is the father[s] of all who believe[t] but have not been cir-
cumcised, in order that righteousness might be credited to them.
12 And he is also the father of the circumcised who not only are cir-
cumcised but who also walk in the footsteps of the faith that our fa-
ther Abraham had before he was circumcised.
13 It was not through law that Abraham and his offspring received
4:13 [u]Gal 3:16,29 [v]Ge 17:4-6 the promise[u] that he would be heir of the world,[v] but through the
righteousness that comes by faith. 14 For if those who live by law are heirs, faith has no value and the prom-
4:14 [w]Gal 3:18 ise is worthless,[w] 15 because law brings wrath.[x] And where there is no law there is no transgression.[y]
4:15 [x]Ro 7:7-25; 1Co 15:56; 2Co 3:7; Gal 3:10; Ro 7:12 [y]Ro 3:20; 7:7 16 Therefore, the promise comes by faith, so that it may be by grace[z] and may be guaranteed[a] to all
Abraham's offspring—not only to those who are of the law but also to those who are of the faith of Abra-
4:16 [z]Ro 3:24 [a]Ro 15:8 ham. He is the father of us all. 17 As it is written: "I have made you a father of many nations."[c][b] He is our
4:17 [b]Ge 17:5 [c]Jn 5:21 [d]Isa 48:13 [e]1Co 1:28 father in the sight of God, in whom he believed—the God who gives life[c] to the dead and calls[d] things
that are not[e] as though they were.
18 Against all hope, Abraham in hope believed and so became the father of many nations,[f] just as it had
4:18 [f]ver 17 [g]Ge 15:5 been said to him, "So shall your offspring be."[d][g] 19 Without weakening in his faith, he faced the fact that his
4:19 [h]Heb 11:11, 12 [i]Ge 17:17 [j]Ge 18:11 body was as good as dead[h]—since he was about a hundred years old[i]—and that Sarah's womb was also
dead.[j] 20 Yet he did not waver through unbelief regarding the promise of God, but was strengthened in his
4:20 [k]Mt 9:8 faith and gave glory to God,[k] 21 being fully persuaded that God had power to do what he had promised.[l]
4:21 [l]Ge 18:14; Heb 11:19

[a] *3* Gen. 15:6; also in verse 22 [b] *8* Psalm 32:1,2 [c] *17* Gen. 17:5 [d] *18* Gen. 15:5

ANCIENT VOICES

Now they had left Trebonius, a member of the conspiracy, to delay Antony at the door with conversation. The others stood about Caesar as he sat in his chair as if they were his friends, but they had concealed daggers. One of their group, Tillius Cimber, approached him to his face and asked for the recall of his banished brother. While Caesar was answering that he was deferring this matter, Cimber seized the purple of Caesar's toga as though pressing his request, pulled back the cloak from his neck, and shouted, "Why wait any longer, friends?" Casca was first; he was standing over Caesar's head and drove his dagger at this throat, but he slipped and struck him in the chest. Caesar snatched his toga from Cimber, grabbed Casca's hand, sprang from his chair and turned back, and then threw down Casca with great force. While Caesar was twisted back like this, someone else thrust a dagger in his side. Cassius stabbed him in the face, Brutus got him in the thigh, and Bucolianus in the back. Caesar turned against each of them, raging and shouting like an animal, but when he recognized that Brutus was striking him, he despaired, wrapped himself in his toga, and fell with dignity beside the statue of Pompey.

—THE HISTORIAN APPIAN ON THE ASSASSINATION OF JULIUS CAESAR
From Appian, *Roman History*, 2.16, trans. by Duane Garrett

See "The Roman Empire" article on page 1845.

4:9–17 In Jewish thought, a distinction remained between Abraham's descendants—covenant participants—and the "other" nations, who also received benefits through Abraham in some unspecified way. Paul broke down that distinction: Gentiles along with Jews are Abraham's "offspring," equal recipients with Jews of God's covenant blessings.

4:11 See "Circumcision in the Ancient World" on page 1840.

A CHRONOLOGICAL HISTORY OF ROME FROM 600 B.C. THROUGH THE END OF THE JEWISH REVOLT IN A.D. 150

	Events	Persons
600 B.C.		
	Overthrow of Etruscan control at Rome and the founding of the republic (509)	
	First consuls appointed (508)	
	First dictator (501)	
500		
	Alliance of Rome and the Latins (493)	
	Twelve Tables (451–450)	
400		
	Rome captured by the Gauls (390)	
	First Samnite War (343–341)	
	The Latin War (340–338)	
	Dissolution of Latin League (338)	
	Second Samnite War (327–304)	
300		
	Third Samnite War (298–290)	
	First Punic War (264–241)	
		Cato the Elder (234–149)
	Roman envoys in Athens and Corinth (228)	
	Second Punic War (218–201)	
	Hannibal's crossing of the Alps (218)	
	First Macedonian War (214–205)	
	Rome's defeat of Carthage at Zama (202)	
200		
	Second Macedonian War: Rome's defeat of Philip V (200–196)	
	Repeal of Oppian Law (195)	
	War with Antiochus III (the Great) (191–189)	
	Third Macedonian War (176–167)	
	Voconian Law (169)	
	Third Punic War: Carthage destroyed (150–146)	
	War with the Achaeans: Corinth destroyed (146)	
	Slave war in Sicily (135–131)	
		Cicero (106–43)
100		
		Cato the Younger (95–46)
	Slave war with Spartacus (73–71)	Catullus (84–54)
	First consulship of Pompey and Crassus (70)	Virgil (70–19)
	Pompey's capture of Jerusalem (63)	
	Consulship of Cicero (63)	Horace (65–8)
	Coalition of Pompey, Caesar and Crassus (60)	
	First consulship of Caesar (59)	Lucretius (60)
	Caesar's Gallic Wars (59–51)	
		Livy (59 B.C.–A.D.17)

	Events	Persons
100 B.C. con't	Cicero exiled (58)	
	Cicero recalled (57)	
	Second consulship of Pompey and Crassus (55)	
	Caesar's invasions of Britain (55–54)	
	Crassus defeated and killed by the Parthians (53)	
	Pompey sole consul (52)	
	Julius Caesar's defeat of Pompey at Pharsalus (49)	
	Caesar's dictatorship (49–44)	
	Assassination of Julius Caesar (March 15, 44)	
	Octavian consul and Antony, Lepidus and Octavian triumvirs (43)	Ovid (43 B.C.–A.D. 17)
	Octavian and Mark Antony's defeat of Brutus and Cassius at Philippi (42)	
	Defeat of Sextus Pompey (36)	
	Parthian War (36)	
	Deaths of Antony and Cleopatra VIII and the annexation of Egypt (30)	
	Octavian Augustus Caesar (27 B.C.–A.D. 14)	
	Annexation of Galatia (25)	
1 B.C.		Seneca (3 B.C.–A.D. 65)
A.D. 1	Campaigns against Germanicus (14–17)	
	Tiberius (14–37)	
		Pliny the Elder (23–79)
	Caligula (37–41)	Lucan (39–65)
		Martial (40–104)
	Claudius (41–54)	
	Invasion and annexation of southern Britain (43)	
	Nero (54–68)	Juvenal (50s after 127)
		Tacitus (56–c. 117)
	Assassination of Agrippina, mother of Nero (59)	
		Pliny the Younger (61–113)
	Fire in Rome; Christians persecuted (64)	
	Vespasian (69–79)	
	Destruction of Jerusalem (70)	
		Suetonius (c. 75–150)
	Titus (79–81)	
	Destruction of Pompeii and Herculaneum (79)	
	Domitian (81–96)	
	Trajan (98–117)	
	Hadrian (117–138)	
	Revolt of the Jews in the East (132–134)	
	Final Jewish revolt against Rome put down (135)	

Chronological and Background Charts of the New Testament, pp. 48–49

22 This is why "it was credited to him as righteousness."[m] 23 The words "it was credited to him" were writ-
ten not for him alone, 24 but also for us,[n] to whom God will credit righteousness—for us who believe in
him[o] who raised Jesus our Lord from the dead.[p] 25 He was delivered over to death for our sins[q] and was
raised to life for our justification.

Peace and Joy

5 Therefore, since we have been justified through faith,[r] we[a] have peace with God through our Lord
Jesus Christ, 2 through whom we have gained access[s] by faith into this grace in which we now stand.[t]
And we[a] rejoice in the hope[u] of the glory of God. 3 Not only so, but we[a] also rejoice in our sufferings,[v] be-
cause we know that suffering produces perseverance;[w] 4 perseverance, character; and character, hope.
5 And hope[x] does not disappoint us, because God has poured out his love into our hearts by the Holy
Spirit,[y] whom he has given us.
6 You see, at just the right time,[z] when we were still powerless, Christ died for the ungodly.[a] 7 Very rare-
ly will anyone die for a righteous man, though for a good man someone might possibly dare to die. 8 But
God demonstrates his own love for us in this: While we were still sinners, Christ died for us.[b]
9 Since we have now been justified by his blood,[c] how much more shall we be saved from God's
wrath[d] through him! 10 For if, when we were God's enemies,[e] we were reconciled[f] to him through the
death of his Son, how much more, having been reconciled, shall we be saved through his life![g] 11 Not
only is this so, but we also rejoice in God through our Lord Jesus Christ, through whom we have now
received reconciliation.

Death Through Adam, Life Through Christ

12 Therefore, just as sin entered the world through one man,[h] and death through sin,[i] and in this way
death came to all men, because all sinned— 13 for before the law was given, sin was in the world. But sin
is not taken into account when there is no law.[j] 14 Nevertheless, death reigned from the time of Adam to
the time of Moses, even over those who did not sin by breaking a command, as did Adam, who was a
pattern of the one to come.[k]
15 But the gift is not like the trespass. For if the many died by the trespass of the one man,[l] how much
more did God's grace and the gift that came by the grace of the one man, Jesus Christ,[m] overflow to the
many! 16 Again, the gift of God is not like the result of the one man's sin: The judgment followed one sin
and brought condemnation, but the gift followed many trespasses and brought justification. 17 For if, by
the trespass of the one man, death[n] reigned through that one man, how much more will those who re-
ceive God's abundant provision of grace and of the gift of righteousness reign in life through the one
man, Jesus Christ.
18 Consequently, just as the result of one trespass was condemnation for all men,[o] so also the result of
one act of righteousness was justification[p] that brings life for all men. 19 For just as through the disobe-
dience of the one man[q] the many were made sinners, so also through the obedience[r] of the one man the
many will be made righteous.
20 The law was added so that the trespass might increase.[s] But where sin increased, grace increased
all the more,[t] 21 so that, just as sin reigned in death,[u] so also grace might reign through righteousness to
bring eternal life through Jesus Christ our Lord.

Dead to Sin, Alive in Christ

6 What shall we say, then? Shall we go on sinning so that grace may increase?[v] 2 By no means! We died
to sin;[w] how can we live in it any longer? 3 Or don't you know that all of us who were baptized[x] into
Christ Jesus were baptized into his death? 4 We were therefore buried with him through baptism into
death in order that, just as Christ was raised from the dead[y] through the glory of the Father, we too may
live a new life.[z]

[a] *1, 2, 3* Or *let us*

4:22 [m]ver 3
4:24 [n]Ro 15:4; 1Co 9:10; 10:11 [o]Ro 10:9 [p]Ac 2:24
4:25 [q]Isa 53:5,6; Ro 5:6,8
5:1 [r]Ro 3:28
5:2 [s]Eph 2:18 [t]1Co 15:1 [u]Heb 3:6
5:3 [v]Mt 5:12 [w]Jas 1:2,3
5:5 [x]Php 1:20 [y]Ac 2:33
5:6 [z]Gal 4:4 [a]Ro 4:25
5:8 [b]Jn 15:13; 1Pe 3:18
5:9 [c]Ro 3:25 [d]Ro 1:18
5:10 [e]Ro 11:28; Col 1:21 [f]2Co 5:18,19; Col 1:20,22 [g]Ro 8:34
5:12 [h]ver 15,16, 17; 1Co 15:21,22 [i]Ge 2:17; 3:19; Ro 6:23
5:13 [j]Ro 4:15
5:14 [k]1Co 15:22, 45
5:15 [l]ver 12,18, 19 [m]Ac 15:11
5:17 [n]ver 12
5:18 [o]ver 12 [p]Ro 4:25
5:19 [q]ver 12 [r]Php 2:8
5:20 [s]Ro 7:7,8; Gal 3:19 [t]1Ti 1:13,14
5:21 [u]ver 12,14
6:1 [v]ver 15; Ro 3:5,8
6:2 [w]Col 3:3,5; 1Pe 2:24
6:3 [x]Mt 28:19
6:4 [y]Col 2:12 [z]Ro 7:6; Gal 6:15; Eph 4:22-24; Col 3:10

4:25 These words, which reflect the Septuagint translation of Isaiah 53:12, are probably quoted from a Christian confessional formula. (See "The Septuagint and Its Use in the New Testament" on p. 1995.)
6:1 For the heresy of antinomianism (the view that the oral law does not apply to Christians, who are under the law of grace), see the note on 3:8.
6:3–4 In New Testament times baptism so closely followed conversion that the two were considered parts of one event (see Ac 2:38; see also "Baptism in the Ancient World" on p. 1562).

The Roman Empire

ROMANS 4 Tradition claims that Rome was founded in 753 B.C. and originally ruled by a series of kings.[1] Located at a cluster of hills on the Tiber River in central Italy, Rome from its earliest years pressed against the Etruscans to the north and the Latin and Greek colonists to the south in a lengthy process of gaining control of the Italian peninsula. The Roman monarchy ended around 509 B.C. and was replaced by the republic. Most of Italy was under Roman control by the mid-third century B.C., and in the latter part of that century Rome fought a series of wars against the North African city of Carthage (the Punic Wars). In the Second Punic War (218–201 B.C.) Rome suffered a series of catastrophic defeats against the Carthaginian Hannibal but ultimately prevailed due to sheer force of will, thereby gaining control of the western Mediterranean. Moving into the eastern Mediterranean, the Romans subdued the Greeks, **Anatolia** (Turkey), Syria and the Holy Land. Egypt's independence ended when the last pharaoh, Cleopatra, committed suicide before the onslaught of Roman forces in 30 B.C.

Meanwhile the government in the Roman Republic, which had been designed with a complex set of checks and balances, became increasingly paralyzed and characterized by political strife. Generals such as Gaius Marius (c. 157–86 B.C.) and Lucius Cornelius Sulla (c. 138–78 B.C.) demonstrated that a successful general could control Roman politics solely with his army.[2] Gaius Julius Caesar (c. 100–44 B.C.) exploited this to the full and, after conquering Gaul (France) and then defeating his rival Pompey the Great (c. 106–48 B.C.) in a civil war, was declared dictator for life in Rome. Conservatives in the Senate assassinated him in an attempt to restore the republic, but it had run its course. In a series of civil wars, Octavian (Augustus Caesar), great-nephew and adopted heir of Julius Caesar, established himself as sole ruler of the Roman world.[3]

This began the period of Roman history known as the Principate (27 B.C.–A.D. 285), during which the Roman world was ruled by a series of emperors. After a long decline, Emperor Diocletian (A.D. 245–316) restored order and divided the empire into four administrative districts. Diocletian's abdication was followed by another period of war and confusion, from which Constantine the Great (c. 280–337) emerged victorious. He moved his capital city to Byzantium, renaming it Constantinople (modern Istanbul), and declared Christianity to be the official religion of the Roman Empire.[4] The western empire declined and collapsed in 476 with the abdication of Romulus Augustulus, but its eastern counterpart survived as the **Byzantine** Empire until Constantinople fell to the Ottoman Turks in 1453.

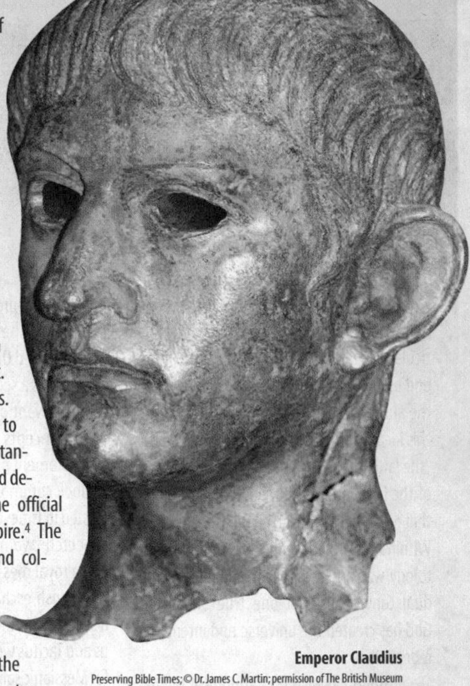
Emperor Claudius

Preserving Bible Times; © Dr. James C. Martin; permission of The British Museum

The Roman Principate provides the political and cultural framework for the writings of the New Testament. Cities that fell under Roman control had various histories of relations with Rome. Tarsus, for instance, was a free city that was not taxed,[5] and Corinth and Philippi, as official Roman colonies, were permitted certain legal benefits.[6] Roman citizenship, although widely extended, was not granted to all who lived under Roman control.[7] An extensive system of roads benefited both the military and commercial pursuits of the empire.[8] With an economy based largely upon agriculture and slavery, the ranks of the lower classes swelled.

The Roman world incorporated a confusing array of religions, cults and superstitions. In addition, Roman emperors were deified at death, and all within the empire were expected to manifest their loyalty to Rome by participating in the imperial cult, paying homage to the current Caesar as lord.[9] When Christians refused to do so, they were accused of treason.[10] Even so, the peaceful conditions that prevailed at this time (the *pax Romana* or "peace of Rome"), the common Greco-Roman culture and the vast transportation system allowed Christianity to flourish.

[1]See "Rome" on page 1838. [2]See "The Roman Army and the Occupation of the Holy Land" on page 1829. [3]See "Caesar Augustus, Emperor of Rome; the Census; and Quirinius, Governor of Syria" on page 1667. [4]See "Constantine and Queen Helena's Roles in Preserving Holy Sites" on page 1758. [5]See "Roman Taxation" on page 1855. [6]See "Corinth" on page 1887 and "Philippi" on page 1927. [7]See "Roman Citizenship" on page 1930. [8]See "Travel in the Greco-Roman World" on page 1946 and "Trade and Mercantilism in the Roman Empire" on page 2070. [9]See "The Imperial Cult" on page 1651. [10]See "The Early Persecution of the Church" on page 2067.

5If we have been united with him like this in his death, we will certainly also be united with him in
his resurrection.[a] 6For we know that our old self[b] was crucified with him[c] so that the body of sin[d] might
be done away with,[a] that we should no longer be slaves to sin— 7because anyone who has died has been
freed from sin.
8Now if we died with Christ, we believe that we will also live with him. 9For we know that since Christ
was raised from the dead,[e] he cannot die again; death no longer has mastery over him.[f] 10The death he
died, he died to sin[g] once for all; but the life he lives, he lives to God.

6:5 [a]2Co 4:10; Php 3:10,11
6:6 [b]Eph 4:22; Col 3:9 [c]Gal 2:20; Col 2:12,20 [d]Ro 7:24
6:9 [e]Ac 2:24 [f]Rev 1:18
6:10 [g]ver 2

[a] 6 Or *be rendered powerless*

Jewish Eschatology in the First Century A.D.

ROMANS 6 Eschatology refers to the "study of the last things" and the ways in which particular religious communities conceive of the end or goal of history. The Bible does not use the abstract term "eschatology" but suggests this idea with phrases like "the coming days," "the latter days," "the end of time" or "the day of the LORD" and its abbreviated version, "on that day" (Dt 4:30; Isa 11:11; Da 2:28; Joel 2:1). Within Judaism and early Christianity, eschatology was a necessary consequence of the dual convictions that one true and living God has created the universe and intends to redeem it.

Although Jewish eschatological beliefs in the first century A.D. were tremendously diverse, certain key concepts were held in common:

- Israel awaited restoration and the divine reversal of all that was wrong in the world.
- Pagan empires and their idols would be cast down and Jerusalem glorified.
- Corrupt leadership within Israel would be removed and the true Davidic King installed.
- Israel's sins would be forgiven, and God would pour out his Spirit upon his people so that the nation would become obedient.
- As a result, light would go forth from Jerusalem and summon all nations to worship the Lord of all the earth.

An important aspect of this general picture is the notion of a personal Redeemer, an authorized representative who mediates the relationship between God and his people. This Anointed One, or Messiah, is understood variously as a second Moses, a royal son, a suffering servant or a chosen high priest. All of these concepts are deeply indebted to the Old Testament prophets and reflect a general outlook common to the diverse groups that existed in Israel. Some Jewish parties actually expected two messiahs: a priestly messiah and a royal messiah.

Jewish eschatological belief was hardly a secret. Even the Roman historians Suetonius and Tacitus were aware of the Jewish hope for Messianic salvation. The synagogue liturgy also included daily prayers that focused on Israel's hope.[1]

Despite the broad unity of Jewish eschatology, a wide array of opinions existed regarding the exact timing and precise manner in which these great events would transpire (1Pe 1:10–12). Individual authors articulated Israel's hope for the future through a range of images and metaphors, the sum total of which can be difficult to reconcile. Different religious groups held widely divergent understandings as to the necessary precursors of the Messianic age, as well as unique perspectives on how their own movements stood in relation to it:

- The Pharisees, who seem to have acknowledged the broadest eschatological scenario, understood faithfulness to the **Torah** as the divine prerequisite for Israel's visitation (Ac 15:5).[2]
- The Sadducees denied the resurrection (Mt 22:23), and their attitude toward eschatology in general remains uncertain.[3]
- The Essenes of **Qumran** believed that their own community was the beginning of the fulfillment of the age of redemption. The Essenes set themselves apart both from Gentile oppressors and from Jewish apostates, with whom they expected a final conflict.
- Josephus considered the Zealots to be a fourth sect within Judaism. Its members thought of themselves as followers of Phinehas, Elijah and the Maccabees in believing that active resistance was the necessary antecedent for the eschatological age.[4]

The diverse interpretations of prophecy in first-century Judaism serve to instill caution in modern interpretations of prophecy. The primary message of the New Testament is that the hope of Israel is fulfilled in Jesus (Mk 1:15; 1Co 10:11; Heb 9:26; 1Pe 1:20), and it was precisely this critical point that many Jewish leaders, despite their close reading of prophecy, failed to recognize. Recent efforts to employ Biblical prophecy to describe with precision how and when the events of the world's end will take place may well prove to be as misguided as those of first-century interpreters.

[1]See "Ancient Synagogues" on page 1783. [2]See "The Pharisees" on page 1566. [3]See "The Sadducees" on page 1600. [4]See "The Zealots and the Essenes" on page 1576.

6:11 [h]ver 2 — 11 In the same way, count yourselves dead to sin[h] but alive to God in Christ Jesus. 12 Therefore do not
let sin reign in your mortal body so that you obey its evil desires. 13 Do not offer the parts of your body
6:13 [i]ver 16,19; Ro 7:5 [j]Ro 12:1; — to sin, as instruments of wickedness,[i] but rather offer yourselves to God, as those who have been brought
1Pe 2:24 — from death to life; and offer the parts of your body to him as instruments of righteousness.[j] 14 For sin
6:14 [k]Gal 5:18 [l]Ro 3:24 — shall not be your master, because you are not under law,[k] but under grace.[l]

Slaves to Righteousness

15 What then? Shall we sin because we are not under law but under grace? By no means! 16 Don't you
know that when you offer yourselves to someone to obey him as slaves, you are slaves to the one whom
6:16 [m]Jn 8:34; 2Pe 2:19 [n]ver 23 — you obey—whether you are slaves to sin,[m] which leads to death,[n] or to obedience, which leads to righ-
6:17 [o]Ro 1:8; 2Co 2:14 — teousness? 17 But thanks be to God[o] that, though you used to be slaves to sin, you wholeheartedly obeyed
[p]2Ti 1:13 — the form of teaching[p] to which you were entrusted. 18 You have been set free from sin[q] and have become
6:18 [q]ver 7,22; Ro 8:2 — slaves to righteousness.
6:19 [r]Ro 3:5 [s]ver 13 — 19 I put this in human terms[r] because you are weak in your natural selves. Just as you used to offer the
parts of your body in slavery to impurity and to ever-increasing wickedness, so now offer them in slav-
6:20 [t]ver 16 — ery to righteousness[s] leading to holiness. 20 When you were slaves to sin,[t] you were free from the control
of righteousness. 21 What benefit did you reap at that time from the things you are now ashamed of? Those
6:21 [u]ver 23 — things result in death![u] 22 But now that you have been set free from sin[v] and have become slaves to God,[w]
6:22 [v]ver 18 [w]1Co 7:22; 1Pe 2:16 — the benefit you reap leads to holiness, and the result is eternal life. 23 For the wages of sin is death,[x] but
6:23 [x]Ge 2:17; Ro 5:12; Gal 6:7, 8; Jas 1:15 [y]Mt 25:46 — the gift of God is eternal life[y] in[a] Christ Jesus our Lord.

An Illustration From Marriage

7:1 [z]Ro 1:13 — 7 Do you not know, brothers[z]—for I am speaking to men who know the law—that the law has au-
thority over a man only as long as he lives? 2 For example, by law a married woman is bound to her
7:2 [a]1Co 7:39 — husband as long as he is alive, but if her husband dies, she is released from the law of marriage.[a] 3 So
then, if she marries another man while her husband is still alive, she is called an adulteress. But if her hus-
band dies, she is released from that law and is not an adulteress, even though she marries another man.
7:4 [b]Ro 8:2; Gal 2:19 [c]Col 1:22 — 4 So, my brothers, you also died to the law[b] through the body of Christ,[c] that you might belong to an-
other, to him who was raised from the dead, in order that we might bear fruit to God. 5 For when we were
7:5 [d]Ro 7:7-11 [e]Ro 6:13 — controlled by the sinful nature,[b] the sinful passions aroused by the law[d] were at work in our bodies,[e] so
that we bore fruit for death. 6 But now, by dying to what once bound us, we have been released from the
7:6 [f]Ro 2:29; 2Co 3:6 — law so that we serve in the new way of the Spirit, and not in the old way of the written code.[f]

Struggling With Sin

7 What shall we say, then? Is the law sin? Certainly not! Indeed I would not have known what sin was
7:7 [g]Ro 3:20; 4:15 [h]Ex 20:17; Dt 5:21 — except through the law.[g] For I would not have known what coveting really was if the law had not said, "Do
not covet."[c h] 8 But sin, seizing the opportunity afforded by the commandment,[i] produced in me every
7:8 [i]ver 11 [j]Ro 4:15; 1Co 15:56 — kind of covetous desire. For apart from law, sin is dead.[j] 9 Once I was alive apart from law; but when the
commandment came, sin sprang to life and I died. 10 I found that the very commandment that was in-
7:10 [k]Lev 18:5; Lk 10:26-28; Ro 10:5; Gal 3:12 — tended to bring life[k] actually brought death. 11 For sin, seizing the opportunity afforded by the command-
7:11 [l]Ge 3:13 — ment, deceived me,[l] and through the commandment put me to death. 12 So then, the law is holy, and the
7:12 [m]1Ti 1:8 — commandment is holy, righteous and good.[m]
13 Did that which is good, then, become death to me? By no means! But in order that sin might be rec-
ognized as sin, it produced death in me through what was good, so that through the commandment sin
might become utterly sinful.
7:14 [n]1Co 3:1 — 14 We know that the law is spiritual; but I am unspiritual,[n] sold[o] as a slave to sin. 15 I do not under-
[o]1Ki 21:20,25; 2Ki 17:17 — stand what I do. For what I want to do I do not do, but what I hate I do.[p] 16 And if I do what I do not want
7:15 [p]ver 19; Gal 5:17 — to do, I agree that the law is good.[q] 17 As it is, it is no longer I myself who do it, but it is sin living in me.[r]
7:16 [q]ver 12 7:17 [r]ver 20 — 18 I know that nothing good lives in me, that is, in my sinful nature.[d s] For I have the desire to do what is
7:18 [s]ver 25 — good, but I cannot carry it out. 19 For what I do is not the good I want to do; no, the evil I do not want to

[a] 23 Or *through* [b] 5 Or *the flesh*; also in verse 25 [c] 7 Exodus 20:17; Deut. 5:21 [d] 18 Or *my flesh*

7:2–3 Some scholars insist that these verses prove that remarriage on any basis other than the death of a spouse is adulterous. But both Roman and Jewish law allowed for remarriage after a legitimate divorce (see "Marriage and Divorce in Ancient Israel" on p. 1548). Paul was not teaching about marriage or divorce but was illustrating the point that believers have "died" to the law.

do—this I keep on doing.[t] 20 Now if I do what I do not want to do, it is no longer I who do it, but it is sin 7:19 [t]ver 15
living in me that does it.[u] 7:20 [u]ver 17
21 So I find this law at work:[v] When I want to do good, evil is right there with me. 22 For in my inner 7:21 [v]ver 23,25
being[w] I delight in God's law;[x] 23 but I see another law at work in the members of my body, waging war[y] 7:22 [w]Eph 3:16 [x]Ps 1:2
against the law of my mind and making me a prisoner of the law of sin at work within my members. 7:23 [y]Gal 5:17; Jas 4:1; 1Pe 2:11
24 What a wretched man I am! Who will rescue me from this body of death?[z] 25 Thanks be to God— 7:24 [z]Ro 6:6; 8:2
through Jesus Christ our Lord!
So then, I myself in my mind am a slave to God's law, but in the sinful nature a slave to the law of sin.

Life Through the Spirit

8 Therefore, there is now no condemnation[a] for those who are in Christ Jesus,[a][b] 2 because through 8:1 [a]ver 34 [b]ver 39; Ro 16:3
Christ Jesus the law of the Spirit of life[c] set me free[d] from the law of sin[e] and death. 3 For what the 8:2 [c]1Co 15:45 [d]Ro 6:18 [e]Ro 7:4
law was powerless[f] to do in that it was weakened by the sinful nature,[b] God did by sending his own Son 8:3 [f]Ac 13:39; Heb 7:18 [g]Php 2:7 [h]Heb 2:14,17
in the likeness of sinful man[g] to be a sin offering.[c][h] And so he condemned sin in sinful man,[d] 4 in order
that the righteous requirements of the law might be fully met in us, who do not live according to the sin-
ful nature but according to the Spirit.[i] 8:4 [i]Gal 5:16
5 Those who live according to the sinful nature have their minds set on what that nature desires;[j] but 8:5 [j]Gal 5:19-21 [k]Gal 5:22-25
those who live in accordance with the Spirit have their minds set on what the Spirit desires.[k] 6 The mind
of sinful man[e] is death, but the mind controlled by the Spirit is life[l] and peace; 7 the sinful mind[f] is hos- 8:6 [l]Gal 6:8
tile to God.[m] It does not submit to God's law, nor can it do so. 8 Those controlled by the sinful nature can- 8:7 [m]Jas 4:4
not please God.
9 You, however, are controlled not by the sinful nature but by the Spirit, if the Spirit of God lives in
you.[n] And if anyone does not have the Spirit of Christ,[o] he does not belong to Christ. 10 But if Christ is in 8:9 [n]1Co 6:19; Gal 4:6 [o]Jn 14:17; 1Jn 4:13
you,[p] your body is dead because of sin, yet your spirit is alive because of righteousness. 11 And if the Spir-
it of him who raised Jesus from the dead[q] is living in you, he who raised Christ from the dead will also 8:10 [p]Gal 2:20; Eph 3:17; Col 1:27
give life to your mortal bodies[r] through his Spirit, who lives in you. 8:11 [q]Ac 2:24 [r]Jn 5:21
12 Therefore, brothers, we have an obligation—but it is not to the sinful nature, to live according to it.
13 For if you live according to the sinful nature, you will die; but if by the Spirit you put to death the mis-
deeds of the body, you will live,[s] 14 because those who are led by the Spirit of God[t] are sons of God.[u] 15 For 8:13 [s]Gal 6:8
you did not receive a spirit that makes you a slave again to fear,[v] but you received the Spirit of sonship.[g] 8:14 [t]Gal 5:18 [u]Jn 1:12; Rev 21:7
And by him we cry, *"Abba,[h]* Father."[w] 16 The Spirit himself testifies with our spirit[x] that we are God's chil- 8:15 [v]2Ti 1:7; Heb 2:15 [w]Mk 14:36; Gal 4:5,6
dren. 17 Now if we are children, then we are heirs[y]—heirs of God and co-heirs with Christ, if indeed we 8:16 [x]Eph 1:13
share in his sufferings in order that we may also share in his glory.[z] 8:17 [y]Ac 20:32; Gal 4:7 [z]1Pe 4:13

Future Glory

18 I consider that our present sufferings are not worth comparing with the glory that will be revealed
in us.[a] 19 The creation waits in eager expectation for the sons of God to be revealed. 20 For the creation 8:18 [a]2Co 4:17; 1Pe 4:13
was subjected to frustration, not by its own choice, but by the will of the one who subjected it,[b] in hope 8:20 [b]Ge 3:17-19
21 that[i] the creation itself will be liberated from its bondage to decay[c] and brought into the glorious free- 8:21 [c]Ac 3:21; 2Pe 3:13; Rev 21:1
dom of the children of God.
22 We know that the whole creation has been groaning[d] as in the pains of childbirth right up to the 8:22 [d]Jer 12:4
present time. 23 Not only so, but we ourselves, who have the firstfruits of the Spirit,[e] groan[f] inwardly as 8:23 [e]2Co 5:5 [f]2Co 5:2,4 [g]Gal 5:5
we wait eagerly[g] for our adoption as sons, the redemption of our bodies. 24 For in this hope we were
saved.[h] But hope that is seen is no hope at all. Who hopes for what he already has? 25 But if we hope for 8:24 [h]1Th 5:8
what we do not yet have, we wait for it patiently.

[a] *1* Some later manuscripts *Jesus, who do not live according to the sinful nature but according to the Spirit,* [b] *3* Or *the flesh*; also in verses 4, 5, 8, 9, 12 and 13 [c] *3* Or *man, for sin* [d] *3* Or *in the flesh* [e] *6* Or *mind set on the flesh* [f] *7* Or *the mind set on the flesh* [g] *15* Or *adoption* [h] *15* Aramaic for *Father* [i] *20,21* Or *subjected it in hope. 21For*

7:25 In the New Testament the word "mind" frequently occurs in an ethical sense (referring to the will and moral disposition of a person), as here and in Colossians 2:18. See "Heart, Breath, Throat and Intestines: Ancient Hebrew Anthropology" on page 968.

8:15 The underlying word of "sonship" is "adoption" (see the NIV text note). Adoption was common among the Greeks and Romans, who granted the adopted son all the privileges of a natural son, including inheritance rights (see "Adoption in the Roman World" on p. 1849).

Abba is the Aramaic word for "father," transliterated into Greek and thence into English. The corresponding Hebrew word is *Ab. Abba* is found three times in the New Testament (see also Mk 14:36; Gal 4:6). For the use of the Aramaic language in New Testament times, see the note on Mark 5:41.

26 In the same way, the Spirit helps us in our weakness. We do not know what we ought to pray for, but
the Spirit himself intercedes for us[i] with groans that words cannot express. 27 And he who searches our
hearts[j] knows the mind of the Spirit, because the Spirit intercedes for the saints in accordance with God's
will.

More Than Conquerors

28 And we know that in all things God works for the good of those who love him,[a] who[b] have been
called[k] according to his purpose. 29 For those God foreknew[l] he also predestined[m] to be conformed to the
likeness of his Son,[n] that he might be the firstborn among many brothers. 30 And those he predestined,[o]
he also called; those he called, he also justified;[p] those he justified, he also glorified.[q]

31 What, then, shall we say in response to this?[r] If God is for us, who can be against us?[s] 32 He who did
not spare his own Son,[t] but gave him up for us all—how will he not also, along with him, graciously give
us all things? 33 Who will bring any charge[u] against those whom God has chosen? It is God who justifies.
34 Who is he that condemns? Christ Jesus, who died[v]—more than that, who was raised to life—is at the

[a] 28 Some manuscripts *And we know that all things work together for good to those who love God* [b] 28 Or *works together with those who love him to bring about what is good—with those who*

8:26 [i]Eph 6:18
8:27 [j]Rev 2:23
8:28 [k]1Co 1:9; 2Ti 1:9
8:29 [l]Ro 11:2 [m]Eph 1:5,11 [n]1Co 15:49; 2Co 3:18; Php 3:21; 1Jn 3:2
8:30 [o]Eph 1:5,11 [p]1Co 6:11 [q]Ro 9:23
8:31 [r]Ro 4:1 [s]Ps 118:6
8:32 [t]Jn 3:16; Ro 4:25; 5:8
8:33 [u]Isa 50:8,9
8:34 [v]Ro 5:6-8

8:26 For commentary on the phrase "groans that words cannot express," see "Tongue-Speaking in Christian and Pagan Worship" on page 1876.
8:31–39 Rhetoric (the art of speaking, and particularly the science of persuasion) was important in the ancient Greco-Roman world (see "Debate and Rhetoric in the Ancient World" on p. 1797). Paul's language in these verses was *rhetorical*—chosen to move or convince the reader. Paul was trying to draw his audience into the discussion.
8:34 For "at the right hand of God," see "The 'Right Hand' in Ancient Thinking" on page 1983.

Adoption in the Roman World

ROMANS 8 Adoption was widely practiced in the ancient world; examples have been found from Mesopotamian, Egyptian, Greek, Roman and ancient Jewish sources. For example, according to Exodus 2:10 Moses was a foundling adopted by Pharaoh's daughter. Generally speaking, only free men (not women or slaves) could adopt, and the adoptee was often an adult rather than a child. Sometimes adoption was undertaken partially for the benefit of the adopter. For example, an older man whose natural children had already died might adopt a younger man as his heir; the adoptee would be responsible to care for the adopter in his old age.[1]

Roman law recognized two kinds of adoption: *adrogatio*, in which a man and all those under his authority were adopted into another family, and *adoptio*, in which an individual was adopted into a family. In *adrogatio* the adopted family in effect ceased to exist as a separate entity and became a part of the adopter's family.

An adopted man or boy no longer belonged to his father's household and legally became a child of the adopter. The adoptee in the Roman world took the adopter's name and rank and became his legal heir. Adoption had to be carried out under a specific protocol (e.g., in the presence of the governor), and a will was often prepared in conjunction with the official process. The association of these two activities reveals the connection between the legal, familial status of the adoptee and his inheritance rights.

Paul embraced the metaphor of adoption in Romans 8 in order to describe the status of Christians in relation to God. God as the Father of his adopted children has authority over them, while they in turn have taken on his identity. Paul also wrote of the inheritance that belongs to believers because God has adopted them as his children (Gal 4:5–7). The redemption of the body is one aspect of the Christian's inheritance that Paul highlighted in Romans 8:23.

[1]See "The Historicity of the Patriarchal Narratives" on page 73 and "Inheritance in the Ancient Near East" on page 250.

right hand of God[w] and is also interceding for us.[x] 35Who shall separate us from the love of Christ? Shall
trouble or hardship or persecution or famine or nakedness or danger or sword?[y] 36As it is written:

> "For your sake we face death all day long;
> we are considered as sheep to be slaughtered."[a][z]

37No, in all these things we are more than conquerors[a] through him who loved us.[b] 38For I am convinced
that neither death nor life, neither angels nor demons,[b] neither the present nor the future, nor any pow-
ers,[c] 39neither height nor depth, nor anything else in all creation, will be able to separate us from the love
of God[d] that is in Christ Jesus our Lord.

God's Sovereign Choice

9 I speak the truth in Christ—I am not lying,[e] my conscience confirms[f] it in the Holy Spirit— 2I have
great sorrow and unceasing anguish in my heart. 3For I could wish that I myself[g] were cursed[h] and
cut off from Christ for the sake of my brothers, those of my own race,[i] 4the people of Israel. Theirs is the
adoption as sons;[j] theirs the divine glory, the covenants,[k] the receiving of the law,[l] the temple worship[m]
and the promises.[n] 5Theirs are the patriarchs, and from them is traced the human ancestry of Christ,[o]
who is God over all,[p] forever praised![c][q] Amen.

6It is not as though God's word had failed. For not all who are descended from Israel are Israel.[r] 7Nor
because they are his descendants are they all Abraham's children. On the contrary, "It is through Isaac that
your offspring will be reckoned."[d][s] 8In other words, it is not the natural children who are God's children,[t]
but it is the children of the promise who are regarded as Abraham's offspring. 9For this was how the
promise was stated: "At the appointed time I will return, and Sarah will have a son."[e][u]

10Not only that, but Rebekah's children had one and the same father, our father Isaac.[v] 11Yet, before the
twins were born or had done anything good or bad—in order that God's purpose[w] in election might
stand: 12not by works but by him who calls—she was told, "The older will serve the younger."[f][x] 13Just as
it is written: "Jacob I loved, but Esau I hated."[g][y]

14What then shall we say? Is God unjust? Not at all![z] 15For he says to Moses,

> "I will have mercy on whom I have mercy,
> and I will have compassion on whom I have compassion."[h][a]

16It does not, therefore, depend on man's desire or effort, but on God's mercy.[b] 17For the Scripture says
to Pharaoh: "I raised you up for this very purpose, that I might display my power in you and that my
name might be proclaimed in all the earth."[i][c] 18Therefore God has mercy on whom he wants to have
mercy, and he hardens whom he wants to harden.[d]

19One of you will say to me:[e] "Then why does God still blame us? For who resists his will?"[f] 20But who
are you, O man, to talk back to God? "Shall what is formed say to him who formed it,[g] 'Why did you make
me like this?' "[j][h] 21Does not the potter have the right to make out of the same lump of clay some pottery
for noble purposes and some for common use?[i]

22What if God, choosing to show his wrath and make his power known, bore with great patience[j] the
objects of his wrath—prepared for destruction? 23What if he did this to make the riches of his glory[k]
known to the objects of his mercy, whom he prepared in advance for glory[l]— 24even us, whom he also
called,[m] not only from the Jews but also from the Gentiles?[n] 25As he says in Hosea:

> "I will call them 'my people' who are not my people;
> and I will call her 'my loved one' who is not my loved one,"[k][o]

8:34 [w]Mk 16:19 [x]Heb 7:25; 9:24; 1Jn 2:1
8:35 [y]1Co 4:11
8:36 [z]Ps 44:22; 2Co 4:11
8:37 [a]1Co 15:57 [b]Gal 2:20; Rev 1:5; 3:9
8:38 [c]Eph 1:21; 1Pe 3:22
8:39 [d]Ro 5:8
9:1 [e]2Co 11:10; Gal 1:20; 1Ti 2:7 [f]Ro 1:9
9:3 [g]Ex 32:32 [h]1Co 12:3; 16:22 [i]Ro 11:14
9:4 [j]Ex 4:22 [k]Ge 17:2; Ac 3:25; Eph 2:12 [l]Ps 147:19 [m]Heb 9:1 [n]Ac 13:32
9:5 [o]Mt 1:1-16 [p]Jn 1:1 [q]Ro 1:25
9:6 [r]Ro 2:28,29; Gal 6:16
9:7 [s]Ge 21:12; Heb 11:18
9:8 [t]Ro 8:14
9:9 [u]Ge 18:10,14
9:10 [v]Ge 25:21
9:11 [w]Ro 8:28
9:12 [x]Ge 25:23
9:13 [y]Mal 1:2,3
9:14 [z]2Ch 19:7
9:15 [a]Ex 33:19
9:16 [b]Eph 2:8
9:17 [c]Ex 9:16
9:18 [d]Ex 4:21
9:19 [e]Ro 11:19 [f]2Ch 20:6; Da 4:35
9:20 [g]Isa 64:8 [h]Isa 29:16
9:21 [i]2Ti 2:20
9:22 [j]Ro 2:4
9:23 [k]Ro 2:4 [l]Ro 8:30
9:24 [m]Ro 8:28 [n]Ro 3:29
9:25 [o]Hos 2:23; 1Pe 2:10

[a] *36* Psalm 44:22 [b] *38* Or *nor heavenly rulers* [c] *5* Or *Christ, who is over all. God be forever praised!* Or *Christ. God who is over all be forever praised!* [d] *7* Gen. 21:12 [e] *9* Gen. 18:10,14 [f] *12* Gen. 25:23 [g] *13* Mal. 1:2,3 [h] *15* Exodus 33:19 [i] *17* Exodus 9:16 [j] *20* Isaiah 29:16; 45:9 [k] *25* Hosea 2:23

9:4 The "people of Israel" refers to the descendants of Jacob (who was named Israel by God; see Ge 32:28). The name was used of the entire nation (see Jdg 5:7), then of the northern kingdom after the nation was divided (see 1Ki 12), the southern kingdom being called Judah. During the intertestamental period and later in New Testament times, Palestinian Jews used the title to indicate that they were the chosen people of God, his adopted "sons" (see "Adoption in the Roman World" on p. 1849).

9:17 God's "name" is synonymous with God himself because it reflects his character (see the note on Jer 16:21).

9:21 Rabbis (including Jesus) regularly used simple illustrations from everyday life to drive home profound theological points. Describing God as a potter illustrates his sovereignty. But analogies were not meant to be exhaustive theological statements. The analogies between God and the potter and between a human being and a pot should not be pressed to the extreme. A human is more than an inanimate object made of clay. (See "Pottery-Making in Bible Times" on p. 1223.)

[26]and,

"It will happen that in the very place where it was said to them,
'You are not my people,'
9:26 [p]Hos 1:10 they will be called 'sons of the living God.' "[a][p]

[27]Isaiah cries out concerning Israel:

9:27 [q]Ge 22:17; Hos 1:10 [r]Ro 11:5 "Though the number of the Israelites be like the sand by the sea,[q]
only the remnant will be saved.[r]
[28]For the Lord will carry out
9:28 [s]Isa 10:22, 23 his sentence on earth with speed and finality."[b][s]

[29]It is just as Isaiah said previously:

9:29 [t]Jas 5:4 [u]Isa 1:9; Dt 29:23; Isa 13:19; Jer 50:40 "Unless the Lord Almighty[t]
had left us descendants,
we would have become like Sodom,
we would have been like Gomorrah."[c][u]

Israel's Unbelief

[30]What then shall we say? That the Gentiles, who did not pursue righteousness, have obtained it, a
9:30 [v]Ro 1:17; 10:6; Gal 2:16; Php 3:9; Heb 11:7 righteousness that is by faith;[v] [31]but Israel, who pursued a law of righteousness,[w] has not attained it.[x]
9:31 [w]Isa 51:1; Ro 10:2,3 [x]Gal 5:4 [32]Why not? Because they pursued it not by faith but as if it were by works. They stumbled over the "stum-
9:32 [y]1Pe 2:8 bling stone."[y] [33]As it is written:

"See, I lay in Zion a stone that causes men to stumble
and a rock that makes them fall,
9:33 [z]Isa 28:16; Ro 10:11 and the one who trusts in him will never be put to shame."[d][z]

10 Brothers, my heart's desire and prayer to God for the Israelites is that they may be saved. [2]For I
10:2 [a]Ac 21:20 can testify about them that they are zealous[a] for God, but their zeal is not based on knowledge.
[3]Since they did not know the righteousness that comes from God and sought to establish their own, they
10:3 [b]Ro 1:17 did not submit to God's righteousness.[b] [4]Christ is the end of the law[c] so that there may be righteousness
10:4 [c]Gal 3:24; Ro 7:1-4 [d]Ro 3:22 for everyone who believes.[d]
[5]Moses describes in this way the righteousness that is by the law: "The man who does these things
10:5 [e]Lev 18:5; Ne 9:29; Eze 20:11,13,21; Ro 7:10 will live by them."[e][e] [6]But the righteousness that is by faith[f] says: "Do not say in your heart, 'Who will as-
cend into heaven?'[f]"[g] (that is, to bring Christ down) [7]"or 'Who will descend into the deep?'[g]" (that is, to
10:6 [f]Ro 9:30 [g]Dt 30:12 bring Christ up from the dead). [8]But what does it say? "The word is near you; it is in your mouth and in
10:8 [h]Dt 30:14 your heart,"[h][h] that is, the word of faith we are proclaiming: [9]That if you confess[i] with your mouth, "Jesus
10:9 [i]Mt 10:32; Lk 12:8 [j]Ac 2:24 is Lord," and believe in your heart that God raised him from the dead,[j] you will be saved. [10]For it is with
your heart that you believe and are justified, and it is with your mouth that you confess and are saved.
10:11 [k]Isa 28:16; Ro 9:33 [11]As the Scripture says, "Anyone who trusts in him will never be put to shame."[i][k] [12]For there is no differ-
10:12 [l]Ro 3:22, 29 [m]Ac 10:36 ence between Jew and Gentile[l]—the same Lord is Lord of all[m] and richly blesses all who call on him,
10:13 [n]Ac 2:21 [o]Joel 2:32 [13]for, "Everyone who calls on the name of the Lord[n] will be saved."[j][o]
[14]How, then, can they call on the one they have not believed in? And how can they believe in the one
of whom they have not heard? And how can they hear without someone preaching to them? [15]And how
can they preach unless they are sent? As it is written, "How beautiful are the feet of those who bring good
10:15 [p]Isa 52:7; Na 1:15 news!"[k][p]
[16]But not all the Israelites accepted the good news. For Isaiah says, "Lord, who has believed our

[a] *26* Hosea 1:10 [b] *28* Isaiah 10:22,23 [c] *29* Isaiah 1:9 [d] *33* Isaiah 8:14; 28:16 [e] *5* Lev. 18:5 [f] *6* Deut. 30:12 [g] *7* Deut. 30:13 [h] *8* Deut. 30:14 [i] *11* Isaiah 28:16 [j] *13* Joel 2:32 [k] *15* Isaiah 52:7

10:7 See "Sheol, Hades, Gehenna, the Abyss and Tartarus: Images of Hell" on page 946.

10:9 The affirmation "Jesus is Lord," the earliest Christian confession of faith (see 1Co 12:3 and its note), was probably used at baptisms. In view of the fact that "Lord" is used over 6,000 times in the Septuagint to translate the name of Israel's God (Yahweh), it is clear that Paul, when using this word of Jesus, was ascribing deity to him. (See "YHWH: The Name of God in the Old Testament" on p. 89.)

In Biblical terms the heart is the seat not only of the emotions and affections, but also of the intellect and will (see Ps 4:7 and its note, as well as "Heart, Breath, Throat and Intestines: Ancient Hebrew Anthropology" on p. 968).

message?"[a][q] 17 Consequently, faith comes from hearing the message,[r] and the message is heard through
the word of Christ.[s] 18 But I ask: Did they not hear? Of course they did:

> "Their voice has gone out into all the earth,
> their words to the ends of the world."[b][t]

19 Again I ask: Did Israel not understand? First, Moses says,

> "I will make you envious[u] by those who are not a nation;
> I will make you angry by a nation that has no understanding."[c][v]

20 And Isaiah boldly says,

> "I was found by those who did not seek me;
> I revealed myself to those who did not ask for me."[d][w]

21 But concerning Israel he says,

> "All day long I have held out my hands
> to a disobedient and obstinate people."[e][x]

The Remnant of Israel

11 I ask then: Did God reject his people? By no means![y] I am an Israelite myself, a descendant of
Abraham,[z] from the tribe of Benjamin.[a] 2 God did not reject his people, whom he foreknew.[b]
Don't you know what the Scripture says in the passage about Elijah—how he appealed to God against
Israel: 3 "Lord, they have killed your prophets and torn down your altars; I am the only one left, and they
are trying to kill me"[f]?[c] 4 And what was God's answer to him? "I have reserved for myself seven thou-
sand who have not bowed the knee to Baal."[g][d] 5 So too, at the present time there is a remnant[e] chosen by
grace. 6 And if by grace, then it is no longer by works;[f] if it were, grace would no longer be grace.[h]
7 What then? What Israel sought so earnestly it did not obtain,[g] but the elect did. The others were
hardened,[h] 8 as it is written:

> "God gave them a spirit of stupor,
> eyes so that they could not see
> and ears so that they could not hear,[i]
> to this very day."[i][j]

9 And David says:

> "May their table become a snare and a trap,
> a stumbling block and a retribution for them.
> 10 May their eyes be darkened so they cannot see,
> and their backs be bent forever."[j][k]

Ingrafted Branches

11 Again I ask: Did they stumble so as to fall beyond recovery? Not at all![l] Rather, because of their trans-
gression, salvation has come to the Gentiles[m] to make Israel envious.[n] 12 But if their transgression means
riches for the world, and their loss means riches for the Gentiles,[o] how much greater riches will their
fullness bring!
13 I am talking to you Gentiles. Inasmuch as I am the apostle to the Gentiles,[p] I make much of my min-
istry 14 in the hope that I may somehow arouse my own people to envy[q] and save[r] some of them. 15 For if
their rejection is the reconciliation[s] of the world, what will their acceptance be but life from the dead?[t]

10:16 [q]Isa 53:1; Jn 12:38 **10:17** [r]Gal 3:2,5 [s]Col 3:16 **10:18** [t]Ps 19:4; Mt 24:14; Col 1:6, 23; 1Th 1:8 **10:19** [u]Ro 11:11, 14 [v]Dt 32:21 **10:20** [w]Isa 65:1; Ro 9:30 **10:21** [x]Isa 65:2 **11:1** [y]1Sa 12:22; Jer 31:37 [z]2Co 11:22 [a]Php 3:5 **11:2** [b]Ro 8:29 **11:3** [c]1Ki 19:10, 14 **11:4** [d]1Ki 19:18 **11:5** [e]Ro 9:27 **11:6** [f]Ro 4:4 **11:7** [g]Ro 9:31 [h]ver 25; Ro 9:18 **11:8** [i]Mt 13:13-15 [j]Dt 29:4; Isa 29:10 **11:10** [k]Ps 69:22, 23 **11:11** [l]ver 1 [m]Ac 13:46 [n]Ro 10:19 **11:12** [o]ver 25 **11:13** [p]Ac 9:15 **11:14** [q]ver 11; Ro 10:19 [r]1Co 1:21; 1Ti 2:4; Tit 3:5 **11:15** [s]Ro 5:10 [t]Lk 15:24,32

[a] *16* Isaiah 53:1 [b] *18* Psalm 19:4 [c] *19* Deut. 32:21 [d] *20* Isaiah 65:1 [e] *21* Isaiah 65:2 [f] *3* 1 Kings 19:10,14 [g] *4* 1 Kings 19:18 [h] *6* Some manuscripts *be grace. But if by works, then it is no longer grace; if it were, work would no longer be work.* [i] *8* Deut. 29:4; Isaiah 29:10 [j] *10* Psalm 69:22,23

11:4 For "Baal," see the note on Judges 2:13 and "The Ugaritic Text of the Myth of Baal" on page 905.

11:5 Central to Jewish tradition was a distinction between corporate (group) and individual election. Deuteronomy 7:6 represented the first—the binding, covenant agreement between God and Israel (as a group). As Israel's history progressed, however, Jews continued to rebel against God. From this came the concept of the "remnant"—those individual Israelites who remained committed to God. Paul intertwined these strands: Only those Jews God had chosen by grace were truly his people—the Israel (individuals) within Israel (the group).

11:16 [u]Lev 23:10,17; 16If the part of the dough offered as firstfruits[u] is holy, then the whole batch is holy; if the root is holy, so
Nu 15:18-21 are the branches.
11:17 [v]Jer 11:16; 17If some of the branches have been broken off,[v] and you, though a wild olive shoot, have been graft-
Jn 15:2 [w]Ac 2:39; ed in among the others[w] and now share in the nourishing sap from the olive root, 18do not boast over
Eph 2:11-13 those branches. If you do, consider this: You do not support the root, but the root supports you.[x] 19You
11:18 [x]Jn 4:22 will say then, "Branches were broken off so that I could be grafted in." 20Granted. But they were broken
11:20 [y]1Co 10:12; off because of unbelief, and you stand by faith.[y] Do not be arrogant,[z] but be afraid.[a] 21For if God did not
2Co 1:24; [z]Ro 12:16; spare the natural branches, he will not spare you either.
1Ti 6:17 22Consider therefore the kindness[b] and sternness of God: sternness to those who fell, but kindness
[a]1Pe 1:17 11:22 [b]Ro 2:4 to you, provided that you continue[c] in his kindness. Otherwise, you also will be cut off.[d] 23And if they
[c]1Co 15:2; Heb 3:6 [d]Jn 15:2 do not persist in unbelief, they will be grafted in, for God is able to graft them in again.[e] 24After all, if
11:23 [e]2Co 3:16 you were cut out of an olive tree that is wild by nature, and contrary to nature were grafted into a cul-
tivated olive tree, how much more readily will these, the natural branches, be grafted into their own ol-
ive tree!

All Israel Will Be Saved

11:25 [f]Ro 1:13 25I do not want you to be ignorant[f] of this mystery,[g] brothers, so that you may not be conceited:[h] Is-
[g]Ro 16:25 [h]Ro 12:16 [i]ver 7; rael has experienced a hardening[i] in part until the full number of the Gentiles has come in.[j] 26And so all
Ro 9:18 [j]Lk 21:24 Israel will be saved, as it is written:

> "The deliverer will come from Zion;
> he will turn godlessness away from Jacob.
> 27And this is[a] my covenant with them
> 11:27 [k]Isa 27:9; Heb 8:10,12 when I take away their sins."[b][k]

11:28 [l]Ro 5:10 [m]Dt 7:8; 10:15; 28As far as the gospel is concerned, they are enemies[l] on your account; but as far as election is con-
Ro 9:5 11:29 [n]Ro 8:28 cerned, they are loved on account of the patriarchs,[m] 29for God's gifts and his call[n] are irrevocable.[o] 30Just
[o]Heb 7:21 11:30 [p]Eph 2:2 as you who were at one time disobedient[p] to God have now received mercy as a result of their disobedi-
ence, 31so they too have now become disobedient in order that they too may now[c] receive mercy as a re-
11:32 [q]Ro 3:9 sult of God's mercy to you. 32For God has bound all men over to disobedience[q] so that he may have mercy
on them all.

Doxology

> 11:33 [r]Ro 2:4 [s]Ps 92:5 33Oh, the depth of the riches[r] of the wisdom and[d] knowledge
> [t]Job 11:7 of God![s]
> How unsearchable his judgments,
> and his paths beyond tracing out![t]
> 34"Who has known the mind of the Lord?
> 11:34 [u]Isa 40:13, 14; Job 15:8; Or who has been his counselor?"[e][u]
> 36:22; 1Co 2:16 35"Who has ever given to God,
> 11:35 [v]Job 35:7 that God should repay him?"[f][v]
> 11:36 [w]1Co 8:6; 36For from him and through him and to him are all things.[w]
> Col 1:16; Heb 2:10 [x]Ro 16:27 To him be the glory forever! Amen.[x]

[a] 27 Or *will be* [b] 27 Isaiah 59:20,21; 27:9; Jer. 31:33,34 [c] 31 Some manuscripts do not have *now.* [d] 33 Or *riches and the wisdom and the* [e] 34 Isaiah 40:13 [f] 35 Job 41:11

11:16 Part of the dough made from the first of the harvested grain (firstfruits) was offered to the Lord. This consecrated the whole batch (see Nu 15:17–21).

11:17 The usual procedure was to insert a shoot or slip of a cultivated tree into a common or wild one. In verses 17–24, however, the metaphor is used of grafting a wild olive branch into the cultivated olive tree. Such a procedure is unnatural (see v. 24 and its note)—which is precisely the point. Normally, such a graft would be unfruitful.

11:24 Obviously, the reasoning in this verse is more theological than horticultural. It would be difficult horticulturally to graft broken branches back into the parent tree, but the Jews really "belong" (historically and theologically) to the parent tree.

11:25 The so-called mystery religions of Paul's day used the Greek word *mysterion* in the sense of something that was to be revealed only to the initiated (see "The Mystery Religions" on p. 1939). Paul used the term to refer to something formerly hidden or obscure but now revealed by God for all to know and understand.

11:26 The Talmud (a Jewish collection of religious instruction) understood Isaiah 59:20 to be a reference to the Messiah, and Paul appears to have used it in this way.

11:36 This concept of God as source, sustainer and goal of all things may reflect Greek Stoic philosophy (see "Greek Philosophical Schools" on p. 1937).

Living Sacrifices

12 Therefore, I urge you,[y] brothers, in view of God's mercy, to offer your bodies as living sacrifices,[z]
holy and pleasing to God—this is your spiritual[a] act of worship. 2 Do not conform[a] any longer
to the pattern of this world,[b] but be transformed by the renewing of your mind.[c] Then you will be able
to test and approve what God's will is[d]—his good, pleasing and perfect will.
3 For by the grace given me[e] I say to every one of you: Do not think of yourself more highly than you
ought, but rather think of yourself with sober judgment, in accordance with the measure of faith God
has given you. 4 Just as each of us has one body with many members, and these members do not all have
the same function,[f] 5 so in Christ we who are many form one body,[g] and each member belongs to all the
others. 6 We have different gifts,[h] according to the grace given us. If a man's gift is prophesying, let him
use it in proportion to his[b] faith.[i] 7 If it is serving, let him serve; if it is teaching, let him teach;[j] 8 if it is en-
couraging, let him encourage;[k] if it is contributing to the needs of others, let him give generously;[l] if it
is leadership, let him govern diligently; if it is showing mercy, let him do it cheerfully.

12:1 [y]Eph 4:1 [z]Ro 6:13,16,19; 1Pe 2:5
12:2 [a]1Pe 1:14 [b]1Jn 2:15 [c]Eph 4:23 [d]Eph 5:17
12:3 [e]Ro 15:15; Gal 2:9; Eph 4:7
12:4 [f]1Co 12:12-14; Eph 4:16
12:5 [g]1Co 10:17
12:6 [h]1Co 7:7; 12:4,8-10 [i]1Pe 4:10,11
12:7 [j]Eph 4:11
12:8 [k]Ac 15:32 [l]2Co 9:5-13

Love

9 Love must be sincere.[m] Hate what is evil; cling to what is good. 10 Be devoted to one another in broth-
erly love.[n] Honor one another above yourselves.[o] 11 Never be lacking in zeal, but keep your spiritual fer-
vor,[p] serving the Lord. 12 Be joyful in hope,[q] patient in affliction,[r] faithful in prayer. 13 Share with God's
people who are in need. Practice hospitality.[s]
14 Bless those who persecute you;[t] bless and do not curse. 15 Rejoice with those who rejoice; mourn
with those who mourn.[u] 16 Live in harmony with one another.[v] Do not be proud, but be willing to asso-
ciate with people of low position.[c] Do not be conceited.[w]
17 Do not repay anyone evil for evil.[x] Be careful to do what is right in the eyes of everybody.[y] 18 If it is
possible, as far as it depends on you, live at peace with everyone.[z] 19 Do not take revenge,[a] my friends, but
leave room for God's wrath, for it is written: "It is mine to avenge; I will repay,"[d][b] says the Lord. 20 On the
contrary:

> "If your enemy is hungry, feed him;
> if he is thirsty, give him something to drink.
> In doing this, you will heap burning coals on his head."[e][c]

21 Do not be overcome by evil, but overcome evil with good.

12:9 [m]1Ti 1:5
12:10 [n]Heb 13:1 [o]Php 2:3
12:11 [p]Ac 18:25
12:12 [q]Ro 5:2 [r]Heb 10:32,36
12:13 [s]1Ti 3:2
12:14 [t]Mt 5:44
12:15 [u]Job 30:25
12:16 [v]Ro 15:5 [w]Jer 45:5; Ro 11:25
12:17 [x]Pr 20:22 [y]2Co 8:21
12:18 [z]Mk 9:50; Ro 14:19
12:19 [a]Lev 19:18; Pr 20:22; 24:29 [b]Dt 32:35
12:20 [c]Pr 25:21,22; Mt 5:44; Lk 6:27

Submission to the Authorities

13 Everyone must submit himself to the governing authorities,[d] for there is no authority except that
which God has established.[e] The authorities that exist have been established by God. 2 Conse-
quently, he who rebels against the authority is rebelling against what God has instituted, and those who
do so will bring judgment on themselves. 3 For rulers hold no terror for those who do right, but for those
who do wrong. Do you want to be free from fear of the one in authority? Then do what is right and he will
commend you.[f] 4 For he is God's servant to do you good. But if you do wrong, be afraid, for he does not
bear the sword for nothing. He is God's servant, an agent of wrath to bring punishment on the wrongdo-
er.[g] 5 Therefore, it is necessary to submit to the authorities, not only because of possible punishment but
also because of conscience.
6 This is also why you pay taxes, for the authorities are God's servants, who give their full time to gov-
erning. 7 Give everyone what you owe him: If you owe taxes, pay taxes;[h] if revenue, then revenue; if respect,
then respect; if honor, then honor.

13:1 [d]Tit 3:1; 1Pe 2:13,14 [e]Da 2:21; Jn 19:11
13:3 [f]1Pe 2:14
13:4 [g]1Th 4:6
13:7 [h]Mt 17:25; 22:17,21; Lk 23:2

[a] *1* Or *reasonable* [b] *6* Or *in agreement with the* [c] *16* Or *willing to do menial work* [d] *19* Deut. 32:35 [e] *20* Prov. 25:21,22

12:1 Scholars claim that in the ancient world religion *was* sacrifice. The popularity of sacrifice in ancient religions, however, often led to abuses. People thought that all they had to do to please their god was to offer a sacrifice, regardless of their sincerity. Both Jewish and pagan authors in Paul's day warned against this attitude.

12:8 "Let him govern" may be a reference to an elder. The Ephesian church had elders by about this time (see Ac 20:17; see also 1Ti 5:17 and its note).

13:1 The "governing authorities" were the civil rulers, all of whom were probably pagans at the time Paul was writing. Christians may have been tempted not to submit to them and to claim allegiance only to Christ (cf. "The Imperial Cult" on p. 1651). Even the possibility of a persecuting state did not shake Paul's conviction that civil government is ordained by God.

13:4 The sword was the symbol of Roman authority on both national and international levels.

13:6 See "Roman Taxation" on page 1855.

Love, for the Day Is Near

[8]Let no debt remain outstanding, except the continuing debt to love one another, for he who loves his
13:8 [i]ver 10; Jn 13:34; Gal 5:14; Col 3:14 fellowman has fulfilled the law.[i] [9]The commandments, "Do not commit adultery," "Do not murder," "Do
13:9 [j]Ex 20:13-15,17; Dt 5:17-19,21 [k]Lev 19:18; Mt 19:19 not steal," "Do not covet,"[a][j] and whatever other commandment there may be, are summed up in this one
rule: "Love your neighbor as yourself."[b][k] [10]Love does no harm to its neighbor. Therefore love is the ful-
13:10 [l]ver 8; Mt 22:39,40 fillment of the law.[l]
[11]And do this, understanding the present time. The hour has come[m] for you to wake up from your
13:11 [m]1Co 7:29-31; 10:11

[a] 9 Exodus 20:13-15,17; Deut. 5:17-19,21 [b] 9 Lev. 19:18

Roman Taxation

A hoard of coins from c. A.D. 66 (probably a delivery of the temple tax intercepted before arriving at the Jerusalem temple at the beginning of the Jewish War)

Preserving Bible Times; © Dr. James C. Martin; permission of Eretz Israel Museum

ROMANS 13 In the Roman Republic the regular tax was called the *vectigalia*, although an extra levy called the *tributum* could also be raised. The Senate annually set the amount of revenue to be collected. With the expansion of Roman power, however, an enormous amount of wealth poured into Rome from the provinces, and the empire was less dependent upon taxes raised from its own citizens. Governors raised taxes for Rome from the provinces, enriching themselves in the process. Provincials suffered grievously under this arrangement, but a governor who showed restraint and fairness could earn the admiration of the local people (as did Cicero when governing Cilicia in Asia Minor).[1]

With the establishment of the empire, Augustus Caesar created a regular bureaucracy for conducting the census and collecting taxes (see Lk 2:1).[2] The provinces were subjected to both a poll tax and a land tax. The revenue supported the army, the imperial household, government salaries, road maintenance and public works, as well as the dole of grain for the Roman masses.

The actual task of gathering revenues in the provinces was farmed out to private companies of tax collectors called *publicani* or *conductores*. These tax collectors accumulated enough money to meet the demands of the state and also to retain a profit for themselves. As the New Testament reflects, *publicani* were hated by the people (Mt 18:17; Lk 18:11). Taxation could be heavy and unfair, and the *publicani* were regarded as greedy traitors serving foreign overlords.

Issues involving taxation appear repeatedly in the New Testament. Jesus himself paid taxes, although his means of raising the money to do so was unusual (see Mt 17:24–27; this tax was levied upon the Jews for the upkeep of the Jerusalem temple). The very image of Caesar on Roman coinage caused something of a religious dilemma for the Jews, although Jesus considered scruples concerning the matter to be more contrived than sincere (Mt 22:15–22).[3] Paul, in Romans 13:6–7, was clear that the collection of taxes by a government is legitimate and the payment of taxes by Christians imperative. Set against the backdrop of the Roman taxation of the times, this was clearly a stand based upon principle and not upon popular satisfaction with the system.

[1]See "The Roman Governor" on page 1824. [2]See also "Caesar Augustus, Emperor of Rome; the Census; and Quirinius, Governor of Syria" on page 1667. [3]See "Coins and Numismatics" on page 1699.

slumber,[n] because our salvation is nearer now than when we first believed. 12 The night is nearly over; the
day is almost here.[o] So let us put aside the deeds of darkness[p] and put on the armor[q] of light. 13 Let us
behave decently, as in the daytime, not in orgies and drunkenness, not in sexual immorality and de-
bauchery, not in dissension and jealousy.[r] 14 Rather, clothe yourselves with the Lord Jesus Christ,[s] and
do not think about how to gratify the desires of the sinful nature.[a]

The Weak and the Strong

14 Accept him whose faith is weak,[t] without passing judgment on disputable matters. 2 One man's
faith allows him to eat everything, but another man, whose faith is weak, eats only vegetables.
3 The man who eats everything must not look down on[u] him who does not, and the man who does not
eat everything must not condemn[v] the man who does, for God has accepted him. 4 Who are you to judge
someone else's servant?[w] To his own master he stands or falls. And he will stand, for the Lord is able to
make him stand.

5 One man considers one day more sacred than another;[x] another man considers every day alike. Each
one should be fully convinced in his own mind. 6 He who regards one day as special, does so to the Lord.
He who eats meat, eats to the Lord, for he gives thanks to God;[y] and he who abstains, does so to the Lord
and gives thanks to God. 7 For none of us lives to himself alone[z] and none of us dies to himself alone. 8 If
we live, we live to the Lord; and if we die, we die to the Lord. So, whether we live or die, we belong to the
Lord.[a]

9 For this very reason, Christ died and returned to life[b] so that he might be the Lord of both the dead
and the living.[c] 10 You, then, why do you judge your brother? Or why do you look down on your brother?
For we will all stand before God's judgment seat.[d] 11 It is written:

> " 'As surely as I live,' says the Lord,
> 'every knee will bow before me;
> every tongue will confess to God.' "[b] [e]

12 So then, each of us will give an account of himself to God.[f]

13 Therefore let us stop passing judgment[g] on one another. Instead, make up your mind not to put any
stumbling block or obstacle in your brother's way. 14 As one who is in the Lord Jesus, I am fully convinced
that no food[c] is unclean in itself.[h] But if anyone regards something as unclean, then for him it is unclean.[i]
15 If your brother is distressed because of what you eat, you are no longer acting in love.[j] Do not by your
eating destroy your brother for whom Christ died.[k] 16 Do not allow what you consider good to be spoken
of as evil.[l] 17 For the kingdom of God is not a matter of eating and drinking,[m] but of righteousness, peace
and joy in the Holy Spirit,[n] 18 because anyone who serves Christ in this way is pleasing to God and ap-
proved by men.[o]

19 Let us therefore make every effort to do what leads to peace[p] and to mutual edification.[q] 20 Do not
destroy the work of God for the sake of food.[r] All food is clean, but it is wrong for a man to eat anything
that causes someone else to stumble.[s] 21 It is better not to eat meat or drink wine or to do anything else
that will cause your brother to fall.[t]

22 So whatever you believe about these things keep between yourself and God. Blessed is the man who
does not condemn[u] himself by what he approves. 23 But the man who has doubts[v] is condemned if he
eats, because his eating is not from faith; and everything that does not come from faith is sin.

15 We who are strong ought to bear with the failings of the weak[w] and not to please ourselves. 2 Each
of us should please his neighbor for his good,[x] to build him up.[y] 3 For even Christ did not please
himself[z] but, as it is written: "The insults of those who insult you have fallen on me."[d] [a] 4 For everything

13:11 [n]Eph 5:14; 1Th 5:5,6
13:12 [o]1Jn 2:8 [p]Eph 5:11 [q]Eph 6:11,13
13:13 [r]Gal 5:20,21
13:14 [s]Gal 3:27; 5:16; Eph 4:24
14:1 [t]Ro 15:1; 1Co 8:9-12
14:3 [u]Lk 18:9 [v]Col 2:16
14:4 [w]Jas 4:12
14:5 [x]Gal 4:10
14:6 [y]Mt 14:19; 1Co 10:30,31; 1Ti 4:3,4
14:7 [z]2Co 5:15; Gal 2:20
14:8 [a]Php 1:20
14:9 [b]Rev 1:18 [c]2Co 5:15
14:10 [d]2Co 5:10
14:11 [e]Isa 45:23; Php 2:10,11
14:12 [f]Mt 12:36; 1Pe 4:5
14:13 [g]Mt 7:1
14:14 [h]Ac 10:15 [i]1Co 8:7
14:15 [j]Eph 5:2 [k]1Co 8:11
14:16 [l]1Co 10:30
14:17 [m]1Co 8:8 [n]Ro 15:13
14:18 [o]2Co 8:21
14:19 [p]Ps 34:14; Ro 12:18; Heb 12:14 [q]Ro 15:2; 2Co 12:19
14:20 [r]ver 15 [s]1Co 8:9-12
14:21 [t]1Co 8:13
14:22 [u]1Jn 3:21
14:23 [v]ver 5
15:1 [w]Ro 14:1; Gal 6:1,2; 1Th 5:14
15:2 [x]1Co 10:33 [y]Ro 14:19
15:3 [z]2Co 8:9 [a]Ps 69:9

[a] 14 Or *the flesh* [b] *11* Isaiah 45:23 [c] *14* Or *that nothing* [d] *3* Psalm 69:9

13:12 This does not mean that the early Christians believed that Jesus would return within a few years. Rather, they regarded the death and resurrection of Christ as the crucial events of history that began the last days.

14:1 Those "whose faith is weak" were probably Jewish Christians at Rome who were unwilling to give up the observance of certain requirements of the law, such as dietary restrictions and the keeping of the Sabbath and other special days. Their concern was not quite the same as that of the Judaizers of Galatia (see the note on Gal 1:7), who thought they could put God in their debt by works of righteousness and were trying to force this heretical teaching on the Galatian churches. The "weak" Roman Christians did neither. They were not yet clear as to the status of Old Testament regulations under the new covenant inaugurated by the coming of Christ.

14:20 On the subject of defilement in the Old and New Testaments, see the note at Song of Songs 5:3.

14:21 See "Wine and Alcoholic Beverages in the Ancient World" on page 2015.

ARCHAEOLOGICAL SITES

POMPEII

ROMANS 14 On August 24, A.D. 79, Mount Vesuvius, a volcano on the western coast of Italy, erupted violently, spewing lava, rock and ash as high as 12 miles (19 km) into the air and burying a number of cities that lay near its base. Among these was Pompeii. The historian Pliny the Younger witnessed the eruption from an island off the coast and described in detail how the daytime sky turned pitch black. Late that night Vesuvius emitted a tremendous pyroclastic surge of noxious gas and ash that covered all but the tops of a few structures and instantly killed anyone who had not yet escaped. The site was abandoned and eventually forgotten. Pompeii was rediscovered briefly in 1594, but regular excavations of the site did not begin until 1748. With a few interruptions, archaeologists have been working continuously there ever since.

What amounted to a tragedy for the original inhabitants turned out to be a boon to Roman archaeology. Beneath its 30-foot layer of ash, Pompeii was wonderfully well preserved. Excavations revealed a large, relatively wealthy city laid out in a grid pattern. Inside the houses researchers uncovered beautiful mosaics, colorful frescoes and even the familiar warning *Cave Canem* ("Beware of dog"). Utensils and artistic objects revealed a great deal about the culture of Pompeii.

Another exciting discovery within the ash was the existence of pockets that had once been occupied by the corpses of those killed by the pyroclastic surge. The bodies had eventually decomposed, leaving cavities within the dried ash. Scientists poured plaster of Paris into these cavities and created three-dimensional casts of the victims' bodies that were so exact that specialists were able to estimate the age, probable occupation and overall level of health of these individuals.

Taken together, these architectural, artistic and human remains have proven to be an invaluable resource for historians in reconstructing life in a Roman city during the New Testament period. Excavations have also commenced below the level of the Roman city, in order to learn more about the development of Pompeii over time. A great deal of effort and expense is being directed toward conservation as well, since pollution and human traffic pose serious threats to these ancient treasures.[1]

[1]For discoveries in Pompeii, see "Triclinia" on page 1748.

Mount Vesuvius behind Pompeii

Photograph: © Todd Bolen/Bible Places.com

that was written in the past was written to teach us,[b] so that through endurance and the encouragement 15:4 [b]Ro 4:23,24
of the Scriptures we might have hope.
5 May the God who gives endurance and encouragement give you a spirit of unity[c] among yourselves 15:5 [c]Ro 12:16; 1Co 1:10
as you follow Christ Jesus, 6 so that with one heart and mouth you may glorify the God and Father[d] of 15:6 [d]Rev 1:6
our Lord Jesus Christ.
7 Accept one another,[e] then, just as Christ accepted you, in order to bring praise to God. 8 For I tell you 15:7 [e]Ro 14:1
that Christ has become a servant of the Jews[a][f] on behalf of God's truth, to confirm the promises[g] made 15:8 [f]Mt 15:24; Ac 3:25,26
to the patriarchs 9 so that the Gentiles[h] may glorify God[i] for his mercy, as it is written: [g]2Co 1:20 15:9 [h]Ro 3:29 [i]Mt 9:8

"Therefore I will praise you among the Gentiles; [j]2Sa 22:50; Ps 18:49
I will sing hymns to your name."[b][j]

10 Again, it says,

"Rejoice, O Gentiles, with his people."[c][k] 15:10 [k]Dt 32:43

11 And again,

"Praise the Lord, all you Gentiles,
and sing praises to him, all you peoples."[d][l] 15:11 [l]Ps 117:1

12 And again, Isaiah says,

"The Root of Jesse[m] will spring up, 15:12 [m]Rev 5:5
one who will arise to rule over the nations; [n]Isa 11:10; Mt 12:21
the Gentiles will hope in him."[e][n]

13 May the God of hope fill you with all joy and peace[o] as you trust in him, so that you may overflow 15:13 [o]Ro 14:17
with hope by the power of the Holy Spirit.[p] [p]ver 19; 1Co 2:4; 1Th 1:5

Paul the Minister to the Gentiles

14 I myself am convinced, my brothers, that you yourselves are full of goodness,[q] complete in knowl- 15:14 [q]Eph 5:9
edge[r] and competent to instruct one another. 15 I have written you quite boldly on some points, as if to [r]2Pe 1:12
remind you of them again, because of the grace God gave me[s] 16 to be a minister of Christ Jesus to the 15:15 [s]Ro 12:3
Gentiles[t] with the priestly duty of proclaiming the gospel of God,[u] so that the Gentiles might become an 15:16 [t]Ac 9:15; Ro 11:13 [u]Ro 1:1
offering[v] acceptable to God, sanctified by the Holy Spirit. [v]Isa 66:20
17 Therefore I glory in Christ Jesus[w] in my service to God.[x] 18 I will not venture to speak of anything 15:17 [w]Php 3:3
except what Christ has accomplished through me in leading the Gentiles[y] to obey God[z] by what I have [x]Heb 2:17 15:18 [y]Ac 15:12; 21:19; Ro 1:5
said and done— 19 by the power of signs and miracles,[a] through the power of the Spirit.[b] So from Jeru- [z]Ro 16:26
salem[c] all the way around to Illyricum, I have fully proclaimed the gospel of Christ. 20 It has always been 15:19 [a]Jn 4:48; Ac 19:11 [b]ver 13
my ambition to preach the gospel where Christ was not known, so that I would not be building on some- [c]Ac 22:17-21
one else's foundation.[d] 21 Rather, as it is written: 15:20 [d]2Co 10:15,16

"Those who were not told about him will see,
and those who have not heard will understand."[f][e] 15:21 [e]Isa 52:15

22 This is why I have often been hindered from coming to you.[f] 15:22 [f]Ro 1:13

Paul's Plan to Visit Rome

23 But now that there is no more place for me to work in these regions, and since I have been longing
for many years to see you,[g] 24 I plan to do so when I go to Spain.[h] I hope to visit you while passing through 15:23 [g]Ac 19:21; Ro 1:10,11
and to have you assist me on my journey there, after I have enjoyed your company for a while. 25 Now, 15:24 [h]ver 28

[a] 8 Greek *circumcision* [b] 9 2 Samuel 22:50; Psalm 18:49 [c] 10 Deut. 32:43 [d] 11 Psalm 117:1 [e] 12 Isaiah 11:10
[f] 21 Isaiah 52:15

15:12 The Gentile mission of the early church was a fulfillment of this prophecy, as is the continuing evangelization of the nations.
15:19 Jerusalem was the home of the mother church, where the gospel originated and its dissemination began (see Ac 1:8; see also "The Church From the Resurrection to the Conversion of Paul" on p. 1766, "Geographic Expansion of the Church Under Persecution" on p. 1781, and "Before the Gentile Expansion: The Jewish Churches in the Holy Land" on p. 1997).

Illyricum was a Roman province north of Macedonia (present-day Albania and Yugoslavia).
15:24 Paul wanted to use the Roman church as a base of operations for a mission to Spain (see also v. 28).

THE NEW TESTAMENT TEXTS

ROMANS 15 No other ancient text is substantiated by such a wealth of ancient textual witnesses as is the New Testament. Roughly 5,500 separate manuscripts are available, variously containing anything from the entire New Testament corpus to a slight fragment of a single verse. There are also hundreds of copies of ancient translations (or **versions**) of the New Testament that reveal the form of the text known to their translators, as well as numerous New Testament quotations in the writings of the early church fathers that disclose the form of the particular texts known to them.

- The oldest known copy of any portion of the New Testament is the John Rylands papyrus, officially designated p[52] and dated to approximately A.D. 125. It contains John 18:31–33, 37–38.[1]
- The oldest complete, or nearly complete, manuscripts of the New Testament are **Codex** Vaticanus and Codex Sinaiticus, both from the fourth century.
- Sixty-five other New Testament partial manuscripts from the fourth century or earlier are also extant, along with many complete manuscripts from later centuries.

A facsimile page of Codex Vaticanus, one of the oldest complete manuscripts of the New Testament

© Dr. James C. Martin. Sola Scriptura. The Van Kampen Collection on display at the Holy Land Experience in Orlando, Florida.

This textual support is far superior to that available for any other ancient documents, such as the classical texts from Greek and Roman writers (e.g., Plato, Aristotle and Cicero). Only partial manuscripts have survived for many works of antiquity, and it is not unusual to find that the only complete manuscript for some ancient writing is a copy dating from 1,000 years after its composition.

The original New Testament manuscripts probably would have been recorded on papyrus, the most common writing material of the time, and would have been read and copied continuously until they were no longer legible.[2] As was invariably the case in antiquity, no two copies of a manuscript were exactly alike, despite meticulous care on the part of copyists. Although we can no longer consult the original manuscripts, the richness and antiquity of those that are at the disposal of scholars are such that it is usually not difficult to determine what the original authors wrote. In most cases we can also discern how and why variations arose in the manuscripts. In no case does a fundamental Christian teaching depend upon accepting one manuscript reading over another.[3]

The history of the manuscript tradition at the end of Paul's letter to the Romans is one of the most complicated in all of the New Testament. The closing benediction found in Romans 16:25–27 appears in three other places in the various manuscripts: either immediately following chapter 14, immediately following chapter 15 or at the end of both chapters 14 and 16. To complicate the situation, some manuscripts do not include the doxology at all. This evidence has led to a wide array of suggestions about the history of the writing of Romans:

- Some scholars conclude that the letter originally had only 14 or 15 chapters, ending with the doxology. They hold that the remainder was added later, probably by Paul himself when sending a later edition of the Roman letter to another church.
- Most scholars, however, concur that the letter originally included all 16 chapters but that shortened versions were circulated among some churches.

Some believe that the doxology itself was a later addition, originally written to provide an appropriate ending to one of the shorter forms but subsequently added to the end of the other forms as well.

It is just as likely, however, that the doxology was the original ending of Romans and that it was later moved to the end of the shorter versions, leading to the complicated situation found in the history of the manuscript tradition.

For information on Old Testament texts, see "Texts of the Old Testament" on page 1491 and "The Ancient Translations" on page 1492.

[1]See "John Rylands Papyrus (p[52])" on page 1755. [2]See "Writing Materials in the Ancient World" on page 2037 and "Scrolls, Seals and Codices" on page 2053. [3]See also "Textual Criticism" on page 1151.

however, I am on my way to Jerusalem[i] in the service[j] of the saints there. 26 For Macedonia[k] and Achaia[l]
were pleased to make a contribution for the poor among the saints in Jerusalem. 27 They were pleased to
do it, and indeed they owe it to them. For if the Gentiles have shared in the Jews' spiritual blessings, they
owe it to the Jews to share with them their material blessings.[m] 28 So after I have completed this task and
have made sure that they have received this fruit, I will go to Spain and visit you on the way. 29 I know
that when I come to you,[n] I will come in the full measure of the blessing of Christ.

30 I urge you, brothers, by our Lord Jesus Christ and by the love of the Spirit,[o] to join me in my strug-
gle by praying to God for me.[p] 31 Pray that I may be rescued[q] from the unbelievers in Judea and that my
service in Jerusalem may be acceptable to the saints there, 32 so that by God's will[r] I may come to you[s] with
joy and together with you be refreshed.[t] 33 The God of peace[u] be with you all. Amen.

Personal Greetings

16 I commend[v] to you our sister Phoebe, a servant[a] of the church in Cenchrea.[w] 2 I ask you to receive
her in the Lord[x] in a way worthy of the saints and to give her any help she may need from you,
for she has been a great help to many people, including me.

3 Greet Priscilla[b] and Aquila,[y] my fellow workers in Christ Jesus.[z] 4 They risked their lives for me. Not
only I but all the churches of the Gentiles are grateful to them.

5 Greet also the church that meets at their house.[a]

Greet my dear friend Epenetus, who was the first convert[b] to Christ in the province of Asia.

6 Greet Mary, who worked very hard for you.

7 Greet Andronicus and Junias, my relatives[c] who have been in prison with me. They are outstanding
among the apostles, and they were in Christ before I was.

8 Greet Ampliatus, whom I love in the Lord.

9 Greet Urbanus, our fellow worker in Christ,[d] and my dear friend Stachys.

10 Greet Apelles, tested and approved in Christ.

Greet those who belong to the household of Aristobulus.

11 Greet Herodion, my relative.[e]

Greet those in the household of Narcissus who are in the Lord.

12 Greet Tryphena and Tryphosa, those women who work hard in the Lord.

Greet my dear friend Persis, another woman who has worked very hard in the Lord.

13 Greet Rufus, chosen in the Lord, and his mother, who has been a mother to me, too.

14 Greet Asyncritus, Phlegon, Hermes, Patrobas, Hermas and the brothers with them.

15 Greet Philologus, Julia, Nereus and his sister, and Olympas and all the saints[f] with them.[g]

16 Greet one another with a holy kiss.[h]

All the churches of Christ send greetings.

[a] *1* Or *deaconess* [b] *3* Greek *Prisca,* a variant of *Priscilla*

15:25 [i]Ac 19:21 [j]Ac 24:17
15:26 [k]Ac 16:9; 2Co 8:1 [l]Ac 18:12
15:27 [m]1Co 9:11
15:29 [n]Ro 1:10, 11
15:30 [o]Gal 5:22 [p]2Co 1:11; Col 4:12
15:31 [q]2Th 3:2
15:32 [r]Ac 18:21 [s]Ro 1:10,13 [t]1Co 16:18
15:33 [u]Ro 16:20; 2Co 13:11; Php 4:9; 1Th 5:23; Heb 13:20
16:1 [v]2Co 3:1 [w]Ac 18:18
16:2 [x]Php 2:29
16:3 [y]Ac 18:2 [z]ver 7,9,10
16:5 [a]1Co 16:19; Col 4:15; Phm 2 [b]1Co 16:15
16:7 [c]ver 11,21
16:9 [d]ver 3
16:11 [e]ver 7,21
16:15 [f]ver 2 [g]ver 14
16:16 [h]1Co 16:20; 2Co 13:12; 1Th 5:26

15:26 For "Macedonia and Achaia," see the note on 1 Thessalonians 1:7–8.

15:30–32 The prayer at the end of Romans 15 is not to be taken as the conclusion of a letter but only as the appropriate conclusion of a particular topic. Paul had been telling of his itinerary. He was deeply moved as he contemplated the perils of his impending visit to Jerusalem and strongly implored the prayers of the saints in Rome with respect to the matter.

16:1 Phoebe was probably the carrier of the letter to Rome (cf. v. 2). She is called a "servant" (see the NIV text note), one who serves or ministers in any way. When church-related, as it is here, it probably refers to a specific office—a female deacon or deaconess.

Cenchrea was a port located about 6 miles (nearly 10 km) east of Corinth on the Saronic Gulf.

16:3–24 Most of the people represented by the names in this list of greetings were Gentiles, freed slaves or descendants of freed slaves (see "Labor and Welfare in the Ancient World" on p. 1952 and "Slavery in the Greco-Roman World" on p. 1979). Paul specifically mentioned at least two groups of slaves: the household servants of Aristobulus and those of Narcissus. What little evidence we have suggests that a large percentage of early Christians came from the "lower" classes.

Of the 27 Christians Paul greeted, 10 were women. Women made up a significant part of the early Christian church and engaged in significant ministry. Paul commended six of them—Phoebe, Priscilla, Junias, Tryphena, Tryphosa and Persis—for their labor in the Lord.

16:3 Priscilla and Aquila were close friends of Paul who worked in the same trade of tent-making.

16:5 See "House Churches and Early Church Buildings" on page 2033.

16:7 The more common reading of the Greek text is Junia (not Junias, as in the NIV), a feminine name. Andronicus and Junia may have been husband and wife.

16:10 Aristobulus may have been the grandson of Herod the Great and the brother of Herod Agrippa I.

16:11 Narcissus is sometimes identified with Tiberius Claudius Narcissus, a wealthy freedman of the Roman emperor Tiberius.

16:12 Tryphena and Tryphosa may have been sisters, perhaps even twins, because it was common for such persons to be given names from the same root.

Persis means "Persian woman."

16:14–15 None of these persons can be further identified, except that they were slaves or freedmen (men who had been emancipaed from slavery) in the Roman church (see "Labor and Welfare in the Ancient World" on p. 1952 and "Slavery in the Greco-Roman World" on p. 1979.)

16:16 Justin Martyr (A.D. 150) stated that the holy kiss was a regular part of the worship service in his day. This is still a practice in some churches. (See "The Jewish Custom of Kissing" on p. 1682.)

[17]I urge you, brothers, to watch out for those who cause divisions and put obstacles in your way that
are contrary to the teaching you have learned.[i] Keep away from them.[j] [18]For such people are not serving
our Lord Christ, but their own appetites.[k] By smooth talk and flattery they deceive[l] the minds of naive
people. [19]Everyone has heard[m] about your obedience, so I am full of joy over you; but I want you to be
wise about what is good, and innocent about what is evil.[n]
[20]The God of peace[o] will soon crush[p] Satan under your feet.
The grace of our Lord Jesus be with you.[q]

16:17 [i]Gal 1:8,9; 1Ti 1:3; 6:3 [j]2Th 3:6,14; 2Jn 10
16:18 [k]Php 3:19 [l]Col 2:4
16:19 [m]Ro 1:8 [n]Mt 10:16; 1Co 14:20
16:20 [o]Ro 15:33 [p]Ge 3:15 [q]1Th 5:28

ANCIENT TEXTS AND ARTIFACTS

The Erastus Inscription

The Erastus Inscription
Preserving Bible Times; © Dr. James C. Martin

ROMANS 16 Erastus was a first-century Christian who worked with Paul. The earliest mention of him is in Acts 19:22: Paul, at Ephesus on his third missionary journey around A.D. 53–55, "sent two of his helpers, Timothy and Erastus, to Macedonia." Then, in Romans 16:23, Paul wrote (probably from Corinth around the year 57) that "Erastus, who [was] the city's director of public works," sent greetings. Finally, in 2 Timothy 4:20, when Paul was writing from prison in Rome toward the end of his life (around 66–67), he gave a status report on his coworkers, including the statement that "Erastus stayed in Corinth." It appears that Erastus was a resident of Corinth and, if so, most likely became a believer as a result of Paul's 18-month ministry in that city on his second missionary journey, around A.D. 50–52 (Ac 18:1–17).[1]

In 1929 an inscription was discovered at Corinth mentioning an Erastus who may have been the same one referred to in the New Testament.[2] Located in a paved area northeast of the theater and dated to the mid-first century A.D., it reads, "Erastus in return for his aedileship laid [the pavement] at his own expense." An *aedile*, an elected official, was a city business manager responsible for such property as streets, public buildings and markets, as well as for the revenue gleaned from them. He was also a judge who decided most of the city's commercial and financial litigation. In addition, an aedile was responsible for the public games taking place within a city.

Thus, Paul's term "director of public works" in Romans 16:23 probably describes Erastus's position as an aedile. Some have argued that since the Greek word Paul used, *oikonomos*, may not have been the exact equivalent of the Latin *aedile*, Erastus may have held a lower position at the time of Paul's writing. On the other hand, it is possible that Paul first encountered Erastus while he was discharging his fiscal responsibilities and thus perceived him primarily in this role. Also, Corinth was distinctive in that the games there were run not by the aedile but by a different set of officials. Thus, the aedile at Corinth basically functioned as a city treasurer (the rendering used in some translations, such as the NASB).

[1]See also "The Missionary Journeys of Paul" on page 1795 and "Imprisonment in the Roman World: In Prison Versus House Arrest" on page 1826. [2]See "Corinth" on page 1884.

[21]Timothy,[r] my fellow worker, sends his greetings to you, as do Lucius,[s] Jason[t] and Sosipater, my rel-
atives.[u]
[22]I, Tertius, who wrote down this letter, greet you in the Lord.
[23]Gaius, whose hospitality I and the whole church here enjoy, sends you his greetings.
Erastus,[v] who is the city's director of public works, and our brother Quartus send you their greet-
ings.[a]
[25]Now to him who is able[w] to establish you by my gospel[x] and the proclamation of Jesus Christ, ac-
cording to the revelation of the mystery[y] hidden for long ages past, [26]but now revealed and made known
through the prophetic writings by the command of the eternal God, so that all nations might believe and
obey him— [27]to the only wise God be glory forever through Jesus Christ! Amen.[z]

16:21 [r]Ac 16:1 [s]Ac 13:1 [t]Ac 17:5 [u]ver 7,11
16:23 [v]Ac 19:22
16:25 [w]Eph 3:20 [x]Ro 2:16 [y]Eph 1:9; Col 1:26,27
16:27 [z]Ro 11:36

[a] 23 Some manuscripts *their greetings.* [24]*May the grace of our Lord Jesus Christ be with all of you. Amen.*

16:21–22 This is a letter, not a treatise; as such, it was not intended to be a formal literary product. In the midst of greetings from friends who were with the author as he wrote, Tertius, the scribe to whom the letter was dictated, inserted his own personal greeting. This personal touch reminds us that the people of the Bible were human beings under human circumstances, and the letter means more to us because this is so.
16:21 This Jason may have been the individual by that name mentioned in Acts 17:5–9. Sosipater was probably Sopater, the son of Pyrrhus, from Berea (see Ac 20:4).
16:22 Tertius had functioned as Paul's secretary.
16:23 Gaius is usually identified with Titius Justus, a God-fearer (see the notes on Jn 12:20; Ac 10:2; cf. "converts" in the note on Ac 2:11) in whose house Paul stayed while in Corinth (see Ac 18:7; 1Co 1:14). His full name would be Gaius Titius Justus.

At Corinth archaeologists have discovered a reused block of stone in a paved square, with the Latin inscription: "Erastus, commissioner of public works, bore the expense of this pavement" (see "The Erastus Inscription" on p. 1861). This may refer to the Erastus mentioned here. If it does, it is the earliest reference to a Christian by name outside the New Testament. He may also be the same person referred to in Acts 19:22 and 2 Timothy 4:20, though it is difficult to be certain because the name was fairly common.
16:25–27 Various manuscripts show this closing benediction at different locations within the book of Romans—and some manuscripts do not include it at all (see "The New Testament Texts" on p. 1859).

INTRODUCTION TO 1 *Corinthians*

AUTHOR, PLACE AND DATE OF WRITING

Early church fathers (e.g., Clement of Rome, as early as A.D. 96), as well as the letter itself (1:1), acknowledge Paul as the author of 1 Corinthians.

Most scholars date the letter to A.D. 54–55 on the grounds of a chronology for Acts that places Paul's first visit to Corinth during the time of Gallio, A.D. 51–52 (see "Gallio, Proconsul of Achaia" on p. 1806).

Paul wrote his letter from Ephesus (16:8). On the difficult chronology of the Corinthian visits and correspondence, see "Paul's Visits and Letters to Corinth" on page 1888.

AUDIENCE

Paul directed this letter to the believers in Corinth.

CULTURAL FACTS AND HIGHLIGHTS

Corinth was a thriving, cosmopolitan city, known for its diversity, culture, commerce, paganism, immorality and great wealth (see "Corinth" on p. 1887). As founder of the church of Corinth, Paul was vitally concerned about its spiritual health. He wrote 1 Corinthians in response to a formidable number of problems that had arisen. He had been "officially" informed of some of these issues (5:1) but was made aware of others on the basis of questions from the Corinthian believers (7:1). There were factions in the church (ch. 1), elitism and conflict over spiritual gifts (chs. 2; 12–13), sexual immorality (chs. 5–6; 10), challenges to Paul's authority (ch. 9), nascent heresy about the resurrection (ch. 15), aberrant practices in the worship services (ch. 11) and questions about proper Christian behavior (chs. 7–8).

TIMELINE

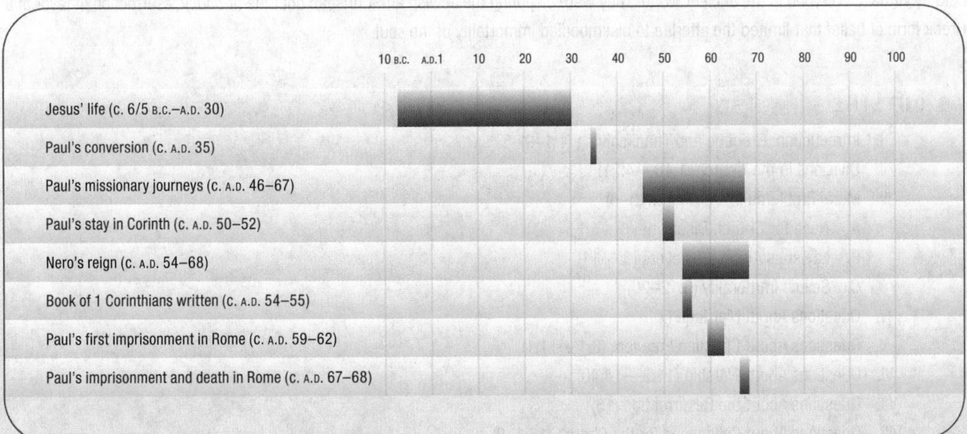

AS YOU READ

Look for general principles and practical information that can be applied to Christian living and modern church relationships. Note Paul's advice regarding divisiveness, marriage, Christian freedom, worship, spiritual gifts and church unity. Study and find encouragement in his argument that Jesus' resurrection was a factual, historical event.

DID YOU KNOW?

- The term "household" generally included family members, servants or anyone else who lived in a house (1:16).
- The emperor Nero sometimes clothed Christians in the skins of beasts when he exposed them to wild beasts (4:9).
- The Roman orator Cicero asserted that incest was practically unheard of in Roman society (5:1).
- In the culture of Paul's day men uncovered their heads in worship to signify their respect for and submission to deity (11:4).
- The central Christian confession, "Jesus is Lord," was a particular problem in the Roman Empire, because the affirmation of the sovereignty of Jesus was a direct challenge to the claim of absolute rule on the part of the Roman emperor (12:3).

THEMES

First Corinthians includes the following themes:

1. *Divisions.* Corinthian society was riddled with competitive individualism, an attitude that spilled over into the church. Feuding groups developed around rival leading figures who may have hosted different house churches. Paul admonished those who fancied themselves "spiritual" (3:1), "mature" (2:6) and "wise" (3:18; 4:10), reminding them that God uses the lowly, despised and weak in the world to bring about change in the wise and the strong (1:18–31).

2. *Christian conduct.* Correct living is rooted in correct thinking. Paul addressed the problem of sexual immorality and the dangers and advantages of sexual asceticism (5:1–13; 6:12—7:40). He pointed out the detrimental effects of Christians suing one another in secular courts (6:1–11) and the evils of idolatry (8:1—11:1).

3. *Worship.* Paul addressed practices in worship (11:2–16; 14:26–40), the character of the Lord's Supper (11:17–34) and the nature and use of spiritual gifts (12:1—14:40). Worship is to be orderly, God-honoring, uplifting and unifying.

4. *Resurrection.* In denying the resurrection, the Corinthians almost certainly were not denying life after death; belief in the afterlife was held by virtually everyone in the ancient world. They were disputing the Jewish and Christian doctrine of *bodily* resurrection in favor of a Greek form of belief that limited the afterlife to disembodied immortality of the soul.

OUTLINE

I. Introduction: Greeting and Thanksgiving (1:1–9)
II. Divisions in the Church (1:10—4:21)
III. Moral Problems in the Church (5–6)
   A. Need for Church Discipline (5)
   B. Lawsuits Among Believers (6:1–11)
   C. Sexual Immorality (6:12–20)
IV. Questions About Marriage (7)
V. Questions About Christian Freedom (8:1—11:1)
VI. Questions About Worship (11:2—14:40)
VII. Questions About the Resurrection (15)
VIII. Questions About Collections for the Church (16:1–9)
IX. Conclusion (16:10–24)

1:1 [a]Ro 1:1; Eph 1:1 [b]2Co 1:1 [c]Ac 18:17 1 Paul, called to be an apostle[a] of Christ Jesus by the will of God,[b] and our brother Sosthenes,[c]
1:2 [d]Ac 18:1 [e]Ro 1:7 2To the church of God in Corinth,[d] to those sanctified in Christ Jesus and called[e] to be holy, together
with all those everywhere who call on the name of our Lord Jesus Christ—their Lord and ours:
1:3 [f]Ro 1:7 3Grace and peace to you from God our Father and the Lord Jesus Christ.[f]

Thanksgiving

1:4 [g]Ro 1:8 4I always thank God for you[g] because of his grace given you in Christ Jesus. 5For in him you have been
1:5 [h]2Co 9:11 [i]2Co 8:7 enriched[h] in every way—in all your speaking and in all your knowledge[i]— 6because our testimony[j]
1:6 [j]Rev 1:2 about Christ was confirmed in you. 7Therefore you do not lack any spiritual gift as you eagerly wait for
1:7 [k]Php 3:20; Tit 2:13; 2Pe 3:12 our Lord Jesus Christ to be revealed.[k] 8He will keep you strong to the end, so that you will be blameless[l]
1:8 [l]1Th 3:13 on the day of our Lord Jesus Christ. 9God, who has called you into fellowship with his Son Jesus Christ
1:9 [m]1Jn 1:3 [n]Isa 49:7; 1Th 5:24 our Lord,[m] is faithful.[n]

Divisions in the Church

10I appeal to you, brothers, in the name of our Lord Jesus Christ, that all of you agree with one anoth-
er so that there may be no divisions among you and that you may be perfectly united in mind and
thought. 11My brothers, some from Chloe's household have informed me that there are quarrels among
1:12 [o]1Co 3:4,22 [p]Ac 18:24 [q]Jn 1:42 you. 12What I mean is this: One of you says, "I follow Paul";[o] another, "I follow Apollos";[p] another, "I fol-
low Cephas*[a]*";[q] still another, "I follow Christ."
1:13 [r]Mt 28:19 13Is Christ divided? Was Paul crucified for you? Were you baptized into*[b]* the name of Paul?[r] 14I am
1:14 [s]Ac 18:8; Ro 16:23 [t]Ac 19:29 thankful that I did not baptize any of you except Crispus[s] and Gaius,[t] 15so no one can say that you were
baptized into my name. 16(Yes, I also baptized the household of Stephanas;[u] beyond that, I don't remem-
1:16 [u]1Co 16:15 ber if I baptized anyone else.) 17For Christ did not send me to baptize,[v] but to preach the gospel—not
1:17 [v]Jn 4:2 [w]1Co 2:1,4,13 with words of human wisdom,[w] lest the cross of Christ be emptied of its power.

Christ the Wisdom and Power of God

1:18 [x]2Co 2:15 [y]Ro 1:16 18For the message of the cross is foolishness to those who are perishing,[x] but to us who are being
saved it is the power of God.[y] 19For it is written:

> "I will destroy the wisdom of the wise;
> 1:19 [z]Isa 29:14 the intelligence of the intelligent I will frustrate."*[c]*[z]

a 12 That is, Peter *b 13* Or *in*; also in verse 15 *c 19* Isaiah 29:14

1:1–3 Paul partially broke with the normal conventions for first-century letters (see "Letter Writing in Greco-Roman Antiquity" on p. 1889) to introduce the concerns that he would address in this letter.

1:2 Corinth was the chief city of Greece, both commercially and politically. Located just off the Corinthian isthmus, it was a bustling trading port of 100,000 (see "Corinth" on p. 1887). Today it is a small village.

1:10 For "brothers," see the note on Romans 1:13.

Paul called for unity despite the great sociological divisions of the ancient Middle East: Jew versus Gentile, slave versus free, men versus women.

1:11 Information may have come to Paul via a letter no longer in existence (see "The 'Missing' Letter From the Corinthians to Paul" on p. 1870).

1:12 Apollos, an Alexandrian by birth, was a Jewish Christian with notable intellectual and oratorical abilities. Luke wrote that "he was a learned man, with a thorough knowledge of the Scriptures" (Ac 18:24). We also know that Apollos was associated with Paul in the early years of the church in Corinth (1Co 3:4–6,22). He worked in the established church, teaching and encouraging the converts Paul had won.

Cephas is Aramaic for *Peter* (Greek). Those who followed Cephas in Corinth were probably Jewish Christians.

1:13 In Bible times the notion of "name" had a significance it does not carry today, when it is usually an otherwise unmeaning personal label (see "Naming of Children" on p. 28). When a person gave his own name to another, it signified the joining of the two in close unity, as when God gave his name to Israel (Dt 28:9–10). To be baptized into someone else's name accordingly meant to pass into new ownership (Mt 28:19; Ac 8:16; 1Co 1:15). In the Scriptures there is the closest possible relationship between a person and his or her name, the two being practically equivalent.

1:14 Crispus was probably the synagogue ruler (see the notes on Mk 5:22; Lk 8:41) mentioned in Acts 18:8.

1:16 The term "household" generally included family members, servants or anyone else who lived in the house.

1:17–31 For false doctrines, see the note on Colossians 2:8–23.

1:17 Paul's mission was not to couch the gospel in the language of a trained orator, who applied the special rhetorical techniques of persuasion that had been developed by the rabbis among the Jews and by the sophists among the Greeks (see "Debate and Rhetoric in the Ancient World" on p. 1797).

1:18—2:16 The word "philosophy" with its related terms is generally used in a derogatory sense in the Bible. It was not a genuine love of wisdom that Paul deprecated in Colossians 2:8 but "hollow and deceptive philosophy, which depends on human tradition and the basic principles of this world rather than on Christ." The same thought is expressed in the discussion of "wisdom" here in 1 Corinthians, where Paul not only emphasized the inadequacy of worldly wisdom but asserted, "We . . . speak a message of wisdom among the mature" (1 Co 2:6), a wisdom based on revelation. This is similar to the "wisdom" doctrine of Job, Ecclesiastes, certain psalms and especially Proverbs.

1:19 The Athenian statesman Aristides (530–468 B.C.) asserted that on every street in Corinth one met a so-called wise man who had his own solutions to humanity's problems.

20Where is the wise man?[a] Where is the scholar? Where is the philosopher of this age? Has not God
made foolish[b] the wisdom of the world? 21For since in the wisdom of God the world through its wisdom
did not know him, God was pleased through the foolishness of what was preached to save those who be-
lieve. 22Jews demand miraculous signs[c] and Greeks look for wisdom, 23but we preach Christ crucified: a
stumbling block[d] to Jews and foolishness[e] to Gentiles, 24but to those whom God has called,[f] both Jews
and Greeks, Christ the power of God and the wisdom of God.[g] 25For the foolishness[h] of God is wiser than
man's wisdom, and the weakness[i] of God is stronger than man's strength.
26Brothers, think of what you were when you were called. Not many of you were wise by human stan-
dards; not many were influential; not many were of noble birth. 27But God chose[j] the foolish[k] things of
the world to shame the wise; God chose the weak things of the world to shame the strong. 28He chose the
lowly things of this world and the despised things—and the things that are not[l]—to nullify the things
that are, 29so that no one may boast before him.[m] 30It is because of him that you are in Christ Jesus, who
has become for us wisdom from God—that is, our righteousness,[n] holiness and redemption.[o] 31There-
fore, as it is written: "Let him who boasts boast in the Lord."[a][p]

2 When I came to you, brothers, I did not come with eloquence or superior wisdom[q] as I proclaimed
to you the testimony about God.[b] 2For I resolved to know nothing while I was with you except Jesus
Christ and him crucified.[r] 3I came to you[s] in weakness and fear, and with much trembling. 4My message
and my preaching were not with wise and persuasive words, but with a demonstration of the Spirit's
power,[t] 5so that your faith might not rest on men's wisdom, but on God's power.[u]

Wisdom From the Spirit

6We do, however, speak a message of wisdom among the mature,[v] but not the wisdom of this age[w] or
of the rulers of this age, who are coming to nothing. 7No, we speak of God's secret wisdom, a wisdom that
has been hidden and that God destined for our glory before time began. 8None of the rulers of this age un-
derstood it, for if they had, they would not have crucified the Lord of glory.[x] 9However, as it is written:

"No eye has seen,
no ear has heard,
no mind has conceived
what God has prepared for those who love him"[c][y]—

10but God has revealed[z] it to us by his Spirit.[a]
The Spirit searches all things, even the deep things of God. 11For who among men knows the thoughts
of a man[b] except the man's spirit[c] within him? In the same way no one knows the thoughts of God ex-
cept the Spirit of God. 12We have not received the spirit[d] of the world[e] but the Spirit who is from God, that
we may understand what God has freely given us. 13This is what we speak, not in words taught us by hu-
man wisdom[f] but in words taught by the Spirit, expressing spiritual truths in spiritual words.[d] 14The
man without the Spirit does not accept the things that come from the Spirit of God, for they are foolish-
ness[g] to him, and he cannot understand them, because they are spiritually discerned. 15The spiritual
man makes judgments about all things, but he himself is not subject to any man's judgment:

16"For who has known the mind of the Lord
that he may instruct him?"[e][h]

But we have the mind of Christ.[i]

1:20 [a]Isa 19:11, 12 [b]Job 12:17; Ro 1:22
1:22 [c]Mt 12:38
1:23 [d]Lk 2:34; Gal 5:11 [e]1Co 2:14
1:24 [f]Ro 8:28 [g]ver 30; Col 2:3
1:25 [h]ver 18 [i]2Co 13:4
1:27 [j]Jas 2:5 [k]ver 20
1:28 [l]Ro 4:17
1:29 [m]Eph 2:9
1:30 [n]Jer 23:5,6; 2Co 5:21 [o]Ro 3:24; Eph 1:7, 14
1:31 [p]Jer 9:23, 24; 2Co 10:17
2:1 [q]1Co 1:17
2:2 [r]Gal 6:14; 1Co 1:23
2:3 [s]Ac 18:1-18
2:4 [t]Ro 15:19
2:5 [u]2Co 4:7; 6:7
2:6 [v]Eph 4:13; Php 3:15; Heb 5:14 [w]1Co 1:20
2:8 [x]Ac 7:2; Jas 2:1
2:9 [y]Isa 64:4; 65:17
2:10 [z]Mt 13:11; Eph 3:3,5 [a]Jn 14:26
2:11 [b]Jer 17:9 [c]Pr 20:27
2:12 [d]Ro 8:15 [e]1Co 1:20,27
2:13 [f]1Co 1:17
2:14 [g]1Co 1:18
2:16 [h]Isa 40:13 [i]Jn 15:15

[a] *31* Jer. 9:24 [b] *1* Some manuscripts *as I proclaimed to you God's mystery* [c] *9* Isaiah 64:4 [d] *13* Or *Spirit, interpreting spiritual truths to spiritual men* [e] *16* Isaiah 40:13

1:20 "Wise man" is a probable reference to Gentile philosophers in general (see "Greek Philosophical Schools" on p. 1937).

"Scholar" is most likely a reference to Jewish teachers of the law (see the notes on Mt 2:4; Lk 5:17).

"Philosopher of this age" probably refers to the Greek sophists, who engaged in long and subtle disputes (see "Debate and Rhetoric in the Ancient World" on p. 1797 and "Greek Philosophical Schools" on p. 1937).

1:22 Greeks specifically looked for insight into the workings of the world that would relieve humanity's problems.

1:23 Greeks and Romans were certain that no reputable person would be crucified, so it was unthinkable to them that a crucified criminal could be the world's Savior.

2:1 "When I came to you" is a reference to Paul's initial trip to Corinth (c. A.D. 51).

For "eloquence or superior wisdom," see the note on 1 Co 1:17.

2:4 Paul's letters reveal a great deal of knowledge in many areas of learning, and his eloquence is apparent in his address before the Areopagus (see Ac 17:22–31; see also "The Areopagus" on p. 1802). Paul's point was that his confidence as a preacher did not rest on intellectual or oratorical ability, as did that of the Jewish rabbis and the Greek orators (see the note on 1 Co 1:17); rather, his confidence was in the power of the Holy Spirit.

2:6 Greek society was preoccupied with wisdom, looking to philosophers and rulers as the fount of insight (see "Greek Philosophical Schools" on p. 1937).

On Divisions in the Church

3 Brothers, I could not address you as spiritual[j] but as worldly[k]—mere infants[l] in Christ. 2 I gave you milk, not solid food,[m] for you were not yet ready for it.[n] Indeed, you are still not ready. 3 You are still worldly. For since there is jealousy and quarreling[o] among you, are you not worldly? Are you not acting like mere men? 4 For when one says, "I follow Paul," and another, "I follow Apollos,"[p] are you not mere men?

5 What, after all, is Apollos? And what is Paul? Only servants, through whom you came to believe—as the Lord has assigned to each his task. 6 I planted the seed,[q] Apollos watered it, but God made it grow. 7 So neither he who plants nor he who waters is anything, but only God, who makes things grow. 8 The man who plants and the man who waters have one purpose, and each will be rewarded according to his own labor.[r] 9 For we are God's fellow workers;[s] you are God's field,[t] God's building.[u]

10 By the grace God has given me,[v] I laid a foundation[w] as an expert builder, and someone else is building on it. But each one should be careful how he builds. 11 For no one can lay any foundation other than the one already laid, which is Jesus Christ.[x] 12 If any man builds on this foundation using gold, silver, costly stones, wood, hay or straw, 13 his work will be shown for what it is,[y] because the Day[z] will bring it to light. It will be revealed with fire, and the fire will test the quality of each man's work. 14 If what he has built survives, he will receive his reward. 15 If it is burned up, he will suffer loss; he himself will be saved, but only as one escaping through the flames.[a]

16 Don't you know that you yourselves are God's temple[b] and that God's Spirit lives in you? 17 If anyone destroys God's temple, God will destroy him; for God's temple is sacred, and you are that temple.

18 Do not deceive yourselves. If any one of you thinks he is wise[c] by the standards of this age, he should become a "fool" so that he may become wise. 19 For the wisdom of this world is foolishness[d] in God's sight. As it is written: "He catches the wise in their craftiness"[a];[e] 20 and again, "The Lord knows that the thoughts of the wise are futile."[b][f] 21 So then, no more boasting about men![g] All things are yours,[h] 22 whether Paul or Apollos or Cephas[c][i] or the world or life or death or the present or the future[j]—all are yours, 23 and you are of Christ,[k] and Christ is of God.

Apostles of Christ

4 So then, men ought to regard us as servants of Christ and as those entrusted[l] with the secret things[m] of God. 2 Now it is required that those who have been given a trust must prove faithful. 3 I care very little if I am judged by you or by any human court; indeed, I do not even judge myself. 4 My conscience is clear, but that does not make me innocent.[n] It is the Lord who judges me. 5 Therefore judge nothing[o] before the appointed time; wait till the Lord comes. He will bring to light what is hidden in darkness and will expose the motives of men's hearts. At that time each will receive his praise from God.[p]

6 Now, brothers, I have applied these things to myself and Apollos for your benefit, so that you may learn from us the meaning of the saying, "Do not go beyond what is written."[q] Then you will not take pride in one man over against another.[r] 7 For who makes you different from anyone else? What do you have that you did not receive?[s] And if you did receive it, why do you boast as though you did not?

8 Already you have all you want! Already you have become rich![t] You have become kings—and that without us! How I wish that you really had become kings so that we might be kings with you! 9 For it seems to me that God has put us apostles on display at the end of the procession, like men condemned to die[u] in the arena. We have been made a spectacle[v] to the whole universe, to angels as well as to men. 10 We are fools for Christ,[w] but you are so wise in Christ![x] We are weak, but you are strong![y] You are honored, we are dishonored! 11 To this very hour we go hungry and thirsty, we are in rags, we are brutally treated, we are homeless.[z] 12 We work hard with our own hands.[a] When we are cursed, we bless;[b] when we are persecuted, we endure it; 13 when we are slandered, we answer kindly. Up to this moment we have become the scum of the earth, the refuse[c] of the world.

3:1 [j]1Co 2:15 [k]Ro 7:14; 1Co 2:14 [l]Heb 5:13
3:2 [m]Heb 5:12-14; 1Pe 2:2 [n]Jn 16:12
3:3 [o]1Co 1:11; Gal 5:20
3:4 [p]1Co 1:12
3:6 [q]Ac 18:4-11
3:8 [r]Ps 62:12
3:9 [s]2Co 6:1 [t]Isa 61:3 [u]Eph 2:20-22; 1Pe 2:5
3:10 [v]Ro 12:3 [w]Ro 15:20
3:11 [x]Isa 28:16; Eph 2:20
3:13 [y]1Co 4:5 [z]2Th 1:7-10
3:15 [a]Jude 23
3:16 [b]1Co 6:19; 2Co 6:16
3:18 [c]Isa 5:21; 1Co 8:2
3:19 [d]1Co 1:20, 27 [e]Job 5:13
3:20 [f]Ps 94:11
3:21 [g]1Co 4:6 [h]Ro 8:32
3:22 [i]1Co 1:12 [j]Ro 8:38
3:23 [k]1Co 15:23; 2Co 10:7; Gal 3:29
4:1 [l]1Co 9:17; Tit 1:7 [m]Ro 16:25
4:4 [n]Ro 2:13
4:5 [o]Mt 7:1,2; Ro 2:1 [p]Ro 2:29
4:6 [q]1Co 1:19,31; 3:19,20 [r]1Co 1:12
4:7 [s]Jn 3:27; Ro 12:3,6
4:8 [t]Rev 3:17,18
4:9 [u]Ro 8:36 [v]Heb 10:33
4:10 [w]1Co 1:18; Ac 17:18 [x]1Co 3:18 [y]1Co 2:3
4:11 [z]Ro 8:35; 2Co 11:23-27
4:12 [a]Ac 18:3 [b]1Pe 3:9
4:13 [c]La 3:45

[a] *19* Job 5:13 [b] *20* Psalm 94:11 [c] *22* That is, Peter

---

3:1 For "brothers," see the note on Romans 1:13.
3:4 For "Apollos," see the note on 1:12.
3:9 Paul's choice of metaphors accords with the fact that in the ancient world planting the land and building a house (or city or temple) were traditionally the two basic focal points of human industry.
4:1 The Greek underlying the phrase "those entrusted" means "house manager" or "steward" (see the notes on Lk 12:42; 16:1).
4:9 When a Roman general returned home victorious, he led his army in a triumphal procession, at the end of which trailed the captives who were condemned to fight with beasts. Paul felt that, in contrast to the proud Corinthians, the apostles had been put "on display at the end of the procession, like men condemned to die in the arena." God had made them a spectacle to be gazed at and made sport of in the arena of the world. The emperor Nero used to clothe the Christians in the skins of beasts when he exposed them to the wild beasts (cf. 2 Ti 4:17).
4:12 Paul was a tentmaker by trade (see Ac 18:3 and its note).

[14]I am not writing this to shame you, but to warn you, as my dear children.[d] [15]Even though you have ten thousand guardians in Christ, you do not have many fathers, for in Christ Jesus I became your father through the gospel.[e] [16]Therefore I urge you to imitate me.[f] [17]For this reason I am sending to you Timothy, my son[g] whom I love, who is faithful in the Lord. He will remind you of my way of life in Christ Jesus, which agrees with what I teach everywhere in every church.[h]

[18]Some of you have become arrogant, as if I were not coming to you. [19]But I will come to you very soon,[i] if the Lord is willing,[j] and then I will find out not only how these arrogant people are talking, but what power they have. [20]For the kingdom of God is not a matter of talk but of power. [21]What do you prefer? Shall I come to you with a whip,[k] or in love and with a gentle spirit?

4:14 [d]1Th 2:11
4:15 [e]1Co 9:12, 14,18,23
4:16 [f]1Co 11:1; Php 3:17; 1Th 1:6; 2Th 3:7,9
4:17 [g]1Ti 1:2 [h]1Co 7:17
4:19 [i]2Co 1:15, 16 [j]Ac 18:21
4:21 [k]2Co 1:23; 13:2,10

Expel the Immoral Brother!

5 It is actually reported that there is sexual immorality among you, and of a kind that does not occur even among pagans: A man has his father's wife.[l] [2]And you are proud! Shouldn't you rather have been filled with grief[m] and have put out of your fellowship the man who did this? [3]Even though I am not physically present, I am with you in spirit.[n] And I have already passed judgment on the one who did this, just as if I were present. [4]When you are assembled in the name of our Lord Jesus[o] and I am with you in spirit, and the power of our Lord Jesus is present, [5]hand this man over[p] to Satan, so that the sinful nature[a] may be destroyed and his spirit saved on the day of the Lord.

[6]Your boasting is not good.[q] Don't you know that a little yeast[r] works through the whole batch of dough?[s] [7]Get rid of the old yeast that you may be a new batch without yeast—as you really are. For Christ, our Passover lamb, has been sacrificed.[t] [8]Therefore let us keep the Festival, not with the old yeast, the yeast of malice and wickedness, but with bread without yeast,[u] the bread of sincerity and truth.

[9]I have written you in my letter not to associate[v] with sexually immoral people— [10]not at all meaning the people of this world[w] who are immoral, or the greedy and swindlers, or idolaters. In that case you would have to leave this world. [11]But now I am writing you that you must not associate with anyone who calls himself a brother but is sexually immoral or greedy, an idolater[x] or a slanderer, a drunkard or a swindler. With such a man do not even eat.

[12]What business is it of mine to judge those outside[y] the church? Are you not to judge those inside?[z] [13]God will judge those outside. "Expel the wicked man from among you."[b][a]

5:1 [l]Lev 18:8; Dt 22:30
5:2 [m]2Co 7:7-11
5:3 [n]Col 2:5
5:4 [o]2Th 3:6
5:5 [p]1Ti 1:20
5:6 [q]Jas 4:16 [r]Mt 16:6,12 [s]Gal 5:9
5:7 [t]Mk 14:12; 1Pe 1:19
5:8 [u]Ex 12:14,15; Dt 16:3
5:9 [v]Eph 5:11; 2Th 3:6,14
5:10 [w]1Co 10:27
5:11 [x]1Co 10:7, 14
5:12 [y]Mk 4:11 [z]ver 3-5; 1Co 6:1-4
5:13 [a]Dt 13:5

Lawsuits Among Believers

6 If any of you has a dispute with another, dare he take it before the ungodly for judgment instead of before the saints?[b] [2]Do you not know that the saints will judge the world?[c] And if you are to judge the world, are you not competent to judge trivial cases? [3]Do you not know that we will judge angels? How much more the things of this life! [4]Therefore, if you have disputes about such matters, appoint as judges even men of little account in the church![c] [5]I say this to shame you.[d] Is it possible that there is nobody among you wise enough to judge a dispute between believers?[e] [6]But instead, one brother goes to law against another—and this in front of unbelievers![f]

6:1 [b]Mt 18:17
6:2 [c]Mt 19:28; Lk 22:30
6:5 [d]1Co 4:14 [e]Ac 1:15
6:6 [f]2Co 6:14,15

[a] 5 *Or that his body;* or *that the flesh* [b] 13 Deut. 17:7; 19:19; 21:21; 22:21,24; 24:7 [c] 4 *Or matters, do you appoint as judges men of little account in the church?*

4:15 For "guardians," see the note on Galatians 3:24.

5:1—6:20 For the heresy of antinomianism (the view that the oral law does not apply to Christians, who are under the law of grace), see the note on Romans 3:8.

5:1–5 For commentary on excommunication, see the note on 1 Timothy 1:20.

5:1 The Roman orator Cicero asserted that incest was practically unheard of in Roman society.

"His father's wife" implies that the woman was his stepmother. The Old Testament explicitly prohibited such sexual relations (see Lev 18:8; Dt 22:30).

5:2 "Put out of your fellowship" means excommunicated from the church (see the note on Jn 9:22).

5:6 Paul was alluding to the prohibition against the use of leaven (or yeast) in the bread eaten in the Passover feast (see "The Festivals of Israel" on p. 186 and "The Passover" on p. 656). Leaven (or yeast) in Scripture usually symbolizes evil or sin (see the note on Mk 8:15), and the church here was called upon to rid itself of the yeast of sin because its members constituted an unleavened batch of dough—new creations in Christ.

5:7 This may refer to the Passover custom of sweeping all of the (leavened) bread crumbs out of one's house before preparing the Passover meal.

5:8 The "Festival" is here the Feast of Unleavened Bread, which actually followed the Passover (see the notes on Mt 26:17; Mk 14:1; see also "The Festivals of Israel" on p. 186).

5:9 Paul here clarified a previous letter (evidently not preserved). Some in the Corinthian church mistook that letter to imply that, upon separating from sin, they should disassociate themselves from all immoral persons, including non-Christians. Instead, Paul meant that they should separate from immoral persons who were affiliated with the church (see vv. 10–11).

6:1 Paul warned against the Corinthian practice of suing fellow Christians in secular courts. The apostle seems to have been talking about civil court cases, not criminal cases that should have been handled by the state (Ro 13:3–4). The Corinthians were to take their civil cases before the church for informal, out-of-court settlements.

7 The very fact that you have lawsuits among you means you have been completely defeated already.
6:7 [g]Mt 5:39,40 Why not rather be wronged? Why not rather be cheated?[g] 8 Instead, you yourselves cheat and do wrong,
6:8 [h]1Th 4:6 and you do this to your brothers.[h]
6:9 [i]Gal 5:21 9 Do you not know that the wicked will not inherit the kingdom of God?[i] Do not be deceived:[j] Neither
[j]1Co 15:33; the sexually immoral nor idolaters nor adulterers nor male prostitutes nor homosexual offenders 10 nor
Jas 1:16 thieves nor the greedy nor drunkards nor slanderers nor swindlers will inherit the kingdom of God.
6:11 [k]Eph 2:2 11 And that is what some of you were.[k] But you were washed,[l] you were sanctified,[m] you were justified in
[l]Ac 22:16 [m]1Co 1:2 the name of the Lord Jesus Christ and by the Spirit of our God.

Sexual Immorality

6:12 [n]1Co 10:23 12 "Everything is permissible for me"—but not everything is beneficial.[n] "Everything is permissible
for me"—but I will not be mastered by anything. 13 "Food for the stomach and the stomach for food"—
6:13 [o]Col 2:22 but God will destroy them both.[o] The body is not meant for sexual immorality, but for the Lord, and the
6:14 [p]Ro 6:5; Lord for the body. 14 By his power God raised the Lord from the dead, and he will raise us also.[p] 15 Do you
Eph 1:19,20 not know that your bodies are members of Christ himself?[q] Shall I then take the members of Christ and
6:15 [q]Ro 12:5 unite them with a prostitute? Never! 16 Do you not know that he who unites himself with a prostitute is
6:16 [r]Ge 2:24; one with her in body? For it is said, "The two will become one flesh."[a r] 17 But he who unites himself with
Mt 19:5; Eph 5:31 **6:17** [s]Jn 17:21- the Lord is one with him in spirit.[s]
23; Gal 2:20 **6:18** [t]2Co 12:21; 18 Flee from sexual immorality.[t] All other sins a man commits are outside his body, but he who sins
1Th 4:3,4; Heb 13:4 sexually sins against his own body.[u] 19 Do you not know that your body is a temple[v] of the Holy Spirit, who
[u]Ro 6:12 **6:19** [v]Jn 2:21 is in you, whom you have received from God? You are not your own;[w] 20 you were bought at a price.[x] There-
[w]Ro 14:7,8 **6:20** [x]Ac 20:28; fore honor God with your body.
1Co 7:23; 1Pe 1:18,19; Rev 5:9

Marriage

7:1 [y]ver 8,26 **7** Now for the matters you wrote about: It is good for a man not to marry.[b y] 2 But since there is so much
immorality, each man should have his own wife, and each woman her own husband. 3 The husband
7:3 [z]Ex 21:10; should fulfill his marital duty to his wife,[z] and likewise the wife to her husband. 4 The wife's body does
1Pe 3:7 not belong to her alone but also to her husband. In the same way, the husband's body does not belong to
7:5 [a]Ex 19:15; him alone but also to his wife. 5 Do not deprive each other except by mutual consent and for a time,[a] so
1Sa 21:4,5 [b]Mt 4:10 [c]1Th 3:5 that you may devote yourselves to prayer. Then come together again so that Satan[b] will not tempt you[c]
7:6 [d]2Co 8:8 because of your lack of self-control. 6 I say this as a concession, not as a command.[d] 7 I wish that all men
7:7 [e]ver 8; were as I am.[e] But each man has his own gift from God; one has this gift, another has that.[f]
1Co 9:5 [f]Mt 19:11,12; 8 Now to the unmarried and the widows I say: It is good for them to stay unmarried, as I am.[g] 9 But if
Ro 12:6; 1Co 12:4,11 they cannot control themselves, they should marry,[h] for it is better to marry than to burn with passion.
7:8 [g]ver 1,26 **7:9** [h]1Ti 5:14 10 To the married I give this command (not I, but the Lord): A wife must not separate from her hus-
7:10 [i]Mal 2:14- band.[i] 11 But if she does, she must remain unmarried or else be reconciled to her husband. And a husband
16; Mt 5:32; 19:3-9; Mk 10:11; must not divorce his wife.
Lk 16:18 **7:12** [j]ver 6,10; 12 To the rest I say this (I, not the Lord):[j] If any brother has a wife who is not a believer and she is will-
2Co 11:17 ing to live with him, he must not divorce her. 13 And if a woman has a husband who is not a believer and
he is willing to live with her, she must not divorce him. 14 For the unbelieving husband has been sanc-
tified through his wife, and the unbelieving wife has been sanctified through her believing husband.
7:14 [k]Mal 2:15 Otherwise your children would be unclean, but as it is, they are holy.[k]
15 But if the unbeliever leaves, let him do so. A believing man or woman is not bound in such cir-
7:15 [l]Ro 14:19; 1Co 14:33 cumstances; God has called us to live in peace.[l] 16 How do you know, wife, whether you will save[m] your
7:16 [m]Ro 11:14 [n]1Pe 3:1 husband?[n] Or, how do you know, husband, whether you will save your wife?

[a] 16 Gen. 2:24 [b] 1 Or *"It is good for a man not to have sexual relations with a woman."*

6:9 Paul identified three kinds of sexually immoral persons: adulterers, male prostitutes (see "Prostitution in the Ancient World" on p. 284) and males who practiced homosexuality (see "Homosexuality in the Ancient World" on p. 1836). In Romans 1:26 he added the category of females who practiced homosexuality.

6:15 Corinth was infamous for prostitution (see the notes on v. 18; 7:2; see also "Prostitution in the Ancient World" on p. 284).

6:18 The Greek word translated "flee" suggests that one must continually run away from sexual sinning (advice particularly needed in Corinth). The prostitutes of Corinth were dedicated to the service of Aphrodite, the goddess of love and sex (see the note on 7:2).

7:1 The Corinthians had written Paul, asking him a number of vexing questions (see "The 'Missing' Letter From the Corinthians to Paul" on p. 1870).

7:2 Examples of immorality in Corinth included the temple to Aphrodite on the Acrocorinth, the rocky eminence above Corinth, which at one time had in its service 1,000 priestess prostitutes (see the note on 6:18).

7:14 See "Marriage and Divorce in Ancient Israel" on page 1548.

THE "MISSING" LETTER FROM THE CORINTHIANS TO PAUL

1 CORINTHIANS 7 Before composing 1 Corinthians Paul received information about the Corinthian church. He mentioned personal reports "from Chloe's household" (1Co 1:11) and spoke of a letter from the Corinthians that Stephanas, Fortunatus and Achaicus had probably delivered (7:1). No copies of this missing letter apparently remain extant, but it likely included questions about marriage, food sacrificed to idols, worship, resurrection, Paul's collection for Jerusalem relief, and Apollos. Paul answered the Corinthian believers' questions on each of these matters, utilizing the phrases "Now for ..." or "Now about" when taking up a new topic (v. 1; 8:1; 12:1; 16:1,12). In some cases it is unclear whether Paul was quoting the Corinthians' own statements in order to correct them (7:1b; 8:1b) or whether these phrases reflect his own teaching.

As an apostle responsible for the care of churches spread across the Roman Empire,[1] Paul no doubt carried on a lively correspondence with those churches throughout his career.[2] When we recognize that his letters were not written as abstract theological treatises but often as responses to specific problems within the context of specific church situations, we can better understand the lessons these letters contain. It is pointless to speculate on the possible significance of finding one of Paul's lost letters. The chances of this happening are minuscule, and the canon of the New Testament, at any rate, is closed.[3]

[1]See "The Missionary Journeys of Paul" on page 1795. [2]See "Letter Writing in the Greco-Roman World" on page 1889. [3]See "The New Testament Canon" on page 2022.

[17]Nevertheless, each one should retain the place in life that the Lord assigned to him and to which
God has called him.[o] This is the rule I lay down in all the churches.[p] [18]Was a man already circumcised
when he was called? He should not become uncircumcised. Was a man uncircumcised when he was
called? He should not be circumcised.[q] [19]Circumcision is nothing and uncircumcision is nothing.[r] Keep-
ing God's commands is what counts. [20]Each one should remain in the situation which he was in when
God called him.[s] [21]Were you a slave when you were called? Don't let it trouble you—although if you can
gain your freedom, do so. [22]For he who was a slave when he was called by the Lord is the Lord's freed-
man;[t] similarly, he who was a free man when he was called is Christ's slave.[u] [23]You were bought at a price;[v]
do not become slaves of men. [24]Brothers, each man, as responsible to God, should remain in the situa-
tion God called him to.[w]

[25]Now about virgins: I have no command from the Lord,[x] but I give a judgment as one who by the
Lord's mercy[y] is trustworthy. [26]Because of the present crisis, I think that it is good for you to remain as
you are.[z] [27]Are you married? Do not seek a divorce. Are you unmarried? Do not look for a wife. [28]But if

7:17 [o]Ro 12:3 [p]1Co 4:17; 14:33; 2Co 8:18; 11:28
7:18 [q]Ac 15:1,2
7:19 [r]Ro 2:25-27; Gal 5:6; 6:15; Col 3:11
7:20 [s]ver 24
7:22 [t]Jn 8:32,36; Phm 16 [u]Eph 6:6
7:23 [v]1Co 6:20
7:24 [w]ver 20
7:25 [x]ver 6; 2Co 8:8 [y]2Co 4:1; 1Ti 1:13,16
7:26 [z]ver 1,8

7:18 See "Circumcision in the Ancient World" on page 1840.
7:21 In the social and economic sphere, Christian slaves were to live contentedly in their situation, realizing that they had become free in Christ. However, if Christian slaves were given an opportunity to attain their freedom, they were to take advantage of it. In the Roman Empire slaves were sometimes freed by Roman patricians (see "Slavery in the Greco-Roman World" on p. 1979).
7:22 "Freedman" or "free woman" translates two slightly different Greek words: (1) *Apeleutheros,* as here, refers to a slave who had received his freedom, although this verse concerns one who had received spiritual freedom from the Lord. (2) *Eleutheros,* as used in Galatians 4:22–23 and 30, Revelation 6:15, refers to a free woman or man, as opposed to a slave.

you do marry, you have not sinned; and if a virgin marries, she has not sinned. But those who marry will
face many troubles in this life, and I want to spare you this.
7:29 [a]ver 31; 29 What I mean, brothers, is that the time is short.[a] From now on those who have wives should live as
Ro 13:11,12 if they had none; 30 those who mourn, as if they did not; those who are happy, as if they were not; those
who buy something, as if it were not theirs to keep; 31 those who use the things of the world, as if not en-
7:31 [b]1Jn 2:17 grossed in them. For this world in its present form is passing away.[b]
32 I would like you to be free from concern. An unmarried man is concerned about the Lord's af-
7:32 [c]1Ti 5:5 fairs[c]—how he can please the Lord. 33 But a married man is concerned about the affairs of this world—
how he can please his wife— 34 and his interests are divided. An unmarried woman or virgin is con-
7:34 [d]Lk 2:37 cerned about the Lord's affairs: Her aim is to be devoted to the Lord in both body and spirit.[d] But a
married woman is concerned about the affairs of this world—how she can please her husband. 35 I am
7:35 [e]Ps 86:11 saying this for your own good, not to restrict you, but that you may live in a right way in undivided[e]
devotion to the Lord.
36 If anyone thinks he is acting improperly toward the virgin he is engaged to, and if she is getting
7:36 [f]ver 28 along in years and he feels he ought to marry, he should do as he wants. He is not sinning.[f] They should
get married. 37 But the man who has settled the matter in his own mind, who is under no compulsion
but has control over his own will, and who has made up his mind not to marry the virgin—this man also
7:38 [g]Heb 13:4 does the right thing. 38 So then, he who marries the virgin does right,[g] but he who does not marry her does
even better.[a]
7:39 [h]Ro 7:2,3 39 A woman is bound to her husband as long as he lives.[h] But if her husband dies, she is free to mar-
[i]2Co 6:14
7:40 [j]ver 25 ry anyone she wishes, but he must belong to the Lord.[i] 40 In my judgment,[j] she is happier if she stays as
she is—and I think that I too have the Spirit of God.

[a] 36-38 Or *36 If anyone thinks he is not treating his daughter properly, and if she is getting along in years, and he feels she ought to marry, he should do as he wants. He is not sinning. He should let her get married. 37 But the man who has settled the matter in his own mind, who is under no compulsion but has control over his own will, and who has made up his mind to keep the virgin unmarried—this man also does the right thing. 38 So then, he who gives his virgin in marriage does right, but he who does not give her in marriage does even better.*

7:29 For "brothers," see the note on Romans 1:13.

"Temple Restaurants" and Food Sacrificed to Idols

1 CORINTHIANS 8 In many ancient cultures people routinely sacrificed animals to their gods and then ate the meat. In the Greco-Roman world temples would often contain dining areas in which groups of people could feast together. The temple of Asclepius at Corinth ("Map 13"), for example, had three dining rooms, each with space for 11 guests on couches lining the walls. It is uncertain whether these particular dining rooms were in use during Paul's day, but some such arrangement seems to have been behind Paul's discussion in 1 Corinthians 8–10. Corinth also included a temple for the goddess Demeter and her daughter Kore, as well as sanctuaries associated with Egyptian gods and Roman emperors.[1] Although meals at these shrines were often more social occasions than religious ceremonies, no one could deny that there was in them a religious element. The presence of a Christian at a meal associated with such a pagan context was repugnant to Paul.

Excess meat from the temples may have found its way to the market. If such meat, which may or may not have been associated with idol worship, was presented to a believer in someone else's home, Paul permitted the Christian to eat it. If, however, the host openly declared that the meat had come from a pagan shrine, the believer was to abstain for the sake of "weaker" brothers, whose consciences might still be sensitive to idolatrous practices.[2]

[1] See "The Gods of the Greeks and Romans" on page 1908 and "The Imperial Cult" on page 1651. [2] See also "Jewish Meals and Meal Customs" on page 1575.

Food Sacrificed to Idols

8 Now about food sacrificed to idols:[k] We know that we all possess knowledge.[a][l] Knowledge puffs up, but love builds up. 2 The man who thinks he knows something[m] does not yet know as he ought to know.[n] 3 But the man who loves God is known by God.[o]

4 So then, about eating food sacrificed to idols:[p] We know that an idol is nothing at all in the world[q] and that there is no God but one.[r] 5 For even if there are so-called gods,[s] whether in heaven or on earth (as indeed there are many "gods" and many "lords"), 6 yet for us there is but one God, the Father,[t] from whom all things came[u] and for whom we live; and there is but one Lord,[v] Jesus Christ, through whom all things came[w] and through whom we live.

7 But not everyone knows this. Some people are still so accustomed to idols that when they eat such food they think of it as having been sacrificed to an idol, and since their conscience is weak,[x] it is defiled. 8 But food does not bring us near to God;[y] we are no worse if we do not eat, and no better if we do.

9 Be careful, however, that the exercise of your freedom does not become a stumbling block[z] to the weak.[a] 10 For if anyone with a weak conscience sees you who have this knowledge eating in an idol's temple, won't he be emboldened to eat what has been sacrificed to idols? 11 So this weak brother, for whom Christ died, is destroyed[b] by your knowledge. 12 When you sin against your brothers[c] in this way and wound their weak conscience, you sin against Christ. 13 Therefore, if what I eat causes my brother to fall into sin, I will never eat meat again, so that I will not cause him to fall.[d]

The Rights of an Apostle

9 Am I not free? Am I not an apostle?[e] Have I not seen Jesus our Lord?[f] Are you not the result of my work in the Lord?[g] 2 Even though I may not be an apostle to others, surely I am to you! For you are the seal[h] of my apostleship in the Lord.

3 This is my defense to those who sit in judgment on me. 4 Don't we have the right to food and drink?[i] 5 Don't we have the right to take a believing wife[j] along with us, as do the other apostles and the Lord's brothers[k] and Cephas[b]? 6 Or is it only I and Barnabas[l] who must work for a living?

7 Who serves as a soldier at his own expense? Who plants a vineyard[m] and does not eat of its grapes? Who tends a flock and does not drink of the milk? 8 Do I say this merely from a human point of view? Doesn't the Law say the same thing? 9 For it is written in the Law of Moses: "Do not muzzle an ox while it is treading out the grain."[c][n] Is it about oxen that God is concerned?[o] 10 Surely he says this for us, doesn't he? Yes, this was written for us,[p] because when the plowman plows and the thresher threshes, they ought to do so in the hope of sharing in the harvest.[q] 11 If we have sown spiritual seed among you, is it too much if we reap a material harvest from you?[r] 12 If others have this right of support from you, shouldn't we have it all the more?

But we did not use this right.[s] On the contrary, we put up with anything rather than hinder[t] the gospel of Christ. 13 Don't you know that those who work in the temple get their food from the temple, and those who serve at the altar share in what is offered on the altar?[u] 14 In the same way, the Lord has commanded that those who preach the gospel should receive their living from the gospel.[v]

15 But I have not used any of these rights.[w] And I am not writing this in the hope that you will do such things for me. I would rather die than have anyone deprive me of this boast.[x] 16 Yet when I preach the gospel, I cannot boast, for I am compelled to preach.[y] Woe to me if I do not preach the gospel! 17 If I preach voluntarily, I have a reward;[z] if not voluntarily, I am simply discharging the trust committed to me.[a]

8:1 [k]Ac 15:20 [l]Ro 15:14
8:2 [m]1Co 3:18 [n]1Co 13:8,9,12; 1Ti 6:4
8:3 [o]Ro 8:29; Gal 4:9
8:4 [p]ver 1,7,10 [q]1Co 10:19 [r]Dt 6:4; Eph 4:6
8:5 [s]2Th 2:4
8:6 [t]Mal 2:10 [u]Ro 11:36 [v]Eph 4:5 [w]Jn 1:3
8:7 [x]Ro 14:14; 1Co 10:28
8:8 [y]Ro 14:17
8:9 [z]Gal 5:13 [a]Ro 14:1
8:11 [b]Ro 14:15, 20
8:12 [c]Mt 18:6
8:13 [d]Ro 14:21
9:1 [e]2Co 12:12 [f]1Co 15:8 [g]1Co 3:6; 4:15
9:2 [h]2Co 3:2,3
9:4 [i]1Th 2:6
9:5 [j]1Co 7:7,8 [k]Mt 12:46
9:6 [l]Ac 4:36
9:7 [m]Dt 20:6; Pr 27:18
9:9 [n]Dt 25:4; 1Ti 5:18 [o]Dt 22:1-4
9:10 [p]Ro 4:23,24 [q]2Ti 2:6
9:11 [r]Ro 15:27
9:12 [s]Ac 18:3 [t]2Co 11:7-12
9:13 [u]Lev 6:16, 26; Dt 18:1
9:14 [v]Mt 10:10; 1Ti 5:18
9:15 [w]Ac 18:3 [x]2Co 11:9,10
9:16 [y]Ro 1:14; Ac 9:15
9:17 [z]1Co 3:8,14 [a]Gal 2:7; Col 1:25

[a] 1 Or *"We all possess knowledge," as you say* [b] 5 That is, Peter [c] 9 Deut. 25:4

8:1 Most meat sold in the Corinthian marketplace (see "The Ancient City" on p. 1790 and "The Ancient Agora" on p. 1799) came from sacrificial animals that had been slaughtered at pagan temple ceremonies. The Corinthian Christians had questions regarding whether such meat could be eaten—and if so, under what conditions. (See "'Temple Restaurants' and Food Sacrificed to Idols" on p. 1871.) For false doctrines, see the note on Colossians 2:8–23.
8:5 See "The Gods of the Greeks and Romans" on page 1908.
8:7 Those with a "weak" conscience thought that in eating meat sacrificed on pagan altars they were involving themselves in pagan worship and thus sinning against Christ.
8:10 At the site of ancient Corinth archaeologists have found two temples containing rooms apparently used for pagan feasts where meat offered to idols was eaten. Christians may have been invited to such feasts by their pagan friends (see "'Temple Restaurants' and Food Sacrificed to Idols" on p. 1871).
9:9 For a discussion of the threshing floor, see the note on Ruth 3:4–7. See also "The Threshing Floor" on page 608.
9:11–18 Unlike itinerant Greco-Roman philosophers and religious teachers, Paul did not accept payment for his services but supported himself through various means, including tent-making.
9:11 For "reaping," see the note on Galatians 6:7–8.

[18]What then is my reward? Just this: that in preaching the gospel I may offer it free of charge,[b] and so not make use of my rights in preaching it.

[19]Though I am free[c] and belong to no man, I make myself a slave to everyone,[d] to win as many as possible.[e] [20]To the Jews I became like a Jew, to win the Jews.[f] To those under the law I became like one under the law (though I myself am not under the law), so as to win those under the law. [21]To those not having the law I became like one not having the law[g] (though I am not free from God's law but am under Christ's law), so as to win those not having the law. [22]To the weak I became weak, to win the weak. I have become all things to all men[h] so that by all possible means I might save some.[i] [23]I do all this for the sake of the gospel, that I may share in its blessings.

[24]Do you not know that in a race all the runners run, but only one gets the prize? Run[j] in such a way as to get the prize. [25]Everyone who competes in the games goes into strict training. They do it to get a crown that will not last; but we do it to get a crown that will last forever.[k] [26]Therefore I do not run like a man running aimlessly; I do not fight like a man beating the air. [27]No, I beat my body[l] and make it my slave so that after I have preached to others, I myself will not be disqualified for the prize.

Warnings From Israel's History

10 For I do not want you to be ignorant of the fact, brothers, that our forefathers were all under the cloud[m] and that they all passed through the sea.[n] [2]They were all baptized into Moses in the cloud and in the sea. [3]They all ate the same spiritual food [4]and drank the same spiritual drink; for they drank from the spiritual rock[o] that accompanied them, and that rock was Christ. [5]Nevertheless, God was not pleased with most of them; their bodies were scattered over the desert.[p]

[6]Now these things occurred as examples[a] to keep us from setting our hearts on evil things as they did. [7]Do not be idolaters,[q] as some of them were; as it is written: "The people sat down to eat and drink and got up to indulge in pagan revelry."[b][r] [8]We should not commit sexual immorality, as some of them did—and in one day twenty-three thousand of them died.[s] [9]We should not test the Lord, as some of them did—and were killed by snakes.[t] [10]And do not grumble, as some of them did[u]—and were killed[v] by the destroying angel.[w]

[11]These things happened to them as examples and were written down as warnings for us, on whom the fulfillment of the ages has come.[x] [12]So, if you think you are standing firm,[y] be careful that you don't fall! [13]No temptation has seized you except what is common to man. And God is faithful;[z] he will not let you be tempted beyond what you can bear.[a] But when you are tempted, he will also provide a way out so that you can stand up under it.

Idol Feasts and the Lord's Supper

[14]Therefore, my dear friends, flee from idolatry. [15]I speak to sensible people; judge for yourselves what I say. [16]Is not the cup of thanksgiving for which we give thanks a participation in the blood of Christ? And

9:18 [b]2Co 11:7; 12:13
9:19 [c]ver 1 [d]Gal 5:13 [e]Mt 18:15; 1Pe 3:1
9:20 [f]Ac 16:3; 21:20-26; Ro 11:14
9:21 [g]Ro 2:12,14
9:22 [h]1Co 10:33 [i]Ro 11:14
9:24 [j]Gal 2:2; 2Ti 4:7; Heb 12:1
9:25 [k]Jas 1:12; Rev 2:10
9:27 [l]Ro 8:13
10:1 [m]Ex 13:21 [n]Ex 14:22,29
10:4 [o]Ex 17:6; Nu 20:11; Ps 78:15
10:5 [p]Nu 14:29; Heb 3:17
10:7 [q]ver 14 [r]Ex 32:4,6,19
10:8 [s]Nu 25:1-9
10:9 [t]Nu 21:5,6
10:10 [u]Nu 16:41 [v]Nu 16:49 [w]Ex 12:23
10:11 [x]Ro 13:11
10:12 [y]Ro 11:20
10:13 [z]1Co 1:9 [a]2Pe 2:9

[a] 6 Or *types*; also in verse 11 [b] 7 Exodus 32:6

9:20–22 For the sake of the Jews ("those under the law") Paul conformed to the Jewish law. For the sake of the Gentiles ("those not having the law") the apostle accommodated himself to Gentile culture when doing so did not violate his allegiance to Christ. For the sake of the "weak," Paul did not exercise his Christian freedom in such matters as eating meat sacrificed to idols (see 8:9,13).

9:24–27 In these verses Paul alluded to the Isthmian games, which were celebrated every two years on the Isthmus of Corinth. Held in honor of the Greek gods, the festival consisted of foot races, horse races, chariot contests, jumping, wrestling, boxing and throwing the discus and javelin. The prizes in these games were perishable wreathes. To the Greeks these were events of patriotic pride, a passion rather than a pastime, and thus they made a suitable image of earnestness in the Christian race (cf. 2Ti 2:5; 1Pe 1:4). Other allusions in the New Testament to the language of games are found in Acts 20:24, Ephesians 6:12, Philippians 3:12–14, 1 Timothy 6:12; 2 Timothy 4:7, Hebrews 12:1–2, James 1:12 and Revelation 2:10.

9:24 The clearest uses of the Greek words *agôn* and *stadion* (most frequently translated "a foot race") are in this verse, 2 Timothy 4:7 and Hebrews 12:1, although other passages may well allude to such a race: Galatians 5:7, Philippians 2:16. The Greek race was one of a series of highly competitive games. It consisted of (1) the goal, a square pillar opposite the entrance to the course, marking the end of the track; (2) the herald, whose duty it was to announce the name and the country of each competitor, as well as the name and family of the victor; (3) the prize, the crown or wreath that was awarded the winner (cf. 1Co 9:25; 2Ti 2:5); and (4) the judges (2Ti 4:8). The Lord is viewed as the righteous judge who bestows the wreath on those who have truly run well.

9:25 For a discussion of asceticism in the believer's life, see the note on Leviticus 10:9.

10:8 Paul stated the number of the dead as 23,000, while the Hebrew and Greek (Septuagint) texts of Numbers 25:9 both indicate 24,000. It is clear that Paul was not striving for exactness but only speaking approximately. First-century writers were not as concerned about precision as twenty-first-century authors typically are.

10:14 Corinthian Christians had emerged from a background of paganism. Temples for the worship of Apollo, Asclepius, Demeter, Aphrodite and other pagan gods and goddesses (see "The Gods of the Greeks and Romans" on p. 1908) were seen daily by the Corinthians as they engaged in the activities of everyday life. The worship of Aphrodite was a particularly strong temptation (see the note on 6:18).

10:16 The "cup of thanksgiving" refers to the cup of wine that Christians drink during the celebration of the Lord's Supper.

is not the bread that we break a participation in the body of Christ?[b] 17 Because there is one loaf, we, who
are many, are one body,[c] for we all partake of the one loaf.
18 Consider the people of Israel: Do not those who eat the sacrifices[d] participate in the altar? 19 Do I
mean then that a sacrifice offered to an idol is anything, or that an idol is anything?[e] 20 No, but the sac-
rifices of pagans are offered to demons,[f] not to God, and I do not want you to be participants with de-
mons. 21 You cannot drink the cup of the Lord and the cup of demons too; you cannot have a part in both
the Lord's table and the table of demons.[g] 22 Are we trying to arouse the Lord's jealousy?[h] Are we stron-
ger than he?[i]

The Believer's Freedom

23 "Everything is permissible"—but not everything is beneficial.[j] "Everything is permissible"—but
not everything is constructive. 24 Nobody should seek his own good, but the good of others.[k]
25 Eat anything sold in the meat market without raising questions of conscience,[l] 26 for, "The earth is
the Lord's, and everything in it."[a][m]
27 If some unbeliever invites you to a meal and you want to go, eat whatever is put before you[n] with-
out raising questions of conscience. 28 But if anyone says to you, "This has been offered in sacrifice," then
do not eat it, both for the sake of the man who told you and for conscience' sake[b][o]— 29 the other man's
conscience, I mean, not yours. For why should my freedom[p] be judged by another's conscience? 30 If I
take part in the meal with thankfulness, why am I denounced because of something I thank God for?[q]

10:16 [b]Mt 26:26-28
10:17 [c]Ro 12:5; 1Co 12:27
10:18 [d]Lev 7:6, 14,15
10:19 [e]1Co 8:4
10:20 [f]Dt 32:17; Ps 106:37; Rev 9:20
10:21 [g]2Co 6:15, 16
10:22 [h]Dt 32:16, 21 [i]Ecc 6:10; Isa 45:9
10:23 [j]1Co 6:12
10:24 [k]ver 33; Ro 15:1,2; 1Co 13:5; Php 2:4,21
10:25 [l]Ac 10:15; 1Co 8:7
10:26 [m]Ps 24:1
10:27 [n]Lk 10:7
10:28 [o]1Co 8:7, 10-12
10:29 [p]Ro 14:16; 1Co 9:1,19
10:30 [q]Ro 14:6

[a] 26 Psalm 24:1 [b] 28 Some manuscripts *conscience' sake, for "the earth is the Lord's and everything in it"*

10:18–20 When the people of Israel ate part of the sacrifice made at the altar (Lev 7:15; 8:31; Dt 12:17–18), they were participating with the altar in consuming the sacrifices; that which was consumed on the altar (with fire) was Yahweh's portion.

God's people were warned that, in a similar way, if they did eat meat sacrificed to idols they should refrain from eating it with pagans in their temple feasts; to do so would be to become "participants with demons." (See "'Temple Restaurants' and Food Sacrificed to Idols" on p. 1871.)

10:25 Christians could eat anything sold in the meat market, even if it had been sacrificed to an idol, because out in the public market it had lost its pagan religious significance.

10:26 This quotation from Psalm 24:1 was used at Jewish mealtimes as a blessing.

10:27 Whether or not the meat might have been sacrificed to idols, the believers were to ask no questions. As long as the subject was not brought up, they were free to eat the meat.

The Love Feast

1 CORINTHIANS 11 Sharing meals together was a crucial part of early church life. Jesus set an example by welcoming to the table fellowship all who would come. The early church continued this practice and members often met together in people's homes to share food (e.g., Ac 2:42). Certain Jewish and Greco-Roman religious associations also met for common meals,[1] and at times behavior at pagan communal meals could be extremely disorderly.[2] For Christians, however, the shared meal was such a powerful emblem of their love in Christ that it came to be called a "love feast" (Greek *agape*; lit., "a love"). The word is used in this manner in the New Testament only in Jude 12.

Jesus also instituted the Eucharist (or "Lord's Supper"), and it is difficult to ascertain the relationship between the Eucharist and the "love feast." Were they one and the same or two different events? The most likely answer is that in the early church no firm distinction was made between the two. The Eucharist was probably celebrated in the context of a church meal, just as the first Eucharist was commemorated in the context of a Passover supper. It soon became evident, however, that it was unwise to combine the two (1Co 11:20–21: "When you come together, it is not the Lord's Supper you eat, for as you eat, each of you goes ahead without waiting for anybody else. One remains hungry, another gets drunk." In later centuries the Lord's Supper was separated from the common meal, and the tradition of the "love feast" began to disappear.

[1]See "Jewish Meals and Meal Customs" on page 1575. [2]See "'Temple Restaurants' and Food Sacrificed to Idols" on page 1871.

31 So whether you eat or drink or whatever you do, do it all for the glory of God.[r] 32 Do not cause anyone to stumble,[s] whether Jews, Greeks or the church of God[t]— 33 even as I try to please everybody in every way.[u] For I am not seeking my own good but the good of many, so that they may be saved.[v]

11 1 Follow my example,[w] as I follow the example of Christ.

Propriety in Worship

2 I praise you[x] for remembering me in everything[y] and for holding to the teachings,[a] just as I passed them on to you.[z]

3 Now I want you to realize that the head of every man is Christ,[a] and the head of the woman is man,[b] and the head of Christ is God.[c] 4 Every man who prays or prophesies with his head covered dishonors his head. 5 And every woman who prays or prophesies[d] with her head uncovered dishonors her head—it is just as though her head were shaved.[e] 6 If a woman does not cover her head, she should have her hair cut off; and if it is a disgrace for a woman to have her hair cut or shaved off, she should cover her head. 7 A man ought not to cover his head,[b] since he is the image[f] and glory of God; but the woman is the glory of man. 8 For man did not come from woman, but woman from man;[g] 9 neither was man created for woman, but woman for man.[h] 10 For this reason, and because of the angels, the woman ought to have a sign of authority on her head.

11 In the Lord, however, woman is not independent of man, nor is man independent of woman. 12 For as woman came from man, so also man is born of woman. But everything comes from God.[i] 13 Judge for yourselves: Is it proper for a woman to pray to God with her head uncovered? 14 Does not the very nature of things teach you that if a man has long hair, it is a disgrace to him, 15 but that if a woman has long hair, it is her glory? For long hair is given to her as a covering. 16 If anyone wants to be contentious about this, we have no other practice—nor do the churches of God.[j]

The Lord's Supper

17 In the following directives I have no praise for you,[k] for your meetings do more harm than good. 18 In the first place, I hear that when you come together as a church, there are divisions[l] among you, and to some extent I believe it. 19 No doubt there have to be differences among you to show which of you have God's approval.[m] 20 When you come together, it is not the Lord's Supper you eat, 21 for as you eat, each of you goes ahead without waiting for anybody else.[n] One remains hungry, another gets drunk. 22 Don't you have homes to eat and drink in? Or do you despise the church of God[o] and humiliate those who have nothing?[p] What shall I say to you? Shall I praise you[q] for this? Certainly not!

23 For I received from the Lord[r] what I also passed on to you:[s] The Lord Jesus, on the night he was betrayed, took bread, 24 and when he had given thanks, he broke it and said, "This is my body, which is for you; do this in remembrance of me." 25 In the same way, after supper he took the cup, saying, "This cup is the new covenant[t] in my blood;[u] do this, whenever you drink it, in remembrance of me." 26 For whenever you eat this bread and drink this cup, you proclaim the Lord's death until he comes.

27 Therefore, whoever eats the bread or drinks the cup of the Lord in an unworthy manner will be guilty of sinning against the body and blood of the Lord.[v] 28 A man ought to examine himself[w] before he eats of the bread and drinks of the cup. 29 For anyone who eats and drinks without recognizing the body of the

10:31 [r]Col 3:17; 1Pe 4:11 **10:32** [s]Ac 24:16 [t]Ac 20:28 **10:33** [u]Ro 15:2; 1Co 9:22 [v]Ro 11:14 **11:1** [w]1Co 4:16 **11:2** [x]ver 17,22 [y]1Co 4:17 [z]1Co 15:2,3; 2Th 2:15 **11:3** [a]Eph 1:22 [b]Ge 3:16; Eph 5:23 [c]1Co 3:23 **11:5** [d]Ac 21:9 [e]Dt 21:12 **11:7** [f]Ge 1:26; Jas 3:9 **11:8** [g]Ge 2:21-23; 1Ti 2:13 **11:9** [h]Ge 2:18 **11:12** [i]Ro 11:36 **11:16** [j]1Co 7:17 **11:17** [k]ver 2,22 **11:18** [l]1Co 1:10-12; 3:3 **11:19** [m]1Jn 2:19 **11:21** [n]2Pe 2:13; Jude 12 **11:22** [o]1Co 10:32 [p]Jas 2:6 [q]ver 2, 17 **11:23** [r]Gal 1:12 [s]1Co 15:3 **11:25** [t]Lk 22:20 [u]1Co 10:16 **11:27** [v]Heb 10:29 **11:28** [w]2Co 13:5

[a] 2 Or *traditions* [b] 4-7 Or *4Every man who prays or prophesies with long hair dishonors his head. 5And every woman who prays or prophesies with no covering ⌊of hair⌋ on her head dishonors her head—she is just like one of the "shorn women." 6If a woman has no covering, let her be for now with short hair, but since it is a disgrace for a woman to have her hair shorn or shaved, she should grow it again. 7A man ought not to have long hair*

11:4 In the culture of Paul's day men uncovered their heads in worship to signify their respect for and submission to deity. When a man prayed or prophesied with his head covered, he failed to show the proper attitude toward Christ.

11:5–6 Based on their newfound freedom in Christ, women in the Corinthian church were praying and prophesying. Christian tradition from Pentecost on had approved of such practice (Ac 2:17–18), and it readily fit Paul's emphasis on freedom. But these women, as they spoke in worship, were apparently flaunting social convention by sending ambiguous signals about their sexuality or religious commitment through inappropriate hairstyles or the lack of headdresses. Paul encouraged them to exercise restraint.

11:15 A woman's covering of her head is mentioned in the Bible only in this verse. In the preceding verses Paul stated that women should have their heads covered in public worship. At that time in Greece only immoral women were seen with their heads uncovered. Paul was saying that Christian women could not afford to disregard social convention, as this would hurt their testimony. In Paul's view, in giving them long hair, a natural veil, God through "nature" teaches the lesson that women are not to be unveiled in public assemblies. For a discussion of literal and figurative references to hair in the Bible, see the note at Psalm 40:12. See also "Beards and Hairstyles in the Biblical World" on page 1084.

11:21 The early church held the *agape* ("love") feast in connection with the Lord's Supper (see "The Love Feast" on p. 1874). Perhaps the meal was something like a present-day potluck dinner. But some in the church gorged themselves and got drunk at the expense of those who came later or had less. Jude 12 addresses a similar problem.

11:23 See "The Last Supper and the Passover" on page 1611.

11:24 Giving thanks was the Jewish practice at meals (see "Jewish Meals and Meal Customs" on p. 1575).

Lord eats and drinks judgment on himself. 30 That is why many among you are weak and sick, and a num-
ber of you have fallen asleep. 31 But if we judged ourselves, we would not come under judgment.[x] 32 When
we are judged by the Lord, we are being disciplined[y] so that we will not be condemned with the world.
33 So then, my brothers, when you come together to eat, wait for each other. 34 If anyone is hungry,[z] he
should eat at home,[a] so that when you meet together it may not result in judgment.
And when I come[b] I will give further directions.

11:31 [x]Ps 32:5; 1Jn 1:9 **11:32** [y]Ps 94:12; Heb 12:7-10; Rev 3:19 **11:34** [z]ver 21 [a]ver 22 [b]1Co 4:19

11:33 The phrase "come together to eat" is another reference to the *agape* fellowship meal (see the note on v. 21).

Tongue-Speaking in Christian and Pagan Worship

1 CORINTHIANS 12 Speaking in tongues was a recognized part of the life of the early church. In Acts 2 tongues are identified as foreign languages understood by the various pilgrims in Jerusalem. In 1 Corinthians, however, it is unclear whether tongues were unlearned foreign languages, angelic languages or inarticulate groanings "that words cannot express" (Ro 8:26). Whatever the case may have been, Paul desired that tongues be translated so that all present might benefit.

The god Pan

Preserving Bible Times; © Dr. James C. Martin; permission of The British Museum

Some argue that there were parallels to tongue-speaking in the pagan world, but these supposed correspondences can be misleading. It is true that other cultures knew of - various sorts of ecstatic speech, which could sometimes include either unintelligible speech or foreign words and phrases. Some pagan rites (with the aid of alcohol or drugs) worked people into a state of delirium. At pagan oracles, ecstatic priestesses sometimes delivered messages purported to be from gods. People would describe these priestesses as "raving," but that usually referred to the fact that their meaning was obscure. A pagan oracle might have been delivered in everyday Greek, but its meaning might still have been puzzling or confusing, even to a Greek-speaking audience. The words were understandable, but their message was unclear.

A famous example concerns the legend of Croesus, king of Lydia, who sought the advice of the oracle at Delphi regarding whether or not he should wage war against **Persia**.[1] He was told that if he did, a great kingdom would fall. Croesus attacked, believing that the oracle was signifying his own victory, but he was defeated and his own kingdom fell. Thus, although the priestess at Delphi may have spoken in an ecstatic manner, the real issue was the ambiguity of her message.

This form of ecstatic speech must be distinguished from the Christian practice, in which the unknown tongue would evidently be immediately translated into speech understood by the congregation. Of course, the unrestrained use of tongues in worship may at times have resembled the rantings of pagan worshipers.[2] This may have accounted for Paul's concern in 1 Corinthians 14:23, where he pointed out that an unbeliever might enter the service and hear uninterpreted tongues and "say that you are out of your mind."

[1]See Glossary on page 2080 for definitions of bolded words. [2]See "Magic in the Greco-Roman World" on page 1911.

Spiritual Gifts

12 Now about spiritual gifts,[c] brothers, I do not want you to be ignorant. 2 You know that when you
were pagans,[d] somehow or other you were influenced and led astray to mute idols.[e] 3 Therefore
I tell you that no one who is speaking by the Spirit of God says, "Jesus be cursed,"[f] and no one can say,
"Jesus is Lord,"[g] except by the Holy Spirit.[h]
4 There are different kinds of gifts, but the same Spirit.[i] 5 There are different kinds of service, but the
same Lord. 6 There are different kinds of working, but the same God[j] works all of them in all men.
7 Now to each one the manifestation of the Spirit is given for the common good.[k] 8 To one there is giv-
en through the Spirit the message of wisdom,[l] to another the message of knowledge[m] by means of the
same Spirit, 9 to another faith[n] by the same Spirit, to another gifts of healing[o] by that one Spirit, 10 to an-
other miraculous powers,[p] to another prophecy, to another distinguishing between spirits,[q] to another
speaking in different kinds of tongues,[a][r] and to still another the interpretation of tongues.[a] 11 All these
are the work of one and the same Spirit,[s] and he gives them to each one, just as he determines.

One Body, Many Parts

12 The body is a unit, though it is made up of many parts; and though all its parts are many, they form
one body.[t] So it is with Christ.[u] 13 For we were all baptized by[b] one Spirit[v] into one body—whether Jews
or Greeks, slave or free[w]—and we were all given the one Spirit to drink.[x]
14 Now the body is not made up of one part but of many. 15 If the foot should say, "Because I am not a
hand, I do not belong to the body," it would not for that reason cease to be part of the body. 16 And if the
ear should say, "Because I am not an eye, I do not belong to the body," it would not for that reason cease
to be part of the body. 17 If the whole body were an eye, where would the sense of hearing be? If the whole
body were an ear, where would the sense of smell be? 18 But in fact God has arranged[y] the parts in the
body, every one of them, just as he wanted them to be.[z] 19 If they were all one part, where would the body
be? 20 As it is, there are many parts, but one body.[a]
21 The eye cannot say to the hand, "I don't need you!" And the head cannot say to the feet, "I don't need
you!" 22 On the contrary, those parts of the body that seem to be weaker are indispensable, 23 and the parts
that we think are less honorable we treat with special honor. And the parts that are unpresentable are
treated with special modesty, 24 while our presentable parts need no special treatment. But God has com-
bined the members of the body and has given greater honor to the parts that lacked it, 25 so that there
should be no division in the body, but that its parts should have equal concern for each other. 26 If one part
suffers, every part suffers with it; if one part is honored, every part rejoices with it.
27 Now you are the body of Christ,[b] and each one of you is a part of it.[c] 28 And in the church[d] God has
appointed first of all apostles,[e] second prophets, third teachers, then workers of miracles, also those hav-
ing gifts of healing,[f] those able to help others, those with gifts of administration,[g] and those speaking in
different kinds of tongues.[h] 29 Are all apostles? Are all prophets? Are all teachers? Do all work miracles?
30 Do all have gifts of healing? Do all speak in tongues[c]?[i] Do all interpret? 31 But eagerly desire[d][j] the great-
er gifts.

Love

And now I will show you the most excellent way.
13 If I speak in the tongues[e][k] of men and of angels, but have not love, I am only a resounding gong
or a clanging cymbal. 2 If I have the gift of prophecy and can fathom all mysteries[l] and all knowl-
edge, and if I have a faith[m] that can move mountains,[n] but have not love, I am nothing. 3 If I give all I pos-
sess to the poor[o] and surrender my body to the flames,[f][p] but have not love, I gain nothing.

12:1 [c]Ro 1:11; 1Co 14:1,37 **12:2** [d]Eph 2:11, 12; 1Pe 4:3 [e]Ps 115:5; Jer 10:5; Hab 2:18,19; 1Th 1:9 **12:3** [f]Ro 9:3 [g]Jn 13:13 [h]1Jn 4:2,3 **12:4** [i]Ro 12:4-8; Eph 4:11; Heb 2:4 **12:6** [j]Eph 4:6 **12:7** [k]Eph 4:12 **12:8** [l]1Co 2:6 [m]2Co 8:7 **12:9** [n]Mt 17:19, 20; 2Co 4:13 [o]ver 28,30 **12:10** [p]Gal 3:5 [q]1Jn 4:1 [r]Mk 16:17 **12:11** [s]ver 4
12:12 [t]Ro 12:5 [u]ver 27 **12:13** [v]Eph 2:18 [w]Gal 3:28; Col 3:11 [x]Jn 7:37-39
12:18 [y]ver 28 [z]ver 11
12:20 [a]ver 12,14
12:27 [b]Eph 1:23; 4:12; Col 1:18,24 [c]Ro 12:5 **12:28** [d]1Co 10:32 [e]Eph 4:11 [f]ver 9 [g]Ro 12:6-8 [h]ver 10 **12:30** [i]ver 10 **12:31** [j]1Co 14:1, 39
13:1 [k]ver 8 **13:2** [l]1Co 14:2 [m]1Co 12:9 [n]Mt 17:20; 21:21 **13:3** [o]Mt 6:2 [p]Da 3:28

[a] *10* Or *languages;* also in verse 28 [b] *13* Or *with;* or *in* [c] *30* Or *other languages* [d] *31* Or *But you are eagerly desiring*
[e] *1* Or *languages* [f] *3* Some early manuscripts *body that I may boast*

12:3 The same Greek word for "Lord" is used in the Septuagint to translate the Hebrew name *Yahweh* ("the LORD"; see the note on Ro 10:9; see also "YHWH: The Name of God in the Old Testament" on p. 89). The central Christian confession, "Jesus is Lord," was a particular problem in the Roman Empire, because the affirmation of the sovereignty of Jesus was a direct challenge to the claim of absolute rule on the part of the Roman emperor (see "The Imperial Cult" on p. 1651).

12:10 For "tongues," see "Tongue-Speaking in Christian and Pagan Worship" on page 1876.

12:12 The believers in Corinth, and elsewhere in the ancient world, came from diverse ethnic and socioeconomic backgrounds. But in Christ there is no ethnic, cultural or social distinction.

13:3 Many early Christians experienced martyrdom through being burned at the stake (see "The Early Persecution of the Church" on p. 2067).

4 Love is patient,[q] love is kind. It does not envy, it does not boast, it is not proud. 5 It is not rude, it is not self-seeking,[r] it is not easily angered, it keeps no record of wrongs. 6 Love does not delight in evil[s] but rejoices with the truth.[t] 7 It always protects, always trusts, always hopes, always perseveres.

8 Love never fails. But where there are prophecies,[u] they will cease; where there are tongues,[v] they will be stilled; where there is knowledge, it will pass away. 9 For we know in part[w] and we prophesy in part, 10 but when perfection comes,[x] the imperfect disappears. 11 When I was a child, I talked like a child, I thought like a child, I reasoned like a child. When I became a man, I put childish ways behind me. 12 Now we see but a poor reflection as in a mirror; then we shall see face to face.[y] Now I know in part; then I shall know fully, even as I am fully known.[z]

13 And now these three remain: faith, hope and love.[a] But the greatest of these is love.[b]

Gifts of Prophecy and Tongues

14 Follow the way of love[c] and eagerly desire[d] spiritual gifts,[e] especially the gift of prophecy. 2 For anyone who speaks in a tongue[a][f] does not speak to men but to God. Indeed, no one understands him; he utters mysteries[g] with his spirit.[b] 3 But everyone who prophesies speaks to men for their strengthening,[h] encouragement and comfort. 4 He who speaks in a tongue[i] edifies himself, but he who prophesies[j] edifies the church. 5 I would like every one of you to speak in tongues,[c] but I would rather have you prophesy.[k] He who prophesies is greater than one who speaks in tongues,[d] unless he interprets, so that the church may be edified.

6 Now, brothers, if I come to you and speak in tongues, what good will I be to you, unless I bring you some revelation[l] or knowledge or prophecy or word of instruction?[m] 7 Even in the case of lifeless things that make sounds, such as the flute or harp, how will anyone know what tune is being played unless there is a distinction in the notes? 8 Again, if the trumpet does not sound a clear call, who will get ready for battle?[n] 9 So it is with you. Unless you speak intelligible words with your tongue, how will anyone know what you are saying? You will just be speaking into the air. 10 Undoubtedly there are all sorts of languages in the world, yet none of them is without meaning. 11 If then I do not grasp the meaning of what someone is saying, I am a foreigner to the speaker, and he is a foreigner to me. 12 So it is with you. Since you are eager to have spiritual gifts, try to excel in gifts that build up the church.

13 For this reason anyone who speaks in a tongue should pray that he may interpret what he says. 14 For if I pray in a tongue, my spirit prays, but my mind is unfruitful. 15 So what shall I do? I will pray with my spirit, but I will also pray with my mind; I will sing[o] with my spirit, but I will also sing with my mind. 16 If you are praising God with your spirit, how can one who finds himself among those who do not understand[e] say "Amen"[p] to your thanksgiving,[q] since he does not know what you are saying? 17 You may be giving thanks well enough, but the other man is not edified.

18 I thank God that I speak in tongues more than all of you. 19 But in the church I would rather speak five intelligible words to instruct others than ten thousand words in a tongue.

20 Brothers, stop thinking like children.[r] In regard to evil be infants,[s] but in your thinking be adults. 21 In the Law[t] it is written:

> "Through men of strange tongues
> and through the lips of foreigners
> I will speak to this people,
> but even then they will not listen to me,"[f][u]
> says the Lord.

22 Tongues, then, are a sign, not for believers but for unbelievers; prophecy,[v] however, is for believers, not for unbelievers. 23 So if the whole church comes together and everyone speaks in tongues, and some who do not understand[g] or some unbelievers come in, will they not say that you are out of your mind?[w]

13:4 [q]1Th 5:14
13:5 [r]1Co 10:24
13:6 [s]2Th 2:12 [t]2Jn 4; 3Jn 3,4
13:8 [u]ver 2 [v]ver 1
13:9 [w]ver 12; 1Co 8:2
13:10 [x]Php 3:12
13:12 [y]Ge 32:30; 2Co 5:7; 1Jn 3:2 [z]1Co 8:3
13:13 [a]Gal 5:5,6 [b]1Co 16:14
14:1 [c]1Co 16:14 [d]ver 39; 1Co 12:31 [e]1Co 12:1
14:2 [f]Mk 16:17 [g]1Co 13:2
14:3 [h]ver 4,5,12, 17,26; Ro 14:19
14:4 [i]Mk 16:17 [j]1Co 13:2
14:5 [k]Nu 11:29
14:6 [l]ver 26; Eph 1:17 [m]Ro 6:17
14:8 [n]Nu 10:9; Jer 4:19
14:15 [o]Eph 5:19; Col 3:16
14:16 [p]Dt 27:15-26; 1Ch 16:36; Ne 8:6; Ps 106:48; Rev 5:14; 7:12 [q]1Co 11:24
14:20 [r]Eph 4:14; Heb 5:12,13; 1Pe 2:2 [s]Ro 16:19
14:21 [t]Jn 10:34 [u]Isa 28:11,12
14:22 [v]ver 1
14:23 [w]Ac 2:13

[a] 2 Or *another language*; also in verses 4, 13, 14, 19, 26 and 27 [b] 2 Or *by the Spirit* [c] 5 Or *other languages*; also in verses 6, 18, 22, 23 and 39 [d] 5 Or *other languages*; also in verses 6, 18, 22, 23 and 39 [e] 16 Or *among the inquirers* [f] 21 Isaiah 28:11,12 [g] 23 Or *some inquirers*

13:8 For false doctrines, see the note on Colossians 2:8–23.
13:12 The imagery is of a polished metal (probably bronze) mirror in which one could perceive only an imperfect reflection.
14:2 For "tongue," see "Tongue-Speaking in Christian and Pagan Worship" on page 1876.
14:7 Flutes and harps were well known in Greece.
14:8 All Greeks would have been acquainted with the use of the trumpet for battle signals (see "Trumpets in the Ancient World" on p. 2057, and the Jews would have been familiar with the use of the ram's horn (see "The Shofar" on p. 898).
14:23 See "Tongue-Speaking in Christian and Pagan Worship" on page 1876.

24 But if an unbeliever or someone who does not understand[a] comes in while everybody is prophesying,
he will be convinced by all that he is a sinner and will be judged by all, 25 and the secrets of his heart will
14:25 [x]Isa 45:14; Zec 8:23 be laid bare. So he will fall down and worship God, exclaiming, "God is really among you!"[x]

Orderly Worship

14:26 [y]1Co 12:7-10 [z]Eph 5:19 [a]ver 6 [b]Ro 14:19 26 What then shall we say, brothers? When you come together, everyone[y] has a hymn,[z] or a word of in-
struction,[a] a revelation, a tongue or an interpretation. All of these must be done for the strengthening[b]
of the church. 27 If anyone speaks in a tongue, two—or at the most three—should speak, one at a time,
and someone must interpret. 28 If there is no interpreter, the speaker should keep quiet in the church and
speak to himself and God.
14:29 [c]1Co 12:10 29 Two or three prophets should speak, and the others should weigh carefully what is said.[c] 30 And if a
revelation comes to someone who is sitting down, the first speaker should stop. 31 For you can all proph-
esy in turn so that everyone may be instructed and encouraged. 32 The spirits of prophets are subject to
14:32 [d]1Jn 4:1 the control of prophets.[d] 33 For God is not a God of disorder[e] but of peace.
14:33 [e]ver 40 [f]Ac 9:13 As in all the congregations of the saints,[f] 34 women should remain silent in the churches. They are not
14:34 [g]1Ti 2:11, 12 [h]Ge 3:16 allowed to speak, but must be in submission,[g] as the Law[h] says. 35 If they want to inquire about something,
they should ask their own husbands at home; for it is disgraceful for a woman to speak in the church.
36 Did the word of God originate with you? Or are you the only people it has reached? 37 If anybody
14:37 [i]2Co 10:7 [j]1Jn 4:6 thinks he is a prophet[i] or spiritually gifted, let him acknowledge that what I am writing to you is the
Lord's command.[j] 38 If he ignores this, he himself will be ignored.[b]
14:39 [k]1Co 12:31 39 Therefore, my brothers, be eager[k] to prophesy, and do not forbid speaking in tongues. 40 But every-
14:40 [l]ver 33 thing should be done in a fitting and orderly[l] way.

[a] 24 Or *or some inquirer* [b] 38 Some manuscripts *If he is ignorant of this, let him be ignorant*

14:26 This verse includes the elements that made up the worship service at Corinth. Some of them (the hymn and the word of instruction) were carryovers from Old Testament and synagogue worship. (See "Early Christian Hymnody" on p. 2007.)

14:34–35 Paul had already noted that God had gifted women with the capacity to prophesy and pray in public (11:5). So rather than intending to silence women totally in the church, Paul may have been referring to interfering chatter or to the promotion of false teaching. (See "The Role of Women in Religious Life in the Greco-Roman World" on p. 1897, "Husbands and Wives: Family Life in the Greco-Roman World" on p. 1922 and "The Demeanor of Wives" on p. 2013.)

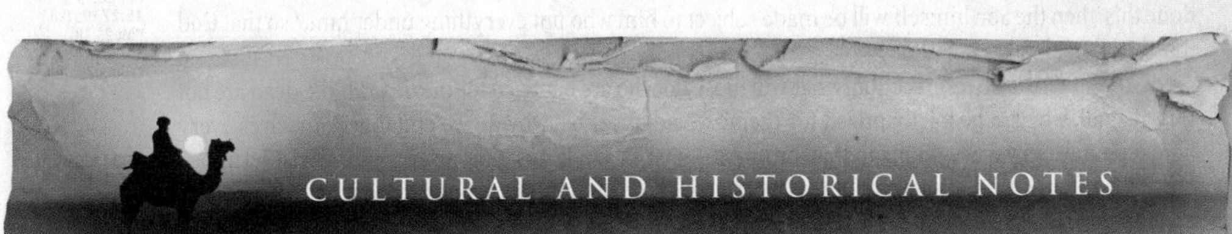

The Role of Women in Religious Life in the Greco-Roman World

1 CORINTHIANS 14 The religious activities of women in the Greco-Roman world spanned a wide range and exhibited enormous diversity. Some mystery cults included ecstatic, orgiastic worship in which women played a prominent role, and priestesses were common in the worship of Greek goddesses.[1] Some religious festivals in Greece were exclusively for women; an example is the Thesmophoria, which honored the goddess Demeter. The Bacchae, a play by the Greek poet Euripides (fifth century B.C.), tells of frenzied religious celebration of the god Dionysus by women who followed his cult.[2] Other pagan religions created space for significant sexual expression during religious festivals, and fertility cults employed women for the purpose of ritual or sacred prostitution.[3] On the other hand, within Judaism women's access to the inner courts of the Jerusalem temple was restricted, and scholars debate whether the synagogues of the time displayed gender segregation.

In 1 Corinthians 14 Paul provided guidelines for orderly worship, including some instructions specifically addressing the activities of women in worship (vv. 33–35). Evidence from Corinth[4] reveals that the city contained several temples to Aphrodite and Apollo, and Paul's readers would have been familiar with these and with other cults that were widespread in the Greco-Roman world.

[1]See "Magic in the Greco-Roman World" on page 1911 and "The Mystery Religions" on page 1939. [2]See "The Cult of Dionysus" on page 1921. [3]See "Prostitution in the Ancient World" on page 284. [4]See "Corinth" on page 1887.

The Resurrection of Christ

15 Now, brothers, I want to remind you of the gospel[m] I preached to you, which you received and on
which you have taken your stand. 2 By this gospel you are saved,[n] if you hold firmly[o] to the word
I preached to you. Otherwise, you have believed in vain.
3 For what I received[p] I passed on to you[q] as of first importance[a]: that Christ died for our sins[r] accord-
ing to the Scriptures,[s] 4 that he was buried, that he was raised[t] on the third day[u] according to the Scrip-
tures,[v] 5 and that he appeared to Peter,[b][w] and then to the Twelve.[x] 6 After that, he appeared to more than
five hundred of the brothers at the same time, most of whom are still living, though some have fallen
asleep. 7 Then he appeared to James, then to all the apostles,[y] 8 and last of all he appeared to me also,[z] as
to one abnormally born.
9 For I am the least of the apostles[a] and do not even deserve to be called an apostle, because I perse-
cuted[b] the church of God. 10 But by the grace of God I am what I am, and his grace to me[c] was not with-
out effect. No, I worked harder than all of them[d]—yet not I, but the grace of God that was with me.[e]
11 Whether, then, it was I or they, this is what we preach, and this is what you believed.

The Resurrection of the Dead

12 But if it is preached that Christ has been raised from the dead, how can some of you say that there
is no resurrection of the dead?[f] 13 If there is no resurrection of the dead, then not even Christ has been
raised. 14 And if Christ has not been raised,[g] our preaching is useless and so is your faith. 15 More than that,
we are then found to be false witnesses about God, for we have testified about God that he raised Christ
from the dead.[h] But he did not raise him if in fact the dead are not raised. 16 For if the dead are not raised,
then Christ has not been raised either. 17 And if Christ has not been raised, your faith is futile; you are
still in your sins.[i] 18 Then those also who have fallen asleep in Christ are lost. 19 If only for this life we have
hope in Christ, we are to be pitied more than all men.[j]
20 But Christ has indeed been raised from the dead,[k] the firstfruits[l] of those who have fallen asleep.[m]
21 For since death came through a man,[n] the resurrection of the dead comes also through a man. 22 For
as in Adam all die, so in Christ all will be made alive.[o] 23 But each in his own turn: Christ, the firstfruits;[p]
then, when he comes,[q] those who belong to him. 24 Then the end will come, when he hands over the
kingdom[r] to God the Father after he has destroyed all dominion, authority and power.[s] 25 For he must
reign until he has put all his enemies under his feet.[t] 26 The last enemy to be destroyed is death.[u] 27 For
he "has put everything under his feet."[c][v] Now when it says that "everything" has been put under him,
it is clear that this does not include God himself, who put everything under Christ.[w] 28 When he has
done this, then the Son himself will be made subject to him who put everything under him,[x] so that God
may be all in all.[y]
29 Now if there is no resurrection, what will those do who are baptized for the dead? If the dead are not
raised at all, why are people baptized for them? 30 And as for us, why do we endanger ourselves every
hour?[z] 31 I die every day[a]—I mean that, brothers—just as surely as I glory over you in Christ Jesus our
Lord. 32 If I fought wild beasts[b] in Ephesus[c] for merely human reasons, what have I gained? If the dead
are not raised,

> "Let us eat and drink,
> for tomorrow we die."[d][d]

15:1 [m]Ro 2:16
15:2 [n]Ro 1:16 [o]Ro 11:22
15:3 [p]Gal 1:12 [q]1Co 11:23 [r]Isa 53:5; 1Pe 2:24 [s]Lk 24:27; Ac 26:22,23
15:4 [t]Ac 2:24 [u]Mt 16:21 [v]Ac 2:25,30,31
15:5 [w]Lk 24:34 [x]Mk 16:14
15:7 [y]Lk 24:33, 36,37; Ac 1:3,4
15:8 [z]Ac 9:3-6, 17; 1Co 9:1
15:9 [a]Eph 3:8; 1Ti 1:15 [b]Ac 8:3
15:10 [c]Ro 12:3 [d]2Co 11:23 [e]Php 2:13
15:12 [f]Ac 17:32; 23:8; 2Ti 2:18
15:14 [g]1Th 4:14
15:15 [h]Ac 2:24
15:17 [i]Ro 4:25
15:19 [j]1Co 4:9
15:20 [k]1Pe 1:3 [l]ver 23; Ac 26:23; Rev 1:5 [m]ver 6,18
15:21 [n]Ro 5:12
15:22 [o]Ro 5:14-18
15:23 [p]ver 20 [q]ver 52
15:24 [r]Da 7:14, 27 [s]Ro 8:38
15:25 [t]Ps 110:1; Mt 22:44
15:26 [u]2Ti 1:10; Rev 20:14; 21:4
15:27 [v]Ps 8:6 [w]Mt 28:18
15:28 [x]Php 3:21 [y]1Co 3:23
15:30 [z]2Co 11:26
15:31 [a]Ro 8:36
15:32 [b]2Co 1:8 [c]Ac 18:19 [d]Isa 22:13; Lk 12:19

[a] 3 Or *you at the first* [b] 5 Greek *Cephas* [c] 27 Psalm 8:6 [d] 32 Isaiah 22:13

15:1 For "brothers," see the note on Romans 1:13.
15:3 Here Paul linked himself with early Christian tradition. He was not its originator, nor did he receive it directly from the Lord. His source was other Christians.
15:4 The Jews counted parts of days as whole days. Thus the three days would have included part of Friday afternoon, all of Saturday, and Sunday morning.
15:7 Since this James is listed in addition to the apostles, he was neither James, the son of Zebedee, nor James, the son of Alphaeus (Mt 10:2–3). This was James, the half brother of Jesus (Mt 13:55; see "The Family of Joseph, Mary and Jesus" on p. 1581), who did not believe in Christ before the resurrection (Jn 7:5) but afterward joined the apostolic band (Ac 1:14) and later became prominent in the Jerusalem church (Ac 15:13).
15:9 For "persecuted," see "The Early Persecution of the Church" on page 2067.
15:20 "Firstfruits" refers to the first sheaf of the harvest given to the Lord as a token that all of the harvest belonged to him and would be dedicated to him through committed lives (see Ex 23:19; Lev 2:12).
15:25 "Under his feet" is an Old Testament expression for complete conquest (see the note on Ps 110:1).
15:29 The present tense suggests that at Corinth people were currently being baptized for the dead. But because Paul did not offer any additional information about the practice, many attempts have been made to interpret the concept (see "Baptism for the Dead" on p. 1881).
15:32 See the note on 4:9.

33 Do not be misled: "Bad company corrupts good character." 34 Come back to your senses as you ought,
and stop sinning; for there are some who are ignorant of God—I say this to your shame.

The Resurrection Body

35 But someone may ask,[e] "How are the dead raised? With what kind of body will they come?"[f] 36 How
foolish![g] What you sow does not come to life unless it dies.[h] 37 When you sow, you do not plant the body

15:35 [e]Ro 9:19
[f]Eze 37:3
15:36 [g]Lk 11:40
[h]Jn 12:24

15:33 This quotation is from the Greek comedy *Thais*, written by the familiar Greek poet Menander.

Baptism for the Dead

1 CORINTHIANS 15 Numerous proposals have been offered for the meaning of "baptized for the dead" in 1 Corinthians 15:29. Every theory has some problems, but some are more plausible than others:

- One explanation holds that Paul was alluding to some form of "proxy baptism" (an individual being baptized to secure the salvation of ancestors, relatives or friends who had died without Christ). There is no indication in this text, however, that Corinthians were being baptized for their ancestors or for other dead pagans—and no evidence that this was ever practiced in the early church.
- Some suggest that the term refers to baptism for believers who had died unbaptized; others that it may have been some ritual rooted in a superstitious belief that baptism itself had almost magical, life-giving powers. The Corinthian believers may have been influenced by a local cult of the dead at Corinth. On the other hand, if such a pagan background were behind this practice, we would expect Paul to have voiced his disapproval.
- Still others propose that the phrase actually means "baptized in the place of the dead" in the sense of taking the place of Christian martyrs who had lost their lives for the faith. This kind of baptism would thus have been a rite whereby a living believer symbolically took the place of his or her fallen brother or sister. This interpretation has some support in the context, since Paul immediately spoke in the following verses (vv. 30–32)[1] of his own endurance of persecution.

[1]See also "Baptism in the Ancient World" on page 1562.

Roman era mummy

Preserving Bible Times; © Dr. James C. Martin; permission of Musée de Louvre

that will be, but just a seed, perhaps of wheat or of something else. 38But God gives it a body as he has
determined, and to each kind of seed he gives its own body.[i] 39All flesh is not the same: Men have one
kind of flesh, animals have another, birds another and fish another. 40There are also heavenly bodies and
there are earthly bodies; but the splendor of the heavenly bodies is one kind, and the splendor of the
earthly bodies is another. 41The sun has one kind of splendor, the moon another and the stars another;
and star differs from star in splendor.

42So will it be[j] with the resurrection of the dead. The body that is sown is perishable, it is raised im-
perishable; 43it is sown in dishonor, it is raised in glory;[k] it is sown in weakness, it is raised in power; 44it
is sown a natural body, it is raised a spiritual body.[l]

If there is a natural body, there is also a spiritual body. 45So it is written: "The first man Adam became
a living being"[a];[m] the last Adam,[n] a life-giving spirit.[o] 46The spiritual did not come first, but the natural,
and after that the spiritual. 47The first man was of the dust of the earth,[p] the second man from heaven.[q]
48As was the earthly man, so are those who are of the earth; and as is the man from heaven, so also are
those who are of heaven.[r] 49And just as we have borne the likeness of the earthly man,[s] so shall we[b] bear
the likeness of the man from heaven.[t]

50I declare to you, brothers, that flesh and blood[u] cannot inherit the kingdom of God, nor does the
perishable inherit the imperishable. 51Listen, I tell you a mystery:[v] We will not all sleep, but we will all be
changed[w]— 52in a flash, in the twinkling of an eye, at the last trumpet. For the trumpet will sound,[x] the
dead[y] will be raised imperishable, and we will be changed. 53For the perishable must clothe itself with
the imperishable,[z] and the mortal with immortality. 54When the perishable has been clothed with the im-
perishable, and the mortal with immortality, then the saying that is written will come true: "Death has
been swallowed up in victory."[c][a]

55"Where, O death, is your victory?
Where, O death, is your sting?"[d][b]

56The sting of death is sin,[c] and the power of sin is the law.[d] 57But thanks be to God![e] He gives us the
victory through our Lord Jesus Christ.[f]

58Therefore, my dear brothers, stand firm. Let nothing move you. Always give yourselves fully to the
work of the Lord,[g] because you know that your labor in the Lord is not in vain.

The Collection for God's People

16 Now about the collection[h] for God's people:[i] Do what I told the Galatian[j] churches to do. 2On the
first day of every week,[k] each one of you should set aside a sum of money in keeping with his in-
come, saving it up, so that when I come no collections will have to be made.[l] 3Then, when I arrive, I will
give letters of introduction to the men you approve[m] and send them with your gift to Jerusalem. 4If it
seems advisable for me to go also, they will accompany me.

Personal Requests

5After I go through Macedonia, I will come to you[n]—for I will be going through Macedonia.[o] 6Per-
haps I will stay with you awhile, or even spend the winter, so that you can help me on my journey,[p] wher-
ever I go. 7I do not want to see you now and make only a passing visit; I hope to spend some time with

15:38 [i]Ge 1:11
15:42 [j]Da 12:3; Mt 13:43
15:43 [k]Php 3:21; Col 3:4
15:44 [l]ver 50
15:45 [m]Ge 2:7 [n]Ro 5:14 [o]Jn 5:21; Ro 8:2
15:47 [p]Ge 2:7; 3:19 [q]Jn 3:13,31
15:48 [r]Php 3:20, 21
15:49 [s]Ge 5:3 [t]Ro 8:29
15:50 [u]Jn 3:3,5
15:51 [v]1Co 13:2 [w]Php 3:21
15:52 [x]Mt 24:31 [y]Jn 5:25
15:53 [z]2Co 5:2,4
15:54 [a]Isa 25:8; Rev 20:14
15:55 [b]Hos 13:14
15:56 [c]Ro 5:12 [d]Ro 4:15
15:57 [e]2Co 2:14 [f]Ro 8:37
15:58 [g]1Co 16:10
16:1 [h]Ac 24:17 [i]Ac 9:13 [j]Ac 16:6
16:2 [k]Ac 20:7 [l]2Co 9:4,5
16:3 [m]2Co 8:18, 19
16:5 [n]1Co 4:19 [o]Ac 19:21
16:6 [p]Ro 15:24

[a] 45 Gen. 2:7 [b] 49 Some early manuscripts *so let us* [c] 54 Isaiah 25:8 [d] 55 Hosea 13:14

15:50 For "brothers," see the note on Romans 1:13.
15:52 See "Trumpets in the Ancient World" on page 2057.
16:1 "God's people" refers to his people at Jerusalem. Many Jewish Christians in Jerusalem were impoverished—perhaps because of the famine recorded in Acts 11:28 (c. A.D. 44 or 46) or on account of the persecution of Jerusalem Christians (cf. Ac 8:1, as well as "The Early Persecution of the Church" on p. 2067)—and Paul spent considerable energy on his third missionary journey raising funds on their behalf from various Gentile churches. Paul undoubtedly saw the collection as an opportunity to promote unity and to pay a spiritual debt the Gentile congregations owed their "mother church" in Jerusalem (see Ro 15:26–27). Paul also hoped to demonstrate the genuineness of Gentile Christianity to skeptical Jewish Christians (cf. Ac 24:17).
16:2 Every Sunday ("the first day of every week") believers were to bring what they had set aside for the Lord's work—an amount proportionate to their income. Since it was to be brought on Sunday, the day when Christians gathered for worship (see Ac 20:7; Rev 1:10), it was probably collected at the worship service rather than at home. Justin Martyr indicated that in his time (c. A.D. 150) offerings were brought to the church on Sundays (*Apology*, 1.67–68).
16:6 Paul's desire to spend a full winter in Corinth may have been realized, even if it was delayed by a year. The winter stay is probably the three-month visit to Greece mentioned in Acts 20:3. His motivation was at least twofold: (1) He wanted a significant period of time with the Corinthians in the hope of improving the situation in the church. (2) He desired to avoid having to travel in treacherous weather during the winter season, a time when the high seas were generally impassable and travel overland was arduous (see the note on Ac 27:9; see also "Travel in the Greco-Roman World" on p. 1946).

16:7 [q]Ac 18:21
16:8 [r]Ac 18:19
[s]Ac 2:1
16:9 [t]Ac 14:27
16:10 [u]Ac 16:1
[v]1Co 15:58
16:11 [w]1Ti 4:12
[x]Ac 15:33
16:12 [y]Ac 18:24; 1Co 1:12
16:13 [z]Gal 5:1; Php 1:27; 1Th 3:8; 2Th 2:15
[a]Eph 6:10
16:14 [b]1Co 14:1
16:15 [c]1Co 1:16
[d]Ro 16:5
[e]Ac 18:12
16:16 [f]Heb 13:17
16:17 [g]2Co 11:9; Php 2:30
16:18 [h]Phm 7
[i]Php 2:29
16:19 [j]Ac 18:2
[k]Ro 16:5
16:20 [l]Ro 16:16
16:21 [m]Gal 6:11; Col 4:18
16:22 [n]Eph 6:24
[o]Ro 9:3
[p]Rev 22:20
16:23 [q]Ro 16:20

you, if the Lord permits.[q] 8 But I will stay on at Ephesus[r] until Pentecost,[s] 9 because a great door for ef-
fective work has opened to me,[t] and there are many who oppose me.
10 If Timothy[u] comes, see to it that he has nothing to fear while he is with you, for he is carrying on the
work of the Lord,[v] just as I am. 11 No one, then, should refuse to accept him.[w] Send him on his way in
peace[x] so that he may return to me. I am expecting him along with the brothers.
12 Now about our brother Apollos:[y] I strongly urged him to go to you with the brothers. He was quite
unwilling to go now, but he will go when he has the opportunity.
13 Be on your guard; stand firm[z] in the faith; be men of courage; be strong.[a] 14 Do everything in love.[b]
15 You know that the household of Stephanas[c] were the first converts[d] in Achaia,[e] and they have de-
voted themselves to the service of the saints. I urge you, brothers, 16 to submit[f] to such as these and to
everyone who joins in the work, and labors at it. 17 I was glad when Stephanas, Fortunatus and Achaicus
arrived, because they have supplied what was lacking from you.[g] 18 For they refreshed[h] my spirit and
yours also. Such men deserve recognition.[i]

Final Greetings

19 The churches in the province of Asia send you greetings. Aquila and Priscilla[a][j] greet you warmly in
the Lord, and so does the church that meets at their house.[k] 20 All the brothers here send you greetings.
Greet one another with a holy kiss.[l]
21 I, Paul, write this greeting in my own hand.[m]
22 If anyone does not love the Lord[n]—a curse[o] be on him. Come, O Lord[b]![p]
23 The grace of the Lord Jesus be with you.[q]
24 My love to all of you in Christ Jesus. Amen.[c]

[a] *19* Greek *Prisca,* a variant of *Priscilla* [b] *22* In Aramaic the expression *Come, O Lord* is *Marana tha.* [c] *24* Some manuscripts do not have *Amen.*

16:8 Pentecost was commemorated on the fiftieth day after Passover (see the note on Ac 2:1, as well as "Pentecost" on p. 275), when the Jews celebrated the Feast of Firstfruits (Lev 23:10–16)—in the late spring.
16:9 These opponents were probably the pagan craftsmen who made the silver shrines of Artemis, as well as the general populace whom they had stirred up (see Ac 19:23–34).
16:12 For "Apollos," see the note on 1:12.
16:15 Those of the household of Stephanas were among the first converts in Achaia (Greece), along with the few individuals in Athens who had believed a short time earlier (Ac 17:34). They were among the few people Paul had baptized at Corinth (1 Co 1:16).
16:17 These men were probably the ones who had brought Paul the letter from the Corinthians referred to in 7:1 (see "The 'Missing' Letter From the Corinthians to Paul" on p. 1870).
16:19 The "province of Asia" refers to the Roman province (presently in western Turkey) in which Ephesus and the surrounding cities were located. The churches of Colosse, Laodicea and Hierapolis, which were located on the border of the province of Asia, may have been included in the greetings, along with the other churches of Revelation 2–3.

While Christians at first continued to worship in temple and synagogue, from the beginning they also met in private homes (Ac 1:13; 2:2,46). Worship in homes was a well-established pattern in Paul's ministry (see also Ro 16:5; Col 4:15; Phm 2), and special buildings for Christian churches did not appear in the New Testament. The family had been the religious unit from the beginning of creation, and worship had centered in the house, from tent to palace. Tabernacle and temple were, in contrast, "the house of God." In the New Testament the house where a Christian family lived was open to other Christian brothers and sisters to worship together, and when the temple was destroyed and the synagogue closed to Christians the church in the home became the sole refuge for the believers until special buildings were later erected (see "House Churches and Early Church Buildings" on p. 2033).
16:20 The "holy kiss" was the kiss of mutual respect and love in the Lord that was evidently the public practice of early Christians—from a practice that was customary in the ancient Near East (see "The Jewish Custom of Kissing" on p. 1682). Such a practice may have been used in the first-century A.D. synagogue—men kissing men, and women kissing women—and it would have been natural for the practice to have been continued in the early Jewish-Gentile churches.
16:21 Paul signed this letter, as was his habit, as a mark of its authenticity. Someone else had been penning the letter for him up to this point. (See "Letter Writing in the Greco-Roman World" on p. 1889 and "Writing Materials in the Ancient World" on p. 2037.)

INTRODUCTION TO 2 *Corinthians*

AUTHOR, PLACE AND DATE OF WRITING

Paul's authorship of this letter (1:1) is not disputed, although many scholars are vexed by 2 Corinthians because of its abrupt changes in tone and topics. They wonder whether what we call "2 Corinthians" is in fact an accumulation of several different letters from Paul to Corinth.

Some scholars have broken up 2 Corinthians into several smaller, hypothetical letters and have tried to relate them to each other, to 1 Corinthians and to what we know from Acts of Paul's dealings with the Corinthian church. For example, some argue that the letter written with many tears mentioned in 2 Corinthians 2:4 was actually 2 Corinthians 10:1—13:10. Put another way, they hypothesize that 2 Corinthians 10:1—13:10 was a separate epistle written before the letter of reconciliation found in 2 Corinthians 1:1—2:13 (and in a few other portions of 2 Corinthians).

Against this, we have no manuscript evidence for breaking up 2 Corinthians into several smaller letters. It is possible that 2 Corinthians was one letter that was written over a relatively lengthy period and that circumstances changed while Paul was midway through the letter. On the assumption that 2 Corinthians is a unified letter, however, readers can relate it to Paul's travels and other letters (see "Paul's Visits and Letters to Corinth" on p. 1888). It was probably written from Macedonia around A.D. 55.

AUDIENCE

Paul wrote this letter to the believers in Corinth.

CULTURAL FACTS AND HIGHLIGHTS

Like 1 Corinthians, 2 Corinthians was Paul's response to diverse situations in the Corinthian church. On the one hand, the Corinthians had heeded his rebukes in several areas, and he wanted to share his relief and thanks (2Co 1:1—2:13). But on the other, he found it necessary to encourage the Corinthian believers to avoid being "yoked with unbelievers" (6:14—7:1) and to rebuke those who had submitted to the religious tyranny of the "super-apostles" (10:1—13:10). He also wanted to teach these believers the true nature of Christian ministry (2:14—7:4) and to encourage their generosity (chs. 8–9). In short, Paul was continuing the work of trying to bring his church to maturity and stability.

TIMELINE

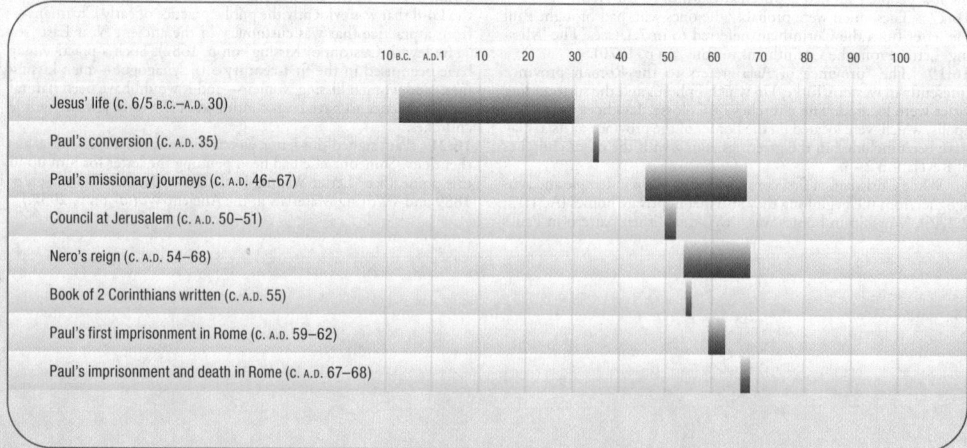

AS YOU READ

Note the personal nature of this letter. What types of conflicts are addressed? What advice did Paul give regarding contentious interpersonal relationships within the church? Watch for new information about Paul that appears nowhere else in Scripture.

DID YOU KNOW?

- Ink applied to parchment or papyrus documents tended to fade and was easily erased or blocked out (3:3).
- Treasures were frequently concealed in clay jars, which had little value or beauty in themselves and did not attract attention (4:7).
- In the ancient secular world "reconciliation" was a diplomatic term referring to the harmony established between enemies by peace treaties (5:18).

THEMES

Second Corinthians includes the following themes:

1. *Ministry of Reconciliation.* Paul's love for the Corinthians was evidenced by his joy at their repentance and renewed commitment to him (7:9), his pride in them (1:14; 7:4) and his hope for their future (1:7). Paul's desire and goal was reconciliation—between himself and the Corinthians; among the Corinthian church members; and most importantly, between God and human beings.

2. *Generosity in giving.* Paul encouraged the Corinthians to renew their commitment to the collection for the believers in Jerusalem (8:1—9:15). The apostle taught that charity is an act of obedience, resulting in eternal reward and bringing glory to God. God often rewards magnanimity with material abundance to make possible additional generosity.

3. *Defense of Paul's apostleship.* Some in the Corinthian church had become alienated from Paul by the presence and influence of boastful rivals. Paul defended his apostleship and made a fervent appeal for them to renew their commitment to him. The breach between Paul and some Corinthians was not simply over theological issues but had its roots in Corinthian cultural mores that clashed with Christian values.

OUTLINE

I. Introduction: Greeting and Thanksgiving (1:1–11)
II. Paul's Explanation of His Conduct and Apostolic Ministry (1:12—7:16)
  A. Paul's Integrity (1:12—2:4)
  B. The Need for Forgiveness (2:5–11)
  C. Ministers of the New Covenant (2:12–17)
  D. Ministers Made Competent by the Spirit (3:1–11)
  E. Transformed Into His Likeness (3:12—4:6)
  F. Treasure in Jars of Clay (4:7–16a)
  G. The Prospects of Our Heavenly Dwelling (4:16b—5:10)
  H. The Ministry of Reconciliation (5:11—6:10)
  I. Paul's Appeal to the Corinthians (6:11—7:4)
  J. Titus's Good Report (7:5–16)
III. The Collection for the Christians at Jerusalem (8–9)
IV. Paul's Vindication of His Apostolic Authority (10–13)
  A. Defense of His Ministry (10)
  B. Paul Compared to False Apostles (11–12)
  C. Final Warnings (13:1–10)
V. Conclusion (13:11–14)

1 Paul, an apostle of Christ Jesus by the will of God,[a] and Timothy our brother, 1:1 [a]1Co 1:1; Eph 1:1; Col 1:1; 2Ti 1:1

To the church of God[b] in Corinth, together with all the saints throughout Achaia:[c] [b]1Co 10:32 [c]Ac 18:12

2 Grace and peace to you from God our Father and the Lord Jesus Christ.[d] 1:2 [d]Ro 1:7

The God of All Comfort

3 Praise be to the God and Father of our Lord Jesus Christ,[e] the Father of compassion and the God of 1:3 [e]Eph 1:3; 1Pe 1:3
all comfort, 4 who comforts us[f] in all our troubles, so that we can comfort those in any trouble with the 1:4 [f]2Co 7:6,7,13
comfort we ourselves have received from God. 5 For just as the sufferings of Christ flow over into our
lives,[g] so also through Christ our comfort overflows. 6 If we are distressed, it is for your comfort and sal- 1:5 [g]2Co 4:10; Col 1:24
vation;[h] if we are comforted, it is for your comfort, which produces in you patient endurance of the same 1:6 [h]2Co 4:15
sufferings we suffer. 7 And our hope for you is firm, because we know that just as you share in our suffer-
ings,[i] so also you share in our comfort. 1:7 [i]Ro 8:17
8 We do not want you to be uninformed, brothers, about the hardships we suffered[j] in the province of 1:8 [j]1Co 15:32
Asia. We were under great pressure, far beyond our ability to endure, so that we despaired even of life.
9 Indeed, in our hearts we felt the sentence of death. But this happened that we might not rely on our-
selves but on God,[k] who raises the dead. 10 He has delivered us from such a deadly peril,[l] and he will de- 1:9 [k]Jer 17:5,7
liver us. On him we have set our hope that he will continue to deliver us, 11 as you help us by your prayers.[m] 1:10 [l]Ro 15:31 1:11 [m]Ro 15:30; Php 1:19
Then many will give thanks[n] on our[a] behalf for the gracious favor granted us in answer to the prayers of [n]2Co 4:15
many.

Paul's Change of Plans

12 Now this is our boast: Our conscience[o] testifies that we have conducted ourselves in the world, 1:12 [o]Ac 23:1
and especially in our relations with you, in the holiness and sincerity[p] that are from God. We have [p]2Co 2:17
done so not according to worldly wisdom[q] but according to God's grace. 13 For we do not write you [q]1Co 2:1,4,13
anything you cannot read or understand. And I hope that, 14 as you have understood us in part, you
will come to understand fully that you can boast of us just as we will boast of you in the day of the
Lord Jesus.[r] 1:14 [r]1Co 1:8
15 Because I was confident of this, I planned to visit you[s] first so that you might benefit twice.[t] 16 I 1:15 [s]1Co 4:19 [t]Ro 1:11,13; 15:29
planned to visit you on my way[u] to Macedonia and to come back to you from Macedonia, and then to have
you send me on my way to Judea. 17 When I planned this, did I do it lightly? Or do I make my plans in a 1:16 [u]1Co 16:5-7
worldly manner[v] so that in the same breath I say, "Yes, yes" and "No, no"? 1:17 [v]2Co 10:2,3
18 But as surely as God is faithful,[w] our message to you is not "Yes" and "No." 19 For the Son of God, 1:18 [w]1Co 1:9
Jesus Christ, who was preached among you by me and Silas[b] and Timothy, was not "Yes" and "No," but in
him it has always[x] been "Yes." 20 For no matter how many promises[y] God has made, they are "Yes" in 1:19 [x]Heb 13:8
Christ. And so through him the "Amen"[z] is spoken by us to the glory of God. 21 Now it is God who makes 1:20 [y]Ro 15:8 [z]1Co 14:16
both us and you stand firm in Christ. He anointed[a] us, 22 set his seal of ownership on us, and put his Spir- 1:21 [a]1Jn 2:20, 27
it in our hearts as a deposit, guaranteeing what is to come.[b] 1:22 [b]2Co 5:5

[a] *11* Many manuscripts *your* [b] *19* Greek *Silvanus,* a variant of *Silas*

1:1 There were two kinds of apostles in the early church: (1) the original "twelve apostles" (called disciples in the Gospels), sent out by Jesus during his ministry and later confirmed by the resurrected Christ, and (2) those "apostles" sent out by churches. Such missionaries received their authority from the other apostles and the sending churches. Paul was unique in that he stood in, or between, these classes (see Ac 13:1–3). But this combination caused him problems. Those rejecting his apostleship denied his calling by the resurrected Christ and discredited his authority.

Greece in Paul's day was divided into two Roman provinces: Achaia in the south (which included Athens and the capital city of Corinth; see the note on 1 Corinthians 1:2) and Macedonia in the north (which included Berea, Philippi and the capital city of Thessalonica).

1:8 For "brothers," see the note on Romans 1:13.

Asia was a Roman province in western Asia Minor, now Turkish territory.

1:15 Originally Paul had planned to cross by sea from Ephesus to Corinth, visiting the Corinthians before traveling north to Macedonia, and then, returning from Macedonia, to visit them a second time, thus giving them the benefit of two short visits. What probably occurred was that he paid the Corinthians a quick visit directly from Ephesus, a visit he had not contemplated and that proved to be "painful" (2:1). See "Paul's Visits and Letters to Corinth" on page 1888.

1:16 For "Macedonia," see the note on 1:1.

1:17 Paul's opponents in Corinth had been attempting to persuade the Christians there that Paul's change of plan was evidence that his word was not to be trusted and that he was fickle and unreliable.

1:20 "Amen" was uttered by the congregation at the end of an offering of prayer or praise.

1:22 A seal denoted ownership and security (see "Scrolls, Seals and Codices" on p. 2053).

A deposit was a part given as a guarantee that the whole would be forthcoming. The first installment of an inherited sum of money, for example, assured the recipient that the entire amount would be forthcoming.

ARCHAEOLOGICAL SITES

CORINTH

The Acrocorinth at the Site of Corinth
Preserving Bible Times; © Dr. James C. Martin

2 CORINTHIANS 1 The ancient city of Corinth lay on an isthmus between the Greek mainland and the Peloponnese, the southwestern corner of Greece ("Map 13"). The isthmus was about 6,562 yards (6,000 m) wide at its narrowest point, which led many to consider digging a canal there (a dream not realized until modern times). Two harbors were nearby: Lechaeum to the north, on the Gulf of Corinth, and Cenchrea to the south, on the Saronic Gulf. Corinth's location made the city a site of great strategic and economic importance. Ships often preferred to sail into Corinth and transport their goods overland across the isthmus on the portage road rather than risk the wild seas around the Peloponnese. This brought lively trade to the city—along with the vices often associated with bustling commercial centers. It is not surprising, therefore, that ancient Corinth became a byword for sexual immorality.

Corinth's history may be divided into two distinct periods: its long duration as one of the major cities of classical Greek civilization and its subsequent years after the Roman conquest as a cosmopolitan crossroads. The classical city was at one time a major player in the politics of Greece[1] and was particularly important in the long history of competition between Athens and Sparta (Corinth was usually on the side of Sparta). Later, as head of the Achaean League (a coalition of Greek cities), it led resistance to Roman aggression. Its role as host of the Isthmian games (second only to the Olympic games in prestige) greatly enhanced Corinth's ancient status. This city, however, was destroyed in 146 B.C. by the Roman general Lucius Mummius. While some inhabitants stayed in the vicinity of Corinth, the city did not rise to prominence again until 44 B.C., when Julius Caesar refounded it as a Roman colony.[2]

The new city was Roman in its administration and architecture, with the majority of its settlers being freedmen. The natural advantages of the site, coupled with the entrepreneurial vigor of the freedmen, soon led to renewed prosperity. The Corinth of the New Testament era was reputed to be one of the most beautiful cities of the Greco-Roman world. Its importance in trade and its status as a Roman administrative center made Corinth a significant city in Paul's day.

Corinth had a mixed, cosmopolitan populace, as reflected in its many religious shrines:

- Visitors to Corinth can still find archaeological evidence of votive offerings made to Asclepius, the god of medicine, in gratitude for healings. These offerings were clay models of body parts (often arms, legs or sexual organs) the god had supposedly healed, hung around the temple as tributes to Asclepius.[3]
- Corinth was home to a famous temple to Aphrodite that supposedly employed 1,000 temple prostitutes. While this number may be an exaggeration, scholars can hardly doubt that this port city supported a thriving prostitution industry, probably centered around such a shrine.[4]
- There were also temples to other Greek gods, such as to Poseidon, god of the sea (appropriate for a port city), and to Demeter and Kore, goddesses of an ancient Greek fertility cult.[5]
- The cosmopolitan nature of Corinth is reflected in the fact that it also had numerous places of worship for foreign deities, such as a shrine to the Egyptian goddess Isis—as well as a Jewish synagogue.[6]

With its cultural diversity, wealth, paganism and infamous debauchery, Corinth was perhaps not the place onlookers would have expected the church to flourish. Yet it was precisely here that Paul enjoyed one of his most successful ministries—and also here that he experienced some of his greatest challenges with early converts to Christianity.

[1]See "Greece: From the Prehistoric Period Through the Mycenaean Empire" on page 1810 and "Greece: From Independent City-states Through Alexander the Great" on page 1814. [2]See "Greece: Roman Domination and the Growth of Christianity" on page 1816. [3]See "Disease and Medicine in the Ancient World" on page 1674. [4]See "Prostitution in the Ancient World" on page 284. [5]See "The Gods of the Greeks and Romans" on page 1908. [6]See "Ancient Synagogues" on page1783.

23 I call God as my witness[c] that it was in order to spare you[d] that I did not return to Corinth. 24 Not
2 that we lord it over[e] your faith, but we work with you for your joy, because it is by faith you stand
firm.[f] 1 So I made up my mind that I would not make another painful visit to you.[g] 2 For if I grieve
you,[h] who is left to make me glad but you whom I have grieved? 3 I wrote as I did[i] so that when I came I

1:23 [c]Ro 1:9 [d]1Co 4:21
1:24 [e]1Pe 5:3 [f]Ro 11:20
2:1 [g]2Co 1:23
2:2 [h]2Co 7:8
2:3 [i]2Co 7:8,12 [j]2Co 12:21

2:1 The former, "painful" visit mentioned here could not have been the one Paul had made to Corinth at the time when the church there was founded in response to the preaching of the gospel (cf. Ac 18). Therefore he must have paid the church a second visit; this is confirmed by 12:14 and 13:1, in which he stated that the visit he was about to make would be his third. The second probably took place between the writing of 1 and 2 Corinthians, although some scholars hold that it occurred before 1 Corinthians was written. See "Paul's Visits and Letters to Corinth," on page 1887.

Paul's Visits and Letters to Corinth

2 CORINTHIANS 2 The chronology of Paul's visits and letters to Corinth[1] is difficult to track and somewhat disputed, but the following sequence is a reasonable interpretation of the Biblical record:

✣ *First Visit* (A.D. 50–52): Paul visited Corinth ("Map 13") during his second missionary journey, staying on for almost two years with Aquila and Priscilla, who were refugees from Italy because of Emperor Claudius's decree in A.D. 49 expelling the Jews from Rome (Ac 18:1–18).[2] Paul was summoned before the proconsul Lucius Junius Gallio in the summer of A.D. 51.[3]

✣ In A.D. 52 Paul, in the company of Priscilla and Aquila, left Corinth, moving his center of ministry to Ephesus, where he labored for about three years (Ac 18:18—19:41).[4] During his absence Apollos visited Corinth on Paul's behalf.

✣ Paul wrote his first letter (now lost) to Corinth; it included a warning against associating with immoral people (1Co 5:9–11).[5]

✣ Paul dispatched Timothy and Erastus to Corinth (Ac 19:22; 1Co 4:17; 16:10) and received from Chloe's household news about quarreling within the church (1Co 1:11), as well as questions from the congregation, delivered by Stephanas, Fortunatus and Achaicus (1Co 16:17).

✣ From Ephesus (c. A.D. 55/56) Paul sent a second letter (1Co) to the church there, including instructions on collecting money for needy Christians in Jerusalem (1Co 16:1–3). Aquila and Priscilla remained in Ephesus, and Titus and Timothy returned to Paul from Corinth (both are mentioned in 2Co 1:1; 12:18).

✣ *Second Visit* (A.D. 56): Paul experienced a "painful" visit to Corinth (1Co 4:19; 2Co 2:1–2).

✣ Shortly after this visit he wrote a third letter (also lost), sending it via Titus as a letter of "many tears," pleading with the Corinthians to change their behavior (2:3–9,13; 7:6–15; 8:6). Some scholars believe that this letter of "tears" was either 1 Corinthians or 2 Corinthians 10–13.

✣ Paul proceeded to the seaport of Troas in Asia, where he expected to meet Titus, who failed to arrive (Ac 20:1; 2Co 2:13). Paul later found him in Macedonia. Titus reported some success with the Corinthians: The congregation had dealt with their offender (vv. 7–8; 7:5–16), but their submission to Paul's leadership had declined (10:1—13:10).

✣ Paul dispatched a fourth letter (probably 2Co) to Corinth via Titus, who oversaw the collection for Jerusalem and prepared for Paul's visit (8:6–24; 13:1–10). This letter was written approximately one year after 1 Corinthians. The churches throughout Macedonia donated generously for the needy in Jerusalem (2 Co 8:1–2).

✣ *Third Visit*: Paul stayed in Corinth for three months to finalize the collection and reconcile with the church (Ac 20:2–3; 2Co 12:14; 13:1). Priscilla and Aquila returned to Rome, while Timothy remained with Paul (Ac 20:4; Ro 16:3,21). The Achaean churches contributed for the poor in Jerusalem (Ro 15:26).

✣ Around A.D. 57–61 Paul delivered the relief gift in Jerusalem, after which he found himself imprisoned in Caesarea and Rome (Ac 21:15—28:31).[6] In approximately A.D. 61 Paul was released from prison and set out once again to preach (Php 1:25–26; 2:24; Phm 22).

[1]See "Corinth" on page 1887. [2]See "Claudius, Emperor of Rome" on page 1788. [3]See "Gallio, Proconsul of Achaia" on page 1806. [4]See "Ephesus During the Time of Paul" on page 1968. [5]See "The 'Missing' Letter From the Corinthians to Paul" on page 1870. [6]See "Imprisonment in the Roman World: In Prison Versus House Arrest" on page 1826.

should not be distressed[j] by those who ought to make me rejoice. I had confidence[k] in all of you, that
you would all share my joy. 4 For I wrote you[l] out of great distress and anguish of heart and with many
tears, not to grieve you but to let you know the depth of my love for you.

Forgiveness for the Sinner

5 If anyone has caused grief,[m] he has not so much grieved me as he has grieved all of you, to some ex-
tent—not to put it too severely. 6 The punishment[n] inflicted on him by the majority is sufficient for him.
7 Now instead, you ought to forgive and comfort him,[o] so that he will not be overwhelmed by excessive
sorrow. 8 I urge you, therefore, to reaffirm your love for him. 9 The reason I wrote you was to see if you
would stand the test and be obedient in everything.[p] 10 If you forgive anyone, I also forgive him. And what
I have forgiven—if there was anything to forgive—I have forgiven in the sight of Christ for your sake,
11 in order that Satan[q] might not outwit us. For we are not unaware of his schemes.[r]

Ministers of the New Covenant

12 Now when I went to Troas[s] to preach the gospel of Christ[t] and found that the Lord had opened a
door[u] for me, 13 I still had no peace of mind,[v] because I did not find my brother Titus[w] there. So I said
good-by to them and went on to Macedonia.
14 But thanks be to God,[x] who always leads us in triumphal procession in Christ and through us spreads
everywhere the fragrance[y] of the knowledge of him. 15 For we are to God the aroma of Christ among those
who are being saved and those who are perishing.[z] 16 To the one we are the smell of death;[a] to the other,
the fragrance of life. And who is equal to such a task?[b] 17 Unlike so many, we do not peddle the word of
God for profit.[c] On the contrary, in Christ we speak before God with sincerity,[d] like men sent from God.[e]

2:3 [k]2Co 8:22
2:4 [l]2Co 7:8,12
2:5 [m]1Co 5:1,2
2:6 [n]1Co 5:4,5
2:7 [o]Gal 6:1; Eph 4:32
2:9 [p]2Co 10:6
2:11 [q]Mt 4:10 [r]Lk 22:31; 2Co 4:4; 1Pe 5:8,9
2:12 [s]Ac 16:8 [t]Ro 1:1 [u]Ac 14:27
2:13 [v]2Co 7:5 [w]2Co 7:6,13; 12:18
2:14 [x]Ro 6:17 [y]Eph 5:2; Php 4:18
2:15 [z]1Co 1:18
2:16 [a]Lk 2:34 [b]2Co 3:5,6
2:17 [c]2Co 4:2 [d]1Co 5:8 [e]2Co 1:12

2:7–9 For commentary on excommunication, see the note on 1 Timothy 1:20.
2:12 For "Troas," see the note on Acts 16:8.
2:14 In Roman times a magnificent procession would be hosted in honor of a victorious general, the highest military honor he could obtain. He would enter the city in a chariot, followed by the senate and magistrates, musicians, the spoils of his victory and the captives in chains. Sacrifices were made to Jupiter, and incense was burned by the priests. Paul undoubtedly had such a triumphal procession in mind when he wrote these words.
2:17 False teachers who were insincere, self-sufficient and boastful had artfully presented themselves in a persuasive manner to the Corinthian church. Their chief interest was to obtain money from gullible church members. Paul, by contrast, had preached the gospel sincerely and free of charge, taking care not to be a financial burden to the Corinthian believers (see 1Co 9:11–15).

Letter Writing in the Greco-Roman World

2 CORINTHIANS 3 In the Greco-Roman world letters allowed people to maintain contact with others across great distances. Various letter types have been identified, including family letters and letters of friendship, praise or blame, exhortation, and recommendation. The Greco-Roman letter typically consisted of several parts, beginning with an introduction identifying the writer and recipients and expressing greetings. A short statement of thanksgiving often followed the introduction, after which the author would present the main body of the letter. The writer would conclude with wishes for good health and a statement of farewell. Students in Greek schools were instructed in the conventions of letter writing, and scribes trained in the art of writing were available to help others compose letters.

The traditional letter form is visible in Paul's letters, although he adapted it in several ways:

- He transformed the Greek greeting into an invocation of grace and peace.
- He often extended the thanksgiving section by including prayers to God.
- He employed a benediction in place of the traditional farewell.

In the use of this style, we see that God chose to communicate the New Testament message in a form familiar to its first recipients.

3 Are we beginning to commend ourselves[f] again? Or do we need, like some people, letters of recom-
mendation[g] to you or from you? 2 You yourselves are our letter, written on our hearts, known and
read by everybody.[h] 3 You show that you are a letter from Christ, the result of our ministry, written not with
ink but with the Spirit of the living God, not on tablets of stone[i] but on tablets of human hearts.[j]
4 Such confidence[k] as this is ours through Christ before God. 5 Not that we are competent in ourselves
to claim anything for ourselves, but our competence comes from God.[l] 6 He has made us competent as
ministers of a new covenant[m]—not of the letter but of the Spirit; for the letter kills, but the Spirit gives
life.[n]

The Glory of the New Covenant

7 Now if the ministry that brought death, which was engraved in letters on stone, came with glory, so
that the Israelites could not look steadily at the face of Moses because of its glory,[o] fading though it was,
8 will not the ministry of the Spirit be even more glorious? 9 If the ministry that condemns men[p] is glo-
rious, how much more glorious is the ministry that brings righteousness![q] 10 For what was glorious has
no glory now in comparison with the surpassing glory. 11 And if what was fading away came with glory,
how much greater is the glory of that which lasts!
12 Therefore, since we have such a hope, we are very bold.[r] 13 We are not like Moses, who would put a
veil over his face[s] to keep the Israelites from gazing at it while the radiance was fading away. 14 But their
minds were made dull,[t] for to this day the same veil remains when the old covenant[u] is read.[v] It has not
been removed, because only in Christ is it taken away. 15 Even to this day when Moses is read, a veil cov-
ers their hearts. 16 But whenever anyone turns to the Lord,[w] the veil is taken away.[x] 17 Now the Lord is the
Spirit,[y] and where the Spirit of the Lord is, there is freedom.[z] 18 And we, who with unveiled faces all re-
flect[a][a] the Lord's glory,[b] are being transformed into his likeness[c] with ever-increasing glory, which comes
from the Lord, who is the Spirit.

Treasures in Jars of Clay

4 Therefore, since through God's mercy[d] we have this ministry, we do not lose heart. 2 Rather, we have
renounced secret and shameful ways;[e] we do not use deception, nor do we distort the word of God.[f]
On the contrary, by setting forth the truth plainly we commend ourselves to every man's conscience[g] in
the sight of God. 3 And even if our gospel[h] is veiled,[i] it is veiled to those who are perishing.[j] 4 The god[k] of
this age has blinded[l] the minds of unbelievers, so that they cannot see the light of the gospel of the glo-
ry of Christ, who is the image of God. 5 For we do not preach ourselves,[m] but Jesus Christ as Lord, and our-
selves as your servants[n] for Jesus' sake. 6 For God, who said, "Let light shine out of darkness,"[b][o] made his
light shine in our hearts[p] to give us the light of the knowledge of the glory of God in the face of Christ.
7 But we have this treasure in jars of clay[q] to show that this all-surpassing power is from God[r] and not
from us. 8 We are hard pressed on every side,[s] but not crushed; perplexed, but not in despair; 9 persecut-
ed,[t] but not abandoned;[u] struck down, but not destroyed.[v] 10 We always carry around in our body the
death of Jesus, so that the life of Jesus may also be revealed in our body.[w] 11 For we who are alive are al-
ways being given over to death for Jesus' sake,[x] so that his life may be revealed in our mortal body. 12 So
then, death is at work in us, but life is at work in you.[y]
13 It is written: "I believed; therefore I have spoken."[c][z] With that same spirit of faith we also believe and
therefore speak, 14 because we know that the one who raised the Lord Jesus from the dead will also raise
us with Jesus[a] and present us with you in his presence.[b] 15 All this is for your benefit, so that the grace that
is reaching more and more people may cause thanksgiving[c] to overflow to the glory of God.
16 Therefore we do not lose heart. Though outwardly we are wasting away, yet inwardly[d] we are being
renewed[e] day by day. 17 For our light and momentary troubles are achieving for us an eternal glory that
far outweighs them all.[f] 18 So we fix our eyes not on what is seen, but on what is unseen.[g] For what is seen
is temporary, but what is unseen is eternal.

3:1 [f]2Co 5:12; 12:11 [g]Ac 18:27
3:2 [h]1Co 9:2
3:3 [i]Ex 24:12 [j]Pr 3:3; Jer 31:33; Eze 11:19
3:4 [k]Eph 3:12
3:5 [l]1Co 15:10
3:6 [m]Lk 22:20 [n]Jn 6:63
3:7 [o]Ex 34:29-35
3:9 [p]ver 7 [q]Ro 1:17; 3:21,22
3:12 [r]Eph 6:19
3:13 [s]ver 7; Ex 34:33
3:14 [t]Ro 11:7,8 [u]Ac 13:15 [v]ver 6
3:16 [w]Ro 11:23 [x]Ex 34:34
3:17 [y]Isa 61:1,2 [z]Jn 8:32
3:18 [a]1Co 13:12 [b]2Co 4:4,6 [c]Ro 8:29
4:1 [d]1Co 7:25
4:2 [e]1Co 4:5 [f]2Co 2:17 [g]2Co 5:11
4:3 [h]2Co 2:12 [i]2Co 3:14 [j]1Co 1:18
4:4 [k]Jn 12:31 [l]2Co 3:14
4:5 [m]1Co 1:13 [n]1Co 9:19
4:6 [o]Ge 1:3 [p]2Pe 1:19
4:7 [q]Job 4:19; 2Co 5:1 [r]1Co 2:5
4:8 [s]2Co 7:5
4:9 [t]Jn 15:20 [u]Heb 13:5 [v]Ps 37:24
4:10 [w]Ro 6:5
4:11 [x]Ro 8:36
4:12 [y]2Co 13:9
4:13 [z]Ps 116:10
4:14 [a]1Th 4:14 [b]Eph 5:27
4:15 [c]2Co 1:11
4:16 [d]Ro 7:22 [e]Col 3:10
4:17 [f]Ro 8:18; 1Pe 1:6,7
4:18 [g]Ro 8:24; Heb 11:1

[a] *18* Or *contemplate* [b] *6* Gen. 1:3 [c] *13* Psalm 116:10

3:1 The appearance of vagrant impostors led to the need for "letters of recommendation." Paul needed no such confirmation; but others, including the Corinthian intruders, did need authentication and often resorted to unscrupulous methods for obtaining or forging such letters.

3:3 The ink written on parchment or papyrus documents faded and was easily erased or blocked out (see "Writing Materials in the Ancient World" on p. 2037).

4:7 Treasures were frequently concealed in clay jars, which had little value or beauty in themselves and did not attract attention. Here they represent Paul's human frailty and unworthiness.

5:1 [h]1Co 15:47 [i]2Pe 1:13,14 5:2 [j]ver 4; Ro 8:23 [k]1Co 15:53,54

Our Heavenly Dwelling

5 Now we know that if the earthly[h] tent[i] we live in is destroyed, we have a building from God, an eter-
nal house in heaven, not built by human hands. 2Meanwhile we groan,[j] longing to be clothed with
our heavenly dwelling,[k] 3because when we are clothed, we will not be found naked. 4For while we are in
this tent, we groan and are burdened, because we do not wish to be unclothed but to be clothed with our

5:4 Paul reversed the age-old imagery of death and the grave as being the great swallower (see Ps 49:14 and its note; see also "Sheol, Hades, Gehenna, the Abyss and Tartarus: Images of Hell" on p. 946).

CULTURAL AND HISTORICAL NOTES

The Judgment Seat

The *bema* or "judgment seat" of Corinth
Preserving Bible Times; © Dr. James C. Martin

A Judge From the Roman era
Preserving Bible Times; © Dr. James C. Martin; permission of The Istanbul Archaeological Museum

2 CORINTHIANS 5 Paul stated in 2 Corinthians 5:10, "We must all appear before the judgment seat of Christ" (cf. Ro 14:10). The Greek word translated "judgment seat" is *bema*. A bema, referred to numerous times in classical literature, was a raised speaker's platform from which proclamations were read and on which citizens stood to appear before officials. Three bemas are referred to in the New Testament:

- Pilate tried Jesus at the bema in Jerusalem (Mt 27:19; Jn 19:13).[1]
- King Herod Agrippa I was struck by an angel of the Lord while making a speech at the bema in Caesarea (Ac 12:21–23), and Paul later appeared before Governor Porcius Festus there (Ac 25:1–12).
- The Jews of Corinth ("Map 13") brought Paul to the bema to be tried by Governor Gallio (Ac 18:12–17).[2]

The Corinthian bema where Paul was tried has been excavated. It is a large stone structure at the side of the *agora*, or public market, rising some 7.5 feet (2.3 m) above the pavement and originally covered with beautifully carved marble. A partially reconstructed Latin inscription found nearby reads, "He revetted the rostra and paid personally the expense of making all its marble." (The word *rostra* is the Latin equivalent of *bema.*)

[1]See "Pontius Pilate" on page 1714. [2]See "Gallio, Proconsul of Achaia" on page 1806.

heavenly dwelling,[l] so that what is mortal may be swallowed up by life. [5]Now it is God who has made us
for this very purpose and has given us the Spirit as a deposit, guaranteeing what is to come.[m]
[6]Therefore we are always confident and know that as long as we are at home in the body we are away
from the Lord. [7]We live by faith, not by sight.[n] [8]We are confident, I say, and would prefer to be away from
the body and at home with the Lord.[o] [9]So we make it our goal to please him,[p] whether we are at home
in the body or away from it. [10]For we must all appear before the judgment seat of Christ, that each one
may receive what is due him[q] for the things done while in the body, whether good or bad.

The Ministry of Reconciliation

[11]Since, then, we know what it is to fear the Lord,[r] we try to persuade men. What we are is plain to God,
and I hope it is also plain to your conscience.[s] [12]We are not trying to commend ourselves to you again,[t]
but are giving you an opportunity to take pride in us,[u] so that you can answer those who take pride in
what is seen rather than in what is in the heart. [13]If we are out of our mind,[v] it is for the sake of God; if
we are in our right mind, it is for you. [14]For Christ's love compels us, because we are convinced that one
died for all, and therefore all died.[w] [15]And he died for all, that those who live should no longer live for
themselves[x] but for him who died for them and was raised again.
[16]So from now on we regard no one from a worldly[y] point of view. Though we once regarded Christ
in this way, we do so no longer. [17]Therefore, if anyone is in Christ, he is a new creation;[z] the old has gone,
the new has come![a] [18]All this is from God, who reconciled us to himself through Christ[b] and gave us the
ministry of reconciliation: [19]that God was reconciling the world to himself in Christ, not counting men's
sins against them.[c] And he has committed to us the message of reconciliation. [20]We are therefore Christ's
ambassadors,[d] as though God were making his appeal through us. We implore you on Christ's behalf: Be
reconciled to God. [21]God made him who had no sin[e] to be sin[*a*] for us, so that in him we might become
the righteousness of God.[f]

6 As God's fellow workers[g] we urge you not to receive God's grace in vain. [2]For he says,

> "In the time of my favor I heard you,
> and in the day of salvation I helped you."[*b*][h]

I tell you, now is the time of God's favor, now is the day of salvation.

Paul's Hardships

[3]We put no stumbling block in anyone's path,[i] so that our ministry will not be discredited. [4]Rather,
as servants of God we commend ourselves in every way: in great endurance; in troubles, hardships and
distresses; [5]in beatings, imprisonments[j] and riots; in hard work, sleepless nights and hunger;[k] [6]in puri-
ty, understanding, patience and kindness; in the Holy Spirit[l] and in sincere love; [7]in truthful speech[m]
and in the power of God; with weapons of righteousness[n] in the right hand and in the left; [8]through glo-
ry and dishonor,[o] bad report and good report; genuine, yet regarded as impostors;[p] [9]known, yet regard-
ed as unknown; dying,[q] and yet we live on;[r] beaten, and yet not killed; [10]sorrowful, yet always rejoicing;[s]
poor, yet making many rich;[t] having nothing, and yet possessing everything.[u]
[11]We have spoken freely to you, Corinthians, and opened wide our hearts to you.[v] [12]We are not with-
holding our affection from you, but you are withholding yours from us. [13]As a fair exchange—I speak
as to my children[w]—open wide your hearts also.

Do Not Be Yoked With Unbelievers

[14]Do not be yoked together[x] with unbelievers. For what do righteousness and wickedness have in

5:4 [l]1Co 15:53, 54
5:5 [m]Ro 8:23; 2Co 1:22
5:7 [n]1Co 13:12
5:8 [o]Php 1:23
5:9 [p]Ro 14:18
5:10 [q]Mt 16:27; Ro 14:10; Eph 6:8
5:11 [r]Heb 10:31; Jude 23 [s]2Co 4:2
5:12 [t]2Co 3:1 [u]2Co 1:14
5:13 [v]2Co 11:1, 16,17
5:14 [w]Gal 2:20
5:15 [x]Ro 14:7-9
5:16 [y]2Co 11:18
5:17 [z]Gal 6:15 [a]Isa 65:17; Rev 21:4,5
5:18 [b]Ro 5:10; Col 1:20
5:19 [c]Ro 4:8
5:20 [d]2Co 6:1; Eph 6:20
5:21 [e]Heb 4:15; 1Pe 2:22,24; 1Jn 3:5 [f]Ro 1:17
6:1 [g]1Co 3:9; 2Co 5:20
6:2 [h]Isa 49:8
6:3 [i]Ro 14:13,20; 1Co 9:12; 10:32
6:5 [j]2Co 11:23-25 [k]1Co 4:11
6:6 [l]1Th 1:5
6:7 [m]2Co 4:2 [n]2Co 10:4; Eph 6:10-18
6:8 [o]1Co 4:10 [p]Mt 27:63
6:9 [q]Ro 8:36 [r]2Co 1:8-10; 4:10,11
6:10 [s]2Co 7:4 [t]2Co 8:9 [u]Ro 8:32; 1Co 3:21
6:11 [v]2Co 7:3
6:13 [w]1Co 4:14
6:14 [x]1Co 5:9,10

a 21 Or *be a sin offering* *b* 2 Isaiah 49:8

5:11 See "Debate and Rhetoric in the Ancient World" on page 1797.
5:18 Some scholars believe that Paul's use of the word "reconciliation" came from the ancient secular world, where it was a diplomatic term referring to the harmony established between enemies by peace treaties. As "Christ's ambassadors" (v. 20), Christians are sent to announce that God has established a "peace treaty" with his enemies.
5:20 The word *ambassador(s)* in the New Testament comes from the Greek *presbeuein,* meaning "to be, work or travel as an envoy." Today's concept of an ambassador as a resident representative of a foreign state is somewhat alien to the Biblical concept of an ambassador as a messenger. See also Ephesians 6:20.
6:5 See "Imprisonment in the Roman World: In Prison Versus House Arrest" on page 1826.
6:14 Paul pleaded with the Corinthians not to be "yoked together" with unbelievers. He was referring to any kind of association that might significantly form an individual's identity. Determining whether someone is "yoked together" with another is a judgment call. The answer depends upon the degree, significance, purpose and level of self-identification involved in one person's relationship with another.

THE RELIABILITY OF THE BIBLE

CHRISTIANITY'S FOUNDER: PAUL OR JESUS?

2 CORINTHIANS 7 In modern times it has been popular among some groups to argue that Paul took the simple message of Jesus and created from it something totally different: "Christianity." This argument is flawed. While there are certainly different emphases in the teachings of Jesus and Paul, these are largely due to their unique ministry environments. Jesus operated within Palestinian Judaism, where the Law of Moses was widely taught, while Paul functioned mainly among pagans, who were powerfully influenced by the surrounding Greco-Roman cultures. In any event, the points of convergence between the two vastly outweigh the differences.

The most crucial point of agreement is Jesus' identity as the Messiah. Today many argue that Jesus and the primitive church held to a "low Christology" that regarded the Messiah as little more than a great man, whereas Paul and other second-century **Hellenistic**[1] Christians developed a "high Christology," in which Jesus is declared to be a divine figure. It is true that Jesus himself kept his Messianic identity quiet throughout much of his ministry, but this was not because of any self-doubt regarding his identity or mission. Rather, he realized that people would fundamentally misunderstand the true calling of the Messiah. The events surrounding the last week of his life (the Triumphal Entry, the action in the temple, the Last Supper, etc.)[2] demonstrate that he understood himself to be the Messiah. Furthermore, Jesus frequently and without hesitation claimed for himself divine prerogatives, such as the right to dictate the Law, as God had done at Sinai (Mt 7:24–29) and to forgive sin (Mt 9:2). Also, the ex-Pharisee Paul could hardly use the title *Christos* (Greek for "Messiah") outside of a Jewish pattern of thinking.

Equally important is the convergence between Jesus and Paul in terms of the characteristics of kingdom life. Where did Paul learn the absolute centrality of the love commandment (1Co 13; Gal 5:6,14)? Where did he learn that Christians are to love even their enemies (Ro 12:14–21)? Where indeed did he learn to overthrow the traditional values of society and joyfully take on the role of a servant (1Co 1:26–31)? Where, in short, did he learn that the cross was God's paradoxical path to victory (1Co 1:23; Gal 6:14; Php 2:5–11), the means by which God would bring new life to the world? The obvious answer to all of these questions: from the teachings of Jesus, the author of our faith.

[1]See Glossary on page 2080 for definitions of bolded words. [2]See "The Last Supper and the Passover" on page 1611.

6:14 [y]Eph 5:7,11; 1Jn 1:6
6:15 [z]Ac 5:14
6:16 [a]1Co 3:16 [b]Lev 26:12; Jer 32:38; Eze 37:27
6:17 [c]Rev 18:4 [d]Isa 52:11
6:18 [e]Isa 43:6
7:1 [f]2Co 6:17,18

common? Or what fellowship can light have with darkness?[y] 15What harmony is there between Christ
and Belial[a]? What does a believer[z] have in common with an unbeliever? 16What agreement is there be-
tween the temple of God and idols? For we are the temple[a] of the living God. As God has said: "I will live
with them and walk among them, and I will be their God, and they will be my people."[b b]

17 "Therefore come out from them[c]
and be separate,
says the Lord.
Touch no unclean thing,
and I will receive you."[c d]
18 "I will be a Father to you,
and you will be my sons and daughters,[e]
says the Lord Almighty."[d]

7 Since we have these promises,[f] dear friends, let us purify ourselves from everything that contami-
nates body and spirit, perfecting holiness out of reverence for God.

[a] 15 Greek *Beliar*, a variant of *Belial* [b] 16 Lev. 26:12; Jer. 32:38; Ezek. 37:27 [c] 17 Isaiah 52:11; Ezek. 20:34,41
[d] 18 2 Samuel 7:14; 7:8

6:15 Belial is Satan.
6:16 This verse contains terminology used in the supreme Old Testament affirmation of the covenant relationship between God and his people (see "Deuteronomy and the Covenant Treaty Form" on p. 255).

Paul's Joy

2Make room for us in your hearts.[g] We have wronged no one, we have corrupted no one, we have ex- **7:2** [g]2Co 6:12,13
ploited no one. 3I do not say this to condemn you; I have said before that you have such a place in our
hearts[h] that we would live or die with you. 4I have great confidence in you; I take great pride in you. I am **7:3** [h]2Co 6:11,12
greatly encouraged; in all our troubles my joy knows no bounds.[i] **7:4** [i]2Co 6:10
5For when we came into Macedonia,[j] this body of ours had no rest, but we were harassed at every **7:5** [j]2Co 2:13
turn[k]—conflicts on the outside, fears within.[l] 6But God, who comforts the downcast,[m] comforted us by [k]2Co 4:8 [l]Dt 32:25
the coming of Titus,[n] 7and not only by his coming but also by the comfort you had given him. He told us **7:6** [m]2Co 1:3,4 [n]ver 13; 2Co 2:13
about your longing for me, your deep sorrow, your ardent concern for me, so that my joy was greater than
ever.
8Even if I caused you sorrow by my letter,[o] I do not regret it. Though I did regret it—I see that my let- **7:8** [o]2Co 2:2,4
ter hurt you, but only for a little while— 9yet now I am happy, not because you were made sorry, but be-
cause your sorrow led you to repentance. For you became sorrowful as God intended and so were not
harmed in any way by us. 10Godly sorrow brings repentance that leads to salvation[p] and leaves no re- **7:10** [p]Ac 11:18
gret, but worldly sorrow brings death. 11See what this godly sorrow has produced in you: what earnest-
ness, what eagerness to clear yourselves, what indignation, what alarm, what longing, what concern,[q] **7:11** [q]ver 7
what readiness to see justice done. At every point you have proved yourselves to be innocent in this mat-
ter. 12So even though I wrote to you,[r] it was not on account of the one who did the wrong[s] or of the in- **7:12** [r]ver 8;
jured party, but rather that before God you could see for yourselves how devoted to us you are. 13By all 2Co 2:3,9 [s]1Co 5:1,2
this we are encouraged.
In addition to our own encouragement, we were especially delighted to see how happy Titus[t] was, be- **7:13** [t]ver 6;
cause his spirit has been refreshed by all of you. 14I had boasted to him about you,[u] and you have not 2Co 2:13 **7:14** [u]ver 4 [v]ver 6
embarrassed me. But just as everything we said to you was true, so our boasting about you to Titus[v] has
proved to be true as well. 15And his affection for you is all the greater when he remembers that you were
all obedient,[w] receiving him with fear and trembling.[x] 16I am glad I can have complete confidence in **7:15** [w]2Co 2:9
you.[y] [x]Php 2:12 **7:16** [y]2Co 2:3

Generosity Encouraged

8 And now, brothers, we want you to know about the grace that God has given the Macedonian[z] church- **8:1** [z]Ac 16:9
es. 2Out of the most severe trial, their overflowing joy and their extreme poverty welled up in rich
generosity. 3For I testify that they gave as much as they were able,[a] and even beyond their ability. Entire- **8:3** [a]1Co 16:2
ly on their own, 4they urgently pleaded with us for the privilege of sharing in this service[b] to the saints.[c] **8:4** [b]Ac 24:17
5And they did not do as we expected, but they gave themselves first to the Lord and then to us in keeping [c]Ro 15:25; 2Co 9:1
with God's will. 6So we urged[d] Titus,[e] since he had earlier made a beginning, to bring also to completion[f] **8:6** [d]ver 17;
this act of grace on your part. 7But just as you excel in everything[g]—in faith, in speech, in knowledge,[h] 2Co 12:18 [e]ver 16,23 [f]ver 10,11
in complete earnestness and in your love for us[a]—see that you also excel in this grace of giving. **8:7** [g]2Co 9:8 [h]1Co 1:5
8I am not commanding you,[i] but I want to test the sincerity of your love by comparing it with the ear- **8:8** [i]1Co 7:6
nestness of others. 9For you know the grace of our Lord Jesus Christ,[j] that though he was rich, yet for **8:9** [j]2Co 13:14
your sakes he became poor,[k] so that you through his poverty might become rich. [k]Mt 20:28; Php 2:6-8
10And here is my advice[l] about what is best for you in this matter: Last year you were the first not only **8:10** [l]1Co 7:25,
to give but also to have the desire to do so.[m] 11Now finish the work, so that your eager willingness[n] to do 40 [m]1Co 16:2,3; 2Co 9:2
it may be matched by your completion of it, according to your means. 12For if the willingness is there, the **8:11** [n]2Co 9:2
gift is acceptable according to what one has,[o] not according to what he does not have. **8:12** [o]Mk 12:43,
13Our desire is not that others might be relieved while you are hard pressed, but that there might be 44; Lk 21:3
equality. 14At the present time your plenty will supply what they need,[p] so that in turn their plenty will **8:14** [p]2Co 9:12
supply what you need. Then there will be equality, 15as it is written: "He who gathered much did not have
too much, and he who gathered little did not have too little."[b][q] **8:15** [q]Ex 16:18

Titus Sent to Corinth

16I thank God,[r] who put into the heart[s] of Titus[t] the same concern I have for you. 17For Titus not only **8:16** [r]2Co 2:14 [s]Rev 17:17
welcomed our appeal, but he is coming to you with much enthusiasm and on his own initiative.[u] 18And [t]2Co 2:13 **8:17** [u]ver 6

[a] 7 Some manuscripts *in our love for you* [b] 15 Exodus 16:18

7:5 For "Macedonia," see the note on 1:1. **7:8** See "Paul's Visits and Letters to Corinth" on page 1888.

we are sending along with him the brother[v] who is praised by all the churches[w] for his service to the gospel.[x] 19What is more, he was chosen by the churches to accompany us[y] as we carry the offering, which we administer in order to honor the Lord himself and to show our eagerness to help.[z] 20We want to avoid any criticism of the way we administer this liberal gift. 21For we are taking pains to do what is right, not only in the eyes of the Lord but also in the eyes of men.[a]

22In addition, we are sending with them our brother who has often proved to us in many ways that he is zealous, and now even more so because of his great confidence in you. 23As for Titus, he is my partner[b] and fellow worker[c] among you; as for our brothers,[d] they are representatives of the churches and an honor to Christ. 24Therefore show these men the proof of your love and the reason for our pride in you,[e] so that the churches can see it.

9 There is no need[f] for me to write to you about this service to the saints.[g] 2For I know your eagerness to help, and I have been boasting[h] about it to the Macedonians, telling them that since last year[i] you in Achaia[j] were ready to give; and your enthusiasm has stirred most of them to action. 3But I am sending the brothers in order that our boasting about you in this matter should not prove hollow, but that you may be ready, as I said you would be.[k] 4For if any Macedonians[l] come with me and find you unprepared, we—not to say anything about you—would be ashamed of having been so confident. 5So I thought it necessary to urge the brothers to visit you in advance and finish the arrangements for the generous gift you had promised. Then it will be ready as a generous gift,[m] not as one grudgingly given.[n]

Sowing Generously

6Remember this: Whoever sows sparingly will also reap sparingly, and whoever sows generously will also reap generously.[o] 7Each man should give what he has decided in his heart to give,[p] not reluctantly or under compulsion,[q] for God loves a cheerful giver.[r] 8And God is able[s] to make all grace abound to you, so that in all things at all times, having all that you need,[t] you will abound in every good work. 9As it is written:

"He has scattered abroad his gifts to the poor;
his righteousness endures forever."[a][u]

10Now he who supplies seed to the sower and bread for food[v] will also supply and increase your store of seed and will enlarge the harvest of your righteousness.[w] 11You will be made rich[x] in every way so that you can be generous on every occasion, and through us your generosity will result in thanksgiving to God.[y]

12This service that you perform is not only supplying the needs[z] of God's people but is also overflowing in many expressions of thanks to God.[a] 13Because of the service[b] by which you have proved yourselves, men will praise God[c] for the obedience that accompanies your confession of the gospel of Christ,[d] and for your generosity in sharing with them and with everyone else. 14And in their prayers for you their hearts will go out to you, because of the surpassing grace God has given you. 15Thanks be to God[e] for his indescribable gift![f]

Paul's Defense of His Ministry

10 By the meekness and gentleness[g] of Christ, I appeal to you—I, Paul,[h] who am "timid" when face to face with you, but "bold" when away! 2I beg you that when I come I may not have to be as bold[i] as I expect to be toward some people who think that we live by the standards of this world. 3For though we live in the world, we do not wage war as the world does. 4The weapons we fight with[j] are not the weapons of the world. On the contrary, they have divine power[k] to demolish strongholds.[l] 5We demolish arguments and every pretension that sets itself up against the knowledge of God,[m] and we take captive every thought to make it obedient[n] to Christ. 6And we will be ready to punish every act of disobedience, once your obedience is complete.[o]

7You are looking only on the surface of things.[b][p] If anyone is confident that he belongs to Christ,[q] he should consider again that we belong to Christ just as much as he.[r] 8For even if I boast somewhat freely

8:18 [v]2Co 12:18 [w]1Co 7:17 [x]2Co 2:12
8:19 [y]1Co 16:3,4 [z]ver 11,12
8:21 [a]Ro 12:17; 14:18
8:23 [b]Phm 17 [c]Php 2:25 [d]ver 18,22
8:24 [e]2Co 7:4,14; 9:2
9:1 [f]1Th 4:9 [g]2Co 8:4
9:2 [h]2Co 7:4,14 [i]2Co 8:10 [j]Ac 18:12
9:3 [k]1Co 16:2
9:4 [l]Ro 15:26
9:5 [m]Php 4:17 [n]2Co 12:17,18
9:6 [o]Pr 11:24,25; 22:9; Gal 6:7,9
9:7 [p]Ex 25:2; 2Co 8:12 [q]Dt 15:10 [r]Ro 12:8
9:8 [s]Eph 3:20 [t]Php 4:19
9:9 [u]Ps 112:9
9:10 [v]Isa 55:10 [w]Hos 10:12
9:11 [x]1Co 1:5 [y]2Co 1:11
9:12 [z]2Co 8:14 [a]2Co 1:11
9:13 [b]2Co 8:4 [c]Mt 9:8 [d]2Co 2:12
9:15 [e]2Co 2:14 [f]Ro 5:15,16
10:1 [g]Mt 11:29 [h]Gal 5:2
10:2 [i]1Co 4:21; 2Co 13:2,10
10:4 [j]2Co 6:7 [k]1Co 2:5 [l]Jer 1:10; 2Co 13:10
10:5 [m]Isa 2:11, 12; 1Co 1:19 [n]2Co 9:13
10:6 [o]2Co 2:9; 7:15
10:7 [p]Jn 7:24 [q]1Co 1:12; 3:23; 14:37 [r]2Co 11:23

[a] 9 Psalm 112:9 [b] 7 Or *Look at the obvious facts*

8:23 These "representatives" were duly elected delegates of the churches at large (so that they could not be dismissed as cronies chosen by Paul alone).

9:2 For information on Macedonia and Achaia, see the note on 1:1.

about the authority the Lord gave us for building you up rather than pulling you down,[s] I will not be
ashamed of it. 9I do not want to seem to be trying to frighten you with my letters. 10For some say, "His
letters are weighty and forceful, but in person he is unimpressive[t] and his speaking amounts to noth-
ing."[u] 11Such people should realize that what we are in our letters when we are absent, we will be in our
actions when we are present.
12We do not dare to classify or compare ourselves with some who commend themselves.[v] When they
measure themselves by themselves and compare themselves with themselves, they are not wise. 13We,
however, will not boast beyond proper limits, but will confine our boasting to the field God has assigned
to us,[w] a field that reaches even to you. 14We are not going too far in our boasting, as would be the case
if we had not come to you, for we did get as far as you[x] with the gospel of Christ.[y] 15Neither do we go be-
yond our limits by boasting of work done by others.[a][z] Our hope is that, as your faith continues to grow,[a]
our area of activity among you will greatly expand, 16so that we can preach the gospel in the regions be-
yond you.[b] For we do not want to boast about work already done in another man's territory. 17But, "Let
him who boasts boast in the Lord."[b][c] 18For it is not the one who commends himself[d] who is approved,
but the one whom the Lord commends.[e]

10:8 [s]2Co 13:10
10:10 [t]1Co 2:3; Gal 4:13,14 [u]1Co 1:17
10:12 [v]2Co 3:1
10:13 [w]ver 15,16
10:14 [x]1Co 3:6 [y]2Co 2:12
10:15 [z]Ro 15:20 [a]2Th 1:3
10:16 [b]Ac 19:21
10:17 [c]Jer 9:24; 1Co 1:31
10:18 [d]ver 12 [e]Ro 2:29; 1Co 4:5

[a] 13-15 Or *13We, however, will not boast about things that cannot be measured, but we will boast according to the standard of measurement that the God of measure has assigned us—a measurement that relates even to you. 14 . . . 15Neither do we boast about things that cannot be measured in regard to the work done by others.* [b] 17 Jer. 9:24

10:10 Paul's adversaries used a professional type of oratory designed to extract money from their gullible audiences. But Paul's manner of speaking was plain, straightforward and free from artificiality—as well as "free of charge" (11:7).

10:13 The assigned "field" may be a picture of an athletic contest in which lanes are marked out for the different runners.

10:16 "Regions beyond" may be a reference to Spain.

Early Christian Heresies

2 CORINTHIANS 10 In his New Testament epistles, Paul frequently warned his readers to be on guard against false teaching (e.g., 2Co 11:3–4). These cautions reveal that from an early point Christianity was open to distortions and heresies that took many forms through overemphasis on some and denial of other central Christian teachings.

The "super-apostles" who opposed Paul in 11:5 appear to have erred by overemphasizing their own righteousness (11:15) and boasting about revelations they had purportedly received (12:1). Perhaps they were similar to the Judaizing opponents Paul faced in Galatia,[1] whose teaching required the continuation of Jewish customs and led to an imposition of circumcision and dietary laws upon Gentiles.[2] Paul condemned those who distorted the gospel through the addition of Jewish requirements (Gal 1:8) and preached salvation on the basis of faith rather than works. Montanism was a later heresy that placed strict emphasis on law observance. It arose during the second century and encouraged excessive prophetic utterances in the hope of speeding Christ's return.

Other early Christian heresies that denied central Christian beliefs included Gnosticism, Docetism, Ebionism and Arianism.

✣ *Gnostics* were a diverse group, but the main tenet of their philosophy was that the material world was by nature evil and that by knowledge one could ascend to the pure spirituality of the heavenly realm.[3]

✣ *Docetists*, a subgroup of the Gnostics, affirmed the deity of Jesus but denied his humanity, believing that a divine being was incapable of suffering and concluding that Jesus merely appeared to be human and to experience pain.

✣ At the opposite extreme, beginning at the end of the first century A.D., a Jewish Christian sect known as the *Ebionites* denied the deity of Jesus, preferring to uphold him as a human being who perfectly obeyed the law and was rewarded by being made Messiah.

✣ Similarly, in the fourth century *Arians* denied the divinity of Jesus, demoting him to the status of a demigod (a being with more power than a mortal but less than a god, or a person so outstanding as to seem to approach the divine). They argued that upholding the divinity of Jesus would contradict a belief in the oneness and immutability of God.

The creeds composed by the early church were an attempt to combat heresy and identify orthodox teaching. They emphasize the uniqueness of Jesus Christ, who is simultaneously fully God and fully man.

[1]See "Which Galatia?" on page 1903; see also "Map 13." [2]See "Circumcision in the Ancient World" on page 1840 and "Jewish Meals and Meal Customs" on page 1575.
[3]See "The Gnostics and Their Scriptures" on page 2029.

Paul and the False Apostles

11 I hope you will put up with[f] a little of my foolishness;[g] but you are already doing that. 2I am
jealous for you with a godly jealousy. I promised you to one husband,[h] to Christ, so that I might
present you[i] as a pure virgin to him. 3But I am afraid that just as Eve was deceived by the serpent's
cunning,[j] your minds may somehow be led astray from your sincere and pure devotion to Christ. 4For
if someone comes to you and preaches a Jesus other than the Jesus we preached,[k] or if you receive a
different spirit[l] from the one you received, or a different gospel[m] from the one you accepted, you put
up with it easily enough. 5But I do not think I am in the least inferior to those "super-apostles."[n] 6I
may not be a trained speaker,[o] but I do have knowledge.[p] We have made this perfectly clear to you in
every way.

7Was it a sin[q] for me to lower myself in order to elevate you by preaching the gospel of God to you
free of charge?[r] 8I robbed other churches by receiving support from them[s] so as to serve you. 9And when
I was with you and needed something, I was not a burden to anyone, for the brothers who came from
Macedonia supplied what I needed. I have kept myself from being a burden to you[t] in any way, and will
continue to do so. 10As surely as the truth of Christ is in me,[u] nobody in the regions of Achaia[v] will stop
this boasting[w] of mine. 11Why? Because I do not love you? God knows I do![x] 12And I will keep on doing
what I am doing in order to cut the ground from under those who want an opportunity to be considered
equal with us in the things they boast about.

13For such men are false apostles,[y] deceitful[z] workmen, masquerading as apostles of Christ.[a] 14And
no wonder, for Satan himself masquerades as an angel of light. 15It is not surprising, then, if his servants
masquerade as servants of righteousness. Their end will be what their actions deserve.[b]

Paul Boasts About His Sufferings

16I repeat: Let no one take me for a fool.[c] But if you do, then receive me just as you would a fool, so
that I may do a little boasting. 17In this self-confident boasting I am not talking as the Lord would,[d] but
as a fool. 18Since many are boasting in the way the world does, I too will boast.[e] 19You gladly put up with
fools since you are so wise![f] 20In fact, you even put up with anyone who enslaves you[g] or exploits you or
takes advantage of you or pushes himself forward or slaps you in the face. 21To my shame I admit that
we were too weak[h] for that!

What anyone else dares to boast about—I am speaking as a fool—I also dare to boast about.[i] 22Are
they Hebrews? So am I.[j] Are they Israelites? So am I.[k] Are they Abraham's descendants? So am I. 23Are
they servants of Christ? (I am out of my mind to talk like this.) I am more. I have worked much harder,[l]
been in prison more frequently,[m] been flogged more severely, and been exposed to death again and again.
24Five times I received from the Jews the forty lashes[n] minus one. 25Three times I was beaten with rods,[o]
once I was stoned,[p] three times I was shipwrecked, I spent a night and a day in the open sea, 26I have
been constantly on the move. I have been in danger from rivers, in danger from bandits, in danger from
my own countrymen,[q] in danger from Gentiles; in danger in the city,[r] in danger in the country, in dan-
ger at sea; and in danger from false brothers.[s] 27I have labored and toiled and have often gone without
sleep; I have known hunger and thirst and have often gone without food;[t] I have been cold and naked.
28Besides everything else, I face daily the pressure of my concern for all the churches. 29Who is weak,
and I do not feel weak? Who is led into sin, and I do not inwardly burn?

30If I must boast, I will boast of the things that show my weakness.[u] 31The God and Father of the Lord

11:1 [f]ver 4,19, 20; Mt 17:17 [g]ver 16,17,21; 2Co 5:13
11:2 [h]Hos 2:19; Eph 5:26,27 [i]2Co 4:14
11:3 [j]Ge 3:1-6, 13; Jn 8:44; 1Ti 2:14; Rev 12:9
11:4 [k]1Co 3:11 [l]Ro 8:15 [m]Gal 1:6-9
11:5 [n]2Co 12:11; Gal 2:6
11:6 [o]1Co 1:17 [p]Eph 3:4
11:7 [q]2Co 12:13 [r]1Co 9:18
11:8 [s]Php 4:15, 18
11:9 [t]2Co 12:13, 14,16
11:10 [u]Ro 9:1 [v]Ac 18:12 [w]1Co 9:15
11:11 [x]2Co 12:15
11:13 [y]2Pe 2:1 [z]Tit 1:10 [a]Rev 2:2
11:15 [b]Php 3:19
11:16 [c]ver 1
11:17 [d]1Co 7:12, 25
11:18 [e]Php 3:3,4
11:19 [f]1Co 4:10
11:20 [g]Gal 2:4
11:21 [h]2Co 10:1, 10 [i]Php 3:4
11:22 [j]Php 3:5 [k]Ro 9:4
11:23 [l]1Co 15:10 [m]Ac 16:23; 2Co 6:4,5
11:24 [n]Dt 25:3
11:25 [o]Ac 16:22 [p]Ac 14:19
11:26 [q]Ac 9:23; 14:5 [r]Ac 21:31 [s]Gal 2:4
11:27 [t]1Co 4:11, 12; 2Co 6:5
11:30 [u]1Co 2:3

11:5 "Super-apostles" were the false apostles who had infiltrated the Corinthian church and who were in reality not apostles at all (see "Early Christian Heresies" on p. 1896).

11:6 Paul intentionally remained an "amateur" when it came to public speaking. He viewed his calling to be proclamation, not persuasion or manipulation. He did whatever it took not to be confused with the professional rhetoricians of the ancient world (see "Debate and Rhetoric in The Ancient World" on p. 1797).

11:7 The false teachers' method of operation was to demand payment for their "professional" services. Paul, his enemies accused, was lowering himself by breaking the rule that teachers should receive payment in proportion to the worth of their performance.

11:10 For "Achaia," see the note on 1:1.

11:22 The claims implied here on the part of the false apostles indicate that they were Jews who felt superior to Gentile Christians. It is probable, in fact, that they were Judaizers (see the note on Gal 1:7), who wished to impose distinctive Jewish practices on Gentile converts.

11:24–25 Eight floggings are mentioned here, five at the hands of Jewish authorities and three at the hands of Romans. The three floggings by the Romans were beatings with rods (not the scourge) that took place despite the fact that Paul, a Roman citizen, was legally protected from such punishment (see "Roman Citizenship" on p. 1930).

11:25 Stoning was a traditional manner of Jewish execution.

Only one shipwreck is recorded in Acts, but it took place after the writing of this letter. The three shipwrecks referred to here must have occurred during earlier voyages (see "Travel in the Greco-Roman World" on p. 1946).

Aretas IV of Nabatea and Petra

2 CORINTHIANS 11 Aretas IV ruled the desert kingdom of Nabatea ("Map 14") from 9 B.C. to A.D. 40. With its capital at Petra, this nation included southern Syria, Jordan, the Negev of Israel, the Sinai Peninsula, portions of the eastern deserts of Egypt and the northwestern region of Saudi Arabia. Beginning during the fourth century B.C. Nabatea began to amass great wealth through caravan trade in luxury goods from the East.

Aretas IV, although a usurper with only a marginal claim to the throne, became the most powerful ruler of Nabatea, eventually winning official recognition from Caesar Augustus.[1] During his reign the kingdom reached its zenith commercially, culturally and artistically. Numerous coins minted by Aretas IV have survived, many of them bearing his image.[2]

One of Aretas IV's daughters married Herod Antipas, the son of Herod the Great and the ruler of Galilee and Perea in Transjordan from 4 B.C. to A.D. 39. Herod Antipas later divorced Aretas's daughter in order to marry Herodias, the wife of his half brother Herod Philip I. John the Baptist spoke out against this, warning Herod Antipas, "It is not lawful for you to have your brother's wife" (Mk 6:18). John was imprisoned and eventually executed at the request of Herodias (Mt 14:1–12; Mk 6:14–29). As there was also a dispute between Aretas IV and Antipas regarding rule over a territory called Gamalitis, Aretas used Antipas's rejection of his Nabatean wife as an occasion to wage war. The Jewish historian Josephus recorded that when Aretas IV destroyed much of Antipas's army a few years afterward, many Jews viewed this as divine retribution for John's execution (*Antiquities*, 18.5.2).

The most famous Nabatean site is Petra, located in modern Jordan in what was once Edomite territory. It lay near the **King's Highway**, one of the important trade routes on the eastern side of the Jordan River. The site occupies an area approximately 1 mile(1.6 km) long and slightly less distance in width. Magnificent tombs and funerary banquet halls had been carved into the sandstone mountains surrounding the area, the most famous of which are the Treasury of the Pharaoh and the Royal Tombs. An ancient cultic site sitting atop one of the surrounding peaks features one of the best preserved altars from antiquity. Petra may possibly be identified as the Old Testament site of Sela, captured by Amaziah of Judah (2Ki 14:7). By 312 B.C., when the Greeks took control of the Near East, Petra was the capital of the Nabateans, who may have migrated from the Persian Gulf.

The "Kazneh" at Petra (perhaps the tomb of Aretas IV)
Photograph: © Todd Bolen/Bible Places.com

After Paul began preaching in the synagogues of Damascus,[3] the local Jews, with the support of the Roman ethnarch under Aretas IV, attempted to kill him, but he was able to escape (Ac 9:23–25; 2Co 11:32–33). This incident indicates that both Rome and Aretas IV had political power in Damascus.

[1]See "Caesar Augustus, Emperor of Rome; the Census; and Quirinius, Governor of Syria" on page 1667. [2]See "Coins and Numismatics" on page 1699. [3]See "Damascus" on page 1087.

11:31 [v]Ro 9:5 Jesus, who is to be praised forever,[v] knows that I am not lying. 32 In Damascus the governor under King
11:32 [w]Ac 9:24 Aretas had the city of the Damascenes guarded in order to arrest me.[w] 33 But I was lowered in a basket
11:33 [x]Ac 9:25 from a window in the wall and slipped through his hands.[x]

Paul's Vision and His Thorn

12:1 [y]2Co 11:16, 30 [z]ver 7 **12** I must go on boasting.[y] Although there is nothing to be gained, I will go on to visions and reve-
lations[z] from the Lord. 2 I know a man in Christ who fourteen years ago was caught up[a] to the
12:2 [a]Ac 8:39 [b]Eph 4:10 [c]2Co 11:11 third heaven.[b] Whether it was in the body or out of the body I do not know—God knows.[c] 3 And I know
that this man—whether in the body or apart from the body I do not know, but God knows— 4 was
12:4 [d]Lk 23:43; Rev 2:7 caught up to paradise.[d] He heard inexpressible things, things that man is not permitted to tell. 5 I will
boast about a man like that, but I will not boast about myself, except about my weaknesses. 6 Even if I
12:6 [e]2Co 11:16 should choose to boast, I would not be a fool,[e] because I would be speaking the truth. But I refrain, so
no one will think more of me than is warranted by what I do or say.
7 To keep me from becoming conceited because of these surpassingly great revelations, there was giv-
12:7 [f]Nu 33:55 en me a thorn in my flesh,[f] a messenger of Satan, to torment me. 8 Three times I pleaded with the Lord
12:8 [g]Mt 26:39, 44 to take it away from me.[g] 9 But he said to me, "My grace is sufficient for you, for my power[h] is made per-
12:9 [h]Php 4:13 fect in weakness." Therefore I will boast all the more gladly about my weaknesses, so that Christ's pow-
12:10 [i]2Co 6:4 er may rest on me. 10 That is why, for Christ's sake, I delight in weaknesses, in insults, in hardships,[i] in per-
[j]Ro 5:3; 2Th 1:4 [k]2Co 13:4 secutions,[j] in difficulties. For when I am weak, then I am strong.[k]

Paul's Concern for the Corinthians

12:11 [l]2Co 11:1 11 I have made a fool of myself,[l] but you drove me to it. I ought to have been commended by you, for I
[m]2Co 11:5 [n]1Co 15:9,10 am not in the least inferior to the "super-apostles,"[m] even though I am nothing.[n] 12 The things that mark
12:12 [o]Jn 4:48 an apostle—signs, wonders and miracles[o]—were done among you with great perseverance. 13 How were
12:13 [p]1Co 9:12, 18 [q]2Co 11:7 you inferior to the other churches, except that I was never a burden to you?[p] Forgive me this wrong![q]
12:14 [r]2Co 13:1 14 Now I am ready to visit you for the third time,[r] and I will not be a burden to you, because what I want
[s]1Co 4:14,15 [t]Pr 19:14 is not your possessions but you. After all, children should not have to save up for their parents,[s] but par-
ents for their children.[t] 15 So I will very gladly spend for you everything I have and expend myself as
12:15 [u]Php 2:17; 1Th 2:8 well.[u] If I love you more, will you love me less? 16 Be that as it may, I have not been a burden to you.[v] Yet,
12:16 [v]2Co 11:9 crafty fellow that I am, I caught you by trickery! 17 Did I exploit you through any of the men I sent you?
12:18 [w]2Co 8:6, 16 [x]2Co 8:18 18 I urged[w] Titus to go to you and I sent our brother[x] with him. Titus did not exploit you, did he? Did we
not act in the same spirit and follow the same course?
19 Have you been thinking all along that we have been defending ourselves to you? We have been speak-
12:19 [y]Ro 9:1 [z]2Co 10:8 ing in the sight of God[y] as those in Christ; and everything we do, dear friends, is for your strengthening.[z]
12:20 [a]2Co 2:1-4 20 For I am afraid that when I come[a] I may not find you as I want you to be, and you may not find me as
[b]1Co 4:21 [c]1Co 1:11; 3:3 you want me to be.[b] I fear that there may be quarreling,[c] jealousy, outbursts of anger, factions,[d] slander,
[d]Gal 5:20 [e]Ro 1:29 gossip,[e] arrogance and disorder.[f] 21 I am afraid that when I come again my God will humble me before
[f]1Co 14:33 12:21 [g]2Co 2:1,4 you, and I will be grieved[g] over many who have sinned earlier[h] and have not repented of the impurity,
[h]2Co 13:2 sexual sin and debauchery in which they have indulged.

Final Warnings

13:1 [i]2Co 12:14 [j]Dt 19:15; Mt 18:16 **13** This will be my third visit to you.[i] "Every matter must be established by the testimony of two
or three witnesses."[a][j] 2 I already gave you a warning when I was with you the second time. I now

[a] *1* Deut. 19:15

11:32 For "Damascus," see the note on Acts 9:2.

Aretas IV, the father-in-law of Herod Antipas, ruled over the Nabatean Arabs from about 9 B.C. to A.D. 40 (see the note on Ac 9:23, as well as "Aretas IV of Nabatea and Petra" on p. 1898). The Roman emperor Caligula may have given Damascus back to Aretas, since it was once part of his territory.

11:33 See "The Ancient City" on page 1790.

12:2 "Fourteen years ago" refers to a point early in Paul's ministry, before his first missionary journey.

The "third heaven" apparently designates a place beyond the immediate "heaven" of Earth's atmosphere and the farther "heaven" of outer space—into the presence of God himself. See the note on ancient cosmology at Ezekiel 32:7–8.

12:4 A word of Persian origin, the Greek *paradeisos,* meaning "park" but transliterated "paradise" three times in the New Testament (here; Lk 23:43; Rev 2:7), refers in each instance to heaven. There was a similar word in the Hebrew Old Testament, *pardçs,* translated "forest," "orchard" or "park" (Ne 2:8, Ecc 2:5; SS 4:13).

12:14 For commentary on the parent-child relationship, see the note on Ephesians 6:4.

12:16 Paul sarcastically echoed the accusation of the false teachers that he had organized the collection for the poverty-stricken Christians in Jerusalem only so that the monies could end up in his own pocket.

12:20 The church at Corinth was immature, unspiritual, disorganized and schismatic.

repeat it while absent: On my return I will not spare[k] those who sinned earlier[l] or any of the others,
3 since you are demanding proof that Christ is speaking through me.[m] He is not weak in dealing with
you, but is powerful among you. 4 For to be sure, he was crucified in weakness,[n] yet he lives by God's
power.[o] Likewise, we are weak[p] in him, yet by God's power we will live with him to serve you.
5 Examine yourselves[q] to see whether you are in the faith; test yourselves.[r] Do you not realize that
Christ Jesus is in you[s]—unless, of course, you fail the test? 6 And I trust that you will discover that we have
not failed the test. 7 Now we pray to God that you will not do anything wrong. Not that people will see
that we have stood the test but that you will do what is right even though we may seem to have failed. 8 For
we cannot do anything against the truth, but only for the truth. 9 We are glad whenever we are weak but
you are strong; and our prayer is for your perfection.[t] 10 This is why I write these things when I am ab-
sent, that when I come I may not have to be harsh in my use of authority—the authority the Lord gave
me for building you up, not for tearing you down.[u]

Final Greetings

11 Finally, brothers,[v] good-by. Aim for perfection, listen to my appeal, be of one mind, live in peace.[w]
And the God of love and peace[x] will be with you.
12 Greet one another with a holy kiss.[y] 13 All the saints send their greetings.[z]
14 May the grace of the Lord Jesus Christ,[a] and the love of God,[b] and the fellowship of the Holy Spir-
it[c] be with you all.

13:2 [k]2Co 1:23 [l]2Co 12:21
13:3 [m]Mt 10:20; 1Co 5:4
13:4 [n]Php 2:7,8; 1Pe 3:18 [o]Ro 1:4; 6:4 [p]ver 9
13:5 [q]1Co 11:28 [r]Jn 6:6 [s]Ro 8:10
13:9 [t]ver 11
13:10 [u]2Co 10:8
13:11 [v]1Th 4:1; 2Th 3:1 [w]Mk 9:50 [x]Ro 15:33; Eph 6:23
13:12 [y]Ro 16:16
13:13 [z]Php 4:22
13:14 [a]Ro 16:20; 2Co 8:9 [b]Ro 5:5; Jude 21 [c]Php 2:1

13:11 For "brothers," see the note on Romans 1:13.

13:12 For "holy kiss," see the note on 1 Corinthians 16:20.

INTRODUCTION TO *Galatians*

AUTHOR, PLACE AND DATE OF WRITING

The apostle Paul wrote Galatians (1:1). The date for the letter's composition depends upon whether the Galatians to whom Paul addressed the letter were located in the northern part of the province of Galatia (the "North Galatian" theory) or the southern part (the "South Galatian" theory). The North Galatian theory maintains that Galatians was written from Ephesus or Macedonia in the mid–50s. Of those subscribing to the South Galatian theory, some believe that Galatians was written from Syrian Antioch in 48–49, while others assert that it was drafted in Syrian Antioch or in Corinth between 51 and 53. Today most scholars accept the South Galatian theory and the earlier date for the letter (see "Which Galatia?" on p. 1903).

AUDIENCE

As indicated above, the original recipients of this letter are uncertain. The addressees may have been believers in northern Galatia in the region of Ancyra (these churches would have been founded by Paul during his second missionary journey; see Ac 16:6; 18:23) or churches founded by Paul and Barnabas (Ac 14:1–23) during Paul's first missionary journey into southern Galatia (Iconium, Lystra and Derbe)—the more widely accepted view.

CULTURAL FACTS AND HIGHLIGHTS

Judaizers were Jewish Christians who believed that a number of ceremonial practices of the Old Testament were still binding on the New Testament church. This thorny issue, in various forms, dogged Paul throughout his ministry (see "Paul's Jewish Opponents" on p. 1907). Paul wrote Galatians to convince his readers that this perspective was no less than an abandonment of the principle of salvation by grace through faith.

TIMELINE

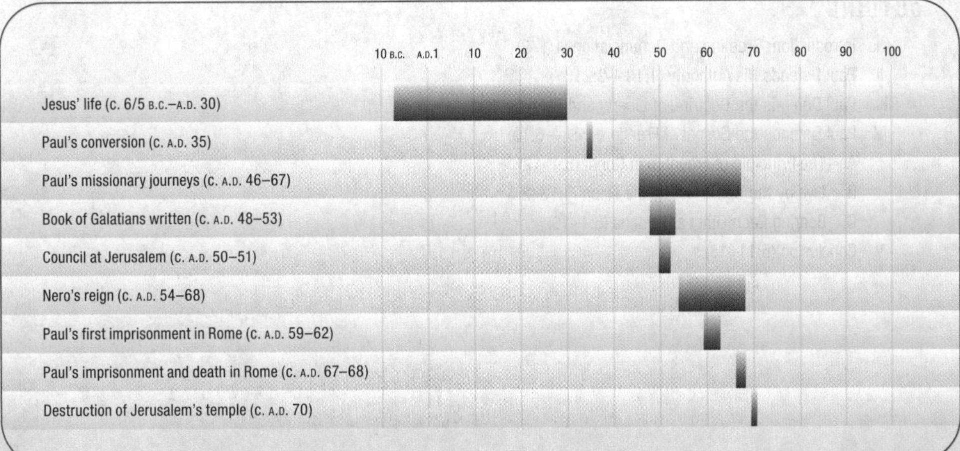

AS YOU READ

Note the accusations leveled against Paul and the vigorous arguments he put forth to defend the gospel of grace and freedom in Christ that he preached. Apply the truths laid out by Paul to your own (or your church's) battles with legalism. Identify Paul's explanation of the doctrine of justification by faith.

DID YOU KNOW?

- To "live like a Gentile" meant to disregard Jewish customs, especially dietary restrictions (2:14).
- The expression "put in charge" refers to the personal slave-attendant who accompanied a freeborn boy wherever he went and exercised a certain amount of discipline over him. His function was more like that of a baby-sitter than a teacher (3:24).
- In ancient times the Greek word for "mark" was used for the brand that identified slaves or animals (6:17).

THEMES

Galatians includes the following themes:

1. *Paul's apostleship.* Paul vigorously defended his apostolic calling (1:1,15; 2:1–10) and his gospel (1:11–12). He was not trying to protect his wounded reputation as an apostle but was defending the truth of the gospel as it had been revealed to him by Christ.
2. *Salvation by faith alone.* Paul's definition of the truth of the gospel affirms God's universal grace for all people: In Christ there is "neither Jew nor Greek, slave nor free, male nor female, for . . . all [are] one in Christ Jesus" (3:28). Justification by faith, a doctrine central to this letter, creates harmonious community.
3. *Legalism versus freedom.* Believers do not need to be under the law to lead ethical lives (5:1—6:16). The Spirit, whom they receive when they believe (3:1–3), empowers them to live the way God wants (5:16–17,22–25). The law can neither produce the fruit of the Spirit (5:22–23) nor restrain people from sinning. Its function is to identify sin and pronounce God's judgment (3:19–24), and it is through the believer's union with Christ that he or she is truly set free. This liberation is not freedom to sin, but freedom to "serve one another in love" (5:13).
4. *A Spirit-empowered life.* Believers are not to rely on their own power to live the Christian life. The Spirit-led Christian does not live for self (5:16) but allows the fruit of the Spirit shine through his or her everyday activities (5:22–23).

OUTLINE

I. Introduction: Greeting and Denunciation (1:1–9)
II. Paul Defends His Authority (1:10—2:21)
III. Paul Defends the Doctrine of Liberty and Faith (3–4)
IV. Paul Defends the Gospel of Freedom (5:1—6:10)
  A. The Principle of Freedom in Christ (5:1–12)
  B. Live by the Spirit, Not by the Flesh (5:13–26)
  C. Bearing Each Other's Burdens (6:1–10)
V. Conclusion (6:11–18)

1:1 [a]Ac 9:15 [b]Ac 2:24
1:2 [c]Php 4:21 [d]Ac 16:6; 1Co 16:1
1:3 [e]Ro 1:7
1:4 [f]Mt 20:28; Ro 4:25; Gal 2:20 [g]Php 4:20
1:5 [h]Ro 11:36
1:6 [i]Gal 5:8 [j]2Co 11:4
1:7 [k]Ac 15:24; Gal 5:10

1 Paul, an apostle—sent not from men nor by man, but by Jesus Christ[a] and God the Father, who
raised him from the dead[b]— 2and all the brothers with me,[c]

To the churches in Galatia:[d]

3Grace and peace to you from God our Father and the Lord Jesus Christ,[e] 4who gave himself for our
sins[f] to rescue us from the present evil age, according to the will of our God and Father,[g] 5to whom be
glory for ever and ever. Amen.[h]

No Other Gospel

6I am astonished that you are so quickly deserting the one who called[i] you by the grace of Christ and
are turning to a different gospel[j]— 7which is really no gospel at all. Evidently some people are throwing
you into confusion[k] and are trying to pervert the gospel of Christ. 8But even if we or an angel from heaven

---

1:1 For "apostle," see the note on 2 Corinthians 1:1.
1:2 For "brothers," see the note on Romans 1:13.
This was a circular letter to several congregations ("churches").
The term "Galatia" is uncertain. In 1 Peter 1:1 it refers to the northern area of Asia Minor, occupied by the Gauls. Here (and in 1Co 16:1) Paul probably used the term to refer to the Roman province of Galatia (in modern central Turkey) and an additional area to the south, through which he traveled on his first missionary journey. See "Which Galatia?" on page 1903.
1:7 "Some people" refers to the Judaizers, Jewish Christians who believed, among other things, that a number of the ceremonial practices of the Old Testament were still binding on the New Testament church. They insisted that Gentile converts to Christianity abide by certain Old Testament rites, especially circumcision. They may have been motivated by a desire to avoid the persecution of Zealot Jews who objected to their fraternizing with Gentiles (6:12). The Judaizers argued that Paul was not an authentic apostle and that out of a desire to make the message more appealing to Gentiles he had removed from the gospel certain legal requirements. (See "Early Christian Heresies" on p. 1896.)
1:8–9 For expressions of vengeful attitudes toward enemies, see the note on Psalm 69:22–28. See also "Curses and Imprecations" on page 883.
1:8 "Eternally condemned" comes from the Greek word *anathema,* which originally referred to a pagan temple offering in payment for a vow. Later it came to represent a curse.

Which Galatia?

GALATIANS 1 At the time Paul wrote his letter to "the churches in Galatia" (Gal 1:2), the Roman province by that name extended from north-central **Asia Minor**[1] (Turkey), where the Gauls (Galatians) had settled centuries earlier, to south-central Asia Minor, which had been incorporated into the province at the end of the first century B.C. Did Paul address his letter to believers in the north, who would have been ethnic Galatians, or to those living in the southern part of the Roman province?[2]

Acts indicates that Paul traveled to Pisidian Antioch, Iconium, Lystra and Derbe during his first missionary journey (Ac 13:14—14:21).[3] Although Luke did not refer to them as Galatian cities, they did belong to the southern part of that province. If Paul wrote this letter to believers in those cities shortly after that first journey, this would have been his first letter—and probably the oldest document in the New Testament. On the other hand, Acts 16:6 and 18:23 may indicate that Paul also traveled through northern Galatia during his second and third missionary journeys. If so, he may have addressed this letter to churches he had founded at that time.

This issue is important for determining the destination and date of Paul's letter to the Galatians, as well as for interpreting crucial passages that relate to the apostle's life. The "South Galatian theory" dates the letter to about A.D. 49–50 and the "North Galatian theory" to the mid–50s. Some scholars believe that Galatians 2:1–10 refers to the Jerusalem council of Acts 15, while others see it as a reference to the famine visit of Acts 11.

Many scholars doubt that Paul would have referred to his readers as "Galatians" (Gal 3:1) if they were not *ethnically* Galatians. Others feel that it would have been the most appropriate term for believers of various ethnic backgrounds who all lived in that Roman province. Some interpreters argue that, in describing geographic locations and ethnic groups, Paul would have used the same terms that his contemporary and fellow Jew Josephus used. This famous historian appears to have considered all of the inhabitants of the Roman province of Galatia to be "Galatians."

Today most scholars hold to the "South Galatian theory," believing that the letter refers to the churches Paul evangelized in that region (Pisidian Antioch, Iconium, Lystra and Derbe). In fact, there is no clear evidence that Paul ever evangelized the northern Galatian region.

[1]See Glossary on page 2080 for definitions of bolded words. [2]See also "Letter Writing in the Greco-Roman World" on page 1889. [3]See "The Missionary Journeys of Paul" on page 1795 and "Map 13."

should preach a gospel other than the one we preached to you,[l] let him be eternally condemned![m] 9 As
we have already said, so now I say again: If anybody is preaching to you a gospel other than what you ac-
cepted,[n] let him be eternally condemned!
10 Am I now trying to win the approval of men, or of God? Or am I trying to please men?[o] If I were still
trying to please men, I would not be a servant of Christ.

Paul Called by God

11 I want you to know, brothers,[p] that the gospel I preached is not something that man made up. 12 I did
not receive it from any man,[q] nor was I taught it; rather, I received it by revelation[r] from Jesus Christ.

1:8 [l]2Co 11:4 [m]Ro 9:3
1:9 [n]Ro 16:17
1:10 [o]Ro 2:29; 1Th 2:4
1:11 [p]1Co 15:1
1:12 [q]ver 1 [r]ver 16

ARCHAEOLOGICAL SITES

ANTIOCH OF SYRIA, CENTER OF CHRISTIANITY

GALATIANS 2 There are two cities in the New Testament by the name of Antioch: Antioch of Pisidia in **Asia Minor**, evangelized by Paul (Ac 13:14–50), and Antioch in Syria, an early center of Christianity. Antioch of Syria was located on the Orontes River, about 15 miles (24 km) from the Mediterranean coast. Today this is the site of Antakya in southern Turkey, close to the border with Syria. Due to its status as a major commercial center at the junction of trade routes running eastward to Mesopotamia, westward to the Aegean and south to Damascus, Palestine and Egypt, it was one of the greatest cities in the ancient world.

Stone carving from Syrian Antioch
Preserving Bible Times; © Dr. James C. Martin

Paul, in Galatians 2:11–14, provided us with a look at church life in this early center of Christianity, a place where Jewish and Gentile believers came together. It became the base of the early church as a result of persecution, which forced followers of Jesus to flee there from Judea during the first century (Ac 11:19). Paul and Barnabas spent much time in Antioch preaching and teaching (Ac 11:25–26; 15:35); Paul embarked upon his missionary journeys from there (Ac 13:1–3; 15:36–41; 18:23);[1] and it was there that believers in Jesus were first called Christians (Ac 11:26). Excavations from 1932 to 1939 revealed the main street of first-century Antioch, flanked by broad walkways, temples, shops and baths. Herod the Great paved the street with marble, and Tiberius later added colonnades.[2]

A street and theater at Pisidian Antioch
Preserving Bible Times; © Dr. James C. Martin

[1]See "The Missionary Journeys of Paul" on page 1795. [2]See "Herod the Great" on page 1627 and "Tiberius Caesar, the Caesar of Jesus' Ministry" on page 1708.

1:13 [s]Ac 26:4,5 [t]Ac 8:3 [13]For you have heard of my previous way of life in Judaism,[s] how intensely I persecuted the church
of God and tried to destroy it.[t] [14]I was advancing in Judaism beyond many Jews of my own age and was
1:14 [u]Mt 15:2 extremely zealous for the traditions of my fathers.[u] [15]But when God, who set me apart from birth[a][v] and
1:15 [v]Isa 49:1,5; Jer 1:5 [w]Ac 9:15 called me[w] by his grace, was pleased [16]to reveal his Son in me so that I might preach him among the
1:16 [x]Gal 2:9 [y]Mt 16:17 Gentiles,[x] I did not consult any man,[y] [17]nor did I go up to Jerusalem to see those who were apostles be-
fore I was, but I went immediately into Arabia and later returned to Damascus.
1:18 [z]Ac 9:22,23 [18]Then after three years,[z] I went up to Jerusalem[a] to get acquainted with Peter[b] and stayed with him
[a]Ac 9:26,27 1:19 [b]Mt 13:55 fifteen days. [19]I saw none of the other apostles—only James,[b] the Lord's brother. [20]I assure you before
1:20 [c]Ro 9:1 1:21 [d]Ac 6:9 God that what I am writing you is no lie.[c] [21]Later I went to Syria and Cilicia.[d] [22]I was personally unknown
1:22 [e]1Th 2:14 to the churches of Judea[e] that are in Christ. [23]They only heard the report: "The man who formerly perse-
1:23 [f]Ac 6:7 1:24 [g]Mt 9:8 cuted us is now preaching the faith[f] he once tried to destroy." [24]And they praised God[g] because of me.

Paul Accepted by the Apostles

2:1 [h]Ac 15:2 **2** Fourteen years later I went up again to Jerusalem,[h] this time with Barnabas. I took Titus along also.
2:2 [i]Ac 15:4,12 [j]1Co 9:24; [2]I went in response to a revelation and set before them the gospel that I preach among the Gentiles.[i]
Php 2:16 But I did this privately to those who seemed to be leaders, for fear that I was running or had run my race[j]
2:3 [k]2Co 2:13 [l]Ac 16:3; in vain. [3]Yet not even Titus,[k] who was with me, was compelled to be circumcised, even though he was a
1Co 9:21 2:4 [m]2Co 11:26 Greek.[l] [4]⌞This matter arose⌟ because some false brothers[m] had infiltrated our ranks to spy on[n] the free-
[n]Jude 4 [o]Ac 15:1; Gal 5:1,13 dom[o] we have in Christ Jesus and to make us slaves. [5]We did not give in to them for a moment, so that
2:5 [p]ver 14 the truth of the gospel[p] might remain with you.
2:6 [q]Gal 6:3 [6]As for those who seemed to be important[q]—whatever they were makes no difference to me; God
[r]Ac 10:34 does not judge by external appearance[r]—those men added nothing to my message. [7]On the contrary,
2:7 [s]1Th 2:4; 1Ti 1:11 [t]Ac 9:15 they saw that I had been entrusted with the task[s] of preaching the gospel to the Gentiles,[c][t] just as Peter[u]
[u]ver 9,11,14 2:8 [v]Ac 1:25 had been to the Jews.[d] [8]For God, who was at work in the ministry of Peter as an apostle[v] to the Jews, was
2:9 [w]ver 7,11,14 [x]1Ti 3:15 [y]Ac 4:36 also at work in my ministry as an apostle to the Gentiles. [9]James, Peter[e][w] and John, those reputed to be
[z]Ro 12:3 pillars,[x] gave me and Barnabas[y] the right hand of fellowship when they recognized the grace given to
me.[z] They agreed that we should go to the Gentiles, and they to the Jews. [10]All they asked was that we
2:10 [a]Ac 24:17 should continue to remember the poor,[a] the very thing I was eager to do.

Paul Opposes Peter

2:11 [b]ver 7,9,14 [c]Ac 11:19 [11]When Peter[b] came to Antioch,[c] I opposed him to his face, because he was clearly in the wrong. [12]Be-
2:12 [d]Ac 11:3 fore certain men came from James, he used to eat with the Gentiles.[d] But when they arrived, he began to

[a] 15 Or *from my mother's womb* [b] 18 Greek *Cephas* [c] 7 Greek *uncircumcised* [d] 7 Greek *circumcised*; also in verses 8 and 9
[e] 9 Greek *Cephas*; also in verses 11 and 14

1:13 Judaism is the term for the Jewish faith and way of life that developed during the period between the Old and New Testaments (see "The Intertestamental Period" on p. 1551). The term is derived from Judah, the southern kingdom that came to an end in the sixth century, B.C. with the exile into Babylonia.

1:14 For "the traditions of my fathers," compare "the tradition of the elders" (see the note on Mt 15:2).

1:16 "Gentiles" (lit., "nations" or "peoples") was a common designation for foreigners—pagans. The term was applied indiscriminately to the entire non-Jewish world.

1:17 Jerusalem played just as crucial a role in first-century Christianity as it did in ancient Judaism. The apostles were based there much of the time, and in that city resided much of the authority and knowledge needed for the development of Christian thinking.

Damascus (see the note on Ac 9:2) was the capital of ancient Syria. Paul had been converted en route from Jerusalem to Damascus.

1:19 For information on James, see the note on Acts 21:18.

1:20 An oath is an appeal to God to witness the truth of a statement or of the binding character of a promise (see also Ge 21:23; 31:53; Heb 6:16). By the time of Christ the Old Testament law regarding oaths (Ex 22:11) had been much perverted by the scribes, and our Lord therefore condemned indiscriminate and light oath taking, stating that people should be so transparently honest that oaths between them are unnecessary. The lawfulness of oaths was recognized by the apostles, who called on God to witness to the truth of what they said (see also 2Co 11:31, as well as "Oaths in Jewish and Christian Practice on p. 1988).

1:21 Syria and Cilicia were provinces in Asia Minor. Specifically, Paul went to Tarsus, his hometown (see the note on Ac 22:3).

1:22 See "Before the Gentile Expansion: The Jewish Churches in the Holy Land" on page 1997.

2:1–10 The meeting of delegates of the church in Antioch with the apostles and elders in Jerusalem (see also Ac 15) is usually called the "Council of Jerusalem," although the text does not contain the word *council.*

2:1 For information on Barnabas, see the note on Acts 13:1–2.

Titus, one of Paul's converts, was an uncircumcised Gentile Christian who served as Paul's delegate to Corinth. He was later left in Crete to oversee the church there. The last word we hear about him in the New Testament is that he went on an assignment to Dalmatia (see 2Ti 4:10), also known as Illyricum (see the note on Ro 15:19).

2:4 "False brothers" refers to the Judaizers (see the note on 1:7).

2:7 Paul's ministry was not exclusively to the Gentiles. In fact, he regularly went first to the synagogue when arriving in a new location (see the note on Ac 13:14). He did, however, consider himself to be foremost an apostle to the Gentiles (see Ro 11:13).

2:9 For information on James, see the note on Acts 21:18. His name may have been mentioned first because he played a dominant role in the Jerusalem council (Ac 15:12–21).

"Pillars" is a common metaphor for those who represent and strongly support an institution.

A common practice among both Jews and Greeks, the "right hand of fellowship" indicated a pledge of friendship.

2:11–12 Antioch (see the note on Ac 11:19, as well as "Antioch of Syria, Center of Christianity" on p. 1904) was the leading city of Roman Syria and the third leading city of the empire (after Rome and Alexandria).

Peter was "in the wrong" because, although he had been willing to shed the laws of Judaism (food and table restrictions) in Antioch in order to enjoy a newfound fellowship with Gentile Christians, he draw back and separate himself from the Gentiles because he was afraid of those who belonged to the circumcision group.[e] 13 The other Jews joined him in his hypocrisy, so that by their hypocrisy even Barnabas[f] was led astray.

14 When I saw that they were not acting in line with the truth of the gospel,[g] I said to Peter[h] in front of them all, "You are a Jew, yet you live like a Gentile and not like a Jew.[i] How is it, then, that you force Gentiles to follow Jewish customs?

15 "We who are Jews by birth[j] and not 'Gentile sinners'[k] 16 know that a man is not justified by observing the law, but by faith in Jesus Christ.[l] So we, too, have put our faith in Christ Jesus that we may be justified by faith in Christ and not by observing the law, because by observing the law no one will be justified.

17 "If, while we seek to be justified in Christ, it becomes evident that we ourselves are sinners,[m] does that mean that Christ promotes sin? Absolutely not![n] 18 If I rebuild what I destroyed, I prove that I am a lawbreaker. 19 For through the law I died to the law[o] so that I might live for God.[p] 20 I have been crucified with Christ[q] and I no longer live, but Christ lives in me.[r] The life I live in the body, I live by faith in the Son of God,[s] who loved me[t] and gave himself for me.[u] 21 I do not set aside the grace of God, for if righteousness could be gained through the law,[v] Christ died for nothing!"[a]

Faith or Observance of the Law

3 You foolish Galatians! Who has bewitched you?[w] Before your very eyes Jesus Christ was clearly portrayed as crucified.[x] 2 I would like to learn just one thing from you: Did you receive the Spirit by observing the law, or by believing what you heard?[y] 3 Are you so foolish? After beginning with the Spirit, are you now trying to attain your goal by human effort? 4 Have you suffered so much for nothing—if it really was for nothing? 5 Does God give you his Spirit and work miracles[z] among you because you observe the law, or because you believe what you heard?

6 Consider Abraham: "He believed God, and it was credited to him as righteousness."[b][a] 7 Understand, then, that those who believe[b] are children of Abraham. 8 The Scripture foresaw that God would justify the Gentiles by faith, and announced the gospel in advance to Abraham: "All nations will be blessed through you."[c][c] 9 So those who have faith[d] are blessed along with Abraham, the man of faith.

10 All who rely on observing the law are under a curse, for it is written: "Cursed is everyone who does not continue to do everything written in the Book of the Law."[d][e] 11 Clearly no one is justified before God by the law, because, "The righteous will live by faith."[e][f] 12 The law is not based on faith; on the contrary, "The man who does these things will live by them."[f][g] 13 Christ redeemed us from the curse of the law[h] by becoming a curse for us, for it is written: "Cursed is everyone who is hung on a tree."[g][i] 14 He redeemed us in order that the blessing given to Abraham might come to the Gentiles through Christ Jesus,[j] so that by faith we might receive the promise of the Spirit.[k]

The Law and the Promise

15 Brothers, let me take an example from everyday life. Just as no one can set aside or add to a human covenant that has been duly established, so it is in this case. 16 The promises were spoken to Abraham and to his seed.[l] The Scripture does not say "and to seeds," meaning many people, but "and to your seed,"[h] meaning one person, who is Christ. 17 What I mean is this: The law, introduced 430 years[m] later, does not set aside the covenant previously established by God and thus do away with the promise. 18 For if the inheritance depends on the law, then it no longer depends on a promise;[n] but God in his grace gave it to Abraham through a promise.

2:12 [e] Ac 11:2
2:13 [f] ver 1; Ac 4:36
2:14 [g] ver 5 [h] ver 7,9,11 [i] Ac 10:28
2:15 [j] Php 3:4,5 [k] 1Sa 15:18
2:16 [l] Ac 13:39; Ro 9:30
2:17 [m] ver 15 [n] Gal 3:21
2:19 [o] Ro 7:4 [p] Ro 6:10,11,14; 2Co 5:15
2:20 [q] Ro 6:6 [r] 1Pe 4:2 [s] Mt 4:3 [t] Ro 8:37 [u] Gal 1:4
2:21 [v] Gal 3:21
3:1 [w] Gal 5:7 [x] 1Co 1:23
3:2 [y] Ro 10:17
3:5 [z] 1Co 12:10
3:6 [a] Ge 15:6; Ro 4:3
3:7 [b] ver 9
3:8 [c] Ge 12:3; Ac 3:25
3:9 [d] ver 7; Ro 4:16
3:10 [e] Dt 27:26; Jer 11:3
3:11 [f] Hab 2:4; Gal 2:16; Heb 10:38
3:12 [g] Lev 18:5; Ro 10:5
3:13 [h] Gal 4:5 [i] Dt 21:23; Ac 5:30
3:14 [j] Ro 4:9,16 [k] ver 2; Joel 2:28; Ac 2:33
3:16 [l] Lk 1:55; Ro 4:13,16
3:17 [m] Ge 15:13, 14; Ex 12:40
3:18 [n] Ro 4:14

a 21 Some interpreters end the quotation after verse 14. *b* 6 Gen. 15:6 *c* 8 Gen. 12:3; 18:18; 22:18 *d* 10 Deut. 27:26
e 11 Hab. 2:4 *f* 12 Lev. 18:5 *g* 13 Deut. 21:23 *h* 16 Gen. 12:7; 13:15; 24:7

had later abandoned this stance to pacify the Judaizers (see the note on 1:7). The sharing of a common meal (see "Jewish Meals and Meal Customs" on p. 1575) was a visible and powerful symbol of what Paul was teaching young churches: "You are all one in Christ Jesus" (3:28). But this symbol was publicly damaged by Peter's return to an insistence that Gentile Christians live like Jews.

The "circumcision group" refers to the Judaizers (see the note on 1:7 and "Circumcision in the Ancient World" on p. 1840).

2:13 "Other Jews" refers to Jewish Christians not associated with the circumcision party but whom Peter's behavior had led astray.

2:14 To "live like a Gentile" meant to disregard Jewish customs, especially dietary restrictions.

3:1 See "Which Galatia?" on page 1903.

3:7 Abraham was the physical and spiritual father of the Jewish race. Here all believers (Jews and Gentiles alike) are called his spiritual children.

3:13 "Tree" is used in classical Greek of stocks and poles on which bodies were impaled (cf. Est 2:23 and its note); here it refers to the cross.

3:15 For "brothers," see the note on Romans 1:13.

The Greek word translated "human covenant" normally indicates a last will or testament, which is probably the legal instrument Paul was referring to here. But in the Septuagint it had been widely used of God's covenant with his people.

3:17 God did not give the law to Moses until 430 years *after* his original covenant with Abraham. So the Abrahamic covenant had been established solely by faith.

3:19 ºRo 5:20 ᵖver 16 ᵠAc 7:53 ʳEx 20:19
3:20 ˢHeb 8:6; 9:15; 12:24
3:21 ᵗGal 2:17 ᵘGal 2:21

[19]What, then, was the purpose of the law? It was added because of transgressions[o] until the Seed[p] to
whom the promise referred had come. The law was put into effect through angels[q] by a mediator.[r] [20]A me-
diator,[s] however, does not represent just one party; but God is one.
[21]Is the law, therefore, opposed to the promises of God? Absolutely not![t] For if a law had been given
that could impart life, then righteousness would certainly have come by the law.[u] [22]But the Scripture

3:19 For "through angels," see the note on Acts 7:38.

Paul's Jewish Opponents

GALATIANS 3 Throughout his Christian ministry Paul was dogged by Jewish opponents who sought to undermine his message. Some of these challengers were Jews who rejected the Messianic claims of Jesus and sought to halt the growth of the church by open persecution (Ac 13:45; 14:19), just as Paul himself had once done. On other occasions, however, Paul seems to have been opposed by Jews who were perhaps offended not so much by the fact that Paul preached Christ but that he did not require Gentiles to become proselytes (i.e., to embrace the ways of Judaism, such as circumcision, observance of the Sabbath and avoidance of non-kosher foods).[1] It appears that the Christians in Galatia had been persuaded not to turn away from Christ but to become proselytes. For Paul this was an alarming development because it undercut the core message of the gospel; if salvation could not be attained without embracing Judaism, then the death of Christ was insufficient.

Scholars have become vitally interested in understanding Paul's Jewish adversaries, because this issue is key to understanding Paul. The traditional Protestant view is that Paul's Jewish opponents were "legalists" who believed that salvation is not received by grace through faith but must be earned by "good works" (which in this case meant adherence to the ritual laws of Judaism).

Against this, some have recently argued that first-century Judaism was not really "legalistic" at all but that it held to the belief that forgiveness was obtained purely by the mercy of God. These scholars charge that Protestants have judged ancient Jews out of the context of the Protestant Reformation, when Luther faced the legalism of Roman Catholic masses and indulgences, rather than truly listening to the first-century Jews themselves. To the contrary, such critics insist, faithful Jews believed that God had chosen them purely on the basis of his grace and that he required only that they regulate their lives according to the terms of his covenant. The "rules" of Judaism, according to this perspective, helped Jews to preserve their identity and faithfulness but were not a means for acquiring God's favor.

This viewpoint on Judaism has led to an altered perspective on Paul. If the early Jews were not in fact legalistic, then our interpretation of some of Paul's words needs significant revision. On the other hand, many believe that it is valid to claim that many first-century Jews did embrace an excessively moralistic and institutionalized view of religion and that Paul was reacting against this code. Scholars are currently involved in research to try to determine exactly what these early Jews believed about how God's favor was to be obtained.

Even so, it is probably unnecessary to prove that first-century Judaism was formally and theologically legalistic in order to demonstrate that many of Paul's opponents were legalistic in their approach to their religion. When Jesus opposed the Jewish leadership, he was concerned not so much with debating the Pharisees over hypothetical elements of theology as with their lack of repentance (e.g., Mt 23).[2] When religious people are unrepentant, they often become harsh and judgmental, adhering to a letter-of-the-law code of moral and ethical standards. Their ability to perform religious rites and duties becomes a substitute for an authentic and personal knowledge of God. This is true in Christian communities as well, notwithstanding the fact that no one in these communities disputes that Christianity holds to salvation "by grace and not by works" as one of its core teachings. Thus, even though many of Paul's opponents may have formally accepted that forgiveness depends entirely upon the mercy of God, in their practical religious lives they may well have been legalistic.

[1]See "Circumcision in the Ancient World" on page 1840 and "Jewish Meals and Meal Customs" on page 1575. [2]See "The Pharisees" on page 1566.

The Gods of the Greeks and Romans

GALATIANS 4 The "religious marketplace" was extremely crowded during the **Hellenistic** era. The Olympian deities (and their Roman equivalents) still held a place in popular religion: mighty Zeus and his consort Hera, warlike Ares, erotic Aphrodite, prophetic Apollo, the virgin warrior Athena, Artemis the huntress,[1] Hermes the messenger of the gods, Hephaestus the smith, Poseidon of the sea, Demeter of the field and Hestia of the hearth. Pluto, the grim god of the underworld, was not always listed among the "Twelve" but retained a significant place in religious thinking. While these deities were certainly reverenced, they were seldom seen as admirable characters. To the contrary, myths described them as violent and lustful, as well as capricious and conniving in their dealings with humans and with one another (as is seen in Homer's *Iliad* and *Odyssey* and in Ovid's *Metamorphoses*).

It is not surprising, then, that these deities and their stories were later sanitized by the philosophers.[2] In some systems, for example, Zeus was equated with the organizing principle of the universe (examples are Cleanthes' *Hymn to Zeus* and Aratus's *Phaenomena*). This transformation of the idea of Zeus was so thorough that Jews and Christians could sometimes make use of material related to Zeus in their apologetic teaching in the Hellenistic world (as in Paul's reference to a poem by the stoic Aratus in Ac 17).

Nereid temple of Xanthos

Preserving Bible Times; © Dr. James C. Martin; permission of The British Museum

Foreign cults also proliferated in Greece and Rome during the Hellenistic age. The worship of the god Sarapis was particularly popular, even though it appears that he was invented as late as the third century B.C., drawing together characteristics from various Greek and Egyptian deities. Widespread stories of his offering help to his followers (deliverance from shipwreck, healing, etc.) compensated for his lack of a long history. Isis and Osiris, other Egyptian dieties, were also popular objects of worship.

In addition to these major deities, there remained a host of local spirits and gods that attractedveneration throughout the empire. Household gods, preserving hearth and home, were especially popular among the Romans. Naiads were described as water-nymphs associated with fountains, just as Dryads were associated with trees and Nereids with the sea. Various spirits connected with the earth were thought to bring fertility to crops, as well as to be associated with death and the underworld. The terrifying goddess Hekate was particularly prominent and was frequently invoked in magic spells.[3] Finally, heroes from the past, most notably Hercules, were thought to aid people in distress and sometimes to serve as spiritual mentors.

See also "The Imperial Cult" on page 1651, the discussion of Asclepius in "Disease and Medicine in the Ancient World" on page 1674, "The Cult of Dionysus" on page 1921 and "The Mystery Religions" on page 1939.

[1]See "Artemis of the Ephesians" on page1808. [2]See "Greek Philosophical Schools" on page 1937. [3]See "Magic in the Greco-Roman World" on page 1911.

3:22 [v]Ro 3:9-19; declares that the whole world is a prisoner of sin,[v] so that what was promised, being given through faith
11:32 in Jesus Christ, might be given to those who believe.
3:23 [w]Ro 11:32 23 Before this faith came, we were held prisoners[w] by the law, locked up until faith should be revealed.
3:24 [x]Ro 10:4 24 So the law was put in charge to lead us to Christ[a][x] that we might be justified by faith.[y] 25 Now that faith
[y]Gal 2:16 has come, we are no longer under the supervision of the law.

Sons of God

3:26 [z]Ro 8:14 3:27 [a]Mt 28:19; 26 You are all sons of God[z] through faith in Christ Jesus, 27 for all of you who were baptized into Christ[a]
Ro 6:3 [b]Ro 13:14 3:28 [c]Col 3:11 have clothed yourselves with Christ.[b] 28 There is neither Jew nor Greek, slave nor free,[c] male nor female,
[d]Jn 10:16; 17:11; Eph 2:14,15 for you are all one in Christ Jesus.[d] 29 If you belong to Christ,[e] then you are Abraham's seed, and heirs ac-
3:29 [e]1Co 3:23 cording to the promise.[f]
[f]ver 16 4 What I am saying is that as long as the heir is a child, he is no different from a slave, although he
owns the whole estate. 2 He is subject to guardians and trustees until the time set by his father. 3 So
4:3 [g]Gal 2:4 [h]Col 2:8,20 also, when we were children, we were in slavery[g] under the basic principles of the world.[h] 4 But when the
4:4 [i]Mk 1:15; Eph 1:10 [j]Jn 1:14 time had fully come,[i] God sent his Son, born of a woman,[j] born under law,[k] 5 to redeem those under law,
[k]Lk 2:27 that we might receive the full rights[l] of sons. 6 Because you are sons, God sent the Spirit of his Son into
4:5 [l]Jn 1:12 4:6 [m]Ro 5:5 our hearts,[m] the Spirit who calls out, "*Abba*,[b] Father."[n] 7 So you are no longer a slave, but a son; and since
[n]Ro 8:15,16 4:7 [o]Ro 8:17 you are a son, God has made you also an heir.[o]

Paul's Concern for the Galatians

4:8 [p]1Co 1:21; Eph 2:12; 1Th 4:5 8 Formerly, when you did not know God,[p] you were slaves to those who by nature are not gods.[q] 9 But
[q]2Ch 13:9; Isa 37:19 now that you know God—or rather are known by God[r]—how is it that you are turning back to those
4:9 [r]1Co 8:3 [s]ver 3 [t]Col 2:20 weak and miserable principles? Do you wish to be enslaved[s] by them all over again?[t] 10 You are observ-
4:10 [u]Ro 14:5 ing special days and months and seasons and years![u] 11 I fear for you, that somehow I have wasted my ef-
4:11 [v]1Th 3:5 forts on you.[v]
4:12 [w]Gal 6:18 12 I plead with you, brothers,[w] become like me, for I became like you. You have done me no wrong.
4:13 [x]1Co 2:3 13 As you know, it was because of an illness[x] that I first preached the gospel to you. 14 Even though my ill-
ness was a trial to you, you did not treat me with contempt or scorn. Instead, you welcomed me as if I were
4:14 [y]Mt 10:40 an angel of God, as if I were Christ Jesus himself.[y] 15 What has happened to all your joy? I can testify that,
if you could have done so, you would have torn out your eyes and given them to me. 16 Have I now become
4:16 [z]Am 5:10 your enemy by telling you the truth?[z]
17 Those people are zealous to win you over, but for no good. What they want is to alienate you ⌊from
us⌋, so that you may be zealous for them. 18 It is fine to be zealous, provided the purpose is good, and to
4:18 [a]ver 13,14 4:19 [b]1Co 4:15 be so always and not just when I am with you.[a] 19 My dear children,[b] for whom I am again in the pains
[c]Eph 4:13 of childbirth until Christ is formed in you,[c] 20 how I wish I could be with you now and change my tone,
because I am perplexed about you!

Hagar and Sarah

21 Tell me, you who want to be under the law, are you not aware of what the law says? 22 For it is written

[a] 24 Or *charge until Christ came* [b] 6 Aramaic for *Father*

3:24 The expression "put in charge" translates the Greek *paidagogos* (from which *pedagogue* is derived). It refers to the personal slave-attendant who accompanied a freeborn boy wherever he went and exercised a certain amount of discipline over him. His function was more like that of a baby-sitter than a teacher. (The Greek term is translated "guardians" in 1Co 4:15.)
3:26–29 Faith in Christ makes a person a "son of God." This gives people, regardless of race, class or gender (v. 28; see "Slavery in the Greco-Roman World" on p. 1979), a new identity—that of Jesus Christ, with whom they share "sonship." By adoption (see "Adoption in the Roman World" on p. 1849), the justified believer is an heir in God's family, with all the attendant rights and privileges. (See "Genealogies in Ancient Israel" on p. 1559.)
4:2 "Guardians" is a broader term than "[those] put in charge" in 3:24.
4:5 For "full rights of sons," see the note on 3:26–29.
4:6 *Abba* is the Aramaic word for "father," transliterated into Greek and thence into English. The corresponding Hebrew word is *Ab*. *Abba* is found three times in the New Testament (see also Mk 14:36; Ro 8:15). For the use of the Aramaic language in New Testament times, see the note on Mark 5:41. Jewish children used the term *Abba* to show both intimacy with and respect toward their fathers.
4:10 "Special days" refers to days such as the Sabbath and the Day of Atonement (see "The Day of Atonement" on p. 176).
"Months and seasons" refers to New Moons (see the note on 1Sa 20:5), Passover (see "The Passover" on p. 656) and Firstfruits (see "The Festivals of Israel" on p. 186).
"Years" refers to the sabbath year (see "Sabbath, Sabbath Year and the Jubilee" on p. 189).
The Pharisees (see the notes on Mt 3:7; Lk 5:17) meticulously observed all of these in an attempt to gain merit before God.
4:12 For "brothers," see the note on Romans 1:13.
4:13 Paul's "illness" has not been identified. Some suggest that it was eye trouble, while others have suggested malaria or epilepsy.
4:17 "Those people" refer to the Judaizers (see the note on 1:7).
4:22–23 The "two sons" were Ishmael, born to the slave woman, Hagar (Ge 16:1–16); and Isaac, born to the free woman, Sarah (Ge 21:2–5).

GRECO-ROMAN DEITIES

Greek Name	Roman Name	Position	Scripture Reference
Aphrodite	Venus	Goddess of love	
Apollo	Sol (also identified with Helias)	Shepherd-god; sun-god; associated with poetry, music, prophecy and hunting	
Ares	Mars	War-god; also linked with agriculture; Areopagus (Mars Hill) named after him	Acts 17:22
Artemis	Diana	Goddess of fertility	Acts 19:21–40
Asklepios (Asclepius)		Goddess of medicine	
Athena	Minerva	Goddess of wisdom, fertility and war; guardian of Athens	
Cronus	Saturn	Father of Zeus; agriculture	
Dike		Justice	Acts 28:4
Demeter	Ceres	Corn-goddess; guardian of marriage	
Dionys(i)us	Bacchus (Liber)	Phrygian god; associated with nature, wine and revelry	
Hades	Pluto (Dis)	God of the underworld	
Hephaistos (Hephaestus)	Vulcan	God of fire; patron of craftsmen	
Hera	Juno	Goddess of women	
Hermes	Mercury	God of heralds	Acts 14:12
Hestia	Vesta	Goddess of fire; cf. vestal virgins	
Pan	Faunus	Goat-god of shepherds	
Poseidon	Neptune	Water-god; also linked with earthquakes	
Prometheus		God of fire; created man from clay	
Tyche	Fortuna	God of destiny	
Zeus	Jupiter	Sky-god; controller of weather; ruler of all gods and men	Acts 14:12,13
	Cybele	Mother-earth	
	Emperor	Julius Caesar and Augustus Caesar were deified posthumously; Caligula, Nero and Domitian demanded worship during their lifetimes.	

Olympian gods are in bold type.

Chronological and Background Charts of the New Testament, p. 57

4:22 [d]Ge 16:15 that Abraham had two sons, one by the slave woman[d] and the other by the free woman.[e] 23 His son by the
[e]Ge 21:2 4:23 [f]Ro 9:7,8 slave woman was born in the ordinary way;[f] but his son by the free woman was born as the result of a
[g]Ge 18:10-14; Heb 11:11 promise.[g]
24 These things may be taken figuratively, for the women represent two covenants. One covenant is
from Mount Sinai and bears children who are to be slaves: This is Hagar. 25 Now Hagar stands for Mount
Sinai in Arabia and corresponds to the present city of Jerusalem, because she is in slavery with her chil-
4:26 [h]Heb 12:22; Rev 3:12 dren. 26 But the Jerusalem that is above[h] is free, and she is our mother. 27 For it is written:

> "Be glad, O barren woman,
> who bears no children;
> break forth and cry aloud,
> you who have no labor pains;
> because more are the children of the
> desolate woman
> than of her who has a husband."[a][i]

4:27 [i]Isa 54:1

28 Now you, brothers, like Isaac, are children of promise. 29 At that time the son born in the ordinary
4:29 [j]ver 23 [k]Ge 21:9 way[j] persecuted the son born by the power of the Spirit.[k] It is the same now. 30 But what does the Scrip-
ture say? "Get rid of the slave woman and her son, for the slave woman's son will never share in the in-
4:30 [l]Ge 21:10 heritance with the free woman's son."[b][l] 31 Therefore, brothers, we are not children of the slave woman,
but of the free woman.

[a] *27* Isaiah 54:1 [b] *30* Gen. 21:10

4:24 The Sarah-Hagar account is an allegory, not because it was non-historical but in the sense that Paul used the events to illustrate a theological truth.

Mount Sinai is the site at which the old covenant was established (see "The Location of Mount Sinai" on p. 123).

4:25 Jerusalem can be equated with Mount Sinai because it represents the center of Judaism.

4:26 Rabbinical teaching held that the "Jerusalem that is above" was the heavenly archetype that in the Messianic period would be let down to Earth. Here it refers to the heavenly city of God, in which Christ reigns and of which Christians are citizens, in contrast to the "present city of Jerusalem" (v. 25).

4:30 Sarah's words in Genesis 21:10 were used by Paul as the Scriptural basis for teaching the Galatians to put the Judaizers (see the note on 1:7) out of the church. (For information on excommunication, see the note on Jn 9:22.)

Magic in the Greco-Roman World

GALATIANS 5 Various types of magical practice flourished in the Greco-Roman world. Spells, charms, **amulets**, potions and even voodoo-type dolls were used to procure the favor of supernatural powers. The borders of magic were fluid; some "magical potions" may have been legitimate attempts at pharmacology,[1] while certain "magical spells" had a strong component of prayer and worship. Nonetheless, the idea of magic as manipulating supernatural beings for one's personal benefit still accurately represents this underground spirituality.

Various substances—anything from bits of the hair of a desired lover to baboon dung or drowned field mice—were employed in spells. These substances, combined with the "right" ritual practices and the proper magic words, supposedly guaranteed the compliance of the deity who was to accomplish the task. The words might be nonsense syllables or secret names of the gods. It was not unusual for such spells to end with an abrupt command such as "Quick! Quick! Do it! Do it!" While practitioners commonly called upon evil spirits of the underworld to do their bidding, any divinity was likely to be invoked. Some magicians even attempted to manipulate the God of Israel. Indeed, he is invoked frequently in the magical papyri, generally under the name "Lao," a possible mispronunciation of the name **Yahweh**.[2]

[1] See "Disease and Medicine in the Ancient World" on page 1674. [2] See also "Miracle Workers and Magicians in the First Century A.D." on page 1706.

ANCIENT VOICES

I adjure you, Evangelos, by Anubis and Hermes and all the rest down below; attract and bind / Sarapias whom Helen bore, to this Herais, whom Thermoutharin bore, now, now; quickly, quickly. By her soul and heart / attract Sarapias herself...

—A MAGICAL LOVE SPELL FOR A WOMAN TO HELP HER WIN THE AFFECTION OF ANOTHER WOMAN

From Hans Dieter Betz, ed., *The Greek Magical Papyri in Translation* (Univ. of Chicago Press, 1986), 266. Trans. by E. N. O'Neil

See "Magic in the Greco-Roman World" article on the previous page.

Freedom in Christ

5 It is for freedom that Christ has set us free.[m] Stand firm,[n] then, **5:1** [m]Jn 8:32 [n]1Co 16:13 [o]Ac 15:10; Gal 2:4
and do not let yourselves be burdened again by a yoke of
slavery.[o]
2 Mark my words! I, Paul, tell you that if you let yourselves be cir-
cumcised,[p] Christ will be of no value to you at all. 3 Again I declare **5:2** [p]Ac 15:1
to every man who lets himself be circumcised that he is obligated
to obey the whole law.[q] 4 You who are trying to be justified by law **5:3** [q]Gal 3:10
have been alienated from Christ; you have fallen away from grace.[r] **5:4** [r]Heb 12:15; 2Pe 3:17
5 But by faith we eagerly await through the Spirit the righteousness
for which we hope.[s] 6 For in Christ Jesus neither circumcision nor **5:5** [s]Ro 8:23,24
uncircumcision has any value.[t] The only thing that counts is faith **5:6** [t]1Co 7:19 [u]1Th 1:3
expressing itself through love.[u]
7 You were running a good race.[v] Who cut in on you[w] and kept **5:7** [v]1Co 9:24 [w]Gal 3:1
you from obeying the truth? 8 That kind of persuasion does not come
from the one who calls you.[x] 9 "A little yeast works through the whole **5:8** [x]Ro 8:28; Gal 1:6
batch of dough."[y] 10 I am confident[z] in the Lord that you will take no **5:9** [y]1Co 5:6 **5:10** [z]2Co 2:3 [a]Php 3:15
other view.[a] The one who is throwing you into confusion[b] will pay the penalty, whoever he may be. [b]Gal 1:7
11 Brothers, if I am still preaching circumcision, why am I still being persecuted?[c] In that case the of- **5:11** [c]Gal 4:29; 6:12 [d]1Co 1:23
fense[d] of the cross has been abolished. 12 As for those agitators,[e] I wish they would go the whole way and **5:12** [e]ver 10
emasculate themselves!
13 You, my brothers, were called to be free. But do not use your freedom to indulge the sinful nature[a];[f] **5:13** [f]1Co 8:9; 1Pe 2:16 [g]1Co 9:19; Eph 5:21
rather, serve one another[g] in love. 14 The entire law is summed up in a single command: "Love your neigh-
bor as yourself."[b][h] 15 If you keep on biting and devouring each other, watch out or you will be destroyed **5:14** [h]Lev 19:18; Mt 22:39
by each other.

Life by the Spirit

16 So I say, live by the Spirit,[i] and you will not gratify the desires of the sinful nature.[j] 17 For the sinful **5:16** [i]Ro 8:2,4-6, 9,14 [j]ver 24
nature desires what is contrary to the Spirit, and the Spirit what is contrary to the sinful nature.[k] They **5:17** [k]Ro 8:5-8 [l]Ro 7:15-23
are in conflict with each other, so that you do not do what you want.[l] 18 But if you are led by the Spirit, you
are not under law.[m] **5:18** [m]Ro 6:14; 1Ti 1:9
19 The acts of the sinful nature are obvious: sexual immorality,[n] impurity and debauchery; 20 idolatry **5:19** [n]1Co 6:18
and witchcraft; hatred, discord, jealousy, fits of rage, selfish ambition, dissensions, factions 21 and envy;
drunkenness, orgies, and the like.[o] I warn you, as I did before, that those who live like this will not inher- **5:21** [o]Ro 13:13
it the kingdom of God.
22 But the fruit[p] of the Spirit is love,[q] joy, peace, patience, kindness, goodness, faithfulness, 23 gentle- **5:22** [p]Mt 7:16-20; Eph 5:9 [q]Col 3:12-15
ness and self-control.[r] Against such things there is no law. 24 Those who belong to Christ Jesus have cru- **5:23** [r]Ac 24:25
cified the sinful nature[s] with its passions and desires.[t] 25 Since we live by the Spirit, let us keep in step with **5:24** [s]Ro 6:6 [t]ver 16,17
the Spirit. 26 Let us not become conceited,[u] provoking and envying each other. **5:26** [u]Php 2:3

Doing Good to All

6 Brothers, if someone is caught in a sin, you who are spiritual[v] should restore him gently. But watch **6:1** [v]1Co 2:15
yourself, or you also may be tempted. 2 Carry each other's burdens, and in this way you will fulfill
the law of Christ.[w] 3 If anyone thinks he is something[x] when he is nothing, he deceives himself. 4 Each **6:2** [w]Ro 15:1; Jas 2:8
one should test his own actions. Then he can take pride in himself, without comparing himself to some- **6:3** [x]Ro 12:3; 1Co 8:2
body else, 5 for each one should carry his own load.
6 Anyone who receives instruction in the word must share all good things with his instructor.[y] **6:6** [y]1Co 9:11,14

[a] *13* Or *the flesh*; also in verses 16, 17, 19 and 24 [b] *14* Lev. 19:18

5:1 The freedom spoken of here is freedom from the yoke of the law (see the note on Mt 11:28–30).
5:6 See "Circumcision in the Ancient World" on page 1840.
5:7 For "[foot] race," see the note on 1 Corinthians 9:24–27.
5:9 For "yeast," see the note on Mark 8:15.
5:11 For "brothers," see the note on Romans 1:13.
5:23 For a discussion of asceticism in the believer's life, see the note on Leviticus 10:9.
5:24 For the heresy of antinomianism (the view that the oral law does not apply to Christians, who are under the law of grace), see the note on Romans 3:8.

6:7 [z]1Co 6:9 [a]2Co 9:6
6:8 [b]Job 4:8; Hos 8:7 [c]Jas 3:18
6:9 [d]1Co 15:58 [e]Rev 2:10
6:10 [f]Pr 3:27 [g]Eph 2:19

7 Do not be deceived:[z] God cannot be mocked. A man reaps what he sows.[a] 8 The one who sows to
please his sinful nature, from that nature[a] will reap destruction;[b] the one who sows to please the Spirit,
from the Spirit will reap eternal life.[c] 9 Let us not become weary in doing good,[d] for at the proper time
we will reap a harvest if we do not give up.[e] 10 Therefore, as we have opportunity, let us do good[f] to all peo-
ple, especially to those who belong to the family[g] of believers.

Not Circumcision but a New Creation

6:11 [h]1Co 16:21
6:12 [i]Ac 15:1 [j]Gal 5:11
6:13 [k]Ro 2:25 [l]Php 3:3
6:14 [m]Ro 6:2,6
6:15 [n]1Co 7:19 [o]2Co 5:17
6:17 [p]Isa 44:5; 2Co 1:5
6:18 [q]Ro 16:20 [r]2Ti 4:22

11 See what large letters I use as I write to you with my own hand![h]
12 Those who want to make a good impression outwardly are trying to compel you to be circumcised.[i]
The only reason they do this is to avoid being persecuted[j] for the cross of Christ. 13 Not even those who
are circumcised obey the law,[k] yet they want you to be circumcised that they may boast about your flesh.[l]
14 May I never boast except in the cross of our Lord Jesus Christ, through which[b] the world has been cru-
cified to me, and I to the world.[m] 15 Neither circumcision nor uncircumcision means anything;[n] what
counts is a new creation.[o] 16 Peace and mercy to all who follow this rule, even to the Israel of God.
17 Finally, let no one cause me trouble, for I bear on my body the marks[p] of Jesus.
18 The grace of our Lord Jesus Christ[q] be with your spirit,[r] brothers. Amen.

[a] 8 Or *his flesh, from the flesh* [b] 14 Or *whom*

6:7–8 Reaping in ancient times consisted in either pulling up the grain by the roots or cutting it with a sickle. The stalks were then bound into bundles and taken to the threshing floor (see the note on Rev 1:22; see also "The Threshing Floor" on p. 608). In Bible lands cutting and binding are still practiced. The reaper sometimes wears pieces of cane on his or her fingers to prevent being cut by the sharp spears of wheat or the sickle. Strict laws for reaping were imposed on Israel (Lev 19:9; 23:10; 25:11; Dt 16:9). Samuel cautioned that reaping would be a duty that the nation's newly chosen king, Saul, would demand of the people (1Sa 8:12). The figurative usage of the term speaks of deeds that produce their own harvest (see also Pr 22:8: Hos 8:7; 1Co 9:11).

6:10 The practice of assisting the poor was so ingrained in the early Christian church that it often required only the briefest of reminders in the Epistles.

6:11 The letter up to this point had probably been dictated to a scribe, after which Paul took the pen in his own hand and finished the writing (see "Writing Materials in the Ancient World" on p. 2037). The "large letters" may have been for emphasis or, as some have suggested, because Paul struggled with poor eyesight (see the note on 4:13).

6:17 In ancient times the Greek word for "mark" was used for the brand that identified slaves or animals.

6:18 For "brothers," see the note on Romans 1:13.

"Amen" is a word of confirmation often used at the close of a doxology or benediction.

INTRODUCTION TO *Ephesians*

AUTHOR, PLACE AND DATE OF WRITING

It appears that the apostle Paul wrote Ephesians (1:1; 3:1; but see "The Authorship of Ephesians" on p. 1919) between A.D. 60 and 62, while he was imprisoned in Rome (3:1; 4:1; 6:20), and that Tychicus delivered the letter (6:21–22).

AUDIENCE

A number of churches in the province of Asia, including the one in Ephesus, most likely read this letter. Evidently Paul had not met all of the Christians in areas where this epistle circulated, but he had heard about their faith and was aware that news of his ministry had reached them (see 1:15; 3:2).

CULTURAL FACTS AND HIGHLIGHTS

During Paul's day Ephesus was a thriving urban center and the capital of the province of Asia (see "Ephesus During the Time of Paul" on p. 1968). Rivaling Rome, Antioch, Alexandria and Corinth in importance, Ephesus' strategic location at the center of trade routes attracted people from all over the known world.

Today the ruins of Ephesus (in modern-day Turkey) still proclaim its former magnificence. In Paul's day thousands of people traveled there to worship in the temple of Artemis (Diana), one of the seven wonders of the ancient world. Activities in three gymnasiums, public baths and a theater that seated 25,000 people provided some of the local entertainment and recreation.

TIMELINE

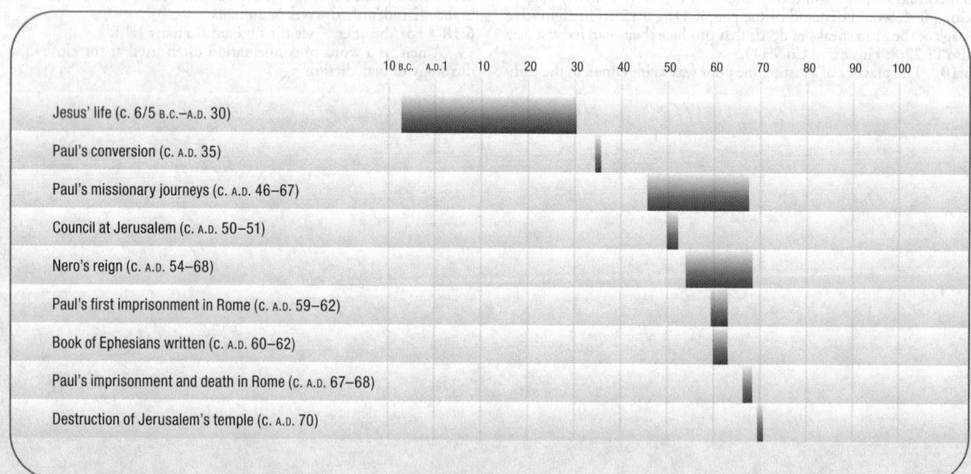

AS YOU READ

Watch for Paul's frequent use of the phrase "in Christ" to explain the believer's new relationship to the Lord. Note Paul's systematic enumeration of the many blessings Christians possess in Christ. Look for the clear statement of God's ultimate purpose for the universe (see 1:10) and his plan for the church. Finally, notice the word pictures Paul used to describe the church and the importance of unity.

DID YOU KNOW?

- The Ephesians were familiar with the Greco-Roman practice of redemption. Slaves were freed by the payment of a ransom (1:7).
- The right hand was the symbolic place of highest honor and authority (1:20).
- Ancient Greek culture often viewed humility, meekness, gentleness and self-sacrifice in negative terms, as weaknesses (4:2).
- In the Greek and Roman world, slavery was considered an economic and practical necessity, an assumed part of life (6:5–9).
- The large Roman shield was covered with leather, which could be soaked in water and used to extinguish flame-tipped arrows (6:16).

THEMES

Paul's letter to the Ephesians focuses on two aspects of unity:

1. *The basis for unity.* God's eternal purpose—"to bring all things in heaven and on earth together under one head, even Christ" (1:10)—is evidenced in, and accomplished through, the church. Christians are chosen to be "holy and blameless" before God (1:4), were created in Christ Jesus "to do good works" (2:10) and have been called to be members of a united "household" (2:19). By his death Christ destroyed every "barrier" (2:14) that separated human beings, so believers can have true unity as members of "one body" (3:6). Through the church the "mystery" (1:9; 3:3–6) that all believers share a common identity as the one family of God is revealed and fulfilled (3:9–10).

2. *Maintaining unity.* Church unity is more than just an ideal; it is a reality to be experienced. Paul gave practical instructions for realizing and maintaining this unity. Old patterns of thinking and behavior, which were characterized by futility, darkness and sensuality (4:17–19), had to be "put off" (4:25). Instead, believers were to live in a manner consistent with their salvation in Christ (4:1).

OUTLINE

- I. Greeting (1:1–2)
- II. The Divine Purpose (1:3—3:21)
  - A. Made Alive in Christ by Grace (1:3—2:10)
  - B. Jew and Gentile Made One in Christ (2:11–18)
  - C. Jew and Gentile United in One Household in Christ (2:19–22)
  - D. Paul as a Minister to the Gentiles (3:1–13)
  - E. Paul's Prayer for the Ephesians (3:14–21)
- III. Practical Instruction (4:1—6:20)
- IV. Conclusion (6:21–24)

1 Paul, an apostle[a] of Christ Jesus by the will of God,[b] 1:1 [a]1Co 1:1 [b]2Co 1:1 [c]Col 1:2

To the saints in Ephesus,[a] the faithful[b][c] in Christ Jesus:

2 Grace and peace to you from God our Father and the Lord Jesus Christ.[d] 1:2 [d]Ro 1:7

Spiritual Blessings in Christ

3 Praise be to the God and Father of our Lord Jesus Christ,[e] who has blessed us in the heavenly realms[f] 1:3 [e]2Co 1:3 [f]Eph 2:6; 3:10;
with every spiritual blessing in Christ. 4 For he chose us in him before the creation of the world to be holy 6:12
and blameless[g] in his sight. In love[h] 5 he[c] predestined[i] us to be adopted as his sons through Jesus Christ, 1:4 [g]Eph 5:27;
in accordance with his pleasure[j] and will— 6 to the praise of his glorious grace, which he has freely giv- Col 1:22 [h]Eph 4:2, 15,16
en us in the One he loves.[k] 7 In him we have redemption[l] through his blood, the forgiveness of sins, in ac- 1:5 [i]Ro 8:29,30 [j]1Co 1:21
cordance with the riches of God's grace 8 that he lavished on us with all wisdom and understanding. 9 And 1:6 [k]Mt 3:17 1:7 [l]Ro 3:24
he[d] made known to us the mystery[m] of his will according to his good pleasure, which he purposed in 1:9 [m]Ro 16:25
Christ, 10 to be put into effect when the times will have reached their fulfillment[n]—to bring all things in 1:10 [n]Gal 4:4 [o]Col 1:20
heaven and on earth together under one head, even Christ.[o]
11 In him we were also chosen,[e] having been predestined according to the plan of him who works out
everything in conformity with the purpose[p] of his will, 12 in order that we, who were the first to hope in 1:11 [p]Eph 3:11; Heb 6:17
Christ, might be for the praise of his glory.[q] 13 And you also were included in Christ when you heard the 1:12 [q]ver 6,14
word of truth,[r] the gospel of your salvation. Having believed, you were marked in him with a seal,[s] the 1:13 [r]Col 1:5 [s]Eph 4:30
promised Holy Spirit, 14 who is a deposit guaranteeing our inheritance[t] until the redemption of those 1:14 [t]Ac 20:32
who are God's possession—to the praise of his glory.

Thanksgiving and Prayer

15 For this reason, ever since I heard about your faith in the Lord Jesus and your love for all the saints,[u] 1:15 [u]Col 1:4
16 I have not stopped giving thanks for you,[v] remembering you in my prayers. 17 I keep asking that the 1:16 [v]Ro 1:8
God of our Lord Jesus Christ, the glorious Father,[w] may give you the Spirit[f] of wisdom[x] and revelation, 1:17 [w]Jn 20:17 [x]Col 1:9
so that you may know him better. 18 I pray also that the eyes of your heart may be enlightened[y] in order 1:18 [y]Ac 26:18; 2Co 4:6
that you may know the hope to which he has called you, the riches of his glorious inheritance in the
saints, 19 and his incomparably great power for us who believe. That power[z] is like the working of his 1:19 [z]Col 1:29 [a]Eph 6:10
mighty strength,[a] 20 which he exerted in Christ when he raised him from the dead[b] and seated him at 1:20 [b]Ac 2:24
his right hand in the heavenly realms, 21 far above all rule and authority, power and dominion, and every
title[c] that can be given, not only in the present age but also in the one to come. 22 And God placed all 1:21 [c]Php 2:9,10
things under his feet[d] and appointed him to be head[e] over everything for the church, 23 which is his body, 1:22 [d]Mt 28:18 [e]Eph 4:15; 5:23
the fullness of him who fills everything in every way.

Made Alive in Christ

2 As for you, you were dead in your transgressions and sins,[f] 2 in which you used to live[g] when you 2:1 [f]ver 5; Col 2:13
followed the ways of this world and of the ruler of the kingdom of the air,[h] the spirit who is now at 2:2 [g]Col 3:7 [h]Jn 12:31;
work in those who are disobedient.[i] 3 All of us also lived among them at one time, gratifying the cravings Eph 6:12 [i]Eph 5:6
of our sinful nature[g][j] and following its desires and thoughts. Like the rest, we were by nature objects of 2:3 [j]Gal 5:16
wrath. 4 But because of his great love for us, God, who is rich in mercy, 5 made us alive with Christ even
when we were dead in transgressions[k]—it is by grace you have been saved.[l] 6 And God raised us up with 2:5 [k]ver 1 [l]ver 8; Ac 15:11

[a] 1 Some early manuscripts do not have *in Ephesus.* [b] 1 Or *believers who are* [c] 4,5 Or *sight in love.* [5]*He* [d] 8,9 Or *us. With all wisdom and understanding,* [9]*he* [e] 11 Or *were made heirs* [f] 17 Or *a spirit* [g] 3 Or *our flesh*

1:1–2 Letters in the ancient world followed a set form (see "Letter Writing in the Greco-Roman World" on p. 1889). Instead of the standard greeting (*chairein*), through a play on words Paul here changed his greeting to read "grace" (*charis*).
1:1 The book of Ephesians may have been intended as a circular letter to several churches, including the one at Ephesus. Ephesus was at the time a city of 200,000, renowned for its traders and silversmiths. Today the Turkish city of Selcuk occupies the site. (See "Early History of Ephesus" on p. 1965 and "Ephesus During the Time of Paul" on p. 1968.)
1:3 Jewish people used the word "bless" to express both God's kindness to them and their thanks and praise to him.
1:5 For "adopted," see the note on Romans 8:15.
1:7 The Ephesians were familiar with the Greco-Roman practice of redemption. Slaves were freed by the payment of a ransom. Similarly, the ransom necessary to free sinners from the bondage of sin and the resulting curse imposed by the law (Gal 3:13) was the death of Jesus Christ ("his blood").
1:9 For "mystery," see the note on Romans 11:25.
1:13 In those days a seal denoted ownership and security (see "Scrolls, Seals and Codices" on p. 2053).
1:20 The right hand was the symbolic place of highest honor and authority (see "The 'Right Hand' in Ancient Thinking" on p. 1983).
1:22 For "under his feet," see the note on 1 Corinthians 15:25.

2:6 [m]Eph 1:20
[n]Eph 1:3
2:7 [o]Tit 3:4
2:8 [p]ver 5
2:9 [q]2Ti 1:9
[r]1Co 1:29
2:10 [s]Eph 4:24
[t]Tit 2:14

Christ and seated us with him[m] in the heavenly realms[n] in Christ Jesus, 7in order that in the coming ages
he might show the incomparable riches of his grace, expressed in his kindness[o] to us in Christ Jesus.
8For it is by grace you have been saved,[p] through faith—and this not from yourselves, it is the gift of
God— 9not by works,[q] so that no one can boast.[r] 10For we are God's workmanship, created[s] in Christ
Jesus to do good works,[t] which God prepared in advance for us to do.

2:10 The Greek word translated "workmanship" sometimes carries the connotation of a "work of art."

ANCIENT TEXTS AND ARTIFACTS

The Dividing Wall of the "Court of the Gentiles" in Herod's Temple

EPHESIANS 2 Gentiles were allowed to enter the outer temple enclosure in Jerusalem. This large, paved area surrounding the temple and its inner courts was enclosed by a double colonnade of pillars standing 37 feet (10 m) high. The perimeter of this area measured three-quarters of a mile (1.2 km). This outer court was also called the court of the Gentiles.

But Gentiles were physically prevented access to the inner courts of the temple by a 4.5 foot (1.4 m) high barrier (Paul's "dividing wall of hostility" in 2:14). The Jewish historian Josephus pointed out that 13 stone slabs with writing in both Greek and Latin were placed at intervals on the barrier, warning Gentiles not to enter.[1] In Josephus's words, "There was a partition made of stone ... Its construction was very elegant; upon it stood pillars, at equal distances from one another, declaring the law of purity, some in Greek, and some in Roman letters, that 'no foreigner should go within that sanctuary'" (*Wars*, 5.5.2). Archaeologists have discovered two of these warning slabs, which state: "No foreigner is allowed to enter within the balustrade surrounding the sanctuary and the court enclosed. Whoever is caught will be personally responsible for his ensuing death."

This dividing wall had great significance for Paul, who was arrested in Jerusalem for reportedly bringing a Gentile into the inner court of the temple (see Ac 21:16–30). Paul and other Jewish followers of Christ recognized that the God who had previously resided in the temple had entered humanity in the person of Jesus, the Messiah. Jesus' death on the cross and his resurrection had in effect broken down the dividing wall, effecting spiritual unity between Jews and Gentiles. As a result, Paul knew, all people have been granted access to God through saving faith in Jesus Christ.

[1]See "Herod's Temple" on page 1648.

Warning inscription from the Jerusalem temple
Preserving Bible Times; © Dr. James C. Martin; permission of The Israel Museum

One in Christ

11Therefore, remember that formerly you who are Gentiles by birth and called "uncircumcised" by
those who call themselves "the circumcision" (that done in the body by the hands of men)[u]— 12remem-
ber that at that time you were separate from Christ, excluded from citizenship in Israel and foreigners to
the covenants of the promise,[v] without hope[w] and without God in the world. 13But now in Christ Jesus
you who once were far away have been brought near[x] through the blood of Christ.[y]
14For he himself is our peace, who has made the two one[z] and has destroyed the barrier, the dividing
wall of hostility, 15by abolishing in his flesh[a] the law with its commandments and regulations.[b] His pur-
pose was to create in himself one[c] new man out of the two, thus making peace, 16and in this one body to
reconcile both of them to God through the cross,[d] by which he put to death their hostility. 17He came and
preached peace to you who were far away and peace to those who were near.[e] 18For through him we both
have access[f] to the Father[g] by one Spirit.[h]
19Consequently, you are no longer foreigners and aliens,[i] but fellow citizens[j] with God's people and
members of God's household,[k] 20built on the foundation[l] of the apostles and prophets, with Christ Jesus
himself as the chief cornerstone.[m] 21In him the whole building is joined together and rises to become a
holy temple[n] in the Lord. 22And in him you too are being built together to become a dwelling in which
God lives by his Spirit.

Paul the Preacher to the Gentiles

3 For this reason I, Paul, the prisoner[o] of Christ Jesus for the sake of you Gentiles—
2Surely you have heard about the administration of God's grace that was given to me[p] for you, 3that
is, the mystery[q] made known to me by revelation,[r] as I have already written briefly. 4In reading this, then,
you will be able to understand my insight[s] into the mystery of Christ, 5which was not made known to men
in other generations as it has now been revealed by the Spirit to God's holy apostles and prophets.[t] 6This
mystery is that through the gospel the Gentiles are heirs[u] together with Israel, members together of one
body,[v] and sharers together in the promise in Christ Jesus.
7I became a servant of this gospel[w] by the gift of God's grace given me through the working of his
power.[x] 8Although I am less than the least of all God's people,[y] this grace was given me: to preach to
the Gentiles the unsearchable riches of Christ, 9and to make plain to everyone the administration of
this mystery,[z] which for ages past was kept hidden in God, who created all things. 10His intent was that
now, through the church, the manifold wisdom of God[a] should be made known[b] to the rulers and au-
thorities[c] in the heavenly realms, 11according to his eternal purpose which he accomplished in Christ
Jesus our Lord. 12In him and through faith in him we may approach God[d] with freedom and confi-
dence.[e] 13I ask you, therefore, not to be discouraged because of my sufferings for you, which are your
glory.

A Prayer for the Ephesians

14For this reason I kneel[f] before the Father, 15from whom his whole family[a] in heaven and on earth
derives its name. 16I pray that out of his glorious riches he may strengthen you with power[g] through his
Spirit in your inner being,[h] 17so that Christ may dwell in your hearts[i] through faith. And I pray that you,
being rooted[j] and established in love, 18may have power, together with all the saints, to grasp how wide
and long and high and deep[k] is the love of Christ, 19and to know this love that surpasses knowledge—
that you may be filled[l] to the measure of all the fullness of God.[m]

2:11 [u]Col 2:11
2:12 [v]Gal 3:17 [w]1Th 4:13
2:13 [x]ver 17; Ac 2:39 [y]Col 1:20
2:14 [z]1Co 12:13
2:15 [a]Col 1:21,22 [b]Col 2:14 [c]Gal 3:28
2:16 [d]Col 1:20,22
2:17 [e]Ps 148:14; Isa 57:19
2:18 [f]Eph 3:12 [g]Col 1:12 [h]1Co 12:13
2:19 [i]ver 12 [j]Php 3:20 [k]Gal 6:10
2:20 [l]Mt 16:18; Rev 21:14 [m]1Pe 2:4-8
2:21 [n]1Co 3:16, 17
3:1 [o]Ac 23:18; Eph 4:1
3:2 [p]Col 1:25
3:3 [q]Ro 16:25 [r]1Co 2:10
3:4 [s]2Co 11:6
3:5 [t]Ro 16:26
3:6 [u]Gal 3:29 [v]Eph 2:15,16
3:7 [w]1Co 3:5 [x]Eph 1:19
3:8 [y]1Co 15:9
3:9 [z]Ro 16:25
3:10 [a]1Co 2:7 [b]1Pe 1:12 [c]Eph 1:21
3:12 [d]Eph 2:18 [e]Heb 4:16
3:14 [f]Php 2:10
3:16 [g]Col 1:11 [h]Ro 7:22
3:17 [i]Jn 14:23 [j]Col 1:23
3:18 [k]Job 11:8,9
3:19 [l]Col 2:10 [m]Eph 1:23

[a] 15 Or *whom all fatherhood*

2:11 Most of the Ephesians were Gentiles. The rite of circumcision was applied to all Jewish male babies; so this physical act ("done in the body by the hands of men") was a clear mark of distinction between Jew and Gentile, in which Jewish people naturally took pride (see "Circumcision in the Ancient World" on p. 1840).
2:14 The "dividing wall" may be an allusion to the barricade in the Jerusalem temple area that marked the limit to how far a Gentile might go (see "The Dividing Wall of the 'Court of the Gentiles' in Herod's Temple" on p. 1917). Paul used it here to describe the total religious isolation Jews and Gentiles experienced from each other.
2:19 The household in ancient times included what we today might call an "extended family."
3:1 Apparently Paul was under house arrest—possibly in Rome—at this time (see Ac 28:16,30; see also "Imprisonment in the Roman World: In Prison Versus House Arrest" on p. 1826).
3:3 For "mystery," see the note on Romans 11:25.
3:14 Kneeling expressed deep emotion and reverence; people in Paul's day ordinarily stood to pray.
3:15 The Greek word translated "family" is similar to the word for "father," so it can be said that the "family" derives its name (and being) from the father.
3:17 The heart was for people of Paul's day synonymous with an individual's whole inner being (see the note on Ps 4:7).

THE AUTHORSHIP OF EPHESIANS

EPHESIANS 4 Did Paul truly write the letter to the Ephesians? The answer has great significance for the letter's canonical authority. In Ephesians 3:1–7 Paul placed great emphasis on his apostolic authority (see also 1Co 9:1–2; 2Co 12:11–12; Gal 1:1). So rejection of Pauline authorship would significantly diminish the letter's authority.[1]

Eastern aerial view of Ephesus, including the theater and central street of the city

© Dr. James C. Martin

Some scholars question Paul's authorship of this book because its vocabulary differs somewhat from his other letters and its sentences are unusually long and complex. The theology of Ephesians also incorporates the idea of the church universal, suggesting that this letter might be dated to a time after the apostle's death, when the church was better established and theology was more developed (although Paul certainly espoused this concept). The letters of Ephesians and Colossians are in fact quite similar, raising the possibility that Ephesians was modeled after Colossians but written later and by a different author.

Other evidence, however, does support Pauline authorship:

◆ The letter itself twice claims Paul as its author (1:1; 3:1) and contains biographical material corresponding to Paul's life (3:1–13).

◆ Personal remarks are in keeping with Pauline authorship (see 6:21–22).

◆ Centuries of church tradition support this premise. The letter's authenticity was never questioned by the early church.

◆ Analyzing the writing style of Ephesians is too subjective a process to be a serious basis for disputing Pauline authorship. No doubt Paul was capable of employing variety in his writing style. Throughout this letter he created a worshipful context, particularly in Ephesians 1–3, and the elevated style of writing was appropriate in light of the book's portrayal of believers' exaltation in Christ.

◆ The suggestion that Ephesians may have been written as a circular letter (i.e., intended for multiple churches rather than addressing a specific crisis in a specific church) may also help to account for its stylistic distinctives. Since this epistle was not written to address a particular controversy, it lacks the direct, hard-hitting and sometimes harsh tone found in the books of 1 Corinthians and Galatians.

◆ The structure of Ephesians, which moves from a doctrinal foundation (chs. 1–3) to practical exhortation (chs. 4–6), is also found in letters that are indisputably Pauline, such as Romans and Galatians.

◆ The theology of Ephesians is consistent with Paul's message elsewhere. For example, the description of Gentile sin in Ephesians 4:17–19 is similar to that found in Romans 1:21–23.

◆ Slight differences between Ephesians and other letters may actually support Pauline authorship of Ephesians, where Paul sometimes took familiar ideas in new directions. For example, the picture of the church as the body of Christ (4:15–16) is expressed differently from what we read in Romans 12:3–5, but both passages are examples of what for Paul was a standard image of the church. An imitator of Paul would most likely not have taken this idea in a new direction but would have slavishly followed Paul's use of the image found in Romans.

On the other hand, similarities between Ephesians and Colossians do not suggest non-Pauline authorship. The same author could quite possibly have written two letters with similar style and content at about the same time. Paul may simply have addressed similar thoughts to different audiences.

[1]See also "The Authorship of the Pastoral Epistles" on page 1957 and "Letter Writing in the Greco-Roman World" on page 1889.

20 Now to him who is able[n] to do immeasurably more than all we ask or imagine, according to his **3:20** [n]Ro 16:25
power that is at work within us, 21 to him be glory in the church and in Christ Jesus throughout all gen-
erations, for ever and ever! Amen.[o] **3:21** [o]Ro 11:36

Unity in the Body of Christ

4 As a prisoner[p] for the Lord, then, I urge you to live a life worthy[q] of the calling you have received. 2 Be **4:1** [p]Eph 3:1 [q]Php 1:27; Col 1:10
completely humble and gentle; be patient, bearing with one another[r] in love.[s] 3 Make every effort to **4:2** [r]Col 3:12,13 [s]Eph 1:4
keep the unity[t] of the Spirit through the bond of peace. 4 There is one body and one Spirit[u]—just as you **4:3** [t]Col 3:14
were called to one hope when you were called— 5 one Lord, one faith, one baptism; 6 one God and Father **4:4** [u]1Co 12:13
of all, who is over all and through all and in all.[v] **4:6** [v]Ro 11:36
7 But to each one of us[w] grace has been given[x] as Christ apportioned it. 8 This is why it[a] says: **4:7** [w]1Co 12:7,11 [x]Ro 12:3

> "When he ascended on high,
> he led captives[y] in his train
> and gave gifts to men."[b][z] **4:8** [y]Col 2:15 [z]Ps 68:18

9 (What does "he ascended" mean except that he also descended to the lower, earthly regions[c]? 10 He who
descended is the very one who ascended higher than all the heavens, in order to fill the whole universe.)
11 It was he who gave some to be apostles,[a] some to be prophets, some to be evangelists,[b] and some to be **4:11** [a]1Co 12:28 [b]Ac 21:8
pastors and teachers, 12 to prepare God's people for works of service, so that the body of Christ[c] may be **4:12** [c]1Co 12:27
built up 13 until we all reach unity[d] in the faith and in the knowledge of the Son of God and become ma- **4:13** [d]ver 3,5 [e]Col 1:28
ture,[e] attaining to the whole measure of the fullness of Christ.
14 Then we will no longer be infants,[f] tossed back and forth by the waves,[g] and blown here and there **4:14** [f]1Co 14:20 [g]Jas 1:6 [h]Eph 6:11
by every wind of teaching and by the cunning and craftiness of men in their deceitful scheming.[h] 15 In-
stead, speaking the truth in love, we will in all things grow up into him who is the Head,[i] that is, Christ. **4:15** [i]Eph 1:22
16 From him the whole body, joined and held together by every supporting ligament, grows[j] and builds **4:16** [j]Col 2:19
itself up in love, as each part does its work.

Living as Children of Light

17 So I tell you this, and insist on it in the Lord, that you must no longer live as the Gentiles do, in the
futility of their thinking.[k] 18 They are darkened in their understanding[l] and separated from the life of **4:17** [k]Ro 1:21 **4:18** [l]Ro 1:21
God[m] because of the ignorance that is in them due to the hardening of their hearts.[n] 19 Having lost all [m]Eph 2:12 [n]2Co 3:14
sensitivity,[o] they have given themselves over[p] to sensuality[q] so as to indulge in every kind of impurity, **4:19** [o]1Ti 4:2 [p]Ro 1:24 [q]Col 3:5
with a continual lust for more.
20 You, however, did not come to know Christ that way. 21 Surely you heard of him and were taught in him
in accordance with the truth that is in Jesus. 22 You were taught, with regard to your former way of life, to
put off[r] your old self,[s] which is being corrupted by its deceitful desires; 23 to be made new in the attitude **4:22** [r]1Pe 2:1 [s]Ro 6:6
of your minds;[t] 24 and to put on the new self,[u] created to be like God in true righteousness and holiness.[v] **4:23** [t]Col 3:10 **4:24** [u]Ro 6:4 [v]Eph 2:10
25 Therefore each of you must put off falsehood and speak truthfully[w] to his neighbor, for we are all mem- **4:25** [w]Zec 8:16 [x]Ro 12:5
bers of one body.[x] 26 "In your anger do not sin"[d]: Do not let the sun go down while you are still angry, 27 and
do not give the devil a foothold. 28 He who has been stealing must steal no longer, but must work,[y] doing **4:28** [y]Ac 20:35 [z]1Th 4:11
something useful with his own hands,[z] that he may have something to share with those in need.[a] [a]Lk 3:11
29 Do not let any unwholesome talk come out of your mouths,[b] but only what is helpful for building **4:29** [b]Col 3:8
others up according to their needs, that it may benefit those who listen. 30 And do not grieve the Holy
Spirit of God,[c] with whom you were sealed for the day of redemption.[d] 31 Get rid of all bitterness, rage and **4:30** [c]1Th 5:19 [d]Ro 8:23
anger, brawling and slander, along with every form of malice.[e] 32 Be kind and compassionate to one an- **4:31** [e]Col 3:8
other, forgiving each other, just as in Christ God forgave you.[f] **4:32** [f]Mt 6:14,15

[a] 8 Or *God* [b] 8 Psalm 68:18 [c] 9 Or *the depths of the earth* [d] 26 Psalm 4:4

4:1 For "prisoner," see the note on 3:1.
4:2 Ancient Greek culture often viewed humility, meekness, gentleness and self-sacrifice in negative terms, as weaknesses. But Paul taught that the love experienced in Christ is to be extended to others.
4:5 "Baptism" in this context probably refers to water baptism, not to the baptism of the Spirit. (See "Baptism in the Ancient World" on p. 1562.)
4:14 There were many distorted teachings and heresies that might easily have thrown the immature off course (see "Early Christian Heresies" on p. 1896).
4:22–23 Because some ancient Greeks believed that desires corrupted and destroyed life, they sought to be free of desire. In fact, they viewed passions as diseases of the mind. Living free of desire was considered the mark of wisdom and maturity. But no one can achieve this status. The solution is not the rejection of desires but their subjection to God.
4:30 For "sealed," see the note on 1:13.

5:1 gLk 6:36 5 Be imitators of God,[g] therefore, as dearly loved children 2and live a life of love, just as Christ loved
5:2 hGal 1:4 i2Co 2:15; Heb 7:27 us and gave himself up for us[h] as a fragrant offering and sacrifice to God.[i]
3But among you there must not be even a hint of sexual immorality, or of any kind of impurity, or of
5:3 jCol 3:5 greed,[j] because these are improper for God's holy people. 4Nor should there be obscenity, foolish talk or
5:4 kver 20 coarse joking, which are out of place, but rather thanksgiving.[k] 5For of this you can be sure: No immoral,

5:2 In the Old Testament the offering of a sacrifice pleased the Lord so much that it was described as a "pleasing aroma" (Ge 8:21; Ex 29:18,25,41).

The Cult of Dionysus

EPHESIANS 5 The cult of Dionysus, the god of wine, also called Bacchus, appears to have emigrated from Asia to ancient Greece. Dionysus worship was notorious for its unrestrained, orgiastic character, involving wine, music, dance and sex (although festivals officially sanctioned by Greek cities tended to downplay some of the wilder elements).

Euripides, the ancient Greek playwright, included a memorable account of Dionysus worship in his play *Bacchae*. This play highlights the efforts of Pentheus, king of Thebes, to stifle Dionysus worship in his city. At the end of the play, frenzied female devotees of Dionysus (a group that included Pentheus's mother) tore the unfortunate king limb from limb.

The cult remained popular throughout the Hellenistic age. Although suppressed in Rome during the second century B.C., Dionysus worship experienced a resurgence, becoming an authorized religion of the Roman Empire. Outsiders sometimes confused Jewish worship with that of Dionysus, possibly for the following reasons:

- Prior to the Jewish Maccabean revolt, which began in 167 B.C., Greek overlords forced their Jewish slaves to participate in Dionysus worship (See 2Mc 6:7).[1,2] Observers may have believed that these Jews had become involved in the Dionysus cult voluntarily.
- Jewish society used symbols also associated with Dionysus worship (such as the vine leaf, grape cluster and cup).
- Ecstatic worshipers of Dionysus often shouted out a meaningless exclamation, *Euoe Saboe!* This could have been confused with the Jewish term for God, *Yahweh Sabaoth*, which was sometimes pronounced *Iao Sabaoth*.

Dionysian drunkenness was more than mere self-indulgence; it was a counterfeit spirituality.[3] In the frenzied and ecstatic Dionysiac rituals, intoxication with wine was equated with being filled with the spirit of Dionysus. Some of the new believers in Asia Minor were probably carrying this form of worship with them into the church by associating wine with the filling of the Holy Spirit. Paul did not want anyone to confuse a drunken frenzy with the power of the Spirit. He repudiated this notion by denouncing drunkenness and associating Spirit filling with other activities.

[1]Second Maccabees is an Apocryphal book never accepted into the standard Protestant canon. [2]See also the "The Intertestamental Period" on page 1551. [3]See also "The Gods of the Greeks and Romans" on page 1908 and "The Mystery Religions" on page 1939.

The Greek god Dionysus

Preserving Bible Times; © Dr. James C. Martin; permission of The Seljuk Museum

impure or greedy person—such a man is an idolater[l]—has any inheritance in the kingdom of Christ 5:5 [l]Col 3:5
and of God.[a][m] [6]Let no one deceive you with empty words, for because of such things God's wrath[n] comes [m]1Co 6:9 5:6 [n]Ro 1:18
on those who are disobedient. [7]Therefore do not be partners with them.
[8]For you were once[o] darkness, but now you are light in the Lord. Live as children of light[p] [9](for the 5:8 [o]Eph 2:2
fruit[q] of the light consists in all goodness, righteousness and truth) [10]and find out what pleases the Lord. [p]Lk 16:8 5:9 [q]Gal 5:22
[11]Have nothing to do with the fruitless deeds of darkness, but rather expose them. [12]For it is shameful

[a] 5 Or *kingdom of the Christ and God*

Husbands and Wives: Family Life in the Greco-Roman World

EPHESIANS 6 The Latin phrase *pater familias*, which means "father of the family," signified the Roman father's place as the head of the family.[1] Roman writers commonly discussed family life in terms of three sets of fundamental relationships: husbands and wives, parents and children, and masters and slaves.[2] This organizational pattern, called the "household code," was strictly hierarchical. By following the code, the patriarch/ householder adhered to the generally accepted, "proper way" to rule his household. In Roman culture people understood that society's structure and stability were rooted in the family's structure and stability. The empire itself was viewed as a great family in which the Roman emperor stood at the top and everyone else had a predetermined, designated place.

Fathers were expected to provide for their families, although mothers often imparted the most direct moral influence on young children. As a son grew up, however, the father would assume primary responsibility for his education and discipline.

The Roman mother held a place of high honor in society and was expected to behave with honor and chastity. She handled day-to-day responsibilities of her household, held the household keys and managed any domestic servants. Beginning with the Augustan Age, a Roman woman who had at least three children was free to conduct business on her own. Some Roman women were renowned for their wisdom and virtue. For example, the Roman statesman Cicero read and admired the letters of a famous Roman matron named Cornelia.

Modern Bible students do well to be cautious of popular but false generalizations stating that women and girls, even in the upper echelons of Roman society, were regarded as little more than property, on a par with domestic animals, or that Roman men had no love for their wives and daughters. Roman women definitely had fewer legal rights than men, but they and their children (including to some extent their daughters) still had rights and often enjoyed deep affection from their husbands and fathers. Cicero maintained a close relationship with his daughter Tullia and was devastated when she died. Pliny the Younger, another Roman, wrote tender love letters to his wife, Calpurnia.

Greek and Roman epitaphs often record great sorrow and affection for deceased wives and daughters, and epitaphs written for departed husbands are often equally tender. One mourning widow described how she and her husband had been bound by love from the moment they met.

We are unwise to attempt to project attitudes/cultural perspectives onto ancient people simply because their social order was hierarchical or their marriages often arranged. For additional information on women during the New Testament period, see "The Role of Women in Religious Life in the Greco-Roman World" on page 1879 and "The Demeanor of Wives" on page 2013.

Paul, in Ephesians 5:25—6:8, not surprisingly assumed a top-down, male-dominated social order. Still, people of the Roman world would not have perceived his injunction that a husband was to love his wife (5:25–33) as contrived, peculiar or revolutionary.

[1]See also "The Role of the Patriarch in Family Life" on page 30. [2]See "Slavery in the Greco-Roman World" on page 1979.

5:13 [r]Jn 3:20,21 even to mention what the disobedient do in secret. [13]But everything exposed by the light[r] becomes vis-
ible, [14]for it is light that makes everything visible. This is why it is said:

5:14 [s]Ro 13:11 "Wake up, O sleeper,[s]
[t]Jn 5:25 [u]Isa 60:1 rise from the dead,[t]
and Christ will shine on you."[u]

[15]Be very careful, then, how you live—not as unwise but as wise, [16]making the most of every oppor-
5:16 [v]Col 4:5 [w]Eph 6:13 tunity,[v] because the days are evil.[w] [17]Therefore do not be foolish, but understand what the Lord's will
5:17 [x]Ro 12:2; 1Th 4:3 is.[x] [18]Do not get drunk on wine,[y] which leads to debauchery. Instead, be filled with the Spirit.[z] [19]Speak
5:18 [y]Pr 20:1 [z]Lk 1:15 to one another with psalms, hymns and spiritual songs.[a] Sing and make music in your heart to the Lord,
5:19 [a]Ac 16:25; Col 3:16 [20]always giving thanks[b] to God the Father for everything, in the name of our Lord Jesus Christ.
5:20 [b]Ps 34:1 5:21 [c]Gal 5:13 [21]Submit to one another[c] out of reverence for Christ.

Wives and Husbands

5:22 [d]Ge 3:16; 1Pe 3:1,5,6 [22]Wives, submit to your husbands[d] as to the Lord.[e] [23]For the husband is the head of the wife as Christ
[e]Eph 6:5 is the head of the church,[f] his body, of which he is the Savior. [24]Now as the church submits to Christ, so
5:23 [f]1Co 11:3; Eph 1:22 also wives should submit to their husbands in everything.
5:25 [g]Col 3:19 [h]ver 2 [25]Husbands, love your wives,[g] just as Christ loved the church and gave himself up for her[h] [26]to make
5:26 [i]Ac 22:16 her holy, cleansing[a] her by the washing[i] with water through the word, [27]and to present her to himself as
5:27 [j]Eph 1:4; Col 1:22 a radiant church, without stain or wrinkle or any other blemish, but holy and blameless.[j] [28]In this same
5:28 [k]ver 25 way, husbands ought to love their wives[k] as their own bodies. He who loves his wife loves himself. [29]Af-
ter all, no one ever hated his own body, but he feeds and cares for it, just as Christ does the church—
5:30 [l]1Co 12:27 [30]for we are members of his body.[l] [31]"For this reason a man will leave his father and mother and be unit-
5:31 [m]Ge 2:24; Mt 19:5; 1Co 6:16 ed to his wife, and the two will become one flesh."[b][m] [32]This is a profound mystery—but I am talking
5:33 [n]ver 25 about Christ and the church. [33]However, each one of you also must love his wife[n] as he loves himself, and
the wife must respect her husband.

Children and Parents

6:1 [o]Col 3:20 6 Children, obey your parents in the Lord, for this is right.[o] [2]"Honor your father and mother"—which
is the first commandment with a promise— [3]"that it may go well with you and that you may enjoy
6:3 [p]Ex 20:12 long life on the earth."[c][p]
6:4 [q]Col 3:21 [r]Ge 18:19; Dt 6:7 [4]Fathers, do not exasperate your children;[q] instead, bring them up in the training and instruction of
the Lord.[r]

Slaves and Masters

6:5 [s]1Ti 6:1 [t]Col 3:22 [5]Slaves, obey your earthly masters with respect[s] and fear, and with sincerity of heart,[t] just as you
[u]Eph 5:22 would obey Christ.[u] [6]Obey them not only to win their favor when their eye is on you, but like slaves of

[a] 26 Or *having cleansed* [b] 31 Gen. 2:24 [c] 3 Deut. 5:16

5:14 This quotation may well be from a hymn used by early Christians (see "Early Christian Hymnody" on p. 2007).
5:18 See "Wine and Alcoholic Beverages in the Ancient World" on page 2015.
5:22—6:9 "House codes" is the label assigned to those sections of Ephesians, Colossians and 1 Peter that give instructions to wives and husbands, children and parents, and slaves and masters. Unlike secular "house codes" of the day, those in the New Testament focused on the responsibilities of the more powerful persons in society (husbands, parents and masters) toward the dependent and vulnerable. (See "Husbands and Wives: Family Life in the Greco-Roman World" on p. 1922 and "The Demeanor of Wives" on p. 2013.)
5:23 For Jesus as Savior, see the note on Luke 2:11.
5:32 The Latin Vulgate translates the word "mystery" here as *sacramentum.* In classical times *sacramentum* was used in two chief senses: (1) as a technical legal term to denote the sum of money that the two parties to a suit deposited in a temple, of which the winner had his part returned, while the loser forfeited his to the temple treasury; or (2) as a technical military term to designate the oath of obedience of a soldier to his commanding officer. In the Greek New Testament there is no word corresponding to *sacrament,* nor do we find the word used in the earliest history of Christianity to refer to certain rites of the church. Pliny the Younger (c. A.D. 112) used the term in connection with Christianity in a famous letter in which he stated that the Christians of Bithynia bound themselves "by a sacramentum to commit no kind of crime," but it is doubtful that he was using the word with any special Christian nuance of meaning. The word *sacramentum* was used with a distinctively Christian meaning for the first time in the Old Latin Bible and in Tertullian (end of the second century). In the Old Latin and in the Vulgate it was employed, as here, to translate the Greek *mystērion,* "mystery" (see also 1Ti 3:16; Rev 1:20; 17:7). For a long time the word was used to refer not only to religious rites but also to doctrines and facts. For "mystery," see also the note on Romans 11:25.
6:1 In the Bible, "parents" (Greek: *goneis*) is a distinctly New Testament word, occurring only in the plural. Although this English word occurs only infrequently in the NIV Old Testament (and not at all in the KJV), there is much instruction there about the parent-child relationship. Children were to honor their parents (Ex 20:12) and to obey and reverence them (Lev 19:3; Dt 5:16). Failure to do so on the child's part could be punished by death (Dt 21:18–21). The same high regard for parents was expected of children in the New Testament (see also Col 3:20). Parents were in turn to love their children, to care and provide for them and to avoid provoking them to wrath (see also 2Co 12:14; Col 3:21).
6:5–9 In the Greek and Roman world, slavery was considered an economic and practical necessity, an assumed part of life. It is possible

Christ, doing the will of God from your heart. [7]Serve wholeheartedly, as if you were serving the Lord, not men,[v] [8]because you know that the Lord will reward everyone for whatever good he does,[w] whether he is slave or free.

[9]And masters, treat your slaves in the same way. Do not threaten them, since you know that he who is both their Master and yours[x] is in heaven, and there is no favoritism with him.

The Armor of God

[10]Finally, be strong in the Lord[y] and in his mighty power.[z] [11]Put on the full armor of God[a] so that you can take your stand against the devil's schemes. [12]For our struggle is not against flesh and blood, but against the rulers, against the authorities,[b] against the powers[c] of this dark world and against the spiritual forces of evil in the heavenly realms.[d] [13]Therefore put on the full armor of God, so that when the day of evil comes, you may be able to stand your ground, and after you have done everything, to stand. [14]Stand firm then, with the belt of truth buckled around your waist,[e] with the breastplate of righteousness in place,[f] [15]and with your feet fitted with the readiness that comes from the gospel of peace.[g] [16]In addition to all this, take up the shield of faith,[h] with which you can extinguish all the flaming arrows of the evil one. [17]Take the helmet of salvation[i] and the sword of the Spirit, which is the word of God.[j] [18]And pray in the Spirit on all occasions[k] with all kinds of prayers and requests.[l] With this in mind, be alert and always keep on praying for all the saints.

[19]Pray also for me,[m] that whenever I open my mouth, words may be given me so that I will fearlessly[n] make known the mystery of the gospel, [20]for which I am an ambassador[o] in chains.[p] Pray that I may declare it fearlessly, as I should.

Final Greetings

[21]Tychicus,[q] the dear brother and faithful servant in the Lord, will tell you everything, so that you also may know how I am and what I am doing. [22]I am sending him to you for this very purpose, that you may know how we are,[r] and that he may encourage you.

[23]Peace[s] to the brothers, and love with faith from God the Father and the Lord Jesus Christ. [24]Grace to all who love our Lord Jesus Christ with an undying love.

6:7 [v]Col 3:23
6:8 [w]Col 3:24
6:9 [x]Job 31:13, 14
6:10 [y]1Co 16:13 [z]Eph 1:19
6:11 [a]Ro 13:12
6:12 [b]Eph 1:21 [c]Ro 8:38 [d]Eph 1:3
6:14 [e]Isa 11:5 [f]Isa 59:17
6:15 [g]Isa 52:7
6:16 [h]1Jn 5:4
6:17 [i]Isa 59:17 [j]Heb 4:12
6:18 [k]Lk 18:1 [l]Mt 26:41; Php 1:4
6:19 [m]1Th 5:25 [n]Ac 4:29; 2Co 3:12
6:20 [o]2Co 5:20 [p]Ac 21:33
6:21 [q]Ac 20:4
6:22 [r]Col 4:7-9
06:23 [s]Gal 6:16; 1Pe 5:14

---

that up to one-third of the people living in Greece and Rome were slaves in Paul's day. People became slaves through birth, parental sale or abandonment, captivity in war, inability to pay debts or voluntary attempts to better their situations. Race was not a factor.

Both the Old and New Testaments included regulations governing societal realities such as slavery and divorce (see "Slavery in the Greco-Roman World" on p. 1979 and "Marriage and Divorce in Ancient Israel" on p. 1548). Such regulations did not encourage or condone such situations but were divinely-given, practical ways of dealing with them.

The directions Paul gave to slaves did not upset the cultural order but nevertheless subverted the concept of slavery. Slave owners were losing control, as Christian slaves now held to a higher allegiance than to their owners. They had become slaves of Christ, serving him and doing God's will. Furthermore, Christian owners were to treat their slaves the same way the slaves were to treat their masters.
the Isthmian games, see the note on 1 Corinthians 9:24–27.

6:13–14 Standing firm in this context is imagery not of a massive invasion of the domain of evil but of individual soldiers withstanding assault.

6:15 Whereas the description of the messenger's feet in Isaiah 52:7 reflects the custom of running barefoot, here the message of the gospel is picturesquely connected with the protective and supportive footgear of the Roman soldier.

6:16 This verse describes the large Roman shield covered with leather, which could be soaked in water and used to extinguish flame-tipped arrows.

6:17 The helmet protected the soldier and, under certain circumstances, provided a striking symbol of military victory.

6:19 For "mystery," see the note on Romans 11:25.

6:20 For "ambassador," see the note on 2 Corinthians 5:20.

6:21 Tychicus was an associate of Paul who traveled as his representative.

6:23 For "brothers," see the note on Romans 1:13.

INTRODUCTION TO 

AUTHOR, PLACE AND DATE OF WRITING

The author identified himself as Paul, and this has been accepted with little dissent. However, some interpreters consider Philippians to be a composite of several of Paul's letters to the Philippian church. Polycarp, bishop of Smyrna, mentioned in a letter to Philippi that Paul had sent "letters" to this church. Philippians does seem somewhat disjointed—the change in tone at 3:2 seems particularly abrupt—and this has led to the suggestion that the current book contains parts of several letters. However, it seems most likely that Philippians is one of several letters Paul wrote to Philippi, not a composite of several letters.

Candidates for the place and date of origination of this letter include Rome (c. 60–63), Ephesus (c. 54–57), Corinth (c. 50) and Caesarea (c. 58–60). It is clear that Paul was imprisoned at the time at or near a praetorium (1:13). There is no doubt that Paul endured multiple periods of confinement (2Co 11:23).

AUDIENCE

Paul wrote this letter to the believers in Philippi (see "Philippi" on p. 1927). The city was located at the gateway between Europe and Asia and was like a miniature Rome, with a large number of Roman citizens.

CULTURAL FACTS AND HIGHLIGHTS

The Philippians were proud of their Roman heritage (see Ac 16:21). They dressed like Romans (see "Dress and Fashion in the Greco-Roman World" on p. 2004) and often spoke Latin. Many Philippians were retired military men who had been given land in the vicinity and who in turn served as a military presence there.

There does not appear to be a single overriding concern behind this epistle. For the most part, this is simply a pastoral communication between Paul and a church that was especially dear to him.

TIMELINE

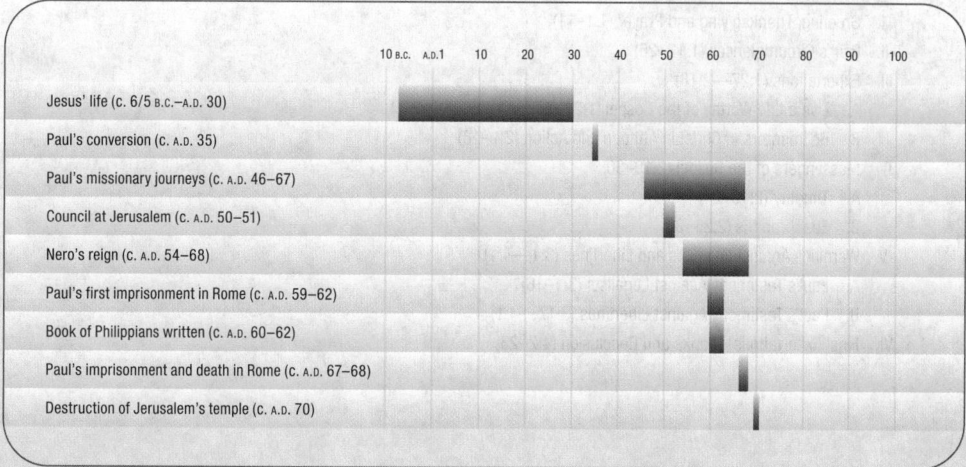

AS YOU READ

Watch for the repeated use of the words "joy" and "rejoice" throughout this letter. Note Paul's ability to find joy and contentment in any circumstance. Look for clues to the source of his joy. Notice that Paul held up Christ as the model for Christians to follow and included a beautiful psalm of praise to Jesus (2:5–11).

DID YOU KNOW?

- Philippi was a wealthy town because of nearby gold and silver mines (1:1).
- The "whole palace guard" was a contingent of soldiers numbering several thousand, many of whom would have had personal contact with Paul or would have been assigned individually to guard him during the course of his imprisonment (1:13).
- The winner of the Greek races received a wreath of leaves and sometimes a cash award (3:14).
- "Those who belong to Caesar's household" were not blood relatives of the emperor but those employed (as slaves or freedmen) in or around the palace area (4:22).

THEMES

Philippians includes the following themes:

1. *Joy.* Paul modeled joy in the midst of suffering and guided the Philippians in their situation of persecution (1:27–30; 2:14–16). His joy derived from his union with Christ (3:8; 4:12–13), his communion with other Christians (1:4–5) and the promise of the resurrection (3:10–11,20–21).

2. *Humility.* Believers are to imitate Christ, who modeled humility (2:3–4) by emptying himself in order to obey God and serve others, even to the point of death on the cross (2:8). Both Timothy and Epaphroditus exemplified the selfless attitude Paul wanted the community to emulate (2:19–30). In contrast, Euodia and Syntyche were at odds with one another (4:2–3).

3. *Thanksgiving.* Paul commended Epaphroditus for his life-endangering service to the apostle. He also acknowledged and thanked the Philippians for their missionary partnership and gift to himself. Paul had served them sacrificially (2:17), and they had responded in kind. He commended them for their Christian maturity, affirmed that they had received spiritual benefits from giving and assured them of God's reward.

OUTLINE

- I. Greeting, Thanksgiving and Prayer (1:1–11)
- II. Paul's Circumstances (1:12–26)
- III. Exhortations (1:27—2:18)
  - A. Live a Life Worthy of the Gospel (1:27–30)
  - B. Be Imitators of Christ in Attitude and Action (2:1–18)
- IV. Messengers of the Gospel (2:19–30)
  - A. Timothy (2:19–24)
  - B. Epaphroditus (2:25–30)
- V. Warnings Against Legalists and Libertines (3:1—4:1)
  - A. Paul's Testimony Against Legalists (3:1–16)
  - B. Paul's Testimony Against Libertines (3:17—4:1)
- VI. Final Exhortations, Thanks and Conclusion (4:2–23)

1:1 [a]Ac 16:1; 2Co 1:1 [b]Ac 9:13 [c]Ac 16:12 [d]1Ti 3:1 [e]1Ti 3:8
1:2 [f]Ro 1:7
1:3 [g]Ro 1:8
1:4 [h]Ro 1:10
1:5 [i]Ac 2:42; Php 4:15 [j]Ac 16:12-40
1:6 [k]ver 10; 1Co 1:8
1:7 [l]2Pe 1:13 [m]2Co 7:3 [n]ver 13, 14,17; Ac 21:33 [o]ver 16
1:8 [p]Ro 1:9
1:9 [q]1Th 3:12
1:10 [r]ver 6; 1Co 1:8
1:11 [s]Jas 3:18

1 Paul and Timothy,[a] servants of Christ Jesus,

To all the saints[b] in Christ Jesus at Philippi,[c] together with the overseers[a][d] and deacons:[e]

2 Grace and peace to you from God our Father and the Lord Jesus Christ.[f]

Thanksgiving and Prayer

3 I thank my God every time I remember you.[g] 4 In all my prayers for all of you, I always pray[h] with joy
5 because of your partnership[i] in the gospel from the first day[j] until now, 6 being confident of this, that he
who began a good work in you will carry it on to completion until the day of Christ Jesus.[k]
7 It is right[l] for me to feel this way about all of you, since I have you in my heart;[m] for whether I am in
chains[n] or defending[o] and confirming the gospel, all of you share in God's grace with me. 8 God can tes-
tify[p] how I long for all of you with the affection of Christ Jesus.
9 And this is my prayer: that your love[q] may abound more and more in knowledge and depth of insight,
10 so that you may be able to discern what is best and may be pure and blameless until the day of Christ,[r]
11 filled with the fruit of righteousness[s] that comes through Jesus Christ—to the glory and praise of God.

[a] 1 Traditionally *bishops*

1:1–2 As in all his epistles, Paul basically followed the conventional letter format of his day (see "Letter Writing in the Greco-Roman World" on p. 1889).

1:1 For information on Timothy, see the note on Acts 16:1. He is identified as Paul's associate, but not as the coauthor of this letter. Philippi was a wealthy town because of nearby gold and silver mines. Today the Greek city of Kavalla is located 9 miles (14.5 km) from its ruins. (See "Philippi" on p. 1927.)

For "overseers," see the note on 1 Timothy 3:1–7 and for "deacons" the note on 1 Timothy 3:8–13.

ARCHAEOLOGICAL SITES

PHILIPPI

PHILIPPIANS 1 The city of Philippi ("Map 13") in Paul's day boasted a remarkably colorful history:

- In 359 B.C. the orator Callistratus and some Greek colonists from the island of Thasos founded a colony called Krenides in northern Greece near Macedonia and Thrace.
- In 356 B.C. Philip II of Macedon seized the gold mines near the site, fortified the city wall, drained the nearby marshes, constructed a theater, increased the city's size and renamed it after himself.
- Alexander the Great (the son of Philip II) used Philippi as a base for his conquests.
- In the second century B.C. Macedonia was captured by the Romans and Philippi became a Roman outpost.
- In 42 B.C., in the civil war following Julius Caesar's assassination, Octavian (Augustus)[1] and Mark Antony defeated the forces of Cassius and Brutus at a major battle near Philippi.
- Octavian, also victorious in a subsequent war against Mark Antony and Cleopatra, renamed the city Colonia Julia Augusta Philippensis and settled a number of Roman veterans there.
- Paul's missionary work in Europe began at Philippi, and it was there that the first baptisms in Europe took place (Ac 16:9–33).[2]

Situated near the Via Egnatia, Philippi lay between Asia and Europe and was thus an excellent base of operations for Lydia, a dealer in purple cloth (Ac 16:14–15), since she could acquire this commodity from the east and sell it to Romans and Greeks in the west.[3] Acts 16:12 is sometimes taken to mean that Philippi was the administrative center of the district of Macedonia, but the Greek text of this verse is uncertain and may actually mean that Philippi was "a city of the first district of Macedonia." Evidence from Pliny the Elder (*Natural History*, 4.38) indicates that the capital city of this region was Amphipolis. A theater that was in use in Paul's day can still be found in Philippi, and a stone crypt near the forum is traditionally identified as Paul's jail (Ac 16:23), although this tradition has not been verified.

The Philippi of Paul's day was essentially a Roman city in Greece. Its Roman citizens enjoyed the same legal rights as those in Italy, and Latin became the common language of the city. The heavy Roman presence in Philippi may account for the greeting from "Caesar's household" in Philippians 4:22. Still, Paul reminded his Christian readers, their citizenship was in heaven (Php 3:20).

[1]See "Caesar Augustus, Emperor of Rome; the Census; and Quirinius, Governor of Syria" on page 1667. [2]See "The Missionary Journeys of Paul" on page 1795. [3]See "Trade and Mercantilism in the Roman Empire" on page 2070.

Paul's Chains Advance the Gospel

12 Now I want you to know, brothers, that what has happened to me has really served to advance the
gospel. 13 As a result, it has become clear throughout the whole palace guard[a] and to everyone else that I
am in chains[t] for Christ. 14 Because of my chains,[u] most of the brothers in the Lord have been encouraged **1:13** [t] ver 7,14,17
to speak the word of God more courageously and fearlessly. **1:14** [u] ver 7,13,17
15 It is true that some preach Christ out of envy and rivalry, but others out of goodwill. 16 The latter do
so in love, knowing that I am put here for the defense of the gospel.[v] 17 The former preach Christ out of **1:16** [v] ver 7,12
selfish ambition,[w] not sincerely, supposing that they can stir up trouble for me while I am in chains.[b][x] **1:17** [w] Php 2:3
18 But what does it matter? The important thing is that in every way, whether from false motives or true, [x] ver 7,13,14
Christ is preached. And because of this I rejoice.
Yes, and I will continue to rejoice, 19 for I know that through your prayers[y] and the help given by the **1:19** [y] 2Co 1:11
Spirit of Jesus Christ,[z] what has happened to me will turn out for my deliverance.[c] 20 I eagerly expect[a] [z] Ac 16:7 **1:20** [a] Ro 8:19
and hope that I will in no way be ashamed, but will have sufficient courage[b] so that now as always Christ [b] ver 14 [c] 1Co 6:20
will be exalted in my body,[c] whether by life or by death.[d] 21 For to me, to live is Christ[e] and to die is gain. [d] Ro 14:8 **1:21** [e] Gal 2:20
22 If I am to go on living in the body, this will mean fruitful labor for me. Yet what shall I choose? I do not
know! 23 I am torn between the two: I desire to depart[f] and be with Christ,[g] which is better by far; 24 but **1:23** [f] 2Ti 4:6
it is more necessary for you that I remain in the body. 25 Convinced of this, I know that I will remain, and [g] Jn 12:26; 2Co 5:8
I will continue with all of you for your progress and joy in the faith, 26 so that through my being with you
again your joy in Christ Jesus will overflow on account of me.
27 Whatever happens, conduct yourselves in a manner worthy[h] of the gospel of Christ. Then, wheth- **1:27** [h] Eph 4:1
er I come and see you or only hear about you in my absence, I will know that you stand firm[i] in one [i] 1Co 16:13
spirit, contending[j] as one man for the faith of the gospel 28 without being frightened in any way by those [j] Jude 3
who oppose you. This is a sign to them that they will be destroyed, but that you will be saved—and
that by God. 29 For it has been granted to you[k] on behalf of Christ not only to believe on him, but also to **1:29** [k] Mt 5:11,12
suffer[l] for him, 30 since you are going through the same struggle[m] you saw[n] I had, and now hear[o] that I [l] Ac 14:22 **1:30** [m] Col 2:1; 1Th 2:2
still have. [n] Ac 16:19-40 [o] ver 13

Imitating Christ's Humility

2 If you have any encouragement from being united with Christ, if any comfort from his love, if any
fellowship with the Spirit,[p] if any tenderness and compassion,[q] 2 then make my joy complete[r] by be- **2:1** [p] 2Co 13:14 [q] Col 3:12
ing like-minded,[s] having the same love, being one[t] in spirit and purpose. 3 Do nothing out of selfish am- **2:2** [r] Jn 3:29 [s] Php 4:2
bition or vain conceit,[u] but in humility consider others better than yourselves.[v] 4 Each of you should look [t] Ro 12:16
not only to your own interests, but also to the interests of others. **2:3** [u] Gal 5:26 [v] Ro 12:10; 1Pe 5:5
5 Your attitude should be the same as that of Christ Jesus:[w] **2:5** [w] Mt 11:29

6 Who, being in very nature[d] God,[x] **2:6** [x] Jn 1:1 [y] Jn 5:18
did not consider equality with God[y] something to be grasped,
7 but made himself nothing,
taking the very nature[e] of a servant,[z] **2:7** [z] Mt 20:28
being made in human likeness.[a] [a] Jn 1:14; Heb 2:17
8 And being found in appearance as a man,
he humbled himself

[a] *13* Or *whole palace* [b] *16,17* Some late manuscripts have verses 16 and 17 in reverse order. [c] *19* Or *salvation* [d] *6* Or *in the form of* [e] *7* Or *the form*

1:12 For "brothers," see the note on Romans 1:13.

It is evident that Paul wrote this letter from prison (see "Imprisonment in the Roman World: In Prison Versus House Arrest" on p. 1826). Some have argued that this imprisonment took place in Ephesus, perhaps about A.D. 54–57. Others place it in Caesarea in about 58–60. The best evidence, however, favors Rome as the place of origin and the date as about 60–63 (see the book introduction on p. 1925).

1:13 *Praetorium,* sometimes spelled *Pretorium,* was the Latin term for the Greek *praitôrion,* which among the Romans could refer to a number of things. Originally it identified the general's tent in the camp of an army station, although sometimes the reference was to the military headquarters in Rome itself or in the provincial capitals. The word also denoted the staff of men in such an establishment or even the session of a planning council. In the Gospels (Mt 27:27; Mk 15:16; Jn 18:28,33), the term refers to the temporary palace or headquarters ("judgment hall") of the Roman governor or procurator while he was in Jerusalem, which was actually Herod's palace, adjacent to the temple (cf. Ac 23:35). This was the scene of Jesus' trial before Pontius Pilate. No doubt the debated reference in this verse (cf. "Caesar's household," Php 4:22) refers to the headquarters of the emperor's bodyguard, which could have been either in Rome or in one of the provincial capitals.

The "whole palace guard" was a contingent of soldiers numbering several thousand, many of whom would have had personal contact with Paul or would have been assigned individually to guard him during the course of his imprisonment.

1:15–16 See the note on 2 Timothy 1:15.

2:6–11 Many view these verses as an early Christian hymn (see "Early Christian Hymnody" on p. 2007), perhaps modified by Paul.

2:8 Crucifixion was the most degrading form of execution that could be inflicted on a person at the time (see "Crucifixion" on p. 1757).

2:8 [b]Mt 26:39; Jn 10:18; Heb 5:8 — and became obedient to death[b]—
even death on a cross!
2:9 [c]Ac 2:33; Heb 2:9 — 9 Therefore God exalted him[c] to the highest place
[d]Eph 1:20,21 — and gave him the name that is above every name,[d]
2:10 [e]Ro 14:11 — 10 that at the name of Jesus every knee should bow,[e]
[f]Mt 28:18 — in heaven and on earth and under the earth,[f]
2:11 [g]Jn 13:13 — 11 and every tongue confess that Jesus Christ is Lord,[g]
to the glory of God the Father.

Shining as Stars

12 Therefore, my dear friends, as you have always obeyed—not only in my presence, but now much
2:12 [h]2Co 7:15 — more in my absence—continue to work out your salvation with fear and trembling,[h] 13 for it is God who
2:13 [i]Ezr 1:5 — works in you[i] to will and to act according to his good purpose.
2:14 [j]1Co 10:10; 1Pe 4:9 — 14 Do everything without complaining[j] or arguing, 15 so that you may become blameless and pure, chil-
2:15 [k]Mt 5:45,48; Eph 5:1 [l]Ac 2:40 — dren of God[k] without fault in a crooked and depraved generation,[l] in which you shine like stars in the uni-
verse 16 as you hold out[a] the word of life—in order that I may boast on the day of Christ that I did not
2:16 [m]1Th 2:19 — run or labor for nothing.[m] 17 But even if I am being poured out like a drink offering[n] on the sacrifice[o]
2:17 [n]2Ti 4:6 [o]Ro 15:16 — and service coming from your faith, I am glad and rejoice with all of you. 18 So you too should be glad and
rejoice with me.

Timothy and Epaphroditus

2:19 [p]ver 23 — 19 I hope in the Lord Jesus to send Timothy to you soon,[p] that I also may be cheered when I receive
2:20 [q]1Co 16:10 — news about you. 20 I have no one else like him,[q] who takes a genuine interest in your welfare. 21 For every-
2:21 [r]1Co 10:24; 13:5 — one looks out for his own interests,[r] not those of Jesus Christ. 22 But you know that Timothy has proved
2:22 [s]1Co 4:17; 1Ti 1:2 — himself, because as a son with his father[s] he has served with me in the work of the gospel. 23 I hope, there-
2:23 [t]ver 19 — fore, to send him as soon as I see how things go with me.[t] 24 And I am confident[u] in the Lord that I my-
2:24 [u]Php 1:25 — self will come soon.

2:25 [v]Php 4:3 — 25 But I think it is necessary to send back to you Epaphroditus, my brother, fellow worker[v] and fellow
[w]Phm 2 [x]Php 4:18 — soldier,[w] who is also your messenger, whom you sent to take care of my needs.[x] 26 For he longs for all of
2:26 [y]Php 1:8 — you[y] and is distressed because you heard he was ill. 27 Indeed he was ill, and almost died. But God had
mercy on him, and not on him only but also on me, to spare me sorrow upon sorrow. 28 Therefore I am
all the more eager to send him, so that when you see him again you may be glad and I may have less anx-
2:29 [z]1Co 16:18; 1Ti 5:17 — iety. 29 Welcome him in the Lord with great joy, and honor men like him,[z] 30 because he almost died for
2:30 [a]1Co 16:17 — the work of Christ, risking his life to make up for the help you could not give me.[a]

No Confidence in the Flesh

3 Finally, my brothers, rejoice in the Lord! It is no trouble for me to write the same things to you again,
and it is a safeguard for you.
3:2 [b]Ps 22:16,20 — 2 Watch out for those dogs,[b] those men who do evil, those mutilators of the flesh. 3 For it is we who are
3:3 [c]Ro 2:28,29; Gal 6:15; Col 2:11 — the circumcision,[c] we who worship by the Spirit of God, who glory in Christ Jesus, and who put no con-
fidence in the flesh— 4 though I myself have reasons for such confidence.
3:5 [d]Lk 1:59 [e]2Co 11:22 — If anyone else thinks he has reasons to put confidence in the flesh, I have more: 5 circumcised[d] on the
[f]Ro 11:1 [g]Ac 23:6 — eighth day, of the people of Israel,[e] of the tribe of Benjamin,[f] a Hebrew of Hebrews; in regard to the law,
3:6 [h]Ac 8:3 [i]Ro 10:5 — a Pharisee;[g] 6 as for zeal, persecuting the church;[h] as for legalistic righteousness,[i] faultless.

[a] 16 Or *hold on to*

2:16 For commentary on running a "[foot] race," see the note on 1 Corinthians 9:24–27.
2:17 A "drink offering" was wine poured out as a sacrifice to the Lord. The reference may be to Paul's entire ministry as one large thanksgiving sacrifice. However, it is more probable that Paul was referring to his present imprisonment, which could have ended in a martyr's death. His life would then have been poured out as a drink offering accompanying the sacrificial service of the Philippians. See also the note on 2 Timothy 4:6.
2:19–23 Paul planned to send Timothy (see the note on Ac 16:1), who was with him in Rome, to discover and report on conditions in the Philippian church.
3:2 "Dogs" is a harsh word for Paul's opponents. Their teaching was probably similar to that of the Judaizers (see the note on Gal 1:7). They had so distorted the meaning of circumcision (see "Circumcision in the Ancient World" on p. 1840) that the practice had become nothing more than a useless cutting of the body (a mutilation).
3:5 Paul was born a Jew and was not a proselyte (see "Proselytes in Second Temple Judaism" on p. 1776). His Jewish roots were deep and unambiguous; in language, attitudes and lifestyle, he was a Hebrew. He had also been a Pharisee (see the note on Mt 3:7, as well as "The Pharisees" on p. 1566).

7 But whatever was to my profit I now consider loss[j] for the sake of Christ. 8 What is more, I consider 3:7 [j]Mt 13:44; Lk 14:33
everything a loss compared to the surpassing greatness of knowing[k] Christ Jesus my Lord, for whose 3:8 [k]Eph 4:13; 2Pe 1:2
sake I have lost all things. I consider them rubbish, that I may gain Christ 9 and be found in him, not hav-
ing a righteousness of my own that comes from the law,[l] but that which is through faith in Christ—the 3:9 [l]Ro 10:5 [m]Ro 9:30
righteousness that comes from God and is by faith.[m] 10 I want to know Christ and the power of his res-
urrection and the fellowship of sharing in his sufferings,[n] becoming like him in his death,[o] 11 and so, 3:10 [n]Ro 8:17 [o]Ro 6:3-5
somehow, to attain to the resurrection[p] from the dead. 3:11 [p]Rev 20:5,6

Pressing on Toward the Goal

12 Not that I have already obtained all this, or have already been made perfect,[q] but I press on to take 3:12 [q]1Co 13:10 [r]1Ti 6:12 [s]Ac 9:5,6
hold[r] of that for which Christ Jesus took hold of me.[s] 13 Brothers, I do not consider myself yet to have tak-
en hold of it. But one thing I do: Forgetting what is behind[t] and straining toward what is ahead, 14 I press 3:13 [t]Lk 9:62
on[u] toward the goal to win the prize for which God has called[v] me heavenward in Christ Jesus. 3:14 [u]Heb 6:1 [v]Ro 8:28
15 All of us who are mature[w] should take such a view of things.[x] And if on some point you think dif- 3:15 [w]1Co 2:6 [x]Gal 5:10
ferently, that too God will make clear to you. 16 Only let us live up to what we have already attained.
17 Join with others in following my example,[y] brothers, and take note of those who live according to the 3:17 [y]1Co 4:16; 1Pe 5:3
pattern we gave you. 18 For, as I have often told you before and now say again even with tears,[z] many live 3:18 [z]Ac 20:31 [a]Gal 6:12
as enemies of the cross of Christ.[a] 19 Their destiny is destruction, their god is their stomach,[b] and their 3:19 [b]Ro 16:18

3:12–14 For commentary on the Isthmian games, see the note on 1 Corinthians 9:24–27.

3:14 The winner of the Greek races received a wreath of leaves and sometimes a cash award (see the note on 1 Co 9:24–27).

Roman Citizenship

PHILIPPIANS 3 Paul was acutely aware of his dual citizenship. In Philippians 3:20 he stated clearly that "our citizenship is in heaven," and he made it clear to the Philippian Christians that this, and not a Jewish pedigree, is what really matters before God. But Paul also knew himself to be a Roman citizen, and in Acts 22:25–29 he claimed the rights of a citizen. (Paul further considered himself a citizen of Tarsus—Ac 21:39—as well as, of course, a loyal Jew.) But what precisely did it mean in the first century A.D. to be a Roman citizen?

Roman citizenship carried with it several important privileges, including the right to vote, exemption from certain taxes[1] and certain legal protections (although Rome did at times extend citizenship without voting rights to the residents of certain cities). Ancient legal codes did not strive, even in theory, to achieve equality before the law. For example, Roman citizens were not to be tortured and generally were not executed without a judicial process, while noncitizens (and especially slaves)[2] were summarily tortured by the authorities.

Over the course of its history, Rome gradually extended citizenship more and more broadly. During the early expansion of Roman power, from the third through the first centuries B.C., Italian cities under Roman rule agitated for and eventually won Roman citizenship for their people. By the standards of the times, Rome became quite generous in granting citizenship. Freed slaves of Romans, for example, automatically became citizens. Paul claimed to be a citizen by birthright (Ac 22:28), although we do not know how his parents had acquired citizenship. In A.D. 212 Emperor Caracalla extended citizenship to all freeborn provincials in the "Antonine constitution," but by this time the distinctive rights of Roman citizenship had so eroded that the act had little significance.

In Paul's day, however, possession of Roman citizenship was still vitally important. Even so, Paul's notion of citizenship in heaven was not derived primarily from Roman analogies. Psalm 87 celebrates the fact that, by divine decree, people from Egypt, Babylon and elsewhere are said to have been "born" in Zion (Ps 87:4). Although the term "citizen" is not used there, it could hardly have escaped Paul's notice that this ancient psalm already treated Gentiles as natural-born members of the heavenly kingdom.

[1]See "Roman Taxation" on page 1855. [2]See "Slavery in the Greco-Roman World" on page 1979.

3:19 cRo 6:21 dRo 8:5,6 3:20 eEph 2:19 fCol 3:1 g1Co 1:7 3:21 hEph 1:19 i1Co 15:43-53 jCol 3:4 4:1 kPhp 1:8 l1Co 16:13

glory is in their shame.[c] Their mind is on earthly things.[d] 20 But our citizenship[e] is in heaven.[f] And we ea-
gerly await a Savior from there, the Lord Jesus Christ,[g] 21 who, by the power[h] that enables him to bring ev-
erything under his control, will transform our lowly bodies[i] so that they will be like his glorious body.[j]
4 Therefore, my brothers, you whom I love and long for,[k] my joy and crown, that is how you should
stand firm[l] in the Lord, dear friends!

3:20 Paul stated that he had become a Roman citizen by birth. Either his father or some other ancestor had acquired this right and had transmitted it to his son. Paul was proud of his Roman citizenship and, when occasion demanded, availed himself of his rights. When writing to the Philippians, who were members of a Roman colony and therefore also Roman citizens, Paul emphasized that Christians are citizens of a heavenly commonwealth and ought to live accordingly.

Nero, Persecutor of Christians

PHILIPPIANS 4 Nero was emperor for 14 years, from A.D. 54 to 68. His first five years were considered exemplary, probably because of good advisors, such as the renowned Seneca. During this early period Nero demonstrated more respect for the Senate than had his predecessors and reversed some of the cruelty and excesses of power that former emperors had exercised. After Nero's initial five years as emperor, however, one of his trusted advisors died and another retired to private life. Thereafter, the emperor sank into immorality and crime, to the point of being implicated in the murders of his own mother and cousin.

In A.D. 64 fire destroyed much of Rome. Many attributed the blaze to Nero himself, for it quickly became known that he intended to build his new palace on the site of the burned quarters, seizing a good deal of private property for the state. To avoid charges, Nero shifted blame to the Christians. It is reported that Nero burned Christians alive, using them as human torches during his circus races.

In 66, after the district had endured a series of harsh governors, rebellion broke out in Judea, and Nero sent his general Vespasian to suppress the Jews. Meanwhile, he traveled to Greece to compete in the festivals there. His trip culminated in his declaration that Greece was henceforth free from Roman rule and taxation, an act that won him the lasting goodwill of the Greeks.[1] The following year Nero committed suicide in a country villa, while rebellion intensified within the Senate and aristocracy. In the aftermath of Nero's death in A.D. 68, Vespasian left Judea to seize the throne in Rome. Titus, Vespasian's son, took charge of the Roman army in Judea and went on to destroy Jerusalem in A.D. 70, fulfilling the prophecy of Jesus (Mt 24:1–2; Mk 13:1–2; Lk 21:5–6).

Gladiator's helmet
Preserving Bible Times; © Dr. James C. Martin; permission of The British Museum

Paul's imprisonment and subsequent trial in Caesarea probably took place around 57–59; thus, all of the references to "Caesar" in Acts 25–28 are to Nero. Paul was transferred to Rome and spent at least two years there as a prisoner during Nero's reign (Ac 28:30). Throughout the years of Paul's missionary journeys, Christianity was rapidly making inroads in Rome. By the time the apostle himself arrived, there were already many there who followed "the Way" (Ac 9:2; 19:23; 22:4; 24:14,22), including numerous individuals employed in the imperial palace. Philippians was likely written in Rome while Paul was under house arrest there.[2] At the end of the letter he sent greetings from the saints, "especially those who belong to Caesar's household" (Php 4:22).

While Nero began his career with distinction and merit, even winning the love and gratitude of the commoners through the many games and festivals he sponsored, he is remembered most for instigating the Roman persecution of Christians. This policy of persecuting Christians was continued by Roman authorities until the fourth century.[3]

[1]See "Roman Taxation" on page 1855. [2]See "Imprisonment in the Roman World: In Prison Versus House Arrest" on page 1826. [3]See "The Geographic Expansion of the Church Under Persecution" on page 1781 and "The Early Persecution of the Church" on page 2067.

Exhortations

2 I plead with Euodia and I plead with Syntyche to agree with each other[m] in the Lord. 3 Yes, and I ask 4:2 [m]Php 2:2
you, loyal yokefellow,[a] help these women who have contended at my side in the cause of the gospel, along
with Clement and the rest of my fellow workers, whose names are in the book of life.
4 Rejoice in the Lord always. I will say it again: Rejoice![n] 5 Let your gentleness be evident to all. The 4:4 [n]Ro 12:12; Php 3:1
Lord is near.[o] 6 Do not be anxious about anything,[p] but in everything, by prayer and petition, with thanks- 4:5 [o]Heb 10:37; Jas 5:8,9
giving, present your requests to God.[q] 7 And the peace of God,[r] which transcends all understanding, will 4:6 [p]Mt 6:25-34 [q]Eph 6:18
guard your hearts and your minds in Christ Jesus. 4:7 [r]Isa 26:3; Jn 14:27; Col 3:15
8 Finally, brothers, whatever is true, whatever is noble, whatever is right, whatever is pure, whatever is
lovely, whatever is admirable—if anything is excellent or praiseworthy—think about such things.
9 Whatever you have learned or received or heard from me, or seen in me—put it into practice.[s] And the 4:9 [s]Php 3:17 [t]Ro 15:33
God of peace[t] will be with you.

Thanks for Their Gifts

10 I rejoice greatly in the Lord that at last you have renewed your concern for me.[u] Indeed, you have 4:10 [u]2Co 11:9
been concerned, but you had no opportunity to show it. 11 I am not saying this because I am in need, for
I have learned to be content[v] whatever the circumstances. 12 I know what it is to be in need, and I know 4:11 [v]1Ti 6:6,8
what it is to have plenty. I have learned the secret of being content in any and every situation, whether
well fed or hungry,[w] whether living in plenty or in want.[x] 13 I can do everything through him who gives 4:12 [w]1Co 4:11 [x]2Co 11:9
me strength.[y] 4:13 [y]2Co 12:9
14 Yet it was good of you to share[z] in my troubles. 15 Moreover, as you Philippians know, in the early 4:14 [z]Php 1:7
days[a] of your acquaintance with the gospel, when I set out from Macedonia, not one church shared with 4:15 [a]Php 1:5 [b]2Co 11:8,9
me in the matter of giving and receiving, except you only;[b] 16 for even when I was in Thessalonica,[c] you 4:16 [c]Ac 17:1 [d]1Th 2:9
sent me aid again and again when I was in need.[d] 17 Not that I am looking for a gift, but I am looking for
what may be credited to your account.[e] 18 I have received full payment and even more; I am amply sup- 4:17 [e]1Co 9:11, 12
plied, now that I have received from Epaphroditus[f] the gifts you sent. They are a fragrant[g] offering, an 4:18 [f]Php 2:25 [g]2Co 2:14
acceptable sacrifice, pleasing to God. 19 And my God will meet all your needs[h] according to his glorious 4:19 [h]Ps 23:1; 2Co 9:8 [i]Ro 2:4
riches[i] in Christ Jesus.
20 To our God and Father[j] be glory for ever and ever. Amen.[k] 4:20 [j]Gal 1:4 [k]Ro 11:36

Final Greetings

21 Greet all the saints in Christ Jesus. The brothers who are with me[l] send greetings. 22 All the saints[m] 4:21 [l]Gal 1:2 4:22 [m]Ac 9:13
send you greetings, especially those who belong to Caesar's household.
23 The grace of the Lord Jesus Christ[n] be with your spirit. Amen.[b] 4:23 [n]Ro 16:20

[a] 3 Or *loyal Syzygus* [b] 23 Some manuscripts do not have *Amen.*

4:3 The Greek *syzygos* ("yoked together") was common among Greek writers in referring to those united by close bonds, as in marriage, labor, etc. It is found only here in the New Testament, and its meaning is not clear. Some feel that Paul was referring here to a fellow worker, while others think the word was the proper name of the man he was addressing, Syzygus.

4:7 This verse depicts a military sentry standing guard.

4:8 See "Speech Ethics" on page 2005.

4:14–15 The church at Philippi in ancient Macedonia was the first European church founded by Paul and thus represents the first major penetration of the gospel into Europe. The events leading to the founding of the congregation are related in Acts 16:9–40. The apostle Paul, accompanied by his coworkers Silas, Timothy and Luke, was on his second missionary journey through Asia Minor. Forbidden by the Holy Spirit to preach in Asia and in Bithynia to the north, they made their way to Troas, the farthest port of Asia on the Aegean Sea. In Troas Paul received a vision from the Lord, instructing him to take the gospel to Europe. A man stood before him, a Greek from Macedonia, begging him, "Come over to Macedonia and help us" (Ac 16:9). Paul and his companions immediately answered this divine call and set sail from the nearest port—Neopolis of Philippi, named after Phillip II of Macedon, the father of Alexander the Great.

Philippi had been thoroughly colonized by the Romans after 30 B.C., but the city was still more Greek than Roman in culture. Also, it was the first station on the Egnation Way and the gateway to the East. Luke described the city as follows: "From there we traveled to Philippi, a Roman colony and the leading city of that district of Macedonia" (Ac 16:12).

4:15 Macedonia was the northern part of modern-day Greece, where Berea, Philippi and the capital city of Thessalonica were located.

4:16 See "Thessalonica" on page 1944.

4:18 The "fragrant offering" has its background is the Old Testament sacrifice—not a sacrifice of atonement for sin, but one of thanksgiving and praise (see the notes on Ro 12:1; Eph 5:2).

4:22 Those "who belong to Caesar's household" were not blood relatives of the emperor but those employed (as slaves or freedmen) in or around the palace area (cf. "palace guard," 1:13).

INTRODUCTION TO 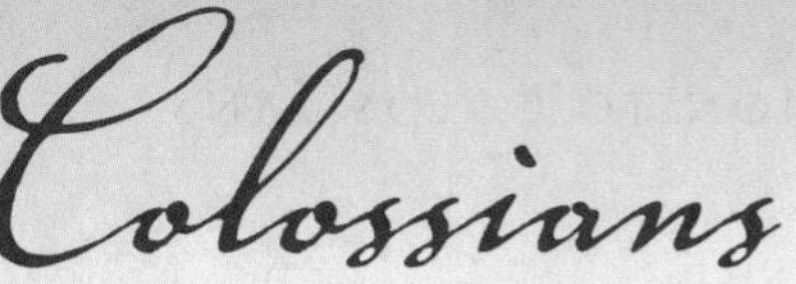

AUTHOR, PLACE AND DATE OF WRITING

This letter presents itself as being from Paul. Today, however, a number of scholars consider it to be pseudonymous (a forgery attributed to Paul). Some have argued that the letter's style is unlike Paul's—an argument that is difficult to demonstrate in so short an epistle. Some point out that the exalted and cosmic language used of Christ in 1:15–20 goes beyond what we see in Paul's other letters, but in reality such ideas appear in passages such as 1 Corinthians 8:6. Other objections to Pauline authorship of Colossians (e.g., that it lacks Paul's emphasis on faith versus works) are weak.

Similarities to Ephesians suggest that Paul wrote the two letters at nearly the same time. Colosse was in the Lycus valley, inland from Ephesus and not far from Laodicea, and Paul evidently sent out the letters to a number of churches in the area, with Ephesians perhaps being a circular letter (see "The Letter From the Laodiceans" on p. 1940 and "The Authorship of Ephesians" on p. 1919). Paul was in prison at the time Colossians was written (4:3)—most likely in Rome but possibly in Caesarea. A date of writing of about A.D. 60 seems probable.

AUDIENCE

This letter was written to the believers in Colosse. The church there had been planted by Paul's coworker Epaphras (1:7; 4:12), who joined Paul while he was under house arrest in Rome (4:12; Phm 23; see Ac 28:16–31), during which time the apostle likely wrote this letter.

CULTURAL FACTS AND HIGHLIGHTS

Epaphras had just brought a report to Paul on the situation of the churches in the Lycus Valley. Although much of the news was good, certain matters concerned Paul. A brand of false teaching had arisen in Colosse, but it is unclear whether this was a unified body of false doctrine or an amalgam of errors, superstitions and misunderstandings. Elements included taboos about food and holy days, devotion to angelic beings and a pseudo-sophisticated theology that may have had something to do with the later Gnostic heresies (ch. 2). A large portion of the letter, however, is taken up with general exhortations to Christian living (see especially chs. 3–4).

TIMELINE

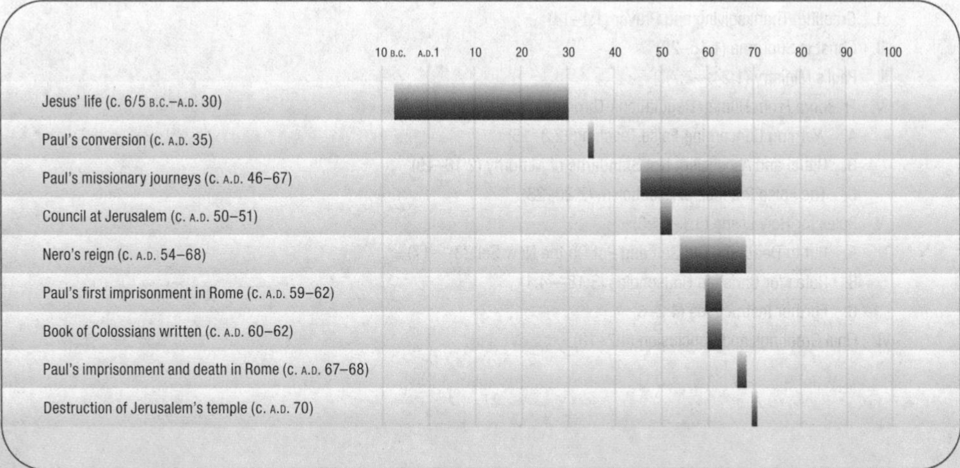

AS YOU READ

Look for an eloquent passage on the supremacy of Christ, note the basic standards for Christian living and family interactions and take to heart Paul's warning against mixing elements from various religions.

DID YOU KNOW?

- "Written code" was a business term, referring to a certificate of indebtedness in the debtor's own handwriting (2:14).
- Disarming the enemy is a picture of conquered soldiers stripped of their clothing and weapons to symbolize their total defeat (2:15).
- The central error of the Colossian heresy was a defective view of Christ, in that he was believed to be less than deity (2:19).
- A "barbarian" referred to someone who did not speak Greek and was on that basis thought to be uncivilized (3:11).

THEMES

Colossians includes the following themes:

1. *A warning against heresy.* Paul labeled the Colossian heresy a vain deceit based on human tradition and the "basic principles of this world" (2:8,20). It denied Christ's sufficiency and belittled Christian hope in his finished work on the cross.

2. *The supremacy of Christ.* Paul affirmed that: (a) Christ is God (1:15; 2:9); (b) he is the Creator of *all* things (1:16); (c) all the fullness of God dwells in him (1:19; 2:9); (d) Christ is superior to the angels (2:10,15); (e) Christ is the head of the church (1:18), through whom believers have "fullness" (2:10); (f) in Christ all the requirements of the Mosaic Law have been met (2:11,16–17); (g) asceticism has no value (2:23), while a life "hidden in Christ" (3:3) brings glory (3:4); and (h) Christ himself is the "mystery of God" (2:2; see 1:25–27; 4:3); no other secret knowledge is necessary.

3. *Christian living.* Paul insisted that the believer's union with Christ (3:1–4) results in holy living. He outlined clear standards (3:5–17) that prescribe attitudes that are to govern relationships within family and church. Leadership is to be exercised, but domination is unacceptable.

OUTLINE

I. Greeting, Thanksgiving and Prayer (1:1–14)
II. Christ Is Supreme (1:15–23)
III. Paul's Ministry (1:24—2:7)
IV. Freedom From Human Regulations Through Life in Christ (2:8–23)
  A. Warning Concerning False Teaching (2:8–15)
  B. Ritual and Asceticism Not Standards of Maturity (2:16–19)
  C. The False Practice of Asceticism (2:20–23)
V. Rules for Holy Living (3:1—4:6)
  A. Put to Death the Old Self and Put On the New Self (3:1–17)
  B. Rules for Christian Households (3:18—4:1)
  C. Further Instructions (4:2–6)
VI. Final Greetings and Conclusion (4:7–18)

1:1 [a]1Co 1:1 [b]2Co 1:1 **1** Paul, an apostle[a] of Christ Jesus by the will of God,[b] and Timothy our brother,

2 To the holy and faithful[a] brothers in Christ at Colosse:

1:2 [c]Col 4:18 [d]Ro 1:7 Grace[c] and peace to you from God our Father.[bd]

Thanksgiving and Prayer

1:3 [e]Ro 1:8 3 We always thank God,[e] the Father of our Lord Jesus Christ, when we pray for you, 4 because we have
1:4 [f]Gal 5:6 [g]Eph 1:15 heard of your faith in Christ Jesus and of the love[f] you have for all the saints[g]— 5 the faith and love that
1:5 [h]1Th 5:8; Tit 1:2 [i]1Pe 1:4 spring from the hope[h] that is stored up for you in heaven[i] and that you have already heard about in the
1:6 [j]Ro 10:18 [k]Jn 15:16 word of truth, the gospel 6 that has come to you. All over the world[j] this gospel is bearing fruit[k] and grow-
ing, just as it has been doing among you since the day you heard it and understood God's grace in all its
1:7 [l]Phm 23 [m]Col 4:7 truth. 7 You learned it from Epaphras,[l] our dear fellow servant, who is a faithful minister[m] of Christ on
1:8 [n]Ro 15:30 our[c] behalf, 8 and who also told us of your love in the Spirit.[n]
1:9 [o]Eph 1:15 [p]Eph 5:17 [q]Eph 1:17 9 For this reason, since the day we heard about you,[o] we have not stopped praying for you and asking
God to fill you with the knowledge of his will[p] through all spiritual wisdom and understanding.[q] 10 And

[a] 2 Or *believing* [b] 2 Some manuscripts *Father and the Lord Jesus Christ* [c] 7 Some manuscripts *your*

1:1–2 Ancient letters typically began with a simple identification of the sender and the recipients, followed by a greeting (see "Letter Writing in the Greco-Roman World" on p. 1889).

1:1 For "apostle," see the note on 2 Corinthians 1:1.
For "Timothy," see the note on Acts 16:1.

1:2 For "brothers," see the note on Romans 1:13.
Colosse was known for its soft wool and dyed cloth. The site housing the city's ruins is located near the modern-day Turkish village of Honaz (see "Colosse" on p. 1935).

ARCHAEOLOGICAL SITES

COLOSSE

COLOSSIANS 1 Colosse (or Colossae) was located in the Roman province of **Asia Minor**[1] in the Lycus valley about 120 miles (194 km) east of Ephesus in today's southwestern Turkey.[2] An ancient city of Phrygia, it was situated on the southern bank of the Lycus River, about 11 miles (18 km) from Laodicea and 13 miles (21 km) from Hierapolis. The site is currently unoccupied and has not been excavated, although a few surface inscriptions have been found. What little we know of Colosse comes from numismatics (the study of coins and related objects) and from comments made by ancient writers,[3] but until the city can be excavated our understanding of its history will remain clouded.

The historian Herodotus (*History*, 7.30) referred in 480 B.C. to Colosse as "a great city of Phrygia," and Xenophon (*Anabasis*, 1.2.6) described it in 400 B.C. as large and prosperous. Colosse, standing on the most important trade route from Ephesus to the Euphrates, was a place of great importance from early times. The Persian king Xerxes visited it in 481 B.C., as did Cyrus the Younger in 401. By the time of Paul the city may have diminished somewhat in significance. Its economy depended upon trade and textiles, and particularly on a distinctive purple wool called *colossinus*.

The church at Colosse was established on Paul's third missionary journey, during his three years in Ephesus, not by Paul himself (2:1) but by Epaphras (1:7,12–13), a native of Colosse and an evangelist in nearby Laodicea and Hierapolis (see 4:13). Paul loved and admired him, calling him "our dear fellow servant," "a faithful minister of Christ" and a "fellow prisoner" (Phm 23). Epaphras was the one who told Paul at Rome about the Colossian church problem and thereby stimulated Paul to write this letter. The name Epaphras is a shortened form of Epaphroditus (from "Aphrodite," the Greek goddess of love), suggesting that he was a convert from paganism. He is not the Epaphroditus of Philippians 2:24 and 4:18. Archippus also exercised a fruitful ministry in Colosse (Col 4:17; Phm 2). Philemon was an active member of this church, as was Onesimus (Col 4:9).

Colosse lost its importance due to a change of the road system, after which Laodicea became the greater city. During the seventh and eighth centuries its open position exposed it to the terrible raids of the Saracens, and the people moved to Chonae (now called Chonas), a fortress on the slope of Mount Cadmus, about three miles (five km) farther south. During the twelfth century A.D. the Turks destroyed the city. Archaeologists have unearthed ruins of an ancient church.

[1] See Glossary on page 2080 for definitions of bolded words. [2] See "Early History of Ephesus" on page 1965 and "Ephesus During the Time of Paul" on page 1968; see also "Map 13." [3] See "Coins and Numismatics" on page 1699.

we pray this in order that you may live a life worthy[r] of the Lord and may please him in every way: bear-
ing fruit in every good work, growing in the knowledge of God, 11 being strengthened with all power[s] ac-
cording to his glorious might so that you may have great endurance and patience,[t] and joyfully 12 giving
thanks to the Father,[u] who has qualified you[a] to share in the inheritance[v] of the saints in the kingdom
of light. 13 For he has rescued us from the dominion of darkness[w] and brought us into the kingdom[x] of
the Son he loves,[y] 14 in whom we have redemption,[b][z] the forgiveness of sins.[a]

The Supremacy of Christ

15 He is the image[b] of the invisible God,[c] the firstborn over all creation. 16 For by him all things were
created:[d] things in heaven and on earth, visible and invisible, whether thrones or powers or rulers or au-
thorities;[e] all things were created by him and for him.[f] 17 He is before all things,[g] and in him all things
hold together. 18 And he is the head[h] of the body, the church; he is the beginning and the firstborn from
among the dead,[i] so that in everything he might have the supremacy. 19 For God was pleased[j] to have all
his fullness[k] dwell in him, 20 and through him to reconcile[l] to himself all things, whether things on earth
or things in heaven,[m] by making peace through his blood,[n] shed on the cross.

21 Once you were alienated from God and were enemies[o] in your minds[p] because of[c] your evil behav-
ior. 22 But now he has reconciled you by Christ's physical body[q] through death to present you holy in his
sight, without blemish and free from accusation[r]— 23 if you continue in your faith, established[s] and firm,
not moved from the hope[t] held out in the gospel. This is the gospel that you heard and that has been pro-
claimed to every creature under heaven,[u] and of which I, Paul, have become a servant.[v]

Paul's Labor for the Church

24 Now I rejoice in what was suffered for you, and I fill up in my flesh what is still lacking in regard to
Christ's afflictions,[w] for the sake of his body, which is the church. 25 I have become its servant[x] by the com-
mission God gave me[y] to present to you the word of God in its fullness— 26 the mystery[z] that has been kept
hidden for ages and generations, but is now disclosed to the saints. 27 To them God has chosen to make
known[a] among the Gentiles the glorious riches of this mystery, which is Christ in you, the hope of glory.

28 We proclaim him, admonishing[b] and teaching everyone with all wisdom,[c] so that we may present
everyone perfect[d] in Christ. 29 To this end I labor,[e] struggling[f] with all his energy, which so powerfully
works in me.[g]

2 I want you to know how much I am struggling[h] for you and for those at Laodicea,[i] and for all who
have not met me personally. 2 My purpose is that they may be encouraged in heart[j] and united in
love, so that they may have the full riches of complete understanding, in order that they may know the
mystery of God, namely, Christ, 3 in whom are hidden all the treasures of wisdom and knowledge.[k] 4 I tell
you this so that no one may deceive you by fine-sounding arguments.[l] 5 For though I am absent from you
in body, I am present with you in spirit[m] and delight to see how orderly[n] you are and how firm[o] your
faith in Christ is.

Freedom From Human Regulations Through Life With Christ

6 So then, just as you received Christ Jesus as Lord,[p] continue to live in him, 7 rooted[q] and built up in
him, strengthened in the faith as you were taught, and overflowing with thankfulness.

1:10 [r]Eph 4:1
1:11 [s]Eph 3:16 [t]Eph 4:2
1:12 [u]Eph 5:20 [v]Ac 20:32
1:13 [w]Ac 26:18 [x]Eph 6:12; 2Pe 1:11 [y]Mt 3:17
1:14 [z]Ro 3:24 [a]Eph 1:7
1:15 [b]2Co 4:4 [c]Jn 1:18
1:16 [d]Jn 1:3 [e]Eph 1:20,21 [f]Ro 11:36
1:17 [g]Jn 1:2
1:18 [h]Eph 1:22 [i]Ac 26:23; Rev 1:5
1:19 [j]Eph 1:5 [k]Jn 1:16
1:20 [l]2Co 5:18 [m]Eph 1:10 [n]Eph 2:13
1:21 [o]Ro 5:10 [p]Eph 2:3
1:22 [q]Ro 7:4 [r]Eph 5:27
1:23 [s]Eph 3:17 [t]ver 5 [u]Ro 10:18 [v]ver 25; 1Co 3:5
1:24 [w]2Co 1:5
1:25 [x]ver 23 [y]Eph 3:2
1:26 [z]Ro 16:25
1:27 [a]Mt 13:11
1:28 [b]Col 3:16 [c]1Co 2:6,7 [d]Eph 5:27
1:29 [e]1Co 15:10 [f]Col 2:1 [g]Eph 1:19
2:1 [h]Col 1:29; 4:12 [i]Rev 1:11
2:2 [j]Col 4:8
2:3 [k]Ro 11:33; 1Co 1:24,30
2:4 [l]Ro 16:18
2:5 [m]1Th 2:17 [n]1Co 14:40 [o]1Pe 5:9
2:6 [p]Col 1:10
2:7 [q]Eph 3:17

[a] 12 Some manuscripts *us* [b] 14 A few late manuscripts *redemption through his blood* [c] 21 Or *minds, as shown by*

1:15–20 These verses may have been the lyrics to an early Christian hymn on the supremacy of Christ (see "Early Christian Hymnody" on p. 2007).
1:15 Just as the firstborn son had certain privileges and rights in the Biblical world (see "The Rights of the Firstborn" on p. 43), so also Christ has certain rights in relation to all creation—priority, preeminence and sovereignty (see vv. 16–18).
1:16 The terms "thrones," "powers," "rulers" and "authorities" are references to angels. An angelic hierarchy figured prominently in the Colossian heresy.
1:26 In the pagan religious environment of Colosse, the word "mystery" referred to rites and symbols hidden from the uninitiated (see "The Mystery Religions" on p. 1939). Paul used the word in a more Jewish sense, with reference to God's secret plans for the last days. The Christian mystery is not secret knowledge for a few. It is a revelation of divine truths—once hidden but now openly proclaimed.
1:27 Paul summed up the secret of the cosmos, which all philosophers, sages, wise men and religious seekers have pursued since the beginning: "Christ in you, the hope of glory."
1:28 "Perfect," or "fully mature," was a term employed by the mystery religions (see "The Mystery Religions" on p. 1939) and the Gnostics (see "Early Christian Heresies" on p. 1896 and "The Gnostics and Their Scriptures" on p. 2029) to describe those who had become possessors of the secrets or knowledge boasted of by adherents to the particular religion.
2:1 This letter was to have been read to the church in Laodicea (near present-day Denizli, Turkey).
2:2 For "mystery," see the note on 1:26.
2:3 Paul stressed knowledge in this letter because he was refuting a heresy that emphasized knowledge as the means of salvation
2:6–8 A certain contingent in the Colossian church was promoting a philosophy of asceticism (strict self-denial as a form of spiritual discipline).

2:8 [r]1Ti 6:20 [s]Gal 4:3
2:10 [t]Eph 1:22
2:11 [u]Ro 2:29; Php 3:3 [v]Gal 5:24
2:12 [w]Ro 6:5 [x]Ac 2:24
2:13 [y]Eph 2:1,5
2:14 [z]Eph 2:15

[8]See to it that no one takes you captive through hollow and deceptive philosophy,[r] which depends on
human tradition and the basic principles of this world[s] rather than on Christ.
[9]For in Christ all the fullness of the Deity lives in bodily form, [10]and you have been given fullness in
Christ, who is the head[t] over every power and authority. [11]In him you were also circumcised,[u] in the put-
ting off of the sinful nature,[a][v] not with a circumcision done by the hands of men but with the circumci-
sion done by Christ, [12]having been buried with him in baptism and raised with him[w] through your faith
in the power of God, who raised him from the dead.[x]
[13]When you were dead in your sins[y] and in the uncircumcision of your sinful nature,[b] God made you[c]
alive with Christ. He forgave us all our sins, [14]having canceled the written code, with its regulations,[z] that

[a] 11 Or *the flesh* [b] 13 Or *your flesh* [c] 13 Some manuscripts *us*

2:8–23 Within the New Testament there are references to claims of knowledge and wisdom (e.g., 1Co 1:17–31; 8:1; 13:8) that could have been the roots that led to the development of Gnosticism (see "The Gnostics and Their Scriptures" on p. 2029). There was a heresy in the church of Colosse, as well as false teaching in the churches Timothy knew (1Ti 1:3–11; 4:3–16; 2Ti 2:18; 3:5–7), that may be termed a false *gnôsis* (1Ti 6:20). Then in the epistles of John there are references to false teaching about the reality of Jesus' humanity (1Jn 4:3; 2Jn 7). But there is nothing in the New Testament of the developed kind of Gnostic doctrines that the teachers of the church would face a century or so later.

2:8 The Greek term*stoicheia,* translated "basic principles of this world" ("elementary truths" in Heb 5:12), in this context denotes false, worldly, elementary teachings (see "Greek Philosophical Schools" on p. 1937). Paul was counteracting the Colossian heresy, which, in part, taught that for salvation one needed to combine faith in Christ with secret knowledge and with human regulations concerning such physical and external practices as circumcision, eating and drinking and observance of the religious festivals. See the note on "philosophy" at 1 Corinthians 1:18—2:16.

2:9 The declaration that the very essence of deity was present in totality in Jesus' human body was a direct refutation of Gnostic teaching.

2:11 See "Circumcision in the Ancient World" on page 1840.

2:12 See the note on Romans 6:3–4.

2:14 The "written code" is a business term, meaning a certificate of indebtedness in the debtor's own handwriting. Paul used this language to designate the Mosaic Law, with all its regulations, under which everyone is a debtor to God.

Greek Philosophical Schools

COLOSSIANS 2 Hellenistic (Greek) philosophy may be divided into several schools or traditions in the first century A.D.:

✣ *Classical philosophy:* Plato was still deeply influential. Those who adhered most closely to his teachings (among whom Philo of Alexandria is most notable) are known today as Middle Platonists. Aristotle's followers, known as the Peripatetics, were also still active.

✣ *The Skeptics:* The linear descendants of Plato's Academy took a more negative view about the possibility of gaining true knowledge and accordingly became known as the Skeptics. This tradition is said to have begun with Pyrrho of Elis (fourth century B.C.); hence the designation of Skepticism as Pyrrhonism. While some Skeptics determined that "suspension of judgment" was the most reasonable approach to philosophy, others modified this to include a measure of probability.

✣ *The Stoics:* The Skeptics were highly critical of the most influential school of **Hellenistic** philosophy, the Stoics (named after the *stoa*, or colonnade, from which their founder, Zeno of Citium, taught). Known for their high moral standards and devotion to duty, the Stoics taught that reality is ultimately material and that it is governed by a *logos*, a kind of fiery, divine substance that pervades the cosmos and confers upon it order and direction. This logos, in their view, is also resident within people, enabling them to make sense of the universe. The goal for Stoics was thus a life lived "in accordance with Nature." There was ultimately little difference in Stoic discourse between nature, logos and God.[1]

✣ *The Epicureans:* This school of philosophy was founded by Epicurus (fourth century B.C.). Its adherents sought to counter traditional views of the gods, relegating them to the *intermundia*, the region "between the worlds," from which they were assumed to take no notice of human affairs. Followers of Epicurus anticipated modern evolutionists in their belief in a closed universe emerging from the chance collision of atoms within a void. In terms of ethics, they regarded pleasure as the ultimate good. Pleasure for them did not signify devotion to sensual excess but a life lived in moderation, since the traditional virtues of prudence and justice in their view yielded true happiness.

[1]See "The *Logos* in Greek and Jewish Literature" on page 1721.

was against us and that stood opposed to us; he took it away, nailing it to the cross.[a] 15And having disarmed
the powers and authorities,[b] he made a public spectacle of them, triumphing over them[c] by the cross.[a]
16Therefore do not let anyone judge you[d] by what you eat or drink,[e] or with regard to a religious fes-
tival,[f] a New Moon celebration[g] or a Sabbath day.[h] 17These are a shadow of the things that were to come;[i]
the reality, however, is found in Christ. 18Do not let anyone who delights in false humility[j] and the wor-
ship of angels disqualify you for the prize.[k] Such a person goes into great detail about what he has seen,
and his unspiritual mind puffs him up with idle notions. 19He has lost connection with the Head,[l] from
whom the whole body, supported and held together by its ligaments and sinews, grows as God causes it
to grow.[m]
20Since you died with Christ to the basic principles of this world,[n] why, as though you still belonged
to it, do you submit to its rules:[o] 21"Do not handle! Do not taste! Do not touch!"? 22These are all destined
to perish[p] with use, because they are based on human commands and teachings.[q] 23Such regulations in-
deed have an appearance of wisdom, with their self-imposed worship, their false humility and their harsh
treatment of the body, but they lack any value in restraining sensual indulgence.

Rules for Holy Living

3 Since, then, you have been raised with Christ, set your hearts on things above, where Christ is seat-
ed at the right hand of God. 2Set your minds on things above, not on earthly things.[r] 3For you died,[s]
and your life is now hidden with Christ in God. 4When Christ, who is your[b] life, appears,[t] then you also
will appear with him in glory.[u]
5Put to death, therefore, whatever belongs to your earthly nature: sexual immorality, impurity, lust, evil
desires and greed,[v] which is idolatry.[w] 6Because of these, the wrath of God[x] is coming.[c] 7You used to walk
in these ways, in the life you once lived.[y] 8But now you must rid yourselves[z] of all such things as these:
anger, rage, malice, slander,[a] and filthy language from your lips.[b] 9Do not lie to each other,[c] since you
have taken off your old self with its practices 10and have put on the new self, which is being renewed[d] in
knowledge in the image of its Creator.[e] 11Here there is no Greek or Jew,[f] circumcised or uncircumcised,[g]
barbarian, Scythian, slave or free,[h] but Christ is all,[i] and is in all.
12Therefore, as God's chosen people, holy and dearly loved, clothe yourselves with compassion, kind-
ness, humility,[j] gentleness and patience.[k] 13Bear with each other[l] and forgive whatever grievances you
may have against one another. Forgive as the Lord forgave you.[m] 14And over all these virtues put on love,[n]
which binds them all together in perfect unity.[o]
15Let the peace of Christ[p] rule in your hearts, since as members of one body you were called to peace.
And be thankful. 16Let the word of Christ[q] dwell in you richly as you teach and admonish one another
with all wisdom,[r] and as you sing psalms, hymns and spiritual songs with gratitude in your hearts to

2:14 [a]1Pe 2:24
2:15 [b]Eph 6:12 [c]Lk 10:18
2:16 [d]Ro 14:3,4 [e]Ro 14:17 [f]Ro 14:5 [g]1Ch 23:31 [h]Gal 4:10
2:17 [i]Heb 8:5
2:18 [j]ver 23 [k]Php 3:14
2:19 [l]Eph 1:22 [m]Eph 4:16
2:20 [n]Gal 4:3,9 [o]ver 14,16
2:22 [p]1Co 6:13 [q]Isa 29:13; Mt 15:9; Tit 1:14
3:2 [r]Php 3:19,20
3:3 [s]Ro 6:2; 2Co 5:14
3:4 [t]1Co 1:7 [u]1Pe 1:13; 1Jn 3:2
3:5 [v]Eph 5:3 [w]Eph 5:5
3:6 [x]Ro 1:18
3:7 [y]Eph 2:2
3:8 [z]Eph 4:22 [a]Eph 4:31 [b]Eph 4:29
3:9 [c]Eph 4:22,25
3:10 [d]Ro 12:2; Eph 4:23 [e]Eph 2:10
3:11 [f]Ro 10:12 [g]1Co 7:19 [h]Gal 3:28 [i]Eph 1:23
3:12 [j]Php 2:3 [k]2Co 6:6; Gal 5:22,23
3:13 [l]Eph 4:2 [m]Eph 4:32
3:14 [n]1Co 13:1-13 [o]Eph 4:3
3:15 [p]Jn 14:27
3:16 [q]Ro 10:17 [r]Col 1:28

[a] 15 Or *them in him* [b] 4 Some manuscripts *our* [c] 6 Some early manuscripts *coming on those who are disobedient*

2:15 Disarming the enemy is a picture of conquered soldiers stripped of their clothing, as well as of their weapons, to symbolize their total defeat.

The triumphal procession is a metaphor that recalls victorious Roman general leading his captives through the streets of his city for all the citizens to see.

2:18 Second-century Gnosticism conceived of a list of spirit beings who had emanated from God and through whom the Gnostics believed God might be approached.

In the New Testament the word "mind" frequently occurs in an ethical sense, as here and in Romans 7:25. See "Heart, Breath, Throat and Intestines: Ancient Hebrew Anthropology" on page 968.

2:19 The central error of the Colossian heresy was a defective view of Christ, in that he was believed to be less than deity.

2:20 For "basic principles of this world," see the note on verse 8.

2:21 The strict ascetic nature of the Colossian heresy is seen here. These prohibitions seem to carry Old Testament ceremonial laws to the extreme.

2:23 This verse contains a detailed analysis of the Colossian heresy: (1) It appeared to set forth an impressive system of religious philosophy. (2) It was a system created by the false teachers themselves ("self-imposed"), rather than being of divine origin. (3) The false teachers paraded their humility. (4) This may have been accomplished through a harsh asceticism that brutally misused the body.

3:1 See "The 'Right Hand' in Ancient Thinking" on page 1983.

3:11 A "barbarian" referred to someone who did not speak Greek and was on that basis thought to be uncivilized.

The name "Scythian" was used by classical writers as a general term for the barbarians of the steppes. In common parlance it was a term for the savage and uncivilized. Scythia was the name given by the Greeks to an ill-defined area between the Carpathians and the Don, the western portion of which included the black earth wheatlands of the modern Ukraine. The steppe land was wide open to nomadic invasion, and the Indo-European tribes who occupied it in the seventh century B.C. are those to whom the term Scythian is most properly applied. There must have been a considerable "folk-wandering" about this time, because Scythians appeared in upper Mesopotamia and Syria between 650 and 620 B.C., and another force reached the middle Danube. South Russia, to speak in modern geographical terms, was firmly occupied. The nomads were formidable soldiers, swift archer cavalry versed in the tactics of desert warfare and mobile strategy. By a "scorched-earth" policy and by their elusive defense they frustrated an attack by Darius in 512 B.C. and similarly beat off Alexander's general Zopyrion in 325. They exploited the labor of the earlier inhabitants and were exporters of large quantities of wheat to the Greek Black Sea colonies. Greek pottery and metal work were given in exchange, and the tombs of the chiefs have produced a rich profusion of such articles. The Celts and Samaritans seem to have displaced the Scythians during the last three centuries before Christ.

3:16 Some of the most important early Christian doctrines were expressed in hymns (see "Early Christian Hymnody" on p. 2007).

3:16 [s]Eph 5:19
3:17 [t]1Co 10:31
[u]Eph 5:20

God.[s] 17And whatever you do,[t] whether in word or deed, do it all in the name of the Lord Jesus, giving
thanks[u] to God the Father through him.

Rules for Christian Households

3:18 [v]Eph 5:22

18Wives, submit to your husbands,[v] as is fitting in the Lord.
19Husbands, love your wives and do not be harsh with them.

3:18—4:1 See the note on Ephesians 5:22—6:9.

The Mystery Religions

COLOSSIANS 3 Mystery religions were secret cults that flourished during the Greco-Roman period and involved the worship of deities from Greece, Egypt and the Near East. Unlike official religions (such as the imperial cult),[1] which involved little more than pledges of loyalty, these religions offered personal salvation and a sense of belonging to a community. Members participated in rituals and were expected to keep both the rites and the teachings secret; hence the designation "mystery religions." Famous examples are the Greek Eleusinian and Dionysian mysteries,[2] the Mithras mysteries and the Egyptian cult of Isis and Osiris.

Each cult was distinct, but many mystery cults shared a motif of death and afterlife. The Eleusinian mysteries centered upon the myth of the annual descent of Persephone, the daughter of Demeter, into Hades and her subsequent return to the land of the living. The cult of Isis and Osiris was similar. In Egyptian religion Osiris, the lord of the dead, was also believed to be a source of life and renewal. Osiris had been murdered by his brother Set, but his wife/sister, Isis, had located his scattered remains and effected for him a kind of resurrection.

Some cults focused on cosmic power. The Mithras cult, which became popular with Roman men around the second century A.D., is widely thought to have been **Persian** in origin, but recent research indicates that its teachings may have been indigenous to the Greco-Roman world. Worship was carried out in a small, cavelike chamber called a Mithraeum, which contained cryptic inscriptions and symbols, the primary clues to the nature of the religion. The central motif centered around a man, Mithras, who had purportedly slain a bull. In the iconography Mithras is accompanied by a dog, a snake, a raven and a scorpion. All of these creatures equate to constellations (Taurus, Canis Minor, Hydra, Corvus and Scorpio, respectively), and thus the cult may have been astrological in orientation and based upon the belief that Mithras was the ruler of the cosmos. Members of the cult ascended through a hierarchy of seven ranks, corresponding to the seven planets; solar and lunar icons are invariably found in a Mithraeum.

The cults frequently focused upon fertility, were often accompanied by erotic symbolism and included secret rituals that were sometimes either gory or orgiastic. The Dionysian mysteries, which involved a kind of ecstatic madness, were in fact for a time outlawed by the Roman Senate. Popular fear of and fascination with the bacchanalian frenzy is reflected in ancient literary works such as *The Bacchae* by Euripides and the *Metamorphoses* by Ovid. In many mystery religions the initiate underwent a ritual death and rebirth through either ecstatic frenzy or secret ritual. One inscription in a Mithraeum describes the initiate as having been "piously reborn."

Some have suggested that Paul may have been influenced by these cults in his understanding of the "mystery" of the gospel of Christ. It is more likely, however, that the apostle used the term "mystery" to refer to the fact that the Old Testament prophecies, which include much that is mysterious, find their meaning and fulfillment in Christ. Certainly nothing indicates that converts to Christianity were sworn to keep its tenets or practices a secret. In addition, Paul probably did want to communicate to his Gentile converts that the true way to rebirth and resurrection is through Christ, and the word "mystery" helped him to convey that reality.

[1]See "The Imperial Cult" on page 1651. [2]See "The Cult of Dionysus" on page 1921.

THE LETTER FROM THE LAODICEANS

COLOSSIANS 4 In Colossians 4:16 Paul instructed the Colossians to read the "letter from Laodicea." Most likely Paul was referring to a letter he had written to the believers in that city. Attempts to identify this letter have included suggestions that it was an **Apocryphal** Latin document, Paul's letter to the Ephesians or a text that no longer exists.

◆ The Latin "Epistle to the Laodiceans" strings together many Pauline phrases found in Philippians and Galatians and then directs the readers to exchange letters with Colosse. It is doubtful that Paul wrote this document and likely that its true author forged the letter on the basis of Colossians 4:16.

◆ Some scholars identify the book of Ephesians as the "letter from Laodicea" because Marcion, a second-century heretic, referred to the book of Ephesians by this name. Additionally, some early manuscripts of Ephesians do not specify Ephesus as the destination of that letter at Ephesians 1:1.[1] Paul may have intended to circulate Ephesians among several churches throughout the Lycus Valley, including Laodicea and Colosse. This does not require, however, that we regard Ephesians as the missing letter of Colossians 4:16.

◆ Many of Paul's letters have been lost to us. It is therefore quite possible that the letter referred to in Colossians 4:16 simply has not survived.[2]

[1]See "The Authorship of Ephesians" on page 1919. [2]See "The 'Missing' Letter From the Corinthians to Paul" on page 1870 and "Paul's Visits and Letters to Corinth" on page 1888.

Ruins of Laodicea, located in the Lycus Valley

© Dr. James C. Martin

20 Children, obey your parents in everything, for this pleases the Lord.
21 Fathers, do not embitter your children, or they will become discouraged.
22 Slaves, obey your earthly masters in everything; and do it, not only when their eye is on you and to
win their favor, but with sincerity of heart and reverence for the Lord. 23 Whatever you do, work at it with
all your heart, as working for the Lord, not for men, 24 since you know that you will receive an inheri-
tance[w] from the Lord as a reward. It is the Lord Christ you are serving. 25 Anyone who does wrong will
be repaid for his wrong, and there is no favoritism.[x]

4 Masters, provide your slaves with what is right and fair, because you know that you also have a Mas-
ter in heaven.

Further Instructions

2 Devote yourselves to prayer,[y] being watchful and thankful. 3 And pray for us, too, that God may open
a door[z] for our message, so that we may proclaim the mystery of Christ, for which I am in chains.[a] 4 Pray
that I may proclaim it clearly, as I should. 5 Be wise[b] in the way you act toward outsiders;[c] make the most
of every opportunity.[d] 6 Let your conversation be always full of grace,[e] seasoned with salt,[f] so that you may
know how to answer everyone.[g]

Final Greetings

7 Tychicus[h] will tell you all the news about me. He is a dear brother, a faithful minister and fellow ser-
vant[i] in the Lord. 8 I am sending him to you for the express purpose that you may know about our[a] cir-
cumstances and that he may encourage your hearts.[j] 9 He is coming with Onesimus,[k] our faithful and
dear brother, who is one of you. They will tell you everything that is happening here.
10 My fellow prisoner Aristarchus[l] sends you his greetings, as does Mark, the cousin of Barnabas.[m]
(You have received instructions about him; if he comes to you, welcome him.) 11 Jesus, who is called Jus-
tus, also sends greetings. These are the only Jews among my fellow workers for the kingdom of God, and
they have proved a comfort to me. 12 Epaphras,[n] who is one of you and a servant of Christ Jesus, sends
greetings. He is always wrestling in prayer for you,[o] that you may stand firm in all the will of God, ma-
ture[p] and fully assured. 13 I vouch for him that he is working hard for you and for those at Laodicea[q] and
Hierapolis. 14 Our dear friend Luke,[r] the doctor, and Demas[s] send greetings. 15 Give my greetings to the
brothers at Laodicea, and to Nympha and the church in her house.[t]
16 After this letter has been read to you, see that it is also read[u] in the church of the Laodiceans and
that you in turn read the letter from Laodicea.
17 Tell Archippus:[v] "See to it that you complete the work you have received in the Lord."[w]
18 I, Paul, write this greeting in my own hand.[x] Remember[y] my chains. Grace be with you.[z]

[a] 8 Some manuscripts *that he may know about your*

3:24 [w]Ac 20:32
3:25 [x]Ac 10:34
4:2 [y]Lk 18:1
4:3 [z]Ac 14:27 [a]Eph 6:19,20
4:5 [b]Eph 5:15 [c]Mk 4:11 [d]Eph 5:16
4:6 [e]Eph 4:29 [f]Mk 9:50 [g]1Pe 3:15
4:7 [h]Ac 20:4 [i]Eph 6:21,22
4:8 [j]Eph 6:21,22
4:9 [k]Phm 10
4:10 [l]Ac 19:29 [m]Ac 4:36
4:12 [n]Col 1:7; Phm 23 [o]Ro 15:30 [p]1Co 2:6
4:13 [q]Col 2:1
4:14 [r]2Ti 4:11; Phm 24 [s]2Ti 4:10
4:15 [t]Ro 16:5
4:16 [u]2Th 3:14
4:17 [v]Phm 2 [w]2Ti 4:5
4:18 [x]1Co 16:21 [y]Heb 13:3 [z]1Ti 6:21; 2Ti 4:22; Tit 3:15; Heb 13:25

3:20–21 For commentary on the parent-child relationship, see the note on Ephesians 6:1.

3:22—4:1 Paul neither condoned slavery nor sanctioned revolt against masters. Rather, he called on both slaves and masters to demonstrate Christian principles in their relationship and thus to attempt to transform the institution from within (see "Slavery in the Greco-Roman World" on p. 1979).

4:3 For "mystery," see the note on 1:26.

4:6 For "salt," see the note on Matthew 5:13.

4:9 Onesimus, a slave belonging to Philemon, had apparently stolen from his master (Phm 18) and then run away, a crime that under Roman law was punishable by death. But Onesimus met Paul and through his ministry became a Christian (Phm 10). When Onesimus agreed to return to his master, Paul wrote a letter to Philemon requesting that he accept Onesimus back as a Christian brother (Phm 16).

4:10 Aristarchus, a Macedonian, was with Paul during the Ephesian riot (Ac 19:29) and therefore was known in Colosse. He also accompanied the apostle to Greece (Ac 20:4), as well as on his trip to Rome (Ac 27:2).

Mark, also called John Mark, wrote the second Gospel. He was a close associate of Peter and a cousin of Barnabas (see the note on Ac 13:1–2). Although Mark was at the center of a dispute between Paul and Barnabas (see Ac 15:36–40), Paul later asserted that he was "helpful to [him] in [his] ministry" (2Ti 4:11).

4:13 For "Laodicea," see the note on 2:1.

Hierapolis was a town in Asia Minor (present-day Turkey), about 6 miles (9.7 km) from Laodicea and 14 miles (22.5 km) from Colosse. Its church may have been founded during Paul's three-year stay in Ephesus (Ac 19), but probably not by Paul himself.

4:14 Luke wrote about Paul in the book of Acts, having often accompanied him on his travels (see the note on Ac 16:10). He was with Paul in Rome during his imprisonment (Ac 28), from which this letter was written.

4:15 New Testament examples of individuals hosting home churches are Priscilla and Aquila (Ro 16:5; 1Co 16:19), Philemon (Phm 2) and Mary the mother of John (Ac 12:12). See "House Churches and Early Church Buildings" on page 2033, as well as the note on 1 Corinthians 16:19.

4:16 The practice of the early church was to read Paul's letters aloud to the assembled congregation.

4:18 Paul's custom was to dictate his letters and then to add a few greetings himself. His personal signature guaranteed the genuineness of the letter. (See "Writing Materials in the Ancient World" on p. 2037.)

INTRODUCTION TO 1 Thessalonians

AUTHOR, PLACE AND DATE OF WRITING

This letter identifies its author as Paul (and his associates Silas and Timothy; 1:1). Despite the fact that a few critics have denied Paul's authorship of this letter, the vast majority of scholars remain convinced that it is Pauline.

Two factors suggest a date of about A.D. 51–52: The letter fits with what we know of Paul's missionary work from Acts 17–18, and the Gallio inscription is evidence that Timothy's visit to Corinth took place during that time period (see "Gallio, Proconsul of Achaia" on p. 1806).

AUDIENCE

Paul wrote to the new believers in Thessalonica, a major military and commercial port located along the Egnatian Way (an important Roman road connecting Asia Minor with the Adriatic Sea). Thessalonica had a population of about 200,000, making it the largest city in Macedonia (see "Thessalonica" on p. 1944).

CULTURAL FACTS AND HIGHLIGHTS

After having planted a church in Thessalonica, Paul was abruptly forced out of the city (Ac 17:1–10), leaving the new Christians there with only minimal teaching in Christian doctrine. Paul dispatched Timothy to check on the Thessalonian Christians while he himself remained in Athens (1Th 3:1–2). Upon his return Timothy found the apostle in Corinth (Ac 18:1–5). Although Timothy could report that the Thessalonians were steadfast in the faith, he relayed the need for additional teaching in matters of Christian ethics and eschatology (matters relating to the end times). Paul wrote this letter to assure the Thessalonian Christians that his abrupt departure had not signified lack of love for these believers (1Th 2–3), to encourage them to avoid sexual immorality (4:1–8) and to clear up confusion in some of their minds regarding the resurrection and second advent of Christ (4:13—5:3).

TIMELINE

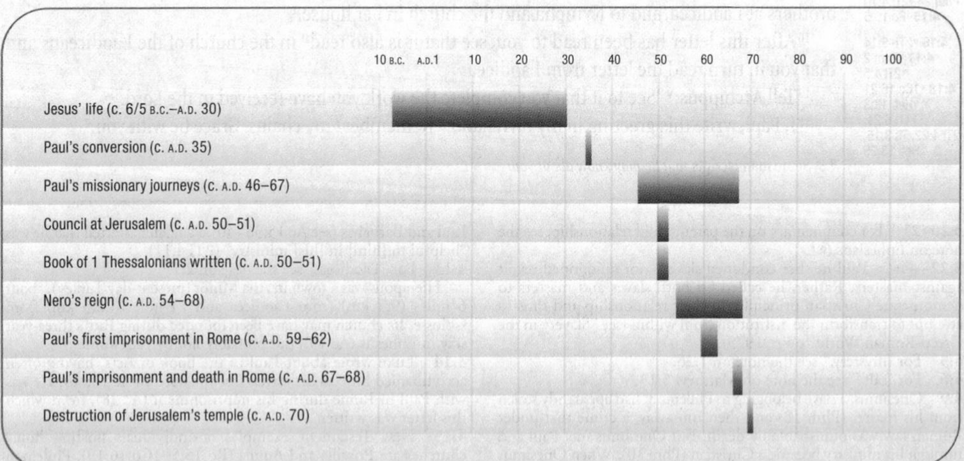

AS YOU READ

Note the repeated references to God's faithfulness, and list truths from this letter regarding the end times and Christ's second coming. Watch for practical advice on living the Christian life within the context of an immoral culture that is hostile to Christian values.

DID YOU KNOW?

- Greeks despised manual labor and viewed it as fit only for slaves (2:9).
- A wide range of sexual values and practices existed in Paul's day in both Greek and Roman society; moral standards were generally low, and chastity was regarded as an unreasonable restriction (4:3).
- Inscriptions on tombs and references in literature demonstrate that first-century pagans viewed death with horror (4:13).

THEMES

First Thessalonians includes the following themes:

1. *Persecution.* Paul applauded the Thessalonians for their progress in the faith and urged them to stay the course (4:1,10; 5:11), asserting that the trials believers endure because of their faith are not just chance happenings. On the contrary, suffering for the faith is to be expected (3:3).

2. *Christ's return.* Paul assured the Thessalonians that believers who have died will be raised first at Christ's return. Regarding the time and date of this event, Paul likened it to the unexpected coming of a thief in the night (5:2) and to the certain, but often sudden, arrival of a baby (5:3).

3. *Christian living.* While believers await the Lord's coming, they are to live quiet, respectful, holy and productive lives (4:1–12), to encourage and help each other and to be patient and kind to everyone (5:14). While a moral life is not a precondition for acceptance by God, an immoral lifestyle is irreconcilable with the Christian faith.

OUTLINE

- I. Greeting and Thanksgiving (1)
  - A. Thanksgiving for Their Faith (1:1–4)
  - B. Thanksgiving for Their Faithfulness and Witness (1:5–10)
- II. Paul Defends His Actions and Absence (2–3)
  - A. The Integrity of His Ministry (2:1–16)
  - B. The Reason for His Absence (2:17—3:10)
  - C. Prayer (3:11–13)
- III. Exhortations (4:1—5:22)
  - A. Live to Please God (4:1–12)
  - B. Take Hope in the Promise of Christ's Coming (4:13—5:11)
  - C. Final Instructions (5:12–22)
- IV. Concluding Prayer, Greeting and Benediction (5:23–28)

1 Paul, Silas[a] and Timothy,[a] **1:1** [a]Ac 16:1; 2Th 1:1 [b]Ac 17:1 [c]Ro 1:7

To the church of the Thessalonians[b] in God the Father and the Lord Jesus Christ:

Grace and peace to you.[bc]

Thanksgiving for the Thessalonians' Faith

2 We always thank God for all of you,[d] mentioning you in our prayers. 3 We continually remember be- **1:2** [d]Ro 1:8
fore our God and Father your work produced by faith,[e] your labor prompted by love, and your endurance **1:3** [e]2Th 1:11
inspired by hope in our Lord Jesus Christ.
4 For we know, brothers loved by God, that he has chosen you, 5 because our gospel[f] came to you not **1:5** [f]2Th 2:14
simply with words, but also with power, with the Holy Spirit and with deep conviction. You know how we
lived among you for your sake. 6 You became imitators of us[g] and of the Lord; in spite of severe suffer- **1:6** [g]1Co 4:16 [h]Ac 17:5-10
ing,[h] you welcomed the message with the joy given by the Holy Spirit.[i] 7 And so you became a model to [i]Ac 13:52

[a] *1* Greek *Silvanus*, a variant of *Silas* [b] *1* Some early manuscripts *you from God our Father and the Lord Jesus Christ*

1:1 This verse forms a complete unit, identifying the senders and recipients and conveying Paul's greeting (see "Letter Writing in the Greco-Roman World" on p. 1889).

For "Paul," see the note on Philippians 3:5, for "Silas" the note on Acts 15:22 and for "Timothy" the note on Acts 16:1.

Thessalonica was a thriving metropolis of 200,000 (see "Thessalonica" on p. 1944). The city still exists today as the Greek city of Thessaloníki, population 750,000.

1:7–8 In New Testament times Achaia was a Roman province that included the Peloponnesus and northern Greece south of Illyricum, Epirus and Thessaly, which were districts of Macedonia. Corinth was the capital. Used together, "Macedonia and Achaia" generally meant all of Greece (see also Ac 19:21; Ro 15:26, as well as the note on 2 Co 1:1).

ARCHAEOLOGICAL SITES

THESSALONICA

1 THESSALONIANS 1 The city of Thessalonica ("Map 13") was founded in 315 B.C. at the head of the Thermaic Gulf on the Aegean Sea. Thessalonica was a military and commercial port that became the capital of the Macedonian province in 146 B.C. Paul wrote letters to churches in at least two Macedonian cities, Thessalonica and Philippi.[1] Thessalonica became a free city in 42 B.C. as a reward for assisting Mark Antony and Octavian (later called Augustus) in a military engagement with Brutus and Cassius, the leading assassins of Julius Caesar, at the battle of Philippi. As a port city located on the Via Egnatia, a road that ran through the major cities of Macedonia, Thessalonica became a major center for trade and the arts. It had both a large Roman and a sizable Jewish population.

Paul's first letter to the Thessalonian believers hints that the Christians there suffered persecution from their own countrymen (1Th 2:14). Whether this persecution came primarily at the hands of Jews or Gentiles in the region is uncertain.[2] Archaeological and historical records indicate the presence of temples to Roman gods and various oriental cults.[3] Inscriptions discovered in the city also give evidence of Jewish settlements there during the **Roman period**.[4,5]

Because an active, modern city (Thessaloniki) exists on the site, little remains of the ancient city (or is available for excavation). The Arch of Galerius commemorates a Roman victory over the **Persians**, dating to the late third century A.D., but only one section of the original remains. A Roman forum has been unearthed, but it may have been in use no earlier than the second century A.D. Archaeologists are aware, however, that a first-century A.D. arch, called the Vandar Arch, once existed in Thessaloniki. It was torn down in 1867, but an inscription from the arch is now on display in the British Museum. It mentions officials called *politarches*, a Greek word Luke used to designate the Thessalonian officials (Ac 17:6). Since no previous usage of this word had been found in Greek literature, scholars had once wondered whether Luke's usage of the term was an error. In light of this controversy, the location of the inscription proved to be a significant step in illustrating the precision of Luke's account;[6] a fair number of occurrences of this otherwise elusive word in inscriptions from the general area have since been documented.

[1]See "Philippi" on page 1927. [2]See also "The Geographic Expansion of the Church Under Persecution" on page 1781, "Nero, Persecutor of Christians" on page 1931 and "The Early Persecution of the Church" on page 2067. [3]See "The Gods of the Greeks and Romans" on page 1908. [4]See Glossary on page 2080 for definitions of bolded words. [5]See "The Jewish Diaspora in the First Century A.D." on page 1769. [6]See "The Historical Value of Luke–Acts" on page 1697.

all the believers in Macedonia and Achaia. 8The Lord's message rang out from you not only in Macedo-
1:8 jRo 1:8; 10:18 nia and Achaia—your faith in God has become known everywhere.[j] Therefore we do not need to say
anything about it, 9for they themselves report what kind of reception you gave us. They tell how you
1:9 k1Co 12:2; Gal 4:8 turned to God from idols[k] to serve the living and true God, 10and to wait for his Son from heaven, whom
1:10 lAc 2:24 mRo 5:9 he raised from the dead[l]—Jesus, who rescues us from the coming wrath.[m]

Paul's Ministry in Thessalonica

2:1 n1Th 1:5,9 **2** You know, brothers, that our visit to you[n] was not a failure. 2We had previously suffered[o] and been
2:2 oAc 16:22; Php 1:30 insulted in Philippi, as you know, but with the help of our God we dared to tell you his gospel in spite
2:3 p2Co 2:17 of strong opposition. 3For the appeal we make does not spring from error or impure motives,[p] nor are
we trying to trick you. 4On the contrary, we speak as men approved by God to be entrusted with the gos-
2:4 qGal 2:7 rGal 1:10 pel.[q] We are not trying to please men[r] but God, who tests our hearts. 5You know we never used flattery,
2:5 sAc 20:33 tRo 1:9 nor did we put on a mask to cover up greed[s]—God is our witness.[t] 6We were not looking for praise from
men, not from you or anyone else.

2:6 u1Co 9:1,2 As apostles[u] of Christ we could have been a burden to you, 7but we were gentle among you, like a
2:7 vver 11 mother caring for her little children.[v] 8We loved you so much that we were delighted to share with you
2:8 w2Co 12:15; 1Jn 3:16 not only the gospel of God but our lives as well,[w] because you had become so dear to us. 9Surely you re-
2:9 xAc 18:3 y2Th 3:8 member, brothers, our toil and hardship; we worked[x] night and day in order not to be a burden to any-
one[y] while we preached the gospel of God to you.

2:10 z1Th 1:5 a2Co 1:12 10You are witnesses,[z] and so is God, of how holy,[a] righteous and blameless we were among you who
2:11 bver 7; 1Co 4:14 believed. 11For you know that we dealt with each of you as a father deals with his own children,[b] 12en-
2:12 cEph 4:1 couraging, comforting and urging you to live lives worthy[c] of God, who calls you into his kingdom and
glory.

2:13 d1Th 1:2 eHeb 4:12 13And we also thank God continually[d] because, when you received the word of God,[e] which you heard
from us, you accepted it not as the word of men, but as it actually is, the word of God, which is at work
2:14 fGal 1:22 gAc 17:5; 2Th 1:4 in you who believe. 14For you, brothers, became imitators of God's churches in Judea,[f] which are in Christ
Jesus: You suffered from your own countrymen[g] the same things those churches suffered from the Jews,
2:15 hAc 2:23 iMt 5:12 15who killed the Lord Jesus[h] and the prophets[i] and also drove us out. They displease God and are hostile
2:16 jAc 13:45, 50 kMt 23:32 to all men 16in their effort to keep us from speaking to the Gentiles[j] so that they may be saved. In this way
they always heap up their sins to the limit.[k] The wrath of God has come upon them at last.[a]

Paul's Longing to See the Thessalonians

2:17 l1Co 5:3; Col 2:5 m1Th 3:10 17But, brothers, when we were torn away from you for a short time (in person, not in thought),[l] out of
our intense longing we made every effort to see you.[m] 18For we wanted to come to you—certainly I, Paul,
2:18 nMt 4:10 oRo 1:13; 15:22 did, again and again—but Satan[n] stopped us.[o] 19For what is our hope, our joy, or the crown[p] in which
2:19 pPhp 4:1 q2Co 1:14 we will glory[q] in the presence of our Lord Jesus when he comes?[r] Is it not you? 20Indeed, you are our glo-
rMt 16:27; 1Th 3:13 ry[s] and joy.
2:20 s2Co 1:14 3:1 tver 5 **3** So when we could stand it no longer,[t] we thought it best to be left by ourselves in Athens.[u] 2We sent
uAc 17:15 Timothy, who is our brother and God's fellow worker[b] in spreading the gospel of Christ, to strength-
en and encourage you in your faith, 3so that no one would be unsettled by these trials. You know quite
3:3 vAc 9:16; 14:22 well that we were destined for them.[v] 4In fact, when we were with you, we kept telling you that we would
3:4 w1Th 2:14 be persecuted. And it turned out that way, as you well know.[w] 5For this reason, when I could stand it no
3:5 xver 1 yMt 4:3 zGal 2:2; Php 2:16 longer,[x] I sent to find out about your faith. I was afraid that in some way the tempter[y] might have tempt-
ed you and our efforts might have been useless.[z]

[a] 16 Or *them fully* [b] 2 Some manuscripts *brother and fellow worker*; other manuscripts *brother and God's servant*

2:3 The Greek for "trick" was originally used of a lure for catching fish, but the term came to be used of any sort of cunning used for profit.
2:4 For "hearts," see the note on Psalm 4:7.
2:9 Greeks despised manual labor and viewed it as fit only for slaves, but Paul was not ashamed of doing any sort of work that would help further the gospel.
2:14 At the time of Paul's initial visit to Thessalonica, persecution instigated by the Jews was apparently being carried out against the church by unbelieving Gentiles (see Ac 17:5–9; see also "Before the Gentile Expansion: The Jewish Churches in the Holy Land" on p. 1997).
2:17—3:5 In Paul's day, a "superior" could write a letter to an "inferior" as a basis for making a request. Thus Paul's words not only expressed to the Thessalonians his feelings for them but also prepared the way for the rest of his letter.
2:19 The "crown" was a wreath used on festive occasions or as a prize in the Greek games.
3:1 See "Athens" on page 1804.
3:2 In Greek classical literature the word "strengthen" was generally used in the literal sense of putting a buttress on a building. In the New Testament it is mainly used figuratively, as here.
3:3 "Trials" is a reference to the opposition and persecution suffered by the Thessalonian converts (see "The Early Persecution of the Church" on p. 2067).

Timothy's Encouraging Report

6But Timothy has just now come to us from you[a] and has brought good news about your faith and 3:6 [a]Ac 18:5
love.[b] He has told us that you always have pleasant memories of us and that you long to see us, just as we [b]1Th 1:3
also long to see you. 7Therefore, brothers, in all our distress and persecution we were encouraged about
you because of your faith. 8For now we really live, since you are standing firm[c] in the Lord. 9How can we 3:8 [c]1Co 16:13
thank God enough for you[d] in return for all the joy we have in the presence of our God because of you? 3:9 [d]1Th 1:2
10Night and day we pray[e] most earnestly that we may see you again[f] and supply what is lacking in your 3:10 [e]2Ti 1:3
faith. [f]1Th 2:17

11Now may our God and Father himself and our Lord Jesus clear the way for us to come to you. 12May
the Lord make your love increase and overflow for each other[g] and for everyone else, just as ours does 3:12 [g]1Th 4:9,10
for you. 13May he strengthen your hearts so that you will be blameless[h] and holy in the presence of our 3:13 [h]1Co 1:8
God and Father when our Lord Jesus comes[i] with all his holy ones. [i]1Th 2:19

Living to Please God

4 Finally, brothers,[j] we instructed you how to live in order to please God,[k] as in fact you are living. 4:1 [j]2Co 13:11
Now we ask you and urge you in the Lord Jesus to do this more and more. 2For you know what in- [k]2Co 5:9
structions we gave you by the authority of the Lord Jesus.

3It is God's will that you should be sanctified: that you should avoid sexual immorality;[l] 4that each of 4:3 [l]1Co 6:18

4:3 A wide range of sexual values and practices existed in Paul's day in Greek and Roman society; moral standards were generally low, and chastity was regarded as an unreasonable restriction. Paul offered people from diverse backgrounds a sexual standard based on what they shared—a relationship with God.

Travel in the Greco-Roman World

1 THESSALONIANS 3 Travelers in the Greco-Roman world could choose to journey either by foot or by sea. Although the opportunities for travel greatly increased under the Roman Empire, journeys continued to be treacherous and slow. The vast expanse of the empire led of necessity to the construction and improvement of an intricate network of roads in order to connect cities from east to west. Major arteries, such as the Via Egnatia (which passed through Thessalonica),[1] conveyed an enormous amount of traffic, and cities along these routes became prosperous and cosmopolitan. These well-developed and maintained roads were necessary for both military operations and trade purposes.[2] Amazingly, the quality of their construction was so high that many of them remain intact to this day.

Voyage by sea put the traveler at the risk of shipwreck and intervention by buccaneers, but the presence of Roman fleets on the seas lessened the fears of piracy. With the exception of the dangerous winter season, running from mid-November until early March, such voyages were significantly less expensive and faster than travel by land. Scholars used to think that ships in classical times hugged the shoreline and never ventured into deep water, but recent research has proved this to be false.[3]

The mobility made possible by the Roman Empire contributed greatly to the spread of Christianity in the Greco-Roman world. Paul and his coworkers traveled extensively, both by foot and by sea, in their efforts to spread the gospel and to maintain contact with the churches they had established (1Th 3:2,6). Reflecting upon his own travels, Paul mentioned three shipwrecks and other dangers that he had faced (2Co 11:25–26). Scholars estimate from the journeys recorded in Acts that Paul must have covered over 10,000 miles during his missionary career.[4]

[1]See "Thessalonica" on page 1944. [2]See "The Roman Army and the Occupation of the Holy Land" on page 1829 and "Trade and Mercantilism in the Roman Empire" on page 2070. [3]See "Seafaring in the Ancient World" on page 1473. [4]See "The Missionary Journeys of Paul" on page 1795.

you should learn to control his own body[a][m] in a way that is holy and honorable, 5 not in passionate lust[n]
like the heathen,[o] who do not know God; 6 and that in this matter no one should wrong his brother or take
advantage of him.[p] The Lord will punish men for all such sins,[q] as we have already told you and warned
you. 7 For God did not call us to be impure, but to live a holy life.[r] 8 Therefore, he who rejects this instruc-
tion does not reject man but God, who gives you his Holy Spirit.[s]

9 Now about brotherly love[t] we do not need to write to you,[u] for you yourselves have been taught by
God to love each other.[v] 10 And in fact, you do love all the brothers throughout Macedonia.[w] Yet we urge
you, brothers, to do so more and more.[x]

11 Make it your ambition to lead a quiet life, to mind your own business and to work with your hands,[y]
just as we told you, 12 so that your daily life may win the respect of outsiders[z] and so that you will not be
dependent on anybody.

The Coming of the Lord

13 Brothers, we do not want you to be ignorant about those who fall asleep, or to grieve like the rest of
men, who have no hope.[a] 14 We believe that Jesus died and rose again and so we believe that God will
bring with Jesus those who have fallen asleep in him.[b] 15 According to the Lord's own word, we tell you
that we who are still alive, who are left till the coming of the Lord, will certainly not precede those who
have fallen asleep.[c] 16 For the Lord himself will come down from heaven, with a loud command, with the
voice of the archangel and with the trumpet call of God,[d] and the dead in Christ will rise first.[e] 17 After
that, we who are still alive and are left[f] will be caught up together with them in the clouds[g] to meet the
Lord in the air. And so we will be with the Lord[h] forever. 18 Therefore encourage each other with these
words.

5 Now, brothers, about times and dates[i] we do not need to write to you,[j] 2 for you know very well that
the day of the Lord[k] will come like a thief in the night.[l] 3 While people are saying, "Peace and safety,"
destruction will come on them suddenly, as labor pains on a pregnant woman, and they will not escape.

4 But you, brothers, are not in darkness[m] so that this day should surprise you like a thief. 5 You are all
sons of the light and sons of the day. We do not belong to the night or to the darkness. 6 So then, let us not
be like others, who are asleep,[n] but let us be alert and self-controlled. 7 For those who sleep, sleep at night,
and those who get drunk, get drunk at night.[o] 8 But since we belong to the day, let us be self-controlled,
putting on faith and love as a breastplate,[p] and the hope of salvation[q] as a helmet.[r] 9 For God did not ap-
point us to suffer wrath but to receive salvation through our Lord Jesus Christ.[s] 10 He died for us so that,
whether we are awake or asleep, we may live together with him.[t] 11 Therefore encourage one another and
build each other up, just as in fact you are doing.

Final Instructions

12 Now we ask you, brothers, to respect those who work hard among you, who are over you in the Lord[u]
and who admonish you. 13 Hold them in the highest regard in love because of their work. Live in peace
with each other.[v] 14 And we urge you, brothers, warn those who are idle,[w] encourage the timid, help the
weak,[x] be patient with everyone. 15 Make sure that nobody pays back wrong for wrong,[y] but always try
to be kind to each other[z] and to everyone else.

16 Be joyful always;[a] 17 pray continually; 18 give thanks in all circumstances, for this is God's will for you
in Christ Jesus.

19 Do not put out the Spirit's fire;[b] 20 do not treat prophecies[c] with contempt. 21 Test everything.[d] Hold
on to the good. 22 Avoid every kind of evil.

4:4 [m]1Co 7:2,9 **4:5** [n]Ro 1:26 [o]Eph 4:17 **4:6** [p]1Co 6:8 [q]Heb 13:4 **4:7** [r]Lev 11:44; 1Pe 1:15 **4:8** [s]Ro 5:5; Gal 4:6 **4:9** [t]Ro 12:10 [u]1Th 5:1 [v]Jn 13:34 **4:10** [w]1Th 1:7 [x]1Th 3:12 **4:11** [y]Eph 4:28; 2Th 3:10-12 **4:12** [z]Mk 4:11 **4:13** [a]Eph 2:12 **4:14** [b]1Co 15:18 **4:15** [c]1Co 15:52 **4:16** [d]Mt 24:31 [e]1Co 15:23; 2Th 2:1 **4:17** [f]1Co 15:52 [g]Ac 1:9; Rev 11:12 [h]Jn 12:26 **5:1** [i]Ac 1:7 [j]1Th 4:9 **5:2** [k]1Co 1:8 [l]2Pe 3:10 **5:4** [m]Ac 26:18; 1Jn 2:8 **5:6** [n]Ro 13:11 **5:7** [o]Ac 2:15; 2Pe 2:13 **5:8** [p]Eph 6:14 [q]Ro 8:24 [r]Eph 6:17 **5:9** [s]2Th 2:13,14 **5:10** [t]2Co 5:15 **5:12** [u]1Ti 5:17; Heb 13:17 **5:13** [v]Mk 9:50 **5:14** [w]2Th 3:6,7, 11 [x]Ro 14:1 **5:15** [y]1Pe 3:9 [z]Gal 6:10; Eph 4:32 **5:16** [a]Php 4:4 **5:19** [b]Eph 4:30 **5:20** [c]1Co 14:1-40 **5:21** [d]1Co 14:29; 1Jn 4:1

[a] 4 Or *learn to live with his own wife*; or *learn to acquire a wife*

4:11 The Greeks in general thought manual labor degrading and fit only for slaves (see the note on 2:9). Christians took seriously the need for earning their own living, but some of the Thessalonians, perhaps as a result of their belief in the imminent return of Christ (see 2Th 3:11), were neglecting work and relying on others to support them.

4:13 For the Christian, sleep is a particularly apt metaphor for death, since death's finality and horror are removed by the assurance of resurrection. Inscriptions on tombs and references in literature show that first-century pagans viewed death with horror, as the end of everything.

4:16–17 The only named archangel in the Bible is Michael (Jude 9; see Da 10:13). In Scripture, Gabriel is simply called an angel (Lk 1:19,26). See "Angels and Guardian Spirits in the Bible and the Ancient Near East" on page 1529.

See "Trumpets in the Ancient World" on page 2057.

See also "Storm Gods, Storm Imagery and Theophany" on page 808.

5:8 Paul did not consistently attach a particular virtue to each piece of armor; the general idea of equipment for battle is pictured.

5:11 The verb "build up" was basically applied to building houses, but Paul frequently used it for Christians being edified.

[23]May God himself, the God of peace,[e] sanctify you through and through. May your whole spirit, soul
and body be kept blameless at the coming of our Lord Jesus Christ. [24]The one who calls you is faithful[f]
and he will do it.

[25]Brothers, pray for us.[g] [26]Greet all the brothers with a holy kiss.[h] [27]I charge you before the Lord to have
this letter read to all the brothers.[i]
[28]The grace of our Lord Jesus Christ be with you.[j]

5:23 [e]Ro 15:33
5:24 [f]1Co 1:9
5:25 [g]Eph 6:19
5:26 [h]Ro 16:16
5:27 [i]Col 4:16
5:28 [j]Ro 16:20

5:14 See the note on 4:11.

5:26 For "holy kiss," see the note on 1 Corinthians 16:20 and "The Jewish Custom of Kissing" on page 1682.

INTRODUCTION TO 2 *Thessalonians*

AUTHOR, PLACE AND DATE OF WRITING

Although this letter declares itself to be from Paul and fits perfectly well as a sequel to 1 Thessalonians, many scholars have been skeptical about its authenticity. The letter's vocabulary and style have been subjected to minute analysis, but statistics in this regard are of dubious value for so short a letter. Idiosyncrasies in its style, though real, are not substantial enough to overthrow Pauline authorship, and there are many similarities between the two letters. Another argument is that the eschatology of 2 Thessalonians differs from that of Paul's earlier epistle to this congregation. While 2 Thessalonians implies that the coming of the Lord will be preceded by an observable event—the appearance of the "man of lawlessness" (2Th 2:3)—the argument goes, 1 Thessalonians teaches that Christ's return will be sudden and unexpected (1Th 5:1–4). In fact, however, 1 Thessalonians 5 indicates that the end will be unanticipated by unbelievers, but not by believers. Both letters are brief responses to problems among the Thessalonians, and the two should not be set against each other.

It appears that 2 Thessalonians was written soon after 1 Thessalonians, probably after Paul had received a response to his first letter. Thus, 2 Thessalonians was likely written from Corinth in about A.D. 51–52.

AUDIENCE

Paul wrote to the new believers in Thessalonica, a major military and commercial port located along the Egnatian Way (see "Thessalonica" on p. 1944).

CULTURAL FACTS AND HIGHLIGHTS

Second Thessalonians was clearly a response to ongoing issues among the Thessalonians. On the one hand, these believers were enduring in the faith despite persecution (2Th 1:4). On the other, some had become frantic about the return of the Lord (ch. 2), while others had taken to living off the largesse of their fellow believers (3:6–15). Paul wanted to set the record straight.

TIMELINE

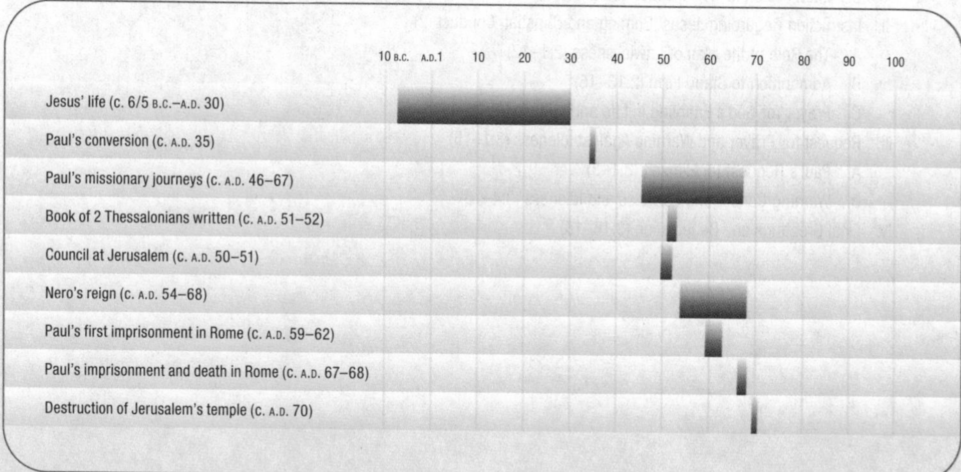

AS YOU READ

Note Paul's words of encouragement to those experiencing persecution and his concern for the Thessalonians as expressed in his prayers. What lessons can be learned about perseverance in suffering? Make a list of the truths set forth by Paul concerning the end times and Christ's second coming.

DID YOU KNOW?

- "Powerful angels" may refer to a class of angels (such a group is mentioned in apocalyptic writings) endowed with special power to do God's will (1:7).
- Until the New Testament was written, essential Christian teaching was passed on in the "traditions" (2:15).
- Paul normally dictated his letters, but toward the end of some of them he added a brief word in his own handwriting (3:17).

THEMES

Second Thessalonians includes the following themes:

1. *Christ's return.* Some of the Thessalonians had developed an unhealthy anxiety about Christ's return and had been duped by those who claimed this event had already occurred (2:2). Paul stated that Christ's coming will be preceded by the arrival of an antichrist figure, who will unleash a season of unprecedented hostility to God, incite widespread rebellion and delude many through satanic signs and wonders. He will be a self-deifying figure who will exalt himself over other deities, seek to destroy Christ's work and beguile those who are perishing (2:4–12).

2. *Vigilance until Christ's return.* Paul reminded this church that it had been chosen for salvation through sanctification by God and that it must stand firm to the end (2:13–17). Since God is the One who will inflict vengeance on those who afflict the faithful, Christians are to wait patiently and faithfully for Christ's return. Watchfulness is expressed by diligent work for Christ.

OUTLINE

I. Greeting, Thanksgiving and Prayer (1)
   A. Greeting (1:1–2)
   B. Thanksgiving for the Thessalonians' Perseverance Under Persecution (1:3–10)
   C. Intercession for Their Continued Growth and Fruitfulness (1:11–12)

II. Instruction Regarding Jesus' Coming and Christian Conduct (2)
   A. The Role of the Man of Lawlessness (2:1–12)
   B. Admonition to Stand Firm (2:13–15)
   C. Prayer for God's Enabling in Life and Ministry (2:16–17)

III. Request for Prayer and Warning Against Idleness (3:1–15)
   A. Paul's Request for Himself (3:1–3)
   B. Warning Concerning Laziness and Idleness (3:4–15)

IV. Final Greetings and Benediction (3:16–18)

1:1 [a]Ac 16:1; 1Th 1:1 1 Paul, Silas[a] and Timothy,[a]

To the church of the Thessalonians in God our Father and the Lord Jesus Christ:

1:2 [b]Ro 1:7 [2]Grace and peace to you from God the Father and the Lord Jesus Christ.[b]

Thanksgiving and Prayer

[3]We ought always to thank God for you, brothers, and rightly so, because your faith is growing more
1:3 [c]1Th 3:12 and more, and the love every one of you has for each other is increasing.[c] [4]Therefore, among God's
1:4 [d]2Co 7:14 [e]1Th 1:3 churches we boast[d] about your perseverance and faith[e] in all the persecutions and trials you are en-
[f]1Th 2:14 during.[f]

1:5 [g]Php 1:28 [5]All this is evidence[g] that God's judgment is right, and as a result you will be counted worthy of the
kingdom of God, for which you are suffering. [6]God is just: He will pay back trouble to those who trouble
1:6 [h]Col 3:25; Rev 6:10 you[h] [7]and give relief to you who are troubled, and to us as well. This will happen when the Lord Jesus is
1:7 [i]1Th 4:16; Jude 14 revealed from heaven in blazing fire with his powerful angels.[i] [8]He will punish those who do not know
1:8 [j]Gal 4:8 [k]Ro 2:8 God[j] and do not obey the gospel of our Lord Jesus.[k] [9]They will be punished with everlasting destruc-
1:9 [l]Php 3:19; 2Pe 3:7 [m]2Th 2:8 tion[l] and shut out from the presence of the Lord and from the majesty of his power[m] [10]on the day[n] he
1:10 [n]1Co 3:13 [o]Jn 17:10 comes to be glorified[o] in his holy people and to be marveled at among all those who have believed. This
[p]1Co 1:6 includes you, because you believed our testimony to you.[p]

1:11 [q]ver 5 [r]1Th 1:3 [11]With this in mind, we constantly pray for you, that our God may count you worthy[q] of his calling,
and that by his power he may fulfill every good purpose of yours and every act prompted by your faith.[r]
1:12 [s]Php 2:9-11 [12]We pray this so that the name of our Lord Jesus may be glorified in you,[s] and you in him, according to
the grace of our God and the Lord Jesus Christ.[b]

The Man of Lawlessness

2:1 [t]Mk 13:27; 1Th 4:15-17 2 Concerning the coming of our Lord Jesus Christ and our being gathered to him,[t] we ask you, broth-
2:2 [u]2Th 3:17 [v]1Co 1:8 ers, [2]not to become easily unsettled or alarmed by some prophecy, report or letter[u] supposed to have
2:3 [w]Eph 5:6-8 [x]Da 7:25; 8:25; come from us, saying that the day of the Lord[v] has already come. [3]Don't let anyone deceive you[w] in any
11:36; Rev 13:5,6 way, for ⌊that day will not come⌋ until the rebellion occurs and the man of lawlessness[c] is revealed,[x] the
2:4 [y]1Co 8:5 [z]Isa 14:13,14; man doomed to destruction. [4]He will oppose and will exalt himself over everything that is called God[y]
Eze 28:2 or is worshiped, so that he sets himself up in God's temple, proclaiming himself to be God.[z]

[5]Don't you remember that when I was with you I used to tell you these things? [6]And now you know
what is holding him back, so that he may be revealed at the proper time. [7]For the secret power of law-
lessness is already at work; but the one who now holds it back will continue to do so till he is taken out
of the way. [8]And then the lawless one will be revealed, whom the Lord Jesus will overthrow with the
2:8 [a]Isa 11:4; Rev 19:15 breath of his mouth[a] and destroy by the splendor of his coming. [9]The coming of the lawless one will be
2:9 [b]Mt 24:24; Jn 4:48 in accordance with the work of Satan displayed in all kinds of counterfeit miracles, signs and wonders,[b]
2:10 [c]1Co 1:18 [10]and in every sort of evil that deceives those who are perishing.[c] They perish because they refused to
2:11 [d]Ro 1:28 love the truth and so be saved. [11]For this reason God sends them[d] a powerful delusion so that they will
believe the lie [12]and so that all will be condemned who have not believed the truth but have delighted in
2:12 [e]Ro 1:32 wickedness.[e]

Stand Firm

[13]But we ought always to thank God for you, brothers loved by the Lord, because from the beginning
2:13 [f]Eph 1:4 [g]1Th 5:9 [h]1Pe 1:2 God chose you[d][f] to be saved[g] through the sanctifying work of the Spirit[h] and through belief in the truth.
[14]He called you to this through our gospel, that you might share in the glory of our Lord Jesus Christ.
2:15 [i]1Co 16:13 [j]1Co 11:2 [15]So then, brothers, stand firm[i] and hold to the teachings[e] we passed on to you,[j] whether by word of
mouth or by letter.

[a] *1* Greek *Silvanus,* a variant of *Silas* [b] *12* Or *God and Lord, Jesus Christ* [c] *3* Some manuscripts *sin* [d] *13* Some manuscripts *because God chose you as his firstfruits* [e] *15* Or *traditions*

1:7 "Powerful angels" may refer to a class of angels (such a group is mentioned in apocalyptic writings) endowed with special power to do God's will (see "Angels and Guardian Spirits in the Bible and the Ancient Near East" on p. 1529).

1:12 In ancient times one's name was often more than a personal label; it summed up what a person was.

2:2 The Greek for "unsettled" was often used of a ship adrift from its mooring, suggesting lack of stability.

2:15 "Teachings" is literally "traditions." Until the New Testament was written, essential Christian teaching was passed on in the "traditions," just as was Rabbinic law (see the note on Mt 15:2).

16 May our Lord Jesus Christ himself and God our Father, who loved us[k] and by his grace gave us eternal
encouragement and good hope, 17 encourage[l] your hearts and strengthen[m] you in every good deed and word.

2:16 [k]Jn 3:16
2:17 [l]1Th 3:2 [m]2Th 3:3

Request for Prayer

3 Finally, brothers,[n] pray for us[o] that the message of the Lord[p] may spread rapidly and be honored, just
as it was with you. 2 And pray that we may be delivered from wicked and evil men,[q] for not every-
one has faith. 3 But the Lord is faithful,[r] and he will strengthen and protect you from the evil one.[s] 4 We

3:1 [n]1Th 4:1 [o]1Th 5:25 [p]1Th 1:8
3:2 [q]Ro 15:31
3:3 [r]1Co 1:9 [s]Mt 5:37

3:2 These "wicked and evil men" were people who maliciously obstructed the gospel, like those in Thessalonica who had instigated a riot to hinder Paul from preaching the gospel when he had first visited the city (see Ac 17:5).

Labor and Welfare in the Ancient World

2 THESSALONIANS 3 In the ancient world there were three classes of laborers: freemen, slaves and a middle group, serfs, who were bound to work the soil or to perform other menial tasks on behalf of some state or institution. Slaves and serfs naturally labored under the direction of their overlords,[1] but freemen were obliged to find means of providing for themselves. Most men learned their trade from their fathers, just as most women acquired domestic skills from their mothers.

The varieties of occupations an individual might follow involved both skilled and unskilled labor. Jesus' parable of the unjust steward (Lk 16:1–9) illustrates two extremes: stewards (educated people who managed the financial affairs of others) and those who dug ditches or even begged. A remarkable Egyptian document called *Dua-Khety*, or "The Satire on the Trades," lists a wide variety of possible occupations: jewelers, carpenters, barbers, smiths, potters, agricultural workers, couriers, cobblers and others. Any and all of these jobs, this text asserts, were miserable occupations in comparison with the work of the scribe.[2]

Autograph and self-portrait of an artist who worked in the Valley of the Kings; Egypt, 1307–1070 B.C.

© The Schøyen Collection; photography courtesy of Mr. Martin Schøyen

The rise of the Roman Empire[3] also gave rise to a class of citizens that to some degree lived off the public dole: During the period of the Roman Republic, politicians sought to gain the votes of the masses by periodically giving people a supply of grain, either freely or at a greatly reduced price. C. Sempronius Gracchus (d. 122 B.C.) made this a regular feature of Roman life by establishing a monthly ration of grain at a set price. In 58 B.C. P. Clodius Pulcher made this ration free. At the beginning of the empire, Augustus reorganized the system of public dole, instituting the tradition of providing "bread and circuses" for the masses.[4]

Apart from the state welfare system for the Romans, Christians were encouraged to donate freely to the poor, especially to fellow believers in need. Such generosity could be—and invariably was—abused. Already in 2 Thessalonians 3 Paul found it necessary to rebuke those who were content to live off the charity of other Christians, confronting them with the maxim, "If a man will not work, he shall not eat" (v. 10). In 1 Timothy 5:3–15 Paul provided guidelines for providing assistance to widows who were indeed needy, in contrast to those who should not have been living off the beneficence of the churches. Brought up in the Jewish tradition in which every son learned a trade, Paul supported himself as a tentmaker (Ac 18:2–3), and he expected other Christians to work for their livings as well.

[1]See "Slavery in the Greco-Roman World" on page 1979. [2]See "The Scribe" on page 682. [3]See "The Roman Empire" on page 1845. [4]See also "The 'Benefactor'" on page 1711.

3:4 [t]2Co 2:3 have confidence[t] in the Lord that you are doing and will continue to do the things we command. 5May
3:5 [u]1Ch 29:18 the Lord direct your hearts[u] into God's love and Christ's perseverance.

Warning Against Idleness

3:6 [v]1Co 5:4 [w]Ro 16:17 [x]ver 7, 6In the name of the Lord Jesus Christ,[v] we command you, brothers, to keep away from[w] every broth-
11 [y]1Co 11:2 er who is idle[x] and does not live according to the teaching[a] you received from us.[y] 7For you yourselves
3:7 [z]1Co 4:16 know how you ought to follow our example.[z] We were not idle when we were with you, 8nor did we eat
3:8 [a]Ac 18:3; Eph 4:28 anyone's food without paying for it. On the contrary, we worked[a] night and day, laboring and toiling so
that we would not be a burden to any of you. 9We did this, not because we do not have the right to such
3:9 [b]1Co 9:4-14 [c]ver 7 help,[b] but in order to make ourselves a model for you to follow.[c] 10For even when we were with you,[d] we
3:10 [d]1Th 3:4 [e]1Th 4:11 gave you this rule: "If a man will not work,[e] he shall not eat."
3:11 [f]ver 6,7; 1Ti 5:13 11We hear that some among you are idle. They are not busy; they are busybodies.[f] 12Such people we
3:12 [g]1Th 4:1 [h]1Th 4:11; command and urge in the Lord Jesus Christ[g] to settle down and earn the bread they eat.[h] 13And as for
Eph 4:28 you, brothers, never tire of doing what is right.[i]
3:13 [i]Gal 6:9 14If anyone does not obey our instruction in this letter, take special note of him. Do not associate with
3:14 [j]ver 6 him,[j] in order that he may feel ashamed. 15Yet do not regard him as an enemy, but warn him as a brother.[k]
3:15 [k]Gal 6:1; 1Th 5:14

Final Greetings

3:16 [l]Ro 15:33 [m]Ru 2:4 16Now may the Lord of peace[l] himself give you peace at all times and in every way. The Lord be with
all of you.[m]
3:17 [n]1Co 16:21 17I, Paul, write this greeting in my own hand,[n] which is the distinguishing mark in all my letters. This
is how I write.
3:18 [o]Ro 16:20 18The grace of our Lord Jesus Christ be with you all.[o]

[a] 6 Or *tradition*

3:5 For "hearts," see the note on Psalm 4:7.
3:6 For "the name," see the note on 1:12. For "idle," see the note on 1 Thessalonians 4:11.
3:15 For "brother," see the note on Romans 1:13.

3:17 Paul normally dictated his letters, but toward the end of some of them he added a brief word in his own handwriting. Here he stated that this practice was his distinguishing mark. (See "Writing Materials in the Ancient World" on p. 2037.)

INTRODUCTION TO 1 Timothy

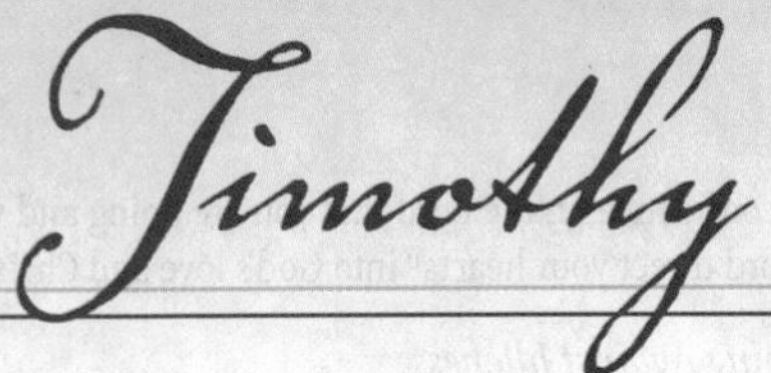

AUTHOR, PLACE AND DATE OF WRITING

Paul wrote this letter to his disciple Timothy, whom he had left in Ephesus to oversee the work there. Today many scholars deny Pauline authorship of 1 and 2 Timothy and Titus, but much evidence supports the traditional view that Paul did indeed write these letters (see "The Authorship of the Pastoral Epistles" on p. 1957).

First Timothy was written after Paul's release from Roman imprisonment (Ac 28:16–31), in about 63–65 and possibly from Macedonia.

AUDIENCE

Paul wrote to Timothy, whom he had sent to the church in Ephesus to combat the false teaching that had arisen there. Timothy occupied a special place in Paul's heart as his coworker, emissary, traveling companion and "true son in the faith" (1:2).

CULTURAL FACTS AND HIGHLIGHTS

First Timothy is essentially a letter of encouragement to Paul's aide, Timothy. This is not to say, however, that it is entirely personal. Paul seems to have used the occasion to construct a letter on the nature of Christian ministry in the face of opposition and heresy. Paul viewed the opposition his younger protégé was enduring from a prophetic perspective, pointing out that the Spirit had foretold such apostasy (4:1). Paul instructed Timothy to refute false teachers and to promote good order and godliness in the church.

TIMELINE

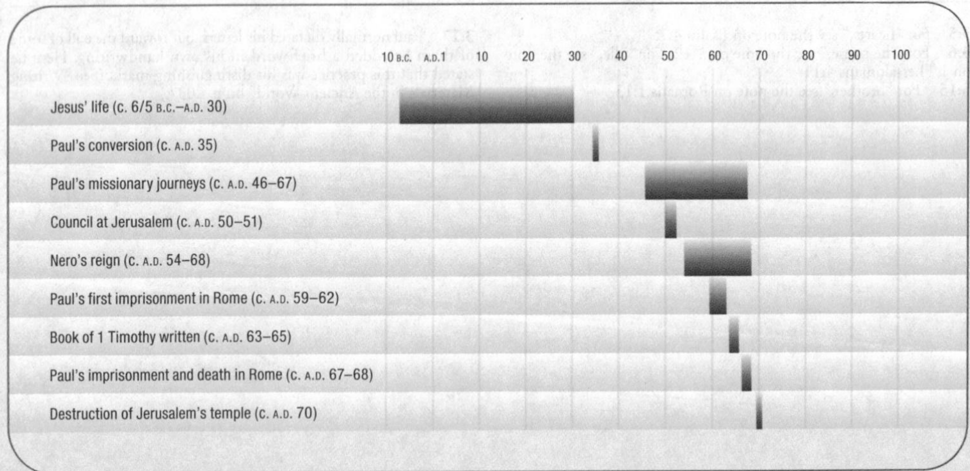

AS YOU READ

Note the types of problems about which Paul alerted Timothy. Are there modern correlations? Identify Paul's advice for dealing with leadership responsibilities and combating heresy.

DID YOU KNOW?

- In Greek culture the word "overseer" was used of a presiding official in a civic or religious organization (3:1–7).
- In ancient Rome life expectancy was much lower than it is today. We may assume that there were more unmarried women than available men in the Ephesian congregation and that some of these women had become financially destitute (5:3–5).
- Paul gave instructions to Timothy about the care of widows by the church. The only widows included were those who were at least sixty years of age, had been married only once and had a reputation for good works (5:4).

THEMES

First Timothy includes the following themes:

1. *Sound doctrine.* False teachers who showed an unhealthy fascination with myths and genealogies (1:4; 4:7) and a preoccupation with the law (1:7) had infiltrated the church in Ephesus. They prohibited marriage and the eating of certain foods (4:3) and taught that the final resurrection had already taken place (1:20; see 2Ti 2:18). In contrast, Timothy was to teach only what was trustworthy, sound and good (1Ti 1:9–11; 3:9; 4:6; 6:3–4).

2. *Right living.* The false teachers were intent on stirring up controversy and prone to speculation (1:4,6; 6:4,20), deception (4:1–2) and greed (6:5). Paul instructed Timothy to "set an example for the believers in speech, in life, in love, in faith and in purity" (4:12).

3. *Evangelism.* Paul's concern for the church's successful evangelism lay at the heart of his commands. The conduct of Christians is to be above reproach because it has a direct effect on the success of their evangelistic efforts.

4. *Church leaders.* Church leaders need to reach for even higher standards than what is expected of persons holding similarly important positions in contemporary society. Warnings against immoral practices and materialism, however, apply to all members (6:7–10,17–19).

OUTLINE

I. Greeting (1:1–2)
II. Warning Against False Teachers (1:3–11)
III. The Lord's Grace to Paul (1:12–17)
IV. The Purpose of Paul's Instructions to Timothy (1:18–20)
V. Instructions Concerning the Church (2:1—4:5)
   A. Guidelines for Public Worship (2:1–15)
   B. Qualifications for Overseers and Deacons (3:1–13)
   C. The Purpose of the Letter (3:14–16)
   D. Dealing With False Teaching (4:1–5)
VI. Timothy's Responsibilities (4:6—6:19)
   A. Personal Life (4:6–16)
   B. Relationships With Others (5:1—6:2)
   C. More on False Teachers (6:3–5)
   D. The Love of Money (6:6–10)
   E. Paul's Charge to Timothy (6:11–16)
   F. Command to the Rich (6:17–19)
VII. Conclusion (6:20–21)

1 Paul, an apostle of Christ Jesus by the command of God[a] our Savior and of Christ Jesus our hope,[b] **1:1** [a]Tit 1:3 [b]Col 1:27

2 To Timothy[c] my true son[d] in the faith: **1:2** [c]Ac 16:1 [d]2Ti 1:2; Tit 1:4

Grace, mercy and peace from God the Father and Christ Jesus our Lord.

Warning Against False Teachers of the Law

3 As I urged you when I went into Macedonia, stay there in Ephesus[e] so that you may command cer- **1:3** [e]Ac 18:19
tain men not to teach false doctrines[f] any longer 4 nor to devote themselves to myths[g] and endless gene- [f]Gal 1:6,7 **1:4** [g]1Ti 4:7;
alogies. These promote controversies[h] rather than God's work—which is by faith. 5 The goal of this com- Tit 1:14 [h]1Ti 6:4
mand is love, which comes from a pure heart[i] and a good conscience and a sincere faith.[j] 6 Some have **1:5** [i]2Ti 2:22
wandered away from these and turned to meaningless talk. 7 They want to be teachers of the law, but they [j]2Ti 1:5
do not know what they are talking about or what they so confidently affirm.
8 We know that the law is good[k] if one uses it properly. 9 We also know that law[a] is made not for the righ- **1:8** [k]Ro 7:12
teous but for lawbreakers and rebels,[l] the ungodly and sinful, the unholy and irreligious; for those who **1:9** [l]Gal 3:19
kill their fathers or mothers, for murderers, 10 for adulterers and perverts, for slave traders and liars and
perjurers—and for whatever else is contrary to the sound doctrine[m] 11 that conforms to the glorious **1:10** [m]2Ti 4:3; Tit 1:9
gospel of the blessed God, which he entrusted to me.[n] **1:11** [n]Gal 2:7

The Lord's Grace to Paul

12 I thank Christ Jesus our Lord, who has given me strength,[o] that he considered me faithful, appoint- **1:12** [o]Php 4:13
ing me to his service. 13 Even though I was once a blasphemer and a persecutor[p] and a violent man, I was **1:13** [p]Ac 8:3
shown mercy because I acted in ignorance and unbelief.[q] 14 The grace of our Lord was poured out on me [q]Ac 26:9
abundantly,[r] along with the faith and love that are in Christ Jesus.[s] **1:14** [r]Ro 5:20 [s]2Ti 1:13
15 Here is a trustworthy saying[t] that deserves full acceptance: Christ Jesus came into the world to save **1:15** [t]1Ti 3:1;
sinners—of whom I am the worst. 16 But for that very reason I was shown mercy[u] so that in me, the worst 2Ti 2:11; Tit 3:8 **1:16** [u]ver 13
of sinners, Christ Jesus might display his unlimited patience as an example for those who would believe **1:17** [v]Rev 15:3
on him and receive eternal life. 17 Now to the King[v] eternal, immortal, invisible,[w] the only God, be honor [w]Col 1:15 [x]Ro 11:36
and glory for ever and ever. Amen.[x]
18 Timothy, my son, I give you this instruction in keeping with the prophecies once made about you,[y] **1:18** [y]1Ti 4:14
so that by following them you may fight the good fight,[z] 19 holding on to faith and a good conscience. [z]2Ti 2:3
Some have rejected these and so have shipwrecked their faith.[a] 20 Among them are Hymenaeus[b] and Al- **1:19** [a]1Ti 6:21 **1:20** [b]2Ti 2:17
exander,[c] whom I have handed over to Satan[d] to be taught not to blaspheme. [c]2Ti 4:14 [d]1Co 5:5

Instructions on Worship

2 I urge, then, first of all, that requests, prayers, intercession and thanksgiving be made for everyone—
2 for kings and all those in authority,[e] that we may live peaceful and quiet lives in all godliness and **2:2** [e]Ezr 6:10; Ro 13:1
holiness. 3 This is good, and pleases God our Savior, 4 who wants[f] all men[g] to be saved and to come to a **2:4** [f]Eze 18:23,32 [g]Tit 2:11

[a] 9 Or *that the law*

1:1 For "Paul," see the note on Philippians 3:5 and for "apostle" the note on 2 Corinthians 1:1.
1:2 The ancient Greek usage of the word "grace" implied a "superior" welcoming and accepting of a "subordinate" into intimate relationship and favor.
1:3–11 For false doctrines, see the note on Colossians 2:8–23.
1:3 For "Macedonia," see the note on Philippians 4:15 and for "Ephesus" the note on Ephesians 1:1; see also "Early History of Ephesus" on page 1965 and "Ephesus During the Time of Paul" on page 1968.
1:4 "Myths" may refer to mythical stories built upon Old Testament history ("genealogies") that later developed into intricate Gnostic philosophical systems (see "Early Christian Heresies" on p. 1896 and "The Gnostics and Their Scriptures" on p. 2029).
1:18 In the early church God revealed his will in various matters through prophets (see Ac 13:1–3, where prophets had an active role in sending Paul and Barnabas on their mission to the Gentiles). In Timothy's case a prophecy may have occurred at the time of or before his ordination (1 Ti 4:14), perhaps about 12 years earlier on Paul's second missionary journey (see Ac 16:1–3).
1:20 The Jews had two forms of excommunication (disciplinary exclusion from church fellowship), apparently alluded to in Luke 6:22 by Jesus: "Blessed are you . . . when they exclude you [the Jewish *middûy,* for 30, 60 or 90 days] and . . . reject your name as evil [the Jewish *ḥęrem,* a formally pronounced, perpetual cutting off from the community], because of the Son of Man." Christian excommunication was both commanded by the Lord (Mt 18:15–18) and followed by apostolic precept and practice (1Co 5:11; Tit 3:10). "Being handed over to Satan" (see also 1Co 5:5) seems to mean being cast out of the church into the world that lies in the power of the wicked one (Eph 6:12; 1Jn 5:19). The object of excommunication is the good of the offender (1Co 5:5) and the moral well-being of the sound church members (2Ti 2:17). Its subjects are those guilty of heresy or great immorality (here and in 1Co 5:1–5). This penalty is inflicted by the church and its representative ministers (1Co 5:1,3–4; Tit 3:10). Paul's inspired words, however, give no warrant for uninspired ministers claiming the same right to direct the church to excommunicate at will (2Co 2:7–9).
2:1–2 The notorious Roman emperor Nero (A.D. 54–68) was in power when Paul wrote these words (see "Nero, Persecutor of Christians" on p. 1931).

THE AUTHORSHIP OF THE PASTORAL EPISTLES

1 TIMOTHY 1 First and Second Timothy and Titus, the **Pastoral epistles**,[1] claim Paul as their author (1Ti 1:1; 2Ti 1:1; Tit 1:1). These unique letters include biographical material (2Ti 1:8,15–18), as well as personal requests (2Ti 4:9–13,19–21; Tit 3:12) appropriate to Paul. Nonetheless, many scholars maintain that the Pastorals are **pseudepigraphical**—falsely written in Paul's name. Several arguments are commonly made in defense of this viewpoint:

- It is sometimes difficult to relate the incidents the Pastorals describe (such as church work in Crete, mentioned in Titus) to the history of Paul's missionary work as recorded in Acts.[2]
- There is evidence in these letters of a church structure that seems to have been too highly developed to have come from Paul's lifetime.
- The Pastorals contain vocabulary and style that does not seem to match what we otherwise know of Paul.

Much evidence, however, supports the traditional view of Pauline authorship:

- Writings from the second century support the belief that Paul was released from his first Roman imprisonment (Ac 28),[3] allowing for subsequent activity in Crete and Ephesus prior to his final arrest and martyrdom.[4] If this was indeed the case, it might not be surprising that the Pastorals would have few parallels in Acts, since they would have come from a later period of Paul's life.
- Although the Pastoral Epistles display significant interest in the qualifications for church leaders, this does not necessitate a highly developed church structure along the lines of the later Roman Catholic Church. Paul alluded to "overseers and deacons" in his earlier writings (Php 1:1), making invalid the assumption that the earliest churches lacked structure. Indeed, the very first congregation, the one at Jerusalem, very quickly felt the need for a more developed structure and for several distinct types of offices within the church (apostles, deacons and elders; Ac 6:1–6; 11:30). The variety of "gifts" Paul described for the churches indicates a variety of offices (1Co 12:28–29), and the presence of false teachers in leadership positions in Ephesus and Crete warranted Paul's focus on the establishment of sound church leadership.
- The vocabulary and style of the Pastoral Epistles are well within Paul's range, and the variations can be explained in light of the context of these letters. Writing in the face of particular false teachings (1Ti 1:4,6–7; 2Ti 2:18; Tit 1:10,14; 3:9), Paul freely appropriated the language of his opponents for his own purposes. Furthermore, he wrote to his coworkers, Timothy and Titus, assuming their familiarity with his teaching, which allowed him to dispense with the fundamentals and focus instead upon urgent practical matters.
- The early church, which rejected pseudonymous letters, declining to accept into the **canon** letters that falsely claimed to be Pauline, fully embraced the Pastorals.[5]

The Mamertime Prison, said to have housed both Peter and Paul (Peter's traditional upside-down cross is depicted on the altar)

Preserving Bible Times; © Dr. James C. Martin; on licence Ministero per i Beni le Attivita Culturali-Soprintendza Archeologica di Roma

[1]See Glossary on page 2080 for definitions of bolded words. [2]See "The Missionary Journeys of Paul" on page 1795. [3]See "Imprisonment in the Roman World: In Prison Versus House Arrest" on page 1826. [4]See "Crete" on page 1972. [5]See also "The Bible and Pseudepigraphical Literature" on page 2041.

knowledge of the truth.[h] 5For there is one God[i] and one mediator[j] between God and men, the man Christ Jesus, 6who gave himself as a ransom for all men—the testimony[k] given in its proper time.[l] 7And for this purpose I was appointed a herald and an apostle—I am telling the truth, I am not lying—and a teacher[m] of the true faith to the Gentiles.[n]

8I want men everywhere to lift up holy hands[o] in prayer, without anger or disputing.

9I also want women to dress modestly, with decency and propriety, not with braided hair or gold or pearls or expensive clothes,[p] 10but with good deeds, appropriate for women who profess to worship God.

11A woman should learn in quietness and full submission.[q] 12I do not permit a woman to teach or to have authority over a man; she must be silent. 13For Adam was formed first, then Eve.[r] 14And Adam was not the one deceived; it was the woman who was deceived and became a sinner.[s] 15But women[a] will be saved[b] through childbearing—if they continue in faith, love[t] and holiness with propriety.

Overseers and Deacons

3 Here is a trustworthy saying:[u] If anyone sets his heart on being an overseer,[c][v] he desires a noble task. 2Now the overseer must be above reproach,[w] the husband of but one wife, temperate, self-controlled, respectable, hospitable,[x] able to teach,[y] 3not given to drunkenness, not violent but gentle, not quarrelsome,[z] not a lover of money.[a] 4He must manage his own family well and see that his children obey him with proper respect.[b] 5(If anyone does not know how to manage his own family, how can he take care of God's church?)[c] 6He must not be a recent convert, or he may become conceited[d] and fall under the same judgment as the devil. 7He must also have a good reputation with outsiders, so that he will not fall into disgrace and into the devil's trap.[e]

8Deacons,[f] likewise, are to be men worthy of respect, sincere, not indulging in much wine,[g] and not pursuing dishonest gain. 9They must keep hold of the deep truths of the faith with a clear conscience.[h] 10They must first be tested; and then if there is nothing against them, let them serve as deacons.

11In the same way, their wives[d] are to be women worthy of respect, not malicious talkers[i] but temperate and trustworthy in everything.

12A deacon must be the husband of but one wife and must manage his children and his household well.[j] 13Those who have served well gain an excellent standing and great assurance in their faith in Christ Jesus.

14Although I hope to come to you soon, I am writing you these instructions so that, 15if I am delayed, you will know how people ought to conduct themselves in God's household, which is the church[k]

2:4 [h]2Ti 2:25
2:5 [i]Ro 3:29,30 [j]Gal 3:20
2:6 [k]1Co 1:6 [l]1Ti 6:15
2:7 [m]2Ti 1:11 [n]Ac 9:15; Eph 3:7,8
2:8 [o]Ps 134:2; Lk 24:50
2:9 [p]1Pe 3:3
2:11 [q]1Co 14:34
2:13 [r]Ge 2:7,22; 1Co 11:8
2:14 [s]Ge 3:1-6, 13; 2Co 11:3
2:15 [t]1Ti 1:14
3:1 [u]1Ti 1:15 [v]Ac 20:28
3:2 [w]Tit 1:6-8 [x]Ro 12:13 [y]2Ti 2:24
3:3 [z]2Ti 2:24 [a]Heb 13:5; 1Pe 5:2
3:4 [b]Tit 1:6
3:5 [c]1Co 10:32
3:6 [d]1Ti 6:4
3:7 [e]2Ti 2:26
3:8 [f]Php 1:1 [g]Tit 2:3
3:9 [h]1Ti 1:19
3:11 [i]2Ti 3:3; Tit 2:3
3:12 [j]ver 4
3:15 [k]ver 5; Eph 2:21

[a] *15* Greek *she* [b] *15* Or *restored* [c] *1* Traditionally *bishop*; also in verse 2 [d] *11* Or *way, deaconesses*

2:5 The belief that "there is one God" is the basic tenet of Judaism, which every Jew confessed daily in the *Shema* (see the notes on Dt 6:4–9; Mk 12:29).

2:6 For "ransom," see the note on Matthew 20:28.

2:7 For "apostle," see the note on 2 Corinthians 1:1.

2:8 In this case the Greek word for "men" refers not to humankind in general but to males, as distinct from females. Women also prayed in public, however.

2:9 This was not a total ban on the wearing of jewelry or on braided hair. Rather, Paul was expressing caution in a society in which such things were viewed as signs of extravagant luxury and proud personal display (see "Dress and Fashion in the Greco-Roman World" on p. 2004 and "The Demeanor of Wives" on p. 2013).

2:12–14 Some believe that Paul in these verses restricted women in all circumstances and cultures from teaching or exercising authority over men, while others hold that Paul prohibited teaching only by women who had not themselves been properly instructed (i.e., by the women at Ephesus). Still others maintain that Paul's teaching here was historically conditioned.

Paul's restriction on women teaching certainly made sense in a world that refused to give women teachers a hearing and in which most women were uneducated. The New Testament had not yet been completed, so people were dependent on the authoritative, spoken word.

3:1–7 In Greek culture the word "overseer" was used of a presiding official in a civic or religious organization. Here it refers to a man who oversaw a local congregation. The equivalent word from the Jewish background of Christianity is "elder" (see the next paragraph for a discussion of the related terms "presbyter" and "bishop"). The terms "overseer" and "elder" are often used interchangeably in the Bible (see Ac 20:17,28; Tit 1:5–7; 1Pe 5:1–2). The duties of an overseer were to teach and preach (1 Ti 3:2; 5:17), to direct the affairs of the church (3:5; 5:17), to shepherd ("pastor") the flock of God and to guard the church from error (Ac 20:28–31).

The titles "elder" ("overseer") or "presbyter" appear to apply to the same office, with "elder" referring to the bearer's age and dignity and "bishop" to his work of superintendence. As the churches multiplied, the bishop of a larger church would often be given special honor, and so gradually there grew up a hierarchy, all the way from presiding elders to bishops (over groups of churches), to archbishops.

3:8–13 The diaconate, as a church office, is inferred from Acts 6:1–8, but at least two of the seven men in this instance were also evangelists. Ignatius, a contemporary of the apostle John, declared that the deacons were not mere servers of meat and drink, although the seven in Acts 6 did serve (*diakonein*) tables so that the apostles could devote themselves to the ministry (*diakonia*). First Timothy 3 shows that deacons were not considered ordinary lay members of the church, and Paul's mention of deacons in connection with bishops (Php 1:1) supports this view. Clement of Rome based the office on the two classes of synagogue workers mentioned in Isaiah 60:17 in the Septuagint translation—"pastors and helpers." The same Greek word, used of Phoebe in Romans 16:1, is translated as "servant" ("deaconess" in some versions). Certain women had ministered (*diakonein*) to Jesus (Lk 8:2–3). It does not appear from the Scripture or early church literature, however, that deaconesses were ever church officers.

3:11 The Greek for the phrase "their wives" simply means "the women" and therefore could refer either to the deacons' wives or to deaconesses.

3:14 See "Letter Writing in the Greco-Roman World" on page 1889 and "Writing Materials in the Ancient World" on page 2037.

of the living God, the pillar and foundation of the truth. [16]Beyond all question, the mystery[l] of godliness is great:

> He[a] appeared in a body,[b][m]
> was vindicated by the Spirit,
> was seen by angels,
> was preached among the nations,[n]
> was believed on in the world,
> was taken up in glory.[o]

Instructions to Timothy

4 The Spirit[p] clearly says that in later times[q] some will abandon the faith and follow deceiving spirits[r] and things taught by demons. [2]Such teachings come through hypocritical liars, whose consciences have been seared as with a hot iron.[s] [3]They forbid people to marry[t] and order them to abstain from certain foods,[u] which God created[v] to be received with thanksgiving[w] by those who believe and who know the truth. [4]For everything God created is good,[x] and nothing is to be rejected if it is received with thanksgiving, [5]because it is consecrated by the word of God and prayer.

[6]If you point these things out to the brothers, you will be a good minister of Christ Jesus, brought up in the truths of the faith[y] and of the good teaching that you have followed. [7]Have nothing to do with godless myths and old wives' tales;[z] rather, train yourself to be godly. [8]For physical training is of some value, but godliness has value for all things,[a] holding promise for both the present life[b] and the life to come.

[9]This is a trustworthy saying[c] that deserves full acceptance [10](and for this we labor and strive), that we have put our hope in the living God, who is the Savior of all men, and especially of those who believe. [11]Command and teach these things.[d] [12]Don't let anyone look down on you because you are young, but set an example[e] for the believers in speech, in life, in love, in faith[f] and in purity. [13]Until I come, devote yourself to the public reading of Scripture, to preaching and to teaching. [14]Do not neglect your gift, which was given you through a prophetic message[g] when the body of elders laid their hands on you.[h]

[15]Be diligent in these matters; give yourself wholly to them, so that everyone may see your progress. [16]Watch your life and doctrine closely. Persevere in them, because if you do, you will save both yourself and your hearers.

Advice About Widows, Elders and Slaves

5 Do not rebuke an older man[i] harshly,[j] but exhort him as if he were your father. Treat younger men[k] as brothers, [2]older women as mothers, and younger women as sisters, with absolute purity.

[3]Give proper recognition to those widows who are really in need.[l] [4]But if a widow has children or grandchildren, these should learn first of all to put their religion into practice by caring for their own family and so repaying their parents and grandparents,[m] for this is pleasing to God.[n] [5]The widow who is really in need[o] and left all alone puts her hope in God[p] and continues night and day to pray[q] and to ask God for help. [6]But the widow who lives for pleasure is dead even while she lives.[r] [7]Give the people these instructions,[s] too, so that no one may be open to blame. [8]If anyone does not provide for his relatives, and especially for his immediate family, he has denied[t] the faith and is worse than an unbeliever.

[a] 16 Some manuscripts *God* [b] 16 Or *in the flesh*

3:16 [l]Ro 16:25 [m]Jn 1:14 [n]Col 1:23 [o]Mk 16:19
4:1 [p]Jn 16:13 [q]2Ti 3:1 [r]2Th 2:3
4:2 [s]Eph 4:19
4:3 [t]Heb 13:4 [u]Col 2:16 [v]Ge 1:29 [w]Ro 14:6
4:4 [x]Ro 14:14-18
4:6 [y]1Ti 1:10
4:7 [z]2Ti 2:16
4:8 [a]1Ti 6:6 [b]Ps 37:9,11; Mk 10:29,30
4:9 [c]1Ti 1:15
4:11 [d]1Ti 5:7; 6:2
4:12 [e]Tit 2:7; 1Pe 5:3 [f]1Ti 1:14
4:14 [g]1Ti 1:18 [h]Ac 6:6; 2Ti 1:6
5:1 [i]Tit 2:2 [j]Lev 19:32 [k]Tit 2:6
5:3 [l]ver 5,16
5:4 [m]Eph 6:1,2 [n]1Ti 2:3
5:5 [o]ver 3,16 [p]1Co 7:34; 1Pe 3:5 [q]Lk 2:37
5:6 [r]Lk 15:24
5:7 [s]1Ti 4:11
5:8 [t]2Pe 2:1; Jude 4; Tit 1:16

3:16 For "mystery," see the note on Romans 11:25.
This verse includes a hymn (see "Early Christian Hymnody" on p. 2007).

4:3 This unbiblical asceticism arose out of the mistaken notion that the material world was evil—a central belief of the Gnostic heresy (see "The Gnostics and Their Scriptures" on p. 2029).

4:7 For "myths," see the note on 1:4.

4:12 Timothy was probably in his mid-thirties or younger at this time, and in that day such an influential position was not usually held by a man so young. For this reason, his leadership ability had been called into question.
For the names by which early Christians were known (here "believers"), see the note on 1 Peter 4:16.

4:14 For a discussion of the rite of laying on of hands, see the notes on Acts 6:6 and 2 Timothy 1:6. Here it is an act of commissioning to service.

5:3–5 In ancient Rome life expectancy was much less than it is today. We may assume that there were more unmarried women than available men in the Ephesian congregation and that some of these women had become financially destitute. Widows were particularly vulnerable in ancient societies because pensions, government assistance, life insurance, and the like were not available. Paul defined widows who were "really in need" (v. 5) as those who had no family members to care for them, who trusted God and who did not live for worldly pleasure. (See "The Care of Widows and Orphans in the Bible and the Ancient Near East" on p. 285.)

5:4 Paul gave instructions to Timothy about the care of widows by the church, but only those were included who were at least sixty years of age, had been married only once and had a reputation for good works (vv. 9–10). In the second and third centuries there was an order of widows in the church, assigned to look after the needs of women of the congregation. This order was abolished by the Synod of Laodicea in A.D. 364.

5:8 Apostolic teaching emphasized social responsibility. In the pagan world of that time people generally took care of their own family members.

9No widow may be put on the list of widows unless she is over sixty, has been faithful to her husband,[a] 10and is well known for her good deeds,[u] such as bringing up children, showing hospitality, washing the feet[v] of the saints, helping those in trouble[w] and devoting herself to all kinds of good deeds.

11As for younger widows, do not put them on such a list. For when their sensual desires overcome their dedication to Christ, they want to marry. 12Thus they bring judgment on themselves, because they have broken their first pledge. 13Besides, they get into the habit of being idle and going about from house to house. And not only do they become idlers, but also gossips and busybodies,[x] saying things they ought not to. 14So I counsel younger widows to marry,[y] to have children, to manage their homes and to give the enemy no opportunity for slander.[z] 15Some have in fact already turned away to follow Satan.[a]

16If any woman who is a believer has widows in her family, she should help them and not let the church be burdened with them, so that the church can help those widows who are really in need.[b]

17The elders[c] who direct the affairs of the church well are worthy of double honor,[d] especially those whose work is preaching and teaching. 18For the Scripture says, "Do not muzzle the ox while it is treading out the grain,"[b][e] and "The worker deserves his wages."[c][f] 19Do not entertain an accusation against an elder[g] unless it is brought by two or three witnesses.[h] 20Those who sin are to be rebuked[i] publicly, so that the others may take warning.[j]

21I charge you, in the sight of God and Christ Jesus[k] and the elect angels, to keep these instructions without partiality, and to do nothing out of favoritism.

22Do not be hasty in the laying on of hands,[l] and do not share in the sins of others.[m] Keep yourself pure.

23Stop drinking only water, and use a little wine[n] because of your stomach and your frequent illnesses.

24The sins of some men are obvious, reaching the place of judgment ahead of them; the sins of others trail behind them. 25In the same way, good deeds are obvious, and even those that are not cannot be hidden.

6 All who are under the yoke of slavery should consider their masters worthy of full respect,[o] so that God's name and our teaching may not be slandered.[p] 2Those who have believing masters are not to show less respect for them because they are brothers.[q] Instead, they are to serve them even better, because those who benefit from their service are believers, and dear to them. These are the things you are to teach and urge on them.[r]

Love of Money

3If anyone teaches false doctrines[s] and does not agree to the sound instruction[t] of our Lord Jesus Christ and to godly teaching, 4he is conceited and understands nothing. He has an unhealthy interest in controversies and quarrels about words[u] that result in envy, strife, malicious talk, evil suspicions 5and constant friction between men of corrupt mind, who have been robbed of the truth[v] and who think that godliness is a means to financial gain.

6But godliness with contentment[w] is great gain.[x] 7For we brought nothing into the world, and we can take nothing out of it.[y] 8But if we have food and clothing, we will be content with that.[z] 9People who want to get rich[a] fall into temptation and a trap[b] and into many foolish and harmful desires that plunge men into ruin and destruction. 10For the love of money[c] is a root of all kinds of evil. Some people, eager for money, have wandered from the faith[d] and pierced themselves with many griefs.

5:10 [u]Ac 9:36; 1Ti 6:18; 1Pe 2:12 [v]Lk 7:44 [w]ver 16
5:13 [x]2Th 3:11
5:14 [y]1Co 7:9 [z]1Ti 6:1
5:15 [a]Mt 4:10
5:16 [b]ver 3-5
5:17 [c]Ac 11:30 [d]Php 2:29; 1Th 5:12
5:18 [e]Dt 25:4; 1Co 9:7-9 [f]Lk 10:7; Lev 19:13; Dt 24:14,15; Mt 10:10; 1Co 9:14
5:19 [g]Ac 11:30 [h]Mt 18:16
5:20 [i]2Ti 4:2; Tit 1:13 [j]Dt 13:11
5:21 [k]1Ti 6:13; 2Ti 4:1
5:22 [l]Ac 6:6 [m]Eph 5:11
5:23 [n]1Ti 3:8
6:1 [o]Eph 6:5; Tit 2:9; 1Pe 2:18 [p]Tit 2:5,8
6:2 [q]Phm 16 [r]1Ti 4:11
6:3 [s]1Ti 1:3 [t]1Ti 1:10
6:4 [u]2Ti 2:14
6:5 [v]Tit 1:15
6:6 [w]Php 4:11; Heb 13:5 [x]1Ti 4:8
6:7 [y]Job 1:21; Ecc 5:15
6:8 [z]Heb 13:5
6:9 [a]Pr 15:27 [b]1Ti 3:7
6:10 [c]1Ti 3:3 [d]Jas 5:19

[a] 9 Or *has had but one husband* [b] *18* Deut. 25:4 [c] *18* Luke 10:7

5:9 The church in Ephesus seems to have maintained a "list of widows" supported by the church.
5:10 Washing the feet of guests was a menial task, the duty of the lowliest servant (see the note on Jn 13:5), but it was necessary in New Testament times because of dusty roads and the wearing of sandals.
5:14 The remarriage of widows was frowned upon by some during the apostolic period, although Paul here seems to have been more lenient on the matter.
5:17 All elders were to exercise leadership (3:4–5), teach and preach (3:2) and receive honor. But those who excelled in leadership were to be counted "worthy of double honor."
5:18 The application of the term "Scripture" to both an Old Testament (Dt 25:4) and a New Testament (Lk 10:7) passage shows that by this time portions of the New Testament (or what would ultimately become the New Testament) were considered to be equal in authority to the Old Testament Scriptures. (See "The Old Testament Canon" on p. 1552, "The Old Testament of the Early Church" on p. 1967 and "The New Testament Canon" on p. 2022.)
5:22 For "laying on of hands," see the note on Acts 6:6. Paul was here speaking about the ordination of elders.
5:23 In view of Timothy's physical ailments, and perhaps because safe drinking water was often difficult to find, Paul advised him to drink "a little wine" (see "Wine and Alcoholic Beverages in the Ancient World" on p. 2015).
6:1 For "slavery," see the notes on Ephesians 6:5–9 and Colossians 3:22—4:1; see also "Slavery in the Greco-Roman World" on page 1979.

Paul's Charge to Timothy

6:11 [e]2Ti 3:17 [f]2Ti 2:22 [11]But you, man of God,[e] flee from all this, and pursue righteousness, godliness, faith, love,[f] endur-
6:12 [g]1Co 9:25, 26; 1Ti 1:18 ance and gentleness. [12]Fight the good fight[g] of the faith. Take hold of[h] the eternal life to which you were
[h]Php 3:12 called when you made your good confession in the presence of many witnesses. [13]In the sight of God, who
6:13 [i]Jn 18:33-37 [j]1Ti 5:21 gives life to everything, and of Christ Jesus, who while testifying before Pontius Pilate[i] made the good con-
fession, I charge you[j] [14]to keep this command without spot or blame until the appearing of our Lord
6:15 [k]1Ti 1:11 [l]1Ti 1:17 Jesus Christ, [15]which God will bring about in his own time—God, the blessed[k] and only Ruler,[l] the King
[m]Rev 17:14; 19:16 of kings and Lord of lords,[m] [16]who alone is immortal[n] and who lives in unapproachable light, whom no
6:16 [n]1Ti 1:17 [o]Jn 1:18 one has seen or can see.[o] To him be honor and might forever. Amen.

[17]Command those who are rich in this present world not to be arrogant nor to put their hope in
6:17 [p]Lk 12:20, 21 [q]1Ti 4:10 wealth,[p] which is so uncertain, but to put their hope in God,[q] who richly provides us with everything for
[r]Ac 14:17 6:18 [s]1Ti 5:10 our enjoyment.[r] [18]Command them to do good, to be rich in good deeds,[s] and to be generous and will-
[t]Ro 12:8,13 6:19 [u]Mt 6:20 ing to share.[t] [19]In this way they will lay up treasure for themselves[u] as a firm foundation for the coming
age, so that they may take hold of the life that is truly life.

6:20 [v]2Ti 1:12,14 [w]2Ti 2:16 [20]Timothy, guard what has been entrusted[v] to your care. Turn away from godless chatter[w] and the op-
posing ideas of what is falsely called knowledge, [21]which some have professed and in so doing have wan-
6:21 [x]2Ti 2:18 [y]Col 4:18 dered from the faith.[x]

Grace be with you.[y]

6:13 See "Pontius Pilate" on page 1714.

6:17 Early Christian churches did not lack members of the upper, wealthier class. Regardless of how they had gained their wealth, they needed instruction on how to use those resources in a Christian manner.

6:20 "Opposing ideas of what is falsely called knowledge" may be a reference to an early form of the heresy of Gnosticism (see "The Gnostics and Their Scriptures" on p. 2029, as well as the note on Col 2:8–23), which taught that an individual may be saved on the basis of his or her knowledge.

INTRODUCTION TO 2 *Timothy*

AUTHOR, PLACE AND DATE OF WRITING

As with the other two Pastoral Letters (1 Timothy and Titus), this epistle purports to have been written by Paul, but that claim is once again denied by many scholars today. Nevertheless, the book may be regarded as authentically Pauline (see "The Authorship of the Pastoral Epistles" on p. 1957).

It appears that after the close of the book of Acts Paul was released from his first Roman imprisonment (c. A.D. 62), that he traveled to Spain and then back east, where he conducted missionary work in Crete and in various cities around the Aegean. Most scholars believe that Paul wrote 2 Timothy after the end of this last missionary journey, after which he traveled back to Rome and was again imprisoned. This scenario suggests a date of about A.D. 67 for the letter.

AUDIENCE

Paul wrote this letter from prison (1:16; 2:9) to his disciple and coworker Timothy (1:2), who was still in Ephesus (see 4:19) where Paul had previously left him (1Ti 1:3).

CULTURAL FACTS AND HIGHLIGHTS

Paul wrote this letter both for personal reasons and out of concern for the churches. On the one hand he was isolated in prison and feeling abandoned (2Ti 4:10), aware that he was soon to die (4:6–8). In this situation, the apostle was eager that Timothy, for whom he felt a special affection, get to him as soon as possible (4:9). On the other hand, Paul was alarmed at how quickly heresy and factionalism had grown in the churches (3:1–5; 4:2–3,14–15) and sensed that severe persecutions were soon to begin (2:3). He used this letter as a final occasion to exhort Timothy and other ministers to be faithful in preaching, to oppose false doctrine and cultic teachers and to promote genuine godliness among the churches.

TIMELINE

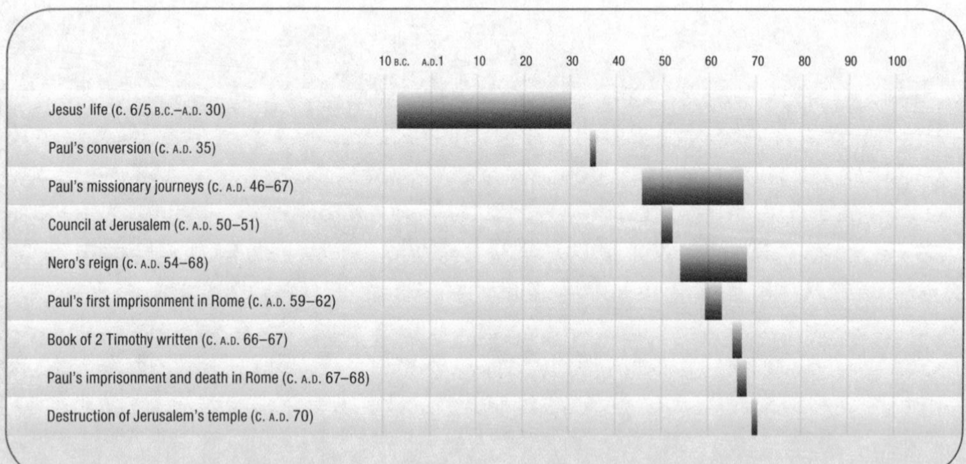

AS YOU READ

Look for clues about Paul's loneliness, suffering and future martyrdom—and for his hymn of hope. Even as he suffered, he continued his role as mentor to Timothy by encouraging the younger man and offering practical advice regarding Timothy's role and responsibilities as pastor-teacher in the church.

DID YOU KNOW?

- Before Jesus came, the certainty of life after death was somewhat shrouded in darkness (1:10).
- According to Jewish tradition Jannes and Jambres were the Egyptian court magicians who had opposed Moses (3:8).
- A Jewish boy formally began studying the Old Testament when he was only five years old (3:15).
- As a Roman citizen Paul could not be thrown to the lions in the amphitheater (4:17).

THEMES

Second Timothy includes the following themes:

1. *Encouragement to persevere.* Paul encouraged Timothy to continue the mission of evangelism (4:2). He directed his young protégé to hold fast to the traditions he had received (1:3–14; 2:1–9; 3:14–15) and set himself up as a model for Timothy to emulate (1:8,13; 2:3; 3:10–11; 4:6–8). This letter teaches that the truth is not just something to believe but a path to follow (cf. 2:18).

2. *Reliance on the authority of Scripture.* Timothy had been trained from early childhood in the Scriptures (3:14), which helped him respond to the truth of Jesus Christ. Paul emphasized correct handling of Scripture (2:15), its authority (3:16) and its importance in developing disciples capable of serving others (3:16–17).

3. *Warning against false teachers.* Paul warned Timothy about false teachers who stir up quarrels over senseless controversies (2:23) and seek to deceive (3:6). They indulge in "godless chatter" (2:16) and propagate muddy theology. In contrast, the Lord's servants are to hold to sound doctrine and to avoid pointless quarrels. They are to be kind to everyone, promote sound doctrine and gently and patiently instruct opponents in the truth, rather than seeking to crush them (2:24–26).

OUTLINE

- I. Introduction (1:1–4)
- II. Paul's Concern for Timothy (1:5–14)
- III. Paul's Situation (1:15–18)
- IV. Special Instructions to Timothy (2)
  - A. Charge to Be Strong (2:1–13)
  - B. Charge to Be a Workman Approved by God (2:14–26)
- V. Warning About the Last Days (3)
  - A. Evil Times of the Last Days (3:1–9)
  - B. Holding to the Truth in Evil Times (3:10–17)
- VI. Paul's Departing Remarks (4:1–8)
  - A. Final Charge to Timothy (4:1–5)
  - B. The Waiting Crown of Righteousness (4:6–8)
- VII. Final Requests, Greetings, and Benediction (4:9–22)

1 Paul, an apostle of Christ Jesus by the will of God,[a] according to the promise of life that is in Christ
Jesus,[b]

2 To Timothy,[c] my dear son:[d]

Grace, mercy and peace from God the Father and Christ Jesus our Lord.

Encouragement to Be Faithful

3 I thank God,[e] whom I serve, as my forefathers did, with a clear conscience, as night and day I con-
stantly remember you in my prayers.[f] 4 Recalling your tears,[g] I long to see you,[h] so that I may be filled with
joy. 5 I have been reminded of your sincere faith,[i] which first lived in your grandmother Lois and in your
mother Eunice[j] and, I am persuaded, now lives in you also. 6 For this reason I remind you to fan into flame
the gift of God, which is in you through the laying on of my hands.[k] 7 For God did not give us a spirit of
timidity,[l] but a spirit of power, of love and of self-discipline.
8 So do not be ashamed[m] to testify about our Lord, or ashamed of me his prisoner.[n] But join with me
in suffering for the gospel,[o] by the power of God, 9 who has saved us and called[p] us to a holy life—not
because of anything we have done but because of his own purpose and grace. This grace was given us in
Christ Jesus before the beginning of time, 10 but it has now been revealed[q] through the appearing of our
Savior, Christ Jesus, who has destroyed death[r] and has brought life and immortality to light through the
gospel. 11 And of this gospel I was appointed a herald and an apostle and a teacher.[s] 12 That is why I am
suffering as I am. Yet I am not ashamed, because I know whom I have believed, and am convinced that
he is able to guard[t] what I have entrusted to him for that day.[u]
13 What you heard from me, keep[v] as the pattern of sound teaching, with faith and love in Christ
Jesus.[w] 14 Guard the good deposit that was entrusted to you—guard it with the help of the Holy Spirit who
lives in us.[x]
15 You know that everyone in the province of Asia has deserted me,[y] including Phygelus and Hermog-
enes.
16 May the Lord show mercy to the household of Onesiphorus,[z] because he often refreshed me and
was not ashamed of my chains. 17 On the contrary, when he was in Rome, he searched hard for me until
he found me. 18 May the Lord grant that he will find mercy from the Lord on that day! You know very well
in how many ways he helped me[a] in Ephesus.

2 You then, my son, be strong[b] in the grace that is in Christ Jesus. 2 And the things you have heard me
say[c] in the presence of many witnesses[d] entrust to reliable men who will also be qualified to teach
others. 3 Endure hardship with us like a good soldier[e] of Christ Jesus. 4 No one serving as a soldier gets
involved in civilian affairs—he wants to please his commanding officer. 5 Similarly, if anyone competes
as an athlete, he does not receive the victor's crown[f] unless he competes according to the rules. 6 The
hardworking farmer should be the first to receive a share of the crops. 7 Reflect on what I am saying, for
the Lord will give you insight into all this.
8 Remember Jesus Christ, raised from the dead,[g] descended from David.[h] This is my gospel,[i] 9 for
which I am suffering[j] even to the point of being chained like a criminal. But God's word is not chained.
10 Therefore I endure everything[k] for the sake of the elect, that they too may obtain the salvation that is
in Christ Jesus, with eternal glory.[l]

1:1 [a]2Co 1:1 [b]Eph 3:6; 1Ti 6:19
1:2 [c]Ac 16:1 [d]1Ti 1:2
1:3 [e]Ro 1:8 [f]Ro 1:10
1:4 [g]Ac 20:37 [h]2Ti 4:9
1:5 [i]1Ti 1:5 [j]Ac 16:1
1:6 [k]1Ti 4:14
1:7 [l]Ro 8:15
1:8 [m]Mk 8:38; Ro 1:16 [n]Eph 3:1 [o]2Ti 2:3,9; 4:5
1:9 [p]Ro 8:28
1:10 [q]Eph 1:9 [r]1Co 15:26,54
1:11 [s]1Ti 2:7
1:12 [t]1Ti 6:20 [u]ver 18
1:13 [v]Tit 1:9 [w]1Ti 1:14
1:14 [x]Ro 8:9
1:15 [y]2Ti 4:10, 11,16
1:16 [z]2Ti 4:19
1:18 [a]Heb 6:10
2:1 [b]Eph 6:10
2:2 [c]2Ti 1:13 [d]1Ti 6:12
2:3 [e]1Ti 1:18
2:5 [f]1Co 9:25
2:8 [g]Ac 2:24 [h]Mt 1:1 [i]Ro 2:16
2:9 [j]Ac 9:16
2:10 [k]Col 1:24 [l]2Co 4:17

1:1 For "Paul," see the note on Philippians 3:5 and for "apostle" the note on 2 Corinthians 1:1.
1:5 According to Acts 16:1, Timothy's mother was a Jewish Christian. Here we learn that his grandmother, too, had been converted to Christianity. Timothy's father, however, was a Greek and apparently an unbeliever.
1:6 Ordination in the sense of setting aside officers of the church for a certain work by the laying on of hands was practiced in apostolic times (see also 1Ti 4:14), but it is nowhere described or enjoined. No great emphasis was placed on this rite. See also the note on Acts 6:6.
1:7 Apparently lack of confidence was a serious problem for Timothy.
1:10 This verse implies that before Jesus came, the certainty of life after death was somewhat shrouded in darkness. For information on the ancients' view of the afterlife, see the note on Psalm 6:5 and "Sheol, Hades, Gehenna, the Abyss and Tartarus: Images of Hell" on page 946.
1:15 Timothy was then in Ephesus (see the note on Eph 1:1), the capital of the province of Asia.
Paul mentioned Phygelus and Hermogenes by name as being among those Christians of Asia (the western province of Asia Minor) who had turned away from the apostle. From the context (2 Ti 1:13–14) we may assume that their apostasy included the repudiation of Paul's doctrine. If we connect Phygelus with 4:16 ("at my first defense, no one came to my support"), we may infer that he, being in Rome, forsook Paul's personal cause in the Roman courts at a crucial time when his testimony could have meant much for the future of the church. Some scholars feel that Phygelus may also have been one of the leaders of a group of wayward Christians in Rome (Php 1:15–16).
1:17 See "Rome" on page 1838.
2:5 For "victor's crown," see the note on 1 Thessalonians 2:19.
2:9 Apparently Paul was awaiting execution.

ARCHAEOLOGICAL SITES

EARLY HISTORY OF EPHESUS

2 TIMOTHY 1 Ephesus ("Maps 13–14") was at the center of Paul's missionary work. He visited there while on his second and third missionary journeys and maintained exceptionally close ties to the Christians at this location (Ac 20:17–38).[1] Toward the end of his ministry, the apostle left Timothy in Ephesus to care for the Ephesian Christians (1Ti 1:3), and at the very end of his life he continued to show concern for the church there (2Ti 1:18; 4:12).

Ephesus was situated on the Aegean coast by the Cayster River (in the southwestern corner of modern Turkey), but its specific location shifted slightly through the centuries. The city was originally founded by Greeks in approximately 1000 B.C.

Ephesus was captured by Cyrus the Great of **Persia**[2] in 546 B.C.[3] After Persia's disastrously failed invasion of Greece, however, Ephesus came in 454 B.C.[4] under the control of Athens, against which it rebelled during the Peloponnesian War (431–404 B.C.),[5] joining instead the Spartan alliance. After the fall of Athens, Ephesus again came under Persian control, but this ended with the conquest of the region in 333 B.C. by Alexander the Great.

After Alexander's death his general Lysimachus emerged victorious in a struggle for power in **Asia Minor**. Lysimachus moved the city a short distance from its original site and constructed a 6-mile-long (10 km) wall around its new boundaries (c. 286–281 B.C.). Ephesus then came under **Seleucid** rule, which lasted until Rome defeated Antiochus III in 189 B.C.[6] Rome placed Ephesus under the control of the Attalids, the rulers of nearby Pergamum, but took direct control of the city in 133 B.C. Emperor Augustus honored Ephesus as the first city of Roman Asia.[7]

(photos from top to bottom) **A street in Ephesus; a domestic neighborhood in Ephesus; the theater of Ephesus**
Preserving Bible Times; © Dr. James C. Martin

[1]See "The Missionary Journeys of Paul" on page 1795. [2]See Glossary on page 2080 for definitions of bolded words. [3]See "Cyrus the Great" on page 669. [4]See "Athens" on page 1804. [5]See "Greece: From Independent City-states Through Alexander the Great" on page 1814. [6]See "The History of the Holy Land" on page xxi. [7]See "Caesar Augustus, Emperor of Rome; the Census; and Quirinius, Governor of Syria" on page 1667.

11 Here is a trustworthy saying:

If we died with him,
we will also live with him;[m] 2:11 [m]Ro 6:2-11
12 if we endure,
we will also reign with him.[n] 2:12 [n]Ro 8:17; 1Pe 4:13
If we disown him, [o]Mt 10:33
he will also disown us;[o]
13 if we are faithless,
he will remain faithful,[p] 2:13 [p]Nu 23:19; Ro 3:3
for he cannot disown himself.

A Workman Approved by God

14 Keep reminding them of these things. Warn them before God against quarreling about words;[q] it is 2:14 [q]1Ti 6:4
of no value, and only ruins those who listen. 15 Do your best to present yourself to God as one approved,
a workman who does not need to be ashamed and who correctly handles the word of truth.[r] 16 Avoid 2:15 [r]Eph 1:13; Jas 1:18
godless chatter,[s] because those who indulge in it will become more and more ungodly. 17 Their teaching 2:16 [s]Tit 3:9
will spread like gangrene. Among them are Hymenaeus[t] and Philetus, 18 who have wandered away from 2:17 [t]1Ti 1:20
the truth. They say that the resurrection has already taken place, and they destroy the faith of some.[u] 2:18 [u]1Ti 1:19
19 Nevertheless, God's solid foundation stands firm,[v] sealed with this inscription: "The Lord knows those 2:19 [v]Isa 28:16
who are his,"[a][w] and, "Everyone who confesses the name of the Lord[x] must turn away from wickedness." [w]Jn 10:14 [x]1Co 1:2
20 In a large house there are articles not only of gold and silver, but also of wood and clay; some are for
noble purposes and some for ignoble.[y] 21 If a man cleanses himself from the latter, he will be an instru- 2:20 [y]Ro 9:21
ment for noble purposes, made holy, useful to the Master and prepared to do any good work.[z] 2:21 [z]2Ti 3:17
22 Flee the evil desires of youth, and pursue righteousness, faith, love[a] and peace, along with those 2:22 [a]1Ti 1:14; 6:11 [b]1Ti 1:5
who call on the Lord out of a pure heart.[b] 23 Don't have anything to do with foolish and stupid argu-
ments, because you know they produce quarrels. 24 And the Lord's servant must not quarrel; instead, he
must be kind to everyone, able to teach, not resentful.[c] 25 Those who oppose him he must gently in- 2:24 [c]1Ti 3:2,3
struct, in the hope that God will grant them repentance leading them to a knowledge of the truth,[d] 26 and 2:25 [d]1Ti 2:4
that they will come to their senses and escape from the trap of the devil,[e] who has taken them captive 2:26 [e]1Ti 3:7
to do his will.

Godlessness in the Last Days

3 But mark this: There will be terrible times in the last days.[f] 2 People will be lovers of themselves, lov- 3:1 [f]1Ti 4:1
ers of money,[g] boastful, proud,[h] abusive, disobedient to their parents,[i] ungrateful, unholy, 3 without 3:2 [g]1Ti 3:3 [h]Ro 1:30 [i]Ro 1:30
love, unforgiving, slanderous, without self-control, brutal, not lovers of the good, 4 treacherous, rash, con-
ceited,[j] lovers of pleasure rather than lovers of God— 5 having a form of godliness but denying its pow- 3:4 [j]1Ti 3:6
er. Have nothing to do with them.
6 They are the kind who worm their way[k] into homes and gain control over weak-willed women, who 3:6 [k]Jude 4
are loaded down with sins and are swayed by all kinds of evil desires, 7 always learning but never able to
acknowledge the truth. 8 Just as Jannes and Jambres opposed Moses,[l] so also these men oppose[m] the 3:8 [l]Ex 7:11 [m]Ac 13:8 [n]1Ti 6:5
truth—men of depraved minds,[n] who, as far as the faith is concerned, are rejected. 9 But they will not get
very far because, as in the case of those men,[o] their folly will be clear to everyone. 3:9 [o]Ex 7:12

Paul's Charge to Timothy

10 You, however, know all about my teaching,[p] my way of life, my purpose, faith, patience, love, endurance, 3:10 [p]1Ti 4:6

[a] *19* Num. 16:5 (see Septuagint)

2:11–13 These verses were probably an early Christian hymn (see "Early Christian Hymnody" on p. 2007).

2:14–18 The wording of these verses indicates that the heresy mentioned here was an early form of Gnosticism (see "The Gnostics and Their Scriptures" on p. 2029).

2:17 Like several other men named in the Scriptures—Judas Iscariot, Alexander, Demas and Hymenaeus, to name a few—Philetus is remembered only for the evil he did. Paul alone mentioned him as a false teacher in the church of Ephesus who, together with Hymenaeus, held that "the resurrection has already taken place" (v. 18); although Hymenaeus did not radically deny a doctrine of the resurrection, he allegorized it into a spiritual awakening or conversion and not a bodily resurrection, as Paul had taught in 1 Corinthians 15.

For commentary on excommunication, see the note on 1 Timothy 1:20.

2:18 For false doctrines, see the note on Colossians 2:8–23.

2:19 For "sealed," see the note on Ephesians 1:13.

3:8 According to Jewish tradition Jannes and Jambres were the Egyptian court magicians who had opposed Moses (see Ex 7:11).

3:11 [q]Ac 13:14, 50 [r]2Co 11:23-27 [s]Ps 34:19
3:12 [t]Ac 14:22
3:13 [u]2Ti 2:16
3:14 [v]2Ti 1:13
3:15 [w]2Ti 1:5 [x]Jn 5:39 [y]Ps 119:98,99
3:16 [z]2Pe 1:20, 21 [a]Ro 4:23,24
3:17 [b]1Ti 6:11 [c]2Ti 2:21
4:1 [d]Ac 10:42 [e]1Ti 5:21
4:2 [f]1Ti 4:13 [g]Gal 6:6 [h]1Ti 5:20; Tit 1:13; 2:15
4:3 [i]1Ti 1:10
4:4 [j]1Ti 1:4
4:5 [k]2Ti 1:8 [l]Ac 21:8

11 persecutions, sufferings—what kinds of things happened to me in Antioch,[q] Iconium and Lystra, the
persecutions I endured.[r] Yet the Lord rescued me from all of them.[s] 12 In fact, everyone who wants to live
a godly life in Christ Jesus will be persecuted,[t] 13 while evil men and impostors will go from bad to worse,[u]
deceiving and being deceived. 14 But as for you, continue in what you have learned and have become con-
vinced of, because you know those from whom you learned it,[v] 15 and how from infancy[w] you have known
the holy Scriptures,[x] which are able to make you wise[y] for salvation through faith in Christ Jesus. 16 All
Scripture is God-breathed[z] and is useful for teaching,[a] rebuking, correcting and training in righteous-
ness, 17 so that the man of God[b] may be thoroughly equipped for every good work.[c]

4 In the presence of God and of Christ Jesus, who will judge the living and the dead,[d] and in view of
his appearing and his kingdom, I give you this charge:[e] 2 Preach[f] the Word;[g] be prepared in season
and out of season; correct, rebuke[h] and encourage—with great patience and careful instruction. 3 For the
time will come when men will not put up with sound doctrine.[i] Instead, to suit their own desires, they
will gather around them a great number of teachers to say what their itching ears want to hear. 4 They will
turn their ears away from the truth and turn aside to myths.[j] 5 But you, keep your head in all situations,
endure hardship,[k] do the work of an evangelist,[l] discharge all the duties of your ministry.

3:11 For "Antioch," see the note on Acts 11:19 and for "Iconium" the note on Acts 13:51. For "Lystra," see the note on Acts 14:6. All three cities were in the Roman province of Galatia, which Paul visited on his first and second missionary journeys.
3:15 A Jewish boy formally began studying the Old Testament when he was five years old. Timothy had been taught at home by his mother and grandmother even before he reached this age.
3:16 "All Scripture" is primarily a reference to the Old Testament, since some of the New Testament books had not even been written at this time. But Peter's mention of Paul's writings among the "Scriptures" (2Pe 3:16) shows that the early church already viewed such apostolic letters to be as authoritative as the Old Testament. (See "The Old Testament Canon" on p. 1552, "The Old Testament of the Early Church" on p. 1967 and "The New Testament Canon" on p. 2022.)
4:4 For "myths," see the note on 1 Timothy 1:4.

ANCIENT TEXTS AND ARTIFACTS

The Old Testament of the Early Church

2 TIMOTHY 3 The first Christians referred to the Old Testament as "the Holy Scriptures" (Lk 24:44; Jn 1:45; Ac 28:23; Ro 1:2; 2Ti 3:15) and, despite the fact that it was not explicitly "Christian," as their fundamental source of doctrinal and moral teaching (Ro 3:21; 2Ti 3:1–17).

The Old Testament of the first century was divided into two or three sections in early Jewish and Christian thought. The two-part division of the Old Testament into "the Law and the Prophets" was the most common (Mt 22:40; Ac 13:15; Ro 3:21; see also 2Mc 15:9).[1] Already in the second century B.C. some authors began to refer to a threefold division of the Old Testament similar to that used by Jews to this day: the Law, the Prophets and the Writings. The prologue to Ecclesiasticus in the **Apocrypha** refers to the "Law, the Prophets and the other books," while a **Dead Sea Scrolls** text (4QMMT) speaks of "the Book of Moses and the words of the Prophets and of David." Here "David" serves as a title for the third division, since it began with his Psalms. Similarly, in Luke 24:44 Jesus stated that "everything must be fulfilled that is written about me in the Law of Moses, the Prophets and the Psalms." This way of referring to Scripture combines with other evidence to strongly suggest that the Old Testament **canon** had been firmly established before the middle of the second century A.D.[2]

It is important to note that the books of the "Law and the Prophets" were the same as the 39 books of the Christian Old Testament. Rabbis had developed different ways of counting the number of books (for example, the 12 "Minor Prophets" are often simply called "The Twelve" and counted as a single book in Jewish sources), but the content was the same. There is no evidence that either first-century Jews or Christians regarded any other religious books of the Jews, including the so-called Apocryphal books and the numerous **pseudepigraphal** books, as canonical.[3] Over against such groups as the Sadducees and the Samaritans, by contrast, mainstream Jews and Christians did not restrict the canon to the Law (Pentateuch) only.[4] Finally, the outright rejection of the Old Testament in some Christian circles, such as by the followers of Marcion and the early Gnostics, was plainly a heterodox aberration.[5]

[1]Second Maccabees is an Apocryphal book, never accepted as a part of the traditional Protestant canon. [2]See "The Old Testament Canon" on page 1552, "Texts of the Old Testament" on page 1491 and "The Ancient Translations" on page 1492. [3]See "The Apocrypha" on page 1973 and "The Bible and Pseudepigraphical Literature" on page 2041. [4]See "The Sadducees" on page 1600 and "The Samaritans" on page 1737. [5]See "Early Christian Heresies" on page 1896.

[6]For I am already being poured out like a drink offering,[m] and the time has come for my departure.[n]
[7]I have fought the good fight,[o] I have finished the race,[p] I have kept the faith. [8]Now there is in store for
me[q] the crown of righteousness, which the Lord, the righteous Judge, will award to me on that day[r]—
and not only to me, but also to all who have longed for his appearing.

4:6 [m]Php 2:17 [n]Php 1:23 4:7 [o]1Ti 1:18 [p]1Co 9:24 4:8 [q]Col 1:5 [r]2Ti 1:12

4:6 A "drink offering" or libation involved the pouring out of a liquid, such as wine, water or oil (but generally wine) as an offering to a deity. Libations were common among the heathen nations (Dt 32:38), and drink offerings accompanied many Old Testament sacrifices (Ex 29:40–41; Lev 23:13,18,37; Nu 15:4–10,24; 28:7–10). Here and in Philippians 2:17 (see the note there), Paul pictured his death as a drink offering, a pouring out of his life as an offering to Christ.

4:7 For "[foot] race," the note on 1 Corinthians 9:24–27.

4:8 For "crown," see the note on 1 Thessalonians 2:19.

ARCHAEOLOGICAL SITES

EPHESUS DURING THE TIME OF PAUL

2 TIMOTHY 4 By the time of Paul, Ephesus had become enormously wealthy due to its status and position as a major port city of Asia Minor. It boasted a number of major public buildings, including gymnasiums, theaters and a triumphal arch constructed in 3 B.C. In addition, the Ephesian temple of Artemis was lauded as one of the seven wonders of the ancient world and was already then a significant source of income (Ac 19:23–27).[1]

Ephesus became a major center of the Christian faith. Although Paul probably wrote his epistle to the Ephesians as a circular letter, the church of Ephesus was a major focus of his ministry.[2] The apostle John also wrote to this church in Revelation 2:1–7, and during the first five centuries A.D. several church councils were convened there. By the medieval period, however, silt from the Cayster River had extended the coastline so far to the west that Ephesus had ceased to be a port city and was abandoned.

The desertion of Ephesus was a boon for modern archaeology, since it meant that the unoccupied city was open for excavation. Today Ephesus exists as one of the most magnificent ruins of the ancient world. Under the direction of Austrian and Turkish archaeologists, the city has reappeared. Important finds include the following:

✣ *The Temple of Artemis*. Little remains of the temple today (it was sacked by Goths in A.D. 262), but it was a sacred site for over 1,200 years and was at the center of the controversy between pagans and early Christians.

✣ *Other Temples*. Several other Roman-era temples and shrines have been discovered there. Evidence indicates that Ephesus was home to a wide variety of pagan cults, including a temple to the Egyptian god Serapis.[3]

✣ *The Great Theater*. This theater, which could seat 25,000 persons, was the location of the tumultuous protest against Paul's preaching related in Acts 19. Although Paul wanted to address the crowd gathered there, the disciples restrained him (Ac 19:30).

✣ *The Agoras*. Two *agoras*, or public squares, have been located in Ephesus. One was the Civic Agora (perhaps the location of the temple to Augustus) and the other was the Square or Commercial Agora (near the harbor and the site of numerous shops).

✣ *The Celsus Library*. One of the great libraries of the ancient world, it was built in A.D. 115–125 and so was not yet in existence in New Testament times.

✣ *The Gymnasiums, Baths and Public Latrines*. Several gymnasium and bath complexes have been identified in Ephesus, although a few date to later than the New Testament period. Archaeologists are often able to identify a gymnasium's changing room, exercise room, swimming pool, frigidarium (cold-water bath), caldarium (hot-water bath) and unctorium (oil-massage room). The public latrines also give modern visitors an obvious connection to ordinary life in an ancient city.

✣ *Private Homes*. Residential areas of Ephesus have been excavated, and several upper-class homes have been unearthed. Frescoes (paintings done on freshly spread, moist lime plaster) have been recovered and kitchens, bathrooms and bedrooms identified.

✣ *The Basilica of Saint John*. This structure obviously postdates the New Testament, but, according to second-century tradition, the apostle John spent his last years in Ephesus there and was buried under what is now the apse of this church, which also features a fine example of an early Christian baptistery.[4] According to tradition Jesus' mother, Mary, may have died in Ephesus; therefore, there is also a church of the Virgin Mary (the site of the ecumenical council of Ephesus in A.D. 431).

The population of New Testament Ephesus is unknown, but it is clear that the city at that time was a thriving, cosmopolitan center of trade, religion and recreation. Its remains provide a rare look at an ancient city that was also important as a setting for the apostolic mission and the rise of Christianity. Perhaps more than any other archaeological site, Ephesus affords the reader of Acts a sense of context. Since there is no modern city there, the remains of Ephesus distinctively allow visitors to enter vicariously into the ancient world.

[1]See "Artemis of the Ephesians" on page 1808. [2]See "The Authorship of Ephesians" on page 1919. [3]See "The Gods of the Greeks and Romans" on page 1908.
[4]See "Baptism in the Ancient World" on page 1562.

Personal Remarks

4:10 [s]Col 4:14 [t]1Jn 2:15 [u]Ac 16:6 4:11 [v]Col 4:14 [w]2Ti 1:15 [x]Ac 12:12 4:12 [y]Ac 20:4

[9]Do your best to come to me quickly, [10]for Demas,[s] because he loved this world,[t] has deserted me and
has gone to Thessalonica. Crescens has gone to Galatia,[u] and Titus to Dalmatia. [11]Only Luke[v] is with me.[w]
Get Mark[x] and bring him with you, because he is helpful to me in my ministry. [12]I sent Tychicus[y] to Eph-
esus. [13]When you come, bring the cloak that I left with Carpus at Troas, and my scrolls, especially the
parchments.

4:14 [z]Ac 19:33 [a]Ro 12:19

[14]Alexander[z] the metalworker did me a great deal of harm. The Lord will repay him for what he has
done.[a] [15]You too should be on your guard against him, because he strongly opposed our message.

4:16 [b]Ac 7:60 4:17 [c]Ac 23:11 [d]Ac 9:15 4:18 [e]Ps 121:7 [f]Ro 11:36

[16]At my first defense, no one came to my support, but everyone deserted me. May it not be held against
them.[b] [17]But the Lord stood at my side[c] and gave me strength, so that through me the message might be
fully proclaimed and all the Gentiles might hear it.[d] And I was delivered from the lion's mouth. [18]The
Lord will rescue me from every evil attack[e] and will bring me safely to his heavenly kingdom. To him be
glory for ever and ever. Amen.[f]

Final Greetings

4:19 [g]Ac 18:2 4:20 [h]Ac 19:22 [i]Ac 20:4 4:21 [j]ver 9

[19]Greet Priscilla[a] and Aquila[g] and the household of Onesiphorus. [20]Erastus[h] stayed in Corinth, and I
left Trophimus[i] sick in Miletus. [21]Do your best to get here before winter.[j] Eubulus greets you, and so do
Pudens, Linus, Claudia and all the brothers.

4:22 [k]Gal 6:18; Phm 25 [l]Col 4:18

[22]The Lord be with your spirit.[k] Grace be with you.[l]

[a] *19* Greek *Prisca,* a variant of *Priscilla*

4:10 For "Thessalonica," see the note on 1 Thessalonians 1:1.

"Galatia" was either the northern area of Asia Minor (Gaul) or a Roman province in what is now central Turkey (see the note on Gal 1:2, as well as "Which Galatia?" on p. 1903).

Titus, an uncircumcised Gentile (Gal 2:3), was one of Paul's converts and a considerable help to the apostle in his ministry. After Paul's release from his first Roman imprisonment (Ac 28), he and Titus worked together briefly in Crete, after which Paul commissioned Titus to remain there as his representative. Titus is here said to have left on a mission to Dalmatia (this is the last word we hear about him in the New Testament).

For information on Dalmatia, also known as Illyricum, see the note on Romans 15:19.

4:11 For information on Mark, also known as John Mark, see the note on Colossians 4:10.

4:12 Tychicus was Paul's trusted coworker, who on various occasions traveled with or for Paul (see Ac 20:4; Eph 6:21).

For "Ephesus," see the note on Ephesians 1:1.

4:13 A cloak was worn for protection against cold and damp weather conditions. This was probably a heavy, sleeveless outer garment, circular in shape, with a hole in the middle for the head (see "Dress and Fashion in the Greco-Roman World" on p. 2004).

For "Troas," see the note on Acts 16:8.

Scrolls were made of leather or papyrus, while parchments were made of the skins of animals (see the note on Ex 17:14 and "Scrolls, Seals and Codices" on p. 2053). The latter may have been copies of parts of the Old Testament.

4:17 Since, as a Roman citizen (see "Roman Citizenship" on p. 1930), Paul could not have been thrown to the lions in the amphitheater, this must be a figurative way of saying that his first hearing did not result in an immediate "guilty" verdict. For commentary on persecution in the arena, see the note on 1 Corinthians 4:9.

4:19 Priscilla and Aquila were close friends of Paul who worked in the same trade of tentmaking. They helped Paul found the church at Corinth and ministered to the church at Ephesus.

4:20 For information on Erastus, see the note on Romans 16:23 and "The Erastus Inscription" on page 1861. For "Corinth," see the note on 1 Corinthians 1:2.

Miletus was a seaport off the coast of Asia Minor about 35 miles (56 km) south of Ephesus.

4:21 Early tradition says that Linus was bishop of Rome after the deaths of Peter and Paul.

For "brothers," see the note on Romans 1:13.

INTRODUCTION TO 

AUTHOR, PLACE AND DATE OF WRITING

Today many scholars deny that the Pastoral Epistles (1 and 2 Timothy and Titus) are Pauline, but arguments against Paul's authorship are not sufficiently compelling to overthrow the clear claim of the epistles themselves (see "The Authorship of the Pastoral Epistles" on p. 1957).

The letter to Titus was probably written from Nicopolis (3:12) in western Greece. It was delivered by Zenas and Apollos, who were on a journey that took them through Crete (3:13).

AUDIENCE

This letter was written by Paul to one of his associates, Titus, a Gentile Christian (see Gal 2:1–3) who had probably been converted through Paul's ministry and was presently overseeing the churches on Crete. Titus had traveled with Paul and become his trusted associate. After Paul's release from his first Roman imprisonment (Ac 28), he and Titus had ministered briefly on Crete. When Paul departed he left Titus behind to continue the ministry, organize the churches and appoint elders (Tit 1:5).

CULTURAL FACTS AND HIGHLIGHTS

Paul plainly stated that he had left Titus on Crete in order to set the churches there in order, both organizationally and doctrinally. The letter was intended to encourage Titus and to give him further instruction for accomplishing this task. Paul apparently regarded the Cretans as a particularly difficult group to work with (see "Crete" on p. 1972). In New Testament times life on Crete had sunk to a deplorable moral level. Those who had become Christians were immature in their faith and needed basic instruction concerning immorality and Christian conduct. In addition, false teachings of various kinds were troubling the Cretan churches (1:10–16).

TIMELINE

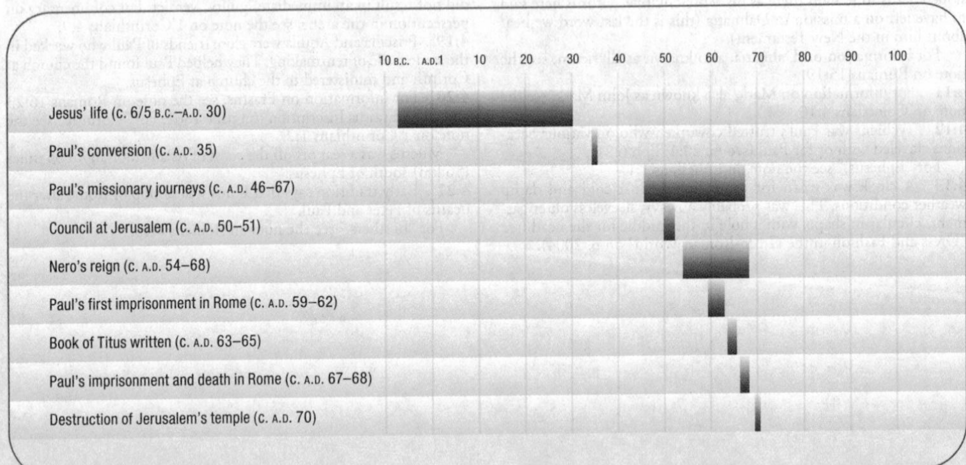

AS YOU READ

List Paul's qualifications for effective church leaders. Note his instructions for living a godly life, including his guidelines for successful relationships with family, friends and community. Note that specific groups had special responsibilities but that every individual was accountable to live a life characterized by self-control, integrity and grace.

DID YOU KNOW?

- Crete, the fourth largest island in the Mediterranean Sea, was a Roman province populated primarily by farmers and fruit growers (1:5).
- Roman slaves had no legal rights, their fates being entirely in their masters' hands (2:9–10).
- In the Jewish sense the term "lawyer" referred to an expert in the Mosaic Law, while in the Gentile context it referred to a Roman jurist (3:13).

THEMES

Titus includes the following themes:

1. *Church leaders.* Cretan culture was known for its moral decadence (1:12), and Paul instructed Titus that leaders in the church must be above reproach, as examples to others of the Christian life. When Christians are guilty of immoral behavior, they discredit the truth of the very gospel they proclaim.

2. *Self-control and integrity make the gospel attractive.* Paul instructed Titus on directing various other groups besides leaders—older men (2:2); older women, who also taught younger women (2:3–5); younger men (2:6)—all were to exhibit self-control. Slaves (2:9–10) were to be respectful and honest. The gospel has a civilizing effect on all aspects of a Christian's life (2:11–14), including relationships within the home (2:4–5).

3. *False teachers.* Like, Timothy, Titus had to contend with false teachers, about whom Paul spoke harshly (1:10–16). Paul clearly valued unity within the community and condemned anyone who threatened it.

OUTLINE

- I. Greeting (1:1–4)
- II. Concerning Elders (1:5–9)
  - A. Where to Appoint Elders (1:5)
  - B. Qualifications of Elders (1:6–9)
- III. Concerning False Teachers (1:10–16)
- IV. Concerning Various Groups in the Congregation (2)
  - A. Teaching for Different Groups (2:1–10)
  - B. Grace as the Foundation for Christian Living (2:11–14)
  - C. Charge to Titus (2:15)
- V. Concerning Believers in General (3:1–8)
  - A. Believers as Citizens (3:1–2)
  - B. Doing What Is Good (3:3–8)
- VI. Concerning Response to Spiritual Error (3:9–11)
- VII. Conclusion (3:12–15)

Ancient Voices

Let us then praise famous men
And our fathers, who were famous in their generation.
The Lord ordained great glory for them,
And ages ago ordained his majesty for them.
They were rulers in their kingdoms
And were renowned men in power;
They gave counsel by their insight
And gave oracles through their prophetic powers.
They led a people by their counsels
And a people by their scribal insight;
The words of their instruction were wise.
They sought out musical melodies
And arranged verses in a written text.
They were wealthy men well-supplied with resources,
And they lived peaceably in their homes.
All these men were honored in their generations,
And they were the pride of their days.

—In Praise of Jewish Heroes of Bygone Days
From Sirach 44:1–7 (Rahlfs' Septuagint), trans. by Duane Garrett

See "The Apocrypha" article.

1 Paul, a servant of God[a] and an apostle of Jesus Christ for the 1:1 [a]Ro 1:1
faith of God's elect and the knowledge of the truth[b] that leads [b]1Ti 2:4
to godliness— 2 a faith and knowledge resting on the hope of eter-
nal life,[c] which God, who does not lie, promised before the begin- 1:2 [c]2Ti 1:1
ning of time,[d] 3 and at his appointed season[e] he brought his word to [d]2Ti 1:9 1:3 [e]1Ti 2:6
light[f] through the preaching entrusted to me[g] by the command of [f]2Ti 1:10 [g]1Ti 1:11
God our Savior,[h] [h]Lk 1:47

4 To Titus,[i] my true son in our common faith: 1:4 [i]2Co 2:13

Grace and peace from God the Father and Christ Jesus our Savior.

Titus's Task on Crete

5 The reason I left you in Crete[j] was that you might straighten out 1:5 [j]Ac 27:7
what was left unfinished and appoint[*a*] elders[k] in every town, as I di- [k]Ac 11:30
rected you. 6 An elder must be blameless,[l] the husband of but one 1:6 [l]1Ti 3:2
wife, a man whose children believe and are not open to the charge
of being wild and disobedient. 7 Since an overseer[*b*][m] is entrusted 1:7 [m]1Ti 3:1

[*a*] 5 Or *ordain* [*b*] 7 Traditionally *bishop*

1:1 For "Paul," see the note on Philippians 3:5 and for "apostle" the note on 2 Corinthians 1:1.
1:4 Paul had left Titus (see the note on 2Ti 4:10) on the island of Crete to organize the church there and deal with a crisis situation of false teachers who had infiltrated its ranks. Titus, like Timothy (see the notes on Ac 16:1), had been converted through Paul's ministry.
1:5 Crete, the fourth largest island in the Mediterranean Sea, was a Roman province populated primarily by farmers and fruit growers. Today this Greek island, which is 156 miles (252 km) long and lies directly south of the Aegean Sea (see "Crete" on p. 1972), is home to approximately 600,000 people.
1:6 Since elders, by definition, were chosen from among the older men of the congregation, Paul assumed that most of these individuals were already married and had children. A qualified unmarried man was not necessarily barred.
1:7 The terms "overseer" and "elder" were used interchangeably (see the note on 1Ti 3:1-7). "Elder" indicates qualification (maturity and

ARCHAEOLOGICAL SITES

CRETE

TITUS 1 Crete ("Map 14"), about 170 miles (274 km) south of the Greek mainland, is the largest of the Greek islands, at 156 miles (252 km) long (from east to west) and, at most, 35 miles (56 km) wide (from north to south). It was home to the Minoan civilization, a Mediterranean culture that reached its high point around 1500 B.C. but collapsed at the end of the **Bronze Age**,[1] in around 1200 B.C.[2] The most spectacular remains of this civilization may be viewed at Knossos. Crete is referred to in the Old Testament as Caphtor (Dt 2:23; Jer 47:4), and the Philistines came to Canaan by way of Crete (Am 9:7). Crete does not figure significantly in history during the classical period, although the island is said to have been a base for pirates. It was brought under Roman rule in 67 B.C.

The island had a substantial Jewish population during the New Testament period (cf. Ac 2:11), and Paul was troubled by the negative influence of some of these Jews on the early Christians (Tit 1:14). The Cretan poet who labeled his fellow Cretans as liars and lazy gluttons (v. 12) is supposed to have been Epimenides, although the original text is no longer available.

[1]See Glossary on page 2080 for definitions of bolded words. [2]For more information, see "Greece: From the Prehistoric Period Through the Mycenaean Empire" on page 1810.

1:7 [n]1Co 4:1 [o]1Ti 3:3,8 with God's work,[n] he must be blameless—not overbearing, not quick-tempered, not given to drunken-
1:8 [p]1Ti 3:2 [q]2Ti 3:3 ness, not violent, not pursuing dishonest gain.[o] [8]Rather he must be hospitable,[p] one who loves what is
1:9 [r]1Ti 1:19 [s]1Ti 1:10 good,[q] who is self-controlled, upright, holy and disciplined. [9]He must hold firmly[r] to the trustworthy
message as it has been taught, so that he can encourage others by sound doctrine[s] and refute those who
oppose it.
1:10 [t]1Ti 1:6 [u]Ac 11:2 [10]For there are many rebellious people, mere talkers[t] and deceivers, especially those of the circumci-
1:11 [v]2Ti 3:6 sion group.[u] [11]They must be silenced, because they are ruining whole households[v] by teaching things
1:12 [w]Ac 17:28 [x]Ac 2:11 they ought not to teach—and that for the sake of dishonest gain. [12]Even one of their own prophets[w] has
1:13 [y]2Co 13:10 [z]Tit 2:2 said, "Cretans[x] are always liars, evil brutes, lazy gluttons." [13]This testimony is true. Therefore, rebuke[y]
1:14 [a]1Ti 1:4 [b]Col 2:22 them sharply, so that they will be sound in the faith[z] [14]and will pay no attention to Jewish myths[a] or to
the commands[b] of those who reject the truth. [15]To the pure, all things are pure, but to those who are cor-
1:15 [c]Ro 14:14, 23 rupted and do not believe, nothing is pure.[c] In fact, both their minds and consciences are corrupted.
1:16 [d]1Jn 2:4 [16]They claim to know God, but by their actions they deny him.[d] They are detestable, disobedient and
unfit for doing anything good.

---

experience), while "overseer" connotes responsibility (watching over God's flock).

1:8 For a discussion of asceticism in the believer's life, see the note at Leviticus 10:9.

1:10–16 These verses introduce the false teachers who had to be opposed by doctrinally informed elders. The presence of Jews throughout the ancient world, many of whom bought into "Jewish myths" (v. 14; see also the note on 1Ti 1:4), provided a network through which those who taught nonbiblical stories and other deviant teachings could circulate their errors.

These troublemakers had three main characteristics: (1) They belonged to the "circumcision group" (Tit 1:10), like the Judaizers (see the note on Gal 1:7; see also "Circumcision in the Ancient World" on p. 1840). (2) They held to unscriptural "Jewish myths" (v. 14; see the note on 1Ti 1:4). (3) They promoted a philosophy of asceticism (strict self-denial as a form of spiritual discipline).

1:12 The quotation is from the poet Epimenides, a sixth-century B.C. native of Crete, who was held in high esteem by the Cretans. He was credited with several predictions that were in fact later fulfilled.

ANCIENT TEXTS AND ARTIFACTS

The Apocrypha

TITUS 2 As the early church developed, Gentile believers needed to be taught "sound doctrine" (Tit 2:1). Although Paul and the apostles exclusively used the Old Testament as their **canonical** Bible, Gentiles also encountered many other Jewish religious texts among the Greek scrolls of the Scriptures. Many Gentile believers no doubt embraced these books as authoritative, and debate over their place in the churches has raged ever since.

The term "Apocrypha" (meaning "hidden away") refers broadly to a grouping of noncanonical books. However, the collection commonly called the Apocrypha is limited to 14 or 15 documents that were for the most part written during the last two centuries B.C. and the first century A.D. The Apocrypha actually represents only a small portion of the extant noncanonical Jewish literature from this period. Second Esdras 14:45–46 explicitly refers to the large amount of such material known at that time. In this passage a distinction is made between the canonical books of the Hebrew Old Testament—to be published for everyone—and "the seventy books which were written later"—to be reserved for the wise among the people.

The early manuscripts of the Greek Bible (the **Septuagint**) included the books now known as the Apocrypha. During the early Christian centuries Apocryphal texts were widely read and came to be regarded by some as canonical (cf. Augustine, *The City of God*, 18:36). Christian scholars, however, were aware of the discrepancies between the Greek and the Hebrew Bible. When Jerome published his Latin translation of the Bible (the **Vulgate**), he worked directly from the Hebrew Bible and carefully distinguished between what he considered canonical writings and the grouping of writings that he first designated as "the Apocrypha." Martin Luther (sixteenth century A.D.) opposed certain Apocryphal passages, such as 2 Maccabees 12:45–46, which had been used by the Roman Catholic Church to support the doctrine of purgatory and the selling of indulgences. In his 1534 German translation, Luther printed the books of the Apocrypha together in a separate appendix, rather than interspersing them among the canonical books. The Roman Catholic Council of Trent in 1546 rejected Luther's distinction by decreeing that the books of the Apocrypha are "Deuterocanonical" (belonging to the "second canon"). The Roman Catholic Deuterocanonical books, which remain a part of the Catholic Old Testament canon, are roughly equivalent to the Protestant Apocrypha.

Several books of the Apocrypha are pseudonymous, meaning that they purport to have been authored by a famous character of the Old Testament, such as Jeremiah, but were in fact written much later than the time of the alleged author.

What Must Be Taught to Various Groups

2 You must teach what is in accord with sound doctrine.[e] 2 Teach the older men to be temperate, wor- 2:1 e1Ti 1:10
thy of respect, self-controlled, and sound in faith,[f] in love and in endurance. 2:2 fTit 1:13
3 Likewise, teach the older women to be reverent in the way they live, not to be slanderers or addicted
to much wine,[g] but to teach what is good. 4 Then they can train the younger women to love their husbands 2:3 g1Ti 3:8

2:3 See "Wine and Alcoholic Beverages in the Ancient World" on page 2015.

ANCIENT TEXTS AND ARTIFACTS

The Books of the Apocrypha

TITUS 2 The books of the Apocrypha are as follows:

✣ *Tobit*: Set during the **Assyrian** exile, Tobit is an implausible narrative about a pious Jew. Tobit, taken into exile in Nineveh, goes blind as a result of sparrow droppings falling into his eyes. He dispatches his son Tobias to Media to retrieve a stash of money, providing a guide, Azariah, who turns out to be the angel Raphael. Raphael instructs Tobias to catch a large fish and to preserve its liver, heart and gall because of their magical powers. The two encounter a lovely Jewess, Sarah, whose seven grooms have died on their respective wedding nights because of the demon Asmodeus. Raphael instructs Tobias in how to thwart Asmodeus through ritual magic. Tobias then marries Sarah, retrieves the money, returns to Nineveh and heals Tobit with the fish gall.

✣ *Judith*: This nonhistorical tale describes how a pious Jewish woman effects deliverance for her people. Written during the latter part of the second century B.C., it was unaccountably set in the days of "Nebuchadnezzar, king of the Assyrians" (Nebuchadnezzar was king of Babylon).[1]

✣ *Ecclesiasticus/Sirach*: This book is fundamentally a collection of hymns, prayers and instructions upholding traditional Jewish piety and wisdom. Written in approximately 180 B.C., it includes some justly celebrated passages, such as its catalogue of heroes of the faith (Eccus/Sir 44:1—49:16).

✣ *Wisdom of Solomon*: Written at the earliest during the first century B.C., this work exhorts the reader to pursue wisdom and right behavior.

✣ *Baruch*: Although purported to have been authored by Baruch, Jeremiah's scribe, the book was probably written long after Baruch's day.[2] Drawing upon diverse parts of the Old Testament, it contains prayers, hymns and a passage that praises wisdom and claims it to be the special possession of Israel (Bar 3:9—4:4).

✣ *First and Second Maccabees*: These historical texts recount the persecution inflicted upon the Jews by Antiochus IV and the desecration of the temple that ignited the Maccabean revolt. First Maccabees was probably written around 100 B.C., while its counterpart may actually have come from a somewhat earlier date. Although the books are propagandistic in nature, they are a vital source for the history and religion of this period.[3]

✣ *First Esdras*: Written around 100 B.C., this is a loose retelling of Biblical history from Josiah's celebration of the Passover to Ezra's reforms. One part not copied from canonical Scripture is 1 Esdras 3:1—5:6, which records how a young Jewish man at the court of Darius solves a riddle about the strongest thing in the world (women are strongest, but truth conquers all). This Jewish man turns out to be Zerubbabel (Ezr 2:2).

✣ *Second Esdras*: This book is a composite of three writings, the latest of which may have been penned as recently as the third century A.D. Apocalyptic in nature,[4] it includes a reaction to the A.D. 70 destruction of the Jerusalem temple by the Romans.[5] The central portion of the book (2Es 3:1—14:48), dated to about A.D. 100, is a fictitious series of visions supposedly given by the angel Uriel to Ezra and dealing with such issues as the justice of God. A Christian appendix (2Es 15:1—16:78) was added during the third century A.D.

✣ *Epistle of Jeremiah*: Loosely based on Jeremiah 29, this short, pseudonymous essay denounces the folly of idolatry. The writing most likely came from the third century B.C. or later.

✣ *Prayer of Manasseh*: A pseudonymous, penitential prayer beseeching God to cancel Israel's exile, this book claims to be the prayer of Manasseh mentioned in 2 Chronicles 33:12–13; it comes in fact from the second or first century B.C. The writing draws upon a number of Biblical texts, especially Psalm 51.[6]

✣ *Additions to Esther*: This includes six supplements to Esther, adding pious language and motifs in an evident attempt to make up for the fact that the canonical book never mentions God.

✣ *Additions to Daniel*: These supplements to Daniel include the Prayer of Azariah, the Song of the Three Young Men, Susanna, and Bel and the Dragon (or Serpent). The dates of composition are unknown.

1See "Nebuchadnezzar" on page 571. 2See "Baruch, Scribe of Jeremiah" on page 1248. 3See "The Intertestamental Period" on page 1551. 4See "Apocalyptic Literature Outside the Bible" on page 2048. 5See also "Josephus and the Fall of Jerusalem" on page 1606. 6See "The Seal of Manasseh" on page 565.

SELECTED JEWISH AND CHRISTIAN LITERATURE

APOCRYPHA	Epistle/Letter of Jeremiah (317 B.C.)
	Tobit (250–175 B.C.)
	Baruch (200 B.C.–A.D. 70)
	Ecclesiasticus/Sirach (190 B.C.)
	Additions to Esther (180–145 B.C.)
	Judith (175–110 B.C.)
	The Song of the Three Children/Young Men (167–163 B.C.?)
	1 Esdras (c. 150 B.C.)
	Bel and the Dragon (150–100 B.C.?)
	Prayer of Manasseh/Serpent (150–50 B.C.?)
	Wisdom of Solomon (150 B.C.—A.D. 40)
	1 Maccabees (103–63 B.C.)
	2 Maccabees (c. 100 B.C.)
	Susanna (c. 100 B.C.?)
	2 Esdras (A.D. 70–135)
PSEUDEPIGRAPHA*	Enoch (200–63 B.C.)
	Letter of Aristeas (170–130 B.C.)
	Book of Jubilees (150–100 B.C.)
	Testaments of the Twelve Patriarchs (c. 130 B.C.)
	3 Maccabees (1st century B.C.)
	4 Maccabees (?)
	The Sibylline Oracles (c. 80 B.C.–A.D. 130)
	Psalms of Solomon (c. 40 B.C.)
	Book of Adam and Eve (1st century A.D.)
	Lives of the Prophets (1st century A.D.)
	Assumption of Moses (A.D. 1–30)
	2 Baruch (A.D. 70–100)
	Ascension of Isaiah (2nd century A.D.)
APOSTOLIC FATHERS	1 Clement (A.D. 95–96)
	Ignatius (A.D. 110–117)
	The Didache (A.D. 100–130?)
	Shepherd of Hermas (A.D. 100–140)
	Epistle of Barnabas (C. A.D. 132)
	Polycarp (before 155 A.D.)

*See "The Bible and Pseudepigraphical Literature" on page 2041 and "Apocalyptic Literature Outside the Bible" on page 2048. The list in the chart is not inclusive and varies from those in the articles.

Chronological and Background Charts of the New Testament, p. 58

and children, 5to be self-controlled and pure, to be busy at home, to be kind, and to be subject to their
husbands,[h] so that no one will malign the word of God.[i]
6Similarly, encourage the young men[j] to be self-controlled. 7In everything set them an example[k] by
doing what is good. In your teaching show integrity, seriousness 8and soundness of speech that cannot
be condemned, so that those who oppose you may be ashamed because they have nothing bad to say
about us.[l]
9Teach slaves to be subject to their masters in everything,[m] to try to please them, not to talk back to
them, 10and not to steal from them, but to show that they can be fully trusted, so that in every way they
will make the teaching about God our Savior attractive.[n]
11For the grace of God that brings salvation has appeared to all men.[o] 12It teaches us to say "No" to un-
godliness and worldly passions,[p] and to live self-controlled, upright and godly lives[q] in this present age,
13while we wait for the blessed hope—the glorious appearing of our great God and Savior, Jesus Christ,[r]
14who gave himself for us to redeem us from all wickedness and to purify for himself a people that are
his very own,[s] eager to do what is good.[t]
15These, then, are the things you should teach. Encourage and rebuke with all authority. Do not let
anyone despise you.

Doing What Is Good

3 Remind the people to be subject to rulers and authorities,[u] to be obedient, to be ready to do what-
ever is good,[v] 2to slander no one,[w] to be peaceable and considerate, and to show true humility to-
ward all men.
3At one time we too were foolish, disobedient, deceived and enslaved by all kinds of passions and
pleasures. We lived in malice and envy, being hated and hating one another. 4But when the kindness[x] and
love of God our Savior appeared,[y] 5he saved us, not because of righteous things we had done,[z] but be-
cause of his mercy. He saved us through the washing of rebirth and renewal[a] by the Holy Spirit, 6whom
he poured out on us[b] generously through Jesus Christ our Savior, 7so that, having been justified by his
grace,[c] we might become heirs[d] having the hope[e] of eternal life.[f] 8This is a trustworthy saying.[g] And I
want you to stress these things, so that those who have trusted in God may be careful to devote them-
selves to doing what is good.[h] These things are excellent and profitable for everyone.
9But avoid foolish controversies and genealogies and arguments and quarrels[i] about the law, because
these are unprofitable and useless. 10Warn a divisive person once, and then warn him a second time. Af-
ter that, have nothing to do with him.[j] 11You may be sure that such a man is warped and sinful; he is self-
condemned.

Final Remarks

12As soon as I send Artemas or Tychicus[k] to you, do your best to come to me at Nicopolis, because I
have decided to winter there.[l] 13Do everything you can to help Zenas the lawyer and Apollos[m] on their
way and see that they have everything they need. 14Our people must learn to devote themselves to doing
what is good,[n] in order that they may provide for daily necessities and not live unproductive lives.
15Everyone with me sends you greetings. Greet those who love us in the faith.[o]
Grace be with you all.[p]

2:5 [h]Eph 5:22 [i]1Ti 6:1
2:6 [j]1Ti 5:1
2:7 [k]1Ti 4:12
2:8 [l]1Pe 2:12
2:9 [m]Eph 6:5
2:10 [n]Mt 5:16
2:11 [o]1Ti 2:4
2:12 [p]Tit 3:3 [q]2Ti 3:12
2:13 [r]2Pe 1:1
2:14 [s]Ex 19:5 [t]Eph 2:10
3:1 [u]Ro 13:1 [v]2Ti 2:21
3:2 [w]Eph 4:31; 2Ti 2:24
3:4 [x]Eph 2:7 [y]Tit 2:11
3:5 [z]Eph 2:9 [a]Ro 12:2
3:6 [b]Ro 5:5
3:7 [c]Ro 3:24 [d]Ro 8:17 [e]Ro 8:24 [f]Tit 1:2
3:8 [g]1Ti 1:15 [h]Tit 2:14
3:9 [i]1Ti 1:4; 2Ti 2:14
3:10 [j]Ro 16:17
3:12 [k]Ac 20:4 [l]2Ti 4:9,21
3:13 [m]Ac 18:24
3:14 [n]ver 8
3:15 [o]1Ti 1:2 [p]Col 4:18

2:9–10 Slavery was a basic element of Roman society (see "Slavery in the Greco-Roman World" on p. 1979), and the impact of Christianity upon slaves was a vital concern. Guidance for the conduct of Christian slaves was essential.

The Greek for "masters" (v. 9), from which our English term "despot" is derived, indicates the owner's absolute authority over his slave. Roman slaves had no legal rights, their fates being entirely in their masters' hands.

3:9 For "genealogies," see the note on 1 Timothy 1:4.

3:10 For commentary on excommunication, see the note on 1 Timothy 1:20.

3:12 Artemas is mentioned only here in the Bible, but tradition has it that he was a bishop of Lystra. For "Tychicus," see the note on 2 Timothy 4:12.

Several cities of Paul's day bore the name Nicopolis, but the reference here is apparently to the city in the district of Epirus on the western shore of Greece. An ancient city, Nicopolis ("city of victory"), which is situated on the Gulf of Actium (modern Gulf of Arta), was founded by Augustus Caesar to celebrate his decisive victory over Mark Antony in 31 B.C. At the time Paul wrote his letter to Titus, in the interval between the apostle's first and his final imprisonment under Nero at Rome, he had determined to winter there.

3:13 If "Zenas the lawyer" was a Jewish convert, "lawyer" implies that he was an expert in the Mosaic Law. If he was a Gentile convert, "lawyer" indicates that he was a Roman jurist.

For "Apollos," see the note on 1 Corinthians 1:12.

INTRODUCTION TO 

AUTHOR, PLACE AND DATE OF WRITING

Paul's authorship of this letter is virtually unquestioned. The apostle was apparently in prison in Rome when he wrote to Philemon (v. 9), and a composition of this letter around the same time as Colossians, about A.D. 60, seems reasonable.

AUDIENCE

Paul wrote this letter primarily to Philemon, a believer in Colosse, but it is also addressed to Apphia (possibly Philemon's wife), Archippus (see Col 4:17) and the members of the church in Colosse (Phm 2).

CULTURAL FACTS AND HIGHLIGHTS

This is a personal letter, in that Paul wrote to Philemon to plead with him to be lenient with his runaway slave, Onesimus. Under Roman law Philemon could have punished Onesimus with almost any degree of severity, including death, but Paul wanted Philemon not only to forgive Onesimus but to grant him manumission (vv. 14–16; see also "Slavery in the Greco-Roman World" on p. 1979). Paul had not visited Colosse but seems to have been responsible for Philemon's conversion (v. 19). Onesimus had apparently robbed Philemon and made his way to Paul in Rome, where he had confessed his crime and himself been converted.

TIMELINE

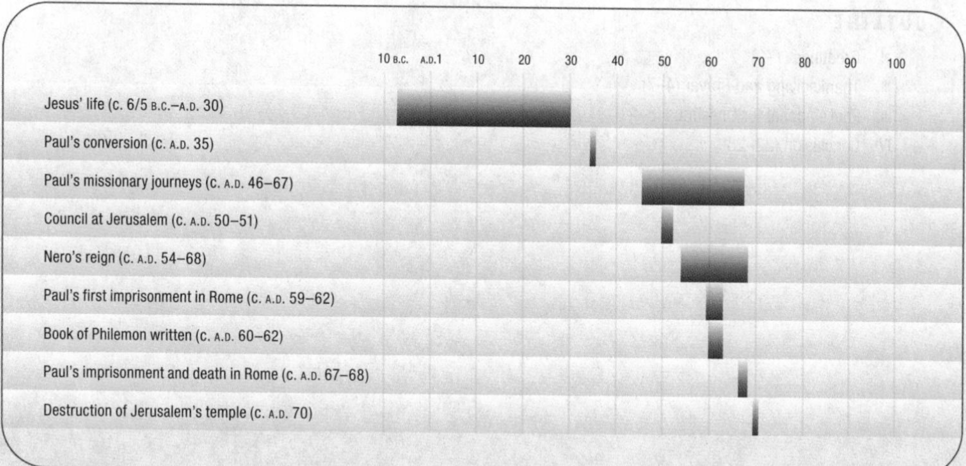

AS YOU READ

Look for glimpses into Paul's relationships with Onesimus and Philemon. Note the way Paul described the transformation that occurs in a person's relationships when he or she becomes a believer (v. 16–17). Examine Paul's view of Onesimus, and consider how radical it must have seemed in Paul's day (see v. 16).

DID YOU KNOW?

- Approximately one-third of the first-century Roman population was made up of slaves (v. 12).
- Slaves had no legal status, and a runaway could be severely whipped, branded on the face, chained, forced to wear an iron neck collar or restrained by having his or her legs broken. Slaves could also be sold to the mines or sentenced to death (v. 14).
- The aristocratic historian Sallust described the Rome of Paul's day as "the common cesspool of the world" (v. 24).

THEMES

Philemon includes the following themes:

1. *Forgiveness.* Paul asked Philemon to accept his formerly troublesome slave as he would accept Paul himself, extending the same forgiving love to Onesimus that he himself had received from God (see Col 3:13). Their reconciliation was so important that it took precedence over Paul's desire to have Onesimus remain with himself (v. 13). This brief letter speaks of failure, intercession, repentance, forgiveness and restoration.

2. *Equality in Christ.* Paul did not overtly challenge the slavery system, but neither did he sanctify it as part of God's design. Instead, he focused on how conversion fundamentally transforms personal relationships with others and with God. He laid down universal principles that, when taken seriously, ultimately topple the foundations of injustice in any form.

OUTLINE

I. Greetings (1–3)
II. Thanksgiving and Prayer (4–7)
III. Paul's Appeal for Onesimus (8–21)
IV. Conclusion (22–25)

1:1 [a]ver 9,23; Eph 3:1 [b]2Co 1:1 [c]Php 2:25
1:2 [d]Col 4:17 [e]Php 2:25 [f]Ro 16:5

1 Paul, a prisoner[a] of Christ Jesus, and Timothy our brother,[b]

To Philemon our dear friend and fellow worker,[c] 2 to Apphia our sister, to Archippus[d] our fellow soldier[e] and to the church that meets in your home:[f]

3 Grace to you and peace from God our Father and the Lord Jesus Christ.

---

1 For "Paul," see the note on Philippians 3:5 and for "Timothy" the note on Acts 16:1.
Philemon, a member of the church at Colosse, was a slave owner (see "Slavery in the Greco-Roman World" on p. 1979 and "Labor and Welfare in the Ancient World" on p. 1952).

2 Apphia was probably Philemon's wife.
House churches were common in this early period (see "House Churches and Early Church Buildings" on p. 2033, as well as the note on 1Co 16:19).

Slavery in the Greco-Roman World

PHILEMON Slavery was practiced throughout the Greco-Roman world, and there were several categories of slaves:

✣ The *helot* was a citizen of a city that was in permanent subordination to another state. A famous example is Messenia, a Greek city-state subdued by Sparta and then reduced to peasant status and forced to serve the needs of Sparta's military culture. The people of Gibeon are an analogous example from Israelite history; they served as menial workers for the sanctuary (Jos 9).

✣ The indentured servant was reduced to slavery by debt but could obtain remission by working off that liability.

✣ The chattel-slave was quite simply the property of his or her master.

People fell into slavery by various means and for various reasons. As mentioned above, unresolved debt could lead to this condition. Large numbers of people became slaves through conquest. Victorious armies would sell captured people into slavery, and these wretched souls typically never again saw their homelands. Frequently slavers would simply kidnap people, take them far away and sell them. Ancient pirates regularly practiced this, and the Roman government from time to time sought to clear the seas of pirate fleets. In addition, the children of a slave woman were born into slavery, regardless of the status of their father. Slavery was not racially based, although people generally preferred not to enslave others of their own ethnic group (e.g., Greeks typically enslaved non-Greeks, whom they considered "barbarians").

The degree of hardship related to slavery also varied considerably. No doubt the worst lot fell to those who worked in mines and similar labor-intensive industries. Slightly better was the situation of peasant-farmers, with household slaves experiencing an easier life still. The most desirable position for a slave was that of a teacher, scribe or clerk, but even such a situation could be miserable if the master was harsh. Slaves were considered nonpersons and thus enjoyed no rights—including privacy or control over their own sexual lives. Not surprisingly, an enormous number of slaves ran away, particularly if they had no hope of obtaining manumission. The flight of Philemon's slave Onesimus, then, was not a peculiar occurrence. Occasionally outright rebellion occurred, the most spectacular example being that of the Spartacus slave revolt of 73 B.C. Passive resistance (e.g., by working slowly) was more common.[1]

The New Testament does not condemn slavery outright or demand that Christian slaveholders emancipate their slaves. On the other hand, the pressure Paul applied to Philemon to release Onesimus was exemplary, and Paul elsewhere urged Christian slaves to obtain manumission if at all possible (1Co 7:21). Paul undermined the foundation of slavery—the notion that slaves were nonentities—when he made the declaration that in Christ there is no distinction between slave and free (Gal 3:28).

[1]See also "Slavery and Labor Law in the Ancient Near East" on page 127 and "Labor and Welfare in the Ancient World" on page 127.

Thanksgiving and Prayer

4 I always thank my God[g] as I remember you in my prayers, 5 because I hear about your faith in the — **1:4** [g]Ro 1:8
Lord Jesus and your love for all the saints.[h] 6 I pray that you may be active in sharing your faith, so that — **1:5** [h]Eph 1:15; Col 1:4
you will have a full understanding of every good thing we have in Christ. 7 Your love has given me great — **1:7** [i]2Co 7:4,13 [j]ver 20
joy and encouragement,[i] because you, brother, have refreshed[j] the hearts of the saints.

Paul's Plea for Onesimus

8 Therefore, although in Christ I could be bold and order you to do what you ought to do, 9 yet I appeal
to you on the basis of love. I then, as Paul—an old man and now also a prisoner[k] of Christ Jesus— 10 I — **1:9** [k]ver 1,23
appeal to you for my son[l] Onesimus,[a][m] who became my son while I was in chains. 11 Formerly he was — **1:10** [l]1Co 4:15 [m]Col 4:9
useless to you, but now he has become useful both to you and to me.
12 I am sending him—who is my very heart—back to you. 13 I would have liked to keep him with me
so that he could take your place in helping me while I am in chains for the gospel. 14 But I did not want
to do anything without your consent, so that any favor you do will be spontaneous and not forced.[n] 15 Per- — **1:14** [n]2Co 9:7; 1Pe 5:2
haps the reason he was separated from you for a little while was that you might have him back for good—
16 no longer as a slave, but better than a slave, as a dear brother.[o] He is very dear to me but even dearer to — **1:16** [o]Mt 23:8; 1Ti 6:2
you, both as a man and as a brother in the Lord.
17 So if you consider me a partner,[p] welcome him as you would welcome me. 18 If he has done you any — **1:17** [p]2Co 8:23
wrong or owes you anything, charge it to me. 19 I, Paul, am writing this with my own hand. I will pay it
back—not to mention that you owe me your very self. 20 I do wish, brother, that I may have some bene-
fit from you in the Lord; refresh[q] my heart in Christ. 21 Confident[r] of your obedience, I write to you, know- — **1:20** [q]ver 7 **1:21** [r]2Co 2:3
ing that you will do even more than I ask.
22 And one thing more: Prepare a guest room for me, because I hope to be[s] restored to you in answer — **1:22** [s]Php 1:25; 2:24 [t]2Co 1:11
to your prayers.[t]

23 Epaphras,[u] my fellow prisoner in Christ Jesus, sends you greetings. 24 And so do Mark,[v] Aristar- — **1:23** [u]Col 1:7 **1:24** [v]Ac 12:12 [w]Ac 19:29 [x]Col 4:14
chus,[w] Demas[x] and Luke, my fellow workers.
25 The grace of the Lord Jesus Christ be with your spirit.[y] — **1:25** [y]2Ti 4:22

[a] *10 Onesimus* means *useful.*

---

7 There is a celebrated letter of the Roman writer Pliny on a similar subject, written perhaps 40 years after Paul's appeal to Philemon. It is interesting to compare Pliny's language of humane generosity with Paul's words of brotherly affection. Pliny voiced his plea for forgiveness on humanitarian and philosophical grounds, while Paul focused on Christian fellowship (vv. 16,20). Paul wrote with exquisite tact and with words of praise before referring to obligation. The word "brother" comes like a friendly handclasp at the end of this verse, and "my son Onesimus" adds a curiously poignant appeal at the close of verse 10.

Paul, the ambassador, might well have spoken of duty. An imperial legate had a right to speak for the emperor, and the analogy would not have been lost on Philemon. Instead, Paul reminded Philemon that, in respect to bondage, Paul's own position was similar to that of the man for whom he pleaded. Onesimus was both a fellow bondsman and a son. The Talmud states, "If one teaches the son of his neighbor the Law, this is the same as if he had begotten him." Paul evidently had this rabbinical saying in mind.

10 Onesimus was one of Philemon's slaves. He had apparently stolen from Philemon and then run away, which under Roman law was punishable by death. But Onesimus met Paul and through his ministry became a Christian. Now Onesimus was willing to return to his master, and Paul wrote this personal appeal to ask that he be accepted as a Christian brother (v. 16).

11 The name Onesimus (most likely a common nickname for a slave) means "useful," and Paul made a play on the word here, proceeding immediately to point to the sacrifice he himself was making. Onesimus was "briefly" parted from Philemon, Paul pointed out, going on to strongly hint that manumission might be the truest mark of brotherliness. With a closing touch of humor Paul offered to pay Philemon back for anything the runaway owed, discounting, as he returned to seriousness, Philemon's own deep debt.

12 In sending Onesimus back to his owner, Paul appeared at first glance to be endorsing the practice of slavery (see "Slavery in the Greco-Roman World" on p. 1979). With possibly one-third of the Roman population enslaved, Paul had to be tactful in how he approached this subject. In a few brief words, Paul effectively undermined the entire system of slavery, stressing that he, too, was a prisoner in chains (v. 10), accused of violating the laws and subject to the authority of Rome. The reconciliation of a disloyal slave with his master as brothers in Christ recasts all relationships and reflects Christ's reconciliation of all things.

14 The Roman imperial economy depended on slaves for labor. Any concern for a slave's welfare was usually practical, motivated by the owner's self-interest.

19 The letter up to this point had probably been dictated to a scribe, after which Paul took the pen in his own hand and finished the letter (see "Writing Materials in the Ancient World" on p. 2037).

22–25 The letter ends on a note of intimacy. There was something truly Greek about Paul. The great Greek orators and authors seldom placed the climax of their speech or writing in their closing words, ending on a minor note designed to bring the excited audience back to a state of normalcy and rest.

24 For "Mark," see the note on Colossians 4:10.

Rome was the frequent goal of fugitives such as Onesimus; the city was called by the aristocratic historian Sallust "the common cesspool of the world." Some Ephesian or Colossian individual in Rome, perhaps Aristarchus (Ac 27:2; Col 4:10–14; Phm 24) or Epaphras (Col 1:7; 4:12–13; Phm 23), seems to have recognized the man and brought him to Paul in his captivity. Onesimus became a Christian and was persuaded to return to his master. From that incident came this exquisite letter, which demonstrates so vividly the social solvent that Christianity had brought into the world. It appears that Onesimus left Rome in company with Tychicus, carrying the letter to Philemon, along with Paul's letters to the Ephesian and Colossian churches. Nothing more is known about Onesimus, and a tradition that he became the martyr bishop of Berea is of doubtful authenticity.

INTRODUCTION TO 

AUTHOR, PLACE AND DATE OF WRITING

The letter to the Hebrews is anonymous. The tradition of Pauline authorship is not reliable, and there are in fact serious reasons to contest this assertion. Luke, Clement of Rome, Barnabas, Apollos, Epaphras, Silas, Priscilla and others have been suggested, but in reality we simply do not know who wrote this book (see "Who Wrote Hebrews?" on p. 1985). We are aware that the author was well schooled in the Old Testament, acquainted with his audience, capable of writing excellent Greek and a friend of Timothy (13:23).

Hebrews was almost certainly written before the fall of Jerusalem in A.D. 70. In light of the author's determination to demonstrate Christ's superiority over the Aaronic priesthood and the temple sacrifices, it seems inconceivable that no mention would have been made of the destruction of the temple, the ultimate sign of its rejection by God, had that event already occurred. We know too that the book was written at a time when persecution was becoming a serious concern (13:3). While it is true that imprisonment of Christian leaders took place in the early years of church history (Ac 4:3), on balance this suggests a later date for Hebrews; A.D. 60–70 is probable.

AUDIENCE

If there is uncertainty about the author of the letter, there is also ambiguity about the addressees. The title, Hebrews (or "To the Hebrews"), was not part of the original text and thus is of questionable value, but most interpreters do believe that the letter was written to Jewish Christians who spoke Greek and probably used the Septuagint.

CULTURAL FACTS AND HIGHLIGHTS

The author appears to have been especially concerned that some of these Christians might "shrink back" (10:38), although there seems to have been no danger of their espousing paganism. Hebrews everywhere stresses the superiority of Christ to the glory of the old covenant; thus, it seems more likely that at least some of the readers were tempted to revert to Second Temple Judaism. Against the magnificence of Herod's temple, the worship service carried out in house churches must have seemed paltry indeed. The author of Hebrews, however, sought to warn his struggling audience that the glory of the earthly temple was but a shadow, soon to disappear.

TIMELINE

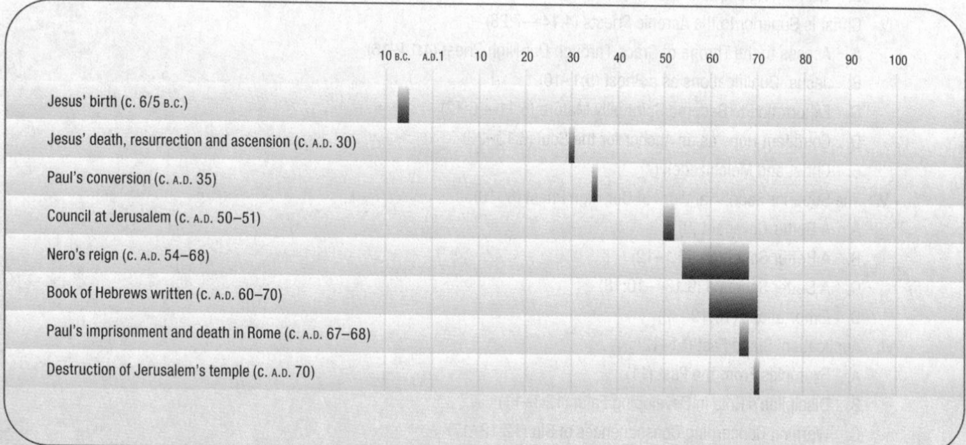

AS YOU READ

Examine the five warnings the author gave the readers regarding their spiritual condition (2:1; 3:7; 5:11; 10:26; 12:25). Note the writer's statements about Jewish customs and his explanation that Jesus brought a new covenant (of grace through faith) that is infinitely better than the old one (of obedience to the law). Pay attention to the repeated use of the words "better" and "superior."

DID YOU KNOW?

- In the Law of Moses the priestly function was restricted to the family of Aaron from the tribe of Levi, but Jesus came from the non-priestly tribe of Judah (7:16).
- The priceless treasures of the Egyptian King Tutankhamen's tomb included several thousand pounds of pure gold (11:26).

THEMES

The book of Hebrews includes the following themes:

1. *The superiority of Christ.* Hebrews presents Christ as superior to the prophets (1:1–2), angels (1:4–6), Moses (3:3), Joshua (4:8), the Old Testament priesthood and the high priest (4:14—5:10; 7:1–28), the sacrificial system and the sanctuary (8:1—10:18).
2. *Perseverance.* Believers are called to a heavenward journey (3:1) but must first undergo testing.
3. *Faith pleases God.* Hebrews 11 emphasizes a faith that is exercised in numerous large and small ways.
4. *Discipline comes to God's children.* Hardship is the means God uses to discipline his children.
5. *Christian living.* Christians are to show hospitality (13:1–3), refrain from sexual immorality (13:4), guard against the love of money (13:5), do good and share with others (13:16), obey their leaders (13:17) and pray (13:18–19).

OUTLINE

I. The Superiority of God's New Revelation (1:1–4)
II. Christ Is Superior to the Angels (1:5—2:18)
  A. Biblical Evidence of Christ's Superiority (1:5–14)
  B. The Danger of Neglecting the Truth About Christ (2:1–4)
  C. Further Biblical Evidence of Christ's Superiority (2:5–18)
III. Christ Is Superior to Moses (3:1—4:13)
  A. Christ the Son; Moses the Servant (3:1–6)
  B. Warning Against Unbelief (3:7—4:13)
IV. Christ Is Superior to the Aaronic Priests (4:14—7:28)
  A. Access to the Throne of Grace Through Our High Priest (4:14–16)
  B. Jesus' Qualifications as a Priest (5:1–10)
  C. Exhortation to Become Spiritually Mature (5:11—6:12)
  D. Confident Hope as an Anchor for the Soul (6:13–20)
  E. Christ and Melchizedek (7)
V. The Superior Sacrificial Work of Our High Priest (8–10)
  A. A Better Covenant (8)
  B. A Better Sanctuary (9:1–12)
  C. A Better Sacrifice (9:13—10:18)
  D. Exhortations (10:19–39)
VI. Application: Stand Fast (11–12)
  A. Examples From the Past (11)
  B. Discipline's Role in Developing Faith (12:1–11)
  C. Warning Concerning Consequences of Sin (12:12–17)
  D. Danger of Refusing This Message (12:18–29)
VII. Conclusion (13)

The Son Superior to Angels

1:1 [a]Jn 9:29; Heb 2:2,3 [b]Ac 2:30 [c]Nu 12:6,8
1:2 [d]Ps 2:8 [e]Jn 1:3
1:3 [f]Jn 1:14 [g]Col 1:17 [h]Heb 7:27 [i]Mk 16:19
1:4 [j]Eph 1:21; Php 2:9,10
1:5 [k]Ps 2:7 [l]2Sa 7:14

1 In the past God spoke[a] to our forefathers through the prophets[b] at many times and in various ways,[c]
2 but in these last days he has spoken to us by his Son, whom he appointed heir[d] of all things, and
through whom[e] he made the universe. 3 The Son is the radiance of God's glory[f] and the exact represen-
tation of his being, sustaining all things[g] by his powerful word. After he had provided purification for
sins,[h] he sat down at the right hand of the Majesty in heaven.[i] 4 So he became as much superior to the an-
gels as the name he has inherited is superior to theirs.[j]
5 For to which of the angels did God ever say,

> "You are my Son;
> today I have become your Father"[a][b][k]

Or again,

> "I will be his Father,
> and he will be my Son"[c][l]

[a] 5 Or *have begotten you* [b] 5 Psalm 2:7 [c] 5 2 Samuel 7:14; 1 Chron. 17:13

1:1–14 Hebrews may well have been a sermon crafted by someone accustomed to worshiping in a Greek-speaking synagogue and educated in the Greek and Roman institutions of the day. Both the Greek and Roman traditions emphasized an appropriate beginning, in which the speaker was to present the main topic(s) of his speech or sermon and seek to rivet the audience's attention.

1:3 See "The 'Right Hand' in Ancient Thinking" on page 1983.

1:4 To most Jews angels were exalted beings, especially revered because they had been involved in the giving of the Law, which to the Jews was God's supreme revelation. According to some Jewish writings, four archangels (Michael, Raphael, Gabriel and Phanuel) are always present before the throne of God. (See "Angels and Guardian Spirits in the Bible and the Ancient Near East" on p. 1529.)

The "Right Hand" in Ancient Thinking

HEBREWS 1 The hand was symbolic in the ancient world. It was believed that from it one either bestowed grace or pronounced punishment. In addition, the hand represented the authority of an individual, the instrument of carrying out a person's intentions. The right hand, in particular, was special for two reasons. First, the left hand was universally acknowledged to be the one used for sanitation purposes and, therefore, was less respected than its counterpart. Secondly, since most people were right-handed, the right hand was considered to have innately superior strength and capability.

Because of its special physical status, the right hand was assigned important metaphorical significance, frequently expressing blessing, fellowship or comfort. Certain acts of ritual cleansing, as well as the ordination of the Aaronic priesthood, involved the right hand or the right-hand side.[1] The right hand was also used in taking vows in judicial matters, since it was believed to represent the character, will and actions of the individual taking the vow. In literature, it personified a king or deity's character and deeds,[2] while in the Hebrew Bible the right hand represented God's ultimate strength and provision for his people.

To be seated at the right hand of a ruler or host meant occupying a place of high honor. The position itself was considered an indicator of the power and authority of the one holding it. Someone who sat at the king's right hand was, as in the modern English idiom, his "right-hand man,"—the one acting as the principal agent of the king's authority, through whom he carried out his most important work. In addition, sitting at the right hand was a statement of fellowship and favor between the central figure and the individual so honored. Jesus Christ is depicted several times in the Bible as sitting at the right hand of God the Father for eternity (Ps 110:1; Ac 2:33–35; 5:31; Ro 8:34; Eph 1:20; Col 3:1; Heb 1:3,13; 8:1; 10:12; 12:2; 1Pe 3:22).

[1] See "The Levites and the Priests" on page 648 and "Ritual Purity in Israel and the Ancient Near East" on page 166. [2] See "The Ancient Near Eastern King" on page 839.

6 And again, when God brings his firstborn into the world,[m] he says,

"Let all God's angels worship him."[a][n]

1:6 [m]Heb 10:5 [n]Dt 32:43 (LXX and DSS); Ps 97:7

7 In speaking of the angels he says,

"He makes his angels winds,
his servants flames of fire."[b][o]

1:7 [o]Ps 104:4

8 But about the Son he says,

"Your throne, O God, will last for ever and ever,
and righteousness will be the scepter of your kingdom.
9 You have loved righteousness and hated wickedness;
therefore God, your God, has set you above your companions[p]
by anointing you with the oil[q] of joy."[c]

1:9 [p]Php 2:9 [q]Isa 61:1,3

10 He also says,

"In the beginning, O Lord, you laid the foundations of the earth,
and the heavens are the work of your hands.
11 They will perish, but you remain;
they will all wear out like a garment.[r]
12 You will roll them up like a robe;
like a garment they will be changed.
But you remain the same,[s]
and your years will never end."[d][t]

1:11 [r]Isa 34:4
1:12 [s]Heb 13:8 [t]Ps 102:25-27

13 To which of the angels did God ever say,

"Sit at my right hand
until I make your enemies
a footstool[u] for your feet"[e]?[v]

14 Are not all angels ministering spirits[w] sent to serve those who will inherit salvation?[x]

1:13 [u]Jos 10:24; Heb 10:13 [v]Ps 110:1
1:14 [w]Ps 103:20 [x]Heb 5:9

Warning to Pay Attention

2 We must pay more careful attention, therefore, to what we have heard, so that we do not drift away.
2 For if the message spoken[y] by angels[z] was binding, and every violation and disobedience received
its just punishment,[a] 3 how shall we escape if we ignore such a great salvation?[b] This salvation, which
was first announced by the Lord,[c] was confirmed to us by those who heard him.[d] 4 God also testified to
it by signs, wonders and various miracles,[e] and gifts of the Holy Spirit[f] distributed according to his will.[g]

2:2 [y]Heb 1:1 [z]Dt 33:2; Ac 7:53 [a]Heb 10:28
2:3 [b]Heb 10:29 [c]Heb 1:2 [d]Lk 1:2
2:4 [e]Jn 4:48 [f]1Co 12:4 [g]Eph 1:5

Jesus Made Like His Brothers

5 It is not to angels that he has subjected the world to come, about which we are speaking. 6 But there
is a place where someone has testified:

"What is man that you are mindful of him,
the son of man that you care for him?[h]
7 You made him a little[f] lower than the angels;
you crowned him with glory and honor
8 and put everything under his feet."[g][i]

2:6 [h]Job 7:17
2:8 [i]Ps 8:4-6; 1Co 15:25

In putting everything under him, God left nothing that is not subject to him. Yet at present we do not see
everything subject to him. 9 But we see Jesus, who was made a little lower than the angels, now crowned

[a] *6* Deut. 32:43 (see Dead Sea Scrolls and Septuagint) [b] *7* Psalm 104:4 [c] *9* Psalm 45:6,7 [d] *12* Psalm 102:25-27
[e] *13* Psalm 110:1 [f] *7* Or *him for a little while*; also in verse 9 [g] *8* Psalm 8:4-6

1:7 Psalm 104:4 speaks of the wind and the lightning as agents of God's purposes (see the note on Eze 1:4; see also "Storm Gods, Storm Imagery and Theophany" on p. 808). The Septuagint, which the author of Hebrews quoted as the version familiar to his readers, reflects the developing doctrine of angels during the period between the Old Testament and New Testament (see "The Septuagint and Its Use in the New Testament" on p. 1995).

WHO WROTE HEBREWS?

HEBREWS 2 Almost since its origin, the authorship of the epistle to the Hebrews has been a matter of speculation. The earliest complete copy of Hebrews (in the Chester Beatty papyrus) is situated squarely within the Pauline corpus, immediately after Romans. Although Pauline authorship did for some time become a traditional view, there are serious and ancient reasons for resisting this conclusion:

◆ The book of Hebrews is anonymous, whereas the other 13 Pauline texts each begins explicitly with the name Paul.[1]

◆ It is also unlikely that Paul, who unambiguously considered himself an apostle and "eyewitness" of the resurrected Jesus (1Co 15:8–9; Gal 1:11–2), would have referred to himself as a second-generation believer (Heb 2:3).

◆ The theological perspective of Hebrews (an emphasis on Jesus Christ as high priest and the use of sacrificial categories to explain the significance of his death) are uncharacteristic of Paul's other known writings.

◆ There are striking stylistic differences between Hebrews and the letters of Paul. The language of Hebrews is breathtaking in its eloquence and structural vision. The author employed a studied, elevated prose, together with rich rhetorical embellishment. In contrast, Paul explicitly stated that he lacked this quality in his writing and speech (1Co 1:17; 2:1; 2Co 11:6).

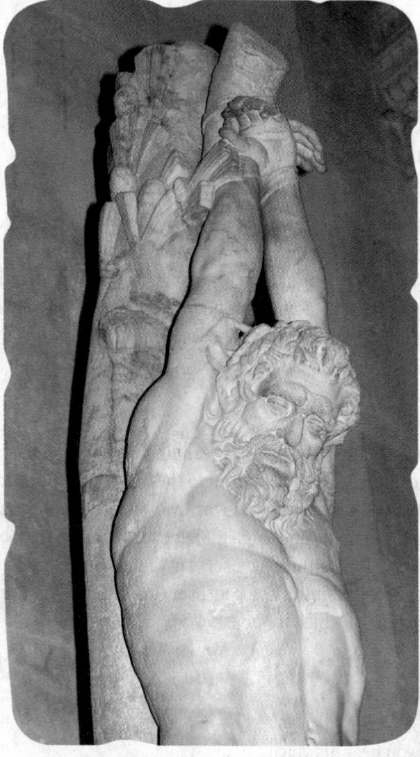

This replica of a Roman original (Figure of Marsyas) portrays a Roman hanging—a reminder of the suffering of Christians referred to in Hebrews

© Dr. James C. Martin; Musée de Louvre; Autorisation de photographer et de filmer - LOUVRE. Photographed by permission.

Interpreters throughout Christian history have wrestled with the issue of the authorship of Hebrews, and many have tried to account for these discrepancies between Hebrews and the "other" Pauline writings in various ways:

◆ Clement of Alexandria (c. A.D. 150–215) theorized that Paul wrote in Hebrew to the Hebrews and that Luke later translated the text into an elevated Greek (cf. Ro 16:22; 1Pe 5:12).

◆ Origen (A.D. 185–253) struggled with whether Hebrews could have come from Paul but confessed uncertainty regarding the identity of the writer, merely reporting that some suggest Luke or Clement of Rome.

◆ Tertullian (c. A.D. 155–220) first suggested Barnabas as an alternative author, since his Levitical background (Ac 4:36) would explain certain points of emphasis in Hebrews, as well as the fact that his name (meaning "son of encouragement") corresponds well to the Greek expression behind Hebrews 13:22.

◆ Martin Luther (A.D. 1483–1546) proposed Apollos as the writer—a "learned man" from Alexandria who had a "thorough knowledge of the Scriptures" (Ac 18:24).

◆ Modern scholars have expanded the list of candidates to include Priscilla, Silas, Epaphras and several others.

While the named identity of the author of Hebrews remains uncertain, a number of affirmations can be made on the basis of the existing text:

◆ The author of Hebrews was almost certainly a second-generation Christian (Heb 2:3).

◆ He was a profound thinker who wrote with an impressive style, vocabulary and cogency and who knew the Greek language well (there are some 151 Greek words unique to Hebrews within the New Testament).

◆ He was intimately acquainted with the **Septuagint**[2] in its Alexandrian form, as well as with Jewish customs and modes of Scriptural interpretation.[3]

◆ Above all, he wrote with a studied conviction that God had climactically made himself known to humanity in his Son Jesus (1:1–2).

[1]See "Letter Writing in the Greco-Roman World" on page 1889. [2]See Glossary on page 2080 for definitions of bolded words. [3]See "The Septuagint and Its Use in the New Testament" on page 1995 and "Biblical Interpretation at Qumran and Among the Early Rabbis" on page 1603.

with glory and honor[j] because he suffered death,[k] so that by the grace of God he might taste death for
everyone.[l]
10 In bringing many sons to glory, it was fitting that God, for whom and through whom everything
exists,[m] should make the author of their salvation perfect through suffering.[n] 11 Both the one who makes
men holy and those who are made holy[o] are of the same family. So Jesus is not ashamed to call them
brothers.[p] 12 He says,

> "I will declare your name to my brothers;
> in the presence of the congregation I will sing your praises."[a][q]

13 And again,

> "I will put my trust in him."[b][r]

And again he says,

> "Here am I, and the children God has given me."[c][s]

14 Since the children have flesh and blood, he too shared in their humanity[t] so that by his death he
might destroy[u] him who holds the power of death—that is, the devil[v]— 15 and free those who all their
lives were held in slavery by their fear[w] of death. 16 For surely it is not angels he helps, but Abraham's de-
scendants. 17 For this reason he had to be made like his brothers[x] in every way, in order that he might be-
come a merciful[y] and faithful high priest[z] in service to God,[a] and that he might make atonement for[d] the
sins of the people. 18 Because he himself suffered when he was tempted, he is able to help those who are
being tempted.[b]

Jesus Greater Than Moses

3 Therefore, holy brothers,[c] who share in the heavenly calling, fix your thoughts on Jesus, the apostle
and high priest[d] whom we confess.[e] 2 He was faithful to the one who appointed him, just as Moses
was faithful in all God's house.[f] 3 Jesus has been found worthy of greater honor than Moses, just as the
builder of a house has greater honor than the house itself. 4 For every house is built by someone, but God
is the builder of everything. 5 Moses was faithful as a servant[g] in all God's house,[h] testifying to what
would be said in the future. 6 But Christ is faithful as a son[i] over God's house. And we are his house,[j] if we
hold on[k] to our courage and the hope[l] of which we boast.

Warning Against Unbelief

7 So, as the Holy Spirit says:[m]

> "Today, if you hear his voice,
> 8 do not harden your hearts
> as you did in the rebellion,
> during the time of testing in the desert,
> 9 where your fathers tested and tried me
> and for forty years saw what I did.[n]
> 10 That is why I was angry with that generation,
> and I said, 'Their hearts are always going astray,
> and they have not known my ways.'
> 11 So I declared on oath in my anger,
> 'They shall never enter my rest.'[o]"[e][p]

12 See to it, brothers, that none of you has a sinful, unbelieving heart that turns away from the living
God. 13 But encourage one another daily,[q] as long as it is called Today, so that none of you may be hard-

2:9 [j]Ac 2:33; 3:13; Php 2:9 [k]Php 2:7-9 [l]Jn 3:16; 2Co 5:15
2:10 [m]Ro 11:36 [n]Lk 24:26; Heb 7:28
2:11 [o]Heb 10:10 [p]Mt 28:10; Jn 20:17
2:12 [q]Ps 22:22
2:13 [r]Isa 8:17 [s]Isa 8:18; Jn 10:29
2:14 [t]Jn 1:14 [u]1Co 15:54-57; 2Ti 1:10 [v]1Jn 3:8
2:15 [w]2Ti 1:7
2:17 [x]Php 2:7 [y]Heb 5:2 [z]Heb 4:14,15; 7:26,28 [a]Heb 5:1
2:18 [b]Heb 4:15
3:1 [c]Heb 2:11 [d]Heb 2:17 [e]Heb 4:14
3:2 [f]Nu 12:7
3:5 [g]Ex 14:31 [h]ver 2; Nu 12:7
3:6 [i]Heb 1:2 [j]1Co 3:16 [k]Ro 11:22 [l]Ro 5:2
3:7 [m]Heb 9:8
3:9 [n]Ac 7:36
3:11 [o]Heb 4:3,5 [p]Ps 95:7-11
3:13 [q]Heb 10:24, 25

[a] *12* Psalm 22:22 [b] *13* Isaiah 8:17 [c] *13* Isaiah 8:18 [d] *17* Or *and that he might turn aside God's wrath, taking away*
[e] *11* Psalm 95:7-11

2:10 The Greek word for "author" often expresses the idea of "originator" or "founder." This term was also applied to a leader, ruler or prince. In the present context it may have had the sense of "champion"—of one who came to the aid of the enslaved.

2:17 For "high priest," see the note on 6:19.

3:11 See "Oaths in Jewish and Christian Practice" on page 1988.

3:13 rEph 4:22 ened by sin's deceitfulness.[r] 14We have come to share in Christ if we hold firmly[s] till the end the confi-
3:14 sver 6 dence we had at first. 15As has just been said:

> "Today, if you hear his voice,
> do not harden your hearts
> 3:15 tver 7,8; Ps 95:7,8 as you did in the rebellion."[a][t]

3:16 uNu 14:2 16Who were they who heard and rebelled? Were they not all those Moses led out of Egypt?[u] 17And
with whom was he angry for forty years? Was it not with those who sinned, whose bodies fell in the des-
3:17 vNu 14:29; Ps 106:26 ert?[v] 18And to whom did God swear that they would never enter his rest[w] if not to those who disobeyed[b]?[x]
3:18 wNu 14:20-23 xHeb 4:6 3:19 yJn 3:36 19So we see that they were not able to enter, because of their unbelief.[y]

A Sabbath-Rest for the People of God

4 Therefore, since the promise of entering his rest still stands, let us be careful that none of you be
4:1 zHeb 12:15 found to have fallen short of it.[z] 2For we also have had the gospel preached to us, just as they did; but
4:2 a1Th 2:13 the message they heard was of no value to them, because those who heard did not combine it with faith.[c][a]
3Now we who have believed enter that rest, just as God has said,

> "So I declared on oath in my anger,
> 4:3 bPs 95:11; Heb 3:11 'They shall never enter my rest.' "[d][b]

And yet his work has been finished since the creation of the world. 4For somewhere he has spoken about
4:4 cGe 2:2,3; Ex 20:11 the seventh day in these words: "And on the seventh day God rested from all his work."[e][c] 5And again in
4:5 dPs 95:11 the passage above he says, "They shall never enter my rest."[d]
6It still remains that some will enter that rest, and those who formerly had the gospel preached to
4:6 eHeb 3:18 them did not go in, because of their disobedience.[e] 7Therefore God again set a certain day, calling it To-
day, when a long time later he spoke through David, as was said before:

> "Today, if you hear his voice,
> 4:7 fPs 95:7,8; Heb 3:7,8,15 do not harden your hearts."[a][f]

4:8 gJos 22:4 8For if Joshua had given them rest,[g] God would not have spoken[h] later about another day. 9There re-
hHeb 1:1 mains, then, a Sabbath-rest for the people of God; 10for anyone who enters God's rest also rests from his
4:10 iver 4 own work, just as God did from his.[i] 11Let us, therefore, make every effort to enter that rest, so that no
4:11 jHeb 3:18 one will fall by following their example of disobedience.[j]
4:12 k1Pe 1:23 12For the word of God[k] is living and active.[l] Sharper than any double-edged sword,[m] it penetrates
lJer 23:29 mEph 6:17; Rev 1:16 even to dividing soul and spirit, joints and marrow; it judges the thoughts and attitudes of the heart.[n]
n1Co 14:24,25 4:13 oPs 33:13-15 13Nothing in all creation is hidden from God's sight.[o] Everything is uncovered and laid bare before the
eyes of him to whom we must give account.

Jesus the Great High Priest

4:14 pHeb 6:20 14Therefore, since we have a great high priest who has gone through the heavens,[f][p] Jesus the Son of
qHeb 3:1 God, let us hold firmly to the faith we profess.[q] 15For we do not have a high priest who is unable to sym-
4:15 rHeb 2:18 pathize with our weaknesses, but we have one who has been tempted in every way, just as we are[r]—yet
s2Co 5:21 was without sin.[s] 16Let us then approach the throne of grace with confidence, so that we may receive
mercy and find grace to help us in our time of need.
5 Every high priest is selected from among men and is appointed to represent them in matters relat-
5:1 tHeb 8:3 uHeb 7:27 ed to God, to offer gifts and sacrifices[t] for sins.[u] 2He is able to deal gently with those who are igno-
5:2 vHeb 2:18 wHeb 7:28 rant and are going astray,[v] since he himself is subject to weakness.[w] 3This is why he has to offer sacri-
5:3 xHeb 7:27; 9:7 fices for his own sins, as well as for the sins of the people.[x]

[a] 15,7 Psalm 95:7,8 [b] 18 Or *disbelieved* [c] 2 Many manuscripts *because they did not share in the faith of those who obeyed*
[d] 3 Psalm 95:11; also in verse 5 [e] 4 Gen. 2:2 [f] 14 Or *gone into heaven*

4:12 The word "soul" is commonly used in the Bible to designate the inner self of a human being in its ordinary relationships with earthly and physical things. The "mind" (*nous*) is used to refer to the self in its rational functions. Another word, *phronęma* (also "mind"), focuses on the mind in the process of thinking. "Heart" (*kardia*) is used in the sense of the self manifesting a complex of attitudes. The precise meaning of "spirit" (*pneuma*) is difficult to determine. The term's most basic meaning is "breeze," but here it represents a nonmaterial life force. God is spirit, and angelic beings can be called "spirits." Used of humans, the term may represent an individual's life and selfhood, as received from God. See "Heart, Breath, Throat and Intestines: Ancient Hebrew Anthropology" on page 968.

5:1 See "Sacrifices and Offerings in the Bible and the Ancient Near East" on page 158.

4No one takes this honor upon himself; he must be called by God, just as Aaron was.[y] 5So Christ also did not take upon himself the glory[z] of becoming a high priest. But God said[a] to him,

5:4 [y]Ex 28:1
5:5 [z]Jn 8:54 [a]Heb 1:1 [b]Ps 2:7

"You are my Son;
today I have become your Father.[a]"[b]

6And he says in another place,

"You are a priest forever,
in the order of Melchizedek."[c]

5:6 [c]Ps 110:4; Heb 7:17,21

[a] 5 Or *have begotten you* [b] 5 Psalm 2:7 [c] 6 Psalm 110:4

Oaths in Jewish and Christian Practice

HEBREWS 6 By means of oaths people in New Testament times affirmed that they would keep their promises or that their words were true, and in oaths people called down curses upon themselves should their pledges prove false. These commonly took the form of *executor-type* oaths ("May God do such-and-such to me if I do not perform this act") or *surety-type* oaths ("May my life be forfeit if this does not happen").

In early Judaism people often substituted something else for the name of God when making a vow. Thus one might swear by the temple, by heaven and Earth or by Jerusalem. This practice may have come into vogue in part to avoid the threat of divine retribution should the oath not be fulfilled. But there was also a concern to prevent God's holy name from being tainted by association with rash oaths and false promises. Jewish writers like Philo, Josephus and Sirach all expressed concern about the use of God's name in oaths and considered such oaths to be violations of the third commandment.

Considerable attention was also devoted to the means by which a person might be extricated from an oath that would prove difficult or impossible to fulfill. In light of the widespread abuse of oaths in his society, Jesus taught that it was best to avoid them altogether (Mt 5:33–37; cf. Jas 5:12). The use of substitutes would not soften the blow of unfulfilled oaths, since sacred objects like the temple or Jerusalem shared in God's holiness. Moreover, persons of integrity had no need to resort to oaths; others could trust that their "no" meant "no" and their "yes" meant "yes" without the invocation of a third party.

God's oath, however, is wholly unlike that of a mere human being. Knowing that his word will be fulfilled, he can swear by the highest authority—himself—that he will do something without any possibility of failure or change of heart. Therefore, the use of an oath in Hebrews 6:17 is a powerful way for God to express "the unchanging nature of his purpose." God's use of an oath can also be considered an accommodation to our weakness; he does not need to swear an oath, but the oath conveys strong assurance to weak and doubting humans.

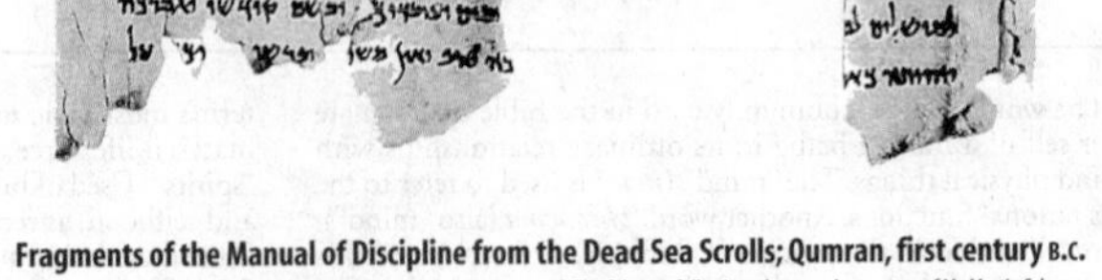

Fragments of the Manual of Discipline from the Dead Sea Scrolls; Qumran, first century B.C.

© The Schøyen Collection; photography courtesy of Mr. Martin Schøyen

5:7 [d]Mt 27:46,50 [7]During the days of Jesus' life on earth, he offered up prayers and petitions with loud cries and tears[d]
[e]Mk 14:36 to the one who could save him from death, and he was heard because of his reverent submission.[e] [8]Al-
5:8 [f]Php 2:8 though he was a son, he learned obedience from what he suffered[f] [9]and, once made perfect,[g] he became
5:9 [g]Heb 2:10 5:10 [h]ver 5 [i]ver 6 the source of eternal salvation for all who obey him [10]and was designated by God to be high priest[h] in
the order of Melchizedek.[i]

Warning Against Falling Away

[11]We have much to say about this, but it is hard to explain because you are slow to learn. [12]In fact,
5:12 [j]Heb 6:1 though by this time you ought to be teachers, you need someone to teach you the elementary truths[j] of
[k]1Co 3:2; 1Pe 2:2 God's word all over again. You need milk, not solid food![k] [13]Anyone who lives on milk, being still an in-
5:13 [l]1Co 14:20 5:14 [m]1Co 2:6 fant,[l] is not acquainted with the teaching about righteousness. [14]But solid food is for the mature,[m] who
[n]Isa 7:15 by constant use have trained themselves to distinguish good from evil.[n]
6:1 [o]Php 3:12-14 [p]Heb 5:12 **6** Therefore let us leave[o] the elementary teachings[p] about Christ and go on to maturity, not laying
[q]Heb 9:14 again the foundation of repentance from acts that lead to death,[a][q] and of faith in God, [2]instruction
6:2 [r]Jn 3:25 about baptisms,[r] the laying on of hands,[s] the resurrection of the dead,[t] and eternal judgment. [3]And God
[s]Ac 6:6 [t]Ac 17:18, 32 permitting,[u] we will do so.
6:3 [u]Ac 18:21 6:4 [v]Heb 10:32 [4]It is impossible for those who have once been enlightened,[v] who have tasted the heavenly gift,[w] who
[w]Eph 2:8 [x]Gal 3:2 have shared in the Holy Spirit,[x] [5]who have tasted the goodness of the word of God and the powers of the
6:6 [y]2Pe 2:21; coming age, [6]if they fall away, to be brought back to repentance,[y] because[b] to their loss they are crucify-
1Jn 5:16 ing the Son of God all over again and subjecting him to public disgrace.
[7]Land that drinks in the rain often falling on it and that produces a crop useful to those for whom it
is farmed receives the blessing of God. [8]But land that produces thorns and thistles is worthless and is in
6:8 [z]Ge 3:17,18; Isa 5:6 danger of being cursed.[z] In the end it will be burned.
6:9 [a]1Co 10:14 [9]Even though we speak like this, dear friends,[a] we are confident of better things in your case—things
that accompany salvation. [10]God is not unjust; he will not forget your work and the love you have shown
6:10 [b]Mt 10:40, 42; 25:40; him as you have helped his people and continue to help them.[b] [11]We want each of you to show this same
1Th 1:3 diligence to the very end, in order to make your hope[c] sure. [12]We do not want you to become lazy, but to
6:11 [c]Heb 3:6 6:12 [d]Heb 13:7 imitate[d] those who through faith and patience[e] inherit what has been promised.[f]
[e]2Th 1:4; Jas 1:3; Rev 13:10 [f]Heb 10:36

The Certainty of God's Promise

[13]When God made his promise to Abraham, since there was no one greater for him to swear by, he
6:13 [g]Ge 22:16; Lk 1:73 swore by himself,[g] [14]saying, "I will surely bless you and give you many descendants."[c][h] [15]And so after
6:14 [h]Ge 22:17 6:15 [i]Ge 21:5 waiting patiently, Abraham received what was promised.[i]
[16]Men swear by someone greater than themselves, and the oath confirms what is said and puts an
6:16 [j]Ex 22:11 6:17 [k]Ps 110:4 end to all argument.[j] [17]Because God wanted to make the unchanging[k] nature of his purpose very clear
[l]Heb 11:9 to the heirs of what was promised,[l] he confirmed it with an oath. [18]God did this so that, by two unchange-
6:18 [m]Nu 23:19; able things in which it is impossible for God to lie,[m] we who have fled to take hold of the hope[n] offered
Tit 1:2 [n]Heb 3:6 to us may be greatly encouraged. [19]We have this hope as an anchor for the soul, firm and secure. It en-
6:19 [o]Lev 16:2; Heb 9:2,3,7 ters the inner sanctuary behind the curtain,[o] [20]where Jesus, who went before us, has entered on our be-
6:20 [p]Heb 4:14 half.[p] He has become a high priest[q] forever, in the order of Melchizedek.[r]
[q]Heb 2:17 [r]Heb 5:6

Melchizedek the Priest

7:1 [s]Mk 5:7 **7** This Melchizedek was king of Salem and priest of God Most High.[s] He met Abraham returning from
[t]Ge 14:18-20 the defeat of the kings and blessed him,[t] [2]and Abraham gave him a tenth of everything. First, his
name means "king of righteousness"; then also, "king of Salem" means "king of peace." [3]Without father

[a] *1* Or *from useless rituals* [b] *6* Or *repentance while* [c] *14* Gen. 22:17

6:2 "Instruction about baptisms" probably had in mind different forms of baptism with which the readers were familiar, such as Jewish baptism of proselytes, John the Baptist's baptism and the baptism commanded by Jesus (see Mt 28:19). See "Baptism in the Ancient World" on page 1562.

For "laying on of hands," see the note on Acts 6:6.

6:13–17 See the note on Galatians 1:20; see also "Oaths in Jewish and Christian Practice" on page 1988.

6:19 "The inner sanctuary behind the curtain" refers to the Most Holy Place, the place of God's presence. Under the old covenant only the high priest could step behind the curtain in the tabernacle (later temple) separating the outer area of the Holy Place from the inner—and then only once a year on the Day of Atonement. This barrier was torn away in the new covenant.

7:1–2 For "Melchizedek," see Genesis 14:18–20, as well as the note on Genesis 14:19. Salem was the name of the city of which Melchizedek was king (Ge 14:18). Josephus noted that Jewish writers generally regarded "Salem" as a synonym for Jerusalem, and it is apparently so regarded in Psalm 76:2.

or mother, without genealogy,[u] without beginning of days or end of life, like the Son of God[v] he remains 7:3 [u]ver 6 [v]Mt 4:3
a priest forever.
4Just think how great he was: Even the patriarch[w] Abraham gave him a tenth of the plunder![x] 5Now 7:4 [w]Ac 2:29 [x]Ge 14:20
the law requires the descendants of Levi who become priests to collect a tenth from the people[y]—that 7:5 [y]Nu 18:21,26
is, their brothers—even though their brothers are descended from Abraham. 6This man, however, did
not trace his descent from Levi, yet he collected a tenth from Abraham and blessed[z] him who had the 7:6 [z]Ge 14:19,20 [a]Ro 4:13
promises.[a] 7And without doubt the lesser person is blessed by the greater. 8In the one case, the tenth is
collected by men who die; but in the other case, by him who is declared to be living.[b] 9One might even 7:8 [b]Heb 5:6; 6:20
say that Levi, who collects the tenth, paid the tenth through Abraham, 10because when Melchizedek met
Abraham, Levi was still in the body of his ancestor.

Jesus Like Melchizedek

11If perfection could have been attained through the Levitical priesthood (for on the basis of it the law
was given to the people),[c] why was there still need for another priest to come[d]—one in the order of Mel- 7:11 [c]ver 18,19; Heb 8:7
chizedek,[e] not in the order of Aaron? 12For when there is a change of the priesthood, there must also be [d]Heb 10:1 [e]ver 17
a change of the law. 13He of whom these things are said belonged to a different tribe,[f] and no one from 7:13 [f]ver 11
that tribe has ever served at the altar.[g] 14For it is clear that our Lord descended from Judah,[h] and in re- [g]ver 14 7:14 [h]Isa 11:1; Mt 1:3; Lk 3:33
gard to that tribe Moses said nothing about priests. 15And what we have said is even more clear if anoth-
er priest like Melchizedek appears, 16one who has become a priest not on the basis of a regulation as to
his ancestry but on the basis of the power of an indestructible life. 17For it is declared:

> "You are a priest forever,
> in the order of Melchizedek."[a][i] 7:17 [i]Ps 110:4; ver 21; Heb 5:6

18The former regulation is set aside because it was weak and useless[j] 19(for the law made nothing 7:18 [j]Ro 8:3
perfect),[k] and a better hope is introduced, by which we draw near to God.[l] 7:19 [k]Ac 13:39; Ro 3:20; Heb 9:9
20And it was not without an oath! Others became priests without any oath, 21but he became a priest [l]Heb 4:16
with an oath when God said to him:

> "The Lord has sworn
> and will not change his mind:[m] 7:21 [m]1Sa 15:29
> 'You are a priest forever.' "[a][n] [n]Ps 110:4

22Because of this oath, Jesus has become the guarantee of a better covenant.[o] 7:22 [o]Heb 8:6
23Now there have been many of those priests, since death prevented them from continuing in office;
24but because Jesus lives forever, he has a permanent priesthood.[p] 25Therefore he is able to save com- 7:24 [p]ver 28
pletely[b] those who come to God[q] through him, because he always lives to intercede for them.[r] 7:25 [q]ver 19 [r]Ro 8:34
26Such a high priest meets our need—one who is holy, blameless, pure, set apart from sinners,[s] ex- 7:26 [s]2Co 5:21
alted above the heavens.[t] 27Unlike the other high priests, he does not need to offer sacrifices[u] day after [t]Heb 4:14 7:27 [u]Heb 5:1
day, first for his own sins,[v] and then for the sins of the people. He sacrificed for their sins once for all[w] [v]Heb 5:3 [w]Heb 9:12,26,28
when he offered himself.[x] 28For the law appoints as high priests men who are weak;[y] but the oath, which [x]Eph 5:2; Heb 9:14,28
came after the law, appointed the Son,[z] who has been made perfect[a] forever. 7:28 [y]Heb 5:2 [z]Heb 1:2 [a]Heb 2:10

The High Priest of a New Covenant

8 The point of what we are saying is this: We do have such a high priest,[b] who sat down at the right 8:1 [b]Heb 2:17
hand of the throne of the Majesty in heaven, 2and who serves in the sanctuary, the true tabernacle[c] 8:2 [c]Heb 9:11,24
set up by the Lord, not by man.
3Every high priest is appointed to offer both gifts and sacrifices,[d] and so it was necessary for this one 8:3 [d]Heb 5:1 [e]Heb 9:14
also to have something to offer.[e] 4If he were on earth, he would not be a priest, for there are already men

[a] *17,21* Psalm 110:4 [b] *25* Or *forever*

7:4 Since Melchizedek was a priest of the Most High, we can be certain that by Abraham's day the giving of tithes had been recognized as a holy deed.
7:16 In the Law of Moses the priestly function was restricted to the family of Aaron from the tribe of Levi (see "The Levites and the Priests" on p. 648), but Jesus came from the non-priestly tribe of Judah.
7:21–22 See "Oaths in Jewish and Christian Practice" on page 1988.
7:27 "Day after day" is a reference to the endless repetition of sacrifices throughout the year (see Ex 29:36–42), recognition that these sacrifices never effectively and finally atoned for sin.
8:1 See "The 'Right Hand' in Ancient Thinking" on page 1983.
8:3 For "sacrifices," see "Sacrifices and Offerings in the Bible and the Ancient Near East" on page 158.
8:4 The present tense of the verb "offer," here and elsewhere in this letter, indicates that the temple in Jerusalem was still standing. The book of Hebrews, therefore, must have been written prior to the temple's destruction in A.D. 70.

who offer the gifts prescribed by the law.[f] 5 They serve at a sanctuary that is a copy[g] and shadow[h] of what
is in heaven. This is why Moses was warned[i] when he was about to build the tabernacle: "See to it that
you make everything according to the pattern shown you on the mountain."[a][j] 6 But the ministry Jesus
has received is as superior to theirs as the covenant[k] of which he is mediator[l] is superior to the old one,
and it is founded on better promises.

7 For if there had been nothing wrong with that first covenant, no place would have been sought for
another.[m] 8 But God found fault with the people and said[b]:

"The time is coming, declares the Lord,
when I will make a new covenant[n]
with the house of Israel
and with the house of Judah.
9 It will not be like the covenant
I made with their forefathers[o]
when I took them by the hand
to lead them out of Egypt,
because they did not remain faithful to my covenant,
and I turned away from them,
declares the Lord.
10 This is the covenant I will make with the house of Israel
after that time, declares the Lord.
I will put my laws in their minds
and write them on their hearts.[p]
I will be their God,
and they will be my people.[q]
11 No longer will a man teach his neighbor,
or a man his brother, saying, 'Know the Lord,'
because they will all know me,[r]
from the least of them to the greatest.
12 For I will forgive their wickedness
and will remember their sins no more.[s]"[c][t]

13 By calling this covenant "new," he has made the first one obsolete;[u] and what is obsolete and aging
will soon disappear.

Worship in the Earthly Tabernacle

9 Now the first covenant had regulations for worship and also an earthly sanctuary.[v] 2 A tabernacle[w]
was set up. In its first room were the lampstand,[x] the table[y] and the consecrated bread;[z] this was
called the Holy Place. 3 Behind the second curtain was a room called the Most Holy Place,[a] 4 which had
the golden altar of incense[b] and the gold-covered ark of the covenant.[c] This ark contained the gold jar
of manna,[d] Aaron's staff that had budded,[e] and the stone tablets of the covenant. 5 Above the ark were the
cherubim of the Glory,[f] overshadowing the atonement cover.[d] But we cannot discuss these things in detail now.

8:4 [f]Heb 5:1 8:5 [g]Heb 9:23 [h]Col 2:17; Heb 10:1 [i]Heb 11:7; 12:25 [j]Ex 25:40 8:6 [k]Lk 22:20 [l]Heb 7:22 8:7 [m]Heb 7:11,18 8:8 [n]Jer 31:31 8:9 [o]Ex 19:5,6 8:10 [p]2Co 3:3; Heb 10:16 [q]Zec 8:8 8:11 [r]Isa 54:13; Jn 6:45 8:12 [s]Heb 10:17 [t]Ro 11:27 8:13 [u]2Co 5:17 9:1 [v]Ex 25:8 9:2 [w]Ex 25:8,9 [x]Ex 25:31-39 [y]Ex 25:23-29 [z]Lev 24:5-8 9:3 [a]Ex 26:31-33 9:4 [b]Ex 30:1-5 [c]Ex 25:10-22 [d]Ex 16:32,33 [e]Nu 17:10 9:5 [f]Ex 25:17-19

[a] 5 Exodus 25:40 [b] 8 Some manuscripts may be translated *fault and said to the people.* [c] 12 Jer. 31:31-34 [d] 5 Traditionally *the mercy seat*

9:1 The "first covenant" refers to the covenant made at Sinai.
9:2 The lampstand was composed of hammered gold and placed at the south side of the Holy Place (see Ex 40:24). Its seven lamps were kept burning day and night.

The table, constructed of acacia wood overlaid with gold (see Ex 25:23–30), stood on the north side of the Holy Place (see Ex 40:22). On it were twelve loaves, replaced every Sabbath and arranged in two rows of six each (see Lev 24:5–8).

See "The Tabernacle and the Ark" on page 153.

9:4 Although the altar of incense stood in the Holy Place, the author described it as belonging to the Most Holy Place. His evident purpose was to indicate its close relationship to the inner sanctuary and to the ark of the covenant. On the Day of Atonement (see "The Day of Atonement" on p. 176) the high priest took incense from this altar, along with the blood of the sin offering, into the Most Holy Place (see Lev 16:12–14).

The ark was a chest made of acacia wood, overlaid inside and out with gold (see Ex 25:10–16).

9:5 The "cherubim of the Glory" were two winged figures made of pure gold, of one piece with the atonement cover, or mercy seat, and standing at either end of it. Between them the glory of God's Presence appeared (see Ex 25:17–22; Lev 16:2; Nu 7:89; see also the note on Ex 25:18 and "Angels and Guardian Spirits in the Bible and the Ancient Near East" on p. 1529).

The atonement cover, or mercy seat, was a slab of pure gold on which the blood of the sin offering was sprinkled by the high priest on the Day of Atonement (see Lev 16:14–15).

6 When everything had been arranged like this, the priests entered regularly[g] into the outer room to 9:6 [g]Nu 28:3
carry on their ministry. 7 But only the high priest entered[h] the inner room, and that only once a year,[i] and 9:7 [h]Lev 16:11-19 [i]Lev 16:34
never without blood, which he offered for himself[j] and for the sins the people had committed in igno- [j]Heb 5:2,3
rance. 8 The Holy Spirit was showing[k] by this that the way[l] into the Most Holy Place had not yet been dis- 9:8 [k]Heb 3:7
closed as long as the first tabernacle was still standing. 9 This is an illustration for the present time, in- [l]Jn 14:6; Heb 10:19,20
dicating that the gifts and sacrifices being offered[m] were not able to clear the conscience of the worshiper. 9:9 [m]Heb 5:1
10 They are only a matter of food[n] and drink[o] and various ceremonial washings—external regulations[p] 9:10 [n]Lev 11:2-23 [o]Col 2:16
applying until the time of the new order. [p]Heb 7:16

The Blood of Christ

11 When Christ came as high priest[q] of the good things that are already here,[a r] he went through the 9:11 [q]Heb 2:17 [r]Heb 10:1
greater and more perfect tabernacle[s] that is not man-made, that is to say, not a part of this creation. 12 He [s]Heb 8:2
did not enter by means of the blood of goats and calves;[t] but he entered the Most Holy Place[u] once for 9:12 [t]Heb 10:4
all[v] by his own blood, having obtained eternal redemption. 13 The blood of goats and bulls and the ash- [u]ver 24 [v]Heb 7:27
es of a heifer[w] sprinkled on those who are ceremonially unclean sanctify them so that they are outward- 9:13 [w]Nu 19:9,17,18
ly clean. 14 How much more, then, will the blood of Christ, who through the eternal Spirit[x] offered him- 9:14 [x]1Pe 3:18
self unblemished to God, cleanse our consciences[y] from acts that lead to death,[b z] so that we may serve [y]Tit 2:14; Heb 10:2,22
the living God! [z]Heb 6:1

15 For this reason Christ is the mediator[a] of a new covenant, that those who are called may receive the 9:15 [a]1Ti 2:5
promised eternal inheritance—now that he has died as a ransom to set them free from the sins com- [b]Heb 7:22
mitted under the first covenant.[b]

16 In the case of a will,[c] it is necessary to prove the death of the one who made it, 17 because a will is
in force only when somebody has died; it never takes effect while the one who made it is living. 18 This
is why even the first covenant was not put into effect without blood.[c] 19 When Moses had proclaimed 9:18 [c]Ex 24:6-8
every commandment of the law to all the people, he took the blood of calves, together with water, scar-
let wool and branches of hyssop, and sprinkled the scroll and all the people.[d] 20 He said, "This is the 9:19 [d]Ex 24:6-8
blood of the covenant, which God has commanded you to keep."[d e] 21 In the same way, he sprinkled 9:20 [e]Ex 24:8; Mt 26:28
with the blood both the tabernacle and everything used in its ceremonies. 22 In fact, the law requires
that nearly everything be cleansed with blood,[f] and without the shedding of blood there is no forgive- 9:22 [f]Lev 8:15 [g]Lev 17:11
ness.[g]

23 It was necessary, then, for the copies[h] of the heavenly things to be purified with these sacrifices, but 9:23 [h]Heb 8:5
the heavenly things themselves with better sacrifices than these. 24 For Christ did not enter a man-made
sanctuary that was only a copy of the true one;[i] he entered heaven itself, now to appear for us in God's 9:24 [i]Heb 8:2
presence. 25 Nor did he enter heaven to offer himself again and again, the way the high priest enters the
Most Holy Place[j] every year with blood that is not his own.[k] 26 Then Christ would have had to suffer many 9:25 [j]Heb 10:19 [k]ver 7,8
times since the creation of the world.[l] But now he has appeared once for all[m] at the end of the ages to do 9:26 [l]Heb 4:3 [m]Heb 7:27
away with sin by the sacrifice of himself. 27 Just as man is destined to die once,[n] and after that to face 9:27 [n]Ge 3:19
judgment,[o] 28 so Christ was sacrificed once to take away the sins of many people; and he will appear a sec- [o]2Co 5:10
ond time,[p] not to bear sin,[q] but to bring salvation to those who are waiting for him.[r] 9:28 [p]Tit 2:13 [q]1Pe 2:24 [r]1Co 1:7

Christ's Sacrifice Once for All

10 The law is only a shadow[s] of the good things[t] that are coming—not the realities themselves.[u] 10:1 [s]Heb 8:5 [t]Heb 9:11
For this reason it can never, by the same sacrifices repeated endlessly year after year, make per- [u]Heb 9:23 [v]Heb 7:19
fect[v] those who draw near to worship. 2 If it could, would they not have stopped being offered? For the wor-

[a] *11* Some early manuscripts *are to come* [b] *14* Or *from useless rituals* [c] *16* Same Greek word as *covenant*; also in verse 17
[d] *20* Exodus 24:8

9:7 The high priest entered the Most Holy Place only once a year, on the Day of Atonement (*Yom Kippur*), the tenth day of the seventh month (see Lev 16:29,34).
9:13 For "ashes of a heifer," see "The Red Heifer" on page 222.
9:15 For "ransom," see the note on Matthew 20:28.
9:16 "Will" translates the same Greek word elsewhere rendered "covenant" (e.g., v. 15), but here and in verse 17 it is used in the sense of a last will and testament. (Verse 18 returns to the concept of covenant.) A will may be defined as a testament, oral or written, which a law court puts into effect, by which property may be disposed of after the testator's death. Covenants between living persons can be bilateral, with each party making promises, or unilateral, an agreement by one party that the other may accept or reject but may not alter. Wills grew out of the latter. In early times among the Hebrews, as among others, property descended according to the laws of inheritance, without wills. The only clear Biblical reference to a will is in this passage.
9:19 For "branches of hyssop," see "Hyssop and the Rituals of Cleansing" on page 847.
9:28 The Israelites on the Day of Atonement waited for the high priest to reappear after ministering in the Most Holy Place, so that they could receive assurance that their sins had been atoned for.

shipers would have been cleansed once for all, and would no longer have felt guilty for their sins. 3But
those sacrifices are an annual reminder of sins,[w] 4because it is impossible for the blood of bulls and
goats[x] to take away sins.
5Therefore, when Christ came into the world,[y] he said:

> "Sacrifice and offering you did not desire,
> but a body you prepared for me;[z]
> 6with burnt offerings and sin offerings
> you were not pleased.
> 7Then I said, 'Here I am—it is written about me in the scroll[a]—
> I have come to do your will, O God.' "[a][b]

8First he said, "Sacrifices and offerings, burnt offerings and sin offerings you did not desire, nor were you
pleased with them"[c] (although the law required them to be made). 9Then he said, "Here I am, I have come
to do your will."[d] He sets aside the first to establish the second. 10And by that will, we have been made
holy[e] through the sacrifice of the body[f] of Jesus Christ once for all.[g]
11Day after day every priest stands and performs his religious duties; again and again he offers the
same sacrifices,[h] which can never take away sins.[i] 12But when this priest had offered for all time one sac-
rifice for sins, he sat down at the right hand of God. 13Since that time he waits for his enemies to be made
his footstool,[j] 14because by one sacrifice he has made perfect[k] forever those who are being made holy.
15The Holy Spirit also testifies[l] to us about this. First he says:

> 16"This is the covenant I will make with them
> after that time, says the Lord.
> I will put my laws in their hearts,
> and I will write them on their minds."[b][m]

17Then he adds:

> "Their sins and lawless acts
> I will remember no more."[c][n]

18And where these have been forgiven, there is no longer any sacrifice for sin.

A Call to Persevere

19Therefore, brothers, since we have confidence to enter the Most Holy Place[o] by the blood of Jesus,
20by a new and living way[p] opened for us through the curtain,[q] that is, his body, 21and since we have a
great priest[r] over the house of God, 22let us draw near to God[s] with a sincere heart in full assurance of
faith, having our hearts sprinkled to cleanse us from a guilty conscience[t] and having our bodies washed
with pure water. 23Let us hold unswervingly to the hope[u] we profess, for he who promised is faithful.[v]
24And let us consider how we may spur one another on toward love and good deeds. 25Let us not give up
meeting together,[w] as some are in the habit of doing, but let us encourage one another[x]—and all the
more as you see the Day approaching.
26If we deliberately keep on sinning[y] after we have received the knowledge of the truth, no sacrifice
for sins is left, 27but only a fearful expectation of judgment and of raging fire[z] that will consume the en-
emies of God. 28Anyone who rejected the law of Moses died without mercy on the testimony of two or
three witnesses.[a] 29How much more severely do you think a man deserves to be punished who has tram-
pled the Son of God under foot,[b] who has treated as an unholy thing the blood of the covenant[c] that
sanctified him, and who has insulted the Spirit[d] of grace?[e][e] 30For we know him who said, "It is mine to
avenge; I will repay,"[d][f] and again, "The Lord will judge his people."[e][g] 31It is a dreadful thing to fall into the
hands of the living God.[h]
32Remember those earlier days after you had received the light,[i] when you stood your ground in a

10:3 wHeb 9:7
10:4 xHeb 9:12, 13
10:5 yHeb 1:6 z1Pe 2:24
10:7 aJer 36:2 bPs 40:6-8
10:8 cver 5,6; Mk 12:33
10:9 dver 7
10:10 eJn 17:19 fHeb 2:14; 1Pe 2:24 gHeb 7:27
10:11 hHeb 5:1 iver 1,4
10:13 jHeb 1:13
10:14 kver 1
10:15 lHeb 3:7
10:16 mJer 31:33; Heb 8:10
10:17 nHeb 8:12
10:19 oEph 2:18; Heb 9:8,12,25
10:20 pHeb 9:8 qHeb 9:3
10:21 rHeb 2:17
10:22 sHeb 7:19 tEze 36:25; Heb 9:14
10:23 uHeb 3:6 v1Co 1:9
10:25 wAc 2:42 xHeb 3:13
10:26 yNu 15:30; 2Pe 2:20
10:27 zIsa 26:11; 2Th 1:7; Heb 9:27
10:28 aDt 17:6,7; Heb 2:2
10:29 bHeb 6:6 cMt 26:28 dEph 4:30; Heb 6:4 eHeb 2:3
10:30 fDt 32:35; Ro 12:19 gDt 32:36
10:31 hMt 16:16
10:32 iHeb 6:4

[a] *7* Psalm 40:6-8 (see Septuagint) [b] *16* Jer. 31:33 [c] *17* Jer. 31:34 [d] *30* Deut. 32:35 [e] *30* Deut. 32:36; Psalm 135:14

10:5–6 The different terms used for Levitical sacrifices represent four of the five types of offerings prescribed by the Mosaic Law, namely, fellowship, grain, burnt and sin (see Lev 1–7; see also "Sacrifices and Offerings in the Bible and the Ancient Near East" on p. 158).

10:12 See "The 'Right Hand' in Ancient Thinking" on page 1983.
10:22 Very likely both "hearts sprinkled" and "bodies washed" allude to Christian baptism (see "Baptism in the Ancient World" on p. 1562).

great contest in the face of suffering.[j] 33 Sometimes you were publicly exposed to insult and persecution;[k]
at other times you stood side by side with those who were so treated.[l] 34 You sympathized with those in
prison[m] and joyfully accepted the confiscation of your property, because you knew that you yourselves
had better and lasting possessions.[n]
35 So do not throw away your confidence; it will be richly rewarded. 36 You need to persevere[o] so that
when you have done the will of God, you will receive what he has promised. 37 For in just a very little while,

> "He who is coming[p] will come and will not delay.[q]
> 38 But my righteous one[a] will live by faith.[r]
> And if he shrinks back,
> I will not be pleased with him."[b]

39 But we are not of those who shrink back and are destroyed, but of those who believe and are saved.

By Faith

11 Now faith is being sure of what we hope for and certain of what we do not see.[s] 2 This is what the
ancients were commended for.[t]
3 By faith we understand that the universe was formed at God's command,[u] so that what is seen was
not made out of what was visible.
4 By faith Abel offered God a better sacrifice than Cain did. By faith he was commended as a righteous
man, when God spoke well of his offerings.[v] And by faith he still speaks, even though he is dead.[w]
5 By faith Enoch was taken from this life, so that he did not experience death; he could not be found,
because God had taken him away.[x] For before he was taken, he was commended as one who pleased God.
6 And without faith it is impossible to please God, because anyone who comes to him[y] must believe that
he exists and that he rewards those who earnestly seek him.
7 By faith Noah, when warned about things not yet seen, in holy fear built an ark[z] to save his family.[a]
By his faith he condemned the world and became heir of the righteousness that comes by faith.
8 By faith Abraham, when called to go to a place he would later receive as his inheritance,[b] obeyed and
went,[c] even though he did not know where he was going. 9 By faith he made his home in the promised
land[d] like a stranger in a foreign country; he lived in tents,[e] as did Isaac and Jacob, who were heirs with
him of the same promise.[f] 10 For he was looking forward to the city[g] with foundations,[h] whose architect
and builder is God.
11 By faith Abraham, even though he was past age—and Sarah herself was barren[i]—was enabled to
become a father[j] because he[c] considered him faithful who had made the promise. 12 And so from this
one man, and he as good as dead,[k] came descendants as numerous as the stars in the sky and as count-
less as the sand on the seashore.[l]
13 All these people were still living by faith when they died. They did not receive the things promised;[m]
they only saw them and welcomed them from a distance.[n] And they admitted that they were aliens and
strangers on earth.[o] 14 People who say such things show that they are looking for a country of their own.
15 If they had been thinking of the country they had left, they would have had opportunity to return.[p]
16 Instead, they were longing for a better country—a heavenly one.[q] Therefore God is not ashamed[r] to
be called their God,[s] for he has prepared a city[t] for them.
17 By faith Abraham, when God tested him, offered Isaac as a sacrifice.[u] He who had received the prom-
ises was about to sacrifice his one and only son, 18 even though God had said to him, "It is through Isaac
that your offspring[d] will be reckoned."[e][v] 19 Abraham reasoned that God could raise the dead,[w] and figu-
ratively speaking, he did receive Isaac back from death.
20 By faith Isaac blessed Jacob and Esau in regard to their future.[x]
21 By faith Jacob, when he was dying, blessed each of Joseph's sons,[y] and worshiped as he leaned on
the top of his staff.
22 By faith Joseph, when his end was near, spoke about the exodus of the Israelites from Egypt and
gave instructions about his bones.[z]

10:32 [j]Php 1:29, 30
10:33 [k]1Co 4:9 [l]Php 4:14; 1Th 2:14
10:34 [m]Heb 13:3 [n]Heb 11:16
10:36 [o]Lk 21:19; Heb 12:1
10:37 [p]Mt 11:3 [q]Rev 22:20
10:38 [r]Ro 1:17; Gal 3:11
11:1 [s]Ro 8:24; 2Co 4:18
11:2 [t]ver 4,39
11:3 [u]Ge 1; Jn 1:3; 2Pe 3:5
11:4 [v]Ge 4:4; 1Jn 3:12 [w]Heb 12:24
11:5 [x]Ge 5:21-24
11:6 [y]Heb 7:19
11:7 [z]Ge 6:13-22 [a]1Pe 3:20
11:8 [b]Ge 12:7 [c]Ge 12:1-4; Ac 7:2-4
11:9 [d]Ac 7:5 [e]Ge 12:8; 18:1,9 [f]Heb 6:17
11:10 [g]Heb 12:22; 13:14 [h]Rev 21:2, 14
11:11 [i]Ge 17:17-19; 18:11-14 [j]Ge 21:2
11:12 [k]Ro 4:19 [l]Ge 22:17
11:13 [m]ver 39 [n]Mt 13:17 [o]Ge 23:4; Ps 39:12; 1Pe 1:17
11:15 [p]Ge 24:6-8
11:16 [q]2Ti 4:18 [r]Mk 8:38 [s]Ex 3:6, 15 [t]Heb 13:14
11:17 [u]Ge 22:1-10; Jas 2:21
11:18 [v]Ge 21:12; Ro 9:7
11:19 [w]Ro 4:21
11:20 [x]Ge 27:27-29,39,40
11:21 [y]Ge 48:1, 8-22
11:22 [z]Ge 50:24, 25; Ex 13:19

[a] 38 One early manuscript *But the righteous* [b] 38 Hab. 2:3,4 [c] 11 Or *By faith even Sarah, who was past age, was enabled to bear children because she* [d] 18 Greek *seed* [e] 18 Gen. 21:12

11:14 "Country" and "city" were virtually interchangeable, since a country was viewed as an extension of the royal city.

11:21 For "on the top of his staff," see "The Septuagint and Its Use in the New Testament" on page 1995.

THE RELIABILITY OF THE BIBLE

THE SEPTUAGINT USE IN THE NEW TESTAMENT

The Greek text of Leviticus; Egypt, second century A.D.

© The Schøyen Collection; photography courtesy of Mr. Martin Schøyen

HEBREWS 11 Christian readers are often puzzled when they read a quotation from the Old Testament in the New Testament and then, in looking up the actual Old Testament text, discover that it is somewhat different from the cited quotation. Often, this difference is based on the fact that the Old Testament was translated from the standard version of the Hebrew Bible (the **Masoretic text**), whereas the New Testament is citing the same passage as it appears in the early Greek translation of the Old Testament known as the **Septuagint**.[1]

The Septuagint was used by **Hellenistic** Jews and by the early church. Most scholars believe that the Greek translation of the **Pentateuch** was produced by Jewish scholars in the mid-third century B.C. in Alexandria, Egypt. The rest of the Old Testament (along with some other books, including the **Apocrypha**) was completed during the following century or two. Some parts of the Septuagint reflect a more literal approach to translation, while others provide a freer rendition. Some portions are also more skillfully translated than others. Sometimes the Septuagint translators began with a Hebrew text that differed slightly from the standard, Masoretic text of the Hebrew Bible.

The Septuagint is the version of the Old Testament with which early Greek-speaking Christians would have been familiar. Naturally, then, most of the Old Testament quotations found in the New Testament reflect its influence. In the vast majority of instances the Septuagint agrees with the Masoretic text—if not word-for-word, at least in basic thrust. In a few cases the Septuagint may even reflect the original Hebrew text better than the Masoretic text does. The Masoretic text may, for instance, contain a copyist's error, so that it does not at a given point accurately reflect the original Hebrew text.[2] Sometimes in such cases the Greek reading in the Septuagint allows scholars to reconstruct what was in the original Hebrew manuscript (most modern translations of the Old Testament are based on the Masoretic text, with occasional emendations drawn from the Septuagint).[3]

When a New Testament author followed the Septuagint, the validity of his argument is not usually dependent upon peculiarities of the Septuagint rendering as over against the Masoretic text. In other words, the New Testament writers did not cite the Septuagint because it said what they wanted it to say, while the Hebrew text did not, nor were they implying that the Septuagint is superior to the Hebrew. Rather, they cited the Septuagint because their readers were familiar with it—as well as, in general, with the Greek language. It was important to bear in mind that the Septuagint was prepared not by Christians but by Jewish scholars before the coming of Christ. Therefore, when the authors of the New Testament quoted the Septuagint, they could not be accused of using a translation that was prepared with their vested interests in mind.

When Hebrews 11:21 states that "by faith Jacob, when he was dying, blessed each of Joseph's sons, and worshiped as he leaned on the top of his staff," the last clause agrees perfectly with the Septuagint rendering of Genesis 47:31. The Masoretic text, on the other hand, states that Jacob worshiped "on the top of his bed." The author of Hebrews quoted the version of Scripture known to his readers to make the point that Jacob was a man of faith and that, even as he lay dying, his faith led him to bless his sons (trusting that God would fulfill the blessing). Whether Jacob was leaning on his staff or lying on his bed is not essential to the argument in Hebrews. Citing the text in the form known to the author's contemporary readership would not have diminished its validity but rather would have made it easier for the audience to recognize a Scriptural citation.[4]

[1]See "Texts of the Old Testament" on page 1491 and "The Ancient Translations" on page 1492. [2]See "The Septuagint and the Masoretic Text" on page 1254.
[3]See "Textual Criticism" on page 1151. [4]See "The Old Testament of the Early Church" on page 1967.

23 By faith Moses' parents hid him for three months after he was born,[a] because they saw he was no ordinary child, and they were not afraid of the king's edict.[b]

24 By faith Moses, when he had grown up, refused to be known as the son of Pharaoh's daughter.[c] 25 He chose to be mistreated[d] along with the people of God rather than to enjoy the pleasures of sin for a short time. 26 He regarded disgrace[e] for the sake of Christ as of greater value than the treasures of Egypt, because he was looking ahead to his reward.[f] 27 By faith he left Egypt,[g] not fearing the king's anger; he persevered because he saw him who is invisible. 28 By faith he kept the Passover and the sprinkling of blood, so that the destroyer of the firstborn would not touch the firstborn of Israel.[h]

29 By faith the people passed through the Red Sea[a] as on dry land; but when the Egyptians tried to do so, they were drowned.[i]

30 By faith the walls of Jericho fell, after the people had marched around them for seven days.[j]

31 By faith the prostitute Rahab, because she welcomed the spies, was not killed with those who were disobedient.[b][k]

32 And what more shall I say? I do not have time to tell about Gideon, Barak,[l] Samson, Jephthah, David,[m] Samuel[n] and the prophets, 33 who through faith conquered kingdoms,[o] administered justice, and gained what was promised; who shut the mouths of lions,[p] 34 quenched the fury of the flames, and escaped the edge of the sword; whose weakness was turned to strength;[q] and who became powerful in battle and routed foreign armies.[r] 35 Women received back their dead, raised to life again.[s] Others were tortured and refused to be released, so that they might gain a better resurrection. 36 Some faced jeers and flogging,[t] while still others were chained and put in prison.[u] 37 They were stoned[c];[v] they were sawed in two; they were put to death by the sword.[w] They went about in sheepskins and goatskins,[x] destitute, persecuted and mistreated— 38 the world was not worthy of them. They wandered in deserts and mountains, and in caves[y] and holes in the ground.

39 These were all commended[z] for their faith, yet none of them received what had been promised.[a] 40 God had planned something better for us so that only together with us would they be made perfect.

11:23 [a]Ex 2:2 [b]Ex 1:16,22
11:24 [c]Ex 2:10, 11
11:25 [d]ver 37
11:26 [e]Heb 13:13 [f]Heb 10:35
11:27 [g]Ex 12:50, 51
11:28 [h]Ex 12:21-23
11:29 [i]Ex 14:21-31
11:30 [j]Jos 6:12-20
11:31 [k]Jos 2:1,9-14; 6:22-25; Jas 2:25
11:32 [l]Jdg 4-5 [m]1Sa 16:1,13 [n]1Sa 1:20
11:33 [o]2Sa 7:11; 8:1-3 [p]Da 6:22
11:34 [q]2Ki 20:7 [r]Jdg 15:8
11:35 [s]1Ki 17:22, 23
11:36 [t]Jer 20:2 [u]Ge 39:20
11:37 [v]2Ch 24:21 [w]1Ki 19:10 [x]2Ki 1:8
11:38 [y]1Ki 18:4
11:39 [z]ver 2,4 [a]ver 13

God Disciplines His Sons

12 Therefore, since we are surrounded by such a great cloud of witnesses, let us throw off everything that hinders and the sin that so easily entangles, and let us run[b] with perseverance[c] the race marked out for us. 2 Let us fix our eyes on Jesus, the author and perfecter of our faith, who for the joy set before him endured the cross,[d] scorning its shame,[e] and sat down at the right hand of the throne of God. 3 Consider him who endured such opposition from sinful men, so that you will not grow weary[f] and lose heart.

4 In your struggle against sin, you have not yet resisted to the point of shedding your blood.[g] 5 And you have forgotten that word of encouragement that addresses you as sons:

> "My son, do not make light of the Lord's discipline,
> and do not lose heart when he rebukes you,
> 6 because the Lord disciplines those he loves,[h]
> and he punishes everyone he accepts as a son."[d][i]

7 Endure hardship as discipline; God is treating you as sons.[j] For what son is not disciplined by his father? 8 If you are not disciplined (and everyone undergoes discipline),[k] then you are illegitimate children and not true sons. 9 Moreover, we have all had human fathers who disciplined us and we respected them for it. How much more should we submit to the Father of our spirits[l] and live![m] 10 Our fathers disciplined us for a little while as they thought best; but God disciplines us for our good, that we may share in his holiness.[n] 11 No discipline seems pleasant at the time, but painful. Later on, however, it produces a harvest of righteousness and peace[o] for those who have been trained by it.

12:1 [b]1Co 9:24 [c]Heb 10:36
12:2 [d]Php 2:8,9 [e]Heb 13:13
12:3 [f]Gal 6:9
12:4 [g]Heb 10:32-34
12:6 [h]Ps 94:12; Rev 3:19 [i]Pr 3:11, 12
12:7 [j]Dt 8:5
12:8 [k]1Pe 5:9
12:9 [l]Nu 16:22 [m]Isa 38:16
12:10 [n]2Pe 1:4
12:11 [o]Isa 32:17; Jas 3:17,18

[a] 29 That is, Sea of Reeds [b] 31 Or *unbelieving* [c] 37 Some early manuscripts *stoned; they were put to the test;*
[d] 6 Prov. 3:11,12

11:26 The priceless treasures of King Tutankhamen's tomb alone included several thousand pounds of pure gold.
11:30 See "The Walls of Jericho" on page 312.
11:31 For "prostitute," see "Prostitution in the Ancient World" on page 284.
11:36 For "prison," see "Imprisonment in the Roman World: In Prison Versus House Arrest" on page 1826
12:1–2 For commentary on running a "[foot] race," see the note on 1 Corinthians 9:24–27.
12:1 The Greek word translated "witnesses"—the origin of the English *martyr*—means "testifiers." These individuals bear testimony to the power of faith and to God's faithfulness.
12:2 See "The 'Right Hand' in Ancient Thinking" on page 1983.

12:12 [p]Isa 35:3
12:13 [q]Pr 4:26
[r]Gal 6:1

12 Therefore, strengthen your feeble arms and weak knees.[p] 13 "Make level paths for your feet,"[a][q] so
that the lame may not be disabled, but rather healed.[r]

Warning Against Refusing God

12:14 [s]Ro 14:19
[t]Ro 6:22 [u]Mt 5:8
12:15 [v]Gal 5:4;
Heb 3:12

14 Make every effort to live in peace with all men[s] and to be holy;[t] without holiness no one will see
the Lord.[u] 15 See to it that no one misses the grace of God[v] and that no bitter root grows up to cause

[a] *13* Prov. 4:26

Before the Gentile Expansion: The Jewish Churches in the Holy Land

HEBREWS 12 The majority of the earliest believers in Christ were Jews. Although the Jewish people as a whole did not accept the claims of Jesus, the earliest Christian documents do bear witness to a significant Jewish response to gospel preaching. Luke reported that 3,000 people responded to Peter's Pentecost sermon (Ac 2:41) and that about 5,000 believed at a slightly later time (Ac 4:4). When the apostle Paul went up to Jerusalem around A.D. 58, the leaders of the Jerusalem church informed him of "how many thousands of Jews have believed" (Ac 21:20). Since the population of Jerusalem at the time of Jesus was only around 40,000 people, these figures testify to the growth and historical existence of Jewish Christianity.[1]

The existence of Jewish churches finds explicit testimony in diverse sources (Ac 8:1; Gal 1:22; 1Th 2:14), and archaeological excavations have revealed synagogues with Christian symbolism at Nazareth and Capernaum.[2] These church communities endured a series of persecutions in the midst of a tumultuous era in Jewish history. Early leaders were arrested (Ac 4:1–3; 12:3), people were ostracized from synagogues because of their faith in Christ (Lk 6:22; Jn 9:22; 16:2), and some suffered physically and endured the seizure of their property (Heb 10:32–34). One of the leading instigators of persecution appears to have been Saul of Tarsus (Ac 9:1; Php 3:6). In A.D. 62 the leader of the church in Jerusalem, James the brother of Jesus, was publicly executed by the reigning high priest Ananus (Josephus, *Antiquities*, 20.9.1; Eusebius, *Ecclesiastical History*, 2.23.21–28).[3] Despite such external pressures, the Jewish churches continued to expand and witness.[4]

At the outbreak of the first Jewish revolt against Rome, the Jewish-Christian community refused to participate in the conflict. This refusal reflected a profound change in the Jewish-Christian understanding of its purpose and mission. According to Eusebius, the church of Jerusalem was warned through an oracle to flee the city and seek refuge across the Jordan in a city named Pella (*Ecclesiastical History*, 3.5.3; cf. Lk 21:20–21; Rev 12:6). Some in the Jewish-Christian community returned after the war under the leadership of Simeon, the cousin of Jesus (*Ecclesiastical History*, 4.22.4).

In theology and practice Jewish Christianity possessed certain characteristics that set it apart from the emerging Gentile Christianity:

- Jewish Christianity may have had distinctive Christological emphases, such as referring to Jesus prominently as the prophet like Moses (cf. Dt 18:15,18).
- It produced a significant body of **Apocryphal** literature. Unfortunately, most of this is known only in fragmentary form.[5]
- Most significant is the Judeo-Christian veneration of the Law of Moses. For Jewish Christians, faith in Christ was consistent with adherence to traditional practices such as circumcision, Sabbath keeping and dietary restrictions (Ac 15:1,5). Church leaders in Jerusalem described Jewish believers as "zealous for the law" (Ac 21:20). For these reasons Paul's preaching that Christ, not the law, was the center of all things (Col 2:2–3) was often regarded with suspicion and even hostility (Ac 21:21), and Paul had to defend this message throughout his writings (Ro 3:31). As late as the second century A.D., the Christian apologist Justin Martyr still distinguished Christians of Jewish origin who demanded that Gentiles observe traditional commandments from those who were ready to accept those Gentiles who did not.[6]

[1]See "The Church From the Resurrection to the Conversion of Paul" on page 1766. [2]See "The Capernaum Synagogue" on page 1591. [3]See "The High Priests Annas and Caiaphas" on page 1772. [4]See "The Geographic Expansion of the Church Under Persecution" on page 1781. [5]See "The Apocrypha" on page 1973. [6]See "Proselytes in Second Temple Judaism" on page 1776.

trouble and defile many. 16See that no one is sexually immoral, or is godless like Esau, who for a single
meal sold his inheritance rights as the oldest son.[w] 17Afterward, as you know, when he wanted to inher-
it this blessing, he was rejected. He could bring about no change of mind, though he sought the blessing
with tears.[x]

18You have not come to a mountain that can be touched and that is burning with fire; to darkness,
gloom and storm;[y] 19to a trumpet blast[z] or to such a voice speaking words that those who heard it begged
that no further word be spoken to them,[a] 20because they could not bear what was commanded: "If even
an animal touches the mountain, it must be stoned."[a][b] 21The sight was so terrifying that Moses said, "I
am trembling with fear."[b]

22But you have come to Mount Zion, to the heavenly Jerusalem,[c] the city[d] of the living God. You have
come to thousands upon thousands of angels in joyful assembly, 23to the church of the firstborn, whose
names are written in heaven.[e] You have come to God, the judge of all men,[f] to the spirits of righteous
men made perfect,[g] 24to Jesus the mediator of a new covenant, and to the sprinkled blood that speaks a
better word than the blood of Abel.[h]

25See to it that you do not refuse him who speaks. If they did not escape when they refused him who
warned[i] them on earth, how much less will we, if we turn away from him who warns us from heaven?[j]
26At that time his voice shook the earth,[k] but now he has promised, "Once more I will shake not only the
earth but also the heavens."[c][l] 27The words "once more" indicate the removing of what can be shaken[m]—
that is, created things—so that what cannot be shaken may remain.

28Therefore, since we are receiving a kingdom that cannot be shaken,[n] let us be thankful, and so wor-
ship God acceptably with reverence and awe,[o] 29for our "God is a consuming fire."[d][p]

Concluding Exhortations

13 Keep on loving each other as brothers.[q] 2Do not forget to entertain strangers,[r] for by so doing
some people have entertained angels without knowing it.[s] 3Remember those in prison[t] as if you
were their fellow prisoners, and those who are mistreated as if you yourselves were suffering.

4Marriage should be honored by all, and the marriage bed kept pure, for God will judge the adulter-
er and all the sexually immoral.[u] 5Keep your lives free from the love of money and be content with what
you have,[v] because God has said,

> "Never will I leave you;
> never will I forsake you."[e][w]

6So we say with confidence,

> "The Lord is my helper; I will not be afraid.
> What can man do to me?"[f]

7Remember your leaders,[x] who spoke the word of God to you. Consider the outcome of their way of
life and imitate[y] their faith. 8Jesus Christ is the same yesterday and today and forever.[z]

9Do not be carried away by all kinds of strange teachings.[a] It is good for our hearts to be strength-
ened[b] by grace, not by ceremonial foods,[c] which are of no value to those who eat them. 10We have an al-
tar from which those who minister at the tabernacle have no right to eat.[d]

11The high priest carries the blood of animals into the Most Holy Place as a sin offering, but the bod-
ies are burned outside the camp.[e] 12And so Jesus also suffered outside the city gate[f] to make the people
holy through his own blood. 13Let us, then, go to him outside the camp, bearing the disgrace he bore.[g]
14For here we do not have an enduring city, but we are looking for the city that is to come.[h]

12:16 [w]Ge 25:29-34
12:17 [x]Ge 27:30-40
12:18 [y]Ex 19:12-22; Dt 4:11
12:19 [z]Ex 20:18 [a]Ex 20:19; Dt 5:5,25
12:20 [b]Ex 19:12,13
12:22 [c]Gal 4:26 [d]Heb 11:10
12:23 [e]Lk 10:20 [f]Ps 94:2 [g]Php 3:12
12:24 [h]Ge 4:10; Heb 11:4
12:25 [i]Heb 8:5; 11:7 [j]Heb 2:2,3
12:26 [k]Ex 19:18 [l]Hag 2:6
12:27 [m]1Co 7:31; 2Pe 3:10
12:28 [n]Da 2:44 [o]Heb 13:15
12:29 [p]Dt 4:24
13:1 [q]Ro 12:10; 1Pe 1:22
13:2 [r]Mt 25:35 [s]Ge 18:1-33
13:3 [t]Mt 25:36; Col 4:18
13:4 [u]1Co 6:9
13:5 [v]Php 4:11 [w]Dt 31:6,8; Jos 1:5
13:7 [x]ver 17,24 [y]Heb 6:12
13:8 [z]Heb 1:12
13:9 [a]Eph 4:14 [b]Col 2:7 [c]Col 2:16
13:10 [d]1Co 9:13; 10:18
13:11 [e]Ex 29:14; Lev 16:27
13:12 [f]Jn 19:17
13:13 [g]Heb 11:26
13:14 [h]Php 3:20; Heb 12:22

[a] *20* Exodus 19:12,13 [b] *21* Deut. 9:19 [c] *26* Haggai 2:6 [d] *29* Deut. 4:24 [e] *5* Deut. 31:6 [f] *6* Psalm 118:6,7

12:16–17 See "The Rights of the Firstborn" on page 43.
12:22 "Mount Zion" is a reference not to the literal Zion (Jerusalem, or its southeast portion) but to the heavenly city of God and to those who dwell there with him.
13:2 Travelers in ancient times depended on the hospitality of strangers (see Ex 2:20; Jdg 19:15–21; 2Ki 4:8; Ac 28:7), as inns in the modern sense were uncommon. The Hebrew word for "inn" means a "night resting place" and could apply to any place where there was encampment for the night, whether by caravans, individuals or even armies. The presence of a building was not implied (the same situation held true during the New Testament era). A very early "inn" was in all likelihood only a piece of level ground near a spring where carriers of merchandise could, with their animals, pass the night.
13:3 For "prison," see "Imprisonment in the Roman World: In Prison Versus House Arrest" on page 1826.
13:4 See "Marriage and Divorce in Ancient Israel" on page 1548.
13:9 "Ceremonial foods" is a reference to the legalistic teachings of the Judaizers (see the note on Gal 1:7). The old Mosaic order was rendered obsolete at the cross.
13:10 The "altar" of this text is probably Christ as received through the Eucharist (Lord's Supper or communion).

[15]Through Jesus, therefore, let us continually offer to God a sacrifice[i] of praise—the fruit of lips[j] that
confess his name. [16]And do not forget to do good and to share with others,[k] for with such sacrifices[l] God
is pleased.
[17]Obey your leaders and submit to their authority. They keep watch over you[m] as men who must give
an account. Obey them so that their work will be a joy, not a burden, for that would be of no advantage
to you.
[18]Pray for us.[n] We are sure that we have a clear conscience[o] and desire to live honorably in every way.
[19]I particularly urge you to pray so that I may be restored to you soon.[p]
[20]May the God of peace,[q] who through the blood of the eternal covenant[r] brought back from the dead[s]
our Lord Jesus, that great Shepherd of the sheep,[t] [21]equip you with everything good for doing his will,
and may he work in us[u] what is pleasing to him,[v] through Jesus Christ, to whom be glory for ever and
ever. Amen.[w]
[22]Brothers, I urge you to bear with my word of exhortation, for I have written you only a short letter.[x]
[23]I want you to know that our brother Timothy[y] has been released. If he arrives soon, I will come with
him to see you.
[24]Greet all your leaders[z] and all God's people. Those from Italy[a] send you their greetings.
[25]Grace be with you all.[b]

13:15 [i]1Pe 2:5 [j]Hos 14:2
13:16 [k]Ro 12:13 [l]Php 4:18
13:17 [m]Isa 62:6; Ac 20:28
13:18 [n]1Th 5:25 [o]Ac 23:1
13:19 [p]Phm 22
13:20 [q]Ro 15:33 [r]Isa 55:3; Eze 37:26; Zec 9:11 [s]Ac 2:24 [t]Jn 10:11
13:21 [u]Php 2:13 [v]1Jn 3:22 [w]Ro 11:36
13:22 [x]1Pe 5:12
13:23 [y]Ac 16:1
13:24 [z]ver 7,17 [a]Ac 18:2
13:25 [b]Col 4:18

13:22 For "brothers," see the note on Romans 1:13.

13:23 For information on Timothy, see the note on Acts 16:1.

13:24 The Greek term for "leaders," or rulers, is *hoi hēgoumenoi* (see also vv. 7,17), a technical phrase not found elsewhere in the New Testament, but other writings coming from Rome and the West use the same terminology (cf. 1 Clement 1:3; 21:6; Shepherd of Hermas 2:6; 9:7 [where *proēgoumenoi* is used]). The original leaders seem to have died (13:7), and their successors were continually engaged in the task of watching over the flock (v. 17). To these the writer sent greetings.

This letter was first known in Rome and the West. Its original readers were probably Jewish Christians who both spoke and wrote Greek. The brief statement "Those from Italy send you their greetings" certainly favors the suggestion of the readers' being located there. If the writer had personally been in Italy, he would no doubt have named his precise location. Hence, it appears that there were Italian Christians with the writer somewhere outside of Italy as he penned this letter—and that the writer knew his future readers well (see 5:11–14; 6:9–10; 10:32–36).

Many roads led to Rome. The believers to whom this letter was addressed may have been in a city nearer or farther from the capital. Paul himself spent seven days with the brothers in Puteoli (Ac 28:13–14), which could have been near Rome or in its suburbs. As the writer penned this letter, Timothy had departed from him and was absent—very likely on some tour of churches. Were he to return soon, the writer and Timothy together intended to pay a visit to the recipients of this letter (Heb 13:23).

INTRODUCTION TO *James*

AUTHOR, PLACE AND DATE OF WRITING

There are several Christian leaders named James in the New Testament, and thus the author of this epistle could have been one of several different men. James the son of Zebedee and the brother of John is an unlikely candidate, however, since he died about A.D. 44 (Ac 12:2), almost certainly too early for this epistle. Most interpreters regard Jesus' half brother James to have been the author of this letter. Against this, some have argued that, being an Aramaic-speaking son of a Galilean carpenter, the Lord's brother could not have mastered Greek. However, in light of the wide acceptance of James's leadership in Jerusalem, it seems reasonable to assume that he was able to speak articulately to the large and diverse Jewish Christian community of the first century A.D.

Some scholars date James in the early 60s, but others think it was written earlier, perhaps before A.D. 50. The letter's distinctive Jewish nature, the simple church order described, the use of the Greek term for *synagogue* and the lack of reference to the issue of Gentile circumcision all seem to point to an early date. It is probable that the letter was written from Jerusalem.

AUDIENCE

The letter lacks any personal references or greetings to individuals and is addressed to the "twelve tribes" of the Diaspora (1:1). While this could be read metaphorically as referring to the (Gentile) Christian church, most surmise that James intended his epistle as a general, circular letter for Jewish believers throughout the Roman world.

CULTURAL FACTS AND HIGHLIGHTS

James's purpose was to encourage his readers, who were not only scattered (see Ac 11:19) but also largely poor and oppressed (Jas 2:6; 5:1–6). The letter has a strongly moral tone; it is filled with exhortations to the readers to live in a pious and upright manner.

TIMELINE

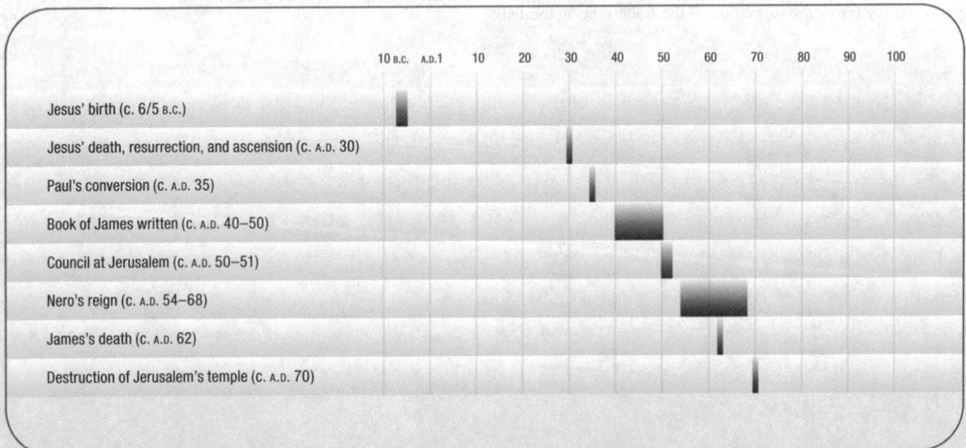

AS YOU READ

Note the diverse groups James addressed and his instructions to each. Look for his emphasis on vital Christianity that is characterized by good deeds and a faith that works. Compare James's commands with Jesus' teachings found in the Sermon on the Mount (e.g., cf. Jas 2:5 with Mt 5:3; Jas 3:10–12 with Mt 7:15–20; Jas 3:18 with Mt 5:9; and Jas 5:2–3 with Mt 6:19–20; 5:12 with Mt 5:33–37). Take to heart James's no-nonsense teaching about the tongue.

DID YOU KNOW?

- The Greek word for "crown" was the usual term for the wreath placed on the head of a victorious athlete or military leader (1:12).
- "There is one God" is a declaration of monotheism that reflects the well-known Jewish creed called the *Shema* (2:19).
- As a common greeting or blessing, *shalom* expressed a wish for prosperity, physical health, salvation and harmonious relationships (3:18).
- In the ancient world, rural land holdings and their produce were the source of real wealth. A prosperous landowner in James's culture was, by definition, an exploiter of the poor (5:1–6).

THEMES

The book of James includes the following themes:

1. *Genuine faith.* James's statement that "a person is justified by what he does and not by faith alone" is not a contradiction of Paul's teaching that salvation is based solely on faith (see Gal 3:6–14). A "faith" that knows for certain that God exists but fails to trust him or to manifest itself in a transformed life is not faith at all.

2. *Good deeds.* "Deeds" in James is another term for "fruit"—acts of Christian love that inevitably accompany a genuine faith.

3. *Genuine wisdom.* James contrasted two kinds of wisdom. False wisdom produces envy and selfish ambition (3:14), whereas genuine wisdom results in humility, deeds of mercy and right conduct (3:13). Wisdom helps Christians control their speech (3:1–12) and promotes peace, consideration, submission, mercy, good deeds, impartiality and sincerity (3:17).

OUTLINE

I. Greeting (1:1)
II. Trials and Temptations (1:2–18)
   A. Facing Trials and Temptations (1:2–12)
   B. God as the Giver of Good Gifts, Not as Tempter (1:13–18)
III. Listening and Doing (1:19–27)
IV. Favoritism Forbidden (2:1–13)
V. Faith and Deeds (2:14–26)
VI. Taming the Tongue (3:1–12)
VII. Two Kinds of Wisdom (3:13–18)
VIII. Warning Against Worldliness (4:1—5:6)
   A. Selfishness (4:1–3)
   B. Friendship With the World (4:4)
   C. Pride (4:5–10)
   D. Slander (4:11–12)
   E. Boasting (4:13–17)
   F. Selfishness (5:1–6)
IX. Miscellaneous Exhortations (5:7–20)

1

1 James,[a] a servant of God[b] and of the Lord Jesus Christ, 1:1 [a]Ac 15:13 [b]Tit 1:1 [c]Ac 26:7 [d]Dt 32:26; Jn 7:35; 1Pe 1:1

To the twelve tribes[c] scattered[d] among the nations:

Greetings.

Trials and Temptations

2Consider it pure joy, my brothers, whenever you face trials of many kinds,[e] 3because you know that 1:2 [e]Mt 5:12; 1Pe 1:6
the testing of your faith develops perseverance. 4Perseverance must finish its work so that you may be
mature and complete, not lacking anything. 5If any of you lacks wisdom, he should ask God,[f] who gives 1:5 [f]1Ki 3:9,10; Pr 2:3-6 [g]Mt 7:7
generously to all without finding fault, and it will be given to him.[g] 6But when he asks, he must believe
and not doubt,[h] because he who doubts is like a wave of the sea, blown and tossed by the wind. 7That man 1:6 [h]Mk 11:24
should not think he will receive anything from the Lord; 8he is a double-minded man,[i] unstable in all he 1:8 [i]Jas 4:8
does.
9The brother in humble circumstances ought to take pride in his high position. 10But the one who is
rich should take pride in his low position, because he will pass away like a wild flower.[j] 11For the sun ris- 1:10 [j]1Co 7:31; 1Pe 1:24
es with scorching heat and withers[k] the plant; its blossom falls and its beauty is destroyed.[l] In the same 1:11 [k]Ps 102:4, 11 [l]Isa 40:6-8
way, the rich man will fade away even while he goes about his business.
12Blessed is the man who perseveres under trial, because when he has stood the test, he will receive
the crown of life[m] that God has promised to those who love him.[n] 1:12 [m]1Co 9:25 [n]Jas 2:5
13When tempted, no one should say, "God is tempting me." For God cannot be tempted by evil, nor
does he tempt anyone; 14but each one is tempted when, by his own evil desire, he is dragged away and
enticed. 15Then, after desire has conceived, it gives birth to sin;[o] and sin, when it is full-grown, gives birth 1:15 [o]Job 15:35; Ps 7:14 [p]Ro 6:23
to death.[p]
16Don't be deceived,[q] my dear brothers.[r] 17Every good and perfect gift is from above,[s] coming down 1:16 [q]1Co 6:9 [r]ver 19
from the Father of the heavenly lights, who does not change[t] like shifting shadows. 18He chose to give us 1:17 [s]Jn 3:27 [t]Nu 23:19; Mal 3:6
birth[u] through the word of truth, that we might be a kind of firstfruits[v] of all he created. 1:18 [u]Jn 1:13 [v]Eph 1:12; Rev 14:4

Listening and Doing

19My dear brothers, take note of this: Everyone should be quick to listen, slow to speak[w] and slow to 1:19 [w]Pr 10:19
become angry, 20for man's anger does not bring about the righteous life that God desires. 21Therefore,
get rid of[x] all moral filth and the evil that is so prevalent and humbly accept the word planted in you,[y] 1:21 [x]Eph 4:22 [y]Eph 1:13
which can save you.
22Do not merely listen to the word, and so deceive yourselves. Do what it says. 23Anyone who listens
to the word but does not do what it says is like a man who looks at his face in a mirror 24and, after look-
ing at himself, goes away and immediately forgets what he looks like. 25But the man who looks intently
into the perfect law that gives freedom,[z] and continues to do this, not forgetting what he has heard, but 1:25 [z]Jas 2:12 [a]Jn 13:17
doing it—he will be blessed in what he does.[a]

1:1 The author of this letter referred to himself as "James, a servant of God and of the Lord Jesus Christ." The New Testament mentions five men who bore the name of James, but tradition attributes the authorship of this letter to James the brother of the Lord, who had probably been favored with a special appearance of the risen Christ (1Co 15:7) and who from a very early date occupied a leading position in the church at Jerusalem (Ac 12:17; Gal 1:19). Paul named him first among the three pillars of the church whom he saw on his second visit to the city after his conversion (Gal 2:9), and in Acts 15 James is described as the leader and chief spokesman of the apostolic council. All that is known of him reflects that he was highly esteemed not only by Christians but also by Jews. According to Josephus, James was put to death by the high priest during the period between the death of Festus and the arrival of his successor, Albinus, in A.D. 62. See the note on James at Acts 21:18.

For the names by which early Christians were known (here "servant[s]"), see the note on 1 Peter 4:16.

James addressed his letter to "the twelve tribes scattered among the nations." This ambiguous expression could conceivably be interpreted in a number of ways: (1) The Jews of the Diaspora in general, who were living throughout the Mediterranean world outside Palestine. This meaning is ruled out, for the writer was addressing Christians. (2) The Jewish Christians of the Diaspora. (3) The Christian church as the new people of God, living far from their heavenly homeland. Early Christians regarded themselves as the true Israel (Gal 6:16), the true circumcision (Php 3:3) and the seed of Abraham (Ro 4:16; Gal 3:29), so it would not be surprising if they also thought of themselves as "the twelve tribes." We cannot however, be certain of James's intended meaning.

1:2 For "brothers," see the note on Romans 1:13.

1:12 The Greek for "crown" was the usual term for the wreath placed on the head of a victorious athlete or military leader. For commentary on the Isthmian games, see the note on 1 Corinthians 9:24–27.

1:14 The words "dragged away" and "enticed" were commonly used to describe hunting methods. Here they metaphorically describe how evil desires operate.

1:18 Just as the first sheaf of the harvest ("firstfruits") was an indication that the whole harvest would eventually follow, so the early Christians were a sign that a great number of people would eventually espouse the Christian faith.

1:23–24 Any smooth or polished surface that reflected images could be referred to as a mirror. The mirrors of the serving women were made of brass (Ex 38:8) and so could be used as material for the laver. Similarly, Elihu in Job 37:18 spoke of the sky as resembling "a mirror of cast bronze." Paul mentioned the inadequacy of these ancient mirrors in 1 Corinthians 13:12.

1:26 [b]Ps 34:13; 1Pe 3:10 26 If anyone considers himself religious and yet does not keep a tight rein on his tongue,[b] he deceives
himself and his religion is worthless. 27 Religion that God our Father accepts as pure and faultless is this:
1:27 [c]Mt 25:36 [d]Isa 1:17,23 [e]Ro 12:2 to look after[c] orphans and widows[d] in their distress and to keep oneself from being polluted by the
world.[e]

Favoritism Forbidden

2:1 [f]1Co 2:8 [g]Lev 19:15 **2** My brothers, as believers in our glorious[f] Lord Jesus Christ, don't show favoritism.[g] 2 Suppose a man
comes into your meeting wearing a gold ring and fine clothes, and a poor man in shabby clothes
also comes in. 3 If you show special attention to the man wearing fine clothes and say, "Here's a good seat
for you," but say to the poor man, "You stand there" or "Sit on the floor by my feet," 4 have you not dis-
2:4 [h]Jn 7:24 criminated among yourselves and become judges[h] with evil thoughts?
2:5 [i]Jas 1:16,19 [j]1Co 1:26-28 5 Listen, my dear brothers:[i] Has not God chosen those who are poor in the eyes of the world[j] to be rich
[k]Lk 12:21 [l]Jas 1:12 in faith[k] and to inherit the kingdom he promised those who love him?[l] 6 But you have insulted the poor.[m]
2:6 [m]1Co 11:22 [n]Ac 8:3 Is it not the rich who are exploiting you? Are they not the ones who are dragging you into court?[n] 7 Are
they not the ones who are slandering the noble name of him to whom you belong?
2:8 [o]Lev 19:18 8 If you really keep the royal law found in Scripture, "Love your neighbor as yourself,"[a][o] you are doing
2:9 [p]ver 1 [q]Dt 1:17 right. 9 But if you show favoritism,[p] you sin and are convicted by the law as lawbreakers.[q] 10 For whoever
2:10 [r]Mt 5:19; Gal 3:10 keeps the whole law and yet stumbles at just one point is guilty of breaking all of it.[r] 11 For he who said,
2:11 [s]Ex 20:14; Dt 5:18 [t]Ex 20:13; Dt 5:17 "Do not commit adultery,"[b][s] also said, "Do not murder."[c][t] If you do not commit adultery but do commit
murder, you have become a lawbreaker.
2:12 [u]Jas 1:25 12 Speak and act as those who are going to be judged by the law that gives freedom,[u] 13 because judg-
2:13 [v]Mt 5:7; 18:32-35 ment without mercy will be shown to anyone who has not been merciful.[v] Mercy triumphs over judg-
ment!

Faith and Deeds

2:14 [w]Mt 7:26; Jas 1:22-25 14 What good is it, my brothers, if a man claims to have faith but has no deeds?[w] Can such faith save
2:15 [x]Mt 25:35, 36 him? 15 Suppose a brother or sister is without clothes and daily food.[x] 16 If one of you says to him, "Go, I
2:16 [y]1Jn 3:17, 18 wish you well; keep warm and well fed," but does nothing about his physical needs, what good is it?[y] 17 In
the same way, faith by itself, if it is not accompanied by action, is dead.
18 But someone will say, "You have faith; I have deeds."
2:18 [z]Ro 3:28 [a]Jas 3:13 Show me your faith without deeds,[z] and I will show you my faith by what I do.[a] 19 You believe that
2:19 [b]Dt 6:4 [c]Mt 8:29; Lk 4:34 there is one God.[b] Good! Even the demons believe that[c]—and shudder.
2:20 [d]ver 17,26 20 You foolish man, do you want evidence that faith without deeds is useless[d]?[d] 21 Was not our ances-
2:21 [e]Ge 22:9,12 tor Abraham considered righteous for what he did when he offered his son Isaac on the altar?[e] 22 You see
2:22 [f]Heb 11:17 [g]1Th 1:3 that his faith and his actions were working together,[f] and his faith was made complete by what he did.[g]
23 And the scripture was fulfilled that says, "Abraham believed God, and it was credited to him as righ-
2:23 [h]Ge 15:6; Ro 4:3 [i]2Ch 20:7; Isa 41:8 teousness,"[e][h] and he was called God's friend.[i] 24 You see that a person is justified by what he does and not
by faith alone.
25 In the same way, was not even Rahab the prostitute considered righteous for what she did when she
2:25 [j]Heb 11:31 gave lodging to the spies and sent them off in a different direction?[j] 26 As the body without the spirit is
2:26 [k]ver 17,20 dead, so faith without deeds is dead.[k]

Taming the Tongue

3:2 [l]1Ki 8:46; Jas 2:10 [m]1Pe 3:10 [n]Mt 12:37 [o]Jas 1:26 **3** Not many of you should presume to be teachers, my brothers, because you know that we who teach
will be judged more strictly. 2 We all stumble[l] in many ways. If anyone is never at fault in what he
says,[m] he is a perfect man,[n] able to keep his whole body in check.[o]

[a] *8* Lev. 19:18 [b] *11* Exodus 20:14; Deut. 5:18 [c] *11* Exodus 20:13; Deut. 5:17 [d] *20* Some early manuscripts *dead*
[e] *23* Gen. 15:6

1:26–27 *Thrçskeia* ("religious") in the New Testament means the outward expression of religion and the content of faith. James here made a distinction between the sham and the reality of religious expression.
1:27 See "The Care of Widows and Orphans in the Bible and the Ancient Near East" on page 285.
2:2 The Greek for "meeting" is the origin of the English word "synagogue" (see the notes on Mk 1:21; Lk 21:12; see also "Ancient Synagogues" on p. 1783).

For information on clothing, see "Dress and Fashion in the Greco-Roman World" on page 2004.
2:19 "There is one God" is a declaration of monotheism that reflects the well-known Jewish creed called the Shema (see the notes on Dt 6:4–9; Mk 12:29).
2:25 See "Prostitution in the Ancient World" on page 284.

Dress and Fashion in the Greco-Roman World

JAMES 2 In the Greco-Roman world clothing basically fit into two categories: the tunic and the mantle. The tunic was something like the modern T-shirt, but very long (of knee or ankle length), made of wool or linen, with or without sleeves. In ancient terminology one "entered into" a tunic to put it on. A mantle was something like a large blanket wrapped around a person.

The tunic (or *chiton*) was the basic article of clothing for virtually all people, serving as a linen undergarment worn next to the skin. The only item of clothing the poorest people may have owned, it was often quite dirty.

✣ The average Roman man added a girdle and an *abolla*, a rectangular woolen mantle worn in a double fold over the right shoulder and fastened with a pin.

✣ Upper-class men wore a second undergarment over the tunic, in addition to the girdle.

✣ Prosperous Romans donned the familiar toga, a long, oval-shaped (or semicircular) woolen mantle draped over the body in a series of complicated folds. Although the toga originated among the Romans, it soon found wide acceptance by wealthy citizens throughout the empire and remained the standard formal dress for Roman citizens until the late **Roman period**.[1]

✣ Alternative garments for upper-class men included the *himation*, a mantle of a Greek style more popular in the eastern part of the empire, and the *chlamys*, a short, woolen mantle (like a cape), often associated with soldiers.

Lower-class women often wore only an ankle-length tunic, gathered by a belt across the upper abdomen, while women of higher economic status added a mantle—often either a *himation* or a *peplos*—over the tunic. These garments were held in place by ornate "safety-pins" called *fibula*.

✣ The *himation* for women was smaller than that for men. It was sometimes dyed in various colors or adorned with a pattern, although coloration and patterning were simple by modern standards. But the patterns and coloring, as well as the size, did distinguish whether a *himation* was intended for a man or a woman. A woman's *himation* was often pleated and could be worn in a wide variety of styles (over the shoulder, as a cape, as a hood, diagonally across the upper body, etc.).

✣ The *peplos* was a single, large rectangle of cloth, distinguished from the *himation* by its size and especially by the way it was folded: The *peplos* always used a cuff-like overfold called an *apotygma*. A woman's *peplos* was typically as long as the distance from her shoulders to her feet, plus about 12 inches (30.5 cm) for the *apotygma*. The fold for the *apotygma* was approximately at the shoulders, from which it draped outward and down over the upper body. The fold could be worn as a hood over the head as a sign of modesty when a woman was walking in the streets or taking part in certain religious ceremonies (cf. 1Co 11:6).[2]

Clothes were draped over the body rather than fitted; indeed, this draping effect is part of the classical ideal of dignity and serenity. At night, one's clothing (especially the mantle) could also serve as a blanket. Leather sandals were the standard footwear for all ranks of society.

In ancient sculpture people often appear wearing only a mantle (if anything at all). This is because of the classical ideal of beauty and does not reflect ordinary dress. In fact, people almost always donned tunics under their mantles, and men ordinarily wore loincloths as underwear as well. A scene from Pompeii[3] depicts two female athletes wearing garments similar to a modern two-piece swim suit, suggesting that women of means had a fairly wide variety of underwear and outerwear available to them.

Upper-class Roman women often frequently sported exotic hairstyles, often with an outlandish display of curls. Dyeing the hair and wearing expensive cosmetics were popular with women (cf. 1Pe 3:3), who also wore decorative tiaras, pins and nets with their hair. The wearing of rings and other jewelry by both men and women contributed to the display of wealth. James warned his readers not to be so dazzled by the finery of the rich that they showed partiality to wealthy believers over their less fortunate Christian brothers and sisters.[4]

(above) **Roman era caryatide (statue of a woman used as a column), illustrating the wearing of a mantle over a tunic; *(top right)* Second-century A.D. Roman marble statue of Cleopatra (note overfold or *apotygma* of dress)**

Preserving Bible Times; © Dr. James C. Martin; permission of The Istanbul Archaeological Museum

[1]See Glossary on page 2080 for definitions of bolded words. [2]See "The Role of Women in Religious Life in the Greco-Roman World" on page 1879. [3]See "Pompeii" on page 1857. [4]Confer "Ancient Israelite Clothing and Jewelry" on page 1059.

3:3 [p]Ps 32:9 3When we put bits into the mouths of horses to make them obey us, we can turn the whole animal.[p]
4Or take ships as an example. Although they are so large and are driven by strong winds, they are steered
by a very small rudder wherever the pilot wants to go. 5Likewise the tongue is a small part of the body,
3:5 [q]Ps 12:3,4 but it makes great boasts.[q] Consider what a great forest is set on fire by a small spark. 6The tongue also
3:6 [r]Pr 16:27 is a fire,[r] a world of evil among the parts of the body. It corrupts the whole person,[s] sets the whole course
[s]Mt 15:11,18,19 of his life on fire, and is itself set on fire by hell.
7All kinds of animals, birds, reptiles and creatures of the sea are being tamed and have been tamed
3:8 [t]Ps 140:3; Ro 3:13 by man, 8but no man can tame the tongue. It is a restless evil, full of deadly poison.[t]
9With the tongue we praise our Lord and Father, and with it we curse men, who have been made in
3:9 [u]Ge 1:26,27; 1Co 11:7 God's likeness.[u] 10Out of the same mouth come praise and cursing. My brothers, this should not be. 11Can
both fresh water and salt[a] water flow from the same spring? 12My brothers, can a fig tree bear olives, or
3:12 [v]Mt 7:16 a grapevine bear figs?[v] Neither can a salt spring produce fresh water.

Two Kinds of Wisdom

3:13 [w]Jas 2:18 13Who is wise and understanding among you? Let him show it[w] by his good life, by deeds done in the
3:14 [x]ver 16 humility that comes from wisdom. 14But if you harbor bitter envy and selfish ambition[x] in your hearts,
[y]Jas 5:19
3:15 [z]Jas 1:17 do not boast about it or deny the truth.[y] 15Such "wisdom" does not come down from heaven[z] but is earth-
[a]1Ti 4:1 ly, unspiritual, of the devil.[a] 16For where you have envy and selfish ambition, there you find disorder and
every evil practice.
3:17 [b]1Co 2:6 17But the wisdom that comes from heaven[b] is first of all pure; then peace-loving, considerate, sub-
[c]Lk 6:36 [d]Ro 12:9 missive, full of mercy[c] and good fruit, impartial and sincere.[d] 18Peacemakers who sow in peace raise a
3:18 [e]Pr 11:18; Isa 32:17 harvest of righteousness.[e]

[a] *11* Greek *bitter* (see also verse 14)

3:5 See "Speech Ethics," below.
3:6 For "hell," see the note on Matthew 5:22.
3:18 When James encouraged his readers to "sow in peace," he was referring to the Old Testament notion of *shalom*, a state of wholeness, health and completion. As a common greeting or blessing, it expressed a wish for prosperity, physical health, salvation and harmonious relationships.

Speech Ethics

JAMES 3 James's guidelines on speech ethics, while rooted in the Old Testament and the teachings of Jesus, were also in harmony with widespread social conventions in the ancient world. The comparison of the tongue to the rudder of a ship (Jas 3:4), for example, had been made generations earlier by the ancient Egyptian sage Amenemope.[1] The image of the tongue as a destructive fire (v. 6) has parallels in **Hellenistic** literature (e.g., in the writings of Seneca and Plutarch). The same may be said for the importance of being slow to speak (1:19) and for the need to match words with deeds (1:22); the Roman Cicero also affirmed this ideal. James's absolute prohibition against oaths (5:12; cf. Mt 5:33–37) was a Christian distinctive, but even here Greco-Roman writers agreed that a person's character ought to be so blameless that oaths were not strictly necessary (such ideas are expressed by the classical writers Epictetus and Diogenes Laertius).[2]

It is important to realize that these standards of Christian behavior have parallels in the best ethical literature of the ancient world. This reminds us, first, that the Bible does not claim to be presenting new moral standards. The morality it proclaims is for the most part ancient and universal. Second, the parallels remind us that the Biblical texts affirmed what was good and true in the culture around the writers and their audiences. Biblical authors did not perceive themselves to be invariably opposed to the norms of their day (see Php 4:8).

[1]See "The Teaching of Amenemope" on page 994. [2]See also "Oaths in Jewish and Christian Practice" on page 1988.

Submit Yourselves to God

4 What causes fights and quarrels[f] among you? Don't they come from your desires that battle[g] with- 4:1 [f]Tit 3:9
in you? 2 You want something but don't get it. You kill and covet, but you cannot have what you want. [g]Ro 7:23
You quarrel and fight. You do not have, because you do not ask God. 3 When you ask, you do not receive,[h] 4:3 [h]Ps 18:41
because you ask with wrong motives,[i] that you may spend what you get on your pleasures. [i]1Jn 3:22; 5:14
4 You adulterous people, don't you know that friendship with the world[j] is hatred toward God?[k] Any- 4:4 [j]Jas 1:27
one who chooses to be a friend of the world becomes an enemy of God.[l] 5 Or do you think Scripture says [k]1Jn 2:15 [l]Jn 15:19
without reason that the spirit he caused to live in us envies intensely?[a] 6 But he gives us more grace. That
is why Scripture says:

> "God opposes the proud
> but gives grace to the humble."[b][m] 4:6 [m]Ps 138:6; Pr 3:34; Mt 23:12

7 Submit yourselves, then, to God. Resist the devil,[n] and he will flee from you. 8 Come near to God and 4:7 [n]Eph 4:27; 1Pe 5:6-9
he will come near to you.[o] Wash your hands,[p] you sinners, and purify your hearts, you double-minded.[q] 4:8 [o]2Ch 15:2
9 Grieve, mourn and wail. Change your laughter to mourning and your joy to gloom.[r] 10 Humble your- [p]Isa 1:16 [q]Jas 1:8 4:9 [r]Lk 6:25
selves before the Lord, and he will lift you up.
11 Brothers, do not slander one another.[s] Anyone who speaks against his brother or judges him[t] speaks 4:11 [s]1Pe 2:1
against the law and judges it. When you judge the law, you are not keeping it,[u] but sitting in judgment on [t]Mt 7:1 [u]Jas 1:22
it. 12 There is only one Lawgiver and Judge, the one who is able to save and destroy.[v] But you—who are 4:12 [v]Mt 10:28
you to judge your neighbor?[w] [w]Ro 14:4

Boasting About Tomorrow

13 Now listen, you who say, "Today or tomorrow we will go to this or that city, spend a year there, car-
ry on business and make money."[x] 14 Why, you do not even know what will happen tomorrow. What is your 4:13 [x]Pr 27:1
life? You are a mist that appears for a little while and then vanishes.[y] 15 Instead, you ought to say, "If it is 4:14 [y]Job 7:7;
the Lord's will,[z] we will live and do this or that." 16 As it is, you boast and brag. All such boasting is evil.[a] Ps 102:3 4:15 [z]Ac 18:21
17 Anyone, then, who knows the good he ought to do and doesn't do it, sins.[b] 4:16 [a]1Co 5:6 4:17 [b]Lk 12:47; Jn 9:41

Warning to Rich Oppressors

5 Now listen, you rich people,[c] weep and wail because of the misery that is coming upon you. 2 Your 5:1 [c]Lk 6:24
wealth has rotted, and moths have eaten your clothes.[d] 3 Your gold and silver are corroded. Their cor- 5:2 [d]Job 13:28; Mt 6:19,20
rosion will testify against you and eat your flesh like fire. You have hoarded wealth in the last days.[e] 4 Look! 5:3 [e]ver 7,8
The wages you failed to pay the workmen[f] who mowed your fields are crying out against you. The cries[g] 5:4 [f]Lev 19:13
of the harvesters have reached the ears of the Lord Almighty.[h] 5 You have lived on earth in luxury and [g]Dt 24:15 [h]Ro 9:29
self-indulgence. You have fattened yourselves[i] in the day of slaughter.[c][j] 6 You have condemned and mur- 5:5 [i]Am 6:1
dered innocent men,[k] who were not opposing you. [j]Jer 12:3; 25:34 5:6 [k]Heb 10:38

Patience in Suffering

7 Be patient, then, brothers, until the Lord's coming. See how the farmer waits for the land to yield its
valuable crop and how patient he is for the autumn and spring rains.[l] 8 You too, be patient and stand firm, 5:7 [l]Dt 11:14; Jer 5:24
because the Lord's coming is near.[m] 9 Don't grumble against each other, brothers,[n] or you will be judged. 5:8 [m]Ro 13:11;
The Judge[o] is standing at the door![p] 1Pe 4:7 5:9 [n]Jas 4:11
10 Brothers, as an example of patience in the face of suffering, take the prophets[q] who spoke in the name [o]1Co 4:5; 1Pe 4:5 [p]Mt 24:33 5:10 [q]Mt 5:12

[a] 5 Or *that God jealously longs for the spirit that he made to live in us*; or *that the Spirit he caused to live in us longs jealously*
[b] 6 Prov. 3:34 [c] 5 Or *yourselves as in a day of feasting*

4:8 Before the Old Testament priests approached God at the tabernacle, they had to wash their hands and feet at the bronze basin as a symbol of spiritual cleansing (see Ex 30:17–21; see also "Bathing" on p. 456).
4:9 See "Sackcloth and Ashes: Rituals of Lamentation" on page 820.
4:13–17 James addressed some traveling merchants within the church. He was not arguing against making money but against their arrogant attitudes.
5:1–6 These verses, which are similar to Old Testament declarations of judgment against pagan nations, are addressed to wealthy landowners and concern their improper use of wealth. In the ancient world, rural land holdings and their produce were the source of real wealth. A prosperous landowner in James's culture was, by definition, an exploiter of the poor.
5:2 Clothes were a form of wealth in the ancient world (see "Ancient Israelite Clothing and Jewelry" on p. 1059 and "Dress and Fashion in the Greco-Roman World" on p. 2004).
5:6 The injustice described here probably occurred through control of the courts by the rich and powerful.
5:7 In Israel the autumn rain comes in October and November, soon after the grain is sown, while the spring rain comes in March and April, just prior to the harvest.

5:11 [r]Mt 5:10 [s]Job 1:21,22; 2:10 [t]Job 42:10, 12-17 [u]Nu 14:18

5:12 [v]Mt 5:34-37

of the Lord. 11 As you know, we consider blessed[r] those who have persevered. You have heard of Job's perse-
verance[s] and have seen what the Lord finally brought about.[t] The Lord is full of compassion and mercy.[u]
12 Above all, my brothers, do not swear—not by heaven or by earth or by anything else. Let your "Yes"
be yes, and your "No," no, or you will be condemned.[v]

The Prayer of Faith

5:13 [w]Ps 50:15 [x]Col 3:16
5:14 [y]Mk 6:13
5:16 [z]Mt 3:6 [a]1Pe 2:24 [b]Jn 9:31
5:17 [c]Ac 14:15 [d]1Ki 17:1; Lk 4:25
5:18 [e]1Ki 18:41-45
5:19 [f]Jas 3:14 [g]Mt 18:15
5:20 [h]Ro 11:14 [i]1Pe 4:8

13 Is any one of you in trouble? He should pray.[w] Is anyone happy? Let him sing songs of praise.[x] 14 Is
any one of you sick? He should call the elders of the church to pray over him and anoint him with oil[y] in
the name of the Lord. 15 And the prayer offered in faith will make the sick person well; the Lord will raise
him up. If he has sinned, he will be forgiven. 16 Therefore confess your sins[z] to each other and pray for each
other so that you may be healed.[a] The prayer of a righteous man is powerful and effective.[b]
17 Elijah was a man just like us.[c] He prayed earnestly that it would not rain, and it did not rain on the
land for three and a half years.[d] 18 Again he prayed, and the heavens gave rain, and the earth produced
its crops.[e]
19 My brothers, if one of you should wander from the truth[f] and someone should bring him back,[g]
20 remember this: Whoever turns a sinner from the error of his way will save[h] him from death and cover
over a multitude of sins.[i]

5:12 See "Oaths in Jewish and Christian Practice" on page 1988.
5:13 See "Early Christian Hymnody," below.
5:14 For "elders," see the note on 1 Timothy 3:1 and for "church" the note on Matthew 16:18.

Referred to by Philo, Pliny and the physician Galen, oil was one of the best-known ancient medicines (see "Disease and Medicine in the Ancient World" on p. 1674) and "Perfumes and Anointing Oils" on p. 1746). Some believe that James may have been using the term medicinally in this passage, while others regard its use here as an aid to faith.
5:19 For "brothers," see the note on Romans 1:13.

Early Christian Hymnody

JAMES 5 Pliny the Younger, in a famous letter sent to Emperor Trajan in around A.D. 110 (*Epistle*, 10.96), described his encounter with Christians and reported on their practices. Among other remarks, this historian mentioned that the followers of Christ gathered early in the morning to "chant a song to Christ as if to a god." It is not surprising that singing became a standard Christian practice; James 5:13 commands Christians to "sing songs of praise" as an expression of joy, and similar exhortations to and examples of singing praise are found elsewhere in the New Testament (Mt 26:30; Lk 1:46–55; Ac 16:25; Eph 5:19; Col 3:16; Rev 5:9–10).

Paul, in Ephesians 5:19, spoke of "psalms, hymns and spiritual songs" in the Christian church. It is uncertain how or even whether these three should be differentiated, although "psalms" certainly refers to the singing either of Biblical psalms or of songs modeled after them. Mary's Magnificat (Lk 1:46–55), although not an Old Testament psalm, is obviously psalm-like.

It is also difficult to ascertain the musical style of these early hymns. It is likely that the earliest Christian singing was heavily influenced by Jewish singing and liturgy; the medieval plainchant or "Gregorian chant" may preserve something of that style. It may be that the early Christians wanted a musical style that distinguished their hymns from the clapping, dancing and boisterous style of contemporary pagan music. The old music of the Armenian, Coptic and other ancient churches may preserve something of the flavor of early Christian singing. A few pieces of early Christian music have survived even in the modern, Western church. The words of the "Gloria Patri," for example, go back to the first century A.D.

Some scholars suggest that fragments of early Christian hymns are included in certain New Testament epistles. Philippians 2:6–11 is often regarded as such, and other possible examples include Ephesians 5:14, 1 Timothy 3:16 and 2 Timothy 2:11–13. None of these texts is obviously poetic, however, and the suggestion that they are hymns remains speculative.[1]

Terra-cotta lamp in the form of an organist sitting at a water organ
Preserving Bible Times; © Dr. James C. Martin; permission of The British Museum

[1]See also "Ancient Musical Instruments" on page 797 and "Ancient Israelite Poets and Singers" on page 869.

INTRODUCTION TO 1 Peter

AUTHOR, PLACE AND DATE OF WRITING

The authorship of 1 and 2 Peter is disputed today, with many denying that Peter wrote either epistle. However, substantial evidence, both internal and from the early church, favors Petrine authorship of these letters (see "The Authorship of Peter's Epistles" on p. 2011).

Fairly strong tradition asserts that Peter was martyred under Nero about A.D. 66 (after the great fire in Rome of A.D. 64 but before Nero's death in A.D. 68). In addition, Peter demonstrated familiarity with Colossians and Ephesians (see 2Pe 3:15; cf. 1Pe 1:1–3 with Eph 1:1–3 and 1Pe 2:18 with Col 3:22). These letters of Paul are dated to A.D. 60 at the earliest; thus 1 Peter must be dated between 60 and 64, before the beginning of the persecutions under Nero.

First Peter 5:13 states that Peter wrote from "Babylon." Although several places have been suggested as Peter's "Babylon," only two seem reasonable: the actual Babylon, in Mesopotamia (a premier center of Jewish culture), or a metaphorical Babylon (Rome), although the context of 5:13 does not appear to be figurative or cryptic.

AUDIENCE

The letter was addressed to Christians in "Pontus, Galatia, Cappadocia, Asia and Bithynia" (1:1). This would seem to include most of Asia Minor (modern Turkey), although Peter may have used the terms in a more restricted sense. Believers in those areas were suffering persecution for their faith (1:6; 4:12–19; 5:9–10), and Peter described his recipients as God's elect in Diaspora (1:1), terms normally reserved for Jews. On the other hand, he stated that his recipients had formerly followed the empty manner of life they had inherited from their forefathers (1:18; cf. 4:3–5). From this it appears that Peter's original readers were Gentiles who had come to Christ and were therefore metaphorically strangers and aliens (2:11) in this world.

CULTURAL FACTS AND HIGHLIGHTS

Peter did not address some specific issue or crisis but offered counsel regarding the fundamentals of the Christian life. The letter is in effect a pamphlet on Christian living, written for the benefit of believers in many different places and circumstances.

TIMELINE

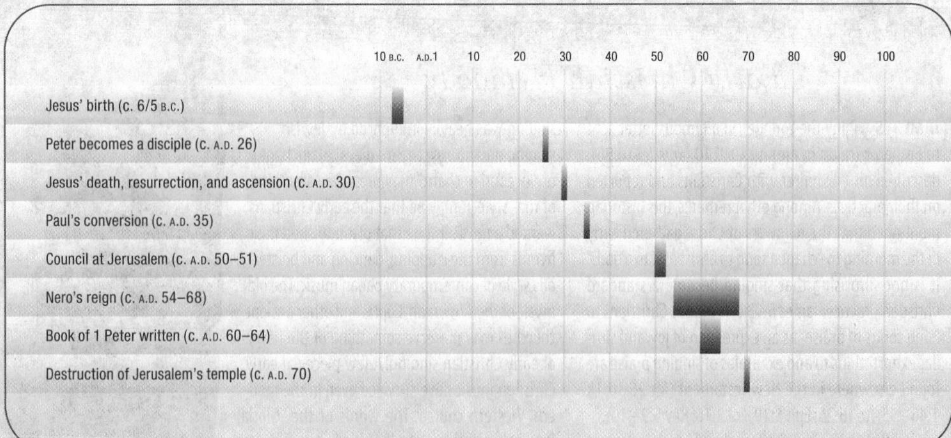

AS YOU READ

Watch for general principles regarding the problematic issues of pain, suffering and persecution, and note Peter's reason for hope. Observe Peter's style and his blending of doctrine and practical guidelines for Christian living. Study his teaching on submission to authority and its ramifications.

DID YOU KNOW?

- In the language of the first century, "prepare . . . for action" literally suggested that the readers should gather up their long, flowing garments and be ready for physical activity (1:13).
- In the Greek world slaves could be redeemed by a monetary payment, made either by someone else or by the slave on his or her own behalf (1:18).
- "Slaves" referred to household servants, whatever their particular training or functions (2:18).

THEMES

First Peter includes the following themes:

1. *The believer's new identity.* Peter's goal was to encourage Christians enduring persecution. Because of God's great mercy (1:3), believers have been given new life (1:3), a "living hope" (1:3; see also 1:13,21; 3:15) and an eternal inheritance (1:4). They are now "the people of God" (2:10). As such they are to rejoice (1:6,8; 4:13) and be encouraged in the midst of suffering.

2. *Suffering for doing good.* Although believers may experience "all kinds of trials" (1:6), they are to stand firm in the faith (5:9). Suffering acts as a purifying fire to prove the genuineness of faith (1:7). It also gives Christians an opportunity to give witness to their hope (3:15). When they suffer unjustly, they are to follow Christ's example (2:21).

3. *Christian living.* Christians are to live lives befitting their conversion. Peter pictured salvation as a process (1:9; 2:2) into which believers grow from their daily faithfulness under pressure. They are to strive toward personal holiness (1:13–21) out of reverent fear of God (1:17–21) and to display their faith by loving others (1:22).

OUTLINE

- I. Greeting (1:1–12)
- II. Exhortations to Holy Living (1:13—5:11)
  - A. Self-Control and Holiness (1:13—2:3)
  - B. The Conduct of the People of God (2:4–12)
  - C. Submission to Authority (2:13—3:7)
  - D. Suffering for Doing Good (3:8–17)
  - E. Armed With the Attitude of Christ (3:18—4:6)
  - F. Conduct in View of the End of All Things (4:7–11)
  - G. Suffering for Being a Christian (4:12–19)
  - H. Exhortations to Elders (5:1–4)
  - I. Exhortations to Young Men (5:5–11)
- III. The Purpose of the Letter (5:12)
- IV. Closing Greeting (5:13–14)

1

Peter, an apostle of Jesus Christ,[a]

To God's elect,[b] strangers in the world, scattered throughout Pontus, Galatia, Cappadocia, Asia and
Bithynia,[c] 2who have been chosen according to the foreknowledge[d] of God the Father, through the sanc-
tifying work of the Spirit,[e] for obedience to Jesus Christ and sprinkling by his blood:[f]

Grace and peace be yours in abundance.

Praise to God for a Living Hope

3Praise be to the God and Father of our Lord Jesus Christ![g] In his great mercy[h] he has given us new
birth into a living hope through the resurrection of Jesus Christ from the dead,[i] 4and into an inheritance
that can never perish, spoil or fade—kept in heaven for you,[j] 5who through faith are shielded by God's
power[k] until the coming of the salvation that is ready to be revealed in the last time. 6In this you great-
ly rejoice,[l] though now for a little while[m] you may have had to suffer grief in all kinds of trials.[n] 7These
have come so that your faith—of greater worth than gold, which perishes even though refined by fire[o]—
may be proved genuine[p] and may result in praise, glory and honor when Jesus Christ is revealed.[q]
8Though you have not seen him, you love him; and even though you do not see him now, you believe in
him[r] and are filled with an inexpressible and glorious joy, 9for you are receiving the goal of your faith, the
salvation of your souls.[s]
10Concerning this salvation, the prophets, who spoke[t] of the grace that was to come to you, searched
intently and with the greatest care,[u] 11trying to find out the time and circumstances to which the Spirit
of Christ[v] in them was pointing when he predicted the sufferings of Christ and the glories that would
follow. 12It was revealed to them that they were not serving themselves but you, when they spoke of the
things that have now been told you by those who have preached the gospel to you[w] by the Holy Spirit
sent from heaven. Even angels long to look into these things.

Be Holy

13Therefore, prepare your minds for action; be self-controlled; set your hope fully on the grace to be
given you when Jesus Christ is revealed. 14As obedient children, do not conform[x] to the evil desires you
had when you lived in ignorance.[y] 15But just as he who called you is holy, so be holy in all you do;[z] 16for
it is written: "Be holy, because I am holy."[a][a]
17Since you call on a Father who judges each man's work impartially,[b] live your lives as strangers here
in reverent fear.[c] 18For you know that it was not with perishable things such as silver or gold that you
were redeemed[d] from the empty way of life handed down to you from your forefathers, 19but with the pre-
cious blood of Christ, a lamb[e] without blemish or defect.[f] 20He was chosen before the creation of the
world,[g] but was revealed in these last times[h] for your sake. 21Through him you believe in God,[i] who raised
him from the dead and glorified him, and so your faith and hope are in God.
22Now that you have purified[j] yourselves by obeying the truth so that you have sincere love for your

1:1 [a]2Pe 1:1 [b]Mt 24:22 [c]Ac 16:7
1:2 [d]Ro 8:29 [e]2Th 2:13 [f]Heb 10:22; 12:24
1:3 [g]2Co 1:3; Eph 1:3 [h]Tit 3:5; Jas 1:18 [i]1Co 15:20
1:4 [j]Col 1:5
1:5 [k]Jn 10:28
1:6 [l]Ro 5:2 [m]1Pe 5:10 [n]Jas 1:2
1:7 [o]Job 23:10; Ps 66:10; Pr 17:3 [p]Jas 1:3 [q]Ro 2:7
1:8 [r]Jn 20:29
1:9 [s]Ro 6:22
1:10 [t]Mt 26:24 [u]Mt 13:17
1:11 [v]2Pe 1:21
1:12 [w]ver 25
1:14 [x]Ro 12:2 [y]Eph 4:18
1:15 [z]2Co 7:1; 1Th 4:7
1:16 [a]Lev 11:44, 45
1:17 [b]Ac 10:34 [c]Heb 12:28
1:18 [d]Mt 20:28; 1Co 6:20
1:19 [e]Jn 1:29 [f]Ex 12:5
1:20 [g]Eph 1:4 [h]Heb 9:26
1:21 [i]Ro 4:24
1:22 [j]Jas 4:8

[a] *16* Lev. 11:44,45; 19:2

1:1 The term "strangers" in this context refers to people in lowly conditions, those who reside in an area without the legal protection and rights provided to citizens or who stay in one place for only a brief time. The Christians of Asia Minor were considered strangers either because (1) they were from already marginalized social castes or (2) by becoming Christians they were joining a disenfranchised group.

Jewish and Gentile Christians were scattered throughout much of Asia Minor. People from this area were in Jerusalem on the day of Pentecost (see the note on Ac 2:9–11), and Paul preached and taught in some of these provinces.

The name Galatia also occurs in Acts 16:6 ("Galatian"), 18:23, 1 Corinthians 16:1, Galatians 1:2 and Timothy 4:10. In Acts 16:6 and 18:23 the name is an adjective for the Galatian country or region. Luke was apparently referring to the region, not the province, since in Acts, when speaking of Asia Minor, he used the old ethnographic designations. The context in 1 Peter 1:1 seems clearly to indicate that the province was meant. Paul's general practice of using political designations points to the usage also in 1 Corinthians 16:1 and Galatians 1:2.

1:10–12 See "Jewish Eschatology in the First Century A.D." on page 1846.

1:13 In the language of the first century, "prepare . . . for action" meant that the readers should literally gather up their long, flowing garments and be ready for physical activity.

1:14 Christians, born into the family of God, are children of their heavenly Father. Believers are also described as being adopted into God's family (see Ro 8:15 and its note).

1:18 In the Bible, to redeem means to free someone from something bad by paying a penalty or a ransom. Likewise, in the Greek world slaves could be redeemed by the payment of a price, either by someone else or by the slave on his or her own behalf.

Some maintain that "your forefathers" implies that the recipients must have been pagans, based upon the New Testament stress on the emptiness of pagan life (see Ro 1:21; Eph 4:17). Others think that the recipients were Jews, since Jews were traditionalists who stressed the influence of the father as teacher in the home. In the light of the context of the whole letter, it is probable that both Jews and Gentiles were being addressed.

1:19 The Old Testament sacrifices were types (foreshadowings) of Christ (see "Sacrifices and Offerings in the Bible and the Ancient Near East" on p. 158).

1:22 For "brothers," see the note on Romans 1:13.

THE AUTHORSHIP OF PETER'S EPISTLES

1 PETER 1 First and Second Peter both claim authorship by Peter, an apostle of Jesus Christ (1Pe 1:1; 2Pe 1:1,17–18) and "a fellow elder, a witness of Christ's sufferings and one who also will share in the glory to be revealed" (1Pe 5:1). The early church unhesitatingly received 1 Peter as authentic. Some examples:

◆ Papias (A.D. 60–135) noted that "Mark is mentioned by Peter in his first epistle" (Eusebius, *History*, 2.15).

◆ Clement of Rome (A.D. 30–101); *The Didache* (an anonymous, early-second-century A.D. work dealing with a variety of doctrinal and practical matters of import to the early Christian church); and Polycarp (A.D. 69–156) all quoted from 1 Peter.

◆ Irenaeus (A.D. 130–200) cited 1 Peter, using the apostle's name (*Against Heresies*, 4.9.2; 4.16.5).

◆ Eusebius summarized the **canonical**[1] discussion by placing letters in four categories (*History*, 3.25):

> those recognized as genuine by all Christians (e.g., 1Pe);
>
> those that, though disputed, were still recognized as authentic by the church as a whole and were familiar to most Christians (e.g., 2Pe);
>
> spurious, noncanonical works that were yet familiar;
>
> and those that were generally acknowledged as outright heretical.

Despite strong historical evidence supporting Peter as the author of the two letters that bear his name, some commentators hesitate to accept Petrine authorship for several reasons:

◆ Nero's persecution of Christians in Rome (Tacitus, *Annals*, 15.44) set a precedent for Roman officials in all the provinces to consider Christians as criminals.[2] First Peter includes several references to the persecution of Christians outside Rome (1:6; 2:15; 3:15–16; 4:12–13; 5:8–9). Since all scholars agree that Peter died during Nero's reign (A.D. 64–68; cf. Eusebius, *History*, 2.25), and since persecution outside of Rome began after Nero's reign,[3] many New Testament commentators hold that both 1 and 2 Peter are pseudonymous works (falsely attributed to Peter). Their language, however, does not necessarily refer to a large-scale, official persecution and thus does not demand a date subsequent to Nero's reign. The suffering Peter referred to was local and sporadic rather than universal and under imperial mandate. Indeed, Peter spoke more of Christians suffering verbal abuse and social ostracism than he did of martyrdom.

◆ The enormous geographical area represented by the audience addressed in 1 Peter 1:1 (i.e., believers in Pontus, Galatia, Cappadocia, Asia and Bithynia) suggests to many scholars that these epistles were not composed until well after the 60s. They argue that enough time would have had to elapse after Paul's missionary journeys to allow for the growth of Christianity in these areas (especially since we have no record that Paul even visited Pontus, Cappadocia or Bithynia). As reflected in the book of Acts and in Paul's letters, however, Christian churches were often founded in short periods of time, and Peter may have first met some of his readers when they came to Jerusalem at Pentecost (Ac 2:9–10).

◆ First and Second Peter demonstrate a refined vocabulary and rich literary style. Since Peter and John are called "unschooled, ordinary men" in Acts 4:13, many think it unlikely that Peter would have possessed the skill to write these epistles. However, the Greek word used in Acts 4:13 (*agrammatos*) most likely means something like "without an advanced education" rather than "illiterate." The Jews prided themselves upon the education of their children (cf. Josephus, *Against Apion*, 1.12; 2.26). Peter evidently lacked the Talmud or "college" level of training. However, as a businessman in the fishing industry, he would have had to know how to read and probably would have been fluent in Greek, the language of common, public discourse. The picture of Peter that is frequently put forth today in popular expositions of Scripture—the notion that he was something of a buffoon—is most certainly invalid. In addition, 1 Peter 5:12 tells us that Silas assisted in the writing of the letter, indicating that Peter was not above seeking to make certain his letters read well.

The weight of evidence is in favor of the authenticity of these two letters. In addition, the early church did not on principle approve of books written under false names. For example, the church father Tertullian (*On Baptism*, 17) indicated that the elder who wrote the pseudonymous Acts of Paul in order to augment "Paul's fame" was defrocked, and the so-called Gospel of Peter was criticized as false (Eusebius, *History*, 6.12). Moreover, pseudonymous materials tend to be drastically different from 1 and 2 Peter.

[1]See Glossary on page 2080 for definitions of bolded words. [2]See "Nero, Persecutor of Christians" on page 1931. [3]See "The Early Persecution of the Church" on page 2067.

brothers, love one another deeply,[k] from the heart.[a] 23For you have been born again,[l] not of perishable
seed, but of imperishable, through the living and enduring word of God.[m] 24For,

> "All men are like grass,
> and all their glory is like the flowers of the field;
> the grass withers and the flowers fall,
> 25 but the word of the Lord stands forever."[b][n]

And this is the word that was preached to you.

2 Therefore, rid yourselves[o] of all malice and all deceit, hypocrisy, envy, and slander[p] of every kind.
2Like newborn babies, crave pure spiritual milk,[q] so that by it you may grow up[r] in your salvation,
3now that you have tasted that the Lord is good.[s]

The Living Stone and a Chosen People

4As you come to him, the living Stone[t]—rejected by men but chosen by God and precious to him—
5you also, like living stones, are being built[u] into a spiritual house[v] to be a holy priesthood,[w] offering
spiritual sacrifices acceptable to God through Jesus Christ.[x] 6For in Scripture it says:

> "See, I lay a stone in Zion,
> a chosen and precious cornerstone,[y]
> and the one who trusts in him
> will never be put to shame."[c][z]

7Now to you who believe, this stone is precious. But to those who do not believe,[a]

> "The stone the builders rejected
> has become the capstone,[d]"[e][b]

8and,

> "A stone that causes men to stumble
> and a rock that makes them fall."[f][c]

They stumble because they disobey the message—which is also what they were destined for.[d]
9But you are a chosen people,[e] a royal priesthood, a holy nation,[f] a people belonging to God, that you
may declare the praises of him who called you out of darkness into his wonderful light.[g] 10Once you were
not a people, but now you are the people of God;[h] once you had not received mercy, but now you have re-
ceived mercy.
11Dear friends, I urge you, as aliens and strangers in the world, to abstain from sinful desires,[i] which
war against your soul.[j] 12Live such good lives among the pagans that, though they accuse you of doing
wrong, they may see your good deeds[k] and glorify God[l] on the day he visits us.

Submission to Rulers and Masters

13Submit yourselves for the Lord's sake to every authority[m] instituted among men: whether to the king,
as the supreme authority, 14or to governors, who are sent by him to punish those who do wrong[n] and to
commend those who do right.[o] 15For it is God's will[p] that by doing good you should silence the ignorant talk
of foolish men.[q] 16Live as free men,[r] but do not use your freedom as a cover-up for evil; live as servants of
God.[s] 17Show proper respect to everyone: Love the brotherhood of believers,[t] fear God, honor the king.[u]
18Slaves, submit yourselves to your masters with all respect,[v] not only to those who are good and con-
siderate,[w] but also to those who are harsh. 19For it is commendable if a man bears up under the pain of

1:22 [k]Jn 13:34; Heb 13:1
1:23 [l]Jn 1:13 [m]Heb 4:12
1:25 [n]Isa 40:6-8
2:1 [o]Eph 4:22 [p]Jas 4:11
2:2 [q]1Co 3:2 [r]Eph 4:15,16
2:3 [s]Heb 6:5
2:4 [t]ver 7
2:5 [u]1Co 3:9 [v]1Ti 3:15 [w]Isa 61:6 [x]Php 4:18; Heb 13:15
2:6 [y]Eph 2:20 [z]Isa 28:16
2:7 [a]2Co 2:16 [b]Ps 118:22
2:8 [c]Isa 8:14; 1Co 1:23 [d]Ro 9:22
2:9 [e]Dt 10:15 [f]Isa 62:12 [g]Ac 26:18
2:10 [h]Hos 1:9,10
2:11 [i]Gal 5:16 [j]Jas 4:1
2:12 [k]Php 2:15; 1Pe 3:16 [l]Mt 5:16; 9:8
2:13 [m]Ro 13:1
2:14 [n]Ro 13:4 [o]Ro 13:3
2:15 [p]1Pe 3:17 [q]ver 12
2:16 [r]Jn 8:32 [s]Ro 6:22
2:17 [t]Ro 12:10 [u]Ro 13:7
2:18 [v]Eph 6:5 [w]Jas 3:17

[a] 22 Some early manuscripts *from a pure heart* [b] 25 Isaiah 40:6-8 [c] 6 Isaiah 28:16 [d] 7 Or *cornerstone*
[e] 7 Psalm 118:22 [f] 8 Isaiah 8:14

2:6 The cornerstone, which determined the design and orientation of a building, was the most significant stone in the structure. Here it is an obvious reference to Christ.

2:13 The meaning of "submit" in the Greek is "to order oneself under, or according to, a given relationship" or "to live according to the governmental order." Clearly here the notion of submitting to the government is secondary to that of obeying God (1:2,14,22) and doing his will (2:15).

When Peter wrote, the emperor ("king") was the brutal Nero, who ruled from A.D. 54 to 68 (see "Nero, Persecutor of Christians" on p. 1931).

2:16 For the various names by which early Christians were known, see the note on 4:16.

2:18 "Slaves" is a reference to household servants, whatever their particular training and functions (see "Labor and Welfare in the Ancient World" on p. 1952 and "Slavery in the Greco-Roman World" on p. 1979). The context indicates that Peter was addressing Christian slaves.

2:19 [x]1Pe 3:14, 17 unjust suffering because he is conscious of God.[x] 20 But how is it to your credit if you receive a beating
for doing wrong and endure it? But if you suffer for doing good and you endure it, this is commendable
2:20 [y]1Pe 3:17 2:21 [z]Ac 14:22 before God.[y] 21 To this[z] you were called, because Christ suffered for you, leaving you an example,[a] that you
[a]Mt 16:24 should follow in his steps.

> 22 "He committed no sin,
> 2:22 [b]Isa 53:9 and no deceit was found in his mouth."[a][b]

2:23 [c]Isa 53:7 23 When they hurled their insults at him, he did not retaliate; when he suffered, he made no threats.[c] In-
[d]Lk 23:46 2:24 [e]Heb 9:28 stead, he entrusted himself[d] to him who judges justly. 24 He himself bore our sins[e] in his body on the tree,
[f]Ro 6:2 [g]Isa 53:5; Heb 12:13; so that we might die to sins[f] and live for righteousness; by his wounds you have been healed.[g] 25 For you
Jas 5:16 2:25 [h]Isa 53:6 were like sheep going astray,[h] but now you have returned to the Shepherd[i] and Overseer of your souls.
[i]Jn 10:11

Wives and Husbands

3:1 [j]1Pe 2:18 [k]Eph 5:22 **3** Wives, in the same way be submissive[j] to your husbands[k] so that, if any of them do not believe the
[l]1Co 7:16; 9:19 word, they may be won over[l] without words by the behavior of their wives, 2 when they see the purity

[a] *22* Isaiah 53:9

2:25 Throughout the Old Testament and the ancient Near East, the term "shepherd" was often applied to rulers (see 2Sa 5:2; Jer 23:2; see also the note on Ps 23:1 and "Shepherding in the Ancient World" on p. 1363). Here it is a reference to Christ.

For "Overseer" (again a reference to Christ), see the note on 1 Timothy 3:1–7. Elders are to be both shepherds and overseers.

3:1 Peter no doubt encountered and associated with a large number of women whose husbands were not yet Christians. His call to "be submissive" was followed by the reason: to win their spouses to faith on the basis of their behavior. The same Greek verb translated "be submissive" is used in 2:13 and 18 as a call for submission to a recognized authority. Here the context is the hierarchical structure of the

The Demeanor of Wives

1 PETER 3 First Peter 3:1–7 develops the theme that Christians are to conduct themselves honorably among the Gentiles by being submissive to human institutions, so that Gentiles may observe Christian behavior, be converted and glorify God. A woman who was married to an unbelieving husband was to use her Christian demeanor to win over her husband to Christ.

Hand-mirror from Qumran

Preserving Bible Times; © Dr. James C. Martin; permission of The Israel Museum/Shrine of the Book

Peter specifically exhorted women to a beauty that exuded from the heart rather than one based solely upon external appearance. Verse 3 may be translated simply as "gold-braided hair" rather than "braided hair and the wearing of gold jewelry." Women in Peter's day would often braid their hair, interweaving into it golden spangles and threads that glittered and tinkled with every movement of the head. One ancient writer, Xenophon of Ephesus, described women with hair braided in such a way in a procession for the goddess Artemis as erotically attractive.[1] This was not to be the way of Christian women.

The theme of Christian conduct continues as the discussion turns to Sarah, "who obeyed Abraham and called him her master" (v. 6). The same word rendered here as "master" is translated in John 12:21 as "sir," a common, deferential mode of address. Husbands were likewise expected to demonstrate respect for their wives (1Pe 3:7).[2]

[1]See "Artemis of the Ephesians" on page 1808.
[2]See also "Husbands and Wives: Family Life in the Greco-Roman World" on page 1922.

and reverence of your lives. 3Your beauty should not come from outward adornment, such as braided
hair and the wearing of gold jewelry and fine clothes.[m] 4Instead, it should be that of your inner self,[n] the
unfading beauty of a gentle and quiet spirit, which is of great worth in God's sight. 5For this is the way
the holy women of the past who put their hope in God[o] used to make themselves beautiful. They were
submissive to their own husbands, 6like Sarah, who obeyed Abraham and called him her master.[p] You are
her daughters if you do what is right and do not give way to fear.

7Husbands,[q] in the same way be considerate as you live with your wives, and treat them with respect
as the weaker partner and as heirs with you of the gracious gift of life, so that nothing will hinder your
prayers.

Suffering for Doing Good

8Finally, all of you, live in harmony with one another; be sympathetic, love as brothers,[r] be compas-
sionate and humble.[s] 9Do not repay evil with evil[t] or insult with insult,[u] but with blessing, because to this[v]
you were called so that you may inherit a blessing.[w] 10For,

"Whoever would love life
　　and see good days
must keep his tongue from evil
　　and his lips from deceitful speech.
11He must turn from evil and do good;
　　he must seek peace and pursue it.
12For the eyes of the Lord are on the righteous
　　and his ears are attentive to their prayer,
but the face of the Lord is against those who do evil."[a][x]

13Who is going to harm you if you are eager to do good?[y] 14But even if you should suffer for what is
right, you are blessed.[z] "Do not fear what they fear[b]; do not be frightened."[c][a] 15But in your hearts set apart
Christ as Lord. Always be prepared to give an answer[b] to everyone who asks you to give the reason for
the hope that you have. But do this with gentleness and respect, 16keeping a clear conscience,[c] so that
those who speak maliciously against your good behavior in Christ may be ashamed of their slander.[d]
17It is better, if it is God's will,[e] to suffer for doing good[f] than for doing evil. 18For Christ died for sins[g]
once for all, the righteous for the unrighteous, to bring you to God. He was put to death in the body[h] but
made alive by the Spirit,[i] 19through whom[d] also he went and preached to the spirits in prison[j] 20who dis-
obeyed long ago when God waited patiently in the days of Noah while the ark was being built.[k] In it only
a few people, eight in all, were saved[l] through water, 21and this water symbolizes baptism that now saves
you[m] also—not the removal of dirt from the body but the pledge[e] of a good conscience toward God. It
saves you by the resurrection of Jesus Christ,[n] 22who has gone into heaven and is at God's right hand[o]—
with angels, authorities and powers in submission to him.[p]

Living for God

4 Therefore, since Christ suffered in his body, arm yourselves also with the same attitude, because he
who has suffered in his body is done with sin. 2As a result, he does not live the rest of his earthly
life for evil human desires,[q] but rather for the will of God. 3For you have spent enough time in the past[r]

3:3 [m]Isa 3:18-23; 1Ti 2:9
3:4 [n]Ro 7:22
3:5 [o]1Ti 5:5
3:6 [p]Ge 18:12
3:7 [q]Eph 5:25-33
3:8 [r]Ro 12:10 [s]1Pe 5:5
3:9 [t]Ro 12:17 [u]1Pe 2:23 [v]1Pe 2:21 [w]Heb 6:14
3:12 [x]Ps 34:12-16
3:13 [y]Pr 16:7
3:14 [z]1Pe 2:19, 20; 4:15,16 [a]Isa 8:12,13
3:15 [b]Col 4:6
3:16 [c]Heb 13:18 [d]1Pe 2:12,15
3:17 [e]1Pe 2:15 [f]1Pe 2:20
3:18 [g]1Pe 2:21 [h]Col 1:22; 1Pe 4:1 [i]1Pe 4:6
3:19 [j]1Pe 4:6
3:20 [k]Ge 6:3,5, 13,14 [l]Heb 11:7
3:21 [m]Tit 3:5 [n]1Pe 1:3
3:22 [o]Mk 16:19 [p]Ro 8:38
4:2 [q]Ro 6:2
4:3 [r]Eph 2:2

[a] *12* Psalm 34:12-16 [b] *14* Or *not fear their threats* [c] *14* Isaiah 8:12 [d] *18,19* Or *alive in the spirit, 19through which*
[e] *21* Or *response*

ancient household. When a woman joined a religion different from her husband's, the action could be seen as evidence of insubordination. (See "Husbands and Wives: Family Life in the Greco-Roman World" on p. 1922 and "The Demeanor of Wives" on p. 2013.)

3:3 Christian women, stated Peter, were not to rely on extreme coiffures, gaudy exhibits of jewelry or expensive garments for their beauty (see "Dress and Fashion in the Greco-Roman World" on p. 2004).

3:5–7 See "Husbands and Wives: Family Life in the Greco-Roman World" on page 1922.

3:19 The familiar Apostles' Creed affirmation that Jesus descended into hell is based chiefly on two references from 1 Peter, one of which (3:19) is more direct than the other (4:6), supported by implications to be taken from two other New Testament verses (Ac 2:27; Ro 10:7). The term is in harmony also with the language of Paul, where he spoke of Christ's descending "to the lower, earthly regions" (Eph 4:9), and with John's mention of "the First and the Last," who holds "the keys of death and Hades" (Rev 1:17–18). The lowest regions were recognized as the habitation of the disembodied spirits of the dead, but 1 Peter 4:6 may instead refer to fallen angels (cf. Jude 6). See "Sheol, Hades, Gehenna, the Abyss and Tartarus: Images of Hell" on page 946.

3:21 See "Baptism in the Ancient World" on page 1562.

3:22 See "The 'Right Hand' in Ancient Thinking" on page 1983.

4:3 The terms "pagans" (lit., "the Gentiles") and "idolatry" suggest that at least some of Peter's readers were Gentiles who had converted from a pagan lifestyle (see "Proselytes in Second Temple Judaism" on p. 1776).

doing what pagans choose to do—living in debauchery, lust, drunkenness, orgies, carousing and de-
testable idolatry. 4 They think it strange that you do not plunge with them into the same flood of dissi-
4:4 s1Pe 3:16 pation, and they heap abuse on you.s 5 But they will have to give account to him who is ready to judge
4:5 tAc 10:42; 2Ti 4:1 the living and the dead.t 6 For this is the reason the gospel was preached even to those who are now
4:6 u1Pe 3:19 dead,u so that they might be judged according to men in regard to the body, but live according to God
in regard to the spirit.
4:7 vRo 13:11 7 The end of all things is near.v Therefore be clear minded and self-controlled so that you can pray.

Wine and Alcoholic Beverages in the Ancient World

1 PETER 4 Wine, the most widely used fermented drink in the ancient world, was present at religious rituals, in festive celebrations and in everyday life in Mediterranean culture. It was, in fact, celebrated in pagan culture. Libations of wine were commonly poured out to gods, and deities such as Dionysus (the god of wine) had many followers.[1] Even in Israel, however, wine was used in religious rituals (Nu 15:7), and viticulture (the cultivation of grapes for wine making) continues to be a significant agricultural industry for the modern nation of Israel.

Then as now, there were many varieties of wine, including red, white and mixed wines. The Old Testament employs a number of words for different kinds of wine. Precise translations for the Hebrew words are elusive since we do not know exactly how they differ from each other, but translators regularly use terms such as "wine," "new wine," "spiced wine" and "sweet wine." Passages such as Hosea 4:11 make clear that these wines were alcoholic and intoxicating; there is no basis for suggesting that either the Greek or the Hebrew terms for wine refer to unfermented grape juice.

The production of wine, of course, required vineyards. Watchtowers were constructed to protect the vines (Isa 5:1–2; Mk 12:1); of particular concern were foxes, who were prone to eat the grapes (SS 2:15). In the Greek world boys would hunt foxes to keep them from the vineyards. After the grapes had been harvested, the *must* (grape juice for fermenting) would be produced by treading out the grapes in a vat.[2] The must would be strained and the fermentation process begun. The mixed wines were created by combining the fermented juice of the grape with other elements, including other wines, spices, honey or strong drink created from other fruits or grains. Wine diluted with water was obviously considered to be of inferior quality (Isa 1:22), although the Greeks, considering the drinking of pure wine to be an excess, routinely diluted their wine. Mixed wines served in a number of applications: Wine mixed with barley made good vinegar and, when blended with myrrh, served as an anesthetic. This last type was offered to Jesus on the cross (Mk 15:23).

Mosaic from Paphos (inscription says "The First Winedrinkers")

Preserving Bible Times; © Dr. James C. Martin

Priests were not to drink wine while ministering at the sanctuary (Lev 10:9), and ordinary people were to avoid wine and grape products in any form while under the restrictions of a Nazirite vow (Nu 6:4). Other than these few exceptions, however, Biblical references make it clear that wine was a common, everyday part of a regular diet (Ge 14:18; 1Sa 16:20). Scripture, however, repeatedly emphasizes moderation and the dangers of excess (Pr 20:1; 23:20; Isa 5:11). See also "Food and Agriculture" on page 390.

[1]See "The Cult of Dionysus" on page 1921. [2]See "The Winepress" on page 1171.

8 Above all, love each other deeply,[w] because love covers over a multitude of sins.[x] 9 Offer hospitality to one another without grumbling.[y] 10 Each one should use whatever gift he has received to serve others,[z] faithfully[a] administering God's grace in its various forms. 11 If anyone speaks, he should do it as one speaking the very words of God. If anyone serves, he should do it with the strength God provides,[b] so that in all things God may be praised[c] through Jesus Christ. To him be the glory and the power for ever and ever. Amen.

Suffering for Being a Christian

12 Dear friends, do not be surprised at the painful trial you are suffering,[d] as though something strange were happening to you. 13 But rejoice that you participate in the sufferings of Christ, so that you may be overjoyed when his glory is revealed.[e] 14 If you are insulted because of the name of Christ, you are blessed,[f] for the Spirit of glory and of God rests on you. 15 If you suffer, it should not be as a murderer or thief or any other kind of criminal, or even as a meddler. 16 However, if you suffer as a Christian, do not be ashamed, but praise God that you bear that name.[g] 17 For it is time for judgment to begin with the family of God;[h] and if it begins with us, what will the outcome be for those who do not obey the gospel of God?[i] 18 And,

> "If it is hard for the righteous to be saved,
> what will become of the ungodly and the sinner?"[a][j]

19 So then, those who suffer according to God's will should commit themselves to their faithful Creator and continue to do good.

To Elders and Young Men

5 To the elders among you, I appeal as a fellow elder,[k] a witness[l] of Christ's sufferings and one who also will share in the glory to be revealed:[m] 2 Be shepherds of God's flock[n] that is under your care, serving as overseers—not because you must, but because you are willing, as God wants you to be; not greedy for money,[o] but eager to serve; 3 not lording it over[p] those entrusted to you, but being examples[q] to the flock. 4 And when the Chief Shepherd appears, you will receive the crown of glory[r] that will never fade away.

5 Young men, in the same way be submissive[s] to those who are older. All of you, clothe yourselves with humility toward one another, because,

> "God opposes the proud
> but gives grace to the humble."[b][t]

6 Humble yourselves, therefore, under God's mighty hand, that he may lift you up in due time.[u] 7 Cast all your anxiety on him[v] because he cares for you.[w]

8 Be self-controlled and alert. Your enemy the devil prowls around[x] like a roaring lion looking for someone to devour. 9 Resist him,[y] standing firm in the faith,[z] because you know that your brothers throughout the world are undergoing the same kind of sufferings.[a]

10 And the God of all grace, who called you to his eternal glory[b] in Christ, after you have suffered a little while, will himself restore you and make you strong,[c] firm and steadfast. 11 To him be the power for ever and ever. Amen.[d]

4:8 [w]1Pe 1:22 [x]Pr 10:12
4:9 [y]Php 2:14
4:10 [z]Ro 12:6,7 [a]1Co 4:2
4:11 [b]Eph 6:10 [c]1Co 10:31
4:12 [d]1Pe 1:6,7
4:13 [e]Ro 8:17
4:14 [f]Mt 5:11
4:16 [g]Ac 5:41
4:17 [h]Jer 25:29 [i]2Th 1:8
4:18 [j]Pr 11:31; Lk 23:31
5:1 [k]Ac 11:30 [l]Lk 24:48 [m]1Pe 1:5,7; Rev 1:9
5:2 [n]Jn 21:16 [o]1Ti 3:3
5:3 [p]Eze 34:4 [q]Php 3:17
5:4 [r]1Co 9:25
5:5 [s]Eph 5:21 [t]Pr 3:34; Jas 4:6
5:6 [u]Jas 4:10
5:7 [v]Ps 37:5; Mt 6:25 [w]Heb 13:5
5:8 [x]Job 1:7
5:9 [y]Jas 4:7 [z]Col 2:5 [a]Ac 14:22
5:10 [b]2Co 4:17 [c]2Th 2:17
5:11 [d]Ro 11:36

[a] *18* Prov. 11:31 [b] *5* Prov. 3:34

4:16 The Biblical meaning of the name "Christian" is "adherent of Christ." The disciples were formally called Christians first in Antioch (Ac 11:26), and later Agrippa recognized that to believe what Paul preached would have made him a Christian (Ac 26:28). Peter accepted the name as in itself a basis for persecution. Thus gradually a name imposed by Gentiles was adopted by the disciples of Jesus. Some Jews had referred to Christ's followers as "the Nazarene sect" (Ac 24:5), and Paul, when he was himself a persecutor, had identified them as those "who belonged to the Way" (Ac 9:2). The Latin suffix *-ianus* was often used with the name of the slave's owner (e.g., a slave of Iulius might be called Iulianus). This implication occurs in the New Testament (e.g., Ro 6:22; 1Pe 2:16). The apostles wrote of themselves as "servants" (slaves) of Christ (Ro 1:1; Jas 1:1; 2Pe 1:1; Jude 1; Rev 1:1), and the New Testament variously calls the followers of Christ "brothers" (Ac 14:2), "disciples" (Ac 6:1–2), "saints" (Ac 9:13; Ro 1:7; 2Co 1:2), "believers" (1Ti 4:12), "the church of God" (Ac 20:28) and "all who call on the [Lord's] name" (Ac 9:14; see Ro 10:12–13). See also the note on Christians at Acts 11:26.

5:1 By using the term "fellow elder," Peter identified himself with the elders of the church. This would have been heartening to them in light of their great responsibilities and the difficult situation faced by the churches. The churches for which these elders were responsible were scattered across much of Asia Minor, so if Peter functioned as a local church officer, he must have been officially related to one of them.

5:2 For "shepherds" and "overseers," see the note on 2:25. Here it applies to the elders of the church.

Final Greetings

5:12 [e]2Co 1:19 [f]Heb 13:22 [12]With the help of Silas,[a][e] whom I regard as a faithful brother, I have written to you briefly,[f] encour-
aging you and testifying that this is the true grace of God. Stand fast in it.
[13]She who is in Babylon, chosen together with you, sends you her greetings, and so does my son
5:13 [g]Ac 12:12 5:14 [h]Ro 16:16 [i]Eph 6:23 Mark.[g] [14]Greet one another with a kiss of love.[h]
Peace[i] to all of you who are in Christ.

[a] 12 Greek *Silvanus*, a variant of *Silas*

5:12 Silas (see the note on Ac 15:22) may have been the bearer of the letter. He may also have been the scribe who recorded what Peter dictated or who aided, as an informed and intelligent secretary, in the phrasing of Peter's thoughts.

5:13 Because Old Testament Babylon was a notorious place of sin, that city's name had become shorthand for any place known for its wickedness. Peter may also have used the name here to describe any place to which Christians had been deported from their homeland of Judea. In either case, the description fits Rome, and early Christian tradition indicates that Peter wrote from there.

Peter regarded Mark (see the note on Col 4:10) with such warmth and affection that he called him his son. It is possible that Peter had led Mark to Christ (cf. 1Ti 1:2). In any event, early Christian tradition closely associates the two.

INTRODUCTION TO *2 Peter*

AUTHOR, PLACE AND DATE OF WRITING

Second Peter explicitly claims to have been written by the apostle Peter, yet today this claim is widely rejected in scholarship. Those who reject Petrine authorship do so for the following reasons: (1) There is a lack of early support for 2 Peter by the church fathers. (2) The letter draws heavily on the epistle of Jude. (3) Its content deals with second-century A.D. problems and issues, such as Gnosticism and the delay in Christ's return. (4) Second Peter 3:15–16 mentions that a collection of Paul's letters was already known in the churches. (5) Some argue that 2 Peter is so transparently not by Peter that the early readers would have seen this claim as no more than a literary device.

There are other reasons, however, for maintaining Peter's authorship: (1) While 2 Peter 2 and Jude have a great deal in common, the fact that their texts are similar has no bearing on the inspiration or authorship of either. (2) Second Peter contains no direct reference to any second-century church issue or institution, and concern over the delay of Christ's return appears already in 1 Thessalonians (written c. A.D. 50–51). (3) The passing reference to Paul's letters may only indicate that the practice of circulating his letters had begun. (4) Early Christians were quick to repudiate pseudo-apostolic texts and in particular renounced books falsely claiming to have been from Peter (e.g., the Apocalypse of Peter, the Gospel of Peter, the Acts of Peter, and the Letter of Peter to Philip).

Peter, according to strong tradition, died about A.D. 64–68 under Nero. Thus, his authorship requires a date earlier than this. It has been suggested that Peter wrote this letter from Rome.

AUDIENCE

This epistle was addressed to Christians to warn them against false teaching (2:1). If 3:1 is a reference to 1 Peter, then Christians in Asia Minor were the recipients of both letters. Otherwise, the identity of 2 Peter's addressees is uncertain.

CULTURAL FACTS AND HIGHLIGHTS

Second Peter is an appeal to faith and godliness from the apostle to the churches. Its message does refer to enemies of the faith, but in such broad terms that it is hard to imagine that Peter had a specific heresy in view. The letter is probably a general exhortation to the churches from the apostle as he approached his death.

TIMELINE

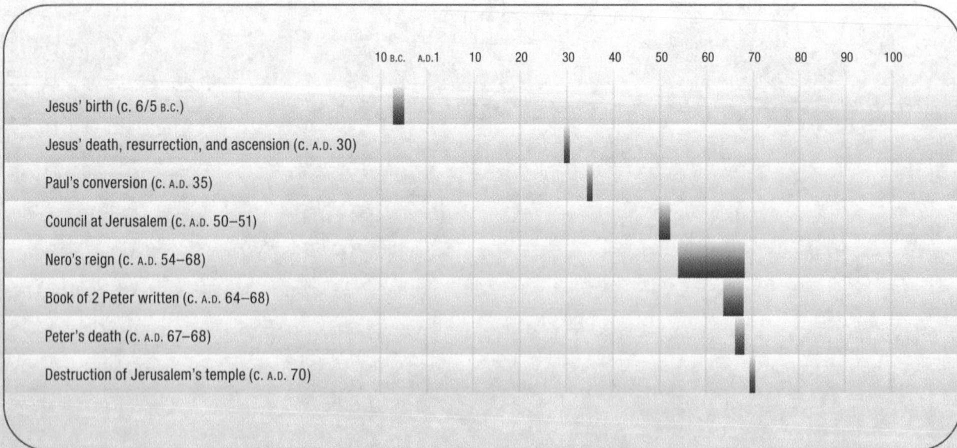

AS YOU READ

Note Peter's instruction to grow in godly virtues and Christian character. Watch for his repeated emphasis on truth, which includes not only his warning against false teachers but also his certainty of Christ's return.

DID YOU KNOW?

- New Testament authors adapted literary forms from their culture as they communicated the gospel (1:5–7).
- The Greek term for "seduce" depicts a fisherman who attempts to lure and catch fish with bait (2:14).
- In the first century A.D. the term "elements" referred to such entities as earth, air, fire and water (3:10).

THEMES

Second Peter includes the following themes:

1. *Spiritual Growth.* As Peter faced the end of his life (1:13–15), he predicted impending calamities and expressed concern about his readers remaining faithful and continuing to grow in discipleship.

2. *False teaching.* Peter sounded the alarm about false teachers, who posed a major threat to the faithfulness of believers.

3. *The certainty of Christ's return.* Peter warned against scoffers who abandon the hope of Christ's coming in judgment (3:3–4). The delay of divine judgment is a revelation of God's patience, in that he is allowing time for repentance (3:9). Since the return of the Lord Jesus is certain, believers are to prepare themselves through faithful, ethical living (3:11–16).

OUTLINE

I. Introduction (1:1–2)

II. Knowing God (1:3–21)
   - A. Know Your Calling (1:3–11)
   - B. Know the Scriptures (1:12–21)

III. Warning Against False Teachers (2)
   - A. Their Coming Predicted (2:1–3a)
   - B. God Will Judge Them (2:3b–9)
   - C. Some Characteristics (2:10–22)

IV. The Fact of Christ's Return (3:1–16)
   - A. Peter's Purpose in Writing Restated (3:1–2)
   - B. The Coming of Scoffers (3:3–7)
   - C. The Certainty of Christ's Return (3:8–10)
   - D. Exhortations Based on the Fact of Christ's Return (3:11–16)

V. Concluding Remarks (3:17–18)

1 Simon Peter, a servant[a] and apostle of Jesus Christ,[b]

To those who through the righteousness[c] of our God and Savior Jesus Christ[d] have received a faith as
precious as ours:

2 Grace and peace be yours in abundance through the knowledge of God and of Jesus our Lord.[e]

Making One's Calling and Election Sure

3 His divine power[f] has given us everything we need for life and godliness through our knowledge of
him who called us[g] by his own glory and goodness. 4 Through these he has given us his very great and
precious promises,[h] so that through them you may participate in the divine nature[i] and escape the cor-
ruption in the world caused by evil desires.[j]
5 For this very reason, make every effort to add to your faith goodness; and to goodness, knowledge;[k]
6 and to knowledge, self-control;[l] and to self-control, perseverance; and to perseverance, godliness;[m] 7 and
to godliness, brotherly kindness; and to brotherly kindness, love.[n] 8 For if you possess these qualities in
increasing measure, they will keep you from being ineffective and unproductive[o] in your knowledge of
our Lord Jesus Christ. 9 But if anyone does not have them, he is nearsighted and blind,[p] and has forgot-
ten that he has been cleansed from his past sins.[q]
10 Therefore, my brothers, be all the more eager to make your calling and election sure. For if you do
these things, you will never fall,[r] 11 and you will receive a rich welcome into the eternal kingdom of our
Lord and Savior Jesus Christ.

Prophecy of Scripture

12 So I will always remind you of these things,[s] even though you know them and are firmly established
in the truth you now have. 13 I think it is right to refresh your memory as long as I live in the tent of this
body,[t] 14 because I know that I will soon put it aside,[u] as our Lord Jesus Christ has made clear to me.[v] 15 And
I will make every effort to see that after my departure[w] you will always be able to remember these things.
16 We did not follow cleverly invented stories when we told you about the power and coming of our
Lord Jesus Christ, but we were eyewitnesses of his majesty.[x] 17 For he received honor and glory from God
the Father when the voice came to him from the Majestic Glory, saying, "This is my Son, whom I love; with
him I am well pleased."[a][y] 18 We ourselves heard this voice that came from heaven when we were with him
on the sacred mountain.[z]
19 And we have the word of the prophets made more certain, and you will do well to pay attention to
it, as to a light[a] shining in a dark place, until the day dawns and the morning star[b] rises in your hearts.
20 Above all, you must understand that no prophecy of Scripture came about by the prophet's own inter-
pretation. 21 For prophecy never had its origin in the will of man, but men spoke from God[c] as they were
carried along by the Holy Spirit.[d]

False Teachers and Their Destruction

2 But there were also false prophets[e] among the people, just as there will be false teachers among you.[f]
They will secretly introduce destructive heresies, even denying the sovereign Lord[g] who bought
them[h]—bringing swift destruction on themselves. 2 Many will follow their shameful ways and will bring

1:1 [a]Ro 1:1 [b]1Pe 1:1 [c]Ro 3:21-26 [d]Tit 2:13
1:2 [e]Php 3:8
1:3 [f]1Pe 1:5 [g]1Th 2:12
1:4 [h]2Co 7:1 [i]Eph 4:24; Heb 12:10; 1Jn 3:2 [j]2Pe 2:18-20
1:5 [k]Col 2:3
1:6 [l]Ac 24:25 [m]ver 3
1:7 [n]1Th 3:12
1:8 [o]Jn 15:2; Tit 3:14
1:9 [p]1Jn 2:11 [q]Eph 5:26
1:10 [r]2Pe 3:17
1:12 [s]Php 3:1; 1Jn 2:21
1:13 [t]2Co 5:1,4
1:14 [u]2Ti 4:6 [v]Jn 21:18,19
1:15 [w]Lk 9:31
1:16 [x]Mt 17:1-8
1:17 [y]Mt 3:17
1:18 [z]Mt 17:6
1:19 [a]Ps 119:105 [b]Rev 22:16
1:21 [c]2Ti 3:16 [d]2Sa 23:2; Ac 1:16; 1Pe 1:11
2:1 [e]Dt 13:1-3 [f]1Ti 4:1 [g]Jude 4 [h]1Co 6:20

[a] *17* Matt. 17:5; Mark 9:7; Luke 9:35

1:1 For the various names by which early Christians were known, see the note on 1 Peter 4:16.
1:3 If 2 Peter was written to combat an incipient Gnosticism (see "The Gnostics and Their Scriptures" on p. 2029), the apostle may have been insisting that the knowledge derived from the apostles was entirely adequate to meet their spiritual needs. No secret, esoteric knowledge is necessary for salvation.
1:5–7 New Testament authors adapted literary forms from their culture as they communicated the gospel. One of these, the *sorites*, linked together virtues or vices in a series (see, e.g., Ro 5:3–4). An ancient writer did not necessarily list the vices or virtues in any particular order. All of the virtues in these verses are important, and Christians were and are to exhibit each of them "in increasing measure" (2Pe 1:8).
1:6 For a discussion of asceticism in the believer's life, see the note on Leviticus 10:9.
1:8 Christians' knowledge should affect the way they live. It does not set them free from moral restraints, as the heretics taught. The heresy to which Peter referred may have been an early form of second-century Gnosticism (see "The Gnostics and Their Scriptures" on p. 2029) that claimed to possess special, esoteric knowledge.
1:10 For "brothers," see the note on Romans 1:13.
1:12–15 Many scholars classify 2 Peter as a "testament"—a book, or part of a book, in which a person makes a final speech from his or her deathbed.
1:16 Peter's message was based on his eyewitness account of the supernatural events that marked the life of Jesus—not made up of myths and imaginative stories as was the message of the heretics (see 2:3).
1:18 For "sacred mountain," see the note on Luke 9:28.

2:3 [i]2Co 2:17; the way of truth into disrepute. 3In their greed these teachers will exploit you[i] with stories they have
1Th 2:5 made up. Their condemnation has long been hanging over them, and their destruction has not been
sleeping.
4For if God did not spare angels when they sinned, but sent them to hell,[a] putting them into gloomy
2:4 [j]Jude 6; dungeons[b] to be held for judgment;[j] 5if he did not spare the ancient world[k] when he brought the flood
Rev 20:1,2 2:5 [k]2Pe 3:6 on its ungodly people, but protected Noah, a preacher of righteousness, and seven others;[l] 6if he con-
[l]Heb 11:7; 1Pe 3:20 demned the cities of Sodom and Gomorrah by burning them to ashes,[m] and made them an example[n] of
2:6 [m]Ge 19:24,25 [n]Nu 26:10; Jude 7 what is going to happen to the ungodly; 7and if he rescued Lot,[o] a righteous man, who was distressed by
2:7 [o]Ge 19:16 [p]2Pe 3:17 the filthy lives of lawless men[p] 8(for that righteous man, living among them day after day, was torment-
ed in his righteous soul by the lawless deeds he saw and heard)— 9if this is so, then the Lord knows
2:9 [q]1Co 10:13 how to rescue godly men from trials[q] and to hold the unrighteous for the day of judgment, while con-
2:10 [r]2Pe 3:3 tinuing their punishment.[c] 10This is especially true of those who follow the corrupt desire[r] of the sinful
[s]Jude 8 nature[d] and despise authority.
Bold and arrogant, these men are not afraid to slander celestial beings;[s] 11yet even angels, although
they are stronger and more powerful, do not bring slanderous accusations against such beings in the
2:11 [t]Jude 9 presence of the Lord.[t] 12But these men blaspheme in matters they do not understand. They are like brute
2:12 [u]Jude 10 beasts, creatures of instinct, born only to be caught and destroyed, and like beasts they too will perish.[u]
13They will be paid back with harm for the harm they have done. Their idea of pleasure is to carouse
2:13 [v]Ro 13:13 in broad daylight.[v] They are blots and blemishes, reveling in their pleasures while they feast with you.[e][w]
[w]1Co 11:20,21; Jude 12 14With eyes full of adultery, they never stop sinning; they seduce[x] the unstable; they are experts in
2:14 [x]ver 18 [y]ver 3 [z]Eph 2:3 greed[y]—an accursed brood![z] 15They have left the straight way and wandered off to follow the way of Ba-
2:15 [a]Nu 22:4-20; Jude 11 laam[a] son of Beor, who loved the wages of wickedness. 16But he was rebuked for his wrongdoing by a don-
2:16 [b]Nu 22:21-30 key—a beast without speech—who spoke with a man's voice and restrained the prophet's madness.[b]
2:17 [c]Jude 12 17These men are springs without water[c] and mists driven by a storm. Blackest darkness is reserved
[d]Jude 13 2:18 [e]Jude 16 for them.[d] 18For they mouth empty, boastful words[e] and, by appealing to the lustful desires of sinful
human nature, they entice people who are just escaping from those who live in error. 19They promise
them freedom, while they themselves are slaves of depravity—for a man is a slave to whatever has mas-
2:19 [f]Jn 8:34; Ro 6:16 tered him.[f] 20If they have escaped the corruption of the world by knowing[g] our Lord and Savior Jesus
2:20 [g]2Pe 1:2 Christ and are again entangled in it and overcome, they are worse off at the end than they were at the
[h]Mt 12:45 beginning.[h] 21It would have been better for them not to have known the way of righteousness, than to
2:21 [i]Heb 6:4-6 have known it and then to turn their backs on the sacred command that was passed on to them.[i] 22Of
2:22 [j]Pr 26:11 them the proverbs are true: "A dog returns to its vomit,"[f][j] and, "A sow that is washed goes back to her
wallowing in the mud."

The Day of the Lord

3:1 [k]2Pe 1:13 3 Dear friends, this is now my second letter to you. I have written both of them as reminders[k] to stim-
3:3 [l]1Ti 4:1 ulate you to wholesome thinking. 2I want you to recall the words spoken in the past by the holy
[m]2Pe 2:10; Jude 18 prophets and the command given by our Lord and Savior through your apostles.
3:4 [n]Isa 5:19; 3First of all, you must understand that in the last days[l] scoffers will come, scoffing and following their
Eze 12:22; Mt 24:48 own evil desires.[m] 4They will say, "Where is this 'coming' he promised?[n] Ever since our fathers died,

[a] 4 Greek *Tartarus* [b] 4 Some manuscripts *into chains of darkness* [c] 9 Or *unrighteous for punishment until the day of judgment* [d] 10 Or *the flesh* [e] 13 Some manuscripts *in their love feasts* [f] 22 Prov. 26:11

2:4 Some believe the angels' sin was the one referred to in Genesis 6:2, where the sons of God are said to have intermarried with the daughters of men, meaning (according to this view) that angels married human women. The offspring of those marriages are said to have been the Nephilim (see "Who Were the Nephilim?" on p. 215). Others believe the angels' sin probably occurred before the fall of Adam and Eve. Those who fell became the devil and the evil angels (probably the demons and evil spirits referred to in the New Testament).

For "hell," see "Sheol, Hades, Gehenna, the Abyss and Tartarus: Images of Hell" on page 946.

2:5 "A preacher of righteousness" is a description of Noah found nowhere else in Scripture. However, similar descriptions are used of him in Josephus (*Antiquities*, 1.3.1), *1 Clement* (7.6; 9.4) and the *Sibylline Oracles* (1.128–29).

2:6 See "The Destruction of Sodom and Gomorrah" on page 32.

2:13 "Feast" no doubt refers to "love feasts," as in Jude 12 (see "The Love Feast" on p. 1874).

2:14 The Greek for "seduce" depicts a fisherman who attempts to lure and catch fish with bait. For a parallel use, see James 1:14 and its note.

2:17 For "blackest darkness," see "Sheol, Hades, Gehenna, the Abyss and Tartarus: Images of Hell" on page 946.

2:18 "People who are just escaping" refers to new converts who had just broken away from pagan friends. The depraved, false teachers preyed on new converts who had not yet had an opportunity to develop spiritual resistance.

2:21 In its early days, Christianity was known as "the Way" (see Ac 9:2).

3:3 These "scoffers" may have been the Gnostics (see "The Gnostics and Their Scriptures" on p. 2029), who resisted the ideas of a time of judgment and of moral accountability.

THE NEW TESTAMENT CANON

2 PETER 3 The process of determining which texts would comprise the Biblical **canon**[1] (the standard of authoritative and normative teaching for the church) took place over several centuries. Beginning in the first century A.D., Christian communities recognized the authority of texts that they gathered into collections for circulation and use in public worship.[2] Second Peter already suggests a familiarity with multiple letters of Paul and goes so far as to place them on par with the Hebrew Scriptures (3:16). Evidence reveals that during public worship Christians in the earliest centuries read from the texts that would become the New Testament, just as they did from the Hebrew Scriptures.

Scholars often attribute the creation of the New Testament canon to the heretic Marcion, who accepted only the authority of Paul's letters and of Luke. In reality, the churches already accepted these texts as authoritative, and Marcion was attempting to exclude the acceptance of any others. The Muratorian Canon (date uncertain), an early attempt to establish a list of canonical books, did not include most of the general epistles. By the fourth century the churches were seeking to compile a definitive list of New Testament books. Eusebius, Athanasius and the Councils of Laodicea (363), Hippo (393) and Carthage (397) created such lists (both of the latter two accepted the 27 books of the New Testament the church now acknowledges). In some sense these lists merely ratified the church's practice by identifying the texts that were already functioning in an authoritative manner. Twenty-seven writings, including the Gospels, Acts and the New Testament letters, formed the New Testament canon and ultimately defined the church's identity.

The selection process considered three key criteria for the acceptance of a particular text as canonical:

◆ Writings in the canon had to reflect orthodox teaching. Texts that were determined to contain teaching incongruent with that of the earliest Christians were not to be included.[3]

◆ The canon sought to include the earliest, most accurate accounts about Jesus and about the early church by selecting texts that had been written either by the apostles themselves or by those who were closely associated with them. Texts claiming apostolic authorship were critically inspected, and if the authorship claim was suspect, the were rejected. The Gospels of Mark and Luke received canonical status because they were written by a companion of Peter and a coworker of Paul, respectively. The book of Acts, also written by Luke, was also accepted as canonical. The other two Gospels, the Epistles and the book of Revelation all have clear apostolic connections.[4]

◆ Texts that were popular in only one region were viewed as doubtful, while those that had found widespread acceptance, both in the east and in Rome, were included in the canon. The writings chosen for the canon were understood to have universal application. For instance, although Paul addressed his letters to specific communities, others quickly acknowledged that his teaching was relevant to them as well.

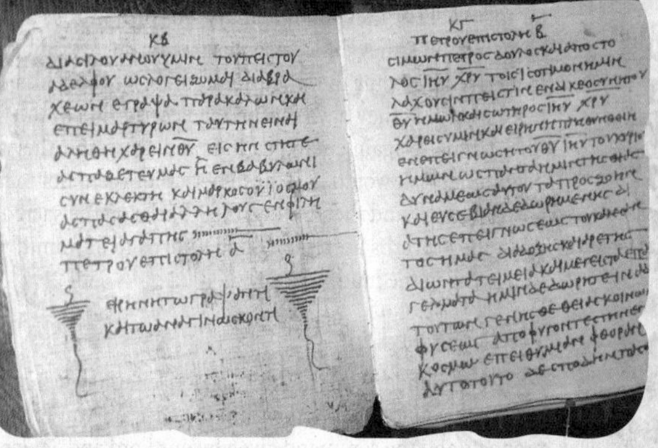

Facsimile leaf of the second letter of Peter on papyrus (p[72]); C. A.D. 200

© Dr. James C. Martin

Other Christian writings circulated alongside the canonical texts. Among these, the Shepherd of Hermas and the Epistle to Barnabas were held in high esteem by some Christians but were eventually rejected from the canon because of their distance from the apostles and the apostolic age. Although these texts were not canonized for reading in the public assembly of the church, they were not condemned as heretical. Texts of this sort continued to be used by Christians for personal devotions and reflections, but without the same authority as the canonical writings.[5]

[1]See Glossary on page 2080 for definitions of bolded words. [2]See "The New Testament Texts" on page 1859. [3]See "Early Christian Heresies" on page 1896. [4]See "The Historical Value of Luke–Acts" on page 1697, "Can John's Gospel Be Trusted?" on page 1761 and "Who Wrote Revelation?" on page 2060. [5]For other noncanonical texts by early Christians, see also "The Bible and Pseudepigraphical Literature" on page 2041.

everything goes on as it has since the beginning of creation."[o] 5But they deliberately forget that long ago
by God's word[p] the heavens existed and the earth was formed out of water and by water.[q] 6By these wa-
ters also the world of that time was deluged and destroyed.[r] 7By the same word the present heavens and
earth are reserved for fire,[s] being kept for the day of judgment and destruction of ungodly men.
8But do not forget this one thing, dear friends: With the Lord a day is like a thousand years, and a
thousand years are like a day.[t] 9The Lord is not slow in keeping his promise,[u] as some understand slow-
ness. He is patient[v] with you, not wanting anyone to perish, but everyone to come to repentance.[w]
10But the day of the Lord will come like a thief.[x] The heavens will disappear with a roar; the elements
will be destroyed by fire, and the earth and everything in it will be laid bare.[a][y]
11Since everything will be destroyed in this way, what kind of people ought you to be? You ought to live
holy and godly lives 12as you look forward[z] to the day of God and speed its coming.[b][a] That day will bring
about the destruction of the heavens by fire, and the elements will melt in the heat.[b] 13But in keeping with
his promise we are looking forward to a new heaven and a new earth,[c] the home of righteousness.
14So then, dear friends, since you are looking forward to this, make every effort to be found spotless,
blameless[d] and at peace with him. 15Bear in mind that our Lord's patience[e] means salvation,[f] just as our
dear brother Paul also wrote you with the wisdom that God gave him.[g] 16He writes the same way in all
his letters, speaking in them of these matters. His letters contain some things that are hard to under-
stand, which ignorant and unstable[h] people distort, as they do the other Scriptures,[i] to their own de-
struction.
17Therefore, dear friends, since you already know this, be on your guard[j] so that you may not be car-
ried away by the error[k] of lawless men and fall from your secure position.[l] 18But grow in the grace and
knowledge of our Lord and Savior Jesus Christ.[m] To him be glory both now and forever! Amen.

3:4 [o]Mk 10:6
3:5 [p]Ge 1:6,9; Heb 11:3 [q]Ps 24:2
3:6 [r]Ge 7:21,22
3:7 [s]ver 10,12; 2Th 1:7
3:8 [t]Ps 90:4
3:9 [u]Hab 2:3; Heb 10:37 [v]Ro 2:4 [w]1Ti 2:4
3:10 [x]Lk 12:39; 1Th 5:2 [y]Mt 24:35; Rev 21:1
3:12 [z]1Co 1:7 [a]Ps 50:3 [b]ver 10
3:13 [c]Isa 65:17; 66:22; Rev 21:1
3:14 [d]1Th 3:13
3:15 [e]Ro 2:4 [f]ver 9 [g]Eph 3:3
3:16 [h]2Pe 2:14 [i]ver 2
3:17 [j]1Co 10:12 [k]2Pe 2:18 [l]Rev 2:5
3:18 [m]2Pe 1:11

[a] 10 Some manuscripts *be burned up* [b] 12 Or *as you wait eagerly for the day of God to come*

3:10 In the first century A.D. the term "elements" referred to such entities as earth, air, fire and water.

3:15 It has been suggested that what Paul wrote to the recipients of 2 Peter may have been a copy of Romans, which would have been sent to the churches as a circular letter.

3:16 Peter placed Paul's letters on the same level of authority as the inspired writings of the Old Testament. (See "The Old Testament Canon" on p. 1552 and "The New Testament Canon" on p. 2022.)

INTRODUCTION TO 1 John

AUTHOR, PLACE AND DATE OF WRITING

First John does not name its author but has an enormous number of similarities to the Gospel of John (e.g., cf. 1Jn 1:1 and Jn 1:1; 1Jn 1:4 and Jn 16:24; 1Jn 2:7 and Jn 13:34–35; 1Jn 4:6 and Jn 8:47; 1Jn 5:12 and Jn 3:36). Although some scholars have sought to point out differences between the Gospel and the epistle, the commonalities far outweigh the dissimilarities. In addition, the author of the epistle declared himself to have seen and touched Jesus (1:1).

There is no indication of when the book was written. However, since the author appears to have been elderly (note his repeatedly reference to his original readers as "children"; see 2:1; 3:7), many believe that this letter was written near the end of the first century. The possibility that the epistle was written to oppose an early form of Gnosticism, a second-century heresy, supports this dating. Ephesus has been suggested as the place of writing.

AUDIENCE

First John was apparently intended to be a circular letter; it does not specify any recipients or refer to any geographic locations. The earliest confirmed use of 1 John was in the Roman province of Asia (in modern Turkey), where Ephesus was located.

CULTURAL FACTS AND HIGHLIGHTS

First John 4:2 is the clearest indication that a kind of proto-Gnostic teaching may have been the heresy John was confronting. Because Gnostics considered physical matter to be innately evil, they could not comprehend the incarnation. For them, the divine *Logos* ("Word") could not possibly have become flesh. Gnosticism denies the need for an incarnation or an atonement (the implied assertion that Jesus had a physical body in 1Jn 1:1 may also be set against Gnostic teaching; see "The Gnostics and Their Scriptures" on p. 2029).

If John were confronting Gnosticism, however, readers might expect a more complete refutation of its doctrines. First John is surely nothing like the anti-Gnostic texts we see from the second century (such as Irenaeus's *Against Heresies*). It seems best to suggest that John was aware of a rising tendency toward anti-incarnational thinking among some who called themselves Christians but that his letter is a general exhortation toward godliness.

TIMELINE

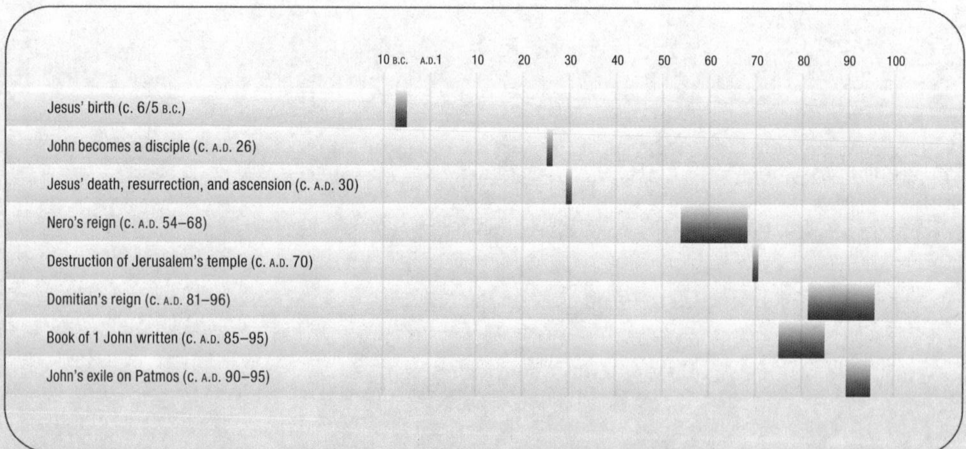

AS YOU READ

Look for John's call for Christians to live in a godly manner: turning from sin, obeying God's commands, showing love to other believers, abandoning worldly glory and holding fast to orthodox teachings about Jesus Christ.

DID YOU KNOW?

- The Gnostics denied that their immoral actions were sinful (1:10).
- The Gnostics insisted that the teaching of the apostles was to be supplemented with the "higher knowledge" they claimed to possess (2:27).
- The Gnostics taught that the divine Christ came upon the human Jesus at his baptism and then left him at the cross, so that it was only the man Jesus who died (4:2).

THEMES

First John includes the following themes:

1. *The incarnation.* John wrote this epistle to warn Christians of false teachers, or "antichrists" (2:18), from within the church who denied that Jesus had come in the flesh (2:22; 4:2–3). John insisted that Christ is not some supernatural apparition disguised as a human but a historical person, Jesus of Nazareth. The test of Biblical Christianity is belief in the full humanity and full divinity of Jesus Christ.

2. *Love.* The key command of this beautiful little book is the call to love (3:11,23; 4:11,21). Christians are to follow Christ's example by loving one another (3:10–11) and caring for those in need (3:17), even to the point of laying down their lives for one another (3:16). Since "love comes from God" (4:7), genuine love can only be expressed as God lives in us (4:12) and we in him (4:16).

3. *Christian certainties.* John asserted that Christians can be certain of the following: (1) Jesus is the Son of God (5:5). (2) Believers have eternal life through him (5:11). (3) God hears and answers their prayers (5:14). (4) They are no longer in bondage to sin but are kept safe by God from the evil one (5:18). (5) They are children of God (5:19). (6) They can know God through his Son, Jesus Christ (5:20). (7) Jesus is "the true God" (5:20).

OUTLINE

- I. The Reality of the Incarnation (1:1–4)
- II. Fellowship With the Father and the Son (1:5—2:28)
  - A. Walking in the Light as the Basis of Fellowship (1:5—2:11)
  - B. A Digression (2:12–14)
  - C. Love of the World as a Hindrance to Fellowship (2:15–17)
  - D. Denial of Christ as a Hindrance to Fellowship (2:18–28)
- III. Children of God (2:29—4:6)
  - A. What a Child of God Looks Like (2:29—3:24)
  - B. What a Child of God Knows (4:1–6)
- IV. God Is Love (4:7—5:12)
- V. Great Christian Certainties (5:13–21)

The Word of Life

1 That which was from the beginning,[a] which we have heard, which we have seen with our eyes,[b]
which we have looked at and our hands have touched[c]—this we proclaim concerning the Word of
life. 2 The life appeared;[d] we have seen it and testify to it, and we proclaim to you the eternal life, which
was with the Father and has appeared to us. 3 We proclaim to you what we have seen and heard, so that
you also may have fellowship with us. And our fellowship is with the Father and with his Son, Jesus
Christ.[e] 4 We write this[f] to make our[*a*] joy complete.[g]

Walking in the Light

5 This is the message we have heard[h] from him and declare to you: God is light; in him there is no
darkness at all. 6 If we claim to have fellowship with him yet walk in the darkness,[i] we lie and do not live
by the truth.[j] 7 But if we walk in the light, as he is in the light, we have fellowship with one another, and
the blood of Jesus, his Son, purifies us from all[*b*] sin.[k]
8 If we claim to be without sin,[l] we deceive ourselves and the truth is not in us.[m] 9 If we confess our sins,
he is faithful and just and will forgive us our sins[n] and purify us from all unrighteousness. 10 If we claim
we have not sinned, we make him out to be a liar[o] and his word has no place in our lives.[p]
2 My dear children,[q] I write this to you so that you will not sin. But if anybody does sin, we have one
who speaks to the Father in our defense[r]—Jesus Christ, the Righteous One. 2 He is the atoning sac-
rifice for our sins,[s] and not only for ours but also for[*c*] the sins of the whole world.
3 We know that we have come to know him if we obey his commands.[t] 4 The man who says, "I know
him," but does not do what he commands is a liar, and the truth is not in him.[u] 5 But if anyone obeys his
word,[v] God's love[*d*] is truly made complete in him.[w] This is how we know we are in him: 6 Whoever claims
to live in him must walk as Jesus did.[x]
7 Dear friends, I am not writing you a new command but an old one, which you have had since the
beginning.[y] This old command is the message you have heard. 8 Yet I am writing you a new command;[z]
its truth is seen in him and you, because the darkness is passing[a] and the true light[b] is already shining.[c]
9 Anyone who claims to be in the light but hates his brother is still in the darkness. 10 Whoever loves
his brother lives in the light,[d] and there is nothing in him[*e*] to make him stumble. 11 But whoever hates his
brother is in the darkness and walks around in the darkness; he does not know where he is going, be-
cause the darkness has blinded him.[e]

12 I write to you, dear children,
because your sins have been forgiven on account of his name.
13 I write to you, fathers,
because you have known him who is from the beginning.
I write to you, young men,
because you have overcome the evil one.[f]
I write to you, dear children,
because you have known the Father.
14 I write to you, fathers,
because you have known him who is from the beginning.
I write to you, young men,
because you are strong,[g]

1:1 [a]Jn 1:2 [b]Jn 1:14; 2Pe 1:16 [c]Jn 20:27
1:2 [d]Jn 1:1-4; 1Ti 3:16
1:3 [e]1Co 1:9
1:4 [f]1Jn 2:1 [g]Jn 3:29
1:5 [h]1Jn 3:11
1:6 [i]2Co 6:14 [j]Jn 3:19-21
1:7 [k]Heb 9:14; Rev 1:5
1:8 [l]Pr 20:9; Jas 3:2 [m]1Jn 2:4
1:9 [n]Ps 32:5; 51:2
1:10 [o]1Jn 5:10 [p]1Jn 2:14
2:1 [q]ver 12,13,28 [r]Ro 8:34; Heb 7:25
2:2 [s]Ro 3:25
2:3 [t]Jn 14:15
2:4 [u]1Jn 1:6,8
2:5 [v]Jn 14:21,23 [w]1Jn 4:12
2:6 [x]Mt 11:29; 1Pe 2:21
2:7 [y]1Jn 3:11,23; 2Jn 5,6
2:8 [z]Jn 13:34 [a]Ro 13:12 [b]Jn 1:9 [c]Eph 5:8; 1Th 5:5
2:10 [d]1Jn 3:14
2:11 [e]Jn 12:35
2:13 [f]ver 14
2:14 [g]Eph 6:10

[*a*] 4 Some manuscripts *your* [*b*] 7 Or *every* [*c*] 2 Or *He is the one who turns aside God's wrath, taking away our sins, and not only ours but also* [*d*] 5 Or *word, love for God* [*e*] 10 Or *it*

1:1 At the outset, John contracted the heresy of the Gnostics (see the note on 2:3) by testifying that the one who has existed from eternity "became flesh" (Jn 1:14).

1:10 The Gnostics (see the note on 2:3) denied that their immoral actions were sinful.

2:3 Forty-two times John used two Greek verbs ordinarily translated "know." One of these verbs is related to the name of the Gnostics, the heretical sect that claimed to have a special knowledge (Greek *gnosis*) of God (see "The Gnostics and Their Scriptures" on p. 2029).

2:7 We cannot be sure whether this letter was written before or after John's Gospel. Tradition says that the Gospel was written late in the life of John, toward the end of the first century. Evidences of a late date for the letter are (1) that Christianity had apparently been so long in existence that its precepts could be spoken of as an "old command" and (2) signs that the Gnostic movement had begun, although it was not yet fully developed.

2:9 For "brother," see the note on Romans 1:13.

2:12–14 "Dear children" (v. 12–13), as elsewhere in this letter, probably refers to all of John's readers, including fathers and young men. The terms "fathers" and "young men" may, however, describe two different levels of spiritual maturity. Some hold that all three terms refer to degrees of maturity in the faith.

2:14 [h]Jn 5:38; 1Jn 1:10 [i]ver 13

and the word of God lives in you,[h]
and you have overcome the evil one.[i]

Do Not Love the World

2:15 [j]Ro 12:2 [k]Jas 4:4
2:16 [l]Ro 13:14 [m]Pr 27:20
2:17 [n]1Co 7:31

15 Do not love the world or anything in the world.[j] If anyone loves the world, the love of the Father is
not in him.[k] 16 For everything in the world—the cravings of sinful man,[l] the lust of his eyes[m] and the
boasting of what he has and does—comes not from the Father but from the world. 17 The world and its
desires pass away,[n] but the man who does the will of God lives forever.

Warning Against Antichrists

2:18 [o]ver 22; 1Jn 4:3; 2Jn 7 [p]1Jn 4:1
2:19 [q]Ac 20:30 [r]1Co 11:19
2:20 [s]2Co 1:21 [t]Mk 1:24 [u]Jn 14:26
2:21 [v]2Pe 1:12; Jude 5
2:22 [w]2Jn 7
2:23 [x]Jn 8:19; 1Jn 4:15
2:24 [y]Jn 14:23
2:26 [z]2Jn 7
2:27 [a]ver 20

18 Dear children, this is the last hour; and as you have heard that the antichrist is coming,[o] even now
many antichrists have come.[p] This is how we know it is the last hour. 19 They went out from us,[q] but they
did not really belong to us. For if they had belonged to us, they would have remained with us; but their
going showed that none of them belonged to us.[r]
20 But you have an anointing[s] from the Holy One,[t] and all of you know the truth.[a][u] 21 I do not write to
you because you do not know the truth, but because you do know it[v] and because no lie comes from the
truth. 22 Who is the liar? It is the man who denies that Jesus is the Christ. Such a man is the antichrist—
he denies the Father and the Son.[w] 23 No one who denies the Son has the Father; whoever acknowledges
the Son has the Father also.[x]
24 See that what you have heard from the beginning remains in you. If it does, you also will remain in
the Son and in the Father.[y] 25 And this is what he promised us—even eternal life.
26 I am writing these things to you about those who are trying to lead you astray.[z] 27 As for you, the
anointing[a] you received from him remains in you, and you do not need anyone to teach you. But as his
anointing teaches you about all things and as that anointing is real, not counterfeit—just as it has taught
you, remain in him.

Children of God

2:28 [b]ver 1 [c]1Jn 3:2 [d]1Jn 4:17 [e]1Th 2:19
2:29 [f]1Jn 3:7

28 And now, dear children,[b] continue in him, so that when he appears[c] we may be confident[d] and un-
ashamed before him at his coming.[e]
29 If you know that he is righteous,[f] you know that everyone who does what is right has been born of
him.

3:1 [g]Jn 3:16 [h]Jn 1:12 [i]Jn 16:3
3:2 [j]Ro 8:29; 2Pe 1:4 [k]2Co 3:18
3:3 [l]2Co 7:1; 2Pe 3:13,14
3:4 [m]1Jn 5:17
3:5 [n]2Co 5:21
3:6 [o]ver 9 [p]3Jn 11 [q]1Jn 2:4
3:7 [r]1Jn 2:1 [s]1Jn 2:26 [t]1Jn 2:29
3:8 [u]Jn 8:44
3:9 [v]Jn 1:13 [w]1Jn 5:18 [x]1Pe 1:23
3:10 [y]1Jn 4:8

3 How great is the love[g] the Father has lavished on us, that we should be called children of God![h] And
that is what we are! The reason the world does not know us is that it did not know him.[i] 2 Dear
friends, now we are children of God, and what we will be has not yet been made known. But we know that
when he appears,[b] we shall be like him,[j] for we shall see him as he is.[k] 3 Everyone who has this hope in
him purifies himself,[l] just as he is pure.
4 Everyone who sins breaks the law; in fact, sin is lawlessness.[m] 5 But you know that he appeared so that
he might take away our sins. And in him is no sin.[n] 6 No one who lives in him keeps on sinning.[o] No one
who continues to sin has either seen him[p] or known him.[q]
7 Dear children,[r] do not let anyone lead you astray.[s] He who does what is right is righteous, just as he
is righteous.[t] 8 He who does what is sinful is of the devil,[u] because the devil has been sinning from the be-
ginning. The reason the Son of God appeared was to destroy the devil's work. 9 No one who is born of God[v]
will continue to sin,[w] because God's seed[x] remains in him; he cannot go on sinning, because he has been
born of God. 10 This is how we know who the children of God are and who the children of the devil are: Any-
one who does not do what is right is not a child of God; nor is anyone who does not love[y] his brother.

Love One Another

3:11 [z]1Jn 1:5 [a]Jn 13:34,35; 2Jn 5
3:12 [b]Ge 4:8

11 This is the message you heard[z] from the beginning: We should love one another.[a] 12 Do not be like
Cain, who belonged to the evil one and murdered his brother.[b] And why did he murder him? Because

[a] 20 Some manuscripts *and you know all things* [b] 2 Or *when it is made known*

2:18 With other New Testament writers, John viewed the whole period beginning with Christ's first coming as the last days (see "Jewish Eschatology in the First Century A.D." on p. 1846).
2:23 See 2 John 9 and its note.
2:27 Gnostic teachers insisted that the teaching of the apostles was to be supplemented with the "higher knowledge" that they (see the note on 2:3) claimed to possess. John's response was that what his readers had been taught under the Spirit's ministry through the apostles was not only adequate but constituted the only reliable truth.
3:1 For "children of God," see the note on Romans 8:15.

his own actions were evil and his brother's were righteous. 13 Do not be surprised, my brothers, if the
world hates you.[c] 14 We know that we have passed from death to life,[d] because we love our brothers. Any-
one who does not love remains in death.[e] 15 Anyone who hates his brother is a murderer,[f] and you know
that no murderer has eternal life in him.[g]

16 This is how we know what love is: Jesus Christ laid down his life for us. And we ought to lay down
our lives for our brothers.[h] 17 If anyone has material possessions and sees his brother in need but has no
pity on him,[i] how can the love of God be in him?[j] 18 Dear children,[k] let us not love with words or tongue
but with actions and in truth.[l] 19 This then is how we know that we belong to the truth, and how we set
our hearts at rest in his presence 20 whenever our hearts condemn us. For God is greater than our hearts,
and he knows everything.

21 Dear friends, if our hearts do not condemn us, we have confidence before God[m] 22 and receive from
him anything we ask,[n] because we obey his commands and do what pleases him.[o] 23 And this is his com-
mand: to believe[p] in the name of his Son, Jesus Christ, and to love one another as he commanded us.[q]
24 Those who obey his commands live in him,[r] and he in them. And this is how we know that he lives in
us: We know it by the Spirit he gave us.[s]

3:13 [c]Jn 15:18, 19; 17:14
3:14 [d]Jn 5:24 [e]1Jn 2:9
3:15 [f]Mt 5:21,22; Jn 8:44 [g]Gal 5:20, 21
3:16 [h]Jn 15:13
3:17 [i]Dt 15:7,8 [j]1Jn 4:20
3:18 [k]1Jn 2:1 [l]Eze 33:31; Ro 12:9
3:21 [m]1Jn 5:14
3:22 [n]Mt 7:7 [o]Jn 8:29
3:23 [p]Jn 6:29 [q]Jn 13:34
3:24 [r]1Jn 2:6 [s]1Jn 4:13

Test the Spirits

4 Dear friends, do not believe every spirit, but test the spirits to see whether they are from God, be-
cause many false prophets have gone out into the world.[t] 2 This is how you can recognize the Spirit
of God: Every spirit that acknowledges that Jesus Christ has come in the flesh[u] is from God,[v] 3 but every
spirit that does not acknowledge Jesus is not from God. This is the spirit of the antichrist,[w] which you
have heard is coming and even now is already in the world.

4 You, dear children, are from God and have overcome them, because the one who is in you[x] is great-
er than the one who is in the world.[y] 5 They are from the world[z] and therefore speak from the viewpoint
of the world, and the world listens to them. 6 We are from God, and whoever knows God listens to us; but
whoever is not from God does not listen to us.[a] This is how we recognize the Spirit[a] of truth[b] and the spir-
it of falsehood.

4:1 [t]2Pe 2:1; 1Jn 2:18
4:2 [u]Jn 1:14; 1Jn 2:23 [v]1Co 12:3
4:3 [w]1Jn 2:22; 2Jn 7
4:4 [x]Ro 8:31 [y]Jn 12:31
4:5 [z]Jn 15:19
4:6 [a]Jn 8:47 [b]Jn 14:17

God's Love and Ours

7 Dear friends, let us love one another,[c] for love comes from God.
Everyone who loves has been born of God and knows God.[d] 8 Who-
ever does not love does not know God, because God is love.[e] 9 This
is how God showed his love among us: He sent his one and only Son[b]
into the world that we might live through him.[f] 10 This is love: not
that we loved God, but that he loved us[g] and sent his Son as an aton-
ing sacrifice for[c] our sins.[h] 11 Dear friends, since God so loved us,[i]
we also ought to love one another. 12 No one has ever seen God;[j] but
if we love one another, God lives in us and his love is made complete
in us.[k]

13 We know that we live in him and he in us, because he has giv-
en us of his Spirit.[l] 14 And we have seen and testify[m] that the Father
has sent his Son to be the Savior of the world.[n] 15 If anyone acknowl-
edges that Jesus is the Son of God,[o] God lives in him and he in God.
16 And so we know and rely on the love God has for us.

God is love.[p] Whoever lives in love lives in God, and God in him.[q]
17 In this way, love is made complete[r] among us so that we will have
confidence on the day of judgment, because in this world we are like

4:7 [c]1Jn 3:11 [d]1Jn 2:4
4:8 [e]ver 7,16
4:9 [f]Jn 3:16,17; 1Jn 5:11
4:10 [g]Ro 5:8,10 [h]1Jn 2:2
4:11 [i]Jn 3:16
4:12 [j]Jn 1:18; 1Ti 6:16 [k]1Jn 2:5
4:13 [l]1Jn 3:24
4:14 [m]Jn 15:27 [n]Jn 3:17
4:15 [o]Ro 10:9
4:16 [p]ver 8 [q]1Jn 3:24
4:17 [r]1Jn 2:5

[a] 6 Or *spirit* [b] 9 Or *his only begotten Son* [c] 10 Or *as the one who would turn aside his wrath, taking away*

ANCIENT VOICES

Some people make a habit of going about bearing the Name, but with evil deceit: They do things that are unworthy of God. You must turn from these as you would turn from wild beasts, for they are ravenous dogs that bite secretly. You must be on guard against them; they are almost incurable. There is one physician: He is both flesh and spirit; he is born and unborn; he is God in man; he is true life in death; he is from Mary and from God; he first suffered and then was beyond suffering; he is Jesus Christ our lord.

—IGNATIUS OF ANTIOCH ON FALSE TEACHERS AND ON THE DOCTRINE THAT CHRIST IS BOTH GOD AND MAN

From Ignatius of Antioch (d. c. A.D. 107), *Letter to the Ephesians*, 6, trans. by Duane Garrett

See "The Gnostics and Their Scriptures" article.

3:13 For "brothers," see the note on Romans 1:13.
4:1 False prophets, such as the Gnostics of John's day (see "The Gnostics and Their Scriptures" on p. 2029), speak under the influence of spirits alienated from God.
4:2 The Gnostics taught that the divine Christ came upon the human Jesus at his baptism and then left him at the cross, so that it was only the man Jesus who died.
4:3 For false doctrines, see the note on Colossians 2:8–23.
4:14 For Jesus as Savior, see the note on Luke 2:11.

THE RELIABILITY OF THE BIBLE

THE GNOSTICS AND THEIR SCRIPTURES

1 JOHN 4 Gnosticism was one of the earliest Christian heresies. Gnostic writings are many and varied, frequently drawing upon Platonic concepts, imagery from the New Testament and pagan myth. A number of Gnostic texts were discovered at Nag Hammadi in Egypt in 1945. Many were pseudo-apostolic—falsely ascribed to apostles. Examples include the Gospel of Thomas, the Apocryphon of James and the Letter of Peter to Philip. Certain broad observations can be made of Gnostic literature:

◆ From the Greek word *gnosis*, meaning "knowledge," Gnosticism was a movement that claimed to provide secret knowledge about God. Its adherents considered the Biblical God, the Creator of the world, to be an inferior god. In Gnostic teaching the material world was innately evil and thus its Creator a lesser deity.

◆ The Gnostic Savior, rather than providing atonement for sin, brought the knowledge of humanity's "true" divine origins, thus freeing people from their ignorance and enslavement to the material world.

◆ Some Gnostics believed that "the Christ" (a kind of spiritual anointing or presence) came upon the man Jesus at his baptism and departed before his crucifixion—thus, that there was no lasting union of divine and human natures in Jesus. In their view, the true Christ had no physical body.

◆ One particular brand of Gnostics, called "Docetists," believed that Jesus was actually a divine spirit who only appeared to be physical: His body, they argued, was not truly flesh but was only an illusion. First John 4:2 ("Every spirit that acknowledges that Jesus Christ has come in the flesh is from God") refutes this teaching. Possibly those whom John countered were forerunners of the groups that later wrote the Gnostic texts.

John's warnings indicate that heresy can come in many forms, often in the guise of apostolic teaching. Those who deny the humanity of Jesus are equally as heretical as those who deny his deity. In addition, any doctrine that understands the created, material world to be intrinsically evil is dangerous and misguided.[1]

[1]See also "Early Christian Heresies" on page 1896.

4:18 [s]Ro 8:15 him. 18There is no fear in love. But perfect love drives out fear,[s] because fear has to do with punishment.
The one who fears is not made perfect in love.
4:19 [t]ver 10 **4:20** [u]1Jn 2:9 19We love because he first loved us.[t] 20If anyone says, "I love God," yet hates his brother,[u] he is a liar.[v]
[v]1Jn 2:4 [w]1Jn 3:17 [x]ver 12 For anyone who does not love his brother, whom he has seen,[w] cannot love God, whom he has not seen.[x]
4:21 [y]Mt 5:43 21And he has given us this command: Whoever loves God must also love his brother.[y]

Faith in the Son of God

5:1 [z]1Jn 2:22 [a]Jn 1:13; 5 Everyone who believes that Jesus is the Christ[z] is born of God,[a] and everyone who loves the father
1Jn 2:23 [b]Jn 8:42 loves his child as well.[b] 2This is how we know that we love the children of God: by loving God and
5:3 [c]Jn 14:15; carrying out his commands. 3This is love for God: to obey his commands.[c] And his commands are not
2Jn 6 [d]Mt 11:30 burdensome,[d] 4for everyone born of God overcomes[e] the world. This is the victory that has overcome
5:4 [e]Jn 16:33 the world, even our faith. 5Who is it that overcomes the world? Only he who believes that Jesus is the Son
of God.
5:6 [f]Jn 19:34 [g]Jn 14:17 6This is the one who came by water and blood[f]—Jesus Christ. He did not come by water only, but by
5:7 [h]Mt 18:16 water and blood. And it is the Spirit who testifies, because the Spirit is the truth.[g] 7For there are three[h]

5:1 John wrote at a time when members of a family were closely associated as a unit under the headship of the father. He therefore used the family as an illustration to show that anyone who loves God the Father will naturally love God's children.

5:6 The majority of interpreters see water and blood as summing up the totality of Jesus' humanity and ministry on Earth. His baptism (water) and crucifixion (blood) frame his ministry. John was reacting to the Gnostic heretics of his day who taught that the heavenly Christ descended upon the man Jesus at baptism but departed before he was crucified. Hence, John explained, Jesus came not only by baptismal water but also through the blood of the cross.

that testify: 8 the[a] Spirit, the water and the blood; and the three are in agreement. 9 We accept man's tes-
timony,[i] but God's testimony is greater because it is the testimony of God,[j] which he has given about his
Son. 10 Anyone who believes in the Son of God has this testimony in his heart.[k] Anyone who does not be-
lieve God has made him out to be a liar,[l] because he has not believed the testimony God has given about
his Son. 11 And this is the testimony: God has given us eternal life, and this life is in his Son.[m] 12 He who
has the Son has life; he who does not have the Son of God does not have life.[n]

Concluding Remarks

13 I write these things to you who believe in the name of the Son of God[o] so that you may know that
you have eternal life.[p] 14 This is the confidence[q] we have in approaching God: that if we ask anything ac-
cording to his will, he hears us.[r] 15 And if we know that he hears us—whatever we ask—we know[s] that
we have what we asked of him.

16 If anyone sees his brother commit a sin that does not lead to death, he should pray and God will
give him life.[t] I refer to those whose sin does not lead to death. There is a sin that leads to death.[u] I am
not saying that he should pray about that.[v] 17 All wrongdoing is sin,[w] and there is sin that does not lead
to death.[x]

18 We know that anyone born of God does not continue to sin; the one who was born of God keeps
him safe, and the evil one cannot harm him.[y] 19 We know that we are children of God,[z] and that the whole
world is under the control of the evil one.[a] 20 We know also that the Son of God has come and has given
us understanding,[b] so that we may know him who is true.[c] And we are in him who is true—even in his
Son Jesus Christ. He is the true God and eternal life.[d]

21 Dear children, keep yourselves from idols.[e]

5:9 [i]Jn 5:34 [j]Mt 3:16,17; Jn 8:17,18
5:10 [k]Ro 8:16; Gal 4:6 [l]Jn 3:33
5:11 [m]Jn 1:4; 1Jn 2:25
5:12 [n]Jn 3:15,16, 36
5:13 [o]1Jn 3:23 [p]Jn 20:31; 1Jn 1:1,2
5:14 [q]1Jn 3:21 [r]Mt 7:7
5:15 [s]ver 18,19, 20
5:16 [t]Jas 5:15 [u]Heb 6:4-6; 10:26 [v]Jer 7:16
5:17 [w]1Jn 3:4 [x]1Jn 2:1
5:18 [y]Jn 14:30
5:19 [z]1Jn 4:6 [a]Gal 1:4
5:20 [b]Lk 24:45 [c]Jn 17:3 [d]ver 11
5:21 [e]1Co 10:14; 1Th 1:9

[a] 7,8 Late manuscripts of the Vulgate *testify in heaven: the Father, the Word and the Holy Spirit, and these three are one. 8 And there are three that testify on earth: the* (not found in any Greek manuscript before the fourteenth century)

5:7 The Old Testament law required "two or three witnesses" (Dt 17:6). At the end of this verse, some older English versions add the words found in the NIV text note. But the addition is not found in any Greek manuscript or New Testament translation prior to the fourteenth century. (See "Early Scribal Emendation" on p. 448 and "Textual Criticism" on p. 1151.)

5:16 In the context of this letter, directed against Gnostic teaching, which denied the incarnation and threw off all moral restraints, it is probable that the "sin that leads to death" is a reference to the Gnostics' adamant and persistent denial of the truth and to their shameless immorality.

INTRODUCTION TO 2 John

AUTHOR, PLACE AND DATE OF WRITING

Ancient tradition holds that this letter was written by the apostle John. Second John identifies its author only as the "elder," but the letter has clear affinities with the Gospel of John, as well as with 1 John (e.g., cf. 2Jn 14:23 with 1Jn 5:3). All in all, there is no reason to doubt John's authorship.

The date of composition is unknown, but this short letter was probably written in the late first century A.D. Ephesus has been suggested as the place of writing.

AUDIENCE

This letter is addressed to "the chosen lady" (v. 1), also called "dear lady" (v. 5). This address may be a reference to a particular Christian woman and her family or to an individual, female leader of a house church (see Col 4:15). In the Greek text of verse 8, however, the author referred to the addressee using a masculine plural pronoun, which strongly suggests that the "chosen lady" of verse 1 may be a metaphorical reference to a sister church in a nearby town. In this case, the "children of your chosen sister" (v. 13) would refer to the members of another local church.

CULTURAL FACTS AND HIGHLIGHTS

During the first two centuries the gospel was spread by traveling evangelists and teachers. Since inns were not readily available, believers customarily took these missionaries into their homes and supplied them with provisions for their journey when they were about to leave. John asked his readers to refuse hospitality to false teachers moving about among the churches who did not "acknowledge Jesus Christ as coming in the flesh" (v. 7). This may refer to a very early form of Gnostic teaching (see "The Gnostics and Their Scriptures" on p. 2029).

TIMELINE

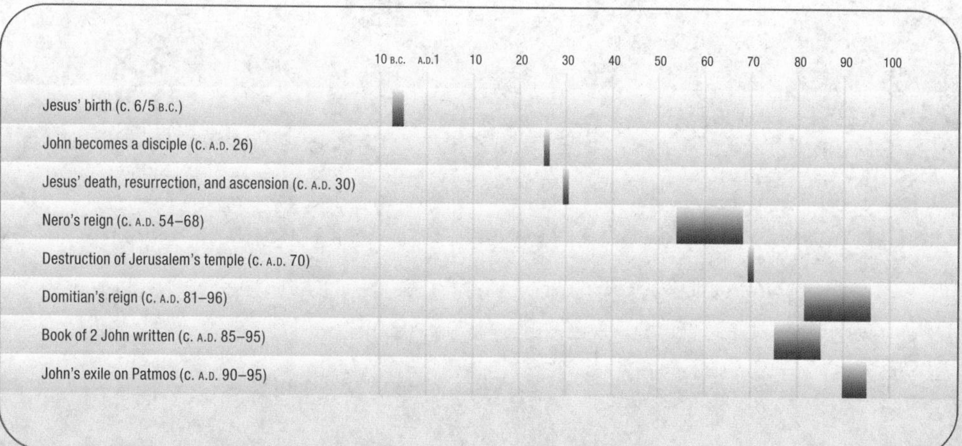

AS YOU READ

Pay attention to John's emphasis on truth and love, and note his warning against false teaching and deceivers.

DID YOU KNOW?

- In his later years the apostle John functioned as an elder, perhaps of the Ephesian church (v. 1).
- The paper of John's day was made from papyrus reeds, which were readily available and inexpensive (v. 12).
- Ink (the Greek term comes from a word that means "black") was made by mixing carbon, water and gum or oil (v. 12).

THEMES

Second John includes the following themes:

1. *Warning against false teaching.* This epistle cautions Christians against the same false teaching John opposed in his first letter (see the introduction to 1Jn).

2. *Truth.* Truth is an important theme in the writings of John—mentioned 52 times in his Gospel and 22 times in his three short epistles.

3. *Love.* Like 1 John, this letter emphasizes the command to love one another—the test of a true believer. John's command to love does not contradict his directive to refuse hospitality to false teachers. Issues of truth are too important to compromise.

OUTLINE

I. Greeting (1–3)
II. Commendation (4)
III. Counsel and Warning (5–11)
IV. Conclusion (12–13)

1:1 [a]3Jn 1 [b]Ro 16:13 [c]Jn 8:32 1 The elder,[a]

To the chosen[b] lady and her children, whom I love in the truth—and not I only, but also all who know
1:2 [d]2Pe 1:12 [e]1Jn 1:8 the truth[c]— 2 because of the truth,[d] which lives in us[e] and will be with us forever:

1:3 [f]Ro 1:7 3 Grace, mercy and peace from God the Father and from Jesus Christ,[f] the Father's Son, will be with
us in truth and love.

1:4 [g]3Jn 3,4 4 It has given me great joy to find some of your children walking in the truth,[g] just as the Father com-
manded us. 5 And now, dear lady, I am not writing you a new command but one we have had from the be-
1:5 [h]1Jn 2:7; 3:11 ginning.[h] I ask that we love one another. 6 And this is love:[i] that we walk in obedience to his commands.
1:6 [i]1Jn 2:5 As you have heard from the beginning, his command is that you walk in love.
1:7 [j]1Jn 2:22; 4:2,3 [k]1Jn 4:1 7 Many deceivers, who do not acknowledge Jesus Christ[j] as coming in the flesh, have gone out into the
[l]1Jn 2:18 world.[k] Any such person is the deceiver and the antichrist.[l] 8 Watch out that you do not lose what you
1:8 [m]1Co 3:8 have worked for, but that you may be rewarded fully.[m] 9 Anyone who runs ahead and does not continue
in the teaching of Christ does not have God; whoever continues in the teaching has both the Father and
1:9 [n]1Jn 2:23 the Son.[n] 10 If anyone comes to you and does not bring this teaching, do not take him into your house or
1:10 [o]Ro 16:17 welcome him.[o] 11 Anyone who welcomes him shares[p] in his wicked work.
1:11 [p]1Ti 5:22 12 I have much to write to you, but I do not want to use paper and ink. Instead, I hope to visit you and
1:12 [q]3Jn 13,14 talk with you face to face,[q] so that our joy may be complete.

1:13 [r]ver 1 13 The children of your chosen[r] sister send their greetings.

---

1 For "elder," see the note on 1 Timothy 3:1. In his later years John functioned as an elder, perhaps of the Ephesian church. The apostle Peter held a similar position (see 1Pe 5:1 and its note).

Second John is addressed to "the chosen lady and her children." Many suppose that the reference is to a church and its spiritual children, while others hold that a particular individual named *Kyria* (Greek for *lady*) is intended.

7–11 This section deals with the basic Gnostic heresy attacked in 1 John (see "The Gnostics and Their Scriptures" on p. 2029): that the Son of God did not become flesh but that he temporarily came upon the man Jesus between his baptism and crucifixion (see the notes on 1Jn 4:2; 5:6).

7 For false doctrines, see the note on Colossians 2:8–23.

9 "The teaching of Christ" probably refers not to teaching given by Christ but to true teaching about Christ.

10 See "House Churches and Early Church Buildings" on page 2033.

12 Paper was made from papyrus reeds, which were readily available and cheap. The ink (the Greek comes from a word that means "black") was made by mixing carbon, water and gum or oil. (See "Writing Materials in the Ancient World" on p. 2037.

House Churches and Early Church Buildings

2 JOHN The earliest Christians gathered for worship and fellowship in private homes. Affluent Christians with more spacious homes generally opened them to their brothers and sisters in Christ. In a context in which Christians frequently faced persecution, there were obvious advantages to meeting in a private setting.[1] This practice is also consistent with kinship language found in the Bible.[2] The New Testament letters mention several of the house churches in which believers congregated:

- Romans 16:5 speaks of several house churches in Rome, and the households mentioned in Romans 16:10–11, as well as the groups in 16:14–15, might indicate the identities of the various homeowners.
- First Corinthians 16:19 tells of a church that met in the house of Aquila and Priscilla.
- Colossians 4:15 reveals that a church gathered in Nympha's home.
- Philemon 2 contains Paul's greetings to the church that met in the home of Philemon, Apphia or Archippus.
- Second John 10–11 warned its readers against bringing false teachers into their houses. This warning may have been a more comprehensive admonition to be cautious not to accept false teachers into the church.[3]

[1]See "The Geographic Expansion of the Church Under Persecution" on page 1781 and "The Early Persecution of the Church" on page 2067. [2]See "Adoption in the Roman World" on page 1849 and "The Love Feast" on page 1874. [3]See "Early Christian Heresies" on page 1896.

INTRODUCTION TO 3 John

AUTHOR, PLACE AND DATE OF WRITING

This brief letter, which is quite similar to 2 John, has traditionally been understood as the work of the apostle John, and there is no reason to doubt the validity of this tradition. Like 1 and 2 John, it was probably written in the late first century from Ephesus.

AUDIENCE

John addressed this letter to his friend Gaius. Gaius was a common Roman name, and it is not known whether the Gaius addressed here is to be identified with any other New Testament individual bearing that name (see Ac 19:29; 20:4; Ro 16:23; 1Co 1:14).

CULTURAL FACTS AND HIGHLIGHTS

Some of John's aides had been commissioned by him to go out and teach in various churches, and they required lodging from the believers in the places where they ministered. Demetrius (v. 12), evidently one of those itinerant ministers, may have been the bearer of John's letter.

In one church, however, a local leader named Diotrephes had refused to admit John's emissaries. John was writing to Gaius, a believer whose loyalty he trusted, to contend that he expected better treatment of his disciples. If Gaius was part of the same congregation as Diotrephes, he was to speak up and put a halt to Diotrephes' domination of the church. If, however, Gaius belonged to another congregation, he was to see to it that Diotrephes' attitude did not gain a foothold in his own church. There is an implied warning that John might come and confront Diotrephes himself—no doubt a potential source of embarrassment to the church.

TIMELINE

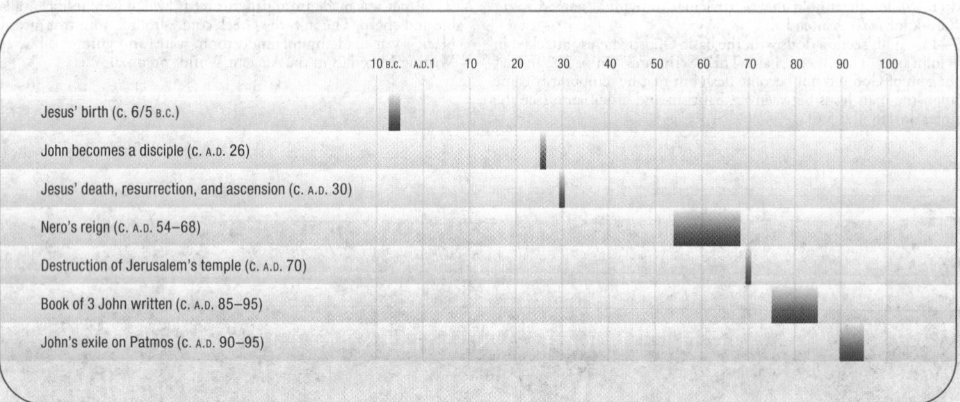

AS YOU READ

Look both for John's commendation of Gaius for his past hospitality and his condemnation of Diotrephes for his mistreatment of fellow believers.

DID YOU KNOW?

- Modern Orthodox Jews often address God by the title *Ha-Shem*, meaning "The Name" (v. 7).

THEMES

Third John includes the following themes:

1. *Hospitality.* John praised Gaius for his hospitality and condemned Diotrephes for refusing to show hospitality to "the brothers." Diotrephes' behavior may, in fact, have been part of what John had in mind when he referred in 1 John 3:15–17 to hating fellow Christians. Itinerant Christian preachers were dependent upon the hospitality of Christians among whom they ministered. This built up networks between the scattered churches and fostered a sense of solidarity. The local churches saw themselves as belonging to the one church, united around the foundational truth of the gospel.
2. *Truth.* Demetrius, who is otherwise unknown, was probably the bearer of this letter. He was to be received, stated John, because he manifested the truth (v. 12). We may assume that Demetrius had passed the ethical tests of faith outlined in 1 John. For further information on John's theme of truth, see the themes listed in the introduction to 2 John.

OUTLINE

I. Greeting (1–2)
II. Commendation of Gaius (3–8)
III. Exhortation to Gaius (9–12)
  A. Diotrephes: a Bad Example (9–11)
  B. Demetrius: a Good Example (12)
IV. Conclusion (13–14)

1 The elder,[a] 1:1 [a]2Jn 1

To my dear friend Gaius, whom I love in the truth.

2 Dear friend, I pray that you may enjoy good health and that all may go well with you, even as your
soul is getting along well. 3 It gave me great joy to have some brothers[b] come and tell about your faithful- 1:3 [b]ver 5,10
ness to the truth and how you continue to walk in the truth.[c] 4 I have no greater joy than to hear that my [c]2Jn 4
children[d] are walking in the truth. 1:4 [d]1Co 4:15;
5 Dear friend, you are faithful in what you are doing for the brothers, even though they are strangers 1Jn 2:1
to you.[e] 6 They have told the church about your love. You will do well to send them on their way in a man- 1:5 [e]Ro 12:13;
ner worthy of God. 7 It was for the sake of the Name[f] that they went out, receiving no help from the pa- Heb 13:2 1:7 [f]Jn 15:21
gans.[g] 8 We ought therefore to show hospitality to such men so that we may work together for the truth. [g]Ac 20:33,35
9 I wrote to the church, but Diotrephes, who loves to be first, will have nothing to do with us. 10 So if I
come,[h] I will call attention to what he is doing, gossiping maliciously about us. Not satisfied with that, 1:10 [h]2Jn 12
he refuses to welcome the brothers.[i] He also stops those who want to do so and puts them out of the [i]ver 5 [j]Jn 9:22,34
church.[j]
11 Dear friend, do not imitate what is evil but what is good.[k] Anyone who does what is good is from 1:11 [k]Ps 37:27
God.[l] Anyone who does what is evil has not seen God.[m] 12 Demetrius is well spoken of by everyone[n]— [l]1Jn 2:29 [m]1Jn 3:6,9,10
and even by the truth itself. We also speak well of him, and you know that our testimony is true.[o] 1:12 [n]1Ti 3:7 [o]Jn 21:24
13 I have much to write you, but I do not want to do so with pen and ink. 14 I hope to see you soon, and
we will talk face to face.[p] 1:14 [p]2Jn 12 [q]Jn 10:3

Peace to you. The friends here send their greetings. Greet the friends there by name.[q]

---

1 For "elder," see the note on 2 John 1.
Gaius was a common Roman name. This particular Gaius, a Christian in one of the churches of the province of Asia, was standing firm while his community was struggling under the pressure of a single antagonist, Diotrephes, a powerful church leader who had gained control and rejected John's authority. The Christian community under John's influence was evidently made up of scattered congregations that had brought in some converts who had no knowledge of apostolic tradition. When a source of authority—like the apostle John—stepped forward, some resisted submitting.

4 "My children" may refer either to John's converts or to believers currently under his spiritual guidance.

7 For "the Name," see the note on Jeremiah 16:21. Today Orthodox Jews often address God by the title *Ha-Shem* ("The Name").

9 John was alluding to a previous letter from himself that is now lost.
Diotrephes must have had considerable influence since he was able to exclude people from the church fellowship (see v. 10).

10 "Puts them out of the church" refers to excommunication (see the notes on Jn 9:22; 1Ti 1:20).

12 Demetrius may have been the bearer of this letter.

Writing Materials in the Ancient World

3 JOHN John's statement that he was writing "with pen and ink" (3Jn 13) sounds modern, but in fact ancient people used writing materials that were far removed from what we think of as pen and paper. Ancient texts were written on the following materials:

✣ *Stone*. This could be ordinary limestone or sandstone, or, for a small inscription, a semiprecious stone such as amethyst, turquoise or opal. The writing tool could be a chisel or metal stylus, but sometimes people wrote on stone with ink. In some instances the stone was covered with a coat of plaster, as in Deuteronomy 27:2–3. Stone, including marble, was widely used for monumental inscriptions describing the feats of kings,[1] but simple graffiti was also cut into stone.

✣ *Metal*. This material was primarily used for commemorative and decorative objects, such as for inscriptions on a silver bowl. Two silver **amulets**[2] inscribed with the text of Numbers 6:24–27 were discovered near Jerusalem,[3] while a copper scroll was located at **Qumran**.

✣ *Wooden Tablets*. These could be coated with wax or stucco for the writing surface. Wax was especially useful since one could inscribe it with a pointed stylus and then rub out the writing and reuse the tablet.

✣ *Clay Tablets*. Clay was the medium for **cuneiform**. While still moist, it would be inscribed with a sharpened stick to create the distinctive, wedge-shaped cuneiform script. If baked, tablets became virtually indestructible, and thus many have survived through the centuries.[4]

Inkwell from the Scriptorium of Khirbet, Qumran (site of the Dead Sea Scrolls); pre-A.D. 68

© The Schøyen Collection; photography courtesy of Mr. Martin Schøyen

✣ *Ostraca*. An ostracon is a common potsherd (a broken piece of pottery). It could be inscribed with a metal stylus or written on with ink.[5] Ostraca were handy for short notes and letters. In Athens voters used them to write down the name of a citizen they wanted to send into exile or to "ostracize" (hence the name).

✣ *Leather*. Leather pages are often referred to as vellum or parchment. In Israel leather was the medium of choice for writing the books of the Scriptures. The Isaiah scroll from Qumran, for example, is composed of leather, with the writing done in black ink.[6]

✣ *Papyrus*. This was the closest thing to paper from the ancient world. The Egyptian **papyrus** plant was cut into strips and pressed into sheets that were then glued together. This made for a strong, smooth writing surface, and papyrus naturally became very popular in the ancient world.[7] The ink on a papyrus could be erased and the papyrus reused; an erased and reused papyrus document is called a *palimpsest*.

✣ *Scrolls and Codices*. For almost all of Biblical history, papyrus or leather was formed into long strips and rolled up on scrolls. However, around the first century A.D. people began to stitch together one side of a group of papyrus or leather leaves to create the equivalent of the modern book, called a **codex**. The early Christians adopted the idea of the codex, and thus most early Christian Bibles are in the form of codices rather than scrolls.[8]

Ink pot from Qumran

Preserving Bible Times; © Dr. James C. Martin; permission of The Amman Museum

✣ *Ink*. John specifically mentioned "ink." In the ancient world ink was usually black, made from carbon mixed with a natural gum. Red ink, however, was also widely used.

The literacy rate was especially high in the Greco-Roman world, and writing materials, although difficult to work with by modern standards, were widely available. Letter writing was common,[9] and the relative ease of communication facilitated the missionary and pastoral work of the apostles.

[1]See "The Mesha (Moabite) Stone" on page 530. [2]See Glossary on page 2080 for definitions of bolded words. [3]See "The Ketef Hinnom Amulets" on page 204. [4]See "Cuneiform and Clay Tablets in the Ancient Near East" on page 1108. [5]See "The Samaria Ostraca" on page 550. [6]See "The Great Isaiah Scroll" on page 1115. [7]See "John Rylands Papyrus (p^{52})" on page 1755. [8]See "Scrolls, Seals and Codices" on page 2053. [9]See "Letter Writing in the Greco-Roman World" on page 1889.

INTRODUCTION TO *Jude*

AUTHOR, PLACE AND DATE OF WRITING

The author of Jude called himself "a brother of James" (v. 1). The most well-known James of the early church was James, the Lord's brother (see the introduction to the book of James). Mark 6:3 mentions both James and Jude (Greek "Judas") among the members of Jesus' immediate family (see "The Family of Joseph, Mary and Jesus" on p. 1581). It should be noted that neither James nor Jude ever referred to himself as Jesus' brother (most likely a demonstration of reverence), but others did not hesitate to speak of them in this way (see Mt 13:55; Jn 7:3–10; Ac 1:14; 1Co 9:5; Gal 1:19).

Some Biblical scholars deny that Jude wrote this letter, primarily on the grounds that its Greek is too articulate to have come from a Galilean, but this falsely assumes that the Galileans were semiliterate and lacking in contact with Hellenistic culture. Tiberias, on the western shore of the Sea of Galilee, was a thoroughly Hellenistic city, and its presence in the region illustrates that the broader culture of the Greco-Roman world was never far away.

Many believe that 2 Peter borrowed and modified material from Jude (see the introduction to 2Pe). If this was indeed the case, and if 2 Peter was written about A.D. 64–68, as appears probable, then Jude was obviously written before A.D. 68. The apparent borrowing, however, may have gone the other way around.

AUDIENCE

All that is known of the original recipients of this letter is that they were Christians (v. 1). Verse 3 may indicate that Jude knew them personally; from this some infer that the letter was more than simply a pamphlet addressed to a number of churches or to all Christians everywhere.

CULTURAL FACTS AND HIGHLIGHTS

The tone of the letter suggests that its author was alarmed, and verse 3 indicates that the epistle was written in some haste. Jude clearly wanted to warn his readers to beware of false brothers who were infiltrating the churches, creating an irreverent atmosphere, causing divisions and disseminating doubt and cynicism. Their motivation was greed and lust.

Interpreters have naturally tried to identify these false brothers, but Jude was not specific about them. It may be that he was dismayed over an increasing trend toward worldliness and the presence of a significant number of unconverted people within the churches.

AS YOU READ

Notice the similarities between Jude and 2 Peter. Watch for references to the noncanonical works titled the Testament of Moses (also called the Assumption of Moses; v. 9) and the book of Enoch (v. 14). For a better understanding of these texts, see "The Bible and Pseudepigraphical Literature" on page 2041.

DID YOU KNOW?

- The book of Jude was regarded by the second-century church father Origen as "of but few verses yet full of mighty words of heavenly wisdom" (vv. 1–12).
- Jude, like his brothers, did not believe in Jesus during his earthly ministry but became his follower after the resurrection (v. 1).
- Both James and Jude in the opening of their New Testament lettters referred to themselves as servants of Jesus Christ rather than as his brothers in the flesh (v. 1).
- Two of Jude's grandsons were brought before the emperor Domitian as descendants of David, but both were dismissed as harmless peasants (v. 1).

THEMES

The book of Jude includes the following themes:

1. *Warning against false teachers.* Jude's primary focus was the ethical dangers posed by false teachers who denied Christ's lordship by using Christian freedom and God's grace as a "license for immorality" (v. 4). These false teachers were "grumblers and faultfinders" (v. 16), scoffers who followed their own ungodly desires and natural instincts (vv. 18–19).

2. *Christian behavior.* Jude's letter emphasizes the lordship of Christ (vv. 4,9,14–15,25). Christian freedom is not a hall pass to do whatever one wishes. Christians are to build themselves up in the foundational teachings of the faith, pray, remain faithful to God and be merciful to others.

OUTLINE

I. Introduction (1–2)
II. Occasion for the Letter (3–4)
III. Warning Against False Teachers (5–16)
IV. Exhortation to Believers (17–23)
V. Concluding Doxology (24–25)

ANCIENT VOICES

Azazel taught people to make swords and weapons and shields and breastplates (these were the teachings of angels) and showed them mines and the working of them, as well as bracelets, cosmetics, eyeshadow and beautification for the eyelids, and all kinds of precious stones, and all materials useful for making dyes. And much ungodliness came about. They committed fornication and were led astray, and they became corrupt in all their ways. Semiaza taught enchantments and the use of root-cuttings, Armaros taught the undoing of enchantments, Barakial taught astrology, Chochiel taught the interpretation of signs, Sathiel taught the observation of stars, and Sariel taught the phases of the moon. Then the outcry of people who were perishing went up to heaven.

—HOW DEMONS TAUGHT ARTS AND CRAFTS TO HUMANS, ACCORDING TO 1 ENOCH
From 1 Enoch 8:1–4, trans. by Duane Garrett

See "The Bible and Pseudepigraphical Literature" article.

1 Jude,[a] a servant of Jesus Christ and a brother of James,

To those who have been called,[b] who are loved by God the Father
and kept by[a] Jesus Christ:[c]

2 Mercy, peace and love be yours in abundance.[d]

The Sin and Doom of Godless Men

3 Dear friends, although I was very eager to write to you about the
salvation we share,[e] I felt I had to write and urge you to contend[f] for
the faith that was once for all entrusted to the saints. 4 For certain
men whose condemnation was written about[b] long ago have secret-
ly slipped in among you.[g] They are godless men, who change the
grace of our God into a license for immorality and deny Jesus Christ
our only Sovereign and Lord.[h]
5 Though you already know all this, I want to remind you that the
Lord[c] delivered his people out of Egypt, but later destroyed those
who did not believe.[i] 6 And the angels who did not keep their posi-
tions of authority but abandoned their own home—these he has
kept in darkness, bound with everlasting chains for judgment on the
great Day.[j] 7 In a similar way, Sodom and Gomorrah and the sur-
rounding towns[k] gave themselves up to sexual immorality and per-
version. They serve as an example of those who suffer the punish-
ment of eternal fire.[l]
8 In the very same way, these dreamers pollute their own bodies,
reject authority and slander celestial beings.[m] 9 But even the arch-
angel Michael,[n] when he was disputing with the devil about the
body of Moses, did not dare to bring a slanderous accusation against him, but said, "The Lord rebuke
you!"[o] 10 Yet these men speak abusively against whatever they do not understand; and what things they
do understand by instinct, like unreasoning animals—these are the very things that destroy them.[p]
11 Woe to them! They have taken the way of Cain;[q] they have rushed for profit into Balaam's error;[r]
they have been destroyed in Korah's rebellion.[s]
12 These men are blemishes at your love feasts,[t] eating with you without the slightest qualm—shep-
herds who feed only themselves. They are clouds without rain,[u] blown along by the wind;[v] autumn trees,

1:1 [a]Mt 13:55; Ac 1:13 [b]Ro 1:6,7 [c]Jn 17:12
1:2 [d]2Pe 1:2
1:3 [e]Tit 1:4 [f]1Ti 6:12
1:4 [g]Gal 2:4 [h]Tit 1:16; 2Pe 2:1
1:5 [i]Nu 14:29; Ps 106:26
1:6 [j]2Pe 2:4,9
1:7 [k]Dt 29:23 [l]2Pe 2:6
1:8 [m]2Pe 2:10
1:9 [n]Da 10:13,21 [o]Zec 3:2
1:10 [p]2Pe 2:12
1:11 [q]Ge 4:3-8; 1Jn 3:12 [r]2Pe 2:15 [s]Nu 16:1-3,31-35
1:12 [t]2Pe 2:13; 1Co 11:20-22 [u]Pr 25:14; 2Pe 2:17 [v]Eph 4:14

[a] *1* Or *for*; or *in* [b] *4* Or *men who were marked out for condemnation* [c] *5* Some early manuscripts *Jesus*

1-12 The book of Jude was regarded by the second-century church father Origen as "of but few verses yet full of mighty words of heavenly wisdom."

1 There are six different persons named Judas (the Greek form of the Hebrew name Judah or Jude) in the New Testament, but the author of this letter was almost certainly Jesus' brother (see Mk 6:3, where he is called "Judas"; see also "The Family of Joseph, Mary and Jesus" on p. 1581). Both James and Jude in the opening of their New Testament letters demonstrated their Christian humility and their faith in the deity of Jesus by referring to themselves as servants of Jesus Christ, rather than as his brothers in the flesh. Beyond this we know of Jude from Scripture only that, like his brothers, he did not believe in Jesus during his earthly ministry (Jn 7:5) but became his follower after the resurrection (Ac 1:14). Hegesippus (c. A.D. 11–c. 180) stated that two of Jude's grandsons were brought before the emperor Domitian as descendants of David but that both were dismissed as harmless peasants.

4 Jude implied that the false teachers claimed to be Christian but noted that they somehow abused the grace of God in Christ. Accusations about their immoral lifestyle lay at the heart of his critique.

6 A popular tradition about angels who had sinned was associated with the reference in Genesis 6:1–4 to the "sons of God" who had come down to Earth and cohabitated with the "daughters of men" (see the note on 2Pe 2:4). Jewish interpreters had built an extensive story, identifying the "sons of God" as angels and attributing much evil in our world to their influence. These stories were elaborated in 1 Enoch, a pseudepigraphical book (see the note on vv. 14–15 and "The Bible and Pseudepigraphical Literature" on p. 2041). Since Jude quoted from that book in verses 14–15, verse 6 is perhaps best interpreted in light of that passage.

Jude's dependence upon Jewish sources apart from the Old Testament has been a cause of controversy. In addition to quoting 1 Enoch in verses 14–15, in verse 9 Jude cited a story from another noncanonical book (The Testament of Moses or The Assumption of Moses; see the note on v. 9). Jude may have viewed the story as legend and used it as illustration.

7 God destroyed Sodom and Gomorrah by pouring down "burning sulfur" (Ge 19:24; see "The Destruction of Sodom and Gomorrah" on p. 32)—a foretaste of the eternal fire that is to come.

8 "Pollute their own bodies" may be a reference to the homosexual practices of Sodom and Gomorrah (see vv. 4,7 and the note on v. 7; see also "Homosexuality in the Ancient World" on p. 1836).

9 According to several church fathers, this verse is based upon a noncanonical work called The Assumption of Moses or The Testament of Moses (from approximately the first century A.D.; see the note on v. 6 and "The Bible and Pseudepigraphical Literature" on p. 2041). Other New Testament quotations from, or allusions to, nonbiblical works include Paul's quotations of Aratus (see Ac 17:28 and its note), Menander (see 1Co 15:33 and its note) and Epimenides (see Tit 1:12 and its note). Such usage in no way suggests that the quotations, or the books from which they were taken, are divinely inspired. It only means that the Biblical author found the quotations to be a helpful confirmation, clarification or illustration.

12 For "love feasts," see "The Love Feast" on page 1874.

For "shepherds," see the note on 1 Peter 2:25. Here it refers to the false teachers.

THE BIBLE AND PSEUDEPIGRAPHICAL LITERATURE

JUDE **Pseudepigrapha**,[1] meaning "false title," refers to Jewish books that falsely claimed to have been written by Moses, Enoch, Abraham or some other ancient hero of the faith. Most pseudepigrapha were written between 250 B.C. and A.D. 200. A few examples are as follows:

◆ *Testaments of the Twelve Patriarchs*: A series of documents claiming to be the "testaments" of the patriarchs of the tribes of Israel, in which they by turn give exhortations to their descendants. This work was probably written in the second century B.C., but its present form seems to reflect revision by a Christian. Depending upon interpretation, it may present a doctrine of two messiahs: a priestly messiah (from Levi) and a royal messiah (from Judah). In a manner typical of **intertestamental** Judaism,[2] this work describes the Mosaic Law as the wisdom of God but reflects also the influence of Stoicism, a **Hellenistic** school of philosophy.[3]

◆ *Testament of Solomon*: An outlandish tale, in which Solomon receives a magical[4] ring from the archangel Michael and uses it to control demons, the book may have been written during the first or second century A.D.

◆ *Testament of Moses*: A text in which Moses purportedly predicts the history of Israel from the conquest under Joshua to the postexilic period, the book's principal concern is the apostasy of Hellenistic Jews. The date of its composition is disputed; some suggest that it was composed during the first century A.D.

◆ *Psalms of Solomon*: This is a first-century B.C. collection of psalms written in reaction to the Roman occupation of Palestine.[5] These psalms anticipated the coming of a "Lord Messiah" who would lead pious Jews to overthrow the Roman forces occupying the land. They are important for illustrating the Messianic fervor and religious turmoil that prevailed among the Jews in the days prior to Jesus' birth.[6]

◆ *Jubilees*: Claiming Mosaic authorship, this work, essentially a retelling of Genesis and Exodus written between the second century B.C. and the first century A.D., has some curious emphases. For example, it devotes a great deal of attention to Rebekah and considers the slaughter of Shechem (Ge 34) to have been a praiseworthy event. The book is also intensely concerned with priestly matters.

Top row right 1Q17, "Jubilees"; top row left 1Q18, "Jubilees"; center and bottom rows 1Q20, "Genesis Apocryphon"

© Dr. James C. Martin; The Amman Archaeological Museum; photographed by permission

◆ *First Enoch*: Early mystics of both Jewish and Christian background were fascinated by Enoch, the man who, after having walked with God, "was no more" (Ge 5:24). First Enoch is the first of many "accounts" detailing Enoch's ascent into heaven, but even this work is a composite of texts written from approximately the third century B.C. to the first century A.D. The narrative is highly fantastic in nature. For example, 1 Enoch 6–11 describes the rebellion of the "watchers," the angels who, according to Genesis 6:1–4 (cf. Jude 6) took the daughters of men to be their wives. In 1 Enoch 72–82, a section referred to as the Astronomical Book of Enoch, Enoch is given a tour of the heavens by the angel Uriel and sees the gates out of which the sun and moon rise and set. This section is also highly concerned with calendar issues.

As a rule the New Testament authors avoided this material, but Jude appears to have made use of it in two places. In verse 9 he alluded to a story concerning Michael and the devil that is found in a version of The Assumption of Moses (as noted by Clement and Origen; the actual text is lost). Also, in verse 14 Jude quoted from 1 Enoch 1:9: "See, the Lord is coming with thousands upon thousands of his holy ones." It is possible that through God's providence some pseudepigrapha have preserved some genuine traditions and that Jude was able to discern the true from the false. Given the nature of these books, however, it would be perilous to treat them as reliable sources. It is also helpful to keep in mind that citation of a given work by a Biblical author does not in and of itself imply endorsement. Paul cited pagan poets (Ac 17:28; 1Co 15:33; Tit 1:12), and Jude's references to 1 Enoch do not imply that he thought the book had canonical authority.

[1]See Glossary on page 2080 for definitions of bolded words. [2]See "The Intertestamental Period" on page 1551. [3]See "Greek Philosophical Schools" on page 1937. [4]See "Magic in the Greco-Roman World" on page 1911. [5]See "The Roman Army and the Occupation of the Holy Land" on page 1829. [6]See also "Jewish Eschatology in the First Century A.D." on page 1846.

Ancient Voices

And the angel opened the gates of heaven to me, and I saw the holy temple and the Most High upon a throne of glory. And He said to me, "Levi, I have given you the blessings of the priesthood until I come and dwell in the midst of Israel." Then the angel brought me to earth and gave me a weapon and a sword and said, "Carry out vengeance on Shechem in behalf of your sister, Dinah. And I will be with you, for the Lord has sent me." And at that time I destroyed the sons of Hamor, as it is written on the heavenly tablets. And I said to him, "Please, Lord, tell me your name so that I can call upon you in a day of trouble." And he said, "I am the angel who intercedes for the nation of Israel, that they may not be completely struck down, for every evil spirit attacks it."

—How an Angel Gave Levi the Priesthood and Ordered Him to Destroy Shechem, According to the "Testament of Levi" in the *Testament of the Twelve Patriarchs*.

From *Testament of Levi*, 5:1–6, trans. by Duane Garrett

See "The Bible and Pseudepigraphical Literature" article on the previous page.

without fruit and uprooted[w]—twice dead. 13They are wild waves of
the sea,[x] foaming up their shame;[y] wandering stars, for whom black-
est darkness has been reserved forever.[z]
14Enoch,[a] the seventh from Adam, prophesied about these men:
"See, the Lord is coming with thousands upon thousands of his holy
ones[b] 15to judge[c] everyone, and to convict all the ungodly of all the
ungodly acts they have done in the ungodly way, and of all the harsh
words ungodly sinners have spoken against him."[d] 16These men are
grumblers and faultfinders; they follow their own evil desires; they
boast[e] about themselves and flatter others for their own advantage.

A Call to Persevere

17But, dear friends, remember what the apostles of our Lord Jesus
Christ foretold.[f] 18They said to you, "In the last times[g] there will be
scoffers who will follow their own ungodly desires."[h] 19These are the
men who divide you, who follow mere natural instincts and do not
have the Spirit.[i]
20But you, dear friends, build yourselves up[j] in your most holy
faith and pray in the Holy Spirit.[k] 21Keep yourselves in God's love as
you wait[l] for the mercy of our Lord Jesus Christ to bring you to eter-
nal life.
22Be merciful to those who doubt; 23snatch others from the fire
and save them;[m] to others show mercy, mixed with fear—hating
even the clothing stained by corrupted flesh.[n]

Doxology

24To him who is able[o] to keep you from falling and to present you
before his glorious presence[p] without fault[q] and with great joy—
25to the only God[r] our Savior be glory, majesty, power and authority, through Jesus Christ our Lord, be-
fore all ages, now and forevermore![s] Amen.[t]

1:12 [w]Mt 15:13
1:13 [x]Isa 57:20 [y]Php 3:19 [z]2Pe 2:17
1:14 [a]Ge 5:18, 21-24 [b]Dt 33:2; Da 7:10
1:15 [c]2Pe 2:6-9 [d]1Ti 1:9
1:16 [e]2Pe 2:18
1:17 [f]2Pe 3:2
1:18 [g]1Ti 4:1 [h]2Pe 2:1
1:19 [i]1Co 2:14, 15
1:20 [j]Col 2:7 [k]Eph 6:18
1:21 [l]Tit 2:13; 2Pe 3:12
1:23 [m]Am 4:11; Zec 3:2-5 [n]Rev 3:4
1:24 [o]Ro 16:25 [p]2Co 4:14 [q]Col 1:22
1:25 [r]Jn 5:44; 1Ti 1:17 [s]Heb 13:8 [t]Ro 11:36

13 The ancient Hebrews were not a sea people. The sea in the Bible is symbolic of restlessness, instability and death (see also Isa 57:20; Jer 49:23; Jas 1:6; Rev 13:1).
14–15 This quotation is from the book of Enoch, which purports to have been written by the Enoch of Genesis 5 but actually did not appear until the first century B.C. (see "The Bible and Pseudepigraphical Literature" on p. 2041).

INTRODUCTION TO Revelation

AUTHOR, PLACE AND DATE OF WRITING

This book identifies its author as "John" (1:1,4,9; 22:8)—traditionally understood to be the apostle John, the son of Zebedee and the author of the Gospel by that name. Today, however, many conservative scholars hold to the view of Dionysius, the third-century bishop of Alexandria, that the book was written by another John, a certain "John the Elder." Other scholars regard the book as pseudonymous (falsely attributed to John) and probably a composite of several texts. Overall, there are valid historical and literary reasons for believing that Revelation was written by the apostle John (see "Who Wrote Revelation?" on p. 2060).

Although some hold that Revelation was written in A.D. 68–69, shortly after the death of the infamous emperor Nero, most believe it to have originated late in the first century. Irenaeus (*Against Heresies*, 5.30.3) stated that the apostle John saw his revelation at the close of Domitian's reign (A.D. 81–96). This is widely accepted today, and many believe that the persecutions carried out by Domitian were behind the writing of Revelation.

The author stated that he was writing from Patmos (1:9), a small, rocky island in the Aegean Sea off the coast of modern Turkey that served as a Roman penal settlement. Eusebius (A.D. 265–340) reported that John was ultimately released from Patmos under the emperor Nerva (96–98).

AUDIENCE

Revelation is addressed to seven churches in Asia Minor (modern Turkey)—Ephesus, Smyrna, Pergamum, Thyatira, Sardis, Philadelphia and Laodicea. Roman persecution of Christians (1:9; 2:10,13; 3:10) was widespread at the time, and false teachings were prominent in the churches.

CULTURAL FACTS AND HIGHLIGHTS

The book of Revelation was written at a time when the Roman authorities were beginning to enforce emperor worship (see "The Imperial Cult" on p. 1651). Christians, who held that "Jesus is Lord" (Ro 10:9), faced increasing persecution, including martyrdom (Rev 2:13; 6:9). The apostle John had been exiled to the island of Patmos for his activities as a Christian missionary (1:9), and believers were being warned against coming opposition and oppression (2:10; 3:10). Some Christians were advocating compromise with the Roman government (2:14–14,20), and John wrote in part to encourage believers to stand firm in the trying days ahead.

TIMELINE

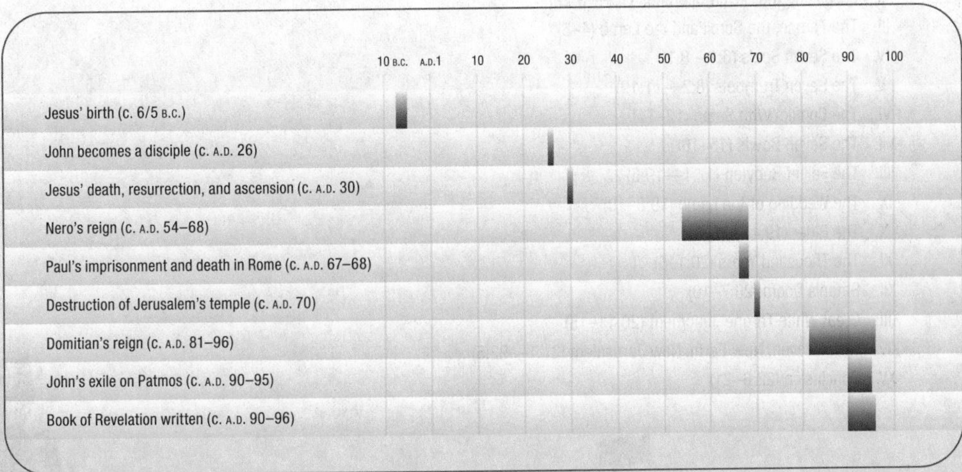

AS YOU READ

As you read chapters 2–3, watch for clues about the conditions within the churches addressed. As you move further into the book, try not to get bogged down by the timetable of events, the symbolism or the obscure details. Remember to view this book not only as history and prophecy but also as a source of encouragement and hope for Christians of all times who may be undergoing persecution.

DID YOU KNOW?

- Wormwood, a plant with a strong, bitter taste, is used here as a metaphor for calamity and sorrow. Though not poisonous, its bitterness does suggest death (8:11).
- The ancients believed that the Abyss was the subterranean abode of demonic hordes (9:1).
- Belief in statues that could speak is widely attested in ancient literature. Sometimes the image at a shrine would be hollow, enabling a priest to hide within the statue and speak for the god (13:15).
- Ancients typically diluted every part of wine with two parts water, except when their aim was to become drunk (14:8).

THEMES

The book of Revelation includes the following themes:

1. *God is in control.* John's visions penetrate the barrier that separates the heavenly realm from the earthly world and reveal the heavenly reality that will triumph over earthly illusion. Knowledge of the Old Testament is helpful for understanding Revelation's symbolism, for events in the Old Testament are seen as reflecting recurring patterns in history.

2. *Jesus will return.* The final deliverance will occur at Christ's return. This will be preceded by a period of unprecedented distress, symbolized by images of childbirth; military conflict; and supernatural, cosmic catastrophes. The new age will not come as the result of human activity nor evolve from this present age but will result from God's direct intervention. Revelation warns its readers to evaluate the present in light of the future age, in which evil will be judged and destroyed and the righteous rewarded.

3. *Salvation is for all who will receive it.* Salvation is not exclusive to any people group or nation.

OUTLINE

I. Introduction (1:1–8)
II. Jesus and the Seven Churches (1:9—3:22)
III. The Throne, the Scroll and the Lamb (4–5)
IV. The Seven Seals (6:1—8:1)
V. The Seven Trumpets (8:2—11:19)
VI. The Conflict With Satan (12–14)
VII. The Seven Bowls (15–16)
VIII. The Fall of Babylon (17:1—19:5)
IX. The Wedding of the Lamb (19:6–10)
X. The Rider (19:11–21)
XI. The Thousand Years (20:1–6)
XII. Satan's Doom (20:7–10)
XIII. Great White Throne Judgment (20:11–15)
XIV. New Heaven, New Earth, New Jerusalem (21:1—22:5)
XV. Conclusion (22:6–21)

Prologue

1 The revelation of Jesus Christ, which God gave him to show his servants what must soon take place.
1:1 [a]Rev 22:16 He made it known by sending his angel[a] to his servant John, 2who testifies to everything he saw—
1:2 [b]1Co 1:6; Rev 12:17 that is, the word of God and the testimony of Jesus Christ.[b] 3Blessed is the one who reads the words of
1:3 [c]Lk 11:28 this prophecy, and blessed are those who hear it and take to heart what is written in it,[c] because the time
is near.

Greetings and Doxology

4John,

To the seven churches in the province of Asia:

1:4 [d]Rev 3:1; 4:5 Grace and peace to you from him who is, and who was, and who is to come, and from the seven spirits[a][d]
1:5 [e]Rev 3:14 [f]Col 1:18 before his throne, 5and from Jesus Christ, who is the faithful witness,[e] the firstborn from the dead,[f] and
[g]Rev 17:14 the ruler of the kings of the earth.[g]

To him who loves us and has freed us from our sins by his blood, 6and has made us to be a kingdom
1:6 [h]1Pe 2:5 [i]Ro 11:36 and priests[h] to serve his God and Father—to him be glory and power for ever and ever! Amen.[i]

1:7 [j]Da 7:13 [k]Zec 12:10 7Look, he is coming with the clouds,[j]
and every eye will see him,
even those who pierced him;
and all the peoples of the earth will mourn[k]
because of him.
So shall it be! Amen.

1:8 [l]Rev 21:6 [m]Rev 4:8 8"I am the Alpha and the Omega,"[l] says the Lord God, "who is, and who was, and who is to come, the
Almighty."[m]

One Like a Son of Man

1:9 [n]Php 4:14 [o]2Ti 2:12 9I, John, your brother and companion in the suffering[n] and kingdom and patient endurance[o] that are
ours in Jesus, was on the island of Patmos because of the word of God and the testimony of Jesus. 10On
1:10 [p]Rev 4:2 [q]Rev 4:1 the Lord's Day I was in the Spirit,[p] and I heard behind me a loud voice like a trumpet,[q] 11which said:
1:11 [r]ver 4,20 [s]Rev 3:1 "Write on a scroll what you see and send it to the seven churches:[r] to Ephesus, Smyrna, Pergamum, Thy-
atira, Sardis,[s] Philadelphia and Laodicea."
1:12 [t]Ex 25:31-40; Zec 4:2 12I turned around to see the voice that was speaking to me. And when I turned I saw seven gold-
1:13 [u]Eze 1:26; Da 7:13; 10:16 en lampstands,[t] 13and among the lampstands was someone "like a son of man,"[b][u] dressed in a robe

[a] 4 Or *the sevenfold Spirit* [b] 13 Daniel 7:13

1:1 Though an apostle, John identified himself not in terms of his authority over the churches but as a servant of God, a title often applied to Old Testament prophets (see, e.g., Jer 29:19; see also the note on 1Pe 4:16). This title could reflect honor as well as submission: Servants of powerful masters like Caesar often enjoyed more prestige than aristocrats. (See "Who Wrote Revelation?" on p. 2060.)

1:4 The leading council of Asiarchs (cf. "officials of the province" at Ac 19:31) met each year in a revolving succession of seven strategic Asian cities. These were the same cities to which John wrote, with the exception that he replaced Cyzicus, far to the north, with the more central Thyatira. These seven churches were located about 50 miles (80 km) apart, forming a circle in the Roman province of Asia (modern western Turkey), moving clockwise north from Ephesus and coming around full circle to Laodicea, east of Ephesus (see "The Seven Churches of Asia Minor" on p. 2051). They may have been postal centers serving seven geographic regions. Apparently the entire book of Revelation was sent to each church (see v. 11).

"Who is, and who was, and who is to come" is a paraphrase of the divine name from Exodus 3:14–15 (see "YHWH: The Name of God in the Old Testament" on p. 89).

1:10 The "Lord's Day" is a technical term for the first day of the week—so named because Jesus rose from the dead on that day. It was also the day on which the Christians met (see Ac 20:7) and took up collections (see 1Co 16:2).

1:11 A scroll contained pieces of papyrus or parchment sewn together and rolled on a spindle (see the note on Ex 17:14; see also "Writing Materials in the Ancient World" on p. 2037 and "Scrolls, Seals and Codices" on p. 2053).

1:12 Throughout the Mediterranean world, a seven-branched lampstand, or menorah, stood as a recognizable symbol of Israel and Judaism. The fact that each of the seven local congregations (Ephesus, Smyrna, Pergamum, Thyatira, Sardis, Philadelphia and Laodicea) was symbolized by a lampstand likely suggested to John the larger church, the full people of God.

1:13 Why Jesus decided to call himself "son of man" (82 times in the Gospels; see also Ac 7:56; Rev 14:14) is not known, despite much scholarly debate on the question. Often he put his statements about himself in the third person, evidently to infuse his teachings with added force. Whenever he did this he used this phrase as a name for himself—no doubt taken from the prophecy in Daniel 7:13, with which the Jews were familiar. Jesus, in assuming this title, may in effect have been saying to the Jews, "I am the son of man in that prophecy." This title emphasized his union with humankind and was also a name no one would criticize. Jesus could not openly refer to himself as the Son of God or as the Messiah, as the Jews would not have accepted him as such, but they did not object to the "son of man." On the other hand, we have no record of anyone else ever calling Jesus by that name.

The high priest wore a full-length robe (Ex 28:4; 29:5). Reference to Christ as high priest is supported by the reference to the golden sash around his chest.

reaching down to his feet and with a golden sash around his chest.[v] 14His head and hair were white
like wool, as white as snow, and his eyes were like blazing fire.[w] 15His feet were like bronze glowing
in a furnace,[x] and his voice was like the sound of rushing waters.[y] 16In his right hand he held seven
stars,[z] and out of his mouth came a sharp double-edged sword.[a] His face was like the sun shining in
all its brilliance.

17When I saw him, I fell at his feet[b] as though dead. Then he placed his right hand on me and said:
"Do not be afraid. I am the First and the Last.[c] 18I am the Living One; I was dead,[d] and behold I am alive
for ever and ever![e] And I hold the keys of death and Hades.[f]

19"Write, therefore, what you have seen, what is now and what will take place later. 20The mystery of
the seven stars that you saw in my right hand and of the seven golden lampstands[g] is this: The seven
stars are the angels[a] of the seven churches,[h] and the seven lampstands are the seven churches.[i]

[a] 20 Or *messengers*

1:13 [v]Da 10:5; Rev 15:6
1:14 [w]Da 7:9; 10:6; Rev 19:12
1:15 [x]Da 10:6 [y]Eze 43:2; Rev 14:2
1:16 [z]Rev 2:1; 3:1 [a]Isa 49:2; Heb 4:12; Rev 2:12,16
1:17 [b]Eze 1:28; Da 8:17,18 [c]Isa 41:4; 44:6; 48:12; Rev 22:13
1:18 [d]Ro 6:9 [e]Rev 4:9,10 [f]Rev 20:1
1:20 [g]Zec 4:2 [h]ver 4,11 [i]Mt 5:14,15

1:16 "Sword" here is likely a reference to a long Thracian sword (also in 2:12,16; 6:8; 19:15,21), while the one in 6:4 and 13:10 and 14 is a small sword or dagger. The sword symbolizes divine judgment.
1:17 To fall at someone's feet was a sign of the greatest respect and awe.

The right hand represented the authority of an individual (see "The 'Right Hand' in Ancient Thinking" on p. 1983).
1:18 In ancient palaces, the one holding the keys was an important official—the only person controlling access into the king's presence.

"Death and Hades" together represent death's power (see "Sheol, Hades, Gehenna, the Abyss and Tartarus: Images of Hell" on p. 946). Because of his victory on the cross, Jesus holds these powerful keys. In the book of Revelation death and Hades are four times associated (see also 6:8; 20:13–14), being treated as almost synonymous terms. In the last verse mentioned, death and Hades are together to be cast into the lake of fire—doomed to utter destruction.

ARCHAEOLOGICAL SITES

PATMOS

REVELATION 1 Only 25 miles (40 km) in circumference, Patmos ("Map 13") is a small island off the coast of **Asia Minor**,[1] approximately 36 miles (58 km) southwest of Miletus. It has a bare, mountainous terrain, with Mount Elias, at 800 feet (243 m), as its highest point. Patmos served as a place of banishment during the **Roman period**. Tradition holds that the apostle John, by that time an old man, was exiled to Patmos during the fourteenth year of the reign of Emperor Domitian (Eusebius, *Ecclesiastical History*, 3:18–20). Since it was on this isle that John received his revelation (Rev 1:9–10), Patmos has been held in awe by many Christians from the Roman period to the present. In 1088 Saint John's Cloister was constructed by Saint Christodoulos upon the site of John's Grotto. Today a great **Byzantine** library there holds the work produced by the numerous monasteries and churches that have existed on Patmos over the centuries. The island has changed political hands several times over time; since 1947 it has belonged to Greece.

[1]See Glossary on page 2080 for definitions of bolded words.

The harbor of Patmos
Photograph: © Todd Bolen/Bible Places.com

To the Church in Ephesus

2 "To the angel[a] of the church in Ephesus write:
These are the words of him who holds the seven stars in his right hand[j] and walks among the
seven golden lampstands:[k] 2 I know your deeds,[l] your hard work and your perseverance. I know
that you cannot tolerate wicked men, that you have tested[m] those who claim to be apostles but are
not, and have found them false.[n] 3 You have persevered and have endured hardships for my name,[o]
and have not grown weary.
4 Yet I hold this against you: You have forsaken your first love.[p] 5 Remember the height from
which you have fallen! Repent[q] and do the things you did at first. If you do not repent, I will come
to you and remove your lampstand[r] from its place. 6 But you have this in your favor: You hate the
practices of the Nicolaitans,[s] which I also hate.
7 He who has an ear, let him hear[t] what the Spirit says to the churches. To him who overcomes,
I will give the right to eat from the tree of life,[u] which is in the paradise[v] of God.

2:1 [j]Rev 1:16 [k]Rev 1:12,13 **2:2** [l]Rev 3:1,8,15 [m]1Jn 4:1 [n]2Co 11:13 **2:3** [o]Jn 15:21 **2:4** [p]Mt 24:12 **2:5** [q]ver 16,22 [r]Rev 1:20 **2:6** [s]ver 15 **2:7** [t]Mt 11:15; Rev 3:6,13,22 [u]Ge 2:9; Rev 22:2,14,19 [v]Lk 23:43

To the Church in Smyrna

8 "To the angel of the church in Smyrna[w] write:
These are the words of him who is the First and the Last,[x] who died and came to life again.[y]
9 I know your afflictions and your poverty—yet you are rich![z] I know the slander of those who
say they are Jews and are not,[a] but are a synagogue of Satan.[b] 10 Do not be afraid of what you are
about to suffer. I tell you, the devil will put some of you in prison to test you,[c] and you will suffer
persecution for ten days.[d] Be faithful,[e] even to the point of death, and I will give you the crown
of life.
11 He who has an ear, let him hear what the Spirit says to the churches. He who overcomes will
not be hurt at all by the second death.[f]

2:8 [w]Rev 1:11 [x]Rev 1:17 [y]Rev 1:18 **2:9** [z]Jas 2:5 [a]Rev 3:9 [b]Mt 4:10 **2:10** [c]Rev 3:10 [d]Da 1:12,14 [e]ver 13 **2:11** [f]Rev 20:6,14; 21:8

[a] *1* Or *messenger*; also in verses 8, 12 and 18

2:1–7 Proconsular Asia in New Testament times was the Roman province that contained the southwestern part of Asia Minor, and in particular "the seven churches in the province of Asia" (1:4) addressed in the first three chapters of Revelation. In the New Testament the word "Asia" occurs 19 times, always referring to this division, not to the whole continent or even to Anatolia. Its capital was Ephesus, where both Paul and John had labored. For information on the city of Ephesus, see "Early History of Ephesus" on page 1965 and "Ephesus During the Time of Paul" on page 1968.

2:6 The Nicolaitans were a heretical sect within the church that had worked out a compromise with the pagan society. They apparently taught that spiritual liberty allowed them to practice idolatry and immorality. Tradition identifies them with Nicolas, the proselyte of Antioch who was purported to be one of the first seven deacons in the Jerusalem church (Ac 6:5), though the evidence for this claim is merely circumstantial. A similar group at Pergamum held to the teaching of the Old Testament Balaam (Rev 2:14–15) through whose influence the Israelites had eaten food sacrificed to idols and committed fornication; others at Thyatira were followers of the wicked queen Jezebel (v. 20). From their heretical tendencies it would appear that all three groups were Nicolaitans. A sect of Nicolaitans existed later among the Gnostics in the third century, as is known from church fathers of the time (Irenaeus, Clement of Alexandria and Tertullian). It probably had its origin in the group condemned in Revelation.

2:7 See "The Tree of Life in Jewish Imagery" on page 2075.

"Paradise" was originally a Persian word for a pleasure garden. In Revelation it symbolizes the eschatological state in which God and believers are restored to the perfect fellowship that existed before sin entered the world.

2:8–11 Most of the cities of Old Testament "Asia" (see the note on vv. 1–7) have disappeared, but Smyrna remains a great city even now (Izmir in modern Turkey), and Philadelphia remained in existence until the Middle Ages.

The Smyrna of John's day was a port on the western coast of Asia Minor at the head of the gulf into which the Hermus River flows, a well-protected harbor and the natural terminal of a great inland trade route up the Hermus Valley. Smyrna's early history was checkered. The city was destroyed by the Lydians in 627 B.C. and for three centuries was little more than a village. It was refounded in the middle of the fourth century before Christ, after Alexander's capture of Sardis, and rapidly became the chief city of Asia. Smyrna was shrewd enough to mark the rising star of Rome. A common danger, the aggression of Antiochus the Great of Syria, united Smyrna with Rome at the end of the third century before Christ, and the bond then formed remained unbroken. Smyrna was, indeed, the handiest of the bridgeheads, balancing the naval power of Rhodes in the Aegean Sea. Smyrna referred to its ancient alliance with Rome when, in A.D. 26, the city petitioned Tiberius to allow the community to build a temple to his deity. Permission was granted, and Smyrna constructed the second Asian temple to the emperor. The city had worshiped Rome as a spiritual power since 195 B.C.; hence Smyrna's historical pride in her Caesar cult (see "The Imperial Cult" on p. 1651).

Smyrna was famous for science, medicine and the majesty of its buildings. Apollonius of Tyana referred to its "crown of porticoes," a circle of beautiful public buildings that ringed the summit of Mount Pagos like a diadem; hence John's reference in v. 10. Polycarp, Smyrna's martyred bishop of A.D. 155, had been a disciple of John.

2:9 For "synagogue of Satan," see the note on 3:9 and "The Seven Churches of Asia Minor" on page 2051.

2:10 See "The Early Persecution of the Church" on page 2067.

"Crown" does not refer to a royal crown (12:3; 13:1; 19:12) but to the garland or wreath awarded to the winner in athletic contests (3:11; 4:4,10; 6:2; 9:7; 12:1; 14:14; see the note on 1Co 9:24–27). For commentary on the meaning of the "crown" as it specifically applied to Smyrna, see the note on 2:8-11. For a comparison between the victory crown and the royal crown, see the note of 2:3.

2:11 In Smyrna "overcoming" meant withstanding persecution (see "The Early Percution of the Church" on p. 2067). Jewish teaching already identified martyrdom with overcoming, but Revelation underlined the image of the triumphant Lion as a slain Lamb (5:5–6,9,12).

APOCALYPTIC LITERATURE OUTSIDE THE BIBLE

REVELATION 2 Some of the religious literature from early Jewish and Christian sources is referred to as "apocalyptic literature." Such writings are characterized by visions and revelations given by God to great saints; often these visions are filled with strange symbols. Apocalyptic literature originated in Old Testament times and may be seen in parts of Ezekiel and Zechariah, and especially in Daniel. Revelation is the last great apocalyptic book of the Bible, but there are many nonbiblical apocalyptic texts, which are referred to as "pseudo-apocalyptic" because they are imitations of Biblical apocalyptic works such as Daniel and Revelation. Important examples are the books of Enoch, the Sibylline Oracles, 2 Baruch, 4 Ezra and the Apocalypse of Abraham:

- First Enoch, which in its present form consists of 108 chapters of various visions involving the patriarch Enoch, was a tremendously popular book in early Jewish and Christian communities. It is particularly noteworthy for its elaboration of Genesis 6, a narrative Enoch interprets as an angelic interbreeding with human women. Enoch's expansion of the Genesis 6 narrative includes a vivid description of the places of judgment (e.g., 1 Enoch 21–22) and of the coming of God's kingdom (1 Enoch 45; 93).
- The Sibylline Oracles, which likewise enjoyed widespread use, consist of oracles of looming judgment written in the style of Greek prophecy but drawn from Biblical texts.
- Fourth Ezra and 2 Baruch deal with (among other things) the theological questions raised by the fall of Jerusalem in A.D. 70.[1] Both adopt the convention of having been written shortly after the **Babylonian captivity**, but contextual clues make it clear that they are post-A.D. 70 works. Fourth Ezra is remarkable for its concern over the problem of evil, as Ezra relentlessly pressed God's angel to explain why the wicked nations appeared to triumph over God's chosen people.
- The Apocalypse of Abraham is ostensibly a narrative of a heavenly journey by the forefather of the Jewish people.

The word *apocalyptic* comes from the Greek word for "unveiling." The key feature of apocalyptic literature, which was common in early Judaism, was the unveiling of secrets by heavenly mediators. Often these secrets concerned the end times, when God would come to judge the world,[2] but in nonbiblical texts these visions could also include matters such as pseudoscientific descriptions of the paths of the stars or other "mysteries" of the natural world. Sometimes the recipient of the visionary secrets would be caught up into heaven, while on other occasions an angel might descend with the revelation (e.g., 2 Baruch 6:5–6). Although vivid and sometimes bizarre imagery appears in Jewish apocalyptic literature, the book of Revelation is especially noteworthy for its heavy concentration of such symbolism.

John's Revelation is not an isolated work; it is clear that it is in some ways similar to the nonbiblical literature described above. On the other hand, Revelation does not draw upon the nonbiblical apocalyptic material, although it does directly appropriate other Biblical apocalyptic images, especially those from Daniel. The key question, of course, is not whether Revelation is unique in style but whether it reflects authentic revelation. Some books simply mimic a Biblical style by including fantastic images or by repeating some stock phrases from the Bible. Most pseudo-apocalyptic works were also pseudepigraphical, falsely claiming ancient heroes, such as Abraham or Baruch, as their authors.[3] But in originality, in breadth of vision, in the subtle way it draws together a massive amount of Old Testament and New Testament theology and in the profound nature of its visions, Revelation has no equal.

The "Vision of Daniel" parchment discovered in the Cairo Geniza, a one-leaf apocalyptic Hebrew text of the tenth century Byzantium Empire containing prophesies said to have been given to Daniel

© The Israel Museum, Jerusalem

[1]See "Josephus and the Fall of Jerusalem" on page 1606. [2]See "Jewish Eschatology in the First Century A.D." on page 1846. [3]See "The Bible and Pseudepigraphical Literature" on page 2041.

To the Church in Pergamum

2:12 [g]Rev 1:11 [h]Rev 1:16 12“To the angel of the church in Pergamum[g] write:

These are the words of him who has the sharp, double-edged sword.[h] 13I know where you live—
where Satan has his throne. Yet you remain true to my name. You did not renounce your faith in
2:13 [i]Rev 14:12 [j]ver 9,24 me,[i] even in the days of Antipas, my faithful witness, who was put to death in your city—where
Satan lives.[j]
2:14 [k]ver 20 [l]2Pe 2:15 [m]1Co 6:13 14Nevertheless, I have a few things against you:[k] You have people there who hold to the teach-
ing of Balaam,[l] who taught Balak to entice the Israelites to sin by eating food sacrificed to idols and
by committing sexual immorality.[m] 15Likewise you also have those who hold to the teaching of
2:15 [n]ver 6 the Nicolaitans.[n] 16Repent therefore! Otherwise, I will soon come to you and will fight against them
2:16 [o]2Th 2:8; Rev 1:16 with the sword of my mouth.[o]
17He who has an ear, let him hear what the Spirit says to the churches. To him who overcomes,
2:17 [p]Jn 6:49,50 [q]Isa 62:2 [r]Rev 19:12 I will give some of the hidden manna.[p] I will also give him a white stone with a new name[q] writ-
ten on it, known only to him who receives it.[r]

To the Church in Thyatira

2:18 [s]Rev 1:11 [t]Rev 1:14,15 18“To the angel of the church in Thyatira[s] write:

These are the words of the Son of God, whose eyes are like blazing fire and whose feet are like
2:19 [u]ver 2 burnished bronze.[t] 19I know your deeds,[u] your love and faith, your service and perseverance, and
that you are now doing more than you did at first.
2:20 [v]1Ki 16:31; 21:25; 2Ki 9:7 20Nevertheless, I have this against you: You tolerate that woman Jezebel,[v] who calls herself a
prophetess. By her teaching she misleads my servants into sexual immorality and the eating of
2:21 [w]Ro 2:4 [x]Rev 9:20 food sacrificed to idols. 21I have given her time[w] to repent of her immorality, but she is unwilling.[x]
2:22 [y]Rev 17:2; 18:9 22So I will cast her on a bed of suffering, and I will make those who commit adultery[y] with her
2:23 [z]1Sa 16:7; Jer 11:20; Ac 1:24; Ro 8:27 suffer intensely, unless they repent of her ways. 23I will strike her children dead. Then all the
churches will know that I am he who searches hearts and minds,[z] and I will repay each of you

---

2:12–17 Pergamum (modern Bergama), was located in the Caicus Valley, 15 miles (25 km) inland. Royally situated on a cone-shaped hill rising 1,000 feet (305 m) above the surrounding valley, its name in Greek means “citadel.” Pergamum was the capital of the region until the last of the Pergemenian kings bequeathed his realm to Rome in 133 B.C., after which it became the chief town of the new province of Asia and the site of the first temple of the Caesar cult, erected to Rome and Augustus in 29 B.C (see “The Imperial Cult” on p. 1651). A second shrine was later dedicated to Trajan, and the multiplication of such honor marked the prestige of Pergamum in pagan Asia. The worship of Asclepius and Zeus were also widespread (see “The Gods of the Greeks and Romans” on p. 1908). The symbol of the former was a serpent, and Pausanias described his cult image “with a staff in one hand and the other on the head of a serpent.” Pergamenian coins illustrate the importance that the community attached to this cult. Caracalla is shown on one coin, saluting a serpent twined around a bending sapling.

On the crag above Pergamum stood a thronelike altar to Zeus (v. 13), which is now in the Berlin Museum. It commemorated the defeat of a Gallic inroad and was decorated with a representation of the conflict between the gods and the giants, the latter depicted as monsters with snakelike tails. To deepen Christian horror at Pergamum's obsession with the serpent-image, Zeus was called in this connection “Zeus the Savior.” It is natural that the “Nicolaitans” (see the note on v. 6) should have flourished in a place where politics and paganism were so closely allied (v. 15) and where pressure upon Christians to compromise must have been heavy.

Pergamum, an ancient seat of culture, possessed a library that rivaled Alexandria's. Parchment (*charta Pergamena*) was invented at Pergamum to free the library from Egypt's jealous ban on the export of papyrus.

The sword here is the long sword (see the note on 1:16).

2:13 Antipas was the first martyr of Asia. According to tradition he was slowly roasted to death in a bronze kettle during the reign of Domitian (A.D. 81–96).

2:15 For “Nicolaitans,” see the note on verse 6.

2:16 The sword here is the long sword (see the note on 1:16).

2:17 Certain kinds of stones were used as tokens for various purposes. In the context of a Messianic banquet, the white stone was probably for the purpose of admission.

For “new name,” see the notes on Genesis 1:5 and 17:5.

2:18–29 Thyatira (modern Akhisar), a city in the province of Asia on the boundary of Lydia and Mysia, has no illustrious history and is scarcely mentioned by ancient writers. It was founded by Seleucus I (311–280 B.C.) as a military outpost. Coinage suggests that, lying as it did on a great highway linking two river valleys, Thyatira was a garrison town for many centuries. Its ancient Anatolian deity was a warlike figure armed with a battle-ax and mounted on a charger. An odd coin or two depicts a female deity wearing a battlemented crown.

The city was a center of commerce, and its records preserve references to more trade guilds than those listed for any other Asian city. Lydia, whom Paul met in Philippi, was a Thyatiran seller of “turkey red,” the product of the madder root (Ac 16:14). It is curious to find another woman, Jezebel, nicknamed after the princess who by marriage sealed Ahab's trading partnership with the Phoenicians, leading a party of compromise in the Thyatiran church (Rev 2:20–24; see the note on v. 20). The necessity of membership in a trade guild invited the Christians of Thyatira to compromise and opened the door to many temptations. Thyatira played a significant role in the later history of the church.

2:20 Shopkeepers or craftsmen risked loss of income by refusing to join guilds, whose meetings included common meals dedicated to patron deities (see “‘Temple Restaurants' and Food Sacrificed to Idols” on p. 1871 and “The Early Persecution of the Church” on p. 2067). Aspects of emperor worship also affected nearly every guild (see “The Imperial Cult” on p. 1651). This situation likely contributed to “Jezebel's” appeal. This false prophetess, claiming to offer “deep secrets” (v. 24), deceived and misled God's people, advocating participation in local civic and commercial life despite the inevitable compromise with paganism.

2:22 Disease was often considered an appropriate punishment for sin.

2:23 The “mind” (lit., “kidney”) often referred to the will and the affections, while the “heart” designated the center of rational life (see the notes on Ps 7:9; 139:13, as well as “Heart, Breath, Throat and Intestines: Ancient Hebrew Anthropology” on p. 968).

according to your deeds. 24 Now I say to the rest of you in Thyatira, to you who do not hold to her
teaching and have not learned Satan's so-called deep secrets (I will not impose any other burden
on you):[a] 25 Only hold on to what you have[b] until I come. 2:24 [a]Ac 15:28
26 To him who overcomes and does my will to the end, I will give authority over the nations[c]— 2:25 [b]Rev 3:11 2:26 [c]Ps 2:8; Rev 3:21

27 'He will rule them with an iron scepter;[d] 2:27 [d]Rev 12:5 [e]Isa 30:14; Jer 19:11
he will dash them to pieces like pottery'[a][e]—

just as I have received authority from my Father. 28 I will also give him the morning star.[f] 29 He who 2:28 [f]Rev 22:16
has an ear, let him hear[g] what the Spirit says to the churches. 2:29 [g]ver 7

To the Church in Sardis

3 "To the angel[b] of the church in Sardis write:

These are the words of him who holds the seven spirits[c][h] of God and the seven stars.[i] I know 3:1 [h]Rev 1:4
your deeds;[j] you have a reputation of being alive, but you are dead.[k] 2 Wake up! Strengthen what [i]Rev 1:16 [j]Rev 2:2 [k]1Ti 5:6
remains and is about to die, for I have not found your deeds complete in the sight of my God. 3 Re-
member, therefore, what you have received and heard; obey it, and repent.[l] But if you do not wake 3:3 [l]Rev 2:5
up, I will come like a thief,[m] and you will not know at what time I will come to you. [m]2Pe 3:10
4 Yet you have a few people in Sardis who have not soiled their clothes.[n] They will walk with me, 3:4 [n]Jude 23
dressed in white,[o] for they are worthy. 5 He who overcomes will, like them, be dressed in white. I will [o]Rev 4:4; 6:11; 7:9,13,14
never blot out his name from the book of life,[p] but will acknowledge his name before my Father[q] 3:5 [p]Rev 20:12 [q]Mt 10:32
and his angels. 6 He who has an ear, let him hear[r] what the Spirit says to the churches. 3:6 [r]Rev 2:7

To the Church in Philadelphia

7 "To the angel of the church in Philadelphia[s] write: 3:7 [s]Rev 1:11 [t]1Jn 5:20

These are the words of him who is holy and true,[t] who holds the key of David.[u] What he opens [u]Isa 22:22; Mt 16:19
no one can shut, and what he shuts no one can open. 8 I know your deeds. See, I have placed before
you an open door[v] that no one can shut. I know that you have little strength, yet you have kept my 3:8 [v]Ac 14:27
word and have not denied my name.[w] 9 I will make those who are of the synagogue of Satan,[x] who [w]Rev 2:13 3:9 [x]Rev 2:9
claim to be Jews though they are not, but are liars—I will make them come and fall down at your [y]Isa 49:23
feet[y] and acknowledge that I have loved you.[z] 10 Since you have kept my command to endure pa- [z]Isa 43:4
tiently, I will also keep you[a] from the hour of trial that is going to come upon the whole world to 3:10 [a]2Pe 2:9
test[b] those who live on the earth.[c] [b]Rev 2:10 [c]Rev 6:10; 17:8
11 I am coming soon. Hold on to what you have,[d] so that no one will take your crown.[e] 12 Him 3:11 [d]Rev 2:25 [e]Rev 2:10
who overcomes I will make a pillar[f] in the temple of my God. Never again will he leave it. I will 3:12 [f]Gal 2:9

[a] 27 Psalm 2:9 [b] 1 Or *messenger*; also in verses 7 and 14 [c] 1 Or *the sevenfold Spirit*

2:24 Later Gnosticism (see "The Gnostics and Their Scriptures" on p. 2029) taught that in order to defeat Satan one had to enter his stronghold—to experience evil deeply.
2:27 "Rule" is literally "shepherd," a common metaphor for rulers (see the notes on Ps 23:1; Isa 44:28).
3:1–6 Sardis (modern Sart), the capital of the ancient kingdom of Lydia, was a city of great wealth and fame. Its acropolis, a natural citadel on the northern spur of Mount Tmolus, rose 1,500 feet (457 m) above the lower valley. Sardis was full of sophisticated paganism. The lack of mention of persecution probably reflects the secure position of its Jewish community. Jesus' followers evidently coexisted peacefully with the synagogue community and city establishment. Unaccustomed to opposition, they had grown comfortable in their relationship with the world. Their spiritual state (deadness) prevented them from realizing that Jesus' resurrection power was available to them.
3:7–13 Philadelphia (modern Alashehir) was a Lydian city founded by Attalus II Philadelphus (220–130 B.C.), who was known for his devotion to his brother Eumenes. His name (meaning "brotherly love") was perpetuated by the city. Philadelphia was a city of commercial importance, conveniently located as the gateway to the high central plateau of the Roman province of Asia in Asia Minor. Philadelphia, an outpost of Hellenism in native Anatolia, lay under Mount Tmolus in a wide vale that opens into the Hermus Valley and along which the post road ran. Its location on a broad, low, easily defended hill explains the city's long stand against the Turks.

The district is disastrously seismic, and the great earthquake of A.D. 17 ruined it completely. Placed directly above the fault, Philadelphia was tormented by 20 years of recurrent quakes after that calamity. Hence, stated the Biblical historian Ramsay, is derived the imagery of verse 12. The "new name" in this verse is certainly a reference to the proposal to rename the city Neocaesarea in gratitude for Tiberius's generous earthquake relief.

The district was an area of vine growing and wine production and therefore a center for the worship of Dionysus, the god of wine and fertility (see "The Cult of Dionysus" on p. 1921).

The believers of the Philadelphian church were like the Jewish Christians for whom John wrote his Gospel. Many had likely been expelled from their synagogues (see the notes on Jn 9:22; 1Ti 1:20). A Christian witness, despite Muslim invasion and pressure, was maintained in Philadelphia through medieval and into modern times.
3:9 "Synagogue of Satan" is a bold metaphor directed against unbelieving and hostile Jews (see 2:9; see also "The Seven Churches of Asia Minor" on p. 2051). The Jewish synagogue was a gathering place for worship, study and communal activities (see the notes on Mk 1:21; Lk 21:12).

To fall at someone's feet was an appropriate act of submission in the Near East.
3:12 For "pillar in the temple," see the note on 7:15.

Names revealed character. Christ's new name symbolizes all that he is by virtue of his redemptive work for humankind.

The Seven Churches of Asia Minor

REVELATION 3 The seven churches mentioned in Revelation 1–3 were all located within the Roman province of Asia (in western Turkey), opposite the island of Patmos where John received his revelation.[1] Although there were almost certainly other churches in the area at this time, it appears that John chose these seven because they formed a natural route for a circuit rider, starting in Ephesus[2] and moving on in a counterclockwise direction through Smyrna, Pergamum, Thyatira, Sardis, Philadelphia and Laodicea (all on "Map 13"). At the same time, given John's interest in numbers, it is hardly a coincidence that he chose seven churches. The number seven is often symbolic in Scripture of totality or completeness (as in the seven days of the creation week), and the implication here is that John's message was not intended simply for these seven individual churches but was relevant to the church universal.

Arches at Smyrna
Preserving Bible Times; © Dr. James C. Martin

Efforts have been made to tie items in the seven messages to the precise historical setting of each city. For the most part John's language is too general (and too laden with Old Testament imagery) to allow for such exact identification. But archaeology and history can shed light on some matters:

✣ The reference to the "synagogue of Satan" (2:9, 3:9) was not a general attack on Judaism but a reference to Jews who had denounced Christians to the Roman government as not being "true Jews." Since the Jews enjoyed legal exemption from participation in the imperial cult (worship of the emperor as a god), this left the Christians open to prosecution for their nonparticipation.[3] John affirmed that although they were disowned by the "official" synagogue, God would acknowledge the faithful Christians as his people.

✣ The "throne" of Satan in Pergamum (2:13) likely referred to the city's status as center of the imperial cult (some suggest that the imperial temple looked like a throne).

✣ Philadelphia had suffered a massive earthquake in A.D. 17, the effects of which had been so severe that people lived in the countryside outside the city for years afterward. The promise to the Philadelphians, "I will make [him] a pillar in the temple of my God. Never again will he leave it" (3:12), would have had obvious significance in the light of this historical background.

✣ In verse 3:16 the Laodicean church was denounced as "lukewarm," neither hot nor cold. There were well-known hot springs in Hieropolis, just 6 miles (9.7 km) from Laodicea, and a good supply of cold running water in nearby Colosse.[4] Laodicea itself, however, appears to have had a tepid and barely potable water supply. This would have been a potent symbol for this congregation of its church's ineffectiveness.

The temple to Serapis at Pergamum
Photograph: © Todd Bolen/Bible Places.com

[1]See "Patmos" on page 2046. [2]See "Early History of Ephesus" on page1965 and "Ephesus During the Time of Paul" on page 1968. [3]See "The Imperial Cult" on page 1651. [4]See "Colosse" on page 1935.

write on him the name of my God[g] and the name of the city of my God, the new Jerusalem,[h] which
is coming down out of heaven from my God; and I will also write on him my new name. 13 He who
has an ear, let him hear what the Spirit says to the churches.

3:12 gRev 14:1; 22:4 hRev 21:2,10

To the Church in Laodicea

14 "To the angel of the church in Laodicea write:

These are the words of the Amen, the faithful and true witness, the ruler of God's creation.[i] 15 I
know your deeds, that you are neither cold nor hot.[j] I wish you were either one or the other! 16 So,
because you are lukewarm—neither hot nor cold—I am about to spit you out of my mouth. 17 You
say, 'I am rich; I have acquired wealth and do not need a thing.'[k] But you do not realize that you are
wretched, pitiful, poor, blind and naked. 18 I counsel you to buy from me gold refined in the fire, so
you can become rich; and white clothes to wear, so you can cover your shameful nakedness;[l] and
salve to put on your eyes, so you can see.

19 Those whom I love I rebuke and discipline.[m] So be earnest, and repent.[n] 20 Here I am! I stand
at the door[o] and knock. If anyone hears my voice and opens the door,[p] I will come in[q] and eat with
him, and he with me.

21 To him who overcomes, I will give the right to sit with me on my throne,[r] just as I overcame[s]
and sat down with my Father on his throne. 22 He who has an ear, let him hear[t] what the Spirit says
to the churches."

3:14 iCol 1:16,18
3:15 jRo 12:11
3:17 kHos 12:8; 1Co 4:8
3:18 lRev 16:15
3:19 mPr 3:12; Heb 12:5,6 nRev 2:5
3:20 oMt 24:33 pLk 12:36 qJn 14:23
3:21 rMt 19:28 sRev 5:5
3:22 tRev 2:7

The Throne in Heaven

4 After this I looked, and there before me was a door standing open in heaven. And the voice I had
first heard speaking to me like a trumpet[u] said, "Come up here,[v] and I will show you what must take
place after this."[w] 2 At once I was in the Spirit,[x] and there before me was a throne in heaven[y] with some-
one sitting on it. 3 And the one who sat there had the appearance of jasper and carnelian. A rainbow,[z] re-
sembling an emerald, encircled the throne. 4 Surrounding the throne were twenty-four other thrones,
and seated on them were twenty-four elders.[a] They were dressed in white[b] and had crowns of gold on
their heads. 5 From the throne came flashes of lightning, rumblings and peals of thunder.[c] Before the
throne, seven lamps[d] were blazing. These are the seven spirits[a][e] of God. 6 Also before the throne there
was what looked like a sea of glass,[f] clear as crystal.

In the center, around the throne, were four living creatures,[g] and they were covered with eyes, in front
and in back. 7 The first living creature was like a lion, the second was like an ox, the third had a face like

4:1 uRev 1:10 vRev 11:12 wRev 1:19
4:2 xRev 1:10 yIsa 6:1; Eze 1:26-28; Da 7:9
4:3 zEze 1:28
4:4 aRev 11:16 bRev 3:4,5
4:5 cRev 8:5; 16:18 dZec 4:2 eRev 1:4
4:6 fRev 15:2 gEze 1:5

[a] 5 Or *the sevenfold Spirit*

3:14–22 A city in Asia Minor founded by Antiochus II (261–246 B.C.), Laodicea (near modern Denizli) was the wealthiest city in Phrygia during Roman times and the head of the "circuit" of "the seven churches in the province of Asia" (1:4). The city lay on one of the great Asian trade routes, and this ensured its commercial prosperity. Laodicea was a leading banking center (in 51 B.C. Cicero, en route to his Cilician province, cashed drafts there), and it was no doubt the rich banking firms that in A.D. 60 financed the reconstruction of the city after the great earthquake that had destroyed it. Self-sufficient Laodicea refused the Senate's earthquake relief.

The Lycus Valley produced a glossy black wool, the source of black cloaks and carpets, for which the city was renowned. Laodicea was also the home of a medical school and the manufacture of collyrium, a famous eye salve. The scornful imagery of the apocalyptic letter to Laodicea was obviously based on these activities. It also made reference to the soda-laden, lukewarm water piped in from Hierapolis, whose thermal springs ran into the Maeander.

Sir William Ramsey suggested that the city's exposed position and easy wealth caused the growth in the community of that spirit of compromise and worldly mindedness castigated in Revelation. Under Diocletian, Laodicea, still prosperous, was made the chief city of the province of Phrygia.

3:16 "Hot" most likely refers to the tepid, medicinal waters of nearby Hierapolis (see "The Seven Churches of Asia Minor" on p. 2051, as well as the note on vv. 14–22). By the time the water was piped from Hierapolis o Laodicea, it was lukewarm.

3:18 This verse refers to the three items in which Laodicea took great pride: financial wealth, an extensive textile industry and a famous eye salve (see the note on vv. 14–22).

3:20 Jesus did not reject these believers. He wanted in fact to dine with them—an image associated with intimacy in the ancient world (see "Jewish Meals and Meal Customs" on p. 1575). Inviting Jesus in for a meal during his ministry years would have been a gesture of hospitality not uncommon even from an acquaintance.

4:2 The depiction of God ruling from his throne in heaven is a regular feature of the Old Testament (e.g., Ps 47:8; see "Thrones in the Ancient World" on p. 899).

4:3 See "Precious Stones of the Biblical World" on page 1156.

4:5 Awe-inspiring natural phenomena are symbolic of the majesty and power of God (see "Storm Gods, Storm Imagery and Theophany" on p. 808).

4:6 The "sea of glass" may be the basin in the heavenly temple, whose counterpart in the earthly temple was referred to as the Sea (1Ki 7:23–25). Other features of the temple in heaven are: the lamps (Rev 4:5), the altar (6:9), the altar of incense (8:3) and the ark of the covenant (11:19). (See "The Tabernacle and the Ark" on p. 153, "Solomon's Temple and Other Ancient Temples" on p. 620, "The Horned Altar" on p. 924 and "Herod's Temple" on p. 1648.)

For "clear as crystal," see the note on Job 28:17.

Ezekiel in a vision also saw four living creatures (see Eze 1:6,10 and the note on Eze 1:5), which he called cherubim in Ezekiel 10:15. Here in Revelation, the four living creatures are said to have six wings each (Rev. 4:8), a characteristic of the seraphs of Isaiah 6:2–3. The four living creatures, with features of the cherubim and the seraphs, are portrayed as an exalted order of angelic beings whose task it is to guard the heavenly throne and to lead in the worship and adoration of God (see "Angels and Guardian Spirits in the Bible and the Ancient Near East" on p. 1529).

4:7 [h]Eze 1:10; 10:14
4:8 [i]Isa 6:2 [j]Isa 6:3; Rev 1:8 [k]Rev 1:4

a man, the fourth was like a flying eagle.[h] 8 Each of the four living creatures had six wings[i] and was cov-
ered with eyes all around, even under his wings. Day and night they never stop saying:

"Holy, holy, holy
is the Lord God Almighty,[j]
who was, and is, and is to come."[k]

4:9 [l]Ps 47:8
4:10 [m]ver 4 [n]Rev 5:8,14 [o]ver 2

9 Whenever the living creatures give glory, honor and thanks to him who sits on the throne[l] and who lives
for ever and ever, 10 the twenty-four elders[m] fall down before him[n] who sits on the throne,[o] and worship
him who lives for ever and ever. They lay their crowns before the throne and say:

4:11 [p]Rev 5:12 [q]Rev 10:6

11 "You are worthy, our Lord and God,
to receive glory and honor and power,[p]
for you created all things,
and by your will they were created
and have their being."[q]

4:11 Jewish tradition suggested that God created the world for the sake of humanity or specifically for Israel, but Christians see his ultimate purpose in Christ's saving work. The emperor Domitian expected worship as "lord and god," but the heavenly choirs of angels and the redeemed people hail the true "Lord and God"—the One who created and rules over his universe.

ANCIENT TEXTS AND ARTIFACTS

Scrolls, Seals and Codices

REVELATION 5 What is the "book" mentioned in Revelation 5? Codices (singular *codex*) are similar to modern books, having spines and leaves. They existed at the time John was writing and were particularly popular within the Christian community. Sheets of either **papyrus** or parchment were folded over and stitched together to produce the codex.[1]

But in John's time a book still generally referred to a scroll, made either of papyrus or parchment, and this is almost certainly what John was referring to in Revelation 5. Sheets of papyrus (usually 20 or so) were glued together to form a roll approximately 30 feet (9 m) long. From the expression "with writing on both sides" (v. 1; cf. Eze 2:10, to which John was alluding), we may gather that this was an *opisthograph* (a scroll with writing on both the front and the back).

To prevent tampering and unwanted reading, scrolls were often sealed with clay impressed with the owner's mark. John may have had in mind Roman wills, which were sometimes witnessed (and sealed) by seven witnesses and put into effect only upon the death of the testator. It is also possible, however, that the number seven ("seven seals"; Rev 5:1) in this context may simply have allowed for a dramatic unfolding of events.

[1]See "Writing Materials in the Ancient World" on page 2037.

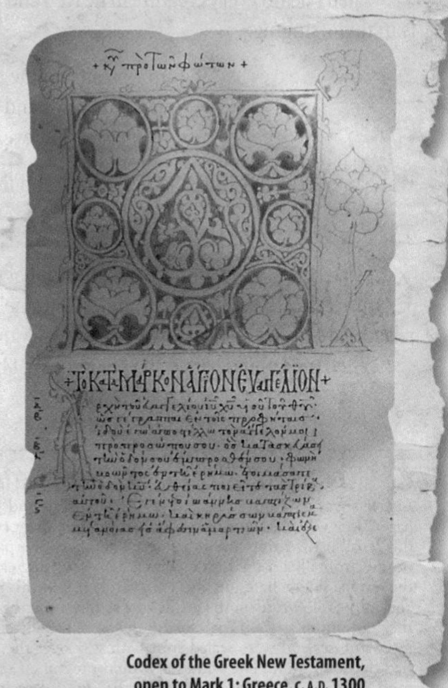

Codex of the Greek New Testament, open to Mark 1; Greece, C. A.D. 1300

© The Schøyen Collection; photography courtesy of Mr. Martin Schøyen

The Scroll and the Lamb

5 Then I saw in the right hand of him who sat on the throne[r] a scroll with writing on both sides[s] and — 5:1 [r]ver 7,13 [s]Eze 2:9,10
sealed[t] with seven seals. 2And I saw a mighty angel proclaiming in a loud voice, "Who is worthy to — [t]Isa 29:11;
break the seals and open the scroll?" 3But no one in heaven or on earth or under the earth could open the — Da 12:4
scroll or even look inside it. 4I wept and wept because no one was found who was worthy to open the
scroll or look inside. 5Then one of the elders said to me, "Do not weep! See, the Lion[u] of the tribe of Ju- — 5:5 [u]Ge 49:9
dah, the Root of David,[v] has triumphed. He is able to open the scroll and its seven seals." — [v]Isa 11:1,10; Ro 15:12; Rev 22:16
6Then I saw a Lamb,[w] looking as if it had been slain, standing in the center of the throne, encircled — 5:6 [w]Jn 1:29
by the four living creatures and the elders. He had seven horns and seven eyes,[x] which are the seven spir- — [x]Zec 4:10
its[a] of God sent out into all the earth. 7He came and took the scroll from the right hand of him who sat
on the throne.[y] 8And when he had taken it, the four living creatures and the twenty-four elders fell down — 5:7 [y]ver 1
before the Lamb. Each one had a harp[z] and they were holding golden bowls full of incense, which are the — 5:8 [z]Rev 14:2
prayers[a] of the saints. 9And they sang a new song:[b] — [a]Ps 141:2 5:9 [b]Ps 40:3 [c]Rev 4:11 [d]Heb 9:12 [e]1Co 6:20

"You are worthy[c] to take the scroll
and to open its seals,
because you were slain,
and with your blood[d] you purchased[e] men for God
from every tribe and language and people and nation.
10You have made them to be a kingdom and priests[f] to — 5:10 [f]1Pe 2:5
serve our God,
and they will reign on the earth."

11Then I looked and heard the voice of many angels, numbering thousands upon thousands, and ten
thousand times ten thousand.[g] They encircled the throne and the living creatures and the elders. 12In a — 5:11 [g]Da 7:10; Heb 12:22
loud voice they sang:

"Worthy is the Lamb, who was slain,
to receive power and wealth and wisdom and strength
and honor and glory and praise!"[h] — 5:12 [h]Rev 4:11

13Then I heard every creature in heaven and on earth and under the earth[i] and on the sea, and all that — 5:13 [i]ver 3; Php 2:10
is in them, singing: — [j]Rev 6:16 [k]1Ch 29:11

"To him who sits on the throne and to the Lamb[j]
be praise and honor and glory and power,
for ever and ever!"[k]

14The four living creatures said, "Amen,"[l] and the elders fell down and worshiped.[m] — 5:14 [l]Rev 4:9 [m]Rev 4:10; 19:4

The Seals

6 I watched as the Lamb[n] opened the first of the seven seals.[o] Then I heard one of the four living crea- — 6:1 [n]Rev 5:6 [o]Rev 5:1 [p]Rev 4:6,7
tures[p] say in a voice like thunder,[q] "Come!" 2I looked, and there before me was a white horse![r] Its — [q]Rev 14:2; 19:6 6:2 [r]Zec 6:3;
rider held a bow, and he was given a crown,[s] and he rode out as a conqueror bent on conquest.[t] — Rev 19:11 [s]Zec 6:11; Rev 14:14
3When the Lamb opened the second seal, I heard the second living creature[u] say, "Come!" 4Then an- — [t]Ps 45:4 6:3 [u]Rev 4:7

[a] 6 Or *the sevenfold Spirit*

5:1 For "scroll," see the note on 1:11, "Writing Materials in the Ancient World" on page 2037 and "Scrolls, Seals and Codices" on page 2053. Like the stone tablets of the Old Testament covenant law, this scroll had writing on both sides. The fibers of a papyrus scroll run horizontally on the inside, which makes writing easier than on the reverse side (where the fibers are vertical). For this reason, most ancient people wrote on the inside of a scroll, using the back only if they ran out of space. Legal documents were usually closed by listing witnesses and were sealed shut with wax over the threads that tied the scroll shut. The witnesses would press their seals into this wax. Seals reserved the contents for the rightful recipient(s)—as authenticated and attested by the witnesses.

5:6 The idea of the lamb as a victorious military leader seems to have come from the apocalyptic tradition (1 Enoch 90:9; Testament of Joseph 19:8). See "Apocalyptic Literature Outside the Bible" on page 2048.

The horn is an ancient Jewish symbol for power or strength (cf. Dt 33:17). Seven horns would have symbolized full strength.

5:8 The ancient harp was a stringed instrument used especially to accompany songs (see Ps 33:2, as well as "Ancient Musical Instruments" on p. 797).

The bowl referred to was a flat, shallow cup. Here it was used to hold incense, a normal feature of Hebrew ritual (see "Incense" on p. 1209).

In later Jewish thought, such as in Tobit 12:15 and 3 Baruch 11 (both Apocryphal books), angels were often depicted as presenting the prayers of the saints to God.

5:9–10 See "Early Christian Hymnody" on page 2007.

6:4 [v]Zec 6:2 [w]Mt 10:34
6:5 [x]Rev 4:7 [y]Zec 6:2
6:6 [z]Rev 4:6,7 [a]Rev 9:4
6:7 [b]Rev 4:7
6:8 [c]Zec 6:3 [d]Hos 13:14 [e]Jer 15:2,3; Eze 5:12,17
6:9 [f]Rev 14:18; 16:7 [g]Rev 20:4
6:10 [h]Zec 1:12 [i]Rev 3:7 [j]Rev 19:2
6:11 [k]Rev 3:4 [l]Heb 11:40
6:12 [m]Rev 16:18 [n]Mt 24:29
6:13 [o]Mt 24:29; Rev 8:10; 9:1 [p]Isa 34:4
6:14 [q]Jer 4:24; Rev 16:20
6:15 [r]Isa 2:10,19,21
6:16 [s]Hos 10:8; Lk 23:30
6:17 [t]Zep 1:14,15; Rev 16:14 [u]Ps 76:7
7:1 [v]Da 7:2
7:3 [w]Rev 6:6 [x]Eze 9:4; Rev 22:4
7:4 [y]Rev 9:16 [z]Rev 14:1,3

other horse came out, a fiery red one.[v] Its rider was given power to take peace from the earth[w] and to
make men slay each other. To him was given a large sword.

5 When the Lamb opened the third seal, I heard the third living creature[x] say, "Come!" I looked, and
there before me was a black horse![y] Its rider was holding a pair of scales in his hand. 6 Then I heard what
sounded like a voice among the four living creatures,[z] saying, "A quart[a] of wheat for a day's wages,[b] and
three quarts of barley for a day's wages,[b] and do not damage[a] the oil and the wine!"

7 When the Lamb opened the fourth seal, I heard the voice of the fourth living creature[b] say, "Come!"
8 I looked, and there before me was a pale horse![c] Its rider was named Death, and Hades[d] was following
close behind him. They were given power over a fourth of the earth to kill by sword, famine and plague,
and by the wild beasts of the earth.[e]

9 When he opened the fifth seal, I saw under the altar[f] the souls of those who had been slain[g] be-
cause of the word of God and the testimony they had maintained. 10 They called out in a loud voice,
"How long,[h] Sovereign Lord, holy and true,[i] until you judge the inhabitants of the earth and avenge
our blood?"[j] 11 Then each of them was given a white robe,[k] and they were told to wait a little longer,
until the number of their fellow servants and brothers who were to be killed as they had been was
completed.[l]

12 I watched as he opened the sixth seal. There was a great earthquake.[m] The sun turned black[n] like
sackcloth made of goat hair, the whole moon turned blood red, 13 and the stars in the sky fell to earth,[o]
as late figs drop from a fig tree[p] when shaken by a strong wind. 14 The sky receded like a scroll, rolling up,
and every mountain and island was removed from its place.[q]

15 Then the kings of the earth, the princes, the generals, the rich, the mighty, and every slave and ev-
ery free man hid in caves and among the rocks of the mountains.[r] 16 They called to the mountains and
the rocks, "Fall on us[s] and hide us from the face of him who sits on the throne and from the wrath of the
Lamb! 17 For the great day[t] of their wrath has come, and who can stand?"[u]

144,000 Sealed

7 After this I saw four angels standing at the four corners of the earth, holding back the four winds[v]
of the earth to prevent any wind from blowing on the land or on the sea or on any tree. 2 Then I saw
another angel coming up from the east, having the seal of the living God. He called out in a loud voice to
the four angels who had been given power to harm the land and the sea: 3 "Do not harm[w] the land or the
sea or the trees until we put a seal on the foreheads[x] of the servants of our God." 4 Then I heard the num-
ber[y] of those who were sealed: 144,000[z] from all the tribes of Israel.

5 From the tribe of Judah 12,000 were sealed,
from the tribe of Reuben 12,000,
from the tribe of Gad 12,000,
6 from the tribe of Asher 12,000,
from the tribe of Naphtali 12,000,
from the tribe of Manasseh 12,000,

[a] 6 Greek *a choinix* (probably about a liter) [b] 6 Greek *a denarius*

6:4 For "sword," see the note on 1:16.
6:5 The "pair of scales" was a balance beam with scales hung from either end. Weights were originally stones (see the note on Pr 16:11).
6:6 One quart of wheat would have been enough for only one person, while three quarts of the less nutritious barley would have been barely enough for a small family. Famine had inflated prices to at least ten times their normal level.
6:8 For "Hades," see "Sheol, Hades, Gehenna, the Abyss and Tartarus: Images of Hell" on page 946. See also the note on "death and Hades" at 1:18.
The sword referred to here is the long sword (see the note on 1:16).
6:9 In Old Testament ritual the blood of the slaughtered animal was poured out at the base of the altar (Ex 29:12; Lev 4:7).
6:10 For expressions of vengeful attitudes toward enemies, see the note on Psalm 69:22–28. See also "Curses and Imprecations" on page 883.
6:11 Jewish thought held that God rules the world according to a predetermined time schedule (2Es 4:35–37, an Apocyrphal book never accepted into the standard Protestant canon) and that the end awaits the death of a certain number of the righteous (1 Enoch 47:4).
For "brothers," see the note on Romans 1:13.
6:12 See the note on sackcloth at Job 16:15, as well as "Sackcloth and Ashes: Rituals of Lamentation" on page 820.
6:13 Late figs are green figs appearing in the winter; they are easily blown from the tree, which at that season has no leaves.
6:15 A general was a Roman officer who commanded a cohort of about 1,000 men. For "freeman," see "Labor and Welfare in the Ancient Word" on page 1952.
7:2 Ancient documents were folded and tied, and a lump of clay was pressed over the knot. The sender would then stamp the hardening clay with his signet ring or roll it with a cylinder seal, which authenticated and protected the contents (see "Scrolls, Seals and Codices" on p. 2053). The sealing in chapter 7 results in the name of the Lord being stamped on the forehead of each of his followers (see 9:4; 14:1; cf. 22:4). For the background, see Ezekiel 9:4, where the mark was the Hebrew letter *Taw,* made like an *x* or + (see the note on this verse). Its primary purpose here is to protect the people of God in the coming judgments.

[7] from the tribe of Simeon 12,000,
from the tribe of Levi 12,000,
from the tribe of Issachar 12,000,
[8] from the tribe of Zebulun 12,000,
from the tribe of Joseph 12,000,
from the tribe of Benjamin 12,000.

The Great Multitude in White Robes

[9] After this I looked and there before me was a great multitude that no one could count, from every na-
tion, tribe, people and language,[a] standing before the throne[b] and in front of the Lamb. They were wear-
ing white robes and were holding palm branches in their hands. [10] And they cried out in a loud voice:

"Salvation belongs to our God,[c]
who sits on the throne,
and to the Lamb."

[11] All the angels were standing around the throne and around the elders[d] and the four living creatures.[e]
They fell down on their faces[f] before the throne and worshiped God, [12] saying:

"Amen!
Praise and glory
and wisdom and thanks and honor
and power and strength
be to our God for ever and ever.
Amen!"[g]

[13] Then one of the elders asked me, "These in white robes—who are they, and where did they come
from?"

7:9 [a]Rev 5:9 [b]ver 15
7:10 [c]Ps 3:8; Rev 12:10; 19:1
7:11 [d]Rev 4:4 [e]Rev 4:6 [f]Rev 4:10
7:12 [g]Rev 5:12-14

7:9 See "Palm Branches in Israel," below.

7:11 For information on the four living creatures, see the note on 4:6.

Palm Branches in Israel

REVELATION 7 The branches of the date palm appear in the symbolism of Greek, Roman and Jewish cultures:

✣ Palms were a longstanding sign of victory in the Greek world, and the Roman authors Livy, Virgil and Cicero made use of them based upon this significance as well.

✣ Palm branches were associated with the Jewish Feast of Tabernacles (Lev 23:40).[1]

✣ Together with the myrtle, willow and citron, they formed the *lulab*, an object the rabbis tell us was shaken at the recitation of Psalm 118:25: "O LORD, save us!" (Hebrew, *Hosanna!*). In John 12:13 the crowds waved their palm branches while shouting this same verse.

✣ The Maccabees used palm branches as part of the rededication ceremony for the temple (2Mc 10:7)[2] and minted coins picturing palm trees along with the inscription "For the redemption of Zion."[3]

✣ These symbols were also employed by the Jews of the failed Bar Kokhba rebellion when they attempted to overthrow the Romans and set up a Messianic kingdom.

Palm branches thus vividly depicted God's victory and the deliverance of his people. Revelation 7:9 portrays Christians who have overcome the persecutions of this world as waving palm branches and wearing white robes. The symbolism of the palm branches would have been meaningful to any ancient reader, but especially to one familiar with the place of palm branches in Jewish tradition and worship.

[1]See "The Festivals of Israel" on page 186. [2]Second Maccabees is an Apocryphal book. [3]For information on the Maccabees, see "The Intertestamental Period" on page 1551.

[14]I answered, "Sir, you know."

7:14 [h]Rev 22:14 [i]Heb 9:14; 1Jn 1:7

And he said, "These are they who have come out of the great tribulation; they have washed their robes[h]
and made them white in the blood of the Lamb.[i] [15]Therefore,

7:15 [j]ver 9 [k]Rev 22:3 [l]Rev 11:19 [m]Isa 4:5,6; Rev 21:3

"they are before the throne of God[j]
and serve him[k] day and night in his temple;[l]
and he who sits on the throne will spread his tent
over them.[m]
[16]Never again will they hunger;
never again will they thirst.
The sun will not beat upon them,
nor any scorching heat.[n]
[17]For the Lamb at the center of the throne will be their
shepherd;[o]
he will lead them to springs of living water.
And God will wipe away every tear from their eyes."[p]

7:16 [n]Isa 49:10

7:17 [o]Ps 23:1; Jn 10:11 [p]Isa 25:8; Rev 21:4

7:15 All 16 references to the temple in Revelation use the word that designates the temple proper—the place where God's presence dwelled—rather than its larger precincts. No longer may only one tribe (the Levites) enter into God's presence, for all believers have been made priests in God's service (see 1:6; 5:10; 20:6).

7:17 Ancient kings often referred to themselves as shepherds of their people (see Ps 23:1 and its note).

Trumpets in the Ancient World

REVELATION 8 Both Jewish and Greco-Roman cultures made use of trumpets, which played a variety of roles in the ancient world. In addition to their musical function, trumpets could be used to signal various public gatherings, from theatrical performances to coronations to worship services.

The Old Testament, more than Greco-Roman culture, provides the background for the New Testament's use of the "trumpet." Prior to the birth of Jesus, Israel used two basic kinds of trumpets: long, metallic instruments and the ram's horn (*shofar*).[1] The New Testament uses one word to translate both kinds. Common uses for the trumpet in the Old Testament were as follows:

- They were blown to ready troops for battle (Nu 10:9; Jdg 3:27). Paul employed this image in 1 Corinthians 14:8.
- Priests sounded trumpets at the time of the destruction of **Jericho** (Jos 6:16).[2]
- Particularly important is the Old Testament's association of trumpets with theophany (a manifest appearing of God). For example, when Moses led the people of Israel to meet with God at Sinai, a trumpet blast was heard (Ex 19:16).
- A special ritual of trumpet blasts on the first day of the seventh calendar month inaugurated a sacred month that included the Day of Atonement and the Feast of Tabernacles or Booths (Nu 29:1–6).[3]

The trumpet in the New Testament is connected in Matthew 24:31, 1 Corinthians 15:52 and 1 Thessalonians 4:16 with God's appearing to the world at the end of history (already anticipated in Isa 27:13 and Zec 9:14). In a similar way the seven trumpets in Revelation 8–11 serve as warnings to people on Earth and signal the advent of God's kingdom. The parallels with the seven trumpets at the fall of Jericho are striking in light of the "collapse" of the great city in Revelation 11:13.

[1]See "Ancient Musical Instruments" on page 797 and "The Shofar" on page 898. [2]See "The Walls of Jericho" on page 312. [3]See "The Festivals of Israel" on page 186.

The Seventh Seal and the Golden Censer

8 When he opened the seventh seal,[q] there was silence in heaven for about half an hour.
2 And I saw the seven angels[r] who stand before God, and to them were given seven trumpets.
3 Another angel,[s] who had a golden censer, came and stood at the altar. He was given much incense
to offer, with the prayers of all the saints,[t] on the golden altar[u] before the throne. 4 The smoke of the in-
cense, together with the prayers of the saints, went up before God[v] from the angel's hand. 5 Then the an-
gel took the censer, filled it with fire from the altar,[w] and hurled it on the earth; and there came peals of
thunder,[x] rumblings, flashes of lightning and an earthquake.[y]

The Trumpets

6 Then the seven angels who had the seven trumpets[z] prepared to sound them.
7 The first angel sounded his trumpet, and there came hail and fire[a] mixed with blood, and it was
hurled down upon the earth. A third[b] of the earth was burned up, a third of the trees were burned up,
and all the green grass was burned up.[c]
8 The second angel sounded his trumpet, and something like a huge mountain,[d] all ablaze, was thrown
into the sea. A third[e] of the sea turned into blood,[f] 9 a third[g] of the living creatures in the sea died, and a
third of the ships were destroyed.
10 The third angel sounded his trumpet, and a great star, blazing like a torch, fell from the sky[h] on a
third of the rivers and on the springs of water[i]— 11 the name of the star is Wormwood.[a] A third[j] of the
waters turned bitter, and many people died from the waters that had become bitter.[k]
12 The fourth angel sounded his trumpet, and a third of the sun was struck, a third of the moon, and
a third of the stars, so that a third[l] of them turned dark.[m] A third of the day was without light, and also
a third of the night.
13 As I watched, I heard an eagle that was flying in midair[n] call out in a loud voice: "Woe! Woe! Woe[o]
to the inhabitants of the earth, because of the trumpet blasts about to be sounded by the other three
angels!"

9 The fifth angel sounded his trumpet, and I saw a star that had fallen from the sky to the earth.[p] The
star was given the key to the shaft of the Abyss.[q] 2 When he opened the Abyss, smoke rose from it like
the smoke from a gigantic furnace.[r] The sun and sky were darkened[s] by the smoke from the Abyss. 3 And
out of the smoke locusts[t] came down upon the earth and were given power like that of scorpions[u] of the
earth. 4 They were told not to harm[v] the grass of the earth or any plant or tree,[w] but only those people who
did not have the seal of God on their foreheads.[x] 5 They were not given power to kill them, but only to
torture them for five months.[y] And the agony they suffered was like that of the sting of a scorpion[z] when
it strikes a man. 6 During those days men will seek death, but will not find it; they will long to die, but
death will elude them.[a]
7 The locusts looked like horses prepared for battle.[b] On their heads they wore something like crowns
of gold, and their faces resembled human faces.[c] 8 Their hair was like women's hair, and their teeth were
like lions' teeth.[d] 9 They had breastplates like breastplates of iron, and the sound of their wings was like

8:1 [q]Rev 6:1
8:2 [r]ver 6-13; Rev 9:1,13; 11:15
8:3 [s]Rev 7:2 [t]Rev 5:8 [u]Ex 30:1-6; Heb 9:4; Rev 9:13
8:4 [v]Ps 141:2
8:5 [w]Lev 16:12,13 [x]Rev 4:5 [y]Rev 6:12
8:6 [z]ver 2
8:7 [a]Eze 38:22 [b]ver 7-12; Rev 9:15,18; 12:4 [c]Rev 9:4
8:8 [d]Jer 51:25 [e]ver 7 [f]Rev 16:3
8:9 [g]ver 7
8:10 [h]Isa 14:12; Rev 6:13; 9:1 [i]Rev 14:7; 16:4
8:11 [j]ver 7 [k]Jer 9:15; 23:15
8:12 [l]ver 7 [m]Ex 10:21-23; Rev 6:12,13
8:13 [n]Rev 14:6; 19:17 [o]Rev 9:12; 11:14
9:1 [p]Rev 8:10 [q]ver 2,11; Lk 8:31
9:2 [r]Ge 19:28; Ex 19:18 [s]Joel 2:2,10
9:3 [t]Ex 10:12-15 [u]ver 5,10
9:4 [v]Rev 6:6 [w]Rev 8:7 [x]Rev 7:2,3
9:5 [y]ver 10 [z]ver 3
9:6 [a]Job 3:21; Jer 8:3; Rev 6:16
9:7 [b]Joel 2:4 [c]Da 7:8
9:8 [d]Joel 1:6

[a] *11* That is, Bitterness

8:2 In Old Testament times the trumpet served to announce important events and to give signals in time of war (see "Trumpets in the Ancient World" on p. 2057).
8:3 A censer was a firepan used to hold live charcoal for the burning of incense (cf. Ex 27:3; 1Ki 7:50; see "Incense" on p. 1209).
8:4 See "Angels and Guardian Spirits in the Bible and the Ancient Near East" on p. 1529.
8:5 See the note on 4:5.
8:7–8,10,12–13 See "Trumpets in the Ancient World" on page 2057.
8:11 Wormwood, a plant with a strong, bitter taste, is used here as a metaphor for calamity and sorrow. It is not poisonous, but its bitterness does suggest death.
9:1 The ancients believed that the Abyss was the subterranean abode of demonic hordes. This Greek word, meaning "very deep" or "bottomless," is used in the Septuagint to translate the Hebrew word for the primeval deep (see Ge 1:2; 7:11; Pr 8:28; see also the note on Lk 8:31 and "Sheol, Hades, Gehenna, the Abyss and Tartarus: Images of Hell" on p. 946).
9:3 Locusts traveling in enormous swarms could strip a land of all vegetation. As recently as 1866, 200,000 people died in a famine in Algiers following a locust plague. (See "Locusts in the Ancient Near East" on p. 1438.)

Scorpions are large, spider-like organisms that injure or kill by means of a poisonous barb in the tail.
9:4 For "the seal of God on their foreheads," see the note on 7:2.
9:5 "Five months" is a limited period of time suggested by the life cycle of the locust or the duration of the dry season (spring through late summer, about five months), in which the danger of a locust invasion is always present in this part of the world.
9:6 Cornelius Gallus, a Roman poet living in the first century B.C., wrote: "Worse than any wound is the wish to die and yet not be able to do so."
9:8 For a discussion of literal and figurative references to hair in the Bible, see the note on Psalm 40:12. See also "Beards and Hairstyles in the Biblical World" on page 1084.
9:9 The breastplate was a coat of mail that protected the wearer's midsection. "Breastplates of iron" is a reference to thin iron pieces riveted to a leather base.

9:9 [e]Joel 2:5 the thundering of many horses and chariots rushing into battle.[e] 10 They had tails and stings like scor-
9:10 [f]ver 3,5,19 pions, and in their tails they had power to torment people for five months.[f] 11 They had as king over them
9:11 [g]ver 1,2 the angel of the Abyss,[g] whose name in Hebrew is Abaddon, and in Greek, Apollyon.[a]
9:12 [h]Rev 8:13 12 The first woe is past; two other woes are yet to come.[h]
9:13 [i]Ex 30:1-3 13 The sixth angel sounded his trumpet, and I heard a voice coming from the horns[b][i] of the golden al-
[j]Rev 8:3 tar that is before God.[j] 14 It said to the sixth angel who had the trumpet, "Release the four angels who are
9:14 [k]Rev 16:12 bound at the great river Euphrates."[k] 15 And the four angels who had been kept ready for this very hour
9:15 [l]ver 18 and day and month and year were released to kill a third of mankind.[l] 16 The number of the mounted
9:16 [m]Rev 5:11; 7:4 troops was two hundred million. I heard their number.[m]
17 The horses and riders I saw in my vision looked like this: Their breastplates were fiery red, dark
9:17 [n]Rev 11:5 blue, and yellow as sulfur. The heads of the horses resembled the heads of lions, and out of their mouths[n]
[o]ver 18 9:18 [p]ver 15 came fire, smoke and sulfur.[o] 18 A third of mankind was killed[p] by the three plagues of fire, smoke and
[q]ver 17 sulfur[q] that came out of their mouths. 19 The power of the horses was in their mouths and in their tails;
for their tails were like snakes, having heads with which they inflict injury.
9:20 [r]Dt 31:29 20 The rest of mankind that were not killed by these plagues still did not repent of the work of their
[s]1Co 10:20 [t]Ps 115:4-7; hands;[r] they did not stop worshiping demons,[s] and idols of gold, silver, bronze, stone and wood—idols
135:15-17; Da 5:23 that cannot see or hear or walk.[t] 21 Nor did they repent[u] of their murders, their magic arts,[v] their sexual
9:21 [u]Rev 2:21 [v]Rev 18:23 [w]Rev 17:2,5 immorality[w] or their thefts.

The Angel and the Little Scroll

10:1 [x]Rev 5:2 [y]Mt 17:2; Rev 1:16 10 Then I saw another mighty angel[x] coming down from heaven. He was robed in a cloud, with a
[z]Rev 1:15 rainbow above his head; his face was like the sun,[y] and his legs were like fiery pillars.[z] 2 He was
holding a little scroll, which lay open in his hand. He planted his right foot on the sea and his left foot on
the land, 3 and he gave a loud shout like the roar of a lion. When he shouted, the voices of the seven thun-
10:3 [a]Rev 4:5 ders[a] spoke. 4 And when the seven thunders spoke, I was about to write; but I heard a voice from heaven
10:4 [b]Da 8:26; 12:4,9; Rev 22:10 say, "Seal up what the seven thunders have said and do not write it down."[b]
10:5 [c]Da 12:7 5 Then the angel I had seen standing on the sea and on the land raised his right hand to heaven.[c] 6 And
he swore by him who lives for ever and ever, who created the heavens and all that is in them, the earth
10:6 [d]Rev 4:11; 14:7 [e]Rev 16:17 and all that is in it, and the sea and all that is in it,[d] and said, "There will be no more delay![e] 7 But in the
10:7 [f]Ro 16:25 days when the seventh angel is about to sound his trumpet, the mystery[f] of God will be accomplished,
just as he announced to his servants the prophets."
10:8 [g]ver 4 8 Then the voice that I had heard from heaven[g] spoke to me once more: "Go, take the scroll that lies
open in the hand of the angel who is standing on the sea and on the land."
9 So I went to the angel and asked him to give me the little scroll. He said to me, "Take it and eat it. It
10:9 [h]Jer 15:16; Eze 2:8-3:3 will turn your stomach sour, but in your mouth it will be as sweet as honey."[h] 10 I took the little scroll
from the angel's hand and ate it. It tasted as sweet as honey in my mouth, but when I had eaten it, my
10:11 [i]Eze 37:4,9 stomach turned sour. 11 Then I was told, "You must prophesy[i] again about many peoples, nations, lan-
guages and kings."

The Two Witnesses

11:1 [j]Eze 40:3; Rev 21:15 11 I was given a reed like a measuring rod[j] and was told, "Go and measure the temple of God and
11:2 [k]Eze 40:17,20 the altar, and count the worshipers there. 2 But exclude the outer court;[k] do not measure it,

[a] *11 Abaddon* and *Apollyon* mean *Destroyer.* [b] *13* That is, projections

9:10 For "five months," see the note on verse 5.
9:13 See "Trumpets in the Ancient World" on page 2057.
The horns were projections at the four corners of an altar (Ex 27:2; see also "The Horned Altar" on p. 924). Those fleeing judgment could seek mercy by taking hold of these horns (see 1Ki 1:50–51; 2:28; see also the note on Am 3:14).
9:14 See "The Tigris and Euphrates Rivers" on page 604.
9:17 For "breastplates," see the note on verse 9.
9:21 The magic arts involved the mixing of various ingredients for magical purposes. Believers at Ephesus publicly burned their books of magic, valued at 50,000 drachmas (Ac 19:19). (A drachma was a silver coin worth about a day's wages.)
10:5–6 Raising one's right hand was a part of oath taking (see Ge 14:22–23; Dt 32:40; see also "The 'Right Hand' in Ancient Thinking" on p. 1983 and "Oaths in Jewish and Christian Practice" on p. 1988).
10:7 In apocalyptic thought mysteries were secrets preserved in heaven and revealed to the apocalyptist (see "Apocalyptic Literature Outside the Bible" on p. 2048). Here the mystery is that God has won the victory over the forces of evil and will reign for ever and ever.
10:9 Honey is used in the Bible as a standard of comparison for pleasant things, whether they are ultimately good or bad (see also Pr 5:3; 16:24; SS 4:11; 5:1; Eze 3:3).
11:1 "Reed" refers to a bamboo-like cane that often reached a height of 20 feet (6 m) and grew in abundance in the waters along the banks of the Jordan. Straight and light, the reed was a convenient measuring rod (see Eze 40:3; Zec 2:1–2).
11:2 The "outer court" was the court of the Gentiles, encompassing approximately 26 acres.

WHO WROTE REVELATION?

REVELATION 10 Unlike nonbiblical apocalyptic works, Revelation is not attributed to a hero of the distant past.[1] The author identified himself as John (1:1) and informed his readership that he was writing from the island of Patmos, where he had apparently been exiled because of his testimony to Christ.[2] The author was clearly Jewish, based upon the numerous Old Testament quotations and allusions in the book and on his evident familiarity with the symbolic world of **Second Temple** Judaism.[3] The traditional view, held from the early second century forward, is that this was the same John (John the apostle) who wrote the Gospel of John, as well as 1, 2 and 3 John.

The common view that John the apostle wrote Revelation was challenged, however, in the third century by Dionysius, the bishop of Alexandria, because he was disturbed at the millenarianism (a belief in a 1,000 year reign of Christ on Earth; 20:2) that had arisen in his church as a result of reading the book in a literal fashion. Seeking, perhaps, to diminish the authority of Revelation, he claimed that the apostle could not possibly have written it, noting that the author of Revelation did not claim to be the beloved disciple, that the style of the book is markedly dissimilar to that of John's Gospel and that there was in fact another early Christian leader named John. Eusebius (*Ecclesiastical History*, 3.39.1–7), in a citation of the church father Papias, affirmed that there had been two church leaders by this name, the second of whom was known simply as "John the Elder." John was indeed a common name in Jewish circles, and it would not have been surprising to find two significant figures in the early church bearing this name (some have even ascribed Revelation to John Mark, author of the Gospel of Mark). As a result of these criticisms, the authority of the book of Revelation in the eastern churches was greatly diminished, to the point that some came to deny that it was **canonical**.

Another reason for denying that John the apostle wrote Revelation is 21:14, which states that the foundations of the New Jerusalem have inscribed upon them the names of the 12 apostles. This wording may suggest that the author was not himself an apostle and that the age of apostles was indeed past. Nonetheless, there are strong reasons for holding to the traditional view:

◆ Papias's implied assertion that there was a "John the Elder" is controversial.

We have only the citation of Papias (C. A.D. 130), found in Eusebius (C. A.D. 263–339), to work with. It is true that Papias's statement as we have it appears to imply the presence of a second John, but the evidence would be more compelling if it were not found only in a secondary citation.

The author of Revelation never called himself "the elder," a surprising fact if he were indeed this second John, known in the churches by this designation.

John the apostle, widely regarded to be the author of 2 and 3 John, referred to himself as "the elder" in both of these epistles. Thus it may be that John the Elder and the apostle John were in reality the same individual.

It would be surprising, if this profound book were written by this later "John the Elder," for this individual to have been widely known and revered in the churches of Asia and yet almost entirely forgotten until his name was recovered by the scholarly diligence of Eusebius.

Neither Papias nor Eusebius claimed that the second John wrote Revelation. The Papias quote says nothing about Revelation, and Eusebius stated only that if one were unwilling to ascribe Revelation to John the apostle, he or she could alternatively opt to ascribe it to the second John.

◆ Justin Martyr (mid-second century A.D.) and other church fathers, such as Irenaeus, Tertullian and Clement of Alexandria, all believed that John the apostle wrote Revelation.

◆ Despite their very different literary styles, there are thematic similarities between the Gospel of John and Revelation: Christ is the "Word" in both John 1:1 and Revelation 19:13, and in both works he is also both the "Lamb" (Jn 1:29; Rev 5:6) and the "shepherd" (Jn 10:11; Rev 7:17).

◆ Both Revelation and John strongly contrast truth and falsehood, light and darkness, etc.

◆ Scholars cannot demonstrate that John the apostle did not write Revelation on the basis of a simple observation that the style of Revelation is unlike that of the Gospel. The Gospel was probably based upon sermons John had been delivering throughout his career and thus had a polished, oratorical style. The Apocalypse, a report of visions, is on the other hand in a genre unlike that of any other New Testament book. It is unreasonable to expect that Revelation would read like either a Gospel or an epistle.

◆ Against the view that 21:14 requires a post-apostolic author, it is clear from Paul that the apostles were well aware of the high significance of their office (1Co 9:1–2; 12:28; Eph 2:20; 1Th 2:6).

◆ The author of Revelation implicitly presented himself as one of great authority. In Revelation 10:10 he symbolically ate a scroll (as did Ezekiel in Eze 3:1), and in Revelation 22:18–19 he conferred upon his own book an authority similar to that of the law in Deuteronomy 4:2. It would have been strange indeed for an obscure Jewish Christian to have made such claims of authority for his own book.

[1]See "Apocalyptic Literature Outside of the Bible" on page 2048. [2]See "Patmos" on page 2046. [3]See "The Tree of Life in Jewish Imagery" on page 2075.

because it has been given to the Gentiles.[l] They will trample on the holy city[m] for 42 months.[n] 3And I will give power to my two witnesses,[o] and they will prophesy for 1,260 days, clothed in sackcloth."[p] 4These are the two olive trees[q] and the two lampstands that stand before the Lord of the earth.[r] 5If anyone tries to harm them, fire comes from their mouths and devours their enemies.[s] This is how anyone who wants to harm them must die.[t] 6These men have power to shut up the sky so that it will not rain during the time they are prophesying; and they have power to turn the waters into blood[u] and to strike the earth with every kind of plague as often as they want.

7Now when they have finished their testimony, the beast[v] that comes up from the Abyss will attack them,[w] and overpower and kill them. 8Their bodies will lie in the street of the great city, which is figuratively called Sodom[x] and Egypt, where also their Lord was crucified.[y] 9For three and a half days men from every people, tribe, language and nation will gaze on their bodies and refuse them burial.[z] 10The inhabitants of the earth[a] will gloat over them and will celebrate by sending each other gifts,[b] because these two prophets had tormented those who live on the earth.

11But after the three and a half days a breath of life from God entered them,[c] and they stood on their feet, and terror struck those who saw them. 12Then they heard a loud voice from heaven saying to them, "Come up here."[d] And they went up to heaven in a cloud,[e] while their enemies looked on.

13At that very hour there was a severe earthquake[f] and a tenth of the city collapsed. Seven thousand people were killed in the earthquake, and the survivors were terrified and gave glory[g] to the God of heaven.[h]

14The second woe has passed; the third woe is coming soon.[i]

The Seventh Trumpet

15The seventh angel sounded his trumpet,[j] and there were loud voices[k] in heaven, which said:

> "The kingdom of the world has become the kingdom of
> our Lord and of his Christ,[l]
> and he will reign for ever and ever."[m]

16And the twenty-four elders,[n] who were seated on their thrones before God, fell on their faces and worshiped God, 17saying:

> "We give thanks to you, Lord God Almighty,[o]
> the One who is and who was,
> because you have taken your great power
> and have begun to reign.[p]
> 18The nations were angry;[q]
> and your wrath has come.
> The time has come for judging the dead,
> and for rewarding your servants the prophets[r]
> and your saints and those who reverence your name,
> both small and great[s]—
> and for destroying those who destroy the earth."

19Then God's temple[t] in heaven was opened, and within his temple was seen the ark of his covenant. And there came flashes of lightning, rumblings, peals of thunder, an earthquake and a great hailstorm.[u]

The Woman and the Dragon

12 A great and wondrous sign appeared in heaven: a woman clothed with the sun, with the moon under her feet and a crown of twelve stars on her head. 2She was pregnant and cried out in pain[v]

11:2 [l]Lk 21:24 [m]Rev 21:2 [n]Da 7:25; Rev 13:5
11:3 [o]Rev 1:5 [p]Ge 37:34
11:4 [q]Ps 52:8; Jer 11:16; Zec 4:3,11 [r]Zec 4:14
11:5 [s]2Ki 1:10; Jer 5:14 [t]Nu 16:29,35
11:6 [u]Ex 7:17,19
11:7 [v]Rev 13:1-4 [w]Da 7:21
11:8 [x]Isa 1:9 [y]Heb 13:12
11:9 [z]Ps 79:2,3
11:10 [a]Rev 3:10 [b]Est 9:19,22
11:11 [c]Eze 37:5,9,10,14
11:12 [d]Rev 4:1 [e]2Ki 2:11; Ac 1:9
11:13 [f]Rev 6:12 [g]Rev 14:7 [h]Rev 16:11
11:14 [i]Rev 8:13
11:15 [j]Rev 10:7 [k]Rev 16:17; 19:1 [l]Rev 12:10 [m]Da 2:44; 7:14,27
11:16 [n]Rev 4:4
11:17 [o]Rev 1:8 [p]Rev 19:6
11:18 [q]Ps 2:1 [r]Rev 10:7 [s]Rev 19:5
11:19 [t]Rev 15:5,8 [u]Rev 16:21
12:2 [v]Gal 4:19

11:3 See the note on sackcloth at Job 16:15, as well as "Sackcloth and Ashes: Rituals of Lamentation" on p. 820.
11:8–9 In the Near East the denial of burial was considered a flagrant violation of decency (see the note on Ps 63:10).
11:15 Trumpets were blown when a new king ascended his throne (see "Trumpets in the Ancient World" on p. 2057).
11:19 The Old Testament ark was a chest of acacia wood (see Dt 10:1–2, as well as "The Tabernacle and the Ark" on p. 153) symbolizing the throne or presence of God among his people. It was probably destroyed when Nebuzaradan razed the temple in Jerusalem (see 2Ki 25:8–10). In the New Testament it symbolizes God's faithfulness in keeping covenant with his people.

Awe-inspiring natural phenomena, such as lightning, thunder, earthquakes and hailstorms, are symbolic of the majesty and power of God (see "Storm Gods, Storm Imagery and Theophany" on p. 808).
12:1 For John the woman probably represented Israel or its faithful remnant, since the prophets often pictured righteous Israel as the

as she was about to give birth. 3Then another sign appeared in heaven: an enormous red dragon with sev-
en heads and ten horns[w] and seven crowns[x] on his heads. 4His tail swept a third[y] of the stars out of the
sky and flung them to the earth.[z] The dragon stood in front of the woman who was about to give birth,
so that he might devour her child[a] the moment it was born. 5She gave birth to a son, a male child, who
will rule all the nations with an iron scepter.[b] And her child was snatched up to God and to his throne.
6The woman fled into the desert to a place prepared for her by God, where she might be taken care of
for 1,260 days.[c]

7And there was war in heaven. Michael and his angels fought against the dragon,[d] and the dragon
and his angels fought back. 8But he was not strong enough, and they lost their place in heaven. 9The great
dragon was hurled down—that ancient serpent[e] called the devil,[f] or Satan, who leads the whole world
astray.[g] He was hurled to the earth,[h] and his angels with him.

10Then I heard a loud voice in heaven[i] say:

"Now have come the salvation and the power and the kingdom of our God,
and the authority of his Christ.
For the accuser of our brothers,[j]
who accuses them before our God day and night,
has been hurled down.
11They overcame him
by the blood of the Lamb[k]
and by the word of their testimony;[l]
they did not love their lives so much
as to shrink from death.[m]
12Therefore rejoice, you heavens[n]
and you who dwell in them!
But woe[o] to the earth and the sea,[p]
because the devil has gone down to you!
He is filled with fury,
because he knows that his time is short."

13When the dragon[q] saw that he had been hurled to the earth, he pursued the woman who had given
birth to the male child.[r] 14The woman was given the two wings of a great eagle,[s] so that she might fly to
the place prepared for her in the desert, where she would be taken care of for a time, times and half a
time,[t] out of the serpent's reach. 15Then from his mouth the serpent spewed water like a river, to over-
take the woman and sweep her away with the torrent. 16But the earth helped the woman by opening its
mouth and swallowing the river that the dragon had spewed out of his mouth. 17Then the dragon was en-
raged at the woman and went off to make war[u] against the rest of her offspring[v]—those who obey God's
13 commandments[w] and hold to the testimony of Jesus.[x] 1And the dragon[a] stood on the shore of
the sea.

The Beast out of the Sea

And I saw a beast coming out of the sea.[y] He had ten horns and seven heads,[z] with ten crowns on his
horns, and on each head a blasphemous name.[a] 2The beast I saw resembled a leopard,[b] but had feet like

a *1* Some late manuscripts *And I*

12:3 [w]Da 7:7,20; Rev 13:1 [x]Rev 19:12
12:4 [y]Rev 8:7 [z]Da 8:10 [a]Mt 2:16
12:5 [b]Ps 2:9; Rev 2:27
12:6 [c]Rev 11:2
12:7 [d]ver 3
12:9 [e]Ge 3:1-7 [f]Mt 25:41 [g]Rev 20:3,8,10 [h]Lk 10:18; Jn 12:31
12:10 [i]Rev 11:15 [j]Job 1:9-11; Zec 3:1
12:11 [k]Rev 7:14 [l]Rev 6:9 [m]Lk 14:26
12:12 [n]Ps 96:11; Isa 49:13; Rev 18:20 [o]Rev 8:13 [p]Rev 10:6
12:13 [q]ver 3 [r]ver 5
12:14 [s]Ex 19:4 [t]Da 7:25
12:17 [u]Rev 11:7 [v]Ge 3:15 [w]Rev 14:12 [x]Rev 1:2
13:1 [y]Da 7:1-6; Rev 15:2 [z]Rev 12:3 [a]Da 11:36; Rev 17:3
13:2 [b]Da 7:6

mother of the restored future remnant (see Isa 54:1; 66:7–10; Mic 4:9–10; 5:3)—an image they mixed with that of Israel as a bride (see Isa 62:5). In Jewish tradition Zion or Jerusalem often appeared as a mother. In one passage God promised the suffering, pregnant Israel that she would truly bear new life in the time of the resurrection, the day of God's wrath in which he would slay the serpent (see Isa 26:17—27:1).

12:3 Dragons abound in the mythology of ancient peoples (Leviathan in Canaanite lore and Set-Typhon, the red crocodile, in Egypt). In the Old Testament they were normally used metaphorically to depict the enemies of God and of Israel (see Ps 74:13–15; Isa 27:1; Eze 29:3 and their notes).

The word *diadem* does not occur in the NIV, but the Greek *diadçma* is used three times in Revelation (12:3; 13:1; 19:12) as an emblem of absolute power, distinguishable from the "crown" (Greek *stephanos*) mentioned elsewhere in the New Testament. The *stephanos* was awarded to victorious athletes, generals and early emperors of Rome, until Diocletian (c. A.D. 284–305) adopted the diadem as a symbol of his autocracy. Our Lord, too, will wear the diadem, as opposed to an ordinary crown (19:12).

12:7 Michael is an archangel who defeats Satan in heavenly warfare. In Daniel 12:1 he is the protector of Israel, who will deliver her from tribulation in the last days. (See "Angels and Guardian Spirits in the Bible and the Ancient Near East" on p. 1529.)

13:1 Multiple horns on one animal denote successive nations or rulers (see also Da 7:7–14; 8:3–22; Rev 17:3–16).

For "crown" ("diadem"), see the note on 12:3.

Roman emperors tended to assume titles of deity. Domitian, for example, was addressed as *Dominus et Deus noster* ("Our Lord and God")—a "blasphemous name." Emperor worship was compulsory (see "The Imperial Cult" on p. 1651).

those of a bear[c] and a mouth like that of a lion.[d] The dragon gave the beast his power and his throne and
great authority.[e] 3One of the heads of the beast seemed to have had a fatal wound, but the fatal wound
had been healed.[f] The whole world was astonished[g] and followed the beast. 4Men worshiped the drag-
on because he had given authority to the beast, and they also worshiped the beast and asked, "Who is like[h]
the beast? Who can make war against him?"

5The beast was given a mouth to utter proud words and blasphemies[i] and to exercise his authority for
forty-two months.[j] 6He opened his mouth to blaspheme God, and to slander his name and his dwelling
place and those who live in heaven.[k] 7He was given power to make war[l] against the saints and to conquer
them. And he was given authority over every tribe, people, language and nation.[m] 8All inhabitants of the
earth[n] will worship the beast—all whose names have not been written in the book of life[o] belonging to
the Lamb that was slain from the creation of the world.[a][p]

9He who has an ear, let him hear.[q]

> 10If anyone is to go into captivity,
> into captivity he will go.
> If anyone is to be killed[b] with the sword,
> with the sword he will be killed.[r]

This calls for patient endurance and faithfulness[s] on the part of the saints.[t]

The Beast out of the Earth

11Then I saw another beast, coming out of the earth. He had two horns like a lamb, but he spoke like
a dragon. 12He exercised all the authority[u] of the first beast on his behalf,[v] and made the earth and its in-
habitants worship the first beast,[w] whose fatal wound had been healed.[x] 13And he performed great and
miraculous signs,[y] even causing fire to come down from heaven[z] to earth in full view of men. 14Because
of the signs[a] he was given power to do on behalf of the first beast, he deceived[b] the inhabitants of the
earth. He ordered them to set up an image in honor of the beast who was wounded by the sword and yet
lived. 15He was given power to give breath to the image of the first beast, so that it could speak and cause
all who refused to worship the image to be killed.[c] 16He also forced everyone, small and great,[d] rich and
poor, free and slave, to receive a mark on his right hand or on his forehead,[e] 17so that no one could buy
or sell unless he had the mark,[f] which is the name of the beast or the number of his name.[g]

18This calls for wisdom.[h] If anyone has insight, let him calculate the number of the beast, for it is
man's number.[i] His number is 666.

The Lamb and the 144,000

14 Then I looked, and there before me was the Lamb,[j] standing on Mount Zion,[k] and with him
144,000[l] who had his name and his Father's name[m] written on their foreheads. 2And I heard
a sound from heaven like the roar of rushing waters[n] and like a loud peal of thunder. The sound I heard
was like that of harpists playing their harps.[o] 3And they sang a new song[p] before the throne and before

13:2 [c]Da 7:5 [d]Da 7:4 [e]Rev 16:10
13:3 [f]ver 12,14 [g]Rev 17:8
13:4 [h]Ex 15:11
13:5 [i]Da 7:8,11,20,25; 11:36; 2Th 2:4 [j]Rev 11:2
13:6 [k]Rev 12:12
13:7 [l]Da 7:21; Rev 11:7 [m]Rev 5:9
13:8 [n]Rev 3:10 [o]Rev 3:5; 20:12 [p]Mt 25:34
13:9 [q]Rev 2:7
13:10 [r]Jer 15:2; 43:11 [s]Heb 6:12 [t]Rev 14:12
13:12 [u]ver 4 [v]ver 14 [w]Rev 14:9,11 [x]ver 3
13:13 [y]Mt 24:24 [z]1Ki 18:38; Rev 20:9
13:14 [a]2Th 2:9,10 [b]Rev 12:9
13:15 [c]Da 3:3-6
13:16 [d]Rev 19:5 [e]Rev 14:9
13:17 [f]Rev 14:9 [g]Rev 14:11; 15:2
13:18 [h]Rev 17:9 [i]Rev 15:2; 21:17
14:1 [j]Rev 5:6 [k]Ps 2:6 [l]Rev 7:4 [m]Rev 3:12
14:2 [n]Rev 1:15 [o]Rev 5:8
14:3 [p]Rev 5:9

[a] 8 *Or written from the creation of the world in the book of life belonging to the Lamb that was slain* [b] 10 Some manuscripts *anyone kills*

13:10 The sword depicted here is the small sword or dagger (see the note on 1:16).
13:11–12 Most interpreters see a connection between the second beast and the emperor worship of John's day (see "The Imperial Cult" on p. 1651).
13:14 The sword here is the small sword or dagger (see the note on 1:16).
13:15 Belief in statues that could speak is widely attested in ancient literature. Sometimes the image at a shrine would be hollow, enabling a priest to hide inside the statue and speak for the god. Ventriloquism and other forms of deception were also common.
13:16 Whatever its origin—possibly the branding of slaves or enemy soldiers, the sealing and stamping of official documents or the sign of the cross on the forehead of a new Christian—the mark of the beast apparently symbolized allegiance to the demands of emperor worship (see "The Imperial Cult" on p. 1651). In the final days of the antichrist it will be the ultimate test of loyalty.

The right hand had metaphorical significance in the ancient world (see "The 'Right Hand' in Ancient Thinking" on p. 1983).

13:17 In ancient times the letters of the alphabet served for numbers. Riddles using numerical equivalents for names were popular.
13:18 Some scholars surmise that the significance of the number associated with the beast was readily apparent to John's original audience. The fact that the hearers were invited to interpret the riddle implies that the answer was available to believers in the seven churches. Various schemes for decoding these numbers result in such names as Euanthas, Lateinos and Nero Caesar. Others take 666 as a symbol for the trinity of evil and imperfection—each digit falls short of the perfect number 7.
14:1 In the Old Testament, Mount Zion was first the fortress of the pre-Israelite city of Jerusalem (see 2Sa 5:6–7 and the note on 2Sa 5:6) and later became a virtual synonym for Jerusalem (see "Jerusalem" on p. 1911). In Revelation, as in Hebrews 12:22–24, it signifies the heavenly Jerusalem, the eternal dwelling place of God and his people (see "Zaphon, Olympus, Sinai and Zion: The Mountain of God" on p. 843).
14:2 For "harps," see "Ancient Musical Instruments" on page 797.

the four living creatures and the elders. No one could learn the song except the 144,000[q] who had been
redeemed from the earth. 4These are those who did not defile themselves with women, for they kept
themselves pure.[r] They follow the Lamb wherever he goes. They were purchased from among men[s] and
offered as firstfruits[t] to God and the Lamb. 5No lie was found in their mouths;[u] they are blameless.[v]

The Three Angels

6Then I saw another angel flying in midair,[w] and he had the eternal gospel to proclaim to those who
live on the earth[x]—to every nation, tribe, language and people.[y] 7He said in a loud voice, "Fear God[z] and
give him glory,[a] because the hour of his judgment has come. Worship him who made the heavens, the
earth, the sea and the springs of water."[b]

8A second angel followed and said, "Fallen! Fallen is Babylon the Great,[c] which made all the nations
drink the maddening wine of her adulteries."[d]

9A third angel followed them and said in a loud voice: "If anyone worships the beast and his image[e]
and receives his mark on the forehead or on the hand, 10he, too, will drink of the wine of God's fury,[f]
which has been poured full strength into the cup of his wrath.[g] He will be tormented with burning sul-
fur in the presence of the holy angels and of the Lamb. 11And the smoke of their torment rises for ever
and ever.[h] There is no rest day or night for those who worship the beast and his image, or for anyone who
receives the mark of his name." 12This calls for patient endurance on the part of the saints[i] who obey
God's commandments and remain faithful to Jesus.

13Then I heard a voice from heaven say, "Write: Blessed are the dead who die in the Lord[j] from now on."
"Yes," says the Spirit, "they will rest from their labor, for their deeds will follow them."

The Harvest of the Earth

14I looked, and there before me was a white cloud, and seated on the cloud was one "like a son of
man"[a][k] with a crown[l] of gold on his head and a sharp sickle in his hand. 15Then another angel came out
of the temple and called in a loud voice to him who was sitting on the cloud, "Take your sickle[m] and reap,
because the time to reap has come, for the harvest[n] of the earth is ripe." 16So he who was seated on the
cloud swung his sickle over the earth, and the earth was harvested.

17Another angel came out of the temple in heaven, and he too had a sharp sickle. 18Still another an-
gel, who had charge of the fire, came from the altar and called in a loud voice to him who had the sharp
sickle, "Take your sharp sickle and gather the clusters of grapes from the earth's vine, because its grapes
are ripe." 19The angel swung his sickle on the earth, gathered its grapes and threw them into the great
winepress of God's wrath.[o] 20They were trampled in the winepress[p] outside the city,[q] and blood flowed
out of the press, rising as high as the horses' bridles for a distance of 1,600 stadia.[b]

14:3 [q]ver 1
14:4 [r]2Co 11:2; Rev 3:4 [s]Rev 5:9 [t]Jas 1:18
14:5 [u]Ps 32:2; Zep 3:13 [v]Eph 5:27
14:6 [w]Rev 8:13 [x]Rev 3:10 [y]Rev 13:7
14:7 [z]Rev 15:4 [a]Rev 11:13 [b]Rev 8:10
14:8 [c]Isa 21:9; Jer 51:8 [d]Rev 17:2,4; 18:3,9
14:9 [e]Rev 13:14
14:10 [f]Isa 51:17; Jer 25:15 [g]Rev 18:6
14:11 [h]Isa 34:10; Rev 19:3
14:12 [i]Rev 13:10
14:13 [j]1Co 15:18; 1Th 4:16
14:14 [k]Da 7:13; Rev 1:13 [l]Rev 6:2
14:15 [m]Joel 3:13 [n]Jer 51:33
14:19 [o]Rev 19:15
14:20 [p]Isa 63:3 [q]Heb 13:12; Rev 11:8

[a] *14* Daniel 7:13 [b] *20* That is, about 180 miles (about 300 kilometers)

14:4 As a portrait of God's army ready for holy war (see "*Herem*, Holy War" on p. 419), the 144,000 resemble Israel's troops who kept themselves from women prior to battle (cf. Dt 23:10; 1Sa 21:5; 2Sa 11:11). Revelation also portrays unrepentant humanity as a prostitute (Rev 17:1–5) and those faithful to Christ as a pure spouse (19:7; 21:2,9). These 144,000 have refused to commit immorality with Babylon.
14:6 The term "gospel" may not simply refer to the "Good News." In the prophetic tradition, "good news" included announcements of judgment on the enemies of God's people (Na 1:15).
14:8 Ancient Babylon in Mesopotamia was the political, commercial and religious center of a world empire (see "Babylon" on p. 1077) noted for its luxury and moral decadence. The title "Babylon the Great" is taken from Daniel 4:30. According to some it is used in Revelation to signify Rome as the center of opposition to God and his people, while others believe that it represents the whole political and religious system of the world in general under the rule of the antichrist. In the view of still others it is to be understood as literal Babylon—rebuilt and restored.

The Greek word translated "maddening" here and in Revalation 18:3 can mean passion, but normally in Revelation it refers to anger (cf. 12:12; 15:1,7; 16:1). God's wine can be seen as righteous anger (judgment) against the "adulteries" Babylon has brought upon the nations. Ancients typically diluted every part of wine with two parts of water, except when their aim was to become drunk. But God administers this wine of his anger at "full strength" (14:10).
14:10 In the Old Testament God's wrath is commonly pictured as a cup of wine to be drunk (see Ps 75:8; Isa 51:17; Jer 25:15; see also the note on v. 8).

Sodom and Gomorrah were destroyed by a rain of burning sulfur (see "The Destruction of Sodom and Gomorrah" on p. 32).
14:14 The "crown of gold" refers to a victory wreath of gold. See the notes on 2:10 and 12:3 for the comparison between the victory crown and the royal crown.

The Israelite sickle used for cutting grain was normally a flint or iron blade attached to a curved shaft of wood or bone (see the note on Mk 4:29).
14:18 This "sickle," in contrast to the one of verse 14, refers to the smaller grape-knife with which the farmer cut the clusters of grapes from the vine.
14:19 See "The Winepress" on page 1171. The treading of grapes was a common Old Testament figure for the execution of divine wrath (see Isa 63:3; La 1:15; Joel 3:13).
14:20 The approximate length of the Holy Land from north to south was 1,600 stadia or about 180 miles (300 km).

Seven Angels With Seven Plagues

15 I saw in heaven another great and marvelous sign:[r] seven angels[s] with the seven last plagues[t]—last, because with them God's wrath is completed. 2 And I saw what looked like a sea of glass[u] mixed with fire and, standing beside the sea, those who had been victorious over the beast and his image[v] and over the number of his name. They held harps given them by God 3 and sang the song of Moses[w] the servant of God and the song of the Lamb:

"Great and marvelous are your deeds,[x]
 Lord God Almighty.
Just and true are your ways,[y]
 King of the ages.
4 Who will not fear you, O Lord,[z]
 and bring glory to your name?
For you alone are holy.
All nations will come
 and worship before you,[a]
for your righteous acts have been revealed."

5 After this I looked and in heaven the temple,[b] that is, the tabernacle of the Testimony,[c] was opened. 6 Out of the temple[d] came the seven angels with the seven plagues.[e] They were dressed in clean, shining linen and wore golden sashes around their chests.[f] 7 Then one of the four living creatures[g] gave to the seven angels seven golden bowls filled with the wrath of God, who lives for ever and ever. 8 And the temple was filled with smoke[h] from the glory of God and from his power, and no one could enter the temple[i] until the seven plagues of the seven angels were completed.

The Seven Bowls of God's Wrath

16 Then I heard a loud voice from the temple saying to the seven angels,[j] "Go, pour out the seven bowls of God's wrath on the earth."

2 The first angel went and poured out his bowl on the land,[k] and ugly and painful sores[l] broke out on the people who had the mark of the beast and worshiped his image.[m]

3 The second angel poured out his bowl on the sea, and it turned into blood like that of a dead man, and every living thing in the sea died.[n]

4 The third angel poured out his bowl on the rivers and springs of water,[o] and they became blood.[p] 5 Then I heard the angel in charge of the waters say:

"You are just in these judgments,[q]
 you who are and who were,[r] the Holy One,[s]
 because you have so judged;
6 for they have shed the blood of your saints and
  prophets,
 and you have given them blood to drink[t] as
  they deserve."

7 And I heard the altar[u] respond:

"Yes, Lord God Almighty,
 true and just are your judgments."[v]

8 The fourth angel[w] poured out his bowl on the sun, and the sun was given power to scorch people with fire.[x] 9 They were seared by the intense heat and they cursed the name of God,[y] who had control over these plagues, but they refused to repent[z] and glorify him.[a]

10 The fifth angel poured out his bowl on the throne of the beast,[b] and his kingdom was plunged into darkness.[c] Men gnawed their tongues in agony 11 and cursed[d] the God of heaven[e] because of their pains and their sores,[f] but they refused to repent of what they had done.[g]

15:1 [r]Rev 12:1,3 [s]Rev 16:1 [t]Lev 26:21
15:2 [u]Rev 4:6 [v]Rev 13:14
15:3 [w]Ex 15:1; Dt 32:4 [x]Ps 111:2 [y]Ps 145:17
15:4 [z]Jer 10:7 [a]Isa 66:23
15:5 [b]Rev 11:19 [c]Nu 1:50
15:6 [d]Rev 14:15 [e]ver 1 [f]Rev 1:13
15:7 [g]Rev 4:6
15:8 [h]Isa 6:4 [i]Ex 40:34,35; 1Ki 8:10,11; 2Ch 5:13,14
16:1 [j]Rev 15:1
16:2 [k]Rev 8:7 [l]Ex 9:9-11 [m]Rev 13:15-17
16:3 [n]Ex 7:17-21; Rev 8:8,9
16:4 [o]Rev 8:10 [p]Ex 7:17-21
16:5 [q]Rev 15:3 [r]Rev 1:4 [s]Rev 15:4
16:6 [t]Isa 49:26; Rev 17:6
16:7 [u]Rev 6:9 [v]Rev 15:3; 19:2
16:8 [w]Rev 8:12 [x]Rev 14:18
16:9 [y]ver 11,21 [z]Rev 2:21 [a]Rev 11:13
16:10 [b]Rev 13:2 [c]Rev 9:2
16:11 [d]ver 9,21 [e]Rev 11:13 [f]ver 2 [g]Rev 2:21

15:2 For "number of his name," see the notes on 13:17–18; for "harps," see the note on 5:8.

16:2 For "mark of the beast," see the note on 13:16.

12 The sixth angel poured out his bowl on the great river Euphrates,[h] and its water was dried up to
prepare the way for the kings from the East.[i] 13 Then I saw three evil[a] spirits that looked like frogs; they
came out of the mouth of the dragon,[j] out of the mouth of the beast[k] and out of the mouth of the false
prophet.[l] 14 They are spirits of demons[m] performing miraculous signs, and they go out to the kings of
the whole world, to gather them for the battle[n] on the great day of God Almighty.
15 "Behold, I come like a thief! Blessed is he who stays awake[o] and keeps his clothes with him, so that
he may not go naked and be shamefully exposed."
16 Then they gathered the kings together to the place that in Hebrew[p] is called Armageddon.[q]
17 The seventh angel poured out his bowl into the air,[r] and out of the temple[s] came a loud voice[t] from
the throne, saying, "It is done!"[u] 18 Then there came flashes of lightning, rumblings, peals of thunder[v]
and a severe earthquake.[w] No earthquake like it has ever occurred since man has been on earth,[x] so tre-
mendous was the quake. 19 The great city[y] split into three parts, and the cities of the nations collapsed.
God remembered[z] Babylon the Great[a] and gave her the cup filled with the wine of the fury of his wrath.[b]
20 Every island fled away and the mountains could not be found.[c] 21 From the sky huge hailstones[d] of
about a hundred pounds each fell upon men. And they cursed God on account of the plague of hail,[e] be-
cause the plague was so terrible.

The Woman on the Beast

17 One of the seven angels[f] who had the seven bowls[g] came and said to me, "Come, I will show you
the punishment[h] of the great prostitute,[i] who sits on many waters.[j] 2 With her the kings of the
earth committed adultery and the inhabitants of the earth were intoxicated with the wine of her adul-
teries."[k]
3 Then the angel carried me away in the Spirit into a desert.[l] There I saw a woman sitting on a scarlet
beast that was covered with blasphemous names[m] and had seven heads and ten horns.[n] 4 The woman
was dressed in purple and scarlet, and was glittering with gold, precious stones and pearls.[o] She held a
golden cup[p] in her hand, filled with abominable things and the filth of her adulteries. 5 This title was
written on her forehead:

MYSTERY
BABYLON THE GREAT[q]
THE MOTHER OF PROSTITUTES
AND OF THE ABOMINATIONS OF THE EARTH.

6 I saw that the woman was drunk with the blood of the saints,[r] the blood of those who bore testimony
to Jesus.
When I saw her, I was greatly astonished. 7 Then the angel said to me: "Why are you astonished? I will
explain to you the mystery[s] of the woman and of the beast she rides, which has the seven heads and ten
horns.[t] 8 The beast, which you saw, once was, now is not, and will come up out of the Abyss and go to his
destruction.[u] The inhabitants of the earth[v] whose names have not been written in the book of life[w] from
the creation of the world will be astonished[x] when they see the beast, because he once was, now is not,
and yet will come.
9 "This calls for a mind with wisdom.[y] The seven heads are seven hills on which the woman sits. 10 They
are also seven kings. Five have fallen, one is, the other has not yet come; but when he does come, he must

16:12 [h]Rev 9:14 [i]Isa 41:2
16:13 [j]Rev 12:3 [k]Rev 13:1 [l]Rev 19:20
16:14 [m]1Ti 4:1 [n]Rev 17:14
16:15 [o]Lk 12:37
16:16 [p]Rev 9:11 [q]2Ki 23:29,30
16:17 [r]Eph 2:2 [s]Rev 14:15 [t]Rev 11:15 [u]Rev 21:6
16:18 [v]Rev 4:5 [w]Rev 6:12 [x]Da 12:1
16:19 [y]Rev 17:18 [z]Rev 18:5 [a]Rev 14:8 [b]Rev 14:10
16:20 [c]Rev 6:14
16:21 [d]Rev 11:19 [e]Ex 9:23-25
17:1 [f]Rev 15:1 [g]Rev 21:9 [h]Rev 16:19 [i]Rev 19:2 [j]Jer 51:13
17:2 [k]Rev 14:8; 18:3
17:3 [l]Rev 12:6,14 [m]Rev 13:1 [n]Rev 12:3
17:4 [o]Rev 18:16 [p]Jer 51:7; Rev 18:6
17:5 [q]Rev 14:8
17:6 [r]Rev 18:24
17:7 [s]ver 5 [t]ver 3
17:8 [u]Rev 13:10 [v]Rev 3:10 [w]Rev 13:8 [x]Rev 13:3
17:9 [y]Rev 13:18

[a] 13 Greek *unclean*

16:12 See "The Tigris and Euphrates Rivers" on page 604.
The "kings from the East" were apparently Parthian rulers (17:15—18:24), to be distinguished from the "kings of the whole world" (16:14) who will wage the final war against Christ and the armies of heaven (19:11–21).
16:13 The frog is classified as an unclean animal (Lev 11:10). The imagery suggests the deceptive propaganda that will, in the last days, lead people to accept and support the cause of evil.
16:16 "Armageddon" probably stands for Har Mageddon, "the mountain of Megiddo" (see the note on Jdg 5:19; see also "Megiddo" on p. 1541). Many see no specific geographical reference in the designation and take it to be a symbol of the final overthrow of evil by God.
17:1 Ancient coins and other artwork depict many an ancient city as a wealthy goddess enthroned beside a river. Literal Babylon lived by "many waters" (Jer 51:13; see "Babylon" on p. 1077), as did most other ancient cities, including Rome. The "waters" may symbolize international power.
17:4 In more ways than one, Babylon was "dressed to kill." Her purple and scarlet clothing indicated wealth, and the gold, precious stones and pearls further contributed to her splendor. John pictured a high-class prostitute who had intoxicated the nations with her hard-to-resist immorality (v. 2) but was herself drunk with the blood of the saints (v. 6).
17:7 For "mystery," see the note on 10:7.
17:8 For "Abyss," see the note on 9:1.
17:9 It may be significant that Rome began as a network of seven hill settlements on the eastern bank of the Tiber River. Her designation as the city on seven hills is commonplace among Roman writers (e.g., Virgil, Martial, Cicero).

The Early Persecution of the Church

REVELATION 17 Persecution was a fact of life for the early Christians. The book of Acts documents the martyrdoms of Stephen (Ac 7) and James, the brother of John (Ac 12:2), and describes Saul/Paul as breathing "murderous threats" against the church prior to his conversion (Ac 9:1).[1] Outside the Holy Land the frequent opposition of the synagogue Jews to Christianity was matched by growing concern among non-Jews. The staunch monotheism of the early Christians would have offended many pagans, who were accustomed to accommodating different gods from all over the world.[2] When the livelihood of pagan religious practitioners was challenged by the testimony of the gospel, persecution was the consequence (Ac 19). Early Christians were persecuted by Jews for claiming that Jesus of Nazareth was the Messiah and by some Christian Jews for accepting Gentile converts without requiring them to become Jewish proselytes,[3] and they were criticized by Gentiles for their monotheism (Gentiles had accepted Judaism as a legitimate, if peculiar, religion and thus did not officially engage in persecution of Jews).

The central Christian confession "Jesus is Lord" was a particular problem in the Roman Empire, because the affirmation of the sovereignty of Jesus was a direct challenge to the absolute rule of the Roman emperor. When the emperor or his representatives called for people to honor the emperor as a deity, Christians could not comply in good conscience.[4] It was inevitable that the Christians' allegiance to Jesus would trouble the Roman authorities, and the situation finally erupted under the emperor Nero in A.D. 64. Searching for a scapegoat for the fires that had plagued the city, Nero seized upon the Christians. The Roman historian Tacitus (*Annals*, 15.44) reported that large numbers of Christians were arrested and killed; some were dressed in animal skins and torn apart by dogs, others crucified and set on fire to serve as outdoor lamps. The abuse was so severe that even those hostile to Christianity criticized Nero's actions.[5]

The colosseum of Rome
Preserving Bible Times; © Dr. James C. Martin

After Nero the persecution of the church appears to have been more sporadic. While the emperor Domitian is sometimes blamed for broad attacks upon the church, the evidence for such a wide-scale persecution during his reign is insubstantial. (Such systematic persecutions, however, did occur during the ensuing centuries up to the time of Constantine.)

Nonetheless, at least one martyrdom is reported in the book of Revelation (that of Antipas in Rev 2:13), with a strong implication that more deaths were coming. A few decades after Revelation was written, the Roman governor Pliny wrote to the emperor Trajan for instructions on the parameters for punishing confessed Christians. Although Trajan's reply focused on procedural matters and did not specify the extent of punishment, it is clear that Christianity was perceived as a serious threat to the social order of the early-second-century Roman Empire.

The early Christians no doubt experienced trouble for confessing their faith in their daily lives as well. In the province of Asia, for example, trade guilds would often adopt a pagan god as their patron. Meetings of the guild would thus have involved the worship of this deity, and Christians who refused to participate in that worship might have compromised their livelihood. Many scholars believe that this is the background to Revelation 13:17, in which those who did not have the mark of the beast could neither buy not sell. Ridicule from neighbors, family tensions and concern over government harassment no doubt contributed to the fear of mistreatment and worse for the early Christians.

[1]See "The Geographic Expansion of the Church Under Persecution" on page 1781. [2]See "The Gods of the Greeks and Romans" on page 1908 and "The Mystery Religions" on page1939. [3]See "Proselytes in Second Temple Judaism" on page 1776. [4]See "The Imperial Cult" on page 1651. [5]See "Nero, Persecutor of Christians" on page 1931.

MAJOR EVENTS IN NEW TESTAMENT HISTORY IN THE FIRST CENTURY A.D.

	Roman	Jewish	Christian
B.C.	Reign of Augustus as emperor (27 B.C.–A.D. 14)	Reign of Herod the Great (37–4 B.C.) Beginning of Herod's temple (20 B.C.) Death of Herod the Great (4 B.C.)	Birth of Jesus Christ (6–4 B.C.)
A.D.	First census ordered by Quirinius, governor of Syria (6 A.D.)		
10	Reign of Tiberius (14–37)	Anointing of Caiaphas as high priest (18)	
20	Appointment of Pilate as procurator over Judea (26)		John the Baptist's ministry (26–27) Jesus' ministry (26–29)
30	Dismissal of Pilate by Rome (36) Reign of Caligula (37–41)	Reign of Herod Agrippa I (37–44)	Crucifixion of Christ (30–33) Pentecost (30–33) Martyrdom of Stephen (32–35) Conversion of Paul (33–35)
40	Reign of Claudius (41–54)	Death of Herod Agrippa I (44) Expelling of Jews from Rome (49)	Martyrdom of James and imprisonment of Peter (41–44) Judean famine and Paul's relief visit (46–47) Paul's first missionary journey (47–49) Jerusalem Council (49) Paul's second missionary journey (49–51)
50	Reign of Nero (54–68)	Appointment of Felix as procurator (52–59) Appointment of Festus as procurator (59–61)	Paul's third missionary journey (52–57) Paul's arrest (56–57) Paul before Festus and Agrippa II; his appeal to Caesar (58–59)
60	Great fire of Rome; Christians blamed and persecuted (64) Reign of Vespasian (69–79)	Jewish revolt against Rome (66) Flight of Jerusalem Christians to Pella, east of Jordan (66)	Paul in Rome (60) Martyrdom of James, the Lord's brother (62) Martyrdom of Paul and Peter (64–68)
70	Reign of Titus (79–81)	Fall of Jerusalem (70) Fall of Masada (73)	
80	Reign of Domitian (81–96)		Great Roman persecution of the church (81–96)
90			Banishment of John the Beloved to Patmos (93–96) Death of John (c. 98)

Chronological and Background Charts of the New Testament, pp. 118–119

17:11 [z]ver 8 remain for a little while. [11]The beast who once was, and now is not,[z] is an eighth king. He belongs to the
seven and is going to his destruction.
17:12 [a]Rev 12:3 [12]"The ten horns[a] you saw are ten kings who have not yet received a kingdom, but who for one hour[b]
[b]Rev 18:10,17,19 will receive authority as kings along with the beast. [13]They have one purpose and will give their power
17:13 [c]ver 17 and authority to the beast.[c] [14]They will make war[d] against the Lamb, but the Lamb will overcome them
17:14 [d]Rev 16:14 [e]1Ti 6:15; because he is Lord of lords and King of kings[e]—and with him will be his called, chosen[f] and faithful
Rev 19:16 [f]Mt 22:14 followers."
17:15 [g]Isa 8:7 [15]Then the angel said to me, "The waters[g] you saw, where the prostitute sits, are peoples, multitudes,
[h]Rev 13:7 nations and languages.[h] [16]The beast and the ten horns you saw will hate the prostitute. They will bring
17:16 [i]Rev 18:17,19 her to ruin[i] and leave her naked;[j] they will eat her flesh[k] and burn her with fire.[l] [17]For God has put it into
[j]Eze 16:37,39 [k]Rev 19:18 their hearts to accomplish his purpose by agreeing to give the beast their power to rule, until God's words
[l]Rev 18:8 17:17 [m]Rev 10:7 17:18 [n]Rev 16:19 are fulfilled.[m] [18]The woman you saw is the great city[n] that rules over the kings of the earth."

The Fall of Babylon

18:1 [o]Rev 17:1 [p]Rev 10:1 **18** After this I saw another angel[o] coming down from heaven.[p] He had great authority, and the earth
[q]Eze 43:2 was illuminated by his splendor.[q] [2]With a mighty voice he shouted:

18:2 [r]Rev 14:8 [s]Isa 13:21,22; Jer 50:39 "Fallen! Fallen is Babylon the Great![r]
She has become a home for demons
and a haunt for every evil[a] spirit,
a haunt for every unclean and detestable bird.[s]
[3]For all the nations have drunk
18:3 [t]Rev 14:8 the maddening wine of her adulteries.[t]
[u]Rev 17:2 [v]Eze 27:9-25 [w]ver 7,9 The kings of the earth committed adultery with her,[u]
and the merchants of the earth grew rich[v] from her
excessive luxuries."[w]

[4]Then I heard another voice from heaven say:

18:4 [x]Isa 48:20; Jer 50:8; 2Co 6:17 "Come out of her, my people,[x]
so that you will not share in her sins,
so that you will not receive any of her plagues;
18:5 [y]Jer 51:9 [z]Rev 16:19 [5]for her sins are piled up to heaven,[y]
and God has remembered[z] her crimes.
[6]Give back to her as she has given;
18:6 [a]Ps 137:8; Jer 50:15,29 [b]Rev 14:10; 16:19 pay her back[a] double for what she has done.
Mix her a double portion from her own cup.[b]
[7]Give her as much torture and grief
18:7 [c]Eze 28:2-8 [d]Isa 47:7,8; Zep 2:15 as the glory and luxury she gave herself.[c]
In her heart she boasts,
'I sit as queen; I am not a widow,
and I will never mourn.'[d]
18:8 [e]ver 10; Isa 47:9; Jer 50:31,32 [f]Rev 17:16 [8]Therefore in one day[e] her plagues will overtake her:
death, mourning and famine.
She will be consumed by fire,[f]
for mighty is the Lord God who judges her.

18:9 [g]Rev 17:2,4 [h]ver 18; Rev 19:3 [9]"When the kings of the earth who committed adultery with her[g] and shared her luxury see the smoke
[i]Eze 26:17,18 18:10 [j]ver 15,17 of her burning,[h] they will weep and mourn over her.[i] [10]Terrified at her torment, they will stand far off[j]
and cry:

[a] 2 Greek *unclean*

18:1–24 The exiled Jewish Christian prophet John wrote a funeral dirge over the mightiest empire in the world. This thinly veiled attack on Rome could have brought the early church unwanted scrutiny and more persecution. John's act must have appeared to his contemporary believers as courageous and full of faith—or as an invitation to mass martyrdom.

18:3 For "the maddening wine of her adulteries," see the note on 14:8.

Rome's mercantile empire had made it rich (see "Trade and Mercantilism in the Roman Empire on p. 2070). Most of its people, though poor themselves, were seduced by its greatness.

" 'Woe! Woe, O great city,[k]
O Babylon, city of power!
In one hour[l] your doom has come!' 18:10 [k]ver 16,19 [l]Rev 17:12

11"The merchants[m] of the earth will weep and mourn over her because no one buys their cargoes any 18:11
more[n]— 12cargoes of gold, silver, precious stones and pearls; fine linen, purple, silk and scarlet cloth; ev- [m]Eze 27:27 [n]ver 3
ery sort of citron wood, and articles of every kind made of ivory, costly wood, bronze, iron and marble;[o] 18:12 [o]Rev 17:4
13cargoes of cinnamon and spice, of incense, myrrh and frankincense, of wine and olive oil, of fine flour
and wheat; cattle and sheep; horses and carriages; and bodies and souls of men.[p] 18:13
14"They will say, 'The fruit you longed for is gone from you. All your riches and splendor have vanished, [p]Eze 27:13; 1Ti 1:10
never to be recovered.' 15The merchants who sold these things and gained their wealth from her[q] will 18:15 [q]ver 3
stand far off, terrified at her torment. They will weep and mourn[r] 16and cry out: [r]Eze 27:31

" 'Woe! Woe, O great city,
dressed in fine linen, purple and scarlet,
and glittering with gold, precious stones and pearls![s] 18:16 [s]Rev 17:4
17In one hour[t] such great wealth has been brought to ruin!'[u] 18:17 [t]ver 10 [u]Rev 17:16 [v]Eze 27:28-30

"Every sea captain, and all who travel by ship, the sailors, and all who earn their living from the sea,[v]
will stand far off. 18When they see the smoke of her burning, they will exclaim, 'Was there ever a city like
this great city?'[w] 19They will throw dust on their heads,[x] and with weeping and mourning cry out: 18:18 [w]Eze 27:32; Rev 13:4

" 'Woe! Woe, O great city, 18:19 [x]Jos 7:6; Eze 27:30
where all who had ships on the sea [y]Rev 17:16
became rich through her wealth!
In one hour she has been brought to ruin![y]

18:12–13 Rome's problem may have been not its wealth per se but unequal opportunity. The luxury items listed here represent status symbols or a squandering of resources at the expense of others' essential needs.

18:12 Purple was an expensive dye since it was extracted a drop at a time from the murex shellfish.

Citron wood was a costly dark wood from north Africa—used for inlay work in luxurious furniture.

Marble was used to decorate public buildings and the homes of the very rich.

18:13 Myrrh and frankincense had been brought by the Magi as gifts for the infant Jesus (see Mt 2:11 and its note; see also "Incense" on p. 1209).

18:19 Throwing dust on one's head was an act of sorrow and dismay (see "Sackcloth and Ashes: Rituals of Lamentation" on p. 820).

Trade and Mercantilism in the Roman Empire

REVELATION 18 Economic gain was the driving force of Rome's imperial expansion. Egypt, for instance, supplied much of the grain for Rome, while Judea provided items such as processed fish and balsam. Colonial governance, military peacekeeping efforts and the extensive system of Roman roads were all designed for Rome's material benefit. Local people who joined forces with Rome also profited from the imperial enterprise. Thus Revelation 18:11 notes that the merchants would weep and mourn over Babylon (Rome) because no one would purchase their cargo any longer.

In Revelation John was especially concerned about Roman economic exploitation through the trade in luxury goods. John's list of goods in verses 18:12–13 was modeled upon the listing of cargoes mentioned in the lament for the city of Tyre in Ezekiel 27, but he adapted it to the realities of the Roman Empire. Items like gold, silver, cinnamon and citron wood were luxuries, not necessities, for the Roman elite. Taken in this light, Revelation was not only a prediction of doom for the wicked kingdom of "Babylon" but also a challenge to any nation that focuses on wealth and luxury while rejecting the rule of God.

18:20 [z]Jer 51:48; Rev 12:12 [a]Rev 19:2

20 Rejoice over her, O heaven![z]
Rejoice, saints and apostles and prophets!
God has judged her for the way she treated you.' "[a]

18:21 [b]Rev 5:2 [c]Jer 51:63

21 Then a mighty angel[b] picked up a boulder the size of a large millstone and threw it into the sea,[c] and
said:

"With such violence
the great city of Babylon will be thrown down,
never to be found again.
22 The music of harpists and musicians, flute players and trumpeters,
will never be heard in you again.[d]
No workman of any trade
will ever be found in you again.
The sound of a millstone
will never be heard in you again.[e]
23 The light of a lamp
will never shine in you again.
The voice of bridegroom and bride
will never be heard in you again.[f]
Your merchants were the world's great men.[g]
By your magic spell[h] all the nations were led astray.
24 In her was found the blood of prophets and of the saints,[i]
and of all who have been killed on the earth."[j]

18:22 [d]Isa 24:8; Eze 26:13 [e]Jer 25:10
18:23 [f]Jer 7:34; 16:9; 25:10 [g]Isa 23:8 [h]Na 3:4
18:24 [i]Rev 16:6; 17:6 [j]Jer 51:49

Hallelujah!

19 After this I heard what sounded like the roar of a great multitude[k] in heaven shouting:

"Hallelujah!
Salvation[l] and glory and power[m] belong to our God,
2 for true and just are his judgments.
He has condemned the great prostitute
who corrupted the earth by her adulteries.
He has avenged on her the blood of his servants."[n]

3 And again they shouted:

"Hallelujah!
The smoke from her goes up for ever and ever."[o]

4 The twenty-four elders[p] and the four living creatures[q] fell down[r] and worshiped God, who was seat-
ed on the throne. And they cried:

"Amen, Hallelujah!"

5 Then a voice came from the throne, saying:

"Praise our God,
all you his servants,[s]
you who fear him,
both small and great!"[t]

19:1 [k]Rev 11:15 [l]Rev 7:10 [m]Rev 4:11
19:2 [n]Dt 32:43; Rev 6:10
19:3 [o]Isa 34:10; Rev 14:11
19:4 [p]Rev 4:4 [q]Rev 4:6 [r]Rev 5:14
19:5 [s]Ps 134:1 [t]Rev 11:18; 20:12

18:20 For expressions of vengeful attitudes toward enemies, see the note on Psalm 69:22–28. See also "Curses and Imprecations" on page 883.
18:21 The "large millstone" here is reminiscent of the one in Mark 9:42 (see the note there). It was actually a "donkey millstone" (one large enough to require a donkey to turn it). A millstone cast into the sea was symbolic of absolute destruction.
19:1–6 For expressions of vengeful attitudes toward enemies, see the note on Psalm 69:22–28. See also "Curses and Imprecations" on page 883.

19:1 "Hallelujah" is a word of praise found in most of the languages into which the Bible has been translated. The word, often rendered "Praise the Lord," was used by the writers of various psalms to invite all to join them in praising God (Ps 104:35; 105:45; 106:1,48; 111:1; 112:1; 113:1,9; 115:18; 116:19; 117:2; 135:1,21; the first and last verses of Ps 146 to 150). The term in Revelation 19:1, 3, 4 and 6 is borrowed from these psalms.

6 Then I heard what sounded like a great multitude,[u] like the roar of rushing waters and like loud peals
of thunder, shouting:

"Hallelujah!
  For our Lord God Almighty reigns.
7 Let us rejoice and be glad
  and give him glory!
For the wedding of the Lamb[v] has come,
  and his bride[w] has made herself ready.
8 Fine linen, bright and clean,
  was given her to wear."

(Fine linen stands for the righteous acts[x] of the saints.)

9 Then the angel said to me,[y] "Write:[z] 'Blessed are those who are invited to the wedding supper of the
Lamb!' "[a] And he added, "These are the true words of God."[b]
10 At this I fell at his feet to worship him.[c] But he said to me, "Do not do it! I am a fellow servant with
you and with your brothers who hold to the testimony of Jesus. Worship God![d] For the testimony of Jesus[e]
is the spirit of prophecy."

The Rider on the White Horse

11 I saw heaven standing open and there before me was a white horse, whose rider[f] is called Faithful
and True.[g] With justice he judges and makes war.[h] 12 His eyes are like blazing fire,[i] and on his head are
many crowns.[j] He has a name written on him that no one knows but he himself.[k] 13 He is dressed in a robe
dipped in blood,[l] and his name is the Word of God.[m] 14 The armies of heaven were following him, riding
on white horses and dressed in fine linen,[n] white and clean. 15 Out of his mouth comes a sharp sword[o]
with which to strike down[p] the nations. "He will rule them with an iron scepter."[a][q] He treads the wine-
press[r] of the fury of the wrath of God Almighty. 16 On his robe and on his thigh he has this name written:[s]

KING OF KINGS AND LORD OF LORDS.[t]

17 And I saw an angel standing in the sun, who cried in a loud voice to all the birds[u] flying in midair,[v]
"Come,[w] gather together for the great supper of God, 18 so that you may eat the flesh of kings, generals,
and mighty men, of horses and their riders, and the flesh of all people,[x] free and slave, small and great."
19 Then I saw the beast and the kings of the earth[y] and their armies gathered together to make war
against the rider on the horse and his army. 20 But the beast was captured, and with him the false prophet[z]
who had performed the miraculous signs on his behalf.[a] With these signs he had deluded those who had
received the mark of the beast and worshiped his image. The two of them were thrown alive into the fi-
ery lake[b] of burning sulfur.[c] 21 The rest of them were killed with the sword[d] that came out of the mouth
of the rider on the horse,[e] and all the birds[f] gorged themselves on their flesh.

The Thousand Years

20 And I saw an angel coming down out of heaven,[g] having the key[h] to the Abyss and holding in his
hand a great chain. 2 He seized the dragon, that ancient serpent, who is the devil, or Satan,[i] and
bound him for a thousand years.[j] 3 He threw him into the Abyss, and locked and sealed[k] it over him, to
keep him from deceiving the nations[l] anymore until the thousand years were ended. After that, he must
be set free for a short time.
4 I saw thrones[m] on which were seated those who had been given authority to judge. And I saw the

19:6 [u]Rev 11:15
19:7 [v]Mt 22:2; 25:10; Eph 5:32 [w]Rev 21:2,9
19:8 [x]Rev 15:4
19:9 [y]ver 10 [z]Rev 1:19 [a]Lk 14:15 [b]Rev 21:5; 22:6
19:10 [c]Rev 22:8 [d]Ac 10:25,26; Rev 22:9 [e]Rev 12:17
19:11 [f]Rev 6:2 [g]Rev 3:14 [h]Isa 11:4
19:12 [i]Rev 1:14 [j]Rev 6:2 [k]Rev 2:17
19:13 [l]Isa 63:2,3 [m]Jn 1:1
19:14 [n]ver 8
19:15 [o]Rev 1:16 [p]Isa 11:4; 2Th 2:8 [q]Ps 2:9; Rev 2:27 [r]Rev 14:20
19:16 [s]ver 12 [t]Rev 17:14
19:17 [u]ver 21 [v]Rev 8:13 [w]Eze 39:17
19:18 [x]Eze 39:18-20
19:19 [y]Rev 16:14,16
19:20 [z]Rev 16:13 [a]Rev 13:12 [b]Da 7:11; Rev 20:10,14,15; 21:8 [c]Rev 14:10
19:21 [d]ver 15 [e]ver 11,19 [f]ver 17
20:1 [g]Rev 10:1 [h]Rev 1:18
20:2 [i]Rev 12:9 [j]2Pe 2:4
20:3 [k]Da 6:17 [l]Rev 12:9
20:4 [m]Da 7:9

[a] *15* Psalm 2:9

19:7–8 The imagery of a wedding to express the intimate relationship between God and his people ("his bride") has its roots in the prophetic literature of the Old Testament (e.g., Isa 54:5–7; Hos 2:19; see also "Weddings in Ancient Israel" on p. 1039). Compare the New Testament usage at Matthew 22:2–14 and Ephesians 5:32.
19:10 For "fell at his feet," see the note on 1:17. The angel disallowed John's worship and declared that he, too, was simply acting as God's messenger. Many of John's Jewish contemporaries believed that the Spirit of prophecy had been suppressed but would return during the Messianic age.
19:12 For "crown" (*diadem*), see the note on 12:3.
19:15 For "sharp sword," see the note on 1:16. For "winepress," see "The Winepress" on page 1171.
19:20 Punishment by fire is prominent in both Biblical (see, e.g., La 1:13) and nonbiblical Jewish writings (e.g., 1 Enoch 54:1). Although the designation *gehenna* is not used here, this is what John was referring to (see the note on Mt 5:22).
19:21 The sword here is the long sword (see the note on 1:16).
20:1 For "Abyss," see the note on 9:1.
20:4 For "his mark," see the note on 13:16.

20:4 [n]Rev 6:9 souls of those who had been beheaded[n] because of their testimony for Jesus and because of the word of
[o]Rev 13:12 God. They had not worshiped the beast[o] or his image and had not received his mark on their foreheads
[p]Rev 13:16 or their hands.[p] They came to life and reigned with Christ a thousand years. 5(The rest of the dead did
20:5 [q]Lk 14:14; Php 3:11 not come to life until the thousand years were ended.) This is the first resurrection.[q] 6Blessed[r] and holy
20:6 [r]Rev 14:13 [s]Rev 2:11 are those who have part in the first resurrection. The second death[s] has no power over them, but they will
[t]Rev 1:6 [u]ver 4 be priests[t] of God and of Christ and will reign with him[u] for a thousand years.

Satan's Doom

20:7 [v]ver 2 7When the thousand years are over,[v] Satan will be released from his prison 8and will go out to de-
20:8 [w]ver 3,10 [x]Eze 38:2; 39:1 ceive the nations[w] in the four corners of the earth—Gog and Magog[x]—to gather them for battle.[y] In
[y]Rev 16:14 [z]Heb 11:12 number they are like the sand on the seashore.[z] 9They marched across the breadth of the earth and sur-
20:9 [a]Eze 38:9,16 rounded[a] the camp of God's people, the city he loves. But fire came down from heaven[b] and devoured
[b]Eze 38:22; 39:6 20:10 [c]Rev 19:20 them. 10And the devil, who deceived them,[c] was thrown into the lake of burning sulfur, where the beast
[d]Rev 14:10,11 and the false prophet had been thrown. They will be tormented day and night for ever and ever.[d]

The Dead Are Judged

20:11 [e]Rev 4:2 11Then I saw a great white throne[e] and him who was seated on it. Earth and sky fled from his pres-
ence, and there was no place for them. 12And I saw the dead, great and small, standing before the throne,
20:12 [f]Da 7:10 [g]Rev 3:5 and books were opened.[f] Another book was opened, which is the book of life.[g] The dead were judged
[h]Jer 17:10; Mt 16:27; according to what they had done[h] as recorded in the books. 13The sea gave up the dead that were in it,
Rev 2:23 20:13 [i]Rev 6:8 and death and Hades[i] gave up the dead[j] that were in them, and each person was judged according to
[j]Isa 26:19 what he had done. 14Then death[k] and Hades were thrown into the lake of fire. The lake of fire is the sec-
20:14 [k]1Co 15:26 20:15 [l]ver 12 ond death. 15If anyone's name was not found written in the book of life,[l] he was thrown into the lake of
fire.

The New Jerusalem

21:1 [m]Isa 65:17; 2Pe 3:13 21 Then I saw a new heaven and a new earth,[m] for the first heaven and the first earth had passed
away, and there was no longer any sea. 2I saw the Holy City, the new Jerusalem, coming down out
21:2 [n]Heb 11:10; 12:22; Rev 3:12 of heaven from God,[n] prepared as a bride beautifully dressed for her husband. 3And I heard a loud voice
from the throne saying, "Now the dwelling of God is with men, and he will live with them. They will be
21:3 [o]2Co 6:16 his people, and God himself will be with them and be their God.[o] 4He will wipe every tear from their
21:4 [p]Rev 7:17 [q]1Co 15:26; eyes.[p] There will be no more death[q] or mourning or crying or pain,[r] for the old order of things has passed
Rev 20:14 [r]Isa 35:10; 65:19 away."
21:5 [s]Rev 4:9; 20:11 [t]Rev 19:9 5He who was seated on the throne[s] said, "I am making everything new!" Then he said, "Write this
down, for these words are trustworthy and true."[t]
21:6 [u]Rev 16:17 [v]Rev 1:8; 22:13 6He said to me: "It is done.[u] I am the Alpha and the Omega,[v] the Beginning and the End. To him who
[w]Jn 4:10 is thirsty I will give to drink without cost from the spring of the water of life.[w] 7He who overcomes will
inherit all this, and I will be his God and he will be my son. 8But the cowardly, the unbelieving, the vile,
21:8 [x]1Co 6:9 [y]Rev 2:11 the murderers, the sexually immoral, those who practice magic arts, the idolaters and all liars[x]—their
place will be in the fiery lake of burning sulfur. This is the second death."[y]
21:9 [z]Rev 15:1,6,7 9One of the seven angels who had the seven bowls full of the seven last plagues[z] came and said to me,
[a]Rev 19:7 21:10 [b]Rev 17:3 "Come, I will show you the bride,[a] the wife of the Lamb." 10And he carried me away[b] in the Spirit[c] to a
[c]Rev 1:10 mountain great and high, and showed me the Holy City, Jerusalem, coming down out of heaven from
21:11 [d]Rev 15:8; 22:5 God. 11It shone with the glory of God,[d] and its brilliance was like that of a very precious jewel, like a jas-
[e]Rev 4:6 per, clear as crystal.[e] 12It had a great, high wall with twelve gates, and with twelve angels at the gates. On

---

20:7 Some scholars have suggested that Satan's release represents his own "second coming," mocking Jesus' future return to Earth. If so, in God's providence it becomes merely the stage for his final destruction.
20:8 Gog and Magog symbolize the nations of the world as they band together for a final assault on God. The Old Testament background is Ezekiel 38–39 (see the note on Eze 38:2). Revelation draws on the warning in Ezekiel 39:6 that God will hurl fire on Magog, and especially on the threat of 38:22 that he will cast hailstones and burning sulfur on Gog's army. Magog was a son of Japheth (Ge 10:2; 1Ch 1:5). Josephus applied this name to the Scythians (see the note on Col 3:11), but there is no evidence to support this identification.
20:13–14 See "Sheol, Hades, Gehenna, the Abyss and Tartarus: Images of Hell" on page 946, as well as the note on "death and Hades" at 1:18.
20:14–15 For "lake of fire," see the note on 19:20.
21:6 For "the Alpha and the Omega," etc., see the note on 1:8.
21:8 The magic arts in ancient times called for the mixing of various herbs to ward off evil.
For "fiery lake of burning sulfur," see the note on 19:20.
21:11 See the note on crystal at Job 28:17.

the gates were written the names of the twelve tribes of Israel.[f] [13]There were three gates on the east, three on the north, three on the south and three on the west. [14]The wall of the city had twelve foundations, and on them were the names of the twelve apostles of the Lamb.

[15]The angel who talked with me had a measuring rod[g] of gold to measure the city, its gates and its walls. [16]The city was laid out like a square, as long as it was wide. He measured the city with the rod and found it to be 12,000 stadia[a] in length, and as wide and high as it is long. [17]He measured its wall and it was 144 cubits[b] thick,[c] by man's measurement, which the angel was using. [18]The wall was made of jasper,[h] and the city of pure gold, as pure as glass.[i] [19]The foundations of the city walls were decorated with every kind of precious stone.[j] The first foundation was jasper, the second sapphire, the third chalcedony, the fourth emerald, [20]the fifth sardonyx, the sixth carnelian,[k] the seventh chrysolite, the eighth beryl, the ninth topaz, the tenth chrysoprase, the eleventh jacinth, and the twelfth amethyst.[d] [21]The twelve gates were twelve pearls, each gate made of a single pearl. The great street of the city was of pure gold, like transparent glass.[l]

[22]I did not see a temple[m] in the city, because the Lord God Almighty[n] and the Lamb[o] are its temple. [23]The city does not need the sun or the moon to shine on it, for the glory of God gives it light,[p] and the Lamb is its lamp. [24]The nations will walk by its light, and the kings of the earth will bring their splendor into it.[q] [25]On no day will its gates ever be shut,[r] for there will be no night there.[s] [26]The glory and honor of the nations will be brought into it. [27]Nothing impure will ever enter it, nor will anyone who does what is shameful or deceitful,[t] but only those whose names are written in the Lamb's book of life.

The River of Life

22 Then the angel showed me the river of the water of life, as clear as crystal,[u] flowing[v] from the throne of God and of the Lamb [2]down the middle of the great street of the city. On each side of the river stood the tree of life,[w] bearing twelve crops of fruit, yielding its fruit every month. And the leaves of the tree are for the healing of the nations.[x] [3]No longer will there be any curse.[y] The throne of God and of the Lamb will be in the city, and his servants will serve him.[z] [4]They will see his face,[a] and his name will be on their foreheads.[b] [5]There will be no more night.[c] They will not need the light of a lamp or the light of the sun, for the Lord God will give them light.[d] And they will reign for ever and ever.[e]

[6]The angel said to me,[f] "These words are trustworthy and true.[g] The Lord, the God of the spirits of the prophets,[h] sent his angel[i] to show his servants the things that must soon take place."

Jesus Is Coming

[7]"Behold, I am coming soon![j] Blessed[k] is he who keeps the words of the prophecy in this book."

[8]I, John, am the one who heard and saw these things.[l] And when I had heard and seen them, I fell down to worship at the feet[m] of the angel who had been showing them to me. [9]But he said to me, "Do not do it! I am a fellow servant with you and with your brothers the prophets and of all who keep the words of this book.[n] Worship God!"[o]

[10]Then he told me, "Do not seal up[p] the words of the prophecy of this book, because the time is near.[q] [11]Let him who does wrong continue to do wrong; let him who is vile continue to be vile; let him who does right continue to do right; and let him who is holy continue to be holy."[r]

[12]"Behold, I am coming soon![s] My reward is with me,[t] and I will give to everyone according to what he has done. [13]I am the Alpha and the Omega,[u] the First and the Last,[v] the Beginning and the End.[w]

[14]"Blessed are those who wash their robes, that they may have the right to the tree of life[x] and may go

21:12 [f]Eze 48:30-34
21:15 [g]Rev 11:1
21:18 [h]ver 11 [i]ver 21
21:19 [j]Isa 54:11,12
21:20 [k]Rev 4:3
21:21 [l]ver 18
21:22 [m]Jn 4:21,23 [n]Rev 1:8 [o]Rev 5:6
21:23 [p]Isa 24:23; 60:19,20; Rev 22:5
21:24 [q]Isa 60:3,5
21:25 [r]Isa 60:11 [s]Zec 14:7; Rev 22:5
21:27 [t]Isa 52:1; Joel 3:17; Rev 22:14,15
22:1 [u]Rev 4:6 [v]Eze 47:1; Zec 14:8
22:2 [w]Rev 2:7 [x]Eze 47:12
22:3 [y]Zec 14:11 [z]Rev 7:15
22:4 [a]Mt 5:8 [b]Rev 14:1
22:5 [c]Rev 21:25 [d]Rev 21:23 [e]Da 7:27; Rev 20:4
22:6 [f]Rev 1:1 [g]Rev 19:9; 21:5 [h]Heb 12:9 [i]ver 16
22:7 [j]Rev 3:11 [k]Rev 1:3
22:8 [l]Rev 1:1 [m]Rev 19:10
22:9 [n]ver 10,18,19 [o]Rev 19:10
22:10 [p]Da 8:26; Rev 10:4 [q]Rev 1:3
22:11 [r]Eze 3:27; Da 12:10
22:12 [s]ver 7,20 [t]Isa 40:10
22:13 [u]Rev 1:8 [v]Rev 1:17 [w]Rev 21:6
22:14 [x]Rev 2:7

[a] *16* That is, about 1,400 miles (about 2,200 kilometers) [b] *17* That is, about 200 feet (about 65 meters) [c] *17* Or *high*
[d] *20* The precise identification of some of these precious stones is uncertain.

21:16 The city was a perfect cube, as was the Most Holy Place of both the tabernacle and the later temple (see 1Ki 6:19–20). The entire city will be the place where believers will experience God's presence.
21:18–21 See "Precious Stones of the Biblical World" on page 1156.
22:1 See the note on crystal at Job 28:17.
22:2 For "tree of life," see "The Tree of Life in Jewish Imagery" on page 2075.
22:4 In ancient times criminals were banished from the presence of the king (see Est 7:8; cf. 2Sa 14:24).
22:8 See the note on 1:17.
22:10 See "Scrolls, Seals and Codices" on page 2053.
22:13 For "the Alpha and the Omega," etc., see the note on 1:8.
22:14 See "The Tree of Life in Jewish Imagery" on page 2075 and "The City Gate" on page 392.

through the gates[y] into the city.[z] 15 Outside[a] are the dogs,[b] those who practice magic arts, the sexually
immoral, the murderers, the idolaters and everyone who loves and practices falsehood.
16 "I, Jesus,[c] have sent my angel to give you[a] this testimony for the churches.[d] I am the Root[e] and the
Offspring of David, and the bright Morning Star."[f]

[a] 16 The Greek is plural.

22:14 [y]Rev 21:12 [z]Rev 21:27 **22:15** [a]1Co 6:9,10; Gal 5:19-21; Col 3:5,6 [b]Php 3:2 **22:16** [c]Rev 1:1 [d]Rev 1:4 [e]Rev 5:5 [f]2Pe 1:19; Rev 2:28

22:15 The term "dogs" applied to all types of ceremonially impure persons.

The Tree of Life in Jewish Imagery

REVELATION 22 The tree of life in Revelation 22 depicts the healing of humanity from the effects of the fall, the most terrible effect being death itself. This image is found elsewhere in the Bible and is widely appropriated in early Jewish religious language and art. The tree of life in Genesis 2–3 represented the eternal life that humanity lost in the fall. In Ezekiel 47 trees with healing fruit grew alongside the river that flowed from the temple in the kingdom of God.[1] The menorah, the lampstand placed in the temple, may have been an abstract representation of the tree of life. In Biblical Wisdom texts such as Psalm 1, the righteous are compared to a tree planted by rivers of water. And in Proverbs 3:18 wisdom is described as a tree of life to those who take hold of her.

Outside of the Bible Jewish sources abound with references to the tree of life:

✣ Trees appear regularly in Jewish artwork. They are especially common in funerary settings, in this context almost certainly representing the tree of life as a symbol of immortality.

✣ The tree of life was common in early Jewish religious literature.

A text called the Targum Neofiti says, "The Law is a [or the] Tree of Life to all who study in it, and those who guard its commandments will live and rise up like a Tree of Life in the world to come."

In 4 Ezra 51–52 Ezra is told that God will open paradise for the righteous: It is for them that the tree of life was planted.[2]

In 1 Enoch 24–25 Enoch saw the tree of life on a journey to the ends of the earth; it was planted on God's mountain throne and was marvelously beautiful and fragrant.[3]

Rabbinic tradition suggested that the tree of life was so tall that it required a 500-year journey to scale it and reach the top.

There are many other such texts from Judaism. Collectively they tell us that the symbol of the tree of life powerfully evoked yearning for life and spiritual healing among ancient Jews, providing a Biblical symbol that they readily embraced. John was in effect saying that the only way to the true tree of life is through Jesus Christ.

Menorah in a stone carving from a synagogue frieze, third–fourth centuries A.D., from Eshtemoa near Hebron
Preserving Bible Times; © Dr. James C. Martin

[1]See "The Geography of Ezekiel 47" on page 1378. [2]For a description of 4 Ezra, also known as 2 Esdras, see "The Apocrypha" on page 1973. [3]For a description of 1 Enoch, see "The Bible and Pseudepigraphical Literature" on page 2041.

17 The Spirit[g] and the bride say, "Come!" And let him who hears say, "Come!" Whoever is thirsty, let him
come; and whoever wishes, let him take the free gift of the water of life.

18 I warn everyone who hears the words of the prophecy of this book: If anyone adds anything to
them,[h] God will add to him the plagues described in this book.[i] 19 And if anyone takes words away[j] from
this book of prophecy, God will take away from him his share in the tree of life and in the holy city, which
are described in this book.

20 He who testifies to these things[k] says, "Yes, I am coming soon."

Amen. Come, Lord Jesus.[l]

21 The grace of the Lord Jesus be with God's people.[m] Amen.

22:17 [g]Rev 2:7
22:18 [h]Dt 4:2; Pr 30:6 [i]Rev 15:6-16:21
22:19 [j]Dt 4:2
22:20 [k]Rev 1:2 [l]1Co 16:22
22:21 [m]Ro 16:20

22:19 See "The Tree of Life in Jewish Imagery" on page 2075.

Study Helps

Table OF WEIGHTS AND MEASURES

	BIBLICAL UNIT	APPROXIMATE AMERICAN EQUIVALENT	APPROXIMATE METRIC EQUIVALENT
Weights	talent (60 minas)	75 pounds	34 kilograms
	mina (50 shekels)	1¼ pounds	0.6 kilogram
	shekel (2 bekas)	⅖ ounce	11.5 grams
	pim (⅔ shekel)	⅓ ounce	7.6 grams
	beka (10 gerahs)	⅕ ounce	5.5 grams
	gerah	1/50 ounce	0.6 gram
Length	cubit	18 inches	0.5 meter
	span	9 inches	23 centimeters
	handbreadth	3 inches	8 centimeters
Capacity			
Dry Measure	cor [homer] (10 ephahs)	6 bushels	220 liters
	lethek (5 ephahs)	3 bushels	110 liters
	ephah (10 omers)	⅗ bushel	22 liters
	seah (⅓ ephah)	7 quarts	7.3 liters
	omer (1/10 ephah)	2 quarts	2 liters
	cab (1/18 ephah)	1 quart	1 liter
Liquid Measure	bath (1 ephah)	6 gallons	22 liters
	hin (⅙ bath)	4 quarts	4 liters
	log (1/72 bath)	⅓ quart	0.3 liter

The figures of the table are calculated on the basis of a shekel equaling 11.5 grams, a cubit equaling 18 inches and an ephah equaling 22 liters. The quart referred to is either a dry quart (slightly larger than a liter) or a liquid quart (slightly smaller than a liter), whichever is applicable. The ton referred to in the footnotes is the American ton of 2,000 pounds.

This table is based upon the best available information, but it is not intended to be mathematically precise; like the measurement equivalents in the footnotes, it merely gives approximate amounts and distances. Weights and measures differed somewhat at various times and places in the ancient world. There is uncertainty particularly about the ephah and the bath; further discoveries may shed more light on these units of capacity.

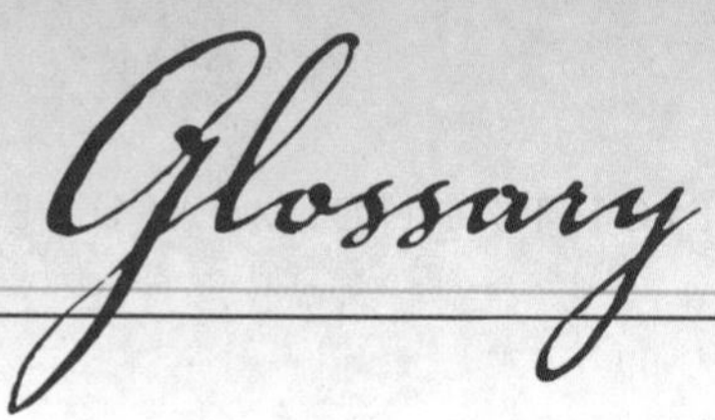

Achaemenid The ruling dynasty of the Persian Empire from 550 B.C. to 330 B.C. Founded by Cyrus the Great, the dynasty reached its peak under the rule of Darius the Great when the empire stretched from the Indus River in the east to modern day Libya in the west.

acropolis The uppermost part of a city in Hellenistic culture, often reserved for religious and cultic practice. The most significant acropolis is that in Athens, a level area of 300 by 150 meters (328 x 164 yd) that overlooks the city. It has played a significant role in the area for over three millennia. Construction of the temple system began in the eighth century B.C. and continued for three centuries. The pinnacle of this system is the grand Parthenon, constructed during the fifth century B.C. and dedicated to the goddess Athena. See "Athens" on page 1804.

Ai (Heb., "heap" or "ruin"); A town in central Palestine, most likely in the area of Jericho and Jerusalem, east of Bethel. The Israelites, under Joshua, defeated the city after initially having been repulsed. The victory was secured only after Achan's sin had been punished by God. See "Ai" on page 316.

Akkad The northern section of the southern Mesopotamian plain.

Akkadian(s) A third through first millennium B.C. Semitic language written in cuneiform. Originally from Mesopotamia, Akkadian became the official diplomatic language of the entire ancient Near East. The two primary known dialects were Assyrian and Babylonian.

Amarna The premier city of Pharaoh Amenhotep IV (fourteenth century B.C.). It is located 180 miles south of present day Cairo on the east side of the Nile. Hundreds of cuneiform letters have been found here from the reign of Amenhotep III (mid-fourteenth century B.C.). Many describe the political conditions in the Levant at a time when Habiru were attacking Canaanite city-states. See "The Amarna Tablets and the Habiru" on page 347.

Amenhotep IV (Akhenaten) (r. 1352–1336 B.C.); The "heretic" pharaoh who tried to replace traditional Egyptian religion with a near monotheistic worship of Aten. His reign also left behind an important set of Akkadian texts called the Amarna Letters.

Amorite(s) One of the nations that inhabited Canaan prior to the Israelite conquest. The Amorites may perhaps be identified with the Amurru named in cuneiform documents as overrunning Mesopotamia in the late third through early second millennia B.C. and forming the First Babylonian dynasty.

amphora A tall, two-handed vessel used in ancient Rome and Greece to store oil, honey, wine or corn.

amulet(s) A charm that is either carried or worn, generally with inscriptions of figures or characters. It was used to protect the carrier from sickness or witchcraft.

Anatolia The area that is today the Asian portion of the nation of Turkey. It served as a crossroads for the ancient Mediterranean world and thus had numerous significant cultural contacts with Syro-Palestine and its inhabitants. See "Anatolia and the Hittites" on page 144.

Apocrypha; Apocryphal The term *Apocrypha* means "hidden away" and refers to noncanonical books relevant to either the Old Testament or the New Testament. However, the collection commonly called the Apocrypha refers to 14 or 15 documents that were for the most part written between the last two centuries B.C. and the first century A.D. The term was first coined by Jerome in the fifth century A.D. to refer to those books that were part of the Septuagint (the Greek translation of the Old Testament) but not of the Hebrew Bible. Protestants do not view these books as canonical. See "The Apocrypha" on page 1973.

Aramaic A Semitic language closely related to Hebrew. It developed during the second millennium B.C. and later became the lingua franca of the Middle East. At the time of Christ it was the dominant language used by Jews in Palestine. Christ spoke and taught in Aramaic, and parts of the Old Testament were written in this language.

Ashdod An ancient city that was one of the five major political centers of the Philistines in the eleventh century B.C. The city saw conflicts between the Philistines and the Israelites and eventually came under Israelite control. The contemporary city of Ashdod is located three miles (nearly five km) north of the ancient site.

ashlar(s) A type of masonry that uses carefully cut stones set together with closed joints.

Asia Minor An area that is roughly represented by the nation of Turkey or the Anatolian peninsula. Civilization in this area has been dated back to 9000 B.C.

Asiatic(s) A native or descendent of Asia, which in Near Eastern studies refers to the Middle East. The Egyptians called Semitic peoples from Syria-Palestine "Asiatics."

Asshur The first capital of Assyria, located on the western bank of the Tigris River in modern Iraq. The city wall dates to the third millennium B.C.

Assyria; Assyrian(s) An ancient country situated in today's northern Iraq, with agricultural areas in the eastern portion. The area had been inhabited as early as the Paleolithic Age, but civilization appeared here around 6500 B.C. Assyrians were closely related in many ways to their southern neighbors, the Sumerians and later the Babylonians. See the articles on Assyria on pages 1501 and 1502.

Babylon; Babylonia; Babylonian(s) ("Gate of the gods"); Babylon was one of the most important cities of the ancient world and the capital of Babylonia during the second and first millennia B.C. Its location along the primary trade route between the Persian Gulf and the Mediterranean added to its significance. It was located 56 miles (90 km) south of present day Baghdad. During the Neo-Babylonian Empire it was the largest city in the known world, covering 2,500 acres. See "Babylon" on page 1077.

Babylonian captivity Also known as the Babylonian exile, this refers to the period between the deportation of the Israelites under Nebuchadnezzar II in the early sixth century B.C. and their release roughly 70 years later by Cyrus the Great. The exile was accomplished by two deportations, one in 597 B.C. and the second after the destruction of Jerusalem in 586. Most Israelites never returned to the area later called Palestine and became part of the Diaspora. See "The Jewish Diaspora in the First Century A.D." on page 1769.

Babylonian Talmud One of two compilations of the Talmud, the other being the Palestinian or Jerusalem Talmud. The Talmud is a collection of Jewish laws, including commentaries on the Torah. It is comprised of the Mishnah, a codification of rulings based on the Law of Moses, and a commentary on the Mishnah, also known as the Gemara.

Bethel (Heb., "House of God"); A historic city of great religious and ceremonial significance, located 11 miles (nearly 18 km) north of Jerusalem in present-day Jordan. Abraham built an altar, and Jacob had his vision of the ladder here. See "Bethel" on page 59.

Bronze Age(s) (3300–1200 B.C.; Early, Middle, Late); The period during which bronze alloys were the primary metals used to make tools. Scholars differ somewhat as to the dates assigned to these periods, and the terminology is not altogether uniform. The Early Bronze period lasted from approximately 3300–2100 B.C., The Middle Bronze period from around 2100–1550 B.C. and the Late Bronze period from about 1600–1200 B.C.

bulla(e) A lump of clay that has a seal impression or impressions on it. Bullae were used for sealing shut documents of papyrus.

Byzantine Pertaining to the eastern half of the Roman Empire, which survived the breakup of the western empire in the fifth century A.D. Its capital, Constantinople, was first given prominence by the Emperor Constantine, who in A.D. 330 made it the capital of the Roman Empire. Its language was primarily Greek, but its cultural influence was clearly Roman. The empire combined Roman and Greek influence with Christian Orthodoxy.

cache A hidden stash of items.

Canaan; Canaanite(s) The name associated with Palestine in the Old Testament; the land west of the Jordan River and east of the Mediterranean Sea. It was named after the father of the Canaanites, the original inhabitants. The Israelites systematically conquered this region during the second millennium B.C.

canon; canonical ("standard" or "rule"); The list of books that are considered authoritative by the Christian church. The Protestant canon contains fewer books than does the Catholic canon, which incorporates the books of the Apocrypha (called by Catholics the Deuterocanonicals). See "The Old Testament Canon" on page 1552 and "The New Testament Canon" on page 2022.

carinated A descriptive term for the sharp curves on some pottery vessels.

cartouche An oval-shaped box in which personal names were written in Egyptian hieroglyphs.

casemate wall(s) A type of city wall made of two parallel walls joined by crosswalls at regular intervals.

Chalcolithic Age The period between the Neolithic and Bronze Ages, running from approximately 4300–3300 B.C. and characterized by the use of stone and copper tools.

church fathers The men whose writings helped interpret Scripture and who established the doctrines of the Christian church. The Western church fathers include Augustine, Jerome, Ambrose, Gregory I and Tertullian, while their Eastern counterparts include Origen, Justin Martyr and Clement of Alexandria.

Code of Hammurabi (see Hammurabi, Code of).

codex An early form of book, replacing the scroll, in which several sheets of papyrus or parchment were stitched together and attached by thongs to thin wooden boards. See "Writing Materials in the Ancient World" on page 2037.

colophon Material at the end of a written work, usually giving the name of the author or scribe and the occasion for the writing. Ancient colophons frequently contained blessing or curse formulae.

cuneiform A writing system using a wedge-shaped stylus pressed into wet clay, which later hardened. The wedge-shaped characters of cuneiform also appear incised in metal, stone and other media. This form of writing was invented by the Sumerians before 3000 B.C. and adopted by the Akkadians, through whom it was carried throughout the Near East.

Dagon A fertility god worshiped in the Near East, including Philistia. His name may derive from the Semitic word for "grain."

Dead Sea Scrolls Manuscripts found, beginning in 1947, at the site of Qumran to the northwest of the Dead Sea. The collection of approximately 600 manuscripts contains portions of every Old Testament book except for Esther, in addition to numerous other works (hymnals, apocalyptic material, rulebooks, etc.). See "Biblical Interpretation at Qumran and Among the Early Rabbis" on page 1603.

Decapolis The area east of the Jordan River and the Sea of Galilee, dominated by ten Hellenic cities, some of which date back to the reign of Alexander the Great. These cities were distributed to different provinces during the reign of Trajan in the early second century A.D., so that the administrative district of the Decapolis ceased to exist.

demotic A cursive form of Egyptian hieroglyphics used from the seventh century B.C. to the fifth century A.D.

Deuterocanonical A term used among Roman Catholics for the Jewish texts written during the period between the Old Testament and the New Testament, including such works as Tobit and Maccabees. This same collection is called the Apocrypha by Protestants. See "The Apocrypha" on page 1973 and "The Books of the Apocrypha" on page 1974.

Diaspora The dispersion of the Jews away from Judea. Beginning with the Babylonian Captivity (586 B.C.), Jews emigrated from Judea. Some through forced deportations ended up in Babylon, while other fled as refugees to Egypt and other areas in the Middle East. After the destruction of Jerusalem in A.D. 70 many others were taken to Rome as captives. The Diaspora allowed Paul to visit and convert many Jews in several cities around the Mediterranean, thus planting Christian churches throughout the Roman Empire.

divided monarchy The period after the death of Solomon during which the Israelite kingdom was split into the northern kingdom of Israel (whose capital was later established at Samaria) and Judah (whose capital was at Jerusalem). The divided monarchy began when Israel, under the leadership of Jeroboam, rebelled against Rehoboam in 930 B.C.

divination The attempt to gain knowledge about events by consulting the gods through various means (e.g., dreams, interpreting natural phenomena as omens, inspecting the entrails of sacrificed animals, etc.). See "Akkadian Divination" on page 277.

Early Bronze Age (see Bronze Age)

Ebla An important city in northern Syria which has yielded a wealth of third-millennium B.C. cuneiform texts. See "Ebla" on page 19.

Elam; Elamite(s) An ancient kingdom located east of the Tigris River and north of the Persian Gulf. One of the earliest civilizations, dating back to the sixth millennium B.C., Elam was eventually defeated by the Assyrians in the seventh century B.C. Elamite, the language of Elam, was first written with pictograms and later by cuneiform. Small enclaves of Elamite speakers were still in existence in Iran during the tenth century A.D.

Elohim The general Hebrew term for deities, used in particular for the God of Israel. It is translated as "God" or "gods."

Enlightenment The eighteenth-century A.D. movement that prized human reason, progress, nature and the scientific process, rejecting the miraculous and supernatural, battling the institutional Christian church and instituting a religious system based primarily upon the reasonable ethical behavior of humanity.

epigraphy; epigraphic The study of inscriptions.

execration text(s) Texts that demonstrate the Egyptian practice of formally cursing persons and cities, attested from the Old Kingdom to the New Kingdom periods. The ritual most often involved writing the name of the person or city on a ceramic bowl, after which the curse was spoken and the bowl smashed.

exile(s); exilic period The Assyrian exile began with the first deportation of Israelites (from the northern kingdom) in 734 B.C., and the second deportation occurred after the destruction of Samaria in 722. These captives were forcibly migrated to other parts of the Assyrian Empire, including Nineveh. The Babylonian exile (or captivity) began in 608 B.C., when Nebuchadnezzar II deported some of the nobility and learned men of Judah. Subsequent deportations followed, until Nebuchadnezzar destroyed Jerusalem in 586 and led captives away to southern Mesopotamia. In 538 B.C., when Cyrus the Persian defeated the Babylonian Empire, he allowed the Jews to return to Jerusalem.

exodus, the; exodus period The Israelites' escape from slavery in Egypt, led by Moses. This event may be seen as the most significant in Israel's history. Although there is some debate as to the date of the exodus, most conservative scholars place it in the mid-fifteenth century B.C. See "The Date of the Exodus" on page 106.

glacis A slope at the base of a fortification wall, often found in Middle Bronze Age levels in Syria-Palestine.

Hammurabi A king of Babylonia during the eighteenth century B.C. (1792–1950, according to middle chronology dates). Hammurabi greatly expanded the First Babylonian Empire, even reaching the Mediterranean Sea.

Hammurabi, Code of The earliest complete collection of laws that has been discovered to date. It was commissioned by King Hammurabi of Babylonia and engraved on a black basalt stone 7.5 feet (2.3 m) tall.

Hasmonean(s) A prominent Jewish family of rulers (named for their ancestor Hasmon) during the second and first centuries B.C. Also known as the Maccabees, they led the Jews in rebellion against Syria.

Hazor An ancient Canaanite city that stood at the crossroads of two main trade routes north of the Sea of Galilee. Hazor became a strategic Israelite city and was fortified by Solomon. See "Hazor" on page 322.

hieroglyphs; hieroglyphics A system of writing, employed by Egyptians and Hittites, in which pictures represent words and syllables.

Hellenism; Hellenize(d); Hellenization; Hellenistic period The period from Alexander the Great (356–323 B.C.) to Roman rule (early first century B.C.). The term "Hellenistic" generally refers to Greek culture and its adoption by non-Greeks.

Hittite(s) A people of Indo-European descent who migrated into Anatolia by the second millennium B.C. The Old Assyrian name for the Anatolia region was Hatti. See "Anatolia and the Hittites" on page 144.

Horeb Another name for Mount Sinai. See "The Location of Mount Sinai" on page 123.

Hurrian(s) A people who migrated into the Near East from the north during the third millennium B.C. As the Hurrian population increased in the Near East, these people formed the powerful kingdom of Mitanni during the late second millennium. There is evidence of Hurrians residing in Syria and Canaan as well. See "The Hurrians" on page 57.

Hyksos A mixed group (mostly Semitic) that infiltrated Egypt in the Middle Bronze Age and took over control of the country. Their role in the exodus is still debated among scholars. See "The Hyksos and the Exodus" on page 99 and "The Hyksos and the Old Testament" on page 121.

Idumea; Idumeans The area comprised of Samaria and Edom. It was subjected to the Hasmonean kingdom under John Hyrcanus during the second century B.C., at which time the Idumeans were compelled to accept Judaism.

Intertestamental period The roughly 400-year period between the closing of the Old Testament and the beginning of the New Testament. See "The Intertestamental Period" on page 1551.

Iron Age (c. 1200–332 B.C.); The period of history in Syria-Palestine when iron tools began to be used (although bronze tools and weapons were actually still in wide usage).

Jericho A town located in the Jordan Valley, north of the Dead Sea and west of the Jordan River. It is the oldest known settlement, dating back to 8000 B.C. See "The Walls of Jericho" on page 312 and "New Testament Jericho" on page 1646.

Johannine Refers to the New Testament literature written by the apostle John.

Josephus (c. A.D. 37–101); A Jewish historian who was part of both the Jewish and Roman cultures. As a Pharisee, he reportedly fought against the Romans only to later enjoy imperial patronage under Emperor Titus. Josephus witnessed firsthand the destruction of Jerusalem in A.D. 70. His writings are of great significance in first-century Jewish and Christian studies. See "Josephus and the Fall of Jerusalem" on page 1606.

Judah/Judea The tribe of Judah was part of the kingdom of Israel until the period of the divided monarchy. After the secession of the northern tribes, Judah became the kingdom of Judah or the "southern kingdom," until the Babylonians conquered it in the sixth century B.C. After the exile the Jewish resettlement at Jerusalem eventually became known as "Yehud" or Judea. The boundaries of the region are roughly Jerusalem in the north, the Jordan River in the east, the Mediterranean Sea in the west and the Negev Desert in the south.

Kadesh Barnea A site in the Sinai where the Israelites camped during their wilderness wandering. Miriam died there, and it was there that Moses disobeyed God by striking the rock to produce water. See "Kadesh Barnea" on page 214.

Kassites Invaders of the northern regions of Babylonia during the seventeenth century B.C. Because of the early sixteen-century invasion of the Hittites, the Babylonians were susceptible to the Kassites' power and were overthrown. The Kassites established a dynasty that ruled until 1155 B.C. During this period, however, they lost their own cultural identity and became absorbed into the Babylonian culture.

King's Highway A strategic trade route that joined Arabia and the Mediterranean Sea.

lacuna(e) A term describing gaps that exist within ancient writings. The cause of these breaks is often the deterioration of the medium upon which the text was inscribed. For example, as a papyrus document rots away, portions of the text written on it become illegible.

Late Bronze Age (see Bronze Age).

Maccabean revolt A Jewish revolt in response to the attempts of the Syrian rulers of Palestine to replace Judaism with Hellenism. The tension reached its zenith in 168 B.C. when the Seleucid ruler replaced the temple altar to Yahweh with an altar to Zeus. The revolt was lead by a Jewish priest, Mattathias, and his sons, known as the Maccabees. The Maccabees were ultimately successful, and Israel enjoyed a new status as an independent nation under Maccabean (also called Hasmonean) rule.

Madaba map The earliest known map of Palestine, dating to approximately A.D. 560–565. It is designed into the floor mosaic of a Byzantine Church in Madaba, Jordan.

Marduk In Babylonian religion the god of thunderstorms. He defeated Tiamat and Kingu, the dragons of chaos, and thus assumed the mantle of supreme deity in the Babylonian pantheon. Believed to be the creator of the universe and thus of humanity, he had roughly 50 titles but was ultimately known as Bel or "Lord." See "A Prayer of Confession to Marduk" on page 831.

Mari An important Mesopotamian city in the third millennium B.C., located on the Euphrates River. The site has yielded tens of thousands of cuneiform documents relating to political and cultural issues during that time. See "Mari" on page 54.

Masoretic text The standard version of the Hebrew Old Testament, produced by the Masoretes, a group of Jewish scholars dating from the early Christian period until the Middle Ages. The Masoretes punctuated the text and added vowels (the original Hebrew text included only consonants). The standard for Hebrew Bibles printed today is a Masoretic text from A.D. 1088, currently housed in the Saint Petersburg Public Library.

material culture Archaeological finds in the form of tangible objects, such as pottery, figurines, cultic items, artwork, etc.

matriarch(s) The wives of the Biblical patriarchs: Sarah, Rebekah, Leah and Rachel.

Megiddo An important Israelite city in the Jezreel Valley that was fortified by Solomon. See "Megiddo" on page 1541.

Mesopotamia; Mesopotamian(s) (Gr., "between the rivers"); The area of land between the Tigris and Euphrates Rivers in present-day Iraq and Syria, Mesopotamia was one of the earliest centers of civilization. Civilization began to flourish here in the sixth millennium B.C., with major cities appearing in the fourth millennium B.C. The oldest settlement in Mesopotamia is Eridu, dating to the fifth millennium. See "The Patriarchal Period: Mesopotamia During the Time of Abraham" on page 26.

Middle Bronze Age (see Bronze Age).

Middle Kingdom (Egypt) A period of Egyptian history covering the Eleventh and Twelfth Dynasties, or the period from 2106–1786 B.C. During this time the central government of the pharaohs reasserted itself and local lords began to lose power. Joseph may have played a significant role in bringing about the end of feudal power.

Midrash/midrashic The word *midrash* stems from the Hebrew verb *darash* ("to explain") and came to refer to an interpretation or exposition of a Biblical text. The term *midrashic* is used to describe a distinctive mode of interpretation employed by early rabbis.

miqveh A Jewish ritual bath or pool.

Mishnah Meaning "repetition," the term refers to a collection of rabbinical discussions on the correct interpretation of the Law of Moses, compiled at the turn of the second and third centuries A.D. by Rabbi Judah. Mishnaic teaching became the most prominent form of instruction in Judaism. The text in its current version represents centuries of development.

Mitanni; Mitannians A Mesopotamian (Hurrian) kingdom that existed from the fifteenth until the thirteenth centuries B.C.

Moab An ancient country that was located east of the Dead Sea in present-day Jordan. The Moabites often oppressed the Israelites during the period of the judges but were subjects of Israel during the time of the Davidic kingdom. Ruth was a Moabite. See "Moab" on page 292.

monarchic period; monarchy The period in Israel's history between the judges and the exile, when either the united or the divided monarchy existed (eleventh–sixth centuries B.C.).

Nebuchadnezzar II (r. 605–562 B.C.); A king of the Chaldean, or Neo-Babylonian, Empire, Nebuchadnezzar is credited with having greatly extended the boundaries of the empire and overseeing an ambitious building program throughout Babylon. He took Jerusalem in 597 B.C. and exiled King Jehoiachin and many of his subjects to Babylonia. See "Nebuchadnezzar" on page 571.

necropolis A city's burial area.

Neo-Babylonian A Chaldean empire, founded by Nabopolassar, the father of Nebuchadnezzar, during the seventh century B.C., that regained great prestige for the Babylonian Empire. However, its short history came to an end in 539 B.C. with the defeat of Babylon by the Persian Cyrus the Great.

Neolithic Age (period) The New Stone Age, characterized by the use of stone tools and agricultural advances, as well as the development of pottery making and weaving. Dates for the Neolithic period are not uniformly established, but for Egypt and the Near East they encompass roughly the two centuries from 8000–6000 B.C.

New Kingdom (Egypt) A period of Egyptian history (Eighteenth to Twentieth Dynasties; 1550–1069 B.C.) that can be considered the high point of Egyptian power. The New Kingdom was established by Pharaoh Ahmose, who drove out the last of the Hyksos. This is the era during which Israel escaped Egyptian slavery. The New Kingdom would become an empire that reached through Canaan into Syria. See "A Breakdown of Ancient Egyptian History" on page 104.

noncanonical Any book or portion of a book that does not belong to the 66 canonical books of the Christian Bible. Examples include the Gospel of Thomas and the letters of Clement.

Nuzi An ancient city in present-day northern Iraq. Excavation of this site has produced tablets that reveal fifteenth-century B.C. legal customs that parallel those of the Biblical patriarchs. See "Nuzi" on page 52.

offset-inset wall A defensive wall that, instead of being flat, protruded at regular intervals.

Old Babylonian Empire The initial period of Babylonian dominance, beginning around 2017 B.C. and lasting until the Kassites captured Babylon in 1595 B.C.

Old Kingdom (Egypt) A period of Egyptian history (Third to Sixth Dynasties; 2700–2160 B.C.) during which the pyramids and the great sphinx were constructed. The study of medicine also flourished, and works such as the Proverbs of Ptahhotep were produced. Pharaohs ventured outside Egypt on military campaigns to the Sinai and to Libya. See "A Breakdown of Ancient Egyptian History" on page 104.

orthostat(s) Large stone slabs, inscribed or carved in relief and painted, used to adorn ancient Near Eastern palaces and temples.

ossuary; pl. ossuaries A box, often of clay or metal, for holding the bones of the dead.

ostracon; pl. ostraca A broken fragment of pottery used as writing material. Messages, lists and school exercises were written on ostraca. The Athenians used this medium to record the names of persons they wished to send into exile from the city, thus giving us the word *ostracize*.

paleography; paleographic The study of ancient writing.

paleo-Hebrew An early form of Hebrew, closely related to Canaanite.

papyrus; pl. papyri Writing material made from the papyrus plant, first used in Egypt. From this term we get our word *paper*.

Pastoral epistles First and Second Timothy and Titus, so named for their content.

Patriarchal Age (period) The period in the Old Testament narrative, during the first half of the second millennium B.C., starting with Abraham and ending with the establishment of the sons of Jacob as the 12 tribes of Israel.

patrimony Land inherited from one's father.

Pentateuch The Greek term for the first five books of the Old Testament. The word was coined by Origen during the early Christian period.

Persia; Persian(s); Persian Empire/Persian period The Persian Empire was established by Cyrus the Great in the middle of the sixth century B.C. The empire reached its pinnacle under Darius the Great, who ruled in the late sixth and early fifth centuries. He expanded Persia's borders and established it as a world power but was defeated by the Greeks at the Battle of Marathon in 490 B.C. His son, Xerxes I, succeeded him to the throne, but neither he nor his son, Artaxerxes I, managed to restore the kingdom to its former glory. See the articles on Persia on pages 717 and 718.

Peshitta A first-century A.D. Syriac version of the Old Testament.

Phoenicia; Phoenician(s) An ancient nation on the eastern shore of the Mediterranean Sea in present-day Lebanon, whose first civilizations are dated to approximately 2500 B.C. The Phoenicians were conquered by the Egyptians around 1800 B.C. and remained under Egyptian rule until about 1200 B.C. They were excellent sailors, using this skill for trade and for the establishment of colonies along the Mediterranean Sea. See "Phoenicia" on page 488.

Pithom One of the Egyptian store cities built by the Israelites, possibly modern Tell el-Rataba. See "The Store Cities of Pithom and Rameses" on page 86.

portico A colonnade or covered walkway. Architecture employing the portico was popular in the classical Greek and Roman periods.

postexilic period The more than 500 years from the Persian conquest of Babylon until the beginning of the New Testament Age. This period saw the rebuilding of the wall and temple in Jerusalem.

potsherd (see sherd).

pre-monarchic period The period before Israel's monarchy was established (with Saul being the first king), during which Israel was led by judges.

proto-Canaanite The language of Canaan/Israel during the Late Bronze Age and Iron Age I; the proto-Canaanite script is the writing system used for this language.

pseudepigrapha; pseudepigraphal A collection of noncanonical books by both Jewish and Christian writers, dating from approximately 200 B.C. to well into the Christian period. The books were falsely attributed to great religious figures of the Jewish and Christian religions (e.g., Abraham, Moses, Job, Solomon). See "The Bible and Pseudepigraphical Literature" on page 2041.

Ptolemaic/Ptolemies/Ptolemy A Macedonian empire, established by Ptolemy (a general of Alexander), that existed in Egypt and Africa from the fourth through the first centuries B.C. With its capital at Alexandria in Egypt, the empire was dominated by Greek thought and custom, although it did participate in Egyptian religious ceremonies. The empire faced constant rebellion from the Egyptian population.

Q source An unidentified document or documents that many scholars have proposed is a second document source to the Gospels of Matthew and Luke. In the "Two Document Hypothesis," the Gospel of Mark is the first source upon which Matthew and Luke drew; Q is the second. See "The Synoptic Problem and 'Q'" on page 1685.

Qumran An ancient Jewish settlement on the northwestern shore of the Dead Sea, inhabited by the Essenes, a Jewish sect that had broken away from mainline Judaism to live an ascetic life in the caves around Qumran. The Dead Sea Scrolls were discovered here. See "Qumran and the New Testament" on page 1679.

Rameses II The grandson of Rameses I and the Egyptian pharaoh from 1290–1224 B.C. Rameses fought to regain much land that Egypt had lost. His primary enemy was the Hittite nation, and the major battle of this war was fought at Kadesh in 1274 B.C. Although Rameses claimed a great victory, there was no clear winner, and a subsequent treaty divided the disputed area. His reign was characterized by ambitious building projects, such as the great hall at the Temple of Amon, as well as the Temple at Abu Simbel.

Ras Shamra Ancient Ugarit. See Ugarit.

register(s) Panels or rows (one on top of the other) inside of which inscriptions, carvings or other decorations are made.

relief(s) A raised design that protrudes slightly from a flat surface.

retaining wall A wall constructed to support an area of land or a mound. The Wailing Wall in Jerusalem was built by Herod the Great as a retaining wall for the temple mount.

Roman period The period beginning when Pompey seized Jerusalem in 63 B.C. The Empire lasted another five centuries and saw the rise of Christianity as the prominent religion. Much of Rome's institutions were Hellenistic in origin.

Rosetta Stone A trilingual stone discovered in 1799 that led to the decipherment of hieroglyphics. See "The Rosetta Stone and the Deciphering of Hieroglyphs" on page 101.

Samaria; Samarian The capital of the northern kingdom (i.e., Israel). Founded by Omri near the beginning of the ninth century B.C., Samaria was destroyed by Shalmaneser III and Sargon II in 721 B.C. During the postexilic period the name Samaria was given to the region north of Judah. See "Omri and Samaria" on page 512.

sarcophagus; pl. sarcophagi A coffin that was placed above ground. The term means "flesh eating" in Greek and refers to the use of limestone sarcophagi that reportedly consumed a corpse with the exception of the teeth within 40 days. Most sarcophagi were made of stone. The oldest known examples are Egyptian.

Sargon the Great A Semitic ruler (c. 2335–2279 B.C.) and the founder of the dynasty of Akkad. Sargon united the regions of Akkad and Sumer, conquered all of Mesopotamia and commanded all of the trade routes. He instituted Akkadian as the official language, taking the place of Sumerian.

scarab(s) Either the sacred beetle of Egypt or a carving of this beetle inscribed on its underside and used as an amulet.

scribe A person trained in the skill of writing who kept records or copied manuscripts professionally. See "The Scribe" on page 682.

Sea Peoples Invaders of Egypt and the Levant in the thirteenth–twelfth centuries B.C., they were part of a larger movement of peoples responsible for much destruction in the Aegean, Anatolia and Syria-Palestine.

Second Intermediate period (Egypt) A period in Egyptian history (Thirteenth to Seventeenth Dynasties; 1786–1550 B.C.) when central authority collapsed. The Hyksos (foreign, Semitic rulers) took control of Lower Egypt during this time. See "A Breakdown of Ancient Egyptian History" on page 104.

Second Temple The period from the construction of the postexilic temple in 515 B.C. to the destruction of the Herodian temple by the Romans in A.D. 70. See "The Intertestamental Period" on page 1551.

Seleucid(s) A kingdom that included Syria and neighboring areas, created when the domain of Alexander the Great was divided. The Seleucid Empire extended eastward from present-day Turkey into present-day Pakistan, lasting from the fourth through the first centuries B.C. See "The Seleucids" on page 1408.

Septuagint The Greek translation of the Old Testament, containing additional books not found in the Hebrew text. Legend holds that 70 elders, working independently of one another, each produced an identical translation of the Hebrew. The Septuagint is named after these 70.

Shalmaneser III An Assyrian king (858–824 B.C.) who invaded Syria-Palestine. Although the Bible does not mention him, his victory stele, known as the Black Obelisk, depicts Jehu of Israel paying homage to him. See "Jehu/The Black Obelisk of Shalmaneser III" on page 544.

Shechem A city 65 miles (105 km) north of Jerusalem in the central hill country, occupied by the tribes of Ephraim and Manasseh. See "Shechem" on page 340.

shekel The primary Hebrew weight and coin. See "Weights and Measures" on page 1459.

Shephelah The foothills between the Judean high country and the coastal plain on the Mediterranean Sea.

sherd(s) A broken piece of pottery.

Sinai The wilderness area located between the two fingers of the Red Sea, traditionally seen as the location of Mount Sinai (although this is debatable). See "The Location of Mount Sinai" on page 123.

stele A stone monument, usually inscribed and carved with images celebrating a ruler's victories.

Sumer; Sumerian The southernmost part of the Mesopotamian alluvial plain. It is debated whether the Sumerians were the original inhabitants of the area or whether they migrated from the Indus region. See "Sumer" on page 10.

superscript; superscription(s) An explanatory title at the beginning of many psalms and other ancient works, often giving the author's name and the occasion of the writing, as well as musical instructions for the piece.

Suppiluliumas I An able Hittite king (c. 1350–1325 B.C.) who consolidated Hittite power in Anatolia and expanded Hittite hegemony over Mitanni and over states in Syria-Palestine that had once been dominated by Egypt.

suzerain An overlord, or king, who had power over an inferior king or state.

Synoptic Gospels Matthew, Mark and Luke. The three Synoptic Gospels have much material in common and can be compared easily.

Syriac A dialect of Aramaic. The Syriac version of the Bible, known as the Peshitta, was produced toward the end of the fourth century A.D.

Talmud; Talmudic Meaning "study," the term refers to collections of commentary on the Mishnah, rabbinical discussions and explanations of the Law of Moses. While there are two Talmuds, the Palestinian and the Babylonian, which contain different content, "Talmud" usually refers to the Babylonian compilation. The Palestinian Talmud was completed at the end of the fourth century A.D., while the Babylonian Talmud was completed during the following century.

Targum(s) An Aramaic translation of the Old Testament, produced by many translators over the course of the first few centuries A.D. In places the translation is a paraphrase, often accompanied by explanatory material.

tel; tell A mound that rises higher than the surrounding area, beneath which are found layers of occupational or other human activity. As edifices, streets, fortifications, etc. were destroyed, rebuilt or renovated, the new constructions were often built directly over the previous levels. Thus, the tel (Hebrew) or tell (Arabic) began to become elevated above its surroundings. When conducting surface surveys, archaeologists can often determine the best places to dig simply by locating the site of a tel/tell.

tetrarch The head over one fourth of a given region. Eventually the term came to designate simply a lesser ruler, lower than a king.

textual criticism The study and comparison of ancient Biblical versions to determine the original reading of the text. See "Textual Criticism" on page 1151.

theodicy A system of theological justification for the problem of evil; i.e., an explanation for the existence of evil, given the realities that God is both omnipotent and loving.

Tigris The eastern river that, together with the Euphrates, formed the alluvial plain in Mesopotamia. Flooding in the late spring, the Tigris originates in the Zagros mountains to the north and flows through what is modern Iraq before emptying into the Persian Gulf. See "The Tigris and Euphrates Rivers" on page 604.

Torah The Pentateuch, or first five books of the Old Testament.

Transjordan; Transfordanian Territory on the eastern side of the Jordan River, encompassing the regions of Bashon, Gilead, Ammon, Moab and Edom. The Israelite tribes of Gad and Reuben and part of the tribe of Manasseh settled here.

Ugarit; Ugaritic Located at modern Ras Shamra, this important coastal city in northern Syria has yielded a wealth of texts that help us to understand the region's history and the Canaanite religion. See "Ugarit/Ras Shamra" on page 819.

united kingdom (see united monarchy).

united monarchy The period constituting the reigns of Saul, David and Solomon. When Rehoboam succeeded Solomon in 930 B.C., Israel rebelled under the leadership of Jeroboam, and two kingdoms resulted: Israel (the northern kingdom) and Judah (the southern).

Uruk A Mesopotamian city, also known as Warka, on the lower Euphrates, which was occupied for 5,000 years before being abandoned in the third century B.C. It was an important religious center, at which several temples and beautiful cultic items have been discovered.

vassal(s) In the ancient Near East a vassal was a king or state subordinate to an overlord. Treaties between a vassal and the superior usually stipulated that the overlord would protect the vassal from enemies, while the vassal would pay annual tribute and provide soldiers or laborers for the superior.

version(s) Translations of the Bible. The primary ancient versions are the Greek (Septuagint), Syriac (Peshitta), Coptic and Latin (Vulgate).

Via Maris ("the way of the sea"); An important ancient land trade route that hugged the Mediterranean coastline from Egypt to Syria. It turned inland through the Valley of Jezreel as it made its way north.

Vulgate The Latin translation of the Bible, produced in the fourth century A.D. by Jerome.

wadi A riverbed that is dry for most of the year, except during the rainy season. Wadis are found throughout the Middle East and North Africa.

Yahweh/YHWH The personal name of the God of Israel, translated as "the LORD" in most English texts. God used this name for himself when addressing Moses from the burning bush (Ex 3:14). Many scholars and laypersons believe that it means "I am," but see "YHWH: The Name of God in the Old Testament" on page 89.

SUBJECT INDEX TO *Articles*

List OF ARTICLES IN ALPHABETICAL ORDER

List OF ARTICLES BY SCRIPTURE REFERENCE

Concordance

This NIV Concordance is a condensation of *The NIV Complete Concordance*, taking over 35,000 references from the latter's 250,000. These 35,000 references have been selected as the most helpful for the average Bible student or layperson.

When determining whether or not to include a verse reference, we gave careful consideration to the passage in which the verse is located. We also encourage you to always consider the larger context of the passage, giving special attention to the flow of the thought from beginning to end. Whenever you look up a verse, your goal should be to discover the intended meaning of the verse in context. Do not use this concordance, or any concordance, merely as a *verse-finder*; it should also be used as a *passage-finder*. The contexts surrounding each entry are longer than those usually found in concordances; but even so, the context excerpts are too brief for study purposes. They serve only to help you locate familiar verses.

In some cases the usual short contextual phrases are ineffective in helping you locate a passage. This is especially true in studying key events in a Bible character's life. Therefore, we have incorporated 260 "block entries" in which we use descriptive phrases that mark the breadth of a passage containing episodes of that person's life. The descriptive phrases replace the brief context surrounding each occurrence of the name.

Often more than one Bible character has the same name. For example, there are more than thirty Zechariahs in the Bible. In these cases we have given the name a block entry, assigning each person a number (1), (2), etc., and have included a descriptive phrase to distinguish each. Insignificant names are not included.

In this concordance there are 1,239 key word entries that have an exhaustive list of every appearance of that word. When this occurs, the word or block entry is marked with an asterisk (*).

Two entries are marked with a dagger (†) and two with a double-dagger (‡). LORD† and LORD'S† list occurrences of the title "Lord," spelled "Lord" and "lord," "Lord's" and "lord's" in the NIV. LORD‡ and LORD'S‡ list occurrences of the proper name of God, *Yahweh,* spelled "LORD" and "LORD's" in the NIV. See the Preface to the New International Version on page xiv.

This mini-concordance includes some words not found in *The NIV Complete Concordance.* These words include: boy, boy's, boys, daughter, daughters, girl, man, man's, men, men's, people, peoples, woman, and women.

Since this concordance can only serve one translation—the New International Version—it is difficult for readers familiar with the Authorized Version to make the transition from its older, more archaic language to that of the NIV. We have tried, therefore, to make this transition a bit easier by including some forty-four prominent Authorized Version words and linking them to NIV words that have taken their place. We wish to thank Dr. Daniel E. Sauerwein of Multnomah Bible College for supplying the data for these additional words.

We pray that this concordance will be used by NIV readers to introduce them to the full scope of God's truth in every book of the Bible.

John R. Kohlenberger III

Edward W. Goodrick

AARON
Genealogy of (Ex 6:16–20; Jos 21:4, 10; 1Ch 6:3–15).
Priesthood of (Ex 28:1; Nu 17; Heb 5:1–4; 7), garments (Ex 28; 39), consecration (Ex 29), ordination (Lev 8).
Spokesman for Moses (Ex 4:14–16, 27–31; 7:1–2). Supported Moses' hands in battle (Ex 17:8–13). Built golden calf (Ex 32; Dt 9:20). Talked against Moses (Nu 12). Priesthood opposed (Nu 16); staff budded (Nu 17). Forbidden to enter land (Nu 20:1–12). Death (Nu 20:22–29; 33:38–39).

ABADDON*
Rev 9: 11 whose name in Hebrew is *A*,

ABANDON (ABANDONED)
Dt 4: 31 he will not *a* or destroy you
1Ki 6: 13 and will not *a* my people Israel."
Ne 9: 19 compassion you did not *a* them
9: 31 an end to them or *a* them,
Ps 16: 10 you will not *a* me to the grave,
Ac 2: 27 you will not *a* me to the grave,
1Ti 4: 1 in later times some will *a* the faith

ABANDONED (ABANDON)
Ge 24: 27 who has not *a* his kindness
2Co 4: 9 persecuted, but not *a*; struck down,

ABBA*
Mk 14: 36 "*A*, Father," he said, "everything is
Ro 8: 15 And by him we cry, "*A*, Father."
Gal 4: 6 the Spirit who calls out, "*A*, Father

ABEDNEGO
Deported to Babylon with Daniel (Da 1:1–6). Name changed from Azariah (Da 1:7). Refused defilement by food (Da 1:8–20). Refused idol worship (Da 3:1–12); saved from furnace (Da 3:13–30).

ABEL
Second son of Adam (Ge 4:2). Offered proper sacrifice (Ge 4:4; Heb 11:4). Murdered by Cain (Ge 4:8; Mt 23:35; Lk 11:51; 1Jn 3:12).

ABHOR (ABHORS)
Lev 26: 30 of your idols, and I will *a* you.
Dt 7: 26 Utterly *a* and detest it,
Ps 26: 5 I *a* the assembly of evildoers
119:163 I hate and *a* falsehood
139: 21 and *a* those who rise up against you
Am 6: 8 "I *a* the pride of Jacob
Ro 2: 22 You who *a* idols, do you rob

ABHORS (ABHOR)
Pr 11: 1 The LORD *a* dishonest scales,

ABIATHAR
High priest in days of Saul and David (1Sa 22; 2Sa 15; 1Ki 1–2; Mk 2:26). Escaped Saul's slaughter of priests (1Sa 22:18–23). Supported David in Absalom's revolt (2Sa 15:24–29). Supported Adonijah (1Ki 1:7–42); deposed by Solomon (1Ki 2:22–35; cf. 1Sa 2:31–35).

ABIGAIL
1. Sister of David (1Ch 2:16–17).
2. Wife of Nabal (1Sa 25:30); pled for his life with David (1Sa 25:14–35). Became David's wife after Nabal's death (1Sa 25:36–42); bore him Kileab (2Sa 3:3) also known as Daniel (1Ch 3:1).

ABIHU
Son of Aaron (Ex 6:23; 24:1, 9); killed for offering unauthorized fire (Lev 10; Nu 3:2–4; 1Ch 24:1–2).

ABIJAH
1. Second son of Samuel (1Ch 6:28); a corrupt judge (1Sa 8:1–5).
2. An Aaronic priest (1Ch 24:10; Lk 1:5).
3. Son of Jeroboam I of Israel; died as prophesied by Ahijah (1Ki 14:1–18).
4. Son of Rehoboam; king of Judah who fought Jeroboam I attempting to reunite the kingdom (1Ki 14:31–15:8; 2Ch 12:16–14:1; Mt 1:7).

ABILITY (ABLE)
Ex 35: 34 tribe of Dan, the *a* to teach others.
Dt 8: 18 for it is he who gives you the *a*
Ezr 2: 69 According to their *a* they gave
Mt 25: 15 one talent, each according to his *a*.
Ac 11: 29 disciples, each according to his *a*,
2Co 1: 8 far beyond our *a* to endure,
8: 3 were able, and even beyond their *a*.

ABIMELECH
1. King of Gerar who took Abraham's wife Sarah, believing her to be his sister (Ge 20). Later made a covenant with Abraham (Ge 21:22–33).
2. King of Gerar who took Isaac's wife Rebekah, believing her to be his sister (Ge 26:1–11). Later made a covenant with Isaac (Ge 26:12–31).
3. Son of Gideon (Jdg 8:31). Attempted to make himself king (Jdg 9).

ABISHAG*
Shunammite virgin; attendant of David in his old age (1Ki 1:1–15; 2:17–22).

ABISHAI
Son of Zeruiah, David's sister (1Sa 26:6; 1Ch 2:16). One of David's chief warriors (1Ch 11:15–21): against Edom (1Ch 18:12–13), Ammon (2Sa 10), Absalom (2Sa 18), Sheba (2Sa 20). Wanted to kill Saul (1Sa 26), killed Abner (2Sa 2:18–27; 3:22–39), wanted to kill Shimei (2Sa 16:5–13; 19:16–23).

ABLE (ABILITY ENABLE ENABLED ENABLES ENABLING)
Nu 14: 16 'The LORD was not *a*
1Ch 29: 14 that we should be *a* to give
2Ch 2: 6 who is *a* to build a temple for him,
Eze 7: 19 and gold will not be *a* to save them
Da 3: 17 the God we serve is *a* to save us
4: 37 walk in pride he is *a* to humble.
Mt 9: 28 "Do you believe that I am *a*
Lk 13: 24 will try to enter and will not be *a* to
14: 30 to build and was not *a* to finish.'
21: 15 none of your adversaries will be *a*
21: 36 and that you may be *a* to stand
Ac 5: 39 you will not be *a* to stop these men;
Ro 8: 39 will be *a* to separate us
14: 4 for the Lord is *a* to make him stand
16: 25 to him who is *a* to establish you
2Co 9: 8 God is *a* to make all grace abound
Eph 3: 20 him who is *a* to do immeasurably
6: 13 you may be *a* to stand your ground,
1Ti 3: 2 respectable, hospitable, *a* to teach,
2Ti 1: 12 and am convinced that he is *a*
2: 24 kind to everyone, *a* to teach,
3: 15 which are *a* to make you wise
Heb 2: 18 he is *a* to help those who are being
7: 25 he is *a* to save completely
Jas 3: 2 *a* to keep his whole body in check.
Jude : 24 To him who is *a* to keep you
Rev 5: 5 He is *a* to open the scroll

ABNER
Cousin of Saul and commander of his army (1Sa 14:50; 17:55–57; 26). Made Ish-Bosheth king after Saul (2Sa 2:8–10), but later defected to David (2Sa 3:6–21). Killed Asahel (2Sa 2:18–32), for which he was killed by Joab and Abishai (2Sa 3:22–39).

ABOLISH (ABOLISHED ABOLISHING)
Hos 2: 18 I will *a* from the land,
Mt 5: 17 that I have come to *a* the Law

ABOLISHED (ABOLISH)
Gal 5: 11 the offense of the cross has been *a*.

ABOLISHING* (ABOLISH)
Eph 2: 15 by *a* in his flesh the law

ABOMINATION*
Da 11: 31 set up the *a* that causes desolation.
12: 11 *a* that causes desolation is set up,
Mt 24: 15 the holy place 'the *a* that causes
Mk 13: 14 you see 'the *a* that causes

ABOUND (ABOUNDING)
2Co 9: 8 able to make all grace *a* to you,
9: 8 you will *a* in every good work.
Php 1: 9 that your love may *a* more

ABOUNDING (ABOUND)
Ex 34: 6 slow to anger, *a* in love
Nu 14: 18 *a* in love and forgiving sin
Ne 9: 17 slow to anger and *a* in love.
Ps 86: 5 *a* in love to all who call to you.
86: 15 slow to anger, *a* in love
103: 8 slow to anger, *a* in love.
Joel 2: 13 slow to anger and *a* in love,
Jnh 4: 2 slow to anger and *a* in love,

ABRAHAM
Abram, son of Terah (Ge 11:26–27), husband of Sarah (Ge 11:29).
Covenant relation with the LORD (Ge 12:1–3; 13:14–17; 15; 17; 22:15–18; Ex 2:24; Ne 9:8; Ps 105; Mic 7:20; Lk 1:68–75; Ro 4; Heb 6:13–15).
Called from Ur, via Haran, to Canaan (Ge 12:1; Ac 7:2–4; Heb 11:8–10). Moved to Egypt, nearly lost Sarah to Pharoah (Ge 12:10–20). Divided the land with Lot; settled in Hebron (Ge 13). Saved Lot from four kings (Ge 14:1–16); blessed by Melchizedek (Ge 14:17–20; Heb 7:1–20). Declared righteous by faith (Ge 15:6; Ro 4:3; Gal 3:6–9). Fathered Ishmael by Hagar (Ge 16).
Name changed from Abram (Ge 17:5; Ne 9:7). Circumcised (Ge 17; Ro 4:9–12). Entertained three visitors (Ge 18); promised a son by Sarah (Ge 18:9–15; 17:16). Questioned destruction of Sodom and Gomorrah (Ge 18:16–33). Moved to Gerar; nearly lost Sarah to Abimelech (Ge 20). Fathered Isaac by Sarah (Ge 21:1–7; Ac 7:8; Heb 11:11–12); sent away Hagar and Ishmael (Ge 21:8–21; Gal 4:22–30). Covenant with Abimelech (Ge 21:22–32). Tested by offering Isaac (Ge 22; Heb 11:17–19; Jas 2:21–24). Sarah died; bought field of Ephron for burial (Ge 23). Secured wife for Isaac (Ge 24). Fathered children by Keturah (Ge 25:1–6; 1Ch 1:32–33). Death (Ge 25:7–11).
Called servant of God (Ge 26:24), friend of God (2Ch 20:7; Isa 41:8; Jas 2:23), prophet (Ge 20:7), father of Israel (Ex 3:15; Isa 51:2; Mt 3:9; Jn 8:39–58).

ABSALOM
Son of David by Maacah (2Sa 3:3; 1Ch 3:2). Killed Amnon for rape of his sister Tamar; banished by David (2Sa 13). Returned to Jerusalem; received by David (2Sa 14). Rebelled against David; siezed kingdom (2Sa 15–17). Killed (2Sa 18).

ABSENT
Col 2: 5 though I am *a* from you in body,

ABSOLUTE*
1Ti 5: 2 women as sisters, with *a* purity.

ABSTAIN (ABSTAINS)
Ex 19: 15 *A* from sexual relations."
Nu 6: 3 he must *a* from wine and other
Ac 15: 20 them to *a* from food polluted
1Pe 2: 11 to *a* from sinful desires,

ABSTAINS* (ABSTAIN)
Ro 14: 6 thanks to God; and he who *a*,

ABUNDANCE (ABUNDANT)
Ge 41: 29 Seven years of great *a* are coming
Job 36: 31 and provides food in *a*.
Ps 66: 12 but you brought us to a place of *a*.
Ecc 5: 12 but the *a* of a rich man
Isa 66: 11 and delight in her overflowing *a*."
Jer 2: 22 and use an *a* of soap,
Mt 13: 12 given more, and he will have an *a*.
25: 29 given more, and he will have an *a*.
Lk 12: 15 consist in the *a* of his possessions."
1Pe 1: 2 Grace and peace be yours in *a*.
2Pe 1: 2 yours in *a* through the knowledge
Jude : 2 peace and love be yours in *a*.

ABUNDANT (ABUNDANCE)
Dt 28: 11 will grant you *a* prosperity—
32: 2 like *a* rain on tender plants.
Job 36: 28 and *a* showers fall on mankind.
Ps 68: 9 You gave *a* showers, O God;
78: 15 gave them water as *a* as the seas;
132: 15 I will bless her with *a* provisions;
145: 7 will celebrate your *a* goodness
Pr 12: 11 works his land will have *a* food,

28: 19 works his land will have *a* food,
Jer 33: 9 and will tremble at the *a* prosperity
Ro 5: 17 who receive God's *a* provision

ABUSIVE
2Ti 3: 2 *a*, disobedient to their parents,

ABYSS*
Lk 8: 31 not to order them to go into the *A*.
Rev 9: 1 the key to the shaft of the *A*.
9: 2 When he opened the *A*, smoke rose
9: 2 darkened by the smoke from the *A*.
9: 11 king over them the angel of the *A*,
11: 7 up from the *A* will attack them,
17: 8 and will come up out of the *A*
20: 1 having the key to the *A*
20: 3 He threw him into the *A*,

ACCEPT (ACCEPTABLE ACCEPTANCE ACCEPTED ACCEPTS)
Ex 23: 8 "Do not *a* a bribe,
Dt 16: 19 Do not *a* a bribe, for a bribe blinds
Job 42: 8 and I will *a* his prayer and not deal
Pr 10: 8 The wise in heart *a* commands,
19: 20 Listen to advice and *a* instruction,
Ro 15: 7 *A* one another, then, just
Jas 1: 21 humbly *a* the word planted in you,

ACCEPTABLE (ACCEPT)
Pr 21: 3 is more *a* to the LORD

ACCEPTANCE* (ACCEPT)
Ro 11: 15 what will their *a* be but life
1Ti 1: 15 saying that deserves full *a*:
4: 9 saying that deserves full *a*

ACCEPTED (ACCEPT)
Ge 4: 7 will you not be *a*? But if you do not
Job 42: 9 and the LORD *a* Job's prayer.
Lk 4: 24 "no prophet is *a* in his hometown.
Gal 1: 9 you a gospel other than what you *a*,

ACCEPTS (ACCEPT)
Ps 6: 9 the LORD *a* my prayer.
Jn 13: 20 whoever *a* anyone I send *a* me;
13: 20 whoever *a* me *a* the one who sent

ACCESS
Ro 5: 2 through whom we have gained *a*
Eph 2: 18 For through him we both have *a*

ACCOMPANIED (ACCOMPANY)
1Co 10: 4 from the spiritual rock that *a* them,
Jas 2: 17 if it is not *a* by action, is dead.

ACCOMPANIES (ACCOMPANY)
2Co 9: 13 obedience that *a* your confession

ACCOMPANY (ACCOMPANIED ACCOMPANIES)
Dt 28: 2 *a* you if you obey the LORD your
Mk 16: 17 these signs will *a* those who believe
Heb 6: 9 your case—things that *a* salvation.

ACCOMPLISH
Ecc 2: 2 And what does pleasure *a*?"
Isa 44: 28 and will *a* all that I please;
55: 11 but will *a* what I desire

ACCORD
Nu 24: 13 not do anything of my own *a*,
Jn 10: 18 but I lay it down of my own *a*.
12: 49 For I did not speak of my own *a*,

ACCOUNT (ACCOUNTABLE)
Ge 2: 4 This is the *a* of the heavens
5: 1 This is the written *a* of Adam's line
6: 9 This is the *a* of Noah.
10: 1 This is the *a* of Shem, Ham
11: 10 This is the *a* of Shem.
11: 27 This is the *a* of Terah.
25: 12 This is the *a* of Abraham's son
25: 19 This is the *a* of Abraham's son
36: 1 This is the *a* of Esau (that is, Edom
36: 9 This is the *a* of Esau the father
37: 2 This is the *a* of Jacob.
Mt 12: 36 to give *a* on the day of judgment
Lk 16: 2 Give an *a* of your management,
Ro 14: 12 each of us will give an *a* of himself
Heb 4: 13 of him to whom we must give *a*.

ACCOUNTABLE* (ACCOUNT)
Eze 3: 18 and I will hold you *a* for his blood.
3: 20 and I will hold you *a* for his blood.
33: 6 but I will hold the watchman *a*
33: 8 and I will hold you *a* for his blood.
34: 10 and will hold them *a* for my flock.
Da 6: 2 The satraps were made *a* to them
Jnh 1: 14 Do not hold us *a* for killing
Ro 3: 19 and the whole world held *a* to God.

ACCURATE
Dt 25: 15 You must have *a* and honest
Pr 11: 1 but *a* weights are his delight.

ACCURSED (CURSE)
2Pe 2: 14 experts in greed—an *a* brood!

ACCUSATION (ACCUSE)
1Ti 5: 19 Do not entertain an *a*

ACCUSATIONS (ACCUSE)
2Pe 2: 11 do not bring slanderous *a*

ACCUSE (ACCUSATION ACCUSATIONS ACCUSER ACCUSES ACCUSING)
Pr 3: 30 Do not *a* a man for no reason—
Lk 3: 14 and don't *a* people falsely—

ACCUSER (ACCUSE)
Jn 5: 45 Your *a* is Moses, on whom your
Rev 12: 10 For the *a* of our brothers,

ACCUSES (ACCUSE)
Job 40: 2 Let him who *a* God answer him!"
Rev 12: 10 who *a* them before our God day

ACCUSING (ACCUSE)
Ro 2: 15 and their thoughts now *a*,

ACHAN*
Sin at Jericho caused defeat at Ai; stoned (Jos 7; 22:20; 1Ch 2:7).

ACHE*
Pr 14: 13 Even in laughter the heart may *a*,

ACHIEVE
Isa 55: 11 *a* the purpose for which I sent it.

ACHISH
King of Gath before whom David feigned insanity (1Sa 21:10–15). Later "ally" of David (2Sa 27–29).

ACKNOWLEDGE (ACKNOWLEDGED ACKNOWLEDGES)
Pr 3: 6 in all your ways *a* him,
Jer 3: 13 Only *a* your guilt—
Hos 6: 3 let us press on to *a* him.
Mt 10: 32 *a* him before my Father in heaven.
Lk 12: 8 *a* him before the angels of God.
1Jn 4: 3 spirit that does not *a* Jesus is not

ACKNOWLEDGED (ACKNOWLEDGE)
Lk 7: 29 *a* that God's way was right,

ACKNOWLEDGES* (ACKNOWLEDGE)
Ps 91: 14 for he *a* my name.
Mt 10: 32 "Whoever *a* me before men,
Lk 12: 8 whoever *a* me before men,
1Jn 2: 23 whoever *a* the Son has the Father
4: 2 Every spirit that *a* that Jesus Christ
4: 15 If anyone *a* that Jesus is the Son

ACQUIRES (ACQUIRING)
Pr 18: 15 of the discerning *a* knowledge;

ACQUIRING* (ACQUIRES)
Pr 1: 3 for *a* a disciplined and prudent life,

ACQUIT (ACQUITTING)
Ex 23: 7 to death, for I will not *a* the guilty.

ACQUITTING* (ACQUIT)
Dt 25: 1 *a* the innocent and condemning
Pr 17: 15 *A* the guilty and condemning

ACT (ACTION ACTIONS ACTIVE ACTIVITY ACTS)
Ps 119:126 It is time for you to *a*, O LORD;

ACTION (ACT)
2Co 9: 2 has stirred most of them to *a*.
Jas 2: 17 if it is not accompanied by *a*,
1Pe 1: 13 minds for *a*; be self-controlled;

ACTIONS (ACT)
Mt 11: 19 wisdom is proved right by her *a*."
Gal 6: 4 Each one should test his own *a*.
Tit 1: 16 but by their *a* they deny him.

ACTIVE* (ACT)
Phm : 6 I pray that you may be *a*
Heb 4: 12 For the word of God is living and *a*

ACTIVITY (ACT)
Ecc 3: 1 a season for every *a* under heaven:
3: 17 for there will be a time for every *a*,

ACTS (ACT)
1Ch 16: 9 tell of all his wonderful *a*.
Ps 71: 16 proclaim your mighty *a*,
71: 24 tell of your righteous *a*
105: 2 tell of all his wonderful *a*.
106: 2 Who can proclaim the mighty *a*
145: 4 they will tell of your mighty *a*.
145: 12 all men may know of your mighty *a*
150: 2 Praise him for his *a* of power;
Isa 64: 6 all our righteous *a* are like filthy
Mt 6: 1 not to do your '*a* of righteousness'

ADAM
1. First man (Ge 1:26–2:25; Ro 5:14; 1Ti 2:13). Sin of (Ge 3; Hos 6:7; Ro 5:12–21). Children of (Ge 4:1–5:5). Death of (Ge 5:5; Ro 5:12–21; 1Co 15:22).
2. City (Jos 3:16).

ADD (ADDED)
Dt 4: 2 Do not *a* to what I command you
12: 32 do not *a* to it or take away from it.
Pr 1: 5 let the wise listen and *a*
9: 9 he will *a* to his learning.
30: 6 Do not *a* to his words,
Mt 6: 27 by worrying can *a* a single hour
Lk 12: 25 by worrying can *a* a single hour
Rev 22: 18 God will *a* to him the plagues

ADDED (ADD)
Ecc 3: 14 nothing can be *a* to it and nothing
Ac 2: 47 Lord *a* to their number daily those
Ro 5: 20 The law was *a* so that the trespass
Gal 3: 19 It was *a* because of transgressions

ADDICTED*
Tit 2: 3 to be slanderers or *a* to much wine,

ADMINISTRATION*
1Co 12: 28 with gifts of *a*, and those speaking
Eph 3: 2 Surely you have heard about the *a*
3: 9 to everyone the *a* of this mystery,

ADMIRABLE*
Php 4: 8 whatever is lovely, whatever is *a*—

ADMIT
Hos 5: 15 until they *a* their guilt.

ADMONISH* (ADMONISHING)
Col 3: 16 and *a* one another with all wisdom,
1Th 5: 12 you in the Lord and who *a* you.

ADMONISHING* (ADMONISH)
Col 1: 28 *a* and teaching everyone

ADONIJAH
1. Son of David by Haggith (2Sa 3:4; 1Ch 3:2). Attempted to be king after David; killed by Solomon's order (1Ki 1–2).
2. Levite; teacher of the Law (2Ch 17:8).

ADOPTED (ADOPTION)
Eph 1: 5 In love he predestined us to be *a*

ADOPTION* (ADOPTED)
Ro 8: 23 as we wait eagerly for our *a* as sons,
9: 4 Theirs is the *a* as sons; theirs

ADORE*
SS 1: 4 How right they are to *a* you!

ADORNMENT* (ADORNS)
1Pe 3: 3 should not come from outward *a*,

ADORNS* (ADORNMENT)
Ps 93: 5 holiness *a* your house
Isa 61: 10 as a bride *a* herself with her jewels.
61: 10 bridegroom *a* his head like a priest,

ADULTERER (ADULTERY)
Lev 20: 10 both the *a* and the adulteress must
Heb 13: 4 for God will judge the *a*

ADULTERERS (ADULTERY)
1Co 6: 9 idolaters nor *a* nor male prostitutes
1Ti 1: 10 for murderers, for *a* and perverts,

ADULTERESS (ADULTERY)
Hos 3: 1 she is loved by another and is an *a.*

ADULTERIES (ADULTERY)
Jer 3: 8 sent her away because of all her *a.*

ADULTEROUS (ADULTERY)
Mk 8: 38 in this *a* and sinful generation,
Jas 4: 4 You *a* people, don't you know that

ADULTERY (ADULTERER ADULTERERS ADULTERESS ADULTERIES ADULTEROUS)
Ex 20: 14 "You shall not commit *a.*
Dt 5: 18 "You shall not commit *a.*
Mt 5: 27 that it was said, 'Do not commit *a.*'
5: 28 lustfully has already committed *a*
5: 32 the divorced woman commits *a.*
15: 19 murder, *a,* sexual immorality, theft
19: 9 marries another woman commits *a*
19: 18 do not commit *a,* do not steal,
Mk 7: 21 theft, murder, *a,* greed, malice,
10: 11 marries another woman commits *a*
10: 12 another man, she commits *a.*"
10: 19 do not commit *a,* do not steal,
Lk 16: 18 a divorced woman commits *a.*
16: 18 marries another woman commits *a*
18: 20 'Do not commit *a,* do not murder,
Jn 8: 4 woman was caught in the act of *a.*
Rev 18: 3 of the earth committed *a* with her,

ADULTS*
1Co 14: 20 but in your thinking be *a.*

ADVANCE (ADVANCED)
Ps 18: 29 With your help I can *a*
Php 1: 12 has really served to *a* the gospel.

ADVANCED (ADVANCE)
Job 32: 7 *a* years should teach wisdom.'

ADVANTAGE
Ex 22: 22 "Do not take *a* of a widow
Dt 24: 14 Do not take *a* of a hired man who is
Ro 3: 1 What *a,* then, is there
2Co 11: 20 or exploits you or takes *a* of you
1Th 4: 6 should wrong his brother or take *a*

ADVERSITY*
Pr 17: 17 and a brother is born for *a.*
Isa 30: 20 the Lord gives you the bread of *a*

ADVICE (ADVISERS)
1Ki 12: 8 rejected the *a* the elders
12: 14 he followed the *a* of the young men
2Ch 10: 8 rejected the *a* the elders
Pr 12: 5 but the *a* of the wicked is deceitful.
12: 15 but a wise man listens to *a.*
19: 20 Listen to *a* and accept instruction,
20: 18 Make plans by seeking *a;*

ADVISERS (ADVICE)
Pr 11: 14 but many *a* make victory sure.

ADVOCATE*
Job 16: 19 my *a* is on high.

AFFLICTED (AFFLICTION)
Job 2: 7 and *a* Job with painful sores
36: 6 but gives the *a* their rights.
Ps 9: 12 he does not ignore the cry of the *a.*
9: 18 nor the hope of the *a* ever perish.
119: 67 Before I was *a* I went astray,
119: 71 It was good for me to be *a*
119: 75 and in faithfulness you have *a* me.
Isa 49: 13 will have compassion on his *a* ones.
53: 4 smitten by him, and *a.*
53: 7 He was oppressed and *a,*
Na 1: 12 Although I have *a* you, ›O Judah,‹

AFFLICTION (AFFLICTED AFFLICTIONS)
Dt 16: 3 bread of *a,* because you left Egypt
Ps 107: 41 he lifted the needy out of their *a*
Isa 30: 20 of adversity and the water of *a,*
48: 10 in the furnace of *a.*
La 3: 33 For he does not willingly bring *a*
Ro 12: 12 patient in *a,* faithful in prayer.

AFFLICTIONS (AFFLICTION)
Col 1: 24 lacking in regard to Christ's *a,*

AFRAID (FEAR)
Ge 3: 10 and I was *a* because I was naked;
26: 24 Do not be *a,* for I am with you;
Ex 2: 14 Then Moses was *a* and thought,
3: 6 because he was *a* to look at God.
Dt 1: 21 Do not be *a;* do not be discouraged
1: 29 "Do not be terrified; do not be *a*
20: 1 do not be *a* of them,
20: 3 Do not be fainthearted or *a;*
2Ki 25: 24 "Do not be *a* of the Babylonian
1Ch 13: 12 David was *a* of God that day
Ps 27: 1 of whom shall I be *a?*
56: 3 When I am *a,* / I will trust in you.
56: 4 in God I trust; I will not be *a.*
Pr 3: 24 lie down, you will not be *a;*
Isa 10: 24 do not be *a* of the Assyrians,
12: 2 I will trust and not be *a.*
44: 8 Do not tremble, do not be *a.*
Jer 1: 8 Do not be *a* of them, for I am
Mt 8: 26 You of little faith, why are you so *a*
10: 28 be *a* of the One who can destroy
10: 31 So don't be *a;* you are worth more
Mk 5: 36 "Don't be *a;* just believe."
Lk 9: 34 and they were *a* as they entered
Jn 14: 27 hearts be troubled and do not be *a.*
Ac 27: 24 beside me and said, 'Do not be *a,*
Ro 11: 20 Do not be arrogant, but be *a.*
Heb 13: 6 Lord is my helper; I will not be *a.*

AGAG (AGAGITE)
King of Amalekites not killed by Saul (1Sa 15).

AGAGITE (AGAG)
Est 8: 3 to the evil plan of Haman the *A,*

AGED (AGES)
Job 12: 12 Is not wisdom found among the *a?*
Pr 17: 6 children are a crown to the *a,*

AGES (AGED)
Ro 16: 25 the mystery hidden for long *a* past,
Eph 2: 7 that in the coming *a* he might show
3: 9 which for *a* past was kept hidden
Col 1: 26 that has been kept hidden for *a*
Rev 15: 3 King of the *a.*

AGONY
Lk 16: 24 because I am in *a* in this fire.'
Rev 16: 10 Men gnawed their tongues in *a*

AGREE (AGREEMENT AGREES)
Mt 18: 19 on earth *a* about anything you ask
Ro 7: 16 want to do, I *a* that the law is good.
Php 4: 2 with Syntyche to *a* with each other

AGREEMENT (AGREE)
2Co 6: 16 What *a* is there between the temple

AGREES* (AGREE)
Ac 7: 42 This *a* with what is written
24: 14 I believe everything that *a*
1Co 4: 17 which *a* with what I teach

AGRIPPA*
Descendant of Herod; king before whom Paul pled his case in Caesarea (Ac 25:13–26:32).

AHAB
1. Son of Omri; king of Israel (1Ki 16:28–22:40), husband of Jezebel (1Ki 16:31). Promoted Baal worship (1Ki 16:31–33); opposed by Elijah (1Ki 17:1; 18; 21), a prophet (1Ki 20:35–43), Micaiah (1Ki 22:1–28). Defeated Ben-Hadad (1Ki 20). Killed for failing to kill Ben-Hadad and for murder of Naboth (1Ki 20:35–21:40).
2. A false prophet (Jer 29:21–22).

AHAZ
1. Son of Jotham; king of Judah, (2Ki 16; 2Ch 28). Idolatry of (2Ki 16:3–4, 10–18; 2Ch 28:1–4, 22–25). Defeated by Aram and Israel (2Ki 16:5–6; 2Ch 28:5–15). Sought help from Assyria rather than the LORD (2Ki 16:7–9; 2Ch 28:16–21; Isa 7).
2. Benjamite, descendant of Saul (1Ch 8:35–36).

AHAZIAH
1. Son of Ahab; king of Israel (1Ki 22:51–2Ki 1:18; 2Ch 20:35–37). Made an unsuccessful alliance with Jehoshaphat of Judah (2Ch 20:35–37). Died for seeking Baal rather than the LORD (2Ki 1).
2. Son of Jehoram; king of Judah (2Ki 8:25–29; 9:14–29), also called Jehoahaz (2Ch 21:17–22:9; 25:23). Killed by Jehu while visiting Joram (2Ki 9:14–29; 2Ch 22:1–9).

AHIJAH
1Sa 14: 18 Saul said to *A,* "Bring the ark
1Ki 14: 2 *A* the prophet is there—the one

AHIMELECH
1. Priest who helped David in his flight from Saul (1Sa 21–22).
2. One of David's warriors (1Sa 26:6).

AHITHOPHEL
One of David's counselors who sided with Absalom (2Sa 15:12, 31–37; 1Ch 27:33–34); committed suicide when his advice was ignored (2Sa 16:15–17:23).

AI
Jos 7: 4 they were routed by the men of *A,*
8: 28 So Joshua burned *A* and made it

AID
Isa 38: 14 troubled; O Lord, come to my *a!*"
Php 4: 16 you sent me *a* again and again

AIM
1Co 7: 34 Her *a* is to be devoted to the Lord
2Co 13: 11 *A* for perfection, listen

AIR
Mt 8: 20 and birds of the *a* have nests,
Lk 9: 58 and birds of the *a* have nests,
1Co 9: 26 not fight like a man beating the *a.*
14: 9 You will just be speaking into the *a*
Eph 2: 2 of the ruler of the kingdom of the *a,*
1Th 4: 17 clouds to meet the Lord in the *a.*

ALABASTER*
Mt 26: 7 came to him with an *a* jar
Mk 14: 3 a woman came with an *a* jar
Lk 7: 37 she brought an *a* jar of perfume,

ALARM (ALARMED)
2Co 7: 11 indignation, what *a,* what longing,

ALARMED (ALARM)
Mk 13: 7 and rumors of wars, do not be *a.*
2Th 2: 2 not to become easily unsettled or *a*

ALERT*
Jos 8: 4 All of you be on the *a.*
Ps 17: 11 with eyes *a,* to throw me
Isa 21: 7 let him be *a,* / fully *a.*"
Mk 13: 33 Be *a!* You do not know
Eph 6: 18 be *a* and always keep on praying
1Th 5: 6 but let us be *a* and self-controlled.
1Pe 5: 8 Be self-controlled and *a.*

ALIEN (ALIENATED ALIENS)
Ex 22: 21 "Do not mistreat an *a*
Lev 24: 22 are to have the same law for the *a*
Ps 146: 9 The LORD watches over the *a*

ALIENATED (ALIEN)
Gal 5: 4 by law have been *a* from Christ;
Col 1: 21 Once you were *a* from God

ALIENS (ALIEN)
Ex 23: 9 know how it feels to be *a,*
1Pe 2: 11 as *a* and strangers in the world,

ALIVE (LIVE)
1Sa 2: 6 LORD brings death and makes *a;*
Lk 24: 23 vision of angels, who said he was *a.*
Ac 1: 3 convincing proofs that he was *a.*
Ro 6: 11 but *a* to God in Christ Jesus.
1Co 15: 22 so in Christ all will be made *a.*
Eph 2: 5 made us *a* with Christ

ALMIGHTY (MIGHT)
Ge 17: 1 “I am God *A;* walk before me
Ex 6: 3 to Isaac and to Jacob as God *A,*
Ru 1: 20 the *A* has made my life very bitter.
Job 11: 7 Can you probe the limits of the *A?*
33: 4 the breath of the *A* gives me life.
Ps 89: 8 O LORD God *A,* who is like you?
91: 1 will rest in the shadow of the *A.*
Isa 6: 3 “Holy, holy, holy is the LORD *A;*
45: 13 says the LORD *A.*”
47: 4 the LORD *A* is his name—
48: 2 the LORD *A* is his name:
51: 15 the LORD *A* is his name.
54: 5 the LORD *A* is his name—
Am 5: 14 the LORD God *A* will be with you,
5: 15 the LORD God *A* will have mercy
Rev 4: 8 holy is the Lord God *A,* who was,
19: 6 For our Lord God *A* reigns.

ALPHA*
Rev 1: 8 “I am the *A* and the Omega,”
21: 6 I am the *A* and the Omega,
22: 13 I am the *A* and the Omega,

ALTAR
Ge 8: 20 Then Noah built an *a* to the LORD
12: 7 So he built an *a* there to the LORD
13: 18 where he built an *a* to the LORD.
22: 9 Abraham built an *a* there
22: 9 his son Isaac and laid him on the *a,*
26: 25 Isaac built an *a* there and called
35: 1 and build an *a* there to God,
Ex 17: 15 Moses built an *a* and called it
27: 1 “Build an *a* of acacia wood,
30: 1 “Make an *a* of acacia wood
37: 25 They made the *a* of incense out
Dt 27: 5 an *a* to the LORD your God, an *a*
Jos 8: 30 on Mount Ebal an *a* to the LORD,
22: 10 built an imposing *a* there
Jdg 6: 24 So Gideon built an *a* to the LORD
21: 4 the next day the people built an *a*
1Sa 7: 17 he built an *a* there to the LORD.
14: 35 Then Saul built an *a* to the LORD;
2Sa 24: 25 David built an *a* to the LORD
1Ki 12: 33 sacrifices on the *a* he had built
13: 2 “O *a, a!* This is what the LORD
16: 32 He set up an *a* for Baal
18: 30 and he repaired the *a* of the LORD
2Ki 16: 11 So Uriah the priest built an *a*
1Ch 21: 26 David built an *a* to the LORD
2Ch 4: 1 made a bronze *a* twenty cubits
4: 19 the golden *a;* the tables
15: 8 He repaired the *a* of the LORD
32: 12 ‘You must worship before one *a*
33: 16 he restored the *a* of the LORD
Ezr 3: 2 to build the *a* of the God of Israel
Isa 6: 6 taken with tongs from the *a.*
Eze 40: 47 the *a* was in front of the temple.
Mt 5: 23 if you are offering your gift at the *a*
Ac 17: 23 found an *a* with this inscription:
Heb 13: 10 We have an *a* from which those
Rev 6: 9 I saw under the *a* the souls

ALTER*
Ps 89: 34 or *a* what my lips have uttered.

ALWAYS
Dt 15: 11 There will *a* be poor people
Ps 16: 8 I have set the LORD *a* before me.
51: 3 and my sin is *a* before me.
Pr 23: 7 who is *a* thinking about the cost.
Mt 26: 11 The poor you will *a* have with you,
28: 20 And surely I am with you *a,*
Mk 14: 7 The poor you will *a* have with you,
Jn 12: 8 You will *a* have the poor
1Co 13: 7 *a* protects, *a* trusts, *a* hopes, *a*
Php 4: 4 Rejoice in the Lord *a.*
1Pe 3: 15 *A* be prepared to give an answer

AMALEKITES
Ex 17: 8 *A* came and attacked the Israelites
1Sa 15: 2 ‘I will punish the *A*

AMASA
Nephew of David (1Ch 2:17). Commander of Absalom’s forces (2Sa 17:24–27). Returned to David (2Sa 19:13). Killed by Joab (2Sa 20:4–13).

AMASSES*
Pr 28: 8 *a* it for another, who will be kind

AMAZED
Mt 7: 28 the crowds were *a* at his teaching,
Mk 6: 6 And he was *a* at their lack of faith.
10: 24 The disciples were *a* at his words.
Ac 2: 7 Utterly *a,* they asked: “Are not all
13: 12 for he was *a* at the teaching about

AMAZIAH
1. Son of Joash; king of Judah (2Ki 14; 2Ch 25). Defeated Edom (2Ki 14:7; 2Ch 25:5–13); defeated by Israel for worshiping Edom’s gods (2Ki 14:8–14; 2Ch 25:14–24).
2. Idolatrous priest who opposed Amos (Am 7:10–17).

AMBASSADOR* (AMBASSADORS)
Eph 6: 20 for which I am an *a* in chains.

AMBASSADORS (AMBASSADOR)
2Co 5: 20 We are therefore Christ’s *a,*

AMBITION*
Ro 15: 20 It has always been my *a*
Gal 5: 20 fits of rage, selfish *a,* dissensions,
Php 1: 17 preach Christ out of selfish *a,*
2: 3 Do nothing out of selfish *a*
1Th 4: 11 Make it your *a* to lead a quiet life,
Jas 3: 14 and selfish *a* in your hearts,
3: 16 where you have envy and selfish *a,*

AMENDS
Pr 14: 9 Fools mock at making *a* for sin,

AMNON
Firstborn of David (2Sa 3:2; 1Ch 3:1). Killed by Absalom for raping his sister Tamar (2Sa 13).

AMON
1. Son of Manasseh; king of Judah (2Ki 21:18–26; 1Ch 3:14; 2Ch 33:21–25).
2. Ruler of Samaria under Ahab (1Ki 22:26; 2Ch 18:25).

AMOS
1. Prophet from Tekoa (Am 1:1; 7:10–17).
2. Ancestor of Jesus (Lk 3:25).

ANAK (ANAKITES)
Nu 13: 28 even saw descendants of *A* there.

ANAKITES (ANAK)
Dt 1: 28 We even saw the *A* there.’ ”
2: 10 and numerous, and as tall as the *A.*
9: 2 “Who can stand up against the *A?*”

ANANIAS
1. Husband of Sapphira; died for lying to God (Ac 5:1–11).
2. Disciple who baptized Saul (Ac 9:10–19).
3. High priest at Paul’s arrest (Ac 22:30–24:1).

ANCESTORS (ANCESTRY)
1Ki 19: 4 I am no better than my *a.*”

ANCESTRY (ANCESTORS)
Ro 9: 5 from them is traced the human *a*

ANCHOR
Heb 6: 19 We have this hope as an *a*

ANCIENT
Da 7: 9 and the *A* of Days took his seat.
7: 13 He approached the *A* of Days
7: 22 until the *A* of Days came

ANDREW*
Apostle; brother of Simon Peter (Mt 4:18; 10:2; Mk 1:16–18, 29; 3:18; 13:3; Lk 6:14; Jn 1:35–44; 6:8–9; 12:22; Ac 1:13).

ANGEL (ANGELS ARCHANGEL)
Ge 16: 7 The *a* of the LORD found Hagar
22: 11 But the *a* of the LORD called out
Ex 23: 20 I am sending an *a* ahead of you
Nu 22: 23 When the donkey saw the *a*
Jdg 2: 1 The *a* of the LORD went up
6: 22 Gideon realized that it was the *a*
13: 15 Manoah said to the *a* of the LORD
2Sa 24: 16 The *a* of the LORD was then
1Ki 19: 7 The *a* of the LORD came back
2Ki 19: 35 That night the *a* of the LORD went
Ps 34: 7 The *a* of the LORD encamps
Hos 12: 4 He struggled with the *a*
Mt 2: 13 an *a* of the Lord appeared
28: 2 for an *a* of the Lord came
Lk 1: 26 God sent the *a* Gabriel
2: 9 An *a* of the Lord appeared to them,
22: 43 An *a* from heaven appeared to him
Ac 6: 15 his face was like the face of an *a.*
12: 7 Suddenly an *a* of the Lord
2Co 11: 14 Satan himself masquerades as an *a*
Gal 1: 8 or an *a* from heaven should preach

ANGELS (ANGEL)
Ps 91: 11 command his *a* concerning you
Mt 4: 6 command his *a* concerning you,
13: 39 of the age, and the harvesters are *a.*
13: 49 The *a* will come and separate
18: 10 For I tell you that their *a*
25: 41 prepared for the devil and his *a.*
Lk 4: 10 command his *a* concerning you
20: 36 for they are like the *a.*
1Co 6: 3 you not know that we will judge *a?*
13: 1 in the tongues of men and of *a,*
Col 2: 18 and the worship of *a* disqualify you
Heb 1: 4 as much superior to the *a*
1: 6 “Let all God’s *a* worship him.”
1: 7 “He makes his *a* winds,
1: 14 Are not all *a* ministering spirits
2: 7 made him a little lower than the *a;*
2: 9 was made a little lower than the *a,*
13: 2 some people have entertained *a*
1Pe 1: 12 Even *a* long to look
2Pe 2: 4 For if God did not spare *a*
Jude : 6 *a* who did not keep their positions

ANGER (ANGERED ANGRY)
Ex 15: 7 You unleashed your burning *a;*
22: 24 My *a* will be aroused, and I will kill
32: 10 alone so that my *a* may burn
32: 11 “why should your *a* burn
32: 12 Turn from your fierce *a;* relent
32: 19 his *a* burned and he threw
34: 6 slow to *a,* abounding in love
Lev 26: 28 then in my *a* I will be hostile
Nu 14: 18 slow to *a,* abounding in love
25: 11 has turned my *a* away
32: 10 LORD’s *a* was aroused that day
32: 13 The LORD’s *a* burned
Dt 9: 19 I feared the *a* and wrath
29: 28 In furious *a* and in great wrath
Jdg 14: 19 Burning with *a,* he went up
2Sa 12: 5 David burned with *a*
2Ki 22: 13 Great is the LORD’s *a* that burns
Ne 9: 17 slow to *a* and abounding in love.
Ps 30: 5 For his *a* lasts only a moment,
78: 38 Time after time he restrained his *a*
86: 15 slow to *a,* abounding in love
90: 7 We are consumed by your *a*
103: 8 slow to *a,* abounding in love.
Pr 15: 1 but a harsh word stirs up *a.*
29: 11 A fool gives full vent to his *a,*
30: 33 so stirring up *a* produces strife.”
Jnh 4: 2 slow to *a* and abounding in love,
Eph 4: 26 “In your *a* do not sin”: Do not let
Jas 1: 20 for man’s *a* does not bring about

ANGERED (ANGER)
Pr 22: 24 do not associate with one easily *a,*
1Co 13: 5 it is not easily *a,* it keeps no record

ANGRY (ANGER)
Ps 2: 12 Kiss the Son, lest he be *a*
95: 10 For forty years I was *a*
Pr 29: 22 An *a* man stirs up dissension,
Mt 5: 22 But I tell you that anyone who is *a*
Jas 1: 19 slow to speak and slow to become *a*

ANGUISH
Ps 118: 5 In my *a* I cried to the LORD,
Jer 4: 19 Oh, my *a*, my *a!*
Zep 1: 15 a day of distress and *a*,
Lk 21: 25 nations will be in *a* and perplexity
22: 44 in *a*, he prayed more earnestly,
Ro 9: 2 and unceasing *a* in my heart.

ANIMALS
Ge 1: 24 wild *a*, each according to its kind."
7: 16 The *a* going in were male
Dt 14: 4 These are the *a* you may eat: the ox
Job 12: 7 ask the *a*, and they will teach you,
Isa 43: 20 The wild *a* honor me,

ANNOUNCE (ANNOUNCED)
Mt 6: 2 give to the needy, do not *a* it

ANNOUNCED (ANNOUNCE)
Isa 48: 5 before they happened I *a* them
Gal 3: 8 and *a* the gospel in advance

ANNOYANCE*
Pr 12: 16 A fool shows his *a* at once,

ANNUAL*
Ex 30: 10 This *a* atonement must be made
Jdg 21: 19 there is the *a* festival of the LORD
1Sa 1: 21 family to offer the *a* sacrifice
2: 19 husband to offer the *a* sacrifice.
20: 6 an *a* sacrifice is being made there
2Ch 8: 13 New Moons and the three *a* feasts
Heb 10: 3 those sacrifices are an *a* reminder

ANOINT (ANOINTED ANOINTING)
Ex 30: 26 use it to *a* the Tent of Meeting,
30: 30 "*A* Aaron and his sons
1Sa 9: 16 *A* him leader over my people Israel
15: 1 to *a* you king over his people Israel;
2Ki 9: 3 what the LORD says: I *a* you king
Ps 23: 5 You *a* my head with oil;
Da 9: 24 prophecy and to *a* the most holy.
Jas 5: 14 and *a* him with oil in the name

ANOINTED (ANOINT)
1Ch 16: 22 "Do not touch my *a* ones;
Ps 105: 15 "Do not touch my *a* ones;
Isa 61: 1 because the LORD has *a* me
Da 9: 26 the *A* One will be cut off
Lk 4: 18 because he has *a* me
Ac 10: 38 how God *a* Jesus of Nazareth

ANOINTING (ANOINT)
Lev 8: 12 some of the *a* oil on Aaron's head
1Ch 29: 22 *a* him before the LORD to be ruler
Ps 45: 7 by *a* you with the oil of joy.
Heb 1: 9 by *a* you with the oil of joy."
1Jn 2: 20 you have an *a* from the Holy One,
2: 27 about all things and as that *a* is real,

ANT* (ANTS)
Pr 6: 6 Go to the *a*, you sluggard;

ANTICHRIST* (ANTICHRISTS)
1Jn 2: 18 have heard that the *a* is coming,
2: 22 a man is the *a*— he denies
4: 3 of the *a*, which you have heard is
2Jn : 7 person is the deceiver and the *a*.

ANTICHRISTS* (ANTICHRIST)
1Jn 2: 18 even now many *a* have come.

ANTIOCH
Ac 11: 26 were called Christians first at *A*.

ANTS* (ANT)
Pr 30: 25 *A* are creatures of little strength,

ANXIETIES* (ANXIOUS)
Lk 21: 34 drunkenness and the *a* of life,

ANXIETY (ANXIOUS)
1Pe 5: 7 Cast all your *a* on him

ANXIOUS (ANXIETIES ANXIETY)
Pr 12: 25 An *a* heart weighs a man down,
Php 4: 6 Do not be *a* about anything,

APOLLOS*
Christian from Alexandria, learned in the Scriptures; instructed by Aquila and Priscilla (Ac 18:24–28). Ministered at Corinth (Ac 19:1; 1Co 1:12; 3; Tit 3:13).

APOLLYON*
Rev 9: 11 is Abaddon, and in Greek, *A*.

APOSTLE (APOSTLES APOSTLES')
Ro 11: 13 as I am the *a* to the Gentiles,
1Co 9: 1 Am I not an *a?* Have I not seen
2Co 12: 12 The things that mark an *a*— signs,
Gal 2: 8 of Peter as an *a* to the Jews,
1Ti 2: 7 was appointed a herald and an *a*—
2Ti 1: 11 I was appointed a herald and an *a*
Heb 3: 1 *a* and high priest whom we confess.

APOSTLES (APOSTLE)
See also Andrew, Bartholomew, James, John, Judas, Matthew, Matthias, Nathanael, Paul, Peter, Philip, Simon, Thaddaeus, Thomas.
Mk 3: 14 twelve—designating them *a*—
Lk 11: 49 'I will send them prophets and *a*,
Ac 1: 26 so he was added to the eleven *a*.
2: 43 signs were done by the *a*.
1Co 12: 28 God has appointed first of all *a*,
15: 9 For I am the least of the *a*
2Co 11: 13 masquerading as *a* of Christ.
Eph 2: 20 built on the foundation of the *a*
4: 11 It was he who gave some to be *a*,
Rev 21: 14 names of the twelve *a* of the Lamb.

APOSTLES' (APOSTLE)
Ac 5: 2 the rest and put it at the *a'* feet.
8: 18 at the laying on of the *a'* hands,

APPEAL
Ac 25: 11 *I a* to Caesar!" After Festus had
Phm : 9 yet I *a* to you on the basis of love.

APPEAR (APPEARANCE APPEARANCES APPEARED APPEARING APPEARS)
Ge 1: 9 to one place, and let dry ground *a*."
Lev 16: 2 I *a* in the cloud over the atonement
Mt 24: 30 of the Son of Man will *a* in the sky,
Mk 13: 22 false prophets will *a* and perform
Lk 19: 11 of God was going to *a* at once.
2Co 5: 10 we must all *a* before the judgment
Col 3: 4 also will *a* with him in glory.
Heb 9: 24 now to *a* for us in God's presence.
9: 28 and he will *a* a second time,

APPEARANCE (APPEAR)
1Sa 16: 7 Man looks at the outward *a*,
Isa 52: 14 his *a* was so disfigured beyond that
53: 2 in his *a* that we should desire him.
Gal 2: 6 God does not judge by external *a*—

APPEARANCES* (APPEAR)
Jn 7: 24 Stop judging by mere *a*,

APPEARED (APPEAR)
Nu 14: 10 glory of the LORD *a* at the Tent
Mt 1: 20 an angel of the Lord *a* to him
Lk 2: 9 An angel of the Lord *a* to them,
1Co 15: 5 and that he *a* to Peter,
Heb 9: 26 now he has *a* once for all at the end

APPEARING (APPEAR)
1Ti 6: 14 until the *a* of our Lord Jesus Christ,
2Ti 1: 10 through the *a* of our Savior,
4: 8 to all who have longed for his *a*.
Tit 2: 13 the glorious *a* of our great God

APPEARS (APPEAR)
Mal 3: 2 Who can stand when he *a?*
Col 3: 4 When Christ, who is your life, *a*,
1Pe 5: 4 And when the Chief Shepherd *a*,
1Jn 3: 2 But we know that when he *a*,

APPETITE
Pr 16: 26 The laborer's *a* works for him;
Ecc 6: 7 yet his *a* is never satisfied.
Jer 50: 19 his *a* will be satisfied

APPLES
Pr 25: 11 is like *a* of gold in settings of silver.

APPLY (APPLYING)
Pr 22: 17 *a* your heart to what I teach,
23: 12 *A* your heart to instruction

APPLYING (APPLY)
Pr 2: 2 and *a* your heart to understanding,

APPOINT (APPOINTED)
Ps 61: 7 *a* your love and faithfulness
1Th 5: 9 For God did not *a* us
Tit 1: 5 and *a* elders in every town,

APPOINTED (APPOINT)
Dt 1: 15 *a* them to have authority over you
Pr 8: 23 I was *a* from eternity,
Da 11: 27 an end will still come at the *a* time.
Hab 2: 3 For the revelation awaits an *a* time;
Jn 15: 16 Chose you and *a* you to go
Ro 9: 9 "At the *a* time I will return,

APPROACH (APPROACHING)
Ex 24: 2 but Moses alone is to *a* the LORD;
Eph 3: 12 in him we may *a* God with freedom
Heb 4: 16 Let us then *a* the throne of grace

APPROACHING (APPROACH)
Heb 10: 25 all the more as you see the Day *a*.
1Jn 5: 14 is the confidence we have in *a* God:

APPROPRIATE
1Ti 2: 10 *a* for women who profess

APPROVAL (APPROVE)
Jdg 18: 6 Your journey has the LORD's *a*."
Jn 6: 27 the Father has placed his seal of *a*."
1Co 11: 19 to show which of you have God's *a*
Gal 1: 10 trying to win the *a* of men,

APPROVE (APPROVAL APPROVED APPROVES)
Ro 2: 18 if you know his will and *a*
12: 2 and *a* what God's will is—

APPROVED* (APPROVE)
Ro 14: 18 pleasing to God and *a* by men.
16: 10 Greet Apelles, tested and *a*
2Co 10: 18 who commends himself who is *a*,
1Th 2: 4 as men *a* by God to be entrusted
2Ti 2: 15 to present yourself to God as one *a*,

APPROVES* (APPROVE)
Ro 14: 22 not condemn himself by what he *a*.

APT*
Pr 15: 23 A man finds joy in giving an *a* reply

AQUILA*
Husband of Priscilla; co-worker with Paul, instructor of Apollos (Ac 18; Ro 16:3; 1Co 16:19; 2Ti 4:19).

ARABIA
Gal 1: 17 but I went immediately into *A*
4: 25 Hagar stands for Mount Sinai in *A*

ARARAT
Ge 8: 4 came to rest on the mountains of *A*.

ARAUNAH
2Sa 24: 16 threshing floor of *A* the Jebusite.

ARBITER* (ARBITRATE)
Lk 12: 14 who appointed me a judge or an *a*

ARBITRATE* (ARBITER)
Job 9: 33 If only there were someone to *a*

ARCHANGEL* (ANGEL)
1Th 4: 16 with the voice of the *a*
Jude : 9 *a* Michael, when he was disputing

ARCHER
Pr 26: 10 Like an *a* who wounds at random

ARCHIPPUS*
Col 4: 17 Tell *A:* "See to it that you complete
Phm : 2 to *A* our fellow soldier

ARCHITECT*
Heb 11: 10 whose *a* and builder is God.

AREOPAGUS*
Ac 17: 19 brought him to a meeting of the *A*,
17: 22 up in the meeting of the *A*
17: 34 of the *A*, also a woman named

ARGUE (ARGUMENT ARGUMENTS)
Job 13: 3 and to *a* my case with God.
13: 8 Will you *a* the case for God?
Pr 25: 9 If you *a* your case with a neighbor,

ARGUMENT (ARGUE)
Heb 6: 16 is said and puts an end to all *a.*

ARGUMENTS (ARGUE)
Isa 41: 21 "Set forth your *a,*" says Jacob's
Col 2: 4 you by fine-sounding *a.*
2Ti 2: 23 to do with foolish and stupid *a,*
Tit 3: 9 and *a* and quarrels about the law,

ARK
Ge 6: 14 So make yourself an *a*
Ex 25: 21 and put in the *a* the Testimony,
Dt 10: 5 put the tablets in the *a* I had made,
1Sa 4: 11 The *a* of God was captured,
7: 2 that the *a* remained at Kiriath
2Sa 6: 17 They brought the *a* of the LORD
1Ki 8: 9 There was nothing in the *a*
1Ch 13: 9 out his hand to steady the *a,*
2Ch 35: 3 "Put the sacred *a* in the temple that
Heb 9: 4 This *a* contained the gold jar
11: 7 in holy fear built an *a*
Rev 11: 19 within his temple was seen the *a*

ARM (ARMY)
Nu 11: 23 "Is the LORD's *a* too short?
Dt 4: 34 hand and an outstretched *a,*
7: 19 mighty hand and outstretched *a,*
Ps 44: 3 it was your right hand, your *a,*
98: 1 his right hand and his holy *a*
Jer 27: 5 outstretched *a* I made the earth
1Pe 4: 1 *a* yourselves also with the same

ARMAGEDDON*
Rev 16: 16 that in Hebrew is called *A.*

ARMIES (ARMY)
1Sa 17: 26 Philistine that he should defy the *a*
Rev 19: 14 *a* of heaven were following him,

ARMOR (ARMY)
1Ki 20: 11 on his *a* should not boast like one
Jer 46: 4 put on your *a!*
Ro 13: 12 deeds of darkness and put on the *a*
Eph 6: 11 Put on the full *a* of God
6: 13 Therefore put on the full *a* of God,

ARMS (ARMY)
Dt 33: 27 underneath are the everlasting *a.*
Ps 18: 32 It is God who *a* me with strength
Pr 31: 17 her *a* are strong for her tasks.
31: 20 She opens her *a* to the poor
Isa 40: 11 He gathers the lambs in his *a*
Mk 10: 16 And he took the children in his *a,*
Heb 12: 12 strengthen your feeble *a*

ARMY (ARM ARMIES ARMOR ARMS)
Ps 33: 16 No king is saved by the size of his *a*
Joel 2: 2 a large and mighty *a* comes,
2: 5 like a mighty *a* drawn up for battle.
2: 11 thunders at the head of his *a;*
Rev 19: 19 the rider on the horse and his *a.*

AROMA
Ge 8: 21 The LORD smelled the pleasing *a*
Ex 29: 18 a pleasing *a,* an offering made
Lev 3: 16 made by fire, a pleasing *a.*
2Co 2: 15 For we are to God the *a* of Christ

AROUSE (AROUSED)
Ro 11: 14 I may somehow *a* my own people

AROUSED (AROUSE)
Ps 78: 58 they *a* his jealousy with their idols.

ARRANGED
1Co 12: 18 But in fact God has *a* the parts

ARRAYED*
Ps 110: 3 *A* in holy majesty,
Isa 61: 10 and *a* me in a robe of righteousness

ARREST
Mt 10: 19 But when they *a* you, do not worry

ARROGANCE (ARROGANT)
1Sa 2: 3 or let your mouth speak such *a,*
Pr 8: 13 I hate pride and *a,*
Mk 7: 22 lewdness, envy, slander, *a* and folly
2Co 12: 20 slander, gossip, *a* and disorder.

ARROGANT (ARROGANCE)
Ps 5: 5 The *a* cannot stand
119: 78 May the *a* be put to shame
Pr 17: 7 *A* lips are unsuited to a fool—
21: 24 *a* man—"Mocker" is his name;
Ro 1: 30 God-haters, insolent, *a*
11: 20 Do not be *a,* but be afraid.
1Ti 6: 17 in this present world not to be *a*

ARROW (ARROWS)
Ps 91: 5 nor the *a* that flies by day,
Pr 25: 18 Like a club or a sword or a sharp *a*

ARROWS (ARROW)
Ps 64: 3 and aim their words like deadly *a.*
64: 7 But God will shoot them with *a;*
127: 4 Like *a* in the hands of a warrior
Pr 26: 18 firebrands or deadly *a*
Eph 6: 16 you can extinguish all the flaming *a*

ARTAXERXES
King of Persia; allowed rebuilding of temple under Ezra (Ezr 4; 7), and of walls of Jerusalem under his cupbearer Nehemiah (Ne 2; 5:14; 13:6).

ARTEMIS
Ac 19: 28 "Great is *A* of the Ephesians!"

ASA
King of Judah (1Ki 15:8–24; 1Ch 3:10; 2Ch 14–16). Godly reformer (2Ch 15); in later years defeated Israel with help of Aram, not the LORD (1Ki 15:16–22; 2Ch 16).

ASAHEL
1. Nephew of David, one of his warriors (2Sa 23:24; 1Ch 2:16; 11:26; 27:7). Killed by Abner (2Sa 2); avenged by Joab (2Sa 3:22–39).
2. Levite; teacher (2Ch 17:8).

ASAPH
1. Recorder to Hezekiah (2Ki 18:18, 37; Isa 36:3, 22).
2. Levitical musician (1Ch 6:39; 15:17–19; 16:4–7, 37). Sons of (1Ch 25; 2Ch 5:12; 20:14; 29:13; 35:15; Ezr 2:41; 3:10; Ne 7:44; 11:17; 12:27–47). Psalms of (2Ch 29:30; Ps 50; 73–83).

ASCEND* (ASCENDED ASCENDING)
Dt 30: 12 "Who will *a* into heaven to get it
Ps 24: 3 Who may *a* the hill of the LORD?
Isa 14: 13 "I will *a* to heaven;
14: 14 I will *a* above the tops of the clouds
Jn 6: 62 of Man *a* to where he was before!
Ac 2: 34 For David did not *a* to heaven,
Ro 10: 6 'Who will *a* into heaven?' " (that is,

ASCENDED (ASCEND)
Ps 68: 18 When you *a* on high,
Eph 4: 8 "When he *a* on high,

ASCENDING (ASCEND)
Ge 28: 12 and the angels of God were *a*
Jn 1: 51 and the angels of God *a*

ASCRIBE*
1Ch 16: 28 *A* to the LORD, O families
16: 28 *a* to the LORD glory and strength,
16: 29 *a* to the LORD the glory due his
Job 36: 3 I will *a* justice to my Maker.
Ps 29: 1 *A* to the LORD, O mighty ones,
29: 1 *a* to the LORD glory and strength.
29: 2 *A* to the LORD the glory due his
96: 7 *A* to the LORD, O families
96: 7 *a* to the LORD glory and strength.
96: 8 *A* to the LORD the glory due his

ASHAMED (SHAME)
Mk 8: 38 If anyone is *a* of me and my words
Lk 9: 26 If anyone is *a* of me and my words,
Ro 1: 16 I am not *a* of the gospel,
2Ti 1: 8 So do not be *a* to testify about our
2: 15 who does not need to be *a*

ASHER
Son of Jacob by Zilpah (Ge 30:13; 35:26; 46:17; Ex 1:4; 1Ch 2:2). Tribe of blessed (Ge 49:20; Dt 33:24–25), numbered (Nu 1:40–41; 26:44–47), allotted land (Jos 10:24–31; Eze 48:2), failed to fully possess (Jdg 1:31–32), failed to support Deborah (Jdg 5:17), supported Gideon (Jdg 6:35; 7:23) and David (1Ch 12:36), 12,000 from (Rev 7:6).

ASHERAH (ASHERAHS)
Ex 34: 13 and cut down their *A* poles.
1Ki 18: 19 the four hundred prophets of *A,*

ASHERAHS* (ASHERAH)
Jdg 3: 7 and served the Baals and the *A.*

ASHES
Job 42: 6 and repent in dust and *a.*"
Mt 11: 21 ago in sackcloth and *a.*

ASHTORETHS
Jdg 2: 13 and served Baal and the *A.*
1Sa 7: 4 put away their Baals and *A,*

ASLEEP (SLEEP)
1Co 15: 18 who have fallen *a* in Christ are lost.
1Th 4: 13 be ignorant about those who fall *a,*

ASSEMBLY
Ps 1: 5 nor sinners in the *a* of the righteous
35: 18 I will give you thanks in the great *a*
82: 1 God presides in the great *a;*
149: 1 his praise in the *a* of the saints.

ASSIGNED
1Ki 7: 14 and did all the work *a* to him.
Mk 13: 34 with his *a* task, and tells the one
1Co 3: 5 as the Lord has *a* to each his task.
7: 17 place in life that the Lord *a* to him
2Co 10: 13 to the field God has *a* to us,

ASSOCIATE
Pr 22: 24 do not *a* with one easily angered,
Jn 4: 9 (For Jews do not *a* with Samaritans
Ac 10: 28 law for a Jew to *a* with a Gentile
Ro 12: 16 but be willing to *a* with people
1Co 5: 9 to *a* with sexually immoral people
5: 11 am writing you that you must not *a*
2Th 3: 14 Do not *a* with him,

ASSURANCE (ASSURED)
Heb 10: 22 with a sincere heart in full *a* of faith

ASSURED (ASSURANCE)
Col 4: 12 the will of God, mature and fully *a.*

ASTRAY
Ps 119: 67 Before I was afflicted I went *a,*
Pr 10: 17 ignores correction leads others *a.*
20: 1 whoever is led *a* by them is not
Isa 53: 6 We all, like sheep, have gone *a,*
Jer 50: 6 their shepherds have led them *a*
Jn 16: 1 you so that you will not go *a.*
1Pe 2: 25 For you were like sheep going *a,*
1Jn 3: 7 do not let anyone lead you *a.*

ASTROLOGERS
Isa 47: 13 Let your *a* come forward,
Da 2: 2 *a* to tell him what he had dreamed.

ATE (EAT)
Ge 3: 6 wisdom, she took some and *a* it.
27: 25 Jacob brought it to him and he *a;*
2Sa 9: 11 Mephibosheth *a* at David's table
Ps 78: 25 Men *a* the bread of angels;
Jer 15: 16 When your words came, I *a* them;
Eze 3: 3 So I *a* it, and it tasted as sweet
Mt 14: 20 They all *a* and were satisfied,
15: 37 They all *a* and were satisfied.
Mk 6: 42 They all *a* and were satisfied,
Lk 9: 17 They all *a* and were satisfied,

ATHALIAH
Granddaughter of Omri; wife of Jehoram and mother of Ahaziah; encouraged their evil ways (2Ki 8:18, 27; 2Ch 22:2). At death of Ahaziah she made herself queen, killing all his sons but Joash (2Ki 11:1–3; 2Ch 22:10–12); killed six years later when Joash was revealed (2Ki 11:4–16; 2Ch 23:1–15).

ATHLETE*
2Ti 2: 5 if anyone competes as an *a,*

ATONE* (ATONEMENT)
Ex 30: 15 to the LORD to *a* for your lives.
2Ch 29: 24 for a sin offering to *a* for all Israel,

Da 9: 24 an end to sin, to *a* for wickedness,
ATONED* (ATONEMENT)
Dt 21: 8 And the bloodshed will be *a* for.
1Sa 3: 14 guilt of Eli's house will never be *a*
Pr 16: 6 faithfulness sin is *a* for;
Isa 6: 7 guilt is taken away and your sin *a*
22: 14 your dying day this sin will not be *a*
27: 9 then, will Jacob's guilt be *a* for,
ATONEMENT (ATONE ATONED)
Ex 25: 17 "Make an *a* cover of pure gold—
30: 10 Once a year Aaron shall make *a*
Lev 17: 11 it is the blood that makes *a*
23: 27 this seventh month is the Day of *A*.
Nu 25: 13 and made *a* for the Israelites."
Ro 3: 25 presented him as a sacrifice of *a*,
Heb 2: 17 that he might make *a* for the sins
ATTACK
Ps 109: 3 they *a* me without cause.
ATTAINED
Php 3: 16 up to what we have already *a*.
Heb 7: 11 If perfection could have been *a*
ATTENTION (ATTENTIVE)
Pr 4: 1 pay *a* and gain understanding.
4: 20 My son, pay *a* to what I say;
5: 1 My son, pay *a* to my wisdom,
7: 24 pay *a* to what I say.
22: 17 Pay *a* and listen to the sayings
Ecc 7: 21 Do not pay *a* to every word people
Isa 42: 20 many things, but have paid no *a*;
Tit 1: 14 and will pay no *a* to Jewish myths
Heb 2: 1 We must pay more careful *a*,
ATTENTIVE (ATTENTION)
Ne 1: 11 let your ear be *a* to the prayer
1Pe 3: 12 and his ears are *a* to their prayer,
ATTITUDE (ATTITUDES)
Eph 4: 23 new in the *a* of your minds;
Php 2: 5 Your *a* should be the same
1Pe 4: 1 yourselves also with the same *a*,
ATTITUDES (ATTITUDE)
Heb 4: 12 it judges the thoughts and *a*
ATTRACTIVE
Tit 2: 10 teaching about God our Savior *a*.
AUDIENCE
Pr 29: 26 Many seek an *a* with a ruler,
AUTHORITIES (AUTHORITY)
Ro 13: 1 *a* that exist have been established
13: 5 it is necessary to submit to the *a*,
13: 6 for the *a* are God's servants,
Eph 3: 10 and *a* in the heavenly realms,
6: 12 but against the rulers, against the *a*,
Col 1: 16 thrones or powers or rulers or *a*;
2: 15 having disarmed the powers and *a*,
Tit 3: 1 people to be subject to rulers and *a*,
1Pe 3: 22 *a* and powers in submission to him.
AUTHORITY (AUTHORITIES)
Mt 7: 29 because he taught as one who had *a*
9: 6 the Son of Man has *a* on earth
28: 18 "All *a* in heaven and on earth has
Mk 1: 22 he taught them as one who had *a*,
2: 10 the Son of Man has *a* on earth
Lk 4: 32 because his message had *a*.
5: 24 the Son of Man has *a* on earth
Jn 10: 18 *a* to lay it down and *a*
Ac 1: 7 the Father has set by his own *a*.
Ro 7: 1 that the law has *a* over a man only
13: 1 for there is no *a* except that which
13: 2 rebels against the *a* is rebelling
1Co 11: 10 to have a sign of *a* on her head.
15: 24 he has destroyed all dominion, *a*
1Ti 2: 2 for kings and all those in *a*,
2: 12 to teach or to have *a* over a man;
Tit 2: 15 Encourage and rebuke with all *a*.
Heb 13: 17 your leaders and submit to their *a*.
AUTUMN*
Dt 11: 14 both *a* and spring rains,
Ps 84: 6 the *a* rains also cover it with pools.
Jer 5: 24 who gives *a* and spring rains
Joel 2: 23 both *a* and spring rains, as before.
Jas 5: 7 and how patient he is for the *a*
Jude : 12 blown along by the wind; *a* trees,
AVENGE (VENGEANCE)
Lev 26: 25 sword upon you to *a* the breaking
Dt 32: 35 It is mine to *a*; I will repay.
32: 43 for he will *a* the blood
Ro 12: 19 "It is mine to *a*; I will repay,"
Heb 10: 30 "It is mine to *a*; I will repay,"
Rev 6: 10 of the earth and *a* our blood?"
AVENGER (VENGEANCE)
Nu 35: 27 the *a* of blood may kill the accused
Jos 20: 3 find protection from the *a* of blood.
Ps 8: 2 to silence the foe and the *a*.
AVENGES (VENGEANCE)
Ps 94: 1 O LORD, the God who *a*,
AVENGING (VENGEANCE)
1Sa 25: 26 and from *a* yourself with your own
Na 1: 2 The LORD is a jealous and *a* God;
AVOID (AVOIDS)
Pr 4: 15 *A* it, do not travel on it;
20: 3 It is to a man's honor to *a* strife,
20: 19 so *a* a man who talks too much.
Ecc 7: 18 who fears God will *a* all ›extremes‹.
1Th 4: 3 you should *a* sexual immorality;
5: 22 *A* every kind of evil.
2Ti 2: 16 *A* godless chatter, because those
Tit 3: 9 But *a* foolish controversies
AVOIDS* (AVOID)
Pr 16: 6 of the LORD a man *a* evil.
16: 17 The highway of the upright *a* evil;
AWAITS (WAIT)
Pr 15: 10 Stern discipline *a* him who leaves
28: 22 and is unaware that poverty *a* him.
AWAKE (WAKE)
Ps 17: 15 when I *a*, I will be satisfied
Pr 6: 22 when you *a*, they will speak to you.
AWARD*
2Ti 4: 8 will *a* to me on that day—
AWARE
Ex 34: 29 he was not *a* that his face was
Mt 24: 50 and at an hour he is not *a* of.
Lk 12: 46 and at an hour he is not *a* of.
AWE* (AWESOME OVERAWED)
1Sa 12: 18 So all the people stood in *a*
1Ki 3: 28 they held the king in *a*,
Job 25: 2 "Dominion and *a* belong to God;
Ps 119:120 I stand in *a* of your laws.
Ecc 5: 7 Therefore stand in *a* of God.
Isa 29: 23 will stand in *a* of the God of Israel.
Jer 2: 19 and have no *a* of me,"
33: 9 they will be in *a* and will tremble
Hab 3: 2 I stand in *a* of your deeds,
Mal 2: 5 and stood in *a* of my name.
Mt 9: 8 they were filled with *a*;
Lk 1: 65 The neighbors were all filled with *a*
5: 26 They were filled with *a* and said,
7: 16 They were all filled with *a*
Ac 2: 43 Everyone was filled with *a*,
Heb 12: 28 acceptably with reverence and *a*,
AWESOME* (AWE)
Ge 28: 17 and said, "How *a* is this place!
Ex 15: 11 *a* in glory,
34: 10 among will see how *a* is the work
Dt 4: 34 or by great and *a* deeds,
7: 21 is among you, is a great and *a* God.
10: 17 the great God, mighty and *a*,
10: 21 and *a* wonders you saw
28: 58 revere this glorious and *a* name—
34: 12 performed the *a* deeds that Moses
Jdg 13: 6 like an angel of God, very *a*.
2Sa 7: 23 *a* wonders by driving out nations
1Ch 17: 21 *a* wonders by driving out nations
Ne 1: 5 of heaven, the great and *a* God,
4: 14 and *a*, and fight for your brothers,
9: 32 the great, mighty and *a* God,
Job 10: 16 again display your *a* power
37: 22 God comes in *a* majesty.
Ps 45: 4 let your right hand display *a* deeds.
47: 2 How *a* is the LORD Most High,
65: 5 us with *a* deeds of righteousness,
66: 3 to God, "How *a* are your deeds!
66: 5 how *a* his works in man's behalf!
68: 35 You are *a*, O God,
89: 7 he is more *a* than all who surround
99: 3 praise your great and *a* name—
106: 22 and *a* deeds by the Red Sea.
111: 9 holy and *a* is his name.
145: 6 of the power of your *a* works,
Isa 64: 3 when you did *a* things that we did
Eze 1: 18 Their rims were high and *a*,
1: 22 expanse, sparkling like ice, and *a*.
Da 2: 31 dazzling statue, *a* in appearance.
9: 4 "O Lord, the great and *a* God,
Zep 2: 11 The LORD will be *a* to them
AX
Mt 3: 10 The *a* is already at the root
Lk 3: 9 The *a* is already at the root
BAAL
Jdg 6: 25 Tear down your father's altar to *B*
1Ki 16: 32 *B* in the temple of *B* that he built
18: 25 Elijah said to the prophets of *B*,
19: 18 knees have not bowed down to *B*
2Ki 10: 28 Jehu destroyed *B* worship in Israel.
Jer 19: 5 places of *B* to burn their sons
Ro 11: 4 have not bowed the knee to *B*."
BAASHA
King of Israel (1Ki 15:16–16:7; 2Ch 16:1–6).
BABBLER* (BABBLING)
Ac 17: 18 "What is this *b* trying to say?"
BABBLING* (BABBLER)
Mt 6: 7 do not keep on *b* like pagans,
BABIES* (BABY)
Ge 25: 22 The *b* jostled each other within her
Ex 2: 6 "This is one of the Hebrew *b*,"
Lk 18: 15 also bringing *b* to Jesus
Ac 7: 19 them to throw out their newborn *b*
1Pe 2: 2 Like newborn *b*, crave pure
BABY* (BABIES BABY'S)
Ex 2: 6 She opened it and saw the *b*.
2: 7 women to nurse the *b* for you?"
2: 9 So the woman took the *b*
2: 9 "Take this *b* and nurse him for me,
1Ki 3: 17 I had a *b* while she was there
3: 18 was born, this woman also had a *b*.
3: 26 give her the living *b*! Don't kill him
3: 27 Give the living *b* to the first woman
Isa 49: 15 "Can a mother forget the *b*
Lk 1: 41 the *b* leaped in her womb,
1: 44 the *b* in my womb leaped for joy.
1: 57 time for Elizabeth to have her *b*,
2: 6 the time came for the *b* to be born,
2: 12 You will find a *b* wrapped in strips
2: 16 the *b*, who was lying in the manger.
Jn 16: 21 but when her *b* is born she forgets
BABY'S* (BABY)
Ex 2: 8 the girl went and got the *b* mother.
BABYLON
Ps 137: 1 By the rivers of *B* we sat and wept
Jer 29: 10 seventy years are completed for *B*,
51: 37 *B* will be a heap of ruins,
Rev 14: 8 "Fallen! Fallen is *B* the Great,
17: 5 MYSTERY *B* THE GREAT
BACKS
2Pe 2: 21 and then to turn their *b*
BACKSLIDING* (BACKSLIDINGS)
Jer 2: 19 your *b* will rebuke you.
3: 22 I will cure you of *b*."
14: 7 For our *b* is great;
15: 6 "You keep on *b*.
Eze 37: 23 them from all their sinful *b*,

BACKSLIDINGS* (BACKSLIDING)
Jer 5: 6 and their *b* many.

BALAAM
Prophet who attempted to curse Israel (Nu 22–24; Dt 23:4–5; 2Pe 2:15; Jude 11). Killed in Israel's vengeance on Midianites (Nu 31:8; Jos 13:22).

BALAK
Moabite king who hired Balaam to curse Israel (Nu 22–24; Jos 24:9).

BALDHEAD
2Ki 2: 23 "Go on up, you *b!*" they said.

BALM
Jer 8: 22 Is there no *b* in Gilead?

BANISH (BANISHED)
Jer 25: 10 I will *b* from them the sounds of joy

BANISHED (BANISH)
Dt 30: 4 Even if you have been *b*

BANNER
Ex 17: 15 and called it The LORD is my *B.*
SS 2: 4 and his *b* over me is love.
Isa 11: 10 the Root of Jesse will stand as a *b*

BANQUET
SS 2: 4 He has taken me to the *b* hall,
Lk 14: 13 when you give a *b*, invite the poor,

BAPTISM* (BAPTIZE)
Mt 21: 25 John's *b*— where did it come from?
Mk 1: 4 and preaching a *b* of repentance
10: 38 baptized with the *b* I am baptized
10: 39 baptized with the *b* I am baptized
11: 30 John's *b*— was it from heaven,
Lk 3: 3 preaching a *b* of repentance
12: 50 But I have a *b* to undergo,
20: 4 John's *b*— was it from heaven,
Ac 1: 22 beginning from John's *b*
10: 37 after the *b* that John preached—
13: 24 and *b* to all the people of Israel.
18: 25 though he knew only the *b* of John.
19: 3 did you receive?" "John's *b*,"
19: 3 "Then what *b* did you receive?"
19: 4 "John's *b* was a *b* of repentance.
Ro 6: 4 with him through *b* into death
Eph 4: 5 one Lord, one faith, one *b*;
Col 2: 12 having been buried with him in *b*
1Pe 3: 21 this water symbolizes *b* that now

BAPTISMS* (BAPTIZE)
Heb 6: 2 instruction about *b*, the laying

BAPTIZE* (BAPTISM BAPTISMS BAPTIZED BAPTIZING)
Mt 3: 11 He will *b* you with the Holy Spirit
3: 11 "I *b* you with water for repentance.
Mk 1: 8 I *b* you with water, but he will
1: 8 he will *b* you with the Holy Spirit."
Lk 3: 16 He will *b* you with the Holy Spirit
3: 16 John answered them all, "I *b* you
Jn 1: 25 "Why then do you *b*
1: 26 nor the Prophet?" "I *b* with water,"
1: 33 and remain is he who will *b*
1: 33 me to *b* with water told me,
1Co 1: 14 I am thankful that I did not *b* any
1: 17 For Christ did not send me to *b*,

BAPTIZED* (BAPTIZE)
Mt 3: 6 they were *b* by him in the Jordan
3: 13 to the Jordan to be *b* by John.
3: 14 saying, "I need to be *b* by you,
3: 16 as Jesus was *b*, he went up out
Mk 1: 5 they were *b* by him in the Jordan
1: 9 and was *b* by John in the Jordan.
10: 38 or be *b* with the baptism I am
10: 38 with the baptism I am *b* with?"
10: 39 and be *b* with the baptism I am
10: 39 with the baptism I am *b* with,
16: 16 believes and is *b* will be saved,
Lk 3: 7 to the crowds coming out to be *b*
3: 12 Tax collectors also came to be *b*.
3: 21 were being *b*, Jesus was *b* too.
7: 29 because they had been *b* by John.
7: 30 they had not been *b* by John.)
Jn 3: 22 spent some time with them, and *b*.
3: 23 were constantly coming to be *b*.
4: 2 in fact it was not Jesus who *b*,
Ac 1: 5 For John *b* with water,
1: 5 but in a few days you will be *b*
2: 38 Repent and be *b*, every one of you,
2: 41 who accepted his message were *b*,
8: 12 they were *b*, both men and women.
8: 13 Simon himself believed and was *b*.
8: 16 they had simply been *b*
8: 36 Why shouldn't I be *b?*"
8: 38 into the water and Philip *b* him.
9: 18 was *b*, and after taking some food,
10: 47 people from being *b* with water?
10: 48 So he ordered that they be *b*
11: 16 what the Lord had said, 'John *b*
11: 16 you will be *b* with the Holy Spirit.'
16: 15 members of her household were *b*,
16: 33 he and all his family were *b*.
18: 8 heard him believed and were *b*.
19: 5 they were *b* into the name
22: 16 be *b* and wash your sins away,
Ro 6: 3 *b* into Christ Jesus were *b*
1Co 1: 13 Were you *b* into the name of Paul?
1: 15 so no one can say that you were *b*
1: 16 I also *b* the household of Stephanas
1: 16 I don't remember if I *b* anyone else
10: 2 They were all *b* into Moses
12: 13 For we were all *b* by one Spirit
15: 29 what will those do who are *b*
15: 29 why are people *b* for them?
Gal 3: 27 all of you who were *b*

BAPTIZING* (BAPTIZE)
Mt 3: 7 coming to where he was *b*,
28: 19 *b* them in the name of the Father
Mk 1: 4 *b* in the desert region
Jn 1: 28 of the Jordan, where John was *b*.
1: 31 but the reason I came *b*
3: 23 also was *b* at Aenon near Salim,
3: 26 he is *b*, and everyone is going
4: 1 and *b* more disciples than John,
10: 40 to the place where John had been *b*

BAR-JESUS*
Ac 13: 6 and false prophet named *B*,

BARABBAS
Mt 27: 26 Then he released *B* to them.

BARAK*
Judge who fought with Deborah against Canaanites (Jdg 4–5; 1Sa 12:11; Heb 11:32).

BARBARIAN*
Col 3: 11 circumcised or uncircumcised, *b*,

BARBS*
Nu 33: 55 allow to remain will become *b*

BARE
Hos 2: 3 as *b* as on the day she was born;
Heb 4: 13 and laid *b* before the eyes of him

BARNABAS*
Disciple, originally Joseph (Ac 4:36), prophet (Ac 13:1), apostle (Ac 14:14). Brought Paul to apostles (Ac 9:27), Antioch (Ac 11:22–29; Gal 2:1–13), on the first missionary journey (Ac 13–14). Together at Jerusalem Council, they separated over John Mark (Ac 15). Later co-workers (1Co 9:6; Col 4:10).

BARREN
Ge 11: 30 Sarai was *b;* she had no children.
29: 31 her womb, but Rachel was *b*.
Ps 113: 9 He settles the *b* woman
Isa 54: 1 "Sing, O *b* woman,
Lk 1: 7 children, because Elizabeth was *b;*
Gal 4: 27 "Be glad, O *b* woman,
Heb 11: 11 and Sarah herself was *b*—

BARTHOLOMEW*
Apostle (Mt 10:3; Mk 3:18; Lk 6:14; Ac 1:13). Possibly also known as Nathanael (Jn 1:45–49; 21:2).

BARUCH
Jeremiah's secretary (Jer 32:12–16; 36; 43:1–6; 45:1–2).

BARZILLAI
1. Gileadite who aided David during Absalom's revolt (2Sa 17:27; 19:31–39).
2. Son-in-law of 1. (Ezr 2:61; Ne 7:63).

BASHAN
Jos 22: 7 Moses had given land in *B*,
Ps 22: 12 strong bulls of *B* encircle me.

BASIN
Ex 30: 18 "Make a bronze *b*,

BASKET
Ex 2: 3 she got a papyrus *b* for him
Ac 9: 25 him in a *b* through an opening
2Co 11: 33 I was lowered in a *b* from a window

BATCH*
Ro 11: 16 then the whole *b* is holy;
1Co 5: 6 through the whole *b* of dough?
5: 7 old yeast that you may be a new *b*
Gal 5: 9 through the whole *b* of dough."

BATH (BATHING)
Jn 13: 10 person who has had a *b* needs only

BATHING (BATH)
2Sa 11: 2 From the roof he saw a woman *b*.

BATHSHEBA*
Wife of Uriah who committed adultery with and became wife of David (2Sa 11), mother of Solomon (2Sa 12:24; 1Ki 1–2; 1Ch 3:5).

BATTLE (BATTLES)
1Sa 17: 47 for the *b* is the LORD's,
2Ch 20: 15 For the *b* is not yours, but God's.
Ps 24: 8 the LORD mighty in *b*.
Ecc 9: 11 or the *b* to the strong,
Isa 31: 4 down to do *b* on Mount Zion
Eze 13: 5 in the *b* on the day of the LORD.
Rev 16: 14 them for the *b* on the great day
20: 8 and Magog—to gather them for *b*.

BATTLES* (BATTLE)
1Sa 8: 20 to go out before us and fight our *b*."
18: 17 and fight the *b* of the LORD."
25: 28 because he fights the LORD's *b*.
2Ch 32: 8 God to help us and to fight our *b*."

BEAR (BEARING BEARS BIRTH BIRTHRIGHT BORE BORN CHILDBEARING CHILDBIRTH FIRSTBORN NEWBORN REBIRTH)
Ge 4: 13 punishment is more than I can *b*.
Ps 38: 4 like a burden too heavy to *b*.
Isa 11: 7 The cow will feed with the *b*,
53: 11 and he will *b* their iniquities.
Da 7: 5 beast, which looked like a *b*.
Mt 7: 18 A good tree cannot *b* bad fruit,
Jn 15: 2 branch that does *b* fruit he prunes
15: 8 glory, that you *b* much fruit,
15: 16 appointed you to go and *b* fruit—
Ro 7: 4 in order that we might *b* fruit
15: 1 ought to *b* with the failings
1Co 10: 13 tempted beyond what you can *b*.
Col 3: 13 *B* with each other and forgive

BEARD
Lev 19: 27 or clip off the edges of your *b*.
Isa 50: 6 to those who pulled out my *b;*

BEARING (BEAR)
Eph 4: 2 *b* with one another in love.
Col 1: 10 *b* fruit in every good work,
Heb 13: 13 outside the camp, *b* the disgrace he

BEARS (BEAR)
1Ki 8: 43 house I have built *b* your Name.
Ps 68: 19 who daily *b* our burdens.

BEAST (BEASTS)
Rev 13: 18 him calculate the number of the *b*,
16: 2 people who had the mark of the *b*
19: 20 who had received the mark of the *b*

BEASTS (BEAST)
Da 7: 3 Four great *b*, each different
1Co 15: 32 If I fought wild *b* in Ephesus

BEAT (BEATEN BEATING BEATINGS)
Isa 2: 4 They will *b* their swords

Joel 3: 10 B your plowshares into swords
Mic 4: 3 They will b their swords
1Co 9: 27 I b my body and make it my slave

BEATEN (BEAT)
Lk 12: 47 do what his master wants will be b
12: 48 deserving punishment will be b
2Co 11: 25 Three times I was b with rods,

BEATING (BEAT)
1Co 9: 26 I do not fight like a man b the air.
1Pe 2: 20 if you receive a b for doing wrong

BEATINGS (BEAT)
Pr 19: 29 and b for the backs of fools.

BEAUTIFUL* (BEAUTY)
Ge 6: 2 that the daughters of men were b,
12: 11 "I know what a b woman you are.
12: 14 saw that she was a very b woman.
24: 16 The girl was very b, a virgin;
26: 7 of Rebekah, because she is b."
29: 17 Rachel was lovely in form, and b.
49: 21 that bears b fawns.
Nu 24: 5 "How b are your tents, O Jacob,
Dt 21: 11 among the captives a b woman
Jos 7: 21 saw in the plunder a b robe
1Sa 25: 3 was an intelligent and b woman,
2Sa 11: 2 The woman was very b,
13: 1 the b sister of Absalom son
14: 27 and she became a b woman.
1Ki 1: 3 throughout Israel for a b girl
1: 4 The girl was very b; she took care
Est 2: 2 for b young virgins for the king.
2: 3 realm to bring all these b girls
Job 38: 31 "Can you bind the b Pleiades?
42: 15 land were there found women as b
Ps 48: 2 It is b in its loftiness,
Pr 11: 22 is a b woman who shows no
24: 4 filled with rare and b treasures.
Ecc 3: 11 He has made everything b
SS 1: 8 Lover If you do not know, most b
1: 10 Your cheeks are b with earrings,
1: 15 Oh, how b!
1: 15 Lover How b you are, my darling!
2: 10 my b one, and come with me.
2: 13 my b one, come with me."
4: 1 How b you are, my darling!
4: 1 Oh, how b!
4: 7 All b you are, my darling;
5: 9 most b of women?
6: 1 most b of women?
6: 4 Lover You are b, my darling,
7: 1 How b your sandaled feet,
7: 6 How b you are and how pleasing,
Isa 4: 2 of the LORD will be b
28: 5 a b wreath
52: 7 How b on the mountains
Jer 3: 19 the most b inheritance
6: 2 so b and delicate.
11: 16 with fruit b in form.
46: 20 "Egypt is a b heifer,
Eze 7: 20 They were proud of their b jewelry
16: 7 and became the most b of jewels.
16: 12 and a b crown on your head.
16: 13 You became very b and rose
20: 6 and honey, the most b of all lands.
20: 15 and honey, most b of all lands—
23: 42 and b crowns on their heads.
27: 24 traded with you b garments,
31: 3 with b branches overshadowing
31: 9 I made it b
33: 32 who sings love songs with a b voice
Da 4: 12 Its leaves were b, its fruit abundant
4: 21 with b leaves and abundant fruit,
8: 9 to the east and toward the B Land.
11: 16 will establish himself in the B Land
11: 41 He will also invade the B Land.
11: 45 the seas at the b holy mountain.
Zec 9: 17 How attractive and b they will be!
Mt 23: 27 which look b on the outside
26: 10 She has done a b thing to me.
Mk 14: 6 She has done a b thing to me.
Lk 21: 5 temple was adorned with b stones
Ac 3: 2 carried to the temple gate called B,
3: 10 at the temple gate called B,
Ro 10: 15 "How b are the feet
1Pe 3: 5 in God used to make themselves b.

BEAUTY* (BEAUTIFUL)
Est 1: 11 order to display her b to the people
2: 3 let b treatments be given to them.
2: 9 her with her b treatments
2: 12 months of b treatments prescribed
Ps 27: 4 to gaze upon the b of the LORD
37: 20 LORD's enemies will be like the b
45: 11 The king is enthralled by your b;
50: 2 From Zion, perfect in b,
Pr 6: 25 lust in your heart after her b
31: 30 is deceptive, and b is fleeting;
Isa 3: 24 instead of b, branding.
28: 1 to the fading flower, his glorious b,
28: 4 That fading flower, his glorious b,
33: 17 Your eyes will see the king in his b
53: 2 He had no b or majesty
61: 3 to bestow on them a crown of b
La 2: 15 the perfection of b,
Eze 16: 14 had given you made your b perfect,
16: 14 the nations on account of your b,
16: 15 passed by and your b became his.
16: 15 " 'But you trusted in your b
16: 25 lofty shrines and degraded your b,
27: 3 "I am perfect in b."
27: 4 your builders brought your b
27: 11 they brought your b to perfection.
28: 7 draw their swords against your b
28: 12 full of wisdom and perfect in b.
28: 17 proud on account of your b,
31: 7 It was majestic in b,
31: 8 could match its b.
Jas 1: 11 blossom falls and its b is destroyed.
1Pe 3: 3 Your b should not come
3: 4 the unfading b of a gentle

BED (SICKBED)
Isa 28: 20 The b is too short to stretch out on,
Lk 11: 7 and my children are with me in b.
17: 34 night two people will be in one b;
Heb 13: 4 and the marriage b kept pure,

BEELZEBUB*
Mt 10: 25 of the house has been called B,
12: 24 "It is only by B, the prince
12: 27 And if I drive out demons by B,
Mk 3: 22 possessed by B! By the prince
Lk 11: 15 "By B, the prince of demons,
11: 18 claim that I drive out demons by B.
11: 19 Now if I drive out demons by B,

BEER
Pr 20: 1 Wine is a mocker and b a brawler;

BEERSHEBA
Ge 21: 14 and wandered in the desert of B.
Jdg 20: 1 all the Israelites from Dan to B
1Sa 3: 20 to B recognized that Samuel was
2Sa 3: 10 and Judah from Dan to B."
17: 11 Let all Israel, from Dan to B—
24: 2 the tribes of Israel from Dan to B
24: 15 of the people from Dan to B died.
1Ki 4: 25 from Dan to B, lived in safety,
1Ch 21: 2 count the Israelites from B to Dan.
2Ch 30: 5 throughout Israel, from B to Dan,

BEFALLS*
Pr 12: 21 No harm b the righteous,

BEGGING
Ps 37: 25 or their children b bread.
Ac 16: 9 of Macedonia standing and b him,

BEGINNING
Ge 1: 1 In the b God created the heavens
Ps 102: 25 In the b you laid the foundations
111: 10 of the LORD is the b of wisdom;
Pr 1: 7 of the LORD is the b of knowledge
9: 10 of the LORD is the b of wisdom,
Ecc 3: 11 fathom what God has done from b
Isa 40: 21 Has it not been told you from the b
46: 10 I make known the end from the b,
Mt 24: 8 All these are the b of birth pains.
Lk 1: 3 investigated everything from the b,
Jn 1: 1 In the b was the Word,
1Jn 1: 1 That which was from the b,
Rev 21: 6 and the Omega, the B and the End.
22: 13 and the Last, the B and the End.

BEHAVE (BEHAVIOR)
Ro 13: 13 Let us b decently, as in the daytime

BEHAVIOR (BEHAVE)
1Pe 3: 1 without words by the b of their wives,
3: 16 maliciously against your good b

BEHEMOTH*
Job 40: 15 "Look at the b,

BELIEVE (BELIEVED BELIEVER BELIEVERS BELIEVES BELIEVING)
Ex 4: 1 "What if they do not b me
1Ki 10: 7 I did not b these things until I came
2Ch 9: 6 But I did not b what they said
Ps 78: 32 of his wonders, they did not b.
Hab 1: 5 that you would not b,
Mt 18: 6 one of these little ones who b in me
21: 22 If you b, you will receive whatever
27: 42 from the cross, and we will b in him
Mk 1: 15 Repent and b the good news!"
5: 36 ruler, "Don't be afraid; just b."
9: 24 "I do b; help me overcome my
9: 42 one of these little ones who b in me
11: 24 b that you have received it,
15: 32 the cross, that we may see and b."
16: 16 but whoever does not b will be
16: 17 signs will accompany those who b:
Lk 8: 12 so that they may not b and be saved.
8: 13 They b for a while, but in the time
8: 50 just b, and she will be healed."
22: 67 you will not b me,
24: 25 to b all that the prophets have
Jn 1: 7 that through him all men might b.
3: 18 does not b stands condemned
4: 42 "We no longer b just
5: 38 for you do not b the one he sent.
5: 46 believed Moses, you would b me,
6: 29 to b in the one he has sent."
6: 69 We b and know that you are
7: 5 his own brothers did not b in him.
8: 24 if you do not b that I am ›the one I
9: 35 "Do you b in the Son of Man?"
9: 36 "Tell me so that I may b in him."
9: 38 "Lord, I b," and he worshiped him.
10: 26 you do not b because you are not
10: 37 Do not b me unless I do what my
10: 38 you do not b me, b the miracles,
11: 27 "I b that you are the Christ,
12: 37 they still would not b in him.
12: 39 For this reason they could not b,
12: 44 in me, he does not b in me only,
13: 19 does happen you will b that I am
14: 10 Don't you b that I am in the Father
14: 11 B me when I say that I am
14: 11 or at least b on the evidence
16: 30 This makes us b that you came
16: 31 "You b at last!" Jesus answered.
17: 21 that the world may b that you have
19: 35 he testifies so that you also may b.
20: 27 Stop doubting and b."
20: 31 written that you may b that Jesus is
Ac 16: 31 They replied, "B in the Lord Jesus,
19: 4 the people to b in the one coming
24: 14 I b everything that agrees
26: 27 Agrippa, do you b the prophets?
Ro 3: 22 faith in Jesus Christ to all who b.
4: 11 he is the father of all who b
10: 9 b in your heart that God raised him
10: 10 For it is with your heart that you b
10: 14 And how can they b in the one
16: 26 so that all nations might b

1Co 1: 21 preached to save those who *b.*
Gal 3: 22 might be given to those who *b.*
Php 1: 29 of Christ not only to *b* on him,
1Th 4: 14 We *b* that Jesus died and rose again
2Th 2: 11 delusion so that they will *b* the lie
1Ti 4: 10 and especially of those who *b.*
Tit 1: 6 a man whose children *b*
Heb 11: 6 comes to him must *b* that he exists
Jas 1: 6 But when he asks, he must *b*
2: 19 Even the demons *b* that—
2: 19 You *b* that there is one God.
1Pe 2: 7 to you who *b,* this stone is precious
1Jn 3: 23 to *b* in the name of his Son,
4: 1 Dear friends, do not *b* every spirit,
5: 13 things to you who *b* in the name

BELIEVED (BELIEVE)
Ge 15: 6 Abram *b* the LORD, and he
Ex 4: 31 signs before the people, and they *b.*
Isa 53: 1 Who has *b* our message
Jnh 3: 5 The Ninevites *b* God.
Lk 1: 45 is she who has *b* that what the Lord
Jn 1: 12 to those who *b* in his name,
2: 22 Then they *b* the Scripture
3: 18 because he has not *b* in the name
5: 46 If you *b* Moses, you would believe
7: 39 whom those who *b*
11: 40 "Did I not tell you that if you *b,*
12: 38 "Lord, who has *b* our message
20: 8 He saw and *b.*
20: 29 who have not seen and yet have *b.*"
Ac 13: 48 were appointed for eternal life *b.*
19: 2 the Holy Spirit when you *b?*"
Ro 4: 3 Scripture say? "Abraham *b* God,
10: 14 call on the one they have not *b* in?
10: 16 "Lord, who has *b* our message?"
1Co 15: 2 Otherwise, you have *b* in vain.
Gal 3: 6 Consider Abraham: "He *b* God,
2Th 2: 12 who have not *b* the truth
1Ti 3: 16 was *b* on in the world,
2Ti 1: 12 because I know whom I have *b,*
Jas 2: 23 that says, "Abraham *b* God,

BELIEVER* (BELIEVE)
1Ki 18: 3 (Obadiah was a devout *b*
Ac 16: 1 whose mother was a Jewess and a *b*
16: 15 "If you consider me a *b* in the Lord
1Co 7: 12 brother has a wife who is not a *b*
7: 13 has a husband who is not a *b*
2Co 6: 15 What does a *b* have in common
1Ti 5: 16 any woman who is a *b* has widows

BELIEVERS* (BELIEVE)
Jn 4: 41 of his words many more became *b.*
Ac 1: 15 among the *b* (a group numbering
2: 44 All the *b* were together
4: 32 All the *b* were one in heart
5: 12 And all the *b* used to meet together
9: 41 he called the *b* and the widows
10: 45 The circumcised *b* who had come
11: 2 the circumcised *b* criticized him
15: 2 along with some other *b,*
15: 5 Then some of the *b* who belonged
15: 23 To the Gentile *b* in Antioch,
21: 25 for the Gentile *b,* we have written
1Co 6: 5 to judge a dispute between *b?*
14: 22 is for *b,* not for unbelievers.
14: 22 not for *b* but for unbelievers;
Gal 6: 10 who belong to the family of *b.*
1Th 1: 7 a model to all the *b* in Macedonia
1Ti 4: 12 set an example for the *b* in speech,
6: 2 benefit from their service are *b,*
Jas 2: 1 *b* in our glorious Lord Jesus Christ,
1Pe 2: 17 Love the brotherhood of *b,*

BELIEVES* (BELIEVE)
Pr 14: 15 A simple man *b* anything,
Mk 9: 23 is possible for him who *b.*"
11: 23 *b* that what he says will happen,
16: 16 Whoever *b* and is baptized will be
Jn 3: 15 that everyone who *b*
3: 16 that whoever *b* in him shall not
3: 18 Whoever *b* in him is not
3: 36 Whoever *b* in the Son has eternal
5: 24 *b* him who sent me has eternal life
6: 35 and he who *b* in me will never be
6: 40 and *b* in him shall have eternal life,
6: 47 he who *b* has everlasting life.
7: 38 Whoever *b* in me, as the Scripture
11: 25 He who *b* in me will live, even
11: 26 and *b* in me will never die.
12: 44 Jesus cried out, "When a man *b*
12: 46 so that no one who *b*
Ac 10: 43 about him that everyone who *b*
13: 39 him everyone who *b* is justified
Ro 1: 16 for the salvation of everyone who *b*
10: 4 righteousness for everyone who *b.*
1Jn 5: 1 Everyone who *b* that Jesus is
5: 5 Only he who *b* that Jesus is the Son
5: 10 Anyone who *b* in the Son

BELIEVING* (BELIEVE)
Jn 20: 31 and that by *b* you may have life
Ac 9: 26 not *b* that he really was a disciple.
1Co 7: 14 sanctified through her *b* husband.
7: 15 A *b* man or woman is not bound
9: 5 right to take a *b* wife along with us,
Gal 3: 2 or by *b* what you heard? Are you
1Ti 6: 2 Those who have *b* masters are not

BELLY
Ge 3: 14 You will crawl on your *b*
Da 2: 32 its *b* and thighs of bronze,
Mt 12: 40 three nights in the *b* of a huge fish,

BELONG (BELONGING BELONGS)
Ge 40: 8 "Do not interpretations *b* to God?
Lev 25: 55 for the Israelites *b* to me
Dt 10: 14 LORD your God *b* the heavens,
29: 29 The secret things *b*
Job 12: 13 "To God *b* wisdom and power;
12: 16 To him *b* strength and victory;
25: 2 "Dominion and awe *b* to God;
Ps 47: 9 for the kings of the earth *b* to God;
95: 4 and the mountain peaks *b* to him.
115: 16 The highest heavens *b*
Jer 5: 10 for these people do not *b*
Jn 8: 44 You *b* to your father, the devil,
15: 19 As it is, you do not *b* to the world,
Ro 1: 6 called to *b* to Jesus Christ.
7: 4 that you might *b* to another,
8: 9 of Christ, he does not *b* to Christ.
14: 8 we live or die, we *b* to the Lord.
1Co 7: 39 but he must *b* to the Lord.
15: 23 when he comes, those who *b*
Gal 3: 29 If you *b* to Christ, then you are
5: 24 Those who *b* to Christ Jesus have
1Th 5: 5 We do not *b* to the night
5: 8 But since we *b* to the day, let us be
1Jn 3: 19 then is how we know that we *b*

BELONGING (BELONG)
1Pe 2: 9 a holy nation, a people *b* to God,

BELONGS (BELONG)
Lev 27: 30 *b* to the LORD; it is holy
Dt 1: 17 of any man, for judgment *b* to God.
Job 41: 11 Everything under heaven *b* to me.
Ps 22: 28 for dominion *b* to the LORD
89: 18 Indeed, our shield *b* to the LORD,
111: 10 To him *b* eternal praise.
Eze 18: 4 For every living soul *b* to me,
Jn 8: 47 He who *b* to God hears what God
Ro 12: 5 each member *b* to all the others.
Rev 7: 10 "Salvation *b* to our God,

BELOVED* (LOVE)
Dt 33: 12 "Let the *b* of the LORD rest secure
SS 5: 9 How is your *b* better than others,
5: 9 *Friends* How is your *b* better
Jer 11: 15 "What is my *b* doing in my temple

BELSHAZZAR
King of Babylon in days of Daniel (Da 5).

BELT
Ex 12: 11 with your cloak tucked into your *b,*
1Ki 18: 46 and, tucking his cloak into his *b,*
2Ki 4: 29 "Tuck your cloak into your *b,*
9: 1 "Tuck your cloak into your *b,*
Isa 11: 5 Righteousness will be his *b*
Eph 6: 14 with the *b* of truth buckled

BENEFICIAL* (BENEFIT)
1Co 6: 12 for me"—but not everything is *b.*
10: 23 but not everything is *b.*

BENEFIT (BENEFICIAL BENEFITS)
Job 22: 2 "Can a man be of *b* to God?
Isa 38: 17 Surely it was for my *b*
Ro 6: 22 the *b* you reap leads to holiness,
2Co 4: 15 All this is for your *b,*

BENEFITS (BENEFIT)
Ps 103: 2 and forget not all his *b.*
Jn 4: 38 you have reaped the *b* of their labor

BENJAMIN
Twelfth son of Jacob by Rachel (Ge 35:16–24; 46:19–21; 1Ch 2:2). Jacob refused to send him to Egypt, but relented (Ge 42–45). Tribe of blessed (Ge 49:27; Dt 33:12), numbered (Nu 1:37; 26:41), allotted land (Jos 18:11–28; Eze 48:23), failed to fully possess (Jdg 1:21), nearly obliterated (Jdg 20–21), sided with Ish-Bosheth (2Sa 2), but turned to David (1Ch 12:2, 29). 12,000 from (Rev 7:8).

BEREANS*
Ac 17: 11 the *B* were of more noble character

BESTOWING* (BESTOWS)
Pr 8: 21 *b* wealth on those who love me

BESTOWS (BESTOWING)
Ps 84: 11 the LORD *b* favor and honor;

BETHANY
Mk 11: 1 and *B* at the Mount of Olives,

BETHEL
Ge 28: 19 He called that place *B,*

BETHLEHEM
Ru 1: 19 went on until they came to *B.*
1Sa 16: 1 I am sending you to Jesse of *B.*
2Sa 23: 15 from the well near the gate of *B!*"
Mic 5: 2 "But you, *B* Ephrathah,
Mt 2: 1 After Jesus was born in *B* in Judea,
2: 6 " 'But you, *B,* in the land of Judah,

BETHPHAGE
Mt 21: 1 came to *B* on the Mount of Olives,

BETHSAIDA
Jn 12: 21 who was from *B* in Galilee,

BETRAY (BETRAYED BETRAYS)
Ps 89: 33 nor will I ever *b* my faithfulness.
Pr 25: 9 do not *b* another man's confidence,
Mt 10: 21 "Brother will *b* brother to death,
26: 21 the truth, one of you will *b* me."

BETRAYED (BETRAY)
Mt 27: 4 "for I have *b* innocent blood."

BETRAYS (BETRAY)
Pr 11: 13 A gossip *b* a confidence,
20: 19 A gossip *b* a confidence;

BEULAH*
Isa 62: 4 and your land *B;*

BEWITCHED*
Gal 3: 1 foolish Galatians! Who has *b* you?

BEZALEL
Judahite craftsman in charge of building the tabernacle (Ex 31:1–11; 35:30–39:31).

BIDDING*
Ps 103: 20 you mighty ones who do his *b,*
148: 8 stormy winds that do his *b,*

BILDAD
One of Job's friends (Job 8; 18; 25).

BILHAH
Servant of Rachel, mother of Jacob's sons Dan and Naphtali (Ge 30:1–7; 35:25; 46:23–25).

BIND (BINDS BOUND)
Dt 6: 8 and *b* them on your foreheads.

Pr 3: 3 *b* them around your neck,
6: 21 *B* them upon your heart forever;
7: 3 *B* them on your fingers;
Isa 61: 1 me to *b* up the brokenhearted,
Mt 16: 19 whatever you *b* on earth will be

BINDS (BIND)
Ps 147: 3 and *b* up their wounds.
Isa 30: 26 when the LORD *b* up the bruises

BIRD (BIRDS)
Pr 27: 8 Like a *b* that strays from its nest
Ecc 10: 20 a *b* of the air may carry your words,

BIRDS (BIRD)
Mt 8: 20 and *b* of the air have nests,
Lk 9: 58 and *b* of the air have nests,

BIRTH (BEAR)
Ps 51: 5 Surely I was sinful at *b*,
58: 3 Even from *b* the wicked go astray;
Isa 26: 18 but we gave *b* to wind.
Mt 1: 18 This is how the *b* of Jesus Christ
24: 8 these are the beginning of *b* pains.
Jn 3: 6 Flesh gives *b* to flesh, but the Spirit
1Pe 1: 3 great mercy he has given us new *b*

BIRTHRIGHT (BEAR)
Ge 25: 34 So Esau despised his *b*.

BITTEN
Nu 21: 8 anyone who is *b* can look at it

BITTER (BITTERNESS EMBITTER)
Ex 12: 8 along with *b* herbs, and bread made
Pr 27: 7 what is *b* tastes sweet.

BITTERNESS (BITTER)
Pr 14: 10 Each heart knows its own *b*,
17: 25 and *b* to the one who bore him.
Ro 3: 14 full of cursing and *b*."
Eph 4: 31 Get rid of all *b*, rage and anger,

BLACK
Zec 6: 6 The one with the *b* horses is going
Rev 6: 5 and there before me was a *b* horse!

BLAMELESS* (BLAMELESSLY)
Ge 6: 9 *b* among the people of his time,
17: 1 walk before me and be *b*.
Dt 18: 13 You must be *b* before the LORD
2Sa 22: 24 I have been *b* before him
22: 26 to the *b* you show yourself *b*,
Job 1: 1 This man was *b* and upright;
1: 8 one on earth like him; he is *b*
2: 3 one on earth like him; he is *b*
4: 6 and your *b* ways your hope?
8: 20 God does not reject a *b* man
9: 20 if I were *b*, it would pronounce me
9: 21 "Although I am *b*,
9: 22 'He destroys both the *b*
12: 4 though righteous and *b*!
22: 3 gain if your ways were *b*?
31: 6 and he will know that I am *b*—
Ps 15: 2 He whose walk is *b*
18: 23 I have been *b* before him
18: 25 to the *b* you show yourself *b*,
19: 13 Then will I be *b*,
26: 1 for I have led a *b* life;
26: 11 But I lead a *b* life;
37: 18 The days of the *b* are known
37: 37 Consider the *b*, observe the upright
84: 11 from those whose walk is *b*.
101: 2 I will be careful to lead a *b* life—
101: 2 house with *b* heart.
101: 6 he whose walk is *b*
119: 1 Blessed are they whose ways are *b*,
119: 80 May my heart be *b*
Pr 2: 7 a shield to those whose walk is *b*,
2: 21 and the *b* will remain in it;
11: 5 of the *b* makes a straight way
11: 20 in those whose ways are *b*.
19: 1 Better a poor man whose walk is *b*
20: 7 The righteous man leads a *b* life;
28: 6 Better a poor man whose walk is *b*
28: 10 *b* will receive a good inheritance.
28: 18 He whose walk is *b* is kept safe,
Eze 28: 15 You were *b* in your ways
1Co 1: 8 so that you will be *b* on the day
Eph 1: 4 world to be holy and *b* in his sight.
5: 27 any other blemish, but holy and *b*.
Php 1: 10 and *b* until the day of Christ,
2: 15 so that you may become *b* and pure
1Th 2: 10 and *b* we were among you who
3: 13 hearts so that you will be *b*
5: 23 and body be kept *b* at the coming
Tit 1: 6 An elder must be *b*, the husband of
1: 7 he must be *b*— not overbearing,
Heb 7: 26 *b*, pure, set apart from sinners,
2Pe 3: 14 effort to be found spotless, *b*
Rev 14: 5 found in their mouths; they are *b*.

BLAMELESSLY* (BLAMELESS)
Lk 1: 6 commandments and regulations *b*.

BLASPHEME* (BLASPHEMED BLASPHEMER BLASPHEMES BLASPHEMIES BLASPHEMING BLASPHEMOUS BLASPHEMY)
Ex 22: 28 "Do not *b* God or curse the ruler
Ac 26: 11 and I tried to force them to *b*.
1Ti 1: 20 over to Satan to be taught not to *b*.
2Pe 2: 12 these men *b* in matters they do not
Rev 13: 6 He opened his mouth to *b* God,

BLASPHEMED* (BLASPHEME)
Lev 24: 11 of the Israelite woman *b* the Name
2Ki 19: 6 of the king of Assyria have *b* me.
19: 22 Who is it you have insulted and *b*?
Isa 37: 6 of the king of Assyria have *b* me.
37: 23 Who is it you have insulted and *b*?
52: 5 my name is constantly *b*.
Eze 20: 27 your fathers *b* me by forsaking me:
Ac 19: 37 robbed temples nor *b* our goddess.
Ro 2: 24 name is *b* among the Gentiles

BLASPHEMER* (BLASPHEME)
Lev 24: 14 "Take the *b* outside the camp.
24: 23 they took the *b* outside the camp
1Ti 1: 13 I was once a *b* and a persecutor

BLASPHEMES* (BLASPHEME)
Lev 24: 16 anyone who *b* the name
24: 16 native-born, when he *b* the Name,
Nu 15: 30 native-born or alien, *b* the LORD,
Mk 3: 29 whoever *b* against the Holy Spirit
Lk 12: 10 but anyone who *b* against the Holy

BLASPHEMIES* (BLASPHEME)
Ne 9: 18 or when they committed awful *b*.
9: 26 to you; they committed awful *b*.
Mk 3: 28 and *b* of men will be forgiven them.
Rev 13: 5 and *b* and to exercise his authority

BLASPHEMING* (BLASPHEME)
Mt 9: 3 "This fellow is *b*!" Knowing their
Mk 2: 7 He's *b*! Who can forgive sins

BLASPHEMOUS* (BLASPHEME)
Rev 13: 1 and on each head a *b* name.
17: 3 that was covered with *b* names

BLASPHEMY* (BLASPHEME)
Mt 12: 31 and *b* will be forgiven men,
12: 31 the *b* against the Spirit will not be
26: 65 Look, now you have heard the *b*.
26: 65 "He has spoken *b*! Why do we
Mk 14: 64 "You have heard the *b*.
Lk 5: 21 "Who is this fellow who speaks *b*?
Jn 10: 33 replied the Jews, "but for *b*,
10: 36 Why then do you accuse me of *b*
Ac 6: 11 words of *b* against Moses

BLAST*
Ex 15: 8 By the *b* of your nostrils
19: 13 horn sounds a long *b* may they go
19: 16 and a very loud trumpet *b*.
Nu 10: 5 When a trumpet *b* is sounded,
10: 6 At the sounding of a second *b*,
10: 6 The *b* will be the signal
10: 9 sound a *b* on the trumpets.
Jos 6: 5 you hear them sound a long *b*
6: 16 the priests sounded the trumpet *b*,
2Sa 22: 16 at the *b* of breath from his nostrils.
Job 4: 9 at the *b* of his anger they perish.
39: 25 At the *b* of the trumpet he snorts,
Ps 18: 15 the *b* of breath from your nostrils.
98: 6 and the *b* of the ram's horn—
147: 17 Who can withstand his icy *b*?
Isa 27: 8 with his fierce *b* he drives her out,
Eze 22: 20 a furnace to melt it with a fiery *b*,
Am 2: 2 tumult amid war cries and the *b*
Heb 12: 19 to a trumpet *b* or to such a voice

BLEATING*
1Sa 15: 14 "What then is this *b* of sheep

BLEMISH (BLEMISHES)
Lev 22: 21 be without defect or *b*
Eph 5: 27 or wrinkle or any other *b*,
Col 1: 22 without *b* and free from accusation
1Pe 1: 19 a lamb without *b* or defect.

BLEMISHES* (BLEMISH)
2Pe 2: 13 and *b*, reveling in their pleasures
Jude : 12 These men are *b* at your love feasts

BLESS (BLESSED BLESSES BLESSING BLESSINGS)
Ge 12: 3 I will *b* those who *b* you,
32: 26 not let you go unless you *b* me."
Dt 7: 13 He will love you and *b* you
33: 11 *B* all his skills, O LORD,
Ps 72: 15 and *b* him all day long.
Ro 12: 14 Bless those who persecute you; *b*

BLESSED (BLESS)
Ge 1: 22 God *b* them and said, "Be fruitful
2: 3 And God *b* the seventh day
22: 18 nations on earth will be *b*,
Nu 24: 9 "May those who bless you be *b*
1Ch 17: 27 have *b* it, and it will be *b* forever."
Ps 1: 1 *B* is the man
2: 12 *B* are all who take refuge in him.
32: 2 *B* is the man
33: 12 *B* is the nation whose God is
40: 4 *B* is the man
41: 1 *B* is he who has regard for the weak
84: 5 *B* are those whose strength is
89: 15 *B* are those who have learned
94: 12 *B* is the man you discipline,
106: 3 *B* are they who maintain justice,
112: 1 *B* is the man who fears the LORD,
118: 26 *B* is he who comes in the name
119: 1 *B* are they whose ways are
119: 2 *B* are they who keep his statutes
127: 5 *B* is the man
Pr 3: 13 *B* is the man who finds wisdom,
8: 34 *B* is the man who listens to me,
28: 20 A faithful man will be richly *b*,
29: 18 but *b* is he who keeps the law.
31: 28 Her children arise and call her *b*;
Isa 30: 18 *B* are all who wait for him!
Mal 3: 12 Then all the nations will call you *b*,
3: 15 But now we call the arrogant *b*.
Mt 5: 3 saying: "*B* are the poor in spirit,
5: 4 *B* are those who mourn,
5: 5 *B* are the meek,
5: 6 *B* are those who hunger
5: 7 *B* are the merciful,
5: 8 *B* are the pure in heart,
5: 9 *B* are the peacemakers,
5: 10 *B* are those who are persecuted
5: 11 "*B* are you when people insult you,
Lk 1: 48 on all generations will call me *b*,
Jn 12: 13 "*B* is he who comes in the name
Ac 20: 35 'It is more *b* to give than to receive
Tit 2: 13 while we wait for the *b* hope—
Jas 1: 12 *B* is the man who perseveres
Rev 1: 3 *B* is the one who reads the words
22: 7 *B* is he who keeps the words
22: 14 "*B* are those who wash their robes,

BLESSES (BLESS)
Ps 29: 11 the LORD *b* his people with peace.
Ro 10: 12 and richly *b* all who call on him,

BLESSING (BLESS)
Ge 27: 4 so that I may give you my *b*

Dt 23: 5 turned the curse into a *b* for you,
33: 1 This is the *b* that Moses the man
Pr 10: 22 The *b* of the LORD brings wealth,
Eze 34: 26 there will be showers of *b*.

BLESSINGS (BLESS)
Dt 11: 29 proclaim on Mount Gerizim the *b*,
Jos 8: 34 all the words of the law—the *b*
Pr 10: 6 *B* crown the head of the righteous,
Ro 15: 27 shared in the Jews' spiritual *b*,

BLIND (BLINDED)
Mt 15: 14 a *b* man leads a *b* man, both will fall
23: 16 "Woe to you, *b* guides! You say,
Mk 10: 46 a *b* man, Bartimaeus (that is,
Lk 6: 39 "Can a *b* man lead a *b* man?
Jn 9: 25 I was *b* but now I see!"

BLINDED (BLIND)
Jn 12: 40 elsewhere: "He has *b* their eyes
2Co 4: 4 The god of this age has *b* the minds

BLOOD (BLOODSHED BLOODTHIRSTY)
Ge 4: 10 Your brother's *b* cries out to me
9: 6 "Whoever sheds the *b* of man,
Ex 12: 13 and when I see the *b*, I will pass
24: 8 "This is the *b* of the covenant that
Lev 16: 15 and take its *b* behind the curtain
17: 11 For the life of a creature is in the *b*,
Dt 12: 23 eat the *b*, because the *b* is the life,
Ps 72: 14 for precious is their *b* in his sight.
Pr 6: 17 hands that shed innocent *b*,
Isa 1: 11 pleasure in the *b* of bulls and lambs
Mt 26: 28 This is my *b* of the covenant,
27: 24 "I am innocent of this man's *b*,"
Mk 14: 24 "This is my *b* of the covenant,
Lk 22: 44 drops of *b* falling to the ground.
Jn 6: 53 of the Son of Man and drink his *b*,
Ac 15: 20 of strangled animals and from *b*.
20: 26 innocent of the *b* of all men.
Ro 3: 25 of atonement, through faith in his *b*
5: 9 have now been justified by his *b*,
1Co 11: 25 cup is the new covenant in my *b*;
Eph 1: 7 we have redemption through his *b*,
2: 13 near through the *b* of Christ.
Col 1: 20 by making peace through his *b*,
Heb 9: 7 once a year, and never without *b*,
9: 12 once for all by his own *b*,
9: 20 "This is the *b* of the covenant,
9: 22 of *b* there is no forgiveness.
12: 24 word than the *b* of Abel.
1Pe 1: 19 but with the precious *b* of Christ,
1Jn 1: 7 and the *b* of Jesus, his Son,
Rev 1: 5 has freed us from our sins by his *b*,
5: 9 with your *b* you purchased men
7: 14 white in the *b* of the Lamb.
12: 11 him by the *b* of the Lamb
19: 13 He is dressed in a robe dipped in *b*,

BLOODSHED (BLOOD)
Jer 48: 10 on him who keeps his sword from *b*
Eze 35: 6 did not hate *b*, *b* will pursue you.
Hab 2: 12 to him who builds a city with *b*

BLOODTHIRSTY* (BLOOD)
Ps 5: 6 *b* and deceitful men
26: 9 my life with *b* men,
55: 23 *b* and deceitful men
59: 2 and save me from *b* men.
139: 19 Away from me, you *b* men!
Pr 29: 10 *B* men hate a man of integrity

BLOSSOM
Isa 35: 1 the wilderness will rejoice and *b*.

BLOT (BLOTS)
Ex 32: 32 then *b* me out of the book you have
Ps 51: 1 *b* out my transgressions.
Rev 3: 5 I will never *b* out his name

BLOTS (BLOT)
Isa 43: 25 "I, even I, am he who *b* out

BLOWN
Eph 4: 14 and *b* here and there by every wind
Jas 1: 6 doubts is like a wave of the sea, *b*
Jude : 12 without rain, *b* along by the wind;

BLUSH
Jer 6: 15 they do not even know how to *b*.

BOAST (BOASTS)
1Ki 20: 11 armor should not *b* like one who
Ps 34: 2 My soul will *b* in the LORD;
44: 8 In God we make our *b* all day long,
Pr 27: 1 Do not *b* about tomorrow,
Jer 9: 23 or the rich man *b* of his riches,
1Co 1: 31 Let him who boasts *b* in the Lord."
2Co 10: 17 Let him who boasts *b* in the Lord."
11: 30 I do not inwardly burn? If I must *b*,
Gal 6: 14 May I never *b* except in the cross
Eph 2: 9 not by works, so that no one can *b*.

BOASTS (BOAST)
Jer 9: 24 but let him who *b* boast about this:

BOAZ
Wealthy Bethlehemite who showed favor to Ruth (Ru 2), married her (Ru 4). Ancestor of David (Ru 4:18–22; 1Ch 2:12–15), Jesus (Mt 1:5–16; Lk 3:23–32).

BODIES (BODY)
Isa 26: 19 their *b* will rise.
Ro 12: 1 to offer your *b* as living sacrifices,
1Co 6: 15 not know that your *b* are members
Eph 5: 28 to love their wives as their own *b*.

BODILY (BODY)
Col 2: 9 of the Deity lives in *b* form,

BODY (BODIES BODILY EMBODIMENT)
Zec 13: 6 What are these wounds on your *b*?'
Mt 10: 28 afraid of those who kill the *b*
26: 26 saying, "Take and eat; this is my *b*
26: 41 spirit is willing, but the *b* is weak."
Mk 14: 22 saying, "Take it; this is my *b*."
Lk 22: 19 saying, "This is my *b* given for you;
Jn 13: 10 wash his feet; his whole *b* is clean.
Ro 6: 13 Do not offer the parts of your *b*
12: 4 us has one *b* with many members,
1Co 6: 19 not know that your *b* is a temple
6: 20 Therefore honor God with your *b*.
11: 24 "This is my *b*, which is for you;
12: 12 The *b* is a unit, though it is made up
12: 13 baptized by one Spirit into one *b*—
15: 44 a natural *b*, it is raised a spiritual *b*.
Eph 1: 23 which is his *b*, the fullness
4: 25 for we are all members of one *b*.
5: 30 for we are members of his *b*.
Php 1: 20 Christ will be exalted in my *b*,
Col 1: 24 sake of his *b*, which is the church.

BOLD (BOLDNESS)
Ps 138: 3 you made me *b* and stouthearted.
Pr 21: 29 A wicked man puts up a *b* front,
28: 1 but the righteous are as *b* as a lion.

BOLDNESS* (BOLD)
Lk 11: 8 of the man's *b* he will get up
Ac 4: 29 to speak your word with great *b*.

BONDAGE
Ezr 9: 9 God has not deserted us in our *b*.

BONES
Ge 2: 23 "This is now bone of my *b*
Ps 22: 14 and all my *b* are out of joint.
22: 17 I can count all my *b*;
Eze 37: 1 middle of a valley; it was full of *b*.
Jn 19: 36 "Not one of his *b* will be broken,"

BOOK (BOOKS)
Ex 32: 33 against me I will blot out of my *b*.
Jos 1: 8 Do not let this *B* of the Law depart
2Ki 22: 8 "I have found the *B* of the Law
2Ch 34: 15 "I have found the *B* of the Law
Ne 8: 8 They read from the *B* of the Law
Ps 69: 28 May they be blotted out of the *b*
Da 12: 1 name is found written in the *b*—
Jn 20: 30 which are not recorded in this *b*.
Php 4: 3 whose names are in the *b* of life.
Rev 3: 5 never blot out his name from the *b*
20: 12 *b* was opened, which is the *b*
20: 15 was not found written in the *b*
21: 27 written in the Lamb's *b* of life.
22: 18 him the plagues described in this *b*.

BOOKS* (BOOK)
Ecc 12: 12 Of making many *b* there is no end,
Da 7: 10 and the *b* were opened.
Jn 21: 25 for the *b* that would be written.
Rev 20: 12 the throne, and *b* were opened.
20: 12 they had done as recorded in the *b*.

BORE (BEAR)
Isa 53: 12 For he *b* the sin of many,
1Pe 2: 24 He himself *b* our sins in his body

BORN (BEAR)
Ecc 3: 2 a time to be *b* and a time to die,
Isa 9: 6 For to us a child is *b*,
66: 8 Can a country be *b* in a day
Lk 2: 11 of David a Savior has been *b* to you
Jn 3: 3 see the kingdom of God unless he is *b* again.
3: 4 How can a man be *b* when he is old
3: 5 unless he is *b* of water
3: 7 at my saying, 'You must be *b* again
3: 8 it is with everyone *b* of the Spirit."
1Pe 1: 23 For you have been *b* again,
1Jn 3: 9 because he has been *b* of God.
4: 7 Everyone who loves has been *b*
5: 1 believes that Jesus is the Christ is *b*
5: 4 for everyone *b* of God overcomes
5: 18 We know that anyone *b*

BORROWER
Pr 22: 7 and the *b* is servant to the lender.

BOTHER (BOTHERING)
Lk 11: 7 one inside answers, 'Don't *b* me.

BOTHERING (BOTHER)
Lk 18: 5 yet because this widow keeps *b* me,

BOUGHT (BUY)
Ac 20: 28 which he *b* with his own blood.
1Co 6: 20 You are not your own; you were *b*
7: 23 You were *b* at a price; do not
2Pe 2: 1 the sovereign Lord who *b* them—

BOUND (BIND)
Is 56: 3 Let no foreigner who has *b* himself
Mt 16: 19 bind on earth will be *b* in heaven,
18: 18 bind on earth will be *b* in heaven,
Ro 7: 2 by law a married woman is *b*
1Co 7: 39 A woman is *b* to her husband
Jude : 6 *b* with everlasting chains
Rev 20: 2 and *b* him for a thousand years.

BOUNDARY (BOUNDS)
Nu 34: 3 your southern *b* will start
Pr 23: 10 Do not move an ancient *b* stone
Hos 5: 10 who move *b* stones.

BOUNDS (BOUNDARY)
2Co 7: 4 all our troubles my joy knows no *b*.

BOUNTY*
Ge 49: 26 than the *b* of the age-old hills.
Dt 28: 12 heavens, the storehouse of his *b*,
1Ki 10: 13 he had given her out of his royal *b*.
Ps 65: 11 You crown the year with your *b*,
68: 10 from your *b*, O God, you provided
Jer 31: 12 rejoice in the *b* of the LORD—
31: 14 my people will be filled with my *b*

BOW (BOWED BOWS)
Dt 5: 9 You shall not *b* down to them
1Ki 22: 34 But someone drew his *b* at random
Ps 5: 7 in reverence will I *b* down
44: 6 I do not trust in my *b*,
95: 6 Come, let us *b* down in worship,
138: 2 I will *b* down toward your holy
Isa 44: 19 Shall I *b* down to a block of wood?"
45: 23 Before me every knee will *b*;
Ro 14: 11 'every knee will *b* before me;
Php 2: 10 name of Jesus every knee should *b*,

BOWED (BOW)
Ps 145: 14 and lifts up all who are *b* down.
146: 8 the LORD lifts up those who are *b*

2Pe 1: 7 and to godliness, *b* kindness;
1: 7 kindness; and to *b* kindness,

BROTHERS (BROTHER)
Jos 1: 14 You are to help your *b*
Ps 133: 1 is when *b* live together in unity!
Pr 6: 19 who stirs up dissension among *b*.
Mt 12: 49 "Here are my mother and my *b*.
19: 29 everyone who has left houses or *b*
25: 40 one of the least of these *b* of mine,
Mk 3: 33 "Who are my mother and my *b*?"
10: 29 or *b* or sisters or mother or father
Lk 21: 16 will be betrayed even by parents, *b*,
22: 32 turned back, strengthen your *b*."
Jn 7: 5 his own *b* did not believe in him.
Ac 15: 32 to encourage and strengthen the *b*.
Ro 9: 3 off from Christ for the sake of my *b*
1Co 8: 12 sin against your *b* in this way
2Co 11: 26 and in danger from false *b*.
Gal 2: 4 some false *b* had infiltrated our
1Th 4: 10 you do love all the *b*
5: 26 Greet all the *b* with a holy kiss.
1Ti 6: 2 for them because they are *b*.
Heb 2: 11 Jesus is not ashamed to call them *b*.
2: 17 to be made like his *b* in every way,
13: 1 Keep on loving each other as *b*.
1Pe 1: 22 you have sincere love for your *b*,
3: 8 be sympathetic, love as *b*,
1Jn 3: 14 death to life, because we love our *b*.
3: 16 to lay down our lives for our *b*.
3Jn : 10 he refuses to welcome the *b*.
Rev 12: 10 For the accuser of our *b*,

BROW
Ge 3: 19 By the sweat of your *b*

BRUISED (BRUISES)
Isa 42: 3 A *b* reed he will not break,
Mt 12: 20 A *b* reed he will not break,

BRUISES (BRUISED)
Isa 30: 26 when the LORD binds up the *b*

BRUTAL (BRUTE)
2Ti 3: 3 slanderous, without self-control, *b*,

BRUTE* (BRUTAL)
Ps 73: 22 I was a *b* beast before you.
2Pe 2: 12 They are like *b* beasts, creatures

BUBBLING*
Pr 18: 4 the fountain of wisdom is a *b* brook
Isa 35: 7 the thirsty ground *b* springs.

BUCKET*
Isa 40: 15 the nations are like a drop in a *b*;

BUCKLED* (BUCKLER)
Eph 6: 14 belt of truth *b* around your waist,

BUCKLER* (BUCKLED)
Ps 35: 2 Take up shield and *b*;

BUD (BUDDED)
Isa 27: 6 Israel will *b* and blossom

BUDDED (BUD)
Heb 9: 4 Aaron's staff that had *b*,

BUILD (BUILDER BUILDERS BUILDING BUILDS BUILT REBUILD REBUILT)
2Sa 7: 5 Are you the one to *b* me a house
1Ki 6: 1 he began to *b* the temple
Ecc 3: 3 a time to tear down and a time to *b*,
Mt 16: 18 and on this rock I will *b* my church,
Ac 20: 32 which can *b* you up and give you
Ro 15: 2 neighbor for his good, to *b* him up.
1Co 14: 12 excel in gifts that *b* up the church.
1Th 5: 11 one another and *b* each other up,
Jude : 20 *b* yourselves up in your most holy

BUILDER* (BUILD)
1Co 3: 10 I laid a foundation as an expert *b*,
Heb 3: 3 the *b* of a house has greater honor
3: 4 but God is the *b* of everything.
11: 10 whose architect and *b* is God.

BUILDERS (BUILD)
Ps 118: 22 The stone the *b* rejected
Mt 21: 42 " 'The stone the *b* rejected
Mk 12: 10 " 'The stone the *b* rejected
Lk 20: 17 " 'The stone the *b* rejected
Ac 4: 11 " 'the stone you *b* rejected,
1Pe 2: 7 "The stone the *b* rejected

BUILDING (BUILD)
Ezr 3: 8 to supervise the *b* of the house
Ne 4: 17 of Judah who were *b* the wall.
Ro 15: 20 so that I would not be *b*
1Co 3: 9 you are God's field, God's *b*.
2Co 5: 1 we have a *b* from God, an eternal
10: 8 us for *b* you up rather
13: 10 the Lord gave me for *b* you up,
Eph 2: 21 him the whole *b* is joined together
4: 29 helpful for *b* others up according

BUILDS (BUILD)
Ps 127: 1 Unless the LORD *b* the house,
Pr 14: 1 The wise woman *b* her house,
1Co 3: 10 one should be careful how he *b*.
3: 12 If any man *b* on this foundation
8: 1 Knowledge puffs up, but love *b* up.
Eph 4: 16 grows and *b* itself up in love,

BUILT (BUILD)
1Ki 6: 14 So Solomon *b* the temple
Mt 7: 24 is like a wise man who *b* his house
Lk 6: 49 is like a man who *b* a house
Ac 17: 24 does not live in temples *b* by hands.
1Co 3: 14 If what he has *b* survives, he will
2Co 5: 1 in heaven, not *b* by human hands.
Eph 2: 20 *b* on the foundation of the apostles
4: 12 the body of Christ may be *b* up
Col 2: 7 live in him, rooted and *b* up in him,
1Pe 2: 5 are being *b* into a spiritual house

BULL (BULLS)
Lev 4: 3 bring to the LORD a young *b*

BULLS (BULL)
1Ki 7: 25 The Sea stood on twelve *b*,
Heb 10: 4 it is impossible for the blood of *b*

BURDEN (BURDENED BURDENS BURDENSOME)
Ps 38: 4 like a *b* too heavy to bear.
Ecc 1: 13 What a heavy *b* God has laid
Mt 11: 30 my yoke is easy and my *b* is light."
Ac 15: 28 to us not to *b* you with anything
2Co 11: 9 from being a *b* to you in any way,
12: 14 and I will not be a *b* to you,
1Th 2: 9 day in order not to be a *b* to anyone
2Th 3: 8 so that we would not be a *b* to any
Heb 13: 17 not a *b*, for that would be

BURDENED* (BURDEN)
Isa 43: 23 have not *b* you with grain offerings
43: 24 But you have *b* me with your sins
Mic 6: 3 How have I *b* you? Answer me.
Mt 11: 28 all you who are weary and *b*,
2Co 5: 4 are in this tent, we groan and are *b*,
Gal 5: 1 do not let yourselves be *b* again
1Ti 5: 16 not let the church be *b* with them,

BURDENS (BURDEN)
Ps 68: 19 who daily bears our *b*.
Lk 11: 46 down with *b* they can hardly carry,
Gal 6: 2 Carry each other's *b*,

BURDENSOME (BURDEN)
1Jn 5: 3 And his commands are not *b*,

BURIED (BURY)
Ru 1: 17 die I will die, and there I will be *b*.
Ro 6: 4 *b* with him through baptism
1Co 15: 4 that he was *b*, that he was raised
Col 2: 12 having been *b* with him in baptism

BURN (BURNING BURNT)
Dt 7: 5 and *b* their idols in the fire.
Ps 79: 5 long will your jealousy *b* like fire?
1Co 7: 9 to marry than to *b* with passion.

BURNING (BURN)
Ex 27: 20 so that the lamps may be kept *b*.
Lev 6: 9 the fire must be kept *b* on the altar.
Ps 18: 28 You, O LORD, keep my lamp *b*;
Pr 25: 22 you will heap *b* coals on his head,
Ro 12: 20 you will heap *b* coals on his head."
Rev 19: 20 alive into the fiery lake of *b* sulfur.

BURNISHED*
1Ki 7: 45 of the LORD were of *b* bronze.
Eze 1: 7 and gleamed like *b* bronze.
Da 10: 6 and legs like the gleam of *b* bronze,
Rev 2: 18 and whose feet are like *b* bronze.

BURNT (BURN)
Ge 8: 20 he sacrificed *b* offerings on it.
22: 2 as a *b* offering on one
Ex 10: 25 and *b* offerings to present
18: 12 brought a *b* offering and other
40: 6 Place the altar of *b* offering in front
Lev 1: 3 " 'If the offering is a *b* offering
Jos 8: 31 offered to the LORD *b* offerings
Jdg 6: 26 offer the second bull as a *b* offering
13: 16 But if you prepare a *b* offering,
1Ki 3: 4 offered a thousand *b* offerings
9: 25 year Solomon sacrificed *b* offerings
10: 5 and the *b* offerings he made
Ezr 3: 2 Israel to sacrifice *b* offerings on it,
Eze 43: 18 for sacrificing *b* offerings

BURST
Ps 98: 4 *b* into jubilant song with music;
Isa 44: 23 *B* into song, you mountains,
49: 13 *b* into song, O mountains!
52: 9 *B* into songs of joy together,
54: 1 *b* into song, shout for joy,
55: 12 will *b* into song before you,

BURY (BURIED)
Mt 8: 22 and let the dead *b* their own dead."
Lk 9: 60 "Let the dead *b* their own dead,

BUSH
Ex 3: 2 the *b* was on fire it did not burn up.
Mk 12: 26 the account of the *b*, how God said
Lk 20: 37 But in the account of the *b*,
Ac 7: 35 who appeared to him in the *b*.

BUSINESS
Ecc 4: 8 a miserable *b*!
Da 8: 27 and went about the king's *b*.
1Co 5: 12 What *b* is it of mine to judge those
1Th 4: 11 to mind your own *b* and to work
Jas 1: 11 even while he goes about his *b*.

BUSY*
1Ki 18: 27 Perhaps he is deep in thought, or *b*,
20: 40 While your servant was *b* here
Isa 32: 6 his mind is *b* with evil:
Hag 1: 9 of you is *b* with his own house.
2Th 3: 11 They are not *b*; they are
Tit 2: 5 to be *b* at home, to be kind,

BUSYBODIES*
2Th 3: 11 They are not busy; they are *b*.
1Ti 5: 13 *b*, saying things they ought not to.

BUY (BOUGHT BUYS)
Pr 23: 23 *B* the truth and do not sell it;
Isa 55: 1 Come, *b* wine and milk
Rev 13: 17 so that no one could *b* or sell

BUYS (BUY)
Pr 31: 16 She considers a field and *b* it;

BYWORD (WORD)
1Ki 9: 7 Israel will then become a *b*
Ps 44: 14 You have made us a *b*
Joel 2: 17 a *b* among the nations.

CAESAR
Mt 22: 21 "Give to *C* what is Caesar's,

CAIN
Firstborn of Adam (Ge 4:1), murdered brother Abel (Ge 4:1–16; 1Jn 3:12).

CAKE
Hos 7: 8 Ephraim is a flat *c* not turned over.

CALEB
Judahite who spied out Canaan (Nu 13:6); allowed to enter land because of faith (Nu 13:30–14:38; Dt 1:36). Possessed Hebron (Jos 14:6–15:19).

CALF
Ex 32: 4 into an idol cast in the shape of a *c*,
Pr 15: 17 than a fattened *c* with hatred.
Lk 15: 23 Bring the fattened *c* and kill it.
Ac 7: 41 made an idol in the form of a *c*.

CALL (CALLED CALLING CALLS)
1Ki 18: 24 I will *c* on the name of the LORD.
2Ki 5: 11 *c* on the name of the LORD his
1Ch 16: 8 to the LORD, *c* on his name;
Ps 105: 1 to the LORD, *c* on his name;
116: 13 and *c* on the name of the LORD.
116: 17 and *c* on the name of the LORD.
145: 18 near to all who *c* on him,
Pr 31: 28 children arise and *c* her blessed;
Isa 5: 20 Woe to those who *c* evil good
12: 4 to the LORD, *c* on his name;
55: 6 *c* on him while he is near.
65: 24 Before they *c* I will answer;
Jer 33: 3 '*C* to me and I will answer you
Zep 3: 9 that all of them may *c* on the name
Zec 13: 9 They will *c* on my name
Mt 9: 13 come to *c* the righteous,
Mk 2: 17 I have not come to *c* the righteous,
Lk 5: 32 I have not come to *c* the righteous,
Ac 2: 39 all whom the Lord our God will *c*."
9: 14 to arrest all who *c* on your name."
9: 21 among those who *c* on this name?
Ro 10: 12 and richly blesses all who *c* on him,
11: 29 gifts and his *c* are irrevocable.
1Co 1: 2 with all those everywhere who *c*
1Th 4: 7 For God did not *c* us to be impure,
2Ti 2: 22 along with those who *c*

CALLED (CALL)
Ge 2: 23 she shall be *c* 'woman,'
5: 2 he blessed them and *c* them "man
12: 8 and *c* on the name of the LORD.
21: 33 and there he *c* upon the name
26: 25 and *c* on the name of the LORD.
1Sa 3: 5 and said, "Here I am; you *c* me."
2Ch 7: 14 if my people, who are *c*
Ps 34: 6 This poor man *c*, and the LORD
116: 4 Then I *c* on the name of the LORD
Isa 56: 7 for my house will be *c*
La 3: 55 I *c* on your name, O LORD,
Hos 11: 1 and out of Egypt I *c* my son.
Mt 1: 16 was born Jesus, who is *c* Christ.
2: 15 "Out of Egypt I *c* my son."
21: 13 " 'My house will be *c* a house
Mk 11: 17 " 'My house will be *c*
Lk 1: 32 will be *c* the Son of the Most High.
1: 35 to be born will be *c* the Son of God.
Ro 1: 1 *c* to be an apostle and set apart
1: 6 among those who are *c* to belong
1: 7 loved by God and *c* to be saints:
8: 28 who have been *c* according
8: 30 And those he predestined, he also *c*
1Co 1: 1 *c* to be an apostle of Christ Jesus
1: 2 in Christ Jesus and *c* to be holy,
1: 24 but to those whom God has *c*,
1: 26 of what you were when you were *c*.
7: 15 God has *c* us to live in peace.
7: 17 and to which God has *c* him.
Gal 1: 6 deserting the one who *c* you
1: 15 from birth and *c* me by his grace,
5: 13 You, my brothers, were *c* to be free
Eph 1: 18 the hope to which he has *c* you,
4: 4 as you were *c* to one hope
Col 3: 15 of one body you were *c* to peace.
2Th 2: 14 He *c* you to this through our gospel
1Ti 6: 12 life to which you were *c*
2Ti 1: 9 who has saved us and *c* us
Heb 9: 15 that those who are *c* may receive
1Pe 1: 15 But just as he who *c* you is holy,
2: 9 of him who *c* you out of darkness
3: 9 to this you were *c* so that you may
5: 10 who *c* you to his eternal glory
2Pe 1: 3 of him who *c* us by his own glory
Jude : 1 To those who have been *c*,

CALLING (CALL)
Isa 40: 3 A voice of one *c*:
Mt 3: 3 "A voice of one *c* in the desert,
Mk 1: 3 "a voice of one *c* in the desert,
10: 49 Cheer up! On your feet! He's *c* you
Lk 3: 4 "A voice of one *c* in the desert,
Jn 1: 23 I am the voice of one *c* in the desert
Ac 22: 16 wash your sins away, *c* on his name
Eph 4: 1 worthy of the *c* you have received.
2Th 1: 11 may count you worthy of his *c*,
2Pe 1: 10 all the more eager to make your *c*

CALLOUS* (CALLOUSED)
Ps 17: 10 They close up their *c* hearts,
73: 7 From their *c* hearts comes iniquity;
119: 70 Their hearts are *c* and unfeeling,

CALLOUSED* (CALLOUS)
Isa 6: 10 Make the heart of this people *c*;
Mt 13: 15 this people's heart has become *c*;
Ac 28: 27 this people's heart has become *c*;

CALLS (CALL)
Ps 147: 4 and *c* them each by name.
Isa 40: 26 and *c* them each by name.
Joel 2: 32 And everyone who *c*
Mt 22: 43 speaking by the Spirit, *c* him 'Lord
Jn 10: 3 He *c* his own sheep by name
Ac 2: 21 And everyone who *c*
Ro 10: 13 "Everyone who *c* on the name
1Th 2: 12 who *c* you into his kingdom
5: 24 The one who *c* you is faithful

CALM (CALMS)
Ps 107: 30 They were glad when it grew *c*,
Isa 7: 4 keep *c* and don't be afraid.
Eze 16: 42 I will be *c* and no longer angry.

CALMS* (CALM)
Pr 15: 18 but a patient man *c* a quarrel.

CAMEL
Mt 19: 24 it is easier for a *c* to go
23: 24 strain out a gnat but swallow a *c*.
Mk 10: 25 It is easier for a *c* to go
Lk 18: 25 it is easier for a *c* to go

CAMP (ENCAMPS)
Heb 13: 13 outside the *c*, bearing the disgrace

CANAAN (CANAANITE CANAANITES)
Ge 10: 15 *C* was the father of Sidon his
Lev 14: 34 "When you enter the land of *C*,
25: 38 of Egypt to give you the land of *C*
Nu 13: 2 men to explore the land of *C*,
33: 51 'When you cross the Jordan into *C*,
Jdg 4: 2 a king of *C*, who reigned in Hazor.
1Ch 16: 18 "To you I will give the land of *C*
Ps 105: 11 "To you I will give the land of *C*
Ac 13: 19 he overthrew seven nations in *C*

CANAANITE (CANAAN)
Ge 10: 18 Later the *C* clans scattered
28: 1 "Do not marry a *C* woman.
Jos 5: 1 all the *C* kings along the seacoast
Jdg 1: 32 lived among the *C* inhabitants

CANAANITES (CANAAN)
Ex 33: 2 before you and drive out the *C*,

CANCEL (CANCELED)
Dt 15: 1 seven years you must *c* debts.

CANCELED (CANCEL)
Mt 18: 27 pity on him, *c* the debt
Lk 7: 42 so he *c* the debts of both.
Col 2: 14 having *c* the written code,

CANDLESTICKS see LAMPSTANDS

CANOPY*
2Sa 22: 12 He made darkness his *c*
2Ki 16: 18 away the Sabbath *c* that had been
Ps 18: 11 made darkness his covering, his *c*
Isa 4: 5 over all the glory will be a *c*.
40: 22 stretches out the heavens like a *c*,
Jer 43: 10 he will spread his royal *c*

CAPERNAUM
Mt 4: 13 Nazareth, he went and lived in *C*,
Jn 6: 59 teaching in the synagogue in *C*.

CAPITAL
Dt 21: 22 guilty of a *c* offense is put to death

CAPSTONE* (STONE)
Ps 118: 22 has become the *c*;
Zec 4: 7 he will bring out the *c* to shouts
Mt 21: 42 has become the *c*;
Mk 12: 10 has become the *c*;
Lk 20: 17 has become the *c*'?
Ac 4: 11 which has become the *c*.'
1Pe 2: 7 has become the *c*,"

CAPTIVATE* (CAPTIVE)
Pr 6: 25 or let her *c* you with her eyes,

CAPTIVATED* (CAPTIVE)
Pr 5: 19 may you ever be *c* by her love.
5: 20 Why be *c*, my son, by an adulteress

CAPTIVE (CAPTIVATE CAPTIVATED CAPTIVES CAPTIVITY CAPTURED)
Ac 8: 23 full of bitterness and *c* to sin."
2Co 10: 5 and we take *c* every thought
Col 2: 8 See to it that no one takes you *c*
2Ti 2: 26 who has taken them *c* to do his will.

CAPTIVES (CAPTIVE)
Ps 68: 18 you led *c* in your train;
Isa 61: 1 to proclaim freedom for the *c*
Eph 4: 8 he led *c* in his train

CAPTIVITY (CAPTIVE)
Dt 28: 41 because they will go into *c*.
2Ki 25: 21 So Judah went into *c*, away
Jer 30: 3 Israel and Judah back from *c*
52: 27 So Judah went into *c*, away
Eze 29: 14 I will bring them back from *c*

CAPTURED (CAPTIVE)
1Sa 4: 11 The ark of God was *c*,
2Sa 5: 7 David *c* the fortress of Zion,
2Ki 17: 6 the king of Assyria *c* Samaria

CARCASS
Jdg 14: 9 taken the honey from the lion's *c*.
Mt 24: 28 there is a *c*, there the vultures

CARE (CAREFUL CARES CARING)
Ps 8: 4 the son of man that you *c* for him?
65: 9 You *c* for the land and water it;
144: 3 what is man that you *c* for him,
Pr 29: 7 The righteous *c* about justice
Mk 5: 26 deal under the *c* of many doctors
Lk 10: 34 him to an inn and took *c* of him.
18: 4 I don't fear God or *c* about men,
Jn 21: 16 Jesus said, "Take *c* of my sheep."
1Ti 3: 5 how can he take *c* of God's church
6: 20 what has been entrusted to your *c*.
Heb 2: 6 the son of man that you *c* for him?
1Pe 5: 2 of God's flock that is under your *c*,

CAREFUL* (CARE)
Ge 31: 24 "Be *c* not to say anything to Jacob,
31: 29 'Be *c* not to say anything to Jacob,
Ex 19: 12 'Be *c* that you do not go up
23: 13 "Be *c* to do everything I have said
34: 12 Be *c* not to make a treaty
34: 15 "Be *c* not to make a treaty
Lev 18: 4 and be *c* to follow my decrees.
25: 18 " 'Follow my decrees and be *c*
26: 3 and are *c* to obey my commands,
Dt 2: 4 afraid of you, but be very *c*.
4: 9 before you today? Only be *c*,
4: 23 Be *c* not to forget the covenant
5: 32 So be *c* to do what the LORD your
6: 3 be *c* to obey so that it may go well
6: 12 be *c* that you do not forget
6: 25 And if we are *c* to obey all this law
7: 12 attention to these laws and are *c*
8: 1 Be *c* to follow every command I am
8: 11 Be *c* that you do not forget
11: 16 Be *c*, or you will be enticed
12: 1 and laws you must be *c* to follow
12: 13 Be *c* not to sacrifice your burnt
12: 19 Be *c* not to neglect the Levites

12: 28 Be *c* to obey all these regulations I
12: 30 be *c* not to be ensnared
15: 5 are *c* to follow all these commands
15: 9 Be *c* not to harbor this wicked
17: 10 Be *c* to do everything they direct
24: 8 cases of leprous diseases be very *c*
Jos 1: 7 Be *c* to obey all the law my servant
1: 8 so that you may be *c*
22: 5 But be very *c* to keep
23: 6 be *c* to obey all that is written
23: 11 be very *c* to love the LORD your
1Ki 8: 25 if only your sons are *c* in all they do
2Ki 10: 31 Yet Jehu was not *c* to keep the law
17: 37 You must always be *c*
21: 8 if only they will be *c*
1Ch 22: 13 if you are *c* to observe the decrees
28: 8 Be *c* to follow all the commands
2Ch 6: 16 if only your sons are *c* in all they do
33: 8 if only they will be *c*
Ezr 4: 22 Be *c* not to neglect this matter.
Job 36: 18 Be *c* that no one entices you
Ps 101: 2 I will be *c* to lead a blameless life—
Pr 13: 24 he who loves him is *c*
27: 23 give *c* attention to your herds;
Isa 7: 4 Be *c*, keep calm and don't be afraid.
Jer 17: 21 Be *c* not to carry a load
17: 24 But if you are *c* to obey me,
22: 4 For if you are *c* to carry out these
Eze 11: 20 will follow my decrees and be *c*
18: 19 has been *c* to keep all my decrees,
20: 19 follow my decrees and be *c*
20: 21 they were not *c* to keep my laws—
36: 27 you to follow my decrees and be *c*
37: 24 and be *c* to keep my decrees.
Mic 7: 5 be *c* of your words.
Hag 1: 5 "Give *c* thought to your ways.
1: 7 "Give *c* thought to your ways.
2: 15 give *c* thought to this from this day
2: 18 Give *c* thought: Is there yet any
2: 18 give *c* thought to the day
Mt 2: 8 and make a *c* search for the child.
6: 1 "Be *c* not to do your 'acts
16: 6 "Be *c*," Jesus said to them.
Mk 8: 15 "Be *c*," Jesus warned them.
Lk 21: 34 Be *c*, or your hearts will be weighed
Ro 12: 17 Be *c* to do what is right in the eyes
1Co 3: 10 each one should be *c* how he builds
8: 9 Be *c*, however, that the exercise
10: 12 standing firm, be *c* that you don't
Eph 5: 15 Be very *c*, then, how you live—
2Ti 4: 2 great patience and *c* instruction.
Tit 3: 8 may be *c* to devote themselves
Heb 2: 1 We must pay more *c* attention,
4: 1 let us be *c* that none

CARELESS*
Mt 12: 36 for every *c* word they have spoken.

CARES* (CARE)
Dt 11: 12 It is a land the LORD your God *c*
Job 39: 16 she *c* not that her labor was in vain,
Ps 55: 22 Cast your *c* on the LORD
142: 4 no one *c* for my life.
Pr 12: 10 A righteous man *c* for the needs
Ecc 5: 3 when there are many *c*,
Jer 12: 11 because there is no one who *c*.
30: 17 Zion for whom no one *c*.'
Na 1: 7 He *c* for those who trust in him,
Jn 10: 13 and *c* nothing for the sheep.
Eph 5: 29 but he feeds and *c* for it, just
1Pe 5: 7 on him because he *c* for you.

CARING* (CARE)
1Th 2: 7 like a mother *c* for her little
1Ti 5: 4 practice by *c* for their own family

CARPENTER (CARPENTER'S)
Mk 6: 3 does miracles! Isn't this the *c*?

CARPENTER'S* (CARPENTER)
Mt 13: 55 "Isn't this the *c* son? Isn't his

CARRIED (CARRY)
Ex 19: 4 and how I *c* you on eagles' wings
Dt 1: 31 how the LORD your God *c* you,
Isa 53: 4 and *c* our sorrows,
63: 9 he lifted them up and *c* them
Mt 8: 17 and *c* our diseases."
Heb 13: 9 Do not be *c* away by all kinds
2Pe 1: 21 as they were *c* along by the Holy
3: 17 so that you may not be *c* away

CARRIES (CARRY)
Dt 32: 11 and *c* them on its pinions.
Isa 40: 11 and *c* them close to his heart;

CARRY (CARRIED CARRIES CARRYING)
Lev 16: 22 goat will *c* on itself all their sins
26: 15 and fail to *c* out all my commands
Isa 46: 4 I have made you and I will *c* you;
Lk 14: 27 anyone who does not *c* his cross
Gal 6: 2 *C* each other's burdens,
6: 5 for each one should *c* his own load.

CARRYING (CARRY)
Jn 19: 17 *C* his own cross, he went out
1Jn 5: 2 loving God and *c* out his

CARVED (CARVES)
Nu 33: 52 Destroy all their *c* images
Mic 5: 13 I will destroy your *c* images

CARVES* (CARVED)
Dt 27: 15 "Cursed is the man who *c* an image

CASE
Pr 18: 17 to present his *c* seems right,
22: 23 for the LORD will take up their *c*
23: 11 he will take up their *c* against you.

CAST (CASTING)
Ex 34: 17 "Do not make *c* idols.
Lev 16: 8 He is to *c* lots for the two goats—
Ps 22: 18 and *c* lots for my clothing.
55: 22 *C* your cares on the LORD
Pr 16: 33 The lot is *c* into the lap,
Ecc 11: 1 *C* your bread upon the waters,
Jn 19: 24 and *c* lots for my clothing."
1Pe 5: 7 *C* all your anxiety on him

CASTING (CAST)
Pr 18: 18 *C* the lot settles disputes
Mt 27: 35 divided up his clothes by *c* lots.

CATCH (CATCHES CAUGHT)
Lk 5: 4 and let down the nets for a *c*."
5: 10 from now on you will *c* men."

CATCHES (CATCH)
Job 5: 13 He *c* the wise in their craftiness,
1Co 3: 19 "He *c* the wise in their craftiness";

CATTLE
Ps 50: 10 and the *c* on a thousand hills.

CAUGHT (CATCH)
Ge 22: 13 there in a thicket he saw a ram *c*
2Co 12: 2 who fourteen years ago was *c* up
1Th 4: 17 and are left will be *c* up together with them

CAUSE (CAUSES)
Pr 24: 28 against your neighbor without *c*,
Ecc 8: 3 Do not stand up for a bad *c*,
Mt 18: 7 of the things that *c* people to sin!
Ro 14: 21 else that will *c* your brother
1Co 10: 32 Do not *c* anyone to stumble,

CAUSES (CAUSE)
Ps 7: 16 The trouble he *c* recoils on himself;
Isa 8: 14 a stone that *c* men to stumble
Mt 5: 29 If your right eye *c* you to sin,
5: 30 And if your right hand *c* you to sin,
18: 6 if anyone *c* one of these little ones
18: 8 or your foot *c* you to sin,
Ro 14: 20 to eat anything that *c* someone else
1Co 8: 13 if what I eat *c* my brother to fall
1Pe 2: 8 "A stone that *c* men to stumble

CAUTIOUS*
Pr 12: 26 A righteous man is *c* in friendship,

CEASE
Ps 46: 9 He makes wars *c* to the ends

CELEBRATE*
Ex 10: 9 we are to *c* a festival to the LORD
12: 14 generations to come you shall *c* it
12: 17 *C* this day as a lasting ordinance
12: 17 "*C* the Feast of Unleavened Bread,
12: 47 community of Israel must *c* it.
12: 48 to *c* the LORD's Passover must
23: 14 are to *c* a festival to me.
23: 15 "*C* the Feast of Unleavened Bread;
23: 16 "*C* the Feast of Harvest
23: 16 "*C* the Feast of Ingathering
34: 18 "*C* the Feast of Unleavened Bread.
34: 22 "*C* the Feast of Weeks
Lev 23: 39 *c* the festival to the LORD
23: 41 *C* this as a festival to the LORD
23: 41 for the generations to come; *c* it
Nu 9: 2 "Have the Israelites *c* the Passover
9: 3 *C* it at the appointed time,
9: 4 told the Israelites to *c* the Passover,
9: 6 of them could not *c* the Passover
9: 10 they may still *c* the LORD's
9: 11 are to *c* it on the fourteenth day
9: 12 When they *c* the Passover,
9: 13 on a journey fails to *c* the Passover,
9: 14 to *c* the LORD's Passover must do
29: 12 *C* a festival to the LORD
Dt 16: 1 *c* the Passover of the LORD your
16: 10 Then *c* the Feast of Weeks
16: 13 *C* the Feast of Tabernacles
16: 15 For seven days *c* the Feast
Jdg 16: 23 to Dagon their god and to *c*,
2Sa 6: 21 the LORD's people Israel—I will *c*
2Ki 23: 21 "*C* the Passover to the LORD your
2Ch 30: 1 and *c* the Passover to the LORD,
30: 2 decided to *c* the Passover
30: 3 able to *c* it at the regular time
30: 5 and *c* the Passover to the LORD,
30: 13 in Jerusalem to *c* the Feast
30: 23 to *c* the festival seven more days;
Ne 8: 12 of food and to *c* with great joy,
12: 27 to *c* joyfully the dedication
Est 9: 21 to have them *c* annually
Ps 145: 7 They will *c* your abundant
Isa 30: 29 as on the night you *c* a holy festival
Na 1: 15 *C* your festivals, O Judah,
Zec 14: 16 and to *c* the Feast of Tabernacles.
14: 18 up to *c* the Feast of Tabernacles.
14: 19 up to *c* the Feast of Tabernacles.
Mt 26: 18 I am going to *c* the Passover
Lk 15: 23 Let's have a feast and *c*.
15: 24 So they began to *c*.
15: 29 goat so I could *c* with my friends.
15: 32 But we had to *c* and be glad,
Rev 11: 10 will *c* by sending each other gifts,

CELESTIAL*
2Pe 2: 10 afraid to slander *c* beings;
Jude : 8 authority and slander *c* beings.

CENSER (CENSERS)
Lev 16: 12 is to take a *c* full of burning coals
Rev 8: 3 Another angel, who had a golden *c*,

CENSERS (CENSER)
Nu 16: 6 Take *c* and tomorrow put fire

CENTURION
Mt 8: 5 had entered Capernaum, a *c* came
27: 54 When the *c* and those
Mk 15: 39 And when the *c*, who stood there
Lk 7: 3 The *c* heard of Jesus and sent some
23: 47 The *c*, seeing what had happened,
Ac 10: 1 a *c* in what was known
27: 1 handed over to a *c* named Julius,

CEPHAS* (PETER)
Jn 1: 42 You will be called *C*" (which,
1Co 1: 12 another, "I follow *C*"; still another,
3: 22 Paul or Apollos or *C* or the world
9: 5 and the Lord's brothers and *C*?

CEREMONIAL* (CEREMONY)
Lev 14: 2 at the time of his *c* cleansing,
15: 13 off seven days for his *c* cleansing;

Mk 7: 3 they give their hands a *c* washing,
Jn 2: 6 used by the Jews for *c* washing,
3: 25 Jew over the matter of *c* washing.
11: 55 to Jerusalem for their *c* cleansing
18: 28 to avoid *c* uncleanness the Jews did
Heb 9: 10 drink and various *c* washings—
13: 9 not by *c* foods, which are

CEREMONIALLY* (CEREMONY)
Lev 4: 12 outside the camp to a place *c* clean,
5: 2 touches anything *c* unclean—
6: 11 the camp to a place that is *c* clean.
7: 19 anyone *c* clean may eat it.
7: 19 touches anything *c* unclean must
10: 14 Eat them in a *c* clean place;
11: 4 not have a split hoof; it is *c* unclean
12: 2 birth to a son will be *c* unclean
12: 7 and then she will be *c* clean
13: 3 he shall pronounce him *c* unclean.
14: 8 with water; then he will be *c* clean.
15: 28 and after that she will be *c* clean.
15: 33 lies with a woman who is *c* unclean.
17: 15 he will be *c* unclean till evening.
21: 1 must not make himself *c* unclean
22: 3 of your descendants is *c* unclean
27: 11 he vowed is a *c* unclean animal—
Nu 5: 2 who is *c* unclean because of a dead
6: 7 must not make himself *c* unclean
8: 6 Israelites and make them *c* clean.
9: 6 they were *c* unclean on account
9: 13 But if a man who is *c* clean
18: 11 household who is *c* clean may eat
18: 13 household who is *c* clean may eat
19: 7 but he will be *c* unclean till evening
19: 9 and put them in a *c* clean place
19: 18 Then a man who is *c* clean is
Dt 12: 15 Both the *c* unclean and the clean
12: 22 Both the *c* unclean and the clean
14: 7 they are *c* unclean for you.
15: 22 Both the *c* unclean and the clean
1Sa 20: 26 to David to make him *c* unclean—
2Ch 13: 11 the bread on the *c* clean table
30: 17 for all those who were not *c* clean
Ezr 6: 20 themselves and were all *c* clean.
Ne 12: 30 Levites had purified themselves *c*,
Isa 66: 20 of the LORD in *c* clean vessels.
Eze 22: 10 period, when they are *c* unclean.
Ac 24: 18 I was *c* clean when they found me
Heb 9: 13 those who are *c* unclean sanctify

CEREMONY* (CEREMONIAL CEREMONIALLY)
Ge 50: 11 Egyptians are holding a solemn *c*
Ex 12: 25 as he promised, observe this *c*.
12: 26 'What does this *c* mean to you?'
13: 5 are to observe this *c* in this month:

CERTAIN (CERTAINTY)
2Pe 1: 19 word of the prophets made more *c*,

CERTAINTY* (CERTAIN)
Lk 1: 4 so that you may know the *c*
Jn 17: 8 They knew with *c* that I came

CERTIFICATE* (CERTIFIED)
Dt 24: 1 and he writes her a *c* of divorce,
24: 3 and writes her a *c* of divorce,
Isa 50: 1 "Where is your mother's *c*
Jer 3: 8 I gave faithless Israel her *c*
Mt 5: 31 divorces his wife must give her a *c*
19: 7 that a man give his wife a *c*
Mk 10: 4 a man to write a *c* of divorce

CERTIFIED* (CERTIFICATE)
Jn 3: 33 has accepted it has *c* that God is

CHAFF
Ps 1: 4 They are like *c*
35: 5 May they be like *c* before the wind,
Da 2: 35 became like *c* on a threshing floor
Mt 3: 12 up the *c* with unquenchable fire."

CHAINED (CHAINS)
2Ti 2: 9 But God's word is not *c*.

CHAINS (CHAINED)
Eph 6: 20 for which I am an ambassador in *c*.
Col 4: 18 Remember my *c*.
2Ti 1: 16 and was not ashamed of my *c*.
Jude : 6 with everlasting *c* for judgment

CHAMPION
Ps 19: 5 like a *c* rejoicing to run his course.

CHANCE
Ecc 9: 11 but time and *c* happen to them all.

CHANGE (CHANGED)
1Sa 15: 29 of Israel does not lie or *c* his mind;
Ps 110: 4 and will not *c* his mind:
Jer 7: 5 If you really *c* your ways
Mal 3: 6 "I the LORD do not *c*.
Mt 18: 3 unless you *c* and become like little
Heb 7: 21 and will not *c* his mind:
Jas 1: 17 who does not *c* like shifting

CHANGED (CHANGE)
1Sa 10: 6 you will be *c* into a different person
Hos 11: 8 My heart is *c* within me;
1Co 15: 51 but we will all be *c*— in a flash,

CHARACTER*
Ru 3: 11 that you are a woman of noble *c*.
Pr 12: 4 of noble *c* is her husband's crown,
31: 10 A wife of noble *c* who can find?
Ac 17: 11 noble *c* than the Thessalonians,
Ro 5: 4 perseverance, *c*; and *c*, hope.
1Co 15: 33 "Bad company corrupts good *c*."

CHARGE (CHARGES)
Job 34: 13 him in *c* of the whole world?
Ro 8: 33 Who will bring any *c*
1Co 9: 18 the gospel I may offer it free of *c*,
2Co 11: 7 the gospel of God to you free of *c*?
2Ti 4: 1 I give you this *c*: Preach the Word;
Phm : 18 or owes you anything, *c* it to me.

CHARGES (CHARGE)
Isa 50: 8 Who then will bring *c* against me?

CHARIOT (CHARIOTS)
2Ki 2: 11 suddenly a *c* of fire and horses
Ps 104: 3 He makes the clouds his *c*
Ac 8: 28 sitting in his *c* reading the book

CHARIOTS (CHARIOT)
2Ki 6: 17 and *c* of fire all around Elisha.
Ps 20: 7 Some trust in *c* and some in horses,
68: 17 The *c* of God are tens of thousands

CHARM* (CHARMING)
Pr 17: 8 bribe is a *c* to the one who gives it;
31: 30 *C* is deceptive, and beauty is

CHARMING* (CHARM)
Pr 26: 25 his speech is *c*, do not believe
SS 1: 16 Oh, how *c*!

CHASE (CHASES)
Lev 26: 8 Five of you will *c* a hundred,

CHASES* (CHASE)
Pr 12: 11 he who *c* fantasies lacks judgment.
28: 19 one who *c* fantasies will have his

CHASM*
Lk 16: 26 and you a great *c* has been fixed,

CHATTER* (CHATTERING)
1Ti 6: 20 Turn away from godless *c*
2Ti 2: 16 Avoid godless *c*, because those

CHATTERING* (CHATTER)
Pr 10: 8 but a *c* fool comes to ruin.
10: 10 and a *c* fool comes to ruin.

CHEAT* (CHEATED CHEATING CHEATS)
Mal 1: 14 "Cursed is the *c* who has
1Co 6: 8 you yourselves *c* and do wrong,

CHEATED* (CHEAT)
Ge 31: 7 yet your father has *c* me
1Sa 12: 3 Whom have I *c*? Whom have I
12: 4 "You have not *c* or oppressed us,"
Lk 19: 8 if I have *c* anybody out of anything,
1Co 6: 7 Why not rather be *c*? Instead,

CHEATING* (CHEAT)
Am 8: 5 and *c* with dishonest scales,

CHEATS* (CHEAT)
Lev 6: 2 or if he *c* him, or if he finds lost

CHEEK (CHEEKS)
Mt 5: 39 someone strikes you on the right *c*,
Lk 6: 29 If someone strikes you on one *c*,

CHEEKS (CHEEK)
Isa 50: 6 my *c* to those who pulled out my

CHEERFUL* (CHEERS)
Pr 15: 13 A happy heart makes the face *c*,
15: 15 but the *c* heart has a continual feast
15: 30 A *c* look brings joy to the heart,
17: 22 A *c* heart is good medicine,
2Co 9: 7 for God loves a *c* giver.

CHEERS (CHEERFUL)
Pr 12: 25 but a kind word *c* him up.

CHEMOSH
2Ki 23: 13 for *C* the vile god of Moab,

CHERISH (CHERISHED CHERISHES)
Ps 17: 14 You still the hunger of those you *c*;

CHERISHED (CHERISH)
Ps 66: 18 If I had *c* sin in my heart,

CHERISHES* (CHERISH)
Pr 19: 8 he who *c* understanding prospers.

CHERUB (CHERUBIM)
Ex 25: 19 Make one *c* on one end
Eze 28: 14 You were anointed as a guardian *c*,

CHERUBIM (CHERUB)
Ge 3: 24 side of the Garden of Eden *c*
1Sa 4: 4 who is enthroned between the *c*.
2Sa 6: 2 enthroned between the *c* that are
22: 11 He mounted the *c* and flew;
1Ki 6: 23 a pair of *c* of olive wood,
2Ki 19: 15 of Israel, enthroned between the *c*,
1Ch 13: 6 who is enthroned between the *c*—
Ps 18: 10 He mounted the *c* and flew;
80: 1 who sit enthroned between the *c*,
99: 1 he sits enthroned between the *c*,
Isa 37: 16 of Israel, enthroned between the *c*,
Eze 10: 1 was over the heads of the *c*.

CHEST
Ex 25: 10 "Have them make a *c*
2Ki 12: 9 Jehoiada the priest took a *c*
Da 2: 32 its *c* and arms of silver, its belly
Rev 1: 13 with a golden sash around his *c*.

CHEWS
Lev 11: 3 divided and that *c* the cud.

CHIEF
1Pe 5: 4 And when the *C* Shepherd appears,

CHILD (CHILDISH CHILDREN CHILDREN'S GRANDCHILDREN)
Pr 20: 11 Even a *c* is known by his actions,
22: 6 Train a *c* in the way he should go,
22: 15 Folly is bound up in the heart of a *c*
23: 13 not withhold discipline from a *c*;
29: 15 *c* left to himself disgraces his mother.
Isa 7: 14 The virgin will be with *c*
9: 6 For to us a *c* is born,
11: 6 and a little *c* will lead them.
66: 13 As a mother comforts her *c*,
Mt 1: 23 "The virgin will be with *c*
18: 2 He called a little *c* and had him
Lk 1: 42 and blessed is the *c* you will bear!
1: 80 And the *c* grew and became strong
1Co 13: 11 When I was a *c*, I talked like a *c*,
1Jn 5: 1 who loves the father loves his *c*

CHILDBEARING (BEAR)
Ge 3: 16 greatly increase your pains in *c*;

CHILDBIRTH (BEAR)
Gal 4: 19 the pains of *c* until Christ is formed

CHILDISH* (CHILD)
1Co 13: 11 When I became a man, I put *c* ways

CHILDREN (CHILD)
Ex 20: 5 punishing the *c* for the sin
Dt 4: 9 Teach them to your *c*

1: 16 and coming of our Lord Jesus *C*,
1Jn 2: 1 Jesus *C*, the Righteous One.
2: 22 man who denies that Jesus is the *C*.
3: 16 Jesus *C* laid down his life for us.
3: 23 in the name of his Son, Jesus *C*,
4: 2 that Jesus *C* has come
5: 1 believes that Jesus is the *C* is born
5: 20 even in his Son Jesus *C*.
2Jn : 9 teaching of *C* does not have God;
Jude : 4 deny Jesus *C* our only Sovereign
Rev 1: 1 The revelation of Jesus *C*,
1: 5 from Jesus *C*, who is the faithful
11: 15 kingdom of our Lord and of his *C*,
20: 4 reigned with *C* a thousand years.
20: 6 they will be priests of God and of *C*

CHRIST'S (CHRIST)
1Co 9: 21 from God's law but am under *C* law
2Co 5: 14 For *C* love compels us,
5: 20 We are therefore *C* ambassadors,
12: 9 so that *C* power may rest on me.
Col 1: 22 by *C* physical body through death

CHRISTIAN* (CHRIST)
Ac 26: 28 you can persuade me to be a *C*?"
1Pe 4: 16 as a *C*, do not be ashamed,

CHRISTIANS* (CHRIST)
Ac 11: 26 The disciples were called *C* first

CHRISTS* (CHRIST)
Mt 24: 24 For false *C* and false prophets will
Mk 13: 22 For false *C* and false prophets will

CHURCH
Mt 16: 18 and on this rock I will build my *c*,
18: 17 if he refuses to listen even to the *c*,
Ac 20: 28 Be shepherds of the *c* of God,
1Co 5: 12 of mine to judge those outside the *c*
14: 4 but he who prophesies edifies the *c*.
14: 12 to excel in gifts that build up the *c*.
14: 26 done for the strengthening of the *c*.
15: 9 because I persecuted the *c* of God.
Gal 1: 13 how intensely I persecuted the *c*
Eph 5: 23 as Christ is the head of the *c*,
Col 1: 18 he is the head of the body, the *c*;
1: 24 the sake of his body, which is the *c*.

CHURNING
Pr 30: 33 For as *c* the milk produces butter,

CIRCLE
Isa 40: 22 enthroned above the *c* of the earth,

CIRCUMCISE (CIRCUMCISED CIRCUMCISION)
Dt 10: 16 *C* your hearts, therefore,

CIRCUMCISED (CIRCUMCISE)
Ge 17: 10 Every male among you shall be *c*.
17: 12 who is eight days old must be *c*,
Jos 5: 3 and *c* the Israelites at Gibeath
Gal 5: 2 that if you let yourselves be *c*,

CIRCUMCISION (CIRCUMCISE)
Ro 2: 25 *C* has value if you observe the law,
2: 29 and *c* is *c* of the heart, by the Spirit,
1Co 7: 19 *C* is nothing and uncircumcision is

CIRCUMSTANCES
Php 4: 11 to be content whatever the *c*.
1Th 5: 18 continually; give thanks in all *c*,

CITIES (CITY)
Lk 19: 17 small matter, take charge of ten *c*.'
19: 19 'You take charge of five *c*.'

CITIZENS (CITIZENSHIP)
Eph 2: 19 but fellow *c* with God's people

CITIZENSHIP* (CITIZENS)
Ac 22: 28 "I had to pay a big price for my *c*."
Eph 2: 12 excluded from *c* in Israel
Php 3: 20 But our *c* is in heaven.

CITY (CITIES)
Mt 5: 14 A *c* on a hill cannot be hidden.
Ac 18: 10 I have many people in this *c*."
Heb 13: 14 here we do not have an enduring *c*,
Rev 21: 2 saw the Holy *C*, the new

CIVILIAN*
2Ti 2: 4 a soldier gets involved in *c* affairs—

CLAIM (CLAIMS RECLAIM)
Pr 25: 6 do not *c* a place among great men;
1Jn 1: 6 If we *c* to have fellowship
1: 8 If we *c* to be without sin, we
1: 10 If we *c* we have not sinned,

CLAIMS (CLAIM)
Jas 2: 14 if a man *c* to have faith
1Jn 2: 6 Whoever *c* to live in him must walk
2: 9 Anyone who *c* to be in the light

CLANGING*
1Co 13: 1 a resounding gong or a *c* cymbal.

CLAP* (CLAPPED CLAPS)
Job 21: 5 *c* your hand over your mouth.
Ps 47: 1 *C* your hands, all you nations;
98: 8 Let the rivers *c* their hands,
Pr 30: 32 *c* your hand over your mouth!
Isa 55: 12 will *c* their hands.
La 2: 15 *c* their hands at you;

CLAPPED* (CLAP)
2Ki 11: 12 and the people *c* their hands
Eze 25: 6 Because you have *c* your hands

CLAPS* (CLAP)
Job 27: 23 It *c* its hands in derision
34: 37 scornfully he *c* his hands among us
Na 3: 19 *c* his hands at your fall,

CLASSIFY*
2Co 10: 12 dare to *c* or compare ourselves

CLAUDIUS
Ac 11: 28 happened during the reign of *C*.)
18: 2 because *C* had ordered all the Jews

CLAY
Isa 45: 9 Does the *c* say to the potter,
64: 8 We are the *c*, you are the potter;
Jer 18: 6 "Like *c* in the hand of the potter,
La 4: 2 are now considered as pots of *c*,
Da 2: 33 partly of iron and partly of baked *c*.
Ro 9: 21 of the same lump of *c* some pottery
2Co 4: 7 we have this treasure in jars of *c*
2Ti 2: 20 and *c*; some are for noble purposes

CLEAN (CLEANNESS CLEANSE CLEANSED CLEANSES CLEANSING)
Ge 7: 2 seven of every kind of *c* animal,
Lev 4: 12 the camp to a place ceremonially *c*,
16: 30 you will be *c* from all your sins.
Ps 24: 4 He who has *c* hands and a pure
51: 7 with hyssop, and I will be *c*;
Pr 20: 9 I am *c* and without sin"?
Eze 36: 25 I will sprinkle *c* water on you,
Mt 8: 2 are willing, you can make me *c*."
12: 44 the house unoccupied, swept *c*
23: 25 You *c* the outside of the cup
Mk 7: 19 Jesus declared all foods "*c*.")
Jn 13: 10 to wash his feet; his whole body is *c*
15: 3 are already *c* because of the word
Ac 10: 15 impure that God has made *c*."
Ro 14: 20 All food is *c*, but it is wrong

CLEANNESS (CLEAN)
2Sa 22: 25 according to my *c* in his sight.

CLEANSE (CLEAN)
Ps 51: 2 and *c* me from my sin.
51: 7 *C* me with hyssop, and I will be
Pr 20: 30 Blows and wounds *c* away evil,
Heb 9: 14 *c* our consciences from acts that
10: 22 having our hearts sprinkled to *c* us

CLEANSED (CLEAN)
Heb 9: 22 requires that nearly everything be *c*
2Pe 1: 9 has forgotten that he has been *c*

CLEANSES* (CLEAN)
2Ti 2: 21 If a man *c* himself from the latter,

CLEANSING (CLEAN)
Eph 5: 26 *c* her by the washing with water

CLEFT*
Ex 33: 22 I will put you in a *c* in the rock

CLEVER
Isa 5: 21 and *c* in their own sight.

CLING
Ro 12: 9 Hate what is evil; *c* to what is good.

CLINGS
Ps 63: 8 My soul *c* to you;

CLOAK
Ex 12: 11 with your *c* tucked into your belt,
2Ki 4: 29 "Tuck your *c* into your belt,
9: 1 "Tuck your *c* into your belt,
Mt 5: 40 let him have your *c* as well.

CLOSE (CLOSER CLOSES)
2Ki 11: 8 Stay *c* to the king wherever he goes
2Ch 23: 7 Stay *c* to the king wherever he goes
Ps 34: 18 LORD is *c* to the brokenhearted
148: 14 of Israel, the people *c* to his heart.
Isa 40: 11 and carries them *c* to his heart;
Jer 30: 21 himself to be *c* to me?'

CLOSER (CLOSE)
Ex 3: 5 "Do not come any *c*," God said.
Pr 18: 24 there is a friend who sticks *c*

CLOSES (CLOSE)
Pr 28: 27 he who *c* his eyes to them receives

CLOTHE (CLOTHED CLOTHES CLOTHING)
Ps 45: 3 *c* yourself with splendor
Isa 52: 1 *c* yourself with strength.
Ro 13: 14 *c* yourselves with the Lord Jesus
Col 3: 12 *c* yourselves with compassion,
1Pe 5: 5 *c* yourselves with humility

CLOTHED (CLOTHE)
Ps 30: 11 removed my sackcloth and *c* me
104: 1 you are *c* with splendor
Pr 31: 22 she is *c* in fine linen and purple.
31: 25 She is *c* with strength and dignity;
Isa 61: 10 For he has *c* me with garments
Lk 24: 49 until you have been *c* with power
Gal 3: 27 into Christ have *c* yourselves

CLOTHES (CLOTHE)
Dt 8: 4 Your *c* did not wear out
Mt 6: 25 the body more important than *c*?
6: 28 "And why do you worry about *c*?
27: 35 they divided up his *c* by casting lots
Jn 11: 44 Take off the grave *c* and let him go

CLOTHING (CLOTHE)
Dt 22: 5 A woman must not wear men's *c*,
Job 29: 14 I put on righteousness as my *c*;
Ps 22: 18 and cast lots for my *c*.
Mt 7: 15 They come to you in sheep's *c*,
1Ti 6: 8 But if we have food and *c*,

CLOUD (CLOUDS)
Ex 13: 21 them in a pillar of *c* to guide them
1Ki 18: 44 *c* as small as a man's hand is rising
Pr 16: 15 his favor is like a rain *c* in spring.
Isa 19: 1 See, the LORD rides on a swift *c*
Lk 21: 27 of Man coming in a *c* with power
Heb 12: 1 by such a great *c* of witnesses,
Rev 14: 14 seated on the *c* was one "like a son

CLOUDS (CLOUD)
Dt 33: 26 and on the *c* in his majesty.
Ps 68: 4 extol him who rides on the *c*—
104: 3 He makes the *c* his chariot
Pr 25: 14 Like *c* and wind without rain
Da 7: 13 coming with the *c* of heaven.
Mt 24: 30 of Man coming on the *c* of the sky,
26: 64 and coming on the *c* of heaven."
Mk 13: 26 coming in *c* with great power
1Th 4: 17 with them in the *c* to meet the Lord
Rev 1: 7 Look, he is coming with the *c*,

CLUB
Pr 25: 18 Like a *c* or a sword or a sharp arrow

CO-HEIRS* (INHERIT)
Ro 8: 17 heirs of God and *c* with Christ,

COALS
Pr 25: 22 you will heap burning *c* on his head
Ro 12: 20 you will heap burning *c* on his head

COARSE*
Eph 5: 4 or *c* joking, which are out of place,
CODE*
Ro 2: 27 even though you have the written *c*
2: 29 by the Spirit, not by the written *c*.
7: 6 not in the old way of the written *c*.
Col 2: 14 having canceled the written *c*,
COINS
Mt 26: 15 out for him thirty silver *c*.
Lk 15: 8 suppose a woman has ten silver *c*
COLD
Pr 25: 25 Like *c* water to a weary soul
Mt 10: 42 if anyone gives even a cup of *c* water
24: 12 the love of most will grow *c*,
COLLECTION
1Co 16: 1 Now about the *c* for God's people:
COLT
Zec 9: 9 on a *c*, the foal of a donkey.
Mt 21: 5 on a *c*, the foal of a donkey.' "
COMB
Ps 19: 10 than honey from the *c*.
COMFORT* (COMFORTED COMFORTER COMFORTERS COMFORTING COMFORTS)
Ge 5: 29 "He will *c* us in the labor
37: 35 and daughters came to *c* him,
Ru 2: 13 "You have given me *c*
1Ch 7: 22 and his relatives came to *c* him.
Job 2: 11 sympathize with him and *c* him.
7: 13 When I think my bed will *c* me
16: 5 *c* from my lips would bring you
36: 16 to the *c* of your table laden
Ps 23: 4 rod and your staff, they *c* me.
71: 21 and *c* me once again.
119: 50 My *c* in my suffering is this:
119: 52 and I find *c* in them.
119: 76 May your unfailing love be my *c*,
119: 82 I say, "When will you *c* me?"
Isa 40: 1 *C*, *c* my people,
51: 3 The LORD will surely *c* Zion
51: 19 who can *c* you?—
57: 18 I will guide him and restore *c*
61: 2 to *c* all who mourn,
66: 13 so will I *c* you;
Jer 16: 7 food to *c* those who mourn
31: 13 I will give them *c* and joy instead
La 1: 2 there is none to *c* her.
1: 9 there was none to *c* her.
1: 16 No one is near to *c* me,
1: 17 but there is no one to *c* her.
1: 21 but there is no one to *c* me.
2: 13 that I may *c* you,
Eze 16: 54 all you have done in giving them *c*.
Na 3: 7 Where can I find anyone to *c* you?"
Zec 1: 17 and the LORD will again *c* Zion
10: 2 they give *c* in vain.
Lk 6: 24 you have already received your *c*.
Jn 11: 19 and Mary to *c* them in the loss
1Co 14: 3 encouragement and *c*.
2Co 1: 3 of compassion and the God of all *c*,
1: 4 so that we can *c* those
1: 4 with the *c* we ourselves have
1: 5 through Christ our *c* overflows.
1: 6 if we are comforted, it is for your *c*,
1: 6 it is for your *c* and salvation;
1: 7 so also you share in our *c*.
2: 7 you ought to forgive and *c* him,
7: 7 also by the *c* you had given him.
Php 2: 1 if any *c* from his love,
Col 4: 11 and they have proved a *c* to me.
COMFORTED* (COMFORT)
Ge 24: 67 Isaac was *c* after his mother's death
37: 35 comfort him, but he refused to be *c*.
2Sa 12: 24 Then David *c* his wife Bathsheba,
Job 42: 11 They *c* and consoled him
Ps 77: 2 and my soul refused to be *c*.
86: 17 have helped me and *c* me.
Isa 12: 1 and you have *c* me.
52: 9 for the LORD has *c* his people,
54: 11 lashed by storms and not *c*,
66: 13 and you will be *c* over Jerusalem."
Jer 31: 15 and refusing to be *c*,
Mt 2: 18 and refusing to be *c*,
5: 4 for they will be *c*.
Lk 16: 25 but now he is *c* here and you are
Ac 20: 12 man home alive and were greatly *c*.
2Co 1: 6 if we are *c*, it is for your comfort,
7: 6 *c* us by the coming of Titus,
COMFORTER* (COMFORT)
Ecc 4: 1 and they have no *c*;
4: 1 and they have no *c*.
Jer 8: 18 O my *C* in sorrow,
COMFORTERS* (COMFORT)
Job 16: 2 miserable *c* are you all!
Ps 69: 20 for *c*, but I found none.
COMFORTING* (COMFORT)
Isa 66: 11 satisfied at her *c* breasts;
Zec 1: 13 *c* words to the angel who talked
Jn 11: 31 *c* her, noticed how quickly she got
1Th 2: 12 *c* and urging you to live lives
COMFORTS* (COMFORT)
Job 29: 25 I was like one who *c* mourners.
Isa 49: 13 For the LORD *c* his people
51: 12 "I, even I, am he who *c* you.
66: 13 As a mother *c* her child,
2Co 1: 4 who *c* us in all our troubles,
7: 6 But God, who *c* the downcast,
COMMAND (COMMANDED COMMANDING COMMANDMENT COMMANDMENTS COMMANDS)
Ex 7: 2 You are to say everything I *c* you,
Nu 14: 41 are you disobeying the LORD's *c*?
24: 13 to go beyond the *c* of the LORD—
Dt 4: 2 Do not add to what I *c* you
8: 1 to follow every *c* I am giving you
12: 32 See that you do all I *c* you;
15: 11 I *c* you to be openhanded
30: 16 For I *c* you today to love
32: 46 so that you may *c* your children
Ps 91: 11 For he will *c* his angels concerning
Pr 13: 13 but he who respects a *c* is rewarded
Ecc 8: 2 Obey the king's *c*, I say,
Jer 1: 7 you to and say whatever I *c* you.
1: 17 and say to them whatever I *c* you.
7: 23 Walk in all the ways I *c* you,
11: 4 Obey me and do everything I *c* you
26: 2 Tell them everything I *c* you;
Joel 2: 11 mighty are those who obey his *c*.
Mt 4: 6 He will *c* his angels concerning you
15: 3 why do you break the *c* of God
Lk 4: 10 " 'He will *c* his angels concerning
Jn 14: 15 love me, you will obey what I *c*.
15: 12 My *c* is this: Love each other
15: 14 friends if you do what I *c*.
15: 17 This is my *c*: Love each other.
1Co 14: 37 writing to you is the Lord's *c*.
Gal 5: 14 law is summed up in a single *c*:
1Ti 1: 5 goal of this *c* is love, which comes
6: 14 to you keep this *c* without spot
6: 17 *C* those who are rich
Heb 11: 3 universe was formed at God's *c*,
2Pe 2: 21 on the sacred *c* that was passed
3: 2 and the *c* given by our Lord
1Jn 2: 7 I am not writing you a new *c*
3: 23 this is his *c*: to believe in the name
4: 21 And he has given us this *c*:
2Jn : 6 his *c* is that you walk in love.
COMMANDED (COMMAND)
Ge 2: 16 And the LORD God *c* the man,
7: 5 Noah did all that the LORD *c* him.
50: 12 Jacob's sons did as he had *c* them:
Ex 7: 6 did just as the LORD *c* them.
19: 7 all the words the LORD had *c* him
Dt 4: 5 laws as the LORD my God *c* me,
6: 24 The LORD *c* us to obey all these
Jos 1: 9 Have I not *c* you? Be strong
1: 16 Whatever you have *c* us we will do,
2Sa 5: 25 So David did as the LORD *c* him,
2Ki 17: 13 the entire Law that I *c* your fathers
21: 8 careful to do everything I *c* them
2Ch 33: 8 do everything I *c* them concerning
Ps 33: 9 he *c*, and it stood firm.
78: 5 which he *c* our forefathers
148: 5 for he *c* and they were created.
Mt 28: 20 to obey everything I have *c* you.
1Co 9: 14 Lord has *c* that those who preach
1Jn 3: 23 and to love one another as he *c* us.
2Jn : 4 in the truth, just as the Father *c* us.
COMMANDING (COMMAND)
2Ti 2: 4 he wants to please his *c* officer.
COMMANDMENT* (COMMAND)
Jos 22: 5 But be very careful to keep the *c*
Mt 22: 36 which is the greatest *c* in the Law?"
22: 38 This is the first and greatest *c*.
Mk 12: 31 There is no *c* greater than these."
Lk 23: 56 the Sabbath in obedience to the *c*.
Jn 13: 34 "A new *c* I give you: Love one
Ro 7: 8 the opportunity afforded by the *c*,
7: 9 when the *c* came, sin sprang to life
7: 10 that the very *c* that was intended
7: 11 and through the *c* put me to death.
7: 11 the opportunity afforded by the *c*,
7: 12 and the *c* is holy, righteous
7: 13 through the *c* sin might become
13: 9 and whatever other *c* there may be,
Eph 6: 2 which is the first *c* with a promise
Heb 9: 19 Moses had proclaimed every *c*
COMMANDMENTS* (COMMAND)
Ex 20: 6 who love me and keep my *c*.
34: 28 of the covenant—the Ten *C*.
Dt 4: 13 to you his covenant, the Ten *C*,
5: 10 who love me and keep my *c*.
5: 22 These are the *c* the LORD
6: 6 These *c* that I give you today are
9: 10 were all the *c* the LORD
10: 4 The Ten *C* he had proclaimed
Ecc 12: 13 Fear God and keep his *c*,
Mt 5: 19 one of the least of these *c*
19: 17 If you want to enter life, obey the *c*
22: 40 the Prophets hang on these two *c*."
Mk 10: 19 You know the *c*: 'Do not murder,
12: 28 "Of all the *c*, which is the most
Lk 1: 6 observing all the Lord's *c*
18: 20 You know the *c*: 'Do not commit
Ro 13: 9 The *c*, "Do not commit adultery,"
Eph 2: 15 in his flesh the law with its *c*
Rev 12: 17 those who obey God's *c*
14: 12 part of the saints who obey God's *c*
COMMANDS (COMMAND)
Ex 24: 12 and *c* I have written for their
25: 22 give you all my *c* for the Israelites.
34: 32 gave them all the *c* the LORD had
Lev 22: 31 "Keep my *c* and follow them.
Nu 15: 39 and so you will remember all the *c*
Dt 7: 9 those who love him and keep his *c*.
7: 11 Therefore, take care to follow the *c*
11: 1 decrees, his laws and his *c* always.
11: 27 the blessing if you obey the *c*
28: 1 carefully follow all his *c* I give you
30: 10 LORD your God and keep his *c*
Jos 22: 5 to walk in all his ways, to obey his *c*
1Ki 2: 3 and keep his decrees and *c*,
8: 58 in all his ways and to keep the *c*,
8: 61 to live by his decrees and obey his *c*
1Ch 28: 7 unswerving in carrying out my *c*
29: 19 devotion to keep your *c*,
2Ch 31: 21 in obedience to the law and the *c*,
Ne 1: 5 those who love him and obey his *c*,
Ps 78: 7 but would keep his *c*.
112: 1 who finds great delight in his *c*.
119: 10 do not let me stray from your *c*.
119: 32 I run in the path of your *c*,
119: 35 Direct me in the path of your *c*,
119: 47 for I delight in your *c*

119: 48 I lift up my hands to your *c*,
119: 73 me understanding to learn your *c*.
119: 86 All your *c* are trustworthy;
119: 96 but your *c* are boundless.
119: 98 Your *c* make me wiser
119:115 that I may keep the *c* of my God!
119:127 Because I love your *c*
119:131 longing for your *c*.
119:143 but your *c* are my delight.
119:151 and all your *c* are true.
119:172 for all your *c* are righteous.
119:176 for I have not forgotten your *c*.
Pr 2: 1 and store up my *c* within you,
3: 1 but keep my *c* in your heart,
6: 23 For these *c* are a lamp,
10: 8 The wise in heart accept *c*,
Isa 48: 18 you had paid attention to my *c*,
Da 9: 4 all who love him and obey his *c*,
Mt 5: 19 teaches these *c* will be called great
Mk 7: 8 You have let go of the *c* of God
7: 9 way of setting aside the *c* of God
Jn 14: 21 Whoever has my *c* and obeys them,
15: 10 If you obey my *c*, you will remain
Ac 17: 30 but now he *c* all people everywhere
1Co 7: 19 Keeping God's *c* is what counts.
1Jn 2: 3 come to know him if we obey his *c*.
2: 4 but does not do what he *c* is a liar,
3: 22 we obey his *c* and do what pleases
3: 24 Those who obey his *c* live in him,
5: 2 loving God and carrying out his *c*.
5: 3 And his *c* are not burdensome,
5: 3 This is love for God: to obey his *c*.
2Jn : 6 that we walk in obedience to his *c*.

COMMEMORATE
Ex 12: 14 "This is a day you are to *c*;

COMMEND* (COMMENDABLE COMMENDED COMMENDS)
Ps 145: 4 One generation will *c* your works
Ecc 8: 15 So I *c* the enjoyment of life,
Ro 13: 3 do what is right and he will *c* you.
16: 1 I *c* to you our sister Phoebe,
2Co 3: 1 beginning to *c* ourselves again?
4: 2 the truth plainly we *c* ourselves
5: 12 trying to *c* ourselves to you again,
6: 4 as servants of God we *c* ourselves
10: 12 with some who *c* themselves.
1Pe 2: 14 and to *c* those who do right.

COMMENDABLE* (COMMEND)
1Pe 2: 19 For it is *c* if a man bears up
2: 20 you endure it, this is *c* before God.

COMMENDED* (COMMEND)
Ne 11: 2 The people *c* all the men who
Job 29: 11 and those who saw me *c* me,
Lk 16: 8 master *c* the dishonest manager
Ac 15: 40 *c* by the brothers to the grace
2Co 12: 11 I ought to have been *c* by you,
Heb 11: 2 This is what the ancients were *c* for
11: 4 By faith he was *c* as a righteous
11: 5 he was *c* as one who pleased God.
11: 39 These were all *c* for their faith,

COMMENDS* (COMMEND)
Pr 15: 2 of the wise *c* knowledge,
2Co 10: 18 but the one whom the Lord *c*.
10: 18 not the one who *c* himself who is

COMMIT (COMMITS COMMITTED)
Ex 20: 14 "You shall not *c* adultery.
Dt 5: 18 "You shall not *c* adultery.
1Sa 7: 3 and *c* yourselves to the LORD
Ps 31: 5 Into your hands I *c* my spirit;
37: 5 *C* your way to the LORD;
Pr 16: 3 *C* to the LORD whatever you do,
Mt 5: 27 that it was said, 'Do not *c* adultery.'
5: 32 causes her to *c* adultery,
19: 18 do not *c* adultery, do not steal,
Mk 10: 19 do not *c* adultery, do not steal,
Lk 18: 20 'Do not *c* adultery, do not murder,
23: 46 into your hands I *c* my spirit."
Ac 20: 32 I *c* you to God and to the word
Ro 2: 22 do you *c* adultery? You who abhor
2: 22 that people should not *c* adultery,
13: 9 "Do not *c* adultery,"
1Co 10: 8 We should not *c* sexual immorality,
Jas 2: 11 do not *c* adultery but do *c* murder,
1Pe 4: 19 to God's will should *c* themselves
Rev 2: 22 I will make those who *c* adultery

COMMITS (COMMIT)
Pr 6: 32 man who *c* adultery lacks
29: 22 a hot-tempered one *c* many sins.
Ecc 8: 12 a wicked man *c* a hundred crimes
Eze 18: 12 He *c* robbery.
18: 14 who sees all the sins his father *c*,
18: 24 from his righteousness and *c* sin
18: 26 from his righteousness and *c* sin,
22: 11 you one man *c* a detestable offense
Mt 5: 32 the divorced woman *c* adultery.
19: 9 marries another woman *c* adultery
Mk 10: 11 marries another woman *c* adultery
10: 12 another man, she *c* adultery."
Lk 16: 18 a divorced woman *c* adultery.
16: 18 marries another woman *c* adultery,

COMMITTED (COMMIT)
Nu 5: 7 and must confess the sin he has *c*.
1Ki 8: 61 But your hearts must be fully *c*
15: 14 Asa's heart was fully *c*
2Ch 16: 9 those whose hearts are fully *c*
Mt 5: 28 lustfully has already *c* adultery
11: 27 "All things have been *c* to me
Lk 10: 22 "All things have been *c* to me
Ac 14: 23 *c* them to the Lord,
14: 26 where they had been *c* to the grace
1Co 9: 17 I am simply discharging the trust *c*
2Co 5: 19 And he has *c* to us the message
1Pe 2: 22 "He *c* no sin,
Rev 17: 2 the kings of the earth *c* adultery
18: 3 of the earth *c* adultery with her,
18: 9 kings of the earth who *c* adultery

COMMON
Ge 11: 1 had one language and a *c* speech.
Lev 10: 10 between the holy and the *c*,
Pr 22: 2 Rich and poor have this in *c*:
29: 13 the oppressor have this in *c*:
Ac 2: 44 together and had everything in *c*.
1Co 10: 13 has seized you except what is *c*
2Co 6: 14 and wickedness have in *c*?

COMPANION (COMPANIONS)
Ps 55: 13 my *c*, my close friend,
55: 20 My *c* attacks his friends;
Pr 13: 20 but a *c* of fools suffers harm.
28: 7 a *c* of gluttons disgraces his father.
29: 3 *c* of prostitutes squanders his
Rev 1: 9 your brother and *c* in the suffering

COMPANIONS (COMPANION)
Ps 45: 7 your God, has set you above your *c*
Pr 18: 24 A man of many *c* may come to ruin
Heb 1: 9 your God, has set you above your *c*

COMPANY
Ps 14: 5 present in the *c* of the righteous.
Pr 21: 16 comes to rest in the *c* of the dead.
24: 1 do not desire their *c*;
Jer 15: 17 I never sat in the *c* of revelers,
1Co 15: 33 "Bad *c* corrupts good character."

COMPARE* (COMPARED COMPARING COMPARISON)
Job 28: 17 Neither gold nor crystal can *c*
28: 19 The topaz of Cush cannot *c* with it;
39: 13 but they cannot *c* with the pinions
Ps 86: 8 no deeds can *c* with yours.
89: 6 skies above can *c* with the LORD?
Pr 3: 15 nothing you desire can *c* with her.
8: 11 nothing you desire can *c* with her.
Isa 40: 18 To whom, then, will you *c* God?
40: 18 What image will you *c* him to?
40: 25 "To whom will you *c* me?
46: 5 "To whom will you *c* me
La 2: 13 With what can I *c* you,
Eze 31: 8 *c* with its branches—
Da 1: 13 Then *c* our appearance with that
Mt 11: 16 "To what can I *c* this generation?
Lk 7: 31 I *c* the people of this generation?
13: 18 What shall I *c* it to? It is like
13: 20 What shall I *c* the kingdom of God
2Co 10: 12 and *c* themselves with themselves,
10: 12 or *c* ourselves with some who

COMPARED* (COMPARE)
Jdg 8: 2 What have I accomplished *c* to you
8: 3 What was I able to do *c* to you?"
Isa 46: 5 you liken me that we may be *c*?
Eze 31: 2 Who can be *c* with you in majesty?
31: 18 the trees of Eden can be *c* with you
Php 3: 8 I consider everything a loss *c*

COMPARING* (COMPARE)
Ro 8: 18 present sufferings are not worth *c*
2Co 8: 8 the sincerity of your love by *c* it
Gal 6: 4 without *c* himself to somebody else

COMPARISON* (COMPARE)
2Co 3: 10 now in *c* with the surpassing glory.

COMPASSION* (COMPASSIONATE COMPASSIONS)
Ex 33: 19 I will have *c* on whom I will have *c*.
Dt 13: 17 he will show you mercy, have *c*
28: 54 man among you will have no *c*
30: 3 restore your fortunes and have *c*
32: 36 and have *c* on his servants
Jdg 2: 18 for the LORD had *c* on them
1Ki 3: 26 son was alive was filled with *c*
2Ki 13: 23 and had *c* and showed concern
2Ch 30: 9 and your children will be shown *c*
Ne 9: 19 of your great *c* you did not
9: 27 and in your great *c* you gave them
9: 28 in your *c* you delivered them time
Ps 51: 1 according to your great *c*
77: 9 Has he in anger withheld his *c*?"
90: 13 Have *c* on your servants.
102: 13 You will arise and have *c* on Zion,
103: 4 and crowns you with love and *c*.
103: 13 As a father has *c* on his children,
103: 13 so the LORD has *c*
116: 5 our God is full of *c*.
119: 77 Let your *c* come to me that I may
119:156 Your *c* is great, O LORD;
135: 14 and have *c* on his servants.
145: 9 he has *c* on all he has made.
Isa 13: 18 will they look with *c* on children.
14: 1 The LORD will have *c* on Jacob;
27: 11 so their Maker has no *c* on them,
30: 18 he rises to show you *c*.
49: 10 He who has *c* on them will guide
49: 13 and will have *c* on his afflicted ones
49: 15 and have no *c* on the child she has
51: 3 and will look with *c* on all her ruins
54: 7 with deep *c* I will bring you back.
54: 8 I will have *c* on you,"
54: 10 says the LORD, who has *c* on you.
60: 10 in favor I will show you *c*.
63: 7 to his *c* and many kindnesses.
63: 15 and *c* are withheld from us.
Jer 12: 15 I will again have *c* and will bring
13: 14 *c* to keep me from destroying them
15: 6 I can no longer show *c*.
21: 7 show them no mercy or pity or *c*.'
30: 18 and have *c* on his dwellings;
31: 20 I have great *c* for him,"
33: 26 restore their fortunes and have *c*
42: 12 I will show you *c* so that he will
42: 12 so that he will have *c* on you
La 3: 32 he brings grief, he will show *c*,
Eze 9: 5 without showing pity or *c*.
16: 5 or had *c* enough to do any
39: 25 and will have *c* on all the people
Hos 2: 19 in love and *c*.
11: 8 all my *c* is aroused.
13: 14 "I will have no *c*,
14: 3 for in you the fatherless find *c*."

Am 1: 11 stifling all *c*,
Jnh 3: 9 with *c* turn from his fierce anger
3: 10 he had *c* and did not bring
Mic 7: 19 You will again have *c* on us;
Zec 7: 9 show mercy and *c* to one another.
10: 6 because I have *c* on them.
Mal 3: 17 as in *c* a man spares his son who
Mt 9: 36 When he saw the crowds, he had *c*
14: 14 he had *c* on them and healed their
15: 32 "I have *c* for these people;
20: 34 Jesus had *c* on them and touched
Mk 1: 41 with *c*, Jesus reached out his hand
6: 34 and saw a large crowd, he had *c*
8: 2 "I have *c* for these people;
Lk 15: 20 and was filled with *c* for him;
Ro 9: 15 and I will have *c* on whom I have *c*
2Co 1: 3 the Father of *c* and the God
Php 2: 1 and *c*, then make my joy complete
Col 3: 12 clothe yourselves with *c*, kindness,
Jas 5: 11 The Lord is full of *c* and mercy.

COMPASSIONATE* (COMPASSION)
Ex 22: 27 out to me, I will hear, for I am *c*.
34: 6 the LORD, the *c* and gracious God
2Ch 30: 9 LORD your God is gracious and *c*.
Ne 9: 17 gracious and *c*, slow to anger
Ps 86: 15 O Lord, are a *c* and gracious God,
103: 8 The LORD is *c* and gracious,
111: 4 the LORD is gracious and *c*.
112: 4 the gracious and *c* and righteous
145: 8 The LORD is gracious and *c*,
La 4: 10 With their own hands *c* women
Joel 2: 13 for he is gracious and *c*,
Jnh 4: 2 that you are a gracious and *c* God,
Eph 4: 32 Be kind and *c* to one another,
1Pe 3: 8 love as brothers, be *c* and humble.

COMPASSIONS* (COMPASSION)
La 3: 22 for his *c* never fail.

COMPELLED (COMPULSION)
Ac 20: 22 "And now, *c* by the Spirit,
1Co 9: 16 I cannot boast, for I am *c* to preach.

COMPELS (COMPULSION)
Job 32: 18 and the spirit within me *c* me;
2Co 5: 14 For Christ's love *c* us, because we

COMPETENCE* (COMPETENT)
2Co 3: 5 but our *c* comes from God.

COMPETENT* (COMPETENCE)
Ro 15: 14 and *c* to instruct one another.
1Co 6: 2 are you not *c* to judge trivial cases?
2Co 3: 5 Not that we are *c* in ourselves to claim
3: 6 He has made us *c* as ministers

COMPETES*
1Co 9: 25 Everyone who *c* in the games goes
2Ti 2: 5 Similarly, if anyone *c* as an athlete,
2: 5 unless he *c* according to the rules.

COMPLACENCY* (COMPLACENT)
Pr 1: 32 and the *c* of fools will destroy them
Eze 30: 9 ships to frighten Cush out of her *c*.

COMPLACENT* (COMPLACENCY)
Isa 32: 9 You women who are so *c*,
32: 11 Tremble, you *c* women;
Am 6: 1 Woe to you who are *c* in Zion,
Zep 1: 12 and punish those who are *c*,

COMPLAINING*
Php 2: 14 Do everything without *c* or arguing

COMPLETE
Dt 16: 15 your hands, and your joy will be *c*.
Jn 3: 29 That joy is mine, and it is now *c*.
15: 11 and that your joy may be *c*.
16: 24 will receive, and your joy will be *c*.
17: 23 May they be brought to *c* unity
Ac 20: 24 *c* the task the Lord Jesus has given
Php 2: 2 then make my joy *c*
Col 4: 17 to it that you *c* the work you have
Jas 1: 4 so that you may be mature and *c*,
2: 22 his faith was made *c* by what he did
1Jn 1: 4 We write this to make our joy *c*.
2: 5 God's love is truly made *c* in him.
4: 12 and his love is made *c* in us.
4: 17 love is made *c* among us
2Jn : 12 to face, so that our joy may be *c*.

COMPLIMENTS*
Pr 23: 8 and will have wasted your *c*.

COMPREHEND* (COMPREHENDED)
Job 28: 13 Man does not *c* its worth;
Ecc 8: 17 No one can *c* what goes
8: 17 he knows, he cannot really *c* it.

COMPREHENDED* (COMPREHEND)
Job 38: 18 Have you *c* the vast expanses

COMPULSION (COMPELLED COMPELS)
2Co 9: 7 not reluctantly or under *c*,

CONCEAL (CONCEALED CONCEALS)
Ps 40: 10 I do not *c* your love and your truth
Pr 25: 2 It is the glory of God to *c* a matter;

CONCEALED (CONCEAL)
Jer 16: 17 nor is their sin *c* from my eyes.
Mt 10: 26 There is nothing *c* that will not be
Mk 4: 22 and whatever is *c* is meant
Lk 8: 17 nothing *c* that will not be known
12: 2 There is nothing *c* that will not be

CONCEALS* (CONCEAL)
Pr 10: 18 He who *c* his hatred has lying lips,
28: 13 He who *c* his sins does not prosper,

CONCEIT* (CONCEITED CONCEITS)
Isa 16: 6 her overweening pride and *c*,
Jer 48: 29 her overweening pride and *c*,
Php 2: 3 out of selfish ambition or vain *c*,

CONCEITED* (CONCEIT)
1Sa 17: 28 I know how *c* you are and how
Ro 11: 25 brothers, so that you may not be *c*:
12: 16 Do not be *c*.
2Co 12: 7 To keep me from becoming *c*
Gal 5: 26 Let us not become *c*, provoking
1Ti 3: 6 or he may become *c* and fall
6: 4 he is *c* and understands nothing.
2Ti 3: 4 of the good, treacherous, rash, *c*,

CONCEITS* (CONCEIT)
Ps 73: 7 evil *c* of their minds know no

CONCEIVED (CONCEIVES)
Ps 51: 5 from the time my mother *c* me.
Mt 1: 20 what is *c* in her is from the Holy
1Co 2: 9 no mind has *c*
Jas 1: 15 after desire has *c*, it gives birth

CONCEIVES* (CONCEIVED)
Ps 7: 14 *c* trouble gives birth

CONCERN* (CONCERNED)
Ge 39: 6 he did not *c* himself with anything
39: 8 "my master does not *c* himself
1Sa 23: 21 "The LORD bless you for your *c*
2Ki 13: 23 and had compassion and showed *c*
Job 9: 21 I have no *c* for myself;
19: 4 my error remains my *c* alone.
Ps 131: 1 I do not *c* myself with great matters
Pr 29: 7 but the wicked have no such *c*.
Eze 36: 21 I had *c* for my holy name, which
Ac 15: 14 God at first showed his *c* by taking
18: 17 But Gallio showed no *c* whatever.
1Co 7: 32 I would like you to be free from *c*.
12: 25 that its parts should have equal *c*
2Co 7: 7 your deep sorrow, your ardent *c*
7: 11 what alarm, what longing, what *c*,
8: 16 of Titus the same *c* I have for you.
11: 28 of my *c* for all the churches.
Php 4: 10 at last you have renewed your *c*

CONCERNED (CONCERN)
Ex 2: 25 Israelites and was *c* about them.
Ps 142: 4 no one is *c* for me.
Jnh 4: 10 "You have been *c* about this vine,
4: 11 Should I not be *c* about that great
1Co 7: 32 An unmarried man is *c* about
9: 9 Is it about oxen that God is *c*?
Php 4: 10 you have been *c*, but you had no

CONCESSION*
1Co 7: 6 I say this as a *c*, not as a command.

CONDEMN* (CONDEMNATION CONDEMNED CONDEMNING CONDEMNS)
Job 9: 20 innocent, my mouth would *c* me;
10: 2 I will say to God: Do not *c* me,
34: 17 Will you *c* the just and mighty One
34: 29 if he remains silent, who can *c* him?
40: 8 Would you *c* me to justify yourself?
Ps 94: 21 and *c* the innocent to death.
109: 7 and may his prayers *c* him.
109: 31 from those who *c* him.
Isa 50: 9 Who is he that will *c* me?
Mt 12: 41 with this generation and *c* it;
12: 42 with this generation and *c* it;
20: 18 They will *c* him to death
Mk 10: 33 They will *c* him to death
Lk 6: 37 Do not *c*, and you will not be
11: 31 men of this generation and *c* them;
11: 32 with this generation and *c* it;
Jn 3: 17 Son into the world to *c* the world,
7: 51 "Does our law *c* anyone
8: 11 "Then neither do I *c* you,"
12: 48 very word which I spoke will *c* him
Ro 2: 27 yet obeys the law will *c* you who,
14: 3 everything must not *c* the man who
14: 22 is the man who does not *c* himself
2Co 7: 3 this to *c* you; I have said
1Jn 3: 20 presence whenever our hearts *c* us.
3: 21 if our hearts do not *c* us,

CONDEMNATION* (CONDEMN)
Jer 42: 18 of *c* and reproach; you will never
44: 12 and horror, of *c* and reproach.
Ro 3: 8 may result"? Their *c* is deserved.
5: 16 followed one sin and brought *c*,
5: 18 of one trespass was *c* for all men,
8: 1 there is now no *c* for those who are
2Pe 2: 3 Their *c* has long been hanging
Jude : 4 certain men whose *c* was written

CONDEMNED* (CONDEMN)
Dt 13: 17 of those *c* things shall be found
Job 32: 3 to refute Job, and yet had *c* him.
Ps 34: 21 the foes of the righteous will be *c*.
34: 22 will be *c* who takes refuge in him.
37: 33 let them be *c* when brought to trial.
79: 11 preserve those *c* to die.
102: 20 and release those *c* to death."
Mt 12: 7 you would not have *c* the innocent.
12: 37 and by your words you will be *c*."
23: 33 How will you escape being *c* to hell
27: 3 betrayed him, saw that Jesus was *c*,
Mk 14: 64 They all *c* him as worthy of death.
16: 16 whoever does not believe will be *c*.
Lk 6: 37 condemn, and you will not be *c*.
Jn 3: 18 Whoever believes in him is not *c*,
3: 18 does not believe stands *c* already
5: 24 has eternal life and will not be *c*;
5: 29 who have done evil will rise to be *c*.
8: 10 Has no one *c* you?" "No one, sir,"
16: 11 prince of this world now stands *c*.
Ac 25: 15 against him and asked that he be *c*.
Ro 3: 7 why am I still *c* as a sinner?"
8: 3 And so he *c* sin in sinful man,
14: 23 But the man who has doubts is *c*
1Co 4: 9 like men *c* to die in the arena.
11: 32 disciplined so that we will not be *c*
Gal 1: 8 let him be eternally *c*! As we have
1: 9 let him be eternally *c*! Am I now
2Th 2: 12 that all will be *c* who have not
Tit 2: 8 of speech that cannot be *c*,
Heb 11: 7 By his faith he *c* the world
Jas 5: 6 You have *c* and murdered innocent
5: 12 and your "No," no, or you will be *c*
2Pe 2: 6 if he *c* the cities of Sodom
Rev 19: 2 He has *c* the great prostitute

CONDEMNING* (CONDEMN)
Dt 25: 1 the innocent and *c* the guilty.
1Ki 8: 32 *c* the guilty and bringing

Pr 17: 15 the guilty and *c* the innocent—
Ac 13: 27 yet in *c* him they fulfilled the words
Ro 2: 1 judge the other, you are *c* yourself,

CONDEMNS* (CONDEMN)
Job 15: 6 Your own mouth *c* you, not mine;
Pr 12: 2 but the LORD *c* a crafty man.
Ro 8: 34 Who is he that *c*? Christ Jesus,
2Co 3: 9 the ministry that *c* men is glorious,

CONDITION
Pr 27: 23 Be sure you know the *c*

CONDUCT (CONDUCTED CONDUCTS)
Pr 10: 23 A fool finds pleasure in evil *c*,
20: 11 by whether his *c* is pure and right.
21: 8 but the *c* of the innocent is upright.
Ecc 6: 8 how to *c* himself before others?
Jer 4: 18 "Your own *c* and actions
17: 10 to reward a man according to his *c*,
Eze 7: 3 I will judge you according to your *c*
Php 1: 27 *c* yourselves in a manner worthy
1Ti 3: 15 to *c* themselves in God's household

CONDUCTED* (CONDUCT)
2Co 1: 12 testifies that we have *c* ourselves

CONDUCTS* (CONDUCT)
Ps 112: 5 who *c* his affairs with justice.

CONFESS* (CONFESSED CONFESSES CONFESSING CONFESSION)
Lev 5: 5 he must *c* in what way he has
16: 21 and *c* over it all the wickedness
26: 40 " 'But if they will *c* their sins
Nu 5: 7 must *c* the sin he has committed.
1Ki 8: 33 back to you and *c* your name,
8: 35 toward this place and *c* your name
2Ch 6: 24 they turn back and *c* your name,
6: 26 toward this place and *c* your name
Ne 1: 6 I *c* the sins we Israelites, including
Ps 32: 5 I said, "I will *c*
38: 18 I *c* my iniquity;
Jn 1: 20 fail to *c*, but confessed freely,
12: 42 they would not *c* their faith
Ro 10: 9 That if you *c* with your mouth,
10: 10 it is with your mouth that you *c*
14: 11 every tongue will *c* to God.' "
Php 2: 11 every tongue *c* that Jesus Christ is
Heb 3: 1 and high priest whom we *c*.
13: 15 the fruit of lips that *c* his name.
Jas 5: 16 Therefore *c* your sins to each other
1Jn 1: 9 If we *c* our sins, he is faithful

CONFESSED* (CONFESS)
1Sa 7: 6 day they fasted and there they *c*,
Ne 9: 2 in their places and *c* their sins
Da 9: 4 to the LORD my God and *c*:
Jn 1: 20 but *c* freely, "I am not the Christ."
Ac 19: 18 and openly *c* their evil deeds.

CONFESSES* (CONFESS)
Pr 28: 13 whoever *c* and renounces them
2Ti 2: 19 and, "Everyone who *c* the name

CONFESSING* (CONFESS)
Ezr 10: 1 While Ezra was praying and *c*,
Da 9: 20 *c* my sin and the sin
Mt 3: 6 *C* their sins, they were baptized
Mk 1: 5 *C* their sins, they were baptized

CONFESSION* (CONFESS)
Ezr 10: 11 Now make *c* to the LORD,
Ne 9: 3 and spent another quarter in *c*
2Co 9: 13 obedience that accompanies your *c*
1Ti 6: 12 called when you made your good *c*
6: 13 Pontius Pilate made the good *c*,

CONFIDENCE* (CONFIDENT)
Jdg 9: 26 and its citizens put their *c* in him.
2Ki 18: 19 On what are you basing this *c*
2Ch 32: 8 And the people gained *c*
32: 10 On what are you basing your *c*,
Job 4: 6 Should not your piety be your *c*
Ps 71: 5 my *c* since my youth.
Pr 3: 26 for the LORD will be your *c*
3: 32 but takes the upright into his *c*.
11: 13 A gossip betrays a *c*,
20: 19 A gossip betrays a *c*;
25: 9 do not betray another man's *c*,
31: 11 Her husband has full *c* in her
Isa 32: 17 will be quietness and *c* forever.
36: 4 On what are you basing this *c*
Jer 17: 7 whose *c* is in him.
49: 31 which lives in *c*,"
Eze 29: 16 a source of *c* for the people of Israel
Mic 7: 5 put no *c* in a friend.
2Co 2: 3 I had *c* in all of you, that you would
3: 4 Such *c* as this is ours
7: 4 I have great *c* in you; I take great
7: 16 I am glad I can have complete *c*
8: 22 so because of his great *c* in you.
Eph 3: 12 God with freedom and *c*.
Php 3: 3 and who put no *c* in the flesh—
3: 4 I myself have reasons for such *c*.
3: 4 reasons to put *c* in the flesh,
2Th 3: 4 We have *c* in the Lord that you are
Heb 3: 14 till the end the *c* we had at first.
4: 16 the throne of grace with *c*,
10: 19 since we have *c* to enter the Most
10: 35 So do not throw away your *c*;
13: 6 So we say with *c*,
1Jn 3: 21 we have *c* before God and receive
4: 17 us so that we will have *c* on the day
5: 14 This is the *c* we have

CONFIDENT* (CONFIDENCE)
Job 6: 20 because they had been *c*;
Ps 27: 3 even then will I be *c*.
27: 13 I am still *c* of this:
Lk 18: 9 To some who were *c*
2Co 1: 15 Because I was *c* of this, I planned
5: 6 Therefore we are always *c*
5: 8 We are *c*, I say, and would prefer
9: 4 ashamed of having been so *c*.
10: 7 If anyone is *c* that he belongs
Gal 5: 10 I am *c* in the Lord that you will
Php 1: 6 day until now, being *c* of this,
2: 24 I am *c* in the Lord that I myself will
Phm : 21 *C* of your obedience, I write to you,
Heb 6: 9 we are *c* of better things
1Jn 2: 28 that when he appears we may be *c*

CONFIDES*
Ps 25: 14 The LORD *c* in those who fear him

CONFORM* (CONFORMED CONFORMITY CONFORMS)
Ro 12: 2 Do not *c* any longer to the pattern
1Pe 1: 14 do not *c* to the evil desires you had

CONFORMED* (CONFORM)
Eze 5: 7 *c* to the standards of the nations
11: 12 but have *c* to the standards
Ro 8: 29 predestined to be *c* to the likeness

CONFORMITY* (CONFORM)
Eph 1: 11 in *c* with the purpose of his will,

CONFORMS* (CONFORM)
1Ti 1: 11 to the sound doctrine that *c*

CONQUEROR* (CONQUERORS)
Mic 1: 15 I will bring a *c* against you
Rev 6: 2 he rode out as a *c* bent on conquest.

CONQUERORS (CONQUEROR)
Ro 8: 37 than *c* through him who loved us.

CONSCIENCE* (CONSCIENCE-STRICKEN CONSCIENCES CONSCIENTIOUS)
Ge 20: 5 I have done this with a clear *c*
20: 6 I know you did this with a clear *c*,
1Sa 25: 31 have on his *c* the staggering burden
Job 27: 6 my *c* will not reproach me as long
Ac 23: 1 to God in all good *c* to this day."
24: 16 to keep my *c* clear before God
Ro 9: 1 my *c* confirms it in the Holy Spirit
13: 5 punishment but also because of *c*.
1Co 4: 4 My *c* is clear, but that does not
8: 7 since their *c* is weak, it is defiled.
8: 10 with a weak *c* sees you who have
8: 12 in this way and wound their weak *c*
10: 25 without raising questions of *c*,
10: 27 you without raising questions of *c*.
10: 28 man who told you and for *c'* sake—
10: 29 freedom be judged by another's *c*?
10: 29 the other man's *c*, I mean,
2Co 1: 12 Our *c* testifies that we have
4: 2 to every man's *c* in the sight of God
5: 11 and I hope it is also plain to your *c*.
1Ti 1: 5 and a good *c* and a sincere faith.
1: 19 holding on to faith and a good *c*.
3: 9 truths of the faith with a clear *c*.
2Ti 1: 3 as my forefathers did, with a clear *c*
Heb 9: 9 able to clear the *c* of the worshiper.
10: 22 to cleanse us from a guilty *c*
13: 18 We are sure that we have a clear *c*
1Pe 3: 16 and respect, keeping a clear *c*,
3: 21 the pledge of a good *c* toward God.

CONSCIENCE-STRICKEN* (CONSCIENCE)
1Sa 24: 5 David was *c* for having cut
2Sa 24: 10 David was *c* after he had counted

CONSCIENCES* (CONSCIENCE)
Ro 2: 15 their *c* also bearing witness,
1Ti 4: 2 whose *c* have been seared
Tit 1: 15 their minds and *c* are corrupted.
Heb 9: 14 cleanse our *c* from acts that lead

CONSCIENTIOUS* (CONSCIENCE)
2Ch 29: 34 for the Levites had been more *c*

CONSCIOUS*
Ro 3: 20 through the law we become *c* of sin
1Pe 2: 19 of unjust suffering because he is *c*

CONSECRATE (CONSECRATED)
Ex 13: 2 "*C* to me every firstborn male.
40: 9 *c* it and all its furnishings,
Lev 20: 7 " '*C* yourselves and be holy,
25: 10 *C* the fiftieth year and proclaim
1Ch 15: 12 fellow Levites are to *c* yourselves

CONSECRATED (CONSECRATE)
Ex 29: 43 and the place will be *c* by my glory.
Lev 8: 30 So he *c* Aaron and his garments
2Ch 7: 16 *c* this temple so that my Name may
Lk 2: 23 is to be *c* to the Lord"),
1Ti 4: 5 because it is *c* by the word of God

CONSENT
1Co 7: 5 except by mutual *c* and for a time,

CONSIDER (CONSIDERATE CONSIDERED CONSIDERS)
1Sa 12: 24 *c* what great things he has done
16: 7 "Do not *c* his appearance
2Ch 19: 6 "*C* carefully what you do,
Job 37: 14 stop and *c* God's wonders.
Ps 8: 3 When I *c* your heavens,
77: 12 and *c* all your mighty deeds.
107: 43 and *c* the great love of the LORD.
143: 5 and *c* what your hands have done.
Pr 6: 6 *c* its ways and be wise!
20: 25 and only later to *c* his vows.
Ecc 7: 13 *C* what God has done:
Lk 12: 24 *C* the ravens: They do not sow
12: 27 about the rest? "*C* how the lilies
Php 2: 3 but in humility *c* others better
3: 8 I *c* everything a loss compared
Heb 10: 24 And let us *c* how we may spur one
Jas 1: 2 *C* it pure joy, my brothers,

CONSIDERATE* (CONSIDER)
Tit 3: 2 to be peaceable and *c*,
Jas 3: 17 then peace-loving, *c*, submissive,
1Pe 2: 18 only to those who are good and *c*,
3: 7 in the same way be *c* as you live

CONSIDERED (CONSIDER)
Job 1: 8 "Have you *c* my servant Job?
2: 3 "Have you *c* my servant Job?
Ps 44: 22 we are *c* as sheep to be slaughtered.
Isa 53: 4 yet we *c* him stricken by God,
Ro 8: 36 we are *c* as sheep to be slaughtered

CONSIDERS (CONSIDER)
Pr 31: 16 She *c* a field and buys it;

Ro 14: 5 One man *c* one day more sacred
Jas 1: 26 If anyone *c* himself religious

CONSIST (CONSISTS)
Lk 12: 15 a man's life does not *c*

CONSISTS (CONSIST)
Eph 5: 9 fruit of the light *c* in all goodness,

CONSOLATION
Ps 94: 19 your *c* brought joy to my soul.

CONSPIRE
Ps 2: 1 Why do the nations *c*

CONSTANT
Dt 28: 66 You will live in *c* suspense,
Pr 19: 13 wife is like a *c* dripping.
27: 15 a *c* dripping on a rainy day;
Ac 27: 33 "you have been in *c* suspense
Heb 5: 14 by *c* use have trained themselves

CONSTRUCTIVE*
1Co 10: 23 but not everything is *c*.

CONSULT
Pr 15: 12 he will not *c* the wise.
Gal 1: 16 I did not *c* any man, nor did I go up

CONSUME (CONSUMES CONSUMING)
Jn 2: 17 "Zeal for your house will *c* me."

CONSUMES (CONSUME)
Ps 69: 9 for zeal for your house *c* me,

CONSUMING (CONSUME)
Dt 4: 24 For the LORD your God is a *c* fire,
Heb 12: 29 and awe, for our "God is a *c* fire."

CONTAIN* (CONTAINED CONTAINS)
1Ki 8: 27 the highest heaven, cannot *c* you.
2Ch 2: 6 the highest heavens, cannot *c* him?
6: 18 the highest heavens, cannot *c* you.
Ecc 8: 8 power over the wind to *c* it;
2Pe 3: 16 His letters *c* some things that are

CONTAINED (CONTAIN)
Heb 9: 4 This ark *c* the gold jar of manna,

CONTAINS (CONTAIN)
Pr 15: 6 of the righteous *c* great treasure,

CONTAMINATES*
2Co 7: 1 from everything that *c* body

CONTEMPT
Pr 14: 31 He who oppresses the poor shows *c*
17: 5 He who mocks the poor shows *c*
18: 3 When wickedness comes, so does *c*
Da 12: 2 others to shame and everlasting *c*.
Mal 1: 6 O priests, who show *c* for my name.
Ro 2: 4 Or do you show *c* for the riches
Gal 4: 14 you did not treat me with *c*
1Th 5: 20 do not treat prophecies with *c*.

CONTEND (CONTENDED CONTENDING CONTENTIOUS)
Ge 6: 3 "My Spirit will not *c*
Ps 35: 1 *C*, O LORD, with those who
Isa 49: 25 I will *c* with those who *c* with you,
Jude : 3 you to *c* for the faith that was once

CONTENDED (CONTEND)
Php 4: 3 help these women who have *c*

CONTENDING* (CONTEND)
Php 1: 27 *c* as one man for the faith

CONTENT* (CONTENTMENT)
Jos 7: 7 If only we had been *c* to stay
Pr 13: 25 The righteous eat to their hearts' *c*,
19: 23 one rests *c*, untouched by trouble.
Ecc 4: 8 yet his eyes were not *c*
Lk 3: 14 don't accuse people falsely—be *c*
Php 4: 11 to be *c* whatever the circumstances
4: 12 I have learned the secret of being *c*
1Ti 6: 8 and clothing, we will be *c* with that.
Heb 13: 5 and be *c* with what you have,

CONTENTIOUS* (CONTEND)
1Co 11: 16 If anyone wants to be *c* about this,

CONTENTMENT* (CONTENT)
Job 36: 11 and their years in *c*.
SS 8: 10 like one bringing *c*.

1Ti 6: 6 But godliness with *c* is great gain.

CONTEST*
Heb 10: 32 in a great *c* in the face of suffering.

CONTINUAL (CONTINUE)
Pr 15: 15 but the cheerful heart has a *c* feast.
Eph 4: 19 of impurity, with a *c* lust for more.

CONTINUE (CONTINUAL CONTINUES CONTINUING)
1Ki 8: 23 servants who *c* wholeheartedly
2Ch 6: 14 servants who *c* wholeheartedly
Ps 36: 10 *C* your love to those who know you
Ac 13: 43 urged them to *c* in the grace of God
Ro 11: 22 provided that you *c* in his kindness.
Gal 3: 10 Cursed is everyone who does not *c*
Php 2: 12 *c* to work out your salvation
Col 1: 23 if you *c* in your faith, established
2: 6 received Christ Jesus as Lord, *c*
1Ti 2: 15 if they *c* in faith, love and holiness
2Ti 3: 14 *c* in what you have learned
1Jn 2: 28 And now, dear children, *c* in him,
3: 9 born of God will *c* to sin,
5: 18 born of God does not *c* to sin;
2Jn : 9 and does not *c* in the teaching
Rev 22: 11 and let him who is holy *c* to be holy
22: 11 let him who does right *c* to do right;

CONTINUES (CONTINUE)
Ps 100: 5 *c* through all generations.
119: 90 Your faithfulness *c*
2Co 10: 15 Our hope is that, as your faith *c*
1Jn 3: 6 No one who *c* to sin has

CONTINUING (CONTINUE)
Ro 13: 8 the *c* debt to love one another,

CONTRIBUTION (CONTRIBUTIONS)
Ro 15: 26 pleased to make a *c* for the poor

CONTRIBUTIONS (CONTRIBUTION)
2Ch 24: 10 all the people brought their *c* gladly
31: 12 they faithfully brought in the *c*,

CONTRITE*
Ps 51: 17 a broken and *c* heart,
Isa 57: 15 also with him who is *c* and lowly
57: 15 and to revive the heart of the *c*.
66: 2 he who is humble and *c* in spirit,

CONTROL (CONTROLLED CONTROLS SELF-CONTROL SELF-CONTROLLED)
Pr 29: 11 a wise man keeps himself under *c*.
1Co 7: 9 But if they cannot *c* themselves,
7: 37 but has *c* over his own will,
1Th 4: 4 you should learn to *c* his own body

CONTROLLED (CONTROL)
Ps 32: 9 but must be *c* by bit and bridle
Ro 8: 6 but the mind *c* by the Spirit is life
8: 8 Those *c* by the sinful nature cannot

CONTROLS* (CONTROL)
Job 37: 15 you know how God *c* the clouds
Pr 16: 32 a man who *c* his temper

CONTROVERSIES*
Ac 26: 3 with all the Jewish customs and *c*.
1Ti 1: 4 These promote *c* rather
6: 4 He has an unhealthy interest in *c*
Tit 3: 9 But avoid foolish *c* and genealogies

CONVERSATION
Col 4: 6 Let your *c* be always full of grace,

CONVERT
1Ti 3: 6 He must not be a recent *c*,

CONVICT (CONVICTION)
Pr 24: 25 with those who *c* the guilty,
Jn 16: 8 he will *c* the world of guilt in regard
Jude : 15 and to *c* all the ungodly

CONVICTION* (CONVICT)
1Th 1: 5 the Holy Spirit and with deep *c*.

CONVINCE* (CONVINCED CONVINCING)
Ac 28: 23 and tried to *c* them about Jesus

CONVINCED* (CONVINCE)
Ge 45: 28 "I'm *c*! My son Joseph is still alive.

Lk 16: 31 will not be *c* even if someone rises
Ac 19: 26 and hear how this fellow Paul has *c*
26: 9 "I too was *c* that I ought
26: 26 I am *c* that none of this has escaped
28: 24 Some were *c* by what he said,
Ro 2: 19 if you are *c* that you are a guide
8: 38 For I am *c* that neither death
14: 5 Each one should be fully *c*
14: 14 I am fully *c* that no food is unclean
15: 14 I myself am *c*, my brothers,
1Co 14: 24 he will be *c* by all that he is a sinner
2Co 5: 14 we are *c* that one died for all,
Php 1: 25 *C* of this, I know that I will remain,
2Ti 1: 12 and am *c* that he is able
3: 14 have learned and have become *c*

CONVINCING* (CONVINCE)
Ac 1: 3 and gave many *c* proofs that he was

COOLNESS*
Pr 25: 13 Like the *c* of snow at harvest time

COPIES (COPY)
Heb 9: 23 for the *c* of the heavenly things

COPY (COPIES)
Dt 17: 18 for himself on a scroll a *c* of this law
Heb 8: 5 They serve at a sanctuary that is a *c*
9: 24 sanctuary that was only a *c*

CORBAN*
Mk 7: 11 received from me is *C*' (that is,

CORD (CORDS)
Jos 2: 18 you have tied this scarlet *c*
Ecc 4: 12 *c* of three strands is not quickly

CORDS (CORD)
Pr 5: 22 the *c* of his sin hold him fast.
Isa 54: 2 lengthen your *c*,
Hos 11: 4 them with *c* of human kindness,

CORINTH
Ac 18: 1 Paul left Athens and went to *C*.
1Co 1: 2 To the church of God in *C*,
2Co 1: 1 To the church of God in *C*,

CORNELIUS*
Roman to whom Peter preached; first Gentile Christian (Ac 10).

CORNER (CORNERS)
Ru 3: 9 "Spread the *c* of your garment
Pr 21: 9 Better to live on a *c* of the roof
25: 24 Better to live on a *c* of the roof
Ac 26: 26 because it was not done in a *c*.

CORNERS (CORNER)
Mt 6: 5 on the street *c* to be seen by men.
22: 9 Go to the street *c* and invite

CORNERSTONE* (STONE)
Job 38: 6 or who laid its *c*—
Isa 28: 16 a precious *c* for a sure foundation;
Jer 51: 26 rock will be taken from you for a *c*,
Zec 10: 4 From Judah will come the *c*,
Eph 2: 20 Christ Jesus himself as the chief *c*.
1Pe 2: 6 a chosen and precious *c*,

CORRECT* (CORRECTED CORRECTING CORRECTION CORRECTIONS CORRECTS)
Job 6: 26 Do you mean to *c* what I say,
40: 2 contends with the Almighty *c* him?
Jer 10: 24 *C* me, LORD, but only with justice
2Ti 4: 2 *c*, rebuke and encourage—

CORRECTED* (CORRECT)
Pr 29: 19 A servant cannot be *c*

CORRECTING* (CORRECT)
2Ti 3: 16 *c* and training in righteousness,

CORRECTION* (CORRECT)
Lev 26: 23 things you do not accept my *c*
Job 36: 10 He makes them listen to *c*
Pr 5: 12 How my heart spurned *c*!
10: 17 whoever ignores *c* leads others
12: 1 but he who hates *c* is stupid.
13: 18 but whoever heeds *c* is honored.
15: 5 whoever heeds *c* shows prudence.
15: 10 he who hates *c* will die.

COVET* (COVETED COVETING COVETOUS)
Ex 20: 17 You shall not *c* your neighbor's
20: 17 "You shall not *c* your neighbor's
34: 24 and no one will *c* your land
Dt 5: 21 "You shall not *c* your neighbor's
7: 25 Do not *c* the silver and gold
Mic 2: 2 They *c* fields and seize them,
Ro 7: 7 if the law had not said, "Do not *c*."
13: 9 "Do not steal," "Do not *c*,"
Jas 4: 2 *c*, but you cannot have what you

COVETED* (COVET)
Jos 7: 21 weighing fifty shekels, I *c* them
Ac 20: 33 I have not *c* anyone's silver or gold

COVETING
Ro 7: 7 what *c* really was if the law

COVETOUS* (COVET)
Ro 7: 8 in me every kind of *c* desire.

COWARDLY*
Rev 21: 8 But the *c*, the unbelieving, the vile,

COWS
Ge 41: 2 of the river there came up seven *c*,
Ex 25: 5 skins dyed red and hides of sea *c*;
Nu 4: 6 are to cover this with hides of sea *c*,
1Sa 6: 7 Hitch the *c* to the cart,

CRAFTINESS* (CRAFTY)
Job 5: 13 He catches the wise in their *c*,
1Co 3: 19 "He catches the wise in their *c*";
Eph 4: 14 and *c* of men in their deceitful

CRAFTSMAN
Pr 8: 30 Then I was the *c* at his side.

CRAFTY* (CRAFTINESS)
Ge 3: 1 the serpent was more *c* than any
1Sa 23: 22 They tell me he is very *c*.
Job 5: 12 He thwarts the plans of the *c*,
15: 5 you adopt the tongue of the *c*.
Pr 7: 10 like a prostitute and with *c* intent.
12: 2 but the LORD condemns a *c* man.
14: 17 and a *c* man is hated.
2Co 12: 16 *c* fellow that I am, I caught you

CRAVE* (CRAVED CRAVES CRAVING CRAVINGS)
Nu 11: 4 with them began to *c* other food,
Dt 12: 20 you *c* meat and say, "I would like
Pr 23: 3 Do not *c* his delicacies,
23: 6 do not *c* his delicacies;
31: 4 not for rulers to *c* beer,
Mic 7: 1 none of the early figs that I *c*.
1Pe 2: 2 newborn babies, *c* pure spiritual

CRAVED* (CRAVE)
Nu 11: 34 the people who had *c* other food.
Ps 78: 18 by demanding the food they *c*.
78: 29 for he had given them what they *c*.
78: 30 turned from the food they *c*,

CRAVES* (CRAVE)
Pr 13: 4 The sluggard *c* and gets nothing,
21: 10 The wicked man *c* evil;
21: 26 All day long he *c* for more,

CRAVING* (CRAVE)
Job 20: 20 he will have no respite from his *c*;
Ps 106: 14 In the desert they gave in to their *c*;
Pr 10: 3 but he thwarts the *c* of the wicked.
13: 2 the unfaithful have a *c* for violence.
21: 25 The sluggard's *c* will be the death
Jer 2: 24 sniffing the wind in her *c*—

CRAVINGS* (CRAVE)
Ps 10: 3 He boasts of the *c* of his heart;
Eph 2: 3 gratifying the *c* of our sinful nature
1Jn 2: 16 in the world—the *c* of sinful man,

CRAWL
Ge 3: 14 You will *c* on your belly

CREATE* (CREATED CREATES CREATING CREATION CREATOR)
Ps 51: 10 *C* in me a pure heart, O God,
Isa 4: 5 Then the LORD will *c* over all
45: 7 I bring prosperity and *c* disaster;
45: 7 I form the light and *c* darkness,
45: 18 he did not *c* it to be empty,
65: 17 "Behold, I will *c* / new heavens
65: 18 for I will *c* Jerusalem to be a delight
65: 18 forever in what I will *c*,
Jer 31: 22 The LORD will *c* a new thing
Mal 2: 10 one Father? Did not one God *c* us?
Eph 2: 15 His purpose was to *c*

CREATED* (CREATE)
Ge 1: 1 In the beginning God *c* the heavens
1: 21 God *c* the great creatures of the sea
1: 27 So God *c* man in his own image,
1: 27 in the image of God he *c* him;
1: 27 male and female he *c* them.
2: 4 and the earth when they were *c*.
5: 1 When God *c* man, he made him
5: 2 He *c* them male and female
5: 2 when they were *c*, he called them
6: 7 whom I have *c*, from the face
Dt 4: 32 from the day God *c* man
Ps 89: 12 You *c* the north and the south;
89: 47 what futility you have *c* all men!
102: 18 a people not yet *c* may praise
104: 30 you send your Spirit, / they are *c*,
139: 13 For you *c* my inmost being;
148: 5 for he commanded and they were *c*
Isa 40: 26 Who *c* all these?
41: 20 that the Holy One of Israel has *c* it.
42: 5 he who *c* the heavens and stretched
43: 1 he who *c* you, O Jacob,
43: 7 whom I *c* for my glory,
45: 8 I, the LORD, have *c* it.
45: 12 and *c* mankind upon it.
45: 18 he who *c* the heavens,
48: 7 They are *c* now, and not long ago;
54: 16 And it is I who have *c* the destroyer
54: 16 "See, it is I who *c* the blacksmith
57: 16 the breath of man that I have *c*.
Eze 21: 30 In the place where you were *c*,
28: 13 the day you were *c* they were
28: 15 ways from the day you were *c*
Mk 13: 19 when God *c* the world, until now—
Ro 1: 25 and served *c* things rather
1Co 11: 9 neither was man *c* for woman,
Eph 2: 10 *c* in Christ Jesus to do good works,
3: 9 hidden in God, who *c* all things.
4: 24 *c* to be like God in true
Col 1: 16 For by him all things were *c*:
1: 16 all things were *c* by him
1Ti 4: 3 which God *c* to be received
4: 4 For everything God *c* is good,
Heb 12: 27 *c* things—so that what cannot be
Jas 1: 18 a kind of firstfruits of all he *c*.
Rev 4: 11 and by your will they were *c*
4: 11 for you *c* all things,
10: 6 who *c* the heavens and all that is

CREATES* (CREATE)
Am 4: 13 *c* the wind,

CREATING* (CREATE)
Ge 2: 3 the work of *c* that he had done.
Isa 57: 19 *c* praise on the lips of the mourners

CREATION* (CREATE)
Hab 2: 18 he who makes it trusts in his own *c*;
Mt 13: 35 hidden since the *c* of the world."
25: 34 for you since the *c* of the world.
Mk 10: 6 of *c* God 'made them male
16: 15 and preach the good news to all *c*.
Jn 17: 24 me before the *c* of the world.
Ro 1: 20 For since the *c* of the world God's
8: 19 The *c* waits in eager expectation
8: 20 For the *c* was subjected
8: 21 in hope that the *c* itself will be
8: 22 that the whole *c* has been groaning
8: 39 depth, nor anything else in all *c*,
2Co 5: 17 he is a new *c*; the old has gone,
Gal 6: 15 anything; what counts is a new *c*.
Eph 1: 4 us in him before the *c* of the world
Col 1: 15 God, the firstborn over all *c*.
Heb 4: 3 finished since the *c* of the world.
4: 13 Nothing in all *c* is hidden
9: 11 that is to say, not a part of this *c*.
9: 26 times since the *c* of the world.
1Pe 1: 20 chosen before the *c* of the world,
2Pe 3: 4 as it has since the beginning of *c*."
Rev 3: 14 true witness, the ruler of God's *c*.
13: 8 slain from the *c* of the world.
17: 8 life from the *c* of the world will be

CREATOR* (CREATE)
Ge 14: 19 *C* of heaven and earth.
14: 22 God Most High, *C* of heaven
Dt 32: 6 Is he not your Father, your *C*,
Ecc 12: 1 Remember your *C*
Isa 27: 11 and their *C* shows them no favor.
40: 28 the *C* of the ends of the earth.
43: 15 Israel's *C*, your King."
Mt 19: 4 the beginning the *C* 'made them
Ro 1: 25 created things rather than the *C*—
Col 3: 10 in knowledge in the image of its *C*.
1Pe 4: 19 themselves to their faithful *C*

CREATURE (CREATURES)
Lev 17: 11 For the life of a *c* is in the blood,
17: 14 the life of every *c* is its blood.
Ps 136: 25 and who gives food to every *c*.
Eze 1: 15 beside each *c* with its four faces.
Rev 4: 7 The first living *c* was like a lion,

CREATURES (CREATURE)
Ge 6: 19 bring into the ark two of all living *c*,
8: 21 again will I destroy all living *c*,
Ps 104: 24 the earth is full of your *c*.
Eze 1: 5 was what looked like four living *c*.

CREDIT (CREDITED CREDITOR CREDITS)
Lk 6: 33 what *c* is that to you? Even
Ro 4: 24 to whom God will *c* righteousness
1Pe 2: 20 it to your *c* if you receive a beating

CREDITED (CREDIT)
Ge 15: 6 and he *c* it to him as righteousness.
Ps 106: 31 This was *c* to him as righteousness
Eze 18: 20 of the righteous man will be *c*
Ro 4: 3 and it was *c* to him as righteousness
4: 4 his wages are not *c* to him as a gift,
4: 5 his faith is *c* as righteousness.
4: 9 saying that Abraham's faith was *c*
4: 23 The words "it was *c*
Gal 3: 6 and it was *c* to him as righteousness
Php 4: 17 for what may be *c* to your account.
Jas 2: 23 and it was *c* to him as righteousness

CREDITOR (CREDIT)
Dt 15: 2 Every *c* shall cancel the loan he has

CREDITS (CREDIT)
Ro 4: 6 whom God *c* righteousness apart

CRETANS (CRETE)
Tit 1: 12 "*C* are always liars, evil brutes,

CRETE (CRETANS)
Ac 27: 12 harbor in *C*, facing both southwest

CRIED (CRY)
Ex 2: 23 groaned in their slavery and *c* out,
14: 10 They were terrified and *c* out
Nu 20: 16 but when we *c* out to the LORD,
Jos 24: 7 But they *c* to the LORD for help,
Jdg 3: 9 But when they *c* out to the LORD,
3: 15 Again the Israelites *c* out
4: 3 they *c* to the LORD for help.
6: 6 the Israelites that they *c* out
10: 12 Maonites oppressed you and you *c*
1Sa 7: 9 He *c* out to the LORD
12: 8 they *c* to the LORD for help,
12: 10 They *c* out to the LORD and said,
Ps 18: 6 I *c* to my God for help.

CRIMINALS
Lk 23: 32 both *c*, were also led out with him

CRIMSON
Isa 1: 18 though they are red as *c*,
63: 1 with his garments stained *c*?

CRIPPLED
2Sa 9: 3 of Jonathan; he is *c* in both feet."
Mk 9: 45 better for you to enter life *c*

CRISIS*
1Co 7: 26 of the present *c*, I think that it is

CRITICISM*
2Co 8: 20 We want to avoid any *c*

CROOKED*
Dt 32: 5 but a warped and *c* generation.
2Sa 22: 27 to the *c* you show yourself shrewd.
Ps 18: 26 to the *c* you show yourself shrewd.
125: 5 But those who turn to *c* ways
Pr 2: 15 whose paths are *c*
5: 6 her paths are *c*, but she knows it
8: 8 none of them is *c* or perverse.
10: 9 he who takes *c* paths will be found
Ecc 7: 13 what he has made *c*?
Isa 59: 8 have turned them into *c* roads;
La 3: 9 he has made my paths *c*.
Lk 3: 5 The *c* roads shall become straight,
Php 2: 15 children of God without fault in a *c*

CROP (CROPS)
Mt 13: 8 where it produced a *c*— a hundred,
21: 41 share of the *c* at harvest time."

CROPS (CROP)
Pr 3: 9 with the firstfruits of all your *c*;
10: 5 He who gathers *c* in summer is
28: 3 like a driving rain that leaves no *c*.
2Ti 2: 6 the first to receive a share of the *c*.

CROSS (CROSSED CROSSING)
Dt 4: 21 swore that I would not *c* the Jordan
12: 10 But you will *c* the Jordan
Mt 10: 38 and anyone who does not take his *c*
16: 24 and take up his *c* and follow me.
Mk 8: 34 and take up his *c* and follow me.
Lk 9: 23 take up his *c* daily and follow me.
14: 27 anyone who does not carry his *c*
Jn 19: 17 Carrying his own *c*, he went out
Ac 2: 23 to death by nailing him to the *c*.
1Co 1: 17 lest the *c* of Christ be emptied
1: 18 the message of the *c* is foolishness
Gal 5: 11 offense of the *c* has been abolished.
6: 12 persecuted for the *c* of Christ.
6: 14 in the *c* of our Lord Jesus Christ,
Eph 2: 16 both of them to God through the *c*,
Php 2: 8 even death on a *c*!
3: 18 as enemies of the *c* of Christ.
Col 1: 20 through his blood, shed on the *c*.
2: 14 he took it away, nailing it to the *c*.
2: 15 triumphing over them by the *c*.
Heb 12: 2 set before him endured the *c*,

CROSSED (CROSS)
Jos 4: 7 When it *c* the Jordan, the waters
Jn 5: 24 he has *c* over from death to life.

CROSSING (CROSS)
Ge 48: 14 he was the younger, and *c* his arms,

CROSSROADS (ROAD)
Jer 6: 16 "Stand at the *c* and look;

CROUCHING
Ge 4: 7 sin is *c* at your door; it desires

CROWD (CROWDS)
Ex 23: 2 Do not follow the *c* in doing wrong.

CROWDS (CROWD)
Mt 9: 36 he saw the *c*, he had compassion

CROWED (CROWS)
Mt 26: 74 the man!" Immediately a rooster *c*.

CROWN (CROWNED CROWNS)
Pr 4: 9 present you with a *c* of splendor."
10: 6 Blessings *c* the head
12: 4 noble character is her husband's *c*,
16: 31 Gray hair is a *c* of splendor;
17: 6 Children's children are a *c*
Isa 35: 10 everlasting joy will *c* their heads.
51: 11 everlasting joy will *c* their heads.
61: 3 to bestow on them a *c* of beauty
62: 3 You will be a *c* of splendor
Eze 16: 12 and a beautiful *c* on your head.
Zec 9: 16 like jewels in a *c*.
Mt 27: 29 and then twisted together a *c* of thorns
Mk 15: 17 then twisted together a *c* of thorns
Jn 19: 2 The soldiers twisted together a *c*
19: 5 When Jesus came out wearing the *c*
1Co 9: 25 it to get a *c* that will last forever.
9: 25 it to get a *c* that will not last;
Php 4: 1 and long for, my joy and *c*,
1Th 2: 19 or the *c* in which we will glory
2Ti 2: 5 he does not receive the victor's *c*
4: 8 store for me the *c* of righteousness,
Jas 1: 12 he will receive the *c*
1Pe 5: 4 you will receive the *c*
Rev 2: 10 and I will give you the *c* of life.
3: 11 so that no one will take your *c*.
14: 14 a son of man" with a *c* of gold

CROWNED* (CROWN)
Ps 8: 5 and *c* him with glory and honor.
Pr 14: 18 the prudent are *c* with knowledge.
SS 3: 11 crown with which his mother *c* him
Heb 2: 7 you *c* him with glory and honor
2: 9 now *c* with glory and honor

CROWNS (CROWN)
Ps 103: 4 and *c* me with love and compassion
149: 4 he *c* the humble with salvation.
Pr 11: 26 blessing *c* him who is willing to sell.
Rev 4: 4 and had *c* of gold on their heads.
4: 10 They lay their *c* before the throne
12: 3 ten horns and seven *c* on his heads.
19: 12 and on his head are many *c*.

CROWS (CROWED)
Mt 26: 34 this very night, before the rooster *c*

CRUCIFIED* (CRUCIFY)
Mt 20: 19 to be mocked and flogged and *c*.
26: 2 of Man will be handed over to be *c*
27: 26 and handed him over to be *c*.
27: 35 When they had *c* him, they divided
27: 38 Two robbers were *c* with him,
27: 44 same way the robbers who were *c*
28: 5 looking for Jesus, who was *c*.
Mk 15: 15 and handed him over to be *c*.
15: 24 And they *c* him.
15: 25 the third hour when they *c* him.
15: 27 They *c* two robbers with him,
15: 32 Those *c* with him also heaped
16: 6 for Jesus the Nazarene, who was *c*.
Lk 23: 23 insistently demanded that he be *c*,
23: 33 *c* him, along with the criminals—
24: 7 be *c* and on the third day be raised
24: 20 sentenced to death, and they *c* him;
Jn 19: 16 him over to them to be *c*.
19: 18 Here they *c* him, and with him two
19: 20 for the place where Jesus was *c* was
19: 23 When the soldiers *c* Jesus,
19: 32 of the first man who had been *c*
19: 41 At the place where Jesus was *c*,
Ac 2: 36 whom you *c*, both Lord and Christ
4: 10 whom you *c* but whom God raised
Ro 6: 6 For we know that our old self was *c*
1Co 1: 13 Is Christ divided? Was Paul *c*
1: 23 but we preach Christ *c*: a stumbling
2: 2 except Jesus Christ and him *c*.
2: 8 they would not have *c* the Lord
2Co 13: 4 to be sure, he was *c* in weakness,
Gal 2: 20 I have been *c* with Christ
3: 1 Christ was clearly portrayed as *c*.
5: 24 Christ Jesus have *c* the sinful
6: 14 which the world has been *c*
Rev 11: 8 where also their Lord was *c*.

CRUCIFY* (CRUCIFIED CRUCIFYING)
Mt 23: 34 Some of them you will kill and *c*;
27: 22 They all answered, "*C* him!" "Why
27: 23 they shouted all the louder, "*C* him
27: 31 Then they led him away to *c* him.
Mk 15: 13 "*C* him!" they shouted.
15: 14 they shouted all the louder, "*C* him
15: 20 Then they led him out to *c* him.
Lk 23: 21 they kept shouting, "*C* him! *C* him
Jn 19: 6 they shouted, "*C*! *C*!"
19: 6 "You take him and *c* him.
19: 10 either to free you or to *c* you?"
19: 15 Crucify him!" "Shall I *c* your king
19: 15 away! Take him away! *C* him!"

CRUCIFYING* (CRUCIFY)
Heb 6: 6 to their loss they are *c* the Son

CRUSH (CRUSHED)
Ge 3: 15 he will *c* your head,
Isa 53: 10 it was the LORD's will to *c* him
Ro 16: 20 The God of peace will soon *c* Satan

CRUSHED (CRUSH)
Ps 34: 18 and saves those who are *c* in spirit.
Pr 17: 22 but a *c* spirit dries up the bones.
18: 14 but a *c* spirit who can bear?
Isa 53: 5 he was *c* for our iniquities;
2Co 4: 8 not *c*; perplexed, but not in despair;

CRY (CRIED)
Ex 2: 23 *c* for help because of their slavery
Ps 5: 2 Listen to my *c* for help,
34: 15 and his ears are attentive to their *c*;
40: 1 he turned to me and heard my *c*.
130: 1 Out of the depths I *c* to you,
Pr 21: 13 to the *c* of the poor,
La 2: 18 *c* out to the Lord.
Hab 2: 11 The stones of the wall will *c* out,
Lk 19: 40 keep quiet, the stones will *c* out."

CUNNING
2Co 11: 3 deceived by the serpent's *c*,
Eph 4: 14 and by the *c* and craftiness of men

CUP
Ps 23: 5 my *c* overflows.
Isa 51: 22 from that *c*, the goblet of my wrath,
51: 22 the *c* that made you stagger;
Mt 10: 42 if anyone gives even a *c* of cold water
20: 22 "Can you drink the *c* I am going
23: 25 You clean the outside of the *c*
23: 26 First clean the inside of the *c*
26: 27 Then he took the *c*, gave thanks
26: 39 may this *c* be taken from me.
26: 42 possible for this *c* to be taken away
Mk 9: 41 anyone who gives you a *c* of water
10: 38 "Can you drink the *c* I drink
10: 39 "You will drink the *c* I drink
14: 23 Then he took the *c*, gave thanks
14: 36 Take this *c* from me.
Lk 11: 39 Pharisees clean the outside of the *c*
22: 17 After taking the *c*, he gave thanks
22: 20 after the supper he took the *c*,
22: 20 "This *c* is the new covenant
22: 42 if you are willing, take this *c*
Jn 18: 11 I not drink the *c* the Father has
1Co 10: 16 Is not the *c* of thanksgiving
10: 21 the *c* of the Lord and the *c*
11: 25 after supper he took the *c*, saying,
11: 25 "This *c* is the new covenant

CUPBEARER
Ge 40: 1 the *c* and the baker of the king
Ne 1: 11 I was *c* to the king.

CURE (CURED)
Jer 17: 9 and beyond *c*.
30: 15 your pain that has no *c*?
Hos 5: 13 But he is not able to *c* you,
Lk 9: 1 out all demons and to *c* diseases,

CURED (CURE)
Mt 11: 5 those who have leprosy are *c*,
Lk 6: 18 troubled by evil spirits were *c*,

CURSE (ACCURSED CURSED CURSES CURSING)
Ge 4: 11 Now you are under a *c*
8: 21 "Never again will I *c* the ground
12: 3 and whoever curses you I will *c*;
Dt 11: 26 before you today a blessing and a *c*
11: 28 the *c* if you disobey the commands
21: 23 hung on a tree is under God's *c*.

23: 5 turned the *c* into a blessing for you,
Job 1: 11 he will surely *c* you to your face."
2: 5 he will surely *c* you to your face."
2: 9 *C* God and die!" He replied,
Ps 109: 28 They may *c*, but you will bless;
Pr 3: 33 The LORD's *c* is on the house
24: 24 peoples will *c* him and nations
Mal 2: 2 and I will *c* your blessings.
Lk 6: 28 bless those who *c* you, pray
Ro 12: 14 persecute you; bless and do not *c*.
Gal 3: 10 on observing the law are under a *c*,
3: 13 of the law by becoming a *c* for us,
Jas 3: 9 with it we *c* men, who have been
Rev 22: 3 No longer will there be any *c*.

CURSED (CURSE)
Ge 3: 17 "*C* is the ground because of you;
Dt 27: 15 "*C* is the man who carves an image
27: 16 "*C* is the man who dishonors his
27: 17 "*C* is the man who moves his
27: 18 "*C* is the man who leads the blind
27: 19 *C* is the man who withholds justice
27: 20 "*C* is the man who sleeps
27: 21 "*C* is the man who has sexual
27: 22 "*C* is the man who sleeps
27: 23 "*C* is the man who sleeps
27: 24 "*C* is the man who kills his
27: 25 "*C* is the man who accepts a bribe
27: 26 "*C* is the man who does not uphold
Jer 17: 5 "*C* is the one who trusts in man,
Mal 1: 14 "*C* is the cheat who has
Ro 9: 3 I could wish that I myself were *c*
1Co 4: 12 When we are *c*, we bless;
12: 3 "Jesus be *c*," and no one can say,
Gal 3: 10 "*C* is everyone who does not
3: 13 *C* is everyone who is hung on a tree

CURSES (CURSE)
Ex 21: 17 "Anyone who *c* his father
Lev 20: 9 " 'If anyone *c* his father or mother,
Nu 5: 23 is to write these *c* on a scroll
Jos 8: 34 the blessings and the *c*— just
Pr 20: 20 If a man *c* his father or mother,
28: 27 to them receives many *c*.
Mt 15: 4 and 'Anyone who *c* his father
Mk 7: 10 and, 'Anyone who *c* his father

CURSING (CURSE)
Ps 109: 18 He wore *c* as his garment;
Ro 3: 14 "Their mouths are full of *c*
Jas 3: 10 the same mouth come praise and *c*.

CURTAIN
Ex 26: 31 "Make a *c* of blue, purple
26: 33 The *c* will separate the Holy Place
Mt 27: 51 At that moment the *c*
Mk 15: 38 The *c* of the temple was torn in two
Lk 23: 45 the *c* of the temple was torn in two.
Heb 6: 19 the inner sanctuary behind the *c*,
9: 3 Behind the second *c* was a room
10: 20 opened for us through the *c*,

CUSTOM
Job 1: 5 This was Job's regular *c*.
Mk 10: 1 and as was his *c*, he taught them.
Lk 4: 16 into the synagogue, as was his *c*.
Ac 17: 2 As his *c* was, Paul went

CUT
Lev 19: 27 " 'Do not *c* the hair at the sides
21: 5 of their beards or *c* their bodies.
1Ki 3: 25 "*C* the living child in two
Isa 51: 1 to the rock from which you were *c*
53: 8 For he was *c* off from the land
Da 2: 45 of the rock *c* out of a mountain,
9: 26 the Anointed One will be *c* off
Mt 3: 10 not produce good fruit will be *c*
24: 22 If those days had not been *c* short,
1Co 11: 6 for a woman to have her hair *c*

CYMBAL* (CYMBALS)
1Co 13: 1 a resounding gong or a clanging *c*.

CYMBALS (CYMBAL)
1Ch 15: 16 instruments: lyres, harps and *c*.
2Ch 5: 12 dressed in fine linen and playing *c*,
Ps 150: 5 praise him with resounding *c*.

CYRUS
Persian king who allowed exiles to return (2Ch 36:22–Ezr 1:8), to rebuild temple (Ezr 5:13–6:14), as appointed by the LORD (Isa 44:28–45:13).

DAGON
Jdg 16: 23 offer a great sacrifice to *D* their god
1Sa 5: 2 Dagon's temple and set it beside *D*.

DAMASCUS
Ac 9: 3 As he neared *D* on his journey,

DAN
1. Son of Jacob by Bilhah (Ge 30:4–6; 35:25; 46:23). Tribe of blessed (Ge 49:16–17; Dt 33:22), numbered (Nu 1:39; 26:43), allotted land (Jos 19:40–48; Eze 48:1), failed to fully possess (Jdg 1:34–35), failed to support Deborah (Jdg 5:17), possessed Laish/Dan (Jdg 18).
2. Northernmost city in Israel (Ge 14:14; Jdg 18; 20:1).

DANCE (DANCED DANCING)
Ecc 3: 4 a time to mourn and a time to *d*,
Mt 11: 17 and you did not *d*;

DANCED (DANCE)
2Sa 6: 14 *d* before the LORD
Mk 6: 22 of Herodias came in and *d*,

DANCING (DANCE)
Ps 30: 11 You turned my wailing into *d*;
149: 3 Let them praise his name with *d*

DANGER
Pr 22: 3 A prudent man sees *d*
27: 12 The prudent see *d* and take refuge,
Mt 5: 22 will be in *d* of the fire of hell.
Ro 8: 35 famine or nakedness or *d* or sword?
2Co 11: 26 I have been in *d* from rivers,

DANIEL
1. Hebrew exile to Babylon, name changed to Belteshazzar (Da 1:6–7). Refused to eat unclean food (Da 1:8–21). Interpreted Nebuchadnezzar's dreams (Da 2; 4), writing on the wall (Da 5). Thrown into lion's den (Da 6). Visions of (Da 7–12).
2. Son of David (1Ch 3:1).

DARIUS
1. King of Persia (Ezr 4:5), allowed rebuilding of temple (Ezr 5–6).
2. Mede who conquered Babylon (Da 5:31).

DARK (DARKENED DARKENS DARKNESS)
Job 34: 22 There is no *d* place, no deep
Ps 18: 9 *d* clouds were under his feet.
Pr 31: 15 She gets up while it is still *d*;
SS 1: 6 Do not stare at me because I am *d*,
Jn 12: 35 in the *d* does not know where he is
Ro 2: 19 a light for those who are in the *d*,
2Pe 1: 19 as to a light shining in a *d* place,

DARKENED (DARK)
Joel 2: 10 the sun and moon are *d*,
Mt 24: 29 " 'the sun will be *d*,
Ro 1: 21 and their foolish hearts were *d*.
Eph 4: 18 They are *d* in their understanding

DARKENS (DARK)
Job 38: 2 "Who is this that *d* my counsel

DARKNESS (DARK)
Ge 1: 2 *d* was over the surface of the deep,
1: 4 he separated the light from the *d*.
Ex 10: 22 and total *d* covered all Egypt
20: 21 approached the thick *d* where God
2Sa 22: 29 the LORD turns my *d* into light.
Ps 18: 28 my God turns my *d* into light.
91: 6 the pestilence that stalks in the *d*,
112: 4 Even in *d* light dawns
139: 12 even the *d* will not be dark to you;
Pr 4: 19 the way of the wicked is like deep *d*
Isa 5: 20 and light for *d*,
42: 16 I will turn the *d* into light
45: 7 I form the light and create *d*,
58: 10 then your light will rise in the *d*,
61: 1 and release from *d*,
Joel 2: 31 The sun will be turned to *d*
Mt 4: 16 the people living in *d*
6: 23 how great is that *d*! "No one can
Lk 11: 34 are bad, your body also is full of *d*.
23: 44 and *d* came over the whole land
Jn 1: 5 The light shines in the *d*,
3: 19 but men loved *d* instead of light
Ac 2: 20 The sun will be turned to *d*
2Co 4: 6 who said, "Let light shine out of *d*
6: 14 fellowship can light have with *d*?
Eph 5: 8 For you were once *d*, but now you
5: 11 to do with the fruitless deeds of *d*,
1Pe 2: 9 out of *d* into his wonderful light.
2Pe 2: 17 Blackest *d* is reserved for them.
1Jn 1: 5 in him there is no *d* at all.
2: 9 but hates his brother is still in the *d*.
Jude : 6 in *d*, bound with everlasting chains
: 13 for whom blackest *d* has been

DASH
Ps 2: 9 you will *d* them to pieces like

DAUGHTER (DAUGHTERS)
Ex 1: 10 she took him to Pharaoh's *d*
Jdg 11: 40 to commemorate the *d* of Jephthah
Est 2: 7 Mordecai had taken her as his own *d*
Ps 9: 14 praises in the gates of the *D* of Zion
137: 8 O *D* of Babylon, doomed
Isa 62: 11 "Say to the *D* of Zion,
Zec 9: 9 Shout, *D* of Jerusalem!
Mk 5: 34 "*D*, your faith has healed you.
7: 29 the demon has left your *d*.

DAUGHTERS (DAUGHTER)
Ge 6: 2 the *d* of men were beautiful,
19: 36 Lot's *d* became pregnant
Nu 36: 10 Zelophehad's *d* did as the LORD
Joel 2: 28 sons and *d* will prophesy,

DAVID
Son of Jesse (Ru 4:17–22; 1Ch 2:13–15), ancestor of Jesus (Mt 1:1–17; Lk 3:31). Wives and children (1Sa 18; 25:39–44; 2Sa 3:2–5; 5:13–16; 11:27; 1Ch 3:1–9).
Anointed king by Samuel (1Sa 16:1–13). Musician to Saul (1Sa 16:14–23; 18:10). Killed Goliath (1Sa 17). Relation with Jonathan (1Sa 18:1–4; 19–20; 23:16–18; 2Sa 1). Disfavor of Saul (1Sa 18:6–23:29). Spared Saul's life (1Sa 24; 26). Among Philistines (1Sa 21:10–14; 27–30). Lament for Saul and Jonathan (2Sa 1).
Anointed king of Judah (2Sa 2:1–11). Conflict with house of Saul (2Sa 2–4). Anointed king of Israel (2Sa 5:1–4; 1Ch 11:1–3). Conquered Jerusalem (2Sa 5:6–10; 1Ch 11:4–9). Brought ark to Jerusalem (2Sa 6; 1Ch 13; 15–16). The LORD promised eternal dynasty (2Sa 7; 1Ch 17; Ps 132). Showed kindness to Mephibosheth (2Sa 9). Adultery with Bathsheba, murder of Uriah (2Sa 11–12). Son Amnon raped daughter Tamar; killed by Absalom (2Sa 13). Absalom's revolt (2Sa 14–17); death (2Sa 18). Sheba's revolt (2Sa 20). Victories: Philistines (2Sa 5:17–25; 1Ch 14:8–17; 2Sa 21:15–22; 1Ch 20:4–8), Ammonites (2Sa 10; 1Ch 19), various (2Sa 8; 1Ch 18). Mighty men (2Sa 23:8–39; 1Ch 11–12). Punished for numbering army (2Sa 24; 1Ch 21). Appointed Solomon king (1Ki 1:28–2:9). Prepared for building of temple (1Ch 22–29). Last words (2Sa 23:1–7). Death (1Ki 2:10–12; 1Ch 29:28).
Psalmist (Mt 22:43–45), musician (Am 6:5), prophet (2Sa 23:2–7; Ac 1:16; 2:30).
Psalms of: 2 (Ac 4:25), 3–32, 34–41, 51–65, 68–70, 86, 95 (Heb 4:7), 101, 103, 108–110, 122, 124, 131, 133, 138–145.

DAWN (DAWNED DAWNS)
Ps 37: 6 your righteousness shine like the *d*,
Pr 4: 18 is like the first gleam of *d*,
Isa 14: 12 O morning star, son of the *d*!
Am 4: 13 he who turns *d* to darkness,
5: 8 who turns blackness into *d*

DAWNED (DAWN)
Isa 9: 2 a light has *d*.

Mt 4: 16 a light has *d.*"

DAWNS* (DAWN)
Ps 65: 8 where morning *d* and evening
112: 4 in darkness light *d* for the upright,
Hos 10: 15 When that day *d,*
2Pe 1: 19 until the day *d* and the morning

DAY (DAYS)
Ge 1: 5 God called the light "*d,*"
1: 5 and there was morning—the first *d*
1: 8 there was morning—the second *d.*
1: 13 there was morning—the third *d.*
1: 19 there was morning—the fourth *d.*
1: 23 there was morning—the fifth *d.*
1: 31 there was morning—the sixth *d.*
2: 2 so on the seventh *d* he rested
8: 22 *d* and night
Ex 16: 30 the people rested on the seventh *d.*
20: 8 "Remember the Sabbath *d*
Lev 16: 30 on this *d* atonement will be made
23: 28 because it is the *D* of Atonement,
Nu 14: 14 before them in a pillar of cloud by *d*
Jos 1: 8 meditate on it *d* and night,
2Ki 7: 9 This is a *d* of good news
25: 30 *D* by *d* the king gave Jehoiachin
1Ch 16: 23 proclaim his salvation *d* after *d.*
Ne 8: 18 *D* after *d,* from the first *d*
Ps 84: 10 Better is one *d* in your courts
96: 2 proclaim his salvation *d* after *d.*
118: 24 This is the *d* the LORD has made;
Pr 27: 1 not know what a *d* may bring forth.
Isa 13: 9 a cruel *d,* with wrath and fierce
Jer 46: 10 But that *d* belongs to the Lord,
50: 31 "for your *d* has come,
Eze 30: 2 "Alas for that *d!*"
Joel 1: 15 "Alas for that *d!*
2: 31 and dreadful *d* of the LORD.
Am 3: 14 On the *d* I punish Israel for her sins
5: 20 Will not the *d* of the LORD be
Ob : 15 "The *d* of the LORD is near
Zep 1: 14 The great *d* of the LORD is near—
Zec 2: 11 joined with the LORD in that *d*
14: 1 A *d* of the LORD is coming
14: 7 It will be a unique *d,*
Mal 4: 5 dreadful *d* of the LORD comes.
Mt 24: 38 up to the *d* Noah entered the ark;
Lk 11: 3 Give us each *d* our daily bread.
17: 24 in his *d* will be like the lightning,
Ac 5: 42 *D* after *d,* in the temple courts
17: 11 examined the Scriptures every *d*
17: 17 as in the marketplace *d* by *d*
Ro 14: 5 man considers every *d* alike.
1Co 5: 5 his spirit saved on the *d* of the Lord
2Co 4: 16 we are being renewed *d* by *d.*
11: 25 I spent a night and a *d*
1Th 5: 2 for you know very well that the *d*
5: 4 so that this *d* should surprise you
2Th 2: 2 saying that the *d* of the Lord has
Heb 7: 27 need to offer sacrifices *d* after *d,*
2Pe 3: 8 With the Lord a *d* is like
3: 10 *d* of the Lord will come like a thief.
Rev 6: 17 For the great *d* of their wrath has
16: 14 on the great *d* of God Almighty.

DAYS (DAY)
Dt 17: 19 he is to read it all the *d* of his life
32: 7 Remember the *d* of old;
Ps 23: 6 all the *d* of my life,
34: 12 and desires to see many good *d,*
39: 5 have made my *d* a mere
90: 10 The length of our *d* is seventy years
90: 12 Teach us to number our *d* aright,
103: 15 As for man, his *d* are like grass,
128: 5 all the *d* of your life;
Pr 31: 12 all the *d* of her life.
Ecc 9: 9 all the *d* of this meaningless life
12: 1 Creator in the *d* of your youth,
Isa 38: 20 all the *d* of our lives
Da 7: 9 and the Ancient of *D* took his seat.
7: 13 He approached the Ancient of *D*
7: 22 until the Ancient of *D* came
Hos 3: 5 and to his blessings in the last *d.*
Joel 2: 29 I will pour out my Spirit in those *d.*
Mic 4: 1 In the last *d*
Lk 19: 43 The *d* will come upon you
Ac 2: 17 by the prophet Joel: " 'In the last *d,*
2Ti 3: 1 will be terrible times in the last *d.*
Heb 1: 2 in these last *d* he has spoken to us
2Pe 3: 3 that in the last *d* scoffers will come,

DAZZLING*
Da 2: 31 *d* statue, awesome in appearance.
Mk 9: 3 His clothes became *d* white,

DEACON* (DEACONS)
1Ti 3: 12 A *d* must be the husband of

DEACONS* (DEACON)
Php 1: 1 together with the overseers and *d:*
1Ti 3: 8 *D,* likewise, are to be men worthy
3: 10 against them, let them serve as *d.*

DEAD (DIE)
Lev 17: 15 who eats anything found *d*
Dt 18: 11 or spiritist or who consults the *d.*
Isa 8: 19 Why consult the *d* on behalf
Mt 8: 22 and let the *d* bury their own *d.*"
28: 7 'He has risen from the *d*
Lk 15: 24 For this son of mine was *d*
24: 46 rise from the *d* on the third day,
Ro 6: 11 count yourselves *d* to sin
1Co 15: 29 do who are baptized for the *d?*
Eph 2: 1 you were *d* in your transgressions
1Th 4: 16 and the *d* in Christ will rise first.
Jas 2: 17 is not accompanied by action, is *d.*
2: 26 so faith without deeds is *d.*
Rev 14: 13 Blessed are the *d* who die
20: 12 And I saw the *d,* great and small,

DEADENED* (DIE)
Jn 12: 40 and *d* their hearts,

DEAR* (DEARER)
2Sa 1: 26 you were very *d* to me.
Ps 102: 14 For her stones are *d*
Jer 31: 20 Is not Ephraim my *d* son,
Jn 2: 4 "*D* woman, why do you involve me
19: 26 he said to his mother, "*D* woman,
Ac 15: 25 to you with our *d* friends Barnabas
Ro 16: 5 Greet my *d* friend Epenetus,
16: 9 in Christ, and my *d* friend Stachys.
16: 12 Greet my *d* friend Persis, another
1Co 4: 14 but to warn you, as my *d* children.
10: 14 my *d* friends, flee from idolatry.
15: 58 Therefore, my *d* brothers,
2Co 7: 1 we have these promises, *d* friends,
12: 19 and everything we do, *d* friends,
Gal 4: 19 My *d* children, for whom I am
Eph 6: 21 the *d* brother and faithful servant
Php 2: 12 my *d* friends, as you have always
4: 1 firm in the Lord, *d* friends!
Col 1: 7 Epaphras, our *d* fellow servant,
4: 7 He is a *d* brother, a faithful
4: 9 our faithful and *d* brother,
4: 14 Our *d* friend Luke, the doctor,
1Th 2: 8 because you had become so *d* to us.
1Ti 6: 2 their service are believers, and *d*
2Ti 1: 2 To Timothy, my *d* son: Grace,
Phm : 1 To Philemon our *d* friend
: 16 He is very *d* to me but
: 16 better than a slave, as a *d* brother.
Heb 6: 9 we speak like this, *d* friends,
Jas 1: 16 Don't be deceived, my *d* brothers.
1: 19 My *d* brothers, take note of this:
2: 5 thoughts? Listen, my *d* brothers:
1Pe 2: 11 *D* friends, I urge you, as aliens
4: 12 *D* friends, do not be surprised
2Pe 3: 1 *D* friends, this is now my second
3: 8 not forget this one thing, *d* friends:
3: 14 *d* friends, since you are looking
3: 15 just as our *d* brother Paul
3: 17 *d* friends, since you already know
1Jn 2: 1 My *d* children, I write this to you
2: 7 *D* friends, I am not writing you
2: 12 I write to you, *d* children,
2: 13 I write to you, *d* children,
2: 18 *D* children, this is the last hour;
2: 28 *d* children, continue in him,
3: 2 *D* friends, now we are children
3: 7 *D* children, do not let anyone lead
3: 18 love of God be in him? *D* children,
3: 21 *D* friends, if our hearts do not
4: 1 *D* friends, do not believe every
4: 4 *d* children, are from God
4: 7 *D* friends, let us love one another,
4: 11 *D* friends, since God so loved us,
5: 21 *D* children, keep yourselves
2Jn : 5 *d* lady, I am not writing you a new
3Jn : 1 The elder, To my *d* friend Gaius,
: 2 *D* friend, I pray that you may enjoy
: 5 *D* friend, you are faithful
: 11 *D* friend, do not imitate what is evil
Jude : 3 *D* friends, although I was very
: 17 But, *d* friends, remember what
: 20 *d* friends, build yourselves up

DEARER* (DEAR)
Phm : 16 dear to me but even *d* to you,

DEATH (DIE)
Ex 21: 12 kills him shall surely be put to *d.*
Nu 35: 16 the murderer shall be put to *d.*
Dt 30: 19 set before you life and *d,*
Ru 1: 17 if anything but *d* separates you
2Ki 4: 40 O man of God, there is *d* in the pot
Job 26: 6 *D* is naked before God;
Ps 23: 4 the valley of the shadow of *d,*
44: 22 for your sake we face *d* all day long
89: 48 What man can live and not see *d,*
116: 15 is the *d* of his saints.
Pr 8: 36 all who hate me love *d.*"
11: 19 he who pursues evil goes to his *d.*
14: 12 but in the end it leads to *d.*
15: 11 *D* and Destruction lie open
16: 25 but in the end it leads to *d.*
18: 21 tongue has the power of life and *d,*
19: 18 do not be a willing party to his *d.*
23: 14 and save his soul from *d.*
Ecc 7: 2 for *d* is the destiny of every man;
Isa 25: 8 he will swallow up *d* forever.
53: 12 he poured out his life unto *d,*
Eze 18: 23 pleasure in the *d* of the wicked?
18: 32 pleasure in the *d* of anyone,
33: 11 pleasure in the *d* of the wicked,
Hos 13: 14 Where, O *d,* are your plagues?
Jn 5: 24 he has crossed over from *d* to life.
Ro 4: 25 delivered over to *d* for our sins
5: 12 and in this way *d* came to all men,
5: 14 *d* reigned from the time of Adam
6: 3 Jesus were baptized into his *d?*
6: 23 For the wages of sin is *d,*
7: 24 me from this body of *d?*
8: 13 put to *d* the misdeeds of the body,
8: 36 your sake we face *d* all day long;
1Co 15: 21 For since *d* came through a man,
15: 26 The last enemy to be destroyed is *d*
15: 55 Where, O *d,* is your sting?"
2Ti 1: 10 who has destroyed *d* and has
Heb 2: 14 him who holds the power of *d*—
1Jn 5: 16 There is a sin that leads to *d.*
Rev 1: 18 And I hold the keys of *d* and Hades
2: 11 hurt at all by the second *d.*
20: 6 The second *d* has no power
20: 14 The lake of fire is the second *d.*
20: 14 Then *d* and Hades were thrown
21: 4 There will be no more *d*
21: 8 This is the second *d.*"

DEBAUCHERY*
Ro 13: 13 not in sexual immorality and *d,*
2Co 12: 21 and *d* in which they have indulged.
Gal 5: 19 impurity and *d;* idolatry
Eph 5: 18 drunk on wine, which leads to *d.*
1Pe 4: 3 living in *d,* lust, drunkenness,

DEBORAH*
1. Prophetess who led Israel to victory over Canaanites (Jdg 4–5).

2. Rebekah's nurse (Ge 35:8).

DEBT* (DEBTOR DEBTORS DEBTS)
Dt 15: 3 must cancel any *d* your brother
24: 6 the upper one—as security for a *d*,
1Sa 22: 2 or in *d* or discontented gathered
Job 24: 9 of the poor is seized for a *d*.
Mt 18: 25 that he had be sold to repay the *d*.
18: 27 canceled the *d* and let him go.
18: 30 into prison until he could pay the *d*.
18: 32 'I canceled all that *d* of yours
Lk 7: 43 who had the bigger *d* canceled."
Ro 13: 8 Let no *d* remain outstanding,
13: 8 continuing *d* to love one another,

DEBTOR* (DEBT)
Isa 24: 2 for *d* as for creditor.

DEBTORS* (DEBT)
Hab 2: 7 Will not your *d* suddenly arise?
Mt 6: 12 as we also have forgiven our *d*.
Lk 16: 5 called in each one of his master's *d*.

DEBTS* (DEBT)
Dt 15: 1 seven years you must cancel *d*.
15: 2 time for canceling *d* has been
15: 9 the year for canceling *d*, is near,"
31: 10 in the year for canceling *d*,
2Ki 4: 7 "Go, sell the oil and pay your *d*.
Ne 10: 31 the land and will cancel all *d*.
Pr 22: 26 or puts up security for *d*;
Mt 6: 12 Forgive us our *d*,
Lk 7: 42 so he canceled the *d* of both.

DECAY*
Ps 16: 10 will you let your Holy One see *d*.
49: 9 and not see *d*.
49: 14 their forms will *d* in the grave,
Pr 12: 4 a disgraceful wife is like *d*
Isa 5: 24 so their roots will *d*
Hab 3: 16 *d* crept into my bones,
Ac 2: 27 will you let your Holy One see *d*.
2: 31 to the grave, nor did his body see *d*.
13: 34 never to *d*, is stated in these words:
13: 35 will not let your Holy One see *d*.'
13: 37 raised from the dead did not see *d*.
Ro 8: 21 liberated from its bondage to *d*

DECEIT (DECEIVE)
Ps 5: 9 with their tongue they speak *d*.
Isa 53: 9 nor was any *d* in his mouth.
Da 8: 25 He will cause *d* to prosper,
Zep 3: 13 nor will *d* be found in their mouths.
Mk 7: 22 greed, malice, *d*, lewdness, envy,
Ac 13: 10 You are full of all kinds of *d*
Ro 1: 29 murder, strife, *d* and malice.
3: 13 their tongues practice *d*."
1Pe 2: 1 yourselves of all malice and all *d*,
2: 22 and no *d* was found in his mouth."

DECEITFUL (DECEIVE)
Jer 17: 9 The heart is *d* above all things
Hos 10: 2 Their heart is *d*,
2Co 11: 13 men are false apostles, *d* workmen,
Eph 4: 14 of men in their *d* scheming.
4: 22 is being corrupted by its *d* desires;
1Pe 3: 10 and his lips from *d* speech.
Rev 21: 27 who does what is shameful or *d*,

DECEITFULNESS* (DECEIVE)
Ps 119:118 for their *d* is in vain.
Mt 13: 22 and the *d* of wealth choke it,
Mk 4: 19 the *d* of wealth and the desires
Heb 3: 13 of you may be hardened by sin's *d*.

DECEIVE (DECEIT DECEITFUL DECEITFULNESS DECEIVED DECEIVER DECEIVERS DECEIVES DECEIVING DECEPTION DECEPTIVE)
Lev 19: 11 " 'Do not *d* one another.
Pr 14: 5 A truthful witness does not *d*,
24: 28 or use your lips to *d*.
Jer 37: 9 Do not *d* yourselves, thinking,
Zec 13: 4 garment of hair in order to *d*.
Mt 24: 5 'I am the Christ,' and will *d* many.
24: 11 will appear and *d* many people.
24: 24 and miracles to *d* even the elect—
Mk 13: 6 'I am he,' and will *d* many.
13: 22 and miracles to *d* the elect—
Ro 16: 18 and flattery they *d* the minds
1Co 3: 18 Do not *d* yourselves.
Eph 5: 6 Let no one *d* you with empty words
Col 2: 4 this so that no one may *d* you
2Th 2: 3 Don't let anyone *d* you in any way,
Jas 1: 22 to the word, and so *d* yourselves.
1Jn 1: 8 we *d* ourselves and the truth is not
Rev 20: 8 and will go out to *d* the nations

DECEIVED (DECEIVE)
Ge 3: 13 "The serpent *d* me, and I ate."
Lk 21: 8 "Watch out that you are not *d*.
1Co 6: 9 the kingdom of God? Do not be *d*:
2Co 11: 3 Eve was *d* by the serpent's cunning
Gal 6: 7 Do not be *d*: God cannot be
1Ti 2: 14 And Adam was not the one *d*;
2Ti 3: 13 to worse, deceiving and being *d*.
Tit 3: 3 *d* and enslaved by all kinds
Jas 1: 16 Don't be *d*, my dear brothers.
Rev 13: 14 he *d* the inhabitants of the earth.
20: 10 And the devil, who *d* them,

DECEIVER (DECEIVE)
Mt 27: 63 while he was still alive that *d* said,
2Jn : 7 Any such person is the *d*

DECEIVERS* (DECEIVE)
Ps 49: 5 when wicked *d* surround me—
Tit 1: 10 and *d*, especially those
2Jn : 7 Many *d*, who do not acknowledge

DECEIVES (DECEIVE)
Pr 26: 19 is a man who *d* his neighbor
Mt 24: 4 "Watch out that no one *d* you.
Mk 13: 5 "Watch out that no one *d* you.
Gal 6: 3 when he is nothing, he *d* himself.
2Th 2: 10 sort of evil that *d* those who are
Jas 1: 26 he *d* himself and his religion is

DECEIVING* (DECEIVE)
Lev 6: 2 by *d* his neighbor about something
1Ti 4: 1 follow *d* spirits and things taught
2Ti 3: 13 go from bad to worse, *d*
Rev 20: 3 him from *d* the nations anymore

DECENCY* (DECENTLY)
1Ti 2: 9 women to dress modestly, with *d*

DECENTLY* (DECENCY)
Ro 13: 13 Let us behave *d*, as in the daytime,

DECEPTION (DECEIVE)
Pr 14: 8 but the folly of fools is *d*.
26: 26 His malice may be concealed by *d*,
Mt 27: 64 This last *d* will be worse
2Co 4: 2 we do not use *d*, nor do we distort

DECEPTIVE (DECEIVE)
Pr 11: 18 The wicked man earns *d* wages,
31: 30 Charm is *d*, and beauty is fleeting;
Jer 7: 4 Do not trust in *d* words and say,
Col 2: 8 through hollow and *d* philosophy,

DECIDED (DECISION)
2Co 9: 7 man should give what he has *d*

DECISION (DECIDED)
Ex 28: 29 heart on the breastpiece of *d*
Joel 3: 14 multitudes in the valley of *d*!

DECLARE (DECLARED DECLARING)
1Ch 16: 24 *D* his glory among the nations,
Ps 19: 1 The heavens *d* the glory of God;
96: 3 *D* his glory among the nations,
Isa 42: 9 and new things I *d*;

DECLARED (DECLARE)
Mk 7: 19 Jesus *d* all foods "clean.")
Ro 2: 13 the law who will be *d* righteous.
3: 20 no one will be *d* righteous

DECLARING (DECLARE)
Ps 71: 8 *d* your splendor all day long.
Ac 2: 11 we hear them *d* the wonders

DECREE (DECREED DECREES)
Ex 15: 25 There the LORD made a *d*
1Ch 16: 17 He confirmed it to Jacob as a *d*,
Ps 2: 7 I will proclaim the *d* of the LORD:
7: 6 Awake, my God; *d* justice.
81: 4 this is a *d* for Israel,
148: 6 he gave a *d* that will never pass
Da 4: 24 and this is the *d* the Most High has
Lk 2: 1 Augustus issued a *d* that a census
Ro 1: 32 know God's righteous *d* that those

DECREED (DECREE)
Ps 78: 5 He *d* statutes for Jacob
Jer 40: 2 LORD your God *d* this disaster
La 3: 37 happen if the Lord has not *d* it?
Da 9: 24 "Seventy 'sevens' are *d*
9: 26 and desolations have been *d*.
Lk 22: 22 Son of Man will go as it has been *d*,

DECREES (DECREE)
Ge 26: 5 my commands, my *d* and my laws
Ex 15: 26 to his commands and keep all his *d*,
18: 16 inform them of God's *d* and laws."
18: 20 Teach them the *d* and laws,
Lev 10: 11 Israelites all the *d* the LORD has
18: 4 and be careful to follow my *d*.
18: 5 Keep my *d* and laws,
18: 26 you must keep my *d* and my laws.
Ps 119: 12 teach me your *d*.
119: 16 I delight in your *d*;
119: 48 and I meditate on your *d*.
119:112 My heart is set on keeping your *d*

DEDICATE (DEDICATED DEDICATION)
Nu 6: 12 He must *d* himself to the LORD
Pr 20: 25 for a man to *d* something rashly

DEDICATED (DEDICATE)
Lev 21: 12 he has been *d* by the anointing oil
Nu 6: 9 thus defiling the hair he has *d*,
6: 18 shave off the hair that he *d*.
18: 6 *d* to the LORD to do the work
1Ki 8: 63 and all the Israelites *d* the temple
2Ch 29: 31 "You have now *d* yourselves
Ne 3: 1 They *d* it and set its doors in place,

DEDICATION (DEDICATE)
Nu 6: 19 shaved off the hair of his *d*,
Jn 10: 22 came the Feast of *D* at Jerusalem.
1Ti 5: 11 sensual desires overcome their *d*

DEED (DEEDS)
Jer 32: 10 and sealed the *d*, had it witnessed,
32: 16 After I had given the *d* of purchase
Col 3: 17 you do, whether in word or *d*,
2Th 2: 17 and strengthen you in every good *d*

DEEDS (DEED)
Dt 3: 24 or on earth who can do the *d*
4: 34 or by great and awesome *d*,
34: 12 the awesome *d* that Moses
1Sa 2: 3 and by him *d* are weighed.
1Ch 16: 24 his marvelous *d* among all peoples.
Job 34: 25 Because he takes note of their *d*,
Ps 26: 7 and telling of all your wonderful *d*.
45: 4 right hand display awesome *d*.
65: 5 with awesome *d* of righteousness,
66: 3 "How awesome are your *d*!
71: 17 day I declare your marvelous *d*.
72: 18 who alone does marvelous *d*.
73: 28 I will tell of all your *d*.
75: 1 men tell of your wonderful *d*.
77: 11 I will remember the *d* of the LORD
77: 12 and consider all your mighty *d*.
78: 4 the praiseworthy *d* of the LORD,
78: 7 and would not forget his *d*
86: 8 no *d* can compare with yours.
86: 10 you are great and do marvelous *d*;
88: 12 or your righteous *d* in the land
90: 16 May your *d* be shown
92: 4 For you make me glad by your *d*,
96: 3 his marvelous *d* among all peoples.
107: 8 and his wonderful *d* for men,
107: 15 and his wonderful *d* for men,
107: 21 and his wonderful *d* for men.
107: 24 his wonderful *d* in the deep.

107: 31 and his wonderful *d* for men.
111: 3 Glorious and majestic are his *d,*
145: 6 and I will proclaim your great *d.*
Jer 32: 19 purposes and mighty are your *d.*
Hab 3: 2 I stand in awe of your *d,* O LORD.
Mt 5: 16 that they may see your good *d*
Lk 1: 51 He has performed mighty *d*
23: 41 we are getting what our *d* deserve.
Ac 26: 20 prove their repentance by their *d.*
1Ti 6: 18 rich in good *d,* and to be generous
Heb 10: 24 on toward love and good *d.*
Jas 2: 14 claims to have faith but has no *d?*
2: 18 Show me your faith without *d,*
2: 20 faith without *d* is useless?
2: 26 so faith without *d* is dead.
1Pe 2: 12 they may see your good *d*
Rev 2: 19 I know your *d,* your love and faith,
2: 23 each of you according to your *d.*
3: 1 I know your *d;* you have
3: 2 I have not found your *d* complete
3: 8 I know your *d.*
3: 15 I know your *d,* that you are neither
14: 13 for their *d* will follow them."
15: 3 "Great and marvelous are your *d,*

DEEP (DEPTH DEPTHS)
Ge 1: 2 was over the surface of the *d,*
8: 2 Now the springs of the *d*
Ps 42: 7 *D* calls to *d*
Lk 5: 4 to Simon, "Put out into *d* water,
1Co 2: 10 all things, even the *d* things
1Ti 3: 9 hold of the *d* truths of the faith

DEER
Ps 42: 1 As the *d* pants for streams of water,

DEFAMED*
Isa 48: 11 How can I let myself be *d?*

DEFEATED
1Co 6: 7 have been completely *d* already.

DEFEND (DEFENDED DEFENDER DEFENDING DEFENDS DEFENSE)
Ps 72: 4 He will *d* the afflicted
74: 22 Rise up, O God, and *d* your cause;
82: 2 "How long will you *d* the unjust
82: 3 *D* the cause of the weak
119:154 *D* my cause and redeem me;
Pr 31: 9 *d* the rights of the poor and needy
Isa 1: 17 *D* the cause of the fatherless,
1: 23 They do not *d* the cause
Jer 5: 28 they do not *d* the rights of the poor.
50: 34 He will vigorously *d* their cause

DEFENDED (DEFEND)
Jer 22: 16 He *d* the cause of the poor

DEFENDER (DEFEND)
Ex 22: 2 the *d* is not guilty of bloodshed;
Ps 68: 5 to the fatherless, a *d* of widows,
Pr 23: 11 for their *D* is strong;

DEFENDING (DEFEND)
Ps 10: 18 *d* the fatherless and the oppressed,
Ro 2: 15 now accusing, now even *d* them.)
Php 1: 7 or *d* and confirming the gospel,

DEFENDS* (DEFEND)
Dt 10: 18 He *d* the cause of the fatherless
33: 7 With his own hands he *d* his cause.
Isa 51: 22 your God, who *d* his people:

DEFENSE (DEFEND)
Ps 35: 23 Awake, and rise to my *d!*
Php 1: 16 here for the *d* of the gospel.
1Jn 2: 1 speaks to the Father in our *d*—

DEFERRED*
Pr 13: 12 Hope *d* makes the heart sick,

DEFIED
1Sa 17: 45 armies of Israel, whom you have *d.*
1Ki 13: 26 the man of God who *d* the word

DEFILE (DEFILED)
Da 1: 8 Daniel resolved not to *d* himself
Rev 14: 4 are those who did not *d* themselves

DEFILED (DEFILE)
Isa 24: 5 The earth is *d* by its people;

DEFRAUD
Lev 19: 13 Do not *d* your neighbor or rob him.
Mk 10: 19 do not *d,* honor your father

DEITY*
Col 2: 9 of the *D* lives in bodily form,

DELAY
Ecc 5: 4 vow to God, do not *d* in fulfilling it.
Isa 48: 9 my own name's sake I *d* my wrath;
Heb 10: 37 is coming will come and will not *d.*
Rev 10: 6 and said, "There will be no more *d!*

DELICACIES
Ps 141: 4 let me not eat of their *d.*
Pr 23: 3 Do not crave his *d,*
23: 6 do not crave his *d;*

DELICIOUS*
Pr 9: 17 food eaten in secret is *d!"*

DELIGHT* (DELIGHTED DELIGHTFUL DELIGHTING DELIGHTS)
Lev 26: 31 and I will take no *d* in the pleasing
Dt 30: 9 The LORD will again *d* in you
1Sa 2: 1 for I *d* in your deliverance.
15: 22 "Does the LORD *d*
Ne 1: 11 the prayer of your servants who *d*
Job 22: 26 Surely then you will find *d*
27: 10 Will he find *d* in the Almighty?
Ps 1: 2 But his *d* is in the law of the LORD
16: 3 in whom is all my *d.*
35: 9 and *d* in his salvation.
35: 27 those who *d* in my vindication
37: 4 *D* yourself in the LORD
43: 4 to God, my joy and my *d.*
51: 16 You do not *d* in sacrifice,
51: 19 whole burnt offerings to *d* you;
62: 4 they take *d* in lies.
68: 30 Scatter the nations who *d* in war.
111: 2 by all who *d* in them.
112: 1 who finds great *d* in his commands.
119: 16 I *d* in your decrees;
119: 24 Your statutes are my *d;*
119: 35 for there I find *d.*
119: 47 for I *d* in your commands
119: 70 but I *d* in your law.
119: 77 for your law is my *d.*
119: 92 If your law had not been my *d,*
119:143 but your commands are my *d.*
119:174 and your law is my *d.*
147: 10 nor his *d* in the legs of a man;
149: 4 For the LORD takes *d*
Pr 1: 22 How long will mockers *d*
2: 14 who *d* in doing wrong
8: 30 I was filled with *d* day after day,
11: 1 but accurate weights are his *d.*
29: 17 he will bring *d* to your soul.
Ecc 2: 10 My heart took *d* in all my work,
SS 1: 4 We rejoice and *d* in you;
2: 3 I *d* to sit in his shade,
Isa 5: 7 are the garden of his *d.*
11: 3 he will *d* in the fear of the LORD.
13: 17 and have no *d* in gold.
32: 14 the *d* of donkeys, a pasture
42: 1 my chosen one in whom I *d;*
55: 2 and your soul will *d* in the richest
58: 13 if you call the Sabbath a *d*
61: 10 I *d* greatly in the LORD;
62: 4 for the LORD will take *d* in you,
65: 18 for I will create Jerusalem to be a *d*
65: 19 and take *d* in my people;
66: 3 their souls *d* in their abominations;
66: 11 *d* in her overflowing abundance."
Jer 9: 24 for in these I *d,"*
15: 16 they were my joy and my heart's *d,*
31: 20 the child in whom I *d?*
49: 25 the town in which I *d?*
Eze 24: 16 away from you the *d* of your eyes.
24: 21 in which you take pride, the *d*
24: 25 and glory, the *d* of their eyes,
Hos 7: 3 *d* the king with their wickedness,
Mic 1: 16 for the children in whom you *d;*
7: 18 but *d* to show mercy.
Zep 3: 17 He will take great *d* in you,
Mt 12: 18 the one I love, in whom I *d;*
Mk 12: 37 large crowd listened to him with *d.*
Lk 1: 14 He will be a joy and *d* to you,
Ro 7: 22 in my inner being I *d* in God's law;
1Co 13: 6 Love does not *d* in evil
2Co 12: 10 for Christ's sake, I *d* in weaknesses,
Col 2: 5 and *d* to see how orderly you are

DELIGHTED (DELIGHT)
2Sa 22: 20 he rescued me because he *d* in me.
1Ki 10: 9 who has *d* in you and placed you
2Ch 9: 8 who has *d* in you and placed you
Ps 18: 19 he rescued me because he *d* in me.
Lk 13: 17 but the people were *d* with all

DELIGHTFUL* (DELIGHT)
Ps 16: 6 surely I have a *d* inheritance.
SS 1: 2 for your love is more *d* than wine.
4: 10 How *d* is your love, my sister,
Mal 3: 12 for yours will be a *d* land,"

DELIGHTING* (DELIGHT)
Pr 8: 31 and *d* in mankind.

DELIGHTS (DELIGHT)
Est 6: 6 for the man the king *d* to honor?"
Ps 22: 8 since he *d* in him."
35: 27 who *d* in the well-being
36: 8 from your river of *d.*
37: 23 if the LORD *d* in a man's way
147: 11 the LORD *d* in those who fear him,
Pr 3: 12 as a father the son he *d* in.
10: 23 of understanding *d* in wisdom.
11: 20 he *d* in those whose ways are
12: 22 but he *d* in men who are truthful.
14: 35 A king *d* in a wise servant,
18: 2 but *d* in airing his own opinions.
23: 24 he who has a wise son *d* in him.
Col 2: 18 Do not let anyone who *d*

DELILAH*
Woman who betrayed Samson (Jdg 16:4–22).

DELIVER (DELIVERANCE DELIVERED DELIVERER DELIVERS)
Dt 32: 39 and no one can *d* out of my hand.
Ps 22: 8 Let him *d* him,
72: 12 For he will *d* the needy who cry out
79: 9 *d* us and forgive our sins
109: 21 of the goodness of your love, *d* me.
119:170 *d* me according to your promise.
Mt 6: 13 but *d* us from the evil one.'
2Co 1: 10 hope that he will continue to *d* us,

DELIVERANCE (DELIVER)
1Sa 2: 1 for I delight in your *d.*
Ps 3: 8 From the LORD comes *d.*
32: 7 and surround me with songs of *d.*
33: 17 A horse is a vain hope for *d;*
Ob : 17 But on Mount Zion will be *d;*

DELIVERED (DELIVER)
Ps 34: 4 he *d* me from all my fears.
107: 6 and he *d* them from their distress.
116: 8 have *d* my soul from death,
Da 12: 1 written in the book—will be *d.*
Ro 4: 25 He was *d* over to death for our sins

DELIVERER* (DELIVER)
Jdg 3: 9 for them a *d,* Othniel son of Kenaz,
3: 15 and he gave them a *d*— Ehud,
2Sa 22: 2 is my rock, my fortress and my *d;*
2Ki 13: 5 The LORD provided a *d* for Israel,
Ps 18: 2 is my rock, my fortress and my *d;*
40: 17 You are my help and my *d;*
70: 5 You are my help and my *d;*
140: 7 O Sovereign LORD, my strong *d,*
144: 2 my stronghold and my *d,*
Ac 7: 35 sent to be their ruler and *d*
Ro 11: 26 "The *d* will come from Zion;

DELIVERS (DELIVER)
Ps 34: 17 he *d* them from all their troubles.

34: 19 but the LORD *d* him from them all
37: 40 The LORD helps them and *d* them
37: 40 he *d* them from the wicked

DELUSION*
2Th 2: 11 God sends them a powerful *d*

DEMAND (DEMANDED)
Lk 6: 30 belongs to you, do not *d* it back.

DEMANDED (DEMAND)
Lk 12: 20 This very night your life will be *d*
12: 48 been given much, much will be *d;*

DEMETRIUS
Ac 19: 24 A silversmith named *D,* who made

DEMON* (DEMONS)
Mt 9: 33 And when the *d* was driven out,
11: 18 and they say, 'He has a *d.*'
17: 18 Jesus rebuked the *d,* and it came
Mk 7: 26 to drive the *d* out of her daughter.
7: 29 the *d* has left your daughter."
7: 30 lying on the bed, and the *d* gone.
Lk 4: 33 there was a man possessed by a *d,*
4: 35 Then the *d* threw the man
7: 33 wine, and you say, 'He has a *d.*'
8: 29 driven by the *d* into solitary places.
9: 42 the *d* threw him to the ground
11: 14 When the *d* left, the man who had
11: 14 was driving out a *d* that was mute.
Jn 8: 49 "I am not possessed by a *d,*"
10: 21 Can a *d* open the eyes of the blind
10: 21 sayings of a man possessed by a *d.*

DEMON-POSSESSED* (DEMON-POSSESSION)
Mt 4: 24 those suffering severe pain, the *d,*
8: 16 many who were *d* were brought
8: 28 two *d* men coming
8: 33 what had happened to the *d* men.
9: 32 man who was *d* and could not talk
12: 22 they brought him a *d* man who was
Mk 1: 32 brought to Jesus all the sick and *d.*
5: 16 what had happened to the *d* man—
5: 18 the man who had been *d* begged
Lk 8: 27 met by a *d* man from the town.
8: 36 the people how the *d* man had been
Jn 7: 20 "You are *d,*" the crowd answered.
8: 48 that you are a Samaritan and *d?*"
8: 52 "Now we know that you are *d!*
10: 20 Many of them said, "He is *d*
Ac 19: 13 Jesus over those who were *d.*

DEMON-POSSESSION* (DEMON-POSSESSED)
Mt 15: 22 is suffering terribly from *d.*"

DEMONS* (DEMON)
Dt 32: 17 to *d,* which are not God—
Ps 106: 37 and their daughters to *d.*
Mt 7: 22 and in your name drive out *d*
8: 31 *d* begged Jesus, "If you drive us
9: 34 prince of *d* that he drives out *d.*"
10: 8 who have leprosy, drive out *d.*
12: 24 of *d,* that this fellow drives out
12: 24 that this fellow drives out *d.*"
12: 27 And if I drive out *d* by Beelzebub,
12: 28 if I drive out *d* by the Spirit of God,
Mk 1: 34 He also drove out many *d,*
1: 34 but he would not let the *d* speak
1: 39 their synagogues and driving out *d.*
3: 15 to have authority to drive out *d.*
3: 22 the prince of *d* he is driving out *d.*"
5: 12 The *d* begged Jesus, "Send us
5: 15 possessed by the legion of *d,*
6: 13 They drove out many *d*
9: 38 "we saw a man driving out *d*
16: 9 out of whom he had driven seven *d*
16: 17 In my name they will drive out *d;*
Lk 4: 41 *d* came out of many people,
8: 2 from whom seven *d* had come out;
8: 30 because many *d* had gone into him.
8: 32 The *d* begged Jesus to let them go
8: 33 When the *d* came out of the man,
8: 35 from whom the *d* had gone out,
8: 38 from whom the *d* had gone out
9: 1 and authority to drive out all *d*
9: 49 "we saw a man driving out *d*
10: 17 the *d* submit to us in your name."
11: 15 the prince of *d,* he is driving out *d.*"
11: 18 you claim that I drive out *d*
11: 19 Now if I drive out *d* by Beelzebub,
11: 20 if I drive out *d* by the finger of God,
13: 32 'I will drive out *d* and heal people
Ro 8: 38 neither angels nor *d,* neither
1Co 10: 20 of pagans are offered to *d,*
10: 20 you to be participants with *d.*
10: 21 of the Lord and the cup of *d* too;
10: 21 the Lord's table and the table of *d.*
1Ti 4: 1 spirits and things taught by *d.*
Jas 2: 19 Good! Even the *d* believe that—
Rev 9: 20 they did not stop worshiping *d,*
16: 14 of *d* performing miraculous signs,
18: 2 She has become a home for *d*

DEMONSTRATE* (DEMONSTRATES DEMONSTRATION)
Ro 3: 25 He did this to *d* his justice,
3: 26 he did it to *d* his justice

DEMONSTRATES* (DEMONSTRATE)
Ro 5: 8 God *d* his own love for us in this:

DEMONSTRATION* (DEMONSTRATE)
1Co 2: 4 but with a *d* of the Spirit's power,

DEN
Da 6: 16 and threw him into the lions' *d.*
Mt 21: 13 you are making it a '*d* of robbers.' "
Mk 11: 17 you have made it 'a *d* of robbers.' "
Lk 19: 46 but you have made it 'a *d* of robbers

DENARII* (DENARIUS)
Mt 18: 28 who owed him a hundred *d.*
Lk 7: 41 One owed him five hundred *d,*

DENARIUS (DENARII)
Mt 20: 2 agreed to pay them a *d* for the day
Mk 12: 15 Bring me a *d* and let me look at it."

DENIED (DENY)
Mt 26: 70 But he *d* it before them all.
Mk 14: 68 But he *d* it.
Lk 22: 57 But he *d* it.
Jn 18: 25 He *d* it, saying, "I am not."
1Ti 5: 8 he has *d* the faith and is worse
Rev 3: 8 my word and have not *d* my name.

DENIES (DENY)
1Jn 2: 22 It is the man who *d* that Jesus is
2: 23 No one who *d* the Son has

DENY (DENIED DENIES DENYING)
Ex 23: 6 "Do not *d* justice to your poor
Job 27: 5 till I die, I will not *d* my integrity.
Isa 5: 23 but *d* justice to the innocent.
La 3: 35 to *d* a man his rights
Am 2: 7 and *d* justice to the oppressed.
Mt 16: 24 he must *d* himself and take up his
Mk 8: 34 he must *d* himself and take up his
Lk 9: 23 he must *d* himself and take up his
22: 34 you will *d* three times that you
Ac 4: 16 miracle, and we cannot *d* it.
Tit 1: 16 but by their actions they *d* him.
Jas 3: 14 do not boast about it or *d* the truth.
Jude : 4 *d* Jesus Christ our only Sovereign

DENYING* (DENY)
Eze 22: 29 mistreat the alien, *d* them justice.
2Ti 3: 5 a form of godliness but *d* its power.
2Pe 2: 1 *d* the sovereign Lord who bought

DEPART (DEPARTED DEPARTS DEPARTURE)
Ge 49: 10 The scepter will not *d* from Judah,
Job 1: 21 and naked I will *d.*
Mt 25: 41 '*D* from me, you who are cursed,
Php 1: 23 I desire to *d* and be with Christ,

DEPARTED (DEPART)
1Sa 4: 21 "The glory has *d* from Israel"—
Ps 119:102 I have not *d* from your laws,

DEPARTS (DEPART)
Ecc 5: 15 and as he comes, so he *d.*

DEPARTURE (DEPART)
Lk 9: 31 spoke about his *d,* which he was
2Ti 4: 6 and the time has come for my *d.*
2Pe 1: 15 after my *d* you will always be able

DEPEND
Ps 62: 7 My salvation and my honor *d*

DEPOSES*
Da 2: 21 he sets up kings and *d* them.

DEPOSIT
Mt 25: 27 money on *d* with the bankers,
Lk 19: 23 didn't you put my money on *d,*
2Co 1: 22 put his Spirit in our hearts as a *d,*
5: 5 and has given us the Spirit as a *d,*
Eph 1: 14 who is a *d* guaranteeing our
2Ti 1: 14 Guard the good *d* that was

DEPRAVED* (DEPRAVITY)
Eze 16: 47 ways you soon became more *d*
23: 11 and prostitution she was more *d*
Ro 1: 28 he gave them over to a *d* mind,
Php 2: 15 fault in a crooked and *d* generation,
2Ti 3: 8 oppose the truth—men of *d* minds,

DEPRAVITY* (DEPRAVED)
Ro 1: 29 of wickedness, evil, greed and *d.*
2Pe 2: 19 they themselves are slaves of *d*—

DEPRIVE
Dt 24: 17 Do not *d* the alien or the fatherless
Pr 18: 5 or to *d* the innocent of justice.
31: 5 *d* all the oppressed of their rights.
Isa 10: 2 to *d* the poor of their rights
29: 21 with false testimony *d* the innocent
La 3: 36 to *d* a man of justice—
1Co 7: 5 Do not *d* each other
9: 15 die than have anyone *d* me

DEPTH (DEEP)
Ro 8: 39 any powers, neither height nor *d,*
11: 33 the *d* of the riches of the wisdom

DEPTHS (DEEP)
Ps 130: 1 Out of the *d* I cry to you, O LORD;

DERIDES*
Pr 11: 12 who lacks judgment *d* his neighbor,

DERIVES*
Eph 3: 15 in heaven and on earth *d* its name.

DESCEND (DESCENDED DESCENDING)
Ro 10: 7 "or 'Who will *d* into the deep?' "

DESCENDED (DESCEND)
Eph 4: 9 except that he also *d* to the lower,
Heb 7: 14 For it is clear that our Lord *d*

DESCENDING (DESCEND)
Ge 28: 12 of God were ascending and *d* on it.
Mt 3: 16 the Spirit of God *d* like a dove
Mk 1: 10 and the Spirit *d* on him like a dove.
Jn 1: 51 and *d* on the Son of Man."

DESECRATING*
Ne 13: 17 you are doing—*d* the Sabbath day?
13: 18 against Israel by *d* the Sabbath."
Isa 56: 2 who keeps the Sabbath without *d* it
56: 6 who keep the Sabbath without *d* it
Eze 44: 7 *d* my temple while you offered me

DESERT
Nu 32: 13 wander in the *d* forty years,
Dt 8: 16 He gave you manna to eat in the *d,*
29: 5 years that I led you through the *d,*
Ne 9: 19 you did not abandon them in the *d.*
Ps 78: 19 "Can God spread a table in the *d?*
78: 52 led them like sheep through the *d.*
Pr 21: 19 Better to live in a *d*
Isa 32: 2 like streams of water in the *d*
32: 15 and the *d* becomes a fertile field,
35: 6 and streams in the *d.*
43: 20 because I provide water in the *d*
Mk 1: 3 "a voice of one calling in the *d,*
1: 13 and he was in the *d* forty days,
Rev 12: 6 fled into the *d* to a place prepared

DESERTED (DESERTS)
Ezr 9: 9 our God has not *d* us

Mt 26: 56 all the disciples *d* him and fled.
2Ti 1: 15 in the province of Asia has *d* me,

DESERTING (DESERTS)
Gal 1: 6 are so quickly *d* the one who called

DESERTS (DESERTED DESERTING)
Zec 11: 17 who *d* the flock!

DESERVE* (DESERVED DESERVES)
Ge 40: 15 to *d* being put in a dungeon."
Lev 26: 21 times over, as your sins *d*.
Jdg 20: 10 it can give them what they *d*
1Sa 26: 16 you and your men *d* to die,
1Ki 2: 26 You *d* to die, but I will not put you
Ps 28: 4 bring back upon them what they *d*.
94: 2 pay back to the proud what they *d*.
103: 10 he does not treat us as our sins *d*
Pr 3: 27 from those who *d* it,
Ecc 8: 14 men who get what the righteous *d*,
8: 14 men who get what the wicked *d*,
Isa 66: 6 repaying his enemies all they *d*.
Jer 14: 16 out on them the calamity they *d*.
17: 10 according to what his deeds *d*."
21: 14 I will punish you as your deeds *d*,
32: 19 to his conduct and as his deeds *d*.
49: 12 "If those who do not *d*
La 3: 64 Pay them back what they *d*,
Eze 16: 59 I will deal with you as you *d*,
Zec 1: 6 to us what our ways and practices *d*
Mt 8: 8 I do not *d* to have you come
22: 8 those I invited did not *d* to come.
Lk 7: 6 for I do not *d* to have you come
23: 15 he has done nothing to *d* death.
23: 41 for we are getting what our deeds *d*
Ro 1: 32 those who do such things *d* death,
1Co 15: 9 even *d* to be called an apostle,
16: 18 Such men *d* recognition.
2Co 11: 15 end will be what their actions *d*.
Rev 16: 6 blood to drink as they *d*."

DESERVED* (DESERVE)
2Sa 19: 28 descendants *d* nothing
Ezr 9: 13 less than our sins have *d*
Job 33: 27 but I did not get what I *d*.
Ac 23: 29 charge against him that *d* death
Ro 3: 8 Their condemnation is *d*.

DESERVES* (DESERVE)
Nu 35: 31 the life of a murderer, who *d* to die.
Dt 25: 2 If the guilty man *d* to be beaten,
25: 2 the number of lashes his crime *d*,
Jdg 9: 16 and if you have treated him as he *d*
2Sa 12: 5 the man who did this *d* to die!
Job 34: 11 upon him what his conduct *d*.
Jer 51: 6 he will pay her what she *d*.
Lk 7: 4 "This man *d* to have you do this,
10: 7 for the worker *d* his wages.
Ac 26: 31 is not doing anything that *d* death
1Ti 1: 15 saying that *d* full acceptance:
4: 9 saying that *d* full acceptance
5: 18 and "The worker *d* his wages."
Heb 10: 29 severely do you think a man *d*

DESIGNATED
Lk 6: 13 also *d* apostles: Simon (whom he
Heb 5: 10 and was *d* by God to be high priest

DESIRABLE* (DESIRE)
Ge 3: 6 and also *d* for gaining wisdom,
Pr 22: 1 A good name is more *d*
Jer 3: 19 and give you a *d* land,

DESIRE* (DESIRABLE DESIRED DESIRES)
Ge 3: 16 Your *d* will be for your husband,
Dt 5: 21 You shall not set your *d*
1Sa 9: 20 to whom is all the *d* of Israel turned
2Sa 19: 38 anything you *d* from me I will do
23: 5 and grant me my every *d*?
1Ch 29: 18 keep this *d* in the hearts
2Ch 1: 11 "Since this is your heart's *d*
9: 8 and his *d* to uphold them forever,
Job 13: 3 But I *d* to speak to the Almighty
21: 14 We have no *d* to know your ways.
Ps 10: 17 O LORD, the *d* of the afflicted;
20: 4 May he give you the *d*
21: 2 You have granted him the *d*
27: 12 me over to the *d* of my foes,
40: 6 Sacrifice and offering you did not *d*
40: 8 I *d* to do your will, O my God;
40: 14 may all who *d* my ruin
41: 2 him to the *d* of his foes.
51: 6 Surely you *d* truth
70: 2 may all who *d* my ruin
73: 25 earth has nothing I *d* besides you
Pr 3: 15 nothing you *d* can compare
8: 11 and nothing you *d* can compare
10: 24 what the righteous *d* will be
11: 23 The *d* of the righteous ends only
12: 12 The wicked *d* the plunder
17: 16 since he has no *d* to get wisdom?
24: 1 do not *d* their company;
Ecc 12: 5 and *d* no longer is stirred.
SS 6: 12 my *d* set me among the royal
7: 10 and his *d* is for me.
Isa 26: 8 are the *d* of our hearts.
53: 2 appearance that we should *d* him.
55: 11 but will accomplish what I *d*
Eze 24: 25 delight of their eyes, their heart's *d*,
Hos 6: 6 For I *d* mercy, not sacrifice,
Mic 7: 3 the powerful dictate what they *d*—
Mal 3: 1 whom you *d*, will come," says
Mt 9: 13 learn what this means: 'I *d* mercy,
12: 7 what these words mean, 'I *d* mercy,
Jn 8: 44 want to carry out your father's *d*.
Ro 7: 8 in me every kind of covetous *d*.
7: 18 For I have the *d* to do what is good,
9: 16 depend on man's *d* or effort,
10: 1 my heart's *d* and prayer to God
1Co 12: 31 But eagerly *d* the greater gifts.
14: 1 and eagerly *d* spiritual gifts,
2Co 8: 10 but also to have the *d* to do so.
8: 13 Our *d* is not that others might be
Php 1: 23 I *d* to depart and be with Christ,
Heb 10: 5 Sacrifice and offering you did not *d*
10: 8 and sin offerings you did not *d*,
13: 18 *d* to live honorably in every way.
Jas 1: 14 by his own evil *d*, he is dragged
1: 15 Then, after *d* has conceived,
2Pe 2: 10 of those who follow the corrupt *d*

DESIRED (DESIRE)
Hag 2: 7 and the *d* of all nations will come,
Lk 22: 15 "I have eagerly *d* to eat this

DESIRES* (DESIRE)
Ge 4: 7 at your door; it *d* to have you,
41: 16 will give Pharaoh the answer he *d*."
2Sa 3: 21 rule over all that your heart *d*."
1Ki 11: 37 rule over all that your heart *d*;
Job 17: 11 and so are the *d* of my heart.
31: 16 "If I have denied the *d* of the poor
Ps 34: 12 and *d* to see many good days,
37: 4 he will give you the *d* of your heart.
103: 5 who satisfies your *d* with good things,
140: 8 do not grant the wicked their *d*,
145: 16 satisfy the *d* of every living thing.
145: 19 He fulfills the *d* of those who fear
Pr 11: 6 the unfaithful are trapped by evil *d*.
13: 4 *d* of the diligent are fully satisfied.
19: 22 What a man *d* is unfailing love;
Ecc 6: 2 so that he lacks nothing his heart *d*,
SS 2: 7 or awaken love / until it so *d*.
3: 5 or awaken love / until it so *d*.
8: 4 or awaken love / until it so *d*.
Hab 2: 4 his *d* are not upright—
Mk 4: 19 and the *d* for other things come in
Ro 1: 24 over in the sinful *d* of their hearts
6: 12 body so that you obey its evil *d*.
8: 5 set on what that nature *d*;
8: 5 set on what the Spirit *d*.
13: 14 to gratify the *d* of the sinful nature.
Gal 5: 16 and you will not gratify the *d*
5: 17 the sinful nature *d* what is contrary
5: 24 nature with its passions and *d*.
Eph 2: 3 and following its *d* and thoughts.
4: 22 being corrupted by its deceitful *d*;
Col 3: 5 impurity, lust, evil *d* and greed,
1Ti 3: 1 an overseer, he *d* a noble task.
5: 11 their sensual *d* overcome their
6: 9 and harmful *d* that plunge men
2Ti 2: 22 Flee the evil *d* of youth,
3: 6 are swayed by all kinds of evil *d*,
4: 3 Instead, to suit their own *d*,
Jas 1: 20 about the righteous life that God *d*.
4: 1 from your *d* that battle within you?
1Pe 1: 14 conform to the evil *d* you had
2: 11 to abstain from sinful *d*, which war
4: 2 of his earthly life for evil human *d*,
2Pe 1: 4 in the world caused by evil *d*.
2: 18 to the lustful *d* of sinful human
3: 3 and following their own evil *d*.
1Jn 2: 17 The world and its *d* pass away,
Jude : 16 they follow their own evil *d*;
: 18 will follow their own ungodly *d*."

DESOLATE (DESOLATION)
Isa 54: 1 are the children of the *d* woman
Gal 4: 27 are the children of the *d* woman

DESOLATION (DESOLATE)
Da 11: 31 up the abomination that causes *d*.
12: 11 abomination that causes *d* is set up,
Mt 24: 15 'the abomination that causes *d*,'

DESPAIR (DESPAIRED)
Isa 61: 3 instead of a spirit of *d*.
2Co 4: 8 perplexed, but not in *d*; persecuted,

DESPAIRED* (DESPAIR)
2Co 1: 8 ability to endure, so that we *d*

DESPERATE*
2Sa 12: 18 He may do something *d*."
Ps 60: 3 have shown your people *d* times;
79: 8 for we are in *d* need.
142: 6 for I am in *d* need;

DESPISE (DESPISED DESPISES)
2Sa 12: 9 Why did you *d* the word
Job 5: 17 so do not *d* the discipline
36: 5 God is mighty, but does not *d* men;
42: 6 Therefore I *d* myself
Ps 51: 17 O God, you will not *d*.
102: 17 he will not *d* their plea.
Pr 1: 7 but fools *d* wisdom and discipline.
3: 11 do not *d* the LORD's discipline
6: 30 Men do not *d* a thief if he steals
23: 22 do not *d* your mother
Jer 14: 21 of your name do not *d* us;
Am 5: 10 and *d* him who tells the truth.
5: 21 "I hate, I *d* your religious feasts;
Mt 6: 24 devoted to the one and *d* the other.
Lk 16: 13 devoted to the one and *d* the other.
1Co 11: 22 Or do you *d* the church of God
Tit 2: 15 Do not let anyone *d* you.
2Pe 2: 10 of the sinful nature and *d* authority.

DESPISED (DESPISE)
Ge 25: 34 So Esau *d* his birthright.
Ps 22: 6 by men and *d* by the people.
Pr 12: 8 but men with warped minds are *d*.
Isa 53: 3 He was *d* and rejected by men,
53: 3 he was *d*, and we esteemed him not
1Co 1: 28 of this world and the *d* things—

DESPISES (DESPISE)
Pr 14: 21 He who *d* his neighbor sins,
15: 20 but a foolish man *d* his mother.
15: 32 who ignores discipline *d* himself,
Zec 4: 10 "Who *d* the day of small things?

DESTINED (DESTINY)
Lk 2: 34 "This child is *d* to cause the falling
1Co 2: 7 and that God *d* for our glory
Col 2: 22 These are all *d* to perish with use,
1Th 3: 3 know quite well that we were *d*
Heb 9: 27 Just as man is *d* to die once,
1Pe 2: 8 which is also what they were *d* for.

DESTINY* (DESTINED PREDESTINED)
Job 8: 13 Such is the *d* of all who forget God;
Ps 73: 17 then I understood their final *d*.

Ecc 7: 2 for death is the *d* of every man;
9: 2 share a common *d*— the righteous
9: 3 the sun: The same *d* overtakes all.
Isa 65: 11 and fill bowls of mixed wine for *D*,
Php 3: 19 Their *d* is destruction, their god is

DESTITUTE
Ps 102: 17 to the prayer of the *d*;
Pr 31: 8 for the rights of all who are *d*.
Heb 11: 37 *d*, persecuted and mistreated—

DESTROY (DESTROYED DESTROYING DESTROYS DESTRUCTION DESTRUCTIVE)
Ge 6: 17 floodwaters on the earth to *d* all life
9: 11 will there be a flood to *d* the earth."
Pr 1: 32 complacency of fools will *d* them;
Mt 10: 28 of the One who can *d* both soul
Mk 14: 58 'I will *d* this man-made temple
Lk 4: 34 to *d* us? I know who you are—
Jn 10: 10 only to steal and kill and *d*;
Ac 8: 3 But Saul began to *d* the church.
Rev 11: 18 destroying those who *d* the earth."

DESTROYED (DESTROY)
Dt 8: 19 you today that you will surely be *d*.
Job 19: 26 And after my skin has been *d*,
Pr 6: 15 he will suddenly be *d*—
11: 3 the unfaithful are *d*
21: 28 listens to him will be *d* forever.
29: 1 will suddenly be *d*—
Isa 55: 13 which will not be *d*."
Da 2: 44 up a kingdom that will never be *d*,
6: 26 his kingdom will not be *d*,
1Co 5: 5 so that the sinful nature may be *d*
8: 11 for whom Christ died, is *d*
15: 24 Father after he has *d* all dominion,
15: 26 The last enemy to be *d* is death.
2Co 4: 9 abandoned; struck down, but not *d*.
5: 1 if the earthly tent we live in is *d*,
Gal 5: 15 or you will be *d* by each other.
Eph 2: 14 the two one and has *d* the barrier,
2Ti 1: 10 who has *d* death and has brought
Heb 10: 39 of those who shrink back and are *d*,
2Pe 2: 12 born only to be caught and *d*,
3: 10 the elements will be *d* by fire,
3: 11 Since everything will be *d*
Jude : 5 later *d* those who did not believe.
: 11 have been *d* in Korah's rebellion.

DESTROYING (DESTROY)
Jer 23: 1 "Woe to the shepherds who are *d*

DESTROYS (DESTROY)
Pr 6: 32 whoever does so *d* himself.
11: 9 mouth the godless *d* his neighbor,
18: 9 is brother to one who *d*.
28: 24 he is partner to him who *d*.
Ecc 9: 18 but one sinner *d* much good.
1Co 3: 17 If anyone *d* God's temple,

DESTRUCTION (DESTROY)
Nu 32: 15 and you will be the cause of their *d*
Pr 16: 18 Pride goes before *d*,
17: 19 he who builds a high gate invites *d*.
24: 22 for those two will send sudden *d*
Hos 13: 14 Where, O grave, is your *d*?
Mt 7: 13 broad is the road that leads to *d*,
Lk 6: 49 it collapsed and its *d* was complete
Jn 17: 12 except the one doomed to *d*
Ro 9: 22 of his wrath—prepared for *d*?
Gal 6: 8 from that nature will reap *d*;
Php 3: 19 Their destiny is *d*, their god is their
1Th 5: 3 *d* will come on them suddenly,
2Th 1: 9 punished with everlasting *d*
2: 3 is revealed, the man doomed to *d*.
1Ti 6: 9 that plunge men into ruin and *d*.
2Pe 2: 1 bringing swift *d* on themselves.
2: 3 and their *d* has not been sleeping.
3: 7 of judgment and *d* of ungodly men.
3: 12 That day will bring about the *d*
3: 16 other Scriptures, to their own *d*.
Rev 17: 8 out of the Abyss and go to his *d*.
17: 11 to the seven and is going to his *d*.

DESTRUCTIVE (DESTROY)
2Pe 2: 1 will secretly introduce *d* heresies,

DETERMINED (DETERMINES)
Job 14: 5 Man's days are *d*;
Isa 14: 26 This is the plan *d* for the whole
Da 11: 36 for what has been *d* must take place
Ac 17: 26 and he *d* the times set for them

DETERMINES* (DETERMINED)
Ps 147: 4 He *d* the number of the stars
Pr 16: 9 but the LORD *d* his steps.
1Co 12: 11 them to each one, just as he *d*.

DETEST (DETESTABLE DETESTED DETESTS)
Lev 11: 10 in the water—you are to *d*.
Pr 8: 7 for my lips *d* wickedness.
13: 19 but fools *d* turning from evil.
16: 12 Kings *d* wrongdoing,
24: 9 and men *d* a mocker.
29: 27 The righteous *d* the dishonest;
29: 27 the wicked *d* the upright.

DETESTABLE (DETEST)
Pr 6: 16 seven that are *d* to him:
21: 27 The sacrifice of the wicked is *d*—
28: 9 even his prayers are *d*.
Isa 1: 13 Your incense is *d* to me.
41: 24 he who chooses you is *d*.
44: 19 Shall I make a *d* thing
Jer 44: 4 'Do not do this *d* thing that I hate!'
Eze 8: 13 doing things that are even more *d*."
Lk 16: 15 among men is *d* in God's sight.
Tit 1: 16 They are *d*, disobedient
1Pe 4: 3 orgies, carousing and *d* idolatry.

DETESTED* (DETEST)
Zec 11: 8 The flock *d* me, and I grew weary

DETESTS* (DETEST)
Dt 22: 5 LORD your God *d* anyone who
23: 18 the LORD your God *d* them both.
25: 16 LORD your God *d* anyone who
Pr 3: 32 for the LORD *d* a perverse man
11: 20 The LORD *d* men
12: 22 The LORD *d* lying lips,
15: 8 The LORD *d* the sacrifice
15: 9 The LORD *d* the way
15: 26 The LORD *d* the thoughts
16: 5 The LORD *d* all the proud of heart
17: 15 the LORD *d* them both.
20: 10 the LORD *d* them both.
20: 23 The LORD *d* differing weights,

DEVIATE*
2Ch 8: 15 They did not *d* from the king's

DEVICES*
Ps 81: 12 to follow their own *d*.

DEVIL* (DEVIL'S)
Mt 4: 1 the desert to be tempted by the *d*.
4: 5 the *d* took him to the holy city
4: 8 *d* took him to a very high mountain
4: 11 the *d* left him, and angels came
13: 39 the enemy who sows them is the *d*.
25: 41 the eternal fire prepared for the *d*
Lk 4: 2 forty days he was tempted by the *d*.
4: 3 *d* said to him, "If you are the Son
4: 5 The *d* led him up to a high place
4: 9 The *d* led him to Jerusalem
4: 13 When the *d* had finished all this
8: 12 then the *d* comes and takes away
Jn 6: 70 of you is a *d*!" (He meant Judas,
8: 44 You belong to your father, the *d*,
13: 2 the *d* had already prompted Judas
Ac 10: 38 were under the power of the *d*,
13: 10 "You are a child of the *d*
Eph 4: 27 and do not give the *d* a foothold.
1Ti 3: 6 under the same judgment as the *d*.
2Ti 2: 26 and escape from the trap of the *d*,
Heb 2: 14 the *d*— and free those who all their
Jas 3: 15 but is earthly, unspiritual, of the *d*.
4: 7 Resist the *d*, and he will flee
1Pe 5: 8 Your enemy the *d* prowls
1Jn 3: 8 because the *d* has been sinning
3: 8 who does what is sinful is of the *d*,
3: 10 and who the children of the *d* are:
Jude : 9 with the *d* about the body of Moses
Rev 2: 10 the *d* will put some of you in prison
12: 9 that ancient serpent called the *d*
12: 12 the *d* has gone down to you!
20: 2 that ancient serpent, who is the *d*,
20: 10 And the *d*, who deceived them,

DEVIL'S* (DEVIL)
Eph 6: 11 stand against the *d* schemes.
1Ti 3: 7 into disgrace and into the *d* trap.
1Jn 3: 8 was to destroy the *d* work.

DEVIOUS*
Pr 2: 15 and who are *d* in their ways.
14: 2 he whose ways are *d* despises him.
21: 8 The way of the guilty is *d*,

DEVOTE* (DEVOTED DEVOTING DEVOTION DEVOUT)
1Ch 22: 19 Now *d* your heart and soul
2Ch 31: 4 Levites so they could *d* themselves
Job 11: 13 "Yet if you *d* your heart to him
Jer 30: 21 for who is he who will *d* himself
Mic 4: 13 You will *d* their ill-gotten gains
1Co 7: 5 so that you may *d* yourselves
Col 4: 2 *D* yourselves to prayer, being
1Ti 1: 4 nor to *d* themselves to myths
4: 13 *d* yourself to the public reading
Tit 3: 8 may be careful to *d* themselves
3: 14 people must learn to *d* themselves

DEVOTED (DEVOTE)
1Ki 11: 4 and his heart was not fully *d*
Ezr 7: 10 For Ezra had *d* himself to the study
Ps 86: 2 Guard my life, for I am *d* to you.
Mt 6: 24 or he will be *d* to the one
Mk 7: 11 from me is Corban' (that is, a gift *d*
Ac 2: 42 They *d* themselves
18: 5 Paul *d* himself exclusively
Ro 12: 10 Be *d* to one another
1Co 7: 34 Her aim is to be *d* to the Lord
16: 15 and they have *d* themselves
2Co 7: 12 for yourselves how *d* to us you are.

DEVOTING* (DEVOTE)
1Ti 5: 10 *d* herself to all kinds of good deeds.

DEVOTION* (DEVOTE)
2Ki 20: 3 and with wholehearted *d* and have
1Ch 28: 9 and serve him with wholehearted *d*
29: 3 in my *d* to the temple
29: 19 son Solomon the wholehearted *d*
2Ch 32: 32 and his acts of *d* are written
35: 26 of Josiah's reign and his acts of *d*,
Job 6: 14 despairing man should have the *d*
15: 4 and hinder *d* to God.
Isa 38: 3 and with wholehearted *d* and have
Jer 2: 2 " 'I remember the *d* of your youth,
Eze 33: 31 With their mouths they express *d*,
1Co 7: 35 way in undivided *d* to the Lord.
2Co 11: 3 from your sincere and pure *d*

DEVOUR (DEVOURED DEVOURING DEVOURS)
2Sa 2: 26 "Must the sword *d* forever?
Mk 12: 40 They *d* widows' houses
1Pe 5: 8 lion looking for someone to *d*.

DEVOURED (DEVOUR)
Jer 30: 16 But all who devour you will be *d*;

DEVOURING (DEVOUR)
Gal 5: 15 keep on biting and *d* each other,

DEVOURS (DEVOUR)
2Sa 11: 25 the sword *d* one as well as another.
Pr 21: 20 but a foolish man *d* all he has.

DEVOUT* (DEVOTE)
1Ki 18: 3 (Obadiah was a *d* believer
Isa 57: 1 *d* men are taken away,
Lk 2: 25 Simeon, who was righteous and *d*.
Ac 10: 2 his family were *d* and God-fearing;
10: 7 a *d* soldier who was one of his attendants
13: 43 and *d* converts to Judaism followed
22: 12 He was a *d* observer of the law

DEW
Jdg 6: 37 If there is *d* only on the fleece

DICTATED
Jer 36: 4 and while Jeremiah *d* all the words

DIE (DEAD DEADENED DEATH DIED DIES DYING)
Ge 2: 17 when you eat of it you will surely *d*
3: 3 you must not touch it, or you will *d*
3: 4 will not surely *d*," the serpent said
Ex 11: 5 Every firstborn son in Egypt will *d*,
Ru 1: 17 Where you *d* I will *d*, and there I
2Ki 14: 6 each is to *d* for his own sins."
Job 2: 9 Curse God and *d*!" He replied,
Pr 5: 23 He will *d* for lack of discipline,
10: 21 but fools *d* for lack of judgment.
15: 10 he who hates correction will *d*.
23: 13 with the rod, he will not *d*.
Ecc 3: 2 a time to be born and a time to *d*,
Isa 22: 13 "for tomorrow we *d*!"
66: 24 their worm will not *d*, nor will their
Jer 31: 30 everyone will *d* for his own sin;
Eze 3: 18 that wicked man will *d* for his sin,
3: 19 he will *d* for his sin; but you will
3: 20 block before him, he will *d*.
18: 4 soul who sins is the one who will *d*.
18: 20 soul who sins is the one who will *d*.
18: 31 Why will you *d*, O house of Israel?
33: 8 'O wicked man, you will surely *d*,'
Mt 26: 52 "for all who draw the sword will *d*
Mk 9: 48 " 'their worm does not *d*,
Jn 8: 21 and you will *d* in your sin.
11: 26 and believes in me will never *d*.
Ro 5: 7 Very rarely will anyone *d*
14: 8 and if we *d*, we *d* to the Lord.
1Co 15: 22 in Adam all *d*, so in Christ all will
15: 31 I *d* every day—I mean that,
15: 32 for tomorrow we *d*."
Php 1: 21 to live is Christ and to *d* is gain.
Heb 9: 27 Just as man is destined to *d* once,
1Pe 2: 24 so that we might *d* to sins
Rev 14: 13 Blessed are the dead who *d*

DIED (DIE)
1Ki 16: 18 So he *d*, because of the sins he had
1Ch 1: 51 Hadad also *d*.
10: 13 Saul *d* because he was unfaithful
Lk 16: 22 "The time came when the beggar *d*
Ro 5: 6 we were still powerless, Christ *d*
5: 8 we were still sinners, Christ *d*
6: 2 By no means! We *d* to sin;
6: 7 anyone who has *d* has been freed
6: 8 if we *d* with Christ, we believe that
6: 10 The death he *d*, he *d* to sin once
14: 9 Christ *d* and returned to life
14: 15 brother for whom Christ *d*.
1Co 8: 11 for whom Christ *d*, is destroyed
15: 3 that Christ *d* for our sins according
2Co 5: 14 *d* for all, and therefore all *d*.
5: 15 he *d* for all, that those who live
Col 2: 20 Since you *d* with Christ
3: 3 For you *d*, and your life is now
1Th 4: 14 We believe that Jesus *d*
5: 10 He *d* for us so that, whether we are
2Ti 2: 11 If we *d* with him,
Heb 9: 15 now that he has *d* as a ransom
9: 17 in force only when somebody has *d*
1Pe 3: 18 For Christ *d* for sins once for all,
Rev 2: 8 who *d* and came to life again.

DIES (DIE)
Job 14: 14 If a man *d*, will he live again?
Pr 11: 7 a wicked man *d*, his hope perishes;
26: 20 without gossip a quarrel *d* down.
Jn 11: 25 in me will live, even though he *d*;
12: 24 But if it *d*, it produces many seeds.
Ro 7: 2 but if her husband *d*, she is released
14: 7 and none of us *d* to himself alone.
1Co 7: 39 But if her husband *d*, she is free
15: 36 does not come to life unless it *d*.

DIFFERENCE* (DIFFERENT)
2Sa 19: 35 Can I tell the *d* between what is
2Ch 12: 8 so that they may learn the *d*
Eze 22: 26 they teach that there is no *d*
44: 23 are to teach my people the *d*
Ro 3: 22 There is no *d*, for all have sinned
10: 12 For there is no *d* between Jew
Gal 2: 6 whatever they were makes no *d*

DIFFERENCES* (DIFFERENT)
1Co 11: 19 to be *d* among you to show which

DIFFERENT* (DIFFERENCE DIFFERENCES DIFFERING DIFFERS)
Lev 19: 19 " 'Do not mate *d* kinds of animals.
Nu 14: 24 my servant Caleb has a *d* spirit
1Sa 10: 6 you will be changed into a *d* person
Est 1: 7 each one *d* from the other,
3: 8 whose customs are *d* from those
Da 7: 3 Four great beasts, each *d*
7: 7 It was *d* from all the former beasts,
7: 19 which was *d* from all the others
7: 23 It will be *d* from all the other
7: 24 them another king will arise, *d*
11: 29 but this time the outcome will be *d*
Mk 16: 12 Jesus appeared in a *d* form
Ro 12: 6 We have *d* gifts, according
1Co 4: 7 For who makes you *d*
12: 4 There are *d* kinds of gifts,
12: 5 There are *d* kinds of service,
12: 6 There are *d* kinds of working,
12: 10 speaking in *d* kinds of tongues,
12: 28 and those speaking in *d* kinds
2Co 11: 4 or a *d* gospel from the one you
11: 4 or if you receive a *d* spirit
Gal 1: 6 and are turning to a *d* gospel—
4: 1 he is no *d* from a slave,
Heb 7: 13 are said belonged to a *d* tribe,
Jas 2: 25 and sent them off in a *d* direction?

DIFFERING* (DIFFERENT)
Dt 25: 13 Do not have two *d* weights
25: 14 Do not have two *d* measures
Pr 20: 10 Differing weights and *d* measures
20: 10 *D* weights and differing measures
20: 23 The LORD detests *d* weights,

DIFFERS* (DIFFERENT)
1Co 15: 41 and star *d* from star in splendor.

DIFFICULT (DIFFICULTIES)
Ex 18: 22 but have them bring every *d* case
Dt 30: 11 commanding you today is not too *d*
2Ki 2: 10 "You have asked a *d* thing,"
Eze 3: 5 of obscure speech and *d* language,
Ac 15: 19 that we should not make it *d*

DIFFICULTIES* (DIFFICULT)
Dt 31: 17 and *d* will come upon them,
31: 21 when many disasters and *d* come
2Co 12: 10 in hardships, in persecutions, in *d*.

DIGNITY
Pr 31: 25 She is clothed with strength and *d*;

DIGS
Pr 26: 27 If a man *d* a pit, he will fall into it;

DILIGENCE (DILIGENT)
Ezr 5: 8 The work is being carried on with *d*
Heb 6: 11 to show this same *d* to the very end

DILIGENT (DILIGENCE)
Pr 10: 4 but *d* hands bring wealth.
12: 24 *D* hands will rule,
12: 27 the *d* man prizes his possessions.
13: 4 of the *d* are fully satisfied.
21: 5 The plans of the *d* lead to profit
1Ti 4: 15 Be *d* in these matters; give yourself

DINAH*
Only daughter of Jacob, by Leah (Ge 30:21; 46:15). Raped by Shechem; avenged by Simeon and Levi (Ge 34).

DINE
Pr 23: 1 When you sit to *d* with a ruler,

DIOTREPHES*
3Jn : 9 but *D*, who loves to be first,

DIRECT (DIRECTED DIRECTIVES DIRECTS)
Ge 18: 19 so that he will *d* his children
Dt 17: 10 to do everything they *d* you to do.
Ps 119: 35 *D* me in the path of your
119:133 *D* my footsteps according
Jer 10: 23 it is not for man to *d* his steps.
2Th 3: 5 May the Lord *d* your hearts
1Ti 5: 17 The elders who *d* the affairs

DIRECTED (DIRECT)
Ge 24: 51 master's son, as the LORD has *d*."
Nu 16: 40 as the LORD *d* him through Moses
Dt 2: 1 Sea, as the LORD had *d* me.
6: 1 laws the LORD your God *d* me
Jos 11: 9 did to them as the LORD had *d*:
11: 23 just as the LORD had *d* Moses,
Pr 20: 24 A man's steps are *d* by the LORD.
Jer 13: 2 as the LORD *d*, and put it
Ac 7: 44 It had been made as God *d* Moses,
Tit 1: 5 elders in every town, as I *d* you.

DIRECTIVES* (DIRECT)
1Co 11: 17 In the following *d* I have no praise

DIRECTS (DIRECT)
Ps 42: 8 By day the LORD *d* his love,
Isa 48: 17 who *d* you in the way you should

DIRGE*
Mt 11: 17 we sang a *d*,
Lk 7: 32 we sang a *d*,

DISABLED*
Jn 5: 3 number of *d* people used to lie—
Heb 12: 13 so that the lame may not be *d*,

DISAGREEMENT*
Ac 15: 39 had such a sharp *d* that they parted

DISAPPEAR (DISAPPEARED DISAPPEARS)
Mt 5: 18 will by any means *d* from the Law
Lk 16: 17 earth to *d* than for the least stroke
Heb 8: 13 is obsolete and aging will soon *d*.
2Pe 3: 10 The heavens will *d* with a roar;

DISAPPEARED (DISAPPEAR)
1Ki 20: 40 busy here and there, the man *d*."

DISAPPEARS (DISAPPEAR)
1Co 13: 10 perfection comes, the imperfect *d*.

DISAPPOINT* (DISAPPOINTED)
Ro 5: 5 And hope does not *d* us,

DISAPPOINTED (DISAPPOINT)
Ps 22: 5 in you they trusted and were not *d*.

DISAPPROVE*
Pr 24: 18 or the LORD will see and *d*

DISARMED*
Col 2: 15 And having *d* the powers

DISASTER
Ex 32: 12 and do not bring *d* on your people.
Ps 57: 1 wings until the *d* has passed.
Pr 1: 26 I in turn will laugh at your *d*;
3: 25 Have no fear of sudden *d*
6: 15 Therefore *d* will overtake him
16: 4 even the wicked for a day of *d*.
17: 5 over *d* will not go unpunished.
27: 10 house when *d* strikes you—
Isa 45: 7 I bring prosperity and create *d*;
Jer 17: 17 you are my refuge in the day of *d*.
Eze 7: 5 An unheard-of *d* is coming.

DISCERN (DISCERNED DISCERNING DISCERNMENT)
Ps 19: 12 Who can *d* his errors?
139: 3 You *d* my going out and my lying
Php 1: 10 you may be able to *d* what is best

DISCERNED (DISCERN)
1Co 2: 14 because they are spiritually *d*.

DISCERNING (DISCERN)
1Ki 3: 9 So give your servant a *d* heart
3: 12 I will give you a wise and *d* heart,
Pr 1: 5 and let the *d* get guidance—
8: 9 To the *d* all of them are right;

10: 13 on the lips of the *d*,
14: 6 knowledge comes easily to the *d*.
14: 33 in the heart of the *d*
15: 14 The *d* heart seeks knowledge,
16: 21 The wise in heart are called *d*,
17: 24 A *d* man keeps wisdom in view,
17: 28 and *d* if he holds his tongue.
18: 15 heart of the *d* acquires knowledge;
19: 25 rebuke a *d* man, and he will gain
28: 7 He who keeps the law is a *d* son,

DISCERNMENT (DISCERN)
Ps 119:125 I am your servant; give me *d*
Pr 3: 21 preserve sound judgment and *d*,
17: 10 A rebuke impresses a man of *d*
28: 11 a poor man who has *d* sees

DISCHARGED* (DISCHARGING)
Ecc 8: 8 As no one is *d* in time of war,

DISCHARGING* (DISCHARGED)
1Co 9: 17 I am simply *d* the trust committed

DISCIPLE (DISCIPLES DISCIPLES')
Mt 10: 42 these little ones because he is my *d*,
Lk 14: 26 his own life—he cannot be my *d*.
14: 27 and follow me cannot be my *d*.
14: 33 everything he has cannot be my *d*.
Jn 13: 23 of them, the *d* whom Jesus loved,
19: 26 and the *d* whom he loved standing
21: 7 Then the *d* whom Jesus loved said
21: 20 saw that the *d* whom Jesus loved

DISCIPLES (DISCIPLE)
Mt 10: 1 He called his twelve *d* to him
26: 56 Then all the *d* deserted him
28: 19 Therefore go and make *d*
Mk 3: 7 withdrew with his *d* to the lake,
16: 20 Then the *d* went out and preached
Lk 6: 13 he called his *d* to him and chose
Jn 2: 11 and his *d* put their faith in him.
6: 66 many of his *d* turned back
8: 31 to my teaching, you are really my *d*
12: 16 At first his *d* did not understand all
13: 35 men will know that you are my *d*
15: 8 showing yourselves to be my *d*.
20: 20 The *d* were overjoyed
Ac 6: 1 the number of *d* was increasing,
11: 26 The *d* were called Christians first
14: 22 strengthening the *d*
18: 23 Phrygia, strengthening all the *d*.

DISCIPLES' (DISCIPLE)
Jn 13: 5 and began to wash his *d* feet,

DISCIPLINE* (DISCIPLINED DISCIPLINES SELF-DISCIPLINE)
Dt 4: 36 made you hear his voice to *d* you.
11: 2 and experienced the *d*
21: 18 listen to them when they *d* him,
Job 5: 17 so do not despise the *d*
Ps 6: 1 or *d* me in your wrath.
38: 1 or *d* me in your wrath.
39: 11 You rebuke and *d* men for their sin;
94: 12 Blessed is the man you *d*, O LORD
Pr 1: 2 for attaining wisdom and *d*;
1: 7 but fools despise wisdom and *d*.
3: 11 do not despise the LORD's *d*
5: 12 You will say, "How I hated *d*!
5: 23 He will die for lack of *d*,
6: 23 and the corrections of *d*
10: 17 He who heeds *d* shows the way
12: 1 Whoever loves *d* loves knowledge,
13: 18 He who ignores *d* comes to poverty
13: 24 who loves him is careful to *d* him.
15: 5 A fool spurns his father's *d*,
15: 10 Stern *d* awaits him who leaves
15: 32 He who ignores *d* despises himself,
19: 18 *D* your son, for in that there is hope
22: 15 the rod of *d* will drive it far
23: 13 Do not withhold *d* from a child;
23: 23 get wisdom, *d* and understanding.
29: 17 *D* your son, and he will give you
Jer 17: 23 would not listen or respond to *d*.
30: 11 I will *d* you but only with justice;
32: 33 would not listen or respond to *d*.
46: 28 I will *d* you but only with justice;
Hos 5: 2 I will *d* all of them.
Heb 12: 5 do not make light of the Lord's *d*,
12: 7 as *d*; God is treating you
12: 8 (and everyone undergoes *d*),
12: 11 No *d* seems pleasant at the time,
Rev 3: 19 Those whom I love I rebuke and *d*.

DISCIPLINED* (DISCIPLINE)
Pr 1: 3 for acquiring a *d* and prudent life,
Isa 26: 16 when you *d* them,
Jer 31: 18 and I have been *d*.
31: 18 'You *d* me like an unruly calf,
1Co 11: 32 we are being *d* so that we will not
Tit 1: 8 upright, holy and *d*.
Heb 12: 7 For what son is not *d* by his father?
12: 8 you are not *d* (and everyone
12: 9 all had human fathers who *d* us
12: 10 Our fathers *d* us for a little while

DISCIPLINES* (DISCIPLINE)
Dt 8: 5 your heart that as a man *d* his son,
8: 5 so the LORD your God *d* you.
Ps 94: 10 Does he who *d* nations not punish?
Pr 3: 12 the LORD *d* those he loves,
Heb 12: 6 because the Lord *d* those he loves,
12: 10 but God *d* us for our good,

DISCLOSED
Lk 8: 17 is nothing hidden that will not be *d*,
Col 1: 26 and generations, but is now *d*
Heb 9: 8 Holy Place had not yet been *d*

DISCORD
Gal 5: 20 idolatry and witchcraft; hatred, *d*,

DISCOURAGED* (DISCOURAGEMENT)
Nu 32: 9 they *d* the Israelites
Dt 1: 21 Do not be afraid; do not be *d*."
31: 8 Do not be afraid; do not be *d*."
Jos 1: 9 Do not be terrified; do not be *d*,
8: 1 "Do not be afraid; do not be *d*.
10: 25 "Do not be afraid; do not be *d*.
1Ch 22: 13 Do not be afraid or *d*.
28: 20 or *d*, for the LORD God,
2Ch 20: 15 or *d* because of this vast army.
20: 17 Do not be afraid; do not be *d*.
32: 7 or *d* because of the king of Assyria
Job 4: 5 to you, and you are *d*;
Isa 42: 4 he will not falter or be *d*
Eph 3: 13 to be *d* because of my sufferings
Col 3: 21 children, or they will become *d*.

DISCOURAGEMENT* (DISCOURAGED)
Ex 6: 9 of their *d* and cruel bondage.

DISCOVERED
2Ki 23: 24 book that Hilkiah the priest had *d*

DISCREDIT* (DISCREDITED)
Ne 6: 13 would give me a bad name to *d* me.
Job 40: 8 "Would you *d* my justice?

DISCREDITED (DISCREDIT)
2Co 6: 3 so that our ministry will not be *d*.

DISCRETION*
1Ch 22: 12 May the LORD give you *d*
Pr 1: 4 knowledge and *d* to the young—
2: 11 *D* will protect you,
5: 2 that you may maintain *d*
8: 12 I possess knowledge and *d*.
11: 22 a beautiful woman who shows no *d*.

DISCRIMINATED*
Jas 2: 4 have you not *d* among yourselves

DISEASE (DISEASES)
Mt 4: 23 and healing every *d* and sickness
9: 35 and healing every *d* and sickness.
10: 1 and to heal every *d* and sickness.

DISEASES (DISEASE)
Ps 103: 3 and heals all my *d*;
Mt 8: 17 and carried our *d*."
Mk 3: 10 those with *d* were pushing forward
Lk 9: 1 drive out all demons and to cure *d*,

DISFIGURE* (DISFIGURED)
Mt 6: 16 for they *d* their faces

DISFIGURED (DISFIGURE)
Isa 52: 14 his appearance was so *d*

DISGRACE (DISGRACEFUL DISGRACES)
Ps 44: 15 My *d* is before me all day long,
52: 1 you who are a *d* in the eyes of God?
74: 21 not let the oppressed retreat in *d*;
Pr 6: 33 Blows and *d* are his lot,
11: 2 When pride comes, then comes *d*,
14: 34 but sin is a *d* to any people.
19: 26 is a son who brings shame and *d*.
Mt 1: 19 want to expose her to public *d*,
Ac 5: 41 of suffering *d* for the Name.
1Co 11: 6 and if it is a *d* for a woman
11: 14 it is a *d* to him, but that
1Ti 3: 7 so that he will not fall into *d*
Heb 6: 6 and subjecting him to public *d*.
11: 26 He regarded *d* for the sake
13: 13 the camp, bearing the *d* he bore.

DISGRACEFUL (DISGRACE)
Pr 10: 5 during harvest is a *d* son.
12: 4 a *d* wife is like decay in his bones.
17: 2 wise servant will rule over a *d* son,
1Co 14: 35 for it is *d* for a woman to speak

DISGRACES (DISGRACE)
Pr 28: 7 of gluttons *d* his father.
29: 15 but a child left to himself *d* his mother

DISGUISES*
Pr 26: 24 A malicious man *d* himself

DISH
Pr 19: 24 sluggard buries his hand in the *d*;
Mt 23: 25 the outside of the cup and *d*,

DISHONEST*
Ex 18: 21 trustworthy men who hate *d* gain
Lev 19: 35 " 'Do not use *d* standards
1Sa 8: 3 They turned aside after *d* gain
Pr 11: 1 The LORD abhors *d* scales,
13: 11 *D* money dwindles away,
20: 23 and *d* scales do not please him.
29: 27 The righteous detest the *d*;
Jer 22: 17 are set only on *d* gain,
Eze 28: 18 By your many sins and *d* trade
Hos 12: 7 The merchant uses *d* scales;
Am 8: 5 and cheating with *d* scales,
Mic 6: 11 Shall I acquit a man with *d* scales,
Lk 16: 8 master commended the *d* manager
16: 10 whoever is *d* with very little will
16: 10 with very little will also be *d*
1Ti 3: 8 wine, and not pursuing *d* gain.
Tit 1: 7 not violent, not pursuing *d* gain.
1: 11 and that for the sake of *d* gain.

DISHONOR* (DISHONORED DISHONORS)
Lev 18: 7 " 'Do not *d* your father
18: 8 wife; that would *d* your father.
18: 10 daughter; that would *d* you.
18: 14 " 'Do not *d* your father's brother
18: 16 that would *d* your brother.
20: 19 for that would *d* a close relative;
Dt 22: 30 he must not *d* his father's bed.
Pr 30: 9 and so *d* the name of my God.
Jer 14: 21 do not *d* your glorious throne.
20: 11 their *d* will never be forgotten.
La 2: 2 princes down to the ground in *d*.
Eze 22: 10 are those who *d* their fathers' bed;
Jn 8: 49 I honor my Father and you *d* me.
Ro 2: 23 do you *d* God by breaking the law?
1Co 15: 43 it is sown in *d*, it is raised in glory;
2Co 6: 8 through glory and *d*, bad report

DISHONORED* (DISHONOR)
Lev 20: 11 father's wife, he has *d* his father.
20: 17 He has *d* his sister and will be held
20: 20 with his aunt, he has *d* his uncle.
20: 21 of impurity; he has *d* his brother.
Dt 21: 14 as a slave, since you have *d* her.
Ezr 4: 14 proper for us to see the king *d*,

1Co 4: 10 You are honored, we are *d!*

DISHONORS* (DISHONOR)
Dt 27: 16 Cursed is the man who *d* his father
27: 20 for he *d* his father's bed."
Job 20: 3 I hear a rebuke that *d* me,
Mic 7: 6 For a son *d* his father,
1Co 11: 4 with his head covered *d* his head.
11: 5 her head uncovered *d* her head—

DISILLUSIONMENT*
Ps 7: 14 conceives trouble gives birth to *d.*

DISMAYED
Isa 28: 16 the one who trusts will never be *d.*
41: 10 do not be *d,* for I am your God.

DISOBEDIENCE* (DISOBEY)
Jos 22: 22 in rebellion or *d* to the LORD,
Jer 43: 7 So they entered Egypt in *d*
Ro 5: 19 as through the *d* of the one man
11: 30 mercy as a result of their *d,*
11: 32 to *d* so that he may have mercy
2Co 10: 6 ready to punish every act of *d,*
Heb 2: 2 and *d* received its just punishment,
4: 6 go in, because of their *d.*
4: 11 fall by following their example of *d.*

DISOBEDIENT* (DISOBEY)
Ne 9: 26 "But they were *d* and rebelled
Lk 1: 17 and the *d* to the wisdom
Ac 26: 19 I was not *d* to the vision
Ro 10: 21 hands to a *d* and obstinate people."
11: 30 as you who were at one time *d*
11: 31 so they too have now become *d*
Eph 2: 2 now at work in those who are *d.*
5: 6 comes on those who are *d.*
5: 12 to mention what the *d* do in secret.
2Ti 3: 2 proud, abusive, *d* to their parents,
Tit 1: 6 to the charge of being wild and *d.*
1: 16 *d* and unfit for doing anything
3: 3 At one time we too were foolish, *d,*
Heb 11: 31 killed with those who were *d.*

DISOBEY* (DISOBEDIENCE DISOBEDIENT DISOBEYED DISOBEYING DISOBEYS)
Dt 11: 28 the curse if you *d* the commands
2Ch 24: 20 'Why do you *d* the LORD's
Est 3: 3 Why do you *d* the king's command
Jer 42: 13 and so *d* the LORD your God,
Ro 1: 30 they *d* their parents; they are
1Pe 2: 8 because they *d* the message—

DISOBEYED* (DISOBEY)
Nu 14: 22 and in the desert but who *d* me
27: 14 both of you *d* my command
Jdg 2: 2 Yet you have *d* me.
Ne 9: 29 arrogant and *d* your commands.
Isa 24: 5 they have *d* the laws,
Jer 43: 4 and all the people *d* the LORD's
Lk 15: 29 for you and never *d* your orders.
Heb 3: 18 rest if not to those who *d?*
1Pe 3: 20 the spirits in prison who *d* long ago

DISOBEYING* (DISOBEY)
Nu 14: 41 "Why are you *d* the LORD's

DISOBEYS* (DISOBEY)
Eze 33: 12 man will not save him when he *d,*

DISORDER
1Co 14: 33 For God is not a God of *d*
2Co 12: 20 slander, gossip, arrogance and *d.*
Jas 3: 16 there you find *d* and every evil

DISOWN (DISOWNS)
Pr 30: 9 I may have too much and *d* you
Mt 10: 33 I will *d* him before my Father
26: 35 to die with you, I will never *d* you."
2Ti 2: 12 If we *d* him,

DISOWNS (DISOWN)
Lk 12: 9 he who *d* me before men will be

DISPENSATION see ADMINISTRATION, TRUST

DISPLACES
Pr 30: 23 a maidservant who *d* her mistress.

DISPLAY (DISPLAYED DISPLAYS)
Ps 45: 4 your right hand *d* awesome deeds.
Eze 39: 21 I will *d* my glory among the nations
Ro 9: 17 that I might *d* my power in you
1Co 4: 9 on *d* at the end of the procession,
1Ti 1: 16 Christ Jesus might *d* his unlimited

DISPLAYED (DISPLAY)
Jn 9: 3 work of God might be *d* in his life.
2Th 2: 9 the work of Satan *d* in all kinds

DISPLAYS (DISPLAY)
Isa 44: 23 he *d* his glory in Israel.

DISPLEASE (DISPLEASED)
1Th 2: 15 They *d* God and are hostile

DISPLEASED (DISPLEASE)
2Sa 11: 27 David had done *d* the LORD.

DISPUTABLE* (DISPUTE)
Ro 14: 1 passing judgment on *d* matters.

DISPUTE (DISPUTABLE DISPUTES DISPUTING)
Pr 17: 14 before a *d* breaks out.
1Co 6: 1 If any of you has a *d* with another,

DISPUTES (DISPUTE)
Pr 18: 18 Casting the lot settles *d*

DISPUTING (DISPUTE)
1Ti 2: 8 in prayer, without anger or *d.*

DISQUALIFIED*
1Co 9: 27 I myself will not be *d* for the prize.

DISREPUTE*
2Pe 2: 2 will bring the way of truth into *d.*

DISSENSION* (DISSENSIONS)
Pr 6: 14 he always stirs up *d.*
6: 19 and a man who stirs up *d*
10: 12 Hatred stirs up *d,*
15: 18 A hot-tempered man stirs up *d,*
16: 28 A perverse man stirs up *d,*
28: 25 A greedy man stirs up *d,*
29: 22 An angry man stirs up *d,*
Ro 13: 13 debauchery, not in *d* and jealousy.

DISSENSIONS* (DISSENSION)
Gal 5: 20 selfish ambition, *d,* factions

DISSIPATION*
Lk 21: 34 will be weighed down with *d,*
1Pe 4: 4 with them into the same flood of *d,*

DISTINCTION
Ac 15: 9 He made no *d* between us

DISTINGUISH (DISTINGUISHING)
1Ki 3: 9 and to *d* between right and wrong.
Heb 5: 14 themselves to *d* good from evil.

DISTINGUISHING
1Co 12: 10 the *d* between spirits,

DISTORT
Ac 20: 30 and *d* the truth in order
2Co 4: 2 nor do we *d* the word of God.
2Pe 3: 16 ignorant and unstable people *d,*

DISTRACTED*
Lk 10: 40 But Martha was *d* by all

DISTRESS (DISTRESSED)
2Ch 15: 4 in their *d* they turned to the LORD
Ps 18: 6 In my *d* I called to the LORD;
81: 7 In your *d* you called and I rescued
120: 1 I call on the LORD in my *d,*
Jnh 2: 2 "In my *d* I called to the LORD,
Mt 24: 21 For then there will be great *d,*
Jas 1: 27 after orphans and widows in their *d*

DISTRESSED (DISTRESS)
Lk 12: 50 how *d* I am until it is completed!
Ro 14: 15 If your brother is *d*

DIVIDE (DIVIDED DIVIDING DIVISION DIVISIONS DIVISIVE)
Ps 22: 18 They *d* my garments among them

DIVIDED (DIVIDE)
Mt 12: 25 household *d* against itself will not
Lk 23: 34 they *d* up his clothes by casting lots
1Co 1: 13 Is Christ *d?* Was Paul crucified

DIVIDING (DIVIDE)
Eph 2: 14 destroyed the barrier, the *d* wall
Heb 4: 12 it penetrates even to *d* soul

DIVINATION
Lev 19: 26 " 'Do not practice *d* or sorcery.

DIVINE
Ro 1: 20 his eternal power and *d* nature—
2Co 10: 4 they have *d* power
2Pe 1: 4 you may participate in the *d* nature

DIVISION (DIVIDE)
Lk 12: 51 on earth? No, I tell you, but *d.*
1Co 12: 25 so that there should be no *d*

DIVISIONS (DIVIDE)
Ro 16: 17 to watch out for those who cause *d*
1Co 1: 10 another so that there may be no *d*
11: 18 there are *d* among you,

DIVISIVE* (DIVIDE)
Tit 3: 10 Warn a *d* person once,

DIVORCE* (DIVORCED DIVORCES)
Dt 22: 19 he must not *d* her as long as he lives
22: 29 He can never *d* her as long
24: 1 and he writes her a certificate of *d,*
24: 3 and writes her a certificate of *d,*
Isa 50: 1 is your mother's certificate of *d*
Jer 3: 8 faithless Israel her certificate of *d*
Mal 2: 16 "I hate *d,*" says the LORD God
Mt 1: 19 he had in mind to *d* her quietly.
5: 31 must give her a certificate of *d.*'
19: 3 for a man to *d* his wife for any
19: 7 man give his wife a certificate of *d*
19: 8 permitted you to *d* your wives
Mk 10: 2 Is it lawful for a man to *d* his wife?"
10: 4 a man to write a certificate of *d*
1Co 7: 11 And a husband must not *d* his wife.
7: 12 to live with him, he must not *d* her.
7: 13 to live with her, she must not *d* him
7: 27 Are you married? Do not seek a *d.*

DIVORCED* (DIVORCE)
Lev 21: 7 or *d* from their husbands,
21: 14 not marry a widow, a *d* woman,
22: 13 daughter becomes a widow or is *d,*
Nu 30: 9 or *d* woman will be binding on her.
Dt 24: 4 then her first husband, who *d* her,
1Ch 8: 8 after he had *d* his wives Hushim
Eze 44: 22 not marry widows or *d* women;
Mt 5: 32 marries the *d* woman commits adultery.
Lk 16: 18 who marries a *d* woman commits

DIVORCES* (DIVORCE)
Jer 3: 1 "If a man *d* his wife
Mt 5: 31 'Anyone who *d* his wife must give
5: 32 tell you that anyone who *d* his wife,
19: 9 tell you that anyone who *d* his wife,
Mk 10: 11 "Anyone who *d* his wife
10: 12 And if she *d* her husband
Lk 16: 18 "Anyone who *d* his wife

DOCTOR
Mt 9: 12 "It is not the healthy who need a *d,*

DOCTRINE* (DOCTRINES)
1Ti 1: 10 to the sound *d* that conforms
4: 16 Watch your life and *d* closely.
2Ti 4: 3 men will not put up with sound *d.*
Tit 1: 9 can encourage others by sound *d*
2: 1 is in accord with sound *d.*

DOCTRINES* (DOCTRINE)
1Ti 1: 3 not to teach false *d* any longer
6: 3 If anyone teaches false *d*

DOEG*
Edomite; Saul's head shepherd; responsible for murder of priests at Nob (1Sa 21:7; 22:6–23; Ps 52).

DOG (DOGS)
Pr 26: 11 As a *d* returns to its vomit,
Ecc 9: 4 a live *d* is better off than a dead lion
2Pe 2: 22 "A *d* returns to its vomit," and,

35: 2 and *e* them in the service
Eze 13: 22 you *e* the wicked not to turn
Ac 9: 31 It was strengthened; and *e*
11: 23 and *e* them all to remain true
16: 40 met with the brothers and *e* them.
18: 27 the brothers *e* him and wrote
27: 36 They were all *e* and ate some food
28: 15 men Paul thanked God and was *e.*
Ro 1: 12 and I may be mutually *e*
1Co 14: 31 everyone may be instructed and *e.*
2Co 7: 4 I am greatly *e;* in all our troubles
7: 13 By all this we are *e.*
Php 1: 14 brothers in the Lord have been *e*
Col 2: 2 My purpose is that they may be *e*
1Th 3: 7 persecution we were *e* about you
Heb 6: 18 offered to us may be greatly *e.*

ENCOURAGEMENT* (ENCOURAGE)
Ac 4: 36 Barnabas (which means Son of *E*),
13: 15 a message of *e* for the people,
20: 2 speaking many words of *e*
Ro 15: 4 *e* of the Scriptures we might have
15: 5 and *e* give you a spirit of unity
1Co 14: 3 to men for their strengthening, *e*
2Co 7: 13 to our own *e,* we were especially
Php 2: 1 If you have any *e* from being united
2Th 2: 16 and by his grace gave us eternal *e*
Phm : 7 love has given me great joy and *e,*
Heb 12: 5 word of *e* that addresses you

ENCOURAGES* (ENCOURAGE)
Isa 41: 7 The craftsman *e* the goldsmith,

ENCOURAGING* (ENCOURAGE)
Ac 14: 22 *e* them to remain true to the faith.
15: 31 and were glad for its *e* message.
20: 1 for the disciples and, after *e* them,
Ro 12: 8 if it is *e,* let him encourage;
1Th 2: 12 *e,* comforting and urging you
1Pe 5: 12 *e* you and testifying that this is

ENCROACH
Pr 23: 10 or *e* on the fields of the fatherless,

END (ENDS)
Ps 119: 33 then I will keep them to the *e.*
119:112 to the very *e.*
Pr 1: 19 Such is the *e* of all who go
5: 4 but in the *e* she is bitter as gall,
5: 11 At the *e* of your life you will groan,
14: 12 but in the *e* it leads to death.
14: 13 and joy may *e* in grief.
16: 25 but in the *e* it leads to death.
19: 20 and in the *e* you will be wise.
20: 21 will not be blessed at the *e.*
23: 32 In the *e* it bites like a snake
25: 8 for what will you do in the *e*
28: 23 in the *e* gain more favor
29: 21 he will bring grief in the *e.*
Ecc 3: 11 done from beginning to *e.*
7: 8 The *e* of a matter is better
12: 12 making many books there is no *e,*
Eze 7: 2 The *e!* The *e* has come
Mt 10: 22 firm to the *e* will be saved.
24: 13 firm to the *e* will be saved.
24: 14 nations, and then the *e* will come.
Lk 21: 9 but the *e* will not come right away
Ro 10: 4 Christ is the *e* of the law
1Co 15: 24 the *e* will come, when he hands
Rev 21: 6 Omega, the Beginning and the *E.*
22: 13 the Last, the Beginning and the *E.*

ENDS (END)
Ps 19: 4 their words to the *e* of the world.
Pr 20: 17 he *e* up with a mouth full of gravel.
Isa 49: 6 salvation to the *e* of the earth."
62: 11 proclamation to the *e* of the earth:
Ac 13: 47 salvation to the *e* of the earth.' "
Ro 10: 18 their words to the *e* of the world."

ENDURANCE* (ENDURE)
Ro 15: 4 through *e* and the encouragement
15: 5 May the God who gives *e*
2Co 1: 6 which produces in you patient *e*
6: 4 in great *e;* in troubles, hardships
Col 1: 11 might so that you may have great *e*
1Th 1: 3 and your *e* inspired by hope
1Ti 6: 11 faith, love, *e* and gentleness.
2Ti 3: 10 patience, love, *e,* persecutions,
Tit 2: 2 and sound in faith, in love and in *e.*
Rev 1: 9 and patient *e* that are ours in Jesus,
13: 10 This calls for patient *e*
14: 12 This calls for patient *e* on the part

ENDURE (ENDURANCE ENDURED ENDURES ENDURING)
Ps 72: 17 May his name *e* forever;
Pr 12: 19 Truthful lips *e* forever,
27: 24 for riches do not *e* forever,
Ecc 3: 14 everything God does will *e* forever;
Da 2: 44 to an end, but it will itself *e* forever.
Mal 3: 2 who can *e* the day of his coming?
1Co 4: 12 when we are persecuted, we *e* it;
2Co 1: 8 far beyond our ability to *e,*
2Ti 2: 3 *E* hardship with us like a good
2: 10 Therefore I *e* everything
2: 12 if we *e,* / we will also reign
4: 5 head in all situations, *e* hardship,
Heb 12: 7 *E* hardship as discipline; God is
1Pe 2: 20 a beating for doing wrong and *e* it?
2: 20 suffer for doing good and you *e* it,
Rev 3: 10 kept my command to *e* patiently,

ENDURED* (ENDURE)
Ps 123: 3 for we have *e* much contempt.
123: 4 We have *e* much ridicule
132: 1 and all the hardships he *e.*
Ac 13: 18 and *e* their conduct forty years
2Ti 3: 11 and Lystra, the persecutions I *e.*
Heb 12: 2 set before him *e* the cross,
12: 3 him who *e* such opposition
Rev 2: 3 and have *e* hardships for my name,

ENDURES (ENDURE)
Ps 102: 12 renown *e* through all generations.
112: 9 his righteousness *e* forever;
136: 1 *His love e forever.*
Da 9: 15 made for yourself a name that *e*
2Co 9: 9 his righteousness *e* forever."

ENDURING (ENDURE)
2Th 1: 4 persecutions and trials you are *e.*
1Pe 1: 23 through the living and *e* word

ENEMIES (ENEMY)
Ps 23: 5 in the presence of my *e.*
110: 1 hand until I make your *e*
Pr 16: 7 his *e* live at peace with him.
Isa 59: 18 wrath to his *e*
Mic 7: 6 a man's *e* are the members
Mt 5: 44 Love your *e* and pray
10: 36 a man's *e* will be the members
Lk 6: 27 Love your *e,* do good
6: 35 But love your *e,* do good to them,
20: 43 hand until I make your *e*
Ro 5: 10 For if, when we were God's *e,*
1Co 15: 25 reign until he has put all his *e*
Php 3: 18 many live as *e* of the cross of Christ
Heb 1: 13 hand until I make your *e*
10: 13 for his *e* to be made his footstool,

ENEMY (ENEMIES ENMITY)
Pr 24: 17 Do not gloat when your *e* falls;
25: 21 If your *e* is hungry, give him food
27: 6 but an *e* multiplies kisses.
29: 24 of a thief is his own *e;*
Lk 10: 19 to overcome all the power of the *e;*
Ro 12: 20 "If your *e* is hungry, feed him;
1Co 15: 26 The last *e* to be destroyed is death.
1Ti 5: 14 and to give the *e* no opportunity
1Pe 5: 8 Your *e* the devil prowls

ENERGY*
Col 1: 29 struggling with all his *e,* which

ENGRAVED
Isa 49: 16 I have *e* you on the palms
2Co 3: 7 which was *e* in letters on stone,

ENHANCES*
Ro 3: 7 my falsehood *e* God's truthfulness

ENJOY (JOY)
Dt 6: 2 and so that you may *e* long life.
Ps 37: 3 dwell in the land and *e* safe pasture.
Pr 28: 16 ill-gotten gain will *e* a long life.
Ecc 3: 22 better for a man than to *e* his work,
Eph 6: 3 and that you may *e* long life
Heb 11: 25 rather than to *e* the pleasures of sin
3Jn : 2 I pray that you may *e* good health

ENJOYMENT (JOY)
Ecc 4: 8 and why am I depriving myself of *e*
1Ti 6: 17 us with everything for our *e.*

ENLARGE (ENLARGES)
2Co 9: 10 *e* the harvest of your righteousness.

ENLARGES (ENLARGE)
Dt 33: 20 Blessed is he who *e* Gad's domain!

ENLIGHTENED* (LIGHT)
Eph 1: 18 that the eyes of your heart may be *e*
Heb 6: 4 for those who have once been *e,*

ENMITY* (ENEMY)
Ge 3: 15 And I will put *e*

ENOCH
1. Son of Cain (Ge 4:17–18).
2. Descendant of Seth; walked with God and taken by him (Ge 5:18–24; Heb 11:5). Prophet (Jude 14).

ENSLAVED (SLAVE)
Gal 4: 9 Do you wish to be *e* by them all
Tit 3: 3 and *e* by all kinds of passions

ENSNARE (SNARE)
Pr 5: 22 of a wicked man *e* him;
Ecc 7: 26 but the sinner she will *e.*

ENSNARED* (SNARE)
Dt 7: 25 for yourselves, or you will be *e* by it
12: 30 be careful not to be *e*
Ps 9: 16 the wicked are *e* by the work
Pr 6: 2 *e* by the words of your mouth,
22: 25 and get yourself *e.*

ENTANGLED (ENTANGLES)
2Pe 2: 20 and are again *e* in it and overcome,

ENTANGLES* (ENTANGLED)
Heb 12: 1 and the sin that so easily *e,*

ENTER (ENTERED ENTERING ENTERS ENTRANCE)
Ps 95: 11 "They shall never *e* my rest."
100: 4 *E* his gates with thanksgiving
Pr 2: 10 For wisdom will *e* your heart,
Mt 5: 20 will certainly not *e* the kingdom
7: 13 "*E* through the narrow gate.
7: 21 Lord,' will *e* the kingdom of heaven
18: 3 you will never *e* the kingdom
18: 8 It is better for you to *e* life maimed
19: 17 to *e* life, obey the commandments
19: 23 man to *e* the kingdom of heaven.
Mk 9: 43 It is better for you to *e* life maimed
9: 45 It is better for you to *e* life crippled
9: 47 for you to *e* the kingdom of God
10: 15 like a little child will never *e* it."
10: 23 is for the rich to *e* the kingdom
Lk 13: 24 will try to *e* and will not be able to.
13: 24 "Make every effort to *e*
18: 17 like a little child will never *e* it."
18: 24 is for the rich to *e* the kingdom
Jn 3: 5 no one can *e* the kingdom of God.
Heb 3: 11 'They shall never *e* my rest.' "
4: 11 make every effort to *e* that rest,

ENTERED (ENTER)
Ps 73: 17 me till I *e* the sanctuary of God;
Eze 4: 14 meat has ever *e* my mouth."
Ac 11: 8 or unclean has ever *e* my mouth.'
Ro 5: 12 as sin *e* the world through one man,
Heb 9: 12 but he *e* the Most Holy Place once

ENTERING (ENTER)
Mt 21: 31 the prostitutes are *e* the kingdom

Lk 11: 52 have hindered those who were *e*."
Heb 4: 1 the promise of *e* his rest still stands,

ENTERS (ENTER)
Mk 7: 18 you see that nothing that *e* a man
Jn 10: 2 The man who *e* by the gate is

ENTERTAIN* (ENTERTAINED ENTERTAINMENT)
Jdg 16: 25 "Bring out Samson to *e* us."
Mt 9: 4 "Why do you *e* evil thoughts
1Ti 5: 19 Do not *e* an accusation
Heb 13: 2 Do not forget to *e* strangers,

ENTERTAINED* (ENTERTAIN)
Ac 28: 7 and for three days *e* us hospitably.
Heb 13: 2 so doing some people have *e* angels

ENTERTAINMENT* (ENTERTAIN)
Da 6: 18 without any *e* being brought to him

ENTHRALLED*
Ps 45: 11 The king is *e* by your beauty;

ENTHRONED* (THRONE)
1Sa 4: 4 who is *e* between the cherubim.
2Sa 6: 2 who is *e* between the cherubim that
2Ki 19: 15 of Israel, *e* between the cherubim,
1Ch 13: 6 who is *e* between the cherubim—
Ps 2: 4 The One *e* in heaven laughs;
9: 11 to the LORD, *e* in Zion;
22: 3 Yet you are *e* as the Holy One;
29: 10 The LORD sits *e* over the flood;
29: 10 the LORD is *e* as King forever.
55: 19 God, who is *e* forever,
61: 7 May he be *e* in God's presence
80: 1 who sit *e* between the cherubim,
99: 1 he sits *e* between the cherubim,
102: 12 But you, O LORD, sit *e* forever;
113: 5 the One who sits *e* on high,
132: 14 here I will sit *e*, for I have desired it
Isa 14: 13 I will sit *e* on the mount
37: 16 of Israel, *e* between the cherubim,
40: 22 He sits *e* above the circle
52: 2 rise up, sit *e*, O Jerusalem.

ENTHRONES* (THRONE)
Job 36: 7 he *e* them with kings

ENTHUSIASM*
2Co 8: 17 he is coming to you with much *e*
9: 2 and your *e* has stirred most of them

ENTICE* (ENTICED ENTICES)
Pr 1: 10 My son, if sinners *e* you,
2Pe 2: 18 they *e* people who are just escaping
Rev 2: 14 who taught Balak to *e* the Israelites

ENTICED* (ENTICE)
Dt 4: 19 do not be *e* into bowing
11: 16 or you will be *e* to turn away
2Ki 17: 21 Jeroboam *e* Israel away
Job 31: 9 If my heart has been *e* by a woman,
31: 27 so that my heart was secretly *e*
Jas 1: 14 desire, he is dragged away and *e*.

ENTICES* (ENTICE)
Dt 13: 6 your closest friend secretly *e* you,
Job 36: 18 Be careful that no one *e* you
Pr 16: 29 A violent man *e* his neighbor

ENTIRE
Gal 5: 14 The *e* law is summed up

ENTRANCE (ENTER)
Mt 27: 60 stone in front of the *e* to the tomb
Mk 15: 46 a stone against the *e* of the tomb.
16: 3 away from the *e* of the tomb?"
Jn 11: 38 cave with a stone laid across the *e*.
20: 1 had been removed from the *e*.

ENTRUST (TRUST)
Jn 2: 24 Jesus would not *e* himself to them,
2Ti 2: 2 the presence of many witnesses *e*

ENTRUSTED (TRUST)
Jer 13: 20 Where is the flock that was *e* to you
Jn 5: 22 but has *e* all judgment to the Son,
Ro 3: 2 they have been *e* with the very
6: 17 of teaching to which you were *e*.
1Co 4: 1 as those *e* with the secret things
1Th 2: 4 by God to be *e* with the gospel.
1Ti 1: 11 of the blessed God, which he *e*
6: 20 guard what has been *e* to your care.
2Ti 1: 12 able to guard what I have *e* to him
1: 14 Guard the good deposit that was *e*
Tit 1: 3 light through the preaching *e* to me
1: 7 Since an overseer is *e*
1Pe 2: 23 he *e* himself to him who judges
5: 3 not lording it over those *e* to you,
Jude : 3 once for all *e* to the saints.

ENVIES
Jas 4: 5 spirit he caused to live in us *e*

ENVIOUS (ENVY)
Dt 32: 21 I will make them *e*
Pr 24: 19 or be *e* of the wicked,
Ro 10: 19 "I will make you *e*

ENVOY
Pr 13: 17 but a trustworthy *e* brings healing.

ENVY (ENVIOUS ENVYING)
Pr 3: 31 Do not *e* a violent man
14: 30 but *e* rots the bones.
23: 17 Do not let your heart *e* sinners,
24: 1 Do not *e* wicked men,
Mk 7: 22 malice, deceit, lewdness, *e*, slander
Ro 1: 29 They are full of *e*, murder, strife,
11: 14 arouse my own people to *e*
1Co 13: 4 It does not *e*, it does not boast,
Gal 5: 21 factions and *e*; drunkenness, orgies
Php 1: 15 that some preach Christ out of *e*
1Ti 6: 4 and quarrels about words that result in *e*,
Tit 3: 3 lived in malice and *e*, being hated
Jas 3: 14 But if you harbor bitter *e*
3: 16 where you have *e* and selfish
1Pe 2: 1 *e*, and slander of every kind.

ENVYING* (ENVY)
Gal 5: 26 provoking and *e* each other.

EPHAH
Eze 45: 11 The *e* and the bath are

EPHESUS
Ac 18: 19 at *E*, where Paul left Priscilla
19: 1 the interior and arrived at *E*.
Eph 1: 1 To the saints in *E*, the faithful
Rev 2: 1 the angel of the church in *E* write:

EPHRAIM
1. Second son of Joseph (Ge 41:52; 46:20). Blessed as firstborn by Jacob (Ge 48). Tribe of numbered (Nu 1:33; 26:37), blessed (Dt 33:17), allotted land (Jos 16:4–9; Eze 48:5), failed to fully possess (Jos 16:10; Jdg 1:29).
2. Synonymous with Northern Kingdom (Isa 7:17; Hos 5).

EQUAL (EQUALITY EQUITY)
Dt 33: 25 and your strength will *e* your days.
1Sa 9: 2 without *e* among the Israelites—
Isa 40: 25 who is my *e*?" says the Holy One.
46: 5 you compare me or count me *e*?
Da 1: 19 and he found none *e* to Daniel,
Jn 5: 18 making himself *e* with God.
1Co 12: 25 that its parts should have *e* concern
2Co 2: 16 And who is *e* to such a task?

EQUALITY* (EQUAL)
2Co 8: 13 pressed, but that there might be *e*.
8: 14 Then there will be *e*, as it is written:
Php 2: 6 did not consider *e*

EQUIP* (EQUIPPED)
Heb 13: 21 *e* you with everything good

EQUIPPED (EQUIP)
2Ti 3: 17 man of God may be thoroughly *e*

EQUITY* (EQUAL)
Ps 96: 10 he will judge the peoples with *e*.
98: 9 and the peoples with *e*.
99: 4 you have established *e*;

ERODES*
Job 14: 18 "But as a mountain *e* and crumbles

ERROR (ERRORS)
Jas 5: 20 Whoever turns a sinner from the *e*
2Pe 2: 18 escaping from those who live in *e*.

ERRORS* (ERROR)
Ps 19: 12 Who can discern his *e*?
Ecc 10: 4 calmness can lay great *e* to rest.

ESAU
Firstborn of Isaac, twin of Jacob (Ge 25:21–26). Also called Edom (Ge 25:30). Sold Jacob his birthright (Ge 25:29–34); lost blessing (Gen 27). Married Hittites (Ge 26:34), Ishmaelites (Ge 28:6–9). Reconciled to Jacob (Gen 33). Genealogy (Ge 36). The LORD chose Jacob over Esau (Mal 1:2–3), but gave Esau land (Dt 2:2–12). Descendants eventually obliterated (Ob 1–21; Jer 49:7–22).

ESCAPE (ESCAPED ESCAPES ESCAPING)
Ps 68: 20 from the Sovereign LORD comes *e*
Pr 11: 9 through knowledge the righteous *e*.
Ro 2: 3 think you will *e* God's judgment?
1Th 5: 3 woman, and they will not *e*.
2Ti 2: 26 and *e* from the trap of the devil,
Heb 2: 3 how shall we *e* if we ignore such
12: 25 If they did not *e* when they refused
2Pe 1: 4 and *e* the corruption in the world

ESCAPED (ESCAPE)
2Pe 2: 20 If they have *e* the corruption

ESCAPES (ESCAPE)
Pr 12: 13 but a righteous man *e* trouble.

ESCAPING (ESCAPE)
1Co 3: 15 only as one *e* through the flames.
2Pe 2: 18 they entice people who are just *e*

ESTABLISH (ESTABLISHED ESTABLISHES)
Ge 6: 18 But I will *e* my covenant with you,
17: 21 But my covenant I will *e* with Isaac
2Sa 7: 11 the LORD himself will *e* a house
1Ki 9: 5 I will *e* your royal throne
1Ch 28: 7 I will *e* his kingdom forever
Ps 90: 17 *e* the work of our hands for us—
Isa 26: 12 LORD, you *e* peace for us;
Ro 10: 3 God and sought to *e* their own,
16: 25 able to *e* you by my gospel
Heb 10: 9 sets aside the first to *e* the second.

ESTABLISHED (ESTABLISH)
Ge 9: 17 the sign of the covenant I have *e*
Ex 6: 4 also *e* my covenant with them
Pr 16: 12 a throne is *e* through righteousness.

ESTABLISHES (ESTABLISH)
Job 25: 2 he *e* order in the heights of heaven.
Isa 42: 4 till he *e* justice on earth.

ESTATE
Ps 136: 23 who remembered us in our low *e*

ESTEEMED
Pr 22: 1 to be *e* is better than silver or gold.
Isa 53: 3 he was despised, and we *e* him not.

ESTHER
Jewess, originally named Hadassah, who lived in Persia; cousin of Mordecai (Est 2:7). Chosen queen of Xerxes (Est 2:8–18). Persuaded by Mordecai to foil Haman's plan to exterminate the Jews (Est 3–4). Revealed Haman's plans to Xerxes, resulting in Haman's death (Est 7), the Jews' preservation (Est 8–9), Mordecai's exaltation (Est 8:15; 9:4; 10). Decreed celebration of Purim (Est 9:18–32).

ETERNAL* (ETERNALLY ETERNITY)
Ge 21: 33 the name of the LORD, the *E* God.
Dt 33: 27 The *e* God is your refuge,
1Ki 10: 9 of the LORD's *e* love for Israel,
Ps 16: 11 with *e* pleasures at your right hand.
21: 6 you have granted him *e* blessings
111: 10 To him belongs *e* praise.
119: 89 Your word, O LORD, is *e*;
119:160 all your righteous laws are *e*.
Ecc 12: 5 Then man goes to his *e* home
Isa 26: 4 LORD, the LORD, is the Rock *e*.
47: 7 the *e* queen!'
Jer 10: 10 he is the living God, the *e* King.

Da 4: 3 His kingdom is an *e* kingdom;
4: 34 His dominion is an *e* dominion;
Hab 3: 6 His ways are *e*.
Mt 18: 8 two feet and be thrown into *e* fire.
19: 16 good thing must I do to get *e* life?"
19: 29 as much and will inherit *e* life.
25: 41 into the *e* fire prepared for the devil
25: 46 but the righteous to *e* life."
25: 46 they will go away to *e* punishment,
Mk 3: 29 be forgiven; he is guilty of an *e* sin."
10: 17 "what must I do to inherit *e* life?"
10: 30 and in the age to come, *e* life.
Lk 10: 25 "what must I do to inherit *e* life?"
16: 9 will be welcomed into *e* dwellings.
18: 18 what must I do to inherit *e* life?"
18: 30 and, in the age to come, *e* life."
Jn 3: 15 believes in him may have *e* life.
3: 16 him shall not perish but have *e* life.
3: 36 believes in the Son has *e* life,
4: 14 spring of water welling up to *e* life."
4: 36 now he harvests the crop for *e* life,
5: 24 believes him who sent me has *e* life
5: 39 that by them you possess *e* life.
6: 27 but for food that endures to *e* life,
6: 40 believes in him shall have *e* life,
6: 54 and drinks my blood has *e* life,
6: 68 You have the words of *e* life.
10: 28 I give them *e* life, and they shall
12: 25 in this world will keep it for *e* life.
12: 50 that his command leads to *e* life.
17: 2 all people that he might give *e* life
17: 3 this is *e* life: that they may know
Ac 13: 46 yourselves worthy of *e* life,
13: 48 were appointed for *e* life believed.
Ro 1: 20 his *e* power and divine nature—
2: 7 and immortality, he will give *e* life.
5: 21 righteousness to bring *e* life
6: 22 to holiness, and the result is *e* life.
6: 23 but the gift of God is *e* life
16: 26 by the command of the *e* God,
2Co 4: 17 for us an *e* glory that far outweighs
4: 18 temporary, but what is unseen is *e*.
5: 1 from God, an *e* house in heaven,
Gal 6: 8 from the Spirit will reap *e* life.
Eph 3: 11 to his *e* purpose which he
2Th 2: 16 his grace gave us *e* encouragement
1Ti 1: 16 believe on him and receive *e* life.
1: 17 Now to the King *e*, immortal,
6: 12 Take hold of the *e* life
2Ti 2: 10 is in Christ Jesus, with *e* glory.
Tit 1: 2 resting on the hope of *e* life,
3: 7 heirs having the hope of *e* life.
Heb 5: 9 he became the source of *e* salvation
6: 2 of the dead, and *e* judgment.
9: 12 having obtained *e* redemption.
9: 14 through the *e* Spirit offered himself
9: 15 the promised *e* inheritance—
13: 20 of the *e* covenant brought back
1Pe 5: 10 you to his *e* glory in Christ,
2Pe 1: 11 into the *e* kingdom of our Lord
1Jn 1: 2 and we proclaim to you the *e* life,
2: 25 what he promised us—even *e* life.
3: 15 know that no murderer has *e* life
5: 11 God has given us *e* life,
5: 13 you may know that you have *e* life.
5: 20 He is the true God and *e* life.
Jude : 7 who suffer the punishment of *e* fire.
: 21 Christ to bring you to *e* life.
Rev 14: 6 and he had the *e* gospel to proclaim

ETERNALLY* (ETERNAL)
Gal 1: 8 let him be *e* condemned! As we
1: 9 let him be *e* condemned! Am I now

ETERNITY* (ETERNAL)
Ps 93: 2 you are from all *e*.
Pr 8: 23 I was appointed from *e*,
Ecc 3: 11 also set *e* in the hearts of men;

ETHIOPIAN*
Jer 13: 23 Can the *E* change his skin
Ac 8: 27 and on his way he met an *E* eunuch

EUNUCH (EUNUCHS)
Ac 8: 27 on his way he met an Ethiopian *e*,

EUNUCHS (EUNUCH)
Isa 56: 4 "To the *e* who keep my Sabbaths,
Mt 19: 12 For some are *e* because they were

EUTYCHUS*
Ac 20: 9 was a young man named *E*,

EVANGELIST* (EVANGELISTS)
Ac 21: 8 stayed at the house of Philip the *e*,
2Ti 4: 5 hardship, do the work of an *e*,

EVANGELISTS* (EVANGELIST)
Eph 4: 11 some to be prophets, some to be *e*,

EVE*
Ge 3: 20 Adam named his wife *E*,
4: 1 Adam lay with his wife *E*,
2Co 11: 3 as *E* was deceived by the serpent's
1Ti 2: 13 For Adam was formed first, then *E*

EVEN-TEMPERED* (TEMPER)
Pr 17: 27 and a man of understanding is *e*.

EVENING
Ge 1: 5 there was *e*, and there was morning

EVER (EVERLASTING FOREVER FOREVERMORE)
Ex 15: 18 LORD will reign for *e* and *e*."
Dt 8: 19 If you *e* forget the LORD your
1Ki 3: 12 anyone like you, nor will there *e* be.
Job 4: 7 were the upright *e* destroyed?
Ps 5: 11 let them *e* sing for joy.
10: 16 The LORD is King for *e* and *e*;
21: 4 length of days, for *e* and *e*.
25: 3 will *e* be put to shame,
25: 15 My eyes are *e* on the LORD,
26: 3 for your love is *e* before me,
45: 6 O God, will last for *e* and *e*;
45: 17 nations will praise you for *e* and *e*.
48: 14 For this God is our God for *e* and *e*;
52: 8 God's unfailing love for *e* and *e*.
61: 8 will I *e* sing praise to your name
71: 6 I will *e* praise you.
84: 4 they are *e* praising you.
89: 33 nor will I *e* betray my faithfulness.
111: 8 They are steadfast for *e* and *e*,
119: 44 your law, for *e* and *e*.
119: 98 for they are *e* with me.
132: 12 sit on your throne for *e* and *e*."
145: 1 I will praise your name for *e* and *e*.
145: 2 and extol your name for *e* and *e*.
145: 21 his holy name for *e* and *e*.
Pr 4: 18 shining *e* brighter till the full light
5: 19 may you *e* be captivated
Isa 66: 8 Who has *e* heard of such a thing?
66: 8 Who has *e* seen such things?
Jer 7: 7 I gave your forefathers for *e* and *e*.
25: 5 and your fathers for *e* and *e*.
31: 36 the descendants of Israel *e* cease
Da 2: 20 be to the name of God for *e* and *e*;
7: 18 it forever—yes, for *e* and *e*.'
12: 3 like the stars for *e* and *e*.
Mic 4: 5 our God for *e* and *e*.
Mt 13: 14 you will be *e* seeing but never
13: 14 " 'You will be *e* hearing
Mk 4: 12 *e* hearing but never understanding;
Jn 1: 18 No one has *e* seen God,
Gal 1: 5 to whom be glory for *e* and *e*.
Eph 3: 21 all generations, for *e* and *e*!
Php 4: 20 and Father be glory for *e* and *e*.
1Ti 1: 17 be honor and glory for *e* and *e*.
2Ti 4: 18 To him be glory for *e* and *e*.
Heb 1: 8 O God, will last for *e* and *e*,
13: 21 to whom be glory for *e* and *e*.
1Pe 4: 11 the glory and the power for *e* and *e*.
5: 11 To him be the power for *e* and *e*.
1Jn 4: 12 No one has *e* seen God;
Rev 1: 6 him be glory and power for *e* and *e*!
1: 18 and behold I am alive for *e* and *e*!
21: 27 Nothing impure will *e* enter it,
22: 5 And they will reign for *e* and *e*.

EVER-INCREASING* (INCREASE)
Ro 6: 19 to impurity and to *e* wickedness,
2Co 3: 18 into his likeness with *e* glory,

EVERLASTING* (EVER)
Ge 9: 16 and remember the *e* covenant
17: 7 an *e* covenant between me and you
17: 8 I will give as an *e* possession to you
17: 13 in your flesh is to be an *e* covenant.
17: 19 an *e* covenant for his descendants
48: 4 *e* possession to your descendants
Nu 18: 19 It is an *e* covenant of salt
Dt 33: 15 and the fruitfulness of the *e* hills;
33: 27 and underneath are the *e* arms.
2Sa 23: 5 made with me an *e* covenant,
1Ch 16: 17 to Israel as an *e* covenant:
16: 36 from *e* to *e*.
29: 10 from *e* to *e*.
Ezr 9: 12 to your children as an *e* inheritance
Ne 9: 5 your God, who is from *e* to *e*."
Ps 41: 13 from *e* to *e*.
52: 5 God will bring you down to *e* ruin:
74: 3 toward these *e* ruins,
78: 66 he put them to *e* shame.
90: 2 from *e* to *e* you are God.
103: 17 But from *e* to *e*
105: 10 to Israel as an *e* covenant:
106: 48 from *e* to *e*.
119:142 Your righteousness is *e*
139: 24 and lead me in the way *e*.
145: 13 Your kingdom is an *e* kingdom,
Isa 9: 6 *E* Father, Prince of Peace.
24: 5 and broken the *e* covenant.
30: 8 it may be an *e* witness.
33: 14 Who of us can dwell with *e* burning
35: 10 *e* joy will crown their heads.
40: 28 The LORD is the *e* God,
45: 17 the LORD with an *e* salvation;
45: 17 to ages *e*.
51: 11 *e* joy will crown their heads.
54: 8 but with *e* kindness
55: 3 I will make an *e* covenant with you,
55: 13 for an *e* sign,
56: 5 I will give them an *e* name
60: 15 I will make you the *e* pride
60: 19 for the LORD will be your *e* light,
60: 20 the LORD will be your *e* light,
61: 7 and *e* joy will be theirs.
61: 8 and make an *e* covenant with them.
63: 12 to gain for himself *e* renown,
Jer 5: 22 an *e* barrier it cannot cross.
23: 40 I will bring upon you *e* disgrace—
23: 40 *e* shame that will not be forgotten."
25: 9 of horror and scorn, and an *e* ruin.
31: 3 "I have loved you with an *e* love;
32: 40 I will make an *e* covenant
50: 5 the LORD in an *e* covenant
Eze 16: 60 and I will establish an *e* covenant
37: 26 with them; it will be an *e* covenant.
Da 7: 14 dominion is an *e* dominion that will
7: 27 His kingdom will be an *e* kingdom,
9: 24 to bring in *e* righteousness,
12: 2 others to shame and *e* contempt.
12: 2 some to *e* life, others to shame
Mic 6: 2 you *e* foundations of the earth.
Hab 1: 12 O LORD, are you not from *e*?
Jn 6: 47 the truth, he who believes has *e* life.
2Th 1: 9 punished with *e* destruction
Jude : 6 bound with *e* chains for judgment

EVER-PRESENT*
Ps 46: 1 an *e* help in trouble

EVIDENCE (EVIDENT)
Jn 14: 11 on the *e* of the miracles themselves.
Ac 11: 23 and saw the *e* of the grace of God,
2Th 1: 5 All this is *e* that God's judgment is
Jas 2: 20 do you want *e* that faith

EVIDENT (EVIDENCE)
Php 4: 5 Let your gentleness be *e* to all.

EVIL (EVILDOER EVILDOERS EVILS)
Ge 2: 9 of the knowledge of good and *e.*
3: 5 be like God, knowing good and *e.*"
6: 5 of his heart was only *e* all the time.
Ex 32: 22 how prone these people are to *e.*
Jdg 2: 11 Then the Israelites did *e* in the eyes
3: 7 The Israelites did *e* in the eyes
3: 12 Once again the Israelites did *e*
4: 1 the Israelites once again did *e*
6: 1 Again the Israelites did *e*
10: 6 Again the Israelites did *e*
13: 1 Again the Israelites did *e*
1Ki 11: 6 So Solomon did *e* in the eyes
16: 25 But Omri did *e* in the eyes
2Ki 15: 24 Pekahiah did *e* in the eyes
Job 1: 1 he feared God and shunned *e.*
1: 8 a man who fears God and shuns *e.*"
34: 10 Far be it from God to do *e,*
36: 21 Beware of turning to *e,*
Ps 5: 4 not a God who takes pleasure in *e;*
23: 4 I will fear no *e,*
34: 13 keep your tongue from *e*
34: 14 Turn from *e* and do good;
34: 16 is against those who do *e,*
37: 1 Do not fret because of *e* men
37: 8 do not fret—it leads only to *e.*
37: 27 Turn from *e* and do good;
49: 5 fear when *e* days come,
51: 4 and done what is *e* in your sight,
97: 10 those who love the LORD hate *e,*
101: 4 I will have nothing to do with *e.*
141: 4 not my heart be drawn to what is *e,*
Pr 4: 27 keep your foot from *e.*
8: 13 To fear the LORD is to hate *e;*
10: 23 A fool finds pleasure in *e* conduct,
11: 19 he who pursues *e* goes to his death.
11: 27 *e* comes to him who searches for it.
14: 16 man fears the LORD and shuns *e,*
17: 13 If a man pays back *e* for good,
20: 30 Blows and wounds cleanse away *e,*
24: 19 Do not fret because of *e* men
24: 20 for the *e* man has no future hope,
26: 23 are fervent lips with an *e* heart.
28: 5 *E* men do not understand justice,
29: 6 An *e* man is snared by his own sin,
Ecc 12: 14 whether it is good or *e.*
Isa 5: 20 Woe to those who call *e* good
13: 11 I will punish the world for its *e,*
55: 7 and the *e* man his thoughts.
Jer 4: 14 wash the *e* from your heart
18: 8 nation I warned repents of its *e,*
18: 11 So turn from your *e* ways,
Eze 33: 11 Turn! Turn from your *e* ways!
33: 13 he will die for the *e* he has done.
33: 15 and does no *e,* he will surely live;
Am 5: 13 for the times are *e.*
Hab 1: 13 Your eyes are too pure to look on *e;*
Zec 8: 17 do not plot *e* against your neighbor,
Mt 5: 45 He causes his sun to rise on the *e*
6: 13 but deliver us from the *e* one.'
7: 11 If you, then, though you are *e,*
12: 34 you who are *e* say anything good?
12: 35 and the *e* man brings *e* things out
12: 35 out of the *e* stored up in him.
12: 43 "When an *e* spirit comes out
15: 19 out of the heart come *e* thoughts,
Mk 7: 21 come *e* thoughts, sexual
Lk 6: 45 and the *e* man brings *e* things out
11: 13 If you then, though you are *e,*
Jn 3: 19 of light because their deeds were *e.*
3: 20 Everyone who does *e* hates
17: 15 you protect them from the *e* one.
Ro 1: 30 they invent ways of doing *e;*
2: 8 who reject the truth and follow *e,*
2: 9 for every human being who does *e:*
3: 8 "Let us do *e* that good may result"?
6: 12 body so that you obey its *e* desires.
7: 19 no, the *e* I do not want to do—
7: 21 to do good, *e* is right there with me.
12: 9 Hate what is *e;* cling
12: 17 Do not repay anyone *e* for *e.*
12: 21 Do not be overcome by *e,*
14: 16 good to be spoken of as *e.*
16: 19 and innocent about what is *e.*
1Co 13: 6 Love does not delight in *e*
14: 20 In regard to *e* be infants,
Eph 5: 16 because the days are *e.*
6: 12 forces of *e* in the heavenly realms.
6: 16 all the flaming arrows of the *e* one.
Col 3: 5 impurity, lust, *e* desires and greed,
1Th 5: 22 Avoid every kind of *e.*
2Th 3: 3 and protect you from the *e* one.
1Ti 6: 10 of money is a root of all kinds of *e.*
2Ti 2: 22 Flee the *e* desires of youth,
3: 6 are swayed by all kinds of *e* desires,
3: 13 while *e* men and impostors will go
Heb 5: 14 to distinguish good from *e.*
Jas 1: 13 For God cannot be tempted by *e,*
1: 21 and the *e* that is so prevalent,
3: 6 a world of *e* among the parts
3: 8 It is a restless *e,* full
1Pe 2: 16 your freedom as a cover-up for *e;*
3: 9 Do not repay *e* with *e* or insult
3: 10 must keep his tongue from *e*
3: 17 for doing good than for doing *e.*
1Jn 2: 13 you have overcome the *e* one.
2: 14 and you have overcome the *e* one.
3: 12 who belonged to the *e* one
5: 18 and the *e* one cannot harm him.
5: 19 is under the control of the *e* one.
3Jn : 11 do not imitate what is *e*

EVILDOER* (EVIL)
2Sa 3: 39 the LORD repay the *e* according
Ps 101: 8 I will cut off every *e*
Mal 4: 1 and every *e* will be stubble,

EVILDOERS* (EVIL)
1Sa 24: 13 saying goes, 'From *e* come evil
Job 8: 20 or strengthen the hands of *e.*
34: 8 He keeps company with *e;*
34: 22 where *e* can hide.
Ps 14: 4 Will *e* never learn—
14: 6 You *e* frustrate the plans
26: 5 I abhor the assembly of *e*
36: 12 See how the *e* lie fallen—
53: 4 Will the *e* never learn—
59: 2 Deliver me from *e*
64: 2 from that noisy crowd of *e.*
92: 7 and all *e* flourish,
92: 9 all *e* will be scattered.
94: 4 all the *e* are full of boasting.
94: 16 will take a stand for me against *e?*
119:115 Away from me, you *e,*
125: 5 the LORD will banish with the *e.*
141: 4 deeds with men who are *e;*
141: 5 ever against the deeds of *e;*
141: 9 from the traps set by *e.*
Pr 21: 15 but terror to *e.*
Isa 1: 4 a brood of *e,*
31: 2 against those who help *e.*
Jer 23: 14 They strengthen the hands of *e,*
Hos 10: 9 the *e* in Gibeah?
Mal 3: 15 Certainly the *e* prosper, and
Mt 7: 23 you *e!*' "Therefore everyone who
Lk 13: 27 Away from me, all you *e!*'
18: 11 *e,* adulterers—or even like this tax

EVILS* (EVIL)
Mk 7: 23 All these *e* come from inside

EWE
2Sa 12: 3 one little *e* lamb he had bought.

EXACT*
Ge 43: 21 the *e* weight—in the mouth
Est 4: 7 including the *e* amount
Mt 2: 7 from them the *e* time the star had
Jn 4: 53 realized that this was the *e* time
Ac 17: 26 the *e* places where they should live.
Heb 1: 3 the *e* representation of his being,

EXALT* (EXALTED EXALTS)
Ex 15: 2 my father's God, and I will *e* him.
Jos 3: 7 begin to *e* you in the eyes
1Sa 2: 10 and *e* the horn of his anointed."
1Ch 25: 5 the promises of God to *e* him.
29: 12 power to *e* and give strength to all.
Job 19: 5 If indeed you would *e* yourselves
Ps 30: 1 I will *e* you, O LORD,
34: 3 let us *e* his name together.
35: 26 may all who *e* themselves over me
37: 34 He will *e* you to inherit the land;
38: 16 *e* themselves over me
75: 6 or from the desert can *e* a man.
89: 17 and by your favor you *e* our horn.
99: 5 *E* the LORD our God
99: 9 *E* the LORD our God
107: 32 Let them *e* him in the assembly
118: 28 you are my God, and I will *e* you.
145: 1 I will *e* you, my God the King;
Pr 4: 8 Esteem her, and she will *e* you;
25: 6 Do not *e* yourself in the king's
Isa 24: 15 *e* the name of the LORD, the God
25: 1 I will *e* you and praise your name,
Eze 29: 15 and will never again *e* itself
Da 4: 37 *e* and glorify the King of heaven,
11: 36 He will *e* and magnify himself
11: 37 but will *e* himself above them all.
Hos 11: 7 he will by no means *e* them.
2Th 2: 4 will *e* himself over everything that is

EXALTED* (EXALT)
Ex 15: 1 for he is highly *e.*
15: 21 for he is highly *e.*
Nu 24: 7 their kingdom will be *e.*
Jos 4: 14 That day the LORD *e* Joshua
2Sa 5: 12 and had *e* his kingdom for the sake
22: 47 *E* be God, the Rock, my Savior!
22: 49 You *e* me above my foes;
23: 1 of the man *e* by the Most High,
1Ch 14: 2 that his kingdom had been highly *e*
17: 17 as though I were the most *e* of men,
29: 11 you are *e* as head over all.
29: 25 The LORD highly *e* Solomon
Ne 9: 5 and may it be *e* above all blessing
Job 24: 24 For a little while they are *e,*
36: 22 "God is *e* in his power.
37: 23 beyond our reach and *e* in power;
Ps 18: 46 *E* be God my Savior!
18: 48 You *e* me above my foes;
21: 13 Be *e,* O LORD, in your strength;
27: 6 Then my head will be *e*
35: 27 they always say, "The LORD be *e,*
40: 16 "The LORD be *e!*"
46: 10 I will be *e* among the nations,
46: 10 I will be *e* in the earth."
47: 9 he is greatly *e.*
57: 5 Be *e,* O God, above the heavens;
57: 11 Be *e,* O God, above the heavens;
70: 4 "Let God be *e!*"
89: 13 hand is strong, your right hand *e.*
89: 19 I have *e* a young man
89: 24 through my name his horn will be *e*
89: 27 the most *e* of the kings of the earth.
89: 42 You have *e* the right hand
92: 8 But you, O LORD, are *e* forever.
92: 10 You have *e* my horn like that
97: 9 you are *e* far above all gods.
99: 2 he is *e* over all the nations.
108: 5 Be *e,* O God, above the heavens,
113: 4 The LORD is *e* over all the nations
138: 2 for you have *e* above all things
148: 13 for his name alone is *e;*
Pr 11: 11 of the upright a city is *e,*
30: 32 have played the fool and *e* yourself,
Isa 2: 11 the LORD alone will be *e*
2: 12 for all that is *e*
2: 17 the LORD alone will be *e*
5: 16 the LORD Almighty will be *e*
6: 1 *e,* and the train of his robe filled
12: 4 and proclaim that his name is *e.*

24: 4 the *e* of the earth languish.
33: 5 The LORD is *e*, for he dwells
33: 10 "Now will I be *e*;
52: 13 be raised and lifted up and highly *e*.
Jer 17: 12 A glorious throne, *e*
La 2: 17 he has *e* the horn of your foes.
Eze 21: 26 The lowly will be *e* and the *e* will be
Hos 13: 1 he was *e* in Israel.
Mic 6: 6 and bow down before the *e* God?
Mt 23: 12 whoever humbles himself will be *e*.
Lk 14: 11 he who humbles himself will be *e*."
18: 14 he who humbles himself will be *e*."
Ac 2: 33 *E* to the right hand of God,
5: 31 God *e* him to his own right hand
Php 1: 20 always Christ will be *e* in my body,
2: 9 Therefore God *e* him
Heb 7: 26 from sinners, *e* above the heavens.

EXALTS* (EXALT)
1Sa 2: 7 he humbles and he *e*.
Job 36: 7 and *e* them forever.
Ps 75: 7 He brings one down, he *e* another.
Pr 14: 34 Righteousness *e* a nation,
Mt 23: 12 For whoever *e* himself will be
Lk 14: 11 For everyone who *e* himself will be
18: 14 For everyone who *e* himself will be

EXAMINE (EXAMINED EXAMINES)
Ps 11: 4 his eyes *e* them.
17: 3 you probe my heart and *e* me
26: 2 *e* my heart and my mind;
Jer 17: 10 and *e* the mind,
20: 12 Almighty, you who *e* the righteous
La 3: 40 Let us *e* our ways and test them,
1Co 11: 28 A man ought to *e* himself
2Co 13: 5 *E* yourselves to see whether you

EXAMINED (EXAMINE)
Job 13: 9 Would it turn out well if he *e* you?
Ac 17: 11 *e* the Scriptures every day to see

EXAMINES (EXAMINE)
Ps 11: 5 The LORD *e* the righteous,
Pr 5: 21 and he *e* all his paths.

EXAMPLE* (EXAMPLES)
2Ki 14: 3 In everything he followed the *e*
Ecc 9: 13 also saw under the sun this *e*
Eze 14: 8 and make him an *e* and a byword.
Jn 13: 15 have set you an *e* that you should
Ro 7: 2 as long as he lives? For *e*,
1Co 11: 1 Follow my *e*, as I follow
11: 1 as I follow the *e* of Christ.
Gal 3: 15 let me take an *e* from everyday life.
Php 3: 17 Join with others in following my *e*,
2Th 3: 7 how you ought to follow our *e*.
1Ti 1: 16 as an *e* for those who would believe
4: 12 set an *e* for the believers in speech,
Tit 2: 7 In everything set them an *e*
Heb 4: 11 fall by following their *e*
Jas 3: 4 Or take ships as an *e*.
5: 10 as an *e* of patience in the face
1Pe 2: 21 leaving you an *e*, that you should
2Pe 2: 6 made them an *e* of what is going
Jude : 7 as an *e* of those who suffer

EXAMPLES* (EXAMPLE)
1Co 10: 6 Now these things occurred as *e*
10: 11 as *e* and were written down
1Pe 5: 3 to you, but being *e* to the flock.

EXASPERATE*
Eph 6: 4 Fathers, do not *e* your children;

EXCEL* (EXCELLENT)
Ge 49: 4 as the waters, you will no longer *e*,
1Co 14: 12 to *e* in gifts that build up the church
2Co 8: 7 But just as you *e* in everything—
8: 7 also *e* in this grace of giving.

EXCELLENT (EXCEL)
1Co 12: 31 now I will show you the most *e* way
Php 4: 8 if anything is *e* or praiseworthy—
1Ti 3: 13 have served well gain an *e* standing
Tit 3: 8 These things are *e* and profitable

EXCESSIVE
Eze 18: 8 or take *e* interest.
2Co 2: 7 not be overwhelmed by *e* sorrow.

EXCHANGE (EXCHANGED)
Mt 16: 26 Or what can a man give in *e*
Mk 8: 37 Or what can a man give in *e*
2Co 6: 13 As a fair *e*— I speak

EXCHANGED (EXCHANGE)
Ps 106: 20 They *e* their Glory
Jer 2: 11 But my people have *e* their Glory
Hos 4: 7 they *e* their Glory
Ro 1: 23 *e* the glory of the immortal God
1: 25 They *e* the truth of God for a lie,
1: 26 their women *e* natural relations

EXCLAIM
Ps 35: 10 My whole being will *e*,

EXCUSE* (EXCUSES)
Ps 25: 3 who are treacherous without *e*.
Lk 14: 18 Please *e* me.'
14: 19 Please *e* me.'
Jn 15: 22 they have no *e* for their sin.
Ro 1: 20 so that men are without *e*.
2: 1 You, therefore, have no *e*,

EXCUSES* (EXCUSE)
Lk 14: 18 "But they all alike began to make *e*.

EXERTED*
Eph 1: 20 which he *e* in Christ

EXHORT*
1Ti 5: 1 but *e* him as if he were your father.

EXILE
2Ki 17: 23 taken from their homeland into *e*
25: 11 into *e* the people who remained

EXISTED* (EXISTS)
2Pe 3: 5 ago by God's word the heavens *e*

EXISTS (EXISTED)
Heb 2: 10 and through whom everything *e*,
11: 6 to him must believe that he *e*

EXPANSE
Ge 1: 7 So God made the *e* and separated
1: 8 God called the *e* "sky."

EXPECT (EXPECTATION EXPECTED EXPECTING)
Mt 24: 44 at an hour when you do not *e* him.
Lk 12: 40 at an hour when you do not *e* him."
Php 1: 20 I eagerly *e* and hope that I will

EXPECTATION (EXPECT)
Ro 8: 19 waits in eager *e* for the sons
Heb 10: 27 but only a fearful *e* of judgment

EXPECTED (EXPECT)
Pr 11: 7 all he *e* from his power comes
Hag 1: 9 "You *e* much, but see, it turned out

EXPECTING (EXPECT)
Lk 6: 35 and lend to them without *e*

EXPEL* (EXPELLED)
1Co 5: 13 *E* the wicked man from among you

EXPELLED (EXPEL)
Eze 28: 16 and I *e* you, O guardian cherub,

EXPENSE (EXPENSIVE)
1Co 9: 7 Who serves as a soldier at his own *e*

EXPENSIVE* (EXPENSE)
Mt 26: 7 jar of very *e* perfume,
Mk 14: 3 jar of very *e* perfume,
Lk 7: 25 those who wear *e* clothes
Jn 12: 3 a pint of pure nard, an *e* perfume;
1Ti 2: 9 or gold or pearls or *e* clothes,

EXPERT
1Co 3: 10 I laid a foundation as an *e* builder,

EXPLAINING (EXPLAINS)
Ac 17: 3 *e* and proving that the Christ had

EXPLAINS* (EXPLAINING)
Ac 8: 31 he said, "unless someone *e* it to me

EXPLOIT* (EXPLOITED EXPLOITING EXPLOITS)
Pr 22: 22 Do not *e* the poor because they are
Isa 58: 3 and *e* all your workers.
2Co 12: 17 Did I *e* you through any
12: 18 Titus did not *e* you, did he?
2Pe 2: 3 greed these teachers will *e* you

EXPLOITED* (EXPLOIT)
2Co 7: 2 no one, we have *e* no one.

EXPLOITING* (EXPLOIT)
Jas 2: 6 Is it not the rich who are *e* you?

EXPLOITS (EXPLOIT)
2Co 11: 20 or *e* you or takes advantage of you

EXPLORE
Nu 13: 2 "Send some men to *e* the land

EXPOSE (EXPOSED)
1Co 4: 5 will *e* the motives of men's hearts.
Eph 5: 11 of darkness, but rather *e* them.

EXPOSED (EXPOSE)
Jn 3: 20 for fear that his deeds will be *e*.
Eph 5: 13 everything *e* by the light becomes

EXPRESS (EXPRESSING)
Ro 8: 26 us with groans that words cannot *e*.

EXPRESSING* (EXPRESS)
1Co 2: 13 *e* spiritual truths in spiritual words.
Gal 5: 6 thing that counts is faith *e* itself

EXTENDS (EXTENT)
Pr 31: 20 and *e* her hands to the needy.
Lk 1: 50 His mercy *e* to those who fear him,

EXTENT (EXTENDS)
Jn 13: 1 he now showed them the full *e*

EXTERNAL
Gal 2: 6 judge by *e* appearance—

EXTINGUISH (EXTINGUISHED)
Eph 6: 16 which you can *e* all the flaming

EXTINGUISHED (EXTINGUISH)
2Sa 21: 17 the lamp of Israel will not be *e*."

EXTOL*
Job 36: 24 Remember to *e* his work,
Ps 34: 1 I will *e* the LORD at all times;
68: 4 *e* him who rides on the clouds—
95: 2 and *e* him with music and song.
109: 30 mouth I will greatly *e* the LORD;
111: 1 I will *e* the LORD with all my heart
115: 18 it is we who *e* the LORD,
117: 1 *e* him, all you peoples.
145: 2 and *e* your name for ever and ever.
145: 10 your saints will *e* you.
147: 12 *E* the LORD, O Jerusalem;

EXTORT*
Lk 3: 14 "Don't *e* money and don't accuse

EXTRAORDINARY*
Ac 19: 11 God did *e* miracles through Paul,

EXTREME (EXTREMES)
2Co 8: 2 and their *e* poverty welled up

EXTREMES* (EXTREME)
Ecc 7: 18 who fears God will avoid all ›*ef*.

EXULT
Ps 89: 16 they *e* in your righteousness.
Isa 45: 25 will be found righteous and will *e*.

EYE (EYES)
Ge 3: 6 good for food and pleasing to the *e*,
Ex 21: 24 you are to take life for life, *e* for *e*,
Dt 19: 21 life for life, *e* for *e*, tooth for tooth,
Ps 94: 9 Does he who formed the *e* not see?
Mt 5: 29 If your right *e* causes you to sin,
5: 38 '*E* for *e*, and tooth for tooth.'
6: 22 "The *e* is the lamp of the body.
7: 3 of sawdust in your brother's *e*
1Co 2: 9 "No *e* has seen,
12: 16 I am not an *e*, I do not belong
15: 52 of an *e*, at the last trumpet.
Eph 6: 6 favor when their *e* is on you,
Col 3: 22 not only when their *e* is on you
Rev 1: 7 and every *e* will see him,

EYES (EYE)
Nu 15: 39 the lusts of your own hearts and *e*.

33: 55 remain will become barbs in your *e*
Dt 11: 12 the *e* of the LORD your God are
12: 25 right in the *e* of the LORD.
16: 19 for a bribe blinds the *e* of the wise
Jos 23: 13 on your backs and thorns in your *e*,
1Sa 15: 17 you were once small in your own *e*,
1Ki 10: 7 I came and saw with my own *e*.
2Ki 9: 30 heard about it, she painted her *e*,
2Ch 16: 9 For the *e* of the LORD range
Job 31: 1 "I made a covenant with my *e*
36: 7 He does not take his *e*
Ps 25: 15 My *e* are ever on the LORD,
36: 1 God before his *e*.
101: 6 My *e* will be on the faithful
118: 23 and it is marvelous in our *e*.
119: 18 Open my *e* that I may see
119: 37 my *e* away from worthless things;
121: 1 I lift up my *e* to the hills—
123: 1 I lift up my *e* to you,
139: 16 your *e* saw my unformed body.
141: 8 But my *e* are fixed on you,
Pr 3: 7 Do not be wise in your own *e*;
4: 25 Let your *e* look straight ahead,
15: 3 The *e* of the LORD are everywhere
17: 24 a fool's *e* wander to the ends
Isa 6: 5 and my *e* have seen the King,
33: 17 Your *e* will see the king
42: 7 to open *e* that are blind,
Jer 24: 6 My *e* will watch over them
Hab 1: 13 Your *e* are too pure to look on evil;
Mt 6: 22 If your *e* are good, your whole
21: 42 and it is marvelous in our *e*?
Lk 16: 15 ones who justify yourselves in the *e*
24: 31 Then their *e* were opened
Jn 4: 35 open your *e* and look at the fields!
Ac 1: 9 he was taken up before their very *e*,
2Co 4: 18 So we fix our *e* not on what is seen,
8: 21 not only in the *e* of the Lord but
Eph 1: 18 also that the *e* of your heart may be
Heb 12: 2 Let us fix our *e* on Jesus, the author
Jas 2: 5 poor in the *e* of the world to be rich
1Pe 3: 12 For the *e* of the Lord are
Rev 7: 17 wipe away every tear from their *e*."
21: 4 He will wipe every tear from their *e*

EYEWITNESSES* (WITNESS)
Lk 1: 2 by those who from the first were *e*
2Pe 1: 16 but we were *e* of his majesty.

EZEKIEL*
Priest called to be prophet to the exiles (Eze 1–3). Symbolically acted out destruction of Jerusalem (Eze 4–5; 12; 24).

EZRA*
Priest and teacher of the Law who led a return of exiles to Israel to reestablish temple and worship (Ezr 7–8). Corrected intermarriage of priests (Ezr 9–10). Read Law at celebration of Feast of Tabernacles (Ne 8). Participated in dedication of Jerusalem's walls (Ne 12).

FACE (FACES)
Ge 32: 30 "It is because I saw God *f* to *f*,
Ex 3: 6 Moses hid his *f*, because he was
33: 11 would speak to Moses *f* to *f*,
33: 20 But," he said, "you cannot see my *f*
34: 29 was not aware that his *f* was radiant
Nu 6: 25 the LORD make his *f* shine
12: 8 With him I speak *f* to *f*,
14: 14 O LORD, have been seen *f* to *f*,
Dt 5: 4 The LORD spoke to you *f* to *f* out
31: 17 I will hide my *f* from them,
34: 10 whom the LORD knew *f* to *f*,
Jdg 6: 22 the angel of the LORD *f* to *f*!"
2Ki 14: 8 challenge: "Come, meet me *f* to *f*."
1Ch 16: 11 seek his *f* always.
2Ch 7: 14 and seek my *f* and turn
25: 17 of Israel: "Come, meet me *f* to *f*."
Ezr 9: 6 and disgraced to lift up my *f* to you,
Ps 4: 6 Let the light of your *f* shine upon us
27: 8 Your *f*, LORD, I will seek.
31: 16 Let your *f* shine on your servant;
44: 3 and the light of your *f*,
44: 22 Yet for your sake we *f* death all day
51: 9 Hide your *f* from my sins
67: 1 and make his *f* shine upon us; *Selah*
80: 3 make your *f* shine upon us,
105: 4 seek his *f* always.
119:135 Make your *f* shine
SS 2: 14 and your *f* is lovely.
Isa 50: 7 Therefore have I set my *f* like flint,
50: 8 Let us *f* each other!
54: 8 I hid my *f* from you for a moment,
Jer 32: 4 and will speak with him *f* to *f*
34: 3 and he will speak with you *f* to *f*.
Eze 1: 10 Each of the four had the *f* of a man,
20: 35 *f* to *f*, I will execute judgment
Mt 17: 2 His *f* shone like the sun,
18: 10 angels in heaven always see the *f*
Lk 9: 29 the appearance of his *f* changed,
Ro 8: 36 "For your sake we *f* death all day
1Co 13: 12 mirror; then we shall see *f* to *f*.
2Co 3: 7 could not look steadily at the *f*
4: 6 the glory of God in the *f* of Christ.
10: 1 who am "timid" when *f* to *f*
1Pe 3: 12 but the *f* of the Lord is
2Jn : 12 to visit you and talk with you *f* to *f*,
3Jn : 14 see you soon, and we will talk *f* to *f*.
Rev 1: 16 His *f* was like the sun shining
22: 4 They will see his *f*, and his name

FACES (FACE)
2Co 3: 18 who with unveiled *f* all reflect

FACTIONS
2Co 12: 20 outbursts of anger, *f*, slander,
Gal 5: 20 selfish ambition, dissensions, *f*

FADE (FADING)
Jas 1: 11 the rich man will *f* away
1Pe 5: 4 of glory that will never *f* away.

FADING (FADE)
2Co 3: 7 *f* though it was, will not
3: 11 if what was *f* away came with glory,
3: 13 at it while the radiance was *f* away.

FAIL (FAILED FAILING FAILINGS FAILS FAILURE)
Lev 26: 15 and *f* to carry out all my commands
1Ki 2: 4 you will never *f* to have a man
1Ch 28: 20 He will not *f* you or forsake you
2Ch 34: 33 they did not *f* to follow the LORD,
Ps 89: 28 my covenant with him will never *f*.
Pr 15: 22 Plans *f* for lack of counsel,
Isa 51: 6 my righteousness will never *f*.
La 3: 22 for his compassions never *f*.
Lk 22: 32 Simon, that your faith may not *f*.
2Co 13: 5 unless, of course, you *f* the test?

FAILED (FAIL)
Jos 23: 14 has been fulfilled; not one has *f*.
1Ki 8: 56 Not one word has *f*
Ps 77: 8 Has his promise *f* for all time?
Ro 9: 6 as though God's word had *f*.
2Co 13: 6 discover that we have not *f* the test.

FAILING (FAIL)
1Sa 12: 23 sin against the LORD by *f* to pray

FAILINGS (FAIL)
Ro 15: 1 ought to bear with the *f* of the weak

FAILS (FAIL)
Jer 14: 6 their eyesight *f*
Joel 1: 10 the oil *f*.
1Co 13: 8 Love never *f*.

FAILURE* (FAIL)
1Th 2: 1 that our visit to you was not a *f*.

FAINT
Isa 40: 31 they will walk and not be *f*.

FAINTHEARTED* (HEART)
Dt 20: 3 Do not be *f* or afraid; do not be
20: 8 shall add, "Is any man afraid or *f*?

FAIR (FAIRNESS)
Pr 1: 3 doing what is right and just and *f*;
Col 4: 1 slaves with what is right and *f*,

FAIRNESS* (FAIR)
Pr 29: 14 If a king judges the poor with *f*,

FAITH* (FAITHFUL FAITHFULLY FAITHFULNESS FAITHLESS)
Ex 21: 8 because he has broken *f* with her.
Dt 32: 51 both of you broke *f* with me
Jos 22: 16 'How could you break *f*
Jdg 9: 16 and in good *f* when you made
9: 19 and in good *f* toward Jerub-Baal
1Sa 14: 33 "You have broken *f*," he said.
2Ch 20: 20 Have *f* in the LORD your God
20: 20 have *f* in his prophets and you will
Isa 7: 9 If you do not stand firm in your *f*,
26: 2 the nation that keeps *f*.
Hab 2: 4 but the righteous will live by his *f*—
Mal 2: 10 by breaking *f* with one another?
2: 11 one another? Judah has broken *f*.
2: 14 because you have broken *f* with her
2: 15 and do not break *f* with the wife
2: 16 in your spirit, and do not break *f*.
Mt 6: 30 O you of little *f*? So do not worry,
8: 10 anyone in Israel with such great *f*.
8: 26 He replied, "You of little *f*,
9: 2 When Jesus saw their *f*, he said
9: 22 he said, "your *f* has healed you."
9: 29 According to your *f* will it be done
13: 58 there because of their lack of *f*.
14: 31 of little *f*," he said, "why did you
15: 28 "Woman, you have great *f*!
16: 8 Jesus asked, "You of little *f*,
17: 20 if you have *f* as small as a mustard
17: 20 "Because you have so little *f*.
21: 21 if you have *f* and do not doubt,
24: 10 many will turn away from the *f*
Mk 2: 5 When Jesus saw their *f*, he said
4: 40 still have no *f*?" They were
5: 34 "Daughter, your *f* has healed you.
6: 6 he was amazed at their lack of *f*.
10: 52 said Jesus, "your *f* has healed you."
11: 22 "Have *f* in God," Jesus answered.
16: 14 he rebuked them for their lack of *f*
Lk 5: 20 When Jesus saw their *f*, he said,
7: 9 I have not found such great *f*
7: 50 the woman, "Your *f* has saved you;
8: 25 "Where is your *f*?" he asked his
8: 48 "Daughter, your *f* has healed you.
12: 28 will he clothe you, O you of little *f*!
17: 5 "Increase our *f*!" He replied,
17: 6 "If you have *f* as small
17: 19 your *f* has made you well."
18: 8 will he find *f* on the earth?"
18: 42 your sight; your *f* has healed you."
22: 32 Simon, that your *f* may not fail.
Jn 2: 11 and his disciples put their *f* in him.
7: 31 in the crowd put their *f* in him.
8: 30 he spoke, many put their *f* in him.
11: 45 had seen what Jesus did, put their *f*
12: 11 to Jesus and putting their *f* in him.
12: 42 they would not confess their *f*
14: 12 anyone who has *f* in me will do
Ac 3: 16 By *f* in the name of Jesus, this man
3: 16 *f* that comes through him that has
6: 5 full of *f* and of the Holy Spirit;
6: 7 of priests became obedient to the *f*.
11: 24 full of the Holy Spirit and *f*,
13: 8 to turn the proconsul from the *f*.
14: 9 saw that he had *f* to be healed
14: 22 them to remain true to the *f*.
14: 27 the door of *f* to the Gentiles.
15: 9 for he purified their hearts by *f*.
16: 5 were strengthened in the *f*
20: 21 and have *f* in our Lord Jesus.
24: 24 as he spoke about *f* in Christ Jesus.
26: 18 those who are sanctified by *f*
27: 25 for I have *f* in God that it will
Ro 1: 5 to the obedience that comes from *f*.
1: 8 because your *f* is being reported all
1: 12 encouraged by each other's *f*.

1: 17 is by *f* from first to last,
1: 17 "The righteous will live by *f*."
3: 3 What if some did not have *f*?
3: 3 lack of *f* nullify God's faithfulness?
3: 22 comes through *f* in Jesus Christ
3: 25 a sacrifice of atonement, through *f*
3: 26 one who justifies those who have *f*
3: 27 the law? No, but on that of *f*.
3: 28 by *f* apart from observing the law.
3: 30 through that same *f*.
3: 30 will justify the circumcised by *f*
3: 31 nullify the law by this *f*? Not at all!
4: 5 his *f* is credited as righteousness.
4: 9 that Abraham's *f* was credited
4: 11 had by *f* while he was still
4: 12 of the *f* that our father Abraham
4: 13 the righteousness that comes by *f*.
4: 14 *f* has no value and the promise is
4: 16 Therefore, the promise comes by *f*,
4: 16 are of the *f* of Abraham.
4: 19 Without weakening in his *f*,
4: 20 but was strengthened in his *f*
5: 1 we have been justified through *f*,
5: 2 access by *f* into this grace
9: 30 a righteousness that is by *f*;
9: 32 Because they pursued it not by *f*
10: 6 the righteousness that is by *f* says:
10: 8 the word of *f* we are proclaiming:
10: 17 *f* comes from hearing the message,
11: 20 of unbelief, and you stand by *f*.
12: 3 measure of *f* God has given you.
12: 6 let him use it in proportion to his *f*.
14: 1 Accept him whose *f* is weak,
14: 2 One man's *f* allows him
14: 2 but another man, whose *f* is weak,
14: 23 because his eating is not from *f*;
14: 23 that does not come from *f* is sin.
1Co 2: 5 so that your *f* might not rest
12: 9 to another *f* by the same Spirit,
13: 2 and if I have a *f* that can move
13: 13 And now these three remain: *f*,
15: 14 is useless and so is your *f*.
15: 17 has not been raised, your *f* is futile;
16: 13 stand firm in the *f*; be men
2Co 1: 24 Not that we lord it over your *f*,
1: 24 because it is by *f* you stand firm.
4: 13 With that same spirit of *f* we
5: 7 We live by *f*, not by sight.
8: 7 in *f*, in speech, in knowledge,
10: 15 as your *f* continues to grow,
13: 5 to see whether you are in the *f*;
Gal 1: 23 now preaching the *f* he once tried
2: 16 Jesus that we may be justified by *f*
2: 16 but by *f* in Jesus Christ.
2: 16 have put our *f* in Christ Jesus that
2: 20 I live by *f* in the Son of God,
3: 8 would justify the Gentiles by *f*,
3: 9 So those who have *f* are blessed
3: 9 along with Abraham, the man of *f*.
3: 11 "The righteous will live by *f*."
3: 12 based on *f*; on the contrary,
3: 14 by *f* we might receive the promise
3: 22 being given through *f*
3: 23 Before this *f* came, we were held
3: 23 up until *f* should be revealed.
3: 24 that we might be justified by *f*.
3: 25 that *f* has come, we are no longer
3: 26 of God through *f* in Christ Jesus,
5: 5 But by *f* we eagerly await
5: 6 that counts is *f* expressing itself
Eph 1: 15 ever since I heard about your *f*
2: 8 through *f*— and this not
3: 12 through *f* in him we may approach
3: 17 dwell in your hearts through *f*.
4: 5 one Lord, one *f*, one baptism;
4: 13 up until we all reach unity in the *f*
6: 16 to all this, take up the shield of *f*,
6: 23 love with *f* from God the Father
Php 1: 25 for your progress and joy in the *f*,
1: 27 as one man for the *f* of the gospel
2: 17 and service coming from your *f*,
3: 9 comes from God and is by *f*.
3: 9 that which is through *f* in Christ—
Col 1: 4 heard of your *f* in Christ Jesus
1: 5 the *f* and love that spring
1: 23 continue in your *f*, established
2: 5 and how firm your *f* in Christ is.
2: 7 in the *f* as you were taught,
2: 12 him through your *f* in the power
1Th 1: 3 Father your work produced by *f*,
1: 8 your *f* in God has become known
3: 2 and encourage you in your *f*,
3: 5 I sent to find out about your *f*.
3: 6 brought good news about your *f*
3: 7 about you because of your *f*.
3: 10 supply what is lacking in your *f*.
5: 8 on *f* and love as a breastplate,
2Th 1: 3 because your *f* is growing more
1: 4 and *f* in all the persecutions
1: 11 and every act prompted by your *f*.
3: 2 evil men, for not everyone has *f*.
1Ti 1: 2 To Timothy my true son in the *f*:
1: 4 than God's work—which is by *f*.
1: 5 a good conscience and a sincere *f*.
1: 14 along with the *f* and love that are
1: 19 and so have shipwrecked their *f*.
1: 19 on to *f* and a good conscience.
2: 7 of the true *f* to the Gentiles.
2: 15 if they continue in *f*, love
3: 9 of the *f* with a clear conscience.
3: 13 assurance in their *f* in Christ Jesus.
4: 1 later times some will abandon the *f*
4: 6 brought up in the truths of the *f*
4: 12 in life, in love, in *f* and in purity.
5: 8 he has denied the *f* and is worse
6: 10 have wandered from the *f*
6: 11 pursue righteousness, godliness, *f*,
6: 12 Fight the good fight of the *f*.
6: 21 so doing have wandered from the *f*.
2Ti 1: 5 been reminded of your sincere *f*,
1: 13 with *f* and love in Christ Jesus.
2: 18 and they destroy the *f* of some.
2: 22 and pursue righteousness, *f*,
3: 8 as far as the *f* is concerned,
3: 10 my purpose, *f*, patience, love,
3: 15 wise for salvation through *f*
4: 7 finished the race, I have kept the *f*.
Tit 1: 1 Christ for the *f* of God's elect
1: 2 a *f* and knowledge resting
1: 4 my true son in our common *f*:
1: 13 so that they will be sound in the *f*
2: 2 self-controlled, and sound in *f*,
3: 15 Greet those who love us in the *f*.
Phm : 5 because I hear about your *f*
: 6 may be active in sharing your *f*,
Heb 4: 2 heard did not combine it with *f*.
4: 14 firmly to the *f* we profess.
6: 1 and of *f* in God, instruction about
6: 12 but to imitate those who through *f*
10: 22 heart in full assurance of *f*,
10: 38 But my righteous one will live by *f*.
11: 1 *f* is being sure of what we hope for
11: 3 By *f* we understand that
11: 4 And by *f* he still speaks, even
11: 4 By *f* Abel offered God a better
11: 4 By *f* he was commended
11: 5 By *f* Enoch was taken from this life
11: 6 And without *f* it is impossible
11: 7 By his *f* he condemned the world
11: 7 By *f* Noah, when warned about
11: 7 the righteousness that comes by *f*.
11: 8 By *f* Abraham, when called to go
11: 9 By *f* he made his home
11: 11 By *f* Abraham, even though he was
11: 13 living by *f* when they died.
11: 17 By *f* Abraham, when God tested
11: 20 By *f* Isaac blessed Jacob
11: 21 By *f* Jacob, when he was dying,
11: 22 By *f* Joseph, when his end was near
11: 23 By *f* Moses' parents hid him
11: 24 By *f* Moses, when he had grown up
11: 27 By *f* he left Egypt, not fearing
11: 28 By *f* he kept the Passover
11: 29 By *f* the people passed
11: 30 By *f* the walls of Jericho fell,
11: 31 By *f* the prostitute Rahab,
11: 33 through *f* conquered kingdoms,
11: 39 were all commended for their *f*,
12: 2 the author and perfecter of our *f*,
13: 7 way of life and imitate their *f*.
Jas 1: 3 of your *f* develops perseverance.
2: 5 the eyes of the world to be rich in *f*
2: 14 has no deeds? Can such *f* save him?
2: 14 if a man claims to have *f*
2: 17 In the same way, *f* by itself,
2: 18 I will show you my *f* by what I do.
2: 18 Show me your *f* without deeds,
2: 18 "You have *f*; I have deeds."
2: 20 do you want evidence that *f*
2: 22 You see that his *f* and his actions
2: 22 and his *f* was made complete
2: 24 by what he does and not by *f* alone.
2: 26 so *f* without deeds is dead.
5: 15 in *f* will make the sick person well;
1Pe 1: 5 who through *f* are shielded
1: 7 These have come so that your *f*—
1: 9 you are receiving the goal of your *f*,
1: 21 and so your *f* and hope are in God.
5: 9 Resist him, standing firm in the *f*,
2Pe 1: 1 Jesus Christ have received a *f*
1: 5 effort to add to your *f* goodness;
1Jn 5: 4 overcome the world, even our *f*.
Jude : 3 to contend for the *f* that was once
: 20 up in your most holy *f*
Rev 2: 13 You did not renounce your *f* in me,
2: 19 your love and *f*, your service

FAITHFUL* (FAITH)
Nu 12: 7 he is *f* in all my house.
Dt 7: 9 your God is God; he is the *f* God,
32: 4 A *f* God who does no wrong,
1Sa 2: 35 I will raise up for myself a *f* priest,
2Sa 20: 19 We are the peaceful and *f* in Israel.
22: 26 "To the *f* you show yourself *f*,
1Ki 3: 6 because he was *f* to you
2Ch 31: 18 were *f* in consecrating themselves.
31: 20 and *f* before the LORD his God.
Ne 9: 8 You found his heart *f* to you,
Ps 12: 1 the *f* have vanished
18: 25 To the *f* you show yourself *f*,
25: 10 of the LORD are loving and *f*
31: 23 The LORD preserves the *f*,
33: 4 he is *f* in all he does.
37: 28 and will not forsake his *f* ones.
78: 8 whose spirits were not *f* to him.
78: 37 they were not *f* to his covenant.
89: 19 to your *f* people you said:
89: 24 My *f* love will be with him,
89: 37 the *f* witness in the sky."
97: 10 for he guards the lives of his *f* ones
101: 6 My eyes will be on the *f* in the land,
111: 7 The works of his hands are *f*
145: 13 The LORD is *f* to all his promises
146: 6 the LORD, who remains *f* forever.
Pr 2: 8 and protects the way of his *f* ones.
20: 6 but a *f* man who can find?
28: 20 A *f* man will be richly blessed,
31: 26 and *f* instruction is on her tongue.
Isa 1: 21 See how the *f* city has become
1: 26 the *F* City."
49: 7 because of the LORD, who is *f*,
55: 3 my *f* love promised to David.
Jer 42: 5 *f* witness against us if we do not act
Eze 43: 11 so that they may be *f* to its design
48: 11 who were *f* in serving me
Hos 11: 12 even against the *f* Holy One.
Zec 8: 8 I will be *f* and righteous to them
Mt 24: 45 Who then is the *f* and wise servant,

25: 21 'Well done, good and *f* servant!
25: 21 You have been *f* with a few things;
25: 23 You have been *f* with a few things;
25: 23 'Well done, good and *f* servant!
Lk 12: 42 then is the *f* and wise manager,
Ro 12: 12 patient in affliction, *f* in prayer.
1Co 1: 9 his Son Jesus Christ our Lord, is *f*.
4: 2 been given a trust must prove *f*.
4: 17 my son whom I love, who is *f*
10: 13 And God is *f*; he will not let you be
2Co 1: 18 no"? But as surely as God is *f*,
Eph 1: 1 in Ephesus, the *f* in Christ Jesus:
6: 21 the dear brother and *f* servant
Col 1: 2 and *f* brothers in Christ at Colosse:
1: 7 who is a *f* minister of Christ
4: 7 a *f* minister and fellow servant
4: 9 He is coming with Onesimus, our *f*
1Th 5: 24 The one who calls you is *f*
2Th 3: 3 the Lord is *f*, and he will strengthen
1Ti 1: 12 he considered me *f*, appointing me
5: 9 has been *f* to her husband,
2Ti 2: 13 he will remain *f*,
Heb 2: 17 and *f* high priest in service to God,
3: 2 He was *f* to the one who appointed
3: 2 as Moses was *f* in all God's house.
3: 5 Moses was *f* as a servant
3: 6 But Christ is *f* as a son
8: 9 because they did not remain *f*
10: 23 for he who promised is *f*.
11: 11 he considered him *f* who had made
1Pe 4: 19 themselves to their *f* Creator
5: 12 whom I regard as a *f* brother,
1Jn 1: 9 he is *f* and just and will forgive us
3Jn : 5 you are *f* in what you are doing
Rev 1: 5 who is the *f* witness, the firstborn
2: 10 Be *f*, even to the point of death,
2: 13 the days of Antipas, my *f* witness,
3: 14 the words of the Amen, the *f*
14: 12 commandments and remain *f*
17: 14 his called, chosen and *f* followers."
19: 11 whose rider is called *F* and True.

FAITHFULLY* (FAITH)
Dt 11: 13 if you *f* obey the commands I am
Jos 2: 14 *f* when the LORD gives us the land
1Sa 12: 24 and serve him *f* with all your heart;
1Ki 2: 4 and if they walk *f* before me
2Ki 20: 3 how I have walked before you *f*
22: 7 because they are acting *f*."
2Ch 19: 9 must serve *f* and wholeheartedly
31: 12 they *f* brought in the contributions,
31: 15 and Shecaniah assisted him *f*
32: 1 all that Hezekiah had so *f* done,
34: 12 The men did the work *f*.
Ne 9: 33 you have acted *f*, while we did
13: 14 so *f* done for the house of my God
Isa 38: 3 how I have walked before you *f*
Jer 23: 28 one who has my word speak it *f*.
Eze 18: 9 and *f* keeps my laws.
44: 15 and who *f* carried out the duties
1Pe 4: 10 *f* administering God's grace

FAITHFULNESS* (FAITH)
Ge 24: 27 not abandoned his kindness and *f*
24: 49 if you will show kindness and *f*
32: 10 and *f* you have shown your servant.
47: 29 you will show me kindness and *f*.
Ex 34: 6 *f*, maintaining love to thousands,
Jos 24: 14 the LORD and serve him with all *f*.
1Sa 26: 23 man for his righteousness and *f*.
2Sa 2: 6 now show you kindness and *f*,
15: 20 May kindness and *f* be with you."
Ps 30: 9 Will it proclaim your *f*?
36: 5 your *f* to the skies.
40: 10 I speak of your *f* and salvation.
54: 5 in your *f* destroy them.
57: 3 God sends his love and his *f*.
57: 10 your *f* reaches to the skies.
61: 7 appoint your love and *f*
71: 22 the harp for your *f*, O my God;
85: 10 Love and *f* meet together;
85: 11 *F* springs forth from the earth,
86: 15 to anger, abounding in love and *f*.
88: 11 your *f* in Destruction?
89: 1 mouth I will make your *f* known
89: 2 that you established your *f*
89: 5 your *f* too, in the assembly
89: 8 and your *f* surrounds you.
89: 14 love and *f* go before you.
89: 33 nor will I ever betray my *f*.
89: 49 which in your *f* you swore to David
91: 4 his *f* will be your shield
92: 2 and your *f* at night,
98: 3 and his *f* to the house of Israel;
100: 5 *f* continues through all
108: 4 your *f* reaches to the skies.
111: 8 done in *f* and uprightness.
115: 1 because of your love and *f*.
117: 2 the *f* of the LORD endures forever.
119: 75 and in *f* you have afflicted me.
119: 90 *f* continues through all
138: 2 name for your love and your *f*,
143: 1 in your *f* and righteousness
Pr 3: 3 Let love and *f* never leave you;
14: 22 plan what is good find love and *f*.
16: 6 Through love and *f* sin is atoned for
20: 28 Love and *f* keep a king safe;
Isa 11: 5 and *f* the sash around his waist.
16: 5 in *f* a man will sit on it—
25: 1 for in perfect *f*
38: 18 cannot hope for your *f*.
38: 19 about your *f*.
42: 3 In *f* he will bring forth justice;
61: 8 In my *f* I will reward them
La 3: 23 great is your *f*.
Hos 2: 20 I will betroth you in *f*,
4: 1 "There is no *f*, no love,
Mt 23: 23 of the law—justice, mercy and *f*.
Ro 3: 3 lack of faith nullify God's *f*?
Gal 5: 22 patience, kindness, goodness, *f*,
3Jn : 3 and tell about your *f* to the truth
Rev 13: 10 and *f* on the part of the saints.

FAITHLESS* (FAITH)
Ps 78: 57 fathers they were disloyal and *f*,
101: 3 The deeds of *f* men I hate;
119:158 I look on the *f* with loathing,
Pr 14: 14 The *f* will be fully repaid
Jer 3: 6 you seen what *f* Israel has done?
3: 8 I gave *f* Israel her certificate
3: 11 "*F* Israel is more righteous
3: 12 *f* Israel,' declares the LORD,
3: 14 *f* people," declares the LORD,
3: 22 "Return, *f* people;
12: 1 Why do all the *f* live at ease?
Ro 1: 31 they are senseless, *f*, heartless,
2Ti 2: 13 if we are *f*,

FALL (FALLEN FALLING FALLS)
Ps 37: 24 though he stumble, he will not *f*,
55: 22 he will never let the righteous *f*.
69: 9 of those who insult you *f* on me.
145: 14 The LORD upholds all those who *f*
Pr 11: 28 Whoever trusts in his riches will *f*,
Isa 40: 7 The grass withers and the flowers *f*,
Mt 7: 25 yet it did not *f*, because it had its
Lk 10: 18 "I saw Satan *f* like lightning
11: 17 a house divided against itself will *f*.
23: 30 say to the mountains, "*F* on us!"
Ro 3: 23 and *f* short of the glory of God,
Heb 6: 6 if they *f* away, to be brought back

FALLEN (FALL)
2Sa 1: 19 How the mighty have *f*!
Isa 14: 12 How you have *f* from heaven,
1Co 11: 30 and a number of you have *f* asleep.
15: 6 though some have *f* asleep.
15: 18 who have *f* asleep in Christ are lost.
15: 20 of those who have *f* asleep.
Gal 5: 4 you have *f* away from grace.
1Th 4: 15 precede those who have *f* asleep.

FALLING (FALL)
Jude : 24 able to keep you from *f*

FALLS (FALL)
Pr 11: 14 For lack of guidance a nation *f*,
24: 17 Do not gloat when your enemy *f*;
28: 14 he who hardens his heart *f*
Mt 13: 21 of the word, he quickly *f* away.
21: 44 He who *f* on this stone will be
Jn 12: 24 a kernel of wheat *f* to the ground
Ro 14: 4 To his own master he stands or *f*.

FALSE (FALSEHOOD FALSELY)
Ex 20: 16 "You shall not give *f* testimony
23: 1 "Do not spread *f* reports.
23: 7 Have nothing to do with a *f* charge
Dt 5: 20 "You shall not give *f* testimony
Pr 12: 17 but a *f* witness tells lies.
13: 5 The righteous hate what is *f*,
14: 5 but a *f* witness pours out lies.
14: 25 but a *f* witness is deceitful.
19: 5 A *f* witness will not go unpunished,
19: 9 A *f* witness will not go unpunished,
21: 28 A *f* witness will perish,
25: 18 is the man who gives *f* testimony
Isa 44: 25 who foils the signs of *f* prophets
Jer 23: 16 they fill you with *f* hopes.
Mt 7: 15 "Watch out for *f* prophets.
15: 19 theft, *f* testimony, slander.
19: 18 not steal, do not give *f* testimony,
24: 11 and many *f* prophets will appear
24: 24 For *f* Christs and *f* prophets will
Mk 10: 19 do not give *f* testimony, do not
13: 22 For *f* Christs and *f* prophets will
Lk 6: 26 their fathers treated the *f* prophets.
18: 20 not steal, do not give *f* testimony,
Jn 1: 47 in whom there is nothing *f*."
1Co 15: 15 found to be *f* witnesses about God,
2Co 11: 13 For such men are *f* apostles,
11: 26 and in danger from *f* brothers.
Gal 2: 4 some *f* brothers had infiltrated our
Php 1: 18 whether from *f* motives or true,
Col 2: 18 anyone who delights in *f* humility
2: 23 their *f* humility and their harsh
1Ti 1: 3 not to teach *f* doctrines any longer
6: 3 If anyone teaches *f* doctrines
2Pe 2: 1 also *f* prophets among the people,
2: 1 there will be *f* teachers among you.
1Jn 4: 1 many *f* prophets have gone out
Rev 16: 13 out of the mouth of the *f* prophet.
19: 20 with him the *f* prophet who had
20: 10 and the *f* prophet had been thrown.

FALSEHOOD* (FALSE)
Job 21: 34 left of your answers but *f*!"
31: 5 "If I have walked in *f*
Ps 52: 3 *f* rather than speaking the truth.
119:163 I hate and abhor *f*
Pr 30: 8 Keep *f* and lies far from me;
Isa 28: 15 and *f* our hiding place."
Ro 3: 7 "If my *f* enhances God's
Eph 4: 25 each of you must put off *f*
1Jn 4: 6 Spirit of truth and the spirit of *f*.
Rev 22: 15 everyone who loves and practices *f*

FALSELY (FALSE)
Lev 19: 12 " 'Do not swear *f* by my name
Mt 5: 11 *f* say all kinds of evil against you
Lk 3: 14 and don't accuse people *f*—
1Ti 6: 20 ideas of what is *f* called knowledge,

FALTER*
Pr 24: 10 If you *f* in times of trouble,
Isa 42: 4 he will not *f* or be discouraged

FAME
Jos 9: 9 of the *f* of the LORD your God.
Isa 66: 19 islands that have not heard of my *f*
Hab 3: 2 LORD, I have heard of your *f*;

FAMILIES (FAMILY)
Ps 68: 6 God sets the lonely in *f*,

FAMILY (FAMILIES)
Pr 15: 27 greedy man brings trouble to his *f*,
31: 15 she provides food for her *f*
Mk 5: 19 to your *f* and tell them how much

Lk 9: 61 go back and say good-by to my f."
12: 52 in one f divided against each other,
Ac 10: 2 He and all his f were devout
16: 33 and all his f were baptized.
16: 34 he and his whole f.
1Ti 3: 4 He must manage his own f well
3: 5 how to manage his own f,
5: 4 practice by caring for their own f
5: 8 and especially for his immediate f,

FAMINE
Ge 12: 10 Now there was a f in the land,
26: 1 Now there was a f in the land—
41: 30 seven years of f will follow them.
Ru 1: 1 the judges ruled, there was a f
1Ki 18: 2 Now the f was severe in Samaria,
Am 8: 11 but a f of hearing the words
Ro 8: 35 or persecution or f or nakedness

FAN*
2Ti 1: 6 you to f into flame the gift of God,

FANTASIES*
Ps 73: 20 you will despise them as f.
Pr 12: 11 but he who chases f lacks judgment
28: 19 one who chases f will have his fill

FAST (FASTING)
Dt 10: 20 Hold f to him and take your oaths
11: 22 in all his ways and to hold f to him
13: 4 serve him and hold f to him.
30: 20 to his voice, and hold f to him.
Jos 22: 5 to hold f to him and to serve him
23: 8 to hold f to the LORD your God,
2Ki 18: 6 He held f to the LORD
Ps 119: 31 I hold f to your statutes, O LORD;
139: 10 your right hand will hold me f.
Mt 6: 16 "When you f, do not look somber
1Pe 5: 12 Stand f in it.

FASTING (FAST)
Ps 35: 13 and humbled myself with f.
Ac 13: 2 were worshiping the Lord and f,
14: 23 and f, committed them to the Lord

FATHER (FATHER'S FATHERED FATHERLESS FATHERS FOREFATHERS)
Ge 2: 24 this reason a man will leave his f
17: 4 You will be the f of many nations.
Ex 20: 12 "Honor your f and your mother,
21: 15 "Anyone who attacks his f
21: 17 "Anyone who curses his f
Lev 18: 7 " 'Do not dishonor your f
19: 3 you must respect his mother and f,
20: 9 " 'If anyone curses his f or mother,
Dt 1: 31 carried you, as a f carries his son,
5: 16 "Honor your f and your mother,
21: 18 son who does not obey his f
32: 6 Is he not your F, your Creator,
2Sa 7: 14 I will be his f, and he will be my son
1Ch 17: 13 I will be his f, and he will be my son
22: 10 will be my son, and I will be his f.
28: 6 to be my son, and I will be his f.
Job 38: 28 Does the rain have a f?
Ps 2: 7 today I have become your F.
27: 10 Though my f and mother forsake
68: 5 A f to the fatherless, a defender
89: 26 to me, 'You are my F,
103: 13 As a f has compassion
Pr 3: 12 as a f the son he delights in.
10: 1 A wise son brings joy to his f,
17: 21 there is no joy for the f of a fool.
17: 25 A foolish son brings grief to his f
23: 22 Listen to your f, who gave you life,
23: 24 f of a righteous man has great joy;
28: 7 of gluttons disgraces his f.
28: 24 He who robs his f or mother
29: 3 loves wisdom brings joy to his f,
Isa 9: 6 Everlasting F, Prince of Peace.
45: 10 Woe to him who says to his f,
63: 16 But you are our F,
Jer 2: 27 They say to wood, 'You are my f,'
3: 19 I thought you would call me 'F'
31: 9 because I am Israel's f,
Eze 18: 19 the son not share the guilt of his f?'
Mic 7: 6 For a son dishonors his f,
Mal 1: 6 If I am a f, where is the honor due
2: 10 we not all one F? Did not one God
Mt 3: 9 'We have Abraham as our f.'
5: 16 and praise your F in heaven.
6: 9 " 'Our F in heaven,
6: 26 yet your heavenly F feeds them.
10: 37 "Anyone who loves his f
11: 27 no one knows the F except the Son
15: 4 'Honor your f and mother'
18: 10 the face of my F in heaven.
19: 5 this reason a man will leave his f
19: 19 honor your f and mother,'
19: 29 or brothers or sisters or f or mother
23: 9 And do not call anyone on earth 'f,'
Mk 7: 10 'Honor your f and your mother,' and,
Lk 9: 59 "Lord, first let me go and bury my f
12: 53 f against son and son against f,
14: 26 and does not hate his f and mother,
18: 20 honor your f and mother.' "
23: 34 Jesus said, "F, forgive them,
Jn 3: 35 The F loves the Son and has placed
4: 21 you will worship the F neither
5: 17 "My F is always at his work
5: 18 he was even calling God his own F,
5: 20 For the F loves the Son
6: 44 the F who sent me draws him,
6: 46 No one has seen the F
8: 19 "You do not know me or my F,"
8: 28 speak just what the F has taught me
8: 41 The only F we have is God himself
8: 42 God were your F, you would love
8: 44 You belong to your f, the devil,
10: 17 reason my F loves me is that I lay
10: 30 I and the F are one."
10: 38 and understand that the F is in me,
14: 6 No one comes to the F
14: 9 who has seen me has seen the F.
14: 28 for the F is greater than I.
15: 9 "As the F has loved me,
15: 23 He who hates me hates my F
20: 17 'I am returning to my F and your F,
Ac 13: 33 today I have become your F.'
Ro 4: 11 he is the f of all who believe
4: 16 He is the f of us all.
8: 15 And by him we cry, "Abba, F."
1Co 4: 15 for in Christ Jesus I became your f
2Co 6: 18 "I will be a F to you,
Eph 5: 31 this reason a man will leave his f
6: 2 "Honor your f and mother"—
Php 2: 11 to the glory of God the F.
Heb 1: 5 today I have become your F"?
12: 7 what son is not disciplined by his f?
1Jn 1: 3 And our fellowship is with the F
2: 15 the love of the F is not in him.
2: 22 he denies the F and the Son.

FATHER'S (FATHER)
Pr 13: 1 A wise son heeds his f instruction,
15: 5 A fool spurns his f discipline,
19: 13 A foolish son is his f ruin,
Mt 16: 27 going to come in his F glory
Lk 2: 49 had to be in my F house?"
Jn 2: 16 How dare you turn my F house
10: 29 can snatch them out of my F hand.
14: 2 In my F house are many rooms;
15: 8 to my F glory, that you bear much

FATHERED (FATHER)
Dt 32: 18 You deserted the Rock, who f you;

FATHERLESS (FATHER)
Dt 10: 18 He defends the cause of the f
14: 29 the f and the widows who live
24: 17 Do not deprive the alien or the f
24: 19 Leave it for the alien, the f
26: 12 the alien, the f and the widow,
Ps 68: 5 A father to the f, a defender
82: 3 Defend the cause of the weak and f
Pr 23: 10 or encroach on the fields of the f,

FATHERS (FATHER)
Ex 20: 5 for the sin of the f to the third
Jer 31: 29 'The f have eaten sour grapes,
Mal 4: 6 the hearts of the children to their f;
Lk 1: 17 the hearts of the f to their children
11: 11 "Which of you f, if your son asks
Jn 4: 20 Our f worshiped on this mountain,
1Co 4: 15 you do not have many f,
Eph 6: 4 F, do not exasperate your children;
Col 3: 21 F, do not embitter your children,
Heb 12: 9 all had human f who disciplined us

FATHOM* (FATHOMED)
Job 11: 7 "Can you f the mysteries of God?
Ps 145: 3 his greatness no one can f.
Ecc 3: 11 yet they cannot f what God has
Isa 40: 28 and his understanding no one can f
1Co 13: 2 and can f all mysteries and all

FATHOMED* (FATHOM)
Job 5: 9 performs wonders that cannot be f,
9: 10 performs wonders that cannot be f,

FATTENED
Pr 15: 17 than a f calf with hatred.
Lk 15: 23 Bring the f calf and kill it.

FAULT (FAULTS)
1Sa 29: 3 I have found no f in him."
Mt 18: 15 and show him his f, just
Php 2: 15 of God without f in a crooked
Jas 1: 5 generously to all without finding f,
Jude : 24 his glorious presence without f

FAULTFINDERS*
Jude : 16 These men are grumblers and f;

FAULTLESS*
Pr 8: 9 they are f to those who have
Php 3: 6 as for legalistic righteousness, f.
Jas 1: 27 Father accepts as pure and f is this:

FAULTS* (FAULT)
Job 10: 6 that you must search out my f
Ps 19: 12 Forgive my hidden f.

FAVOR (FAVORITISM)
Ge 4: 4 The LORD looked with f on Abel
6: 8 But Noah found f in the eyes
Ex 33: 12 and you have found f with me.'
34: 9 if I have found f in your eyes,"
Lev 26: 9 " 'I will look on you with f
Nu 11: 15 if I have found f in your eyes—
Jdg 6: 17 "If now I have found f in your eyes,
1Sa 2: 26 in f with the LORD and with men.
2Sa 2: 6 and I too will show you the same f
2Ki 13: 4 Jehoahaz sought the LORD's f,
2Ch 33: 12 In his distress he sought the f
Est 7: 3 "If I have found f with you, O king,
Ps 90: 17 May the f of the Lord our God rest
Pr 8: 35 and receives f from the LORD.
18: 22 and receives f from the LORD.
19: 6 Many curry f with a ruler,
Isa 61: 2 proclaim the year of the LORD's f
Zec 11: 7 called one F and the other Union,
Lk 1: 30 Mary, you have found f with God.
2: 14 to men on whom his f rests."
2: 52 and in f with God and men.
4: 19 to proclaim the year of the Lord's f
2Co 6: 2 now is the time of God's f,

FAVORITISM* (FAVOR)
Ex 23: 3 and do not show f to a poor man
Lev 19: 15 to the poor or f to the great,
Ac 10: 34 true it is that God does not show f
Ro 2: 11 For God does not show f.
Eph 6: 9 and there is no f with him.
Col 3: 25 for his wrong, and there is no f.
1Ti 5: 21 and to do nothing out of f.
Jas 2: 1 Lord Jesus Christ, don't show f.
2: 9 But if you show f, you sin

FEAR (AFRAID FEARED FEARS FRIGHTENED GOD-FEARING)
Dt 6: 13 F the LORD your God, serve him
10: 12 but to f the LORD your God,
31: 12 and learn to f the LORD your God

31: 13 and learn to *f* the LORD your God
Jos 4: 24 you might always *f* the LORD
24: 14 "Now *f* the LORD and serve him
1Sa 12: 14 If you *f* the LORD and serve
12: 24 But be sure to *f* the LORD
2Sa 23: 3 when he rules in the *f* of God,
2Ch 19: 7 let the *f* of the LORD be upon you.
26: 5 who instructed him in the *f* of God.
Job 1: 9 "Does Job *f* God for nothing?"
Ps 2: 11 Serve the LORD with *f*
19: 9 The *f* of the LORD is pure,
23: 4 I will *f* no evil,
27: 1 whom shall I *f*?
33: 8 Let all the earth *f* the LORD;
34: 7 around those who *f* him,
34: 9 *F* the LORD, you his saints,
46: 2 Therefore we will not *f*,
86: 11 that I may *f* your name.
90: 11 great as the *f* that is due you.
91: 5 You will not *f* the terror of night,
111: 10 *f* of the LORD is the beginning
118: 4 Let those who *f* the LORD say:
128: 1 Blessed are all who *f* the LORD,
145: 19 of those who *f* him;
147: 11 delights in those who *f* him,
Pr 1: 7 *f* of the LORD is the beginning
1: 33 and be at ease, without *f* of harm."
8: 13 To *f* the LORD is to hate evil;
9: 10 *f* of the LORD is the beginning
10: 27 The *f* of the LORD adds length
14: 27 The *f* of the LORD is a fountain
15: 33 *f* of the LORD teaches a man
16: 6 through the *f* of the LORD a man
19: 23 The *f* of the LORD leads to life:
22: 4 Humility and the *f* of the LORD
29: 25 *F* of man will prove to be a snare,
31: 21 she has no *f* for her household;
Ecc 12: 13 *F* God and keep his
Isa 11: 3 delight in the *f* of the LORD.
33: 6 the *f* of the LORD is the key
35: 4 "Be strong, do not *f*;
41: 10 So do not *f*, for I am with you;
41: 13 and says to you, Do not *f*;
43: 1 "*F* not, for I have redeemed you;
51: 7 Do not *f* the reproach of men
54: 14 you will have nothing to *f*.
Jer 17: 8 It does not *f* when heat comes;
Lk 12: 5 I will show you whom you should *f*:
2Co 5: 11 we know what it is to *f* the Lord,
Php 2: 12 to work out your salvation with *f*
1Jn 4: 18 But perfect love drives out *f*,
Jude : 23 to others show mercy, mixed with *f*
Rev 14: 7 "*F* God and give him glory,

FEARED (FEAR)
Job 1: 1 he *f* God and shunned evil.
Ps 76: 7 You alone are to be *f*.
Mal 3: 16 those who *f* the LORD talked

FEARS (FEAR)
Job 1: 8 a man who *f* God and shuns evil."
2: 3 a man who *f* God and shuns evil.
Ps 34: 4 he delivered me from all my *f*.
112: 1 is the man who *f* the LORD,
Pr 14: 16 A wise man *f* the LORD
14: 26 He who *f* the LORD has a secure
31: 30 a woman who *f* the LORD is
2Co 7: 5 conflicts on the outside, *f* within.
1Jn 4: 18 The one who *f* is not made perfect

FEAST (FEASTING FEASTS)
Pr 15: 15 the cheerful heart has a continual *f*.
2Pe 2: 13 pleasures while they *f* with you.

FEASTING (FEAST)
Pr 17: 1 than a house full of *f*, with strife.

FEASTS (FEAST)
Am 5: 21 "I hate, I despise your religious *f*;
Jude : 12 men are blemishes at your love *f*,

FEATHERS
Ps 91: 4 He will cover you with his *f*,

FEEBLE
Job 4: 3 you have strengthened *f* hands.
Isa 35: 3 Strengthen the *f* hands,
Heb 12: 12 strengthen your *f* arms

FEED (FEEDS)
Jn 21: 15 Jesus said, "*F* my lambs."
21: 17 Jesus said, "*F* my sheep.
Ro 12: 20 "If your enemy is hungry, *f* him;
Jude : 12 shepherds who *f* only themselves.

FEEDS (FEED)
Pr 15: 14 but the mouth of a fool *f* on folly.
Mt 6: 26 yet your heavenly Father *f* them.
Jn 6: 57 so the one who *f* on me will live

FEEL
Jdg 16: 26 me where I can *f* the pillars that
Ps 115: 7 they have hands, but cannot *f*,

FEET (FOOT)
Ru 3: 8 discovered a woman lying at his *f*.
Ps 8: 6 you put everything under his *f*:
22: 16 have pierced my hands and my *f*.
40: 2 he set my *f* on a rock
56: 13 and my *f* from stumbling,
66: 9 and kept our *f* from slipping.
73: 2 as for me, my *f* had almost slipped;
110: 1 a footstool for your *f*."
119:105 Your word is a lamp to my *f*
Pr 4: 26 Make level paths for your *f*
Isa 52: 7 are the *f* of those who bring good
Da 2: 33 its *f* partly of iron and partly
Na 1: 15 the *f* of one who brings good news,
Mt 10: 14 shake the dust off your *f*
22: 44 enemies under your *f*." '
Lk 1: 79 to guide our *f* into the path of peace
20: 43 a footstool for your *f*." '
24: 39 Look at my hands and my *f*.
Jn 13: 5 and began to wash his disciples' *f*,
13: 14 also should wash one another's *f*.
Ro 3: 15 "Their *f* are swift to shed blood;
10: 15 "How beautiful are the *f*
16: 20 will soon crush Satan under your *f*.
1Co 12: 21 And the head cannot say to the *f*,
15: 25 has put all his enemies under his *f*.
Eph 1: 22 God placed all things under his *f*
1Ti 5: 10 washing the *f* of the saints,
Heb 1: 13 a footstool for your *f*"?
2: 8 and put everything under his *f*."
12: 13 "Make level paths for your *f*,"
Rev 1: 15 His *f* were like bronze glowing

FELIX
Governor before whom Paul was tried (Ac 23:23–24:27).

FELLOWSHIP
Ex 20: 24 burnt offerings and *f* offerings,
Lev 3: 1 If someone's offering is a *f* offering,
1Co 1: 9 who has called you into *f*
5: 2 out of your *f* the man who did this?
2Co 6: 14 what *f* can light have with darkness
13: 14 and the *f* of the Holy Spirit be
Gal 2: 9 and Barnabas the right hand of *f*
Php 2: 1 if any *f* with the Spirit,
3: 10 the *f* of sharing in his sufferings,
1Jn 1: 3 And our *f* is with the Father
1: 3 so that you also may have *f* with us.
1: 6 claim to have *f* with him yet walk
1: 7 we have *f* with one another,

FEMALE
Ge 1: 27 male and *f* he created them.
5: 2 He created them male and *f*
Mt 19: 4 Creator 'made them male and *f*,'
Mk 10: 6 God 'made them male and *f*.'
Gal 3: 28 *f*, for you are all one in Christ Jesus

FEROCIOUS
Mt 7: 15 but inwardly they are *f* wolves.

FERTILE (FERTILIZE)
Isa 32: 15 and the desert becomes a *f* field,
Jer 2: 7 I brought you into a *f* land

FERTILIZE* (FERTILE)
Lk 13: 8 and I'll dig around it and *f* it.

FERVOR*
Ac 18: 25 and he spoke with great *f*
Ro 12: 11 but keep your spiritual *f*, serving

FESTIVAL
1Co 5: 8 Therefore let us keep the *F*,
Col 2: 16 or with regard to a religious *f*,

FESTUS
Successor of Felix; sent Paul to Caesar (Ac 25–26).

FEVER
Job 30: 30 my body burns with *f*.
Mt 8: 14 mother-in-law lying in bed with a *f*.
Lk 4: 38 was suffering from a high *f*,
Jn 4: 52 "The *f* left him yesterday
Ac 28: 8 suffering from *f* and dysentery.

FIELD (FIELDS)
Ge 4: 8 Abel, "Let's go out to the *f*."
Lev 19: 9 reap to the very edges of your *f*
19: 19 Do not plant your *f* with two kinds
Pr 31: 16 She considers a *f* and buys it;
Isa 40: 6 glory is like the flowers of the *f*.
Mt 6: 28 See how the lilies of the *f* grow.
6: 30 how God clothes the grass of the *f*,
13: 38 *f* is the world, and the good seed
13: 44 is like treasure hidden in a *f*.
Lk 14: 18 I have just bought a *f*, and I must go
1Co 3: 9 you are God's *f*, God's building.
1Pe 1: 24 glory is like the flowers of the *f*;

FIELDS (FIELD)
Ru 2: 2 go to the *f* and pick up the leftover
Lk 2: 8 were shepherds living out in the *f*
Jn 4: 35 open your eyes and look at the *f*!

FIG (FIGS SYCAMORE-FIG)
Ge 3: 7 so they sewed *f* leaves together
Jdg 9: 10 "Next, the trees said to the *f* tree,
1Ki 4: 25 man under his own vine and *f* tree.
Pr 27: 18 He who tends a *f* tree will eat its
Mic 4: 4 and under his own *f* tree,
Zec 3: 10 to sit under his vine and *f* tree,'
Mt 21: 19 Seeing a *f* tree by the road,
Lk 13: 6 "A man had a *f* tree, planted
Jas 3: 12 brothers, can a *f* tree bear olives,
Rev 6: 13 drop from a *f* tree when shaken

FIGHT (FIGHTING FIGHTS FOUGHT)
Ex 14: 14 The LORD will *f* for you; you need
Dt 1: 30 going before you, will *f* for you,
3: 22 the LORD your God himself will *f*
Ne 4: 20 Our God will *f* for us!"
Ps 35: 1 *f* against those who *f* against me.
Jn 18: 36 my servants would *f*
1Co 9: 26 I do not *f* like a man beating the air.
2Co 10: 4 The weapons we *f*
1Ti 1: 18 them you may *f* the good *f*,
6: 12 Fight the good *f* of the faith.
2Ti 4: 7 fought the good *f*, I have finished

FIGHTING (FIGHT)
Jos 10: 14 Surely the LORD was *f* for Israel!

FIGHTS (FIGHT)
Jos 23: 10 the LORD your God *f* for you,
1Sa 25: 28 because he *f* the LORD's battles.
Jas 4: 1 What causes *f* and quarrels

FIGS (FIG)
Lk 6: 44 People do not pick *f*
Jas 3: 12 grapevine bear *f*? Neither can a salt

FILL (FILLED FILLING FILLS FULL FULLNESS FULLY)
Ge 1: 28 and increase in number; *f* the earth
Ps 16: 11 you will *f* me with joy
81: 10 wide your mouth and I will *f* it.
Pr 28: 19 who chases fantasies will have his *f*
Hag 2: 7 and I will *f* this house with glory,'
Jn 6: 26 you ate the loaves and had your *f*.
Ac 2: 28 you will *f* me with joy
Ro 15: 13 the God of hope *f* you with all joy

FILLED (FILL)
Ex 31: 3 I have *f* him with the Spirit of God,
35: 31 he has *f* him with the Spirit of God,
Dt 34: 9 son of Nun was *f* with the spirit
1Ki 8: 10 the cloud *f* the temple
8: 11 glory of the LORD *f* his temple.
2Ch 5: 14 of the LORD *f* the temple of God.
7: 1 the glory of the LORD *f* the temple
Ps 72: 19 may the whole earth be *f*
119: 64 The earth is *f* with your love,
Isa 6: 4 and the temple was *f* with smoke.
Eze 10: 3 and a cloud *f* the inner court.
10: 4 The cloud *f* the temple,
43: 5 the glory of the LORD *f* the temple
Hab 2: 14 For the earth will be *f*
3: 3 and his praise *f* the earth.
Mt 5: 6 for they will be *f*.
Lk 1: 15 and he will be *f* with the Holy Spirit
1: 41 and Elizabeth was *f* with the Holy
1: 67 His father Zechariah was *f*
2: 40 and became strong; he was *f*
Jn 12: 3 the house was *f* with the fragrance
Ac 2: 2 *f* the whole house where they were
2: 4 All of them were *f*
4: 8 Then Peter, *f* with the Holy Spirit,
4: 31 they were all *f* with the Holy Spirit
9: 17 and be *f* with the Holy Spirit."
13: 9 called Paul, *f* with the Holy Spirit,
Eph 5: 18 Instead, be *f* with the Spirit.
Php 1: 11 *f* with the fruit of righteousness
Rev 15: 8 And the temple was *f* with smoke

FILLING (FILL)
Eze 44: 4 the glory of the LORD *f* the temple

FILLS (FILL)
Nu 14: 21 of the LORD *f* the whole earth,
Ps 107: 9 and *f* the hungry with good things.
Eph 1: 23 fullness of him who *f* everything

FILTH (FILTHY)
Isa 4: 4 The Lord will wash away the *f*
Jas 1: 21 rid of all moral *f* and the evil that is

FILTHY (FILTH)
Isa 64: 6 all our righteous acts are like *f* rags;
Col 3: 8 and *f* language from your lips.
2Pe 2: 7 by the *f* lives of lawless men

FINAL (FINALITY)
Ps 73: 17 then I understood their *f* destiny.

FINALITY* (FINAL)
Ro 9: 28 on earth with speed and *f*."

FINANCIAL*
1Ti 6: 5 that godliness is a means to *f* gain.

FIND (FINDS FOUND)
Nu 32: 23 be sure that your sin will *f* you out.
Dt 4: 29 you will *f* him if you look for him
1Sa 23: 16 and helped him *f* strength in God.
Job 23: 3 If only I knew where to *f* him;
Ps 36: 7 *f* refuge in the shadow
62: 5 *F* rest, O my soul, in God alone;
91: 4 under his wings you will *f* refuge;
Pr 8: 17 and those who seek me *f* me.
14: 22 those who plan what is good *f* love
20: 6 but a faithful man who can *f*?
24: 14 if you *f* it, there is a future hope
31: 10 A wife of noble character who can *f*
Jer 6: 16 and you will *f* rest for your souls.
29: 13 and *f* me when you seek me
Mt 7: 7 seek and you will *f*; knock
11: 29 and you will *f* rest for your souls.
16: 25 loses his life for me will *f* it.
22: 9 invite to the banquet anyone you *f*.'
Lk 11: 9 seek and you will *f*; knock
18: 8 will he *f* faith on the earth?"
Jn 10: 9 come in and go out, and *f* pasture.

FINDS (FIND)
Ps 62: 1 My soul *f* rest in God alone;
112: 1 who *f* great delight
119:162 like one who *f* great spoil.
Pr 3: 13 Blessed is the man who *f* wisdom,
8: 35 For whoever *f* me *f* life
11: 27 He who seeks good *f* good will,
18: 22 He who *f* a wife *f* what is good
Mt 7: 8 he who seeks *f*; and to him who
10: 39 Whoever *f* his life will lose it,
Lk 11: 10 he who seeks *f*; and to him who
12: 37 whose master *f* them watching
12: 43 servant whom the master *f* doing
15: 4 go after the lost sheep until he *f* it?
15: 8 and search carefully until she *f* it?

FINE-SOUNDING* (SOUND)
Col 2: 4 may deceive you by *f* arguments.

FINGER
Ex 8: 19 to Pharaoh, "This is the *f* of God."
31: 18 of stone inscribed by the *f* of God.
Dt 9: 10 two stone tablets inscribed by the *f*
Lk 11: 20 But if I drive out demons by the *f*
16: 24 to dip the tip of his *f* in water
Jn 8: 6 to write on the ground with his *f*.
20: 25 and put my *f* where the nails were,

FINISH (FINISHED)
Jn 4: 34 him who sent me and to *f* his work.
5: 36 that the Father has given me to *f*,
Ac 20: 24 if only I may *f* the race
2Co 8: 11 Now *f* the work, so that your eager
Jas 1: 4 Perseverance must *f* its work

FINISHED (FINISH)
Ge 2: 2 seventh day God had *f* the work he
Jn 19: 30 the drink, Jesus said, "It is *f*."
2Ti 4: 7 I have *f* the race, I have kept

FIRE
Ex 3: 2 in flames of *f* from within a bush.
13: 21 in a pillar of *f* to give them light,
Lev 6: 12 *f* on the altar must be kept burning;
9: 24 *F* came out from the presence
1Ki 18: 38 Then the *f* of the LORD fell
2Ki 2: 11 suddenly a chariot of *f*
Isa 5: 24 as tongues of *f* lick up straw
30: 27 and his tongue is a consuming *f*.
Jer 23: 29 my word like *f*," declares
Da 3: 25 four men walking around in the *f*,
Zec 3: 2 stick snatched from the *f*?"
Mal 3: 2 For he will be like a refiner's *f*
Mt 3: 11 you with the Holy Spirit and with *f*.
3: 12 the chaff with unquenchable *f*."
5: 22 will be in danger of the *f* of hell.
18: 8 and be thrown into eternal *f*.
25: 41 into the eternal *f* prepared
Mk 9: 43 where the *f* never goes out.
9: 48 and the *f* is not quenched.'
9: 49 Everyone will be salted with *f*.
Lk 3: 16 you with the Holy Spirit and with *f*.
12: 49 I have come to bring *f* on the earth,
Ac 2: 3 to be tongues of *f* that separated
1Co 3: 13 It will be revealed with *f*,
1Th 5: 19 Do not put out the Spirit's *f*;
Heb 12: 29 for our "God is a consuming *f*."
Jas 3: 5 set on *f* by a small spark.
3: 6 also is a *f*, a world of evil
2Pe 3: 10 the elements will be destroyed by *f*,
Jude : 7 suffer the punishment of eternal *f*.
: 23 snatch others from the *f*
Rev 1: 14 and his eyes were like blazing *f*.
20: 14 The lake of *f* is the second death.

FIRM*
Ex 14: 13 Stand *f* and you will see
15: 8 surging waters stood *f* like a wall;
Jos 3: 17 the covenant of the LORD stood *f*
2Ch 20: 17 stand *f* and see the deliverance
Ezr 9: 8 giving us a *f* place in his sanctuary,
Job 11: 15 you will stand *f* and without fear.
36: 5 he is mighty, and *f* in his purpose.
41: 23 they are *f* and immovable.
Ps 20: 8 but we rise up and stand *f*.
30: 7 you made my mountain stand *f*;
33: 9 he commanded, and it stood *f*.
33: 11 of the LORD stand *f* forever,
37: 23 he makes his steps *f*;
40: 2 and gave me a *f* place to stand.
75: 3 it is I who hold its pillars *f*.
78: 13 made the water stand *f* like a wall.
89: 2 that your love stands *f* forever,
89: 4 and make your throne *f*
93: 5 Your statutes stand *f*;
119: 89 it stands *f* in the heavens.
Pr 4: 26 and take only ways that are *f*.
10: 25 but the righteous stand *f* forever.
12: 7 the house of the righteous stands *f*.
Isa 7: 9 If you do not stand *f* in your faith,
22: 17 about to take *f* hold of you
22: 23 drive him like a peg into a *f* place;
22: 25 into the *f* place will give way;
Eze 13: 5 so that it will stand *f* in the battle
Zec 8: 23 nations will take *f* hold of one Jew
Mt 10: 22 he who stands *f* to the end will be
24: 13 he who stands *f* to the end will be
Mk 13: 13 he who stands *f* to the end will be
Lk 21: 19 By standing *f* you will gain life.
1Co 10: 12 So, if you think you are standing *f*,
15: 58 my dear brothers, stand *f*.
16: 13 on your guard; stand *f* in the faith;
2Co 1: 7 for you is *f*, because we know that
1: 21 who makes both us and you stand *f*
1: 24 because it is by faith you stand *f*.
Gal 5: 1 Stand *f*, then, and do not let
Eph 6: 14 Stand *f* then, with the belt
Php 1: 27 I will know that you stand *f*
4: 1 that is how you should stand *f*
Col 1: 23 in your faith, established and *f*,
2: 5 and how *f* your faith in Christ is.
4: 12 that you may stand *f* in all the will
1Th 3: 8 since you are standing *f* in the Lord
2Th 2: 15 stand *f* and hold to the teachings
1Ti 6: 19 a *f* foundation for the coming age,
2Ti 2: 19 God's solid foundation stands *f*,
Heb 6: 19 an anchor for the soul, *f* and secure
Jas 5: 8 You too, be patient and stand *f*,
1Pe 5: 9 Resist him, standing *f* in the faith,
5: 10 make you strong, *f* and steadfast.

FIRST
Ge 1: 5 and there was morning—the *f* day.
13: 4 and where he had *f* built an altar.
Ex 34: 19 *f* offspring of every womb belongs
1Ki 22: 5 "*F* seek the counsel of the LORD."
Pr 18: 17 *f* to present his case seems right,
Isa 44: 6 I am the *f* and I am the last;
48: 12 I am the *f* and I am the last.
Mt 5: 24 *F* go and be reconciled
6: 33 But seek *f* his kingdom
7: 5 *f* take the plank out
19: 30 But many who are *f* will be last,
20: 16 last will be *f*, and the *f* will be last."
20: 27 wants to be *f* must be your slave—
22: 38 This is the *f* and greatest
23: 26 *F* clean the inside of the cup
Mk 9: 35 to be *f*, he must be the very last,
10: 31 are *f* will be last, and the last *f*."
10: 44 wants to be *f* must be slave
13: 10 And the gospel must *f* be preached
Lk 13: 30 will be *f*, and *f* who will be last."
Jn 8: 7 let him be the *f* to throw a stone
Ac 11: 26 disciples were called Christians *f*
Ro 1: 16 *f* for the Jew, then for the Gentile.
1: 17 is by faith from *f* to last,
2: 9 *f* for the Jew, then for the Gentile;
2: 10 *f* for the Jew, then for the Gentile.
1Co 12: 28 in the church God has appointed *f*
15: 45 "The *f* man Adam became a living
2Co 8: 5 they gave themselves *f* to the Lord
Eph 6: 2 which is the *f* commandment
1Th 4: 16 and the dead in Christ will rise *f*.
1Ti 2: 13 For Adam was formed *f*, then Eve.
Heb 10: 9 He sets aside the *f*
Jas 3: 17 comes from heaven is *f* of all pure;
1Jn 4: 19 We love because he *f* loved us.
3Jn : 9 but Diotrephes, who loves to be *f*,
Rev 1: 17 I am the *F* and the Last.

2: 4 You have forsaken your f love.
22: 13 and the Omega, the F and the Last,

FIRSTBORN (BEAR)
Ex 11: 5 Every f son in Egypt will die,
34: 20 Redeem all your f sons.
Ps 89: 27 I will also appoint him my f,
Lk 2: 7 and she gave birth to her f, a son.
Ro 8: 29 that he might be the f
Col 1: 15 image of the invisible God, the f
1: 18 and the f from among the dead,
Heb 1: 6 when God brings his f
12: 23 of the f, whose names are written
Rev 1: 5 who is the faithful witness, the f

FIRSTFRUITS
Ex 23: 16 the Feast of Harvest with the f
23: 19 "Bring the best of the f of your soil
Ro 8: 23 who have the f of the Spirit,
1Co 15: 23 Christ, the f; then, when he comes,
Rev 14: 4 offered as f to God and the Lamb.

FISH (FISHERS)
Ge 1: 26 let them rule over the f of the sea
Jnh 1: 17 But the LORD provided a great f
Mt 7: 10 asks for a f, will give him a snake?
12: 40 three nights in the belly of a huge f,
14: 17 loaves of bread and two f,"
Mk 6: 38 they said, "Five—and two f."
Lk 5: 6 of f that their nets began to break.
9: 13 loaves of bread and two f—
Jn 6: 9 small barley loaves and two small f,
21: 5 haven't you any f?" "No,"
21: 11 It was full of large f, 153, but

FISHERMEN
Mk 1: 16 a net into the lake, for they were f.

FISHERS (FISH)
Mt 4: 19 "and I will make you f of men."
Mk 1: 17 "and I will make you f of men."

FISHHOOK*
Job 41: 1 pull in the leviathan with a f

FISTS
Mt 26: 67 and struck him with their f.

FIT (FITTING)
Jdg 17: 6 no king; everyone did as he saw f.
21: 25 no king; everyone did as he saw f.

FITTING* (FIT)
Ps 33: 1 it is f for the upright to praise him.
147: 1 how pleasant and f to praise him!
Pr 10: 32 of the righteous know what is f,
19: 10 It is not f for a fool to live in luxury
26: 1 honor is not f for a fool.
1Co 14: 40 everything should be done in a f
Col 3: 18 to your husbands, as is f in the Lord
Heb 2: 10 sons to glory, it was f that God,

FIX* (FIXED)
Dt 11: 18 F these words of mine
Job 14: 3 Do you f your eye on such a one?
Pr 4: 25 f your gaze directly before you.
Isa 46: 8 "Remember this, f it in mind,
Am 9: 4 I will f my eyes upon them
2Co 4: 18 we f our eyes not on what is seen,
Heb 3: 1 heavenly calling, f your thoughts
12: 2 Let us f our eyes on Jesus,

FIXED* (FIX)
2Ki 8: 11 stared at him with a f gaze
Job 38: 10 when I f limits for it
Ps 141: 8 my eyes are f on you, O Sovereign
Pr 8: 28 f securely the fountains of the deep
Jer 33: 25 and night and the f laws of heaven
Lk 16: 26 and you a great chasm has been f,

FLAME (FLAMES FLAMING)
2Ti 1: 6 you to fan into f the gift of God,

FLAMES (FLAME)
1Co 3: 15 only as one escaping through the f.
13: 3 and surrender my body to the f,

FLAMING (FLAME)
Eph 6: 16 you can extinguish all the f arrows

FLANK
Eze 34: 21 Because you shove with f

FLASH
1Co 15: 52 in a f, in the twinkling of an eye,

FLATTER* (FLATTERING FLATTERS FLATTERY)
Job 32: 21 nor will I f any man;
Ps 78: 36 But then they would f him
Jude : 16 f others for their own advantage.

FLATTERING* (FLATTER)
Ps 12: 2 their f lips speak with deception.
12: 3 May the LORD cut off all f lips
Pr 26: 28 and a f mouth works ruin.
28: 23 than he who has a f tongue.
Eze 12: 24 or f divinations among the people

FLATTERS* (FLATTER)
Ps 36: 2 For in his own eyes he f himself
Pr 29: 5 Whoever f his neighbor

FLATTERY* (FLATTER)
Job 32: 22 for if I were skilled in f,
Da 11: 32 With f he will corrupt those who
Ro 16: 18 and f they deceive the minds
1Th 2: 5 You know we never used f,

FLAWLESS*
2Sa 22: 31 the word of the LORD is f.
Job 11: 4 You say to God, 'My beliefs are f
Ps 12: 6 And the words of the LORD are f,
18: 30 the word of the LORD is f.
Pr 30: 5 "Every word of God is f;
SS 5: 2 my dove, my f one.

FLEE (FLEES)
Ps 139: 7 Where can I f from your presence?
1Co 6: 18 F from sexual immorality.
10: 14 my dear friends, f from idolatry.
1Ti 6: 11 But you, man of God, f from all this
2Ti 2: 22 F the evil desires of youth,
Jas 4: 7 Resist the devil, and he will f

FLEECE
Jdg 6: 37 I will place a wool f

FLEES (FLEE)
Pr 28: 1 The wicked man f though no one

FLEETING*
Job 14: 2 like a f shadow, he does not endure
Ps 39: 4 let me know how f is my life.
89: 47 Remember how f is my life.
144: 4 his days are like a f shadow.
Pr 21: 6 is a f vapor and a deadly snare.
31: 30 Charm is deceptive, and beauty is f

FLESH
Ge 2: 23 and f of my f;
2: 24 and they will become one f.
2Ch 32: 8 With him is only the arm of f,
Job 19: 26 yet in my f I will see God;
Eze 11: 19 of stone and give them a heart of f.
36: 26 of stone and give you a heart of f.
Mt 19: 5 and the two will become one f'?
Mk 10: 8 and the two will become one f.'
Jn 1: 14 The Word became f and made his
6: 51 This bread is my f, which I will give
1Co 6: 16 "The two will become one f."
15: 39 All f is not the same: Men have one
Eph 5: 31 and the two will become one f."
6: 12 For our struggle is not against f
Php 3: 2 do evil, those mutilators of the f.
1Jn 4: 2 come in the f is from God,
Jude : 23 the clothing stained by corrupted f.

FLIGHT
Dt 32: 30 or two put ten thousand to f,

FLINT
Isa 50: 7 Therefore have I set my face like f,
Zec 7: 12 They made their hearts as hard as f

FLIRTING*
Isa 3: 16 f with their eyes,

FLOCK (FLOCKS)
Ps 77: 20 You led your people like a f
78: 52 he brought his people out like a f;
95: 7 the f under his care.
Isa 40: 11 He tends his f like a shepherd:
Jer 10: 21 and all their f is scattered.
23: 2 "Because you have scattered my f
31: 10 watch over his f like a shepherd.'
Eze 34: 2 not shepherds take care of the f?
Zec 11: 17 who deserts the f!
Mt 26: 31 the sheep of the f will be scattered.'
Lk 12: 32 little f, for your Father has been
Jn 10: 16 shall be one f and one shepherd.
Ac 20: 28 all the f of which the Holy Spirit
1Co 9: 7 Who tends a f and does not drink
1Pe 5: 2 Be shepherds of God's f that is
5: 3 but being examples to the f.

FLOCKS (FLOCK)
Lk 2: 8 keeping watch over their f at night.

FLOG (FLOGGED FLOGGING)
Pr 19: 25 F a mocker, and the simple will
Ac 22: 25 to f a Roman citizen who hasn't

FLOGGED (FLOG)
Jn 19: 1 Pilate took Jesus and had him f.
Ac 5: 40 the apostles in and had them f.
16: 23 After they had been severely f,
2Co 11: 23 frequently, been f more severely,

FLOGGING (FLOG)
Heb 11: 36 f, while still others were chained

FLOOD (FLOODGATES)
Ge 7: 7 ark to escape the waters of the f.
Mal 2: 13 You f the LORD's altar with tears.
Mt 24: 38 For in the days before the f,
2Pe 2: 5 world when he brought the f

FLOODGATES (FLOOD)
Ge 7: 11 the f of the heavens were opened.
Mal 3: 10 see if I will not throw open the f

FLOOR
Jas 2: 3 or "Sit on the f by my feet,"

FLOUR
Lev 2: 1 his offering is to be of fine f.
Nu 7: 13 filled with fine f mixed with oil
28: 9 of an ephah of fine f mixed with oil.

FLOURISH (FLOURISHES FLOURISHING)
Ps 72: 7 In his days the righteous will f;
92: 7 and all evildoers f,
92: 12 The righteous will f like a palm tree
Pr 14: 11 but the tent of the upright will f.

FLOURISHES (FLOURISH)
Pr 12: 12 but the root of the righteous f.

FLOURISHING (FLOURISH)
Ps 52: 8 f in the house of God;

FLOW (FLOWING)
Nu 13: 27 and it does f with milk and honey!
Jn 7: 38 streams of living water will f

FLOWER (FLOWERS)
Job 14: 2 up like a f and withers away;
Ps 103: 15 he flourishes like a f of the field;
Jas 1: 10 he will pass away like a wild f.

FLOWERS (FLOWER)
Isa 40: 6 and all their glory is like the f
40: 7 The grass withers and the f fall,
1Pe 1: 24 and all their glory is like the f

FLOWING (FLOW)
Ex 3: 8 a land f with milk and honey—
33: 3 Go up to the land f with milk
Nu 16: 14 us into a land f with milk
Jos 5: 6 a land f with milk and honey.
Ps 107: 33 f springs into thirsty ground,
107: 35 the parched ground into f springs;
Jer 32: 22 a land f with milk and honey.
Eze 20: 6 a land f with milk and honey,
Rev 22: 1 f from the throne of God

FLUTE
Ps 150: 4 praise him with the strings and f,
Mt 11: 17 " 'We played the f for you,
1Co 14: 7 that make sounds, such as the f

FOAL*
Zec 9: 9 on a colt, the *f* of a donkey.
Mt 21: 5 on a colt, the *f* of a donkey.' "

FOILS*
Ps 33: 10 The LORD *f* the plans
Isa 44: 25 who *f* the signs of false prophets

FOLDING* (FOLDS)
Pr 6: 10 a little *f* of the hands to rest—
24: 33 a little *f* of the hands to rest—

FOLDS (FOLDING)
Ecc 4: 5 The fool *f* his hands

FOLLOW (FOLLOWED FOLLOWING FOLLOWS)
Ex 23: 2 Do not *f* the crowd in doing wrong.
Lev 18: 4 and be careful to *f* my decrees.
Dt 5: 1 Learn them and be sure to *f* them.
17: 19 *f* carefully all the words of this law
1Ki 11: 6 he did not *f* the LORD completely,
2Ch 34: 33 they did not fail to *f* the LORD,
Ps 23: 6 Surely goodness and love will *f* me
119:166 and I *f* your commands.
Mt 4: 19 *f* me," Jesus said, "and I will make
8: 19 I will *f* you wherever you go."
8: 22 But Jesus told him, "*F* me,
16: 24 and take up his cross and *f* me.
19: 27 "We have left everything to *f* you!
Lk 9: 23 take up his cross daily and *f* me.
9: 61 Still another said, "I will *f* you,
Jn 10: 4 his sheep *f* him because they know
10: 5 But they will never *f* a stranger;
10: 27 I know them, and they *f* me.
12: 26 Whoever serves me must *f* me;
21: 19 Then he said to him, "*F* me!"
1Co 1: 12 One of you says, "I *f* Paul";
11: 1 *F* my example, as I follow
14: 1 *F* the way of love and eagerly
2Th 3: 9 ourselves a model for you to *f*.
1Pe 2: 21 that you should *f* in his steps.
Rev 14: 4 They *f* the Lamb wherever he goes.

FOLLOWED (FOLLOW)
Nu 32: 11 they have not *f* me wholeheartedly,
Dt 1: 36 he *f* the LORD wholeheartedly."
Jos 14: 14 he *f* the LORD, the God of Israel,
2Ch 10: 14 he *f* the advice of the young men
Mt 4: 20 once they left their nets and *f* him.
9: 9 and Matthew got up and *f* him.
26: 58 But Peter *f* him at a distance,
Lk 18: 43 he received his sight and *f* Jesus,

FOLLOWING (FOLLOW)
Ps 119: 14 I rejoice in *f* your statutes
Php 3: 17 Join with others in *f* my example,
1Ti 1: 18 by *f* them you may fight the good

FOLLOWS (FOLLOW)
Jn 8: 12 Whoever *f* me will never walk

FOLLY (FOOL)
Pr 14: 29 a quick-tempered man displays *f*.
19: 3 A man's own *f* ruins his life,
Ecc 10: 1 so a little *f* outweighs wisdom
Mk 7: 22 envy, slander, arrogance and *f*.
2Ti 3: 9 their *f* will be clear to everyone.

FOOD (FOODS)
Ge 1: 30 I give every green plant for *f*."
Pr 12: 9 to be somebody and have no *f*.
12: 11 his land will have abundant *f*,
20: 13 you will have *f* to spare.
20: 17 *F* gained by fraud tastes sweet
21: 20 of the wise are stores of choice *f*
22: 9 for he shares his *f* with the poor.
23: 3 for that *f* is deceptive.
23: 6 Do not eat the *f* of a stingy man,
25: 21 If your enemy is hungry, give him *f*
31: 14 bringing her *f* from afar.
31: 15 she provides *f* for her family
Isa 58: 7 not to share your *f* with the hungry
Eze 18: 7 but gives his *f* to the hungry
Da 1: 8 to defile himself with the royal *f*
Mt 3: 4 His *f* was locusts and wild honey.
6: 25 Is not life more important than *f*,
Jn 4: 32 "I have *f* to eat that you know
4: 34 have brought him *f*?" "My *f*,"
6: 27 Do not work for *f* that spoils,
6: 55 my flesh is real *f* and my blood is
Ac 15: 20 to abstain from *f* polluted by idols,
Ro 14: 14 fully convinced that no *f* is unclean
1Co 8: 1 Now about *f* sacrificed to idols:
8: 8 But *f* does not bring us near to God
2Co 11: 27 and have often gone without *f*;
1Ti 6: 8 But if we have *f* and clothing,
Heb 5: 14 But solid *f* is for the mature,
Jas 2: 15 sister is without clothes and daily *f*.

FOODS (FOOD)
Mk 7: 19 Jesus declared all *f* "clean.")

FOOL (FOLLY FOOL'S FOOLISH FOOLISHNESS FOOLS)
1Sa 25: 25 his name is *F*, and folly goes
Ps 14: 1 The *f* says in his heart,
Pr 10: 10 and a chattering *f* comes to ruin.
10: 18 and whoever spreads slander is a *f*.
12: 15 The way of a *f* seems right to him,
12: 16 A *f* shows his annoyance at once,
14: 16 but a *f* is hotheaded and reckless.
15: 5 A *f* spurns his father's discipline,
17: 12 than a *f* in his folly.
17: 16 use is money in the hand of a *f*,
17: 21 To have a *f* for a son brings grief;
17: 28 Even a *f* is thought wise
18: 2 A *f* finds no pleasure
20: 3 but every *f* is quick to quarrel.
23: 9 Do not speak to a *f*,
24: 7 Wisdom is too high for a *f*;
26: 4 Do not answer a *f* according
26: 5 Answer a *f* according to his folly,
26: 7 is a proverb in the mouth of a *f*.
26: 11 so a *f* repeats his folly.
26: 12 for a *f* than for him.
27: 22 Though you grind a *f* in a mortar,
28: 26 He who trusts in himself is a *f*,
29: 11 A *f* gives full vent to his anger,
29: 20 for a *f* than for him.
Mt 5: 22 But anyone who says, 'You *f*!'
Lk 12: 20 "But God said to him, 'You *f*!
1Co 3: 18 he should become a "*f*"
2Co 11: 21 I am speaking as a *f*— I

FOOL'S (FOOL)
Pr 14: 3 A *f* talk brings a rod to his back,
18: 7 A *f* mouth is his undoing,

FOOLISH (FOOL)
Pr 10: 1 but a *f* son grief to his mother.
14: 1 her own hands the *f* one tears hers
15: 20 but a *f* man despises his mother.
17: 25 A *f* son brings grief to his father
19: 13 A *f* son is his father's ruin,
Mt 7: 26 practice is like a *f* man who built
25: 2 of them were *f* and five were wise.
Lk 11: 40 You *f* people! Did not the one who
24: 25 He said to them, "How *f* you are,
1Co 1: 20 Has not God made *f* the wisdom
1: 27 God chose the *f* things of the world
Gal 3: 1 died for nothing!" You *f* Galatians!
Eph 5: 4 should there be obscenity, *f* talk
5: 17 Therefore do not be *f*,
Tit 3: 9 But avoid *f* controversies

FOOLISHNESS (FOOL)
1Co 1: 18 of the cross is *f* to those who are
1: 21 through the *f* of what was preached
1: 23 block to Jews and *f* to Gentiles,
1: 25 For the *f* of God is wiser
2: 14 for they are *f* to him, and he cannot
3: 19 of this world is *f* in God's sight.

FOOLS (FOOL)
Pr 1: 7 but *f* despise wisdom and discipline
3: 35 but *f* he holds up to shame.
12: 23 but the heart of *f* blurts out folly.
13: 19 but *f* detest turning from evil.
13: 20 but a companion of *f* suffers harm.
14: 9 *F* mock at making amends for sin,
14: 24 but the folly of *f* yields folly.
Ecc 7: 5 than to listen to the song of *f*.
7: 6 so is the laughter of *f*.
10: 6 *F* are put in many high positions,
Mt 23: 17 You blind *f*! Which is greater:
Ro 1: 22 they became *f* and exchanged
1Co 4: 10 We are *f* for Christ, but you are

FOOT (FEET FOOTHOLD)
Jos 1: 3 every place where you set your *f*,
Ps 121: 3 He will not let your *f* slip—
Pr 3: 23 and your *f* will not stumble;
4: 27 keep your *f* from evil.
25: 17 Seldom set *f* in your neighbor's
Isa 1: 6 From the sole of your *f* to the top
Mt 18: 8 or your *f* causes you to sin,
Lk 4: 11 so that you will not strike your *f*
1Co 12: 15 If the *f* should say, "Because I am
Rev 10: 2 He planted his right *f* on the sea

FOOTHOLD* (FOOT)
Ps 69: 2 where there is no *f*.
73: 2 I had nearly lost my *f*.
Eph 4: 27 and do not give the devil a *f*.

FOOTSTEPS (STEP)
Ps 119:133 Direct my *f* according

FOOTSTOOL
Ps 99: 5 and worship at his *f*;
110: 1 a *f* for your feet."
Isa 66: 1 and the earth is my *f*.
Mt 5: 35 for it is his *f*; or by Jerusalem,
Ac 7: 49 and the earth is my *f*.
Heb 1: 13 a *f* for your feet"?
10: 13 for his enemies to be made his *f*,

FORBEARANCE*
Ro 3: 25 because in his *f* he had left the sins

FORBID
1Co 14: 39 and do not *f* speaking in tongues.
1Ti 4: 3 They *f* people to marry

FORCE (FORCED FORCEFUL FORCES FORCING)
Jn 6: 15 to come and make him king by *f*,
Ac 26: 11 and I tried to *f* them to blaspheme.
Gal 2: 14 that you *f* Gentiles

FORCED (FORCE)
Mt 27: 32 and they *f* him to carry the cross.
Phm : 14 do will be spontaneous and not *f*.

FORCEFUL* (FORCE)
Mt 11: 12 forcefully advancing, and *f* men lay
2Co 10: 10 "His letters are weighty and *f*,

FORCES (FORCE)
Mt 5: 41 If someone *f* you to go one mile,
Eph 6: 12 and against the spiritual *f* of evil

FORCING (FORCE)
Lk 16: 16 and everyone is *f* his way into it.

FOREFATHERS (FATHER)
Heb 1: 1 spoke to our *f* through the prophets
1Pe 1: 18 handed down to you from your *f*,

FOREHEAD (FOREHEADS)
Ex 13: 9 a reminder on your *f* that the law
13: 16 on your *f* that the LORD brought
1Sa 17: 49 and struck the Philistine on the *f*.
Rev 13: 16 a mark on his right hand or on his *f*,

FOREHEADS (FOREHEAD)
Dt 6: 8 hands and bind them on your *f*.
Rev 9: 4 not have the seal of God on their *f*.
14: 1 his Father's name written on their *f*

FOREIGN (FOREIGNER FOREIGNERS)
Ge 35: 2 "Get rid of the *f* gods you have
2Ch 14: 3 He removed the *f* altars
33: 15 He got rid of the *f* gods
Isa 28: 11 with *f* lips and strange tongues

FOREIGNER (FOREIGN)
Lk 17: 18 give praise to God except this *f*?"
1Co 14: 11 I am a *f* to the speaker,

FOREIGNERS (FOREIGN)
Eph 2: 12 *f* to the covenants of the promise,

2: 19 you are no longer *f* and aliens,

FOREKNEW* (KNOW)
Ro 8: 29 For those God *f* he
11: 2 not reject his people, whom he *f*.

FOREKNOWLEDGE* (KNOW)
Ac 2: 23 to you by God's set purpose and *f*;
1Pe 1: 2 to the *f* of God the Father,

FORESAW*
Gal 3: 8 Scripture *f* that God would justify

FOREST
Jas 3: 5 Consider what a great *f* is set

FOREVER (EVER)
Ge 3: 22 the tree of life and eat, and live *f*."
6: 3 Spirit will not contend with man *f*,
Ex 3: 15 This is my name *f*, the name
2Sa 7: 26 so that your name will be great *f*.
1Ki 2: 33 may there be the LORD's peace *f*."
9: 3 by putting my Name there *f*.
1Ch 16: 15 He remembers his covenant *f*,
16: 34 his love endures *f*.
16: 41 "for his love endures *f*."
17: 24 and that your name will be great *f*.
2Ch 5: 13 his love endures *f*."
20: 21 for his love endures *f*."
Ps 9: 7 The LORD reigns *f*;
23: 6 dwell in the house of the LORD *f*.
28: 9 be their shepherd and carry them *f*.
29: 10 the LORD is enthroned as King *f*.
33: 11 the plans of the LORD stand firm *f*
37: 28 They will be protected *f*,
44: 8 and we will praise your name *f*.
61: 4 I long to dwell in your tent *f*
72: 19 Praise be to his glorious name *f*;
73: 26 and my portion *f*.
77: 8 Has his unfailing love vanished *f*?
79: 13 will praise you *f*;
81: 15 and their punishment would last *f*.
86: 12 I will glorify your name *f*.
89: 1 of the LORD's great love *f*;
92: 8 But you, O LORD, are exalted *f*.
100: 5 is good and his love endures *f*;
102: 12 But you, O LORD, sit enthroned *f*;
104: 31 of the LORD endure *f*;
107: 1 his love endures *f*.
110: 4 "You are a priest *f*,
111: 3 and his righteousness endures *f*.
112: 6 man will be remembered *f*.
117: 2 of the LORD endures *f*.
118: 1 his love endures *f*.
119:111 Your statutes are my heritage *f*;
119:152 that you established them to last *f*.
136: 1 *His love endures* f.
146: 6 the LORD, who remains faithful *f*.
Pr 10: 25 but the righteous stand firm *f*.
27: 24 for riches do not endure *f*,
Isa 25: 8 he will swallow up death *f*.
26: 4 Trust in the LORD *f*,
32: 17 will be quietness and confidence *f*.
40: 8 but the word of our God stands *f*."
51: 6 But my salvation will last *f*,
51: 8 But my righteousness will last *f*,
57: 15 he who lives *f*, whose name is holy:
59: 21 from this time on and *f*,"
Jer 33: 11 his love endures *f*."
Eze 37: 26 put my sanctuary among them *f*.
Da 2: 44 to an end, but it will itself endure *f*.
3: 9 live *f*! You have issued a decree,
Jn 6: 51 eats of this bread, he will live *f*.
14: 16 Counselor to be with you *f*—
Ro 9: 5 who is God over all, *f* praised!
16: 27 to the only wise God be glory *f*
1Co 9: 25 it to get a crown that will last *f*.
1Th 4: 17 And so we will be with the Lord *f*.
Heb 5: 6 "You are a priest *f*,
7: 17 "You are a priest *f*,
7: 24 Jesus lives *f*, he has a permanent
13: 8 same yesterday and today and *f*.
1Pe 1: 25 but the word of the Lord stands *f*."
1Jn 2: 17 who does the will of God lives *f*.
2Jn : 2 lives in us and will be with us *f*:

FOREVERMORE (EVER)
Ps 113: 2 both now and *f*.

FORFEIT
Mk 8: 36 the whole world, yet *f* his soul?
Lk 9: 25 and yet lose or *f* his very self?

FORGAVE (FORGIVE)
Ps 32: 5 and you *f*
65: 3 you *f* our transgressions
78: 38 you *f* their iniquities
Eph 4: 32 just as in Christ God *f* you.
Col 2: 13 He *f* us all our sins, having
3: 13 Forgive as the Lord *f* you.

FORGET (FORGETS FORGETTING FORGOT FORGOTTEN)
Dt 4: 23 Be careful not to *f* the covenant
6: 12 that you do not *f* the LORD,
2Ki 17: 38 Do not *f* the covenant I have made
Ps 9: 17 all the nations that *f* God.
10: 12 Do not *f* the helpless.
50: 22 "Consider this, you who *f* God,
78: 7 and would not *f* his deeds
103: 2 and *f* not all his benefits.
119: 93 I will never *f* your precepts,
137: 5 may my right hand *f* ›its skill‹.
Pr 3: 1 My son, do not *f* my teaching,
4: 5 do not *f* my words or swerve
Isa 49: 15 "Can a mother *f* the baby
51: 13 that you *f* the LORD your Maker,
Jer 2: 32 Does a maiden *f* her jewelry,
23: 39 I will surely *f* you and cast you out
Heb 6: 10 he will not *f* your work
13: 2 Do not *f* to entertain strangers,
13: 16 And do not *f* to do good
2Pe 3: 8 But do not *f* this one thing,

FORGETS (FORGET)
Jn 16: 21 her baby is born she *f* the anguish
Jas 1: 24 immediately *f* what he looks like.

FORGETTING* (FORGET)
Php 3: 13 *F* what is behind and straining
Jas 1: 25 to do this, not *f* what he has heard,

FORGIVE* (FORGAVE FORGIVENESS FORGIVES FORGIVING)
Ge 50: 17 I ask you to *f* your brothers the sins
50: 17 please *f* the sins of the servants
Ex 10: 17 Now *f* my sin once more
23: 21 he will not *f* your rebellion,
32: 32 But now, please *f* their sin—
34: 9 *f* our wickedness and our sin,
Nu 14: 19 with your great love, *f* the sin
Dt 29: 20 will never be willing to *f* him;
Jos 24: 19 He will not *f* your rebellion
1Sa 15: 25 *f* my sin and come back with me,
25: 28 Please *f* your servant's offense,
1Ki 8: 30 place, and when you hear, *f*.
8: 34 and *f* the sin of your people Israel
8: 36 and *f* the sin of your servants,
8: 39 *F* and act; deal with each man
8: 50 *f* all the offenses they have
8: 50 *f* your people, who have sinned
2Ki 5: 18 But may the LORD *f* your servant
5: 18 may the LORD *f* your servant
24: 4 and the LORD was not willing to *f*.
2Ch 6: 21 place; and when you hear, *f*.
6: 25 and *f* the sin of your people Israel
6: 27 and *f* the sin of your servants,
6: 30 *F*, and deal with each man
6: 39 *f* your people, who have sinned
7: 14 will *f* their sin and will heal their
Job 7: 21 and *f* my sins?
Ps 19: 12 *F* my hidden faults.
25: 11 *f* my iniquity, though it is great.
79: 9 deliver us and *f* our sins
Isa 2: 9 do not *f* them.
Jer 5: 1 I will *f* this city.
5: 7 "Why should I *f* you?
18: 23 Do not *f* their crimes
31: 34 "For I will *f* their wickedness
33: 8 and will *f* all their sins of rebellion
36: 3 then I will *f* their wickedness
50: 20 for I will *f* the remnant I spare.
Da 9: 19 O Lord, listen! O Lord, *f*! O Lord,
Hos 1: 6 that I should at all *f* them.
14: 2 "*F* all our sins
Am 7: 2 *f*! How can Jacob survive?
Mt 6: 12 *F* us our debts,
6: 14 For if you *f* men when they sin
6: 14 heavenly Father will also *f* you.
6: 15 But if you do not *f* men their sins,
6: 15 your Father will not *f* your sins.
9: 6 authority on earth to *f* sins..
18: 21 many times shall I *f* my brother
18: 35 you *f* your brother from your heart
Mk 2: 7 Who can *f* sins but God alone?"
2: 10 authority on earth to *f* sins
11: 25 anything against anyone, *f* him,
11: 25 in heaven may *f* you your sins."
Lk 5: 21 Who can *f* sins but God alone?"
5: 24 authority on earth to *f* sins..
6: 37 *F*, and you will be forgiven.
11: 4 *F* us our sins,
11: 4 *f* everyone who sins against us.
17: 3 rebuke him, and if he repents, *f* him
17: 4 and says, 'I repent,' *f* him."
23: 34 Jesus said, "Father, *f* them,
Jn 20: 23 If you *f* anyone his sins, they are
20: 23 if you do not *f* them, they are not
Ac 8: 22 Perhaps he will *f* you
2Co 2: 7 you ought to *f* and comfort him,
2: 10 If you *f* anyone, I also *f* him.
2: 10 if there was anything to *f*—
12: 13 a burden to you? *F* me this wrong!
Col 3: 13 and *f* whatever grievances you may
3: 13 *F* as the Lord forgave you.
Heb 8: 12 For I will *f* their wickedness
1Jn 1: 9 and just and will *f* us our sins

FORGIVENESS* (FORGIVE)
Ps 130: 4 But with you there is *f*;
Mt 26: 28 out for many for the *f* of sins.
Mk 1: 4 of repentance for the *f* of sins.
Lk 1: 77 salvation through the *f* of their sins,
3: 3 of repentance for the *f* of sins.
24: 47 and *f* of sins will be preached
Ac 5: 31 that he might give repentance and *f*
10: 43 believes in him receives *f* of sins
13: 38 that through Jesus the *f*
26: 18 so that they may receive *f* of sins
Eph 1: 7 through his blood, the *f* of sins,
Col 1: 14 in whom we have redemption, the *f*
Heb 9: 22 the shedding of blood there is no *f*.

FORGIVES* (FORGIVE)
Ps 103: 3 He *f* all my sins
Mic 7: 18 pardons sin and *f* the transgression
Lk 7: 49 "Who is this who even *f* sins?"

FORGIVING* (FORGIVE)
Ex 34: 7 and *f* wickedness, rebellion and sin.
Nu 14: 18 abounding in love and *f* sin
Ne 9: 17 But you are a *f* God, gracious
Ps 86: 5 You are *f* and good, O Lord,
99: 8 you were to Israel a *f* God,
Da 9: 9 The Lord our God is merciful and *f*
Eph 4: 32 to one another, *f* each other,

FORGOT (FORGET)
Dt 32: 18 you *f* the God who gave you birth.
Ps 78: 11 They *f* what he had done,
106: 13 But they soon *f* what he had done

FORGOTTEN (FORGET)
Job 11: 6 God has even *f* some of your sin.
Ps 44: 20 If we had *f* the name of our God
Isa 17: 10 You have *f* God your Savior;
Hos 8: 14 Israel has *f* his Maker
Lk 12: 6 Yet not one of them is *f* by God.
2Pe 1: 9 and has *f* that he has been cleansed

FORM (FORMED)
Isa 52: 14 *f* marred beyond human likeness—
2Ti 3: 5 having a *f* of godliness

FORMED (FORM)
Ge 2: 7 —the LORD God *f* the man
2: 19 Now the LORD God had *f* out
Ps 103: 14 for he knows how we are *f*,
Ecc 11: 5 or how the body is *f* in a mother's
Isa 29: 16 Shall what is *f* say to him who *f* it,
45: 18 but *f* it to be inhabited—
49: 5 he who *f* me in the womb
Jer 1: 5 "Before I *f* you in the womb I knew
Ro 9: 20 "Shall what is *f* say to him who *f* it,
Gal 4: 19 of childbirth until Christ is *f* in you,
1Ti 2: 13 For Adam was *f* first, then Eve.
Heb 11: 3 understand that the universe was *f*
2Pe 3: 5 and the earth was *f* out of water

FORMLESS*
Ge 1: 2 Now the earth was *f* and empty,
Jer 4: 23 and it was *f* and empty;

FORSAKE (FORSAKEN)
Dt 31: 6 he will never leave you nor *f* you."
Jos 1: 5 I will never leave you nor *f* you.
24: 16 "Far be it from us to *f* the LORD
2Ch 15: 2 but if you *f* him, he will *f* you.
Ps 27: 10 Though my father and mother *f* me
94: 14 he will never *f* his inheritance.
Isa 55: 7 Let the wicked *f* his way
Heb 13: 5 never will I *f* you."

FORSAKEN (FORSAKE)
Ps 22: 1 my God, why have you *f* me?
37: 25 I have never seen the righteous *f*
Mt 27: 46 my God, why have you *f* me?"
Rev 2: 4 You have *f* your first love.

FORTRESS
2Sa 22: 2 "The LORD is my rock, my *f*
Ps 18: 2 The LORD is my rock, my *f*
31: 2 a strong *f* to save me.
59: 16 for you are my *f*,
71: 3 for you are my rock and my *f*.
Pr 14: 26 who fears the LORD has a secure *f*,

FORTUNE-TELLING*
Ac 16: 16 deal of money for her owners by *f*.

FORTY
Ge 7: 4 on the earth for *f* days and *f* nights,
18: 29 "What if only *f* are found there?"
Ex 16: 35 The Israelites ate manna *f* years,
24: 18 on the mountain *f* days and *f* nights
Nu 14: 34 For *f* years—one year for each
Jos 14: 7 I was *f* years old when Moses
1Sa 4: 18 He had led Israel *f* years.
2Sa 5: 4 king, and he reigned *f* years.
1Ki 19: 8 he traveled *f* days and *f* nights
2Ki 12: 1 and he reigned in Jerusalem *f* years
2Ch 9: 30 in Jerusalem over all Israel *f* years.
Eze 29: 12 her cities will lie desolate *f* years
Jnh 3: 4 "*F* more days and Nineveh will be
Mt 4: 2 After fasting *f* days and *f* nights,

FOUGHT (FIGHT)
1Co 15: 32 If I *f* wild beasts in Ephesus
2Ti 4: 7 I have *f* the good fight, I have

FOUND (FIND)
2Ki 22: 8 "I have *f* the Book of the Law
1Ch 28: 9 If you seek him, he will be *f* by you;
2Ch 15: 15 sought God eagerly, and he was *f*
Isa 55: 6 Seek the LORD while he may be *f*;
65: 1 I was *f* by those who did not seek
Da 5: 27 on the scales and *f* wanting.
Mt 1: 18 she was *f* to be with child
Lk 15: 6 with me; I have *f* my lost sheep.'
15: 9 with me; I have *f* my lost coin.'
15: 24 is alive again; he was lost and is *f*.'
Ac 4: 12 Salvation is *f* in no one else,
Ro 10: 20 "I was *f* by those who did not seek
Jas 2: 8 If you really keep the royal law *f*
Rev 5: 4 no one was *f* who was worthy

FOUNDATION (FOUNDATIONS FOUNDED)
Isa 28: 16 a precious cornerstone for a sure *f*;
Mt 7: 25 because it had its *f* on the rock.
Lk 14: 29 For if he lays the *f* and is not able
Ro 15: 20 building on someone else's *f*.
1Co 3: 10 I laid a *f* as an expert builder,
3: 11 For no one can lay any *f* other
Eph 2: 20 built on the *f* of the apostles
1Ti 3: 15 the pillar and *f* of the truth.
2Ti 2: 19 God's solid *f* stands firm,
Heb 6: 1 not laying again the *f* of repentance

FOUNDATIONS (FOUNDATION)
Ps 102: 25 In the beginning you laid the *f*
Heb 1: 10 O Lord, you laid the *f* of the earth,

FOUNDED (FOUNDATION)
Jer 10: 12 he *f* the world by his wisdom
Heb 8: 6 and it is *f* on better promises.

FOUNTAIN
Ps 36: 9 For with you is the *f* of life;
Pr 14: 27 The fear of the LORD is a *f* of life,
18: 4 the *f* of wisdom is a bubbling brook.
Zec 13: 1 "On that day a *f* will be opened

FOX (FOXES)
Lk 13: 32 He replied, "Go tell that *f*,

FOXES (FOX)
SS 2: 15 the little *f*
Mt 8: 20 "*F* have holes and birds

FRAGRANCE (FRAGRANT)
Ex 30: 38 it to enjoy its *f* must be cut
Jn 12: 3 filled with the *f* of the perfume.
2Co 2: 14 us spreads everywhere the *f*
2: 16 of death; to the other, the *f* of life.

FRAGRANT (FRAGRANCE)
Eph 5: 2 as a *f* offering and sacrifice to God.
Php 4: 18 They are a *f* offering, an acceptable

FREE (FREED FREEDOM FREELY)
Ge 2: 16 "You are *f* to eat from any tree
Ps 118: 5 and he answered by setting me *f*.
119: 32 for you have set my heart *f*.
146: 7 The LORD sets prisoners *f*,
Pr 6: 3 then do this, my son, to *f* yourself,
Jn 8: 32 and the truth will set you *f*."
8: 36 if the Son sets you *f*, you will be *f*
Ro 6: 18 You have been set *f* from sin
8: 2 of life set me *f* from the law of sin
1Co 12: 13 whether Jews or Greeks, slave or *f*
Gal 3: 28 slave nor *f*, male nor female,
5: 1 for freedom that Christ has set us *f*.
1Pe 2: 16 *f* men, but do not use your freedom

FREED (FREE)
Ps 116: 16 you have *f* me from my chains.
Ro 6: 7 anyone who has died has been *f*
Rev 1: 5 has *f* us from our sins by his blood,

FREEDOM (FREE)
Ps 119: 45 I will walk about in *f*,
Isa 61: 1 to proclaim *f* for the captives
Lk 4: 18 me to proclaim *f* for the prisoners
Ro 8: 21 into the glorious *f* of the children
1Co 7: 21 although if you can gain your *f*,
2Co 3: 17 the Spirit of the Lord is, there is *f*.
Gal 2: 4 ranks to spy on the *f* we have
5: 13 But do not use your *f* to indulge
Jas 1: 25 into the perfect law that gives *f*,
1Pe 2: 16 but do not use your *f* as a cover-up

FREELY (FREE)
Isa 55: 7 and to our God, for he will *f* pardon
Mt 10: 8 Freely you have received, *f* give.
Ro 3: 24 and are justified *f* by his grace
Eph 1: 6 which he has *f* given us

FRESH
Jas 3: 11 Can both *f* water and salt water

FRET*
Ps 37: 1 Do not *f* because of evil men
37: 7 do not *f* when men succeed
37: 8 do not *f*— it leads only to evil.
Pr 24: 19 Do not *f* because of evil men

FRICTION
1Ti 6: 5 and constant *f* between men

FRIEND (FRIENDS FRIENDSHIP)
Ex 33: 11 as a man speaks with his *f*.
2Ch 20: 7 descendants of Abraham your *f*?
Pr 17: 17 A *f* loves at all times,
18: 24 there is a *f* who sticks closer
27: 6 Wounds from a *f* can be trusted
27: 10 Do not forsake your *f* and the *f*
Isa 41: 8 you descendants of Abraham my *f*,
Mt 11: 19 a *f* of tax collectors and "sinners."'
Lk 11: 8 him the bread because he is his *f*,
Jn 19: 12 "If you let this man go, you are no *f*
Jas 2: 23 and he was called God's *f*.
4: 4 Anyone who chooses to be a *f*

FRIENDS (FRIEND)
Pr 16: 28 and a gossip separates close *f*.
17: 9 the matter separates close *f*.
Zec 13: 6 given at the house of my *f*.'
Jn 15: 13 that he lay down his life for his *f*.
15: 14 You are my *f* if you do what I

FRIENDSHIP (FRIEND)
Jas 4: 4 don't you know that *f*

FRIGHTENED (FEAR)
Php 1: 28 gospel without being *f* in any way
1Pe 3: 14 fear what they fear; do not be *f*."

FROGS
Ex 8: 2 plague your whole country with *f*.
Rev 16: 13 three evil spirits that looked like *f*;

FRUIT (FRUITFUL)
Jdg 9: 11 'Should I give up my *f*, so good
Ps 1: 3 which yields its *f* in season
Pr 11: 30 The *f* of the righteous is a tree
12: 14 From the *f* of his lips a man is filled
27: 18 He who tends a fig tree will eat its *f*
Isa 11: 1 from his roots a Branch will bear *f*.
27: 6 and fill all the world with *f*.
32: 17 The *f* of righteousness will be peace
Jer 17: 8 and never fails to bear *f*."
Hos 10: 12 reap the *f* of unfailing love,
14: 2 that we may offer the *f* of our lips.
Am 8: 1 showed me: a basket of ripe *f*.
Mt 3: 8 Produce *f* in keeping
3: 10 does not produce good *f* will be cut
7: 16 By their *f* you will recognize them.
7: 17 good *f*, but a bad tree bears bad *f*.
7: 20 by their *f* you will recognize them.
12: 33 a tree good and its *f* will be good,
Lk 3: 9 does not produce good *f* will be cut
6: 43 nor does a bad tree bear good *f*.
13: 6 and he went to look for *f* on it,
Jn 15: 2 branch in me that bears no *f*,
15: 16 and bear *f*—*f* that will last.
Ro 7: 4 in order that we might bear *f*
Gal 5: 22 But the *f* of the Spirit is love, joy,
Php 1: 11 with the *f* of righteousness that
Col 1: 10 bearing *f* in every good work,
Heb 13: 15 the *f* of lips that confess his name.
Jas 3: 17 and good *f*, impartial and sincere.
Jude : 12 autumn trees, without *f*
Rev 22: 2 of *f*, yielding its *f* every month.

FRUITFUL (FRUIT)
Ge 1: 22 "Be *f* and increase in number
9: 1 "Be *f* and increase in number
35: 11 be *f* and increase in number.
Ex 1: 7 the Israelites were *f* and multiplied
Ps 128: 3 Your wife will be like a *f* vine
Jn 15: 2 prunes so that it will be even more *f*.
Php 1: 22 this will mean *f* labor for me.

FRUITLESS*
Eph 5: 11 to do with the *f* deeds of darkness,

FRUSTRATION
Ro 8: 20 For the creation was subjected to *f*,

FUEL
Isa 44: 19 "Half of it I used for *f*;

FULFILL (FULFILLED FULFILLMENT FULFILLS)
Nu 23: 19 Does he promise and not *f*?
Ps 61: 8 and *f* my vows day after day.

116: 14 I will *f* my vows to the LORD
138: 8 The LORD will *f* his purpose
Ecc 5: 5 than to make a vow and not *f* it.
Isa 46: 11 far-off land, a man to *f* my purpose.
Jer 33: 14 'when I will *f* the gracious promise
Mt 1: 22 place to *f* what the Lord had said
3: 15 us to do this to *f* all righteousness."
4: 14 *f* what was said
5: 17 come to abolish them but to *f* them.
8: 17 This was to *f* what was spoken
12: 17 This was to *f* what was spoken
21: 4 place to *f* what was spoken
Jn 12: 38 This was to *f* the word
13: 18 But this is to *f* the scripture:
15: 25 But this is to *f* what is written
1Co 7: 3 husband should *f* his marital duty

FULFILLED (FULFILL)
Jos 21: 45 of Israel failed; every one was *f*.
23: 14 Every promise has been *f*;
Pr 13: 12 but a longing *f* is a tree of life.
13: 19 A longing *f* is sweet to the soul,
Mt 2: 15 so was *f* what the Lord had said
2: 17 the prophet Jeremiah was *f*:
2: 23 So was *f* what was said
13: 14 In them is *f* the prophecy of Isaiah:
13: 35 So was *f* what was spoken
26: 54 would the Scriptures be *f* that say it
26: 56 of the prophets might be *f*."
27: 9 by Jeremiah the prophet was *f*:
Mk 13: 4 that they are all about to be *f*?"
14: 49 But the Scriptures must be *f*."
Lk 4: 21 "Today this scripture is *f*
18: 31 about the Son of Man will be *f*.
24: 44 Everything must be *f* that is
Jn 18: 9 words he had spoken would be *f*:
19: 24 the Scripture might be *f* which said,
19: 28 and so that the Scripture would be *f*
19: 36 so that the Scripture would be *f*:
Ac 1: 16 to be *f* which the Holy Spirit spoke
Ro 13: 8 loves his fellowman has *f* the law.
Jas 2: 23 And the scripture was *f* that says,

FULFILLMENT (FULFILL)
Ro 13: 10 Therefore love is the *f* of the law.

FULFILLS (FULFILL)
Ps 57: 2 to God, who *f* his purpose for me.
145: 19 He *f* the desires of those who fear

FULL (FILL)
2Ch 24: 10 them into the chest until it was *f*.
Ps 127: 5 whose quiver is *f* of them.
Pr 27: 7 He who is *f* loathes honey,
31: 11 Her husband has *f* confidence
Isa 6: 3 the whole earth is *f* of his glory."
11: 9 for the earth will be *f*
Lk 4: 1 Jesus, *f* of the Holy Spirit,
Jn 10: 10 may have life, and have it to the *f*.
Ac 6: 3 known to be *f* of the Spirit
6: 5 a man *f* of faith and of the Holy
7: 55 But Stephen, *f* of the Holy Spirit,
11: 24 *f* of the Holy Spirit and faith,

FULL-GROWN* (GROW)
Jas 1: 15 when it is *f*, gives birth to death.

FULLNESS* (FILL)
Dt 33: 16 gifts of the earth and its *f*
Jn 1: 16 From the *f* of his grace we have all
Ro 11: 12 greater riches will their *f* bring!
Eph 1: 23 the *f* of him who fills everything
3: 19 to the measure of all the *f* of God.
4: 13 to the whole measure of the *f*
Col 1: 19 to have all his *f* dwell in him,
1: 25 to you the word of God in its *f*—
2: 9 in Christ all the *f* of the Deity lives
2: 10 and you have been given *f* in Christ

FULLY (FILL)
1Ki 8: 61 your hearts must be *f* committed
2Ch 16: 9 whose hearts are *f* committed
Ps 119: 4 that are to be *f* obeyed.
119:138 they are *f* trustworthy.
Pr 13: 4 of the diligent are *f* satisfied.
Lk 6: 40 everyone who is *f* trained will be
Ro 4: 21 being *f* persuaded that God had
14: 5 Each one should be *f* convinced
1Co 13: 12 shall know *f*, even as I am *f* known.
15: 58 Always give yourselves *f*
2Ti 4: 17 the message might be *f* proclaimed

FURIOUS (FURY)
Dt 29: 28 In *f* anger and in great wrath
Jer 32: 37 where I banish them in my *f* anger

FURNACE
Isa 48: 10 in the *f* of affliction.
Da 3: 6 be thrown into a blazing *f*."
Mt 13: 42 will throw them into the fiery *f*,

FURY (FURIOUS)
Isa 14: 6 and in *f* subdued nations
Jer 21: 5 and a mighty arm in anger and *f*
Rev 14: 10 will drink of the wine of God's *f*,
16: 19 with the wine of the *f* of his wrath.
19: 15 the winepress of the *f* of the wrath

FUTILE (FUTILITY)
Mal 3: 14 You have said, 'It is *f* to serve God.
1Co 3: 20 that the thoughts of the wise are *f*."

FUTILITY (FUTILE)
Eph 4: 17 in the *f* of their thinking.

FUTURE
Ps 37: 37 there is a *f* for the man of peace.
Pr 23: 18 There is surely a *f* hope for you,
Ecc 7: 14 anything about his *f*.
8: 7 Since no man knows the *f*,
Jer 29: 11 plans to give you hope and a *f*.
31: 17 So there is hope for your *f*,"
Ro 8: 38 neither the present nor the *f*,
1Co 3: 22 life or death or the present or the *f*

GABRIEL*
Angel who interpreted Daniel's visions (Da 8:16–26; 9:20–27); announced births of John (Lk 1:11–20), Jesus (Lk 1:26–38).

GAD
1. Son of Jacob by Zilpah (Ge 30:9–11; 35:26; 1Ch 2:2). Tribe of blessed (Ge 49:19; Dt 33:20–21), numbered (Nu 1:25; 26:18), allotted land east of the Jordan (Nu 32; 34:14; Jos 18:7; 22), west (Eze 48:27–28), 12,000 from (Rev 7:5).
2. Prophet; seer of David (1Sa 22:5; 2Sa 24:11–19; 1Ch 29:29).

GAIN (GAINED GAINS)
Ex 14: 17 And I will *g* glory through Pharaoh
Ps 60: 12 With God we will *g* the victory,
Pr 4: 1 pay attention and *g* understanding.
8: 5 You who are simple, *g* prudence;
28: 16 he who hates ill-gotten *g* will enjoy
28: 23 in the end *g* more favor
Isa 63: 12 to *g* for himself everlasting renown
Da 2: 8 that you are trying to *g* time,
Mk 8: 36 it for a man to *g* the whole world,
Lk 9: 25 it for a man to *g* the whole world,
21: 19 standing firm you will *g* life.
1Co 13: 3 but have not love, I *g* nothing.
Php 1: 21 to live is Christ and to die is *g*.
3: 8 that I may *g* Christ and be found
1Ti 3: 13 have served well *g* an excellent
6: 5 godliness is a means to financial *g*.
6: 6 with contentment is great *g*.

GAINED (GAIN)
Jer 32: 20 have *g* the renown that is still yours
Ro 5: 2 through whom we have *g* access

GAINS (GAIN)
Pr 3: 13 the man who *g* understanding,
11: 16 A kindhearted woman *g* respect,
15: 32 heeds correction *g* understanding.
29: 23 but a man of lowly spirit *g* honor.
Mt 16: 26 for a man if he *g* the whole world,

GALILEE
Isa 9: 1 but in the future he will honor *G*
Mt 4: 15 *G* of the Gentiles—
26: 32 I will go ahead of you into *G*."
28: 10 Go and tell my brothers to go to *G*;

GALL
Mt 27: 34 mixed with *g*; but after tasting it,

GALLIO
Ac 18: 12 While *G* was proconsul of Achaia,

GALLOWS
Est 7: 10 Haman on the *g* he had prepared

GAMALIEL
Ac 5: 34 But a Pharisee named *G*, a teacher

GAMES
1Co 9: 25 in the *g* goes into strict training.

GAP
Eze 22: 30 stand before me in the *g* on behalf

GAPE*
Ps 35: 21 They *g* at me and say, "Aha! Aha!

GARDEN (GARDENER)
Ge 2: 8 the LORD God had planted a *g*
2: 15 put him in the *G* of Eden to work it
SS 4: 12 You are a *g* locked up, my sister,
Isa 58: 11 You will be like a well-watered *g*,
Jer 31: 12 They will be like a well-watered *g*,
Eze 28: 13 the *g* of God;
31: 9 Eden in the *g* of God.

GARDENER (GARDEN)
Jn 15: 1 true vine, and my Father is the *g*.

GARLAND*
Pr 1: 9 They will be a *g* to grace your head
4: 9 She will set a *g* of grace

GARMENT (GARMENTS)
Ps 102: 26 they will all wear out like a *g*.
Isa 50: 9 They will all wear out like a *g*;
51: 6 the earth will wear out like a *g*
61: 3 and a *g* of praise
Mt 9: 16 of unshrunk cloth on an old *g*,
Jn 19: 23 This *g* was seamless, woven
Heb 1: 11 they will all wear out like a *g*.

GARMENTS (GARMENT)
Ge 3: 21 The LORD God made *g* of skin
Ex 28: 2 Make sacred *g* for your brother
Lev 16: 23 and take off the linen *g* he put
16: 24 holy place and put on his regular *g*.
Isa 61: 10 me with *g* of salvation
63: 1 with his *g* stained crimson?
Joel 2: 13 and not your *g*.
Zec 3: 4 and I will put rich *g* on you."
Jn 19: 24 "They divided my *g* among them

GATE (GATES)
Ps 118: 20 This is the *g* of the LORD
Pr 31: 23 husband is respected at the city *g*,
31: 31 works bring her praise at the city *g*.
Mt 7: 13 For wide is the *g* and broad is
7: 13 "Enter through the narrow *g*.
Jn 10: 1 not enter the sheep pen by the *g*,
10: 2 enters by the *g* is the shepherd
10: 7 "I tell you the truth, I am the *g*
10: 9 I am the *g*; whoever enters
Heb 13: 12 also suffered outside the city *g*
Rev 21: 21 each *g* made of a single pearl.

GATES (GATE)
Ps 24: 7 Lift up your heads, O you *g*;
24: 9 Lift up your heads, O you *g*;
100: 4 Enter his *g* with thanksgiving
118: 19 Open for me the *g* of righteousness
Isa 60: 11 Your *g* will always stand open,
60: 18 and your *g* Praise.
62: 10 Pass through, pass through the *g*!
Mt 16: 18 the *g* of Hades will not overcome it
Rev 21: 12 On the *g* were written the names
21: 21 The twelve *g* were twelve pearls,
21: 25 On no day will its *g* ever be shut,
22: 14 may go through the *g* into the city.

GATH
1Sa 17: 23 the Philistine champion from *G*,
2Sa 1: 20 "Tell it not in *G*,

Mic 1: 10 Tell it not in G;

GATHER (GATHERED GATHERS)
Ps 106: 47 and g us from the nations,
Isa 11: 12 and g the exiles of Israel;
Jer 3: 17 and all nations will g in Jerusalem
23: 3 "I myself will g the remnant
31: 10 who scattered Israel will g them
Zep 2: 1 G together, g together,
3: 20 At that time I will g you;
Zec 14: 2 I will g all the nations to Jerusalem
Mt 12: 30 he who does not g with me scatters
13: 30 then g the wheat and bring it
23: 37 longed to g your children together,
24: 31 and they will g his elect
25: 26 g where I have not scattered seed?
Mk 13: 27 and g his elect from the four winds,
Lk 3: 17 and to g the wheat into his barn,
11: 23 and he who does not g with me,
13: 34 longed to g your children together,

GATHERED (GATHER)
Ex 16: 18 and he who g little did not have too
Pr 30: 4 Who has g up the wind
Mt 25: 32 All the nations will be g before him
2Co 8: 15 and he who g little did not have too
2Th 2: 1 Lord Jesus Christ and our being g
Rev 16: 16 Then they g the kings together

GATHERS (GATHER)
Ps 147: 2 he g the exiles of Israel.
Pr 10: 5 He who g crops in summer is a wise
Isa 40: 11 He g the lambs in his arms
Mt 23: 37 a hen g her chicks under her wings,

GAVE (GIVE)
Ge 2: 20 man g names to all the livestock,
3: 6 She also g some to her husband,
14: 20 Abram g him a tenth of everything.
28: 4 the land God g to Abraham."
35: 12 The land I g to Abraham
39: 23 g him success in whatever he did.
47: 11 g them property in the best part
Ex 4: 11 to him, "Who g man his mouth?
31: 18 he g him the two tablets
Dt 2: 12 did in the land the LORD g them
2: 36 The LORD our God g us all
3: 12 I g the Reubenites and the Gadites
3: 13 I g to the half tribe of Manasseh.
3: 15 And I g Gilead to Makir.
3: 16 Gadites I g the territory extending
8: 16 He g you manna to eat in the desert
26: 9 us to this place and g us this land,
32: 8 the Most High g the nations their
Jos 11: 23 and he g it as an inheritance
13: 14 tribe of Levi he g no inheritance,
14: 13 g him Hebron as his inheritance.
21: 44 The LORD g them rest
24: 13 I g you a land on which you did not
1Sa 27: 6 So on that day Achish g him Ziklag
2Sa 12: 8 I g you the house of Israel
1Ki 4: 29 God g Solomon wisdom
5: 12 The LORD g Solomon wisdom,
Ezr 2: 69 According to their ability they g
Ne 9: 15 In their hunger you g them bread
9: 20 You g your good Spirit
9: 22 You g them kingdoms and nations,
9: 27 compassion you g them deliverers,
Job 1: 21 LORD g and the LORD has taken
42: 10 prosperous again and g him twice
Ps 69: 21 and g me vinegar for my thirst.
135: 12 he g their land as an inheritance,
Ecc 12: 7 the spirit returns to God who g it.
Eze 3: 2 and he g me the scroll to eat.
Mt 1: 25 And he g him the name Jesus.
25: 35 and you g me something to drink,
25: 42 and you g me nothing to drink,
26: 26 Jesus took bread, g thanks
27: 50 in a loud voice, he g up his spirit.
Mk 6: 7 g them authority over evil spirits.
Jn 1: 12 he g the right to become children
3: 16 so loved the world that he g his one
17: 4 by completing the work you g me
17: 6 you g them to me and they have
19: 30 bowed his head and g up his spirit.
Ac 1: 3 g many convincing proofs that he
2: 45 they g to anyone as he had need.
11: 17 g them the same gift as he g us,
Ro 1: 24 Therefore God g them
1: 26 God g them over to shameful lusts.
1: 28 he g them over to a depraved mind,
8: 32 not spare his own Son, but g him up
2Co 5: 18 g us the ministry of reconciliation:
8: 3 For I testify that they g as much
8: 5 they g themselves first to the Lord
Gal 1: 4 who g himself for our sins
2: 20 who loved me and g himself for me
Eph 4: 8 and g gifts to men."
5: 2 as Christ loved us and g himself up
5: 25 and g himself up for her
2Th 2: 16 and by his grace g us eternal
1Ti 2: 6 who g himself as a ransom
Tit 2: 14 who g himself for us to redeem us
1Jn 3: 24 We know it by the Spirit he g us.

GAZE
Ps 27: 4 to g upon the beauty of the LORD
Pr 4: 25 fix your g directly before you.

GEDALIAH
Governor of Judah appointed by Nebuchadnezzar (2Ki 25:22–26; Jer 39–41).

GEHAZI*
Servant of Elisha (2Ki 4:12–5:27; 8:4–5).

GENEALOGIES
1Ti 1: 4 themselves to myths and endless g.
Tit 3: 9 avoid foolish controversies and g

GENERATION (GENERATIONS)
Ex 3: 15 am to be remembered from g to g.
Nu 32: 13 until the whole g of those who had
Dt 1: 35 of this evil g shall see the good land
Jdg 2: 10 After that whole g had been
Ps 24: 6 Such is the g of those who seek him
48: 13 tell of them to the next g.
71: 18 I declare your power to the next g,
78: 4 we will tell the next g
102: 18 Let this be written for a future g,
112: 2 the g of the upright will be blessed
145: 4 One g will commend your works
La 5: 19 your throne endures from g to g.
Da 4: 3 his dominion endures from g to g.
4: 34 his kingdom endures from g to g.
Joel 1: 3 and their children to the next g.
Mt 12: 39 adulterous g asks for a miraculous
17: 17 "O unbelieving and perverse g,"
23: 36 all this will come upon this g.
24: 34 this g will certainly not pass away
Mk 9: 19 "O unbelieving g," Jesus replied,
13: 30 this g will certainly not pass away
Lk 1: 50 who fear him, from g to g.
11: 29 Jesus said, "This is a wicked g.
11: 30 will the Son of Man be to this g.
11: 50 Therefore this g will be held
21: 32 this g will certainly not pass away
Ac 2: 40 Save yourselves from this corrupt g
Php 2: 15 fault in a crooked and depraved g,

GENERATIONS (GENERATION)
Ge 9: 12 a covenant for all g to come:
17: 7 after you for the g to come,
17: 9 after you for the g to come.
Ex 20: 6 a thousand g of those
31: 13 and you for the g to come,
Dt 7: 9 covenant of love to a thousand g
32: 7 consider the g long past.
1Ch 16: 15 he commanded, for a thousand g,
Job 8: 8 "Ask the former g
Ps 22: 30 future g will be told about the Lord
33: 11 of his heart through all g.
45: 17 your memory through all g;
89: 1 faithfulness known through all g.
90: 1 throughout all g.
100: 5 continues through all g.
102: 12 your renown endures through all g.
105: 8 he commanded, for a thousand g,
119: 90 continues through all g;
135: 13 renown, O LORD, through all g.
145: 13 dominion endures through all g.
146: 10 your God, O Zion, for all g.
Pr 27: 24 and a crown is not secure for all g.
Isa 41: 4 forth the g from the beginning?
51: 8 my salvation through all g."
Lk 1: 48 now on all g will call me blessed,
Eph 3: 5 not made known to men in other g
3: 21 in Christ Jesus throughout all g,
Col 1: 26 been kept hidden for ages and g,

GENEROSITY* (GENEROUS)
2Co 8: 2 poverty welled up in rich g.
9: 11 and through us your g will result
9: 13 and for your g in sharing with them

GENEROUS* (GENEROSITY)
Ps 37: 26 They are always g and lend freely;
112: 5 Good will come to him who is g
Pr 11: 25 A g man will prosper;
22: 9 A g man will himself be blessed,
Mt 20: 15 Or are you envious because I am g
2Co 9: 5 Then it will be ready as a g gift,
9: 5 for the g gift you had promised.
9: 11 way so that you can be g
1Ti 6: 18 and to be g and willing to share.

GENTILE (GENTILES)
Ac 21: 25 As for the G believers, we have
Ro 1: 16 first for the Jew, then for the G.
2: 9 first for the Jew, then for the G;
2: 10 first for the Jew, then for the G.
10: 12 difference between Jew and G—

GENTILES (GENTILE)
Isa 42: 6 and a light for the G,
49: 6 also make you a light for the G,
49: 22 "See, I will beckon to the G,
Lk 2: 32 a light for revelation to the G
21: 24 on by the G until the times
Ac 9: 15 to carry my name before the G
10: 45 been poured out even on the G.
11: 18 granted even the G repentance unto
13: 16 and you G who worship God,
13: 46 of eternal life, we now turn to the G
13: 47 I have made you a light for the G,
14: 27 opened the door of faith to the G.
15: 14 by taking from the G a people
18: 6 From now on I will go to the G."
22: 21 I will send you far away to the G.' "
26: 20 and in all Judea, and to the G also,
28: 28 salvation has been sent to the G,
Ro 2: 14 when G, who do not have the law,
3: 9 and G alike are all under sin.
3: 29 Is he not the God of G too? Yes,
9: 24 from the Jews but also from the G?
11: 11 to the G to make Israel envious.
11: 12 their loss means riches for the G,
11: 13 as I am the apostle to the G,
15: 9 I will praise you among the G;
15: 9 so that the G may glorify God
1Co 1: 23 block to Jews and foolishness to G,
Gal 1: 16 I might preach him among the G,
2: 2 gospel that I preach among the G.
2: 8 my ministry as an apostle to the G.
2: 9 agreed that we should go to the G,
3: 8 that God would justify the G
3: 14 to the G through Christ Jesus,
Eph 3: 6 the gospel the G are heirs together
3: 8 to the G the unsearchable riches
Col 1: 27 among the G the glorious riches
1Ti 2: 7 a teacher of the true faith to the G.
2Ti 4: 17 and all the G might hear it.

GENTLE* (GENTLENESS)
Dt 28: 54 Even the most g and sensitive man
28: 56 The most g and sensitive woman
28: 56 and g that she would not venture
2Sa 18: 5 Be g with the young man Absalom
1Ki 19: 12 And after the fire came a g whisper

Job 41: 3 Will he speak to you with *g* words?
Pr 15: 1 A *g* answer turns away wrath,
25: 15 and a *g* tongue can break a bone.
Jer 11: 19 I had been like a *g* lamb led
Zec 9: 9 *g* and riding on a donkey,
Mt 11: 29 for I am *g* and humble in heart,
21: 5 *g* and riding on a donkey,
Ac 27: 13 When a *g* south wind began
1Co 4: 21 or in love and with a *g* spirit?
Eph 4: 2 Be completely humble and *g*;
1Th 2: 7 but we were *g* among you,
1Ti 3: 3 not violent but *g*, not quarrelsome,
1Pe 3: 4 the unfading beauty of a *g*

GENTLENESS* (GENTLE)
2Co 10: 1 By the meekness and *g* of Christ,
Gal 5: 23 faithfulness, *g* and self-control.
Php 4: 5 Let your *g* be evident to all.
Col 3: 12 kindness, humility, *g* and patience.
1Ti 6: 11 faith, love, endurance and *g*.
1Pe 3: 15 But do this with *g* and respect,

GENUINE*
2Co 6: 8 *g*, yet regarded as impostors;
Php 2: 20 who takes a *g* interest
1Pe 1: 7 may be proved *g* and may result

GERIZIM
Dt 27: 12 on Mount *G* to bless the people:

GERSHOM
Ex 2: 22 and Moses named him *G*, saying,

GETHSEMANE*
Mt 26: 36 disciples to a place called *G*,
Mk 14: 32 They went to a place called *G*,

GHOST see also SPIRIT
Lk 24: 39 a *g* does not have flesh and bones,

GIBEON
Jos 10: 12 "O sun, stand still over *G*,

GIDEON*
Judge, also called Jerub-Baal; freed Israel from Midianites (Jdg 6–8; Heb 11:32). Given sign of fleece (Jdg 6:36–40).

GIFT (GIFTED GIFTS)
Pr 18: 16 A *g* opens the way for the giver
21: 14 A *g* given in secret soothes anger,
Ecc 3: 13 in all his toil—this is the *g* of God.
Mt 5: 23 if you are offering your *g*
Jn 4: 10 "If you knew the *g* of God
Ac 1: 4 wait for the *g* my Father promised,
2: 38 And you will receive the *g*
11: 17 So if God gave them the same *g*
Ro 6: 23 but the *g* of God is eternal life
12: 6 If a man's *g* is prophesying,
1Co 7: 7 each man has his own *g* from God;
2Co 8: 12 the *g* is acceptable according
9: 15 be to God for his indescribable *g*!
Eph 2: 8 it is the *g* of God—not by works,
1Ti 4: 14 not neglect your *g*, which was
2Ti 1: 6 you to fan into flame the *g* of God,
Heb 6: 4 who have tasted the heavenly *g*,
Jas 1: 17 and perfect *g* is from above,
1Pe 3: 7 with you of the gracious *g* of life,
4: 10 should use whatever *g* he has
Rev 22: 17 let him take the free *g* of the water

GIFTED* (GIFT)
1Co 14: 37 he is a prophet or spiritually *g*,

GIFTS (GIFT)
Ps 76: 11 bring *g* to the One to be feared.
112: 9 He has scattered abroad his *g*
Pr 25: 14 of *g* he does not give.
Mt 2: 11 and presented him with *g* of gold
7: 11 Father in heaven give good *g*
7: 11 to give good *g* to your children,
Lk 11: 13 to give good *g* to your children,
Ac 10: 4 and *g* to the poor have come up
Ro 11: 29 for God's *g* and his call are
12: 6 We have different *g*, according
1Co 12: 1 Now about spiritual *g*, brothers,
12: 4 There are different kinds of *g*,
12: 28 those with *g* of administration,
12: 30 all work miracles? Do all have *g*
12: 31 But eagerly desire the greater *g*.
14: 1 and eagerly desire spiritual *g*,
14: 12 eager to have spiritual *g*,
14: 12 excel in *g* that build up the church.
2Co 9: 9 "He has scattered abroad his *g*
Eph 4: 8 and gave *g* to men."
Heb 2: 4 and *g* of the Holy Spirit distributed
9: 9 indicating that the *g* and sacrifices

GILEAD
1Ch 27: 21 the half-tribe of Manasseh in *G*:
Jer 8: 22 Is there no balm in *G*?
46: 11 "Go up to *G* and get balm,

GILGAL
Jos 5: 9 So the place has been called *G*

GIRD*
Ps 45: 3 *G* your sword upon your side,

GIRL
Ge 24: 16 *g* was very beautiful, a virgin;
2Ki 5: 2 a young *g* from Israel.
Mk 5: 41 Little *g*, I say to you, get up!

GIVE (GAVE GIVEN GIVER GIVES GIVING LIFE-GIVING)
Ge 28: 4 you and your descendants the blessing *g* to Abraham
28: 22 that you *g* me I will *g* you a tenth."
Ex 20: 16 "You shall not *g* false testimony
30: 15 The rich are not to *g* more
Nu 6: 26 and *g* you peace." '
Dt 5: 20 "You shall not *g* false testimony
15: 10 *G* generously to him and do
15: 14 *G* to him as the LORD your God
1Sa 1: 11 then I will *g* him to the LORD
1: 28 So now I *g* him to the LORD.
2Ch 15: 7 be strong and do not *g* up,
Pr 21: 26 but the righteous *g* without sparing
23: 26 My son, *g* me your heart
25: 21 if he is thirsty, *g* him water to drink
30: 8 but *g* me only my daily bread.
31: 31 *G* her the reward she has earned,
Ecc 3: 6 a time to search and a time to *g* up,
Isa 42: 8 I will not *g* my glory to another
Eze 36: 26 I will *g* you a new heart
Mt 6: 11 *G* us today our daily bread.
7: 11 know how to *g* good gifts
10: 8 Freely you have received, freely *g*.
16: 19 I will *g* you the keys
22: 21 "*G* to Caesar what is Caesar's,
Mk 8: 37 Or what can a man *g* in exchange
10: 19 not steal, do not *g* false testimony,
Lk 6: 38 *G*, and it will be given to you.
11: 3 *G* us each day our daily bread.
11: 13 Father in heaven *g* the Holy Spirit
14: 33 who does not *g* up everything he
Jn 10: 28 I *g* them eternal life, and they shall
13: 34 "A new commandment I *g* you:
14: 16 he will *g* you another Counselor
14: 27 I do not *g* to you as the world gives.
14: 27 leave with you; my peace I *g* you.
17: 2 people that he might *g* eternal life
Ac 20: 35 blessed to *g* than to receive.' "
Ro 2: 7 immortality, he will *g* eternal life.
8: 32 with him, graciously *g* us all things
12: 8 let him *g* generously;
13: 7 *G* everyone what you owe him:
14: 12 each of us will *g* an account
2Co 9: 7 Each man should *g* what he has
Gal 2: 5 We did not *g* in to them
6: 9 reap a harvest if we do not *g* up.
Heb 10: 25 Let us not *g* up meeting together,
Rev 14: 7 "Fear God and *g* him glory,

GIVEN (GIVE)
Nu 8: 16 are to be *g* wholly to me.
Dt 26: 11 things the LORD your God has *g*
Job 3: 23 Why is life *g* to a man
Ps 115: 16 but the earth he has *g* to man.
Isa 9: 6 to us a son is *g*,
Mt 6: 33 and all these things will be *g* to you
7: 7 "Ask and it will be *g* to you;
13: 12 Whoever has will be *g* more,
22: 30 people will neither marry nor be *g*
25: 29 everyone who has will be *g* more,
Lk 6: 38 Give, and it will be *g* to you.
8: 10 kingdom of God has been *g* to you,
11: 9 Ask and it will be *g* to you;
22: 19 saying, "This is my body *g* for you;
Jn 3: 27 man can receive only what is *g* him
15: 7 you wish, and it will be *g* you.
17: 24 I want those you have *g* me to be
17: 24 the glory you have *g* me
18: 11 the cup the Father has *g* me?"
Ac 5: 32 whom God has *g* to those who
20: 24 the task the Lord Jesus has *g* me—
Ro 5: 5 the Holy Spirit, whom he has *g* us.
1Co 4: 2 those who have been *g* a trust must
11: 24 and when he had *g* thanks,
12: 13 we were all *g* the one Spirit to drink
2Co 5: 5 and has *g* us the Spirit as a deposit,
Eph 1: 6 which he has freely *g* us
4: 7 to each one of us grace has been *g*
1Ti 4: 14 was *g* you through a prophetic
1Jn 4: 13 because he has *g* us of his Spirit.

GIVER* (GIVE)
Pr 18: 16 A gift opens the way for the *g*
2Co 9: 7 for God loves a cheerful *g*.

GIVES (GIVE)
Job 35: 10 who *g* songs in the night,
Ps 119:130 The unfolding of your words *g* light;
Pr 3: 34 but *g* grace to the humble.
11: 24 One man *g* freely, yet gains
14: 30 A heart at peace *g* life to the body,
15: 30 good news *g* health to the bones.
19: 6 of a man who *g* gifts.
25: 26 is a righteous man who *g* way
28: 27 He who *g* to the poor will lack
29: 4 justice a king *g* a country stability,
Isa 40: 29 He *g* strength to the weary
Hab 2: 15 "Woe to him who *g* drink
Mt 10: 42 if anyone *g* even a cup of cold water
Jn 5: 21 even so the Son *g* life to whom he is
6: 63 The Spirit *g* life; the flesh counts
1Co 15: 57 He *g* us the victory
2Co 3: 6 the letter kills, but the Spirit *g* life.
1Th 4: 8 who *g* you his Holy Spirit.
Jas 1: 25 into the perfect law that *g* freedom,
4: 6 but *g* grace to the humble."
1Pe 5: 5 but *g* grace to the humble."

GIVING (GIVE)
Ne 8: 8 *g* the meaning so that the people
Est 9: 19 a day for *g* presents to each other.
Ps 19: 8 *g* joy to the heart.
Pr 15: 23 A man finds joy in *g* an apt reply—
Mt 6: 4 so that your *g* may be in secret.
24: 38 marrying and *g* in marriage,
Ac 15: 8 them by *g* the Holy Spirit to them,
2Co 8: 7 also excel in this grace of *g*.
Php 4: 15 shared with me in the matter of *g*

GLAD* (GLADDENS GLADNESS)
Ex 4: 14 his heart will be *g* when he sees you
Jos 22: 33 They were *g* to hear the report
Jdg 8: 25 "We'll be *g* to give them."
18: 20 household?" Then the priest was *g*.
1Sa 19: 5 and you saw it and were *g*.
2Sa 1: 20 daughters of the Philistines be *g*,
1Ki 8: 66 *g* in heart for all the good things
1Ch 16: 31 heavens rejoice, let the earth be *g*;
2Ch 7: 10 and *g* in heart for the good things
Ps 5: 11 let all who take refuge in you be *g*;
9: 2 I will be *g* and rejoice in you;
14: 7 let Jacob rejoice and Israel be *g*!
16: 9 Therefore my heart is *g*
21: 6 made him *g* with the joy
31: 7 I will be *g* and rejoice in your love,
32: 11 Rejoice in the LORD and be *g*,
40: 16 rejoice and be *g* in you;

45: 8 music of the strings makes you g.
46: 4 whose streams make g the city
48: 11 the villages of Judah are g
53: 6 let Jacob rejoice and Israel be g!
58: 10 The righteous will be g
67: 4 May the nations be g and sing
68: 3 But may the righteous be g
69: 32 The poor will see and be g—
70: 4 rejoice and be g in you;
90: 14 for joy and be g all our days.
90: 15 Make us g for as many days
92: 4 For you make me g by your deeds,
96: 11 heavens rejoice, let the earth be g;
97: 1 LORD reigns, let the earth be g;
97: 8 and the villages of Judah are g
105: 38 Egypt was g when they left,
107: 30 They were g when it grew calm,
118: 24 let us rejoice and be g in it.
149: 2 of Zion be g in their King.
Pr 23: 15 then my heart will be g;
23: 25 May your father and mother be g;
29: 6 a righteous one can sing and be g.
Ecc 8: 15 sun than to eat and drink and be g.
Isa 25: 9 let us rejoice and be g
35: 1 and the parched land will be g;
65: 18 But be g and rejoice forever
66: 10 with Jerusalem and be g for her,
Jer 20: 15 who made him very g, saying,
31: 13 Then maidens will dance and be g,
41: 13 were with him, they were g.
50: 11 "Because you rejoice and are g,
La 4: 21 be g, O Daughter of Edom,
Joel 2: 21 be g and rejoice.
2: 23 Be g, O people of Zion,
Hab 1: 15 and so he rejoices and is g.
Zep 3: 14 Be g and rejoice with all your heart
Zec 2: 10 and be g, O Daughter of Zion.
8: 19 will become joyful and g occasions
10: 7 their hearts will be g as with wine.
Mt 5: 12 be g, because great is your reward
Lk 15: 32 But we had to celebrate and be g,
Jn 4: 36 and the reaper may be g together.
8: 56 my day; he saw it and was g."
11: 15 for your sake I am g I was not there
14: 28 you would be g that I am going
Ac 2: 26 Therefore my heart is g
2: 46 together with g and sincere hearts,
11: 23 he was g and encouraged them all
13: 48 they were g and honored the word
15: 3 news made all the brothers very g.
15: 31 were g for its encouraging message.
1Co 16: 17 was g when Stephanas, Fortunatus
2Co 2: 2 who is left to make me g
7: 16 I am g I can have complete
13: 9 We are g whenever we are weak
Gal 4: 27 "Be g, O barren woman,
Php 2: 17 I am g and rejoice with all of you.
2: 18 So you too should be g and rejoice
2: 28 you see him again you may be g
Rev 19: 7 Let us rejoice and be g

GLADDENS* (GLAD)
Ps 104: 15 wine that g the heart of man,

GLADNESS* (GLAD)
2Ch 29: 30 So they sang praises with g
Est 8: 16 a time of happiness and joy, g
8: 17 there was joy and g
Job 3: 22 who are filled with g
Ps 35: 27 shout for joy and g;
45: 15 They are led in with joy and g;
51: 8 Let me hear joy and g;
65: 12 the hills are clothed with g.
100: 2 Worship the LORD with g;
Ecc 5: 20 God keeps him occupied with g
9: 7 Go, eat your food with g,
Isa 16: 10 g are taken away from the orchards
35: 10 G and joy will overtake them,
51: 3 Joy and g will be found in her,
51: 11 G and joy will overtake them,
61: 3 the oil of g / instead of mourning,
Jer 7: 34 and g and to the voices of bride
16: 9 and g and to the voices of bride
25: 10 from them the sounds of joy and g,
31: 13 I will turn their mourning into g;
33: 11 once more the sounds of joy and g,
48: 33 Joy and g are gone
Joel 1: 16 joy and g

GLAZE*
Pr 26: 23 of g over earthenware

GLEAM*
Pr 4: 18 of the righteous is like the first g
Da 10: 6 legs like the g of burnished bronze,

GLOAT (GLOATS)
Pr 24: 17 Do not g when your enemy falls;

GLOATS* (GLOAT)
Pr 17: 5 whoever g over disaster will not go

GLORIES* (GLORY)
1Pe 1: 11 and the g that would follow.

GLORIFIED* (GLORY)
Isa 66: 5 'Let the LORD be g,
Eze 39: 13 day I am g will be a memorable day
Da 4: 34 and g him who lives forever.
Jn 7: 39 since Jesus had not yet been g.
11: 4 glory so that God's Son may be g
12: 16 after Jesus was g did they realize
12: 23 come for the Son of Man to be g.
12: 28 "I have g it, and will glorify it again
13: 31 Son of Man g and God is g in him.
13: 32 If God is g in him, God will glorify
Ac 3: 13 our fathers, has g his servant Jesus.
Ro 1: 21 they neither g him as God
8: 30 those he justified, he also g.
2Th 1: 10 comes to be g in his holy people
1: 12 of our Lord Jesus may be g in you,
1Pe 1: 21 him from the dead and g him,

GLORIFIES* (GLORY)
Lk 1: 46 My soul g the Lord
Jn 8: 54 as your God, is the one who g me.

GLORIFY* (GLORY)
Ps 34: 3 G the LORD with me;
63: 3 my lips will g you.
69: 30 and g him with thanksgiving.
86: 12 I will g your name forever.
Isa 60: 13 and I will g the place of my feet.
Da 4: 37 and exalt and g the King of heaven,
Jn 8: 54 Jesus replied, "If I g myself,
12: 28 glorified it, and will g it again."
12: 28 g your name!" Then a voice came
13: 32 God will g the Son in himself,
13: 32 in himself, and will g him at once.
17: 1 G your Son, that your Son may
17: 1 your Son, that your Son may g you.
17: 5 g me in your presence
21: 19 death by which Peter would g God.
Ro 15: 6 and mouth you may g the God
15: 9 so that the Gentiles may g God
1Pe 2: 12 and g God on the day he visits us.
Rev 16: 9 they refused to repent and g him.

GLORIFYING* (GLORY)
Lk 2: 20 g and praising God

GLORIOUS* (GLORY)
Dt 28: 58 not revere this g and awesome
33: 29 and your g sword.
1Ch 29: 13 and praise your g name.
Ne 9: 5 "Blessed be your g name,
Ps 16: 3 they are the g ones
45: 13 All g is the princess
66: 2 make his praise g.
72: 19 Praise be to his g name forever;
87: 3 G things are said of you,
111: 3 G and majestic are his deeds,
145: 5 of the g splendor of your majesty,
145: 12 the g splendor of your kingdom.
Isa 3: 8 defying his g presence.
4: 2 the LORD will be beautiful and g,
11: 10 and his place of rest will be g.
12: 5 for he has done g things;
28: 1 to the fading flower, his g beauty,
28: 4 That fading flower, his g beauty,
28: 5 will be a g crown,
42: 21 to make his law great and g.
60: 7 and I will adorn my g temple.
63: 12 who sent his g arm of power
63: 14 to make for yourself a g name.
63: 15 from your lofty throne, holy and g.
64: 11 g temple, where our fathers praised
Jer 13: 18 for your g crowns
14: 21 do not dishonor your g throne.
17: 12 A g throne, exalted
48: 17 how broken the g staff!'
Mt 19: 28 the Son of Man sits on his g throne,
Lk 9: 31 appeared in g splendor, talking
Ac 2: 20 of the great and g day of the Lord.
Ro 8: 21 and brought into the g freedom
2Co 3: 8 of the Spirit be even more g?
3: 9 how much more g is the ministry
3: 9 ministry that condemns men is g,
3: 10 For what was g has no glory now
Eph 1: 6 to the praise of his g grace,
1: 17 g Father, may give you the Spirit
1: 18 the riches of his g inheritance
3: 16 of his g riches he may strengthen
Php 3: 21 so that they will be like his g body.
4: 19 to his g riches in Christ Jesus.
Col 1: 11 all power according to his g might
1: 27 among the Gentiles the g riches
1Ti 1: 11 to the g gospel of the blessed God,
Tit 2: 13 the g appearing of our great God
Jas 2: 1 believers in our g Lord Jesus Christ
1Pe 1: 8 with an inexpressible and g joy,
Jude : 24 before his g presence without fault

GLORIOUSLY* (GLORY)
Isa 24: 23 and before its elders, g.

GLORY (GLORIES GLORIFIED GLORIFIES GLORIFY GLORIFYING GLORIOUS GLORIOUSLY)
Ex 14: 4 But I will gain g for myself
14: 17 And I will gain g through Pharaoh
15: 11 awesome in g,
16: 10 and there was the g of the LORD
24: 16 and the g of the LORD settled
33: 18 Moses said, "Now show me your g
40: 34 and the g of the LORD filled
Nu 14: 21 the g of the LORD fills the whole
Dt 5: 24 LORD our God has shown us his g
Jos 7: 19 "My son, give g to the LORD,
1Sa 4: 21 "The g has departed from Israel"—
1Ch 16: 10 G in his holy name;
16: 24 Declare his g among the nations,
16: 28 ascribe to the LORD g
29: 11 and the g and the majesty
Ps 8: 1 You have set your g
8: 5 and crowned him with g and honor
19: 1 The heavens declare the g of God;
24: 7 that the King of g may come in.
26: 8 the place where your g dwells.
29: 1 ascribe to the LORD g
29: 9 And in his temple all cry, "G!"
57: 5 let your g be over all the earth.
66: 2 Sing the g of his name;
72: 19 the whole earth be filled with his g.
96: 3 Declare his g among the nations,
102: 15 of the earth will revere your g.
108: 5 and let your g be over all the earth.
149: 9 This is the g of all his saints.
Pr 19: 11 it is to his g to overlook an offense.
25: 2 It is the g of God to conceal
Isa 4: 5 over all the g will be a canopy.
6: 3 the whole earth is full of his g."
24: 16 "G to the Righteous One."
26: 15 You have gained g for yourself;
35: 2 they will see the g of the LORD,
40: 5 the g of the LORD will be revealed
42: 8 I will not give my g to another
42: 12 Let them give g to the LORD
43: 7 whom I created for my g,

3: 12 And *G* said, "I will be with you.
3: 14 what shall I tell them?" *G* said
4: 27 he met Moses at the mountain of *G*
6: 7 own people, and I will be your *G*.
8: 10 is no one like the Lord our *G*.
10: 16 sinned against the Lord your *G*
13: 18 So *G* led the people
15: 2 He is my *G*, and I will praise him,
16: 12 that I am the Lord your *G*.' "
17: 9 with the staff of *G* in my hands."
18: 5 camped near the mountain of *G*.
19: 3 Then Moses went up to *G*,
20: 1 And *G* spoke all these words:
20: 2 the Lord your *G*, who brought
20: 5 the Lord your *G*, am a jealous *G*,
20: 7 the name of the Lord your *G*,
20: 10 a Sabbath to the Lord your *G*.
20: 12 the Lord your *G* is giving you.
20: 19 But do not have *G* speak to us
20: 20 the fear of *G* will be with you
22: 20 "Whoever sacrifices to any *g* other
22: 28 "Do not blaspheme *G*
23: 19 to the house of the Lord your *G*.
31: 18 inscribed by the finger of *G*.
34: 6 the compassionate and gracious *G*,
34: 14 name is Jealous, is a jealous *G*.
Lev 2: 13 salt of the covenant of your *G* out
11: 44 the Lord your *G*; consecrate
18: 21 not profane the name of your *G*.
19: 2 the Lord your *G*, am holy.
20: 7 because I am the Lord your *G*.
21: 6 They must be holy to their *G*
22: 33 out of Egypt to be your *G*.
26: 12 walk among you and be your *G*,
Nu 15: 40 and will be consecrated to your *G*.
22: 18 the command of the Lord my *G*.
22: 38 I must speak only what *G* puts
23: 19 *G* is not a man, that he should lie,
25: 13 zealous for the honor of his *G*
Dt 1: 17 for judgment belongs to *G*.
1: 21 the Lord your *G* has given you
1: 30 The Lord your *G*, who is going
3: 22 Lord your *G* himself will fight
3: 24 For what *g* is there in heaven
4: 24 is a consuming fire, a jealous *G*.
4: 29 there you seek the Lord your *G*,
4: 31 the Lord your *G* is a merciful *G*;
4: 39 heart this day that the Lord is *G*
5: 9 the Lord your *G*, am a jealous *G*,
5: 11 the name of the Lord your *G*,
5: 12 the Lord your *G* has commanded
5: 14 a Sabbath to the Lord your *G*.
5: 15 the Lord your *G* brought you out
5: 16 the Lord your *G* has commanded
5: 16 the Lord your *G* is giving you.
5: 24 Lord our *G* has shown us his
5: 26 of the living *G* speaking out of fire,
6: 2 them may fear the Lord your *G*
6: 4 Lord our *G*, the Lord is one.
6: 5 Love the Lord your *G*
6: 13 the Lord your *G*, serve him only
6: 16 Do not test the Lord your *G*
7: 6 holy to the Lord your *G*.
7: 9 your *G* is *G*; he is the faithful *G*,
7: 12 the Lord your *G* will keep his
7: 19 Lord your *G* will do the same
7: 21 is a great and awesome *G*.
8: 5 the Lord your *G* disciplines you.
8: 11 do not forget the Lord your *G*,
8: 18 But remember the Lord your *G*,
9: 10 inscribed by the finger of *G*.
10: 12 but to fear the Lord your *G*,
10: 14 the Lord your *G* belong
10: 17 For the Lord your *G* is *G* of gods
10: 21 He is your praise; he is your *G*,
11: 1 Love the Lord your *G*
11: 13 to love the Lord your *G*
12: 12 rejoice before the Lord your *G*,
12: 28 in the eyes of the Lord your *G*.
13: 3 The Lord your *G* is testing you
13: 4 the Lord your *G* you must
15: 6 the Lord your *G* will bless you
15: 19 the Lord your *G* every firstborn
16: 11 rejoice before the Lord your *G*
16: 17 the Lord your *G* has blessed you.
18: 13 before the Lord your *G*.
18: 15 The Lord your *G* will raise up
19: 9 to love the Lord your *G*
22: 5 the Lord your *G* detests anyone
23: 5 the Lord your *G* loves you.
23: 14 the Lord your *G* moves about
23: 21 a vow to the Lord your *G*,
25: 16 the Lord your *G* detests anyone
26: 5 declare before the Lord your *G*:
29: 13 that he may be your *G*
29: 29 belong to the Lord our *G*,
30: 2 return to the Lord your *G*
30: 4 the Lord your *G* will gather you
30: 6 The Lord your *G* will circumcise
30: 16 today to love the Lord your *G*,
30: 20 you may love the Lord your *G*,
31: 6 for the Lord your *G* goes
32: 3 Oh, praise the greatness of our *G*!
32: 4 A faithful *G* who does no wrong,
33: 27 The eternal *G* is your refuge,
Jos 1: 9 for the Lord your *G* will be
14: 8 the Lord my *G* wholeheartedly.
14: 9 the Lord my *G* wholeheartedly.'
14: 14 the *G* of Israel, wholeheartedly.
22: 5 to love the Lord your *G*,
22: 22 The Mighty One, *G*, the Lord!
22: 34 Between Us that the Lord is *G*.
23: 8 to hold fast to the Lord your *G*,
23: 11 careful to love the Lord your *G*.
23: 14 the Lord your *G* gave you has
23: 15 of the Lord your *G* has come true
24: 19 He is a holy *G*; he is a jealous *G*.
24: 23 to the Lord, the *G* of Israel."
Jdg 5: 3 to the Lord, the *G* of Israel.
16: 28 O *G*, please strengthen me just
Ru 1: 16 be my people and your *G* my *G*.
2: 12 by the Lord, the *G* of Israel,
1Sa 2: 2 there is no Rock like our *G*.
2: 3 for the Lord is a *G* who knows,
2: 25 another man, *G* may mediate
10: 26 men whose hearts *G* had touched.
12: 12 the Lord your *G* was your king.
16: 15 spirit from *G* is tormenting you.
17: 26 defy the armies of the living *G*?"
17: 36 defied the armies of the living *G*.
17: 45 the *G* of the armies of Israel,
17: 46 world will know that there is a *G*
23: 16 and helped him find strength in *G*.
28: 15 and *G* has turned away from me.
30: 6 strength in the Lord his *G*.
2Sa 7: 22 and there is no *G* but you,
7: 23 on earth that *G* went out to redeem
14: 14 But *G* does not take away life;
21: 14 *G* answered prayer in behalf
22: 3 my *G* is my rock, in whom I take
22: 31 "As for *G*, his way is perfect;
22: 32 And who is the Rock except our *G*
22: 33 It is *G* who arms me with strength
22: 47 Exalted be *G*, the Rock, my Savior!
1Ki 2: 3 what the Lord your *G* requires:
4: 29 *G* gave Solomon wisdom
5: 5 for the Name of the Lord my *G*,
8: 23 there is no *G* like you in heaven
8: 27 "But will *G* really dwell on earth?
8: 60 may know that the Lord is *G*
8: 61 committed to the Lord our *G*,
10: 24 to hear the wisdom *G* had put
15: 30 he provoked the Lord, the *G*
18: 21 If the Lord is *G*, follow him;
18: 36 it be known today that you are *G*
18: 37 are *G*, and that you are turning
20: 28 a *g* of the hills and not a *g*
2Ki 5: 15 "Now I know that there is no *G*
18: 5 in the Lord, the *G* of Israel.
19: 15 *G* of Israel, enthroned
19: 19 Now, O Lord our *G*, deliver us
1Ch 12: 18 for your *G* will help you."
13: 2 if it is the will of the Lord our *G*,
16: 35 Cry out, "Save us, O *G* our Savior;
17: 20 and there is no *G* but you,
17: 24 the *G* over Israel, is Israel's *G*!'
21: 8 said to *G*, "I have sinned greatly
22: 1 house of the Lord *G* is to be here,
22: 19 soul to seeking the Lord your *G*.
28: 2 for the footstool of our *G*,
28: 9 acknowledge the *G* of your father,
28: 20 for the Lord *G*, my *G*, is with you
29: 1 not for man but for the Lord *G*.
29: 2 provided for the temple of my *G*—
29: 3 of my *G* I now give my personal
29: 10 *G* of our father Israel,
29: 13 Now, our *G*, we give you thanks,
29: 16 O Lord our *G*, as for all this
29: 17 my *G*, that you test the heart
29: 18 *G* of our fathers Abraham,
2Ch 2: 4 for the Name of the Lord my *G*
5: 14 of the Lord filled the temple of *G*
6: 4 be to the Lord, the *G* of Israel,
6: 14 there is no *G* like you in heaven
6: 18 "But will *G* really dwell on earth
10: 15 for this turn of events was from *G*,
13: 12 *G* is with us; he is our leader.
15: 3 was without the true *G*,
15: 12 the *G* of their fathers,
15: 15 They sought *G* eagerly,
18: 13 I can tell him only what my *G* says
19: 3 have set your heart on seeking *G*."
19: 7 with the Lord our *G* there is no
20: 6 are you not the *G* who is in heaven?
20: 20 Have faith in the Lord your *G*
25: 8 for *G* has the power to help
26: 5 sought the Lord, *G* gave him
30: 9 for the Lord your *G* is gracious
30: 19 who sets his heart on seeking *G*—
31: 21 he sought his *G* and worked
32: 31 *G* left him to test him
33: 12 the favor of the Lord his *G*
34: 33 fail to follow the Lord, the *G*
Ezr 6: 21 to seek the Lord, the *G* of Israel.
7: 18 accordance with the will of your *G*.
7: 23 Whatever the *G* of heaven has
8: 22 "The gracious hand of our *G* is
8: 31 The hand of our *G* was on us,
9: 6 "O my *G*, I am too ashamed
9: 9 our *G* has not deserted us
9: 13 our *G*, you have punished us less
9: 15 *G* of Israel, you are righteous!
Ne 1: 5 the great and awesome *G*,
5: 9 fear of our *G* to avoid the reproach
5: 15 for *G* I did not act like that.
7: 2 feared *G* more than most men do.
8: 8 from the Book of the Law of *G*,
8: 18 from the Book of the Law of *G*.
9: 5 and praise the Lord your *G*,
9: 17 But you are a forgiving *G*,
9: 31 you are a gracious and merciful *G*.
9: 32 the great, mighty and awesome *G*,
10: 29 oath to follow the Law of *G* given
10: 39 not neglect the house of our *G*."
12: 43 *G* had given them great joy.
13: 11 Why is the house of *G* neglected?"
13: 26 He was loved by his *G*,
13: 31 Remember me with favor, O my *G*.
Job 1: 1 he feared *G* and shunned evil.
1: 22 by charging *G* with wrongdoing.
2: 10 Shall we accept good from *G*,
4: 17 a mortal be more righteous than *G*?
5: 17 is the man whom *G* corrects;
8: 3 Does *G* pervert justice?
8: 20 "Surely *G* does not reject
9: 2 a mortal be righteous before *G*?
11: 7 Can you fathom the mysteries of *G*

12: 13 “To *G* belong wisdom and power;
16: 7 Surely, O *G*, you have worn me out
19: 26 yet in my flesh I will see *G*;
21: 19 ‘*G* stores up a man's punishment
21: 22 Can anyone teach knowledge to *G*,
22: 12 “Is not *G* in the heights of heaven?
22: 13 Yet you say, ‘What does *G* know?
22: 21 “Submit to *G* and be at peace
25: 2 “Dominion and awe belong to *G*;
25: 4 can a man be righteous before *G*?
26: 6 Death is naked before *G*;
30: 20 O *G*, but you do not answer;
31: 6 let *G* weigh me in honest scales
31: 14 do when *G* confronts me?
32: 13 let *G* refute him, not man.’
33: 6 I am just like you before *G*;
33: 14 For *G* does speak—now one way,
33: 26 He prays to *G* and finds favor
34: 10 Far be it from *G* to do evil,
34: 12 is unthinkable that *G* would do
34: 23 *G* has no need to examine men
34: 33 Should *G* then reward you
36: 5 “*G* is mighty, but does not despise
36: 26 is *G*— beyond our understanding!
37: 22 *G* comes in awesome majesty.
Ps 5: 4 You are not a *G* who takes pleasure
7: 11 *G* is a righteous judge,
10: 14 O *G*, do see trouble and grief;
14: 5 for *G* is present in the company
18: 2 my *G* is my rock, in whom I take
18: 28 my *G* turns my darkness into light.
18: 30 As for *G*, his way is perfect;
18: 31 And who is the Rock except our *G*
18: 32 It is *G* who arms me with strength
18: 46 Exalted be *G* my Savior!
19: 1 The heavens declare the glory of *G*;
22: 1 *G*, my *G*, why have you forsaken
22: 10 womb you have been my *G*.
27: 9 O *G* my Savior.
29: 3 the *G* of glory thunders,
31: 5 redeem me, O LORD, the *G*
31: 14 I say, “You are my *G*.”
33: 12 the nation whose *G* is the LORD,
35: 24 righteousness, O LORD my *G*;
37: 31 The law of his *G* is in his heart;
40: 3 a hymn of praise to our *G*.
40: 8 I desire to do your will, O my *G*;
42: 1 so my soul pants for you, O *G*.
42: 2 thirsts for *G*, for the living *G*.
42: 5 Put your hope in *G*,
42: 8 a prayer to the *G* of my life.
42: 11 Put your hope in *G*,
43: 4 to *G*, my joy and my delight.
44: 8 In *G* we make our boast all day
45: 6 O *G*, will last for ever and ever;
45: 7 therefore *G*, your *G*, has set you
46: 1 *G* is our refuge and strength,
46: 5 *G* will help her at break of day.
46: 10 “Be still, and know that I am *G*;
47: 1 shout to *G* with cries of joy.
47: 6 Sing praises to *G*, sing praises;
47: 7 For *G* is the King of all the earth;
48: 9 Within your temple, O *G*,
49: 7 or give to *G* a ransom for him—
50: 2 *G* shines forth.
50: 3 Our *G* comes and will not be silent;
51: 1 Have mercy on me, O *G*,
51: 10 Create in me a pure heart, O *G*,
51: 17 O *G*, you will not despise.
53: 2 any who seek *G*.
54: 4 Surely *G* is my help;
55: 19 *G*, who is enthroned forever,
56: 4 In *G*, whose word I praise,
56: 10 In *G*, whose word I praise,
56: 13 that I may walk before *G*
57: 3 *G* sends his love and his
57: 7 My heart is steadfast, O *G*,
59: 17 are my fortress, my loving *G*.
62: 1 My soul finds rest in *G* alone;
62: 7 my honor depend on *G*;
62: 8 for *G* is our refuge.
62: 11 One thing *G* has spoken,
63: 1 O *G*, you are my *G*,
65: 5 O *G* our Savior,
66: 1 Shout with joy to *G*, all the earth!
66: 3 Say to *G*, “How awesome are your
66: 5 Come and see what *G* has done,
66: 16 listen, all you who fear *G*;
66: 20 Praise be to *G*,
68: 4 Sing to *G*, sing praise to his name,
68: 6 *G* sets the lonely in families,
68: 20 Our *G* is a *G* who saves;
68: 24 has come into view, O *G*,
68: 35 You are awesome, O *G*,
69: 5 You know my folly, O *G*;
70: 1 Hasten, O *G*, to save me;
70: 4 “Let *G* be exalted!”
70: 5 come quickly to me, O *G*.
71: 17 my youth, O *G*, you have taught
71: 18 do not forsake me, O *G*,
71: 19 reaches to the skies, O *G*,
71: 22 harp for your faithfulness, O my *G*;
73: 17 me till I entered the sanctuary of *G*;
73: 26 but *G* is the strength of my heart
76: 11 Make vows to the LORD your *G*
77: 13 What *g* is so great as our God?
77: 14 You are the *G* who performs
78: 19 Can *G* spread a table in the desert?
79: 9 Help us, O *G* our Savior,
81: 1 Sing for joy to *G* our strength;
82: 1 *G* presides in the great assembly;
84: 2 out for the living *G*.
84: 10 a doorkeeper in the house of my *G*
84: 11 For the LORD *G* is a sun
86: 12 O Lord my *G*, with all my heart;
86: 15 a compassionate and gracious *G*,
87: 3 O city of *G*: *Selah*
89: 7 of the holy ones *G* is greatly feared;
90: 2 to everlasting you are *G*.
91: 2 my *G*, in whom I trust.”
94: 22 my *G* the rock in whom I take
95: 7 for he is our *G*
99: 8 you were to Israel a forgiving *G*,
99: 9 Exalt the LORD our *G*
100: 3 Know that the LORD is *G*.
108: 1 My heart is steadfast, O *G*;
113: 5 Who is like the LORD our *G*,
115: 3 Our *G* is in heaven;
116: 5 our *G* is full of compassion.
123: 2 look to the LORD our *G*,
136: 2 Give thanks to the *G* of gods.
136: 26 Give thanks to the *G* of heaven.
139: 17 to me are your thoughts, O *G*!
139: 23 Search me, O *G*, and know my
143: 10 for you are my *G*;
144: 2 He is my loving *G* and my fortress,
147: 1 is to sing praises to our *G*,
Pr 3: 4 in the sight of *G* and man.
14: 31 to the needy honors *G*.
25: 2 of *G* to conceal a matter;
30: 5 “Every word of *G* is flawless;
Ecc 2: 26 *G* gives wisdom, knowledge
3: 11 cannot fathom what *G* has done
3: 13 in all his toil—this is the gift of *G*.
3: 14 *G* does it so that men will revere him.
5: 4 When you make a vow to *G*,
5: 19 in his work—this is a gift of *G*.
8: 12 who are reverent before *G*.
11: 5 cannot understand the work of *G*,
12: 7 the spirit returns to *G* who gave it.
12: 13 Fear *G* and keep his
Isa 5: 16 the holy *G* will show himself holy
9: 6 Wonderful Counselor, Mighty *G*,
12: 2 Surely *G* is my salvation;
25: 9 “Surely this is our *G*;
28: 11 *G* will speak to this people,
29: 23 will stand in awe of the *G* of Israel.
30: 18 For the LORD is a *G* of justice.
35: 4 your *G* will come,
37: 16 you alone are *G* over all
40: 1 says your *G*.
40: 3 a highway for our *G*.
40: 8 the word of our *G* stands forever.”
40: 18 then, will you compare *G*?
40: 28 The LORD is the everlasting *G*,
41: 10 not be dismayed, for I am your *G*.
41: 13 For I am the LORD, your *G*,
43: 10 Before me no *g* was formed,
44: 6 apart from me there is no *G*.
44: 15 he also fashions a *g* and worships it;
45: 18 he is *G*;
48: 17 “I am the LORD your *G*,
52: 7 “Your *G* reigns!”
52: 12 *G* of Israel will be your rear guard.
55: 7 to our *G*, for he will freely pardon.
57: 21 says my *G*, “for the wicked.”
59: 2 you from your *G*;
60: 19 and your *G* will be your glory.
61: 2 and the day of vengeance of our *G*,
61: 10 my soul rejoices in my *G*.
62: 5 so will your *G* rejoice over you.
Jer 7: 23 I will be your *G* and you will be my
10: 10 But the LORD is the true *G*;
10: 12 But *G* made the earth by his power;
23: 23 “Am I only a *G* nearby,”
23: 36 distort the words of the living *G*,
31: 33 I will be their *G*,
32: 27 “I am the LORD, the *G*
42: 6 for we will obey the LORD our *G*.”
51: 10 what the LORD our *G* has done.’
51: 56 For the LORD is a *G* of retribution
Eze 28: 13 the garden of *G*;
34: 31 and I am your *G*, declares
Da 2: 28 there is a *G* in heaven who reveals
3: 17 the *G* we serve is able to save us
3: 29 for no other *g* can save in this way
6: 16 “May your *G*, whom you serve
9: 4 O Lord, the great and awesome *G*,
10: 12 to humble yourself before your *G*,
11: 36 things against the *G* of gods.
Hos 1: 9 my people, and I am not your *G*.
1: 10 will be called ‘sons of the living *G*.’
4: 6 you have ignored the law of your *G*
6: 6 acknowledgment of *G* rather
9: 8 The prophet, along with my *G*,
12: 6 and wait for your *G* always.
Joel 2: 13 Return to the LORD your *G*,
2: 23 rejoice in the LORD your *G*,
Am 4: 12 prepare to meet your *G*, O Israel.”
4: 13 the LORD *G* Almighty is his name
Jnh 1: 6 Get up and call on your *g*!
4: 2 a gracious and compassionate *G*,
Mic 6: 8 and to walk humbly with your *G*.
7: 7 I wait for *G* my Savior;
7: 18 Who is a *G* like you,
Na 1: 2 LORD is a jealous and avenging *G*;
Hab 3: 18 I will be joyful in *G* my Savior.
Zep 3: 17 The LORD your *G* is with you,
Zec 14: 5 Then the LORD my *G* will come,
Mal 2: 10 Father? Did not one *G* create us?
2: 16 says the LORD *G* of Israel,
3: 8 Will a man rob *G*? Yet you rob me.
Mt 1: 23 which means, “*G* with us.”
4: 4 comes from the mouth of *G*.’ ”
4: 7 ‘Do not put the Lord your *G*
4: 10 ‘Worship the Lord your *G*,
5: 8 for they will see *G*.
6: 24 You cannot serve both *G*
19: 6 Therefore what *G* has joined
19: 26 but with *G* all things are possible.”
22: 21 and to *G* what is God's.”
22: 32 He is not the *G* of the dead
22: 37 “ ‘Love the Lord your *G*
27: 46 which means, “My *G*, my *G*,
Mk 2: 7 Who can forgive sins but *G* alone?”
7: 13 Thus you nullify the word of *G*
10: 6 of creation *G* ‘made them male

13: 26 of Abraham, and you *G* Gentiles,
13: 50 But the Jews incited the *G* women
17: 4 as did a large number of *G* Greeks
17: 17 with the Jews and the *G* Greeks,

GOD-HATERS* (HATE)
Ro 1: 30 They are gossips, slanderers, *G,*

GOD'S (GOD)
2Ch 20: 15 For the battle is not yours, but *G.*
Job 37: 14 stop and consider *G* wonders.
Ps 52: 8 I trust in *G* unfailing love
69: 30 I will praise *G* name in song
Mk 3: 35 Whoever does *G* will is my brother
Jn 7: 17 If anyone chooses to do *G* will,
10: 36 'I am *G* Son'? Do not believe me
Ro 2: 3 think you will escape *G* judgment?
2: 4 not realizing that *G* kindness leads
3: 3 lack of faith nullify *G* faithfulness?
7: 22 in my inner being I delight in *G* law
9: 16 or effort, but on *G* mercy.
11: 29 for *G* gifts and his call are
12: 2 and approve what *G* will is—
12: 13 Share with *G* people who are
13: 6 for the authorities are *G* servants,
1Co 7: 19 Keeping *G* commands is what
2Co 6: 2 now is the time of *G* favor,
Eph 1: 7 riches of *G* grace that he lavished
1Th 4: 3 It is *G* will that you should be sanctified;
5: 18 for this is *G* will for you
1Ti 6: 1 so that *G* name and our teaching
2Ti 2: 19 *G* solid foundation stands firm,
Tit 1: 7 overseer is entrusted with *G* work,
Heb 1: 3 The Son is the radiance of *G* glory
9: 24 now to appear for us in *G* presence.
11: 3 was formed at *G* command,
1Pe 2: 15 For it is *G* will that
3: 4 which is of great worth in *G* sight.
1Jn 2: 5 *G* love is truly made complete

GODLESS
Job 20: 5 the joy of the *g* lasts but a moment.
1Ti 6: 20 Turn away from *g* chatter

GODLINESS (GOD)
1Ti 2: 2 and quiet lives in all *g* and holiness.
4: 8 but *g* has value for all things,
6: 5 and who think that *g* is a means
6: 6 *g* with contentment is great gain.
6: 11 and pursue righteousness, *g,* faith,
2Pe 1: 6 and to perseverance, *g;*

GODLY (GOD)
Ps 4: 3 that the LORD has set apart the *g*
2Co 7: 10 *G* sorrow brings repentance that
11: 2 jealous for you with a *g* jealousy.
2Ti 3: 12 everyone who wants to live a *g* life
2Pe 3: 11 You ought to live holy and *g* lives

GODS (GOD)
Ex 20: 3 "You shall have no other *g*
Dt 5: 7 "You shall have no other *g*
1Ch 16: 26 For all the *g* of the nations are idols
Ps 82: 6 "I said, 'You are "*g*";
Jn 10: 34 have said you are *g*'? If he called
Ac 19: 26 He says that man-made *g* are no *g*

GOG
Eze 38: 18 When *G* attacks the land of Israel,
Rev 20: 8 *G* and Magog—to gather them

GOLD
1Ki 20: 3 'Your silver and *g* are mine,
Job 22: 25 then the Almighty will be your *g,*
23: 10 tested me, I will come forth as *g.*
28: 15 cannot be bought with the finest *g,*
31: 24 "If I have put my trust in *g*
Ps 19: 10 They are more precious than *g,*
119:127 more than *g,* more than pure *g,*
Pr 3: 14 and yields better returns than *g.*
22: 1 esteemed is better than silver or *g.*
Hag 2: 8 The silver is mine and the *g* is mine
Mt 2: 11 and presented him with gifts of *g*
Rev 3: 18 to buy from me *g* refined in the fire,

GOLGOTHA*
Mt 27: 33 to a place called *G* (which means
Mk 15: 22 to the place called *G* (which means
Jn 19: 17 (which in Aramaic is called *G).*

GOLIATH
Philistine giant killed by David (1Sa 17; 21:9).

GOMORRAH
Ge 19: 24 sulfur on Sodom and *G*—
Mt 10: 15 and *G* on the day of judgment
2Pe 2: 6 and *G* by burning them to ashes,
Jude : 7 *G* and the surrounding towns gave

GOOD
Ge 1: 4 God saw that the light was *g,*
1: 10 And God saw that it was *g.*
1: 12 And God saw that it was *g.*
1: 18 And God saw that it was *g.*
1: 21 And God saw that it was *g.*
1: 25 And God saw that it was *g.*
1: 31 he had made, and it was very *g.*
2: 9 and the tree of the knowledge of *g*
2: 9 pleasing to the eye and *g* for food.
2: 18 "It is not *g* for the man to be alone.
3: 22 become like one of us, knowing *g*
50: 20 but God intended it for *g*
2Ch 7: 3 "He is *g;* / his love endures
31: 20 doing what was *g* and right
Job 2: 10 Shall we accept *g* from God,
Ps 14: 1 there is no one who does *g.*
34: 8 Taste and see that the LORD is *g;*
34: 14 Turn from evil and do *g;*
37: 3 Trust in the LORD and do *g;*
37: 27 Turn from evil and do *g;*
52: 9 for your name is *g.*
53: 3 there is no one who does *g,*
84: 11 no *g* thing does he withhold
86: 5 You are forgiving and *g,* O Lord
100: 5 For the LORD is *g* and his love
103: 5 satisfies your desires with *g* things,
112: 5 *G* will come to him who is
119: 68 You are *g,* and what you do is *g;*
133: 1 How *g* and pleasant it is
145: 9 The LORD is *g* to all;
147: 1 How *g* it is to sing praises
Pr 3: 4 you will win favor and a *g* name
3: 27 Do not withhold *g*
11: 27 He who seeks *g* finds *g* will,
13: 22 A *g* man leaves an inheritance
14: 22 those who plan what is *g* find love
15: 3 on the wicked and the *g.*
15: 23 and how *g* is a timely word!
15: 30 *g* news gives health to the bones.
17: 22 A cheerful heart is *g* medicine,
18: 22 He who finds a wife finds what is *g*
19: 2 It is not *g* to have zeal
22: 1 A *g* name is more desirable
31: 12 She brings him *g,* not harm,
Ecc 12: 14 whether it is *g* or evil.
Isa 5: 20 Woe to those who call evil *g*
40: 9 You who bring *g* tidings
52: 7 the feet of those who bring *g* news,
61: 1 me to preach *g* news to the poor.
Jer 6: 16 ask where the *g* way is,
13: 23 Neither can you do *g*
32: 39 the *g* of their children after them.
Eze 34: 14 I will tend them in a *g* pasture,
Mic 6: 8 has showed you, O man, what is *g.*
Na 1: 15 the feet of one who brings *g* news,
Mt 5: 45 sun to rise on the evil and the *g,*
7: 11 Father in heaven give *g* gifts
7: 17 Likewise every *g* tree bears *g* fruit,
7: 18 A *g* tree cannot bear bad fruit,
12: 35 The *g* man brings *g* things out
13: 8 Still other seed fell on *g* soil,
13: 24 is like a man who sowed *g* seed
13: 48 and collected the *g* fish in baskets,
19: 17 "There is only One who is *g.*
22: 10 both *g* and bad, and the wedding
25: 21 'Well done, *g* and faithful servant!
Mk 1: 15 Repent and believe the *g* news!"
3: 4 lawful on the Sabbath: to do *g*
4: 8 Still other seed fell on *g* soil.
8: 36 What *g* is it for a man
10: 18 "No one is *g*— except God alone.
16: 15 preach the *g* news to all creation.
Lk 2: 10 I bring you *g* news
3: 9 does not produce *g* fruit will be
6: 27 do *g* to those who hate you,
6: 43 nor does a bad tree bear *g* fruit.
6: 45 The *g* man brings *g* things out
8: 8 Still other seed fell on *g* soil.
9: 25 What *g* is it for a man
14: 34 "Salt is *g,* but if it loses its saltiness,
18: 19 "No one is *g*— except God alone.
19: 17 " 'Well done, my *g* servant!'
Jn 10: 11 "I am the *g* shepherd.
Ro 3: 12 there is no one who does *g,*
7: 12 is holy, righteous and *g.*
7: 16 want to do, I agree that the law is *g.*
7: 18 I have the desire to do what is *g,*
8: 28 for the *g* of those who love him,
10: 15 feet of those who bring *g* news!"
12: 2 his *g,* pleasing and perfect will.
12: 9 Hate what is evil; cling to what is *g.*
13: 4 For he is God's servant to do you *g*
16: 19 you to be wise about what is *g,*
1Co 7: 1 It is *g* for a man not to marry.
10: 24 should seek his own *g,* but the *g*
15: 33 Bad company corrupts *g* character
2Co 9: 8 you will abound in every *g* work.
Gal 4: 18 provided the purpose is *g,*
6: 9 us not become weary in doing *g,*
6: 10 as we have opportunity, let us do *g*
Eph 2: 10 in Christ Jesus to do *g* works,
6: 8 everyone for whatever *g* he does,
Php 1: 6 that he who began a *g* work
Col 1: 10 bearing fruit in every *g* work,
1Th 5: 21 Hold on to the *g.*
1Ti 3: 7 have a *g* reputation with outsiders,
4: 4 For everything God created is *g,*
6: 12 Fight the *g* fight of the faith.
6: 18 them to do *g,* to be rich in *g* deeds,
2Ti 3: 17 equipped for every *g* work.
4: 7 I have fought the *g* fight, I have
Tit 1: 8 loves what is *g,* who is
2: 7 an example by doing what is *g.*
2: 14 his very own, eager to do what is *g.*
Heb 5: 14 to distinguish *g* from evil.
10: 24 on toward love and *g* deeds.
12: 10 but God disciplines us for our *g,*
13: 16 do not forget to do *g* and to share
Jas 4: 17 who knows the *g* he ought to do
1Pe 2: 3 you have tasted that the Lord is *g.*
2: 12 Live such *g* lives among the pagans
2: 18 not only to those who are *g*
3: 17 to suffer for doing *g*

GOODS
Ecc 5: 11 As *g* increase,

GORGE
Pr 23: 20 or *g* themselves on meat,

GOSHEN
Ge 45: 10 You shall live in the region of *G*
Ex 8: 22 differently with the land of *G,*

GOSPEL
Ro 1: 16 I am not ashamed of the *g,*
15: 16 duty of proclaiming the *g* of God,
15: 20 to preach the *g* where Christ was
1Co 1: 17 to preach the *g*— not with words
9: 12 rather than hinder the *g* of Christ.
9: 14 who preach the *g* should receive
9: 16 Woe to me if I do not preach the *g!*
15: 1 you of the *g* I preached to you,
15: 2 By this *g* you are saved,
2Co 4: 4 light of the *g* of the glory of Christ,
9: 13 your confession of the *g*
Gal 1: 7 a different *g*— which is really no *g*
Eph 6: 15 comes from the *g* of peace.
Php 1: 27 in a manner worthy of the *g*

Col 1: 23 This is the *g* that you heard
1Th 2: 4 by God to be entrusted with the *g*.
2Th 1: 8 do not obey the *g* of our Lord Jesus
2Ti 1: 10 immortality to light through the *g*.
Rev 14: 6 he had the eternal *g* to proclaim

GOSSIP*
Pr 11: 13 A *g* betrays a confidence,
16: 28 and a *g* separates close friends.
18: 8 of a *g* are like choice morsels;
20: 19 A *g* betrays a confidence;
26: 20 without *g* a quarrel dies down.
26: 22 of a *g* are like choice morsels;
2Co 12: 20 slander, *g*, arrogance and disorder.

GOVERN (GOVERNMENT)
Ge 1: 16 the greater light to *g* the day
Job 34: 17 Can he who hates justice *g*?
Ro 12: 8 it is leadership, let him *g* diligently;

GOVERNMENT (GOVERN)
Isa 9: 6 and the *g* will be on his shoulders.

GRACE* (GRACIOUS)
Ps 45: 2 lips have been anointed with *g*,
Pr 1: 9 will be a garland to *g* your head
3: 22 an ornament to *g* your neck.
3: 34 but gives *g* to the humble.
4: 9 She will set a garland of *g*
Isa 26: 10 Though *g* is shown to the wicked,
Jnh 2: 8 forfeit the *g* that could be theirs.
Zec 12: 10 of Jerusalem a spirit of *g*
Lk 2: 40 and the *g* of God was upon him.
Jn 1: 14 who came from the Father, full of *g*
1: 16 of his *g* we have all received one
1: 17 *g* and truth came through Jesus
Ac 4: 33 and much *g* was upon them all.
6: 8 a man full of God's *g* and power,
11: 23 saw the evidence of the *g* of God,
13: 43 them to continue in the *g* of God.
14: 3 message of his *g* by enabling them
14: 26 they had been committed to the *g*
15: 11 We believe it is through the *g*
15: 40 by the brothers to the *g* of the Lord
18: 27 to those who by *g* had believed.
20: 24 testifying to the gospel of God's *g*.
20: 32 to God and to the word of his *g*,
Ro 1: 5 we received *g* and apostleship
1: 7 *G* and peace to you
3: 24 and are justified freely by his *g*
4: 16 be by *g* and may be guaranteed
5: 2 access by faith into this *g*
5: 15 came by the *g* of the one man,
5: 15 how much more did God's *g*
5: 17 God's abundant provision of *g*
5: 20 where sin increased, *g* increased all
5: 21 also *g* might reign
6: 1 on sinning so that *g* may increase?
6: 14 you are not under law, but under *g*.
6: 15 we are not under law but under *g*?
11: 5 there is a remnant chosen by *g*.
11: 6 if by *g*, then it is no longer by works
11: 6 if it were, *g* would no longer be *g*.
12: 3 For by the *g* given me I say
12: 6 according to the *g* given us.
15: 15 because of the *g* God gave me
16: 20 The *g* of our Lord Jesus be
1Co 1: 3 *G* and peace to you
1: 4 of his *g* given you in Christ Jesus.
3: 10 By the *g* God has given me,
15: 10 But by the *g* of God I am what I am
15: 10 but the *g* of God that was with me.
15: 10 his *g* to me was not without effect.
16: 23 The *g* of the Lord Jesus be with you
2Co 1: 2 *G* and peace to you
1: 12 wisdom but according to God's *g*.
4: 15 so that the *g* that is reaching more
6: 1 not to receive God's *g* in vain.
8: 1 to know about the *g* that God has
8: 6 also to completion this act of *g*
8: 7 also excel in this *g* of giving.
8: 9 For you know the *g*
9: 8 able to make all *g* abound to you,
9: 14 of the surpassing *g* God has given
12: 9 "My *g* is sufficient for you,
13: 14 May the *g* of the Lord Jesus Christ,
Gal 1: 3 *G* and peace to you
1: 6 the one who called you by the *g*
1: 15 from birth and called me by his *g*,
2: 9 when they recognized the *g* given
2: 21 I do not set aside the *g* of God,
3: 18 God in his *g* gave it to Abraham
5: 4 you have fallen away from *g*.
6: 18 The *g* of our Lord Jesus Christ be
Eph 1: 2 *G* and peace to you
1: 6 to the praise of his glorious *g*,
1: 7 riches of God's *g* that he lavished
2: 5 it is by *g* you have been saved.
2: 7 the incomparable riches of his *g*,
2: 8 For it is by *g* you have been saved,
3: 2 of God's *g* that was given to me
3: 7 by the gift of God's *g* given me
3: 8 God's people, this *g* was given me:
4: 7 to each one of us *g* has been given
6: 24 *G* to all who love our Lord Jesus
Php 1: 2 *G* and peace to you
1: 7 all of you share in God's *g* with me.
4: 23 The *g* of the Lord Jesus Christ be
Col 1: 2 *G* and peace to you
1: 6 understood God's *g* in all its truth.
4: 6 conversation be always full of *g*,
4: 18 *G* be with you.
1Th 1: 1 and the Lord Jesus Christ: *G*
5: 28 The *g* of our Lord Jesus Christ be
2Th 1: 2 *G* and peace to you
1: 12 according to the *g* of our God
2: 16 and by his *g* gave us eternal
3: 18 The *g* of our Lord Jesus Christ be
1Ti 1: 2 my true son in the faith: *G*,
1: 14 The *g* of our Lord was poured out
6: 21 *G* be with you.
2Ti 1: 2 To Timothy, my dear son: *G*,
1: 9 This *g* was given us in Christ Jesus
1: 9 because of his own purpose and *g*.
2: 1 be strong in the *g* that is
4: 22 *G* be with you.
Tit 1: 4 *G* and peace from God the Father
2: 11 For the *g* of God that brings
3: 7 having been justified by his *g*,
3: 15 *G* be with you all.
Phm : 3 *G* to you and peace
: 25 The *g* of the Lord Jesus Christ be
Heb 2: 9 that by the *g* of God he might taste
4: 16 find *g* to help us in our time of need
4: 16 the throne of *g* with confidence,
10: 29 and who has insulted the Spirit of *g*
12: 15 See to it that no one misses the *g*
13: 9 hearts to be strengthened by *g*,
13: 25 *G* be with you all.
Jas 4: 6 but gives *g* to the humble."
4: 6 But he gives us more *g*. That is why
1Pe 1: 2 *G* and peace be yours in abundance
1: 10 who spoke of the *g* that was
1: 13 fully on the *g* to be given you
4: 10 faithfully administering God's *g*
5: 5 but gives *g* to the humble."
5: 10 the God of all *g*, who called you
5: 12 and testifying that this is the true *g*
2Pe 1: 2 *G* and peace be yours in abundance
3: 18 But grow in the *g* and knowledge
2Jn : 3 and will be with us forever: *G*,
Jude : 4 who change the *g* of our God
Rev 1: 4 *G* and peace to you
22: 21 The *g* of the Lord Jesus be

GRACIOUS (GRACE)
Ex 34: 6 the compassionate and *g* God,
Nu 6: 25 and be *g* to you;
Ne 9: 17 But you are a forgiving God, *g*
Ps 67: 1 May God be *g* to us and bless us
Pr 22: 11 a pure heart and whose speech is *g*
Isa 30: 18 Yet the LORD longs to be *g* to you

GRAIN
Lev 2: 1 When someone brings a *g* offering
Lk 17: 35 women will be grinding *g* together;
1Co 9: 9 ox while it is treading out the *g*."

GRANDCHILDREN (CHILD)
1Ti 5: 4 But if a widow has children or *g*,

GRANDMOTHER (MOTHER)
2Ti 1: 5 which first lived in your *g* Lois

GRANT (GRANTED)
Ps 20: 5 May the LORD *g* all your requests
51: 12 *g* me a willing spirit, to sustain me.

GRANTED (GRANT)
Pr 10: 24 what the righteous desire will be *g*.
Mt 15: 28 great faith! Your request is *g*."
Php 1: 29 For it has been *g* to you on behalf

GRAPES
Nu 13: 23 branch bearing a single cluster of *g*.
Jer 31: 29 'The fathers have eaten sour *g*,
Eze 18: 2 " 'The fathers eat sour *g*,
Mt 7: 16 Do people pick *g* from thornbushes
Rev 14: 18 and gather the clusters of *g*

GRASPED
Php 2: 6 with God something to be *g*,

GRASS
Ps 103: 15 As for man, his days are like *g*,
Isa 40: 6 "All men are like *g*,
Mt 6: 30 If that is how God clothes the *g*
1Pe 1: 24 "All men are like *g*,

GRASSHOPPERS
Nu 13: 33 We seemed like *g* in our own eyes,

GRATIFY* (GRATITUDE)
Ro 13: 14 think about how to *g* the desires
Gal 5: 16 and you will not *g* the desires

GRATITUDE (GRATIFY)
Col 3: 16 and spiritual songs with *g*

GRAVE (GRAVES)
Nu 19: 16 who touches a human bone or a *g*,
Dt 34: 6 day no one knows where his *g* is.
Ps 5: 9 Their throat is an open *g*;
49: 15 will redeem my life from the *g*;
Pr 7: 27 Her house is a highway to the *g*,
Hos 13: 14 Where, O *g*, is your destruction?
Jn 11: 44 "Take off the *g* clothes
Ac 2: 27 you will not abandon me to the *g*,

GRAVES (GRAVE)
Eze 37: 12 I am going to open your *g*
Jn 5: 28 are in their *g* will hear his voice
Ro 3: 13 "Their throats are open *g*;

GRAY
Pr 16: 31 *G* hair is a crown of splendor;
20: 29 *g* hair the splendor of the old.

GREAT (GREATER GREATEST GREATNESS)
Ge 12: 2 I will make your name *g*,
12: 2 "I will make you into a *g* nation
Ex 32: 11 out of Egypt with *g* power
Nu 14: 19 In accordance with your *g* love,
Dt 4: 32 so *g* as this ever happened,
10: 17 the *g* God, mighty and awesome,
29: 28 in *g* wrath the LORD uprooted
Jos 7: 9 do for your own *g* name?"
Jdg 16: 5 you the secret of his *g* strength
2Sa 7: 22 "How *g* you are, O Sovereign
22: 36 you stoop down to make me *g*.
24: 14 for his mercy is *g*; but do not let me
1Ch 17: 19 made known all these *g* promises.
Ps 18: 35 you stoop down to make me *g*.
19: 11 in keeping them there is *g* reward.
47: 2 the *g* King over all the earth!
57: 10 For *g* is your love, reaching
68: 11 and *g* was the company
89: 1 of the LORD's *g* love forever;
103: 11 so *g* is his love for those who fear
107: 43 consider the *g* love of the LORD.
108: 4 For *g* is your love, higher
117: 2 For *g* is his love toward us,
119:165 *G* peace have they who love your

145: 3 *G* is the LORD and most worthy
Pr 22: 1 is more desirable than *g* riches;
23: 24 of a righteous man has *g* joy;
Isa 42: 21 to make his law *g* and glorious.
Jer 27: 5 With my *g* power and outstretched
32: 19 *g* are your purposes and mighty are
La 3: 23 *g* is your faithfulness.
Da 9: 4 "O Lord, the *g* and awesome God,
Joel 2: 11 The day of the LORD is *g*;
2: 20 Surely he has done *g* things.
Zep 1: 14 "The *g* day of the LORD is near—
Mal 1: 11 My name will be *g*
4: 5 the prophet Elijah before that *g*
Mt 20: 26 whoever wants to become *g*
Mk 10: 43 whoever wants to become *g*
Lk 6: 23 because *g* is your reward in heaven.
6: 35 Then your reward will be *g*,
21: 27 in a cloud with power and *g* glory.
Eph 1: 19 and his incomparably *g* power
2: 4 But because of his *g* love for us,
1Ti 6: 6 with contentment is *g* gain.
Tit 2: 13 glorious appearing of our *g* God
Heb 2: 3 if we ignore such a *g* salvation?
1Jn 3: 1 How *g* is the love the Father has
Rev 6: 17 For the *g* day of their wrath has
20: 11 Then I saw a *g* white throne

GREATER (GREAT)
Mt 11: 11 there has not risen anyone *g*
12: 6 I tell you that one *g*
12: 41 and now one *g* than Jonah is here.
12: 42 now one *g* than Solomon is here.
Mk 12: 31 There is no commandment *g*
Jn 1: 50 You shall see *g* things than that."
3: 30 He must become *g*; I must become
14: 12 He will do even *g* things than these
15: 13 *G* love has no one than this,
1Co 12: 31 But eagerly desire the *g* gifts.
2Co 3: 11 how much *g* is the glory
Heb 3: 3 the builder of a house has *g* honor
3: 3 worthy of *g* honor than Moses,
7: 7 lesser person is blessed by the *g*.
11: 26 as of *g* value than the treasures
1Jn 3: 20 For God is *g* than our hearts,
4: 4 is in you is *g* than the one who is

GREATEST (GREAT)
Mt 22: 38 is the first and *g* commandment.
23: 11 *g* among you will be your servant.
Lk 9: 48 least among you all—he is the *g*."
1Co 13: 13 But the *g* of these is love.

GREATNESS* (GREAT)
Ex 15: 7 In the *g* of your majesty
Dt 3: 24 to show to your servant your *g*
32: 3 Oh, praise the *g* of our God!
1Ch 29: 11 O LORD, is the *g* and the power
2Ch 9: 6 half the *g* of your wisdom was told
Est 10: 2 account of the *g* of Mordecai
Ps 145: 3 his *g* no one can fathom.
150: 2 praise him for his surpassing *g*.
Isa 63: 1 forward in the *g* of his strength?
Eze 38: 23 I will show my *g* and my holiness,
Da 4: 22 your *g* has grown until it reaches
5: 18 and *g* and glory and splendor.
7: 27 and *g* of the kingdoms
Mic 5: 4 will live securely, for then his *g*
Lk 9: 43 And they were all amazed at the *g*
Php 3: 8 compared to the surpassing *g*

GREED (GREEDY)
Lk 12: 15 on your guard against all kinds of *g*
Ro 1: 29 kind of wickedness, evil, *g*
Eph 5: 3 or of any kind of impurity, or of *g*,
Col 3: 5 evil desires and *g*, which is idolatry
2Pe 2: 14 experts in *g*— an accursed brood!

GREEDY (GREED)
Pr 15: 27 A *g* man brings trouble
1Co 6: 10 nor thieves nor the *g* nor drunkards
Eph 5: 5 No immoral, impure or *g* person—
1Pe 5: 2 not *g* for money, but eager to serve;

GREEK (GREEKS)
Gal 3: 28 There is neither Jew nor *G*,
Col 3: 11 Here there is no *G* or Jew,

GREEKS (GREEK)
1Co 1: 22 miraculous signs and *G* look

GREEN
Ps 23: 2 makes me lie down in *g* pastures,

GREW (GROW)
Lk 1: 80 And the child *g* and became strong
2: 52 And Jesus *g* in wisdom and stature,
Ac 9: 31 by the Holy Spirit, it *g* in numbers,
16: 5 in the faith and *g* daily in numbers.

GRIEF (GRIEFS GRIEVANCES GRIEVE GRIEVED)
Ps 10: 14 O God, do see trouble and *g*;
Pr 10: 1 but a foolish son *g* to his mother.
14: 13 and joy may end in *g*.
17: 21 To have a fool for a son brings *g*;
Ecc 1: 18 the more knowledge, the more *g*.
La 3: 32 Though he brings *g*, he will show
Jn 16: 20 but your *g* will turn to joy.
1Pe 1: 6 had to suffer *g* in all kinds of trials.

GRIEFS* (GRIEF)
1Ti 6: 10 pierced themselves with many *g*.

GRIEVANCES* (GRIEF)
Col 3: 13 forgive whatever *g* you may have

GRIEVE (GRIEF)
Eph 4: 30 do not *g* the Holy Spirit of God,
1Th 4: 13 or to *g* like the rest of men,

GRIEVED (GRIEF)
Isa 63: 10 and *g* his Holy Spirit.

GRINDING
Lk 17: 35 women will be *g* grain together;

GROAN (GROANING GROANS)
Ro 8: 23 *g* inwardly as we wait eagerly
2Co 5: 4 For while we are in this tent, we *g*

GROANING (GROAN)
Ex 2: 24 God heard their *g* and he
Eze 21: 7 'Why are you *g*?' you shall say,
Ro 8: 22 that the whole creation has been *g*

GROANS (GROAN)
Ro 8: 26 with *g* that words cannot express.

GROUND
Ge 1: 10 God called the dry *g* "land,"
3: 17 "Cursed is the *g* because of you;
4: 10 blood cries out to me from the *g*.
Ex 3: 5 where you are standing is holy *g*."
15: 19 walked through the sea on dry *g*.
Isa 53: 2 and like a root out of dry *g*.
Mt 10: 29 fall to the *g* apart from the will
25: 25 and hid your talent in the *g*.
Jn 8: 6 to write on the *g* with his finger.
Eph 6: 13 you may be able to stand your *g*,

GROW (FULL-GROWN GREW GROWING GROWS)
Pr 13: 11 by little makes it *g*.
20: 13 not love sleep or you will *g* poor;
Isa 40: 31 they will run and not *g* weary,
Mt 6: 28 See how the lilies of the field *g*.
1Co 3: 6 watered it, but God made it *g*.
2Pe 3: 18 But *g* in the grace and knowledge

GROWING (GROW)
Col 1: 6 this gospel is bearing fruit and *g*,
1: 10 *g* in the knowledge of God,
2Th 1: 3 your faith is *g* more and more,

GROWS (GROW)
Eph 4: 16 *g* and builds itself up in love,
Col 2: 19 *g* as God causes it to grow.

GRUMBLE (GRUMBLED GRUMBLERS GRUMBLING)
1Co 10: 10 And do not *g*, as some of them did
Jas 5: 9 Don't *g* against each other,

GRUMBLED (GRUMBLE)
Ex 15: 24 So the people *g* against Moses,
Nu 14: 29 and who has *g* against me.

GRUMBLERS* (GRUMBLE)
Jude : 16 These men are *g* and faultfinders;

GRUMBLING (GRUMBLE)
Jn 6: 43 "Stop *g* among yourselves,"
1Pe 4: 9 to one another without *g*.

GUARANTEE (GUARANTEEING)
Heb 7: 22 Jesus has become the *g*

GUARANTEEING* (GUARANTEE)
2Co 1: 22 as a deposit, *g* what is to come.
5: 5 as a deposit, *g* what is to come.
Eph 1: 14 who is a deposit *g* our inheritance

GUARD (GUARDS)
1Sa 2: 9 He will *g* the feet of his saints,
Ps 141: 3 Set a *g* over my mouth, O LORD;
Pr 2: 11 and understanding will *g* you.
4: 13 *g* it well, for it is your life.
4: 23 Above all else, *g* your heart,
7: 2 *g* my teachings as the apple
Isa 52: 12 the God of Israel will be your rear *g*
Mk 13: 33 Be on *g*! Be alert! You do not know
Lk 12: 1 "Be on your *g* against the yeast
12: 15 Be on your *g* against all kinds
Ac 20: 31 So be on your *g*! Remember that
1Co 16: 13 Be on your *g*; stand firm in the faith
Php 4: 7 will *g* your hearts and your minds
1Ti 6: 20 *g* what has been entrusted
2Ti 1: 14 *G* the good deposit that was

GUARDS (GUARD)
Pr 13: 3 He who *g* his lips *g* his life,
19: 16 who obeys instructions *g* his life,
21: 23 He who *g* his mouth and his tongue
22: 5 he who *g* his soul stays far

GUIDANCE (GUIDE)
Pr 1: 5 and let the discerning get *g*—
11: 14 For lack of *g* a nation falls,
24: 6 for waging war you need *g*,

GUIDE (GUIDANCE GUIDED GUIDES)
Ex 13: 21 of cloud to *g* them on their way
15: 13 In your strength you will *g* them
Ne 9: 19 cease to *g* them on their path,
Ps 25: 5 *g* me in your truth and teach me,
43: 3 let them *g* me;
48: 14 he will be our *g* even to the end.
67: 4 and *g* the nations of the earth.
73: 24 You *g* me with your counsel,
139: 10 even there your hand will *g* me,
Pr 4: 11 I *g* you in the way of wisdom
6: 22 When you walk, they will *g* you;
Isa 58: 11 The LORD will *g* you always;
Jn 16: 13 comes, he will *g* you into all truth.

GUIDED (GUIDE)
Ps 107: 30 he *g* them to their desired haven.

GUIDES (GUIDE)
Ps 23: 3 He *g* me in paths of righteousness
25: 9 He *g* the humble in what is right
Pr 11: 3 The integrity of the upright *g* them,
16: 23 A wise man's heart *g* his mouth,
Mt 23: 16 "Woe to you, blind *g*! You say,
23: 24 You blind *g*! You strain out a gnat

GUILT (GUILTY)
Lev 5: 15 It is a *g* offering.
Ps 32: 5 the *g* of my sin.
38: 4 My *g* has overwhelmed me
Isa 6: 7 your *g* is taken away and your sin
Jer 2: 22 the stain of your *g* is still before me
Eze 18: 19 'Why does the son not share the *g*

GUILTY (GUILT)
Ex 34: 7 does not leave the *g* unpunished;
Mk 3: 29 Spirit will never be forgiven; he is *g*
Jn 8: 46 Can any of you prove me *g* of sin?
1Co 11: 27 in an unworthy manner will be *g*
Heb 10: 2 and would no longer have felt *g*
10: 22 to cleanse us from a *g* conscience
Jas 2: 10 at just one point is *g* of breaking all

HABAKKUK*
Prophet to Judah (Hab 1:1; 3:1).

HABIT
1Ti 5: 13 they get into the *h* of being idle
Heb 10: 25 as some are in the *h* of doing,

HADAD
Edomite adversary of Solomon (1Ki 11:14–25).

HADES*
Mt 16: 18 the gates of *H* will not overcome it.
Rev 1: 18 And I hold the keys of death and *H*
6: 8 *H* was following close behind him.
20: 13 and *H* gave up the dead that were
20: 14 *H* were thrown into the lake of fire.

HAGAR
Servant of Sarah, wife of Abraham, mother of Ishmael (Ge 16:1–6; 25:12). Driven away by Sarah while pregnant (Ge 16:5–16); after birth of Isaac (Ge 21:9–21; Gal 4:21–31).

HAGGAI*
Post-exilic prophet who encouraged rebuilding of the temple (Ezr 5:1; 6:14; Hag 1–2).

HAIL
Ex 9: 19 the *h* will fall on every man
Rev 8: 7 and there came *h* and fire mixed

HAIR (HAIRS HAIRY)
Lev 19: 27 " 'Do not cut the *h* at the sides
Nu 6: 5 he must let the *h* of his head grow
Pr 16: 31 Gray *h* is a crown of splendor;
20: 29 gray *h* the splendor of the old.
Lk 7: 44 and wiped them with her *h*.
21: 18 But not a *h* of your head will perish
Jn 11: 2 and wiped his feet with her *h*.
12: 3 and wiped his feet with her *h*.
1Co 11: 6 for a woman to have her *h* cut
11: 6 she should have her *h* cut off;
11: 14 that if a man has long *h*,
11: 15 For long *h* is given to her
11: 15 but that if a woman has long *h*,
1Ti 2: 9 not with braided *h* or gold or pearls
1Pe 3: 3 as braided *h* and the wearing
Rev 1: 14 and *h* were white like wool,

HAIRS (HAIR)
Mt 10: 30 even the very *h* of your head are all
Lk 12: 7 the very *h* of your head are all

HAIRY (HAIR)
Ge 27: 11 "But my brother Esau is a *h* man,

HALF
Ex 30: 13 This *h* shekel is an offering
Jos 8: 33 *H* of the people stood in front
1Ki 3: 25 give *h* to one and *h* to the other."
10: 7 Indeed, not even *h* was told me;
Est 5: 3 Even up to *h* the kingdom,
Da 7: 25 him for a time, times and *h* a time.
Mk 6: 23 up to *h* my kingdom."

HALF-TRIBE (TRIBE)
Nu 32: 33 and the *h* of Manasseh son

HALLELUJAH*
Rev 19: 1, 3, 4, 6.

HALLOWED* (HOLY)
Mt 6: 9 *h* be your name,
Lk 11: 2 *h* be your name,

HALT
Job 38: 11 here is where your proud waves *h*?

HALTER*
Pr 26: 3 for the horse, a *h* for the donkey,

HAM
Son of Noah (Ge 5:32; 1Ch 1:4), father of Canaan (Ge 9:18; 10:6–20; 1Ch 1:8–16). Saw Noah's nakedness (Ge 9:20–27).

HAMAN
Agagite nobleman honored by Xerxes (Est 3:1–2). Plotted to exterminate the Jews because of Mordecai (Est 3:3–15). Forced to honor Mordecai (Est 5–6). Plot exposed by Esther (Est 5:1–8; 7:1–8). Hanged (Est 7:9–10).

HAMPERED*
Pr 4: 12 you walk, your steps will not be *h*;

HAND (HANDED HANDFUL HANDS OPENHANDED)
Ge 24: 2 "Put your *h* under my thigh.
47: 29 put your *h* under my thigh
Ex 13: 3 out of it with a mighty *h*.
15: 6 Your right *h*, O LORD,
33: 22 and cover you with my *h*
Dt 12: 7 in everything you have put your *h*
1Ki 8: 42 and your mighty *h* and your
13: 4 But the *h* he stretched out
1Ch 29: 14 you only what comes from your *h*.
29: 16 it comes from your *h*, and all
2Ch 6: 15 with your *h* you have fulfilled it—
Ne 4: 17 materials did their work with one *h*
Job 40: 4 I put my *h* over my mouth.
Ps 16: 8 Because he is at my right *h*,
32: 4 your *h* was heavy upon me;
37: 24 the LORD upholds him with his *h*.
44: 3 it was your right *h*, your arm,
45: 9 at your right *h* is the royal bride
63: 8 your right *h* upholds me.
75: 8 In the *h* of the LORD is a cup
91: 7 ten thousand at your right *h*,
98: 1 his right *h* and his holy arm
109: 31 at the right *h* of the needy one,
110: 1 "Sit at my right *h*
137: 5 may my right *h* forget ›its skill‹.
139: 10 even there your *h* will guide me,
145: 16 You open your *h*
Pr 27: 16 or grasping oil with the *h*.
Ecc 5: 15 that he can carry in his *h*.
9: 10 Whatever your *h* finds to do,
Isa 11: 8 the young child put his *h*
40: 12 the waters in the hollow of his *h*,
41: 13 who takes hold of your right *h*
44: 5 still another will write on his *h*,
48: 13 My own *h* laid the foundations
64: 8 we are all the work of your *h*.
La 3: 3 he has turned his *h* against me
Da 10: 10 *h* touched me and set me trembling
Jnh 4: 11 people who cannot tell their right *h*
Hab 3: 4 rays flashed from his *h*,
Mt 5: 30 if your right *h* causes you to sin,
6: 3 know what your right *h* is doing,
12: 10 a man with a shriveled *h* was there.
18: 8 If your *h* or your foot causes you
22: 44 "Sit at my right *h*
26: 64 at the right *h* of the Mighty One
Mk 3: 1 a man with a shriveled *h* was there.
9: 43 If your *h* causes you to sin, cut it off
12: 36 "Sit at my right *h*
16: 19 and he sat at the right *h* of God.
Lk 6: 6 there whose right *h* was shriveled.
20: 42 "Sit at my right *h*
22: 69 at the right *h* of the mighty God."
Jn 10: 28 one can snatch them out of my *h*.
20: 27 Reach out your *h* and put it
Ac 7: 55 Jesus standing at the right *h* of God
1Co 12: 15 I am not a *h*, I do not belong
Heb 1: 13 "Sit at my right *h*
Rev 13: 16 to receive a mark on his right *h*

HANDED (HAND)
Da 7: 25 The saints will be *h* over to him
1Ti 1: 20 whom I have *h* over to Satan

HANDFUL (HAND)
Ecc 4: 6 Better one *h* with tranquillity

HANDLE (HANDLES)
Col 2: 21 "Do not *h*! Do not taste! Do not

HANDLES (HANDLE)
2Ti 2: 15 who correctly *h* the word of truth.

HANDS (HAND)
Ge 27: 22 but the *h* are the *h* of Esau."
Ex 17: 11 As long as Moses held up his *h*,
29: 10 his sons shall lay their *h* on its head
Dt 6: 8 Tie them as symbols on your *h*
Jdg 7: 6 lapped with their *h* to their mouths.
2Ki 11: 12 and the people clapped their *h*
2Ch 6: 4 who with his *h* has fulfilled what he
Ps 22: 16 they have pierced my *h*
24: 4 He who has clean *h* and a pure
31: 5 Into your *h* I commit my spirit;
31: 15 My times are in your *h*;
47: 1 Clap your *h*, all you nations;
63: 4 and in your name I will lift up my *h*
Pr 10: 4 Lazy *h* make a man poor,
21: 25 because his *h* refuse to work.
31: 13 and works with eager *h*.
31: 20 and extends her *h* to the needy.
Ecc 10: 18 if his *h* are idle, the house leaks.
Isa 35: 3 Strengthen the feeble *h*,
49: 16 you on the palms of my *h*;
55: 12 will clap their *h*.
65: 2 All day long I have held out my *h*
La 3: 41 Let us lift up our hearts and our *h*
Lk 23: 46 into your *h* I commit my spirit."
Ac 6: 6 who prayed and laid their *h*
8: 18 at the laying on of the apostles' *h*,
13: 3 they placed their *h* on them
19: 6 When Paul placed his *h* on them,
28: 8 placed his *h* on him and healed him
1Th 4: 11 and to work with your *h*,
1Ti 2: 8 to lift up holy *h* in prayer,
4: 14 body of elders laid their *h* on you.
5: 22 hasty in the laying on of *h*,
2Ti 1: 6 you through the laying on of my *h*.
Heb 6: 2 the laying on of *h*, the resurrection

HANDSOME*
Ge 39: 6 Now Joseph was well-built and *h*,
1Sa 16: 12 a fine appearance and *h* features.
17: 42 ruddy and *h*, and he despised him.
2Sa 14: 25 praised for his *h* appearance
1Ki 1: 6 also very *h* and was born next
SS 1: 16 *Beloved* How *h* you are, my lover!
Eze 23: 6 all of them *h* young men,
23: 12 horsemen, all *h* young men.
23: 23 with them, *h* young men,
Da 1: 4 without any physical defect, *h*,
Zec 11: 13 the *h* price at which they priced me

HANG (HANGED HANGING HUNG)
Mt 22: 40 and the Prophets *h* on these two

HANGED (HANG)
Mt 27: 5 Then he went away and *h* himself.

HANGING (HANG)
Ac 10: 39 They killed him by *h* him on a tree,

HANNAH*
Wife of Elkanah, mother of Samuel (1Sa 1). Prayer at dedication of Samuel (1Sa 2:1–10). Blessed (1Sa 2:18–21).

HAPPIER (HAPPY)
Mt 18: 13 he is *h* about that one sheep
1Co 7: 40 she is *h* if she stays as she is—

HAPPINESS* (HAPPY)
Dt 24: 5 bring *h* to the wife he has married.
Est 8: 16 For the Jews it was a time of *h*
Job 7: 7 my eyes will never see *h* again.
Ecc 2: 26 gives wisdom, knowledge and *h*,
Mt 25: 21 Come and share your master's *h*!'
25: 23 Come and share your master's *h*!'

HAPPY* (HAPPIER HAPPINESS)
Ge 30: 13 The women will call me *h*."
30: 13 Then Leah said, "How *h* I am!
1Ki 4: 20 they drank and they were *h*.
10: 8 How *h* your men must be!
10: 8 men must be! How *h* your officials,
2Ch 9: 7 How *h* your men must be!
9: 7 men must be! How *h* your officials,
Est 5: 9 Haman went out that day *h*
5: 14 the king to the dinner and be *h*."
Ps 10: 6 I'll always be *h* and never have
68: 3 may they be *h* and joyful.
113: 9 as a *h* mother of children.
137: 8 *h* is he who repays you
Pr 15: 13 A *h* heart makes the face cheerful,

Ecc 3: 12 better for men than to be *h*
5: 19 to accept his lot and be *h*
7: 14 When times are good, be *h;*
11: 9 Be *h,* young man, while you are
Jnh 4: 6 Jonah was very *h* about the vine.
Zec 8: 19 and glad occasions and *h* festivals
1Co 7: 30 those who are *h,* as if they were not
2Co 7: 9 yet now I am *h,* not because you
7: 13 delighted to see how *h* Titus was,
Jas 5: 13 Is anyone *h?* Let him sing songs

HARD (HARDEN HARDENED HARDENING HARDENS HARDER HARDSHIP HARDSHIPS)
Ge 18: 14 Is anything too *h* for the LORD?
1Ki 10: 1 came to test him with *h* questions.
Pr 14: 23 All *h* work brings a profit,
Jer 32: 17 Nothing is too *h* for you.
Zec 7: 12 They made their hearts as *h* as flint
Mt 19: 23 it is *h* for a rich man
Mk 10: 5 your hearts were *h* that Moses
Jn 6: 60 disciples said, "This is a *h* teaching.
Ac 20: 35 of *h* work we must help the weak,
26: 14 It is *h* for you to kick
Ro 16: 12 woman who has worked very *h*
1Co 4: 12 We work *h* with our own hands.
2Co 6: 5 imprisonments and riots; in *h* work
1Th 5: 12 to respect those who work *h*
Rev 2: 2 your *h* work and your

HARDEN (HARD)
Ex 4: 21 I will *h* his heart so that he will not
Ps 95: 8 do not *h* your hearts as you did
Ro 9: 18 he hardens whom he wants to *h.*
Heb 3: 8 do not *h* your hearts

HARDENED (HARD)
Ex 10: 20 But the LORD *h* Pharaoh's heart,

HARDENING* (HARD)
Ro 11: 25 Israel has experienced a *h* in part
Eph 4: 18 in them due to the *h* of their hearts.

HARDENS* (HARD)
Pr 28: 14 he who *h* his heart falls into trouble
Ro 9: 18 and he *h* whom he wants to harden.

HARDER (HARD)
1Co 15: 10 No, I worked *h* than all of them—
2Co 11: 23 I have worked much *h,* been

HARDHEARTED* (HEART)
Dt 15: 7 do not be *h* or tightfisted

HARDSHIP (HARD)
Ro 8: 35 Shall trouble or *h* or persecution
2Ti 2: 3 Endure *h* with us like a good
4: 5 endure *h,* do the work
Heb 12: 7 Endure *h* as discipline; God is

HARDSHIPS (HARD)
Ac 14: 22 go through many *h* to enter
2Co 6: 4 in troubles, *h* and distresses;
12: 10 in insults, in *h,* in persecutions,
Rev 2: 3 and have endured *h* for my name,

HARM (HARMS)
1Ch 16: 22 do my prophets no *h.*"
Ps 105: 15 do my prophets no *h.*"
121: 6 the sun will not *h* you by day,
Pr 3: 29 not plot *h* against your neighbor,
12: 21 No *h* befalls the righteous,
31: 12 She brings him good, not *h,*
Jer 10: 5 they can do no *h*
29: 11 to prosper you and not to *h* you,
Ro 13: 10 Love does no *h* to its neighbor.
1Co 11: 17 for your meetings do more *h*
1Jn 5: 18 the evil one cannot *h* him.

HARMONY*
Zec 6: 13 there will be *h* between the two.'
Ro 12: 16 Live in *h* with one another.
2Co 6: 15 What *h* is there between Christ
1Pe 3: 8 live in *h* with one another;

HARMS* (HARM)
Pr 8: 36 whoever fails to find me *h* himself;

HARP (HARPS)
Ge 4: 21 the father of all who play the *h*
1Sa 16: 23 David would take his *h* and play.
Ps 33: 2 Praise the LORD with the *h;*
98: 5 with the *h* and the sound of singing
150: 3 praise him with the *h* and lyre,
Rev 5: 8 Each one had a *h* and they were

HARPS (HARP)
Ps 137: 2 we hung our *h,*

HARSH
Pr 15: 1 but a *h* word stirs up anger.
Col 2: 23 and their *h* treatment of the body,
3: 19 and do not be *h* with them.
1Pe 2: 18 but also to those who are *h.*
Jude : 15 of all the *h* words ungodly sinners

HARVEST (HARVESTERS)
Ge 8: 22 seedtime and *h,*
Ex 23: 16 the Feast of *H* with the firstfruits
Dt 16: 15 God will bless you in all your *h*
Pr 10: 5 during *h* is a disgraceful son.
Jer 8: 20 "The *h* is past,
Joel 3: 13 for the *h* is ripe.
Mt 9: 37 *h* is plentiful but the workers are
Lk 10: 2 He told them, "The *h* is plentiful,
Jn 4: 35 at the fields! They are ripe for *h.*
1Co 9: 11 if we reap a material *h* from you?
2Co 9: 10 the *h* of your righteousness.
Gal 6: 9 at the proper time we will reap a *h*
Heb 12: 11 it produces a *h* of righteousness
Jas 3: 18 in peace raise a *h* of righteousness.
Rev 14: 15 for the *h* of the earth is ripe."

HARVESTERS (HARVEST)
Ru 2: 3 to glean in the fields behind the *h.*

HASTE (HASTEN HASTY)
Ex 12: 11 it in *h;* it is the LORD's Passover.
Pr 21: 5 as surely as *h* leads to poverty.
29: 20 Do you see a man who speaks in *h?*

HASTEN (HASTE)
Ps 70: 1 *H,* O God, to save me;
119: 60 I will *h* and not delay

HASTY* (HASTE)
Pr 19: 2 nor to be *h* and miss the way.
Ecc 5: 2 do not be *h* in your heart
1Ti 5: 22 Do not be *h* in the laying

HATE (GOD-HATERS HATED HATES HATING HATRED)
Lev 19: 17 " 'Do not *h* your brother
Ps 5: 5 you *h* all who do wrong.
36: 2 too much to detect or *h* his sin.
45: 7 righteousness and *h* wickedness;
97: 10 those who love the LORD *h* evil,
119:104 therefore I *h* every wrong path.
119:163 I *h* and abhor falsehood
139: 21 Do I not *h* those who *h* you,
Pr 8: 13 To fear the LORD is to *h* evil;
9: 8 rebuke a mocker or he will *h* you;
13: 5 The righteous *h* what is false,
25: 17 too much of you, and he will *h* you.
29: 10 Bloodthirsty men *h* a man
Ecc 3: 8 a time to love and a time to *h,*
Isa 61: 8 I *h* robbery and iniquity.
Eze 35: 6 Since you did not *h* bloodshed,
Am 5: 15 *H* evil, love good;
Mal 2: 16 "I *h* divorce," says the LORD God
Mt 5: 43 your neighbor and *h* your enemy.'
10: 22 All men will *h* you because of me,
Lk 6: 22 Blessed are you when men *h* you,
6: 27 do good to those who *h* you,
14: 26 does not *h* his father and mother,
Ro 12: 9 *H* what is evil; cling to what is good

HATED (HATE)
Mal 1: 3 loved Jacob, but Esau I have *h,*
Jn 15: 18 keep in mind that it *h* me first.
Ro 9: 13 "Jacob I loved, but Esau I *h.*"
Eph 5: 29 no one ever *h* his own body,
Heb 1: 9 righteousness and *h* wickedness;

HATES (HATE)
Pr 6: 16 There are six things the LORD *h,*
13: 24 He who spares the rod *h* his son,
15: 27 but he who *h* bribes will live.
26: 28 A lying tongue *h* those it hurts,
Jn 3: 20 Everyone who does evil *h* the light,
12: 25 while the man who *h* his life
1Jn 2: 9 *h* his brother is still in the darkness.
4: 20 "I love God," yet *h* his brother,

HATING (HATE)
Jude : 23 *h* even the clothing stained

HATRED (HATE)
Pr 10: 12 *H* stirs up dissension,
15: 17 than a fattened calf with *h.*
Jas 4: 4 with the world is *h* toward God?

HAUGHTY
Pr 6: 17 detestable to him: / *h* eyes,
16: 18 a *h* spirit before a fall.

HAVEN
Ps 107: 30 he guided them to their desired *h.*

HAY
1Co 3: 12 costly stones, wood, *h* or straw,

HEAD (HEADS HOTHEADED)
Ge 3: 15 he will crush your *h,*
Nu 6: 5 no razor may be used on his *h.*
Jdg 16: 17 If my *h* were shaved, my strength
1Sa 9: 2 a *h* taller than any of the others.
2Sa 18: 9 Absalom's *h* got caught in the tree.
Ps 23: 5 You anoint my *h* with oil;
133: 2 is like precious oil poured on the *h,*
Pr 10: 6 Blessings crown the *h*
25: 22 will heap burning coals on his *h,*
Isa 59: 17 and the helmet of salvation on his *h*
Eze 33: 4 his blood will be on his own *h.*
Mt 8: 20 of Man has no place to lay his *h.*"
Jn 19: 2 crown of thorns and put it on his *h.*
Ro 12: 20 will heap burning coals on his *h.*"
1Co 11: 3 and the *h* of Christ is God.
11: 5 her *h* uncovered dishonors her *h*—
12: 21 And the *h* cannot say to the feet,
Eph 1: 22 him to be *h* over everything
5: 23 For the husband is the *h* of the wife
Col 1: 18 And he is the *h* of the body,
2Ti 4: 5 keep your *h* in all situations,
Rev 14: 14 with a crown of gold on his *h*
19: 12 and on his *h* are many crowns.

HEADS (HEAD)
Lev 26: 13 you to walk with *h* held high.
Ps 22: 7 they hurl insults, shaking their *h:*
24: 7 Lift up your *h,* O you gates;
Isa 35: 10 everlasting joy will crown their *h.*
51: 11 everlasting joy will crown their *h.*
Mt 27: 39 shaking their *h* and saying,
Lk 21: 28 stand up and lift up your *h,*
Ac 18: 6 "Your blood be on your own *h!*
Rev 4: 4 and had crowns of gold on their *h.*

HEAL* (HEALED HEALING HEALS)
Nu 12: 13 please *h* her!" The LORD replied
Dt 32: 39 I have wounded and I will *h,*
2Ki 20: 5 and seen your tears; I will *h* you.
20: 8 the sign that the LORD will *h* me
2Ch 7: 14 their sin and will *h* their land.
Job 5: 18 he injures, but his hands also *h.*
Ps 6: 2 *h* me, for my bones are in agony.
41: 4 *h* me, for I have sinned against you
Ecc 3: 3 a time to kill and a time to *h,*
Isa 19: 22 he will strike them and *h* them.
19: 22 respond to their pleas and *h* them.
57: 18 seen his ways, but I will *h* him;
57: 19 "And I will *h* them."
Jer 17: 14 *H* me, O LORD, and I will be
30: 17 and *h* your wounds,'
33: 6 I will *h* my people and will let them
La 2: 13 Who can *h* you?
Hos 5: 13 not able to *h* your sores.
6: 1 but he will *h* us;
7: 1 whenever I would *h* Israel,
14: 4 "I will *h* their waywardness
Na 3: 19 Nothing can *h* your wound;
Zec 11: 16 or seek the young, or *h* the injured,

Mt 8: 7 said to him, "I will go and *h* him."
10: 1 to *h* every disease and sickness.
10: 8 *H* the sick, raise the dead,
12: 10 "Is it lawful to *h* on the Sabbath?"
13: 15 and turn, and I would *h* them.'
17: 16 but they could not *h* him."
Mk 3: 2 if he would *h* him on the Sabbath.
6: 5 on a few sick people and *h* them.
Lk 4: 23 to me: 'Physician, *h* yourself!
5: 17 present for him to *h* the sick.
6: 7 to see if he would *h* on the Sabbath.
7: 3 him to come and *h* his servant.
8: 43 years, but no one could *h* her.
9: 2 kingdom of God and to *h* the sick.
10: 9 *H* the sick who are there
13: 32 and *h* people today and tomorrow,
14: 3 "Is it lawful to *h* on the Sabbath
Jn 4: 47 begged him to come and *h* his son,
12: 40 nor turn—and I would *h* them."
Ac 4: 30 Stretch out your hand to *h*
28: 27 and turn, and I would *h* them.'

HEALED* (HEAL)
Ge 20: 17 to God, and God *h* Abimelech,
Ex 21: 19 and see that he is completely *h.*
Lev 13: 37 hair has grown in it, the itch is *h.*
14: 3 If the person has been *h*
Jos 5: 8 were in camp until they were *h.*
1Sa 6: 3 you will be *h,* and you will know
2Ki 2: 21 LORD says: 'I have *h* this water.
2Ch 30: 20 heard Hezekiah and *h* the people.
Ps 30: 2 and you *h* me.
107: 20 He sent forth his word and *h* them;
Isa 6: 10 and turn and be *h.*"
53: 5 and by his wounds we are *h.*
Jer 14: 19 us so that we cannot be *h?*
17: 14 Heal me, O LORD, and I will be *h;*
51: 8 perhaps she can be *h.*
51: 9 but she cannot be *h;*
51: 9 " 'We would have *h* Babylon,
Eze 34: 4 the weak or *h* the sick
Hos 11: 3 it was I who *h* them.
Mt 4: 24 and the paralyzed, and he *h* them.
8: 8 the word, and my servant will be *h.*
8: 13 his servant was *h* at that very hour.
8: 16 with a word and *h* all the sick.
9: 21 If I only touch his cloak, I will be *h*
9: 22 he said, "your faith has *h* you."
9: 22 woman was *h* from that moment.
12: 15 him, and he *h* all their sick,
12: 22 Jesus *h* him, so that he could both
14: 14 on them and *h* their sick.
14: 36 and all who touched him were *h.*
15: 28 And her daughter was *h*
15: 30 laid them at his feet; and he *h* them
17: 18 and he was *h* from that moment.
19: 2 followed him, and he *h* them there.
21: 14 to him at the temple, and he *h* them
Mk 1: 34 and Jesus *h* many who had various
3: 10 For he had *h* many, so that those
5: 23 hands on her so that she will be *h*
5: 28 If I just touch his clothes, I will be *h*
5: 34 "Daughter, your faith has *h* you.
6: 13 people with oil and *h* them.
6: 56 and all who touched him were *h.*
10: 52 said Jesus, "your faith has *h* you."
Lk 4: 40 hands on each one, he *h* them.
5: 15 and to be *h* of their sicknesses.
6: 18 and to be *h* of their diseases.
7: 7 the word, and my servant will be *h.*
8: 47 and how she had been instantly *h.*
8: 48 "Daughter, your faith has *h* you.
8: 50 just believe, and she will be *h.*"
9: 11 and *h* those who needed healing.
9: 42 *h* the boy and gave him back
13: 14 Jesus had *h* on the Sabbath,
13: 14 So come and be *h* on those days,
14: 4 he *h* him and sent him away.
17: 15 when he saw he was *h,* came back,
18: 42 your sight; your faith has *h* you."
22: 51 touched the man's ear and *h* him.
Jn 5: 10 said to the man who had been *h,*
5: 13 man who was *h* had no idea who it
Ac 4: 9 and are asked how he was *h,*
4: 10 stands before you *h.*
4: 14 who had been *h* standing there
4: 22 man who was miraculously *h* was
5: 16 evil spirits, and all of them were *h.*
8: 7 paralytics and cripples were *h.*
14: 9 saw that he had faith to be *h*
28: 8 placed his hands on him and *h* him.
Heb 12: 13 may not be disabled, but rather *h.*
Jas 5: 16 for each other so that you may be *h*
1Pe 2: 24 by his wounds you have been *h.*
Rev 13: 3 but the fatal wound had been *h.*
13: 12 whose fatal wound had been *h.*

HEALING* (HEAL)
2Ch 28: 15 food and drink, and *h* balm.
Pr 12: 18 but the tongue of the wise brings *h.*
13: 17 but a trustworthy envoy brings *h.*
15: 4 The tongue that brings *h* is a tree
16: 24 sweet to the soul and *h* to the bones
Isa 58: 8 and your *h* will quickly appear;
Jer 8: 15 for a time of *h*
8: 22 Why then is there no *h*
14: 19 for a time of *h*
30: 12 your injury beyond *h.*
30: 13 no *h* for you.
33: 6 I will bring health and *h* to it;
46: 11 there is no *h* for you.
Eze 30: 21 It has not been bound up for *h*
47: 12 for food and their leaves for *h.*"
Mal 4: 2 rise with *h* in its wings.
Mt 4: 23 and *h* every disease and sickness
9: 35 and *h* every disease and sickness.
Lk 6: 19 coming from him and *h* them all.
9: 6 gospel and *h* people everywhere.
9: 11 and healed those who needed *h.*
Jn 7: 23 angry with me for *h* the whole man
Ac 3: 16 him that has given this complete *h*
10: 38 *h* all who were under the power
1Co 12: 9 to another gifts of *h*
12: 28 also those having gifts of *h,*
12: 30 Do all have gifts of *h?* Do all speak
Rev 22: 2 are for the *h* of the nations.

HEALS* (HEAL)
Ex 15: 26 for I am the LORD, who *h* you."
Lev 13: 18 a boil on his skin and it *h,*
Ps 103: 3 and *h* all your diseases;
147: 3 He *h* the brokenhearted
Isa 30: 26 and *h* the wounds he inflicted.
Ac 9: 34 said to him, "Jesus Christ *h* you.

HEALTH* (HEALTHIER HEALTHY)
1Sa 25: 6 And good *h* to all that is yours!
25: 6 Good *h* to you and your household
Ps 38: 3 of your wrath there is no *h*
38: 7 there is no *h* in my body.
Pr 3: 8 This will bring *h* to your body
4: 22 and *h* to a man's whole body.
15: 30 and good news gives *h* to the bones
Isa 38: 16 You restored me to *h*
Jer 30: 17 But I will restore you to *h*
33: 6 I will bring *h* and healing to it;
3Jn : 2 I pray that you may enjoy good *h*

HEALTHIER* (HEALTH)
Da 1: 15 end of the ten days they looked *h*

HEALTHY* (HEALTH)
Ge 41: 5 Seven heads of grain, *h* and good,
41: 7 of grain swallowed up the seven *h,*
Ps 73: 4 their bodies are *h* and strong.
Zec 11: 16 or heal the injured, or feed the *h,*
Mt 9: 12 "It is not the *h* who need a doctor,
Mk 2: 17 "It is not the *h* who need a doctor,
Lk 5: 31 "It is not the *h* who need a doctor,

HEAP
Pr 25: 22 you will *h* burning coals
Ro 12: 20 you will *h* burning coals

HEAR (HEARD HEARING HEARS)
Ex 15: 14 The nations will *h* and tremble;
22: 27 I will *h,* for I am compassionate.
Nu 14: 13 Then the Egyptians will *h* about it!
Dt 1: 16 *H* the disputes between your
4: 36 heaven he made you *h* his voice
6: 4 *H,* O Israel: The LORD our God,
19: 20 The rest of the people will *h* of this
31: 13 must *h* it and learn
Jos 7: 9 of the country will *h* about this
1Ki 8: 30 *H* the supplication of your servant
2Ki 19: 16 O LORD, and *h;* open your eyes,
2Ch 7: 14 then will I *h* from heaven
Job 31: 35 ("Oh, that I had someone to *h* me!
Ps 94: 9 he who implanted the ear not *h?*
95: 7 Today, if you *h* his voice,
Ecc 7: 21 or you may *h* your servant cursing
Isa 21: 3 I am staggered by what I *h,*
29: 18 that day the deaf will *h* the words
30: 21 your ears will *h* a voice behind you,
51: 7 *H* me, you who know what is right,
59: 1 nor his ear too dull to *h.*
65: 24 while they are still speaking I will *h*
Jer 5: 21 who have ears but do not *h:*
Eze 33: 7 so *h* the word I speak and give
37: 4 'Dry bones, *h* the word
Mt 11: 5 the deaf *h,* the dead are raised,
11: 15 He who has ears, let him *h.*
13: 17 and to *h* what you *h* but did not *h* it
Mk 12: 29 answered Jesus, "is this: '*H,*
Lk 7: 22 the deaf *h,* the dead are raised,
Jn 8: 47 reason you do not *h* is that you do
Ac 13: 7 he wanted to *h* the word of God.
13: 44 gathered to *h* the word of the Lord.
17: 32 "We want to *h* you again
Ro 2: 13 is not those who *h* the law who are
10: 14 they *h* without someone preaching
2Ti 4: 3 what their itching ears want to *h.*
Heb 3: 7 "Today, if you *h* his voice,
Rev 1: 3 and blessed are those who *h* it

HEARD (HEAR)
Ex 2: 24 God *h* their groaning and he
Dt 4: 32 has anything like it ever been *h* of?
2Sa 7: 22 as we have *h* with our own ears.
Job 42: 5 My ears had *h* of you
Isa 40: 21 Have you not *h?*
40: 28 Have you not *h?*
66: 8 Who has ever *h* of such a thing?
Jer 18: 13 Who has ever *h* anything like this?
Da 10: 12 your words were *h,* and I have
12: 8 I *h,* but I did not understand.
Hab 3: 16 I *h* and my heart pounded,
Mt 5: 21 "You have *h* that it was said
5: 27 "You have *h* that it was said,
5: 33 you have *h* that it was said
5: 38 "You have *h* that it was said,
5: 43 "You have *h* that it was said,
Lk 12: 3 in the dark will be *h* in the daylight,
Jn 8: 26 and what I have *h* from him I tell
Ac 2: 6 because each one *h* them speaking
1Co 2: 9 no ear has *h,*
2Co 12: 4 He *h* inexpressible things,
1Th 2: 13 word of God, which you *h* from us,
2Ti 1: 13 What you *h* from me, keep
Jas 1: 25 not forgetting what he has *h,*
Rev 22: 8 am the one who *h* and saw these

HEARING (HEAR)
Isa 6: 9 Be ever *h,* but never understanding
Mt 13: 14 will be ever *h* but never
Mk 4: 12 ever *h* but never understanding;
Ac 28: 26 will be ever *h* but never
Ro 10: 17 faith comes from *h* the message,
1Co 12: 17 where would the sense of *h* be?

HEARS (HEAR)
Jn 5: 24 whoever *h* my word and believes
1Jn 5: 14 according to his will, he *h* us.
Rev 3: 20 If anyone *h* my voice and opens

HEART (BROKENHEARTED FAINT-HEARTED HARDHEARTED HEART'S HEARTACHE HEARTS KINDHEARTED SIMPLEHEARTED STOUTHEARTED WHOLEHEARTED WHOLEHEARTEDLY)

Ge 6: 5 of his *h* was only evil all the time.
Ex 4: 21 But I will harden his *h*
25: 2 each man whose *h* prompts him
35: 21 and whose *h* moved him came
Lev 19: 17 Do not hate your brother in your *h*.
Dt 4: 9 or let them slip from your *h* as long
4: 29 if you look for him with all your *h*
6: 5 LORD your God with all your *h*
10: 12 LORD your God with all your *h*
11: 13 and to serve him with all your *h*
13: 3 you love him with all your *h*
15: 10 and do so without a grudging *h;*
26: 16 observe them with all your *h*
29: 18 you today whose *h* turns away
30: 2 and obey him with all your *h*
30: 6 you may love him with all your *h*
30: 10 LORD your God with all your *h*
Jos 22: 5 and to serve him with all your *h*
23: 14 You know with all your *h*
1Sa 10: 9 God changed Saul's *h,*
12: 20 serve the LORD with all your *h*.
12: 24 serve him faithfully with all your *h;*
13: 14 sought out a man after his own *h*
14: 7 I am with you *h* and soul."
16: 7 but the LORD looks at the *h*."
17: 32 "Let no one lose *h* on account
1Ki 2: 4 faithfully before me with all their *h*
3: 9 So give your servant a discerning *h*
3: 12 give you a wise and discerning *h,*
8: 48 back to you with all their *h*
9: 3 and my *h* will always be there.
9: 4 walk before me in integrity of *h*
10: 24 the wisdom God had put in his *h*.
11: 4 and his *h* was not fully devoted
14: 8 and followed me with all his *h,*
15: 14 Asa's *h* was fully committed
2Ki 22: 19 Because your *h* was responsive
23: 3 with all his *h* and all his soul,
1Ch 28: 9 for the LORD searches every *h*
2Ch 6: 38 back to you with all their *h*
7: 16 and my *h* will always be there.
15: 12 of their fathers, with all their *h*
15: 17 Asa's *h* was fully committed
17: 6 His *h* was devoted to the ways
22: 9 sought the LORD with all his *h*."
34: 31 with all his *h* and all his soul,
36: 13 stiff-necked and hardened his *h*
Ezr 1: 5 everyone whose *h* God had moved
Ne 4: 6 the people worked with all their *h*.
Job 19: 27 How my *h* yearns within me!
22: 22 and lay up his words in your *h*.
37: 1 "At this my *h* pounds
Ps 9: 1 you, O LORD, with all my *h;*
14: 1 The fool says in his *h,*
16: 9 Therefore my *h* is glad
19: 14 and the meditation of my *h*
20: 4 he give you the desire of your *h*
24: 4 who has clean hands and a pure *h,*
26: 2 examine my *h* and my mind;
37: 4 will give you the desires of your *h*.
37: 31 The law of his God is in his *h;*
44: 21 since he knows the secrets of the *h*
45: 1 My *h* is stirred by a noble theme
51: 10 Create in me a pure *h,* O God,
51: 17 a broken and contrite *h,*
53: 1 The fool says in his *h,*
66: 18 If I had cherished sin in my *h,*
73: 1 to those who are pure in *h*.
73: 26 My flesh and my *h* may fail,
86: 11 give me an undivided *h,*
90: 12 that we may gain a *h* of wisdom.
97: 11 and joy on the upright in *h*.
108: 1 My *h* is steadfast, O God;
109: 22 and my *h* is wounded within me.
111: 1 will extol the LORD with all my *h*
112: 7 his *h* is steadfast, trusting
112: 8 His *h* is secure, he will have no fear
119: 2 and seek him with all their *h*.
119: 10 I seek you with all my *h;*
119: 11 I have hidden your word in my *h*
119: 30 I have set my *h* on your laws.
119: 32 for you have set my *h* free.
119: 34 and obey it with all my *h*.
119: 36 Turn my *h* toward your statutes
119: 58 sought your face with all my *h;*
119: 69 I keep your precepts with all my *h*.
119:111 they are the joy of my *h*.
119:112 My *h* is set on keeping your
119:145 I call with all my *h;* answer me,
125: 4 to those who are upright in *h*.
138: 1 you, O LORD, with all my *h;*
139: 23 Search me, O God, and know my *h*
Pr 2: 2 applying your *h* to understanding,
3: 1 but keep my commands in your *h,*
3: 3 write them on the tablet of your *h*.
3: 5 Trust in the LORD with all your *h*
4: 4 hold of my words with all your *h;*
4: 21 keep them within your *h;*
4: 23 Above all else, guard your *h,*
6: 21 Bind them upon your *h* forever;
7: 3 write them on the tablet of your *h*.
10: 8 The wise in *h* accept commands,
13: 12 Hope deferred makes the *h* sick,
14: 13 Even in laughter the *h* may ache,
14: 30 A *h* at peace gives life to the body,
15: 13 A happy *h* makes the face cheerful,
15: 15 the cheerful *h* has a continual feast.
15: 28 *h* of the righteous weighs its
15: 30 A cheerful look brings joy to the *h,*
16: 23 A wise man's *h* guides his mouth,
17: 22 A cheerful *h* is good medicine,
20: 9 can say, "I have kept my *h* pure;
22: 11 He who loves a pure *h*
22: 17 apply your *h* to what I teach,
22: 18 when you keep them in your *h*
23: 15 My son, if your *h* is wise,
23: 19 and keep your *h* on the right path.
23: 26 My son, give me your *h*
24: 17 stumbles, do not let your *h* rejoice,
27: 19 so a man's *h* reflects the man.
Ecc 5: 2 do not be hasty in your *h*
8: 5 wise *h* will know the proper time
11: 10 banish anxiety from your *h*
SS 3: 1 I looked for the one my *h* loves;
4: 9 You have stolen my *h,* my sister,
5: 2 *Beloved* I slept but my *h* was awake
5: 4 my *h* began to pound for him.
8: 6 Place me like a seal over your *h,*
Isa 6: 10 Make the *h* of this people calloused
40: 11 and carries them close to his *h;*
57: 15 and to revive the *h* of the contrite.
66: 14 you see this, your *h* will rejoice
Jer 3: 15 give you shepherds after my own *h,*
4: 14 wash the evil from your *h*
9: 26 of Israel is uncircumcised in *h*."
17: 9 The *h* is deceitful above all things
20: 9 is in my *h* like a fire,
24: 7 I will give them a *h* to know me,
29: 13 when you seek me with all your *h*.
32: 39 I will give them singleness of *h*
32: 41 them in this land with all my *h*
51: 46 Do not lose *h* or be afraid
Eze 11: 19 I will give them an undivided *h*
18: 31 and get a new *h* and a new spirit.
36: 26 I will give you a new *h*
44: 7 foreigners uncircumcised in *h*
Da 7: 4 and the *h* of a man was given to it.
Joel 2: 12 "return to me with all your *h,*
2: 13 Rend your *h*
Zep 3: 14 Be glad and rejoice with all your *h,*
Mt 5: 8 Blessed are the pure in *h,*
5: 28 adultery with her in his *h*.
6: 21 treasure is, there your *h* will be
11: 29 for I am gentle and humble in *h,*
12: 34 of the *h* the mouth speaks.
13: 15 For this people's *h* has become
15: 18 out of the mouth come from the *h,*
15: 19 For out of the *h* come evil thoughts
18: 35 forgive your brother from your *h*."
22: 37 the Lord your God with all your *h*
Mk 11: 23 and does not doubt in his *h*
12: 30 the Lord your God with all your *h*
12: 33 To love him with all your *h,*
Lk 2: 19 and pondered them in her *h*.
2: 51 treasured all these things in her *h*.
6: 45 out of the good stored up in his *h,*
6: 45 overflow of his *h* his mouth speaks.
8: 15 for those with a noble and good *h,*
10: 27 the Lord your God with all your *h*
12: 34 treasure is, there your *h* will be
Jn 12: 27 "Now my *h* is troubled,
Ac 1: 24 "Lord, you know everyone's *h*.
2: 37 they were cut to the *h*
4: 32 All the believers were one in *h*
8: 21 your *h* is not right before God.
15: 8 who knows the *h,* showed that he
16: 14 The Lord opened her *h* to respond
28: 27 For this people's *h* has become
Ro 1: 9 with my whole *h* in preaching
2: 29 is circumcision of the *h,*
10: 9 in your *h* that God raised him
10: 10 is with your *h* that you believe
15: 6 with one *h* and mouth you may
1Co 14: 25 the secrets of his *h* will be laid bare.
2Co 2: 4 anguish of *h* and with many tears,
4: 1 this ministry, we do not lose *h*.
4: 16 Therefore we do not lose *h*.
9: 7 give what he has decided in his *h*
Eph 1: 18 eyes of your *h* may be enlightened
5: 19 make music in your *h* to the Lord,
6: 5 and with sincerity of *h,* just
6: 6 doing the will of God from your *h*.
Php 1: 7 since I have you in my *h;* for
Col 2: 2 is that they may be encouraged in *h*
3: 22 but with sincerity of *h*
3: 23 work at it with all your *h,*
1Ti 1: 5 which comes from a pure *h*
3: 1 If anyone sets his *h*
2Ti 2: 22 call on the Lord out of a pure *h*.
Phm : 12 who is my very *h*— back to you.
: 20 in the Lord; refresh my *h* in Christ.
Heb 4: 12 the thoughts and attitudes of the *h*.
1Pe 1: 22 one another deeply, from the *h*.

HEART'S* (HEART)

2Ch 1: 11 "Since this is your *h* desire
Jer 15: 16 they were my joy and my *h* delight,
Eze 24: 25 delight of their eyes, their *h* desire,
Ro 10: 1 my *h* desire and prayer to God

HEARTACHE* (HEART)

Pr 15: 13 but *h* crushes the spirit.

HEARTLESS*

La 4: 3 but my people have become *h*
Ro 1: 31 they are senseless, faithless, *h,*

HEARTS (HEART)

Lev 26: 41 their uncircumcised *h* are humbled
Dt 6: 6 are to be upon your *h*.
10: 16 Circumcise your *h,* therefore,
11: 18 Fix these words of mine in your *h*
30: 6 your God will circumcise your *h*
Jos 11: 20 himself who hardened their *h*
24: 23 and yield your *h* to the LORD,
1Sa 7: 3 to the LORD with all your *h,*
10: 26 valiant men whose *h* God had
2Sa 15: 6 and so he stole the *h* of the men
1Ki 8: 39 for you alone know the *h* of all men
8: 61 your *h* must be fully committed
18: 37 are turning their *h* back again."
1Ch 29: 18 and keep their *h* loyal to you.
2Ch 6: 30 (for you alone know the *h* of men),
11: 16 tribe of Israel who set their *h*
29: 31 all whose *h* were willing brought

Ps 7: 9 who searches minds and *h*,
33: 21 In him our *h* rejoice,
62: 8 pour out your *h* to him,
95: 8 do not harden your *h* as you did
Ecc 3: 11 also set eternity in the *h* of men;
Isa 26: 8 are the desire of our *h*.
29: 13 but their *h* are far from me.
35: 4 say to those with fearful *h*,
51: 7 people who have my law in your *h*:
63: 17 harden our *h* so we do not revere
65: 14 out of the joy of their *h*,
Jer 4: 4 circumcise your *h*,
12: 2 but far from their *h*.
17: 1 on the tablets of their *h*
31: 33 and write it on their *h*.
Mal 4: 6 He will turn the *h* of the fathers
Mt 15: 8 but their *h* are far from me.
Mk 6: 52 the loaves; their *h* were hardened.
7: 6 but their *h* are far from me.
7: 21 out of men's *h*, come evil thoughts,
Lk 1: 17 to turn the *h* of the fathers
16: 15 of men, but God knows your *h*.
24: 32 "Were not our *h* burning within us
Jn 5: 42 not have the love of God in your *h*.
14: 1 "Do not let your *h* be troubled.
14: 27 Do not let your *h* be troubled
Ac 7: 51 with uncircumcised *h* and ears!
11: 23 true to the Lord with all their *h*.
15: 9 for he purified their *h* by faith.
28: 27 understand with their *h*
Ro 1: 21 and their foolish *h* were darkened.
2: 15 of the law are written on their *h*,
5: 5 love into our *h* by the Holy Spirit,
8: 27 who searches our *h* knows
1Co 4: 5 will expose the motives of men's *h*.
2Co 1: 22 put his Spirit in our *h* as a deposit,
3: 2 written on our *h*, known
3: 3 but on tablets of human *h*.
4: 6 shine in our *h* to give us the light
6: 11 and opened wide our *h* to you.
6: 13 to my children—open wide your *h*
7: 2 Make room for us in your *h*.
Gal 4: 6 the Spirit of his Son into our *h*,
Eph 3: 17 dwell in your *h* through faith.
Php 4: 7 will guard your *h* and your minds
Col 3: 1 set your *h* on things above,
3: 15 the peace of Christ rule in your *h*,
3: 16 with gratitude in your *h* to God.
1Th 2: 4 men but God, who tests our *h*.
3: 13 May he strengthen your *h*
2Th 2: 17 encourage your *h* and strengthen
Phm : 7 have refreshed the *h* of the saints.
Heb 3: 8 do not harden your *h*
8: 10 and write them on their *h*.
10: 16 I will put my laws in their *h*,
10: 22 having our *h* sprinkled
Jas 4: 8 purify your *h*, you double-minded.
2Pe 1: 19 the morning star rises in your *h*.
1Jn 3: 20 For God is greater than our *h*,

HEAT
Ps 19: 6 nothing is hidden from its *h*.
2Pe 3: 12 and the elements will melt in the *h*.

HEAVEN (HEAVENLY HEAVENS HEAVENWARD)
Ge 14: 19 Creator of *h* and earth.
28: 12 with its top reaching to *h*,
Ex 16: 4 rain down bread from *h* for you.
20: 22 that I have spoken to you from *h*:
Dt 26: 15 from *h*, your holy dwelling place,
30: 12 "Who will ascend into *h* to get it
1Ki 8: 27 the highest *h*, cannot contain you.
8: 30 Hear from *h*, your dwelling place,
22: 19 the host of *h* standing around him
2Ki 2: 1 up to *h* in a whirlwind,
19: 15 You have made *h* and earth.
2Ch 7: 14 then will I hear from *h*
Isa 14: 12 How you have fallen from *h*,
66: 1 "*H* is my throne,
Da 7: 13 coming with the clouds of *h*.
Mt 3: 2 for the kingdom of *h* is near."
3: 16 At that moment *h* was opened,
4: 17 for the kingdom of *h* is near."
5: 12 because great is your reward in *h*,
5: 19 great in the kingdom of *h*.
6: 9 " 'Our Father in *h*,
6: 10 done on earth as it is in *h*.
6: 20 up for yourselves treasures in *h*,
7: 21 Lord,' will enter the kingdom of *h*,
16: 19 bind on earth will be bound in *h*,
18: 3 will never enter the kingdom of *h*.
18: 18 bind on earth will be bound in *h*,
19: 14 the kingdom of *h* belongs to such
19: 21 and you will have treasure in *h*.
19: 23 man to enter the kingdom of *h*.
23: 13 the kingdom of *h* in men's faces.
24: 35 *H* and earth will pass away,
26: 64 and coming on the clouds of *h*."
28: 18 "All authority in *h*
Mk 1: 10 he saw *h* being torn open
10: 21 and you will have treasure in *h*.
13: 31 *H* and earth will pass away,
14: 62 and coming on the clouds of *h*."
16: 19 he was taken up into *h*
Lk 3: 21 *h* was opened and the Holy Spirit
10: 18 saw Satan fall like lightning from *h*.
10: 20 that your names are written in *h*."
12: 33 in *h* that will not be exhausted,
15: 7 in *h* over one sinner who repents
18: 22 and you will have treasure in *h*.
21: 33 *H* and earth will pass away,
24: 51 left them and was taken up into *h*.
Jn 3: 13 No one has ever gone into *h*
6: 38 down from *h* not to do my will
12: 28 Then a voice came from *h*,
Ac 1: 11 has been taken from you into *h*,
7: 49 the prophet says: " '*H* is my
7: 55 looked up to *h* and saw the glory
9: 3 a light from *h* flashed around him.
26: 19 disobedient to the vision from *h*.
Ro 10: 6 'Who will ascend into *h*?' " (that is,
1Co 15: 47 the earth, the second man from *h*.
2Co 5: 1 an eternal house in *h*, not built
12: 2 ago was caught up to the third *h*.
Eph 1: 10 to bring all things in *h*
Php 2: 10 *h* and on earth and under the earth,
3: 20 But our citizenship is in *h*.
Col 1: 16 things in *h* and on earth, visible
4: 1 that you also have a Master in *h*.
1Th 1: 10 and to wait for his Son from *h*,
4: 16 himself will come down from *h*,
Heb 1: 3 hand of the Majesty in *h*.
8: 5 and shadow of what is in *h*.
9: 24 he entered *h* itself, now to appear
12: 23 whose names are written in *h*.
1Pe 1: 4 spoil or fade—kept in *h* for you,
3: 22 who has gone into *h* and is
2Pe 3: 13 we are looking forward to a new *h*
Rev 5: 13 Then I heard every creature in *h*
11: 19 God's temple in *h* was opened,
12: 7 And there was war in *h*.
15: 5 this I looked and in *h* the temple,
19: 1 of a great multitude in *h* shouting:
19: 11 I saw *h* standing open and there
21: 1 Then I saw a new *h* and a new earth
21: 10 coming down out of *h* from God.

HEAVENLY (HEAVEN)
Ps 8: 5 him a little lower than the *h* beings
2Co 5: 2 to be clothed with our *h* dwelling,
Eph 1: 3 in the *h* realms with every spiritual
1: 20 at his right hand in the *h* realms,
2Ti 4: 18 bring me safely to his *h* kingdom.
Heb 12: 22 to the *h* Jerusalem, the city

HEAVENS (HEAVEN)
Ge 1: 1 In the beginning God created the *h*
11: 4 with a tower that reaches to the *h*,
Dt 33: 26 who rides on the *h* to help you
1Ki 8: 27 The *h*, even the highest heaven,
2Ch 2: 6 since the *h*, even the highest
Ezr 9: 6 and our guilt has reached to the *h*.
Ne 9: 6 You made the *h*, even the highest
Job 11: 8 They are higher than the *h*—
38: 33 Do you know the laws of the *h*?
Ps 8: 3 When I consider your *h*,
19: 1 The *h* declare the glory of God;
33: 6 of the LORD were the *h* made,
57: 5 Be exalted, O God, above the *h*;
102: 25 the *h* are the work of your hands.
103: 11 as high as the *h* are above the earth,
108: 4 is your love, higher than the *h*;
115: 16 The highest *h* belong to the LORD
119: 89 it stands firm in the *h*.
135: 6 in the *h* and on the earth,
139: 8 If I go up to the *h*, you are there;
148: 1 Praise the LORD from the *h*,
Isa 40: 26 Lift your eyes and look to the *h*:
45: 8 "You *h* above, rain
51: 6 Lift up your eyes to the *h*,
55: 9 "As the *h* are higher than the earth,
65: 17 new *h* and a new earth.
Jer 31: 37 if the *h* above can be measured
32: 17 you have made the *h* and the earth
Eze 1: 1 *h* were opened and I saw visions
Da 12: 3 shine like the brightness of the *h*,
Joel 2: 30 I will show wonders in the *h*
Mt 24: 31 from one end of the *h* to the other.
Mk 13: 27 of the earth to the ends of the *h*.
Eph 4: 10 who ascended higher than all the *h*,
Heb 4: 14 priest who has gone through the *h*,
7: 26 from sinners, exalted above the *h*.
2Pe 3: 5 ago by God's word the *h* existed
3: 10 The *h* will disappear with a roar;

HEAVENWARD (HEAVEN)
Php 3: 14 for which God has called me *h*

HEAVIER (HEAVY)
Pr 27: 3 provocation by a fool is *h* than both

HEAVY (HEAVIER)
1Ki 12: 4 and the *h* yoke he put on us,
Ecc 1: 13 What a *h* burden God has laid
Isa 47: 6 you laid a very *h* yoke.
Mt 23: 4 They tie up *h* loads and put them

HEBREW (HEBREWS)
Ge 14: 13 and reported this to Abram the *H*.
2Ki 18: 26 speak to us in *H* in the hearing
Php 3: 5 tribe of Benjamin, a *H* of Hebrews;

HEBREWS (HEBREW)
Ex 9: 1 of the *H*, says: "Let my people go,
2Co 11: 22 Are they *H*? So am I.

HEBRON
Ge 13: 18 near the great trees of Mamre at *H*,
23: 2 died at Kiriath Arba (that is, *H*)
Jos 14: 13 and gave him *H* as his inheritance.
20: 7 *H*) in the hill country of Judah.
21: 13 the priest they gave *H* (a city
2Sa 2: 11 king in *H* over the house

HEDGE
Job 1: 10 "Have you not put a *h* around him

HEED (HEEDS)
Ecc 7: 5 It is better to *h* a wise man's rebuke

HEEDS (HEED)
Pr 13: 1 wise son *h* his father's instruction,
13: 18 whoever *h* correction is honored.
15: 5 whoever *h* correction shows
15: 32 whoever *h* correction gains

HEEL
Ge 3: 15 and you will strike his *h*."

HEIR (INHERIT)
Gal 4: 7 God has made you also an *h*.
Heb 1: 2 whom he appointed *h* of all things,

HEIRS (INHERIT)
Ro 8: 17 then we are *h*— *h* of God
Gal 3: 29 and *h* according to the promise.
Eph 3: 6 gospel the Gentiles are *h* together
1Pe 3: 7 as *h* with you of the gracious gift

HELD (HOLD)
Ex 17: 11 As long as Moses *h* up his hands,
Dt 4: 4 but all of you who *h* fast
2Ki 18: 6 He *h* fast to the LORD
SS 3: 4 I *h* him and would not let him go
Isa 65: 2 All day long I have *h* out my hands
Ro 10: 21 day long I have *h* out my hands
Col 2: 19 and *h* together by its ligaments

HELL*
Mt 5: 22 will be in danger of the fire of *h.*
5: 29 body to be thrown into *h.*
5: 30 for your whole body to go into *h.*
10: 28 destroy both soul and body in *h.*
18: 9 and be thrown into the fire of *h.*
23: 15 as much a son of *h* as you are.
23: 33 you escape being condemned to *h?*
Mk 9: 43 than with two hands to go into *h,*
9: 45 have two feet and be thrown into *h.*
9: 47 two eyes and be thrown into *h,*
Lk 12: 5 has power to throw you into *h.*
16: 23 In *h,* where he was in torment,
Jas 3: 6 and is itself set on fire by *h.*
2Pe 2: 4 but sent them to *h,* putting them

HELMET
Isa 59: 17 and the *h* of salvation on his head;
Eph 6: 17 Take the *h* of salvation
1Th 5: 8 and the hope of salvation as a *h.*

HELP (HELPED HELPER HELPFUL HELPING HELPLESS HELPS)
Ex 23: 5 leave it there; be sure you *h* him
Lev 25: 35 *h* him as you would an alien
Dt 33: 26 who rides on the heavens to *h* you
2Ch 16: 12 even in his illness he did not seek *h*
Ps 18: 6 I cried to my God for *h.*
30: 2 my God, I called to you for *h*
33: 20 he is our *h* and our shield.
46: 1 an ever-present *h* in trouble.
72: 12 the afflicted who have no one to *h.*
79: 9 *H* us, O God our Savior,
108: 12 for the *h* of man is worthless.
115: 9 he is their *h* and shield.
121: 1 where does my *h* come from?
Ecc 4: 10 his friend can *h* him up.
Isa 41: 10 I will strengthen you and *h* you;
Jnh 2: 2 depths of the grave I called for *h,*
Mk 9: 24 *h* me overcome my unbelief!"
Lk 11: 46 will not lift one finger to *h* them.
Ac 16: 9 Come over to Macedonia and *h* us
18: 27 he was a great *h* to those who
20: 35 of hard work we must *h* the weak,
26: 22 I have had God's *h* to this very day,
1Co 12: 28 those able to *h* others, those
2Co 9: 2 For I know your eagerness to *h,*
1Ti 5: 16 she should *h* them and not let

HELPED (HELP)
1Sa 7: 12 "Thus far has the LORD *h* us."

HELPER (HELP)
Ge 2: 18 I will make a *h* suitable for him."
Ps 10: 14 you are the *h* of the fatherless.
Heb 13: 6 Lord is my *h;* I will not be afraid.

HELPFUL (HELP)
Eph 4: 29 only what is *h* for building others

HELPING (HELP)
Ac 9: 36 always doing good and *h* the poor.
1Ti 5: 10 *h* those in trouble and devoting

HELPLESS (HELP)
Ps 10: 12 Do not forget the *h.*
Mt 9: 36 because they were harassed and *h,*

HELPS (HELP)
Ro 8: 26 the Spirit *h* us in our weakness.

HEN
Mt 23: 37 as a *h* gathers her chicks
Lk 13: 34 as a *h* gathers her chicks

HERALD
1Ti 2: 7 for this purpose I was appointed a *h*
2Ti 1: 11 of this gospel I was appointed a *h*

HERBS
Ex 12: 8 with bitter *h,* and bread made

HERITAGE (INHERIT)
Ps 61: 5 you have given me the *h*
119:111 Your statutes are my *h* forever;
127: 3 Sons are a *h* from the LORD,

HEROD
1. King of Judea who tried to kill Jesus (Mt 2; Lk 1:5).
2. Son of 1. Tetrarch of Galilee who arrested and beheaded John the Baptist (Mt 14:1–12; Mk 6:14–29; Lk 3:1, 19–20; 9:7–9); tried Jesus (Lk 23:6–15).
3. Grandson of 1. King of Judea who killed James (Ac 12:2); arrested Peter (Ac 12:3–19). Death (Ac 12:19–23).

HERODIAS
Wife of Herod the Tetrarch who persuaded her daughter to ask for John the Baptist's head (Mt 14:1–12; Mk 6:14–29).

HEWN
Isa 51: 1 the quarry from which you were *h;*

HEZEKIAH
King of Judah. Restored the temple and worship (2Ch 29–31). Sought the LORD for help against Assyria (2Ki 18–19; 2Ch 32:1–23; Isa 36–37). Illness healed (2Ki 20:1–11; 2Ch 32:24–26; Isa 38). Judged for showing Babylonians his treasures (2Ki 20:12–21; 2Ch 32:31; Isa 39).

HID (HIDE)
Ge 3: 8 and they *h* from the LORD God
Ex 2: 2 she *h* him for three months.
Jos 6: 17 because she *h* the spies we sent.
1Ki 18: 13 I *h* a hundred of the LORD's
2Ch 22: 11 she *h* the child from Athaliah
Isa 54: 8 I *h* my face from you for a moment,
Mt 13: 44 When a man found it, he *h* it again,
25: 25 and *h* your talent in the ground.
Heb 11: 23 By faith Moses' parents *h* him

HIDDEN (HIDE)
1Sa 10: 22 has *h* himself among the baggage."
Job 28: 11 and brings *h* things to light.
Ps 19: 12 Forgive my *h* faults.
78: 2 I will utter *h* things, things from of old—
119: 11 I have *h* your word in my heart
Pr 2: 4 and search for it as for *h* treasure,
27: 5 rebuke than *h* love.
Isa 59: 2 your sins have *h* his face from you,
Da 2: 22 He reveals deep and *h* things;
Mt 5: 14 A city on a hill cannot be *h.*
10: 26 or *h* that will not be made known.
11: 25 because you have *h* these things
13: 35 I will utter things *h*
13: 44 of heaven is like treasure *h*
Mk 4: 22 For whatever is *h* is meant
Ro 16: 25 of the mystery *h* for long ages past,
1Co 2: 7 a wisdom that has been *h*
Eph 3: 9 for ages past was kept *h* in God,
Col 1: 26 the mystery that has been kept *h*
2: 3 in whom are *h* all the treasures
3: 3 and your life is now *h* with Christ

HIDE (HID HIDDEN HIDING)
Dt 31: 17 I will *h* my face from them,
Ps 17: 8 *h* me in the shadow of your wings
27: 5 he will *h* me in the shelter
143: 9 for I *h* myself in you.
Isa 53: 3 one from whom men *h* their faces

HIDING (HIDE)
Ps 32: 7 You are my *h* place;
Pr 28: 12 to power, men go into *h.*

HIGH
Ge 14: 18 He was priest of God Most *H,*
14: 22 God Most *H,* Creator of heaven
Ps 21: 7 the unfailing love of the Most *H*
82: 6 you are all sons of the Most *H.'*
Isa 14: 14 I will make myself like the Most *H*
Da 4: 17 know that the Most *H* is sovereign
Mk 5: 7 Jesus, Son of the Most *H* God?
Heb 7: 1 and priest of God Most *H.*

HIGHWAY
Isa 40: 3 a *h* for our God.

HILL (HILLS)
Ps 24: 3 ascend the *h* of the LORD?
Isa 40: 4 every mountain and *h* made low;
Mt 5: 14 A city on a *h* cannot be hidden.
Lk 3: 5 every mountain and *h* made low.

HILLS (HILL)
1Ki 20: 23 "Their gods are gods of the *h.*
Ps 50: 10 and the cattle on a thousand *h.*
121: 1 I lift up my eyes to the *h*—
Hos 10: 8 and to the *h,* "Fall on us!"
Lk 23: 30 and to the *h,* "Cover us!" '
Rev 17: 9 The seven heads are seven *h*

HINDER (HINDERED HINDERS)
1Sa 14: 6 Nothing can *h* the LORD
Mt 19: 14 come to me, and do not *h* them,
1Co 9: 12 anything rather than *h* the gospel
1Pe 3: 7 so that nothing will *h* your prayers.

HINDERED (HINDER)
Lk 11: 52 and you have *h* those who were

HINDERS (HINDER)
Heb 12: 1 let us throw off everything that *h*

HINT*
Eph 5: 3 even a *h* of sexual immorality,

HIP
Ge 32: 32 socket of Jacob's *h* was touched

HIRAM
King of Tyre; helped David build his palace (2Sa 5:11–12; 1Ch 14:1); helped Solomon build the temple (1Ki 5; 2Ch 2) and his navy (1Ki 9:10–27; 2Ch 8).

HIRED
Lk 15: 15 and *h* himself out to a citizen
Jn 10: 12 *h* hand is not the shepherd who

HOARDED (HOARDS)
Ecc 5: 13 wealth *h* to the harm of its owner,
Jas 5: 3 You have *h* wealth in the last days.

HOARDS (HOARDED)
Pr 11: 26 People curse the man who *h* grain,

HOLD (HELD HOLDS)
Ex 20: 7 LORD will not *h* anyone guiltless
Lev 19: 13 " 'Do not *h* back the wages
Dt 5: 11 LORD will not *h* anyone guiltless
11: 22 in all his ways and to *h* fast to him
13: 4 serve him and *h* fast to him.
30: 20 listen to his voice, and *h* fast to him
Jos 22: 5 to *h* fast to him and to serve him
2Ki 4: 16 "you will *h* a son in your arms."
Ps 18: 16 from on high and took *h* of me;
73: 23 you *h* me by my right hand.
Pr 4: 4 "Lay *h* of my words
Isa 41: 13 who takes *h* of your right hand
54: 2 do not *h* back;
Eze 3: 18 and I will *h* you accountable
3: 20 and I will *h* you accountable
33: 6 I will *h* the watchman accountable
Zec 8: 23 nations will take firm *h* of one Jew
Mk 11: 25 if you *h* anything against anyone,
Jn 20: 17 Jesus said, "Do not *h* on to me,
Php 2: 16 as you *h* out the word of life—
3: 12 but I press on to take *h* of that
Col 1: 17 and in him all things *h* together.
1Th 5: 21 *H* on to the good.
1Ti 6: 12 Take *h* of the eternal life
Heb 10: 23 Let us *h* unswervingly

HOLDS (HOLD)
Pr 10: 19 but he who *h* his tongue is wise.
17: 28 and discerning if he *h* his tongue.

HOLES
Hag 1: 6 to put them in a purse with *h* in it."
Mt 8: 20 "Foxes have *h* and birds

HOLINESS* (HOLY)
Ex 15: 11 majestic in *h,*

Dt 32: 51 because you did not uphold my *h*
1Ch 16: 29 the LORD in the splendor of his *h*.
2Ch 20: 21 him for the splendor of his *h*
Ps 29: 2 in the splendor of his *h*.
89: 35 Once for all, I have sworn by my *h*
93: 5 *h* adorns your house
96: 9 in the splendor of his *h*;
Isa 29: 23 they will acknowledge the *h*
35: 8 it will be called the Way of *H*.
Eze 36: 23 I will show the *h* of my great name,
38: 23 I will show my greatness and my *h*,
Am 4: 2 LORD has sworn by his *h*:
Lk 1: 75 fear in *h* and righteousness
Ro 1: 4 the Spirit of *h* was declared
6: 19 to righteousness leading to *h*.
6: 22 the benefit you reap leads to *h*,
1Co 1: 30 our righteousness, *h*
2Co 1: 12 in the *h* and sincerity that are
7: 1 perfecting *h* out of reverence
Eph 4: 24 God in true righteousness and *h*.
1Ti 2: 2 quiet lives in all godliness and *h*.
2: 15 love and *h* with propriety.
Heb 12: 10 that we may share in his *h*.
12: 14 without *h* no one will see the Lord.

HOLY (HALLOWED HOLINESS)
Ge 2: 3 the seventh day and made it *h*,
Ex 3: 5 you are standing is *h* ground."
16: 23 a *h* Sabbath to the LORD.
19: 6 kingdom of priests and a *h* nation.'
20: 8 the Sabbath day by keeping it *h*.
26: 33 Place from the Most *H* Place.
26: 33 curtain will separate the *H* Place
28: 36 seal: *H* TO THE LORD.
29: 37 Then the altar will be most *h*,
30: 10 It is most *h* to the LORD."
30: 29 them so they will be most *h*,
31: 13 I am the LORD, who makes you *h*.
40: 9 all its furnishings, and it will be *h*.
Lev 10: 3 I will show myself *h*;
10: 10 must distinguish between the *h*
10: 13 in a *h* place, because it is your share
11: 44 and be *h*, because I am *h*.
11: 45 therefore be *h*, because I am *h*.
19: 2 'Be *h* because I, the LORD your
19: 8 he has desecrated what is *h*
19: 24 the fourth year all its fruit will be *h*,
20: 3 and profaned my *h* name.
20: 7 " 'Consecrate yourselves and be *h*,
20: 8 I am the LORD, who makes you *h*.
20: 26 You are to be *h* to me because I,
21: 6 They must be *h* to their God
21: 8 Consider them *h*, because I
22: 9 am the LORD, who makes them *h*.
22: 32 Do not profane my *h* name.
25: 12 For it is a jubilee and is to be *h*
27: 9 given to the LORD becomes *h*.
Nu 4: 15 they must not touch the *h* things
6: 5 He must be *h* until the period
20: 12 as *h* in the sight of the Israelites,
20: 13 and where he showed himself *h*
Dt 5: 12 the Sabbath day by keeping it *h*,
23: 14 Your camp must be *h*,
26: 15 from heaven, your *h* dwelling place
33: 2 He came with myriads of *h* ones
Jos 5: 15 place where you are standing is *h*."
24: 19 He is a *h* God; he is a jealous God.
1Sa 2: 2 "There is no one *h* like the LORD;
6: 20 of the LORD, this *h* God?
21: 5 even on missions that are not *h*.
2Ki 4: 9 often comes our way is a *h* man
1Ch 16: 10 Glory in his *h* name;
16: 35 may give thanks to your *h* name,
29: 3 I have provided for this *h* temple:
2Ch 30: 27 heaven, his *h* dwelling place.
Ezr 9: 2 and have mingled the *h* race
Ne 11: 1 the *h* city, while the remaining nine
Job 6: 10 not denied the words of the *H* One.
Ps 2: 6 King on Zion, my *h* hill."
11: 4 The LORD is in his *h* temple;
16: 10 will you let your *H* One see decay.
22: 3 you are enthroned as the *H* One;
24: 3 Who may stand in his *h* place?
30: 4 praise his *h* name.
77: 13 Your ways, O God, are *h*.
78: 54 to the border of his *h* land,
99: 3 he is *h*.
99: 5 he is *h*.
99: 9 for the LORD our God is *h*.
105: 3 Glory in his *h* name;
111: 9 *h* and awesome is his name.
Pr 9: 10 of the *H* One is understanding.
Isa 5: 16 the *h* God will show himself *h*
6: 3 *H*, *h*, *h* is the LORD Almighty;
8: 13 is the one you are to regard as *h*,
29: 23 they will keep my name *h*;
40: 25 who is my equal?" says the *H* One.
43: 3 the *H* One of Israel, your Savior;
54: 5 *H* One of Israel is your Redeemer;
57: 15 who lives forever, whose name is *h*:
58: 13 and the LORD's *h* day honorable,
Jer 17: 22 but keep the Sabbath day *h*,
Eze 20: 41 I will show myself *h* among you
22: 26 to my law and profane my *h* things;
28: 22 and show myself *h* within her.
28: 25 I will show myself *h* among them
36: 20 nations they profaned my *h* name,
38: 16 when I show myself *h* through you
44: 23 the difference between the *h*
Da 9: 24 prophecy and to anoint the most *h*.
Hab 2: 20 But the LORD is in his *h* temple;
Zec 14: 5 and all the *h* ones with him.
14: 20 On that day *H* TO THE LORD
Mt 24: 15 in the *h* place 'the abomination
Mk 1: 24 the *H* One of God!" "Be quiet!"
Lk 1: 35 the *h* one to be born will be called
1: 49 *h* is his name.
4: 34 the *H* One of God!" "Be quiet!"
Jn 6: 69 and know that you are the *H* One
Ac 2: 27 will you let your *H* One see decay.
13: 35 will not let your *H* One see decay.'
Ro 1: 2 prophets in the *H* Scriptures
7: 12 and the commandment is *h*,
11: 16 if the root is *h*, so are the branches.
12: 1 as living sacrifices, *h* and pleasing
1Co 1: 2 in Christ Jesus and called to be *h*,
7: 14 be unclean, but as it is, they are *h*.
Eph 1: 4 the creation of the world to be *h*
2: 21 and rises to become a *h* temple
3: 5 by the Spirit to God's *h* apostles
5: 3 improper for God's *h* people.
5: 26 up for her to make her *h*,
Col 1: 22 death to present you *h* in his sight,
1Th 2: 10 and so is God, of how *h*,
3: 13 and *h* in the presence of our God
3: 13 comes with all his *h* ones.
4: 7 us to be impure, but to live a *h* life.
2Th 1: 10 to be glorified in his *h* people
1Ti 2: 8 to lift up *h* hands in prayer,
2Ti 1: 9 saved us and called us to a *h* life—
2: 21 for noble purposes, made *h*,
3: 15 you have known the *h* Scriptures,
Tit 1: 8 upright, *h* and disciplined.
Heb 2: 11 Both the one who makes men *h*
7: 26 one who is *h*, blameless, pure,
10: 10 we have been made *h*
10: 14 those who are being made *h*.
10: 19 to enter the Most *H* Place
12: 14 in peace with all men and to be *h*;
13: 12 gate to make the people *h*
1Pe 1: 15 But just as he who called you is *h*,
1: 16 is written: "Be *h*, because I am *h*."
2: 5 house to be a *h* priesthood,
2: 9 a royal priesthood, a *h* nation,
3: 5 For this is the way the *h* women
2Pe 3: 11 You ought to live *h* and godly lives
Jude : 14 upon thousands of his *h* ones
Rev 3: 7 are the words of him who is *h*
4: 8 "*H*, *h*, *h* is the Lord God
15: 4 For you alone are *h*.
20: 6 and *h* are those who have part
22: 11 let him who is *h* continue to be *h*."

HOME (HOMES)
Dt 6: 7 Talk about them when you sit at *h*
11: 19 about them when you sit at *h*
20: 5 Let him go *h*, or he may die
24: 5 is to be free to stay at *h*
Ru 1: 11 "Return *h*, my daughters.
2Sa 7: 10 them so that they can have a *h*
1Ch 16: 43 and David returned *h* to bless his
Ps 84: 3 Even the sparrow has found a *h*,
113: 9 settles the barren woman in her *h*
Pr 3: 33 but he blesses the *h* of the righteous
27: 8 is a man who strays from his *h*.
Ecc 12: 5 Then man goes to his eternal *h*
Eze 36: 8 for they will soon come *h*.
Mic 2: 2 They defraud a man of his *h*,
Mt 1: 24 and took Mary *h* as his wife.
Mk 10: 29 "no one who has left *h* or brothers
Lk 10: 38 named Martha opened her *h*
Jn 14: 23 to him and make our *h* with him.
19: 27 this disciple took her into his *h*.
Ac 16: 15 baptized, she invited us to her *h*.
Tit 2: 5 to be busy at *h*, to be kind,

HOMELESS*
1Co 4: 11 we are brutally treated, we are *h*.

HOMES (HOME)
Ne 4: 14 daughters, your wives and your *h*."
Isa 32: 18 in secure *h*,
Mk 10: 30 as much in this present age (*h*,
1Ti 5: 14 to manage their *h* and to give

HOMETOWN
Mt 13: 57 "Only in his *h*
Lk 4: 24 "no prophet is accepted in his *h*.

HOMOSEXUAL*
1Co 6: 9 male prostitutes nor *h* offenders

HONEST (HONESTY)
Lev 19: 36 Use *h* scales and *h* weights,
Dt 25: 15 and *h* weights and measures,
Job 31: 6 let God weigh me in *h* scales
Pr 12: 17 truthful witness gives *h* testimony,

HONESTY (HONEST)
2Ki 12: 15 they acted with complete *h*.

HONEY (HONEYCOMB)
Ex 3: 8 a land flowing with milk and *h*—
Jdg 14: 8 a swarm of bees and some *h*,
1Sa 14: 26 they saw the *h* oozing out,
Ps 19: 10 than *h* from the comb.
119:103 sweeter than *h* to my mouth!
Pr 25: 16 If you find *h*, eat just enough—
SS 4: 11 milk and *h* are under your tongue.
Isa 7: 15 and *h* when he knows enough
Eze 3: 3 it tasted as sweet as *h* in my mouth.
Mt 3: 4 His food was locusts and wild *h*.
Rev 10: 9 mouth it will be as sweet as *h*."

HONEYCOMB (HONEY)
SS 4: 11 Your lips drop sweetness as the *h*,
5: 1 I have eaten my *h* and my honey;

HONOR (HONORABLE HONORABLY HONORED HONORS)
Ex 20: 12 "*H* your father and your mother,
Nu 20: 12 trust in me enough to *h* me
25: 13 he was zealous for the *h* of his God
Dt 5: 16 "*H* your father and your mother,
Jdg 4: 9 going about this, the *h* will not be
1Sa 2: 8 and has them inherit a throne of *h*.
2: 30 Those who *h* me I will *h*,
1Ch 29: 12 Wealth and *h* come from you;
2Ch 1: 11 or *h*, nor for the death
18: 1 had great wealth and *h*,
Est 6: 6 for the man the king delights to *h*
Ps 8: 5 and crowned him with glory and *h*.
45: 11 *h* him, for he is your lord.
84: 11 the LORD bestows favor and *h*;
Pr 3: 9 *H* the LORD with your wealth,
3: 35 The wise inherit *h*,

15: 33 and humility comes before *h.*
18: 12 but humility comes before *h.*
20: 3 It is to a man's *h* to avoid strife,
25: 27 is it honorable to seek one's own *h.*
Isa 29: 13 and *h* me with their lips,
Jer 33: 9 and *h* before all nations
Mt 13: 57 own house is a prophet without *h.*"
15: 4 '*H* your father and mother'
15: 8 These people *h* me with their lips,
19: 19 *h* your father and mother,'
23: 6 they love the place of *h* at banquets
Mk 6: 4 own house is a prophet without *h.*"
Lk 14: 8 do not take the place of *h,*
Jn 5: 23 that all may *h* the Son just
7: 18 does so to gain *h* for himself,
12: 26 My Father will *h* the one who
Ro 12: 10 *H* one another above yourselves.
1Co 6: 20 Therefore *h* God with your body.
Eph 6: 2 "*H* your father and mother"—
1Ti 5: 17 well are worthy of double *h,*
Heb 2: 7 you crowned him with glory and *h*
Rev 4: 9 *h* and thanks to him who sits

HONORABLE (HONOR)
1Th 4: 4 body in a way that is holy and *h,*

HONORABLY (HONOR)
Heb 13: 18 and desire to live *h* in every way.

HONORED (HONOR)
Ps 12: 8 when what is vile is *h* among men.
Pr 13: 18 but whoever heeds correction is *h.*
Da 4: 34 I *h* and glorified him who lives
1Co 12: 26 if one part is *h,* every part rejoices
Heb 13: 4 Marriage should be *h* by all,

HONORS (HONOR)
Ps 15: 4 but *h* those who fear the LORD,
Pr 14: 31 to the needy *h* God.

HOOF
Ex 10: 26 not a *h* is to be left behind.

HOOKS
Isa 2: 4 and their spears into pruning *h.*
Joel 3: 10 and your pruning *h* into spears.
Mic 4: 3 and their spears into pruning *h.*

HOPE (HOPES)
Job 13: 15 Though he slay me, yet will I *h*
Ps 25: 3 No one whose *h* is in you
33: 17 A horse is a vain *h* for deliverance;
33: 18 on those whose *h* is
42: 5 Put your *h* in God,
62: 5 my *h* comes from him.
119: 74 for I have put my *h* in your word.
130: 5 and in his word I put my *h.*
130: 7 O Israel, put your *h* in the LORD,
146: 5 whose *h* is in the LORD his God,
147: 11 who put their *h* in his unfailing love
Pr 13: 12 *H* deferred makes the heart sick,
23: 18 There is surely a future *h* for you,
Isa 40: 31 but those who *h* in the LORD
Jer 29: 11 plans to give you *h* and a future.
La 3: 21 and therefore I have *h:*
Zec 9: 12 to your fortress, O prisoners of *h;*
Ro 5: 4 character; and character, *h.*
8: 20 in *h* that the creation itself will be
8: 24 But *h* that is seen is no *h* at all.
8: 25 if we *h* for what we do not yet have,
12: 12 Be joyful in *h,* patient in affliction,
15: 4 of the Scriptures we might have *h.*
15: 13 May the God of *h* fill you
1Co 13: 13 now these three remain: faith, *h*
15: 19 for this life we have *h* in Christ,
Eph 2: 12 without *h* and without God
Col 1: 27 Christ in you, the *h* of glory.
1Th 1: 3 and your endurance inspired by *h*
5: 8 and the *h* of salvation as a helmet.
1Ti 4: 10 that we have put our *h*
6: 17 but to put their *h* in God,
Tit 1: 2 resting on the *h* of eternal life,
2: 13 while we wait for the blessed *h*—
Heb 6: 19 We have this *h* as an anchor
10: 23 unswervingly to the *h* we profess,
11: 1 faith is being sure of what we *h* for
1Jn 3: 3 Everyone who has this *h*

HOPES (HOPE)
1Co 13: 7 always *h,* always perseveres.

HORN (HORNS)
Ex 19: 13 when the ram's *h* sounds a long
27: 2 Make a *h* at each of the four
Da 7: 8 This *h* had eyes like the eyes

HORNS (HORN)
Da 7: 24 ten *h* are ten kings who will come
Rev 5: 6 He had seven *h* and seven eyes,
12: 3 and ten *h* and seven crowns
13: 1 He had ten *h* and seven heads,
17: 3 and had seven heads and ten *h.*

HORRIBLE (HORROR)
Jer 5: 30 "A *h* and shocking thing

HORROR (HORRIBLE)
Jer 2: 12 and shudder with great *h,*"

HORSE
Ps 147: 10 not in the strength of the *h,*
Pr 26: 3 A whip for the *h,* a halter
Zec 1: 8 before me was a man riding a red *h*
Rev 6: 2 and there before me was a white *h!*
6: 4 Come!" Then another *h* came out,
6: 5 and there before me was a black *h!*
6: 8 and there before me was a pale *h!*
19: 11 and there before me was a white *h,*

HOSANNA
Mt 21: 9 "*H* in the highest!"
Mk 11: 9 "*H!*"
Jn 12: 13 "*H!*"

HOSEA
Prophet whose wife and family pictured the unfaithfulness of Israel (Hos 1–3).

HOSHEA (JOSHUA)
1. Original name of Joshua (Nu 13:16).
2. Last king of Israel (2Ki 15:30; 17:1–6).

HOSPITABLE* (HOSPITALITY)
1Ti 3: 2 self-controlled, respectable, *h,*
Tit 1: 8 Rather he must be *h,* one who loves

HOSPITABLY* (HOSPITALITY)
Ac 28: 7 and for three days entertained us *h.*

HOSPITALITY* (HOSPITABLE HOSPITABLY)
Ro 12: 13 Practice *h.*
16: 23 whose *h* I and the whole church
1Ti 5: 10 as bringing up children, showing *h,*
1Pe 4: 9 Offer *h* to one another
3Jn : 8 therefore to show *h* to such men

HOSTILE (HOSTILITY)
Ro 8: 7 the sinful mind is *h* to God.

HOSTILITY (HOSTILE)
Eph 2: 14 wall of *h,* by abolishing
2: 16 by which he put to death their *h.*

HOT
1Ti 4: 2 have been seared as with a *h* iron.
Rev 3: 15 that you are neither cold nor *h.*

HOT-TEMPERED (TEMPER)
Pr 15: 18 A *h* man stirs up dissension,
19: 19 A *h* man must pay the penalty;
22: 24 Do not make friends with a *h* man,
29: 22 and a *h* one commits many sins.

HOTHEADED (HEAD)
Pr 14: 16 but a fool is *h* and reckless.

HOUR
Ecc 9: 12 knows when his *h* will come:
Mt 6: 27 you by worrying can add a single *h*
Lk 12: 40 the Son of Man will come at an *h*
Jn 12: 23 The *h* has come for the Son of Man
12: 27 for this very reason I came to this *h*

HOUSE (HOUSEHOLD HOUSEHOLDS HOUSES STOREHOUSE)
Ex 12: 22 the door of his *h* until morning.
20: 17 shall not covet your neighbor's *h.*
Nu 12: 7 he is faithful in all my *h.*
Dt 5: 21 desire on your neighbor's *h*
2Sa 7: 11 LORD himself will establish a *h*
1Ch 17: 23 and his *h* be established forever.
Ne 10: 39 "We will not neglect the *h*
Ps 23: 6 I will dwell in the *h* of the LORD
27: 4 dwell in the *h* of the LORD
69: 9 for zeal for your *h* consumes me,
84: 10 a doorkeeper in the *h* of my God
122: 1 "Let us go to the *h* of the LORD."
127: 1 Unless the LORD builds the *h,*
Pr 7: 27 Her *h* is a highway to the grave,
21: 9 than share a *h* with a quarrelsome
Isa 56: 7 a *h* of prayer for all nations."
Jer 7: 11 Has this *h,* which bears my Name,
18: 2 "Go down to the potter's *h,*
Eze 33: 7 made you a watchman for the *h*
Joel 3: 18 will flow out of the LORD's *h*
Zec 13: 6 given at the *h* of my friends.'
Mt 7: 24 is like a wise man who built his *h*
10: 11 and stay at his *h* until you leave.
12: 29 can anyone enter a strong man's *h*
21: 13 My *h* will be called a *h* of prayer,'
Mk 3: 25 If a *h* is divided against itself,
11: 17 " 'My *h* will be called
Lk 6: 48 He is like a man building a *h,*
10: 7 Do not move around from *h* to *h.*
11: 17 a *h* divided against itself will fall.
11: 24 'I will return to the *h* I left.'
15: 8 sweep the *h* and search carefully
19: 9 Today salvation has come to this *h,*
Jn 2: 16 How dare you turn my Father's *h*
2: 17 "Zeal for your *h* will consume me."
12: 3 the *h* was filled with the fragrance
14: 2 In my Father's *h* are many rooms;
Ac 20: 20 you publicly and from *h* to *h.*
Ro 16: 5 the church that meets at their *h.*
Heb 3: 3 the builder of a *h* has greater honor
1Pe 2: 5 built into a spiritual *h* to be a holy

HOUSEHOLD (HOUSE)
Ex 12: 3 lamb for his family, one for each *h.*
Jos 24: 15 my *h,* we will serve the LORD."
Pr 31: 21 it snows, she has no fear for her *h;*
31: 27 over the affairs of her *h*
Mic 7: 6 are the members of his own *h.*
Mt 10: 36 will be the members of his own *h.*'
12: 25 or *h* divided against itself will not
Ac 16: 31 you will be saved—you and your *h*
Eph 2: 19 people and members of God's *h,*
1Ti 3: 12 manage his children and his *h* well.
3: 15 to conduct themselves in God's *h,*

HOUSEHOLDS (HOUSE)
Tit 1: 11 because they are ruining whole *h*

HOUSES (HOUSE)
Ex 12: 27 passed over the *h* of the Israelites
Mt 19: 29 everyone who has left *h* or brothers

HOVERING* (HOVERS)
Ge 1: 2 of God was *h* over the waters.
Isa 31: 5 Like birds *h* overhead,

HOVERS* (HOVERING)
Dt 32: 11 and *h* over its young,

HULDAH*
Prophetess inquired by Hilkiah for Josiah (2Ki 22; 2Ch 34:14–28).

HUMAN (HUMANITY)
Lev 24: 17 If anyone takes the life of a *h* being,
Isa 52: 14 his form marred beyond *h* likeness
Jn 8: 15 You judge by *h* standards;
Ro 1: 3 as to his *h* nature was a descendant
9: 5 from them is traced the *h* ancestry
1Co 1: 17 not with words of *h* wisdom,
1: 26 of you were wise by *h* standards;
2: 13 not in words taught us by *h* wisdom
2Co 3: 3 of stone but on tablets of *h* hearts.
Gal 3: 3 to attain your goal by *h* effort?
2Pe 2: 18 lustful desires of sinful *h* nature,

INTEREST (INTERESTS)
Lev 25: 36 Do not take *i* of any kind from him,
Dt 23: 20 You may charge a foreigner *i*,
Mt 25: 27 would have received it back with *i*.
Php 2: 20 who takes a genuine *i*

INTERESTS (INTEREST)
1Co 7: 34 his wife—and his *i* are divided.
Php 2: 4 only to your own *i*, but also to the *i*
2: 21 everyone looks out for his own *i*,

INTERFERE*
Ezr 6: 7 Do not *i* with the work

INTERMARRY (MARRY)
Dt 7: 3 Do not *i* with them.
Ezr 9: 14 and *i* with the peoples who commit

INTERPRET (INTERPRETATION INTERPRETER INTERPRETS)
Ge 41: 15 "I had a dream, and no one can *i* it.
Mt 16: 3 you cannot *i* the signs of the times.
1Co 12: 30 Do all *i*? But eagerly desire
14: 13 pray that he may *i* what he says.
14: 27 one at a time, and someone must *i*.

INTERPRETATION (INTERPRET)
1Co 12: 10 and to still another the *i* of tongues.
14: 26 a revelation, a tongue or an *i*.
2Pe 1: 20 about by the prophet's own *i*.

INTERPRETER (INTERPRET)
1Co 14: 28 If there is no *i*, the speaker should

INTERPRETS (INTERPRET)
1Co 14: 5 he *i*, so that the church may be

INVADED
2Ki 17: 5 king of Assyria *i* the entire land,
24: 1 king of Babylon *i* the land,

INVENT* (INVENTED)
Ro 1: 30 boastful; they *i* ways of doing evil;

INVENTED* (INVENT)
2Pe 1: 16 We did not follow cleverly *i* stories

INVESTIGATED
Lk 1: 3 I myself have carefully *i* everything

INVISIBLE*
Ro 1: 20 of the world God's *i* qualities—
Col 1: 15 He is the image of the *i* God,
1: 16 and on earth, visible and *i*,
1Ti 1: 17 immortal, *i*, the only God,
Heb 11: 27 because he saw him who is *i*.

INVITE (INVITED INVITES)
Mt 22: 9 *i* to the banquet anyone you find.'
25: 38 did we see you a stranger and *i* you
Lk 14: 12 do not *i* your friends, your brothers
14: 13 you give a banquet, *i* the poor,

INVITED (INVITE)
Zep 1: 7 he has consecrated those he has *i*.
Mt 22: 14 For many are *i*, but few are chosen
25: 35 I was a stranger and you *i* me in,
Lk 14: 10 But when you are *i*, take the lowest
Rev 19: 9 'Blessed are those who are *i*

INVITES (INVITE)
Pr 18: 6 and his mouth *i* a beating.
1Co 10: 27 If some unbeliever *i* you to a meal

INVOLVED
2Ti 2: 4 a soldier gets *i* in civilian affairs—

IRON
2Ki 6: 6 threw it there, and made the *i* float.
Ps 2: 9 will rule them with an *i* scepter;
Pr 27: 17 As *i* sharpens *i*,
Da 2: 33 and thighs of bronze, its legs of *i*,
1Ti 4: 2 have been seared as with a hot *i*.
Rev 2: 27 He will rule them with an *i* scepter;
12: 5 all the nations with an *i* scepter.
19: 15 He will rule them with an *i* scepter

IRRELIGIOUS*
1Ti 1: 9 and sinful, the unholy and *i*;

IRREVOCABLE*
Ro 11: 29 for God's gifts and his call are *i*.

ISAAC
Son of Abraham by Sarah (Ge 17:19; 21:1–7; 1Ch 1:28). Abrahamic covenant perpetuated through (Ge 17:21; 26:2–5). Offered up by Abraham (Ge 22; Heb 11:17–19). Rebekah taken as wife (Ge 24). Inherited Abraham's estate (Ge 25:5). Fathered Esau and Jacob (Ge 25:19–26; 1Ch 1:34). Nearly lost Rebekah to Abimelech (Ge 26:1–11). Covenant with Abimelech (Ge 26:12–31). Tricked into blessing Jacob (Ge 27). Death (Ge 35:27–29). Father of Israel (Ex 3:6; Dt 29:13; Ro 9:10).

ISAIAH
Prophet to Judah (Isa 1:1). Called by the LORD (Isa 6). Announced judgment to Ahaz (Isa 7), deliverance from Assyria to Hezekiah (2Ki 19; Isa 36–37), deliverance from death to Hezekiah (2Ki 20:1–11; Isa 38). Chronicler of Judah's history (2Ch 26:22; 32:32).

ISH-BOSHETH*
Son of Saul who attempted to succeed him as king (2Sa 2:8–4:12; 1Ch 8:33).

ISHMAEL
Son of Abraham by Hagar (Ge 16; 1Ch 1:28). Blessed, but not son of covenant (Ge 17:18–21; Gal 4:21–31). Sent away by Sarah (Ge 21:8–21). Children (Ge 25:12–18; 1Ch 1:29–31). Death (Ge 25:17).

ISLAND
Rev 1: 9 was on the *i* of Patmos
16: 20 Every *i* fled away

ISRAEL (ISRAEL'S ISRAELITE ISRAELITES)
1. Name given to Jacob (see JACOB).
2. Corporate name of Jacob's descendants; often specifically Northern Kingdom.
Ex 28: 11 Engrave the names of the sons of *I*
28: 29 of the sons of *I* over his heart
Nu 24: 17 a scepter will rise out of *I*.
Dt 6: 4 Hear, O *I*: The LORD our God,
10: 12 O *I*, what does the LORD your
Jos 4: 22 *I* crossed the Jordan on dry ground
Jdg 17: 6 In those days *I* had no king;
Ru 2: 12 of *I*, under whose wings you have
1Sa 3: 20 *I* from Dan to Beersheba
4: 21 "The glory has departed from *I*"—
14: 23 So the LORD rescued *I* that day,
15: 26 has rejected you as king over *I*!"
17: 46 will know that there is a God in *I*.
18: 16 But all *I* and Judah loved David,
2Sa 5: 2 'You will shepherd my people *I*,
5: 3 they anointed David king over *I*.
14: 25 In all *I* there was not a man
1Ki 1: 35 I have appointed him ruler over *I*
10: 9 of the LORD's eternal love for *I*,
18: 17 "Is that you, you troubler of *I*?"
19: 18 Yet I reserve seven thousand in *I*—
2Ki 5: 8 know that there is a prophet in *I*."
1Ch 17: 22 made your people *I* your very own
21: 1 incited David to take a census of *I*.
29: 25 Solomon in the sight of all *I*
2Ch 9: 8 of the love of your God for *I*
Ps 73: 1 Surely God is good to *I*,
81: 8 if you would but listen to me, O *I*!
98: 3 his faithfulness to the house of *I*;
99: 8 you were to *I* a forgiving God,
Isa 11: 12 and gather the exiles of *I*;
27: 6 *I* will bud and blossom
44: 21 O *I*, I will not forget you.
46: 13 my splendor to *I*.
Jer 2: 3 *I* was holy to the LORD,
23: 6 and *I* will live in safety.
31: 2 I will come to give rest to *I*."
31: 10 'He who scattered *I* will gather
31: 31 covenant with the house of *I*
33: 17 sit on the throne of the house of *I*,
Eze 3: 17 you a watchman for the house of *I*;
33: 7 you a watchman for the house of *I*;
34: 2 prophesy against the shepherds of *I*
37: 28 that I the LORD make *I* holy,
39: 23 of *I* went into exile for their sin,
Da 9: 20 my sin and the sin of my people *I*
Hos 11: 1 "When *I* was a child, I loved him,
Am 4: 12 prepare to meet your God, O *I*."
7: 11 and *I* will surely go into exile,
8: 2 "The time is ripe for my people *I*;
9: 14 I will bring back my exiled people *I*
Mic 5: 2 one who will be ruler over *I*,
Zep 3: 13 The remnant of *I* will do no wrong;
Zec 11: 14 brotherhood between Judah and *I*.
Mal 1: 5 even beyond the borders of *I*!'
Mt 2: 6 be the shepherd of my people *I*.' "
10: 6 Go rather to the lost sheep of *I*.
15: 24 only to the lost sheep of *I*."
Mk 12: 29 'Hear, O *I*, the Lord our God,
Lk 22: 30 judging the twelve tribes of *I*.
Ac 1: 6 going to restore the kingdom to *I*?"
9: 15 and before the people of *I*.
Ro 9: 4 of my own race, the people of *I*.
9: 6 all who are descended from *I* are *I*.
9: 31 but *I*, who pursued a law
11: 7 What *I* sought so earnestly it did
11: 26 And so all *I* will be saved,
Gal 6: 16 who follow this rule, even to the *I*
Eph 2: 12 excluded from citizenship in *I*
3: 6 Gentiles are heirs together with *I*,
Heb 8: 8 covenant with the house of *I*
Rev 7: 4 144,000 from all the tribes of *I*.
21: 12 the names of the twelve tribes of *I*.

ISRAEL'S (ISRAEL)
Jdg 10: 16 he could bear *I* misery no longer.
2Sa 23: 1 *I* singer of songs:
Isa 44: 6 *I* King and Redeemer, the LORD
Jer 3: 9 Because *I* immorality mattered
31: 9 because I am *I* father,
Jn 3: 10 "You are *I* teacher," said Jesus,

ISRAELITE (ISRAEL)
Ex 16: 1 The whole *I* community set out
35: 29 All the *I* men and women who
Nu 8: 16 offspring from every *I* woman.
20: 1 the whole *I* community arrived
20: 22 The whole *I* community set out
Jn 1: 47 "Here is a true *I*, in whom there is
Ro 11: 1 I am an *I* myself, a descendant

ISRAELITES (ISRAEL)
Ex 1: 7 the *I* were fruitful and multiplied
2: 23 The *I* groaned in their slavery
3: 9 the cry of the *I* has reached me,
12: 35 The *I* did as Moses instructed
12: 37 The *I* journeyed from Rameses
14: 22 and the *I* went through the sea
16: 12 I have heard the grumbling of the *I*.
16: 35 The *I* ate manna forty years,
24: 17 To the *I* the glory of the LORD
28: 30 decisions for the *I* over his heart
29: 45 Then I will dwell among the *I*
31: 16 The *I* are to observe the Sabbath,
33: 5 "Tell the *I*, 'You are a stiff-necked
39: 42 The *I* had done all the work just
Lev 22: 32 be acknowledged as holy by the *I*.
25: 46 rule over your fellow *I* ruthlessly.
25: 55 for the *I* belong to me as servants.
Nu 2: 32 These are the *I*, counted according
6: 23 'This is how you are to bless the *I*.
9: 2 "Have the *I* celebrate the Passover
9: 17 the *I* set out; wherever the cloud
10: 12 Then the *I* set out from the Desert
14: 2 All the *I* grumbled against Moses
20: 12 as holy in the sight of the *I*,
21: 6 they bit the people and many *I* died
26: 65 had told those *I* they would surely
27: 12 and see the land I have given the *I*.
33: 3 The *I* set out from Rameses
35: 10 "Speak to the *I* and say to them:
Dt 33: 1 on the *I* before his death.
Jos 1: 2 about to give to them—to the *I*.
5: 6 The *I* had moved about
7: 1 the *I* acted unfaithfully in regard
8: 32 There in the presence of the *I*,
18: 1 of the *I* gathered at Shiloh
21: 3 the *I* gave the Levites the following

22: 9 of Manasseh left the *I* at Shiloh
Jdg 2: 11 Then the *I* did evil in the eyes
3: 12 Once again the *I* did evil
4: 1 the *I* once again did evil in the eyes
6: 1 Again the *I* did evil in the eyes
10: 6 Again the *I* did evil in the eyes
13: 1 Again the *I* did evil in the eyes
1Sa 17: 2 Saul and the *I* assembled
1Ki 8: 63 and all the *I* dedicated the temple
9: 22 did not make slaves of any of the *I;*
12: 1 for all the *I* had gone there
12: 17 But as for the *I* who were living
2Ki 17: 24 towns of Samaria to replace the *I.*
1Ch 9: 2 in their own towns were some *I,*
10: 1 fought against Israel; the *I* fled
11: 4 and all the *I* marched to Jerusalem,
2Ch 7: 6 and all the *I* were standing.
Ne 1: 6 the sins we *I,* including myself
Jer 16: 14 who brought the *I* up out of Egypt,'
Hos 1: 10 "Yet the *I* will be like the sand
3: 1 Love her as the LORD loves the *I,*
Am 4: 5 boast about them, you *I,*
Mic 5: 3 return to join the *I.*
Ro 9: 27 the number of the *I* be like the sand
10: 1 for the *I* is that they may be saved.
10: 16 But not all the *I* accepted the good
2Co 11: 22 Are they *I?* So am I.

ISSACHAR

Son of Jacob by Leah (Ge 30:18; 35:23; 1Ch 2:1). Tribe of blessed (Ge 49:14–15; Dt 33:18–19), numbered (Nu 1:29; 26:25), allotted land (Jos 19:17–23; Eze 48:25), assisted Deborah (Jdg 5:15), 12,000 from (Rev 7:7).

ISSUING*

Da 9: 25 From the *i* of the decree to restore

ITALY

Ac 27: 1 decided that we would sail for *I,*
Heb 13: 24 from *I* send you their greetings.

ITCHING*

2Ti 4: 3 to say what their *i* ears want to hear

ITHAMAR

Son of Aaron (Ex 6:23; 1Ch 6:3). Duties at tabernacle (Ex 38:21; Nu 4:21–33; 7:8).

ITTAI

2Sa 15: 19 The king said to *I* the Gittite,

IVORY

1Ki 10: 22 silver and *i,* and apes and baboons.
22: 39 the palace he built and inlaid with *i*

JABBOK

Ge 32: 22 and crossed the ford of the *J.*
Dt 3: 16 and out to the *J* River,

JABESH

1Sa 11: 1 And all the men of *J* said to him,
31: 12 wall of Beth Shan and went to *J,*
1Ch 10: 12 and his sons and brought them to *J.*

JABESH GILEAD

Jdg 21: 8 that no one from *J* had come to
2Sa 2: 4 the men of *J* who had buried Saul,
1Ch 10: 11 the inhabitants of *J* heard

JACOB

Second son of Isaac, twin of Esau (Ge 25:21–26; 1Ch 1:34). Bought Esau's birthright (Ge 25:29–34); tricked Isaac into blessing him (Ge 27:1–37). Fled to Haran (Ge 28:1–5). Abrahamic covenant perpetuated through (Ge 28:13–15; Mal 1:2). Vision at Bethel (Ge 28:10–22). Served Laban for Rachel and Leah (Ge 29:1–30). Children (Ge 29:31–30:24; 35:16–26; 1Ch 2–9). Flocks increased (Ge 30:25–43). Returned to Canaan (Ge 31). Wrestled with God; name changed to Israel (Ge 32:22–32). Reconciled to Esau (Ge 33). Returned to Bethel (Ge 35:1–15). Favored Joseph (Ge 37:3). Sent sons to Egypt during famine (Ge 42–43). Settled in Egypt (Ge 46). Blessed Ephraim and Manasseh (Ge 48). Blessed sons (Ge 49:1–28; Heb 11:21). Death (Ge 49:29–33). Burial (Ge 50:1–14).

JAEL*

Woman who killed Canaanite general, Sisera (Jdg 4:17–22; 5:24–27).

JAIR

Judge from Gilead (Jdg 10:3–5).

JAIRUS*

Synagogue ruler whose daughter Jesus raised (Mk 5:22–43; Lk 8:41–56).

JAMES

1. Apostle; brother of John (Mt 4:21–22; 10:2; Mk 3:17; Lk 5:1–10). At transfiguration (Mt 17:1–13; Mk 9:1–13; Lk 9:28–36). Killed by Herod (Ac 12:2).

2. Apostle; son of Alphaeus (Mt 10:3; Mk 3:18; Lk 6:15).

3. Brother of Jesus (Mt 13:55; Mk 6:3; Lk 24:10; Gal 1:19) and Judas (Jude 1). With believers before Pentecost (Ac 1:13). Leader of church at Jerusalem (Ac 12:17; 15; 21:18; Gal 2:9, 12). Author of epistle (Jas 1:1).

JAPHETH

Son of Noah (Ge 5:32; 1Ch 1:4–5). Blessed (Ge 9:18–28). Sons of (Ge 10:2–5).

JAR (JARS)

Ge 24: 14 let down your *j* that I may have
1Ki 17: 14 'The *j* of flour will not be used up
Jer 19: 1 "Go and buy a clay *j* from a potter.
Lk 8: 16 hides it in a *j* or puts it under a bed.

JARS (JAR)

Jn 2: 6 Nearby stood six stone water *j,*
2Co 4: 7 we have this treasure in *j* of clay

JASPER

Ex 28: 20 row a chrysolite, an onyx and a *j.*
Eze 28: 13 chrysolite, onyx and *j,*
Rev 4: 3 sat there had the appearance of *j*
21: 19 The first foundation was *j,*

JAVELIN

1Sa 17: 45 me with sword and spear and *j,*

JAWBONE

Jdg 15: 15 Finding a fresh *j* of a donkey,

JEALOUS (JEALOUSY)

Ex 20: 5 the LORD your God, am a *j* God,
34: 14 whose name is Jealous, is a *j* God.
Dt 4: 24 God is a consuming fire, a *j* God.
6: 15 is a *j* God and his anger will burn
32: 21 They made me *j* by what is no god
Jos 24: 19 He is a holy God; he is a *j* God.
Eze 16: 38 of my wrath and *j* anger.
16: 42 my *j* anger will turn away from you
23: 25 I will direct my *j* anger against you,
36: 6 in my *j* wrath because you have
Joel 2: 18 the LORD will be *j* for his land
Na 1: 2 LORD is a *j* and avenging God;
Zep 3: 8 consumed by the fire of my *j* anger.
Zec 1: 14 I am very *j* for Jerusalem and Zion,
8: 2 "I am very *j* for Zion; I am burning
2Co 11: 2 I am *j* for you with a godly jealousy

JEALOUSY (JEALOUS)

Ps 79: 5 How long will your *j* burn like fire?
Pr 6: 34 for *j* arouses a husband's fury,
27: 4 but who can stand before *j?*
SS 8: 6 its *j* unyielding as the grave.
Zep 1: 18 In the fire of his *j*
Zec 8: 2 I am burning with *j* for her."
Ro 13: 13 debauchery, not in dissension and *j*
1Co 3: 3 For since there is *j* and quarreling
10: 22 trying to arouse the Lord's *j?*
2Co 11: 2 I am jealous for you with a godly *j.*
12: 20 *j,* outbursts of anger, factions,
Gal 5: 20 hatred, discord, *j,* fits of rage,

JEERS*

Heb 11: 36 Some faced *j* and flogging,

JEHOAHAZ

1. Son of Jehu; king of Israel (2Ki 13:1–9).

2. Son of Josiah; king of Judah (2Ki 23:31–34; 2Ch 36:1–4).

JEHOASH

1. See JOASH.

2. Son of Jehoahaz; king of Israel. Defeat of Aram prophesied by Elisha (2Ki 13:10–25). Defeated Amaziah in Jerusalem (2Ki 14:1–16; 2Ch 25:17–24).

JEHOIACHIN

Son of Jehoiakim; king of Judah exiled by Nebuchadnezzar (2Ki 24:8–17; 2Ch 36:8–10; Jer 22:24–30; 24:1). Raised from prisoner status (2Ki 25:27–30; Jer 52:31–34).

JEHOIADA

Priest who sheltered Joash from Athaliah (2Ki 11–12; 2Ch 22:11–24:16).

JEHOIAKIM

Son of Josiah; made king of Judah by Pharaoh Neco (2Ki 23:34–24:6; 2Ch 36:4–8; Jer 22:18–23). Burned scroll of Jeremiah's prophecies (Jer 36).

JEHORAM

1. Son of Jehoshaphat; king of Judah (2Ki 8:16–24). Prophesied against by Elijah; killed by the LORD (2Ch 21).

2. See JORAM.

JEHOSHAPHAT

Son of Asa; king of Judah. Strengthened his kingdom (2Ch 17). Joined with Ahab against Aram (2Ki 22; 2Ch 18). Established judges (2Ch 19). Joined with Joram against Moab (2Ki 3; 2Ch 20).

JEHU

1. Prophet against Baasha (2Ki 16:1–7).

2. King of Israel. Anointed by Elijah to obliterate house of Ahab (1Ki 19:16–17); anointed by servant of Elisha (2Ki 9:1–13). Killed Joram and Ahaziah (2Ki 9:14–29; 2Ch 22:7–9), Jezebel (2Ki 9:30–37), relatives of Ahab (2Ki 10:1–17), ministers of Baal (2Ki 10:18–29). Death (2Ki 10:30–36).

JEPHTHAH

Judge from Gilead who delivered Israel from Ammon (Jdg 10:6–12:7). Made rash vow concerning his daughter (Jdg 11:30–40).

JEREMIAH

Prophet to Judah (Jer 1:1–3). Called by the LORD (Jer 1). Put in stocks (Jer 20:1–3). Threatened for prophesying (Jer 11:18–23; 26). Opposed by Hananiah (Jer 28). Scroll burned (Jer 36). Imprisoned (Jer 37). Thrown into cistern (Jer 38). Forced to Egypt with those fleeing Babylonians (Jer 43).

JERICHO

Nu 22: 1 along the Jordan across from *J.*
Jos 3: 16 the people crossed over opposite *J.*
5: 10 camped at Gilgal on the plains of *J,*
Lk 10: 30 going down from Jerusalem to *J,*
Heb 11: 30 By faith the walls of *J* fell,

JEROBOAM

1. Official of Solomon; rebelled to become first king of Israel (1Ki 11:26–40; 12:1–20; 2Ch 10). Idolatry (1Ki 12:25–33); judgment for (1Ki 13–14; 2Ch 13).

2. Son of Jehoash; king of Israel (1Ki 14:23–29).

JERUSALEM

Jos 10: 1 of *J* heard that Joshua had taken Ai
15: 8 of the Jebusite city (that is, *J*).
Jdg 1: 8 The men of Judah attacked *J* also
1Sa 17: 54 head and brought it to *J,*
2Sa 5: 5 and in *J* he reigned over all Israel
5: 6 and his men marched to *J*
9: 13 And Mephibosheth lived in *J,*
11: 1 But David remained in *J.*
15: 29 took the ark of God back to *J*
24: 16 stretched out his hand to destroy *J,*
1Ki 3: 1 the LORD, and the wall around *J.*
9: 15 the wall of *J,* and Hazor, Megiddo
9: 19 whatever he desired to build in *J,*
10: 26 cities and also with him in *J.*
10: 27 as common in *J* as stones,
11: 7 of *J,* Solomon built a high place
11: 13 my servant and for the sake of *J,*

11: 36 always have a lamp before me in *J*,
11: 42 Solomon reigned in *J*
12: 27 at the temple of the LORD in *J*,
14: 21 and he reigned seventeen years in *J*
14: 25 Shishak king of Egypt attacked *J*.
15: 2 and he reigned in *J* three years.
15: 10 and he reigned in *J* forty-one years.
22: 42 he reigned in *J* twenty-five years.
2Ki 8: 17 and he reigned in *J* eight years.
8: 26 and he reigned in *J* one year.
12: 1 and he reigned in *J* forty years.
12: 17 Then he turned to attack *J*.
14: 2 he reigned in *J* twenty-nine years.
14: 13 Then Jehoash went to *J*
15: 2 and he reigned in *J* fifty-two years.
15: 33 and he reigned in *J* sixteen years.
16: 2 and he reigned in *J* sixteen years.
16: 5 Israel marched up to fight against *J*
18: 2 he reigned in *J* twenty-nine years.
18: 17 Lachish to King Hezekiah at *J*.
19: 31 For out of *J* will come a remnant,
21: 1 and he reigned in *J* fifty-five years.
21: 12 going to bring such disaster on *J*
21: 19 and he reigned in *J* two years.
22: 1 he reigned in *J* thirty-one years.
23: 27 and I will reject *J*, the city I chose,
23: 31 and he reigned in *J* three months.
23: 36 and he reigned in *J* eleven years.
24: 8 and he reigned in *J* three months.
24: 10 king of Babylon advanced on *J*
24: 14 He carried into exile all *J*:
24: 18 and he reigned in *J* eleven years.
24: 20 anger that all this happened to *J*
25: 1 king of Babylon marched against *J*
25: 9 royal palace and all the houses of *J*.
1Ch 11: 4 and all the Israelites marched to *J*,
21: 16 sword in his hand extended over *J*.
2Ch 1: 4 he had pitched a tent for it in *J*.
3: 1 the LORD in *J* on Mount Moriah,
6: 6 now I have chosen *J* for my Name
9: 1 she came to *J* to test him
20: 15 and all who live in Judah and *J*!
20: 27 and *J* returned joyfully to *J*,
29: 8 LORD has fallen on Judah and *J*;
36: 19 and broke down the wall of *J*;
Ezr 1: 2 a temple for him at *J* in Judah.
2: 1 to Babylon (they returned to *J*
3: 1 people assembled as one man in *J*.
4: 12 up to us from you have gone to *J*
4: 24 of God in *J* came to a standstill
6: 12 or to destroy this temple in *J*.
7: 8 Ezra arrived in *J* in the fifth month
9: 9 a wall of protection in Judah and *J*.
10: 7 for all the exiles to assemble in *J*.
Ne 1: 2 the exile, and also about *J*.
1: 3 The wall of *J* is broken down,
2: 11 to *J*, and after staying there three
2: 17 Come, let us rebuild the wall of *J*,
2: 20 you have no share in *J* or any claim
3: 8 They restored *J* as far as the Broad
4: 8 fight against *J* and stir up trouble
11: 1 leaders of the people settled in *J*,
12: 27 At the dedication of the wall of *J*,
12: 43 in *J* could be heard far away.
Ps 51: 18 build up the walls of *J*.
79: 1 they have reduced *J* to rubble.
122: 2 in your gates, O *J*.
122: 3 *J* is built like a city
122: 6 Pray for the peace of *J*:
125: 2 As the mountains surround *J*,
128: 5 may you see the prosperity of *J*,
137: 5 If I forget you, O *J*,
147: 2 The LORD builds up *J*;
147: 12 Extol the LORD, O *J*;
SS 6: 4 lovely as *J*,
Isa 1: 1 and *J* that Isaiah son of Amoz saw
2: 1 saw concerning Judah and *J*:
3: 1 is about to take from *J* and Judah
3: 8 *J* staggers,

4: 3 recorded among the living in *J*.
8: 14 And for the people of *J* he will be
27: 13 LORD on the holy mountain in *J*.
31: 5 the LORD Almighty will shield *J*;
33: 20 your eyes will see *J*,
40: 2 Speak tenderly to *J*,
40: 9 You who bring good tidings to *J*,
52: 1 O *J*, the holy city.
52: 2 rise up, sit enthroned, O *J*.
62: 6 on your walls, O *J*;
62: 7 give him no rest till he establishes *J*
65: 18 for I will create *J* to be a delight
Jer 2: 2 and proclaim in the hearing of *J*:
3: 17 time they will call *J* The Throne
4: 5 and proclaim in *J* and say:
4: 14 O *J*, wash the evil from your heart
5: 1 "Go up and down the streets of *J*,
6: 6 and build siege ramps against *J*.
8: 5 Why does *J* always turn away?
9: 11 "I will make *J* a heap of ruins,
13: 27 Woe to you, O *J*!
23: 14 And among the prophets of *J*
24: 1 into exile from *J* to Babylon
26: 18 *J* will become a heap of rubble,
32: 2 of Babylon was then besieging *J*,
33: 10 the streets of *J* that are deserted,
39: 1 This is how *J* was taken: In
51: 50 and think on *J*."
52: 14 broke down all the walls around *J*.
La 1: 7 *J* remembers all the treasures
Eze 14: 21 send against *J* my four dreadful
16: 2 confront *J* with her detestable
Da 6: 10 the windows opened toward *J*.
9: 2 of *J* would last seventy years.
9: 12 done like what has been done to *J*.
9: 25 and rebuild *J* until the Anointed
Joel 3: 1 restore the fortunes of Judah and *J*,
3: 16 and thunder from *J*;
3: 17 *J* will be holy;
Am 2: 5 will consume the fortresses of *J*."
Ob : 11 and cast lots for *J*,
Mic 1: 5 Is it not *J*?
4: 2 the word of the LORD from *J*.
Zep 3: 16 On that day they will say to *J*,
Zec 1: 14 'I am very jealous for *J* and Zion,
1: 17 comfort Zion and choose *J*.' "
2: 2 He answered me, "To measure *J*,
2: 4 '*J* will be a city without walls
8: 3 I will return to Zion and dwell in *J*.
8: 8 I will bring them back to live in *J*;
8: 15 determined to do good again to *J*
8: 22 powerful nations will come to *J*
9: 9 Shout, Daughter of *J*!
9: 10 and the war-horses from *J*,
12: 3 I will make *J* an immovable rock
12: 10 the inhabitants of *J* a spirit of grace
14: 2 the nations to *J* to fight against it;
14: 8 living water will flow out from *J*,
14: 16 that have attacked *J* will go up
Mt 16: 21 to his disciples that he must go to *J*
20: 18 said to them, "We are going up to *J*
21: 10 When Jesus entered *J*, the whole
23: 37 "O *J*, *J*, you who kill the prophets
Mk 10: 33 "We are going up to *J*," he said,
Lk 2: 22 Mary took him to *J* to present him
2: 41 Every year his parents went to *J*
2: 43 the boy Jesus stayed behind in *J*,
4: 9 The devil led him to *J*
9: 31 about to bring to fulfillment at *J*.
9: 51 Jesus resolutely set out for *J*,
13: 34 die outside *J*! "O *J*, *J*,
18: 31 told them, "We are going up to *J*,
19: 41 As he approached *J* and saw
21: 20 "When you see *J* being surrounded
21: 24 *J* will be trampled
24: 47 name to all nations, beginning at *J*.
Jn 4: 20 where we must worship is in *J*."
Ac 1: 4 this command: "Do not leave *J*,
1: 8 and you will be my witnesses in *J*,

6: 7 of disciples in *J* increased rapidly,
20: 22 by the Spirit, I am going to *J*,
23: 11 As you have testified about me in *J*
Ro 15: 19 So from *J* all the way
Gal 4: 25 corresponds to the present city of *J*
4: 26 But the *J* that is above is free,
Heb 12: 22 to the heavenly *J*, the city
Rev 3: 12 the new *J*, which is coming
21: 2 I saw the Holy City, the new *J*,
21: 10 and showed me the Holy City, *J*,

JESSE

Father of David (Ru 4:17–22; 1Sa 16; 1Ch 2:12–17).

JESUS

LIFE: Genealogy (Mt 1:1–17; Lk 3:21–37). Birth announced (Mt 1:18–25; Lk 1:26–45). Birth (Mt 2:1–12; Lk 2:1–40). Escape to Egypt (Mt 2:13–23). As a boy in the temple (Lk 2:41–52). Baptism (Mt 3:13–17; Mk 1:9–11; Lk 3:21–22; Jn 1:32–34). Temptation (Mt 4:1–11; Mk 1:12–13; Lk 4:1–13). Ministry in Galilee (Mt 4:12–18:35; Mk 1:14–9:50; Lk 4:14–13:9; Jn 1:35–2:11; 4; 6), Transfiguration (Mt 17:1–8; Mk 9:2–8; Lk 9:28–36), on the way to Jerusalem (Mt 19–20; Mk 10; Lk 13:10–19:27), in Jerusalem (Mt 21–25; Mk 11–13; Lk 19:28–21:38; Jn 2:12–3:36; 5; 7–12). Last supper (Mt 26:17–35; Mk 14:12–31; Lk 22:1–38; Jn 13–17). Arrest and trial (Mt 26:36–27:31; Mk 14:43–15:20; Lk 22:39–23:25; Jn 18:1–19:16). Crucifixion (Mt 27:32–66; Mk 15:21–47; Lk 23:26–55; Jn 19:28–42). Resurrection and appearances (Mt 28; Mk 16; Lk 24; Jn 20–21; Ac 1:1–11; 7:56; 9:3–6; 1Co 15:1–8; Rev 1:1–20).

MIRACLES. Healings: official's son (Jn 4:43–54), demoniac in Capernaum (Mk 1:23–26; Lk 4:33–35), Peter's mother-in-law (Mt 8:14–17; Mk 1:29–31; Lk 4:38–39), leper (Mt 8:2–4; Mk 1:40–45; Lk 5:12–16), paralytic (Mt 9:1–8; Mk 2:1–12; Lk 5:17–26), cripple (Jn 5:1–9), shriveled hand (Mt 12:10–13; Mk 3:1–5; Lk 6:6–11), centurion's servant (Mt 8:5–13; Lk 7:1–10), widow's son raised (Lk 7:11–17), demoniac (Mt 12:22–23; Lk 11:14), Gadarene demoniacs (Mt 8:28–34; Mk 5:1–20; Lk 8:26–39), woman's bleeding and Jairus' daughter (Mt 9:18–26; Mk 5:21–43; Lk 8:40–56), blind man (Mt 9:27–31), mute man (Mt 9:32–33), Canaanite woman's daughter (Mt 15:21–28; Mk 7:24–30), deaf man (Mk 7:31–37), blind man (Mk 8:22–26), demoniac boy (Mt 17:14–18; Mk 9:14–29; Lk 9:37–43), ten lepers (Lk 17:11–19), man born blind (Jn 9:1–7), Lazarus raised (Jn 11), crippled woman (Lk 13:11–17), man with dropsy (Lk 14:1–6), two blind men (Mt 20:29–34; Mk 10:46–52; Lk 18:35–43), Malchus' ear (Lk 22:50–51). Other Miracles: water to wine (Jn 2:1–11), catch of fish (Lk 5:1–11), storm stilled (Mt 8:23–27; Mk 4:37–41; Lk 8:22–25), 5,000 fed (Mt 14:15–21; Mk 6:35–44; Lk 9:10–17; Jn 6:1–14), walking on water (Mt 14:25–33; Mk 6:48–52; Jn 6:15–21), 4,000 fed (Mt 15:32–39; Mk 8:1–9), money from fish (Mt 17:24–27), fig tree cursed (Mt 21:18–22; Mk 11:12–14), catch of fish (Jn 21:1–14).

MAJOR TEACHING: Sermon on the Mount (Mt 5–7; Lk 6:17–49), to Nicodemus (Jn 3), to Samaritan woman (Jn 4), Bread of Life (Jn 6:22–59), at Feast of Tabernacles (Jn 7–8), woes to Pharisees (Mt 23; Lk 11:37–54), Good Shepherd (Jn 10:1–18), Olivet Discourse (Mt 24–25; Mk 13; Lk 21:5–36), Upper Room Discourse (Jn 13–16).

PARABLES: Sower (Mt 13:3–23; Mk 4:3–25; Lk 8:5–18), seed's growth (Mk 4:26–29), wheat and weeds (Mt 13:24–30, 36–43), mustard seed (Mt 13:31–32; Mk 4:30–32), yeast (Mt 13:33; Lk 13:20–21), hidden treasure (Mt 13:44), valuable pearl (Mt 13:45–46), net (Mt 13:47–51), house owner (Mt 13:52), good Samaritan (Lk 10:25–37), unmerciful servant (Mt 18:15–35), lost sheep (Mt 18:10–14; Lk 15:4–7), lost coin (Lk 15:8–10), lost son (Lk 15:11–32), dishonest manager (Lk 16:1–13), rich man and Lazarus (Lk 16:19–31), persistent widow (Lk 18:1–8), Pharisee and tax collector (Lk 18:9–14), payment of workers (Mt 20:1–16), tenants and the vineyard (Mt 21:28–46; Mk 12:1–12; Lk 20:9–19), wedding banquet (Mt 22:1–14), faithful servant (Mt 24:45–51), ten virgins (Mt 25:1–13), talents (Mt 25:14–30; Lk 19:12–27).

DISCIPLES see APOSTLES. Call of (Jn 1:35–51; Mt 4:18–22; 9:9; Mk 1:16–20; 2:13–14; Lk 5:1–11, 27–28). Named Apostles (Mk 3:13–19; Lk 6:12–16). Twelve sent out (Mt 10; Mk 6:7–11; Lk 9:1–5). Seventy sent out (Lk 10:1–24). Defection of (Jn 6:60–71; Mt 26:56; Mk 14:50–52). Final commission (Mt 28:16–20; Jn 21:15–23; Ac 1:3–8).

Ac 2: 32 God has raised this *J* to life,
9: 5 "I am *J*, whom you are persecuting
9: 34 said to him, "*J* Christ heals you.
15: 11 of our Lord *J* that we are saved,
16: 31 "Believe in the Lord *J*,
20: 24 the task the Lord *J* has given me—
Ro 3: 24 redemption that came by Christ *J*.
5: 17 life through the one man, *J* Christ.
8: 1 for those who are in Christ *J*,
1Co 1: 7 for our Lord *J* Christ to be revealed
2: 2 except *J* Christ and him crucified.
6: 11 in the name of the Lord *J* Christ
8: 6 and there is but one Lord, *J* Christ,
12: 3 and no one can say, "*J* is Lord,"
2Co 4: 5 not preach ourselves, but *J* Christ
13: 5 Do you not realize that Christ *J* is
Gal 2: 16 but by faith in *J* Christ.
3: 28 for you are all one in Christ *J*.
5: 6 in Christ *J* neither circumcision
6: 17 bear on my body the marks of *J*.
Eph 1: 5 as his sons through *J* Christ,
2: 10 created in Christ *J*
2: 20 with Christ *J* himself as the chief
Php 1: 6 until the day of Christ *J*.
2: 5 be the same as that of Christ *J*:
2: 10 name of *J* every knee should bow,
Col 3: 17 do it all in the name of the Lord *J*,
1Th 1: 10 whom he raised from the dead—*J*,
4: 14 We believe that *J* died
5: 23 at the coming of our Lord *J* Christ.
2Th 1: 7 when the Lord *J* is revealed
2: 1 the coming of our Lord *J* Christ
1Ti 1: 15 Christ *J* came into the world
2Ti 1: 10 appearing of our Savior, Christ *J*,
2: 3 us like a good soldier of Christ *J*.
3: 12 life in Christ *J* will be persecuted,
Tit 2: 13 our great God and Savior, *J* Christ,
Heb 2: 9 But we see *J*, who was made a little
2: 11 So *J* is not ashamed to call them
3: 1 fix your thoughts on *J*, the apostle
3: 3 *J* has been found worthy
4: 14 through the heavens, *J* the Son
6: 20 where *J*, who went before us,
7: 22 *J* has become the guarantee
7: 24 but because *J* lives forever,
8: 6 But the ministry *J* has received is
12: 2 Let us fix our eyes on *J*, the author
12: 24 to *J* the mediator of a new
1Pe 1: 3 the resurrection of *J* Christ
2Pe 1: 16 and coming of our Lord *J* Christ,
1Jn 1: 7 and the blood of *J*, his Son,
2: 1 *J* Christ, the Righteous One.
2: 6 to live in him must walk as *J* did.
4: 15 anyone acknowledges that *J* is
Rev 1: 1 The revelation of *J* Christ,
22: 16 *J*, have sent my angel
22: 20 Come, Lord *J*.

JETHRO

Father-in-law and adviser of Moses (Ex 3:1; 18). Also known as Reuel (Ex 2:18).

JEW (JEWS JEWS' JUDAISM)
Est 2: 5 of Susa a *J* of the tribe of Benjamin,
Zec 8: 23 of one *J* by the hem of his robe
Ac 21: 39 "I am a *J*, from Tarsus in Cilicia,
Ro 1: 16 first for the *J*, then for the Gentile.
2: 28 A man is not a *J* if he is only one
10: 12 there is no difference between *J*
1Co 9: 20 To the Jews I became like a *J*,
Gal 2: 14 "You are a *J*, yet you live like
3: 28 There is neither *J* nor Greek,
Col 3: 11 Here there is no Greek or *J*,

JEWEL (JEWELRY JEWELS)
Pr 20: 15 that speak knowledge are a rare *j*.
SS 4: 9 with one *j* of your necklace.
Rev 21: 11 that of a very precious *j*,

JEWELRY (JEWEL)
Ex 35: 22 and brought gold *j* of all kinds:
Jer 2: 32 Does a maiden forget her *j*,
Eze 16: 11 you with *j*: I put bracelets
1Pe 3: 3 wearing of gold *j* and fine clothes.

JEWELS (JEWEL)
Isa 54: 12 your gates of sparkling *j*,
61: 10 as a bride adorns herself with her *j*.
Zec 9: 16 like *j* in a crown.

JEWS (JEW)
Ne 4: 1 He ridiculed the *J*,
Est 3: 13 kill and annihilate all the *J*—
4: 14 and deliverance for the *J* will arise
Mt 2: 2 who has been born king of the *J*?
27: 11 "Are you the king of the *J*?" "Yes,
Jn 4: 9 (For *J* do not associate
4: 22 for salvation is from the *J*.
19: 3 saying, "Hail, king of the *J*!"
Ac 20: 21 I have declared to both *J*
Ro 3: 29 Is God the God of *J* only?
9: 24 not only from the *J* but
15: 27 they owe it to the *J* to share
1Co 1: 22 *J* demand miraculous signs
9: 20 To the *J* I became like a Jew,
12: 13 whether *J* or Greeks, slave or free
Gal 2: 8 of Peter as an apostle to the *J*,
Rev 2: 9 slander of those who say they are *J*
3: 9 claim to be *J* though they are not,

JEWS' (JEW)
Ro 15: 27 shared in the *J* spiritual blessings,

JEZEBEL

Sidonian wife of Ahab (1Ki 16:31). Promoted Baal worship (1Ki 16:32–33). Killed prophets of the LORD (1Ki 18:4, 13). Opposed Elijah (1Ki 19:1–2). Had Naboth killed (1Ki 21). Death prophesied (1Ki 21:17–24). Killed by Jehu (2Ki 9:30–37).

JEZREEL
2Ki 9: 36 at *J* dogs will devour Jezebel's flesh
10: 7 and sent them to Jehu in *J*.
Hos 1: 4 house of Jehu for the massacre at *J*,

JOAB

Nephew of David (1Ch 2:16). Commander of his army (2Sa 8:16). Victorious over Ammon (2Sa 10; 1Ch 19), Rabbah (2Sa 11; 1Ch 20), Jerusalem (1Ch 11:6), Absalom (2Sa 18), Sheba (2Sa 20). Killed Abner (2Sa 3:22–39), Amasa (2Sa 20:1–13). Numbered David's army (2Sa 24; 1Ch 21). Sided with Adonijah (1Ki 1:17, 19). Killed by Benaiah (1Ki 2:5–6, 28–35).

JOASH

Son of Ahaziah; king of Judah. Sheltered from Athaliah by Jehoiada (2Ki 11; 2Ch 22:10–23:21). Repaired temple (2Ki 12; 2Ch 24).

JOB

Wealthy man from Uz; feared God (Job 1:1–5). Righteousness tested by disaster (Job 1:6–22), personal affliction (Job 2). Maintained innocence in debate with three friends (Job 3–31), Elihu (Job 32–37). Rebuked by the LORD (Job 38–41). Vindicated and restored to greater stature by the LORD (Job 42). Example of righteousness (Eze 14:14, 20).

JOCHEBED*

Mother of Moses and Aaron (Ex 6:20; Nu 26:59).

JOEL

Prophet (Joel 1:1; Ac 2:16).

JOHN

1. Son of Zechariah and Elizabeth (Lk 1). Called the Baptist (Mt 3:1–12; Mk 1:2–8). Witness to Jesus (Mt 3:11–12; Mk 1:7–8; Lk 3:15–18; Jn 1:6–35; 3:27–30; 5:33–36). Doubts about Jesus (Mt 11:2–6; Lk 7:18–23). Arrest (Mt 4:12; Mk 1:14). Execution (Mt 14:1–12; Mk 6:14–29; Lk 9:7–9). Ministry compared to Elijah (Mt 11:7–19; Mk 9:11–13; Lk 7:24–35).

2. Apostle; brother of James (Mt 4:21–22; 10:2; Mk 3:17; Lk 5:1–10). At transfiguration (Mt 17:1–13; Mk 9:1–13; Lk 9:28–36). Desire to be greatest (Mk 10:35–45). Leader of church at Jerusalem (Ac 4:1–3; Gal 2:9). Elder who wrote epistles (2Jn 1; 3Jn 1). Prophet who wrote Revelation (Rev 1:1; 22:8).

3. Cousin of Barnabas, co-worker with Paul, (Ac 12:12–13:13; 15:37), see MARK.

JOIN (JOINED JOINS)
Ne 10: 29 all these now *j* their brothers
Pr 23: 20 Do not *j* those who drink too much
24: 21 and do not *j* with the rebellious,
Jer 3: 18 of Judah will *j* the house of Israel,
Eze 37: 17 *J* them together into one stick
Da 11: 34 who are not sincere will *j* them.
Ro 15: 30 to *j* me in my struggle by praying
2Ti 1: 8 *j* with me in suffering for the gospel

JOINED (JOIN)
Zec 2: 11 "Many nations will be *j*
Mt 19: 6 Therefore what God has *j* together,
Mk 10: 9 Therefore what God has *j* together,
Ac 1: 14 They all *j* together constantly
Eph 2: 21 him the whole building is *j* together
4: 16 *j* and held together

JOINS (JOIN)
1Co 16: 16 and to everyone who *j* in the work,

JOINT (JOINTS)
Ps 22: 14 and all my bones are out of *j*.

JOINTS (JOINT)
Heb 4: 12 even to dividing soul and spirit, *j*

JOKING*
Ge 19: 14 his sons-in-law thought he was *j*.
Pr 26: 19 and says, "I was only *j*!"
Eph 5: 4 or coarse *j*, which are out of place,

JONAH

Prophet in days of Jeroboam II (2Ki 14:25). Called to Nineveh; fled to Tarshish (Jnh 1:1–3). Cause of storm; thrown into sea (Jnh 1:4–16). Swallowed by fish (Jnh 1:17). Prayer (Jnh 2). Preached to Nineveh (Jnh 3). Attitude reproved by the LORD (Jnh 4). Sign of (Mt 12:39–41; Lk 11:29–32).

JONATHAN

Son of Saul (1Sa 13:16; 1Ch 8:33). Valiant warrior (1Sa 13–14). Relation to David (1Sa 18:1–4; 19–20; 23:16–18). Killed at Gilboa (1Sa 31). Mourned by David (2Sa 1).

JOPPA
Ezr 3: 7 logs by sea from Lebanon to *J*,
Jnh 1: 3 to *J*, where he found a ship bound
Ac 9: 43 Peter stayed in *J* for some time

JORAM

1. Son of Ahab; king of Israel. Fought with Jehoshaphat against Moab (2Ki 3). Killed with Ahaziah by Jehu (2Ki 8:25–29; 9:14–26; 2Ch 22:5–9).

2. See JEHORAM.

JORDAN
Ge 13: 10 plain of the *J* was well watered,
Nu 22: 1 and camped along the *J*
34: 12 boundary will go down along the *J*
Dt 3: 27 you are not going to cross this *J*.
Jos 1: 2 get ready to cross the *J* River
3: 11 go into the *J* ahead of you.
3: 17 ground in the middle of the *J*,
4: 22 Israel crossed the *J* on dry ground.'
2Ki 2: 7 and Elisha had stopped at the *J*.
2: 13 and stood on the bank of the *J*.
5: 10 wash yourself seven times in the *J*,
6: 4 They went to the *J* and began
Ps 114: 3 the *J* turned back;

Isa 9: 1 along the *J*— The people walking
Jer 12: 5 manage in the thickets by the *J*?
Mt 3: 6 baptized by him in the *J* River.
4: 15 the way to the sea, along the *J*,
Mk 1: 9 and was baptized by John in the *J*.

JOSEPH

1. Son of Jacob by Rachel (Ge 30:24; 1Ch 2:2). Favored by Jacob, hated by brothers (Ge 37:3–4). Dreams (Ge 37:5–11). Sold by brothers (Ge 37:12–36). Served Potiphar; imprisoned by false accusation (Ge 39). Interpreted dreams of Pharaoh's servants (Ge 40), of Pharaoh (Ge 41:4–40). Made greatest in Egypt (Ge 41:41–57). Sold grain to brothers (Ge 42–45). Brought Jacob and sons to Egypt (Ge 46–47). Sons Ephraim and Manasseh blessed (Ge 48). Blessed (Ge 49:22–26; Dt 33:13–17). Death (Ge 50:22–26; Ex 13:19; Heb 11:22). 12,000 from (Rev 7:8).

2. Husband of Mary, mother of Jesus (Mt 1:16–24; 2:13–19; Lk 1:27; 2; Jn 1:45).

3. Disciple from Arimathea, who gave his tomb for Jesus' burial (Mt 27:57–61; Mk 15:43–47; Lk 24:50–52).

4. Original name of Barnabas (Ac 4:36).

JOSHUA (HOSHEA)

1. Son of Nun; name changed from Hoshea (Nu 13:8, 16; 1Ch 7:27). Fought Amalekites under Moses (Ex 17:9–14). Servant of Moses on Sinai (Ex 24:13; 32:17). Spied Canaan (Nu 13). With Caleb, allowed to enter land (Nu 14:6, 30). Succeeded Moses (Dt 1:38; 31:1–8; 34:9).

Charged Israel to conquer Canaan (Jos 1). Crossed Jordan (Jos 3–4). Circumcised sons of wilderness wanderings (Jos 5). Conquered Jericho (Jos 6), Ai (Jos 7–8), five kings at Gibeon (Jos 10:1–28), southern Canaan (Jos 10:29–43), northern Canaan (Jos 11–12). Defeated at Ai (Jos 7). Deceived by Gibeonites (Jos 9). Renewed covenant (Jos 8:30–35; 24:1–27). Divided land among tribes (Jos 13–22). Last words (Jos 23). Death (Jos 24:28–31).

2. High priest during rebuilding of temple (Hag 1–2; Zec 3:1–9; 6:11).

JOSIAH

Son of Amon; king of Judah (2Ki 21:26; 1Ch 3:14). Prophesied (1Ki 13:2). Book of Law discovered during his reign (2Ki 22; 2Ch 34:14–31). Reforms (2Ki 23:1–25; 2Ch 34:1–13; 35:1–19). Killed by Pharaoh Neco (2Ki 23:29–30; 2Ch 35:20–27).

JOTHAM

1. Son of Gideon (Jdg 9).

2. Son of Azariah (Uzziah); king of Judah (2Ki 15:32–38; 2Ch 26:21–27:9).

JOURNEY

Dt 1: 33 who went ahead of you on your *j*,
2: 7 over your *j* through this vast desert
Jdg 18: 6 Your *j* has the LORD's approval."
Ezr 8: 21 and ask him for a safe *j* for us
Job 16: 22 before I go on the *j* of no return.
Isa 35: 8 The unclean will not *j* on it;
Mt 25: 14 it will be like a man going on a *j*,
Ro 15: 24 to have you assist me on my *j* there

JOY* (ENJOY ENJOYMENT JOYFUL JOYOUS OVERJOYED REJOICE REJOICES REJOICING)

Ge 31: 27 so I could send you away with *j*
Lev 9: 24 shouted for *j* and fell facedown.
Dt 16: 15 and your *j* will be complete.
Jdg 9: 19 may Abimelech be your *j*,
1Ch 12: 40 and sheep, for there was *j* in Israel.
16: 27 strength and *j* in his dwelling place.
16: 33 sing for *j* before the LORD,
29: 17 with *j* how willingly your people
29: 22 drank with great *j* in the presence
2Ch 30: 26 There was great *j* in Jerusalem,
Ezr 3: 12 while many others shouted for *j*.
3: 13 of the shouts of *j* from the sound
6: 16 of the house of God with *j*.
6: 22 with *j* by changing the attitude
6: 22 *j* the Feast of Unleavened Bread,
Ne 8: 10 for the *j* of the LORD is your
8: 12 and to celebrate with great *j*,
8: 17 And their *j* was very great.
12: 43 God had given them great *j*.
Est 8: 16 a time of happiness and *j*,
8: 17 there was *j* and gladness
9: 17 and made it a day of feasting and *j*.
9: 18 and made it a day of feasting and *j*.
9: 19 as a day of *j* and feasting,
9: 22 and *j* and giving presents of food
9: 22 their sorrow was turned into *j*
Job 3: 7 may no shout of *j* be heard in it.
6: 10 my *j* in unrelenting pain—
8: 21 and your lips with shouts of *j*.
9: 25 they fly away without a glimpse of *j*
10: 20 from me so I can have a moment's *j*
20: 5 the *j* of the godless lasts
33: 26 he sees God's face and shouts for *j*;
38: 7 and all the angels shouted for *j*?
Ps 4: 7 have filled my heart with greater *j*
5: 11 let them ever sing for *j*.
16: 11 me with *j* in your presence,
19: 8 giving *j* to the heart.
20: 5 We will shout for *j*
21: 1 How great is his *j* in the victories
21: 6 with the *j* of your presence.
27: 6 will I sacrifice with shouts of *j*;
28: 7 My heart leaps for *j*
30: 11 sackcloth and clothed me with *j*,
33: 3 play skillfully, and shout for *j*.
35: 27 shout for *j* and gladness;
42: 4 with shouts of *j* and thanksgiving
43: 4 to God, my *j* and my delight.
45: 7 by anointing you with the oil of *j*.
45: 15 They are led in with *j* and gladness;
47: 1 shout to God with cries of *j*.
47: 5 God has ascended amid shouts of *j*,
48: 2 the *j* of the whole earth.
51: 8 Let me hear *j* and gladness;
51: 12 to me the *j* of your salvation
65: 8 you call forth songs of *j*.
65: 13 they shout for *j* and sing.
66: 1 Shout with *j* to God, all the earth!
67: 4 the nations be glad and sing for *j*,
71: 23 My lips will shout for *j*
81: 1 Sing for *j* to God our strength;
86: 4 Bring *j* to your servant,
89: 12 Hermon sing for *j* at your name.
90: 14 for *j* and be glad all our days.
92: 4 I sing for *j* at the works
94: 19 your consolation brought *j*
95: 1 let us sing for *j* to the LORD;
96: 12 the trees of the forest will sing for *j*;
97: 11 and *j* on the upright in heart.
98: 4 for *j* to the LORD, all the earth,
98: 6 shout for *j* before the LORD,
98: 8 the mountains sing together for *j*;
100: 1 for *j* to the LORD, all the earth.
105: 43 his chosen ones with shouts of *j*;
106: 5 share in the *j* of your nation
107: 22 and tell of his works with songs of *j*
118: 15 Shouts of *j* and victory
119:111 they are the *j* of my heart.
126: 2 our tongues with songs of *j*.
126: 3 and we are filled with *j*.
126: 5 will reap with songs of *j*.
126: 6 will return with songs of *j*,
132: 9 may your saints sing for *j*."
132: 16 and her saints will ever sing for *j*.
137: 3 tormentors demanded songs of *j*;
137: 6 my highest *j*.
149: 5 and sing for *j* on their beds.
Pr 10: 1 A wise son brings *j* to his father,
10: 28 The prospect of the righteous is *j*,
11: 10 wicked perish, there are shouts of *j*.
12: 20 but *j* for those who promote peace.
14: 10 and no one else can share its *j*.
14: 13 and *j* may end in grief.
15: 20 A wise son brings *j* to his father,
15: 23 A man finds *j* in giving an apt reply
15: 30 A cheerful look brings *j*
17: 21 there is no *j* for the father of a fool.
21: 15 it brings *j* to the righteous
23: 24 of a righteous man has great *j*;
27: 9 incense bring *j* to the heart,
27: 11 my son, and bring *j* to my heart;
29: 3 A man who loves wisdom brings *j*
Ecc 8: 15 Then *j* will accompany him
11: 9 let your heart give you *j* in the days
Isa 9: 3 and increased their *j*;
12: 3 With *j* you will draw water
12: 6 Shout aloud and sing for *j*,
16: 9 shouts of *j* over your ripened fruit
16: 10 *J* and gladness are taken away
22: 13 But see, there is *j* and revelry,
24: 11 all *j* turns to gloom,
24: 14 raise their voices, they shout for *j*;
26: 19 wake up and shout for *j*.
35: 2 will rejoice greatly and shout for *j*.
35: 6 the mute tongue shout for *j*.
35: 10 Gladness and *j* will overtake them,
35: 10 everlasting *j* will crown their heads
42: 11 Let the people of Sela sing for *j*;
44: 23 Sing for *j*, O heavens,
48: 20 Announce this with shouts of *j*
49: 13 Shout for *j*, O heavens;
51: 3 *J* and gladness will be found in her,
51: 11 Gladness and *j* will overtake them,
51: 11 everlasting *j* will crown their heads
52: 8 together they shout for *j*.
52: 9 Burst into songs of *j* together,
54: 1 burst into song, shout for *j*,
55: 12 You will go out in *j*
56: 7 give them *j* in my house of prayer.
58: 14 then you will find your *j*
60: 5 heart will throb and swell with *j*;
60: 15 and the *j* of all generations.
61: 7 and everlasting *j* will be theirs.
65: 14 out of the *j* of their hearts,
65: 18 and its people a *j*.
66: 5 that we may see your *j*!'
Jer 7: 34 will bring an end to the sounds of *j*
15: 16 they were my *j* and my heart's
16: 9 will bring an end to the sounds of *j*
25: 10 banish from them the sounds of *j*
31: 7 "Sing with *j* for Jacob;
31: 12 shout for *j* on the heights of Zion;
31: 13 give them comfort and *j* instead
33: 9 this city will bring me renown, *j*,
33: 11 be heard once more the sounds of *j*
48: 33 *J* and gladness are gone
48: 33 no one treads them with shouts of *j*
48: 33 they are not shouts of *j*.
51: 48 will shout for *j* over Babylon,
La 2: 15 the *j* of the whole earth?"
5: 15 *J* is gone from our hearts;
Eze 7: 7 not *j*, upon the mountains.
24: 25 their *j* and glory, the delight
Joel 1: 12 Surely the *j* of mankind
1: 16 *j* and gladness
Mt 13: 20 and at once receives it with *j*.
13: 44 in his *j* went and sold all he had
28: 8 afraid yet filled with *j*,
Mk 4: 16 and at once receive it with *j*.
Lk 1: 14 He will be a *j* and delight to you,
1: 44 the baby in my womb leaped for *j*.
1: 58 great mercy, and they shared her *j*.
2: 10 news of great *j* that will be
6: 23 "Rejoice in that day and leap for *j*,
8: 13 the word with *j* when they hear it,
10: 17 The seventy-two returned with *j*
10: 21 full of *j* through the Holy Spirit,
24: 41 still did not believe it because of *j*
24: 52 returned to Jerusalem with great *j*.
Jn 3: 29 That *j* is mine, and it is now
3: 29 full of *j* when he hears
15: 11 and that your *j* may be complete.
15: 11 this so that my *j* may be in you

16: 20 but your grief will turn to *j.*
16: 21 because of her *j* that a child is born
16: 22 and no one will take away your *j.*
16: 24 and your *j* will be complete.
17: 13 measure of my *j* within them.
Ac 2: 28 with *j* in your presence.'
8: 8 So there was great *j* in that city.
13: 52 And the disciples were filled with *j*
14: 17 and fills your hearts with *j.*"
16: 34 he was filled with *j* because he had come
Ro 14: 17 peace and *j* in the Holy Spirit,
15: 13 the God of hope fill you with all *j*
15: 32 will I may come to you with *j*
16: 19 so I am full of *j* over you;
2Co 1: 24 but we work with you for your *j,*
2: 3 that you would all share my *j.*
7: 4 our troubles my *j* knows no
7: 7 so that my *j* was greater than ever.
8: 2 their overflowing *j* and their
Gal 4: 15 What has happened to all your *j?*
5: 22 *j,* peace, patience, kindness,
Php 1: 4 I always pray with *j*
1: 25 for your progress and *j* in the faith,
1: 26 being with you again your *j*
2: 2 then make my *j* complete
2: 29 him in the Lord with great *j,*
4: 1 and long for, my *j* and crown,
1Th 1: 6 with the *j* given by the Holy Spirit.
2: 19 For what is our hope, our *j,*
2: 20 Indeed, you are our glory and *j.*
3: 9 you in return for all the *j* we have
2Ti 1: 4 so that I may be filled with *j.*
Phm : 7 Your love has given me great *j*
Heb 1: 9 by anointing you with the oil of *j.*"
12: 2 for the *j* set before him endured
13: 17 them so that their work will be a *j,*
Jas 1: 2 Consider it pure *j,* my brothers,
4: 9 to mourning and your *j* to gloom.
1Pe 1: 8 with an inexpressible and glorious *j*
1Jn 1: 4 this to make our *j* complete.
2Jn : 4 It has given me great *j* to find some
: 12 so that our *j* may be complete.
3Jn : 3 It gave me great *j* to have some
: 4 I have no greater *j*
Jude : 24 without fault and with great *j*—

JOY * (JOY)
Dt 16: 14 Be *j* at your Feast—you, your sons
1Sa 18: 6 with *j* songs and with tambourines
1Ki 8: 66 *j* and glad in heart
1Ch 15: 16 as singers to sing *j* songs,
2Ch 7: 10 *j* and glad in heart
Ps 68: 3 may they be happy and *j.*
100: 2 come before him with *j* songs.
Ecc 9: 7 and drink your wine with a *j* heart,
Isa 24: 8 the *j* harp is silent.
Jer 31: 4 and go out to dance with the *j.*
Hab 3: 18 I will be *j* in God my Savior.
Zec 8: 19 and tenth months will become *j*
10: 7 Their children will see it and be *j;*
Ro 12: 12 Be *j* in hope, patient in affliction,
1Th 5: 16 Be *j* always; pray continually;
Heb 12: 22 thousands of angels in *j* assembly,

JOYOUS* (JOY)
Est 8: 15 the city of Susa held a *j* celebration.

JUBILANT
Ps 96: 12 let the fields be *j,* and everything
98: 4 burst into *j* song with music;

JUBILEE
Lev 25: 11 The fiftieth year shall be a *j* for you;

JUDAH (JUDEA)
1. Son of Jacob by Leah (Ge 29:35; 35:23; 1Ch 2:1). Did not want to kill Joseph (Ge 37:26–27). Among Canaanites, fathered Perez by Tamar (Ge 38). Tribe of blessed as ruling tribe (Ge 49:8–12; Dt 33:7), numbered (Nu 1:27; 26:22), allotted land (Jos 15; Eze 48:7), failed to fully possess (Jos 15:63; Jdg 1:1–20).

2. Name used for people and land of Southern Kingdom.
Ru 1: 7 take them back to the land of *J.*
2Sa 2: 4 king over the house of *J.*
Isa 1: 1 The vision concerning *J*
3: 8 *J* is falling;
Jer 13: 19 All *J* will be carried into exile,
30: 3 bring my people Israel and *J* back
Hos 1: 7 I will show love to the house of *J;*
Zec 10: 4 From *J* will come the cornerstone,
Mt 2: 6 least among the rulers of *J;*
Heb 7: 14 that our Lord descended from *J,*
8: 8 and with the house of *J.*
Rev 5: 5 of the tribe of *J,* the Root of David,

JUDAISM (JEW)
Ac 13: 43 devout converts to *J* followed Paul
Gal 1: 13 of my previous way of life in *J,*
1: 14 advancing in *J* beyond many Jews

JUDAS
1. Apostle; son of James (Lk 6:16; Jn 14:22; Ac 1:13). Probably also called Thaddaeus (Mt 10:3; Mk 3:18).
2. Brother of James and Jesus (Mt 13:55; Mk 6:3), also called Jude (Jude 1).
3. Christian prophet (Ac 15:22–32).
4. Apostle, also called Iscariot, who betrayed Jesus (Mt 10:4; 26:14–56; Mk 3:19; 14:10–50; Lk 6:16; 22:3–53; Jn 6:71; 12:4; 13:2–30; 18:2–11). Suicide of (Mt 27:3–5; Ac 1:16–25).

JUDEA (JUDAH)
Mt 2: 1 born in Bethlehem in *J,*
24: 16 are in *J* flee to the mountains.
Lk 3: 1 Pontius Pilate was governor of *J,*
Ac 1: 8 and in all *J* and Samaria,
9: 31 Then the church throughout *J,*
1Th 2: 14 imitators of God's churches in *J,*

JUDGE (JUDGED JUDGES JUDGING JUDGMENT JUDGMENTS)
Ge 16: 5 May the LORD *j* between you
18: 25 Will not the *J* of all the earth do
Lev 19: 15 but *j* your neighbor fairly.
Dt 1: 16 between your brothers and *j* fairly,
17: 12 man who shows contempt for the *j*
32: 36 The LORD will *j* his people
Jdg 2: 18 Whenever the LORD raised up a *j*
1Sa 2: 10 the LORD will *j* the ends
3: 13 that I would *j* his family forever
7: 15 *j* over Israel all the days of his life.
24: 12 May the LORD *j* between you
1Ki 8: 32 *J* between your servants,
1Ch 16: 33 for he comes to *j* the earth.
2Ch 6: 23 *J* between your servants, repaying
19: 7 *J* carefully, for with the LORD our
Job 9: 15 plead with my *J* for mercy.
Ps 7: 8 *J* me, O LORD, according
7: 8 let the LORD *j* the peoples.
7: 11 God is a righteous *j,*
9: 8 He will *j* the world in righteousness
50: 6 for God himself is *j.*
51: 4 and justified when you *j.*
75: 2 it is I who *j* uprightly.
76: 9 when you, O God, rose up to *j,*
82: 8 Rise up, O God, *j* the earth,
94: 2 Rise up, O *J* of the earth;
96: 10 he will *j* the peoples with equity.
96: 13 He will *j* the world in righteousness
98: 9 He will *j* the world in righteousness
110: 6 He will *j* the nations, heaping up
Pr 31: 9 Speak up and *j* fairly;
Isa 2: 4 He will *j* between the nations
3: 13 he rises to *j* the people.
11: 3 He will not *j* by what he sees
33: 22 For the LORD is our *j,*
Jer 11: 20 Almighty, you who *j* righteously
Eze 7: 3 I will *j* you according
7: 27 by their own standards I will *j* them
18: 30 O house of Israel, I will *j* you,
20: 36 so I will *j* you, declares
22: 2 "Son of man, will you *j* her?
34: 17 I will *j* between one sheep
Joel 3: 12 sit to *j* all the nations on every side.
Mic 3: 11 Her leaders *j* for a bribe,
4: 3 He will *j* between many peoples
Mt 7: 1 Do not *j,* or you too will be judged.
Lk 6: 37 "Do not *j,* and you will not be
18: 2 there was a *j* who neither feared
Jn 5: 27 And he has given him authority to *j*
5: 30 By myself I can do nothing; I *j* only
8: 16 But if I do *j,* my decisions are right,
12: 47 For I did not come to *j* the world,
12: 48 There is a *j* for the one who rejects
Ac 10: 42 as *j* of the living and the dead.
17: 31 a day when he will *j* the world
Ro 2: 16 day when God will *j* men's secrets
3: 6 how could God *j* the world?
14: 10 then, why do you *j* your brother?
1Co 4: 3 indeed, I do not even *j* myself.
4: 5 Therefore *j* nothing
6: 2 And if you are to *j* the world,
6: 2 that the saints will *j* the world?
Gal 2: 6 not *j* by external appearance—
Col 2: 16 Therefore do not let anyone *j* you
2Ti 4: 1 who will *j* the living and the dead,
4: 8 which the Lord, the righteous *J,*
Heb 10: 30 "The Lord will *j* his people."
12: 23 come to God, the *j* of all men,
13: 4 for God will *j* the adulterer
Jas 4: 12 There is only one Lawgiver and *J,*
4: 12 who are you to *j* your neighbor?
1Pe 4: 5 to him who is ready to *j* the living
Rev 20: 4 who had been given authority to *j.*

JUDGED (JUDGE)
Mt 7: 1 "Do not judge, or you too will be *j.*
1Co 4: 3 I care very little if I am *j* by you
10: 29 For why should my freedom be *j*
11: 31 But if we *j* ourselves, we would not
14: 24 all that he is a sinner and will be *j*
Jas 3: 1 who teach will be *j* more strictly.
Rev 20: 12 The dead were *j* according

JUDGES (JUDGE)
Jdg 2: 16 Then the LORD raised up *j,*
Job 9: 24 he blindfolds its *j.*
Ps 58: 11 there is a God who *j* the earth."
75: 7 But it is God who *j:*
Pr 29: 14 If a king *j* the poor with fairness,
Jn 5: 22 Moreover, the Father *j* no one,
1Co 4: 4 It is the Lord who *j* me.
Heb 4: 12 it *j* the thoughts and attitudes
1Pe 1: 17 on a Father who *j* each man's work
2: 23 himself to him who *j* justly.
Rev 19: 11 With justice he *j* and makes war.

JUDGING (JUDGE)
Ps 9: 4 on your throne, *j* righteously.
Pr 24: 23 To show partiality in *j* is not good:
Isa 16: 5 one who in *j* seeks justice
Mt 19: 28 *j* the twelve tribes of Israel.
Jn 7: 24 Stop *j* by mere appearances,

JUDGMENT (JUDGE)
Nu 33: 4 for the LORD had brought *j*
Dt 1: 17 of any man, for *j* belongs to God.
32: 41 and my hand grasps it in *j,*
1Sa 25: 33 May you be blessed for your good *j*
Ps 1: 5 the wicked will not stand in the *j,*
9: 7 he has established his throne for *j.*
76: 8 From heaven you pronounced *j,*
82: 1 he gives *j* among the "gods":
119: 66 Teach me knowledge and good *j,*
143: 2 Do not bring your servant into *j,*
Pr 3: 21 preserve sound *j* and discernment,
6: 32 man who commits adultery lacks *j;*
8: 14 Counsel and sound *j* are mine;
10: 21 but fools die for lack of *j.*
11: 12 man who lacks *j* derides his
12: 11 but he who chases fantasies lacks *j.*
17: 18 A man lacking in *j* strikes hands
18: 1 he defies all sound *j.*

28: 16 A tyrannical ruler lacks *j*,
Ecc 12: 14 God will bring every deed into *j*,
Isa 3: 14 The LORD enters into *j*
28: 6 justice to him who sits in *j*,
53: 8 By oppression and *j* he was taken
66: 16 the LORD will execute *j*
Jer 2: 35 But I will pass *j* on you
25: 31 he will bring *j* on all mankind
51: 18 when their *j* comes, they will
Eze 11: 10 and I will execute *j* on you
Da 7: 22 pronounced *j* in favor of the saints
Am 7: 4 Sovereign LORD was calling for *j*
Zec 8: 16 and sound *j* in your courts;
Mal 3: 5 "So I will come near to you for *j*.
Mt 5: 21 who murders will be subject to *j*.'
5: 22 with his brother will be subject to *j*.
10: 15 on the day of *j* than for that town.
11: 24 on the day of *j* than for you."
12: 36 have to give account on the day of *j*
12: 41 up at the *j* with this generation
Jn 5: 22 but has entrusted all *j* to the Son,
5: 30 as I hear, and my *j* is just,
7: 24 appearances, and make a right *j*."
8: 26 "I have much to say in *j* of you.
9: 39 "For *j* I have come into this world,
12: 31 Now is the time for *j* on this world;
16: 8 to sin and righteousness and *j*:
16: 11 in regard to *j*, because the prince
Ac 24: 25 self-control and the *j* to come,
Ro 2: 1 you who pass *j* on someone else,
2: 2 Now we know that God's *j*
5: 16 The *j* followed one sin
12: 3 rather think of yourself with sober *j*
14: 10 stand before God's *j* seat.
14: 13 Therefore let us stop passing *j*
1Co 7: 40 In my *j*, she is happier if she stays
11: 29 body of the Lord eats and drinks *j*
2Co 5: 10 appear before the *j* seat of Christ,
2Th 1: 5 is evidence that God's *j* is right,
1Ti 3: 6 fall under the same *j* as the devil.
5: 12 Thus they bring *j* on themselves,
Heb 6: 2 of the dead, and eternal *j*.
9: 27 to die once, and after that to face *j*,
10: 27 but only a fearful expectation of *j*
Jas 2: 13 *j* without mercy will be shown
4: 11 are not keeping it, but sitting in *j*
1Pe 4: 17 For it is time for *j* to begin
2Pe 2: 9 the unrighteous for the day of *j*,
3: 7 being kept for the day of *j*
1Jn 4: 17 have confidence on the day of *j*,
Jude : 6 bound with everlasting chains for *j*
Rev 14: 7 because the hour of his *j* has come.

JUDGMENTS (JUDGE)
Jer 1: 16 I will pronounce my *j* on my people
Da 9: 11 and sworn *j* written in the Law
Hos 6: 5 my *j* flashed like lightning
Ro 11: 33 How unsearchable his *j*,
1Co 2: 15 spiritual man makes *j* about all
Rev 16: 7 true and just are your *j*."

JUG
1Sa 26: 12 and water *j* near Saul's head,
1Ki 17: 12 of flour in a jar and a little oil in a *j*.

JUST* (JUSTICE JUSTIFICATION JUSTIFIED JUSTIFIES JUSTIFY JUSTIFYING JUSTLY)
Ge 18: 19 LORD by doing what is right and *j*,
Dt 2: 12 *j* as Israel did in the land
6: 3 *j* as the LORD, the God
27: 3 and honey, *j* as the LORD,
30: 9 *j* as he delighted in your fathers,
32: 4 and all his ways are *j*.
32: 4 upright and *j* is he.
32: 47 They are not *j* idle words for you—
32: 50 *j* as your brother Aaron died
2Sa 8: 15 doing what was *j* and right
1Ch 18: 14 doing what was *j* and right
2Ch 12: 6 and said, "The LORD is *j*."
Ne 9: 13 and laws that are *j* and right,
9: 33 you have been *j*; you have acted
Job 34: 17 Will you condemn the *j*
35: 2 Elihu said: "Do you think this is *j*?
Ps 37: 28 For the LORD loves the *j*
37: 30 and his tongue speaks what is *j*.
99: 4 what is *j* and right.
111: 7 of his hands are faithful and *j*;
119:121 I have done what is righteous and *j*;
Pr 1: 3 doing what is right and *j* and fair;
2: 8 for he guards the course of the *j*
2: 9 will understand what is right and *j*
8: 8 All the words of my mouth are *j*;
8: 15 and rulers make laws that are *j*;
12: 5 The plans of the righteous are *j*,
21: 3 To do what is right and *j*
Isa 32: 7 even when the plea of the needy is *j*
58: 2 They ask me for *j* decisions
Jer 4: 2 if in a truthful, *j* and righteous way
22: 3 what the LORD says: Do what is *j*
22: 15 He did what was right and *j*,
23: 5 do what is *j* and right in the land.
33: 15 he will do what is *j* and right
Eze 18: 5 who does what is *j* and right.
18: 19 Since the son has done what is *j*
18: 21 and does what is *j* and right,
18: 25 'The way of the Lord is not *j*.'
18: 27 and does what is *j* and right,
18: 29 'The way of the Lord is not *j*.'
33: 14 and does what is *j* and right—
33: 16 He has done what is *j* and right;
33: 17 But it is their way that is not *j*.
33: 17 'The way of the Lord is not *j*.'
33: 19 and does what is *j* and right,
33: 20 'The way of the Lord is not *j*.'
45: 9 and oppression and do what is *j*
Da 4: 37 does is right and all his ways are *j*.
Jn 5: 30 as I hear, and my judgment is *j*,
Ro 3: 26 as to be *j* and the one who justifies
2Th 1: 6 God is *j*: He will pay back trouble
Heb 2: 2 received its *j* punishment,
1Jn 1: 9 and *j* and will forgive us our sins
Rev 15: 3 *J* and true are your ways,
16: 5 "You are *j* in these judgments,
16: 7 true and *j* are your judgments."
19: 2 for true and *j* are his judgments.

JUSTICE* (JUST)
Ge 49: 16 "Dan will provide *j* for his people
Ex 23: 2 do not pervert *j* by siding
23: 6 "Do not deny *j* to your poor people
Lev 19: 15 " 'Do not pervert *j*; do not show
Dt 16: 19 Do not pervert *j* or show partiality.
16: 20 Follow *j* and *j* alone,
24: 17 the alien or the fatherless of *j*,
27: 19 Cursed is the man who withholds *j*
1Sa 8: 3 accepted bribes and perverted *j*.
2Sa 15: 4 and I would see that he gets *j*."
15: 6 came to the king asking for *j*,
1Ki 3: 11 for discernment in administering *j*,
3: 28 wisdom from God to administer *j*.
7: 7 the Hall of *J*, where he was to judge
10: 9 to maintain *j* and righteousness."
2Ch 9: 8 to maintain *j* and righteousness."
Ezr 7: 25 and judges to administer *j*
Est 1: 13 experts in matters of law and *j*,
Job 8: 3 Does God pervert *j*?
9: 19 matter of *j*, who will summon him?
19: 7 though I call for help, there is no *j*.
27: 2 as God lives, who has denied me *j*,
29: 14 *j* was my robe and my turban.
31: 13 "If I have denied *j*
34: 5 but God denies me *j*.
34: 12 that the Almighty would pervert *j*.
34: 17 Can he who hates *j* govern?
36: 3 I will ascribe *j* to my Maker.
36: 17 *j* have taken hold of you.
37: 23 in his *j* and great righteousness,
40: 8 "Would you discredit my *j*?
Ps 7: 6 Awake, my God; decree *j*.
9: 8 he will govern the peoples with *j*.
9: 16 The LORD is known by his *j*;
11: 7 he loves *j*;
33: 5 LORD loves righteousness and *j*;
36: 6 your *j* like the great deep.
37: 6 *j* of your cause like the noonday
45: 6 a scepter of *j* will be the scepter
72: 1 Endow the king with your *j*, O God
72: 2 your afflicted ones with *j*.
89: 14 *j* are the foundation of your throne;
97: 2 *j* are the foundation of his throne.
99: 4 The King is mighty, he loves *j*—
101: 1 I will sing of your love and *j*;
103: 6 and *j* for all the oppressed.
106: 3 Blessed are they who maintain *j*,
112: 5 who conducts his affairs with *j*.
140: 12 I know that the LORD secures *j*
Pr 8: 20 along the paths of *j*,
16: 10 and his mouth should not betray *j*.
17: 23 to pervert the course of *j*.
18: 5 or to deprive the innocent of *j*.
19: 28 A corrupt witness mocks at *j*,
21: 15 When *j* is done, it brings joy
28: 5 Evil men do not understand *j*,
29: 4 By *j* a king gives a country stability
29: 7 The righteous care about *j*
29: 26 from the LORD that man gets *j*.
Ecc 3: 16 place of *j*— wickedness was there.
5: 8 poor oppressed in a district, and *j*
Isa 1: 17 Seek *j*,
1: 21 She once was full of *j*;
1: 27 Zion will be redeemed with *j*,
5: 7 he looked for *j*, but saw bloodshed;
5: 16 Almighty will be exalted by his *j*,
5: 23 but deny *j* to the innocent.
9: 7 it with *j* and righteousness
10: 2 and withhold *j* from the oppressed of
11: 4 with *j* he will give decisions
16: 5 one who in judging seeks *j*
28: 6 He will be a spirit of *j*
28: 17 I will make *j* the measuring line
29: 21 deprive the innocent of *j*.
30: 18 For the LORD is a God of *j*.
32: 1 and rulers will rule with *j*.
32: 16 *J* will dwell in the desert
33: 5 with *j* and righteousness.
42: 1 and he will bring *j* to the nations.
42: 3 In faithfulness he will bring forth *j*;
42: 4 till he establishes *j* on earth.
51: 4 my *j* will become a light
51: 5 my arm will bring *j* to the nations.
56: 1 "Maintain *j*
59: 4 No one calls for *j*;
59: 8 there is no *j* in their paths.
59: 9 So *j* is far from us,
59: 11 We look for *j*, but find none;
59: 14 So *j* is driven back,
59: 15 that there was no *j*.
61: 8 "For I, the LORD, love *j*;
Jer 9: 24 *j* and righteousness on earth,
10: 24 Correct me, LORD, but only with *j*
12: 1 speak with you about your *j*:
21: 12 " 'Administer *j* every morning;
30: 11 I will discipline you but only with *j*;
46: 28 I will discipline you but only with *j*;
La 3: 36 to deprive a man of *j*—
Eze 22: 29 mistreat the alien, denying them *j*.
34: 16 I will shepherd the flock with *j*.
Hos 2: 19 you in righteousness and *j*,
12: 6 maintain love and *j*,
Am 2: 7 and deny *j* to the oppressed.
5: 7 You who turn *j* into bitterness
5: 12 and you deprive the poor of *j*
5: 15 maintain *j* in the courts.
5: 24 But let *j* roll on like a river,
6: 12 But you have turned *j* into poison
Mic 3: 1 Should you not know *j*,
3: 8 and with *j* and might,
3: 9 who despise *j*
Hab 1: 4 and *j* never prevails.
1: 4 so that *j* is perverted.
Zep 3: 5 by morning he dispenses his *j*,

Zec 7: 9 'Administer true *j*; show mercy
Mal 2: 17 or "Where is the God of *j*?"
3: 5 and deprive aliens of *j*,
Mt 12: 18 he will proclaim *j* to the nations.
12: 20 till he leads *j* to victory.
23: 23 important matters of the law—*j*,
Lk 11: 42 you neglect *j* and the love of God.
18: 3 'Grant me *j* against my adversary.'
18: 5 I will see that she gets *j*,
18: 7 And will not God bring about *j*
18: 8 he will see that they get *j*,
Ac 8: 33 humiliation he was deprived of *j*.
17: 31 with *j* by the man he has appointed.
28: 4 *J* has not allowed him to live."
Ro 3: 25 He did this to demonstrate his *j*,
3: 26 it to demonstrate his *j*
2Co 7: 11 what readiness to see *j* done.
Heb 11: 33 administered *j*, and gained what
Rev 19: 11 With *j* he judges and makes war.

JUSTIFICATION* (JUST)
Eze 16: 52 for you have furnished some *j*
Ro 4: 25 and was raised to life for our *j*.
5: 16 many trespasses and brought *j*.
5: 18 of righteousness was *j* that brings

JUSTIFIED* (JUST)
Ps 51: 4 and *j* when you judge.
Lk 18: 14 rather than the other, went home *j*
Ac 13: 39 from everything you could not be *j*
13: 39 him everyone who believes is *j*
Ro 3: 24 and are *j* freely by his grace
3: 28 For we maintain that a man is *j*
4: 2 If, in fact, Abraham was *j* by works,
5: 1 since we have been *j* through faith,
5: 9 Since we have now been *j*
8: 30 those he called, he also *j*; those he *j*,
10: 10 heart that you believe and are *j*,
1Co 6: 11 you were *j* in the name
Gal 2: 16 in Christ Jesus that we may be *j*
2: 16 observing the law no one will be *j*.
2: 16 sinners' know that a man is not *j*
2: 17 "If, while we seek to be *j* in Christ,
3: 11 Clearly no one is *j* before God
3: 24 to Christ that we might be *j* by faith
5: 4 to be *j* by law have been alienated
Tit 3: 7 so that, having been *j* by his grace,
Jas 2: 24 You see that a person is *j*

JUSTIFIES* (JUST)
Ro 3: 26 one who *j* those who have faith
4: 5 but trusts God who *j* the wicked,
8: 33 God has chosen? It is God who *j*.

JUSTIFY* (JUST)
Est 7: 4 such distress would *j* disturbing
Job 40: 8 you condemn me to *j* yourself?
Isa 53: 11 my righteous servant will *j* many,
Lk 10: 29 But he wanted to *j* himself,
16: 15 "You are the ones who *j* yourselves
Ro 3: 30 who will *j* the circumcised by faith
Gal 3: 8 that God would *j* the Gentiles

JUSTIFYING* (JUST)
Job 32: 2 angry with Job for *j* himself rather

JUSTLY* (JUST)
Ps 58: 1 Do you rulers indeed speak *j*?
67: 4 for you rule the peoples *j*
Jer 7: 5 and deal with each other *j*,
Mic 6: 8 To act *j* and to love mercy
Lk 23: 41 We are punished *j*,
1Pe 2: 23 himself to him who judges *j*.

KADESH
Nu 20: 1 of Zin, and they stayed at *K*.
Dt 1: 46 And so you stayed in *K* many days

KADESH BARNEA
Nu 32: 8 I sent them from *K* to look over

KEBAR
Eze 1: 1 among the exiles by the *K* River,

KEDORLAOMER
Ge 14: 17 Abram returned from defeating *K*

KEEP (KEEPER KEEPING KEEPS KEPT)
Ge 31: 49 "May the LORD *k* watch
Ex 15: 26 his commands and *k* all his
20: 6 and *k* my commandments.
Lev 15: 31 You must *k* the Israelites separate
Nu 6: 24 and *k* you;
Dt 4: 2 but *k* the commands of the LORD
6: 17 Be sure to *k* the commands
7: 9 who love him and *k* his commands.
7: 12 your God will *k* his covenant
11: 1 your God and *k* his requirements,
13: 4 *K* his commands and obey him;
30: 10 your God and *k* his commands
30: 16 and to *k* his commands, decrees
Jos 22: 5 careful to *k* the commandment
1Ki 8: 58 and to *k* the commands,
2Ki 17: 19 Judah did not *k* the commands
23: 3 the LORD and *k* his commands,
1Ch 29: 18 and *k* their hearts loyal to you.
2Ch 6: 14 you who *k* your covenant of love
34: 31 the LORD and *k* his commands,
Job 14: 16 but not *k* track of my sin.
Ps 18: 28 You, O LORD, *k* my lamp burning
19: 13 *K* your servant also from willful
78: 10 they did not *k* God's covenant
119: 2 Blessed are they who *k* his statutes
119: 9 can a young man *k* his way pure?
121: 7 The LORD will *k* you
141: 3 *k* watch over the door of my lips.
Pr 4: 21 *k* them within your heart;
4: 24 *k* corrupt talk far from your lips.
30: 8 *K* falsehood and lies far from me;
Ecc 3: 6 a time to *k* and a time
12: 13 and *k* his commandments,
Isa 26: 3 You will *k* in perfect peace
42: 6 I will *k* you and will make you
58: 13 "If you *k* your feet
Jer 16: 11 forsook me and did not *k* my law.
Eze 20: 19 and be careful to *k* my laws.
Mt 10: 10 for the worker is worth his *k*.
Lk 12: 35 and *k* your lamps burning,
17: 33 tries to *k* his life will lose it,
Jn 10: 24 How long will you *k* us in suspense
12: 25 in this world will *k* it for eternal life
Ac 2: 24 for death to *k* its hold on him.
18: 9 "Do not be afraid; *k* on speaking,
Ro 7: 19 want to do—this I *k* on doing.
12: 11 but *k* your spiritual fervor,
14: 22 you believe about these things *k*
16: 17 *K* away from them.
1Co 1: 8 He will *k* you strong to the end,
2Co 12: 7 To *k* me from becoming conceited
Gal 5: 25 let us *k* in step with the Spirit.
Eph 4: 3 Make every effort to *k* the unity
2Th 3: 6 to *k* away from every brother who
1Ti 5: 22 *K* yourself pure.
2Ti 4: 5 *k* your head in all situations,
Heb 9: 20 God has commanded you to *k*."
13: 5 *K* your lives free from the love
Jas 1: 26 and yet does not *k* a tight rein
2: 8 If you really *k* the royal law found
3: 2 able to *k* his whole body in check.
2Pe 1: 8 will *k* you from being ineffective
Jude : 21 *K* yourselves in God's love
: 24 able to *k* you from falling
Rev 3: 10 also *k* you from the hour
22: 9 of all who *k* the words of this book.

KEEPER (KEEP)
Ge 4: 9 I my brother's *k*?" The LORD

KEEPING (KEEP)
Ex 20: 8 the Sabbath day by *k* it holy.
Dt 5: 12 the Sabbath day by *k* it holy,
13: 18 *k* all his commands that I am
Ps 19: 11 in *k* them there is great reward.
119:112 My heart is set on *k* your decrees
Pr 15: 3 *k* watch on the wicked
Mt 3: 8 Produce fruit in *k* with repentance.
Lk 2: 8 *k* watch over their flocks at night.
1Co 7: 19 *K* God's commands is what counts.
2Co 8: 5 and then to us in *k* with God's will.
Jas 4: 11 you are not *k* it, but sitting
1Pe 3: 16 and respect, *k* a clear conscience,
2Pe 3: 9 Lord is not slow in *k* his promise,

KEEPS (KEEP)
Ne 1: 5 who *k* his covenant of love
Ps 15: 4 who *k* his oath
Pr 12: 23 A prudent man *k* his knowledge
15: 21 of understanding *k* a straight
17: 28 a fool is thought wise if he *k* silent,
29: 11 a wise man *k* himself under control
Isa 56: 2 who *k* the Sabbath
Da 9: 4 who *k* his covenant of love
Am 5: 13 Therefore the prudent man *k* quiet
Jn 7: 19 Yet not one of you *k* the law.
8: 51 if anyone *k* my word, he will never
1Co 13: 5 is not easily angered, it *k* no record
Jas 2: 10 For whoever *k* the whole law
Rev 22: 7 Blessed is he who *k* the words

KEILAH
1Sa 23: 13 that David had escaped from *K*,

KEPT (KEEP)
Ex 12: 42 Because the LORD *k* vigil that
Dt 7: 8 and *k* the oath he swore
2Ki 18: 6 he *k* the commands the LORD had
Ne 9: 8 You have *k* your promise
Ps 130: 3 If you, O LORD, *k* a record of sins,
Isa 38: 17 In your love you *k* me
Mt 19: 20 these I have *k*," the young man
2Co 11: 9 I have *k* myself from being
2Ti 4: 7 finished the race, I have *k* the faith.
1Pe 1: 4 spoil or fade—*k* in heaven for you,

KERNEL
Mk 4: 28 then the full *k* in the head.
Jn 12: 24 a *k* of wheat falls to the ground

KEY (KEYS)
Isa 33: 6 the fear of the LORD is the *k*
Rev 20: 1 having the *k* to the Abyss

KEYS* (KEY)
Mt 16: 19 I will give you the *k* of the kingdom
Rev 1: 18 And I hold the *k* of death

KICK*
Ac 26: 14 for you to *k* against the goads.'

KILL (KILLED KILLS)
Ecc 3: 3 a time to *k* and a time to heal,
Mt 10: 28 *k* the body but cannot *k* the soul.
17: 23 They will *k* him, and on the third
Mk 9: 31 will *k* him, and after three days
10: 34 spit on him, flog him and *k* him.

KILLED (KILL)
Ge 4: 8 his brother Abel and *k* him.
Ex 2: 12 he *k* the Egyptian and hid him
13: 15 the LORD *k* every firstborn
Nu 35: 11 who has *k* someone accidentally
1Sa 17: 50 down the Philistine and *k* him.
Ne 9: 26 They *k* your prophets, who had
Hos 6: 5 I *k* you with the words
Lk 11: 48 they *k* the prophets, and you build
Ac 3: 15 You *k* the author of life,

KILLS (KILL)
Ex 21: 12 *k* him shall surely be put to death.
Lev 24: 21 but whoever *k* a man must be put
2Co 3: 6 for the letter *k*, but the Spirit gives

KIND (KINDNESS KINDNESSES KINDS)
Ge 1: 24 animals, each according to its *k*."
2Ch 10: 7 "If you will be *k* to these people
Pr 11: 17 A *k* man benefits himself,
12: 25 but a *k* word cheers him up.
14: 21 blessed is he who is *k* to the needy.
14: 31 whoever is *k* to the needy honors
19: 17 He who is *k* to the poor lends
Da 4: 27 by being *k* to the oppressed.
Lk 6: 35 because he is *k* to the ungrateful
1Co 13: 4 Love is patient, love is *k*.
15: 35 With what *k* of body will they
Eph 4: 32 Be *k* and compassionate

1Th 5: 15 but always try to be *k* to each other
2Ti 2: 24 instead, he must be *k* to everyone,
Tit 2: 5 to be busy at home, to be *k*,

KINDHEARTED* (HEART)
Pr 11: 16 A *k* woman gains respect,

KINDNESS (KIND)
Ge 24: 12 and show *k* to my master Abraham
32: 10 I am unworthy of all the *k*
39: 21 he showed him *k* and granted him
Jdg 8: 35 failed to show *k* to the family
Ru 2: 20 has not stopped showing his *k*
2Sa 9: 3 to whom I can show God's *k*?"
22: 51 he shows unfailing *k*
Ps 18: 50 he shows unfailing *k*
141: 5 righteous man strike me—it is a *k*;
Isa 54: 8 but with everlasting *k*
Jer 9: 24 I am the LORD, who exercises *k*,
Hos 11: 4 I led them with cords of human *k*,
Ac 14: 17 He has shown *k* by giving you rain
Ro 11: 22 Consider therefore the *k*
2Co 6: 6 understanding, patience and *k*;
Gal 5: 22 peace, patience, *k*, goodness,
Eph 2: 7 expressed in his *k* to us
Col 3: 12 yourselves with compassion, *k*,
Tit 3: 4 But when the *k* and love
2Pe 1: 7 brotherly *k*; and to brotherly *k*,

KINDNESSES* (KIND)
Ps 106: 7 did not remember your many *k*,
Isa 63: 7 I will tell of the *k* of the LORD,
63: 7 to his compassion and many *k*.

KINDS (KIND)
Ge 1: 12 bearing seed according to their *k*
1Co 12: 4 There are different *k* of gifts,
1Ti 6: 10 of money is a root of all *k* of evil.
1Pe 1: 6 had to suffer grief in all *k* of trials.

KING (KING'S KINGDOM KINGDOMS KINGS)
1. Kings of Judah and Israel: see Saul, David, Solomon.
2. Kings of Judah: see Rehoboam, Abijah, Asa, Jehoshaphat, Jehoram, Ahaziah, Athaliah (Queen), Joash, Amaziah, Azariah (Uzziah), Jotham, Ahaz, Hezekiah, Manasseh, Amon, Josiah, Jehoahaz, Jehoiakim, Jehoiachin, Zedekiah.
3. Kings of Israel: see Jeroboam I, Nadab, Baasha, Elah, Zimri, Tibni, Omri, Ahab, Ahaziah, Joram, Jehu, Jehoahaz, Jehoash, Jeroboam II, Zechariah, Shallum, Menahem, Pekah, Pekahiah, Hoshea.
Ex 1: 8 a new *k*, who did not know about
Dt 17: 14 "Let us set a *k* over us like all
Jdg 17: 6 In those days Israel had no *k*;
1Sa 8: 5 now appoint a *k* to lead us,
11: 15 as *k* in the presence of the LORD.
12: 12 the LORD your God was your *k*.
2Sa 2: 4 and there they anointed David *k*
1Ki 1: 30 Solomon your son shall be *k*
Ps 2: 6 "I have installed my *K*
24: 7 that the *K* of glory may come in.
44: 4 You are my *K* and my God,
47: 7 For God is the *K* of all the earth;
Isa 32: 1 See, a *k* will reign in righteousness
Jer 30: 9 and David their *k*,
Hos 3: 5 their God and David their *k*.
Mic 2: 13 *k* will pass through before them,
Zec 9: 9 See, your *k* comes to you,
Mt 2: 2 is the one who has been born *k*
27: 11 "Are you the *k* of the Jews?" "Yes,
Lk 19: 38 "Blessed is the *k* who comes
23: 3 "Are you the *k* of the Jews?" "Yes,
23: 38 THE *K* OF THE JEWS.
Jn 1: 49 of God; you are the *K* of Israel."
12: 13 "Blessed is the *K* of Israel!"
Ac 17: 7 saying that there is another *k*,
1Ti 1: 17 Now to the *K* eternal, immortal,
6: 15 the *K* of kings and Lord of lords,
Heb 7: 1 This Melchizedek was *k* of Salem
1Pe 2: 13 to the *k*, as the supreme authority,
2: 17 of believers, fear God, honor the *k*.
Rev 15: 3 *K* of the ages.
17: 14 he is Lord of lords and *K* of kings—
19: 16 *K* OF KINGS AND LORD

KING'S (KING)
Pr 21: 1 The *k* heart is in the hand
Ecc 8: 3 in a hurry to leave the *k* presence.

KINGDOM (KING)
Ex 19: 6 you will be for me a *k* of priests
Dt 17: 18 When he takes the throne of his *k*,
2Sa 7: 12 body, and I will establish his *k*.
1Ki 11: 31 to tear the *k* out of Solomon's hand
1Ch 17: 11 own sons, and I will establish his *k*.
29: 11 Yours, O LORD, is the *k*;
Ps 45: 6 justice will be the scepter of your *k*.
103: 19 and his *k* rules over all.
145: 11 They will tell of the glory of your *k*
Eze 29: 14 There they will be a lowly *k*.
Da 2: 39 "After you, another *k* will rise,
4: 3 His *k* is an eternal *k*;
7: 27 His *k* will be an everlasting *k*,
Ob : 21 And the *k* will be the LORD's.
Mt 3: 2 Repent, for the *k* of heaven is near
4: 17 Repent, for the *k* of heaven is near
4: 23 preaching the good news of the *k*,
5: 3 for theirs is the *k* of heaven.
5: 10 for theirs is the *k* of heaven.
5: 19 great in the *k* of heaven.
5: 19 least in the *k* of heaven,
5: 20 you will certainly not enter the *k*
6: 10 your *k* come,
6: 33 But seek first his *k* and his
7: 21 Lord,' will enter the *k* of heaven,
8: 11 Isaac and Jacob in the *k* of heaven.
8: 12 the subjects of the *k* will be thrown
9: 35 preaching the good news of the *k*
10: 7 preach this message: 'The *k*
11: 11 least in the *k* of heaven is greater
11: 12 the *k* of heaven has been forcefully
12: 25 "Every *k* divided against itself will
12: 26 How then can his *k* stand?
12: 28 then the *k* of God has come
13: 11 knowledge of the secrets of the *k*
13: 19 hears the message about the *k*
13: 24 "The *k* of heaven is like a man who
13: 31 *k* of heaven is like a mustard seed,
13: 33 "The *k* of heaven is like yeast that
13: 38 stands for the sons of the *k*.
13: 41 of his *k* everything that causes sin
13: 43 the sun in the *k* of their Father.
13: 44 *k* of heaven is like treasure hidden
13: 45 the *k* of heaven is like a merchant
13: 47 *k* of heaven is like a net that was let
13: 52 has been instructed about the *k*
16: 19 the keys of the *k* of heaven;
16: 28 the Son of Man coming in his *k*."
18: 1 the greatest in the *k* of heaven?"
18: 3 you will never enter the *k*
18: 4 the greatest in the *k* of heaven.
18: 23 the *k* of heaven is like a king who
19: 12 because of the *k* of heaven.
19: 14 for the *k* of heaven belongs to such
19: 23 man to enter the *k* of heaven.
19: 24 for a rich man to enter the *k* of God
20: 1 "For the *k* of heaven is like
20: 21 the other at your left in your *k*."
21: 31 the prostitutes are entering the *k*
21: 43 "Therefore I tell you that the *k*
22: 2 "The *k* of heaven is like a king who
23: 13 You shut the *k* of heaven
24: 7 rise against nation, and *k* against *k*.
24: 14 gospel of the *k* will be preached
25: 1 "At that time the *k*
25: 34 the *k* prepared for you
26: 29 anew with you in my Father's *k*."
Mk 1: 15 "The *k* of God is near.
3: 24 If a *k* is divided against itself,
3: 24 against itself, that *k* cannot stand.
4: 11 "The secret of the *k*
4: 26 "This is what the *k* of God is like.
4: 30 "What shall we say the *k*
6: 23 I will give you, up to half my *k*."
9: 1 before they see the *k* of God come
9: 47 better for you to enter the *k* of God
10: 14 for the *k* of God belongs to such
10: 15 anyone who will not receive the *k*
10: 23 for the rich to enter the *k* of God!"
10: 24 how hard it is to enter the *k* of God
10: 25 for a rich man to enter the *k* of God
11: 10 "Blessed is the coming *k*
12: 34 "You are not far from the *k* of God
13: 8 rise against nation, and *k* against *k*.
14: 25 day when I drink it anew in the *k*
15: 43 who was himself waiting for the *k*
Lk 1: 33 Jacob forever; his *k* will never
4: 43 of the *k* of God to the other towns
6: 20 for yours is the *k* of God.
7: 28 in the *k* of God is greater than he."
8: 1 proclaiming the good news of the *k*
8: 10 knowledge of the secrets of the *k*
9: 2 out to preach the *k* of God
9: 11 spoke to them about the *k* of God,
9: 27 before they see the *k* of God."
9: 60 you go and proclaim the *k* of God
9: 62 fit for service in the *k* of God."
10: 9 'The *k* of God is near you.'
10: 11 sure of this: The *k* of God is near.'
11: 2 your *k* come.
11: 17 "Any *k* divided against itself will
11: 18 himself, how can his *k* stand?
11: 20 then the *k* of God has come to you.
12: 31 seek his *k*, and these things will be
12: 32 has been pleased to give you the *k*.
13: 18 "What is the *k* of God like?
13: 20 What shall I compare the *k* of God
13: 28 all the prophets in the *k* of God,
13: 29 places at the feast in the *k* of God.
14: 15 eat at the feast in the *k* of God."
16: 16 the good news of the *k*
17: 20 when the *k* of God would come,
17: 20 *k* of God does not come with careful
17: 21 because the *k* of God is within you
18: 16 for the *k* of God belongs to such
18: 17 anyone who will not receive the *k*
18: 24 for the rich to enter the *k* of God!
18: 25 for a rich man to enter the *k* of God
18: 29 for the sake of the *k* of God will fail
19: 11 and the people thought that the *k*
21: 10 rise against nation, and *k* against *k*.
21: 31 you know that the *k* of God is near.
22: 16 until it finds fulfillment in the *k*
22: 18 the vine until the *k* of God comes."
22: 29 And I confer on you a *k*, just
22: 30 and drink at my table in my *k*
23: 42 me when you come into your *k*."
23: 51 he was waiting for the *k* of God.
Jn 3: 3 no one can see the *k* of God.
3: 5 no one can enter the *k* of God.
18: 36 now my *k* is from another place."
18: 36 "My *k* is not of this world.
Ac 1: 3 and spoke about the *k* of God.
1: 6 going to restore the *k* to Israel?"
8: 12 he preached the good news of the *k*
14: 22 hardships to enter the *k* of God,"
19: 8 arguing persuasively about the *k*
20: 25 about preaching the *k* will ever see
28: 23 and declared to them the *k* of God
28: 31 hindrance he preached the *k*
Ro 14: 17 For the *k* of God is not a matter
1Co 4: 20 For the *k* of God is not a matter
6: 9 the wicked will not inherit the *k*
6: 10 swindlers will inherit the *k* of God.
15: 24 hands over the *k* to God the Father
15: 50 blood cannot inherit the *k* of God,
Gal 5: 21 live like this will not inherit the *k*
Eph 2: 2 and of the ruler of the *k* of the air,
5: 5 has any inheritance in the *k*
Col 1: 12 of the saints in the *k* of light.
1: 13 and brought us into the *k*
4: 11 among my fellow workers for the *k*

1Th 2: 12 who calls you into his *k* and glory.
2Th 1: 5 will be counted worthy of the *k*
2Ti 4: 1 in view of his appearing and his *k*,
4: 18 bring me safely to his heavenly *k*.
Heb 1: 8 will be the scepter of your *k*.
12: 28 we are receiving a *k* that cannot be
Jas 2: 5 to inherit the *k* he promised those
2Pe 1: 11 into the eternal *k* of our Lord
Rev 1: 6 has made us to be a *k* and priests
1: 9 companion in the suffering and *k*
5: 10 You have made them to be a *k*
11: 15 of the world has become the *k*
11: 15 "The *k* of the world has become
12: 10 the power and the *k* of our God,
16: 10 his *k* was plunged into darkness.
17: 12 who have not yet received a *k*,

KINGDOMS (KING)
2Ki 19: 15 God over all the *k* of the earth.
19: 19 so that all *k* on earth may know
2Ch 20: 6 rule over all the *k* of the nations.
Ps 68: 32 Sing to God, O *k* of the earth,
Isa 37: 16 God over all the *k* of the earth.
37: 20 so that all *k* on earth may know
Eze 29: 15 It will be the lowliest of *k*
37: 22 or be divided into two *k*.
Da 4: 17 Most High is sovereign over the *k*
7: 17 great beasts are four *k* that will rise
Zep 3: 8 to gather the *k*

KINGS (KING)
Ps 2: 2 The *k* of the earth take their stand
47: 9 for the *k* of the earth belong to God
68: 29 *k* will bring you gifts.
72: 11 All *k* will bow down to him
110: 5 he will crush *k* on the day
149: 8 to bind their *k* with fetters,
Pr 16: 12 *K* detest wrongdoing,
Isa 24: 21 and the *k* on the earth below.
52: 15 and *k* will shut their mouths
60: 11 their *k* led in triumphal procession.
Da 2: 21 he sets up *k* and deposes them.
7: 24 ten horns are ten *k* who will come
Lk 21: 12 and you will be brought before *k*
1Co 4: 8 You have become *k*—
1Ti 2: 2 for *k* and all those in authority,
6: 15 the King of *k* and Lord of lords,
Rev 1: 5 and the ruler of the *k* of the earth.
17: 14 he is Lord of lords and King of *k*—
19: 16 KING OF *K* AND LORD

KINSMAN-REDEEMER (REDEEM)
Ru 3: 9 over me, since you are a *k*."
4: 14 day has not left you without a *k*.

KISS (KISSED KISSES)
Ps 2: 12 *K* the Son, lest he be angry
Pr 24: 26 is like a *k* on the lips.
SS 1: 2 *Beloved* Let him *k* me
8: 1 I would *k* you,
Lk 22: 48 the Son of Man with a *k*?"
Ro 16: 16 Greet one another with a holy *k*.
1Co 16: 20 Greet one another with a holy *k*.
2Co 13: 12 Greet one another with a holy *k*.
1Th 5: 26 Greet all the brothers with a holy *k*
1Pe 5: 14 Greet one another with a *k* of love.

KISSED (KISS)
Mk 14: 45 Judas said, "Rabbi!" and *k* him.
Lk 7: 38 *k* them and poured perfume

KISSES* (KISS)
Pr 27: 6 but an enemy multiplies *k*.
SS 1: 2 with the *k* of his mouth—

KNEE (KNEES)
Isa 45: 23 Before me every *k* will bow;
Ro 14: 11 'every *k* will bow before me;
Php 2: 10 name of Jesus every *k* should bow,

KNEEL (KNELT)
Est 3: 2 But Mordecai would not *k* down
Ps 95: 6 let us *k* before the LORD our
Eph 3: 14 For this reason I *k*

KNEES (KNEE)
1Ki 19: 18 all whose *k* have not bowed
Isa 35: 3 steady the *k* that give way;
Da 6: 10 times a day he got down on his *k*
Lk 5: 8 he fell at Jesus' *k* and said,
Heb 12: 12 your feeble arms and weak *k*.

KNELT* (KNEEL)
1Ki 1: 16 Bathsheba bowed low and *k*
2Ch 6: 13 and then *k* down before the whole
7: 3 they *k* on the pavement
29: 29 everyone present with him *k* down
Est 3: 2 officials at the king's gate *k* down
Mt 8: 2 and *k* before him and said,
9: 18 a ruler came and *k* before him
15: 25 The woman came and *k* before him
17: 14 a man approached Jesus and *k*
27: 29 *k* in front of him and mocked him.
Lk 22: 41 *k* down and prayed, "Father,
Ac 20: 36 he *k* down with all of them
21: 5 there on the beach we *k* to pray.

KNEW (KNOW)
2Ch 33: 13 Manasseh *k* that the LORD is God
Job 23: 3 If only I *k* where to find him;
Pr 24: 12 "But we *k* nothing about this,"
Jer 1: 5 you in the womb I *k* you,
Jnh 4: 2 I *k* that you are a gracious
Mt 7: 23 tell them plainly, 'I never *k* you.
12: 25 Jesus *k* their thoughts
Jn 2: 24 himself to them, for he *k* all men.
14: 7 If you really *k* me, you would know

KNIFE
Ge 22: 10 and took the *k* to slay his son.
Pr 23: 2 and put a *k* to your throat

KNOCK* (KNOCKS)
Mt 7: 7 *k* and the door will be opened
Lk 11: 9 *k* and the door will be opened
Rev 3: 20 I am! I stand at the door and *k*.

KNOCKS (KNOCK)
Mt 7: 8 and to him who *k*, the door will be

KNOW (FOREKNEW FOREKNOWLEDGE KNEW KNOWING KNOWLEDGE KNOWN KNOWS)
Ge 22: 12 Now I *k* that you fear God,
Ex 6: 7 you will *k* that I am the LORD
14: 4 and the Egyptians will *k* that I am
33: 13 teach me your ways so I may *k* you
Dt 7: 9 *K* therefore that the LORD your
18: 21 "How can we *k* when a message
Jos 4: 24 of the earth might *k* that the hand
23: 14 You *k* with all your heart
1Sa 17: 46 the whole world will *k* that there is
1Ki 8: 39 heart (for you alone *k* the hearts
Job 11: 6 *K* this: God has even forgotten
19: 25 I *k* that my Redeemer lives,
42: 3 things too wonderful for me to *k*.
Ps 9: 10 Those who *k* your name will trust
46: 10 "Be still, and *k* that I am God;
100: 3 *K* that the LORD is God.
139: 1 and you *k* me.
139: 23 Search me, O God, and *k* my heart;
145: 12 so that all men may *k*
Pr 27: 1 for you do not *k* what a day may
30: 4 Tell me if you *k*!
Ecc 8: 5 wise heart will *k* the proper time
Isa 29: 15 "Who sees us? Who will *k*?"
40: 21 Do you not *k*?
Jer 6: 15 they do not even *k* how to blush.
22: 16 Is that not what it means to *k* me?"
24: 7 I will give them a heart to *k* me,
31: 34 his brother, saying, '*K* the LORD,'
33: 3 unsearchable things you do not *k*.'
Eze 2: 5 they will *k* that a prophet has been
6: 10 they will *k* that I am the LORD;
Da 11: 32 people who *k* their God will firmly
Mt 6: 3 let your left hand *k* what your right
7: 11 *k* how to give good gifts
9: 6 But so that you may *k* that the Son
22: 29 you do not *k* the Scriptures
24: 42 you do not *k* on what day your
26: 74 "I don't *k* the man!" Immediately
Mk 12: 24 you do not *k* the Scriptures
Lk 1: 4 so that you may *k* the certainty
11: 13 *k* how to give good gifts
12: 48 But the one who does not *k*
13: 25 'I don't *k* you or where you come
21: 31 you *k* that the kingdom of God is
23: 34 for they do not *k* what they are
Jn 1: 26 among you stands one you do not *k*
3: 11 we speak of what we *k*,
4: 22 we worship what we do *k*,
4: 42 and we *k* that this man really is
6: 69 and *k* that you are the Holy One
7: 28 You do not *k* him, but I *k* him
8: 14 for I *k* where I came from
8: 19 "You do not *k* me or my Father,"
8: 32 Then you will *k* the truth,
8: 55 Though you do not *k* him, I *k* him.
9: 25 One thing I do *k*.
10: 4 him because they *k* his voice.
10: 14 I *k* my sheep and my sheep *k* me—
10: 27 I *k* them, and they follow me.
12: 35 the dark does not *k* where he is
13: 17 Now that you *k* these things,
13: 35 all men will *k* that you are my
14: 17 you *k* him, for he lives with you
15: 21 for they do not *k* the One who sent
16: 30 we can see that you *k* all things
17: 3 that they may *k* you, the only true
17: 23 to let the world *k* that you sent me
21: 15 he said, "you *k* that I love you."
21: 24 We *k* that his testimony is true.
Ac 1: 7 "It is not for you to *k* the times
1: 24 "Lord, you *k* everyone's heart.
Ro 3: 17 and the way of peace they do not *k*
6: 3 Or don't you *k* that all
6: 6 For we *k* that our old self was
6: 16 Don't you *k* that when you offer
7: 14 We *k* that the law is spiritual;
7: 18 I *k* that nothing good lives in me,
8: 22 We *k* that the whole creation has
8: 26 We do not *k* what we ought to pray
8: 28 we *k* that in all things God works
1Co 1: 21 through its wisdom did not *k* him,
2: 2 For I resolved to *k* nothing
3: 16 Don't you *k* that you yourselves
5: 6 Don't you *k* that a little yeast
6: 2 Do you not *k* that the saints will
6: 15 Do you not *k* that your bodies are
6: 16 Do you not *k* that he who unites
6: 19 Do you not *k* that your body is
7: 16 How do you *k*, wife, whether you
8: 2 does not yet *k* as he ought to *k*.
9: 13 Don't you *k* that those who work
9: 24 Do you not *k* that
13: 9 For we *k* in part and we prophesy
13: 12 Now I *k* in part; then I shall *k* fully,
15: 58 because you *k* that your labor
2Co 5: 1 we *k* that if the earthly tent we live
5: 11 we *k* what it is to fear the Lord,
8: 9 For you *k* the grace
Gal 1: 11 you to *k*, brothers, that the gospel I
2: 16 not 'Gentile sinners' *k* that a man
Eph 1: 17 so that you may *k* him better.
1: 18 in order that you may *k* the hope
6: 8 you *k* that the Lord will reward
6: 9 since you *k* that he who is both
Php 3: 10 I want to *k* Christ and the power
4: 12 I *k* what it is to be in need,
Col 2: 2 order that they may *k* the mystery
4: 1 because you *k* that you
4: 6 so that you may *k* how
1Th 3: 3 You *k* quite well that we were
5: 2 for you *k* very well that the day
2Th 1: 8 punish those who do not *k* God
1Ti 1: 7 they do not *k* what they are talking
3: 5 (If anyone does not *k* how
3: 15 you will *k* how people ought

2Ti 1: 12 because I *k* whom I have believed,
2: 23 you *k* they produce quarrels.
3: 14 you *k* those from whom you
Heb 8: 11 because they will all *k* me,
11: 8 he did not *k* where he was going.
Jas 1: 3 because you *k* that the testing
3: 1 you *k* that we who teach will be
4: 4 don't you *k* that friendship
4: 14 *k* what will happen tomorrow.
1Pe 1: 18 For you *k* that it was not
2Pe 1: 12 even though you *k* them
1Jn 2: 3 We *k* that we have come
2: 4 The man who says, "I *k* him,"
2: 5 This is how we *k* we are in him:
2: 11 he does not *k* where he is going,
2: 20 and all of you *k* the truth.
2: 29 you *k* that everyone who does
3: 1 not *k* us is that it did not *k* him.
3: 2 But we *k* that when he appears,
3: 10 This is how we *k* who the children
3: 14 We *k* that we have passed
3: 16 This is how we *k* what love is:
3: 19 then is how we *k* that we belong
3: 24 We *k* it by the Spirit he gave us.
4: 8 does not love does not *k* God,
4: 13 We *k* that we live in him
4: 16 so we *k* and rely on the love God
5: 2 This is how we *k* that we love
5: 13 so that you may *k* that you have
5: 15 And if we *k* that he hears us—
5: 18 We *k* that anyone born
5: 20 We *k* also that the Son
Rev 2: 2 I *k* your deeds, your hard work
2: 9 I *k* your afflictions and your
2: 19 I *k* your deeds, your love and faith,
3: 3 you will not *k* at what time I will
3: 15 I *k* your deeds, that you are neither

KNOWING (KNOW)
Ge 3: 5 and you will be like God, *k* good
3: 22 now become like one of us, *k* good
Jn 19: 28 *k* that all was now completed,
Php 3: 8 of *k* Christ Jesus my Lord,
Phm : 21 *k* that you will do even more
Heb 13: 2 entertained angels without *k* it.

KNOWLEDGE (KNOW)
Ge 2: 9 the tree of the *k* of good and evil.
2: 17 eat from the tree of the *k* of good
2Ch 1: 10 and *k*, that I may lead this people,
Job 21: 22 "Can anyone teach *k* to God,
38: 2 counsel with words without *k*?
42: 3 obscures my counsel without *k*?'
Ps 19: 2 night after night they display *k*.
73: 11 Does the Most High have *k*?"
94: 10 Does he who teaches man lack *k*?
119: 66 Teach me *k* and good judgment,
139: 6 Such *k* is too wonderful for me,
Pr 1: 4 *k* and discretion to the young—
1: 7 of the LORD is the beginning of *k*,
2: 5 and find the *k* of God.
2: 6 from his mouth come *k*
2: 10 and *k* will be pleasant to your soul.
3: 20 by his *k* the deeps were divided,
8: 10 *k* rather than choice gold,
8: 12 I possess *k* and discretion.
9: 10 *k* of the Holy One is understanding
10: 14 Wise men store up *k*,
12: 1 Whoever loves discipline loves *k*,
12: 23 A prudent man keeps his *k*
13: 16 Every prudent man acts out of *k*,
14: 6 *k* comes easily to the discerning.
15: 7 The lips of the wise spread *k*;
15: 14 The discerning heart seeks *k*,
17: 27 A man of *k* uses words
18: 15 heart of the discerning acquires *k*;
19: 2 to have zeal without *k*,
19: 25 discerning man, and he will gain *k*.
20: 15 lips that speak *k* are a rare jewel.
23: 12 and your ears to words of *k*.
24: 4 through *k* its rooms are filled
Ecc 7: 12 but the advantage of *k* is this:
Isa 11: 2 the Spirit of *k* and of the fear
11: 9 full of the *k* of the LORD
40: 14 Who was it that taught him *k*
Jer 3: 15 who will lead you with *k*
Hos 4: 6 are destroyed from lack of *k*.
Hab 2: 14 filled with the *k* of the glory
Mal 2: 7 lips of a priest ought to preserve *k*,
Mt 13: 11 The *k* of the secrets of the kingdom
Lk 8: 10 The *k* of the secrets of the kingdom
11: 52 you have taken away the key to *k*.
Ac 18: 24 with a thorough *k* of the Scriptures
Ro 1: 28 worthwhile to retain the *k* of God,
10: 2 but their zeal is not based on *k*.
11: 33 riches of the wisdom and *k* of God!
1Co 8: 1 *K* puffs up, but love builds up.
8: 11 Christ died, is destroyed by your *k*.
12: 8 to another the message of *k*
13: 2 can fathom all mysteries and all *k*,
13: 8 where there is *k*, it will pass away.
2Co 2: 14 everywhere the fragrance of the *k*
4: 6 light of the *k* of the glory of God
8: 7 in *k*, in complete earnestness
11: 6 a trained speaker, but I do have *k*.
Eph 3: 19 to know this love that surpasses *k*
4: 13 and in the *k* of the Son of God
Php 1: 9 and more in *k* and depth of insight,
Col 1: 9 God to fill you with the *k* of his will
1: 10 every good work, growing in the *k*
2: 3 all the treasures of wisdom and *k*.
3: 10 which is being renewed in *k*
1Ti 2: 4 and to come to a *k* of the truth.
6: 20 ideas of what is falsely called *k*,
Tit 1: 1 and the *k* of the truth that leads
Heb 10: 26 after we have received the *k*
2Pe 1: 5 and to goodness, *k*; and to *k*,
3: 18 grow in the grace and *k* of our Lord

KNOWN (KNOW)
Ex 6: 3 the LORD I did not make myself *k*
Ps 16: 11 You have made *k* to me the path
89: 1 I will make your faithfulness *k*
98: 2 LORD has made his salvation *k*
105: 1 make *k* among the nations what he
119: 168 for all my ways are *k* to you.
Pr 20: 11 Even a child is *k* by his actions,
Isa 12: 4 make *k* among the nations what he
46: 10 *k* the end from the beginning,
61: 9 Their descendants will be *k*
Eze 38: 23 I will make myself *k* in the sight
39: 7 " 'I will make *k* my holy name
Mt 10: 26 or hidden that will not be made *k*.
24: 43 of the house had *k* at what time
Lk 19: 42 had only *k* on this day what would
Jn 15: 15 from my Father I have made *k*
16: 14 from what is mine and making it *k*
17: 26 I have made you *k* to them,
Ac 2: 28 You have made *k* to me the paths
Ro 1: 19 since what may be *k* about God is
3: 21 apart from law, has been made *k*,
9: 22 his wrath and make his power *k*,
11: 34 "Who has *k* the mind of the Lord?
15: 20 the gospel where Christ was not *k*,
16: 26 and made *k* through the prophetic
1Co 2: 16 "For who has *k* the mind
8: 3 But the man who loves God is *k*
13: 12 know fully, even as I am fully *k*.
2Co 3: 2 written on our hearts, *k*
Gal 4: 9 or rather are *k* by God—
Eph 3: 5 which was not made *k* to men
6: 19 will fearlessly make *k* the mystery
2Ti 3: 15 infancy you have *k* the holy
2Pe 2: 21 than to have *k* it and then

KNOWS (KNOW)
1Sa 2: 3 for the LORD is a God who *k*,
Est 4: 14 And who *k* but that you have come
Job 23: 10 But he *k* the way that I take;
Ps 44: 21 since he *k* the secrets of the heart?
94: 11 The LORD *k* the thoughts of man;
103: 14 for he *k* how we are formed,
Ecc 8: 7 Since no man *k* the future,
8: 17 Even if a wise man claims he *k*,
9: 12 no man *k* when his hour will come:
Isa 29: 16 "He *k* nothing"?
Jer 9: 24 that he understands and *k* me,
Mt 6: 8 for your Father *k* what you need
11: 27 No one *k* the Son
24: 36 "No one *k* about that day or hour,
Lk 12: 47 "That servant who *k* his master's
16: 15 of men, but God *k* your hearts.
Ac 15: 8 who *k* the heart, showed that he
Ro 8: 27 who searches our hearts *k* the mind
1Co 2: 11 who among men *k* the thoughts
8: 2 who thinks he *k* something does
2Ti 2: 19 The Lord *k* those who are his," and
Jas 4: 17 who *k* the good he ought to do
1Jn 4: 6 and whoever *k* God listens to us;
4: 7 born of God and *k* God.

KOHATHITE (KOHATHITES)
Nu 3: 29 The *K* clans were to camp

KOHATHITES (KOHATHITE)
Nu 3: 28 The *K* were responsible
4: 15 *K* are to carry those things that are

KORAH
Levite who led rebellion against Moses and Aaron (Nu 16; Jude 11).

KORAZIN
Mt 11: 21 "Woe to you, *K!* Woe to you,

LABAN
Brother of Rebekah (Ge 24:29), father of Rachel and Leah (Ge 29:16). Received Abraham's servant (Ge 24:29–51). Provided daughters as wives for Jacob in exchange for Jacob's service (Ge 29:1–30). Provided flocks for Jacob's service (Ge 30:25–43). After Jacob's departure, pursued and covenanted with him (Ge 31).

LABOR (LABORING)
Ex 1: 11 to oppress them with forced *l*,
20: 9 Six days you shall *l* and do all your
Dt 5: 13 Six days you shall *l* and do all your
Ps 127: 1 its builders *l* in vain.
128: 2 You will eat the fruit of your *l*;
Pr 12: 24 but laziness ends in slave *l*.
Isa 54: 1 you who were never in *l*;
55: 2 and your *l* on what does not satisfy
Mt 6: 28 They do not *l* or spin.
Jn 4: 38 have reaped the benefits of their *l*."
1Co 3: 8 rewarded according to his own *l*.
15: 58 because you know that your *l*
Gal 4: 27 you who have no *l* pains;
Php 2: 16 day of Christ that I did not run or *l*
Rev 14: 13 "they will rest from their *l*,

LABORING* (LABOR)
2Th 3: 8 *l* and toiling so that we would not

LACK (LACKED LACKING LACKS)
Ps 34: 9 for those who fear him *l* nothing.
Pr 5: 23 He will die for *l* of discipline,
10: 21 but fools die for *l* of judgment.
11: 14 For *l* of guidance a nation falls,
15: 22 Plans fail for *l* of counsel,
28: 27 to the poor will *l* nothing,
Mk 6: 6 he was amazed at their *l* of faith.
16: 14 he rebuked them for their *l* of faith
Ro 3: 3 Will their *l* of faith nullify God's
1Co 1: 7 you do not *l* any spiritual gift
7: 5 because of your *l* of self-control.
Col 2: 23 *l* any value in restraining sensual

LACKED (LACK)
Dt 2: 7 and you have not *l* anything.
Ne 9: 21 them in the desert; they *l* nothing,
1Co 12: 24 honor to the parts that *l* it,

LACKING (LACK)
Pr 17: 18 A man *l* in judgment strikes hands
Ro 12: 11 Never be *l* in zeal, but keep your
Jas 1: 4 and complete, not *l* anything.

LACKS (LACK)
Pr 6: 32 who commits adultery *l* judgment;
11: 12 man who *l* judgment derides his
12: 11 he who chases fantasies *l* judgment
15: 21 delights a man who *l* judgment,
24: 30 of the man who *l* judgment;
25: 28 is a man who *l* self-control.
28: 16 A tyrannical ruler *l* judgment,
31: 11 and *l* nothing of value.
Eze 34: 8 because my flock *l* a shepherd
Jas 1: 5 any of you *l* wisdom, he should ask

LAID (LAY)
Isa 53: 6 and the LORD has *l* on him
Mk 6: 29 took his body and *l* it in a tomb.
Lk 6: 48 and *l* the foundation on rock.
Ac 6: 6 and *l* their hands on them.
1Co 3: 11 other than the one already *l*,
1Ti 4: 14 body of elders *l* their hands on you.
1Jn 3: 16 Jesus Christ *l* down his life for us.

LAKE
Mt 8: 24 a furious storm came up on the *l*,
14: 25 out to them, walking on the *l*.
Mk 4: 1 into a boat and sat in it out on the *l*,
Lk 8: 33 down the steep bank into the *l*
Jn 6: 25 him on the other side of the *l*,
Rev 19: 20 into the fiery *l* of burning sulfur.
20: 14 The *l* of fire is the second death.

LAMB (LAMB'S LAMBS)
Ge 22: 8 "God himself will provide the *l*
Ex 12: 21 and slaughter the Passover *l*.
Nu 9: 11 are to eat the *l*, together
2Sa 12: 4 he took the ewe *l* that belonged
Isa 11: 6 The wolf will live with the *l*,
53: 7 he was led like a *l* to the slaughter,
Mk 14: 12 to sacrifice the Passover *l*,
Jn 1: 29 *L* of God, who takes away the sin
Ac 8: 32 as a *l* before the shearer is silent,
1Co 5: 7 our Passover *l*, has been sacrificed.
1Pe 1: 19 a *l* without blemish or defect.
Rev 5: 6 Then I saw a *L*, looking
5: 12 "Worthy is the *L*, who was slain,
7: 14 white in the blood of the *L*.
14: 4 They follow the *L* wherever he
15: 3 of God and the song of the *L*:
17: 14 but the *L* will overcome them
19: 9 to the wedding supper of the *L*!' "
21: 23 gives it light, and the *L* is its lamp.

LAMB'S (LAMB)
Rev 21: 27 written in the *L* book of life.

LAMBS (LAMB)
Lk 10: 3 I am sending you out like *l*
Jn 21: 15 Jesus said, "Feed my *l*."

LAME
Isa 33: 23 even the *l* will carry off plunder.
35: 6 Then will the *l* leap like a deer,
Mt 11: 5 The blind receive sight, the *l* walk,
15: 31 the *l* walking and the blind seeing.
Lk 14: 21 the crippled, the blind and the *l*.'

LAMENT
2Sa 1: 17 took up this *l* concerning Saul
Eze 19: 1 Take up a *l* concerning the princes

LAMP (LAMPS LAMPSTAND LAMPSTANDS)
2Sa 22: 29 You are my *l*, O LORD;
Ps 18: 28 You, O LORD, keep my *l* burning;
119:105 Your word is a *l* to my feet
132: 17 and set up a *l* for my anointed one.
Pr 6: 23 For these commands are a *l*,
20: 27 *l* of the LORD searches the spirit
31: 18 and her *l* does not go out at night.
Mt 6: 22 "The eye is the *l* of the body.
Lk 8: 16 "No one lights a *l* and hides it
Rev 21: 23 gives it light, and the Lamb is its *l*.
22: 5 They will not need the light of a *l*

LAMPS (LAMP)
Mt 25: 1 be like ten virgins who took their *l*
Lk 12: 35 for service and keep your *l* burning,
Rev 4: 5 the throne, seven *l* were blazing.

LAMPSTAND (LAMP)
Ex 25: 31 "Make a *l* of pure gold
Zec 4: 2 "I see a solid gold *l* with a bowl
4: 11 on the right and the left of the *l*?"
Heb 9: 2 In its first room were the *l*,
Rev 2: 5 and remove your *l* from its place.

LAMPSTANDS (LAMP)
2Ch 4: 7 He made ten gold *l* according
Rev 1: 12 when I turned I saw seven golden *l*,
1: 20 and of the seven golden *l* is this:

LAND (LANDS)
Ge 1: 10 God called the dry ground "*l*,"
1: 11 "Let the *l* produce vegetation:
1: 24 "Let the *l* produce living creatures
12: 1 and go to the *l* I will show you.
12: 7 To your offspring I will give this *l*."
13: 15 All the *l* that you see I will give
15: 18 "To your descendants I give this *l*,
50: 24 out of this *l* to the *l* he promised
Ex 3: 8 a *l* flowing with milk and honey—
6: 8 to the *l* I swore with uplifted hand
33: 3 Go up to the *l* flowing with milk
Lev 25: 23 *l* must not be sold permanently,
Nu 14: 8 us into that *l*, a *l* flowing with milk
35: 33 Do not pollute the *l* where you are.
Dt 1: 8 See, I have given you this *l*.
8: 7 God is bringing you into a good *l*—
11: 10 The *l* you are entering to take
28: 21 you from the *l* you are entering
29: 19 will bring disaster on the watered *l*
34: 1 LORD showed him the whole *l*—
Jos 13: 2 "This is the *l* that remains:
14: 4 Levites received no share of the *l*
14: 9 *l* on which your feet have walked
2Sa 21: 14 answered prayer in behalf of the *l*.
2Ki 17: 5 of Assyria invaded the entire *l*,
24: 1 king of Babylon invaded the *l*,
25: 21 into captivity, away from her *l*.
2Ch 7: 14 their sin and will heal their *l*.
7: 20 then I will uproot Israel from my *l*,
36: 21 The *l* enjoyed its sabbath rests;
Ezr 9: 11 entering to possess is a *l* polluted
Ne 9: 36 in the *l* you gave our forefathers
Ps 37: 11 But the meek will inherit the *l*
37: 29 the righteous will inherit the *l*
136: 21 and gave their *l* as an inheritance,
142: 5 my portion in the *l* of the living."
Pr 2: 21 For the upright will live in the *l*,
12: 11 who works his *l* will have abundant
Isa 6: 13 though a tenth remains in the *l*,
53: 8 cut off from the *l* of the living;
Jer 2: 7 But you came and defiled my *l*
Eze 36: 24 and bring you back into your own *l*.

LANDS (LAND)
Ps 111: 6 giving them the *l* of other nations.
Eze 20: 6 honey, the most beautiful of all *l*.
Zec 10: 9 in distant *l* they will remember me.

LANGUAGE (LANGUAGES)
Ge 11: 1 Now the whole world had one *l*
11: 9 there the LORD confused the *l*
Ps 19: 3 There is no speech or *l*
Jn 8: 44 When he lies, he speaks his native *l*
Ac 2: 6 heard them speaking in his own *l*.
Col 3: 8 slander, and filthy *l* from your lips.
Rev 5: 9 from every tribe and *l* and people
7: 9 every nation, tribe, people and *l*,
14: 6 to every nation, tribe, *l* and people.

LANGUAGES (LANGUAGE)
Zec 8: 23 "In those days ten men from all *l*

LAODICEA
Rev 3: 14 the angel of the church in *L* write:

LAP
Jdg 7: 5 "Separate those who *l* the water

LASHES
Pr 17: 10 more than a hundred *l* a fool.
2Co 11: 24 from the Jews the forty *l* minus one

LAST (LASTING LASTS LATTER)
Ex 14: 24 During the *l* watch of the night
2Sa 23: 1 These are the *l* words of David:
Isa 2: 2 and Jerusalem: In the *l* days
41: 4 and with the *l*— I am he."
44: 6 I am the first and I am the *l*;
48: 12 I am the first and I am the *l*.
Hos 3: 5 and to his blessings in the *l* days.
Mic 4: 1 In the *l* days
Mt 19: 30 But many who are first will be *l*,
20: 8 beginning with the *l* ones hired
21: 37 *L* of all, he sent his son to them.
Mk 9: 35 must be the very *l*, and the servant
10: 31 are first will be *l*, and the *l* first."
15: 37 a loud cry, Jesus breathed his *l*.
Jn 6: 40 and I will raise him up at the *l* day."
15: 16 and bear fruit—fruit that will *l*.
Ac 2: 17 " 'In the *l* days, God says,
Ro 1: 17 is by faith from first to *l*,
1Co 15: 26 *l* enemy to be destroyed is death.
15: 52 of an eye, at the *l* trumpet.
2Ti 3: 1 will be terrible times in the *l* days.
2Pe 3: 3 in the *l* days scoffers will come,
Jude : 18 "In the *l* times there will be
Rev 1: 17 I am the First and the *L*.
22: 13 the First and the *L*, the Beginning

LASTING (LAST)
Ex 12: 14 to the LORD—a *l* ordinance.
Lev 24: 8 of the Israelites, as a *l* covenant.
Nu 25: 13 have a covenant of a *l* priesthood,
Heb 10: 34 had better and *l* possessions.

LASTS (LAST)
Ps 30: 5 For his anger *l* only a moment,
2Co 3: 11 greater is the glory of that which *l*!

LATTER (LAST)
Job 42: 12 The LORD blessed the *l* part
Mt 23: 23 You should have practiced the *l*,
Php 1: 16 *l* do so in love, knowing that I am

LAUGH (LAUGHED LAUGHS LAUGHTER)
Ps 59: 8 But you, O LORD, *l* at them;
Pr 31: 25 she can *l* at the days to come.
Ecc 3: 4 a time to weep and a time to *l*,
Lk 6: 21 for you will *l*.
6: 25 Woe to you who *l* now,

LAUGHED (LAUGH)
Ge 17: 17 Abraham fell facedown; he *l*
18: 12 So Sarah *l* to herself as she thought,

LAUGHS (LAUGH)
Ps 2: 4 The One enthroned in heaven *l*;
37: 13 but the Lord *l* at the wicked,

LAUGHTER (LAUGH)
Ge 21: 6 Sarah said, "God has brought me *l*,
Ps 126: 2 Our mouths were filled with *l*,
Pr 14: 13 Even in *l* the heart may ache,
Jas 4: 9 Change your *l* to mourning

LAVISHED
Eph 1: 8 of God's grace that he *l* on us
1Jn 3: 1 great is the love the Father has *l*

LAW (LAWFUL LAWGIVER LAWS)
Lev 24: 22 are to have the same *l* for the alien
Nu 6: 13 " 'Now this is the *l* for the Nazirite
Dt 1: 5 Moses began to expound this *l*,
6: 25 to obey all this *l* before the LORD
27: 26 of this *l* by carrying them out."
31: 11 you shall read this *l* before them
31: 26 "Take this Book of the *L*
Jos 1: 7 to obey all the *l* my servant Moses
1: 8 of the *L* depart from your mouth;
22: 5 and the *l* that Moses the servant
2Ki 22: 8 of the *L* in the temple of the LORD
2Ch 6: 16 walk before me according to my *l*,
17: 9 the Book of the *L* of the LORD;
34: 14 of the *L* of the LORD that had
Ezr 7: 6 versed in the *L* of Moses,
Ne 8: 2 Ezra the priest brought the *L*
8: 8 from the Book of the *L* of God,
Ps 1: 2 and on his *l* he meditates day

6: 22 the benefit you reap *l* to holiness,
14: 19 effort to do what *l* to peace
2Co 2: 14 always *l* us in triumphal procession
7: 10 sorrow brings repentance that *l*
Tit 1: 1 of the truth that *l* to godliness—

LEAH
Wife of Jacob (Ge 29:16–30); bore six sons and one daughter (Ge 29:31–30:21; 34:1; 35:23).

LEAN (LEANED)
Pr 3: 5 *l* not on your own understanding;

LEANED (LEAN)
Ge 47: 31 as he *l* on the top of his staff.
Jn 21: 20 (This was the one who had *l* back
Heb 11: 21 as he *l* on the top of his staff.

LEAP (LEAPED LEAPS)
Isa 35: 6 Then will the lame *l* like a deer,
Mal 4: 2 *l* like calves released from the stall.
Lk 6: 23 "Rejoice in that day and *l* for joy,

LEAPED (LEAP)
Lk 1: 41 heard Mary's greeting, the baby *l*

LEAPS (LEAP)
Ps 28: 7 My heart *l* for joy

LEARN (LEARNED LEARNING LEARNS)
Dt 4: 10 so that they may *l* to revere me
5: 1 *L* them and be sure to follow them.
31: 12 and *l* to fear the LORD your God
Ps 119: 7 as I *l* your righteous laws.
Isa 1: 17 *l* to do right!
26: 9 of the world *l* righteousness.
Mt 11: 29 yoke upon you and *l* from me,
Jn 14: 31 world must *l* that I love the Father
1Th 4: 4 that each of you should *l*
1Ti 2: 11 A woman should *l* in quietness
5: 4 these should *l* first of all

LEARNED (LEARN)
Ps 119:152 Long ago I *l* from your statutes
Mt 11: 25 things from the wise and *l*,
Php 4: 9 Whatever you have *l* or received
4: 11 for I have *l* to be content whatever
2Ti 3: 14 continue in what you have *l*
Heb 5: 8 he *l* obedience from what he

LEARNING (LEARN)
Pr 1: 5 let the wise listen and add to their *l*,
9: 9 man and he will add to his *l*.
Isa 44: 25 who overthrows the *l* of the wise
Jn 7: 15 "How did this man get such *l*
2Ti 3: 7 always *l* but never able

LEARNS (LEARN)
Jn 6: 45 and *l* from him comes to me.

LEATHER
2Ki 1: 8 and with a *l* belt around his waist."
Mt 3: 4 and he had a *l* belt around his waist

LEAVES
Ge 3: 7 so they sewed fig *l* together
Eze 47: 12 for food and their *l* for healing."
Rev 22: 2 the *l* of the tree are for the healing

LEBANON
Dt 11: 24 from the desert to *L*,
1Ki 4: 33 from the cedar of *L*

LED (LEAD)
Ex 3: 1 and he *l* the flock to the far side
Dt 8: 2 the LORD your God *l* you all
1Ki 11: 3 and his wives *l* him astray.
2Ch 26: 16 his pride *l* to his downfall.
Ne 13: 26 he was *l* into sin by foreign women.
Ps 68: 18 you *l* captives in your train;
78: 52 he *l* them like sheep
Pr 7: 21 persuasive words she *l* him astray;
20: 1 whoever is *l* astray
Isa 53: 7 he was *l* like a lamb to the slaughter
Jer 11: 19 I had been like a gentle lamb *l*
Am 2: 10 and I *l* you forty years in the desert
Mt 4: 1 Then Jesus was *l* by the Spirit
27: 31 they *l* him away to crucify him.
Lk 4: 1 was *l* by the Spirit in the desert,
Ac 8: 32 "He was *l* like a sheep
Ro 8: 14 those who are *l* by the Spirit
2Co 7: 9 your sorrow *l* you to repentance.
Gal 5: 18 But if you are *l* by the Spirit,
Eph 4: 8 he *l* captives in his train

LEEKS*
Nu 11: 5 melons, *l*, onions and garlic.

LEFT
Dt 28: 14 or to the *l*, following other gods
Jos 1: 7 turn from it to the right or to the *l*,
23: 6 aside to the right or to the *l*.
2Ki 22: 2 aside to the right or to the *l*.
Pr 4: 27 Do not swerve to the right or the *l*;
Isa 30: 21 turn to the right or to the *l*,
Mt 6: 3 do not let your *l* hand know what
25: 33 on his right and the goats on his *l*.

LEGALISTIC*
Php 3: 6 as for *l* righteousness, faultless.

LEGION
Mk 5: 9 "My name is *L*," he replied,

LEND (LENDER LENDS MONEYLENDER)
Lev 25: 37 You must not *l* him money
Dt 15: 8 freely *l* him whatever he needs.
Ps 37: 26 are always generous and *l* freely;
Eze 18: 8 He does not *l* at usury
Lk 6: 34 if you *l* to those from whom you

LENDER (LEND)
Pr 22: 7 and the borrower is servant to the *l*.
Isa 24: 2 for borrower as for *l*,

LENDS (LEND)
Ps 15: 5 who *l* his money without usury
112: 5 to him who is generous and *l* freely,
Pr 19: 17 to the poor *l* to the LORD,

LENGTH (LONG)
Ps 90: 10 The *l* of our days is seventy years—
Pr 10: 27 The fear of the LORD adds *l* to life

LENGTHY* (LONG)
Mk 12: 40 and for a show make *l* prayers.
Lk 20: 47 and for a show make *l* prayers.

LEOPARD
Isa 11: 6 the *l* will lie down with the goat,
Da 7: 6 beast, one that looked like a *l*.
Rev 13: 2 The beast I saw resembled a *l*,

LEPROSY (LEPROUS)
Nu 12: 10 toward her and saw that she had *l*;
2Ki 5: 1 was a valiant soldier, but he had *l*.
7: 3 men with *l* at the entrance
2Ch 26: 21 King Uzziah had *l*
Mt 11: 5 those who have *l* are cured,
Lk 17: 12 ten men who had *l* met him.

LEPROUS (LEPROSY)
Ex 4: 6 and when he took it out, it was *l*,

LETTER (LETTERS)
Mt 5: 18 not the smallest *l*, not the least
2Co 3: 2 You yourselves are our *l*, written
3: 6 for the *l* kills, but the Spirit gives
2Th 3: 14 not obey our instruction in this *l*,

LETTERS (LETTER)
2Co 3: 7 which was engraved in *l* on stone,
10: 10 "His *l* are weighty and forceful,
2Pe 3: 16 His *l* contain some things that are

LEVEL
Ps 143: 10 lead me on *l* ground.
Pr 4: 26 Make *l* paths for your feet
Isa 26: 7 The path of the righteous is *l*;
40: 4 the rough ground shall become *l*,
Jer 31: 9 on a *l* path where they will not
Heb 12: 13 "Make *l* paths for your feet,"

LEVI (LEVITE LEVITES LEVITICAL)
1. Son of Jacob by Leah (Ge 29:34; 46:11; 1Ch 2:1). With Simeon avenged rape of Dinah (Ge 34). Tribe of blessed (Ge 49:5–7; Dt 33:8–11), chosen as priests (Nu 3–4), numbered (Nu 3:39; 26:62), allotted cities, but not land (Nu 18; 35; Dt 10:9; Jos 13:14; 21), land (Eze 48:8–22), 12,000 from (Rev 7:7).
2. See MATTHEW.

LEVIATHAN
Job 41: 1 pull in the *l* with a fishhook
Ps 74: 14 you who crushed the heads of *L*
Isa 27: 1 *L* the gliding serpent,

LEVITE (LEVI)
Dt 26: 12 you shall give it to the *L*, the alien,
Jdg 19: 1 a *L* who lived in a remote area

LEVITES (LEVI)
Nu 1: 53 The *L* are to be responsible
3: 12 "I have taken the *L*
8: 6 "Take the *L* from among the other
18: 21 I give to the *L* all the tithes in Israel
35: 7 must give the *L* forty-eight towns,
2Ch 31: 2 assigned the priests and *L*
Mal 3: 3 he will purify the *L* and refine them

LEVITICAL (LEVI)
Heb 7: 11 attained through the *L* priesthood

LEWDNESS
Mk 7: 22 malice, deceit, *l*, envy, slander,

LIAR* (LIE)
Dt 19: 18 and if the witness proves to be a *l*,
Job 34: 6 I am considered a *l*;
Pr 17: 4 *l* pays attention to a malicious
19: 22 better to be poor than a *l*.
30: 6 will rebuke you and prove you a *l*.
Mic 2: 11 If a *l* and deceiver comes and says,
Jn 8: 44 for he is a *l* and the father of lies.
8: 55 I did not, I would be a *l* like you,
Ro 3: 4 Let God be true, and every man a *l*.
1Jn 1: 10 we make him out to be a *l*
2: 4 not do what he commands is a *l*,
2: 22 Who is the *l*? It is the man who
4: 20 yet hates his brother, he is a *l*.
5: 10 God has made him out to be a *l*,

LIARS* (LIE)
Ps 63: 11 the mouths of *l* will be silenced.
116: 11 "All men are *l*."
Isa 57: 4 the offspring of *l*?
Mic 6: 12 her people are *l*
1Ti 1: 10 for slave traders and *l* and perjurers
4: 2 come through hypocritical *l*,
Tit 1: 12 "Cretans are always *l*, evil brutes,
Rev 3: 9 though they are not, but are *l*—
21: 8 magic arts, the idolaters and all *l*—

LIBERATED*
Ro 8: 21 that the creation itself will be *l*

LICENSE
Jude : 4 of our God into a *l* for immorality

LICK
Ps 72: 9 and his enemies will *l* the dust.
Isa 49: 23 they will *l* the dust at your feet.
Mic 7: 17 They will *l* dust like a snake,

LIE (LIAR LIARS LIED LIES LYING)
Lev 18: 22 " 'Do not *l* with a man
19: 11 " 'Do not *l*.
Nu 23: 19 God is not a man, that he should *l*,
Dt 6: 7 when you *l* down and when you get
25: 2 the judge shall make him *l* down
1Sa 15: 29 the Glory of Israel does not *l*
Ps 4: 8 I will *l* down and sleep in peace,
23: 2 me *l* down in green pastures,
89: 35 and I will not *l* to David—
Pr 3: 24 when you *l* down, you will not be
Isa 11: 6 leopard will *l* down with the goat,
28: 15 for we have made a *l* our refuge
Jer 9: 5 They have taught their tongues to *l*
23: 14 They commit adultery and live a *l*.
Eze 13: 6 are false and their divinations a *l*.
34: 14 they will *l* down in good grazing
Ro 1: 25 exchanged the truth of God for a *l*,
Col 3: 9 Do not *l* to each other,
2Th 2: 11 so that they will believe the *l*
Tit 1: 2 which God, who does not *l*,
Heb 6: 18 which it is impossible for God to *l*,
1Jn 2: 21 because no *l* comes from the truth.
Rev 14: 5 No *l* was found in their mouths;

LIED (LIE)
Ac 5: 4 You have not *l* to men but to God."

LIES (LIE)
Lev 6: 3 finds lost property and *l* about it,
Ps 5: 6 You destroy those who tell *l*;
10: 7 His mouth is full of curses and *l*
12: 2 Everyone *l* to his neighbor;
34: 13 and your lips from speaking *l*.
58: 3 they are wayward and speak *l*.
144: 8 whose mouths are full of *l*,
Pr 6: 19 a false witness who pours out *l*
12: 17 but a false witness tells *l*.
19: 5 he who pours out *l* will not go free.
19: 9 and he who pours out *l* will perish.
29: 12 If a ruler listens to *l*,
30: 8 Keep falsehood and *l* far from me;
Isa 59: 3 Your lips have spoken *l*,
Jer 5: 31 The prophets prophesy *l*,
9: 3 like a bow, to shoot *l*;
14: 14 "The prophets are prophesying *l*
Hos 11: 12 Ephraim has surrounded me with *l*,
Jn 8: 44 for he is a liar and the father of *l*.

LIFE (LIVE)
Ge 1: 30 everything that has the breath of *l*
2: 7 into his nostrils the breath of *l*,
2: 9 of the garden were the tree of *l*
6: 17 to destroy all *l* under the heavens,
9: 5 for the *l* of his fellow man.
9: 11 Never again will all *l* be cut
Ex 21: 6 Then he will be his servant for *l*.
21: 23 you are to take *l* for *l*, eye for eye,
23: 26 I will give you a full *l* span.
Lev 17: 14 the *l* of every creature is its blood.
24: 17 " 'If anyone takes the *l*
24: 18 must make restitution—*l* for *l*.
Nu 35: 31 a ransom for the *l* of a murderer,
Dt 4: 42 one of these cities and save his *l*.
12: 23 because the blood is the *l*,
19: 21 Show no pity: *l* for *l*, eye for eye,
30: 15 I set before you today *l*
30: 19 Now choose *l*, so that you
30: 20 For the LORD is your *l*,
32: 39 I put to death and I bring to *l*,
32: 47 words for you—they are your *l*.
1Sa 19: 5 He took his *l* in his hands
Job 2: 6 hands; but you must spare his *l*."
33: 4 of the Almighty gives me *l*.
33: 30 that the light of *l* may shine on him.
Ps 16: 11 known to me the path of *l*;
17: 14 this world whose reward is in this *l*.
23: 6 all the days of my *l*,
27: 1 LORD is the stronghold of my *l*—
34: 12 Whoever of you loves *l*
36: 9 For with you is the fountain of *l*;
39: 4 let me know how fleeting is my *l*.
41: 2 will protect him and preserve his *l*;
49: 7 No man can redeem the *l*
49: 8 the ransom for a *l* is costly,
63: 3 Because your love is better than *l*,
69: 28 they be blotted out of the book of *l*
91: 16 With long *l* will I satisfy him
104: 33 I will sing to the LORD all my *l*;
119: 25 preserve my *l* according to your word
Pr 1: 3 a disciplined and prudent *l*,
3: 2 will prolong your *l* many years
3: 18 of *l* to those who embrace her;
4: 23 for it is the wellspring of *l*.
6: 23 are the way to *l*,
6: 26 adulteress preys upon your very *l*.
7: 23 little knowing it will cost him his *l*.
8: 35 For whoever finds me finds *l*
10: 11 of the righteous is a fountain of *l*,
10: 27 of the LORD adds length to *l*,
11: 30 of the righteous is a tree of *l*,
13: 3 He who guards his lips guards his *l*,
13: 12 but a longing fulfilled is a tree of *l*.
13: 14 of the wise is a fountain of *l*,
14: 27 of the LORD is a fountain of *l*,
15: 4 that brings healing is a tree of *l*,
16: 22 Understanding is a fountain of *l*
19: 3 A man's own folly ruins his *l*,
19: 23 The fear of the LORD leads to *l*:
21: 21 finds *l*, prosperity and honor.
Isa 53: 10 LORD makes his *l* a guilt offering,
53: 11 he will see the light ›of *l*‹
53: 12 he poured out his *l* unto death,
Jer 10: 23 that a man's *l* is not his own;
La 3: 58 you redeemed my *l*.
Eze 18: 27 and right, he will save his *l*.
37: 5 enter you, and you will come to *l*.
Da 12: 2 some to everlasting *l*, others
Jnh 2: 6 you brought my *l* up from the pit,
Mal 2: 5 a covenant of *l* and peace,
Mt 6: 25 Is not *l* more important than food,
7: 14 and narrow the road that leads to *l*,
10: 39 Whoever finds his *l* will lose it,
16: 21 and on the third day be raised to *l*.
16: 25 wants to save his *l* will lose it,
18: 8 better for you to enter *l* maimed
19: 16 thing must I do to get eternal *l*?"
19: 29 as much and will inherit eternal *l*.
20: 28 to give his *l* as a ransom for many."
25: 46 but the righteous to eternal *l*."
Mk 8: 35 but whoever loses his *l* for me
9: 43 better for you to enter *l* maimed
10: 17 "what must I do to inherit eternal *l*
10: 30 and in the age to come, eternal *l*.
10: 45 to give his *l* as a ransom for many."
Lk 6: 9 to save *l* or to destroy it?"
9: 22 and on the third day be raised to *l*."
9: 24 wants to save his *l* will lose it,
12: 15 a man's *l* does not consist
12: 22 do not worry about your *l*,
12: 25 can add a single hour to his *l*?
14: 26 even his own *l*— he cannot be my
17: 33 tries to keep his *l* will lose it,
21: 19 standing firm you will gain *l*.
Jn 1: 4 In him was *l*, and that *l* was
3: 15 believes in him may have eternal *l*.
3: 36 believes in the Son has eternal *l*,
4: 14 of water welling up to eternal *l*."
5: 21 raises the dead and gives them *l*,
5: 24 him who sent me has eternal *l*
5: 26 For as the Father has *l* in himself,
5: 39 that by them you possess eternal *l*.
5: 40 refuse to come to me to have *l*.
6: 27 for food that endures to eternal *l*,
6: 33 down from heaven and gives *l*
6: 35 Jesus declared, "I am the bread of *l*
6: 40 believes in him shall have eternal *l*,
6: 47 he who believes has everlasting *l*.
6: 48 I am the bread of *l*.
6: 51 give for the *l* of the world."
6: 53 and drink his blood, you have no *l*
6: 63 The Spirit gives *l*; the flesh counts
6: 68 You have the words of eternal *l*.
8: 12 but will have the light of *l*."
10: 10 I have come that they may have *l*,
10: 15 and I lay down my *l* for the sheep.
10: 17 loves me is that I lay down my *l*—
10: 28 I give them eternal *l*, and they shall
11: 25 "I am the resurrection and the *l*.
12: 25 The man who loves his *l* will lose it,
12: 50 his command leads to eternal *l*.
13: 37 I will lay down my *l* for you."
14: 6 am the way and the truth and the *l*.
15: 13 lay down his *l* for his friends.
17: 2 people that he might give eternal *l*
17: 3 Now this is eternal *l*: that they may
20: 31 that by believing you may have *l*
Ac 2: 32 God has raised this Jesus to *l*,
3: 15 You killed the author of *l*,
11: 18 the Gentiles repentance unto *l*."
13: 48 appointed for eternal *l* believed.
Ro 2: 7 immortality, he will give eternal *l*.
4: 25 was raised to *l* for our justification.
5: 10 shall we be saved through his *l*!
5: 18 was justification that brings *l*
5: 21 righteousness to bring eternal *l*
6: 4 the Father, we too may live a new *l*.
6: 13 have been brought from death to *l*;
6: 22 holiness, and the result is eternal *l*.
6: 23 but the gift of God is eternal *l*
8: 6 mind controlled by the Spirit is *l*
8: 11 also give *l* to your mortal bodies
8: 38 convinced that neither death nor *l*,
1Co 15: 19 If only for this *l* we have hope
15: 36 What you sow does not come to *l*
2Co 2: 16 to the other, the fragrance of *l*.
3: 6 letter kills, but the Spirit gives *l*.
4: 10 so that the *l* of Jesus may
5: 4 is mortal may be swallowed up by *l*.
Gal 2: 20 The *l* I live in the body, I live
3: 21 had been given that could impart *l*,
6: 8 from the Spirit will reap eternal *l*.
Eph 4: 1 I urge you to live a *l* worthy
Php 2: 16 as you hold out the word of *l*—
4: 3 whose names are in the book of *l*.
Col 1: 10 order that you may live a *l* worthy
3: 3 your *l* is now hidden with Christ
1Th 4: 12 so that your daily *l* may win
1Ti 1: 16 on him and receive eternal *l*.
4: 8 for both the present *l* and the *l*
4: 12 in *l*, in love, in faith and in purity.
4: 16 Watch your *l* and doctrine closely.
6: 12 Take hold of the eternal *l*
6: 19 hold of the *l* that is truly *l*.
2Ti 1: 9 saved us and called us to a holy *l*—
1: 10 destroyed death and has brought *l*
3: 12 to live a godly *l* in Christ Jesus will
Tit 1: 2 resting on the hope of eternal *l*,
3: 7 heirs having the hope of eternal *l*.
Heb 7: 16 of the power of an indestructible *l*.
Jas 1: 12 crown of *l* that God has promised
3: 13 Let him show it by his good *l*,
1Pe 3: 7 with you of the gracious gift of *l*,
3: 10 "Whoever would love *l*
4: 2 rest of his earthly *l* for evil human
2Pe 1: 3 given us everything we need for *l*
1Jn 1: 1 proclaim concerning the Word of *l*.
2: 25 he promised us—even eternal *l*.
3: 14 we have passed from death to *l*,
3: 16 Jesus Christ laid down his *l* for us.
5: 11 has given us eternal *l*, and this *l* is
5: 20 He is the true God and eternal *l*.
Jude : 21 Christ to bring you to eternal *l*.
Rev 2: 7 the right to eat from the tree of *l*,
2: 8 who died and came to *l* again.
2: 10 and I will give you the crown of *l*.
3: 5 name from the book of *l*,
13: 8 written in the book of *l* belonging
17: 8 in the book of *l* from the creation
20: 12 was opened, which is the book of *l*.
20: 15 not found written in the book of *l*,
21: 6 from the spring of the water of *l*.
21: 27 written in the Lamb's book of *l*.
22: 1 me the river of the water of *l*,
22: 2 side of the river stood the tree of *l*,
22: 14 may have the right to the tree of *l*
22: 17 take the free gift of the water of *l*.
22: 19 from him his share in the tree of *l*

LIFE-GIVING (GIVE)
Pr 15: 31 He who listens to a *l* rebuke
1Co 15: 45 being"; the last Adam, a *l* spirit.

LIFETIME (LIVE)
Ps 30: 5 but his favor lasts a *l*;
Lk 16: 25 in your *l* you received your good

LIFT (LIFTED LIFTING LIFTS)
Ps 3: 3 you bestow glory on me and *l*
28: 2 as I *l* up my hands
63: 4 in your name I will *l* up my hands.
91: 12 they will *l* you up in their hands,
121: 1 I *l* up my eyes to the hills—
123: 1 I *l* up my eyes to you,
134: 2 *L* up your hands in the sanctuary
143: 8 for to you I *l* up my soul.
Isa 40: 9 *l* up your voice with a shout,

La 2: 19 *L* up your hands to him
3: 41 Let us *l* up our hearts and our
Mt 4: 6 they will *l* you up in their hands,
Lk 21: 28 stand up and *l* up your heads,
1Ti 2: 8 everywhere to *l* up holy hands
Jas 4: 10 the Lord, and he will *l* you up.
1Pe 5: 6 that he may *l* you up in due time.

LIFTED (LIFT)
Ne 8: 6 and all the people *l* their hands
Ps 24: 7 be *l* up, you ancient doors,
40: 2 He *l* me out of the slimy pit,
41: 9 has *l* up his heel against me.
Isa 52: 13 *l* up and highly exalted.
63: 9 he *l* them up and carried them
Jn 3: 14 Moses *l* up the snake in the desert,
8: 28 "When you have *l* up the Son
12: 32 when I am *l* up from the earth,
12: 34 'The Son of Man must be *l* up'?
13: 18 shares my bread has *l* up his heel

LIFTING (LIFT)
Ps 141: 2 may the *l* up of my hands be like

LIFTS (LIFT)
Ps 113: 7 and *l* the needy from the ash heap;

LIGAMENT* (LIGAMENTS)
Eph 4: 16 held together by every supporting *l*

LIGAMENTS* (LIGAMENT)
Col 2: 19 held together by its *l* and sinews,

LIGHT (ENLIGHTENED LIGHTS)
Ge 1: 3 "Let there be *l*," and there was *l*.
Ex 13: 21 in a pillar of fire to give them *l*,
25: 37 it so that they *l* the space in front
2Sa 22: 29 LORD turns my darkness into *l*.
Job 38: 19 "What is the way to the abode of *l*?
Ps 4: 6 Let the *l* of your face shine upon us
18: 28 my God turns my darkness into *l*.
19: 8 giving *l* to the eyes.
27: 1 LORD is my *l* and my salvation—
36: 9 in your *l* we see *l*.
56: 13 God in the *l* of life.
76: 4 You are resplendent with *l*,
89: 15 who walk in the *l* of your presence,
104: 2 He wraps himself in *l*
119:105 and a *l* for my path.
119:130 The unfolding of your words gives *l*;
139: 12 for darkness is as *l* to you.
Pr 4: 18 till the full *l* of day.
Isa 2: 5 let us walk in the *l* of the LORD.
9: 2 have seen a great *l*;
42: 6 and a *l* for the Gentiles,
45: 7 I form the *l* and create darkness,
49: 6 also make you a *l* for the Gentiles,
53: 11 he will see the *l* of life
60: 1 "Arise, shine, for your *l* has come,
60: 19 LORD will be your everlasting *l*,
Eze 1: 27 and brilliant *l* surrounded him.
Mic 7: 8 the LORD will be my *l*.
Mt 4: 16 have seen a great *l*;
5: 14 "You are the *l* of the world.
5: 15 it gives *l* to everyone in the house.
5: 16 let your *l* shine before men,
6: 22 your whole body will be full of *l*.
11: 30 yoke is easy and my burden is *l*."
17: 2 his clothes became as white as the *l*
24: 29 and the moon will not give its *l*;
Mk 13: 24 and the moon will not give its *l*;
Lk 2: 32 a *l* for revelation to the Gentiles
8: 16 those who come in can see the *l*.
11: 33 those who come in may see the *l*.
Jn 1: 4 and that life was the *l* of men.
1: 5 The *l* shines in the darkness,
1: 7 witness to testify concerning that *l*,
1: 9 The true *l* that gives *l*
3: 19 but men loved darkness instead of *l*
3: 20 Everyone who does evil hates the *l*,
8: 12 he said, "I am the *l* of the world.
9: 5 in the world, I am the *l* of the world
12: 35 Walk while you have the *l*,
12: 46 I have come into the world as a *l*,
Ac 13: 47 " 'I have made you a *l*
Ro 13: 12 darkness and put on the armor of *l*.
2Co 4: 6 made his *l* shine in our hearts
6: 14 Or what fellowship can *l* have
11: 14 masquerades as an angel of *l*.
Eph 5: 8 but now you are *l* in the Lord.
1Th 5: 5 You are all sons of the *l*
1Ti 6: 16 and who lives in unapproachable *l*,
1Pe 2: 9 of darkness into his wonderful *l*.
2Pe 1: 19 as to a *l* shining in a dark place,
1Jn 1: 5 God is *l*; in him there is no
1: 7 But if we walk in the *l*,
2: 9 Anyone who claims to be in the *l*
Rev 21: 23 for the glory of God gives it *l*,
22: 5 for the Lord God will give them *l*.

LIGHTNING
Ex 9: 23 and *l* flashed down to the ground.
20: 18 and *l* and heard the trumpet
Ps 18: 12 with hailstones and bolts of *l*.
Eze 1: 13 it was bright, and *l* flashed out of it.
Da 10: 6 his face like *l*, his eyes like flaming
Mt 24: 27 For as the *l* that comes from the east
28: 3 His appearance was like *l*,
Lk 10: 18 "I saw Satan fall like *l* from heaven.
Rev 4: 5 From the throne came flashes of *l*,

LIGHTS (LIGHT)
Ge 1: 14 "Let there be *l* in the expanse
Lk 8: 16 No one *l* a lamp and hides it in a jar

LIKE-MINDED* (MIND)
Php 2: 2 make my joy complete by being *l*,

LIKENESS
Ge 1: 26 man in our image, in our *l*,
Ps 17: 15 I will be satisfied with seeing your *l*
Isa 52: 14 his form marred beyond human *l*—
Ro 8: 3 Son in the *l* of sinful man
8: 29 to be conformed to the *l* of his Son,
2Co 3: 18 his *l* with ever-increasing glory,
Php 2: 7 being made in human *l*.
Jas 3: 9 who have been made in God's *l*.

LILIES (LILY)
Lk 12: 27 "Consider how the *l* grow.

LILY (LILIES)
SS 2: 1 a *l* of the valleys.
2: 2 *Lover* Like a *l* among thorns

LIMIT
Ps 147: 5 his understanding has no *l*.
Jn 3: 34 for God gives the Spirit without *l*.

LINEN
Lev 16: 4 He is to put on the sacred *l* tunic,
Pr 31: 22 she is clothed in fine *l* and purple.
31: 24 She makes *l* garments
Mk 15: 46 So Joseph bought some *l* cloth,
Jn 20: 6 He saw the strips of *l* lying there,
Rev 15: 6 shining *l* and wore golden sashes
19: 8 Fine *l*, bright and clean,

LINGER
Hab 2: 3 Though it *l*, wait for it;

LION (LION'S LIONS')
Jdg 14: 6 power so that he tore the *l* apart
1Sa 17: 34 When a *l* or a bear came
Isa 11: 7 and the *l* will eat straw like the ox.
65: 25 and the *l* will eat straw like the ox,
Eze 1: 10 right side each had the face of a *l*,
10: 14 the third the face of a *l*,
Da 7: 4 "The first was like a *l*,
1Pe 5: 8 around like a roaring *l* looking
Rev 4: 7 The first living creature was like a *l*
5: 5 See, the *L* of the tribe of Judah,

LION'S (LION)
Ge 49: 9 You are a *l* cub, O Judah;

LIONS' (LION)
Da 6: 7 shall be thrown into the *l* den.

LIPS
Ps 8: 2 From the *l* of children and infants
34: 1 his praise will always be on my *l*.
40: 9 I do not seal my *l*,
63: 3 my *l* will glorify you.
119:171 May my *l* overflow with praise,
140: 3 the poison of vipers is on their *l*.
141: 3 keep watch over the door of my *l*.
Pr 10: 13 on the *l* of the discerning,
10: 18 who conceals his hatred has lying *l*,
10: 32 *l* of the righteous know what is
12: 22 The LORD detests lying *l*,
13: 3 He who guards his *l* guards his life,
14: 7 will not find knowledge on his *l*.
24: 26 is like a kiss on the *l*.
26: 23 are fervent *l* with an evil heart.
27: 2 someone else, and not your own *l*.
Isa 6: 5 For I am a man of unclean *l*,
28: 11 with foreign *l* and strange tongues
29: 13 and honor me with their *l*,
Mal 2: 7 "For the *l* of a priest ought
Mt 15: 8 These people honor me with their *l*
21: 16 " 'From the *l* of children
Lk 4: 22 words that came from his *l*.
Ro 3: 13 "The poison of vipers is on their *l*."
Col 3: 8 and filthy language from your *l*.
Heb 13: 15 the fruit of *l* that confess his name.
1Pe 3: 10 and his *l* from deceitful speech.

LISTEN (LISTENED LISTENING LISTENS)
Dt 18: 15 You must *l* to him.
30: 20 *l* to his voice, and hold fast to him.
1Ki 4: 34 came to *l* to Solomon's wisdom,
2Ki 21: 9 But the people did not *l*.
Pr 1: 5 let the wise *l* and add
Ecc 5: 1 Go near to *l* rather
Eze 2: 5 And whether they *l* or fail to *l*—
Mt 12: 42 earth to *l* to Solomon's wisdom,
Mk 9: 7 *L* to him!" Suddenly,
Jn 10: 27 My sheep *l* to my voice; I know
Ac 3: 22 you must *l* to everything he tells
Jas 1: 19 Everyone should be quick to *l*,
1: 22 Do not merely *l* to the word,
1Jn 4: 6 not from God does not *l* to us.

LISTENED (LISTEN)
Ne 8: 3 And all the people *l* attentively
Isa 66: 4 when I spoke, no one *l*.
Da 9: 6 We have not *l* to your servants

LISTENING (LISTEN)
1Sa 3: 9 Speak, LORD, for your servant is *l*
Pr 18: 13 He who answers before *l*—
Lk 10: 39 at the Lord's feet *l* to what he said.

LISTENS (LISTEN)
Pr 12: 15 but a wise man *l* to advice.
Lk 10: 16 "He who *l* to you *l*
1Jn 4: 6 and whoever knows God *l* to us;

LIVE (ALIVE LIFE LIFETIME LIVES LIVING)
Ge 3: 22 tree of life and eat, and *l* forever."
Ex 20: 12 so that you may *l* long
33: 20 for no one may see me and *l*."
Nu 21: 8 who is bitten can look at it and *l*."
Dt 5: 24 we have seen that a man can *l*
6: 2 as you *l* by keeping all his decrees
8: 3 to teach you that man does not *l*
Job 14: 14 If a man dies, will he *l* again?
Ps 15: 1 Who may *l* on your holy hill?
24: 1 the world, and all who *l* in it;
26: 8 I love the house where you *l*,
119:175 Let me *l* that I may praise you,
Pr 21: 9 Better to *l* on a corner of the roof
21: 19 Better to *l* in a desert
Ecc 9: 4 a *l* dog is better off than a dead lion
Isa 26: 19 But your dead will *l*;
55: 3 hear me, that your soul may *l*.
Eze 17: 19 LORD says: As surely as I *l*,
20: 11 for the man who obeys them will *l*
37: 3 can these bones *l*?" I said,
Am 5: 6 Seek the LORD and *l*,
Hab 2: 4 but the righteous will *l* by his faith
Zec 2: 11 I will *l* among you and you will
Mt 4: 4 'Man does not *l* on bread alone,
Lk 4: 4 'Man does not *l* on bread alone.' "
Jn 14: 19 Because I *l*, you also will *l*.

Ac 17: 24 does not *l* in temples built by hands
17: 28 'For in him we *l* and move
Ro 1: 17 "The righteous will *l* by faith."
2Co 5: 7 We *l* by faith, not by sight.
6: 16 "I will *l* with them and walk
Gal 2: 20 The life I *l* in the body, I *l* by faith
3: 11 "The righteous will *l* by faith."
5: 25 Since we *l* by the Spirit, let us keep
Eph 4: 17 that you must no longer *l*
Php 1: 21 to *l* is Christ and to die is gain.
Col 1: 10 order that you may *l* a life worthy
1Th 4: 1 we instructed you how to *l* in order
5: 13 *L* in peace with each other.
1Ti 2: 2 that we may *l* peaceful
2Ti 3: 12 who wants to *l* a godly life
Tit 2: 12 and to *l* self-controlled, upright
Heb 10: 38 But my righteous one will *l* by faith
12: 14 Make every effort to *l* in peace
1Pe 1: 17 *l* your lives as strangers here
3: 8 *l* in harmony with one another;

LIVES (LIVE)
Ge 45: 7 and to save your *l* by a great
Job 19: 25 I know that my Redeemer *l*,
Pr 1: 19 it takes away the *l*
Isa 57: 15 he who *l* forever, whose name is
Da 3: 28 to give up their *l* rather than serve
Jn 14: 17 for he *l* with you and will be in you.
Ro 6: 10 but the life he *l*, he *l* to God.
7: 18 I know that nothing good *l* in me,
8: 9 if the Spirit of God *l* in you.
14: 7 For none of us *l* to himself alone
1Co 3: 16 and that God's Spirit *l* in you?
Gal 2: 20 I no longer live, but Christ *l* in me.
1Th 2: 8 only the gospel of God but our *l*
1Ti 2: 2 quiet *l* in all godliness and holiness.
Tit 2: 12 and godly *l* in this present age,
Heb 7: 24 but because Jesus *l* forever,
13: 5 Keep your *l* free from the love
1Pe 3: 2 the purity and reverence of your *l*.
2Pe 3: 11 You ought to live holy and godly *l*
1Jn 3: 16 to lay down our *l* for our brothers.
4: 16 Whoever *l* in love *l* in God,

LIVING (LIVE)
Ge 2: 7 and the man became a *l* being.
1Sa 17: 26 defy the armies of the *l* God?"
Isa 53: 8 cut off from the land of the *l*;
Jer 2: 13 the spring of *l* water,
Eze 1: 5 what looked like four *l* creatures.
Zec 14: 8 On that day *l* water will flow out
Mt 22: 32 the God of the dead but of the *l*."
Jn 4: 10 he would have given you *l* water."
6: 51 I am the *l* bread that came
7: 38 streams of *l* water will flow
Ro 8: 11 Jesus from the dead is *l* in you,
12: 1 to offer your bodies as *l* sacrifices,
1Co 9: 14 the gospel should receive their *l*
Heb 4: 12 For the word of God is *l* and active.
10: 20 and *l* way opened for us
10: 31 to fall into the hands of the *l* God.
1Pe 1: 23 through the *l* and enduring word
Rev 1: 18 I am the *L* One; I was dead,
4: 6 the throne, were four *l* creatures,
7: 17 to springs of *l* water.

LOAD (LOADS)
Gal 6: 5 for each one should carry his own *l*.

LOADS (LOAD)
Mt 23: 4 They tie up heavy *l* and put them

LOAF (LOAVES)
1Co 10: 17 for we all partake of the one *l*.

LOAVES (LOAF)
Mk 6: 41 Taking the five *l* and the two fish
8: 6 When he had taken the seven *l*
Lk 11: 5 'Friend, lend me three *l* of bread,

LOCKED
Jn 20: 26 the doors were *l*, Jesus came
Gal 3: 23 *l* up until faith should be revealed.

LOCUSTS
Ex 10: 4 I will bring *l* into your country
Joel 2: 25 you for the years the *l* have eaten—
Mt 3: 4 His food was *l* and wild honey.
Rev 9: 3 And out of the smoke *l* came

LOFTY
Ps 139: 6 too *l* for me to attain.
Isa 57: 15 is what the high and *l* One says—

LONELY
Ps 68: 6 God sets the *l* in families,
Lk 5: 16 Jesus often withdrew to *l* places

LONG (LENGTH LENGTHY LONGED LONGING LONGINGS LONGS)
Ex 17: 11 As *l* as Moses held up his hands,
Nu 6: 5 the hair of his head grow *l*.
1Ki 18: 21 "How *l* will you waver
Ps 119: 97 I meditate on it all day *l*.
119:174 I *l* for your salvation, O LORD,
Hos 7: 13 I *l* to redeem them
Am 5: 18 Why do you *l* for the day
Mt 25: 5 The bridegroom was a *l* time
Jn 9: 4 As *l* as it is day, we must do
1Co 11: 14 that if a man has *l* hair,
Eph 3: 18 to grasp how wide and *l* and high
Php 1: 8 God can testify how I *l* for all
1Pe 1: 12 Even angels *l* to look

LONGED (LONG)
Mt 13: 17 righteous men *l* to see what you see
23: 37 how often I have *l*
Lk 13: 34 how often I have *l*
2Ti 4: 8 to all who have *l* for his appearing.

LONGING* (LONG)
Dt 28: 65 with *l*, and a despairing heart.
Job 7: 2 Like a slave *l* for the evening
Ps 119: 20 My soul is consumed with *l*
119: 81 with *l* for your salvation,
119:131 *l* for your commands.
143: 7 my spirit faints with *l*.
Pr 13: 12 but a *l* fulfilled is a tree of life.
13: 19 A *l* fulfilled is sweet to the soul,
Eze 23: 27 look on these things with *l*
Lk 16: 21 and *l* to eat what fell from the rich
Ro 15: 23 since I have been *l* for many years
2Co 5: 2 *l* to be clothed with our heavenly
7: 7 He told us about your *l* for me,
7: 11 what alarm, what *l*, what concern,
1Th 2: 17 out of our intense *l* we made every
Heb 11: 16 they were *l* for a better country—

LONGINGS* (LONG)
Ps 38: 9 All my *l* lie open before you,
112: 10 the *l* of the wicked will come

LONGS* (LONG)
Ps 63: 1 my body *l* for you,
Isa 26: 9 in the morning my spirit *l* for you.
30: 18 Yet the LORD *l* to be gracious
Php 2: 26 For he *l* for all of you and is

LOOK (LOOKED LOOKING LOOKS)
Ge 19: 17 "Flee for your lives! Don't *l* back,
Ex 3: 6 because he was afraid to *l* at God.
Nu 21: 8 anyone who is bitten can *l* at it
32: 8 Kadesh Barnea to *l* over the land.
Dt 4: 29 you will find him if you *l* for him
1Sa 16: 7 The LORD does not *l*
Job 31: 1 not to *l* lustfully at a girl.
Ps 34: 5 Those who *l* to him are radiant;
105: 4 *L* to the LORD and his strength;
113: 6 who stoops down to *l*
123: 2 As the eyes of slaves *l* to the hand
Pr 1: 28 they will *l* for me but will not find
4: 25 Let your eyes *l* straight ahead,
15: 30 A cheerful *l* brings joy to the heart,
Isa 17: 7 In that day men will *l*
31: 1 do not *l* to the Holy One of Israel,
40: 26 Lift your eyes and *l* to the heavens:
60: 5 Then you will *l* and be radiant,
Jer 3: 3 Yet you have the brazen *l*
6: 16 "Stand at the crossroads and *l*;
Eze 34: 11 for my sheep and *l* after them.
Hab 1: 13 Your eyes are too pure to *l* on evil;
Zec 12: 10 They will *l* on me, the one they
Mt 18: 10 "See that you do not *l* down on one
18: 12 go to *l* for the one that wandered
23: 27 which *l* beautiful on the outside
Mk 13: 21 '*L*, here is the Christ!' or, '*L*,
Lk 6: 41 "Why do you *l* at the speck
24: 39 *L* at my hands and my feet.
Jn 1: 36 he said, "*L*, the Lamb of God!"
4: 35 open your eyes and *l* at the fields!
19: 37 "They will *l* on the one they have
Ro 14: 10 why do you *l* down on your brother
Php 2: 4 Each of you should *l* not only
1Ti 4: 12 Don't let anyone *l* down on you
Jas 1: 27 to *l* after orphans and widows
1Pe 1: 12 long to *l* into these things.
2Pe 3: 12 as you *l* forward to the day of God

LOOKED (LOOK)
Ge 19: 26 Lot's wife *l* back, and she became
Ex 2: 25 So God *l* on the Israelites
1Sa 6: 19 because they had *l* into the ark
SS 3: 1 I *l* for the one my heart loves;
Eze 22: 30 "I *l* for a man among them who
34: 6 and no one searched or *l* for them.
44: 4 I *l* and saw the glory
Da 7: 9 "As I *l*,
10: 5 I *l* up and there before me was
Hab 3: 6 he *l*, and made the nations tremble.
Mt 25: 36 I was sick and you *l* after me,
Lk 18: 9 and *l* down on everybody else,
22: 61 The Lord turned and *l* straight
1Jn 1: 1 which we have *l* at and our hands

LOOKING (LOOK)
Ps 69: 3 *l* for my God.
119: 82 My eyes fail, *l* for your promise;
119:123 My eyes fail, *l* for your salvation,
Mk 16: 6 "You are *l* for Jesus the Nazarene,
2Co 10: 7 You are *l* only on the surface
Php 4: 17 Not that I am *l* for a gift,
1Th 2: 6 We were not *l* for praise from men,
2Pe 3: 13 with his promise we are *l* forward
Rev 5: 6 I saw a Lamb, *l* as if it had been

LOOKS (LOOK)
1Sa 16: 7 Man *l* at the outward appearance,
Ezr 8: 22 is on everyone who *l* to him,
Ps 104: 32 who *l* at the earth, and it trembles;
138: 6 on high, he *l* upon the lowly,
Pr 27: 18 he who *l* after his master will be
Eze 34: 12 As a shepherd *l* after his scattered
Mt 5: 28 But I tell you that anyone who *l*
16: 4 and adulterous generation *l*
Lk 9: 62 and *l* back is fit for service
Jn 6: 40 Father's will is that everyone who *l*
12: 45 When he *l* at me, he sees the one
Php 2: 21 For everyone *l* out
Jas 1: 25 But the man who *l* intently

LOOSE
Isa 33: 23 Your rigging hangs *l*:
Mt 16: 19 and whatever you *l* on earth will be
18: 18 and whatever you *l* on earth will be

LORD† (LORD'S† LORDED LORDING)
Ge 18: 27 been so bold as to speak to the *L*,
Ex 15: 17 O *L*, your hands established.
Nu 16: 13 now you also want to *l* it over us?
Dt 10: 17 God of gods and *L* of lords,
Jos 3: 13 the *L* of all the earth—set foot
1Ki 3: 10 *L* was pleased that Solomon had
Ne 4: 14 Remember the *L*, who is great
Job 28: 28 'The fear of the *L*— that is wisdom,
Ps 37: 13 but the *L* laughs at the wicked,
38: 22 O *L* my Savior.
54: 4 the *L* is the one who sustains me.
62: 12 and that you, O *L*, are loving.
69: 6 O *L*, the LORD Almighty;
86: 5 You are forgiving and good, O *L*,
86: 8 gods there is none like you, O *L*;
89: 49 O *L*, where is your former great

68: 4 his name is the *L*—
68: 18 O *L* God, might dwell there.
68: 20 from the Sovereign *L* comes escape
69: 31 This will please the *L* more
72: 18 Praise be to the *L* God, the God
75: 8 In the hand of the *L* is a cup
78: 4 the praiseworthy deeds of the *L*,
84: 8 my prayer, O *L* God Almighty;
84: 11 For the *L* God is a sun and shield;
85: 7 Show us your unfailing love, O *L*,
86: 11 Teach me your way, O *L*,
87: 2 the *L* loves the gates of Zion
89: 5 heavens praise your wonders, O *L*,
89: 8 O *L* God Almighty, who is like you
91: 2 I will say of the *L*, "He is my refuge
92: 1 It is good to praise the *L*
92: 4 by your deeds, O *L*;
92: 13 planted in the house of the *L*,
93: 1 The *L* reigns, he is robed in majesty
93: 5 house for endless days, O *L*.
94: 1 O *L*, the God who avenges,
94: 12 is the man you discipline, O *L*,
94: 18 your love, O *L*, supported me.
95: 1 Come, let us sing for joy to the *L*;
95: 3 For the *L* is the great God,
95: 6 let us kneel before the *L* our Maker
96: 1 Sing to the *L* a new song;
96: 5 but the *L* made the heavens.
96: 8 to the *L* the glory due his name;
96: 9 Worship the *L* in the splendor
96: 13 they will sing before the *L*,
97: 1 The *L* reigns, let the earth be glad;
97: 9 O *L*, are the Most High
98: 1 Sing to the *L* a new song,
98: 2 *L* has made his salvation known
98: 4 Shout for joy to the *L*, all the earth,
99: 1 The *L* reigns,
99: 2 Great is the *L* in Zion;
99: 5 Exalt the *L* our God
99: 9 Exalt the *L* our God
100: 1 Shout for joy to the *L*, all the earth.
100: 2 Worship the *L* with gladness;
100: 3 Know that the *L* is God.
100: 5 For the *L* is good and his love
101: 1 to you, O *L*, I will sing praise.
102: 12 But you, O *L*, sit enthroned forever
103: 1 Praise the *L*, O my soul;
103: 8 The *L* is compassionate
103: 19 The *L* has established his throne
104: 1 O *L* my God, you are very great;
104: 24 How many are your works, O *L*!
104: 33 I will sing to the *L* all my life;
105: 4 Look to the *L* and his strength;
105: 7 He is the *L* our God;
106: 2 proclaim the mighty acts of the *L*
107: 1 Give thanks to the *L*, for he is good
107: 8 to the *L* for his unfailing love
107: 21 to the *L* for his unfailing love
107: 43 and consider the great love of the *L*
108: 3 I will praise you, O *L*,
109: 26 Help me, O *L* my God;
110: 1 The *L* says to my Lord:
110: 4 The *L* has sworn
111: 2 Great are the works of the *L*;
111: 4 *L* is gracious and compassionate.
111: 10 The fear of the *L* is the beginning
112: 1 Blessed is the man who fears the *L*,
113: 1 Praise, O servants of the *L*,
113: 2 Let the name of the *L* be praised,
113: 4 *L* is exalted over all the nations,
113: 5 Who is like the *L* our God,
115: 1 Not to us, O *L*, not to us
115: 18 it is we who extol the *L*,
116: 12 How can I repay the *L*
116: 15 Precious in the sight of the *L*
117: 1 Praise the *L*, all you nations;
118: 1 Give thanks to the *L*, for he is good
118: 5 In my anguish I cried to the *L*,
118: 8 It is better to take refuge in the *L*
118: 18 The *L* has chastened me severely,
118: 23 the *L* has done this,
118: 24 This is the day the *L* has made;
118: 26 comes in the name of the *L*.
119: 1 to the law of the *L*.
119: 64 with your love, O *L*;
119: 89 Your word, O *L*, is eternal;
119:126 It is time for you to act, O *L*;
119:159 O *L*, according to your love.
120: 1 I call on the *L* in my distress,
121: 2 My help comes from the *L*,
121: 5 The *L* watches over you—
121: 8 the *L* will watch over your coming
122: 1 "Let us go to the house of the *L*."
123: 2 so our eyes look to the *L* our God,
124: 1 If the *L* had not been on our side—
124: 8 Our help is in the name of the *L*,
125: 2 so the *L* surrounds his people
126: 3 The *L* has done great things for us,
126: 4 Restore our fortunes, O *L*,
127: 1 Unless the *L* builds the house,
127: 3 Sons are a heritage from the *L*,
128: 1 Blessed are all who fear the *L*,
130: 1 O *L*; O Lord, hear my voice.
130: 3 If you, O *L*, kept a record of sins,
130: 5 I wait for the *L*, my soul waits,
131: 3 O Israel, put your hope in the *L*
132: 1 O *L*, remember David
132: 13 For the *L* has chosen Zion,
133: 3 For there the *L* bestows his
134: 3 May the *L*, the Maker of heaven
135: 4 For the *L* has chosen Jacob
135: 6 The *L* does whatever pleases him,
136: 1 Give thanks to the *L*, for he is good
137: 4 How can we sing the songs of the *L*
138: 1 I will praise you, O *L*,
138: 8 The *L* will fulfill ›his purpose‹
139: 1 O *L*, you have searched me
140: 1 Rescue me, O *L*, from evil men;
141: 1 O *L*, I call to you; come quickly
141: 3 Set a guard over my mouth, O *L*;
142: 5 I cry to you, O *L*;
143: 9 Rescue me from my enemies, O *L*,
144: 3 O *L*, what is man that you care
145: 3 Great is the *L* and most worthy
145: 8 *L* is gracious and compassionate,
145: 9 The *L* is good to all;
145: 17 The *L* is righteous in all his ways
145: 18 The *L* is near to all who call on him
146: 5 whose hope is in the *L* his God,
146: 7 The *L* sets prisoners free,
147: 2 The *L* builds up Jerusalem;
147: 7 Sing to the *L* with thanksgiving;
147: 11 *L* delights in those who fear him,
147: 12 Extol the *L*, O Jerusalem;
148: 1 Praise the *L* from the heavens,
148: 7 Praise the *L* from the earth,
149: 4 For the *L* takes delight
150: 1 Praise the *L*.
150: 6 that has breath praise the *L*.
Pr 1: 7 The fear of the *L* is the beginning
1: 29 and did not choose to fear the *L*,
2: 5 will understand the fear of the *L*
2: 6 For the *L* gives wisdom,
3: 5 Trust in the *L* with all your heart
3: 7 fear the *L* and shun evil.
3: 9 Honor the *L* with your wealth,
3: 12 the *L* disciplines those he loves,
3: 19 By wisdom the *L* laid the earth's
5: 21 are in full view of the *L*,
6: 16 There are six things the *L* hates,
8: 13 To fear the *L* is to hate evil;
9: 10 "The fear of the *L* is the beginning
10: 27 The fear of the *L* adds length to life
11: 1 The *L* abhors dishonest scales,
12: 22 The *L* detests lying lips,
14: 2 whose walk is upright fears the *L*,
14: 26 He who fears the *L* has a secure
14: 27 The fear of the *L* is a fountain
15: 3 The eyes of the *L* are everywhere,
15: 16 Better a little with the fear of the *L*
15: 33 of the *L* teaches a man wisdom,
16: 2 but motives are weighed by the *L*.
16: 3 Commit to the *L* whatever you do,
16: 4 The *L* works out everything
16: 5 The *L* detests all the proud of heart
16: 9 but the *L* determines his steps.
16: 33 but its every decision is from the *L*.
18: 10 The name of the *L* is a strong tower
18: 22 and receives favor from the *L*.
19: 14 but a prudent wife is from the *L*.
19: 17 to the poor lends to the *L*,
19: 23 The fear of the *L* leads to life:
20: 10 the *L* detests them both.
21: 2 but the *L* weighs the heart.
21: 3 to the *L* than sacrifice.
21: 30 that can succeed against the *L*.
21: 31 but victory rests with the *L*.
22: 2 The *L* is the Maker of them all.
22: 23 for the *L* will take up their case
23: 17 for the fear of the *L*.
24: 18 or the *L* will see and disapprove
24: 21 Fear the *L* and the king, my son,
25: 22 and the *L* will reward you.
28: 14 is the man who always fears the *L*,
29: 26 from the *L* that man gets justice.
30: 7 "Two things I ask of you, O *L*;
31: 30 a woman who fears the *L* is
Isa 2: 3 up to the mountain of the *L*,
2: 10 the ground from dread of the *L*
3: 17 the *L* will make their scalps bald."
4: 2 of the *L* will be beautiful
5: 16 the *L* Almighty will be exalted
6: 3 holy, holy is the *L* Almighty;
9: 7 The zeal of the *L* Almighty
11: 2 The Spirit of the *L* will rest on him
11: 9 full of the knowledge of the *L*
12: 2 The *L*, the *L*, is my strength
18: 7 of the Name of the *L* Almighty.
24: 1 the *L* is going to lay waste the earth
25: 1 O *L*, you are my God;
25: 6 this mountain the *L* Almighty will
25: 8 The Sovereign *L* will wipe away
26: 4 Trust in the *L* forever,
26: 8 *L*, walking in the way of your laws,
26: 13 O *L*, our God, other lords
26: 21 the *L* is coming out of his dwelling
27: 1 the *L* will punish with his sword,
27: 12 In that day the *L* will thresh
28: 5 In that day the *L* Almighty
29: 6 the *L* Almighty will come
29: 15 to hide their plans from the *L*,
30: 18 For the *L* is a God of justice.
30: 26 when the *L* binds up the bruises
30: 27 the Name of the *L* comes from afar
30: 30 The *L* will cause men
33: 2 O *L*, be gracious to us;
33: 6 the fear of the *L* is the key
33: 22 For the *L* is our judge,
34: 2 The *L* is angry with all nations;
35: 2 they will see the glory of the *L*,
35: 10 the ransomed of the *L* will return.
38: 7 to you that the *L* will do what he
40: 3 the way for the *L*;
40: 5 the glory of the *L* will be revealed,
40: 7 the breath of the *L* blows on them.
40: 10 the Sovereign *L* comes with power,
40: 14 Whom did the *L* consult
40: 28 The *L* is the everlasting God,
40: 31 but those who hope in the *L*
41: 14 will help you," declares the *L*,
41: 20 that the hand of the *L* has done this
42: 6 the *L*, have called you
42: 8 "I am the *L*; that is my name!
42: 13 The *L* will march out like a mighty
42: 21 It pleased the *L*
43: 3 For I am the *L*, your God,
43: 11 I, even I, am the *L*,

44: 6 "This is what the *L* says—
44: 24 I am the *L*,
45: 5 I am the *L*, and there is no other;
45: 7 I, the *L*, do all these things.
45: 21 Was it not I, the *L*?
48: 17 "I am the *L* your God,
50: 4 Sovereign *L* has given me
50: 10 Who among you fears the *L*
51: 1 and who seek the *L*:
51: 11 The ransomed of the *L* will return.
51: 15 the *L* Almighty is his name.
53: 1 the arm of the *L* been revealed?
53: 6 and the *L* has laid on him
53: 10 and the will of the *L* will prosper
54: 5 the *L* Almighty is his name—
55: 6 Seek the *L* while he may be found;
55: 7 to the *L*, and he will have mercy
56: 6 who bind themselves to the *L*
58: 8 of the *L* will be your rear guard.
58: 11 The *L* will guide you always;
59: 1 the arm of the *L* is not too short
60: 1 the glory of the *L* rises upon you.
60: 16 Then you will know that I, the *L*,
60: 20 the *L* will be your everlasting light,
61: 1 Spirit of the Sovereign *L* is on me,
61: 3 a planting of the *L*
61: 10 I delight greatly in the *L*;
61: 11 so the Sovereign *L* will make
62: 4 for the *L* will take delight in you,
63: 7 I will tell of the kindnesses of the *L*,
64: 8 Yet, O *L*, you are our Father.
66: 15 See, the *L* is coming with fire,
Jer 1: 9 Then the *L* reached out his hand
2: 19 when you forsake the *L* your God
3: 25 sinned against the *L* our God,
4: 4 Circumcise yourselves to the *L*,
8: 7 the requirements of the *L*.
9: 24 I am the *L*, who exercises kindness,
10: 6 No one is like you, O *L*;
10: 10 But the *L* is the true God;
12: 1 You are always righteous, O *L*,
14: 7 O *L*, do something for the sake
14: 20 O *L*, we acknowledge our
16: 15 will say, 'As surely as the *L* lives,
16: 19 O *L*, my strength and my fortress,
17: 7 is the man who trusts in the *L*,
17: 10 "I the *L* search the heart
20: 11 *L* is with me like a mighty warrior;
23: 6 The *L* Our Righteousness.
24: 7 heart to know me, that I am the *L*.
28: 9 as one truly sent by the *L* only
31: 11 For the *L* will ransom Jacob
31: 22 The *L* will create a new thing
31: 34 his brother, saying, 'Know the *L*,'
32: 27 I am the *L*, the God of all mankind.
33: 16 The *L* Our Righteousness.'
36: 6 the words of the *L* that you wrote
40: 3 now the *L* has brought it about;
42: 3 Pray that the *L* your God will tell
42: 4 I will tell you everything the *L* says
42: 6 we will obey the *L* our God,
50: 4 go in tears to seek the *L* their God.
51: 10 " 'The *L* has vindicated us;
51: 56 For the *L* is a God of retribution;
La 3: 24 to myself, "The *L* is my portion;
3: 25 *L* is good to those whose hope is
3: 40 and let us return to the *L*.
Eze 1: 3 the word of the *L* came
1: 28 of the likeness of the glory of the *L*.
4: 14 Sovereign *L*! I have never defiled
10: 4 Then the glory of the *L* rose
15: 7 you will know that I am the *L*.
30: 3 the day of the *L* is near—
36: 23 nations will know that I am the *L*,
37: 4 'Dry bones, hear the word of the *L*!
43: 4 glory of the *L* entered the temple
44: 4 LORD filling the temple of the *L*,
Da 9: 2 to the word of the *L* given
Hos 1: 7 horsemen, but by the *L* their God."
2: 20 and you will acknowledge the *L*.
3: 1 as the *L* loves the Israelites,
3: 5 They will come trembling to the *L*
6: 1 "Come, let us return to the *L*.
6: 3 Let us acknowledge the *L*;
10: 12 for it is time to seek the *L*,
12: 5 the *L* is his name of renown!
14: 1 O Israel, to the *L* your God.
Joel 1: 1 The word of the *L* that came
1: 15 For the day of the *L* is near;
2: 1 for the day of the *L* is coming.
2: 11 The day of the *L* is great;
2: 13 Return to the *L* your God,
2: 23 rejoice in the *L* your God,
2: 31 the great and dreadful day of the *L*.
2: 32 on the name of the *L* will be saved;
3: 14 For the day of the *L* is near
3: 16 the *L* will be a refuge for his people,
Am 4: 13 the *L* God Almighty is his name.
5: 6 Seek the *L* and live,
5: 15 Perhaps the *L* God Almighty will
5: 18 long for the day of the *L*?
7: 15 *L* took me from tending the flock
8: 12 searching for the word of the *L*,
9: 5 The Lord, the *L* Almighty,
Ob : 15 "The day of the *L* is near
Jnh 1: 3 But Jonah ran away from the *L*
1: 4 the *L* sent a great wind on the sea,
1: 17 But the *L* provided a great fish
2: 9 Salvation comes from the *L*."
4: 2 He prayed to the *L*, "O *L*,
4: 6 Then the *L* God provided a vine
Mic 1: 1 The word of the *L* that came to Micah
4: 2 up to the mountain of the *L*,
5: 4 flock in the strength of the *L*,
6: 2 For the *L* has a case
6: 8 And what does the *L* require of you
7: 7 as for me, I watch in hope for the *L*,
Na 1: 2 The *L* takes vengeance on his foes
1: 3 The *L* is slow to anger
Hab 2: 14 knowledge of the glory of the *L*,
2: 20 But the *L* is in his holy temple;
3: 2 I stand in awe of your deeds, O *L*.
Zep 1: 1 The word of the *L* that came
1: 7 for the day of the *L* is near.
3: 17 The *L* your God is with you,
Hag 1: 1 the word of the *L* came
1: 8 and be honored," says the *L*.
2: 23 that day,' declares the *L* Almighty,
Zec 1: 1 the word of the *L* came
1: 17 and the *L* will again comfort Zion
3: 1 standing before the angel of the *L*,
4: 6 by my Spirit,' says the *L* Almighty.
6: 12 and build the temple of the *L*.
8: 21 the *L* and seek the *L* Almighty.
9: 16 The *L* their God will save them
14: 5 Then the *L* my God will come,
14: 9 The *L* will be king
14: 16 the *L* Almighty, and to celebrate
Mal 1: 1 The word of the *L* to Israel
3: 6 "I the *L* do not change.
4: 5 and dreadful day of the *L* comes.

LORD'S‡ (LORD‡)
Ex 4: 14 the *L* anger burned against Moses
12: 11 Eat it in haste; it is the *L* Passover.
34: 34 he entered the *L* presence
Lev 23: 4 " 'These are the *L* appointed feasts,
Nu 9: 23 At the *L* command they encamped
14: 41 you disobeying the *L* command?
32: 13 The *L* anger burned against Israel
Dt 6: 18 is right and good in the *L* sight,
10: 13 and to observe the *L* commands
32: 9 For the *L* portion is his people,
Jos 21: 45 Not one of all the *L* good promises
1Sa 24: 10 because he is the *L* anointed.'
1Ki 10: 9 Because of the *L* eternal love
Ps 24: 1 The earth is the *L*, and everything
32: 10 but the *L* unfailing love
89: 1 of the *L* great love forever;
103: 17 *L* love is with those who fear him,
118: 15 "The *L* right hand has done mighty
Pr 3: 11 do not despise the *L* discipline
19: 21 but it is the *L* purpose that prevails.
Isa 24: 14 west they acclaim the *L* majesty.
30: 9 to listen to the *L* instruction.
49: 4 Yet what is due me is in the *L* hand
53: 10 Yet it was the *L* will to crush him
55: 13 This will be for the *L* renown,
61: 2 to proclaim the year of the *L* favor
62: 3 of splendor in the *L* hand,
Jer 25: 17 So I took the cup from the *L* hand
48: 10 lax in doing the *L* work!
51: 7 was a gold cup in the *L* hand;
La 3: 22 of the *L* great love we are not
Eze 7: 19 them in the day of the *L* wrath.
Joel 3: 18 will flow out of the *L* house
Ob : 21 And the kingdom will be the *L*.
Mic 4: 1 of the *L* temple will be established
6: 2 O mountains, the *L* accusation;
Hab 2: 16 from the *L* right hand is coming
Zep 2: 3 sheltered on the day of the *L* anger.

LOSE (LOSES LOSS LOST)
Dt 1: 28 Our brothers have made us *l* heart.
1Sa 17: 32 "Let no one *l* heart on account
Isa 7: 4 Do not *l* heart because of these two
Mt 10: 39 Whoever finds his life will *l* it,
Lk 9: 25 and yet *l* or forfeit his very self?
Jn 6: 39 that I shall *l* none of all that he has
2Co 4: 1 this ministry, we do not *l* heart.
4: 16 Therefore we do not *l* heart.
Heb 12: 3 will not grow weary and *l* heart.
12: 5 do not *l* heart when he rebukes you
2Jn : 8 that you do not *l* what you have

LOSES (LOSE)
Mt 5: 13 But if the salt *l* its saltiness,
Lk 15: 4 you has a hundred sheep and *l* one
15: 8 has ten silver coins and *l* one.

LOSS (LOSE)
Ro 11: 12 and their *l* means riches
1Co 3: 15 he will suffer *l*; he himself will be
Php 3: 8 I consider everything a *l* compared

LOST (LOSE)
Ps 73: 2 I had nearly *l* my foothold.
Jer 50: 6 "My people have been *l* sheep;
Eze 34: 4 the strays or searched for the *l*.
34: 16 for the *l* and bring back the strays.
Mt 18: 14 any of these little ones should be *l*.
Lk 15: 4 go after the *l* sheep until he finds it?
15: 6 with me; I have found my *l* sheep.'
15: 9 with me; I have found my *l* coin.'
15: 24 is alive again; he was *l* and is found
19: 10 to seek and to save what was *l*."
Php 3: 8 for whose sake I have *l* all things.

LOT (LOTS)
Nephew of Abraham (Ge 11:27; 12:5). Chose to live in Sodom (Ge 13). Rescued from four kings (Ge 14). Rescued from Sodom (Ge 19:1–29; 2Pe 2:7). Fathered Moab and Ammon by his daughters (Ge 19:30–38).
Est 3: 7 the *l*) in the presence of Haman
9: 24 the *l*) for their ruin and destruction.
Pr 16: 33 The *l* is cast into the lap,
18: 18 Casting the *l* settles disputes
Ecc 3: 22 his work, because that is his *l*.
Ac 1: 26 Then they cast lots, and the *l* fell

LOTS (LOT)
Jos 18: 10 Joshua then cast *l* for them
Ps 22: 18 and cast *l* for my clothing.
Joel 3: 3 They cast *l* for my people
Ob : 11 and cast *l* for Jerusalem,
Mt 27: 35 divided up his clothes by casting *l*.
Ac 1: 26 Then they cast *l*, and the lot fell

LOVE* (BELOVED LOVED LOVELY LOVER LOVER'S LOVERS LOVES LOVING LOVING-KINDNESS)
Ge 20: 13 'This is how you can show your *l*

22: 2 your only son, Isaac, whom you *l*,
29: 18 Jacob was in *l* with Rachel and said
29: 20 days to him because of his *l* for her.
29: 32 Surely my husband will *l* me now."
Ex 15: 13 "In your unfailing *l* you will lead
20: 6 showing *l* to a thousand generations
20: 6 of those who *l* me
21: 5 'I *l* my master and my wife
34: 6 abounding in *l* and faithfulness,
34: 7 maintaining *l* to thousands,
Lev 19: 18 but *l* your neighbor as yourself.
19: 34 *L* him as yourself,
Nu 14: 18 abounding in *l* and forgiving sin
14: 19 In accordance with your great *l*,
Dt 5: 10 showing *l* to a thousand generations
5: 10 of those who *l* me
6: 5 *L* the LORD your God
7: 9 generations of those who *l* him
7: 9 keeping his covenant of *l*
7: 12 God will keep his covenant of *l*
7: 13 He will *l* you and bless you
10: 12 to walk in all his ways, to *l* him,
10: 19 you are to *l* those who are aliens,
11: 1 *L* the LORD your God
11: 13 to *l* the LORD your God
11: 22 to *l* the LORD your God,
13: 3 you *l* him with all your heart
13: 6 wife you *l*, or your closest friend
19: 9 to *l* the LORD your God
21: 15 the son of the wife he does not *l*,
21: 16 the son of the wife he does not *l*.
30: 6 so that you may *l* him
30: 16 today to *l* the LORD your God,
30: 20 and that you may *l* the LORD your
33: 3 Surely it is you who *l* the people;
Jos 22: 5 to *l* the LORD your God, to walk
23: 11 careful to *l* the LORD your God.
Jdg 5: 31 may they who *l* you be like the sun
14: 16 You hate me! You don't really *l* me
16: 4 he fell in *l* with a woman
16: 15 "How can you say, 'I *l* you,'
1Sa 18: 20 Saul's daughter Michal was in *l*
20: 17 had David reaffirm his oath out of *l*
2Sa 1: 26 Your *l* for me was wonderful,
7: 15 But my *l* will never be taken away
13: 1 son of David fell in *l* with Tamar,
13: 4 said to him, "I'm in *l* with Tamar,
16: 17 "Is this the *l* you show your friend?
19: 6 You *l* those who hate you
19: 6 hate you and hate those who *l* you.
1Ki 3: 3 Solomon showed his *l*
8: 23 you who keep your covenant of *l*
10: 9 of the LORD's eternal *l* for Israel,
11: 2 Solomon held fast to them in *l*.
1Ch 16: 34 his *l* endures forever.
16: 41 "for his *l* endures forever."
17: 13 I will never take my *l* away
2Ch 5: 13 his *l* endures forever."
6: 14 you who keep your covenant of *l*
6: 42 Remember the great *l* promised
7: 3 his *l* endures forever."
7: 6 saying, "His *l* endures forever."
9: 8 Because of the *l* of your God
19: 2 and *l* those who hate the LORD?
20: 21 for his *l* endures forever."
Ezr 3: 11 his *l* to Israel endures forever."
Ne 1: 5 covenant of *l* with those who *l* him
9: 17 slow to anger and abounding in *l*.
9: 32 who keeps his covenant of *l*,
13: 22 to me according to your great *l*.
Job 15: 34 of those who *l* bribes.
19: 19 those I *l* have turned against me.
37: 13 or to water his earth and show his *l*.
Ps 4: 2 How long will you *l* delusions
5: 11 that those who *l* your name may
6: 4 save me because of your unfailing *l*.
11: 5 wicked and those who *l* violence
13: 5 But I trust in your unfailing *l*;
17: 7 Show the wonder of your great *l*,
18: 1 I *l* you, O LORD, my strength.
21: 7 through the unfailing *l*
23: 6 Surely goodness and *l* will follow
25: 6 O LORD, your great mercy and *l*,
25: 7 according to your *l* remember me,
26: 3 for your *l* is ever before me,
26: 8 I *l* the house where you live,
31: 7 I will be glad and rejoice in your *l*,
31: 16 save me in your unfailing *l*.
31: 21 for he showed his wonderful *l*
31: 23 *L* the LORD, all his saints!
32: 10 but the LORD's unfailing *l*
33: 5 the earth is full of his unfailing *l*.
33: 18 whose hope is in his unfailing *l*,
33: 22 May your unfailing *l* rest upon us,
36: 5 Your *l*, O LORD, reaches
36: 7 How priceless is your unfailing *l*!
36: 10 Continue your *l* to those who know
40: 10 I do not conceal your *l*
40: 11 may your *l* and your truth always
40: 16 may those who *l* your salvation
42: 8 By day the LORD directs his *l*,
44: 26 of your unfailing *l*.
45: 7 You *l* righteousness and hate
48: 9 we meditate on your unfailing *l*.
51: 1 according to your unfailing *l*;
52: 3 You *l* evil rather than good,
52: 4 You *l* every harmful word,
52: 8 I trust in God's unfailing *l*
57: 3 God sends his *l* and his faithfulness
57: 10 For great is your *l*, reaching
59: 16 in the morning I will sing of your *l*;
60: 5 that those you *l* may be delivered.
61: 7 appoint your *l* and faithfulness
63: 3 Because your *l* is better than life,
66: 20 or withheld his *l* from me!
69: 13 in your great *l*, O God,
69: 16 out of the goodness of your *l*;
69: 36 and those who *l* his name will dwell
70: 4 may those who *l* your salvation
77: 8 Has his unfailing *l* vanished forever
85: 7 Show us your unfailing *l*, O LORD
85: 10 *L* and faithfulness meet together;
86: 5 abounding in *l* to all who call
86: 13 For great is your *l* toward me;
86: 15 abounding in *l* and faithfulness.
88: 11 Is your *l* declared in the grave,
89: 1 of the LORD's great *l* forever;
89: 2 declare that your *l* stands firm
89: 14 *l* and faithfulness go before you.
89: 24 My faithful *l* will be with him,
89: 28 I will maintain my *l* to him forever,
89: 33 but I will not take my *l* from him,
89: 49 where is your former great *l*,
90: 14 with your unfailing *l*,
92: 2 to proclaim your *l* in the morning
94: 18 your *l*, O LORD, supported me.
97: 10 Let those who *l* the LORD hate
98: 3 He has remembered his *l*
100: 5 is good and his *l* endures forever;
101: 1 I will sing of your *l* and justice;
103: 4 crowns you with *l* and compassion.
103: 8 slow to anger, abounding in *l*.
103: 11 so great is his *l* for those who fear
103: 17 LORD's *l* is with those who fear
106: 1 his *l* endures forever.
106: 45 and out of his great *l* he relented.
107: 1 his *l* endures forever.
107: 8 to the LORD for his unfailing *l*
107: 15 to the LORD for his unfailing *l*
107: 21 to the LORD for his unfailing *l*
107: 31 to the LORD for his unfailing *l*
107: 43 consider the great *l* of the LORD.
108: 4 For great is your *l*, higher
108: 6 that those you *l* may be delivered.
109: 21 out of the goodness of your *l*,
109: 26 save me in accordance with your *l*.
115: 1 because of your *l* and faithfulness.
116: 1 I *l* the LORD, for he heard my
117: 2 For great is his *l* toward us,
118: 1 his *l* endures forever.
118: 2 "His *l* endures forever."
118: 3 "His *l* endures forever."
118: 4 "His *l* endures forever."
118: 29 his *l* endures forever.
119: 41 May your unfailing *l* come to me,
119: 47 because I *l* them.
119: 48 to your commands, which I *l*,
119: 64 The earth is filled with your *l*,
119: 76 May your unfailing *l* be my
119: 88 my life according to your *l*,
119: 97 Oh, how I *l* your law!
119:113 but I *l* your law.
119:119 therefore I *l* your statutes.
119:124 your servant according to your *l*
119:127 Because I *l* your commands
119:132 to those who *l* your name.
119:149 in accordance with your *l*;
119:159 O LORD, according to your *l*.
119:159 See how I *l* your precepts;
119:163 but I *l* your law.
119:165 peace have they who *l* your law,
119:167 for I *l* them greatly.
122: 6 "May those who *l* you be secure.
130: 7 for with the LORD is unfailing *l*
136: 1 -26 *His l endures forever.*
138: 2 for your *l* and your faithfulness,
138: 8 your *l*, O LORD, endures forever
143: 8 of your unfailing *l*,
143: 12 In your unfailing *l*, silence my
145: 8 slow to anger and rich in *l*.
145: 20 over all who *l* him,
147: 11 who put their hope in his unfailing *l*
Pr 1: 22 you simple ones *l* your simple
3: 3 Let *l* and faithfulness never leave
4: 6 *l* her, and she will watch over you.
5: 19 you ever be captivated by her *l*.
7: 18 let's drink deep of *l* till morning;
7: 18 let's enjoy ourselves with *l*!
8: 17 I *l* those who *l* me,
8: 21 wealth on those who *l* me
8: 36 all who hate me *l* death."
9: 8 rebuke a wise man and he will *l* you
10: 12 but *l* covers over all wrongs.
14: 22 those who plan what is good find *l*
15: 17 of vegetables where there is *l*
16: 6 Through *l* and faithfulness sin is
17: 9 over an offense promotes *l*,
18: 21 and those who *l* it will eat its fruit.
19: 22 What a man desires is unfailing *l*;
20: 6 claims to have unfailing *l*,
20: 13 Do not *l* sleep or you will grow
20: 28 *L* and faithfulness keep a king safe;
20: 28 through *l* his throne is made secure
21: 21 who pursues righteousness and *l*
27: 5 rebuke than hidden *l*.
Ecc 3: 8 a time to *l* and a time to hate,
9: 1 but no man knows whether *l*
9: 6 Their *l*, their hate
9: 9 life with your wife, whom you *l*,
SS 1: 2 for your *l* is more delightful
1: 3 No wonder the maidens *l* you!
1: 4 we will praise your *l* more
1: 7 you whom I *l*, where you graze
2: 4 and his banner over me is *l*.
2: 5 for I am faint with *l*.
2: 7 Do not arouse or awaken *l*
3: 5 Do not arouse or awaken *l*
4: 10 How delightful is your *l*, my sister,
4: 10 How much more pleasing is your *l*
5: 8 Tell him I am faint with *l*.
7: 6 O *l*, with your delights!
7: 12 there I will give you my *l*.
8: 4 Do not arouse or awaken *l*
8: 6 for *l* is as strong as death,
8: 7 Many waters cannot quench *l*;
8: 7 all the wealth of his house for *l*,
Isa 1: 23 they all *l* bribes

5: 1 I will sing for the one I *l*
16: 5 In *l* a throne will be established;
38: 17 In your *l* you kept me
43: 4 and because I *l* you,
54: 10 yet my unfailing *l* for you will not
55: 3 my faithful *l* promised to David.
56: 6 to *l* the name of the LORD,
56: 10 they *l* to sleep.
57: 8 a pact with those whose beds you *l*,
61: 8 "For I, the LORD, *l* justice;
63: 9 In his *l* and mercy he redeemed
66: 10 all you who *l* her;
Jer 2: 25 I *l* foreign gods,
2: 33 How skilled you are at pursuing *l*!
5: 31 and my people *l* it this way.
12: 7 I will give the one I *l*
14: 10 "They greatly *l* to wander;
16: 5 my *l* and my pity from this people
31: 3 you with an everlasting *l*;
32: 18 You show *l* to thousands
33: 11 his *l* endures forever."
La 3: 22 of the LORD's great *l* we are not
3: 32 so great is his unfailing *l*.
Eze 16: 8 saw that you were old enough for *l*,
23: 17 of *l*, and in their lust they defiled
33: 32 more than one who sings *l* songs
Da 9: 4 covenant of *l* with all who *l* him
Hos 1: 6 for I will no longer show *l*
1: 7 Yet I will show *l* to the house
2: 4 I will not show my *l* to her children
2: 19 in *l* and compassion.
2: 23 I will show my *l* to the one I called
3: 1 Go, show your *l* to your wife again,
3: 1 and *l* the sacred raisin cakes."
3: 1 *L* her as the LORD loves
4: 1 "There is no faithfulness, no *l*,
4: 18 their rulers dearly *l* shameful ways.
6: 4 Your *l* is like the morning mist,
9: 1 you *l* the wages of a prostitute
9: 15 I will no longer *l* them;
10: 12 reap the fruit of unfailing *l*,
11: 4 with ties of *l*;
12: 6 maintain *l* and justice,
14: 4 and *l* them freely,
Joel 2: 13 slow to anger and abounding in *l*,
Am 4: 5 for this is what you *l* to do,"
5: 15 Hate evil, *l* good;
Jnh 4: 2 slow to anger and abounding in *l*,
Mic 3: 2 you who hate good and *l* evil;
6: 8 To act justly and to *l* mercy
Zep 3: 17 he will quiet you with his *l*,
Zec 8: 17 and do not *l* to swear falsely.
8: 19 Therefore *l* truth and peace."
Mt 3: 17 "This is my Son, whom I *l*;
5: 43 '*L* your neighbor and hate your
5: 44 *L* your enemies and pray
5: 46 you *l* those who *l* you, what reward
6: 5 for they *l* to pray standing
6: 24 he will hate the one and *l* the other,
12: 18 the one I *l*, in whom I delight;
17: 5 "This is my Son, whom I *l*;
19: 19 and '*l* your neighbor as yourself.' "
22: 37 " '*L* the Lord your God
22: 39 '*L* your neighbor as yourself.'
23: 6 they *l* the place of honor
23: 7 they *l* to be greeted
24: 12 the *l* of most will grow cold,
Mk 1: 11 "You are my Son, whom I *l*;
9: 7 "This is my Son, whom I *l*.
12: 30 *L* the Lord your God
12: 31 '*L* your neighbor as yourself.'
12: 33 To *l* him with all your heart,
12: 33 and to *l* your neighbor
Lk 3: 22 "You are my Son, whom I *l*;
6: 27 you who hear me: *L* your enemies,
6: 32 Even 'sinners' *l* those who *l* them.
6: 32 you *l* those who *l* you, what credit
6: 35 *l* your enemies, do good to them,
7: 42 which of them will *l* him more?"
10: 27 and, '*L* your neighbor as yourself
10: 27 " '*L* the Lord your God
11: 42 you neglect justice and the *l* of God
11: 43 you *l* the most important seats
16: 13 he will hate the one and *l* the other,
20: 13 whom I *l*; perhaps they will respect
20: 46 *l* to be greeted in the marketplaces
Jn 5: 42 I know that you do not have the *l*
8: 42 were your Father, you would *l* me,
11: 3 "Lord, the one you *l* is sick."
13: 1 them the full extent of his *l*.
13: 34 I give you: *L* one another.
13: 34 so you must *l* one another.
13: 35 disciples, if you *l* one another."
14: 15 "If you *l* me, you will obey what I
14: 21 I too will *l* him and show myself
14: 23 My Father will *l* him, and we will
14: 24 He who does not *l* me will not obey
14: 31 world must learn that I *l* the Father
15: 9 Now remain in my *l*.
15: 10 commands and remain in his *l*.
15: 10 you will remain in my *l*,
15: 12 *L* each other as I have loved you.
15: 13 Greater *l* has no one than this,
15: 17 This is my command: *L* each other.
15: 19 to the world, it would *l* you
17: 26 known in order that the *l* you have
21: 15 do you truly *l* me more than these
21: 15 he said, "you know that I *l* you."
21: 16 Yes, Lord, you know that I *l* you."
21: 16 do you truly *l* me?" He answered,
21: 17 all things; you know that I *l* you."
21: 17 "Do you *l* me?" He said, "Lord,
21: 17 "Simon son of John, do you *l* me?"
Ro 5: 5 because God has poured out his *l*
5: 8 God demonstrates his own *l* for us
8: 28 for the good of those who *l* him,
8: 35 us from the *l* of Christ?
8: 39 us from the *l* of God that is
12: 9 *L* must be sincere.
12: 10 to one another in brotherly *l*.
13: 8 continuing debt to *l* one another,
13: 9 "*L* your neighbor as yourself."
13: 10 Therefore *l* is the fulfillment
13: 10 *L* does no harm to its neighbor.
14: 15 you are no longer acting in *l*.
15: 30 and by the *l* of the Spirit,
16: 8 Greet Ampliatus, whom I *l*
1Co 2: 9 prepared for those who *l* him"—
4: 17 my son whom I *l*, who is faithful
4: 21 or in *l* and with a gentle spirit?
8: 1 Knowledge puffs up, but *l* builds up
13: 1 have not *l*, I am only a resounding
13: 2 but have not *l*, I am nothing.
13: 3 but have not *l*, I gain nothing.
13: 4 Love is patient, *l* is kind.
13: 4 *L* is patient, love is kind.
13: 6 *L* does not delight in evil
13: 8 *L* never fails.
13: 13 But the greatest of these is *l*.
13: 13 three remain: faith, hope and *l*.
14: 1 way of *l* and eagerly desire spiritual
16: 14 Do everything in *l*.
16: 22 If anyone does not *l* the Lord—
16: 24 My *l* to all of you in Christ Jesus.
2Co 2: 4 to let you know the depth of my *l*
2: 8 therefore, to reaffirm your *l* for him
5: 14 For Christ's *l* compels us,
6: 6 in the Holy Spirit and in sincere *l*;
8: 7 complete earnestness and in your *l*
8: 8 sincerity of your *l* by comparing it
8: 24 show these men the proof of your *l*
11: 11 Why? Because I do not *l* you?
12: 15 If I *l* you more, will you *l* me less?
13: 11 And the God of *l* and peace will be
13: 14 of the Lord Jesus Christ, and the *l*
Gal 5: 6 is faith expressing itself through *l*.
5: 13 rather, serve one another in *l*.
5: 14 "*L* your neighbor as yourself."
5: 22 But the fruit of the Spirit is *l*, joy,
Eph 1: 4 In *l* he predestined us
1: 15 and your *l* for all the saints,
2: 4 But because of his great *l* for us,
3: 17 being rooted and established in *l*,
3: 18 and high and deep is the *l* of Christ,
3: 19 and to know this *l* that surpasses
4: 2 bearing with one another in *l*.
4: 15 Instead, speaking the truth in *l*,
4: 16 grows and builds itself up in *l*,
5: 2 loved children and live a life of *l*,
5: 25 *l* your wives, just as Christ loved
5: 28 husbands ought to *l* their wives
5: 33 each one of you also must *l* his wife
6: 23 *l* with faith from God the Father
6: 24 Christ with an undying *l*.
6: 24 to all who *l* our Lord Jesus Christ
Php 1: 9 that your *l* may abound more
1: 16 so in *l*, knowing that I am put here
2: 1 from his *l*, if any fellowship
2: 2 having the same *l*, being one
4: 1 you whom I *l* and long for,
Col 1: 4 of the *l* you have for all the saints—
1: 5 *l* that spring from the hope that is
1: 8 also told us of your *l* in the Spirit.
2: 2 in heart and united in *l*,
3: 14 And over all these virtues put on *l*,
3: 19 *l* your wives and do not be harsh
1Th 1: 3 your labor prompted by *l*,
3: 6 good news about your faith and *l*.
3: 12 May the Lord make your *l* increase
4: 9 about brotherly *l* we do not need
4: 9 taught by God to *l* each other.
4: 10 you do *l* all the brothers
5: 8 on faith and *l* as a breastplate,
5: 13 them in the highest regard in *l*
2Th 1: 3 and the *l* every one of you has
2: 10 because they refused to *l* the truth
3: 5 direct your hearts into God's *l*
1Ti 1: 5 The goal of this command is *l*,
1: 14 and *l* that are in Christ Jesus.
2: 15 *l* and holiness with propriety.
4: 12 in life, in *l*, in faith and in purity.
6: 10 For the *l* of money is a root
6: 11 faith, *l*, endurance and gentleness.
2Ti 1: 7 of power, of *l* and of self-discipline.
1: 13 with faith and *l* in Christ Jesus.
2: 22 and pursue righteousness, faith, *l*
3: 3 unholy, without *l*, unforgiving,
3: 10 faith, patience, *l*, endurance,
Tit 2: 2 in faith, in *l* and in endurance.
2: 4 women to *l* their husbands
3: 4 and *l* of God our Savior appeared,
3: 15 Greet those who *l* us in the faith.
Phm : 5 and your *l* for all the saints.
: 7 Your *l* has given me great joy
: 9 yet I appeal to you on the basis of *l*.
Heb 6: 10 and the *l* you have shown him
10: 24 may spur one another on toward *l*
13: 5 free from the *l* of money
Jas 1: 12 promised to those who *l* him.
2: 5 he promised those who *l* him?
2: 8 "*L* your neighbor as yourself,"
1Pe 1: 8 you have not seen him, you *l* him;
1: 22 the truth so that you have sincere *l*
1: 22 *l* one another deeply,
2: 17 *L* the brotherhood of believers,
3: 8 be sympathetic, *l* as brothers,
3: 10 "Whoever would *l* life
4: 8 Above all, *l* each other deeply,
4: 8 *l* covers over a multitude of sins.
5: 14 Greet one another with a kiss of *l*.
2Pe 1: 7 and to brotherly kindness, *l*.
1: 17 "This is my Son, whom I *l*;
1Jn 2: 5 God's *l* is truly made complete
2: 15 Do not *l* the world or anything
2: 15 the *l* of the Father is not in him.
3: 1 How great is the *l* the Father has
3: 10 anyone who does not *l* his brother.

3: 11 We should *l* one another.
3: 14 Anyone who does not *l* remains
3: 14 because we *l* our brothers.
3: 16 This is how we know what *l* is:
3: 17 how can the *l* of God be in him?
3: 18 let us not *l* with words or tongue
3: 23 to *l* one another as he commanded
4: 7 Dear friends, let us *l* one another,
4: 7 for *l* comes from God.
4: 8 Whoever does not *l* does not know
4: 8 not know God, because God is *l*.
4: 9 This is how God showed his *l*
4: 10 This is *l*: not that we loved God,
4: 11 we also ought to *l* one another.
4: 12 seen God; but if we *l* one another,
4: 12 and his *l* is made complete in us.
4: 16 God is *l*.
4: 16 Whoever lives in *l* lives in God,
4: 16 and rely on the *l* God has for us.
4: 17 *l* is made complete among us
4: 18 But perfect *l* drives out fear,
4: 18 There is no fear in *l*.
4: 18 who fears is not made perfect in *l*.
4: 19 We *l* because he first loved us.
4: 20 If anyone says, "I *l* God,"
4: 20 anyone who does not *l* his brother,
4: 20 whom he has seen, cannot *l* God,
4: 21 loves God must also *l* his brother.
5: 2 we know that we *l* the children
5: 3 This is *l* for God: to obey his
2Jn : 1 whom I *l* in the truth—
: 3 will be with us in truth and *l*.
: 5 I ask that we *l* one another.
: 6 his command is that you walk in *l*.
: 6 this is *l*: that we walk in obedience
3Jn : 1 To my dear friend Gaius, whom I *l*
: 6 have told the church about your *l*.
Jude : 2 peace and *l* be yours in abundance.
: 12 men are blemishes at your *l* feasts,
: 21 Keep yourselves in God's *l*
Rev 2: 4 You have forsaken your first *l*.
2: 19 I know your deeds, your *l* and faith
3: 19 Those whom I *l* I rebuke
12: 11 they did not *l* their lives so much

LOVED* (LOVE)
Ge 24: 67 she became his wife, and he *l* her;
25: 28 *l* Esau, but Rebekah *l* Jacob.
29: 30 and he *l* Rachel more than Leah.
29: 31 the LORD saw that Leah was not *l*,
29: 33 the LORD heard that I am not *l*,
34: 3 and he *l* the girl and spoke tenderly
37: 3 Now Israel *l* Joseph more than any
37: 4 saw that their father *l* him more
Dt 4: 37 Because he *l* your forefathers
7: 8 But it was because the LORD *l* you
10: 15 on your forefathers and *l* them,
1Sa 1: 5 a double portion because he *l* her,
18: 1 in spirit with David, and he *l* him
18: 3 with David because he *l* him
18: 16 But all Israel and Judah *l* David,
18: 28 that his daughter Michal *l* David,
20: 17 because he *l* him as he *l* himself.
2Sa 1: 23 in life they were *l* and gracious,
12: 24 The LORD *l* him; and
12: 25 and because the LORD *l* him,
13: 15 hated her more than he had *l* her.
1Ki 11: 1 *l* many foreign women
2Ch 11: 21 Rehoboam *l* Maacah daughter
26: 10 in the fertile lands, for he *l* the soil.
Ne 13: 26 He was *l* by his God, and God
Ps 44: 3 light of your face, for you *l* them.
47: 4 the pride of Jacob, whom he *l*.
78: 68 Mount Zion, which he *l*.
88: 18 taken my companions and *l* ones
109: 17 He *l* to pronounce a curse—
Isa 5: 1 My *l* one had a vineyard
Jer 2: 2 how as a bride you *l* me
8: 2 which they have *l* and served
31: 3 "I have *l* you with an everlasting
Eze 16: 37 those you *l* as well as those you
Hos 2: 1 and of your sisters, 'My *l* one.'
2: 23 to the one I called 'Not my *l* one.'
3: 1 though she is *l* by another
9: 10 became as vile as the thing they *l*.
11: 1 "When Israel was a child, I *l* him,
Mal 1: 2 "But you ask, 'How have you *l* us?'
1: 2 "I have *l* you," says the LORD.
1: 2 "Yet I have *l* Jacob, but Esau I
Mk 10: 21 Jesus looked at him and *l* him.
12: 6 left to send, a son, whom he *l*.
Lk 7: 47 been forgiven—for she *l* much.
16: 14 The Pharisees, who *l* money,
Jn 3: 16 so *l* the world that he gave his one
3: 19 but men *l* darkness instead of light
11: 5 Jesus *l* Martha and her sister
11: 36 "See how he *l* him!" But some
12: 43 for they *l* praise from men more
13: 1 Having *l* his own who were
13: 23 the disciple whom Jesus *l*,
13: 34 As I have *l* you, so you must love
14: 21 He who loves me will be *l*
14: 28 If you *l* me, you would be glad that
15: 9 the Father has *l* me, so have I *l* you.
15: 12 Love each other as I have *l* you.
16: 27 loves you because you have *l* me
17: 23 have *l* them even as you have *l* me.
17: 24 you *l* me before the creation
19: 26 the disciple whom he *l* standing
20: 2 one Jesus *l*, and said, "They have
21: 7 the disciple whom Jesus *l* said
21: 20 whom Jesus *l* was following
Ro 1: 7 To all in Rome who are *l* by God
8: 37 conquerors through him who *l* us.
9: 13 "Jacob I *l*, but Esau I hated."
9: 25 her 'my *l* one' who is not my *l* one,"
11: 28 they are *l* on account
Gal 2: 20 who *l* me and gave himself for me.
Eph 5: 1 as dearly *l* children and live a life
5: 2 as Christ *l* us and gave himself up
5: 25 just as Christ *l* the church
Col 3: 12 and dearly *l*, clothe yourselves
1Th 1: 4 For we know, brothers *l* by God,
2: 8 We *l* you so much that we were
2Th 2: 13 for you, brothers *l* by the Lord,
2: 16 who *l* us and by his grace gave us
2Ti 4: 10 for Demas, because he *l* this world,
Heb 1: 9 You have *l* righteousness
2Pe 2: 15 who *l* the wages of wickedness.
1Jn 4: 10 This is love: not that we *l* God,
4: 10 but that he *l* us and sent his Son
4: 11 Dear friends, since God so *l* us,
4: 19 We love because he first *l* us.
Jude : 1 who are *l* by God the Father
Rev 3: 9 and acknowledge that I have *l* you.

LOVELY* (LOVE)
Ge 29: 17 but Rachel was *l* in form,
Est 1: 11 and nobles, for she was *l* to look at.
2: 7 was *l* in form and features,
Ps 84: 1 How *l* is your dwelling place,
SS 1: 5 Dark am I, yet *l*,
2: 14 and your face is *l*.
4: 3 your mouth is *l*.
5: 16 he is altogether *l*.
6: 4 *l* as Jerusalem,
Am 8: 13 *l* young women and strong young
Php 4: 8 whatever is *l*, whatever is

LOVER* (LOVE)
SS 1: 13 My *l* is to me a sachet of myrrh
1: 14 My *l* is to me a cluster
1: 16 How handsome you are, my *l*!
2: 3 is my *l* among the young men.
2: 8 Listen! My *l*!
2: 9 My *l* is like a gazelle or a young
2: 10 My *l* spoke and said to me,
2: 16 *Beloved* My *l* is mine and I am his;
2: 17 turn, my *l*,
4: 16 Let my *l* come into his garden
5: 2 Listen! My *l* is knocking:
5: 4 My *l* thrust his hand
5: 5 I arose to open for my *l*,
5: 6 I opened for my *l*,
5: 6 but my *l* had left; he was gone.
5: 8 if you find my *l*,
5: 10 *Beloved* My *l* is radiant and ruddy,
5: 16 This is my *l*, this my friend,
6: 1 Where has your *l* gone,
6: 1 Which way did your *l* turn,
6: 2 *Beloved* My *l* has gone
6: 3 I am my lover's and my *l* is mine;
7: 9 May the wine go straight to my *l*,
7: 10 I belong to my *l*,
7: 11 my *l*, let us go to the countryside,
7: 13 that I have stored up for you, my *l*.
8: 5 leaning on her *l*?
8: 14 *Beloved* Come away, my *l*,
1Ti 3: 3 not quarrelsome, not a *l* of money.

LOVER'S* (LOVE)
SS 6: 3 I am my *l* and my lover is mine;

LOVERS* (LOVE)
SS 5: 1 drink your fill, O *l*.
Jer 3: 1 as a prostitute with many *l*—
3: 2 the roadside you sat waiting for *l*,
4: 30 Your *l* despise you;
La 1: 2 Among all her *l*
Eze 16: 33 but you give gifts to all your *l*,
16: 36 in your promiscuity with your *l*,
16: 37 I am going to gather all your *l*,
16: 39 Then I will hand you over to your *l*,
16: 41 and you will no longer pay your *l*.
23: 5 she lusted after her *l*, the Assyrians
23: 9 I handed her over to her *l*,
23: 20 There she lusted after her *l*,
23: 22 I will stir up your *l* against you,
Hos 2: 5 She said, 'I will go after my *l*,
2: 7 She will chase after her *l*
2: 10 lewdness before the eyes of her *l*;
2: 12 she said were her pay from her *l*;
2: 13 and went after her *l*,
8: 9 Ephraim has sold herself to *l*.
2Ti 3: 2 People will be *l* of themselves,
3: 2 *l* of money, boastful, proud,
3: 3 without self-control, brutal, not *l*
3: 4 *l* of pleasure rather than *l* of God—

LOVES* (LOVE)
Ge 44: 20 sons left, and his father *l* him.'
Dt 10: 18 and *l* the alien, giving him food
15: 16 because he *l* you and your family
21: 15 and he *l* one but not the other,
21: 16 son of the wife he *l* in preference
23: 5 because the LORD your God *l* you
28: 54 wife he *l* or his surviving children,
28: 56 will begrudge the husband she *l*
33: 12 and the one the LORD *l* rests
Ru 4: 15 who *l* you and who is better to you
2Ch 2: 11 "Because the LORD *l* his people,
Ps 11: 7 he *l* justice;
33: 5 The LORD *l* righteousness
34: 12 Whoever of you *l* life
37: 28 For the LORD *l* the just
87: 2 the LORD *l* the gates of Zion
91: 14 Because he *l* me," says the LORD,
99: 4 The King is mighty, he *l* justice—
119:140 and your servant *l* them.
127: 2 for he grants sleep to those he *l*.
146: 8 the LORD *l* the righteous.
Pr 3: 12 the LORD disciplines those he *l*,
12: 1 Whoever *l* discipline *l* knowledge,
13: 24 he who *l* him is careful
15: 9 he *l* those who pursue
17: 17 A friend *l* at all times,
17: 19 He who *l* a quarrel *l* sin;
19: 8 He who gets wisdom *l* his own soul
21: 17 He who *l* pleasure will become
21: 17 whoever *l* wine and oil will never
22: 11 He who *l* a pure heart and whose
29: 3 A man who *l* wisdom brings joy
Ecc 5: 10 Whoever *l* money never has

5: 10 whoever *l* wealth is never satisfied
SS 3: 1 I looked for the one my heart *l;*
3: 2 I will search for the one my heart *l.*
3: 3 "Have you seen the one my heart *l*
3: 4 when I found the one my heart *l.*
Hos 3: 1 as the LORD *l* the Israelites,
10: 11 that *l* to thresh;
12: 7 he *l* to defraud.
Mal 2: 11 the sanctuary the LORD *l,*
Mt 10: 37 anyone who *l* his son or daughter
10: 37 "Anyone who *l* his father
Lk 7: 5 because he *l* our nation
7: 47 has been forgiven little *l* little."
Jn 3: 35 Father *l* the Son and has placed
5: 20 For the Father *l* the Son
10: 17 reason my Father *l* me is that I lay
12: 25 The man who *l* his life will lose it,
14: 21 He who *l* me will be loved
14: 21 obeys them, he is the one who *l* me.
14: 23 Jesus replied, "If anyone *l* me,
16: 27 the Father himself *l* you
Ro 13: 8 for he who *l* his fellowman has
1Co 8: 3 But the man who *l* God is known
2Co 9: 7 for God *l* a cheerful giver.
Eph 1: 6 has freely given us in the One he *l.*
5: 28 He who *l* his wife *l* himself.
5: 33 must love his wife as he *l* himself,
Col 1: 13 us into the kingdom of the Son he *l,*
Tit 1: 8 one who *l* what is good, who is
Heb 12: 6 the Lord disciplines those he *l,*
1Jn 2: 10 Whoever *l* his brother lives
2: 15 If anyone *l* the world, the love
4: 7 Everyone who *l* has been born
4: 21 Whoever *l* God must also love his
5: 1 who *l* the father *l* his child
3Jn : 9 but Diotrephes, who *l* to be first,
Rev 1: 5 To him who *l* us and has freed us
20: 9 camp of God's people, the city he *l.*
22: 15 and everyone who *l* and practices

LOVING* (LOVE)
Ps 25: 10 All the ways of the LORD are *l*
59: 10 my *l* God.
59: 17 O God, are my fortress, my *l* God.
62: 12 and that you, O Lord, are *l.*
144: 2 He is my *l* God and my fortress,
145: 13 and *l* toward all he has made.
145: 17 and *l* toward all he has made.
Pr 5: 19 A *l* doe, a graceful deer—
Heb 13: 1 Keep on *l* each other as brothers.
1Jn 5: 2 by *l* God and carrying out his

LOVING-KINDNESS* (LOVE)
Jer 31: 3 I have drawn you with *l.*

LOWER
Ps 8: 5 You made him a little *l*
2Co 11: 7 a sin for me to *l* myself in order
Heb 2: 7 You made him a little *l*

LOWING
1Sa 15: 14 What is this *l* of cattle that I hear?"

LOWLY
Job 5: 11 The *l* he sets on high,
Ps 138: 6 on high, he looks upon the *l,*
Pr 29: 23 but a man of *l* spirit gains honor.
Isa 57: 15 also with him who is contrite and *l*
Eze 21: 26 *l* will be exalted and the exalted
1Co 1: 28 He chose the *l* things of this world

LOYAL
1Ch 29: 18 and keep their hearts *l* to you.
Ps 78: 8 whose hearts were not *l* to God,

LUKE*
Co-worker with Paul (Col 4:14; 2Ti 4:11; Phm 24).

LUKEWARM*
Rev 3: 16 So, because you are *l*— neither hot

LUST (LUSTED LUSTS)
Pr 6: 25 Do not *l* in your heart
Eze 20: 30 and *l* after their vile images?
Col 3: 5 sexual immorality, impurity, *l,*
1Th 4: 5 not in passionate *l* like the heathen,
1Pe 4: 3 in debauchery, *l,* drunkenness,
1Jn 2: 16 the *l* of his eyes and the boasting

LUSTED (LUST)
Eze 23: 5 she *l* after her lovers, the Assyrians

LUSTS* (LUST)
Nu 15: 39 yourselves by going after the *l*
Ro 1: 26 God gave them over to shameful *l.*

LUXURY
Jas 5: 5 You have lived on earth in *l*

LYDIA'S*
Ac 16: 40 went to *L* house, where they met

LYING (LIE)
Pr 6: 17 a *l* tongue,
12: 22 The LORD detests *l* lips,
21: 6 A fortune made by a *l* tongue
26: 28 A *l* tongue hates those it hurts,

MACEDONIA
Ac 16: 9 "Come over to *M* and help us."

MAD
Dt 28: 34 The sights you see will drive you *m*

MADE (MAKE)
Ge 1: 7 So God *m* the expanse
1: 16 God *m* two great lights—
1: 16 He also *m* the stars.
1: 25 God *m* the wild animals according
1: 31 God saw all that he had *m,*
2: 22 Then the LORD God *m* a woman
6: 6 was grieved that he had *m* man
9: 6 has God *m* man.
15: 18 that day the LORD *m* a covenant
Ex 20: 11 six days the LORD *m* the heavens
20: 11 the Sabbath day and *m* it holy.
24: 8 the covenant that the LORD has *m*
32: 4 *m* it into an idol cast in the shape
Lev 16: 34 Atonement is to be *m* once a year
Dt 32: 6 who *m* you and formed you?
Jos 24: 25 On that day Joshua *m* a covenant
2Ki 19: 15 You have *m* heaven and earth.
2Ch 2: 12 the God of Israel, who *m* heaven
Ne 9: 6 You *m* the heavens,
9: 10 You *m* a name for yourself,
Ps 33: 6 of the LORD were the heavens *m,*
95: 5 The sea is his, for he *m* it,
96: 5 but the LORD *m* the heavens.
100: 3 It is he who *m* us, and we are his;
118: 24 This is the day the LORD has *m;*
136: 7 who *m* the great lights—
139: 14 I am fearfully and wonderfully *m;*
Ecc 3: 11 He has *m* everything beautiful
Isa 43: 7 whom I formed and *m.*"
45: 12 It is I who *m* the earth
45: 18 he who fashioned and *m* the earth,
66: 2 Has not my hand *m* all these things
Jer 10: 12 But God *m* the earth by his power;
27: 5 and outstretched arm I *m* the earth
32: 17 you have *m* the heavens
33: 2 LORD says, he who *m* the earth,
51: 15 "He *m* the earth by his power;
Eze 3: 17 I have *m* you a watchman
33: 7 I have *m* you a watchman
Am 5: 8 (he who *m* the Pleiades and Orion,
Jnh 1: 9 who *m* the sea and the land."
Mk 2: 27 "The Sabbath was *m* for man,
Jn 1: 3 Through him all things were *m;*
Ac 17: 24 "The God who *m* the world
1Co 3: 6 watered it, but God *m* it grow.
Heb 1: 2 through whom he *m* the universe.
Jas 3: 9 who have been *m* in God's likeness
Rev 14: 7 Worship him who *m* the heavens,

MAGDALENE
Lk 8: 2 Mary (called *M)* from whom seven

MAGI
Mt 2: 1 *M* from the east came to Jerusalem

MAGIC (MAGICIANS)
Eze 13: 20 I am against your *m* charms
Rev 21: 8 those who practice *m* arts,
22: 15 those who practice *m* arts,

MAGICIANS (MAGIC)
Ex 7: 11 the Egyptian *m* also did the same
Da 2: 2 So the king summoned the *m,*

MAGNIFICENCE* (MAGNIFICENT)
1Ch 22: 5 for the LORD should be of great *m*

MAGNIFICENT (MAGNIFICENCE)
1Ki 8: 13 I have indeed built a *m* temple
Isa 28: 29 in counsel and *m* in wisdom.
Mk 13: 1 stones! What *m* buildings!"

MAGOG
Eze 38: 2 of the land of *M,* the chief prince
39: 6 I will send fire on *M*
Rev 20: 8 and *M*— to gather them for battle.

MAIDEN (MAIDENS)
Pr 30: 19 and the way of a man with a *m.*
Isa 62: 5 As a young man marries a *m,*
Jer 2: 32 Does a *m* forget her jewelry,

MAIDENS (MAIDEN)
SS 1: 3 No wonder the *m* love you!

MAIMED
Mt 18: 8 It is better for you to enter life *m*

MAINTAIN (MAINTAINING)
Ps 82: 3 *m* the rights of the poor
106: 3 Blessed are they who *m* justice,
Hos 12: 6 *m* love and justice,
Am 5: 15 *m* justice in the courts.
Ro 3: 28 For we *m* that a man is justified

MAINTAINING* (MAINTAIN)
Ex 34: 7 faithfulness, *m* love to thousands,

MAJESTIC* (MAJESTY)
Ex 15: 6 was *m* in power.
15: 11 *m* in holiness,
Job 37: 4 he thunders with his *m* voice.
Ps 8: 1 how *m* is your name in all the earth
8: 9 how *m* is your name in all the earth
29: 4 the voice of the LORD is *m.*
68: 15 of Bashan are *m* mountains;
76: 4 more *m* than mountains rich
111: 3 Glorious and *m* are his deeds,
SS 6: 4 *m* as troops with banners.
6: 10 *m* as the stars in procession?
Isa 30: 30 men to hear his *m* voice
Eze 31: 7 It was *m* in beauty,
2Pe 1: 17 came to him from the *M* Glory,

MAJESTY* (MAJESTIC)
Ex 15: 7 In the greatness of your *m*
Dt 5: 24 has shown us his glory and his *m,*
11: 2 his *m,* his mighty hand, his
33: 17 In *m* he is like a firstborn bull;
33: 26 and on the clouds in his *m.*
1Ch 16: 27 Splendor and *m* are before him;
29: 11 and the *m* and the splendor,
Est 1: 4 the splendor and glory of his *m.*
7: 3 if it pleases your *m,* grant me my
Job 37: 22 God comes in awesome *m.*
40: 10 and clothe yourself in honor and *m*
Ps 21: 5 on him splendor and *m.*
45: 3 with splendor and *m.*
45: 4 In your *m* ride forth victoriously
68: 34 whose *m* is over Israel,
93: 1 The LORD reigns, he is robed in *m*
93: 1 the LORD is robed in *m*
96: 6 Splendor and *m* are before him;
104: 1 clothed with splendor and *m.*
110: 3 Arrayed in holy *m,*
145: 5 of the glorious splendor of your *m,*
Isa 2: 10 and the splendor of his *m!*
2: 19 and the splendor of his *m,*
2: 21 and the splendor of his *m,*
24: 14 west they acclaim the LORD's *m.*
26: 10 and regard not the *m* of the LORD.
53: 2 or *m* to attract us to him,
Eze 31: 2 can be compared with you in *m?*
31: 18 with you in splendor and *m?*
Da 4: 30 and for the glory of my *m?*"

Mic 5: 4 in the *m* of the name
Zec 6: 13 and he will be clothed with *m*
Ac 19: 27 will be robbed of her divine *m*."
25: 26 to write to His *M* about him.
2Th 1: 9 and from the *m* of his power
Heb 1: 3 hand of the *M* in heaven.
8: 1 of the throne of the *M* in heaven,
2Pe 1: 16 but we were eyewitnesses of his *m*.
Jude : 25 only God our Savior be glory, *m*,

MAKE (MADE MAKER MAKERS MAKES MAKING MAN-MADE)
Ge 1: 26 "Let us *m* man in our image,
2: 18 I will *m* a helper suitable for him."
6: 14 *m* yourself an ark of cypress wood;
12: 2 "I will *m* you into a great nation
Ex 22: 3 thief must certainly *m* restitution,
25: 9 *M* this tabernacle and all its
25: 40 See that you *m* them according
Nu 6: 25 the LORD *m* his face shine
2Sa 7: 9 Now I will *m* your name great,
Job 7: 17 "What is man that you *m* so much
Ps 4: 8 *m* me dwell in safety.
20: 4 and *m* all your plans succeed.
108: 1 *m* music with all my soul.
110: 1 hand until I *m* your enemies
119:165 and nothing can *m* them stumble.
Pr 3: 6 and he will *m* your paths straight.
4: 26 *M* level paths for your feet
20: 18 *M* plans by seeking advice;
Isa 14: 14 I will *m* myself like the Most High
29: 16 "He did not *m* me"?
55: 3 I will *m* an everlasting covenant
61: 8 and *m* an everlasting covenant
Jer 31: 31 "when I will *m* a new covenant
Eze 37: 26 I will *m* a covenant of peace
Mt 3: 3 *m* straight paths for him.' "
28: 19 and *m* disciples of all nations,
Mk 1: 17 "and I will *m* you fishers of men."
Lk 13: 24 "*M* every effort to enter
14: 23 country lanes and *m* them come in,
Ro 14: 19 *m* every effort to do what leads
2Co 5: 9 So we *m* it our goal to please him,
Eph 4: 3 *M* every effort to keep the unity
Col 4: 5 *m* the most of every opportunity.
1Th 4: 11 *M* it your ambition
Heb 4: 11 *m* every effort to enter that rest,
8: 5 it that you *m* everything according
12: 14 *M* every effort to live in peace
2Pe 1: 5 *m* every effort to add
3: 14 *m* every effort to be found spotless,

MAKER* (MAKE)
Job 4: 17 Can a man be more pure than his *M*
9: 9 He is the *M* of the Bear and Orion,
32: 22 my *M* would soon take me away.
35: 10 no one says, 'Where is God my *M*,
36: 3 I will ascribe justice to my *M*.
40: 19 yet his *M* can approach him
Ps 95: 6 kneel before the LORD our *M*;
115: 15 the *M* of heaven and earth.
121: 2 the *M* of heaven and earth.
124: 8 the *M* of heaven and earth.
134: 3 the *M* of heaven and earth,
146: 6 the *M* of heaven and earth,
149: 2 Let Israel rejoice in their *M*;
Pr 14: 31 poor shows contempt for their *M*,
17: 5 poor shows contempt for their *M*;
22: 2 The LORD is the *M* of them all.
Ecc 11: 5 the *M* of all things.
Isa 17: 7 that day men will look to their *M*
27: 11 so their *M* has no compassion
45: 9 to him who quarrels with his *M*,
45: 11 the Holy One of Israel, and its *M*:
51: 13 that you forget the LORD your *M*,
54: 5 For your *M* is your husband—
Jer 10: 16 for he is the *M* of all things,
51: 19 for he is the *M* of all things,
Hos 8: 14 Israel has forgotten his *M*

MAKERS* (MAKE)
Isa 45: 16 All the *m* of idols will be put

MAKES (MAKE)
Ps 23: 2 *m* me lie down in green pastures,
Pr 13: 12 Hope deferred *m* the heart sick,
1Co 3: 7 but only God, who *m* things grow.

MAKING (MAKE)
Ps 19: 7 *m* wise the simple.
Ecc 12: 12 Of *m* many books there is no end,
Jn 5: 18 *m* himself equal with God.
Eph 5: 16 *m* the most of every opportunity,

MALACHI*
Mal 1: 1 of the LORD to Israel through *M*.

MALE
Ge 1: 27 *m* and female he created them.
Ex 13: 2 to me every firstborn *m*.
Nu 8: 16 the first *m* offspring
Mt 19: 4 the Creator 'made them *m*
Gal 3: 28 slave nor free, *m* nor female,

MALICE (MALICIOUS)
Mk 7: 22 adultery, greed, *m*, deceit,
Ro 1: 29 murder, strife, deceit and *m*.
1Co 5: 8 the yeast of *m* and wickedness,
Eph 4: 31 along with every form of *m*.
Col 3: 8 *m*, slander, and filthy language
1Pe 2: 1 rid yourselves of all *m*

MALICIOUS (MALICE)
Pr 26: 24 A *m* man disguises himself
1Ti 3: 11 not *m* talkers but temperate
6: 4 *m* talk, evil suspicions

MALIGN
Tit 2: 5 so that no one will *m* the word

MAN (MAN'S MANKIND MEN MEN'S WOMAN WOMEN)
Ge 1: 26 "Let us make *m* in our image,
2: 7 God formed the *m* from the dust
2: 8 *m* became a living being
2: 15 God took the *m* and put
2: 18 for the *m* to be alone
2: 20 *m* gave names to all the
2: 23 she was taken out of *m*.
2: 25 *m* and his wife were both
3: 9 God called to the *m*,
3: 22 *m* has now become like
4: 1 I have brought forth a *m*.
6: 3 not contend with *m* forever,
6: 6 grieved that he had made *m*
9: 6 Whoever sheds the blood of *m*,
Dt 8: 3 *m* does not live on bread
1Sa 13: 14 a *m* after his own heart
15: 29 he is not a *m* that he
16: 7 at the things *m* looks at.
Job 14: 1 *M* born of woman is of few
14: 14 If a *m* dies, will he live
Ps 1: 1 Blessed is the *m* who does
8: 4 what is *m* that you are
32: 2 Blessed is the *m* whose sin
40: 4 Blessed is the *m* who makes
84: 12 blessed is the *m* who trusts
103: 15 As for *m*, his days are
112: 1 Blessed is the *m* who fears
119: 9 can a young *m* keep his
127: 5 Blessed is the *m* whose quiver
144: 3 what is *m* that you care
Pr 3: 13 Blessed is the *m* who finds
9: 9 Instruct a wise *m*
14: 12 that seems right to a *m*,
30: 19 way of a *m* with a maiden.
Isa 53: 3 a *m* of sorrows,
Jer 17: 5 the one who trusts in *m*,
17: 7 blessed is the *m* who trusts
Eze 22: 30 I looked for a *m*
Mt 4: 4 *M* does not live on bread
19: 5 a *m* will leave his father
Mk 8: 36 What good is it for a *m*
Lk 4: 4 '*M* does not live on bread
Ro 5: 12 entered the world through one *m*
1Co 2: 15 spiritual *m* makes judgments
3: 12 If any *m* builds on this
7: 1 good for a *m* not to marry.
7: 2 each *m* should have his own
11: 3 head of every *m* is Christ,
11: 3 head of woman is *m*
13: 11 When I became a *m*,
15: 21 death came through a *m*,
15: 45 first *m* Adam became a
15: 47 the second *m* from heaven
2Co 12: 2 I know a *m* in Christ
Eph 2: 15 create in himself one new *m*
5: 31 a *m* will leave his father
Php 2: 8 found in appearance as a *m*,
1Ti 2: 5 the *m* Christ Jesus,
2: 12 have authority over a *m*;
2Ti 3: 17 that the *m* of God may be
Heb 2: 6 what is *m* that you are
9: 27 as *m* is destined to die

MAN'S (MAN)
Pr 20: 24 A *m* steps are directed by
Jer 10: 23 a *m* life is not his own;
1Co 1: 25 is wiser than *m* wisdom,

MAN-MADE (MAKE)
Heb 9: 11 perfect tabernacle that is not *m*,
9: 24 not enter a *m* sanctuary that was

MANAGE (MANAGER)
Jer 12: 5 how will you *m* in the thickets
1Ti 3: 4 He must *m* his own family well
3: 12 one wife and must *m* his children
5: 14 to *m* their homes and to give

MANAGER (MANAGE)
Lk 12: 42 Who then is the faithful and wise *m*
16: 1 a rich man whose *m* was accused

MANASSEH
1. Firstborn of Joseph (Ge 41:51; 46:20). Blessed by Jacob but not firstborn (Ge 48). Tribe of blessed (Dt 33:17), numbered (Nu 1:35; 26:34), half allotted land east of Jordan (Nu 32; Jos 13:8–33), half west (Jos 17; Eze 48:4), failed to fully possess (Jos 17:12–13; Jdg 1:27), 12,000 from (Rev 7:6).
2. Son of Hezekiah; king of Judah (2Ki 21:1–18; 2Ch 33:1–20). Judah exiled for his detestable sins (2Ki 21:10–15). Repentance (2Ch 33:12–19).

MANDRAKES
Ge 30: 14 give me some of your son's *m*."

MANGER
Lk 2: 12 in strips of cloth and lying in a *m*."

MANIFESTATION*
1Co 12: 7 to each one the *m* of the Spirit is

MANKIND (MAN)
Ge 6: 7 I will wipe *m*, whom I have created
Ps 33: 13 and sees all *m*;
Pr 8: 31 and delighting in *m*.
Ecc 7: 29 God made *m* upright,
Isa 40: 5 and all *m* together will see it.
45: 12 and created *m* upon it.
Jer 32: 27 "I am the LORD, the God of all *m*.
Zec 2: 13 Be still before the LORD, all *m*,
Lk 3: 6 And all *m* will see God's salvation

MANNA
Ex 16: 31 people of Israel called the bread *m*.
Dt 8: 16 He gave you *m* to eat in the desert,
Jn 6: 49 Your forefathers ate the *m*
Rev 2: 17 I will give some of the hidden *m*.

MANNER
1Co 11: 27 in an unworthy *m* will be guilty
Php 1: 27 conduct yourselves in a *m* worthy

MANSIONS*
Ps 49: 14 far from their princely *m*.
Isa 5: 9 the fine *m* left without occupants.
Am 3: 15 and the *m* will be demolished,"
5: 11 though you have built stone *m*,

MARCH
Jos 6: 4 *m* around the city seven times,
Isa 42: 13 LORD will *m* out like a mighty

MARITAL* (MARRY)
Ex 21: 10 of her food, clothing and *m* rights.

MEETINGS* (MEET)
1Co 11: 17 for your *m* do more harm
MEETS (MEET)
Heb 7: 26 Such a high priest *m* our need—
MELCHIZEDEK
Ge 14: 18 *M* king of Salem brought out bread
Ps 110: 4 in the order of *M*."
Heb 7: 11 in the order of *M*, not in the order
MELT (MELTS)
2Pe 3: 12 and the elements will *m* in the heat.
MELTS (MELT)
Am 9: 5 he who touches the earth and it *m*,
MEMBER (MEMBERS)
Ro 12: 5 each *m* belongs to all the others.
MEMBERS (MEMBER)
Mic 7: 6 a man's enemies are the *m*
Mt 10: 36 a man's enemies will be the *m*
Ro 7: 23 law at work in the *m* of my body,
12: 4 of us has one body with many *m*,
1Co 6: 15 not know that your bodies are *m*
12: 24 But God has combined the *m*
Eph 3: 6 *m* together of one body,
4: 25 for we are all *m* of one body.
5: 30 for we are *m* of his body.
Col 3: 15 as *m* of one body you were called
MEMORABLE* (MEMORY)
Eze 39: 13 day I am glorified will be a *m* day
MEMORIES* (MEMORY)
1Th 3: 6 us that you always have pleasant *m*
MEMORY (MEMORABLE MEMORIES)
Pr 10: 7 *m* of the righteous will be
Mt 26: 13 she has done will also be told, in *m*
MEN (MAN)
Ge 6: 2 daughter of *m* were beautiful,
6: 4 heroes of old, *m* of renown
Ps 9: 20 nations know they are but *m*.
11: 4 He observes the sons of *m*;
Mt 4: 19 will make you fishers of *m*
5: 16 your light shine before *m*
6: 14 if you forgive *m* when
10: 32 acknowledges me before *m*
12: 31 blasphemy will be forgiven *m*,
12: 36 *m* will have to give account
23: 5 is done for *m* to see:
Mk 7: 7 are but rules taught by *m*.
Lk 6: 22 Blessed are you when *m*
6: 26 Woe to you when all *m*
Jn 1: 4 life was the light of *m*.
2: 24 for he knew all *m*.
3: 19 *m* loved darkness instead
12: 32 will draw all *m* to myself
13: 35 all *m* will know that you
Ac 5: 29 obey God rather than *m*!
Ro 1: 18 wickedness of *m*
1: 27 indecent acts with other *m*,
5: 12 death came to all *m*,
1Co 2: 11 among *m* knows the thoughts
3: 3 acting like mere *m*?
3: 21 no more boasting about *m*!
9: 22 all things to all *m*
13: 1 tongues of *m* and of angels
16: 13 be *m* of courage;
16: 18 Such *m* deserve recognition.
2Co 5: 11 we try to persuade *m*.
8: 21 but also in the eyes of *m*.
Gal 1: 1 sent not from *m* nor
1: 10 to win approval of *m*, or
Eph 4: 8 and gave gifts to *m*.
1Th 2: 4 as *m* approved by God
2: 13 not as the word of *m*,
1Ti 2: 4 wants all *m* to be saved
2: 6 as a ransom for all *m*—
4: 10 the Savior of all *m*
5: 2 younger *m* as brothers
2Ti 2: 2 entrust to reliable *m*
Tit 2: 11 has appeared to all *m*.
Heb 5: 1 is selected from among *m*
7: 28 high priests *m* who are weak;
2Pe 1: 21 but *m* spoke from God
Rev 21: 3 dwelling of God is with *m*,
MEN'S (MAN)
2Ki 19: 18 fashioned by *m* hands.
2Ch 32: 19 the work of *m* hands.
1Co 2: 5 not rest on *m* wisdom,
MENAHEM*
King of Israel (2Ki 15:17–22).
MENE
Da 5: 25 that was written: *M*, *M*,
MEPHIBOSHETH
Son of Jonathan shown kindness by David (2Sa 4:4; 9; 21:7). Accused of siding with Absalom (2Sa 16:1–4; 19:24–30).
MERCHANT
Pr 31: 14 She is like the *m* ships,
Mt 13: 45 of heaven is like a *m* looking
MERCIFUL (MERCY)
Dt 4: 31 the LORD your God is a *m* God;
Ne 9: 31 for you are a gracious and *m* God.
Ps 77: 9 Has God forgotten to be *m*?
78: 38 Yet he was *m*;
Jer 3: 12 for I am *m*,' declares the LORD,
Da 9: 9 The Lord our God is *m*
Mt 5: 7 Blessed are the *m*,
Lk 1: 54 remembering to be *m*
6: 36 Be *m*, just as your Father is *m*.
Heb 2: 17 in order that he might become a *m*
Jas 2: 13 to anyone who has not been *m*.
Jude : 22 Be *m* to those who doubt; snatch
MERCY (MERCIFUL)
Ex 33: 19 *m* on whom I will have *m*,
2Sa 24: 14 of the LORD, for his *m* is great;
1Ch 21: 13 for his *m* is very great;
Ne 9: 31 But in your great *m* you did not put
Ps 25: 6 O LORD, your great *m* and love,
28: 6 for he has heard my cry for *m*.
57: 1 Have *m* on me, O God, have *m*
Pr 28: 13 renounces them finds *m*.
Isa 63: 9 and *m* he redeemed them;
Da 9: 18 but because of your great *m*.
Hos 6: 6 For I desire *m*, not sacrifice,
Am 5: 15 LORD God Almighty will have *m*
Mic 6: 8 To act justly and to love *m*
7: 18 but delight to show *m*.
Hab 3: 2 in wrath remember *m*.
Zec 7: 9 show *m* and compassion
Mt 5: 7 for they will be shown *m*.
9: 13 learn what this means: 'I desire *m*,
12: 7 'I desire *m*, not sacrifice,' you
18: 33 Shouldn't you have had *m*
23: 23 justice, *m* and faithfulness.
Lk 1: 50 His *m* extends to those who fear
Ro 9: 15 "I will have *m* on whom I have *m*,
9: 18 Therefore God has *m*
11: 32 so that he may have *m* on them all.
12: 1 brothers, in view of God's *m*,
12: 8 if it is showing *m*, let him do it
Eph 2: 4 who is rich in *m*, made us alive
1Ti 1: 13 I was shown *m* because I acted
1: 16 for that very reason I was shown *m*
Tit 3: 5 we had done, but because of his *m*.
Heb 4: 16 so that we may receive *m*
Jas 2: 13 judgment without *m* will be shown
2: 13 *M* triumphs over judgment!
3: 17 submissive, full of *m* and good fruit
5: 11 full of compassion and *m*.
1Pe 1: 3 In his great *m* he has given us new
2: 10 once you had not received *m*,
Jude : 23 to others show *m*, mixed with fear
MERRY
Lk 12: 19 Take life easy; eat, drink and be *m*
MESHACH
Hebrew exiled to Babylon; name changed from Mishael (Da 1:6–7). Refused defilement by food (Da 1:8–20). Refused to worship idol (Da 3:1–18); saved from furnace (Da 3:19–30).
MESSAGE (MESSENGER)
Isa 53: 1 Who has believed our *m*
Jn 12: 38 "Lord, who has believed our *m*
Ac 5: 20 "and tell the people the full *m*
10: 36 You know the *m* God sent
17: 11 for they received the *m*
Ro 10: 16 who has believed our *m*?"
10: 17 faith comes from hearing the *m*,
1Co 1: 18 For the *m* of the cross is
2: 4 My *m* and my preaching were not
2Co 5: 19 to us the *m* of reconciliation.
2Th 3: 1 pray for us that the *m*
Tit 1: 9 firmly to the trustworthy *m*
Heb 4: 2 the *m* they heard was of no value
1Pe 2: 8 because they disobey the *m*—
MESSENGER (MESSAGE)
Pr 25: 13 is a trustworthy *m*
Mal 3: 1 I will send my *m*, who will prepare
Mt 11: 10 " 'I will send my *m* ahead of you,
2Co 12: 7 a *m* of Satan, to torment me.
MESSIAH*
Jn 1: 41 "We have found the *M*" (that is,
4: 25 "I know that *M*" (called Christ) "is
METHUSELAH
Ge 5: 27 Altogether, *M* lived 969 years,
MICAH
1. Idolater from Ephraim (Jdg 17–18).
2. Prophet from Moresheth (Jer 26:18–19; Mic 1:1).
MICAIAH
Prophet of the LORD who spoke against Ahab (1Ki 22:1–28; 2Ch 18:1–27).
MICHAEL
Archangel (Jude 9); warrior in angelic realm, protector of Israel (Da 10:13, 21; 12:1; Rev 12:7).
MICHAL
Daughter of Saul, wife of David (1Sa 14:49; 18:20–28). Warned David of Saul's plot (1Sa 19). Saul gave her to Paltiel (1Sa 25:44); David retrieved her (2Sa 3:13–16). Criticized David for dancing before the ark (2Sa 6:16–23); 1Ch 15:29).
MIDIAN
Ex 2: 15 Pharaoh and went to live in *M*,
Jdg 7: 2 me to deliver *M* into their hands.
MIDWIVES
Ex 1: 17 The *m*, however, feared God
MIGHT (ALMIGHTY MIGHTIER MIGHTY)
Jdg 16: 30 Then he pushed with all his *m*,
2Sa 6: 5 with all their *m* before the LORD,
6: 14 before the LORD with all his *m*,
2Ch 20: 6 Power and *m* are in your hand,
Ps 21: 13 we will sing and praise your *m*.
54: 1 vindicate me by your *m*.
Isa 63: 15 Where are your zeal and your *m*?
Mic 3: 8 and with justice and *m*,
Zec 4: 6 'Not by *m* nor by power,
Col 1: 11 power according to his glorious *m*
1Ti 6: 16 To him be honor and *m* forever.
MIGHTIER (MIGHT)
Ps 93: 4 *M* than the thunder
MIGHTY (MIGHT)
Ge 49: 24 of the hand of the *M* One of Jacob,
Ex 6: 1 of my *m* hand he will drive them
13: 3 out of it with a *m* hand.
Dt 5: 15 out of there with a *m* hand
7: 8 he brought you out with a *m* hand
10: 17 the great God, *m* and awesome,
34: 12 one has ever shown the *m* power
2Sa 1: 19 How the *m* have fallen!
23: 8 the names of David's *m* men:
Ne 9: 32 the great, *m* and awesome God,
Job 36: 5 God is *m*, but does not despise men
Ps 24: 8 The LORD strong and *m*,
45: 3 upon your side, O *m* one;

50: 1 The *M* One, God, the LORD,
62: 7 he is my *m* rock, my refuge.
68: 33 who thunders with *m* voice.
71: 16 proclaim your *m* acts,
77: 12 and consider all your *m* deeds.
77: 15 With your *m* arm you redeemed
89: 8 You are *m*, O LORD,
93: 4 the LORD on high is *m*.
99: 4 The King is *m*, he loves justice—
110: 2 LORD will extend your *m* scepter
118: 15 right hand has done *m* things!
136: 12 with a *m* hand and outstretched
145: 4 they will tell of your *m* acts.
145: 12 all men may know of your *m* acts
147: 5 Great is our Lord and *m* in power;
SS 8: 6 like a *m* flame.
Isa 9: 6 Wonderful Counselor, *M* God,
60: 16 your Redeemer, the *M* One
63: 1 *m* to save."
Jer 10: 6 and your name is *m* in power.
20: 11 with me like a *m* warrior;
32: 19 your purposes and *m* are your
Eze 20: 33 I will rule over you with a *m* hand
Zep 3: 17 he is *m* to save.
Mt 26: 64 at the right hand of the *M* One
Eph 1: 19 like the working of his *m* strength,
6: 10 in the Lord and in his *m* power.
1Pe 5: 6 therefore, under God's *m* hand,

MILE*
Mt 5: 41 If someone forces you to go one *m*,

MILK
Ex 3: 8 a land flowing with *m* and honey—
23: 19 a young goat in its mother's *m*.
Pr 30: 33 as churning the *m* produces butter,
Isa 55: 1 Come, buy wine and *m*
1Co 3: 2 I gave you *m*, not solid food,
Heb 5: 12 You need *m*, not solid food!
1Pe 2: 2 babies, crave pure spiritual *m*,

MILLSTONE (STONE)
Lk 17: 2 sea with a *m* tied around his neck

MIND (DOUBLE-MINDED LIKE-MINDED MINDED MINDFUL MINDS)
Nu 23: 19 that he should change his *m*.
Dt 28: 65 LORD will give you an anxious *m*,
1Sa 15: 29 Israel does not lie or change his *m*;
1Ch 28: 9 devotion and with a willing *m*,
2Ch 30: 12 the people to give them unity of *m*
Ps 26: 2 examine my heart and my *m*;
110: 4 and will not change his *m*:
Isa 26: 3 him whose *m* is steadfast,
Jer 17: 10 and examine the *m*,
Mt 22: 37 all your soul and with all your *m*.'
Mk 12: 30 with all your *m* and with all your
Lk 10: 27 your strength and with all your *m*';
Ac 4: 32 believers were one in heart and *m*.
Ro 1: 28 he gave them over to a depraved *m*
7: 25 I myself in my *m* am a slave
8: 6 The *m* of sinful man is death,
8: 7 the sinful *m* is hostile to God.
12: 2 by the renewing of your *m*.
14: 13 make up your *m* not
1Co 1: 10 you may be perfectly united in *m*
2: 9 no *m* has conceived
14: 14 spirit prays, but my *m* is unfruitful.
2Co 13: 11 be of one *m*, live in peace.
Php 3: 19 Their *m* is on earthly things.
Col 2: 18 and his unspiritual *m* puffs him up
1Th 4: 11 to *m* your own business
Heb 7: 21 and will not change his *m*:

MINDED* (MIND)
1Pe 4: 7 be clear *m* and self-controlled

MINDFUL* (MIND)
Ps 8: 4 what is man that you are *m* of him,
Lk 1: 48 God my Savior, for he has been *m*
Heb 2: 6 What is man that you are *m* of him,

MINDS (MIND)
Dt 11: 18 of mine in your hearts and *m*;
Ps 7: 9 who searches *m* and hearts,
Jer 31: 33 "I will put my law in their *m*
Lk 24: 38 and why do doubts rise in your *m*?
24: 45 Then he opened their *m*
Ro 8: 5 to the sinful nature have their *m* set
2Co 4: 4 god of this age has blinded the *m*
Eph 4: 23 new in the attitude of your *m*;
Col 3: 2 Set your *m* on things above,
Heb 8: 10 I will put my laws in their *m*
10: 16 and I will write them on their *m*."
1Pe 1: 13 prepare your *m* for action;
Rev 2: 23 I am he who searches hearts and *m*,

MINISTER (MINISTERING MINISTERS MINISTRY)
Ps 101: 6 will *m* to me.
1Ti 4: 6 you will be a good *m*

MINISTERING (MINISTER)
Heb 1: 14 Are not all angels *m* spirits sent

MINISTERS (MINISTER)
2Co 3: 6 as *m* of a new covenant—

MINISTRY (MINISTER)
Ac 6: 4 to prayer and the *m* of the word."
Ro 11: 13 I make much of my *m*
2Co 4: 1 God's mercy we have this *m*,
5: 18 gave us the *m* of reconciliation:
6: 3 so that our *m* will not be
Gal 2: 8 who was at work in the *m* of Peter
2Ti 4: 5 discharge all the duties of your *m*.
Heb 8: 6 But the *m* Jesus has received is

MIRACLE* (MIRACLES MIRACULOUS)
Ex 7: 9 'Perform a *m*,' then say to Aaron,
Mk 9: 39 "No one who does a *m*
Lk 23: 8 hoped to see him perform some *m*.
Jn 7: 21 "I did one *m*, and you are all
Ac 4: 16 they have done an outstanding *m*,

MIRACLES* (MIRACLE)
1Ch 16: 12 his *m*, and the judgments he
Ne 9: 17 to remember the *m* you performed
Job 5: 9 *m* that cannot be counted.
9: 10 *m* that cannot be counted.
Ps 77: 11 I will remember your *m* of long ago
77: 14 You are the God who performs *m*;
78: 12 He did *m* in the sight
105: 5 his *m*, and the judgments he
106: 7 they gave no thought to your *m*;
106: 22 *m* in the land of Ham
Mt 7: 22 out demons and perform many *m*?'
11: 20 most of his *m* had been performed,
11: 21 If the *m* that were performed
11: 23 If the *m* that were performed
13: 58 And he did not do many *m* there
24: 24 and perform great signs and *m*
Mk 6: 2 does *m*! Isn't this the carpenter?
6: 5 He could not do any *m* there,
13: 22 and *m* to deceive the elect—
Lk 10: 13 For if the *m* that were performed
19: 37 for all the *m* they had seen:
Jn 7: 3 disciples may see the *m* you do.
10: 25 *m* I do in my Father's name speak
10: 32 "I have shown you many great *m*
10: 38 do not believe me, believe the *m*,
14: 11 the evidence of the *m* themselves.
15: 24 But now they have seen these *m*,
Ac 2: 22 accredited by God to you by *m*,
8: 13 by the great signs and *m* he saw.
19: 11 God did extraordinary *m*
Ro 15: 19 by the power of signs and *m*,
1Co 12: 28 third teachers, then workers of *m*,
12: 29 Are all teachers? Do all work *m*?
2Co 12: 12 and *m*— were done among you
Gal 3: 5 work *m* among you because you
2Th 2: 9 in all kinds of counterfeit *m*,
Heb 2: 4 it by signs, wonders and various *m*,

MIRACULOUS (MIRACLE)
Dt 13: 1 and announces to you a *m* sign
Mt 12: 39 generation asks for a *m* sign!
13: 54 this wisdom and these *m* powers?"
Jn 2: 11 This, the first of his *m* signs,
2: 23 people saw the *m* signs he was
3: 2 could perform the *m* signs you are
4: 48 "Unless you people see *m* signs
7: 31 will he do more *m* signs
9: 16 "How can a sinner do such *m* signs
12: 37 Jesus had done all these *m* signs
20: 30 Jesus did many other *m* signs
Ac 2: 43 *m* signs were done by the apostles.
5: 12 apostles performed many *m* signs
1Co 1: 22 Jews demand *m* signs and Greeks
12: 10 to another *m* powers,

MIRE
Ps 40: 2 out of the mud and *m*;
Isa 57: 20 whose waves cast up *m* and mud.

MIRIAM
Sister of Moses and Aaron (Nu 26:59). Led dancing at Red Sea (Ex 15:20–21). Struck with leprosy for criticizing Moses (Nu 12). Death (Nu 20:1).

MIRROR
1Co 13: 12 but a poor reflection as in a *m*;
Jas 1: 23 a man who looks at his face in a *m*

MISDEEDS*
Ps 99: 8 though you punished their *m*.
Ro 8: 13 put to death the *m* of the body,

MISERY
Ex 3: 7 "I have indeed seen the *m*
Jdg 10: 16 he could bear Israel's *m* no longer.
Hos 5: 15 in their *m* they will earnestly seek
Ro 3: 16 ruin and *m* mark their ways,
Jas 5: 1 of the *m* that is coming upon you.

MISFORTUNE
Ob : 12 brother in the day of his *m*,

MISLEAD (MISLED)
Isa 47: 10 wisdom and knowledge *m* you

MISLED (MISLEAD)
1Co 15: 33 Do not be *m*: "Bad company

MISS (MISSES)
Pr 19: 2 nor to be hasty and *m* the way.

MISSES (MISS)
Heb 12: 15 See to it that no one *m* the grace

MIST
Hos 6: 4 Your love is like the morning *m*,
Jas 4: 14 You are a *m* that appears for a little

MISTREAT (MISTREATED)
Ex 22: 21 "Do not *m* an alien or oppress him,
Eze 22: 29 and needy and *m* the alien,
Lk 6: 28 pray for those who *m* you.

MISTREATED (MISTREAT)
Eze 22: 7 *m* the fatherless and the widow.
Heb 11: 25 to be *m* along with the people
11: 37 destitute, persecuted and *m*—
13: 3 who are *m* as if you yourselves

MISUSE* (MISUSES)
Ex 20: 7 "You shall not *m* the name
Dt 5: 11 "You shall not *m* the name
Ps 139: 20 your adversaries *m* your name.

MISUSES* (MISUSE)
Ex 20: 7 anyone guiltless who *m* his name.
Dt 5: 11 anyone guiltless who *m* his name.

MIXED (MIXING)
Da 2: 41 even as you saw iron *m* with clay.

MIXING (MIXED)
Isa 5: 22 and champions at *m* drinks,

MOAB (MOABITESS)
Ge 19: 37 she named him *M*; he is the father
Dt 34: 6 He buried him in *M*, in the valley
Ru 1: 1 live for a while in the country of *M*.
Isa 15: 1 An oracle concerning *M*:
Jer 48: 16 "The fall of *M* is at hand;
Am 2: 1 "For three sins of *M*,

MOABITESS (MOAB)
Ru 1: 22 accompanied by Ruth the *M*,

MOAN
Ps 90: 9 we finish our years with a *m.*

MOCK (MOCKED MOCKER MOCKERS MOCKING MOCKS)
Ps 22: 7 All who see me *m* me;
119: 51 The arrogant *m* me
Pr 1: 26 I will *m* when calamity overtakes
14: 9 Fools *m* at making amends for sin,
Mk 10: 34 who will *m* him and spit on him,

MOCKED (MOCK)
Ps 89: 51 with which they have *m* every step
Mt 27: 29 knelt in front of him and *m* him.
27: 41 of the law and the elders *m* him.
Gal 6: 7 not be deceived: God cannot be *m.*

MOCKER (MOCK)
Pr 9: 7 corrects a *m* invites insult;
9: 12 if you are a *m,* you alone will suffer
20: 1 Wine is a *m* and beer a brawler;
22: 10 Drive out the *m,* and out goes strife

MOCKERS (MOCK)
Ps 1: 1 or sit in the seat of *m.*
Pr 29: 8 *M* stir up a city,

MOCKING (MOCK)
Isa 50: 6 face from *m* and spitting.

MOCKS (MOCK)
Pr 17: 5 He who *m* the poor shows
30: 17 "The eye that *m* a father,

MODEL*
Eze 28: 12 " 'You were the *m* of perfection,
1Th 1: 7 And so you became a *m*
2Th 3: 9 to make ourselves a *m* for you

MODESTY*
1Co 12: 23 are treated with special *m,*

MOLDED*
Job 10: 9 Remember that you *m* me like clay

MOLDY
Jos 9: 5 of their food supply was dry and *m.*

MOLECH
Lev 20: 2 of his children to *M* must be put
1Ki 11: 33 and *M* the god of the Ammonites,

MOMENT (MOMENTARY)
Job 20: 5 the joy of the godless lasts but a *m.*
Ps 2: 12 for his wrath can flare up in a *m.*
30: 5 For his anger lasts only a *m,*
Pr 12: 19 but a lying tongue lasts only a *m.*
Isa 54: 7 "For a brief *m* I abandoned you,
66: 8 or a nation be brought forth in a *m?*
Gal 2: 5 We did not give in to them for a *m,*

MOMENTARY* (MOMENT)
2Co 4: 17 and *m* troubles are achieving

MONEY
Pr 13: 11 Dishonest *m* dwindles away,
Ecc 5: 10 Whoever loves *m* never has *m*
Isa 55: 1 and you who have no *m,*
Mt 6: 24 You cannot serve both God and *M.*
27: 5 Judas threw the *m* into the temple
Lk 3: 14 "Don't extort *m* and don't accuse
9: 3 no bread, no *m,* no extra tunic.
16: 13 You cannot serve both God and *M*
Ac 5: 2 part of the *m* for himself,
1Co 16: 2 set aside a sum of *m* in keeping
1Ti 3: 3 not quarrelsome, not a lover of *m.*
6: 10 For the love of *m* is a root
2Ti 3: 2 lovers of *m,* boastful, proud,
Heb 13: 5 free from the love of *m*
1Pe 5: 2 not greedy for *m,* but eager to serve

MONEYLENDER* (LEND)
Ex 22: 25 not be like a *m;* charge him no
Lk 7: 41 men owed money to a certain *m.*

MONTH (MONTHS)
Ex 12: 2 "This *m* is to be for you the first
Eze 47: 12 Every *m* they will bear,
Rev 22: 2 of fruit, yielding its fruit every *m.*

MONTHS (MONTH)
Gal 4: 10 and *m* and seasons and years!
Rev 11: 2 trample on the holy city for 42 *m.*
13: 5 his authority for forty-two *m.*

MOON
Jos 10: 13 and the *m* stopped,
Ps 8: 3 the *m* and the stars,
74: 16 you established the sun and *m.*
89: 37 be established forever like the *m,*
104: 19 The *m* marks off the seasons,
121: 6 nor the *m* by night.
136: 9 the *m* and stars to govern the night;
148: 3 Praise him, sun and *m,*
SS 6: 10 fair as the *m,* bright as the sun,
Joel 2: 31 and the *m* to blood
Hab 3: 11 and *m* stood still in the heavens
Mt 24: 29 and the *m* will not give its light;
Ac 2: 20 and the *m* to blood
1Co 15: 41 *m* another and the stars another;
Col 2: 16 a New *M* celebration or a Sabbath
Rev 6: 12 the whole *m* turned blood red,
21: 23 city does not need the sun or the *m*

MORAL*
Jas 1: 21 rid of all *m* filth and the evil that is

MORDECAI
Benjamite exile who raised Esther (Est 2:5–15). Exposed plot to kill Xerxes (Est 2:19–23). Refused to honor Haman (Est 3:1–6; 5:9–14). Charged Esther to foil Haman's plot against the Jews (Est 4). Xerxes forced Haman to honor Mordecai (Est 6). Mordecai exalted (Est 8–10). Established Purim (Est 9:18–32).

MORIAH*
Ge 22: 2 and go to the region of *M.*
2Ch 3: 1 LORD in Jerusalem on Mount *M,*

MORNING
Ge 1: 5 and there was *m*— the first day.
Dt 28: 67 In the *m* you will say, "If only it
2Sa 23: 4 he is like the light of *m* at sunrise
Ps 5: 3 In the *m,* O LORD,
Pr 27: 14 blesses his neighbor early in the *m,*
Isa 14: 12 O *m* star, son of the dawn!
La 3: 23 They are new every *m;*
2Pe 1: 19 and the *m* star rises in your hearts.
Rev 2: 28 I will also give him the *m* star.
22: 16 of David, and the bright *M* Star."

MORTAL
Ge 6: 3 for he is *m;* his days will be
Job 10: 4 Do you see as a *m* sees?
Ro 8: 11 also give life to your *m* bodies
1Co 15: 53 and the *m* with immortality.
2Co 5: 4 that what is *m* may be swallowed

MOSES
Levite; brother of Aaron (Ex 6:20; 1Ch 6:3). Put in basket into Nile; discovered and raised by Pharaoh's daughter (Ex 2:1–10). Fled to Midian after killing Egyptian (Ex 2:11–15). Married to Zipporah, fathered Gershom (Ex 2:16–22).

Called by the LORD to deliver Israel (Ex 3–4). Pharaoh's resistance (Ex 5). Ten plagues (Ex 7–11). Passover and Exodus (Ex 12–13). Led Israel through Red Sea (Ex 14). Song of deliverance (Ex 15:1–21). Brought water from rock (Ex 17:1–7). Raised hands to defeat Amalekites (Ex 17:8–16). Delegated judges (Ex 18; Dt 1:9–18).

Received Law at Sinai (Ex 19–23; 25–31; Jn 1:17). Announced Law to Israel (Ex 19:7–8; 24; 35). Broke tablets because of golden calf (Ex 32; Dt 9). Saw glory of the LORD (Ex 33–34). Supervised building of tabernacle (Ex 36–40). Set apart Aaron and priests (Lev 8–9). Numbered tribes (Nu 1–4; 26). Opposed by Aaron and Miriam (Nu 12). Sent spies into Canaan (Nu 13). Announced forty years of wandering for failure to enter land (Nu 14). Opposed by Korah (Nu 16). Forbidden to enter land for striking rock (Nu 20:1–13; Dt 1:37). Lifted bronze snake for healing (Nu 21:4–9; Jn 3:14). Final address to Israel (Dt 1–33). Succeeded by Joshua (Nu 27:12–23; Dt 34). Death (Dt 34:5–12).

"Law of Moses" (1Ki 2:3; Ezr 3:2; Mk 12:26; Lk 24:44). "Book of Moses" (2Ch 25:12; Ne 13:1). "Song of Moses" (Ex 15:1–21; Rev 15:3). "Prayer of Moses" (Ps 90).

MOTH
Mt 6: 19 where *m* and rust destroy,

MOTHER (GRANDMOTHER MOTHER-IN-LAW MOTHER'S)
Ge 2: 24 and *m* and be united to his wife,
3: 20 because she would become the *m*
Ex 20: 12 "Honor your father and your *m,*
Lev 20: 9 " 'If anyone curses his father or *m,*
Dt 5: 16 "Honor your father and your *m,*
21: 18 who does not obey his father and *m*
27: 16 who dishonors his father or his *m.*"
Jdg 5: 7 arose a *m* in Israel.
1Sa 2: 19 Each year his *m* made him a little
Ps 113: 9 as a happy *m* of children.
Pr 10: 1 but a foolish son grief to his *m.*
23: 22 do not despise your *m*
23: 25 May your father and *m* be glad;
29: 15 a child left to himself disgraces his *m.*
30: 17 that scorns obedience to a *m,*
31: 1 an oracle his *m* taught him:
Isa 49: 15 "Can a *m* forget the baby
66: 13 As a *m* comforts her child,
Jer 20: 17 with my *m* as my grave,
Mic 7: 6 a daughter rises up against her *m,*
Mt 10: 35 a daughter against her *m,*
10: 37 or *m* more than me is not worthy
12: 48 He replied to him, "Who is my *m,*
15: 4 'Honor your father and *m*'
19: 5 and *m* and be united to his wife,
19: 19 honor your father and *m,*'
Mk 7: 10 'Honor your father and your *m,*' and,
10: 19 honor your father and *m.*' "
Lk 11: 27 "Blessed is the *m* who gave you
12: 53 daughter and daughter against *m,*
18: 20 honor your father and *m.*' "
Jn 19: 27 to the disciple, "Here is your *m.*"
Gal 4: 26 is above is free, and she is our *m.*
Eph 5: 31 and *m* and be united to his wife,
6: 2 "Honor your father and *m*"—
1Th 2: 7 like a *m* caring for her little
2Ti 1: 5 and in your *m* Eunice and,

MOTHER-IN-LAW (MOTHER)
Ru 2: 19 Ruth told her *m* about the one
Mt 10: 35 a daughter-in-law against her *m*—

MOTHER'S (MOTHER)
Job 1: 21 "Naked I came from my *m* womb,
Pr 1: 8 and do not forsake your *m* teaching
Ecc 5: 15 from his *m* womb,
11: 5 the body is formed in a *m* womb,
Jn 3: 4 time into his *m* womb to be born!"

MOTIVE* (MOTIVES)
1Ch 28: 9 and understands every *m*

MOTIVES* (MOTIVE)
Pr 16: 2 but *m* are weighed by the LORD.
1Co 4: 5 will expose the *m* of men's hearts.
Php 1: 18 whether from false *m* or true,
1Th 2: 3 spring from error or impure *m,*
Jas 4: 3 because you ask with wrong *m,*

MOUNT (MOUNTAIN MOUNTAINS MOUNTAINTOPS)
Ps 89: 9 when its waves *m* up, you still them
Isa 14: 13 enthroned on the *m* of assembly,
Eze 28: 14 You were on the holy *m* of God;
Zec 14: 4 stand on the *M* of Olives,

MOUNTAIN (MOUNT)
Ge 22: 14 "On the *m* of the LORD it will be
Ex 24: 18 And he stayed on the *m* forty days
Dt 5: 4 face to face out of the fire on the *m.*
Job 14: 18 "But as a *m* erodes and crumbles
Ps 48: 1 in the city of our God, his holy *m.*
Isa 40: 4 every *m* and hill made low;
Mic 4: 2 let us go up to the *m* of the LORD,
Mt 4: 8 the devil took him to a very high *m*

17: 20 say to this *m*, 'Move from here
Mk 9: 2 with him and led them up a high *m*,
Lk 3: 5 every *m* and hill made low.
Jn 4: 21 the Father neither on this *m*
2Pe 1: 18 were with him on the sacred *m*.

MOUNTAINS (MOUNT)
Ps 36: 6 righteousness is like the mighty *m*,
46: 2 the *m* fall into the heart of the sea,
90: 2 Before the *m* were born
Isa 52: 7 How beautiful on the *m*
54: 10 Though the *m* be shaken
55: 12 the *m* and hills
Eze 34: 6 My sheep wandered over all the *m*
Mt 24: 16 are in Judea flee to the *m*.
Lk 23: 30 they will say to the *m*, "Fall on us!"
1Co 13: 2 if I have a faith that can move *m*,
Rev 6: 16 They called to the *m* and the rocks,

MOUNTAINTOPS (MOUNT)
Isa 42: 11 let them shout from the *m*.

MOURN (MOURNING MOURNS)
Ecc 3: 4 a time to *m* and a time to dance,
Isa 61: 2 to comfort all who *m*,
Mt 5: 4 Blessed are those who *m*,
Ro 12: 15 *m* with those who *m*.

MOURNING (MOURN)
Isa 61: 3 instead of *m*,
Jer 31: 13 I will turn their *m* into gladness;
Rev 21: 4 There will be no more death or *m*

MOURNS (MOURN)
Zec 12: 10 as one *m* for an only child,

MOUTH (MOUTHS)
Nu 22: 38 only what God puts in my *m*."
Dt 8: 3 comes from the *m* of the LORD.
18: 18 I will put my words in his *m*,
30: 14 it is in your *m* and in your heart
Jos 1: 8 of the Law depart from your *m*;
2Ki 4: 34 *m* to *m*, eyes to eyes, hands
Ps 10: 7 His *m* is full of curses and lies
17: 3 resolved that my *m* will not sin.
19: 14 May the words of my *m*
37: 30 *m* of the righteous man utters
40: 3 He put a new song in my *m*,
71: 8 My *m* is filled with your praise,
119:103 sweeter than honey to my *m*!
141: 3 Set a guard over my *m*, O LORD;
Pr 2: 6 and from his *m* come knowledge
4: 24 Put away perversity from your *m*;
10: 11 The *m* of the righteous is a fountain
10: 31 *m* of the righteous brings forth
16: 23 A wise man's heart guides his *m*,
26: 28 and a flattering *m* works ruin.
27: 2 praise you, and not your own *m*;
Ecc 5: 2 Do not be quick with your *m*,
SS 1: 2 with the kisses of his *m*—
5: 16 His *m* is sweetness itself;
Isa 29: 13 come near to me with their *m*
40: 5 For the *m* of the LORD has spoken
45: 23 my *m* has uttered in all integrity
51: 16 I have put my words in your *m*
53: 7 so he did not open his *m*.
55: 11 my word that goes out from my *m*:
59: 21 *m* will not depart from your *m*,
Eze 3: 2 So I opened my *m*, and he gave me
Mal 2: 7 and from his *m* men should seek
Mt 4: 4 comes from the *m* of God.' "
12: 34 overflow of the heart the *m* speaks.
15: 11 into a man's *m* does not make him
15: 18 out of the *m* come from the heart,
Lk 6: 45 overflow of his heart his *m* speaks.
Ro 10: 9 That if you confess with your *m*,
15: 6 and *m* you may glorify the God
1Pe 2: 22 and no deceit was found in his *m*."
Rev 1: 16 and out of his *m* came a sharp
2: 16 them with the sword of my *m*.
3: 16 I am about to spit you out of my *m*.
19: 15 Out of his *m* comes a sharp sword

MOUTHS (MOUTH)
Ps 78: 36 would flatter him with their *m*,
Eze 33: 31 With their *m* they express devotion
Ro 3: 14 "Their *m* are full of cursing
Eph 4: 29 talk come out of your *m*,
Jas 3: 3 bits into the *m* of horses

MOVE (MOVED MOVES)
Dt 19: 14 Do not *m* your neighbor's
Pr 23: 10 Do not *m* an ancient boundary
Ac 17: 28 and *m* and have our being.'
1Co 13: 2 have a faith that can *m* mountains,
15: 58 Let nothing *m* you.

MOVED (MOVE)
Ex 35: 21 and whose heart *m* him came
2Ch 36: 22 the LORD *m* the heart
Ezr 1: 5 everyone whose heart God had *m*
Ps 93: 1 it cannot be *m*.
Jn 11: 33 he was deeply *m* in spirit
Col 1: 23 not *m* from the hope held out

MOVES (MOVE)
Dt 23: 14 For the LORD your God *m* about

MUD (MUDDIED)
Ps 40: 2 out of the *m* and mire;
Isa 57: 20 whose waves cast up mire and *m*.
Jn 9: 6 made some *m* with the saliva,
2Pe 2: 22 back to her wallowing in the *m*."

MUDDIED (MUD)
Pr 25: 26 Like a *m* spring or a polluted well
Eze 32: 13 or *m* by the hoofs of cattle.

MULBERRY*
Lk 17: 6 you can say to this *m* tree,

MULTITUDE (MULTITUDES)
Isa 31: 1 who trust in the *m* of their chariots
Jas 5: 20 and cover over a *m* of sins.
1Pe 4: 8 love covers over a *m* of sins.
Rev 7: 9 me was a great *m* that no one could
19: 1 of a great *m* in heaven shouting:

MULTITUDES (MULTITUDE)
Ne 9: 6 and the *m* of heaven worship you.
Da 12: 2 *M* who sleep in the dust
Joel 3: 14 *M*, *m* in the valley of decision!

MURDER (MURDERED MURDERER MURDERERS)
Ex 20: 13 "You shall not *m*.
Dt 5: 17 "You shall not *m*.
Pr 28: 17 A man tormented by the guilt of *m*
Mt 5: 21 'Do not *m*, and anyone who
15: 19 *m*, adultery, sexual immorality,
Ro 1: 29 *m*, strife, deceit and malice.
13: 9 "Do not *m*," "Do not steal,"
Jas 2: 11 adultery," also said, "Do not *m*."

MURDERED (MURDER)
Mt 23: 31 of those who *m* the prophets.
Ac 7: 52 now you have betrayed and *m* him
1Jn 3: 12 to the evil one and *m* his brother.

MURDERER (MURDER)
Nu 35: 16 he is a *m*; the *m* shall be put
Jn 8: 44 He was a *m* from the beginning,
1Jn 3: 15 who hates his brother is a *m*,

MURDERERS (MURDER)
1Ti 1: 9 for *m*, for adulterers and perverts,
Rev 21: 8 the *m*, the sexually immoral,
22: 15 the sexually immoral, the *m*,

MUSIC* (MUSICAL MUSICIAN MUSICIANS)
Ge 31: 27 singing to the *m* of tambourines
Jdg 5: 3 I will make *m* to the LORD,
1Ch 6: 31 put in charge of the *m* in the house
6: 32 They ministered with *m*
25: 6 fathers for the *m* of the temple
25: 7 and skilled in *m* for the LORD—
Ne 12: 27 and with the *m* of cymbals,
Job 21: 12 They sing to the *m* of tambourine
Ps 27: 6 and make *m* to the LORD.
33: 2 make *m* to him on the ten-stringed
45: 8 the *m* of the strings makes you glad
57: 7 I will sing and make *m*.
81: 2 Begin the *m*, strike the tambourine,
87: 7 As they make *m* they will sing,
92: 1 and make *m* to your name,
92: 3 to the *m* of the ten-stringed lyre
95: 2 and extol him with *m* and song.
98: 4 burst into jubilant song with *m*;
98: 5 make *m* to the LORD
108: 1 make *m* with all my soul.
144: 9 the ten-stringed lyre I will make *m*
147: 7 make *m* to our God on the harp.
149: 3 make *m* to him with tambourine
Isa 30: 32 will be to the *m* of tambourines
La 5: 14 young men have stopped their *m*.
Eze 26: 13 *m* of your harps will be heard no
Da 3: 5 lyre, harp, pipes and all kinds of *m*,
3: 7 and all kinds of *m*, all the peoples,
3: 10 and all kinds of *m* must fall down
3: 15 lyre, harp, pipes and all kinds of *m*,
Am 5: 23 to the *m* of your harps.
Hab 3: 19 For the director of *m*.
Lk 15: 25 came near the house, he heard *m*
Eph 5: 19 make *m* in your heart to the Lord,
Rev 18: 22 The *m* of harpists and musicians,

MUSICAL* (MUSIC)
1Ch 15: 16 accompanied by *m* instruments:
23: 5 with the *m* instruments I have
2Ch 7: 6 with the LORD's *m* instruments,
23: 13 with *m* instruments were leading
34: 12 skilled in playing *m* instruments—
Ne 12: 36 with *m* instruments ›prescribed
Am 6: 5 and improvise on *m* instruments.

MUSICIAN* (MUSIC)
1Ch 6: 33 Heman, the *m*, the son of Joel,

MUSICIANS* (MUSIC)
1Ki 10: 12 to make harps and lyres for the *m*.
1Ch 9: 33 Those who were *m*, heads
15: 19 The *m* Heman, Asaph
2Ch 5: 12 All the Levites who were *m*—
9: 11 to make harps and lyres for the *m*.
35: 15 The *m*, the descendants of Asaph,
Ps 68: 25 are the singers, after them the *m*;
Rev 18: 22 The music of harpists and *m*,

MUSTARD
Mt 13: 31 kingdom of heaven is like a *m* seed,
17: 20 you have faith as small as a *m* seed,
Mk 4: 31 It is like a *m* seed, which is

MUTILATORS*
Php 3: 2 those men who do evil, those *m*

MUTUAL* (MUTUALLY)
Ro 14: 19 leads to peace and to *m* edification.
1Co 7: 5 by *m* consent and for a time,

MUTUALLY* (MUTUAL)
Ro 1: 12 and I may be *m* encouraged

MUZZLE*
Dt 25: 4 Do not *m* an ox while it is treading
Ps 39: 1 I will put a *m* on my mouth
1Co 9: 9 "Do not *m* an ox while it is
1Ti 5: 18 "Do not *m* the ox while it is

MYRRH
Ps 45: 8 All your robes are fragrant with *m*
SS 1: 13 My lover is to me a sachet of *m*
Mt 2: 11 of gold and of incense and of *m*.
Mk 15: 23 offered him wine mixed with *m*,
Jn 19: 39 Nicodemus brought a mixture of *m*
Rev 18: 13 of incense, *m* and frankincense,

MYSTERIES* (MYSTERY)
Job 11: 7 "Can you fathom the *m* of God?
Da 2: 28 a God in heaven who reveals *m*.
2: 29 of *m* showed you what is going
2: 47 Lord of kings and a revealer of *m*,
1Co 13: 2 can fathom all *m* and all knowledge
14: 2 he utters *m* with his spirit.

MYSTERY* (MYSTERIES)
Da 2: 18 God of heaven concerning this *m*,
2: 19 the night the *m* was revealed
2: 27 to the king the *m* he has asked
2: 30 this *m* has been revealed to me,
2: 47 for you were able to reveal this *m*."

4: 9 and no *m* is too difficult for you.
Ro 11: 25 you to be ignorant of this *m,*
16: 25 to the revelation of the *m* hidden
1Co 15: 51 I tell you a *m:* We will not all sleep,
Eph 1: 9 to us the *m* of his will according
3: 3 the *m* made known to me
3: 4 insight into the *m* of Christ,
3: 6 This *m* is that through the gospel
3: 9 the administration of this *m,*
5: 32 This is a profound *m*—
6: 19 I will fearlessly make known the *m*
Col 1: 26 the *m* that has been kept hidden
1: 27 the glorious riches of this *m,*
2: 2 in order that they may know the *m*
4: 3 so that we may proclaim the *m*
1Ti 3: 16 the *m* of godliness is great:
Rev 1: 20 *m* of the seven stars that you saw
10: 7 the *m* of God will be accomplished,
17: 5 written on her forehead: *M*
17: 7 explain to you the *m* of the woman

MYTHS*
1Ti 1: 4 nor to devote themselves to *m*
4: 7 Have nothing to do with godless *m*
2Ti 4: 4 from the truth and turn aside to *m.*
Tit 1: 14 will pay no attention to Jewish *m*

NAAMAN
Aramean general whose leprosy was cleansed by Elisha (2Ki 5).

NABAL
Wealthy Carmelite the LORD killed for refusing to help David (1Sa 25). David married Abigail, his widow (1Sa 25:39–42).

NABOTH*
Jezreelite killed by Jezebel for his vineyard (1Ki 21). Ahab's family destroyed for this (1Ki 21:17–24; 2Ki 9:21–37).

NADAB
1. Firstborn of Aaron (Ex 6:23); killed with Abihu for offering unauthorized fire (Lev 10; Nu 3:4).
2. Son of Jeroboam I; king of Israel (1Ki 15:25–32).

NAHUM
Prophet against Nineveh (Na 1:1).

NAIL* (NAILING)
Jn 20: 25 "Unless I see the *n* marks

NAILING* (NAIL)
Ac 2: 23 him to death by *n* him to the cross.
Col 2: 14 he took it away, *n* it to the cross.

NAIVE
Ro 16: 18 they deceive the minds of *n* people.

NAKED
Ge 2: 25 The man and his wife were both *n,*
Job 1: 21 *N* I came from my mother's womb,
Isa 58: 7 when you see the *n,* to clothe him,
2Co 5: 3 are clothed, we will not be found *n.*

NAME (NAMES)
Ge 2: 19 man to see what he would *n* them;
4: 26 to call on the *n* of the LORD.
11: 4 so that we may make a *n*
12: 2 I will make your *n* great,
32: 29 Jacob said, "Please tell me your *n.*"
Ex 3: 15 This is my *n* forever, the *n*
20: 7 "You shall not misuse the *n*
34: 14 for the LORD, whose *n* is Jealous,
Lev 24: 11 Israelite woman blasphemed the *N*
Dt 5: 11 "You shall not misuse the *n*
12: 11 choose as a dwelling for his *N*—
18: 5 minister in the LORD's *n* always.
25: 6 carry on the *n* of the dead brother
28: 58 this glorious and awesome *n*—
Jos 7: 9 do for your own great *n?*"
Jdg 13: 17 "What is your *n,* so that we may
1Sa 12: 22 of his great *n* the LORD will not
2Sa 6: 2 which is called by the *N,* the name
7: 9 Now I will make your *n* great,
1Ki 5: 5 will build the temple for my *N.*'
8: 29 you said, 'My *N* shall be there,'
1Ch 17: 8 I will make your *n* like the names
2Ch 7: 14 my people, who are called by my *n,*
Ne 9: 10 You made a *n* for yourself,
Ps 8: 1 how majestic is your *n*
9: 10 Those who know your *n* will trust
20: 7 in the *n* of the LORD our God.
29: 2 to the LORD the glory due his *n;*
34: 3 let us exalt his *n* together.
44: 20 If we had forgotten the *n*
66: 2 Sing the glory of his *n;*
68: 4 Sing to God, sing praise to his *n,*
79: 9 for the glory of your *n;*
96: 8 to the LORD the glory due his *n;*
103: 1 my inmost being, praise his holy *n.*
115: 1 but to your *n* be the glory,
138: 2 your *n* and your word.
145: 1 I will praise your *n* for ever
147: 4 and calls them each by *n.*
Pr 3: 4 you will win favor and a good *n*
18: 10 *n* of the LORD is a strong tower;
22: 1 A good *n* is more desirable
30: 4 What is his *n,* and the *n* of his son?
Ecc 7: 1 A good *n* is better
SS 1: 3 your *n* is like perfume poured out.
Isa 12: 4 thanks to the LORD, call on his *n;*
26: 8 your *n* and renown
40: 26 and calls them each by *n.*
42: 8 "I am the LORD; that is my *n!*
56: 5 I will give them an everlasting *n*
57: 15 who lives forever, whose *n* is holy:
63: 14 to make for yourself a glorious *n.*
Jer 14: 7 do something for the sake of your *n*
15: 16 for I bear your *n,*
Eze 20: 9 of my *n* I did what would keep it
20: 14 of my *n* I did what would keep it
20: 22 of my *n* I did what would keep it
Da 12: 1 everyone whose *n* is found written
Hos 12: 5 the LORD is his *n* of renown!
Joel 2: 32 on the *n* of the LORD will be saved
Mic 5: 4 in the majesty of the *n*
Zep 3: 9 call on the *n* of the LORD
Zec 6: 12 is the man whose *n* is the Branch,
14: 9 one LORD, and his *n* the only *n.*
Mal 1: 6 O priests, who show contempt for my *n.*
Mt 1: 21 and you are to give him the *n* Jesus,
6: 9 hallowed be your *n,*
18: 20 or three come together in my *n,*
24: 5 For many will come in my *n,*
28: 19 them in the *n* of the Father
Mk 9: 41 gives you a cup of water in my *n*
Lk 11: 2 hallowed be your *n,*
Jn 10: 3 He calls his own sheep by *n*
14: 13 I will do whatever you ask in my *n,*
16: 24 asked for anything in my *n.*
Ac 2: 21 on the *n* of the Lord will be saved.'
4: 12 for there is no other *n*
Ro 10: 13 "Everyone who calls on the *n*
Php 2: 9 him the *n* that is above every *n,*
2: 10 at the *n* of Jesus every knee should
Col 3: 17 do it all in the *n* of the Lord Jesus,
Heb 1: 4 as the *n* he has inherited is superior
Jas 5: 14 him with oil in the *n* of the Lord.
1Jn 5: 13 believe in the *n* of the Son of God
Rev 2: 17 stone with a new *n* written on it,
3: 5 I will never blot out his *n*
3: 12 I will also write on him my new *n.*
19: 13 and his *n* is the Word of God.
20: 15 If anyone's *n* was not found written

NAMES (NAME)
Ex 28: 9 engrave on them the *n* of the sons
Lk 10: 20 but rejoice that your *n* are written
Php 4: 3 whose *n* are in the book of life.
Heb 12: 23 whose *n* are written in heaven.
Rev 21: 27 but only those whose *n* are written

NAOMI
Wife of Elimelech, mother-in-law of Ruth (Ru 1:2, 4). Left Bethlehem for Moab during famine (Ru 1:1). Returned a widow, with Ruth (Ru 1:6–22). Advised Ruth to seek marriage with Boaz (Ru 2:17–3:4). Cared for Ruth's son Obed (Ru 4:13–17).

NAPHTALI
Son of Jacob by Bilhah (Ge 30:8; 35:25; 1Ch 2:2). Tribe of blessed (Ge 49:21; Dt 33:23), numbered (Nu 1:43; 26:50), allotted land (Jos 19:32–39; Eze 48:3), failed to fully possess (Jdg 1:33), supported Deborah (Jdg 4:10; 5:18), David (1Ch 12:34), 12,000 from (Rev 7:6).

NARROW
Mt 7: 13 "Enter through the *n* gate.
7: 14 and *n* the road that leads to life,

NATHAN
Prophet and chronicler of Israel's history (1Ch 29:29; 2Ch 9:29). Announced the Davidic covenant (2Sa 7; 1Ch 17). Denounced David's sin with Bathsheba (2Sa 12). Supported Solomon (1Ki 1).

NATHANAEL*
Apostle (Jn 1:45–49; 21:2). Probably also called Bartholomew (Mt 10:3).

NATION (NATIONS)
Ge 12: 2 "I will make you into a great *n*
Ex 19: 6 a kingdom of priests and a holy *n.*'
Dt 4: 7 What other *n* is so great
Jos 5: 8 And after the whole *n* had been
2Sa 7: 23 one *n* on earth that God went out
Ps 33: 12 Blessed is the *n* whose God is
Pr 11: 14 For lack of guidance a *n* falls,
14: 34 Righteousness exalts a *n,*
Isa 2: 4 *N* will not take up sword
26: 2 that the righteous *n* may enter,
60: 12 For the *n* or kingdom that will not
65: 1 To a *n* that did not call on my name
66: 8 a *n* be brought forth in a moment?
Mic 4: 3 *N* will not take up sword
Mt 24: 7 *N* will rise against *n,*
Mk 13: 8 *N* will rise against *n,*
1Pe 2: 9 a royal priesthood, a holy *n,*
Rev 5: 9 and language and people and *n.*
7: 9 from every *n,* tribe, people
14: 6 to every *n,* tribe, language

NATIONS (NATION)
Ge 17: 4 You will be the father of many *n.*
18: 18 and all *n* on earth will be blessed
Ex 19: 5 of all *n* you will be my treasured
Lev 20: 26 apart from the *n* to be my own.
Dt 7: 1 drives out before you many *n*—
15: 6 You will rule over many *n*
Jdg 3: 1 These are the *n* the LORD left
2Ch 20: 6 rule over all the kingdoms of the *n.*
Ne 1: 8 I will scatter you among the *n,*
Ps 2: 1 Why do the *n* conspire
2: 8 I will make the *n* your inheritance,
9: 5 You have rebuked the *n*
22: 28 and he rules over the *n.*
46: 10 I will be exalted among the *n,*
47: 8 God reigns over the *n;*
66: 7 his eyes watch the *n*—
67: 2 your salvation among all *n.*
68: 30 Scatter the *n* who delight in war.
72: 17 All *n* will be blessed through him,
96: 3 Declare his glory among the *n,*
99: 2 he is exalted over all the *n.*
106: 35 but they mingled with the *n*
110: 6 He will judge the *n,* heaping up
113: 4 The LORD is exalted over all the *n*
Isa 2: 2 and all *n* will stream to it.
11: 10 the *n* will rally to him,
12: 4 among the *n* what he has done,
40: 15 Surely the *n* are like a drop
42: 1 and he will bring justice to the *n.*
51: 4 justice will become a light to the *n.*
52: 15 so will he sprinkle many *n,*
56: 7 a house of prayer for all *n.*"
60: 3 *N* will come to your light,
66: 18 and gather all *n* and tongues,
Jer 1: 5 you as a prophet to the *n.*"

3: 17 and all *n* will gather in Jerusalem
31: 10 "Hear the word of the LORD, O *n;*
33: 9 and honor before all *n*
46: 28 I completely destroy all the *n*
Eze 22: 4 you an object of scorn to the *n*
34: 13 I will bring them out from the *n*
36: 23 *n* will know that I am the LORD,
37: 22 and they will never again be two *n*
39: 21 I will display my glory among the *n*
Hos 7: 8 "Ephraim mixes with the *n;*
Joel 2: 17 a byword among the *n.*
3: 2 I will gather all *n*
Am 9: 12 and all the *n* that bear my name,"
Zep 3: 8 I have decided to assemble the *n,*
Hag 2: 7 and the desired of all *n* will come,
Zec 8: 13 an object of cursing among the *n,*
8: 23 *n* will take firm hold of one Jew
9: 10 He will proclaim peace to the *n.*
14: 2 I will gather all the *n* to Jerusalem
Mt 12: 18 he will proclaim justice to the *n.*
24: 9 and you will be hated by all *n*
24: 14 whole world as a testimony to all *n,*
25: 32 All the *n* will be gathered
28: 19 and make disciples of all *n,*
Mk 11: 17 a house of prayer for all *n*'?
Ac 4: 25 " 'Why do the *n* rage
Ro 15: 12 who will arise to rule over the *n;*
Gal 3: 8 All *n* will be blessed through you."
1Ti 3: 16 was preached among the *n,*
Rev 15: 4 All *n* will come
21: 24 The *n* will walk by its light,
22: 2 are for the healing of the *n.*

NATURAL (NATURE)
Ro 6: 19 you are weak in your *n* selves.
1Co 15: 44 If there is a *n* body, there is

NATURE (NATURAL)
Ro 1: 20 his eternal power and divine *n*—
7: 18 lives in me, that is, in my sinful *n.*
8: 4 do not live according to the sinful *n*
8: 5 to the sinful *n* have their minds set
8: 8 by the sinful *n* cannot please God.
13: 14 to gratify the desires of the sinful *n.*
Gal 5: 13 freedom to indulge the sinful *n;*
5: 19 The acts of the sinful *n* are obvious:
5: 24 Jesus have crucified the sinful *n*
Php 2: 6 Who, being in very *n* God,
Col 3: 5 whatever belongs to your earthly *n*
2Pe 1: 4 you may participate in the divine *n*

NAZARENE* (NAZARETH)
Mt 2: 23 prophets: "He will be called a *N.*"
Mk 14: 67 "You also were with that *N,* Jesus,"
16: 6 "You are looking for Jesus the *N,*
Ac 24: 5 He is a ringleader of the *N* sect and

NAZARETH (NAZARENE)
Mt 4: 13 Leaving *N,* he went and lived
Lk 4: 16 to *N,* where he had been brought
Jn 1: 46 "*N!* Can anything good come

NAZIRITE
Nu 6: 2 of separation to the LORD as a *N,*
Jdg 13: 7 because the boy will be a *N* of God

NEBO
Dt 34: 1 Then Moses climbed Mount *N*

NEBUCHADNEZZAR
Babylonian king. Subdued and exiled Judah (2Ki 24–25; 2Ch 36; Jer 39). Dreams interpreted by Daniel (Da 2; 4). Worshiped God (Da 3:28–29; 4:34–37).

NECESSARY*
Ac 1: 21 Therefore it is *n* to choose one
Ro 13: 5 it is *n* to submit to the authorities,
2Co 9: 5 I thought it *n* to urge the brothers
Php 1: 24 it is more *n* for you that I remain
2: 25 But I think it is *n* to send back
Heb 8: 3 and so it was *n* for this one
9: 16 it is *n* to prove the death
9: 23 It was *n,* then, for the copies

NECK (STIFF-NECKED)
Pr 3: 22 an ornament to grace your *n.*
6: 21 fasten them around your *n.*
Mt 18: 6 a large millstone hung around his *n*

NECO
Pharaoh who killed Josiah (2Ki 23:29–30; 2Ch 35:20–22), deposed Jehoahaz (2Ki 23:33–35; 2Ch 36:3–4).

NEED (NEEDS NEEDY)
1Ki 8: 59 Israel according to each day's *n,*
Ps 79: 8 for we are in desperate *n.*
116: 6 when I was in great *n,* he saved me.
142: 6 for I am in desperate *n;*
Mt 6: 8 for your Father knows what you *n*
Lk 15: 14 country, and he began to be in *n.*
Ac 2: 45 they gave to anyone as he had *n.*
Ro 12: 13 with God's people who are in *n.*
1Co 12: 21 say to the hand, "I don't *n* you!"
Eph 4: 28 something to share with those in *n.*
1Ti 5: 3 to those widows who are really in *n*
Heb 4: 16 grace to help us in our time of *n.*
1Jn 3: 17 sees his brother in *n* but has no pity

NEEDLE
Mt 19: 24 go through the eye of a *n*

NEEDS (NEED)
Isa 58: 11 he will satisfy your *n*
Php 2: 25 sent to take care of my *n.*
4: 19 God will meet all your *n* according
Jas 2: 16 does nothing about his physical *n,*

NEEDY (NEED)
Dt 15: 11 toward the poor and *n* in your land.
1Sa 2: 8 and lifts the *n* from the ash heap;
Ps 35: 10 and *n* from those who rob them."
69: 33 The LORD hears the *n*
72: 12 he will deliver the *n* who cry out,
140: 12 and upholds the cause of the *n.*
Pr 14: 21 blessed is he who is kind to the *n.*
14: 31 to the *n* honors God.
22: 22 and do not crush the *n* in court,
31: 9 defend the rights of the poor and *n*
31: 20 and extends her hands to the *n.*
Mt 6: 2 "So when you give to the *n,*

NEGLECT* (NEGLECTED)
Dt 12: 19 Be careful not to *n* the Levites
14: 27 And do not *n* the Levites living
Ezr 4: 22 Be careful not to *n* this matter.
Ne 10: 39 We will not *n* the house of our God
Est 6: 10 Do not *n* anything you have
Ps 119: 16 I will not *n* your word.
Lk 11: 42 you *n* justice and the love of God.
Ac 6: 2 for us to *n* the ministry of the word
1Ti 4: 14 Do not *n* your gift, which was

NEGLECTED (NEGLECT)
Mt 23: 23 But you have *n* the more important

NEHEMIAH
Cupbearer of Artaxerxes (Ne 2:1); governor of Israel (Ne 8:9). Returned to Jerusalem to rebuild walls (Ne 2–6). With Ezra, reestablished worship (Ne 8). Prayer confessing nation's sin (Ne 9). Dedicated wall (Ne 12).

NEIGHBOR (NEIGHBOR'S)
Ex 20: 16 give false testimony against your *n.*
20: 17 or anything that belongs to your *n*
Lev 19: 13 Do not defraud your *n* or rob him.
19: 17 Rebuke your *n* frankly
19: 18 but love your *n* as yourself.
Ps 15: 3 who does his *n* no wrong
Pr 3: 29 Do not plot harm against your *n,*
11: 12 who lacks judgment derides his *n,*
14: 21 He who despises his *n* sins,
16: 29 A violent man entices his *n*
24: 28 against your *n* without cause,
25: 18 gives false testimony against his *n.*
27: 10 better a *n* nearby than a brother far
27: 14 If a man loudly blesses his *n*
29: 5 Whoever flatters his *n*
Jer 31: 34 No longer will a man teach his *n,*
Zec 8: 17 do not plot evil against your *n,*
Mt 5: 43 Love your *n* and hate your enemy.'
19: 19 and 'love your *n* as yourself.' "
Mk 12: 31 The second is this: 'Love your *n*
Lk 10: 27 and, 'Love your *n* as yourself.' "
10: 29 who is my *n*?" In reply Jesus said:
Ro 13: 9 "Love your *n* as yourself."
13: 10 Love does no harm to its *n.*
15: 2 Each of us should please his *n*
Gal 5: 14 "Love your *n* as yourself."
Eph 4: 25 and speak truthfully to his *n,*
Heb 8: 11 No longer will a man teach his *n,*
Jas 2: 8 "Love your *n* as yourself,"

NEIGHBOR'S (NEIGHBOR)
Ex 20: 17 You shall not covet your *n* wife,
Dt 5: 21 not set your desire on your *n* house
19: 14 not move your *n* boundary stone
27: 17 who moves his *n* boundary stone."
Pr 25: 17 Seldom set foot in your *n* house—

NESTS
Mt 8: 20 and birds of the air have *n,*

NET (NETS)
Pr 1: 17 How useless to spread a *n*
Hab 1: 15 he catches them in his *n,*
Mt 13: 47 of heaven is like a *n* that was let
Jn 21: 6 "Throw your *n* on the right side

NETS (NET)
Ps 141: 10 Let the wicked fall into their own *n*
Mt 4: 20 At once they left their *n*
Lk 5: 4 and let down the *n* for a catch."

NEVER-FAILING*
Am 5: 24 righteousness like a *n* stream!

NEW
Ps 40: 3 He put a *n* song in my mouth,
98: 1 Sing to the LORD a *n* song,
Ecc 1: 9 there is nothing *n* under the sun.
Isa 42: 9 and *n* things I declare;
62: 2 you will be called by a *n* name
65: 17 *n* heavens and a *n* earth.
66: 22 "As the *n* heavens and the *n* earth
Jer 31: 31 "when I will make a *n* covenant
La 3: 23 They are *n* every morning;
Eze 11: 19 undivided heart and put a *n* spirit
18: 31 and get a *n* heart and a *n* spirit.
36: 26 give you a *n* heart and put a *n* spirit
Zep 3: 5 and every *n* day he does not fail,
Mt 9: 17 Neither do men pour *n* wine
Mk 16: 17 they will speak in *n* tongues;
Lk 5: 39 after drinking old wine wants the *n*
22: 20 "This cup is the *n* covenant
Jn 13: 34 "A *n* commandment I give you:
Ac 5: 20 the full message of this *n* life."
Ro 6: 4 the Father, we too may live a *n* life.
1Co 5: 7 old yeast that you may be a *n* batch
11: 25 "This cup is the *n* covenant
2Co 3: 6 as ministers of a *n* covenant—
5: 17 he is a *n* creation; the old has gone,
Gal 6: 15 what counts is a *n* creation.
Eph 4: 23 to be made *n* in the attitude
4: 24 and to put on the *n* self, created
Col 3: 10 and have put on the *n* self,
Heb 8: 8 when I will make a *n* covenant
9: 15 is the mediator of a *n* covenant,
10: 20 by a *n* and living way opened for us
12: 24 Jesus the mediator of a *n* covenant,
1Pe 1: 3 great mercy he has given us *n* birth
2Pe 3: 13 to a *n* heaven and a *n* earth,
1Jn 2: 8 Yet I am writing you a *n* command;
Rev 2: 17 stone with a *n* name written on it,
3: 12 the *n* Jerusalem, which is coming
21: 1 I saw a *n* heaven and a *n* earth,

NEWBORN (BEAR)
1Pe 2: 2 Like *n* babies, crave pure spiritual

NEWS
2Ki 7: 9 This is a day of good *n*
Ps 112: 7 He will have no fear of bad *n;*
Pr 15: 30 good *n* gives health to the bones.
25: 25 is good *n* from a distant land.
Isa 52: 7 the feet of those who bring good *n,*

61: 1 me to preach good *n* to the poor.
Na 1: 15 the feet of one who brings good *n*,
Mt 4: 23 preaching the good *n*
9: 35 preaching the good *n*
11: 5 the good *n* is preached to the poor.
Mk 1: 15 Repent and believe the good *n*!"
16: 15 preach the good *n* to all creation.
Lk 1: 19 and to tell you this good *n*.
2: 10 I bring you good *n*
3: 18 and preached the good *n* to them.
4: 43 "I must preach the good *n*
8: 1 proclaiming the good *n*
16: 16 the good *n* of the kingdom
Ac 5: 42 proclaiming the good *n* that Jesus
10: 36 telling the good *n* of peace
14: 7 continued to preach the good *n*.
14: 21 They preached the good *n*
17: 18 preaching the good *n* about Jesus
Ro 10: 15 feet of those who bring good *n*!"

NICODEMUS*
Pharisee who visited Jesus at night (Jn 3). Argued fair treatment of Jesus (Jn 7:50–52). With Joseph, prepared Jesus for burial (Jn 19:38–42).

NIGHT (NIGHTS NIGHTTIME)
Ge 1: 5 and the darkness he called "*n*."
1: 16 and the lesser light to govern the *n*.
Ex 13: 21 and by *n* in a pillar of fire
14: 24 During the last watch of the *n*.
Dt 28: 66 filled with dread both *n* and day,
Jos 1: 8 and *n*, so that you may be careful
Job 35: 10 who gives songs in the *n*,
Ps 1: 2 on his law he meditates day and *n*.
19: 2 *n* after *n* they display knowledge.
42: 8 at *n* his song is with me—
63: 6 of you through the watches of the *n*
77: 6 I remembered my songs in the *n*.
90: 4 or like a watch in the *n*.
91: 5 You will not fear the terror of *n*,
119:148 through the watches of the *n*,
121: 6 nor the moon by *n*.
136: 9 the moon and stars to govern the *n*;
Pr 31: 18 and her lamp does not go out at *n*.
Isa 21: 11 Watchman, what is left of the *n*?"
58: 10 and your *n* will become like
Jer 33: 20 and my covenant with the *n*,
Lk 2: 8 watch over their flocks at *n*.
6: 12 and spent the *n* praying to God.
Jn 3: 2 He came to Jesus at *n* and said,
9: 4 *N* is coming, when no one can work
1Th 5: 2 Lord will come like a thief in the *n*.
5: 5 We do not belong to the *n*
Rev 21: 25 for there will be no *n* there.

NIGHTS (NIGHT)
Jnh 1: 17 the fish three days and three *n*.
Mt 4: 2 After fasting forty days and forty *n*
12: 40 three *n* in the belly of a huge fish,
2Co 6: 5 in hard work, sleepless *n*

NIGHTTIME* (NIGHT)
Zec 14: 7 or *n*— a day known to the LORD.

NIMROD
Ge 10: 9 "Like *N*, a mighty hunter

NINEVEH
Jnh 1: 2 "Go to the great city of *N*
Na 1: 1 An oracle concerning *N*.
Mt 12: 41 The men of *N* will stand up

NOAH
Righteous man (Eze 14:14,20) called to build ark (Ge 6–8; Heb 11:7; 1Pe 3:20; 2Pe 2:5). God's covenant with (Ge 9:1–17). Drunkenness of (Ge 9:18–23). Blessed sons, cursed Canaan (Ge 9:24–27).

NOBLE
Ru 3: 11 you are a woman of *n* character.
Ps 45: 1 My heart is stirred by a *n* theme
Pr 12: 4 of *n* character is her husband's
31: 10 A wife of *n* character who can find?
31: 29 "Many women do *n* things,
Isa 32: 8 But the *n* man makes *n* plans,
Lk 8: 15 good soil stands for those with a *n*
Ro 9: 21 of clay some pottery for *n* purposes
Php 4: 8 whatever is *n*, whatever is right,
2Ti 2: 20 some are for *n* purposes

NOSTRILS
Ge 2: 7 and breathed into his *n* the breath
Ex 15: 8 By the blast of your *n*
Ps 18: 15 at the blast of breath from your *n*.

NOTE
Ac 4: 13 and they took *n* that these men had
Php 3: 17 take *n* of those who live according

NOTHING
2Sa 24: 24 offerings that cost me *n*."
Ne 9: 21 in the desert; they lacked *n*,
Ps 73: 25 earth has *n* I desire besides you
Jer 32: 17 *N* is too hard for you
Jn 15: 5 apart from me you can do *n*.

NOURISH
Pr 10: 21 The lips of the righteous *n* many,

NULLIFY
Mt 15: 6 Thus you *n* the word of God
Ro 3: 31 Do we, then, *n* the law by this faith

OATH
Ex 33: 1 up to the land I promised on *o*
Nu 30: 2 or takes an *o* to obligate himself
Dt 6: 18 promised on *o* to your forefathers,
7: 8 and kept the *o* he swore
29: 12 you this day and sealing with an *o*,
Ps 95: 11 So I declared on *o* in my anger,
119:106 I have taken an *o* and confirmed it,
132: 11 The LORD swore an *o* to David,
Ecc 8: 2 because you took an *o* before God.
Mt 5: 33 'Do not break your *o*, but keep
Heb 7: 20 And it was not without an *o*!

OBADIAH
1. Believer who sheltered 100 prophets from Jezebel (1Ki 18:1–16).
2. Prophet against Edom (Ob 1).

OBEDIENCE* (OBEY)
Ge 49: 10 and the *o* of the nations is his.
Jdg 2: 17 of *o* to the LORD's commands.
1Ch 21: 19 So David went up in *o*
2Ch 31: 21 in *o* to the law and the commands,
Pr 30: 17 that scorns *o* to a mother,
Lk 23: 56 Sabbath in *o* to the commandment.
Ac 21: 24 but that you yourself are living in *o*
Ro 1: 5 to the *o* that comes from faith.
5: 19 also through the *o* of the one man
6: 16 to *o*, which leads to righteousness?
16: 19 Everyone has heard about your *o*,
2Co 9: 13 for the *o* that accompanies your
10: 6 once your *o* is complete.
Phm : 21 Confident of your *o*, I write to you,
Heb 5: 8 he learned *o* from what he suffered
1Pe 1: 2 for *o* to Jesus Christ and sprinkling
2Jn : 6 that we walk in *o* to his commands.

OBEDIENT* (OBEY)
Dt 30: 17 heart turns away and you are not *o*,
Isa 1: 19 If you are willing and *o*,
Lk 2: 51 with them and was *o* to them.
Ac 6: 7 of priests became *o* to the faith.
2Co 2: 9 if you would stand the test and be *o*
7: 15 he remembers that you were all *o*,
10: 5 thought to make it *o* to Christ.
Php 2: 8 and became *o* to death—
Tit 3: 1 to be *o*, to be ready
1Pe 1: 14 As *o* children, do not conform

OBEY (OBEDIENCE OBEDIENT OBEYED OBEYING OBEYS)
Ex 12: 24 "*O* these instructions as a lasting
19: 5 Now if you *o* me fully and keep my
24: 7 the LORD has said; we will *o*."
Lev 18: 4 You must *o* my laws and be careful
25: 18 and be careful to *o* my laws,
Nu 15: 40 remember to *o* all my commands
Dt 5: 27 We will listen and *o*."
6: 3 careful to *o* so that it may go well
6: 24 us to *o* all these decrees
11: 13 if you faithfully *o* the commands I
12: 28 to *o* all these regulations I am
13: 4 Keep his commands and *o* him;
21: 18 son who does not *o* his father
28: 1 If you fully *o* the LORD your God
28: 15 if you do not *o* the LORD your
30: 2 and *o* him with all your heart
30: 10 if you *o* the LORD your God
30: 14 and in your heart so you may *o* it.
32: 46 children to *o* carefully all the words
Jos 1: 7 to *o* all the law my servant Moses
22: 5 in all his ways, to *o* his commands,
24: 24 the LORD our God and *o* him."
1Sa 15: 22 To *o* is better than sacrifice,
1Ki 8: 61 by his decrees and *o* his commands
2Ki 17: 13 that I commanded your fathers to *o*
2Ch 34: 31 and to *o* the words of the covenant
Ne 1: 5 who love him and *o* his commands,
Ps 103: 18 and remember to *o* his precepts.
103: 20 who *o* his word.
119: 17 I will *o* your word.
119: 34 and *o* it with all my heart.
119: 57 I have promised to *o* your words.
119: 67 but now I *o* your word.
119:100 for I *o* your precepts.
119:129 therefore I *o* them.
119:167 I *o* your statutes,
Pr 5: 13 I would not *o* my teachers
Jer 7: 23 I gave them this command: *O* me,
11: 4 '*O* me and do everything I
11: 7 and again, saying, "*O* me."
42: 6 we will *o* the LORD our God,
Da 9: 4 who love him and *o* his commands,
Mt 8: 27 the winds and the waves *o* him!"
19: 17 to enter life, *o* the commandments
28: 20 to *o* everything I have commanded
Lk 11: 28 hear the word of God and *o* it."
Jn 14: 15 you will *o* what I command.
14: 23 loves me, he will *o* my teaching.
14: 24 not love me will not *o* my teaching.
15: 10 If you *o* my commands, you will
Ac 5: 29 "We must *o* God rather than men!
5: 32 given to those who *o* him."
Ro 2: 13 it is those who *o* the law who will
6: 12 body so that you *o* its evil desires.
6: 16 slaves to the one whom you *o*—
6: 16 yourselves to someone to *o* him
15: 18 in leading the Gentiles to *o* God
16: 26 nations might believe and *o* him—
Gal 5: 3 obligated to *o* the whole law.
Eph 6: 1 *o* your parents in the Lord,
6: 5 *o* your earthly masters with respect
Col 3: 20 *o* your parents in everything,
3: 22 *o* your earthly masters
2Th 3: 14 anyone does not *o* our instruction
1Ti 3: 4 and see that his children *o* him
Heb 5: 9 eternal salvation for all who *o* him
13: 17 *O* your leaders and submit
1Pe 4: 17 for those who do not *o* the gospel
1Jn 3: 24 Those who *o* his commands live
5: 3 love for God: to *o* his commands.
Rev 12: 17 those who *o* God's commandments
14: 12 the saints who *o* God's

OBEYED (OBEY)
Ge 22: 18 blessed, because you have *o* me."
Jos 1: 17 we fully *o* Moses, so we will obey
Ps 119: 4 that are to be fully *o*.
Da 9: 10 we have not *o* the LORD our God
Jnh 3: 3 Jonah *o* the word of the LORD
Mic 5: 15 the nations that have not *o* me."
Jn 15: 10 as I have *o* my Father's commands
17: 20 If they *o* my teaching, they will
17: 6 and they have *o* your word.
Ac 7: 53 through angels but have not *o* it."
Ro 6: 17 you wholeheartedly *o* the form
Php 2: 12 as you have always *o*— not only
Heb 11: 8 *o* and went, even though he did not
1Pe 3: 6 who *o* Abraham and called him her

OBEYING (OBEY)
1Sa 15: 22 as in *o* the voice of the LORD?
Ps 119: 5 steadfast in *o* your decrees!
Gal 5: 7 and kept you from *o* the truth?
1Pe 1: 22 purified yourselves by *o* the truth

OBEYS (OBEY)
Lev 18: 5 for the man who *o* them will live
Pr 19: 16 He who *o* instructions guards his
Eze 20: 11 for the man who *o* them will live
Jn 14: 21 has my commands and *o* them,
Ro 2: 27 and yet *o* the law will condemn you
1Jn 2: 5 if anyone *o* his word, God's love is

OBLIGATED (OBLIGATION)
Ro 1: 14 I am *o* both to Greeks
Gal 5: 3 himself be circumcised that he is *o*

OBLIGATION (OBLIGATED)
Ro 8: 12 Therefore, brothers, we have an *o*

OBSCENITY*
Eph 5: 4 Nor should there be *o,* foolish talk

OBSCURES*
Job 42: 3 'Who is this that *o* my counsel

OBSERVE (OBSERVING)
Ex 31: 13 'You must *o* my Sabbaths.
Lev 25: 2 the land itself must *o* a sabbath
Dt 4: 6 *O* them carefully, for this will show
5: 12 "*O* the Sabbath day
8: 6 *O* the commands of the LORD
11: 22 If you carefully *o* all these
26: 16 carefully *o* them with all your heart
Ps 37: 37 the blameless, *o* the upright;

OBSERVING (OBSERVE)
Ro 3: 27 principle? On that of *o* the law?
Gal 2: 16 a man is not justified by *o* the law,
3: 2 you receive the Spirit by *o* the law,
3: 10 All who rely on *o* the law are

OBSOLETE
Heb 8: 13 he has made the first one *o;*

OBSTACLE* (OBSTACLES)
Ro 14: 13 or *o* in your brother's way.

OBSTACLES (OBSTACLE)
Ro 16: 17 put *o* in your way that are contrary

OBSTINATE
Isa 65: 2 hands to an *o* people,
Ro 10: 21 to a disobedient and *o* people."

OBTAIN (OBTAINED OBTAINS)
Ro 11: 7 sought so earnestly it did not *o,*
2Ti 2: 10 they too may *o* the salvation that

OBTAINED (OBTAIN)
Ro 9: 30 not pursue righteousness, have *o* it,
Php 3: 12 Not that I have already *o* all this,
Heb 9: 12 having *o* eternal redemption.

OBTAINS* (OBTAIN)
Pr 12: 2 A good man *o* favor

OBVIOUS*
Mt 6: 18 so that it will not be *o*
Gal 5: 19 The acts of the sinful nature are *o:*
1Ti 5: 24 The sins of some men are *o,*
5: 25 In the same way, good deeds are *o,*

OCCASIONS
Eph 6: 18 in the Spirit on all *o* with all kinds

OFFENDED (OFFENSE)
Pr 18: 19 An *o* brother is more unyielding

OFFENDERS* (OFFENSE)
1Co 6: 9 nor homosexual *o* nor thieves

OFFENSE (OFFENDED OFFENDERS OFFENSES OFFENSIVE)
Pr 17: 9 over an *o* promotes love,
19: 11 it is to his glory to overlook an *o.*
Gal 5: 11 In that case the *o* of the cross has

OFFENSES (OFFENSE)
Isa 44: 22 swept away your *o* like a cloud,
59: 12 For our *o* are many in your sight,
Eze 18: 30 Repent! Turn away from all your *o;*
33: 10 "Our *o* and sins weigh us down,

OFFENSIVE (OFFENSE)
Ps 139: 24 See if there is any *o* way in me,

OFFER (OFFERED OFFERING OFFERINGS OFFERS)
Ps 4: 5 *O* right sacrifices
Ro 6: 13 Do not *o* the parts of your body
12: 1 to *o* your bodies as living sacrifices,
Heb 9: 25 he enter heaven to *o* himself again
13: 15 therefore, let us continually *o*

OFFERED (OFFER)
Isa 50: 6 I *o* my back to those who beat me,
1Co 9: 13 share in what is *o* on the altar?
10: 20 of pagans are *o* to demons,
Heb 7: 27 once for all when he *o* himself.
9: 14 the eternal Spirit *o* himself
11: 4 By faith Abel *o* God a better
11: 17 when God tested him, *o* Isaac
Jas 5: 15 prayer *o* in faith will make the sick

OFFERING (OFFER)
Ge 4: 3 of the soil as an *o* to the LORD.
22: 2 a burnt *o* on one of the mountains I
22: 8 provide the lamb for the burnt *o,*
Ex 29: 24 before the LORD as a wave *o.*
29: 40 quarter of a hin of wine as a drink *o.*
Lev 1: 3 If the *o* is a burnt *o* from the herd,
2: 4 " 'If you bring a grain *o* baked
3: 1 " 'If someone's *o* is a fellowship *o,*
4: 3 a sin *o* for the sin he has committed
5: 15 It is a guilt *o.*
7: 37 ordination *o* and the fellowship *o,*
9: 24 and consumed the burnt *o*
22: 18 to fulfill a vow or as a freewill *o,*
22: 21 a special vow or as a freewill *o,*
1Sa 13: 9 And Saul offered up the burnt *o.*
1Ch 21: 26 from heaven on the altar of burnt *o.*
2Ch 7: 1 and consumed the burnt *o*
Ps 40: 6 Sacrifice and *o* you did not desire,
116: 17 I will sacrifice a thank *o* to you
Isa 53: 10 the LORD makes his life a guilt *o,*
Mt 5: 23 if you are *o* your gift at the altar
Ro 8: 3 likeness of sinful man to be a sin *o.*
Eph 5: 2 as a fragrant *o* and sacrifice to God.
Php 2: 17 I am being poured out like a drink *o*
4: 18 are a fragrant *o,* an acceptable
2Ti 4: 6 being poured out like a drink *o,*
Heb 10: 5 "Sacrifice and *o* you did not desire,
1Pe 2: 5 *o* spiritual sacrifices acceptable

OFFERINGS (OFFER)
1Sa 15: 22 Does the LORD delight in burnt *o*
2Ch 35: 7 and goats for the Passover *o,*
Isa 1: 13 Stop bringing meaningless *o!*
Hos 6: 6 of God rather than burnt *o.*
Mal 3: 8 do we rob you?' "In tithes and *o.*
Mk 12: 33 is more important than all burnt *o*
Heb 10: 8 First he said, "Sacrifices and *o,*

OFFERS (OFFER)
Heb 10: 11 and again he *o* the same sacrifices,

OFFICER (OFFICIALS)
2Ti 2: 4 wants to please his commanding *o.*

OFFICIALS (OFFICER)
Ex 5: 21 a stench to Pharaoh and his *o.*
Pr 17: 26 or to flog *o* for their integrity.
29: 12 all his *o* become wicked.

OFFSPRING
Ge 3: 15 and between your *o* and hers;
12: 7 "To your *o* I will give this land."
13: 16 I will make your *o* like the dust
26: 4 and through your *o* all nations
28: 14 blessed through you and your *o.*
Ex 13: 2 The first *o* of every womb
Ru 4: 12 Through the *o* the LORD gives
Isa 44: 3 I will pour out my Spirit on your *o,*
53: 10 he will see his *o* and prolong his
Ac 3: 25 'Through your *o* all peoples
17: 28 own poets have said, 'We are his *o.*'
17: 29 "Therefore since we are God's *o,*
Ro 4: 18 said to him, "So shall your *o* be."
9: 8 who are regarded as Abraham's *o.*

OG
Nu 21: 33 *O* king of Bashan and his whole
Ps 136: 20 and *O* king of Bashan—

OIL
Ex 29: 7 Take the anointing *o* and anoint
30: 25 It will be the sacred anointing *o.*
Dt 14: 23 tithe of your grain, new wine and *o,*
1Sa 10: 1 Then Samuel took a flask of *o*
16: 13 So Samuel took the horn of *o*
1Ki 17: 16 and the jug of *o* did not run dry,
2Ki 4: 6 Then the *o* stopped flowing.
Ps 23: 5 You anoint my head with *o;*
45: 7 by anointing you with the *o* of joy.
104: 15 *o* to make his face shine,
133: 2 It is like precious *o* poured
Pr 21: 17 loves wine and *o* will never be
Isa 1: 6 or soothed with *o.*
61: 3 the *o* of gladness
Mt 25: 3 but did not take any *o* with them.
Heb 1: 9 by anointing you with the *o* of joy."

OLIVE (OLIVES)
Ge 8: 11 beak was a freshly plucked *o* leaf!
Jdg 9: 8 said to the *o* tree, 'Be our king.'
Jer 11: 16 LORD called you a thriving *o* tree
Zec 4: 3 Also there are two *o* trees by it,
Ro 11: 17 and you, though a wild *o* shoot,
11: 24 of an *o* tree that is wild by nature,
Rev 11: 4 These are the two *o* trees

OLIVES (OLIVE)
Zec 14: 4 stand on the Mount of *O,*
Mt 24: 3 sitting on the Mount of *O,*
Jas 3: 12 a fig tree bear *o,* or a grapevine bear

OMEGA*
Rev 1: 8 "I am the Alpha and the *O,*"
21: 6 I am the Alpha and the *O,*
22: 13 I am the Alpha and the *O,*

OMIT*
Jer 26: 2 I command you; do not *o* a word.

OMRI
King of Israel (1Ki 16:21–26).

ONESIMUS*
Col 4: 9 He is coming with *O,* our faithful
Phm : 10 I appeal to you for my son *O,*

ONESIPHORUS*
2Ti 1: 16 mercy to the household of *O,*
4: 19 Aquila and the household of *O.*

ONIONS*
Nu 11: 5 melons, leeks, *o* and garlic.

ONYX
Ex 28: 9 "Take two *o* stones and engrave
28: 20 in the fourth row a chrysolite, an *o*

OPENHANDED* (HAND)
Dt 15: 8 Rather be *o* and freely lend him
15: 11 you to be *o* toward your brothers

OPINIONS*
1Ki 18: 21 will you waver between two *o?*
Pr 18: 2 but delights in airing his own *o.*

OPPONENTS (OPPOSE)
Pr 18: 18 and keeps strong *o* apart.

OPPORTUNE (OPPORTUNITY)
Lk 4: 13 he left him until an *o* time.

OPPORTUNITY* (OPPORTUNE)
1Sa 18: 21 "Now you have a second *o*
Jer 46: 17 he has missed his *o.*'
Mt 26: 16 watched for an *o* to hand him over.
Mk 14: 11 So he watched for an *o* to hand him
Lk 22: 6 and watched for an *o* to hand Jesus
Ac 25: 16 and has had an *o* to defend himself
Ro 7: 8 seizing the *o* afforded
7: 11 seizing the *o* afforded
1Co 16: 12 but he will go when he has the *o.*
2Co 5: 12 are giving you an *o* to take pride
11: 12 from under those who want an *o*
Gal 6: 10 as we have *o,* let us do good

Eph 5: 16 making the most of every *o,*
Php 4: 10 but you had no *o* to show it.
Col 4: 5 make the most of every *o.*
1Ti 5: 14 to give the enemy no *o* for slander.
Heb 11: 15 they would have had *o* to return.

OPPOSE (OPPONENTS OPPOSED OPPOSES OPPOSING OPPOSITION)
Ex 23: 22 and will *o* those who *o* you.
1Sa 2: 10 those who *o* the LORD will be
Job 23: 13 he stands alone, and who can *o* him
Ac 11: 17 I to think that I could *o* God?"
2Ti 2: 25 Those who *o* him he must gently
Tit 1: 9 doctrine and refute those who *o* it.
2: 8 so that those who *o* you may be

OPPOSED (OPPOSE)
Gal 2: 11 to Antioch, I *o* him to his face,
3: 21 therefore, *o* to the promises of God

OPPOSES (OPPOSE)
Jas 4: 6 "God *o* the proud
1Pe 5: 5 because, "God *o* the proud

OPPOSING (OPPOSE)
1Ti 6: 20 the *o* ideas of what is falsely called

OPPOSITION (OPPOSE)
Heb 12: 3 Consider him who endured such *o*

OPPRESS (OPPRESSED OPPRESSES OPPRESSION OPPRESSOR)
Ex 1: 11 masters over them to *o* them
22: 21 "Do not mistreat an alien or *o* him,
Isa 3: 5 People will *o* each other—
Eze 22: 29 they *o* the poor and needy
Da 7: 25 the Most High and *o* his saints
Am 5: 12 You *o* the righteous and take bribes
Zec 7: 10 Do not *o* the widow
Mal 3: 5 who *o* the widows

OPPRESSED (OPPRESS)
Jdg 2: 18 as they groaned under those who *o*
Ps 9: 9 The LORD is a refuge for the *o,*
82: 3 the rights of the poor and *o.*
146: 7 He upholds the cause of the *o*
Pr 16: 19 in spirit and among the *o*
31: 5 and deprive all the *o* of their rights.
Isa 1: 17 encourage the *o.*
53: 7 He was *o* and afflicted,
58: 10 and satisfy the needs of the *o,*
Zec 10: 2 *o* for lack of a shepherd.
Lk 4: 18 to release the *o,*

OPPRESSES (OPPRESS)
Pr 14: 31 He who *o* the poor shows contempt
22: 16 He who *o* the poor
Eze 18: 12 He *o* the poor and needy.

OPPRESSION (OPPRESS)
Ps 12: 5 "Because of the *o* of the weak
72: 14 He will rescue them from *o*
119:134 Redeem me from the *o* of men,
Isa 53: 8 By *o* and judgment he was taken
58: 9 "If you do away with the yoke of *o,*

OPPRESSOR (OPPRESS)
Ps 72: 4 he will crush the *o.*
Isa 51: 13 For where is the wrath of the *o?*
Jer 22: 3 hand of his *o* the one who has been

ORDAINED
Ps 8: 2 you have *o* praise
111: 9 he *o* his covenant forever—
139: 16 All the days *o* for me
Eze 28: 14 for so I *o* you.
Hab 1: 12 you have *o* them to punish.
Mt 21: 16 you have *o* praise'?"

ORDER (ORDERLY ORDERS)
Nu 9: 23 They obeyed the LORD's *o,*
Ps 110: 4 in the *o* of Melchizedek."
Heb 5: 10 priest in the *o* of Melchizedek.
9: 10 until the time of the new *o.*
Rev 21: 4 for the old *o* of things has passed

ORDERLY (ORDER)
1Co 14: 40 done in a fitting and *o* way.
Col 2: 5 and delight to see how *o* you are

ORDERS (ORDER)
Mk 1: 27 He even gives *o* to evil spirits
3: 12 But he gave them strict *o* not
9: 9 Jesus gave them *o* not

ORDINARY
Ac 4: 13 that they were unschooled, *o* men,

ORGIES*
Ro 13: 13 not in *o* and drunkenness,
Gal 5: 21 drunkenness, *o,* and the like.
1Pe 4: 3 *o,* carousing and detestable

ORIGIN (ORIGINATE ORIGINS)
2Pe 1: 21 For prophecy never had its *o*

ORIGINATE* (ORIGIN)
1Co 14: 36 Did the word of God *o* with you?

ORIGINS* (ORIGIN)
Mic 5: 2 whose *o* are from of old,

ORNAMENT* (ORNAMENTED)
Pr 3: 22 an *o* to grace your neck.
25: 12 of gold or an *o* of fine gold

ORNAMENTED (ORNAMENT)
Ge 37: 3 and he made a richly *o* robe for him

ORPHAN* (ORPHANS)
Ex 22: 22 advantage of a widow or an *o.*

ORPHANS (ORPHAN)
Jn 14: 18 will not leave you as *o;* I will come
Jas 1: 27 to look after *o* and widows

OTHNIEL
Nephew of Caleb (Jos 15:15–19; Jdg 1:12–15). Judge who freed Israel from Aram (Jdg 3:7–11).

OUTBURSTS*
2Co 12: 20 jealousy, *o* of anger, factions,

OUTCOME
Heb 13: 7 Consider the *o* of their way of life
1Pe 4: 17 what will the *o* be for those who do

OUTNUMBER
Ps 139: 18 they would *o* the grains of sand.

OUTSIDERS*
Col 4: 5 wise in the way you act toward *o;*
1Th 4: 12 daily life may win the respect of *o*
1Ti 3: 7 also have a good reputation with *o,*

OUTSTANDING
SS 5: 10 *o* among ten thousand.
Ro 13: 8 no debt remain *o,*

OUTSTRETCHED
Ex 6: 6 and will redeem you with an *o* arm
Dt 4: 34 by a mighty hand and an *o* arm,
5: 15 with a mighty hand and an *o* arm.
1Ki 8: 42 your mighty hand and your *o* arm
Ps 136: 12 with a mighty hand and *o* arm;
Jer 27: 5 and *o* arm I made the earth
32: 17 by your great power and *o* arm.
Eze 20: 33 an *o* arm and with outpoured wrath

OUTWEIGHS (WEIGH)
2Co 4: 17 an eternal glory that far *o* them all.

OUTWIT*
2Co 2: 11 in order that Satan might not *o* us.

OVERAWED* (AWE)
Ps 49: 16 Do not be *o* when a man grows rich

OVERBEARING*
Tit 1: 7 not *o,* not quick-tempered,

OVERCAME (OVERCOME)
Rev 3: 21 as I *o* and sat down with my Father
12: 11 They *o* him

OVERCOME (OVERCAME OVERCOMES)
Mt 16: 18 and the gates of Hades will not *o* it.
Mk 9: 24 I do believe; help me *o* my unbelief
Lk 10: 19 to *o* all the power of the enemy;
Jn 16: 33 But take heart! I have *o* the world."
Ro 12: 21 Do not be *o* by evil, but *o* evil
2Pe 2: 20 and are again entangled in it and *o,*
1Jn 2: 13 because you have *o* the evil one.
4: 4 are from God and have *o* them,
5: 4 is the victory that has *o* the world,
Rev 17: 14 but the Lamb will *o* them

OVERCOMES* (OVERCOME)
1Jn 5: 4 born of God *o* the world.
5: 5 Who is it that *o* the world?
Rev 2: 7 To him who *o,* I will give the right
2: 11 He who *o* will not be hurt at all
2: 17 To him who *o,* I will give some
2: 26 To him who *o* and does my will
3: 5 He who *o* will, like them, be
3: 12 Him who *o* I will make a pillar
3: 21 To him who *o,* I will give the right
21: 7 He who *o* will inherit all this,

OVERFLOW (OVERFLOWING OVERFLOWS)
Ps 65: 11 and your carts *o* with abundance.
119:171 May my lips *o* with praise,
La 1: 16 and my eyes *o* with tears.
Mt 12: 34 out of the *o* of the heart the mouth
Lk 6: 45 out of the *o* of his heart his mouth
Ro 5: 15 Jesus Christ, *o* to the many! Again,
15: 13 so that you may *o* with hope
2Co 4: 15 to *o* to the glory of God.
1Th 3: 12 *o* for each other and for everyone

OVERFLOWING (OVERFLOW)
Pr 3: 10 then your barns will be filled to *o,*
2Co 8: 2 their *o* joy and their extreme
9: 12 *o* in many expressions of thanks
Col 2: 7 as you were taught, and *o*

OVERFLOWS* (OVERFLOW)
Ps 23: 5 my cup *o.*
2Co 1: 5 also through Christ our comfort *o.*

OVERJOYED* (JOY)
Da 6: 23 The king was *o* and gave orders
Mt 2: 10 they saw the star, they were *o.*
Jn 20: 20 The disciples were *o*
Ac 12: 14 she was so *o* she ran back
1Pe 4: 13 so that you may be *o*

OVERLOOK
Pr 19: 11 it is to his glory to *o* an offense.

OVERSEER* (OVERSEERS)
Pr 6: 7 no *o* or ruler,
1Ti 3: 1 anyone sets his heart on being an *o,*
3: 2 Now the *o* must be above reproach,
Tit 1: 7 Since an *o* is entrusted
1Pe 2: 25 returned to the Shepherd and *O*

OVERSEERS* (OVERSEER)
Ac 20: 28 the Holy Spirit has made you *o.*
Php 1: 1 together with the *o* and deacons:
1Pe 5: 2 as *o*— not because you must,

OVERSHADOW* (OVERSHADOWING)
Lk 1: 35 power of the Most High will *o* you.

OVERSHADOWING (OVERSHADOW)
Ex 25: 20 wings spread upward, *o* the cover
Heb 9: 5 the glory, *o* the atonement cover.

OVERTHROW (OVERTHROWS)
2Th 2: 8 whom the Lord Jesus will *o*

OVERTHROWS (OVERTHROW)
Pr 13: 6 but wickedness *o* the sinner.
Isa 44: 25 who *o* the learning of the wise

OVERWHELMED (OVERWHELMING)
2Sa 22: 5 the torrents of destruction *o* me.
1Ki 10: 5 temple of the LORD, she was *o.*
Ps 38: 4 My guilt has *o* me
65: 3 When we were *o* by sins,
Mt 26: 38 "My soul is *o* with sorrow
Mk 7: 37 People were *o* with amazement.
9: 15 they were *o* with wonder
2Co 2: 7 so that he will not be *o*

OVERWHELMING (OVERWHELMED)
Pr 27: 4 Anger is cruel and fury *o,*
Isa 10: 22 *o* and righteous.
28: 15 When an *o* scourge sweeps by,

OWE
Ro 13: 7 If you *o* taxes, pay taxes; if revenue
Phm : 19 to mention that you *o* me your very

OWNER'S (OWNERSHIP)
Isa 1: 3 the donkey his *o* manger,

OWNERSHIP* (OWNER'S)
2Co 1: 22 He anointed us, set his seal of *o*

OX (OXEN)
Dt 25: 4 Do not muzzle an *o*
Isa 11: 7 and the lion will eat straw like the *o*
Eze 1: 10 and on the left the face of an *o;*
Lk 13: 15 of you on the Sabbath untie his *o*
1Co 9: 9 "Do not muzzle an *o*
1Ti 5: 18 "Do not muzzle the *o*
Rev 4: 7 second was like an *o,* the third had

OXEN (OX)
1Ki 19: 20 Elisha then left his *o* and ran
Lk 14: 19 'I have just bought five yoke of *o,*

PAGAN (PAGANS)
Mt 18: 17 as you would a *p* or a tax collector.
Lk 12: 30 For the *p* world runs

PAGANS* (PAGAN)
Isa 2: 6 and clasp hands with *p.*
Mt 5: 47 Do not even *p* do that? Be perfect,
6: 7 do not keep on babbling like *p,*
6: 32 For the *p* run after all these things,
1Co 5: 1 that does not occur even among *p:*
10: 20 but the sacrifices of *p* are offered
12: 2 You know that when you were *p,*
1Pe 2: 12 such good lives among the *p* that,
4: 3 in the past doing what *p* choose
3Jn : 7 receiving no help from the *p.*

PAID (PAY)
Isa 40: 2 that her sin has been *p* for,
Zec 11: 12 So they *p* me thirty pieces of silver.

PAIN (PAINFUL PAINS)
Ge 3: 16 with *p* you will give birth
6: 6 and his heart was filled with *p.*
Job 6: 10 my joy in unrelenting *p*—
33: 19 may be chastened on a bed of *p*
Jer 4: 19 I writhe in *p.*
15: 18 Why is my *p* unending
Mt 4: 24 suffering severe *p,*
Jn 16: 21 woman giving birth to a child has *p*
1Pe 2: 19 up under the *p* of unjust suffering
Rev 21: 4 or mourning or crying or *p,*

PAINFUL (PAIN)
Ge 3: 17 through *p* toil you will eat of it
5: 29 and *p* toil of our hands caused
Job 6: 25 How *p* are honest words!
Eze 28: 24 neighbors who are *p* briers
2Co 2: 1 I would not make another *p* visit
Heb 12: 11 seems pleasant at the time, but *p.*
1Pe 4: 12 at the *p* trial you are suffering,

PAINS (PAIN)
Ge 3: 16 "I will greatly increase your *p*
Mt 24: 8 these are the beginning of birth *p.*
Ro 8: 22 as in the *p* of childbirth right up
Gal 4: 19 again in the *p* of childbirth
1Th 5: 3 as labor *p* on a pregnant woman,

PAIRS
Ge 7: 8 *P* of clean and unclean animals,

PALACE (PALACES)
2Sa 7: 2 "Here I am, living in a *p* of cedar,
Jer 22: 6 is what the LORD says about the *p*
22: 13 "Woe to him who builds his *p*

PALACES (PALACE)
Mt 11: 8 wear fine clothes are in kings' *p.*
Lk 7: 25 and indulge in luxury are in *p.*

PALE
Isa 29: 22 no longer will their faces grow *p.*
Jer 30: 6 every face turned deathly *p?*
Da 10: 8 my face turned deathly *p*
Rev 6: 8 and there before me was a *p* horse!

PALM (PALMS)
Jn 12: 13 They took *p* branches and went out
Rev 7: 9 and were holding *p* branches

PALMS (PALM)
Isa 49: 16 you on the *p* of my hands;

PAMPERS*
Pr 29: 21 If a man *p* his servant from youth,

PANIC
Dt 20: 3 or give way to *p* before them.
1Sa 14: 15 It was a *p* sent by God.
Eze 7: 7 there is *p,* not joy,
Zec 14: 13 by the LORD with great *p.*

PANTS
Ps 42: 1 As the deer *p* for streams of water,

PARABLES
See also JESUS: PARABLES
Ps 78: 2 I will open my mouth in *p,*
Mt 13: 35 "I will open my mouth in *p,*
Lk 8: 10 but to others I speak in *p,* so that,

PARADISE*
Lk 23: 43 today you will be with me in *p.*"
2Co 12: 4 God knows—was caught up to *p.*
Rev 2: 7 of life, which is in the *p* of God.

PARALYTIC
Mt 9: 2 Some men brought to him a *p,*
Mk 2: 3 bringing to him a *p,* carried by four
Ac 9: 33 a *p* who had been bedridden

PARCHED
Ps 143: 6 my soul thirsts for you like a *p* land.

PARCHMENTS*
2Ti 4: 13 and my scrolls, especially the *p.*

PARDON* (PARDONED PARDONS)
2Ch 30: 18 *p* everyone who sets his heart
Job 7: 21 Why do you not *p* my offenses
Isa 55: 7 and to our God, for he will freely *p.*
Joel 3: 21 I will *p.*"

PARDONED* (PARDON)
Nu 14: 19 as you have *p* them from the time
Joel 3: 21 bloodguilt, which I have not *p,*

PARDONS* (PARDON)
Mic 7: 18 who *p* sin and forgives

PARENTS
Pr 17: 6 and *p* are the pride of their children
19: 14 wealth are inherited from *p,*
Mt 10: 21 children will rebel against their *p*
Lk 18: 29 left home or wife or brothers or *p*
21: 16 You will be betrayed even by *p,* brothers,
Jn 9: 3 Neither this man nor his *p* sinned,"
Ro 1: 30 they disobey their *p;* they are
2Co 12: 14 for their *p,* but *p* for their children.
Eph 6: 1 Children, obey your *p* in the Lord,
Col 3: 20 obey your *p* in everything,
1Ti 5: 4 repaying their *p* and grandparents,
2Ti 3: 2 disobedient to their *p,* ungrateful,

PARTAKE*
1Co 10: 17 for we all *p* of the one loaf.

PARTIAL* (PARTIALITY)
Pr 18: 5 It is not good to be *p* to the wicked

PARTIALITY (PARTIAL)
Lev 19: 15 do not show *p* to the poor
Dt 1: 17 Do not show *p* in judging;
10: 17 who shows no *p* and accepts no
16: 19 Do not pervert justice or show *p.*
2Ch 19: 7 our God there is no injustice or *p*
Job 32: 21 I will show *p* to no one,
34: 19 who shows no *p* to princes
Pr 24: 23 To show *p* in judging is not good:
Mal 2: 9 have shown *p* in matters of the law
Lk 20: 21 and that you do not show *p*
1Ti 5: 21 keep these instructions without *p,*

PARTICIPANTS (PARTICIPATE)
1Co 10: 20 you to be *p* with demons.

PARTICIPATE (PARTICIPANTS PARTICIPATION)
1Pe 4: 13 rejoice that you *p* in the sufferings
2Pe 1: 4 that through them you may *p*

PARTICIPATION (PARTICIPATE)
1Co 10: 16 is not the bread that we break a *p*

PARTNER (PARTNERS PARTNERSHIP)
Pr 2: 17 who has left the *p* of her youth
Mal 2: 14 though she is your *p,* the wife
1Pe 3: 7 them with respect as the weaker *p*

PARTNERS (PARTNER)
Eph 5: 7 Therefore do not be *p* with them.

PARTNERSHIP* (PARTNER)
Php 1: 5 because of your *p* in the gospel

PASS (PASSED PASSER-BY PASSING)
Ex 12: 13 and when I see the blood, I will *p*
33: 19 goodness to *p* in front of you,
1Ki 9: 8 all who *p* by will be appalled
19: 11 for the LORD is about to *p* by."
Ps 90: 10 for they quickly *p,* and we fly away.
105: 19 till what he foretold came to *p,*
Isa 31: 5 he will '*p* over' it and will rescue it
43: 2 When you *p* through the waters,
62: 10 *P* through, *p* through the gates!
Jer 22: 8 "People from many nations will *p*
La 1: 12 to you, all you who *p* by?
Da 7: 14 dominion that will not *p* away,
Am 5: 17 for I will *p* through your midst,"
Mt 24: 34 will certainly not *p* away
24: 35 Heaven and earth will *p* away,
Mk 13: 31 Heaven and earth will *p* away,
Lk 21: 33 Heaven and earth will *p* away,
1Co 13: 8 there is knowledge, it will *p* away.
Jas 1: 10 he will *p* away like a wild flower.
1Jn 2: 17 The world and its desires *p* away,

PASSED (PASS)
Ge 15: 17 a blazing torch appeared and *p*
Ex 33: 22 you with my hand until I have *p* by.
2Ch 21: 20 He *p* away, to no one's regret,
Ps 57: 1 wings until the disaster has *p.*
Lk 10: 32 saw him, *p* by on the other side.
1Co 15: 3 For what I received I *p* on to you
Heb 11: 29 By faith the people *p*

PASSER-BY* (PASS)
Pr 26: 10 is he who hires a fool or any *p.*
26: 17 is a *p* who meddles

PASSING (PASS)
1Co 7: 31 world in its present form is *p* away.
1Jn 2: 8 because the darkness is *p*

PASSION* (PASSIONATE PASSIONS)
Hos 7: 6 Their *p* smolders all night;
1Co 7: 9 better to marry than to burn with *p.*

PASSIONATE* (PASSION)
1Th 4: 5 not in *p* lust like the heathen,

PASSIONS* (PASSION)
Ro 7: 5 the sinful *p* aroused
Gal 5: 24 crucified the sinful nature with its *p*
Tit 2: 12 to ungodliness and worldly *p,*
3: 3 and enslaved by all kinds of *p*

PASSOVER
Ex 12: 11 Eat it in haste; it is the LORD's *P.*
Nu 9: 2 Have the Israelites celebrate the *P*
Dt 16: 1 celebrate the *P* of the LORD your
Jos 5: 10 the Israelites celebrated the *P.*
2Ki 23: 21 "Celebrate the *P* to the LORD
Ezr 6: 19 the exiles celebrated the *P.*
Mk 14: 12 customary to sacrifice the *P* lamb,
Lk 22: 1 called the *P,* was approaching,
1Co 5: 7 our *P* lamb, has been sacrificed.
Heb 11: 28 he kept the *P* and the sprinkling

PAST
Isa 43: 18 do not dwell on the *p.*
65: 16 For the *p* troubles will be forgotten
Ro 15: 4 in the *p* was written to teach us,
16: 25 the mystery hidden for long ages *p,*
Eph 3: 9 which for ages *p* was kept hidden
Heb 1: 1 In the *p* God spoke

PASTORS*
Eph 4: 11 and some to be *p* and teachers,

PASTURE (PASTURES)
Ps 37: 3 dwell in the land and enjoy safe *p.*
95: 7 and we are the people of his *p,*
100: 3 we are his people, the sheep of his *p*
Jer 50: 7 against the LORD, their true *p,*
Eze 34: 13 I will *p* them on the mountains
Zec 11: 4 "*P* the flock marked for slaughter.

Jn 10: 9 come in and go out, and find *p.*

PASTURES (PASTURE)
Ps 23: 2 He makes me lie down in green *p,*

PATCH
Jer 10: 5 Like a scarecrow in a melon *p,*
Mt 9: 16 No one sews a *p* of unshrunk cloth

PATH (PATHS)
Ps 16: 11 known to me the *p* of life;
27: 11 lead me in a straight *p*
119: 32 I run in the *p* of your commands,
119:105 and a light for my *p.*
Pr 2: 9 and fair—every good *p.*
12: 28 along that *p* is immortality.
15: 10 awaits him who leaves the *p;*
15: 19 the *p* of the upright is a highway.
15: 24 The *p* of life leads upward
21: 16 from the *p* of understanding
Isa 26: 7 The *p* of the righteous is level;
Jer 31: 9 on a level *p* where they will not
Mt 13: 4 fell along the *p,* and the birds came
Lk 1: 79 to guide our feet into the *p* of peace
2Co 6: 3 no stumbling block in anyone's *p,*

PATHS (PATH)
Ps 23: 3 He guides me in *p* of righteousness
25: 4 teach me your *p;*
Pr 2: 13 who leave the straight *p*
3: 6 and he will make your *p* straight.
4: 11 and lead you along straight *p.*
4: 26 Make level *p* for your feet
5: 21 and he examines all his *p.*
8: 20 along the *p* of justice,
22: 5 In the *p* of the wicked lie thorns
Isa 2: 3 so that we may walk in his *p.*"
Jer 6: 16 ask for the ancient *p,*
Mic 4: 2 so that we may walk in his *p.*"
Mt 3: 3 make straight *p* for him.' "
Ac 2: 28 to me the *p* of life;
Ro 11: 33 and his *p* beyond tracing out!
Heb 12: 13 "Make level *p* for your feet,"

PATIENCE* (PATIENT)
Pr 19: 11 A man's wisdom gives him *p;*
25: 15 Through *p* a ruler can be persuaded
Ecc 7: 8 and *p* is better than pride.
Isa 7: 13 Is it not enough to try the *p* of men?
7: 13 Will you try the *p* of my God also?
Ro 2: 4 and *p,* not realizing that God's
9: 22 bore with great *p* the objects
2Co 6: 6 understanding, *p* and kindness;
Gal 5: 22 joy, peace, *p,* kindness, goodness,
Col 1: 11 may have great endurance and *p,*
3: 12 humility, gentleness and *p.*
1Ti 1: 16 Jesus might display his unlimited *p*
2Ti 3: 10 my purpose, faith, *p,* love,
4: 2 with great *p* and careful instruction
Heb 6: 12 *p* inherit what has been promised.
Jas 5: 10 as an example of *p* in the face
2Pe 3: 15 that our Lord's *p* means salvation,

PATIENT* (PATIENCE PATIENTLY)
Ne 9: 30 For many years you were *p*
Job 6: 11 What prospects, that I should be *p?*
Pr 14: 29 A *p* man has great understanding,
15: 18 but a *p* man calms a quarrel.
16: 32 Better a *p* man than a warrior,
Mt 18: 26 'Be *p* with me,' he begged,
18: 29 'Be *p* with me, and I will pay you
Ro 12: 12 Be joyful in hope, *p* in affliction,
1Co 13: 4 Love is *p,* love is kind.
2Co 1: 6 produces in you *p* endurance
Eph 4: 2 humble and gentle; be *p,*
1Th 5: 14 help the weak, be *p* with everyone.
Jas 5: 7 Be *p,* then, brothers,
5: 7 and how *p* he is for the autumn
5: 8 You too, be *p* and stand firm,
2Pe 3: 9 He is *p* with you, not wanting
Rev 1: 9 *p* endurance that are ours in Jesus,
13: 10 This calls for *p* endurance
14: 12 This calls for *p* endurance

PATIENTLY* (PATIENT)
Ps 37: 7 still before the LORD and wait *p*
40: 1 I waited *p* for the LORD;
Isa 38: 13 I waited *p* till dawn,
Hab 3: 16 Yet I will wait *p* for the day
Ac 26: 3 I beg you to listen to me *p.*
Ro 8: 25 we do not yet have, we wait for it *p.*
Heb 6: 15 after waiting *p,* Abraham received
1Pe 3: 20 ago when God waited *p* in the days
Rev 3: 10 kept my command to endure *p,*

PATTERN
Ex 25: 40 according to the *p* shown you
Ro 5: 14 who was a *p* of the one to come.
12: 2 longer to the *p* of this world,
2Ti 1: 13 keep as the *p* of sound teaching,
Heb 8: 5 according to the *p* shown you

PAUL

Also called Saul (Ac 13:9). Pharisee from Tarsus (Ac 9:11; Php 3:5). Apostle (Gal 1). At stoning of Stephen (Ac 8:1). Persecuted Church (Ac 9:1–2; Gal 1:13). Vision of Jesus on road to Damascus (Ac 9:4–9; 26:12–18). In Arabia (Gal 1:17). Preached in Damascus; escaped death through the wall in a basket (Ac 9:19–25). In Jerusalem; sent back to Tarsus (Ac 9:26–30).

Brought to Antioch by Barnabas (Ac 11:22–26). First missionary journey to Cyprus and Galatia (Ac 13–14). Stoned at Lystra (Ac 14:19–20). At Jerusalem council (Ac 15). Split with Barnabas over Mark (Ac 15:36–41).

Second missionary journey with Silas (Ac 16–20). Called to Macedonia (Ac 16:6–10). Freed from prison in Philippi (Ac 16:16–40). In Thessalonica (Ac 17:1–9). Speech in Athens (Ac 17:16–33). In Corinth (Ac 18). In Ephesus (Ac 19). Return to Jerusalem (Ac 20). Farewell to Ephesian elders (Ac 20:13–38). Arrival in Jerusalem (Ac 21:1–26). Arrested (Ac 21:27–36). Addressed crowds (Ac 22), Sanhedrin (Ac 23:1–11). Transferred to Caesarea (Ac 23:12–35). Trial before Felix (Ac 24), Festus (Ac 25:1–12). Before Agrippa (Ac 25:13–26:32). Voyage to Rome; shipwreck (Ac 27). Arrival in Rome (Ac 28).

Epistles: Romans, 1 and 2 Corinthians, Galatians, Ephesians, Philippians, Colossians, 1 and 2 Thessalonians, 1 and 2 Timothy, Titus, Philemon.

PAVEMENT
Jn 19: 13 as the Stone *P* (which

PAY (PAID PAYMENT PAYS REPAID REPAY REPAYING)
Lev 26: 43 They will *p* for their sins
Dt 7: 12 If you *p* attention to these laws
Pr 4: 1 *p* attention and gain understanding
4: 20 My son, *p* attention to what I say;
5: 1 My son, *p* attention to my wisdom,
6: 31 if he is caught, he must *p* sevenfold,
19: 19 man must *p* the penalty;
22: 17 *P* attention and listen
24: 29 I'll *p* that man back for what he did
Eze 40: 4 and *p* attention to everything I am
Zec 11: 12 give me my *p;* but if not, keep it."
Mt 20: 2 He agreed to *p* them a denarius
22: 16 you *p* no attention to who they are.
22: 17 Is it right to *p* taxes to Caesar
Lk 3: 14 falsely—be content with your *p.*"
19: 8 I will *p* back four times the amount
Ro 13: 6 This is also why you *p* taxes,
2Pe 1: 19 you will do well to *p* attention to it,

PAYMENT (PAY)
Ps 49: 8 no *p* is ever enough—
Php 4: 18 I have received full *p* and

PAYS (PAY)
Pr 17: 13 If a man *p* back evil for good,
1Th 5: 15 sure that nobody *p* back wrong

PEACE (PEACEABLE PEACEFUL PEACEMAKERS)
Lev 26: 6 " 'I will grant *p* in the land,
Nu 6: 26 and give you *p.*" '
25: 12 him I am making my covenant of *p*
Dt 20: 10 make its people an offer of *p.*
Jdg 3: 11 So the land had *p* for forty years,
3: 30 and the land had *p* for eighty years.
5: 31 Then the land had *p* forty years.
6: 24 and called it The LORD is *P.*
8: 28 the land enjoyed *p* forty years.
1Sa 7: 14 And there was *p* between Israel
2Sa 10: 19 they made *p* with the Israelites
1Ki 2: 33 may there be the LORD's *p* forever
22: 44 also at *p* with the king of Israel.
2Ki 9: 17 come in *p?'* " The horseman rode
1Ch 19: 19 they made *p* with David
22: 9 and I will grant Israel *p*
2Ch 14: 1 and in his days the country was at *p*
20: 30 kingdom of Jehoshaphat was at *p,*
Job 3: 26 I have no *p,* no quietness;
22: 21 to God and be at *p* with him;
Ps 29: 11 LORD blesses his people with *p.*
34: 14 seek *p* and pursue it.
37: 11 and enjoy great *p.*
37: 37 there is a future for the man of *p.*
85: 10 righteousness and *p* kiss each other
119:165 Great *p* have they who love your
120: 7 I am a man of *p;*
122: 6 Pray for the *p* of Jerusalem:
147: 14 He grants *p* to your borders
Pr 12: 20 but joy for those who promote *p.*
14: 30 A heart at *p* gives life to the body,
16: 7 his enemies live at *p* with him.
17: 1 Better a dry crust with *p* and quiet
Ecc 3: 8 a time for war and a time for *p.*
Isa 9: 6 Everlasting Father, Prince of *P.*
14: 7 All the lands are at rest and at *p;*
26: 3 You will keep in perfect *p*
32: 17 The fruit of righteousness will be *p;*
48: 18 your *p* would have been like a river,
48: 22 "There is no *p,*" says the LORD,
52: 7 who proclaim *p,*
53: 5 punishment that brought us *p* was
54: 10 nor my covenant of *p* be removed,"
55: 12 and be led forth in *p;*
57: 2 enter into *p;*
57: 19 *P, p,* to those far and near,"
57: 21 "There is no *p,*" says my God,
59: 8 The way of *p* they do not know;
Jer 6: 14 '*P, p,*' they say,
8: 11 "*P, p,*" . . . there is no *p.*
30: 10 Jacob will again have *p*
46: 27 Jacob will again have *p*
Eze 13: 10 "*P,*" when there is no *p,*
34: 25 " 'I will make a covenant of *p*
37: 26 I will make a covenant of *p*
Mic 5: 5 And he will be their *p.*
Zec 8: 19 Therefore love truth and *p.*"
9: 10 He will proclaim *p* to the nations.
Mal 2: 5 a covenant of life and *p,*
2: 6 He walked with me in *p*
Mt 10: 34 I did not come to bring *p,*
Mk 9: 50 and be at *p* with each other."
Lk 1: 79 to guide our feet into the path of *p*
2: 14 on earth *p* to men on whom his
19: 38 "*P* in heaven and glory
Jn 14: 27 *P* I leave with you; my *p*
16: 33 so that in me you may have *p.*
Ro 1: 7 and *p* to you from God our Father
2: 10 and *p* for everyone who does good:
5: 1 we have *p* with God
8: 6 by the Spirit is life and *p;*
12: 18 on you, live at *p* with everyone.
14: 19 effort to do what leads to *p*
1Co 7: 15 God has called us to live in *p.*
14: 33 a God of disorder but of *p.*
2Co 13: 11 be of one mind, live in *p.*
Gal 5: 22 joy, *p,* patience, kindness,
Eph 2: 14 he himself is our *p,* who has made
2: 15 thus making *p,* and in this one body
2: 17 and *p* to those who were near.

6: 15 comes from the gospel of *p.*
Php 4: 7 the *p* of God, which transcends all
Col 1: 20 by making *p* through his blood,
3: 15 Let the *p* of Christ rule
3: 15 of one body you were called to *p.*
1Th 5: 3 While people are saying, "*P*
5: 13 Live in *p* with each other.
5: 23 the God of *p,* sanctify you through
2Th 3: 16 the Lord of *p* himself give you *p*
2Ti 2: 22 righteousness, faith, love and *p,*
Heb 7: 2 "king of Salem" means "king of *p.*"
12: 11 *p* for those who have been trained
12: 14 effort to live in *p* with all men
13: 20 May the God of *p,* who
1Pe 3: 11 he must seek *p* and pursue it.
2Pe 3: 14 blameless and at *p* with him.
Rev 6: 4 power to take *p* from the earth

PEACEABLE* (PEACE)
Tit 3: 2 to slander no one, to be *p*

PEACEFUL (PEACE)
1Ti 2: 2 that we may live *p* and quiet lives

PEACE-LOVING
Jas 3: 17 then *p,* considerate

PEACEMAKERS* (PEACE)
Mt 5: 9 Blessed are the *p,*
Jas 3: 18 *P* who sow in peace raise a harvest

PEARL* (PEARLS)
Rev 21: 21 each gate made of a single *p.*

PEARLS (PEARL)
Mt 7: 6 do not throw your *p* to pigs.
13: 45 like a merchant looking for fine *p.*
1Ti 2: 9 or gold or *p* or expensive clothes,
Rev 21: 21 The twelve gates were twelve *p,*

PEDDLE*
2Co 2: 17 we do not *p* the word of God

PEG
Jdg 4: 21 She drove the *p* through his temple

PEKAH
King of Israel (2Ki 15:25–31; Isa 7:1).

PEKAHIAH*
Son of Menahem; king of Israel (2Ki 15:22–26).

PEN
Ps 45: 1 my tongue is the *p*
Mt 5: 18 letter, not the least stroke of a *p,*
Jn 10: 1 who does not enter the sheep *p*

PENETRATES*
Heb 4: 12 it *p* even to dividing soul and spirit,

PENNIES* (PENNY)
Lk 12: 6 not five sparrows sold for two *p?*

PENNY* (PENNIES)
Mt 5: 26 out until you have paid the last *p.*
10: 29 Are not two sparrows sold for a *p?*
Mk 12: 42 worth only a fraction of a *p.*
Lk 12: 59 out until you have paid the last *p.*"

PENTECOST*
Ac 2: 1 of *P* came, they were all together
20: 16 if possible, by the day of *P.*
1Co 16: 8 I will stay on at Ephesus until *P,*

PEOPLE (PEOPLES)
Ge 11: 6 as one *p* speaking the same
Ex 5: 1 Let my *p* go,
6: 7 take you as my own *p,*
8: 23 between my *p* and your *p.*
15: 13 the *p* you have redeemed.
19: 8 The *p* all responded together,
24: 3 Moses went and told the *p*
32: 1 When the *p* saw that Moses
32: 9 they are a stiff-necked *p.*
33: 13 this nation is your *p.*
Lev 9: 7 for yourself and the *p:*
16: 24 the burnt offering for the *p,*
26: 12 and you will be my *p.*
Nu 11: 11 burden of all these *p* on
14: 11 *p* treat me with contempt?
14: 19 forgive the sin of these *p,*
22: 5 A *p* has come out of Egypt
Dt 4: 6 a wise and understanding *p.*
4: 20 the *p* of his inheritance,
5: 28 what this *p* said to you.
7: 6 a *p* holy to the LORD
26: 18 that you are his *p,*
31: 7 you must go with this *p*
31: 16 these *p* will soon prostitute
32: 9 the LORD's portion is his *p,*
32: 43 atonement for his land and *p.*
33: 29 a *p* saved by the LORD?
Jos 1: 6 you will lead this *p*
24: 24 the *p* said to Joshua,
Jdg 2: 7 *p* served the LORD throughout
Ru 1: 16 Your *p* will be my *p*
1Sa 8: 7 the *p* are saying to you;
12: 22 LORD will not reject his *p,*
2Sa 5: 2 will shepherd my *p* Israel
7: 10 provide a place for my *p*
1Ki 3: 8 among the *p* you have chosen,
8: 30 your *p* Israel when they pray
8: 56 has given rest to his *p*
18: 39 when all the *p* saw this,
2Ki 23: 3 all the *p* pledged themselves
1Ch 17: 21 to redeem *p* for himself
29: 17 how willingly your *p* who are
2Ch 2: 11 Because the LORD loves his *p,*
7: 5 *p* dedicated the temple
7: 14 if my *p,* who are called
30: 6 "*P* of Israel, return to
36: 16 was aroused against his *p*
Ezr 2: 1 These are the *p* of the
3: 1 *p* assembled as one man
Ne 1: 10 your *p,* whom you redeemed
4: 6 *p* worked with all their heart
8: 1 *p* assembled as one man
Est 3: 6 to destroy all Mordecai's *p,*
Job 12: 2 Doubtless you are the *p,*
Ps 29: 11 gives strength to his *p;*
33: 12 *p* he chose for his inheritance
50: 4 that he may judge his *p*
53: 6 restores the fortunes of his *p,*
81: 13 If my *p* would but listen
94: 14 LORD will not reject his *p;*
95: 7 we are the *p* of his pasture,
95: 10 a *p* whose hearts go astray,
125: 2 the LORD surrounds his *p*
135: 14 LORD will vindicate his *p*
144: 15 *p* whose God is the LORD.
Pr 14: 34 sin is a disgrace to any *p.*
29: 2 righteous thrive, the *p* rejoice
29: 18 the *p* cast off restraint
Isa 1: 3 my *p* do not understand.
1: 4 a *p* loaded with guilt,
5: 13 my *p* will go into exile
6: 10 the heart of this *p* calloused;
9: 2 the *p* walking in darkness
12: 12 will assemble the scattered *p*
19: 25 Blessed be Egypt my *p,*
25: 8 remove the disgrace of his *p*
29: 13 These *p* come near to me
40: 1 Comfort, comfort my *p*
40: 7 Surely the *p* are grass.
42: 6 a covenant for the *p*
49: 13 the LORD comforts his *p*
51: 4 "Listen to me, my *p;*
52: 6 my *p* will know my name;
53: 8 for the transgression of my *p*
60: 21 will all your *p* be righteous
62: 12 will be called the Holy *P,*
65: 23 they will be a *p* blessed
Jer 2: 11 my *p* have exchanged their
2: 13 *p* have committed two sins:
2: 32 my *p* have forgotten me,
4: 22 My *p* are fools;
5: 14 Because the *p* have spoken
5: 31 my *p* love it this way
7: 16 do not pray for this *p*
7: 23 you will be my *p,*
18: 15 my *p* have forgotten me;
30: 3 I will bring my *p* Israel
Eze 13: 23 I will save my *p* from
36: 8 fruit for my *p* Israel,
36: 28 you will be my *p,*
36: 38 be filled with flocks of *p.*
37: 13 Then you, my *p,* will know
38: 14 *p* Israel are living in safety
39: 7 name among my *p* Israel.
Da 7: 27 saints, the *p* of the Most High.
8: 24 mighty men and the holy *p*
9: 19 your *p* bear your name
9: 24 are decreed for your *p*
9: 26 *p* of the ruler who will come
10: 14 will happen to your *p*
11: 32 *p* who know their God will
12: 1 prince who protects your *p.*
Hos 1: 10 'You are not my *p,*'
2: 23 'You are my *p*';
4: 14 a *p* without understanding
Joel 2: 18 and take pity on his *p.*
3: 16 be a refuge for his *p,*
Am 9: 14 back my exiled *p* Israel;
Mic 6: 2 a case against his *p;*
7: 14 Shepherd your *p* with
Hag 1: 12 remnant of the *p* obeyed
Zec 2: 11 and will become my *p.*
8: 7 I will save my *p*
13: 9 will say, 'They are my *p,*'
Mk 7: 6 *p* honor me with their lips
8: 27 "Who do *p* say I am?"
Lk 1: 17 make ready a *p* prepared
1: 68 and has redeemed his *p.*
2: 10 joy that will be for all the *p.*
21: 23 and wrath against this *p.*
Jn 11: 50 one man die for the *p*
18: 14 if one man died for the *p.*
Ac 15: 14 from the Gentiles a *p.*
18: 10 have many *p* in this city.
Ro 9: 25 will call them 'my *p.*'
11: 1 Did God reject his *p?*
15: 10 O Gentiles, with his *p.*"
2Co 6: 16 and they will be my *p.*"
Tit 2: 14 a *p* that are his very own,
Heb 2: 17 for the sins of the *p.*
4: 9 a Sabbath-rest for the *p*
5: 3 for the sins of the *p.*
10: 30 Lord will judge his *p.*
11: 25 mistreated along with the *p*
13: 12 to make the *p* holy
1Pe 2: 9 you are a chosen *p,*
2: 10 Once you were not a *p,*
2: 10 you are the *p* of God;
2Pe 2: 1 false prophets among the *p,*
3: 11 kind of *p* ought you to be?
Rev 18: 4 "Come out of her, my *p,*
21: 3 They will be his *p,*

PEOPLES (PEOPLE)
Ge 17: 16 kings of *p* will come from her
25: 23 two *p* from within you will
27: 29 and *p* bow down to you
28: 3 become a community of *p.*
48: 4 you a community of *p.*
Dt 14: 2 of all the *p* on the face of
28: 10 Then all the *p* on earth
32: 8 set up boundaries for the *p*
Jos 4: 24 all the *p* of the earth might
1Ki 8: 43 all the *p* of the earth may
2Ch 7: 20 of ridicule among all *p.*
Ps 9: 8 he will govern the *p*
67: 5 may all the *p* praise you.
87: 6 in the register of the *p:*
96: 10 he will judge the *p*
Isa 2: 4 settle disputes for many *p.*
17: 12 Oh, the uproar of the *p*—
25: 6 of rich food for all *p,*
34: 1 pay attention, you *p!*
55: 4 him a witness to the *p,*
Jer 10: 3 customs of the *p* are worthless

Da 7: 14 all *p,* nations and men
Mic 4: 1 and *p* will stream to it.
4: 3 will judge between many *p*
5: 7 in the midst of many *p*
Zep 3: 9 purify the lips of the *p,*
3: 20 among all the *p* of the
Zec 8: 20 Many *p* and the inhabitants
12: 2 all the surrounding *p* reeling.
Rev 10: 11 prophesy again about many *p,*
17: 15 the prostitute sits, are *p,*

PEOR
Nu 25: 3 joined in worshiping the Baal of *P.*
Dt 4: 3 who followed the Baal of *P,*

PERCEIVE (PERCEIVING)
Ps 139: 2 you *p* my thoughts from afar.
Pr 24: 12 not he who weighs the heart *p* it?

PERCEIVING* (PERCEIVE)
Isa 6: 9 be ever seeing, but never *p.'*
Mt 13: 14 you will be ever seeing but never *p.*
Mk 4: 12 may be ever seeing but never *p,*
Ac 28: 26 you will be ever seeing but never *p*

PERFECT* (PERFECTER PERFECTING PERFECTION)
Dt 32: 4 He is the Rock, his works are *p,*
2Sa 22: 31 "As for God, his way is *p;*
22: 33 and makes my way *p.*
Job 36: 4 one *p* in knowledge is with you.
37: 16 of him who is *p* in knowledge?
Ps 18: 30 As for God, his way is *p;*
18: 32 and makes my way *p.*
19: 7 The law of the LORD is *p,*
50: 2 From Zion, *p* in beauty,
64: 6 "We have devised a *p* plan!"
SS 6: 9 but my dove, my *p* one, is unique,
Isa 25: 1 for in *p* faithfulness
26: 3 You will keep in *p* peace
Eze 16: 14 had given you made your beauty *p,*
27: 3 "I am *p* in beauty."
28: 12 full of wisdom and *p* in beauty.
Mt 5: 48 Do not even pagans do that? Be *p,*
5: 48 as your heavenly Father is *p.*
19: 21 answered, "If you want to be *p,*
Ro 12: 2 his good, pleasing and *p* will.
2Co 12: 9 for my power is made *p*
Php 3: 12 or have already been made *p,*
Col 1: 28 so that we may present everyone *p*
3: 14 binds them all together in *p* unity.
Heb 2: 10 the author of their salvation *p*
5: 9 what he suffered and, once made *p,*
7: 19 useless (for the law made nothing *p*
7: 28 who has been made *p* forever.
9: 11 and more *p* tabernacle that is not
10: 1 make *p* those who draw
10: 14 he has made *p* forever those who
11: 40 with us would they be made *p.*
12: 23 spirits of righteous men made *p,*
Jas 1: 17 Every good and *p* gift is from above
1: 25 into the *p* law that gives freedom,
3: 2 he is a *p* man, able
1Jn 4: 18 But *p* love drives out fear,
4: 18 The one who fears is not made *p*

PERFECTER* (PERFECT)
Heb 12: 2 the author and *p* of our faith,

PERFECTING* (PERFECT)
2Co 7: 1 *p* holiness out of reverence for God

PERFECTION* (PERFECT)
Ps 119: 96 To all *p* I see a limit;
La 2: 15 the *p* of beauty,
Eze 27: 4 builders brought your beauty to *p.*
27: 11 they brought your beauty to *p.*
28: 12 " 'You were the model of *p,*
1Co 13: 10 but when *p* comes, the imperfect
2Co 13: 9 and our prayer is for your *p.*
13: 11 Aim for *p,* listen to my appeal,
Heb 7: 11 If *p* could have been attained

PERFORM (PERFORMED PERFORMS)
Ex 3: 20 with all the wonders that I will *p*
2Sa 7: 23 to *p* great and awesome wonders
Jn 3: 2 no one could *p* the miraculous

PERFORMED (PERFORM)
Mt 11: 21 If the miracles that were *p*
Jn 10: 41 John never *p* a miraculous

PERFORMS (PERFORM)
Ps 77: 14 You are the God who *p* miracles;

PERFUME
Ecc 7: 1 A good name is better than fine *p,*
SS 1: 3 your name is like *p* poured out.
Mk 14: 3 jar of very expensive *p,*

PERIL
2Co 1: 10 us from such a deadly *p,*

PERISH (PERISHABLE PERISHED PERISHES PERISHING)
Ge 6: 17 Everything on earth will *p.*
Est 4: 16 And if I *p,* I *p."*
Ps 1: 6 but the way of the wicked will *p.*
37: 20 But the wicked will *p:*
73: 27 Those who are far from you will *p;*
102: 26 They will *p,* but you remain;
Pr 11: 10 when the wicked *p,* there are
19: 9 and he who pours out lies will *p.*
21: 28 A false witness will *p,*
28: 28 when the wicked *p,* the righteous
Isa 1: 28 who forsake the LORD will *p.*
29: 14 the wisdom of the wise will *p,*
60: 12 that will not serve you will *p;*
Zec 11: 9 the dying die, and the perishing *p.*
Lk 13: 3 unless you repent, you too will all *p*
13: 5 unless you repent, you too will all *p*
21: 18 But not a hair of your head will *p.*
Jn 3: 16 whoever believes in him shall not *p*
10: 28 eternal life, and they shall never *p;*
Ro 2: 12 apart from the law will also *p* apart
Col 2: 22 These are all destined to *p* with use,
2Th 2: 10 They *p* because they refused
Heb 1: 11 They will *p,* but you remain;
1Pe 1: 4 into an inheritance that can never *p*
2Pe 3: 9 not wanting anyone to *p,*

PERISHABLE (PERISH)
1Co 15: 42 The body that is sown is *p,*
1Pe 1: 18 not with *p* things such
1: 23 not of *p* seed, but of imperishable,

PERISHED (PERISH)
Ps 119: 92 I would have *p* in my affliction.

PERISHES (PERISH)
Job 8: 13 so *p* the hope of the godless.
1Pe 1: 7 which *p* even though refined by fire

PERISHING (PERISH)
1Co 1: 18 foolishness to those who are *p,*
2Co 2: 15 being saved and those who are *p.*
4: 3 it is veiled to those who are *p.*

PERJURERS* (PERJURY)
Mal 3: 5 and *p,* against those who defraud
1Ti 1: 10 for slave traders and liars and *p*—

PERJURY* (PERJURERS)
Jer 7: 9 murder, commit adultery and *p,*

PERMANENT
Heb 7: 24 lives forever, he has a *p* priesthood.

PERMISSIBLE (PERMIT)
1Co 6: 12 "Everything is *p* for me"—
10: 23 "Everything is *p*"— but not

PERMIT (PERMISSIBLE PERMITTED)
Hos 5: 4 "Their deeds do not *p* them
1Ti 2: 12 I do not *p* a woman to teach

PERMITTED (PERMIT)
Mt 19: 8 Moses *p* you to divorce your wives
2Co 12: 4 things that man is not *p* to tell.

PERSECUTE (PERSECUTED PERSECUTION PERSECUTIONS)
Ps 119: 86 for men *p* me without cause.
Mt 5: 11 *p* you and falsely say all kinds
5: 44 and pray for those who *p* you,
Jn 15: 20 they persecuted me, they will *p* you
Ac 9: 4 why do you *p* me?" "Who are you,
Ro 12: 14 Bless those who *p* you; bless

PERSECUTED (PERSECUTE)
Mt 5: 10 Blessed are those who are *p*
5: 12 same way they *p* the prophets who
Jn 15: 20 If they *p* me, they will persecute
1Co 4: 12 when we are *p,* we endure it;
15: 9 because I *p* the church of God.
2Co 4: 9 in despair; *p,* but not abandoned;
1Th 3: 4 kept telling you that we would be *p.*
2Ti 3: 12 life in Christ Jesus will be *p,*
Heb 11: 37 destitute, *p* and mistreated—

PERSECUTION (PERSECUTE)
Mt 13: 21 When trouble or *p* comes
Ro 8: 35 or hardship or *p* or famine

PERSECUTIONS (PERSECUTE)
Mk 10: 30 and with them, *p)* and in the age
2Co 12: 10 in hardships, in *p,* in difficulties.
2Th 1: 4 faith in all the *p* and trials you are
2Ti 3: 11 love, endurance, *p,* sufferings—

PERSEVERANCE* (PERSEVERE)
Ro 5: 3 we know that suffering produces *p;*
5: 4 *p,* character; and character, hope.
2Co 12: 12 were done among you with great *p.*
2Th 1: 4 churches we boast about your *p*
3: 5 into God's love and Christ's *p.*
Heb 12: 1 run with *p* the race marked out
Jas 1: 3 the testing of your faith develops *p.*
1: 4 *P* must finish its work
5: 11 You have heard of Job's *p*
2Pe 1: 6 *p;* and to *p,* godliness;
Rev 2: 2 your hard work and your *p.*
2: 19 and faith, your service and *p,*

PERSEVERE* (PERSEVERANCE PERSEVERED PERSEVERES PERSEVERING)
1Ti 4: 16 *P* in them, because if you do,
Heb 10: 36 You need to *p* so that

PERSEVERED* (PERSEVERE)
Heb 11: 27 he *p* because he saw him who is
Jas 5: 11 consider blessed those who have *p.*
Rev 2: 3 You have *p* and have endured

PERSEVERES* (PERSEVERE)
1Co 13: 7 trusts, always hopes, always *p.*
Jas 1: 12 Blessed is the man who *p*

PERSEVERING* (PERSEVERE)
Lk 8: 15 retain it, and by *p* produce a crop.

PERSIANS
Da 6: 15 law of the Medes and *P* no decree

PERSISTENCE*
Ro 2: 7 To those who by *p*

PERSUADE (PERSUADED PERSUASIVE)
Ac 18: 4 trying to *p* Jews and Greeks.
2Co 5: 11 is to fear the Lord, we try to *p* men.

PERSUADED (PERSUADE)
Ro 4: 21 being fully *p* that God had power

PERSUASIVE (PERSUADE)
1Co 2: 4 not with wise and *p* words,

PERVERSION* (PERVERT)
Lev 18: 23 sexual relations with it; that is a *p.*
20: 12 What they have done is a *p;*
Ro 1: 27 the due penalty for their *p.*
Jude : 7 up to sexual immorality and *p.*

PERVERT (PERVERSION PERVERTED PERVERTS)
Ex 23: 2 do not *p* justice by siding
Dt 16: 19 Do not *p* justice or show partiality.
Job 34: 12 that the Almighty would *p* justice.
Pr 17: 23 to *p* the course of justice.
Gal 1: 7 are trying to *p* the gospel of Christ.

PERVERTED (PERVERT)
1Sa 8: 3 and accepted bribes and *p* justice.

PERVERTS* (PERVERT)
1Ti 1: 10 for murderers, for adulterers and *p,*

PESTILENCE (PESTILENCES)
Ps 91: 6 nor the *p* that stalks in the darkness

PESTILENCES (PESTILENCE)
Lk 21: 11 famines and *p* in various places,

PETER
Apostle, brother of Andrew, also called Simon (Mt 10:2; Mk 3:16; Lk 6:14; Ac 1:13), and Cephas (Jn 1:42). Confession of Christ (Mt 16:13–20; Mk 8:27–30; Lk 9:18–27). At transfiguration (Mt 17:1–8; Mk 9:2–8; Lk 9:28–36; 2Pe 1:16–18). Caught fish with coin (Mt 17:24–27). Denial of Jesus predicted (Mt 26:31–35; Mk 14:27–31; Lk 22:31–34; Jn 13:31–38). Denied Jesus (Mt 26:69–75; Mk 14:66–72; Lk 22:54–62; Jn 18:15–27). Commissioned by Jesus to shepherd his flock (Jn 21:15–23).
Speech at Pentecost (Ac 2). Healed beggar (Ac 3:1–10). Speech at temple (Ac 3:11–26), before Sanhedrin (Ac 4:1–22). In Samaria (Ac 8:14–25). Sent by vision to Cornelius (Ac 10). Announced salvation of Gentiles in Jerusalem (Ac 11; 15). Freed from prison (Ac 12). Inconsistency at Antioch (Gal 2:11–21). At Jerusalem Council (Ac 15).
Epistles: 1–2 Peter.

PETITION (PETITIONS)
1Ch 16: 4 to make *p*, to give thanks,
Php 4: 6 by prayer and *p*, with thanksgiving,

PETITIONS (PETITION)
Heb 5: 7 he offered up prayers and *p*

PHANTOM*
Ps 39: 6 Man is a mere *p* as he goes to

PHARAOH (PHARAOH'S)
Ge 12: 15 her to *P*, and she was taken
41: 14 So *P* sent for Joseph, and he was
Ex 14: 4 glory for myself through *P*
14: 17 And I will gain glory through *P*

PHARAOH'S (PHARAOH)
Ex 7: 3 But I will harden *P* heart, and

PHARISEE (PHARISEES)
Ac 23: 6 brothers, I am a *P*, the son of a *P*.
Php 3: 5 in regard to the law, a *P*; as for zeal,

PHARISEES (PHARISEE)
Mt 5: 20 surpasses that of the *P*
16: 6 guard against the yeast of the *P*
23: 13 of the law and *P*, you hypocrites!
Jn 3: 1 a man of the *P* named Nicodemus,

PHILADELPHIA
Rev 3: 7 the angel of the church in *P* write:

PHILEMON*
Phm : 1 To *P* our dear friend and fellow

PHILIP
1. Apostle (Mt 10:3; Mk 3:18; Lk 6:14; Jn 1:43–48; 14:8; Ac 1:13).
2. Deacon (Ac 6:1–7); evangelist in Samaria (Ac 8:4–25), to Ethiopian (Ac 8:26–40).

PHILIPPI
Ac 16: 12 From there we traveled to *P*,
Php 1: 1 To all the saints in Christ Jesus at *P*

PHILISTINE (PHILISTINES)
Jos 13: 3 of the five *P* rulers in Gaza,
1Sa 14: 1 let's go over to the *P* outpost
17: 26 is this uncircumcised *P* that he
17: 37 me from the hand of this *P*."

PHILISTINES (PHILISTINE)
Jdg 10: 7 them into the hands of the *P*
13: 1 the hands of the *P* for forty years.
16: 5 The rulers of the *P* went to her
1Sa 4: 1 at Ebenezer, and the *P* at Aphek.
5: 8 together all the rulers of the *P*
13: 23 a detachment of *P* had gone out
17: 1 the *P* gathered their forces for war
23: 1 the *P* are fighting against Keilah
27: 1 is to escape to the land of the *P*.
31: 1 Now the *P* fought against Israel;
2Sa 5: 17 When the *P* heard that David had
8: 1 David defeated the *P* and subdued
21: 15 there was a battle between the *P*
2Ki 18: 8 he defeated the *P*, as far as Gaza
Am 1: 8 Ekron till the last of the *P* is dead,"

PHILOSOPHER* (PHILOSOPHY)
1Co 1: 20 Where is the *p* of this age?

PHILOSOPHY* (PHILOSOPHER)
Col 2: 8 through hollow and deceptive *p*,

PHINEHAS
Nu 25: 7 When *P* son of Eleazar, the son
Ps 106: 30 But *P* stood up and intervened,

PHOEBE*
Ro 16: 1 I commend to you our sister *P*,

PHYLACTERIES*
Mt 23: 5 They make their *p* wide

PHYSICAL
Ro 2: 28 merely outward and *p*.
Col 1: 22 by Christ's *p* body through death
1Ti 4: 8 For *p* training is of some value,
Jas 2: 16 but does nothing about his *p* needs,

PICK (PICKED)
Mk 16: 18 they will *p* up snakes

PICKED (PICK)
Lk 14: 7 noticed how the guests *p* the places
Jn 5: 9 he *p* up his mat and walked.

PIECE (PIECES)
Jn 19: 23 woven in one *p* from top to bottom.

PIECES (PIECE)
Ge 15: 17 and passed between the *p*.
Jer 34: 18 and then walked between its *p*.
Zec 11: 12 So they paid me thirty *p* of silver.
Mt 14: 20 of broken *p* that were left over.

PIERCE (PIERCED)
Ex 21: 6 and *p* his ear with an awl.
Pr 12: 18 Reckless words *p* like a sword,
Lk 2: 35 a sword will *p* your own soul too."

PIERCED (PIERCE)
Ps 22: 16 they have *p* my hands and my feet.
40: 6 but my ears you have *p*;
Isa 53: 5 But he was *p* for our transgressions,
Zec 12: 10 look on me, the one they have *p*,
Jn 19: 37 look on the one they have *p*."
Rev 1: 7 even those who *p* him;

PIG'S (PIGS)
Pr 11: 22 Like a gold ring in a *p* snout

PIGEONS
Lev 5: 11 afford two doves or two young *p*,
Lk 2: 24 "a pair of doves or two young *p*."

PIGS (PIG'S)
Mt 7: 6 do not throw your pearls to *p*.
Mk 5: 11 A large herd of *p* was feeding on

PILATE
Governor of Judea. Questioned Jesus (Mt 27:1–26; Mk 15:15; Lk 22:66–23:25; Jn 18:28–19:16); sent him to Herod (Lk 23:6–12); consented to his crucifixion when crowds chose Barabbas (Mt 27:15–26; Mk 15:6–15; Lk 23:13–25; Jn 19:1–10).

PILLAR (PILLARS)
Ge 19: 26 and she became a *p* of salt.
Ex 13: 21 ahead of them in a *p* of cloud
1Ti 3: 15 the *p* and foundation of the truth.
Rev 3: 12 who overcomes I will make a *p*

PILLARS (PILLAR)
Gal 2: 9 and John, those reputed to be *p*,

PINIONS
Dt 32: 11 and carries them on its *p*.

PISGAH
Dt 3: 27 Go up to the top of *P* and look west

PIT
Ps 7: 15 falls into the *p* he has made.
40: 2 He lifted me out of the slimy *p*,
103: 4 who redeems your life from the *p*
Pr 23: 27 for a prostitute is a deep *p*
26: 27 If a man digs a *p*, he will fall into it;
Isa 24: 17 Terror and *p* and snare await you,
38: 17 me from the *p* of destruction;
Mt 15: 14 a blind man, both will fall into a *p*."

PITCH
Ge 6: 14 and coat it with *p* inside and out.
Ex 2: 3 and coated it with tar and *p*.

PITIED (PITY)
1Co 15: 19 we are to be *p* more than all men.

PITY (PITIED)
Ps 72: 13 He will take *p* on the weak
Ecc 4: 10 But *p* the man who falls
Lk 10: 33 when he saw him, he took *p* on him

PLAGUE (PLAGUED PLAGUES)
2Ch 6: 28 "When famine or *p* comes
Ps 91: 6 nor the *p* that destroys at midday.

PLAGUED* (PLAGUE)
Ps 73: 5 they are not *p* by human ills.
73: 14 All day long I have been *p*;

PLAGUES (PLAGUE)
Hos 13: 14 Where, O death, are your *p*?
Rev 21: 9 full of the seven last *p* came
22: 18 to him the *p* described in this book.

PLAIN
Isa 40: 4 the rugged places a *p*.
Ro 1: 19 what may be known about God is *p*

PLAN (PLANNED PLANS)
Ex 26: 30 according to the *p* shown you
Job 42: 2 no *p* of yours can be thwarted.
Pr 14: 22 those who *p* what is good find love
21: 30 is no wisdom, no insight, no *p*
Am 3: 7 nothing without revealing his *p*
Eph 1: 11 predestined according to the *p*

PLANK
Mt 7: 3 attention to the *p* in your own eye?
Lk 6: 41 attention to the *p* in your own eye?

PLANNED (PLAN)
Ps 40: 5 The things you *p* for us
Isa 14: 24 "Surely, as I have *p*, so it will be,
23: 9 The LORD Almighty *p* it,
46: 11 what I have *p*, that will I do.
Heb 11: 40 God had *p* something better for us

PLANS (PLAN)
Ps 20: 4 and make all your *p* succeed.
33: 11 *p* of the LORD stand firm forever,
Pr 15: 22 *P* fail for lack of counsel,
16: 3 and your *p* will succeed.
19: 21 Many are the *p* in a man's heart,
20: 18 Make *p* by seeking advice;
Isa 29: 15 to hide their *p* from the LORD,
30: 1 those who carry out *p* that are not
32: 8 But the noble man makes noble *p*,
2Co 1: 17 Or do I make my *p* in a worldly

PLANT (PLANTED PLANTING PLANTS)
Am 9: 15 I will *p* Israel in their own land,
Mt 15: 13 "Every *p* that my heavenly Father

PLANTED (PLANT)
Ge 2: 8 the LORD God had *p* a garden
Ps 1: 3 He is like a tree *p* by streams
Jer 17: 8 He will be like a tree *p* by the water
Mt 15: 13 Father has not *p* will be pulled
21: 33 was a landowner who *p* a vineyard.
Lk 13: 6 "A man had a fig tree, *p*
1Co 3: 6 I *p* the seed, Apollos watered it,
Jas 1: 21 humbly accept the word *p* in you,

PLANTING (PLANT)
Isa 61: 3 a *p* of the LORD

PLANTS (PLANT)
Pr 31: 16 out of her earnings she *p* a vineyard
1Co 3: 7 So neither he who *p* nor he who
9: 7 Who *p* a vineyard and does not eat

PLATTER
Mk 6: 25 head of John the Baptist on a *p*."

PLAY (PLAYED)
1Sa 16: 23 David would take his harp and *p*.
Isa 11: 8 The infant will *p* near the hole

PLAYED (PLAY)
Lk 7: 32 " 'We p the flute for you,
1Co 14: 7 anyone know what tune is being p

PLEA (PLEAD PLEADED PLEADS)
1Ki 8: 28 to your servant's prayer and his p
Ps 102: 17 he will not despise their p.
La 3: 56 You heard my p: "Do not close

PLEAD (PLEA)
Isa 1: 17 p the case of the widow.

PLEADED (PLEA)
2Co 12: 8 Three times I p with the Lord

PLEADS (PLEA)
Job 16: 21 on behalf of a man he p with God

PLEASANT (PLEASE)
Ge 49: 15 and how p is his land,
Ps 16: 6 for me in p places;
133: 1 How good and p it is
135: 3 sing praise to his name, for that is p
147: 1 how p and fitting to praise him!
Pr 2: 10 knowledge will be p to your soul.
3: 17 Her ways are p ways,
16: 21 and p words promote instruction.
16: 24 P words are a honeycomb,
Isa 30: 10 Tell us p things,
1Th 3: 6 that you always have p memories
Heb 12: 11 No discipline seems p at the time,

PLEASANTNESS* (PLEASE)
Pr 27: 9 the p of one's friend springs

PLEASE (PLEASANT PLEASANTNESS PLEASED PLEASES PLEASING PLEASURE PLEASURES)
Ps 69: 31 This will p the LORD more
Pr 20: 23 and dishonest scales do not p him.
Isa 46: 10 and I will do all that I p.
Jer 6: 20 your sacrifices do not p me."
27: 5 and I give it to anyone I p.
Jn 5: 30 for I seek not to p myself
Ro 8: 8 by the sinful nature cannot p God.
15: 1 of the weak and not to p ourselves.
15: 2 Each of us should p his neighbor
1Co 7: 32 affairs—how he can p the Lord.
10: 33 I try to p everybody in every way.
2Co 5: 9 So we make it our goal to p him,
Gal 1: 10 or of God? Or am I trying to p men
6: 8 the one who sows to p the Spirit,
Col 1: 10 and may p him in every way:
1Th 2: 4 We are not trying to p men
4: 1 how to live in order to p God,
2Ti 2: 4 wants to p his commanding officer.
Tit 2: 9 to try to p them, not to talk back
Heb 11: 6 faith it is impossible to p God,

PLEASED (PLEASE)
Dt 28: 63 as it p the LORD to make you
1Sa 12: 22 LORD was p to make you his own.
1Ki 3: 10 The Lord was p that Solomon had
1Ch 29: 17 that you test the heart and are p
Mic 6: 7 Will the LORD be p
Mal 1: 10 I am not p with you," says
Mt 3: 17 whom I love; with him I am well p
17: 5 whom I love; with him I am well p.
Mk 1: 11 whom I love; with you I am well p
Lk 3: 22 whom I love; with you I am well p
1Co 1: 21 God was p through the foolishness
Col 1: 19 For God was p to have all his
Heb 10: 6 you were not p.
10: 8 nor were you p with them"
10: 38 I will not be p with him."
11: 5 commended as one who p God.
13: 16 for with such sacrifices God is p.
2Pe 1: 17 whom I love; with him I am well p

PLEASES (PLEASE)
Job 23: 13 He does whatever he p.
Ps 115: 3 he does whatever p him.
135: 6 The LORD does whatever p him,
Pr 15: 8 but the prayer of the upright p him.
21: 1 it like a watercourse wherever he p.
Ecc 2: 26 To the man who p him, God gives
7: 26 man who p God will escape her,
Da 4: 35 He does as he p
Jn 3: 8 The wind blows wherever it p.
8: 29 for I always do what p him."
Eph 5: 10 truth) and find out what p the Lord
Col 3: 20 in everything, for this p the Lord.
1Ti 2: 3 This is good, and p God our Savior,
1Jn 3: 22 his commands and do what p him.

PLEASING (PLEASE)
Ge 2: 9 trees that were p to the eye
Lev 1: 9 an aroma p to the LORD.
Ps 19: 14 be p in your sight,
104: 34 May my meditation be p to him,
Pr 15: 26 but those of the pure are p to him.
16: 7 When a man's ways are p
SS 1: 3 P is the fragrance of your perfumes
4: 10 How much more p is your love
7: 6 How beautiful you are and how p,
Ro 12: 1 p to God—this is your spiritual
14: 18 Christ in this way is p to God
Php 4: 18 an acceptable sacrifice, p to God.
1Ti 5: 4 grandparents, for this is p to God.
Heb 13: 21 may he work in us what is p to him,

PLEASURE (PLEASE)
Ps 5: 4 You are not a God who takes p
51: 16 you do not take p in burnt offerings
147: 10 His p is not in the strength
Pr 10: 23 A fool finds p in evil conduct,
18: 2 A fool finds no p in understanding
21: 17 He who loves p will become poor;
Isa 1: 11 I have no p
Jer 6: 10 they find no p in it.
Eze 18: 23 Do I take any p in the death
18: 32 For I take no p in the death
33: 11 I take no p in the death
Lk 10: 21 Father, for this was your good p.
Eph 1: 5 in accordance with his p and will—
1: 9 of his will according to his good p,
1Ti 5: 6 the widow who lives for p is dead
2Ti 3: 4 lovers of p rather than lovers
2Pe 2: 13 Their idea of p is to carouse

PLEASURES* (PLEASE)
Ps 16: 11 with eternal p at your right hand.
Lk 8: 14 and p, and they do not mature.
Tit 3: 3 by all kinds of passions and p.
Heb 11: 25 rather than to enjoy the p of sin
Jas 4: 3 may spend what you get on your p.
2Pe 2: 13 reveling in their p while they feast

PLEDGE
Dt 24: 17 take the cloak of the widow as a p.
1Pe 3: 21 but the p of a good conscience

PLEIADES
Job 38: 31 "Can you bind the beautiful P?
Am 5: 8 (he who made the P and Orion,

PLENTIFUL (PLENTY)
Mt 9: 37 harvest is p but the workers are
Lk 10: 2 harvest is p, but the workers are

PLENTY (PLENTIFUL)
2Co 8: 14 the present time your p will supply
Php 4: 12 whether living in p or in want.

PLOT (PLOTS)
Est 2: 22 Mordecai found out about the p
Ps 2: 1 and the peoples p in vain?
Pr 3: 29 not p harm against your neighbor,
Zec 8: 17 do not p evil against your neighbor,
Ac 4: 25 and the peoples p in vain?

PLOTS (PLOT)
Pr 6: 14 who p evil with deceit in his heart

PLOW (PLOWMAN PLOWSHARES)
Lk 9: 62 "No one who puts his hand to the p

PLOWMAN (PLOW)
1Co 9: 10 because when the p plows

PLOWSHARES (PLOW)
1Sa 13: 20 to the Philistines to have their p,
Isa 2: 4 They will beat their swords into p
Joel 3: 10 Beat your p into swords
Mic 4: 3 They will beat their swords into p

PLUCK
Mk 9: 47 your eye causes you to sin, p it out.

PLUNDER (PLUNDERED)
Ex 3: 22 And so you will p the Egyptians."
Est 3: 13 of Adar, and to p their goods.
8: 11 to p the property of their enemies.
9: 10 did not lay their hands on the p.
Pr 22: 23 and will p those who p them.
Isa 3: 14 the p from the poor is

PLUNDERED (PLUNDER)
Eze 34: 8 lacks a shepherd and so has been p

PLUNGE
1Ti 6: 9 and harmful desires that p men
1Pe 4: 4 think it strange that you do not p

PODS
Lk 15: 16 with the p that the pigs were eating,

POINT
Mt 4: 5 on the highest p of the temple.
26: 38 with sorrow to the p of death.
Jas 2: 10 yet stumbles at just one p is guilty
Rev 2: 10 Be faithful, even to the p of death,

POISON
Ps 140: 3 the p of vipers is on their lips.
Mk 16: 18 and when they drink deadly p,
Ro 3: 13 "The p of vipers is on their lips."
Jas 3: 8 It is a restless evil, full of deadly p.

POLE (POLES)
Nu 21: 8 "Make a snake and put it up on a p;
Dt 16: 21 not set up any wooden Asherah p

POLES (POLE)
Ex 25: 13 Then make p of acacia wood

POLISHED
Isa 49: 2 he made me into a p arrow

POLLUTE* (POLLUTED POLLUTES)
Nu 35: 33 " 'Do not p the land where you are.
Jude : 8 these dreamers p their own bodies,

POLLUTED* (POLLUTE)
Ezr 9: 11 entering to possess is a land p
Pr 25: 26 Like a muddied spring or a p well
Ac 15: 20 to abstain from food p by idols,
Jas 1: 27 oneself from being p by the world.

POLLUTES* (POLLUTE)
Nu 35: 33 Bloodshed p the land,

PONDER (PONDERED)
Ps 64: 9 and p what he has done.
119: 95 but I will p your statutes.

PONDERED (PONDER)
Ps 111: 2 they are p by all who delight
Lk 2: 19 up all these things and p them

POOR (POVERTY)
Lev 19: 10 Leave them for the p and the alien.
23: 22 Leave them for the p and the alien.
27: 8 If anyone making the vow is too p
Dt 15: 4 there should be no p among you,
15: 7 is a p man among your brothers
15: 11 There will always be p people
24: 12 If the man is p, do not go to sleep
24: 14 advantage of a hired man who is p
Job 5: 16 So the p have hope,
24: 4 force all the p of the land
Ps 14: 6 frustrate the plans of the p,
34: 6 This p man called, and the LORD
35: 10 You rescue the p from those too
40: 17 Yet I am p and needy;
68: 10 O God, you provided for the p.
82: 3 maintain the rights of the p
112: 9 scattered abroad his gifts to the p,
113: 7 He raises the p from the dust
140: 12 the LORD secures justice for the p
Pr 10: 4 Lazy hands make a man p,
13: 7 to be p, yet has great wealth.
14: 20 The p are shunned
14: 31 oppresses the p shows contempt
17: 5 who mocks the p shows contempt

19: 1 Better a *p* man whose walk is
19: 17 to the *p* lends to the LORD,
19: 22 better to be *p* than a liar.
20: 13 not love sleep or you will grow *p*;
21: 13 to the cry of the *p*,
21: 17 who loves pleasure will become *p*;
22: 2 Rich and *p* have this in common:
22: 9 for he shares his food with the *p*.
22: 22 not exploit the *p* because they are *p*
28: 6 Better a *p* man whose walk is
28: 27 to the *p* will lack nothing,
29: 7 care about justice for the *p*,
31: 9 defend the rights of the *p*
31: 20 She opens her arms to the *p*
Ecc 4: 13 Better a *p* but wise youth
Isa 3: 14 the plunder from the *p* is
10: 2 to deprive the *p* of their rights
14: 30 of the *p* will find pasture,
25: 4 You have been a refuge for the *p*,
32: 7 schemes to destroy the *p* with lies,
61: 1 me to preach good news to the *p*.
Jer 22: 16 He defended the cause of the *p*
Eze 18: 12 He oppresses the *p* and needy.
Am 2: 7 They trample on the heads of the *p*
4: 1 you women who oppress the *p*
5: 11 You trample on the *p*
Zec 7: 10 or the fatherless, the alien or the *p*.
Mt 5: 3 saying: "Blessed are the *p* in spirit,
11: 5 the good news is preached to the *p*.
19: 21 your possessions and give to the *p*,
26: 11 The *p* you will always have
Mk 12: 42 But a *p* widow came and put
14: 7 The *p* you will always have
Lk 4: 18 me to preach good news to the *p*.
6: 20 "Blessed are you who are *p*,
11: 41 is inside ›the dish‹ to the *p*,
14: 13 invite the *p*, the crippled, the lame,
21: 2 also saw a *p* widow put
Jn 12: 8 You will always have the *p*
Ac 9: 36 doing good and helping the *p*.
10: 4 and gifts to the *p* have come up
24: 17 to bring my people gifts for the *p*
Ro 15: 26 for the *p* among the saints
1Co 13: 3 If I give all I possess to the *p*
2Co 6: 10 sorrowful, yet always rejoicing; *p*,
8: 9 yet for your sakes he became *p*,
Gal 2: 10 continue to remember the *p*,
Jas 2: 2 and a *p* man in shabby clothes
2: 5 not God chosen those who are *p*
2: 6 But you have insulted the *p*.

POPULATION*
Pr 14: 28 A large *p* is a king's glory,

PORTION
Nu 18: 29 as the LORD's *p* the best
Dt 32: 9 For the LORD's *p* is his people,
1Sa 1: 5 But to Hannah he gave a double *p*
2Ki 2: 9 "Let me inherit a double *p*
Ps 73: 26 and my *p* forever.
119: 57 You are my *p*, O LORD;
Isa 53: 12 Therefore I will give him a *p*
Jer 10: 16 He who is the *P* of Jacob is not like
La 3: 24 to myself, "The LORD is my *p*;
Zec 2: 12 LORD will inherit Judah as his *p*

PORTRAIT
Lk 20: 24 Whose *p* and inscription are on it?"

PORTRAYED
Gal 3: 1 very eyes Jesus Christ was clearly *p*

POSITION (POSITIONS)
Ro 12: 16 to associate with people of low *p*.
Jas 1: 9 ought to take pride in his high *p*.
2Pe 3: 17 and fall from your secure *p*.

POSITIONS (POSITION)
2Ch 20: 17 Take up your *p*; stand firm
Jude : 6 the angels who did not keep their *p*

POSSESS (POSSESSED POSSESSING POSSESSION POSSESSIONS)
Nu 33: 53 for I have given you the land to *p*.
Dt 4: 14 you are crossing the Jordan to *p*.
Pr 8: 12 I *p* knowledge and discretion.
Jn 5: 39 that by them you *p* eternal life.

POSSESSED (POSSESS)
Jn 10: 21 the sayings of a man *p* by a demon.

POSSESSING* (POSSESS)
2Co 6: 10 nothing, and yet *p* everything.

POSSESSION (POSSESS)
Ge 15: 7 to give you this land to take *p* of it
Ex 6: 8 I will give it to you as a *p*.
19: 5 nations you will be my treasured *p*.
Nu 13: 30 "We should go up and take *p*
Dt 7: 6 to be his people, his treasured *p*.
Jos 1: 11 take *p* of the land the LORD your
Ps 2: 8 the ends of the earth your *p*.
135: 4 Israel to be his treasured *p*.
Eph 1: 14 of those who are God's *p*—

POSSESSIONS (POSSESS)
Mt 19: 21 go, sell your *p* and give to the poor,
Lk 11: 21 guards his own house, his *p* are safe
12: 15 consist in the abundance of his *p*."
19: 8 now I give half of my *p* to the poor,
Ac 4: 32 any of his *p* was his own,
2Co 12: 14 what I want is not your *p* but you.
Heb 10: 34 yourselves had better and lasting *p*.
1Jn 3: 17 If anyone has material *p*

POSSIBLE
Mt 19: 26 but with God all things are *p*."
26: 39 if it is *p*, may this cup be taken
Mk 9: 23 "Everything is *p* for him who
10: 27 all things are *p* with God."
14: 35 prayed that if *p* the hour might pass
Ro 12: 18 If it is *p*, as far as it depends on you,
1Co 6: 5 Is it *p* that there is nobody
9: 19 to everyone, to win as many as *p*.
9: 22 by all *p* means I might save some.

POT (POTSHERD POTTER POTTER'S POTTERY)
2Ki 4: 40 there is death in the *p*!"
Jer 18: 4 But the *p* he was shaping

POTIPHAR*
Egyptian who bought Joseph (Ge 37:36), set him over his house (Ge 39:1–6), sent him to prison (Ge 39:7–30).

POTSHERD (POT)
Isa 45: 9 a *p* among the potsherds

POTTER (POT)
Isa 29: 16 Can the pot say of the *p*,
45: 9 Does the clay say to the *p*,
64: 8 We are the clay, you are the *p*;
Jer 18: 6 "Like clay in the hand of the *p*,
Zec 11: 13 it to the *p*"— the handsome price
Ro 9: 21 Does not the *p* have the right

POTTER'S (POT)
Mt 27: 7 to use the money to buy the *p* field

POTTERY (POT)
Ro 9: 21 of clay some *p* for noble purposes

POUR (POURED POURS)
Ps 62: 8 *p* out your hearts to him,
Isa 44: 3 I will *p* out my Spirit
Eze 20: 8 So I said I would *p* out my wrath
39: 29 for I will *p* out my Spirit
Joel 2: 28 I will *p* out my Spirit on all people.
Zec 12: 10 I will *p* out on the house of David
Mal 3: 10 *p* out so much blessing that you
Ac 2: 17 I will *p* out my Spirit on all people.

POURED (POUR)
Ps 22: 14 I am *p* out like water,
Isa 32: 15 till the Spirit is *p* upon us
Mt 26: 28 which is *p* out for many
Lk 22: 20 in my blood, which is *p* out for you.
Ac 2: 33 and has *p* out what you now see
10: 45 of the Holy Spirit had been *p* out
Ro 5: 5 because God has *p* out his love
Php 2: 17 even if I am being *p* out like a drink
2Ti 4: 6 I am already being *p* out like
Tit 3: 6 whom he *p* out on us generously
Rev 16: 2 and *p* out his bowl on the land,

POURS (POUR)
Lk 5: 37 And no one *p* new wine

POVERTY* (POOR)
Dt 28: 48 and thirst, in nakedness and dire *p*,
1Sa 2: 7 The LORD sends *p* and wealth;
Pr 6: 11 *p* will come on you like a bandit
10: 15 but *p* is the ruin of the poor.
11: 24 withholds unduly, but comes to *p*.
13: 18 who ignores discipline comes to *p*
14: 23 but mere talk leads only to *p*.
21: 5 as surely as haste leads to *p*.
22: 16 to the rich—both come to *p*.
24: 34 *p* will come on you like a bandit
28: 19 fantasies will have his fill of *p*.
28: 22 and is unaware that *p* awaits him.
30: 8 give me neither *p* nor riches,
31: 7 let them drink and forget their *p*
Ecc 4: 14 born in *p* within his kingdom.
Mk 12: 44 out of her *p*, put in everything—
Lk 21: 4 she out of her *p* put in all she had
2Co 8: 2 and their extreme *p* welled up
8: 9 through his *p* might become rich.
Rev 2: 9 I know your afflictions and your *p*

POWER (POWERFUL POWERS)
Ex 15: 6 was majestic in *p*.
32: 11 out of Egypt with great *p*
Dt 8: 17 "My *p* and the strength
34: 12 one has ever shown the mighty *p*
1Sa 10: 6 LORD will come upon you in *p*,
10: 10 Spirit of God came upon him in *p*,
11: 6 Spirit of God came upon him in *p*,
16: 13 the LORD came upon David in *p*.
1Ch 29: 11 LORD, is the greatness and the *p*
2Ch 20: 6 *P* and might are in your hand,
32: 7 for there is a greater *p* with us
Job 9: 4 wisdom is profound, his *p* is vast.
36: 22 "God is exalted in his *p*.
37: 23 beyond our reach and exalted in *p*;
Ps 20: 6 with the saving *p* of his right hand.
63: 2 and beheld your *p* and your glory.
66: 3 So great is your *p*
68: 34 Proclaim the *p* of God,
77: 14 you display your *p*
89: 13 Your arm is endued with *p*;
145: 6 of the *p* of your awesome works,
147: 5 Great is our Lord and mighty in *p*;
150: 2 Praise him for his acts of *p*;
Pr 3: 27 when it is in your *p* to act.
18: 21 The tongue has the *p* of life
24: 5 A wise man has great *p*,
Isa 11: 2 the Spirit of counsel and of *p*,
40: 10 the Sovereign LORD comes with *p*
40: 26 of his great *p* and mighty strength,
63: 12 who sent his glorious arm of *p*
Jer 10: 6 and your name is mighty in *p*.
10: 12 But God made the earth by his *p*;
27: 5 With my great *p* and outstretched
32: 17 and the earth by your great *p*
Hos 13: 14 from the *p* of the grave;
Na 1: 3 to anger and great in *p*;
Zec 4: 6 nor by *p*, but by my Spirit,'
Mt 22: 29 do not know the Scriptures or the *p*
24: 30 on the clouds of the sky, with *p*
Lk 1: 35 and the *p* of the Most High will
4: 14 to Galilee in the *p* of the Spirit,
9: 1 he gave them *p* and authority
10: 19 to overcome all the *p* of the enemy;
24: 49 clothed with *p* from on high."
Ac 1: 8 you will receive *p* when the Holy
4: 28 They did what your *p* and will had
4: 33 With great *p* the apostles
10: 38 with the Holy Spirit and *p*,
26: 18 and from the *p* of Satan to God,
Ro 1: 16 it is the *p* of God for the salvation
1: 20 his eternal *p* and divine nature—
4: 21 fully persuaded that God had *p*
9: 17 that I might display my *p* in you

15: 13 overflow with hope by the *p*
15: 19 through the *p* of the Spirit.
1Co 1: 17 cross of Christ be emptied of its *p.*
1: 18 to us who are being saved it is the *p*
2: 4 a demonstration of the Spirit's *p,*
6: 14 By his *p* God raised the Lord
15: 24 all dominion, authority and *p.*
15: 56 of death is sin, and the *p*
2Co 4: 7 to show that this all-surpassing *p* is
6: 7 in truthful speech and in the *p*
10: 4 they have divine *p*
12: 9 for my *p* is made perfect
13: 4 weakness, yet he lives by God's *p.*
Eph 1: 19 and his incomparably great *p*
3: 16 you with *p* through his Spirit
3: 20 according to his *p* that is at work
6: 10 in the Lord and in his mighty *p.*
Php 3: 10 and the *p* of his resurrection
3: 21 by the *p* that enables him
Col 1: 11 strengthened with all *p* according
2: 10 who is the head over every *p*
1Th 1: 5 also with *p,* with the Holy Spirit
2Ti 1: 7 but a spirit of *p,* of love
3: 5 form of godliness but denying its *p.*
Heb 2: 14 might destroy him who holds the *p*
7: 16 of the *p* of an indestructible life.
1Pe 1: 5 by God's *p* until the coming
2Pe 1: 3 His divine *p* has given us
Jude : 25 *p* and authority, through Jesus
Rev 4: 11 to receive glory and honor and *p,*
5: 12 to receive *p* and wealth
11: 17 you have taken your great *p*
19: 1 and glory and *p* belong to our God,
20: 6 The second death has no *p*

POWERFUL (POWER)
2Ch 27: 6 Jotham grew *p* because he walked
Est 9: 4 and he became more and more *p.*
Ps 29: 4 The voice of the LORD is *p;*
Jer 32: 18 *p* God, whose name is the LORD
Zec 8: 22 *p* nations will come to Jerusalem
Mk 1: 7 "After me will come one more *p*
Lk 24: 19 *p* in word and deed before God
2Th 1: 7 in blazing fire with his *p* angels.
Heb 1: 3 sustaining all things by his *p* word.
Jas 5: 16 The prayer of a righteous man is *p*

POWERLESS
Ro 5: 6 when we were still *p,* Christ died
8: 3 For what the law was *p* to do

POWERS (POWER)
Da 4: 35 pleases with the *p* of heaven
Ro 8: 38 nor any *p,* neither height nor depth
1Co 12: 10 to another miraculous *p,*
Eph 6: 12 against the *p* of this dark world
Col 1: 16 whether thrones or *p* or rulers
2: 15 And having disarmed the *p*
Heb 6: 5 and the *p* of the coming age,
1Pe 3: 22 and *p* in submission to him.

PRACTICE (PRACTICED PRACTICES)
Lev 19: 26 " 'Do not *p* divination or sorcery.
Ps 119: 56 This has been my *p:*
Eze 33: 31 but they do not put them into *p.*
Mt 7: 24 into *p* is like a wise man who built
23: 3 for they do not *p* what they preach.
Lk 8: 21 hear God's word and put it into *p.*"
Ro 12: 13 *P* hospitality.
Php 4: 9 or seen in me—put it into *p.*
1Ti 5: 4 to put their religion into *p* by caring

PRACTICED (PRACTICE)
Mt 23: 23 You should have *p* the latter,

PRACTICES (PRACTICE)
Ps 101: 7 No one who *p* deceit
Mt 5: 19 but whoever *p* and teaches these
Col 3: 9 taken off your old self with its *p*

PRAISE (PRAISED PRAISES PRAISEWORTHY PRAISING)
Ex 15: 2 He is my God, and I will *p* him,
Dt 10: 21 He is your *p;* he is your God,
26: 19 declared that he will set you in *p,*
32: 3 Oh, *p* the greatness of our God!
Ru 4: 14 said to Naomi: "*P* be to the LORD,
2Sa 22: 4 to the LORD, who is worthy of *p,*
22: 47 The LORD lives! *P* be to my Rock
1Ch 16: 25 is the LORD and most worthy of *p;*
16: 35 that we may glory in your *p.*"
23: 5 four thousand are to *p* the LORD
29: 10 "*P* be to you, O LORD,
2Ch 5: 13 they raised their voices in *p*
20: 21 and to *p* him for the splendor
29: 30 to *p* the LORD with the words
Ezr 3: 10 took their places to *p* the LORD,
Ne 9: 5 and *p* the LORD your God,
Ps 8: 2 you have ordained *p*
9: 1 I will *p* you, O LORD,
16: 7 I will *p* the LORD, who counsels
26: 7 proclaiming aloud your *p*
30: 4 *p* his holy name.
33: 1 it is fitting for the upright to *p* him.
34: 1 his *p* will always be on my lips.
40: 3 a hymn of *p* to our God.
42: 5 for I will yet *p* him,
43: 5 for I will yet *p* him,
45: 17 the nations will *p* you for ever
47: 7 sing to him a psalm of *p.*
48: 1 the LORD, and most worthy of *p,*
51: 15 and my mouth will declare your *p.*
56: 4 In God, whose word I *p,*
57: 9 I will *p* you, O Lord,
63: 4 I will *p* you as long as I live,
65: 1 *P* awaits you, O God, in Zion;
66: 2 make his *p* glorious.
66: 8 *P* our God, O peoples,
68: 19 *P* be to the Lord, to God our Savior
68: 26 *p* the LORD in the assembly
69: 30 I will *p* God's name in song
69: 34 Let heaven and earth *p* him,
71: 8 My mouth is filled with your *p,*
71: 14 I will *p* you more and more.
71: 22 I will *p* you with the harp
74: 21 the poor and needy *p* your name.
86: 12 I will *p* you, O Lord my God,
89: 5 The heavens *p* your wonders,
92: 1 It is good to *p* the LORD
96: 2 Sing to the LORD, *p* his name;
100: 4 and his courts with *p;*
101: 1 to you, O LORD, I will sing *p.*
102: 18 not yet created may *p* the LORD:
103: 1 *P* the LORD, O my soul;
103: 20 *P* the LORD, you his angels,
104: 1 *P* the LORD, O my soul.
105: 2 Sing to him, sing *p* to him;
106: 1 *P* the LORD.
108: 3 I will *p* you, O LORD,
111: 1 *P* the LORD.
113: 1 *P* the LORD.
117: 1 *P* the LORD, all you nations;
119:175 Let me live that I may *p* you,
135: 1 *P* the LORD.
135: 20 you who fear him, *p* the LORD.
138: 1 I will *p* you, O LORD,
139: 14 I *p* you because I am fearfully
144: 1 *P* be to the LORD my Rock,
145: 3 is the LORD and most worthy of *p;*
145: 10 All you have made will *p* you,
145: 21 Let every creature *p* his holy name
146: 1 *P* the LORD, O my soul.
147: 1 how pleasant and fitting to *p* him!
148: 1 *P* the LORD from the heavens,
148: 13 Let them *p* the name of the LORD,
149: 1 his *p* in the assembly of the saints.
149: 6 May the *p* of God be
149: 9 *P* the LORD.
150: 2 *p* him for his surpassing greatness.
150: 6 that has breath *p* the LORD.
Pr 27: 2 Let another *p* you, and not your
27: 21 man is tested by the *p* he receives.
31: 31 let her works bring her *p*
SS 1: 4 we will *p* your love more than wine
Isa 12: 1 "I will *p* you, O LORD.
42: 10 his *p* from the ends of the earth,
61: 3 and a garment of *p*
Jer 33: 9 *p* and honor before all nations
Da 2: 20 "*P* be to the name of God for ever
4: 37 *p* and exalt and glorify the King
Mt 5: 16 and *p* your Father in heaven.
21: 16 you have ordained *p*'?"
Lk 19: 37 to *p* God in loud voices
Jn 5: 44 effort to obtain the *p* that comes
12: 43 for they loved *p* from men more
Ro 2: 29 Such a man's *p* is not from men,
15: 7 in order to bring *p* to God.
2Co 1: 3 *P* be to the God and Father
Eph 1: 3 *P* be to the God and Father
1: 6 to the *p* of his glorious grace,
1: 12 might be for the *p* of his glory.
1: 14 to the *p* of his glory.
1Th 2: 6 We were not looking for *p*
Heb 13: 15 offer to God a sacrifice of *p*—
Jas 3: 9 With the tongue we *p* our Lord
5: 13 happy? Let him sing songs of *p.*
Rev 5: 13 be *p* and honor and glory
7: 12 *P* and glory

PRAISED (PRAISE)
1Ch 29: 10 David *p* the LORD in the presence
Ne 8: 6 Ezra *p* the LORD, the great God;
Job 1: 21 may the name of the LORD be *p.*"
Ps 113: 2 Let the name of the LORD be *p,*
Pr 31: 30 who fears the LORD is to be *p.*
Isa 63: 7 the deeds for which he is to be *p,*
Da 2: 19 Then Daniel *p* the God of heaven
4: 34 Then I *p* the Most High; I honored
Lk 18: 43 the people saw it, they also *p* God.
23: 47 seeing what had happened, *p* God
Ro 9: 5 who is God over all, forever *p!*
Gal 1: 24 And they *p* God because of me.
1Pe 4: 11 that in all things God may be *p*

PRAISES (PRAISE)
2Sa 22: 50 I will sing *p* to your name.
Ps 18: 49 I will sing *p* to your name.
47: 6 Sing *p* to God, sing *p;*
147: 1 How good it is to sing *p* to our God,
Pr 31: 28 her husband also, and he *p* her:
1Pe 2: 9 that you may declare the *p*

PRAISEWORTHY* (PRAISE)
Ps 78: 4 the *p* deeds of the LORD,
Php 4: 8 if anything is excellent or *p*—

PRAISING (PRAISE)
Lk 2: 13 *p* God and saying, "Glory to God
2: 20 *p* God for all the things they had
Ac 2: 47 *p* God and enjoying the favor
10: 46 speaking in tongues and *p* God.
1Co 14: 16 If you are *p* God with your spirit,

PRAY (PRAYED PRAYER PRAYERS PRAYING PRAYS)
Dt 4: 7 is near us whenever we *p* to him?
1Sa 12: 23 the LORD by failing to *p* for you.
1Ki 8: 30 when they *p* toward this place.
2Ch 7: 14 will humble themselves and *p*
Ezr 6: 10 and *p* for the well-being of the king
Job 42: 8 My servant Job will *p* for you,
Ps 5: 2 for to you I *p.*
32: 6 let everyone who is godly *p*
122: 6 *P* for the peace of Jerusalem:
Jer 29: 7 *P* to the LORD for it,
29: 12 upon me and come and *p* to me,
42: 3 *P* that the LORD your God will
Mt 5: 44 and *p* for those who persecute you,
6: 5 "And when you *p,* do not be like
6: 9 "This, then, is how you should *p:*
14: 23 up on a mountainside by himself to *p.*
19: 13 hands on them and *p* for them.
26: 36 Sit here while I go over there and *p*
Lk 6: 28 *p* for those who mistreat you.
11: 1 us to *p,* just as John taught his
18: 1 them that they should always *p*

22: 40 "*P* that you will not fall
Jn 17: 20 I *p* also for those who will believe
Ro 8: 26 do not know what we ought to *p* for,
1Co 14: 13 in a tongue should *p* that he may
Eph 1: 18 I *p* also that the eyes
3: 16 I *p* that out of his glorious riches he
6: 18 And *p* in the Spirit on all occasions
Col 1: 10 we *p* this in order that you may live
4: 3 *p* for us, too, that God may open
1Th 5: 17 Be joyful always; *p* continually;
2Th 1: 11 in mind, we constantly *p* for you,
Jas 5: 13 one of you in trouble? He should *p.*
5: 16 *p* for each other so that you may be
1Pe 4: 7 self-controlled so that you can *p.*
Jude : 20 up in your most holy faith and *p*

PRAYED (PRAY)
1Sa 1: 27 I *p* for this child, and the LORD
1Ki 18: 36 Elijah stepped forward and *p:*
19: 4 under it and *p* that he might die.
2Ki 6: 17 And Elisha *p,* "O LORD,
2Ch 30: 18 But Hezekiah *p* for them, saying,
Ne 4: 9 we *p* to our God and posted a guard
Job 42: 10 After Job had *p* for his friends,
Da 6: 10 got down on his knees and *p,*
9: 4 I *p* to the LORD my God
Jnh 2: 1 From inside the fish Jonah *p*
Mt 26: 39 with his face to the ground and *p,*
Mk 1: 35 off to a solitary place, where he *p.*
14: 35 *p* that if possible the hour might
Lk 22: 41 knelt down and *p,* "Father,
Jn 17: 1 he looked toward heaven and *p:*
Ac 4: 31 After they *p,* the place where they
6: 6 who *p* and laid their hands on them
8: 15 they *p* for them that they might
13: 3 So after they had fasted and *p,*

PRAYER (PRAY)
2Ch 30: 27 for their *p* reached heaven,
Ezr 8: 23 about this, and he answered our *p.*
Ps 4: 1 be merciful to me and hear my *p.*
6: 9 the LORD accepts my *p.*
17: 1 Give ear to my *p*—
17: 6 give ear to me and hear my *p.*
65: 2 O you who hear *p,*
66: 20 who has not rejected my *p*
86: 6 Hear my *p,* O LORD;
Pr 15: 8 but the *p* of the upright pleases him
15: 29 but he hears the *p* of the righteous.
Isa 56: 7 a house of *p* for all nations."
Mt 21: 13 house will be called a house of *p,*'
21: 22 receive whatever you ask for in *p.*"
Mk 9: 29 This kind can come out only by *p.*"
11: 24 whatever you ask for in *p,*
Jn 17: 15 My *p* is not that you take them out
Ac 1: 14 all joined together constantly in *p,*
2: 42 to the breaking of bread and to *p.*
6: 4 and will give our attention to *p*
10: 31 has heard your *p* and remembered
16: 13 expected to find a place of *p.*
Ro 12: 12 patient in affliction, faithful in *p.*
1Co 7: 5 you may devote yourselves to *p.*
2Co 13: 9 and our *p* is for your perfection.
Php 1: 9 this is my *p:* that your love may
4: 6 but in everything, by *p* and petition
Col 4: 2 yourselves to *p,* being watchful
1Ti 2: 8 to lift up holy hands in *p,*
4: 5 by the word of God and *p.*
Jas 5: 15 *p* offered in faith will make the sick
1Pe 3: 12 and his ears are attentive to their *p,*

PRAYERS (PRAY)
1Ch 5: 20 He answered their *p,* because they
Isa 1: 15 even if you offer many *p,*
Mk 12: 40 and for a show make lengthy *p.*
2Co 1: 11 as you help us by your *p.*
Eph 6: 18 on all occasions with all kinds of *p*
1Ti 2: 1 then, first of all, that requests, *p,*
1Pe 3: 7 so that nothing will hinder your *p.*
Rev 5: 8 which are the *p* of the saints.
8: 3 with the *p* of all the saints,

PRAYING (PRAY)
Ge 24: 45 "Before I finished *p* in my heart,
1Sa 1: 12 As she kept on *p* to the LORD,
Mk 11: 25 And when you stand *p,*
Lk 3: 21 as he was *p,* heaven was opened
6: 12 and spent the night *p* to God.
9: 29 As he was *p,* the appearance
Jn 17: 9 I am not *p* for the world,
Ac 9: 11 from Tarsus named Saul, for he is *p*
16: 25 and Silas were *p* and singing hymns
Ro 15: 30 in my struggle by *p* to God for me.
Eph 6: 18 always keep on *p* for all the saints.

PRAYS (PRAY)
1Co 14: 14 my spirit *p,* but my mind is

PREACH (PREACHED PREACHING)
Isa 61: 1 me to *p* good news to the poor.
Mt 10: 7 As you go, *p* this message:
23: 3 they do not practice what they *p.*
Mk 16: 15 and *p* the good news to all creation.
Lk 4: 18 me to *p* good news to the poor.
Ac 9: 20 At once he began to *p*
16: 10 us to *p* the gospel to them.
Ro 1: 15 am so eager to *p* the gospel
10: 15 how can they *p* unless they are sent
15: 20 to *p* the gospel where Christ was
1Co 1: 17 to *p* the gospel—not with words
1: 23 wisdom, but we *p* Christ crucified:
9: 14 that those who *p* the gospel should
9: 16 Woe to me if I do not *p* the gospel!
2Co 4: 5 For we do not *p* ourselves,
10: 16 so that we can *p* the gospel
Gal 1: 8 from heaven should *p* a gospel
2Ti 4: 2 I give you this charge: *P* the Word;

PREACHED (PREACH)
Mt 24: 14 gospel of the kingdom will be *p*
Mk 6: 12 and *p* that people should repent.
13: 10 And the gospel must first be *p*
14: 9 wherever the gospel is *p*
Ac 8: 4 had been scattered *p* the word
28: 31 hindrance he *p* the kingdom
1Co 9: 27 so that after I have *p* to others,
15: 1 you of the gospel I *p* to you,
2Co 11: 4 other than the Jesus we *p,*
Gal 1: 8 other than the one we *p* to you,
Eph 2: 17 *p* peace to you who were far away
Php 1: 18 false motives or true, Christ is *p.*
1Ti 3: 16 was *p* among the nations,
1Pe 1: 25 this is the word that was *p* to you.
3: 19 and *p* to the spirits in prison who

PREACHING (PREACH)
Lk 9: 6 *p* the gospel and healing people
Ac 18: 5 devoted himself exclusively to *p,*
Ro 10: 14 hear without someone *p* to them?
1Co 2: 4 and my *p* were not with wise
9: 18 in *p* the gospel I may offer it free
Gal 1: 9 If anybody is *p* to you a gospel
1Ti 4: 13 the public reading of Scripture, to *p*
5: 17 especially those whose work is *p*

PRECEDE*
1Th 4: 15 will certainly not *p* those who have

PRECEPTS*
Dt 33: 10 He teaches your *p* to Jacob
Ps 19: 8 The *p* of the LORD are right,
103: 18 and remember to obey his *p.*
105: 45 that they might keep his *p*
111: 7 all his *p* are trustworthy.
111: 10 who follow his *p* have good
119: 4 You have laid down *p*
119: 15 I meditate on your *p*
119: 27 understand the teaching of your *p;*
119: 40 How I long for your *p!*
119: 45 for I have sought out your *p.*
119: 56 I obey your *p.*
119: 63 to all who follow your *p.*
119: 69 I keep your *p* with all my heart.
119: 78 but I will meditate on your *p.*
119: 87 but I have not forsaken your *p.*
119: 93 I will never forget your *p,*
119: 94 I have sought out your *p.*
119:100 for I obey your *p.*
119:104 I gain understanding from your *p;*
119:110 but I have not strayed from your *p.*
119:128 because I consider all your *p* right,
119:134 that I may obey your *p.*
119:141 I do not forget your *p.*
119:159 See how I love your *p;*
119:168 I obey your *p* and your statutes,
119:173 for I have chosen your *p.*

PRECIOUS
Ps 19: 10 They are more *p* than gold,
72: 14 for *p* is their blood in his sight.
116: 15 *P* in the sight of the LORD
119: 72 from your mouth is more *p* to me
139: 17 How *p* to me are your thoughts,
Pr 8: 11 for wisdom is more *p* than rubies,
Isa 28: 16 a *p* cornerstone for a sure
1Pe 1: 19 but with the *p* blood of Christ,
2: 4 but chosen by God and *p* to him—
2: 6 a chosen and *p* cornerstone,
2Pe 1: 1 Christ have received a faith as *p*
1: 4 us his very great and *p* promises,

PREDESTINED* (DESTINY)
Ro 8: 29 *p* to be conformed to the likeness
8: 30 And those he *p,* he also called;
Eph 1: 5 In love he *p* us to be adopted
1: 11 having been *p* according

PREDICTED (PREDICTION)
1Sa 28: 17 The LORD has done what he *p*
Ac 7: 52 killed those who *p* the coming
1Pe 1: 11 when he *p* the sufferings of Christ

PREDICTION* (PREDICTED PREDICTIONS)
Jer 28: 9 only if his *p* comes true."

PREDICTIONS (PREDICTION)
Isa 44: 26 and fulfills the *p* of his messengers,

PREGNANT
Ex 21: 22 who are fighting hit a *p* woman
Mt 24: 19 be in those days for *p* women
1Th 5: 3 as labor pains on a *p* woman,

PREPARE (PREPARED)
Ps 23: 5 You *p* a table before me
Isa 25: 6 the LORD Almighty will *p*
40: 3 "In the desert *p*
Am 4: 12 *p* to meet your God, O Israel."
Mal 3: 1 who will *p* the way before me.
Mt 3: 3 '*P* the way for the Lord,
Jn 14: 2 there to *p* a place for you.
Eph 4: 12 to *p* God's people for works
1Pe 1: 13 Therefore, *p* your minds for action;

PREPARED (PREPARE)
Ex 23: 20 to bring you to the place I have *p.*
Mt 25: 34 the kingdom *p* for you
Ro 9: 22 of his wrath—*p* for destruction?
1Co 2: 9 what God has *p* for those who love
Eph 2: 10 which God *p* in advance for us
2Ti 2: 21 and *p* to do any good work.
4: 2 be *p* in season and out of season;
1Pe 3: 15 Always be *p* to give an answer

PRESCRIBED
Ezr 7: 23 Whatever the God of heaven has *p,*

PRESENCE (PRESENT)
Ex 25: 30 Put the bread of the *P* on this table
33: 14 The LORD replied, "My *P* will go
Nu 4: 7 "Over the table of the *P* they are
1Sa 6: 20 in the *p* of the LORD, this
21: 6 of the *P* that had been removed
2Sa 22: 13 Out of the brightness of his *p*
2Ki 17: 23 LORD removed them from his *p,*
23: 27 also from my *p* as I removed Israel,
Ezr 9: 15 one of us can stand in your *p.*"
Ps 16: 11 you will fill me with joy in your *p,*
21: 6 with the joy of your *p.*
23: 5 in the *p* of my enemies.
31: 20 the shelter of your *p* you hide them
41: 12 and set me in your *p* forever.
51: 11 Do not cast me from your *p*

52: 9 in the *p* of your saints.
89: 15 who walk in the light of your *p*,
90: 8 our secret sins in the light of your *p*
114: 7 O earth, at the *p* of the Lord,
139: 7 Where can I flee from your *p*?
Isa 26: 17 so were we in your *p*, O LORD.
Jer 5: 22 "Should you not tremble in my *p*?
Eze 38: 20 of the earth will tremble at my *p*.
Hos 6: 2 that we may live in his *p*.
Na 1: 5 The earth trembles at his *p*,
Mal 3: 16 in his *p* concerning those who
Ac 2: 28 you will fill me with joy in your *p*.'
1Th 3: 9 have in the *p* of our God
3: 13 and holy in the *p* of our God
2Th 1: 9 and shut out from the *p* of the Lord
Heb 9: 24 now to appear for us in God's *p*.
1Jn 3: 19 rest in his *p* whenever our hearts
Jude : 24 before his glorious *p* without fault

PRESENT (PRESENCE)
1Co 3: 22 life or death or the *p* or the future—
7: 26 of the *p* crisis, I think that it is good
2Co 11: 2 so that I might *p* you as a pure
Eph 5: 27 and to *p* her to himself
1Ti 4: 8 holding promise for both the *p* life
2Ti 2: 15 Do your best to *p* yourself to God
Jude : 24 and to *p* you before his glorious

PRESERVE
Lk 17: 33 and whoever loses his life will *p* it.

PRESERVES
Ps 119: 50 Your promise *p* my life.

PRESS (PRESSED PRESSURE)
Php 3: 12 but I *p* on to take hold of that
3: 14 I *p* on toward the goal

PRESSED (PRESS)
Lk 6: 38 *p* down, shaken together

PRESSURE (PRESS)
2Co 1: 8 We were under great *p*, far
11: 28 I face daily the *p* of my concern

PRETENDED
1Sa 21: 13 So he *p* to be insane

PREVAILS
1Sa 2: 9 "It is not by strength that one *p*;
Pr 19: 21 but it is the LORD's purpose that *p*

PRICE (PRICELESS)
Job 28: 18 the *p* of wisdom is beyond rubies.
1Co 6: 20 your own; you were bought at a *p*.
7: 23 bought at a *p*; do not become slaves

PRICELESS* (PRICE)
Ps 36: 7 How *p* is your unfailing love!

PRIDE (PROUD)
Pr 8: 13 I hate *p* and arrogance,
11: 2 When *p* comes, then comes
13: 10 *P* only breeds quarrels,
16: 18 *P* goes before destruction,
29: 23 A man's *p* brings him low,
Isa 25: 11 God will bring down their *p*
Da 4: 37 And those who walk in *p* he is able
Am 8: 7 The LORD has sworn by the *P*
2Co 5: 12 giving you an opportunity to take *p*
7: 4 in you; I take great *p* in you.
8: 24 and the reason for our *p* in you,
Gal 6: 4 Then he can take *p* in himself,
Jas 1: 9 ought to take *p* in his high position.

PRIEST (PRIESTHOOD PRIESTLY PRIESTS)
Ge 14: 18 He was *p* of God Most High,
Nu 5: 10 to the *p* will belong to the *p*.' "
2Ch 13: 9 and seven rams may become a *p*
Ps 110: 4 "You are a *p* forever,
Heb 2: 17 faithful high *p* in service to God,
3: 1 and high *p* whom we confess.
4: 14 have a great high *p* who has gone
4: 15 do not have a high *p* who is unable
5: 6 "You are a *p* forever,
6: 20 He has become a high *p* forever,
7: 3 Son of God he remains a *p* forever.
7: 15 clear if another *p* like Melchizedek
7: 26 Such a high *p* meets our need—
8: 1 We do have such a high *p*,
10: 11 Day after day every *p* stands
13: 11 The high *p* carries the blood

PRIESTHOOD (PRIEST)
Heb 7: 24 lives forever, he has a permanent *p*.
1Pe 2: 5 into a spiritual house to be a holy *p*,
2: 9 you are a chosen people, a royal *p*,

PRIESTLY (PRIEST)
Ro 15: 16 to the Gentiles with the *p* duty

PRIESTS (PRIEST)
Ex 19: 6 you will be for me a kingdom of *p*
Lev 21: 1 "Speak to the *p*, the sons of Aaron,
Eze 42: 13 where the *p* who approach
46: 2 *p* are to sacrifice his burnt offering
Mal 1: 6 O *p*, who show contempt for my name.
Rev 5: 10 to be a kingdom and *p*
20: 6 but they will be *p* of God

PRIME
Isa 38: 10 recovery: I said, "In the *p* of my life

PRINCE (PRINCES PRINCESS)
Isa 9: 6 Everlasting Father, *P* of Peace.
Eze 34: 24 and my servant David will be *p*
37: 25 my servant will be their *p* forever.
Da 8: 25 stand against the *P* of princes.
Jn 12: 31 now the *p* of this world will be
Ac 5: 31 as *P* and Savior that he might give

PRINCES (PRINCE)
Ps 118: 9 than to trust in *p*.
148: 11 you *p* and all rulers on earth,
Isa 40: 23 He brings *p* to naught

PRINCESS* (PRINCE)
Ps 45: 13 All glorious is the *p*

PRISCILLA*
Wife of Aquila; co-worker with Paul (Ac 18; Ro 16:3; 1Co 16:19; 2Ti 4:19); instructor of Apollos (Ac 18:24–28).

PRISON (PRISONER PRISONERS)
Ps 66: 11 You brought us into *p*
142: 7 Set me free from my *p*,
Isa 42: 7 to free captives from *p*
Mt 25: 36 I was in *p* and you came to visit me
2Co 11: 23 been in *p* more frequently,
Heb 11: 36 others were chained and put in *p*.
13: 3 Remember those in *p*
1Pe 3: 19 spirits in *p* who disobeyed long ago
Rev 20: 7 Satan will be released from his *p*

PRISONER (PRISON)
Ro 7: 23 and making me a *p* of the law of sin
Gal 3: 22 declares that the whole world is a *p*
Eph 3: 1 the *p* of Christ Jesus for the sake

PRISONERS (PRISON)
Ps 68: 6 he leads forth the *p* with singing;
79: 11 groans of the *p* come before you;
107: 10 *p* suffering in iron chains,
146: 7 The LORD sets *p* free,
Zec 9: 12 to your fortress, O *p* of hope;
Lk 4: 18 me to proclaim freedom for the *p*
Gal 3: 23 we were held *p* by the law,

PRIVILEGE*
2Co 8: 4 pleaded with us for the *p* of sharing

PRIZE*
1Co 9: 24 Run in such a way as to get the *p*.
9: 24 but only one gets the *p*? Run
9: 27 will not be disqualified for the *p*.
Php 3: 14 on toward the goal to win the *p*
Col 2: 18 of angels disqualify you for the *p*.

PROBE
Job 11: 7 Can you *p* the limits
Ps 17: 3 Though you *p* my heart

PROCEDURE
Ecc 8: 6 For there is a proper time and *p*

PROCESSION
Ps 68: 24 Your *p* has come into view, O God,
118: 27 boughs in hand, join in the festal *p*
1Co 4: 9 on display at the end of the *p*,
2Co 2: 14 us in triumphal *p* in Christ

PROCLAIM (PROCLAIMED PROCLAIMING PROCLAIMS PROCLAMATION)
Ex 33: 19 and I will *p* my name, the LORD,
Lev 25: 10 and *p* liberty throughout the land
Dt 30: 12 and *p* it to us so we may obey it?"
2Sa 1: 20 *p* it not in the streets of Ashkelon,
1Ch 16: 23 *p* his salvation day after day.
Ne 8: 15 and that they should *p* this word
Ps 2: 7 I will *p* the decree of the LORD:
9: 11 *p* among the nations what he has
19: 1 the skies *p* the work of his hands.
22: 31 They will *p* his righteousness
40: 9 I *p* righteousness in the great
50: 6 the heavens *p* his righteousness,
64: 9 they will *p* the works of God
68: 34 *P* the power of God,
71: 16 I will come and *p* your mighty acts,
92: 2 to *p* your love in the morning
96: 2 *p* his salvation day after day.
97: 6 The heavens *p* his righteousness,
106: 2 Who can *p* the mighty acts
118: 17 will *p* what the LORD has done.
145: 6 and I will *p* your great deeds.
Isa 12: 4 and *p* that his name is exalted.
42: 12 and *p* his praise in the islands.
52: 7 who *p* salvation,
61: 1 to *p* freedom for the captives
66: 19 They will *p* my glory
Jer 7: 2 house and there *p* this message:
50: 2 lift up a banner and *p* it;
Hos 5: 9 I *p* what is certain.
Zec 9: 10 He will *p* peace to the nations.
Mt 10: 27 in your ear, *p* from the roofs.
12: 18 and he will *p* justice to the nations.
Lk 4: 18 me to *p* freedom for the prisoners
9: 60 you go and *p* the kingdom of God."
Ac 17: 23 unknown I am going to *p*
20: 27 hesitated to *p* to you the whole will
1Co 11: 26 you *p* the Lord's death
Col 1: 28 We *p* him, admonishing
4: 4 Pray that I may *p* it clearly,
1Jn 1: 1 this we *p* concerning the Word

PROCLAIMED (PROCLAIM)
Ex 9: 16 and that my name might be *p*
34: 5 there with him and *p* his name,
Ps 68: 11 was the company of those who *p* it:
Ro 15: 19 I have fully *p* the gospel of Christ.
Col 1: 23 that has been *p* to every creature
2Ti 4: 17 me the message might be fully *p*

PROCLAIMING (PROCLAIM)
Ps 26: 7 *p* aloud your praise
92: 15 *p*, "The LORD is upright;
Ac 5: 42 and *p* the good news that Jesus is
Ro 10: 8 the word of faith we are *p*:

PROCLAIMS (PROCLAIM)
Dt 18: 22 If what a prophet *p* in the name

PROCLAMATION (PROCLAIM)
Isa 62: 11 The LORD has made *p*

PRODUCE (PRODUCES)
Mt 3: 8 *P* fruit in keeping with repentance.
3: 10 tree that does not *p* good fruit will

PRODUCES (PRODUCE)
Pr 30: 33 so stirring up anger *p* strife."
Ro 5: 3 that suffering *p* perseverance;
Heb 12: 11 it *p* a harvest of righteousness

PROFANE (PROFANED)
Lev 19: 12 and so *p* the name of your God.
22: 32 Do not *p* my holy name.
Mal 2: 10 Why do we *p* the covenant

PROFANED (PROFANE)
Eze 36: 20 the nations they *p* my holy name,

PROFESS*
1Ti 2: 10 for women who *p* to worship God.
Heb 4: 14 let us hold firmly to the faith we *p*.

3: 5 Spirit to God's holy apostles and *p.*
4: 11 some to be *p,* some
Heb 1: 1 through the *p* at many times
1Pe 1: 10 Concerning this salvation, the *p,*
2Pe 1: 19 word of the *p* made more certain,
3: 2 spoken in the past by the holy *p*
1Jn 4: 1 because many false *p* have gone out
Rev 11: 10 these two *p* had tormented those
18: 20 Rejoice, saints and apostles and *p!*

PROPORTION
Dt 16: 10 by giving a freewill offering in *p*
16: 17 Each of you must bring a gift in *p*

PROPRIETY*
1Ti 2: 9 with decency and *p,*
2: 15 in faith, love and holiness with *p.*

PROSPECT*
Pr 10: 28 The *p* of the righteous is joy,

PROSPER (PROSPERED PROSPERITY PROSPEROUS PROSPERS)
Dt 5: 33 so that you may live and *p*
28: 63 pleased the LORD to make you *p*
29: 9 that you may *p* in everything you
1Ki 2: 3 so that you may *p* in all you do
Ezr 6: 14 and *p* under the preaching
Pr 11: 10 When the righteous *p,* the city
11: 25 A generous man will *p;*
17: 20 A man of perverse heart does not *p*
28: 13 who conceals his sins does not *p,*
28: 25 he who trusts in the LORD will *p.*
Isa 53: 10 of the LORD will *p* in his hand.
Jer 12: 1 Why does the way of the wicked *p?*

PROSPERED (PROSPER)
Ge 39: 2 was with Joseph and he *p,*
2Ch 14: 7 So they built and *p.*
31: 21 And so he *p.*

PROSPERITY (PROSPER)
Dt 28: 11 will grant you abundant *p*—
30: 15 I set before you today life and *p,*
Job 36: 11 will spend the rest of their days in *p*
Ps 73: 3 when I saw the *p* of the wicked.
122: 9 I will seek your *p.*
128: 2 blessings and *p* will be yours.
Pr 3: 2 and bring you *p.*
13: 21 but *p* is the reward of the righteous.
21: 21 finds life, *p* and honor.
Isa 45: 7 I bring *p* and create disaster;

PROSPEROUS (PROSPER)
Dt 30: 9 your God will make you most *p*
Jos 1: 8 Then you will be *p* and successful.
Job 42: 10 the LORD made him *p* again

PROSPERS (PROSPER)
Ps 1: 3 Whatever he does *p.*
Pr 16: 20 gives heed to instruction *p,*
19: 8 he who cherishes understanding *p.*

PROSTITUTE (PROSTITUTES PROSTITUTION)
Lev 20: 6 and spiritists to *p* himself
Nu 15: 39 and not *p* yourselves by going
Jos 2: 1 the house of a *p* named Rahab
Pr 6: 26 for the *p* reduces you to a loaf
7: 10 like a *p* and with crafty intent.
23: 27 for a *p* is a deep pit
Eze 16: 15 and used your fame to become a *p.*
23: 7 a *p* to all the elite of the Assyrians
Hos 3: 3 you must not be a *p* or be intimate
1Co 6: 15 of Christ and unite them with a *p?*
6: 16 with a *p* is one with her in body?
Rev 17: 1 you the punishment of the great *p,*

PROSTITUTES (PROSTITUTE)
Pr 29: 3 of *p* squanders his wealth.
Mt 21: 31 and the *p* are entering the kingdom
Lk 15: 30 property with *p* comes home,
1Co 6: 9 male *p* nor homosexual offenders

PROSTITUTION (PROSTITUTE)
Eze 16: 16 where you carried on your *p.*
23: 3 engaging in *p* from their youth.
Hos 4: 10 engage in *p* but not increase,

PROSTRATE
Dt 9: 18 again I fell *p* before the LORD
1Ki 18: 39 they fell *p* and cried, "The LORD

PROTECT (PROTECTED PROTECTION PROTECTS)
Dt 23: 14 about in your camp to *p* you
Ps 25: 21 integrity and uprightness *p* me,
32: 7 you will *p* me from trouble
40: 11 your truth always *p* me.
41: 2 The LORD will *p* him
91: 14 I will *p* him, for he acknowledges
140: 1 *p* me from men of violence,
Pr 2: 11 Discretion will *p* you,
4: 6 forsake wisdom, and she will *p* you;
Jn 17: 11 *p* them by the power of your name
17: 15 that you *p* them from the evil one.
2Th 3: 3 and *p* you from the evil one.

PROTECTED (PROTECT)
Jos 24: 17 He *p* us on our entire journey
1Sa 30: 23 He has *p* us and handed
Ps 37: 28 They will be *p* forever,
Jn 17: 12 I *p* them and kept them safe

PROTECTION (PROTECT)
Ezr 9: 9 he has given us a wall of *p* in Judah
Ps 5: 11 Spread your *p* over them,

PROTECTS (PROTECT)
Ps 116: 6 The LORD *p* the simplehearted;
Pr 2: 8 and *p* the way of his faithful ones.
1Co 13: 7 It always *p,* always trusts,

PROUD (PRIDE)
Ps 31: 23 but the *p* he pays back in full.
101: 5 has haughty eyes and a *p* heart,
138: 6 but the *p* he knows from afar.
Pr 3: 34 He mocks *p* mockers
16: 5 The LORD detests all the *p*
16: 19 than to share plunder with the *p.*
18: 12 his downfall a man's heart is *p,*
21: 4 Haughty eyes and a *p* heart,
Isa 2: 12 store for all the *p* and lofty,
Ro 12: 16 Do not be *p,* but be willing
1Co 13: 4 it does not boast, it is not *p.*
2Ti 3: 2 lovers of money, boastful, *p,*
Jas 4: 6 "God opposes the *p*
1Pe 5: 5 because, "God opposes the *p*

PROVE (PROOF PROVED PROVING)
Pr 29: 25 Fear of man will *p* to be a snare,
Jn 8: 46 Can any of you *p* me guilty of sin?
Ac 26: 20 *p* their repentance by their deeds.
1Co 4: 2 been given a trust must *p* faithful.

PROVED (PROVE)
Ps 51: 4 so that you are *p* right
Mt 11: 19 wisdom is *p* right by her actions."
Ro 3: 4 "So that you may be *p* right
1Pe 1: 7 may be *p* genuine and may result

PROVIDE (PROVIDED PROVIDES PROVISION)
Ge 22: 8 "God himself will *p* the lamb
22: 14 that place "The LORD will *P.*"
Isa 43: 20 because I *p* water in the desert
61: 3 and *p* for those who grieve in Zion
1Co 10: 13 *p* a way out so that you can stand
1Ti 5: 8 If anyone does not *p*
Tit 3: 14 in order that they may *p*

PROVIDED (PROVIDE)
Ps 68: 10 O God, you *p* for the poor.
111: 9 He *p* redemption for his people;
Jnh 1: 17 But the LORD *p* a great fish
4: 6 Then the LORD God *p* a vine
4: 7 dawn the next day God *p* a worm,
4: 8 God *p* a scorching east wind,
Gal 4: 18 to be zealous, *p* the purpose is good
Heb 1: 3 After he had *p* purification for sins,

PROVIDES (PROVIDE)
Ps 111: 5 He *p* food for those who fear him;
Pr 31: 15 she *p* food for her family
Eze 18: 7 and *p* clothing for the naked.
1Ti 6: 17 who richly *p* us with everything
1Pe 4: 11 it with the strength God *p,*

PROVING* (PROVE)
Ac 9: 22 by *p* that Jesus is the Christ.
17: 3 and *p* that the Christ had to suffer
18: 28 *p* from the Scriptures that Jesus

PROVISION (PROVIDE)
Ro 5: 17 who receive God's abundant *p*

PROVOKED
Ecc 7: 9 Do not be quickly *p* in your spirit,
Jer 32: 32 Judah have *p* me by all the evil they

PROWLS
1Pe 5: 8 Your enemy the devil *p*

PRUDENCE* (PRUDENT)
Pr 1: 4 for giving *p* to the simple,
8: 5 You who are simple, gain *p;*
8: 12 "I, wisdom, dwell together with *p;*
15: 5 whoever heeds correction shows *p.*
19: 25 and the simple will learn *p;*

PRUDENT* (PRUDENCE)
Pr 1: 3 acquiring a disciplined and *p* life,
12: 16 but a *p* man overlooks an insult.
12: 23 A *p* man keeps his knowledge
13: 16 Every *p* man acts out of knowledge
14: 8 The wisdom of the *p* is
14: 15 a *p* man gives thought to his steps.
14: 18 the *p* are crowned with knowledge.
19: 14 but a *p* wife is from the LORD.
22: 3 *p* man sees danger and takes
27: 12 The *p* see danger and take refuge,
Jer 49: 7 Has counsel perished from the *p?*
Am 5: 13 Therefore the *p* man keeps quiet

PRUNES (PRUNING)
Jn 15: 2 that does bear fruit he *p*

PRUNING (PRUNES)
Isa 2: 4 and their spears into *p* hooks.
Joel 3: 10 and your *p* hooks into spears.

PSALMS
Eph 5: 19 Speak to one another with *p,*
Col 3: 16 and as you sing *p,* hymns

PUBLICLY
Ac 20: 20 have taught you *p* and from house
1Ti 5: 20 Those who sin are to be rebuked *p,*

PUFFS
1Co 8: 1 Knowledge *p* up, but love builds up

PULLING
2Co 10: 8 building you up rather than *p* you

PUNISH (PUNISHED PUNISHES PUNISHMENT)
Ge 15: 14 But I will *p* the nation they serve
Ex 32: 34 I will *p* them for their sin."
Pr 17: 26 It is not good to *p* an innocent man,
23: 13 if you *p* him with the rod, he will
Isa 13: 11 I will *p* the world for its evil,
Jer 2: 19 Your wickedness will *p* you;
21: 14 I will *p* you as your deeds deserve,
Zep 1: 12 and *p* those who are complacent,
Ac 7: 7 But I will *p* the nation they serve
2Th 1: 8 He will *p* those who do not know
1Pe 2: 14 by him to *p* those who do wrong

PUNISHED (PUNISH)
Ezr 9: 13 you have *p* us less than our sins
Ps 99: 8 though you *p* their misdeeds.
La 3: 39 complain when *p* for his sins?
Mk 12: 40 Such men will be *p* most severely."
Lk 23: 41 the same sentence? We are *p* justly,
2Th 1: 9 be *p* with everlasting destruction
Heb 10: 29 to be *p* who has trampled the Son

PUNISHES (PUNISH)
Heb 12: 6 and he *p* everyone he accepts

PUNISHMENT (PUNISH)
Isa 53: 5 the *p* that brought us peace was
Jer 4: 18 This is your *p.*
Mt 25: 46 Then they will go away to eternal *p*
Lk 12: 48 and does things deserving *p* will be
21: 22 For this is the time of *p*
Ro 13: 4 wrath to bring *p* on the wrongdoer.

Heb 2: 2 disobedience received its just *p,*
2Pe 2: 9 while continuing their *p.*

PURCHASED
Ps 74: 2 Remember the people you *p* of old,
Rev 5: 9 with your blood you *p* men for God

PURE (PURIFICATION PURIFIED PURIFIES PURIFY PURITY)
2Sa 22: 27 to the *p* you show yourself *p,*
Job 14: 4 Who can bring what is *p*
Ps 19: 9 The fear of the LORD is *p,*
24: 4 who has clean hands and a *p* heart,
51: 10 Create in me a *p* heart, O God,
119: 9 can a young man keep his way *p?*
Pr 15: 26 those of the *p* are pleasing to him.
20: 9 can say, "I have kept my heart *p;*
Isa 52: 11 Come out from it and be *p,*
Hab 1: 13 Your eyes are too *p* to look on evil;
Mt 5: 8 Blessed are the *p* in heart,
2Co 11: 2 I might present you as a *p* virgin
Php 4: 8 whatever is *p,* whatever is lovely,
1Ti 1: 5 which comes from a *p* heart
5: 22 Keep yourself *p.*
2Ti 2: 22 call on the Lord out of a *p* heart.
Tit 1: 15 To the *p,* all things are *p,*
2: 5 to be self-controlled and *p,*
Heb 7: 26 blameless, *p,* set apart from sinners
13: 4 and the marriage bed kept *p,*
Jas 1: 27 that God our Father accepts as *p*
3: 17 comes from heaven is first of all *p;*
1Jn 3: 3 him purifies himself, just as he is *p.*

PURGE
Pr 20: 30 and beatings *p* the inmost being.

PURIFICATION (PURE)
Heb 1: 3 After he had provided *p* for sins,

PURIFIED (PURE)
Ac 15: 9 for he *p* their hearts by faith.
1Pe 1: 22 Now that you have *p* yourselves

PURIFIES* (PURE)
1Jn 1: 7 of Jesus, his Son, *p* us from all sin.
3: 3 who has this hope in him *p* himself,

PURIFY (PURE)
Nu 19: 12 He must *p* himself with the water
2Co 7: 1 us *p* ourselves from everything that
Tit 2: 14 to *p* for himself a people that are
Jas 4: 8 you sinners, and *p* your hearts,
1Jn 1: 9 and *p* us from all unrighteousness.

PURIM
Est 9: 26 Therefore these days were called *P*

PURITY* (PURE)
Hos 8: 5 long will they be incapable of *p?*
2Co 6: 6 in *p,* understanding, patience
1Ti 4: 12 in life, in love, in faith and in *p.*
5: 2 as sisters, with absolute *p.*
1Pe 3: 2 when they see the *p* and reverence

PURPLE
Pr 31: 22 she is clothed in fine linen and *p.*
Mk 15: 17 They put a *p* robe on him, then

PURPOSE (PURPOSED PURPOSES)
Ex 9: 16 I have raised you up for this very *p,*
Job 36: 5 he is mighty, and firm in his *p.*
Pr 19: 21 but it is the LORD's *p* that prevails
Isa 46: 10 I say: My *p* will stand,
55: 11 and achieve the *p* for which I sent it
Ac 2: 23 handed over to you by God's set *p*
Ro 8: 28 have been called according to his *p.*
9: 11 in order that God's *p*
9: 17 "I raised you up for this very *p,*
1Co 3: 8 the man who waters have one *p,*
2Co 5: 5 who has made us for this very *p*
Gal 4: 18 be zealous, provided the *p* is good,
Eph 1: 11 in conformity with the *p* of his will,
3: 11 according to his eternal *p* which he
Php 2: 2 love, being one in spirit and *p.*
2: 13 and to act according to his good *p.*
2Ti 1: 9 but because of his own *p* and grace.

PURPOSED (PURPOSE)
Isa 14: 24 and as I have *p,* so it will stand.
14: 27 For the LORD Almighty has *p,*
Eph 1: 9 which he *p* in Christ, to be put

PURPOSES (PURPOSE)
Ps 33: 10 he thwarts the *p* of the peoples.
Jer 23: 20 the *p* of his heart.
32: 19 great are your *p* and mighty are

PURSE (PURSES)
Hag 1: 6 to put them in a *p* with holes in it."
Lk 10: 4 Do not take a *p* or bag or sandals;
22: 36 "But now if you have a *p,* take it,

PURSES (PURSE)
Lk 12: 33 Provide *p* for yourselves that will

PURSUE (PURSUES)
Ps 34: 14 seek peace and *p* it.
Pr 15: 9 he loves those who *p* righteousness
Ro 9: 30 who did not *p* righteousness,
1Ti 6: 11 and *p* righteousness, godliness,
2Ti 2: 22 and *p* righteousness, faith,
1Pe 3: 11 he must seek peace and *p* it.

PURSUES (PURSUE)
Pr 21: 21 He who *p* righteousness and love
28: 1 wicked man flees though no one *p,*

QUAIL
Ex 16: 13 That evening *q* came and covered
Nu 11: 31 and drove *q* in from the sea.

QUALITIES* (QUALITY)
Da 6: 3 by his exceptional *q* that the king
Ro 1: 20 of the world God's invisible *q*—
2Pe 1: 8 For if you possess these *q*

QUALITY (QUALITIES)
1Co 3: 13 and the fire will test the *q*

QUARREL (QUARRELING QUARRELS QUARRELSOME)
Pr 15: 18 but a patient man calms a *q.*
17: 14 Starting a *q* is like breaching a dam;
17: 19 He who loves a *q* loves sin;
20: 3 but every fool is quick to *q.*
26: 17 in a *q* not his own.
26: 20 without gossip a *q* dies down.
2Ti 2: 24 And the Lord's servant must not *q;*
Jas 4: 2 You *q* and fight.

QUARRELING (QUARREL)
1Co 3: 3 For since there is jealousy and *q*
2Ti 2: 14 before God against *q* about words;

QUARRELS (QUARREL)
Pr 13: 10 Pride only breeds *q,*
Isa 45: 9 Woe to him who *q* with his Maker,
2Ti 2: 23 because you know they produce *q.*
Jas 4: 1 What causes fights and *q*

QUARRELSOME (QUARREL)
Pr 19: 13 a *q* wife is like a constant dripping.
21: 9 than share a house with a *q* wife.
26: 21 so is a *q* man for kindling strife.
1Ti 3: 3 not violent but gentle, not *q,*

QUEEN
1Ki 10: 1 When the *q* of Sheba heard about
2Ch 9: 1 When the *q* of Sheba heard
Mt 12: 42 The *Q* of the South will rise

QUENCH (QUENCHED)
SS 8: 7 Many waters cannot *q* love;

QUENCHED (QUENCH)
Isa 66: 24 nor will their fire be *q,*
Mk 9: 48 and the fire is not *q.*'

QUICK-TEMPERED* (TEMPER)
Pr 14: 17 A *q* man does foolish things,
14: 29 but a *q* man displays folly.
Tit 1: 7 not *q,* not given to drunkenness,

QUIET (QUIETNESS)
Ps 23: 2 he leads me beside *q* waters,
Pr 17: 1 Better a dry crust with peace and *q*
Ecc 9: 17 The *q* words of the wise are more
Am 5: 13 Therefore the prudent man keeps *q*
Zep 3: 17 he will *q* you with his love,
Lk 19: 40 he replied, "if they keep *q,*
1Th 4: 11 it your ambition to lead a *q* life,
1Ti 2: 2 we may live peaceful and *q* lives
1Pe 3: 4 beauty of a gentle and *q* spirit,

QUIETNESS (QUIET)
Isa 30: 15 in *q* and trust is your strength,
32: 17 the effect of righteousness will be *q*
1Ti 2: 11 A woman should learn in *q*

QUIVER
Ps 127: 5 whose *q* is full of them.

RACE
Ecc 9: 11 The *r* is not to the swift
Ac 20: 24 if only I may finish the *r*
1Co 9: 24 that in a *r* all the runners run,
Gal 2: 2 that I was running or had run my *r*
5: 7 You were running a good *r.*
2Ti 4: 7 I have finished the *r,* I have kept
Heb 12: 1 perseverance the *r* marked out

RACHEL
Daughter of Laban (Ge 29:16); wife of Jacob (Ge 29:28); bore two sons (Ge 30:22–24; 35:16–24; 46:19). Stole Laban's gods (Ge 31:19, 32–35). Death (Ge 35:19–20).

RADIANCE (RADIANT)
Eze 1: 28 so was the *r* around him.
Heb 1: 3 The Son is the *r* of God's glory

RADIANT (RADIANCE)
Ex 34: 29 he was not aware that his face was *r*
Ps 34: 5 Those who look to him are *r;*
SS 5: 10 *Beloved* My lover is *r* and ruddy,
Isa 60: 5 Then you will look and be *r,*
Eph 5: 27 her to himself as a *r* church,

RAGE
Ac 4: 25 " 'Why do the nations *r*
Col 3: 8 *r,* malice, slander, and filthy

RAGS
Isa 64: 6 our righteous acts are like filthy *r;*

RAHAB
Prostitute of Jericho who hid Israelite spies (Jos 2; 6:22–25; Heb 11:31; Jas 2:25). Mother of Boaz (Mt 1:5).

RAIN (RAINBOW)
Ge 7: 4 from now I will send *r* on the earth
1Ki 17: 1 nor *r* in the next few years
18: 1 and I will send *r* on the land."
Mt 5: 45 and sends *r* on the righteous
Jas 5: 17 it did not *r* on the land for three
Jude : 12 They are clouds without *r,*

RAINBOW (RAIN)
Ge 9: 13 I have set my *r* in the clouds,

RAISE (RISE)
Jn 6: 39 but *r* them up at the last day.
1Co 15: 15 he did not *r* him if in fact the dead

RAISED (RISE)
Isa 52: 13 he will be *r* and lifted up
Mt 17: 23 on the third day he will be *r* to life
Lk 7: 22 the deaf hear, the dead are *r,*
Ac 2: 24 But God *r* him from the dead,
Ro 4: 25 was *r* to life for our justification.
6: 4 as Christ was *r* from the dead
8: 11 And if the Spirit of him who *r* Jesus
10: 9 in your heart that God *r* him
1Co 15: 4 that he was *r* on the third day
15: 20 But Christ has indeed been *r*

RALLY*
Isa 11: 10 the nations will *r* to him,

RAM (RAMS)
Ge 22: 13 there in a thicket he saw a *r* caught
Da 8: 3 before me was a *r* with two horns,

RAMPART*
Ps 91: 4 will be your shield and *r.*

RAMS (RAM)
1Sa 15: 22 to heed is better than the fat of *r.*
Mic 6: 7 pleased with thousands of *r,*

RAN (RUN)
Jnh 1: 3 But Jonah *r* away from the LORD

RANSOM (RANSOMED)
Isa 50: 2 Was my arm too short to *r* you?
Hos 13: 14 "I will *r* them from the power
Mt 20: 28 and to give his life as a *r* for many."
Mk 10: 45 and to give his life as a *r* for many."
1Ti 2: 6 who gave himself as a *r* for all men
Heb 9: 15 as a *r* to set them free

RANSOMED (RANSOM)
Isa 35: 10 and the *r* of the LORD will return.

RARE
Pr 20: 15 that speak knowledge are a *r* jewel.

RAVEN (RAVENS)
Ge 8: 7 made in the ark and sent out a *r*,
Job 38: 41 Who provides food for the *r*

RAVENS (RAVEN)
1Ki 17: 6 The *r* brought him bread
Ps 147: 9 and for the young *r* when they call.
Lk 12: 24 Consider the *r*: They do not sow

READ (READING READS)
Dt 17: 19 he is to *r* it all the days of his life
Jos 8: 34 Joshua *r* all the words of the law—
2Ki 23: 2 He *r* in their hearing all the words
Ne 8: 8 They *r* from the Book of the Law
Jer 36: 6 and *r* to the people from the scroll
2Co 3: 2 known and *r* by everybody.

READING (READ)
1Ti 4: 13 to the public *r* of Scripture,

READS (READ)
Rev 1: 3 Blessed is the one who *r* the words

REAFFIRM
2Co 2: 8 therefore, to *r* your love for him.

REAL* (REALITIES REALITY)
Jn 6: 55 is *r* food and my blood is *r* drink.
1Jn 2: 27 all things and as that anointing is *r*,

REALITIES* (REAL)
Heb 10: 1 are coming—not the *r* themselves.

REALITY* (REAL)
Col 2: 17 the *r*, however, is found in Christ.

REALM (REALMS)
Hab 2: 9 "Woe to him who builds his *r*

REALMS (REALM)
Eph 1: 3 the heavenly *r* with every spiritual
2: 6 in the heavenly *r* in Christ Jesus,

REAP (REAPER REAPS)
Job 4: 8 and those who sow trouble *r* it.
Ps 126: 5 will *r* with songs of joy.
Hos 8: 7 and *r* the whirlwind.
10: 12 *r* the fruit of unfailing love,
Jn 4: 38 you to *r* what you have not worked
Ro 6: 22 the benefit you *r* leads to holiness,
2Co 9: 6 generously will also *r* generously.
Gal 6: 8 from that nature will *r* destruction;

REAPER (REAP)
Jn 4: 36 and the *r* may be glad together.

REAPS (REAP)
Pr 11: 18 who sows righteousness *r* a sure
22: 8 He who sows wickedness *r* trouble,
Gal 6: 7 A man *r* what he sows.

REASON (REASONED)
Ge 2: 24 For this *r* a man will leave his
Isa 1: 18 "Come now, let us *r* together,"
Mt 19: 5 'For this *r* a man will leave his
Jn 12: 27 it was for this very *r* I came
15: 25 'They hated me without *r*.'
1Pe 3: 15 to give the *r* for the hope that you
2Pe 1: 5 For this very *r*, make every effort

REASONED (REASON)
1Co 13: 11 thought like a child, I *r* like a child.

REBEKAH
Sister of Laban, secured as bride for Isaac (Ge 24). Mother of Esau and Jacob (Ge 25:19–26). Taken by Abimelech as sister of Isaac; returned (Ge 26:1–11). Encouraged Jacob to trick Isaac out of blessing (Ge 27:1–17).

REBEL (REBELLED REBELLION REBELS)
Nu 14: 9 Only do not *r* against the LORD.
1Sa 12: 14 and do not *r* against his commands,
Mt 10: 21 children will *r* against their parents

REBELLED (REBEL)
Ps 78: 56 and *r* against the Most High;
Isa 63: 10 Yet they *r*

REBELLION (REBEL)
Ex 34: 7 and forgiving wickedness, *r* and sin
Nu 14: 18 in love and forgiving sin and *r*.
1Sa 15: 23 For *r* is like the sin of divination,
2Th 2: 3 will not come until the *r* occurs

REBELS (REBEL)
Ro 13: 2 he who *r* against the authority is
1Ti 1: 9 but for lawbreakers and *r*,

REBIRTH* (BEAR)
Tit 3: 5 us through the washing of *r*

REBUILD (BUILD)
Ezr 5: 2 set to work to *r* the house of God
Ne 2: 17 let us *r* the wall of Jerusalem,
Ps 102: 16 For the LORD will *r* Zion
Da 9: 25 and *r* Jerusalem until the Anointed
Am 9: 14 they will *r* the ruined cities
Ac 15: 16 Its ruins I will *r*,

REBUILT (BUILD)
Zec 1: 16 and there my house will be *r*.

REBUKE (REBUKED REBUKES REBUKING)
Lev 19: 17 *R* your neighbor frankly
Ps 141: 5 let him *r* me—it is oil on my head.
Pr 3: 11 and do not resent his *r*,
9: 8 *r* a wise man and he will love you.
15: 31 He who listens to a life-giving *r*
17: 10 A *r* impresses a man
19: 25 *r* a discerning man, and he will gain
25: 12 is a wise man's *r* to a listening ear.
27: 5 Better is open *r*
30: 6 or he will *r* you and prove you a liar
Ecc 7: 5 It is better to heed a wise man's *r*
Isa 54: 9 never to *r* you again.
Jer 2: 19 your backsliding will *r* you.
Lk 17: 3 "If your brother sins, *r* him,
1Ti 5: 1 Do not *r* an older man harshly,
2Ti 4: 2 correct, *r* and encourage—
Tit 1: 13 Therefore, *r* them sharply,
2: 15 Encourage and *r* with all authority.
Rev 3: 19 Those whom I love I *r*

REBUKED (REBUKE)
Mk 16: 14 he *r* them for their lack of faith
1Ti 5: 20 Those who sin are to be *r* publicly,

REBUKES (REBUKE)
Job 22: 4 "Is it for your piety that he *r* you
Pr 28: 23 He who *r* a man will
29: 1 remains stiff-necked after many *r*
Heb 12: 5 do not lose heart when he *r* you,

REBUKING (REBUKE)
2Ti 3: 16 *r*, correcting and training

RECEIVE (RECEIVED RECEIVES)
Mt 10: 41 a righteous man will *r* a righteous
Mk 10: 15 anyone who will not *r* the kingdom
Jn 20: 22 and said, "*R* the Holy Spirit.
Ac 1: 8 you will *r* power when the Holy
2: 38 you will *r* the gift of the Holy Spirit
19: 2 "Did you *r* the Holy Spirit
20: 35 'It is more blessed to give than to *r*
1Co 9: 14 the gospel should *r* their living
2Co 6: 17 and I will *r* you."
1Ti 1: 16 believe on him and *r* eternal life.
Jas 1: 7 should not think he will *r* anything
2Pe 1: 11 and you will *r* a rich welcome
1Jn 3: 22 and *r* from him anything we ask,
Rev 4: 11 to *r* glory and honor and power,
5: 12 to *r* power and wealth and wisdom

RECEIVED (RECEIVE)
Mt 6: 2 they have *r* their reward in full.
10: 8 Freely you have *r*, freely give.
Mk 11: 24 believe that you have *r* it,
Jn 1: 12 Yet to all who *r* him,
1: 16 his grace we have all *r* one blessing
Ac 8: 17 and they *r* the Holy Spirit.
10: 47 They have *r* the Holy Spirit just
Ro 8: 15 but you *r* the Spirit of sonship.
1Co 11: 23 For I *r* from the Lord what I
2Co 1: 4 the comfort we ourselves have *r*
Col 2: 6 just as you *r* Christ Jesus as Lord,
1Pe 4: 10 should use whatever gift he has *r*

RECEIVES (RECEIVE)
Pr 18: 22 and *r* favor from the LORD.
27: 21 but man is tested by the praise he *r*.
Mt 7: 8 everyone who asks *r*; he who seeks
10: 40 he who *r* me *r* the one who sent me.
10: 40 "He who *r* you *r* me, and he who
Ac 10: 43 believes in him *r* forgiveness of sins

RECITE
Ps 45: 1 as I *r* my verses for the king;

RECKLESS
Pr 12: 18 *R* words pierce like a sword,
14: 16 but a fool is hotheaded and *r*.

RECKONING
Isa 10: 3 What will you do on the day of *r*,
Hos 9: 7 the days of *r* are at hand.

RECLAIM* (CLAIM)
Isa 11: 11 time to *r* the remnant that is left

RECOGNITION (RECOGNIZE)
1Co 16: 18 Such men deserve *r*.
1Ti 5: 3 Give proper *r* to those widows who

RECOGNIZE (RECOGNITION RECOGNIZED)
Mt 7: 16 By their fruit you will *r* them.
1Jn 4: 2 This is how you can *r* the Spirit
4: 6 This is how we *r* the Spirit of truth

RECOGNIZED (RECOGNIZE)
Mt 12: 33 for a tree is *r* by its fruit.
Ro 7: 13 in order that sin might be *r* as sin,

RECOMPENSE*
Isa 40: 10 and his *r* accompanies him.
62: 11 and his *r* accompanies him.' "

RECONCILE* (RECONCILED RECONCILIATION RECONCILING)
Ac 7: 26 He tried to *r* them by saying, 'Men,
Eph 2: 16 in this one body to *r* both of them
Col 1: 20 him to *r* to himself all things,

RECONCILED* (RECONCILE)
Mt 5: 24 First go and be *r* to your brother;
Lk 12: 58 try hard to be *r* to him on the way,
Ro 5: 10 how much more, having been *r*,
5: 10 we were *r* to him through the death
1Co 7: 11 or else be *r* to her husband.
2Co 5: 18 who *r* us to himself through Christ
5: 20 you on Christ's behalf: Be *r* to God.
Col 1: 22 he has *r* you by Christ's physical

RECONCILIATION* (RECONCILE)
Ro 5: 11 whom we have now received *r*.
11: 15 For if their rejection is the *r*
2Co 5: 18 and gave us the ministry of *r*:
5: 19 committed to us the message of *r*.

RECONCILING* (RECONCILE)
2Co 5: 19 that God was *r* the world to himself

RECORD (RECORDED)
Ps 130: 3 If you, O LORD, kept a *r* of sins,
Hos 13: 12 his sins are kept on *r*.
1Co 13: 5 is not easily angered, it keeps no *r*

RECORDED (RECORD)
Job 19: 23 "Oh, that my words were *r*,
Jn 20: 30 which are not *r* in this book.

RECOUNT*
Ps 40: 5 no one can *r* to you;
79: 13 we will *r* your praise.
119: 13 With my lips I *r*

RED
Ex 15: 4 are drowned in the *R* Sea.

Ps 106: 9 He rebuked the R Sea,
Pr 23: 31 Do not gaze at wine when it is r,
Isa 1: 18 though they are r as crimson,

REDEEM (KINSMAN-REDEEMER REDEEMED REDEEMER REDEEMS REDEMPTION)
Ex 6: 6 will r you with an outstretched arm
2Sa 7: 23 on earth that God went out to r
Ps 44: 26 r us because of your unfailing love.
49: 7 No man can r the life of another
49: 15 God will r my life from the grave;
130: 8 He himself will r Israel
Hos 13: 14 I will r them from death.
Gal 4: 5 under law, to r those under law,
Tit 2: 14 for us to r us from all wickedness

REDEEMED (REDEEM)
Job 33: 28 He r my soul from going
Ps 71: 23 I, whom you have r.
107: 2 Let the r of the LORD say this—
Isa 35: 9 But only the r will walk there,
63: 9 In his love and mercy he r them;
Gal 3: 13 Christ r us from the curse
1Pe 1: 18 or gold that you were r

REDEEMER (REDEEM)
Job 19: 25 I know that my R lives,
Ps 19: 14 O LORD, my Rock and my R.
Isa 44: 6 and R, the LORD Almighty:
48: 17 your R, the Holy One of Israel:
59: 20 "The R will come to Zion,

REDEEMS (REDEEM)
Ps 34: 22 The LORD r his servants;
103: 4 he r my life from the pit

REDEMPTION (REDEEM)
Ps 130: 7 and with him is full r.
Lk 21: 28 because your r is drawing near."
Ro 3: 24 grace through the r that came
8: 23 as sons, the r of our bodies.
1Co 1: 30 our righteousness, holiness and r.
Eph 1: 7 In him we have r through his blood
1: 14 until the r of those who are God's
4: 30 you were sealed for the day of r.
Col 1: 14 in whom we have r, the forgiveness
Heb 9: 12 having obtained eternal r.

REED
Isa 42: 3 A bruised r he will not break,
Mt 12: 20 A bruised r he will not break,

REFINE*
Jer 9: 7 "See, I will r and test them,
Zec 13: 9 I will r them like silver
Mal 3: 3 and r them like gold and silver.

REFLECT (REFLECTS)
2Co 3: 18 unveiled faces all r the Lord's

REFLECTS (REFLECT)
Pr 27: 19 As water r a face,

REFRESH (REFRESHED REFRESHING)
Phm : 20 in the Lord; r my heart in Christ.

REFRESHED (REFRESH)
Pr 11: 25 refreshes others will himself be r.

REFRESHING* (REFRESH)
Ac 3: 19 that times of r may come

REFUGE
Nu 35: 11 towns to be your cities of r,
Dt 33: 27 The eternal God is your r,
Jos 20: 2 to designate the cities of r,
Ru 2: 12 wings you have come to take r."
2Sa 22: 3 God is my rock, in whom I take r,
22: 31 a shield for all who take r in him.
Ps 2: 12 Blessed are all who take r in him.
5: 11 But let all who take r in you be glad
9: 9 The LORD is a r for the oppressed,
16: 1 for in you I take r.
17: 7 those who take r in you
18: 2 God is my rock, in whom I take r.
31: 2 be my rock of r,
34: 8 blessed is the man who takes r
36: 7 find r in the shadow of your wings.
46: 1 God is our r and strength,
62: 8 for God is our r.
71: 1 In you, O LORD, I have taken r;
91: 2 "He is my r and my fortress,
144: 2 my shield, in whom I take r,
Pr 14: 26 and for his children it will be a r.
30: 5 a shield to those who take r in him.
Na 1: 7 a r in times of trouble.

REFUSE (REFUSED)
Jn 5: 40 yet you r to come to me to have life

REFUSED (REFUSE)
2Th 2: 10 because they r to love the truth
Rev 16: 9 but they r to repent and glorify him

REGARD (REGARDS)
1Th 5: 13 Hold them in the highest r in love

REGARDS (REGARD)
Ro 14: 14 But if anyone r something

REGRET
2Co 7: 10 leads to salvation and leaves no r,

REHOBOAM
Son of Solomon (1Ki 11:43; 1Ch 3:10). Harsh treatment of subjects caused divided kingdom (1Ki 12:1–24; 14:21–31; 2Ch 10–12).

REIGN (REIGNED REIGNS)
Ex 15: 18 The LORD will r
Ps 68: 16 mountain where God chooses to r,
Isa 9: 7 He will r on David's throne
24: 23 for the LORD Almighty will r
32: 1 See, a king will r in righteousness
Jer 23: 5 a King who will r wisely
Lk 1: 33 and he will r over the house
Ro 6: 12 Therefore do not let sin r
1Co 15: 25 For he must r until he has put all
2Ti 2: 12 we will also r with him.
Rev 11: 15 and he will r for ever and ever."
20: 6 will r with him for a thousand years
22: 5 And they will r for ever and ever.

REIGNED (REIGN)
Ro 5: 21 so that, just as sin r in death,
Rev 20: 4 and r with Christ a thousand years.

REIGNS (REIGN)
Ps 9: 7 The LORD r forever;
47: 8 God r over the nations;
93: 1 The LORD r, he is robed
96: 10 among the nations, "The LORD r
97: 1 The LORD r, let the earth be glad;
99: 1 The LORD r, / let the nations tremble;
146: 10 The LORD r forever,
Isa 52: 7 "Your God r!"
Rev 19: 6 For our Lord God Almighty r.

REIN
Jas 1: 26 and yet does not keep a tight r

REJECT (REJECTED REJECTION REJECTS)
Ps 94: 14 For the LORD will not r his people
Ro 11: 1 I ask then: Did God r his people?

REJECTED (REJECT)
1Sa 8: 7 it is not you they have r,
1Ki 19: 10 The Israelites have r your covenant
2Ki 17: 15 They r his decrees
Ps 66: 20 who has not r my prayer
118: 22 The stone the builders r
Isa 5: 24 for they have r the law
41: 9 chosen you and have not r you.
53: 3 He was despised and r by men,
Jer 8: 9 Since they have r the word
Mt 21: 42 " 'The stone the builders r
1Ti 4: 4 nothing is to be r if it is received
1Pe 2: 4 r by men but chosen by God
2: 7 "The stone the builders r

REJECTION* (REJECT)
Ro 11: 15 For if their r is the reconciliation

REJECTS (REJECT)
Lk 10: 16 but he who r me r him who sent me
Jn 3: 36 whoever r the Son will not see life,
1Th 4: 8 he who r this instruction does not

REJOICE (JOY)
Dt 12: 7 shall r in everything you have put
1Ch 16: 10 of those who seek the LORD r.
16: 31 Let the heavens r, let the earth be
Ps 2: 11 and r with trembling.
5: 11 those who love your name may r
9: 14 and there r in your salvation.
34: 2 let the afflicted hear and r.
63: 11 But the king will r in God;
66: 6 come, let us r in him.
68: 3 and r before God;
105: 3 of those who seek the LORD r.
118: 24 let us r and be glad in it.
119: 14 I r in following your statutes
119:162 I r in your promise
149: 2 Let Israel r in their Maker;
Pr 5: 18 may you r in the wife of your youth
23: 25 may she who gave you birth r!
24: 17 stumbles, do not let your heart r,
Isa 9: 3 as men r
35: 1 the wilderness will r and blossom.
61: 7 they will r in their inheritance;
62: 5 so will your God r over you.
Jer 31: 12 they will r in the bounty
Zep 3: 17 he will r over you with singing."
Zec 9: 9 R greatly, O Daughter of Zion!
Lk 6: 23 "R in that day and leap for joy,
10: 20 but r that your names are written
15: 6 'R with me; I have found my lost
15: 9 'R with me; I have found my lost
Ro 5: 2 And we r in the hope of the glory
12: 15 Rejoice with those who r; mourn
Php 2: 17 I am glad and r with all of you.
3: 1 Finally, my brothers, r in the Lord!
4: 4 R in the Lord always.
1Pe 4: 13 But r that you participate
Rev 19: 7 Let us r and be glad

REJOICES (JOY)
Ps 13: 5 my heart r in your salvation.
16: 9 my heart is glad and my tongue r;
Isa 61: 10 my soul r in my God.
62: 5 as a bridegroom r over his bride,
Lk 1: 47 and my spirit r in God my Savior,
Ac 2: 26 my heart is glad and my tongue r;
1Co 12: 26 if one part is honored, every part r
13: 6 delight in evil but r with the truth.

REJOICING (JOY)
2Sa 6: 12 to the City of David with r.
Ne 12: 43 r because God had given them
Ps 30: 5 but r comes in the morning.
Lk 15: 7 in the same way there will be more r
Ac 5: 41 r because they had been counted
2Co 6: 10 sorrowful, yet always r; poor,

RELATIVES
Pr 19: 7 A poor man is shunned by all his r
Mk 6: 4 among his r and in his own house is
Lk 21: 16 betrayed even by parents, brothers, r
1Ti 5: 8 If anyone does not provide for his r

RELEASE (RELEASED)
Isa 61: 1 and r from darkness,
Lk 4: 18 to r the oppressed,

RELEASED (RELEASE)
Ro 7: 6 we have been r from the law
Rev 20: 7 Satan will be r from his prison

RELENTED (RELENTS)
Ex 32: 14 the LORD r and did not bring
Ps 106: 45 and out of his great love he r.

RELENTS* (RELENTED)
Joel 2: 13 and he r from sending calamity.
Jnh 4: 2 a God who r from sending calamity

RELIABLE (RELY)
Pr 22: 21 teaching you true and r words,
Jn 8: 26 But he who sent me is r,
2Ti 2: 2 witnesses entrust to r men who will

RELIANCE * (RELY)
Pr 25: 19 is r on the unfaithful in times

RELIED (RELY)
2Ch 13: 18 were victorious because they *r*
16: 8 Yet when you *r* on the LORD,
Ps 71: 6 From birth I have *r* on you;

RELIEF
Job 35: 9 they plead for *r* from the arm
Ps 94: 13 you grant him *r* from days
143: 1 come to my *r.*
La 3: 49 without *r,*
3: 56 to my cry for *r.*"
2Th 1: 7 and give *r* to you who are troubled,

RELIGION* (RELIGIOUS)
Ac 25: 19 dispute with him about their own *r*
26: 5 to the strictest sect of our *r,*
1Ti 5: 4 all to put their *r* into practice
Jas 1: 26 himself and his *r* is worthless.
1: 27 *R* that God our Father accepts

RELIGIOUS (RELIGION)
Jas 1: 26 If anyone considers himself *r*

RELY (RELIABLE RELIANCE RELIED)
Isa 50: 10 and *r* on his God.
Eze 33: 26 you then possess the land? You *r*
2Co 1: 9 this happened that we might not *r*
Gal 3: 10 All who *r* on observing the law are
1Jn 4: 16 and *r* on the love God has for us.

REMAIN (REMAINS)
Nu 33: 55 allow to *r* will become barbs
Ps 102: 27 But you *r* the same,
Jn 1: 32 from heaven as a dove and *r* on him
15: 4 *R* in me, and I will *r* in you.
15: 7 If you *r* in me and my words
15: 9 Now *r* in my love.
Ro 13: 8 Let no debt *r* outstanding,
1Co 13: 13 And now these three *r:* faith,
2Ti 2: 13 he will *r* faithful,
Heb 1: 11 They will perish, but you *r;*
1Jn 2: 27 just as it has taught you, *r* in him.

REMAINS (REMAIN)
Ps 146: 6 the LORD, who *r* faithful forever.
Heb 7: 3 Son of God he *r* a priest forever.

REMEDY
Isa 3: 7 "I have no *r.*

REMEMBER (REMEMBERED REMEMBERS REMEMBRANCE)
Ge 9: 15 I will *r* my covenant between me
Ex 20: 8 "*R* the Sabbath day
33: 13 *R* that this nation is your people."
Dt 5: 15 *R* that you were slaves in Egypt
1Ch 16: 12 *R* the wonders he has done,
Job 36: 24 *R* to extol his work,
Ps 25: 6 *R,* O LORD, your great mercy
63: 6 On my bed I *r* you;
74: 2 *R* the people you purchased of old,
77: 11 I will *r* the deeds of the LORD;
Ecc 12: 1 *R* your Creator
Isa 46: 8 "*R* this, fix it in mind,
Jer 31: 34 and will *r* their sins no more."
Hab 3: 2 in wrath *r* mercy.
Lk 1: 72 and to *r* his holy covenant,
Gal 2: 10 we should continue to *r* the poor,
Php 1: 3 I thank my God every time I *r* you.
2Ti 2: 8 *R* Jesus Christ, raised
Heb 8: 12 and will *r* their sins no more."

REMEMBERED (REMEMBER)
Ex 2: 24 he *r* his covenant with Abraham,
3: 15 am to be *r* from generation
Ps 98: 3 He has *r* his love
106: 45 for their sake he *r* his covenant
111: 4 He has caused his wonders to be *r;*
136: 23 to the One who *r* us
Isa 65: 17 The former things will not be *r,*
Eze 18: 22 offenses he has committed will be *r*
33: 13 things he has done will be *r;*

REMEMBERS (REMEMBER)
Ps 103: 14 he *r* that we are dust.
111: 5 he *r* his covenant forever.
Isa 43: 25 and *r* your sins no more.

REMEMBRANCE (REMEMBER)
Lk 22: 19 given for you; do this in *r* of me."
1Co 11: 24 which is for you; do this in *r* of me
11: 25 whenever you drink it, in *r* of me."

REMIND
Jn 14: 26 will *r* you of everything I have said
2Pe 1: 12 I will always *r* you of these things,

REMNANT
Ezr 9: 8 has been gracious in leaving us a *r*
Isa 11: 11 time to reclaim the *r* that is left
Jer 23: 3 "I myself will gather the *r*
Zec 8: 12 inheritance to the *r* of this people.
Ro 11: 5 the present time there is a *r* chosen

REMOVED
Ps 30: 11 you *r* my sackcloth and clothed me
103: 12 so far has he *r* our transgressions
Jn 20: 1 and saw that the stone had been *r*

REND
Joel 2: 13 *R* your heart

RENEW (RENEWAL RENEWED RENEWING)
Ps 51: 10 and *r* a steadfast spirit within me.
Isa 40: 31 will *r* their strength.

RENEWAL (RENEW)
Isa 57: 10 You found *r* of your strength,
Tit 3: 5 of rebirth and *r* by the Holy Spirit,

RENEWED (RENEW)
Ps 103: 5 that your youth is *r* like the eagle's.
2Co 4: 16 yet inwardly we are being *r* day

RENEWING* (RENEW)
Ro 12: 2 transformed by the *r* of your mind.

RENOUNCE (RENOUNCED RENOUNCES)
Da 4: 27 *R* your sins by doing what is right,

RENOUNCED (RENOUNCE)
2Co 4: 2 we have *r* secret and shameful

RENOUNCES (RENOUNCE)
Pr 28: 13 confesses and *r* them finds

RENOWN*
Ge 6: 4 were the heroes of old, men of *r.*
Ps 102: 12 *r* endures through all generations.
135: 13 *r,* O LORD, through all
Isa 26: 8 your name and *r*
55: 13 This will be for the LORD's *r,*
63: 12 to gain for himself everlasting *r,*
Jer 13: 11 to be my people for my *r* and praise
32: 20 have gained the *r* that is still yours.
33: 9 Then this city will bring me *r,* joy,
49: 25 the city of *r* not been abandoned,
Eze 26: 17 How you are destroyed, O city of *r,*
Hos 12: 5 the LORD is his name of *r!*

REPAID (PAY)
Lk 6: 34 to 'sinners,' expecting to be *r* in full
14: 14 you will be *r* at the resurrection
Col 3: 25 Anyone who does wrong will be *r*

REPAY (PAY)
Dt 7: 10 But those who hate him he will *r*
32: 35 It is mine to avenge; I will *r.*
Ru 2: 12 May the LORD *r* you
Ps 103: 10 or *r* us according to our iniquities.
116: 12 How can I *r* the LORD
Jer 25: 14 I will *r* them according
Ro 12: 17 Do not *r* anyone evil for evil.
12: 19 "It is mine to avenge; I will *r,*"
1Pe 3: 9 Do not *r* evil with evil

REPAYING (PAY)
2Ch 6: 23 *r* the guilty by bringing
1Ti 5: 4 so *r* their parents and grandparents

REPEATED
Heb 10: 1 the same sacrifices *r* endlessly year

REPENT (REPENTANCE REPENTED REPENTS)
1Ki 8: 47 *r* and plead with you in the land
Job 36: 10 commands them to *r* of their evil.
42: 6 and *r* in dust and ashes."
Jer 15: 19 "If you *r,* I will restore you
Eze 18: 30 *R!* Turn away from all your
18: 32 *R* and live! "Take up a lament
Mt 3: 2 "*R,* for the kingdom of heaven is
4: 17 "*R,* for the kingdom of heaven is
Mk 6: 12 and preached that people should *r.*
Lk 13: 3 unless you *r,* you too will all perish.
Ac 2: 38 Peter replied, "*R* and be baptized,
3: 19 *R,* then, and turn to God,
17: 30 all people everywhere to *r.*
26: 20 also, I preached that they should *r*
Rev 2: 5 *R* and do the things you did at first.

REPENTANCE (REPENT)
Isa 30: 15 "In *r* and rest is your salvation,
Mt 3: 8 Produce fruit in keeping with *r.*
Mk 1: 4 a baptism of *r* for the forgiveness
Lk 3: 8 Produce fruit in keeping with *r.*
5: 32 call the righteous, but sinners to *r.*"
24: 47 and *r* and forgiveness of sins will be
Ac 20: 21 that they must turn to God in *r*
26: 20 and prove their *r* by their deeds.
Ro 2: 4 kindness leads you toward *r?*
2Co 7: 10 Godly sorrow brings *r* that leads
2Pe 3: 9 but everyone to come to *r.*

REPENTED (REPENT)
Mt 11: 21 they would have *r* long ago

REPENTS (REPENT)
Lk 15: 7 in heaven over one sinner who *r*
15: 10 of God over one sinner who *r.*"
17: 3 rebuke him, and if he *r,* forgive him

REPORTS
Ex 23: 1 "Do not spread false *r.*

REPOSES*
Pr 14: 33 Wisdom *r* in the heart

REPRESENTATION*
Heb 1: 3 and the exact *r* of his being,

REPROACH
Job 27: 6 my conscience will not *r* me
Isa 51: 7 Do not fear the *r* of men
1Ti 3: 2 Now the overseer must be above *r,*

REPUTATION
1Ti 3: 7 also have a good *r* with outsiders,

REQUESTS
Ps 20: 5 May the LORD grant all your *r.*
Php 4: 6 with thanksgiving, present your *r*

REQUIRE (REQUIRED REQUIRES)
Mic 6: 8 And what does the LORD *r* of you

REQUIRED (REQUIRE)
1Co 4: 2 it is *r* that those who have been

REQUIRES (REQUIRE)
1Ki 2: 3 what the LORD your God *r:*
Heb 9: 22 the law *r* that nearly everything be

RESCUE (RESCUED RESCUES)
Ps 22: 8 let the LORD *r* him.
31: 2 come quickly to my *r;*
69: 14 *R* me from the mire,
91: 14 says the LORD, "I will *r* him;
143: 9 *R* me from my enemies, O LORD,
Da 6: 20 been able to *r* you from the lions?"
Ro 7: 24 Who will *r* me from this body
Gal 1: 4 himself for our sins to *r* us
2Pe 2: 9 how to *r* godly men from trials

RESCUED (RESCUE)
Ps 18: 17 He *r* me from my powerful enemy,
Pr 11: 8 The righteous man is *r*
Col 1: 13 For he has *r* us from the dominion

RESCUES (RESCUE)
Da 6: 27 He *r* and he saves;
1Th 1: 10 who *r* us from the coming wrath.

RESENT* (RESENTFUL RESENTS)
Pr 3: 11 and do not *r* his rebuke,

RESENTFUL* (RESENT)
2Ti 2: 24 to everyone, able to teach, not *r.*

RESENTS* (RESENT)
Pr 15: 12 A mocker *r* correction;

RESERVE (RESERVED)
1Ki 19: 18 Yet I *r* seven thousand in Israel—

RESERVED (RESERVE)
Ro 11: 4 "I have *r* for myself seven

RESIST (RESISTED RESISTS)
Da 11: 32 know their God will firmly *r* him.
Mt 5: 39 I tell you, Do not *r* an evil person.
Lk 21: 15 of your adversaries will be able to *r*
Jas 4: 7 *R* the devil, and he will flee
1Pe 5: 9 *R* him, standing firm in the faith,

RESISTED (RESIST)
Job 9: 4 Who has *r* him and come out

RESISTS* (RESIST)
Ro 9: 19 For who *r* his will?" But who are

RESOLVED
Ps 17: 3 I have *r* that my mouth will not sin.
Da 1: 8 But Daniel *r* not to defile himself
1Co 2: 2 For I *r* to know nothing while I was

RESOUNDING*
Ps 150: 5 praise him with *r* cymbals.
1Co 13: 1 I am only a *r* gong or a clanging

RESPECT (RESPECTABLE RESPECTED RESPECTS)
Lev 19: 3 " 'Each of you must *r* his mother
19: 32 show *r* for the elderly and revere
Pr 11: 16 A kindhearted woman gains *r*,
Mal 1: 6 where is the *r* due me?" says
Eph 5: 33 and the wife must *r* her husband.
6: 5 obey your earthly masters with *r*
1Th 4: 12 so that your daily life may win the *r*
5: 12 to *r* those who work hard
1Ti 3: 4 children obey him with proper *r*.
3: 8 are to be men worthy of *r*, sincere,
3: 11 are to be women worthy of *r*,
6: 1 their masters worthy of full *r*,
Tit 2: 2 worthy of *r*, self-controlled,
1Pe 2: 17 Show proper *r* to everyone:
3: 7 them with *r* as the weaker partner
3: 16 But do this with gentleness and *r*,

RESPECTABLE* (RESPECT)
1Ti 3: 2 self-controlled, *r*, hospitable,

RESPECTED (RESPECT)
Pr 31: 23 Her husband is *r* at the city gate,

RESPECTS (RESPECT)
Pr 13: 13 he who *r* a command is rewarded.

RESPLENDENT*
Ps 76: 4 You are *r* with light,
132: 18 but the crown on his head will be *r*

RESPOND
Ps 102: 17 He will *r* to the prayer
Hos 2: 21 "I will *r* to the skies,

RESPONSIBILITY (RESPONSIBLE)
Ac 18: 6 your own heads! I am clear of my *r*.

RESPONSIBLE (RESPONSIBILITY)
Nu 1: 53 The Levites are to be *r* for the care
1Co 7: 24 Brothers, each man, as *r* to God,

REST (RESTED RESTS SABBATH-REST)
Ex 31: 15 the seventh day is a Sabbath of *r*,
33: 14 go with you, and I will give you *r*."
Lev 25: 5 The land is to have a year of *r*.
Dt 31: 16 going to *r* with your fathers,
Jos 14: 15 Then the land had *r* from war.
21: 44 The LORD gave them *r*
1Ki 5: 4 The LORD my god has given me *r*
1Ch 22: 9 who will be a man of peace and *r*,
Job 3: 17 and there the weary are at *r*.
Ps 16: 9 my body also will *r* secure,
33: 22 May your unfailing love *r* upon us,
62: 1 My soul finds *r* in God alone;
62: 5 Find *r*, O my soul, in God alone;
90: 17 of the Lord our God *r* upon us;
91: 1 will *r* in the shadow
95: 11 "They shall never enter my *r*."
Pr 6: 10 a little folding of the hands to *r*—
Isa 11: 2 Spirit of the LORD will *r* on him—
11: 10 and his place of *r* will be glorious.
30: 15 "In repentance and *r* is your
32: 18 in undisturbed places of *r*.
57: 20 which cannot *r*,
Jer 6: 16 and you will find *r* for your souls.
47: 6 'how long till you *r*?
Mt 11: 28 and burdened, and I will give you *r*.
2Co 12: 9 so that Christ's power may *r* on me
Heb 3: 11 'They shall never enter my *r*.' "
4: 3 'They shall never enter my *r*.' "
4: 10 for anyone who enters God's *r*
Rev 14: 13 "they will *r* from their labor,

RESTED (REST)
Ge 2: 2 so on the seventh day he *r*
Heb 4: 4 "And on the seventh day God *r*

RESTITUTION
Ex 22: 3 "A thief must certainly make *r*,
Lev 6: 5 He must make *r* in full, add a fifth
Nu 5: 8 the *r* belongs to the LORD

RESTORE (RESTORES)
Ps 51: 12 *R* to me the joy of your salvation
80: 3 *R* us, O God;
126: 4 *R* our fortunes, O LORD,
Jer 31: 18 *R* me, and I will return,
La 5: 21 *R* us to yourself, O LORD,
Da 9: 25 From the issuing of the decree to *r*
Na 2: 2 The LORD will *r* the splendor
Gal 6: 1 are spiritual should *r* him gently.
1Pe 5: 10 will himself *r* you and make you

RESTORES (RESTORE)
Ps 23: 3 he *r* my soul.

RESTRAINED (RESTRAINT)
Ps 78: 38 Time after time he *r* his anger

RESTRAINING (RESTRAINT)
Pr 27: 16 *r* her is like *r* the wind
Col 2: 23 value in *r* sensual indulgence.

RESTRAINT (RESTRAINED RESTRAINING)
Pr 17: 27 of knowledge uses words with *r*,
23: 4 have the wisdom to show *r*.
29: 18 no revelation, the people cast off *r*;

RESTS (REST)
Dt 33: 12 and the one the LORD loves *r*
Pr 19: 23 one *r* content, untouched
Lk 2: 14 to men on whom his favor *r*."

RESULT
Lk 21: 13 This will *r* in your being witnesses
Ro 6: 22 to holiness, and the *r* is eternal life.
11: 31 as a *r* of God's mercy to you.
2Co 3: 3 from Christ, the *r* of our ministry,
2Th 1: 5 as a *r* you will be counted worthy
1Pe 1: 7 may be proved genuine and may *r*

RESURRECTION*
Mt 22: 23 who say there is no *r*, came to him
22: 28 at the *r*, whose wife will she be
22: 30 At the *r* people will neither marry
22: 31 But about the *r* of the dead—
27: 53 and after Jesus' *r* they went
Mk 12: 18 who say there is no *r*, came to him
12: 23 At the *r* whose wife will she be,
Lk 14: 14 repaid at the *r* of the righteous."
20: 27 who say there is no *r*, came to Jesus
20: 33 at the *r* whose wife will she be,
20: 35 in the *r* from the dead will neither
20: 36 since they are children of the *r*.
Jn 11: 24 again in the *r* at the last day."
11: 25 Jesus said to her, "I am the *r*
Ac 1: 22 become a witness with us of his *r*."
2: 31 he spoke of the *r* of the Christ,
4: 2 in Jesus the *r* of the dead.
4: 33 to testify to the *r* of the Lord Jesus,
17: 18 good news about Jesus and the *r*.
17: 32 When they heard about the *r*
23: 6 of my hope in the *r* of the dead."
23: 8 Sadducees say that there is no *r*,
24: 15 that there will be a *r*
24: 21 'It is concerning the *r*
Ro 1: 4 Son of God by his *r* from the dead:
6: 5 also be united with him in his *r*.
1Co 15: 12 some of you say that there is no *r*
15: 13 If there is no *r* of the dead,
15: 21 the *r* of the dead comes
15: 29 if there is no *r*, what will those do
15: 42 So will it be with the *r* of the dead.
Php 3: 10 power of his *r* and the fellowship
3: 11 to attain to the *r* from the dead.
2Ti 2: 18 say that the *r* has already taken
Heb 6: 2 on of hands, the *r* of the dead,
11: 35 so that they might gain a better *r*.
1Pe 1: 3 hope through the *r* of Jesus Christ
3: 21 It saves you by the *r* of Jesus Christ
Rev 20: 5 This is the first *r*.
20: 6 those who have part in the first *r*.

RETALIATE*
1Pe 2: 23 he did not *r*; when he suffered,

RETRIBUTION
Ps 69: 22 may it become *r* and a trap.
Jer 51: 56 For the LORD is a God of *r*;
Ro 11: 9 a stumbling block and a *r* for them.

RETURN (RETURNED RETURNS)
Ge 3: 19 and to dust you will *r*."
2Sa 12: 23 go to him, but he will not *r* to me."
2Ch 30: 9 If you *r* to the LORD, then your
Ne 1: 9 but if you *r* to me and obey my
Job 10: 21 joy before I go to the place of no *r*,
16: 22 before I go on the journey of no *r*.
22: 23 If you *r* to the Almighty, you will
Ps 80: 14 *R* to us, O God Almighty!
126: 6 will *r* with songs of joy,
Isa 10: 21 A remnant will *r*, a remnant
35: 10 the ransomed of the LORD will *r*.
55: 11 It will not *r* to me empty,
Jer 24: 7 for they will *r* to me
31: 8 a great throng will *r*.
La 3: 40 and let us *r* to the LORD.
Hos 6: 1 "Come, let us *r* to the LORD.
12: 6 But you must *r* to your God;
14: 1 *R*, O Israel, to the LORD your
Joel 2: 12 "*r* to me with all your heart,
Zec 1: 3 '*R* to me,' declares the LORD
10: 9 and they will *r*.

RETURNED (RETURN)
Ps 35: 13 When my prayers *r*
Am 4: 6 yet you have not *r* to me,"
1Pe 2: 25 now you have *r* to the Shepherd

RETURNS (RETURN)
Pr 3: 14 and yields better *r* than gold.
Isa 52: 8 When the LORD *r* to Zion,
Mt 24: 46 finds him doing so when he *r*.

REUBEN
Firstborn of Jacob by Leah (Ge 29:32; 46:8; 1Ch 2:1). Attempted to rescue Joseph (Ge 37:21–30). Lost birthright for sleeping with Bilhah (Ge 35:22; 49:4). Tribe of blessed (Ge 49:3–4; Dt 33:6), numbered (Nu 1:21; 26:7), allotted land east of Jordan (Nu 32; 34:14; Jos 13:15), west (Eze 48:6), failed to help Deborah (Jdg 5:15–16), supported David (1Ch 12:37), 12,000 from (Rev 7:5).

REVEAL (REVEALED REVEALS REVELATION REVELATIONS)
Mt 11: 27 to whom the Son chooses to *r* him.
Gal 1: 16 was pleased to *r* his Son in me

REVEALED (REVEAL)
Dt 29: 29 but the things *r* belong to us
Isa 40: 5 the glory of the LORD will be *r*,
43: 12 I have *r* and saved and proclaimed
53: 1 the arm of the LORD been *r*?
65: 1 I *r* myself to those who did not ask
Mt 11: 25 and *r* them to little children.
Jn 12: 38 the arm of the Lord been *r*?"
17: 6 "I have *r* you to those whom you
Ro 1: 17 a righteousness from God is *r*,
8: 18 with the glory that will be *r* in us.
10: 20 I *r* myself to those who did not ask
16: 26 but now *r* and made known
1Co 2: 10 but God has *r* it to us by his Spirit.
2Th 1: 7 happen when the Lord Jesus is *r*
2: 3 and the man of lawlessness is *r*,

1Pe 1: 7 and honor when Jesus Christ is *r.*
1: 20 but was *r* in these last times
4: 13 overjoyed when his glory is *r.*

REVEALS* (REVEAL)
Nu 23: 3 Whatever he *r* to me I will tell you
Job 12: 22 He *r* the deep things of darkness
Da 2: 22 He *r* deep and hidden things;
2: 28 a God in heaven who *r* mysteries.
Am 4: 13 and *r* his thoughts to man,

REVELATION* (REVEAL)
2Sa 7: 17 David all the words of this entire *r.*
1Ch 17: 15 David all the words of this entire *r.*
Pr 29: 18 Where there is no *r,* the people cast
Da 10: 1 a *r* was given to Daniel (who was
Hab 2: 2 "Write down the *r*
2: 3 For the *r* awaits an appointed time;
Lk 2: 32 a light for *r* to the Gentiles
Ro 16: 25 according to the *r*
1Co 14: 6 I bring you some *r* or knowledge
14: 26 a *r,* a tongue or an interpretation.
14: 30 And if a *r* comes to someone who is
Gal 1: 12 I received it by *r* from Jesus Christ.
2: 2 I went in response to a *r*
Eph 1: 17 you the Spirit of wisdom and *r,*
3: 3 mystery made known to me by *r,*
Rev 1: 1 *r* of Jesus Christ, which God gave

REVELATIONS* (REVEAL)
2Co 12: 1 on to visions and *r* from the Lord.
12: 7 of these surpassingly great *r,*

REVELED* (REVELRY)
Ne 9: 25 they *r* in your great goodness.

REVELRY (REVELED)
Ex 32: 6 drink and got up to indulge in *r.*
1Co 10: 7 and got up to indulge in pagan *r.*"

REVENGE (VENGEANCE)
Lev 19: 18 " 'Do not seek *r* or bear a grudge
Ro 12: 19 Do not take *r,* my friends,

REVERE* (REVERENCE REVERENT REVERING)
Lev 19: 32 for the elderly and *r* your God.
Dt 4: 10 so that they may learn to *r* me
13: 4 must follow, and him you must *r.*
14: 23 to *r* the LORD your God always.
17: 19 learn to *r* the LORD his God
28: 58 and do not *r* this glorious
Job 37: 24 Therefore, men *r* him,
Ps 22: 23 *R* him, all you descendants
33: 8 let all the people of the world *r* him
102: 15 of the earth will *r* your glory.
Ecc 3: 14 God does it so that men will *r* him.
Isa 25: 3 cities of ruthless nations will *r* you.
59: 19 of the sun, they will *r* his glory.
63: 17 hearts so we do not *r* you?
Jer 10: 7 Who should not *r* you,
Hos 10: 3 because we did not *r* the LORD.
Mal 4: 2 But for you who *r* my name,

REVERENCE (REVERE)
Lev 19: 30 and have *r* for my sanctuary.
Ne 5: 15 of *r* for God I did not act like that.
Ps 5: 7 in *r* will I bow down
Da 6: 26 people must fear and *r* the God
2Co 7: 1 perfecting holiness out of *r* for God
Eph 5: 21 to one another out of *r* for Christ.
Col 3: 22 of heart and *r* for the Lord.
1Pe 3: 2 when they see the purity and *r*
Rev 11: 18 and those who *r* your name,

REVERENT* (REVERE)
Ecc 8: 12 with God-fearing men, who are *r*
Tit 2: 3 women to be *r* in the way they live,
Heb 5: 7 because of his *r* submission.
1Pe 1: 17 as strangers here in *r* fear.

REVERING* (REVERE)
Dt 8: 6 walking in his ways and *r* him.
Ne 1: 11 who delight in *r* your name.

REVERSE*
Isa 43: 13 When I act, who can *r* it?"

REVIVE* (REVIVING)
Ps 80: 18 *r* us, and we will call on your name.
85: 6 Will you not *r* us again,
Isa 57: 15 and to *r* the heart of the contrite.
57: 15 to *r* the spirit of the lowly
Hos 6: 2 After two days he will *r* us;

REVIVING* (REVIVE)
Ps 19: 7 *r* the soul.

REVOKED
Isa 45: 23 a word that will not be *r:*

REWARD (REWARDED REWARDING REWARDS)
Ge 15: 1 your very great *r.*"
1Sa 24: 19 May the LORD *r* you well
Ps 19: 11 in keeping them there is great *r.*
62: 12 Surely you will *r* each person
127: 3 children a *r* from him.
Pr 9: 12 are wise, your wisdom will *r* you;
11: 18 sows righteousness reaps a sure *r.*
13: 21 prosperity is the *r* of the righteous.
19: 17 he will *r* him for what he has done.
25: 22 and the LORD will *r* you.
31: 31 Give her the *r* she has earned,
Isa 40: 10 See, his *r* is with him,
49: 4 and my *r* is with my God."
61: 8 In my faithfulness I will *r* them
62: 11 See, his *r* is with him,
Jer 17: 10 to *r* a man according to his conduct
32: 19 you *r* everyone according
Mt 5: 12 because great is your *r* in heaven,
6: 1 you will have no *r*
6: 5 they have received their *r* in full.
10: 41 a prophet will receive a prophet's *r,*
16: 27 and then he will *r* each person
Lk 6: 23 because great is your *r* in heaven.
6: 35 Then your *r* will be great,
1Co 3: 14 built survives, he will receive his *r.*
Eph 6: 8 know that the Lord will *r* everyone
Col 3: 24 an inheritance from the Lord as a *r.*
Heb 11: 26 he was looking ahead to his *r.*
Rev 22: 12 I am coming soon! My *r* is with me

REWARDED (REWARD)
Ru 2: 12 May you be richly *r* by the LORD,
2Sa 22: 21 of my hands he has *r* me.
2Ch 15: 7 for your work will be *r.*"
Ps 18: 24 The LORD has *r* me according
Pr 13: 13 he who respects a command is *r.*
14: 14 and the good man *r* for his.
Jer 31: 16 for your work will be *r,*"
1Co 3: 8 and each will be *r* according
Heb 10: 35 your confidence; it will be richly *r.*
2Jn : 8 but that you may be *r* fully.

REWARDING* (REWARD)
Rev 11: 18 for *r* your servants the prophets

REWARDS (REWARD)
1Sa 26: 23 The LORD *r* every man
Pr 12: 14 the work of his hands *r* him.
Heb 11: 6 that he *r* those who earnestly seek

RIBS
Ge 2: 21 he took one of the man's *r*

RICH (RICHES RICHEST)
Job 34: 19 does not favor the *r* over the poor,
Ps 49: 16 overawed when a man grows *r,*
145: 8 slow to anger and *r* in love.
Pr 21: 17 loves wine and oil will never be *r.*
22: 2 *R* and poor have this in common:
23: 4 Do not wear yourself out to get *r;*
28: 6 than a *r* man whose ways are
28: 20 to get *r* will not go unpunished.
28: 22 A stingy man is eager to get *r*
Ecc 5: 12 but the abundance of a *r* man
Isa 33: 6 a *r* store of salvation and wisdom
53: 9 and with the *r* in his death,
Jer 9: 23 or the *r* man boast of his riches,
Zec 3: 4 and I will put *r* garments on you."
Mt 19: 23 it is hard for a *r* man
Lk 1: 53 but has sent the *r* away empty.
6: 24 "But woe to you who are *r,*
12: 21 for himself but is not *r* toward God
16: 1 "There was a *r* man whose
21: 1 Jesus saw the *r* putting their gifts
2Co 6: 10 yet making many *r;* having nothing
8: 2 poverty welled up in *r* generosity.
8: 9 he was *r,* yet for your sakes he
9: 11 You will be made *r* in every way
Eph 2: 4 love for us, God, who is *r* in mercy,
1Ti 6: 9 want to get *r* fall into temptation
6: 17 Command those who are *r*
6: 18 to do good, to be *r* in good deeds,
Jas 1: 10 the one who is *r* should take pride
2: 5 the eyes of the world to be *r* in faith
5: 1 you *r* people, weep and wail
Rev 2: 9 and your poverty—yet you are *r!*
3: 18 you can become *r;* and white

RICHES (RICH)
Job 36: 18 that no one entices you by *r;*
Ps 49: 6 and boast of their great *r?*
49: 12 despite his *r,* does not endure;
62: 10 though your *r* increase,
119: 14 as one rejoices in great *r.*
Pr 3: 16 in her left hand are *r* and honor.
11: 28 Whoever trusts in his *r* will fall,
22: 1 is more desirable than great *r;*
27: 24 for *r* do not endure forever,
30: 8 give me neither poverty nor *r,*
Isa 10: 3 Where will you leave your *r?*
60: 5 to you the *r* of the nations will
Jer 9: 23 or the rich man boast of his *r,*
Lk 8: 14 *r* and pleasures, and they do not
Ro 9: 23 to make the *r* of his glory known
11: 33 the depth of the *r* of the wisdom
Eph 2: 7 he might show the incomparable *r*
3: 8 to the Gentiles the unsearchable *r*
Col 1: 27 among the Gentiles the glorious *r*
2: 2 so that they may have the full *r*

RICHEST (RICH)
Isa 55: 2 and your soul will delight in the *r*

RID
Ge 21: 10 "Get *r* of that slave woman
1Co 5: 7 Get *r* of the old yeast that you may
Gal 4: 30 "Get *r* of the slave woman

RIDE (RIDER RIDING)
Ps 45: 4 In your majesty *r* forth victoriously

RIDER (RIDE)
Rev 6: 2 was a white horse! Its *r* held a bow,
19: 11 whose *r* is called Faithful and True.

RIDING (RIDE)
Zec 9: 9 gentle and *r* on a donkey,
Mt 21: 5 gentle and *r* on a donkey,

RIGGING
Isa 33: 23 Your *r* hangs loose:

RIGHT (RIGHTS)
Ge 4: 7 But if you do not do what is *r,*
18: 19 of the LORD by doing what is *r*
18: 25 the Judge of all the earth do *r?*"
48: 13 on his left toward Israel's *r* hand,
Ex 15: 6 Your *r* hand, O LORD,
15: 26 and do what is *r* in his eyes,
Dt 5: 32 do not turn aside to the *r*
6: 18 Do what is *r* and good
13: 18 and doing what is *r* in his eyes.
Jos 1: 7 do not turn from it to the *r*
1Sa 12: 23 you the way that is good and *r.*
1Ki 3: 9 to distinguish between *r* and wrong
15: 5 For David had done what was *r*
2Ki 7: 9 to each other, "We're not doing *r.*
Ne 9: 13 and laws that are just and *r,*
Ps 16: 8 Because he is at my *r* hand,
16: 11 eternal pleasures at your *r* hand.
17: 7 you who save by your *r* hand
18: 35 and your *r* hand sustains me;
19: 8 The precepts of the LORD are *r,*
25: 9 He guides the humble in what is *r*
33: 4 For the word of the LORD is *r*

44: 3 it was your *r* hand, your arm,
45: 4 let your *r* hand display awesome
51: 4 so that you are proved *r*
63: 8 your *r* hand upholds me.
73: 23 you hold me by my *r* hand.
91: 7 ten thousand at your *r* hand,
98: 1 his *r* hand and his holy arm
106: 3 who constantly do what is *r.*
110: 1 "Sit at my *r* hand
118: 15 LORD's *r* hand has done mighty
119:144 Your statutes are forever *r;*
137: 5 may my *r* hand forget ›its skill‹.
139: 10 your *r* hand will hold me fast.
Pr 1: 3 doing what is *r* and just and fair;
4: 27 Do not swerve to the *r* or the left;
14: 12 There is a way that seems *r*
18: 17 The first to present his case seems *r*
Ecc 7: 20 who does what is *r* and never sins.
SS 1: 4 How *r* they are to adore you!
Isa 1: 17 learn to do *r!*
7: 15 reject the wrong and choose the *r.*
30: 10 us no more visions of what is *r!*
30: 21 Whether you turn to the *r*
41: 10 you with my righteous *r* hand.
41: 13 who takes hold of your *r* hand
48: 13 my *r* hand spread out the heavens;
64: 5 to the help of those who gladly do *r*
Jer 23: 5 and do what is just and *r* in the land
Eze 18: 5 who does what is just and *r.*
18: 21 and does what is just and *r,*
33: 14 and does what is just and *r*—
Hos 14: 9 The ways of the LORD are *r;*
Mt 5: 29 If your *r* eye causes you to sin,
6: 3 know what your *r* hand is doing,
22: 44 "Sit at my *r* hand
25: 33 He will put the sheep on his *r*
Jn 1: 12 he gave the *r* to become children
Ac 2: 34 "Sit at my *r* hand
7: 55 Jesus standing at the *r* hand of God
Ro 3: 4 "So that you may be proved *r*
8: 34 is at the *r* hand of God and is
9: 21 Does not the potter have the *r*
12: 17 careful to do what is *r* in the eyes
1Co 9: 4 Don't we have the *r* to food
2Co 8: 21 we are taking pains to do what is *r,*
Eph 1: 20 and seated him at his *r* hand
6: 1 parents in the Lord, for this is *r.*
Php 4: 8 whatever is *r,* whatever is pure,
2Th 3: 13 never tire of doing what is *r.*
Heb 1: 3 down at the *r* hand of the Majesty
Jas 2: 8 as yourself," you are doing *r.*
1Pe 3: 14 if you should suffer for what is *r,*
1Jn 2: 29 who does what is *r* has been born
Rev 2: 7 I will give the *r* to eat from the tree
3: 21 I will give the *r* to sit with me
22: 11 let him who does *r* continue to do *r*

RIGHTEOUS (RIGHTEOUSLY RIGHTEOUSNESS)

Ge 6: 9 Noah was a *r* man, blameless
18: 23 "Will you sweep away the *r*
Nu 23: 10 Let me die the death of the *r,*
Ne 9: 8 your promise because you are *r.*
Job 36: 7 He does not take his eyes off the *r;*
Ps 1: 5 nor sinners in the assembly of the *r.*
5: 12 O LORD, you bless the *r;*
11: 7 For the LORD is *r,*
15: 2 and who does what is *r,*
34: 15 The eyes of the LORD are on the *r*
37: 16 Better the little that the *r* have
37: 21 but the *r* give generously;
37: 25 yet I have never seen the *r* forsaken
37: 30 of the *r* man utters wisdom,
55: 22 he will never let the *r* fall.
64: 10 Let the *r* rejoice in the LORD
68: 3 But may the *r* be glad
112: 4 compassionate and *r* man.
118: 20 through which the *r* may enter.
119: 7 as I learn your *r* laws.
119:137 *R* are you, O LORD,
140: 13 Surely the *r* will praise your name
143: 2 for no one living is *r* before you.
145: 17 The LORD is *r* in all his ways
Pr 3: 33 but he blesses the home of the *r.*
4: 18 of the *r* is like the first gleam
10: 7 of the *r* will be a blessing,
10: 11 The mouth of the *r* is a fountain
10: 16 The wages of the *r* bring them life,
10: 20 The tongue of the *r* is choice silver,
10: 24 what the *r* desire will be granted.
10: 28 The prospect of the *r* is joy,
10: 32 of the *r* know what is fitting,
11: 23 The desire of the *r* ends only
11: 30 The fruit of the *r* is a tree of life,
12: 10 A *r* man cares for the needs
12: 21 No harm befalls the *r,*
13: 9 The light of the *r* shines brightly,
15: 28 of the *r* weighs its answers,
15: 29 but he hears the prayer of the *r.*
16: 31 it is attained by a *r* life.
18: 10 the *r* run to it and are safe.
20: 7 The *r* man leads a blameless life;
21: 15 justice is done, it brings joy to the *r*
23: 24 The father of a *r* man has great joy;
28: 1 but the *r* are as bold as a lion.
29: 6 but a *r* one can sing and be glad.
29: 7 The *r* care about justice
29: 27 The *r* detest the dishonest;
Ecc 7: 20 There is not a *r* man on earth
Isa 26: 7 The path of the *r* is level;
41: 10 you with my *r* right hand.
45: 21 a *r* God and a Savior;
53: 11 his knowledge my *r* servant will
64: 6 and all our *r* acts are like filthy rags
Jer 23: 5 up to David a *r* Branch,
Eze 3: 20 when a *r* man turns
18: 5 "Suppose there is a *r* man
18: 20 of the *r* man will be credited
33: 12 The *r* man, if he sins, will not be
Da 9: 18 requests of you because we are *r,*
Hab 2: 4 but the *r* will live by his faith—
Zec 9: 9 *r* and having salvation,
Mal 3: 18 see the distinction between the *r*
Mt 5: 45 rain on the *r* and the unrighteous.
9: 13 For I have not come to call the *r,*
10: 41 and anyone who receives a *r* man
13: 43 Then the *r* will shine like the sun
13: 49 and separate the wicked from the *r*
25: 37 "Then the *r* will answer him, 'Lord,
25: 46 to eternal punishment, but the *r*
Ac 24: 15 will be a resurrection of both the *r*
Ro 1: 17 as it is written: "The *r* will live
2: 5 when his *r* judgment will be
2: 13 the law who will be declared *r.*
3: 10 "There is no one *r,* not even one;
3: 20 Therefore no one will be declared *r*
5: 19 one man the many will be made *r.*
Gal 3: 11 because, "The *r* will live by faith."
1Ti 1: 9 that law is made not for the *r*
2Ti 4: 8 which the Lord, the *r* Judge,
Tit 3: 5 because of *r* things we had done,
Heb 10: 38 But my *r* one will live by faith.
Jas 5: 16 The prayer of a *r* man is powerful
1Pe 3: 12 the eyes of the Lord are on the *r*
3: 18 the *r* for the unrighteous,
4: 18 "If it is hard for the *r* to be saved,
1Jn 2: 1 defense—Jesus Christ, the *R* One.
3: 7 does what is right is *r,* just as he is *r.*
Rev 19: 8 stands for the *r* acts of the saints.)

RIGHTEOUSLY* (RIGHTEOUS)

Ps 9: 4 on your throne, judging *r.*
Isa 33: 15 He who walks *r*
Jer 11: 20 LORD Almighty, you who judge *r*

RIGHTEOUSNESS (RIGHTEOUS)

Ge 15: 6 and he credited it to him as *r.*
Dt 9: 4 of this land because of my *r.*"
1Sa 26: 23 LORD rewards every man for his *r*
1Ki 10: 9 to maintain justice and *r.*"
Job 37: 23 great *r,* he does not oppress.
Ps 7: 17 to the LORD because of his *r*
9: 8 He will judge the world in *r;*
17: 15 And I—in *r* I will see your face;
23: 3 He guides me in paths of *r*
33: 5 The LORD loves *r* and justice;
35: 28 My tongue will speak of your *r*
36: 6 Your *r* is like the mighty
37: 6 He will make your *r* shine like
40: 9 I proclaim *r* in the great assembly;
45: 4 in behalf of truth, humility and *r;*
45: 7 You love *r* and hate wickedness;
48: 10 your right hand is filled with *r.*
65: 5 us with awesome deeds of *r,*
71: 2 Rescue me and deliver me in your *r*
71: 15 My mouth will tell of your *r,*
71: 19 Your *r* reaches to the skies, O God,
85: 10 *r* and peace kiss each other.
89: 14 *R* and justice are the foundation
96: 13 He will judge the world in *r*
98: 9 He will judge the world in *r*
103: 6 The LORD works *r*
103: 17 his *r* with their children's children
106: 31 This was credited to him as *r*
111: 3 and his *r* endures forever.
118: 19 Open for me the gates of *r;*
132: 9 May your priests be clothed with *r;*
145: 7 and joyfully sing of your *r.*
Pr 11: 5 *r* of the blameless makes a straight
11: 18 he who sows *r* reaps a sure reward.
13: 6 *R* guards the man of integrity,
14: 34 *R* exalts a nation,
16: 8 Better a little with *r*
16: 12 a throne is established through *r.*
21: 21 He who pursues *r* and love
Isa 5: 16 will show himself holy by his *r.*
9: 7 it with justice and *r*
11: 4 but with *r* he will judge the needy,
16: 5 and speeds the cause of *r.*
26: 9 the people of the world learn *r.*
32: 17 The fruit of *r* will be peace;
42: 6 "I, the LORD, have called you in *r;*
42: 21 the LORD for the sake of his *r*
45: 8 "You heavens above, rain down *r;*
51: 1 "Listen to me, you who pursue *r*
51: 6 my *r* will never fail.
51: 8 But my *r* will last forever,
58: 8 then your *r* will go before you,
59: 17 He put on *r* as his breastplate,
61: 10 and arrayed me in a robe of *r,*
63: 1 "It is I, speaking in *r,*
Jer 9: 24 justice and *r* on earth,
23: 6 The LORD Our *R.*
Eze 3: 20 a righteous man turns from his *r*
14: 20 save only themselves by their *r.*
18: 20 The *r* of the righteous man will be
33: 12 *r* of the righteous man will not save
Da 9: 24 to bring in everlasting *r,*
12: 3 and those who lead many to *r,*
Hos 10: 12 Sow for yourselves *r,*
Am 5: 24 *r* like a never-failing stream!
Mic 7: 9 I will see his *r.*
Zep 2: 3 Seek *r,* seek humility;
Mal 4: 2 the sun of *r* will rise with healing
Mt 5: 6 those who hunger and thirst for *r,*
5: 10 who are persecuted because of *r,*
5: 20 unless your *r* surpasses that
6: 1 to do your 'acts of *r*' before men,
6: 33 But seek first his kingdom and his *r*
Jn 16: 8 world of guilt in regard to sin and *r*
Ac 24: 25 Paul discoursed on *r,* self-control
Ro 1: 17 For in the gospel a *r* from God is
3: 5 brings out God's *r* more clearly,
3: 22 This *r* from God comes
4: 3 and it was credited to him as *r.*"
4: 5 wicked, his faith is credited as *r.*
4: 6 man to whom God credits *r* apart
4: 9 faith was credited to him as *r.*
4: 13 through the *r* that comes by faith.
4: 22 why "it was credited to him as *r.*"

5: 18 of *r* was justification that brings life
6: 13 body to him as instruments of *r.*
6: 16 or to obedience, which leads to *r?*
6: 18 and have become slaves to *r.*
6: 19 in slavery to *r* leading to holiness.
8: 10 yet your spirit is alive because of *r.*
9: 30 did not pursue *r,* have obtained it,
10: 3 they did not know the *r* that comes
14: 17 but of *r,* peace and joy
1Co 1: 30 our *r,* holiness and redemption.
2Co 3: 9 is the ministry that brings *r!*
5: 21 that in him we might become the *r*
6: 7 with weapons of *r* in the right hand
6: 14 For what do *r* and wickedness have
9: 9 his *r* endures forever."
Gal 2: 21 for if *r* could be gained
3: 6 and it was credited to him as *r.*"
3: 21 then *r* would certainly have come
Eph 4: 24 created to be like God in true *r*
5: 9 *r* and truth) and find out what
6: 14 with the breastplate of *r* in place,
Php 1: 11 filled with the fruit of *r* that comes
3: 6 as for legalistic *r,* faultless.
3: 9 not having a *r* of my own that
1Ti 6: 11 and pursue *r,* godliness, faith, love,
2Ti 2: 22 and pursue *r,* faith, love and peace,
3: 16 correcting and training in *r,*
4: 8 is in store for me the crown of *r,*
Heb 1: 8 and *r* will be the scepter
5: 13 with the teaching about *r.*
7: 2 his name means "king of *r*";
11: 7 became heir of the *r* that comes
12: 11 it produces a harvest of *r*
Jas 2: 23 and it was credited to him as *r,*"
3: 18 sow in peace raise a harvest of *r.*
1Pe 2: 24 die to sins and live for *r;*
2Pe 2: 21 not to have known the way of *r,*
3: 13 and a new earth, the home of *r.*

RIGHTS (RIGHT)
Ps 82: 3 maintain the *r* of the poor
Pr 31: 8 for the *r* of all who are destitute.
Isa 10: 2 to deprive the poor of their *r*
La 3: 35 to deny a man his *r*
Gal 4: 5 that we might receive the full *r*

RING
Pr 11: 22 Like a gold *r* in a pig's snout
Lk 15: 22 Put a *r* on his finger and sandals

RIOTS
2Co 6: 5 imprisonments and *r;* in hard work,

RIPE
Joel 3: 13 for the harvest is *r.*
Am 8: 1 showed me: a basket of *r* fruit.
Jn 4: 35 at the fields! They are *r* for harvest.
Rev 14: 15 for the harvest of the earth is *r.*"

RISE (RAISE RAISED RISEN ROSE)
Lev 19: 32 " '*R* in the presence of the aged,
Nu 24: 17 a scepter will *r* out of Israel.
Isa 26: 19 their bodies will *r.*
Mal 4: 2 of righteousness will *r* with healing
Mt 27: 63 'After three days I will *r* again.'
Mk 8: 31 and after three days *r* again.
Lk 18: 33 On the third day he will *r* again."
Jn 5: 29 those who have done good will *r*
20: 9 had to *r* from the dead.)
Ac 17: 3 had to suffer and *r* from the dead.
1Th 4: 16 and the dead in Christ will *r* first.

RISEN (RISE)
Mt 28: 6 He is not here; he has *r,* just
Mk 16: 6 He has *r!* He is not here.
Lk 24: 34 The Lord has *r* and has appeared

RIVER (RIVERS)
Ps 46: 4 There is a *r* whose streams make
Isa 66: 12 "I will extend peace to her like a *r,*
Eze 47: 12 grow on both banks of the *r.*
Rev 22: 1 Then the angel showed me the *r*

RIVERS (RIVER)
Ps 137: 1 By the *r* of Babylon we sat

ROAD (CROSSROADS ROADS)
Mt 7: 13 and broad is the *r* that leads

ROADS (ROAD)
Lk 3: 5 crooked *r* shall become straight,

ROARING
1Pe 5: 8 prowls around like a *r* lion looking

ROB (ROBBERS ROBBERY ROBS)
Mal 3: 8 "Will a man *r* God? Yet you *r* me.

ROBBERS (ROB)
Jer 7: 11 become a den of *r* to you?
Mk 15: 27 They crucified two *r* with him,
Lk 19: 46 but you have made it 'a den of *r.*' "
Jn 10: 8 came before me were thieves and *r,*

ROBBERY (ROB)
Isa 61: 8 I hate *r* and iniquity.

ROBE (ROBED ROBES)
Ge 37: 3 and he made a richly ornamented *r*
Isa 6: 1 the train of his *r* filled the temple.
61: 10 arrayed me in a *r* of righteousness,
Rev 6: 11 each of them was given a white *r,*

ROBED (ROBE)
Ps 93: 1 the LORD is *r* in majesty
Isa 63: 1 Who is this, *r* in splendor,

ROBES (ROBE)
Ps 45: 8 All your *r* are fragrant with myrrh
Rev 7: 13 "These in white *r*— who are they,

ROBS* (ROB)
Pr 19: 26 He who *r* his father and drives out
28: 24 He who *r* his father or mother

ROCK
Ge 49: 24 of the Shepherd, the *R* of Israel,
Ex 17: 6 Strike the *r,* and water will come
Nu 20: 8 Speak to that *r* before their eyes
Dt 32: 4 He is the *R,* his works are perfect,
32: 13 him with honey from the *r,*
2Sa 22: 2 "The LORD is my *r,* my fortress
Ps 18: 2 The LORD is my *r,* my fortress
19: 14 O LORD, my *R* and my Redeemer
40: 2 he set my feet on a *r*
61: 2 lead me to the *r* that is higher
92: 15 he is my *R,* and there is no
Isa 26: 4 the LORD, is the *R* eternal.
51: 1 to the *r* from which you were cut
Da 2: 34 you were watching, a *r* was cut out,
Mt 7: 24 man who built his house on the *r.*
16: 18 and on this *r* I will build my church
Ro 9: 33 and a *r* that makes them fall,
1Co 10: 4 the spiritual *r* that accompanied
1Pe 2: 8 and a *r* that makes them fall."

ROD (RODS)
2Sa 7: 14 I will punish him with the *r* of men,
Ps 23: 4 your *r* and your staff,
Pr 13: 24 He who spares the *r* hates his son,
22: 15 the *r* of discipline will drive it far
23: 13 if you punish him with the *r,*
29: 15 *r* of correction imparts wisdom,
Isa 11: 4 the earth with the *r* of his mouth;

RODS (ROD)
2Co 11: 25 Three times I was beaten with *r,*

ROLL (ROLLED)
Mk 16: 3 "Who will *r* the stone away

ROLLED (ROLL)
Lk 24: 2 They found the stone *r* away

ROMAN
Ac 16: 37 even though we are *R* citizens,
22: 25 you to flog a *R* citizen who hasn't

ROOF (ROOFS)
Pr 21: 9 Better to live on a corner of the *r*

ROOFS
Mt 10: 27 in your ear, proclaim from the *r.*

ROOM (ROOMS)
Mt 6: 6 But when you pray, go into your *r,*
Mk 14: 15 He will show you a large upper *r,*
Lk 2: 7 there was no *r* for them in the inn.
Jn 8: 37 because you have no *r* for my word
21: 25 the whole world would not have *r*
2Co 7: 2 Make *r* for us in your hearts.

ROOMS (ROOM)
Jn 14: 2 In my Father's house are many *r;*

ROOSTER
Mt 26: 34 this very night, before the *r* crows,

ROOT (ROOTED ROOTS)
Isa 11: 10 In that day the *R* of Jesse will stand
53: 2 and like a *r* out of dry ground.
Mt 3: 10 already at the *r* of the trees,
13: 21 But since he has no *r,* he lasts only
Ro 11: 16 if the *r* is holy, so are the branches.
15: 12 "The *R* of Jesse will spring up,
1Ti 6: 10 of money is a *r* of all kinds of evil.
Rev 5: 5 the *R* of David, has triumphed.
22: 16 I am the *R* and the Offspring

ROOTED (ROOT)
Eph 3: 17 being *r* and established in love,

ROOTS (ROOT)
Isa 11: 1 from his *r* a Branch will bear fruit.

ROSE (RISE)
SS 2: 1 I am a *r* of Sharon,
1Th 4: 14 believe that Jesus died and *r* again

ROTS
Pr 14: 30 but envy *r* the bones.

ROUGH
Isa 42: 16 and make the *r* places smooth.
Lk 3: 5 the *r* ways smooth.

ROUND
Ecc 1: 6 *r* and *r* it goes,

ROYAL
Ps 45: 9 at your right hand is the *r* bride
Da 1: 8 not to defile himself with the *r* food
Jas 2: 8 If you really keep the *r* law found
1Pe 2: 9 a *r* priesthood, a holy nation,

RUBBISH*
Php 3: 8 I consider them *r,* that I may gain

RUBIES
Job 28: 18 the price of wisdom is beyond *r.*
Pr 3: 15 She is more precious than *r;*
8: 11 for wisdom is more precious than *r,*
31: 10 She is worth far more than *r.*

RUDDER*
Jas 3: 4 by a very small *r* wherever the pilot

RUDDY
1Sa 16: 12 He was *r,* with a fine appearance
SS 5: 10 *Beloved* My lover is radiant and *r,*

RUDE*
1Co 13: 5 It is not *r,* it is not self-seeking,

RUIN (RUINED RUINING RUINS)
Pr 10: 8 but a chattering fool comes to *r.*
10: 10 and a chattering fool comes to *r.*
10: 14 but the mouth of a fool invites *r.*
10: 29 but it is the *r* of those who do evil.
18: 24 many companions may come to *r,*
19: 13 A foolish son is his father's *r,*
26: 28 and a flattering mouth works *r.*
SS 2: 15 that *r* the vineyards,
Eze 21: 27 A *r!* A *r!* I will make it a *r!*
1Ti 6: 9 desires that plunge men into *r*

RUINED (RUIN)
Isa 6: 5 "I am *r!* For I am a man
Mt 9: 17 and the wineskins will be *r.*
12: 25 divided against itself will be *r,*

RUINING* (RUIN)
Tit 1: 11 they are *r* whole households

RUINS (RUIN)
Pr 19: 3 A man's own folly *r* his life,
Ecc 4: 5 and *r* himself.
2Ti 2: 14 and only *r* those who listen.

RULE (RULER RULERS RULES)
Ge 1: 26 let them *r* over the fish of the sea
3: 16 and he will *r* over you."

Jdg 8: 22 said to Gideon, "*R* over us—
1Sa 12: 12 'No, we want a king to *r* over us'—
Ps 2: 9 You will *r* them with an iron
67: 4 for you *r* the peoples justly
119:133 let no sin *r* over me.
Pr 17: 2 A wise servant will *r*
Isa 28: 10 *r* on *r*, *r* on *r*;
Eze 20: 33 I will *r* over you with a mighty
Zec 6: 13 and will sit and *r* on his throne.
9: 10 His *r* will extend from sea to sea
Ro 13: 9 are summed up in this one *r*:
15: 12 arise to *r* over the nations;
1Co 7: 17 This is the *r* I lay down in all
Gal 6: 16 and mercy to all who follow this *r*,
Eph 1: 21 far above all *r* and authority,
Col 3: 15 the peace of Christ *r* in your hearts,
2Th 3: 10 we gave you this *r*: "If a man will
Rev 2: 27 He will *r* them with an iron scepter;
12: 5 who will *r* all the nations
19: 15 He will *r* them with an iron scepter

RULER (RULE)
Ps 8: 6 You made him *r* over the works
Pr 19: 6 Many curry favor with a *r*,
23: 1 When you sit to dine with a *r*,
25: 15 Through patience a *r* can be
29: 26 Many seek an audience with a *r*,
Isa 60: 17 and righteousness your *r*.
Da 9: 25 the *r*, comes, there will be seven
Mic 5: 2 one who will be *r* over Israel,
Mt 2: 6 for out of you will come a *r*
Eph 2: 2 of the *r* of the kingdom of the air,
1Ti 6: 15 God, the blessed and only *R*,
Rev 1: 5 and the *r* of the kings of the earth.

RULERS (RULE)
Ps 2: 2 and the *r* gather together
119:161 *R* persecute me without cause,
Isa 40: 23 reduces the *r* of this world
Da 7: 27 and all *r* will worship and obey him
Mt 20: 25 "You know that the *r*
Ac 13: 27 and their *r* did not recognize Jesus,
Ro 13: 3 For *r* hold no terror
1Co 2: 6 of this age or of the *r* of this age,
Eph 3: 10 should be made known to the *r*
6: 12 the *r*, against the authorities,
Col 1: 16 or powers or *r* or authorities;

RULES (RULE)
Nu 15: 15 is to have the same *r* for you
2Sa 23: 3 when he *r* in the fear of God,
Ps 22: 28 and he *r* over the nations.
66: 7 He *r* forever by his power,
103: 19 and his kingdom *r* over all.
Isa 29: 13 is made up only of *r* taught by men.
40: 10 and his arm *r* for him.
Mt 15: 9 their teachings are but *r* taught
Lk 22: 26 one who *r* like the one who serves.
2Ti 2: 5 he competes according to the *r*.

RUMORS
Jer 51: 46 afraid when *r* are heard in the land;
Mt 24: 6 You will hear of wars and *r* of wars,

RUN (RAN RUNNERS RUNNING RUNS)
Ps 19: 5 champion rejoicing to *r* his course.
Pr 4: 12 when you *r*, you will not stumble.
18: 10 the righteous *r* to it and are safe.
Isa 10: 3 To whom will you *r* for help?
40: 31 they will *r* and not grow weary,
Joel 3: 18 ravines of Judah will *r* with water.
Hab 2: 2 so that a herald may *r* with it.
1Co 9: 24 *R* in such a way as to get the prize.
Gal 2: 2 that I was running or had *r* my race
Php 2: 16 on the day of Christ that I did not *r*
Heb 12: 1 let us *r* with perseverance the race

RUNNERS* (RUN)
1Co 9: 24 that in a race all the *r* run,

RUNNING (RUN)
Ps 133: 2 *r* down on Aaron's beard,
Lk 17: 23 Do not go *r* off after them.
1Co 9: 26 I do not run like a man *r* aimlessly;
Gal 5: 7 You were *r* a good race.

RUNS (RUN)
Jn 10: 12 he abandons the sheep and *r* away.

RUSH
Pr 1: 16 for their feet *r* into sin,
6: 18 feet that are quick to *r* into evil,
Isa 59: 7 Their feet *r* into sin;

RUST
Mt 6: 19 where moth and *r* destroy,

RUTH*
Moabitess; widow who went to Bethlehem with mother-in-law Naomi (Ru 1). Gleaned in field of Boaz; shown favor (Ru 2). Proposed marriage to Boaz (Ru 3). Married (Ru 4:1–12); bore Obed, ancestor of David (Ru 4:13–22), Jesus (Mt 1:5).

RUTHLESS
Pr 11: 16 but *r* men gain only wealth.
Ro 1: 31 are senseless, faithless, heartless, *r*.

SABBATH (SABBATHS)
Ex 20: 8 "Remember the *S* day
31: 14 " 'Observe the *S*, because it is holy
Lev 25: 2 the land itself must observe a *s*
Dt 5: 12 "Observe the *S* day
Isa 56: 2 keeps the *S* without desecrating it,
56: 6 all who keep the *S*
58: 13 if you call the *S* a delight
Jer 17: 21 not to carry a load on the *S* day
Mt 12: 1 through the grainfields on the *S*.
Lk 13: 10 On a *S* Jesus was teaching in one
Col 2: 16 a New Moon celebration or a *S* day

SABBATH-REST* (REST)
Heb 4: 9 then, a *S* for the people of God;

SABBATHS (SABBATH)
2Ch 2: 4 evening and on *S* and New Moons
Eze 20: 12 Also I gave them my *S*

SACKCLOTH
Ps 30: 11 you removed my *s* and clothed me
Da 9: 3 in fasting, and in *s* and ashes.
Mt 11: 21 would have repented long ago in *s*

SACRED
Lev 23: 2 are to proclaim as *s* assemblies.
Mt 7: 6 "Do not give dogs what is *s*;
Ro 14: 5 One man considers one day more *s*
1Co 3: 17 for God's temple is *s*, and you are
2Pe 1: 18 were with him on the *s* mountain.
2: 21 on the *s* command that was

SACRIFICE (SACRIFICED SACRIFICES)
Ge 22: 2 *S* him there as a burnt offering
Ex 12: 27 'It is the Passover *s* to the LORD,
1Sa 15: 22 To obey is better than *s*,
1Ki 18: 38 the LORD fell and burned up the *s*,
1Ch 21: 24 or *s* a burnt offering that costs me
Ps 40: 6 *S* and offering you did not desire,
50: 14 *S* thank offerings to God,
51: 16 You do not delight in *s*,
54: 6 I will *s* a freewill offering to you;
107: 22 Let them *s* thank offerings
141: 2 of my hands be like the evening *s*.
Pr 15: 8 The LORD detests the *s*
21: 3 to the LORD than *s*.
Da 9: 27 the 'seven' he will put an end to *s*
12: 11 time that the daily *s* is abolished
Hos 6: 6 For I desire mercy, not *s*,
Mt 9: 13 this means: 'I desire mercy, not *s*.'
Ro 3: 25 God presented him as a *s*
Eph 5: 2 as a fragrant offering and *s* to God.
Php 4: 18 an acceptable *s*, pleasing to God.
Heb 9: 26 away with sin by the *s* of himself.
10: 5 "*S* and offering you did not desire,
10: 10 holy through the *s* of the body
10: 14 by one *s* he has made perfect
10: 18 there is no longer any *s* for sin.
11: 4 faith Abel offered God a better *s*
13: 15 offer to God a *s* of praise—
1Jn 2: 2 He is the atoning *s* for our sins,
4: 10 as an atoning *s* for our sins.

SACRIFICED (SACRIFICE)
Ac 15: 29 are to abstain from food *s* to idols,
1Co 5: 7 our Passover lamb, has been *s*.
8: 1 Now about food *s* to idols:
Heb 7: 27 He *s* for their sins once for all
9: 28 so Christ was *s* once

SACRIFICES (SACRIFICE)
Ps 51: 17 The *s* of God are a broken spirit;
Mk 12: 33 than all burnt offerings and *s*."
Ro 12: 1 to offer your bodies as living *s*,
Heb 9: 23 with better *s* than these.
13: 16 for with such *s* God is pleased.
1Pe 2: 5 offering spiritual *s* acceptable

SAD
Lk 18: 23 he heard this, he became very *s*,

SADDUCEES
Mt 16: 6 the yeast of the Pharisees and *S*."
Mk 12: 18 *S*, who say there is no resurrection,
Ac 23: 8 *S* say that there is no resurrection,

SAFE (SAVE)
Ps 27: 5 he will keep me *s* in his dwelling;
37: 3 in the land and enjoy *s* pasture.
Pr 18: 10 the righteous run to it and are *s*.
28: 26 he who walks in wisdom is kept *s*.
29: 25 in the LORD is kept *s*.
Jer 12: 5 If you stumble in *s* country,
Jn 17: 12 kept them *s* by that name you gave
1Jn 5: 18 born of God keeps him *s*,

SAFETY (SAVE)
Ps 4: 8 make me dwell in *s*.
Hos 2: 18 so that all may lie down in *s*.
1Th 5: 3 people are saying, "Peace and *s*,"

SAINTS
1Sa 2: 9 He will guard the feet of his *s*,
Ps 16: 3 As for the *s* who are in the land,
30: 4 Sing to the LORD, you *s* of his;
31: 23 Love the LORD, all his *s*!
34: 9 Fear the LORD, you his *s*,
116: 15 is the death of his *s*.
149: 1 his praise in the assembly of the *s*.
149: 5 Let the *s* rejoice in this honor
Da 7: 18 the *s* of the Most High will receive
Ro 8: 27 intercedes for the *s* in accordance
1Co 6: 2 not know that the *s* will judge
Eph 1: 15 Jesus and your love for all the *s*,
1: 18 of his glorious inheritance in the *s*,
6: 18 always keep on praying for all the *s*
Phm : 7 have refreshed the hearts of the *s*.
Rev 5: 8 which are the prayers of the *s*.
19: 8 for the righteous acts of the *s*.)

SAKE (SAKES)
1Sa 12: 22 For the *s* of his great name
Ps 23: 3 righteousness for his name's *s*.
44: 22 Yet for your *s* we face death all day
106: 8 Yet he saved them for his name's *s*,
Isa 42: 21 for the *s* of his righteousness
43: 25 your transgressions, for my own *s*,
48: 9 For my own name's *s* I delay my
48: 11 For my own *s*, for my own *s*,
Jer 14: 7 for the *s* of your name.
14: 21 For the *s* of your name do not
Eze 20: 9 But for the *s* of my name I did what
20: 14 But for the *s* of my name I did what
20: 22 and for the *s* of my name I did what
36: 22 but for the *s* of my holy name,
Da 9: 17 For your *s*, O Lord, look with favor
Mt 10: 39 life for my *s* will find it.
19: 29 for my *s* will receive a hundred
1Co 9: 23 I do all this for the *s* of the gospel,
2Co 12: 10 for Christ's *s*, I delight
Php 3: 7 loss for the *s* of Christ.
Heb 11: 26 He regarded disgrace for the *s*
1Pe 2: 13 for the Lord's *s* to every authority
3Jn : 7 was for the *s* of the Name that they

SAKES* (SAKE)
2Co 8: 9 yet for your *s* he became poor,

SALEM
Ge 14: 18 king of S brought out bread
Heb 7: 2 "king of S" means "king of peace."

SALT
Ge 19: 26 and she became a pillar of s.
Nu 18: 19 covenant of s before the LORD
Mt 5: 13 "You are the s of the earth.
Col 4: 6 with s, so that you may know how
Jas 3: 11 s water flow from the same spring?

SALVATION* (SAVE)
Ex 15: 2 he has become my s.
2Sa 22: 3 my shield and the horn of my s.
23: 5 Will he not bring to fruition my s
1Ch 16: 23 proclaim his s day after day.
2Ch 6: 41 O LORD God, be clothed with s,
Ps 9: 14 and there rejoice in your s.
13: 5 my heart rejoices in your s.
14: 7 that s for Israel would come out
18: 2 is my shield and the horn of my s,
27: 1 The LORD is my light and my s—
28: 8 a fortress of s for his anointed one.
35: 3 "I am your s."
35: 9 and delight in his s.
37: 39 The s of the righteous comes
40: 10 I speak of your faithfulness and s.
40: 16 those who love your s always say,
50: 23 way so that I may show him the s
51: 12 Restore to me the joy of your s
53: 6 that s for Israel would come out
62: 1 my s comes from him.
62: 2 He alone is my rock and my s;
62: 6 He alone is my rock and my s;
62: 7 My s and my honor depend
67: 2 your s among all nations.
69: 13 answer me with your sure s.
69: 27 do not let them share in your s.
69: 29 may your s, O God, protect me.
70: 4 those who love your s always say,
71: 15 of your s all day long,
74: 12 you bring s upon the earth.
85: 7 and grant us your s.
85: 9 Surely his s is near those who fear
91: 16 and show him my s."
95: 1 to the Rock of our s.
96: 2 proclaim his s day after day.
98: 1 have worked s for him.
98: 2 The LORD has made his s known
98: 3 the s of our God.
116: 13 I will lift up the cup of s
118: 14 he has become my s.
118: 21 you have become my s.
119: 41 your s according to your promise;
119: 81 with longing for your s,
119:123 My eyes fail, looking for your s,
119:155 S is far from the wicked,
119:166 I wait for your s, O LORD,
119:174 I long for your s, O LORD,
132: 16 I will clothe her priests with s,
149: 4 he crowns the humble with s.
Isa 12: 2 Surely God is my s;
12: 2 he has become my s."
12: 3 from the wells of s.
25: 9 let us rejoice and be glad in his s."
26: 1 God makes s
26: 18 We have not brought s to the earth;
30: 15 "In repentance and rest is your s,
33: 2 our s in time of distress.
33: 6 a rich store of s and wisdom
45: 8 let s spring up,
45: 17 the LORD with an everlasting s;
46: 13 I will grant s to Zion,
46: 13 and my s will not be delayed.
49: 6 that you may bring my s
49: 8 and in the day of s I will help you;
51: 5 my s is on the way,
51: 6 But my s will last forever,
51: 8 my s through all generations."
52: 7 who proclaim s,
52: 10 the s of our God.
56: 1 for my s is close at hand
59: 16 so his own arm worked s for him,
59: 17 and the helmet of s on his head;
60: 18 but you will call your walls S
61: 10 me with garments of s
62: 1 her s like a blazing torch.
63: 5 so my own arm worked s for me,
Jer 3: 23 is the s of Israel.
La 3: 26 quietly for the s of the LORD.
Jnh 2: 9 S comes from the LORD."
Zec 9: 9 righteous and having s,
Lk 1: 69 He has raised up a horn of s for us
1: 71 of long ago), s from our enemies
1: 77 give his people the knowledge of s
2: 30 For my eyes have seen your s,
3: 6 And all mankind will see God's s
19: 9 "Today s has come to this house,
Jn 4: 22 for s is from the Jews.
Ac 4: 12 S is found in no one else,
13: 26 message of s has been sent.
13: 47 that you may bring s to the ends
28: 28 to know that God's s has been sent
Ro 1: 16 for the s of everyone who believes:
11: 11 s has come to the Gentiles
13: 11 because our s is nearer now
2Co 1: 6 it is for your comfort and s;
6: 2 and in the day of s I helped you."
6: 2 of God's favor, now is the day of s.
7: 10 brings repentance that leads to s
Eph 1: 13 word of truth, the gospel of your s.
6: 17 Take the helmet of s and the sword
Php 2: 12 to work out your s with fear
1Th 5: 8 and the hope of s as a helmet.
5: 9 to receive s through our Lord Jesus
2Ti 2: 10 they too may obtain the s that is
3: 15 wise for s through faith
Tit 2: 11 of God that brings s has appeared
Heb 1: 14 to serve those who will inherit s?
2: 3 This s, which was first announced
2: 3 escape if we ignore such a great s?
2: 10 of their s perfect through suffering.
5: 9 of eternal s for all who obey him
6: 9 case—things that accompany s.
9: 28 to bring s to those who are waiting
1Pe 1: 5 the coming of the s that is ready
1: 9 of your faith, the s of your souls.
1: 10 Concerning this s, the prophets,
2: 2 by it you may grow up in your s,
2Pe 3: 15 that our Lord's patience means s,
Jude : 3 to write to you about the s we share
Rev 7: 10 "S belongs to our God,
12: 10 have come the s and the power
19: 1 S and glory and power belong

SAMARIA (SAMARITAN)
1Ki 16: 24 He bought the hill of S
2Ki 17: 6 the king of Assyria captured S
Jn 4: 4 Now he had to go through S.
4: 5 came to a town in S called Sychar,

SAMARITAN (SAMARIA)
Lk 10: 33 But a S, as he traveled, came where
17: 16 and thanked him—and he was a S.
Jn 4: 7 When a S woman came

SAMSON
Danite judge. Birth promised (Jdg 13). Married to Philistine, but wife given away (Jdg 14). Vengeance on Philistines (Jdg 15). Betrayed by Delilah (Jdg 16:1–22). Death (Jdg 16:23–31). Feats of strength: killed lion (Jdg 14:6), 30 Philistines (Jdg 14:19), 1,000 Philistines with jawbone (Jdg 15:13–17), carried off gates of Gaza (Jdg 16:3), pushed down temple of Dagon (Jdg 16:25–30).

SAMUEL
Ephraimite judge and prophet (Heb 11:32). Birth prayed for (1Sa 1:10–18). Dedicated to temple by Hannah (1Sa 1:21–28). Raised by Eli (1Sa 2:11, 18–26). Called as prophet (1Sa 3). Led Israel to victory over Philistines (1Sa 7). Asked by Israel for a king (1Sa 8). Anointed Saul as king (1Sa 9–10). Farewell speech (1Sa 12). Rebuked Saul for sacrifice (1Sa 13). Announced rejection of Saul (1Sa 15). Anointed David as king (1Sa 16). Protected David from Saul (1Sa 19:18–24). Death (1Sa 25:1). Returned from dead to condemn Saul (1Sa 28).

SANBALLAT
Led opposition to Nehemiah's rebuilding of Jerusalem (Ne 2:10, 19; 4; 6).

SANCTIFIED* (SANCTIFY)
Jn 17: 19 that they too may be truly s.
Ac 20: 32 among all those who are s.
26: 18 among those who are s by faith
Ro 15: 16 to God, s by the Holy Spirit.
1Co 1: 2 to those s in Christ Jesus
6: 11 But you were washed, you were s,
7: 14 and the unbelieving wife has been s
7: 14 the unbelieving husband has been s
1Th 4: 3 It is God's will that you should be s
Heb 10: 29 blood of the covenant that s him,

SANCTIFY* (SANCTIFIED SANCTIFYING)
Jn 17: 17 S them by the truth; your word is
17: 19 For them I s myself, that they too
1Th 5: 23 s you through and through.
Heb 9: 13 are ceremonially unclean s them

SANCTIFYING* (SANCTIFY)
2Th 2: 13 through the s work of the Spirit
1Pe 1: 2 through the s work of the Spirit,

SANCTUARY
Ex 25: 8 "Then have them make a s for me,
Lev 19: 30 and have reverence for my s,
Ps 15: 1 LORD, who may dwell in your s?
63: 2 I have seen you in the s
68: 24 of my God and King into the s.
68: 35 are awesome, O God, in your s;
73: 17 me till I entered the s of God;
102: 19 looked down from his s on high,
134: 2 Lift up your hands in the s
150: 1 Praise God in his s;
Eze 37: 26 I will put my s among them forever
41: 1 the man brought me to the outer s
Da 9: 26 will destroy the city and the s.
Heb 6: 19 It enters the inner s
8: 2 in the s, the true tabernacle set up
8: 5 They serve at a s that is a copy
9: 24 enter a man-made s that was only

SAND
Ge 22: 17 and as the s on the seashore.
Mt 7: 26 man who built his house on s.

SANDAL (SANDALS)
Ru 4: 7 one party took off his s

SANDALS (SANDAL)
Ex 3: 5 off your s, for the place where you
Dt 25: 9 take off one of his s, spit in his face
Jos 5: 15 off your s, for the place where you
Mt 3: 11 whose s I am not fit to carry.

SANG (SING)
Ex 15: 1 and the Israelites s this song
15: 21 Miriam s to them:
Nu 21: 17 Then Israel s this song:
Jdg 5: 1 Barak son of Abinoam s this song:
1Sa 18: 7 As they danced, they s:
2Sa 22: 1 David s to the LORD the words
2Ch 5: 13 in praise to the LORD and s:
29: 30 So they s praises with gladness
Ezr 3: 11 thanksgiving they s to the LORD:
Job 38: 7 while the morning stars s together
Ps 106: 12 and s his praise.
Rev 5: 9 And they s a new song:
5: 12 In a loud voice they s:
14: 3 they s a new song before the throne
15: 3 and s the song of Moses the servant

SAP
Ro 11: 17 share in the nourishing s

SAPPHIRA*
Ac 5: 1 together with his wife S,

SARAH
Wife of Abraham, originally named Sarai; barren (Ge 11:29–31; 1Pe 3:6). Taken by Pharaoh as Abraham's sister; returned (Ge 12:10–20). Gave Hagar to Abraham; sent her away in pregnancy (Ge 16). Name changed; Isaac promised (Ge 17:15–21; 18:10–15; Heb 11:11). Taken by Abimelech as Abraham's sister; returned (Ge 20). Isaac born; Hagar and Ishmael sent away (Ge 21:1–21; Gal 4:21–31). Death (Ge 23).

SARDIS
Rev 3: 1 the angel of the church in *S* write:

SASH (SASHES)
Rev 1: 13 with a golden *s* around his chest.

SASHES (SASH)
Rev 15: 6 wore golden *s* around their chests.

SAT (SIT)
Ps 137: 1 By the rivers of Babylon we *s*
Mk 16: 19 and he *s* at the right hand of God.
Lk 10: 39 who *s* at the Lord's feet listening
Heb 1: 3 he *s* down at the right hand
8: 1 who *s* down at the right hand
10: 12 he *s* down at the right hand of God.
12: 2 and *s* down at the right hand

SATAN
Job 1: 6 and *S* also came with them.
Zec 3: 2 said to *S*, "The LORD rebuke you,
Mt 12: 26 If *S* drives out *S*, he is divided
16: 23 *S*! You are a stumbling block to me;
Mk 4: 15 *S* comes and takes away the word
Lk 10: 18 "I saw *S* fall like lightning
22: 3 *S* entered Judas, called Iscariot,
Ro 16: 20 The God of peace will soon crush *S*
1Co 5: 5 is present, hand this man over to *S*,
2Co 11: 14 for *S* himself masquerades
12: 7 a messenger of *S*, to torment me.
1Ti 1: 20 handed over to *S* to be taught not
Rev 12: 9 serpent called the devil, or *S*,
20: 2 or *S*, and bound him for a thousand
20: 7 *S* will be released from his prison

SATISFIED (SATISFY)
Ps 17: 15 I will be *s* with seeing your likeness
22: 26 The poor will eat and be *s*;
63: 5 My soul will be *s* as with the richest
104: 28 they are *s* with good things.
105: 40 *s* them with the bread of heaven.
Pr 13: 4 the desires of the diligent are fully *s*
30: 15 are three things that are never *s*,
Ecc 5: 10 whoever loves wealth is never *s*
Isa 53: 11 he will see the light ›of life‹ and be *s*
Mt 14: 20 They all ate and were *s*,
Lk 6: 21 for you will be *s*.

SATISFIES* (SATISFY)
Ps 103: 5 who *s* your desires with good things,
107: 9 for he *s* the thirsty
147: 14 and *s* you with the finest of wheat.

SATISFY (SATISFIED SATISFIES)
Ps 90: 14 *S* us in the morning
145: 16 *s* the desires of every living thing.
Pr 5: 19 may her breasts *s* you always,
Isa 55: 2 and your labor on what does not *s*?
58: 10 and *s* the needs of the oppressed,

SAUL
1. Benjamite; anointed by Samuel as first king of Israel (1Sa 9–10). Defeated Ammonites (1Sa 11). Rebuked for offering sacrifice (1Sa 13:1–15). Defeated Philistines (1Sa 14). Rejected as king for failing to annihilate Amalekites (1Sa 15). Soothed from evil spirit by David (1Sa 16:14–23). Sent David against Goliath (1Sa 17). Jealousy and attempted murder of David (1Sa 18:1–11). Gave David Michal as wife (1Sa 18:12–30). Second attempt to kill David (1Sa 19). Anger at Jonathan (1Sa 20:26–34). Pursued David: killed priests at Nob (1Sa 22), went to Keilah and Ziph (1Sa 23), life spared by David at En Gedi (1Sa 24) and in his tent (1Sa 26). Rebuked by Samuel's spirit for consulting witch at Endor (1Sa 28). Wounded by Philistines; took his own life (1Sa 31; 1Ch 10). Lamented by David (2Sa 1:17–27). Children (1Sa 14:49–51; 1Ch 8).
2. See PAUL

SAVAGE
Ac 20: 29 *s* wolves will come in among you

SAVE (SAFE SAFETY SALVATION SAVED SAVES SAVIOR)
Ge 45: 5 to *s* lives that God sent me ahead
1Ch 16: 35 Cry out, "*S* us, O God our Savior;
Job 40: 14 that your own right hand can *s* you.
Ps 17: 7 you who *s* by your right hand
18: 27 You *s* the humble
28: 9 *S* your people and bless your
31: 16 *s* me in your unfailing love.
69: 35 for God will *s* Zion
71: 2 turn your ear to me and *s* me.
72: 13 and *s* the needy from death.
89: 48 or *s* himself from the power
91: 3 Surely he will *s* you
109: 31 to *s* his life from those who
146: 3 in mortal men, who cannot *s*.
Pr 2: 16 will *s* you also from the adulteress,
Isa 35: 4 he will come to *s* you."
38: 20 The LORD will *s* me,
46: 7 it cannot *s* him from his troubles.
59: 1 of the LORD is not too short to *s*,
63: 1 mighty to *s*."
Jer 17: 14 *s* me and I will be saved,
Eze 3: 18 ways in order to *s* his life,
7: 19 able to *s* them in the day
14: 14 they could *s* only themselves
33: 12 of the righteous man will not *s* him
34: 22 I will *s* my flock, and they will no
Da 3: 17 the God we serve is able to *s* us
Hos 1: 7 and I will *s* them—not by bow,
Zep 1: 18 will be able to *s* them
3: 17 he is mighty to *s*.
Zec 8: 7 "I will *s* my people
Mt 1: 21 he will *s* his people from their sins
16: 25 wants to *s* his life will lose it,
Lk 19: 10 to seek and to *s* what was lost."
Jn 3: 17 but to *s* the world through him.
12: 47 come to judge the world, but to *s* it.
Ro 11: 14 people to envy and *s* some of them.
1Co 7: 16 whether you will *s* your husband?
1Ti 1: 15 came into the world to *s* sinners—
Heb 7: 25 to *s* completely those who come
Jas 5: 20 of his way will *s* him from death
Jude : 23 others from the fire and *s* them;

SAVED (SAVE)
Ps 22: 5 They cried to you and were *s*;
33: 16 No king is *s* by the size of his army;
34: 6 he *s* him out of all his troubles.
106: 21 They forgot the God who *s* them,
116: 6 when I was in great need, he *s* me.
Isa 25: 9 we trusted in him, and he *s* us.
45: 22 "Turn to me and be *s*,
64: 5 How then can we be *s*?
Jer 4: 14 from your heart and be *s*.
8: 20 and we are not *s*."
Eze 3: 19 but you will have *s* yourself.
33: 5 warning, he would have *s* himself.
Joel 2: 32 on the name of the LORD will be *s*;
Mt 10: 22 firm to the end will be *s*.
24: 13 firm to the end will be *s*.
Mk 13: 13 firm to the end will be *s*.
16: 16 believes and is baptized will be *s*,
Jn 10: 9 enters through me will be *s*.
Ac 2: 21 on the name of the Lord will be *s*.'
2: 47 daily those who were being *s*.
4: 12 to men by which we must be *s*."
15: 11 of our Lord Jesus that we are *s*,
16: 30 do to be *s*?" They replied,
Ro 5: 9 how much more shall we be *s*
9: 27 only the remnant will be *s*.
10: 1 the Israelites is that they may be *s*.
10: 9 him from the dead, you will be *s*.
10: 13 on the name of the Lord will be *s*."
11: 26 so all Israel will be *s*, as it is written:
1Co 1: 18 to us who are being *s* it is the power
3: 15 will suffer loss; he himself will be *s*,
5: 5 his spirit *s* on the day of the Lord.
10: 33 of many, so that they may be *s*.
15: 2 By this gospel you are *s*,
Eph 2: 5 it is by grace you have been *s*.
2: 8 For it is by grace you have been *s*,
2Th 2: 13 you to be *s* through the sanctifying
1Ti 2: 4 who wants all men to be *s*
2: 15 But women will be *s*
2Ti 1: 9 who has *s* us and called us
Tit 3: 5 He *s* us through the washing
Heb 10: 39 but of those who believe and are *s*.

SAVES (SAVE)
Ps 7: 10 who *s* the upright in heart.
68: 20 Our God is a God who *s*;
145: 19 he hears their cry and *s* them.
1Pe 3: 21 It *s* you by the resurrection

SAVIOR* (SAVE)
Dt 32: 15 and rejected the Rock his *S*.
2Sa 22: 3 stronghold, my refuge and my *s*—
22: 47 Exalted be God, the Rock, my *S*!
1Ch 16: 35 Cry out, "Save us, O God our *S*;
Ps 18: 46 Exalted be God my *S*!
24: 5 and vindication from God his *S*.
25: 5 for you are God my *S*,
27: 9 O God my *S*.
38: 22 O Lord my *S*.
42: 5 my *S* and
42: 11 my *S* and my God.
43: 5 my *S* and my God.
65: 5 O God our *S*,
68: 19 Praise be to the Lord, to God our *S*,
79: 9 Help us, O God our *S*,
85: 4 Restore us again, O God our *S*,
89: 26 my God, the Rock my *S*.'
Isa 17: 10 You have forgotten God your *S*;
19: 20 he will send them a *s* and defender,
43: 3 the Holy One of Israel, your *S*;
43: 11 and apart from me there is no *s*.
45: 15 O God and *S* of Israel.
45: 21 a righteous God and a *S*;
49: 26 that I, the LORD, am your *S*,
60: 16 know that I, the LORD, am your *S*,
62: 11 'See, your *S* comes!
63: 8 and so he became their *S*.
Jer 14: 8 its *S* in times of distress,
Hos 13: 4 no *S* except me.
Mic 7: 7 I wait for God my *S*;
Hab 3: 18 I will be joyful in God my *S*.
Lk 1: 47 and my spirit rejoices in God my *S*,
2: 11 of David a *S* has been born to you;
Jn 4: 42 know that this man really is the *S*
Ac 5: 31 *S* that he might give repentance
13: 23 God has brought to Israel the *S*
Eph 5: 23 his body, of which he is the *S*.
Php 3: 20 we eagerly await a *S* from there,
1Ti 1: 1 by the command of God our *S*
2: 3 This is good, and pleases God our *S*
4: 10 who is the *S* of all men,
2Ti 1: 10 through the appearing of our *S*,
Tit 1: 3 me by the command of God our *S*,
1: 4 the Father and Christ Jesus our *S*.
2: 10 about God our *S* attractive.
2: 13 appearing of our great God and *S*,
3: 4 and love of God our *S* appeared,
3: 6 through Jesus Christ our *S*,
2Pe 1: 1 *S* Jesus Christ have received a faith
1: 11 eternal kingdom of our Lord and *S*
2: 20 and *S* Jesus Christ and are again
3: 2 and *S* through your apostles.
3: 18 and knowledge of our Lord and *S*
1Jn 4: 14 Son to be the *S* of the world.
Jude : 25 to the only God our *S* be glory,

SCALE (SCALES)
Ps 18: 29 with my God I can *s* a wall.

SCALES (SCALE)
Lev 11: 9 may eat any that have fins and *s*.

19: 36 Use honest *s* and honest weights,
Pr 11: 1 The LORD abhors dishonest *s*,
Da 5: 27 You have been weighed on the *s*
Rev 6: 5 Its rider was holding a pair of *s*

SCAPEGOAT (GOAT)
Lev 16: 10 by sending it into the desert as a *s*.

SCARECROW*
Jer 10: 5 Like a *s* in a melon patch,

SCARLET
Jos 2: 21 she tied the *s* cord in the window.
Isa 1: 18 "Though your sins are like *s*,
Mt 27: 28 They stripped him and put a *s* robe

SCATTER (SCATTERED SCATTERS)
Dt 4: 27 The LORD will *s* you
Ne 1: 8 I will *s* you among the nations,
Jer 9: 16 I will *s* them among nations that
30: 11 the nations among which I *s* you,
Zec 10: 9 I *s* them among the peoples,

SCATTERED (SCATTER)
Isa 11: 12 he will assemble the *s* people
Jer 31: 10 'He who *s* Israel will gather them
Zec 2: 6 "for I have *s* you to the four winds
13: 7 and the sheep will be *s*,
Mt 26: 31 and the sheep of the flock will be *s*.'
Jn 11: 52 but also for the *s* children of God,
Ac 8: 4 who had been *s* preached the word
Jas 1: 1 To the twelve tribes *s*
1Pe 1: 1 *s* throughout Pontus, Galatia,

SCATTERS (SCATTER)
Mt 12: 30 he who does not gather with me *s*.

SCEPTER
Ge 49: 10 The *s* will not depart from Judah,
Nu 24: 17 a *s* will rise out of Israel.
Ps 2: 9 You will rule them with an iron *s*;
45: 6 a *s* of justice will be the *s*
Heb 1: 8 and righteousness will be the *s*
Rev 2: 27 'He will rule them with an iron *s*;
12: 5 rule all the nations with an iron *s*.
19: 15 "He will rule them with an iron *s*."

SCHEMES
Pr 6: 18 a heart that devises wicked *s*,
24: 9 The *s* of folly are sin,
2Co 2: 11 For we are not unaware of his *s*.
Eph 6: 11 stand against the devil's *s*.

SCHOLAR*
1Co 1: 20 Where is the *s*? Where is

SCOFFERS
2Pe 3: 3 that in the last days *s* will come,

SCORN (SCORNED SCORNING SCORNS)
Ps 69: 7 For I endure *s* for your sake,
69: 20 *S* has broken my heart
89: 41 he has become the *s*
109: 25 I am an object of *s* to my accusers;
119: 22 Remove from me *s* and contempt,
Mic 6: 16 you will bear the *s* of the nations."

SCORNED (SCORN)
Ps 22: 6 *s* by men and despised

SCORNING (SCORN)
Heb 12: 2 him endured the cross, *s* its shame,

SCORNS (SCORN)
Pr 13: 13 He who *s* instruction will pay for it,
30: 17 that *s* obedience to a mother,

SCORPION
Lk 11: 12 will give him a *s*? If you then,
Rev 9: 5 sting of a *s* when it strikes a man.

SCOUNDREL
Pr 6: 12 A *s* and villain,

SCRIPTURE (SCRIPTURES)
Jn 2: 22 Then they believed the *S*
7: 42 Does not the *S* say that the Christ
10: 35 and the *S* cannot be broken—
Ac 8: 32 was reading this passage of *S*:
1Ti 4: 13 yourself to the public reading of *S*,
2Ti 3: 16 All *S* is God-breathed
2Pe 1: 20 that no prophecy of *S* came about

SCRIPTURES (SCRIPTURE)
Mt 22: 29 because you do not know the *S*
Lk 24: 27 said in all the *S* concerning himself.
24: 45 so they could understand the *S*.
Jn 5: 39 These are the *S* that testify about
Ac 17: 11 examined the *S* every day to see
2Ti 3: 15 you have known the holy *S*,
2Pe 3: 16 as they do the other *S*,

SCROLL
Ps 40: 7 it is written about me in the *s*.
Isa 34: 4 and the sky rolled up like a *s*;
Eze 3: 1 eat what is before you, eat this *s*;
Heb 10: 7 it is written about me in the *s*—
Rev 6: 14 The sky receded like a *s*, rolling up,
10: 8 take the *s* that lies open in the hand

SCUM
1Co 4: 13 this moment we have become the *s*

SEA (SEASHORE)
Ex 14: 16 go through the *s* on dry ground.
Dt 30: 13 "Who will cross the *s* to get it
1Ki 7: 23 He made the *S* of cast metal,
Job 11: 9 and wider than the *s*.
Ps 93: 4 mightier than the breakers of the *s*
95: 5 The *s* is his, for he made it,
Ecc 1: 7 All streams flow into the *s*,
Isa 57: 20 the wicked are like the tossing *s*,
Jnh 1: 4 LORD sent a great wind on the *s*,
Mic 7: 19 iniquities into the depths of the *s*.
Hab 2: 14 as the waters cover the *s*.
Zec 9: 10 His rule will extend from *s* to *s*
Mt 18: 6 drowned in the depths of the *s*.
1Co 10: 1 that they all passed through the *s*.
Jas 1: 6 who doubts is like a wave of the *s*,
Jude : 13 They are wild waves of the *s*,
Rev 10: 2 He planted his right foot on the *s*
13: 1 I saw a beast coming out of the *s*.
20: 13 The *s* gave up the dead that were
21: 1 and there was no longer any *s*.

SEAL (SEALED SEALS)
Ps 40: 9 I do not *s* my lips,
SS 8: 6 Place me like a *s* over your heart,
Da 12: 4 and *s* the words of the scroll
Jn 6: 27 God the Father has placed his *s*
1Co 9: 2 For you are the *s* of my apostleship
2Co 1: 22 set his *s* of ownership on us,
Eph 1: 13 you were marked in him with a *s*,
Rev 6: 3 the Lamb opened the second *s*,
6: 5 When the Lamb opened the third *s*,
6: 7 the Lamb opened the fourth *s*,
6: 9 When he opened the fifth *s*,
6: 12 I watched as he opened the sixth *s*.
8: 1 When he opened the seventh *s*,
9: 4 people who did not have the *s*
22: 10 "Do not *s* up the words

SEALED (SEAL)
Eph 4: 30 with whom you were *s* for the day
2Ti 2: 19 solid foundation stands firm, *s*
Rev 5: 1 on both sides and *s* with seven seals

SEALS (SEAL)
Rev 5: 2 "Who is worthy to break the *s*
6: 1 opened the first of the seven *s*.

SEAMLESS*
Jn 19: 23 This garment was *s*, woven

SEARCH (SEARCHED SEARCHES SEARCHING)
Ps 4: 4 *s* your hearts and be silent.
139: 23 *S* me, O God, and know my heart;
Pr 2: 4 and *s* for it as for hidden treasure,
25: 2 to *s* out a matter is the glory
SS 3: 2 I will *s* for the one my heart loves.
Jer 17: 10 "I the LORD *s* the heart
Eze 34: 11 I myself will *s* for my sheep
34: 16 I will *s* for the lost and bring back
Lk 15: 8 and *s* carefully until she finds it?

SEARCHED (SEARCH)
Ps 139: 1 O LORD, you have *s* me
Ecc 12: 10 The Teacher *s* to find just the right
1Pe 1: 10 *s* intently and with the greatest

SEARCHES (SEARCH)
1Ch 28: 9 for the LORD *s* every heart
Ps 7: 9 who *s* minds and hearts,
Pr 11: 27 but evil comes to him who *s* for it.
20: 27 The lamp of the LORD *s* the spirit
Ro 8: 27 And he who *s* our hearts knows
1Co 2: 10 The Spirit *s* all things,
Rev 2: 23 will know that I am he who *s* hearts

SEARCHING (SEARCH)
Jdg 5: 15 there was much *s* of heart.
Am 8: 12 *s* for the word of the LORD,

SEARED
1Ti 4: 2 whose consciences have been *s*

SEASHORE (SEA)
Jos 11: 4 as numerous as the sand on the *s*.
1Ki 4: 29 as measureless as the sand on the *s*.

SEASON (SEASONED SEASONS)
Lev 26: 4 I will send you rain in its *s*,
Ps 1: 3 which yields its fruit in *s*
2Ti 4: 2 be prepared in *s* and out of *s*;

SEASONED* (SEASON)
Col 4: 6 full of grace, *s* with salt,

SEASONS (SEASON)
Ge 1: 14 signs to mark *s* and days and years,
Gal 4: 10 and months and *s* and years!

SEAT (SEATED SEATS)
Ps 1: 1 or sit in the *s* of mockers.
Pr 31: 23 where he takes his *s*
Da 7: 9 and the Ancient of Days took his *s*.
Lk 14: 9 say to you, 'Give this man your *s*.'
2Co 5: 10 before the judgment *s* of Christ,

SEATED (SEAT)
Ps 47: 8 God is *s* on his holy throne.
Isa 6: 1 I saw the Lord *s* on a throne,
Lk 22: 69 of Man will be *s* at the right hand
Eph 1: 20 and *s* him at his right hand
2: 6 and *s* us with him in the heavenly
Col 3: 1 where Christ is *s* at the right hand
Rev 14: 14 *s* on the cloud was one "like a son
20: 11 white throne and him who was *s*

SEATS (SEAT)
Lk 11: 43 you love the most important *s*

SECLUSION*
Lk 1: 24 and for five months remained in *s*.

SECRET (SECRETLY SECRETS)
Dt 29: 29 The *s* things belong
Jdg 16: 6 Tell me the *s* of your great strength
Ps 90: 8 our *s* sins in the light
139: 15 when I was made in the *s* place.
Pr 11: 13 but a trustworthy man keeps a *s*.
21: 14 A gift given in *s* soothes anger,
Jer 23: 24 Can anyone hide in *s* places
Mt 6: 4 so that your giving may be in *s*.
6: 18 who sees what is done in *s*,
Mk 4: 11 "The *s* of the kingdom
1Co 2: 7 No, we speak of God's *s* wisdom,
4: 1 entrusted with the *s* things of God.
2Co 4: 2 we have renounced *s* and shameful
Eph 5: 12 what the disobedient do in *s*.
Php 4: 12 I have learned the *s*

SECRETLY (SECRET)
2Pe 2: 1 They will *s* introduce destructive
Jude : 4 about long ago have *s* slipped

SECRETS (SECRET)
Ps 44: 21 since he knows the *s* of the heart?
Ro 2: 16 day when God will judge men's *s*
1Co 14: 25 the *s* of his heart will be laid bare.
Rev 2: 24 Satan's so-called deep *s* (I will not

SECURE (SECURITY)
Dt 33: 12 beloved of the LORD rest *s* in him,
Ps 16: 5 you have made my lot *s*.
16: 9 my body also will rest *s*,
112: 8 His heart is *s*, he will have no fear;
Pr 14: 26 fears the LORD has a *s* fortress,
Heb 6: 19 an anchor for the soul, firm and *s*.
2Pe 3: 17 and fall from your *s* position.

SECURITY (SECURE)
Job 31: 24 or said to pure gold, 'You are my *s*,'

SEED (SEEDS SEEDTIME)
Ge 1: 11 on the land that bear fruit with *s*
Isa 55: 10 so that it yields *s* for the sower
Mt 13: 3 "A farmer went out to sow his *s*.
13: 31 of heaven is like a mustard *s*,
17: 20 have faith as small as a mustard *s*,
Lk 8: 11 of the parable: The *s* is the word
1Co 3: 6 I planted the *s*, Apollos watered it,
2Co 9: 10 he who supplies *s* to the sower
Gal 3: 29 then you are Abraham's *s*,
1Pe 1: 23 not of perishable *s*,
1Jn 3: 9 because God's *s* remains in him;

SEEDS (SEED)
Jn 12: 24 But if it dies, it produces many *s*.
Gal 3: 16 Scripture does not say "and to *s*,"

SEEDTIME* (SEED)
Ge 8: 22 *s* and harvest,

SEEK (SEEKING SEEKS SELF-SEEKING SOUGHT)
Lev 19: 18 Do not *s* revenge or bear a grudge
Dt 4: 29 if from there you *s* the LORD your
1Ki 22: 5 "First *s* the counsel of the LORD."
1Ch 28: 9 If you *s* him, he will be found
2Ch 7: 14 themselves and pray and *s* my face
15: 2 If you *s* him, he will be found
Ps 34: 10 those who *s* the LORD lack no
105: 3 of those who *s* the LORD rejoice.
105: 4 *s* his face always.
119: 2 and *s* him with all their heart.
119: 10 I *s* you with all my heart;
119:176 *S* your servant,
Pr 8: 17 and those who *s* me find me.
18: 15 the ears of the wise *s* it out.
25: 27 is it honorable to *s* one's own honor
28: 5 those who *s* the LORD understand
Isa 55: 6 *S* the LORD while he may be
65: 1 found by those who did not *s* me.
Jer 29: 13 You will *s* me and find me
Hos 10: 12 for it is time to *s* the LORD,
Am 5: 4 "*S* me and live;
Zep 2: 3 *S* the LORD, all you humble
Mt 6: 33 But *s* first his kingdom
7: 7 and it will be given to you; *s*
Lk 12: 31 *s* his kingdom, and these things will
19: 10 For the Son of Man came to *s*
Jn 5: 30 for I *s* not to please myself
Ro 10: 20 found by those who did not *s* me;
1Co 7: 27 you married? Do not *s* a divorce.
10: 24 Nobody should *s* his own good,
Heb 11: 6 rewards those who earnestly *s* him.
1Pe 3: 11 he must *s* peace and pursue it.

SEEKING (SEEK)
2Ch 30: 19 who sets his heart on *s* God—
Pr 20: 18 Make plans by *s* advice;
Mal 3: 1 the Lord you are *s* will come
Jn 8: 50 I am not *s* glory for myself;
1Co 10: 33 For I am not *s* my own good

SEEKS (SEEK)
Pr 11: 27 He who *s* good finds good will,
Mt 7: 8 he who *s* finds; and to him who
Jn 4: 23 the kind of worshipers the Father *s*.
Ro 3: 11 no one who *s* God.

SEER
1Sa 9: 9 of today used to be called a *s*.)

SELF-CONTROL* (CONTROL)
Pr 25: 28 is a man who lacks *s*.
Ac 24: 25 *s* and the judgment to come,
1Co 7: 5 you because of your lack of *s*.
Gal 5: 23 faithfulness, gentleness and *s*.
2Ti 3: 3 slanderous, without *s*, brutal,
2Pe 1: 6 and to knowledge, *s*; and to *s*,

SELF-CONTROLLED* (CONTROL)
1Th 5: 6 are asleep, but let us be alert and *s*.
5: 8 let us be *s*, putting on faith and love
1Ti 3: 2 *s*, respectable, hospitable,
Tit 1: 8 who is *s*, upright, holy
2: 2 worthy of respect, *s*, and sound
2: 5 to be *s* and pure, to be busy at home
2: 6 encourage the young men to be *s*.
2: 12 to live *s*, upright and godly lives
1Pe 1: 13 prepare your minds for action; be *s*;
4: 7 and *s* so that you can pray.
5: 8 Be *s* and alert.

SELF-DISCIPLINE* (DISCIPLINE)
2Ti 1: 7 a spirit of power, of love and of *s*.

SELF-INDULGENCE*
Mt 23: 25 inside they are full of greed and *s*.
Jas 5: 5 lived on earth in luxury and *s*.

SELF-SEEKING* (SEEK)
Ro 2: 8 But for those who are *s*
1Co 13: 5 it is not *s*, it is not easily angered,

SELFISH*
Ps 119: 36 and not toward *s* gain.
Pr 18: 1 An unfriendly man pursues *s* ends;
Gal 5: 20 fits of rage, *s* ambition, dissensions,
Php 1: 17 preach Christ out of *s* ambition,
2: 3 Do nothing out of *s* ambition
Jas 3: 14 and *s* ambition in your hearts,
3: 16 you have envy and *s* ambition,

SELL (SELLING SELLS SOLD)
Ge 25: 31 "First *s* me your birthright."
Mk 10: 21 *s* everything you have
Rev 13: 17 or *s* unless he had the mark,

SELLING (SELL)
Lk 17: 28 buying and *s*, planting and building

SELLS (SELL)
Pr 31: 24 makes linen garments and *s* them,

SEND (SENDING SENDS SENT)
Ps 43: 3 *S* forth your light and your truth,
Isa 6: 8 *S* me!" He said, "Go and tell this
Mal 3: 1 "See, I will *s* my messenger,
Mt 9: 38 to *s* out workers into his harvest
24: 31 And he will *s* his angels
Mk 1: 2 I will *s* my messenger ahead of you,
Lk 20: 13 I will *s* my son, whom I love;
Jn 3: 17 For God did not *s* his Son
16: 7 but if I go, I will *s* him to you.
1Co 1: 17 For Christ did not *s* me to baptize,

SENDING (SEND)
Mt 10: 16 I am *s* you out like sheep
Jn 20: 21 Father has sent me, I am *s* you."
Ro 8: 3 God did by *s* his own Son

SENDS (SEND)
Ps 57: 3 God *s* his love and his faithfulness.

SENNACHERIB
Assyrian king whose siege of Jerusalem was overthrown by the LORD following prayer of Hezekiah and Isaiah (2Ki 18:13–19:37; 2Ch 32:1–21; Isa 36–37).

SENSES*
Lk 15: 17 "When he came to his *s*, he said,
1Co 15: 34 Come back to your *s* as you ought,
2Ti 2: 26 and that they will come to their *s*

SENSITIVITY*
Eph 4: 19 Having lost all *s*, they have given

SENSUAL* (SENSUALITY)
Col 2: 23 value in restraining *s* indulgence.
1Ti 5: 11 For when their *s* desires overcome

SENSUALITY* (SENSUAL)
Eph 4: 19 have given themselves over to *s*

SENT (SEND)
Ex 3: 14 to the Israelites: 'I AM has *s* me
Isa 55: 11 achieve the purpose for which I *s* it.
61: 1 He has *s* me to bind up
Jer 28: 9 as one truly *s* by the LORD only
Mt 10: 40 me receives the one who *s* me.
Mk 6: 7 he *s* them out two by two
Lk 4: 18 He has *s* me to proclaim freedom
9: 2 and he *s* them out to preach
10: 16 rejects me rejects him who *s* me."
Jn 1: 6 There came a man who was *s*
4: 34 "is to do the will of him who *s* me
5: 24 believes him who *s* me has eternal
8: 16 I stand with the Father, who *s* me.
9: 4 must do the work of him who *s* me.
16: 5 "Now I am going to him who *s* me,
17: 3 and Jesus Christ, whom you have *s*.
17: 18 As you *s* me into the world,
20: 21 As the Father has *s* me, I am
Ro 10: 15 can they preach unless they are *s*?
Gal 4: 4 God *s* his Son, born of a woman,
1Jn 4: 10 but that he loved us and *s* his Son

SENTENCE
2Co 1: 9 in our hearts we felt the *s* of death.

SEPARATE (SEPARATED SEPARATES SEPARATION)
Mt 19: 6 has joined together, let man not *s*."
Ro 8: 35 Who shall *s* us from the love
1Co 7: 10 wife must not *s* from her husband.
2Co 6: 17 and be *s*, says the Lord.
Eph 2: 12 at that time you were *s* from Christ,

SEPARATED (SEPARATE)
Isa 59: 2 But your iniquities have *s*
Eph 4: 18 in their understanding and *s*

SEPARATES (SEPARATE)
Pr 16: 28 and a gossip *s* close friends.
17: 9 repeats the matter *s* close friends.
Mt 25: 32 as a shepherd *s* the sheep

SEPARATION (SEPARATE)
Nu 6: 2 a vow of *s* to the LORD

SERAPHS*
Isa 6: 2 Above him were *s*, each
6: 6 Then one of the *s* flew to me

SERIOUSNESS*
Tit 2: 7 *s* and soundness of speech that

SERPENT (SERPENT'S)
Ge 3: 1 the *s* was more crafty than any
Isa 27: 1 Leviathan the coiling *s*;
Rev 12: 9 that ancient *s* called the devil
20: 2 that ancient *s*, who is the devil,

SERPENT'S (SERPENT)
2Co 11: 3 Eve was deceived by the *s* cunning,

SERVANT (SERVANTS)
Ex 14: 31 trust in him and in Moses his *s*.
21: 2 "If you buy a Hebrew *s*, he is
1Sa 3: 10 "Speak, for your *s* is listening."
2Sa 7: 19 the future of the house of your *s*.
1Ki 20: 40 While your *s* was busy here
Job 1: 8 "Have you considered my *s* Job?
Ps 19: 11 By them is your *s* warned;
19: 13 Keep your *s* also from willful sins;
31: 16 Let your face shine on your *s*;
89: 3 I have sworn to David my *s*,
Pr 14: 35 A king delights in a wise *s*,
17: 2 wise *s* will rule over a disgraceful
22: 7 and the borrower is *s* to the lender.
31: 15 and portions for her *s* girls.
Isa 41: 8 "But you, O Israel, my *s*,
49: 3 He said to me, "You are my *s*,
53: 11 my righteous *s* will justify
Zec 3: 8 going to bring my *s*, the Branch.
Mal 1: 6 his father, and a *s* his master.
Mt 8: 13 his *s* was healed at that very hour.
20: 26 great among you must be your *s*,
24: 45 Who then is the faithful and wise *s*,
25: 21 'Well done, good and faithful *s*!
Lk 1: 38 I am the Lord's *s*," Mary answered.
16: 13 "No *s* can serve two masters.
Jn 12: 26 and where I am, my *s* also will be.
Ro 1: 1 a *s* of Christ Jesus, called
13: 4 For he is God's *s* to do you good.
Php 2: 7 taking the very nature of a *s*,
Col 1: 23 of which I, Paul, have become a *s*.
2Ti 2: 24 And the Lord's *s* must not quarrel;

SERVANTS (SERVANT)
Lev 25: 55 for the Israelites belong to me as *s*.
2Ki 17: 13 to you through my *s* the prophets."

Ezr 5: 11 "We are the *s* of the God of heaven
Ps 34: 22 The LORD redeems his *s*;
103: 21 you his *s* who do his will.
104: 4 flames of fire his *s*.
Isa 44: 26 who carries out the words of his *s*
65: 8 so will I do in behalf of my *s*;
65: 13 my *s* will drink,
Lk 17: 10 should say, 'We are unworthy *s*;
Jn 15: 15 longer call you *s*, because a servant
Ro 13: 6 for the authorities are God's *s*,
1Co 3: 5 And what is Paul? Only *s*,
Heb 1: 7 his *s* flames of fire."

SERVE (SERVED SERVES SERVICE SERVING)
Dt 10: 12 to *s* the LORD your God
11: 13 and to *s* him with all your heart
13: 4 *s* him and hold fast to him.
28: 47 you did not *s* the LORD your
Jos 22: 5 and to *s* him with all your heart
24: 15 this day whom you will *s*,
24: 18 We too will *s* the LORD,
1Sa 7: 3 to the LORD and *s* him only,
12: 20 but *s* the LORD with all your heart
12: 24 *s* him faithfully with all your heart;
2Ch 19: 9 "You must *s* faithfully
Job 36: 11 If they obey and *s* him,
Ps 2: 11 *S* the LORD with fear
Da 3: 17 the God we *s* is able to save us
Mt 4: 10 Lord your God, and *s* him only.' "
6: 24 "No one can *s* two masters.
20: 28 but to *s*, and to give his life
Ro 12: 7 If it is serving, let him *s*;
Gal 5: 13 rather, *s* one another in love.
Eph 6: 7 *S* wholeheartedly,
1Ti 6: 2 they are to *s* them even better,
Heb 9: 14 so that we may *s* the living God!
1Pe 4: 10 gift he has received to *s* others,
5: 2 greedy for money, but eager to *s*;
Rev 5: 10 kingdom and priests to *s* our God,

SERVED (SERVE)
Mt 20: 28 Son of Man did not come to be *s*,
Jn 12: 2 Martha *s*, while Lazarus was
Ac 17: 25 And he is not *s* by human hands,
Ro 1: 25 and *s* created things rather
1Ti 3: 13 Those who have *s* well gain

SERVES (SERVE)
Lk 22: 26 one who rules like the one who *s*.
22: 27 But I am among you as one who *s*.
Jn 12: 26 Whoever *s* me must follow me;
Ro 14: 18 because anyone who *s* Christ
1Pe 4: 11 If anyone *s*, he should do it

SERVICE (SERVE)
Lk 9: 62 fit for *s* in the kingdom
12: 35 "Be dressed ready for *s*
Ro 15: 17 in Christ Jesus in my *s* to God.
1Co 12: 5 There are different kinds of *s*,
16: 15 themselves to the *s* of the saints.
2Co 9: 12 This *s* that you perform is not only
Eph 4: 12 God's people for works of *s*,
Rev 2: 19 and faith, your *s* and perseverance,

SERVING (SERVE)
Jos 24: 15 if *s* the LORD seems undesirable
2Ch 12: 8 learn the difference between *s* me
Ro 12: 7 If it is *s*, let him serve;
12: 11 your spiritual fervor, *s* the Lord.
16: 18 people are not *s* our Lord Christ,
Eph 6: 7 as if you were *s* the Lord, not men,
Col 3: 24 It is the Lord Christ you are *s*.
2Ti 2: 4 No one *s* as a soldier gets involved

SETH
Ge 4: 25 birth to a son and named him *S*,

SETTLE
Mt 5: 25 "*S* matters quickly
2Th 3: 12 in the Lord Jesus Christ to *s* down

SEVEN (SEVENS SEVENTH)
Ge 7: 2 Take with you *s* of every kind
Jos 6: 4 march around the city *s* times,
1Ki 19: 18 Yet I reserve *s* thousand in Israel—
Pr 6: 16 *s* that are detestable to him:
24: 16 a righteous man falls *s* times,
Isa 4: 1 In that day *s* women
Da 9: 25 comes, there will be *s* 'sevens,'
Mt 18: 21 Up to *s* times?" Jesus answered,
Lk 11: 26 takes *s* other spirits more wicked
Ro 11: 4 for myself *s* thousand who have not
Rev 1: 4 To the *s* churches in the province
6: 1 opened the first of the *s* seals.
8: 2 and to them were given *s* trumpets.
10: 4 And when the *s* thunders spoke,
15: 7 to the *s* angels *s* golden bowls filled

SEVENS* (SEVEN)
Da 9: 24 "Seventy '*s*' are decreed
9: 25 will be seven '*s*,' and sixty-two '*s*.'
9: 26 the sixty-two '*s*,' the Anointed

SEVENTH (SEVEN)
Ge 2: 2 By the *s* day God had finished
Ex 20: 10 but the *s* day is a Sabbath
23: 11 but during the *s* year let the land lie
23: 12 but on the *s* day do not work,
Heb 4: 4 "And on the *s* day God rested

SEVERE
2Co 8: 2 Out of the most *s* trial, their
1Th 1: 6 of the Lord; in spite of *s* suffering,

SEWED (SEWS)
Ge 3: 7 so they *s* fig leaves together

SEWS (SEWED)
Mt 9: 16 No one *s* a patch of unshrunk cloth

SEXUAL (SEXUALLY)
Ex 22: 19 "Anyone who has *s* relations
Lev 18: 6 relative to have *s* relations.
18: 7 father by having *s* relations
18: 20 Do not have *s* relations with
Mt 15: 19 murder, adultery, *s* immorality,
Ac 15: 20 by idols, from *s* immorality,
1Co 5: 1 reported that there is *s* immorality
6: 13 body is not meant for *s* immorality,
6: 18 Flee from *s* immorality.
10: 8 should not commit *s* immorality,
2Co 12: 21 *s* sin and debauchery
Gal 5: 19 *s* immorality, impurity
Eph 5: 3 even a hint of *s* immorality,
Col 3: 5 *s* immorality, impurity, lust,
1Th 4: 3 that you should avoid *s* immorality

SEXUALLY (SEXUAL)
1Co 5: 9 to associate with *s* immoral people
6: 9 Neither the *s* immoral nor idolaters
6: 18 he who sins *s* sins against his own
Heb 12: 16 See that no one is *s* immoral,
13: 4 the adulterer and all the *s* immoral.
Rev 21: 8 the murderers, the *s* immoral,

SHADE
Ps 121: 5 the LORD is your *s*
Isa 25: 4 and a *s* from the heat.

SHADOW
Ps 17: 8 hide me in the *s* of your wings
23: 4 through the valley of the *s* of death,
36: 7 find refuge in the *s* of your wings.
91: 1 will rest in the *s* of the Almighty.
Isa 51: 16 covered you with the *s* of my hand
Col 2: 17 These are a *s* of the things that
Heb 8: 5 and *s* of what is in heaven.
10: 1 The law is only a *s*

SHADRACH
Hebrew exiled to Babylon; name changed from Hananiah (Da 1:6–7). Refused defilement by food (Da 1:8–20). Refused to worship idol (Da 3:1–18); saved from furnace (Da 3:19–30).

SHAKE (SHAKEN SHAKING)
Ps 64: 8 all who see them will *s* their heads
99: 1 let the earth *s*.
Hag 2: 6 I will once more *s* the heavens
Heb 12: 26 "Once more I will *s* not only

SHAKEN (SHAKE)
Ps 16: 8 I will not be *s*.
30: 6 "I will never be *s*."
62: 2 he is my fortress, I will never be *s*.
112: 6 Surely he will never be *s*;
Isa 54: 10 Though the mountains be *s*
Mt 24: 29 and the heavenly bodies will be *s*.'
Lk 6: 38 *s* together and running over,
Ac 2: 25 I will not be *s*.
Heb 12: 27 that what cannot be *s* may remain.

SHAKING* (SHAKE)
Ps 22: 7 they hurl insults, *s* their heads:
Mt 27: 39 insults at him, *s* their heads
Mk 15: 29 *s* their heads and saying, "So!

SHALLUM
King of Israel (2Ki 15:10–16).

SHAME (ASHAMED SHAMED SHAMEFUL)
Ps 25: 3 will ever be put to *s*,
34: 5 their faces are never covered with *s*
69: 6 not be put to *s* because of me,
Pr 13: 18 discipline comes to poverty and *s*,
18: 13 that is his folly and his *s*.
Jer 8: 9 The wise will be put to *s*;
8: 12 No, they have no *s* at all;
Ro 9: 33 trusts in him will never be put to *s*."
10: 11 trusts in him will never be put to *s*."
1Co 1: 27 things of the world to *s* the wise;
Heb 12: 2 endured the cross, scorning its *s*,

SHAMED (SHAME)
Jer 10: 14 every goldsmith is *s* by his idols.
Joel 2: 26 never again will my people be *s*.

SHAMEFUL (SHAME)
2Co 4: 2 have renounced secret and *s* ways;
2Pe 2: 2 Many will follow their *s* ways
Rev 21: 27 nor will anyone who does what is *s*

SHAMGAR
Judge; killed 600 Philistines (Jdg 3:31).

SHAPE (SHAPES SHAPING)
Job 38: 14 The earth takes *s* like clay

SHAPES (SHAPE)
Isa 44: 10 Who *s* a god and casts an idol,

SHAPING (SHAPE)
Jer 18: 4 the pot he was *s* from the clay was

SHARE (SHARED SHARERS SHARES SHARING)
Ge 21: 10 that slave woman's son will never *s*
Lev 19: 17 frankly so you will not *s* in his guilt.
Dt 10: 9 That is why the Levites have no *s*
1Sa 30: 24 All will *s* alike."
Eze 18: 20 The son will not *s* the guilt
Mt 25: 21 and *s* your master's happiness!'
Lk 3: 11 "The man with two tunics should *s*
Ro 8: 17 if indeed we *s* in his sufferings
12: 13 *S* with God's people who are
2Co 1: 7 as you *s* in our sufferings,
Gal 4: 30 the slave woman's son will never *s*
6: 6 in the word must *s* all good things
Eph 4: 28 something to *s* with those in need.
Col 1: 12 you to *s* in the inheritance
2Th 2: 14 that you might *s* in the glory
1Ti 5: 22 and do not *s* in the sins of others.
6: 18 and to be generous and willing to *s*.
2Ti 2: 6 the first to receive a *s* of the crops.
Heb 12: 10 that we may *s* in his holiness.
13: 16 to do good and to *s* with others,
Rev 22: 19 from him his *s* in the tree of life

SHARED (SHARE)
Ps 41: 9 he who *s* my bread,
Ac 4: 32 but they *s* everything they had.
Heb 2: 14 he too *s* in their humanity so that

SHARERS* (SHARE)
Eph 3: 6 and *s* together in the promise

SHARES (SHARE)
Pr 22: 9 for he *s* his food with the poor.
Jn 13: 18 'He who *s* my bread has lifted up

SHARING (SHARE)
1Co 9: 10 so in the hope of *s* in the harvest.
2Co 9: 13 for your generosity in *s* with them

Php 3: 10 the fellowship of *s* in his sufferings,
Phm : 6 you may be active in *s* your faith,

SHARON
SS 2: 1 I am a rose of *S,*

SHARP (SHARPENED SHARPENS SHARPER)
Pr 5: 4 *s* as a double-edged sword.
Isa 5: 28 Their arrows are *s,*
Rev 1: 16 came a *s* double-edged sword.
19: 15 Out of his mouth comes a *s* sword

SHARPENED (SHARP)
Eze 21: 9 *s* and polished—

SHARPENS* (SHARP)
Pr 27: 17 As iron *s* iron,
27: 17 so one man *s* another.

SHARPER* (SHARP)
Heb 4: 12 *S* than any double-edged sword,

SHATTER (SHATTERED SHATTERS)
Jer 51: 20 with you I *s* nations,

SHATTERED (SHATTER)
1Sa 2: 10 who oppose the LORD will be *s.*
Job 16: 12 All was well with me, but he *s* me;
17: 11 days have passed, my plans are *s,*
Ecc 12: 6 before the pitcher is *s* at the spring,

SHATTERS (SHATTER)
Ps 46: 9 he breaks the bow and *s* the spear,

SHAVED
Jdg 16: 17 my head were *s,* my strength would
1Co 11: 5 it is just as though her head were *s.*

SHEAF (SHEAVES)
Lev 23: 11 is to wave the *s* before the LORD

SHEARER* (SHEARERS)
Ac 8: 32 and as a lamb before the *s* is silent,

SHEARERS (SHEARER)
Isa 53: 7 and as a sheep before her *s* is silent,

SHEAVES (SHEAF)
Ge 37: 7 while your *s* gathered around mine
Ps 126: 6 carrying *s* with him.

SHEBA
1. Benjamite who rebelled against David (2Sa 20).
2. See QUEEN.

SHECHEM
1. Raped Jacob's daughter Dinah; killed by Simeon and Levi (Ge 34).
2. City where Joshua renewed the covenant (Jos 24).

SHED (SHEDDING SHEDS)
Ge 9: 6 by man shall his blood be *s;*
Pr 6: 17 hands that *s* innocent blood,
Ro 3: 15 "Their feet are swift to *s* blood;
Col 1: 20 through his blood, *s* on the cross.

SHEDDING (SHED)
Heb 9: 22 without the *s* of blood there is no

SHEDS (SHED)
Ge 9: 6 "Whoever *s* the blood of man,

SHEEP (SHEEP'S SHEEPSKINS)
Nu 27: 17 LORD's people will not be like *s*
Dt 17: 1 a *s* that has any defect or flaw in it,
1Sa 15: 14 "What then is this bleating of *s*
Ps 44: 22 we are considered as *s*
78: 52 led them like *s* through the desert.
100: 3 we are his people, the *s*
119:176 I have strayed like a lost *s.*
SS 4: 2 teeth are like a flock of *s* just shorn,
Isa 53: 6 We all, like *s,* have gone astray,
53: 7 as a *s* before her shearers is silent,
Jer 50: 6 "My people have been lost *s;*
Eze 34: 11 I myself will search for my *s*
Zec 13: 7 and the *s* will be scattered,
Mt 9: 36 helpless, like *s* without a shepherd.
10: 16 I am sending you out like *s*
12: 11 "If any of you has a *s* and it falls
18: 13 he is happier about that one *s*
25: 32 as a shepherd separates the *s*
Jn 10: 1 man who does not enter the *s* pen
10: 3 He calls his own *s* by name
10: 7 the truth, I am the gate for the *s.*
10: 15 and I lay down my life for the *s.*
10: 27 My *s* listen to my voice; I know
21: 17 Jesus said, "Feed my *s.*
1Pe 2: 25 For you were like *s* going astray,

SHEEP'S* (SHEEP)
Mt 7: 15 They come to you in *s* clothing,

SHEEPSKINS* (SHEEP)
Heb 11: 37 They went about in *s* and goatskins

SHEKEL
Ex 30: 13 This half *s* is an offering

SHELTER
Ps 27: 5 me in the *s* of his tabernacle
31: 20 In the *s* of your presence you hide
55: 8 I would hurry to my place of *s,*
61: 4 take refuge in the *s* of your wings.
91: 1 in the *s* of the Most High
Ecc 7: 12 Wisdom is a *s*
Isa 4: 6 It will be a *s* and shade
25: 4 a *s* from the storm
32: 2 Each man will be like a *s*
58: 7 the poor wanderer with *s*—

SHEM
Son of Noah (Ge 5:32; 6:10). Blessed (Ge 9:26). Descendants (Ge 10:21–31; 11:10–32).

SHEPHERD (SHEPHERDS)
Ge 48: 15 the God who has been my *s*
49: 24 because of the *S,* the Rock of Israel
Nu 27: 17 will not be like sheep without a *s.*"
2Sa 7: 7 commanded to *s* my people Israel,
1Ki 22: 17 on the hills like sheep without a *s,*
Ps 23: 1 LORD is my *s,* I shall not be in want.
28: 9 be their *s* and carry them forever.
80: 1 Hear us, O *S* of Israel,
Isa 40: 11 He tends his flock like a *s:*
Jer 31: 10 will watch over his flock like a *s.*'
Eze 34: 5 scattered because there was no *s,*
34: 12 As a *s* looks after his scattered
Zec 11: 9 and said, "I will not be your *s.*
11: 17 "Woe to the worthless *s,*
13: 7 "Strike the *s,*
Mt 2: 6 who will be the *s* of my people
9: 36 and helpless, like sheep without a *s.*
26: 31 " 'I will strike the *s,*
Jn 10: 11 The good *s* lays down his life
10: 14 "I am the good *s;* I know my sheep
10: 16 there shall be one flock and one *s.*
Heb 13: 20 that great *S* of the sheep, equip you
1Pe 5: 4 And when the Chief *S* appears,
Rev 7: 17 of the throne will be their *s;*

SHEPHERDS (SHEPHERD)
Jer 23: 1 "Woe to the *s* who are destroying
50: 6 their *s* have led them astray
Eze 34: 2 prophesy against the *s* of Israel;
Lk 2: 8 there were *s* living out in the fields
Ac 20: 28 Be *s* of the church of God,
1Pe 5: 2 Be *s* of God's flock that is
Jude : 12 *s* who feed only themselves.

SHIBBOLETH*
Jdg 12: 6 No," they said, "All right, say '*S.*' "

SHIELD (SHIELDED SHIELDS)
Ge 15: 1 I am your *s,*
2Sa 22: 3 my *s* and the horn of my salvation.
22: 36 You give me your *s* of victory;
Ps 3: 3 But you are a *s* around me,
5: 12 with your favor as with a *s.*
7: 10 My *s* is God Most High,
18: 2 He is my *s* and the horn
28: 7 LORD is my strength and my *s;*
33: 20 he is our help and our *s.*
84: 11 For the LORD God is a sun and *s;*
91: 4 his faithfulness will be your *s*
115: 9 he is their help and *s.*
119:114 You are my refuge and my *s;*
144: 2 my *s,* in whom I take refuge,
Pr 2: 7 he is a *s* to those whose walk is
30: 5 he is a *s* to those who take refuge
Eph 6: 16 to all this, take up the *s* of faith,

SHIELDED (SHIELD)
1Pe 1: 5 through faith are *s* by God's power

SHIELDS (SHIELD)
Dt 33: 12 for he *s* him all day long,

SHIFTLESS*
Pr 19: 15 and the *s* man goes hungry.

SHIMEI
Cursed David (2Sa 16:5–14); spared (2Sa 19:16–23). Killed by Solomon (1Ki 2:8–9, 36–46).

SHINE (SHINES SHINING SHONE)
Nu 6: 25 the LORD make his face *s*
Job 33: 30 that the light of life may *s* on him.
Ps 4: 6 Let the light of your face *s* upon us,
37: 6 make your righteousness *s* like
67: 1 and make his face *s* upon us; *Selah*
80: 1 between the cherubim, *s* forth
118: 27 and he has made his light *s* upon us.
Isa 60: 1 "Arise, *s,* for your light has come,
Da 12: 3 are wise will *s* like the brightness
Mt 5: 16 let your light *s* before men,
13: 43 the righteous will *s* like the sun
2Co 4: 6 made his light *s* in our hearts
Eph 5: 14 and Christ will *s* on you."
Php 2: 15 in which you *s* like stars

SHINES (SHINE)
Ps 50: 2 God *s* forth.
Pr 13: 9 The light of the righteous *s* brightly
Jn 1: 5 The light *s* in the darkness,

SHINING (SHINE)
Pr 4: 18 *s* ever brighter till the full light
2Pe 1: 19 as to a light *s* in a dark place,
Rev 1: 16 His face was like the sun *s*

SHIPS
Pr 31: 14 She is like the merchant *s,*

SHIPWRECKED*
2Co 11: 25 I was stoned, three times I was *s,*
1Ti 1: 19 and so have *s* their faith.

SHISHAK
1Ki 14: 25 *S* king of Egypt attacked Jerusalem
2Ch 12: 2 *S* king of Egypt attacked Jerusalem

SHOCKING*
Jer 5: 30 "A horrible and *s* thing

SHONE (SHINE)
Mt 17: 2 His face *s* like the sun,
Lk 2: 9 glory of the Lord *s* around them,
Rev 21: 11 It *s* with the glory of God,

SHOOT
Isa 53: 2 up before him like a tender *s,*
Ro 11: 17 and you, though a wild olive *s,*

SHORE
Lk 5: 3 asked him to put out a little from *s.*

SHORT (SHORTENED)
Nu 11: 23 "Is the LORD's arm too *s?*
Isa 50: 2 Was my arm too *s* to ransom you?
59: 1 of the LORD is not too *s* to save,
Mt 24: 22 If those days had not been cut *s,*
Ro 3: 23 and fall *s* of the glory of God,
1Co 7: 29 brothers, is that the time is *s.*
Heb 4: 1 of you be found to have fallen *s* of it
Rev 20: 3 he must be set free for a *s* time.

SHORTENED (SHORT)
Mt 24: 22 of the elect those days will be *s.*

SHOULDER (SHOULDERS)
Zep 3: 9 and serve him *s* to *s.*

SHOULDERS (SHOULDER)
Dt 33: 12 LORD loves rests between his *s.*"
Isa 9: 6 and the government will be on his *s*
Lk 15: 5 he joyfully puts it on his *s*

SHOUT (SHOUTED)
Ps 47: 1 *s* to God with cries of joy.
66: 1 *S* with joy to God, all the earth!
95: 1 let us *s* aloud to the Rock

98: 4 *S* for joy to the LORD, all the earth
100: 1 *S* for joy to the LORD, all the earth
Isa 12: 6 *S* aloud and sing for joy, people
26: 19 wake up and *s* for joy.
35: 6 the mute tongue *s* for joy.
40: 9 lift up your voice with a *s*,
42: 2 He will not *s* or cry out,
44: 23 *s* aloud, O earth beneath.
54: 1 burst into song, *s* for joy,
Zec 9: 9 *S*, Daughter of Jerusalem!

SHOUTED (SHOUT)
Job 38: 7 and all the angels *s* for joy?

SHOW (SHOWED)
Ex 18: 20 and *s* them the way to live
33: 18 Moses said, "Now *s* me your glory
2Sa 22: 26 the faithful you *s* yourself faithful,
1Ki 2: 2 "So be strong, *s* yourself a man,
Ps 17: 7 *S* the wonder of your great love,
25: 4 *S* me your ways, O LORD,
39: 4 "*S* me, O LORD, my life's end
85: 7 *S* us your unfailing love, O LORD,
143: 8 *S* me the way I should go,
Pr 23: 4 have the wisdom to *s* restraint.
SS 2: 14 *s* me your face,
Isa 5: 16 the holy God will *s* himself holy
30: 18 he rises to *s* you compassion.
Eze 28: 25 I will *s* myself holy among them
Joel 2: 30 I will *s* wonders in the heavens
Zec 7: 9 *s* mercy and compassion
Ac 2: 19 I will *s* wonders in the heaven
10: 34 it is that God does not *s* favoritism
1Co 12: 31 now I will *s* you the most excellent
Eph 2: 7 ages he might *s* the incomparable
Tit 2: 7 In your teaching *s* integrity,
Jas 2: 18 I will *s* you my faith by what I do.
Jude : 23 to others *s* mercy, mixed with fear

SHOWED (SHOW)
1Ki 3: 3 Solomon *s* his love for the LORD
Lk 24: 40 he *s* them his hands and feet.
1Jn 4: 9 This is how God *s* his love

SHOWERS
Eze 34: 26 in season; there will be *s* of blessing
Hos 10: 12 and *s* righteousness on you.

SHREWD
2Sa 22: 27 to the crooked you show yourself *s*.
Mt 10: 16 Therefore be as *s* as snakes and

SHRINK (SHRINKS)
Heb 10: 39 But we are not of those who *s* back

SHRINKS* (SHRINK)
Heb 10: 38 And if he *s* back,

SHRIVEL
Isa 64: 6 we all *s* up like a leaf,

SHUDDER
Eze 32: 10 and their kings will *s* with horror

SHUHITE
Job 2: 11 Bildad the *S* and Zophar

SHUN* (SHUNS)
Job 28: 28 and to *s* evil is understanding.' "
Pr 3: 7 fear the LORD and *s* evil.

SHUNS (SHUN)
Job 1: 8 a man who fears God and *s* evil."
Pr 14: 16 man fears the LORD and *s* evil,

SHUT
Ge 7: 16 Then the LORD *s* him in.
Isa 22: 22 what he opens no one can *s*,
60: 11 they will never be *s*, day or night,
Da 6: 22 and he *s* the mouths of the lions.
Heb 11: 33 who *s* the mouths of lions,
Rev 3: 7 no one can *s*, and what he shuts
21: 25 On no day will its gates ever be *s*,

SICK (SICKNESS)
Pr 13: 12 Hope deferred makes the heart *s*,
Eze 34: 4 or healed the *s* or bound up
Mt 9: 12 who need a doctor, but the *s*.
10: 8 Heal the *s*, raise the dead, cleanse
25: 36 I was *s* and you looked after me,
1Co 11: 30 many among you are weak and *s*,
Jas 5: 14 of you *s*? He should call the elders

SICKBED* (BED)
Ps 41: 3 LORD will sustain him on his *s*

SICKLE
Joel 3: 13 Swing the *s*,
Rev 14: 14 gold on his head and a sharp *s*

SICKNESS (SICK)
Mt 4: 23 and healing every disease and *s*

SIDE (SIDES)
Ps 91: 7 A thousand may fall at your *s*,
124: 1 If the LORD had not been on our *s*
Jn 18: 37 Everyone on the *s* of truth listens
20: 20 he showed them his hands and *s*.
2Ti 4: 17 But the Lord stood at my *s*
Heb 10: 33 at other times you stood *s* by *s*

SIDES (SIDE)
Nu 33: 55 in your eyes and thorns in your *s*.

SIFT
Lk 22: 31 Satan has asked to *s* you as wheat.

SIGHING
Isa 35: 10 and sorrow and *s* will flee away.

SIGHT
Ps 51: 4 and done what is evil in your *s*,
90: 4 For a thousand years in your *s*
116: 15 Precious in the *s* of the LORD
Pr 3: 4 in the *s* of God and man.
Mt 11: 5 The blind receive *s*, the lame walk,
Ac 4: 19 right in God's *s* to obey you rather
1Co 3: 19 this world is foolishness in God's *s*.
2Co 5: 7 We live by faith, not by *s*.
1Pe 3: 4 which is of great worth in God's *s*.

SIGN (SIGNS)
Ge 9: 12 "This is the *s* of the covenant I am
17: 11 and it will be the *s* of the covenant
Isa 7: 14 the Lord himself will give you a *s*:
55: 13 for an everlasting *s*,
Eze 20: 12 I gave them my Sabbaths as a *s*
Mt 12: 38 to see a miraculous *s* from you."
24: 3 what will be the *s* of your coming
24: 30 "At that time the *s* of the Son
Lk 2: 12 This will be a *s* to you: You will
11: 29 It asks for a miraculous *s*,
Ro 4: 11 he received the *s* of circumcision,
1Co 11: 10 to have a *s* of authority on her head
14: 22 are a *s*, not for believers

SIGNS (SIGN)
Ge 1: 14 let them serve as *s* to mark seasons
Ps 78: 43 day he displayed his miraculous *s*
105: 27 They performed his miraculous *s*
Da 6: 27 he performs *s* and wonders
Mt 24: 24 and perform great *s* and miracles
Mk 16: 17 these *s* will accompany those who
Jn 3: 2 perform the miraculous *s* you are
20: 30 Jesus did many other miraculous *s*
Ac 2: 19 and *s* on the earth below,
1Co 1: 22 Jews demand miraculous *s*
2Co 12: 12 *s*, wonders and miracles—
2Th 2: 9 *s* and wonders, and in every sort

SIHON
Nu 21: 21 to say to *S* king of the Amorites:
Ps 136: 19 *S* king of the Amorites

SILAS*
Prophet (Ac 15:22–32); co-worker with Paul on second missionary journey (Ac 16–18; 2Co 1:19). Co-writer with Paul (1Th 1:1; 2Th 1:1); Peter (1Pe 5:12).

SILENCE (SILENCED SILENT)
1Pe 2: 15 good you should *s* the ignorant talk
Rev 8: 1 there was *s* in heaven

SILENCED (SILENCE)
Ro 3: 19 so that every mouth may be *s*
Tit 1: 11 They must be *s*, because they are

SILENT (SILENCE)
Est 4: 14 For if you remain *s* at this time,
Ps 30: 12 to you and not be *s*.
32: 3 When I kept *s*,
39: 2 But when I was *s* and still,
Pr 17: 28 a fool is thought wise if he keeps *s*,
Ecc 3: 7 a time to be *s* and a time to speak,
Isa 53: 7 as a sheep before her shearers is *s*,
62: 1 For Zion's sake I will not keep *s*,
Hab 2: 20 let all the earth be *s* before him."
Ac 8: 32 and as a lamb before the shearer is *s*
1Co 14: 34 women should remain *s*
1Ti 2: 12 over a man; she must be *s*.

SILVER
Ps 12: 6 like *s* refined in a furnace of clay,
66: 10 you refined us like *s*.
Pr 2: 4 and if you look for it as for *s*
3: 14 for she is more profitable than *s*
8: 10 Choose my instruction instead of *s*,
22: 1 to be esteemed is better than *s*
25: 4 Remove the dross from the *s*,
25: 11 is like apples of gold in settings of *s*.
Isa 48: 10 I have refined you, though not as *s*;
Eze 22: 18 They are but the dross of *s*.
Da 2: 32 its chest and arms of *s*, its belly
Hag 2: 8 'The *s* is mine and the gold is mine,'
Zec 13: 9 I will refine them like *s*
Ac 3: 6 Peter said, "*S* or gold I do not have,
1Co 3: 12 *s*, costly stones, wood, hay or straw
1Pe 1: 18 not with perishable things such as *s*

SILVERSMITH
Ac 19: 24 A *s* named Demetrius, who made

SIMEON
Son of Jacob by Leah (Ge 29:33; 35:23; 1Ch 2:1). With Levi killed Shechem for rape of Dinah (Ge 34:25–29). Held hostage by Joseph in Egypt (Ge 42:24–43:23). Tribe of blessed (Ge 49:5–7), numbered (Nu 1:23; 26:14), allotted land (Jos 19:1–9; Eze 48:24), 12,000 from (Rev 7:7).

SIMON
1. See PETER.
2. Apostle, called the Zealot (Mt 10:4; Mk 3:18; Lk 6:15; Ac 1:13).
3. Samaritan sorcerer (Ac 8:9–24).

SIMPLE
Ps 19: 7 making wise the *s*.
119: 130 it gives understanding to the *s*.
Pr 8: 5 You who are *s*, gain prudence;
14: 15 A *s* man believes anything,

SIMPLEHEARTED* (HEART)
Ps 116: 6 The LORD protects the *s*;

SIN (SINFUL SINNED SINNER SINNERS SINNING SINS)
Ge 4: 7 *s* is crouching at your door;
Ex 32: 32 please forgive their *s*— but if not,
Nu 5: 7 and must confess the *s* he has
32: 23 be sure that your *s* will find you
Dt 24: 16 each is to die for his own *s*.
1Sa 12: 23 it from me that I should *s*
15: 23 For rebellion is like the *s*
1Ki 8: 46 for there is no one who does not *s*
2Ch 7: 14 and will forgive their *s* and will heal
Job 1: 22 Job did not *s* by charging God
Ps 4: 4 In your anger do not *s*;
17: 3 resolved that my mouth will not *s*.
32: 2 whose *s* the LORD does not count
32: 5 Then I acknowledged my *s* to you
36: 2 too much to detect or hate his *s*.
38: 18 I am troubled by my *s*.
39: 1 and keep my tongue from *s*;
51: 2 and cleanse me from my *s*.
66: 18 If I had cherished *s* in my heart,
119: 11 that I might not *s* against you.
119: 133 let no *s* rule over me.
Pr 5: 22 the cords of his *s* hold him fast.
10: 19 words are many, *s* is not absent,
14: 9 Fools mock at making amends for *s*
16: 6 faithfulness *s* is atoned for;
17: 19 He who loves a quarrel loves *s*;

20: 9 I am clean and without *s*"?
Isa 3: 9 they parade their *s* like Sodom;
6: 7 is taken away and your *s* atoned
64: 5 But when we continued to *s*
Jer 31: 30 everyone will die for his own *s*;
Eze 3: 18 that wicked man will die for his *s*,
18: 26 his righteousness and commits *s*,
33: 8 that wicked man will die for his *s*,
Am 4: 4 "Go to Bethel and *s*;
Mic 6: 7 of my body for the *s* of my soul?
7: 18 who pardons *s* and forgives
Zec 3: 4 "See, I have taken away your *s*,
Mt 18: 6 little ones who believe in me to *s*,
Mk 3: 29 he is guilty of an eternal *s*."
9: 43 If your hand causes you to *s*,
Lk 17: 1 people to *s* are bound to come,
Jn 1: 29 who takes away the *s* of the world!
8: 7 "If any one of you is without *s*,
8: 34 everyone who sins is a slave to *s*.
8: 46 Can any of you prove me guilty of *s*
Ro 2: 12 All who *s* apart from the law will
5: 12 as *s* entered the world
5: 20 where *s* increased, grace increased
6: 2 By no means! We died to *s*;
6: 11 count yourselves dead to *s*
6: 14 For *s* shall not be your master,
6: 23 For the wages of *s* is death,
7: 7 I would not have known what *s* was
7: 25 sinful nature a slave to the law of *s*.
14: 23 that does not come from faith is *s*.
1Co 8: 12 When you *s* against your brothers
15: 56 The sting of death is *s*,
2Co 5: 21 God made him who had no *s* to be *s*
Gal 6: 1 if someone is caught in a *s*,
1Ti 5: 20 Those who *s* are to be rebuked
Heb 4: 15 just as we are—yet was without *s*.
9: 26 to do away with *s* by the sacrifice
11: 25 the pleasures of *s* for a short time.
12: 1 and the *s* that so easily entangles,
Jas 1: 15 it gives birth to *s*; and *s*,
1Pe 2: 22 "He committed no *s*,
1Jn 1: 7 his Son, purifies us from all *s*.
1: 8 If we claim to be without *s*,
2: 1 But if anybody does *s*, we have one
3: 4 in fact, *s* is lawlessness.
3: 5 And in him is no *s*.
3: 6 No one who continues to *s* has
3: 9 born of God will continue to *s*,
5: 16 There is a *s* that leads to death.
5: 17 All wrongdoing is *s*, and there is *s*
5: 18 born of God does not continue to *s*;

SINAI
Ex 19: 20 descended to the top of Mount *S*
31: 18 speaking to Moses on Mount *S*,
Ps 68: 17 from *S* into his sanctuary.

SINCERE* (SINCERITY)
Da 11: 34 many who are not *s* will join them.
Ac 2: 46 ate together with glad and *s* hearts,
Ro 12: 9 Love must be *s*.
2Co 6: 6 in the Holy Spirit and in *s* love;
11: 3 somehow be led astray from your *s*
1Ti 1: 5 a good conscience and a *s* faith.
3: 8 *s*, not indulging in much wine,
2Ti 1: 5 have been reminded of your *s* faith,
Heb 10: 22 near to God with a *s* heart
Jas 3: 17 and good fruit, impartial and *s*.
1Pe 1: 22 the truth so that you have *s* love

SINCERITY* (SINCERE)
1Co 5: 8 bread without yeast, the bread of *s*
2Co 1: 12 in the holiness and *s* that are
2: 17 speak before God with *s*,
8: 8 but I want to test the *s* of your love
Eph 6: 5 and with *s* of heart, just
Col 3: 22 but with *s* of heart and reverence

SINFUL (SIN)
Ps 51: 5 Surely I was *s* at birth,
51: 5 *s* from the time my mother
Lk 5: 8 from me, Lord; I am a *s* man!"
Ro 7: 5 we were controlled by the *s* nature,
7: 18 lives in me, that is, in my *s* nature.
7: 25 but in the *s* nature a slave to the law
8: 3 Son in the likeness of *s* man
8: 4 not live according to the *s* nature
8: 7 the *s* mind is hostile to God.
8: 8 by the *s* nature cannot please God.
8: 9 are controlled not by the *s* nature
8: 13 if you live according to the *s* nature
13: 14 to gratify the desires of the *s* nature
1Co 5: 5 so that the *s* nature may be
Gal 5: 13 freedom to indulge the *s* nature;
5: 16 gratify the desires of the *s* nature.
5: 19 The acts of the *s* nature are obvious
5: 24 Jesus have crucified the *s* nature
6: 8 sows to please his *s* nature,
Col 2: 11 in the putting off of the *s* nature,
Heb 3: 12 brothers, that none of you has a *s*,
1Pe 2: 11 abstain from *s* desires, which war
1Jn 3: 8 He who does what is *s* is

SING (SANG SINGER SINGING SINGS SONG SONGS SUNG)
Ex 15: 1 "I will *s* to the LORD,
Ps 5: 11 let them ever *s* for joy.
13: 6 I will *s* to the LORD,
30: 4 *S* to the LORD, you saints of his;
33: 1 *S* joyfully to the LORD, you
47: 6 *S* praises to God, *s* praises;
57: 7 I will *s* and make music.
59: 16 But I will *s* of your strength,
63: 7 I *s* in the shadow of your wings.
66: 2 *S* to the glory of his name;
89: 1 I will *s* of the LORD's great love
95: 1 Come, let us *s* for joy to the LORD
96: 1 *S* to the LORD a new song;
98: 1 *S* to the LORD a new song,
101: 1 I will *s* of your love and justice;
108: 1 I will *s* and make music
137: 3 "*S* us one of the songs of Zion!"
147: 1 is to *s* praises to our God,
149: 1 *S* to the LORD a new song,
Isa 54: 1 "*S*, O barren woman,
1Co 14: 15 also pray with my mind; I will *s*
Eph 5: 19 *S* and make music in your heart
Col 3: 16 and as you *s* psalms, hymns
Jas 5: 13 Is anyone happy? Let him *s* songs

SINGER* (SING)
2Sa 23: 1 Israel's *s* of songs:

SINGING (SING)
Ps 63: 5 with *s* lips my mouth will praise
68: 6 he leads forth the prisoners with *s*;
98: 5 with the harp and the sound of *s*,
Isa 35: 10 They will enter Zion with *s*;
Zep 3: 17 he will rejoice over you with *s*."
Ac 16: 25 Silas were praying and *s* hymns
Rev 5: 13 on the sea, and all that is in them, *s*:

SINGLE
Ex 23: 29 I will not drive them out in a *s* year,
Mt 6: 27 you by worrying can add a *s* hour
Gal 5: 14 law is summed up in a *s* command:

SINGS (SING)
Eze 33: 32 more than one who *s* love songs

SINNED (SIN)
Lev 5: 5 confess in what way he has *s*
1Sa 15: 24 Then Saul said to Samuel, "I have *s*
2Sa 12: 13 "I have *s* against the LORD."
24: 10 I have *s* greatly in what I have done
2Ch 6: 37 'We have *s*, we have done wrong
Job 1: 5 "Perhaps my children have *s*
33: 27 'I *s*, and perverted what was right,
Ps 51: 4 Against you, you only, have I *s*
Jer 2: 35 because you say, 'I have not *s*.'
14: 20 we have indeed *s* against you.
Da 9: 5 we have *s* and done wrong.
Mic 7: 9 Because I have *s* against him,
Mt 27: 4 "I have *s*," he said,
Lk 15: 18 I have *s* against heaven
Ro 3: 23 for all have *s* and fall short
5: 12 all *s*— for before the law was given,
2Pe 2: 4 did not spare angels when they *s*,
1Jn 1: 10 claim we have not *s*, we make him

SINNER (SIN)
Ecc 9: 18 but one *s* destroys much good.
Lk 15: 7 in heaven over one *s* who repents
18: 13 'God, have mercy on me, a *s*.'
1Co 14: 24 convinced by all that he is a *s*
Jas 5: 20 Whoever turns a *s* from the error
1Pe 4: 18 become of the ungodly and the *s*?"

SINNERS (SIN)
Ps 1: 1 or stand in the way of *s*
37: 38 But all *s* will be destroyed;
Pr 1: 10 My son, if *s* entice you,
23: 17 Do not let your heart envy *s*,
Mt 9: 13 come to call the righteous, but *s*."
Ro 5: 8 While we were still *s*, Christ died
Gal 2: 17 evident that we ourselves are *s*,
1Ti 1: 15 came into the world to save *s*—
Heb 7: 26 set apart from *s*, exalted

SINNING (SIN)
Ex 20: 20 be with you to keep you from *s*."
1Co 15: 34 stop *s*; for there are some who are
Heb 10: 26 If we deliberately keep on *s*
1Jn 3: 6 No one who lives in him keeps on *s*
3: 9 go on *s*, because he has been born

SINS (SIN)
Lev 5: 1 " 'If a person *s* because he does not
16: 30 you will be clean from all your *s*.
26: 40 " 'But if they will confess their *s*
Nu 15: 30 " 'But anyone who *s* defiantly,
1Sa 2: 25 If a man *s* against another man,
2Ki 14: 6 each is to die for his own *s*."
Ezr 9: 6 our *s* are higher than our heads
9: 13 less than our *s* have deserved
Ps 19: 13 your servant also from willful *s*;
32: 1 whose *s* are covered.
51: 9 Hide your face from my *s*
79: 9 deliver us and forgive our *s*
85: 2 and covered all their *s*.
103: 3 who forgives all your *s*
103: 10 does not treat us as our *s* deserve
130: 3 O LORD, kept a record of *s*,
Pr 14: 21 He who despises his neighbor *s*,
28: 13 who conceals his *s* does not
29: 22 one commits many *s*.
Ecc 7: 20 who does what is right and never *s*.
Isa 1: 18 "Though your *s* are like scarlet,
38: 17 you have put all my *s*
43: 25 and remembers your *s* no more.
59: 2 your *s* have hidden his face
64: 6 like the wind our *s* sweep us away.
Jer 31: 34 and will remember their *s* no more
La 3: 39 complain when punished for his *s*?
Eze 18: 4 soul who *s* is the one who will die.
33: 10 Our offenses and *s* weigh us down,
36: 33 day I cleanse you from all your *s*,
Hos 14: 1 Your *s* have been your downfall!
Mt 1: 21 he will save his people from their *s*
6: 15 if you do not forgive men their *s*,
9: 6 authority on earth to forgive *s*....."
18: 15 "If your brother *s* against you,
26: 28 for many for the forgiveness of *s*.
Lk 5: 24 authority on earth to forgive *s*....."
11: 4 Forgive us our *s*,
17: 3 "If your brother *s*, rebuke him,
Jn 8: 24 you will indeed die in your *s*."
20: 23 If you forgive anyone his *s*,
Ac 2: 38 for the forgiveness of your *s*.
3: 19 so that your *s* may be wiped out,
10: 43 forgiveness of *s* through his name."
22: 16 be baptized and wash your *s* away,
26: 18 they may receive forgiveness of *s*
Ro 4: 7 whose *s* are covered.
4: 25 delivered over to death for our *s*
1Co 15: 3 died for our *s* according
2Co 5: 19 not counting men's *s* against them.
Gal 1: 4 himself for our *s* to rescue us

Eph 2: 1 dead in your transgressions and *s*,
Col 2: 13 us all our *s*, having canceled
1Ti 5: 22 and do not share in the *s* of others.
Heb 1: 3 he had provided purification for *s*,
2: 17 atonement for the *s* of the people.
7: 27 He sacrificed for their *s* once for all
8: 12 and will remember their *s* no more
9: 28 to take away the *s* of many people;
10: 4 of bulls and goats to take away *s*.
10: 12 for all time one sacrifice for *s*,
10: 26 of the truth, no sacrifice for *s* is left,
Jas 4: 17 ought to do and doesn't do it, *s*.
5: 16 Therefore confess your *s*
5: 20 and cover over a multitude of *s*.
1Pe 2: 24 He himself bore our *s* in his body
3: 18 For Christ died for *s* once for all,
4: 8 love covers over a multitude of *s*.
1Jn 1: 9 If we confess our *s*, he is faithful
2: 2 He is the atoning sacrifice for our *s*,
3: 5 so that he might take away our *s*.
4: 10 as an atoning sacrifice for our *s*.
Rev 1: 5 has freed us from our *s* by his blood

SISERA
Jdg 4: 2 The commander of his army was *S*,
5: 26 She struck *S*, she crushed his head,

SISTER (SISTERS)
Lev 18: 9 have sexual relations with your *s*,
Mk 3: 35 does God's will is my brother and *s*

SISTERS (SISTER)
Mt 19: 29 or brothers or *s* or father or mother
1Ti 5: 2 as *s*, with absolute purity.

SIT (SAT SITS SITTING)
Dt 6: 7 them when you *s* at home
1Ki 8: 25 fail to have a man to *s* before me
Ps 1: 1 or *s* in the seat of mockers.
26: 5 and refuse to *s* with the wicked.
80: 1 you who *s* enthroned
110: 1 "*S* at my right hand
139: 2 You know when I *s* and when I rise
SS 2: 3 I delight to *s* in his shade,
Isa 16: 5 in faithfulness a man will *s* on it—
Mic 4: 4 Every man will *s* under his own
Mt 20: 23 to *s* at my right or left is not for me
22: 44 "*S* at my right hand
Lk 22: 30 in my kingdom and *s* on thrones,
Heb 1: 13 "*S* at my right hand
Rev 3: 21 right to *s* with me on my throne,

SITS (SIT)
Ps 99: 1 *s* enthroned between the cherubim,
Isa 40: 22 He *s* enthroned above the circle
Mt 19: 28 of Man *s* on his glorious throne,
Rev 4: 9 thanks to him who *s* on the throne

SITTING (SIT)
Est 2: 19 Mordecai was *s* at the king's gate.
Mt 26: 64 the Son of Man *s* at the right hand
Rev 4: 2 in heaven with someone *s* on it.

SITUATION (SITUATIONS)
1Co 7: 24 remain in the *s* God called him
Php 4: 12 of being content in any and every *s*,

SITUATIONS* (SITUATION)
2Ti 4: 5 head in all *s*, endure hardship,

SKIES (SKY)
Ps 19: 1 the *s* proclaim the work
71: 19 Your righteousness reaches to the *s*
108: 4 your faithfulness reaches to the *s*.

SKILL (SKILLED SKILLFUL)
Ps 137: 5 may my right hand forget ›its *s*‹.
Ecc 10: 10 but *s* will bring success.

SKILLED (SKILL)
Pr 22: 29 Do you see a man *s* in his work?

SKILLFUL (SKILL)
Ps 45: 1 my tongue is the pen of a *s* writer.
78: 72 with *s* hands he led them.

SKIN (SKINS)
Job 19: 20 with only the *s* of my teeth.
19: 26 And after my *s* has been destroyed,
Jer 13: 23 Can the Ethiopian change his *s*

SKINS (SKIN)
Ex 25: 5 ram *s* dyed red and hides
Lk 5: 37 the new wine will burst the *s*,

SKULL
Mt 27: 33 (which means The Place of the *S*).

SKY (SKIES)
Ge 1: 8 God called the expanse "*s*."
Pr 30: 19 the way of an eagle in the *s*,
Isa 34: 4 and the *s* rolled up like a scroll;
Jer 33: 22 stars of the *s* and as measureless
Mt 24: 29 the stars will fall from the *s*,
24: 30 coming on the clouds of the *s*,
Rev 20: 11 Earth and *s* fled from his presence,

SLACK*
Pr 18: 9 One who is *s* in his work

SLAIN (SLAY)
1Sa 18: 7 "Saul has *s* his thousands,
Eze 37: 9 into these *s*, that they may live.' "
Rev 5: 6 as if it had been *s*, standing
5: 12 "Worthy is the Lamb, who was *s*,
6: 9 the souls of those who had been *s*

SLANDER (SLANDERED SLANDERER SLANDERERS SLANDEROUS)
Lev 19: 16 " 'Do not go about spreading *s*
Ps 15: 3 and has no *s* on his tongue,
Pr 10: 18 and whoever spreads *s* is a fool.
2Co 12: 20 outbursts of anger, factions, *s*,
Eph 4: 31 rage and anger, brawling and *s*,
1Ti 5: 14 the enemy no opportunity for *s*.
Tit 3: 2 to *s* no one, to be peaceable
1Pe 3: 16 in Christ may be ashamed of their *s*
2Pe 2: 10 afraid to *s* celestial beings;

SLANDERED (SLANDER)
1Co 4: 13 when we are *s*, we answer kindly.

SLANDERER (SLANDER)
1Co 5: 11 an idolater or a *s*, a drunkard

SLANDERERS (SLANDER)
Ro 1: 30 They are gossips, *s*, God-haters,
1Co 6: 10 nor the greedy nor drunkards nor *s*
Tit 2: 3 not to be *s* or addicted

SLANDEROUS (SLANDER)
2Ti 3: 3 unforgiving, *s*, without self-control
2Pe 2: 11 do not bring *s* accusations

SLAUGHTER (SLAUGHTERED)
Isa 53: 7 he was led like a lamb to the *s*,
Jer 11: 19 been like a gentle lamb led to the *s*;
Ac 8: 32 "He was led like a sheep to the *s*,

SLAUGHTERED (SLAUGHTER)
Ps 44: 22 we are considered as sheep to be *s*.
Ro 8: 36 we are considered as sheep to be *s*

SLAVE (ENSLAVED SLAVERY SLAVES)
Ge 21: 10 "Get rid of that *s* woman
Mt 20: 27 wants to be first must be your *s*—
Jn 8: 34 everyone who sins is a *s* to sin.
Ro 7: 14 I am unspiritual, sold as a *s* to sin.
1Co 7: 21 Were you a *s* when you were called
12: 13 whether Jews or Greeks, *s* or free
Gal 3: 28 *s* nor free, male nor female,
4: 7 So you are no longer a *s*, but a son;
4: 30 Get rid of the *s* woman and her son
Col 3: 11 barbarian, Scythian, *s* or free,
1Ti 1: 10 for *s* traders and liars and perjurers
Phm : 16 no longer as a *s*, but better than a *s*,
2Pe 2: 19 a man is a *s* to whatever has

SLAVERY (SLAVE)
Ex 2: 23 The Israelites groaned in their *s*
Ro 6: 19 parts of your body in *s* to impurity
Gal 4: 3 were in *s* under the basic principles
1Ti 6: 1 of *s* should consider their masters

SLAVES (SLAVE)
Ps 123: 2 As the eyes of *s* look to the hand
Ecc 10: 7 I have seen *s* on horseback,
Ro 6: 6 that we should no longer be *s* to sin
6: 16 you are *s* to sin, which leads
6: 22 and have become *s* to God,
Gal 2: 4 in Christ Jesus and to make us *s*.
4: 8 you were *s* to those who
Eph 6: 5 *S*, obey your earthly masters
Col 3: 22 *S*, obey your earthly masters
4: 1 provide your *s* with what is right
Tit 2: 9 Teach *s* to be subject

SLAY (SLAIN)
Job 13: 15 Though he *s* me, yet will I hope

SLEEP (ASLEEP SLEEPER SLEEPING SLEEPS)
Ge 2: 21 the man to fall into a deep *s*;
15: 12 Abram fell into a deep *s*,
28: 11 it under his head and lay down to *s*.
Ps 4: 8 I will lie down and *s* in peace,
121: 4 will neither slumber nor *s*.
127: 2 for he grants *s* to those he loves.
Pr 6: 9 When will you get up from your *s*?
Ecc 5: 12 The *s* of a laborer is sweet,
1Co 15: 51 We will not all *s*, but we will all be
1Th 5: 7 For those who *s*, *s* at night,

SLEEPER (SLEEP)
Eph 5: 14 "Wake up, O *s*,

SLEEPING (SLEEP)
Mk 13: 36 suddenly, do not let him find you *s*.

SLEEPLESS*
2Co 6: 5 in hard work, *s* nights and hunger;

SLEEPS (SLEEP)
Pr 10: 5 he who *s* during harvest is

SLIMY
Ps 40: 2 He lifted me out of the *s* pit,

SLING
1Sa 17: 50 over the Philistine with a *s*

SLIP (SLIPPING)
Dt 4: 9 let them *s* from your heart as long
Ps 121: 3 He will not let your foot *s*—

SLIPPING (SLIP)
Ps 66: 9 and kept our feet from *s*.

SLOW
Ex 34: 6 and gracious God, *s* to anger,
Jas 1: 19 *s* to speak and *s* to become angry,
2Pe 3: 9 The Lord is not *s* in keeping his

SLUGGARD
Pr 6: 6 Go to the ant, you *s*;
13: 4 The *s* craves and gets nothing,
20: 4 A *s* does not plow in season;
26: 15 The *s* buries his hand in the dish;

SLUMBER
Ps 121: 3 he who watches over you will not *s*;
Pr 6: 10 A little sleep, a little *s*,
Ro 13: 11 for you to wake up from your *s*,

SLUR
Ps 15: 3 and casts no *s* on his fellow man,

SMELL
Ecc 10: 1 As dead flies give perfume a bad *s*,
2Co 2: 16 To the one we are the *s* of death;

SMITTEN
Isa 53: 4 *s* by him, and afflicted.

SMOKE
Ex 19: 18 Mount Sinai was covered with *s*,
Ps 104: 32 touches the mountains, and they *s*.
Isa 6: 4 and the temple was filled with *s*.
Joel 2: 30 blood and fire and billows of *s*.
Ac 2: 19 blood and fire and billows of *s*.
Rev 15: 8 filled with *s* from the glory

SMYRNA
Rev 2: 8 the angel of the church in *S* write:

SNAKE (SNAKES)
Nu 21: 8 "Make a *s* and put it up on a pole;
Pr 23: 32 In the end it bites like a *s*
Jn 3: 14 Moses lifted up the *s* in the desert,

SNAKES (SNAKE)
Mt 10: 16 as shrewd as *s* and as innocent
Mk 16: 18 they will pick up *s* with their hands;

SNARE (ENSNARE ENSNARED SNARED)
Dt 7: 16 for that will be a *s* to you.
Ps 69: 22 before them become a *s*;
91: 3 from the fowler's *s*
Pr 29: 25 Fear of man will prove to be a *s*,
Ro 11: 9 "May their table become a *s*

SNARED (SNARE)
Pr 3: 26 will keep your foot from being *s*.

SNATCH
Jn 10: 28 no one can *s* them out of my hand.
Jude : 23 *s* others from the fire and save

SNOUT
Pr 11: 22 Like a gold ring in a pig's *s*

SNOW
Ps 51: 7 and I will be whiter than *s*.
Isa 1: 18 they shall be as white as *s*;

SNUFF (SNUFFED)
Isa 42: 3 a smoldering wick he will not *s* out.
Mt 12: 20 a smoldering wick he will not *s* out,

SNUFFED (SNUFF)
Pr 13: 9 but the lamp of the wicked is *s* out.

SOAP
Mal 3: 2 a refiner's fire or a launderer's *s*.

SOAR (SOARED)
Isa 40: 31 They will *s* on wings like eagles;

SOARED (SOAR)
2Sa 22: 11 he *s* on the wings of the wind.

SOBER
Ro 12: 3 think of yourself with *s* judgment,

SODOM
Ge 13: 12 and pitched his tents near *S*.
19: 24 rained down burning sulfur on *S*
Isa 1: 9 we would have become like *S*,
Lk 10: 12 on that day for *S* than for that town
Ro 9: 29 we would have become like *S*,
Rev 11: 8 which is figuratively called *S*

SOIL
Ge 4: 2 kept flocks, and Cain worked the *s*.
Mt 13: 23 on good *s* is the man who hears

SOLD (SELL)
1Ki 21: 25 who *s* himself to do evil in the eyes
Mt 10: 29 Are not two sparrows *s* for a penny
13: 44 then in his joy went and *s* all he had
Ro 7: 14 I am unspiritual, *s* as a slave to sin.

SOLDIER
1Co 9: 7 as a *s* at his own expense?
2Ti 2: 3 with us like a good *s* of Christ Jesus

SOLE
Dt 28: 65 place for the *s* of your foot.
Isa 1: 6 From the *s* of your foot to the top

SOLID
2Ti 2: 19 God's *s* foundation stands firm,
Heb 5: 12 You need milk, not *s* food!

SOLOMON
Son of David by Bathsheba; king of Judah (2Sa 12:24; 1Ch 3:5, 10). Appointed king by David (1Ki 1); adversaries Adonijah, Joab, Shimei killed by Benaiah (1Ki 2). Asked for wisdom (1Ki 3; 2Ch 1). Judged between two prostitutes (1Ki 3:16–28). Built temple (1Ki 5–7; 2Ch 2–5); prayer of dedication (1Ki 8; 2Ch 6). Visited by Queen of Sheba (1Ki 10; 2Ch 9). Wives turned his heart from God (1Ki 11:1–13). Jeroboam rebelled against (1Ki 11:26–40). Death (1Ki 11:41–43; 2Ch 9:29–31).
Proverbs of (1Ki 4:32; Pr 1:1; 10:1; 25:1); psalms of (Ps 72; 127); song of (SS 1:1).

SON (SONS SONSHIP)
Ge 17: 19 your wife Sarah will bear you a *s*,
21: 10 rid of that slave woman and her *s*,
22: 2 "Take your *s*, your only *s*, Isaac,
Ex 11: 5 Every firstborn *s* in Egypt will die,
Dt 1: 31 father carries his *s*, all the way you
6: 20 In the future, when your *s* asks you,
8: 5 as a man disciplines his *s*,
21: 18 rebellious *s* who does not obey his
2Sa 7: 14 be his father, and he will be my *s*.
1Ki 3: 20 and put her dead *s* by my breast.
Ps 2: 7 He said to me, "You are my *S*;
2: 12 Kiss the *S*, lest he be angry
8: 4 the *s* of man that you care for him?
Pr 3: 12 as a father the *s* he delights in.
6: 20 My *s*, keep your father's
10: 1 A wise *s* brings joy to his father,
13: 24 He who spares the rod hates his *s*,
29: 17 Discipline your *s*, and he will give
Isa 7: 14 with child and will give birth to a *s*,
Eze 18: 20 The *s* will not share the guilt
Da 3: 25 the fourth looks like a *s* of the gods
7: 13 before me was one like a *s* of man,
Hos 11: 1 and out of Egypt I called my *s*.
Am 7: 14 neither a prophet nor a prophet's *s*,
Mt 1: 1 of Jesus Christ the *s* of David,
1: 21 She will give birth to a *s*,
2: 15 "Out of Egypt I called my *s*."
3: 17 "This is my *S*, whom I love;
4: 3 "If you are the *S* of God, tell these
8: 20 but the *S* of Man has no place
11: 27 one knows the *S* except the Father,
12: 8 For the *S* of Man is Lord
12: 32 a word against the *S* of Man will be
12: 40 so the *S* of Man will be three days
13: 41 *S* of Man will send out his angels,
13: 55 "Isn't this the carpenter's *s*?
14: 33 "Truly you are the *S* of God."
16: 16 "You are the Christ, the *S*
16: 27 For the *S* of Man is going to come
17: 5 "This is my *S*, whom I love;
19: 28 when the *S* of Man sits
20: 18 and the *S* of Man will be betrayed
20: 28 as the *S* of Man did not come
21: 9 "Hosanna to the *S* of David!"
22: 42 Whose *s* is he?" "The *s* of David,"
24: 27 so will be the coming of the *S*
24: 30 They will see the *S* of Man coming
24: 44 the *S* of Man will come at an hour
25: 31 "When the *S* of Man comes
26: 63 if you are the Christ, the *S* of God."
27: 54 "Surely he was the *S* of God!"
28: 19 and of the *S* and of the Holy Spirit,
Mk 1: 11 "You are my *S*, whom I love;
2: 28 So the *S* of Man is Lord
8: 38 the *S* of Man will be ashamed
9: 7 "This is my *S*, whom I love.
10: 45 even the *S* of Man did not come
13: 32 nor the *S*, but only the Father.
14: 62 you will see the *S* of Man sitting
Lk 1: 32 and will be called the *S*
2: 7 she gave birth to her firstborn, a *s*.
3: 22 "You are my *S*, whom I love;
9: 35 This is my *S*, whom I have chosen;
9: 58 but the *S* of Man has no place
12: 8 the *S* of Man will also acknowledge
15: 20 he ran to his *s*, threw his arms
18: 8 when the *S* of Man comes,
18: 31 written by the prophets about the *S*
19: 10 For the *S* of Man came to seek
Jn 1: 34 I testify that this is the *S* of God."
3: 14 so the *S* of Man must be lifted up,
3: 16 that he gave his one and only *S*,
3: 36 believes in the *S* has eternal life,
5: 19 the *S* can do nothing by himself;
6: 40 is that everyone who looks to the *S*
11: 4 so that God's *S* may be glorified
17: 1 Glorify your *S*, that your *S* may
Ac 7: 56 and the *S* of Man standing
13: 33 " 'You are my *S*;
Ro 1: 4 with power to be the *S* of God
5: 10 to him through the death of his *S*,
8: 3 did by sending his own *S*
8: 29 conformed to the likeness of his *S*,
8: 32 He who did not spare his own *S*,
1Co 15: 28 then the *S* himself will be made
Gal 2: 20 I live by faith in the *S* of God,
4: 4 God sent his *S*, born of a woman,
4: 30 rid of the slave woman and her *s*,
1Th 1: 10 and to wait for his *S* from heaven,
Heb 1: 2 days he has spoken to us by his *S*,
1: 5 "You are my *S*;
2: 6 the *s* of man that you care for him?
4: 14 Jesus the *S* of God, let us hold
5: 5 "You are my *S*;
7: 28 appointed the *S*, who has been
10: 29 punished who has trampled the *S*
12: 6 everyone he accepts as a *s*."
2Pe 1: 17 saying, "This is my *S*, whom I love;
1Jn 1: 3 is with the Father and with his *S*,
1: 7 his *S*, purifies us from all sin.
2: 23 whoever acknowledges the *S* has
3: 8 reason the *S* of God appeared was
4: 9 only *S* into the world that we might
4: 14 that the Father has sent his *S*
5: 5 he who believes that Jesus is the *S*
5: 11 eternal life, and this life is in his *S*.
Rev 1: 13 lampstands was someone "like a *s*
14: 14 on the cloud was one "like a *s*

SONG (SING)
Ex 15: 2 LORD is my strength and my *s*;
Ps 40: 3 He put a new *s* in my mouth,
69: 30 I will praise God's name in *s*
96: 1 Sing to the LORD a new *s*;
98: 4 burst into jubilant *s* with music;
119: 54 Your decrees are the theme of my *s*
149: 1 Sing to the LORD a new *s*,
Isa 49: 13 burst into *s*, O mountains!
55: 12 will burst into *s* before you,
Rev 5: 9 And they sang a new *s*:
15: 3 and sang the *s* of Moses the servant

SONGS (SING)
2Sa 23: 1 Israel's singer of *s*:
Job 35: 10 who gives *s* in the night,
Ps 100: 2 come before him with joyful *s*.
126: 6 will return with *s* of joy,
137: 3 "Sing us one of the *s* of Zion!"
Eph 5: 19 with psalms, hymns and spiritual *s*.
Jas 5: 13 Is anyone happy? Let him sing *s*

SONS (SON)
Ge 6: 2 the *s* of God saw that the daughters
10: 20 These are the *s* of Ham
Ru 4: 15 who is better to you than seven *s*,
Ps 127: 3 *S* are a heritage from the LORD,
132: 12 if your *s* keep my covenant
Hos 1: 10 they will be called '*s*
Joel 2: 28 Your *s* and daughters will prophesy
Mt 5: 9 for they will be called *s* of God.
Lk 6: 35 and you will be *s* of the Most High,
Jn 12: 36 so that you may become *s* of light."
Ro 8: 14 by the Spirit of God are *s* of God.
9: 26 they will be called '*s*
2Co 6: 18 and you will be my *s* and daughters
Gal 3: 26 You are all *s* of God through faith
4: 5 we might receive the full rights of *s*.
4: 6 Because you are *s*, God sent
Heb 12: 7 discipline; God is treating you as *s*.

SONSHIP* (SON)
Ro 8: 15 but you received the Spirit of *s*.

SORCERY
Lev 19: 26 " 'Do not practice divination or *s*.

SORROW (SORROWS)
Ps 6: 7 My eyes grow weak with *s*;
116: 3 I was overcome by trouble and *s*.
Isa 60: 20 and your days of *s* will end.
Jer 31: 12 and they will *s* no more.
Ro 9: 2 I have great *s* and unceasing
2Co 7: 10 Godly *s* brings repentance that

SORROWS (SORROW)
Isa 53: 3 a man of *s*, and familiar

SOUGHT (SEEK)
2Ch 26: 5 As long as he *s* the LORD,
31: 21 he *s* his God and worked
Ps 34: 4 I *s* the LORD, and he answered me

119: 58 I have *s* your face with all my heart;

SOUL (SOULS)
Dt 6: 5 with all your *s* and with all your
10: 12 all your heart and with all your *s*,
30: 6 all your heart and with all your *s*,
Jos 22: 5 with all your heart and all your *s*."
2Ki 23: 25 and with all his *s* and with all his
Ps 23: 3 he restores my *s*.
34: 2 My *s* will boast in the LORD;
42: 1 so my *s* pants for you, O God.
42: 11 Why are you downcast, O my *s*?
62: 5 Find rest, O my *s*, in God alone;
63: 8 My *s* clings to you;
94: 19 consolation brought joy to my *s*.
103: 1 Praise the LORD, O my *s*;
Pr 13: 19 A longing fulfilled is sweet to the *s*,
16: 24 sweet to the *s* and healing
22: 5 he who guards his *s* stays far
Isa 55: 2 your *s* will delight in the richest
La 3: 20 and my *s* is downcast within me.
Eze 18: 4 For every living *s* belongs to me,
Mt 10: 28 kill the body but cannot kill the *s*.
16: 26 yet forfeits his *s*? Or what can
22: 37 with all your *s* and with all your
Heb 4: 12 even to dividing *s* and spirit,
3Jn : 2 even as your *s* is getting along well.

SOULS (SOUL)
Pr 11: 30 and he who wins *s* is wise.
Jer 6: 16 and you will find rest for your *s*.
Mt 11: 29 and you will find rest for your *s*.

SOUND (FINE-SOUNDING)
Ge 3: 8 and his wife heard the *s*
Pr 3: 21 preserve *s* judgment
Eze 3: 12 I heard behind me a loud rumbling *s*
Jn 3: 8 You hear its *s*, but you cannot tell
Ac 2: 2 Suddenly a *s* like the blowing
1Co 14: 8 if the trumpet does not *s* a clear call
15: 52 the trumpet will *s*, the dead will
1Ti 1: 10 to the *s* doctrine that conforms
2Ti 4: 3 men will not put up with *s* doctrine.
Tit 1: 9 can encourage others by *s* doctrine
2: 1 is in accord with *s* doctrine.

SOUR
Eze 18: 2 " 'The fathers eat *s* grapes,

SOURCE
Heb 5: 9 became the *s* of eternal salvation

SOVEREIGN (SOVEREIGNTY)
Ge 15: 2 But Abram said, "O *S* LORD,
2Sa 7: 18 O *S* LORD, and what is my family,
Ps 71: 16 your mighty acts, O *S* LORD;
Isa 25: 8 *S* LORD will wipe away the tears
40: 10 the *S* LORD comes with power,
50: 4 *S* LORD has given me
61: 1 The Spirit of the *S* LORD is on me,
61: 11 so the *S* LORD will make
Jer 32: 17 to the LORD: "Ah, *S* LORD,
Eze 12: 28 fulfilled, declares the *S* LORD.' "
Da 4: 25 that the Most High is *s*
2Pe 2: 1 denying the *s* Lord who bought
Jude : 4 and deny Jesus Christ our only *S*

SOVEREIGNTY (SOVEREIGN)
Da 7: 27 Then the *s*, power and greatness

SOW (SOWER SOWN SOWS)
Job 4: 8 and those who *s* trouble reap it.
Ps 126: 5 Those who *s* in tears
Hos 8: 7 "They *s* the wind
10: 12 *S* for yourselves righteousness,
Mt 6: 26 they do not *s* or reap or store away
13: 3 "A farmer went out to *s* his seed.
1Co 15: 36 What you *s* does not come to life
Jas 3: 18 Peacemakers who *s*
2Pe 2: 22 and, "A *s* that is washed goes back

SOWER (SOW)
Isa 55: 10 so that it yields seed for the *s*
Mt 13: 18 to what the parable of the *s* means:
Jn 4: 36 so that the *s* and the reaper may be
2Co 9: 10 Now he who supplies seed to the *s*

SOWN (SOW)
Mt 13: 8 sixty or thirty times what was *s*.
Mk 4: 15 along the path, where the word is *s*.
1Co 15: 42 The body that is *s* is perishable,

SOWS (SOW)
Pr 11: 18 he who *s* righteousness reaps a sure
22: 8 He who *s* wickedness reaps trouble
2Co 9: 6 Whoever *s* sparingly will
Gal 6: 7 A man reaps what he *s*.

SPARE (SPARES SPARING)
Est 7: 3 *s* my people—this is my request.
Ro 8: 32 He who did not *s* his own Son,
11: 21 natural branches, he will not *s* you
2Pe 2: 4 For if God did not *s* angels
2: 5 if he did not *s* the ancient world

SPARES (SPARE)
Pr 13: 24 He who *s* the rod hates his son,

SPARING (SPARE)
Pr 21: 26 but the righteous give without *s*.

SPARKLE
Zec 9: 16 They will *s* in his land

SPARROW (SPARROWS)
Ps 84: 3 Even the *s* has found a home,

SPARROWS (SPARROW)
Mt 10: 29 Are not two *s* sold for a penny?

SPEAR (SPEARS)
1Sa 19: 10 as Saul drove the *s* into the wall.
Ps 46: 9 breaks the bow and shatters the *s*,

SPEARS (SPEAR)
Isa 2: 4 and their *s* into pruning hooks.
Joel 3: 10 and your pruning hooks into *s*.
Mic 4: 3 and their *s* into pruning hooks.

SPECIAL
Jas 2: 3 If you show *s* attention

SPECK
Mt 7: 3 look at the *s* of sawdust

SPECTACLE
1Co 4: 9 We have been made a *s*
Col 2: 15 he made a public *s* of them,

SPEECH
Ps 19: 3 There is no *s* or language
Pr 22: 11 pure heart and whose *s* is gracious
2Co 8: 7 in faith, in *s*, in knowledge,
1Ti 4: 12 set an example for the believers in *s*

SPEND (SPENT)
Pr 31: 3 do not *s* your strength on women,
Isa 55: 2 Why *s* money on what is not bread,
2Co 12: 15 So I will very gladly *s*

SPENT (SPEND)
Mk 5: 26 many doctors and had *s* all she had,
Lk 6: 12 and *s* the night praying to God.
15: 14 After he had *s* everything,

SPIN
Mt 6: 28 They do not labor or *s*.

SPIRIT (SPIRIT'S SPIRITS SPIRITUAL SPIRITUALLY)
Ge 1: 2 and the *S* of God was hovering
6: 3 "My *S* will not contend
Ex 31: 3 I have filled him with the *S* of God,
Nu 11: 25 and put the *S* on the seventy elders.
Dt 34: 9 filled with the *s* of wisdom
Jdg 6: 34 Then the *S* of the LORD came
11: 29 Then the *S* of the LORD came
13: 25 and the *S* of the LORD began
1Sa 10: 10 the *S* of God came upon him
16: 13 day on the *S* of the LORD came
16: 14 the *S* of the LORD had departed
2Sa 23: 2 "The *S* of the LORD spoke
2Ki 2: 9 inherit a double portion of your *s*,"
Ne 9: 20 You gave your good *S*
9: 30 By your *S* you admonished them
Job 33: 4 The *S* of God has made me;
Ps 31: 5 Into your hands I commit my *s*;
34: 18 saves those who are crushed in *s*.
51: 10 and renew a steadfast *s* within me.
51: 11 or take your Holy *S* from me.
51: 17 sacrifices of God are a broken *s*;
106: 33 rebelled against the *S* of God,
139: 7 Where can I go from your *S*?
143: 10 may your good *S*
Isa 11: 2 The *S* of the LORD will rest
30: 1 an alliance, but not by my *S*,
32: 15 till the *S* is poured upon us
44: 3 I will pour out my *S*
57: 15 him who is contrite and lowly in *s*,
61: 1 The *S* of the Sovereign LORD is
63: 10 and grieved his Holy *S*.
Eze 11: 19 an undivided heart and put a new *s*
13: 3 prophets who follow their own *s*
36: 26 you a new heart and put a new *s*
Da 4: 8 and the *s* of the holy gods is in him
Joel 2: 28 I will pour out my *S* on all people.
Zec 4: 6 but by my *S*,' says the LORD
Mt 1: 18 to be with child through the Holy *S*
3: 11 will baptize you with the Holy *S*
3: 16 he saw the *S* of God descending
4: 1 led by the *S* into the desert
5: 3 saying: "Blessed are the poor in *s*,
10: 20 but the *S* of your Father speaking
12: 31 against the *S* will not be forgiven.
26: 41 *s* is willing, but the body is weak."
28: 19 and of the Son and of the Holy *S*,
Mk 1: 8 he will baptize you with the Holy *S*
Lk 1: 35 "The Holy *S* will come upon you,
1: 80 child grew and became strong in *s*;
3: 16 will baptize you with the Holy *S*
4: 18 "The *S* of the Lord is on me,
11: 13 Father in heaven give the Holy *S*
23: 46 into your hands I commit my *s*."
Jn 1: 33 who will baptize with the Holy *S*.'
3: 5 a man is born of water and the *S*,
4: 24 God is *s*, and his worshipers must
6: 63 The *S* gives life; the flesh counts
7: 39 Up to that time the *S* had not been
14: 26 But the Counselor, the Holy *S*,
16: 13 But when he, the *S* of truth, comes,
20: 22 and said, "Receive the Holy *S*.
Ac 1: 5 will be baptized with the Holy *S*."
1: 8 when the Holy *S* comes on you;
2: 4 of them were filled with the Holy *S*
2: 17 I will pour out my *S* on all people.
2: 38 will receive the gift of the Holy *S*.
4: 31 they were all filled with the Holy *S*
5: 3 that you have lied to the Holy *S*
6: 3 who are known to be full of the *S*
8: 15 that they might receive the Holy *S*,
9: 17 and be filled with the Holy *S*."
11: 16 will be baptized with the Holy *S*.'
13: 2 and fasting, the Holy *S* said,
19: 2 "Did you receive the Holy *S*
Ro 8: 4 nature but according to the *S*.
8: 5 set on what the *S* desires.
8: 9 And if anyone does not have the *S*
8: 13 but if by the *S* you put
8: 16 The *S* himself testifies
8: 23 who have the firstfruits of the *S*,
8: 26 the *S* helps us in our weakness.
1Co 2: 10 God has revealed it to us by his *S*.
2: 14 man without the *S* does not accept
5: 3 present, I am with you in *s*.
6: 19 body is a temple of the Holy *S*,
12: 13 baptized by one *S* into one body—
2Co 1: 22 and put his *S* in our hearts
3: 3 but with the *S* of the living God,
3: 6 the letter kills, but the *S* gives life.
3: 17 Now the Lord is the *S*,
5: 5 and has given us the *S* as a deposit,
7: 1 that contaminates body and *s*,
Gal 3: 2 Did you receive the *S*
5: 16 by the *S*, and you will not gratify
5: 22 But the fruit of the *S* is love, joy,
5: 25 let us keep in step with the *S*.
6: 8 from the *S* will reap eternal life.
Eph 1: 13 with a seal, the promised Holy *S*,

2: 22 in which God lives by his *S.*
4: 4 There is one body and one *S*—
4: 30 do not grieve the Holy *S* of God,
5: 18 Instead, be filled with the *S.*
6: 17 of salvation and the sword of the *S,*
Php 2: 2 being one in *s* and purpose.
1Th 5: 23 May your whole *s,* soul
2Th 2: 13 the sanctifying work of the *S*
1Ti 3: 16 was vindicated by the *S,*
2Ti 1: 7 For God did not give us a *s*
Heb 2: 4 of the Holy *S* distributed according
4: 12 even to dividing soul and *s,*
10: 29 and who has insulted the *S* of grace
1Pe 3: 4 beauty of a gentle and quiet *s,*
2Pe 1: 21 carried along by the Holy *S.*
1Jn 3: 24 We know it by the *S* he gave us.
4: 1 Dear friends, do not believe every *s*
4: 13 because he has given us of his *S.*
Jude : 20 holy faith and pray in the Holy *S.*
Rev 2: 7 let him hear what the *S* says

SPIRIT'S* (SPIRIT)
1Co 2: 4 a demonstration of the *S* power,
1Th 5: 19 not put out the *S* fire; do not treat

SPIRITS (SPIRIT)
1Co 12: 10 to another distinguishing between *s,*
14: 32 The *s* of prophets are subject
1Jn 4: 1 test the *s* to see whether they are

SPIRITUAL (SPIRIT)
Ro 12: 1 to God—this is your *s* act of worship.
12: 11 but keep your *s* fervor, serving
1Co 2: 13 expressing *s* truths in *s* words.
3: 1 I could not address you as *s* but
12: 1 Now about *s* gifts, brothers,
14: 1 of love and eagerly desire *s* gifts,
15: 44 a natural body, it is raised a *s* body.
Gal 6: 1 you who are *s* should restore him
Eph 1: 3 with every *s* blessing in Christ.
5: 19 with psalms, hymns and *s* songs.
6: 12 and against the *s* forces of evil
1Pe 2: 2 newborn babies, crave pure *s* milk,
2: 5 are being built into a *s* house

SPIRITUALLY (SPIRIT)
1Co 2: 14 because they are *s* discerned.

SPIT
Mt 27: 30 They *s* on him, and took the staff
Rev 3: 16 I am about to *s* you out

SPLENDOR
1Ch 16: 29 the LORD in the *s* of his holiness.
29: 11 the glory and the majesty and the *s,*
Job 37: 22 of the north he comes in golden *s;*
Ps 29: 2 in the *s* of his holiness.
45: 3 clothe yourself with *s* and majesty.
96: 6 *S* and majesty are before him;
96: 9 in the *s* of his holiness;
104: 1 you are clothed with *s* and majesty.
145: 5 of the glorious *s* of your majesty,
145: 12 and the glorious *s* of your kingdom.
148: 13 his *s* is above the earth
Pr 4: 9 and present you with a crown of *s.*"
16: 31 Gray hair is a crown of *s;*
20: 29 gray hair the *s* of the old.
Isa 55: 5 for he has endowed you with *s.*"
60: 21 for the display of my *s.*
61: 3 the LORD for the display of his *s.*
63: 1 Who is this, robed in *s,*
Hab 3: 4 His *s* was like the sunrise;
Mt 6: 29 in all his *s* was dressed like one
Lk 9: 31 appeared in glorious *s,* talking
2Th 2: 8 and destroy by the *s* of his coming.

SPOIL (SPOILS)
Ps 119:162 like one who finds great *s.*

SPOILS (SPOIL)
Isa 53: 12 he will divide the *s* with the strong,
Jn 6: 27 Do not work for food that *s,*

SPONTANEOUS*
Phm : 14 so that any favor you do will be *s*

SPOTLESS
2Pe 3: 14 make every effort to be found *s,*

SPOTS (SPOTTED)
Jer 13: 23 or the leopard its *s?*

SPOTTED (SPOTS)
Ge 30: 32 and every *s* or speckled goat.

SPREAD (SPREADING SPREADS)
Ps 78: 19 "Can God *s* a table in the desert?
Ac 6: 7 So the word of God *s.*
12: 24 of God continued to increase and *s.*
13: 49 of the Lord *s* through the whole
19: 20 the word of the Lord *s* widely
2Th 3: 1 message of the Lord may *s* rapidly

SPREADING (SPREAD)
Pr 29: 5 is *s* a net for his feet.
1Th 3: 2 God's fellow worker in *s* the gospel

SPREADS (SPREAD)
Pr 10: 18 and whoever *s* slander is a fool.

SPRING (SPRINGS WELLSPRING)
Jer 2: 13 the *s* of living water,
Jn 4: 14 in him a *s* of water welling up
Jas 3: 12 can a salt *s* produce fresh water.

SPRINGS (SPRING)
2Pe 2: 17 These men are *s* without water

SPRINKLE (SPRINKLED SPRINKLING)
Lev 16: 14 and with his finger *s* it on the front

SPRINKLED (SPRINKLE)
Heb 10: 22 having our hearts *s* to cleanse us

SPRINKLING (SPRINKLE)
1Pe 1: 2 to Jesus Christ and *s* by his blood:

SPROUT
Pr 23: 5 for they will surely *s* wings
Jer 33: 15 I will make a righteous Branch *s*

SPUR*
Heb 10: 24 how we may *s* one another

SPURNS*
Pr 15: 5 A fool *s* his father's discipline,

SPY
Gal 2: 4 ranks to *s* on the freedom we have

SQUANDERED (SQUANDERS)
Lk 15: 13 there *s* his wealth in wild living.

SQUANDERS* (SQUANDERED)
Pr 29: 3 of prostitutes *s* his wealth.

SQUARE
Rev 21: 16 The city was laid out like a *s,*

STABILITY*
Pr 29: 4 By justice a king gives a country *s,*

STAFF
Ge 49: 10 the ruler's *s* from between his feet,
Ex 7: 12 Aaron's *s* swallowed up their staffs.
Nu 17: 6 and Aaron's *s* was among them.
Ps 23: 4 your rod and your *s,*

STAIN (STAINED)
Eph 5: 27 without *s* or wrinkle or any other

STAINED (STAIN)
Isa 63: 1 with his garments *s* crimson?

STAKES
Isa 54: 2 strengthen your *s.*

STAND (STANDING STANDS STOOD)
Ex 14: 13 *S* firm and you will see
Jos 10: 12 "O sun, *s* still over Gibeon,
2Ch 20: 17 *s* firm and see the deliverance
Job 19: 25 in the end he will *s* upon the earth.
Ps 1: 1 or *s* in the way of sinners
1: 5 Therefore the wicked will not *s*
24: 3 Who may *s* in his holy place?
33: 11 of the LORD *s* firm forever,
40: 2 and gave me a firm place to *s.*
76: 7 Who can *s* before you
93: 5 Your statutes *s* firm;
119:120 I *s* in awe of your laws.
130: 3 O Lord, who could *s?*
Ecc 5: 7 Therefore *s* in awe of God.
Isa 7: 9 If you do not *s* firm in your faith,
29: 23 will *s* in awe of the God of Israel.
Eze 22: 30 *s* before me in the gap on behalf
Hab 3: 2 I *s* in awe of your deeds, O LORD.
Zec 14: 4 On that day his feet will *s*
Mal 3: 2 Who can *s* when he appears?
Mt 12: 25 divided against itself will not *s.*
Ro 14: 4 for the Lord is able to make him *s.*
14: 10 we will all *s* before God's judgment
1Co 10: 13 out so that you can *s* up under it.
15: 58 Therefore, my dear brothers, *s* firm
16: 13 Be on your guard; *s* firm in the faith
Gal 5: 1 *S* firm, then, and do not let
Eph 6: 14 *S* firm then, with the belt
2Th 2: 15 *s* firm and hold to the teachings we
Jas 5: 8 You too, be patient and *s* firm,
Rev 3: 20 Here I am! I *s* at the door

STANDING (STAND)
Ex 3: 5 where you are *s* is holy ground."
Jos 5: 15 the place where you are *s* is holy."
Ru 2: 1 a man of *s,* whose name was Boaz.
4: 11 May you have *s* in Ephrathah
Lk 21: 19 By *s* firm you will gain life.
1Ti 3: 13 have served well gain an excellent *s*
1Pe 5: 9 Resist him, *s* firm in the faith,

STANDS (STAND)
Ps 89: 2 that your love *s* firm forever,
119: 89 it *s* firm in the heavens.
Pr 12: 7 the house of the righteous *s* firm.
Isa 40: 8 but the word of our God *s* forever."
Mt 10: 22 but he who *s* firm to the end will be
2Ti 2: 19 God's solid foundation *s* firm,
1Pe 1: 25 but the word of the Lord *s* forever

STAR (STARS)
Nu 24: 17 A *s* will come out of Jacob;
Isa 14: 12 O morning *s,* son of the dawn!
Mt 2: 2 We saw his *s* in the east
2Pe 1: 19 the morning *s* rises in your hearts.
Rev 2: 28 I will also give him the morning *s.*
22: 16 and the bright Morning *S.*"

STARS (STAR)
Ge 1: 16 He also made the *s.*
Job 38: 7 while the morning *s* sang together
Da 12: 3 like the *s* for ever and ever.
Php 2: 15 in which you shine like *s*

STATURE
1Sa 2: 26 boy Samuel continued to grow in *s*
Lk 2: 52 And Jesus grew in wisdom and *s,*

STATUTES
Ps 19: 7 *s* of the LORD are trustworthy,
93: 5 Your *s* stand firm;
119: 2 Blessed are they who keep his *s*
119: 14 I rejoice in following your *s*
119: 24 Your *s* are my delight;
119: 36 Turn my heart toward your *s*
119: 99 for I meditate on your *s.*
119:111 Your *s* are my heritage forever;
119:125 that I may understand your *s.*
119:129 Your *s* are wonderful;
119:138 The *s* you have laid
119:152 Long ago I learned from your *s*
119:167 I obey your *s,*

STEADFAST*
Ps 51: 10 and renew a *s* spirit within me.
57: 7 My heart is *s,* O God,
57: 7 my heart is *s;*
108: 1 My heart is *s,* O God;
111: 8 They are *s* for ever and ever,
112: 7 his heart is *s,* trusting in the LORD
119: 5 Oh, that my ways were *s*
Isa 26: 3 him whose mind is *s,*
1Pe 5: 10 and make you strong, firm and *s.*

STEADY
Isa 35: 3 *s* the knees that give way;

STEAL (STOLEN)
Ex 20: 15 "You shall not *s.*
Lev 19: 11 " 'Do not *s.*

Dt 5: 19 "You shall not *s*.
Mt 19: 18 do not *s*, do not give false
Ro 13: 9 "Do not *s*,""Do not covet,"
Eph 4: 28 has been stealing must *s* no longer,

STEP (FOOTSTEPS STEPS)
Job 34: 21 he sees their every *s*.
Gal 5: 25 let us keep in *s* with the Spirit.

STEPHEN
Deacon (Ac 6:5). Arrested (Ac 6:8–15). Speech to Sanhedrin (Ac 7). Stoned (Ac 7:54–60; 22:20).

STEPS (STEP)
Ps 37: 23 he makes his *s* firm;
Pr 14: 15 prudent man gives thought to his *s*.
16: 9 but the LORD determines his *s*.
20: 24 A man's *s* are directed
Jer 10: 23 it is not for man to direct his *s*.
1Pe 2: 21 that you should follow in his *s*.

STERN (STERNNESS)
Pr 15: 10 *S* discipline awaits him who leaves

STERNNESS* (STERN)
Ro 11: 22 and *s* of God: *s* to those who fell,

STICKS
Pr 18: 24 there is a friend who *s* closer

STIFF-NECKED (NECK)
Ex 34: 9 Although this is a *s* people,
Pr 29: 1 A man who remains *s*

STILL
Jos 10: 13 So the sun stood *s*,
Ps 37: 7 Be *s* before the LORD
46: 10 "Be *s*, and know that I am God;
89: 9 its waves mount up, you *s* them.
Zec 2: 13 Be *s* before the LORD, all mankind
Mk 4: 39 said to the waves, "Quiet! Be *s*!"

STIMULATE*
2Pe 3: 1 as reminders to *s* you

STING
1Co 15: 55 Where, O death, is your *s*?"

STINGY
Pr 28: 22 A *s* man is eager to get rich

STIRRED (STIRS)
Ps 45: 1 My heart is *s* by a noble theme

STIRS (STIRRED)
Pr 6: 19 and a man who *s* up dissension
10: 12 Hatred *s* up dissension,
15: 1 but a harsh word *s* up anger.
15: 18 hot-tempered man *s* up dissension,
16: 28 A perverse man *s* up dissension,
28: 25 A greedy man *s* up dissension,
29: 22 An angry man *s* up dissension,

STOLEN (STEAL)
Lev 6: 4 he must return what he has *s*
SS 4: 9 You have *s* my heart, my sister,

STOMACH
1Co 6: 13 Food for the *s* and the *s* for food"—
Php 3: 19 their god is their *s*, and their glory

STONE (CAPSTONE CORNERSTONE MILLSTONE STONED STONES)
Ex 24: 4 set up twelve *s* pillars representing
28: 10 on one *s* and the remaining six
34: 1 "Chisel out two *s* tablets like
Dt 4: 13 then wrote them on two *s* tablets.
19: 14 your neighbor's boundary *s* set up
1Sa 17: 50 the Philistine with a sling and a *s*;
Ps 91: 12 will not strike your foot against a *s*.
118: 22 The *s* the builders rejected
Pr 22: 28 not move an ancient boundary *s*
Isa 8: 14 a *s* that causes men to stumble
28: 16 "See, I lay a *s* in Zion,
Eze 11: 19 remove from them their heart of *s*
36: 26 remove from you your heart of *s*
Mt 7: 9 will give him a *s*? Or if he asks
21: 42 " 'The *s* the builders rejected
24: 2 not one *s* here will be left
Mk 16: 3 "Who will roll the *s* away
Lk 4: 3 tell this *s* to become bread."
Jn 8: 7 the first to throw a *s* at her."
Ac 4: 11 " 'the *s* you builders rejected,
Ro 9: 32 stumbled over the "stumbling *s*."
2Co 3: 3 not on tablets of *s* but on tablets
1Pe 2: 6 "See, I lay a *s* in Zion,
Rev 2: 17 also give him a white *s*

STONED (STONE)
2Co 11: 25 once I was *s*, three times I was
Heb 11: 37 They were *s*; they were sawed

STONES (STONE)
Ex 28: 21 are to be twelve *s*, one for each
Jos 4: 3 to take up twelve *s* from the middle
1Sa 17: 40 chose five smooth *s*
Mt 3: 9 out of these *s* God can raise up
1Co 3: 12 silver, costly *s*, wood, hay or straw,
1Pe 2: 5 also, like living *s*, are being built

STOOD (STAND)
Jos 10: 13 So the sun *s* still,
Lk 22: 28 You are those who have *s* by me
2Ti 4: 17 But the Lord *s* at my side
Jas 1: 12 because when he has *s* the test,

STOOP (STOOPS)
2Sa 22: 36 you *s* down to make me great.

STOOPS (STOOP)
Ps 113: 6 who *s* down to look

STOP
Job 37: 14 *s* and consider God's wonders.
Isa 1: 13 *S* bringing meaningless offerings!
1: 16 *S* doing wrong,
2: 22 *S* trusting in man,
Jer 32: 40 I will never *s* doing good to them,
Mk 9: 39 "Do not *s* him," Jesus said.
Jn 6: 43 "*S* grumbling among yourselves,"
7: 24 *S* judging by mere appearances,
20: 27 *S* doubting and believe."
Ro 14: 13 Therefore let us *s* passing judgment
1Co 14: 20 Brothers, *s* thinking like children.

STORE (STORED)
Pr 2: 1 and *s* up my commands within you,
7: 1 and *s* up my commands within you.
10: 14 Wise men *s* up knowledge,
Isa 33: 6 a rich *s* of salvation and wisdom
Mt 6: 19 not *s* up for yourselves treasures
6: 26 or reap or *s* away in barns,
2Ti 4: 8 Now there is in *s* for me the crown

STORED (STORE)
Lk 6: 45 out of the good *s* up in his heart,
Col 1: 5 from the hope that is *s* up for you

STOREHOUSE (HOUSE)
Mal 3: 10 Bring the whole tithe into the *s*,

STORIES*
2Pe 1: 16 did not follow cleverly invented *s*
2: 3 you with *s* they have made up.

STORM
Job 38: 1 LORD answered Job out of the *s*.
Ps 107: 29 He stilled the *s* to a whisper;
Lk 8: 24 the *s* subsided, and all was calm.

STOUTHEARTED* (HEART)
Ps 138: 3 you made me bold and *s*.

STRAIGHT
Ps 27: 11 lead me in a *s* path
107: 7 He led them by a *s* way
Pr 2: 13 who leave the *s* paths
3: 6 and he will make your paths *s*.
4: 11 and lead you along *s* paths.
4: 25 Let your eyes look *s* ahead,
11: 5 of the blameless makes a *s* way
15: 21 of understanding keeps a *s* course.
Isa 40: 3 make *s* in the wilderness
Mt 3: 3 make *s* paths for him.' "
Jn 1: 23 'Make *s* the way for the Lord.' "
2Pe 2: 15 They have left the *s* way

STRAIN (STRAINING)
Mt 23: 24 You *s* out a gnat but swallow

STRAINING (STRAIN)
Php 3: 13 and *s* toward what is ahead,

STRANGE (STRANGER STRANGERS)
Isa 28: 11 with foreign lips and *s* tongues
1Co 14: 21 "Through men of *s* tongues
1Pe 4: 4 They think it *s* that you do not

STRANGER (STRANGE)
Ps 119: 19 I am a *s* on earth;
Mt 25: 35 I was a *s* and you invited me in,
Jn 10: 5 But they will never follow a *s*;

STRANGERS (STRANGE)
Heb 13: 2 Do not forget to entertain *s*,
1Pe 2: 11 as aliens and *s* in the world,

STRAW
Isa 11: 7 and the lion will eat *s* like the ox.
1Co 3: 12 silver, costly stones, wood, hay or *s*

STRAYED (STRAYS)
Ps 119:176 I have *s* like a lost sheep.
Jer 31: 19 After I *s*,

STRAYS (STRAYED)
Pr 21: 16 A man who *s* from the path
Eze 34: 16 for the lost and bring back the *s*.

STREAM (STREAMS)
Am 5: 24 righteousness like a never-failing *s*!

STREAMS (STREAM)
Ps 1: 3 He is like a tree planted by *s*
46: 4 is a river whose *s* make glad
Ecc 1: 7 All *s* flow into the sea,
Jn 7: 38 *s* of living water will flow

STREET
Mt 6: 5 on the *s* corners to be seen by men.
22: 9 Go to the *s* corners and invite
Rev 21: 21 The great *s* of the city was of pure gold,

STRENGTH (STRONG)
Ex 15: 2 The LORD is my *s* and my song;
Dt 4: 37 by his Presence and his great *s*,
6: 5 all your soul and with all your *s*.
Jdg 16: 15 told me the secret of your great *s*."
2Sa 22: 33 It is God who arms me with *s*
2Ki 23: 25 with all his soul and with all his *s*,
1Ch 16: 11 Look to the LORD and his *s*;
16: 28 ascribe to the LORD glory and *s*,
29: 12 In your hands are *s* and power
Ne 8: 10 for the joy of the LORD is your *s*."
Ps 18: 1 I love you, O LORD, my *s*.
21: 13 Be exalted, O LORD, in your *s*;
28: 7 The LORD is my *s* and my shield;
29: 11 The LORD gives *s* to his people;
33: 16 no warrior escapes by his great *s*.
46: 1 God is our refuge and *s*,
59: 17 O my *S*, I sing praise to you;
65: 6 having armed yourself with *s*,
73: 26 but God is the *s* of my heart
84: 5 Blessed are those whose *s* is in you,
96: 7 ascribe to the LORD glory and *s*.
105: 4 Look to the LORD and his *s*;
118: 14 The LORD is my *s* and my song;
147: 10 not in the *s* of the horse,
Pr 24: 5 a man of knowledge increases *s*;
30: 25 Ants are creatures of little *s*,
Isa 12: 2 the LORD, is my *s* and my song;
31: 1 and in the great *s* of their horsemen
40: 26 of his great power and mighty *s*,
40: 31 will renew their *s*.
63: 1 forward in the greatness of his *s*?
Jer 9: 23 or the strong man boast of his *s*
Mic 5: 4 flock in the *s* of the LORD,
Hab 3: 19 The Sovereign LORD is my *s*;
Mk 12: 30 all your mind and with all your *s*.'
1Co 1: 25 of God is stronger than man's *s*.
Eph 1: 19 is like the working of his mighty *s*,
Php 4: 13 through him who gives me *s*.
Heb 11: 34 whose weakness was turned to *s*;
1Pe 4: 11 it with the *s* God provides,

STRENGTHEN (STRONG)
2Ch 16: 9 to *s* those whose hearts are fully
Ps 119: 28 *s* me according to your word.
Isa 35: 3 *S* the feeble hands,

SUFFERS (SUFFER)
Pr 13: 20 but a companion of fools *s* harm.
1Co 12: 26 If one part *s*, every part *s* with it;

SUFFICIENT
2Co 12: 9 said to me, "My grace is *s* for you,

SUITABLE
Ge 2: 18 I will make a helper *s* for him."

SUMMED* (SUMS)
Ro 13: 9 there may be, are *s* up
Gal 5: 14 The entire law is *s* up

SUMMONS
Ps 50: 1 speaks and *s* the earth
Isa 45: 3 God of Israel, who *s* you by name.

SUMS* (SUMMED)
Mt 7: 12 for this *s* up the Law

SUN (SUNRISE)
Jos 10: 13 So the *s* stood still,
Jdg 5: 31 may they who love you be like the *s*
Ps 84: 11 For the LORD God is a *s*
121: 6 the *s* will not harm you by day,
136: 8 the *s* to govern the day,
Ecc 1: 9 there is nothing new under the *s*.
Isa 60: 19 The *s* will no more be your light
Mal 4: 2 the *s* of righteousness will rise
Mt 5: 45 He causes his *s* to rise on the evil
13: 43 the righteous will shine like the *s*
17: 2 His face shone like the *s*,
Lk 23: 45 for the *s* stopped shining.
Eph 4: 26 Do not let the *s* go
Rev 1: 16 His face was like the *s* shining
21: 23 The city does not need the *s*

SUNG (SING)
Mt 26: 30 When they had *s* a hymn, they

SUNRISE (SUN)
2Sa 23: 4 he is like the light of morning at *s*
Hab 3: 4 His splendor was like the *s*;

SUPERIOR
Heb 1: 4 he became as much *s* to the angels
8: 6 ministry Jesus has received is as *s*

SUPERVISION
Gal 3: 25 longer under the *s* of the law.

SUPPER
Lk 22: 20 after the *s* he took the cup, saying,
1Co 11: 25 after *s* he took the cup,
Rev 19: 9 to the wedding *s* of the Lamb!' "

SUPPLIED (SUPPLY)
Ac 20: 34 of mine have *s* my own needs
Php 4: 18 and even more; I am amply *s*,

SUPPLY (SUPPLIED SUPPLYING)
2Co 8: 14 your plenty will *s* what they need,
1Th 3: 10 and *s* what is lacking in your faith.

SUPPLYING* (SUPPLY)
2Co 9: 12 you perform is not only *s* the needs

SUPPORT (SUPPORTED SUPPORTING)
Ps 18: 18 but the LORD was my *s*.
Ro 11: 18 consider this: You do not *s* the root
1Co 9: 12 If others have this right of *s*

SUPPORTED (SUPPORT)
Ps 94: 18 your love, O LORD, *s* me.
Col 2: 19 *s* and held together by its ligaments

SUPPORTING (SUPPORT)
Eph 4: 16 held together by every *s* ligament,

SUPPRESS*
Ro 1: 18 wickedness of men who *s* the truth

SUPREMACY* (SUPREME)
Col 1: 18 in everything he might have the *s*.

SUPREME (SUPREMACY)
Pr 4: 7 Wisdom is *s*; therefore get wisdom.

SURE
Nu 28: 31 Be *s* the animals are without defect
32: 23 you may be *s* that your sin will find
Dt 6: 17 Be *s* to keep the commands
14: 22 Be *s* to set aside a tenth
29: 18 make *s* there is no root
Jos 23: 13 then you may be *s* that the LORD
1Sa 12: 24 But be *s* to fear the LORD
Ps 19: 9 The ordinances of the LORD are *s*
132: 11 a *s* oath that he will not revoke:
Pr 27: 23 Be *s* you know the condition
Isa 28: 16 cornerstone for a *s* foundation;
Eph 5: 5 of this you can be *s*: No immoral,
Heb 11: 1 faith is being *s* of what we hope for
2Pe 1: 10 to make your calling and election *s*.

SURFACE
2Co 10: 7 You are looking only on the *s*

SURPASS* (SURPASSED SURPASSES SURPASSING)
Pr 31: 29 but you *s* them all."

SURPASSED* (SURPASS)
Jn 1: 15 'He who comes after me has *s* me
1: 30 man who comes after me has *s* me

SURPASSES* (SURPASS)
Pr 8: 19 what I yield *s* choice silver.
Mt 5: 20 unless your righteousness *s* that
Eph 3: 19 to know this love that *s* knowledge

SURPASSING* (SURPASS)
Ps 150: 2 praise him for his *s* greatness.
2Co 3: 10 in comparison with the *s* glory.
9: 14 of the *s* grace God has given you.
Php 3: 8 the *s* greatness of knowing Christ

SURPRISE (SURPRISED)
1Th 5: 4 that this day should *s* you like

SURPRISED (SURPRISE)
1Pe 4: 12 do not be *s* at the painful trial you
1Jn 3: 13 Do not be *s*, my brothers,

SURRENDER
1Co 13: 3 and *s* my body to the flames,

SURROUND (SURROUNDED SURROUNDS)
Ps 5: 12 you *s* them with your favor
32: 7 and *s* me with songs of deliverance.
89: 7 awesome than all who *s* him.
125: 2 As the mountains *s* Jerusalem,
Jer 31: 22 a woman will *s* a man."

SURROUNDED (SURROUND)
Heb 12: 1 since we are *s* by such a great cloud

SURROUNDS* (SURROUND)
Ps 32: 10 *s* the man who trusts in him.
89: 8 and your faithfulness *s* you.
125: 2 so the LORD *s* his people

SUSA
Ezr 4: 9 and Babylon, the Elamites of *S*,
Ne 1: 1 while I was in the citadel of *S*,

SUSPENDS*
Job 26: 7 he *s* the earth over nothing.

SUSPICIONS*
1Ti 6: 4 evil *s* and constant friction

SUSTAIN (SUSTAINING SUSTAINS)
Ps 55: 22 and he will *s* you;
Isa 46: 4 I am he, I am he who will *s* you.

SUSTAINING* (SUSTAIN)
Heb 1: 3 *s* all things by his powerful word.

SUSTAINS (SUSTAIN)
Ps 18: 35 and your right hand *s* me;
146: 9 and *s* the fatherless and the widow,
147: 6 The LORD *s* the humble
Isa 50: 4 to know the word that *s* the weary.

SWALLOW (SWALLOWED)
Isa 25: 8 he will *s* up death forever.
Jnh 1: 17 provided a great fish to *s* Jonah,
Mt 23: 24 You strain out a gnat but *s* a camel.

SWALLOWED (SWALLOW)
1Co 15: 54 "Death has been *s* up in victory."
2Co 5: 4 so that what is mortal may be *s* up

SWAYED
Mt 11: 7 A reed *s* by the wind? If not,
22: 16 You aren't *s* by men, because you
2Ti 3: 6 are *s* by all kinds of evil desires,

SWEAR (SWORE SWORN)
Lev 19: 12 " 'Do not *s* falsely by my name
Ps 24: 4 or *s* by what is false.
Isa 45: 23 by me every tongue will *s*.
Mt 5: 34 Do not *s* at all: either by heaven,
Jas 5: 12 Above all, my brothers, do not *s*—

SWEAT*
Ge 3: 19 By the *s* of your brow
Lk 22: 44 his *s* was like drops of blood falling

SWEET (SWEETER SWEETNESS)
Job 20: 12 "Though evil is *s* in his mouth
Ps 119:103 How *s* are your words
Pr 9: 17 "Stolen water is *s*;
13: 19 A longing fulfilled is *s* to the soul,
16: 24 *s* to the soul and healing
20: 17 by fraud tastes *s* to a man,
24: 14 also that wisdom is *s* to your soul;
Ecc 5: 12 The sleep of a laborer is *s*,
Isa 5: 20 and *s* for bitter.
Eze 3: 3 it tasted as *s* as honey in my mouth.
Rev 10: 10 It tasted as *s* as honey in my mouth

SWEETER (SWEET)
Ps 19: 10 they are *s* than honey,
119:103 *s* than honey to my mouth!

SWEETNESS* (SWEET)
SS 4: 11 Your lips drop *s* as the honeycomb,
5: 16 His mouth is *s* itself;

SWEPT
Mt 12: 44 finds the house unoccupied, *s* clean

SWERVE*
Pr 4: 5 do not forget my words or *s*
4: 27 Do not *s* to the right or the left;

SWIFT
Pr 1: 16 they are *s* to shed blood.
Ecc 9: 11 The race is not to the *s*
Isa 59: 7 they are *s* to shed innocent blood.
Ro 3: 15 "Their feet are *s* to shed blood;
2Pe 2: 1 bringing *s* destruction

SWINDLER* (SWINDLERS)
1Co 5: 11 or a slanderer, a drunkard or a *s*.

SWINDLERS* (SWINDLER)
1Co 5: 10 or the greedy and *s*, or idolaters.
6: 10 *s* will inherit the kingdom of God.

SWORD (SWORDS)
Ge 3: 24 and a flaming *s* flashing back
Dt 32: 41 when I sharpen my flashing *s*
Jos 5: 13 of him with a drawn *s* in his hand.
1Sa 17: 45 "You come against me with *s*
17: 47 here will know that it is not by *s*
31: 4 so Saul took his own *s* and fell on it.
2Sa 12: 10 therefore, the *s* will never depart
Ps 44: 6 my *s* does not bring me victory;
45: 3 Gird your *s* upon your side,
Pr 12: 18 Reckless words pierce like a *s*,
Isa 2: 4 Nation will not take up *s*
Mic 4: 3 Nation will not take up *s*
Mt 10: 34 come to bring peace, but a *s*.
26: 52 all who draw the *s* will die by the *s*.
Lk 2: 35 a *s* will pierce your own soul too."
Ro 13: 4 for he does not bear the *s*
Eph 6: 17 of salvation and the *s* of the Spirit,
Heb 4: 12 Sharper than any double-edged *s*,
Rev 1: 16 came a sharp double-edged *s*.
19: 15 Out of his mouth comes a sharp *s*

SWORDS (SWORD)
Ps 64: 3 who sharpen their tongues like *s*
Isa 2: 4 They will beat their *s*
Joel 3: 10 Beat your plowshares into *s*

SWORE (SWEAR)
Heb 6: 13 for him to swear by, he *s* by himself

SWORN (SWEAR)
Ps 110: 4 The LORD has *s*
Eze 20: 42 the land I had *s* with uplifted hand
Heb 7: 21 "The Lord has *s*

SYCAMORE-FIG (FIG)
Am 7: 14 and I also took care of *s* trees.

Lk 19: 4 and climbed a *s* tree to see him,

SYMBOLIZES*

1Pe 3: 21 this water *s* baptism that now saves

SYMPATHETIC* (SYMPATHY)

1Pe 3: 8 in harmony with one another; be *s*,

SYMPATHIZED* (SYMPATHY)

Heb 10: 34 You *s* with those in prison

SYMPATHY (SYMPATHETIC SYMPATHIZED)

Ps 69: 20 I looked for *s*, but there was none,

SYNAGOGUE

Lk 4: 16 the Sabbath day he went into the *s*,
Ac 17: 2 custom was, Paul went into the *s*,

TABERNACLE (TABERNACLES)

Ex 40: 34 the glory of the LORD filled the *t*.
Heb 8: 2 the true *t* set up by the Lord,
9: 11 and more perfect *t* that is not
9: 21 sprinkled with the blood both the *t*
Rev 15: 5 that is, the *t* of the Testimony,

TABERNACLES (TABERNACLE)

Lev 23: 34 the LORD's Feast of *T* begins,
Dt 16: 16 Feast of Weeks and the Feast of *T*.
Zec 14: 16 and to celebrate the Feast of *T*.

TABLE (TABLES)

Ex 25: 23 "Make a *t* of acacia wood—
Ps 23: 5 You prepare a *t* before me

TABLES (TABLE)

Jn 2: 15 changers and overturned their *t*.
Ac 6: 2 word of God in order to wait on *t*.

TABLET (TABLETS)

Pr 3: 3 write them on the *t* of your heart.
7: 3 write them on the *t* of your heart.

TABLETS (TABLET)

Ex 31: 18 he gave him the two *t*
Dt 10: 5 and put the *t* in the ark I had made,
2Co 3: 3 not on *t* of stone but on *t*

TAKE (TAKEN TAKES TAKING TOOK)

Ge 15: 7 land to *t* possession of it."
22: 17 Your descendants will *t* possession
Ex 3: 5 "*T* off your sandals,
21: 23 you are to *t* life for life, eye for eye,
22: 22 "Do not *t* advantage of a widow
Lev 10: 17 given to you to *t* away the guilt
25: 14 do not *t* advantage of each other.
Nu 13: 30 and *t* possession of the land,
Dt 1: 8 and *t* possession of the land that
12: 32 do not add to it or *t* away from it.
31: 26 "*T* this Book of the Law
1Sa 8: 11 He will *t* your sons and make them
1Ch 17: 13 I will never *t* my love away
Job 23: 10 But he knows the way that I *t*;
Ps 2: 12 Blessed are all who *t* refuge in him.
25: 18 and *t* away all my sins.
27: 14 be strong and *t* heart
31: 24 Be strong and *t* heart,
49: 17 for he will *t* nothing with him
51: 11 or *t* your Holy Spirit from me.
73: 24 afterward you will *t* me into glory.
118: 8 It is better to *t* refuge in the LORD
Pr 22: 23 for the LORD will *t* up their case
Isa 62: 4 for the LORD will *t* delight in you,
Eze 3: 10 and *t* to heart all the words I speak
33: 11 I *t* no pleasure in the death
Mt 10: 38 anyone who does not *t* his cross
11: 29 *T* my yoke upon you and learn
16: 24 deny himself and *t* up his cross
26: 26 saying, "*T* and eat; this is my body
Mk 14: 36 *T* this cup from me.
1Ti 6: 12 *T* hold of the eternal life

TAKEN (TAKE)

Ge 2: 23 for she was *t* out of man."
Lev 6: 4 must return what he has stolen or *t*
Nu 8: 16 I have *t* them as my own in place
19: 3 it is to be *t* outside the camp
Ecc 3: 14 added to it and nothing *t* from it.
Isa 6: 7 your guilt is *t* away and your sin
Zec 3: 4 "See, I have *t* away your sin,
Mt 13: 12 even what he has will be *t* from him
24: 40 one will be *t* and the other left.
26: 39 may this cup be *t* from me.
Mk 16: 19 he was *t* up into heaven
Ac 1: 9 he was *t* up before their very eyes,
Ro 5: 13 But sin is not *t* into account
1Ti 3: 16 was *t* up in glory.

TAKES (TAKE)

1Ki 20: 11 should not boast like one who *t* it
Ps 5: 4 You are not a God who *t* pleasure
34: 8 blessed is the man who *t* refuge
Lk 6: 30 and if anyone *t* what belongs to you
Jn 1: 29 who *t* away the sin of the world!
10: 18 No one *t* it from me, but I lay it
Rev 22: 19 And if anyone *t* words away

TAKING (TAKE)

Ac 15: 14 by *t* from the Gentiles a people
Php 2: 7 *t* the very nature of a servant,

TALENT

Mt 25: 15 to another one *t*, each according

TALES*

1Ti 4: 7 with godless myths and old wives' *t*

TALL

1Sa 17: 4 He was over nine feet *t*.
1Ch 11: 23 who was seven and a half feet *t*.

TAMAR

1. Wife of Judah's sons Er and Onan (Ge 38:1–10). Tricked Judah into fathering children when he refused her his third son (Ge 38:11–30).

2. Daughter of David, raped by Amnon (2Sa 13).

TAMBOURINE

Ps 150: 4 praise him with *t* and dancing,

TAME* (TAMED)

Jas 3: 8 but no man can *t* the tongue.

TAMED* (TAME)

Jas 3: 7 the sea are being *t* and have been *t*

TARSHISH

Jnh 1: 3 from the LORD and headed for *T*.

TARSUS

Ac 9: 11 ask for a man from *T* named Saul,

TASK (TASKS)

1Ch 29: 1 The *t* is great, because this palatial
Mk 13: 34 each with his assigned *t*,
Ac 20: 24 complete the *t* the Lord Jesus has
1Co 3: 5 the Lord has assigned to each his *t*.
2Co 2: 16 And who is equal to such a *t*?
1Ti 3: 1 an overseer, he desires a noble *t*.

TASKS (TASK)

Pr 31: 17 her arms are strong for her *t*.

TASTE (TASTED TASTY)

Ps 34: 8 *T* and see that the LORD is good;
119:103 sweet are your words to my *t*,
Pr 24: 13 from the comb is sweet to your *t*.
SS 2: 3 and his fruit is sweet to my *t*.
Col 2: 21 Do not *t*! Do not touch!"?
Heb 2: 9 the grace of God he might *t* death

TASTED (TASTE)

Eze 3: 3 it *t* as sweet as honey in my mouth.
1Pe 2: 3 now that you have *t* that the Lord
Rev 10: 10 It *t* as sweet as honey in my mouth,

TASTY (TASTE)

Ge 27: 4 Prepare me the kind of *t* food I like

TATTOO*

Lev 19: 28 or put *t* marks on yourselves.

TAUGHT (TEACH)

1Ki 4: 33 He also *t* about animals and birds,
2Ki 17: 28 *t* them how to worship the LORD.
2Ch 17: 9 They *t* throughout Judah,
Ps 119:102 for you yourself have *t* me.
Pr 4: 4 he *t* me and said,
31: 1 an oracle his mother *t* him:
Isa 29: 13 is made up only of rules *t* by men.
50: 4 ear to listen like one being *t*.
Mt 7: 29 he *t* as one who had authority,
15: 9 their teachings are but rules *t*
Lk 4: 15 He *t* in their synagogues,
Ac 20: 20 have *t* you publicly and from house
1Co 2: 13 but in words *t* by the Spirit,
Gal 1: 12 nor was I *t* it; rather, I received it
1Ti 1: 20 to Satan to be *t* not to blaspheme.
1Jn 2: 27 just as it has *t* you, remain in him.

TAX (TAXES)

Mt 11: 19 a friend of *t* collectors and "sinners
17: 24 of the two-drachma *t* came to Peter

TAXES (TAX)

Mt 22: 17 Is it right to pay *t* to Caesar or not
Ro 13: 7 If you owe *t*, pay *t*; if revenue,

TEACH (TAUGHT TEACHER TEACHERS TEACHES TEACHING TEACHINGS)

Ex 4: 12 and will *t* you what to say."
18: 20 *T* them the decrees and laws,
33: 13 *t* me your ways so I may know you
Lev 10: 11 and you must *t* the Israelites all
Dt 4: 9 *T* them to your children
6: 1 me to *t* you to observe
8: 3 to *t* you that man does not live
11: 19 *T* them to your children, talking
1Sa 12: 23 I will *t* you the way that is good
1Ki 8: 36 *T* them the right way to live,
Job 12: 7 ask the animals, and they will *t* you
Ps 32: 8 *t* you in the way you should go;
34: 11 I will *t* you the fear of the LORD.
51: 13 I will *t* transgressors your ways,
78: 5 forefathers to *t* their children,
90: 12 *T* us to number our days aright,
119: 33 *T* me, O LORD, to follow your
143: 10 *T* me to do your will,
Pr 9: 9 *t* a righteous man and he will add
Jer 31: 34 No longer will a man *t* his neighbor
Mic 4: 2 He will *t* us his ways,
Lk 11: 1 said to him, "Lord, *t* us to pray,
12: 12 for the Holy Spirit will *t* you
Jn 14: 26 will *t* you all things and will remind
Ro 2: 21 who *t* others, do you not *t* yourself?
15: 4 in the past was written to *t* us,
1Ti 2: 12 I do not permit a woman to *t*
3: 2 respectable, hospitable, able to *t*,
2Ti 2: 2 also be qualified to *t* others.
2: 24 kind to everyone, able to *t*,
Tit 2: 1 You must *t* what is in accord
2: 15 then, are the things you should *t*.
Heb 8: 11 No longer will a man *t* his neighbor
Jas 3: 1 know that we who *t* will be judged
1Jn 2: 27 you do not need anyone to *t* you.

TEACHER (TEACH)

Ecc 1: 1 The words of the *T*, son of David,
Mt 10: 24 "A student is not above his *t*,
13: 52 "Therefore every *t*
23: 10 Nor are you to be called '*t*,'
Lk 6: 40 A student is not above his *t*,
Jn 3: 2 we know you are a *t* who has come
13: 14 and *T*, have washed your feet,

TEACHERS (TEACH)

Ps 119: 99 I have more insight than all my *t*,
Pr 5: 13 I would not obey my *t*
Lk 20: 46 "Beware of the *t* of the law.
1Co 12: 28 third *t*, then workers of miracles,
Eph 4: 11 and some to be pastors and *t*,
2Ti 4: 3 around them a great number of *t*
Heb 5: 12 by this time you ought to be *t*,
Jas 3: 1 of you should presume to be *t*,
2Pe 2: 1 as there will be false *t* among you.

TEACHES (TEACH)

Ps 25: 9 and *t* them his way.
94: 10 Does he who *t* man lack
Pr 15: 33 of the LORD *t* a man wisdom,
Isa 48: 17 who *t* you what is best for you,
Mt 5: 19 *t* these commands will be called
1Ti 6: 3 If anyone *t* false doctrines
Tit 2: 12 It *t* us to say "No" to ungodliness
1Jn 2: 27 his anointing *t* you about all things

TEACHING (TEACH)
Ezr 7: 10 to *t* its decrees and laws in Israel.
Pr 1: 8 and do not forsake your mother's *t.*
3: 1 My son, do not forget my *t,*
6: 23 this *t* is a light,
Mt 28: 20 *t* them to obey everything I have
Jn 7: 17 whether my *t* comes from God or
8: 31 to my *t,* you are really my disciples.
14: 23 loves me, he will obey my *t.*
Ac 2: 42 themselves to the apostles' *t*
Ro 12: 7 let him serve; if it is *t,* let him teach;
Eph 4: 14 and there by every wind of *t*
2Th 3: 6 to the *t* you received from us.
1Ti 4: 13 of Scripture, to preaching and to *t.*
5: 17 whose work is preaching and *t.*
6: 3 Lord Jesus Christ and to godly *t,*
2Ti 3: 16 is God-breathed and is useful for *t,*
Tit 1: 11 by *t* things they ought not
2: 7 In your *t* show integrity,
Heb 5: 13 with the *t* about righteousness.
2Jn : 9 and does not continue in the *t*

TEACHINGS (TEACH)
Pr 7: 2 guard my *t* as the apple of your eye.
2Th 2: 15 hold to the *t* we passed on to you,
Heb 6: 1 leave the elementary *t* about Christ

TEAR (TEARS)
Rev 7: 17 God will wipe away every *t*
21: 4 He will wipe every *t*

TEARS (TEAR)
Ps 126: 5 Those who sow in *t*
Isa 25: 8 LORD will wipe away the *t*
Jer 31: 16 and your eyes from *t,*
50: 4 in *t* to seek the LORD their God.
Lk 7: 38 she began to wet his feet with her *t.*
2Co 2: 4 anguish of heart and with many *t,*
Php 3: 18 and now say again even with *t,*

TEETH (TOOTH)
Job 19: 20 with only the skin of my *t.*
Ps 35: 16 they gnashed their *t* at me.
Jer 31: 29 and the children's *t* are set on edge
Mt 8: 12 will be weeping and gnashing of *t.*"

TEMPER (EVEN-TEMPERED HOT-TEMPERED ILL-TEMPERED QUICK-TEMPERED)
Pr 16: 32 a man who controls his *t*

TEMPERANCE see SELF-CONTROL

TEMPERATE*
1Ti 3: 2 *t,* self-controlled, respectable,
3: 11 not malicious talkers but *t*
Tit 2: 2 Teach the older men to be *t,*

TEMPEST
Ps 50: 3 and around him a *t* rages.
55: 8 far from the *t* and storm."

TEMPLE (TEMPLES)
1Ki 6: 1 began to build the *t* of the LORD.
6: 38 the *t* was finished in all its details
8: 10 the cloud filled the *t* of the LORD.
8: 27 How much less this *t* I have built!
2Ch 36: 19 They set fire to God's *t*
36: 23 me to build a *t* for him at Jerusalem
Ezr 6: 14 finished building the *t* according
Ps 27: 4 and to seek him in his *t.*
Isa 6: 1 and the train of his robe filled the *t.*
Eze 10: 4 cloud filled the *t,* and the court was
43: 4 glory of the LORD entered the *t*
Hab 2: 20 But the LORD is in his holy *t;*
Mt 12: 6 that one greater than the *t* is here.
26: 61 'I am able to destroy the *t* of God
27: 51 of the *t* was torn in two from top
Lk 21: 5 about how the *t* was adorned
Jn 2: 14 In the *t* courts he found men selling
1Co 3: 16 that you yourselves are God's *t*
6: 19 you not know that your body is a *t*
2Co 6: 16 For we are the *t* of the living God.
Rev 21: 22 I did not see a *t* in the city,

TEMPLES (TEMPLE)
Ac 17: 24 does not live in *t* built by hands.

TEMPORARY
2Co 4: 18 what is seen is *t,* but what is unseen

TEMPT* (TEMPTATION TEMPTED TEMPTER TEMPTING)
1Co 7: 5 again so that Satan will not *t* you
Jas 1: 13 does he *t* anyone; but each one is

TEMPTATION* (TEMPT)
Mt 6: 13 And lead us not into *t,*
26: 41 pray so that you will not fall into *t.*
Mk 14: 38 pray so that you will not fall into *t.*
Lk 11: 4 And lead us not into *t.*' "
22: 40 "Pray that you will not fall into *t.*"
22: 46 pray so that you will not fall into *t*
1Co 10: 13 No *t* has seized you except what is
1Ti 6: 9 want to get rich fall into *t*

TEMPTED* (TEMPT)
Mt 4: 1 into the desert to be *t* by the devil.
Mk 1: 13 was in the desert forty days, being *t*
Lk 4: 2 for forty days he was *t* by the devil.
1Co 10: 13 But when you are *t,* he will
10: 13 he will not let you be *t*
Gal 6: 1 yourself, or you also may be *t.*
1Th 3: 5 way the tempter might have *t* you
Heb 2: 18 able to help those who are being *t.*
2: 18 he himself suffered when he was *t,*
4: 15 but we have one who has been *t*
Jas 1: 13 For God cannot be *t* by evil,
1: 13 When *t,* no one should say,
1: 14 each one is *t* when, by his own evil

TEMPTER* (TEMPT)
Mt 4: 3 The *t* came to him and said,
1Th 3: 5 some way the *t* might have

TEMPTING* (TEMPT)
Lk 4: 13 the devil had finished all this *t,*
Jas 1: 13 no one should say, "God is *t* me."

TEN (TENTH TITHE TITHES)
Ex 34: 28 covenant—the *T* Commandments.
Lev 26: 8 of you will chase *t* thousand,
Dt 4: 13 covenant, the *T* Commandments,
10: 4 The *T* Commandments he had
Ps 91: 7 *t* thousand at your right hand,
Da 7: 24 *t* horns are *t* kings who will come
Mt 25: 1 will be like *t* virgins who took
25: 28 it to the one who has the *t* talents.
Lk 15: 8 suppose a woman has *t* silver coins
Rev 12: 3 and *t* horns and seven crowns

TENANTS
Mt 21: 34 servants to the *t* to collect his fruit.

TEND
Jer 23: 2 to the shepherds who *t* my people:
Eze 34: 14 I will *t* them in a good pasture,

TENDERNESS*
Isa 63: 15 Your *t* and compassion are
Php 2: 1 fellowship with the Spirit, if any *t*

TENT (TENTMAKER TENTS)
Ex 27: 21 In the *T* of Meeting,
40: 2 "Set up the tabernacle, the *T*
Isa 54: 2 "Enlarge the place of your *t,*
2Co 5: 1 that if the earthly *t* we live
2Pe 1: 13 as long as I live in the *t* of this body,

TENTH (TEN)
Ge 14: 20 Abram gave him a *t* of everything.
Nu 18: 26 you must present a *t* of that tithe
Dt 14: 22 Be sure to set aside a *t*
1Sa 8: 15 He will take a *t* of your grain
Lk 11: 42 you give God a *t* of your mint,
18: 12 I fast twice a week and give a *t*
Heb 7: 4 patriarch Abraham gave him a *t*

TENTMAKER* (TENT)
Ac 18: 3 and because he was a *t* as they were

TENTS (TENT)
Ge 13: 12 and pitched his *t* near Sodom.
Ps 84: 10 than dwell in the *t* of the wicked.

TERAH
Ge 11: 31 *T* took his son Abram, his

TERRIBLE (TERROR)
2Ti 3: 1 There will be *t* times

TERRIFIED (TERROR)
Dt 7: 21 Do not be *t* by them,
20: 3 do not be *t* or give way to panic
Ps 90: 7 and *t* by your indignation.
Mt 14: 26 walking on the lake, they were *t.*
17: 6 they fell facedown to the ground, *t.*
27: 54 they were *t,* and exclaimed,
Mk 4: 41 They were *t* and asked each other,

TERRIFYING (TERROR)
Heb 12: 21 The sight was so *t* that Moses said,

TERRITORY
2Co 10: 16 done in another man's *t.*

TERROR (TERRIBLE TERRIFIED TERRIFYING)
Dt 2: 25 very day I will begin to put the *t*
28: 67 of the *t* that will fill your hearts
Job 9: 34 so that his *t* would frighten me no
Ps 91: 5 You will not fear the *t* of night,
Pr 21: 15 but *t* to evildoers.
Isa 13: 8 *T* will seize them,
24: 17 *T* and pit and snare await you,
51: 13 live in constant *t* every day
54: 14 *T* will be far removed;
Lk 21: 26 Men will faint from *t,* apprehensive
Ro 13: 3 For rulers hold no *t*

TEST (TESTED TESTING TESTS)
Dt 6: 16 Do not *t* the LORD your God
Jdg 3: 1 to *t* all those Israelites who had not
1Ki 10: 1 came to *t* him with hard questions.
1Ch 29: 17 that you *t* the heart and are pleased
Ps 26: 2 *T* me, O LORD, and try me,
78: 18 They willfully put God to the *t*
106: 14 wasteland they put God to the *t.*
139: 23 *t* me and know my anxious
Jer 11: 20 and *t* the heart and mind,
Lk 4: 12 put the Lord your God to the *t.*' "
Ac 5: 9 How could you agree to *t* the Spirit
Ro 12: 2 Then you will be able to *t*
1Co 3: 13 and the fire will *t* the quality
10: 9 We should not *t* the Lord,
2Co 13: 5 unless, of course, you fail the *t?*
1Th 5: 21 *T* everything.
Jas 1: 12 because when he has stood the *t,*
1Jn 4: 1 *t* the spirits to see whether they are

TESTED (TEST)
Ge 22: 1 Some time later God *t* Abraham.
Job 23: 10 when he has *t* me, I will come forth
34: 36 that Job might be *t* to the utmost
Ps 66: 10 For you, O God, *t* us;
Pr 27: 21 man is *t* by the praise he receives.
Isa 28: 16 a *t* stone,
48: 10 I have *t* you in the furnace
1Ti 3: 10 They must first be *t;* and then
Heb 11: 17 By faith Abraham, when God *t* him

TESTIFIES (TESTIFY)
Jn 5: 32 There is another who *t* in my favor,
Ro 8: 16 The Spirit himself *t*

TESTIFY (TESTIFIES TESTIMONY)
Pr 24: 28 Do not *t* against your neighbor
Jn 1: 7 a witness to *t* concerning that light,
1: 34 and I *t* that this is the Son of God."
5: 39 are the Scriptures that *t* about me,
7: 7 because I *t* that what it does is evil.
15: 26 he will *t* about me. And you
Ac 4: 33 continued to *t* to the resurrection
10: 43 All the prophets *t* about him that
2Ti 1: 8 ashamed to *t* about our Lord,
1Jn 4: 14 *t* that the Father has sent his Son
5: 7 For there are three that *t:* the Spirit

TESTIMONY (TESTIFY)
Ex 20: 16 "You shall not give false *t*
31: 18 gave him the two tablets of the *T,*
Nu 35: 30 only on the *t* of witnesses.
Dt 19: 18 giving false *t* against his brother,
Pr 12: 17 A truthful witness gives honest *t,*
Isa 8: 20 and to the *t!* If they do not speak

Mt 15: 19 sexual immorality, theft, false *t*,
24: 14 preached in the whole world as a *t*
Lk 18: 20 not give false *t*, honor your father
Jn 2: 25 He did not need man's *t* about man
21: 24 We know that his *t* is true.
1Jn 5: 9 but God's *t* is greater because it is
Rev 12: 11 and by the word of their *t*;

TESTING (TEST)
Lk 8: 13 but in the time of *t* they fall away.
Heb 3: 8 during the time of *t* in the desert,
Jas 1: 3 because you know that the *t*

TESTS (TEST)
Pr 17: 3 but the LORD *t* the heart.
1Th 2: 4 but God, who *t* our hearts.

THADDAEUS
Apostle (Mt 10:3; Mk 3:18); probably also known as Judas son of James (Lk 6:16; Ac 1:13).

THANK (THANKFUL THANKFULNESS THANKS THANKSGIVING)
Php 1: 3 I *t* my God every time I remember
1Th 3: 9 How can we *t* God enough for you

THANKFUL (THANK)
Col 3: 15 And be *t*.
Heb 12: 28 let us be *t*, and so worship God

THANKFULNESS (THANK)
1Co 10: 30 If I take part in the meal with *t*,
Col 2: 7 taught, and overflowing with *t*.

THANKS (THANK)
1Ch 16: 8 Give *t* to the LORD, call
Ne 12: 31 assigned two large choirs to give *t*.
Ps 7: 17 I will give *t* to the LORD
28: 7 and I will give *t* to him in song.
30: 12 my God, I will give you *t* forever.
35: 18 I will give you *t* in the great
75: 1 we give *t*, for your Name is near;
100: 4 give *t* to him and praise his name.
107: 1 Give *t* to the LORD, for he is good;
118: 28 are my God, and I will give you *t*;
136: 1 Give *t* to the LORD, for he is good.
Ro 1: 21 as God nor gave *t* to him,
1Co 11: 24 when he had given *t*, he broke it
15: 57 *t* be to God! He gives us the victory
2Co 2: 14 *t* be to God, who always leads us
9: 15 *T* be to God for his indescribable
1Th 5: 18 give *t* in all circumstances,
Rev 4: 9 and *t* to him who sits on the throne

THANKSGIVING (THANK)
Ps 95: 2 Let us come before him with *t*
100: 4 Enter his gates with *t*
1Co 10: 16 cup of *t* for which we give thanks
Php 4: 6 by prayer and petition, with *t*,
1Ti 4: 3 created to be received with *t*

THEFT (THIEF)
Mt 15: 19 sexual immorality, *t*, false

THEFTS* (THIEF)
Rev 9: 21 their sexual immorality or their *t*.

THEME*
Ps 45: 1 My heart is stirred by a noble *t*
119: 54 Your decrees are the *t* of my song

THIEF (THEFT THEFTS THIEVES)
Ex 22: 3 A *t* must certainly make restitution
Pr 6: 30 Men do not despise a *t* if he steals
Lk 12: 39 at what hour the *t* was coming,
1Th 5: 2 day of the Lord will come like a *t*
1Pe 4: 15 or *t* or any other kind of criminal,
Rev 16: 15 I come like a *t*! Blessed is he who

THIEVES (THIEF)
Mt 6: 19 and where *t* break in and steal.
Jn 10: 8 who ever came before me were *t*
1Co 6: 10 nor homosexual offenders nor *t*

THINK (THINKING THOUGHT THOUGHTS)
Ps 63: 6 I *t* of you through the watches
Isa 44: 19 No one stops to *t*,
Mt 22: 42 "What do you *t* about the Christ?
Ro 12: 3 Do not *t* of yourself more highly
Php 4: 8 praiseworthy—*t* about such things

THINKING (THINK)
Pr 23: 7 who is always *t* about the cost.
1Co 14: 20 Brothers, stop *t* like children.
2Pe 3: 1 to stimulate you to wholesome *t*.

THIRST (THIRSTS THIRSTY)
Ps 69: 21 and gave me vinegar for my *t*.
Mt 5: 6 Blessed are those who hunger and *t*
Jn 4: 14 the water I give him will never *t*.
2Co 11: 27 I have known hunger and *t*
Rev 7: 16 never again will they *t*.

THIRSTS (THIRST)
Ps 42: 2 My soul *t* for God,

THIRSTY (THIRST)
Ps 107: 9 for he satisfies the *t*
Pr 25: 21 if he is *t*, give him water to drink.
Isa 55: 1 "Come, all you who are *t*,
Mt 25: 35 I was *t* and you gave me something
Jn 7: 37 "If anyone is *t*, let him come to me
Ro 12: 20 if he is *t*, give him something
Rev 21: 6 To him who is *t* I will give to drink
22: 17 Whoever is *t*, let him come;

THOMAS
Apostle (Mt 10:3; Mk 3:18; Lk 6:15; Jn 11:16; 14:5; 21:2; Ac 1:13). Doubted resurrection (Jn 20:24–28).

THONGS
Mk 1: 7 *t* of whose sandals I am not worthy

THORN (THORNBUSHES THORNS)
2Co 12: 7 there was given me a *t* in my flesh,

THORNBUSHES (THORN)
Lk 6: 44 People do not pick figs from *t*,

THORNS (THORN)
Ge 3: 18 It will produce *t* and thistles
Nu 33: 55 in your eyes and *t* in your sides.
Mt 13: 7 fell among *t*, which grew up
27: 29 and then twisted together a crown of *t*
Heb 6: 8 But land that produces *t*

THOUGHT (THINK)
Pr 14: 15 a prudent man gives *t* to his steps.
21: 29 an upright man gives *t* to his ways.
1Co 13: 11 I talked like a child, I *t* like a child,

THOUGHTS (THINK)
1Ch 28: 9 every motive behind the *t*.
Ps 94: 11 The LORD knows the *t* of man;
139: 23 test me and know my anxious *t*.
Isa 55: 8 "For my *t* are not your *t*,
Mt 15: 19 For out of the heart come evil *t*,
1Co 2: 11 among men knows the *t* of a man
Heb 4: 12 it judges the *t* and attitudes

THREE
Ge 6: 10 Noah had *t* sons: Shem, Ham
Ex 23: 14 "*T* times a year you are
Dt 19: 15 the testimony of two or *t* witnesses.
2Sa 23: 8 a Tahkemonite, was chief of the *T*;
Pr 30: 15 "There are *t* things that are never
30: 18 "There are *t* things that are too
30: 21 "Under *t* things the earth trembles,
30: 29 "There are *t* things that are stately
Ecc 4: 12 of *t* strands is not quickly broken.
Da 3: 24 "Weren't there *t* men that we tied up
Am 1: 3 "For *t* sins of Damascus,
Jnh 1: 17 inside the fish *t* days and *t* nights.
Mt 12: 40 so the Son of Man will be *t* days
12: 40 *t* nights in the belly of a huge fish,
12: 40 *t* nights in the heart of the earth.
17: 4 I will put up *t* shelters—one
18: 20 or *t* come together in my name,
26: 34 you will disown me *t* times."
26: 75 you will disown me *t* times."
27: 63 'After *t* days I will rise again.'
Mk 8: 31 and after *t* days rise again.
9: 5 Let us put up *t* shelters—one
14: 30 yourself will disown me *t* times."
Jn 2: 19 and I will raise it again in *t* days."
1Co 13: 13 And now these *t* remain: faith,
14: 27 or at the most *t*— should speak,
2Co 13: 1 testimony of two or *t* witnesses."

1Jn 5: 7 For there are *t* that testify:

THRESHER* (THRESHING)
1Co 9: 10 plowman plows and the *t* threshes,

THRESHING (THRESHER)
Ru 3: 6 So she went down to the *t* floor
2Sa 24: 18 an altar to the LORD on the *t* floor
Lk 3: 17 is in his hand to clear his *t* floor

THREW (THROW)
Da 6: 16 and *t* him into the lions' den.
Jnh 1: 15 took Jonah and *t* him overboard,

THRIVE
Pr 29: 2 When the righteous *t*, the people

THROAT (THROATS)
Ps 5: 9 Their *t* is an open grave;
Pr 23: 2 and put a knife to your *t*

THROATS (THROAT)
Ro 3: 13 "Their *t* are open graves;

THROB*
Isa 60: 5 your heart will *t* and swell with joy;

THRONE (ENTHRONED ENTHRONES THRONES)
2Sa 7: 16 your *t* will be established forever
1Ch 17: 12 and I will establish his *t* forever.
Ps 11: 4 the LORD is on his heavenly *t*.
45: 6 Your *t*, O God, will last for ever
47: 8 God is seated on his holy *t*.
89: 14 justice are the foundation of your *t*;
Isa 6: 1 I saw the Lord seated on a *t*,
66: 1 "Heaven is my *t*,
Eze 28: 2 I sit on the *t* of a god
Da 7: 9 His *t* was flaming with fire,
Mt 19: 28 Son of Man sits on his glorious *t*,
Ac 7: 49 prophet says: " 'Heaven is my *t*,
Heb 1: 8 "Your *t*, O God, will last for ever
4: 16 Let us then approach the *t* of grace
12: 2 at the right hand of the *t* of God.
Rev 3: 21 sat down with my Father on his *t*.
3: 21 the right to sit with me on my *t*,
4: 2 there before me was a *t* in heaven
4: 10 They lay their crowns before the *t*
20: 11 Then I saw a great white *t*
22: 3 *t* of God and of the Lamb will be

THRONES (THRONE)
Mt 19: 28 me will also sit on twelve *t*,
Rev 4: 4 throne were twenty-four other *t*,

THROW (THREW)
Jn 8: 7 the first to *t* a stone at her."
Heb 10: 35 So do not *t* away your confidence;
12: 1 let us *t* off everything that hinders

THUNDER (THUNDERS)
Ps 93: 4 Mightier than the *t*
Mk 3: 17 which means Sons of *T*); Andrew,

THUNDERS (THUNDER)
Job 37: 5 God's voice *t* in marvelous ways;
Ps 29: 3 the God of glory *t*,
Rev 10: 3 the voices of the seven *t* spoke.

THWART* (THWARTED)
Isa 14: 27 has purposed, and who can *t* him?

THWARTED (THWART)
Job 42: 2 no plan of yours can be *t*.

THYATIRA
Rev 2: 18 the angel of the church in *T* write:

TIBNI
King of Israel (1Ki 16:21–22).

TIDINGS
Isa 40: 9 You who bring good *t* to Jerusalem
52: 7 who bring good *t*,

TIES
Hos 11: 4 with *t* of love;
Mt 12: 29 unless he first *t* up the strong man?

TIGHT*
Jas 1: 26 and yet does not keep a *t* rein

TIGHTFISTED*
Dt 15: 7 or *t* toward your poor brother.

Joel 2: 1 Let all who live in the land *t,*
Hab 3: 6 he looked, and made the nations *t.*

TREMBLED (TREMBLE)
Ex 19: 16 Everyone in the camp *t.*
20: 18 in smoke, they *t* with fear.
2Sa 22: 8 "The earth *t* and quaked,
Ac 7: 32 Moses *t* with fear and did not dare

TREMBLES (TREMBLE)
Ps 97: 4 the earth sees and *t.*
104: 32 he who looks at the earth, and it *t,*
Isa 66: 2 and *t* at my word.
Jer 10: 10 When he is angry, the earth *t;*
Na 1: 5 The earth *t* at his presence,

TREMBLING (TREMBLE)
Ps 2: 11 and rejoice with *t.*
Da 10: 10 set me *t* on my hands and knees.
Php 2: 12 out your salvation with fear and *t,*
Heb 12: 21 terrifying that Moses said, "I am *t*

TRESPASS* (TRESPASSES)
Ro 5: 15 But the gift is not like the *t.*
5: 15 died by the *t* of the one man,
5: 17 For if, by the *t* of the one man,
5: 18 result of one *t* was condemnation
5: 20 added so that the *t* might increase.

TRESPASSES* (TRESPASS)
Ro 5: 16 but the gift followed many *t*

TRIAL (TRIALS)
Ps 37: 33 condemned when brought to *t.*
Mk 13: 11 you are arrested and brought to *t,*
2Co 8: 2 most severe *t,* their overflowing
Jas 1: 12 is the man who perseveres under *t,*
1Pe 4: 12 at the painful *t* you are suffering,
Rev 3: 10 you from the hour of *t* that is going

TRIALS* (TRIAL)
Dt 7: 19 saw with your own eyes the great *t,*
29: 3 own eyes you saw those great *t,*
Lk 22: 28 who have stood by me in my *t.*
1Th 3: 3 one would be unsettled by these *t.*
2Th 1: 4 the persecutions and *t* you are
Jas 1: 2 whenever you face *t* of many kinds,
1Pe 1: 6 had to suffer grief in all kinds of *t.*
2Pe 2: 9 how to rescue godly men from *t*

TRIBE (HALF-TRIBE TRIBES)
Heb 7: 13 no one from that *t* has ever served
Rev 5: 5 See, the Lion of the *t* of Judah,
5: 9 God from every *t* and language
11: 9 men from every people, *t,*
14: 6 to every nation, *t,* language

TRIBES (TRIBE)
Ge 49: 28 All these are the twelve *t* of Israel,
Mt 19: 28 judging the twelve *t* of Israel.

TRIBULATION*
Rev 7: 14 who have come out of the great *t;*

TRICKERY*
Ac 13: 10 full of all kinds of deceit and *t.*
2Co 12: 16 fellow that I am, I caught you by *t!*

TRIED (TRY)
Ps 73: 16 When I *t* to understand all this,
95: 9 where your fathers tested and *t* me,
Heb 3: 9 where your fathers tested and *t* me

TRIES (TRY)
Lk 17: 33 Whoever *t* to keep his life will lose

TRIMMED
Mt 25: 7 virgins woke up and *t* their lamps.

TRIUMPH (TRIUMPHAL TRIUMPHED TRIUMPHING TRIUMPHS)
Ps 25: 2 nor let my enemies *t* over me.
54: 7 my eyes have looked in *t*
112: 8 in the end he will look in *t*
118: 7 I will look in *t* on my enemies.
Pr 28: 12 When the righteous *t,* there is great
Isa 42: 13 and will *t* over his enemies.

TRIUMPHAL* (TRIUMPH)
Isa 60: 11 their kings led in *t* procession.
2Co 2: 14 us in *t* procession in Christ

TRIUMPHED (TRIUMPH)
Rev 5: 5 of Judah, the Root of David, has *t.*

TRIUMPHING* (TRIUMPH)
Col 2: 15 of them, *t* over them by the cross.

TRIUMPHS* (TRIUMPH)
Jas 2: 13 Mercy *t* over judgment! What

TROUBLE (TROUBLED TROUBLES)
Ge 41: 51 God has made me forget all my *t*
Jos 7: 25 Why have you brought this *t* on us?
Job 2: 10 good from God, and not *t?"*
5: 7 Yet man is born to *t*
14: 1 is of few days and full of *t.*
42: 11 him over all the *t* the LORD had
Ps 7: 14 conceives *t* gives birth
7: 16 The *t* he causes recoils on himself;
9: 9 a stronghold in times of *t.*
10: 14 But you, O God, do see *t* and grief;
22: 11 for *t* is near
27: 5 For in the day of *t*
32: 7 you will protect me from *t*
37: 39 he is their stronghold in time of *t.*
41: 1 LORD delivers him in times of *t.*
46: 1 an ever-present help in *t.*
50: 15 and call upon me in the day of *t;*
59: 16 my refuge in times of *t.*
66: 14 spoke when I was in *t.*
86: 7 In the day of my *t* I will call to you,
91: 15 I will be with him in *t,*
107: 6 to the LORD in their *t,*
107: 13 they cried to the LORD in their *t,*
116: 3 I was overcome by *t* and sorrow.
119:143 *T* and distress have come upon me,
138: 7 Though I walk in the midst of *t,*
143: 11 righteousness, bring me out of *t.*
Pr 11: 8 righteous man is rescued from *t,*
11: 17 a cruel man brings *t* on himself
11: 29 He who brings *t* on his family will
12: 13 but a righteous man escapes *t.*
12: 21 but the wicked have their fill of *t.*
15: 27 A greedy man brings *t* to his family
19: 23 one rests content, untouched by *t.*
22: 8 He who sows wickedness reaps *t,*
24: 10 If you falter in times of *t,*
25: 19 on the unfaithful in times of *t.*
28: 14 he who hardens his heart falls into *t*
Jer 30: 7 It will be a time of *t* for Jacob,
Na 1: 7 a refuge in times of *t.*
Zep 1: 15 a day of *t* and ruin,
Mt 6: 34 Each day has enough *t* of its own.
13: 21 When *t* or persecution comes
Jn 16: 33 In this world you will have *t.*
Ro 8: 35 Shall *t* or hardship or persecution
2Co 1: 4 those in any *t* with the comfort we
2Th 1: 6 *t* to those who *t* you
Jas 5: 13 one of you in *t?* He should pray.

TROUBLED (TROUBLE)
Ps 38: 18 I am *t* by my sin.
Isa 38: 14 I am *t;* O Lord, come to my aid!"
Mk 14: 33 began to be deeply distressed and *t.*
Jn 14: 1 "Do not let your hearts be *t.*
14: 27 Do not let your hearts be *t*
2Th 1: 7 and give relief to you who are *t,*

TROUBLES (TROUBLE)
Ps 34: 6 he saved him out of all his *t.*
34: 17 he delivers them from all their *t.*
34: 19 A righteous man may have many *t,*
40: 12 For *t* without number surround me
54: 7 he has delivered me from all my *t,*
1Co 7: 28 those who marry will face many *t*
2Co 1: 4 who comforts us in all our *t,*
4: 17 and momentary *t* are achieving
6: 4 in *t,* hardships and distresses;
7: 4 in all our *t* my joy knows no bounds
Php 4: 14 good of you to share in my *t.*

TRUE (TRUTH)
Nu 11: 23 not what I say will come *t* for you."
12: 7 this is not *t* of my servant Moses;
Dt 18: 22 does not take place or come *t,*
Jos 23: 15 of the LORD your God has come *t*
1Sa 9: 6 and everything he says comes *t.*
1Ki 10: 6 and your wisdom is *t.*
2Ch 6: 17 your servant David come *t.*
15: 3 was without the *t* God,
Ps 33: 4 of the LORD is right and *t;*
119:142 and your law is *t.*
119:151 and all your commands are *t.*
119:160 All your words are *t;*
Pr 8: 7 My mouth speaks what is *t,*
22: 21 teaching you *t* and reliable words,
Jer 10: 10 But the LORD is the *t* God;
28: 9 only if his prediction comes *t."*
Eze 33: 33 "When all this comes *t*—
Lk 16: 11 who will trust you with *t* riches?
Jn 1: 9 The *t* light that gives light
4: 23 when the *t* worshipers will worship
6: 32 Father who gives you the *t* bread
7: 28 on my own, but he who sent me is *t*
15: 1 "I am the *t* vine, and my Father is
17: 3 the only *t* God, and Jesus Christ,
19: 35 testimony, and his testimony is *t.*
21: 24 We know that his testimony is *t.*
Ac 10: 34 "I now realize how *t* it is that God
11: 23 all to remain *t* to the Lord
14: 22 them to remain *t* to the faith.
17: 11 day to see if what Paul said was *t.*
Ro 3: 4 Let God be *t,* and every man a liar.
Php 4: 8 whatever is *t,* whatever is noble,
1Jn 2: 8 and the *t* light is already shining.
5: 20 He is the *t* God and eternal life.
Rev 19: 9 "These are the *t* words of God."
22: 6 These words are trustworthy and *t.*

TRUMPET (TRUMPETS)
Isa 27: 13 And in that day a great *t* will sound
Eze 33: 5 Since he heard the sound of the *t*
Zec 9: 14 Sovereign LORD will sound the *t;*
Mt 24: 31 send his angels with a loud *t* call,
1Co 14: 8 if the *t* does not sound a clear call,
15: 52 For the *t* will sound, the dead will
1Th 4: 16 and with the *t* call of God,
Rev 8: 7 The first angel sounded his *t,*

TRUMPETS (TRUMPET)
Jdg 7: 19 They blew their *t* and broke the jars
Rev 8: 2 and to them were given seven *t.*

TRUST* (ENTRUST ENTRUSTED TRUSTED TRUSTFULLY TRUSTING TRUSTS TRUSTWORTHY)
Ex 14: 31 put their *t* in him and in Moses his
19: 9 and will always put their *t* in you."
Nu 20: 12 "Because you did not *t*
Dt 1: 32 you did not *t* in the LORD your
9: 23 You did not *t* him or obey him.
28: 52 walls in which you *t* fall down.
Jdg 11: 20 did not *t* Israel to pass
2Ki 17: 14 who did not *t* in the LORD their
18: 30 to *t* in the LORD when he says,
1Ch 9: 22 to their positions of *t* by David
Job 4: 18 If God places no *t* in his servants,
15: 15 If God places no *t* in his holy ones,
31: 24 "If I have put my *t* in gold
39: 12 Can you *t* him to bring
Ps 4: 5 and *t* in the LORD.
9: 10 Those who know your name will *t*
13: 5 But I *t* in your unfailing love;
20: 7 Some *t* in chariots and some
20: 7 we *t* in the name of the LORD our
22: 4 In you our fathers put their *t;*
22: 9 you made me *t* in you
25: 2 I lift up my soul; in you I *t,*
31: 6 I *t* in the LORD.
31: 14 But I *t* in you, O LORD;
33: 21 for we *t* in his holy name.
37: 3 *T* in the LORD and do good;
37: 5 *t* in him and he will do this:
40: 3 and put their *t* in the LORD.
40: 4 who makes the LORD his *t,*
44: 6 I do not *t* in my bow,
49: 6 those who *t* in their wealth

49: 13 of those who *t* in themselves,
52: 8 I *t* in God's unfailing love
55: 23 But as for me, I *t* in you.
56: 3 I will *t* in you.
56: 4 in God I *t*; I will not be afraid.
56: 11 in God I *t*; I will not be afraid.
62: 8 *T* in him at all times, O people;
62: 10 Do not *t* in extortion
78: 7 Then they would put their *t* in God
78: 22 or *t* in his deliverance.
91: 2 my God, in whom I *t*."
115: 8 and so will all who *t* in them.
115: 9 O house of Israel, *t* in the LORD—
115: 10 O house of Aaron, *t* in the LORD
115: 11 You who fear him, *t* in the LORD
118: 8 than to *t* in man.
118: 9 than to *t* in princes.
119: 42 for I *t* in your word.
125: 1 Those who *t* in the LORD are like
135: 18 and so will all who *t* in them.
143: 8 for I have put my *t* in you.
146: 3 Do not put your *t* in princes,
Pr 3: 5 *T* in the LORD with all your heart
21: 22 the stronghold in which they *t*.
22: 19 So that your *t* may be in the LORD
Isa 8: 17 I will put my *t* in him.
12: 2 I will *t* and not be afraid.
26: 4 *T* in the LORD forever,
30: 15 in quietness and *t* is your strength,
31: 1 who *t* in the multitude
36: 15 to *t* in the LORD when he says,
42: 17 But those who *t* in idols,
50: 10 *t* in the name of the LORD
Jer 2: 37 LORD has rejected those you *t*;
5: 17 the fortified cities in which you *t*.
7: 4 Do not *t* in deceptive words
7: 14 the temple you *t* in, the place I gave
9: 4 do not *t* your brothers.
12: 6 Do not *t* them,
28: 15 you have persuaded this nation to *t*
39: 18 you *t* in me, declares the LORD.'"
48: 7 Since you *t* in your deeds
49: 4 you *t* in your riches and say,
49: 11 Your widows too can *t* in me."
Mic 7: 5 Do not *t* a neighbor;
Na 1: 7 He cares for those who *t* in him,
Zep 3: 2 She does not *t* in the LORD,
3: 12 who *t* in the name of the LORD.
Lk 16: 11 who will *t* you with true riches?
Jn 12: 36 Put your *t* in the light
14: 1 *T* in God; *t* also in me.
Ac 14: 23 Lord, in whom they had put their *t*.
Ro 15: 13 you with all joy and peace as you *t*
1Co 4: 2 been given a *t* must prove faithful.
9: 17 discharging the *t* committed
2Co 13: 6 I *t* that you will discover that we
Heb 2: 13 "I will put my *t* in him."

TRUSTED* (TRUST)
1Sa 27: 12 Achish *t* David and said to himself,
2Ki 18: 5 Hezekiah *t* in the LORD, the God
1Ch 5: 20 their prayers, because they *t*
Job 12: 20 He silences the lips of *t* advisers
Ps 5: 9 from their mouth can be *t*;
22: 4 they *t* and you delivered them.
22: 5 in you they *t* and were not
26: 1 I have *t* in the LORD
41: 9 Even my close friend, whom I *t*,
52: 7 but *t* in his great wealth
Isa 20: 5 Those who *t* in Cush and boasted
25: 9 This is the LORD, we *t* in him;
25: 9 we *t* in him, and he saved us.
47: 10 You have *t* in your wickedness
Jer 13: 25 and *t* in false gods.
38: 22 those *t* friends of yours.
48: 13 ashamed when they *t* in Bethel.
Eze 16: 15 "'But you *t* in your beauty
Da 3: 28 They *t* in him and defied the king's
6: 23 because he had *t* in his God.
Lk 11: 22 the armor in which the man *t*
16: 10 *t* with very little can also be *t*
Ac 12: 20 a *t* personal servant of the king,
Tit 2: 10 but to show that they can be fully *t*,
3: 8 so that those who have *t*

TRUSTFULLY* (TRUST)
Pr 3: 29 who lives *t* near you.

TRUSTING* (TRUST)
Job 15: 31 by *t* what is worthless,
Ps 112: 7 his heart is steadfast, *t*
Isa 2: 22 Stop *t* in man,
Jer 7: 8 you are *t* in deceptive words that

TRUSTS* (TRUST)
Job 8: 14 What he *t* in is fragile;
Ps 21: 7 For the king *t* in the LORD;
22: 8 "He *t* in the LORD;
28: 7 my heart *t* in him, and I am helped.
32: 10 surrounds the man who *t* in him.
84: 12 blessed is the man who *t* in you.
86: 2 who *t* in you.
Pr 11: 28 Whoever *t* in his riches will fall,
16: 20 blessed is he who *t* in the LORD.
28: 25 he who *t* in the LORD will prosper.
28: 26 He who *t* in himself is a fool,
29: 25 whoever *t* in the LORD is kept safe
Isa 26: 3 because he *t* in you.
28: 16 one who *t* will never be dismayed.
Jer 17: 5 "Cursed is the one who *t* in man,
17: 7 blessed is the man who *t*
Eze 33: 13 but then he *t* in his righteousness
Hab 2: 18 For he who makes it *t*
Mt 27: 43 He *t* in God.
Ro 4: 5 but *t* God who justifies the wicked,
9: 33 one who *t* in him will never be put
10: 11 "Anyone who *t* in him will never
1Co 13: 7 always protects, always *t*,
1Pe 2: 6 and the one who *t* in him

TRUSTWORTHY* (TRUST)
Ex 18: 21 *t* men who hate dishonest gain—
2Sa 7: 28 you are God! Your words are *t*,
Ne 13: 13 these men were considered *t*.
Ps 19: 7 The statutes of the LORD are *t*,
111: 7 all his precepts are *t*.
119: 86 All your commands are *t*;
119:138 they are fully *t*.
Pr 11: 13 but a *t* man keeps a secret.
13: 17 but a *t* envoy brings healing.
25: 13 is a *t* messenger to those who send
Da 2: 45 and the interpretation is *t*."
6: 4 he was *t* and neither corrupt
Lk 16: 11 So if you have not been *t*
16: 12 And if you have not been *t*
19: 17 'Because you have been *t*
1Co 7: 25 one who by the Lord's mercy is *t*.
1Ti 1: 15 Here is a *t* saying that deserves full
3: 1 Here is a *t* saying: If anyone sets his
3: 11 but temperate and *t* in everything.
4: 9 This is a *t* saying that deserves full
2Ti 2: 11 Here is a *t* saying:
Tit 1: 9 must hold firmly to the *t* message
3: 8 This is a *t* saying.
Rev 21: 5 for these words are *t* and true."
22: 6 "These words are *t* and true.

TRUTH* (TRUE TRUTHFUL TRUTHFULNESS TRUTHS)
Ge 42: 16 tested to see if you are telling the *t*.
1Ki 17: 24 LORD from your mouth is the *t*."
22: 16 the *t* in the name of the LORD?"
2Ch 18: 15 the *t* in the name of the LORD?"
Ps 15: 2 who speaks the *t* from his heart
25: 5 guide me in your *t* and teach me,
26: 3 and I walk continually in your *t*.
31: 5 redeem me, O LORD, the God of *t*
40: 10 do not conceal your love and your *t*
40: 11 your *t* always protect me.
43: 3 Send forth your light and your *t*,
45: 4 victoriously in behalf of *t*, humility
51: 6 Surely you desire *t*
52: 3 than speaking the *t*.
86: 11 and I will walk in your *t*;
96: 13 and the peoples in his *t*.
119: 30 I have chosen the way of *t*;
119: 43 of *t* from my mouth,
145: 18 to all who call on him in *t*.
Pr 16: 13 they value a man who speaks the *t*.
23: 23 Buy the *t* and do not sell it;
Isa 45: 19 I, the LORD, speak the *t*;
48: 1 but not in *t* or righteousness—
59: 14 *t* has stumbled in the streets,
59: 15 *T* is nowhere to be found,
65: 16 will do so by the God of *t*;
65: 16 will swear by the God of *t*.
Jer 5: 1 who deals honestly and seeks the *t*,
5: 3 do not your eyes look for *t*?
7: 28 *T* has perished; it has vanished
9: 3 it is not by *t*
9: 5 and no one speaks the *t*.
26: 15 for in *t* the LORD has sent me
Da 8: 12 and *t* was thrown to the ground.
9: 13 and giving attention to your *t*.
10: 21 what is written in the Book of *T*.
11: 2 "Now then, I tell you the *t*:
Am 5: 10 and despise him who tells the *t*.
Zec 8: 3 will be called the City of *T*,
8: 16 are to do: Speak the *t* to each other,
8: 19 Therefore love *t* and peace."
Mt 5: 18 I tell you the *t*, until heaven
5: 26 I tell you the *t*, you will not get out
6: 2 I tell you the *t*, they have received
6: 5 I tell you the *t*, they have received
6: 16 I tell you the *t*, they have received
8: 10 "I tell you the *t*, I have not found
10: 15 I tell you the *t*, it will be more
10: 23 I tell you the *t*, you will not finish
10: 42 I tell you the *t*, he will certainly not
11: 11 I tell you the *t*: Among those born
13: 17 For I tell you the *t*, many prophets
16: 28 I tell you the *t*, some who are
17: 20 I tell you the *t*, if you have faith
18: 3 And he said: "I tell you the *t*,
18: 13 And if he finds it, I tell you the *t*,
18: 18 "I tell you the *t*, whatever you bind
19: 23 to his disciples, "I tell you the *t*,
19: 28 "I tell you the *t*, at the renewal
21: 21 Jesus replied, "I tell you the *t*,
21: 31 Jesus said to them, "I tell you the *t*,
22: 16 of God in accordance with the *t*.
23: 36 I tell you the *t*, all this will come
24: 2 "I tell you the *t*, not one stone here
24: 34 I tell you the *t*, this generation will
24: 47 I tell you the *t*, he will put him
25: 12 'I tell you the *t*, I don't know you.'
25: 40 The King will reply, 'I tell you the *t*
25: 45 "He will reply, 'I tell you the *t*,
26: 13 tell you the *t*, wherever this gospel
26: 21 "I tell you the *t*, one
26: 34 "I tell you the *t*," Jesus answered,
Mk 3: 28 I tell you the *t*, all the sins
5: 33 with fear, told him the whole *t*.
8: 12 I tell you the *t*, no sign will be given
9: 1 he said to them, "I tell you the *t*,
9: 41 I tell you the *t*, anyone who gives
10: 15 I tell you the *t*, anyone who will not
10: 29 "I tell you the *t*," Jesus replied,
11: 23 "I tell you the *t*, if anyone says
12: 14 of God in accordance with the *t*.
12: 43 Jesus said, "I tell you the *t*,
13: 30 I tell you the *t*, this generation will
14: 9 I tell you the *t*, wherever the gospel
14: 18 "I tell you the *t*, one
14: 25 "I tell you the *t*, I will not drink
14: 30 "I tell you the *t*," Jesus answered,
Lk 4: 24 "I tell you the *t*," he continued,
9: 27 I tell you the *t*, some who are
12: 37 I tell you the *t*, he will dress himself
12: 44 I tell you the *t*, he will put him
18: 17 I tell you the *t*, anyone who will not
18: 29 I tell you the *t*," Jesus said to them,

20: 21 of God in accordance with the *t*.
21: 3 "I tell you the *t*," he said, "this
21: 32 tell you the *t*, this generation will
23: 43 answered him, "I tell you the *t*,
Jn 1: 14 from the Father, full of grace and *t*.
1: 17 and *t* came through Jesus Christ.
1: 51 "I tell you the *t*, you shall see
3: 3 "I tell you the *t*, no one can see
3: 5 Jesus answered, "I tell you the *t*,
3: 11 I tell you the *t*, we speak
3: 21 But whoever lives by the *t* comes
4: 23 worship the Father in spirit and *t*,
4: 24 must worship in spirit and in *t*."
5: 19 "I tell you the *t*, the Son can do
5: 24 "I tell you the *t*, whoever hears my
5: 25 I tell you the *t*, a time is coming
5: 33 and he has testified to the *t*.
6: 26 "I tell you the *t*, you are looking
6: 32 Jesus said to them, "I tell you the *t*,
6: 47 I tell you the *t*, he who believes has
6: 53 Jesus said to them, "I tell you the *t*,
7: 18 the one who sent him is a man of *t*;
8: 32 Then you will know the *t*,
8: 32 and the *t* will set you free."
8: 34 Jesus replied, "I tell you the *t*,
8: 40 who has told you the *t* that I heard
8: 44 to the *t*, for there is no *t* in him.
8: 45 I tell the *t*, you do not believe me!
8: 46 I am telling the *t*, why don't you
8: 51 I tell you the *t*, if anyone keeps my
8: 58 "I tell you the *t*," Jesus answered,
10: 1 "I tell you the *t*, the man who does
10: 7 "I tell you the *t*, I am the gate
12: 24 I tell you the *t*, unless a kernel
13: 16 I tell you the *t*, no servant is greater
13: 20 tell you the *t*, whoever accepts
13: 21 "I tell you the *t*, one of you is going
13: 38 I tell you the *t*, before the rooster
14: 6 I am the way and the *t* and the life.
14: 12 I tell you the *t*, anyone who has
14: 17 with you forever—the Spirit of *t*.
15: 26 the Spirit of *t* who goes out
16: 7 But I tell you the *t*: It is
16: 13 But when he, the Spirit of *t*, comes,
16: 13 comes, he will guide you into all *t*.
16: 20 I tell you the *t*, you will weep
16: 23 I tell you the *t*, my Father will give
17: 17 them by the *t*; your word is *t*.
18: 23 if I spoke the *t*, why did you strike
18: 37 into the world, to testify to the *t*.
18: 37 on the side of *t* listens to me."
18: 38 "What is *t*?" Pilate asked.
19: 35 He knows that he tells the *t*,
21: 18 I tell you the *t*, when you were
Ac 20: 30 and distort the *t* in order
21: 24 everybody will know there is no *t*
21: 34 commander could not get at the *t*
24: 8 able to learn the *t* about all these
28: 25 "The Holy Spirit spoke the *t*
Ro 1: 18 of men who suppress the *t*
1: 25 They exchanged the *t* of God
2: 2 who do such things is based on *t*.
2: 8 who reject the *t* and follow evil,
2: 20 embodiment of knowledge and *t*—
9: 1 I speak the *t* in Christ—I am not
15: 8 of the Jews on behalf of God's *t*,
1Co 5: 8 the bread of sincerity and *t*.
13: 6 in evil but rejoices with the *t*.
2Co 4: 2 setting forth the *t* plainly we
11: 10 As surely as the *t* of Christ is in me,
12: 6 because I would be speaking the *t*.
13: 8 against the *t*, but only for the *t*.
Gal 2: 5 so that the *t* of the gospel might
2: 14 in line with the *t* of the gospel,
4: 16 enemy by telling you the *t*?
5: 7 and kept you from obeying the *t*?
Eph 1: 13 when you heard the word of *t*,
4: 15 Instead, speaking the *t* in love,
4: 21 him in accordance with the *t* that is
5: 9 and *t*) and find out what pleases
6: 14 with the belt of *t* buckled
Col 1: 5 heard about in the word of *t*,
1: 6 understood God's grace in all its *t*.
2Th 2: 10 because they refused to love the *t*
2: 12 who have not believed the *t*
2: 13 and through belief in the *t*.
1Ti 2: 4 to come to a knowledge of the *t*.
2: 7 I am telling the *t*, I am not lying—
3: 15 the pillar and foundation of the *t*.
4: 3 who believe and who know the *t*.
6: 5 who have been robbed of the *t*
2Ti 2: 15 correctly handles the word of *t*.
2: 18 have wandered away from the *t*.
2: 25 them to a knowledge of the *t*,
3: 7 never able to acknowledge the *t*.
3: 8 so also these men oppose the *t*—
4: 4 will turn their ears away from the *t*
Tit 1: 1 the knowledge of the *t* that leads
1: 14 of those who reject the *t*.
Heb 10: 26 received the knowledge of the *t*,
Jas 1: 18 birth through the word of *t*,
3: 14 do not boast about it or deny the *t*.
5: 19 of you should wander from the *t*
1Pe 1: 22 by obeying the *t* so that you have
2Pe 1: 12 established in the *t* you now have.
2: 2 the way of *t* into disrepute.
1Jn 1: 6 we lie and do not live by the *t*.
1: 8 deceive ourselves and the *t* is not
2: 4 commands is a liar, and the *t* is not
2: 8 its *t* is seen in him and you,
2: 20 and all of you know the *t*.
2: 21 because no lie comes from the *t*.
2: 21 because you do not know the *t*,
3: 18 or tongue but with actions and in *t*.
3: 19 we know that we belong to the *t*,
4: 6 is how we recognize the Spirit of *t*
5: 6 testifies, because the Spirit is the *t*.
2Jn : 1 whom I love in the *t*—
: 2 who know the *t*— because of the *t*,
: 3 will be with us in *t* and love.
: 4 of your children walking in the *t*,
3Jn : 1 friend Gaius, whom I love in the *t*.
: 3 how you continue to walk in the *t*.
: 3 tell about your faithfulness to the *t*
: 4 my children are walking in the *t*.
: 8 we may work together for the *t*.
: 12 everyone—and even by the *t* itself.

TRUTHFUL* (TRUTH)
Pr 12: 17 A *t* witness gives honest testimony,
12: 19 *T* lips endure forever,
12: 22 but he delights in men who are *t*.
14: 5 A *t* witness does not deceive,
14: 25 A *t* witness saves lives,
Jer 4: 2 and if in a *t*, just and righteous way
Jn 3: 33 it has certified that God is *t*.
2Co 6: 7 in *t* speech and in the power

TRUTHFULNESS* (TRUTH)
Ro 3: 7 "If my falsehood enhances God's *t*

TRUTHS* (TRUTH)
1Co 2: 13 expressing spiritual *t*
1Ti 3: 9 hold of the deep *t* of the faith
4: 6 brought up in the *t* of the faith
Heb 5: 12 to teach you the elementary *t*

TRY (TRIED TRIES TRYING)
Ps 26: 2 Test me, O LORD, and *t* me,
Isa 7: 13 enough to *t* the patience of men?
Lk 12: 58 *t* hard to be reconciled to him
13: 24 will *t* to enter and will not be able
1Co 10: 33 even as I *t* to please everybody
14: 12 *t* to excel in gifts that build up
2Co 5: 11 is to fear the Lord, we *t*
1Th 5: 15 always *t* to be kind to each other
Tit 2: 9 to *t* to please them, not to talk back

TRYING (TRY)
2Co 5: 12 We are not *t* to commend ourselves
Gal 1: 10 If I were still *t* to please men,
1Th 2: 4 We are not *t* to please men but God
1Pe 1: 11 *t* to find out the time
1Jn 2: 26 things to you about those who are *t*

TUMORS
1Sa 5: 6 them and afflicted them with *t*.

TUNE
1Co 14: 7 anyone know what *t* is being

TUNIC (TUNICS)
Lk 6: 29 do not stop him from taking your *t*.

TUNICS (TUNIC)
Lk 3: 11 "The man with two *t* should share

TURMOIL
Ps 65: 7 and the *t* of the nations.
Pr 15: 16 than great wealth with *t*.

TURN (TURNED TURNING TURNS)
Ex 32: 12 *T* from your fierce anger; relent
Nu 32: 15 If you *t* away from following him,
Dt 5: 32 do not *t* aside to the right
28: 14 Do not *t* aside from any
30: 10 and *t* to the LORD your God
Jos 1: 7 do not *t* from it to the right
1Ki 8: 58 May he *t* our hearts to him,
2Ch 7: 14 and *t* from their wicked ways,
30: 9 He will not *t* his face from you
Job 33: 30 to *t* back his soul from the pit,
Ps 28: 1 do not *t* a deaf ear to me.
34: 14 *T* from evil and do good;
51: 13 and sinners will *t* back to you.
78: 6 they in *t* would tell their children.
119: 36 *T* my heart toward your statutes
119:132 *T* to me and have mercy on me,
Pr 22: 6 when he is old he will not *t* from it.
Isa 17: 7 *t* their eyes to the Holy One
28: 6 to those who *t* back the battle
29: 16 You *t* things upside down,
30: 21 Whether you *t* to the right
45: 22 "*T* to me and be saved,
55: 7 Let him *t* to the LORD,
Jer 31: 13 I will *t* their mourning
Eze 33: 9 if you do warn the wicked man to *t*
33: 11 *T*! *T* from your evil ways!
Jnh 3: 9 and with compassion *t*
Mal 4: 6 He will *t* the hearts of the fathers
Mt 5: 39 you on the right cheek, *t*
10: 35 For I have come to *t*
Lk 1: 17 to *t* the hearts of the fathers
Jn 12: 40 nor *t*— and I would heal them."
16: 20 but your grief will *t* to joy.
Ac 3: 19 Repent, then, and *t* to God,
26: 18 and *t* them from darkness to light,
1Co 14: 31 For you can all prophesy in *t*
15: 23 But each in his own *t*: Christ,
1Ti 6: 20 *T* away from godless chatter
1Pe 3: 11 He must *t* from evil and do good;

TURNED (TURN)
Dt 23: 5 *t* the curse into a blessing for you,
1Ki 11: 4 his wives *t* his heart
2Ch 15: 4 But in their distress they *t*
Est 9: 1 but now the tables were *t*
9: 22 when their sorrow was *t* into joy
Ps 14: 3 All have *t* aside,
30: 11 You *t* my wailing into dancing;
40: 1 he *t* to me and heard my cry.
Isa 9: 12 for all this, his anger is not *t* away,
53: 6 each of us has *t* to his own way;
Hos 7: 8 Ephraim is a flat cake not *t* over.
Joel 2: 31 The sun will be *t* to darkness
Lk 22: 32 And when you have *t* back,
Ro 3: 12 All have *t* away,

TURNING (TURN)
2Ki 21: 13 wiping it and *t* it upside down.
Pr 2: 2 *t* your ear to wisdom
14: 27 *t* a man from the snares of death.

TURNS (TURN)
2Sa 22: 29 the LORD *t* my darkness into light
Pr 15: 1 A gentle answer *t* away wrath,
Isa 44: 25 and *t* it into nonsense,
Jas 5: 20 Whoever *t* a sinner from the error

TWELVE
Ge 35: 22 Jacob had *t* sons: The sons of Leah:
49: 28 All these are the *t* tribes of Israel,
Mt 10: 1 He called his *t* disciples to him
Lk 9: 17 the disciples picked up *t* basketfuls
Rev 21: 12 the names of the *t* tribes of Israel.
21: 14 of the *t* apostles of the Lamb.

TWIN (TWINS)
Ge 25: 24 there were *t* boys in her womb.

TWINKLING*
1Co 15: 52 in a flash, in the *t* of an eye,

TWINS (TWIN)
Ro 9: 11 before the *t* were born

TWISTING* (TWISTS)
Pr 30: 33 and as *t* the nose produces blood,

TWISTS (TWISTING)
Ex 23: 8 and *t* the words of the righteous.

TYRANNICAL*
Pr 28: 16 A *t* ruler lacks judgment,

TYRE
Eze 28: 12 a lament concerning the king of *T*
Mt 11: 22 it will be more bearable for *T*

UNAPPROACHABLE*
1Ti 6: 16 immortal and who lives in *u* light,

UNASHAMED*
1Jn 2: 28 and *u* before him at his coming.

UNBELIEF* (UNBELIEVER UNBELIEVERS UNBELIEVING)
Mk 9: 24 help me overcome my *u*!"
Ro 4: 20 through *u* regarding the promise
11: 20 they were broken off because of *u*,
11: 23 And if they do not persist in *u*,
1Ti 1: 13 because I acted in ignorance and *u*.
Heb 3: 19 able to enter, because of their *u*.

UNBELIEVER* (UNBELIEF)
1Co 7: 15 But if the *u* leaves, let him do so.
10: 27 If some *u* invites you to a meal
14: 24 if an *u* or someone who does not
2Co 6: 15 have in common with an *u*?
1Ti 5: 8 the faith and is worse than an *u*.

UNBELIEVERS* (UNBELIEF)
Lk 12: 46 and assign him a place with the *u*.
Ro 15: 31 rescued from the *u* in Judea
1Co 6: 6 another—and this in front of *u*!
14: 22 however, is for believers, not for *u*.
14: 22 not for believers but for *u*;
14: 23 do not understand or some *u* come
2Co 4: 4 this age has blinded the minds of *u*,
6: 14 Do not be yoked together with *u*.

UNBELIEVING* (UNBELIEF)
Mt 17: 17 "O *u* and perverse generation,"
Mk 9: 19 "O *u* generation," Jesus replied,
Lk 9: 41 "O *u* and perverse generation,"
1Co 7: 14 For the *u* husband has been
7: 14 and the *u* wife has been sanctified
Heb 3: 12 *u* heart that turns away
Rev 21: 8 But the cowardly, the *u*, the vile,

UNBLEMISHED*
Heb 9: 14 the eternal Spirit offered himself *u*

UNCEASING
Ro 9: 2 and *u* anguish in my heart.

UNCERTAIN*
1Ti 6: 17 which is so *u*, but to put their hope

UNCHANGEABLE* (UNCHANGING)
Heb 6: 18 by two *u* things in which it is

UNCHANGING* (UNCHANGEABLE)
Heb 6: 17 wanted to make the *u* nature

UNCIRCUMCISED
Lev 26: 41 when their *u* hearts are humbled
1Sa 17: 26 Who is this *u* Philistine that he
Jer 9: 26 house of Israel is *u* in heart."
Ac 7: 51 stiff-necked people, with *u* hearts
Ro 4: 11 had by faith while he was still *u*.
1Co 7: 18 Was a man *u* when he was called?
Col 3: 11 circumcised or *u*, barbarian,

UNCIRCUMCISION
1Co 7: 19 is nothing and *u* is nothing.
Gal 5: 6 neither circumcision nor *u* has any

UNCLEAN
Ge 7: 2 and two of every kind of *u* animal,
Lev 10: 10 between the *u* and the clean,
11: 4 it is ceremonially *u* for you.
17: 15 he will be ceremonially *u* till evening.
Isa 6: 5 ruined! For I am a man of *u* lips,
52: 11 Touch no *u* thing!
Mt 15: 11 mouth does not make him '*u*,'
Ac 10: 14 never eaten anything impure or *u*."
Ro 14: 14 fully convinced that no food is *u*
2Co 6: 17 Touch no *u* thing,

UNCLOTHED*
2Co 5: 4 because we do not wish to be *u*

UNCONCERNED*
Eze 16: 49 were arrogant, overfed and *u*;

UNCOVERED
Ru 3: 7 Ruth approached quietly, *u* his feet
1Co 11: 5 with her head *u* dishonors her head
11: 13 to pray to God with her head *u*?
Heb 4: 13 Everything is *u* and laid bare

UNDERGOES* (UNDERGOING)
Heb 12: 8 (and everyone *u* discipline),

UNDERGOING* (UNDERGOES)
1Pe 5: 9 the world are *u* the same kind

UNDERSTAND (UNDERSTANDING UNDERSTANDS UNDERSTOOD)
Ne 8: 8 the people could *u* what was being
Job 38: 4 Tell me, if you *u*.
42: 3 Surely I spoke of things I did not *u*,
Ps 14: 2 men to see if there are any who *u*,
73: 16 When I tried to *u* all this,
119: 27 Let me *u* the teaching
119:125 that I may *u* your statutes.
Pr 2: 5 then you will *u* the fear
2: 9 Then you will *u* what is right
30: 18 four that I do not *u*:
Ecc 7: 25 to *u* the stupidity of wickedness
11: 5 so you cannot *u* the work of God,
Isa 6: 10 *u* with their hearts,
44: 18 know nothing, they *u* nothing;
52: 15 they have not heard, they will *u*.
Jer 17: 9 Who can *u* it?
31: 19 after I came to *u*,
Da 9: 25 and *u* this: From the issuing
Hos 14: 9 Who is discerning? He will *u* them.
Mt 13: 15 *u* with their hearts
24: 15 Daniel—let the reader *u*—
Lk 24: 45 so they could *u* the Scriptures.
Ac 8: 30 "Do you *u* what you are reading?"
Ro 7: 15 I do not *u* what I do.
15: 21 those who have not heard will *u*."
1Co 2: 12 that we may *u* what God has freely
2: 14 and he cannot *u* them,
14: 16 those who do not *u* say "Amen"
Eph 5: 17 but *u* what the Lord's will is.
Heb 11: 3 By faith we *u* that the universe was
2Pe 1: 20 you must *u* that no prophecy
3: 3 you must *u* that in the last days
3: 16 some things that are hard to *u*,

UNDERSTANDING (UNDERSTAND)
1Ki 4: 29 and a breadth of *u* as measureless
Job 12: 12 Does not long life bring *u*?
28: 12 Where does *u* dwell?
28: 28 and to shun evil is *u*.' "
32: 8 of the Almighty, that gives him *u*.
36: 26 How great is God—beyond our *u*!
37: 5 he does great things beyond our *u*.
Ps 111: 10 follow his precepts have good *u*.
119: 34 Give me *u*, and I will keep your law
119:100 I have more *u* than the elders,
119:104 I gain *u* from your precepts;
119:130 it gives *u* to the simple.
136: 5 who by his *u* made the heavens,
147: 5 his *u* has no limit.
Pr 2: 2 and applying your heart to *u*,
2: 6 his mouth come knowledge and *u*.
3: 5 and lean not on your own *u*;
3: 13 the man who gains *u*,
4: 5 Get wisdom, get *u*;
4: 7 Though it cost all you have, get *u*.
7: 4 and call *u* your kinsman;
9: 10 knowledge of the Holy One is *u*.
10: 23 but a man of *u* delights in wisdom.
11: 12 but a man of *u* holds his tongue.
14: 29 A patient man has great *u*,
15: 21 a man of *u* keeps a straight course.
15: 32 whoever heeds correction gains *u*.
16: 16 to choose *u* rather than silver!
16: 22 *U* is a fountain of life
17: 27 and a man of *u* is even-tempered.
18: 2 A fool finds no pleasure in *u*
19: 8 he who cherishes *u* prospers.
20: 5 but a man of *u* draws them out.
23: 23 get wisdom, discipline and *u*.
Isa 11: 2 the Spirit of wisdom and of *u*,
40: 28 and his *u* no one can fathom.
56: 11 They are shepherds who lack *u*;
Jer 3: 15 you with knowledge and *u*.
10: 12 stretched out the heavens by his *u*.
Da 5: 12 a keen mind and knowledge and *u*,
10: 12 that you set your mind to gain *u*
Hos 4: 11 which take away the *u*
Mk 4: 12 and ever hearing but never *u*;
12: 33 with all your *u* and with all your
Lk 2: 47 who heard him was amazed at his *u*
2Co 6: 6 in purity, *u*, patience and kindness;
Eph 1: 8 on us with all wisdom and *u*.
Php 4: 7 of God, which transcends all *u*,
Col 1: 9 through all spiritual wisdom and *u*.
2: 2 have the full riches of complete *u*,
1Jn 5: 20 God has come and has given us *u*,

UNDERSTANDS (UNDERSTAND)
1Ch 28: 9 and *u* every motive
Jer 9: 24 that he *u* and knows me,
Mt 13: 23 man who hears the word and *u* it.
Ro 3: 11 there is no one who *u*,
1Ti 6: 4 he is conceited and *u* nothing.

UNDERSTOOD (UNDERSTAND)
Ne 8: 12 they now *u* the words that had
Ps 73: 17 then I *u* their final destiny.
Isa 40: 13 Who has *u* the mind of the LORD,
40: 21 Have you not *u* since the earth was
Jn 1: 5 but the darkness has not *u* it.
Ro 1: 20 being *u* from what has been made,

UNDESIRABLE*
Jos 24: 15 But if serving the LORD seems *u*

UNDIVIDED*
1Ch 12: 33 to help David with *u* loyalty—
Ps 86: 11 give me an *u* heart,
Eze 11: 19 I will give them an *u* heart
1Co 7: 35 way in *u* devotion to the Lord.

UNDOING
Pr 18: 7 A fool's mouth is his *u*,

UNDYING*
Eph 6: 24 Lord Jesus Christ with an *u* love.

UNEQUALED*
Mt 24: 21 *u* from the beginning of the world
Mk 13: 19 of distress *u* from the beginning,

UNFADING*
1Pe 3: 4 the *u* beauty of a gentle

UNFAILING*
Ex 15: 13 "In your *u* love you will lead
1Sa 20: 14 But show me *u* kindness like that
2Sa 22: 51 he shows *u* kindness
Ps 6: 4 save me because of your *u* love.
13: 5 But I trust in your *u* love;
18: 50 he shows *u* kindness
21: 7 through the *u* love
31: 16 save me in your *u* love.
32: 10 but the LORD's *u* love

33: 5 the earth is full of his *u* love.
33: 18 those whose hope is in his *u* love,
33: 22 May your *u* love rest upon us,
36: 7 How priceless is your *u* love!
44: 26 redeem us because of your *u* love.
48: 9 we meditate on your *u* love.
51: 1 according to your *u* love;
52: 8 I trust in God's *u* love
77: 8 Has his *u* love vanished forever?
85: 7 Show us your *u* love, O LORD,
90: 14 in the morning with your *u* love,
107: 8 thanks to the LORD for his *u* love
107: 15 thanks to the LORD for his *u* love
107: 21 to the LORD for his *u* love
107: 31 to the LORD for his *u* love
119: 41 May your *u* love come to me,
119: 76 May your *u* love be my comfort,
130: 7 for with the LORD is *u* love
143: 8 bring me word of your *u* love,
143: 12 In your *u* love, silence my enemies;
147: 11 who put their hope in his *u* love.
Pr 19: 22 What a man desires is *u* love;
20: 6 Many a man claims to have *u* love,
Isa 54: 10 yet my *u* love for you will not be
La 3: 32 so great is his *u* love.
Hos 10: 12 reap the fruit of *u* love,

UNFAITHFUL (UNFAITHFULNESS)
Lev 6: 2 is *u* to the LORD by deceiving his
Nu 5: 6 and so is *u* to the LORD,
1Ch 10: 13 because he was *u* to the LORD;
Pr 11: 6 the *u* are trapped by evil desires.
13: 2 the *u* have a craving for violence.
13: 15 but the way of the *u* is hard.
22: 12 but he frustrates the words of the *u*.
23: 28 and multiplies the *u* among men.
25: 19 is reliance on the *u* in times
Jer 3: 20 But like a woman *u* to her husband,

UNFAITHFULNESS (UNFAITHFUL)
1Ch 9: 1 to Babylon because of their *u*.
Mt 5: 32 except for marital *u*, causes her
19: 9 for marital *u*, and marries another

UNFIT*
Tit 1: 16 and *u* for doing anything good.

UNFOLDING
Ps 119:130 the *u* of your words gives light;

UNFORGIVING*
2Ti 3: 3 unholy, without love, *u*, slanderous

UNFRIENDLY*
Pr 18: 1 An *u* man pursues selfish ends;

UNFRUITFUL
1Co 14: 14 my spirit prays, but my mind is *u*.

UNGODLINESS (UNGODLY)
Tit 2: 12 It teaches us to say "No" to *u*

UNGODLY (UNGODLINESS)
Ro 5: 6 powerless, Christ died for the *u*.
1Ti 1: 9 the *u* and sinful, the unholy
2Ti 2: 16 in it will become more and more *u*.
2Pe 2: 6 of what is going to happen to the *u*;
Jude : 15 and to convict all the *u*

UNGRATEFUL*
Lk 6: 35 he is kind to the *u* and wicked.
2Ti 3: 2 disobedient to their parents, *u*,

UNHOLY*
1Ti 1: 9 and sinful, the *u* and irreligious;
2Ti 3: 2 ungrateful, *u*, without love,
Heb 10: 29 as an *u* thing the blood

UNINTENTIONALLY
Lev 4: 2 'When anyone sins *u* and does
Nu 15: 22 " 'Now if you *u* fail to keep any
Dt 4: 42 flee if he had *u* killed his neighbor

UNIT
1Co 12: 12 body is a *u*, though it is made up

UNITE (UNITED UNITY)
1Co 6: 15 and *u* them with a prostitute?

UNITED (UNITE)
Ge 2: 24 and mother and be *u* to his wife,
Mt 19: 5 and mother and be *u* to his wife,
Ro 6: 5 If we have been *u* with him like this
Eph 5: 31 and mother and be *u* to his wife,
Php 2: 1 from being *u* with Christ,
Col 2: 2 encouraged in heart and *u* in love,

UNITY* (UNITE)
2Ch 30: 12 the people to give them *u* of mind
Ps 133: 1 is when brothers live together in *u*!
Jn 17: 23 May they be brought to complete *u*
Ro 15: 5 a spirit of *u* among yourselves
Eph 4: 3 effort to keep the *u* of the Spirit
4: 13 up until we all reach *u* in the faith
Col 3: 14 them all together in perfect *u*.

UNIVERSE*
1Co 4: 9 made a spectacle to the whole *u*,
Eph 4: 10 in order to fill the whole *u*.)
Php 2: 15 which you shine like stars in the *u*
Heb 1: 2 and through whom he made the *u*.
11: 3 understand that the *u* was formed

UNJUST
Ro 3: 5 That God is *u* in bringing his wrath
9: 14 What then shall we say? Is God *u*?
1Pe 2: 19 up under the pain of *u* suffering

UNKNOWN
Ac 17: 23 TO AN *U* GOD.

UNLEAVENED
Ex 12: 17 "Celebrate the Feast of *U* Bread,
Dt 16: 16 at the Feast of *U* Bread, the Feast

UNLIMITED*
1Ti 1: 16 Jesus might display his *u* patience

UNLOVED
Pr 30: 23 an *u* woman who is married,

UNMARRIED
1Co 7: 8 It is good for them to stay *u*,
7: 27 Are you *u*? Do not look for a wife.
7: 32 An *u* man is concerned about

UNPLOWED
Ex 23: 11 the seventh year let the land lie *u*
Hos 10: 12 and break up your *u* ground;

UNPRODUCTIVE
Tit 3: 14 necessities and not live *u* lives.
2Pe 1: 8 and *u* in your knowledge

UNPROFITABLE
Tit 3: 9 because these are *u* and useless.

UNPUNISHED
Ex 34: 7 Yet he does not leave the guilty *u*;
Pr 6: 29 no one who touches her will go *u*.
11: 21 of this: The wicked will not go *u*,
19: 5 A false witness will not go *u*,

UNQUENCHABLE
Lk 3: 17 he will burn up the chaff with *u* fire

UNREPENTANT*
Ro 2: 5 stubbornness and your *u* heart,

UNRIGHTEOUS*
Zep 3: 5 yet the *u* know no shame.
Mt 5: 45 rain on the righteous and the *u*.
1Pe 3: 18 the righteous for the *u*, to bring you
2Pe 2: 9 and to hold the *u* for the day

UNSEARCHABLE
Ro 11: 33 How *u* his judgments,
Eph 3: 8 preach to the Gentiles the *u* riches

UNSEEN*
Mt 6: 6 and pray to your Father, who is *u*.
6: 18 who is *u*; and your Father,
2Co 4: 18 on what is seen, but on what is *u*.
4: 18 temporary, but what is *u* is eternal.

UNSETTLED*
1Th 3: 3 so that no one would be *u*
2Th 2: 2 not to become easily *u*

UNSHRUNK
Mt 9: 16 patch of *u* cloth on an old garment,

UNSPIRITUAL*
Ro 7: 14 but I am *u*, sold as a slave to sin.
Col 2: 18 and his *u* mind puffs him up
Jas 3: 15 down from heaven but is earthly, *u*,

UNSTABLE*
Jas 1: 8 he is a double-minded man, *u*
2Pe 2: 14 they seduce the *u*; they are experts
3: 16 ignorant and *u* people distort,

UNTHINKABLE*
Job 34: 12 It is *u* that God would do wrong,

UNTIE
Mk 1: 7 worthy to stoop down and *u*.
Lk 13: 15 each of you on the Sabbath *u* his ox

UNVEILED*
2Co 3: 18 with *u* faces all reflect the Lord's

UNWHOLESOME*
Eph 4: 29 Do not let any *u* talk come out

UNWISE
Eph 5: 15 how you live—not as *u* but as wise,

UNWORTHY*
Ge 32: 10 I am *u* of all the kindness
Job 40: 4 "I am *u*— how can I reply to you?
Lk 17: 10 should say, 'We are *u* servants;
1Co 11: 27 Lord in an *u* manner will be guilty

UPHOLD (UPHOLDS)
Isa 41: 10 I will *u* you with my righteous right
Ro 3: 31 Not at all! Rather, we *u* the law.

UPHOLDS* (UPHOLD)
Ps 37: 17 but the LORD *u* the righteous.
37: 24 for the LORD *u* him with his hand.
63: 8 your right hand *u* me.
140: 12 and *u* the cause of the needy.
145: 14 The LORD *u* all those who fall
146: 7 He *u* the cause of the oppressed

UPRIGHT
Dt 32: 4 *u* and just is he.
Job 1: 1 This man was blameless and *u*;
Ps 7: 10 who saves the *u* in heart.
11: 7 *u* men will see his face.
25: 8 Good and *u* is the LORD;
33: 1 it is fitting for the *u* to praise him.
64: 10 let all the *u* in heart praise him!
92: 15 proclaiming, "The LORD is *u*;
97: 11 and joy on the *u* in heart.
119: 7 I will praise you with an *u* heart
Pr 2: 7 He holds victory in store for the *u*,
3: 32 but takes the *u* into his confidence.
14: 2 whose walk is *u* fears the LORD,
15: 8 but the prayer of the *u* pleases him.
21: 29 an *u* man gives thought to his ways.
Isa 26: 7 O *u* One, you make the way
Tit 1: 8 who is self-controlled, *u*, holy
2: 12 *u* and godly lives in this present

UPROOTED
Dt 28: 63 You will be *u* from the land you are
Jer 31: 40 The city will never again be *u*
Jude : 12 without fruit and *u*— twice dead.

UPSET
Lk 10: 41 are worried and *u* about many

URIAH
Hittite husband of Bathsheba, killed by David's order (2Sa 11).

USEFUL
Eph 4: 28 doing something *u*
2Ti 2: 21 *u* to the Master and prepared
3: 16 Scripture is God-breathed and is *u*
Phm : 11 now he has become *u* both to you

USELESS
1Co 15: 14 our preaching is *u*
Tit 3: 9 these are unprofitable and *u*.
Phm : 11 Formerly he was *u* to you,
Heb 7: 18 *u* (for the law made nothing perfect
Jas 2: 20 faith without deeds is *u*?

USURY
Ne 5: 10 But let the exacting of *u* stop!
Ps 15: 5 who lends his money without *u*

UTMOST
Job 34: 36 that Job might be tested to the *u*

UTTER (UTTERS)
Ps 78: 2 I will *u* hidden things, things from of old—
Mt 13: 35 I will *u* things hidden

UTTERS (UTTER)
1Co 14: 2 he *u* mysteries with his spirit.

UZZIAH
Son of Amaziah; king of Judah also known as Azariah (2Ki 15:1–7; 1Ch 6:24; 2Ch 26). Struck with leprosy because of pride (2Ch 26:16–23).

VAIN
Ps 33: 17 A horse is a *v* hope for deliverance;
73: 13 in *v* have I kept my heart pure;
127: 1 its builders labor in *v*.
Isa 65: 23 They will not toil in *v*
1Co 15: 2 Otherwise, you have believed in *v*.
15: 58 labor in the Lord is not in *v*.
2Co 6: 1 not to receive God's grace in *v*.
Gal 2: 2 running or had run my race in *v*.

VALIANT
1Sa 10: 26 by *v* men whose hearts God had

VALID
Jn 8: 14 my own behalf, my testimony is *v*,

VALLEY (VALLEYS)
Ps 23: 4 walk through the *v* of the shadow
Isa 40: 4 Every *v* shall be raised up,
Joel 3: 14 multitudes in the *v* of decision!

VALLEYS (VALLEY)
SS 2: 1 a lily of the *v*.

VALUABLE (VALUE)
Lk 12: 24 And how much more *v* you are

VALUE (VALUABLE VALUED)
Lev 27: 3 set the *v* of a male between the ages
Pr 16: 13 they *v* a man who speaks the truth.
31: 11 and lacks nothing of *v*.
Mt 13: 46 When he found one of great *v*,
1Ti 4: 8 For physical training is of some *v*,
Heb 11: 26 as of greater *v* than the treasures

VALUED (VALUE)
Lk 16: 15 What is highly *v* among men is

VANISHES
Jas 4: 14 appears for a little while and then *v*.

VASHTI*
Queen of Persia replaced by Esther (Est 1–2).

VAST
Ge 2: 1 completed in all their *v* array.
Dt 1: 19 of the Amorites through all that *v*
8: 15 He led you through the *v*
Ps 139: 17 How *v* is the sum of them!

VEGETABLES
Pr 15: 17 of *v* where there is love
Ro 14: 2 whose faith is weak, eats only *v*.

VEIL
Ex 34: 33 to them, he put a *v* over his face.
2Co 3: 14 for to this day the same *v* remains

VENGEANCE (AVENGE AVENGER AVENGES AVENGING REVENGE)
Nu 31: 3 to carry out the LORD's *v* on them
Isa 34: 8 For the LORD has a day of *v*,
Na 1: 2 The LORD takes *v* on his foes

VERDICT
Jn 3: 19 This is the *v*: Light has come

VICTOR'S* (VICTORY)
2Ti 2: 5 he does not receive the *v* crown

VICTORIES* (VICTORY)
2Sa 22: 51 He gives his king great *v*;
Ps 18: 50 He gives his king great *v*;
21: 1 great is his joy in the *v* you give!
21: 5 Through the *v* you gave, his glory is
44: 4 who decrees *v* for Jacob.

VICTORIOUS (VICTORY)
Ps 20: 5 for joy when you are *v*

VICTORIOUSLY* (VICTORY)
Ps 45: 4 In your majesty ride forth *v*

VICTORY (VICTOR'S VICTORIES VICTORIOUS VICTORIOUSLY)
2Sa 8: 6 gave David *v* wherever he
Ps 44: 6 my sword does not bring me *v*;
60: 12 With God we will gain the *v*,
129: 2 they have not gained the *v* over me.
Pr 11: 14 but many advisers make *v* sure.
1Co 15: 54 "Death has been swallowed up in *v*
15: 57 He gives us the *v* through our Lord
1Jn 5: 4 This is the *v* that has overcome

VIEW
Pr 5: 21 are in full *v* of the LORD,
2Ti 4: 1 and in *v* of his appearing

VILLAGE
Mk 6: 6 went around teaching from *v* to *v*.

VINDICATED (VINDICATION)
Job 13: 18 I know I will be *v*.
1Ti 3: 16 was *v* by the Spirit,

VINDICATION (VINDICATED)
Ps 24: 5 and *v* from God his Savior.

VINE (VINEYARD)
Ps 128: 3 Your wife will be like a fruitful *v*
Isa 36: 16 one of you will eat from his own *v*
Jnh 4: 6 Jonah was very happy about the *v*.
Jn 15: 1 "I am the true *v*, and my Father is

VINEGAR
Pr 10: 26 As *v* to the teeth and smoke
Mk 15: 36 filled a sponge with wine *v*,

VINEYARD (VINE)
1Ki 21: 1 an incident involving a *v* belonging
Pr 31: 16 out of her earnings she plants a *v*.
SS 1: 6 my own *v* I have neglected.
Isa 5: 1 My loved one had a *v*
1Co 9: 7 Who plants a *v* and does not eat

VIOLATION
Heb 2: 2 every *v* and disobedience received

VIOLENCE (VIOLENT)
Ge 6: 11 in God's sight and was full of *v*.
Isa 53: 9 though he had done no *v*,
60: 18 No longer will *v* be heard
Eze 45: 9 Give up your *v* and oppression
Joel 3: 19 of *v* done to the people of Judah,
Jnh 3: 8 give up their evil ways and their *v*.

VIOLENT (VIOLENCE)
Eze 18: 10 "Suppose he has a *v* son, who sheds
1Ti 1: 13 and a persecutor and a *v* man,
3: 3 not *v* but gentle, not quarrelsome,
Tit 1: 7 not *v*, not pursuing dishonest gain.

VIPERS
Ps 140: 3 the poison of *v* is on their lips.
Lk 3: 7 "You brood of *v*! Who warned you
Ro 3: 13 "The poison of *v* is on their lips."

VIRGIN (VIRGINS)
Dt 22: 15 shall bring proof that she was a *v*
Isa 7: 14 The *v* will be with child
Mt 1: 23 "The *v* will be with child
Lk 1: 34 I am a *v*?" The angel answered,
2Co 11: 2 that I might present you as a pure *v*

VIRGINS (VIRGIN)
Mt 25: 1 will be like ten *v* who took their
1Co 7: 25 Now about *v*: I have no command

VIRTUES*
Col 3: 14 And over all these *v* put on love,

VISIBLE
Eph 5: 13 exposed by the light becomes *v*,
Col 1: 16 and on earth, *v* and invisible,

VISION (VISIONS)
Da 9: 24 to seal up *v* and prophecy
Ac 26: 19 disobedient to the *v* from heaven.

VISIONS (VISION)
Nu 12: 6 I reveal myself to him in *v*,
Joel 2: 28 your young men will see *v*.
Ac 2: 17 your young men will see *v*,

VOICE
Dt 30: 20 listen to his *v*, and hold fast to him.
1Sa 15: 22 as in obeying the *v* of the LORD?
Job 40: 9 and can your *v* thunder like his?
Ps 19: 4 Their *v* goes out into all the earth,
29: 3 The *v* of the LORD is
66: 19 and heard my *v* in prayer.
95: 7 Today, if you hear his *v*,
Pr 8: 1 Does not understanding raise her *v*
Isa 30: 21 your ears will hear a *v* behind you,
40: 3 A *v* of one calling:
Mk 1: 3 "a *v* of one calling in the desert,
Jn 5: 28 are in their graves will hear his *v*
10: 3 and the sheep listen to his *v*.
Ro 10: 18 "Their *v* has gone out
Heb 3: 7 "Today, if you hear his *v*,
Rev 3: 20 If anyone hears my *v* and opens

VOMIT
Lev 18: 28 it will *v* you out as it vomited out
Pr 26: 11 As a dog returns to its *v*,
2Pe 2: 22 "A dog returns to its *v*," and,

VOW (VOWS)
Nu 6: 2 a *v* of separation to the LORD
30: 2 When a man makes a *v*
Jdg 11: 30 Jephthah made a *v* to the LORD:

VOWS (VOW)
Ps 116: 14 I will fulfill my *v* to the LORD
Pr 20: 25 and only later to consider his *v*.

VULTURES
Mt 24: 28 is a carcass, there the *v* will gather.

WAGE (WAGES WAGING)
2Co 10: 3 we do not *w* war as the world does.

WAGES (WAGE)
Mal 3: 5 who defraud laborers of their *w*,
Lk 10: 7 for the worker deserves his *w*.
Ro 4: 4 his *w* are not credited to him
6: 23 For the *w* of sin is death,
1Ti 5: 18 and "The worker deserves his *w*."

WAGING (WAGE)
Ro 7: 23 *w* war against the law of my mind

WAILING
Ps 30: 11 You turned my *w* into dancing;

WAIST
2Ki 1: 8 and with a leather belt around his *w*."
Mt 3: 4 he had a leather belt around his *w*.

WAIT (AWAITS WAITED WAITING WAITS)
Ps 27: 14 *W* for the LORD;
130: 5 I *w* for the LORD, my soul waits,
Isa 30: 18 Blessed are all who *w* for him!
Ac 1: 4 *w* for the gift my Father promised,
Ro 8: 23 as we *w* eagerly for our adoption
1Th 1: 10 and to *w* for his Son from heaven,
Tit 2: 13 while we *w* for the blessed hope—

WAITED (WAIT)
Ps 40: 1 I *w* patiently for the LORD;

WAITING (WAIT)
Heb 9: 28 to those who are *w* for him.

WAITS (WAIT)
Ro 8: 19 creation *w* in eager expectation

WAKE (AWAKE WAKENS)
Eph 5: 14 "*W* up, O sleeper,

WAKENS* (WAKE)
Isa 50: 4 He *w* me morning by morning,
50: 4 *w* my ear to listen like one being

WALK (WALKED WALKING WALKS)
Lev 26: 12 I will *w* among you and be your
Dt 5: 33 *W* in all the way that the LORD
6: 7 and when you *w* along the road,
10: 12 to *w* in all his ways, to love him,
11: 19 and when you *w* along the road,
11: 22 to *w* in all his ways and to hold fast
26: 17 and that you will *w* in his ways,
Jos 22: 5 to *w* in all his ways,
Ps 1: 1 who does not *w* in the counsel
15: 2 He whose *w* is blameless
23: 4 Even though I *w*
84: 11 from those whose *w* is blameless.

89: 15 who *w* in the light of your presence
119: 45 I will *w* about in freedom,
Pr 4: 12 When you *w*, your steps will not be
6: 22 When you *w*, they will guide you;
Isa 2: 3 so that we may *w* in his paths."
2: 5 let us *w* in the light of the LORD.
30: 21 saying, "This is the way; *w* in it."
40: 31 they will *w* and not be faint.
57: 2 Those who *w* uprightly
Jer 6: 16 ask where the good way is, and *w*
Da 4: 37 And those who *w* in pride he is able
Am 3: 3 Do two *w* together
Mic 4: 5 All the nations may *w*
6: 8 and to *w* humbly with your God.
Mk 2: 9 'Get up, take your mat and *w*'?
Jn 8: 12 Whoever follows me will never *w*
1Jn 1: 6 with him yet *w* in the darkness,
1: 7 But if we *w* in the light,
2Jn : 6 his command is that you *w* in love.

WALKED (WALK)
Ge 5: 24 Enoch *w* with God; then he was no
Jos 14: 9 which your feet have *w* will be your
Mt 14: 29 *w* on the water and came toward Jesus.

WALKING (WALK)
1Ki 3: 3 love for the LORD by *w* according
Da 3: 25 I see four men *w* around in the fire,
2Jn : 4 of your children *w* in the truth,

WALKS (WALK)
Pr 10: 9 The man of integrity *w* securely,
13: 20 He who *w* with the wise grows wise
Isa 33: 15 He who *w* righteously
Jn 11: 9 A man who *w* by day will not

WALL (WALLS)
Jos 6: 20 *w* collapsed; so every man charged
Ne 2: 17 let us rebuild the *w* of Jerusalem,
Eph 2: 14 the dividing *w* of hostility,
Rev 21: 12 It had a great, high *w*

WALLOWING
2Pe 2: 22 back to her *w* in the mud."

WALLS (WALL)
Isa 58: 12 be called Repairer of Broken *W*,
60: 18 but you will call your *w* Salvation
Heb 11: 30 By faith the *w* of Jericho fell,

WANDER (WANDERED)
Nu 32: 13 he made them *w* in the desert forty
Jas 5: 19 one of you should *w* from the truth

WANDERED (WANDER)
Eze 34: 6 My sheep *w* over all the mountains
Mt 18: 12 go to look for the one that *w* off?
1Ti 6: 10 have *w* from the faith and pierced
2Ti 2: 18 who have *w* away from the truth.

WANT (WANTED WANTING WANTS)
1Sa 8: 19 "We *w* a king over us.
Mt 19: 21 Jesus answered, "If you *w*
Lk 19: 14 'We don't *w* this man to be our king
Ro 7: 15 For what I *w* to do I do not do,
13: 3 Do you *w* to be free from fear
2Co 12: 14 what I *w* is not your possessions
Php 3: 10 I *w* to know Christ and the power

WANTED (WANT)
1Co 12: 18 of them, just as he *w* them to be.
Heb 6: 17 Because God *w* to make

WANTING (WANT)
Da 5: 27 weighed on the scales and found *w*.
2Pe 3: 9 with you, not *w* anyone to perish,

WANTS (WANT)
Mt 5: 42 from the one who *w* to borrow
20: 26 whoever *w* to become great
Mk 8: 35 For whoever *w* to save his life will
10: 43 whoever *w* to become great
Ro 9: 18 he hardens whom he *w* to harden.
1Ti 2: 4 who *w* all men to be saved
1Pe 5: 2 you are willing, as God *w* you to be;

WAR (WARRIOR WARS)
Jos 11: 23 Then the land had rest from *w*.
1Sa 15: 18 make *w* on them until you have
Ps 68: 30 the nations who delight in *w*.
120: 7 but when I speak, they are for *w*.
144: 1 who trains my hands for *w*,
Isa 2: 4 nor will they train for *w* anymore.
Da 9: 26 *W* will continue until the end,
Ro 7: 23 waging *w* against the law
2Co 10: 3 we do not wage *w* as the world does
1Pe 2: 11 which *w* against your soul.
Rev 12: 7 And there was *w* in heaven.
19: 11 With justice he judges and makes *w*

WARN* (WARNED WARNING WARNINGS)
Ex 19: 21 *w* the people so they do not force
Nu 24: 14 let me *w* you of what this people
1Sa 8: 9 but *w* them solemnly and let them
1Ki 2: 42 swear by the LORD and *w* you,
2Ch 19: 10 you are to *w* them not to sin
Ps 81: 8 O my people, and I will *w* you—
Jer 42: 19 I *w* you today that you made a fatal
Eze 3: 18 and you do not *w* him or speak out
3: 19 But if you do *w* the wicked man
3: 20 Since you did not *w* him, he will die
3: 21 if you do *w* the righteous man not
33: 3 blows the trumpet to *w* the people,
33: 6 blow the trumpet to *w* the people
33: 9 if you do *w* the wicked man to turn
Lk 16: 28 Let him *w* them, so that they will
Ac 4: 17 we must *w* these men
1Co 4: 14 but to *w* you, as my dear children.
Gal 5: 21 I *w* you, as I did before, that those
1Th 5: 14 brothers, *w* those who are idle,
2Th 3: 15 an enemy, but *w* him as a brother.
2Ti 2: 14 *W* them before God
Tit 3: 10 and then *w* him a second time.
3: 10 *W* a divisive person once,
Rev 22: 18 I *w* everyone who hears the words

WARNED (WARN)
2Ki 17: 13 The LORD *w* Israel and Judah
Ps 19: 11 By them is your servant *w*;
Jer 22: 21 I *w* you when you felt secure,
Mt 3: 7 Who *w* you to flee
1Th 4: 6 have already told you and *w* you.
Heb 11: 7 when *w* about things not yet seen,
12: 25 they refused him who *w* them

WARNING (WARN)
Jer 6: 8 Take *w*, O Jerusalem,
1Ti 5: 20 so that the others may take *w*.

WARNINGS (WARN)
1Co 10: 11 and were written down as *w* for us,

WARRIOR (WAR)
Ex 15: 3 The LORD is a *w*;
1Ch 28: 3 you are a *w* and have shed blood.'
Pr 16: 32 Better a patient man than a *w*,

WARS (WAR)
Ps 46: 9 He makes *w* cease to the ends
Mt 24: 6 You will hear of *w* and rumors of *w*,

WASH (WASHED WASHING)
Ps 51: 7 *w* me, and I will be whiter
Jer 4: 14 *w* the evil from your heart
Jn 13: 5 and began to *w* his disciples' feet,
Ac 22: 16 be baptized and *w* your sins away,
Jas 4: 8 *W* your hands, you sinners,
Rev 22: 14 Blessed are those who *w* their robes

WASHED (WASH)
Ps 73: 13 in vain have I *w* my hands
1Co 6: 11 you were *w*, you were sanctified,
Heb 10: 22 and having our bodies *w*
2Pe 2: 22 and, "A sow that is *w* goes back
Rev 7: 14 they have *w* their robes

WASHING (WASH)
Eph 5: 26 cleansing her by the *w* with water
1Ti 5: 10 showing hospitality, *w* the feet
Tit 3: 5 us through the *w* of rebirth

WASTED (WASTING)
Jn 6: 12 Let nothing be *w*."

WASTING (WASTED)
2Co 4: 16 Though outwardly we are *w* away,

WATCH (WATCHER WATCHES WATCHING WATCHMAN)
Ge 31: 49 "May the LORD keep *w*
Ps 90: 4 or like a *w* in the night.
141: 3 keep *w* over the door of my lips.
Pr 4: 6 love her, and she will *w* over you.
6: 22 when you sleep, they will *w*
Jer 31: 10 will *w* over his flock like a shepherd
Mic 7: 7 I *w* in hope for the LORD,
Mt 24: 42 "Therefore keep *w*, because you do
26: 41 *W* and pray so that you will not fall
Mk 13: 35 "Therefore keep *w* because you do
Lk 2: 8 keeping *w* over their flocks at night
1Ti 4: 16 *W* your life and doctrine closely.
Heb 13: 17 They keep *w* over you

WATCHER* (WATCH)
Job 7: 20 O *w* of men?

WATCHES* (WATCH)
Nu 19: 5 While he *w*, the heifer is
Job 24: 15 The eye of the adulterer *w* for dusk;
Ps 1: 6 For the LORD *w* over the way
33: 14 from his dwelling place he *w*
63: 6 of you through the *w* of the night.
119:148 through the *w* of the night,
121: 3 he who *w* over you will not slumber
121: 4 indeed, he who *w* over Israel
121: 5 The LORD *w* over you—
127: 1 Unless the LORD *w* over the city,
145: 20 LORD *w* over all who love him,
146: 9 The LORD *w* over the alien
Pr 31: 27 She *w* over the affairs
Ecc 11: 4 Whoever *w* the wind will not plant;
La 2: 19 as the *w* of the night begin;
4: 16 he no longer *w* over them.

WATCHING (WATCH)
Lk 12: 37 whose master finds them *w*

WATCHMAN (WATCH)
Eze 3: 17 I have made you a *w* for the house
33: 6 but I will hold the *w* accountable

WATER (WATERED WATERING WATERS WELL-WATERED)
Ex 7: 20 all the *w* was changed into blood.
17: 1 but there was no *w* for the people
Nu 20: 2 there was no *w* for the community,
Ps 1: 3 like a tree planted by streams of *w*,
22: 14 I am poured out like *w*,
42: 1 As the deer pants for streams of *w*,
Pr 25: 21 if he is thirsty, give him *w* to drink.
Isa 12: 3 With joy you will draw *w*
30: 20 of adversity and the *w* of affliction,
32: 2 like streams of *w* in the desert
49: 10 and lead them beside springs of *w*.
Jer 2: 13 broken cisterns that cannot hold *w*.
17: 8 will be like a tree planted by the *w*
31: 9 I will lead them beside streams of *w*
Eze 36: 25 I will sprinkle clean *w* on you,
Zec 14: 8 On that day living *w* will flow out
Mt 14: 29 walked on the *w* and came toward Jesus.
Mk 9: 41 anyone who gives you a cup of *w*
Lk 5: 4 to Simon, "Put out into deep *w*,
Jn 3: 5 unless he is born of *w* and the Spirit.
4: 10 he would have given you living *w*."
7: 38 streams of living *w* will flow
Eph 5: 26 washing with *w* through the word,
Heb 10: 22 our bodies washed with pure *w*.
1Pe 3: 21 this *w* symbolizes baptism that now
2Pe 2: 17 These men are springs without *w*
1Jn 5: 6 This is the one who came by *w*
5: 6 come by *w* only, but by *w*
5: 8 the Spirit, the *w* and the blood;
Rev 7: 17 to springs of living *w*.
21: 6 cost from the spring of the *w* of life.

WATERED (WATER)
1Co 3: 6 I planted the seed, Apollos *w* it,

WATERING (WATER)
Isa 55: 10 it without *w* the earth

WATERS (WATER)
Ps 23: 2 he leads me beside quiet *w*,
Ecc 11: 1 Cast your bread upon the *w*,
SS 8: 7 Many *w* cannot quench love;
Isa 11: 9 as the *w* cover the sea.
43: 2 When you pass through the *w*,
55: 1 come to the *w*;
58: 11 like a spring whose *w* never fail.
Hab 2: 14 as the *w* cover the sea.
1Co 3: 7 plants nor he who *w* is anything,

WAVE (WAVES)
Lev 23: 11 He is to *w* the sheaf
Jas 1: 6 he who doubts is like a *w* of the sea,

WAVER*
1Ki 18: 21 "How long will you *w*
Ro 4: 20 Yet he did not *w* through unbelief

WAVES (WAVE)
Isa 57: 20 whose *w* cast up mire and mud.
Mt 8: 27 Even the winds and the *w* obey him
Eph 4: 14 tossed back and forth by the *w*,

WAY (WAYS)
Ex 13: 21 of cloud to guide them on their *w*
18: 20 and show them the *w* to live
Dt 1: 33 to show you the *w* you should go.
32: 6 Is this the *w* you repay the LORD,
1Sa 12: 23 I will teach you the *w* that is good
2Sa 22: 31 "As for God, his *w* is perfect;
1Ki 8: 23 wholeheartedly in your *w*.
8: 36 Teach them the right *w* to live,
Job 23: 10 But he knows the *w* that I take;
Ps 1: 1 or stand in the *w* of sinners
32: 8 teach you in the *w* you should go;
37: 5 Commit your *w* to the LORD;
86: 11 Teach me your *w*, O LORD,
119: 9 can a young man keep his *w* pure?
139: 24 See if there is any offensive *w* in me
Pr 4: 11 I guide you in the *w* of wisdom
12: 15 The *w* of a fool seems right to him,
14: 12 There is a *w* that seems right
16: 17 he who guards his *w* guards his life.
19: 2 nor to be hasty and miss the *w*.
22: 6 Train a child in the *w* he should go,
30: 19 and the *w* of a man with a maiden.
Isa 30: 21 saying, "This is the *w*; walk in it."
35: 8 it will be called the *W* of Holiness.
40: 3 the *w* for the LORD;
48: 17 you in the *w* you should go.
53: 6 each of us has turned to his own *w*;
55: 7 Let the wicked forsake his *w*
Jer 5: 31 and my people love it this *w*.
Mal 3: 1 who will prepare the *w* before me.
Mt 3: 3 'Prepare the *w* for the Lord,
Lk 7: 27 who will prepare your *w* before you
Jn 14: 6 "I am the *w* and the truth
Ac 1: 11 in the same *w* you have seen him go
9: 2 any there who belonged to the *W*,
24: 14 of the *W*, which they call a sect.
1Co 10: 13 also provide a *w* out so that you can
12: 31 will show you the most excellent *w*.
14: 1 Follow the *w* of love and eagerly
Col 1: 10 and may please him in every *w*:
Tit 2: 10 that in every *w* they will make
Heb 4: 15 who has been tempted in every *w*,
9: 8 was showing by this that the *w*
10: 20 and living *w* opened for us
13: 18 desire to live honorably in every *w*.

WAYS (WAY)
Ex 33: 13 teach me your *w* so I may know
Dt 10: 12 to walk in all his *w*, to love him,
26: 17 and that you will walk in his *w*,
30: 16 in his *w*, and to keep his commands
32: 4 and all his *w* are just.
Jos 22: 5 in all his *w*, to obey his commands,
2Ch 11: 17 walking in the *w* of David
Job 34: 21 "His eyes are on the *w* of men;
Ps 25: 4 Show me your *w*, O LORD,
25: 10 All the *w* of the LORD are loving
37: 7 fret when men succeed in their *w*,
51: 13 I will teach transgressors your *w*,
77: 13 Your *w*, O God, are holy.
119: 59 I have considered my *w*
139: 3 you are familiar with all my *w*.
145: 17 The LORD is righteous in all his *w*
Pr 3: 6 in all your *w* acknowledge him,
4: 26 and take only *w* that are firm.
5: 21 For a man's *w* are in full view
16: 2 All a man's *w* seem innocent
16: 7 When a man's *w* are pleasing
Isa 2: 3 He will teach us his *w*,
55: 8 neither are your *w* my *w*,"
Eze 28: 15 You were blameless in your *w*
33: 8 out to dissuade him from his *w*,
Hos 14: 9 The *w* of the LORD are right;
Ro 1: 30 they invent *w* of doing evil;
Jas 3: 2 We all stumble in many *w*.

WEAK (WEAKER WEAKNESS WEAKNESSES)
Ps 41: 1 is he who has regard for the *w*;
72: 13 He will take pity on the *w*
82: 3 Defend the cause of the *w*
Eze 34: 4 You have not strengthened the *w*
Mt 26: 41 spirit is willing, but the body is *w*."
Ac 20: 35 of hard work we must help the *w*,
Ro 14: 1 Accept him whose faith is *w*,
15: 1 to bear with the failings of the *w*
1Co 1: 27 God chose the *w* things
8: 9 become a stumbling block to the *w*.
9: 22 To the *w* I became *w*, to win the *w*.
11: 30 That is why many among you are *w*
2Co 12: 10 For when I am *w*, then I am strong.
1Th 5: 14 help the *w*, be patient
Heb 12: 12 your feeble arms and *w* knees.

WEAK-WILLED (WILL)
2Ti 3: 6 and gain control over *w* women,

WEAKER* (WEAK)
2Sa 3: 1 the house of Saul grew *w* and *w*.
1Co 12: 22 seem to be *w* are indispensable,
1Pe 3: 7 them with respect as the *w* partner

WEAKNESS* (WEAK)
La 1: 6 in *w* they have fled
Ro 8: 26 the Spirit helps us in our *w*.
1Co 1: 25 and the *w* of God is stronger
2: 3 I came to you in *w* and fear,
15: 43 it is sown in *w*, it is raised in power;
2Co 11: 30 boast of the things that show my *w*.
12: 9 for my power is made perfect in *w*
13: 4 he was crucified in *w*, yet he lives
Heb 5: 2 since he himself is subject to *w*.
11: 34 whose *w* was turned to strength;

WEAKNESSES* (WEAK)
2Co 12: 5 about myself, except about my *w*.
12: 9 all the more gladly about my *w*,
12: 10 I delight in *w*, in insults,
Heb 4: 15 unable to sympathize with our *w*,

WEALTH
Dt 8: 18 gives you the ability to produce *w*,
2Ch 1: 11 and you have not asked for *w*,
Ps 39: 6 he heaps up *w*, not knowing who
Pr 3: 9 Honor the LORD with your *w*,
10: 4 but diligent hands bring *w*.
11: 4 *W* is worthless in the day of wrath,
13: 7 to be poor, yet has great *w*.
15: 16 than great *w* with turmoil.
22: 4 bring *w* and honor and life.
Ecc 5: 10 whoever loves *w* is never satisfied
5: 13 *w* hoarded to the harm of its owner,
SS 8: 7 all the *w* of his house for love,
Mt 13: 22 and the deceitfulness of *w* choke it,
Mk 10: 22 away sad, because he had great *w*.
12: 44 They all gave out of their *w*; but she
Lk 15: 13 and there squandered his *w*
1Ti 6: 17 nor to put their hope in *w*,
Jas 5: 2 Your *w* has rotted, and moths have
5: 3 You have hoarded *w*

WEAPON (WEAPONS)
Ne 4: 17 work with one hand and held a *w*

WEAPONS (WEAPON)
Ecc 9: 18 Wisdom is better than *w* of war,
2Co 6: 7 with *w* of righteousness
10: 4 The *w* we fight with are not

WEAR (WEARING)
Dt 8: 4 Your clothes did not *w* out
22: 5 nor a man *w* women's clothing,
Ps 102: 26 they will all *w* out like a garment.
Pr 23: 4 Do not *w* yourself out to get rich;
Isa 51: 6 the earth will *w* out like a garment
Heb 1: 11 they will all *w* out like a garment.
Rev 3: 18 and white clothes to *w*,

WEARIES (WEARY)
Ecc 12: 12 and much study *w* the body.

WEARING (WEAR)
Jn 19: 5 When Jesus came out *w* the crown
Jas 2: 3 attention to the man *w* fine clothes
1Pe 3: 3 as braided hair and the *w*
Rev 7: 9 They were *w* white robes

WEARY (WEARIES)
Isa 40: 28 He will not grow tired or *w*,
40: 31 they will run and not grow *w*,
50: 4 know the word that sustains the *w*.
Mt 11: 28 all you who are *w* and burdened,
Gal 6: 9 Let us not become *w* in doing good,
Heb 12: 3 so that you will not grow *w*
Rev 2: 3 my name, and have not grown *w*.

WEDDING
Mt 22: 11 who was not wearing *w* clothes.
Rev 19: 7 For the *w* of the Lamb has come,

WEEDS
Mt 13: 25 and sowed *w* among the wheat,

WEEK
Mt 28: 1 at dawn on the first day of the *w*,
1Co 16: 2 On the first day of every *w*,

WEEP (WEEPING WEPT)
Ecc 3: 4 a time to *w* and a time to laugh,
Lk 6: 21 Blessed are you who *w* now,
23: 28 *w* for yourselves and for your

WEEPING (WEEP)
Ps 30: 5 *w* may remain for a night,
126: 6 He who goes out *w*,
Jer 31: 15 Rachel *w* for her children
Mt 2: 18 Rachel *w* for her children
8: 12 where there will be *w* and gnashing

WEIGH (OUTWEIGHS WEIGHED WEIGHS WEIGHTIER WEIGHTS)
1Co 14: 29 others should *w* carefully what is

WEIGHED (WEIGH)
Job 28: 15 nor can its price be *w* in silver.
Da 5: 27 You have been *w* on the scales
Lk 21: 34 or your hearts will be *w*

WEIGHS (WEIGH)
Pr 12: 25 An anxious heart *w* a man down,
15: 28 of the righteous *w* its answers,
21: 2 but the LORD *w* the heart.
24: 12 not he who *w* the heart perceive

WEIGHTIER* (WEIGH)
Jn 5: 36 "I have testimony *w* than that

WEIGHTS (WEIGH)
Lev 19: 36 Use honest scales and honest *w*,
Dt 25: 13 Do not have two differing *w*
Pr 11: 1 but accurate *w* are his delight.

WELCOME (WELCOMES)
Mk 9: 37 welcomes me does not *w* me
2Pe 1: 11 and you will receive a rich *w*

WELCOMES (WELCOME)
Mt 18: 5 whoever *w* a little child like this
2Jn : 11 Anyone who *w* him shares

WELL (WELLED WELLING WELLS)
Mt 15: 31 crippled made *w*, the lame walking
Lk 14: 5 falls into a *w* on the Sabbath day,
17: 19 your faith has made you *w*."
Jas 5: 15 in faith will make the sick person *w*

WELL-WATERED (WATER)
Isa 58: 11 You will be like a w garden,

WELLED* (WELL)
2Co 8: 2 and their extreme poverty w up

WELLING* (WELL)
Jn 4: 14 of water w up to eternal life."

WELLS (WELL)
Isa 12: 3 from the w of salvation.

WELLSPRING* (SPRING)
Pr 4: 23 for it is the w of life.

WEPT (WEEP)
Ps 137: 1 of Babylon we sat and w
Lk 22: 62 And he went outside and w bitterly
Jn 11: 35 Jesus w.

WEST
Ps 103: 12 as far as the east is from the w,
107: 3 from east and w, from north

WHEAT
Mt 3: 12 gathering his w into the barn
13: 25 and sowed weeds among the w,
Lk 22: 31 Satan has asked to sift you as w.
Jn 12: 24 a kernel of w falls to the ground

WHEELS
Eze 1: 16 appearance and structure of the w:

WHIRLWIND (WIND)
2Ki 2: 1 to take Elijah up to heaven in a w,
Hos 8: 7 and reap the w.
Na 1: 3 His way is in the w and the storm,

WHISPER (WHISPERED)
1Ki 19: 12 And after the fire came a gentle w.
Job 26: 14 how faint the w we hear of him!
Ps 107: 29 He stilled the storm to a w;

WHISPERED (WHISPER)
Mt 10: 27 speak in the daylight; what is w

WHITE (WHITER)
Isa 1: 18 they shall be as w as snow;
Da 7: 9 His clothing was as w as snow;
7: 9 the hair of his head was w like wool
Mt 28: 3 and his clothes were w as snow.
Rev 1: 14 hair were w like wool, as w as snow,
3: 4 dressed in w, for they are worthy.
6: 2 and there before me was a w horse!
7: 13 "These in w robes—who are they,
19: 11 and there before me was a w horse,
20: 11 Then I saw a great w throne

WHITER (WHITE)
Ps 51: 7 and I will be w than snow.

WHOLE
Ge 1: 29 plant on the face of the w earth
2: 6 and watered the w surface
11: 1 Now the w world had one language
Ex 12: 47 The w community
19: 5 Although the w earth is mine,
Lev 16: 17 and the w community of Israel.
Nu 14: 21 of the LORD fills the w earth,
32: 13 until the w generation
Dt 13: 16 w burnt offering to the LORD your
19: 8 gives you the w land he promised
Jos 2: 3 come to spy out the w land."
1Sa 1: 28 For his w life he will be given
17: 46 the w world will know that there is
1Ki 10: 24 The w world sought audience
2Ki 21: 8 and will keep the w Law that my
Ps 72: 19 may the w earth be filled
Pr 4: 22 and health to a man's w body.
8: 31 rejoicing in his w world
Ecc 12: 13 for this is the w duty of man.
Isa 1: 5 Your w head is injured,
6: 3 the w earth is full of his glory."
14: 26 plan determined for the w world;
Eze 34: 6 were scattered over the w earth,
37: 11 these bones are the w house
Da 2: 35 mountain and filled the w earth.
Zep 1: 18 the w world will be consumed,
Zec 14: 9 will be king over the w earth.
Mal 3: 10 the w tithe into the storehouse,
Mt 5: 29 than for your w body to be thrown
6: 22 your w body will be full of light.
16: 26 for a man if he gains the w world,
24: 14 will be preached in the w world
Lk 21: 35 live on the face of the w earth.
Jn 12: 19 Look how the w world has gone
13: 10 to wash his feet; his w body is clean
21: 25 the w world would not have room
Ac 17: 26 they should inhabit the w earth;
20: 27 proclaim to you the w will of God.
Ro 1: 9 whom I serve with my w heart
3: 19 and the w world held accountable
8: 22 know that the w creation has been
1Co 4: 9 made a spectacle to the w universe,
12: 17 If the w body were an ear,
Gal 3: 22 declares that the w world is
5: 3 obligated to obey the w law.
Eph 4: 10 in order to fill the w universe.)
4: 13 attaining to the w measure
1Th 5: 23 May your w spirit, soul
Jas 2: 10 For whoever keeps the w law
1Jn 2: 2 but also for the sins of the w world.
Rev 3: 10 going to come upon the w world

WHOLEHEARTED* (HEART)
2Ki 20: 3 you faithfully and with w devotion
1Ch 28: 9 and serve him with w devotion
29: 19 my son Solomon the w devotion
Isa 38: 3 you faithfully and with w devotion

WHOLEHEARTEDLY* (HEART)
Nu 14: 24 a different spirit and follows me w,
32: 11 they have not followed me w,
32: 12 for they followed the LORD w.'
Dt 1: 36 because he followed the LORD w
Jos 14: 8 followed the LORD my God w.
14: 9 followed the LORD my God w.'
14: 14 the LORD, the God of Israel, w.
1Ki 8: 23 with your servants who continue w
1Ch 29: 9 for they had given freely and w
2Ch 6: 14 with your servants who continue w
15: 15 oath because they had sworn it w.
19: 9 and w in the fear of the LORD.
25: 2 in the eyes of the LORD, but not w
31: 21 he sought his God and worked w.
Ro 6: 17 you w obeyed the form of teaching
Eph 6: 7 Serve w, as if you were serving

WHOLESOME*
2Ki 2: 22 And the water has remained w
2Pe 3: 1 to stimulate you to w thinking.

WICK
Isa 42: 3 a smoldering w he will not snuff out
Mt 12: 20 a smoldering w he will not snuff out

WICKED (WICKEDNESS)
Ge 13: 13 Now the men of Sodom were w
39: 9 How then could I do such a w thing
Ex 23: 1 Do not help a w man
Nu 14: 35 things to this whole w community,
Dt 15: 9 not to harbor this w thought:
Jdg 19: 22 some of the w men
1Sa 2: 12 Eli's sons were w men; they had no
15: 18 completely destroy those w people,
25: 17 He is such a w man that no one can
2Sa 13: 12 in Israel! Don't do this w thing.
2Ki 17: 11 They did w things that provoked
2Ch 7: 14 and turn from their w ways,
19: 2 "Should you help the w
Ne 13: 17 "What is this w thing you are doing
Ps 1: 1 walk in the counsel of the w
1: 5 Therefore the w will not stand
7: 9 to an end the violence of the w
10: 13 Why does the w man revile God?
11: 5 the w and those who love violence
12: 8 The w freely strut about
26: 5 and refuse to sit with the w.
32: 10 Many are the woes of the w,
36: 1 concerning the sinfulness of the w:
37: 13 but the Lord laughs at the w,
49: 5 when w deceivers surround me—
50: 16 But to the w, God says:
58: 3 Even from birth the w go astray;
73: 3 when I saw the prosperity of the w.
82: 2 and show partiality to the w? *Selah*
112: 10 the longings of the w will come
119: 61 Though the w bind me with ropes,
119:155 Salvation is far from the w,
140: 8 do not grant the w their desires,
141: 10 Let the w fall into their own nets,
146: 9 but he frustrates the ways of the w.
Pr 2: 12 you from the ways of w men,
4: 14 Do not set foot on the path of the w
6: 18 a heart that devises w schemes,
9: 7 whoever rebukes a w man incurs
10: 20 the heart of the w is of little value.
10: 28 the hopes of the w come to nothing
11: 5 w are brought down by their own
11: 10 when the w perish, there are shouts
11: 21 The w will not go unpunished,
12: 5 but the advice of the w is deceitful.
12: 10 the kindest acts of the w are cruel.
14: 19 the w at the gates of the righteous.
15: 3 keeping watch on the w
15: 26 detests the thoughts of the w,
21: 10 The w man craves evil;
21: 29 A w man puts up a bold front,
28: 1 w man flees though no one pursues,
28: 4 who forsake the law praise the w,
29: 7 but the w have no such concern.
29: 16 When the w thrive, so does sin,
29: 27 the w detest the upright.
Isa 11: 4 breath of his lips he will slay the w.
13: 11 the w for their sins.
26: 10 Though grace is shown to the w,
48: 22 says the LORD, "for the w."
53: 9 He was assigned a grave with the w
55: 7 Let the w forsake his way
57: 20 But the w are like the tossing sea,
Jer 35: 15 of you must turn from your w ways
Eze 3: 18 that w man will die for his sin,
13: 22 you encouraged the w not to turn
14: 7 and puts a w stumbling block
18: 21 "But if a w man turns away
18: 23 pleasure in the death of the w?
21: 25 " 'O profane and w prince of Israel,
33: 8 When I say to the w, 'O w man,
33: 11 pleasure in the death of the w,
33: 14 to the w man, 'You will surely die,'
33: 19 And if a w man turns away
Da 12: 10 but the w will continue to be w.
Mt 12: 39 w and adulterous generation asks
12: 45 be with this w generation."
12: 45 with it seven other spirits more w
Lk 6: 35 he is kind to the ungrateful and w.
Ac 2: 23 and you, with the help of w men,
Ro 4: 5 but trusts God who justifies the w,
1Co 5: 13 "Expel the w man from among you
6: 9 not know that the w will not inherit
Rev 2: 2 that you cannot tolerate w men,

WICKEDNESS (WICKED)
Ge 6: 5 The LORD saw how great man's w
Ex 34: 7 and forgiving w, rebellion and sin.
Lev 16: 21 and confess over it all the w
19: 29 to prostitution and be filled with w.
Dt 9: 4 it is on account of the w
Ne 9: 2 and confessed their sins and the w
Ps 45: 7 You love righteousness and hate w;
92: 15 he is my Rock, and there is no w
Pr 13: 6 but w overthrows the sinner.
Jer 3: 2 land with your prostitution and w.
8: 6 No one repents of his w,
14: 20 O LORD, we acknowledge our w
Eze 18: 20 the w of the wicked will be charged
28: 15 created till w was found in you.
33: 19 wicked man turns away from his w
Da 4: 27 and your w by being kind
9: 24 to atone for w, to bring
Jnh 1: 2 its w has come up before me."
Mt 24: 12 Because of the increase of w,
Lk 11: 39 inside you are full of greed and w.

Ac 1: 18 (With the reward he got for his *w,*
Ro 1: 18 who suppress the truth by their *w,*
1Co 5: 8 the yeast of malice and *w,*
2Co 6: 14 what do righteousness and *w* have
2Ti 2: 19 of the Lord must turn away from *w*
Tit 2: 14 for us to redeem us from all *w*
Heb 1: 9 loved righteousness and hated *w;*
8: 12 For I will forgive their *w*
2Pe 2: 15 who loved the wages of *w.*

WIDE
Ps 81: 10 Open *w* your mouth and I will fill it
Isa 54: 2 stretch your tent curtains *w,*
Mt 7: 13 For *w* is the gate and broad is
2Co 6: 13 my children—open *w* your hearts
Eph 3: 18 to grasp how *w* and long and high

WIDOW (WIDOWS)
Ex 22: 22 "Do not take advantage of a *w*
Dt 10: 18 cause of the fatherless and the *w,*
Ps 146: 9 sustains the fatherless and the *w,*
Isa 1: 17 plead the case of the *w.*
Lk 21: 2 saw a poor *w* put in two very small
1Ti 5: 4 But if a *w* has children

WIDOWS (WIDOW)
Ps 68: 5 to the fatherless, a defender of *w,*
Ac 6: 1 their *w* were being overlooked
1Co 7: 8 to the unmarried and the *w* I say:
1Ti 5: 3 to those *w* who are really
Jas 1: 27 look after orphans and *w*

WIFE (WIVES WIVES')
Ge 2: 24 and mother and be united to his *w,*
19: 26 But Lot's *w* looked back,
24: 67 she became his *w,* and he loved her;
Ex 20: 17 shall not covet your neighbor's *w,*
Lev 20: 10 adultery with another man's *w*—
Dt 5: 21 shall not covet your neighbor's *w.*
24: 5 happiness to the *w* he has married.
Ru 4: 13 took Ruth and she became his *w.*
Pr 5: 18 in the *w* of your youth.
12: 4 *w* of noble character is her
18: 22 He who finds a *w* finds what is
19: 13 quarrelsome *w* is like a constant
31: 10 *w* of noble character who can find?
Hos 1: 2 take to yourself an adulterous *w*
Mal 2: 14 the witness between you and the *w*
Mt 1: 20 to take Mary home as your *w,*
19: 3 for a man to divorce his *w* for any
Lk 17: 32 Remember Lot's *w!* Whoever tries
18: 29 or *w* or brothers or parents
1Co 7: 2 each man should have his own *w,*
7: 33 how he can please his *w*—
Eph 5: 23 the husband is the head of the *w*
5: 33 must love his *w* as he loves himself,
1Ti 3: 2 husband of but one *w,* temperate,
Rev 21: 9 I will show you the bride, the *w*

WILD
Ge 1: 25 God made the *w* animals according
8: 1 Noah and all the *w* animals
Lk 15: 13 squandered his wealth in *w* living.
Ro 11: 17 and you, though a *w* olive shoot,

WILL (WEAK-WILLED WILLFUL WILLING WILLINGNESS)
Ps 40: 8 I desire to do your *w,* O my God;
143: 10 Teach me to do your *w,*
Isa 53: 10 Yet it was the LORD's *w*
Mt 6: 10 your *w* be done
7: 21 who does the *w* of my Father
10: 29 apart from the *w* of your Father.
12: 50 does the *w* of my Father
26: 39 Yet not as I *w,* but as you *w.*"
26: 42 I drink it, may your *w* be done."
Jn 6: 38 but to do the *w* of him who sent me.
7: 17 If anyone chooses to do God's *w,*
Ac 20: 27 to you the whole *w* of God.
Ro 12: 2 and approve what God's *w* is—
1Co 7: 37 but has control over his own *w,*
Eph 5: 17 understand what the Lord's *w* is.
Php 2: 13 for it is God who works in you to *w*
1Th 4: 3 God's *w* that you should be sanctified:
5: 18 for this is God's *w* for you
2Ti 2: 26 has taken them captive to do his *w.*
Heb 2: 4 distributed according to his *w.*
9: 16 In the case of a *w,* it is necessary
10: 7 I have come to do your *w,* O God
13: 21 everything good for doing his *w,*
Jas 4: 15 "If it is the Lord's *w,*
1Pe 3: 17 It is better, if it is God's *w,*
4: 2 but rather for the *w* of God.
2Pe 1: 21 never had its origin in the *w*
1Jn 5: 14 we ask anything according to his *w,*
Rev 4: 11 and by your *w* they were created

WILLFUL (WILL)
Ps 19: 13 Keep your servant also from *w* sins;

WILLING (WILL)
1Ch 28: 9 devotion and with a *w* mind,
29: 5 who is *w* to consecrate himself
Ps 51: 12 grant me a *w* spirit, to sustain me.
Da 3: 28 were *w* to give up their lives rather
Mt 18: 14 Father in heaven is not *w* that any
23: 37 her wings, but you were not *w.*
26: 41 The spirit is *w,* but the body is weak
1Ti 6: 18 and to be generous and *w* to share.
1Pe 5: 2 but because you are *w,*

WILLINGNESS* (WILL)
2Co 8: 11 so that your eager *w*
8: 12 For if the *w* is there, the gift is

WIN (WINS WON)
1Co 9: 19 myself a slave to everyone, to *w*
Php 3: 14 on toward the goal to *w* the prize
1Th 4: 12 your daily life may *w* the respect

WIND (WHIRLWIND WINDS)
Ps 1: 4 that the *w* blows away.
Ecc 2: 11 meaningless, a chasing after the *w;*
Hos 8: 7 "They sow the *w*
Mk 4: 41 Even the *w* and the waves obey
Jn 3: 8 The *w* blows wherever it pleases.
Eph 4: 14 and there by every *w* of teaching
Jas 1: 6 blown and tossed by the *w.*

WINDOW
Jos 2: 21 she tied the scarlet cord in the *w.*
Ac 20: 9 in a *w* was a young man named
2Co 11: 33 in a basket from a *w* in the wall

WINDS (WIND)
Ps 104: 4 He makes *w* his messengers,
Mt 24: 31 gather his elect from the four *w,*
Heb 1: 7 "He makes his angels *w,*

WINE
Ps 104: 15 *w* that gladdens the heart of man,
Pr 20: 1 *W* is a mocker and beer a brawler;
23: 20 join those who drink too much *w*
23: 31 Do not gaze at *w* when it is red,
31: 6 *w* to those who are in anguish;
SS 1: 2 your love is more delightful than *w.*
Isa 28: 7 And these also stagger from *w*
55: 1 Come, buy *w* and milk
Mt 9: 17 Neither do men pour new *w*
Lk 23: 36 They offered him *w* vinegar
Jn 2: 3 When the *w* was gone, Jesus'
Ro 14: 21 not to eat meat or drink *w*
Eph 5: 18 on *w,* which leads to debauchery.
1Ti 5: 23 a little *w* because of your stomach
Rev 16: 19 with the *w* of the fury of his wrath.

WINEPRESS
Isa 63: 2 like those of one treading the *w?*
Rev 19: 15 He treads the *w* of the fury

WINESKINS
Mt 9: 17 do men pour new wine into old *w.*

WINGS
Ex 19: 4 and how I carried you on eagles' *w*
Ru 2: 12 under whose *w* you have come
Ps 17: 8 hide me in the shadow of your *w*
91: 4 under his *w* you will find refuge;
Isa 6: 2 him were seraphs, each with six *w:*
40: 31 They will soar on *w* like eagles;
Eze 1: 6 of them had four faces and four *w.*
Zec 5: 9 in their *w!* They had *w* like those
Mal 4: 2 rise with healing in its *w.*
Lk 13: 34 hen gathers her chicks under her *w,*
Rev 4: 8 the four living creatures had six *w*

WINS (WIN)
Pr 11: 30 and he who *w* souls is wise.

WINTER
Mk 13: 18 that this will not take place in *w,*

WIPE (WIPED)
Isa 25: 8 The Sovereign LORD will *w* away
Rev 7: 17 God will *w* away every tear
21: 4 He will *w* every tear

WIPED (WIPE)
Lk 7: 38 Then she *w* them with her hair,
Ac 3: 19 so that your sins may be *w* out,

WISDOM (WISE)
Ge 3: 6 and also desirable for gaining *w,*
1Ki 4: 29 God gave Solomon *w* and very
2Ch 1: 10 Give me *w* and knowledge,
Ps 51: 6 you teach me *w* in the inmost place
111: 10 of the LORD is the beginning of *w;*
Pr 2: 6 For the LORD gives *w,*
3: 13 Blessed is the man who finds *w,*
4: 7 *W* is supreme; therefore get
8: 11 for *w* is more precious than rubies,
11: 2 but with humility comes *w.*
13: 10 *w* is found in those who take advice
23: 23 get *w,* discipline and understanding
29: 3 A man who loves *w* brings joy
29: 15 The rod of correction imparts *w,*
31: 26 She speaks with *w,*
Isa 11: 2 Spirit of *w* and of understanding,
28: 29 in counsel and magnificent in *w.*
Jer 10: 12 he founded the world by his *w*
Mic 6: 9 and to fear your name is *w*—
Mt 11: 19 But *w* is proved right by her actions
Lk 2: 52 And Jesus grew in *w* and stature,
Ac 6: 3 known to be full of the Spirit and *w.*
Ro 11: 33 the depth of the riches of the *w*
1Co 1: 17 not with words of human *w,*
1: 30 who has become for us *w* from God
12: 8 through the Spirit the message of *w*
Eph 1: 17 may give you the Spirit of *w*
Col 2: 3 are hidden all the treasures of *w*
2: 23 indeed have an appearance of *w,*
Jas 1: 5 of you lacks *w,* he should ask God,
3: 13 in the humility that comes from *w.*
Rev 5: 12 and wealth and *w* and strength

WISE (WISDOM WISER)
1Ki 3: 12 give you a *w* and discerning heart,
Job 5: 13 He catches the *w* in their craftiness
Ps 19: 7 making *w* the simple.
Pr 3: 7 Do not be *w* in your own eyes;
9: 8 rebuke a *w* man and he will love
10: 1 A *w* son brings joy to his father,
11: 30 and he who wins souls is *w.*
13: 1 A *w* son heeds his father's
13: 20 He who walks with the *w* grows *w,*
16: 23 A *w* man's heart guides his mouth,
17: 28 Even a fool is thought *w*
Ecc 9: 17 The quiet words of the *w* are more
Jer 9: 23 "Let not the *w* man boast
Eze 28: 6 " 'Because you think you are *w,*
Da 2: 21 He gives wisdom to the *w*
12: 3 Those who are *w* will shine like
Mt 11: 25 hidden these things from the *w*
25: 2 them were foolish and five were *w.*
1Co 1: 19 I will destroy the wisdom of the *w;*
1: 27 things of the world to shame the *w;*
3: 19 He catches the *w* in their craftiness
Eph 5: 15 but as *w,* making the most
2Ti 3: 15 able to make you *w* for salvation
Jas 3: 13 Who is *w* and understanding

WISER (WISE)
Pr 9: 9 a wise man and he will be *w* still;
1Co 1: 25 of God is *w* than man's wisdom,

WISH (WISHES)
Jn 15: 7 ask whatever you *w,* and it will be
Ro 9: 3 For I could *w* that I myself were
Rev 3: 15 I *w* you were either one

WISHES (WISH)
Rev 22: 17 let him come; and whoever *w,*

WITCHCRAFT
Dt 18: 10 engages in *w,* or casts spells,
Gal 5: 20 idolatry and *w;* hatred, discord,

WITHDREW
Lk 5: 16 But Jesus often *w* to lonely places

WITHER (WITHERS)
Ps 1: 3 and whose leaf does not *w.*
37: 19 In times of disaster they will not *w;*

WITHERS (WITHER)
Isa 40: 7 The grass *w* and the flowers fall,
1Pe 1: 24 the grass *w* and the flowers fall,

WITHHELD (WITHHOLD)
Ge 22: 12 you have not *w* from me your son,

WITHHOLD (WITHHELD WITHHOLDS)
Ps 84: 11 no good thing does he *w*
Pr 23: 13 Do not *w* discipline from a child;

WITHHOLDS (WITHHOLD)
Dt 27: 19 "Cursed is the man who *w* justice

WITNESS (EYEWITNESSES WITNESSES)
Pr 12: 17 truthful *w* gives honest testimony,
19: 9 A false *w* will not go unpunished,
Jn 1: 8 he came only as a *w* to the light.

WITNESSES (WITNESS)
Dt 19: 15 by the testimony of two or three *w.*
Mt 18: 16 by the testimony of two or three *w.*'
Ac 1: 8 and you will be my *w* in Jerusalem,

WIVES (WIFE)
Eph 5: 22 *W,* submit to your husbands
5: 25 love your *w,* just as Christ loved
1Pe 3: 1 words by the behavior of their *w,*

WIVES' (WIFE)
1Ti 4: 7 with godless myths and old *w* tales

WOE
Isa 6: 5 "*W* to me!" I cried.
Eze 34: 2 *W* to the shepherds
Mt 18: 7 "*W* to the world
23: 13 "*W* to you, teachers of the law
Jude : 11 *W* to them! They have taken

WOLF (WOLVES)
Isa 65: 25 *w* and the lamb will feed together,

WOLVES (WOLF)
Mt 10: 16 you out like sheep among *w.*

WOMAN (MAN)
Ge 2: 22 God made a *w* from
2: 23 she shall be called '*w,*'
3: 6 *w* saw that the fruit
3: 12 The *w* you put here with
3: 15 between you and the *w,*
3: 16 To the *w* he said,
12: 11 a beautiful *w* you are.
20: 3 because of the *w* you have
24: 5 if the *w* is unwilling
Ex 2: 1 married a Levite *w*
3: 22 Every *w* is to ask her
21: 10 If he marries another *w*
21: 22 hit a pregnant *w*
Lev 12: 2 *w* who becomes pregnant
15: 19 *w* has her regular flow
15: 25 a *w* has a discharge
18: 17 sexual relations with both a *w*
20: 13 as one lies with a *w,*
Nu 5: 29 when a *w* goes astray
30: 3 young *w* still living in
30: 9 by a widow or divorced *w*
30: 10 *w* living with her husband
Dt 20: 7 become pledged to a *w*
21: 11 the captives a beautiful *w*
22: 5 *w* must not wear men's
22: 13 married this *w* but when
Jdg 4: 9 hand Sisera over to a *w.*
13: 6 the *w* went to her husband
14: 2 have seen a Philistine *w*
16: 4 he fell in love with a *w*
20: 4 husband of the murdered *w*
Ru 3: 11 a *w* of noble character
1Sa 1: 15 a *w* who is deeply troubled
25: 3 intelligent and beautiful *w,*
28: 7 a *w* who is a medium,
2Sa 11: 2 he saw a *w* bathing
13: 17 "Get this *w* out of here
14: 2 had a wise *w* brought
20: 16 a wise *w* called from
1Ki 3: 18 this *w* also had a baby.
17: 24 the *w* said to Elijah,
2Ki 4: 8 a well-to-do *w* was there,
8: 1 Elisha had said to the *w*
9: 34 "Take care of that cursed *w,*"
Job 14: 1 Man born of *w* is of few
Pr 11: 16 A kindhearted *w* gains respect,
11: 22 a beautiful *w* who shows no
14: 1 a wise *w* builds her house,
30: 23 unloved *w* who is married,
31: 30 a *w* who fears the LORD
Isa 54: 1 O barren *w,* you who never
Mt 5: 28 looks at a *w* lustfully
9: 20 a *w* who had been subject
15: 28 *W* you have great faith!
26: 7 a *w* came to him with
Mk 5: 25 a *w* was there who had
7: 25 a *w* whose little daughter
Lk 7: 39 what kind of a *w* she is
10: 38 a *w* named Martha opened
13: 12 "*W,* you are set free
15: 8 suppose a *w* has ten silver
Jn 2: 4 *w,* why do you involve
4: 7 a Samaritan *w* came
8: 3 a *w* caught in adultery.
19: 26 *w,* here is your son,"
20: 15 *W,* 'he said, "Why are you crying?
Ac 9: 40 Turning toward the dead *w,*
16: 14 was a *w* named Lydia,
Ro 7: 2 a married *w* is bound to
1Co 7: 2 each *w* her own husband
7: 15 a believing man or *w* is
7: 34 an unmarried *w* or virgin
7: 39 *w* is bound to her husband
11: 3 the head of the *w* is man,
11: 7 the *w* is the glory of man
11: 13 a *w* to pray to God with
Gal 4: 4 his Son, born of a *w,*
4: 31 not children of the slave *w,*
1Ti 2: 11 A *w* should learn in
5: 16 any *w* who is a believer
Rev 2: 20 You tolerate that *w* Jezebel,
12: 1 a *w* clothed with the sun
12: 13 he pursued the *w* who had
17: 3 a *w* sitting on a scarlet

WOMEN (MAN)
Mt 11: 11 among those born of *w,*
28: 5 The angel said to the *w,*
Mk 15: 41 Many other *w* who had come
Lk 1: 42 Blessed are you among *w,*
8: 2 also some *w* who had been
23: 27 *w* who mourned and wailed
24: 11 they did not believe the *w,*
Ac 1: 14 along with the *w* and Mary
16: 13 speak to the *w* who had
17: 4 not a few prominent *w.*
Ro 1: 26 *w* exchanged natural relations
1Co 14: 34 *w* should remain silent in
Php 4: 3 help these *w* who have
1Ti 2: 9 want *w* to dress modestly
5: 2 older *w* as mothers,
Tit 2: 3 teach the older *w* to be
2: 4 train the younger *w* to love
Heb 11: 35 *W* received back their dead
1Pe 3: 5 the holy *w* of the past

WOMB
Job 1: 21 Naked I came from my mother's *w,*
Ps 139: 13 in my mother's *w.*
Pr 31: 2 "O my son, O son of my *w,*
Jer 1: 5 you in the *w* I knew you,
Lk 1: 44 the baby in my *w* leaped for joy.
Jn 3: 4 into his mother's *w* to be born!"

WON (WIN)
1Pe 3: 1 they may be *w* over without words

WONDER (WONDERFUL WONDERS)
Ps 17: 7 Show the *w* of your great love,
SS 1: 3 No *w* the maidens love you!

WONDERFUL* (WONDER)
2Sa 1: 26 Your love for me was *w,*
1: 26 more *w* than that of women.
1Ch 16: 9 tell of all his *w* acts.
Job 42: 3 things too *w* for me to know.
Ps 26: 7 and telling of all your *w* deeds.
31: 21 for he showed his *w* love to me
75: 1 men tell of your *w* deeds.
105: 2 tell of all his *w* acts.
107: 8 and his *w* deeds for men,
107: 15 and his *w* deeds for men,
107: 21 and his *w* deeds for men.
107: 24 his *w* deeds in the deep.
107: 31 and his *w* deeds for men.
119: 18 *w* things in your law.
119:129 Your statutes are *w;*
131: 1 or things too *w* for me.
139: 6 Such knowledge is too *w* for me,
139: 14 your works are *w,*
145: 5 I will meditate on your *w* works.
Isa 9: 6 *W* Counselor, Mighty God,
28: 29 *w* in counsel and magnificent
Mt 21: 15 of the law saw the *w* things he did
Lk 13: 17 with all the *w* things he was doing.
1Pe 2: 9 out of darkness into his *w* light.

WONDERS (WONDER)
Ex 3: 20 with all the *w* that I will perform
Dt 10: 21 and awesome *w* you saw
2Sa 7: 23 awesome *w* by driving out nations
Job 37: 14 stop and consider God's *w.*
Ps 9: 1 I will tell of all your *w.*
89: 5 The heavens praise your *w,*
119: 27 then I will meditate on your *w.*
Joel 2: 30 I will show *w* in the heavens
Ac 2: 11 we hear them declaring the *w*
2: 19 I will show *w* in the heaven above
5: 12 many miraculous signs and *w*
2Co 12: 12 that mark an apostle—signs, *w*
2Th 2: 9 and *w,* and in every sort
Heb 2: 4 also testified to it by signs, *w*

WOOD
Isa 44: 19 Shall I bow down to a block of *w?*"
1Co 3: 12 costly stones, *w,* hay or straw,

WOOL
Pr 31: 13 She selects *w* and flax
Isa 1: 18 they shall be like *w.*
Da 7: 9 hair of his head was white like *w.*
Rev 1: 14 and hair were white like *w,*

WORD (BYWORD WORDS)
Nu 30: 2 he must not break his *w*
Dt 8: 3 but on every *w* that comes
2Sa 22: 31 the *w* of the LORD is flawless.
Ps 56: 4 In God, whose *w* I praise,
119: 9 By living according to your *w.*
119: 11 I have hidden your *w* in my heart
119:105 Your *w* is a lamp to my feet
Pr 12: 25 but a kind *w* cheers him up.
15: 1 but a harsh *w* stirs up anger.
25: 11 A *w* aptly spoken
30: 5 "Every *w* of God is flawless;
Isa 55: 11 so is my *w* that goes out
Jer 23: 29 "Is not my *w* like fire," declares
Mt 4: 4 but on every *w* that comes
12: 36 for every careless *w* they have
15: 6 Thus you nullify the *w* of God

WRONG (WRONGDOING WRONGED WRONGS)
Ex 23: 2 Do not follow the crowd in doing *w*
Nu 5: 7 must make full restitution for his *w*,
Dt 32: 4 A faithful God who does no *w*,
Job 34: 12 unthinkable that God would do *w*,
Ps 5: 5 you hate all who do *w*.
Gal 2: 11 to his face, because he was clearly in the *w*.
1Th 5: 15 that nobody pays back *w* for *w*,

WRONGDOING (WRONG)
Job 1: 22 sin by charging God with *w*.
1Jn 5: 17 All *w* is sin, and there is sin that

WRONGED (WRONG)
1Co 6: 7 not rather be *w*? Why not rather

WRONGS (WRONG)
Pr 10: 12 but love covers over all *w*.
1Co 13: 5 angered, it keeps no record of *w*.

WROTE (WRITE)
Ex 34: 28 And he *w* on the tablets the words
Jn 5: 46 for he *w* about me.
8: 8 down and *w* on the ground.

XERXES

King of Persia, husband of Esther. Deposed Vashti; replaced her with Esther (Est 1–2). Sealed Haman's edict to annihilate the Jews (Est 3). Received Esther without having called her (Est 5:1–8). Honored Mordecai (Est 6). Hanged Haman (Est 7). Issued edict allowing Jews to defend themselves (Est 8). Exalted Mordecai (Est 8:1–2, 15; 9:4; 10).

YEAR (YEARS)
Ex 34: 23 Three times a *y* all your men are
Lev 16: 34 to be made once a *y* for all the sins
25: 4 But in the seventh *y* the land is
25: 11 The fiftieth *y* shall be a jubilee
Heb 10: 1 repeated endlessly *y* after *y*,

YEARS (YEAR)
Ge 1: 14 to mark seasons and days and *y*,
Ex 12: 40 lived in Egypt was 430 *y*.
16: 35 The Israelites ate manna forty *y*,
Job 36: 26 of his *y* is past finding out.
Ps 90: 4 For a thousand *y* in your sight
90: 10 The length of our days is seventy *y*
Pr 3: 2 they will prolong your life many *y*
Lk 3: 23 Jesus himself was about thirty *y* old
2Pe 3: 8 the Lord a day is like a thousand *y*,
Rev 20: 2 and bound him for a thousand *y*.

YEAST
Ex 12: 15 are to eat bread made without *y*.
Mt 16: 6 guard against the *y* of the Pharisees
1Co 5: 6 you know that a little *y* works

YESTERDAY
Heb 13: 8 Jesus Christ is the same *y*

YOKE (YOKED)
1Ki 12: 4 and the heavy *y* he put on us,
Mt 11: 29 Take my *y* upon you and learn
Gal 5: 1 be burdened again by a *y*

YOKED (YOKE)
2Co 6: 14 Do not be *y* together

YOUNG (YOUNGER YOUTH)
2Ch 10: 14 he followed the advice of the *y* men
Ps 37: 25 I was *y* and now I am old,
119: 9 How can a *y* man keep his way
Pr 20: 29 The glory of *y* men is their strength
Isa 40: 11 he gently leads those that have *y*.
Joel 2: 28 your *y* men will see visions.
Ac 2: 17 your *y* men will see visions,
7: 58 at the feet of a *y* man named Saul.
1Ti 4: 12 down on you because you are *y*,
Tit 2: 6 encourage the *y* men
1Pe 5: 5 *Y* men, in the same way be
1Jn 2: 13 I write to you, *y* men,

YOUNGER (YOUNG)
1Ti 5: 1 Treat *y* men as brothers, older
Tit 2: 4 Then they can train the *y* women

YOUTH (YOUNG)
Ps 103: 5 so that your *y* is renewed like
Ecc 12: 1 Creator in the days of your *y*,
2Ti 2: 22 Flee the evil desires of *y*,

ZACCHAEUS
Lk 19: 2 A man was there by the name of *Z*;

ZEAL (ZEALOUS)
Ps 69: 9 for *z* for your house consumes me,
Pr 19: 2 to have *z* without knowledge,
Isa 59: 17 and wrapped himself in *z*
Jn 2: 17 "*Z* for your house will consume me
Ro 10: 2 their *z* is not based on knowledge.
12: 11 Never be lacking in *z*,

ZEALOUS (ZEAL)
Nu 25: 13 he was *z* for the honor of his God
Pr 23: 17 always be *z* for the fear
Eze 39: 25 and I will be *z* for my holy name.
Gal 4: 18 fine to be *z*, provided the purpose is

ZEBULUN

Son of Jacob by Leah (Ge 30:20; 35:23; 1Ch 2:1). Tribe of blessed (Ge 49:13; Dt 33:18–19), numbered (Nu 1:31; 26:27), allotted land (Jos 19:10–16; Eze 48:26), failed to fully possess (Jdg 1:30), supported Deborah (Jdg 4:6–10; 5:14, 18), David (1Ch 12:33), 12,000 from (Rev 7:8).

ZECHARIAH

1. Son of Jeroboam II; king of Israel (2Ki 15:8–12).

2. Post-exilic prophet who encouraged rebuilding of temple (Ezr 5:1; 6:14; Zec 1:1).

3. Father of John the Baptist (Lk 1:13; 3:2).

ZEDEKIAH

1. False prophet (1Ki 22:11–24; 2Ch 18:10–23).

2. Mattaniah, son of Josiah (1Ch 3:15), made king of Judah by Nebuchadnezzar (2Ki 24:17–25:7; 2Ch 36:10–14; Jer 37–39; 52:1–11).

ZEPHANIAH

Prophet; descendant of Hezekiah (Zep 1:1).

ZERUBBABEL

Descendant of David (1Ch 3:19; Mt 1:3). Led return from exile (Ezr 2:2; Ne 7:7). Governor of Israel; helped rebuild altar and temple (Ezr 3; Hag 1–2; Zec 4).

ZILPAH

Servant of Leah, mother of Jacob's sons Gad and Asher (Ge 30:9–12; 35:26, 46:16–18).

ZIMRI

King of Israel (1Ki 16:9–20).

ZION
2Sa 5: 7 David captured the fortress of *Z*,
Ps 2: 6 King on *Z*, my holy hill."
9: 11 to the LORD, enthroned in *Z*;
74: 2 Mount *Z*, where you dwelt.
87: 2 the LORD loves the gates of *Z*
102: 13 and have compassion on *Z*,
137: 3 "Sing us one of the songs of *Z*!"
Isa 2: 3 The law will go out from *Z*,
28: 16 "See, I lay a stone in *Z*,
51: 11 They will enter *Z* with singing;
52: 8 When the LORD returns to *Z*,
Jer 50: 5 They will ask the way to *Z*
Joel 3: 21 The LORD dwells in *Z*!
Am 6: 1 to you who are complacent in *Z*,
Mic 4: 2 The law will go out from *Z*,
Zec 9: 9 Rejoice greatly, O Daughter of *Z*!
Ro 9: 33 I lay in *Z* a stone that causes men
11: 26 "The deliverer will come from *Z*;
Heb 12: 22 But you have come to Mount *Z*,
Rev 14: 1 standing on Mount *Z*,

ZIPPORAH*

Daughter of Reuel; wife of Moses (Ex 2:21–22; 4:20–26; 18:1–6).

ZOPHAR

One of Job's friends (Job 11; 20).

INDEX TO *Color Maps*

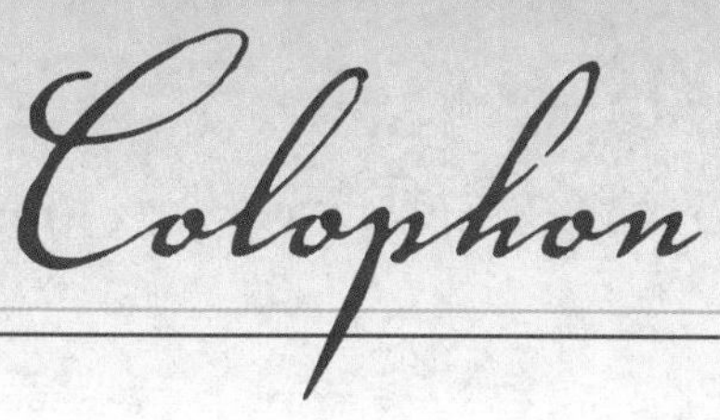

ARCHAEOLOGICAL STUDY BIBLE

President and Executive Editor Gordon-Conwell Theological Seminary:	Dr. Walter C. Kaiser, Jr.
General Editor and Theological Review:	Dr. Duane A. Garrett
Project Management and Editorial:	Donna L. Huisjen
Editorial Management:	Timothy J. Beals Paul Caminiti Michael Vander Klipp
Editorial Development:	Natalie J. Block Stephen W. Sorenson Amy Ballor Carol Postma Julie Zahm Shari VandenBerg
Production Management:	Phil Herich
Project Art Direction and Cover Design:	Jamie DeBruyn
Interior Design:	Kirk DouPonce, DogEared Design
Interior Typesetting:	Nancy Wilson
Additional Interior Assistance:	Mark Sheeres Ruth Bandstra
Design Management:	Ron Huizinga

For Photographic Permissions and Publishing Rights see pages xvii–xviii

GUARANTEE

Zondervan guarantees leather Bibles unconditionally against manufacturing defects for a lifetime and hardcover, softcover and Leather Look™ Bibles for four years. This guarantee does not apply to normal wear. Contact Zondervan Customer Service, 800-727-1309, for replacement instructions.

CARE

We suggest loosening the binding of your new Bible by gently pressing on a small section of pages at a time from the center. To ensure against breakage of the spine, it is best not to bend the cover backward around the spine or to carry study notes, church bulletins, pens, etc., inside the cover. Because a felt-tipped marker will "bleed" through the pages, we recommend use of a ball-point pen or pencil to underline favorite passages. Protecting the gold or silver edges of the paper from moisture will avoid spotting, streaking or fading. Your Bible should not be exposed to excessive heat, cold, or humidity.

Map 1: **WORLD OF THE PATRIARCHS**

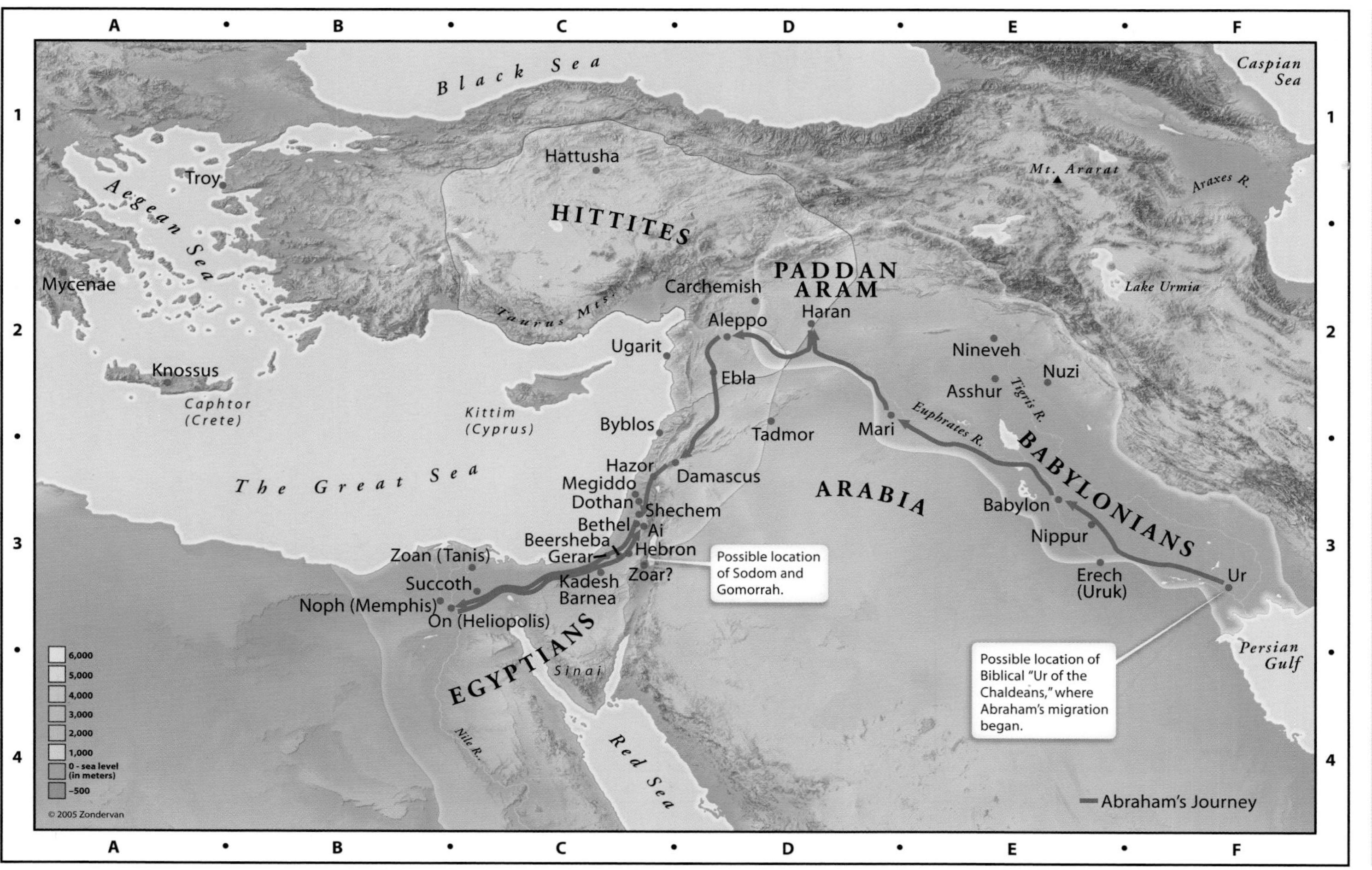

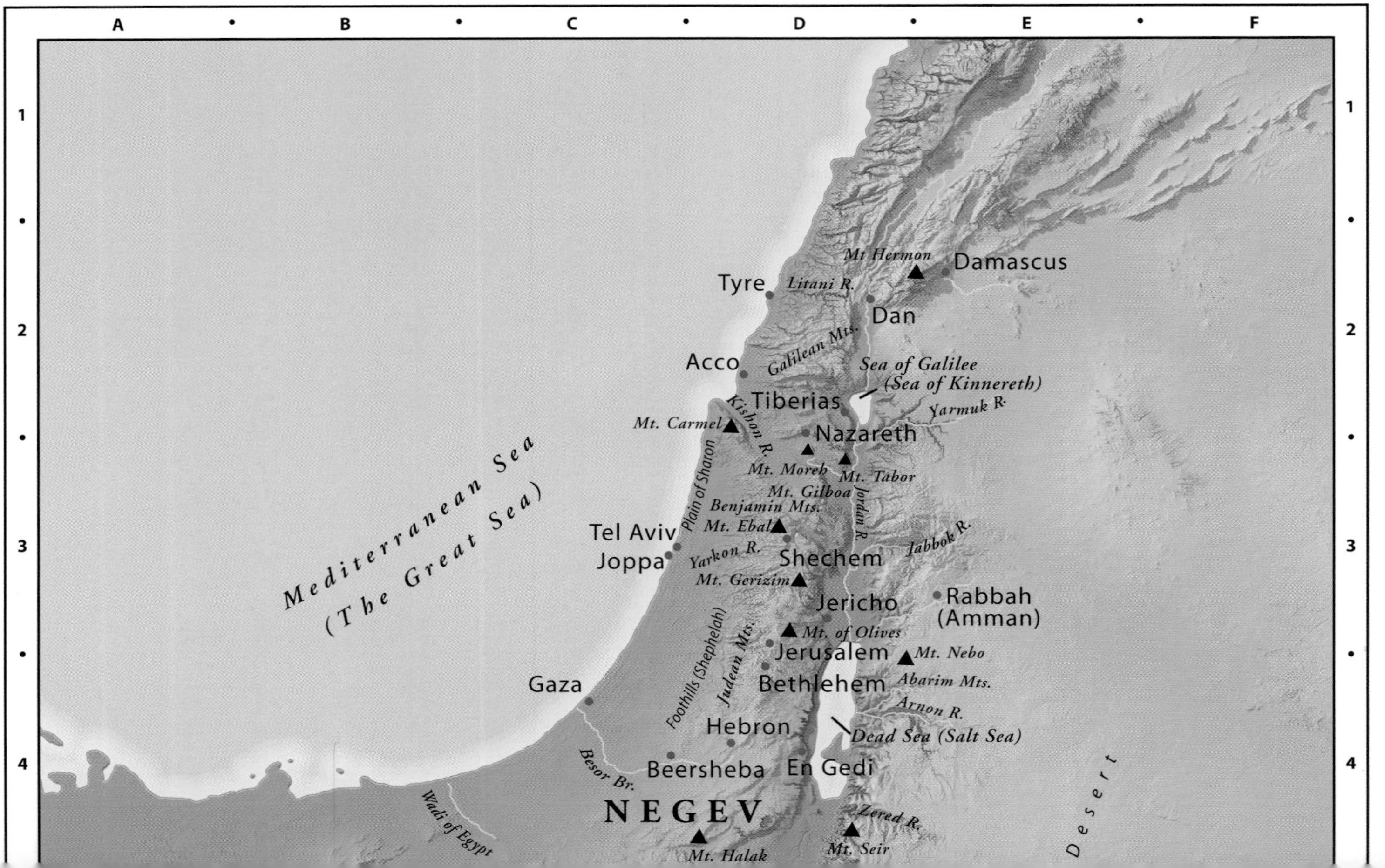
Mt Hermon
Damascus
Tyre
Litani R.
Dan
Acco
Galilean Mts.
Sea of Galilee
(Sea of Kinnereth)
Tiberias
Yarmuk R.
Mt. Carmel
Kishon R.
Nazareth
Mt. Moreh
Mt. Tabor
Mt. Gilboa
Jordan R.
Plain of Sharon
Mediterranean Sea
(The Great Sea)
Benjamin Mts.
Mt. Ebal
Tel Aviv
Joppa
Yarkon R.
Shechem
Jabbok R.
Mt. Gerizim
Jericho
Rabbah
(Amman)
Mt. of Olives
Jerusalem
Mt. Nebo
Foothills (Shephelah)
Judean Mts.
Gaza
Bethlehem
Abarim Mts.
Arnon R.
Hebron
Dead Sea (Salt Sea)
Besor Br.
Beersheba
En Gedi
Wadi of Egypt
NEGEV
Zered R.
Mt. Halak
Mt. Seir
Desert
A
B
C
D
E
F
1
2
3
4

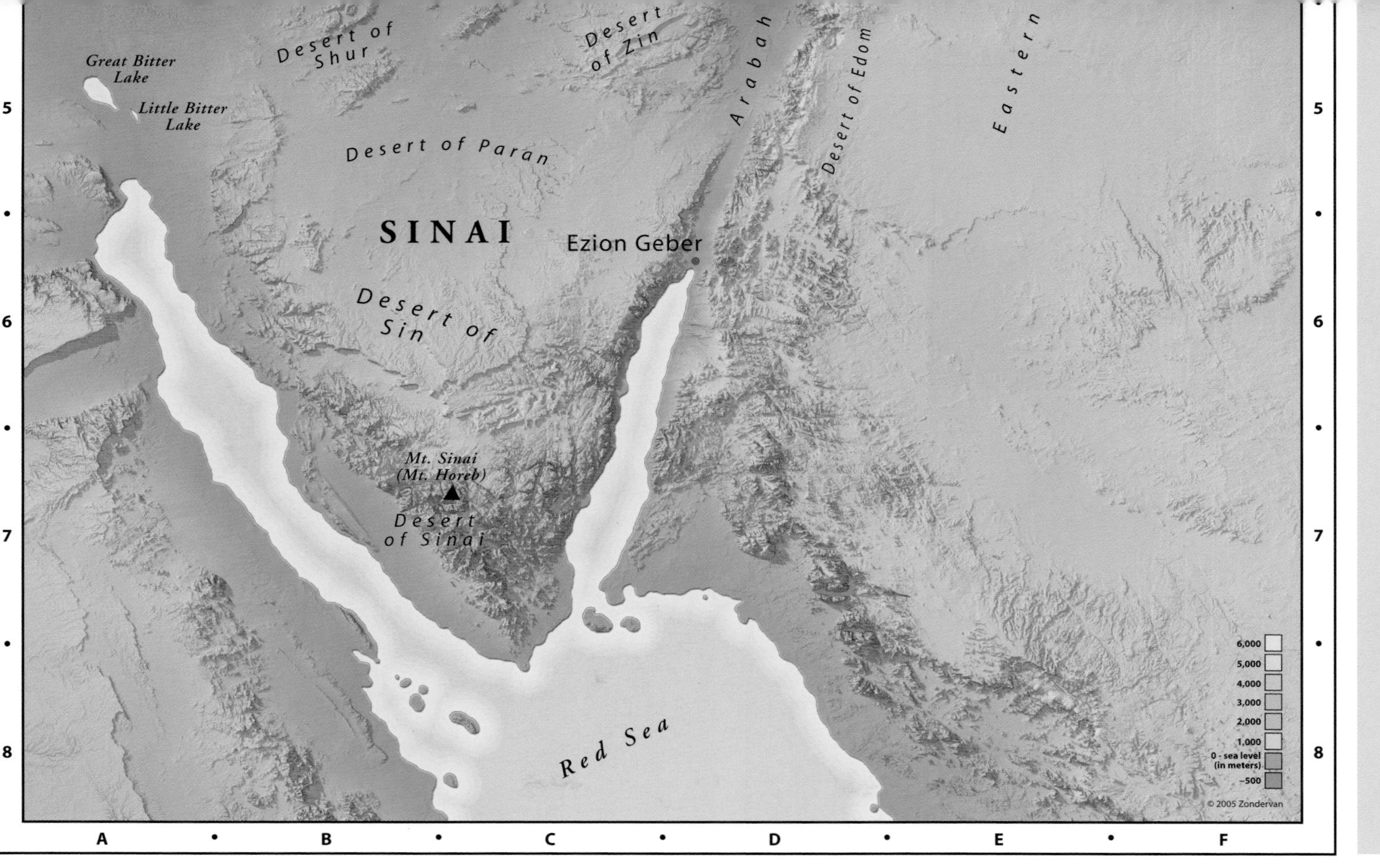

Great Bitter Lake
Little Bitter Lake
Desert of Shur
Desert of Zin
Desert of Paran
Arabah
Desert of Edom
Eastern
SINAI
Ezion Geber
Desert of Sin
Mt. Sinai (Mt. Horeb)
Desert of Sinai
Red Sea
6,000
5,000
4,000
3,000
2,000
1,000
0 - sea level (in meters)
–500
© 2005 Zondervan
A
B
C
D
E
F
5
6
7
8

Map 3: **EXODUS AND CONQUEST OF CANAAN**

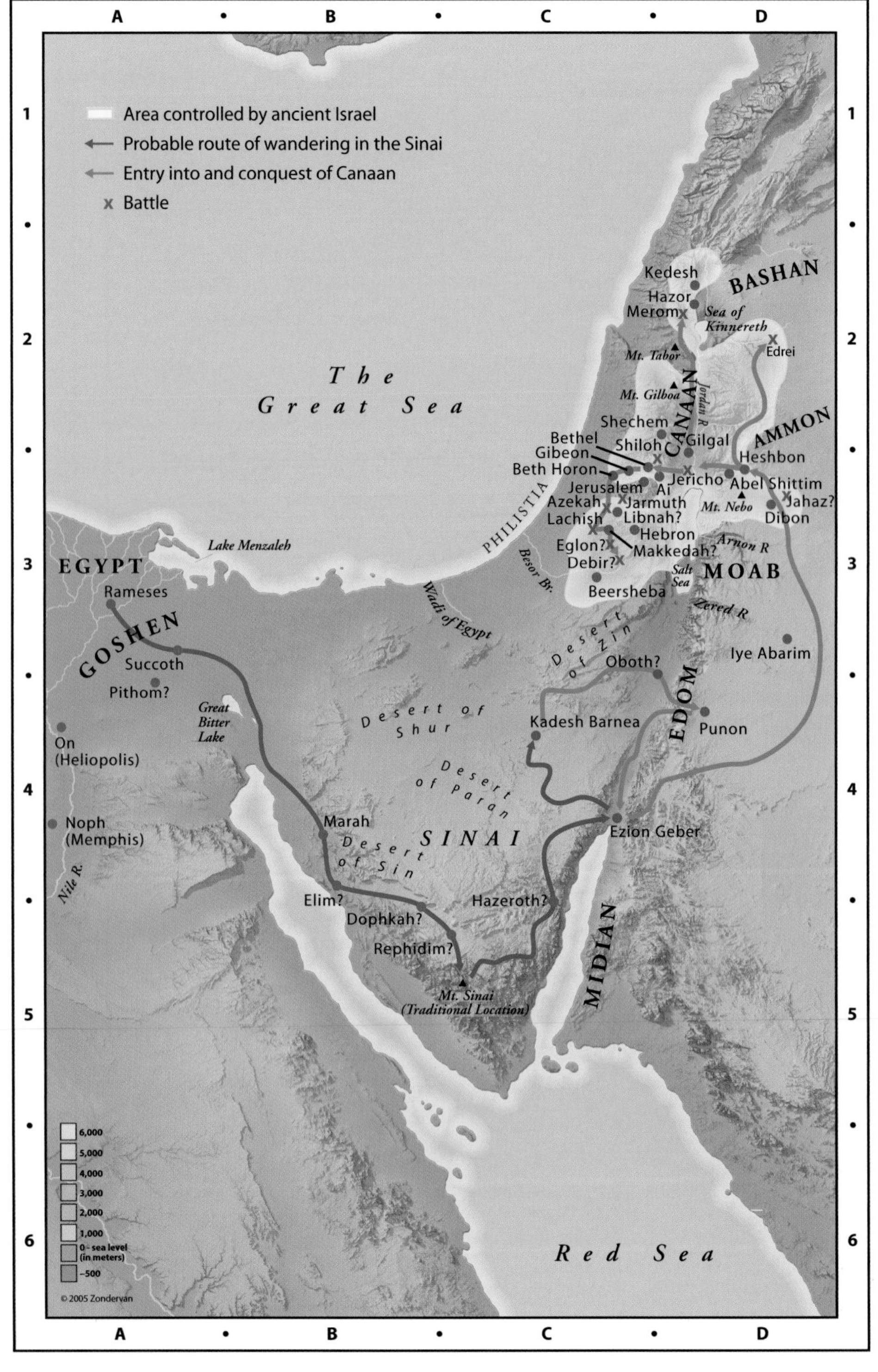

© 2005 Zondervan

Map 4: **LAND OF THE TWELVE TRIBES**

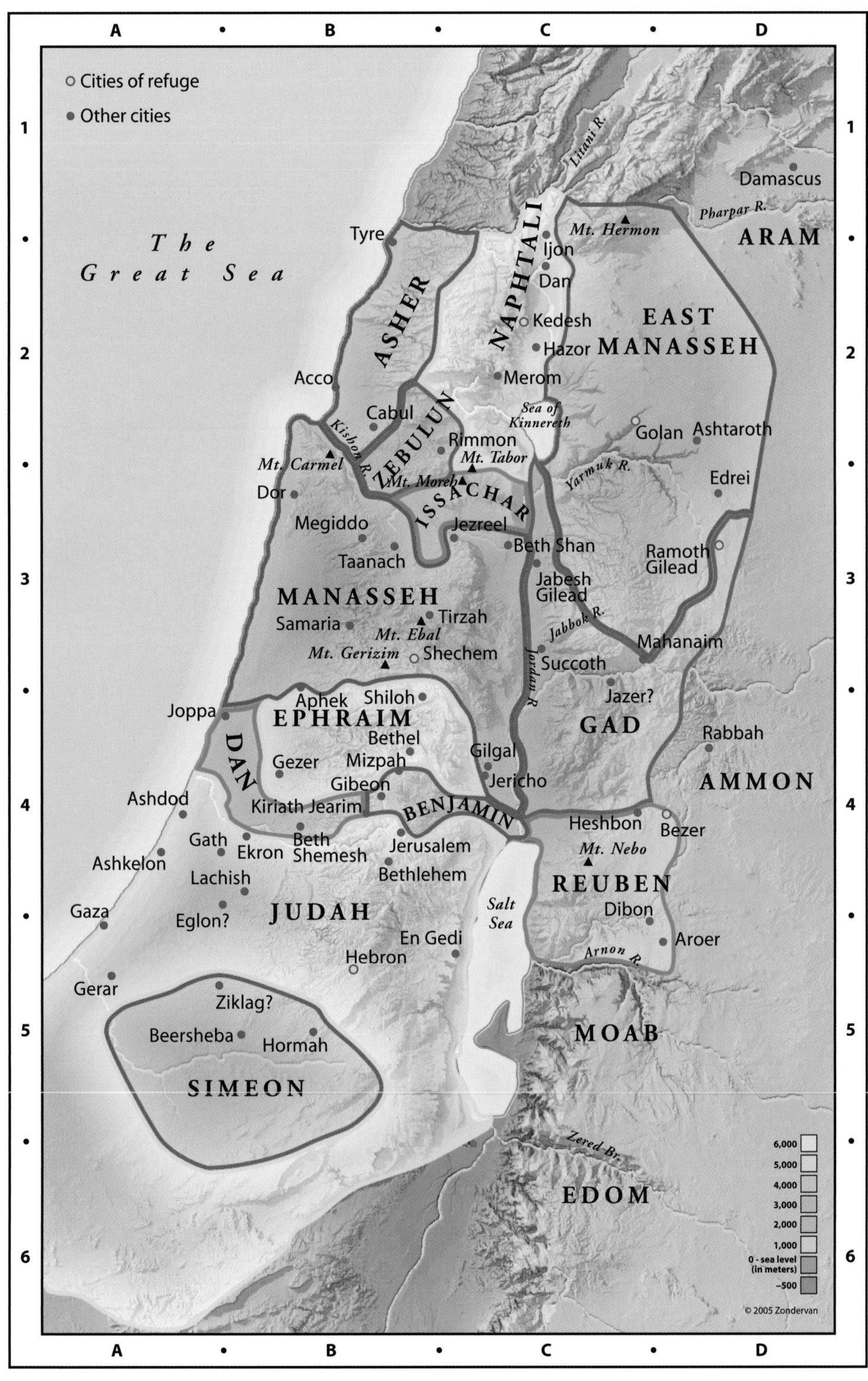

Map 5: **KINGDOM OF DAVID AND SOLOMON**

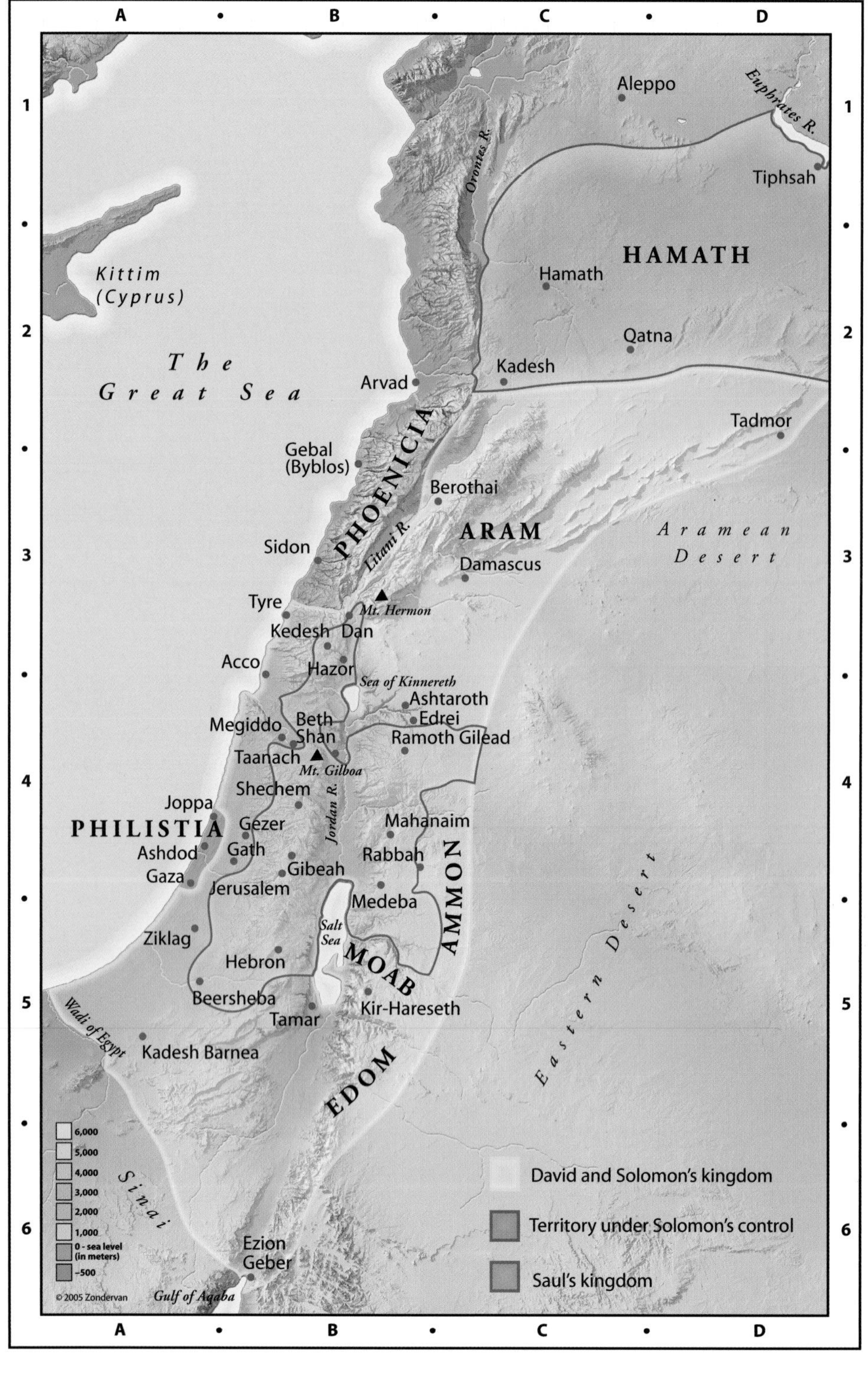

Map 6: **KINGDOMS OF ISRAEL AND JUDAH**

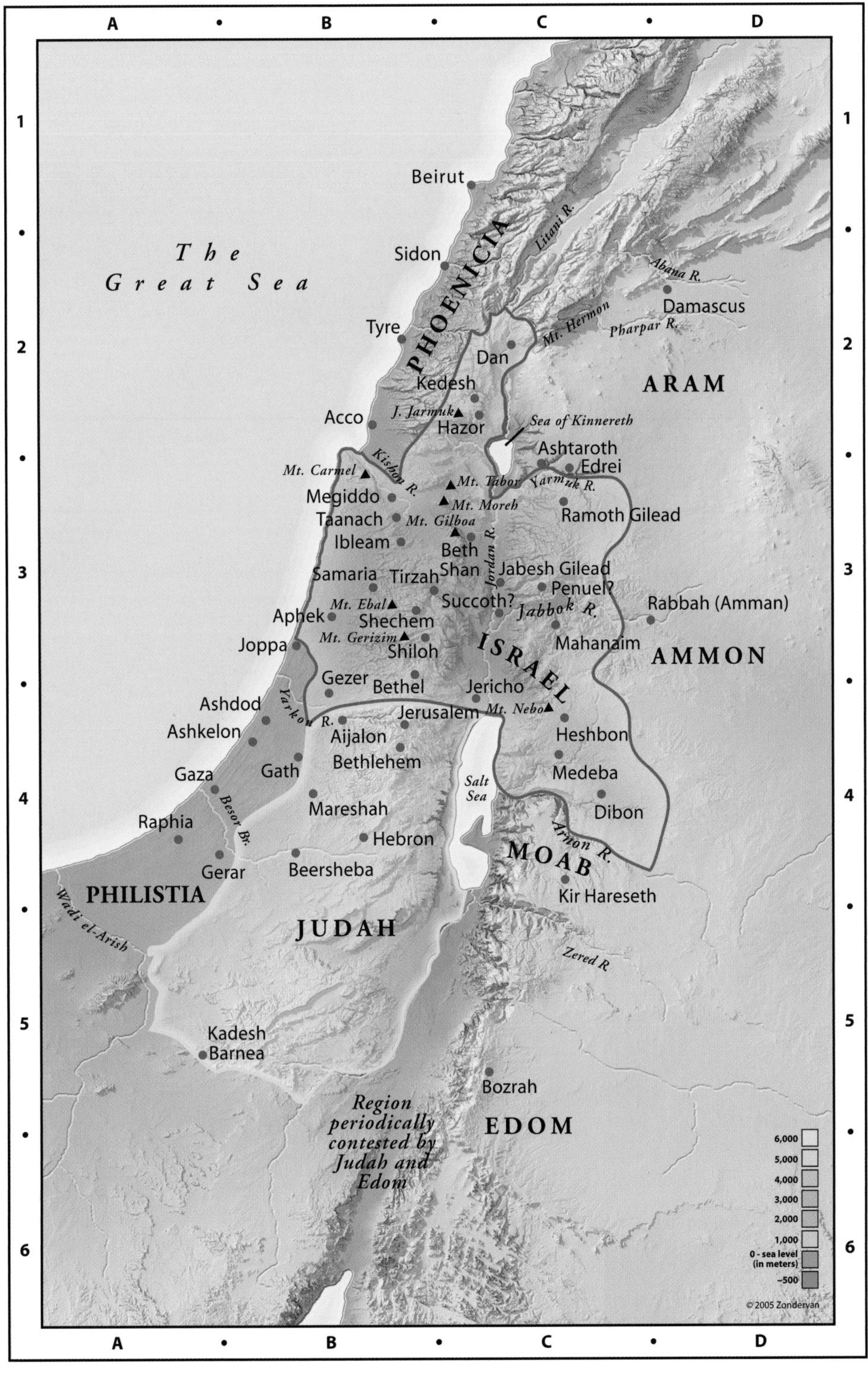

© 2005 Zondervan

Map 7: **PROPHETS IN ISRAEL AND JUDAH**

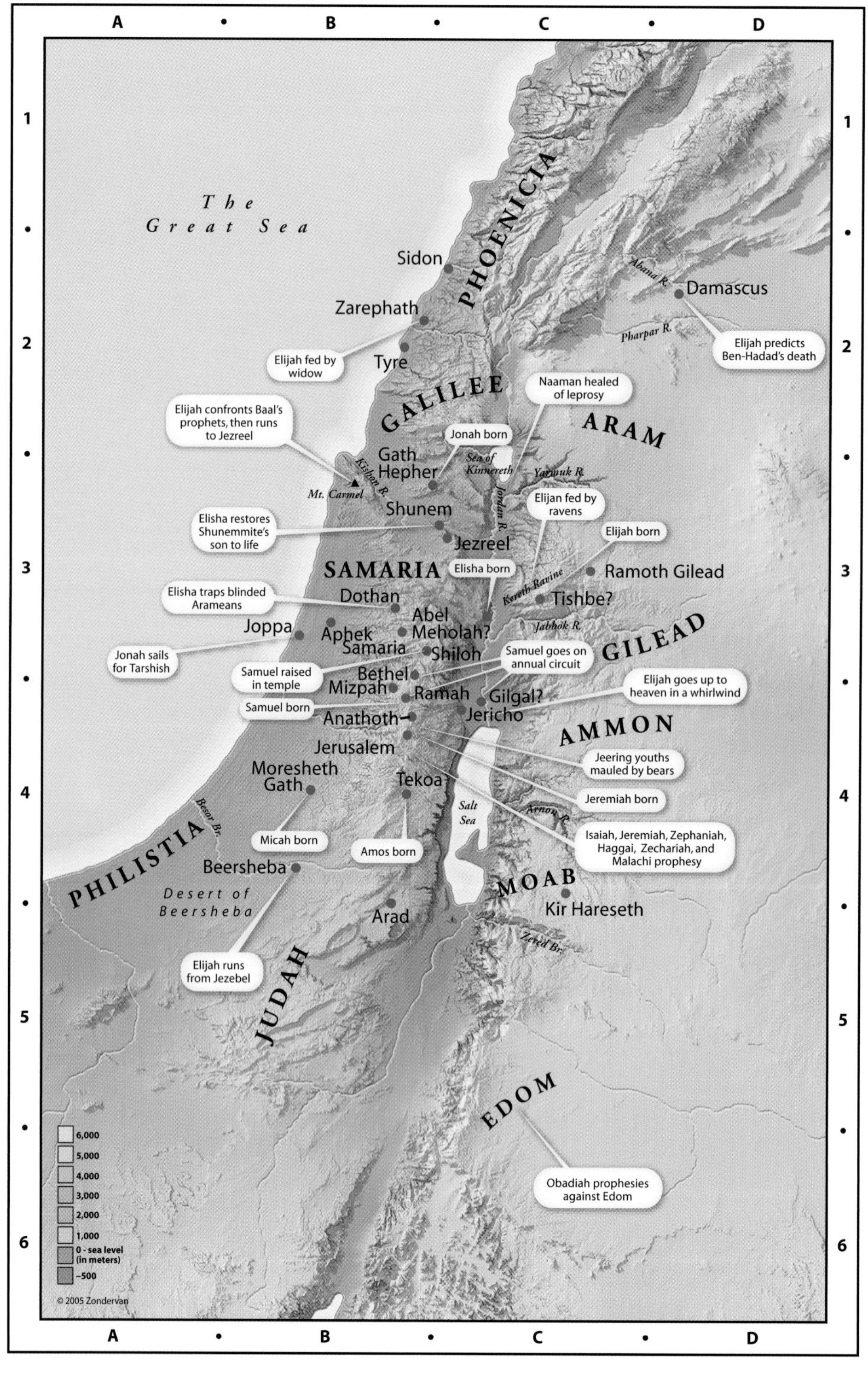

Map 8: **ASSYRIAN AND BABYLONIAN EMPIRES**

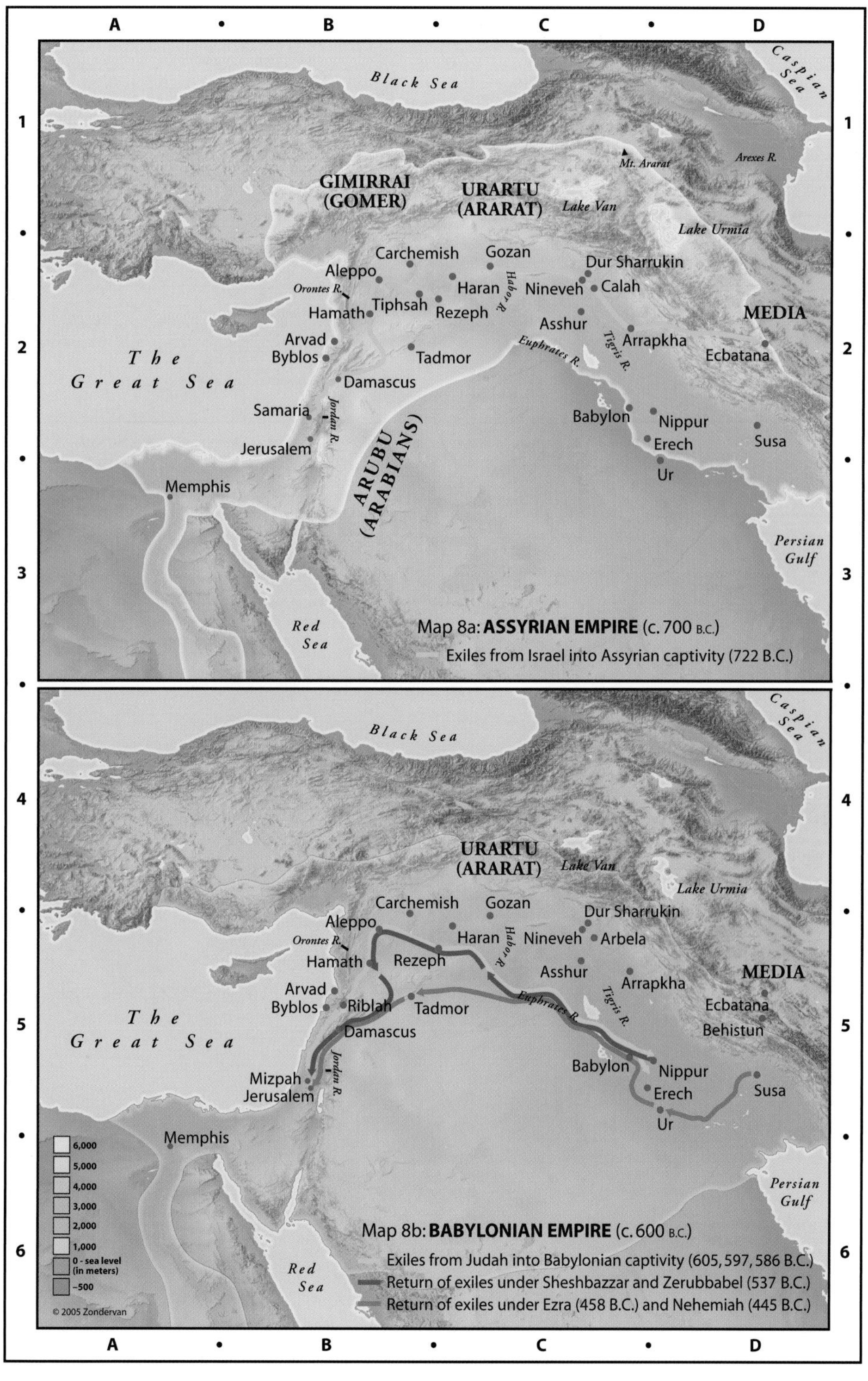

Map 9: **HOLY LAND IN THE TIME OF JESUS**

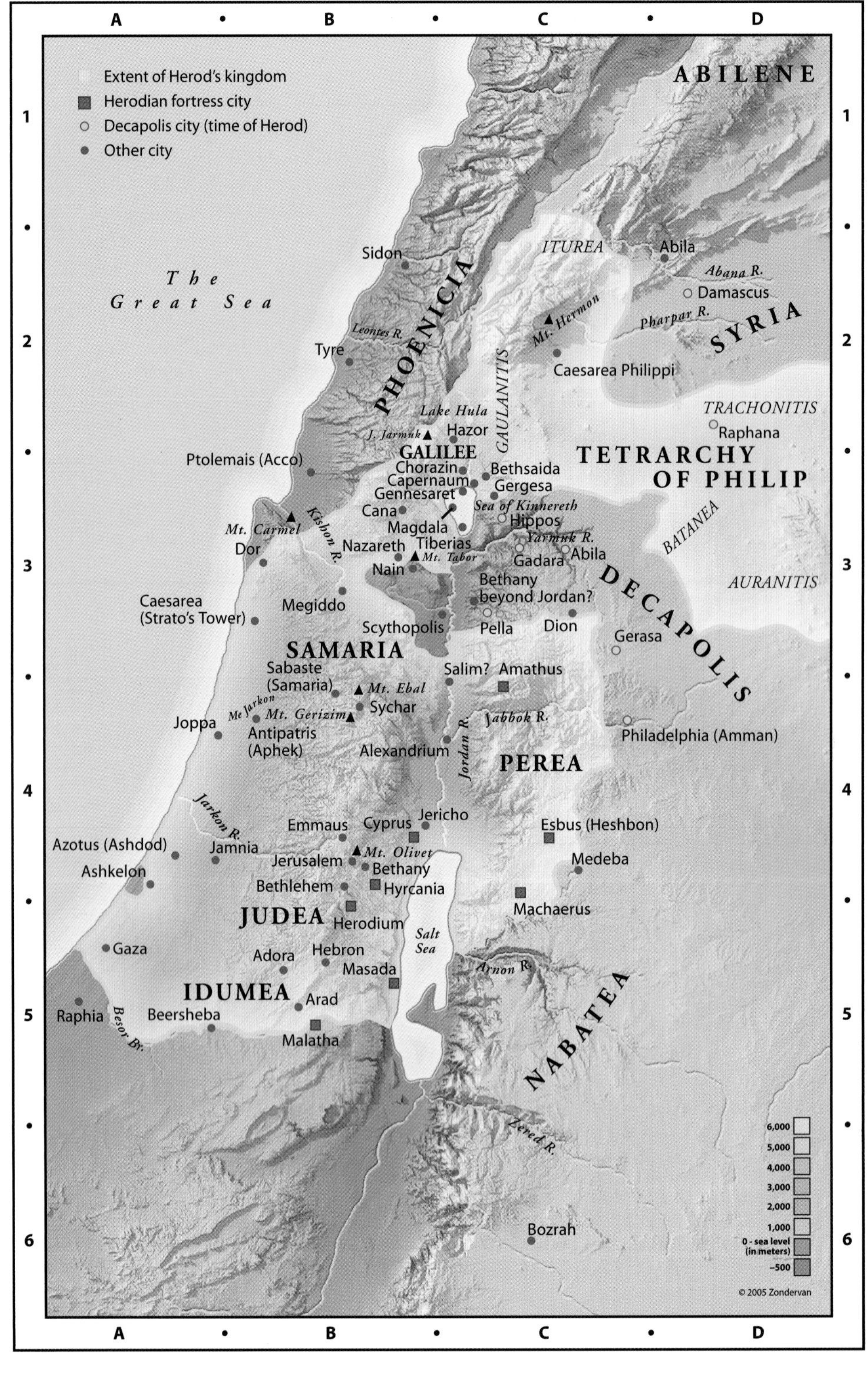

Map 10: **JERUSALEM IN THE TIME OF JESUS**

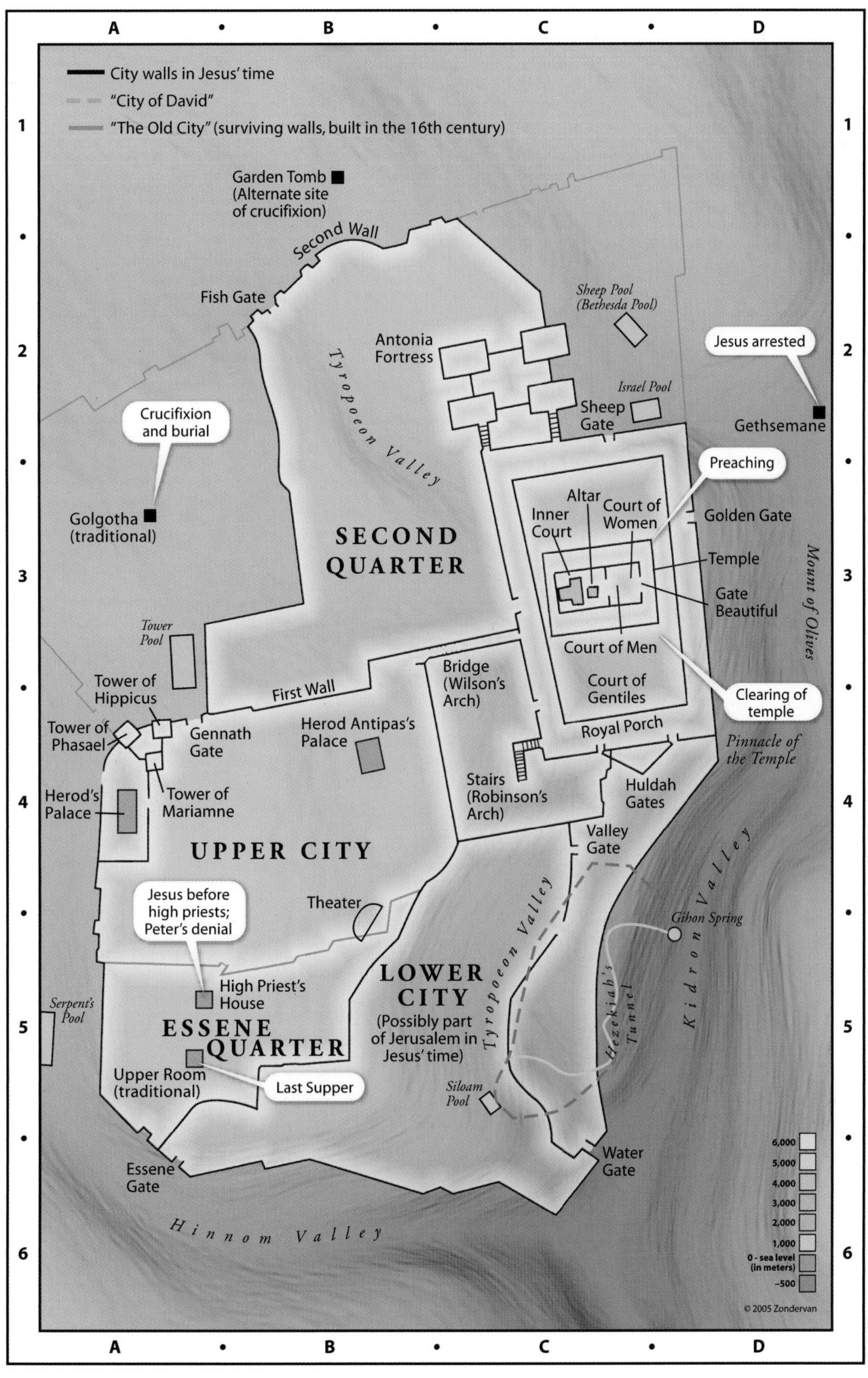

Map 11: **JESUS' MINISTRY**

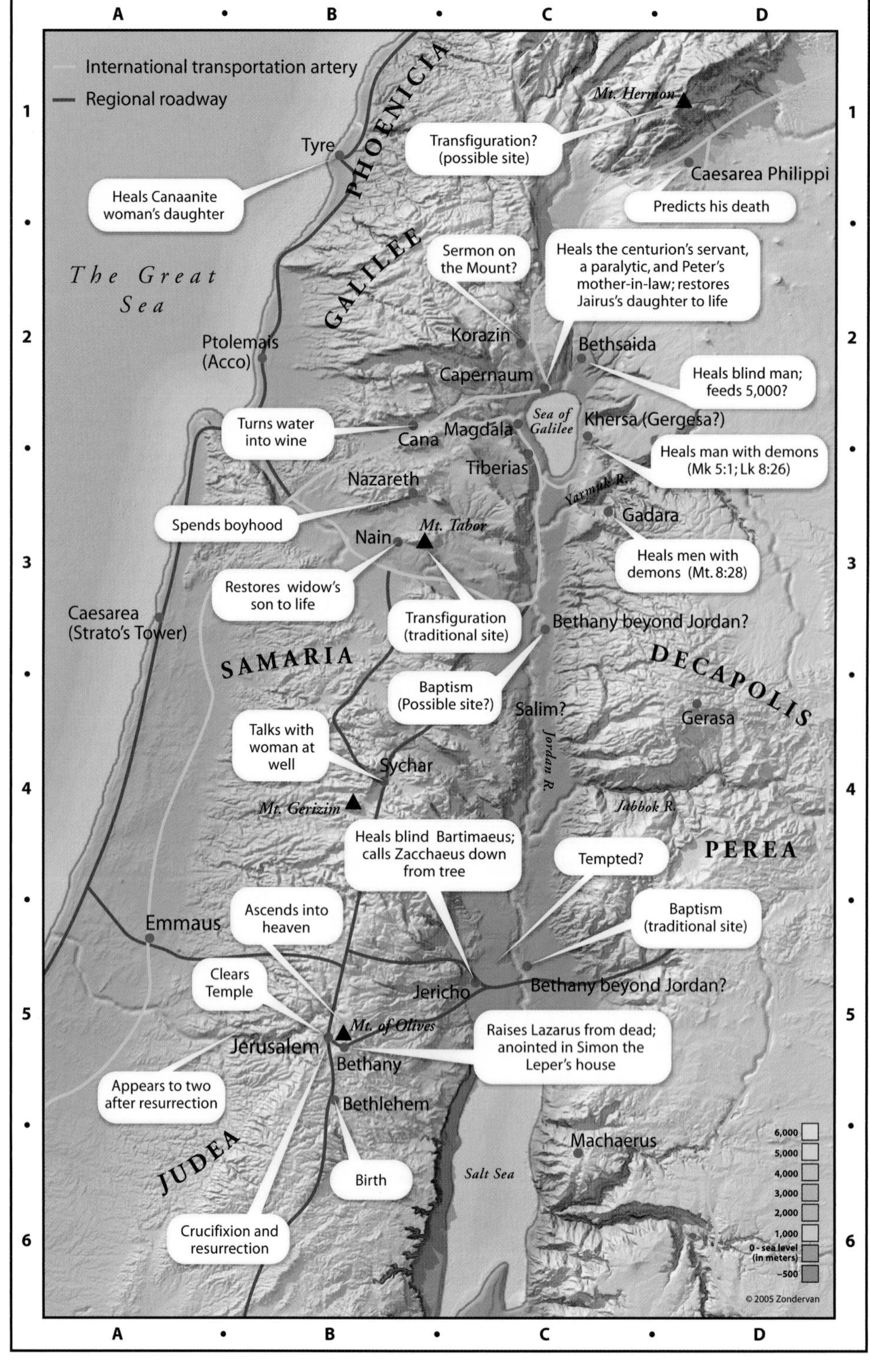

Map 12: **APOSTLES' EARLY TRAVELS**

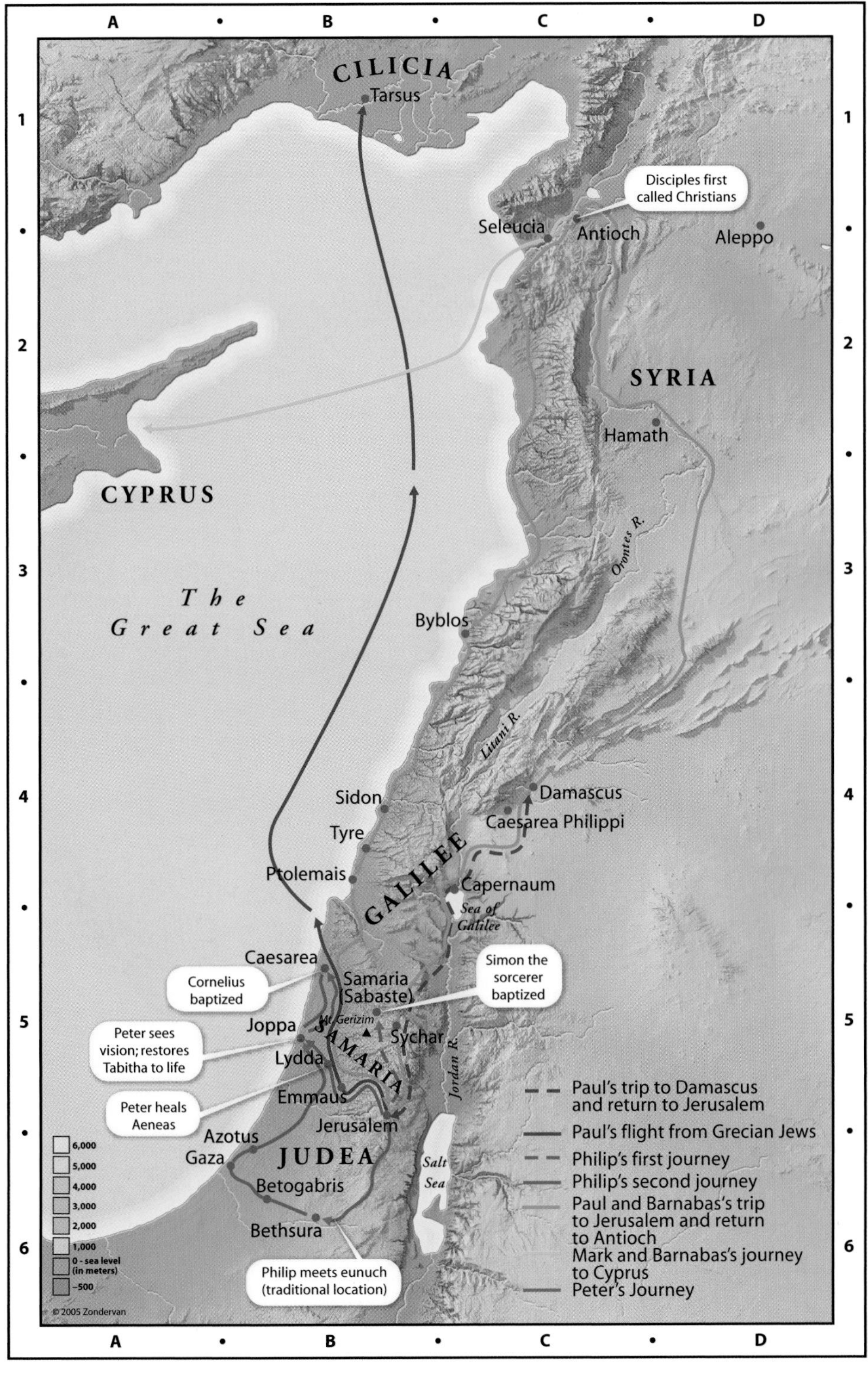

Map 13: **MISSIONARY JOURNEY**

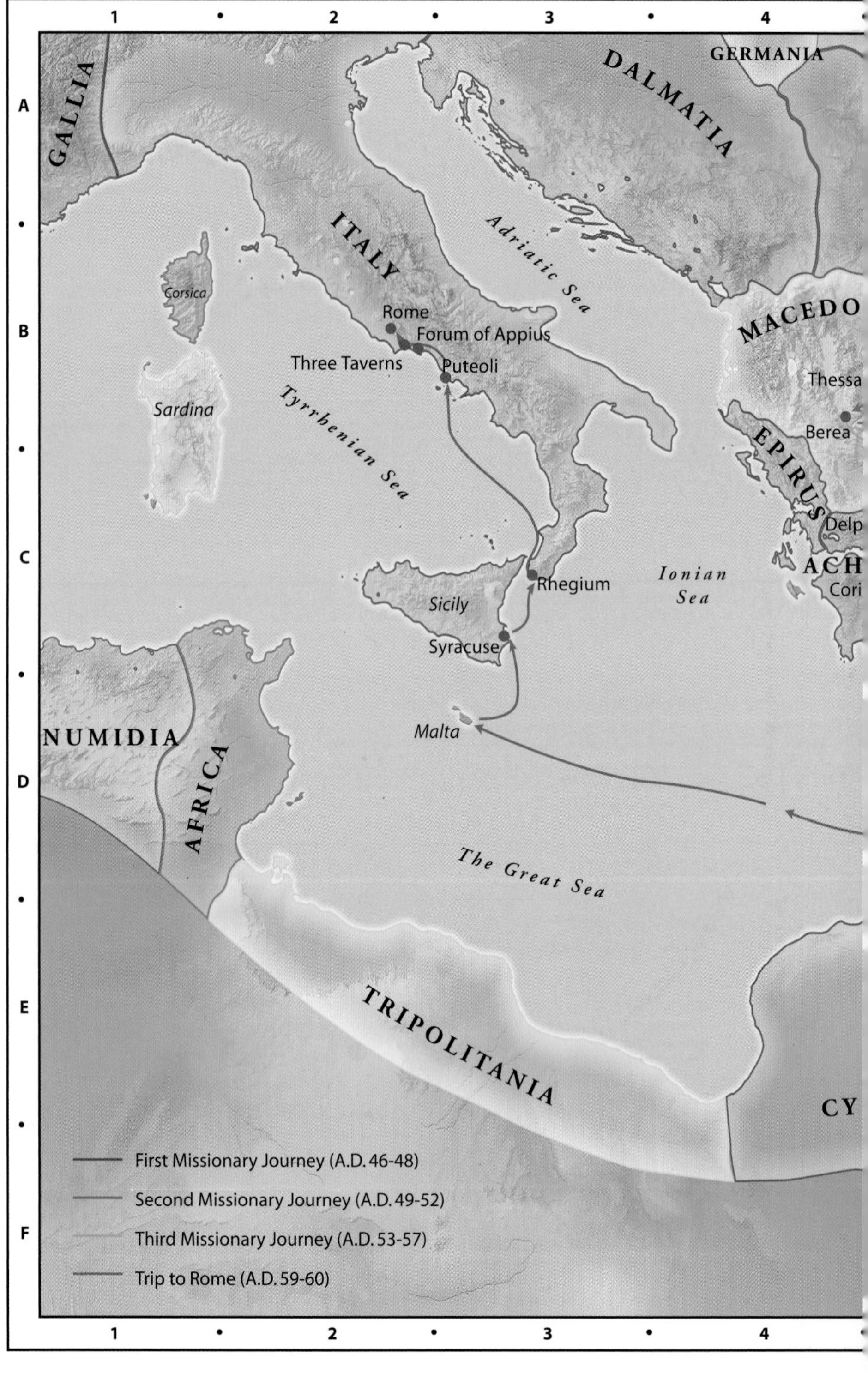

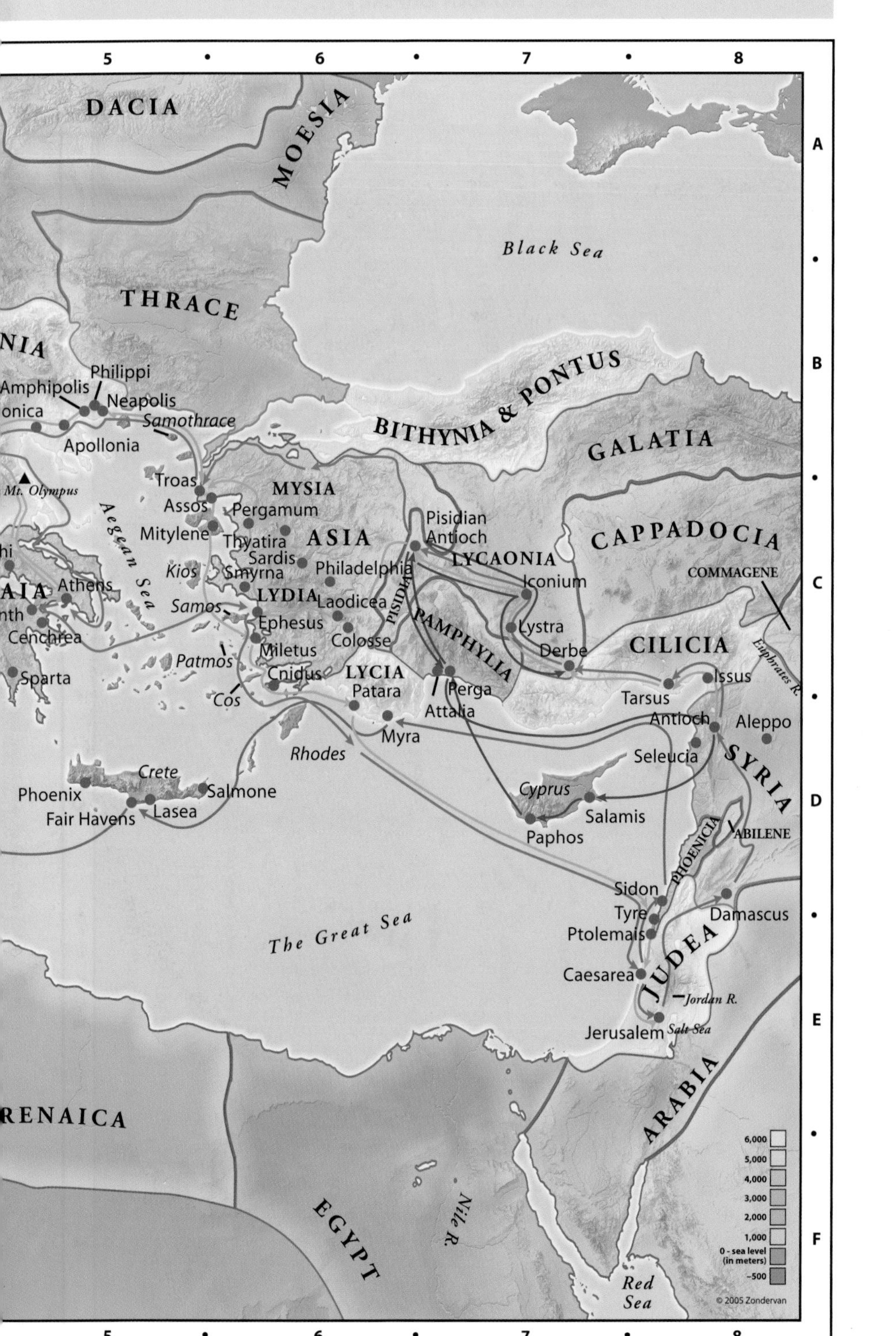

DACIA
MOESIA
THRACE
Black Sea
BITHYNIA & PONTUS
GALATIA
CAPPADOCIA
COMMAGENE
MYSIA
ASIA
LYDIA
LYCAONIA
PISIDIA
PAMPHYLIA
LYCIA
CILICIA
SYRIA
ABILENE
PHOENICIA
JUDEA
ARABIA
EGYPT
RENAICA
AIA
NIA
Philippi
Amphipolis
Neapolis
onica
Samothrace
Apollonia
Mt. Olympus
Troas
Assos
Pergamum
Mitylene
Thyatira
Sardis
Smyrna
Kios
Aegean Sea
Athens
nth
Cenchrea
Sparta
Samos
Ephesus
Miletus
Patmos
Cos
Cnidus
Patara
Myra
Rhodes
Philadelphia
Laodicea
Colosse
Pisidian Antioch
Iconium
Lystra
Derbe
Perga
Attalia
Tarsus
Issus
Antioch
Aleppo
Seleucia
Euphrates R.
Crete
Phoenix
Fair Havens
Lasea
Salmone
Cyprus
Salamis
Paphos
Sidon
Tyre
Ptolemais
Damascus
Caesarea
Jordan R.
Jerusalem
Salt Sea
The Great Sea
Nile R.
Red Sea
5
6
7
8
A
B
C
D
E
F
6,000
5,000
4,000
3,000
2,000
1,000
0 - sea level (in meters)
-500
© 2005 Zondervan